To Daddy

Happy Christmas

Lots of love from

POPPY xxx

Christmas 2005.

RadioTimes GUIDE TO FILMS

Introduction by Barry Norman

Edited by Kilmeny Fane-Saunders

BBC WORLDWIDE LIMITED

Published by BBC Worldwide Limited 80 Wood Lane London W12 0TT
ISBN 0 563 49323 2
First published in the United Kingdom 2000
Sixth edition published in the United Kingdom 2005

Text designed by Ben Cracknell Studios
Typesetting by Polestar Applied Solutions
Printed in the United Kingdom by William Clowes

Contents

Introduction by Barry Norman 4

How to use this guide 5

Contributors and acknowledgements 8

A-Z of films 9

Directors 1401

Actors 1437

Alternative titles 1645

Awards 1665

Five- and four-star films 1689

Introduction
by Barry Norman

One Oscar night in Beverly Hills, around the turn of the century, the screenwriter William Goldman told me, gloomily, that in his view the 1990s had been the worst decade in Hollywood history.

I think he was right. Remakes – always a sign that the movie industry has run out of ideas and courage – had begun to proliferate, as had a new kind of insidiously bad film, the dumbed-down epic.

Titanic, with its daft love story, was one example; *Pearl Harbor*, which continued the trend into the new millennium, was considerably worse. It cost a fortune and, alas, because of its special effects, on which most of the money had been spent, also made a fortune. But it had an even dafter love story, an equally poor screenplay, indifferent direction and acting and was in fact a B-picture dressed up to look like something important – all fur coat and no knickers.

So what with this and those remakes, not only of western classics but also of Oriental horror flicks, I feared that, cinematically, the 00s would be as barren as the 90s.

But then the 2005 Oscar nominations, normally an occasion to reward hype and box-office hits, gave me cause for cheer because the list was packed with serious, grown-up films, the kind you could only appreciate if you engaged your brain while watching. There were *Vera Drake* and *Hotel Rwanda*, *Million Dollar Baby*, *The Aviator*, *Sideways*, *Eternal Sunshine of the Spotless Mind*, *The Motorcycle Diaries*...

Suddenly the industry seemed to have remembered that mature adults, not just sensation-seeking teenagers and early 20-somethings, went to the movies, too. If this trend continues, there may be hope yet.

All the above films are, of course, reviewed in the hefty tome you are now holding in your hands or, if you're sensible, resting on a table.

As you will notice, it's even heavier than last year's and that's because it contains more than 500 new entries. You will also notice that the reviews are no longer anonymous, each now having the critic's initials at the end. This is to let you know whom to blame when you disagree, apoplectically, with the writer's views.

And there's another small but significant change. The definitions of the star ratings, from one to five, have been modified to suggest that even good films may contain flaws and the worst – well, not the worst, but the otherwise negligible – can have some redeeming quality, even if it's only the background music.

This could be helpful – though sprinkling stars, like largesse, over movies is something I always avoided doing. All criticism, amateur or professional, is subjective, but what it should boil down to is simple: is this film good or bad of its kind?

Leave it at that. Because when you start distributing stars there's a danger that personal prejudices may creep in. For example, a critic is reviewing two films – one a musical, and he loves musicals, the other a western, and he hates westerns. (This is hypothetical, of course, because no intelligent person hates westerns.)

Both movies are good of their kind and the critic, honest fellow, acknowledges that. But isn't it possible that, obliged to award stars, he will give more to his beloved musical than to the detested western, thus misleading his readers?

A case in point: a few years ago a well-known critic on a respected national newspaper gave five stars to *Austin Powers: the Spy Who Shagged Me* and only four to *Citizen Kane*. It's true – he did.

Now, OK, maybe he prefers scatological slapstick to serious drama, in which case he's to be pitied. But to suggest, as he did, that *Austin Powers* is actually better than one of the finest films ever made borders on lunacy.

To be fair, after howls of ridicule from his readers, he allotted *Citizen Kane* an extra star the following week, thus suggesting that both films were equally good of their kind.

Well, perhaps they are, but even that is highly debatable. Here, though, is the good news – this sort of thing couldn't happen in the *Radio Times Guide to Films* because its critics tend to be genre specialists. Therefore *Austin Powers* and *Citizen Kane* are reviewed by different people, experts in their respective fields.

And that brings us to one of the strongest appeals of guides like this. Yes, certainly, they're written by people who know their stuff and give a good indication of what's worth watching and what isn't.

But their very opinions, however informed, are likely to get your adrenalin flowing. When I was reviewing films on TV, my brother, Rick, to whom I am very close, watched my programmes carefully and then decided to avoid most of the movies I liked while hurrying to those I didn't. In short, our tastes are different.

So it is with the *Radio Times* guide and me. When you look inside you will see, for example, that it and I disagree seriously over *Titanic*, to which I would award a reluctant two stars only because it perks up when the ship begins to sink – and if in so saying I have spoilt the ending for you, I'm sorry.

But who is right – the guide or me? Well, I am, of course, just as you are when you in turn agree or disagree with both of us. That's part of the fun of the book. Its greatest value, however, lies in the reviews of the films that you have not seen. Read and assess them carefully, acknowledging or ignoring the allotted stars as you will. They could save you wasting a lot of time and, better still, guide you towards a great deal of pleasure.

Above all, though, enjoy.

How to use this guide

The 2006 edition has more than 500 new entries, making for the greatest number of films ever included in the guide: a grand total of 21,284. For the first time, we've also included initials to identify the author of each and every review. (You'll find a list of our contributors on page 8.) Many of our film reviewers are genre specialists, many are film historians, but all of them are experts whose opinions are informed and, we trust, enlightening. We hope you'll find it interesting and useful to know with whom you agree (or disagree)!

The new entries include all films released in UK cinemas during the past 12 months, a selection of straight-to-video titles, and movies made for television which have been screened during the year. And, as always, we aim to be the most up-to-date film guide on the market, with a large number of reviews for movies that hadn't made it to cinemas in the UK at the time of going to press, thanks to the advance work of our dedicated reviewers. Making the way for these new entries are older TV movies and straight-to-video films.

The *Radio Times Guide to Films* covers a wide range of cinema; we haven't limited our selection to mainstream UK and US movies, but also include European films, significant and interesting works of world cinema, and even underground and experimental films – a cross-section of 20th- and 21st-century cinema, rather than a comprehensive guide to a narrower range of movies. Some film series may be represented here selectively, to give you a feel for their character and style. Many straight-to-video movies are included, as are made-for-television films, except for British TV productions, which are treated as dramas, rather than films, by *Radio Times*.

Recommendations and criticisms from our readers are invaluable. We welcome your contributions, and we'd like to hear your comments and suggestions. You can write to: *Radio Times Guide to Films*, Room A1080, BBC Worldwide Ltd, 80 Wood Lane, London W12 0TT; or email us at films.radiotimes@bbc.co.uk.

Kilmeny Fane-Saunders

TITLES

Films are listed under the titles by which we consider them to be best known in the United Kingdom and these titles are listed as they appear on screen. While many foreign-language movies are listed under their English title, others are listed under their original title, especially if they are particularly famous, or were released theatrically or on video/DVD under that title.

Alternative titles If you cannot find the film you are looking for in the main A-Z section, refer to the appendix of alternative titles at the back of the book. You should find a cross-reference to the film you're seeking there. The alternative-title appendix is not a complete index of all the alternative titles and/or foreign-language titles by which a film might be known – it is a selective appendix, designed to help you find the film you're looking for.

Alphabetisation Titles are listed alphabetically, ignoring definite and indefinite articles (a, the, an, including foreign-language articles such as les, das, il, el; place names being the exception, eg Los Angeles). Titles are also listed alphabetically by word, with initials counting as an individual word. For example, *Back to the Future* comes before *Backdraft*; *LA Confidential* before *Labyrinth*. Punctuation, such as apostrophes and colons, is also ignored. A hyphen equals a space (ie *Life-Size* comes before *Life Stinks*, not before *Lifespan*).

STAR RATING

The star rating assigned a film reflects the opinion of the reviewer. Many older films may be considered "difficult" (*The Battleship Potemkin*) or offensive (Leni Riefenstahl's *Triumph of the Will*) by today's audiences but will still have a high star rating because of their importance and/or their technical excellence.

The star ratings also help rank a movie within its genre. For example, a TV movie may be granted five stars in comparison to other TV movies (*The Autobiography of Miss Jane Pittman* versus *Danielle Steel's Fine Things*); but you wouldn't compare it to *Citizen Kane*. Action film *True Lies* rates four stars when compared to *Delta Force 2*, but you wouldn't compare it to *Kiss Me Kate*. And, within each star rating (since we don't give half stars) there may be a band of quality, some two-star movies being better than others. (The handful of "lost films" included in this guide have no star rating, as no prints exist.) Times change, perspectives change and, on occasion, so do our star ratings, as we are constantly reassessing and updating our entries.

As a guideline, the star ratings mean:

★ poor
★★ could be worse
★★★ worth watching
★★★★ very good
★★★★★ outstanding

Films with only one star are probably so bad that most viewers wouldn't want to waste a couple of hours of their time on such efforts. Those that have two will have some points of merit and a number of faults, but may appeal to fans of a certain actor or genre, or as a moderately pleasant time-waster. Granting three stars means that, although a film is not without flaws, the positives definitely outweigh the negatives. Films that have four stars are beyond just being watchable – within their genre, they're special, and any flaws will be minor ones. Those films granted five stars are the outstanding, brilliant few. In fact, there are only 778 in our guide – roughly 3.5 per cent of the total.

GENRE
Set by our editorial team to give you some indication of the type of film, as a guide only. See also the notes regarding the Appendix of Five-and Four-Star Films.

YEAR
Wherever possible, this is the copyright year of the film, not the year in which it was released. When we have been unable to confirm a copyright year, we have used the year of production; if that cannot be confirmed, we have used the year of first release.

COUNTRY OF ORIGIN
The country, or countries, of origin is determined by which country/countries financed the film, not where it was made.

US – United States
UK – United Kingdom
Alg – Algeria
Arg – Argentina
Arm – Armenia
Aus – Australia
Ban – Bangladesh
Bel – Belgium
Bra – Brazil
Bul – Bulgaria
Can – Canada
Chi – China
Chil – Chile
Col – Colombia
Cos R – Costa Rica
Cro – Croatia
Cub – Cuba
Cur – Curaçao
Cyp – Cyprus
Cz – Czechoslovakia (up to 1993)
Cz Rep – Czech Republic (1993 and onwards)
Den – Denmark
E Ger – East Germany (1945-90)
Ecu – Ecuador
Egy – Egypt
Fin – Finland
Fr – France
Ger – Germany (pre-1945, post-1990)
Gr – Greece
HK – Hong Kong
Hun – Hungary
Ice – Iceland
Ind – India
Ire – Republic of Ireland
Is – Israel
It – Italy
Iv C – Ivory Coast
Jam – Jamaica
Jpn – Japan
Kaz – Kazakhstan
Ken – Kenya
Lux – Luxembourg
Mac – Macedonia
Mex – Mexico
Mor – Morocco
Nep – Nepal
Neth – Netherlands
NZ – New Zealand
Nic – Nicaragua
Nor – Norway
Pak – Pakistan
Pan – Panama
Phil – Philippines
Pol – Poland
Por – Portugal
P Ric – Puerto Rico
Rom – Romania
Rus – Russia (pre-1922, post-1996)
S Afr – South Africa
S Kor – South Korea
Sen – Senegal
Ser – Serbia
Sing – Singapore
Sp – Spain
Sri L – Sri Lanka
Swe – Sweden
Swi – Switzerland
Tai – Taiwan
Thai – Thailand
Tun – Tunisia
Tur – Turkey
Urug – Uruguay
USSR – Soviet Union (post-1922, pre-1996)
Viet – Vietnam
W Ger – West Germany (1945-90)
Yug – Yugoslavia
Zim – Zimbabwe

BRITISH BOARD OF FILM CLASSIFICATION CERTIFICATES
Where possible we give the current BBFC video certificate. For post-1982 films not on video in the UK, we list the original UK cinema certificate. Definitions of the current video certificates appear at the foot of each page in the A–Z section of films. We haven't included older cinema certificates (X, AA, A), since we consider them no longer a useful guide. However, films that received a U certificate pre-1982 are listed with that certificate (once a U always a U, but the fact that *Abbott and Costello Meet Dr Jekyll and Mr Hyde* rated an X back in 1953 is amusing but not very helpful).

In 2002, the BBFC introduced a new certificate for cinema only – 12A (children under 12 may view the film, when accompanied by an adult). A film not yet released on video/DVD at the time of going to press may carry this new certificate.

Note: there may be no certificate at all for foreign-language films, made-for-TV movies and films that did not receive a theatrical release in this country.

COLOUR
This refers to the original colour of the film, ie the colour in which it was made: black and white, colour, tinted, sepia or a combination of these. Films that were originally made in black and white but now exist in colourised versions will still be listed as "BW", ie black and white.

RUNNING TIME
Where there is a certificate, the running time relates to that certificate: that is, a video running time if the film is available on video in the UK, or the theatrical running time if not. Made-for-TV movies, unless they have been released on video/DVD, are not given with a running time; and for some more obscure films, it may not have been possible to ascertain the running time so none has been given. In the case of some silent films, we may only have been able to obtain information regarding the number of reels; and since the actual running length could vary dramatically depending on the speed at which the film is screened, no running time is listed.

REVIEWS
These have been written by our team of reviewers, and the opinions expressed in them are their own, based on their expertise and critical judgement.

LANGUAGE INFORMATION
Where applicable, language information has been added to the end of the review. If we have been able to confirm whether a film is available in subtitled or dubbed versions, we have specified. If we have been unable to confirm this information, or if different versions of a film may be available, we have given the language of the film only (ie "A

German language film", versus "In French with English subtitles" and "Italian dialogue dubbed into English").

FAMILY VIEWING

Where available and appropriate, we have included a content warning at the end of the review. Where no advice as to the film's suitability has been given, please be guided by the BBFC certificate and the content of the review itself. For those films without a certificate, the reviewers' comments should give an indication of the content of the movie.

VIDEO AND DVD AVAILABILITY

[video icon] = available on video (Pal)

DVD = available on DVD (Region 2)

The information is correct at the time of going to press and is based on availability in the UK only. Video/DVD availability means that, at some point, the film was released on video/DVD and does not mean that it is currently on a distributor's list. Only those films that have a valid BBFC video certificate are flagged as being available. Encryption technology means that videos and DVDs released in other countries may not be playable on standard equipment in the United Kingdom.

CAST LIST

For each film we have included a selected cast list of actors followed by the characters they play (where known). Famous people, when playing themselves in a film, appear with no character name. Generally, documentaries do not include a cast list.

Some actors are occasionally credited in different ways on different films. For example, early in his career, Charles Bronson used his real surname and was credited as Charles Buchinski. In these cases, we have printed the actor's name as he/she was credited on that film, followed in square brackets by the name under which that actor is listed in our index: eg Charles Buchinski [Charles Bronson].

A number – eg (1), (2) – after a person's name is an indicator that there is another person, of the same name, on our database.

In the case of animated films, the actor credited to a character is providing the voice only.

CREDITS

Each entry includes a director credit and a writer credit. In a small number of cases, we were unable to confirm the writer credit, and so none appears. In some cases we have given additional names of those who have contributed to a screenplay, such as the person responsible for the adaptation or for additional dialogue. There may also be additional credits for cinematography, music, costume design, art direction and others. These have been included if the reviewer has singled out this aspect of a film for special commendation, or if it received an award.

DIRECTORS' AND ACTORS' INDEXES

These are indexes to the films of the actors and directors that appear in this book, not complete filmographies. If an actor does not appear in the cast list for a film in the A–Z, then that film will not appear after the actor's name in the index. And if an actor or a director has only one film listed in the A–Z, his or her name has not been included in the index.

Index entries also include years of birth/death, which we have included where known, and regularly update. These have been exhaustively compiled and researched by consulting editor David Parkinson, who explains: "Dates are the most disputed item in film history. It's hard enough identifying years of release. But when the vanity of stars and the duplicity of studio publicity machines are taken into account, it becomes almost impossible to be 100 per cent accurate all the time. Each one has been checked against at least five reputable sources, with a majority decision accepted in the most contentious cases."

APPENDIX OF ALTERNATIVE TITLES

This is not a complete index of all the alternative titles and/or foreign-language titles by which a film might be known – it is a selective appendix, designed to help you find the film you're looking for.

APPENDIX OF AWARDS

International awards covered are the British Academy Film Awards ("Baftas"), Academy Awards ("Oscars"), Golden Globe Awards (from the Hollywood Foreign Press Association), the Cannes Film Festival and the Berlin Film Festival. Categories in the appendix are: best film, best foreign-language film, best director, best actor, best actress, best supporting actor, best supporting actress and best screenplay. For the Academy Awards, Baftas and Golden Globes, the year of the award relates to the year of the eligible films, not the event. For the Cannes and Berlin festivals, it is the year of the event.

For the Baftas and the Oscars we have included winners and nominees; for other events, winners only.

APPENDIX OF FIVE- AND FOUR-STAR FILMS

This includes all our five- and four-star films, listed by genre, with UK video and DVD availability. The headings under which the films are found are determined by the genre as specified in the individual entries in the A-Z of films. Those films that have multiple genres will appear several times in the appendix. *The English Patient* (1996), for example, appears three times in the appendix: under "War", "Romance" and "Drama". In some cases, a film may have strong enough elements of a certain genre to merit inclusion under additional headings, even when its "official genre" does not mention it: for example, *Titanic* (1997) is listed under "Epic", "Romance" and "Drama" (as per its *RT* genre "Epic romantic drama"), but also appears under "Disaster".

Contributing reviewers

DAVID PARKINSON (DP) has been reviewing for *Radio Times* since 1995. Specialising in foreign-language films, he is also a contributing editor on *Empire*. Among his books are *A History of Film* and *Mornings in the Dark: the Graham Greene Film Reader*.

ANDREW COLLINS (AC) has been the film editor of *Radio Times* since 2001. A former editor of *Empire*, he presented Radio 4's weekly film programme, *Back Row*, for two and a half years. He also co-presented *Collins & Maconie's Movie Club* for ITV.

DAVE ALDRIDGE (DA) is a former editor of *Film Review* magazine. He is currently film and video reviewer for BBC Radio 5 Live and a regular contributor to *Radio Times*.

KEITH BAILEY (KB) is a freelance writer based in Victoria, Canada. He is also the creator of *The Unknown Movies* (www.unknownmovies.com), a website devoted to obscure films.

BRIAN BAXTER (BB) has devoted his career exclusively to film. A former programmer for the National Film Theatre, he was Films Editor for BBC1 and 2. He has worked as a journalist since his teens, and is a regular contributor to *The Guardian*.

RONALD BERGAN (RB) has lectured on literature, theatre and film. A regular contributor to *The Guardian*, his numerous books on the cinema include biographies of the Coen Brothers, Sergei Eisenstein, Jean Renoir, Dustin Hoffman and Katharine Hepburn.

JOANNA BERRY (JB) began her career as a film journalist at the age of 18, writing for *Time Out* and *Film Review* before becoming reviews editor for *Empire*. She is currently film critic and celebrity editor for *eve* magazine.

MAJ CANTON (MC) is the author of the definitive *Complete Reference Guide to Movies and Miniseries Made for TV and Cable 1984-1994* and a second volume covering the years 1994-2001.

JASON CARO (JC) is a devotee of sci-fi, fantasy and thrillers and is a regular contributor to *Film Review* and *Ultimate DVD*, as well as several specialist science-fiction magazines.

ANGIE ERRIGO (AME) is a contributing editor on *Empire* and a Sony Award-winning broadcaster and regular on the BBC Radio 2 Arts programme. Errigo is also on the jury for the *Evening Standard* British Film Awards.

ALLEN EYLES (AE) is a film historian whose many books include studies of such stars as Humphrey Bogart and James Stewart. He founded the magazine *Focus on Film*, is a former editor of *Films and Filming*, and currently edits *Picture House*.

LESLIE FELPERIN (LF) is the film editor of *The Big Issue* and a film critic for *Variety*. She also regularly contributes to *The Independent*, *Empire*, *Heat*, *Uncut* and *Sight & Sound*.

JOHN FERGUSON (JF) has written about film for publications such as the *Daily Mail*, *Film Review* and the *NZ Business Times*. He is now based in New Zealand and writes for publications such as *Billboard* and the Australian video magazine *Screen Print*.

DICK FIDDY (DF) is a freelance writer/researcher and is a member of the programming team at the National Film Theatre. He is also contributing editor on the *Radio Times Guide to Comedy*.

SLOAN FREER (SF) is a film journalist with a passion for horror and alternative culture. She has contributed to publications including *The Observer*, *The Face*, *Total Film* and *Bizarre*.

LORIEN HAYNES (LH) is a celebrity editor at *eve* magazine and a freelance film journalist who reviews and interviews for *Observer Screen*, *Hello!*, *Elle*, *Red* and *Film Review*, among other publications.

STEPHEN HUGHES (StH) is the producer of Radio 4's film programme *Back Row*.

TOM HUTCHINSON (TH) has been reviewing films for newspapers and trade magazines for 30 years. He worked with director J Lee Thompson on several scripts, including *The Men in the Cage*. His most recent book is *Rod Steiger: Memoirs of a Friendship*.

ALAN JONES (AJ) has reviewed fantasy, horror and sci-fi movies for *Radio Times* since 1995. He has written two documentaries on the Italian horror directors Mario Bava and Dario Argento. He also organises London's FrightFest festival.

ROBYN KARNEY (RK) is a former critic and interviewer for *Empire* magazine. Her books include *The Foreign Film Guide* with Ronald Bergan, *A Star Danced: the Life of Audrey Hepburn* and *A Singular Man: Burt Lancaster*.

KAREN KRIZANOVICH (KK) juggles writing about films with producing. She is a regular contributor to *Radio Times*, has her own column in *Ms London* magazine and has reviewed films for *Empire*, *Cosmopolitan* and *The Independent*.

FRANCES LASS (FL) is a film and music journalist who has contributed to *Time Out*, *Radio Times*, *Sunday Times*, *The Times* and the *Daily Mail*.

DAVID MCGILLIVRAY (DM) is a broadcaster and journalist.

BRIAN PENDREIGH (BP) is a former cinema editor of *The Scotsman* and currently writes for a wide range of publications in the UK and overseas, including *The Times* and *Herald*. He won the Ainsworth Film Journalist of the Year award in 1995 and 1999.

ROBERT SELLERS (RS) is an established freelance writer and the author of a number of film biographies. His latest book is *Very Naughty Boys – the Inside Story of HandMade Films*.

SIMON ROSE (SR) is a former film critic of *The Mirror* and author of both *The Essential Film Guide* and *The Classic Film Guide* as well as *Collins Gems Classic Films*.

ADAM SMITH (AS) was deputy editor of *Empire* between 1997 and 2000 and remains the magazine's Senior Features Writer. He is also a freelance journalist and has written about movies for *Q*, *GQ*, *FHM*, *Arena*, *The Observer* and *The Independent*.

ADDITIONAL REVIEWERS
Omar Ahmed (OA), Narinda Flora (NF), Peter Freedman (PF), Ian Freer (IF), John Gammon (JG), Sue George (SG), Scott Hamilton and Chris Holland (ST), Sue Heal (SH), John Marriott (JM), Gareth Moses (GM), David Oppedisano (DO), Stella Papamichael (SP), Chris Pearson (CLP), Jamie Russell (JR), Rupert Smith (RSm), Neil Smith (NS), Rose Thompson (RT), Adrian Turner (AT), Damon Wise (DW), Tom Vallance (TV)

Editorial team

Edited by Kilmeny Fane-Saunders (KFS)
Contributing editors Andrew Collins, David Parkinson
Consulting editor (*Radio Times* Film Unit) Sue Oates (SO)
***Radio Times* Film Unit** Colin Prior, Jeremy Aspinall (JA), Lucy Barrick (LB), John Carroll, Tom Folley, Rupert Frost, Nick Funnell (NPF), Jamie Healy, Tony Peters, Anna Richards (AR), Susannah Straughan (SS)
Additional design Ranjika De Silva
Database designed by Mark Ginns

Sources
Certain data published under licence from Baseline II Inc.
Certain data published under licence from the British Board of Film Classification.
Some material is verified from the Motion Picture Guide, published by Cinebooks, New York, with kind permission.

A-Z of films

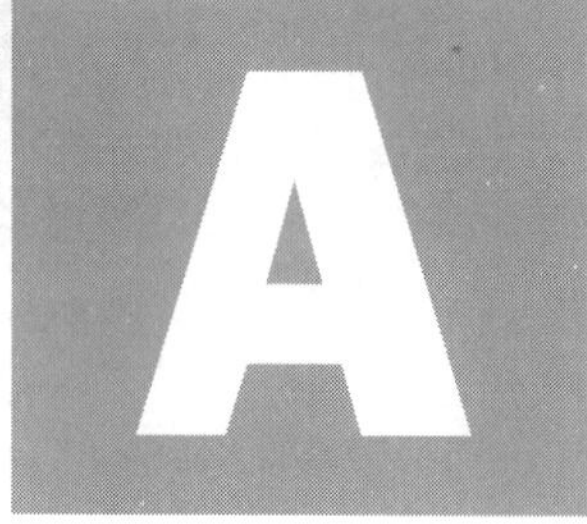

ABC Africa ★★★★

Documentary 2001 · Ir/Fr · Colour · 85mins

Invited by the United Nations to study the endeavours of the Uganda Women's Effort to Save Orphans, director Abbas Kiarostami went to the country merely to scout locations but ended up shooting all the footage for the documentary on unaccustomed digital video. Once more he was working with children, but for the first time it was outside his homeland and using a format with which he was unfamiliar. Nevertheless, Iran's foremost film-maker has succeeded in locating reasons for optimism among the nearly two million orphans left helpless by the ravages of war and Aids. There are tragic tales and images of utter desolation, yet this is an unsentimental documentary about remarkable resilience and compassion. DP. In English and Farsi with subtitles.

Dir Abbas Kiarostami • *Cinematographer* Seifollah Samadian

ABCD ★★★

Drama 1999 · US · Colour · 105mins

With its acronymic title translating as "American-Born Confused Dashi", this is an assured insight into the cultural and generational problems facing Indians resident in the States. Krutin Patel's debut feature hones in on the human drama, but there's also plenty of wry humour at the expense of both traditionalists and progressives, as 20-something accountant Faran Tahir and his ad exec sister Sheetal Sheth try to live their own lives without alienating (too much) their interventionist mother Madhur Jaffrey. DP

Madhur Jaffrey *Anju* • Faran Tahir *Raj* • Sheetal Sheth *Nina* • Aasif Mandvi *Ashok* • David Ari *Brian* ■ *Dir* Krutin Patel • *Scr* James McManus, Krutin Patel, from a story by Krutin Patel

A Bout de Souffle ★★★★★ PG

Drama 1959 · Fr · BW · 86mins

Inspired by *Gun Crazy*, Joseph H Lewis's B-movie *film noir*, and made with the assistance of François Truffaut and Claude Chabrol, this was the keystone of the French New Wave. A homage to such fatalistic heroes as Jean Gabin and Humphrey Bogart, Jean-Luc Godard's masterpiece employed just about every cinematic trick associated with the *nouvelle vague*: location shooting, direct sound, hand-held footage (masterfully shot by Raoul Coutard), jump cuts, in-jokes and visual tributes to master film-makers. Jean-Paul Belmondo is superbly shambolic as the petty thief whose brief dalliance with American newspaper vendor Jean Seberg precipitates his demise. The film's influence is incalculable. DP. In French with English subtitles. DVD

Jean-Paul Belmondo *Michel Poiccard/Laszlo Kovacs* • Jean Seberg *Patricia Franchini* • Van Doude *Journalist* • Daniel Boulanger *Police Inspector* • Henri-Jacques Huet *Antonio Berrutti* • Liliane Robin *Minouche* • Claude Mansard *Claudius Mansard* • Roger Hanin *Carl Zombach* • Jean-Pierre Melville *Parvulesco* • Richard Balducci *Tolmatchoff* • Jean-Luc Godard *Informer* ■ *Dir* Jean-Luc Godard • *Scr* Jean-Luc Godard, from a story by François Truffaut • *Cinematographer* Raoul Coutard

A-Haunting We Will Go ★★ U

Comedy 1942 · US · BW · 63mins

This is the second of the five indifferent pictures Laurel and Hardy made for 20th Century-Fox in the early 1940s. As the script was written while they were on tour, Laurel was denied the opportunity to add some much needed comic genius to this tiresome tale of crooks and coffins. DP

Stan Laurel *Stan* • Oliver Hardy *Ollie* • Harry A Jansen *Dante the magician* • Sheila Ryan *Margo* • John Shelton *Tommy White* • Don Costello (1) *Doc Lake* • Elisha Cook Jr *Frank Lucas* ■ *Dir* Alfred Werker • *Scr* Lou Breslow, from a story by Lou Breslow, Stanley Rauh

AI: Artificial Intelligence ★★★★ 12

Science-fiction fantasy drama
2001 · US · Colour · 139mins

Steven Spielberg's ambitious, dark-toned fable takes the story of Pinocchio, gives it a daring twist and decks it out with terrific special effects. Haley Joel Osment (*The Sixth Sense*) plays an android child, programmed to love and allocated to a couple whose own critically-ill son has been cryogenically frozen. When the real son recovers, the robot boy is left to fend for himself in a brutal world that doesn't want him. In a difficult role, Osment proves once again what a fine young actor he is, while Jude Law gives a showy performance as his guide-cum-protector. This is by far the director's bleakest work and Osment's desperate quest to become a "real" boy and win back the love of his human "mother" is a disturbing one. KFS DVD

Haley Joel Osment *David* • Jude Law *Gigolo Joe* • Frances O'Connor *Monica Swinton* • Brendan Gleeson *Lord Johnson-Johnson* • Sam Robards *Henry Swinton* • William Hurt *Prof Hobby (the Visionary)* • Jake Thomas *Martin Swinton* • Ben Kingsley *Specialist* • Robin Williams *Dr Know* • Meryl Streep *Blue mecha* ■ *Dir* Steven Spielberg • *Scr* Steven Spielberg, from a story by Ian Watson, from the short story *Supertoys Last All Summer Long* by Brian W Aldiss

AKA ★★ 18

Drama based on a true story
2002 · UK · Colour · 118mins

Drawing on his own past, director Duncan Roy seeks to achieve a visual means of conveying the social and emotional crises experienced by a runaway Romford teenager in this ambitious drama, but the end result unfortunately falls short. Matthew Leitch's bid to pass himself off in bohemian Paris as the son of socialite gallery owner Diana Quick seizes the attention, but loosens its grip with the introduction of Texan hustler Peter Youngblood Hills and gay roué George Asprey. DP. Contains swearing and drug abuse. DVD

Matthew Leitch *Dean Page* • Diana Quick *Lady Francine Gryffoyn* • Lindsey Coulson *Georgie Page* • George Asprey *David Glendenning* • Blake Ritson *Alexander Gryffoyn* • Peter Youngblood Hills *Benjamin* • Geoff Bell *Brian Page* • Bill Nighy *Uncle Louis Gryffoyn* ■ *Dir/Scr* Duncan Roy

A la Place du Coeur ★★ 15

Romantic drama 1998 · Fr · Colour · 107mins

Robert Guédiguian's follow-up to his acclaimed breakthrough picture, *Marius et Jeannette*, came as a surprise to many. Yet, for all its good intentions and the committed naturalism of the performances, this slice-of-life tale, about a white teenager (Laure Raoust) who embarks on an affair with a jailed young black (Alexandre Ogou), rings hollow. DP. In French with English subtitles. Contains swearing, nudity and sexual references.

Ariane Ascaride *Marianne* • Christine Brücher *Francine* • Jean-Pierre Darroussin *Joel* • Gérard Meylan *Franck* • Alexandre Ogou *Bébé* • Laure Raoust *Clim* ■ *Dir* Robert Guédiguian • *Scr* Jean-Louis Milesi, Robert Guédiguian, from the novel *If Beale Street Could Talk* by James Baldwin

A l'Attaque! ★★ 15

Comedy 2000 · Fr · Colour · 94mins

Robert Guédiguian's contrived comedy follows a pair of writers trying to lick their story into a successful screenplay. Had he concentrated on the nub of this screenplay – the struggles of a sidestreet garage to compete with the forces of commercialism – this could have been engaging. But the constant intrusion of Jacques Pieiller and Denis Podalydès, as the writers who keep changing their minds about the screenplay's focus, detracts from the film's human core. DP. In French with English subtitles.

Ariane Ascaride *Lola* • Pierre Banderet *Mr Moreau* • Gérard Meylan *Gigi* • Jacques Boudet *Pépé Moliterno* • Jean-Pierre Darroussin *Jean-Do* • Jacques Pieiller *Xavier* • Denis Podalydès *Yvan* ■ *Dir* Robert Guédiguian • *Scr* Jean-Louis Milesi, Robert Guédiguian

A Ma Soeur! ★★ 18

Drama 2001 · Fr/It/Sp · Colour · 81mins

Anaïs Reboux impresses as the grumpily plump 12-year-old envying glamorous Roxane Mesquida's fling with student Libero De Rienzo. This would have been a fascinating insight into corrupted innocence had Catherine Breillat concentrated on the shock of watching their graphically depicted sexual encounters in the sisters' shared holiday bedroom. But she concludes proceedings with a brutal incident of such calculated sensationalism that it devalues all that has gone before. DP. In French and Italian with English subtitles. DVD

Anaïs Reboux *Anaïs* • Roxane Mesquida *Elena* • Libero De Rienzo *Fernando* • Arsinée Khanjian *Mother* • Romain Goupil *Father* ■ *Dir/Scr* Catherine Breillat

A Nous la Liberté ★★★ U

Satire 1931 · Fr · BW · 83mins

Director René Clair's classic satire on modern life tells of an escaped convict who ends up running a gramophone factory and is then blackmailed by his cell-mate. Both end up as vagabonds. Made during the Depression, it chimed with audiences at the time who loved its mixture of music, comedy and radical politics. Clair's imagery of mass production with human automatons, led to the film to being banned by the left-wing government of Hungary and the right-wing government of Portugal. It was also the inspiration for Chaplin's *Modern Times*, and when Clair's producer wanted to take out a legal action for plagiarism, the director refused, saying he felt flattered. AT. In French with English subtitles. DVD

Henri Marchand *Emile* • Raymond Cordy *Louis* • Rolla France *Jeanne* • Paul Olivier *Paul Imaque* • Shelly Jacques *Paul* • André Michaud *Foreman* • Germaine Aussey *Maud* • Alexandre D'Arcy [Alex D'Arcy] *Gigolo* ■ *Dir/Scr* René Clair

A Propos de Nice ★★★★ U

Silent experimental documentary
1930 · Fr · BW · 27mins

At a time when documentarists across Europe were making "city symphonies", the French director Jean Vigo produced this delightful Riviera rhapsody. Vigo was one of the great screen poets, but the inspiration for this playful portrait clearly comes from the montage experiments of cinematographer Boris Kaufman's older brother, Dziga Vertov, the Polish director of the hugely influential *Man with a Movie Camera*. Brilliantly using transitions and parallel cutting, Vigo throws in some superb sequences, such as the sunbather turning into a skeleton and promenaders becoming strutting animals. Most famously, he employed a series of dissolves to strip a woman, a scene that was originally cut by British censors. DP

Dir/Scr Jean Vigo • *Cinematographer* Boris Kaufman

A Toute Vitesse ★★ 18

Drama 1996 · Fr · Colour · 81mins

Gaël Morel's directorial debut adheres closely to the theme of disaffected youth that inspired the film in which he made his name, André Téchiné's *Les Roseaux Sauvages*. He even recruits his co-star, Elodie Bouchez, to hold together a picture that admirably captures the language and attitudes of modern teenagers, before opting for some disappointingly formulaic resolutions. Patchy, but occasionally provocative. DP. In French with English subtitles. Contains swearing, nudity and violence.

Elodie Bouchez *Julie* • Pascal Cervo *Quentin* • Stéphane Rideau *Jimmy* • Meziane Bardadi *Samir* • Romain Auger *Rick* • Salim Kechiouche *Jamel* ■ *Dir* Gaël Morel • *Scr* Gaël Morel, Catherine Corsini

AVP: Alien vs Predator ★★★ 15

Science-fiction action thriller
2004 · US/UK/Cz Rep/Can/Ger · Col · 96m

In director Paul WS Anderson's sometimes inspired melding of two sci-fi horror franchises, an expedition heads for Antarctica after billionaire Lance Henriksen discovers a pyramid under the ice. This proves to be the venue for a Predator vs Alien smackdown, with the expedition's crew as the warm-up. The characterisation is nonexistent, but Sanaa Lathan shines during the thrilling finale. This guilty pleasure is all about slime-covered face-offs between monster-movie icons, and that's where Anderson really delivers. AJ. Contains violence. DVD

Sanaa Lathan *Alexa Woods* • Raoul Bova *Sebastian De Rosa* • Ewen Bremner *Graeme Miller* • Colin Salmon *Maxwell Stafford* • Lance Henriksen *Charles Bishop Weyland* • Tommy Flanagan *Mark Verheiden* • Joseph Rye *Joe Connors* • Agathe de la Boulaye *Adele Rousseau* ■ *Dir* Paul WS Anderson [Paul Anderson] • *Scr* Paul WS Anderson, from a story by Paul WS Anderson, Dan O'Bannon, Ronald Shusett, from characters created by Dan O'Bannon, Ronald Shusett, and from characters created by Jim Thomas, John Thomas

AWOL ★★ 18

Action thriller 1990 · US · Colour · 103mins

Although Jean-Claude Van Damme gawps blankly, at least his director Sheldon Lettich knows how to move the action along in this mildly efficient thriller. Balancing most of the tale between the sentimental, the risible and the hysterically overacted, Van Damme provides volleys of well crafted fisticuffs, and brings a certain humanity to his punch-drunk protagonist, a French legionnaire who's deserted to the States. JM. Contains violence, swearing, nudity. DVD

Jean-Claude Van Damme *Lyon Gaultier* • Harrison Page *Joshua* • Deborah Rennard *Cynthia* • Lisa Pelikan *Helene* • Ashley Johnson *Nicole* • Brian Thompson *Russell* • Voyo *Sergeant Hartog* • Michel Qissi *Moustafa* ■ *Dir* Sheldon Lettich • *Scr* Sheldon Lettich, Jean-Claude Van Damme, RN Warren, from a story by Jean-Claude Van Damme

A

Aaltra ★★★ 15

Black comedy road movie drama
2004 · Bel · BW · 93mins

Benoît Delépine and Gustave Kervern's trans-continental road movie is a grimly amusing and abrasively unpatronising study of physical disability. The co-directors take the lead roles as two resolutely unsympathetic Belgians who head to Finland to demand compensation from the manufacturers of the tractor that crushed them. Their antics have a cruel knockabout quality, as they exhibit cynical selfishness towards each other and those they meet. Dark, daring and very funny. DP. In English, French, Finnish and German with subtitles. Contains swearing and sex scenes.

Benoît Delépine *M Vives, the Commuter* • Gustave Kervern *Agricultural worker* • Aki Kaurismäki *Aaltra boss* • Jason Flemyng *English motocross owner* • Benoît Poelvoorde *Motocross fan* • Noel Godin *Chatty homeless man* • Isabelle Delépine *Wife* ■ *Dir/Scr* Benoît Delépine, Gustave Kervern

Aar Paar ★★★ U

Romantic drama 1954 · Ind · BW · 117mins

This previously overlooked Guru Dutt offering tinkers with the conventions of the Bollywood masala. The songs (many of which have since become standards) are woven more naturally into the fabric of the storyline, peripheral characters participate in the dance routines alongside the principals, and the camera roves more freely around the evocative backdrops. Dutt also headlines as the taxi driver who falls in love with the boss's daughter, played by Shyama. With its roguish humour and larcenous subplots involving kidnappers and safecrackers, this is well worth its overdue recognition. DP. In Hindi with English subtitles. [video] DVD

Guru Dutt *Kalu* • Shyama *Nikki* • Shakila *Dancer (captain's moll)* • Johnny Walker *Rustom* ■ *Dir* Guru Dutt • *Scr* Nabendu Ghosh, Abrar Alvi

Aaron Loves Angela ★★★

Romantic action drama
1975 · US · Colour · 99mins

The son of one of African-American cinema's leading pioneers, Gordon Parks Jr was best known for *Superfly* when he took this unexpected detour from hard-hitting blaxploitation. Set in Harlem, its combination of star-crossed romance, gang rivalry and urban deprivation invites comparisons with *West Side Story*, especially as the girl is a Puerto Rican. But the focus isn't restricted to Irene Cara and her black beau, Kevin Hooks, as the director adds coarse comedy, the music of José Feliciano and uncompromising action to the explosive mixture. DP

Kevin Hooks *Aaron* • Irene Cara *Angela* • Moses Gunn *Ike* • Robert Hooks *Beau* • Ernestine Jackson *Cleo* • Leon Pinkney *Willie* ■ *Dir* Gordon Parks Jr • *Scr* Gerald Sanford

ABBA the Movie ★★★ U

Music documentary
1977 · Swe/Aus · Colour · 96mins

This visual record of the Swedish superstars' 1977 Australian tour shows why they were billed as the most popular group in the world and became the pinnacle of kitsch glam. There is a story, involving a journalist desperate to secure an interview with the band, but really it's just an excuse to hear every major hit, from *Waterloo* to *Dancing Queen*. Sing along and say, "Thank you for the music". AJ [video]

Robert Hughes *Ashley* • Tom Oliver *Bodyguard/Bartender/Taxi driver* • Bruce Barry *Radio station manager* • Stig Anderson *Manager* • Anni-Frid Lyngstad • Benny Andersson • Bjorn Ulvaeus • Agnetha Faltskog ■ *Dir/Scr* Lasse Hallström

Abbott and Costello Go to Mars ★ U

Comedy 1953 · US · BW · 73mins

Having run out of exotic backgrounds on Earth, the duo board a spaceship and think they've landed on Mars when they're in the middle of the New Orleans Mardi Gras. Hijacked by a couple of bank robbers, they escape to Venus, which is populated solely by former Miss Universe contestants under Mari Blanchard as Queen Allura. The stars' comic inventiveness was at a standstill and the tired routines won't have improved with age. AE [video]

Bud Abbott *Lester* • Lou Costello *Orville* • Robert Paige *Dr Wilson* • Mari Blanchard *Allura* • Martha Hyer *Janie* • Horace McMahon *Mugsy* • Anita Ekberg *Venusian woman* ■ *Dir* Charles Lamont • *Scr* DD Beauchamp, John Grant, from a story by Howard Christie, DD Beauchamp

Abbott and Costello in Hollywood ★★ U

Comedy 1945 · US · BW · 82mins

This typical Abbott and Costello vehicle offers some interesting behind-the-scenes glimpses of MGM at work; the film also includes guest appearances by the likes of Lucille Ball, Jackie "Butch" Jenkins and director Robert Z Leonard. The plot has Bud and Lou as a barber and shoeshine boy respectively, attempting to be Hollywood agents, though it's just a peg on which to hang a series of comic routines. TS

Bud Abbott *Buzz Kurtis* • Lou Costello *Abercrombie* • Frances Rafferty *Claire Warren* • Robert Stanton [Bob Haymes] *Jeff Parker* • Jean Porter *Ruthie* • Warner Anderson *Norman Royce* • Mike Mazurki *Klondike Pete* ■ *Dir* S Sylvan Simon • *Scr* Nat Perrin, Lou Breslow

Abbott and Costello in Society ★★

Comedy 1944 · US · BW · 75mins

This very average Abbott and Costello flick relies too much on slapstick gags which don't seem as funny today as they did during the war. The same can be said for the plot, which has Bud and Lou as two dumb plumbers who gatecrash a posh weekend party. There's some charming fluff involving 1940s vocalist Marion Hutton (Betty's sister) as a taxi driver with the hots for Kirby Grant. Substantial footage from the WC Fields classic *Never Give a Sucker an Even Break* was hijacked to boost the production values of the chase sequences. TS

Bud Abbott *Eddie Harrington* • Lou Costello *Albert Mansfield* • Marion Hutton *Elsie Hammerdingle* • Kirby Grant *Peter Evans* • Margaret Irving *Mrs Roger Winthrop* • [Ann Gillis] *Gloria Winthrop* • Arthur Treacher *Pipps* • Thomas Gomez *Drexel* ■ *Dir* Jean Yarbrough • *Scr* John Grant, Edmund L Hartmann, Hal Fimberg, Sid Fields, Clyde Bruckman, from a story by Hugh Wedlock Jr, Howard Snyder

Abbott and Costello in the Foreign Legion ★★ U

Comedy 1950 · US · BW · 76mins

Between meeting Bela Lugosi and the Invisible Man, Abbott and Costello took time out to cavort on existing sets on Universal's backlot, and they could well have done with some scriptwriting help. The duo were also beginning to show their age physically, and Lou in particular was starting to look a little grotesque. TS [video]

Bud Abbott *Jonesy* • Lou Costello *Lou Hotchkiss* • Patricia Medina *Nicole* • Walter Slezak *Axmann* • Douglass Dumbrille *Hamud El Khalid* ■ *Dir* Charles Lamont • *Scr* Leonard Stern, John Grant, Martin Ragaway, from a story by DD Beauchamp

Abbott and Costello Meet Captain Kidd ★★ U

Comedy 1952 · US · Colour · 70mins

A rare colour outing for Bud and Lou as they are shanghaied by pirate Charles Laughton in his race for buried loot with Hillary Brooke's Anne Bonney. Slapsticking way below even their usual standard, the boys are as much use on the treasure hunt as a map without an X, while Laughton shamelessly spoofs his performance as Captain Bligh in the 1935 version of *Mutiny on the Bounty*. DP

Bud Abbott *Rocky Stonebridge* • Lou Costello *Oliver "Puddin' Head" Johnson* • Charles Laughton *Captain Kidd* • Hillary Brooke *Captain Bonney* • Fran Warren *Lady Jane* • Bill Shirley *Bruce Martingale* • Leif Erickson *Morgan* ■ *Dir* Charles Lamont • *Scr* Howard Dimsdale, John Grant

Abbott and Costello Meet Dr Jekyll and Mr Hyde ★★★ PG

Comedy 1953 · US · BW · 73mins

It sounds like the double date from hell, but this is one of Bud and Lou's livelier outings. The boys play a couple of sacked cops who hope to impress Inspector Reginald Denny by capturing the monster that is terrorising London. There are even a couple of laughs in the wax museum and rooftop chase scenes, although the romance between Helen Wescott and Craig Stevens slows things down a touch. Boris Karloff juicily hams up the roles of the mad scientist and his alter ego, making Jekyll seem every bit as sinister as Hyde. DP [video]

Bud Abbott *Slim* • Lou Costello *Tubby* • Boris Karloff *Dr Jekyll/Mr Hyde* • Helen Westcott *Vicky Edwards* • Craig Stevens *Bruce Adams* • Reginald Denny *Inspector* ■ *Dir* Charles Lamont • *Scr* Lee Loeb, John Grant, from the novel *The Strange Case of Dr Jekyll and Mr Hyde* by Robert Louis Stevenson

Abbott and Costello Meet Frankenstein ★★★ PG

Comedy 1948 · US · BW · 79mins

Bud and Lou often just weren't funny enough by themselves. So Universal International set up a series of confrontations from the horror films that had been such a success for the studio in the 1930s. This was one of the naively funniest, with the boys delivering crates to a wax museum (of course) unaware that their consignment contains Count Dracula and Frankenstein's monster. Bela Lugosi and Lon Chaney Jr as the Wolf Man play it straight enough to be naturally comic, so the real comedians end up as stooges. TH [video]

Bud Abbott *Chick* • Lou Costello *Wilbur* • Lon Chaney Jr *Lawrence Talbot/the Wolf Man* • Bela Lugosi *Dracula* • Glenn Strange *The Monster* • Lenore Aubert *Sandra Mornay* • Jane Randolph *Joan Raymond* • Frank Ferguson *Mr McDougal* • Charles Bradstreet *Dr Steven* ■ *Dir* Charles T Barton [Charles Barton] • *Scr* Robert Lees, Frederic Rinaldo, John Grant, from the novel *Frankenstein* by Mary Shelley

Abbott and Costello Meet the Invisible Man ★★ U

Comedy 1951 · US · BW · 78mins

Bungling private eyes Bud and Lou are hired by boxer Arthur Franz to get him off a murder rap in this acceptable timepasser. There is a modicum of mystery beneath the thin layer of comedy, and the highlight is a boxing bout in which Bud gets an invisible hand to hold off the champ. DP [video]

Bud Abbott *Bud Alexander* • Lou Costello *Lou Francis* • Nancy Guild *Helen Gray* • Arthur Franz *Tommy Nelson* • Adele Jergens *Boots Marsden* • Sheldon Leonard *Morgan* • William Frawley *Detective Roberts* • Gavin Muir *Dr Philip Gray* ■ *Dir* Charles Lamont • *Scr* Robert Lees, Frederic I Rinaldo, John Grant, from the novel *The Invisible Man* by HG Wells

Abbott and Costello Meet the Keystone Cops ★★ U

Comedy 1955 · US · BW · 75mins

A meeting some might want to miss. Intimidating Bud and slaphappy Lou are sold a rundown film studio in the early days of Hollywood, though they turn out to be better stuntmen than producers. Inept timing stifles the gags, but the chase finale is up there with the best of the original Keystones. However, the real interest lies in a guest appearance from Mack Sennett – the comedy giant from a time when silence really was golden. TH [video]

Bud Abbott *Harry Pierce* • Lou Costello *Willie Piper* • Fred Clark *Joseph Gorman/Sergei Trumanoff* • Lynn Bari *Leota Van Cleef* • Frank Wilcox *Snavely* • Maxie Rosenbloom *Hinds* • Henry Kulky *Brakeman* • Sam Flint *Conductor* • Mack Sennett ■ *Dir* Charles Lamont • *Scr* John Grant, from a story by Lee Cobb

Abbott and Costello Meet the Killer, Boris Karloff ★★ PG

Comedy mystery 1949 · US · BW · 80mins

This sort of title really should have caught on. Picture, if you will, "Bill and Ted Meet the Terminator, Arnold Schwarzenegger". The only snag is that Boris Karloff is not the killer. In fact, he's scarcely in the movie at all, although his charlatan swami does have the best scenes, notably the one in which he urges the mesmerised Lou Costello to top himself. The rest of this wobbly whodunnit revolves around bellboy Lou being scared out of his ample skin by clues that have vanished before hotel detective Bud Abbott lays eyes on them. DP [video]

Bud Abbott *Casey Edwards* • Lou Costello *Freddie Phillips* • Boris Karloff *Swami Talpur* • Lenore Aubert *Angela Gordon* • Gar Moore *Jeff Wilson* ■ *Dir* Charles T Barton [Charles Barton] • *Scr* Hugh Wedlock Jr, John Grant, Howard Snyder

Abbott and Costello Meet the Mummy ★ U

Comedy 1955 · US · BW · 76mins

Abbott and Costello ended 15 years at Universal with this dismal low-budget attempt to excavate some humour from a story of buried treasure in Egypt. Having run through the rest of the studio's horror gallery earlier, Bud and Lou now stir up the Mummy (here played by minor actor Eddie Parker) who's a rather lifeless figure compared to the likes of Dracula and the Wolf Man. At least character actress Marie Windsor brings waspish authority to her role of villainess. AE [video]

Bud Abbott *Peter* • Lou Costello *Freddie* • Marie Windsor *Madame Rontru* • Michael Ansara *Charlie* • Dan Seymour *Josef* • Kurt Katch *Dr Zomer* • Richard Karlan *Hetsut* • Richard Deacon *Semu* • Eddie Parker *Klaris, the mummy* ■ *Dir* Charles Lamont • *Scr* John Grant, from a story by Lee Loeb

Abby ★★

Blaxploitation horror
1974 · US · Colour · 89mins

Noted Shakespearean actor William Marshall (*Blacula*) unleashes the evil African spirit of Eshu in this virtual copy of *The Exorcist*, made for the blaxploitation market by hack director William Girdler. Following Marshall to America, Eshu possesses minister's wife Carol Speed, who predictably starts talking dirty, sleeping around and vomiting. Successful legal action by Warner Bros makes this sluggish addition to the black-slanted genre a difficult-to-see 1970s artefact. AJ

A

William Marshall (2) *Bishop Garnet Williams* • Carol Speed *Abby Williams* • Terry Carter *Reverend Emmett Williams* • Austin Stoker *Cass Potter* • Juanita Moore *Mama Potter* ■ *Dir* William Girdler • *Scr* G Cornell Layne, from a story by William Girdler, Gordon C Layne [G Cornell Layne]

The Abdication ★★

Historical drama
1974 · UK · Colour · 100mins

Liv Ullmann steps into Garbo's shoes by playing Queen Christina, who abdicates the Swedish throne and heads for Rome, wanting to be accepted as a Catholic and undergoing a searching inquisition from Cardinal Peter Finch. Having already played Pope Joan and fresh from *Lost Horizon*, Ullmann looks as if she's about to break into a schmaltzy song. Anthony Harvey directs, presumably in the hope of turning this piece of stodge into another *Lion in Winter*. AT

Peter Finch *Cardinal Azzolino* • Liv Ullmann *Queen Christina* • Cyril Cusack *Oxenstierna* • Graham Crowden *Cardinal Barberini* • Michael Dunn *The Dwarf* • Lewis Fiander *Father Dominic* • Kathleen Byron *Queen Mother* • James Faulkner *Magnus* • Ania Marson *Ebba Sparre* ■ *Dir* Anthony Harvey • *Scr* Ruth Wolff, from her play

Abduction ★★

Erotic crime drama
1975 · US · Colour · 94mins

A low-budget curiosity, mainly because of its striking similarities with the real-life Patty Hearst case. In this one, Judith-Marie Bergan is a poor little rich girl who gets a radical makeover when she is kidnapped by American urban terrorists. It's exploitational fare, with politics largely taking a back seat, and it's not exactly a high point in the careers of movie veterans Dorothy Malone and Lawrence Tierney. JF

Judith-Marie Bergan *Patricia* • David Pendleton *Dory* • Gregory Rozakis *Frank* • Leif Erickson *Mr Prescott* • Dorothy Malone *Mrs Prescott* • Lawrence Tierney *FBI agent* • Presley Caton *Angie* • Catherine Lacy *Carol* ■ *Dir* Joseph Zito • *Scr* Kent E Carroll, from the book *Black Abductor* by Harrison James

The Abduction Club ★★★ 12

Period adventure
2002 · UK/Fr/Ire/Ger · Colour · 92mins

This romp has a pleasingly anachronistic undertone that prevents it from feeling like a Sunday evening serial. Set in 18th-century Ireland, when second sons were wont to kidnap heiresses in order to persuade them to marry, Stefan Schwartz's boisterous adventure is soon slowed by stereotypical characters and clichéd dialogue. However, Daniel Lapaine and Matthew Rhys are dashing as the headstrong suitors seeking to keep spirited sisters Sophia Myles and Alice Evans out of the clutches of cad Liam Cunningham. DP [VIDEO] DVD

Daniel Lapaine *Byrne* • Matthew Rhys *Strang* • Sophia Myles *Anne Kennedy* • Alice Evans *Catharine Kennedy* • Edward Woodward *Lord Fermoy* • Liam Cunningham *John Power* • Patrick Malahide *Sir Myles* ■ *Dir* Stefan Schwartz • *Scr* Bill Britten, Richard Crawford

Abel ★★★ 15

Black comedy 1986 · Neth · Colour · 102mins

Abel, played by writer/director Alex Van Warmerdam, is a 31-year-old man who has never left home – literally. After failing to make progress with doctors and psychiatrists, his strict father attempts to teach him basic social skills by introducing a female into the household. Abel is accused of having an affair and gets thrown out on to the streets, where he meets a kind-hearted stripper. This weird Dutch film about obsessive family values is a classy rite-of-passage comedy full of whimsical amusement. AJ. In Dutch with English subtitles.

Alex Van Warmerdam *Abel* • Henri Garcin *Abel's father* • Olga Zuiderhoek *Abel's mother* • Annet Malherbe • Loes Luca ■ *Dir/Scr* Alex Van Warmerdam

Abel Gance's Beethoven ★★★

Biographical romance
1936 · Fr · BW · 115mins

Abel Gance, the great Romantic of French cinema, idolised Ludwig van Beethoven, the great Romantic of German music. Unfortunately, the loss of sound for Beethoven and the coming of sound for Gance were almost equally agonising. Gance was not at his best with dialogue, as this rather leaden biopic demonstrates. But it does have the expected visual flourishes, such as the poignant sequence when the hero loses his hearing, revealed by the silent shots of violins, bells and birds singing. The powerful actor Harry Baur is well cast as Beethoven. RB. In French with English subtitles.

Harry Baur *Ludwig van Beethoven* • Annie Ducaux *Thérèse de Brunswick* • Jany Holt *Giulietta Glucciardi* • Jean-Louis Barrault *Karl* • Jane Marken *Esther* • Jean Debucourt *Le Comte Gallenberg* • André Nox *Humpholz* ■ *Dir* Abel Gance • *Scr* Steve Passeur, Abel Gance

Abendland ★★★ 18

Drama
1999 · Ger/Por/Neth · Colour · 146mins

Emasculated by unemployment, Wolfgang Michael wanders his desolate town in an impenetrable torpor that finally drives his girlfriend, Verena Jasch, out of his life and into prostitution. But their everyday tragedy pales beside the Tarkovsky-esque encounter with an eccentric bellmaker, the sight of some paedophiles bidding for a small child and the discovery of her body in the river. The technical accomplishment somewhat undermines the nihilism of the action, but this is still a sobering experience, and puts director Fred Kelemen among Europe's offbeat elite. DP. In German with English subtitles.

Verena Jasch *Leni* • Wolfgang Michael *Anton* • Adolfo Assor *Bell founder* • Isa Hochgerner *Nina* ■ *Dir/Scr* Fred Kelemen

Aberdeen ★★★

Drama 2000 · UK/Nor/Swe · Colour · 113mins

Hinging on a volatile relationship between father and daughter, this is a road trip where the journey is essentially emotional, with Lena Headey and Stellan Skarsgård both excellent as the pair. Sent to Oslo with orders to bring her alcoholic father back to Aberdeen, Headey scuppers what should have been a straightforward trip with a bout of lounge-rage at Oslo airport and they are forbidden a flight. Fuelled by alcohol (Skarsgård), coke (Headey) and anger (both), it's touch and go whether they'll make it without concussing each other with their hefty emotional baggage. LH

Stellan Skarsgård *Tomas* • Lena Headey *Kaisa* • Ian Hart *Clive* • Charlotte Rampling *Helen* • Louise Goodall *Nurse* • Jason Hetherington *Perkins* ■ *Dir* Hans Petter Moland • *Scr* Kristin Amundsen, Hans Petter Moland, from a story by Lars Bill Lundholm

Aberration ★★ 18

Science-fiction horror thriller
1997 · Aus/NZ · Colour · 89mins

This chiller about lethal lizards is a formulaic affair. The setting is a remote wooded area, where the local wildlife has been wiped out by a mysterious force. The culprits turn out to be cunning, mutant reptiles who soon start tucking into human meat as well. Director Tim Boxell lays on lashings of gags and gore, but it is all very derivative. JF. Contains violence, swearing and nudity. [VIDEO]

Pamela Gidley *Amy* • Simon Bossell *Marshall* • Valery Nikolaev *Uri* • Norman Forsey *Mr Peterson* • Helen Moulder *Mrs Miller* ■ *Dir* Tim Boxell • *Scr* Darrin Oura, Scott Lew

Abhijaan ★★★

Drama 1962 · Ind · BW · 150mins

This was the closest cinema pioneer Satyajit Ray ever came to making a mainstream melodrama and even then he only assumed the reins of this dramatisation after Bijoy Chatterjee (who was a personal friend) suffered a crisis of confidence after a single day's shooting. Soumitra Chatterjee reveals a darker side as a cab driver who falls among smugglers after losing his job and finds himself torn between a Catholic schoolteacher (Ruma Guha Thakurta) and a prostitute (Bollywood superstar Waheeda Rehman). DP. In Bengali with English subtitles.

Soumitra Chatterjee *Narsingh* • Waheeda Rehman *Gulabi* • Ruma Guha Thakurta *Neeli* • Gyanesh Mukherjee *Joseph* • Charuprakash Ghosh *Sukhanram* • Robi Ghosh *Rama* ■ *Dir* Satyajit Ray • *Scr* Satyajit Ray, from the novel by Tarashankar Bannerjee

Abie's Irish Rose ★★ U

Silent comedy 1928 · US · BW · 108mins

A maudlin silent version of Anne Nichols's hit Broadway play about an Irish girl who marries a Jewish boy and starts up a feud between their two families. Directed by Victor Fleming, who would make *Gone with the Wind* a decade later, the film was mightily berated by the *New Yorker*, whose critic, the waspish Dorothy Parker, wrote: "They gave me the best view... they put me behind a post." TH

Jean Hersholt *Solomon Levy* • Charles Rogers *Abie Levy* • Nancy Carroll *Rosemary Murphy* • J Farrell MacDonald *Patrick Murphy* • Bernard Gorcey *Isaac Cohen* • Ida Kramer *Mrs Isaac Cohen* • Nick Cogley *Father Whalen* • Camillus Pretal *Rabbi Jacob Samuels* ■ *Dir* Victor Fleming • *Scr* Julian Johnson, Herman Mankiewicz, from the play by Anne Nichols

Abie's Irish Rose ★★ U

Comedy 1946 · US · BW · 96mins

Eighteen years after Victor Fleming's silent version, this tale of a Jewish boy and an Irish girl who fall in love seems even more dumb and sluggish in this mawkish makeover from producer Bing Crosby and director Edward Sutherland. Joanne Dru, Richard Norris and Michael Chekhov head the cast, while the screenplay is by the original playwright, Anne Nichols – not that it helps, though. TH

Joanne Dru *Rosemary* • Richard Norris *Abie* • Michael Chekhov *Solomon Levy* • JM Kerrigan *Patrick Murphy* • George E Stone *Isaac Cohen* • Vera Gordon *Mrs Cohen* • Emory Parnell *Father Whalen* • Art Baker *Rabbi Samuels* • Eric Blore *Hotel manager* ■ *Dir* Edward Sutherland [A Edward Sutherland] • *Scr* Anne Nichols, from her play • *Producer* Bing Crosby

Abilene Town ★★★

Western 1945 · US · BW · 91mins

Randolph Scott made virtually nothing but westerns after the Second World War and in this early example he's the marshal of Abilene, the town where the cattle drives end. Bringing prosperity as well as trouble, the rowdy cowboys dare to disturb the church service with their six-gun salute to Ann Dvorak's singing in the local saloon. Based on a novel by Ernest Haycox (who also co-wrote the screenplay for *Stagecoach*), it's a lively stew of rather familiar confrontations, with a spirited Rhonda Fleming as the grocer's daughter who tries to keep Scott from doing what a man has to do. AE

Randolph Scott *Dan Mitchell* • Ann Dvorak *Rita* • Edgar Buchanan *Bravo Trimble* • Rhonda Fleming *Sherry Balder* • Lloyd Bridges *Henry Dreiser* • Helen Boice *Big Annie* • Howard Freeman *Ed Balder* • Richard Hale *Charlie Fair* • Jack Lambert *Jet Younger* ■ *Dir* Edwin L Marin • *Scr* Harold Shumate, from the novel *Trail Town* by Ernest Haycox

Abjad ★★★ PG

Romantic drama
2003 · Iran/Fr · Colour · 112mins

The Iranian authorities took a dim view of Abolfazl Jalili's autobiographical study of a teenager in constant conflict with his family and Islam. Set during the days before the Islamic Revolution in 1980, the film explores the validity of the arts and the noblest interpretation of the Koran. But equally contentious is Mehdi Morady's crush on Mina Molania, the daughter of a Jewish cinema owner. While the visuals are pretty perfunctory, the performances are creditably strong. DP. In Farsi with English subtitles. Contains some swearing and violence.

Mehdi Morady *Emkan* • Mina Molania *Maassoum* • Abdolreza Akbary ■ *Dir/Scr* Abolfazl Jalili

The Abominable Dr Phibes ★★★★ 15

Horror 1971 · UK · Colour · 90mins

Vincent Price's role as an ex-vaudevillian madman living in a secret underground mechanical world is his only self-originated monster and is superbly tailored for the horror maestro. Phibes is a deformed maniac with a florid sense of style and an inclination to ham, who concocts a divinely ingenious revenge, gruesomely inspired by ancient plagues, on the surgeons he holds responsible for the death of his wife. Full of gaudy Art Deco excess, surprise charm and sardonic violence, this deadpan send-up is a classy delight. Originally billed with the tag-line "Love means never having to say you're ugly"! Price reprised the role the following year in *Dr Phibes Rises Again*. AJ [VIDEO] DVD

Vincent Price *Dr Anton Phibes* • Joseph Cotten *Dr Vesalius* • Hugh Griffith *Rabbi* • Terry-Thomas *Dr Longstreet* • Virginia North *Vulnavia* • Aubrey Woods *Goldsmith* • Susan Travers *Nurse Allan* • Alex Scott (1) *Dr Hargreaves* • Peter Gilmore *Dr Kitaj* • Edward Burnham *Dr Dunwoody* • Peter Jeffrey *Inspector Trout* • Maurice Kaufman *Dr Whitcombe* ■ *Dir* Robert Fuest • *Scr* James Whiton, William Goldstein

The Abominable Snowman ★★★ PG

Horror 1957 · UK · BW · 86mins

Based on Nigel (*Quatermass*) Kneale's television play, this subtle Hammer horror follows two men with opposing views who go on a Yeti expedition to the Himalayas. Gun-runner Forrest Tucker plans to capture and exploit the legendary creature, while botanist Peter Cushing thinks research is more important. The man-beast turns out to have a surprise for both in this gripping slice of monster macabre. Tensely directed by Val Guest, the film uses eerie claustrophobia to convey a taut paranoid atmosphere that makes you overlook the fakeness of the studio-built mountains. AJ [VIDEO] DVD

Forrest Tucker *Tom Friend* • Peter Cushing *Dr John Rollason* • Maureen Connell *Helen Rollason* • Richard Wattis *Peter Fox* • Robert Brown *Ed Shelley* • Michael Brill *Andrew McNee* ■ *Dir* Val Guest • *Scr* Nigel Kneale, from his TV play

U = SUITABLE FOR ALL Uc = SUITABLE FOR ALL, ESPECIALLY FOR YOUNG CHILDREN (VIDEO ONLY) PG = PARENTAL GUIDANCE

Abouna ★★★ PG

Drama 2002 · Chad/Fr · Colour · 80mins

Having considered the impressions of a returning exile in *Bye Bye Africa*, Mahamat-Saleh Haroun examines the plight of those left behind by migrant workers in this wry, occasionally tragic, but ultimately optimistic study of life on the Chad-Cameroon border. Dispelling the sub-Saharan cinematic myth of towns having a purely negative impact on families and communities, the film also dares to be gently critical of conditions in the strict Koranic school to which teenager Ahidjo Mahamat Moussa and his asthmatic younger brother Hamza Moctar Aguid are sent. DP. In Chad Arabic with English subtitles. [VIDEO] DVD

Ahidjo Mahamat Moussa *Tahir Brahim* • Hamza Moctar Aguid *Amine Brahim* • Zara Haroun *Achta Brahim* • Mounira Khalil *Mute girl* • Koulsy Lamko *Mr Brahim* • Garba Issa *Master* ■ *Dir/Scr* Mahamat-Saleh Haroun

About a Boy ★★★★ 12

Romantic comedy drama
2002 · Ger/US/Fr/UK · Colour · 96mins

Nick Hornby's answer to Bridget Jones gets to the big screen via a surprising source, with *American Pie* directors Chris and Paul Weitz at the helm. But, unlike the Americanised version of Hornby's *High Fidelity*, this movie remains on home turf. Hugh Grant is on excellent form as a 30-something, shallow singleton, who intends to use single-parent support groups to pick up women. One of his would-be conquests introduces him to troubled boy Nicholas Hoult and his suicidal mother Toni Collette. All goes surprisingly well until the confirmed bachelor falls for single mother Rachel Weisz, which puts a strain on their friendship. Funny and moving, this is an endearing examination of masculinity. LH [VIDEO] DVD

Hugh Grant *Will* • Toni Collette *Fiona* • Rachel Weisz *Rachel* • Nicholas Hoult *Marcus* • Isabel Brook *Angie* • Sharon Small *Christine* • Victoria Smurfit *Suzie* • Nicholas Hutchison *John* ■ *Dir* Chris Weitz, Paul Weitz • *Scr* Peter Hedges, Chris Weitz, Paul Weitz

About Adam ★★★ 15

Romantic comedy
2000 · Ire/UK /US · Colour · 92mins

Stuart Townsend stars as the charming layabout who bewitches every member of an outwardly respectable family. However, the onus in this multi-perspective tale falls on the siblings who succumb to his charms – bubbly torch singer Kate Hudson, bookish Frances O'Connor, sensible Charlotte Bradley and confused brother Alan Maher. Toning down the amorality of this sly social sitcom with some sparkling dialogue, writer/director Gerard Stembridge is greatly aided in the glossy telling of his tale by a willing cast and Bruno de Keyzer's attractive Dublin-based photography. DP. Contains swearing. [VIDEO] DVD

Stuart Townsend *Adam* • Frances O'Connor *Laura* • Charlotte Bradley *Alice* • Kate Hudson *Lucy Owens* • Alan Maher *David* • Tommy Tiernan *Simon* • Brendan Dempsey *Martin* • Cathleen Bradley *Karen* • Rosaleen Linehan *Peggy* • Roger Gregg *Professor McCormick* ■ *Dir/Scr* Gerard Stembridge

About Last Night... ★★★ 18

Comedy drama 1986 · US · Colour · 108mins

Rob Lowe and Demi Moore star in this 1980s look at the lifestyles and lovestyles of young city professionals. The film is based on David Mamet's play *Sexual Perversity in Chicago*, though you'd hardly know it, since it is a far slicker affair than Mamet would ever produce. Yet it does retain at least some of the playwright's insight and intelligence, while also providing its ration of entertainment. Lowe and Moore do well, although it is James Belushi, in an over-the-top supporting performance, who all but walks off with the show. PF. Contains swearing and nudity. [VIDEO] DVD

Rob Lowe *Danny Martin* • Demi Moore *Debbie Sullivan* • James Belushi *Bernie Litko* • Elizabeth Perkins *Joan* • George DiCenzo *Mr Favio* • Michael Alldredge *Mother Malone* • Robin Thomas *Steve Carlson* • Donna Gibbons *Alex* ■ *Dir* Edward Zwick • *Scr* Tim Kazurinsky, Denise DeClue, from the play *Sexual Perversity in Chicago* by David Mamet

About Mrs Leslie ★★ U

Romantic drama 1954 · US · BW · 103mins

This melodramatic tale tells the story in flashback of a couple of lovers who meet sporadically, spending time together once a year. Trouble is, he's the marvellously rugged Robert Ryan, and audiences may well wonder what on earth he sees in Shirley Booth. Distinguished film historian David Shipman called this "a very special film", but, despite the quality of the playing, this soap opera takes a lot of believing. TS

Shirley Booth *Mrs Vivien Leslie* • Robert Ryan *George Leslie* • Marjie Millar *Nadine Roland* • Alex Nicol *Ian McKay* • Sammy White *Harry Willey* • James Bell *Mr Poole* • Virginia Brissac *Mrs Poole* • Eileen Janssen [Eilene Janssen] *Pixie* ■ *Dir* Daniel Mann • *Scr* Ketti Frings, Hal Kanter, from the novel by Vina Delmar

About Sarah ★★★

Drama 1998 · US · Colour · 93mins

Mary Steenburgen, Kellie Martin and Marion Ross star in a made-for-TV drama about Sarah, a mentally disabled, unmarried woman who lives with her devoted mother. When her parent suddenly dies, Sarah's daughter becomes her legal guardian – a dramatic turn of events that is challenged in court by an aunt. Steenburgen was nominated for a Screen Actors Guild award for her moving performance. MC

Kellie Martin *Mary Beth* • Mary Steenburgen *Sarah* • Diane Baker *Lila* • Nick Searcy *Johnny* • Steven Gilborn *Lew Roth* • Marion Ross *Rose* • Karen Rauch *Grace* ■ *Dir* Susan Rohrer • *Scr* Susan Rohrer, Nancey Silvers, from a story by Susan Rohrer

About Schmidt ★★★★ 15

Satirical comedy drama
2002 · US · Colour · 120mins

In director Alexander Payne's endearing tragicomedy, Jack Nicholson plays a man who feels disconnected from his own life, a mood brought on by forced retirement, the sudden death of his wife and his daughter's impending marriage to a man he regards as a loser. His road trip to her wedding is the start of a very offbeat journey, as a subdued Nicholson gets to grips with new beginnings. It's funnier than it sounds as the film's quirky approach to this late-life crisis is typified by Schmidt's hilarious outpouring of pent-up bitterness in his letters to a Tanzanian orphan he has sponsored. While this is not a movie of great dramatic or comic peaks, the star's poignant performance extracts meaning from the smallest moments. JC. Contains swearing. [VIDEO] DVD

Jack Nicholson *Warren Schmidt* • Hope Davis *Jeannie* • Dermot Mulroney *Randall Hertzel* • Kathy Bates *Roberta Hertzel* • Len Cariou *Ray* • Howard Hesseman *Larry* • June Squibb *Helen Schmidt* • Harry Groener *John* ■ *Dir* Alexander Payne • *Scr* Alexander Payne, Jim Taylor, from the novel by Louis Begley

Above and Beyond ★

Second World War drama
1952 · US · BW · 122mins

Robert Taylor is given the job of dropping the Bomb on Hiroshima while his amour, Eleanor Parker, is moved into an army camp for security reasons, though she moves out because the laundry facilities aren't up to scratch. Poor dear, she hasn't been told what hubby's up to. It's all quite pathetic, really, trivialising a major historic event and patronising to women even in 1952. AT

Robert Taylor (1) *Col Paul Tibbets* • Eleanor Parker *Lucy Tibbets* • James Whitmore *Maj Uanna* • Larry Keating *Maj Gen Vernon C Brent* • Larry Gates *Capt Parsons* • Marilyn Erskine *Marge Bratton* • Stephen Dunne [Steve Dunne] *Maj Harry Bratton* • Robert Burton *Gen Samuel E Roberts* ■ *Dir* Melvin Frank, Norman Panama • *Scr* Beirne Lay Jr, Frank Panama

Above Suspicion ★★★★

Spy drama 1943 · US · BW · 90mins

Joan Crawford's presence is, for once, rather muted in this entertaining spy drama. Not only does she have to share star-billing with Fred MacMurray – they're honeymooning Americans caught up in espionage in pre-war Germany – but she also has to compete with the heel-clicking dynamism of Conrad Veidt and a marvellously villainous Basil Rathbone. So the star who could even upstage herself is considerably controlled, allowing the plot to gain proper prominence. The result is terrifically enjoyable escapism. TH

Joan Crawford *Frances Myles* • Fred MacMurray *Richard Myles* • Conrad Veidt *Hassert Seidel* • Basil Rathbone *Sig Von Aschenhausen* • Reginald Owen *Dr Mespelbrunn* • Richard Ainley *Peter Galt* • Cecil Cunningham *Countess* • Ann Shoemaker *Aunt Ellen* ■ *Dir* Richard Thorpe • *Scr* Keith Winter, Melville Baker, Patricia Coleman, from the novel by Helen MacInnes

Above the Rim ★★ 15

Sports drama 1994 · US · Colour · 93mins

Every hackneyed cliché is depressingly frog-marched before the camera in this sports-themed "gangsta ghetto" fare telling the tired tale of talented high school basketball player Duane Martin, torn between two friends on opposing sides of the law. One is drug-dealer Tupac Shakur who wants him playing on his tough inner-city team. The other is coach Leon, a former champion haunted by the death of his best friend. With no originality to commend it, director Jeff Pollack's saccharine saga relies on energetic basketball action to give it some pep. AJ [VIDEO]

Duane Martin *Kyle* • Leon *Shep* • Tupac Shakur *Birdie* • David Bailey *Rollins* • Tonya Pinkins *Mailika* • Marlon Wayans *Bugaloo* • Bernie Mac *Flip* ■ *Dir* Jeff Pollack • *Scr* Jeff Pollack, Barry Michael Cooper, from a story by Jeff Pollack, Benny Medina

Above Us the Waves ★★ U

Second World War drama
1955 · UK · BW · 95mins

Having failed with torpedoes, John Mills and his rookie crew set out in midget submarines to try to sink the German battleship *Tirpitz* in this rather disappointing Second World War action adventure. Riddled with stiff-upper-lipped stereotypes, this is one of those proud re-creations of an "against the odds" mission that were the staple of postwar British cinema. However, by opting to examine the cramped conditions of his characters rather than go overboard on their heroic exploits, director Ralph Thomas kills the pace of the picture. DP [VIDEO] DVD

John Mills *Commander Frazer* • John Gregson *Lt Alec Duffy* • Donald Sinden *Lt Tom Corbett* • James Robertson-Justice *Admiral Ryder* • Michael Medwin *Smart* • James Kenney *Abercrombie* • OE Hasse *Tirpitz Captain* • William Russell *Ramsey* • Thomas Heathcote *Hutchins* • Lee Patterson *Cox* • Theodore Bikel *German officer* • Anthony Newley *X2 engineer* ■ *Dir* Ralph Thomas • *Scr* Robin Estridge, from a story by CET Warren, James Benson

Abraham Lincoln ★★★ U

Drama 1930 · US · Tinted · 92mins

The last gasp of genius from the great silent film-maker, DW Griffith, this biopic of the American president has too much explanatory detail but boasts some remarkable visual set pieces. Written by Stephen Vincent Benet and Gerrit Lloyd, it stars Walter Huston as Lincoln and Una Merkel as his wife, and shows how the great man entered small-town politics before rising to the highest office in the land. Griffith was accused of racism in *The Birth of a Nation*; here, he shows a capacity for tolerance. TH [VIDEO] DVD

Walter Huston *Abraham Lincoln* • Una Merkel *Ann Rutledge* • Kay Hammond *Mary Todd Lincoln* • E Alyn Warren *Stephen Douglas* • Hobart Bosworth *Gen Robert E Lee* • Fred Warren *Gen US Grant* • Henry B Walthall *Col Marshall* • Frank Campeau *Gen Sheridan* ■ *Dir* DW Griffith • *Scr* Stephen Vincent Benet, Gerrit Lloyd • *Cinematographer* Karl Struss

Abraham Valley ★★★ PG

Drama 1993 · Por/Fr/Swi · Colour · 188mins

Manoel de Oliveira reworks Gustave Flaubert's *Madame Bovary* in this typically stylised outing. In translating the story to a wine-growing region of modern-day Portugal, novelist Augustina Bessa-Luis draws on her own acquaintances for inspiration. However, this is still very much the director's film, sprawling like an epic cinematic poem. As the lame adulteress whose amours scandalise her staid community, Leonor Silveira is deliciously dolorous, while Luís Miguel Cintra is doggedly decent as the doctor she marries after a troubled childhood. DP. In Portuguese with English subtitles.

Mario Barroso *Narrator* • Leonor Silveira *Ema Cardeano* • Cecile Sanz de Alba *Young Ema* • Luis Miguel Cintra *Carlos Paiva* • Rui de Carvalho *Paulino Cardeano* ■ *Dir* Manoel de Oliveira • *Scr* Manoel de Oliveira, from the novel *Vale Abraao* by Augustina Bessa-Luis

Abraxas ★ 15

Science-fiction adventure
1991 · Can · Colour · 86mins

Wrestler-turned-politician Jesse "the Body" Ventura is a 10,000-year-old law enforcer from the future in this cut-rate *Terminator*. His quest is to find renegade cop Sven-Ole Thorsen (doing a terrible Arnold Schwarzenegger impersonation) before he can kill his son who holds the key to universal peace. There's little on offer to either engage or entertain in this Canadian-made time-waster. AJ [VIDEO]

Jesse Ventura *Abraxas* • Sven-Ole Thorsen *Secundus* • Damian Lee *Dar* • Jerry Levitan *Hite* • Marjorie Bransfield *Sonia* • Ken Quinn *Carl* ■ *Dir* Damian Lee • *Scr* Damian Lee, David Mitchell

Abroad with Two Yanks ★★ U

Comedy 1944 · US · BW · 81mins

The two Yanks are loveable William Bendix and straight-up Dennis O'Keefe, and abroad is Australia, where the two marines find themselves competing for the attentions of the same woman, Helen Walker. It's likeable, lightweight stuff, without much substance, given pace and comedic style by veteran Allan Dwan. TS

William Bendix *Biff Koraski* • Helen Walker *Joyce Stuart* • Dennis O'Keefe *Jeff Reardon* • John Loder *Cyril North* • George Cleveland *Roderick Stuart* • Janet Lambert *Alice* • James Flavin *Sergeant Wiggins* • Arthur Hunnicutt *Arkie* ■ *Dir* Allan Dwan • *Scr* Charles Rogers, Wilkie Mahoney, Ted Sills

A

Absence of Malice ★★ PG

Drama 1981 · US · Colour · 111mins

Miami reporter Sally Field defames honest businessman Paul Newman in this big-issue drama, which is too sluggishly worthy to make any real impact. Sydney Pollack's direction is simply monotonous, even if ex-newspaperman Kurt Luedtke's script makes all the right liberal noises as Sally Field's journalist is manipulated by government leaks about Newman's Mafia relatives. But Melinda Dillon's performance as Newman's frightened alibi and the Newman-Field confrontation make this worth the time. TH. Contains swearing and some violence. VIDEO DVD

Paul Newman *Michael Gallagher* • Sally Field *Megan Carter* • Bob Balaban *Elliot Rosen* • Melinda Dillon *Teresa* • Luther Adler *Malderone* • Barry Primus *Waddell* • Josef Sommer *McAdam* • John Harkins *Davidek* ■ *Dir* Sydney Pollack • *Scr* Kurt Luedtke

Absence of the Good ★★★ 15

Thriller 1999 · US · Colour · 94mins

John Flynn is an under-rated and largely unsung action director and here he brings his usual no-frills professionalism to a familiar but quietly satisfying serial killer thriller. Stephen Baldwin (nicely understated for once) is the cop recovering from the accidental death of his son who becomes obsessed with a killer who is leaving a trail of bodies behind him as he searches for his own perfect home. You'll probably guess the identity of killer long before Baldwin does but Flynn sustains a believable air of suspense throughout. JF VIDEO DVD

Stephen Baldwin *Caleb Barnes* • Rob Knepper [Robert Knepper] *Glenn Dwyer* • Shawn Huff *Mary Barnes* • Tyne Daly *Marcia Lyons* • Allen Garfield *Lt Paul Taylor* ■ *Dir* John Flynn • *Scr* James Reid

The Absent-Minded Professor ★★★ U

Fantasy comedy 1961 · US · BW · 95mins

This warm-hearted slice of Walt Disney-style Americana stars likeable Fred MacMurray as the inventor of flying rubber. Wicked Keenan Wynn wants to steal it, and that's about the nub of the flub. The image of the flubber-driven family car crossing the Moon so inspired a young Steven Spielberg that he copied it to provide the most potent shot in *ET*, and eventually used it as the logo of his company, Amblin. A sequel, *Son of Flubber*, followed, as did a TV remake and a big screen offering, *Flubber*, starring Robin Williams. TS VIDEO

Fred MacMurray *Professor Ned Brainard* • Nancy Olson *Betsy Carlisle* • Keenan Wynn *Alonzo Hawk* • Tommy Kirk *Bill Hawk* • Leon Ames *Rufus Daggett* • Elliott Reid *Shelby Ashton* • Edward Andrews *Defence Secretary* • Wally Brown *Coach Elkins* ■ *Dir* Robert Stevenson • *Scr* Bill Walsh, from a story by Samuel W Taylor

Absolute Beginners ★★ 15

Musical 1986 · UK · Colour · 102mins

A dismal attempt to turn Colin MacInnes's cult novel about the birth of the teenage nation in Britain into an 1980s *Expresso Bongo* without the talents of Cliff Richard. Will fashion designer Patsy Kensit choose romance with trendy photographer Eddie O'Connell or toff couturier James Fox in this highly stylised view of 1950s pop culture and changing social mores? Songs by David Bowie, Ray Davies, Sade and the Style Council do help lighten the lively, if vacuous, load. AJ. Contains some swearing. VIDEO

Eddie O'Connell *Colin Young* • Patsy Kensit *Crepe Suzette* • David Bowie *Vendice Partners* • James Fox *Henley of Mayfair* • Ray Davies *Arthur* • Mandy Rice-Davies *Mum* • Steven Berkoff *Fanatic* • Sade *Athene Duncannon* ■ *Dir* Julien Temple • *Scr* Richard Burridge, Christopher Wicking, Don MacPherson, Michael Hamlyn, from the novel by Colin MacInnes

Absolute Power ★★★ 15

Crime drama 1996 · US · Colour · 116mins

Clint Eastwood composes the music (with Lennie Niehaus), directs and stars in this well-paced tale of high-level corruption. Clint plays a master burglar who, while robbing a mansion, witnesses President Gene Hackman indulging in a sadistic sex act that leads to the death of a rich man's wife. Eastwood and his estranged daughter (Laura Linney) must then stay one step ahead of the police and the president's men. Credibility is the main casualty of the piece, but William Goldman's taut script is well realised by thoughtful direction and the high-calibre cast. TH. Contains violence, swearing and sex scenes. VIDEO DVD

Clint Eastwood *Luther Whitney* • Gene Hackman *President Richmond* • Ed Harris *Seth Frank* • Laura Linney *Kate Whitney* • Scott Glenn *Bill Burton* • Dennis Haysbert *Tim Collin* • Judy Davis *Gloria Russell* • EG Marshall *Walter Sullivan* • Alison Eastwood *Art Student* • Kimber Eastwood *White House tour guide* ■ *Dir* Clint Eastwood • *Scr* William Goldman, from the novel by David Baldacci

Absolution ★ 15

Thriller 1978 · UK · Colour · 91mins

Lashings of Catholic guilt pervade this totally bonkers potboiler, with Richard Burton as the priest in a Catholic boarding school for boys whose protégé, Dominic Guard, runs away with hippy Billy Connolly and turns into a killer. Unlike red wine, the three years this movie spent on the shelf did not improve it, and it might never have been released had it not been for the star presence of Burton, the film's only point of interest. AT VIDEO

Richard Burton *Father Goddard* • Dominic Guard *Benjie Stanfield* • Billy Connolly *Blakey* • Andrew Keir *Headmaster* • Dai Bradley [David Bradley (2)] *Arthur Dyson* • Willoughby Gray *Brigadier Walsh* • Preston Lockwood *Father Hibbert* • Brook Williams *Father Clarence* ■ *Dir* Anthony Page • *Scr* Anthony Shaffer

The Abyss ★★★ 15

Science-fiction thriller
1989 · US · Colour · 139mins

For some, this was James Cameron's *Waterworld*, a bloated, sentimental epic from the king of hi-tech thrillers. Some of the criticism was deserved, but it remains a fascinating folly. Ed Harris is the leader of an underwater team working for an oil company that is pressed into service to rescue the crew of a crippled submarine. Harris is great in a rare leading-man role and there is first-rate support from Mary Elizabeth Mastrantonio as his estranged partner. Cameron excels in cranking up the tension within the cramped quarters and the awe-inspiring effects deservedly won an Oscar. JF. Contains violence, swearing. VIDEO DVD

Ed Harris *Bud Brigman* • Mary Elizabeth Mastrantonio *Lindsey Brigman* • Michael Biehn *Lieutenant Coffey* • Leo Burmester *Catfish De Vries* • Todd Graff *Alan "Hippy" Carnes* • John Bedford Lloyd *Jammer Willis* • JC Quinn *"Sonny" Dawson* • Kimberly Scott *Lisa "One Night" Standing* • Captain Kidd Brewer Jr *Lew Finler* • George Robert Klek *Wilhite* • Christopher Murphy *Schoenick* ■ *Dir/Scr* James Cameron • *Special Effects* Joe Unsinn, Joseph Viskocil

Acapulco Gold ★ 15

Action adventure 1976 · US · Colour · 87mins

Marjoe Gortner, a former evangelist turned actor, made his screen debut alongside American TV stalwart Robert Lansing in this barely watchable yarn about drug smugglers. Gortner is best remembered for his role as the psychotic religious freak in *Earthquake*. After that, he became a rather unlikely leading man of cheaply-made action movies and thrillers. AT VIDEO

Marjoe Gortner *Ralph* • Robert Lansing *Carl Solborg* • Ed Nelson *Hollister* • Randi Oakes *Sally* • John Harkins *Morgan Frye* • Lawrence Casey [Lawrence P Casey] *Gordon* ■ *Dir* Burt Brinckerhoff • *Scr* Don Enright, O'Brian Tomalin, from a story by David Lees, Stan Berkowitz

Accattone ★★★★ 15

Drama 1961 · It · BW · 111mins

Pier Paolo Pasolini made his directorial debut with this uncompromising study of life on the mean streets of Rome. Using a cast of actors drawn mostly from the city's slums, he manages to find a raw poetry in the dealings of the pimps, prostitutes and petty thieves who populate a world with which he was very familiar. Franco Citti brings an indolent charm to his portrayal of Accattone, a wastrel who's reluctant to work, yet insufficiently ruthless to live by crime. However, it's Pasolini's ability to re-create the teeming urban bustle, which he ironically counterpoints with the music of Bach, that gives this ultimately tragic tale its authenticity and power. DP. In Italian with English subtitles. VIDEO

Franco Citti *Vittorio Accattone* • Franca Pasut *Stella* • Silvana Corsini *Maddalena* • Paolo Guidi *Ascenza* • Adriana Asti *Amore* • Renato Capogna *Renato* ■ *Dir/Scr* Pier Paolo Pasolini

Accent on Youth ★★★

Romance 1935 · US · BW · 77mins

Paramount made two subsequent versions of Samson Raphaelson's hit Broadway comedy – *Mr Music* (1950) and *But Not for Me* (1959) – though neither had the sparkle of the first, directed with style by Wesley Ruggles (one of the original Keystone Kops). Sylvia Sidney escapes from her usual tragic roles to play a young secretary who falls for her middle-aged employer (the mellifluous-voiced Herbert Marshall). It is rather wordy, but fortunately most of those words are witty and crisply delivered. RB

Sylvia Sidney *Linda Brown* • Herbert Marshall *Steven Gaye* • Philip Reed *Dickie Reynolds* • Astrid Allwyn *Genevieve Lang* • Holmes Herbert *Frank Galloway* • Catherine Doucet *Eleanor Darling* • Ernest Cossart *Flogdell* • Donald Meek *Orville* ■ *Dir* Wesley Ruggles • *Scr* Herbert Fields, Claude Binyon, from the play by Samson Raphaelson

Accident ★★★★★ PG

Drama 1967 · UK · Colour · 100mins

Shimmeringly photographed by Gerry Fisher, Oxford and its surrounding countryside have never looked as beautiful as in this delicious exercise in character assassination. Dirk Bogarde and Stanley Baker seize upon every opportunity presented in Harold Pinter's merciless script, in which donnish civility only thinly veils the disappointment, lust and cruelty of unfulfilled middle age. Michael York, Delphine Seyrig and Vivien Merchant also give impeccable performances as those unfortunate enough to be caught up in Bogarde and Baker's mind games. Joseph Losey's relentless direction leaves the characters with few hiding places, particularly during the squirmingly uncomfortable Sunday supper. Brilliant film-making. DP VIDEO DVD

Dirk Bogarde *Stephen* • Stanley Baker *Charley* • Jacqueline Sassard *Anna* • Delphine Seyrig *Francesca* • Alexander Knox *Provost* • Michael York *William* • Vivien Merchant *Rosalind* • Harold Pinter *Bell* • Ann Firbank *Laura* ■ *Dir* Joseph Losey • *Scr* Harold Pinter, from the novel by Nicholas Mosley

Accidental Hero ★★★★ 15

Comedy drama 1992 · US · Colour · 113mins

Another of Stephen Frears's box-office failures, this was originally released as *Hero* in the States. Clearly influenced by Billy Wilder's *Ace in the Hole*, Frears's film is seriously under-rated, a drama about a plane crash in which Geena Davis's TV reporter is saved by a mystery Good Samaritan. We know it's Dustin Hoffman, but when Andy Garcia claims to be the "Angel of Flight 104" he's swept up in the media hysteria. Sometimes funny, often deeply cynical and pessimistic, it's a clever and brave picture. AT. Contains some swearing. VIDEO DVD

Dustin Hoffman *Bernie Laplante* • Geena Davis *Gale Gayley* • Andy Garcia *John Bubber* • Joan Cusack *Evelyn* • Kevin J O'Connor *Chucky* • Maury Chaykin *Winston* • Stephen Tobolowsky *Wallace* • Christian Clemenson *Conklin* • Tom Arnold *Chick* • Warren Berlinger *Judge Goines* ■ *Dir* Stephen Frears • *Scr* David Webb Peoples, from a story by Laura Ziskin, Alvin Sergent, David Webb Peoples

The Accidental Spy ★★ 12

Action adventure thriller
2001 · HK · Colour · 83mins

Sports equipment salesman Jackie Chan becomes the pawn in a hunt for missing phials of ultra-addictive opium in this pedestrian action adventure. Notable for its horrendous dubbing, this is one of Chan's least exciting projects. Though there's no denying his amazing physical abilities, the plot is patchy, the obligatory slapstick inappropriate, and the fight sequences repetitive. SF. Cantonese, Mandarin, Korean, Turkish and French dialogue dubbed into English. VIDEO DVD

Jackie Chan *Buck Yuen* • Eric Tsang *Many Liu* • Vivian Hsu *Yong* • Wu Hsing-kuo *Mr Zen* • Alfred Cheung *Cheung* • Kim Min-jeong *Carmen Wong* • Anthony Rene Jones *Philip Ashley* ■ *Dir* Teddy Chen • *Scr* Ivy Ho

The Accidental Tourist ★★★★ PG

Comedy drama 1988 · US · Colour · 116mins

The Big Chill may be the crowd-pleaser from director Lawrence Kasdan's portfolio, but this under-rated story remains one of his best. William Hurt is wonderful as the travel writer whose life falls apart when his young son dies and his wife (Kathleen Turner) leaves him; an Oscar-winning Geena Davis is the loopy dog trainer who helps him recover. While there are plenty of laughs along the way, an air of melancholy hangs over the piece as Kasdan movingly probes the emotions Hurt has so successfully buried. JF VIDEO

William Hurt *Macon Leary* • Kathleen Turner *Sarah Leary* • Geena Davis *Muriel Pritchett* • Amy Wright *Rose Leary* • Bill Pullman *Julian Edge* • Robert Gorman [Robert Hy Gorman] *Alexander Pritchett* • David Ogden Stiers *Porter Leary* • Ed Begley Jr *Charles Leary* • Bradley Mott *Mr Loomis* • Seth Granger *Ethan Leary* ■ *Dir* Lawrence Kasdan • *Scr* Frank Galati and Lawrence Kasdan, from the novel by Anne Tyler

Acción Mutante ★★ 18

Science-fiction horror
1993 · Sp · Colour · 94mins

Spanish director Alex de la Iglesia's debut feature begins in crackerjack comic book style as members of a disabled terrorist group in 2012 kidnap a debutante's daughter and hold her to ransom on a distant mining planet. But although gory, nasty and sexy in equal proportion, this Pedro Almodóvar-produced trash peters out into sci-fi on the verge of a nervous breakdown. AJ. In Spanish with English subtitles.

Antonio Resines *Ramón Yarritu* • Alex Angulo *Alex* • Frédérique Feder *Patricia Orujo* • Fernando Guillén [Fernando Guillen-Cuervo] *Orujo* • Enrique San Francisco *Novio Ultrajado* ■ *Dir* Alex de la Iglesia • *Scr* Alex de la Iglesia, Jorge Guerricaechevarría

L'Accompagnatrice

★★★★ PG

Second World War drama
1992 · Fr · Colour · 111mins

The Nazi occupation of France during the Second World War provides the backdrop for this compelling, but not always convincing, story of a young pianist who finds herself playing accompanist both on and off stage to her glamorous employer. François Truffaut's protégé Claude Miller has always excelled at directing young actresses and here he coaxes a bewitching performance from Romane Bohringer, who judges the differing shades of devotion, jealousy, timidity and regret to perfection. Elena Safonova has a ball as the singer torn between her collaborator husband and her Resistance hero lover. DP. In French with English subtitles.

Richard Bohringer *Charles Brice* • Elena Safonova *Irène Brice* • Romane Bohringer *Sophie Vasseur* • Bernard Verley *Jacques Ceniat* • Samuel Lebarthe *Jacques Fabert* • Nelly Borgeaud *Madame Vasseur* • Julien Rassam *Benoit Weizman* • Jean-Pierre Kohut Svelko *General Heller* • Claude Rich *Minister* ■ *Dir* Claude Miller • *Scr* Claude Miller, Luc Béraud, from the novel by Nina Berberova

Account Rendered ★

Crime drama 1957 · UK · BW · 61mins

Griffith Jones plays a city banker who is apparently knocked unconscious when his two-timing wife, Ursula Howells, is murdered. We've heard that one before, say the men from Scotland Yard, so it's up to the hapless Jones to prove his innocence. This sub-standard B-movie, directed by the tireless Peter Graham Scott, is notable only for an early screen appearance by Honor Blackman. AT

Honor Blackman *Sarah Hayward* • Griffith Jones *Robert Ainsworth* • Ursula Howells *Lucille Ainsworth* • Ewen Solon *Inspector Marshall* ■ *Dir* Peter Graham Scott • *Scr* Barbara S Harper, from the book by Pamela Barrington

Accused ★★

Crime drama 1936 · UK · BW · 87mins

In this backstage murder mystery, set in Paris, Douglas Fairbanks Jr and Dolores Del Rio star as a married couple who perform one of those acts in which the man is tied to a revolving table and the woman throws knives at him. There's a whiff of adultery in the air, and the show's spiteful star (Florence Desmond) winds up with a dagger in her heart. It's a modestly enjoyable effort that features Googie Withers in a minor role. AT

Douglas Fairbanks Jr *Tony Seymour* • Dolores Del Rio *Gaby Seymour* • Florence Desmond *Yvette Delange* • Basil Sydney *Eugene Roget* • Athole Stewart *President of Court* • Cecil Humphreys *Prosecuting counsel* • Esme Percy *Morel* • Edward Rigby *Alphonse* • George Moore Marriott *Dubec* • Cyril Raymond *Guy Henry* • Googie Withers *Ninette* ■ *Dir* Thornton Freeland • *Scr* Zoe Akins, George Barraud

The Accused ★★★

Crime drama 1949 · US · BW · 100mins

Loretta Young stars as the emotionally frigid professor of psychology who kills one of her students after he attempts to seduce her on a beach. Making the death look like a drowning accident, Young takes sleeping pills then heads for hospital where a serious case of flashback syndrome assails her, together with the cops and her lawyer. Hollywood was then at the height of its Freudian phase and you need to know what "cyclothymia" means to get the most out of this *noir*-ish drama. AT

Loretta Young *Wilma Tuttle* • Robert Cummings *Warren Ford* • Wendell Corey *Lt Ted Dorgan* • Sam Jaffe *Dr Romley* • Douglas Dick *Bill Perry* • Suzanne Dalbert *Susan Duval* • George Spaulding *Dean Rhodes* • Sara Allgood *Mrs Conner* ■ *Dir* William Dieterle • *Scr* Ketti Frings, from the novel *Be Still, My Love* by June Truesdell

The Accused ★★★★ 18

Drama 1988 · US · Colour · 105mins

Jodie Foster won her first best actress Oscar for her moving performance here as Sarah Tobias, the white-trash waitress who is gang raped in a bar and then endures public scrutiny so her attackers and those who watched can be brought to justice. Jonathan Kaplan's controversial movie raised a storm of protest on its release from those who believed its content veered too close to gratuitous voyeurism – yes, the rape scene is explicit and designed to shock. Both Foster and Kelly McGillis, as the crusading lawyer, are superb and the film raises some pointed questions about an emotive subject. JB. Contains violence, swearing, nudity, drug abuse. DVD

Jodie Foster *Sarah Tobias* • Kelly McGillis *Kathryn Murphy* • Bernie Coulson *Kenneth Joyce* • Leo Rossi *Cliff "Scorpion" Albrecht* • Ann Hearn *Sally Fraser* • Carmen Argenziano *Da Paul Rudolph* • Steve Antin *Bob Joiner* • Tom O'Brien *Larry* • Peter Van Norden *Paulsen* ■ *Dir* Jonathan Kaplan • *Scr* Tom Topor

Accused of Murder ★★

Murder mystery 1956 · US · Colour · 73mins

Poverty-stricken programmer thriller in which nightclub singer Vera Ralston is the prime suspect for the murder of shady lawyer Sidney Blackmer. David Brian, the investigating detective, is convinced of her innocence, while his sergeant Lee Van Cleef thinks she's guilty. A have-it-both-ways ending is the nail in the coffin of a tale which, considering that it was adapted from a novel by the usually reliable WR Burnett (who also co-scripted), is surprisingly weak. RK

David Brian *Lt Roy Hargis* • Vera Ralston *Ilona Vance* • Sidney Blackmer *Hobart* • Virginia Grey *Sandra* • Warren Stevens *Stan* • Lee Van Cleef *Sgt Lackey* ■ *Dir* Joseph Kane • *Scr* WR Burnett, Bob Williams, from the novel *Vanity Row* by WR Burnett

Ace Eli and Rodger of the Skies ★★

Adventure 1973 · US · Colour · 92mins

Stunt pilot Cliff Robertson teaches his son Eric Shea the tricks of his trade during the Roaring Twenties in this mediocre action adventure, notable for being based on a story by Steven Spielberg and for marking the screen debut of Broadway diva Bernadette Peters. Dogged by production problems and re-edited against director John Erman's wishes (the reason the name "Bill Sampson" appears on the credits), it's only worth catching for the breathtaking aerial photography. AJ

Cliff Robertson *Eli* • Pamela Franklin *Shelby* • Eric Shea *Rodger* • Rosemary Murphy *Hannah* • Bernadette Peters *Allison* • Alice Ghostley *Sister Lite* • Kelly Jean Peters *Rachel* • Don Keefer *Mr Parsons* ■ *Dir* Bill Sampson [John Erman] • *Scr* Chips Rosen [Claudia Salter], from a story by Steven Spielberg • *Cinematographer* David M Walsh

Ace High ★★★ 15

Spaghetti western comedy
1968 · It · Colour · 116mins

Eli Wallach is the nominal star of Giuseppe Colizzi's confidently directed spaghetti western – which is also known as *Four Gunmen of Ave Maria*, *Have Gun Will Travel* and *Revenge at El Paso*. However, aficionados will be drawn by the prospect of seeing one of the genre's most enduring double acts, Terence Hill and Bud Spencer – or Mario Girotti and Carlo Pedersoli to give them their proper names. Blonde-haired Hill carries the plot as an outlaw called Cat Stevens, who escapes from a necktie party, only to resume his life of crime while searching for the trio of drifters who landed him in jail in the first place. DP. An English/Italian language film.

Eli Wallach *Cacopoulos* • Terence Hill *Cat Stevens* • Bud Spencer *Hutch Bessy* • Brock Peters *Thomas* • Kevin McCarthy *Drake* ■ *Dir/Scr* Giuseppe Colizzi

Ace in the Hole ★★★★★

Satirical drama 1951 · US · BW · 111mins

"I've met some hard-boiled eggs in my time," says Jan Sterling to Kirk Douglas. "But you – you're 20 minutes!" Sterling's husband gets trapped in a cave; Douglas is the on-the-skids journalist who prolongs the man's agony while turning the accident into a major human interest story. Sterling co-operates with the scheme, making dough from the crowds who show up to watch the rescue operation. Few movies are as tough as this one, which is probably why it flopped at the box office – audiences don't like having their noses rubbed in their own dirt. However, it's one of Hollywood's great masterpieces, filled with Wilder's caustic wit and Douglas's trademark intensity. AT

Kirk Douglas *Chuck Tatum* • Jan Sterling *Lorraine* • Bob Arthur *Herbie Cook* • Porter Hall *Jacob Q Boot* • Frank Cady *Mr Federber* • Richard Benedict *Leo Minosa* • Ray Teal *Sheriff* • Lewis Martin *McCardle* • John Berkes *Papa Minosa* • Frances Dominguez *Mama Minosa* ■ *Dir* Billy Wilder • *Scr* Billy Wilder, Lesser Samuels, Walter Newman

Ace of Aces ★★★

First World War drama
1933 · US · BW · 75mins

This is one of several powerful deglamourisations of war from the pen of John Monk Saunders, who served in the Army Air Corps and won an Oscar for the story of *The Dawn Patrol* (1930). Richard Dix is the sculptor with pacifist leanings, goaded by his girlfriend (Elizabeth Allan) into becoming a First World War pilot. He turns into a cold-blooded ace of the air until a meeting with Allan in Paris leaves him disillusioned and resigned to his fate. Skilfully directed by J Walter Ruben, it may not be subtle but it still reverberates with feeling. AE

Richard Dix *Lt Rex Thorne* • Elizabeth Allan *Nancy Adams* • Ralph Bellamy *Major Blake* • Theodore Newton *Lt Foster Kelly* • Bill Cagney [William Cagney] *Lt Meeker* • Clarence Stroud *Lt Carroll Winstead* ■ *Dir* J Walter Ruben • *Scr* John Monk Saunders, HW Hanemann, from the story *Bird of Prey* by John Monk Saunders

The Ace of Hearts ★★★

Silent crime drama 1921 · US · BW · 75mins

The most celebrated of director Wallace Worsley's five collaborations with Lon Chaney was undoubtedly *The Hunchback of Notre Dame* (1923). But this adaptation is not without interest, even though the "Man of a Thousand Faces" takes something of a back seat, as waiter John Bowers allows sentiment to blunt his terrorist purpose. The introduction of the sinister assassination bureau is splendidly atmospheric, but the action becomes increasingly melodramatic once Bowers falls for co-conspirator Leatrice Joy. DP

Lon Chaney *Mr Farallone* • Leatrice Joy *Lilith* • John Bowers *Mr Forrest* • Hardee Kirkland *Mr Morgridge* • Raymond Hatton *The Menace* • Edwin N Wallock *Chemist* ■ *Dir* Wallace Worsley • *Scr* Ruth Wightman, from a story by Gouverneur Morris

Ace Ventura: Pet Detective ★★★★ 12

Comedy 1993 · US · Colour · 82mins

Doctor Dolittle meets *The Crying Game* in the smash hit that made Jim Carrey an overnight comedy sensation. The rubber-faced star plays a bumbling, Hawaiian-shirted detective hired to find the kidnapped dolphin mascot of the Miami Dolphins football team. Your reaction to the film will largely depend on whether you find Carrey's distinctive style of extremely physical comedy – often compared to that of Jerry Lewis – stupidly hilarious or downright annoying. Tom Shadyac directs with anarchic energy and quirky imagination. AJ. Contains swearing and sexual references. DVD

Jim Carrey *Ace Ventura* • Courteney Cox *Melissa* • Sean Young *Lieutenant Lois Einhorn* • Tone Loc *Emilio* • Dan Marino • Noble Willingham *Riddle* • Troy Evans *Podacter* • Raynor Scheine *Woodstock* • Udo Kier *Camp* • Frank Adonis *Vinnie* • Tiny Ron *Roc* ■ *Dir* Tom Shadyac • *Scr* Jack Bernstein, Tom Shadyac, Jim Carrey, from a story by Jack Bernstein

Ace Ventura: When Nature Calls ★★ PG

Comedy 1995 · US · Colour · 88mins

Even though Jim Carrey has as many detractors as supporters, there's no denying his breakthrough hit *Ace Ventura: Pet Detective* exuded a barmy charm, but this silly sequel is often just plain irritating. For this adventure, Ace is off to Africa where he gets mixed up with warring tribes and the hunt for a rare bat. The slim plot is just the flimsiest of excuses for Carrey's wacky grimaces, while the slapstick is relentlessly juvenile and director Steve Oedekerk's direction lacks the surreal inspiration of the original. JF DVD

Jim Carrey *Ace Ventura* • Ian McNeice *Fulton Greenwall* • Simon Callow *Vincent Cadby* • Maynard Eziashi *Ouda* • Bob Gunton *Burton Quinn* • Sophie Okonedo *Princess* • Tommy Davidson *Tiny warrior* • Adewale Hitu ■ *Dir/Scr* Steve Oedekerk

Aces and Eights ★★ U

Western 1936 · US · BW · 55mins

Poker fans will recognise the title immediately – the infamous "dead man's hand", held by Wild Bill Hickock as he was shot in the back and killed by gambler Jack McCall on the night of 2 August 1876 in Deadwood City. The estimable Tim McCoy is fine as the gambler trying to clear himself of murder. McCoy may defeat the villains, but not the programme-filler plot and slim production values of this run-of-the-mill western. TS

Tim McCoy *Gentleman Tim Madigan* • Luana Walters *Juanita Hernandez* • Rex Lease *Jose Hernandez* • Wheeler Oakman *Arce Morgan* • Charles Stevens *Capt Felipe* • Earl Hodgins [Earle Hodgins] *Marshal* ■ *Dir* Sam Newfield • *Scr* Arthur Durlan

Aces High ★★★ PG

First World War action drama
1976 · UK · Colour · 108mins

Jack Gold's stout antiwar statement actually takes its cue from an early sound film, 1930's *Journey's End*, but transposes the action from the trenches to the skies. It is here that the film finds its conviction, in the form of dogfight sequences that succeed in being both thrilling and horrifying. Back at base, however, where eager First World War flier Peter Firth gradually

A

comes to understand the cynicism of his superior, Malcolm McDowell, events are not as well realised. JM. Contains violence. DVD

Malcolm McDowell *Gresham* • Christopher Plummer *Sinclair* • Simon Ward *Crawford* • Peter Firth *Croft* • John Gielgud *Headmaster* • Trevor Howard *Lt Col Silkin* • Richard Johnson *Colonel Lyle* • Ray Milland *Brigadier Whale* ■ *Dir* Jack Gold • *Scr* Howard Barker, from the film *Journey's End* by James Whale, from the play by RC Sherriff

Aces: Iron Eagle III ★★ 15

Action adventure 1992 · US · Colour · 94mins

A far cry from its predecessors, this was John Glen's first feature after directing five James Bond movies, and the sense of anticlimax is there for all to see. Yet this vaguely silly enterprise is not without its pleasures. Louis Gossett Jr returns as the USAF ace who recruits his pals at a flying circus to deliver a South American village from the clutches of a drug baron. The final *Iron Eagle* appeared in 1995. DP. Contains swearing, violence.

Louis Gossett Jr *Colonel Charles "Chappy" Sinclair* • Rachel McLish *Anna* • Christopher Cazenove *Palmer* • Sonny Chiba *Horikoshi* • Horst Buchholz *Leichman* • Paul Freeman *Kleiss* • Ray Mancini *Chico* ■ *Dir* John Glen • *Scr* Kevin Elders, from characters created by Kevin Elders, Sidney J Furie

Achilles ★★ U

Action adventure 1962 · It · Colour · 117mins

This Italian-made, would-be epic stars Hollywood hunk Gordon Mitchell – a sort of low-rent Steve Reeves – as Achilles, and Gallic "boeufcake" Jacques Bergerac as his arch rival, Hector. If one turns a blind eye to the performances and a deaf ear to the Anglo-American dubbing, this is quite a handsome breeze through parts of Homer's *Iliad*, with some decent battles and nice location work. AT. Italian dialogue dubbed into English.

Gordon Mitchell (1) *Achilles* • Jacques Bergerac *Hector* • Enio Girolami *Patrocles* • Mario Petri *Agamemnon* • Cristina Gajoni *Briseyde* • Gloria Milland *Griseyde* • Eleonora Bianchi *Andromache* ■ *Dir* Marino Girolami • *Scr* Gino De Santis, Vladimiro Cajoli

The Acid House ★★ 18

Drama 1998 · UK · Colour · 106mins

This trio of very dark tales from Irvine Welsh's anthology has a great cast, but these stories are too wild, weird and unpleasant to appeal to anybody other than hardcore fans of Welsh's book. Although the stories – a downtrodden teen meets God and is transformed into a fly, nice guy suffers from the neighbour from hell, and an acid-taking clubber swaps bodies with a newborn baby – all offer dramatic potential, they seem more calculated to shock and offend with graphic sex and in-your-face nastiness than to actually entertain. JC. Contains swearing, nudity, violence. DVD

Stephen McCole *Boab* • Maurice Roëves *God* • Garry Sweeney *Kev ("The Granton Star Cause")* • Jenny McCrindle *Evelyn* • Kevin McKidd *Johnny* • Ewen Bremner *Coco* • Martin Clunes *Rory* • Simon Weir *Tambo* • Alex Howden *Boab Snr* ■ *Dir* Paul McGuigan • *Scr* Irvine Welsh, from his short stories

Acquasanta Joe ★★

Spaghetti western 1971 · It · Colour · 94mins

At the end of the American Civil War Confederate soldiers have their cannon stolen by bandits, who use it to pull off a series of bank raids. But then they make the mistake of stealing the loot stashed by a bounty hunter. The resultant action is a muddled round of ambushes and escapes, thefts and recoveries as all and sundry try to make off with the dough. Director Mario Gariazzo obviously knows his spaghetti, but this is a sloppily served helping. DP. Italian dialogue dubbed into English.

Lincoln Tate *Acquasanta Joe* • Ty Hardin *Donovan* • Silvia Monelli *Estella* ■ *Dir* Mario Gariazzo • *Scr* Franco Poggi, Mario Gariazzo

Across 110th Street ★★ 18

Blaxploitation crime thriller
1972 · US · Colour · 97mins

In New York, the demarcation line between squalor and style, war and peace, was always 110th Street. Below the line was Central Park, above it was Harlem and mayhem. Even if that isn't the case today, in this movie crooked cop Anthony Quinn has a lot of hardware to deal with Harlem's racketeers. Director Barry Shear's picture tries to be hard-edged and aim for realism, but doesn't always succeed. AT. Contains swearing and violence. DVD

Anthony Quinn *Captain Frank Mattelli* • Yaphet Kotto *Detective Lieutenant Pope* • Anthony Franciosa *Nick D'Salvio* • Paul Benjamin *Jim Harris* • Ed Bernard *Joe Logart* • Richard Ward *Doc Johnson* • Norma Donaldson *Gloria Roberts* • Antonio Fargas *Henry J Jackson* ■ *Dir* Barry Shear • *Scr* Luther Davis, from the novel by Wally Ferris

Across the Bridge ★★★★ PG

Thriller 1957 · UK · BW · 99mins

Rod Steiger takes on the ultimate scene-stealer – a small dog – and just about wins in this thriller, adapted from a Graham Greene story. Steiger plays a fraudster on the run who murders a man and assumes his identity, only to discover his victim is also a fugitive. His attempts to escape are further hampered when he becomes attached to the dead man's mangy mongrel. There was friction between director Ken Annakin and his star during production, with Spanish exteriors standing in for Latin American locations. Nevertheless, Steiger gives one of his best and most poignant performances. TH DVD

Rod Steiger *Carl Schaffner* • David Knight *Johnny* • Marla Landi *Mary* • Noel Willman *Chief of Police* • Bernard Lee *Chief Inspector Hadden* • Bill Nagy *Paul Scarff* • Eric Pohlman [Eric Pohlmann] *Police Sergeant* ■ *Dir* Ken Annakin • *Scr* Guy Elmes, Denis Freeman, from a story by Graham Greene

Across the Great Divide ★★ U

Period adventure 1977 · US · Colour · 96mins

Following the success of *The Adventures of the Wilderness Family*, producer Arthur R Dubs and director Stewart Raffill returned to the Rocky Mountains for this old-fashioned rites of passage picture. As the orphans risking all to claim their estate in Salem, Oregan, Heather Rattray and Mark Edward Hall give spirited performances, although conman Robert F Logan hogs nearly all their scenes. For all its visual splendour, the film lacks a sense of period (it's set in 1876) and the perils faced by the trio are predictable and too easily overcome. DP

Robert Logan *Zachariah Coop* • Heather Rattray *Holly Smith* • Mark Edward Hall *Jason Smith* • George "Buck" Flower *Ben* • Hal Bokar *Sternface* ■ *Dir/Scr* Stewart Raffill • *Producer* Arthur R Dubs

Across the Pacific ★★★ U

Spy drama 1942 · US · BW · 96mins

A wartime melodrama that reunited the cast and crew of *The Maltese Falcon*. The original script, written in 1941, described a Japanese plan to attack Pearl Harbor and when that really happened the script was rewritten, set near the Panama Canal and peopled with sundry spies, adventurers and mystery women. Humphrey Bogart plays a spy ordered to keep tabs on Sydney Greenstreet. What happens is purely formulaic, and enjoyable only because of the interplay between Bogart, Greenstreet and Mary Astor. AT

Humphrey Bogart *Rick Leland* • Mary Astor *Alberta Marlow* • Sydney Greenstreet *Dr Lorenz* • Charles Halton *AV Smith* • Victor Sen Yung *Joe Totsuiko* • Roland Got *Sugi* ■ *Dir* John Huston • *Scr* Richard Macaulay, from the serial *Aloha Means Goodbye* by Robert Carson in *The Saturday Evening Post*

Across the Tracks ★★ 15

Drama 1990 · US · Colour · 96mins

Brad Pitt got one of his first opportunities to lead from the front in this below-par tale of sibling rivalry. He certainly looks the part as a clean-cut running star who tries to save cynical brother Rick Schroder from drug peddling by encouraging him to take up athletics. Few demands are made of Pitt's acting ability, as writer/director Sandy Tung's script is awash with clichéd situations and unconvincing sports sequences. However, it's fascinating to watch Pitt and Schroder competing with each other in the acting stakes. DP. Contains swearing and drug abuse.

Rick Schroder *Billy Maloney* • Brad Pitt *Joe Maloney* • Carrie Snodgress *Rosemary Maloney* • David Anthony Marshall *Louie* • Thomas Mikal Ford *Coach Walsh* • John Linton *Brad* • Cyril O'Reilly *Coach Ryder* • Jack McGee *Frank* ■ *Dir/Scr* Sandy Tung

Across the Wide Missouri ★★★ U

Western adventure
1951 · US · Colour · 78mins

A great example of the use of Technicolor (cameraman William C Mellor), as vast landscapes are bloodied by the advance of "civilisation" in the shape of pioneers in the Rocky Mountains of the 1820s. Clark Gable seems uncomfortably cast as real-life trapper Flint Mitchell, and the complex dialogue scenes with the Indians severely hinder the plot's progression, but the movie has genuine scale, and the score is outstanding. TS

Clark Gable *Flint Mitchell* • Ricardo Montalban *Ironshirt* • John Hodiak *Brecan* • Adolphe Menjou *Pierre* • Maria Elena Marques *Kamiah* • J Carrol Naish *Looking Glass* • Jack Holt *Bear Ghost* • Alan Napier *Captain Humberstone Lyon* • Howard Keel *Narrator* ■ *Dir* William Wellman [William A Wellman] • *Scr* Talbot Jennings, from a story by Talbot Jennings, Frank Cavett, from a novel by Bernard DeVoto • *Music* David Raksin

Act of Love ★★★

Drama 1953 · US · BW · 109mins

Along with stars such as Alan Ladd, Kirk Douglas took full advantage of the postwar tax breaks available to American actors working in Europe, and this intense adult romance is a prime example of his output during that period. The late Dany Robin is the girl Douglas falls for, while other cast members include Gene Kelly's *Happy Road* co-star Barbara Laage, and a pretty, pouting youngster awaiting discovery called Brigitte Bardot. An intelligent, mature movie. TS

Kirk Douglas *Robert Teller* • Dany Robin *Lisa* • Barbara Laage *Nina* • Robert Strauss *Blackwood* • Gabrielle Dorziat *Adele* • Grégoire Aslan *Commissaire* • Marthe Mercadier *Young woman* • Brigitte Bardot *Mimi* ■ *Dir* Anatole Litvak • *Scr* Irwin Shaw, from the novel *The Girl on the Via Flaminia* by Alfred Hayes

Act of Necessity ★★★

Documentary drama
1991 · Aus · Colour · 90mins

Although it seems a bit gimmicky to play the trial before a real judge and jury to get an authentic verdict, this docudrama is anything but a contrived melodrama. Angie Milliken gives a towering performance as the young mother who takes on the farmers and the chemical companies of Australia's cotton belt when she realises that the pesticides used in crop-spraying are responsible for her daughter's leukaemia. Passionately scripted by Pamela Williams and directed with Ken Loach-like realism by Ian Munro, this is hard-hitting stuff. DP

Angie Milliken ■ *Dir* Ian Munro • *Scr* Pamela Williams

Act of Piracy ★★ 18

Action thriller 1990 · US · Colour · 100mins

Gary Busey is a popular draw in the straight-to-video stakes nowadays, and this is a typically no-nonsense slice of action hokum. Here he's a Vietnam vet who fights back when Ray Sharkey and some terrorist pals seize his yacht with his children on board. There are echoes of Busey's *Under Siege* in the ocean-bound plotting, but it's not in the same class as that action spectacular. Nevertheless, Busey and Sharkey spark off each other nicely and it makes for undemanding entertainment. JF. Contains swearing, violence and nudity.

Gary Busey *Ted Andrews* • Belinda Bauer *Sandy Andrews* • Ray Sharkey *Jack Wilcox* ■ *Dir* John "Bud" Cardos • *Scr* Hal Reed

Act of the Heart ★★★

Religious drama
1970 · Can · Colour · 103mins

An obsessive love affair within an obsessive religious faith lifts this Canadian movie out of the ordinary. while the acting elevates it even further. Country girl Geneviève Bujold falls desperately in love with priest Donald Sutherland when she goes to his urban parish to sing in the choir. The film is darker in hue than the surface gloss suggests, though non-religious audiences may wonder why everything is so intense. TH

Geneviève Bujold *Martha Hayes* • Donald Sutherland *Father Michael Ferrier* • Monique Leyrac *Johane Foss* • Bill Mitchell *Russell Foss* ■ *Dir/Scr* Paul Almond

Act of Vengeance ★★★ 18

Crime drama 1974 · US · Colour · 87mins

A surprisingly hard-edged slice of B-movie exploitation that manages to come up with a different spin on the familiar vigilante theme. Jo Ann Harris leads a band of rape victims who decide to take the law into their own hands and gain revenge against a serial attacker. The largely unknown cast – *Dallas* regular Steve Kanaly is probably the most recognisable face – gives sterling performances and director Robert Kelljchian succeeds in avoiding the more sensationalist aspects of the story. JF. Contains violence and swearing.

Jo Ann Harris *Linda* • Peter Brown *Jack* • Jennifer Lee (1) *Nancy* • Lisa Moore *Karen* • Connie Strickland *Teresa* • Patricia Estrin *Angie* • Lada Edmund Jr *Tiny* • Steve Kanaly *Tom* ■ *Dir* Robert Kelljchian [Bob Kelljan] • *Scr* Betty Conklin, HR Christian

Act of Violence ★★★

Film noir 1949 · US · BW · 82mins

This fine *film noir* melodrama from MGM allows its talented young contract director Fred Zinnemann to flex his creative muscles. There's a great cast, including two of Hollywood's finest second league heavyweights, Robert Ryan and Van Heflin, the latter particularly good as an officer who, while he was a prisoner of war, betrayed his men. Ryan is his fellow prisoner who seeks revenge.

Janet Leigh is wasted as Heflin's worried wife, but there's a remarkable performance from the redoubtable Mary Astor as a bar-room prostitute. A grim but satisfying movie. TS

Van Heflin *Frank R Enley* • Robert Ryan *Joe Parkson* • Janet Leigh *Edith Enley* • Mary Astor *Pat* • Phyllis Thaxter *Ann* • Berry Kroeger *Johnny* • Taylor Holmes *Gavery* • Harry Antrim *Fred* • Connie Gilchrist *Martha* ■ *Dir* Fred Zinnemann • *Scr* Robert L Richards

Act One ★

Biographical drama 1963 · US · BW · 110mins

The autobiography of playwright Moss Hart who, with George S Kaufman, wrote some of the best comedies ever to come out of America makes an entertaining and fascinating read. This attempt to film it, however, is an abject failure. The movie doesn't find a way of translating Hart's genial account into a suitable narrative, leaving only a series of static scenes and a lot of Broadway name-dropping. RK

George Hamilton *Moss Hart* • Jason Robards Jr [Jason Robards] *George S Kaufman* • Jack Klugman *Joe Hyman* • Sam Levene *Richard Maxwell* • Ruth Ford *Beatrice Kaufman* • Eli Wallach *Warren Stone* • Joseph Leon *Max Siegel* • George Segal *Lester Sweyd* • Martin Wolfson *Mr Hart* ■ *Dir* Dore Schary • *Scr* Dore Schary, from the autobiography by Moss Hart

Action in Arabia ★★★ U

Spy drama 1944 · US · BW · 75mins

Footage from Ernest B Schoedsack and Merian C Cooper's aborted 1933 biopic of Lawrence of Arabia adds some local colour to this otherwise anaemic spy thriller. The film provides a dashing showcase for George Sanders, who, for once, doesn't play the cad, as his intrepid reporter teams up with Virginia Bruce's plucky agent to prevent various Arab tribes rallying to the Nazi cause. It's efficiently directed by Russian-born exile Leonide Moguy, but the movie is held together by Sanders's polished performance. DP

George Sanders *Gordon* • Virginia Bruce *Yvonne* • Lenore Aubert *Mouniran* • Gene Lockhart *Danesco* • Robert Armstrong *Reed* • HB Warner *Rashid* ■ *Dir* Leonide Moguy [Léonide Moguy] • *Scr* Philip MacDonald, Herbert J Biberman

Action in the North Atlantic ★★★

Second World War drama
1943 · US · BW · 127mins

This Second World War flag-waver began as one of many Warner Bros short films designed to salute various aspects of the war effort – this time the merchant marine – but ended up a full-length feature. Humphrey Bogart and Raymond Massey play the courageous seamen who sail from the USA to Murmansk in the Soviet Union, dodging German U-boats and bombers all the way. Ruth Gordon, meanwhile, keeps the home fires burning. Bogart and Massey make a convincing pair of heroes and the action sequences are impressive. AT

Humphrey Bogart *Joe Rossi* • Raymond Massey *Captain Steve Jarvis* • Alan Hale *Boats O'Hara* • Julie Bishop *Pearl* • Ruth Gordon *Mrs Jarvis* • Sam Levene *Chips Abrams* • Dane Clark *Johnny Pulaski* ■ *Dir* Lloyd Bacon • *Scr* John Howard Lawson, from the novel by Guy Gilpatric

Action Jackson ★★★ 18

Action thriller 1988 · US · Colour · 91mins

Rocky star Carl Weathers is smart Detroit cop Jericho "Action" Jackson (he's even got a Harvard law degree!) out to nail evil auto magnate Craig T Nelson in this loud *Commando* clone liberally dosed with outlandish explosions, huge car crashes and stylish shoot-outs. Illogical and incomprehensible it may be most of the time, but the memorable high octane action more than makes up for its plot deficiencies. Featuring an early appearance by Sharon Stone. AJ. Contains graphic violence, nudity, sexual situations and swearing

Carl Weathers *Jericho "Action" Jackson* • Craig T Nelson *Peter Dellaplane* • Vanity *Sydney Ash* • Sharon Stone *Patrice Dellaplane* • Thomas F Wilson *Officer Kornblau* • Bill Duke *Captain Armbruster* • Robert Davi *Tony Moretti* • Jack Thibeau *Detective Kotterwell* ■ *Dir* Craig R Baxley • *Scr* Robert Reneau

Action of the Tiger ★★ U

Adventure 1957 · US · Colour · 96mins

Van Johnson plays an adventurer who smuggles Martine Carol into Albania where the secret police are holding her father. What makes this B-movie rather more interesting now than it was in 1957 is the presence of Sean Connery, who plays Johnson's romantic rival and gets beaten up for his trouble. Director Terence Young thought the film was "dreadful, very badly directed", and Johnson (always a rather weak leading man) is no match for Sean's hulking sexuality. AT

Van Johnson *Carson* • Martine Carol *Tracy* • Herbert Lom *Trifon* • Gustavo Rojo *Henri* • Tony Dawson [Anthony Dawson] *Security officer* • Anna Gerber *Mara* • Yvonne Warren [Yvonne Romain] *Katina* • Helen Haye *The Countess* • Sean Connery *Mike* ■ *Dir* Terence Young • *Scr* Robert Carson, from a novel by James Wellard

The Actors ★★ 15

Crime comedy
2003 · UK/Ire/US/Ger · Colour · 87mins

Michael Caine plays a veteran stage performer tackling the part of Richard III in an amateurish Irish production. Comedian Dylan Moran is the protégé Caine persuades to take on a fake identity in order to con a local gangster. Naturally there are hitches and Moran must adopt two further personas. Although Moran's character transformations are pulled off with reasonable credibility, writer/director Conor McPherson undermines these deceptions with inane plotting and one-dimensional characters. JC. Contains swearing. DVD

Michael Caine *Anthony O'Malley* • Dylan Moran *Tom* • Michael Gambon *Barreller* • Lena Headey *Dolores Barreller* • Miranda Richardson *Mrs Magnani* • Michael McElhatton *Jock* • Aisling O'Sullivan *Rita* ■ *Dir* Conor McPherson • *Scr* Conor McPherson, from a story by Neil Jordan

Actors and Sin ★★★

Comedy drama 1952 · US · BW · 85mins

Two featurettes, glued together: the first is about a grand actor who makes the suicide of his vain, hateful daughter look like murder. The second is a satire about a Hollywood agent who sells a script that everyone thinks is brilliant and turns out to be written by a nine-year-old. Ben Hecht puts all available cynicism into this project but the second story is rivetingly weird as Hecht casts his own daughter as the moppet writer and her lack of acting ability is excruciatingly obvious. AT

Edward G Robinson *Maurice* • Marsha Hunt *Marcia* • Dan O'Herlihy *Alfred O'Shea* • Eddie Albert *Orlando Higgens* • Tracey Roberts *Miss Flannigan* • Jenny Hecht *Daisy Marcher* ■ *Dir/Scr* Ben Hecht

An Actor's Revenge ★★★★ PG

Drama 1963 · Jpn · Colour · 108mins

Having starred in the 1935 version, veteran actor Kazuo Hasegawa reprises the dual role of Yukinojo the female impersonator and Yamitaro, the bandit who befriends him. Revelling in his scheme to destroy the triumvirate responsible for the suicide of his parents – he starts by seducing the daughter of one of the men – Hasegawa gives a performance of rare immersion and control. While remaining faithful to the original, director Kon Ichikawa creates a nice sense of nostalgia and irony by re-creating not only the conventions of Kabuki theatre, but also the look of Japanese painting and the films of the early sound era. DP. In Japanese with English subtitles. DVD

Kazuo Hasegawa *Yamitaro/Yukinojo* • Fujiko Yamamoto *Ohatsu* • Ayako Wakao *Namiji* • Ganjiro Nakamura *Sansai Dobe* ■ *Dir* Kon Ichikawa • *Scr* Teinosuke Kinugasa, Daisuke Ito, Natto Wada

The Actress ★★★★ U

Drama 1953 · US · BW · 90mins

Keeping up with the Jones girl is some feat! As Ruth Jones, aspiring thespian and would-be star, Jean Simmons is an obstinate and headstrong teenager demanding her theatrical rights despite opposition from Spencer Tracy as her seafaring father. Every dad will have his day, but not for very long, in this endearing adaptation of actress Ruth Gordon's play about her Broadway-bound early days in a Massachusetts small town. Anthony Perkins makes a rather timid debut as Ruth's boyfriend, but it's Tracy's movie, although Simmons does stand up to him remarkably well. TH

Spencer Tracy *Clinton Jones* • Jean Simmons *Ruth Gordon Jones* • Teresa Wright *Annie Jones* • Anthony Perkins *Fred Whitmarsh* • Ian Wolfe *Mr Bagley* • Kay Williams *Hazel Dawn* • Mary Wickes *Emma Glavey* • Norma Jean Nilsson *Anna* • Dawn Bender *Katherine* ■ *Dir* George Cukor • *Scr* Ruth Gordon, from her play *Years Ago*

The Actress ★★★

Biographical drama
1992 · HK · Colour · 146mins

Maggie Cheung won Berlin's Best Actress prize for her work in this Brechtian biopic of Ruan Ling Yu, the 1930s Chinese movie star who was driven to suicide at the age of 25 by press criticism of her relationship with a married man. It's an affecting performance, although it loses some of its impact through comparison with footage of the real Ruan in the silent clips with which director Stanley Kwan studs the action. There are also several interviews with friends and colleagues, whose testimony echoes Kwan's contention that this fragile icon was broken by a combination of celebrity and hypocrisy. DP. In Cantonese with English subtitles.

Maggie Cheung Man Yuk [Maggie Cheung] *Ruan Ling Yu* • Tony Leung Ka-Fai [Tony Leung (1)] *Tsai Chu Sheng* • Carina Lau *Lily Li* • Lawrence Ng *Chang Ta Min* • Lee Waise ■ *Dir* Stanley Kwan • *Scr* Chui Tai An- Ping

Actresses ★★★ 15

Drama 1996 · Sp · Colour · 87mins

Intimacy and intensity are the bywords for Ventura Pons's adaptation of JM Benet I Jornet's acclaimed play about the encounters between an ambitious drama student and a legendary diva's favourite pupils. However, such is his emphasis on the mood and language of this essentially theatrical piece, that Pons neglects the cinematic potential of the allusions to *Rashomon* and *All about Eve* that arise as the truth slowly emerges from the embittered trio's well-practised reminiscences. The performances, however, are impeccable. DP. In Catalan and Spanish with English subtitles. Contains swearing.

Núria Espert *Gloria Marc* • Rosa Maria Sarda *Assumpta Roca* • Anna Lizaran *Maria Caminal* • Mercè Pons *Girl* ■ *Dir* Ventura Pons • *Scr* Ventura Pons, JM Benet I Jornet, from the play *ER* by JM Benet I Jornet

Acts of Love ★★ 18

Romantic drama
1995 · US · Colour · 104mins

It's hard to swallow Dennis Hopper as a shy teacher, married (unhappily) to Amy Irving, who lives on a farm with his sick mother (Julie Harris). The plot doesn't get any more credible when his character gets a new lease of life through an affair with a student (Amy Locane). Hopper lurches around with a limp, though that's nothing compared to Ed Jones's script. TH. Contains swearing and sex scenes.

Dennis Hopper *Joseph Svenden* • Amy Irving *Rosealee Henson* • Amy Locane *Catherine Wheeler* • Julie Harris *Joseph's mother* • Gary Busey *Major Nathan Wheeler* • Hal Holbrook *Dr Evans* • Christopher Pettiet *Robert Henson* • Priscilla Pointer *Lily Henson* ■ *Dir* Bruno Barreto • *Scr* Ed Jones, from the novel *Farmer* by Jim Harrison

Ada ★★★

Drama 1961 · US · Colour · 108mins

Susan Hayward stars as former prostitute Ada, the fiery wife of southern politician Dean Martin, in an MGM rags-to-riches tale. Wilfrid Hyde White is Martin's scheming political adviser, who threatens to expose Hayward's colourful past if she continues to appear at her husband's side. Martin Balsam is also effective as Martin's press agent. A mesmerising melodrama from the studio's post-*Ben-Hur* period, when chances were taken with unusual casts and subjects, this was directed with a knowing hand by Daniel Mann. TS

Susan Hayward *Ada* • Dean Martin *Bo Gillis* • Wilfrid Hyde White *Sylvester Marin* • Ralph Meeker *Colonel Yancey* • Martin Balsam *Steve Jackson* • Frank Maxwell *Ronnie Hallerton* • Connie Sawyer *Alice Sweet* • Ford Rainey *Speaker* • Charles Watts *Al Winslow* • Larry Gates *Joe Adams* ■ *Dir* Daniel Mann • *Scr* Arthur Sheekman, William Driskill, from the novel *Ada Dallas* by Wirt Williams

Adalen 31 ★★★

Period drama 1969 · Swe · Colour · 114mins

Bo Widerberg has an eye for lyrical imagery, but such pictorialism seems out of place in the reconstruction of a key moment in Swedish labour history. The 1931 protracted strike by the paper mill workers in an isolated northern town resulted in five people being killed by panicked soldiers. The violence is all the more shocking for the beauty of the visuals. But while we know everything about the striker's son and the plant manager's pregnant daughter, we get little insight into the hardships suffered by their families. DP. In Swedish with English subtitles.

Peter Schildt *Kjell Andersson* • Kerstin Tidelius *Kjell's mother* • Roland Hedlund *Harald Andersson* • Stefan Feierbach *Åke* • Martin Widerberg *Martin* • Marie De Geer *Anna* ■ *Dir/Scr* Bo Widerberg

Adam ★★★★ 15

Drama based on a true story
1983 · US · Colour · 91mins

This moving and classy TV movie stars Daniel J Travanti and JoBeth Williams as parents who suffer the anguish of having their son kidnapped. In the hope of helping other families with missing children, the couple lobby Congress to give parents access to the FBI's national crime computer. Subtly and movingly performed, this is above average, and earned an Emmy nomination for outstanding drama. A weak sequel, *Adam: His Song Continues*, followed. JB

Daniel J Travanti *John Walsh* • JoBeth Williams *Reve Walsh* • Martha Scott *Gram Walsh* • Richard Masur *Jay Howell* • Paul Regina *Joe Walsh* • Mason Adams *Ray Mellette* ■ *Dir* Michael Tuchner

Adam and Evelyne ★★★

Romantic comedy 1949 · UK · BW · 82mins

Stewart Granger and Jean Simmons, who married in real life a year later, first played opposite each other in this pleasing comedy (although they both appeared three years earlier in *Caesar and Cleopatra*). He's a professional gambler who pretends to work on the stock exchange; she's an orphan who thinks he's her father but soon learns differently. Jest, not incest, is the name of this game, exuberantly performed by its two stars. The only thing that lets it down is Harold French's stodgy direction. AT

Stewart Granger *Adam Black* • Jean Simmons *Evelyne Wallace* • Edwin Styles *Bill Murray* • Raymond Young *Roddy Black* • Helen Cherry *Moira* • Beatrice Varley *Mrs Parker* • Joan Swinstead *Molly* • Wilfrid Hyde White *Colonel Bradley* • Irene Handl *Manageress* • Dora Bryan *Store assistant* ■ *Dir* Harold French • *Scr* Noel Langley, Lesley Storm, George Barraud, Nicholas Phipps

Adam & Paul ★★★ 15

Comedy drama 2004 · Ire · Colour · 85mins

Adam and Paul (played by screenwriter Mark O'Halloran and Tom Murphy) are two Dublin junkies. The story follows them over the course of a day as they pursue a fix, encountering en route friends, acquaintances and strangers, most of them hostile. Although watching the physical ravages of heroin withdrawal borders on the nauseating at times, the tone here is quietly observant rather than judgemental. The script and direction extract considerable comedy out of the duo's picaresque adventures, which are spiked by moments of absurdity, coincidence and tenderness. LF. Contains swearing and drug abuse.

Tom Murphy *Paul* • Mark O'Halloran *Adam* • Louise Lewis (2) *Janine* • Gary Egan *Georgie* • Deirdre Molloy *Marian* • Mary Murray *Orla* • Paul Roe *Wayne* ■ *Dir* Lenny Abrahamson • *Scr* Mark O'Halloran

Adam at 6 AM ★★★ 15

Drama 1970 · US · Colour · 90mins

A young Michael Douglas overcomes miscasting with an acceptable performance as a West Coast professor in search of himself and a simpler life in rural America. The film, which offers neither a pulsating plot nor sparkling dialogue, flopped on its first outing. But it does have a certain offbeat appeal, as well as an authentic feel for its Missouri locations, and a strong performance by Joe Don Baker as the foreman of a crew of labourers who employs Douglas. PF

Michael Douglas *Adam Gaines* • Lee Purcell *Jerri Jo Hopper* • Joe Don Baker *Harvey Gavin* • Charles Aidman *Mr Hooper* • Marge Redmond *Cleo* • Louise Latham *Mrs Hopper* • Grayson Hall *Inez Treadley* • Carolyn Conwell *Mavis* • Dana Elcar *Van* • Meg Foster *Joyce* ■ *Dir* Robert Scheerer • *Scr* Stephen Karpf, Elinor Karpf

Adam Had Four Sons ★★★

Melodrama 1941 · US · BW · 108mins

In this powerful melodrama, Ingrid Bergman stars as a governess hired to look after Warner Baxter's family shortly before a family tragedy. There's a cracking turn from up-and-coming Susan Hayward as a girl you wouldn't want to bring home to your parents, but otherwise this would-be sincere drama suffers from serious undercasting. Bergman's star quality keeps you watching and caring. TS

Ingrid Bergman *Emilie Gallatin* • Warner Baxter *Adam Stoddard* • Susan Hayward *Hester* • Fay Wray *Molly Stoddard* • Helen Westley *Cousin Phillipa* • Richard Denning *Jack Stoddard* • Johnny Downs *David Stoddard* • June Lockhart *Vance* ■ *Dir* Gregory Ratoff • *Scr* William Hurlbut, Michael Blankfort, from the novel *Legacy* by Charles Bonner

Adam Sandler's Eight Crazy Nights ★ 12

Animated musical comedy
2003 · US · Colour · mins

Festive cartoon fun gets an adult flavour in this ill-conceived musical comedy. An inane combination of bad-taste humour, flat animation and puerile songs, it's little more than a crude vanity project for Adam Sandler. Co-writer/producer Sandler also voices the film's central characters. Escaping a yuletide prison sentence, Davey gets one last shot at redemption by performing community service as Whitey's assistant. The result is merely a torrent of scatological gags and juvenile sexual innuendo. SF DVD

Adam Sandler *Davey Stone/Whitey/Eleanor* • Austin Stout *Benjamin* • Kevin Nealon *Mayor* • Rob Schneider *Chinese waiter/Narrator* • Norm Crosby *Judge* • Jon Lovitz *Tom Baltezor* ■ *Dir* Seth Kearsley • *Scr* Brooks Arthur, Allen Covert, Brad Isaacs, Adam Sandler

Adam's Rib ★★★★★ U

Classic comedy 1949 · US · BW · 96mins

This witty and sophisticated "battle of the sexes" comedy is a peerless joy. Tailor-made for Spencer Tracy and Katharine Hepburn, it gave the roles of a lifetime to an enduring partnership which first flourished on screen in the 1942 comedy *Woman of the Year*. They face each other as married lawyers on opposing sides in court, as Hepburn defends and Tracy prosecutes Judy Holliday. She almost puts the star couple in the shade as the dizzy blonde accused of a shooting involving her philandering husband Tom Ewell. Here the delightful Oscar-nominated screenplay by Ruth Gordon and Garson Kanin brings out the best in the talented stars, and the subtle direction of George Cukor shows him to be a master of his craft. The sexual politics of the piece are as relevant now as they were prescient then, and the movie stands as a glorious tribute to all involved. TS DVD

Spencer Tracy *Adam Bonner* • Katharine Hepburn *Amanda Bonner* • Judy Holliday *Doris Attinger* • Tom Ewell *Warren Attinger* • David Wayne *Kip Lurie* • Jean Hagen *Beryl Caighn* • Hope Emerson *Olympia La Pere* • Eve March *Grace* • Polly Moran *Mrs McGrath* • Clarence Kolb *Judge Reiser* ■ *Dir* George Cukor • *Scr* Ruth Gordon, Garson Kanin

Adam's Woman ★★

Adventure 1970 · Aus · Colour · 116mins

This well-intentioned drama compromised by the casting of Beau Bridges as an American sailor wrongly sentenced to transportation to the penal colony that is now known as Australia. Bridges is there to lure the American audience (there wasn't one) while alienating the British audience (there wasn't one of those, either, since the film was never released to cinemas). John Mills appears briefly as the Governor. AT

Beau Bridges *Adam* • Jane Merrow *Bess* • James Booth *Dyson* • Andrew Keir *O'Shea* • Tracy Reed *Duchess* • Peter O'Shaughnessy *Barrett* • John Mills *Sir Philip* ■ *Dir* Philip Leacock • *Scr* Richard Fielder, from a story by Lowell Barrington

Adaptation. ★★★★ 15

Satirical comedy drama
2002 · US · Colour · 110mins

Being John Malkovich director Spike Jonze again demonstrates his style and originality with this inventive comedy drama. Based on a screenplay by previous collaborator Charlie Kaufman (who credits his fictitious twin brother Donald as co-writer), the film takes the idea of life imitating art to new extremes. Instead of a straight adaptation of journalist Susan Orlean's non-fiction book *The Orchid Thief*, Jonze presents a surreal version of Kaufman turning the literary work into a screenplay. It's a dark, hilarious and visually intoxicating celluloid trip, made even more appealing by a riveting double turn from Nicolas Cage as both the creatively blocked Charlie and as Donald, who's an aspiring screenwriter of action blockbusters. But it's Meryl Streep who's the biggest revelation in this dazzling and emotionally vibrant movie. SF DVD

Nicolas Cage *Charlie Kaufman/Donald Kaufman* • Meryl Streep *Susan Orlean* • Chris Cooper *John Laroche* • Tilda Swinton *Valerie* • Cara Seymour *Amelia* • Brian Cox *Robert McKee* • Judy Greer *Alice the waitress* • Maggie Gyllenhaal *Caroline* ■ *Dir* Spike Jonze • *Scr* Charlie Kaufman, Donald Kaufman, from the non-fiction book *The Orchid Thief* by Susan Orlean

The Addams Family ★★★★ PG

Comedy horror 1991 · US · Colour · 95mins

Hollywood's plundering of classic TV series has produced its fair share of turkeys, but this is a glorious exception. This is partly owing to director Barry Sonnenfeld's wise decision to stick with the black humour of Charles Addams's original *New Yorker* cartoons and some inspired casting. Anjelica Huston and Raul Julia are note perfect as loving Morticia and Gomez, while Christopher Lloyd was equally born to play Fester. However, these stars are almost surpassed by the astonishingly agile Thing and by Christina Ricci's splendid performance as the young Wednesday. The plot a confidence trickster (Lloyd) poses as Fester to steal the Addams fortune is a tad contrived, but the result is a witty family comedy that has enough sly humour to keep adults chuckling throughout. JF

Anjelica Huston *Morticia Addams* • Raul Julia *Gomez Addams* • Christopher Lloyd *Uncle Fester Addams/Gordon Craven* • Dan Hedaya *Tully Alford* • Elizabeth Wilson *Abigail Craven* • Judith Malina *Granny* • Carel Struycken *Lurch* • Christina Ricci *Wednesday Addams* • Jimmy Workman *Pugsley Addams* • Dana Ivey *Margaret Alford* • Paul Benedict *Judge Womack* ■ *Dir* Barry Sonnenfeld • *Scr* Caroline Thompson, Larry Wilson, from characters created by Charles Addams

Addams Family Reunion ★ PG

Comedy horror 1998 · US · Colour · 87mins

Even the Addams family themselves would be turning in their graves over this one. Carel Struycken aside, none of the original stars of the excellent first two films is back for this cheap TV movie cash-in. Tim Curry and Daryl Hannah take on the Raul Julia and Anjelica Huston roles with enthusiasm, but they can't do anything with the unfunny, childish script, and their spirited performances are further hampered by the slapdash special effects. JF

Tim Curry *Gomez Addams* • Daryl Hannah *Morticia Addams* • Nicole Marie Fugere *Wednesday Addams* • Jerry Messing *Pugsley Addams* • Ray Walston *Walter* • Kevin McCarthy *Grandpa Addams* • Ed Begley Jr *Phillip Adams* ■ *Dir* David Payne [Dave Payne] • *Scr* Scott Sandin, Rob Krechner, from characters created by Charles Addams

Addams Family Values ★★★★ PG

Comedy horror 1993 · US · Colour · 90mins

A delightful follow-up to *The Addams Family*, with a more expansive plot and blessed with an even blacker vein of humour than the original. This time, Gomez and Morticia (Raul Julia and Anjelica Huston) have a new baby, much to the displeasure of their other children, while Fester has fallen under the spell of the youngster's new black widow nanny (Joan Cusack). Once again, the playing is faultless, but it is Christina Ricci who effortlessly steals the show, whether trying to bump off her new sibling or creating havoc at an all-American summer camp. The sets are wonderful, the cinematography exquisite and Barry Sonnenfeld's direction exhilarating. The perfect antidote to more traditional family fare. JF. Contains cartoonish violence and some swearing. DVD

Anjelica Huston *Morticia Addams* • Raul Julia *Gomez Addams* • Christopher Lloyd *Uncle Fester* • Joan Cusack *Debbie Jellinsky* • Christina Ricci *Wednesday Addams* • Carol Kane *Granny* • Jimmy Workman *Pugsley Addams* • Carel Struycken *Lurch* • Peter MacNicol *Gary Granger* • Christine Baranski *Becky Granger* ■ *Dir* Barry Sonnenfeld • *Scr* Paul Rudnick, from characters created by Charles Addams

Addicted to Love ★★★ 15

Romantic black comedy
1997 · US · Colour · 96mins

In this surprisingly dark romantic comedy, the usually sweet Meg Ryan stars as a vengeful ex-girlfriend who spends her waking hours thinking up ways of making life hell for the man who dumped her (Tcheky Karyo). This involves teaming up with the more strait-laced Matthew Broderick, whose childhood sweetheart has dumped him for Meg's ex. A tale of love gone sour from actor-turned-director Griffin Dunne, this has an enjoyably acidic bite. JB. Contains swearing, sex scenes and nudity. DVD

Meg Ryan *Maggie* • Matthew Broderick *Sam* • Kelly Preston *Linda Green* • Tcheky Karyo *Anton Depeaux* • Maureen Stapleton *Nana* • Nesbitt Blaisdell *Ed Green* • Remak Ramsay *Professor Wells* • Lee Wilkof *Carl* ■ *Dir* Griffin Dunne • *Scr* Robert Gordon

The Addiction ★★★ 18

Horror 1994 · US · BW · 82mins

Shot in black and white for that Andy Warhol feel, Abel Ferrara's New Wave tale is his most idiosyncratic film to date. Lili Taylor is the New York University philosophy student-turned-vampire who spends as much time pondering the Nietzschean significance of her gory deeds as she does shooting up blood. Intriguing and stylish, if pretentiously over-intellectualised, the film is hard-hitting if you're in the right frame of mind and can cope with such arch dialogue as "Do you want an apology for ethical relativism?" Otherwise, you should approach with caution. AJ

Lili Taylor *Kathleen Conklin* • Christopher Walken *Peina* • Annabella Sciorra *Casanova* • Edie Falco *Jean* • Paul Calderon *Professor* • Fredro Starr *Black* ■ *Dir* Abel Ferrara • *Scr* Nicholas St John

The Adding Machine ★★★

Fantasy drama
1969 · US/UK · Colour · 104mins

This grim, symbolic fantasy was adapted from Elmer Rice's agitprop play of the 1920s. Milo O'Shea is Mr Zero, an oppressed office drudge who murders his boss, is executed and sent not to hell, but to a heavenly waiting area populated by other killers en route to a new life. Directed by Jerome Epstein, with luminous photography by Water Lassally, it lacks the Expressionist edge that such an allegory needs. There are memorable performances from Phyllis Diller, as the nagging wife, and Sydney Chaplin. TH

Phyllis Diller *Mrs Zero* • Milo O'Shea *Zero* • Billie Whitelaw *Daisy* • Sydney Chaplin *Lieutenant Charles* • Julian Glover *Shrdlu* • Raymond Huntley *Smithers* • Phil Brown *Don* • Libby Morris *Ethel* • Hugh McDermott *Harry* ■ *Dir* Jerome Epstein • *Scr* Jerome Epstein, from the play by Elmer Rice

Address Unknown ★

Second World War drama 1944 · US · BW · 72mins

Paul Lukas plays a German-American art dealer who returns to Germany in 1939 and becomes a card-carrying Nazi. However, his position changes when the Jewishness of his partner's daughter is discovered. Lukas overacts terribly in what is a slow and rather worthy slice of wartime propaganda. Director William Cameron Menzies is better known as the production designer who worked on such classics as *Invaders from Mars* (which he also directed) and *Gone with the Wind*. AT

Paul Lukas *Martin Schulz* • Carl Esmond *Baron von Friesche* • Peter Van Eyck *Heinrich Schulz* • Mady Christians *Elsa* • Morris Carnovsky *Max Eisenstein* • KT Stevens *Griselle* • Mary Young *Mrs Delaney* ■ *Dir* William Cameron Menzies • *Scr* Herbert Dalmas, from a story by Kressman Taylor

Adios Amigo ★

Comedy western 1975 · US · Colour · 87mins

Former football star Fred Williamson stars in, writes, directs and produces this blaxploitation pic, a sort of western about a pair of hopelessly inefficient con artists. As Williamson's partner in crime, Richard Pryor mugs shamelessly, only sometimes revealing an unwillingness to show up Williamson's obvious lack of acting ability. The fact that he can't write or direct very well is beside the point. AT

Richard Pryor *Sam* • Fred Williamson *Ben* • Thalmus Rasulala *Noah* ■ *Dir/Scr* Fred Williamson

Adios Gringo ★★

Western 1965 · It/Fr/Sp · Colour · 99mins

Spaghetti western staple Guiliano Gemma (usually billed as Montgomery Wood) can always be relied on to bring a touch of class to even the most routine cowboy drama. This one needs him more than most. He plays a gunslinger who goes on the run after almost being lynched for a murder he didn't commit. En route he rescues damsel in distress Evelyn Stewart before taking revenge on the cattle rustlers responsible for his plight. AJ

Montgomery Wood [Guiliano Gemma] *Brent Landers* • Evelyn Stewart *Lucy Tillson* • Roberto Camardiel *Dr Barfield* • Jesus Puente *Tex Slaughter* • Max Dean *Avery Ranchester* • Peter Cross *Clayton Ranchester* ■ *Dir* George Finlay [Georgio Stegani] • *Scr* Georgio Stegani, Jose Luis Jerez, Michele Villerot

Adios, Sabata ★★★ 12

Spaghetti western 1970 · It · Colour · 101mins

This is a lesser known but nonetheless competent spaghetti western, set in 19th-century Mexico and starring Yul Brynner. He plays Sabata, the archetypal gunslinger supreme, who teams up with a band of Mexican revolutionaries. This is a quite acceptable offering of its kind, with a few original touches added to the usual body count. PF. Italian dialogue dubbed into English. [VIDEO]

Yul Brynner *Sabata* • Dean Reed *Ballantine* • Pedro Sanchez [Ignazio Spalla] *Escudo* • Gerard Herter *Colonel Skimmel* • Sal Borgese *Septiembre* • Franco Fantasia *Ocano* • Gianni Rizzo *Folgen* • Salvatore Billa *Manuel* • Massimo Carocci *Juan* ■ *Dir* Frank Kramer [Gianfranco Parolini] • *Scr* Renato Izzo, Gianfranco Parolini

The Adjuster ★★★ 18

Drama 1991 · Can · Colour · 97mins

Preoccupied with images and the way in which we perceive them, Atom Egoyan is one of the most intriguing directors working today. Elias Koteas and Arsinée Khanjian are perhaps the perfect Egoyan couple. He studies accident scenes and photographs to assess insurance claims, while she is a porn film censor. He sleeps with his clients, she secretly records the scenes she is paid to withhold from the public. Nothing is what it seems in this teasing film, in which the full picture is as likely to emerge in a close-up as it is in a long shot. DP. Contains sex scenes and nudity. [VIDEO]

Elias Koteas *Noah Render* • Arsinée Khanjian *Hera Render* • Maury Chaykin *Bubba* • Gabrielle Rose *Mimi* • Jennifer Dale *Arianne* • David Hemblen *Bert* • Rose Sarkisyan *Seta* ■ *Dir/Scr* Atom Egoyan

The Admirable Crichton ★★★ U

Comedy adventure 1957 · UK · Colour · 93mins

An agreeably dated version of JM Barrie's play, about the butler to Lord Loam taking over as master when the family is shipwrecked. It's a splendid vehicle for Kenneth More's genial urbanity, though it's Cecil Parker, as the bemused peer, who seems more in touch with turn-of-the-century times. Diane Cilento (Jason Connery's mother) and Sally Ann Howes are the charmers vying for Crichton's impeccable affections. TH

Kenneth More *Crichton* • Diane Cilento *Tweeny* • Cecil Parker *Lord Loam* • Sally Ann Howes *Lady Mary* • Martita Hunt *Lady Brocklehurst* • Jack Watling *Treherne* • Peter Graves (1) *Brocklehurst* • Gerald Harper *Ernest* ■ *Dir* Lewis Gilbert • *Scr* Vernon Harris, from the play by JM Barrie

The Admiral Was a Lady ★★ U

Comedy 1950 · US · BW · 86mins

This sometimes droll, but mostly dull, film attempts to make a comedy of sexual manners out of seafaring Wanda Hendrix's hold over four disparate but somewhat dissolute men. Hendrix is good fun and Edmond O'Brien is watchable as always, but, despite a decent cast that struggles vainly with the poor material, this one fails to ignite from reel one. SH

Edmond O'Brien *Jimmie Stevens* • Wanda Hendrix *Jean Madison* • Rudy Vallee *Peter Pettigrew* • Johnny Sands *Eddie* • Steve Brodie *Mike* • Richard Erdman *Ollie* • Hillary Brooke *Mrs Pettigrew* ■ *Dir* Albert S Rogell • *Scr* Sidney Salkow, John O'Dea

Adolf Hitler – My Part in His Downfall ★★★ PG

Comedy 1972 · UK · Colour · 101mins

Spike Milligan doesn't write the script or play himself in this adaptation of his bestselling wartime memoir; Johnny Byrne does the honours in the first department, while Jim Dale portrays the future Goon. (Milligan puts in a cameo appearance as his own father.) It must have been a near impossible task to turn Milligan's priceless prose into a coherent movie, but this is a pretty fair effort that's bound to ring bells with anyone who survived basic training. The shifts between absurd comedy and sudden tragedy are neatly handled, and the supporting cast more than pass muster. DP DVD

Jim Dale *Spike Milligan* • Arthur Lowe *Major Drysdale* • Bill Maynard *Sergeant Ellis* • Windsor Davies *Sergeant Mackay* • Tony Selby *Bill* • Geoffrey Hughes *Larry* • Jim Norton *Pongo* • David Belcher *Smith* • Spike Milligan *Spike's father* • Pat Coombs *Spike's mother* ■ *Dir* Norman Cohen • *Scr* Johnny Byrne, from the memoir by Spike Milligan

Adorable Lies ★★★★

Satirical drama 1991 · Cub · Colour · 108mins

Robert Redford's Sundance Institute helped with the funding for this scathing Cuban satire, which then ran into difficulties with the Communist censors. It's hardly surprising, considering the barbed implications of this seemingly innocent story about a frustrated screenwriter (Luis Alberto Garcia) who loses touch with reality when his passion for wannabe actress Isabel Santos turns to obsession. Constantly switching the cinematic point-of-view and littering the action with allegorical references and sight gags, Gerardo Chijona has produced a film almost on a par with the early works of those master satirists Tomás Gutiérrez Alea and Humberto Solás. DP. In Spanish with English subtitles.

Isabel Santos • Luis Alberto Garcia • Mirtha Ibarra [Mirta Ibarra] ■ *Dir* Gerardo Chijona • *Scr* Senel Paz

Adrenalin: Fear the Rush ★★ 18

Science-fiction action thriller 1995 · US · Colour · 93mins

Species babe Natasha Henstridge and *Highlander* star Christopher Lambert (credited here as Christophe) join forces as two cops on the trail of a plague-infected serial killer in a so-so science-fiction effort scripted and directed by direct-to-video master Albert Pyun. As viral thrillers go it's an average action package, but the two photogenic stars add solid weight to the budget bravado. AJ. Contains swearing and violence. [VIDEO]

Christophe Lambert [Christopher Lambert] *Lemieux* • Natasha Henstridge *Delon* • Norbert Weisser *Cuzo* • Elizabeth Barondes *Wocek* • Xavier Declie *Volker* • Craig Davis *Suspect* • Nicholas Guest *Rennard* • Andrew Divoff *Sterns* ■ *Dir/Scr* Albert Pyun

Advance to the Rear ★★★

Comedy western 1964 · US · BW · 96mins

This sweet-tempered send-up of Civil War heroics from *Destry Rides Again* director George Marshall has a company of Union misfits sent out of the reach of battle, but still managing to capture a rebel spy (Stella Stevens) and save a vast pay-out in gold. The situations are obvious, but Glenn Ford injects an amused authority into the action so the result is gentle satire that saddles up the usual clichés but for different reasons. TH

Glenn Ford *Captain Jared Heath* • Stella Stevens *Martha Lou* • Melvyn Douglas *Colonel Claude Brackenby* • Jim Backus *General Willoughby* • Joan Blondell *Jenny* ■ *Dir* George Marshall • *Scr* Samuel A Peeples, William Bowers, from the novel *The Company of Cowards* by Jack Schaefer

Adventure ★★

Adventure drama 1945 · US · BW · 128mins

Clark Gable had famously gone off to fight in the Second World War, and was decorated after flying bomb runs over Germany. But in 1945 he returned to Hollywood and made *Adventure*, giving MGM the dreamy advertising slogan, "Gable's back and Garson's got him!". But the movie, so anticipated, was a syrupy romance between a merchant sailor and a priggish bookworm. AT

Clark Gable *Harry Patterson* • Greer Garson *Emily Sears* • Joan Blondell *Helen Melohn* • Thomas Mitchell *Mudgin* • Tom Tully *Gus* • John Qualen *Model T* • Richard Haydn *Limo* ■ *Dir* Victor Fleming • *Scr* Frederick Hazlitt Brennan, Vincent Lawrence, from a novel by Clyde Brion Davis

An Adventure for Two ★★

Drama 1979 · Fr · Colour · 112mins

This rarely seen feature is one of writer/director Claude Lelouch's more puzzling offerings. So much of it seems to have been designed to vex the viewer, particularly in terms of its stuttering structure, its pernickety attention to minor detail and its often dubious incidents. Yet, Lelouch makes arresting use of locations in both the US and Canada and draws credible performances from Jacques Dutronc and Catherine Deneuve as a runaway gangster and his hostage who eventually become lovers. DP. In French with English subtitles.

Catherine Deneuve *Françoise* • Jacques Dutronc *Simon* • Jacques Villeret *Tonton* • Gerard Caillaud *Bliche* • Paul Preboist *Inspector Mimile* • Bernard Crommbey [Bernard Crombey] *Inspector Alain* • Gilberte Genait *Zézette* ■ *Dir/Scr* Claude Lelouch

Adventure in Baltimore ★★ U

Comedy 1949 · US · BW · 88mins

A vehicle supposedly tailored for Shirley Temple, a Hollywood veteran at the age of 21, who retired from the screen soon after this movie was released. The tale of the independent girl who scandalises her home town with her paintings and feminist leanings sits awkwardly with Temple's frothy image. As her father, a pastor who comes round to his daughter's point of view, Robert Young has something of a rehearsal for his role in TV's *Father Knows Best*. TS [VIDEO]

Robert Young (1) *Dr Sheldon* • Shirley Temple *Dinah Sheldon* • John Agar *Tom Wade* • Albert Sharpe *Mr Fletcher* • Josephine Hutchinson *Mrs Sheldon* • Charles Kemper *Mr Steuben* • Johnny Sands *Gene Sheldon* ■ *Dir* Richard Wallace • *Scr* Lionel Houser, from a story by Lesser Samuels, Christopher Isherwood

The Adventure of Sherlock Holmes' Smarter Brother ★★★ PG

Comedy 1975 · US/UK · Colour · 87mins

Gene Wilder's directorial debut owes much to his slapdash, slapstick mentor Mel Brooks, with its hit-and-miss array of jokes. Wilder also stars as a wonderfully supercilious Sigerson Holmes, taking over a blackmail case, involving Madeline Kahn and opera star Dom DeLuise, from his more famous brother Sherlock (Douglas Wilmer), and then becoming entangled with stolen state secrets. In a Victorian London that's a set designer's over-cluttered dream, the best humour is very funny indeed, but, apart from that, the whimsy can be rather tiresome. It's all a bit too elementary. TH. Contains swearing. [VIDEO]

Gene Wilder *Sigerson Holmes* • Madeline Kahn *Jenny* • Marty Feldman *Orville Sacker* • Dom DeLuise *Gambetti* • Leo McKern *Moriarty* • Roy Kinnear *Moriarty's aide* • John Le Mesurier *Lord Redcliff* • Douglas Wilmer *Sherlock Holmes* • Thorley Walters *Dr Watson* ■ *Dir/Scr* Gene Wilder

The Adventurers ★★ U

Adventure 1950 · UK · BW · 77mins

Not the 1970 Harold Robbins fiasco, but a sturdy British would-be action drama set in South Africa about the squabbling members of an expedition searching for a cache of diamonds. Jack Hawkins, on his way to major stardom, is cast against type as a villain, who enlists an unconvincing Dennis Price, a young Peter Hammond and Grégoire Aslan to help him recover the treasure. This could have been

A

quite stirring if it hadn't been morbidly under-directed at a snail's pace by David MacDonald. TS

Jack Hawkins *Pieter Brandt* • Peter Hammond *Hendrik Von Thaal* • Dennis Price *Clive Hunter* • Grégoire Aslan *Dominic* • Charles Paton *Barman* • Siobhan McKenna *Anne Hunter* • Bernard Lee *O'Connell* ■ *Dir* David MacDonald • *Scr* Robert Westerby

The Adventurers ★★ U

Action adventure
1968 · Fr/It · Colour · 101mins

The "adventurers" of the title are Alain Delon and Lino Ventura, whose partnership here was a huge European casting coup. Delon and Ventura play a daredevil and inventor respectively who team up for stunts involving fast cars and a plane they plan to fly under the Arc de Triomphe. Joanna Shimkus briefly introduces a touch of *Jules et Jim* into the proceedings, before they become dominated by a race against the Mafia for hidden treasure. AT. French dialogue dubbed into English.

Alain Delon *Manu* • Lino Ventura *Roland* • Joanna Shimkus *Letitia* ■ *Dir* Robert Enrico • *Scr* Robert Enrico, Pierre Pelegri, José Giovanni, from the novel *Les Aventuriers* by José Giovanni

The Adventurers ★ 18

Action adventure
1970 · US · Colour · 163mins

Lewis Gilbert directs this monumentally bad adaptation of Harold Robbins's potboiler about South American revolution, torrid sex and macho posturing. Bekim Fehmiu, a Yugoslavian actor whose career was deservedly short-lived, is at the top of a bewildering list of international stars. The film's mishmash of orgies, violence, Freudian psycho-babble and jet-set locations makes for entertaining viewing – for the first hour. Alas, there's still two more to go. AT

Bekim Fehmiu *Dax Xenos* • Alan Badel *Rojo* • Candice Bergen *Sue Ann Daley* • Ernest Borgnine *Fat Cat* • Leigh Taylor-Young *Amparo* • Fernando Rey *Jaime Xenox* • Charles Aznavour *Marcel Campion* • Olivia de Havilland *Deborah Hadley* • John Ireland *Mr Hadley* • Rossano Brazzi *Baron de Coyne* • Sydney Tafler *Colonel Gutierrez* • Peter Graves (2) *Trustee banker* • Jaclyn Smith *Belinda* • Lois Maxwell *Woman at Fashion Show* ■ *Dir* Lewis Gilbert • *Scr* Lewis Gilbert, Michael Hastings, from the novel by Harold Robbins

Adventures of a Plumber's Mate ★ 18

Sex comedy 1978 · UK · Colour · 84mins

An example of the British blue-comedy boom of the 1970s, this tatty tale presents wife-beating as slapstick. Christopher Neil is singularly unappealing as the titular hero, whose attempts to settle his debts bring him into contact with endless sex-starved women and gangster William Rushton. DP. Contains swearing, sex scenes, nudity.

Christopher Neil *Sid South* • Arthur Mullard *Blackie* • Elaine Paige *Susie* • Anna Quayle *Loretta Proudfoot* ■ *Dir* Stanley Long • *Scr* Stephen D Frances, Aubrey Cash

Adventures of a Private Eye ★ 18

Sex comedy 1977 · UK · Colour · 92mins

Following on from the surprisingly profitable *Adventures of a Taxi Driver*, this smutty romp sticks to the same formula. Christopher Neil, in the title role, strips at regular intervals to satisfy a blackmailer's demand that he sleep with every pretty girl he meets. Comic stalwarts aside, this is really no more than soft-core pulp. DP

Christopher Neil *Bob West* • Suzy Kendall *Laura Sutton* • Harry H Corbett *Sydney* • Liz Fraser *Violet* • Irene Handl *Miss Friggin* • Ian Lavender *Derek* • Jon Pertwee *Judd Blake* • Adrienne Posta *Lisa Moroni* • Anna Quayle *Medea* • William Rushton *Wilfred* • Diana Dors *Mrs Horne* ■ *Dir* Stanley Long • *Scr* Michael Armstrong

Adventures of a Taxi Driver ★★ 18

Sex comedy 1975 · UK · Colour · 85mins

Back in the 1970s, smutty comedies such as this entry in the *Adventures* series were the order of the day for comedy actors trying to break into movies. Robert Lindsay, Liz Fraser, Ian Lavender and Henry McGee are among the familiar faces who probably squirmed with embarrassment at their performances in this bawdy comedy. Barry Evans, who came to prominence in the *Doctor* TV series, is the nominal leading man. JF. Contains swearing, sex scenes, drug abuse, nudity.

Barry Evans *Joe North* • Judy Geeson *Nikki* • Adrienne Posta *Carol* • Diana Dors *Mrs North* • Liz Fraser *Maisie* • Ian Lavender *Ronald* • Robert Lindsay *Tom* • Henry McGee *Inspector Rogers* ■ *Dir* Stanley A Long [Stanley Long] • *Scr* Suzanne Mercer

The Adventures of Baron Munchausen ★★★★ PG

Fantasy adventure
1988 · UK/W Ger · Colour · 121mins

John Neville plays the legendary liar to perfection in this sumptuous revision of the Rudolph Erich Raspe stories that gives a delicious contemporary relevance to the infamous baron's outlandish exploits. Director Terry Gilliam's grandiose masterpiece visualises a warped world of chaotic Pythonesque extremes that extends from the Moon (with the lunar king played by Robin Williams) to Mount Etna (where Oliver Reed gives a brilliant performance) as the baron reunites his four fantastically talented friends to fight the Turkish army. It's an opulent odyssey that balances romance, comedy and thrills. AJ. Contains violence, swearing, brief nudity. DVD

John Neville *Baron Munchausen* • Eric Idle *Desmond/Berthold* • Sarah Polley *Sally Salt* • Oliver Reed *Vulcan* • Charles McKeown *Rupert/Adolphus* • Winston Dennis *Bill Albrecht* • Jack Purvis *Jeremy/Gustavus* • Valentina Cortese *Queen Ariadne/Violet* • Jonathan Pryce *Horatio Jackson* • Uma Thurman *Venus/Rose* • Bill Paterson *Henry Salt* • Peter Jeffrey *Sultan* • Alison Steadman *Daisy* • Sting *Heroic officer* • Robin Williams *King of the moon* ■ *Dir* Terry Gilliam • *Scr* Charles McKeown, Terry Gilliam, from the stories by Rudolph Erich Raspe

The Adventures of Barry McKenzie ★★★ 15

Comedy 1972 · Aus · Colour · 101mins

This is a scrappy but often hilarious screen version of the *Private Eye* comic strip, with Barry Crocker escorting his Aunt Edna Everage through England's grottiest highways and dirtiest byways, and ending with Humphries "flashing his nasty" in front of Joan Bakewell on a late-night TV show. Words like "chunder" and "tubes of beer" entered the English language and, frankly possums, a lot of it is disgusting. A sequel, *Barry McKenzie Holds His Own*, followed two years later. AT DVD

Barry Crocker *Barry McKenzie* • Barry Humphries *Edna Everage/Hoot/Dr Meyer de Lamphrey* • Paul Bertam *Curly* • Dennis Price *Mr Gort* • Avice Landone *Mrs Gort* • Peter Cook *Dominic* • Mary Anne Severne *Lesley* • Dick Bentley *Detective* • Spike Milligan *Landlord* ■ *Dir* Bruce Beresford • *Scr* Bruce Beresford, Barry Humphries, from the comic strip *The Wonderful World of Barry McKenzie* by Barry Humphries

The Adventures of Buckaroo Banzai across the 8th Dimension ★★ 15

Science-fiction comedy
1984 · US · Colour · 97mins

Comic book hero and rock star Banzai (Peter Weller) crashes his Jet Car through the eighth dimension and unwittingly opens a hole in time. Unless he and his weirdo team of Hong Kong Cavaliers close it, evil aliens will overrun the Earth. Far too clever and quirky for its own good, this esoteric cult movie (the directing debut of WD Richter) is a wacky spaced-out oddity. An amazing cast tries to keep it all accessible but it wilfully degenerates into a huge impenetrable mess. AJ DVD

Peter Weller *Buckaroo Banzai* • John Lithgow *Dr Emilio Lizardo/Lord John Whorfin* • Ellen Barkin *Penny Priddy* • Jeff Goldblum *New Jersey* • Christopher Lloyd *John Bigboote* • Lewis Smith *Perfect Tommy* • Robert Ito *Professor Hikita* ■ *Dir* WD Richter • *Scr* Earl Mac Rauch

The Adventures of Bullwhip Griffin ★★★ U

Comedy adventure
1967 · US · Colour · 105mins

This lively western spoof would have been even more entertaining if the mediocre songs had been dropped and director James Neilson had kept a tighter rein on the action. Roddy McDowall has a ball as the staid Boston butler who gains a reputation as a boxer after he unwillingly joins his young master, Bryan Russell, on the California gold rush. Karl Malden, who has stolen Richard Haydn's treasure map, relishes the chance to play a wicked master of disguise. DP

Roddy McDowall *Bullwhip Griffin* • Suzanne Pleshette *Arabella Flagg* • Karl Malden *Judge Higgins* • Harry Guardino *Sam Trimble* • Bryan Russell *Jack Flagg* • Richard Haydn *Quentin Bartlett* • Liam Redmond *Captain Swain* • Hermione Baddeley *Irene Chesney* • Cecil Kellaway *Mr Pemberton* ■ *Dir* James Neilson • *Scr* Lowell S Hawley, from the novel *By the Great Horn Spoon* by Sid Fleischman

Adventures of Captain Fabian ★★ PG

Adventure 1951 · US/Fr · BW · 100mins

Errol Flynn stars in this mediocre costume melodrama. Although William Marshall was credited as director, the influence of his unbilled assistant, Robert Florey (a maverick whose credentials never quite matched his potential), is evident. Flynn overdoes the dash as he delivers servant Micheline Presle from a murder charge and he's upstaged by both Vincent Price, as the New Orleans fop Presle eventually marries, and the ever-dependable Agnes Moorehead. DP

Errol Flynn *Captain Michael Fabian* • Micheline Presle *Lea Mariotte* • Vincent Price *George Brissac* • Agnes Moorehead *Aunt Jezebel* • Victor Francen *Henri Brissac* • Jim Gérald *Constable* ■ *Dir* William Marshall (1) • *Scr* Errol Flynn, from the novel *Fabulous Ann Madlock* by Robert Shannon

Adventures of Don Juan ★★★ PG

Period adventure
1948 · US · Colour · 110mins

Errol Flynn's career was at a low ebb when Warner Bros gave him a shot at playing Don Juan. He attempts to revive the athleticism and charm of his 1930s swashbucklers, and credit must go to director Vincent Sherman, who tactfully photographs the star from angles that disguise the facial ravages of booze, drugs and women. Despite some fine swordplay, and decent acting from both damsel-in-distress Viveca Lindfors and arch-villain Robert Douglas, the film bombed in America, though it was a hit in Europe, where Flynn ended his career. AT

Errol Flynn *Don Juan* • Viveca Lindfors *Queen Margaret* • Robert Douglas *Duke de Lorca* • Alan Hale *Leporello* • Romney Brent *King Phillip III* • Ann Rutherford *Donna Elena* • Robert Warwick *Count De Polan* • Jerry Austin *Don Sebastian* ■ *Dir* Vincent Sherman • *Scr* George Oppenheimer, Harry Kurnitz, from a story by Herbert Dalmas

The Adventures of Elmo in Grouchland ★★★ U

Musical adventure
1999 · US · Colour · 70mins

Sesame Street has always aimed to entertain adults while teaching children, though this big-screen adaptation – concerning Elmo the muppet chasing his runaway blanket to Grouchland and finding both under the thumb of the selfish Mr Huxley (Mandy Patinkin) – is almost exclusively aimed at the five-and-under crowd. What's left over for grown-ups mostly consists of a few hilarious one-liner and Bert and Ernie's pleasing appearances; perhaps the next *Sesame Street* movie should focus on them. KB

Vanessa L Williams *Queen of Trash* • Mandy Patinkin *Huxley* • Kevin Clash *Elmo/Pestie/Grouch jailer/Grouch cab driver* • Fran Brill *Zoe/Pestie/Prairie Dawn* • Sonia Manzano *Maria* • Roscoe Orman *Gordon* • Stephanie D'Abruzzo *Grizzy/Pestie* ■ *Dir* Gary Halvorson • *Scr* Mitchell Kriegman, Joseph Mazzarino, from a story by Mitchell Kriegman

The Adventures of Ford Fairlane ★★ 18

Action comedy 1990 · US · Colour · 97mins

Controversial sexist comic Andrew Dice Clay crashed and burned in an awkward misstep from action director Renny Harlin. The over-hyped Clay plays a rock 'n' roll detective investigating the death of a heavy metal singer on stage in this crude adventure, big on empty spectacle but very low on honest laughs. Robert Englund turns up as a killer with a bad English accent while Priscilla Presley and Wayne Newton send themselves up as usual. AJ

Andrew Dice Clay *Ford Fairlane* • Wayne Newton *Julian Grendel* • Priscilla Presley *Colleen Sutton* • Morris Day *Don Cleveland* • Lauren Holly *Jazz* • Maddie Corman *Zuzu Petals* • Gilbert Gottfried *Johnny Crunch* • David Patrick Kelly *Sam* • Robert Englund *Smiley* ■ *Dir* Renny Harlin • *Scr* Daniel Waters, James Cappe, David Arnott, from the characters created by Rex Weiner

The Adventures of Gerard ★★

Historical adventure
1970 · UK/It/Swi · Colour · 91mins

Based on the stories of Sir Arthur Conan Doyle, this free-spirited romp through the Napoleonic Wars might well puncture a few inflated ideas about military glory, but director Jerzy Skolimowski seems to have embarked on this campaign with little or no strategy. The jokes are haphazard, the acting veers between the astute and the theatrical, period detail is flouted and the battle scenes are more shambolic than satire intended. DP

Peter McEnery *Colonel Etienne Gerard* • Claudia Cardinale *Countess Teresa* • Eli Wallach *Napoleon* • Jack Hawkins *Millefleurs* • Mark Burns *Colonel Russell* • Norman Rossington *Sgt Papilette* • John Neville *Wellington* ■ *Dir* Jerzy Skolimowski • *Scr* HAL Craig, Henry Lester, Gene Gutowski and Jerzy Skolimowski, from the stories by Sir Arthur Conan Doyle

The Adventures of Hajji Baba ★★

Adventure 1954 · US · Colour · 79mins

An unintentionally hilarious *Arabian Nights*-style fantasy, with the late John Derek, husband of Bo, as scantily clad as all the ladies of the harem. Whether or not Hajji is a relative of Ali Baba isn't clear; but because he's a barber, there's a phonetic logic to it all. Anyway, there's a lot of dashing about, plenty of kissing, some fine carpets, a little torture and, weirdest of all, Nat King Cole crooning on the soundtrack whenever the strapping Mr Derek makes an appearance. AT

John Derek *Hajji Baba* • Elaine Stewart *Princess Fawzia* • Thomas Gomez *Osman Aga* • Paul Picerni *Nur-el-din* • Amanda Blake *Banah* • Rosemarie Bowe *Ayesha* ■ *Dir* Don Weis • *Scr* Richard Collins

The Adventures of Huck Finn ★★★ PG

Adventure 1993 · US · Colour · 107mins

With his wide eyes and refreshingly uncontrived manner, Elijah Wood gives a good account of himself in the title role in this Disney version of the Mark Twain classic, while escaped slave Jim is played with great finesse by Courtney B Vance. If writer/director Stephen Sommers occasionally soft-soaps and over-modernises in an attempt to connect with his audience, he still gets fine performances from a brutish Ron Perlman, and the roguish duo of Jason Robards and Robbie Coltrane. DP [VIDEO] DVD

Elijah Wood *Huck Finn* • Courtney B Vance *Jim* • Robbie Coltrane *The Duke* • Jason Robards *The King* • Ron Perlman *Pap Finn* • Dana Ivey *Widow Douglas* • Anne Heche *Mary Jane Wilks* • James Gammon *Deputy Hines* • Paxton Whitehead *Harvey Wilks* • Tom Aldredge *Dr Robinson* ■ *Dir* Stephen Sommers • *Scr* Stephen Sommers from the novel by Mark Twain

The Adventures of Huckleberry Finn ★★★ U

Adventure 1939 · US · BW · 90mins

This was a showcase for MGM's popular and versatile male star Mickey Rooney, who was Oscar-nominated the same year for *Babes in Arms*. Although lacking the lavish Technicolor of David O Selznick's earlier *The Adventures of Tom Sawyer*, this film does benefit from producer Joseph L Mankiewicz's insistence on filming on authentic river locations. The members of the cast look perfect, as if they had just stepped out of Mark Twain's pages, particularly Rex Ingram as Jim the slave and Elizabeth Risdon as the Widow Douglass. TS

Mickey Rooney *Huckleberry Finn* • Walter Connolly *The King* • William Frawley *The Duke* • Rex Ingram (2) *Jim* • Lynne Carver *Mary Jane* • Jo Ann Sayers *Susan* • Minor Watson *Captain Brandy* • Elisabeth Risdon *Widow Douglass* • Clara Blandick *Miss Watson* ■ *Dir* Richard Thorpe • *Scr* Hugo Butler, from the novel by Mark Twain

The Adventures of Huckleberry Finn ★★★ U

Adventure 1960 · US · Colour · 106mins

For all its Mississippi locations, this version of the great Mark Twain novel doesn't sweep us along in the torrential way it should. Maybe Eddie Hodges, as the mischievous Huck, is too prim, or perhaps director Michael Curtiz cut too many of the book's grimmer aspects. It's still an enjoyable epic, however, with Tony Randall as a superbly roguish conman and lively cameos by Buster Keaton and Andy Devine. As the slave, former light heavyweight boxing world champion Archie Moore is a knockout. TH

Tony Randall *The King* • Eddie Hodges *Huckleberry Finn* • Archie Moore *Jim* • Patty McCormack *Joanna* • Neville Brand *Pap* • Mickey Shaughnessy *The Duke* • Judy Canova *Sheriff's wife* • Andy Devine *Mr Carmody* • Buster Keaton *Lion tamer* • John Carradine *Slave Catcher* • Dean Stanton [Harry Dean Stanton] *Slave Catcher* ■ *Dir* Michael Curtiz • *Scr* James Lee, from the novel by Mark Twain

The Adventures of Ichabod and Mr Toad ★★★ U

Animated adventure
1949 · US/UK · Colour · 65mins

This Disney feature begins with a whimsical version of the Washington Irving story *The Legend of Sleepy Hollow*. The tale of put-upon schoolmaster Ichabod Crane is pleasingly told by Bing Crosby, but it's the adventures of Toad of Toad Hall that capture the imagination. Basil Rathbone provides the narration, while Toad is superbly voiced by Eric Blore, best known as the butler in many of the Rogers–Astaire musicals. DP [VIDEO]

Bing Crosby *Narrator* • Basil Rathbone *Narrator* • Eric Blore *Mr Toad* ■ *Dir* Jack Kinney, Clyde Geronimi, James Algar • *Scr* Erdman Penner, Winston Hibler, Joe Rinaldi, Ted Sears, Homer Brightman, Harry Reeves, from the story *The Legend of Sleepy Hollows* by Washington Irving and from the novel *The Wind in the Willows* by Kenneth Grahame

The Adventures of Marco Polo ★★ U

Historical adventure 1938 · US · BW · 99mins

Gary Cooper is the most unlikely Marco Polo, but that didn't stop producer Samuel Goldwyn from casting him in this would-be tongue-in-cheek spectacular. Trouble is, it's not funny enough, nor at all spectacular, and, with cheesy art direction that cries out for Technicolor, the end result is both silly and dull. Also surprisingly dull is villain Basil Rathbone as Ahmed, his character not helped by director Archie Mayo's lack of imagination. Altogether a misfire, but Lana Turner fans should watch for her brief appearance as a handmaiden. TS [VIDEO]

Gary Cooper *Marco Polo* • Sigrid Gurie *Princess Kukachin* • Basil Rathbone *Ahmed* • Ernest Truex *Binguccio* • George Barbier *Kublai Khan* • Binnie Barnes *Nazama* • Alan Hale *Kaidu* • Lana Turner *Maid* ■ *Dir* Archie Mayo • *Scr* Robert E Sherwood, from a story by NA Pogson

The Adventures of Mark Twain ★★★ U

Biographical drama 1944 · US · BW · 130mins

Fredric March plays the title role in this competent biography of Samuel Clemens, alias Mark Twain, America's greatest humorist. Twain, of course, was the creator of Huckleberry Finn, Tom Sawyer and half the entries in any decent book of quotations. He also had an eventful life, which in turn makes an enjoyable film, despite a script which at times suggests that rumours of Twain's wit must have been greatly exaggerated. PF

Fredric March *Samuel Clemens/Mark Twain* • Alexis Smith *Olivia Langdon* • Donald Crisp *JB Pond* • Alan Hale *Steve Gillis* • C Aubrey Smith *Oxford Chancellor* • John Carradine *Bret Harte* • William Henry *Charles Langdon* • Robert Barrat *Horace E Bixby* ■ *Dir* Irving Rapper • *Scr* Alan LeMay, Harry Chandlee

The Adventures of Michael Strogoff ★★

Adventure drama 1937 · US · BW · 83mins

Before this version, Jules Verne's story had already been filmed twice in the silent era; in addition to this American adaptation, it was filmed four more times in Europe. Anton Walbrook here makes his Hollywood debut as a dashing emissary of the Tsar who is sent from St Petersburg to the frozen wastes of Siberia. The journey involves clashes with Tartars, romantic interludes and an interview with a British journalist. Despite some decent scenes and some lavish detail, what the movie really needs is a director like Michael Curtiz to bring it to life. AT

Anton Walbrook *Strogoff* • Elizabeth Allan *Nadia* • Akim Tamiroff *Ogareff* • Margot Grahame *Zangarra* • Eric Blore *Blount* • Edward Brophy *Packer* • Paul Guilfoyle (1) *Vasiloff* ■ *Dir* George Nichols Jr • *Scr* Mortimer Offner, Anthony Veiller, Anne Morrison Chapin from the novel by Jules Verne

The Adventures of Milo and Otis ★★★ U

Adventure 1986 · Jpn · Colour · 71mins

Owing a huge debt to Disney's 1963 film *The Incredible Journey*, this Japanese live-action animal tale is far superior to the studio's own 1993 remake *Homeward Bound: the Incredible Journey*, as the cat and dog of the title don't "speak" for themselves, making their perilous exploits seem all the more thrilling. Dudley Moore might not have been everyone's choice as narrator, but his lively voiceover gives the action sequences a bit more bite and prevents the gentler moments lapsing into whimsy. DP [VIDEO]

Dudley Moore *Narrator* ■ *Dir* Masanori Hata • *Scr* Mark Saltzman, from a story by Masanori Hata

The Adventures of Mowgli ★★★

Animation 1967 · USSR/US · Colour · 89mins

Originally released a year after Disney made box-office history with *The Jungle Book*, this 1967 Soviet version of Rudyard Kipling's ever-popular classic was re-edited and re-voiced in 1996 for a new generation of cartoon fans. Charlton Heston narrates the story of the foundling who is raised by wolves before embarking upon a series of adventures with the animals of the jungle. As directed by R Davidov, the animation has none of Disney's cuteness, but it was a prestige project for the Soyuzmultfilm studios and the care taken is evident. DP. Russian dialogue dubbed into English.

Charlton Heston *Narrator* • Sam Elliott *Kaa* • Dana Delany *Bagheera* • Ian Corlett *Mowgli* • Scott McNeil *Shere Khan* • Cam Lane *Baloo* ■ *Dir* Terry Klausen, R Davidov • *Scr* L Belokurov, with English adaptation by David Longworth, Cordell Wynne, Harry Kalensky, Allan Stanleigh, from the novel *The Jungle Book* by Kipling Rudyard

The Adventures of Pinocchio ★★ U

Fantasy adventure
1996 · UK/Fr/Ger/Cz Rep · Colour · 90mins

Despite state-of-the-art digital technology and creatures from the Jim Henson workshop, this is a disappointing rendition of Carlo Collodi's enchanting morality tale. Martin Landau brings some melancholic gravitas to the proceedings as Geppetto the woodcarver, and Udo Kier is suitably sinister as the puppeteer who lures little boys to his terrifying theme park. Director Steve Barron overplays his hand, however, so the film feels like a glorified pantomime. DP [VIDEO] DVD

Martin Landau *Geppetto* • Jonathan Taylor Thomas *Pinocchio* • Geneviève Bujold *Leona* • Udo Kier *Lorenzini* • Bebe Neuwirth *Felinet* • Rob Schneider *Volpe* • Corey Carrier *Lampwick* • Marcello Magni *Baker* • Dawn French *Baker's wife* • Griff Rhys Jones *Tino* • John Sessions *Schoolmaster* ■ *Dir* Steve Barron • *Scr* Sherry Mills, Steve Barron, Tom Benedek, Barry Berman, from the novel by Carlo Collodi

The Adventures of Priscilla, Queen of the Desert ★★★★ 15

Comedy drama 1994 · Aus · Colour · 98mins

In this wondrously camp classic, director Stephan Elliott tosses the niceties of sexual politics out of the window of a speeding bus and sets about exposing the soft underbelly of the Australian male. Two drag queens and a transsexual travel across the outback in a dilapidated coach for a gig in that bastion of machismo, Alice Springs, en route finding themselves in all manner of hilarious fish-out-of-water situations. Ingeniously cast against type, Terence Stamp is a revelation as the hard-drinking transsexual. Brilliantly bitchy, fabulously photographed and wonderfully played, this frock opera (the costumes won a well-deserved Oscar) addresses serious issues with satirical accuracy and profound insight. DP. Contains swearing [VIDEO] DVD

Terence Stamp *Bernadette* • Hugo Weaving *Tick/Mitzi* • Guy Pearce *Adam/Felicia* • Bill Hunter *Bob* • Sarah Chadwick *Marion* • Mark Holmes *Benjamin* • Julia Cortez *Cynthia* • Ken Radley *Frank* ■ *Dir/Scr* Stephan Elliott • *Cinematographer* Brian Breheny • *Costume Designer* Lizzy Gardiner, Tim Chappel

The Adventures of Robin Hood ★★★★★ U

Classic swashbuckling adventure
1938 · US · Colour · 101mins

Shot in bright-as-a-button Technicolor, this swashbuckler is an action picture that, over 60 years on, still delights people of all ages, even youngsters weaned on computer games. It was intended to star James Cagney, but seems tailor-made for Errol Flynn as Sherwood's noblest outlaw. Flynn woos Olivia de Havilland and crosses swords with Basil Rathbone and Claude Rains, while Erich Wolfgang Korngold's music goes brassily heraldic. A few weeks into production, studio boss Jack Warner thought the rushes lacked sparkle and replaced director William Keighley with Michael Curtiz. The result was a box-office smash and Oscars for the score, editing and interior decoration. AT [VIDEO] DVD

Errol Flynn *Robin Hood* • Olivia de Havilland *Maid Marian* • Basil Rathbone *Guy of Gisbourne* • Claude Rains *Prince John* • Patric Knowles *Will Scarlet* • Eugene Pallette *Friar Tuck* • Alan Hale *Little John* • Melville Cooper *High Sheriff of Nottingham* • Ian Hunter *King Richard* • Una O'Connor *Bess* ■ *Dir* Michael Curtiz, William Keighley • *Scr* Norman Reilly Raine, Seton I Miller, based on ancient Robin Hood legends, the novel *Ivanhoe* by Sir Walter Scott, and the operetta *Robin Hood* by De Koven-Smith • *Cinematographer* Sol Polito, Tony Gaudio, W Howard Greene • *Editor* Ralph Dawson • *Music* Erich Wolfgang Korngold • *Art Director* Carl Jules Weyl

The Adventures of Robinson Crusoe ★★★★ U

Adventure 1952 · US · Colour · 89mins

Considering what director Luis Buñuel did with *Wuthering Heights*, this is an astonishingly restrained adaptation of Daniel Defoe's classic castaway tale. Gone is the surrealism one expects of Buñuel, and in its place comes a heartfelt optimism about the salvation of humanity. Dan O'Herlihy received an Oscar nomination for his portrayal of the privileged man who comes to a greater understanding of life through his unbearable isolation. The arrival of Friday (Jaime Fernandez), offers an even more strenuous test and he finds himself reverting to his old ways. DP. A Spanish language film.

Dan O'Herlihy *Robinson Crusoe* • Jaime Fernandez *Man Friday* • Felipe de Alba *Captain Oberzo* • Chel Lopez *Bosun* • José Chavez

Mutineer • Emilio Garibay *Mutineer* ■ *Dir* Luis Buñuel • *Scr* Luis Buñuel, Philip Ansell Roll [Hugo Butler], from the novel by Daniel Defoe

The Adventures of Rocky & Bullwinkle ★★★ U

Part-animated comedy
1999 · US/Ger · Colour · 87mins

Robert De Niro plays a cartoon villain intent on world domination in this big-screen revival of a popular US children's series of the 1950s and 60s. Animated heroes Rocky (a squirrel) and Bullwinkle (a moose) are brought out of retirement to do battle with Fearless Leader (De Niro) and his associates (Rene Russo and Jason Alexander), who've been transformed into live-action baddies. It's all fast, fun and gloriously tongue-in-cheek. Rocky and Bullwinkle's antics will please younger viewers, and De Niro gleefully sends himself up. DA [video] DVD

Rene Russo *Natasha Fatale* • Jason Alexander *Boris Badenov* • Piper Perabo *Karen Sympathy* • Randy Quaid *Cappy von Trapment* • Robert De Niro *Fearless Leader* • June Foray *Rocket J "Rocky" Squirrel/Natasha/Narrator's mother* • Keith Scott *Bullwinkle J Moose/Fearless Leader/Boris/Narrator* • Billy Crystal *Travelling mattress salesman* • Whoopi Goldberg *Judge* ■ *Dir* Des McAnuff • *Scr* Kenneth Lonergan, from characters created by Jay Way

The Adventures of Sebastian Cole ★★★ 15

Comedy drama 1998 · US · Colour · 94mins

Told mostly in flashback, Tod Williams's episodic debut turns the rites-of-passage picture on its head. Where else would you encounter a drunkenly irresponsible mother, a motorcycling sister and a fiercely Catholic stepfather who decides to have a sex-change operation? Yet, despite this determined kookiness, there's an almost Andy Hardy feel to the pep talks shared by tousle-haired Adrian Grenier and the bewigged Clark Gregg. Sufficiently confident to leave plot strands untied, this is an authentically fuzzy snapshot of a life in progress. DP [video]

Adrian Grenier *Sebastian Cole* • Clark Gregg *Hark/Henrietta Cole* • Aleksa Palladino *Mary* • Margaret Colin *Joan Cole* • John Shea *Hartley* • Marni Lustig *Jessica* • Famke Jannssen *Fiona* ■ *Dir/Scr* Tod Williams

The Adventures of Sharkboy and Lavagirl in 3-D ★★

Action adventure 2005 · US · Colour · 92mins

Robert Rodriguez's family adventure is all about the power of dreams, specifically those of a meek and bullied boy named Max (Cayden Boyd). Max retreats into his imagination only to discover that the titular superheroes of his fantasies have become real. Most of the film takes place in a CGI world of Max's imaginings, with rivers of milk, giant cookies and an actual brainstorm. The film certainly has an upbeat energy, but this could be a headache-inducing ride, with gaudy art direction and uneven performances. GM

Taylor Lautner *Shark Boy* • Taylor Dooley *Lava Girl* • Cayden Boyd *Max* • George Lopez *Mr Electric/Tobor/Ice Guardian/Mr Electricidad* • David Arquette *Max's dad* • Kristin Davis *Max's mom* • Jacob Davich *Linus/Minus* ■ *Dir* Robert Rodriguez • *Scr* Robert Rodriguez, Marcel Rodriguez, from a story by Robert Rodriguez, Racer Rodriguez

The Adventures of Sherlock Holmes ★★★★ PG

Mystery 1939 · US · BW · 81mins

Following *The Hound of the Baskervilles*, this second teaming of Basil Rathbone and Nigel Bruce as Holmes and Watson is one of the master detective's best screen cases. Borrowing from the stories of Sir Arthur Conan Doyle and the stage play by William Gillette, the film superbly re-creates the atmosphere of 221B Baker Street and Victorian London. Holmes never had a more devilish adversary than George Zucco as Moriarty or a more daring plot to foil than the theft of the Crown Jewels. DP [video] DVD

Basil Rathbone *Sherlock Holmes* • Nigel Bruce *Dr Watson* • Ida Lupino *Ann Brandon* • Alan Marshal *Jerrold Hunter* • Terry Kilburn *Billy* • George Zucco *Professor Moriarty* • Henry Stephenson *Sir Ronald Ramsgate* • EE Clive *Inspector Bristol* • Arthur Hohl *Bassick* • May Beatty *Mrs Jameson* ■ *Dir* Alfred Werker • *Scr* Edwin Blum, William Drake, from the play "Sherlock Holmes" by William Gillette, from the stories of Sir Arthur Conan Doyle

The Adventures of Slappy the Sea Lion ★★ PG

Comedy adventure
1998 · US · Colour · 75mins

This lacklustre animal caper sees a group of practical-joking youngsters get into hot water when they abduct Slappy the sea lion from their local aquarium. Predictable, occasionally comic mayhem ensues, including a more than generous dollop of toilet humour. But it's dull stuff, with only the guaranteed pleasures of animal antics to enliven it. RT [video]

BD Wong *Morgan Brinway* • Bronson Pinchot *Roy* • Sam McMurray *Boccoli* • Jennifer Coolidge *Harriet* • Joseph Ashton *Sonny* ■ *Dir* Barnet Kellman • *Scr* Bob Wolterstorff [Robert Wolterstorff], Mike Scott

The Adventures of Tartu ★★

Second World War spy drama
1943 · UK · BW · 112mins

In order to sabotage a Nazi nerve gas factory, Robert Donat goes undercover in Czechoslovakia as a Romanian ex-diplomat. Valerie Hobson is also undercover, though she's posing as a Nazi. Harold S Bucquet's film is solidly made and reasonably tense, but the casting of Donat can't help reminding viewers of the far superior *The Thirty-Nine Steps*. AT

Robert Donat *Captain Terence Stevenson* • Valerie Hobson *Maruschka* • Walter Rilla *Inspector Otto Vogel* • Glynis Johns *Paula Palacek* • Phyllis Morris *Anna Palacek* ■ *Dir* Harold S Bucquet • *Scr* Howard Emmet Rogers, John Lee Mahin, Miles Malleson, from a story by John C Higgins

The Adventures of the Wilderness Family ★★ U

Adventure 1975 · US · Colour · 98mins

Echoes of *Swiss Family Robinson* reverberate around this encounter with the great outdoors, as an identically named family quits Los Angeles to set up home in the Colorado Rockies. However, the marauding wildlife, suspicious locals and unyielding flora soon prove as irksome as the crime and pollution they have left behind. Stewart Raffill makes the most of his breathtaking locations, but the survivalist angle is all too familiar. DP

Robert F Logan [Robert Logan] *Skip* • Susan Damante Shaw [Susan Shaw] *Pat* • Hollye Holmes *Jenny* • Ham Larsen *Toby* ■ *Dir/Scr* Stewart Raffill

The Adventures of Tom Sawyer ★★★★ U

Adventure 1938 · US · Colour · 90mins

This superb David O Selznick production, made the year before he gave the world *Gone with the Wind*, remains the most entertaining, and most faithful, of all screen adaptations of Mark Twain's tale. The nightmare sequences in the caverns are brilliantly executed, and the use of early Technicolor particularly effective. The pace is fast, the running time taut and the casting impeccable: apart from the two decent boy leads, who could fail to warm to a period romp featuring Walter Brennan, May Robson and Victor Jory. TS [video] DVD

Tommy Kelly *Tom Sawyer* • Jackie Moran *Huckleberry Finn* • Ann Gillis *Becky Thatcher* • May Robson *Aunt Polly* • Walter Brennan *Muff Potter* • Victor Jory *Injun Joe* • David Holt *Sid Sawyer* • Victor Kilian *Sheriff* • Nana Bryant *Mrs Thatcher* • Donald Meek *Superintendent* • Charles Richman *Judge Thatcher* ■ *Dir* Norman Taurog • *Scr* John VA Weaver, from the novel by Mark Twain

The Adventures of Tom Thumb and Thumbelina ★★ U

Animated musical adventure
2002 · US · Colour · 71mins

Once upon a time, children would forgive the shoddy graphics and atrocious songs in a cheaply made animation such as this one because animals talked, there was plenty of slapstick and good triumphed over evil. Jennifer Love Hewitt sings sweetly as she laments being imprisoned by both a French carnival barker and the Mole King, but Elijah Wood is less than convincing as her hero. DP [video] DVD

Jennifer Love Hewitt *Thumbelina* • Elijah Wood *Tom Thumb* • Alexandra Boyd *Bertha Beetle* • Peter Gallagher *Mole King* • Rachel Griffiths *Albertine* • Robert Guillaume *Ben* • Jane Leeves *Margaret Beetle* • Esai Morales *Vergas Mouse* • Bebe Neuwirth *Thumbelina's mother* ■ *Dir* Glenn Chaika

The Adversary ★★★

Drama 1970 · Ind · BW · 109mins

Following his father's death, Dhritiman Chatterjee is forced to abandon his studies and find work to support his family, but cannot compete in the rat race. Satyajit Ray paints a perceptive portrait of an educated but listless character attempting to manage life in the stressful environment of Calcutta. The supporting characters are also incisively drawn in this sharply observed tale, at once amusing, poignant and bitter, from India's master auteur. RB. In Bengali with English subtitles.

Dhritiman Chatterjee *Siddhartha* • Krishna Bose *Sutapa* • Jaysree Roy *Keya* • Debraj Roy *Tunu* ■ *Dir* Satyajit Ray • *Scr* Satyajit Ray, from the novel *Pratidwandi* by Sunil Ganguly • *Music* Satyajit Ray

Advice to the Lovelorn ★★

Comedy drama 1933 · US · BW · 62mins

Lee Tracy was never a frontline star and his fast-talking style has not travelled well down the years. Nevertheless, his films were rarely dull. Here journalist Tracy alienates his rich fiancée and breaks up a drugs ring after being relegated to the lonely-hearts column of his local paper. This mixes comedy, tragedy and thrills, with capable performers such as Sally Blane and Jean Adair left in Tracy's dynamic slipstream. DP

Lee Tracy *Toby Prentiss* • Sally Blane *Louise Boley* • Sterling Holloway *Benny* • Jean Adair *Mrs Prentiss* • Paul Harvey *Gaskell* • Matt Briggs *Richards* • Charles Levison [Charles Lane (2)] *Circulation Manager* • Isabel Jewell *Rose* ■ *Dir* Alfred Werker • *Scr* Leonard Praskins, from the novel *Miss Lonelyhearts* by Nathanael West

Advise and Consent ★★★★ PG

Political drama 1962 · US · BW · 132mins

Otto Preminger's superb study of political shenanigans in Washington provides marvellous roles for Henry Fonda as the liberal politician that ailing president Franchot Tone wants to promote and Charles Laughton, in his last film, as the southern senator opposed to the appointment. This was all but unique among Hollywood movies of the time in using homosexuality as a plot device, and, although it may seem a little tame today, it was significant and shocking enough on its release. TS [video]

Henry Fonda *Robert Leffingwell* • Charles Laughton *Sen Seabright "Seb" Cooley* • Don Murray *Sen Brigham Anderson* • Walter Pidgeon *Sen Bob Munson* • Peter Lawford *Sen Lafe Smith* • George Grizzard *Sen Fred Van Ackerman* • Gene Tierney *Dolly Harrison* • Franchot Tone *President* • Lew Ayres *Vice-President* • Burgess Meredith *Herbert Gelman* ■ *Dir* Otto Preminger • *Scr* Wendell Mayes, from the novel by Allen Drury

Ae Fond Kiss... ★★★ 15

Romantic drama
2004 · UK/Ger/It/Sp/Fr · Colour · 100mins

In Ken Loach's surprisingly sexy modern variation on *Romeo and Juliet*, the star-crossed lovers are a Scots-Pakistani DJ (Atta Yaqub) and an Irish music teacher (Eva Birthistle) living in contemporary Glasgow. Yaqub's parents are planning a traditional arranged marriage for him, but he embarks on a relationship with Birthistle. Loach's film emerges as a touching modern love story that should reach beyond his usual audience. BP. An English/Punjabi language film. Contains swearing, sex scenes. DVD

Atta Yaqub *Casim Khan* • Eva Birthistle *Roisin Hanlon* • Shamshad Akhatar *Sadia Khan* • Ghizala Avan *Rukhsana Khan* • Shabana Bakhsh *Tahara Khan* • Ahmad Riaz *Tariq Khan* • Gerard Kelly *Parish priest* ■ *Dir* Ken Loach • *Scr* Paul Laverty

Aelita ★★★★

Silent science-fiction adventure
1924 · USSR · BW · 81mins

Based on the story by Alexei Tolstoy and shamelessly combining propaganda with escapism, this marks Soviet cinema's entry into the realms of science fiction. Exploiting the theatrical stylisation he had discovered during his post-1917 exile, director Jakov Protazanov leavened the polemic with much good humour, as accidental astronaut Nikolai Zeretelli leads a revolution against the tyrannical queen of Mars, Yulia Solntseva. The acting is energetic, the satire assured, and yet it was Isaak Rabinovich's expressionist sets and Aleksandra Ekster's futuristic costumes that were to have the greatest impact on the genre. DP

Nikolai M Zeretelli *Los* • Yulia Solntseva *Queen Aelita* • Igor Illinski *Busev* ■ *Dir* Jakov A Protazanov • *Scr* Fedor Ozep, Aleksey Fajko, from the story by Alexei Tolstoy

The Affair ★★ PG

Romantic drama 1973 · US · Colour · 70mins

Made for American television, this trifling melodrama was shown theatrically in Europe, where its threadbare production values were painfully obvious. Nevertheless, this tale of a young woman disabled since childhood who finds romance with a sophisticated lawyer is given poignancy by the casting of Natalie Wood opposite her real-life husband, Robert Wagner. Director Gilbert Cates occasionally comes up with a few insights amid the tosh but Wagner's just not in Wood's league. TS [video]

Natalie Wood *Courtney Patterson* • Robert Wagner *Marcus Simon* • Bruce Davison *Jamie Patterson* • Jamie Smith-Jackson *Jennifer* • Pat Harrington *Frank* ■ *Dir* Gilbert Cates • *Scr* Barbara Turner • *Producer* Aaron Spelling, Leonard Goldberg

A

Affair in Havana ★★

Crime drama 1957 · US · BW · 77mins

John Cassavetes plays a songwriter who goes to Cuba in search of great music and instead finds Sara Shane, the wife of repulsive plantation owner Raymond Burr. Shane falls for Cassavetes and is all set to run off with him when Burr promises her his $20 million fortune. Tired of waiting for him to die of natural causes, she shoves him into the swimming pool. Directed by Laslo Benedek, this B-movie melodrama was partly financed by Cuba's tottering government. AT

John Cassavetes *Nick* • Raymond Burr *Mallabee* • Sara Shane *Lorna* • Lila Lazo *Fina* • Sergio Pena *Valdes* ■ *Dir* Laszlo Benedek [Laslo Benedek] • *Scr* Burton Lane, Maurice Zimm, from a story by Janet Green

Affair in Trinidad ★★★

Spy drama 1952 · US · BW · 98mins

Rita Hayworth and Glenn Ford, stars of that electric *film noir Gilda*, are re-united here in yet another spy drama set in a far-flung international Hollywood hotspot. The plot is some nonsense about spy rings, with Ford helping Hayworth find her husband's killer, but who cares when the stars strike such sparks from each other? Alexander Scourby makes an effective villain, and veteran director Vincent Sherman is in his element with this kind of material. Despite its flaws, this is highly entertaining, and Hayworth is simply ravishing in her return to the screen after a four-year break following her marriage to Prince Aly Khan. TS

Rita Hayworth *Chris Emery* • Glenn Ford *Steve Emery* • Alexander Scourby *Max Fabian* • Valerie Bettis *Veronica* • Torin Thatcher *Inspector Smythe* • Howard Wendell *Anderson* ■ *Dir* Vincent Sherman • *Scr* Oscar Saul, James Gunn, from a story by Virginia Van Upp, Berne Giler

The Affair of the Necklace ★★ 12

Period romantic drama
2001 · US · Colour · 112mins

Director Charles Shyer delivers a stodgy period drama, based on a true event that has since been credited as one of the contributory causes of the French Revolution. While that sounds potentially fascinating, the result is actually a turgid and woefully miscast mess, as Hilary Swank fails to look like a delicate French lady trying to regain her noble birthright by meddling in court intrigue. Equally out of their depth and looking far too 21st-century are Adrien Brody and Simon Baker as two of her fellow schemers. So it's left to Jonathan Pryce and Christopher Walken to inject some humour by camping it up. JB [VIDEO] DVD

Hilary Swank *Jeanne de la Motte-Valois* • Jonathan Pryce *Cardinal Louis de Rohan* • Simon Baker *Rétaux de Villette* • Adrien Brody *Nicolas de la Motte* • Brian Cox *Baron de Breteuil* • Joely Richardson *Marie Antoinette* • Christopher Walken *Cagliostro* ■ *Dir* Charles Shyer • *Scr* John Sweet

An Affair to Remember ★★★★ U

Romantic drama
1957 · US · Colour · 109mins

The incomparable Cary Grant is at his slickly arch and urbane best as a wealthy, idle womaniser who meets his match in self-contained, sassy Deborah Kerr aboard a luxury liner. Director Leo McCarey (who also made 1939's *Love Affair* on which this is based) dresses his sophisticated comedy of sexual manners in an atmosphere of rhinestone-encrusted dresses, impeccably pressed dinner suits and raised champagne glasses. The second half slips off the boil somewhat, but this remains a cinematic object lesson in the perfect rapier delivery of cut-and-thrust dialogue. SH [VIDEO] DVD

Cary Grant *Nickie Ferrante* • Deborah Kerr *Terry Mckay* • Richard Denning *Kenneth* • Neva Patterson *Lois* • Cathleen Nesbitt *Grandmother* • Robert Q Lewis *Announcer* • Charles Watts *Hathaway* • Fortunio Bonanova *Courbet* ■ *Dir* Leo McCarey • *Scr* Delmer Daves, Donald Ogden Stewart (uncredited), Leo McCarey, from a story by Leo McCarey, Mildred Cram

Affair with a Stranger ★★★ U

Romantic drama 1953 · US · BW · 86mins

A well-cast Victor Mature and Jean Simmons play a warring couple who adopt a child as their union collapses in this lesson in how not to handle a disintegrating relationship. Director Roy Rowland brings out the best in the stars, who make this crazy premise credible by sheer strength of acting. However, having set everything up, Rowland seems unsure about the direction his characters should take. Watching this is rather like opening a tempting box of chocolates and finding half are missing. SH

Jean Simmons *Carolyn Parker* • Victor Mature *Bill Blakeley* • Mary Jo Tarola *Dolly Murray* • Monica Lewis *Janet Boothe* • Jane Darwell *Ma Stanton* • Dabbs Greer *Happy Murray* • Wally Vernon *Joe* • Nicholas Joy *George Craig* ■ *Dir* Roy Rowland • *Scr* Richard Flournoy

Une Affaire de Femmes ★★★

Second World War drama
1988 · Fr · Colour · 110mins

Isabelle Huppert won the best actress prize at the Venice Film Festival for her portrayal of a mother whose struggle to survive the Nazi Occupation brought her into conflict with the Vichy authorities. Before becoming the last woman in France to be guillotined, Marie Latour performs abortions with a detachment that causes many to label her a monster. But Claude Chabrol refuses to take sides, adopting Jean Renoir's famous maxim that everyone has their reasons, as he dispassionately reconstructs the bleak realities of the early 1940s. DP. In French with English subtitles.

Isabelle Huppert *Marie* • François Cluzet *Paul* • Marie Trintignant *Lulu/Lucie* • Nils Tavernier *Lucien* ■ *Dir* Claude Chabrol • *Scr* Claude Chabrol, Colo Tavernier O'Hagan, from the novel *Une Affaire de Femmes* by Francis Szpiner

Les Affaires Publiques ★★★

Comedy 1934 · Fr · BW · 25mins

Robert Bresson made this short during his 20s, while he was in the thrall of René Clair and Charlie Chaplin. He later disowned this early work, and for many years it was thought to be lost until it was discovered and restored in the mid-1980s. Bresson rejected the term burlesque, preferring to call it a "crazy comedy". The film stars Beby the clown as the dictator in an imaginary country, and follows his not especially comic misadventures over a period of days in a provincial town. It remains significant today only as the aberrant work of a future great director before he radicalised his life and art. BB. In French with English subtitles.

Beby *Chancellor* • Andrée Servilanges *Princess* • Marcel Dalio *Sculptor/Fireman/Radio voice* • Gilles Margaritis *Chauffeur* ■ *Dir* Robert Bresson • *Scr* Robert Bresson, Andre Josset, Paul Weill

The Affairs of Annabel ★★★ U

Satire 1938 · US · BW · 67mins

This good-natured, fast-moving semi-satire on the film industry features wacky Lucille Ball as a star and rueful, lovable Jack Oakie as her inept press agent, who's always cooking up stunts that don't work. The film was popular enough in its day to inspire a limp sequel, *Annabel Takes a Tour*, with the same cast but a different director. Lucille Ball would eventually derive personal satisfaction from buying RKO, the studio where she filmed this trifle, and renaming it Desilu, where *I Love Lucy* was recorded for posterity. TS

Lucille Ball *Annabel Allison* • Jack Oakie *Lanny Morgan* • Ruth Donnelly *Josephine* • Bradley Page *Webb* • Fritz Feld *Vladimir* • Thurston Hall *Major* • Elisabeth Risdon *Mrs Fletcher* • Granville Bates *Mr Fletcher* ■ *Dir* Ben Stoloff • *Scr* Bert Granet, Paul Yawitz from a story by Charles Hoffman

The Affairs of Cellini ★★

Comedy 1934 · US · BW · 84mins

Hopelessly dated, this saunter through a Hollywood Florence initially offers some pleasure, largely thanks to director Gregory La Cava's sense of fun. In the title role, a bearded Fredric March proves he was one of the few stars of the time who looked truly comfortable in costume, and a top-billed Constance Bennett and Oscar-nominated Frank Morgan are enjoyable enough to watch, but the farcical tone does become irritating. Quite saucy in its own pre-censorship way. TS

Constance Bennett *Duchess of Florence* • Fredric March *Benvenuto Cellini* • Frank Morgan *Alessandro, Duke of Florence* • Fay Wray *Angela* • Vince Barnett *Ascanio* • Jessie Ralph *Beatrice* • Louis Calhern *Ottaviano* • Lucille Ball *Lady-in-waiting* ■ *Dir* Gregory La Cava • *Scr* Bess Meredyth, from the play *The Firebrand* by Edwin Justus Mayer

The Affairs of Dobie Gillis ★★★ U

Musical comedy 1953 · US · Colour · 72mins

It's youthful love at first sight when Debbie Reynolds and Bobby Van meet at the freshmen's get-together at Grainbelt College – motto: learn, learn, learn; work, work, work. She's there to do just that, he's there to have fun. True love faces numerous obstacles, especially Reynolds's tyrannical father, Hanley Stafford, in this good-natured and increasingly silly, semi-musical college caper. The appealing and talented Van dances up a storm, as do Reynolds, Bob Fosse before he became famous, and Barbara Ruick. RK

Debbie Reynolds *Pansy Hammer* • Bobby Van *Dobie Gillis* • Barbara Ruick *Lorna Ellingboe* • Bob Fosse *Charlie Trask* • Hanley Stafford *Mr Hammer* • Lurene Tuttle *Mrs Hammer* • Hans Conried *Professor Amos Pomfritt* • Charles Lane (2) *Professor Obispo* ■ *Dir* Don Weis • *Scr* Max Shulman

The Affairs of Martha ★★★ U

Comedy 1942 · US · BW · 66mins

Although he would later become known for *films noirs*, heist hrillers and collaborations with his Greek wife Merlina Mercouri, Jules Dassin directed several light entertainments in his early career. This MGM B-movie, his second feature, proved an admirable showcase for Marsha Hunt as the Swedish maid, who not only writes a pseudonymous account of her life with a society family, but also marries son-and-heir Richard Carlson after a drunken night out. The support cast is splendid, as is the literate screenplay. DP

Marsha Hunt *Martha Lindstrom* • Richard Carlson *Jeff Sommerfield* • Marjorie Main *Mrs McKissick* • Virginia Weidler *Miranda Sommerfield* • Spring Byington *Mrs Sophie Sommerfield* • Allyn Joslyn *Joel Archer* • Barry Nelson *Danny O'Brien* • Frances Drake *Sylvia Norwood* • Margaret Hamilton *Guinevere* ■ *Dir* Jules Dassin • *Scr* Isobel Lennart, Lee Gold

The Affairs of Susan ★★★

Comedy 1945 · US · BW · 109mins

Actress Susan Darell, portrayed by a very effervescent Joan Fontaine, gets to reveal four different personae during a series of flashbacks at fiancé Walter Abel's bachelor party, where he has invited two other suitors plus Susan's previous husband, George Brent. This is a witty and classy Hal Wallis production, which rightly garnered an Oscar nomination for best original story. The real surprise is Fontaine, who proves what a capable actress she is, offering a charming and utterly beguiling star performance in an unfairly neglected comedy. TS

Joan Fontaine *Susan Darell* • George Brent *Roger Berton* • Dennis O'Keefe *Bill Anthony* • Don DeFore *Mike Ward* • Rita Johnson *Mona Kent* • Walter Abel *Richard Aiken* • Byron Barr *Chick* • Mary Field *Nancy* • Francis Pierlot *Uncle Jimmy* ■ *Dir* William A Seiter • *Scr* Laszlo Gorog, Richard Flournoy, Thomas Monroe, from a story by Laszlo Gorog, Thomas Monroe

Affectionately Yours ★★

Comedy 1941 · US · BW · 87mins

Top news correspondent Dennis Morgan rushes home from an overseas assignment to win back his wife Merle Oberon. Rita Hayworth appears as "the other woman", and she's the best thing in a supposed marital comedy that misfires in every direction. Ralph Bellamy is fine as a rival for Oberon's affections, but neither of the stars has the right personality or touch to rescue the weak material. RK

Merle Oberon *Sue Marberry* • Dennis Morgan *Richard "Rickey" Mayberry* • Rita Hayworth *Irene Malcolm* • Ralph Bellamy *Owen Wright* • George Tobias *Pasha* • James Gleason *Chester Phillips* • Hattie McDaniel *Cynthia* • Jerome Cowan *Cullen* • Alexis Smith *Guest* • Butterfly McQueen *Butterfly* ■ *Dir* Lloyd Bacon • *Scr* Edward Kaufman, from a story by Fanya Foss, Aleen Leslie

Affliction ★★★ 15

Drama 1997 · US · Colour · 109mins

Part thriller, part examination of a man in midlife crisis. this is bleak but well-performed. Nick Nolte plays a traffic cop in a small New England town. When his friend Jim True returns from a hunting expedition claiming the businessman he took with him died from a self-inflicted wound, Nolte seeks an escape from his damning ex-wife by turning detective. His subsequent mental disintegration is both painful and powerful to watch. Too black to be mainstream, this is nevertheless a tour de force for Nolte, though it was James Coburn who won the Oscar for his portrayal of Nolte's abusive father. LH. Contains swearing and violence. [VIDEO] DVD

Nick Nolte *Wade Whitehouse* • Sissy Spacek *Margie Fogg* • James Coburn *Glen Whitehouse* • Willem Dafoe *Rolfe Whitehouse* • Mary Beth Hurt *Lillian* • Jim True *Jack Hewitt* ■ *Dir* Paul Schrader • *Scr* Paul Schrader, from the novel by Russell Banks

Afraid of the Dark ★★★ 18

Psychological thriller
1991 · UK/Fr · Colour · 87mins

The directorial debut of Mark Peploe, a regular scriptwriter for his brother-in-law Bernardo Bertolucci, this is an eerily effective exercise in suspense. The always watchable James Fox is a cop trying to protect his small son and his blind wife (Fanny Ardant) from the attentions of a neighbourhood psycho, who may be window cleaner and pornographer Paul McGann. It's a quirky blend of *Wait until Dark* and Michael Powell's shocker *Peeping Tom* that throws up as many surprises as it does artistic pretensions. AT

James Fox *Frank* • Fanny Ardant *Miriam* • Paul McGann *Tony Dalton* • Clare Holman *Rose* • Robert Stephens *Dan Burns* • Susan Woolridge *Lucy Trent* • Ben Keyworth *Lucas* ■ *Dir/Scr* Mark Peploe

L'Afrance ★★★ 15

Drama 2001 · Fr/Sen · Colour · 90mins

Acclaimed on the festival circuit, Alain Gomis's debut feature is a charged, compassionate and uncompromising look at the realities facing sub-Saharan exiles in modern France. Torn between a desire to make a difference in his native Senegal and staying in Paris with girlfriend Delphine Zingg, Djolof Mbengue has to battle with the immigration authorities to extend the visa that will enable him to complete his studies. But while Gomis handles this personal history with tact, his primary focus is on the socio-economic pressures that drive so many young African men to endure dead-end jobs and prejudice. DP. In French with English subtitles.

Djolof Mbengue *El Hadj* • Delphine Zingg *Myriam* • Samir Guesmi *Khalid* • Théophile Moussa Sowié *Demba* • Thierno Ndiaye Doss [Thierno Ndiaye] *Father* ■ *Dir* Alain Gomis • *Scr* Alain Gomis, Pierre Schöller, Marc Wels, Xavier Christiaens, Nathalie Stragier

Africa Screams ★★ U

Comedy 1949 · US · BW · 79mins

Abbott and Costello find themselves at the mercy of rampaging lions, cheeky chimps and hostile locals when bookseller Bud persuades explorer Frank Buck that Lou is the big game hunter he needs for his safari. Using every convention of the *Tarzan* movies, this forgettable comedy is as dense as the jungle, with the biggest laughs being Lou's name (Stanley Livingston) and the scene in which he fights off a frisky kitten. DP DVD

Bud Abbott *Buzz Johnson* • Lou Costello *Stanley Livingston* • Hillary Brooke *Diana Emerson* • Max Baer *Boots* • Buddy Baer *Grappler* ■ *Dir* Charles Barton • *Scr* Earl Baldwin

Africa – Texas Style! ★★ U

Adventure 1967 · US/UK · Colour · 108mins

In this unashamed attempt to replicate Howard Hawks's classic *Hatari!* Hugh O'Brian is the Texan cowboy hired by settler John Mills to round up the Kenyan wildlife. Second unit maestro Andrew Marton, who directed the *Ben-Hur* chariot race and the D-Day landings for *The Longest Day*, has a field day with rhinos, but can't overcome the banal script. A short-lived TV series called *Cowboy in Africa* followed. AT

Hugh O'Brian *Jim Sinclair* • John Mills *Wing Commander Hayes* • Nigel Green *Karl Bekker* • Tom Nardini *John Henry* • Adrienne Corri *Fay Carter* • Ronald Howard *Hugo Copp* • Charles Malinda *Sampson* • Honey Wamala *Mr Oyondi* • Hayley Mills *Girl at airport* ■ *Dir* Andrew Marton • *Scr* Andy White

The African Queen ★★★★★ U

Classic romantic adventure
1951 · UK · Colour · 100mins

What an inspired pairing! And to think, Charlie Allnutt and Rose Sayer were nearly played by David Niven and Bette Davis. Initially, all was not well between Katharine Hepburn and Humphrey Bogart but from the moment she began basing her character on Eleanor Roosevelt, the elements fused into a unique screen chemistry, and a gentle humour (that was noticeably absent from the shooting script) began to seep into the action. With director John Huston distracted by extracurricular safaris, the location work was clearly a strain – look at Bogie's face as he pulls the *Queen* through the leech-infested water. Yet the discord and discomfort resulted in a classic, and a long overdue Oscar for Bogart. DP DVD

Humphrey Bogart *Charlie Allnutt* • Katharine Hepburn *Rose Sayer* • Robert Morley *Reverend Samuel Sayer* • Peter Bull *German Captain* • Theodore Bikel *German First Officer* • Walter Gotell *German Second Officer* • Gerald Onn *Petty Officer* ■ *Dir* John Huston • *Scr* James Agee, John Huston, from the novel by CS Forester • *Producer* SP Eagle [Sam Spiegel] • *Cinematographer* Jack Cardiff

After Dark, My Sweet ★★★★ 18

Crime thriller 1990 · US · Colour · 111mins

A suitably bleak slice of pulp fiction, with a brooding central performance from Jason Patric. He plays a washed up former boxer who gets entangled in a kidnapping being planned by Bruce Dern and sultry Rachel Ward. Director James Foley resists the temptation to put his foot on the throttle and is content to coolly watch the characters as they become locked in a doomed dance of greed and betrayal. JF. Contains violence, swearing, nudity, sex scenes and substance abuse.

Jason Patric *Kevin "Collie" Collins* • Rachel Ward *Fay Anderson* • Bruce Dern *Uncle Bud* • George Dickerson *Doc Goldman* • James Cotton *Charlie* • Corey Carrier *Jack* • Rocky Giordani *Bert* • Jeanie Moore *Nanny* ■ *Dir* James Foley • *Scr* Bob Redlin, from the novel by Jim Thompson

After Darkness ★★ 18

Psychological drama
1985 · UK/Swi · Colour · 103mins

Despite the best efforts of a hard-working cast, this psychological thriller never overcomes the flimsiness of its plot and the transparency of the principal protagonists. In delivering younger brother Julian Sands from an asylum, anthropologist John Hurt seems interested solely in helping him deal with the memory of his twin's death. When student Victoria Abril comes between them, however, it soon becomes clear which sibling is the more troubled. Haunting dreams and mysterious pronouncements litter the action, but the melodramatics aren't persuasive. DP

John Hurt *Peter Huninger* • Julian Sands *Laurence Huninger* • Victoria Abril *Pascale* • Pamela Salem *Elisabeth Huninger* • William Jacques *Dr Coles* ■ *Dir/Scr* Dominique Othenin-Girard, Sergio Guerraz

After Hours ★★★★ 15

Black comedy 1985 · US · Colour · 93mins

Griffin Dunne plays the angst-ridden everyman to manic perfection in this brilliantly original black comedy from director Martin Scorsese. In a spiralling tale of nightmarish persecution and paranoia, Dunne's date with unhinged Rosanna Arquette becomes a roller-coaster ride into urban hell. New York's SoHo district becomes a Kafkaesque labyrinth, populated by avant-garde crazies, bloodthirsty gangsters and flaky *Alice in Wonderland*-style headcases. It's weird, wonderful and wildly funny, and Scorsese won the best director prize at Cannes for his efforts. AJ. Contains violence, swearing, nudity. DVD

Griffin Dunne *Paul Hackett* • Rosanna Arquette *Marcy Franklin* • Verna Bloom *June* • Thomas Chong [Tommy Chong] *Pepe* • Linda Fiorentino *Kiki* • Teri Garr *Julie* • John Heard *Tom the bartender* • Richard "Cheech" Marin *Neil* ■ *Dir* Martin Scorsese • *Scr* Joseph Minion • *Cinematographer* Michael Ballhaus

After Life ★★★★ PG

Fantasy drama 1998 · Jpn · Colour · 113mins

Japanese director Hirokazu Koreeda's vision of heaven has an irresistible simplicity to match its subtle ingenuity. Set in a spartan transit camp, the action focuses on a celestial film unit as it tries to help various recently departed souls re-create the favourite memory that will be their sole solace in eternity. Beautifully acted by a cast that includes several non-professionals, this is a sublime celebration of life and the everyday joys that make it so worthwhile. DP. In Japanese with English subtitles.

Arata *Takashi Mochizuki* • Erika Oda *Shiori Satonaka* • Susumu Terajima *Satoru Kawashima* • Takashi Naito *Takuro Sugie* ■ *Dir/Scr* Hirokazu Koreeda

After Midnight ★★★ 18

Horror 1989 · US · Colour · 88mins

A better-than-average horror anthology featuring three stories which provide a fourth climax. Each tale of terror is told by students on a "psychology of fear" course and involve a haunted mansion, killer dogs, mysterious phone calls (the best section) and zombies. Produced, written and directed by Ken and Jim Wheat (the genre's answer to the Coen brothers), the classic *Dead of Night* format is stirred up with some very convincing special effects to leave the viewer suitably shaken. AJ

Ramy Zeda *Professor Derek* • Jillian McWhirter *Allison* • Pamela Segall *Cheryl* • Nadine Van Der Velde *Joan* • Marc McClure *Kevin* • Marg Helgenberger *Alex* • Billy Ray Sharkey *Ray* ■ *Dir/Scr* Ken Wheat, Jim Wheat

After Midnight ★★

Drama 1990 · UK · Colour · 90mins

This tale of a drunken Dublin hotel nightwatchman starts and ends reasonably well, but too much of what is served up in between is misjudged. Saeed Jaffrey turns in a mischievously maudlin performance as the writer whose reasons for abandoning his craft are a secret. However, while his crooked schemes are amusing enough, his treatment of receptionist Hayley Mills and a Chinese prostitute is every bit as objectionable as his racist rivalry with Egyptian night manager Vladek Sheybal. DP. Contains some swearing.

Saeed Jaffrey *Jas* • Hayley Mills *Sally* • Vladek Sheybal *El-Alfi* • Dhirendra *Ranj* • Ian Dury • Maurice O'Donoghue • Patrick Condren ■ *Dir/Scr* Shani Grewal [Shani S Grewal]

After Office Hours ★★★

Crime comedy drama
1935 · US · BW · 71mins

Clark Gable stars as a newspaper man who, with the aid of his glamorous society-girl-cum-reporter (Constance Bennett), solves a murder. A solidly entertaining example of the then fashionable newsroom genre, when papers were papers and reporters played detective, it was written by Herman J Mankiewicz (later to script *Citizen Kane* with Orson Welles) and directed by one of the studio's slickest craftsmen, Robert Z Leonard. The result is a sparky, witty and fast-moving comedy melodrama. RK

Constance Bennett *Sharon Norwood* • Clark Gable *Jim Branch* • Stuart Erwin *Hank Parr* • Billie Burke *Mrs Norwood* • Harvey Stephens *Tommy Bannister* • Katherine Alexander *Mrs Patterson* • Hale Hamilton *Mr Patterson* • Henry Travers *Cap* ■ *Dir* Robert Z Leonard • *Scr* Herman J Mankiewicz, from a story by Laurence Stallings, Dale Van Every

After the Fox ★★★ U

Comedy 1966 · US/UK/It · Colour · 101mins

Peter Sellers stars as a heist-fumbling supercrook, a master of disguise but not of his criminal career, who breaks out of jail to handle the smuggling of loot and to save his film-starlet sister's honour. The pretence of conning police and villagers into landing stolen gold during a movie "shoot" is a hoot, but the script collapses because the writing styles of New Yorker Neil Simon and Italian Cesare Zavattini clash awkwardly. However, the best joke of all is Victor Mature as a fading beefcake star, sending up his own image – corsets and all. TH DVD

Peter Sellers *Aldo Vanucci* • Victor Mature *Tony Powell* • Britt Ekland *Gina Romantica* • Martin Balsam *Harry* • Akim Tamiroff *Okra* • Paolo Stoppa *Polio* • Tino Buazzeli *Siepi* • Mac Ronay *Carlo* ■ *Dir* Vittorio De Sica • *Scr* Neil Simon, Cesare Zavattini

After the Rehearsal ★★★

Drama 1984 · Swe · Colour · 72mins

This chamber drama was originally filmed for television before finally receiving a theatrical release two years into Ingmar Bergman's "retirement". Dozing on a stage dressed for his production of the play, Erland Josephson has encounters with former mistress Ingrid Thulin and aspiring actress, Lena Olin. It is Olin who hopes an affair will further her career, despite the revelation her mother once had an affair with the director. Sven Nykvist's tight angles intensify the intrigue, as we wonder how autobiographical Bergman's insights into art and emotion really are. While superbly acted and directed with disciplined economy, this is very much a minor Bergman work. DP. In Swedish with English subtitles.

Erland Josephson *Henrik Vogler* • Ingrid Thulin *Rakel Egerman* • Lena Olin *Anna Egerman* ■ *Dir/Scr* Ingmar Bergman • *Cinematographer* Sven Nykvist

After the Storm ★★★

Drama 1990 · Arg/Sp · Colour · 99mins

Realism doesn't get much more brutal than this: in depicting the grinding poverty suffered by a rural family, Argentinian director Tristán Bauer refuses to allow petty sentiment to cloud the issue. Nor does he permit his cast the luxury of easy outbursts of bitterness. Lorenzo Quinteros is the proud working man who would rather tear down the doors of his home than send his father to the grave in an unfinished coffin, but it isn't all gloom and doom, as Ruben Alvarez's script suggests better times lie ahead. DP. In Spanish with English subtitles.

Lorenzo Quinteros • Patricio Contreras • Ana Maria Picchio ■ *Dir* Tristán Bauer • *Scr* Tristán Bauer, Ruben Alvarez, Graciela Maglie

After the Storm ★★ 12

Thriller 2001 · US · Colour · 99mins

Based on a story by Ernest Hemingway, this features a charismatic Benjamin Bratt as a beachcomber grudgingly joining forces with Armand Assante to salvage the rich pickings of a yacht sunk during a vicious storm. The tropical setting is easy on the eye and Bratt and Mili Avital certainly make a handsome couple. Unfortunately, after a decent opening section, the film gets bogged down by tedious plotting. Less static direction would have helped. JC DVD

Benjamin Bratt *Arno* • Armand Assante *Jean-Pierre* • Mili Avital *Conquina* • Simone-Elise Girard *Janine* • Steven Lang *Sgt Major Jim* • Nestor Serrano *Ortega* • Arthur J Nascarella [Arthur Nascarella] *Louie Gavotte* • Jennifer

Beals *Mrs Gavotte* ■ *Dir* Guy Ferland • *Scr* AE Hotchner, from a short story by Ernest Hemingway

After the Sunset ★★★ 12

Crime caper 2004 · US · Colour · 93mins

A jewel thief is tempted to come out of retirement in this entertaining Caribbean-set caper. Pierce Brosnan plays a suave crook, whose idyllic life in a Bahamian paradise – shared with partner-in-crime Salma Hayek – is jeopardised when he sees the chance to steal a famed diamond. Brosnan must also contend with his old nemesis, FBI agent Woody Harrelson. The cast's playfulness works well within the predictable plot and tasteless jokes about suntan-oil application. KK. Contains swearing and sexual references. [VIDEO] DVD

Pierce Brosnan *Max Burdett* • Salma Hayek *Lola Cirillo* • Woody Harrelson *Stanley P Lloyd* • Don Cheadle *Henri Mooré* • Naomie Harris *Sophie St Vincent* • Chris Penn *Rowdy fan* • Mykelti Williamson *Agent Stafford* • Obba Babatundé [Obba Babatunde] *Zacharias* ■ *Dir* Brett Ratner • *Scr* Paul Zbyszewski, Craig Rosenberg, from a story by Paul Zbyszewski

After the Thin Man ★★★

Detective comedy 1936 · US · BW · 112mins

The sequel to *The Thin Man* has William Powell, Myrna Loy and Asta the dog once more waltzing through high society, with our intrepid trio solving three murders between cocktails. There's a minor twist with James Stewart playing a meek and mild ex-lover who suddenly loses his rag, but it might seem far too slight and slow for modern audiences. This was, however, a big hit in 1936 and the stars still have a considerable amount of charm. *Another Thin Man* followed in 1939. AT

William Powell *Nick Charles* • Myrna Loy *Nora Charles* • James Stewart *David Graham* • Elissa Landi *Selma Landis* • Joseph Calleia *Dancer* • Jessie Ralph *Aunt Katherine* • Alan Marshal *Robert* • Teddy Hart *Caspar* ■ *Dir* WS Van Dyke • *Scr* Frances Goodrich, Albert Hackett, from a story by Dashiell Hammett

Afterglow ★★★★ 15

Drama 1997 · US · Colour · 109mins

Writer/director Alan Rudolph here delivers a by turns moving and funny tale of love, loss and relationships for which Julie Christie was nominated for an Oscar. She plays a former B-movie actress who embarks on an affair with a younger man in response to her philandering husband's (Nick Nolte) string of younger lovers. Lara Flynn Boyle and Jonny Lee Miller are the younger couple caught in their own web of adultery and lies, but the show truly belongs to the more seasoned stars, the mesmerising Nolte and Christie, whose performances will wrench your heart. JB. Contains swearing, sexual situations and some mild violence. [VIDEO]

Nick Nolte *Lucky "Fix-It" Mann* • Julie Christie *Phyllis Mann* • Lara Flynn Boyle *Marianne Byron* • Jonny Lee Miller *Jeffrey Byron* • Jay Underwood *Donald Duncan* • Domini Blythe *Helene Pelletier* • Yves Corbeil *Bernard Omay* • Alan Fawcett *Count Falco/Jack Dana* ■ *Dir/Scr* Alan Rudolph

AfterLife ★★ 15

Drama 2003 · UK · Colour · 104mins

In striving to be topical and controversial, debuting director Alison Peebles winds up being merely melodramatic in this dour slice of Scottish life. The film's agenda is established by journalist Kevin McKidd's visit to doctor James Laurenson to investigate his links to a Swiss euthanasia clinic. Thus, the revelation that McKidd's mother has ovarian cancer and that he will become responsible for his Down Syndrome sister comes as no surprise. The cast works hard, but Peebles's storytelling lacks a certain finesse. DP

Kevin McKidd *Kenny Brogan* • Lindsay Duncan *May Brogan* • Paula Sage *Roberta Brogan* • Shirley Henderson *Ruby* • James Laurenson *Professor George Wilkinshaw* ■ *Dir* Alison Peebles • *Scr* Andrea Gibb

Against a Crooked Sky ★★ U

Western 1975 · US · Colour · 88mins

This western was criticised on its limited release for its perceived racism in the age of native American awareness. *Variety* complained the film was more upset at the killing of a pet dog than by the vengeful slaughter of hundreds of Indians. The movie starts with an Indian raid and the kidnapping of a white girl, then gnarled fur trapper Richard Boone and teenager Stewart Petersen head off in pursuit across the desert; the usual stuff happens. AT [VIDEO]

Henry Wilcoxon *Cut Tongue* • Richard Boone *Russian* • Stewart Petersen *Sam Sutter* • Jewel Blanch *Charlotte Sutter* • Gordon Hanson *Shumeki* • Geoffrey Land *Temkai* ■ *Dir* Earl Bellamy • *Scr* Douglas C Stewart, Eleanor Lamb

Against All Flags ★★★ U

Adventure 1952 · US · Colour · 83mins

Errol Flynn is on top late-career form as a British naval officer who gets involved with beautiful buccaneer Maureen O'Hara in a Madagascan pirate stronghold ruled over by the scowling Anthony Quinn. This rollicking costume adventure is generally good fun, with rich Technicolor giving O'Hara's red hair and green eyes an even greater lustre. Though the credited director is George Sherman, it is a little-known fact that Douglas Sirk actually undertook most of the work behind the camera. Remade as *The King's Pirate* with Doug McClure, using footage from this original. TS

Errol Flynn *Brian Hawke* • Maureen O'Hara *Spitfire Stevens* • Anthony Quinn *Captain Roc Brasiliano* • Mildred Natwick *Miss MacGregor* • Alice Kelley *Princess Patma* • Robert Warwick *Captain Kidd* ■ *Dir* George Sherman • *Scr* Aeneas MacKenzie, Joseph Hoffman, from a story by Aeneas MacKenzie

Against All Odds ★★★ 18

Thriller 1984 · US · Colour · 116mins

A loose remake of the Robert Mitchum/Jane Greer *film noir* classic *Build My Gallows High*, with Jeff Bridges in the pay of, then on the run from, minor mobster James Woods. Greer herself appears as the mother of her original character, now played by Rachel Ward, and Richard Widmark, another familiar face from the *film noir* era, also features. Director Taylor Hackford maintains a moody atmosphere as the action takes in the streets of Los Angeles and the spectacular Mayan ruins of Mexico. Phil Collins's theme song received an Oscar nomination. AT. Contains violence, sex scenes, drug abuse and nudity. [VIDEO] DVD

Rachel Ward *Jessie Wyler* • Jeff Bridges *Terry Brogan* • James Woods *Jake Wise* • Alex Karras *Hank Sully* • Jane Greer *Mrs Wyler* • Richard Widmark *Ben Caxton* • Saul Rubinek *Steve Kirsch* • Swoosie Kurtz *Edie* • Dorian Harewood *Tommy* • Pat Corley *Ed Phillips* ■ *Dir* Taylor Hackford • *Scr* Eric Hughes, from the film and novel *Build My Gallows High* by Geoffrey Homes [Daniel Mainwaring]

Against the Ropes ★★ 12

Biographical sports drama
2003 · US/Ger · Colour · 106mins

The life story of boxing promoter Jackie Kallen emerges here as an uncertain, ragged mess, hampered by a simplistic script and a strangely unappealing performance from Meg Ryan. Despite the energy injected by the likeable Omar Epps as the wannabe champ and Tony Shalhoub's enthusiastic hamming as a sexist rival promoter, this remains a featherweight affair. AS. Contains swearing. [VIDEO] DVD

Meg Ryan *Jackie Kallen* • Omar Epps *Luther Shaw* • Tony Shalhoub *Sam LaRocca* • Tim Daly [Timothy Daly] *Gavin Reese* • Charles S Dutton *Felix Reynolds* • Kerry Washington *Renee* • Joe Cortese *Irving Abel* ■ *Dir* Charles S Dutton • *Scr* Cheryl Edwards

Against the Wall ★★★ 18

Prison drama based on a true story
1994 · US · Colour · 110mins

The true story of the Attica prison break in the 1970s is turned into a trim, taut and suspenseful pseudo-documentary thanks to John Frankenheimer's solid direction and great performances by Samuel L Jackson and Kyle MacLachlan. Taking the perspective of a rookie warden appalled by the awful treatment of prisoners in the facility, Frankenheimer accents the convicts' grievances by having the do-gooder held hostage by rioters. A gritty, realistic TV movie. AJ [VIDEO] DVD

Kyle MacLachlan *Michael Smith* • Samuel L Jackson *Jamaal* • Harry Dean Stanton *Hal* • Anne Heche *Sharon* • Clarence Williams III *Chaka* • Frederic Forrest *Weisbad* • Philip Bosco *Corrections Commissioner Russell Oswald* • Tom Bower *Ed* ■ *Dir* John Frankenheimer • *Scr* Ron Hutchinson

Against the Wind ★★★ PG

Spy drama 1947 · UK · BW · 91mins

The screenwriter of several classic Ealing comedies, TEB Clarke could turn his hand to several genres, as this tale of spy-school treachery, co-written with Michael Pertwee, proves. Paying tribute to the contribution of saboteurs to the war effort, the film owes a debt to the pseudo-documentary style of such Hollywood thrillers as *The House on 92nd Street*. Jack Warner and Simone Signoret stand out in a cast of dependable character actors, although they are slightly hampered by director Charles Crichton's preoccupation with authentic detail. DP [VIDEO] DVD

Robert Beatty *Father Phillip* • Simone Signoret *Michele* • Jack Warner *Max Cronk* • Gordon Jackson *Johnny Duncan* • Paul Dupuis *Jacques Picquart* • Gisèle Préville *Julie* • John Slater *Emile Meyer* • James Robertson-Justice *Ackerman* ■ *Dir* Charles Crichton • *Scr* TEB Clarke, Michael Pertwee, from a story by J Elder Wills

Agatha ★★★ PG

Drama 1978 · UK/US · Colour · 100mins

Director Michael Apted's drama is based on a real-life incident in 1926 when crime novelist Agatha Christie disappeared, casting suspicion on her husband and sparking off a nationwide hunt. Vanessa Redgrave is fine as the redoubtable writer of whodunnits, but Dustin Hoffman is less successful as the American journalist on her trail, and his lack of stature in his scenes with Redgrave is often comical. Apted, meanwhile, ladles on the 1920s style, but loses his way when it comes to plot and suspense, though the overall result is entertaining enough. TH [VIDEO]

Vanessa Redgrave *Agatha Christie* • Dustin Hoffman *Wally Stanton* • Timothy Dalton *Archie Christie* • Helen Morse *Evelyn* • Celia Gregory *Nancy Neele* • Tony Britton *William Collins* • Timothy West *Kenward* • Alan Badel *Lord Brackenbury* ■ *Dir* Michael Apted • *Scr* Kathleen Tynan, Arthur Hopcraft, from a story by Kathleen Tynan

Agatha Christie's A Caribbean Mystery ★★ PG

Murder mystery 1983 · US · Colour · 92mins

Helen Hayes appears as Miss Marple in a mystery based on one of Agatha Christie's weaker whodunnits, in which the spinster sleuth investigates the death of an elderly major the morning after he revealed a sensational tale of greed and murder to her. Making the best of her miscasting, the 83-year-old Hayes still compares unfavourably with Margaret Rutherford and Joan Hickson, but this TV movie benefits from not having the all-star cast that spoils the guessing game in so many other Christie adaptations. DP [VIDEO]

Helen Hayes *Miss Jane Marple* • Barnard Hughes *Mr Rafiel* • Jameson Parker *Tim Kendall* • Season Hubley *Molly Kendall* • Swoosie Kurtz *Ruth Walters* • Cassie Yates *Lucky Dyson* • Zakes Mokae *Captain Daventry* • Stephen Macht *Greg Dyson* ■ *Dir* Robert Michael Lewis • *Scr* Sue Grafton, Steven Humphrey, from the novel by Agatha Christie

Agatha Christie's Murder in Three Acts ★★★

Murder mystery 1986 · US · Colour · 100mins

The action may have been shifted from the quiet English resbrt of Loomouth to Acapulco, but this is still just about recognisable as the novel *Three Act Tragedy*. With vicars and neurologists falling like flies, even Hercule Poirot isn't convinced foul play is afoot until he discovers the dangers of colourless nicotine. A splendid cast of suspects lines up for this TV movie, with Tony Curtis, Lisa Eichhorn and Emma Samms giving nothing away. Peter Ustinov engages the "little grey cells" in what isn't a classic Christie, but it should keep you guessing. DP

Peter Ustinov *Hercule Poirot* • Tony Curtis *Charles Cartwright* • Emma Samms *Jennifer "Egg" Eastman* • Jonathan Cecil *Hastings* • Fernando Allende *Ricardo Montoya* • Pedro Armendáriz Jr *Colonel Mateo* • Lisa Eichhorn *Cynthia Dayton* • Dana Elcar *Dr Walter Strange* ■ *Dir* Gary Nelson • *Scr* Scott Swanton, from the novel *Three Act Tragedy* by Agatha Christie

Agatha Christie's Murder with Mirrors ★★★ PG

Murder mystery
1985 · US/UK · Colour · 93mins

Director Dick Lowry makes an efficient job of adapting the Queen of Crime's 1952 thriller, *They Do It With Mirrors*. Making her second appearance as Miss Marple, Helen Hayes brought down the curtain on a 75-year screen career by deducing which of the gallery of eccentrics, gathered at a rambling English mansion, intends bumping off John Mills's beloved wife, Bette Davis. Although not one of Christie's best mysteries, it's certainly one of the busiest with countless characters to keep track of and a rather contrived conclusion. DP [VIDEO]

Helen Hayes *Miss Jane Marple* • Bette Davis *Carrie Louise* • John Mills *Lewis Serrocold* • Leo McKern *Inspector Curry* • Dorothy Tutin *Mildred* • Anton Rodgers *Dr Max Hargrove* • Frances de la Tour *Ms Bellaver* • Tim Roth *Edgar* ■ *Dir* Dick Lowry • *Scr* George Eckstein, from the novel *They Do It With Mirrors* by Agatha Christie

Agatha Christie's Sparkling Cyanide ★★ PG

Murder mystery 1983 · US · Colour · 91mins

One of the attractions for Agatha Christie's American fans is her essential Englishness, so it seems odd to transfer the action to Pasadena. With a couple of fatal toasts as its high points, the twisting plot will certainly keep you guessing. However, the tinkering with the original makes the mystery feel forced, and the

A

resolution is not one of the author's most satisfying. DP

Anthony Andrews *Tony Browne* • Deborah Raffin *Iris Murdoch* • Pamela Bellwood *Ruth Lessing* • Nancy Marchand *Lucilla Drake* • Josef Sommer *George Barton* • David Huffman *Stephan Farraday* • Christine Belford *Rosemary Barton* • June Chadwick *Sandra Farraday* ■ *Dir* Robert Michael Lewis • *Scr* Robert Malcolm Young, Sue Grafton, Steven Humphrey, from the novel by Agatha Christie

L'Age d'Or ★★★★★ 15

Satire 1930 · Fr · BW · 62mins

Having avowed that *Un Chien Andalou*, his previous collaboration with co-writer and surrealist artist Salvador Dali, meant nothing at all, Luis Buñuel declared that this second surrealist outing was "a desperate and passionate call to murder". He certainly got his wish, as the film caused riots when it premiered in Paris and was banned for 49 years at the insistence of the French fascists. Exploring the themes that would sustain his entire career, Buñuel mercilessly pillories the bourgeoisie, with virtually every scene touching on the conflict between sexual desire and religious and political repression. The satire is both erotic and hilarious and still has the power to provoke. DP. In French with English subtitles. Contains violence, sexual references. DVD

Lya Lys *The woman* • Gaston Modot *The man* • Max Ernst *Bandit Chief* • Pierre Prévert *Péman, a bandit* ■ *Dir* Luis Buñuel • *Scr* Luis Buñuel, Salvador Dali • *Cinematographer* Albert Duverger

Age Isn't Everything ★★★

Comedy drama 1991 · US · Colour · 91mins

A twist on the body-swap theme that was so popular in the 1980s has Jonathan Silverman as a disgruntled 25-year-old office worker who turns overnight into an octagenarian with a Yiddish accent. Thoroughly rattled, the young man in an old man's body goes to a host of doctors (including American health guru Dr Joyce Brothers) to see if the effects can be reversed. A strong cast of supporting players, whose faces will be familiar to you even if their names are not, make this dark, if sometimes sentimental, comedy a touch above the average. FL

Jonathan Silverman *Seymour* • Paul Sorvino *Max* • Rita Moreno *Rita* • Robert Prosky *Seymour's grandfather* • Rita Karlin *Seymour's grandmother* • Dr Joyce Brothers ■ *Dir/Scr* Douglas Katz

The Age of Consent ★★★

Romance 1932 · US · BW · 106mins

Not to be confused with Michael Powell's 1969 Australian romp, this is an earnest look at the age-old problem of sex before marriage. Campus student Richard Cromwell wants to do it with his girlfriend, Dorothy Wilson (a non-actress who was discovered in the RKO typing pool). When she refuses, he does it instead with local waitress Arline Judge. Director Gregory La Cava keeps it all extremely tasteful and makes you feel a very real angst on Cromwell's part. Worth a look. TS

Dorothy Wilson *Betty* • Richard Cromwell *Michael* • Eric Linden *Duke* • Arline Judge *Dora* • John Halliday *David* • Aileen Pringle *Barbara* • Reginald Barlow *Swale* ■ *Dir* Gregory La Cava • *Scr* Sarah Y Mason, Francis Cockrell, from the play *Cross Roads* by Martin Flavin

Age of Consent ★★★ 15

Romantic drama 1969 · Aus · Colour · 95mins

Michael Powell's final feature film is about an artist (James Mason) who runs out of inspiration and retreats to the Great Barrier Reef with his young model (Helen Mirren). "The film was full of nudity," wrote Powell, "but it is a painter's nudity." Filmed mainly on Dunk Island (now a pricey resort), it is undeniably beautiful and filled with engaging characters. AT

James Mason *Bradley Morahan* • Helen Mirren *Cora* • Jack MacGowran *Nat Kelly* • Neva Carr-Glyn *Ma Ryan* • Andonia Katsaros *Isabel Marley* • Michael Boddy *Hendricks* • Harold Hopkins *Ted Farrell* • Clarissa Kaye *Meg* ■ *Dir* Michael Powell • *Scr* Peter Yeldham, from the novel by Norman Lindsay

The Age of Innocence ★

Period romantic melodrama
1934 · US · BW · 71mins

A rising young lawyer in late 19th-century New York falls in love with a woman in the throes of a divorce. Prevented from marrying her by high society's moral constraints, he marries someone else, but continues to see his true love. John Boles and Irene Dunne star in this bowdlerisation of Edith Wharton's famous novel, which is reduced to a small-scale and dreary melodrama under the first-time direction of Philip Moeller. RK

Irene Dunne *Countess Ellen Olenska* • John Boles *Newland Archer* • Lionel Atwill *Julius Beaufort* • Laura Hope Crews *Mrs Welland* • Helen Westley *Granny Mingott* • Julie Haydon *May Welland* • Herbert Yost *Mr Welland* • Theresa Maxwell Conover *Mrs Archer* ■ *Dir* Philip Moeller • *Scr* Sarah Y Mason, Victor Heerman, from the novel by Edith Wharton • *Music* Max Steiner

The Age of Innocence ★★★★ U

Period romantic drama
1993 · US · Colour · 132mins

Eyebrows were raised when Martin Scorsese announced he was going to adapt Edith Wharton's Pulitzer Prize-winning novel about polite New York society in the 1870s. Yet, influenced by *The Heiress* and *The Magnificent Ambersons*, this is a directorial triumph, with the camera unobtrusively accumulating the small details that help make the story of Newland Archer and the Countess Olenska so compelling. Credit must also go here to cinematographer Michael Ballhaus and production designer Dante Ferretti. Unfortunately, some of the cast, notably Winona Ryder, seem a little stiff; Daniel Day-Lewis and Michelle Pfeiffer, however, excel in conveying the conflict between their passion and their breeding. DP DVD

Daniel Day-Lewis *Newland Archer* • Michelle Pfeiffer *Ellen Olenska* • Winona Ryder *May Welland* • Alexis Smith *Louisa van der Luyden* • Geraldine Chaplin *Mrs Welland* • Mary Beth Hurt *Regina Beaufort* • Alec McCowen *Sillerton Jackson* • Richard E Grant *Larry Lefferts* • Miriam Margolyes *Mrs Mingott* • Robert Sean Leonard *Ted Archer* • Sian Phillips *Mrs Archer* • Joanne Woodward *Narrator* ■ *Dir* Martin Scorsese • *Scr* Jay Cocks, Martin Scorsese, from the novel by Edith Wharton

Agency ★★

Drama 1981 · Can · Colour · 94mins

It is one of the tragedies of cinema that movie producers failed to find roles worthy of the great Robert Mitchum in his latter years, when his craggy, sleepy-eyed features cried out for a decent film. Here the great Mitch plays a dodgy politician trying to corrupt the world by inserting subliminal messages in TV programmes. Directed by George Kaczender, this is a non-starter. TS

Robert Mitchum *Ted Quinn* • Lee Majors *Philip Morgan* • Valerie Perrine *Brenda Wilcox* • Saul Rubinek *Sam Goldstein* • Alexandra Stewart *Mimi* • Hayward Morse *Tony* • Antony Parr *Charlie* ■ *Dir* George Kaczender • *Scr* Noel Hynd, from the novel by Paul Gottlieb

Agent Cody Banks ★★★ 12

Action comedy adventure
2003 · US · Colour · 97mins

Take the traditional plotline and gadgets of a James Bond movie, add an American TV teen heart-throb, throw in some cheeky laughs and you've got a tasty recipe for a boisterous and enjoyable family romp. *Malcolm in the Middle*'s Frankie Muniz plays a high-school student who's also an undercover CIA agent. His first assignment is to befriend class cutie Hilary Duff and spy on her scientist father (Martin Donovan). Though some of the story elements are a little hard to swallow (particularly Ian McShane as a psychotic villain), there's enough humour and excitement to carry the picture. SF DVD

Frankie Muniz *Cody Banks* • Hilary Duff *Natalie Connors* • Angie Harmon *Ronica Miles* • Keith David *CIA Director* • Cynthia Stevenson *Mrs Banks* • Arnold Vosloo *Molay* • Ian McShane *Brinkman* • Martin Donovan (2) *Dr Connors* ■ *Dir* Harald Zwart • *Scr* Ashley Edward Miller, Zack Stentz, Scott Alexander, Larry Karaszewski, from a story by Jeffrey Jurgensen

Agent Cody Banks 2: Destination London ★★ PG

Action comedy adventure
2003 · US · Colour · 95mins

In this limp, clichéd junior spy caper sequel, director Kevin Allen delivers a hackneyed, picture-postcard vision of Britain. Frankie Muniz returns as the teen CIA operative, this time posing as a gifted pupil at an exclusive music school to track down a mind-control gadget stolen by rogue agent Keith Allen. There are few dramatic visual diversions, and it's littered with low-level humour, but pre-teens may enjoy the chirpy presence of ex-S Club star Hannah Spearritt. SF DVD

Frankie Muniz *Cody Banks* • Anthony Anderson *Derek* • Hannah Spearritt *Emily* • Cynthia Stevenson *Mrs Banks* • Daniel Roebuck *Mr Banks* • Anna Chancellor *Jo Kenworth* • Keith Allen *Diaz* • James Faulkner *Kenworth* ■ *Dir* Kevin Allen • *Scr* Don Rhymer, from a story by Don Rhymer, Dylan Sellers, Harald Zwart, from characters created by Jeffrey Jurgensen

Agent for HARM ★★

Science-fiction spy spoof
1966 · US · Colour · 85mins

This lifeless spy hokum has been executed on a minuscule budget that wouldn't keep James Bond in dry martinis. Mark Richman is the agent assigned by an organisation called HARM – a sort of poor man's UNCLE – to stop the dastardly Russians from getting their hands on a deadly space spore that turns human skin into rotting fungus. Director Gerd Oswald plays it tongue-in-cheek, but it's too routine an affair to grip the imagination, despite a few diverting Bond-style gadgets. RS

Mark Richman [Peter Mark Richman] *Adam Chance* • Wendell Corey *Jim Graff* • Carl Esmond *Professor Janos Steffanic* • Barbara Bouchet *Ava Vestok* • Martin Kosleck *Malko* ■ *Dir* Gerd Oswald • *Scr* Blair Robertson

Agent Red ★★ 18

Action thriller
2000 · US/Can · Colour · 91mins

In this tatty low-budget action thriller, Dolph Lundgren is the special forces ace assigned to escort a lethal chemical bug from the old USSR to the safety of the US. However, Russian terrorists take over the nuclear submarine it is being transported on and it is up Lundgren and ex-girlfriend and naval officer Meilani Paul to retake the craft and its deadly load. Routine stuff with ho-hum action scenes and cringe-inducing dialogue. JF

Dolph Lundgren *Matt Hendricks* • Meilani Paul *Linda Christian* • Alexander Kuznetsov *Kretz* • Natalie Radford *Nadia* • Randolph Mantooth *Admiral Edwards* ■ *Dir* Damian Lee • *Scr* Steve Latshaw, Damian Lee, from a story by Steve Latshaw

The Ages of Lulu ★★★ 18

Erotic thriller 1990 · Sp · Colour · 93mins

This was the first film by Bigas Luna to make an international impact. Having already been rejected by numerous actresses, he found Italian star Francesca Neri willing to accept the challenge of playing the innocent who embarks upon a journey of sexual discovery that takes her into the darkest recesses of her psyche. So explicit it was dismissed by many as tasteless porn, this is a surprisingly moral, if ironic, film. DP. In Spanish with English subtitles. Contains swearing, sex scenes and violence. DVD

Francesca Neri *Lulu* • Oscar Ladoire *Pablo* • Maria Barranco *Ely* • Fernando Guillen-Cuervo • Rosana Pastor • Javier Bardem ■ *Dir* Bigas Luna • *Scr* Bigas Luna, Almudena Grandes, from the novel by Almudena Grandes

Agnes Browne ★★★ 15

Period drama 1999 · US/Ire · Colour · 88mins

Anjelica Huston both directs and stars in this quirky little movie, set in Dublin in 1967. When her husband dies prematurely, Huston and her seven children are catapulted into an emotional maelstrom. Ekeing out an existence selling fruit and veg in the local market, she borrows cash from unpleasant loan shark Ray Winstone and dreams of attending an upcoming Tom Jones concert. Despite being too cute and rather bizarre – it's hard to imagine Huston harbouring fantasies about Jones, for example – this is a watchable slice of whimsy. LH

Anjelica Huston *Agnes Browne* • Marion O'Dwyer *Marion Monks* • Ray Winstone *Mr Billy* • Niall O'Shea *Mark Browne* • Ciaran Owens *Frankie Browne* • Tom Jones ■ *Dir* Anjelica Huston • *Scr* John Goldsmith, Brendan O'Carroll, from the novel *The Mammy* by Brendan O'Carroll

Agnes of God ★★★ 15

Drama 1985 · US · Colour · 94mins

An odd, adult drama from director Norman Jewison, which promises more than it delivers. Jane Fonda is her usual forthright self as the court psychiatrist investigating the case of a novice nun (the waif-like Meg Tilly) accused of murdering her baby. It is thanks to the three lead performances Tilly, Fonda and the always dependable Anne Bancroft that this sustains interest for as long as it does, but even they cannot cover up what is a rather disappointing ending. JB. Contains some swearing. DVD

Jane Fonda *Dr Martha Livingston* • Anne Bancroft *Mother Miriam Ruth* • Meg Tilly *Sister Agnes* • Anne Pitoniak *Dr Livingston's mother* • Winston Rekert *Detective Langevin* • Gratien Gelinas *Father Martineau* • Guy Hoffman *Justice Joseph Leveau* • Gabriel Arcand *Monsignor* ■ *Dir* Norman Jewison • *Scr* John Pielmeier, from his play

Agnus Dei ★★★

Religious drama 1997 · Den · Colour · 90mins

Danish cinema's aptitude for depicting childhood is again to the fore in this wonderfully wide-eyed study of the enticements and terrors of religion. Temporarily abandoned by her mother, pre-teenager Amalie Dollerup is forced to rely on the God in whom she doesn't believe to help her through the trials of late-1950s convent life. Although director Caecilia Holbek Trier deals for the most part in stereotypes, she admirably captures the atmosphere of discipline and devotion. DP. A Danish language film.

Amalie Dollerup *Johanne* • Bodil Jorgensen *Augistina* • Nastja Arcel *Mother* • Cecilia Eliasson *Ingrid* • Helle Fagralid *Marianne* ■ *Dir/Scr* Caecilia Holbek Trier

Agony ★★★

Epic 1975 · USSR · Colour and BW · 148mins

Elem Klimov's take on the last days of the Tsar and the baleful influence of Rasputin blends newly shot colour scenes with archive black-and-white footage from 1916-17. The movie manages to be both documentary and speculation, though that didn't stop the Soviet authorities from banning it in 1975. They allowed it to be shown at the 1981 Moscow Film Festival, however, where it inevitably created a sensation. Klimov went on to run the Russian film studios. AT. In Russian with English subtitles.

Alexei Petrenko *Rasputin* • Velta Linei *Tsarina Alexandra* • Alisa Freindlikh *Anna Vyrubova* • Anatoly Romashin *Tsar Nicholas II* • A Romantsov *Prince Felix* ■ *Dir* Elem Klimov • *Scr* Semion Lungin, Ilya Nusinov

The Agony and the Ecstasy ★★ U

Historical drama
1965 · US · Colour · 127mins

There's no doubting the sincerity of those involved in the making of this monumental epic, based on Irving Stone's biography about Michelangelo and the painting of the Sistine Chapel ceiling. This is particularly evident in the playing, notably a self-effacing performance from Charlton Heston. Heston was the cinema's man of action at the time and he's ill-suited to the role of the neurotic artist, no matter how hard he tries. Likewise Rex Harrison's Pope Julius II is more Rex than pontiff. TS [VIDEO] DVD

Charlton Heston *Michelangelo* • Rex Harrison *Pope Julius II* • Diane Cilento *Contessina de Medici* • Harry Andrews *Bramante* • Alberto Lupo *Duke of Urbino* • Adolfo Celi *Giovanni de Medici* • Venantino Venantini *Paris de Grassis* • John Stacy *Sangallo* ■ *Dir* Carol Reed • *Scr* Philip Dunne, from the novel by Irving Stone • *Cinematographer* Leon Shamroy

The Agronomist ★★ PG

Political documentary
2003 · US · Colour · 87mins

Jonathan Demme here charts the life and violent death of Jean Dominique, a former farming scientist who became owner of an independent radio station in Haiti, and thorn in the side of various ruling elites. Demme's unimaginative style uses interview and some archival footage to chart Haiti's violent past, but the history he presents is thin and uninformative and he's hampered by the fact that Dominique ceased cooperating with the project well before his death. Worthy perhaps, but more than a little dull. AS. In English, French and Creole with subtitles. DVD

Dir Jonathan Demme,

Aguirre, Wrath of God ★★★★★ PG

Period drama 1972 · W Ger · Colour · 90mins

One of the crowning achievements of the New German Cinema, this movie is a typically haunting Werner Herzog picture in which an eccentric character pursues an overpowering obsession in the most inhospitable of environs. Klaus Kinski dominates the action as the 16th-century conquistador who ruinously rebels against his commander in order to continue his fanatical search for the legendary city of El Dorado. As if shooting in the depths of the Peruvian jungle wasn't difficult enough, the cast were never permitted to see the script, and it says much for their improvisational powers that there isn't a single weak performance in the film. DP. In German with English subtitles. [VIDEO] DVD

Klaus Kinski *Don Lope de Aguirre* • Cecilia Rivera *Flores* • Ruy Guerra *Lieutenant Ursua* • Helena Rojo *Inez* • Del Negro *Brother Gaspar* • Peter Berling *Guzman* • Armando Polanah *Armando* • Daniel Ades *Perucho* • Edward Roland *Okello* ■ *Dir/Scr* Werner Herzog

Ah, Wilderness! ★★★

Comedy 1935 · US · BW · 97mins

Directed by Clarence "Capability" Brown from Eugene O'Neill's play, this is a typical piece of MGM Americana that enshrines small-town values while concentrating on a boy's first love affair and the advice he gets from his pop, Lionel Barrymore. Since Mickey Rooney is in the cast as Linden's annoying younger brother, this looks like a dry run for the Andy Hardy series, which started two years later. It was remade in 1948 as the musical *Summer Holiday*, in which Rooney takes over the starring role of the lovestruck Richard Miller. AT

Lionel Barrymore *Nat Miller* • Aline MacMahon *Lily Davis* • Eric Linden *Richard Miller* • Cecilia Parker *Muriel McComber* • Spring Byington *Essie Miller* • Mickey Rooney *Tommy Miller* • Charles Grapewin [Charley Grapewin] *Mr McComber* • Wallace Beery *Uncle Sid* ■ *Dir* Clarence Brown • *Scr* Albert Hackett, Frances Goodrich, from the play by Eugene O'Neill

Aileen: Life and Death of a Serial Killer ★★★ 15

Documentary 2003 · UK · Colour · 90mins

This follow-up to documentary film-maker Nick Broomfield's *Aileen Wuornos: the Selling of a Serial Killer* is an uncomfortable affair. While the original film was an exposé of the garish media circus that surrounded the trial of America's most prolific female serial killer, and an indictment of the vultures that surrounded it, this companion piece comes dangerously close to being part of the problem rather than its solution. Broomfield revisits the story as he testifies in an appeal against the death sentence that Wuornos, who murdered seven men, seems doomed to receive. Broomfield is, to his own obvious discomfort, not in control of this macabre and depressing final act of a ruined, pitiable life, but this documentary may be more admirable than his more recent fare precisely for that reason. AS DVD

Dir Nick Broomfield, Joan Churchill • *Cinematographer* Joan Churchill

Aileen Wuornos: the Selling of a Serial Killer ★★★ 18

Documentary 1992 · UK · Colour · 87mins

It's ironic that Charlize Theron won her Oscar for playing Aileen Wournos in *Monster* on the birthday of "America's first female serial killer". All the more so considering the rumpus caused back in 1991 by the revelation that several people involved in the case had attempted to cash in on its notoriety. Exploiting his trademark on-screen disingenuity, Nick Broomfield exposes the cynical greed of Aileen's lawyer, adoptive mother and numerous Florida cops. He also makes shrewd use of courtroom footage to suggest the Angel of Death was herself a victim. But Broomfield was to prove equally culpable of exploitation in the sequel, *Aileen Wournos: Life and Death of a Serial Killer*. DP. Contains swearing, sexual references. [VIDEO] DVD

Dir Nick Broomfield

Ailsa ★★

Psychological drama
1994 · Ire/Ger/Fr · Colour · 78mins

Paddy Breathnach broke into features with this tale of obsession and indecision. Working from his own short story, screenwriter Joe O'Connor makes liberal use of flashback and off-screen narration to chronicle the passion of young husband Brendan Coyle for Juliette Gruber, the American stranger who moves into a flat in his rundown Dublin townhouse. Moody, but ultimately insubstantial. DP

Brendan Coyle *Miles* • Andrea Irvine *Sara* • Juliette Gruber *Campbell* • Anne McGeown *Mrs Foley* • Darragh Kelly *Sean* • Blanaid Irvine *Vera* • Des Spillane *Old Mr Johnson* • Gary Lydon *Jack* ■ *Dir* Paddy Breathnach • *Scr* Joe O'Connor, from his short story

Aimée and Jaguar ★★★ 15

Second World War romantic drama
1999 · Ger · Colour · 121mins

Based on the true story of the wartime relationship between model mother Lilly Wurst and Jewish lesbian Felice Schragenheim, this study of the indomitability of the lovers and the insidiousness of Nazism might have been more persuasive had debuting director Max Färberböck devoted more time to period authenticity. There may be air raids and Gestapo patrols, but the nitty-gritty of life in 1943 Berlin is missing and this undermines the good efforts of Juliane Köhler and Maria Schrader. Melodramatic, but engrossing. DP. In German with English subtitles. [VIDEO] DVD

Maria Schrader *Felice Schragenheim, " Jaguar"* • Juliane Köhler *Lilly Wust, "Aimée"* • Johanna Wokalek *Ilse* • Heike Makatsch *Klärchen* • Elisabeth Degen *Lotte* • Detlev Buck *Günther Wust* ■ *Dir* Max Färberböck • *Scr* Max Färberböck, Rona Munro, from the novel by Erica Fischer

L'Aîné des Ferchaux ★★★

Crime drama 1963 · Fr/It · Colour · 102mins

Released with the English title *Magnet of Doom*, this is one of Jean-Pierre Melville's lesser known features. Although it opens in Paris, much of the action takes place between New York and New Orleans, as failed boxer Jean-Paul Belmondo seeks the opportunity to swindle his employer, Charles Vanel, out of the ill-gotten gains that have forced the financier to flee France. Although the pair have their adventures on the road, most notably with hitcher Stefania Sandrelli and stripper Michèle Mercier, the emphasis is firmly on the unexpected bond that develops between these unlikely accomplices. DP. In French with English subtitles.

Jean-Paul Belmondo *Michel Maudet* • Charles Vanel *Dieudonné Ferchaux* • Michèle Mercier *Lou* • Malvina Silberberg *Lina* • Stefania Sandrelli *Angie* • Barbara Sommers *Lou's friend* ■ *Dir* Jean-Pierre Melville • *Scr* Jean-Pierre Melville, from the novel by Georges Simenon

Ain't Misbehavin' ★★ U

Musical comedy 1955 · US · Colour · 81mins

Rory Calhoun co-stars with Piper Laurie in this somewhat flimsy excuse for a musical with an unmistakeable nod in the direction of *Pygmalion*. He's a millionaire, she's a chorus girl determined to acquire some education and social polish. Edward Buzzell directs the forgettable but agreeable proceedings. Best of the otherwise long-forgotten songs is Fats Waller's famous number, from which the movie takes its title. RK

Rory Calhoun *Kenneth Post* • Piper Laurie *Sarah Hatfield* • Jack Carson *Hal North* • Mamie Van Doren *Jackie* • Reginald Gardiner *Piermont Rogers* • Barbara Britton *Pat* • Dani Crayne *Millie* • Harris Brown *Randall* ■ *Dir* Edward Buzzell • *Scr* Edward Buzzell, Philip Rapp, Devery Freeman, from the story *Third Girl from the Right* by Robert Carson

Air America ★★★ 15

Action comedy 1990 · US · Colour · 107mins

This was originally conceived as a blackly satirical comedy by *The Stunt Man* director Richard Rush, but that idea went out the window in favour of a more obviously commercial approach. Roger Spottiswoode took over the directorial reins and the result was an amiable, if somewhat patchy, action comedy. Set in Laos during the Vietnam War, the story follows the adventures of a CIA-organised air freight organisation, which was actually smuggling heroin on behalf of the local drug barons. Mel Gibson is the amoral head pilot, with Robert Downey Jr as his wild-card sidekick. JF. Contains violence and swearing [VIDEO] DVD

Mel Gibson *Gene Ryack* • Robert Downey Jr *Billy Covington* • Nancy Travis *Corinne Landreaux* • Ken Jenkins *Major Donald Lemond* • David Marshall Grant *Rob Diehl* • Lane Smith *Senator Davenport* • Art La Fleur [Art LaFleur] *Jack Neely* ■ *Dir* Roger Spottiswoode • *Scr* John Eskow, Richard Rush, from the book by Christopher Robbins

Air Bud ★★★ U

Sports adventure
1997 · US/Lux/Can · Colour · 93mins

Meet Air Bud, the 1990s version of Lassie, in this cute family adventure about a sporty dog who is promoted from team mascot to basketball player. While parents will be more impressed by the animal acrobatics, youngsters will be entertained by the plot, in which a lonely young boy and the dog's abusive owner fight for custody of the talented pooch. With a canine story that's both appealing and amusing, this is particularly suitable for younger viewers. JB [VIDEO] DVD

Michael Jeter *Norm Snively* • Kevin Zegers *Josh Framm* • Wendy Makkena *Jackie Framm* • Bill Cobbs *Arthur Chaney* • Eric Christmas *Judge Cranfield* • Jay Brazeau *Referee No 1* • Nicola Cavendish *Principal Pepper* ■ *Dir* Charles Martin Smith • *Scr* Paul Tamasy, Aaron Mendelsohn, from the character created by Kevin DiCicco

Air Bud: Golden Receiver ★★ U

Sports comedy adventure
1998 · US/Can · Colour · 86mins

Kids who didn't get enough of the basketball-playing dog in the first film will probably get a kick out of this adventure, in which our canine friend and his owner Kevin Zegers take up American football. Adults will probably roll their eyes at the goofy animal-abduction subplot masterminded by Nora Dunn, who could learn some things about acting from the dog. In three further sequels, the pup takes up soccer, baseball and volleyball. ST DVD

Kevin Zegers *Josh Framm* • Cynthia Stevenson *Jackie Framm* • Gregory Harrison *Patrick Sullivan* • Nora Dunn *Natalya* • Perry Anzilotti *Popov* • Robert Costanzo *Coach Fanelli* • Shayn Solberg *Tom* • Tim Conway *Fred Davis* ■ *Dir* Richard Martin (2) • *Scr* Paul Tamasy, Aaron Mendelsohn, from the character created by Kevin DiCicco

Air Cadet ★★ U

Aviation drama 1951 · US · BW · 93mins

Directed with brisk efficiency by Joseph Pevney, this movie about pilots training might have been more interesting had the emphasis been on the cadets' backgrounds and not on cocky Richard Long's affair with major Stephen McNally's estranged wife, Gail Russell. The aerial action is better than anything that occurs at the Texas air base, but there's not enough of it. DP

Stephen McNally *Major Jack Page* • Gail Russell *Janet Page* • Alex Nicol *Joe Czanoczek* • Richard Long *Russ Coulter* • Charles Drake *Captain Sullivan* • Robert Arthur *Walt Carver* ■ *Dir* Joseph Pevney • *Scr* Joseph Hoffman, Robert L Richards, from a story by Robert W Soderberg, Robert L Richards

Un Air de Famille ★★★★ 15

Comedy drama 1996 · Fr · Colour · 105mins

After the zestful chic of *When the Cat's Away*, this bourgeois comedy is something of a departure for director Cédric Klapisch. Adapted by Jean-Pierre Bacri and Agnès Jaoui from their own play, it focuses on the spiteful sparring of three siblings unable to shoulder the responsibility for their own disappointments. Cleverly exploiting his claustrophonic set by keeping camera movements to a minimum, Klapisch relies on neat touches rather than grand flourishes, while his use of reflective surfaces recalls the films of Douglas Sirk and Rainer Werner Fassbinder. The performances are uniformly excellent, though the tipsy Catherine Frot steals the show. DP. In French with English subtitles. Contains some swearing and violence.

Jean-Pierre Bacri *Henri Menard* • Agnès Jaoui *Betty Menard* • Jean-Pierre Darroussin *Denis* • Catherine Frot *Yolande, Philippe's wife* • Claire Maurier *Mother* • Wladimir Yordanoff *Philippe Menard* ■ *Dir* Cédric Klapisch • *Scr* Cédric Klapisch, Agnès Jaoui, Jean-Pierre Bacri, from the play by Agnès Jaoui, Jean-Pierre Bacri

Air Force ★★★★ PG

Second World War drama
1943 · US · BW · 119mins

This marvellous wartime drama from one of Hollywood's greatest directors, Howard Hawks, is not as famous as his *Scarface*, *The Big Sleep* or *Rio Bravo*, but is still a major achievement. It tells the story of the Mary Ann, a Flying Fortress, and the men who operated her in the war against the Japanese. The action sequences are excitingly filmed, though it is the quieter moments, when the members of the crew express their excitement and their fears, that give the film its strength as a study of comradeship in adversity. AT DVD

John Ridgely *Captain Mike Quincannon* • Gig Young *Lt Bill Williams* • Arthur Kennedy *Lt Tommy McMartin* • Charles Drake *Lt Munchauser* • Harry Carey *Sgt Robby White* • George Tobias *Cpl Weinberg* • Ward Wood *Cpl Peterson* • John Garfield *Sgt Joe Winocki* ■ *Dir* Howard Hawks • *Scr* Dudley Nichols

Air Force One ★★★★ 15

Action thriller 1997 · US · Colour · 119mins

Hollywood loves putting the US president into its movies, and who better to play him as an action hero than Indiana Jones himself, Harrison Ford. When the First Family is held hostage on board the Presidential jumbo jet by a ruthless gang of Russian terrorists led by Gary Oldman, Ford decides to fight back and escapes into the plane's hold. Meanwhile Vice President Glenn Close is left to take Oldman's phone calls in Washington. A stunt-filled thriller that's brimming with nasty villains and daring deeds. SO. Contains swearing and violence. DVD

Harrison Ford *President James Marshall* • Gary Oldman *Ivan Korshunov* • Glenn Close *Vice President Kathryn Bennett* • Wendy Crewson *Grace Marshall* • Liesel Matthews *Alice Marshall* • Paul Guilfoyle (2) *Chief of Staff Lloyd Shepherd* • Xander Berkeley *Agent Gibbs* • William H Macy *Major Caldwell* • Dean Stockwell *Defense Secretary Walter Dean* • Jürgen Prochnow *General Radek* ■ *Dir* Wolfgang Petersen • *Scr* Andrew W Marlowe

Air Mail ★★

Adventure 1932 · US · BW · 83mins

Director John Ford is more famous for his westerns, but this is his tribute to the pilots who flew the early air mail service across the West. In fact, this remains a typical Ford western in terms of theme and plot, with planes replacing the old Pony Express. Like the best Ford movies, there are lots of hard drinking and bonhomie on the ground and heroics in the air, but it's all pretty routine. AT

Pat O'Brien *Duke Talbot* • Ralph Bellamy *Mike Miller* • Gloria Stuart *Ruth Barnes* • Lillian Bond *Irene Wilkins* • Russell Hopton *Dizzy Wilkins* • Slim Summerville *Slim McCune* • Frank Albertson *Tommy Bogan* ■ *Dir* John Ford • *Scr* Dale Van Every, Frank W Wead, from a story by Frank W Wead

The Air Up There ★★ PG

Sports comedy 1993 · US · Colour · 107mins

In this so-so basketball movie, Kevin Bacon plays the ambitious coach who heads for Africa to sign up exceptional athlete Charles Gitonga Maina. However, the latter is a local prince and is more interested in protecting his village than shooting hoops. The film is low on belly laughs, despite the plucky playing of Bacon, and the serious bits are just plain mawkish. On the plus side, director Paul Michael Glaser stages the basketball sequences with some style. JF. Contains swearing. DVD

Kevin Bacon *Jimmy Dolan* • Charles Gitonga Maina *Jimmy Saleh* • Yolanda Vazquez *Sister Susan* • Winston Ntshona *Urudu* • Mabutho "Kid" Sithole *Nyaga* • Sean McCann *Coach Ray Fox* • Dennis Patrick *Father O'Hara* ■ *Dir* Paul Michael Glaser • *Scr* Max Apple

Airborne ★★★ PG

Sports drama 1993 · US · Colour · 86mins

Forced to move with his family from California to Cincinnati, laid-back teenager Shane McDermott swaps surfing the waves for rollerblading in the streets to impress his arch-enemy's sister. This formulaic teen comedy plot is given a welcome makeover by a likeable cast, and the stunt work is thrilling, especially a hair-raising downhill rollerblade chase through heavy traffic. AJ

Shane McDermott *Mitchell Goosen* • Seth Green *Wiley* • Brittney Powell *Nikki* • Chris Conrad *Jack* • Edie McClurg *Aunt Irene* • Patrick O'Brien [Patrick Thomas O'Brien] *Uncle Louie* ■ *Dir* Rob Bowman • *Scr* Bill Apablasa, from a story by Stephen McEveety, Bill Apablasa

Airborne ★ 18

Action thriller 1997 · Can · Colour · 89mins

Steve Guttenberg gets all mean and moody as the head of an elite squad of commando types, who is assigned to track down an international crook threatening to hold the world the ransom with some sort of secret virus. However, can they trust their own employers? Sean Bean manages to stay out of sight for most of the movie, but the rest of the cast aren't so lucky. Excruciating tosh. JF. Contains violence and some swearing.

Steve Guttenberg *Bill McNeil* • Kim Coates *Bob Murdoch* • Torri Higginson *Sara Gemmel* • Philip Akin *Romeo Cortez* • David Fraser *Mr Samuels* • Sean Bean *Dave Toombs* ■ *Dir* Julian Grant • *Scr* Tony Johnston, Julian Grant

Airheads ★★★ 15

Comedy 1994 · US · Colour · 88mins

A dumb heavy metal band finds fame by hijacking a local radio station in director Michael Lehmann's broad *Wayne's World*-style comedy that lacks the goofy cleverness of that blockbuster hit. Brendan Fraser ably heads the head-banging brigade, with amusing support from dim-witted Adam Sandler and long-haired Steve Buscemi. Never quite as funny as it thinks it is, the amiable anarchy does sometimes hit the screwball spot. AJ. Contains swearing. DVD

Brendan Fraser *Cazz* • Steve Buscemi *Rex* • Adam Sandler *Pip* • Chris Farley *Wilson* • Joe Mantegna *Ian* • Michael McKean *Milo* • Judd Nelson *Jimmie Wing* • Ernie Hudson *Sergeant O'Malley* • Amy Locane *Kayla* • Nina Siemaszko *Suzzi* ■ *Dir* Michael Lehmann • *Scr* Rich Wilkes

Airplane! ★★★★★ PG

Disaster movie spoof
1980 · US · Colour · 84mins

The first, and still the best, of Zucker, Zucker and Abrahams's wonderful movie send-ups. There's hardly a second that passes without an assault by a wickedly accurate spoof, cringe-inducing pun or inspired sight gag, and the years have not diminished its dumb appeal. Robert Hays and Julie Hagerty are the nominal stars, but the most fun is had by the distinguished supporting cast. It's the film that made a comedy star out of Leslie ("don't call me Shirley") Nielsen, but a whole troupe of veteran character actors also have a hugely enjoyable time sending up their screen personae. JF. Contains some swearing. DVD

Robert Hays *Ted Striker* • Julie Hagerty *Elaine Dickinson* • Leslie Nielsen *Dr Rumack* • Lloyd Bridges *McCroskey* • Robert Stack *Rex Kramer* • Kareem Abdul-Jabbar *Roger Murdock* • Peter Graves (2) *Captain Oveur* ■ *Dir/Scr* Jim Abrahams, David Zucker, Jerry Zucker

Airplane II: the Sequel ★★ 15

Comedy 1982 · US · Colour · 80mins

Airplane! was always going to be a hard act to follow and this time the scattergun approach to the script carries more misfires and duds than normal. Still, the two leads from the original (Robert Hays and Julie Hagerty) are back on board again and the silliness of it all should win people over. This time the flimsy storyline revolves around the first commercial flight to the Moon. JF. Contains some swearing and brief nudity. DVD

Robert Hays *Ted Striker* • Julie Hagerty *Elaine* • Lloyd Bridges *McCroskey* • Peter Graves (2) *Captain Oveur* • William Shatner *Murdock* • Chad Everett *Simon* • Sonny Bono *Bomber* • Raymond Burr *Judge* • Chuck Connors *Sarge* • Jack Jones (2) *Singer* ■ *Dir/Scr* Ken Finkleman

Airport ★★★ PG

Disaster movie 1970 · US · Colour · 128mins

After *Airplane!*, it's almost impossible to keep a straight face through this sprawling drama, particularly since it features George Kennedy, who went on to specialise in sending up the sort of role he plays here, most memorably in the *Naked Gun* series. But he and the rest of the starry cast (including an Oscar-winning Helen Hayes) are commendably serious throughout. The result is competent, soapy entertainment. JF DVD

Burt Lancaster *Mel Bakersfeld* • Dean Martin *Vernon Demerest* • Jean Seberg *Tanya Livingston* • Jacqueline Bisset *Gwen Meighen* • George Kennedy *Joe Patroni* • Helen Hayes *Ada Quonsett* • Van Heflin *DO Guerrero* • Maureen Stapleton *Inez Guerrero* ■ *Dir* George Seaton, Henry Hathaway • *Scr* George Seaton, from the novel by Arthur Hailey

Airport 1975 ★★★ PG

Disaster movie 1974 · US · Colour · 101mins

When a light aircraft makes an unscheduled landing in the cockpit of a jumbo jet – the 747 being aloft at the time – it causes something of a panic among the surviving crew and passengers. Stewardess Karen Black takes the controls while Gloria Swanson, Myrna Loy and Sid Caesar gibber quietly in the back, and a sick child (played by *The Exorcist's* Linda Blair) is soothed by a singing nun. Meanwhile, on the ground, George Kennedy talks into a microphone (his wife just happens to be on board) and Charlton Heston prepares to... Well, parting the Red Sea was nothing compared to this stunt. Mind-boggling stuff. AT. Contains some swearing

Charlton Heston *Alan Murdoch* • Karen Black *Nancy* • George Kennedy *Joseph Patroni* • Gloria Swanson • Helen Reddy *Sister Ruth* • Efrem Zimbalist Jr *Captain Stacy* • Sid Caesar *Barney* • Linda Blair *Janice Abbott* • Dana Andrews *Scott Freeman* • Myrna Loy *Mrs Devaney* ■ *Dir* Jack Smight • *Scr* Don Ingalls

Airport '77 ★★★ PG

Disaster movie 1977 · US · Colour · 108mins

The third in the popular midair disaster series and one of the best, thanks to a stellar cast led by Jack Lemmon, James Stewart, Joseph Cotten and Olivia de Havilland. The veterans simply sit around and look classy, but Lemmon has to work a tad harder as he tackles a hijack attempt led by co-pilot Robert Foxworth. It's not the most nail-biting film you'll ever see, but it's stylish entertainment. The franchise continued with *The Concorde – Airport '79*. DP

Jack Lemmon *Don Gallagher* • Lee Grant *Karen Wallace* • Brenda Vaccaro *Eve Clayton* • Joseph Cotten *Nicholas St Downs III* • Olivia de Havilland *Emily Livingston* • Darren McGavin *Stan Buchek* • Christopher Lee *Martin Wallace* • James Stewart *Philip Stevens* • George Kennedy *Joe Patroni* • Robert Foxworth *Chambers* ■ *Dir* Jerry Jameson • *Scr* Michael Scheff, David Spector, from a story by HAL Craig, Charles Kuenstle

Airport '79: the Concorde ★★ PG

Disaster movie 1979 · US · Colour · 108mins

The fourth *Airport* movie goes supersonic and has more disaster-packed moments than the average genre entry. Taking a chance with the usual inedible in-flight food, pilots George Kennedy and Alain Delon also have to deal with a missile chasing the plane, an emergency landing with no brakes, various explosions and doors coming off, and a crash-landing into snow. It's very silly, of course, but the starry cast manages to be as over-the-top as the effects, making this a fun if mindless way to spend a couple of hours. JB. Contains some swearing

Alain Delon *Captain Paul Metrand* • Robert Wagner *Dr Kevin Harrison* • Susan Blakely *Maggie Whelan* • Sylvia Kristel *Isabelle* • George Kennedy *Joe Patroni* • Eddie Albert *Eli Sande* • Bibi Andersson *Francine* • Charo *Margarita* • John Davidson *Robert Palmer* • Cicely Tyson *Elaine Gilbert* • Mercedes McCambridge *Nelli* • David Warner *Peter O'Neill* ■ *Dir* David Lowell Rich • *Scr* Eric Roth, Jennings Lang, inspired by the novel *Airport* by Arthur Hailey

Airspeed ★ PG

Action adventure 1997 · US · Colour · 84mins

In this low-budget movie, Robert Tinnell takes all the clichés that Jim Abrahams and the Zucker brothers had so mercilessly spoofed in *Airplane!* and plays them dead straight. But you won't be able to keep a straight face for long, as the brattish Elisha Cuthbert takes the controls of daddy Joe Mantegna's private plane after a storm does for the cabin crew. Unmissably awful. DP DVD

Elisha Cuthbert *Nicole Stone* • Joe Mantegna *Raymond Stone* • Andrea Prescott *Bronwen Booth* • Lynne Adams *Marilyn Stone* ■ *Dir* Robert Tinnell • *Scr* Richard Goudreau, Roc Lafortune, from a novel by Andrew Sands

A

Aitraaz ★★★ 12

Courtroom drama
2004 · Ind · Colour · 159mins

This engrossing tale, reminiscent of Barry Levinson's *Disclosure*, is a real change of pace for Akshay Kumar, who stars here as a happily married executive accused of sexual harassment by an old flame, played by former Miss World Priyanka Chopra. The ex-beauty queen is a diabolical delight, slinking and strutting her way through the role of the unscrupulous vamp, while Kumar is both compelling and restrained as the man treated as guilty until proven innocent. OA. In Hindi with English subtitles. Contains sexual references. DVD

Akshay Kumar *Raj Malhotra* • Kareena Kapoor *Priya* • Priyanka Chopra *Sonia Sharma* • Annu Kapoor *Ram Choitrani* • Paresh Rawal *Mr Patel* • Amrish Puri *Ranjit Roy* ■ *Dir* Abbas, Mustan • *Scr* Shyam Goel, Shiraz Ahmed, from their story

Ake and His World ★★★★

Drama 1984 · Swe · Colour · 99mins

The terrors that intrude upon the idylls of childhood are explored in this charming tale of village life, set in 1930s Sweden. Martin Lindström is outstanding as the six-year-old boy convinced by the portent of an extinguished candle that he'll be severely punished for accidentally endangering the life of a neighbour's son. As in *Elvira Madigan*, Jörgen Persson's glossy photography romanticises the action, but this doesn't diminish the film's genuine warmth and humanity. DP. In Swedish with English subtitles.

Martin Lindström *Ake* • Loa Falkman *Father* • Gunnel Fred *Mother* • Katja Blomquist *Sister* • Ulla Sjoblom *Grandma* • Suzanne Ernrup *Anne-Marie* • Bjorn Gustafson *Bergstrom* • Alexander Skarsgård *Kalle* • Stellan Skarsgård *Ebenholtz* ■ *Dir* Allan Edwall • *Scr* Allan Edwall, from the novel by Bertil Malmberg

Akenfield ★★

Documentary drama
1974 · UK · Colour · 97mins

Sir Peter Hall, one of modern theatre's more innovative directors, clearly felt up to adapting Ronald Blythe's memoir of life in a sleepy Suffolk farming community for a full-length film. But while the largely non-professional cast provides some fascinating insights, the contrasts with their Edwardian ancestors often feel laboured. Moreover, Ivan Strasburg's lyrical widescreen imagery and Michael Tippett's lush score seem unsuited to such a simple tale. It's a bold experiment, but too stylised and sentimental to succeed. DP

Garrow Shand *Tom Rouse/Old Tom* • Peggy Cole *Dulcie Rouse* • Barbara Tilney *Jean Quantrill* • Lyn Brooks *Charlotte Rouse* • Ida Page *Aunt Ida* • Ted Dedman *Ted* • Charlie Cornish *Charlie* ■ *Dir* Peter Hall • *Scr* Ronald Blythe, from his book

Akira ★★★★ 15

Animated science-fiction fantasy
1988 · Jpn · Colour · 119mins

One of the jewels of the genre, this is perhaps the best known *manga* movie in this country. Directed, co-scripted and designed by Katsuhiro Otomo from his own comic-strip, it's a pacey, unrelentingly violent post-apocalyptic adventure, in which a gang of Neo-Tokyo slum kids attempts to counter the telekinetic machinations of a rogue buddy. Yet, for all its futuristic elements, this is also a dark and disturbing portrait of contemporary urban life that seeks to expose the lack of empathy between the establishment and modern youth. The cityscapes are awesome, the camerawork is dizzying. If you're new to *manga*, prepare to be converted. (Available in both dubbed and subtitled versions.) DP. A Japanese language film. Contains swearing. [video] DVD

Dir Katsuhiro Otomo • *Scr* Izo Hashimoto, Katsuhiro Otomo

Akira Kurosawa's Dreams ★★ PG

Fantasy drama 1990 · Jpn · Colour · 114mins

This is one of the Japanese master's weakest films, though still demonstrating the stylistic versatility and genius for composition that characterises his previous works. Here, the 80-year-old Kurosawa reveals a regrettable tendency towards self-indulgence and political naivety. Although his environmentalism is heartfelt, the messages contained in the eight vignettes that make up the film are muddled and often pompously expressed. There is great beauty to be found, however, notably in the vibrant colours of the *Crows* segment, featuring Martin Scorsese as Vincent van Gogh. DP. In Japanese with English subtitles. [video]

Akira Terao *"I"* • Mitsuko Baisho *Mother of "I"* • Mieko Harada *Snow fairy* • Yoshitaka Zushi *Private Noguchi* • Martin Scorsese *Vincent van Gogh* • Toshie Negishi *Mother carrying child* • Chosuke Ikariya *Weeping demon* • Chishu Ryu *103-year-old man* ■ *Dir/Scr* Akira Kurosawa

Aks ★★ 15

Thriller 2001 · Ind · Colour · 183mins

This supernatural thriller proved a commercial disappointment, despite debutant Rakesh Omprakash Mehra's ambitious direction and Bollywood superstar Amitabh Bachchan in the starring role. Following the assassination of the Indian defence minister, Bachchan begins a protracted pursuit of murderous mastermind Manoj Bajpai. Some of the action sequences are spectacular, but the pacing is sluggish. DP. In Hindi with English subtitles. Contains violence and swearing. [video] DVD

Amitabh Bachchan *Manu Verma* • Manoj Bajpai *Raghavan* • Nandita Das *Supriya* • Raveena Tandon *Neeta* ■ *Dir* Rakesh Omprakash Mehra • *Scr* Rakesh Omprakash Mehra, from a story by Renzil D'Silva

Al Capone ★★★★ 15

Biographical crime drama
1959 · US · BW · 104mins

Rod Steiger was a natural to play Al Capone, the gangster finally imprisoned for tax evasion rather than slaughter on the streets of Chicago. Steiger, of course, brings all his Method mannerisms to play and it's fascinating to compare his portrayal with later ones by Jason Robards (*The St Valentine's Day Massacre*) and Robert De Niro (Brian De Palma's *The Untouchables*). Directed by Richard Wilson, a former associate of Orson Welles, the picture revived interest in Capone, and led to the TV series of *The Untouchables*. AT [video]

Rod Steiger *Al Capone* • Fay Spain *Maureen Flannery* • Martin Balsam *Keely* • James Gregory *Tom Schaeffer* • Murvyn Vye *Bugs Moran* • Nehemiah Persoff *Johnny Torrio* • Joe De Santis *Big Jim Colosimo* • Lewis Charles *Hymie Weiss* ■ *Dir* Richard Wilson • *Scr* Marvin Wald, Henry Greenberg

Aladdin ★ PG

Fantasy 1986 · It · Colour · 91mins

Released in Italy as *SuperFantaGenio*, this was one of the last films directed by Bruno Corbucci. It's pretty much a bargain basement affair, although it does allow Italian star Bud Spencer to gnaw at the scenery as the Genie who is released by the young Luca Venantini from the magic lamp found in a junk shop. Desperately corny and gushingly sentimental. DP. An Italian language film. [video]

Bud Spencer *Genie* • Luca Venantini *Al Haddin* • Janet Agren *Mrs Haddin* • Umberto Raho • Julian Voloshin *Jeremiah* • Daimy Spencer *Patricia* ■ *Dir* Bruno Corbucci • *Scr* Mario Amendola, Marcello Fondato, Bruno Corbucci

Aladdin ★★★★★ U

Animated musical adventure
1992 · US · Colour · 95mins

For a full-length cartoon featuring some remarkably hip animation, it's amazing how Robin Williams's performance as the Genie steals the show, his ad-lib vocals a perfect match for the beautifully constructed Disney visuals. In this *Arabian Nights* tale, Aladdin (voiced by Scott Weinger) is the street urchin who uses a magical oil lamp and its wish-granting genie to win the love of Princess Jasmine (Linda Larkin, Lea Salonga singing) and defeat the evil Jafar (Jonathan Freeman). Kids will be enchanted by this captivating fable, while adults will appreciate the film's delightful songs and numerous sophisticated references. TH [video] DVD

Scott Weinger *Aladdin* • Robin Williams *Genie* • Linda Larkin *Jasmine* • Jonathan Freeman *Jafar* • Frank Welker *Abu/Narrator* • Gilbert Gottfried *Iago* • Douglas Seale *Sultan* • Lea Salonga *Jasmine* ■ *Dir* John Musker, Ron Clements • *Scr* Ron Clements, John Musker, Ted Elliot, Terry Rossio

Aladdin and the King of Thieves ★★★★ U

Animated adventure
1996 · US · Colour · 78mins

In this sequel to the 1992 Disney animated adventure *Aladdin*, Robin Williams returns to give the same sharp voice characterisation to the Genie, helping young Aladdin when he discovers that his father is actually the leader of the "40 Thieves". Adults will be just as entertained as the youngsters, thanks to a well thought-out plot and witty vocals. JB [video] DVD

Robin Williams *Genie* • Scott Weinger *Aladdin* • Linda Larkin *Jasmine* • John Rhys-Davies *Cassim* • Gilbert Gottfried *Iago* • Jerry Orbach *Sa'luk* • Val Bettin *Sultan* • Frank Welker *Abu* ■ *Dir* Tad Stones • *Scr* Mark McCorkle, Robert Schooley

The Alamo ★★★★ PG

Historical western
1960 · US · Colour · 154mins

A local priest said a prayer for the production on the first day of shooting, and some said John Wayne's directorial debut needed it. Filmed in San Antonio, Texas, site of the actual mission that saw the most famous battle of the Mexican war, this was less a pet project for Wayne and more of an obsession. Taking the role of Davy Crockett only to secure backing, he nonetheless adds heft to an already strong cast. The result, historically sketchy, oozes poignancy and high drama, allowing humour into the mix. Unable to live up to its own publicity, it remains a powerful old-school epic made with passion. AC [video] DVD

John Wayne *Colonel David Crockett* • Richard Widmark *Colonel James Bowie* • Laurence Harvey *Colonel William Travis* • Richard Boone *General Sam Houston* • Frankie Avalon *Smitty* • Patrick Wayne *Captain James Butler Bonham* • Linda Cristal *Flaca* • Joan O'Brien *Mrs Dickinson* • Chill Wills *Beekeeper* • Joseph Calleia *Juan Sequin* ■ *Dir* John Wayne • *Scr* James Edward Grant

The Alamo ★★ 12

Historical war drama
2004 · US · Colour · 131mins

Many are familiar with the bare facts of the Alamo – how, in 1836, a handful of Texans mounted a suicidal defence of a former mission against the Mexican army. It's a crucial episode in US history and part of the national psyche, but it would be hard to divine exactly why from this lengthy account. Heavy on character and light on exposition, this reduces events to a mass of buckskin fringes and big knives. The big-name cast is a draw, however. KK. Contains violence. [video] DVD

Dennis Quaid *Sam Houston* • Billy Bob Thornton *Davy Crockett* • Jason Patric *Jim Bowie* • Patrick Wilson *William Travis* • Emilio Echevarría *Antonio López de Santa Anna* • Jordi Mollà *Juan Seguin* • Leon Rippy *Sergeant William Ward* • Tom Davidson *Colonel Green Jameson* • Marc Blucas *James Bonham* ■ *Dir* John Lee Hancock • *Scr* Leslie Bohem, Stephen Gaghan, John Lee Hancock

Alamo Bay ★★★ 15

Drama based on a true story
1985 · US · Colour · 94mins

French director Louis Malle made a better study of racism in his acclaimed 1987 film *Au Revoir les Enfants*, but he also tackled the subject to decent effect two years earlier. This English-language movie examines the conflict between a group of Vietnamese refugees and a Texan shrimp-fishing community, whose members feel threatened by the competition from the hard-working newcomers. Amy Madigan stands out as the on-again, off-again girlfriend (and real-life wife) of chief racist thug Ed Harris, in this new variation on an old story. PF. Contains some swearing. [video]

Amy Madigan *Glory Scheer* • Ed Harris *Shang Pierce* • Nguyen Ho *Dinh* • Donald Moffat *Wally Scheer* • Tran Truyen V *Ben* • Rudy Young *Skinner* • Cynthia Carle *Honey* • Martino Lasalle [Martin Lasalle] *Luis* • William Frankfather *Mac* • Lucky Mosley *Ab Crankshaw* • Bill Thurman *Sheriff* ■ *Dir* Louis Malle • *Scr* Alice Arlen

Alan & Naomi ★★★ PG

Period drama 1992 · US · Colour · 91mins

A small but touching film in which youngsters Lukas Haas and Vanessa Zaoui are two Jewish children in 1940s New York. Haas is instructed to befriend new neighbour Zaoui, deeply disturbed since she was forced to watch her father's death at the hands of the Nazis. He is initially resistant, but the two children develop a lasting friendship. Debut director Sterling Van Wagenen handles his cast with ease and the result is poignant if a little stagey. LH [video]

Lukas Haas *Alan Drucker Silverman* • Vanessa Zaoui *Naomi Kirschenbaum* • Michael Gross *Sol Silverman* • Amy Aquino *Ruth Silverman* • Kevin Connolly *Shaun Kelly* ■ *Dir* Sterling Van Wagenen • *Scr* Jordan Horowitz, from a novel by Myron Levoy

The Alarmist ★★ 15

Comedy crime drama
1997 · US · Colour · 87mins

Evan Dunsky's indie comedy tries desperately to be wackily black, but uncertain pacing and a surfeit of plot padding make it feel like a neat short that unnecessarily sprawled into mediocrity. David Arquette mugs madly as a home security salesman who becomes convinced that crooked boss Stanley Tucci is responsible for the break-in death of his girlfriend (Kate Capshaw). Tucci revels in his Terry-Thomas villainy, but even he can't enliven the clumsy finale. DP. Contains swearing, sex scenes, violence. [video]

David Arquette *Tommy Hudler* • Stanley Tucci *Heinrich Grigoris* • Kate Capshaw *Gale Ancona* • Mary McCormack *Sally* • Ryan Reynolds *Howard Ancona* • Tricia Vessey *April* • Ruth Miller *Mrs Fielding* • Hoke Howell *Mr Fielding* • Lewis Arquette *Bruce Hudler* • Richmond Arquette *Andrew Hudler* ■ *Dir* Evan Dunsky • *Scr* Evan Dunsky, from the play *Life During Wartime* by Keith Reddin

A

Alaska ★★★ PG

Action adventure
1996 · US · Colour · 104mins

Fraser Heston directs his father Charlton for the second time (they first worked together on *Treasure Island* in 1990) in this well-made family adventure about a young brother and sister searching for their missing dad (played by *The A-Team's* Dirk Benedict) in the Alaskan wilderness. Instead they discover an adorable baby polar bear that's being hunted by a ruthless poacher (Heston). Breathtaking scenery, a deliciously evil portrayal from Chuck and energetic performances from the kids (Thora Birch and Vincent Kartheiser) make this an enjoyable adventure. JB

Thora Birch *Jessie Barnes* • Vincent Kartheiser *Sean Barnes* • Dirk Benedict *Jake Barnes* • Charlton Heston *Perry* • Duncan Fraser *Koontz* • Gordon Tootoosis *Ben* • Ben Cardinal *Charlie* • Ryan Kent *Chip* ■ *Dir* Fraser Heston [Fraser C Heston] • *Scr* Andy Burg, Scott Myers

Alaska Seas ★★ U

Adventure drama 1954 · US · BW · 76mins

A fight brews among the cannery men of Alaska, with bad guy Gene Barry opposed by good guys Robert Ryan and Brian Keith, who has just spent time in prison for poaching salmon. Jan Sterling is the girl in the middle, later upstaged by an iceberg that arrives to sort things out. The actors dress up warmly and huddle about, even though they are obviously in a Hollywood studio in front of a back projection screen. AT

Robert Ryan *Matt Kelly* • Jan Sterling *Nicky* • Brian Keith *Jim Kimmerly* • Gene Barry *Verne Williams* • Richard Shannon *Tom Erickson* • Ralph Dumke *Jackson* • Ross Bagdasarian *Joe* ■ *Dir* Jerry Hopper • *Scr* Geoffrey Homes [Daniel Mainwaring], Walter Doniger, from a story by Barrett Willoughby

Albert, RN ★★★ U

Second World War drama
1953 · UK · BW · 88mins

A PoW drama about a mannequin nicknamed Albert which supposedly stands in for escaped prisoners. A huge hit at the time, it still has bags of charm and a degree of tension, though a starrier cast than the wooden Anthony Steel and American expats such as William Sylvester would have helped considerably. But all is not lost: Anton Diffring plays a Nazi. AT

Anthony Steel *Lt Geoffrey Ainsworth* • Jack Warner *Capt Maddox* • Robert Beatty *Lt Jim Reid* • William Sylvester *Lt "Texas" Norton* • Michael Balfour *Lt Henry Adams* • Guy Middleton *Capt Barton* • Anton Diffring *Hauptmann Schultz* ■ *Dir* Lewis Gilbert • *Scr* Vernon Harris, Guy Morgan, from the play by Guy Morgan, Edward Sammis

Albino Alligator ★★ 18

Crime drama 1996 · US/Fr · Colour · 92mins

Highly acclaimed actor Kevin Spacey turns director in this far too theatrical and cerebral hostage thriller. An amateur gang, led by Matt Dillon, flee a gone-wrong heist and hole up in Dino's Last Chance all-night bar. Tension rises and tempers fray among the low-lifes and drunks being tended to by barmaid Faye Dunaway as the police surround the place and wait for the criminals to buckle. The over-ripe dialogue, full of endless philosophical ramblings, and the claustrophobic confines of the stagey scenario soon become stifling. AJ. Contains swearing and violence.

Matt Dillon *Dova* • Faye Dunaway *Janet Boudreaux* • Gary Sinise *Milo* • Viggo Mortensen *Guy Foucard* • Joe Mantegna *GD Browning* • M Emmet Walsh *Dino* • John Spencer *Jack* • William Fichtner *Law* • Skeet Ulrich *Danny Boudreaux* ■ *Dir* Kevin Spacey • *Scr* Christian Forte

The Alchemist ★ 18

Horror 1981 · US · Colour · 83mins

The gates of hell are opened when an old woman incants an ancient spell to free her father from the curse of eternal youth. And what's on the other side? Two men running around wearing dodgy demon rubber masks and a couple of awful special effects! Robert Ginty stars in this tedious occult nonsense from straight-to-video horror maestro Charles Band. AJ

Lucinda Dooling *Lenora* • Robert Ginty *Aaron* • Robert Glaudini *DenGatto* • John Sanderford • Viola Kate Stimpson ■ *Dir* Charles Band • *Scr* Alan J Adler

Aldrich Ames: Traitor Within ★★★ PG

Spy drama based on a true story
1998 · US · Colour · 97mins

Made for cable, this is a fascinating account of one of the USA's most notorious double agents, who betrayed the CIA for years for money. Frustrated by lack of promotion and ridden with debt, Aldrich Ames (Timothy Hutton) starts selling agents' names to the enemy. Joan Plowright is the methodical investigator on his tail, while Elizabeth Peña plays his unsuspecting wife. British director John Mackenzie cranks up the suspense, but this is really Hutton's show. JF. Contains some swearing.

Timothy Hutton *Aldrich Ames* • Elizabeth Peña *Rosario Ames* • Joan Plowright *Jeanne Vertefeuille* • Eugene Lipinski *Vlad* • Robert Benedetti *Chief of Operations* • C David Johnson *Brooks* • Patricia Carroll Brown *Connie Dru* ■ *Dir* John Mackenzie • *Scr* Michael Burton

Alex & Emma ★★ 12

Romantic comedy
2003 · US · Colour · 91mins

The genesis of Dostoyevsky's novella *The Gambler* is the inspiration for Rob Reiner's feeble romantic comedy. Luke Wilson is utterly devoid of passion, whether as the writer trying to pen a bestseller to pay off his gambling debts to some Cuban thugs or as the hero of his 1920s-set story, who is hopelessly in love with Sophie Marceau's society sophisticate. Kate Hudson overcompensates both as the stenographer helping him meet his deadline and the various maids who bewitch him in the dictation sequences. DP. Contains sex scenes. DVD

Kate Hudson *Emma Dinsmore/Ylva/Elsa/Eldora/Anna* • Luke Wilson *Alex Sheldon/Adam Shipley* • Sophie Marceau *Polina Delacroix* • David Paymer *John Shaw* • Rob Reiner *Wirschafter* • Cloris Leachman *Grandmother* • Rip Taylor *Polina's father* ■ *Dir* Rob Reiner • *Scr* Jeremy Leven

Alex and the Gypsy ★★

Romantic drama 1976 · US · Colour · 98mins

Jack Lemmon stars as a bailbondsman who falls for one of his clients, gypsy Geneviève Bujold, after she's accused of nearly killing her husband. It's a story of two of society's drop-outs and sits comfortably within the counterculture era. Lemmon seems to be reprising his Oscar-winning performance in *Save the Tiger*, while Bujold is no less of a cliché, that of the European free spirit. It might have worked better had it been played for black comedy instead of schmaltz. AT

Jack Lemmon *Alexander Main* • Geneviève Bujold *Maritza* • James Woods *Crainpool* • Gino Ardito *Golfer* • Robert Emhardt *Judge* • Joseph X Flaherty *Morgan* • Todd Martin *Roy Blake* ■ *Dir* John Korty • *Scr* Lawrence B Marcus, from the novella *The Bailbondsman* by Stanley Elkin

Alex in Wonderland ★

Comedy 1970 · US · Colour · 111mins

Paul Mazursky directs this horribly self-indulgent and self-conscious bomb about the far-out dilemma of a hippy director searching for a follow-up to his first successful movie. Donald Sutherland plays the navel-gazing *auteur* who takes LSD for inspiration, pokes fun at 1960s Hollywood and then fantasises about meeting Fellini (who appears as himself, along with Jeanne Moreau). AJ

Donald Sutherland *Alex* • Ellen Burstyn *Beth* • Federico Fellini • Jeanne Moreau • Meg Mazursky *Amy* • Glenna Sergent *Nancy* • Andre Philippe *André* • Michael Lerner *Leo* • Paul Mazursky *Hal Stern* ■ *Dir* Paul Mazursky • *Scr* Larry Tucker, Paul Mazursky

Alexander ★★ 15

Historical biographical drama
2004 · US/Ger/UK/Neth · Colour · 175mins

Director Oliver Stone has spent 15 years trying to bring the story of military genius Alexander the Great to the big screen. How sad then that an obvious labour of love should end up such a pompous and flaccid affair. The film presents key events in the life of the golden-haired Macedonian conqueror (played by Colin Farrell), each lazily linked by the reminiscences of his ageing general, Ptolemy (Anthony Hopkins). The visual detail is meticulous, crowned by two remarkable battle sequences, but this sterling work is undone by preposterous dialogue and some leaden performances. SF. Contains violence.

Colin Farrell (2) *Alexander* • Angelina Jolie *Olympias* • Val Kilmer *Philip* • Anthony Hopkins *Ptolemy* • Jared Leto *Hephaistion* • Rosario Dawson *Roxane* • Christopher Plummer *Aristotle* ■ *Dir* Oliver Stone • *Scr* Oliver Stone, Christopher Kyle, Laeta Kalogridis

Alexander Nevsky ★★★★ PG

Historical epic 1938 · USSR · BW · 104mins

The Soviet equivalent to Laurence Olivier's *Henry V*, this historical epic was to serve as propaganda against Hitler's Reich. However, just as Sergei Eisenstein completed the story of the Teutonic invasion of Russia in the 13th century, Stalin and Hitler signed a non-aggression pact, so the film was withdrawn. Then, when Hitler broke the treaty, Stalin ordered the film into release. It is famous for two things – the battle at the frozen lake, filmed in high summer, and Prokofiev's score. Both are worthy of their reputations, but this is offset by some turgid story-telling and excessively theatrical acting. AT. In Russian with English subtitles. DVD

Nikolai Cherkassov *Prince Alexander Yaroslavich Nevsky* • Nikolai P Okhlopkov *Vassily Buslai* • Alexandr L Abrikossov *Gavrilo Olexich* ■ *Dir* Sergei Eisenstein • *Scr* Sergei Eisenstein, Pyotr Pavlenko • *Cinematographer* Edouard Tissé

Alexander the Great ★★ U

Epic historical drama
1956 · US/Sp · Colour · 129mins

This epic promises more than it delivers, though Richard Burton makes a fair stab at depicting the conqueror of half the known world, even if he remains no match for Fredric March's Philip of Macedonia (Alexander's father). The use of early CinemaScope is superb, as is the deployment of the armies of extras and the key scene of slicing the Gordian knot, but Robert Rossen's long and static movie is wordy and ponderous. TS DVD

Richard Burton *Alexander* • Fredric March *Philip of Macedonia* • Claire Bloom *Barsine* • Danielle Darrieux *Olympias* • Barry Jones *Aristotle* • Harry Andrews *Darius* • Stanley Baker *Attalus* • Peter Cushing *Memnon* • Michael Hordern *Demosthenes* ■ *Dir/Scr* Robert Rossen

Alexander's Ragtime Band ★★★ U

Musical 1938 · US · BW · 101mins

It doesn't matter that handsome Tyrone Power shows no sense of rhythm, or that the plot is pure hokum, or that the First World War is over in a montage that's quicker than a wink. No... what matters is that this is a glorious Irving Berlin songfest, with Alice Faye and a young Ethel Merman belting out some of Tin Pan Alley's best and brightest. Unfortunately, there is a plot, and it's 20th Century-Fox's old triangular one: guess who gets Alice – Ty or his best friend, Don Ameche? Puhleeze... Just relax, and revel in the music. TS

Tyrone Power *Roger Grant* • Alice Faye *Stella Kirby* • Don Ameche *Charlie Dwyer* • Ethel Merman *Jerry Allen* • Jack Haley *Davey Lane* • Jean Hersholt *Professor Heinrich* • Helen Westley *Aunt Sophie* • John Carradine *Taxi driver* ■ *Dir* Henry King • *Scr* Kathryn Scola, Lamar Trotti

Alexandria Encore ★★★★

Documentary drama
1990 · Fr/Egy · Colour · 100mins

Youssef Chahine cinema-inspired work is a dazzling, if occasionally self-indulgent, treatise on the process of film-making. Chahine stars as a director assessing his achievements during a period of creative block brought on by a row with the star of his proposed production of *Hamlet*. With a Hollywood song-and-dance spectacular recalling the night he triumphed at Berlin, and flashbacks to an unrealised musical homage to Alexander the Great, this is a witty yet wistful exploration of age, authorship, cinematic art and popular taste. Elegant and engaging piece. DP. In Arabic with English subtitles.

Youssef Chahine • Yousra • Hussein Fahmy • Amr Abdel Guelil ■ *Dir/Scr* Youssef Chahine

Alexandria Why? ★★★★

Second World War drama
1979 · Egy/Alg · Colour · 132mins

Youssef Chahine, Egypt's most respected film-maker and the man who "discovered" Omar Sharif directs this stylish wartime tale, which won the Special Jury prize at Berlin, it focuses on a movie-mad schoolboy (Moshen Mohiedine), obsessed with Hollywood musicals at a time when everyone else is preoccupied with the advance of Rommel. Packed with cinematic references, the highlights of this study of starstruck ambition include a wonderfully fouled-up school play and Mohiedine's touching friendship with a Jewish girl, Nagla Fathi. DP. In Arabic with English subtitles.

Mohsen Mohiedine *Yehia* • Nagla Fathi *Sarah* • Gerry Sundquist *Tommy* ■ *Dir* Youssef Chahine • *Scr* Youssef Chahine, Mohsen Zayed

Alfie ★★★★ 15

Comedy drama 1966 · UK · Colour · 109mins

Receiving five Oscar nominations and rave reviews, this was one of the most talked-about British movies of the 1960s. Today, the frank discussion of pre-marital sex, adultery and illegitimacy may raise fewer eyebrows and the chirpy cockney banter may sound more than a little old hat, but this drama still has much to say about how differently men and women view intimate relationships, and the abortion scene is particularly harrowing. Michael Caine has rarely bettered his performance here, conveying a charm and a naivety that is as troubling as it is accomplished. Of the wronged women, Julia Foster and Vivien Merchant are outstanding. DP. Contains swearing [VIDEO] DVD

Michael Caine *Alfie* • Shelley Winters *Ruby* • Millicent Martin *Siddie* • Julia Foster *Gilda* • Jane Asher *Annie* • Shirley Anne Field *Carla* • Vivien Merchant *Lily* • Eleanor Bron *Doctor* • Denholm Elliott *Abortionist* ■ *Dir* Lewis Gilbert • *Scr* Bill Naughton, from his play

Alfie ★★ 15

Comedy drama 2004 · US · Colour · 101mins

The 1966 film got by largely on the roguеish charm of Michael Caine as the seducer of the title. Here, Jude Law seems to be struggling to believe his character could be such an unconvincing combination of connivance and dimness. With the action transposed to present-day New York, Alfie has his wicked way with a series of ladies before it begins to dawn on him that maybe an endless string of brief sexual encounters isn't what it's all about. A creaky effort. LF. Contains swearing, nudity and sexual references. [VIDEO] DVD

Jude Law *Alfie Elkins* • Marisa Tomei *Julie* • Omar Epps *Marlon* • Nia Long *Lonette* • Jane Krakowski *Dorie* • Sienna Miller *Nikki* • Susan Sarandon *Liz* ■ *Dir* Charles Shyer • *Scr* Charles Shyer, Elaine Pope, from the film and the play by Bill Naughton

Alfie Darling ★★ 18

Comedy drama 1975 · UK · Colour · 97mins

This follow-up to the Oscar-nominated *Alfie* (1966) finds pop singer Alan Price replacing Michael Caine as the cockney casanova, with director Ken Hughes taking over from Lewis Gilbert. This time around Alfie is a truck driver involved with the usual bevy of beauties, none of whom makes any impact apart from Jill Townsend. Lacking much of the verve and pathos of the original, this is harmless and charmless. TH [VIDEO]

Alan Price *Alfie* • Jill Townsend *Abby* • Joan Collins *Fay* • Rula Lenska *Louise* • Hannah Gordon *Dora* • Vicki Michelle *Bird* • Annie Ross *Claire* • Sheila White *Norma* ■ *Dir* Ken Hughes • *Scr* Ken Hughes, from the character created by Bill Naughton

Alfred the Great ★★★

Historical drama
1969 · UK · Colour · 122mins

1960s' trendy David Hemmings is a rather implausible Prince of Wessex, later the only British king to be called "great", in director Clive Donner's story of the man who not only burnt the cakes but also built the boats to create the British navy. In Donner's film, Alfred is portrayed as someone whose greatness was thrust upon him, a deep thinker who had once wanted to take holy orders. An interesting theme, but true epic status somehow eludes the movie. TH

David Hemmings *Alfred* • Michael York *Guthrum* • Prunella Ransome *Aelhswith* • Colin Blakely *Asher* • Julian Glover *Athelstan* • Ian McKellen *Roger* • Alan Dobie *Ethelred* • Peter Vaughan *Buhrud* • Julian Chagrin *Ivar* • Barry Jackson *Wulfstan* • Vivien Merchant *Freda* • Christopher Timothy *Cedric* • Michael Billington *Offa* ■ *Dir* Clive Donner • *Scr* Ken Taylor, James R Webb

Alfredo Alfredo ★★

Comedy 1971 · It · Colour · 97mins

Ever the Method actor, Dustin Hoffman took the trouble to learn the Italian dialogue for this laborious comedy, only for director Pietro Germi to shoot in English and then dub all the voices in post-production into Italian. A dubbed English version then went on general release in the States. Germi veers between cruel slapstick and broad satire as he chronicles Hoffman's doomed relationship with the demanding Stefania Sandrelli. DP. Italian dialogue dubbed into English.

Dustin Hoffman *Alfredo* • Stefania Sandrelli *Mariarosa* • Carla Gravina *Carolina* • Clara Colosimo *Carolina's mother* • Daniele Patella *Carolina's father* • Danika La Loggia *Mariarosa's mother* • Saro Urzi *Mariarosa's father* ■ *Dir* Pietro Germi • *Scr* Leo Benvenuti, Piero De Bernardi, Tullio Pinelli, Pietro Germi

Alf's Button Afloat ★★★ U

Fantasy comedy 1938 · UK · BW · 89mins

The upstaging talents of "The Crazy Gang" – Bud Flanagan, Chesney Allen, Jimmy Nervo, Teddy Knox, Charles Naughton and Jimmy Gold – have never been in doubt. However, Alastair Sim easily surpasses them as the genie they encounter in this version of WA Darlington's famous farce. As buskers serving in the Marines, the Gang work hard at their music hall routines, but the bumbling Sim steals the show. TH

Bud Flanagan *Alf Higgins* • Chesney Allen *Ches* • Jimmy Nervo *Cecil* • Teddy Knox *Teddy* • Charlie Naughton *Charlie* • Jimmy Gold *Jimmy* • Alastair Sim *Eustace* • Wally Patch *Sergeant Hawkins* • Peter Gawthorne *Captain Driscol* • Glennis Lorimer *Frankie Driscol* ■ *Dir* Marcel Varnel • *Scr* Marriott Edgar, Val Guest, Ralph Smart, from the play *Alf's Button* by WA Darlington

Algiers ★★★

Crime drama 1938 · US · BW · 97mins

This loose remake of the Jean Gabin movie *Pépé le Moko*, has Charles Boyer and Hedy Lamarr clinching in the Casbah, the scene of innumerable shady goings-on from the supporting cast. The hard-boiled dialogue by James M Cain, author of *Double Indemnity*, and the lustrous black-and-white photography give this movie irresistible glamour. Producer Hal B Wallis saw how successful it was and immediately ordered a title change to his new production at Warners called *Everybody Comes to Rick's*. The new title? Why, *Casablanca*, of course. AT

Charles Boyer *Pépé le Moko* • Sigrid Gurie *Ines* • Hedy Lamarr *Gaby* • Joseph Calleia *Slimane* • Gene Lockhart *Regis* • Alan Hale *Grandpère* ■ *Dir* John Cromwell • *Scr* John Howard Lawson, James M Cain, from the novel *Pépé le Moko* by Detective Roger D'Ashelbe [Henri La Barthe] • *Cinematographer* James Wong Howe

Ali ★★★ 15

Biographical sports drama
2001 · US · Colour · 150mins

There's no faulting Will Smith's remarkable impersonation of Muhammad Ali, nor can you underestimate the epic scale and historical authenticity of director Michael Mann's biopic. Where it falls down is in the lack of fresh insight into the enigmatic fighter; familiar events are lavishly re-created (Jon Voight's uncanny transformation into renowned American sportscaster Howard Cosell is one of the highlights) but are not re-examined or explored in any depth. While Mann's bruising approach to the heavyweight contests are riveting, elsewhere the sluggish pace lessens the overall impact of a very lengthy movie. JC. Contains violence and swearing. [VIDEO] DVD

Will Smith *Muhammad Ali/Cassius Clay* • Jamie Foxx *Drew "Bundini" Brown* • Jon Voight *Howard Cosell* • Mario Van Peebles *Malcolm X* • Ron Silver *Angelo Dundee* • Jeffrey Wright *Howard Bingham* • Mykelti Williamson *Don King* • Jada Pinkett Smith *Sonji Roi* ■ *Dir* Michael Mann • *Scr* Stephen J Rivele, Christopher Wilkinson, Eric Roth, Michael Mann, from a story by Gregory Allen Howard

Ali: an American Hero ★★ PG

Biographical drama
2000 · US · Colour · 84mins

Although it betrays its TV origins in almost every frame, director Leon Ichaso's biopic at least attempts to trace a life story (unlike Michael Mann's *Ali* which concentrates on a ten year period). Related largely in flashback, the action covers the fighter's childhood and his triumph, as Cassius Clay, at the 1960 Rome Olympics. Familiar landmarks, such as the fights with Sonny Liston and the "Rumble in the Jungle" appear in due course. However, it's melodramatic and David Ramsey in the title role is gauche. DP [VIDEO]

David Ramsey *Cassius Clay/Muhammad Ali* • Clarence Williams III *Marcellus Clay* • Joe Morton *Malcolm X* • Vondie Curtis-Hall *Drew "Bundini" Brown* ■ *Dir* Leon Ichaso • *Scr* Jamal Joseph

Ali Baba and the Forty Thieves ★★ U

Adventure 1944 · US · Colour · 86mins

Baghdad... and the Mongols have landed, throwing everyone into slavery, except young Master Baba, who escapes into the desert and finds said number of thieves. He grows up to be Jon Hall, and falls for Maria Montez as a princess with attitude. Made by Universal as a follow-up to the money-spinning *Arabian Nights*, this take on an old story has its tongue in its cheek and delivers its cheapo action thrills quite efficiently. AT

Maria Montez *Amara* • Jon Hall *Ali Baba* • Turhan Bey *Jamiel* • Andy Devine *Abdullah* • Kurt Katch *Hulagu Khan* • Frank Puglia *Cassim* • Fortunio Bonanova *Baba* • Moroni Olsen *Caliph* • Ramsay Ames *Nalu* ■ *Dir* Arthur Lubin • *Scr* Edmund L Hartmann

Ali G indahouse ★★★ 15

Comedy
2002 · Ger/US/Fr/UK · Colour · 83mins

While by no means an important piece of film-making, this is still so much better than it ought to have been. As forged on TV by Sacha Baron Cohen (who co-writes here), Ali G – the white kid from Staines who behaves like a black rapper from South Central – is essentially a one-joke creation (albeit a good joke). That joke is stretched to breaking point here, but if you laughed the first time, you'll laugh again. This is largely thanks to the ludicrous plot (Ali becomes an MP, exposes sleaze and saves the planet) and a sparkling turn from co-star Martin Freeman as Ali's sidekick. AC. Contains swearing and drug abuse. [VIDEO] DVD

Sacha Baron Cohen *Ali G/Borat* • Michael Gambon *Prime Minister* • Charles Dance *David Carlton* • Kellie Bright *Julie* • Martin Freeman *Ricky C* • Rhona Mitra *Kate Hedges* • Barbara New *Nan* ■ *Dir* Mark Mylod • *Scr* Sacha Baron Cohen, Dan Mazer

Ali Zaoua ★★★ 15

Drama 2000 · Fr/Mor/Bel · Colour · 98mins

This tale of Casablancan street kids battling poverty and casual brutality in order to give their buddy a decent burial is both touching and perceptive. Contrasting the squalor of the docks and the inner-city wastelands with glossy advertising images and optimistic animated inserts, director Nabil Ayouch celebrates the resilience of the pre-teenage trio, while also suggesting their seemingly inevitable fate. Cinematographer Vincent Mathias gives an unexpected lustre to the neorealist imagery. DP. In French and Arabic with English subtitles.

Mounïm Khab *Kwita* • Mustapha Hansali *Omar* • Hicham Moussoune *Boubker* • Abdelhak Zhayra *Ali Zaoua* • Saïd Taghmaoui *Dib* ■ *Dir* Nabil Ayouch • *Scr* Nathalie Saugeon, Nabil Ayouch

Alias Jesse James ★★★ U

Comedy western 1959 · US · Colour · 92mins

Bob Hope stars in yet another western spoof, this time playing an incompetent insurance salesman determined to retrieve the policy he unwittingly sold to outlaw Jesse James (Wendell Corey). Hope provides the jokes, while Rhonda Fleming supplies the pulchritude. The best moments are in the finale, though, when a host of cowboy stars (Roy Rogers, James Garner, Fess Parker) protect Bob from the killers. TH

Bob Hope *Milford Farnsworth* • Rhonda Fleming *Cora Lee Collins* • Wendell Corey *Jesse James* • Jim Davis *Frank James* • Gloria Talbott *Indian maiden* • Will Wright *Titus Queasley* • James Arness *Matt Dillon* • Ward Bond *Major Seth Adams* • Gary Cooper • Bing Crosby • Gail Davis *Annie Oakley* • Hugh O'Brian *Wyatt Earp* • Fess Parker *Davy Crockett* • Roy Rogers • Jay Silverheels *Tonto* • Gene Autry • James Garner *Bret Maverick* ■ *Dir* Norman Z McLeod • *Scr* William Bowers, Daniel D Beauchamp, from a story by Robert St Aubrey, Bert Lawrence

Alias Nick Beal ★★★

Fantasy crime drama
1949 · US · BW · 92mins

This political allegory relocates the Faust legend to 20th-century America. Ray Milland is the mysterious Nick Beal, who materialises to offer honest politician Thomas Mitchell not only wealth but also the charms of Audrey Totter. The former crusader against crime becomes power hungry under the malign influence of "Old Nick". Milland is the personification of evil, while John Farrow does a characteristically efficient job directing what was then considered daring material. BB

Ray Milland *Nick Beal* • Audrey Totter *Donna Allen* • Thomas Mitchell *Joseph Foster* • George Macready *Rev Thomas Garfield* • Fred Clark *Frankie Faulkner* ■ *Dir* John Farrow • *Scr* Jonathan Latimer, from the story *Dr Joe Faust* by Mindret Lord

Alibi ★★

Crime drama 1929 · US · BW · 75mins

This early gangster movie was made by the maverick independent Roland West who later made *The Bat Whispers*. Now long forgotten, *Alibi* has been credited with being the first film to simultaneously record the sound and show the destruction caused by a tommy-gun. Two interrogation scenes are especially shocking, showing the sadistic techniques used by the cops as utterly normal. Chester Morris, in his first starring role, was among those nominated for the second Oscar ceremony. AT

Chester Morris *Chick Williams* • Harry Stubbs *Buck Bachman* • Mae Busch *Daisy Thomas* • Eleanor Griffith *Joan* • Irma Harrison *Toots* • Regis Toomey *Danny McGann* • Al Hill *Brown* • James Bradbury Jr *Blake* ■ *Dir* Roland West • *Scr* Roland West, C Gardner Sullivan, from the play *Nightstick* by John Wray, JC Nugent, Elaine S Carrington

Alice ★★★★ PG

Animated fantasy
1988 · UK/Swi/W Ger · Colour · 82mins

This stunning modern-day version of the Lewis Carroll story from Czech director, animator and surrealist Jan Svankmajer uses every live action technique in the special effects manual, and contains dashes of startling eroticism. The absurdist universe he creates plays around liberally with the source material, yet remains true to its spirit. Flesh-and-blood actress Krystyna Kohoutova stars with a host of scary fish,

A

skeleton birds and, most unusually, perambulating raw meat. AJ

Kristyna Kohoutova *Alice* ■ *Dir* Jan Svankmajer • *Scr* from the novel *Alice's Adventures in Wonderland* by Lewis Carroll

Alice ★★★ 15

Fantasy comedy 1990 · US · Colour · 102mins

When this was originally released, several critics attacked Woody Allen for making the same film over and over again. But is there another Allen picture in which a woman is helped to confront her past with the help of Chinese herbal teas, gets to meet the ghost of an old flame and spy on her family and friends while invisible? What gives this that familiar feel is the all too predictable performance of Mia Farrow, whose bored Manhattan underachiever undoes a lot of the good work by the excellent supporting cast. DP. Contains swearing and drug abuse. DVD

Mia Farrow *Alice* • William Hurt *Doug* • Alec Baldwin *Ed* • Joe Mantegna *Joe* • Cybill Shepherd *Nancy Brill* • Blythe Danner *Dorothy* • Bernadette Peters *Muse* • Gwen Verdon *Alice's mother* • Patrick O'Neal *Alice's father* ■ *Dir/Scr* Woody Allen

Alice Adams ★★★★ U

Comedy drama 1935 · US · BW · 95mins

Brilliant Hollywood director George Stevens dates this small-town opus as the real start of his career, conveniently neglecting the early comedies that he cut his teeth on. Understandable, really, since his technique, together with a magnificent performance from Katharine Hepburn as Booth Tarkington's titular heroine, make this unforgettable. The dinner table scene, where beau Fred MacMurray comes visiting, is rightly famous, and is a brilliant example of the film-maker's craft, albeit aided by superb casting (in particular Hattie McDaniel's slovenly maid). This is, in fact, a remake of a 1923 silent version which had Florence Vidor in the lead, but it's Hepburn's version that's remembered. TS

Katharine Hepburn *Alice Adams* • Fred MacMurray *Arthur Russell* • Fred Stone *Mr Adams* • Evelyn Venable *Mildred Palmer* • Frank Albertson *Walter Adams* • Ann Shoemaker *Mrs Adams* • Charles Grapewin [Charley Grapewin] *Mr Lamb* • Grady Sutton *Frank Dowling* • Hedda Hopper *Mrs Palmer* • Hattie McDaniel *Malena* ■ *Dir* George Stevens • *Scr* Dorothy Yost, Mortimer Offner, from the novel by Booth Tarkington

Alice Doesn't Live Here Anymore ★★★★ 15

Drama 1974 · US · Colour · 107mins

Ellen Burstyn won an Oscar for her portrayal of bruised widow Alice in this expertly played drama from Martin Scorsese. Hitting the road with her brattish son in order to find herself and dreaming of a new beginning as a singer, Burstyn brilliantly conveys the vulnerability that forces her character first into the arms of the brutal Harvey Keitel and then of taciturn rancher Kris Kristofferson. Scorsese just about keeps the sprawling road movie segment on track, but the film only really comes to life when Burnstyn joins forces with a sassy diner waitress played by Oscar-nominated Diane Ladd. DP. Contains violence and swearing. DVD

Ellen Burstyn *Alice Hyatt* • Kris Kristofferson *David Barrie* • Billy Green Bush *Donald Hyatt* • Diane Ladd *Flo* • Lelia Goldoni *Bea* • Lane Bradbury *Rita* • Vic Tayback *Mel* • Jodie Foster *Audrey* • Harvey Keitel *Ben Eberhart* • Alfred Lutter *Tom Hyatt* ■ *Dir* Martin Scorsese • *Scr* Robert Getchell

Alice et Martin ★★★ 15

Drama 1998 · Fr/Sp/US · Colour · 119mins

André Téchiné directs this coolly assured but coldly uninvolving film, which is further undermined by improbable characterisation and contrived plotting. At the mercy of her emotions, Juliette Binoche is never less than persuasive as the violinist who sacrifices everything for Alexis Loret, an undeserving narcissus. Aided by crisp photography and a lovely score, Téchiné deftly captures the fragility of the relationship, but refuses to allow us to delve too deeply. DP. In French with English subtitles. DVD

Juliette Binoche *Alice* • Alexis Loret *Martin Sauvagnac* • Mathieu Amalric *Benjamin Sauvagnac* • Carmen Maura *Jeanine Sauvagnac* • Jean-Pierre Lorit *Frédéric* • Marthe Villalonga *Lucie* • Pierre Maguelon *Victor Sauvagnac* ■ *Dir* André Téchiné • *Scr* André Téchiné, Gilles Taurand, Olivier Assayas • *Cinematographer* Caroline Champetier • *Music* Philippe Sarde

Alice in the Cities ★★★★ U

Road movie 1974 · W Ger · BW · 107mins

Introducing themes that would recur in *Wrong Move, Kings of the Road* and *Paris, Texas*, Wim Wenders's road movie provides an amusing, affectionate and yet quietly critical portrait of 1970s America. Often employing a subjective camera technique, Wenders places the viewer at the heart of the odyssey so that we can experience the sights and sounds of the eastern seaboard exactly as photojournalist Rüdiger Vogler and his nine-year-old companion Yella Rottlander see them. The search for the girl's grandmother is virtually irrelevant, as it is how this odd couple react to each other and their ever-changing environment that is important. DP. In German with English subtitles.

Rüdiger Vogler *Philip Winter* • Yella Rottlander *Alice Van Damm* • Elisabeth Kreuzer *Lisa Van Damm* • Edda Köchl *Edda* • Didi Petrikat *Girl* • Ernest Bohm *Policeman* • Sam Presti *Car salesman* • Lois Moran *Airline girl* ■ *Dir* Wim Wenders • *Scr* Wim Wenders, Veith von Fürstenberg • *Cinematographer* Robby Müller

Alice in Wonderland ★★ U

Fantasy 1933 · US · BW · 79mins

This laboured attempt to include a vast range of Lewis Carroll's characters from both *Alice's Adventures in Wonderland* and *Alice through the Looking Glass* is of most interest for the appearance of Paramount's top stars. However, because they're clad in masks and costumes based on the John Tenniel drawings, the actors are only recognisable by their voices. AE

Charlotte Henry *Alice* • Richard Arlen *Cheshire Cat* • Roscoe Ates *Fish* • William Austin *Gryphon* • Gary Cooper *White Knight* • Jack Duffy (1) *Leg of Mutton* • Leon Errol *Uncle Gilbert* • Louise Fazenda *White Queen* • WC Fields *Humpty Dumpty* • Cary Grant *Mock Turtle* • Edward Everett Horton *Mad Hatter* • Edna May Oliver *Red Queen* • Charlie Ruggles [Charles Ruggles] *March Hare* ■ *Dir* Norman Z McLeod • *Scr* Joseph L Mankiewicz, William Cameron Menzies, from the books by Lewis Carroll

Alice in Wonderland ★★★ U

Animated fantasy 1951 · US · Colour · 72mins

This brash, colourful and undemanding animated feature contains the best-loved episodes from the Lewis Carroll classic. Where it scores over its live action rivals is in the depiction of the more fantastic figures, such as the White Rabbit, the Caterpillar, the Cheshire Cat, the March Hare and the Dormouse, which, while always more Disney than Carroll, are all engaging creations. Of the humans, Alice resembles her Tenniel original, but the Mad Hatter, the weedy King and the blustering Queen of Hearts are more imaginative and great fun. Not among the studio's best, but certainly well worth a watch. DP DVD

Kathryn Beaumont *Alice* • Ed Wynn *Mad Hatter* • Richard Haydn *Caterpillar* • Sterling Holloway *Cheshire Cat* • Jerry Colonna *March Hare* • Verna Felton *Queen of Hearts* • J Pat O'Malley *Walrus/Carpenter/Tweedledee/Tweedledum* • Bill Thompson *White Rabbit/Dodo* ■ *Dir* Clyde Geronimi, Hamilton Luske, Wilfred Jackson • *Scr* from the books by Lewis Carroll

Alice in Wonderland ★★ U

Fantasy adventure 1999 · US/UK · Colour · 133mins

A galaxy of stars surround Tina Majorino in this small-screen adaptation of Alice's adventures in Wonderland, which also benefits from some wondrous Jim Henson puppetry. Yet, somehow, the combination still falls short of the cherished images taken from those first readings of Lewis Carroll's classic tales. There are standout performances from the likes of Miranda Richardson as the Queen of Hearts and Gene Wilder as the Mock Turtle, but others are too eager to please, among them Martin Short's Mad Hatter. DP DVD

Tina Majorino *Alice* • Martin Short *Mad Hatter* • Miranda Richardson *Queen of Hearts* • Ben Kingsley *Major Caterpillar* • Whoopi Goldberg *Cheshire Cat* • Gene Wilder *Mock Turtle* • George Wendt *Tweedledee* • Robbie Coltrane *Tweedledum* ■ *Dir* Nick Willing • *Scr* Peter Barnes, from the novels *Alice's Adventures in Wonderland/Through the Looking Glass* by Lewis Carroll

Alice, Sweet Alice ★★★★ 18

Horror thriller 1977 · US · Colour · 108mins

This offbeat, multilayered whodunnit first won acclaim for director Alfred Sole's approach (a highly individual blend of pastiche and homage). Later commercial success derived from a brief appearance by Brooke Shields, who went on to cause a sensation in *Pretty Baby*. Sole shot his story of a series of murders in and around a Catholic church in his home town (Paterson, New Jersey) in 1961. The killings (still shockingly realistic) are interspersed with biting portrayals of the dysfunctional family and Catholic ritual. There is also black humour, inspired by Hitchcock, although fans will notice many other influences. DM

Linda Miller *Catherine Spages* • Mildred Clinton *Mrs Tredoni* • Paula Sheppard *Alice Spages* • Niles McMaster *Dominick Spages* • Rudolph Willrich *Father Tom* • Jane Lowry *Aunt Annie* • Alphonso DeNoble *Mr Alphonso* • Brooke Shields *Karen Spages* ■ *Dir* Alfred Sole • *Scr* Rosemary Ritvo, Alfred Sole

Alice's Adventures in Wonderland ★★ U

Fantasy 1972 · UK · Colour · 91mins

This all-star version of the Lewis Carroll classic has syrupy music and lyrics by John Barry and Don Black, and casts Fiona Fullerton as Alice. Fullerton had already made a couple of movies and was promoted as a new Julie Andrews, but she has a hard time not being upstaged by her co-stars: Michael Hordern, Ralph Richardson and Spike Milligan. Peter Sellers caused a minor stir by peevishly slagging the film off before it opened. AT DVD

Fiona Fullerton *Alice* • Peter Sellers *March Hare* • Michael Crawford *White Rabbit* • Robert Helpmann *Mad Hatter* • Michael Hordern *Mock Turtle* • Michael Jayston *Dodgson* • Spike Milligan *Gryphon* • Dudley Moore *Dormouse* • Ralph Richardson *Caterpillar* • Flora Robson *Queen of Hearts* ■ *Dir* William Sterling • *Scr* William Sterling, from the books by Lewis Carroll

Alice's Restaurant ★★★ 15

Comedy drama 1969 · US · Colour · 106mins

Not so much the story of the restaurant in question as an anti-Vietnam hymn celebrating dropouts, this stars folk singer Arlo Guthrie. It is based on his lengthy (more than 18 minutes) hit recording in which he detailed some of his experiences of trying to dodge the draft for a war that he and his comrades didn't believe in. Directed with visual authority by Arthur Penn, it has some saving humour, but its narcissistic self-regard detracts from its undoubted sincerity, which reflects the mood of *Easy Rider*, made in the same year. TH DVD

Arlo Guthrie *Arlo* • Pat Quinn [Patricia Quinn] *Alice* • James Broderick *Ray* • Michael McClanathan *Shelly* • Geoff Outlaw *Roger* • Tina Chen *Mari-Chan* • Kathleen Dabney *Karin* • William Obanhein *Officer Obie* • M Emmet Walsh *Group W sergeant* ■ *Dir* Arthur Penn • *Scr* Venable Herndon, Arthur Penn, from the song *The Alice's Restaurant Massacre* by Arlo Guthrie

Alien ★★★★★ 18

Science-fiction action thriller 1979 · US/UK · Colour · 116mins

This revolutionary "haunted house in space" thrill-ride is the classic business, stunning you with shock after shock, even when the fascinating creature is exposed in all its hideous glory. The top-notch acting (super-astronaut Sigourney Weaver) and imaginative bio-mechanical production design (with the alien created by Swiss artist HR Giger) succeed in flattering a script culled from many cult sci-fi movies. There's also director Ridley Scott's eye for detail and brilliant way of alternating false scares with genuine jolts, which help to create a seamless blend of gothic horror and harrowing science fiction. The director's cut, released in 2003, boasts a remastered sound mix and sequences cut from the original – until now only available on the *Alien* DVD – including a much-discussed cocoon scene. AJ. Contains violence and swearing. DVD

Sigourney Weaver *Ripley* • Tom Skerritt *Captain Dallas* • Veronica Cartwright *Lambert* • Harry Dean Stanton *Brett* • John Hurt *Kane* • Ian Holm *Ash* • Yaphet Kotto *Parker* • Helen Horton *"Mother"* ■ *Dir* Ridley Scott • *Scr* Dan O'Bannon, from a story by Dan O'Bannon, Ronald Shusett

Alien^3 ★★★ 18

Science-fiction action thriller 1992 · US · Colour · 109mins

Given that the first two films stand up as sci-fi classics in their own right, *Se7en* director David Fincher, in his feature film debut, had a virtually impossible act to follow with this second sequel. He makes a good fist of it, developing the maternal themes of first sequel *Aliens* and providing an exhilarating final showdown. Sigourney Weaver returns as Ripley, who this time crash-lands on a prison colony where another lethal alien is let loose. While it isn't in the same class as the first two films, this provides a satisfactory addition to the series. A fourth instalment, *Alien: Resurrection*, was released in 1997. JF. Contains violence and swearing. DVD

Sigourney Weaver *Warrant Officer Ripley* • Charles S Dutton *Dillon* • Charles Dance *Clemens* • Paul McGann *Golic* • Brian Glover *Superintendent Andrews* • Ralph Brown *Aaron* • Danny Webb [Daniel Webb] *Morse* • Christopher John Fields *Rains* • Holt McCallany *Junior* • Lance Henriksen *Bishop II* ■ *Dir* David Fincher • *Scr* David Giler, Walter Hill, Larry Ferguson, from a story by Vincent Ward, from characters created by Dan O'Bannon, Ronald Shusett

The Alien Dead ★

Science-fiction horror
1980 · US · Colour · 73mins

The first movie directed by hack-meister Fred Olen Ray was Buster Crabbe's last. It couldn't be a sadder epitaph for the 1930s *Flash Gordon* star if it tried. Crabbe investigates a crash-landed meteorite in Florida, apparently responsible for turning a houseboat full of teens into raving ghouls. A pretty awful load of old zombie nonsense, complete with cheap special effects and amateur-hour direction. AJ

Buster Crabbe [Larry "Buster" Crabbe] *Sheriff Kowalski* • Ray Roberts *Tom Corman* • Linda Lewis *Shawn Michaels* • George Kelsey *Emmett Michaels* • Mike Bonavia *Miller Haze* ■ *Dir* Fred Olen Ray • *Scr* Martin Alan Nicholas, Fred Olen Ray

Alien Nation ★★★★ 18

Science-fiction thriller
1988 · US · Colour · 86mins

This is the ultimate in buddy-buddy cop movies, but with a difference, as this time the mismatched detectives come from different planets. In the near future, an alien race has been uncomfortably integrated into American society and, against this backdrop, Earthling cop James Caan and alien cop Mandy Patinkin are reluctantly paired together to track down the killers of Caan's old partner. Director Graham Baker expertly combines the sci-fi and thriller elements and is well served by the two leads, particularly Patinkin, who manages to create a moving character while operating under a ton of latex. The movie inspired a rather more humdrum but still popular TV series and five TV movies. JF. Contains violence, swearing, drug abuse and sex scenes. DVD

James Caan *Matthew Sykes* • Mandy Patinkin *Sam Francisco, "George"* • Terence Stamp *William Harcourt* • Kevyn Major Howard *Rudyard Kipling* • Leslie Bevis *Cassandra* • Peter Jason *Fedorchuk* • George Jenesky *Quint* • Jeff Kober *Josh Strader* ■ *Dir* Graham Baker • *Scr* Rockne S O'Bannon

Alien: Resurrection ★★★★ 18

Science-fiction action thriller
1997 · US · Colour · 104mins

This enticing helter-skelter trip through space opera cliché cleverly conceals the fact there really isn't anything new of note here, just neat tangents off the basic *Alien* concept: nasty ETs relentlessly stalking their human prey through a deserted spaceship. Sigourney Weaver's Ripley is cloned 200 years after the action of *Alien 3* because she's carrying a queen foetus. French director Jean-Pierre Jeunet's shock thrill-ride showcases such scintillating set pieces as an underwater battle and a gallery of grotesque clones-gone-wrong. Tense, mordantly funny, very graphic and bloody, with Weaver on great form as clone number eight who's gained some interesting alien influences on her personality. AJ DVD

Sigourney Weaver *Ripley* • Winona Ryder *Call* • Dominique Pinon *Vriess* • Ron Perlman *Johner* • Gary Dourdan *Christie* • Michael Wincott *Elgyn* • Kim Flowers *Hillard* • Dan Hedaya *General Perez* ■ *Dir* Jean-Pierre Jeunet • *Scr* Joss Whedon, from characters created by Dan O'Bannon, Ronald Shusett

Alien Space Avenger ★★★

Science-fiction comedy adventure
1989 · US · Colour · 80mins

This fun B-movie from director Richard W Haines melds science-fiction, soft-core porn, gangster chronicle and prison saga together for a cleverly constructed action thriller packed with gore, laughs and quirky acting. Outlaw aliens take over a pair of flapper-era couples in the 1930s, hide out in a space sphere for 50 years, then emerge in late 1980s Manhattan looking for plutonium to return home. As intergalactic bounty hunters close in, a comic-book artist uses their exploits for inspiration in a "Space Avenger" series. An entertaining collision of fantasy and reality, paying homage to 1950s cult movies. AJ

Robert Prichard • Mike McClerie • Charity Staley • Gina Mastrogiacomo • Angela Nicholas ■ *Dir* Richard W Haines • *Scr* Richard W Haines, Linwood Sawyer, Leslie Delano

Alien Terror ★ 18

Science-fiction thriller
1969 · Mex/US · Colour · 73mins

The last movie made by veteran horror icon Boris Karloff was also the last of a shoddily assembled quartet of creature features made back-to-back in Los Angeles and Mexico. Barely directed by schlock maestro Jack Hill (the Mexico scenes were the work of Juan Ibanez) and badly edited – Karloff is clearly emoting to actors in another time and country – the film involves a molecular ray gun which freaks out observing aliens when its inventor (Boris) accidentally blows a hole in his laboratory roof. AJ

Boris Karloff *Professor John Meyer* • Enrique Guzman *Paul* • Christa Linder *Laura* • Yerye Beirute *Convict* • Maura Monti *Isabel* ■ *Dir* Jack Hill • *Scr* Karl Schanzer, Luis Vergara

Aliens ★★★★★ 18

Science-fiction action thriller
1986 · US · Colour · 137mins

Surpassing its predecessor in terms of sheer spectacle, this sequel to Ridley Scott's outer-space nightmare from director James Cameron is an outstanding science-fiction thriller. Sigourney Weaver wakes up 57 years after the original events unfolded, only to be told that the planet where she first met the alien predator has been colonised. When all contact with the inhabitants is lost, she's sent in with a crack squad of marines, and hurtles headlong into a hi-tech house of horrors that delivers super shocks and nail-biting suspense. Masterfully controlling the tension and moving the involving plot at a lightning pace, Cameron exploits everyone's worst fears and carries them to the riveting extreme in this consummate Oscar-winning fright-fest. AJ. Contains violence and swearing. DVD

Sigourney Weaver *Ripley* • Carrie Henn *Rebecca Jorden, "Newt"* • Michael Biehn *Corporal Hicks* • Paul Reiser *Carter J Burke* • Lance Henriksen *Bishop* • Bill Paxton *Private Hudson* • William Hope *Lieutenant Gorman* • Jenette Goldstein *Private Vasquez* • Al Matthews *Sergeant Apone* ■ *Dir* James Cameron • *Scr* James Cameron, from a story by James Cameron, David Giler, Walter Hill, from characters created by Dan O'Bannon, Ronald Shusett

Alison's Birthday ★ 15

Horror 1979 · Aus · Colour · 94mins

In this muddled hybrid, Joanne Samuel is warned by her dead father during a seance to leave home before her 19th birthday. She doesn't and a female black magic cult try to transfer her soul into the remains of a dead witch so she'll become their leader. Trite and poorly directed by Ian Coughlan, who also wrote this crass concoction and appears in the cast. AJ

Joanne Samuel *Alison Findlay* • Margie McCrae *Chrissie Willis* • Martin Vaughan *Mr Martin* • Robyn Gibbes *Helen McGill* • Lou Brown *Pete Healey* • Ian Coughlin *Dave Ducker* ■ *Dir/Scr* Ian Coughlan

Alive ★★★ 15

Drama based on a true story
1992 · US · Colour · 121mins

This harrowing drama is based on the true story of a South American rugby team whose plane crash-landed in the Andes in 1972, leaving the survivors the choice of starving to death or eating their dead to stay alive. Director Frank Marshall stages the mountaintop crash with a terrifying sequence of special effects and makes sure that the subsequent events are tastefully presented. He's also well served by the convincing performances of his cast. TH. Contains swearing. DVD

Ethan Hawke *Nando Parrado* • Vincent Spano *Antonio Balbi* • Josh Hamilton *Roberto Canessa* • Bruce Ramsay *Carlitos Paez* • John Haymes Newton *Tintin* • David Kriegel *Gustavo Zerbino* • Kevin Breznahan *Roy Harley* • Sam Behrens *Javier Methol* • Illeana Douglas *Lilliana Methol* ■ *Dir* Frank Marshall • *Scr* John Patrick Shanley, from the book by Piers Paul Read

Alive and Kicking ★★★

Comedy 1958 · UK · BW · 94mins

Sybil Thorndike, Kathleen Harrison and Estelle Winwood are a joy to behold as three old ladies who escape from a home and set themselves up on an isolated island as the relatives of millionaire Stanley Holloway. Eyes twinkling with mischief as they carve a niche in the local knitwear trade, they are easily on a par with those other matronly menaces, Josephine Hull and Jean Adair in *Arsenic and Old Lace*. Director Cyril Frankel's engaging piece of Irish whimsy is slight but diverting, and also notable as the film debut of Richard Harris. DP

Sybil Thorndike *Dora* • Kathleen Harrison *Rosie* • Estelle Winwood *Mabel* • Stanley Holloway *MacDonagh* • Liam Redmond *Old man* • Marjorie Rhodes *Old woman* • Richard Harris *Lover* • Olive McFarland *Lover* • John Salew *Solicitor* • Eric Pohlmann *Captain* ■ *Dir* Cyril Frankel • *Scr* Denis Cannan

Alive and Kicking ★★★ 15

Comedy drama 1996 · UK · Colour · 94mins

This is a spirited, if not always cinematic, tale by acclaimed dramatist Martin Sherman (*Bent*). Although rooted in the grand old kitchen sink tradition, director Nancy Meckler's grimly comic film is both clichéd and insightful, sad and uplifting. As the ballet dancer coping with the closure of his company and his HIV-positive status, Jason Flemyng gives an unexpectedly poignant performance. But who could compete with Anthony Sher on top form as the paunchy, bald alcoholic who offers him love? DP. Contains swearing.

Jason Flemyng *Tonio* • Antony Sher *Jack* • Dorothy Tutin *Luna* • Anthony Higgins *Ramon* • Bill Nighy *Tristan* • Philip Voss *Duncan* • Diane Parish *Millie* • Aiden Waters *Vincent* • Natalie Roles *Catherine* ■ *Dir* Nancy Meckler • *Scr* Martin Sherman

All about Eve ★★★★★ U

Classic drama 1950 · US · BW · 132mins

"Fasten your seat belts it's going to be a bumpy night!", and with the acerbic talents of multi-Oscar-winning writer/director Joseph L Mankiewicz and his magnificent cast – the superb Bette Davis (replacing, thankfully, an ailing Claudette Colbert), the acid-tongued George Sanders, Celeste Holm, Thelma Ritter, Marilyn Monroe – it certainly is. On its original release, this tale of the theatre was criticised in some quarters for being over-wordy and arch, though today's audiences revel in its wit and cynicism. The dialogue is especially clever and the performances are first-rate. If the framing flashback structure seems a little contrived, or if Anne Baxter's Eve doesn't quite have the killer instinct required for the role, these are minor blemishes in a classic movie. TS DVD

Bette Davis *Margo Channing* • Anne Baxter *Eve Harrington* • George Sanders *Addison DeWitt* • Celeste Holm *Karen Richards* • Gary Merrill *Bill Sampson* • Hugh Marlowe *Lloyd Richards* • Gregory Ratoff *Max Fabian* • Barbara Bates *Phoebe* • Marilyn Monroe *Miss Casswell* • Thelma Ritter *Birdie Coonan* ■ *Dir* Joseph L Mankiewicz • *Scr* Joseph L Mankiewicz, from the short story *The Wisdom of Eve* by Mary Orr in *Hearst's International-Cosmopolitan*

All about Lily Chou-Chou ★★★★ 15

Drama 2001 · Jpn · Colour · 146mins

Adapted by Shunji Iwai from his own interactive online novel, this is a troubling insight into the impact that the internet, pop culture iconography and isolation have on the impressionable mind. Resplendent with striking imagery, the episodic story details how introspective teenager Hayato Ichihara not only becomes addicted to the titular, fictional pop star, but also becomes enamoured by two classmates – musician Ayumi Ito and the abused Yu Aoi – whose fates are dictated by school bully Shugo Oshinari. The maelstrom of adolescent emotion is thoughtfully explored, but more notable is Iwai's compositional sense and his inspired use of sound and silence. DP. In Japanese with English subtitles. DVD

Hayato Ichihara *Yuichi Hasumi* • Shugo Oshinari *Shusuke Hoshino* • Ayumi Ito *Yoko Kuno* • Yu Aoi *Shiori Tsuda* • Takao Osawa *Tabito Takao* • Miwako Ichikawa *Shimabukurow, guide in Okinawa* ■ *Dir/Scr* Shunji Iwai

All about My Mother ★★★★★ 15

Comedy drama 1999 · Sp/Fr · Colour · 96mins

Mature and moving aren't words usually associated with "King of Kitsch" Pedro Almodóvar, but they certainly apply to this inspired reworking of the Bette Davis classic *All about Eve*. Devastated by the death of her son, hospital worker Cecilia Roth finds a whole new purpose in tending to a pregnant HIV-positive nun (Penélope Cruz) and a *grande dame* of the stage nearing the end of her career (Marisa Paredes). This fond, deliciously flamboyant study of womanhood and friendship is intense without ever being overbearing, touching but never sentimental. It's one of the Spanish director's finest achievements. DP. In Spanish with English subtitles. Contains drug abuse, swearing, sex scenes. DVD

Cecilia Roth *Manuela* • Marisa Paredes *Huma Rojo* • Candela Peña *Niña* • Antonia San Juan *"La Agrado"* • Penélope Cruz *Sister Rosa* • Rosa Maria Sarda *Rosa's mother* • Toni Cantó *Lola, "la Pionera"* • Eloy Azorin *Esteban* ■ *Dir/Scr* Pedro Almodóvar

The All American ★★ U

Drama 1953 · US · BW · 82mins

Tony Curtis stars as a sports hero whose confidence is shaken when his parents are killed en route to watching him play, causing him to abandon glory for serious study – for a time. An unpretentious little film that effectively combines the ingredients of the rah-rah college football movie with a more intimate drama, it showcases the famous pretty-boy good looks that made Curtis a major star. Competently directed by the little known Jesse Hibbs, himself a former professional of the gridiron. RK

Tony Curtis *Nick Bonelli* • Lori Nelson *Sharon Wallace* • Richard Long *Howard Carter* • Mamie Van Doren *Susie Ward* • Gregg Palmer *Cameron* • Paul Cavanagh *Prof Banning* •

A

Herman Hickman *Jumbo* • Stuart Whitman *Zip Parker* ■ *Dir* Jesse Hibbs • *Scr* DD Beauchamp, Robert Yale Libett, from a story by Leonard Freeman

The All-American Boy ★

Sports drama 1973 · US · Colour · 118mins

Jon Voight made this clinker just before his breakthrough in *Midnight Cowboy*, though it sat on the Warner Bros shelf for four years before they re-edited it and released it to an indifferent world. Voight plays a small-town boxer and the movie is artfully structured into six rounds; however, most audiences will have trouble going the distance. AT

Jon Voight *Vic Bealer* • EJ Peaker *Janelle Sharkey* • Ned Glass *Arty* • Anne Archer *Drenna Valentine* • Art Metrano *Jay* • Bob Hastings *Ariel* • Carol Androsky *Rodine* • Gene Borkan *Rockoff* ■ *Dir/Scr* Charles Eastman

All Ashore ★★ U

Musical comedy 1953 · US · Colour · 79mins

This cut-price imitation of the classic musical *On the Town* doesn't make much impression. Directed by Richard Quine from a screenplay he wrote with Blake Edwards, the movie focuses on the shore-leave escapades of three sailors – Mickey Rooney, Dick Haymes, Ray McDonald – and their romantic involvements with Peggy Ryan, Jody Lawrence and Barbara Bates. It falls almost entirely to the diminutive, multi-talented Rooney, as the patsy of the seafaring trio, to provide the fun. RK

Mickey Rooney *Francis "Moby" Dickerson* • Dick Haymes *Joe Carter* • Ray McDonald *Skip Edwards* • Peggy Ryan *Gay Night* • Barbara Bates *Jane Stanton* • Jody Lawrence [Jody Lawrance] *Nancy Flynn* • Fay Roope *Commodore Stanton* ■ *Dir* Richard Quine • *Scr* Blake Edwards, Richard Quine, from a story by Robert Wells, Blake Edwards

All Coppers Are... ★

Comedy 1972 · UK · Colour · 87mins

A comedy misfire about small-time crook Nicky Henson and naive police constable Martin Potter who both fancy Julia Foster. This situation is supposed to be funny but isn't, and none of the ensuing complications raise a smile either. The supporting cast of TV regulars – look out for David Essex in a small role – grin and bear it. AT

Martin Potter *Joe* • Julia Foster *Sue* • Nicky Henson *Barry* • Wendy Allnutt *Peg* • Sandra Dorne *Sue's mother* • Ian Hendry *Sonny Wade* • David Baxter *Fancy Boy* • Glynn Edwards *Jock* • Carmel McSharry *Mrs Briggs* • Queenie Watts *Mrs Malloy* • Eddie Byrne *Malloy* • David Essex *Ronnie Briggs* ■ *Dir* Sidney Hayers • *Scr* Allan Prior

All Creatures Great and Small ★★★ PG

Drama 1974 · UK · Colour · 87mins

We all know the animals are incidental in this screen prequel to TV's popular memoirs of vet James Herriot: what really matters is the Yorkshire folk whose emotions are brought out from behind those gruff exteriors by what happens to their creatures' comfort. Episodic, and fairly sentimental, this has warm-hearted performances by Simon Ward as the young Herriot, Lisa Harrow as his future wife Helen and Anthony Hopkins as local vet Siegfried Farnon. TH [video] DVD

Simon Ward *James Herriot* • Anthony Hopkins *Siegfried Farnon* • Lisa Harrow *Helen Alderson* • Brian Stirner *Tristan Farnon* • Freddie Jones *Cranford* • TP McKenna *Soames* • Brenda Bruce *Miss Harbottle* • John Collin *Mr Alderson* • Christine Buckley *Mrs Hall* ■ *Dir* Claude Whatham • *Scr* Hugh Whitemore, from the books by James Herriot

All Dogs Go to Heaven ★★★ U

Animated adventure
1989 · Ire · Colour · 81mins

Burt Reynolds provides the voice for Charlie B Parkin, a dog in late-1930s Louisiana who is killed by his business partner. Given the choice of remaining in heaven or leaving without being able to return, he decides to go back to Earth to seek revenge. Co-producer/director Don Bluth began his career at Disney so, as you would expect, the animation is excellent, but the story is rather clumsily told and very young children may find some of the darker sequences a bit upsetting. DP [video] DVD

Burt Reynolds *Charlie* • Dom DeLuise *Itchy* • Vic Tayback *Carface* • Judith Barsi *Anne-Marie* • Loni Anderson *Flo* • Melba Moore *Whippet Angel* • Charles Nelson Reilly *Killer* ■ *Dir* Don Bluth • *Scr* David Weiss

All Dogs Go to Heaven 2 ★★ U

Animated adventure
1996 · US/UK · Colour · 79mins

So much plot, so little time. But, sadly, there's also precious little quality in this disappointing sequel. Tired of eternity, Charlie (this time voiced by Charlie Sheen) heads back to earth with his faithful pal Itchy to retrieve Gabriel's Horn, which has fallen into evil hands. There's enough going on to amuse younger viewers but, excepting the energetic villainy of Ernest Borgnine, it's a pretty scrappy affair. DP [video]

Charlie Sheen *Charlie* • Sheena Easton *Sasha* • Ernest Borgnine *Carface* • Dom DeLuise *Itchy Itchiford* • George Hearn *Red* • Bebe Neuwirth *Anabelle* ■ *Dir* Paul Sabella, Larry Leker • *Scr* Arne Olsen, Kelly Ward, Mark Young, from a story by Mark Young, Kelly Ward

All Fall Down ★★★★

Drama 1962 · US · BW · 110mins

The opening shots in Warren Beatty's career created his image as a Hollywood lothario. In this, an intense family saga, he's a loner and a womaniser, idolised by his younger brother Brandon de Wilde – the boy who had idolised Shane and who would later do the same with Paul Newman in *Hud*. Their father, Karl Malden, hits the bottle; their mother, Angela Lansbury, henpecks. And when lodger Eva Marie Saint falls for Beatty, de Wilde looks on, almost eager for a hard lesson in life. Directed by John Frankenheimer and scripted by playwright William Inge, it is now rather dated, but the cast is matchless. AT

Eva Marie Saint *Echo O'Brien* • Warren Beatty *Berry-Berry Willart* • Karl Malden *Ralph Willart* • Angela Lansbury *Annabel Willart* • Brandon de Wilde *Clinton Willart* • Constance Ford *Mrs Mandel* • Barbara Baxley *Schoolteacher* • Evans Evans *Hedy* ■ *Dir* John Frankenheimer • *Scr* William Inge, from the novel by James Leo Herlihy

All for Love ★★ 15

Period drama 1999 · UK · Colour · 85mins

This is a botched attempt to combine swashbuckling adventure with costume romance. Jean-Marc Barr cuts a suitable dash as the French officer who is captured and sent to a remote Scottish PoW camp under the command of Richard E Grant. But director Harry Hook seems uncertain where to place the emphasis once the two men begin competing for the affections of Anna Friel and Barr decides to escape with the assistance of long-lost relations. DP. Contains violence and nudity. [video]

Jean-Marc Barr *Captain Jacques St Ives* • Anna Friel *Flora Gilchrist* • Miranda Richardson *Susan Gilchrist* • Richard E Grant *Major Chevening* • Tim Dutton *François* • Jason Isaacs *Alain St Ives* • Michael Gough *Count* • Vernon Dobtcheff *Bonnefoy* ■ *Dir* Harry Hook • *Scr* Joe Gallagher, Allan Cubitt, from the story *St Ives* by Robert Louis Stevenson

All for Mary ★★ U

Comedy 1955 · UK · Colour · 79mins

In this unfunny comedy, Nigel Patrick and David Tomlinson are rival suitors for the hand of Jill Day, but they contract chickenpox and are forced into quarantine in a Swiss chalet at the mercy of ageing nanny Kathleen Harrison. The invalids become infants as the grown men are brought under control by a dominant female. Sadly, director Wendy Toye takes the joke no further, so all we get is a feeble production that only weakly echoes its successful West End stage origins. TH

Nigel Patrick *Clive Morton* • Kathleen Harrison *Nannie Cartwright* • David Tomlinson *Humpy Miller* • Jill Day *Mary* • David Hurst *M Victor* • Leo McKern *Gaston Nikopopoulos* • Nicholas Phipps *General* • Lionel Jeffries *Maître d'hotel* ■ *Dir* Wendy Toye • *Scr* Peter Blackmore, Paul Soskin, from the play by Harold Brooke, Kay Bannerman

All Hands on Deck ★★ U

Musical comedy 1961 · US · Colour · 98mins

Director Norman Taurog – never one to over-tax the grey matter – ensures this lightweight shipboard comedy has a smooth passage. With Lieutenant Pat Boone excused duties to warble a few inoffensive songs, the time passes pleasantly enough. Given that the chief source of hilarity is the romance between Buddy Hackett's turkey and a pelican, though, it's not surprising the film sometimes goes adrift. DP

Pat Boone *Lt Donald* • Buddy Hackett *Screaming Eagle Garfield* • Dennis O'Keefe *Lt Cdr O'Gara* • Barbara Eden *Sally Hobson* • Warren Berlinger *Ensign Rush* • Gale Gordon *Cdr Bintle* • David Brandon *Lt Kutley* • Joe E Ross *Bosun* • Bartlett Robinson *Lt Cdr Anthony* ■ *Dir* Norman Taurog • *Scr* Jay Sommers, from the novel by Donald R Morris

All I Desire ★★

Period drama 1953 · US · BW · 79mins

Barbara Stanwyck finds herself in a town she left long ago, and pays an unfortunate visit to what's left of her family. This slight tosh is under-directed by melodrama favourite Douglas Sirk, who totally fails to rein in Stanwyck's excesses, so losing all sympathy for her character. This never rises above its double-bill status and is really rather tiresome. TS

Barbara Stanwyck *Naomi Murdoch* • Richard Carlson *Henry Murdoch* • Lyle Bettger *Dutch Heineman* • Marcia Henderson *Joyce Murdoch* • Lori Nelson *Lily Murdoch* • Maureen O'Sullivan *Sara Harper* • Richard Long *Russ Underwood* • Billy Gray *Ted Murdoch* • Lotte Stein *Lena Engstrom* ■ *Dir* Douglas Sirk • *Scr* James Gunn, Robert Blees, Gina Kaus, from the novel *Stopover* by Carol Brink

All I Want for Christmas ★★ U

Seasonal comedy 1991 · US · Colour · 88mins

The only thing Ethan Randall and Thora Birch want for Christmas is for their separated parents to be reconciled. Will they never learn? Lauren Bacall is way over the top as their batty but bountiful granny and everything creaks along, coated liberally in sentiment. This is not meant for cynical adults, but is aimed nearer the 12-year-old market, where it might be received as a passable hoot. SH [video] DVD

Harley Jane Kozak *Catherine O'Fallon* • Jamey Sheridan *Michael O'Fallon* • Ethan Randall [Ethan Embry] *Ethan O'Fallon* • Kevin Nealon *Tony Boer* • Thora Birch *Hallie O'Fallon* • Lauren Bacall *Lillian Brooks* • Amy Oberer *Stephanie* • Leslie Nielsen *Santa* ■ *Dir* Robert Lieberman • *Scr* Richard Kramer, Thom Eberhardt, Gail Parent, Neal Israel

All in a Night's Work ★★★ U

Comedy 1960 · US · Colour · 90mins

Some may be enchanted by this glossily produced, one-gag trifle; others may find it simply smutty. Luckily the bright sheen of 1960s Technicolor makes the shenanigans watchable, despite director Joseph Anthony's occasional lapses of pace and humour. Dean Martin and Shirley MacLaine are both exceedingly adept at this sort of sexy caper, and a fine veteran supporting cast comes along for the ride. Cliff Robertson, meanwhile, makes the most of his thankless role as MacLaine's put-upon fiancé. TS [video]

Dean Martin *Tony Ryder* • Shirley MacLaine *Katie Robbins* • Charles Ruggles *Dr Warren Kingsley Sr* • Cliff Robertson *Warren Kingsley Jr* • Norma Crane *Marge Coombs* • Gale Gordon *Oliver Dunning* • Jerome Cowan *Sam Weaver* • Jack Weston *Lasker* ■ *Dir* Joseph Anthony • *Scr* Edmund Beloin, Maurice Richlin, Sidney Sheldon, from a play by Owen Elford, from a story by Margit Veszi

All Men Are Mortal ★★ 15

Romance
1995 · UK/Neth/Fr · Colour · 86mins

A 1960s-style art movie, based on the novel by Simone de Beauvoir, about a temperamental, very actressy actress (Irène Jacob) who abandons her black musician lover for a mysterious stranger, played by Stephen Rea, who reveals himself to be a 700-year-old immortal prince. It's all very metaphysical, existential, philosophical and, for many viewers, downright pretentious. Set in France in the late 1940s, it was actually filmed in Hungary. AT [video]

Stephen Rea *Fosca* • Irène Jacob *Regina* • Colin Salmon *Chas* • Marianne Sägebrecht *Annie* • Maggie O'Neill *Florence* • Steve Nicolson *Laforet* • Chiara Mastroianni *Françoise* ■ *Dir* Ate De Jong • *Scr* Ate de Jong, Olwen Wymark, Steven Gaydos, from the novel by Simone de Beauvoir

All My Good Countrymen ★★★★

Drama 1968 · Cz · Colour · 126mins

One of four films "banned for ever" by the Czech authorities in the wake of the Prague Spring, this is an acerbic and acutely observed satire that won Vojtech Jasny the best director prize at Cannes. With its intricate blend of comedy, tragedy, fantasy and bitter reality, it chronicles events in a Moravian village from the end of the Second World War to the spring of 1968, exposing the excesses of communist rule by means of four shocking and suspicious deaths that periodically shatter the rural idyll. Played and directed with consummate skill, this provocative picture is as poetic as it is powerful. DP. In Czech with English subtitles.

Vladimir Mensik *Jozka Pyrk* • Radoslav Brozobohaty *Frantisek* • Vlastimil Brodsky *Ocenas* • Vlaclav Babka *Franta Lampa* • Ilja Prachal *Plecmera* • Pavel Pavlovsky *Postman* ■ *Dir/Scr* Vojtech Jasny

All My Sons ★★

Drama 1948 · US · BW · 93mins

The film of Arthur Miller's first play stars Burt Lancaster as the young man who makes the painful discovery that his father, tycoon Edward G Robinson, knowingly sold the US Air Force defective parts for their planes in the Second World War. Seized on by the right-wing as communist propaganda, the movie seems far less contentious today, and its moral debate rather open and shut. Very talkie, too. AT

Edward G Robinson *Joe Keller* • Burt Lancaster *Chris Keller* • Mady Christians *Kate Keller* • Louisa Horton *Ann Deever* • Howard Duff *George Deever* • Frank Conroy *Herbert Deever* • Lloyd Gough *Jim Bayliss* • Arlene Francis *Sue Bayliss* ■ *Dir* Irving Reis • *Scr* Chester Erskine, from the play by Arthur Miller

All Neat in Black Stockings ★

Drama 1969 · UK · Colour · 105mins

There's little to recommend this cheesy mix of peek-a-boo nudity and bawdy humour, even though it boasts that icon of Swinging Sixties sex appeal, Susan George. The pairing of TV playwright Hugh Whitemore and director Christopher Morahan produces little merit. DP

Victor Henry *Ginger* • Susan George *Jill* • Jack Shepherd *Dwyer* • Clare Kelly *Mother* • Anna Cropper *Sis* • Harry Towb *Issur* • Vanessa Forsyth *Carole* ■ *Dir* Christopher Morahan • *Scr* Jane Gaskell, Hugh Whitemore, from the novel by Jane Gaskell

All Night Long ★★ 15

Drama 1961 · UK · Colour · 87mins

The producer/director team of Michael Relph and Basil Dearden (*Sapphire*) had tackle Britain's jazz scene, overlaid with a plot about sexual jealousy that culture vultures may recognise as *Othello*. At the centre of it all is jazz singer Marti Stevens, married to Paul Harris and desired by Patrick McGoohan, jazzmen both. It's shot like a moody *film noir* and its main appeal is the chance to spot hot jazzmen such as Dave Brubeck, Charles Mingus, Tubby Hayes and Britain's own Johnny Dankworth in the frequent musical interludes. AT DVD

Patrick McGoohan *Johnny Cousin* • Marti Stevens *Delia Lane* • Betsy Blair *Emily* • Keith Michell *Cass Michaels* • Richard Attenborough *Rod Hamilton* • Paul Harris *Aurelius Rex* ■ *Dir* Basil Dearden • *Scr* Nel King, Peter Achilles [Paul Jarrico]

All Night Long ★★★ 15

Comedy 1981 · US · Colour · 84mins

Gene Hackman drops his usual intimidating manner to play the confused, middle-aged night-manager of a suburban supermarket, who decides to rebel against his staid existence by having an affair with the kooky wife of his cousin, played by Barbra Streisand. Directed by Frenchman Jean-Claude Tramont, the film's strange domestic focus creates an offbeat view of American city life, though some sequences lack continuity and coherence, and the whole makes for unusual viewing. TH. Contains some swearing [video]

Gene Hackman *George Dupler* • Barbra Streisand *Cheryl Gibbons* • Diane Ladd *Helen Dupler* • Dennis Quaid *Freddie Dupler* • Kevin Dobson *Bobby Gibbons* • William Daniels *Richard H Copleston* • Hamilton Camp *Buggams* • Ann Doran *Grandmother Gibbons* ■ *Dir* Jean-Claude Tramont • *Scr* WD Richter

All of Me ★★★ 15

Comedy 1984 · US · Colour · 87mins

A promising idea and a dynamic performance from Steve Martin aren't enough to distract from this film's shortage of funny moments and an over-reliance on half-baked resolutions. As the lawyer whose body is taken over by the soul of deceased millionairess Lily Tomlin, Martin is effective, combining his trademark exasperation with some amazingly energetic slapstick. Tomlin makes the most of appearing almost exclusively in reflection and Richard Libertini is hilarious as a quack swami, but Victoria Tennant hams shamelessly. DP. Contains violence, swearing. [video] DVD

Steve Martin *Roger Cobb* • Lily Tomlin *Edwina Cutwater* • Victoria Tennant *Terry Hoskins* • Madolyn Smith *Peggy Schuyler* • Richard Libertini *Prahka Lasa* • Dana Elcar *Burton Schuyler* • Jason Bernard *Tyrone Wattell* • Selma Diamond *Margo* ■ *Dir* Carl Reiner • *Scr* Phil Alden Robinson

All or Nothing ★★★★ 18

Comedy drama
2002 · UK/Fr · Colour · 122mins

Dispensing with the caricature that softened the emotional impact of much of his previous work, Mike Leigh delivers a grim and relentless autopsy of working-class life. Beautifully shot and brilliantly acted, the film observes a ragtag group of south London social casualties over a long weekend on a run-down housing estate. The focus is on world-weary minicab driver Timothy Spall (outstanding), his common-law wife Lesley Manville and their two overweight offspring – daughter Alison Garland, who works in an old people's home, and younger son James Corden, an irascible couch potato. It's a poignant and stomach-churning journey into the darkest recesses of human despair, yet, for all its everyday horror, the bittersweet story brims with hope and humanity. SF [video] DVD

Timothy Spall *Phil Bassett* • Lesley Manville *Penny Bassett* • Alison Garland *Rachel Bassett* • James Corden *Rory Bassett* • Ruth Sheen *Maureen* • Marion Bailey *Carol* • Paul Jesson *Ron* • Sam Kelly *Sid* ■ *Dir/Scr* Mike Leigh

All over Me ★★★★ 15

Drama 1996 · US · Colour · 89mins

A haunting, uncompromising snapshot of urban adolescent life, this exceptional debut never gained the same exposure as the similarly themed *kids*, but packs the same raw power to shock. Written and directed (respectively) by Sylvia and Alex Sichel, the film offers a portrait of two teenage girls: Tara Subkoff is hopelessly in love with drug-taking loser Cole Hauser, while Alison Folland is struggling to come to terms with her own sexuality. A brutal murder in their neighbourhood puts the two friends on a collision course. The cast of unknowns is superb, and the brutally frank script helps create a troubled vision of modern American life. JF. Contains swearing and sex scenes [video] DVD

Alison Folland *Claude* • Tara Subkoff *Ellen* • Cole Hauser *Mark* • Wilson Cruz *Jesse* • Ann Dowd *Anne, Claude's mum* • Leisha Hailey *Lucy* ■ *Dir* Alex Sichel • *Scr* Sylvia Sichel

All over the Guy ★★★

Romantic comedy
2001 · US · Colour · 95mins

Dan Bucatinsky and Richard Ruccolo are looking for love as opposed to endless one night stands. Thrown together by mutual mates Sasha Alexander and Adam Goldberg, they are not obvious contenders for "happily ever after" (Ruccolo is a commitment phobe and Bucatinsky wants the wedding dress). While they muddle on, Alexander and Goldberg start successfully simmering over the dating fire. This offers nothing new but the comedic talents of the leads do see you through. LH

Dan Bucatinsky *Eli* • Richard Ruccolo *Tom* • Adam Goldberg *Brett* • Sasha Alexander *Jackie* • Christina Ricci *Rayna* • Lisa Kudrow *Marie* ■ *Dir* Julie Davis • *Scr* Dan Bucatinsky, from his play *I Know You Are, but What Am I?*

All over Town ★★ U

Comedy 1937 · US · BW · 71mins

There's no denying that the comic team of Ole Olsen and Chic Johnson always were an acquired taste, and today the duo are best remembered for their wacky surreal classic of 1941, *Hellzapoppin'*, based on their Broadway success. But they were always very funny, both on stage and screen, and commanded a huge following in their day. This haunted theatre flick has a great deal of typical humour, and should please fans and make converts, even if the Republic studio production values are pretty ropey. TS

Ole Olsen *Olsen* • Chic Johnson *Johnson* • Mary Howard *Joan Eldridge* • Harry Stockwell *Don Fletcher* • Franklin Pangborn *Costumer* • James Finlayson *MacDougal* • Eddie Kane *Bailey* • Stanley Fields *Slug* • Franklin Pangborn *Costumer* ■ *Dir* James Horne [James W Horne] • *Scr* Jack Townley, Jerome Chodorov, from a story by Richard English

All Quiet on the Western Front ★★★★★ PG

Classic war drama
1930 · US · BW and Tinted · 125mins

Today's audiences may feel films such as *Platoon* and *Apocalypse Now* are the definitive war movies, but this classic Oscar-winning tale has lost none of its ability to shock and involve. As a study of the inhumanity of war, it retains all the impact of the novel by Erich Maria Remarque upon which it is so faithfully based. This epic saga of German schoolboys called up during the First World War marked the coming of age of the war movie, and of Carl Laemmle Jr's Universal Studios which produced it. It also demonstrated, as an early talkie, the flexibility of the new technique, with staggering trench sequences brilliantly filmed by director Lewis Milestone, who received his second Academy Award for his work. The performances are also exemplary, but it is primarily a film of great moments – the climactic sequence of the young conscript reaching out for a butterfly in the sun – that, once seen, are never forgotten. TS [video] DVD

Lew Ayres *Paul Baumer* • Louis Wolheim *Katczinsky* • John Wray *Himmelstoss* • Raymond Griffith *Gérard Duval* • George "Slim" Summerville [Slim Summerville] *Tjarden* • Russell Gleason *Müller* • William Bakewell *Albert* • Scott Kolk *Leer* • Walter Browne Rogers *Behm* • Beryl Mercer *Mrs Baumer* ■ *Dir* Lewis Milestone • *Scr* Del Andrews, Maxwell Anderson, George Abbott, from the novel by Erich Maria Remarque • *Cinematographer* Arthur Edeson

All Quiet on the Western Front ★★★ PG

First World War drama
1979 · US · Colour · 122mins

It's a brave man who dares to remake what is still regarded as the most powerful pacifist statement ever committed to celluloid. However, director Delbert Mann does a fine job of adapting Erich Maria Remarque's harrowing study of life in the trenches. In addition to winning Emmys for its editing and special effects, this TV movie also brought nominations for Mann, Patricia Neal and Ernest Borgnine, here cast as the veteran who puts Richard Thomas and his fellow recruits through their paces. While it lacks the immediacy of the 1930 version, this is still a compelling and affecting insight into the hellishness of war. DP [video] DVD

Richard Thomas *Paul Baumer* • Ernest Borgnine *Stanislaus Katczinsky* • Ian Holm *Himmelstoss* • Donald Pleasence *Kantorek* • Patricia Neal *Paul's mother* • Mark Drewry *Tjaden* • Michael Sheard *Paul's Father* ■ *Dir* Delbert Mann • *Scr* Paul Monash, from the novel by Erich Maria Remarque

All That Heaven Allows ★★★★ U

Melodrama 1955 · US · Colour · 88mins

This is a soapy follow-up to the same team's successful *Magnificent Obsession*, which had made a star out of Rock Hudson the previous year. This is almost as daft, but it's revered in some critical circles as director Douglas Sirk's serious commentary on 1950s American values. While Sirk makes the romance between widow Jane Wyman and her gardener Hudson less than likely, the Technicolor photography by Russell Metty is sumptuous, Hudson is remarkably good, and Agnes Moorehead brings some acerbity to the tale. TS

Jane Wyman *Cary Scott* • Rock Hudson *Ron Kirby* • Agnes Moorehead *Sara Warren* • Conrad Nagel *Harvey* • Virginia Grey *Alida Anderson* • Gloria Talbott *Kay Scott* • William Reynolds *Ned Scott* • Jacqueline de Wit *Mona Flash* • Charles Drake *Mick Anderson* ■ *Dir* Douglas Sirk • *Scr* Peggy Fenwick, from a story by Edna Lee, from a story by Harry Lee

All That Jazz ★★★★ 15

Musical drama 1979 · US · Colour · 117mins

Besides being the only musical featuring a surgical operation, this is unique in being heavily autobiographical about its director and co-writer, Bob Fosse. The talented choreographer closely resembles the lead character, Broadway dance-maestro Joe Gideon, whose philandering with women is only surpassed by his flirtations with the Angel of Death – the symbol of self-destructiveness that will eventually kill him. Jessica Lange and Ann Reinking are the women in his angst-fuelled life but it's Roy Scheider, as the driven Joe, who dominates in a film that's as brilliantly egotistical as it is flashily self-indulgent. TH [video] DVD

Roy Scheider *Joe Gideon* • Jessica Lange *Angelique* • Ann Reinking *Kate Jagger* • Leland Palmer *Audrey Paris* • Cliff Gorman *Davis Newman* • Ben Vereen *O'Connor Flood* • Erzsebet Foldi *Michelle* • Michael Tolan *Dr Ballinger* • Sandahl Bergman *Dancer* ■ *Dir* Bob Fosse • *Scr* Bob Fosse, Robert Alan Arthur • *Choreography* Bob Fosse • *Cinematographer* Giuseppe Rotunno • *Editor* Alan Heim • *Music Director* Ralph Burns • *Art Director* Philip Rosenberg, Tony Walton • *Costume Designer* Albert Wolsky

All the Brothers Were Valiant ★★

Adventure 1953 · US · Colour · 95mins

This is a watery yarn about whalers, mutiny, South Seas maidens and exotic pearls. All that's missing is a giant squid and a tidal wave! Robert Taylor and Stewart Granger are on good form at the eponymous siblings, while Lewis Stone – Andy Hardy's dad – puts in an appearance in what was to prove his final film. AT

Robert Taylor (1) *Joel Shore* • Stewart Granger *Mark Shore* • Ann Blyth *Priscilla Holt* • Betta St John *Native girl* • Keenan Wynn *Silva* • James Whitmore *Fetcher* • Kurt Kasznar *Quint* • Lewis Stone *Captain Holt* ■ *Dir* Richard Thorpe • *Scr* Harry Brown, from the novel by Ben Ames Williams

All the Fine Young Cannibals ★★

Drama 1960 · US · Colour · 122mins

A bizarre blend of teenage angst movie and Cassavetes-style drama that has Robert Wagner as Chet Baker in all but name. Jazz trumpeter and protégé of dipso Pearl Bailey, he's also the father of Natalie Wood's baby – though Wood marries George Hamilton when Wagner jilts her. Having Michael Anderson, the British director who made *The Dam Busters* and *Around the World in 80*

A

Days, at the helm ensures a blander ride than the subject merits. AT

Robert Wagner *Chad Bixby* • Natalie Wood *Salome Davis* • Susan Kohner *Catherine McDowall* • George Hamilton *Tony McDowall* • Pearl Bailey *Ruby Jones* • Jack Mullaney *Putney Tinker* • Onslow Stevens *Joshua Davis* • Anne Seymour *Mrs Bixby* ■ *Dir* Michael Anderson • *Scr* Robert Thom, from the novel *The Bixby Girls* by Rosamond Marshall

All the King's Horses ★★

Musical comedy 1935 · US · BW · 84mins

This musical variation of a show that was a cross between *The Prince and the Pauper* and *The Prisoner of Zenda* failed to set the screen alight, and did no favours to the movie careers of popular Carl Brisson or Ivor Novello's leading lady Mary Ellis. They look awkward and stiff in this under-directed Ruritanian farrago about a film star who takes the place of a king. TS

Carl Brisson *Carl Rocco/King Rudolph* • Mary Ellis *Queen Elaine* • Edward Everett Horton *Peppi* • Katherine DeMille *Mimi* • Eugene Pallette *Con Conley* • Arnold Korff *Baron Kraemer* ■ *Dir* Frank Tuttle • *Scr* Frank Tuttle, Frederick Stephani, from the operetta by Laurence Clark, Max Gersberg

All the King's Men ★★★★ U

Political drama 1949 · US · BW · 105mins

A blistering and powerful political drama that deservedly won the best picture Oscar, with the best actor award going to gruff Broderick Crawford in the performance of a lifetime as Willie Stark, a thinly disguised portrait of Louisiana demagogue "Kingfish" Huey Long. Mercedes McCambridge is also superb as a political aide, gaining another well-deserved Oscar as best supporting actress. Today this movie may seem a tad hysterical and over-performed, but it's important to view it in the context of when it was made – a time of extreme corruption and bigotry. Editor (and later director) Robert Parrish was responsible for restructuring director Robert Rossen's cut: Parrish added new scenes and dialogue, making the film worthy of its Oscar. TS DVD

Broderick Crawford *Willie Stark* • Joanne Dru *Anne Stanton* • John Ireland *Jack Burden* • John Derek *Tom Stark* • Mercedes McCambridge *Sadie Burke* • Shepperd Strudwick *Adam Stanton* • Ralph Dumke *Tiny Duffy* • Anne Seymour *Lucy Stark* • Katharine Warren [Katherine Warren] *Mrs Burden* ■ *Dir* Robert Rossen • *Scr* Robert Rossen, from the novel by Robert Penn Warren

All the Little Animals ★★★ 15

Drama 1998 · UK · Colour · 107mins

British producer Jeremy Thomas makes his directorial debut with this odd little drama featuring one of John Hurt's patented quirky performances. Christian Bale stars as a mentally-impaired young man who runs away from his sinister stepfather (Daniel Benzali) and ends up in Cornwall, helping an eccentric hermit (Hurt, of course) collect and bury animals that have been hit by cars. While Thomas never quite settles on a consistent tone, this is still interesting, thanks to the presence of Benzali and Hurt; Bale, however, seems somewhat overwhelmed in their company. JB. Contains violence.

John Hurt *Mr Summers* • Christian Bale *Bobby* • Daniel Benzali *De Winter* • James Faulkner *Mr Whiteside* • John O'Toole *Lorry driver* • Amanda Royle *Des* • Amy Robbins *Bobby's mother* • John Higgins *Dean* ■ *Dir* Jeremy Thomas • *Scr* Eski Thomas, from the novel by Walker Hamilton

All the President's Men ★★★★★ 15

Political thriller 1976 · US · Colour · 132mins

Alan J Pakula's Oscar-winning thriller about the Watergate burglary, with Robert Redford and Dustin Hoffman as the two *Washington Post* reporters (Bob Woodward and Carl Bernstein) whose stubborn digging ultimately brings down President Nixon. William Goldman's script brilliantly clarifies the multilayered labyrinth of corruption, while Pakula's tense direction draws telling parallels between the blazing white, open-plan offices of the *Post* (no secrets here) and the dark, murky world of Washington politics. Great support, too, from Jason Robards as the *Post's* editor, Ben Bradlee, and Hal Holbrook as the creepy informant "Deep Throat". Along with *The Best Man* and *The Manchurian Candidate*, this is one of the best movies ever made about American politics. AT. Contains swearing. DVD

Robert Redford *Bob Woodward* • Dustin Hoffman *Carl Bernstein* • Jack Warden *Harry Rosenfeld* • Martin Balsam *Howard Simons* • Hal Holbrook *Deep Throat* • Jason Robards *Ben Bradlee* • Jane Alexander *Book-keeper* • Meredith Baxter *Debbie Sloan* • Ned Beatty *Dardis* • Stephen Collins *Hugh Sloan Jr* ■ *Dir* Alan J Pakula • *Scr* William Goldman, from the book by Bob Woodward, Carl Bernstein • *Cinematographer* Gordon Willis • *Editor* Robert L Wolfe • *Art Director* George Jenkins

All the Pretty Horses ★★★ 15

Western 2000 · US · Colour · 112mins

Fans of Cormac McCarthy's great modern western novel may not be too enamoured by the overly schematic treatment it has received here under Billy Bob Thornton's measured direction. Despite its many flaws (one being Matt Damon's inability to carry the central emotional load), this retains much of its source novel's power and romantic nostalgia. Finding himself without a home or future when his beloved ranch is sold out from under him by his estranged mother, Damon and his best buddy Henry Thomas head to Mexico to become the cowboys they'd always dreamt of being. AJ. Contains violence and sex scenes. DVD

Matt Damon *John Grady Cole* • Henry Thomas *Lacey Rawlins* • Lucas Black *Jimmy Blevins* • Penélope Cruz *Alejandra* • Rubén Blades *Rocha* • Robert Patrick *Cole* • Bruce Dern *Judge* ■ *Dir* Billy Bob Thornton • *Scr* Ted Tally, from the novel by Cormac McCarthy • *Cinematographer* Barry Markowitz

All the Real Girls ★★★ 15

Romantic drama
2003 · US · Colour · 103mins

This small-town study of love and friendship has the potential to either beguile or bore audiences. Writer/director David Gordon Green captures the awkwardness a fledgeling romance, gaining naturalistic honesty from local stud Paul Schneider and his friend's virginal young sister, Zooey Deschanel. The film has mood, courtesy of some lyrical North Carolina landscape photography and an evocative soundtrack, yet the impression lingers of a movie that thinks a little too highly of itself. JC DVD

Paul Schneider *Paul* • Zooey Deschanel *Noel* • Patricia Clarkson *Elvira Fine* • Benjamin Mouton *Leland* • Maurice Compte *Bo* • Danny McBride *Bust-Ass* • Shea Whigham *Tip* ■ *Dir* David Gordon Green • *Scr* David Gordon Green, from a story by Paul Schneider, David Gordon Green • *Cinematographer* Tim Orr

All the Right Moves ★★★ 15

Sports drama 1983 · US · Colour · 86mins

Respected cinematographer Michael Chapman made his directorial debut with this authentic portrait of college life. Indeed, it's such a well-rounded film that it makes his decision to return to cinematography – following criticism handed out to his follow-up, *The Clan of the Cave Bear* – all the more disappointing. The turbulent relationship between a star footballer (Tom Cruise) and his coach (Craig T Nelson) is convincingly established and the gridiron action smacks of the real thing. DP DVD

Tom Cruise *Stef Djordjevic* • Craig T Nelson *Vern Nickerson* • Lea Thompson *Lisa Lietske* • Charles Cioffi *Pop* • Paul Carafotes *Salvucci* • Christopher Penn [Chris Penn] *Brian* • Sandy Faison *Suzie* ■ *Dir* Michael Chapman • *Scr* Michael Kane

All the Vermeers in New York ★★★★

Romantic drama 1990 · US · Colour · 87mins

Virtually ignored on its original release, this is a subtle and often moving story of unfulfilled love, in which the pace and emptiness of modern life is contrasted with the serenity and beauty of the paintings by Dutch artist Jan Vermeer hanging in New York's art galleries. Proving that the auteur is not yet extinct, versatile Jon Jost not only wrote and directed the film, but also shot, designed and edited it. Jost's imaginative contrasts between art and life and his stylish compositions will linger longest in the memory, and Stephen Lack's passion for Emmanuelle Chaulet will leave you slightly misty-eyed. DP

Emmanuelle Chaulet *Anna* • Katherine Bean *Nicole* • Grace Phillips *Felicity* • Laurel Lee Kiefer *Ariel Ainsworth* • Gracie Mansion • Gordon Joseph Weiss *Gordon* • Stephen Lack *Mark* ■ *Dir/Scr* Jon Jost

All the Way Home ★★★★

Drama 1963 · US · BW · 97mins

This magnificently acted movie is an adaptation of James Agee's autobiographical *A Death in the Family*. The tale of bereavement and its effect on the young Agee in Tennessee in 1915 is seen through the eyes of a boy, played by Michael Kearney, as his father is suddenly and accidentally killed. Jean Simmons is very moving in the role of the mother, and Robert Preston, as the father, also demonstrates what a fine and subtle actor he could be given the right material. TS

Jean Simmons *Mary* • Robert Preston *Jay* • Pat Hingle *Ralph* • Aline MacMahon *Aunt Hannah* • Thomas Chalmers *Joel* • John Cullum *Andrew* • Ronnie Claire Edwards *Sally* • Michael Kearney *Rufus* ■ *Dir* Alex Segal • *Scr* Philip Reisman Jr, from the play by Tad Mosel, from the novel *A Death in the Family* by James Agee

All the Young Men ★★

War drama 1960 · US · BW · 86mins

This desperately tedious Korean War tale, despite its interesting cast, was produced and directed by one of Hollywood's mavericks, Hall Bartlett. It's sad to see Alan Ladd, well past his prime, struggling to hold the screen against sturdy Sidney Poitier and a cast of young Columbia contract artists. TS

Alan Ladd *Kincaid* • Sidney Poitier *Towler* • James Darren *Cotton* • Glenn Corbett *Wade* • Mort Sahl *Crane* • Ana St Clair *Maya* • Joe Gallison *Jackson* • Ingemar Johansson *Torgil* ■ *Dir/Scr* Hall Bartlett

All These Women ★★ PG

Satire 1964 · Swe · Colour · 79mins

Ingmar Bergman's first production in colour is one of his few miscalculations. Co-written with actor Erland Josephson, this clumsy costume comedy seeks both to explore the elusive nature of genius and decry the parasitic insolence of critics, whose only acts of creation depend entirely on the destruction of another's work. Although there are flashes of Mack Sennett, Jacques Tati and Federico Fellini in the humour, biographer Jarl Kulle's encounters with a cellist's female entourage are resolutely unfunny. DP. In Swedish with English subtitles. DVD

Jarl Kulle *Cornelius* • Bibi Andersson *Humlan* • Harriet Andersson *Isolde* • Eva Dahlbeck *Adelaide* ■ *Dir* Ingmar Bergman • *Scr* Erland Josephson, Ingmar Bergman

All Things Fair ★★★ 15

Second World War romantic drama
1995 · Swe/Den · Colour · 124mins

Winner of the Silver Bear at Berlin and recipient of an Oscar nomination for best foreign film, this was something of a return to form for Bo Widerberg, who remains best known outside his native Sweden for *Elvira Madigan*. Set in neutral Malmö during the Second World War, it tells of a lonely teenager who begins an affair with one of his teachers, seemingly with the consent of her drunken husband. The director's son, Johan, takes the lead, and his amenable performance and the customary beauty of the imagery are the main reasons for watching this often incoherent account of first love. DP. In Swedish with English subtitles. Contains swearing, sex scenes and some mild violence.

Johan Widerberg *Stig* • Marika Lagercrantz *Viola* • Tomas von Brömssen *Kjell* • Karin Huldt *Lisbet* • Björn Kjellman *Sigge* • Frida Lindholm *Olga* ■ *Dir/Scr* Bo Widerberg

All This, and Heaven Too ★★★★ U

Romantic drama 1940 · US · BW · 134mins

This sumptuous Warner Bros period melodrama stars Bette Davis as a governess in Paris causing marital problems for her employer Charles Boyer. There's a veritable series of tragedies in scriptwriter Casey Robinson's torrid adaptation of the first half of Rachel Lyman Field's once-popular doorstop *roman à clef*, but Davis is remarkably restrained, and therefore doubly effective, in what must rank as one of her finest screen performances. Despite the length, Anatole Litvak's detailed pacing and Max Steiner's magnificent score render this one unmissable. TS

Bette Davis *Henriette Deluzy Desportes* • Charles Boyer *Duke De Praslin* • Jeffrey Lynn *Reverend Henry Field* • Barbara O'Neil *Duchesse De Praslin* • Virginia Weidler *Louise* • Walter Hampden *Pasquier* • Harry Davenport *Pierre* • Fritz Leiber *Albe* ■ *Dir* Anatole Litvak • *Scr* Casey Robinson, from the novel by Rachel Lyman Field

All through the Night ★★★

Spy drama 1942 · US · BW · 106mins

A standard piece of Warner Bros wartime propaganda, with Humphrey Bogart as a Broadway gambler who discovers a gang of Nazis plotting to sink a US battleship anchored in New York. The tone of the film is rather jokey, though it was released a year after the bombing of Pearl Harbor and consequently no one thought it was very funny. But Bogart is on decent enough form and the usual suspects including Conrad Veidt and Peter Lorre lurk in the shadows. Kaaren Verne does well as the love interest. AT

Humphrey Bogart *Gloves Donahue* • Conrad Veidt *Hall Ebbing* • Kaaren Verne *Leda Hamilton* • Jane Darwell *Ma Donahue* • Frank McHugh *Barney* • Peter Lorre *Pepi* • Judith Anderson *Madame* • William Demarest *Sunshine* • Jackie Gleason *Starchie* • Phil Silvers *Waiter* • Wallace Ford *Spats Hunter* • Barton MacLane *Marty Callahan* ■ *Dir* Vincent

Sherman • *Scr* Leonard Spigelgass, Edwin Gilbert, from a story by Leonard Spigelgass, Leonard Ross

All Tomorrow's Parties ★★

Futuristic drama
2003 · Fr/HK/Neth/Swi · Colour · 96mins

This allegorical assault on the Cultural Revolution sends all manner of mixed messages – most of which will be lost on non-Chinese audiences. Set in a 21st-century dystopia, in which the totalitarian Gui Dao sect holds sway, the film is as much about the responsibility of those enjoying new-found freedom as the cruelty of repression. But whether against the backdrop of the gulag-like Camp Prosperity or the ruins of an industrial metropolis, the narrative involving brothers Diao Yi Nan and Zhao Wei Wei is fractured and impenetrable. DP. In Mandarin with English subtitles.

Cho Yong Won *Xuelan* • Diao Yi Nan *Zhuai* • Zhao Wei Wei *Mian* • Na Ren *Lanlan* ■ *Dir/Scr* Yu Lik Wai [Nelson Lik-Wai Yu]

Allan Quatermain and the Lost City of Gold ★★ PG

Adventure 1987 · US · Colour · 95mins

A sequel to *King Solomon's Mines*, again with Richard Chamberlain and Sharon Stone in search of treasure. If the first film was a remake of a remake that ripped off *Raiders of the Lost Ark*, this one is a remake that rips off *Romancing the Stone*. Lazy direction and hilariously cheap special effects aren't quite awful enough to make it a candidate for the Ed Wood award. AT [VIDEO] DVD

Richard Chamberlain *Allan Quatermain* • Sharon Stone *Jesse Huston* • James Earl Jones *Umslopogaas* • Henry Silva *Agon* • Cassandra Peterson *Sorais* • Robert Donner *Swarma* ■ *Dir* Gary Nelson • *Scr* Gene Quintano, Lee Reynolds, from the novel *Quatermain* by H Rider Haggard

Allegro non Troppo ★★★ PG

Animated musical comedy
1976 · It · BW and Colour · 74mins

Part parody, part homage to Disney's *Fantasia*, Bruno Bozzetto's third feature combines animation and live-action to generally amusing effect. Divided by sections featuring composer Maurizio Nichetti, the best vignettes show the serpent suffering the agony of Eden's apple to the strains of Stravinsky's *Firebird*, a weird menagerie of alien life forms struggling forth from a discarded Coke bottle to Ravel's *Bolero*, and Vivaldi's *Concerto in C Minor* forming the backdrop to a bee's pursuit of pollen in the presence of a courting couple. However, the showpiece is Sibelius's *Valse Triste*, which accompanies a melancholy cat on its nostalgic journey through the ruins of a bombed-out city. DP. An Italian language film. [VIDEO]

Dir Bruno Bozzetto • *Scr* Bruno Bozzetto, Guido Manuli, Maurizio Nichetti • *Animator* Bruno Bozzetto, Guido Manuli

Alligator ★★★★ 15

Horror 1980 · US · Colour · 87mins

The old urban myth about baby alligators thriving in city sewers after being discarded as pets becomes a turbo-driven eco-chiller, thanks to the genuine wit and sardonic wisdom of John Sayles's superb script. Just as he did with *Piranha* and *The Howling* (written with Terence H Winkless), Sayles crafts a monster-on-the-loose scenario that's better than the best of the 1950s movies it resembles. The cast is highly believable and treats the in-jokes with the right amount of tongue-in-cheek deference. Director Lewis Teague (*Cujo*) brings subtle irony to the carnage and infuses the whole radical re-packaging of mutant monster clichés with an immensely likeable sense of insolent fun. AJ [VIDEO] DVD

Robert Forster *Detective David Madison* • Robin Riker *Marisa Kendall* • Dean Jagger *Slade* • Michael Gazzo [Michael V Gazzo] *Police Chief Clark* • Sidney Lassick [Sydney Lassick] *Lou* • Jack Carter *Mayor Ledoux* • Perry Lang *Kelly* • Henry Silva *Col Brock* ■ *Dir* Lewis Teague • *Scr* John Sayles

Alligator II: the Mutation ★★ 15

Horror 1991 · US · Colour · 90mins

The original *Alligator* was a cult delight: John Sayles had a hand in the witty dialogue, while the actors kept theirs tongues firmly in cheek. This sequel reprises the basic plot – mutant reptile wreaks havoc in suburbia – but it's tame stuff, despite a pretty good cast (Joseph Bologna, Dee Wallace Stone, Richard Lynch). The creature isn't particularly scary, either. JF [VIDEO] DVD

Joseph Bologna *David Hodges* • Brock Peters *Chief Speed* • Dee Wallace Stone *Christine Hodges* • Woody Brown *Rich Harmon* • Holly Gagnier *Sheri* • Richard Lynch *Hawkins* • Bill Daily *Anderson* • Steve Railsback *Vincent Brown* ■ *Dir* Jon Hess • *Scr* Curt Allen

Alligator Eyes ★★★ 15

Thriller 1990 · US · Colour · 96mins

This modest but quietly menacing thriller niftily subverts the woman-in-peril scenario. Annabelle Larsen stars as a blind woman who ensnares a trio of holiday-makers in a dangerous web of revenge. Director John Feldman, a documentary film-maker making his feature debut, conjures up an air of brooding suspense and sexual tension, and is rewarded with impressive performances from a largely unknown cast. Classical composer Sheila Silver provides a perfectly cold-blooded score. JF. Contains violence, swearing and nudity. [VIDEO]

Annabelle Larsen *Pauline* • Roger Kabler *Robbie* • John Mackay *Peterson* • Mary McLain *Marjorie* • Allen McCulloch *Lance* ■ *Dir/Scr* John Feldman

An Alligator Named Daisy ★★★ U

Comedy 1955 · UK · Colour · 88mins

A bright, if silly, Rank comic romp for sexy Diana Dors and pompous Donald Sinden, with one of those compulsively watchable period character casts. J Lee Thompson's hand lies a little too heavy over the proceedings and Pinewood's attempt to match Hollywood in pace and style doesn't happen. But Dors reveals a nice sense of comic timing and Stephen Boyd, who is best known for playing Messala in *Ben-Hur*, makes an early impact. TS

Donald Sinden *Peter Weston* • Diana Dors *Vanessa Colebrook* • Jean Carson *Moira* • James Robertson-Justice *Sir James* • Stanley Holloway *General* • Margaret Rutherford *Prudence Croquet* • Roland Culver *Colonel Weston* • Stephen Boyd *Albert* • Richard Wattis *Hoskins* • Henry Kendall *Valet* ■ *Dir* J Lee Thompson • *Scr* Jack Davies

The Alligator People ★

Science-fiction horror
1959 · US · BW · 74mins

1950s "creature features" don't come any sillier or more insane than this. Down in the Louisiana swamplands, doctor George Macready experiments with an alligator serum intended to help amputee victims grow new limbs. Bruce Bennett is a wounded man who takes the serum and turns into an upright reptile, with the help of an ill-fitting rubber suit. Inept in practically every area. AJ

Beverly Garland *Jane Marvin* • Bruce Bennett *Dr Erik Lorimer* • Lon Chaney Jr *Mannon* • George Macready *Dr Mark Sinclair* • Frieda Inescort *Mrs Henry Hawthorne* • Richard Crane *Paul Webster* ■ *Dir* Roy Del Ruth • *Scr* Orville H Hampton, from a story by Charles O'Neal, Orville H Hampton

The Allnighter ★★ PG

Comedy 1987 · US · Colour · 91mins

This attempt to turn The Bangles singer Susanna Hoffs into a movie star fails because she's not a very good actress, and the film isn't that great either. Hoffs and co-star Dedee Pfeiffer are out of their depth, but the performances of the more experienced Joan Cusack and Michael Ontkean help make this a passable, slightly saucy comedy. JB [VIDEO]

Susanna Hoffs *Molly* • Dedee Pfeiffer *Val* • Joan Cusack *Gina* • John Terlesky *CJ* • James Anthony Shanta *Killer* • Michael Ontkean *Mickey Leroi* • Pam Grier *Sgt MacLeish* • Phil Brock *Brad* ■ *Dir/Scr* Tamar Simon Hoffs

All's Fair ★ 15

Comedy 1989 · US · Colour · 85mins

George Segal, once the credible embodiment of harassed middle America, must have been desperate when he agreed to star in this tosh. As chauvinist businessmen take on their wives and female colleagues at a weekend war game, this metaphor for the battle of the sexes is never less than clumsy. A no-laughs comedy saddled with slack direction throughout. JM. Contains swearing. [VIDEO]

George Segal *Colonel* • Sally Kellerman *Florence* • Robert Carradine *Mark* • Jennifer Edwards *Ann* • Jane Kaczmarek *Linda* • John Kapelos *Eddy* • Lou Ferrigno *Klaus* ■ *Dir* Rocky Lang • *Scr* Randee Russell, John Finegan, Tom Rondinella, William Pace, from a story by Watt Tyler, John Finegan

Almost ★ PG

Romantic comedy
1990 · Aus · Colour · 81mins

Wacky housewife Rosanna Arquette regresses into uninspired fantasy through a combination of sheer boredom and constant arguments with her uncaring husband. Director Michael Pattinson's whimsically challenged, unremarkable comedy is short on wit and long on limp laughs. AJ. Contains some swearing and brief nudity. [VIDEO]

Rosanna Arquette *Wendy* • Bruce Spence *Ronnie* • Hugo Weaving *Jake* • Kerry Walker *Deidre* • Doreen Warburton *Elsie* • Desirée Smith *Cynthia* • Susan Lyons *Caroline* ■ *Dir* Michael Pattinson • *Scr* Suzanne Hawley

Almost an Angel ★★ PG

Comedy 1990 · US · Colour · 91mins

Poor Paul ("Crocodile" Dundee) Hogan plays a crook-turned-angel in what is anything but a divine comedy. He only has himself to blame for the feeble wisecracks and fortune cookie philosophy as he wrote the script, and one suspects that he had as much control over the direction as credited John Cornell. Hogan ambles through the action as if his mind was elsewhere, only perking up when joined by real-life wife Linda Kozlowski, who gives a half-decent performance, as does Elias Koteas as her disabled brother. DP. Contains swearing [VIDEO]

Paul Hogan *Terry Dean* • Linda Kozlowski *Rose Garner* • Elias Koteas *Steve Garner* • Doreen Lang *Mrs Garner* • Robert Sutton *Guido* • Travis Venable *Bubba* • Douglas Seale *Father* • Charlton Heston *God* ■ *Dir* John Cornell • *Scr* Paul Hogan

Almost Famous ★★★★ 15

Comedy drama 2000 · US · Colour · 118mins

This funny and touching coming-of-age movie is based on writer/director Cameron Crowe's own experiences as a teenage rock journalist in the early 1970s. Fifteen-year-old William Miller (Patrick Fugit) escapes from the clutches of his delightfully overprotective mother (Frances McDormand) when he's hired to write about rock band Stillwater for *Rolling Stone* magazine. Joining the group on tour, Fugit is sucked into a chaotic world of parties, drugs and clashing egos, falling under the spell of self-styled "band aid" Kate Hudson and lead guitarist Billy Crudup. It loses its way slightly towards the end, but this is still an entertaining and affectionate evocation of growing up in an era before rock 'n' roll was hijacked by marketing men. LH. Contains swearing, brief nudity, drug use. [VIDEO] DVD

Billy Crudup *Russell Hammond* • Frances McDormand *Elaine Miller* • Kate Hudson *Penny Lane* • Jason Lee *Jeff Bebe* • Patrick Fugit *William Miller* • Anna Paquin *Polexia Aphrodisia* • Fairuza Balk *Sapphire* • Noah Taylor *Dick Roswell* • Zooey Deschanel *Anita Miller* ■ *Dir/Scr* Cameron Crowe

Almost Heroes ★★ 12

Comedy adventure
1998 · US · Colour · 86mins

In his final screen outing Chris Farley is paired with Matthew Perry as 19th-century rivals of the legendary explorers Lewis and Clark. Determined to put their names in the history books, they end up falling foul of Indians, the rugged wilderness and each other. Farley is as energetically crude as ever, but both Perry and director Christopher Guest, who was behind the classic *This Is Spinal Tap*, seem uncomfortable with the material. JF. Contains swearing. [VIDEO]

Chris Farley *Bartholomew Hunt* • Matthew Perry *Leslie Edwards* • Bokeem Woodbine *Jonah* • Eugene Levy *Guy Fontenot* • Kevin Dunn *Hidalgo* • Lisa Barbuscia *Shaquinna* • Steven M Porter *Higgins* • David Packer *Bidwell* • Lewis Arquette *Merchant* ■ *Dir* Christopher Guest • *Scr* Boyd Hale, Mark Nutter, Tom Wolfe

Almost Peaceful ★★★ 15

Period drama 2002 · Fr · Colour · 94mins

Michel Deville's film focuses on a group of Jewish tailors toiling in a workshop off the Rue de Soleil in Paris shortly after the war. The ensemble cast evocatively capture the feelings of grief, relief and guilt that pervaded the time, with Zabou Breitman particularly affecting as she realises that she's more attuned to widower Denis Podalydès's melancholy than husband Simon Akbarian's optimism. Much of the action turns around anecdotes and observations, but the scene in which Abkarian encounters the cop who arrested his parents during the war and the climactic picnic give this added resonance. DP. In French with English subtitles. Contains nudity.

Simon Abkarian *Monsieur Albert* • Zabou Breitman [Zabou] *Léa* • Lubna Azabal *Jacqueline* • Clotilde Courau *Simone* • Vincent Elbaz *Léon* • Julie Gayet *Madame Andrée* • Stanislas Merhar *Maurice* • Denis Podalydès *Charles* ■ *Dir* Michel Deville • *Scr* Rosalinde Deville, from the novel *Quoi de Neuf sur la Guerre?* by Robert Bober

An Almost Perfect Affair ★★ 15

Romantic comedy
1979 · US · Colour · 87mins

Michael Ritchie – whose *Smile* was a marvellous satire on Miss Young America beauty pageants – here casts his eye on the Cannes Film Festival. Keith Carradine plays an independent film director who comes to Cannes touting his movie about condemned murderer Gary Gilmore. It's seized by customs, released by Monica Vitti, then bought by an exploitation king who changes the title from *Choice of Ending* to *Shoot Me Before I Kill Again*. There are some nice jokes, but it lacks star power. AT [VIDEO]

Keith Carradine *Hal* • Monica Vitti *Maria* • Raf Vallone *Freddie* • Christian De Sica *Carlo* • Dick Anthony Williams *Jackson* • Henri Garcin *Lieutenant Montand* • Anna Maria Horsford *Amy Zon* ■ *Dir* Michael Ritchie • *Scr* Walter Bernstein, Don Peterson, from a story by Michael Ritchie, Don Peterson

Almost Summer ★★

Romantic drama 1977 · US · Colour · 88mins

High-school elections, the teenage dating game and a feel-good soundtrack combine for an initially bright and breezy satire about youth values. It's when the tone gets too serious and preachy that restlessness is likely to set in. Beach Boy Brian Wilson is credited for the title tune and *It's OK*, while fellow group member Mike Love penned and sings *Cruisin* and *Sad, Sad Summer*. While no great addition to the rock cinema genre, this is good natured enough to get by. AJ

Bruno Kirby *Bobby DeVito* • Lee Purcell *Christine Alexander* • John Friedrich *Darryl Fitzgerald* • Didi Conn *Donna DeVito* • Thomas Carter *Dean Hampton* • Tim Matheson *Kevin Hawkins* ■ *Dir* Martin Davidson • *Scr* Judith Berg, Sandra Berg, Martin Davidson, Marc Reid Rubel

Almost You ★★ 15

Romantic drama 1984 · US · Colour · 92mins

Griffin Dunne stars as the unhappy husband whose wife Brooke Adams is injured in a car accident. It's not long before he's having an affair with nurse Karen Young, hired to look after her, in a drama which suffers from the fact that few of the characters come across as remotely sympathetic. This would be a huge problem were it not for the performance of Dunne, who manages to give his character some credibility and keeps you watching. JB

Brooke Adams *Erica Boyer* • Griffin Dunne *Alex Boyer* • Karen Young *Lisa Willoughby* • Marty Watt *Kevin Danzig* • Christine Estabrook *Maggie* • Josh Mostel *David* • Laura Dean *Jeannie* • Dana Delany *Susan McCall* ■ *Dir* Adam Brooks • *Scr* Mark Horowitz, from a story by Adam Brooks

Aloha, Bobby and Rose ★★★

Crime drama 1975 · US · Colour · 88mins

After making an impact with his role in George Lucas's *American Graffiti*, Paul Le Mat starred in this crime melodrama from director Floyd Mutrux. This is just the kind of rock 'n' roll chase movie that influenced Quentin Tarantino and paved the lethal path towards Oliver Stone's *Natural Born Killers*. Note the use of rock standards and an early appearance from Edward James (billed here as "Eddie") Olmos. TS. Contains violence, swearing.

Paul Le Mat *Bobby* • Dianne Hull *Rose* • Tim McIntire *Buford* • Leigh French *Donna Sue* • Noble Willingham *Uncle Charlie* • Martine Bartlett *Rose's mother* • Robert Carradine *Moxey* • Eddie Olmos [Edward James Olmos] ■ *Dir/Scr* Floyd Mutrux

Aloha Summer ★★★ PG

Drama 1988 · US · Colour · 92mins

The secret of surf movies is to ensure there is plenty of sun and sand, and as many shots of muscular, tanned, teen bodies arching through the breakers as decency will allow. Director Tommy Lee Wallace resists the temptation to tamper with what, essentially, is a winning formula, ensuring that this surfing sextet pass through their rites of passage in an orderly fashion to the sound of rock hits of the day. This being Hawaii in 1959, he is able to slip in a few novel touches, such as the Japanese kid who, while thinking his homeland was hard done by in the war, can't accept his father's traditional code. DP

Chris Makepeace *Mike Tognetti* • Yuji Okumoto *Kenzo Konishi* • Don Michael Paul *Chuck Granville* • Tia Carrere *Lani Kepoo* • Sho Kosugi *Yukinaga Konishi* ■ *Dir* Tommy Lee Wallace • *Scr* Mike Greco, Bob Benedetto, from a story by Mike Greco

Alone in the Dark ★★ 18

Horror 1982 · US · Colour · 89mins

Donald Pleasence is the head of a New Jersey lunatic asylum keeping its really dangerous criminal inmates – among them Jack Palance and Martin Landau – under electronic surveillance. When a power failure occurs, the violent psychos break out and head to the home of the asylum doctor. Aside from a promising opening dream sequence and an interesting "who's really crazy?" denouement, the debut horror feature from director Jack Sholder is below par. AJ

Jack Palance *Frank Hawkes* • Erland Van Lidth *Ronald "Fatty" Elster* • Deborah Hedwall *Nell Potter* • Phillip Clark *Tom Smith/Skagg* • Martin Landau *Bryon "Preacher" Sutcliff* • Dwight Schultz *Dan Potter* ■ *Dir* Jack Sholder • *Scr* Jack Sholder, from a story by Robert Shaye, Michael Harpster, Jack Sholder

Alone in the Woods ★

Comedy 1996 · US · Colour · 92mins

A cheap *Home Alone* cash-in, starring Brady Bluhm as a little brat who becomes separated from his parents but still has a lot of fun tormenting a pair of would-be abductors. Nothing can drown out the irritating sound of barrel being thoroughly scraped. JF

Dan McVicar *Danny Rogers* • Matthias Hues *Kurt* • Chick Vennera *Perry* • Brady Bluhm *Justin Rogers* • Sarah Bibb *Kate Rogers* • Krystee Clark *Chelsea Stuart* ■ *Dir* John Putch • *Scr* J Riley Lagesen

Alone on the Pacific ★★★★

Adventure 1963 · Jpn · Colour · 104mins

In all his major films, from *The Burmese Harp* to *Tokyo Olympiad*, Kon Ichikawa is concerned with men pushed to extremes. Here, a young yachtsman takes three months to sail from Osaka to San Francisco on a 19-foot craft. Based on the true adventures of Kenichi Horie, it seems an impossible subject for a film. But Ichikawa, using widescreen to magnificent effect and integrating flashbacks to the sailor's life on shore, makes even the dull bits of the voyage interesting. The climactic scene, as the Golden Gate bridge looms out of the mist, is genuinely moving. RB. In Japanese with English subtitles.

Yujiro Ishihara *The youth* • Kinuyo Tanaka *His mother* • Masayuki Mori *His father* • Ruriko Asoka *His sister* • Hajime Hana *His friend* ■ *Dir* Kon Ichikawa • *Scr* Natto Wada, from the logbook of Kenichi Horie

Alone with a Stranger ★★

Thriller 2000 · US · Colour · 90mins

Former *Falcon Crest* mainstay William R Moses takes the lead in this decidedly derivative thriller. He simply doesn't have the authority to carry his pivotal double role as twins whose lives have taken very different directions. Director Peter Liapis must take most of the blame for the lack of tension, as he also wrote the screenplay and has a small acting role. JF. Contains swearing.

William R Moses *James/Max Kennington* • Barbara Niven *Sandy Kennington* • Nia Peeples *Beth Jenkins* • Scotty Cox *David Kennington* • Priscilla Barnes *Claire* ■ *Dir* Peter Liapis • *Scr* Peter Liapis, from a story by Peter Liapis, Richard Dana Smith

Along Came a Spider ★★★ 15

Thriller 2001 · US/Ger · Colour · 98mins

A prequel to *Kiss the Girls*, this suspense thriller has Morgan Freeman resuming his role as detective and psychologist Alex Cross. A senator's daughter is being held to ransom, and the Secret Service agent (Monica Potter) who should have been protecting her volunteers to assist Cross. Based on the first of James Patterson's bestselling Cross novels, the film boasts a strong cast assuredly led by Freeman. Yet the pace of the film seems forced in order to fit in too many plot contrivances. JF. Contains violence and swearing. DVD

Morgan Freeman *Alex Cross* • Monica Potter *Secret Service Agent Jezzie Flannigan* • Michael Wincott *Gary Soneji/Jonathan Mercuzio* • Penelope Ann Miller *Elizabeth Rose* • Michael Moriarty *Senator Hank Rose* • Dylan Baker *Special Agent Oliver "Ollie" McArthur* ■ *Dir* Lee Tamahori • *Scr* Marc Moss, from the novel by James Patterson

Along Came Jones ★★★

Comedy western 1945 · US · BW · 89mins

Fans of the Coasters' immortal 1950s record *Along Came Jones* should check out this undervalued film, in which amiable cowpoke Gary Cooper is mistaken for outlaw Dan Duryea. It's a likeable compendium of western clichés, ably handled by former editor Stuart Heisler, who would later direct "Coop" in *Dallas* (1950). There's much to enjoy here, not least a lovely performance from Loretta Young. (She was hand-picked by Cooper, who was also the film's producer.) The title passed into western movie folklore. TS

Gary Cooper *Melody Jones* • Loretta Young *Cherry de Longpre* • William Demarest *George Fury* • Dan Duryea *Monte Jarrad* • Frank Sully *Cherry's brother* • Russell Simpson *Pop de Longpre* • Arthur Loft *Sheriff* ■ *Dir* Stuart Heisler • *Scr* Nunnally Johnson, from a story by Alan LeMay

Along Came Polly ★★ 12

Romantic comedy 2004 · US · Colour · 86mins

In this agreeable romantic comedy, Ben Stiller plays a cautious risk assessor who falls for wild former school friend Jennifer Aniston after his new wife cheats on him during their honeymoon. Stiller and Aniston's performances are reassuringly familiar, demonstrating a comfortable chemistry. However, director John Hamburg insists on throwing in incongruous gross-out humour that would make even the Farrelly Brothers wince. SF DVD

Ben Stiller *Reuben Feffer* • Jennifer Aniston *Polly Prince* • Philip Seymour Hoffman *Sandy Lyle* • Debra Messing *Lisa Kramer* • Hank Azaria *Claude* • Bryan Brown *Leland Van Lew* • Alec Baldwin *Stan Indursky* • Jsu Garcia *Javier* ■ *Dir/Scr* John Hamburg

Along the Great Divide ★★

Western 1951 · US · BW · 87mins

Kirk Douglas, in his memoirs, remembered this standard revenge western with some distaste. "I hated *Along the Great Divide*," he wrote, "I did it just to get my one picture a year obligation [to Warners] out of the way." He recalled the cruelty to the horses, the risks the stuntmen were forced to take and the sadism of the director, Raoul Walsh: "Critics talk about how Walsh movies have such great pace. They have great pace because he was always in a hurry to finish them." AT

Kirk Douglas *Len Merrick* • Virginia Mayo *Ann Keith* • John Agar *Billy Shear* • Walter Brennan *Tim "Pop" Keith* • Ray Teal *Lou Gray* • Hugh Sanders • Morris Ankrum *Ed Roden* • James Anderson (2) *Dan Roden* • Charles Meredith *The Judge* ■ *Dir* Raoul Walsh • *Scr* Walter Doniger, Lewis Meltzer, from a story by Walter Doniger

Along the Rio Grande ★★ U

Western 1941 · US · BW · 64mins

One of cowboy star Tim Holt's RKO series of westerns, featuring a routine plot wherein Tim and two pals join up with an outlaw gang to avenge the murder of their boss. Mind you, it takes some intervention from Sheriff Hal Taliaferro to help our heroes bring the villains to book, but the script is above par for this sort of western. Ray Whitley plays Holt's sidekick Smokey, while leading lady Betty Jane Rhodes is a colourful diversion. TS

Tim Holt *Jeff* • Ray Whitley *Smokey* • Betty Jane Rhodes *Mary Lawry* • Emmett Lynn *Whopper* • Robert Fiske *Doc Randall* • Hal Taliaferro *Sheriff* • Carl Stockdale *Turner* ■ *Dir* Edward Killy • *Scr* Arthur V Jones, Morton Grant, from a story by Stuart Anthony

Alpha Beta ★★★

Drama 1973 · UK · Colour · 66mins

EA Whitehead's play marked Albert Finney's return to the London stage after a six-year absence. The play is a two-hander, and Finney's co-star was Rachel Roberts, who last acted with him in *Saturday Night and Sunday Morning*. In three lacerating acts, the play defines modern marriage as a battlefield; there is caustic wit, bruising, a lot of metaphorical blood and ample opportunity for great acting. Financed by Finney himself and directed by Anthony Page, who also helmed the original Royal Court production, this is a valuable record of the stage original. AT

Albert Finney *Man* • Rachel Roberts (1) *Woman* ■ *Dir* Anthony Page • *Scr* EA Whitehead, from his play

The Alpha Incident ★

Science fiction 1977 · US · Colour · 92mins

A microbe from Mars terrorises people at a rural Wisconsin railroad depot managed by dim-witted Ralph Meeker. Only in sleep does the alien germ take control and destroy the body, so they must stay awake by playing cards and having sex. A micro-budget bore from director Bill Rebane, he of *The Giant Spider Invasion* and *Monster a-Go-Go* infamy, so you can't say you weren't warned. An over-talky feeble fable. AJ

John Alderman *Dr Rogers* • John F Goff *Jack Tiller* • Ralph Meeker *Charlie* • Stafford Morgan *Ted Sorenson* • Carol Irene Newell *Jenny* ■ *Dir* Bill Rebane • *Scr* Ingrid Neumayer

Alphabet City ★★ 18

Crime drama 1984 · US · Colour · 85mins

The most mainstream movie directed by underground film-maker Amos (*Subway Riders*) Poe has style in abundance and a great performance by Vincent Spano but virtually no plot. Tough Spano is a Lower East Side drug dealer with plans to retire until mobsters force him to go on the run. When Spano is centre stage this violent slice-of-life drama crackles with menacing intensity. Otherwise, it's a rather bland affair that goes over too much familiar ground. The music is by Nile Rodgers of Chic fame. AJ

Vincent Spano *Johnny* • Kate Vernon *Angela* • Michael Winslow *Lippy* • Zohra Lampert *Mama* • Jami Gertz *Sophia* • Ray Serra [Raymond Serra] *Gino* ■ *Dir* Amos Poe • *Scr* Amos Poe, Gregory K Heller, Robert Seidman, from a novel by Gregory K Heller

The Alphabet Murders ★ U

Comedy mystery 1966 · UK · BW · 95mins

Having met with cinematic success with Agatha Christie's Miss Marple as played by Margaret Rutherford, MGM

A

turned to another of Christie's detectives, Hercule Poirot, here incarnated in the unlikely personage of Tony Randall. The film's an unfortunate mess, which is doubly sad since talented satirist director Frank Tashlin should be capable of getting a handle on the whole affair. TS

Tony Randall *Hercule Poirot* • Anita Ekberg *Amanda Beatrice Cross* • Robert Morley *Hastings* • Maurice Denham *Inspector Japp* • Guy Rolfe *Duncan Doncaster* • Sheila Allen *Lady Diane* • Margaret Rutherford *Miss Marple* ■ *Dir* Frank Tashlin • *Scr* David Pursall, Jack Seddon, from the novel by Agatha Christie

Alphaville ★★★★ PG

Futuristic detective drama
1965 · Fr · BW · 94mins

This assured blend of sci-fi and *film noir* is perhaps Jean-Luc Godard's most accessible picture: a chilling peek into the future inspired as much by poetry and mythology as pulp fiction. Playing fast and loose with genre conventions, Godard explores themes more readily associated with Michelangelo Antonioni, as world-weary private eye Eddie Constantine searches the far-off metropolis of Alphaville for missing scientist Akim Tamiroff. Anna Karina is genuinely affecting as the robot who discovers emotion, while cinematographer Raoul Coutard miraculously turns Paris into a soulless hell. DP. In French with English subtitles [video] DVD

Eddie Constantine *Lemmy Caution* • Anna Karina *Natacha Von Braun* • Akim Tamiroff *Henri Dickson* • Howard Vernon *Professor Leonard Nosferatu/Von Braun* • Laszlo Szabo *Chief engineer* • Michel Delahaye *Von Braun's assistant* ■ *Dir/Scr* Jean-Luc Godard

Alpine Fire ★★★ 18

Drama 1985 · Swi · Colour · 118mins

Fredi M Murer adapts his own novel with a directorial style as stark as the Alpine landscape, and a power and subtlety usually missing from films about incest. Had the performances not been so innocent and unabashed, however, the realism would have seemed embarrassingly phoney. Johanna Lier impresses as the teenage daughter of a Swiss hill farmer, but it's Thomas Nock who compels as the pubescent deaf-mute who relieves his frustrations by constructing a network of stone monuments. DP. In Swiss German with English subtitles.

Thomas Nock *Boy* • Johanna Lier *Belli* • Dorothea Moritz *Mother* • Rolf Illig *Father* • Tilli Breidenbach *Grandmother* • Joerg Odermatt *Grandfather* ■ *Dir* Fredi M Murer • *Scr* Fredi M Murer, from his novel

Alraune ★★★★

Silent horror 1927 · Ger · BW · 108mins

Twice filmed in 1918 (by Eugen Illes and Michael Curtiz), this is the earliest adaptation to survive. Paul Wegener's crazed scientist unleashes a monster of savage beauty by inseminating a prostitute with the sperm of an executed killer. Having played Maria in *Metropolis*, Brigitte Helm gives another entrancing performance, as screenwriter Henrik Galeen exploits the incestuous father-daughter liaison to explore the nature of evil. Helm reprised the role in 1930, while Hildegarde Neff starred in a 1952 version of the story. DP

Brigitte Helm *Alraune* • Paul Wegener *Prof ten Brinken* • Ivan Petrovich *Frank Braun* ■ *Dir* Henrik Galeen • *Scr* Henrik Galeen, from the novel by Hanns Heinz Ewers

Alsino and the Condor ★★★

Political drama
1982 · Nic/Cub/Mex/Cos R · Colour · 89mins

It's somewhat apt that the first feature produced in Nicaragua under the Sandinistas should have been directed by a Chilean who'd fled the Pinochet regime. Leavening his stylised portrait of the brutal civil war with juvenile escapades and magic realism, Miguel Littin succeeds in fashioning an allegory that, in spite of its anti-American sentiment, received an Oscar nomination for best foreign film. Personifying his nation's need to come of political age, Alan Esquivel is superb as the 12-year-old orphan whose dreams of flying high above the surrounding jungle sustain him through the savagery of the conflict. DP. In Spanish with English subtitles.

Dean Stockwell *Frank* • Alan Esquivel *Alsino* • Carmen Bunster *Alsino's grandmother* • Alejandro Parodi *The Major* ■ *Dir* Miguel Littin • *Scr* Miguel Littín, Isidora Aguirre, Tomas Perez Turrent

Altered States ★★★ 18

Horror fantasy 1980 · US · Colour · 98mins

Scientist William Hurt tinkers with tribal drug rituals and sensory deprivation tanks until they cause him to regress to a primitive killer-simian state of altered consciousness. The deer-eating Neanderthal man mid-section may seem too over-the-top considering the deliberately excessive whole, but, in general, director Ken Russell power-drives his mad doctor update with trademark visual excess and hits the bullseye. Celebrated screenwriter Paddy Chayefsky, who also wrote the novel on which this is based, removed his name from the film in disgust. AJ. Contains violence, swearing and nudity. [video]

William Hurt *Eddie Jessup* • Blair Brown *Emily Jessup* • Bob Balaban *Arthur Rosenberg* • Charles Haid *Mason Parrish* • Thaao Penghlis *Eccheverria* • Miguel Godreau *Primal man* • Dori Brenner *Sylvia Rosenberg* • Peter Brandon *Hobart* • Drew Barrymore *Margaret Jessup* ■ *Dir* Ken Russell • *Scr* Sidney Aaron [Paddy Chayefsky], from his novel

The Alternative Miss World ★★★

Documentary 1980 · UK · Colour · 90mins

Artist Andrew Logan's satirical riposte to the Miss World beauty contest is a real event open to both sexes and all ages. Contestants, many of whom are from Logan's bohemian circle, wear outrageous costumes and generally have a high old time. The Logan show was filmed in its entirety in 1978, when the venue was a circus tent on London's Clapham Common. For lovers of camp humour, Divine, who conducts hilariously banal interviews, is on top form, while the ad-libbed commentary (by judges Molly Parkin and Eric Roberts and contestant Stephen Holt) is also a hoot. DM

Andrew Logan *Master of ceremonies* • Divine *Guest of honour* • Sophie Parkin *Miss Wildlife* • Molly Parkin *Commentator/Judge* • Eric Roberts *Commentator/Judge* • Stephen Holt *Miss Bronx* ■ *Dir/Scr* Richard Gayor

Alucarda ★★★ 18

Horror 1975 · Mex · Colour · 74mins

In this horror tale from Mexican director Juan Lopez Moctezuma (a former assistant to Alejandro Jodorowsky), the action follows a demonically possessed nun as she exacts hideous revenge on the killers of her bosom buddy. Although the movie typically relies on exploitation, Moctezuma gives this rather more style than the average low-budget horror, which serves to make its bizarre events more convincing. DP [video] DVD

Claudio Brook *Dr Oszek/Hunchbacked gypsy* • David Silva *Father Lazaro* • Tina Romero *Alucarda* • Susana Kamini *Justine* • Adriana Roel *Sister Germana* ■ *Dir* Juan Lopez Moctezuma • *Scr* Juan Lopez Moctezuma, Yolanda Lopez Moctezuma, Alexis T Arroyo

Alvarez Kelly ★★★ PG

Western 1966 · US · Colour · 105mins

An oddball American Civil War western, with William Holden as a rancher who delivers a herd of cattle to the Union army and is then kidnapped by the Confederates whose colonel, Richard Widmark, wants Holden to steal back the herd in order to feed his own soldiers. At first it's jokey; then Widmark shoots one of Holden's fingers off and things get rather more serious. Waywardly plotted, it's held together by the terrific rivalry and enmity whipped up by Holden and Widmark. AT. Contains violence and some swearing. [video] DVD

William Holden (2) *Alvarez Kelly* • Richard Widmark *Colonel Tom Rossiter* • Janice Rule *Liz Pickering* • Patrick O'Neal *Major Albert Stedman* • Victoria Shaw *Charity Warwick* • Roger C Carmel *Captain Angus Ferguson* ■ *Dir* Edward Dmytryk • *Scr* Franklin Coen, Elliot Arnold, from a story by Franklin Coen

Alvin Purple ★★

Comedy 1973 · Aus · Colour · 97mins

In this lacklustre Australian romp, Graeme Blundell is so much the sex-object of women's desires – from schoolgirls to bored housewives to kinky ladies – that he's constantly on the run. Eventually, he ends up as a gardener in a convent. The innuendos come thick and fast, but director Tim Burstall's gaudily titled comedy never quite lives up to its promising premise. The film was a box-office blockbuster in its home country, however. TH

Graeme Blundell *Alvin Purple* • Jill Forster *Mrs Horwood* • Elli MacLure *Tina Donovan* • Penne Hackforth-Jones *Dr Liz Sort* • George Whaley *Dr McBurney* • Noel Ferrier *Judge* ■ *Dir* Tim Burstall • *Scr* Alan Hopgood

Always ★★★ 15

Comedy 1985 · US · Colour · 105mins

This distinctive comedy of manners probes the meaning of love and marriage by focusing on three couples, each at different stages of their relationship. Writer/director Henry Jaglom and his former wife Patrice Townsend co-star as a couple about to get divorced; Alan Rachins and Joanna Frank, their best friends in real life, play their best friends on screen; while shooting took place in the house that Jaglom and Townsend shared when they were married. Charming, witty and often perceptive, the film is probably too unconventional in structure to have more than a limited appeal. PF

Henry Jaglom *David* • Patrice Townsend *Judy* • Joanna Frank *Lucy* • Alan Rachins *Eddie* • Melissa Leo *Peggy* • Jonathan Kaufer *Maxwell* • Bud Townsend *Judy's father* • Bob Rafelson *David's neighbour* ■ *Dir/Scr* Henry Jaglom

Always ★★★ PG

Romantic fantasy
1989 · US · Colour · 117mins

This was Steven Spielberg's attempt to make a more grown-up fantasy, after he was criticised for pandering to the child in all of us with *ET* and *Raiders of the Lost Ark*. It's effectively an update of the Spencer Tracy film *A Guy Named Joe*, with Richard Dreyfuss as the firefighter pilot who returns from the dead to watch over the love of his life Holly Hunter. Best pal John Goodman steals the show, and Audrey Hepburn (in her last screen role) gives him a run for his money as an angelic guide, while Hunter and Dreyfuss stave off the syrup to produce a romantic tale of everlasting love. JB [video] DVD

Richard Dreyfuss *Pete Sandich* • Holly Hunter *Dorinda Durston* • Brad Johnson *Ted Baker* • John Goodman *Al Yackey* • Audrey Hepburn *Hap* • Roberts Blossom *Dave* • Keith David *Powerhouse* • Ed Van Nuys *Nails* ■ *Dir* Steven Spielberg • *Scr* Jerry Belson, Diane Thomas, from the film *A Guy Named Joe* by Dalton Trumbo, Frederick Hazlitt Brennan, Chandler Sprague, David Boehm

Always Goodbye ★★

Melodrama 1938 · US · BW · 75mins

This remake of *Gallant Lady* (1934), which starred Ann Harding and Clive Brook, now stars Barbara Stanwyck and Herbert Marshall in the story of an unwed mother who sacrifices her child but then wants him back. Unfortunately, despite the ever-admirable Stanwyck and all the ingredients for a delicious wallow, the movie is directed by Sidney Lanfield with such a heavy overlay of treacle and unsubtle use of close-ups that it ends up an inferior and uninvolving example of the genre. RK

Barbara Stanwyck *Margot Weston* • Herbert Marshall *Jim Howard* • Ian Hunter *Phillip Marshall* • Cesar Romero *Count Giovanni Corini* • Lynn Bari *Jessica Reid* ■ *Dir* Sidney Lanfield • *Scr* Kathryn Scola, Edith Skouras, from a story by Gilbert Emery, Douglas Doty, from the film *Gallant Lady* by Gilbert Emery, Franc Rhodes, Sam Mintz

Always in My Heart ★★ U

Drama 1942 · US · BW · 93mins

An uncomfortable mix of music and drama in which the mother of a teenage daughter with singing aspirations is about to marry for the second time. Complications ensue when her long-lost husband turns up, having served 13 years in jail for a crime he didn't commit. Kay Francis stars as the mother, with singer Gloria Warren as the daughter, but the honours go to the always splendidly sympathetic Walter Huston. The movie is incredibly silly but perfectly agreeable, and boasts an Oscar-nominated title song. RK

Kay Francis *Marjorie Scott* • Walter Huston *MacKenzie Scott* • Gloria Warren *Victoria Scott* • Patty Hale *Dooley* • Frankie Thomas *Martin Scott* • Una O'Connor *Angie* ■ *Dir* Jo Graham • *Scr* Adele Comandini, from the play *Fly Away Home* by Dorothy Bennett, Irving White

Always Leave Them Laughing ★★★ U

Comedy 1949 · US · BW · 115mins

Milton Berle's big feature starring role was not a success in its day, but Miltie went on to greater celebrity in the Golden Era of American television. His face in grimace was not, in truth, well-suited to leading roles on the big cinema screen, but he was perfectly cast in this wry saga of a vaudeville comic who becomes a TV star. There was considerable on-screen competition, though, from vaudeville great Bert Lahr, playing the comedian whose shoes Berle aspires to step into, and who immortalises one of his most famous routines in this movie. TS

Milton Berle *Kip Cooper* • Virginia Mayo *Nancy Egan* • Ruth Roman *Fay Washburn* • Bert Lahr *Eddie Egan* • Alan Hale *Mr Washburn* • Grace Hayes *Mrs Washburn* • Jerome Cowan *Elliot Lewis* ■ *Dir* Roy Del Ruth • *Scr* Jack Rose, Melville Shavelson, from a story by Max Shulman, Richard Mealand

Ama ★★ 15

Fantasy drama
1991 · UK/Ghana · Colour · 105mins

This confused film bravely attempts to transport African mythology to suburban London, but fails to work as either an offbeat drama or a discourse on cultural assimilation. Georgina Ackerman receives dire warnings from her Ghanian ancestors on a golden computer disc – a neat touch – but other promising plot leads are left unpursued. In spite of a feel-good finale at the Notting Hill carnival, this rare British venture into magic realism is an opportunity missed. DP

Thomas Baptiste *Babs* • Anima Misa *Corri* • Roger Griffiths *Joe* • Nii Oma Hunter *Uk* • Joy Elias-Rilwan *Araba* • Georgina Ackerman *Ama* ■ *Dir* Kwesi Owusu, Kwate Nee-Owoo • *Scr* Kwesi Owusu

Amadeus ★★★★★ PG

Biographical drama
1984 · US · Colour · 153mins

The winner of eight Oscars and an unexpected box-office smash, *Amadeus* is simply one of the finest biographical dramas ever made. Reworked rather than simply adapted by Peter Shaffer from his own hit play, the film is as much about the mediocrity and envy of the composer Antonio Salieri as it is about the eccentric genius of his rival Mozart. There is, therefore, a sort of poetic justice in the fact that F Murray Abraham pipped Tom Hulce for the best actor award. Returning to Prague (standing in for Vienna) for the first time since the Soviet invasion in 1968, director Milos Forman and his regular cinematographer Miroslav Ondricek revel in the beauty of the city, but credit must also go to Patrizia von Brandenstein for her superb sets and inspired choice of location interiors. The music is majestic, thanks largely to Neville Marriner's outstanding interpretation of everything from gypsy dances to *Don Giovanni*. DP. Contains some swearing. DVD

F Murray Abraham *Antonio Salieri* • Tom Hulce *Wolfgang Amadeus Mozart* • Elizabeth Berridge *Constanze Mozart* • Simon Callow *Emanuel Schikaneder* • Roy Dotrice *Leopold Mozart* • Christine Ebersole *Katerina Cavalieri* • Jeffrey Jones *Emperor Joseph II* • Charles Kay *Count Orsini-Rosenberg* ■ *Dir* Milos Forman • *Scr* Peter Shaffer, from his stage play

Amandla! A Revolution in Four-Part Harmony ★★★ 12

Documentary
2002 · S Afr/US · Colour · 98mins

Nine years in the making, this inspiring documentary reveals the role played by music in sustaining black South Africa's identity during its half-century struggle against apartheid. Director Lee Hirsch uses archive footage and personal reminiscences to chronicle the key events from 1948-98. But this is more specifically a history of the freedom music of Vuyisile Mini and Vusi Mahlasela – as well as such internationally renowned exiles as Miriam Makeba, Hugh Masekela and Abdullah Ibrahim – that enabled the repressed townships to endure injustice, prejudice and violence even though the outside world seemed to have forgotten them. Moreover, these erudite, evocative songs stand in stark contrast to the triteness of synthetic pop and rap's designer anger. DP. An English and Xhosa language film. Contains violence. DVD

Dir Lee Hirsch

Les Amants ★★★★ 15

Drama 1958 · Fr · BW · 86mins

A *succès de scandale* on its release, Louis Malle's second feature won him the special jury prize at Venice. Although it may no longer have the power to shock, it's still got plenty to admire, first and foremost Henri Decaë's glossy black-and-white photography that sets the film apart from most other French pictures of the New Wave era. Jeanne Moreau is also superb as the seductive socialite who seeks casual affairs to relieve the boredom of her perfect life. The celebrated 20-minute love scene she shares with Jean-Marc Bory looks a little stylised today, but it remains notable for its bold portrayal of passion and rebellion. DP. In French with English subtitles. Contains a sex scene and nudity.

Jeanne Moreau *Jeanne Tournier* • Alain Cuny *Henri Tournier* • Jean-Marc Bory *Bernard Dubois-Lambert* • Judith Magre *Maggy Thiebaut-Leroy* ■ *Dir* Louis Malle • *Scr* Louis Malle, Louise de Vilmorin, from the novel *Point de Lendemain* by Dominique Vivant

Les Amants du Pont-Neuf ★★★ 15

Drama 1990 · Fr · Colour · 120mins

This is a classic example of the kind of flashy French film whose MTV-inspired visuals and sound-bite dialogue earned them the nickname *cinéma du look* for the emphasis on style over content. Writer/director Léos Carax strains to make a grand statement, but ends up trapped between his attempts to explore the social realities of France during the bicentenary of its Revolution, and his genius for opulent set pieces. The scenes on Paris's oldest bridge between Juliette Binoche, an artist losing her sight, and injured fire-eater Denis Lavant are more often pretentious than touching, but the film is still worth a look. DP. In French with English subtitles. Contains some violence and nudity. DVD

Juliette Binoche *Michèle* • Denis Lavant *Alex* • Klaus-Michael Gruber *Hans* • Daniel Buain *Clochard's friend* • Marion Statens *Marion* • Chrichan Larson *Julien* • Paulette Berthonnier *Sailor* • Roger Berthonnier *Sailor* ■ *Dir/Scr* Léos Carax

Amarcord ★★★★★ 15

Comedy drama 1973 · It · Colour · 118mins

Deftly tainting childhood memory with adult insight, Federico Fellini's dazzling blend of autobiography, fantasy and wickedly precise satire won an Oscar for best foreign film. Set in a seaside town not dissimilar to the director's native Rimini, *Amarcord* ("I remember") assembles a wonderful cast of characters, as human as they are grotesque, while mocking Mussolini's regime, Roman Catholicism and the prejudices of the parochial bourgeoisie. Touching, coarse and comic, this is a must for fans and, for those yet to be converted, a superb introduction to the work of a great artist. DP. In Italian with English subtitles. DVD

Puppela Maggio *Miranda Biondi* • Magali Noël *Gradisca* • Bruno Zanin *Titta Biondi* • Armando Brancia *Aurelio Biondi* • Ciccio Ingrassia *Uncle Teo* • Nandino Orfei *Pataca* • Luigi Rossi *Lawyer* • Gianfilippo Carcano *Don Baravelli* ■ *Dir* Federico Fellini • *Scr* Federico Fellini, Tonino Guerra • *Cinematographer* Giuseppe Rotunno • *Art Director* Danilo Donati • *Music* Nino Rota

The Amateur ★★ 15

Spy thriller 1981 · Can · Colour · 106mins

When terrorists take over the US consulate in Munich and kill a female hostage, the girl's boyfriend – computer boffin John Savage – starts plotting revenge. Despite some well-filmed action scenes, the plotting in this thriller is slow and never plausible, while the performances range from the adequate to the laughable (Christopher Plummer's Czech security chief). AT

John Savage *Charles Heller* • Christopher Plummer *Professor Lakos* • Marthe Keller *Elisabeth* • Arthur Hill *Brewer* • Nicholas Campbell *Schraeger* • George Coe *Rutledge* • John Marley *Molton* • Jan Rubes *Kaplan* • Ed Lauter *Anderson* ■ *Dir* Charles Jarrott • *Scr* Robert Littell, Diana Maddox, from the novel by Robert Littell

Amateur ★★★★ 15

Drama 1994 · Fr/UK/US · Colour · 100mins

Given that the central characters are an ex-nun turned professional pornographer and a professional pornographer now suffering from amnesia, it doesn't take a genius to recognise that you are in the world of Hal Hartley, a place where humour is so deadpan it makes *Twin Peaks* look like a celebration of slapstick. Isabelle Huppert gives a marvellous performance of wide-eyed innocence, while Martin Donovan retains that unique expression he saves for Hartley films, one that implies he can't quite fathom why everyone else finds his normal behaviour so eccentric. This is in a league (let alone a world) of its own. DP. Contains violence, swearing and sex scenes.

Isabelle Huppert *Isabelle* • Martin Donovan (2) *Thomas* • Elina Lowensohn *Sofia* • Damian Young *Edward* • Chuck Montgomery *Jan* • David Simonds *Kurt* • Pamela Stewart *Officer Melville* ■ *Dir/Scr* Hal Hartley

The Amazing Captain Nemo ★ U

Fantasy adventure
1978 · US · Colour · 98mins

Seven writers without a worthwhile idea between them collaborated on the script for this ludicrous movie, edited down from a three-part TV series. José Ferrer brings nothing new to the part of the captain, who is awakened after a century in suspended animation and pitched into battle with a mad professor (Burgess Meredith) bent on world domination. DP

José Ferrer *Captain Nemo* • Burgess Meredith *Professor Waldo Cunningham* • Tom Hallick *Commander Tom Franklin* • Burr DeBenning *Lt Jim Porter* • Lynda Day George *Kate* • Mel Ferrer *Dr Robert Cook* • Horst Buchholz *King Tibor* ■ *Dir* Alex March • *Scr* Norman Katkov, Preston Wood, Robert C Dennis, William Keys, Mann Rubin, Robert Bloch, Larry Alexander

The Amazing Colossal Man ★ PG

Science fiction 1957 · US · BW · 79mins

After being exposed to plutonium radiation, Lieutenant Colonel Glen Langan grows ten feet taller per day and rampages through cardboard miniatures on the way to Las Vegas. Truly amazing, because this shoddy *Incredible Shrinking Man* in reverse is considered supremo schlock producer/director Bert I Gordon's best effort. And colossal, because that's exactly what it is – a colossal bore. Amazingly, this spawned a sequel, *War of the Colossal Beast*. AJ

Glen Langan [Glenn Langan] *Lt Col Glenn Manning* • Cathy Downs *Carol Forrest* • William Hudson *Dr Paul Lindstrom* • James Seay *Colonel Hallock* • Larry Thor *Dr Eric Coulter* • Russ Bender *Richard Kingman* • Lyn Osborn *Sergeant Taylor* ■ *Dir* Bert I Gordon • *Scr* Bert I Gordon, Mark Hanna

The Amazing Dobermans ★★

Crime caper 1976 · US · Colour · 96mins

Fred Astaire plays a reformed conman who leads five Doberman pinschers plus one undercover treasury agent (James Franciscus) on the trail of racketeers. This was the final film in a series that began in 1972 with *The Doberman Gang* and continued with *The Daring Dobermans* the following year. All offer the sort of family entertainment Disney churned out in the 60s; by the 70s, however, they seemed strangely anachronistic. AT

Fred Astaire *Daniel Hughes* • James Franciscus *Lucky Vincent* • Barbara Eden *Justine Pirot* • Jack Carter *Solly Kramer* ■ *Dir* Byron Ross Chudnow • *Scr* Michael Kraike, William Goldstein, Richard Chapman, from a story by Michael Kraike, William Goldstein

The Amazing Dr Clitterhouse ★★★

Crime drama 1938 · US · BW · 87mins

Edward G Robinson has a ball in this ingenious gangster picture, co-written by John Huston and directed by Anatole Litvak. Robinson plays a psychiatrist whose study of the criminal mind turns him into a criminal himself, while Humphrey Bogart is the gang leader he studies, emulates and subsequently plans to murder. Morality is very much to the fore, but this is also a first-rate entertainment. AT

Edward G Robinson *Dr Clitterhouse* • Claire Trevor *Jo Keller* • Humphrey Bogart *Rocks Valentine* • Gale Page *Nurse Randolph* • Donald Crisp *Inspector Lane* • Allen Jenkins *Okay* • Thurston Hall *Grant* • Susan Hayward ■ *Dir* Anatole Litvak • *Scr* John Wesley, John Huston, from the play by Barre Lyndon

Amazing Grace and Chuck ★★ PG

Drama 1987 · US · Colour · 110mins

A little league baseball player convinces major athletes on both sides of the Iron Curtain to stop playing sports as a protest over the nuclear arms race in *Four Weddings* director Mike Newell's simple-minded Capra-esque fable. Gregory Peck, as the US President, lends his support to the peacenik effort in a well-intentioned but ultimately squirm-inducing treatise. Jamie Lee Curtis and Boston Celtics player Alex English contribute to the overall embarrassment. AJ

Jamie Lee Curtis *Lynn Taylor* • Alex English *Amazing Grace Smith* • Gregory Peck *President* • William L Petersen *Russell* • Joshua Zuehlke *Chuck Murdock* • Dennis Lipscomb *Johnny B Goode* • Lee Richardson *Jeffries* ■ *Dir* Mike Newell • *Scr* David Field

The Amazing Mr Blunden ★★★ U

Fantasy mystery 1972 · UK · Colour · 94mins

In his later years, character actor Lionel Jeffries had a secondary career as a sympathetic director of films made for and about young people, notably *The Railway Children*. This Antonia Barber period ghost story is also perfectly suitable for adult viewing. There's much to enjoy, especially in the ripe performances from Laurence Naismith in the title role, and from the splendid Diana Dors as Mrs Wickens – gross, warty and every child's nightmare. TS DVD

Laurence Naismith *Mr Blunden* • Lynne Frederick *Lucy Allen* • Garry Miller *Jamie Allen* • Dorothy Alison *Mrs Allen* • Diana Dors *Mrs Wickens* • James Villiers *Uncle Bertie* • Madeline Smith *Bella* • Rosalyn Landor *Sarah* ■ *Dir* Lionel Jeffries • *Scr* Lionel Jeffries, from the story *The Ghosts* by Antonia Barber

The Amazing Mr Williams ★★ U

Screwball comedy mystery
1939 · US · BW · 84mins

Melvyn Douglas is the over-conscientious detective whose workload gets in the way of his romance with long-suffering fiancée Joan Blondell. To keep one date, Douglas arrives with a murderer in tow, and later he is forced into drag to trap a lady killer, which is the most amazing he gets. Though Blondell and Douglas mesh beautifully on their third pairing, the story has a mechanical feel which is not helped by Alexander Hall's uninspired direction. AE

Melvyn Douglas *Kenny Williams* • Joan Blondell *Maxine Carroll* • Clarence Kolb *McGovern* • Ruth Donnelly *Effie* • Edward Brophy *Moseby* • Donald MacBride *Bixler* •

Don Beddoe *Deever* • Jonathan Hale *Mayor* ■ *Dir* Alexander Hall • *Scr* Dwight Taylor, Sy Bartlett, from a story by Sy Bartlett

The Amazing Mrs Holliday ★★ U

Musical adventure 1943 · US · BW · 93mins

The fact that Jean Renoir, the great French director exiled in the US, was considered to be the right man for this sentimental vehicle for the wholesome singing star Deanna Durbin is an example of the mysterious way in which Hollywood works. However, after four weeks work, Renoir decided to withdraw diplomatically on grounds of health. What remains is a superficial film that exploits the theme of war orphans for entertainment. Yet Durbin does well as a missionary in China who smuggles nine Chinese children back to the States. RB [video]

Deanna Durbin *Ruth* • Edmond O'Brien *Tom* • Barry Fitzgerald *Timothy* • Arthur Treacher *Henderson* • Harry Davenport *Commodore* ■ *Dir* Bruce Manning • *Scr* Frank Ryan, John Jacoby from a story by Sonya Levien, adapted by Boris Ingster, Leo Townsend

The Amazing Panda Adventure ★★ PG

Adventure 1995 · US · Colour · 80mins

The panda is cute and the Chinese countryside is gorgeous, but that's all that can be said in this family film's favour. Ryan Slater (Christian's brother) is incredibly annoying as a spoiled American boy who travels to China to visit his father on a panda reserve. Somewhat better is Yi Ding as the young Chinese girl he teams up with to protect a baby panda from poachers. What's really amazing is that the movie has the gall to reuse the same camera shots and few bars of music repeatedly. KB [video]

Stephen Lang *Dr Michael Tyler* • Ryan Slater *Ryan Tyler* • Yi Ding *Ling* • Wang Fei *Chu* ■ *Dir* Chris Cain [Christopher Cain] • *Scr* Jeff Rothberg, Laurice Elehwany, from a story by John Wilcox, Steven Alldredge

The Amazing Quest of Ernest Bliss ★★ U

Comedy 1936 · UK/US · BW · 61mins

An idle millionaire accepts a challenge to earn his living for a year without touching his own means. He takes a serious of humble jobs – greengrocer, chauffeur, salesman and so on – though he decides to lose the bet when his girlfriend's invalid sister needs an operation. A mildly enjoyable, lightweight and light-hearted British film, competently directed by Alfred Zeisler, with the main appeal (then and now) being the presence of imported star Cary Grant. RK DVD

Cary Grant *Ernest Bliss* • Mary Brian *Frances* • Peter Gawthorne *Sir James Aldroyd* • Henry Kendall *Lord Honiton* • Leon M Lion *Dorrington* • John Turnbull *Masters* • Arthur Hardy *Crawley* • Iris Ashley *Clare* ■ *Dir* Alfred Zeisler • *Scr* from the novel *The Amazing Quest of Ernest Bliss* by E Phillips Oppenheim

The Amazing Transparent Man ★ U

Science fiction 1960 · US · BW · 57mins

Bank robber Douglas Kennedy may be transparent, but B-movie maverick Edgar G Ulmer's low-grade *Invisible Man* is hardly amazing. Scientist Ivan Triesault invents a serum to create an army of invisible zombies but when he experiments on convict Kennedy, he unleashes a one-man crime spree. An impoverished quickie. AJ DVD

Marguerite Chapman *Laura* • Douglas Kennedy *Joey Faust* • James Griffith *Krenner* • Ivan Triesault *Dr Ulof* • Boyd "Red" Morgan *Julian* ■ *Dir* Edgar G Ulmer • *Scr* Jack Lewis

Amazon Women on the Moon ★★ 15

Comedy 1987 · US · Colour · 80mins

This collection of comedy sketches spoofing commercials, sexual mores, tabloid television and old movies misses more targets than it hits. However, it's the fabulous cast of cult icons (director Russ Meyer), camp starlets (Sybil Danning) and Hollywood veterans (Ralph Bellamy) that makes this follow-up to *Kentucky Fried Movie* such a delight for cinema trainspotters. AJ [video] DVD

Michelle Pfeiffer *Brenda* • Rosanna Arquette *Karen* • Steve Guttenberg *Jerry* • Steve Forrest *Captain Nelson* • Joey Travolta *Butch* • David Alan Grier *Don Simmons* • Archie Hahn *Harvey Pitnik* • Ed Begley Jr *Griffin* • Matt Adler *George* • Ralph Bellamy *Mr Gower* • Carrie Fisher *Mary Brown* • Sybil Danning • Russ Meyer ■ *Dir* Joe Dante, Carl Gottlieb, Peter Horton, John Landis, Robert K Weiss • *Scr* Michael Barrie, Jim Mulholland

The Ambassador ★★ 18

Political thriller 1984 · US · Colour · 91mins

Elmore Leonard's novel, *52 Pick-Up*, is oddly transposed to Israel where middle-eastern politics, PLO guerrillas and CIA murkiness are added to the cocktail of adultery and blackmail. It's an overstuffed package, though not without its benefits – most of which come in the shape of Robert Mitchum's cuckolded and blackmailed US ambassador. Rock Hudson plays a security expert in what turned out to be his final film. Two years later, John Frankenheimer adapted this Leonard novel rather more faithfully. AT [video]

Robert Mitchum *Peter Hacker* • Ellen Burstyn *Alex Hacker* • Rock Hudson *Frank Stevenson* • Donald Pleasence *Eretz* • Fabio Testi *Mustapha Hashimi* • Michal Bat-Adam *Tova* ■ *Dir* J Lee Thompson • *Scr* Max Jack, from the novel *52 Pick-Up* by Elmore Leonard

The Ambassador's Daughter ★★★ U

Romantic comedy
1956 · US · Colour · 103mins

This old-fashioned comedy, with a plot so featherlight it's in danger of blowing away, is thoroughly enjoyable thanks to glamorous Paris locations, some witty lines and a polished cast that includes Myrna Loy. Written, produced and directed by Norman Krasna, it deals with the adventures that befall the daughter (Olivia de Havilland) of the ambassador (Edward Arnold) when she sets out to disprove visiting senator Adolphe Menjou's contention that the GIs stationed in the city constitute a moral danger. De Havilland is years too old for the role, but carries it off with stylish conviction; and John Forsythe supplies the romancing. RK

Olivia de Havilland *Joan* • John Forsythe *Danny* • Myrna Loy *Mrs Cartwright* • Adolphe Menjou *Senator Cartwright* • Tommy Noonan *Al* • Francis Lederer *Prince Nicholas Obelski* • Edward Arnold *Ambassador Fiske* ■ *Dir/Scr* Norman Krasna

Ambition ★ 15

Psychological drama
1991 · US · Colour · 94mins

Some years after his Oscar-winning role in *The Killing Fields* (1984), Haing S Ngor is the best thing in this rambling indulgence written by and starring Lou Diamond Phillips as a ruthless writer who teams up with a mass murderer. It's almost impossible to suspend disbelief in a wild story that looks as though it was initially intended for television. TH [video]

Lou Diamond Phillips *Mitchell* • Clancy Brown *Albert Merrick* • Cecilia Peck *Julie* • Richard Bradford *Jordan* • Willard Pugh *Freddie* • Grace Zabriskie *Mrs Merrick* • Katherine Armstrong *Roseanne* • JD Cullum [John David Cullum] *Jack* • Haing S Ngor *Tatay* ■ *Dir* Scott D Goldstein • *Scr* Lou Diamond Phillips

The Ambulance ★★★★ 15

Black comedy thriller
1990 · US · Colour · 91mins

A terrific urban paranoia thriller dosed with engaging black comedy, this marvellous B-movie gem from director Larry Cohen is a fright delight. A vintage ambulance roams Manhattan looking for the stricken and injured, only to whisk them off to psychotic surgeon Eric Braeden for illegal medical research. Eric Roberts is the comic artist plunged into a medical nightmare when the girl he's trying to date disappears into thin air. Witty repartee, unpredictable plot twists, Cohen's fast and furious direction and some superb action set pieces make this an instant remedy for boredom and one shock treatment worth undergoing. AJ [video]

Eric Roberts *Josh Baker* • James Earl Jones *Lieutenant Spencer* • Red Buttons *Elias* • Megan Gallagher *Sandy Malloy* • Janine Turner *Cheryl* • Richard Bright *Detective* • Eric Braeden *Doctor* • Stan Lee *Stan Lee, Marvel comics editor* ■ *Dir/Scr* Larry Cohen

Ambush ★★★ U

Western 1949 · US · BW · 88mins

Robert Taylor took up making westerns regularly after this cavalry-versus-Indians story showed how steely-eyed and determined he looked in the saddle. Here he's the scout easily persuaded by glamorous Arlene Dahl to help the army look for her young sister who's been abducted by Apaches. The plot proves cumbersome at times, delving into marital strife at the fort (where Jean Hagen's unhappy wife is carrying on with Don Taylor's lieutenant), but the film scores in its graphic depiction of the Apaches as cunning and merciless enemies. AE

Robert Taylor (1) *Ward Kinsman* • John Hodiak *Capt Ben Lorrison* • Arlene Dahl *Ann Duverall* • Don Taylor *Lt Linus Delaney* • Jean Hagen *Martha Conovan* • Bruce Cowling *Tom Conovan* • Leon Ames *Maj Beverly* ■ *Dir* Sam Wood • *Scr* Marguerite Roberts, from a story by Luke Short

Ambush at Tomahawk Gap ★★

Western adventure
1953 · US · Colour · 72mins

Featuring John Hodiak and John Derek, this has a formula plot in which four ex-cons seek lost loot in a ghost town. There aren't enough sharp twists in the story or characterisations to shake it up, but the swoop of the Apaches is well done. A standard western, certainly, but with some surprising lumps in the usual porridge. TH

John Hodiak *McCord* • John Derek *The Kid* • David Brian *Egan* • Ray Teal *Doc* • Maria Elena Marques *Indian girl* • John Qualen *Jonas P Travis* • Otto Hulett *Stranton* ■ *Dir* Fred F Sears • *Scr* David Lang

Ambush Bay ★★

Second World War adventure
1966 · US · Colour · 109mins

A snare too far and too late for this stalled action movie about a group of US Marines trying to escape a Japanese-controlled island in the Philippines in 1944. Hugh O'Brian and Mickey Rooney at least look as though they mean it, but James Mitchum, son of Robert, gives a performance as lacklustre as that of the film. TH

Hugh O'Brian *First Sergeant Steve Corey* • Mickey Rooney *Sergeant Ernest Wartell* • James Mitchum *Private First Class James Grenier* • Peter Masterson *Sergeant William Maccone* • Harry Lauter *Cpl Alvin Ross* • Greg Amsterdam *Cpl Stanley Parrish* ■ *Dir* Ron Winston • *Scr* Marve Feinberg, Ib Melchior

The Ambushers ★★ PG

Spy spoof 1967 · US · Colour · 97mins

Dean Martin's third Matt Helm romp (after *The Silencers* and *Murderers' Row*) takes him to Mexico to rescue a kidnapped pilot (Janice Rule) who has lost her flying saucer, a top secret gizmo that's vital to western security. Kurt Kasznar is the comic cut-out villain while Senta Berger is the object of Martin's main romantic dalliance. With Martin's gimlet-eyed quips, studio sets and back-projected scenery, the result is a very jaded movie. Martin played Helm again in 1969's *The Wrecking Crew*. AT [video]

Dean Martin *Matt Helm* • Senta Berger *Francesca* • Janice Rule *Sheila* • James Gregory *MacDonald* • Albert Salmi *Ortega* • Kurt Kasznar *Quintana* • Beverly Adams *Lovey Kravezit* ■ *Dir* Henry Levin • *Scr* Herbert Baker, from the novel by Donald Hamilton

Amélie ★★★★★ 15

Romantic comedy drama
2001 · Fr/Ger · Colour · 116mins

Jean-Pierre Jeunet's offering enchants and beguiles with a nostalgic optimism thanks to glorious visuals and ceaseless invention. Audrey Tautou is guaranteed iconic status as Amélie, the Montmartre waitress whose selfless *joie de vivre* leads her to improve the lives of her friends and neighbours. She only takes a break from her role of good fairy to pursue Mathieu Kassovitz, the handsome loner who collects rejected photo-booth snaps for his album of forgotten smiles. It has to be conceded that complaints of uncosmopolitan conservatism made against this film have some justification. But as a love letter to the City of Light – filmed at locations all around Paris yet retaining the stylised magic of a movie set – this is deliciously romantic and ingeniously mischievous. DP. In French with English subtitles. [video] DVD

Audrey Tautou *Amélie Poulain* • Mathieu Kassovitz *Nino Quicampoix* • Rufus *Raphaël Poulain, Amélie's father* • Yolande Moreau *Madeleine Wallace, the concierge* • Artus de Penguern *Hipolito, the writer* • Urbain Cancelier *Collignon, the grocer* • Dominique Pinon *Joseph* ■ *Dir* Jean-Pierre Jeunet • *Scr* Guillaume Laurant, Jean-Pierre Jeunet • *Cinematographer* Bruno Delbonnel

Amen. ★★★ PG

Second World War drama
2002 · Fr/Ger · Colour · 131mins

Costa-Gavras's sincere exposé of the shamefully noncommittal Papal-Allied response to the first news of the Holocaust suffers from being a thriller with a foregone outcome. Moreover, it fails to engage on a human level, despite the percipience of its political insight and the cruel irony of its conclusions. The fact that Kurt Gerstein (Ulrich Tukur), the Christian chemist who unwittingly introduced Zyklon B gas into the concentration camps, is a true-life character, while Mathieu Kassovitz's crusading Jesuit is fictional, also lessens the impact. DP

Ulrich Tukur *Kurt Gerstein* • Mathieu Kassovitz *Riccardo Fontana* • Ulrich Mühe *Doctor* • Michel Duchaussoy *Cardinal* • Ion Caramitru *Count Fontana* • Marcel Iures *Pope* ■ *Dir* Costa-Gavras • *Scr* Costa-Gavras, Jean-Claude Grumberg, from the play *Der Stellvertreter* by Rolf Hochhuth

America ★★★

Silent historical epic
1924 · US · BW · 135mins

Set during the American War of Independence, DW Griffith's failed attempt to repeat the success of *The Birth of a Nation* (1915) is little more than a ponderous patriotic pageant. Claims to historical accuracy are undermined by having George

Washington play cupid to a bland pair of lovers (Neil Hamilton and Carol Dempster, Griffith's then-inamorata). But the battle scenes were filmed magnificently by a team of photographers headed by Billy Bitzer and Hendrik Sartov. RB

Neil Hamilton *Nathan Holden* • Erville Alderson *Justice Montague* • Carol Dempster *Nancy Montague* • Charles Emmett Mack *Charles Philip Edward Montague* • Lee Beggs *Samuel Adams* • John Dunton *John Hancock* • Arthur Donaldson *King George III* • Charles Bennett *William Pitt* • Downing Clarke *Lord Chamberlain* • Lionel Barrymore *Captain Walter Butler* ■ *Dir* DW Griffith • *Scr* John LE Pell, from a story by Robert W Chambers

America ★★

Satirical comedy 1986 · US · Colour · 83mins

In the 1970s, Robert Downey – now probably better known as the father of troubled actor Robert Downey Jr – delivered some enjoyably jaundiced swipes at American institutions. Alas, he lost his way with this amateurish send-up of cable culture. The story focuses on a cheap cable TV station that is propelled on to the international broadcasting stage when its signal gets mistakenly bounced off the Moon. The likes of Michael J Pollard and Richard Belzer give their all, but the satirical barbs are misdirected JF

Zack Norman *Terrence Hackley* • Tammy Grimes *Joy Hackley* • Michael J Pollard *Bob Jolly* • Richard Belzer *Gypsy Beam* • Monroe Arnold *Floyd Praeger* • Liz Torres *Dolores Frantico* • Pablo Ferro *Hector Frantico* • David Kerman *Mr Management* • Robert Downey Jr ■ *Dir* Robert Downey Sr • *Scr* Robert Downey, Sidney Davis

America, America ★★★ PG

Drama 1963 · US · Colour · 161mins

Elia Kazan based this would-be epic on the experiences of his uncle, who fled a perilous existence within the Ottoman empire to start afresh in New York. Whether Stathis Giallelis has the wherewithal to surmount the problems encountered en route is open to debate. Such is the authenticity of everything around him, however, that the hesitancy of his performance almost becomes an advantage. Gene Callahan's turn-of-the-century designs thoroughly deserved their Oscar, while the supporting turns of Paul Mann, Linda Marsh and the wicked Lou Antonio are exemplary. DP

Stathis Giallelis *Stavros Topouzoglou* • Frank Wolff *Vartan Damadian* • Harry Davis *Isaac* • Elena Karam *Vasso* • Estelle Hemsley *Grandmother* • Gregory Rozakis *Hohanness Gardashian* • Lou Antonio *Abdul* • Salem Ludwig *Odysseus* ■ *Dir* Elia Kazan • *Scr* Elia Kazan, from his book

America 3000 ★ 15

Science-fiction comedy
1986 · US · Colour · 89mins

Essentially, this is an update of those chauvinistic all-female tribe movies of the 1950s, with women in charge of the post-apocalypse society and treating men as slaves. Although billed as a comedy, most of it is taken so unenergetically and seriously that there's no fun to be found. KB

Chuck Wagner *Korvis* • Laurene Landon *Vena* • Camilla Sparv *Rhea* • Victoria Barrett *Lakella* • William Wallace *Gruss* • Sue Giosa *Morha* • Galyn Gorg *Lynka* • Shai K Ophir *Lelz* ■ *Dir/Scr* David Engelbach

American Beauty ★★★★★ 18

Black comedy 1999 · US · Colour · 116mins

British theatre director Sam Mendes made an astonishing film debut with this sublime black comedy about midlife crises, starring Kevin Spacey and Annette Bening as a bored couple in suburban America. The sexually frustrated Bening begins an affair with estate agent Peter Gallagher; Spacey, meanwhile, fantasises about Mena Suvari, a teenage friend of his daughter's. Their disparate needs result in a comic tragedy of misunderstanding that combines acute observations with side-splitting scenarios. A truly outstanding film, that deservedly picked up a clutch of Oscars including best picture, best director and best actor. LH. Contains violence, swearing, sex scenes, drug abuse and nudity. DVD

Kevin Spacey *Lester Burnham* • Annette Bening *Carolyn Burnham* • Thora Birch *Jane Burnham* • Wes Bentley *Ricky Fitts* • Mena Suvari *Angela Hayes* • Peter Gallagher *Buddy Kane* • Allison Janney *Barbara Fitts* • Scott Bakula *Jim Olmeyer* • Sam Robards *Jim Berkley* • Chris Cooper *Colonel Fitts* ■ *Dir* Sam Mendes • *Scr* Alan Ball

American Blue Note ★★★ 15

Comedy drama 1989 · US · Colour · 88mins

Neatly capturing the atmosphere of dingy rehearsal rooms and smoky clubs, director Ralph Toporoff strikes the perfect balance between music and drama, and draws a performance of some sensitivity from Peter MacNicol as the jazz bandleader given a year to make it big or settle for a lifetime of disappointment. Striking all the right notes, this is like *The Commitments* in a minor key. DP. Contains some swearing.

Peter MacNicol *Jack* • Charlotte D'Amboise *Benita* • Carl Capotorto *Jerry* • Tim Guinee *Bobby* • Bill Christopher-Myers *Lee* • Jonathan Walker *Tommy* • Zohra Lampert *Louise* ■ *Dir* Ralph Toporoff • *Scr* Gilbert Girion, from a story by Ralph Toporoff

American Boyfriends ★★★ 15

Comedy drama 1989 · Can · Colour · 91mins

The stars and writer/director of the engagingly quirky *My American Cousin* are reunited for this witty sequel. This time, Canadian Margaret Langrick is grappling with adolescence as she heads back to the US to attend her cousin John Wildman's wedding. The two leads once again deliver pleasing performances and Sandy Wilson demonstrates a keen understanding of teenage rites, although the tone here is more melancholy than in the earlier film. JF

Margaret Langrick *Sandy Wilcox* • John Wildman *Butch Wilcox* • Jason Blicker *Marty Kaplan* • Liisa Repo-Martel *Julie La Belle* • Delia Brett *Lizzie* • Michelle Bardeaux *Thelma* • Troy Mallory *Spider* • Scott Anderson *Daryl* ■ *Dir/Scr* Sandy Wilson

American Buffalo ★★★ 15

Drama 1995 · US/UK · Colour · 83mins

Dustin Hoffman returns to the skid row of *Midnight Cowboy's* Ratso Rizzo for this talkfest, scripted by David Mamet from his stage play and directed by Michael Corrente. Hoffman's an aggressive petty thief who decides to muscle in on the burglary plans of ghetto junk dealer Dennis Franz (of *NYPD Blue* fame), at the expense of Franz's teenage sidekick, Sean Nelson. The plot disappears into the Pinteresque pauses, but the dialogue has such power and the acting such conviction, you hang on every word however obscene it is. TH. Contains swearing and some violence. DVD

Dustin Hoffman *Teach* • Dennis Franz *Donny Dubrow* • Sean Nelson *Bobby* ■ *Dir* Michael Corrente • *Scr* David Mamet, from his play

American Cousins ★★★ 15

Crime comedy drama
2003 · UK · Colour · 88mins

These Mafia shenanigans in a Glasgow café have charm, enhanced by performances that always take it seriously enough to convince. After a deal goes sour, New Jersey hoods Danny Nucci and Dan Hedaya flee to Scotland to take refuge with their cousin Gerald Lepkowski, fish fryer by day and stamp collector by night. Director Donald Coutts throws in all sorts of Mafia clichés with total disregard for momentum, but there's a cheerful absurdity about it all that keeps your attention. TH. Contains swearing and violence. DVD

Danny Nucci *Gino* • Shirley Henderson *Alice* • Gerald Lepkowski *Roberto* • Vincent Pastore *Tony* • Dan Hedaya *Settimo* • Russell Hunter *Nonno* • Stevan Rimkus *Jo Jo* • Stephen Graham *Henry* • Jake Abraham *Vince* ■ *Dir* Donald Coutts • *Scr* Sergio Casci

American Desi ★★★ 12

Romantic comedy
2001 · US/Ind · Colour · 99mins

Director Piyush Dinker Pandya's feature debut is a lively campus comedy that explores the socio-cultural problems facing second generation Indian-Americans. By making such mundane matters as fitting in and getting on seem both specific and universal, Pandya appeals to viewers from diverse ethnic backgrounds. He's ably assisted by Deep Katdare's willing performance as the rebel who returns to his roots to woo fellow student Purva Bedi, Ronobir Lahiri, who plays a Sikh weighed down by parental expectation, and Kal Penn as a wannabe disciple of Malcolm X. DP

Deep Katdare *Krishna Reddy* • Purva Bedi *Nina Shah* • Ronobir Lahiri *Jagjit Singh* • Rizwan Manji *Salim Ali Khan* • Kal Penn *Ajay Pandya* • Sunita Param *Farah Saaed* • Anil Kumar *Rakesh Patel* ■ *Dir/Scr* Piyush Dinker Pandya

American Dragons ★★ 15

Crime thriller 1997 · US · Colour · 91mins

Another Hollywood attempt to make a successful crime movie in which mismatched Oriental and American detectives tackle mutual adversaries. However, the racial stereotypes are even more glaring in this mediocre example, with both yakuza and mafiosi being reduced to cyphers engaged in a gun-toting turf war. With Park Joong-Hoon's Korean cop serving as little more than a stooge for his partner's salty insults, Michael Biehn is powerless to rescue the picture. DP. Contains violence and swearing. DVD

Michael Biehn *Detective Tony Luca* • Park Joong-Hoon *Kim* • Cary-Hiroyuki Tagawa *Matsuyama* • Don Stark *Rocco* ■ *Dir* Ralph Hemecker • *Scr* Erik Saltzgaber, Keith W Strandberg

An American Dream ★★★

Drama 1966 · US · Colour · 103mins

This Warner Bros adaptation of one of Norman Mailer's lesser novels is enjoyable enough to watch, despite the ham-fisted direction from actor Robert Gist. It's all Technicolor gloss when it should be lean and mean, though it did receive an X certificate for its release in Britain as *See You in Hell, Darling*. Stuart Whitman is most unappealing as the talk-show host who murders his wife and tries to pass her death off as a suicide. Janet Leigh, as his nosey ex-girlfriend, is much better. TS. Contains some swearing.

Stuart Whitman *Stephen Rojack* • Eleanor Parker *Deborah Kelly Rojack* • Janet Leigh *Cherry McMahon* • Barry Sullivan *Roberts* • Lloyd Nolan *Barney Kelly* • Murray Hamilton *Arthur Kabot* • JD Cannon *Sergeant Leznicki* • Susan Denberg *Ruta* ■ *Dir* Robert Gist • *Scr* Mann Rubin, from the novel by Norman Mailer

American Dreamer ★★★ PG

Comedy adventure
1984 · US · Colour · 105mins

JoBeth Williams throws herself into the part of a bored housewife who bumps her head and regains consciousness convinced that she is the heroine of her own thrill-a-minute tale of romance and intrigue. Tom Conti perhaps overdoes the bemusement as the man she insists is her faithful sidekick, but Giancarlo Giannini looks suitably shifty as her supposed adversary. An enjoyable, sprightly comedy. DP

JoBeth Williams *Cathy Palmer/Rebecca Ryan* • Tom Conti *Alan McMann* • Giancarlo Giannini *Victor Marchand* • Coral Browne *Margaret McMann* • James Staley *Kevin Palmer* • CD Barnes [Christopher Daniel Barnes] *Kevin Palmer Jr* • Huckleberry Fox *Karl Palmer* • Pierre Santini *Klaus* ■ *Dir* Rick Rosenthal • *Scr* Jim Kouf, David Greenwalt, from a story by Ann Biderman

American Flyers ★★ PG

Action drama 1985 · US · Colour · 107mins

This tale of rival cycling siblings competing in a Rocky Mountains endurance race is complicated by David Grant's antagonism towards his sports doctor older brother Kevin Costner. Other distractions in the plot are an anti-Soviet diversion and a terminal illness that Grant may be suffering from. Writer Steve Tesich achieved better results with his more successful *Breaking Away*. TH. Contains swearing and brief nudity.

Kevin Costner *Marcus Sommers* • David Grant [David Marshall Grant] *David Sommers* • Rae Dawn Chong *Sarah* • Alexandra Paul *Becky* • Luca Bercovici *Muzzin* • Robert Townsend *Jerome* • John Amos *Dr Conrad* • John Garber *Belov* • Janice Rule *Mrs Sommers* • Jennifer Grey *Leslie* ■ *Dir* John Badham • *Scr* Steve Tesich

The American Friend ★★★★ 15

Crime drama
1977 · W Ger/Fr · Colour · 120mins

There are enough *film noir* tricks and dark philosophical insights in this adaptation of Patricia Highsmith's *Ripley's Game* for German director Wim Wenders to turn a bleak road movie into a dazzling psychological thriller. Bruno Ganz is the simple Swiss picture framer who, believing he's dying from a blood disease, is lured into killing Mafia kingpins by shady loner Dennis Hopper. Soon the two men from opposite ends of the human spectrum bond, allowing Wenders to explore his existentialist subtext with exciting wit and enjoyable wisdom. The film features cameos from directors Samuel Fuller and Nicholas Ray, to whom Wenders pays visual homage. AJ DVD

Dennis Hopper *Ripley* • Bruno Ganz *Jonathan Zimmermann* • Lisa Kreuzer *Marianne Zimmermann* • Gérard Blain *Raoul Minot* • Nicholas Ray *Derwatt* • Samuel Fuller *American mobster* • Peter Lilienthal *Marcangelo* • Daniel Schmid *Ingraham* ■ *Dir* Wim Wenders • *Scr* Wim Wenders, from the novel *Ripley's Game* by Patricia Highsmith • *Cinematographer* Robby Müller

American Friends ★★★ PG

Romantic drama 1991 · UK · Colour · 91mins

In this delightful, understated personal project, Michael Palin stars as a romantically awkward Oxford don, a character allegedly based on his great-grandfather. The stuffy, frock-coated formality of Victorian varsity life is atmospherically conjured up and the insightful script, co-written by director Tristram Powell and Palin, is used to good effect. There are also some lovely performances, particularly from Trini Alvarado as Palin's bouncy teenage love interest and a consummate Connie Booth as her guardian. SH. Contains nudity. [VIDEO]

Michael Palin *Rev Francis Ashby* • Connie Booth *Miss Caroline Hartley* • Trini Alvarado *Miss Elinor Hartley* • Alfred Molina *Oliver Syme* • David Calder *Pollitt* • Simon Jones *Anderson* • Robert Eddison *Rushden* • Alun Armstrong *Dr Weeks* • Sheila Reid *Mrs Weeks* • Edward Rawle-Hicks *John Weeks* • Roger Lloyd Pack *Dr Butler* • Jonathan Firth *Cable* ■ *Dir* Tristram Powell • *Scr* Michael Palin, Tristram Powell

American Gigolo ★★★ 18

Erotic thriller 1980 · US · Colour · 111mins

Richard Gere romped his way to stardom in this glossy and controversial (for its time) story of a Los Angeles stud who services the bored wives of Beverly Hills. His detached view of life is threatened, however, when he gets caught up in murder and politics. This is probably still director Paul Schrader's biggest hit but it hasn't dated well – it's a beautifully designed but ultimately transparent walk on the wild side. JF. Contains swearing, sex scenes and nudity. [VIDEO] DVD

Richard Gere *Julian Kay* • Lauren Hutton *Michelle Stratton* • Hector Elizondo *Detective Sunday* • Nina Van Pallandt *Anne* • Bill Duke *Leon Jaimes* • Brian Davies *Charles Stratton* • Patti Carr *Judy Rheiman* • Tom Stewart *Mr Rheiman* ■ *Dir/Scr* Paul Schrader

American Gothic ★ 18

Horror 1987 · UK/Can · Colour · 88mins

An uneasy mix of old-fashioned off-screen splatter and humour that's supposed to be black (but ends up being merely ludicrous), this vaguely sick shocker is the worst movie from British-born horror director John Hough. Rod Steiger and Yvonne De Carlo are backwoods nutcases who live on a remote island with their three mentally handicapped adult children. The suspense refuses to build from the moment six campers arrive on the island and become their victims. AJ

Rod Steiger *Pa* • Yvonne De Carlo *Ma* • Sarah Torgov *Cynthia* • Michael J Pollard *Woody* • Fiona Hutchison *Lynn* • William Hootkins *Teddy* ■ *Dir* John Hough • *Scr* John Hough, Terry Lens, Bert Wetanson, Michael Vines

American Graffiti ★★★★★ PG

Comedy drama 1973 · US · Colour · 107mins

A summer night in the lives of a group of small-town Californian teenagers following their graduation from high school in 1962 is brilliantly captured by director George Lucas in this classic coming-of-age saga that virtually invented juke-box nostalgia. Based on Lucas's own youthful exploits, the golden oldie soundtrack is a perfect counterpoint to the sharp and tender comedy, engagingly played by Richard Dreyfuss and Ronny (Ron) Howard, two of a number of future stars in the cast. Wonderfully evoking the feel and spirit of the era, this is one of those rare movies you live through rather than watch. An inferior sequel, *More American Graffiti*, followed in 1979. AJ. Contains swearing. [VIDEO] DVD

Richard Dreyfuss *Curt Henderson* • Ronny Howard [Ron Howard] *Steve Bolander* • Paul Le Mat *John Milner* • Charles Martin Smith *Terry Fields* • Cindy Williams *Laurie* • Candy Clark *Debbie* • Mackenzie Phillips *Carol* • Wolfman Jack *Disc jockey* • Harrison Ford *Bob Falfa* • Bo Hopkins *Joe* • Manuel Padilla Jr *Carlos* ■ *Dir* George Lucas • *Scr* George Lucas, Gloria Katz, Willard Huyck

An American Guerrilla in the Philippines ★★ U

Second World War action adventure
1950 · US · Colour · 103mins

Retitled *I Shall Return* for the UK market, this ultra-patriotic flag-waver is almost unwatchable today, save for the striking Technicolor and the star presence of Tyrone Power, whose dramatic energy alone goes a long way to saving the Filipinos, as he shows them how to build radio stations and organise their resistance against the Japanese. Despite its pacey action sequences, this is rather too slow. TS

Tyrone Power *Ensign Chuck Palmer* • Micheline Presle *Jeanne Martinez* • Tom Ewell *Jim Mitchell* • Bob Patten *Lovejoy* • Tommy Cook *Miguel* • Juan Torena *Juan Martinez* • Jack Elam *Speaker* • Robert Barrat *General Douglas Macarthur* • Carleton Young *Colonel Phillips* ■ *Dir* Fritz Lang • *Scr* Lamar Trotti, from the novel by Ira Wolfert

American Gun ★★★ 15

Murder mystery drama
2002 · US · BW and Colour · 85mins

James Coburn gives his final film more than it deserves. It's a steely investigation into the nature of violent crime in the United States, with Coburn as the father who decides to trace the history of the .357 magnum that killed his daughter (Virginia Madsen) on the streets of his Vermont home. Some of the encounters feel contrived, but the monochrome flashbacks to Coburn's encounters with guns during his childhood and in the Second World War are evocatively staged. DP. Contains swearing, violence and drug abuse.. [VIDEO] DVD

James Coburn *Martin* • Barbara Bain *Anne* • Virginia Madsen *Penny* • Alexandra Holden *Mia* ■ *Dir/Scr* Alan Jacobs

American Heart ★★ 15

Drama 1992 · US · Colour · 114mins

Top-class performances by Jeff Bridges and Edward Furlong add a glossy sheen to this two-dimensional material from Peter Silverman, a writer on the TV shows *Hill Street Blues* and *Moonlighting*. Bridges plays a no-hope drifter who, when released from prison, tries bonding with his alienated teenage son (Furlong), with tragic results. By turns poignant, hard-hitting and annoying, it's only the stars who make director Martin Bell's strained relationship movie work. AJ [VIDEO]

Jeff Bridges *Jack Kelson* • Edward Furlong *Nick Kelson* • Lucinda Jenney *Charlotte* • Don Harvey *Rainey* • Tracey Kapisky *Molly* • Shareen Mitchell *Diane* • Christian Frizzell *Rollie* • Maggie Welsh *Freddie* ■ *Dir* Martin Bell • *Scr* Peter Silverman, from a story by Martin Bell, Peter Silverman, Mary Ellen Mark

American History X ★★★★ 18

Drama 1998 · US · Colour and BW · 113mins

Director Tony Kaye's tough, powerful and uncompromising cautionary tale takes a brutal look at the depths of racial prejudice and the roots of violent hate crimes. Teenager Edward Furlong has been keeping the faith of his older brother Edward Norton, a neo-Nazi white supremacist recently released from jail. However, Norton has undergone a radical transformation through his friendship with a black prison inmate and the moral clarity of solitude. Told in colour with black-and-white flashbacks, Kaye's cutting-edge treatise is a shock to the system filled with unforgettable moments, seriously handled issues and superb acting by Norton, who was deservedly Oscar-nominated. AJ. Contains swearing, nudity and violence. [VIDEO] DVD

Edward Norton *Derek Vinyard* • Edward Furlong *Danny Vinyard* • Beverly D'Angelo *Doris Vinyard* • Jennifer Lien *Davina Vinyard* • Ethan Suplee *Seth* • Fairuza Balk *Stacey* • Avery Brooks *Dr Robert Sweeney* • Elliott Gould *Murray* • Stacy Keach *Cameron Alexander* ■ *Dir* Tony Kaye • *Scr* David McKenna

American Hot Wax ★★★

Biographical drama
1977 · US · Colour · 91mins

DJ Alan Freed was the man credited with introducing white American teenagers to the sounds that their parents considered the Devil's music. With Tim McIntire solid enough as "the Pied Piper of Rock 'n' Roll", this pleasing pop picture makes a fair fist of re-creating the era. You can forgive director Floyd Mutrux for calling on the services of Chuck Berry and Jerry Lee Lewis, but, while their music might be timeless, they are not, and their obvious age and over-polished performances detract from the aura of amateur authenticity. DP

Tim McIntire *Alan Freed* • Fran Drescher *Sheryl* • Jay Leno *Mookie* • Laraine Newman *Louise* • Jeff Altman *Lennie Richfield* • Moosie Drier *Artie Moress* • John Lehne *District Attorney Coleman* • Stewart Steinberg *Stone* ■ *Dir* Floyd Mutrux • *Scr* John Kaye, Art Linson, from a story by John Kaye

An American in Paris ★★★★ U

Musical 1951 · US · Colour · 108mins

This archetypal glamorous MGM musical was the deserved winner of six Oscars, including best picture, collected by genius producer Arthur Freed, with a special Oscar presented to star Gene Kelly for advancing the art of choreography on screen. It still looks pretty good today, with marvellous Technicolored design, athletic dancing from Kelly and a superb Gershwin score, but some sequences have dated. The climactic 17-minute ballet on the theme of the French Impressionists is a little precious and over-staged by today's standards, but much of the movie remains delightful. TS [VIDEO] DVD

Gene Kelly *Jerry Mulligan* • Leslie Caron *Lise* • Oscar Levant *Adam Cook* • Georges Guetary *Henri Baurel* • Nina Foch *Milo Roberts* • Eugene Borden *George Mattieu* • Martha Bamattre *Mathilde Mattieu* ■ *Dir* Vincente Minnelli • *Scr* Alan Jay Lerner • *Cinematographer* John Alton, Alfred Gilks • *Art Director* Cedric Gibbons, Preston Ames • *Costume Designer* Walter Plunkett, Irene Sharaff, Orry-Kelly

American Madness ★★★ U

Period drama 1932 · US · BW · 73mins

Frank Capra was a master of the "feel-good factor", long before the phrase was coined. Populist and simplistic it may be, but this dry run for the financial dilemma of *It's a Wonderful Life* is one of his American fantasies, showing how the "little people" can save big institutions. All bank bosses are perhaps not as dynamic as Walter Huston's, and it's unlikely that small depositors would rally round in real life as they do here, but with Capra you take it on trust. TH [VIDEO]

Walter Huston *Thomas Dickson* • Pat O'Brien *Matt* • Kay Johnson *Mrs Dickson* • Constance Cummings *Helen* • Gavin Gordon *Cluett* ■ *Dir* Frank Capra • *Scr* Robert Riskin

American Me ★★★ 18

Drama 1992 · US · Colour · 120mins

This vivid exploration of three generations of a Hispanic-American family growing up in violence-torn Los Angeles marks the directing debut of actor Edward James Olmos. Low self-esteem and abject poverty inspire the criminal behaviour of Santana, a Chicano underworld kingpin whom Olmos plays as an adult. Against the background of the 1943 Pachuco riots, Santana controls the streets from behind bars in this fact-based drama. Olmos gives the action a brutally violent and raw realism. AJ [VIDEO]

Edward James Olmos *Santana* • William Forsythe *JD* • Pepe Serna *Mundo* • Danny De La Paz *Puppet* • Evelina Fernandez *Julie* • Cary-Hiroyuki Tagawa *El Japo* • Daniel Villarreal *Little Puppet* ■ *Dir* Edward James Olmos • *Scr* Floyd Mutrux, Desmond Nakano, from a story by Floyd Mutrux, Desmond Nakano

American Movie ★★★ 15

Comedy documentary
1999 · US · Colour · 100mins

Wanna make a movie? It's easy, provided you have the patience of Job, a determination bordering on the demented and an 82-year-old uncle with more cents than sense. Less fly-on-the-wall than bug-on-the-rug, Chris Smith's documentary chronicles Wisconsin wannabe Mark Borchardt's production of a cheesy-looking horror short pic called *Coven*, made towards the end of his six-year struggle to fund and film his first feature. This is an intriguing, if overlong insight into the trials and tribulations of no-budget film-making. DA. Contains swearing.

Dir Chris Smith • *Music* Mike Schank

The American Nightmare ★★★★ 18

Documentary
2000 · US/UK · Colour and BW · 70mins

Referencing such horror classics as George Romero's *Night of the Living Dead*, Tobe Hooper's *The Texas Chainsaw Massacre* and David Cronenberg's *Shivers*, this unflinching documentary from Adam Simon wipes away the gore to reveal the dark underside of American society that inspired them. It's hardly revelatory to blame the sexual revolution, Vietnam, racial tension and Watergate for the moral breakdown that fostered the spirit of suspicion and fear that fed these films, but Simon's selection of clips and interviews skilfully supports the thesis. There's a touch too much hindsight, perhaps, but it's still gripping stuff. DP [VIDEO] DVD

Dir/Scr Adam Simon

American Ninja ★★ 18

Martial arts action adventure
1985 · US · Colour · 91mins

At one time Michael Dudikoff was seen as a successor to Chuck Norris, and was a big favourite on tape at the height of the 1980s video boom. This was the one that made his name, and went on to spawn a fair few sequels, most of which didn't stray too far from the blueprint established here. There are some nice fight scenes, but the acting is about as mindless as the action sequences. Dudikoff returned for the first sequel, but not the three others that followed. JF [VIDEO] DVD

Michael Dudikoff *Joe* • Guich Koock *Hickock* • Judie Aronson *Patricia* • Steve James (1) *Jackson* • Don Stewart *Ortega* • John LaMotta *Rinaldo* ■ *Dir* Sam Firstenberg • *Scr* Paul de Mielche, from a story by Avi Kleinberger, Gideon Amir

American Outlaws ★★★ 12

Comedy western 2001 · US · Colour · 90mins

This cowboy film features young gunslingers who would seem more at home popping pimples than pumping pistols – even when they're up against land-grabbing railroad barons. It's yet another re-telling of the Jesse James story, with Colin Farrell as Jesse and Scott Caan as partner Cole Younger. Director Les Mayfield may portray them as mere run-of-the-mill Robin Hoods, but this is all about attracting the *Dawson's Creek* crowd into the cinema. There's welcome support from Kathy Bates and Timothy Dalton. TH. Contains swearing, violence. [VIDEO] DVD

Colin Farrell (2) *Jesse James* • Scott Caan *Cole Younger* • Ali Larter *Zee Mimms* •

Gabriel Macht *Frank James* • Harris Yulin *Thaddeus Rains* • Kathy Bates *Ma James* • Timothy Dalton *Allan Pinkerton* ■ *Dir* Les Mayfield • *Scr* Roderick Taylor, John Rogers, from a story by Roderick Taylor

American Perfekt ★★★ 15

Psychological thriller
1997 · US · Colour · 99mins

The one-letter misspelling in the title of this weird road movie aims to convey the imperfections of the American Dream. Amanda Plummer has a bizarre accident on her way to the town of Peachblossom. Rescued by Robert Forster, a doctor, she then hitches a lift from David Thewlis. As Plummer's sister Fairuza Balk tries to re-trace her movements the plot corkscrews into mania and murder. Terrific performances add colour and momentum, but Paul Chart's lacklustre direction blunts the point and slackens the tension. TH. Contains violence, a sex scene, swearing, nudity. DVD

Robert Forster *Dr Jake Gordon Nyman* • Amanda Plummer *Sandra Thomas* • Fairuza Balk *Alice Thomas* • David Thewlis *Ernest Santini* • Paul Sorvino *Sheriff Frank Noonan* • Geoffrey Lewis *Willy* • Chris Sarandon *Deputy Sheriff Sammy Goodall* • Joanna Gleason *Shirley Dutton* • Jay Patterson *Bernie* ■ *Dir/Scr* Paul Chart

American Pie ★★★★ 15

Comedy 1999 · US · Colour · 91mins

If you thought *Dumb and Dumber* or *There's Something about Mary* plumbed the depths of grossness, hold on to your lunch – you ain't seen nothing yet. This laughter-packed comedy about four teenage boys who pledge to lose their virginity before prom night has enough crass gags to satisfy the most demanding farce fans. Yet it also boasts some spot-on performances from a hip young cast that includes Chris Klein, Mena Suvari, Tara Reid and Natasha Lyonne. Must-see fare for those not easily offended. JB. Contains swearing, sex scenes and nudity. DVD

Jason Biggs *Jim Levenstein* • Chris Klein *Chris "Oz" Ostreicher* • Natasha Lyonne *Jessica* • Thomas Ian Nicholas *Kevin Myers* • Tara Reid *Vicky* • Mena Suvari *Heather* • Eugene Levy *Jim's dad* • Eddie Kaye Thomas *Paul Finch* • Jennifer Coolidge *Stifler's mom* • Seann W Scott [Seann William Scott] *Stifler* • Alyson Hannigan *Michelle Flaherty* ■ *Dir* Paul Weitz • *Scr* Adam Herz

American Pie 2 ★★★ 15

Comedy 2001 · US · Colour · 100mins

Bawdy comedy *American Pie* was an unexpected success in 1999 and the whole cast returned for this sequel. The humour remains the same – rude, crude and lewd – as the gang gets together for lots of beer and sex at a beach house following their first year in college. Sure, the comedy here isn't sophisticated and it's often predictable, but if someone supergluеing his hand to his, erm, member gets you giggling, you'll be laughing too much to notice. JB DVD

Jason Biggs *Jim Levenstein* • Shannon Elizabeth *Nadia* • Alyson Hannigan *Michelle Flaherty* • Chris Klein *Chris "Oz" Ostreicher* • Natasha Lyonne *Jessica* • Thomas Ian Nicholas *Kevin Myers* • Tara Reid *Vicky* • Seann William Scott *Stifler* • Mena Suvari *Heather* • Eugene Levy *Jim's dad* ■ *Dir* James B Rogers • *Scr* Adam Herz, from a story by David H Steinberg, Adam Herz, from characters created by Adam Herz

American Pie: the Wedding ★★★ 15

Comedy 2003 · US/Ger · Colour · 99mins

For some, these adolescent sex comedies are the living proof of how popular cinema has plumbed new depths in taste. For others, they are worthy successors to the classic John Hughes teen-fests of the 1980s. Here, series regulars Jim (Jason Biggs) and Michelle (Alyson Hannigan) attempt to tie the knot. Writer Adam Herz delivers the familiar recipe of successively unpleasant set pieces, together with a shamelessly upbeat and sentimental ending. AS. Contains swearing, sex scenes and nudity. DVD

Jason Biggs *Jim Levenstein* • Alyson Hannigan *Michelle Flaherty* • January Jones *Cadence Flaherty* • Thomas Ian Nicholas *Kevin Myers* • Seann William Scott *Steve Stifler* • Eddie Kaye Thomas *Paul Finch* • Fred Willard *Harold Flaherty* • Eugene Levy *Jim's dad* • Molly Cheek *Jim's mom* ■ *Dir* Jesse Dylan • *Scr* Adam Herz, from his characters

American Pimp ★★★

Documentary 1999 · US · Colour · 86mins

Whether you view Albert and Allen Hughes's documentary as a capitalist allegory or an indictment of the cultural stereotyping of African-Americans, the thing that emerges most clearly is that women are at the bottom of the heap. The attitudes of the pimps become apparent with very little external interference, as they juxtapose outrageously chauvinistic utterances with street situations that depict them as somewhere between blaxploitation characters and rappers. The closing sequences are laced with irony as the pimps' use of smug socio-economic arguments to justify their trade reveals it as callous oppression. DP

Dir Albert Hughes, Allen Hughes

The American President ★★★★ 15

Romantic comedy
1995 · US · Colour · 109mins

A gleaming, witty and irresistible romantic comedy, this was one of several White House-based movies made in the wake of Bill Clinton's election. Michael Douglas is the recently widowed president, the father of a young daughter and in need of female company at official functions. Annette Bening, an eco-lobbyist, fits the bill and, after he dances with her in public, the press go into speculative overdrive. Douglas walks and talks presidentially, while Bening is also terrific. Written by Aaron Sorkin, who went on to create TV's *The West Wing*. AT. Contains swearing. DVD

Michael Douglas *Andrew Shepherd* • Annette Bening *Sydney Ellen Wade* • Michael J Fox *Lewis Rothschild* • David Paymer *Leon Kodak* • Martin Sheen *AJ MacInerney* • Anna Deavere Smith *Robin McCall* • Samantha Mathis *Janie Basdin* • Richard Dreyfuss *Senator Rumson* • John Mahoney *Leo Solomon* • Shawna Waldron *Lucy Shepherd* ■ *Dir* Rob Reiner • *Scr* Aaron Sorkin

American Psycho ★★★★ 18

Satirical black comedy drama
2000 · US/Can · Colour · 97mins

Director Mary Harron fought for Christian Bale to play Bret Easton Ellis's smooth yuppie killer and her decision is totally vindicated. Bale is brilliant as the wealthy, successful and psychotic Patrick Bateman. Despite the novel's skin-crawling reputation, most of the violence takes place off-screen. Moreover, the film's satirical swipes at the materialistic 1980s provide laughs amid the carnage, as does Bale's cheesy, game-show host delivery of Bateman's eccentric cultural observations. Aside from a graphic threesome, this is an admirably restrained adaptation, although its cold, aloof tone lessens the impact of Bateman's actions. JC. Contains violence, swearing, sex scenes, drug abuse and nudity. DVD

Christian Bale *Patrick Bateman* • Willem Dafoe *Donald Kimball* • Jared Leto *Paul Allen* • Reese Witherspoon *Evelyn Williams* • Samantha Mathis *Courtney Rawlinson* • Chloe Sevigny [Chloë Sevigny] *Jean* • Justin Theroux *Timothy Bryce* ■ *Dir* Mary Harron • *Scr* Guinevere Turner, Mary Harron, from the novel by Bret Easton Ellis • *Music* John Cale

American Psycho II: All American Girl ★★ 18

Black comedy horror thriller
2002 · US/Can · Colour · 84mins

This slipshod sequel has very little to do with Mary Harron's adaptation of Bret Easton Ellis's infamous novel. Mila Kunis stars as a girl who, as a child, supposedly slayed the murderous Patrick Bateman, and has become unhealthily fascinated by serial killers. But in chronicling her ruthless bid to become ex-FBI agent William Shatner's teaching assistant, director Morgan J Freeman too often replaces the original's satire with a clumsy brand of gross-out black comedy. DP. Contains violence, swearing. DVD

Mila Kunis *Rachael Newman* • Geraint Wyn Davies *Dr Eric Daniels* • William Shatner *Robert Starkman* • Robin Dunne *Brian Leads* • Lindy Booth *Cassandra Blaire* • Charles Officer *Keith Lawson* ■ *Dir* Morgan J Freeman • *Scr* Karen Craig, Alex Sanger

An American Rhapsody ★★

Drama 2001 · US · Colour and BW · 106mins

Writer/director Eva Gardos charts her amazing life in this careful, but controlled autobiography. The opening section focuses on her parents' escape (without her) from Communist Hungary and her itinerant, but contented existence in the tranquil countryside. But after they've summoned her to the United States, the emphasis shifts to her feuds with her over-compensating mother and the lack of chemistry between Nastassja Kinski and Scarlett Johansson reduces the emotional *frisson* to teleplay melodramatics. DP

Nastassja Kinski *Margit* • Scarlett Johansson *Suzanne* • Tony Goldwyn *Peter* • Mae Whitman *Maria* • Agnes Banfalvy *Helen* • Zoltan Seress *George* ■ *Dir/Scr* Eva Gardos

An American Romance ★★ U

Drama 1944 · US · Colour · 150mins

This epic film by the great pioneering director of the American cinema, King Vidor, is impressive in both scale and technical expertise. Unfortunately, the tale of a European immigrant's rise to the top of industry is an extraordinarily dull affair, curiously devoid of drama or passion. The lead roles are played by the competent but uncharismatic Brian Donlevy and unknown Australian Ann Richards, neither of whose shoulders are big enough to shoulder the weight. RK

Brian Donlevy *Steve Dangos* • Ann Richards *Anna* • Walter Abel *Howard Clinton* • John Qualen *Anton Dubechek* ■ *Dir* King Vidor • *Scr* Herbert Dalmas, William Ludwig, from a story by King Vidor

The American Soldier ★★★★ 15

Crime drama 1970 · W Ger · BW · 76mins

A homage to the visual style of American gangster movies, this is often regarded as the prototype Fassbinder film. Bordering on pastiche, it follows Vietnam veteran Karl Scheydt as he assassinates a gypsy rent boy, a pornographer and his own girlfriend before being wiped out by corrupt cops. Fassbinder was clearly more interested in creating a mood and referencing such film-makers as Samuel Fuller and Rosa von Praunheim than storytelling or social analysis. Yet this brooding non-drama is still highly revelatory of the director's preoccupations: sex and violence are chillingly equated, while emotion and morality are dismissed as fatal flaws. DP. In German with English subtitles.

Karl Scheydt *Ricky* • Elga Sorbas *Rosa von Praunheim* • Jan George *Jan* • Margarethe von Trotta *Maid* • Hark Bohm *Doc* • Ingrid Caven *Singer* • Eva-Ingeborg Scholz *Ricky's mother* • Kurt Raab *Ricky's brother* • Rainer Werner Fassbinder *Franz Walsh* • Ulli Lommel *Gypsy* ■ *Dir/Scr* Rainer Werner Fassbinder

American Splendor ★★★★ 15

Biographical drama
2003 · US · Colour · 97mins

The mundane life of a working-class everyman is celebrated in all its minor detail in this imaginative biopic of American underground comic-book writer Harvey Pekar. It brilliantly captures the humanity and acidic humour of the Cleveland hospital filing clerk who turned his everyday experiences into a cult, autobiographical publication. As well as including authentic archival footage, the directors present the curmudgeonly author in animated form, as his real-life self and, in the picture's main body, as a dramatised character. The combined result is a total delight. SF. Contains swearing. DVD

Paul Giamatti *Harvey Pekar* • Hope Davis *Joyce Brabner* • James Urbaniak *Robert Crumb* • Judah Friedlander *Toby Radloff* • Earl Billings *Mr Boats* • James McCaffrey *Fred* ■ *Dir* Shari Springer Berman, Robert Pulcini • *Scr* Shari Springer Berman, from the comic-book series by Harvey Pekar, from the comic book *Our Cancer Year* by Harvey Pekar, Joyce Brabner

American Strays ★★★

Black comedy crime thriller
1996 · US · Colour · 93mins

Occupying the same surreal niche as the offbeat work of David Lynch, this is a mordantly funny and intensely bizarre study of the meaning of life – and death. It all revolves around Red's Desert Oasis diner, where surly waitress Jennifer Tilly dishes up the very average food and where strangers, travelling salesmen and drifters meet their destinies in anything but average ways. This is a compelling – if perplexing – mystery. Violent and hilarious, it is always intriguing and often likeable. AJ

Jennifer Tilly *Patty Mae* • Eric Roberts *Martin* • John Savage *Dwayne* • Luke Perry *Johnny* • Carol Kane *Helen* • Joe Viterelli *Gene* • James Russo *Harv* • Vonte Sweet *Mondo* • Sam Jones *Exterminator* ■ *Dir/Scr* Michael Covert

The American Success Company ★★

Black comedy drama
1979 · US · Colour · 90mins

Corporate drone Jeff Bridges gives the "success at any price" business world a taste of its own medicine in this offbeat black comedy about ethics and karma. Director William Richert's follow-up to *Winter Kills* is wildly uneven and caustically toned in a way some may find off-putting. When he does hit his targets, however, Richert really pulls no punches. Bianca Jagger's name in the cast list might give you some idea of just how quirky this American Dream satire is. AJ

Jeff Bridges *Harry* • Belinda Bauer *Sarah* • Ned Beatty *Mr Elliot* • Steven Keats *Rick Duprez* • Bianca Jagger *Corinne* • John Glover *Ernst* • Mascha Gonska *Greta* • Michael Durrell *Herman* ■ *Dir* William Richert • *Scr* William Richert, Larry Cohen, from a story by Larry Cohen • *Music* Maurice Jarre

An American Tail ★★★★ U

Animated adventure
1986 · US · Colour · 77mins

Directed by ex-Disney animator Don Bluth and with Steven Spielberg as co-executive producer, this handsome feature has the look and feel of a master cartoonist at work. It's the story of the Mousekewitz family who leave 1880s Russia for the United States because they've heard that the country has no cats and the streets are paved with cheese. This ties in nicely with Bluth's stunning animation and, in true Disney tradition, the Oscar-nominated song *Somewhere Out There* is a major highlight. Children everywhere will love it. DP

Phillip Glasser *Fievel* • Dom DeLuise *Tiger* • Nehemiah Persoff *Papa Mousekewitz* • Erica Yohn *Mama Mousekewitz* • Madeline Kahn *Gussie Mausheimer* • Christopher Plummer *Henri* • Cathianne Blore *Bridget* ■ *Dir* Don Bluth • *Scr* Judy Freudberg, Tony Geiss, from a story by David Kirschner, Judy Freudberg, Tony Geiss

An American Tail: Fievel Goes West ★★ U

Animated adventure
1991 · US · Colour · 71mins

This lacklustre feature following the further adventures of Fievel, the little Russian immigrant mouse. The storyline is practically nonexistent, the songs are unimaginative, and the animation could easily have been done in the 1940s, such is its flat traditionalism. That said, the voiceovers of James Stewart, John Cleese and Dom DeLuise are excellent and they alone earn this poor production its second star. DP

Phillip Glasser *Fievel* • James Stewart *Wylie Burp* • Erica Yohn *Mama Mousekewitz* • John Cleese *Cat R Waul* • Dom DeLuise *Tiger* • Jon Lovitz *TR Chula* • Amy Irving *Miss Kitty* • Nehemiah Persoff *Papa Mousekewitz* • Cathy Cavadini *Tanya Mousekewitz* ■ *Dir* Phil Nibbelink, Simon Wells • *Scr* Flint Dille, from the story by Charles Swenson, from characters created by David Kirschner

An American Tail: the Treasure of Manhattan Island ★★ U

Animated adventure
1998 · US · Colour · 75mins

For all their noble intentions, the first two Fievel movies had a tendency to lay on their message of racial harmony with a trowel. In an increasingly multicultural world, such lessons in tolerance are invaluable, but the solemn sense of decent citizenship borders on the sanctimonious in this direct-to-video offering. Tiny tots will enjoy the story, which sees the immigrant mouse join forces with a band of indigenous rodents to protect a stash of treasure from some avaricious industrialists. DP

Thomas Dekker *Fievel* • Dom DeLuise *Tiger* • Pat Musick *Tony* • Nehemiah Persoff *Papa* • Erica Yohn *Mama* • Lacey Chabert *Tanya* • Ron Perlman *Grasping* • René Auberjonois *Dr Dithering* • David Carradine *Wulisso* ■ *Dir* Larry Latham • *Scr* Len Uhley, from characters created by David Kirschner

An American Tail: the Mystery of the Night Monster ★★ U

Animated adventure
2000 · US · Colour · 72mins

Disappointingly, the fourth adventure featuring Fievel the immigrant mouse contains a number of flagrant racial stereotypes. Moreover, it also includes three dreadful songs and a transparently obvious mystery. Along with his faithful buddies Tony and Tiger, Fievel allies with *The Daily Nibbler*'s ace reporter, Nelly Brie, to investigate a sinister series of mouse-nappings. DP

Thomas Dekker *Fievel Mousekewitz* • Robert Hays *Reed Daley* • Susan Boyd *Nellie Brie* • Pat Musick *Tony Toponi* • Candi Milo *Madame Mousey* • Nehemiah Persoff *Papa Mousekewitz* • Jane Singer *Mama Mousekewitz* • Dom DeLuise *Tiger* • Lacey Chabert *Tanya* ■ *Dir* Larry Latham • *Scr* Len Uhley

An American Tragedy ★★★

Romantic melodrama
1931 · US · BW · 96mins

This is the first film version of Theodore Dreiser's novel about a social climber who murders his pregnant low-born sweetheart when a society girl makes eyes at him. The story is a classic critique of the American Dream, so Hollywood bravely imported the Soviet Union's greatest director and chief propagandist, Sergei Eisenstein, to write and direct it. But Paramount rejected his script and got Josef von Sternberg to take over, much to Dreiser's fury. Sternberg, of course, treats the story as pure melodrama and it's most notable for Sylvia Sidney's touching performance. Fascinating to compare it to the 1951 remake, *A Place in the Sun*. AT

Phillips Holmes *Clyde Griffiths* • Sylvia Sidney *Roberta Alden* • Frances Dee *Sondra Finchley* • Irving Pichel *Orville Mason* • Frederick Burton *Samuel Griffiths* • Claire McDowell *Mrs Samuel Griffiths* ■ *Dir* Josef von Sternberg • *Scr* Samuel Hoffenstein, from the novel by Theodore Dreiser

An American Werewolf in London ★★★★★ 18

Horror comedy 1981 · US · Colour · 92mins

Director John Landis (*The Blues Brothers*) pulls off the difficult trick of revitalising the horror genre while parodying it at the same time. Funny, scary and extremely gory – Griffin Dunne's gradual decomposition is an absolute hoot – this lycanthropic lampoon is also a splendid satire on British life, as seen through American eyes. The special effects and Rick Baker's Oscar-winning make-up established new trends in monster metamorphoses: after this revolutionary movie, no horror transformation was ever the same again. AJ. Contains violence, swearing, sex scenes and nudity. DVD

David Naughton *David Kessler* • Jenny Agutter *Alex Price* • Griffin Dunne *Jack Goodman* • John Woodvine *Dr Hirsch* • Brian Glover *Chess player* • Rik Mayall *Second chess player* • David Schofield *Darts player* • Lila Kaye *Barmaid* ■ *Dir/Scr* John Landis

An American Werewolf in Paris ★★ 15

Horror comedy
1997 · US/Lux/Fr/UK · Colour · 94mins

Made as a belated sequel to the classic *An American Werewolf in London*, director Anthony Waller's watered-down lycanthrope lampoon is frustratingly devoid of the edgy suspense, biting humour and keen visual style of that comedy horror landmark. Three American students go to Paris to bungee jump off the Eiffel Tower and find themselves inducted into a tortured twilight world. Despite the presence of the lovely Julie Delpy as a werewolf, Waller's low-key special effects extravaganza doesn't have the fairy-tale quality of the original. AJ. Contains violence, swearing and nudity. DVD

Tom Everett Scott *Andy* • Julie Delpy *Sérafine* • Vince Vieluf *Brad* • Phil Buckman *Chris* • Julie Bowen *Amy* • Pierre Cosso *Claude* • Thierry Lhermitte *Dr Pigot* • Tom Novembre *Inspector Leduc* ■ *Dir* Anthony Waller • *Scr* Tim Burns, Tom Stern, Anthony Waller, from characters created by John Landis

American Yakuza ★★ 18

Action 1994 · US · Colour · 95mins

In this hard-edged thriller, Viggo Mortensen is FBI man Nick Davis, dispatched to Los Angeles to infiltrate and dismantle the American arm of the Japanese underworld. Adopted by a powerful crime family, he rises through the ranks. Inevitably, however, he finds his loyalties strained between the forces of law and order, his new-found colleagues in the yakuza and the established Mafia, who don't take kindly to interlopers from the other side of the Pacific. JF DVD

Viggo Mortensen *Nick Davis* • Ryo Ishibashi • Michael Nouri • Robert Forster • Franklyn Ajaye ■ *Dir* Frank Cappello • *Scr* Max Strom, John Allen Nelson

American Yakuza 2: Back to Back ★★★ 18

Action thriller 1996 · US · Colour · 87mins

Outside the presence of the excellent Ryo Ishibashi, this quirky and stylish take on what happens when Japanese gangsters run amok in California bears little resemblance to *American Yakuza* (1994). However, it does feature cult comic and *Police Academy* series regular Bobcat Goldthwait, in a brief but bonkers role as a bank-robbing nutcase. The mood is darkly hip as two yakuza – one with an Elvis fixation, the other (Ishibashi) cool and dangerous – hit town on a revenge mission that is thwarted when Goldthwait takes them and a downbeat cop (Michael Rooker) hostage. Slick, explosive and surprisingly original. JF DVD

Michael Rooker *Bob Malone* • Ryo Ishibashi *Koji* • Danielle Harris *Chelsea* • John Laughlin *Dussecq* • Bobcat Goldthwait *Psycho* • Koh Takasugi *Hideo* • Tim Thomerson *Thomas* • Stephen Furst *Jimmy* • Vincent Schiavelli *Leonardo* ■ *Dir* Roger Nygard • *Scr* Roger Nygard, Lloyd Keith

Americana ★★★ 15

Drama 1981 · US · Colour · 86mins

Shot in 1973, when David Carradine and Barbara Hershey (then known as Seagull) were in the middle of their torrid affair, this allegory on faith, morality and the American Way lay in the vaults for several years before post-production was completed. Although some of its relevance had, by then, been lost, there is still much to admire in this portrait of Mid-West, small-town life. Carradine is laudably restrained as the Vietnam veteran who arouses the ire of the locals when he decides to recondition a neglected merry-go-round. As the director, his camera strategies are less inhibited, while Hershey's mute flittings are more irritating than enigmatic. DP

David Carradine *Soldier* • Barbara Seagull [Barbara Hershey] *Girl* • Michael Greene *Garage man* • John Blyth Barrymore *Jack* • Greg Walker *Greg* ■ *Dir* David Carradine • *Scr* Richard Carr, David Carradine, from the novel *The Perfect Round* by Henry Morton Robinson

The Americanization of Emily ★★★★

Comedy drama 1964 · US · BW · 115mins

A surprisingly acerbic and adult comedy from the usually glossy MGM studio. Shot in England and written by the brilliant Paddy Chayefsky from the William Bradford Huie novel, it's magnificently cast. Julie Andrews, in arguably her finest screen role, stars as an English war widow given to comforting US servicemen. James Garner is the cynically treated Yank coward to whom Julie ministers, and the superb supporting players include a very funny James Coburn, obsessed admiral Melvyn Douglas, plus the venerable Joyce Grenfell, perfectly cast as Julie's mum. This is director Arthur Hiller's best work, and his own personal favourite. TS

James Garner *Lt Cmdr Charles Madison* • Julie Andrews *Emily Barham* • Melvyn Douglas *Admiral William Jessup* • James Coburn *Lt Cmdr "Bus" Cummings* • Joyce Grenfell *Mrs Barham* • Liz Fraser *Sheila* • Edward Binns *Admiral Thomas Healy* • Keenan Wynn *Old sailor* • William Windom *Capt Harry Spaulding* ■ *Dir* Arthur Hiller • *Scr* Paddy Chayefsky, from the novel by William Bradford Huie

The Americano ★★ PG

Western 1955 · US · Colour · 81mins

Glenn Ford goes down South America way and meets Frank Lovejoy and Cesar Romero in this amiable western variant, though the Brazilian setting that was a novelty when the film came out may well have lost its appeal by now. Ford's attractive naturalistic style would soon turn him into one of Hollywood's biggest stars. TS

Glenn Ford *Sam Dent* • Frank Lovejoy *Bento Hermanny* • Cesar Romero *Manoel* • Ursula Thiess *Marianna Figuerido* • Abbe Lane *Teresa* • Rodolfo Hoyos Jr [Rodolfo Hoyos] *Christino* • Salvador Baguez *Captain Gonzales* ■ *Dir* William Castle • *Scr* Guy Trosper, from a story by Leslie T White

America's Sweethearts ★★★ 12

Romantic comedy
2001 · US · Colour · 98mins

Catherine Zeta-Jones and John Cusack play the Hollywood couple who've split up since making their last film together. Billy Crystal is the film publicist who has to get the estranged couple together for a press junket. What he can't account for is Zeta-Jones's current wild-card boyfriend, Hank Azaria, and Cusack transferring his affections from his superstar wife to her sister and personal assistant, Julia Roberts. It's all very funny in a daft, predictable kind of way, but Crystal's script lacks the bite that could have made it so much better. LH. Contains swearing. DVD

Julia Roberts *Kiki Harrison* • Billy Crystal *Lee Phillips* • Catherine Zeta-Jones *Gwen Harrison* • John Cusack *Eddie Thomas* • Hank Azaria *Hector* • Stanley Tucci *Dave Kingman* • Christopher Walken *Hal Weidmann* • Alan Arkin *Wellness guide* ■ *Dir* Joe Roth • *Scr* Billy Crystal, Peter Tolan

Americathon ★★ PG

Comedy 1979 · US · Colour · 80mins

Despite a talented, eclectic cast and an inspired premise – the United States is now so poor it has to stage a telethon to bail itself out – this has to go down as a major disappointment. Written by Neal Israel, the man who gave the world *Police Academy*, the film lacks the necessary focus and fails to make the most of its satirical promise. Still, there's fun to be had watching Mel Brooks regular Harvey Korman, future chat-show king Jay Leno and Elvis Costello. JF

Peter Riegert *Eric* • Harvey Korman *Monty Rushmore* • Fred Willard *Vanderhoff* • Zane Buzby *Mouling Jackson* • Nancy Morgan *Lucy Beth* • John Ritter *Chet Roosevelt* • Elvis Costello *Earl Manchester* • Jay Leno *Larry Miller* • Meat Loaf *Oklahoma Roy* ■ *Dir* Neal Israel • *Scr* Neal Israel, Michael Mislove, Monica Johnson, from a play by Peter Bergman, Philip Proctor

Le Amiche ★★★★

Drama 1955 · It · BW · 104mins

After enjoying success as a fashion designer in Rome, Eleonora Rossi-Drago returns to her native Turin and becomes involved in the affairs of four of her upper-middle-class girlfriends. Adapted from a story by Cesare Pavese, the film manages to hold ten characters in almost flawless equilibrium, while simultaneously

A

attending to their individuality and oscillating relationships. Michelangelo Antonioni's gift for positioning actors meaningfully against landscapes is well-demonstrated, notably in an extended afternoon beach sequence. The film demonstrates that Antonioni's greatness was already in evidence before the famous *L'Avventura* five years later. RB. In Italian with English subtitles.

Eleonora Rossi-Drago *Clelia* • Valentina Cortese *Nene* • Yvonne Furneaux *Momina De Stefani* • Gabriele Ferzetti *Lorenzo* • Franco Fabrizi *Cesare Pedoni, the architect* • Ettore Manni *Carlo* ■ *Dir* Michelangelo Antonioni • *Scr* Michelangelo Antonioni, Suso Cecchi D'Amico, Alba De Céspedes, from the story *Tra Donne Sole* by Cesare Pavese

La Amiga ★★★

Drama 1988 · Arg/W Ger · Colour · 110mins

Classical myth, Nazi Germany and the Argentinian junta come together in this rather unfocused drama from Jeanine Meerapfel. As children, Liv Ullmann and Cipe Lincovsky wanted to be actresses, but, while the latter gets to play Antigone on stage, the former takes on the role in real life as she becomes a prominent figure in the "Mothers of the Disappeared". The comparison between the two political situations is adequately made, but, for all her good intentions, Meerapfel doesn't always appear to be in control of her material. The performances, however, are strong and assured. DP. In Spanish with English subtitles.

Liv Ullmann *Maria* • Cipe Lincovsky *Raquel* • Federico Luppi *Pancho* • Victor Laplace *Diego* • Harry Baer *Raquel's friend in Berlin* • Lito Cruz *Chief of Police Tito* • Greger Hansen *"Aleman"* • Nicolas Frei *Chief of Special Commandos* ■ *Dir* Jeanine Meerapfel • *Scr* Jeanine Meerapfel, Alcides Chiesa

Amistad ★★★ 15

Historical courtroom drama
1997 · US · Colour · 148mins

In 1839, a shipload of slaves heading for America overpower their captors, killing all but two crew members needed to navigate them back to Africa. Betrayed, intercepted and charged with murder, the slaves' only hope for justice lies with the Abolitionist movement and an inexperienced lawyer. In this lengthy courtroom drama, director Steven Spielberg fails to ignite the same moral outrage his *Schindler's List* poignantly evoked, despite an all-star cast, an amazing debut by Djimon Hounsou (playing the slaves' leader) and moments of pure visual poetry. AJ. Contains violence. [VIDEO] DVD

Anthony Hopkins *John Quincy Adams* • Matthew McConaughey *Roger Baldwin* • Morgan Freeman *Theodore Joadson* • Djimon Hounsou *Sengbe Pieh, "Cinque"* • Nigel Hawthorne *Martin Van Buren* • David Paymer *Secretary Forsyth* • Pete Postlethwaite *Holabird* • Stellan Skarsgård *Tappan* • Anna Paquin *Queen Isabella* • Jeremy Northam *Judge Coglin* ■ *Dir* Steven Spielberg • *Scr* David Franzoni

The Amityville Horror ★★ 15

Supernatural horror
1979 · US · Colour · 113mins

This only marginally watchable schlock horror is based on Jay Anson's allegedly true bestseller about the Lutz family and their Long Island dream house that's possessed by ghostly squatters. Oozing black mud in the cellar and swarms of flies in the parlour signal a few harrowing moments as valiant James Brolin and Margot Kidder battle evil spirits. Meanwhile, an overblown religious subplot unfolds starring Rod Steiger. Although a baffling box-office hit, this tepid chiller never matches the flesh-crawling terror contained in Anson's book. AJ [VIDEO] DVD

James Brolin *George Lutz* • Margot Kidder *Kathleen Lutz* • Rod Steiger *Father Delaney* • Don Stroud *Father Bolen* • Natasha Ryan *Amy* • KC Martel *Greg* • Meeno Peluce *Matt* • Michael Sacks *Jeff* • Helen Shaver *Carolyn* ■ *Dir* Stuart Rosenberg • *Scr* Sandor Stern, from the non-fiction book by Jay Anson

The Amityville Horror ★★ 15

Supernatural horror
2005 · US · Colour · 89mins

This slick makeover returns to Jay Anson's bestseller for additional material and emphasises the psychological aspects of the notorious – and now clichéd – haunted-house tale. Here, the harrowing month spent by the Lutz family in their new Long Island home focuses on the mental breakdown suffered by patriarch George (an adequate Ryan Reynolds), who apparently becomes the satanic pawn of an ancient evil. Even an increase in the number of action sequences can't cover up the fact that this is aggravatingly ordinary. AJ. Contains swearing and violence.

Ryan Reynolds *George Lutz* • Melissa George *Kathy Lutz* • Jesse James *Billy Lutz* • Jimmy Bennett *Michael Lutz* • Chloë Grace Moretz *Chelsea Lutz* • Rachel Nichols *Lisa* • Philip Baker Hall *Father McNamara* ■ *Dir* Andrew Douglas • *Scr* Scott Kosar, from the film by Sandor Stern, from the non-fiction book by Jay Anson

Amityville II: the Possession ★★★ 18

Horror 1982 · US · Colour · 99mins

Much better overall than the dull first outing, this prequel to *The Amityville Horror* is given a neat European atmosphere by Italian director Damiano Damiani. It tells the full story of the vicious multiple murders that happened a year prior to the Lutz family's infamous tenancy-turned-bestselling book. Standard haunted-house shocks are combined with prowling camerawork for maximum involvement, while unusual imagery and spectacular make-up and special effects make this a handsomely crafted effort. AJ. Contains swearing and violence. [VIDEO] DVD

Burt Young *Anthony Montelli* • Rutanya Alda *Dolores Montelli* • James Olson *Father Adamsky* • Jack Magner *Sonny Montelli* • Diane Franklin *Patricia Montelli* • Andrew Prine *Father Tom* • Leonardo Cimino *Chancellor* • Danny Aiello *First removal man* ■ *Dir* Damiano Damiani • *Scr* Tommy Lee Wallace, from the book *Murder in Amityville* by Hans Holzer

Amityville III: the Demon ★★★ 15

Horror 1983 · US · Colour · 89mins

After exposing a pair of phoney spiritualists based in the notorious Long Island town, journalist Tony Roberts laughs at the legend and moves into the famous cursed Amityville house. Almost immediately, strange manifestations occur, resulting in unexplained deaths among his workmates and family. Decent special effects – originally in highly effective 3-D – dovetail neatly with director Richard Fleischer's creepy, claustrophobic atmosphere. A young Meg Ryan has a small role as a spooked teenager. AJ. Contains violence and swearing. [VIDEO] DVD

Tony Roberts *John Baxter* • Tess Harper *Nancy Baxter* • Robert Joy *Elliot West* • Candy Clark *Melanie* • John Beal *Harold Caswell* • Leora Dana *Emma Caswell* • John Harkins *Clifford Sanders* • Lori Loughlin *Susan Baxter* • Meg Ryan *Lisa* ■ *Dir* Richard Fleischer • *Scr* William Wales

Amityville: the Evil Escapes ★★ 18

Horror 1989 · US · Colour · 95mins

The title conjures up a wonderful image of a detached bungalow loping down the highways to find a new town to terrorise. But, sadly, no, it's only the evil that moves to California, leaving the original house in peace in this third sequel in the series. Director Sandor Stern, who scripted the first film, delivers some neat set pieces, but he is hampered by the constraints of the TV movie format. JF [VIDEO] DVD

Patty Duke *Nancy Evans* • Jane Wyatt *Alice Leacock* • Norman Lloyd *Father Manfred* • Frederic Lehne [Fredric Lehne] *Father Kibbler* • Brandy Gold *Jessica Evans* • Aron Eisenberg *Brian Evans* • Geri Betzler *Amanda Evans* ■ *Dir* Sandor Stern • *Scr* Sandor Stern, from the book by John G Jones

The Amityville Curse ★ 18

Horror 1990 · Can · Colour · 87mins

They must have good estate agents in Amityville because this is yet another tale of someone buying a property, only to discover that it has more than just a damp problem. In this instalment, a young couple snap up an old house to do it up, only to unwittingly unleash supernatural forces which date back to the murder of a priest. One of the weaker additions to the franchise. JF [VIDEO] DVD

Kim Coates *Frank* • Dawna Wrightman *Debbie* • Cassandra Gava *Abigail* • Jan Rubes *Priest* • Helen Hughes *Mrs Moriarty* ■ *Dir* Tom Berry • *Scr* Norvell Rose, Michael Krueger, Doug Olson, from a novel by Hans Holzer

Amityville: a New Generation ★★ 18

Horror 1993 · Can · Colour · 91mins

Following on from *Amityville: It's About Time*, this relocates the action to the city with the portal of evil being a mirror rather than a clock this time around. Ross Partridge is the artist who inherits the evil antique from a sinister street bum. Inevitably, it sparks off a series of mysterious slayings in his apartment block. Predictable stuff but genre fans will appreciate the appearances of David Naughton and Terry O'Quinn. JF [VIDEO] DVD

Ross Partridge *Keyes* • Julia Nickson-Soul *Suki* • David Naughton *Dick Cutler* • Lala Sloatman *Llanie* • Barbara Howard *Jane Cutler* • Richard Roundtree *Pauli* • Terry O'Quinn *Det Clark* ■ *Dir* John Murlowski • *Scr* Christopher DeFaria, Antonio Toro, from the novel *Amityville: the Evil Escapes* by John G Jones

Amityville Dollhouse ★★ 18

Horror 1996 · US · Colour · 92mins

This adds nothing new to the supernatural series which itself merely delivers bland and unremarkable horror homages to innumerable – and far better – efforts in the genre. The Martin family desert the big city rat race for a quiet life in the country. But, when they find a beautifully ornate doll house in their new home, and give it to their daughter, it begins exerting an evil influence over the family – the effects of which will come as little surprise to anyone familiar with the original haunted house shocker. AJ. Contains violence, swearing, sex scenes and brief nudity. [VIDEO] DVD

Robin Thomas *Bill Martin* • Starr Andreeff *Claire* • Allen Cutler *Todd Martin* • Rachel Duncan *Jessica Martin* ■ *Dir* Steve White • *Scr* Joshua Michael Stern

Amnesia ★★★★

Thriller 1994 · Chil · Colour · 90mins

Set in an unspecified country (that is patently Chile around the time of the 1973 coup), this powerful political thriller flashes back to a desert concentration camp and catalogues the crimes of the brutal regime against the inmates. Switching back to the present, a sadistic sergeant becomes the victim of a revenge plot. Seen only by a few privileged festival audiences, but a big box-office hit in Chile, Gonzalo Justiniano's uncompromising picture was cited as one of the ten best films ever made in Chile in a poll specially commissioned for the centenary of cinema. DP. In Spanish with English subtitles.

Julio Jung *Zuniga* • Pedro Vicuna *Ramirez* • Nelson Villagra *The Captain* • Jose Secall *Carrasco* ■ *Dir* Gonzalo Justiniano • *Scr* Gonzalo Justiniano, Gustavo Frias

Among Giants ★★★ 15

Romantic drama 1998 · UK · Colour · 94mins

It may not have quite the same feel-good comedy spin as his hit *The Full Monty*, but writer Simon Beaufoy's look at unemployed Sheffield friends making do buzzes along thanks to his excellent ear for dialogue and his unerring eye for gritty truthfulness. This time, amateur mountain climber Pete Postlethwaite gets the lads to help him paint pylons in the wilds of northern England against an impossible deadline, for cash in hand. When sexy Australian backpacker Rachel Griffiths joins the team, however, romantic competition starts a rift between Postlethwaite and his best mate James Thornton. An always engaging ensemble piece. AJ. Contains swearing, sex scenes and nudity. [VIDEO]

Pete Postlethwaite *Ray* • Rachel Griffiths *Gerry* • James Thornton *Steve* • Lennie James *Shovel* • Andy Serkis *Bob* • Rob Jarvis *Weasel* • Alan Williams *Frank* ■ *Dir* Sam Miller • *Scr* Simon Beaufoy

Among the Living ★★★

Drama 1941 · US · BW · 69mins

In *Dr Cyclops* and this movie, Albert Dekker displayed a remarkable talent that only manifested itself on those rare occasions when he was aptly cast. As a demented twin let loose in a sophisticated world, he is both disturbed and disturbing; ultimately, however, he is let down by the poor production values. Today the film's most interesting elements are its two leading ladies: a nascent Susan Hayward and the tragedy-strewn Frances Farmer, both of whom are excellent. TS

Albert Dekker *John Raden/Paul Raden* • Susan Hayward *Millie Pickens* • Harry Carey *Dr Ben Saunders* • Frances Farmer *Elaine Raden* • Gordon Jones *Bill Oakley* • Jean Phillips *Peggy Nolan* • Maude Eburne *Mrs Pickens* • Frank M Thomas *Sheriff* ■ *Dir* Stuart Heisler • *Scr* Lester Cole, Garrett Fort, from a story by Brian Marlowe, Lester Cole

Amongst Friends ★★ 18

Crime drama 1993 · US · Colour · 83mins

This junior league *Mean Streets* marks a promising enough debut from Rob Weiss, who also appears. The twist here is that the surly teens are from nice wealthy families, who are nevertheless sucked into the world of teenage gangs. It's not long before they are in over their heads, leading to a bloody finale. The young leads (Joseph Lindsey, Patrick McGaw and Steve Parlavecchio) acquit themselves well, although the film is now more notable for providing an early screen role for Mira Sorvino. JF [VIDEO]

Joseph Lindsey *Billy* • Patrick McGaw *Trevor* • Steve Parlavecchio *Andy* • Mira Sorvino *Laura* • Michael Artura *Michael* • Rob Weiss *Bobby* • Chris Santos *Young Andy* • Michael Leb *Young Trevor* • Frank Medrano *Vic* • Louis Lombardi *Eddie* ■ *Dir/Scr* Rob Weiss

El Amor Brujo ★★★

Drama 1986 · Sp · Colour · 100mins

The concluding part of the "flamenco trilogy" that began with *Blood Wedding* and *Carmen* may be the least successful of the three, but there is still much to admire in Carlos Saura's highly stylised production. The tale of doomed gypsy romance has a woman torn between the spirit of her dead husband and the attentions of his convicted murderer. Teo Escamilla's photography enhances both Gerardo Vera's costume designs and Antonio Gades's choreography, but the non-musical passages are heavy-going. DP. In Spanish with English subtitles.

Antonio Gades *Carmelo* • Cristina Hoyos *Candela* • Laura Del Sol *Lucia* • Juan Antonio Jimenez *José* • Emma Penella *Hechicer* • La Polaca *Pastora* • Gomez De Jerez *El Lobo* ■ *Dir* Carlos Saura • *Scr* Antonio Gades, Carlos Saura, from a ballet by Manuel De Falla • *Music* Manuel De Falla

L'Amore ★★★

Drama 1948 · It · BW · 79mins

This film from director Roberto Rossellini, comprising two separate tales, is a paean to the breathtaking talents of Anna Magnani, whose presence is the reason for watching it. The first half, an adaptation of Jean Cocteau's famous one-woman stage monologue *The Human Voice*, has the star as an abandoned society lady attempting to reconcile herself with her lover on the telephone; in *The Miracle*, she is a devout peasant woman seduced by Federico Fellini, who claims to be St Joseph. Rossellini's somewhat over-theatrical departure from neorealism was originally banned in New York and in England on grounds of blasphemy. RB. In Italian with English subtitles.

Anna Magnani *The woman/Nannina* • Federico Fellini *St Joseph* ■ *Dir* Roberto Rossellini • *Scr* Roberto Rossellini, Tullio Pinelli, from the play *La Voix Humaine* by Jean Cocteau and from a story by Federico Fellini

Amore! ★★

Romantic comedy
1993 · US · Colour · 93mins

A starry supporting cast enlivens this otherwise insubstantial slice of movie fluff. Jack Scalia plays a wealthy businessman who rather bizarrely changes his identity and attempts to make it in Hollywood. The plot is ludicrous and Scalia is unconvincing in the lead role, but a string of delightful supporting turns from old troupers such as George Hamilton, Katherine Helmond and Elliott Gould almost make it worthwhile. JF

Jack Scalia *Saul Schwartz* • Kathy Ireland *Taylor Christopher* • George Hamilton *Rudolfo Carbonera* • Norm Crosby *Shlomo Schwartz* • Elliott Gould *George Levine* • Katherine Helmond *Mildred Schwartz* ■ *Dir/Scr* Lorenzo Doumani

L'Amore Molesto ★★★ 15

Thriller 1995 · It · Colour · 98mins

Italian stage star Anna Bonaiuto is directed by her longtime partner Mario Martone in this atmospheric Neapolitan thriller, which was adapted from the acclaimed novel by Elena Ferrante. Returning to investigate the suspicious death of her elderly mother, Bonaiuto is forced to reacquaint herself with the city of her birth and delve into some long suppressed emotions in order to make sense of the clues. Although there is much to intrigue in the Freudian flashbacks and the encounters with the dead woman's male friends, the film's main interest lies in Martone's neorealist portrait of Naples. DP. In Italian with English subtitles. Contains some swearing, sex scenes and nudity. [VIDEO]

Anna Bonaiuto *Delia* • Angela Luce *Amalia* • Carmela Pecoraro *Delia as a child* • Licia Maglietta *Young Amalia* • Gianni Cajafa *Uncle Filippo* • Anna Calato *Mrs De Riso* • Giovanni Viglietti *Nicola Polledro, "Caserta"* ■ *Dir* Mario Martone • *Scr* Mario Martone, from the novel by Elena Ferrante

Amores Perros ★★★★★ 18

Drama 2000 · Mex · Colour · 147mins

With its wealth of hard-bitten characters, intertwining complex plot and nearly three-hour running time, director Alejandro González Iñárritu's internationally acclaimed and multi-award-winning debut feature is a startling original. How a fatal car accident impacts on the disparate lives of a slum teenager (Gael Garcia Bernal) involved in illegal dog fights, a magazine editor (Alvaro Guerrero) who leaves his wife for a perfume campaign model and an ex-con tramp-turned-hired assassin (Emilio Echevarria) is expertly fashioned by Iñárritu into a stunning rumination on the traumas and desperation of love and desire. Shot completely with a hand-held camera, and gaining enormous documentary-style immediacy from this in-your-face device, the film is a truly exhilarating masterpiece. AJ. In Spanish with English subtitles. Contains violence, swearing and sex scenes. [VIDEO] DVD

Emilio Echevarría *El Chivo, the "Goat"* • Gael García Bernal *Octavio* • Goya Toledo *Valeria* • Alvaro Guerrero *Daniel* • Vanessa Bauche *Susana* • Jorge Salinas *Luis* • Marco Perez *Ramiro* • Rodrigo Murray *Gustavo* ■ *Dir* Alejandro González Iñárritu • *Scr* Guillermo Arriaga • *Cinematographer* Rodrigo Prieto

The Amorous Adventures of Moll Flanders ★★

Comedy 1965 · UK · Colour · 132mins

After *Tom Jones* cleaned up at the box office and the Oscars, this rollicking 18th-century yarn was rushed into production, using the same composer (John Addison) with James Bond's director, Terence Young, at the helm. Adapted from the novel by Daniel Defoe, it's a Hollywood concoction that rarely comes off, while Kim Novak isn't anyone's idea of the English workhouse girl who sleeps her way to the gallows and beyond. AT

Kim Novak *Moll Flanders* • Claire Ufland *Young Moll* • Richard Johnson *Jemmy* • Angela Lansbury *Lady Blystone* • Vittorio De Sica *The Count* • Leo McKern *Squint* • George Sanders *The banker* • Lilli Palmer *Dutchy* • Hugh Griffith *Prison governor* ■ *Dir* Terence Young • *Scr* Denis Cannan, Roland Kibbee, from the novel *Moll Flanders* by Daniel Defoe

The Amorous Milkman ★ 18

Sex comedy 1974 · UK · Colour · 86mins

Actor Derren Nesbitt's one and only venture behind the camera is as cheap and cheerful as any soft-core comedy made in the 1970s. Brendan Price does his best to rattle his pintas with panache, but the most significant thing about this bawdy trash is what it says about the state of the British film industry at the time – it's sad that this was the only work Diana Dors, Roy Kinnear and other talented actors could find. DP. Contains sex scenes and nudity. [VIDEO]

Diana Dors *Rita* • Brendan Price *Davy* • Julie Ege *Diana* • Bill Fraser *Gerald* • Roy Kinnear *Sergeant* ■ *Dir* Derren Nesbitt • *Scr* Derren Nesbitt, from his story

The Amorous Prawn ★★★ U

Comedy 1962 · UK · BW · 85mins

Joan Greenwood plays the general's wife who converts her husband's HQ into a hotel in his absence to fleece visiting Americans and raise some cash. Director Anthony Kimmins also wrote the play on which this is based and he hasn't really opened it out too much for the cinema. As a result, the talents of the hugely popular Ian Carmichael – the Hugh Grant of his day – are given little room. However, there's enthusiastic support from Sandra Dorne and Ronald Brittain, the sergeant major who made a media career out of his military bearing and voice. TS [VIDEO]

Joan Greenwood *Lady Fitzadam* • Cecil Parker *General Fitzadam* • Ian Carmichael *Corporal Sidney Green* • Robert Beatty *Larry Hoffman* • Dennis Price *Prawn* • Liz Fraser *Suzie Tidmarsh* • Reg Lye *Uncle Joe* • Bridget Armstrong *Biddy O'Hara* • Derek Nimmo *Willie Maltravers* ■ *Dir* Anthony Kimmins • *Scr* Anthony Kimmins, Nicholas Phipps, from the play by Anthony Kimmins

Amos & Andrew ★★ 15

Comedy 1993 · US · Colour · 95mins

This silly, offbeat comedy begins as a satire of racial stereotyping before stumbling clumsily into buddy-movie territory. Samuel L Jackson is a successful, politically active author who moves into a wealthy (and very white) neighbourhood. His narrow-minded neighbours assume he's a burglar, cops surround the house, and police chief Dabney Coleman comes up with a hair-brained scheme involving small-time criminal Nicolas Cage that might salvage the situation. Writer/director E Max Frye's interesting anti-racist angle is lost in a comic treatment of the issues that totally misses the mark. JC [VIDEO]

Nicolas Cage *Amos Odell* • Samuel L Jackson *Andrew Sterling* • Michael Lerner *Phil Gillman* • Margaret Colin *Judy Gillman* • Dabney Coleman *Chief of Police Cecil Tolliver* • Brad Dourif *Officer Donnie Donaldson* • Chelcie Ross *Earl* ■ *Dir/Scr* E Max Frye

L'Amour Fou ★★★★

Drama 1968 · Fr · BW · 256mins

Of all the French New Wave directors, Jacques Rivette has remained the most uncompromising. He usually goes in for exceptionally long movies, and this one, shot in both 35mm and 16mm, was originally 256 minutes. (The producers, however, initially distributed it in a two-hour version that the director disowned.) Like many of Rivette's pictures, it is about the art of creation: in this case, a theatre group preparing to stage Racine's *Andromaque* while being filmed by a TV team. There is a fascinating interplay between the characters and the play itself, but Rivette's austere style and cerebral preoccupations require some effort on the part of the viewer. RB. A French language film.

Jean-Pierre Kalfon *Sébastien* • Bulle Ogier *Claire* • André Labarthe [André S Labarthe] *André* • Josée Destoops *Marta* ■ *Dir* Jacques Rivette • *Scr* Jacques Rivette, Marilu Tonilini

L'Amour par Terre ★★

Drama 1984 · Fr · Colour · 125mins

A decade after *Celine and Julie Go Boating*, Jacques Rivette returned to similar territory – two women forced to play various roles in a strange house – but with less rewarding results. The director's interest in theatre and literature provides some pleasure (Geraldine Chaplin and Jane Birkin share their names with the Brontë sisters, Charlotte and Emily), as does the chateau setting, but the game-playing becomes tedious after a while. The film is short by Rivette's standards (a mere 125 minutes). RB. In French with English subtitles.

Geraldine Chaplin *Charlotte* • Jane Birkin *Emily* • André Dussollier *Paul* • Jean-Pierre Kalfon *Clément Roquemaure* • Facundo Bo *Silvano* • Laszlo Szabo *Virgil* • Sandra Montaigu *Eléonore* • Isabelle Linnartz *Béatrice* ■ *Dir* Jacques Rivette • *Scr* Pascal Bonitzer, Marilù Parolini, Jacques Rivette, Suzanne Schiffman

The Amsterdam Kill ★★ 15

Thriller 1978 · HK · Colour · 86mins

Robert Mitchum sleepwalks through this Hong Kong-financed thriller about a modern opium war fought out in the Far East and Amsterdam. As a former Drug Enforcement Agency man who was fired for corruption, Mitchum is wholly convincing even when the plot is underdeveloped. Co-stars Bradford Dillman and Leslie Nielsen are given little to work with – beyond counting corpses – and the Chinese actors, stars on their home turf, seem frankly amateurish. Boringly predictable, except for Mitchum. AT [VIDEO] DVD

Robert Mitchum *Quinlan* • Bradford Dillman *Odums* • Richard Egan *Ridgeway* • Leslie Nielsen *Riley Knight* • Keye Luke *Chung Wei* • George Kee Cheung *Jimmy Wong* • Chen Hsing *Assassin* ■ *Dir* Robert Clouse • *Scr* Robert Clouse, Gregory Leifer

Amsterdamned ★★★ 18

Action thriller 1988 · Neth · Colour · 113mins

A maniac frogman, horribly scarred after exposure to toxic chemicals during a botched salvage operation, is haunting Amsterdam's canals to take revenge on the uncaring society he's judged responsible for his plight. Dick Maas's thriller is an unusual mix of police procedural and American stalk-and-slash conventions. Maas – Holland's answer to John Carpenter – both scripts and scores the film, but it's his efficient, no-nonsense direction and humorously etched character studies that set this nuanced Dutch treat apart. AJ. Dutch dialogue dubbed into English. [VIDEO]

Huub Stapel *Eric Visser* • Monique van de Ven *Laura* • Serge-Henri Valcke *Vermeer* • Tanneke Hartsuiker *Potter* • Wim Zomer *John* • Hidde Maas *Martin* • Lou Landré *Chief* ■ *Dir/Scr* Dick Maas • *Music* Dick Maas

Amy ★★ U

Period drama 1981 · US · Colour · 90mins

Disney's inabilty to resist coating the pill undermines this otherwise sincere insight into the educational needs of sight- and hearing-impaired children. Still grieving after the death of her deaf son, Jenny Agutter leaves domineering husband Chris Robinson to work with doctor Barry Newman at a special school, even though such independence was hardly expected of women in the early 1900s. Although aimed at younger viewers, Vincent McEveety's film is carefully made, but over-earnest. DP [VIDEO]

Jenny Agutter *Amy Medford* • Barry Newman *Dr Ben Corcoran* • Kathleen Nolan *Helen Gibbs* • Chris Robinson *Elliot Medford* • Lou Fant *Lyle Ferguson* • Margaret O'Brien *Hazel Johnson* • Nanette Fabray *Malvina* • Otto Rechenberg *Henry Watkins* ■ *Dir* Vincent McEveety • *Scr* Noreen Stone

Amy Foster ★★ 15

Romantic melodrama
1997 · UK/US/Fr · Colour · 108mins

Also known as *Swept from the Sea*, this is a wildly misjudged adaptation of the haunting Joseph Conrad novel. Director Beeban Kidron goes for the overblown romantic (and very heavy-handed) touch in this melodramatic tale of silent Rachel Weisz who falls in love with Vincent Perez, the sole survivor of a shipwreck. However, no amount of craggy scenery, violent storms and mournful looks from the duo can disguise the fact that Kidron has delivered a plodding tragedy. JB. Contains some swearing and violence, and a brief sex scene. [VIDEO] DVD

Rachel Weisz *Amy Foster* • Vincent Perez *Yanko* • Ian McKellen *Dr James Kennedy* • Kathy Bates *Miss Swaffer* • Joss Ackland *Mr Swaffer* • Tony Haygarth *Mr Smith* • Fiona Victory *Mrs Smith* • Tom Bell *Isaac Foster* • Zoë Wanamaker *Mary Foster* ■ *Dir* Beeban Kidron • *Scr* Tim Willocks, from the story by Joseph Conrad

Anaconda ★★★ 15

Horror adventure
1997 · US/Bra · Colour · 85mins

Director Luis Llosa's cheerful slither-fest shows how a documentary film crew sailing up the Amazon gets used as snake-bait by deranged explorer Jon Voight in his obsessive quest to capture a legendary 40ft anaconda. As the competent cast fights a computer-generated garden hose with fangs, and as Voight's performance goes into camp overdrive, the scaly scares shrink while the screams of laughter increase. Daft fun. AJ. Contains swearing and violence. DVD

Jennifer Lopez *Terri Flores* • Ice Cube *Danny Rich* • Jon Voight *Paul Sarone* • Eric Stoltz *Dr Steven Cale* • Jonathan Hyde *Warren Westridge* • Owen Wilson *Gary Dixon* • Kari Wuhrer *Denise Kalberg* • Vincent Castellanos *Mateo* • Danny Trejo *Poacher* ■ *Dir* Luis Llosa • *Scr* Hans Bauer, Jim Cash, Jack Epps Jr

Anacondas: the Hunt for the Blood Orchid ★ 12

Horror adventure 2004 · US · Colour · 92mins

It may have been daft fun, but did 1997's *Anaconda* really warrant a sequel? Watching this bargain-bin film, the answer is a resounding "no". Here the giant serpents prey on scientists who are scouring Borneo for a rare orchid with youth-preserving qualities. For a movie that promises major snake nastiness, it takes an age for the predators to slither into action, and even then abysmal special effects render them ridiculous. SF. Contains swearing. DVD

Johnny Messner *Bill Johnson* • KaDee Strickland *Samantha "Sam" Rogers* • Matthew Marsden *Dr Jack Byron* • Eugene Byrd *Cole Burris* • Salli Richardson-Whitfield [Salli Richardson] *Gail Stern* • Nicholas Gonzalez *Dr Ben Douglas* • Karl Yune *Tran* • Morris Chestnut *Gordon Mitchell* ■ *Dir* Dwight H Little • *Scr* John Claflin, Daniel Zelman, Michael Miner, Ed Neumeier, from a story by Hans Bauer, Jim Cash, Jack Epps Jr

Analyze That ★★ 15

Comedy 2002 · US · Colour · 91mins

Robert De Niro and Billy Crystal – the double act that struck box-office gold with *Analyze This* – return for this sequel, but fail to conjure up the same magic. After faking a breakdown, De Niro's imprisoned mobster is released into the custody of his psychiatrist Crystal. Soon fed up with his houseguest, Crystal gets De Niro a job as a consultant on a TV show. Crystal's quick-witted neuroses still spark effectively off De Niro's slow charm, but that's just not enough. StH. Contains violence, swearing. DVD

Billy Crystal *Ben Sobel* • Robert De Niro *Paul Vitti* • Lisa Kudrow *Laura Sobel* • Joe Viterelli *Jelly* • Reg Rogers *Raoul Berman* • Cathy Moriarty-Gentile [Cathy Moriarty] *Patti LoPresti* • John Finn *Richard Chapin* • Kyle Sabihy *Michael Sobel* ■ *Dir* Harold Ramis • *Scr* Peter Steinfeld, Harold Ramis, Peter Tolan, from characters created by Peter Tolan, Kenneth Lonergan

Analyze This ★★★★ 15

Crime comedy 1999 · US · Colour · 99mins

Robert De Niro gives a great performance in this feel-good Mafia comedy from *Groundhog Day* director Harold Ramis. De Niro stars as a Manhattan Mob boss whose stressful lifestyle causes him to seek undercover therapy from psychiatrist Billy Crystal. De Niro's deadpan responses to the Freudian dissections, together with soon-to-be-married Crystal's increasing entanglement with the "family" business, bring on the laughs. Aided by a clever script packed with fresh repartee, Ramis's skilled timing allows the two dynamic leads to show their full comic potential. AJ. Contains swearing, violence, sex scenes. DVD

Billy Crystal *Ben Sobel* • Robert De Niro *Paul Vitti* • Lisa Kudrow *Laura MacNamara* • Joe Viterelli *Jelly* • Chazz Palminteri *Primo Sindone* • Bill Macy *Isaac Sobel* • Molly Shannon *Caroline* • Max Casella *Nicky Shivers* ■ *Dir* Harold Ramis • *Scr* Peter Tolan, Harold Ramis, Kenneth Lonergan, from a story by Kenneth Lonergan, Peter Tolan

Anari ★★★ U

Drama 1959 · Ind · BW · 156mins

Ever the underdog, Raj Kapoor takes the lead in this outspoken attack on capitalism and medical irresponsibility. It focuses on the plight of a painter, who is accused of murdering his landlady, even though a medicine produced by the company he works for is really to blame. Nutan is charming as the company owner's niece who poses as her own maid to prevent Raj from discovering the extent of her wealth. But the emphasis is clearly as much on the social issues as on escapism, prompting many critics to suggest that Kapoor had as much to do with the direction as Hrishikesh Mukherjee. DP. In Hindi and Urdu with English subtitles. DVD

Raj Kapoor *Raj* • Nutan *Aarti* • Lalita Pawar *Mrs D'Sa* • Motilal *Ramnath* ■ *Dir* Hrishikesh Mukherjee • *Scr* Inder Raj Anand

Anari No 1 ★★ PG

Comedy drama 1999 · Ind · Colour · 161mins

A return to form of sorts for Indian superstar Govinda, though it's clear from the outset that this comedy of errors isn't director Kuku Kohli's forte. Making use of Govinda's undoubted talent at every possible opportunity, Kohli is guilty of not paying enough attention to character development and plot. The result leaves Govinda struggling to carry the film single-handedly. RT. In Hindi with English subtitles.

Govinda *Ruhul Saxena/Raja* • Raveena Tandon *Sapna* • Simran *Sona* • Kader Khan *KK* ■ *Dir/Scr* Kuku Kohli

Anastasia ★★★★ U

Period drama 1956 · US · Colour · 100mins

Ingrid Bergman gives an exceptional, Oscar-winning performance in this gripping tale of a refugee passed off as the Romanov Grand Duchess by cunning Yul Brynner. A clever, insightful script puts flesh on the bones of an already intriguing mystery, but it is Bergman who makes this one a minor classic. She portrays vulnerability and dignity in equal measure with a rare screen intelligence, and Helen Hayes is also very fine as Anastasia's grandmother. SH DVD

Ingrid Bergman *Anastasia/Ana* • Yul Brynner *Bounine* • Helen Hayes *Empress* • Akim Tamiroff *Chernov* • Martita Hunt *Baroness Von Livenbaum* • Felix Aylmer *Russian Chamberlain* • Sacha Pitoeff *Petrovin* • Ivan Desny *Prince Paul* • Natalie Schafer *Lissenskaia* • Gregoire Gromoff *Stepan* • Karel Stepanek *Vlados* ■ *Dir* Anatole Litvak • *Scr* Arthur Laurents, from the play by Marcelle Maurette, adapted by Guy Bolton

Anastasia ★★★ U

Animated musical fantasy
1997 · US · Colour · 90mins

History buffs will despair at the liberal use of fiction in this adventure set around the time of the Russian Revolution. Little girls, however, will be enchanted by the tale of Anastasia, the Tsar's young daughter and the only one to survive after the evil Rasputin puts a curse on her family. Ten years later, without any recollection of her past, she meets her grandmother and discovers her heritage. Sweet stuff. A better-than-average prequel, *Bartok the Magnificent*, followed in 1999. JB DVD

Meg Ryan *Anastasia* • John Cusack *Dimitri* • Kelsey Grammer *Vladimir* • Christopher Lloyd *Rasputin* • Hank Azaria *Bartok* • Bernadette Peters *Sophie* • Kirsten Dunst *Young Anastasia* • Angela Lansbury *Dowager Empress Marie* ■ *Dir* Don Bluth, Gary Goldman • *Scr* Susan Gauthier, Bruce Graham, Bob Tzudiker, Noni White

Anatomy ★★★★ 18

Horror 2000 · Ger · Colour · 95mins

Brilliant but insecure medical student Franka Potente goes to study an anatomy course at the prestigious Heidelberg University and uncovers a sinister secret society infamous for its ruthless research on live bodies. The dissected victims pile up along with the suspenseful shrieks in Austrian director Stefan Ruzowitzky's hugely enjoyable Hammer-style horror that is given a stark hi-tech and contemporary makeover with congealed helpings of pharmaceutical fear and surgical shock on the side. AJ DVD

Franka Potente *Paula Henning* • Benno Fürmann *Hein* • Anna Loos *Gretchen* • Sebastian Blomberg *Casper* • Holger Speckhahn *Phil* • Traugott Buhre *Prof Grombek* ■ *Dir/Scr* Stefan Ruzowitzky

Anatomy of a Murder ★★★★★ 15

Classic courtroom drama
1959 · US · BW · 153mins

Probably the greatest courtroom drama ever made, this features James Stewart's finest screen performance. Controversial in its day for using words such as "panties" and "spermatogenesis", Otto Preminger's film gives you an "irresistible impulse" to watch for nearly three hours as its story about a rape and murder unfolds. As the country hick lawyer (and jazz fan), Stewart is drawn into the case, suckered by it, and comes up against big-town prosecutor George C Scott. Their courtroom duels and stunts are mesmerising as they show us America leaving its traditional old-time moral values behind: this is the America not of apple pie but of *Lolita*. AT. Contains violence and brief nudity. DVD

James Stewart *Paul Biegler* • Lee Remick *Laura Manion* • Ben Gazzara *Lt Frederick Manion* • Arthur O'Connell *Parnell McCarthy* • Eve Arden *Maida* • George C Scott *Claude Dancer* • Kathryn Grant *Mary Pilant* • Joseph N Welch *Judge Weaver* • Duke Ellington *Pie-Eye* ■ *Dir* Otto Preminger • *Scr* Wendell Mayes, from the novel by Robert Traver [John D Voelker]

Anatomy of Hell ★★ 18

Psychological sex drama
2003 · Fr · Colour · 73mins

Catherine Breillat wastes this opportunity to discuss gender politics by settling for pompous platitudes and gimmicky explicitness. Seemingly suicidal Amira Casar picks up Rocco Siffredi in a gay bar and pays him to observe her naked body while she waxes pseudo-poetic on everything from menstruation to misogyny. But even the most open-minded viewer will eventually find their antics with lipsticks, garden implements and tampons a touch tiresome. DP. In French with English subtitles. DVD

Amira Casar *The woman* • Rocco Siffredi *The man* • Catherine Breillat *Narrator* ■ *Dir* Catherine Breillat • *Scr* Catherine Breillat, from her novel *Pornocratie*

Anazapta ★★ 15

Period mystery thriller
2001 · UK · Colour · 110mins

Alberto Sciamma's medieval murder mystery achieves a creditable sense of time and place, considering its meagre budget. But the clumsiness of the dialogue and the tendency of too many cast members to play to the gallery undermine its ambitions. The idea of a mysterious French prisoner from the Hundred Years' War bringing pestilence to an isolated, superstitious settlement is splendid. But as the death toll rises, Sciamma can't decide whether he's making a bodice-ripper or a slasher film. DP. Contains violence and swearing. DVD

Lena Headey *Lady Matilda Mellerby* • David La Haye *Jacques de Saint Amant* • Jason Flemyng *Nicholas* • Christopher Fairbank *Steward* • Anthony O'Donnell *Randall* • Jeff Nuttall *Priest* • Hayley Carmichael *Agnes* • Ian McNeice *Bishop* • Jon Finch *Sir Walter Mellerby* ■ *Dir* Alberto Sciamma • *Scr* Alberto Sciamma, Harriet Sand

Anchoress ★★★ 12

Period drama 1993 · UK/Bel · BW · 108mins

Director Chris Newby's film chronicles the gruesome fate of peasant girl Natalie Morse. Seeking solace from her medieval family and tiny hovel, Morse becomes obsessed with the Virgin Mary and seeks to serve her ad infinitum by being walled up for life in her local church. Almost becoming a deity herself, she is fed by the villagers and sought after as a form of 14th-century guidance counsellor. When her mother is tried and convicted of witchcraft, however, she digs her way out of imprisonment and stands to pay for the action with her life. A haunting film shot in striking monochrome that offers an apt period metaphor for contemporary teenage rebellion. LH

Natalie Morse *Christine Carpenter* • Eugene Bervoets [Gene Bervoets] *Reeve* • Toyah Willcox *Pauline Carpenter* • Peter Postlethwaite [Pete Postlethwaite] *William Carpenter* • Christopher Eccleston *Priest* • Brenda Bertin *Meg Carpenter* • Annette Badland *Mary* ■ *Dir* Chris Newby • *Scr* Christine Watkins, Judith Stanley-Smith

Anchorman: the Legend of Ron Burgundy ★★★ 12

Period comedy 2004 · US · Colour · 90mins

This sporadically amusing but thoroughly dumb 1970s-set comedy stars Will Ferrell as a top news anchorman, who suddenly finds his job under threat from a woman. When ambitious reporter Christina Applegate joins a top-rated but male chauvinistic San Diego news team, she sets her sights on becoming the first female anchor. However, Ferrell has no intention of sharing the limelight and tries to frustrate the plans of his rival. The jokes are puerile in the extreme, but matters are given a lift by a host of cameo appearances. AS. Contains sexual references. DVD

Will Ferrell *Ron Burgundy* • Christina Applegate *Veronica Corningstone* • Paul Rudd *Brian Fantana* • Steve Carell [Steven Carell] *Brick Tamland* • David Koechner *Champ Kind* • Fred Willard *Ed Harken* • Chris Parnell *Garth Holliday* • Kathryn Hahn *Helen* ■ *Dir* Adam McKay • *Scr* Adam McKay, Will Ferrell

Anchors Aweigh ★★★ U

Musical 1945 · US · Colour · 133mins

The musical in which Gene Kelly dances with cartoon mouse Jerry, and Kelly and Frank Sinatra don those oh-so-cute sailor suits, prior to *On the Town*. At times it's schmaltzy and overlong, with cloying moments involving Kathryn Grayson's quest for an interview with conductor José Iturbi, embarrassingly playing himself. However, none of that matters when

U = SUITABLE FOR ALL Uc = SUITABLE FOR ALL, ESPECIALLY FOR YOUNG CHILDREN (VIDEO ONLY) PG = PARENTAL GUIDANCE

Kelly and Sinatra are on the screen. They're a joy to watch, and Sinatra, though not known as a dancer, acquits himself well in his pairings with Kelly. George Sidney's direction is technically clever and assured. TS

Gene Kelly *Joseph Brady* • Frank Sinatra *Clarence Doolittle* • Kathryn Grayson *Susan Abbott* • Dean Stockwell *Donald Martin* • Pamela Britton *Girl from Brooklyn* • Rags Ragland *Police sergeant* • Billy Gilbert *Cafe manager* • Henry O'Neill *Admiral Hammond* • José Iturbi ■ *Dir* George Sidney (2) • *Scr* Isobel Lennart, from a story by Natalie Marcin

And Baby Makes Three ★★

Comedy 1949 · US · BW · 83mins

Barbara Hale is in the family way and about to marry anew, but really wants to stay with divorced first husband Robert Young. Need you ask more? What you could ask is how such a topic appeased the strict US censor's Breen Office, and then enjoy the amazing number of euphemisms used to describe Hale's condition. This is a trifle, nicely played by Barbara Hale, but its tale of a pregnant wife trying to get out of a second marriage to get her first hubby back leaves a strange taste in the mouth. TS

Robert Young (1) *Vernon Walsh* • Barbara Hale *Jacqueline Walsh* • Robert Hutton *Herbert Fletcher* • Janis Carter *Wanda York* • Billie Burke *Mrs Fletcher* • Nicholas Joy *Mr Fletcher* • Lloyd Corrigan *Dr William Parnell* ■ *Dir* Henry Levin • *Scr* Lou Breslow, Joseph Hoffman from their story

And God Created Woman ★★★ PG

Drama 1956 · Fr · Colour · 88mins

This was not Brigitte Bardot's first movie, but it was the one that turned her into the world's ultimate sex symbol. Directed by Roger Vadim, her then husband, the film also turned the little fishing village of St Tropez into a glamorous resort – the kind of place where girls leave their bikini tops on the ironing board, pose provocatively in CinemaScope and go with anything in trousers. Curt Jurgens, Jean-Louis Trintignant and Christian Marquand are three of Bardot's conquests in a movie whose funny attitude towards sex made it seem all the more risqué in the 1950s. AT. In French with English subtitles. DVD

Brigitte Bardot *Juliette Hardy* • Curt Jurgens *Eric Carradine* • Jean-Louis Trintignant *Michel Tardieu* • Christian Marquand *Antoine Tardieu* • Georges Poujouly *Christian Tardieu* • Jean Tissier *M Vigier-Lefranc* • Jeanne Marken [Jane Marken] *Mme Morin* • Marie Glory *Mme Tardieu* ■ *Dir* Roger Vadim • *Scr* Roger Vadim, Raoul J Lévy

And God Created Woman ★ 18

Drama 1988 · US · Colour · 90mins

Director Roger Vadim's sad attempt to reclaim his past glory is a tedious retooling of the sensational 1956 original which made Brigitte Bardot an international sex symbol. Rebecca De Mornay is hardly in the same class as an aspiring rock star who sleeps with electrician Vincent Spano and sundry other high-powered men to get out of jail and achieve her aim. Without Bardot's brand of sexual dynamism, Vadim's contrived fable collapses into a cliché-ridden heap of melodrama and farce. AJ DVD

Rebecca De Mornay *Robin Shay* • Vincent Spano *Billy Moran* • Frank Langella *James Tiernan* • Donovan Leitch *Peter Moran* • Judith Chapman *Alexandra Tiernan* • Jaime McEnnan *Timmy Moran* • Benjamin Mouton *Blue* ■ *Dir* Roger Vadim • *Scr* RJ Stewart

...And God Spoke ★★

Spoof documentary
1993 · US · Colour · 83mins

Though there are some laughs to be had in this mock documentary about two skin flick merchants who decide to make a biblical epic on the cheap – *Spinal Tap* it ain't. Clueless duo Michael Riley and Stephen Rappaport have no idea what they're letting themselves in for, and it's fun to see them treat the Bible like a Jackie Collins bestseller and hire such actors as *The Incredible Hulk*'s Lou Ferrigno and Eve Plumb from *The Brady Bunch*. The gags are few and far between, and the film peters out alarmingly well before the end. AJ

Michael Riley *Clive Walton* • Stephen Rappaport *Marvin Handleman* • Josh Trossman *Ray/Jesus* • Lou Ferrigno *Cain* • Andy Dick *Abel* • Eve Plumb *Mrs Noah* • Fred Kaz *Noah* • Soupy Sales *Moses* • Michael Medved ■ *Dir* Arthur Borman • *Scr* Gregory S Malins, Michael Curtis, from a story by Arthur Borman, Mark Borman

And Hope to Die ★★★

Crime drama 1972 · Fr/US · Colour · 126mins

The penultimate film from veteran French director René Clément is a gangster thriller, filmed mainly in Canada, where fugitive Jean-Louis Trintignant inadvertently finds himself with a million bucks in cash, the price paid by a crime baron (Robert Ryan) to have a state witness assassinated. The plot gets even more complicated when Trintignant is kidnapped by the gang. Clearly intended to rival the crime dramas made by Jean-Pierre Melville, it's undeniably gripping, but not quite in that exalted league. AT. An English/French language film.

Robert Ryan *Charley* • Jean-Louis Trintignant *Tony* • Aldo Ray *Mattone* • Lea Massari *Sugar* • Tisa Farrow *Pepper* • Jean Gaven *Rizzio* • Nadine Nabokov *Majorette* • Andre Lawrence *Gypsy* • Daniel Breton *Paul* ■ *Dir* René Clément • *Scr* Sébastien Japrisot

...And Justice for All ★★★ 15

Courtroom drama
1979 · US · Colour · 116mins

Al Pacino stars as an idealistic young lawyer in this courtroom drama, which takes a scathing look at the American justice system. First seen in prison where he's serving time for contempt, Pacino's attorney is a crusader, fighting corruption within his profession with a zeal that real-life lawyers can only dream of. The script by then husband-and-wife Valerie Curtin and Barry Levinson is, on the whole, solid enough, but the direction by Norman Jewison is rather bloated. AT DVD

Al Pacino *Arthur Kirkland* • Jack Warden *Judge Rayford* • John Forsythe *Judge Fleming* • Lee Strasberg *Grandpa Sam* • Jeffrey Tambor *Jay Porter* • Christine Lahti *Gail Packer* • Sam Levene *Arnie* ■ *Dir* Norman Jewison • *Scr* Valerie Curtin, Barry Levinson

And Life Goes On... ★★★

Documentary drama
1991 · Iran · Colour · 108mins

In keeping with the rest of Iranian director Abbas Kiarostami's canon, this is a deceptively simple study of the enduring link between cinema and life. Following an earthquake in northern Iran, a director (Farhad Kheradmand representing Kiarostami) travels to see whether the cast of his 1987 film *Where Is the Friend's Home?*, survived the disaster. Taking a precarious mountain route, and in the company of his son, he arrives to discuss with the peoples of Rudbar and Rostamabad their plans for the future and how God could have allowed such suffering. Combining simple narrative with unobtrusive documentary, this is a humane, deeply affecting work. DP. In Farsi with English subtitles.

Farhad Kheradmand *Film director* • Buba Bayour *Film director's son* ■ *Dir/Scr* Abbas Kiarostami

And Millions Will Die! ★★

Science-fiction thriller
1973 · US · Colour · 93mins

Leslie Nielsen co-stars with TV regular Richard Baseheart (*Voyage to the Bottom of the Sea*) in this story about an unknown force that threatens to unleash poison gas in Hong Kong. It attempts to cash in on the early 1970s demand for disaster movies, but there is little in the way of either star charisma or suspense. JF. Contains some violence and swearing.

Richard Basehart *Dr Pruitt* • Leslie Nielsen *Gallagher* • Joseph First *Franz Kessler* • Susan Strasberg *Heather Kessler* • Alwyn Kurts *Dr Mitchell* • Shariff Medon *Postman* ■ *Dir* Leslie Martinson [Leslie H Martinson] • *Scr* Michael Fisher

And Now for Something Completely Different ★★★★ PG

Comedy 1971 · UK · Colour · 84mins

Not all that different, though, for British enthusiasts of Monty Python's comic madness, as it's a recycling of some the teams's funniest BBC TV sketches. But this first cinematic celebration was really aimed at American innocents, ignorant of such items as the "Upper Class Twit of the Year Race" and "Hell's Grannies", with Graham Chapman, John Cleese and Terry Gilliam giving vent to a wholly superior form of surrealism. TH. Contains swearing. DVD

Graham Chapman • John Cleese • Terry Gilliam • Eric Idle • Terry Jones • Michael Palin • Carol Cleveland • Connie Booth ■ *Dir* Ian MacNaughton • *Scr* Graham Chapman, John Cleese, Terry Gilliam, Eric Idle, Terry Jones, Michael Palin • *Animation* Terry Gilliam

And Now Miguel ★★ U

Drama 1966 · US · Colour · 94mins

An old-style family entertainment about a little boy in New Mexico who wants to be a shepherd, just like his dad. Much time is spent on what it's like to be a sheep in this part of the world: you stand around, bleat a bit and get sheared once a year. (The humans seem to do much the same thing, only on two legs.) An attack by a pack of wolves comes not a moment too soon. Director James B Clark specialised in this sort of thing. AT

Pat Cardi *Miguel* • Michael Ansara *Blas* • Guy Stockwell *Perez* • Clu Gulager *Johnny* • Joe De Santis *Padre de Chavez* • Pilar Del Rey *Tomasita* • Peter Robbins *Pedro* • Emma Tyson *Faustina* ■ *Dir* James B Clark • *Scr* Ted Sherdeman, Jane Klove, from the novel by Joseph Krumgold

And Now My Love ★★

Drama 1974 · Fr/It · Colour · 121mins

This flamboyant folly from Claude Lelouch astonishingly earned an Oscar nomination for best original screenplay. Wildly overlong and hopelessly self-indulgent, this mammoth picture is interminably dull from our first encounter with a pioneering movie cameraman (Charles Denner) at the turn of the century right through to the moment his granddaughter (Marthe Keller) sets her roguish beau (André Dussollier) on the straight and narrow. DP. In French with English subtitles.

Marthe Keller *Sarah/Her mother/Her grandmother* • André Dussollier *Simon Duroc* • Charles Denner *Cameraman/Sarah's father/Sarah's grandfather* • Carla Gravina *Sarah's Italian friend* • Charles Gerard *Charlot, Simon's friend* • Gilbert Bécaud ■ *Dir* Claude Lelouch • *Scr* Claude Lelouch, Pierre Uytterhoeven

And Now the Screaming Starts! ★★ 15

Horror 1973 · UK · Colour · 90mins

Stephanie Beacham (who cut her soap-acting teeth on horrors such as this) marries Ian Ogilvy and is menaced by a dismembered hand, an axe-wielding farmer and other apparitions thanks to an ancient family curse. The presence of horror veterans Peter Cushing and Herbert Lom gives this formula haunted house material a much needed lift, but there's very little action and too few surprises before the screaming well and truly stops and the yawning starts. AJ DVD

Peter Cushing *Doctor Pope* • Herbert Lom *Henry Fengriffen* • Patrick Magee *Doctor Whittle* • Ian Ogilvy *Charles Fengriffen* • Stephanie Beacham *Catherine Fengriffen* • Geoffrey Whitehead *Silas Jr/Sr* • Guy Rolfe *Maitland* • Rosalie Crutchley *Mrs Luke* ■ *Dir* Roy Ward Baker • *Scr* Roger Marshall, from the novel *Fengriffen* by David Case

And Now Tomorrow ★★

Drama 1944 · US · BW · 84mins

Don't get over-excited by the name Raymond Chandler on the credits of this melodrama. He was only doing it for the money and reserved his best – and least charitable – line until after the movie, describing its star as "a small boy's idea of a tough guy". Actually Ladd deserved better of both writer and film. He plays a doctor with working-class origins who, while working on a cure for deafness caused by meningitis, meets and falls for upper-class Loretta Young. BB

Alan Ladd *Dr Merek Vance* • Loretta Young *Emily Blair* • Susan Hayward *Janice Blair* • Barry Sullivan *Jeff Stoddard* • Beulah Bondi *Aunt Em* • Cecil Kellaway *Dr Weeks* ■ *Dir* Irving Pichel • *Scr* Frank Partos, Raymond Chandler, from the novel by Rachel Field

And Now You're Dead ★★ 18

Action 1998 · HK · Colour · 90mins

Shannon Lee, the daughter of legendary martial artist Bruce Lee, kickboxes and karate chops her way through a threadbare action adventure that clearly doesn't have the budget to match its wild ambitions. She plays a sharpshooter who teams up with her former partner, a professional thief, and two young pickpockets to steal the largest diamond in the Czech Republic. Lee's fine but the espionage double-crossing theatrics and explosive stunts simply aren't in the same league as her fighting proficiency. AJ. Cantonese dialogue dubbed into English. DVD

Shannon Lee *Mandy* • Michael Wong *Marty* • Anita Yuen *Lucy* • Jordan Chan *Tommy* ■ *Dir* Corey Yuen

And Quiet Flows the Don ★★★★

War drama 1957 · USSR · BW · 108mins

Sergei Gerasimov's epic adaptation of Nobel laureate Mikhail Sholokhov's masterpiece has rarely been seen in its sprawling entirety outside the old Soviet bloc. Yet, even in its bowdlerised version, it remains one of the most polished examples of socialist realism. The action initially focuses on Pyotr Glebov's feud with his father, Danilo Ilchenko, who insists he marries Zinaida Kirienko, rather than his lover, Elina Bystritskaya. However, the First World War and the Revolution intervene and change their lives forever. Visually, it's a hugely impressive achievement, although the acting is occasionally bombastic. DP. A Russian language film.

Elina Bystritskaya *Aksinya* • Pyotr Glebov *Grigory* • Zinaida Kirienko *Natalya* • Danilo Ilchenko *Panteleimon Melekhov* ■ *Dir* Sergei Gerasimov • *Scr* Sergei Gerasimov, from the novel *Tikhij Don/And Quiet Flows the Don* by Mikhail Sholokhov

And Quiet Rolls the Dawn ★★★★

Drama 1979 · Ind · Colour · 90mins

Less politically strident than his earlier work, this intense treatise on the role of women in Indian society demonstrates Mrinal Sen's total mastery of his art. Moving between the vast courtyard of a Calcuttan tenement and the crowded apartment in which Satya Bannerjee and his family of seven live, Sen uses the overnight absence of a hard-working daughter to expose the family's indolent dependence on her wage. Interspersing dramatic scenes with speeches to camera, he compels and provokes as he relentlessly probes their middle-class pride and prejudices, as each strives to conceal a concern inspired more by fiscal than familial motives. DP. A Bengali language film.

Satya Bannerjee *Hrishikesh Sen Gupta* • Gita Sen *Mother* • Mamata Shankar *Chinu* • Sreela Majumdar *Minu* • Tapan Das *Tapu* • Umanath Bhattacharya *Landlord* • Arun Mukherjee *Shyamal, the neighbour* ■ *Dir* Mrinal Sen • *Scr* Mrinal Sen, from the story *Abiroto Chene Mukh* by Amalendu Chakravarty

And So They Were Married ★★★

Romantic comedy 1936 · US · BW · 68mins

Widower Melvyn Douglas and his young son Jackie Moran meet widow Mary Astor and her daughter Edith Fellows while vacationing at a winter resort. After a sticky start, the adults fall for each other, but their children set out to sabotage the relationship. A short, neat romantic comedy, directed by the excellent Elliott Nugent, in which the classy expertise of Douglas and Astor is almost buried by the engaging antics of the juveniles. RK

Melvyn Douglas *Hugh "Stephen" Blake* • Mary Astor *Edith Farnham* • Edith Fellows *Brenda Farnham* • Jackie Moran *Tommy Blake* • Donald Meek *Hotel manager* • Dorothy Stickney *Miss Alma Peabody* • Romaine Callender *Mr Ralph P Shirley* • Douglas Scott *Horace* ■ *Dir* Elliott Nugent • *Scr* Doris Anderson, Joseph Anthony, A Laurie Brazee

And Soon the Darkness ★★

Thriller 1970 · UK · Colour · 99mins

One would have thought that writers Brian Clemens (who made his name on series such as *Danger Man* and *The Avengers*) and Terry Nation (doyen of *Doctor Who* scripters) would have come up with something more memorable than this nasty chiller. The voyeuristic approach to both the killer's crimes and the peril in which nurses Pamela Franklin and Michele Dotrice find themselves as they cycle through a French wood is most regrettable, if not downright objectionable. DP

Pamela Franklin *Jane* • Michele Dotrice *Cathy* • Sandor Eles *Paul* • John Nettleton *Gendarme* • Clare Kelly *Schoolmistress* • Hana-Maria Pravda *Madame Lassal* • John Franklyn *Old man* ■ *Dir* Robert Fuest • *Scr* Brian Clemens, Terry Nation

And the Angels Sing ★★ U

Musical comedy 1944 · US · BW · 95mins

Raucous Betty Hutton and glamorous Dorothy Lamour are joined by Diana Lynn and Mimi Chandler to make up a four-girl singing sister act. Their harmonious relationship is fractured by bandleader Fred MacMurray, who helps the quartet to success and finds romance with one of the sisters. This is standard 1940s Hollywood fare, with a good Johnny Burke–Jimmy Van Heusen score that includes the enduring standard, *It Could Happen to You*, a stalwart supporting cast from the Paramount stock company, and a couple of standout numbers from the irrepressible Hutton. RK

Dorothy Lamour *Nancy Angel* • Fred MacMurray *Happy Marshall* • Betty Hutton *Bobby Angel* • Diana Lynn *Josie Angel* • Mimi Chandler *Patti Angel* • Raymond Walburn *Pop Angel* • Eddie Foy Jr *Fuzzy Johnson* ■ *Dir* George Marshall • *Scr* Melvin Frank, Norman Panama, from a story by Claude Binyon

And the Band Played On ★★★ 15

Documentary drama
1993 · US · Colour · 135mins

This made-for-cable adaptation of Randy Shilts's monumental history of Aids is distractingly overloaded with stars, all too willing to prove their political correctness. But, taken as a detective story, this is still a gripping narrative in which French and American scientists search to isolate the virus and seek to find the airline employee who may have brought it from Africa. Matthew Modine's clear-sighted visionary provides the necessary human focus, keeping his integrity while others lose theirs. Director Roger Spottiswoode is hemmed in by too many statistics, yet still produces an absorbing docudrama. TH. Contains some swearing.

Matthew Modine *Dr Don Francis* • Ian McKellen *Bill Kraus* • Lily Tomlin *Dr Selma Dritz* • Richard Gere *Choreographer* • Alan Alda *Dr Robert Gallo* • Glenne Headly *Mary Guinan* • Phil Collins *Eddie Papasano* • Anjelica Huston *Dr Betsy Reisz* • Saul Rubinek *Dr Jim Curran* • Steve Martin *Brother* • Charles Martin Smith *Dr Harold Jaffe* • Elizabeth Taylor ■ *Dir* Roger Spottiswoode • *Scr* Arnold Schulman, from the non-fiction book by Randy Shilts

And the Beat Goes On: the Sonny and Cher Story ★★★ PG

Biographical drama
1999 · US · Colour · 85mins

Based on Sonny Bono's controversial autobiography, this TV biopic of the 1960s odd couple is enjoyably camp without veering too far into the cheap and tacky. Cher – still topping the charts on a regular basis – is played with finesse and respect by lookalike Renee Faia, while Sonny's infectious enthusiasm is ably put across by Jay Underwood. Fans will enjoy the clever soundtrack, which mixes original music from the period with some skilled re-creations. JF

Jay Underwood *Sonny Bono* • Renee Faia *Cher* • Jim Pirri *Buddy Black* • Laura Johnson *Georgia LaPierre* • Christian Leffler *Phil Spector* • Walter Franks *Little Richard* • Bruce Nozick *Art Rupe* • Marie Wilson *Mary Bono* ■ *Dir* David Burton Morris • *Scr* Ellen Weston, from the autobiography by Sonny Bono

And the Same to You ★★ U

Comedy 1960 · UK · BW · 67mins

Any film boasting Sid James, Tommy Cooper and Brian Rix in the cast has to be worth a look, but there are few laughs to be had in this screen version of a popular stage farce. Rix stars as a hopeless boxer who has to keep his career hidden from his disapproving archdeacon uncle. John Paddy Carstairs co-wrote the script with John Junkin, but every punch is pulled. DP
DVD

Brian Rix *Dickie Dreadnought* • William Hartnell *Wally Burton* • Tommy Cooper *Horace Hawkins* • Dick Bentley *George Nibbs* • Vera Day *Cynthia* • Sidney James *Sammy Gatt* • Leo Franklyn *Vicar* • Renee Houston *Mildred* • Miles Malleson *Bishop* ■ *Dir* George Pollock • *Scr* John Paddy Carstairs, John Junkin, from a play by AP Dearsley

And the Ship Sails On ★★★ PG

Comedy drama 1983 · It/Fr · Colour · 128mins

Federico Fellini's idea was to create the last voyage of the old Europe before it was snuffed out by the First World War. So in his mind he builds an ocean liner and lets it sail upon a phoney sea, laden with human cargo – aristocrats, diplomats and a band of opera singers who want to bury a great soprano on an offshore island. The director concocts some stunning moments of surreal beauty and impish humour, and the sudden arrival of Balkan refugees has the required impact. However, the film is still an awkward mishmash, much too long and unevenly acted. AT. Italian dialogue dubbed into English.

Freddie Jones *Mister Orlando* • Barbara Jefford *Ildebranda Cuffari* • Victor Poletti *Aureliano Fuciletto* • Peter Cellier *Sir Reginald Dongby* • Elisa Mainardi *Teresa Valegnani* • Norma West *Lady Violet Dongby* • Janet Suzman *Edmea Tetua* ■ *Dir* Federico Fellini, Mike Hodges • *Scr* Federico Fellini, Tonino Guerra, Catherine Breillat

And Then There Were None ★★★★ U

Crime mystery 1945 · US · BW · 97mins

Of all the adaptations of *Ten Little Niggers*, Agatha Christie's classic who-, what- and why- dunnit, this is the first and the best. French director René Clair, working in Hollywood, provides a distinctly European creepiness to the story of mysteriously invited guests on a deserted Cornish island being killed off one by one and, even without a Poirot or a Miss Marple, the denouement is a real shock. Stalwarts such as Barry Fitzgerald, Walter Huston, Louis Hayward and June Duprez form an ensemble as tetchy is they are terrified. AT DVD

Barry Fitzgerald *Judge Francis J Quincannon* • Walter Huston *Dr Edward G Armstrong* • Louis Hayward *Philip Lombard/Charles Morley* • Roland Young *William H Blore* • June Duprez *Vera Claythorne* • Mischa Auer *Prince Nikita Starloff* • C Aubrey Smith *Gen Sir John Mandrake* • Judith Anderson *Emily Brent* ■ *Dir* René Clair • *Scr* Dudley Nichols, from the novel *Ten Little Niggers* by Agatha Christie

And Then There Were None ★★★ PG

Crime mystery
1974 · Fr/Sp/W Ger/It · Colour · 93mins

This film version of Agatha Christie's whodunnit *Ten Little Niggers* assembles strangers at an isolated Persian palace and bumps them off one by one in retribution. It is lushly filmed by director Peter Collinson in pre-revolutionary Iran, but stars such as Richard Attenborough, Oliver Reed, Elke Sommer and Herbert Lom are given the task of propping up a dubious proposition, helped by the disembodied voice of narrator Orson Welles, who lends the project more weight than it deserves. TH

Oliver Reed *Hugh Lombard* • Richard Attenborough *Judge Cannon* • Elke Sommer *Vera Clyde* • Gert Froebe [Gert Fröbe] *Wilhelm Blore* • Adolfo Celi *General Soule* • Stéphane Audran *Ilona Bergen* • Charles Aznavour *Michel Raven* • Herbert Lom *Dr Armstrong* • Orson Welles *Voice on tape recorder* ■ *Dir* Peter Collinson • *Scr* Erich Krohnke, from the novel *Ten Little Niggers* by Agatha Christie

And Women Shall Weep ★★

Drama 1960 · UK · BW · 65mins

This little British B-movie is given great strength by the leading performance of veteran TV character actress Ruth Dunning. The actress stars as a widow trying to keep her young son Richard O'Sullivan on the straight and narrow. However, her older son Max Butterfield is beyond help. Slight and overplayed, this would have been better as a live TV drama. TS

Ruth Dunning *Mrs Lumsden* • Max Butterfield *Terry Lumsden* • Gillian Vaughan *Brenda Wilkes* • Richard O'Sullivan *Godfrey Lumsden* • Claire Gordon *Sadie MacDougall* ■ *Dir* John Lemont • *Scr* John Lemont, Leigh Vance

And You Thought Your Parents Were Weird ★★ PG

Science-fiction fantasy
1991 · US · Colour · 87mins

A low-budget and fairly weak family sci-fi comedy, rehashing a variety of ideas and gimmicks familiar from films including *Star Wars*, *Short Circuit* and *Forbidden Planet*. The action focuses on two boys who build a multi-talented robot from everyday household items, only to find it contains the spirit of their late father. Inoffensive, but ultimately mediocre. PF

Marcia Strassman *Sarah Carson* • Joshua John Miller *Josh Carson* • Edan Gross *Max Carson* • John Quade *Irwin Kotzwinkle* • Sam Behrens *Steve Franklin* • Richard Libertini *Matthew Carson* • Alan Thicke *Newman the Robot* ■ *Dir/Scr* Tony Cookson

Andaz ★★★★ PG

Drama 1949 · Ind · BW · 150mins

Also known as *A Matter of Style*, this concluded the string of 1940s classics that established Mehboob Khan as one of the key figures in Indian cinema. An allegorical warning to the newly independent state not to lose sight of traditional values, it is a typically knotty melodrama, with ambitious young executive Dilip Kumar coming between his heiress boss Nargis and her feckless husband, Raj Kapoor. The film turned Kumar into a superstar, while also reinforcing the status of his co-stars as the sub-continent's favourite romantic team. DP. In Hindi with English subtitles.

Raj Kapoor *Rajan* • Dilip Kumar *Dilip* • Nargis *Neeta* • Sapru *Badriprasad* ■ *Dir* Mehboob Khan • *Scr* S Ali Raza

The Anderson Tapes ★★★ 15

Crime drama 1971 · US · Colour · 94mins

Sean Connery sets out to burgle a luxury apartment block helped by some notable eccentrics, unaware that his every move is under surveillance from various law enforcement agencies. The implicit ironies – that the agents can't see the larger picture of a major robbery for all their attention to the smaller details – are never quite forged into the intended satire, but director Sidney Lumet does achieve a certain sarcastic humour. Christopher Walken makes one of his first major film appearances. TH. Contains swearing.
DVD

Sean Connery *Duke Anderson* • Dyan Cannon *Ingrid Everleigh* • Martin Balsam *Tommy Haskins* • Ralph Meeker *Delaney* • Alan King *Pat Angelo* • Christopher Walken *The Kid* • Val Avery *Parelli* • Dick Williams [Dick Anthony Williams] *Spencer* • Margaret Hamilton *Miss Kaler* ■ *Dir* Sidney Lumet • *Scr* Frank R Pierson, from the novel by Lawrence Sanders

Andre ★★★ U

Adventure 1994 · US · Colour · 90mins

Set in the early 1960s, this tells the story of the rather cute seal of the title, which is adopted by precocious newcomer Tina Majorino, playing the animal-loving daughter of harbour master Keith Carradine. The local fishing community is worried that Andre will affect their catch, which leads to the inevitable conflict. It's sickly sweet stuff, but Andre (actually played by a sea-lion) is undoubtedly endearing, and youngsters will be enraptured. JF

Keith Carradine *Harry Whitney* • Tina Majorino *Toni Whitney* • Chelsea Field *Thalice Whitney* •

Shane Meier *Steve Whitney* • Aidan Pendleton *Paula Whitney* • Shirley Broderick *Mrs McCann* • Andrea Libman *Mary May* • Joshua Jackson *Mark Baker* ■ *Dir* George Miller (1) • *Scr* Dana Baratta, from the non-fiction book *A Seal Called Andre* by Harry Goodridge, Lew Dietz

Andrei Rublev ★★★★★ 15

Biographical drama
1966 · USSR · Colour and BW · 174mins

Divided into eight episodes and majestically photographed by Vadim Yusov, this is a remarkable study of the artist Andrei Rublev's struggle to overcome both his own doubts, and the poverty and cruelty of his time, to create works of inspirational power and outstanding beauty. Anatoly Solonitsin plays the 15th-century icon painter as a sort of wandering mystic who takes a vow of silence in protest at conditions in Russia under the Tartars. Andrei Tarkovsky includes too much impenetrable symbolism, but the battle, the balloon flight, the snow crucifixion, the casting of the bell and the colour montage from Rublev's work are stunning. DP. In Russian with English subtitles. DVD

Anatoly Solonitsin [Anatoli Solonitsyn] *Andrei Rublev* • Ivan Lapikov *Kirill* • Nikolai Grinko *Daniel Chorny* • Nikolai Sergeyev *Theophanes the Greek* • Irma Rausch *Idiot girl* • Nikolai Burlyaev *Boris* • Yuri Nazarov *The Grand Prince/His brother* ■ *Dir* Andrei Tarkovsky • *Scr* Andrei Tarkovsky, Andrei Mikhalkov-Konchalovsky [Andrei Konchalovsky] • *Cinematographer* Vadim Yusov

Andrew & Jeremy Get Married ★★★ 15

Documentary 2004 · UK · Colour · 72mins

This low-key documentary from writer/director Don Boyd was produced for the BBC's *Storyville* series, which may explain its rather brief running time and small-screen feel. Filmed over the course of a year, it chronicles the relationship between two very different gay men in the run-up to their "wedding". Jeremy is a patrician 69-year-old English professor with connections to London's upper-crust literati, and Andrew is a 49-year-old former bus driver with a history of promiscuity and drug abuse. They're an engaging if odd couple, as Boyd reveals, and their commitment ceremony at London's City Hall, after five years together, is a moving and uplifting experience. DA

Dir/Scr Don Boyd

Androcles and the Lion ★★★ U

Satirical comedy 1952 · US · BW · 96mins

This RKO movie was a long time in the making, and stars Victor Mature and Jean Simmons found greater success with their next foray into Roman history together, *The Robe*. The imported British supporting cast, including Robert Newton, behave like fish out of water under Chester Erskine's shambolic direction, but this is still and interesting and quirky one-off. TS

Jean Simmons *Lavinia* • Alan Young *Androcles* • Victor Mature *Captain* • Robert Newton *Ferrovius* • Maurice Evans *Caesar* • Elsa Lanchester *Megaera* • Reginald Gardiner *Lentulus* • Gene Lockhart *Menagerie keeper* • Alan Mowbray *Editor* ■ *Dir* Chester Erskine • *Scr* Chester Erskine, Ken Englund, from the play by George Bernard Shaw

Android ★★★ 15

Science-fiction fantasy
1982 · US · Colour · 76mins

Three space convicts upset the plans of mad scientist Klaus Kinski to replace his companion android, Max 404, with a perfect female version in a low-key slice of cult science-fiction from the Roger Corman factory. Don Opper's portrayal of Max as a nerdy movie buff clone adds extra pop culture playfulness to the enjoyably exciting proceedings. Neat suspense, a few final reel twists and another eccentric Kinski performance make this low-budget gem a winner. AJ. Contains swearing, violence. DVD

Klaus Kinski *Dr Daniel* • Don Opper *Max 404* • Brie Howard *Maggie* • Norbert Weisser *Keller* • Crofton Hardester *Mendes* • Kendra Kirchner *Cassandra* ■ *Dir* Aaron Lipstadt • *Scr* Don Opper, James Reigle

The Andromeda Strain ★★★★ PG

Science-fiction thriller
1970 · US · Colour · 123mins

This super combination of hi-tech thrills and against-the-clock suspense was the first Michael Crichton novel to be adapted for the big screen. Robert Wise's near-documentary direction keeps tension mounting as desperate scientists race to isolate a fatal alien virus from a fallen satellite. More science fact than fiction, and still powerfully relevant, it's a remarkably faithful account of Crichton's biological invasion bestseller, layered with sophisticated special effects by Douglas Trumbull. AJ DVD

Arthur Hill *Dr Jeremy Stone* • David Wayne *Dr Charles Dutton* • James Olson *Dr Mark Hall* • Kate Reid *Dr Ruth Leavitt* • Paula Kelly *Karen Anson* • George Mitchell *Jackson* • Ramon Bieri *Major Mancheck* • Richard O'Brien *Grimes* ■ *Dir* Robert Wise • *Scr* Nelson Gidding, from the novel by Michael Crichton

Andy Hardy Comes Home ★★ U

Comedy drama 1958 · US · BW · 79mins

A dozen years after his last appearance as Andy Hardy, Mickey Rooney returns to the small town of Carvel and finds himself embroiled in a dishonest property deal over an aircraft factory. Trading heavily on the audience's nostalgia for the series – clips from earlier films are featured – this was intended to herald a brand new run of Andy Hardy movies. Proudly waiting to take up the reins was none other than Mickey's son, Teddy; the series, however, ended here. AT

Mickey Rooney *Andy Hardy* • Patricia Breslin *Jane Hardy* • Fay Holden *Mother Hardy* • Cecilia Parker *Marian* • Sara Haden *Aunt Milly* • Jerry Colonna *Doc* • Frank Ferguson *Mayor Benson* • Teddy Rooney *Andy Hardy Jr* ■ *Dir* Howard W Koch • *Scr* Edward Everett Hutshing, Robert Morris Donley, from characters created by Aurania Rouverol

Andy Hardy Gets Spring Fever ★★ U

Comedy drama 1939 · US · BW · 85mins

Seventh in the series with a new director to marshal the action and those "man to man" talks between Judge Lewis Stone and Mickey Rooney. This time round, Rooney falls for a drama teacher and when it's revealed she's engaged, Andy's regular Ann Rutherford is still there for him. The teacher is played by Helen Gilbert who was a cellist in the MGM studio orchestra until someone gave her a screen test. DP

Lewis Stone *Judge James K Hardy* • Mickey Rooney *Andy Hardy* • Cecilia Parker *Marian Hardy* • Ann Rutherford *Polly Benedict* • Fay Holden *Mrs Emily Hardy* • Sara Haden *Aunt Milly* • Helen Gilbert *Rose Meredith* ■ *Dir* WS Van Dyke II [WS Van Dyke] • *Scr* Kay Van Riper, from characters created by Aurania Rouverol

Andy Hardy Meets Debutante ★★ U

Comedy drama 1940 · US · BW · 87mins

The ninth film in the series sees Mickey Rooney in the Big Apple trying to secure a meeting with a debutante whose photograph he's seen in a magazine. It isn't all Hollywood pap, however: Andy's dad (Lewis Stone) is also in town, tending to the affairs of an orphanage. This entry is notable only for the appearance of Judy Garland, who sings *Alone* and *I'm Nobody's Baby*. She also gives Mickey a peck on the cheek. AT

Lewis Stone *Judge James K Hardy* • Mickey Rooney *Andy Hardy* • Fay Holden *Mrs Emily Hardy* • Cecilia Parker *Marian Hardy* • Judy Garland *Betsy Booth* • Sara Haden *Aunt Milly* • Ann Rutherford *Polly Benedict* • Tom Neal *Aldrich Brown* ■ *Dir* George B Seitz • *Scr* Annalee Whitmore, Thomas Seller, from characters created by Aurania Rouverol

Andy Hardy's Blonde Trouble ★★ U

Comedy drama 1944 · US · BW · 107mins

Mickey Rooney stars in the 14th and penultimate *Andy Hardy* comedy (not counting the straggler made in 1958). As the eternal, archetypal teenager, Rooney enrols in his dad's alma mater but gets into trouble by paying too much attention to girls, mainly Bonita Granville and twin blondes who fancy him and make his life a misery. Awash with those rather cloying MGM family values, plus a few songs, this was the final film of director George B Seitz, a veteran of all but two of the series. AT

Lewis Stone *Judge James K Hardy* • Mickey Rooney *Andy Hardy* • Fay Holden *Mrs Emily Hardy* • Sara Haden *Aunt Milly* • Herbert Marshall *Dr MJ Standish* • Bonita Granville *Kay Wilson* • Jean Porter *Katy Henderson* • Keye Luke *Dr Lee Wong How* ■ *Dir* George B Seitz • *Scr* Harry Ruskin, William Ludwig, Agnes Christine Johnston, from characters created by Aurania Rouverol

Andy Hardy's Double Life ★★ U

Comedy drama 1942 · US · BW · 92mins

This was one of the last films in this ever-popular series, as MGM couldn't stop Mickey Rooney from growing older. Andy Hardy finally gets to go to college, where he gets embroiled with the opposite sex. Rooney's mugging and the sentimental home-town feel was beginning to wear thin, and there would be only two more films in the series, not including *Andy Hardy Comes Home* in 1958. TS

Mickey Rooney *Andy Hardy* • Lewis Stone *Judge James K Hardy* • Esther Williams *Sheila Brooks* • Ann Rutherford *Polly Benedict* • Fay Holden *Mrs Emily Hardy* • Cecilia Parker *Marian Hardy* • Sara Haden *Aunt Milly* • William Lundigan *Jeff Willis* ■ *Dir* George B Seitz • *Scr* Agnes Christine Johnston, from characters created by Aurania Rouverol

Andy Hardy's Private Secretary ★★ U

Comedy drama 1941 · US · BW · 100mins

The gang's all here for this tenth outing, plus 18-year-old Kathryn Grayson making an early screen appearance as the girl Mickey Rooney hires as his secretary as he is about to graduate from high school. She ends up helping him pass his English exam and getting him through high school at the second attempt. Grayson gets to sing and show her star potential (MGM had been grooming her as a rival to Universal's Deanna Durbin), but the formula already shows signs of running out of steam. AT

Lewis Stone *Judge James K Hardy* • Mickey Rooney *Andy Hardy* • Fay Holden *Mrs Emily Hardy* • Ian Hunter *Steven Land* • Ann Rutherford *Polly Benedict* • Kathryn Grayson *Kathryn Land* • Todd Karns *Harry Land* • John Dilson *Mr Davis* ■ *Dir* George B Seitz • *Scr* Jane Murfin, Harry Ruskin, from characters created by Aurania Rouverol

Angel ★★

Drama 1937 · US · BW · 90mins

Marlene Dietrich was already labelled box-office poison when she made this movie for Ernst Lubitsch, a tale of sexual deception that's halfway between romantic melodrama and sophisticated comedy. Dietrich is married to Herbert Marshall, but she still fancies former boyfriend Melvyn Douglas. Things get bogged down by plot and, without Josef von Sternberg's exotic camerawork, Dietrich often looks like a plain Jane. AT

Marlene Dietrich *Maria Barker* • Herbert Marshall *Sir Frederick Barker* • Melvyn Douglas *Anthony Halton* • Edward Everett Horton *Graham* • Ernest Cossart *Walton* • Laura Hope Crews *Grand Duchess Anna Dmitrievna* • Herbert Mundin *Greenwood* • Ivan Lebedeff *Prince Vladimir Gregorovitch* ■ *Dir* Ernst Lubitsch • *Scr* Samson Raphaelson, Guy Bolton, Russell Medcraft, Melchior Lengyel, from the play by Melchior Lengyel

Angel ★★★★ 15

Crime thriller 1982 · Ire · Colour · 88mins

In Neil Jordan's remarkable first feature, Stephen Rea plays a saxophonist who embarks on a bloody trail of revenge after his business manager and a mute girl are gunned down by Irish gangsters. While the Troubles and the sectarian divide are always in the background, Jordan steers a hypnotic and often surreal path through Ulster's underworld, while Rea is perfect as the equivocal hero whose quest becomes almost Arthurian. The actor would later star in Jordan's 1992 Oscar-winner *The Crying Game*. AT DVD

Stephen Rea *Danny* • Alan Devlin *Bill* • Veronica Quilligan *Annie* • Peter Caffrey *Ray* • Honor Heffernan *Deirdre* • Ray McAnally *Bloom* ■ *Dir/Scr* Neil Jordan

Angel ★★

Crime comedy drama
1984 · US · Colour · 92mins

Writer/director Robert Vincent O'Neil tosses some offbeat comedy and a teenage temptress angle into this tacky follow-up to *Vice Squad*. Dick Shawn serves up the former as a gregarious drag queen, while Donna Wilkes does her best to provide the latter as the class-topping student who becomes a fallen angel by night. Other lowlifes include Rory Calhoun as a former cowboy star, Susan Tyrell as a lesbian and John Diehl as the psycho being pursued by cop Cliff Gorman. DP

Cliff Gorman *Lt Andrews* • Susan Tyrrell *Mosler* • Dick Shawn *Mae* • Rory Calhoun *Kit Carson* • John Diehl *Billy Boy* • Donna Wilkes *Angel/Molly* • Robert Acey *Driver/John* ■ *Dir* Robert Vincent O'Neil • *Scr* Robert Vincent O'Neil, Joseph Michael Cala

Angel and the Badman ★★★ U

Western 1947 · US · BW · 95mins

As Republic's one major star, John Wayne flexed his power to make a producing debut with this absorbingly offbeat western on which he promoted his writer buddy, James Edward Grant, to the director's chair. Wayne stars as the injured gunman, nursed back to health by Quakers, who falls for the daughter of the house, Gail Russell. Can Wayne embrace their peaceful ways and avoid firing his six-gun despite the provocation of bad guy Bruce Cabot? Grant's screenplay delivers some gratifying and ingenious twists en route. AE DVD

John Wayne *Quirt Evans* • Gail Russell *Penelope* • Harry Carey *Wistful McClintock* • Bruce Cabot *Laredo Stevens* • Irene Rich *Mrs Worth* • Lee Dixon *Randy McCall* • Stephen Grant *Johnny Worth* • Tom Powers *Dr Mangrum* ■ *Dir/Scr* James Edward Grant

A

Angel, Angel Down We Go ★

Crime drama 1969 · US · Colour · 93mins

Director Robert Thom's staggering folly stars Hollywood legend Jennifer Jones as a porn-movie actress, Roddy McDowall as a rock group member and future soul singer Lou Rawls. It finds rock star Jordan Christopher moving in on a wealthy Hollywood family only to seduce and kill them. Warped, strange and ridiculous, this is an an infamous cult movie disaster. AJ

Jennifer Jones *Astrid Steele* • Jordan Christopher *Bogart* • Roddy McDowall *Santoro* • Holly Near *Tara Nicole Steele* • Lou Rawls *Joe* • Charles Aidman *Willy Steele* • Davey Davison *Anna Livia* ■ *Dir/Scr* Robert Thom

An Angel at My Table ★★★★★ 15

Biographical drama
1990 · NZ/Aus/UK · Colour · 151mins

Director Jane Campion went on to win a screenplay Oscar for *The Piano*, but this perceptive film biography of New Zealand author Janet Frame had already served notice of her remarkable talent. Based on Frame's autobiographies and put together from a three-part TV mini-series it charts the writer's difficult life, including the eight years she spent in a mental hospital after being wrongly diagnosed as schizophrenic. What could so easily have become a sensationalist exposé of mental shock treatment comes across as a small masterpiece about one woman's triumph in breaking out of life's straitjacket. *Shallow Grave's* Kerry Fox and Karen Fergusson give superb performances as the grown-up and teenage Janet. TH. Contains swearing and nudity. [video] DVD

Kerry Fox *Janet Frame* • Karen Fergusson *Teenage Janet* • Alexia Keogh *Young Janet* • Melina Bernecker *Myrtle Frame* • Glynis Angell *Isabel Frame* • Samantha Townsley *Teenage Isabel* • Katherine Murray-Cowper *Young Isabel* • Sarah Smuts Kennedy *June Frame* ■ *Dir* Jane Campion • *Scr* Laura Jones, from the autobiographal books by Janet Frame

Angel Baby ★★★

Drama 1961 · US · BW · 97mins

Notable as Burt Reynolds's big-screen debut, this is a steely look at the effects of a no-holds-barred evangelical ministry on the deeply suspicious backwoods population of America's southern states. There's plenty of hootin', hollerin' and speakin' in tongues, but the movie cleverly avoids the obvious targets, choosing instead to concentrate on what happens to people within their own community when a collective subconscious is uncommonly rattled. Watch for two fine performances from Mercedes McCambridge and Joan Blondell. SH

George Hamilton *Paul Strand* • Mercedes McCambridge *Sarah Strand* • Salome Jens *Angel Baby* • Joan Blondell *Mollie Hays* • Henry Jones *Ben Hays* • Burt Reynolds *Hoke Adams* • Roger Clark *Sam Wilcox* ■ *Dir* Paul Wendkos • *Scr* Orin Borsten, Paul Mason, Samuel Roeca, from the novel *Jenny Angel* by Elsie Oaks Barber

Angel Baby ★★ 15

Romantic drama
1995 · Aus · Colour · 100mins

A tale of doomed love starring John Lynch and Jacqueline McKenzie as two psychiatric patients who decide to live together. The two lovers hit the bottom of mental hell, bouncing off the walls as well as each other and the prognosis does not suggest a happy ending. The film suffers from the fact that the two leads sadly lack the depth to pull it off. LH. Contains some coarse language, nudity and a traumatic childbirth scene. [video]

John Lynch *Harry* • Jacqueline McKenzie *Kate* • Colin Friels *Morris* • Deborra-Lee Furness *Louise* • Daniel Daperis *Sam* • David Argue *Dave* • Geoff Brooks *Rowan* • Humphrey Bower *Frank* ■ *Dir/Scr* Michael Rymer

Angel Dust ★★★ 15

Thriller 1987 · Fr · Colour · 91mins

Edouard Niermans directs this downbeat homage to the Hollywood *film noir*. World-weary cop Bernard Giraudeau pulls his life together to investigate the part played by his wife's new lover in the murder of a prostitute. Trudging through Bernard Lutic's atmospheric cityscapes, Giraudeau gives a suitably hard-boiled performance. But there is plenty of wit here, too, plus a little angelic mystery provided by the victim's impish daughter, Fanny Bastien. DP. In French with English subtitles. Contains violence [video]

Bernard Giraudeau *Simon Blount* • Fanny Bastien *Violetta* • Fanny Cottençon *Martine* • Michel Aumont *Florimont* • Jean-Pierre Sentier *Georges Landry* • Luc Lavandier *Gabriel Spielmacher* ■ *Dir* Edouard Niermans • *Scr* Jacques Audiard, Alain Le Henry, Edouard Niermans, Didier Haudepin

Angel Eyes ★★★ 15

Romantic drama 2001 · US · Colour · 99mins

Whimsy is not usually director Luis Mandoki's cup of tea. He specialises in bringing us realistic love stories such as *When a Man Loves a Woman* and here again he delivers an unconventional romance. Jennifer Lopez is excellent as an embittered Chicago cop who's hopelessly at odds with her father and brother's brutality towards their wives. On the streets, however, she is as aggressive as they are until rescued one day by enigmatic drifter Jim Caviezel. A darker slant makes this intriguing, but it's let down by an appalling finale that reeks of schmaltz. LH [video] DVD

Jennifer Lopez *Sharon Pogue* • Jim Caviezel *Catch* • Terrence Howard *Robby* • Sonia Braga *Josephine Pogue* • Jeremy Sisto *Larry Pogue* • Victor Argo *Carl Pogue* • Shirley Knight *Elanora Davis* ■ *Dir* Luis Mandoki • *Scr* Gerald DiPego

Angel Face ★★★★

Crime drama 1953 · US · BW · 91mins

Jean Simmons was never happy under contract to Howard Hughes, who made her chop off her hair and wear a wig. She also felt Otto Preminger brutalised her during the making of *Angel Face*, taking rather too much enjoyment in showing Robert Mitchum how to slap her around. The film, however, is a near classic, in which Simmons's beauty is a mask for psychopathy. In this Freudian melodrama, she bumps off her dad and stepmother before turning her sights on the chauffeur (Mitchum). Passion has rarely been depicted so chillingly. AT

Robert Mitchum *Frank Jessup* • Jean Simmons *Diane Tremayne* • Mona Freeman *Mary* • Herbert Marshall *Mr Tremayne* • Leon Ames *Fred Barrett* • Barbara O'Neil *Mrs Tremayne* • Kenneth Tobey *Bill* • Raymond Greenleaf *Arthur Vance* • Jim Backus *Judson* ■ *Dir* Otto Preminger • *Scr* Frank Nugent, Oscar Millard, from a story by Chester Erskine

Angel Heart ★★★ 18

Mystery thriller 1987 · US · Colour · 108mins

In Alan Parker's unpleasant, tense thriller set in 1950s New Orleans, Mickey Rourke plays a private detective who's trying to locate a missing person for sinister client Robert De Niro. The trail leads towards voodoo rites. Rourke's naked romp with Lisa Bonet, as blood drips from the ceiling, caused considerable controversy and received attention from the censors. The story is utter nonsense, dressed up by Parker with much visual hype and with Rourke, De Niro and Charlotte Rampling contributing performances just the right side of self-parody. AT. Contains violence, swearing, sex scenes and nudity. [video] DVD

Mickey Rourke *Harry Angel* • Robert De Niro *Louis Cyphre* • Lisa Bonet *Epiphany Proudfoot* • Charlotte Rampling *Margaret Krusemark* • Stocker Fontelieu *Ethan Krusemark* • Brownie McGhee *Toots Sweet* • Michael Higgins *Doctor Fowler* • Elizabeth Whitcraft *Connie* ■ *Dir* Alan Parker • *Scr* Alan Parker, from the novel *Falling Angel* by William Hjortsberg

Angel in Exile ★★★ PG

Western 1948 · US · BW · 86mins

Ex-convict John Carroll heads for Mexico to recover a cache of stolen gold hidden in a disused mine. Plans to work a scam go awry when his "discovery" convinces the local peasantry that God has worked a miracle for their prosperity. Co-directed by veteran Allan Dwan and Philip Ford, with a cast that includes Thomas Gomez as the village doctor and Adele Mara as his daughter, this modest western has an unusual, ironic and appealing message to accompany its otherwise stock ingredients. RK [video]

John Carroll *Charlie Dakin* • Adele Mara *Raquel Chavez* • Thomas Gomez *Dr Esteban Chavez* • Barton MacLane *Max Giorgio* • Alfonso Bedoya *Ysidro Alvarez* • Grant Withers *Sheriff* • Paul Fix *Carl Spitz* • Art Smith *Ernie Coons* ■ *Dir* Allan Dwan, Philip Ford • *Scr* Charles Larson

Angel in My Pocket ★★★

Comedy 1968 · US · Colour · 105mins

Andy Griffith was at his disturbing best in the box-office failure *A Face in the Crowd*, but he seldom went beyond the safe character he developed in his TV series. This lightweight trifle is an extension of that soft-hearted soul, though Griffith is acted off the screen by Jerry Van Dyke's performance as the most revolting brother-in-law in movie history. The tale of a new minister trying to win over his resentful new community is given some scale by the Techniscope process, but it's very American in theme and outlook. TS

Andy Griffith *Samuel D Whitehead* • Jerry Van Dyke *Bubba* • Kay Medford *Racine* • Edgar Buchanan *Axel Gresham* • Gary Collins *Art Shields* • Lee Meriwether *Mary Elizabeth* • Henry Jones *Will Sinclair* • Parker Fennelly *Calvin* ■ *Dir* Alan Rafkin • *Scr* James Fritzell, Everett Greenbaum

The Angel Levine ★★

Fantasy drama 1970 · US · Colour · 105mins

An exhaustingly tiresome parable about Jewish tailor Zero Mostel, forever complaining to God about his bad luck, who finds that black angel Harry Belafonte has been assigned to his case. But even the heavenly presence gets bored with the grumbles – as do we. Some admirable performances, but as an affirmation of faith it comes across in a very negative fashion. TH

Zero Mostel *Morris Mishkin* • Harry Belafonte *Alexander Levine* • Ida Kaminska *Fanny Mishkin* • Milo O'Shea *Dr Arnold Berg* • Gloria Foster *Sally* • Barbara Ann Teer *Welfare lady* • Eli Wallach *Store clerk* ■ *Dir* Jan Kadar • *Scr* Bill Gunn, Ronald Ribman, from the story by Bernard Malamud

Angel of Fury ★ 18

Martial arts horror
1991 · US · Colour · 90mins

This may be one of Cynthia Rothrock's worst efforts to date. She plays a security agent attempting to safely deliver a hi-tech computer from an evil terrorist (described twice in the film as, "Bolt – the terrorist that strikes like lightning"). Rothrock can certainly fight and she looks great in those tight-fitting clothes, but extensive editing ruins the brawling scenes. KB [video]

Cynthia Rothrock *Nancy Bollins* • Chris Barnes • Peter O'Brian • Roy Marten • Tanaka • Jurek Klyne ■ *Dir* Ackyl Anwary • *Scr* Christopher Mitchum, from a story by Deddy Armand

Angel of Mercy ★★

Romantic war drama
1993 · Cz · Colour · 95mins

With a fine classical score and stylishly filmed by Vladimir Hollos, this period piece might have been more convincing had it not succumbed to melodramatic contrivance. Not that Miloslav Luther's film is without its plus points. Ingrid Timkova is particularly impressive as the loyal wife whose shock at finding her soldier husband suffering from extensive burns drives her into the arms of Juraj Simko, a PoW at the military hospital where she nurses. DP. In Czech with English subtitles.

Ingrid Timkova *Anezka* • Juraj Simko *Krystof* • Josef Vajnar *Horecky* • Peter Simun *Fero* • Juraj Mokry *Sylvio* ■ *Dir* Miloslav Luther • *Scr* Vladimir Korner, Marian Puobis

Angel on My Shoulder ★★★

Fantasy drama 1946 · US · BW · 101mins

One of those whimsical fantasies beloved of Hollywood in the 1940s, this time with Paul Muni as a murdered gangster sent back to Earth to seek revenge in a deal with ultra-urbane Devil Claude Rains. The uncharacteristically cast Muni enjoys himself in the brash leading role, and Anne Baxter is simply delightful as the confused fiancée of the crusading judge whom Rains is trying to discredit. Veteran director Archie Mayo keeps the action moving along and makes good use of the story by Harry Segall. TS

Paul Muni *Eddie Kagle/Judge Parker* • Anne Baxter *Barbara Foster* • Claude Rains *Nick/the Devil* • Onslow Stevens *Dr Matt Higgins* • George Cleveland *Albert* • Hardie Albright *Smiley Williams* • James Flavin *Bellamy* • Erskine Sanford *Minister* ■ *Dir* Archie Mayo • *Scr* Harry Segall, Roland Kibbee, from a story by Harry Segall • *Music* Dimitri Tiomkin [Dmitri Tiomkin]

Angel on the Right ★★★ 12

Comedy drama
2002 · Fr/It/Swi/Tajikistan · Colour · 88mins

Combining the grim realities of post-Soviet Tajikistan with the morality of an old Islamic fable, Djamshed Usmonov's disarmingly offbeat comedy is set in his home village of Asht and bathed in washed-out tones. It's something of a family affair, with the director's brother and mother (Maruf Pulodzoda and Uktamoi Miyasarova) headlining the story of a petty hood who is lured into visiting his ailing parent only to be ensnared by irate creditors, who duly proceed to offer him assistance when he's pursued by a vengeful Moscow mobster. Dark and deadpan. DP. In Tajik with English subtitles. Contains violence. DVD

Uktamoi Miyasarova *Halima* • Maruf Pulodzoda *Hamro* • Kova Tilavpur *Yatim* • Mardonquol Qulbobo *The Mayor* ■ *Dir/Scr* Djamshed Usmonov

Angel Sharks ★★★★ 15

Romantic drama 1997 · Fr · Colour · 93mins

Echoes of Jacques Demy and Pier Paolo Pasolini ring teasingly around this tale of teenage driftwood. Yet Manuel Pradal's imagery and structuring are so singular, and his handling of the non-professional cast so impressive, that such comparisons do him a disservice. Not only does the writer/director refuse to sanitise the actions of Frédéric Malgras and his fellow "angel sharks"; he also avoids patronising him when he hooks up with the equally dispossessed Vahina Giocante, who's been rejected by both the local kids and the American sailors she hoped to exploit. Peering into the darker coves of the Côte d'Azur, this is as raw as it is poetic. DP. In French with English subtitles. Contains swearing and violence.

Nicolas Welbers *Goran* • Amira Casar *Young woman* • Swan Carpio *Jurec* • Jamie Harris *Jimmy* • Frédéric Malgras *Orso* • Vahina Giocante *Marie* • Andrew Clover *Andy* ■ *Dir/Scr* Manuel Pradal

Angel Square ★★

Period adventure
1990 · Can · Colour · 106mins

Jeremy Radick stars as a schoolboy who sets out to uncover the truth behind the assault of his best friend's father in this likeable movie, set during the Christmas of 1945. Veteran Hollywood character actor Ned Beatty is a familiar face, and among the cast of youngsters both Radick and Marie Stefan Guadry give pleasing performances. The attention to period detail is also commendable, and, despite the *Boys' Own* plot, the film still manages to push all the right liberal buttons. JB

Ned Beatty *Officer Ozzie O'Driscoll/Santa Claus* • Jeremy Radick *Tommy Doyle* • Marie Stefane Gaudry *Fleurette* • Guillaume Lemay-Thivierge *Coco* • Leon Pownall *Blue Cheeks* • Nicola Cavendish *Aunt Dottie* • Sarah Meyette *Loretta* • Michel Barrette *Frank* ■ *Dir* Anne Wheeler • *Scr* James DeFelice, Anne Wheeler

The Angel Who Pawned Her Harp ★★ U

Fantasy comedy 1954 · UK · BW · 76mins

In one of her first roles, Australian actress Diane Cilento plays an angel sent on a goodwill mission to Earth. Landing in the Angel, Islington, she pawns her harp, wins some dosh on the greyhounds and sets about sorting out the problems of the ordinary folk she encounters. What this dash of whimsy needs is a modicum of tension or humour, but it hopes to survive purely on charm and the attractiveness of Miss Cilento, who later became Mrs Sean Connery. AT

Diane Cilento *The Angel* • Felix Aylmer *Joshua Webman* • Jerry Desmonde *Parker* • Robert Eddison *The Voice* • Sheila Sweet *Jenny Lane* • Alfie Bass *Lennox* • Joe Linnane *Ned Sullivan* • Philip Guard *Len Burrows* ■ *Dir* Alan Bromly • *Scr* Charles Terrot, Sidney Cole, from the novel by Charles Terrot

The Angel Wore Red ★★

Romantic drama 1960 · US · BW · 98mins

One of the few features to deal with the Spanish Civil War, this improbable romantic drama suffers from confused ideas and unsuitable casting; no wonder it barely saw the light of day in cinemas, being released a year or so after it was filmed. Dirk Bogarde is the priest who falls for prostitute Ava Gardner, but, despite their off-screen friendship, no real romantic sparks are struck and as a result the movie suffers a crippling blow. Joseph Cotten and Vittorio de Sica do lend the film gravitas, though. TS

Ava Gardner *Soledad* • Dirk Bogarde *Arturo Carrera* • Joseph Cotten *Hawthorne* • Vittorio De Sica *General Clave* • Aldo Fabrizi *Canon Rota* • Arnoldo Foà *Insurgent Major* • Finlay Currie *Bishop* • Rossana Rory *Mercedes* ■ *Dir/Scr* Nunnally Johnson

Angela ★★

Drama 1955 · US/It · BW · 91mins

Hollywood actor Dennis O'Keefe found himself increasingly in Europe towards the end of his career, and it was there that he wrote, directed and starred in this low-key combination of *Double Indemnity* and *The Postman Always Rings Twice*. Shot entirely on location in Rome, it was one of the movies that brought Italian heart-throb Rossano Brazzi to the attention of the world. O'Keefe does a workmanlike job, and he has a real chemistry with sexy Mara Lane in the title role. TS

Dennis O'Keefe *Steve Catlett* • Mara Lane *Angela Towne* • Rossano Brazzi *Nino* • Arnoldo Foà *Captain Ambrosi* • Galeazzo Benti *Gustavo Venturi* • Enzo Fiermonte *Sergeant Collins* ■ *Dir* Dennis O'Keefe • *Scr* Jonathan Rix [Dennis O'Keefe], Edoardo Anton, from a story by Steven Carruthers

Angela ★★★ 15

Romantic crime drama
2002 · It · Colour · 87mins

Roberta Torre radically departs from the musical comedies with which she began her career, in this intense, fact-based tale of forbidden passion among the Sicilian Mafia. Torn between loyalty to husband Mario Pupella and lust for handsome newcomer Andrea Di Stefano, debutante Donatella Finocchiaro shatters the stereotype of the gangland consort, while remaining true to its rigid code of honour. With Daniele Cipri's brooding photography intensifying the sense of danger that envelops the affair, this is also a compelling insight into the Mob's status within Palermo society. DP. In Italian with English subtitles. DVD

Donatella Finocchiaro *Angela* • Andrea Di Stefano *Masino* • Mario Pupella *Saro* • Erasmo Lo Bello *Mimmo* • Tony Gambino *Santino* • Matteo Gulino *Paolino* ■ *Dir/Scr* Roberta Torre

Angela's Ashes ★★★ 15

Biographical drama
1999 · US/Ire · Colour · 139mins

Frank McCourt's bestselling, Pulitzer Prize-winning memoir is brought vividly to the screen by Alan Parker with a good cast and top-of-the-line production values. The result is a faithful, sometimes pedestrian movie. Parker's decision to film the terrible poverty of the McCourt family – first in America, then in Ireland – with artistic, anaesthetising cinematography is a touch misguided, and Robert Carlyle as Frank's alcoholic dad has much less to do than Emily Watson. But the three boys playing Frank at various ages are all good, and McCourt's early memories of school and church provide some humorous respite. JC DVD

Emily Watson *Angela* • Robert Carlyle *Dad* • Joe Breen *Young Frank* • Ciaran Owens *Middle Frank* • Michael Legge *Older Frank* • Ronnie Masterson *Grandma Sheehan* • Pauline McLynn *Aunt Aggie* • Liam Carney *Uncle Pa Keating* • Eanna MacLiam *Uncle Pat* ■ *Dir* Alan Parker • *Scr* Laura Jones, Alan Parker, from the book by Frank McCourt • *Music* John Williams • *Cinematographer* Michael Seresin

Angèle ★★★★

Melodrama 1934 · Fr · BW · 164mins

As with his famous rural trilogy *Marius, Fanny, Cèsar*, director Marcel Pagnol is here concerned with the problems of illegitimate pregnancy. The setting is again the Marseille region where he grew up and began work as a teacher. Peasant girl Orane Demazis (then having an affair with the director) is abandoned by her lover and heads for the city where she has their baby and resorts to prostitution to survive. A complex story develops into a representation of feminism within a realistic docudrama that was well ahead of its time. BB. In French with English subtitles.

Orane Demazis *Angèle* • Henri Poupon *Clarius Barbaroux* • Fernandel *Saturnin* • Jean Servais *Albin* • Edouard Delmont *Amédée* ■ *Dir* Marcel Pagnol • *Scr* Marcel Pagnol, from the novel *Un de Baumugnes* by Jean Glono

The Angelic Conversation ★★ PG

Experimental drama
1985 · UK · Colour and BW · 77mins

Gay icon director Derek Jarman takes Shakespeare's sonnets back to their homoerotic roots in his highbrow rumination on the objectivity of desire. As young male figures wash, decorate and make love to each other on rocky seaside coastlines, a female narrator (Judi Dench) explores the subtext of the playwright's poetry in gay terms. Beautifully shot with painterly textures, Jarman's academic treatise will either bore or delight, depending on one's openness to the subject matter. AJ

Judi Dench *Narrator* ■ *Dir* Derek Jarman • *Music* Benjamin Britten, Coil

Angels and Insects ★★ 18

Period drama
1995 · UK/US · Colour · 112mins

In this precious adaptation of AS Byatt's novella *Morpho Eugenia*, director Philip Haas and his co-writer Belinda Haas have got some pretty tricky ideas to convey (such as Darwinism and the notion that humans are little more than specimens in a celestial laboratory), but they do so in such a pompous manner that the already stilted performances of Mark Rylance and Patsy Kensit border on the comic. Only Kristin Scott Thomas, playing against type as a mousey governess, emerges with any credit. DP DVD

Mark Rylance *William Adamson* • Patsy Kensit *Eugenia Alabaster* • Saskia Wickham *Rowena Alabaster* • Chris Larkin *Robin Swinnerton* • Douglas Henshall *Edgar Alabaster* • Annette Badland *Lady Alabaster* • Kristin Scott Thomas *Matty Crompton* • Jeremy Kemp *Sir Harald Alabaster* ■ *Dir* Philip Haas • *Scr* Philip Haas, Belinda Haas, from the novella *Morpho Eugenia* by AS Byatt

Angel's Dance ★ 15

Black comedy thriller
1999 · US · Colour · 98mins

Thrillers don't get much more stupid or obnoxious than this jumbled tale of master hitman James Belushi running rookie Kyle Chandler through his paces. The target is eccentric wallflower Sheryl Lee, who wears an ill-fitting dark wig for the first half, so she can make a dramatic (and ludicrous) transformation to cropped blonde avenger when she decides to strike back. JC DVD

James Belushi *Stevie Rosellini* • Sheryl Lee *Angelica Chaste* • Kyle Chandler *Tony "The Rock" Greco* • Jon Polito *Uncle Vinnie* • Frank John Hughes *Nick* ■ *Dir/Scr* David L Corley [David Corley]

Angels in the Outfield ★★ U

Sports fantasy 1951 · US · BW · 98mins

The rough-tongued and ill-tempered manager of a baseball team in need of success calls on celestial help; Paul Douglas heads a cast that includes Janet Leigh. An odd mix of comedy, whimsy and fantasy, this may appeal to those who like their laughs laced with sentimentality. Distinguished Clarence Brown directs but his expertise is wasted on the material. RK

Paul Douglas *Guffy McGovern* • Janet Leigh *Jennifer Paige* • Keenan Wynn *Fred Bayles* • Donna Corcoran *Bridget White* • Lewis Stone *Arnold P Hapgood* • Spring Byington *Sister Edwitha* • Bruce Bennett *Saul Hellman* • Marvin Kaplan *Timothy Durney* ■ *Dir* Clarence Brown • *Scr* Dorothy Kingsley, George Wells, from a story by Richard Conlin

Angels in the Outfield ★★ U

Sports fantasy 1994 · US · Colour · 93mins

This is a flimsy, overly sentimental baseball comedy that wastes the talents of such respected performers as Danny Glover, Christopher Lloyd and Brenda Fricker. Joseph Gordon-Levitt is the nominal star, playing a baseball fan who seeks divine intervention to win back his estranged father (Dermot Mulroney) and help his struggling team end its losing streak. It's sickly sweet, but children may be entertained. A sequel of sorts, *Angels in the Endzone*, followed. JF

Danny Glover *George Knox* • Brenda Fricker *Maggie Nelson* • Tony Danza *Mel Clark* • Christopher Lloyd *Al the Angel* • Ben Johnson *Hank Murphy* • Jay O Sanders *Ranch Wilder* • Joseph Gordon-Levitt *Roger* • Milton Davis Jr *J P* • Matthew McConaughey *Ben Williams* • Dermot Mulroney *Roger's father* ■ *Dir* William Dear • *Scr* Dorothy Kingsley, George Wells, Holly Goldberg Sloan

Angels One Five ★★★ U

Second World War drama
1952 · UK · BW · 93mins

Jack Hawkins, John Gregson and Michael Denison do well in this low-key, intelligent Second World War drama that attempts to show the reality of service life during the Battle of Britain. Director George More O'Ferrall draws on his first-hand knowledge of the subject gained during his own wartime RAF service to probe the emotions behind the British stiff upper lip. A big hit in its day, and still worth the time now. PF

Jack Hawkins *Group Captain "Tiger" Small* • Michael Denison *Squadron Leader Peter Moon* • Dulcie Gray *Nadine Clinton* • John Gregson *Pilot Officer "Septic" Baird* • Cyril Raymond *Squadron Leader Barry Clinton* • Veronica Hurst *Betty Carfax* • Harold Goodwin (2) *Wailes* ■ *Dir* George More O'Ferrall • *Scr* Derek Twist, from a story by Pelham Groom

Angels over Broadway ★★★ U

Drama 1940 · US · BW · 75mins

This is an intriguing, tongue-in-cheek blackly comic drama, in which Douglas Fairbanks Jr tries to embroil a suicidal conman in a poker game with the frantically paced help of Rita Hayworth and Thomas Mitchell, playing a mouthy alcoholic with a big idea. The whole film is not as good as the sum of its many diverse parts, although Mitchell gives a truly terrific performance and takes over the screen whenever he appears. SH

Douglas Fairbanks Jr *Bill O'Brien* • Rita Hayworth *Nina Barona* • Thomas Mitchell *Gene Gibbons* • John Qualen *Charles Engle* • George Watts *Hopper* • Ralph Theodore *Dutch Enright* • Eddie Foster *Louie Artino* • Jack Roper *Eddie Burns* ■ *Dir* Ben Hecht, Lee Garmes • *Scr* Ben Hecht

Angels Wash Their Faces ★★★

Drama 1939 · US · BW · 85mins

This is a follow-up, as you might have guessed from the rather arch title, to the previous year's classic *Angels with Dirty Faces*, though sadly bereft of that film's stars James Cagney and Pat O'Brien, not to mention director Michael Curtiz. So here's Ann Sheridan, who appeared in the original but in a different role, trying to keep her brother away from those pesky Dead End Kids in a sentimental social opus. It's expertly made, nattily paced and beautifully acted. TS

Ann Sheridan *Joy Ryan* • Ronald Reagan *Pat Remson* • Billy Halop *Billy Shafter* • Bonita Granville *Peggy Finnigan* • Frankie Thomas *Gabe Ryan* • Bobby Jordan *Bernie* • Bernard Punsley *Sleepy Arkelian* • Leo Gorcey *Lee Finegan* • Huntz Hall *Huntz* • Gabriel Dell *Luigi* • Henry O'Neill *Mr Remson Sr* ■ *Dir* Ray Enright • *Scr* Michael Fessier, Niven Busch, Robert Buckner, from an idea by Jonathan Finn

A

Angels with Dirty Faces ★★★★★ PG

Classic crime drama 1938 · US · BW · 93mins

This is the definitive Warner Bros gangster movie, starring James Cagney in his image-defining role. It's a knockdown, knockout, fast-paced, gritty melodrama, which, though much copied and even parodied, has never been bettered. The tale of two men – one good, one bad – is given extra weight by the casting of the Dead End Kids, headed by Leo Gorcey and Huntz Hall, as Cagney's would-be disciples, and the moral of the story is still valid today. Michael Curtiz directs with great élan, and the ending, as Cagney walks the famous last "mile" to his execution, is particularly well acted and directed. TS DVD

James Cagney *"Rocky" Sullivan* • Pat O'Brien *Jerry Connelly* • Humphrey Bogart *James Frazier* • Ann Sheridan *Laury Ferguson* • George Bancroft *Mac Keefer* • Billy Halop *"Soapy"* • Bobby Jordan *"Swing"* • Leo Gorcey *"Bim"* • Gabriel Dell *"Pasty"* • Huntz Hall *"Crab"* ■ *Dir* Michael Curtiz • *Scr* John Wexley, Warren Duff, from a story by Rowland Brown

Anger Management ★★★ 15

Comedy 2003 · US · Colour · 100mins

Adam Sandler gives a relatively restrained performance here as a mild-mannered businessman who, after a misunderstanding regarding some in-flight headphones, is ordered into anger management under the counsel of spirited shrink Jack Nicholson. Nicholson's methods are unusual, to say the least – he moves in with Sandler while making a move on his girlfriend Marisa Tomei – but director Peter Segal never really mines the comedy that this pairing and premise deserve. However, this does get by on true star power, Nicholson being one of the very few Hollywood actors who can out-shout Sandler. IF DVD

Adam Sandler *Dave Buznik* • Jack Nicholson *Dr Buddy Rydell* • Marisa Tomei *Linda* • Luis Guzman *Lou* • Lynne Thigpen *Judge Daniels* • Woody Harrelson *Galaxia/Security guard* • John Turturro *Chuck* • Kurt Fuller *Frank Head* • Jonathan Loughran *Nate* ■ *Dir* Peter Segal • *Scr* David Dorfman

Les Anges du Péché ★★★★★

Drama 1943 · Fr · BW · 73mins

Robert Bresson's remarkable directorial debut set the tone for his entire career. It's an intense study of spirituality about a young novice (Renée Fauré) who sacrifices herself for the moral redemption of an ex-prisoner (Jany Holt) who murders her lover immediately on release. Set mainly in the confines of a convent, the film details the devotional aspects of the nuns' lives while depicting the relationship between the two women, one damned, the other divine. Bresson's later work became increasingly pared-down and austere, but this first outing is almost melodramatic; and, while nothing specifically sexual occurs, it's suffused with an eerie, unspoken eroticism. AT. In French with English subtitles.

Renée Fauré *Anne-Marie* • Jany Holt *Thérèse* • Sylvie *Prioress* • Mila Parely *Madeleine* • Marie-Hélène Dasté *Mother St John* ■ *Dir* Robert Bresson • *Scr* Robert Bresson, Jean Giraudoux, RL Brückberger

Angi Vera ★★★★ 12

Political drama 1980 · Hun · Colour · 92mins

Set in 1948, as Stalinism tightened its grip on Hungary, this handsome drama provides an unsettling insight into political indoctrination. Veronika Papp is wholly convincing as the spirited teenage nurse who is sentenced to a Party correction centre after complaining about hospital conditions and then slowly succumbs to the allure of belonging and the illusion of status. The ease with which she betrays both her ideals and her lover is chilling, but Pal Gabor's stealthy direction leaves no doubt where the blame lies. DP. In Hungarian with English subtitles. VIDEO

Veronika Papp *Vera Angi* • Erzsi Pasztor *Anna Trajan* • Eva Szabo *Maria Muskat* • Tamas Dunai *Istvan Andre* • Laszlo Halasz *Comrade Sas* ■ *Dir* Pal Gabor • *Scr* Pal Gabor, from the novel by Endre Veszi

Angie ★★ 15

Comedy drama 1994 · US · Colour · 103mins

This should have been the perfect showcase for the talents of Geena Davis. However, Todd Graff's script is such an unconvincing blend of episode and narrative, comedy and melodrama, that she often seems to be acting in a vacuum. Her search for the mother who abandoned her as a child robs the plot of any momentum gained from the ruckus that occurs when she ditches longtime fiancé James Gandolfini for new beau Stephen Rea. DP. Contains swearing and nudity. VIDEO

Geena Davis *Angie Scacciapensieri* • Stephen Rea *Noel* • James Gandolfini *Vinnie* • Aida Turturro *Tina* • Philip Bosco *Frank* • Jenny O'Hara *Kathy* • Michael Rispoli *Jerry* ■ *Dir* Martha Coolidge • *Scr* Todd Graff, from the novel *Angie, I Says* by Avra Wing

The Angry Hills ★★

Second World War spy drama
1959 · UK · BW · 114mins

This adaptation of Leon Uris's novel casts Robert Mitchum as an American war correspondent trapped by a Nazi advance in Greece after agreeing to spy for British intelligence. Most of the time he poses in front of olive groves, tries to avoid Gestapo officer Stanley Baker and dallies with Gia Scala. Apart from Mitchum's unavoidable and irrepressible charisma, this war frolic has little to commend it. AT

Robert Mitchum *Mike Morrison* • Stanley Baker *Konrad Heisler* • Elisabeth Mueller *Lisa Kyriakides* • Gia Scala *Eleftheria* • Theodore Bikel *Tassos* • Sebastian Cabot *Chesney* • Peter Illing *Leonides* • Leslie Phillips *Ray Taylor* ■ *Dir* Robert Aldrich • *Scr* AI Bezzerides, from the novel by Leon Uris

The Angry Red Planet ★★ PG

Science fiction 1959 · US · Colour · 79mins

A female astronaut under the influence of drugs recalls an expedition to Mars where her team are greeted by giant man-eating plants, three-eyed Martians, Cyclopean blobs, giant bat-spiders and assorted bad vibes. The expressionistic special effects are red-tinted thanks to the film process "Cinemagic" to approximate the distorted, dream-like quality of Nora Hayden's reminiscences. Renowned science fiction director Ib Melchior gives a diverting spin to the familiar Saturday morning serial antics. AJ VIDEO

Gerald Mohr *O'Banion* • Nora Hayden *Iris Ryan* • Les Tremayne *Professor Gettell* • Jack Kruschen *Sergeant Jacobs* • Paul Hahn *General Treegar* • J Edward McKinley *Professor Weiner* • Tom Daly *Dr Gordon* • Edward Innes *General Prescott* ■ *Dir* Ib Melchior • *Scr* Ib Melchior, Sid Pink, from a story by Sid Pink

The Angry Silence ★★★ PG

Drama 1960 · UK · BW · 90mins

Although this fascinating melodrama was made over 40 years ago, its attitudes to trade unionism and industrial action are curiously contemporary. Screenwriter Bryan Forbes explores a range of political issues, but the practised rhetoric sounds false in the mouths of the rank and file, and the best moments are not the confrontations between strike-breaker Richard Attenborough and his workmates, but those depicting the pressures on his marriage. Attenborough gives a sterling performance, but the acting honours go to Pier Angeli as his distraught wife and Alfred Burke as the devious *agent provocateur*. DP VIDEO DVD

Richard Attenborough *Tom Curtis* • Pier Angeli *Anna Curtis* • Michael Craig *Joe Wallace* • Bernard Lee *Bert Connolly* • Alfred Burke *Travers* • Geoffrey Keen *Davis* • Laurence Naismith *Martindale* • Oliver Reed *Mick* ■ *Dir* Guy Green • *Scr* Bryan Forbes, from a story by Michael Craig, Richard Gregson

Anguish ★★★★ 18

Horror 1986 · Sp · Colour · 80mins

Catalan director Bigas Luna ventures into experimental horror with this extraordinary study in complicit voyeurism that makes the viewer part of the on-screen mayhem. As a grim Oedipal fable unfolds – a maniac hospital orderly (Michael Lerner) is hypnotised by his loony mother (*Poltergeist*'s Zelda Rubinstein) into gouging out eyeballs – the camera pulls back to reveal the audience watching this movie and then follows a killer aping Lerner's actions. A blackly comic, metaphorical and metaphysical nightmare. AJ VIDEO

Zelda Rubinstein *Alice Pressman/Mother* • Michael Lerner *John Pressman* • Paul Talia *Patty* • Angel Jove *Killer* • Clara Pastor *Linda* ■ *Dir/Scr* Bigas Luna

Angus ★★★ 12

Comedy drama 1995 · US · Colour · 86mins

It may not be a classic, but there's no way you can watch this charming rites-of-passage picture and not end up smiling. Perfectly pitched without a hint of condescension, this will be an inspiration to all those children who have suffered at school because of their weight. Charlie Talbert gives a truly vibrant performance as the amiable, resilient teenager, who not only overcomes the snide teasing of physique fascist James Van Der Beek, but also steals his girl at the prom. With George C Scott growling out grandfatherly advice, this is funny, touching and hugely reassuring. DP VIDEO

Kathy Bates *Meg* • George C Scott *Ivan* • Charlie Talbert *Angus* • Ariana Richards *Melissa Lefevre* • Chris Owen *Troy Wedberg* • Rita Moreno *Madame Rulenska* • Lawrence Pressman *Principal Metcalf* • Anna Thomson [Anna Levine] *April Thomas* ■ *Dir* Patrick Read Johnson • *Scr* Jill Gordon, from a short story by Chris Crutcher

Aniki-Bobó ★★★★

Drama 1942 · Por · BW · 70mins

Manoel de Oliveira's first feature is a portrait of Oporto street life that is both poetic and highly political. There's a deep irony in the way the kids play cops and robbers without appreciating how the game presages their futures. But their hopes and fears are also touchingly conveyed by the non-professional cast. Yet, despite much of the action being shot from a juvenile perspective, this is more an exercise in innocence than realism. DP. In Portuguese with English subtitles.

Fernanda Matos *Teresinha* • Horacio Silva *Carlitos* • Antonio Santos *Eduardinho* • Antonio Morais Soares *Pistarim* ■ *Dir* Manoel de Oliveira • *Scr* Manoel de Oliveira, Antonio Lopes Ribeiro, Nascimento Fernandes, from the story *Meninos Milionarios* by Joao Rodrigues de Freitas

The Animal ★ 12

Comedy 2001 · US · Colour · 79mins

This gross-out comedy is so dumbed down it's tongue-tied. Although it doesn't contain as many flatulence jokes as some, it does get a lot of mileage from hints about bestiality. Rob Schneider is an inept cop who's seriously injured when his car goes over a cliff. But a mad scientist Michael Caton stitches him together with animal parts and so, before long, Schneider has the olfactory ability of a dog, the sexual urges of a stallion and aquatic skills worthy of Flipper. Beastly. TH VIDEO DVD

Rob Schneider *Marvin Mange* • Colleen Haskell *Rianna* • John C McGinley *Sgt Sisk* • Edward Asner *Chief Wilson* • Michael Caton *Dr Wilder* • Louis Lombardi *Fatty* • Guy Torry *Miles* • Adam Sandler *Townie* ■ *Dir* Luke Greenfield • *Scr* Tom Brady, Rob Schneider, from a story by Tom Brady

Animal Attraction ★★ 12

Romantic comedy
2001 · US · Colour · 93mins

Ashley Judd – displaying no real flair for this sort of comedy – plays a TV talent agent who's let down in love and vents her spleen by writing an article in a men's magazine that likens the male of the species to bulls. Support for her hypothesis is provided by her randy roommate – a serial lothario of the "love-'em-and-leave-'em" variety – played by Hugh Jackman. Rising star Jackman is watchable but he has little to sink his teeth into here. DA VIDEO DVD

Ashley Judd *Jane Goodale* • Greg Kinnear *Ray Brown* • Hugh Jackman *Eddie Alden* • Marisa Tomei *Liz* • Ellen Barkin *Diane Roberts* ■ *Dir* Tony Goldwyn • *Scr* Elizabeth Chandler, from the novel *Animal Husbandry* by Laura Zigman

Animal Behavior ★★ PG

Romantic comedy
1989 · US · Colour · 88mins

An excellent cast can do little with this weak romantic comedy set on a college campus. Karen Allen is the psychologist studying animal communication who finds it more difficult to get on with her own species, particularly musician Armand Assante. There appears to be little chemistry between Allen and Assante and they are hardly helped by the indecisive script and ill-focused direction. JF. Contains some swearing VIDEO

Karen Allen *Alex Bristow* • Armand Assante *Mark Mathias* • Holly Hunter *Coral Grable* • Josh Mostel *Mel Gorsky* • Richard Libertini *Dr Parrish* • Alexa Kenin *Sheila Sandusky* • Jon Mathews *Tyler Forbes* • Nan Martin *Mrs Norton* ■ *Dir* H Anne Riley [Jenny Bowen], H Anne Riley [Kjehl Rasmussen] • *Scr* Susan Rice

Animal Crackers ★★★★ U

Comedy 1930 · US · BW · 92mins

"Hooray for Captain Spaulding, the African explorer!". "Did someone call me schnorrer?" asks Groucho Marx, making one the movies' greatest entrances. This was the Marx Brothers' first Hollywood movie (the earlier two were both shot in New York; one's now lost), and is a relatively straightforward film version of their Broadway hit of the same name. The requirements of early sound recording render the action somewhat static, but the clowning is irresistible and Margaret Dumont is a perfect foil. TS VIDEO DVD

Groucho Marx *Captain Jeffrey Spaulding* • Harpo Marx *Professor* • Chico Marx *Signor Emanuel Ravelli* • Zeppo Marx *Horatio Jamison* • Lillian Roth *Arabella Rittenhouse* • Margaret Dumont *Mrs Rittenhouse* ■ *Dir* Victor Heerman • *Scr* Morris Ryskind, from the play by Morris Ryskind, George S Kaufman

Animal Factory ★★ 15

Prison drama 2000 · US · Colour · 90mins

Steve Buscemi's straightforward version of Edward Bunker's novel gets by on the fine performances of all concerned. Basically it charts the growing father-son relationship between hardened convict Willem

Dafoe – the big cheese at a hard-boiled penitentiary – as he teaches new inmate Edward Furlong about the power zones in the prison's perilous infrastructure. Overly subtle and unsentimental in its depiction of life behind bars, it consistently feels dramatically undernourished because of this refined stance. AJ [VIDEO] DVD

Willem Dafoe *Earl Copen* • Edward Furlong *Ron Decker* • John Heard *James Decker* • Tom Arnold *Buck Rowan* • Mickey Rourke *Jan the Actress* • Seymour Cassel *Lt Seeman* • Edward Bunker *Buzzard* • Danny Trejo *Vito* • Steve Buscemi *AR Hosspack* ■ *Dir* Steve Buscemi • *Scr* Edward Bunker, John Steppling, from the novel by Edward Bunker

Animal Farm ★★★★ U

Animated political satire
1954 · UK · Colour · 69mins

Made by the award-winning husband-and-wife team of John Halas and Joy Batchelor, this adaptation of George Orwell's searing political allegory was the first feature-length cartoon produced in Britain. Having decided to target an adult audience, the directors had to create characters that were not only faithful to the novel, but were also capable of arousing emotions without resorting to Disney cuteness. Their success in bringing to life the dictatorial Napoleon, the idealistic Snowball and the noble Boxer is aided by the amazingly individual voices provided by one man, Maurice Denham. This provocative and polished production is an all-too-rare attempt to make an intelligent and entertaining animation for adults. DP [VIDEO] DVD

Maurice Denham *Voices* • Gordon Heath *Narrator* ■ *Dir* John Halas, Joy Batchelor • *Scr* John Halas, Joy Batchelor, Lothar Wolff, Borden Mace, Philip Stapp, from the novel by George Orwell

Animal Farm ★★ PG

Political satire 1999 · US · Colour · 87mins

In its original literary form, George Orwell's 1946 satire of Stalinist Russia provoked readers' minds with its power and intelligence. Here turned into a TV movie, the political allegory falls flat, losing its impact to show-off animatronics and a "guess the celebrity voice" cast. This story of downtrodden farm animals revolting against their master is relentlessly bleak and often too disturbing and ideologically complex for the youngsters it will attract. SF [VIDEO] DVD

Pete Postlethwaite *Farmer Jones* • Kelsey Grammer *Snowball* • Ian Holm *Squealer* • Julia Louis-Dreyfus *Mollie* • Julia Ormond *Jessie* • Paul Scofield *Boxer* • Patrick Stewart *Napoleon* • Peter Ustinov *Old Major* ■ *Dir* John Stephenson • *Scr* Martyn Burke, Alan Janes, from the novel by George Orwell

The Animal Kingdom ★★★★

Drama 1932 · US · BW · 90mins

This highly sophisticated piece might almost be called a "drawing-room drama". A wealthy and unconventional publisher (Leslie Howard), marries an unsuitably conventional and shallow wife (Myrna Loy) to the detriment of his ideals, his lifestyle and his most precious relationship, with an artist (Ann Harding). An unusual approach and the lightest of touches elevates a seemingly well-worn storyline to something special. Credit is due to the impeccable screenplay, the elegance of the accomplished cast, David O Selznick's A-grade production values, and Edward H Griffith's direction. RK

Ann Harding *Daisy Sage* • Leslie Howard *Tom Collier* • Myrna Loy *Cecilia Henry* • Neil Hamilton *Owen* • William Gargan *Regan* • Henry Stephenson *Rufus Collier* • Ilka Chase *Grace* • Leni Stengel *Franc* • Donald Dillaway *Joe* ■ *Dir* Edward H Griffith • *Scr* Horace Jackson, from the play by Philip Barry

Animalympics ★★ U

Animated comedy
1979 · US · Colour · 78mins

A cartoon feature that spoofs the Olympics by having animals as athletes. It's a good idea, but the dull story could have done with more jokes and a little less preaching about taking part being more important than winning. Uninspired animation means that the characters are a pretty resistible bunch and not even the voices of Gilda Radner and Billy Crystal can liven them up. DP [VIDEO]

Gilda Radner • Billy Crystal • Harry Shearer • Michael Fremer ■ *Dir* Steven Lisberger

Anita ★★★ 18

Drama 1973 · Swe/Fr · Colour · 87mins

Directed with boundless sensitivity by Torgny Wickham and played with aching intensity, this has certainly not worn well. But while it's easy to poke fun at the pat solutions student Stellan Skarsgård proposes to rid Christina Lindberg's psyche of the loathing that drives her to promiscuity, there is an attempt made to explore the extent to which sexual liberation has become socially acceptable in the aftermath of the more permissive 1960s. DP. Swedish dialogue dubbed into English. [VIDEO]

Christina Lindberg *Anita* • Stellan Skarsgård *Erik* • Michael David *Anita's father* • Danièle Vlaminck *Anita's mother* ■ *Dir/Scr* Torgny Wickman

Anita & Me ★★★ 12

Comedy drama 2002 · UK · Colour · 88mins

Although its light-hearted depiction of a Punjabi family settling in a small Midlands village in the early 1970s is rarely more than one-dimensional, Meera Syal's adaptation of her own novel is consistently amusing. At the heart of the story is Asian teenager Meena (Chandeep Uppal), and her relationship with her white neighbour Anita (Anna Brewster), whose sexual maturity and rebellious behaviour alarm Meena's traditionalist family. The above-average supporting cast adds comedic lustre to this enjoyable, if inconsequential movie. JC [VIDEO] DVD

Chandeep Uppal *Meena* • Anna Brewster *Anita Rutter* • Sanjeev Bhaskar *Papa* • Ayesha Dharker *Mama* • Lynn Redgrave *Mrs Ormerod* • Mark Williams *Uncle Alan* • Max Beesley *Hairy Neddy* • Alex Freeborn *Sam Lowbridge* • Kathy Burke *Deidre Rutter* • Meera Syal *Auntie Shaila* ■ *Dir* Metin Hüseyin • *Scr* Meera Syal, from on her novel

Ankur ★★★★ 15

Drama 1974 · Ind · Colour · 125mins

Shyam Benegal (nephew of Bollywood director Guru Dutt) made his feature debut with this astute drama, a key work in the politically committed alternative to mainstream escapism known as Parallel Cinema. Beautifully capturing the sights and sounds of the countryside, Benegal denounces the caste system and provides a fascinating contrast between urban and rural mores in southern India. Shabana Azmi gives a star-making performance as the married servant girl who is seduced by her employer, Anant Nag. DP. In Hindi with English subtitles. [VIDEO]

Shabana Azmi *Laxmi* • Anant Nag *Surya* • Sadhu Meher *Kishtaya* • Priya Tendulkar *Saroj* ■ *Dir* Shyam Benegal • *Scr* Shyam Benegal, Satyadev Dubey

Anlat Istanbul ★★★ 15

Fantasy drama 2005 · Tur · Colour · 99mins

Screenwriter Umit Unal and his four fellow co-directors relocate a quintet of classic fairy tales to modern Istanbul in this sinuous drama that never quite fulfils the promise of its premise. Snow White becomes a mobster's daughter who is rescued by a single female dwarf; the Pied Piper is a cuckolded gypsy clarinettist; Sleeping Beauty is a neurotic in a shabby palace whose prince resembles a confused Kurdish migrant; Cinderella is a transsexual with a fairy godfather; and Red Riding Hood is a courier for a wolfish smuggler who is protected by the spirit of her aborted daughter. Flawed, but intriguing. DP. In Turkish with English subtitles. Contains swearing, violence.

Altan Erkekli *Hilmi* • Azra Akin *Idil* • Guven Kirac *Mimi* ■ *Dir* Selim Demirdelen, Kudret Sabanci, Umit Unal, Yucel Yolcu, Omur Atay • *Scr* Umit Unal

Ann Vickers ★★★

Drama 1933 · US · BW · 74mins

Expertly directed by the always reliable John Cromwell as a starring vehicle for Irene Dunne, this manages to combine themes of feminism, social conscience, political comment and romance to absorbing effect. Dunne, dignified as ever, shines as a reforming social worker who surmounts life's knocks to gain fame for her humane approach to prison reform, while Walter Huston manages to win her heart. Gritty entertainment, albeit with an element of soapy melodrama – though that, too, has its appeal. RK

Irene Dunne *Ann Vickers* • Walter Huston *Barney Dolphin* • Conrad Nagel *Lindsay* • Bruce Cabot *Resnick* • Edna May Oliver *Malvina* • Sam Hardy *Russell Spaulding* • Mitchell Lewis *Capt Waldo* • Helen Eby-Rock *Kitty Cignac* • Gertrude Michael *Mona Dolphin* ■ *Dir* John Cromwell • *Scr* Jane Murfin, from the novel by Sinclair Lewis

Anna ★★★ 15

Drama 1987 · US · Colour · 95mins

Sally Kirkland landed an Oscar nomination for her performance as a fading Czech actress in this beautifully observed but little seen film. Scripted by the Polish director Agnieszka Holland, it is essentially a reworking of *All about Eve*. Kirkland does a nice line in mournful self-effacement, but she's nowhere near as convincing once she becomes jealous of the adoring hopeful (played by debuting supermodel Paulina Porizkova) she has turned into a star. Director Yurek Bogayevicz handles the cast well, but rather loses his grip on the story. DP. Contains swearing and nudity. [VIDEO]

Sally Kirkland *Anna* • Robert Fields *Daniel* • Paulina Porizkova *Krystyna* • Gibby Brand *1st director* • John Robert Tillotson *2nd director* • Julianne Gilliam *Woman author* • Joe Aufiery *Stage manager* • Charles Randall *Agent* • Mimi Wedell *Agent's secretary* • Larry Pine *Baskin* ■ *Dir* Yurek Bogayevicz • *Scr* Agnieszka Holland, from a story by Yurek Bogayevicz, Agnieszka Holland

Anna and the King ★★★ 12

Period drama based on a true story
1999 · US · Colour · 142mins

With so many versions of this tale already on film, who doesn't know the story of the Victorian widow who travels with her son to tutor the children of the King of Siam? Here Jodie Foster, boasting an immaculate English accent, stars as the plucky governess who melts the heart of the king, played by a surprisingly sweet-natured Chow Yun-Fat. With a heavy emphasis on complicated political machinations and the odd gruesome scene, it's hardly suitable for young ones. Nonetheless, this is a heartwarming yarn that builds to a great action climax. SR [VIDEO] DVD

Jodie Foster *Anna Leonowens* • Chow Yun-Fat *King Mongkut* • Bai Ling *Tuptim* • Tom Felton *Louis Leonowens* • Alwi Syed *The Kralahome* • Randall Duk Kim *General Alak* • Lim Kay Siu *Prince Chowfa* • Melissa Campbell *Princess Fa-Ying* ■ *Dir* Andy Tennant • *Scr* Peter Krikes, Steve Meerson, from diaries of Anna Leonowens

Anna and the King of Siam ★★★

Period drama based on a true story
1946 · US · BW · 128mins

Before Deborah Kerr and Yul Brynner were *The King and I* in the musical version of the story, Irene Dunne and Rex Harrison starred in a stolid (if expensive) 20th Century-Fox adaptation of Margaret Landon's bestseller about English schoolteacher Anna Leonowens. While Dunne was born to play a governess, Harrison is miscast, with facial features more appropriate to Hampstead than Thailand. John Cromwell's direction suffers in comparison to the liveliness of the musical version and the art direction is relentlessly Hollywood Siam, but the sets won an Oscar, as did Arthur Miller's camerawork. TS

Irene Dunne *Anna* • Rex Harrison *The King* • Linda Darnell *Tuptin* • Lee J Cobb *Kralahome* • Gale Sondergaard *Lady Thiang* • Mikhail Rasumny *Alak* • Dennis Hoey *Sir Edward* • Tito Renaldo *Prince, as a man* • Richard Lyon *Louis Owens* • William Edmunds *Monshee* • Mickey Roth *Prince, as a boy* ■ *Dir* John Cromwell • *Scr* Talbot Jennings, Sally Benson, from the non-fiction book by Margaret Landon • *Set Designer* Lyle Wheeler, William Darling, Thomas Little, Frank E Hughes

Anna Boleyn ★★★★

Silent biographical drama
1920 · Ger · Tinted · 100mins

Recently restored with the original colour tinting, this sumptuous film has a fine cast headed by Henny Porten, Germany's first superstar, and Emil Jannings as a sensual and cruel Henry VIII. Before German-born Ernst Lubitsch went to Hollywood in 1923, he made his reputation with several ironic historical romances like this one, which led to his first being described as having the "Lubitsch Touch". RB

Henny Porten *Anna Boleyn* • Emil Jannings *King Henry VIII* • Paul Hartmann *Sir Henry Norris* • Ludwig Hartau *Duke of Norfolk* • Aud Egede Nissen *Jane Seymour* • Hedwig Pauly *Queen Catherine* • Hilde Müller *Princess Marie* ■ *Dir* Ernst Lubitsch • *Scr* Norbert Falk [Fred Orbing], Hans Kräly

Anna Christie ★★★ U

Drama 1930 · US · BW · 85mins

"Gif me a whiskey, ginger ale on the side – and don't be stingy, baby." These were the first words spoken on the screen in this, her first talkie, by the great Greta Garbo. She's perfectly cast as Eugene O'Neill's lady with a past in this turgid seafront drama, which plays more than a little creaky today. The Swedish *grande dame* also talked in the simultaneously-shot but shorter German language version of this film, and director Jacques Feyder was much more in sympathy with her angst than was this version's director, Clarence Brown. TS [VIDEO]

Greta Garbo *Anna Christie* • Charles Bickford *Matt Burke* • George F Marion *Producer* • Marie Dressler *Marthy Owen* • James T Mack [James Mack] • Lee Phelps *Larry, barman* ■ *Dir* Clarence Brown • *Scr* Frances Marion, from the play by Eugene O'Neill

Anna Karenina ★★★★ U

Period romantic drama
1935 · US · BW · 89mins

The great Greta Garbo in one of her best-remembered roles, a fine mating of artist and character. This was her second attempt at *Karenina*, having starred with John Gilbert in a notable silent version of the tale in 1927, retitled *Love*. This is very much a *Reader's Digest* version of the great novel, paring the plot down to the

A

bone; it is also overdependent on a splendid, but sometimes disconcertingly multi-accented cast. Garbo's favourite cameraman William Daniels gives a dynamic sheen to the famous final station scene, but the noted MGM production values look a shade creaky today. TS DVD

Greta Garbo *Anna Karenina* • Fredric March *Vronsky* • Freddie Bartholomew *Sergei* • Maureen O'Sullivan *Kitty* • May Robson *Countess Vronsky* • Basil Rathbone *Karenin* • Reginald Owen *Stiva* • Reginald Denny *Yashvin* • Phoebe Foster *Dolly* • Gyles Isham *Levin* ■ *Dir* Clarence Brown • *Scr* Clemence Dane, Salka Viertel, SN Behrman, from the novel by Leo Tolstoy • *Production Designer* Cedric Gibbons • *Costume Designer* Adrian

Anna Karenina ★★★ PG

Period romantic drama
1947 · UK · BW · 133mins

The sumptuous production values of this film, combined with the dazzling beauty of Vivien Leigh as Tolstoy's famously doomed heroine, are not enough to prevent it being ultimately a disappointment. It is too long to support the screenplay and the miscasting of a pretty but dull Kieron Moore as Vronsky robs the drama of weight and conviction. Leigh does her best and there are some affecting moments (notably the scenes between Anna and her child), but only Ralph Richardson, superbly unbending as Karenin, has the measure of the material. RK DVD

Vivien Leigh *Anna Karenina* • Ralph Richardson *Alexei Karenin* • Kieron Moore *Count Vronsky* • Sally Ann Howes *Kitty Scherbatsky* • Niall MacGinnis *Levin* • Martita Hunt *Princess Betty Tversky* • Marie Lohr *Princess Scherbatsky* • Michael Gough *Nicholai* • Hugh Dempster *Stefan Oblonsky* ■ *Dir* Julien Duvivier • *Scr* Jean Anouilh, Guy Morgan, Julien Duvivier, from the novel by Leo Tolstoy • *Cinematographer* Henri Alekan • *Costume Designer* Cecil Beaton

Anna Karenina ★★ 12

Period romantic drama
1997 · US · Colour · 103mins

Despite being the first film adaptation to benefit from authentic locations in St Petersburg and Moscow, this is a fairly negligible version of the classic novel. The problem lies in the leaden script and the Euro-pudding casting. Sophie Marceau is pretty but vacuous in the lead, and only James Fox creates any lasting impression as her cuckolded husband. AT

Sophie Marceau *Anna Karenina* • Sean Bean *Vronsky* • Alfred Molina *Levin* • Mia Kirshner *Kitty* • James Fox *Karenin* • Fiona Shaw *Lydia* • Danny Huston *Stiva* • Phyllida Law *Vronskaya* ■ *Dir* Bernard Rose • *Scr* Bernard Rose, from the novel by Leo Tolstoy

Anna Lucasta ★★★

Melodrama 1949 · US · BW · 85mins

The luscious Paulette Goddard stars as Anna, gone to the bad in Brooklyn after being thrown out by her Polish immigrant father (Oscar Homolka). She is lured back to her coarse, poor and feckless family in the Midwest who plot to marry her off for money, but the plans go awry. It's directed with a sure hand by Irving Rapper and there's a standout supporting performance from Broderick Crawford as her scheming brother-in-law. Solid entertainment that deftly signals the subtexts of incestuous desire and prostitution. RK

Paulette Goddard *Anna Lucasta* • William Bishop *Rudolf Strobel* • Oscar Homolka *Joe Lucasta* • John Ireland *Danny Johnson* • Broderick Crawford *Frank* • Will Geer *Noah* • Gale Page *Katie* • Mary Wickes *Stella* • Whit Bissell *Stanley* ■ *Dir* Irving Rapper • *Scr* Philip Yordan, Arthur Laurents, from the play by Philip Yordan

Anna Lucasta ★★

Drama 1958 · US · BW · 96mins

Philip Yordan's Broadway play, about a girl whose shady past as a sailors' whore catches up with her and almost destroys her chance of a fresh start, was originally staged with an all-black cast. Columbia filmed it in 1949 as an all-white drama and, here, United Artists had Yordan adapt it again, casting Eartha Kitt as Anna with an all-black cast. Kitt acquits herself reasonably well, but Arnold Laven's direction is stagey and the film is utterly lacking in conviction. RK

Eartha Kitt *Anna Lucasta* • Sammy Davis Jr *Danny Johnson* • Frederick O'Neal *Frank* • Henry Scott *Rudolph Slocum* • Rex Ingram (2) *Joe Lucasta* • Georgia Burke *Theresa* • James Edwards *Eddie* ■ *Dir* Arnold Laven • *Scr* Philip Yordan, from his play

Annabel Takes a Tour ★★ U

Comedy 1938 · US · BW · 66mins

Earlier in 1938, RKO's *The Affairs of Annabel* launched a proposed B-comedy series for Lucille Ball, starring her as a giddy movie actress whose press agent (Jack Oakie) dreams up a series of screwball publicity stunts. Bright and fast-moving, the movie drew the punters, and this first sequel followed hot on its heels. It was also the last. A laboured and less amusing retread of the first film, it lost money and the studio cancelled the series. However, Ball's high-octane appeal is intact. RK

Lucille Ball *Annabel* • Jack Oakie *Lanny Morgan* • Ruth Donnelly *Josephine* • Bradley Page *Webb* • Ralph Forbes *Viscount* • Frances Mercer *Natalie* • Donald MacBride *Thompson* ■ *Dir* Lew Landers • *Scr* Bert Granet, Olive Cooper, from a story by Joe Bigelow, from characters created by Charles Hoffman

Annabelle Partagée ★ 18

Drama 1990 · Fr · Colour · 76mins

Although it made censorship history after the BBFC decided to pass the opening image of an ejaculating penis, this dreary melange is the kind of movie that gives art house a bad name. About a provincial in Paris who toys with both an architect friend of her father's and a handsome layabout, its aim is to depict a woman taking control of her own sexual destiny. But Francesca Comencini succeeds only in subjecting Delphine Zingg's body to the camera's dispassionate gaze, and the viewer to some interminably dull conversations about the meaning of life. DP. In French with English subtitles.

Delphine Zingg *Annabelle* • François Marthouret *Richard* • Jean-Claude Adelin *Luca* ■ *Dir/Scr* Francesca Comencini

An Annapolis Story ★★★

Wartime romance
1955 · US · Colour · 81mins

Director Don Siegel makes the most of this tale of two brothers (John Derek and Kevin McCarthy), both cadets at the Annapolis naval academy, who fall out over a girl (Diana Lynn). Their relationship is temporarily poisoned, but the boys eventually settle their differences while on active service in Korea. The personal drama is lent veracity by authentic location filming at Annapolis (complete with flag-waving passing-out parades) and on board a real aircraft carrier. RK

John Derek *Tony Scott* • Diana Lynn *Peggy Lord* • Kevin McCarthy *Jim Scott* • Alvy Moore *Willie* • Pat Conway *Dooley* • LQ Jones *Watson* • John Kirby *Macklin* • Barbara Brown *Mrs Scott* ■ *Dir* Don Siegel • *Scr* Daniel B Ullman, Geoffrey Homes [Daniel Mainwaring], from a story by Daniel B Ullman

Anne and Muriel ★★★★ 15

Romantic drama 1971 · Fr · Colour · 124mins

Inspired by his fascination with the Brontës, François Truffaut reverses the situation in *Jules et Jim* – also adapted from a novel by Henri-Pierre Roché – with this elegiac tale of doomed love. An unbearably sad film, this is as much about the passion of creativity as it is about romance, as Jean-Pierre Léaud's art critic is capable only of appreciating the beauty of English sisters Kika Markham and Stacey Tendeter rather than being captivated by it. Shot in desaturated colour to convey the turn-of-the-century atmosphere, the film also employs written material, voiceovers and a range of cinematic devices to enhance the intimacy of the story. DP. In French with English subtitles.

Jean-Pierre Léaud *Claude Roc* • Kika Markham *Anne Brown* • Stacey Tendeter *Muriel Brown* • Sylvia Marriott *Mrs Brown* • Marie Mansart *Madame Roc* • Philippe Léotard *Diurka* • François Truffaut *Narration* ■ *Dir* François Truffaut • *Scr* Jean Gruault, François Truffaut, from the novel by Henri-Pierre Roché

Anne Devlin ★★★ PG

Historical drama 1984 · Ire · Colour · 121mins

Pat Murphy's film is a fitting tribute to Anne Devlin, the peasant's daughter who, as Robert Emmett's confidante, played a key role in the struggle for Irish independence in the early 19th century. Deftly equating political liberation with female emancipation, Murphy is content to focus on character rather than events, and she's helped by the affecting simplicity of Thaddeus O'Sullivan's photography and Brid Brennan's committed performance. Her pacing is a touch too deliberate, however. DP

Brid Brennan *Anne Devlin* • Bosco Hogan *Robert Emmett* • Des McAleer • Gillian Hackett ■ *Dir* Pat Murphy • *Scr* Pat Murphy, from journals by Anne Devlin

Anne of Green Gables ★★★ U

Drama 1934 · US · BW · 77mins

This is the definitive movie version (it had been filmed before in 1919) of LM Montgomery's popular tale about the teenage orphan. Child actress Dawn O'Day changed her professional name to that of the film's character, and as Anne Shirley delivered an exquisite, utterly charming performance. This is a real one-off: the 1940 sequel *Anne of Windy Poplars* is feeble by comparison, and Shirley was not nearly as beguiling as a grown-up, though she did continue a useful screen career. TS

Dawn O'Day [Anne Shirley] *Anne Shirley* • Tom Brown *Gilbert Blythe* • OP Heggie *Matthew Cuthbert* • Helen Westley *Marilla Cuthbert* • Sara Haden *Mrs Barry* • Murray Kinnell *Mr Phillips* • Gertrude Messinger *Diana* • June Preston *Mrs Blewett's daughter* • Charley Grapewin *Dr Tatum* • Hilda Vaughn *Mrs Blewett* ■ *Dir* George Nichols Jr • *Scr* Sam Mintz, from the novel by LM Montgomery

Anne of the Indies ★★★ U

Swashbuckling adventure
1951 · US · Colour · 79mins

Aha, me hearties, 'tis rollicking Jean Peters as the swashbuckling scourge of the Caribbean, surrounded by old reliables James Robertson-Justice as the first mate, Herbert Marshall as the rummy doc and Thomas Gomez as Blackbeard himself. Louis Jourdan is the dashing Frenchman who is forced into luring the pirate queen into a treasure-baited trap, while 1950s icon Debra Paget plays Jourdan's kidnapped wife. Director Jacques Tourneur seems more than comfortable with this splendid seafaring tale. TS

Jean Peters *Anne* • Louis Jourdan *Captain Pierre François La Rochelle* • Debra Paget *Molly* • Herbert Marshall *Dr Jameson* • Thomas Gomez *Blackbeard* • James Robertson-Justice *Red Dougal* • Francis Pierlot *Herkimer* • Sean McClory *Hackett* • Holmes Herbert *English sea captain* ■ *Dir* Jacques Tourneur • *Scr* Phillip Dunne, Arthur Caesar, from a story by Herbert Ravenel Sass

Anne of the Thousand Days ★★★ PG

Historical drama
1969 · US · Colour · 139mins

Producer Hal Wallis's inventive and flamboyant slice of English history was a surprising hit, reviving a moribund genre and providing marvellous showcases for Richard Burton, as a roistering but soulful Henry VIII, and Geneviève Bujold, touchingly well cast as Anne Boleyn. The period interiors, largely re-created at Shepperton studios, are beautifully designed and detailed. Margaret Furse's costumes rightly won an Oscar; a shame, then, that Charles Jarrott's direction is insipid and poorly paced. Nevertheless, this is a respectable piece of film-making. TS

Richard Burton *King Henry VIII* • Geneviève Bujold *Anne Boleyn* • Irene Papas *Catherine of Aragon* • Anthony Quayle *Cardinal Wolsey* • John Colicos *Cromwell* • Michael Hordern *Thomas Boleyn* • Katharine Blake *Elizabeth Boleyn* • Peter Jeffrey *Norfolk* • William Squire *Thomas More* • Valerie Gearon *Mary Boleyn* • Elizabeth Taylor *Courtesan* ■ *Dir* Charles Jarrott • *Scr* Bridget Boland, John Hale, Richard Sokolove (adaptation), from the play by Maxwell Anderson • *Cinematographer* Arthur Ibbetson • *Art Director* Maurice Carter, Lionel Couch, Patrick McLoughlin

Anne of Windy Poplars ★★ U

Drama 1940 · US · BW · 85mins

Six years after the charming film version of author LM Montgomery's popular *Anne of Green Gables* came this routine sequel, with the now grown-up Anne teaching in one of those small towns where everyone (except kindly old folks) is hypocritical or corrupt, or both. Anne Shirley is once again played by Anne Shirley, the former Dawn O'Day, who changed her name to that of her character. TS

Anne Shirley • James Ellison *Tony Pringle* • Henry Travers *Matey* • Patric Knowles *Gilbert Blythe* • Slim Summerville *Jabez Monkman* • Elizabeth Patterson *Rebecca* • Louise Campbell *Katherine Pringle* • Joan Carroll *Betty Grayson* ■ *Dir* Jack Hively • *Scr* Michael Kanin, Jerry Cady [Jerome Cady], from the novel by LM Montgomery

Anne Trister ★★★

Drama 1986 · Can · Colour · 115mins

Partly inspired by her own experiences, director Léa Pool follows an aspiring painter (Albane Guilhe) from her Swiss home to Montreal, where she fulfils both her artistic and emotional destinies. Liberated from the influence of her father and her boyfriend (Hugues Quester), Guilhe embarks upon a vast mural that reflects her growing attraction to Louise Marleau, the psychologist with whom she is living. Pool successfully gets under the skins of her characters, although her pacing is occasionally ponderous. DP. In French with English subtitles. Contains sex scenes.

Albane Guilhe *Anne Trister* • Louise Marleau *Alix* • Lucie Laurier *Sarah* • Guy Thauvette *Thomas* • Hugues Quester *Pierre* • Nuvit Ozdogru *Simon* ■ *Dir* Léa Pool • *Scr* Léa Pool, Marcel Beaulieu

Annie ★★★ U

Musical 1982 · US · Colour · 122mins

John Huston was the wrong director for this long-winded version of the

U = SUITABLE FOR ALL Uc = SUITABLE FOR ALL, ESPECIALLY FOR YOUNG CHILDREN (VIDEO ONLY) PG = PARENTAL GUIDANCE

Broadway musical based on the popular American comic strip. He lacks the necessary light touch that might have made this the equal of the stage production, and he's not helped by the casting of heavyweight Albert Finney as bald Daddy Warbucks and grimacing Tim Curry as a villain. However, Carol Burnett is a zesty Miss Hannigan and Aileen Quinn is appealing as the moppet of the title, while real class is brought to the proceedings by Broadway divas Bernadette Peters and Ann Reinking. TS [VIDEO] DVD

Albert Finney *Daddy Warbucks* • Carol Burnett *Miss Hannigan* • Bernadette Peters *Lily* • Ann Reinking *Grace Farrell* • Tim Curry *Rooster* • Aileen Quinn *Annie* • Geoffrey Holder *Punjab* • Roger Minami *Asp* ■ *Dir* John Huston • *Scr* Carol Sobieski, from the musical by Thomas Meehan, Charles Strouse, Martin Charnin, from the comic strip *Little Orphan Annie* by Harold Gray

Annie ★★★ U

Musical 1999 · US · Colour · 88mins

The musical that gives thousands of showbiz mums the chance to push their little darlings on the stage gets the Walt Disney treatment in this occasionally saccharine but enjoyably bumptious TV movie. Newcomer Alicia Morton is little orphan Annie, who gradually thaws the heart of millionaire Daddy Warbucks (Victor Garber). As usual, though, it's the baddie who steals the show, and Kathy Bates is a memorable Miss Hannigan. (She received a Golden Globe nomination for her performance.) JF [VIDEO] DVD

Victor Garber *Daddy Warbucks* • Kathy Bates *Miss Hannigan* • Audra McDonald *Grace Farrell* • Kristin Chenoweth *Lily* • Alan Cumming *Rooster* • Alicia Morton *Annie* ■ *Dir* Rob Marshall • *Scr* Irene Mecchi, from the musical by Thomas Meehan, Charles Strouse, Martin Charnin, from the comic strip *Little Orphan Annie* by Harold Gray

Annie: a Royal Adventure ★ U

Drama 1995 · US · Colour · 88mins

Most sequels are disappointing, but few plumb the depths of this right royal mess. Devoid of the cheerful songs that made *Annie* so popular, it relies on a preposterous plot in which the flame-haired heroine comes to London to see Daddy Warbucks receive his knighthood and ends up taking on the evil aristocrat who plans to blow up Buckingham Palace. DP [VIDEO] DVD

Ashley Johnson *Annie* • George Hearn *"Daddy" Oliver Warbucks* • Joan Collins *Lady Edwina Hogbottom* • Ian McDiarmid *Professor Eli Eon* • Emily Ann Lloyd *Hannah Apple* • Camilla Belle *Molly* • Crispin Bonham-Carter *Rupert* • Perry Benson *Murphy* ■ *Dir* Ian Toynton • *Scr* Trish Soodik, from the comic strip *Little Orphan Annie* by Harold Gray

Annie Get Your Gun ★★★★★ U

Musical western
1950 · US · Colour · 103mins

MGM's wonderfully zesty film of Irving Berlin's Broadway smash stars a perfectly cast Betty Hutton as Annie Oakley, replacing an ailing (and, to tell the truth, unsuitable) Judy Garland. George Sidney's bravura direction gets the most out of a marvellous score, which includes such classics as *Anything You Can Do (I Can Do Better)* and *There's No Business Like Show Business*. Handsome newcomer Howard Keel makes an impressive movie musical debut as sharp-shooting Frank Butler, and the Technicolor and costume design are particularly ravishing. It's hard to see how this could have been any better. TS [VIDEO] DVD

Betty Hutton *Annie Oakley* • Howard Keel *Frank Butler* • Louis Calhern *Buffalo Bill* • J Carrol Naish *Chief Sitting Bull* • Edward Arnold *Pawnee Bill* • Keenan Wynn *Charlie Davenport* • Benay Venuta *Dolly Tate* • Clinton Sundberg *Foster Wilson* ■ *Dir* George Sidney (2) • *Scr* Sidney Sheldon, from the play by Herbert Fields, Dorothy Fields • *Cinematographer* Charles Rosher • *Music/lyrics* Irving Berlin • *Music* Adolph Deutsch, Roger Edens

Annie Hall ★★★★★ 15

Romantic comedy
1977 · US · Colour · 89mins

Although Woody Allen had still to acquire great technical strength as a film-maker, this was the movie where he found his own singular voice, a voice that echoes across events with a mixture of exuberance and introspection. Peppered with hilarious, snappy insights into the meaning of life, love, psychiatry, ambition, art and New York, this comic delight also gains considerably from the spirited playing of Diane Keaton as the kooky innocent from the Midwest, and Woody himself as the fumbling New York neurotic. The narrative runs parallel to the real-life relationship between the two leads (Keaton's father's name was Hall), and the film scooped four Oscars, including best film and screenplay (co-written with Marshall Brickman) for Allen, and best actress for Keaton. JM. Contains mild swearing. [VIDEO] DVD

Woody Allen *Alvy Singer* • Diane Keaton *Annie Hall* • Tony Roberts *Rob* • Carol Kane *Allison* • Paul Simon *Tony Lacey* • Shelley Duvall *Pam* • Janet Margolin *Robin* • Colleen Dewhurst *Mom Hall* • Christopher Walken *Duane Hall* • Donald Symington *Dad Hall* • Helen Ludlam *Grammy Hall* • Mordecai Lawner *Alvy's dad* • Joan Newman *Alvy's mom* • Jonathan Munk *Alvy aged nine* ■ *Dir* Woody Allen • *Scr* Woody Allen, Marshall Brickman

Annie Laurie ★★★

Silent romantic melodrama
1927 · US · BW and Colour

Because Lillian Gish's sweet image was out of step with the vogue for flappers and jazz babies, it was said that MGM humiliated her by giving her this, which one critic called "soggy haggis". This tale of clan warfare, in which a governor's daughter has to choose between a Campbell and a MacDonald, is rather tritely handled, yet Gish is as radiant as ever. There is some splendid camerawork, and the recently restored two-tone Technicolor scenes are lovely, but the picture was a failure. RB

Lillian Gish *Annie Laurie* • Norman Kerry *Ian MacDonald* • Creighton Hale *Donald* • Joseph Striker *Alastair* • Hobart Bosworth *The MacDonald Chieftain* • Patricia Avery *Enid* • Russell Simpson *Sandy* • Brandon Hurst *The Campbell Chieftain* ■ *Dir* John S Robertson • *Scr* Josephine Lovett, Marian Ainslee (titles), Ruth Cummings (titles), from a story by Josephine Lovett • *Cinematographer* Jack Parker

Annie Oakley ★★★ U

Western 1935 · US · BW · 86mins

The story of America's most famous female sharpshooter here becomes a vehicle for Barbara Stanwyck. It was her first western, and she copes well enough, though she seems far too contemporary in looks and attitude for the fiesty Ms Oakley. However, this is a still a thoroughly enjoyable early work from George Stevens, who went on to direct such classics as *A Place in the Sun* (1951), *Shane* (1953) and *Giant* (1956). Suave Melvyn Douglas and handsome Preston Foster both score highly in a film that studiously ignores history throughout. TS [VIDEO]

Barbara Stanwyck *Annie Oakley* • Preston Foster *Toby Walker* • Melvyn Douglas *Jeff Hogarth* • Moroni Olsen *Buffalo Bill* • Pert Kelton *Vera Delmar* • Andy Clyde *Macivor* • Chief Thundercloud *Sitting Bull* • Margaret Armstrong *Mrs Oakley* • Delmar Watson *Wesley Oakley* ■ *Dir* George Stevens • *Scr* Joel Sayre, John Twist, from a story by Joseph A Fields, Ewart Adamson

Annie's Coming Out ★★ PG

Drama based on a true story
1984 · Aus · Colour · 88mins

A cerebral palsy victim is confined to a state mental institution despite being highly intelligent, and has to fight to prove she is more than a vegetable. An interesting premise – based on a true story – ends up as TV-movie-of-the-week fodder thanks to a cumbersome soundtrack and an annoying tendency to raise questions without actually providing any answers to them. While it never quite rises above a run-of-the-mill weepie, this nonetheless features solid performances from the leads. JB [VIDEO]

Angela Punch McGregor *Jessica Hathaway* • Drew Forsythe *David Lewis* • Tina Arhondis *Annie O'Farrell* • Monica Maughan *Vera Peters* • Mark Butler *Dr John Monroe* • Philippa Baker *Sister Waterman* ■ *Dir* Gil Brealey • *Scr* John Patterson, Chris Borthwick, from the book by Rosemary Crossley

The Anniversary ★★★ PG

Black comedy 1968 · UK · Colour · 90mins

Here, Hollywood *grande dame* Bette Davis provides the scenes, and some laughs, as an eyepatch-wearing virago ruling an ill-assorted family in England's suburbia. The rest of the cast is no match for Davis, but Sheila Hancock, Jack Hedley and, particularly, James Cossins, hold their own. This Hammer slice of *Grand Guignol* was based on a play and, despite *Brighton Rock* cinematographer Harry Waxman's excellent colour photography, the atmosphere is resolutely theatrical. Still, Davis is always watchable. TS [VIDEO]

Bette Davis *Mrs Taggart* • Sheila Hancock *Karen Taggart* • Jack Hedley *Terry Taggart* • James Cossins *Henry Taggart* • Christian Roberts *Tom Taggart* • Elaine Taylor *Shirley Blair* • Timothy Bateson *Mr Bird* • Arnold Diamond *Headwaiter* ■ *Dir* Roy Ward Baker • *Scr* Jimmy Sangster, from the play by Bill MacIlwraith

The Anniversary Party ★★★★ 18

Drama 2001 · US · Colour · 110mins

British actor Alan Cumming and American star Jennifer Jason Leigh wrote and directed this tale of marriage and Hollywood set at the sixth anniversary party of an actress (Leigh) and her writer/director husband (Cumming). It's superb stuff, packed with revelations (some fuelled by the ecstasy some of the guests indulge in as the evening goes sour) and terrific improvisations by the A-grade cast. JB. Contains swearing, sex scenes and drug abuse. [VIDEO] DVD

Alan Cumming *Joe Therrian* • Jennifer Jason Leigh *Sally Nash* • Gwyneth Paltrow *Skye Davidson* • Kevin Kline *Cal Gold* • Phoebe Cates *Sophia Gold* • Jane Adams (2) *Clair Forsyth* • John C Reilly *Mac Forsythe* • John Benjamin Hickey *Jerry Adams* • Parker Posey *Judy Adams* ■ *Dir/Scr* Alan Cumming, Jennifer Jason Leigh

Another Country ★★★★ 15

Drama 1984 · UK · Colour · 86mins

This is the film that should have made Rupert Everett a bigger star than he is. His electrifying performance, as a homosexual public schoolboy barred from an exclusive prefects' society, is at once endearing and arrogant. Directed by Marek Kanievska, from Julian Mitchell's adaptation of his own play about the background to the Burgess/MacLean spy scandal, the tale only clicks into credibility when Everett goes into outsider mode. A wonderfully flamboyant exposure of the making of a traitor, this deserved more acclaim than it got. TH. Contains swearing and a sex scene. [VIDEO]

Rupert Everett *Guy Bennett* • Colin Firth *Tommy Judd* • Michael Jenn *Barclay* • Robert Addie *Delahay* • Anna Massey *Imogen Bennett* • Betsy Brantley *Julie Schofield* • Rupert Wainwright *Devenish* • Tristan Oliver *Fowler* • Cary Elwes *Harcourt* ■ *Dir* Marek Kanievska • *Scr* Julian Mitchell, from the play by Julian Mitchell

Another Dawn ★★

Romantic adventure 1937 · US · BW · 74mins

Errol Flynn made some classic adventure movies in the 1930s, but this isn't one of them. Everyone involved seems to be treading water: his co-star this time is Kay Francis, who was one of Warner's highest paid female stars until Bette Davis came on the scene. The story is a love triangle, with Francis marrying Ian Hunter yet lusting after Flynn, a British army officer. The Arabs, meanwhile, cause the Empire problems whenever the story gets bogged down. AT

Errol Flynn *Captain Denny Roark* • Kay Francis *Julia Ashton* • Ian Hunter *Colonel John Wister* • Frieda Inescort *Grace Roark* • Herbert Mundin *Wilkins* • Billy Bevan *Hawkins* • Kenneth Hunter *Sir Charles Benton* ■ *Dir* William Dieterle • *Scr* Laird Doyle

Another Day ★★

Fantasy drama
2001 · Can/US · Colour · 90mins

Shannen Doherty stars in this mawkish TV movie as a woman who gets a second chance at life and love. Having seen the father of her unborn child die in a fire, Doherty's wannabe medical student is involved in a boating accident that pitches her back in time to two days before the blaze. But her reunion with Max Martini is more complicated than it first seems, not least because of her relationship with neighbour Julian McMahon. Doherty overindulges in every emotion. DP

Shannen Doherty *Kate Walker* • Max Martini *Paul Marshall* • Kristina Nicoll *Gabby* • Courtney Kidd *Meghan Walker* • Julian McMahon *David Cameron* ■ *Dir* Jeffrey Reiner • *Scr* Helen Frost, Don MacLeod

Another Day in Paradise ★★★★ 18

Drama 1998 · US · Colour · 101mins

Director Larry Clark's compelling glimpse into outlaw life in the American Midwest during the 1970s is not as controversial as his first feature, *kids*, but it's just as grim and gritty. In this disturbing look at thug bravado, a charismatic drugs dealer (James Woods) persuades a teenage runaway (Vincent Kartheiser) and his junkie girlfriend (Natasha Gregson Wagner) to help him pull a bank heist. It's when things go horribly wrong and the dysfunctional "family" is torn apart that this devastating road movie really hits home. As Woods's heroin-addicted lover, Melanie Griffith gives the performance of her career in a shocking tale. AJ. Contains violence, swearing and drug abuse. [VIDEO] DVD

James Woods *Mel* • Melanie Griffith *Sid* • Vincent Kartheiser *Bobbie* • Natasha Gregson Wagner *Rosie* • James Otis *Reverend* • Branden Williams *Danny* • Brent Briscoe *Clem* • Peter Sarsgaard *Ty* • Lou Diamond Phillips *Jules* ■ *Dir* Larry Clark • *Scr* Christopher Landon, Stephen Chin, from the novel by Eddie Little

Another 48 HRS ★★ 18

Comedy thriller 1990 · US · Colour · 95mins

Although the original stars of *48 HRS*, Eddie Murphy and Nick Nolte, are reunited with director Walter Hill, all three seem to be going through the motions. Nolte is the same rough and ready cop who is forced to team up

A

again with con Murphy, this time in a bid to salvage his career. Murphy here verges on self-parody, but the action is spectacular enough. JF. Contains swearing, violence, nudity. DVD

Eddie Murphy *Reggie Hammond* • Nick Nolte *Jack Cates* • Brion James *Ben Kehoe* • Kevin Tighe *Blake Wilson* • Ed O'Ross *Frank Cruise* • David Anthony Marshall *Willy Hickok* • Andrew Divoff *Cherry Ganz* • Bernie Casey *Kirkland Smith* ■ *Dir* Walter Hill • *Scr* John Fasano, Jeb Stuart, Larry Gross, from a story by Fred Braughton, from characters created by Roger Spottiswoode, Walter Hill, Larry Gross, Steven E de Souza

Another Life ★★ 15

Period drama 2000 · UK · Colour · 101mins

Back in the early 1920s, the Edith Thompson case was a *cause célèbre*, with thousands signing a petition for leniancy after her sailor beau, Freddy Bywaters, murdered her intransigent husband, Percy. However, little of that drama surfaces in Philip Goodhew's unpersuasive period piece. Natasha Little plays Edith with spirit, but neither Ioan Gruffudd nor his victim, Nick Moran, are up to the task. DP

Natasha Little *Edie Thompson* • Nick Moran *Percy Thompson* • Ioan Gruffudd *Freddy Bywaters* • Imelda Staunton *Ethel Graydon* • Rachael Stirling *Avis Graydon* ■ *Dir/Scr* Philip Goodhew

Another Man, Another Chance ★★★

Period romantic drama
1977 · Fr/US · Colour · 127mins

This French take on the American western by Claude Lelouch is also a retake, 11 years on, of his most romantic movie of the 1960s, *Un Homme et une Femme*, as the lives of widow Geneviève Bujold, a 19th-century French settler, and widower James Caan, a Yankee vet, intersect. A bit long for what it has to say, but there are some deliciously wry moments Caan demonstrating he's a worse shot than his young son, for example and a feeling that people are worth the effort. TH

James Caan *David Williams* • Geneviève Bujold *Jeanne* • Francis Huster *Francis Leroy* • Jennifer Warren *Mary* • Susan Tyrrell *Debbie/ "Miss Alice"* • Rossie Harris *Simon* • Linda Lee Lyons *Sarah* ■ *Dir/Scr* Claude Lelouch

Another Man's Poison ★

Crime melodrama 1951 · UK · BW · 90mins

Bette Davis crossed the Atlantic with her *Now, Voyager* director Irving Rapper and her husband Gary Merrill for this tale of a lady novelist residing on the Yorkshire moors. Engaged in an affair with her secretary's fiancé (Anthony Steel), she is provoked by her husband's return into murdering him. How could Davis, even in villainess mode, appear in such drivel? RK

Bette Davis *Janet Frobisher* • Gary Merrill *George Bates* • Emlyn Williams *"Dr" Henderson* • Anthony Steel *Larry Stevens* • Barbara Murray *Chris Dale* • Reginald Beckwith *Mr Bigley* • Edna Morris *Mrs Bunting* ■ *Dir* Irving Rapper • *Scr* Val Guest, from a play by Leslie Sands

Another $9\frac{1}{2}$ Weeks ★★ 18

Erotic drama 1997 · US · Colour · 100mins

Mickey Rourke returns to the role that made him (in)famous but he really shouldn't have bothered – this is an utterly pointless and flaccid affair. Here, moody rich bloke Rourke is still pining for Elizabeth (Kim Basinger in the original) and travels to Paris where he hooks up with a fashion designer (Angie Everhart). Director Anne Goursaud gives it a glossy surface sheen, but Rourke sleepwalks through the film. JF. Contains swearing, violence and sex scenes.

Mickey Rourke *John* • Angie Everhart *Lea* • Agathe de la Fontaine *Claire* • Steven Berkoff *Vittorio* • Dougray Scott *Charlie* ■ *Dir* Anne Goursaud • *Scr* Mick Davis, from a character created by Elizabeth McNeil

Another Part of the Forest ★★

Drama 1948 · US · BW · 106mins

Lillian Hellman's prequel to *The Little Foxes* (which was filmed in 1941), shows how the awful Hubbard brood clawed and insinuated their way into Southern high society. The movie's stage origins are evident in every static scene, while the social criticism points to left-wing views for which director Michael Gordon was later blacklisted. There are some good performances, though, notably from Fredric March and from Ann Blyth in the role Bette Davis played seven years earlier. AT

Fredric March *Marcus Hubbard* • Ann Blyth *Regina Hubbard* • Edmond O'Brien *Ben Hubbard* • Florence Eldridge *Lavinia Hubbard* • Dan Duryea *Oscar Hubbard* • John Dall *John Bagtry* • Dona Drake *Laurette* ■ *Dir* Michael Gordon • *Scr* Vladimir Pozner, from the play by Lillian Hellman

Another Shore ★★

Comedy 1948 · UK · BW · 91mins

This is one of the least distinguished films produced by Ealing during its golden age. Part of the problem lies in the unbearable whimsy of the plot, in which customs official Robert Beatty's dreams of living on a South Sea island are brought within touching distance by rich dipsomaniac Stanley Holloway. However, the real problem is the failure of Charles Crichton and his design team to re-create the atmosphere of postwar Dublin. DP

Robert Beatty *Gulliver Shiels* • Stanley Holloway *Alastair McNeil* • Moira Lister *Jennifer Stockley* • Michael Medwin *Yellow Bingham* • Maureen Delaney *Mrs Gleason* • Fred O'Donovan *Coghlan* • Sheila Manahan *Nora* • Wilfrid Brambell *Moore* ■ *Dir* Charles Crichton • *Scr* Walter Meade, from the novel by Kenneth Reddin

Another Stakeout ★★ PG

Action comedy 1993 · US · Colour · 104mins

Richard Dreyfuss and Emilio Estevez are reteamed for a sequel to the box office smash *Stakeout*, but here the chemistry is missing. Once again, the two bickering cops find themselves on surveillance duty, this time watching a potential witness in a Mob trial, played by Cathy Moriarty, and with feisty Assistant DA Rosie O'Donnell along for the ride. The comic playing between the three leads can't be faulted, but this is just a retread. JF. Contains violence and swearing. DVD

Richard Dreyfuss *Chris Lecce* • Emilio Estevez *Bill Reimers* • Rosie O'Donnell *Gina Garrett* • Madeleine Stowe *Maria* • Dennis Farina *Brian O'Hara* • Marcia Strassman *Pam O'Hara* • Cathy Moriarty *Lu Delano* • Miguel Ferrer *Tony Castellano* ■ *Dir* John Badham • *Scr* Jim Kouf, from his characters

Another Thin Man ★★

Detective comedy 1939 · US · BW · 102mins

The third in the massively popular series appeared after a two-year gap in which star William Powell had been absent from MGM through illness. This reunion with Myrna Loy, Asta the dog and director WS Van Dyke is very much the formula as before – witty and sophisticated Nick and Nora Charles trade wisecracks in between solving a few murders – with the addition of a baby, Nick Jr, over whom the couple occasionally coo. Lacking the edge and, of course, the novelty, of its predecessors, it signals the decline of the series (there were three more to come). *Shadow of the Thin Man* continued the series in 1941. RK

William Powell *Nick Charles* • Myrna Loy *Nora Charles* • Virginia Grey *Lois MacFay* • Otto Kruger *Van Slack* • C Aubrey Smith *Colonel MacFay* • Ruth Hussey *Dorothy Waters* • Nat Pendleton *Lt Guild* • Patric Knowles *Dudley Horn* ■ *Dir* WS Van Dyke • *Scr* Frances Goodrich, Albert Hackett, from a story by Dashiell Hammett

Another Time, Another Place ★

Second World War melodrama
1958 · UK · BW · 98mins

This tale casts the glamorous Lana Turner as an unlikely American news reporter in England during the Second World War, who becomes embroiled in a love affair with married war correspondent Sean Connery (yet to find stardom). Tragedy strikes, and Lana spends the rest of director Lewis Allan's turgid film consoling his widow (Glynis Johns) in the unconvincing setting of a Cornish village. RK

Lana Turner *Sara Scott* • Sean Connery *Mark Trevor* • Barry Sullivan *Carter Reynolds* • Glynis Johns *Kay Trevor* ■ *Dir* Lewis Allen • *Scr* Stanley Mann, from the novel by Lenore Coffee

Another Time, Another Place ★★★★ 15

Second World War drama
1983 · UK · Colour · 91mins

This was one of the first *Film on Fours*, and it set a precedent for the innovative work to come. It also marked the directorial debut of Michael Radford, whose glorious *Il Postino* was nominated for a slew of Oscars in 1996. This fascinating, thoughtful Second World War drama takes a sharp but sympathetic look at a lonely young woman who becomes fascinated by the Italian prisoners of war incarcerated nearby. Phyllis Logan and Gregor Fisher (better known as Rab C Nesbitt) give sterling performances in a film that subtly avoids the story's obvious pitfalls. SH DVD

Phyllis Logan *Janie* • Giovanni Mauriello *Luigi* • Gian Luca Favilla *Umberto* • Claudio Rosini *Paolo* • Paul Young *Dougal* • Gregor Fisher *Beel* • Tom Watson *Finlay* • Jennifer Piercey *Kirsty* • Denise Coffey *Meg* • Yvonne Gilan *Jess* ■ *Dir* Michael Radford • *Scr* Michael Radford, from the novel by Jessie Kesson

Another Woman ★★★★ PG

Drama 1988 · US · Colour · 77mins

One of the few Woody Allen movies to have disappeared swiftly on release, this complex, highly structured look at the great questions of life, love and death contains a stunning performance from Gena Rowlands as a rather smug, self-absorbed college professor who is forced to question her assumed truths. This is Allen at his most serious, often verging on pretentiousness, but there is plenty of food for thought and some able support from Ian Holm, Gene Hackman and Mia Farrow before the infamous parting. SH DVD

Gena Rowlands *Marion Post* • Mia Farrow *Hope* • Ian Holm *Ken Post* • Blythe Danner *Lydia* • Gene Hackman *Larry* • Betty Buckley *Kathy* • Martha Plimpton *Laura Post* • John Houseman *Marion's father* • Sandy Dennis *Claire* • David Ogden Stiers *Young Marion's father* ■ *Dir/Scr* Woody Allen

Another You ★ 15

Comedy 1991 · US · Colour · 90mins

Richard Pryor (who has a well-documented history of substance abuse, as well as multiple sclerosis) looks very ill indeed in this lame comedy. The combined talents of the stars can't paper over a nondescript plot and lacklustre dialogue. There are numerous tasteless jokes about mental illness – Gene Wilder has just been released from the local sanatorium – but nothing can disguise Pryor's deep-seated problems. SH. Contains swearing. DVD

Gene Wilder *George/Abe Fielding* • Richard Pryor *Eddie Dash* • Mercedes Ruehl *Elaine/ Mimi Kravitz* • Stephen Lang *Dibbs* • Vanessa Williams [Vanessa L Williams] *Gloria* • Jerry Houser *Tim* • Kevin Pollak *Phil* ■ *Dir* Maurice Phillips • *Scr* Ziggy Steinberg

Anthony Adverse ★★★★

Period swashbuckling drama
1936 · US · BW · 142mins

A mammoth epic based on an even more mammoth popular novel, this splendid Warner Bros period melodrama offers many rewards, most notably the spectacle of a studio in its prime using all its facilities to the utmost. Unsurprisingly, this movie won Oscars for best cinematography, best editing and best score. Apply those elements to a rousing swashbuckler about a hero (an effective Fredric March) whose one true love (Olivia de Havilland at her peak) is swept away from him, and the result is very satisfying. The tale takes its time to unfold, but stick with it, especially for Gale Sondergaard's Oscar-winning debut performance. TS

Fredric March *Anthony Adverse* • Olivia de Havilland *Angela Guessippi* • Edmund Gwenn *John Bonnyfeather* • Claude Rains *Don Luis* • Anita Louise *Maria* • Louis Hayward *Denis Moore* • Gale Sondergaard *Faith Paleologus* • Steffi Duna *Neleta* • Billy Mauch *Anthony as a child* • Donald Woods *Vincent Nolte* • Akim Tamiroff *Carlo Cibo* • Rollo Lloyd *Napoleon Bonaparte* ■ *Dir* Mervyn LeRoy • *Scr* Sheridan Gibney, from the novel by Hervey Allen • *Cinematographer* Tony Gaudio • *Music* Erich Wolfgang Korngold • *Editor* Ralph Dawson

Antitrust ★★ 12

Thriller 2001 · US · Colour · 104mins

Ryan Phillippe stars as a computer whizzkid who abandons his idealism to work for giant software corporation NURV. However, he discovers that there is a link between the suspicious deaths of computer programmers outside NURV and the ground-breaking new codes that NURV is developing. Tim Robbins's performance as a corporate software executive is worthy of a better film, while Phillippe needs more than a pair of glasses to prove his acting credentials. RT DVD

Ryan Phillippe *Milo Hoffman* • Rachael Leigh Cook *Lisa Calighan* • Claire Forlani *Alice Poulson* • Tim Robbins *Gary Winston* • Douglas McFerran *Rob Shrot* • Richard Roundtree *Lyle Barton* ■ *Dir* Peter Howitt • *Scr* Howard Franklin

Antonia's Line ★★★ 15

Drama 1995 · Bel/UK/Neth · Colour · 98mins

Combining pastoral fantasy and magic realism, feminist polemic and humanist compassion, Marleen Gorris's vibrant drama won the Oscar for best foreign film, albeit in a poor year. Sprawling over five decades, the action boasts a spirited start, in which Willeke van Ammelrooy returns to her home village after the war and introduces us to a gallery of eccentric characters. The tale then loses its way, as the opening's life-affirming joy is replaced with a stiff sense of moral rectitude. DP. In Dutch with English subtitles. Contains violence, swearing, sex scenes and nudity. DVD

Willeke van Ammelrooy *Antonia* • Els Dottermans *Danielle, Antonia's daughter* • Jan Decleir *Bas* • Marina de Graaf *Deedee* • Mil Seghers *Crooked Finger* • Fran Waller Zeper *Olga* • Jakob Beks *Farmer Daan* • Jan Steen *Loony Lips* ■ *Dir/Scr* Marleen Gorris

Antonio das Mortes ★★★★

Political drama 1969 · Bra · Colour · 100mins

Returning to the barren *sertao* plain, Glauber Rocha's sequel to *Black God,*

White Devil (1964) was one of the key films in the second phase of the Brazilian *cinema nôvo* revival, known as "cannibal-tropicalist" for its heavy emphasis on allegorical symbolism. Rocha won the best director prize at Cannes for his first colour feature, but the decision to turn Antonio (Maurício do Valle) from an establishment assassin into a revolutionary hero of the downtrodden peasantry did not impress the junta, and he was hounded into decade-long European exile. Almost politicising the spaghetti western, this is highly stylised yet highly effective film-making. DP. In Portuguese with English subtitles.

Mauricio do Valle *Antonio das Mortes* • Hugo Carvana *Police Chief Mattos* • Odete Lara *Laura* • Othon Bastos *Professor* • Jofre Soares *Colonel Horacio* • Lorival Pariz *Coirana* ■ *Dir/Scr* Glauber Rocha

Antony and Cleopatra ★★★

Historical drama
1972 · UK · Colour · 168mins

Charlton Heston played Mark Antony in 1949, then again in 1970, both times in film versions of *Julius Caesar*. Here he begs comparisons with Olivier by directing and starring in an adaptation of the other Shakespeare play in which the character appears. Heston's long experience in epic movies holds him in good stead: the picture has grandeur, while the English cast members are all excellent. But Chuck's Antony is a bit of a pontificating bore, and Hildegard Neil isn't up to the role of Cleopatra. AT

Charlton Heston *Antony* • Hildegard Neil *Cleopatra* • Eric Porter *Enobarbus* • John Castle *Octavius Caesar* • Fernando Rey *Lepidus* • Juan Luis Galiardo *Alexas* • Carmen Sevilla *Octavia* • Freddie Jones *Pompey* • Jane Lapotaire *Charmian* ■ *Dir* Charlton Heston • *Scr* Charlton Heston, from the play by William Shakespeare

Antwone Fisher ★★★ 15

Drama based on a true story
2002 · US · Colour · 115mins

Actor Denzel Washington made his directorial debut with this powerful drama, in which he also stars. It's an often harrowing tale of child abuse and its lifelong effects. Derek Luke puts in a compelling performance as the adult Antwone Fisher, a young black sailor whose deep-rooted problems manifest themselves in violent outbursts. When he's forced to seek help from a naval psychiatrist (played by Washington), he learns to face up to his horrific past. Crisply directed and beautifully shot, Washington's tear-jerking drama has the odd mawkish moment, but is still a balanced film. SF [VIDEO] DVD

Derek Luke *Antwone Fisher* • Joy Bryant *Cheryl Smolley* • Denzel Washington *Jerome Davenport* • Salli Richardson *Berta Davenport* • Earl Billings *James* • Kevin Connolly *Slim* • Viola Davis *Eva* • James Brolin *Fisher's commanding officer* ■ *Dir* Denzel Washington • *Scr* Antwone Fisher, from his autobiography *Finding Fish: a Memoir*

Antz ★★★★★ PG

Animated fantasy adventure
1998 · US · Colour · 83mins

This hugely charming and witty animated adventure is perhaps even more appealing to adults than it is to children, who are nevertheless sure to be enchanted. Woody Allen is the perfect choice for the voice of Z, an ant who feels insignificant among millions. He sets out to achieve something in his life by winning the heart of Princess Bala (sexily voiced by Sharon Stone). Helping him in his quest for fulfilment is a butch soldier ant (Sylvester Stallone), while Gene Hackman and Christopher Walken give voice to the sinister General Mandible and his sidekick Cutter, who are plotting dastardly things for the colony. Beautifully produced by DreamWorks, with a sparkling script. JB [VIDEO] DVD

Woody Allen *Z* • Sharon Stone *Bala* • Sylvester Stallone *Weaver* • Gene Hackman *Mandible* • Christopher Walken *Cutter* • Jane Curtin *Muffy* • Jennifer Lopez *Azteca* • John Mahoney *Drunk Scout* • Paul Mazursky *Psychologist* • Anne Bancroft *Queen* • Dan Aykroyd *Chip* • Danny Glover *Barbatus* ■ *Dir* Eric Darnell, Tim Johnson • *Scr* Todd Alcott, Chris Weitz, Paul Weitz

Any Given Sunday ★★★★ 15

Sports drama 1999 · US · Colour · 150mins

Oliver Stone offers his multi-camera perspective on American football in this bruising "us and them" drama. Essentially it's *North Dallas Forty* with a racial subtext, coated in *Jerry Maguire* sentimentality. But this ensemble masterclass is also a hybrid of *Platoon* and *Wall Street*, with Al Pacino even delivering a teamwork variation on Michael Douglas's "Greed is Good" speech. It's no accident that the tin-helmeted players thunder into encounters resembling the beach sequence in *Saving Private Ryan*, for Stone considers them the cannon fodder in a militaristic stratagem. Overlong, but with moments of explosive inspiration. DP. Contains violence, swearing, drug abuse and nudity. [VIDEO] DVD

Al Pacino *Tony D'Amato* • Cameron Diaz *Christina Pagniacci* • Dennis Quaid *Jack "Cap" Rooney* • James Woods *Dr Harvey Mandrake* • Jamie Foxx *Willie Beamen* • LL Cool J *Julian Washington* • Matthew Modine *Dr Ollie Powers* • Jim Brown *Montezuma Monroe* • Charlton Heston *AFFA football commissioner* • Ann-Margret *Margaret Pagniacci* • Aaron Eckhart *Nick Crozier* ■ *Dir* Oliver Stone • *Scr* John Logan, Oliver Stone, from a story by Daniel Pyne, John Logan

Any Man's Death ★★ 15

Drama 1990 · S Afr · Colour · 104mins

A morality drama with John Savage as a journalist who, while working in Africa, stumbles upon a scientist who once masterminded medical experiments in the Nazi death camps. But the doctor's work now helps humanity. What's a poor reporter to do? Mia Sara and Ernest Borgnine help Savage wrestle with his conscience. The result is a film that raises pertinent questions, but cops out of answering them. DA [VIDEO]

John Savage *Leon* • William Hickey *Schiller* • Mia Sara *Gerline* • Ernest Borgnine *Gantz* • Michael Lerner *Denner* • James Ryan *Caplan* • Damarob *Oskar* • Tobie Cronje *Johann* ■ *Dir* Tom Clegg • *Scr* Iain Roy, Chris Kelly

Any Number Can Play ★★★

Drama 1949 · US · BW · 102mins

Clark Gable runs a casino, much to the embarrassment of his son – until he starts winning, of course. Director Mervyn LeRoy's movie seems to say that gambling will make a man of you and cure family problems. Since it won't do much for your heart condition, however, quit now while you're ahead. There's a weird moral here, though the gangster subplot is more conventional. The solid supporting cast includes Mary Astor and Lewis Stone. AT

Clark Gable *Charley Enley Kyng* • Alexis Smith *Lon Kyng* • Wendell Corey *Robbin Elcott* • Audrey Totter *Alice Elcott* • Frank Morgan *Jim Kurstyn* • Mary Astor *Ada* • Lewis Stone *Ben Gavery Snelerr* • Barry Sullivan *Tycoon* ■ *Dir* Mervyn LeRoy • *Scr* Richard Brooks, from the novel by Edward Harris Heth

Any Number Can Win ★★★

Crime drama 1963 · Fr/It · BW · 112mins

Despite the rise of the French New Wave, such competent directors as Henri Verneuil continued to make traditional genre movies like this entertaining, albeit familiar heist yarn. This time the Cannes casino is the target of an ageing ex-con and a younger crook. What made it a hit in France was the co-starring of Jean Gabin, a huge box-office star of the 1930s, with Alain Delon, as big a name in the 1960s. RB. In French with English subtitles.

Jean Gabin *Charles* • Alain Delon *Francis* • Viviane Romance *Ginette* • Maurice Biraud *Louis* • Carla Marlier *Brigitte* • José-Luis De Villalonga *Grimp* • Germaine Montero *Francis's mother* ■ *Dir* Henri Verneuil • *Scr* Albert Simonin, Michel Audiard, Henri Verneuil, from the novel *The Big Grab* by John Trinian

Any Wednesday ★★★

Comedy 1966 · US · Colour · 109mins

From the bimbo Barbarella via political activist to mogul-mate Jane Fonda has been a moll for all seasons. This is an eager-to-please sex farce with Jason Robards as the married executive whose mid-weekly liaisons with mindless mistress Fonda have become a ritual even his wife (Rosemary Murphy) knows about. Dean Jones, seeking true love, tries to find a way to break the habit so that it all ends happily. Originally cut and called *Bachelor Girl Apartment*, it works better with the risqué bits back in. TH

Jane Fonda *Ellen Gordon* • Jason Robards *John Cleves* • Dean Jones *Cass Henderson* • Rosemary Murphy *Dorothy Cleves* • Ann Prentiss *Miss Linsley* • Jack Fletcher *Felix* • Kelly Jean Peters *Girl in Museum* ■ *Dir* Robert Ellis Miller • *Scr* Julius J Epstein, from the play *Son of Any Wednesday* by Muriel Resnik

Any Which Way You Can ★★★ 15

Action comedy 1980 · US · Colour · 110mins

This sequel to *Every Which Way but Loose* typifies the kind of comic vehicles that paid Clint Eastwood's rent in the late 1970s and early 1980s. Short on plot, long on slapstick humour and featuring real-life girlfriend Sondra Locke as his love interest and the likeable Geoffrey Lewis as his best buddy, it has a lightweight charm that makes up for the insignificance of the story. Eastwood plays a car repair mechanic pushed back into bare-knuckle boxing for one last fight by the Mafia. Destructive orang-utan Clyde steals scenes like an old pro. JC. Contains violence, swearing. [VIDEO]

Clint Eastwood *Philo Beddoe* • Sondra Locke *Lynn Halsey-Taylor* • Geoffrey Lewis *Orville Boggs* • William Smith *Jack Wilson* • Harry Guardino *James Beekman* • Ruth Gordon *Ma Boggs* ■ *Dir* Buddy Van Horn • *Scr* Stanford Sherman, from characters created by Jeremy Joe Kronsberg

Anybody's Woman ★★★

Romantic comedy 1930 · US · BW · 80mins

A case has been made for this movie's seeming honesty because it was directed by a woman, Dorothy Arzner, who empathised with the plight of a woman who married an alcoholic. The film's strengths are in its depiction of the couple's sleaze-ridden life, and the remarkably strong performances of the fine Clive Brook as the drunken lawyer and the splendid Ruth Chatterton as the cheap stripper he marries. Age has not worn this film well, but it retains its inherent interest and – dare one say it? – its topicality. TS

Ruth Chatterton *Pansy Gray* • Clive Brook *Neil Dunlap* • Paul Lukas *Gustav Saxon* • Huntley Gordon *Grant Crosby* • Virginia Hammond *Katherine Malcolm* • Tom Patricola *Eddie Calcio* • Juliette Compton *Ellen* • Cecil Cunningham *Dot* ■ *Dir* Dorothy Arzner • *Scr* Zoe Akins, Doris Anderson, from a story by Gouverneur Morris

Anything Can Happen ★★ U

Comedy 1952 · US · BW · 96mins

Two years after his Oscar-winning performance as Cyrano de Bergerac, José Ferrer played a Russian immigrant in this comedy of manners and language, based on the real-life experiences of George and Helen Papashvily. Falling for a court stenographer (Kim Hunter), Ferrer follows her to California, gets married and starts an orange farm. Director George Seaton's film offers some episodic, fitfully amusing entertainment, though its real aim is to portray America as a haven for the dispossessed of Eastern Europe. AT

José Ferrer *Giorgi* • Kim Hunter *Helen Watson* • Kurt Kasznar *Nuri Bey* • Eugenie Leontovich *Anna Godiedze* • Oscar Karlweis *Uncle Besso* • Oscar Beregi *Uncle John* • Mikhail Rasumny *Tariel Godiedze* • Nick Dennis *Chancho* ■ *Dir* George Seaton • *Scr* George Seaton, George Oppenheimer, from the memoirs of George Papashvily, Helen Papashvily

Anything Else ★★★ 15

Romantic comedy
2003 · US · Colour · 104mins

Woody Allen revisits many of the themes explored in *Annie Hall* in this typically acerbic film, but would-be writer Jason Biggs's disintegrating relationship with aspiring actress Christina Ricci departs in several ways from the director's trusted formula. The action filmed in CinemaScope, and it's also darker than usual, with Allen's teacher-cum-gagsmith fixating on firearms and the Holocaust, while the depiction of both Ricci and her wannabe-singer mother (Stockard Channing) is scathing. Fitfully amusing, but disconcerting. DP. Contains drug abuse and sexual references. [VIDEO] DVD

Woody Allen *David Dobel* • Jason Biggs *Jerry Falk* • Christina Ricci *Amanda* • Stockard Channing *Paula* • Danny DeVito *Harvey* • Jimmy Fallon *Bob* • KaDee Strickland *Brooke* • Erica Leerhsen *Connie* ■ *Dir/Scr* Woody Allen

Anything Goes ★★★ U

Musical 1936 · US · BW · 91mins

PG Wodehouse co-wrote the book for the original Cole Porter stage smash on which this is based. This shipboard story of a romantic stowaway who's forced to pose as a criminal is pretty lightweight, but there's still plenty to enjoy, particularly with Ethel Merman repeating her Broadway triumph by belting out such classic tunes as *I Get a Kick Out of You* and the title song. A relaxed Bing Crosby and a radiant Ida Lupino play the lovers, while Charles Ruggles enjoys himself enormously as "Public Enemy #13". DP

Bing Crosby *Billy Crockett* • Ethel Merman *Reno Sweeney* • Charlie Ruggles [Charles Ruggles] *Rev Dr Moon* • Ida Lupino *Hope Harcourt* • Grace Bradley *Bonnie Le Tour* • Arthur Treacher *Sir Evelyn Oakleigh* • Robert McWade *Elisha J Whitney* • Richard Carle *Bishop Dobson* ■ *Dir* Lewis Milestone • *Scr* Howard Lindsay, Russel Crouse, from the musical by Guy Bolton (book), PG Wodehouse (book), Cole Porter (music/lyrics) • *Source • Story* Cole Porter

Anything Goes ★★ U

Musical 1956 · US · Colour · 105mins

Having already starred in the 1936 film version of Cole Porter's hit musical, Bing Crosby came aboard this Sidney Sheldon-scripted reworking, which is far too loose to be considered a genuine remake. Donald O'Connor co-stars as the vaudevillian who hires showgirl Mitzi Gaynor, unaware that Crosby has already signed up Zizi Jeanmaire. Crosby revels in the exceptional songbook, while Jeanmaire impresses in a ballet choreographed by her husband, Roland Petit. Yet it all remains stubbornly flat. DP

Bing Crosby *Bill Benson* • Donald O'Connor *Ted Adams* • Zizi Jeanmaire *Gaby Duval* • Mitzi Gaynor *Patsy Blair* • Phil Harris *Steve Blair* • Kurt Kasznar *Victor Lawrence* ■ *Dir* Robert Lewis (1) • *Scr* Sidney Sheldon, from the musical by PG Wodehouse, Guy Bolton • *Music* Cole Porter, Jimmy Van Heusen • *Lyrics* Cole Porter, Sammy Cahn

Anywhere but Here ★★★ 12

Comedy drama 1999 · US · Colour · 109mins

Flighty Susan Sarandon and her rebellious daughter Natalie Portman go on a turbulent voyage of self-discovery in an old-fashioned tear-jerker from director Wayne Wang. Familial tension mounts as they drive to Hollywood to fulfil the acting dreams Sarandon has for her embarrassed daughter, though the sudsy script eventually allows its emotional themes to bubble to the surface. Portman breathes fresh life into the over-familiar, soap-opera plot with grace, charm and wit. AJ. Contains sexual references. DVD

Susan Sarandon *Adele August* • Natalie Portman *Ann August* • Eileen Ryan *Lillian* • Ray Baker *Ted* • John Diehl *Jimmy* • Shawn Hatosy *Benny* • Bonnie Bedelia *Carol* • Faran Tahir *Hisham* ■ *Dir* Wayne Wang • *Scr* Alvin Sargent, from the novel by Mona Simpson

Anzio ★★ PG

Second World War drama
1968 · It · Colour · 112mins

In this epic Second World War drama, Robert Mitchum stars as an American war correspondent covering the Allied Forces' landing at Anzio Beach in Italy and their costly and bloody march on Rome. This is one of those war movies that poses thunderous moral questions at every turn and gives ordinary Joes statements rather than dialogue. It's a long haul, in every respect. Predictably, Mitchum and the odd cameo by the likes of Robert Ryan and Arthur Kennedy are the only things worth your attention. AT

Robert Mitchum *Dick Ennis* • Peter Falk *Corporal Rabinoff* • Arthur Kennedy *General Lesly* • Robert Ryan *General Carson* • Earl Holliman *Sergeant Stimler* • Mark Damon *Richardson* • Reni Santoni *Movie* • Joseph Walsh *Doyle* • Thomas Hunter *Andy* • Giancarlo Giannini *Cellini* • Anthony Steel *General Marsh* ■ *Dir* Edward Dmytryk • *Scr* Harry AL Craig, from the novel by Wynford Vaughan-Thomas, adapted by Frank DeFelitta, Duilio Coletti, Giuseppe Mangione, Canestri

Apa ★★★★

Drama 1966 · Hun · BW · 91mins

Described by sophomore director István Szabó as "the autobiography of a generation", this is a visually audacious, yet highly personal, study of the uneasy relationship between postwar Hungary and its past. The fragmentary structure enables Szabó to explore the themes of reputation, heroism and paternalism as student Andras Balint gradually discovers the truth about his deceased partisan father. Committedly played and meticulously constructed, the film gains additional power and authenticity from cinematographer Sándor Sára's inspired photographic pastiches of *film noir* and State-sponsored newsreel. DP. In Hungarian with English subtitles.

Andras Balint *Tako* • Miklos Gabor *Father* • Klari Tolnay *Mother* • Dani Erdelyi *Tako, as a child* • Kati Solyom *Anni* ■ *Dir/Scr* István Szabó • *Cinematographer* Sandor Sara

Apache ★★★★ U

Western 1954 · US · Colour · 87mins

This courageous (for its day) film was directed by newcomer Robert Aldrich, who rose to the challenge and turned in a fine and intelligent western with splendid set pieces. He is helped immeasurably by the dynamic athletic presence of Lancaster in the lead as Massai, the last noble Apache, who tried to hold out against the overwhelming forces of the US Army, and so passed into legend. The showing of the so-called growth of western civilisation through Massai's eyes is superbly directed, and the film, though brutal, presents a realistic and wholly sympathetic viewpoint, despite being compromised by the happy ending insisted upon by the distributors. TS DVD

Burt Lancaster *Massai* • Jean Peters *Nalinle* • John McIntire *Al Sieber* • Charles Buchinsky [Charles Bronson] *Hondo* • John Dehner *Weddle* • Paul Guilfoyle (1) *Santos* • Ian MacDonald *Clagg* • Walter Sande *Lt Col Beck* • Morris Ankrum *Dawson* • Monte Blue *Geronimo* ■ *Dir* Robert Aldrich • *Scr* James R Webb, from the novel *Bronco Apache* by Paul I Wellman

Apache Drums ★★★ U

Western 1951 · US · Colour · 74mins

The fact that this is a darker than usual western is perhaps not too surprising, since it was horror producer Val Lewton's last film. Stephen McNally is excellent as the ne'er-do-well who's run out of town, then returns to help defend the community from an Apache attack, and *Red River's* Coleen Gray also acquits herself well. Argentinian director Hugo Fregonese isn't daunted by the movie's low budget, and the short running time helps keep the tension taut. TS

Stephen McNally *Sam Leeds* • Coleen Gray *Sally* • Arthur Shields *Rev Griffin* • Willard Parker *Joe Madden* • James Griffith *Lt Glidden* • Armando Silvestre *Pedro-Peter* • Georgia Backus *Mrs Keon* • Clarence Muse *Jehu* ■ *Dir* Hugo Fregonese • *Scr* David Chandler, from the story *Stand at Spanish Boot* by Harry Brown

Apache Rifles ★ U

Western drama 1964 · US · Colour · 91mins

Provoked by gold miners invading their homeland, the Apaches go on the warpath. Audie Murphy's cavalry captain brings about a peace that lasts until the murder of a new Indian agent is blamed on the tribe and the ruthless tactics of officer John Archer make matters worse. Unpolished, with a weak supporting cast. AE

Audie Murphy *Jeff Stanton* • Michael Dante *Red Hawk* • Linda Lawson *Dawn Gillis* • LQ Jones *Mike Greer* • Ken Lynch *Hodges* • Joseph Vitale *Victorio* • Robert Brubaker *Sergeant Cobb* • J Pat O'Malley *Captain Thatcher* • John Archer *Colonel Perry* ■ *Dir* William Witney • *Scr* Charles B Smith, from a story by Kenneth Gamet, Richard Schayer, from the 1951 film *Indian Uprising* by Richard Schayer

Apache Trail ★★ U

Western 1942 · US · BW · 65mins

This routine but reliable B-western has a pair of estranged brothers (William Lundigan and Lloyd Nolan) thrown together by an Apache uprising. Donna Reed provides the love interest, while Chill Wills supplies the corncob philosophising, but there are very few surprises on this well-rutted cowboy trail. Richard Thorpe's film was later remade as *Apache War Smoke*. TH

Lloyd Nolan *Trigger Bill* • Donna Reed *Rosalia Martinez* • William Lundigan *Tom Folliard* • Ann Ayars *Constance Selden* • Connie Gilchrist *Senora Martinez* • Chill Wills *"Pike" Skelton* • Miles Mander *James V Thorne* ■ *Dir* Richard Thorpe • *Scr* Maurice Geraghty, from a story by Ernest Haycox

Apache Uprising ★★ U

Western 1965 · US · Colour · 91mins

Curiosity may have drawn audiences in 1965 to see what had become of stars like Rory Calhoun, Corinne Calvet, Lon Chaney Jr, Richard Arlen and Johnny Mack Brown. Unfortunately it's an utterly routine affair which pits hero Calhoun against Apaches and outlaws. John Russell makes an excellent deep-dyed villain, and DeForest Kelley also scores as a paranoid henchman, but it would be kinder to catch the others when they were in their prime. AE

Rory Calhoun *Jim Walker* • Corinne Calvet *Janice MacKenzie* • John Russell *Vance Buckner* • Lon Chaney [Lon Chaney Jr] *Charlie Russell* • Gene Evans *Jess Cooney* • Richard Arlen *Captain Gannon* • Arthur Hunnicutt *Bill Gibson* • DeForest Kelley *Toby Jack Saunders* • Johnny Mack Brown *Sheriff Ben Hall* • Jean Parker *Mrs Hawkes* • Donald Barry *Henry Belden* ■ *Dir* RG Springsteen • *Scr* Harry Sanford, Max Lamb, from the novel *Way Station* by Max Steeber, Harry Sanford

Apache War Smoke ★★ U

Western 1952 · US · BW · 67mins

It was said that MGM's B-pictures looked like other studios' A-features, and this is a good example, with only the absence of star names giving away its modest pretensions. This features an assortment of stage passengers and Apaches on the warpath. Charismatic bandit Gilbert Roland joins the group under siege at a way station run by his long-lost son, Robert Horton. Ace editor Harold Kress, on one of his occasional turns at directing, draws a virile performance from Horton. A remake of 1942's *Apache Trail*. AE

Gilbert Roland *Peso* • Glenda Farrell *Fanny Webson* • Robert Horton *Tom Herrera* • Barbara Ruick *Nancy Dekker* • Gene Lockhart *Cyril R Snowden* • Henry Morgan [Harry Morgan] *Ed Cotten* • Douglas Dumbrille [Douglass Dumbrille] *Maj Dekker* ■ *Dir* Harold Kress • *Scr* Jerry Davis, from a story by Ernest Haycox

Apache Woman ★★ U

Western 1955 · US · Colour · 83mins

Celebrated B-movie producer/director Roger Corman is perhaps best known for his 1960s' adaptations of Edgar Allan Poe stories. He also made notable, if often tacky, contributions to the sci-fi and gangster genres, but westerns like this weren't really his thing, although the story in which Lloyd Bridges is a government agent sent to investigate crimes supposedly committed by a group of renegade Apaches has some surprises. TH

Lloyd Bridges *Rex Moffet* • Joan Taylor *Anne Libeau* • Lance Fuller *Armand* • Morgan Jones *Macey* • Paul Birch *Sheriff* ■ *Dir* Roger Corman • *Scr* Lou Rusoff

Aparajito ★★★★ U

Drama 1956 · Ind · BW · 104mins

This central part of Satyajit Ray's celebrated Apu trilogy won the Golden Lion at the Venice Film Festival. Continuing the story started in *Pather Panchali*, it focuses on Apu's relationship with his mother and the sharp contrasts between his simple country background and the bustle of city life. With his camera scarcely still for a second, Ray paints a fascinating picture of Indian life, considering the clash between western and traditional ideas with the same humanism that characterises all his work. While it lacks some of the poignancy of its predecessor, this is still a remarkable and deeply felt film. DP. In Bengali with English subtitles. DVD

Pinaki Sen Gupta *Apu, as a boy* • Smaran Ghoshal *Apu, as an adolescent* • Karuna Bannerjee *Mother* • Kanu Bannerjee *Father* ■ *Dir* Satyajit Ray • *Scr* Satyajit Ray, from the novels by Bibhutibhushan Bannerjee

The Apartment ★★★★★ PG

Comedy drama 1960 · US · BW · 122mins

Billy Wilder's classic film cleverly veils its darker side and operates as a light romantic comedy, in which Jack Lemmon's put-upon, snuffling insurance clerk CC Baxter basically pimps his apartment to his superiors so that they can indulge in extramarital trysts. That he does it in return for promotions that never come makes "Buddy Boy" Baxter a sad case indeed. But in Lemmon's articulate hands, he instantly earns our sympathy, and redemption comes when Shirley MacLaine's elevator girl – mistress of unscrupulous boss Fred MacMurray – attempts suicide and he comes to her aid. From such potentially edgy material Wilder and co-writer IAL Diamond sculpt an unforgettable romance that won five Oscars. AC DVD

Jack Lemmon *CC "Bud" Baxter* • Shirley MacLaine *Fran Kubelik* • Fred MacMurray *JD Sheldrake* • Ray Walston *Mr Dobisch* • David Lewis (1) *Mr Kirkeby* • Jack Kruschen *Dr Dreyfuss* • Joan Shawlee *Sylvia* • Edie Adams *Miss Olsen* • Hope Holiday *Margie MacDougall* ■ *Dir* Billy Wilder • *Scr* Billy Wilder, IAL Diamond • *Cinematographer* Joseph LaShelle • *Editor* Daniel Mandell • *Art Director* Alexandre Trauner

Apartment for Peggy ★★★

Drama 1948 · US · Colour · 96mins

Jeanne Crain and William Holden star as the young married couple trying to find a place to live in the era of postwar housing shortages in this shamelessly sentimental opus. Crain and Holden play off each other nicely, but both leads are given a run for their money by veterans Edmund Gwenn and Gene Lockhart. Professor Gwenn's transformation from suicidal depressive into hopeful optimist does take some swallowing, though the movie's worth perservering with for the period Technicolor and the charming performances. TS

Jeanne Crain *Peggy* • William Holden (2) *Jason* • Edmund Gwenn *Professor Henry Barnes* • Gene Lockhart *Professor Edward Bell* • Griff Barnett *Dr Conway* • Randy Stuart *Dorothy* ■ *Dir/Scr* George Seaton

Apartment Zero ★★ 15

Psychological thriller
1988 · UK · Colour · 119mins

Colin Firth stars as the manager of a Buenos Aires cinema. Twitchy, timid and totally unconvincing, he falls under the spell of dynamic lodger Hart Bochner. This occasionally intriguing mix of *The Lady from Shanghai* and *The Servant* is often too clever for its own good, and runs out of steam long before the inevitable "housemate from hell" plot kicks in. DP. Contains swearing, nudity.

Colin Firth *Adrian LeDuc* • Hart Bochner *Jack Carney* • Dora Bryan *Margaret McKinney* • Liz Smith *Mary Louise McKinney* • Fabrizio Bentivoglio *Carlos Sanchez-Verne* • James Telfer *"Vanessa"* • Mirella D'Angelo *Laura Werpachowsky* • Juan Vitali *Alberto Werpachowsky* • Francesca D'Aloja *Claudia* ■ *Dir* Martin Donovan (1) • *Scr* Martin Donovan, David Koepp, from a story by Martin Donovan

The Ape ★

Horror 1940 · US · BW · 62mins

This has to be the daftest B-movie horror king Boris Karloff ever appeared in. After polio claims the life of his child, Karloff searches for a cure. He discovers his prototype serum will only work if it contains human spinal fluid; so he kills an escaped circus ape, skins it and, disguised in the animal's hide, hunts for more of the precious liquid. A ridiculously dumb potboiler. AJ

Boris Karloff *Dr Bernard Adrian* • Maris Wrixon *Frances Clifford* • Gertrude W Hoffman

Housekeeper • Henry Hall (1) *Sheriff* ■ *Dir* William Nigh • *Scr* Richard Carroll, Kurt Siodmak [Curt Siodmak], from the play by Adam Hull Shirk

APEX ★★ 15

Science-fiction adventure
1994 · US · Colour · 98mins

Richard Keats visits the past, gets trapped there, makes alterations and returns to 2073, with a killer cyborg in hot pursuit, to find an alternate universe thanks to a deadly virus he may have unleashed. Although efficiently directed with some notable moments (the best being the cyborg mating with a heavy metal CD), Phillip J Roth doesn't have the budget, wit or imagination to pull off such an ambitious concept. JF. Contains violence and swearing. [video] DVD

Richard Keats *Nicholas Sinclair* • Mitchell Cox *Shepherd* • Lisa Ann Russell *Natasha Sinclair* • Marcus Aurelius *Taylor* • Adam Lawson *Rasheed* • David Jean Thomas *Dr Elgin* • Brian Richard Peck *Desert Rat* • Anna B Choi *Mishima* ■ *Dir* Phillip J Roth • *Scr* Phillip J Roth, Ronald Schmidt, from a story by Gian Carlo Scandiuzzi, Phillip J Roth

Aphrodite Goddess of Love ★★

Period drama 1957 · It · Colour · 94mins

Mario Bonnard began directing in 1917 and had trotted out dozens of adaptations and costume dramas by the time he came to this sword-and-sandal adventure. The great Sergio Leone had a hand in the script for this overwrought melodrama set in Corinth in the reign of the Emperor Nero. While corrupt officials sell the poor into slavery to acquire a new canal for their valley, two women, one rich and the other a Christian, vie for the attentions of a handsome artist. The stars look good, but they can't act. DP. In Italian with English subtitles.

Isabelle Corey • Irene Turc • Ivo Garrani • Anthony Steffen ■ *Dir* Mario Bonnard • *Scr* Damiano Damiani

Apocalypse Now ★★★★★ 15

Epic war drama 1979 · US · Colour · 194mins

Direcor Francis Coppola inherited a modest movie about the Vietnam War from writer John Milius and turned it into this phantasmagorical ride, in which Martin Sheen travels up the Mekong river to terminate Marlon Brando's rebel command "with extreme prejudice". Working under difficult conditions in the Philippines and running way over budget, Coppola delivered a harrowing masterwork that bursts with malarial, mystical images. Coppola restored a whopping 50 minutes of extra footage for *Apocalypse Now Redux*, which was released in 2001. Whether the additional scenes greatly enhance an already exhilirating experience is debatable, but they were certainly worth the wait. AT. Contains violence, swearing, drug abuse. [video] DVD

Martin Sheen *Captain Willard* • Marlon Brando *Colonel Kurtz* • Robert Duvall *Lt Col Kilgore* • Frederic Forrest *Chef* • Albert Hall *Chief* • Sam Bottoms *Lance* • Larry Fishburne [Laurence Fishburne] *Clean* • Dennis Hopper *Photo journalist* • GD Spradlin *General* • Harrison Ford *Colonel* • Scott Glenn *Captain Richard Colby* • Bill Graham *Agent* • Christian Marquand *Hubert DeMarais* • Aurore Clément *Roxanne Sarrault* ■ *Dir* Francis Coppola [Francis Ford Coppola] • *Scr* Francis Coppola [Francis Ford Coppola], John Milius, from the novella *Heart of Darkness* by Joseph Conrad • *Cinematographer* Vittorio Storaro

Apollo 13 ★★★★ PG

Space drama based on a true story
1995 · US · Colour · 140mins

In April 1970, astronaut Jim Lovell contacted mission control with the words: "Houston, we have a problem." It was a classic understatement, signalling a huge, complex problem to be solved. Lovell and his crew, Jack Swigert and Fred Haise, were bound for the Moon when an oxygen tank exploded in their craft, leaving them potentially marooned. It gave Nasa's scientists the biggest headache of the space-age so far and kept Americans – by then blasé about the space programme – glued to their TVs. Lovell is played by Tom Hanks, whose very ordinariness is the essence of astronaut-man, while Kevin Bacon and Bill Paxton offer welcome contrasts, as does the superb Ed Harris as the chain-smoking mission controller. Filmed in genuine weightless conditions, Ron Howard's movie is a technical tour de force. AT. Contains swearing. [video] DVD

Tom Hanks *Jim Lovell* • Bill Paxton *Fred Haise* • Kevin Bacon *Jack Swigert* • Gary Sinise *Ken Mattingly* • Ed Harris *Gene Kranz* • Kathleen Quinlan *Marilyn Lovell* • Mary Kate Schellhardt *Barbara Lovell* • Emily Ann Lloyd *Susan Lovell* • Joe Spano *Nasa director* • Xander Berkeley *Henry Hurt* ■ *Dir* Ron Howard • *Scr* William Broyles Jr, Al Reinert, from the non-fiction book *Lost Moon* by Jim Lovell, Jeffrey Kluger

The Apostle ★★★★ 12

Drama 1997 · US · Colour · 128mins

Robert Duvall writes, produces, directs and stars in this beautifully detailed character study of a Pentecostal preacher on a quest for atonement. The journey begins when his wife (Farrah Fawcett) has an affair with a younger minister, forcing him to take a long, hard look at his own life, the rural Texan community he serves and the Word of God itself. Expertly using little-seen Bible Belt locations and a great supporting cast, Duvall then proceeds to act everybody else off the screen. The result is an engrossing labour of love and a literal tour de force. AJ. Contains violence. [video]

Robert Duvall *Euliss "Sonny" Dewey, the Apostle EF* • Farrah Fawcett *Jessie Dewey* • Todd Allen *Horace* • John Beasley *Brother Blackwell* • June Carter Cash *Mrs Dewey Sr* • Walton Goggins *Sam* • Billy Joe Shaver *Joe* • Billy Bob Thornton *Troublemaker* • Miranda Richardson *Toosie* ■ *Dir/Scr* Robert Duvall

L'Appartement ★★★★ 15

Romantic mystery drama
1996 · Fr/Sp/It · Colour · 111mins

One of the most visually audacious French films of the 1990s, this intricate thriller clearly owes a debt to Hitchcock and Truffaut. Debutant writer/director Gilles Mimouni isn't just a cinematic magpie, however, as these homages are an ingenious means of making us identify with Vincent Cassel's high-flying executive. Suspecting that a long-vanished girlfriend has reappeared, he's duped into a web of deceit and desire, with every icon and flashback drawing him deeper into the mystery. We follow not so much out of a desire to solve the puzzle, but more because we're spellbound by the dazzling imagery. DP. In French with English subtitles. Contains sex scenes. [video] DVD

Romane Bohringer *Alice* • Vincent Cassel *Max* • Jean-Philippe Ecoffey *Lucien* • Monica Bellucci *Lisa* • Sandrine Kiberlain *Muriel* • Olivier Granier *Daniel* • Paul Pavel *Jeweller* ■ *Dir/Scr* Gilles Mimouni

Applause ★★★★

Musical drama 1929 · US · BW · 80mins

This very early talkie should be seen for the heart-rending performance of the legendary stage singer Helen Morgan. Not yet 30, she allowed herself, in her first dramatic film role, to be deglamourised and aged to play the boozy burlesque artiste who sacrifices herself for her teenage daughter. Imaginatively directed by Rouben Mamoulian, *Applause* remains equally notable for being one of the first films to throw off the restrictions on camera movement that the microphone had imposed and to use sound creatively, mixing dialogue with atmospheric background noise. AE

Helen Morgan (1) *Kitty Darling* • Joan Peers *April Darling* • Fuller Mellish Jr *Hitch Nelson* • Henry Wadsworth *Tony* • Jack Cameron *Joe King* ■ *Dir* Rouben Mamoulian • *Scr* Garrett Fort, from the novel by Beth Brown

The Apple ★

Science-fiction musical
1980 · US · Colour · 91mins

Set in the New York of the future (well, 1994) and borrowing shamelessly from *The Rocky Horror Picture Show*, this follows the foot-tapping efforts of tunesmiths Catherine Mary Stewart and George Gilmour to deliver the world from drug-peddling villain Mr Boogalow and his demonic dance craze, the "Bim". This discordant drivel is best forgotten. DP

Catherine Mary Stewart *Bibi* • George Gilmour *Alphie* • Grace Kennedy *Pandi* • Alan Love *Dandi* • Joss Ackland *Mr Topps* • Ray Shell *Shake/Snake* • Miriam Margolyes *Landlady* ■ *Dir* Menahem Golan • *Scr* Menahem Golan, Coby Recht, Iris Recht, from a story by Coby Recht, Iris Recht

The Apple ★★★★ PG

Drama based on a true story
1998 · Iran/Fr · Colour · 81mins

In her first feature, 17-year-old Samira Makhmalbaf makes a quietly ambitious assault on social injustice and sexual discrimination. Scripted by her director father, Mohsen, it's inspired by a scandal that shocked Iran. The tale of 12-year-old twin sisters who finally experience the world after being imprisoned since birth by their ultra-conservative father is re-enacted by the real-life people involved. Demonstrating an astonishing ease before the camera, Zahra and Massoumeh Naderi stand in wonderfully mischievous contrast to the shame and regret of their father, Ghorban Ali-Naderi. DP. In Farsi with English subtitles. [video] DVD

Massoumeh Naderi • Zahra Naderi • Ghorban Ali-Naderi • Zahra Sagharisaz • Amir Hossein Khosrojerdi • Azizeh Mohamadi ■ *Dir* Samira Makhmalbaf • *Scr* Mohsen Makhmalbaf

The Apple Dumpling Gang ★★★ U

Comedy western 1974 · US · Colour · 96mins

A charming comedy western from the Disney stable, driven by some fine comic performances. Bill Bixby, best known for his TV roles in *The Magician* and *The Incredible Hulk*, heads a cast full of amiable and refreshingly believable characters. An inferior sequel *The Apple Dumpling Gang Rides Again* was made in 1979. NF [video]

Bill Bixby *Russel Donovan* • Susan Clark *Magnolia Dusty Clydesdale* • Don Knotts *Theodore Ogelvie* • Tim Conway *Amos Tucker* • David Wayne *Colonel TR Clydesdale* • Slim Pickens *Frank Stillwell* • Harry Morgan *Sheriff Homer McCoy* • Brad Savage *Clovis Bradley* ■ *Dir* Norman Tokar • *Scr* Don Tait, from the novel by Jack M Bickham

The Apple Dumpling Gang Rides Again ★ U

Comedy western 1979 · US · Colour · 85mins

Don Knotts and Tim Conway, who formed an enduring Disney partnership in the original *Apple Dumpling* adventure, return as the "Hash Knife Outfit" in this substandard sequel. Their buffoonery raises the odd smile, but there's little else to recommend this tiresome tale. DP [video]

Tim Conway *Amos* • Don Knotts *Theodore* • Tim Matheson *Private Jeff Reid* • Kenneth Mars *Marshall* • Elyssa Davalos *Millie* • Jack Elam *Big Mac* • Robert Pine *Lt Ravencroft* • Harry Morgan *Major Gaskill* ■ *Dir* Vincent McEveety • *Scr* Don Tait

The Appointment ★

Romantic melodrama
1968 · US · Colour · 114mins

Sidney Lumet went all Euro-arty for this dismal melodrama, quite the worst film he ever made.Omar Sharif plays a lawyer in Rome and Anouk Aimée is his wife who may or may not be a high-class call girl. This leads to a thriller of sorts in which Sharif becomes insanely jealous and worries about the meaning of love and existence as if he's seen one too many Michelangelo Antonioni movies. Gobsmackingly awful. AT

Omar Sharif *Federico Fendi* • Anouk Aimée *Carla* • Lotte Lenya *Emma Valadier* • Fausto Tozzi *Renzo* • Ennio Balbo *Ugo Perino* • Didi Perego *Nany* ■ *Dir* Sidney Lumet • *Scr* James Salter, from a story by Antonio Leonviola

The Appointment ★

Horror thriller 1981 · UK · Colour · 90mins

This is an underfunded British horror thriller in which any sense of suspense is undermined by the amateurishness of the special effects. However, the director Lindsey C Vickers is primarily responsible for this being such a lacklustre picture, with many of the incidents during classical musician Samantha Weyson's murderous reign of terror bordering on the risible. Edward Woodward tries to bring a bit of steel to the proceedings. DP

Edward Woodward *Ian Fowler* • Jane Merrow *Diane Fowler* • Samantha Weyson *Joanne Fowler* ■ *Dir/Scr* Lindsey C Vickers

Appointment for Love ★★ U

Romantic comedy 1941 · US · BW · 88mins

Hollywood's favourite Frenchman of the 1940s, Charles Boyer, and the luminously talented and touching Margaret Sullavan (who would die of an overdose at the age of 49), star in this romantic comedy about a playwright (he) and a doctor (she) who marry, only to be plunged into near-terminal misunderstandings and suspicion. They have separate apartments on honeymoon, and only meet once a day, at 7am. Thin and superficial, the movie gets by thanks to the polished expertise of the stars and the glossy direction. RK

Charles Boyer *Andre Casall* • Margaret Sullavan *Jane Alexander* • Rita Johnson *Nancy Benson* • Eugene Pallette *George Hastings* • Ruth Terry *Edith Meredith* • Reginald Denny *Michael Dailey* • Cecil Kellaway *OLeary* • JM Kerrigan *Timothy* ■ *Dir* William A Seiter • *Scr* Bruce Manning, Felix Jackson, from the story by Ladislaus Bus-Fekete

Appointment in Honduras ★★★ U

Adventure 1953 · US · Colour · 79mins

A furiously fast, all-action jungle drama with Glenn Ford at his most nobly heroic, bristling with brio and derring-do as an adventurer en route to save the president of Honduras. Director Jacques Tourneur fashions an intelligent, multilayered romp, which on first sight may appear to be little more than "man wrestles baddies and requisite troop of snarling beasts", but opens out to display great performances from all concerned. SH

Glenn Ford *Corbett* • Ann Sheridan *Sylvia Sheppard* • Zachary Scott *Harry Sheppard* • Rodolfo Acosta *Reyes* • Jack Elam *Castro* • Ric Roman *Jiminez* ■ *Dir* Jacques Tourneur • *Scr* Karen De Wolfe

A

Appointment in London

★★ U

Second World War drama
1952 · UK · BW · 92mins

A routine mission for the reliable Dirk Bogarde, who is slightly off-form as a Second World War pilot grounded on doctor's orders. His determination to continue flying is deflected momentarily by his love for widow Dinah Sheridan and the disappearance of comrade Bryan Forbes. It's all much as you'd expect, but a little more insight into the lives of the air crews would have filled in the gaps left by the absence of flag-waving propaganda. DP

Dirk Bogarde *Wing Commander Tim Mason* • Ian Hunter *Captain Logan* • Dinah Sheridan *Eve Canyon* • Bill Kerr *Flight Lieutenant Bill Brown* • Bryan Forbes *Pilot Officer Greeno* • William Sylvester *Mac* ■ *Dir* Philip Leacock • *Scr* John Wooldridge, Robert Westerby

Appointment with Danger

★★★

Film noir 1950 · US · BW · 89mins

This nifty little B-thriller finds Alan Ladd working for the Post Office's detective branch, tracking down the murderers of a colleague and foiling a robbery by posing as a corrupt cop. Phyllis Calvert plays a nun on the run who witnessed the murder. Moodily shot by master cameraman John F Seitz, the *film noir* proceedings are smartly handled by Lewis Allen, who directed that minor classic, *Suddenly*. AT

Alan Ladd *Al Goddard* • Phyllis Calvert *Sister Augustine* • Paul Stewart *Earl Boettiger* • Jan Sterling *Dodie* • Jack Webb *Joe Regas* • Stacy Harris *Paul Ferrar* • Henry Morgan [Harry Morgan] *George Soderquist* • David Wolfe *David Goodman* ■ *Dir* Lewis Allen • *Scr* Richard Breen [Richard L Breen], Warren Duff

Appointment with Death

★★ PG

Crime mystery 1988 · US · Colour · 98mins

Peter Ustinov as Hercule Poirot travels to Palestine where a murder awaits a twist of his waxed moustache. The usual assortment of glamorous suspects are on hand, including John Gielgud and Lauren Bacall. Michael Winner was the director, so a good time was probably had by the stars, but with Ustinov making his sixth appearance as Poirot, the formula looks stale to say the least, though some mild amusement can be had from the cast and trying to guess whodunnit. AT. Contains violence.

Peter Ustinov *Hercule Poirot* • Lauren Bacall *Lady Westholme* • Carrie Fisher *Nadine Boynton* • John Gielgud *Colonel Carbury* • Piper Laurie *Mrs Emily Boynton* • Hayley Mills *Miss Quinton* • Jenny Seagrove *Dr Sarah King* • David Soul *Jefferson Cope* • Nicholas Guest *Lennox Boynton* ■ *Dir* Michael Winner • *Scr* Anthony Shaffer, Peter Buckman, Michael Winner, from the novel by Agatha Christie

Appointment with Murder

★★

Detective mystery 1948 · US · BW · 67mins

This is far from the best of the Falcon's screen outings, with magician John Calvert paling beside his predecessors George Sanders and Tom Conway. Hamstrung by a minuscule budget, director Jack Bernhard struggles to persuade us that part of the action takes place in Italy. But Jack Reitzen shows well as the mastermind behind a series of art thefts from curator Catherine Craig's gallery. The series ground to a halt with 1949's *Search for Danger*. DP

John Calvert *Michael Waring/"The Falcon"* • Catherine Craig *Lorraine W Brinckley* • Jack Reitzen *Norton Benedict* • Lyle Talbot *Fred Muller* • Peter Brocco *Giuseppe Donatti* ■ *Dir* Jack Bernhard • *Scr* Don Martin, from a story by Joel Malone, Harold Swanton, from the character created by Michael Arlen

Appointment with Venus

★★★ U

Second World War comedy adventure
1951 · UK · BW · 87mins

Venus is a pedigree cow that has to be shipped off the German-occupied Channel Island of Armorel by major David Niven, with help from Glynis Johns, during the Second World War. If you can forget the real-life horrors, this light comedy adventure is more than passable. The supporting cast is a *Who's Who* of British cinema, including Kenneth More in an early role, showing real star potential. TS

David Niven *Major Valentine Morland* • Glynis Johns *Nicola Fallaize* • George Coulouris *Captain Weiss* • Kenneth More *Lionel Fallaize* • Noel Purcell *Trawler Langley* • Barry Jones *Provost* • Bernard Lee *Brigadier* • Richard Wattis *Higher executive* ■ *Dir* Ralph Thomas • *Scr* Nicholas Phipps, from the novel *Transit of Venus* by Jerrard Tickell Black

Apprentice to Murder

★★ 15

Mystery thriller
1988 · US/Can · Colour · 88mins

Fire and brimstone preacher Donald Sutherland – known locally as the Pow Wow Doctor – is sure a hex has been placed on him by Knut Husebo as an emissary from Satan. With help from the young Chad Lowe, who he's training to detect such evil, the maniac mystic kills Husebo. Both religious fanatics are then given a jail sentence. Loosely based on a true-life murder case, this is initially intriguing, but it's very slow in presenting the offbeat facts of the story. Norwegian locations stand in for rural Pennsylvania. AJ

Donald Sutherland *John Reese* • Chad Lowe *Billy Kelly* • Mia Sara *Alice Spangler* • Knut Husebo *Lars Hoeglin* • Rutanya Alda *Elma Kelly* • Eddie Jones *Tom Kelly* • Adrian Sparks *Irwin Meyers* ■ *Dir* RL Thomas [Ralph L Thomas] • *Scr* Alan Scott, Wesley Moore

The Apprenticeship of Duddy Kravitz

★★★★ 15

Drama 1974 · Can · Colour · 120mins

Richard Dreyfuss confirmed his star quality in this adaptation of Mordecai Richler's novel. As Duddy, a no-holds-barred hustler in 1948 Montreal, he alienates friends and family in his quest to get rich and make his mark. Directed by former TV director Ted Kotcheff, the comic highlights include Denholm Elliott's down-at-heel film director setting up a bar mitzvah as an artsy-fartsy work of art. TH

Richard Dreyfuss *Duddy* • Micheline Lanctôt *Yvette* • Jack Warden *Max* • Randy Quaid *Virgil* • Joseph Wiseman *Uncle Benjy* • Denholm Elliott *Friar* • Henry Ramer *Dingleman* • Joe Silver *Farber* ■ *Dir* Ted Kotcheff • *Scr* Mordecai Richler, Lionel Chetwynd, from the novel by Mordecai Richler

Les Apprentis

★★★ 15

Comedy 1995 · Fr · Colour · 93mins

Guillaume Depardieu gave notice that he had finally emerged from the shadow of his famous father Gérard with this César-winning performance. As Fred, the indolent flatmate, he brings some much-needed sanity to the proceedings, as his neurotic buddy François Cluzet comes close to madness wrestling with his literary aspirations. This odd-couple comedy may be short on incident, but it's packed with quirky humour and sly insights into the character of the modern French male. DP. In French with English subtitles. Contains violence, swearing and nudity.

François Cluzet *Antoine* • Guillaume Depardieu *Fred* • Judith Henry *Sylvie* • Claire Laroche *Agnes* • Philippe Girard *Nicolas* • Bernard Yerles *Patrick* • Jean-Pol Brissard *Magazine editor* • Marie Trintignant *Lorette* ■ *Dir* Pierre Salvadori • *Scr* Pierre Salvadori, Philippe Harel

Après l'Amour

★★★ 15

Drama 1992 · Fr · Colour · 100mins

An air of detached amusement hangs over this assured discourse on the sexual mores of today's sophisticated Parisians, exemplified by novelist Isabelle Huppert and her dalliances with architect Bernard Giraudeau and pop star Hippolyte Girardot. Employing her trademark mix of naturalism and keen social insight, director Diane Kurys suggests that, where love is concerned, liberation is just another form of entanglement. Occasionally struggling for significance, the film is perhaps too insular, but the casting is apposite and Huppert is outstanding. DP. In French with English subtitles.

Isabelle Huppert *Lola* • Bernard Giraudeau *David* • Hippolyte Girardot *Tom* • Lio *Marianne* • Yvan Attal *Romain* • Judith Reval *Rachel* • Ingrid Held *Anne* ■ *Dir* Diane Kurys • *Scr* Diane Kurys, Antoine Lacomblez

The April Fools

★★★★

Romantic drama 1969 · US · Colour · 94mins

The oddball teaming of Jack Lemmon, the quintessential neurotic American, with Catherine Deneuve, the epitome of cool French charm, might seem like a seasonal hoax played on cinema audiences. But it works extraordinarily well, with the two stars playing refugees from tedious New York marriages escaping to Paris and self-discovery. Stuart Rosenberg's direction desperately tries to be 1960s' trendy, but there's dramatic poignancy to be experienced all the same. TH

Jack Lemmon *Howard Brubaker* • Catherine Deneuve *Catherine Gunther* • Peter Lawford *Ted Gunther* • Jack Weston *Potter Shrader* • Myrna Loy *Grace Greenlaw* • Charles Boyer *André Greenlaw* • Harvey Korman *Benson* • Sally Kellerman *Phyllis Brubaker* • Melinda Dillon *Leslie Hopkins* • Kenneth Mars *Don Hopkins* • David Doyle *Walters* ■ *Dir* Stuart Rosenberg • *Scr* Hal Dresner

April Fool's Day

★★★ 18

Horror 1986 · US · Colour · 85mins

Responsible for the seminal stalk-and-slash movie *When a Stranger Calls*, director Fred Walton made a belated return to the much-maligned genre he helped create with this amusing diversion. Who's the insane maniac gruesomely reducing the ranks of practical joker Deborah Foreman's college pals as they party on her island retreat? There's a surprising twist in the tail of this wittily inventive whodunnit. AJ. Contains swearing, violence and sex scenes. DVD

Deborah Foreman *Muffy St John/Buffy* • Deborah Goodrich *Nikki* • Ken Olandt *Rob* • Griffin O'Neal *Skip* • Mike Nomad *Buck* • Leah King Pinsent [Leah Pinsent] *Nan* ■ *Dir* Fred Walton • *Scr* Danilo Bach

April in Paris

★ U

Musical comedy romance
1952 · US · Colour · 95mins

This is a leaden would-be romance that never gets off the backlot. The film pairs a hard-working Doris Day with a most unlikely leading man in Ray Bolger and the pair are lumbered with a dud of a plot. The 1950s Technicolor is attractive, but the art direction is garish, the dumb script wastes every opportunity for wit or satire, and the songs are weak. TS DVD

Doris Day *Ethel Dynamite* • *Jackson* • Ray Bolger *S Winthrop Putnam* • Claude Dauphin *Philippe Fouquet* • Eve Miller *Marcia* • George Givot *François* • Paul Harvey *Secretary Sherman* • Herbert Farjeon *Joshua Stevens* • Wilson Millar *Sinclair Wilson* ■ *Dir* David Butler • *Scr* Jack Rose, Melville Shavelson

April Love

★★★

Romantic musical
1957 · US · Colour · 99mins

A harmless remake of *Home in Indiana*, this musical romance is dressed up as a star vehicle for 1950s' teen heart-throb Pat Boone, once considered a serious threat to Elvis Presley. The controversy at the time was that clean-livin' Boone wouldn't take part in love scenes, and, true to form, the moment when he actually plants a peck on co-star Shirley Jones doesn't exactly raise the temperature. However, Boone and Jones make a very likeable pair and this is mighty pleasant. TS

Pat Boone *Nick Conover* • Shirley Jones *Liz Templeton* • Dolores Michaels *Fran* • Arthur O'Connell *Jed* • Matt Crowley *Dan Templeton* • Jeanette Nolan *Henrietta* • Brad Jackson *Al Turner* ■ *Dir* Henry Levin • *Scr* Winston Miller, from the novel by George Agnew Chamberlain

Aprile

★★★ 15

Comedy drama 1998 · It/Fr · Colour · 74mins

Having reinforced his auteur status with *Dear Diary*, Nanni Moretti opted for more of the same in this teasing blend of fact and fiction. Musing on aspects of his own life, as well as the state of Italian politics, this is more calculated and less charming than its predecessor, with the highly personal insights into nationhood, fatherhood and the frustrations of being a film director making for intriguing viewing. The genial honesty of the project keeps you hooked until the bizarre finale, in which Moretti finally succeeds in mounting part of his musical about a politicised pastry cook. DP. In Italian with English subtitles. Contains a scene of drug abuse.

Nanni Moretti • Andrea Molaiolo • Silvio Orlando • Silvia Nono • Pietro Moretti • Nuria Schoenberg ■ *Dir/Scr* Nanni Moretti

Apt Pupil

★★★★ 15

Drama 1997 · US/Fr · Colour · 106mins

The third work taken from Stephen King's 1982 anthology *Different Seasons* outlines the terrible consequences of a gifted Californian teenager's obsession with the Holocaust and his strange relationship with a Nazi war criminal living in secret in his home town. In a tale that's almost the equal of its predecessors *Stand by Me* and *The Shawshank Redemption*, director Bryan Singer uses smart visual fluency to suggest the appalling and shocking nature of his core story. Ian McKellen gives a stupendous performance as the former SS death-camp officer and the film provides unsettling viewing that occasionally crosses the bad taste barrier. AJ. Contains swearing and violence. DVD

Brad Renfro *Todd Bowden* • Ian McKellen *Kurt Dussander* • Joshua Jackson *Joey* • Mickey Cottrell *Sociology teacher* • Michael Reid MacKay *Nightmare victim* • Ann Dowd *Monica Bowden* • Bruce Davison *Richard Bowden* • James Karen *Victor Bowden* • David Schwimmer *Edward French* ■ *Dir* Bryan Singer • *Scr* Brandon Boyce, from the novella by Stephen King

The Arab

★★★

Silent adventure 1924 · US · BW

Having played a key part in the emergence of Rudolph Valentino by directing *The Four Horsemen of the Apocalypse*, Irish firebrand director Rex Ingram drew inspiration from the silent superstar's best-known film, *The Sheik*, for this tempestuous desert romance. However, he had to settle for Hollywood's second-string Latin lover

U = SUITABLE FOR ALL   Uc = SUITABLE FOR ALL, ESPECIALLY FOR YOUNG CHILDREN (VIDEO ONLY)   PG = PARENTAL GUIDANCE

Ramon Novarro, instead of Valentino, to play the disgraced son of a Bedouin chief, now a tour guide, who smoulders missionary Alice Terry into submission. Unusually for the time, this overwrought Metro melodrama was shot on location in North Africa. DP

Ramon Novarro *Jamil Abdullah Azam* • Alice Terry *Mary Hilbert* • Gerald Robertshaw *Dr Hilbert* • Maxudian *Governor* • Count Jean de Limur *Hossein, governor's aide* • Adelqui Millar *Abdulla* ■ *Dir* Rex Ingram (1) • *Scr* Rex Ingram, from the play by Edgar Selwyn

Arabella ★★★

Comedy 1967 · US/It · Colour · 87mins

This bizarre and often very funny comedy has Virna Lisi – a minor goddess of the 1960s – trying to raise money so that her eccentric grandmother (Margaret Rutherford) can pay a fortune in back taxes. Naturally, Lisi hasn't the slightest intention of raising the cash legally. It's all done in episodic fashion with quite a flourish, mainly due to the cast. Rutherford is a cigar-chomping joy, and so is Terry-Thomas in each of his four roles. AT

Virna Lisi *Arabella Danesi* • James Fox *Giorgio* • Margaret Rutherford *Princess Ilaria* • Terry-Thomas *Hotel manager/General/Duke/ Insurance agent* • Paola Borboni *Duchess Moretti* • Antonio Casagrande *Filberto* ■ *Dir* Mauro Bolognini • *Scr* Adriano Baracco

Arabesque ★★★ 12

Spy drama 1966 · US/UK · Colour · 105mins

In the wake of the box-office smash *Charade*, this glamorous trawl through 1960s international post-Bond espionage has the same director, Stanley Donen. This film stars Gregory Peck and Sophia Loren, lit by ace cinematographer Chris Challis in ravishing Panavisioned Technicolor. The plot is some nonsense about Arab espionage which doesn't really matter, but Alan Badel and Kieron Moore provide fine support. This is lush, mindless and expertly-crafted matinée fare. TS [VIDEO]

Sophia Loren *Yasmin Azir* • Gregory Peck *David Pollock* • Alan Badel *Beshraavi* • Kieron Moore *Yussef Kassim* • Carl Duering *Hassan Jena* • John Merivale *Sloane* • Duncan Lamont *Webster* • George Coulouris *Ragheeb* ■ *Dir* Stanley Donen • *Scr* Julian Mitchell, Stanley Price, Pierre Martin, from the novel *The Cipher* by Gordon Cotler

Arabian Adventure ★★ U

Fantasy adventure
1979 · US · Colour · 93mins

Former editor-turned-director Kevin Connor here lacks the imagination needed to conjure up the magic of the *Arabian Nights* tales, and he's not helped by a weak turn from Oliver Tobias as the prince battling Christopher Lee's wicked caliph. The eclectic cast keeps it watchable, but the special effects look cheap and rather let down the whole affair. TS [VIDEO]

Christopher Lee *Alquazar* • Milo O'Shea *Khasim* • Oliver Tobias *Prince Hasan* • Emma Samms *Princess Zuleira* • John Ratzenberger *Achmed* • Peter Cushing *Wazir Al Wuzara* • Capucine *Vahishta* • Mickey Rooney *Daad El Shur* • Athar Malik [Art Malik] *Mahmoud* ■ *Dir* Kevin Connor • *Scr* Brian Hayles

Arabian Knight ★

Animated fantasy 1995 · UK · Colour · 81mins

The quirky, jagged style of this animated feature will probably not appeal to younger viewers. Unfortunately, that's the audience this simple tale is aimed at. Peppered with a few forgettable songs, it's about a young princess who falls for a rather unexciting cobbler. Only notable for featuring one of the last vocal performances by Vincent Price, this is eminently missable. JB

Vincent Price *Zigzag* • Matthew Broderick *Tack the Cobbler* • Jennifer Beals *Princess Yum Yum* • Eric Bogosian *Phido* • Toni Collette *Nurse/Witch* • Jonathan Winters *The Thief* • Clive Revill *King Nod* • Kevin Dorsey *One-Eye* • Donald Pleasence *Additional voice* ■ *Dir* Richard Williams • *Scr* Richard Williams, Margaret French

Arabian Nights ★★★

Adventure 1942 · US · Colour · 86mins

This piece of Hollywood exotica, made to cash in on the success of *The Thief of Bagdad*, stars Jon Hall as the Caliph, Sabu as his best buddy and Maria Montez as his suitor. The actors have their tongues firmly in their cheeks and the whole show is on the brink of send-up, which is exactly where it should be. Producer Walter Wanger was one of Tinseltown's more enterprising independents, though he was later brought to his knees by the crippling costs of *Cleopatra*. AT

Jon Hall *Haroun al Raschid* • Sabu *Ali Ben Ali* • Maria Montez *Sherazad* • Leif Erickson *Kamar* • Shemp Howard *Sinbad* • "Wee Willie" Davis [William "Wee Willie" Davis] *Valda* • John Qualen *Aladdin* • Turhan Bey *Captain* • Richard Lane *Corporal* ■ *Dir* John Rawlins • *Scr* Michael Hogan, True Boardman, from stories by Sir Richard Burton

The Arabian Nights ★★★★ 18

Fantasy adventure
1974 · It/Fr · Colour · 125mins

Italian director Pier Paolo Pasolini took almost two years to complete this final, and most polished, offering in his trilogy of great story cycles, the others being *The Decameron* (1970) and *The Canterbury Tales* (1971). *The Arabian Nights* features ten interwoven stories of love, potions and betrayal, connected by the tale of Mur-El-Din (Franco Merli) searching for his kidnapped slave girl. Filmed in Eritrea, Iran, Nepal and Yemen, it reveals the captivating beauty of those countries, while the ribald spirit of the original tales remains thankfully unshackled by Freudian or religious guilt. RB. Italian dialogue dubbed in English. [VIDEO] DVD

Ninetto Davoli *Aziz* • Ines Pellegrini *Zumurrud* • Franco Citti *Demon* • Franco Merli *Mur-El-Din* ■ *Dir* Pier Paolo Pasolini • *Scr* Pier Paolo Pasolini, Danilo Donati

Arachnid ★ 15

Horror 2001 · Sp · Colour · 91mins

An air force jet crashes into a UFO and the zoological alien cargo is showered over a South Pacific island. A research team, investigating the outbreak of an unknown virus on the island, find themselves fighting mutant bugs instead, culminating in a battle royal with a giant spider. Saddled with a stupid story, an equally stupid script and duff special effects, director Jack Sholder aims squarely for rapid-fire incident but even that desperate tangent fails to excite. AJ [VIDEO] DVD

Chris Potter *Valentine* • Alex Reid *Mercer* • José Sancho *Samuel Léon* • Neus Asensi *Susana* • Ravil Isyanov [Ravil Issyanov] *Capri* ■ *Dir* Jack Sholder • *Scr* Mark Sevi

Arachnophobia ★★★★ PG

Comedy horror 1990 · US · Colour · 104mins

Steven Spielberg's longtime producer Frank Marshall turned director for this tongue-in-cheek creepy-crawly about deadly tropical spiders invading the small California town where phobic doctor Jeff Daniels has just started up a practice. Marshall shows much of his mentor's touch (Spielberg acted as co-executive producer with Marshall), spinning a tension-laden web full of solid scares and well-timed wit in what is virtually *The Birds* with eight legs. The black humour mixes with the black widows surprisingly well, and John Goodman's exterminator provides some lovely moments. AJ [VIDEO] DVD

Jeff Daniels *Dr Ross Jennings* • Harley Jane Kozak *Molly Jennings* • John Goodman *Delbert McClintock* • Julian Sands *Dr James Atherton* • Stuart Pankin *Sheriff Parsons* • Brian McNamara *Chris Collins* • Mark L Taylor *Jerry Manley* • Henry Jones *Dr Sam Metcalf* ■ *Dir* Frank Marshall • *Scr* Don Jakoby, Wesley Strick, from a story by Don Jakoby, Al Williams

Ararat ★★★ 15

Drama 2002 · Can/Fr · Colour · 110mins

How can the crime of genocide be so easily forgotten? That's the question posed by this angry diatribe against the actions of Turkey which, in 1915, slaughtered over a million of its ethnic Armenian population. Until now, the world has overlooked the tragedy, which is here brought to our attention by Atom Egoyan (who is of Armenian descent). Beginning with a film-maker's attempts to shoot a movie about the massacre in Turkey, Egoyan fashions a complex story that flashes back and forth in time, revealing the events leading up to the slaughter and its impact on subsequent generations. The movie-within-a-movie storyline has a morbid grip, but the labyrinthine plot tends to diminish our emotional response to the outrage. TH. Contains violence, swearing and a sex scene. DVD

David Alpay *Raffi* • Charles Aznavour *Edward Saroyan* • Eric Bogosian *Rouben* • Brent Carver *Philip* • Marie-Josée Croze *Celia* • Bruce Greenwood *Martin/Clarence Ussher* • Arsinée Khanjian *Ani* • Elias Koteas *Ali/Jevdet Bey* • Christopher Plummer *David* ■ *Dir* Atom Egoyan • *Scr* Atom Egoyan, from the non-fiction book *An American Physician in Turkey* by Clarence Ussher

Arch of Triumph ★ U

Romantic drama 1948 · US · BW · 126mins

Despite the reteaming of the two stars of *Gaslight* (Ingrid Bergman and Charles Boyer) and the directorial skills of Lewis Milestone, this was a costly failure, sinking its distinguished production company (Enterprise) and failing to find an audience in any of its many re-edited or shortened versions. There's no chemistry between Bergman and Boyer, while the overall pace is deadly and the re-creation of Paris is totally without atmosphere. TS [VIDEO]

Ingrid Bergman *Joan Madou* • Charles Boyer *Dr Ravic* • Charles Laughton *Haake* • Louis Calhern *Morosow* • Ruth Warrick *Kate Hegstroem* • Roman Bohnen *Dr Weber* • Stephen Bekassy *Alex* • Ruth Nelson *Madame Fessier* ■ *Dir* Lewis Milestone • *Scr* Harry Brown, Lewis Milestone, from the novel by Erich Maria Remarque

L'Arche du Désert ★★★ 12

Political drama
1997 · Alg/Fr/Ger/Swi · Colour · 89mins

There's a depressing universality about this tale of bigotry, which valiantly puts the case for co-operation to a world seemingly hellbent on conquest as the only form of co-existence. Ironically, it's love that proves the undoing of this particular interdependent desert community, as Myriam Aouffen and Messaouda Adami's forbidden romance sets the various tribes on a pitiless path to self-destruction. Fascinating in its detail but weak in characterisation, Mohamed Chouikh's powerful film pulls no punches in its depiction of the senseless violence. DP. In Algerian with English subtitles.

Myriam Aouffen *Myriam* • Messaouda Adami *Houria du Ksar* • Hacen Abdou *Amin* • Shyraz Aliane *Cousin* • Amin Chouikh *The child* • Abdelkader Belmokadem *Sage Omar* • Fatyha Nesserine *Myriam's mother* • Lynda Fares *Myriam's aunt* ■ *Dir/Scr* Mohamed Chouikh

Archipelago ★★

Drama 1991 · Chil · Colour · 85mins

Drawing comparisons between the Chono Indians slaughtered by 16th-century conquistadores and protestors killed while demonstrating against present day political repression, this is earnest, but heavy handed. Director Pablo Perelman overloads his imagery with oblique angles to reinforce the dislocation experienced by professor Sergio Schmied, who, escapes from Santiago to an archipelago undergoing deforestation to facilitate the building of a bridge to the mainland. DP. In Spanish with English subtitles.

Hector Noguera *Architect* • Sergio Schmied *Professor* ■ *Dir/Scr* Pablo Perelman

Are We There Yet? ★★ PG

Road movie comedy
2005 · US · Colour · 90mins

A family-friendly mix of sassy dialogue, slapstick and sight gags, this stars Ice Cube as a love-struck singleton who's trying to woo attractive divorcee Nia Long. When he offers to transport her two monstrous children to see her on a business trip, everything that could go wrong does. The clashes and cartoon-style violence that ensue are enjoyable, but the film founders when it becomes overly sentimental, and the youngsters are just too obnoxious. SF DVD

Ice Cube *Nick Persons* • Nia Long *Suzanne Kingston* • Jay Mohr *Marty* • MC Gainey *Al* • Aleisha Allen *Lindsey Kingston* • Philip Daniel Bolden *Kevin Kingston* • Tracy Morgan *Satchel Paige* • Nichelle Nichols *Miss Mable* ■ *Dir* Brian Levant • *Scr* Steven Gary Banks, Claudia Grazioso, J David Stern, David N Weiss from a story by Steven Gary Banks, Claudia Grazioso

Are You Being Served? ★ PG

Comedy 1977 · UK · Colour · 91mins

Grace Brothers opened for business as part of the BBC's *Comedy Playhouse* in the early 1970s, but never in its ten-year history were the shelves as bare as they are in this feeble feature. Abandoning the clothing department for the Costa Plonka, the staff are soon engaging in the usual smutty banter as sun, sand and booze take their toll. Why did the makers of these spin-offs always insist on breaking with the winning sitcom formula? DP [VIDEO] DVD

Mollie Sugden *Mrs Slocombe* • John Inman *Mr Humphries* • Frank Thornton *Captain Peacock* • Trevor Bannister *Mr Lucas* • Wendy Richard *Miss Brahms* • Arthur Brough *Mr Grainger* • Nicholas Smith *Mr Rumbold* • Arthur English *Harman* • Harold Bennett *Young Mr Grace* • Andrew Sachs *Don Bernardo* ■ *Dir* Bob Kellett • *Scr* Jeremy Lloyd, David Croft

Are You with It? ★★ U

Musical comedy 1948 · US · BW · 89mins

This is a hotch-potch of humdrum hokum veers from the sublime (Donald O'Connor's restaurant dance) to the ridiculous (Louis Da Pron's climactic ballet). O'Connor's humourless insurance bod is fired for misplacing a decimal point and seeks solace at the carnival, where he falls for the exotic Olga San Juan, who persuades him to use his mathematical nous to rescue barker Lew Parker's bacon. Musical mediocrity par excellence. DP

Donald O'Connor *Milton Haskins* • Olga San Juan *Vivian Reilly* • Martha Stewart *Bunny LaFleur* • Lew Parker *John Goldie McGoldrick* • Walter Catlett *Jason "Pop" Carter* • Pat Dane [Patricia Dane] *Sally* • Louis Da Pron *Bartender* ■ *Dir* Jack Hively • *Scr* Oscar Brodney, from the musical comedy by Sam Perrin, George Balzer, Harry Revel, from the novel *Slightly Perfect* by George Malcolm-Smith

A

Arena ★★

Western drama 1953 · US · Colour · 83mins

Sadly no gladiators, for this melodrama concerns itself with rodeo riders and bucking broncos. Gig Young is the seasoned rodeo star thinking of quitting, but thinking mostly about his girlfriend and his wife who wants a divorce. Then his best mate gets killed in the arena and Gig gets very gloomy indeed. Filmed in 3-D – hence the frequency of shots in which the bulls snort into the camera lens. AT

Gig Young *Bob Danvers* • Jean Hagen *Meg Hutchins* • Polly Bergen *Ruth Danvers* • Henry Morgan [Harry Morgan] *Lew Hutchins* • Barbara Lawrence *Sylvia Morgan* • Robert Horton *Jackie Roach* • Lee Van Cleef *Smitty* ■ *Dir* Richard Fleischer • *Scr* Harold Jack Bloom, from a story by Arthur Loew Jr

L'Argent ★★★★★ PG

Crime drama 1983 · Fr/Swi · Colour · 80mins

Adhering rigidly to the spirit of a Tolstoy short story, Robert Bresson's final feature is as uncompromising as (but much less admired than) his earlier study of the preordained consequences of crime, *Pickpocket* (1959). Starting with the mischievous exchange of a forged 500 franc note, an inexorable sequence of events culminates in a man murdering his family with an axe. It's a brutal climax to Christian Patey's descent from decency to degradation. Yet, it's hard to accuse Bresson of manipulation, as he views each chillingly logical stage with a dispassion that distressingly echoes that of an even less compassionate society. DP. In French with English subtitles. [video] DVD

Christian Patey *Yvon Targe* • Sylvie van den Elsen *Woman* • Michel Briguet *Woman's father* • Caroline Lang *Elise Targe* • Vincent Risterucci *Lucien* ■ *Dir* Robert Bresson • *Scr* Robert Bresson, from the story *The False Note* by Leo Tolstoy

Argentine Nights ★★ U

Comedy musical 1940 · US · BW · 74mins

A low-budget B-musical with the focus fairly divided by some cheerful but largely unremembered songs and a clutch of fairly crude comic turns. A trio of girl singers, accompanied by their managers (conveniently also numbering three) decamp to Argentina to escape their creditors. Notable for marking the screen debut of immensely popular vocalists the Andrews Sisters, and the Universal debut of former Fox stars, the Ritz Brothers. RK

Laverne Andrews *Laverne* • Maxene Andrews *Maxine* • Patty Andrews *Patty* • Al Ritz *Al* • Harry Ritz *Harry* • Jimmy Ritz *Jimmy* • Constance Moore *Bonnie Brooks* • George Reeves *Eduardo* • Peggy Moran *Peggy* • Anne Nagel *Linda* • Kathryn Adams *Carol* ■ *Dir* Albert S Rogell • *Scr* Arthur T Horman, Ray Golden, sid Kuller

Aria ★★★ 18

Opera anthology 1987 · UK · Colour · 85mins

This is the cinematic equivalent of the *Three Tenors* concerts: hummable slices of opera, here interpreted visually by an eclectic selection of film directors. Understandably, it's an uneven affair but, although the true opera buff will be horrified, there are some little gems. The pick of the vignettes is Franc Roddam's take on the *Liebestod* from Wagner's *Tristan und Isolde*, with Bridget Fonda (in her film debut) and James Mathers as a pair of beautiful, tragic lovers. Honourable mention, too, for Robert Altman's segment from *Les Boréades* (with the camera focused entirely on an audience seemingly made up of inmates from an asylum) and Julien Temple's trashy and kitsch version of Verdi's *Rigoletto*. JF. Contains sex scenes and nudity. [video]

John Hurt • Sophie Ward • Theresa Russell • Jackson Kyle • Marianne McLoughlin [Marian McLoughlin] • Buck Henry • Beverly D'Angelo • Anita Morris • Elizabeth Hurley • Peter Birch • Julie Hagerty • Genevieve Page • Bridget Fonda • James Mathers • Linzi Drew • Andreas Wisniewski • Amy Johnson • Tilda Swinton ■ *Dir* Nicolas Roeg, Jean-Luc Godard, Robert Altman, Derek Jarman, Charles Sturridge, Julien Temple, Bruce Beresford, Franc Roddam, Ken Russell, Bill Bryden • *Scr* Nicolas Roeg, Jean-Luc Godard, Robert Altman, Derek Jarman, Charles Sturridge, Julien Temple, Bruce Beresford, Franc Roddam, Ken Russell, Bill Bryden, Don Boyd

Ariane ★★★

Drama 1931 · Ger · BW · 78mins

The sixth collaboration between the soon-to-be husband-and-wife team of Hungarian director Paul Czinner and Polish-born actress Elizabeth Bergner was their first venture into talkies. She is positively radiant as the Russian émigrée who is distracted from her studies by sophisticated businessman Rudolf Forster, whose boast that he prefers experienced women prompts her to invent a string of affairs that only alienate his affections. Filmed in both German and English (as *The Loves of Ariane*), the action is as deliciously light as Billy Wilder's 1957 remake *Love in the Afternoon*. DP. In German with English subtitles.

Elisabeth Bergner *Ariane* • Rudolf Forster *Konstantin* • Annemarie Steinsieck *Tante Warwara* • Hertha Guthmar *Olga* • Theodor Loos *The teacher* • Nikolas Wassilieff *The student* • Alfred Gerasch *The doctor* ■ *Dir* Paul Czinner • *Scr* Paul Czinner, Carl Mayer, from a novel by Claude Anet

Ariel ★★★★ 15

Comedy drama 1988 · Fin · Colour · 69mins

Aki Kaurismäki puts his habitually offbeat slant on the *film noir* road movie. Quitting Lapland in his Cadillac to seek pastures new, tin miner Turo Pajala makes a typically lugubrious Kaurismäki hero, stumbling into increasingly dangerous situations almost as accidentally as he takes up with single-mom meter maid Susanna Haavisto. The deceptively simple style may seem to subvert traditional social realism, but there's a barbed satirical intent at work here, which blends with the subtle character comedy to pass copious pertinent comments on modern-day Finland. DP. In Finnish with English subtitles. Contains some swearing and moderate violence. [video]

Turo Pajala *Taisto Kasurinen* • Susanna Haavisto *Irmeli* • Matti Pellonpaa *Mikkonen* • Eetu Hilkamo *Riku* • Erkki Pajala *Miner* • Matti Jaaranen *Mugger* ■ *Dir/Scr* Aki Kaurismäki

Arise, My Love ★★★★

Wartime romantic comedy
1940 · US · BW · 111mins

Claudette Colbert and Ray Milland co-star in this superior comedy-drama-romance from Paramount, which won several Oscar nominations and the award itself for its story, although not, surprisingly for the polished screenplay by the team of Billy Wilder and Charles Brackett. It audaciously combines wit and a love story with headline events of the Spanish Civil War and then the Second World War, both of which Paris-based newswoman Colbert is reporting while becoming involved with Milland. The film is sophisticated and gripping entertainment with a serious theme, and Mitchell Leisen's direction perfectly catches the nuances. RK

Claudette Colbert *Augusta Nash* • Ray Milland *Tom Martin* • Dennis O'Keefe *Shep* • Walter Abel *Phillips* • Dick Purcell *Pink* • George Zucco *Prison Governor* • Frank Puglia *Father Jacinto* ■ *Dir* Mitchell Leisen • *Scr* Charles Brackett, Billy Wilder, from the story by Benjamin Glazer, John S Toldy

The Aristocats ★★★★ U

Animated adventure
1970 · US · Colour · 75mins

The delight in Wolfgang Reitherman's turn-of-the-century movie, set in a charmingly detailed Paris, is the brilliant matching of voices to visuals. Hermione Baddeley voices the aristo-owner of elegant feline Duchess (Eva Gabor) who, with her three kittens, is befriended by Phil Harris's alley cat after the butler, Edgar (Roddy Maude-Roxby), has tried to do away with them because the old lady has left everything to the cats in her will. The Sherman brothers' songs are out of the top drawer. TH [video] DVD

Phil Harris *J Thomas O'Malley* • Eva Gabor *Duchess* • Sterling Holloway *Roquefort* • Scatman Crothers *Scat Cat* • Paul Winchell *Chinese Cat* • Tim Hudson *English Cat* • Vito Scotti *Italian Cat* • Thurl Ravenscroft *Russian Cat* • Hermione Baddeley *Madame Bonfamille* • Roddy Maude-Roxby *Butler* ■ *Dir* Wolfgang Reitherman • *Scr* Larry Clemmons, Vance Gerry, Ken Anderson, Frank Thomas, Eric Cleworth, Julius Svendsen, Ralph Wright, Tom Rowe, Tom McGowan • *Animation Director* Frank Thomas

Arizona ★★★ U

Western 1940 · US · BW · 116mins

Wesley Ruggles directs this account of pioneering life in Tucson. Jean Arthur plays the first lady settler there, battling it out with the rogues trying to control her rail freight business. Femininity asserts itself when she falls in love with William Holden, passing through on his travels. Distinguished by Arthur's performance and outstanding photography and action set pieces which reflect the film's then massive production budget, it contains all the ingredients that became standard to the frontier western. RK [video]

Jean Arthur *Phoebe Titus* • William Holden (2) *Peter Muncie* • Warren William *Jefferson Carteret* • Porter Hall *Lazarus Ward* • Paul Harvey *Solomon Warner* • George Chandler *Haley* • Byron Foulger *Pete Kitchen* • Regis Toomey *Grant Oury* ■ *Dir* Wesley Ruggles • *Scr* Claude Binyon, from a story by Clarence Budington Kelland • *Cinematographer* Joseph Walker, Harry Hallenberger, Fayte Browne

Arizona Bushwhackers ★

Western 1968 · US · Colour · 87mins

Producer AC Lyles's series of plodding westerns stuffed with veteran stars was looking as tired as its principal players when this entry hobbled into release. Lyles coaxed James Cagney out of retirement to speak the narration and the film also introduced Roy Rogers Jr in a small supporting role. Otherwise, there's little pleasure now in the convoluted plot about gunrunning under the anonymous direction of Lesley Selander. AE

Howard Keel *Lee Travis* • Yvonne De Carlo *Jill Wyler* • John Ireland *Dan Shelby* • Marilyn Maxwell *Molly* • Scott Brady *Tom Rile* • Brian Donlevy *Major Smith* • Barton MacLane *Sheriff Grover* • James Craig *Ike Clanton* • Roy Rogers Jr *Roy* • James Cagney *Narrator* ■ *Dir* Lesley Selander • *Scr* Steve Fisher, from a story by Steve Fisher, Andrew Craddock

Arizona Dream ★★★ 15

Drama 1991 · Fr · Colour · 134mins

Talented European directors often fail to succeed in transferring their specific view of life to English-language cinema, and this sprawling eccentric drama from Bosnian film-maker Emir Kusturica is a case in point. Nevertheless, it remains mesmerisingly watchable, largely owing to the superb performances of an eclectic cast, particularly the marvellous Faye Dunaway in one of her best roles as the emotional wreck that drifter Johnny Depp falls for, and the cleverly cast Jerry Lewis as Depp's uncle. Despite their efforts, it still doesn't really work. TS. Contains swearing. [video] DVD

Johnny Depp *Axel Backmar* • Jerry Lewis *Leo Sweetie* • Faye Dunaway *Elaine Stalker* • Lili Taylor *Grace Stalker* • Paulina Porizkova *Millie* • Vincent Gallo *Paul Backmar* • Michael J Pollard *Fabian* ■ *Dir* Emir Kusturica • *Scr* David Atkins, Emir Kusturica

The Arizona Kid ★★

Western 1939 · US · BW · 61mins

In 1939, Roy Rogers became the third most popular western star in America; Gene Autry came top, while William "Hopalong Cassidy" Boyd was second. With his trademark white hat, twin holsters and gee-tar, Rogers rode, shot and crooned his way through scores of B-westerns like this one: a Civil War yarn in which our hero, a Confederate captain, must kill his best friend when he realises they have been fighting on the wrong side of the moral fence. AT

Roy Rogers *Roy* • George "Gabby" Hayes *Gabby Whittaker* • Sally March *Laura Radford* • Stuart Hamblen *McBride* • Dorothy Sebastian *Bess Warren* • Earl Dwire *Dr Radford* ■ *Dir* Joseph Kane • *Scr* Luci Ward, Gerald Geraghty, from a story by Luci Ward

Arizona Legion ★ U

Western 1939 · US · BW · 58mins

In this poor series western for RKO, George O'Brien goes undercover as the leader of a band of secret agents and infiltrates the outlaw gang who have taken over a town. Of course, his activities lead to problems with girlfriend Laraine Johnson, (who would become a big star as Laraine Day). By contrast, O'Brien's career had seen much better days. AE

George O'Brien *Boone Yeager* • Laraine Johnson [Laraine Day] *Letty Meade* • Carlyle Moore Jr *Lt Ives* • Chill Wills *Whopper Hatch* • Edward Le Saint *Judge Meade* • Harry Cording *Whiskey Joe* ■ *Dir* David Howard • *Scr* Oliver Drake, from a story by Bernard McConville

Arizona Raiders ★★

Western 1965 · US · Colour · 89mins

Audie Murphy and Ben Cooper are convicted members of Quantrill's Raiders, who agree to help Buster Crabbe and the newly formed Arizona Rangers round up the remainder of the gang who are still on the loose and causing mayhem. This by-the-numbers western is a new version of the 1951 George Montgomery picture *The Texas Rangers*, which helps explain why it seems so old hat. AE

Audie Murphy *Clint* • Michael Dante *Brady* • Ben Cooper *Willie Martin* • Buster Crabbe [Larry "Buster" Crabbe] *Captain Andrews* • Gloria Talbott *Martina* • Ray Stricklyn *Danny Bonner* ■ *Dir* William Witney • *Scr* Alex Gottlieb, Willard Willingham, Mary Willingham, from a story by Frank Gruber, Richard Schayer

The Arizona Ranger ★★

Western 1948 · US · BW · 64mins

Tim Holt, who had just proved once again what a fine actor he was as one of the gold prospectors in John Huston's *The Treasure of the Sierra Madre*, returns to the world of formula B-westerns in this RKO feature. Here at least there was some added interest as Tim was cast as the son of his real-life father, the former western star Jack Holt. Holt Jr falls in love with the wife of abusive Steve Brodie, before reconciling with Dad and returning to the family ranch. AE

Tim Holt *Bob Wade* • Jack Holt *Rawhide* • Nan Leslie *Laura Butler* • Richard Martin (1) *Chito Rafferty* • Steve Brodie *Quirt* ■ *Dir* John Rawlins • *Scr* Norman Houston

The Arizonian ★★★ U

Western 1935 · US · BW · 75mins

An excellent screenplay by Dudley Nichols (who also wrote *Stagecoach*) enlivens a western which these days rather shows its age. Richard Dix is a marshal working with reformed outlaw Preston Foster to rid Silver City of corrupt Louis Calhern. Nichols won a best screenplay Oscar for his next film, *The Informer*, which also featured Margot Grahame. TS

Richard Dix *Clay Tallant* • Margot Grahame *Kitty Rivers* • Preston Foster *Tex Randolph* • Louis Calhern *Jake Mamien* • James Bush *Orin Tallant* • Ray Mayer *McClosky* ■ *Dir* Charles Vidor • *Scr* Dudley Nichols

Arlington Road ★★★★ 15

Thriller 1998 · US/UK · Colour · 112mins

Is college professor Jeff Bridges's new neighbour Tim Robbins an urban terrorist planning to bomb a government target? Or is that theory fuelled by Bridges's paranoia following the death of his FBI agent wife? Director Mark Pellington audaciously chips away at the American psyche to deliver a gripping psychological thriller, powered by a totally sympathetic and believable performance by Bridges. The suspense comes from never letting the viewer in on the supposed conspiracy theory right up to the stunning finale. This is seat-edge stuff, with a sobering message. AJ. Contains violence and swearing. [video] DVD

Jeff Bridges *Michael Faraday* • Tim Robbins *Oliver Lang* • Joan Cusack *Cheryl Lang* • Hope Davis *Brooke Wolf* • Robert Gossett *FBI Agent Whit Carver* • Mason Gamble *Brady Lang* • Spencer Treat Clark *Grant Faraday* • Stanley Anderson *Dr Archer Scobee* ■ *Dir* Mark Pellington • *Scr* Ehren Kruger

Armaan ★★★ U

Musical romantic drama
2003 · Ind · Colour · 158mins

Honey Irani makes her directorial bow with this stellar melodrama scripted with ex-husband and prolific lyricist, Javed Akhtar. Amitabh Bachchan stars as a doctor determined to build a new hospital for his patients, but he dies before his ambition is fulfilled and son Anil Kapoor has to resolve his romantic crisis with Preity Zinta and Gracy Singh before realising his father's dream. With the emphasis more on filial than civic duty, this is a solid, but formulaic drama that also boasts a cameo from Hrithik Roshan. DP. In Hindi with English subtitles. [video] DVD

Amitabh Bachchan *Dr Siddharth Sinha* • Anil Kapoor *Dr Akash Sinha* • Preity Zinta *Soniya Kapoor* • Gracy Singh *Dr Neha Mathur* • Hrithik Roshan ■ *Dir* Honey Irani • *Scr* Honey Irani, Javed Akhtar, from a story by Honey Irani

Armageddon ★★★ 15

Science-fiction action adventure
1998 · US · Colour · 144mins

In this megabucks popcorn-spiller from producer Jerry Bruckheimer and director Michael Bay, there's a meteor "the size of Texas" heading for Earth – as indeed there was in *Deep Impact*, released the same year. It's up to Bruce Willis and his motley oil-drilling gang ("the Wrong Stuff") to blast off and save us all. In hallmark Bruckheimer style, it's flashy, overwrought and excessive, but there's a knowing irony in the committee-written script and in the performances of Willis, Billy Bob Thornton and Steve Buscemi. The love subplot is a low-point, but within such an expert thrill-ride, it's not the end of the world. AC. Contains violence, swearing. [video] DVD

Bruce Willis *Harry S Stamper* • Billy Bob Thornton *Dan Truman* • Ben Affleck *AJ Frost* • Liv Tyler *Grace Stamper* • Keith David *General Kimsey* • Chris Ellis *Walter Clark* • Jason Isaacs *Ronald Quincy* • Will Patton *Charles "Chick" Chapple* • Steve Buscemi *Rockhound* • Charlton Heston *Narrator* ■ *Dir* Michael Bay • *Scr* Jonathan Hensleigh, Jeffrey Abrams, from a story by Jonathan Hensleigh, Robert Roy Pool, adapted by Tony Gilroy, Shane Salerno

Armaguedon ★★★

Crime thriller 1976 · Fr/It · Colour · 95mins

Wrongly dismissed on its original release, Alain Jessua's slow-burning psychological thriller is not only exciting, but also a critique of the cult of celebrity and the power of television. As the shrink called in by detective Michel Duchaussoy to avert a disaster, Alain Delon is nominally the star. But the action is dominated by Jean Yanne's eerily sympathetic performance as a seemingly harmless Everyman who bids to rouse society from its lethargy by threatening to detonate a bomb in a crowded auditorium. DP. In French with English subtitles.

Alain Delon *Ambrose* • Jean Yanne *Carrier* • Renato Salvatori *Einstein* • Michel Duchaussoy *Viven* ■ *Dir* Alain Jessua • *Scr* Alain Jessua, from a novel by David Lippincott

Armed and Dangerous ★ 15

Comedy 1986 · US · Colour · 83mins

John Candy often showed very suspect judgement when it came to leading roles and this moronic comedy was a depressing waste of his talents. Teaming up with old chum Eugene Levy, this finds the unlikely duo causing chaos at a private security company and coming up against cartoonish gangster Robert Loggia. JF [video]

John Candy *Frank Dooley* • Eugene Levy *Norman Kane* • Robert Loggia *Michael Carlino* • Kenneth McMillan *Clarence O'Connell* • Meg Ryan *Maggie Cavanaugh* • Brion James *Anthony Lazarus* • Jonathan Banks *Clyde Klepper* • Don Stroud *Sergeant Rizzo* ■ *Dir* Mark L Lester • *Scr* Harold Ramis, Peter Torokvei, from a story by Brian Grazer, Harold Ramis, James Keach

Armed Response ★★ 18

Action crime drama
1986 · US · Colour · 82mins

Hardworking Fred Olen Ray is best known for cheap and sleazy exploitation hits, but this early effort is a much more mainstream affair. David Carradine teams up with spaghetti western icon Lee Van Cleef to play a father and son who go head to head with the Japanese yakuza, led by Mako. JF [video]

David Carradine *Jim Roth* • Lee Van Cleef *Burt Roth* • Mako *Akira Tanaka* • Lois Hamilton *Sara Roth* • Ross Hagen *Cory Thorton* • Brent Huff *Tommy Roth* • Laurene Landon *Deborah Silverstein* • Dick Miller *Steve* • Michael Berryman *FC* ■ *Dir* Fred Olen Ray • *Scr* TL Lankford, from a story by Paul Hertzberg, Fred Olen Ray, TL Lankford

L'Armée des Ombres ★★★★★

Second World War drama
1969 · Fr/It · Colour · 143mins

Jean-Pierre Melville's reputation rests largely on American-style gangster movies such as *Le Deuxième Souffle* and *Le Samouraï*, but *L'Armée des Ombres* may be his greatest film. In this long but utterly mesmerising vengeance thriller, set during the Second World War, Lino Ventura plays a Resistance fighter searching for the man who betrayed him to the Nazis. With its superb cast, moody photography, marvellous use of Lyons locations and doom-laden flashbacks, this is a war drama *par excellence* that draws on the director's own experience as a member of the Maquis. AT

Lino Ventura *Philippe Gerbier* • Paul Meurisse *Luc Jardie* • Simone Signoret *Mathilde* • Jean-Pierre Cassel *Jean-François* • Claude Mann *Le Masque* • Christian Barbier *Le Bison* • Serge Reggiani *Barber* • Alain Libolt *Paul Dounat* • Paul Crauchet *Felix* ■ *Dir* Jean-Pierre Melville • *Scr* Jean-Pierre Melville, from the novel *Army of Shadows* by Joseph Kessel • *Cinematographer* Pierre Lhomme

Armored Car Robbery ★★

Crime drama 1950 · US · BW · 67mins

This B-movie thriller about a robbery that goes horribly wrong vaguely resembles *The Asphalt Jungle*, which was made the same year, while its ironic climax was copied by Stanley Kubrick for his 1956 movie *The Killing*. Director Richard Fleischer is clearly working on a shoestring, but that doesn't hinder his creation of suspense or atmosphere. The cast, alas, is distinctly third-rate. AT

Charles McGraw *Cordell* • Adele Jergens *Yvonne* • William Talman *Purvus* • Douglas Fowley *Benny* • Steve Brodie *Mapes* • Don McGuire *Ryan* • Don Haggerty *Cuyler* ■ *Dir* Richard Fleischer • *Scr* Earl Fenton, Gerald Drayson Adams, from a story by Robert Angus, Robert Leeds

Armored Command ★★

Second World War spy drama
1961 · US · BW · 98mins

This potentially interesting but bungled wartime drama has Tina Louise as a sort of Mata Hari figure who infiltrates a group of GIs to discover the Allied Forces' strength and tactics. The soldiers squabble for her favours, but the leader remains sceptical. Louise looks good but lacks the dramatic range to carry off the role, and she's not helped by a script that deals strictly in clichés. AT

Howard Keel *Colonel Devlin* • Tina Louise *Alexandra Bastegar* • Warner Anderson *Lt Col Wilson* • Earl Holliman *Sergeant Mike* • Carleton Young *Captain Macklin* • Burt Reynolds *Skee* • Marty Ingels *Pinhead* ■ *Dir* Byron Haskin • *Scr* Ron W Alcorn, Ernest Haller

The Armour of God ★★ 15

Martial arts adventure
1986 · HK · Colour · 84mins

Although he has never reached the kung fu heights of Bruce Lee, Jackie Chan's high-vaulting, low-swiping action movies have an endearing humour that almost amounts to wit. This *Raiders of the Lost Ark* rip-off exports him to Europe, where he seeks out a crusader's relic and battles some lethal monks. As director as well as star, his style is not so much cramped as numbed. A sequel, *Operation Condor: the Armour of God* II, followed in 1990. TH. Cantonese dialogue dubbed into English. [video] DVD

Jackie Chan *Jackie* • Alan Tam *Alan* • Rosamund Kwan *Lorelei* • Lola Forner *May* • Bozidar Smilianic *Bannon* • Ken Boyle *Grand Wizard* • John Ladalski *Chief Lama* • Robert O'Brien (2) *Witch doctor* ■ *Dir* Jackie Chan • *Scr* Edward Tang, Szeto Chuek-Hun, Ken Lowe, John Sheppard, from a story by Barry Wong

Arms and the Man ★★ U

Comedy 1958 · W Ger · Colour · 86mins

Although Jacques Tati's *Mon Oncle* would have won the Oscar for best foreign film in just about any year, only a shortage of suitable submissions could explain why this stilted West German adaptation of George Bernard Shaw's play was even nominated. It's a highly stagebound production, with Franz Peter Wirth restricting his camera to spectating rather than playing an active part in the encounter between fleeing Swiss mercenary OW Fischer and Lisolette Pulver, the fiancée of his adversary. Respectful, but dull. DP. A German language film.

OW Fischer *Captain Bluntschli* • Liselotte Pulver *Raina Petkoff* • Ellen Schwiers *Louka* • Jan Hendriks *Sergius Saranoff* • Ljuba Welitsch *Katharina* • Kurt Kasznar *Petkoff* • Manfred Inger *Nicola* ■ *Dir* Franz Peter Wirth • *Scr* Johanna Sibelius, Eberhard Keindorff, from the play by George Bernard Shaw

Army of Darkness ★★ 15

Horror fantasy comedy
1993 · US · Colour · 84mins

Director Sam Raimi's juvenile second sequel to his classic *Evil Dead* is a vapid exercise in watered-down horror kitsch. After a recap of the first two movies, Bruce Campbell battles with pit monsters, sword-wielding skeletons and his evil clone to find the sacred "Book of the Dead" that will help him escape the Dark Ages and return to the present. There's plenty of in-jokes for the discerning horror buff but little actual horror. AJ [video]

Bruce Campbell *Ash/Evil Ash* • Embeth Davidtz *Sheila/Evil Sheila* • Marcus Gilbert *Arthur* • Ian Abercrombie *Wiseman* • Richard Grove *Duke Henry* • Michael Earl Reid *Gold Tooth* • Bridget Fonda *Linda* • Ivan Raimi *Fake Shemp* ■ *Dir* Sam Raimi • *Scr* Sam Raimi, Ivan Raimi

Army of One ★★ 18

Action thriller 1993 · US · Colour · 96mins

Dolph Lundgren stars in this slam-bam adventure that also goes under the title of *Joshua Tree*, while George Segal is slumming in a movie that seems to have been designed solely to exhibit Lundgren's fighting skills. Seeking the man who framed him, Lundgren rips through the American Southwest like one of Ray Harryhausen's stop-motion animated statues. Strictly for fans. DP. Contains swearing, violence and nudity. [video]

Dolph Lundgren *Wellman Santee* • George Segal *Severence* • Kristian Alfonso *Rita* • Geoffrey Lewis *Cepeda* • Michelle Phillips *Esther* • Matt Battaglia *Michael Agnos* ■ *Dir* Vic Armstrong • *Scr* Steven Pressfield

The Arnelo Affair ★

Mystery melodrama 1947 · US · BW · 87mins

The guilty party in this glossy but less than hypnotic mystery is writer/director Arch Oboler, whose radio background explains the emphasis on talk and the static camera set-ups. The lacklustre line-up of MGM's second-rank stars doesn't help: John Hodiak as a shady nightclub proprietor, George Murphy as a Chicago attorney and Frances Gifford as his neglected wife, whose affair with Hodiak involves her in murder. AE

John Hodiak *Tony Arnelo* • Frances Gifford *Anne Parkson* • George Murphy *Ted Parkson* • Dean Stockwell *Ricky Parkson* • Eve Arden *Vivian Delwyn* • Lowell Gillmore *Avery Border* ■ *Dir/Scr* Arch Oboler

Arnold ★★ 15

Comedy thriller 1973 · US · Colour · 90mins

The oddball cast is the sole attraction here. Stella Stevens plays a gold-digger who marries an aristocrat for his money. The thing is, the poor man is lying in his coffin throughout the ceremony! This makes the reading of the will a rather tricky business, and wastrel brother Roddy MacDowall and sister Elsa Lanchester are miffed to say the least. Others involved in this black comedy are Farley Granger, Victor Buono and British cabaret singer Shani Wallis as the dead aristocrat's widow. Left out of the will, she gets to sing the title number instead. AT [video]

Stella Stevens *Karen* • Roddy McDowall *Robert* • Elsa Lanchester *Hester* • Shani Wallis *Jocelyn* • Farley Granger *Evan Lyons* • Victor Buono *Minister* • John McGiver *Governor* ■ *Dir* Georg Fenady • *Scr* Jameson Brewer, John Fenton Murray

Around the Bend ★★★ 15

Road movie drama
2004 · US · Colour · 83mins

This labour of love from first-time writer/director Jordan Roberts centres on a quartet of men bonding across four generations. Michael Caine plays the ailing great-grandfather being cared for by his grandson (Josh Lucas) and great-grandson (Jonah Bobo). Then, out of the blue, son Christopher Walken returns home for the first time in 30 years. Following Caine's death, the three men take a road trip to Albequerque. Its quirkiness feels rather forced and it lacks tension, but this heartfelt film is well acted and satisfyingly subtle. KK. Contains swearing.

Christopher Walken *Turner Lair* • Josh Lucas *Jason Lair* • Michael Caine *Henry Lair* • Glenne Headly *Katrina* • Jonah Bobo *Zach Lair* • Norbert Weisser *Walter* ■ *Dir/Scr* Jordan Roberts

Around the World in 80 Days ★★★★ U

Adventure 1956 · US · Colour · 174mins

An epic very much of its time, this vastly entertaining, star-studded travelogue was produced (with some difficulty) by the great showman and charismatic producer Michael Todd (best known today for marrying Elizabeth Taylor), who was awarded the best picture Oscar for his considerable pains. The cast, led by the ultra-urbane David Niven, couldn't be bettered, nor could the use of worldwide locations – 13 countries in all. Todd persuaded 46 guest stars to appear in supporting roles, and spotting them is a delight. TS [video] DVD

David Niven *Phileas Fogg* • Cantinflas *Passepartout* • Shirley MacLaine *Princess Aouda* • Robert Newton *Inspector Fix* • Noël Coward *Hesketh-Baggott* • Trevor Howard *Fallentin* • Robert Morley *Ralph* • Hermione Gingold *Sporting lady* • Marlene Dietrich *Dance hall girl, Barbary Coast saloon* • Peter Lorre *Steward* • John Mills *Cabby* • George Raft *Bouncer, Barbary Coast saloon* • Frank Sinatra *Pianist, Barbary Coast saloon* • Buster Keaton *Train conductor* • John Gielgud *Foster* ■ *Dir* Michael Anderson • *Scr* SJ Perelman, James Poe, from the novel by Jules Verne • *Cinematographer* Lionel Lindon • *Music* Victor Young

Around the World in 80 Days ★★ PG

Comedy adventure
2004 · US/Ger/Ire/UK · Colour · 115mins

Inventor Phileas Fogg (Steve Coogan) and his valet Passepartout (Jackie Chan) endeavour to circumnavigate the globe in record time to win a wager set by the villainous Lord Kelvin (Jim Broadbent). Chan delivers his trademark martial arts rough and tumble along the way, but a redundant subplot involving a stolen jade Buddha only serves to slow the action down. The broad comedy is perhaps more suited to Chan's pratfalls than Coogan's wit, but big-name cameos to help pass the time on this laboured journey. GM [video] DVD

Jackie Chan *Passepartout/Lao Xing* • Steve Coogan *Phileas Fogg* • Cécile de France *Monique La Roche* • Jim Broadbent *Lord Kelvin* • Kathy Bates *Queen Victoria* • Arnold Schwarzenegger *Prince Hapi* • John Cleese *Grizzled sergeant* • Owen Wilson *Wilbur Wright* • Luke Wilson *Orville Wright* ■ *Dir* Frank Coraci • *Scr* David Titcher, David Benullo, David Goldstein, from the novel by Jules Verne

Around the World under the Sea ★★ U

Adventure 1965 · US · Colour · 110mins

Lloyd Bridges, master scuba diver in the TV series *Sea Hunt*, spits into his mask again before investigating a series of underwater volcanic eruptions. There's some scientific chat about earthquakes and the end of the world, but mostly it's a daft yarn with a giant squid, a friendly dolphin and Shirley Eaton as the only woman in sight. It was flmed on the Great Barrier Reef and in the Bahamas by veteran director Andrew Marton. AT

Lloyd Bridges *Dr Doug Standish* • Shirley Eaton *Dr Maggie Hanford* • Brian Kelly (1) *Dr Craig Mosby* • David McCallum *Dr Phil Volker* • Keenan Wynn *Hank Stahl* • Marshall Thompson *Dr Orin Hillyard* ■ *Dir* Andrew Marton • *Scr* Arthur Weiss, Art Arthur

The Arousers ★★

Horror 1970 · US · Colour · 75mins

1950s dreamboat Tab Hunter plays the Catherine Deneuve role in a rehash of Polanski's classic psycho shocker, *Repulsion*. Hunter is compelling as a personal trainer who is not the stud he appears, but an impotent, mother-fixated psychopath who kills whenever sex rears its head. The film is an early soft-core slasher with lots of female victims naked and dead. DM

Tab Hunter *Eddie Collins* • Cherie Latimer *Lauren Powers* • Linda Leider *Vickie* • Isabel Jewell *Mrs Cole* • Nadyne Turney *Barbara* ■ *Dir/Scr* Curtis Hanson

The Arrangement ★★ 15

Drama 1969 · US · Colour · 120mins

This rather distasteful film from director Elia Kazan is taken from his own novel about a successful New York advertising man, played by Kirk Douglas, who becomes totally disenchanted with his cosy, privileged world and decides to jettison work, marriage and respectability in one foul swoop. A starry cast struggles with a rather old-fashioned premise, while Kazan promotes the abdication of all personal responsibility. SH. Contains swearing. [video]

Kirk Douglas *Eddie Anderson* • Faye Dunaway *Gwen* • Deborah Kerr *Florence Anderson* • Richard Boone *Sam Anderson* • Hume Cronyn *Arthur* • Michael Higgins *Michael* • John Randolph Jones *Charles* ■ *Dir* Elia Kazan • *Scr* Elia Kazan, from his novel

The Arrival ★★★ 12

Science-fiction thriller
1996 · US · Colour · 110mins

Director David Twohy skilfully reworks a number of science fiction clichés (as well as ideas from his *Waterworld* and *The Fugitive* scripts) to deliver a highly polished entry in the alien invasion sweepstakes. Charlie Sheen plays an astronomer who goes on the run after he discovers an extraterrestrial conspiracy to change the Earth's climate and prepare it for colonisation. He faces stylish computer-generated effects at every turn, but still emerges as the winner in this pleasing, if low-key, B-movie. AJ [video] DVD

Charlie Sheen *Zane Ziminski* • Ron Silver *Gordian* • Lindsay Crouse *Ilana Green* • Teri Polo *Char* • Richard Schiff *Calvin* • Tony T Johnson *Kiki* ■ *Dir/Scr* David Twohy

Arrow in the Dust ★★ U

Western 1954 · US · Colour · 80mins

Prolific director Lesley Selander was one of the unsung heroes of the western, whose feature output embraced such cowboy icons as Buck Jones, Hopalong Cassidy and Tim Holt. This perfectly workmanlike programme filler stars Sterling Hayden as a deserter masquerading as an officer to help out a wagon train. Lee Van Cleef makes an early appearance. TS

Sterling Hayden *Bart Laish* • Coleen Gray *Christella* • Keith Larsen *Lt King* • Tom Tully *Crowshaw* • Jimmy Wakely *Carqueville* • Tudor Owen *Tillotson* • Lee Van Cleef *Crew boss* ■ *Dir* Lesley Selander • *Scr* Don Martin, from the novel by LL Foreman

Arrowhead ★★ U

Western 1953 · US · Colour · 105mins

This western derives considerable force from its depiction of the intense hatred between Charlton Heston, as the army scout who was raised by the Apaches, and Jack Palance as the college-educated son of the chief. The government wants peace but Heston is sure the Apaches can't be trusted. While Palance is chillingly ruthless as the native American, Heston remains monotonously grim. The film is distinctly unpleasant in the crude way it deals with a delicate subject. AE

Charlton Heston *Ed Bannon* • Jack Palance *Toriano* • Katy Jurado *Nita* • Brian Keith *Capt North* • Mary Sinclair *Lee* • Milburn Stone *Sandy MacKinnon* • Richard Shannon *Lieutenant Kirk* ■ *Dir* Charles Marquis Warren • *Scr* Charles Marquis Warren, from the novel *Adobe Walls* by WR Burnett

Arrowsmith ★★★

Drama 1931 · US · BW · 102mins

John Ford wasn't, perhaps, the ideal director for the work of Sinclair Lewis, but this sturdy adaptation of Lewis's novel benefits from a marvellous performance by Ronald Colman as the idealistic doctor of the title who's seeking a cure for bubonic plague. Colman brings a vivid, idealistic freshness to the part and single-handedly justifies this Samuel Goldwyn production. Helen Hayes suffers nobly as his wife and a pre-stardom Myrna Loy excels as the bored society girl with whom Colman has a fling. TS

Ronald Colman *Dr Martin Arrowsmith* • Helen Hayes *Leora* • AC Anson *Professor Gottlieb* • Richard Bennett *Sondelius* • Claude King *Dr Tubbs* • Beulah Bondi *Mrs Tozer* • Myrna Loy *Joyce Lanyon* • Russell Hopton *Terry Wickett* ■ *Dir* John Ford • *Scr* Sidney Howard, from the novel by Sinclair Lewis

The Arsenal Stadium Mystery ★★★ PG

Crime drama 1939 · UK · BW · 82mins

This far from baffling murder mystery may not be premier league stuff, but it has become something of a cult item in art-house circles. There's plenty to enjoy as maverick Scotland Yard inspector Leslie Banks tries to find out who murdered star player Anthony Bushell during a friendly match, not least the chance to see members of the 1937/38 Arsenal championship-winning side in action. Director Thorold Dickinson reveals a talent for authentic detail and there's also a pleasing lightness about the action. DP [video]

Leslie Banks *Inspector Slade* • Greta Gynt *Gwen Lee* • Ian MacLean *Sergeant Clinton* • Esmond Knight *Raille* • Liane Linden *Inga* • Brian Worth *Philip Morring* • Anthony Bushell *Jack Dyce* ■ *Dir* Thorold Dickinson • *Scr* Thorold Dickinson, Donald Bull, from the novel by Leonard Gribble

Arsene Lupin ★★★

Crime adventure 1932 · US · BW · 84mins

The names of John and Lionel Barrymore sharing the marquee guaranteed big audiences for this well-upholstered version of Maurice Leblanc's master criminal. It was the first time the two brothers had starred together on film and that prospect created fireworks in 1932, though today the picture inevitably lacks that resonance and creaks a little. John plays the thief, Lionel the detective on his trail, and director Jack Conway sacrifices plot (the theft of the Mona Lisa from the Louvre) for some elaborate thesping. AT

John Barrymore *Duke of Charmerace* • Lionel Barrymore *Guerchard* • Karen Morley *Sonia* • John Miljan *Prefect of Police* • Tully Marshall *Gourney-Martin* ■ *Dir* Jack Conway • *Scr* Carey Wilson, Bayard Veiller, Lenore Coffee, from the play by Maurice LeBlanc, Francis de Croisset [François Wiener]

Arsène Lupin ★★★

Period crime adventure
2004 · Fr/UK/Sp/It · Colour · 131mins

Maurice Leblanc's notorious *fin-de-siècle* cracksman has already been played on screen by such luminaries as Jules Berry and John Barrymore. But no previous outing can boast the lavish settings and sweeping storyline of Jean-Paul Salomé's rousing adventure, which opens with the daring theft of a necklace that belonged to Marie Antoinette and becomes increasingly complex and compelling as master of disguise Romain Duris meets his match in the darkly seductive Kristin Scott Thornas. Duris is well supported by a cracking gallery of rogues and a director who knows the difference between spectacle and excess. DP. In French with English subtitles.

Romain Duris *Arsène Lupin* • Kristin Scott Thomas *Joséphine* • Pascal Greggory *Beaumagnan* • Eva Green *Clarisse* • Robin Renucci *Dreux-Soubise* • Patrick Toomey *Léonard* • Mathieu Carrière *Duc d'Orléans* • Philippe Magnan *Bonnetot* • Marie Bunel *Henriette Lupin* • Philippe Lemaire *Cardinal d'Etigues* ■ *Dir* Jean-Paul Salomé • *Scr* Jean-Paul Salomé, Laurent Vachaud, from the novel *La Comtesse de Cagliostro* by Maurice Leblanc

Arsene Lupin Returns ★★★

Crime adventure 1938 · US · BW · 80mins

The glamorous criminal was first personified by John Barrymore in 1932, memorably pitted against his brother Lionel, and the ultra-sophisticated thief went down a treat with American audiences. Six years later the same studio, MGM, decided to revive him, this time played by the equally debonair Melvyn Douglas. Trouble is, the quintessential French flavour of the original has been relentlessly Americanised here, with a plot involving Warren William as an overly publicity conscious ex-FBI man. TS

Melvyn Douglas *Rene Farrand* • Virginia Bruce *Lorraine Degrissac* • Warren William *Steve Emerson* • John Halliday *Count Degrissac* • Nat Pendleton *Joe Doyle* • Monty Woolley *Georges Bouchet* • EE Clive *Alf* • George Zucco *Prefect of Police* ■ *Dir* George Fitzmaurice • *Scr* James Kevin McGuiness, Howard Emmett Rogers, George Harmon Coxe • *Music* Franz Waxman

Arsenic and Old Lace ★★★★★ PG

Classic black comedy
1944 · US · BW · 113mins

From the moment he saw Joseph Kesselring's hit play, Frank Capra was determined to bring it to the screen. Although forced to settle for Raymond Massey after he failed to get Boris Karloff to repeat his stage triumph, Capra was blessed with a sparkling cast. Cary Grant only agreed to take the lead as it gave him the chance to reunite with Jean Adair, but he then proceeded to insist on changes to the script, costumes, sets and the lighting. Grant ended up donating his fee to a range of war charities and rarely spoke of the picture with any fondness. A shame, really, as he hurls himself into the part of the decent nephew who discovers that his respectable aunts (played with hilarious dottiness by Josephine Hull and Adair) are serial killers. Spookily lit and very funny, the film is unmissable, with Grant's wonderful double-takes lightening the pitch-black humour. DP [video] DVD

Cary Grant *Mortimer Brewster* • Priscilla Lane *Elaine Harper* • Raymond Massey *Jonathan Brewster* • Jack Carson *O'Hara* • Edward Everett Horton *Mr Witherspoon* • Peter Lorre *Dr Einstein* • James Gleason *Lt Rooney* •

Josephine Hull *Abby Brewster* • Jean Adair *Martha Brewster* • John Alexander *"Teddy Roosevelt" Brewster* • Grant Mitchell *Reverend Harper* • Edward McNamara *Brophy* • Garry Owen *Taxi cab driver* ■ *Dir* Frank Capra • *Scr* Julius J Epstein, Philip G Epstein, from the play by Joseph Kesselring • *Cinematographer* Sol Polito

Art Deco Detective ★★

Detective comedy
1994 · US · Colour · 102mins

John Dennis Johnson is Art Deco, a hard-boiled gumshoe who becomes embroiled in a terrorist conspiracy set-up while investigating the murder of movie star Rena Riffel in which he is implicated as the killer. A game cast is wasted in a lame satire on Hollywood fame and wheeler-dealing. It was written and directed by the Australian director of a couple of *Howling* sequels, Philippe Mora. AJ

John Dennis Johnston *Arthur "Art" Decowitz* • Stephen McHattie *Hyena* • Brion James *Jim Wexler* • Joe Santos *Detective Guy Lean* • Rena Riffel *Julie/Meg Hudson* • Sonia Cole *Irina Bordat* ■ *Dir/Scr* Philippe Mora

Art of Love ★★★ U

Comedy 1965 · US · Colour · 98mins

Glossy, very silly but nonetheless enjoyable example of the Technicolor Universal 1960s style as produced by Ross Hunter. Like his *Pillow Talk*, this is bedecked with likeable stars and is a jolly pleasant way to pass the time. The would-be adult plot involves James Garner and Dick Van Dyke as struggling artists in Paris, with the ultra-glamorous Angie Dickinson and Elke Sommer as their chicks and the great Ethel Merman as a singing madame. What's really strange, though, is how the undeniably talented Norman Jewison's direction is just so, well, anonymous. TS

James Garner *Casey* • Dick Van Dyke *Paul* • Elke Sommer *Nikki* • Angie Dickinson *Laurie* • Ethel Merman *Madame Coco* • Carl Reiner *Rodin* • Pierre Olaf *Carnot* ■ *Dir* Norman Jewison • *Scr* Carl Reiner, from a story by Richard Alan Simmons, William Sackheim

The Art of Love ★★ 18

Sex comedy 1983 · Fr/It · Colour · 93mins

Quite what stars of the magnitude of Laura Betti and Michele Placido are doing in this pretentious soft-core is hard to imagine. But even more distressing is the fact that a director such as Walerian Borowczyk should be wasting his talents on such tawdry erotica. Set in 6AD, the much-censored action focuses on Marina Pierro, whose idea of relaxation – when not servicing her husband and lover – is to listen to the poet Ovid spouting a mix of pith and platitude in a Roman amphitheatre. DP. Italian dialogue dubbed into English. [video]

Marina Pierro *Claudia* • Michele Placido *Macarius* • Massimo Girotti *Publius Ovidius Naso* • Laura Betti *Clio* • Milena Vukotic *Modestina* ■ *Dir* Walerian Borowczyk • *Scr* Walerian Borowczyk, Wilhelm Buchhelm, Enzo Ungari

The Art of Murder ★★

Thriller 1999 · US · Colour · 100mins

Polish-born Joanna Pacula certainly deserves better than this tepid thriller, in which she's blackmailed by slimy Peter Onorati, who threatens to show her wealthy, sozzled husband Michael Moriarty explicit pictures of her cavortings with his supposedly loyal lieutenant, Boyd Kestner. There's a couple of twists that just about pass muster, but you might not consider them worth waiting for. DP

Michael Moriarty *Cole* • Joanna Pacula *Elizabeth Sheridan* • Boyd Kestner *Tony Blanchard* • Peter Onorati *Willie* ■ *Dir* Ruben Preuss • *Scr* Sean Smith, Anthony Stark

The Art of War ★★ 18

Action thriller
2000 · Can/US · Colour · 112mins

This fails to rise above the ordinary, despite a substantial budget and some star names. The daft and hackneyed plot has Wesley Snipes as a United Nations "dirty tricks" operative who finds himself framed for the assassination of the Chinese ambassador. Snipes only gets really animated in some so-so martial arts sequences, but that's an improvement on Donald Sutherland and Anne Archer, who have rarely looked so bored and listless. DA. Contains violence, swearing, drug abuse. [video] DVD

Wesley Snipes *Neil Shaw* • Anne Archer *Eleanor Hooks* • Maury Chaykin *Cappella* • Marie Matiko *Julia Fang* • Cary-Hiroyuki Tagawa *David Chan* • Michael Biehn *Bly* • Donald Sutherland *Douglas Thomas* • Liliana Komorowska *Novak* • James Hong *Ambassador Wu* ■ *Dir* Christian Duguay • *Scr* Wayne Beach, Simon Davis Barry, from a story by Wayne Beach

Artemisia ★★★ 18

Biographical drama
1997 · Fr/Ger/It · Colour · 91mins

The 17th-century painter Artemisia Gentileschi emerges from this sumptuous biopic as the doomed heroine of a Gothic melodrama rather than a courageous artist who challenged the conventions of her day. However, while director Agnès Merlet's approach has appalled purists and feminists alike, she has nevertheless produced a moving portrayal that captures both the flavour of the times and the tragic fate of a passionate artist. Valentina Cervi conveys sensuality rather than creative zest in the title role, but this still succeeds in being a vibrant portrait. DP. In French and Italian with English subtitles. Contains nudity and sex scenes. [video]

Michel Serrault *Orazio Gentileschi* • Valentina Cervi *Artemisia Gentileschi* • Miki Manojlovic *Agostino Tassi* • Luca Zingaretti *Cosimo* • Brigitte Catillon *Tuzia* • Frédéric Pierrot *Roberto* ■ *Dir* Agnès Merlet • *Scr* Agnès Merlet, Christine Miller

Arthur ★★★★ 15

Screwball comedy
1981 · US · Colour · 93mins

While Dudley Moore's drunken millionaire is outclassed by John Gielgud's disdainful butler, he's not the dud he might have been in this boozy variation on Jeeves and Wooster. As he tries to change his layabout lifestyle for love of working girl Liza Minnelli, Moore displays the charm and timing that helped to make *10* a hit, though his character is sometimes too clichéd. The ever-adaptable Gielgud delivers his lines with such wonderful aplomb that he won an Oscar; the veteran actor was tempted back to the role for a brief appearance in the inferior sequel. TH. Contains some swearing. [video] DVD

Dudley Moore *Arthur Bach* • Liza Minnelli *Linda Marolla* • John Gielgud *Hobson* • Geraldine Fitzgerald *Martha Bach* • Jill Eikenberry *Susan Johnson* • Stephen Elliot [Stephen Elliott] *Burt Johnson* • Ted Ross *Bitterman* ■ *Dir/Scr* Steve Gordon

Arthur 2: On the Rocks ★ PG

Romantic comedy
1988 · US · Colour · 108mins

Seven years after the charming if one-joke original, Dudley Moore returned to the role of the drunken millionaire in this disastrous comedy sequel. After a financial takeover by the father of his former girlfriend, Moore is left penniless and has to save his marriage to Liza Minnelli and regain his fortune before the end credits. You know things are getting bad when John Gielgud is resurrected as a ghost. Believe it or not, things get even worse. JB. Contains swearing. [video]

Dudley Moore *Arthur Bach* • Liza Minnelli *Linda Marolla Bach* • John Gielgud *Hobson* • Geraldine Fitzgerald *Martha Bach* • Stephen Elliott *Burt Johnson* • Paul Benedict *Fairchild* • Kathy Bates *Mrs Canby* ■ *Dir* Bud Yorkin • *Scr* Andy Breckman, from characters created by Steve Gordon

Arthur's Dyke ★★ 15

Comedy drama 2001 · UK · Colour · 103mins

This Ealingesque comedy about the eccentricity of the British character doesn't really make the grade. Offa's Dyke provides the magnificent setting for the midlife reunion of college pals Robert Daws, Nicholas Farrell and Richard Graham. Pauline Quirke tops the bill as the woman on a soul-searching mission of her own who travels with the three men. Ribald and occasionally poignant, but without social insight. DP [video] DVD

Pauline Quirke *Janet* • Robert Daws *Arthur* • Nicholas Farrell *Geoffrey* • Richard Graham (2) *Andy* • Rebecca Lacey *Phillipa* • Dennis Waterman *Doubleday* • Brian Conley *Dave* • Warren Clarke *Doug* ■ *Dir* Gerry Poulson • *Scr* Jackie Robb, Bernie Stringle

Arthur's Hallowed Ground ★★

Drama 1985 · UK · Colour · 84mins

The Arthur of the title (Jimmy Jewel) is an indispensable school groundsman whose main ambition in life is to create the perfect cricket pitch. Cue much fiddling with antiquated machinery, which is as slow-moving as the film itself. This is the directorial debut of the distinguished cinematographer Freddie Young, then 82 years old, but his experience doesn't seem to have helped him succeed as director. LH

Jimmy Jewel *Arthur* • Jean Boht *Betty* • David Swift *Lionel* • Michael Elphick *Len* • Derek Benfield *Eric* • Vas Blackwood *Henry* • John Flanagan *Norman* • Bernard Gallagher *George* ■ *Dir* Freddie Young • *Scr* Peter Gibbs

Article 99 ★ 15

Comedy drama 1992 · US · Colour · 96mins

This sets out with three aims, but fails to accomplish any one of them. Firstly, it wants to make us angry that Washington neglects the war veterans in its hospitals. Secondly, it seeks to reproduce the gallows humour of *MASH* by having the cast quip endlessly through each crisis. And, finally, it sets out to prove that Ray Liotta has a gift for comedy. An unrelieved failure. DP. Contains violence and swearing. [video] DVD

Ray Liotta *Dr Richard Sturgess* • Kiefer Sutherland *Dr Peter Morgan* • Forest Whitaker *Dr Sid Handleman* • Lea Thompson *Dr Robin Van Dorn* • John C McGinley *Dr Rudy Bobrick* • John Mahoney *Dr Henry Dreyfoos* • Keith David *Luther Jerome* • Kathy Baker *Dr Diane Walton* • Eli Wallach *Sam Abrams* ■ *Dir* Howard Deutch • *Scr* Ron Cutler

Artists and Models ★★★ U

Musical 1937 · US · BW · 97mins

Jack Benny's first starring vehicle was made at the height of his radio fame. While the Louis Armstrong and Martha Raye blackface sequences seem tasteless and offensive today, this is a raucous funfest that fairly zips along under Raoul Walsh's canny direction. There's a lovely plot-driving performance from young co-star Ida Lupino that's a joy to watch, and sturdy Richard Arlen also registers strongly. A sequel, *Artists and Models Abroad*, followed in 1938. TS

Jack Benny *Mac Brewster* • Ida Lupino *Paula* • Richard Arlen *Alan Townsend* • Gail Patrick *Cynthia* • Ben Blue *Jupiter Pluvius* • Judy Canova *Toots* • Donald Meek *Dr Zimmer* • Louis Armstrong • Martha Raye ■ *Dir* Raoul Walsh • *Scr* Walter DeLeon, Francis Martin, from a story by Sig Herzig, Gene Thackrey • *Choreographer* Vincente Minnelli, LeRoy Prinz • *Music* Victor Young

Artists and Models ★★★★ U

Musical comedy 1955 · US · Colour · 108mins

This superior Dean Martin and Jerry Lewis vehicle is gloriously photographed in some brilliant Technicolor. Of course, appreciation really depends on how one feels about Martin and Lewis, here expertly cast as a cartoonist and wacky fantasist, respectively, Dean using Jerry's dreams for inspiration. What gives this lunacy credence is that it's the work of Frank Tashlin, himself a noted cartoon artist, and there's a wonderful stylistic boldness to the design. As in Tashlin's masterpiece, *The Girl Can't Help It*, the humour may seem sexist today. TS

Dean Martin *Rick Todd* • Jerry Lewis *Eugene Fullstack* • Shirley MacLaine *Bessie Sparrowbush* • Dorothy Malone *Abigail Parker* • Eddie Mayehoff *Mr Murdock* • Eva Gabor *Sonia* • Anita Ekberg *Anita* • George Winslow *Richard Stilton* • Jack Elam *Ivan* ■ *Dir* Frank Tashlin • *Scr* Frank Tashlin, Hal Kanter, Herbert Baker, from a play by Norman Lessing, Michael Davidson • *Cinematographer* Daniel L Fapp

Artists and Models Abroad ★★

Musical 1938 · US · BW · 90mins

This follow-up to Paramount's 1937 hit musical comedy *Artists and Models* is more of the same, only with a French setting. Jack Benny schemes to save his untalented American theatrical troupe when it becomes stranded in Paris, but the story's merely a link between songs and fashion shows. AE

Jack Benny *Buck Boswell* • Joan Bennett *Patricia Harper* • Mary Boland *Mrs Isabel Channing* • Charley Grapewin *James Harper* • Joyce Compton *Chickie* ■ *Dir* Mitchell Leisen • *Scr* Howard Lindsay, Russell Crouse, Ken England, from a story by Howard Lindsay, from an idea by JP McEvoy • *Costume Designer* Edith Head

As Good as It Gets ★★★★ 15

Romantic comedy drama
1997 · US · Colour · 138mins

Ostensibly, James L Brooks's movie is about Jack Nicholson. He plays Melvin Udall, a homophobic bigot who insults everyone, lives alone, writes trashy novels for a living and has an obsessive-compulsive disorder. However, the movie is really about Helen Hunt, who plays that corniest of Hollywood characters – the lonely, frustrated waitress with a problem child. Yet Hunt, who was offered the role when Holly Hunter turned it down and, like Nicholson, won an Oscar for her pains, breathes life into the part, trouncing her co-star and his trademark grouchy act. The picture, though, is a mixed blessing: it's lazily directed and far too long, but Hunt is a revelation and the reason to stick with the film. AT. Contains violence, swearing, and drug abuse. [video] DVD

Jack Nicholson *Melvin Udall* • Helen Hunt *Carol Connelly* • Greg Kinnear *Simon Bishop* • Cuba Gooding Jr *Frank Sachs* • Skeet Ulrich *Vincent* • Shirley Knight *Beverly* • Yeardley Smith *Jackie* • Lupe Ontiveros *Nora* ■ *Dir* James L Brooks • *Scr* Mark Andrus, James L Brooks, from a story by Mark Andrus

As If It Were Raining ★★

Thriller 1963 · Fr/Sp · BW · 84mins

Shamefully wasting the beauties of Madrid and allowing the action to amble along rather than involve and

A

confuse us, José Luis Monter has made rather a mess of this Franco-Spanish co-production. French film icon Eddie Constantine plays an American author whose chance encounter with a damsel in distress leads to his involvement in shady, and ultimately deadly, dealings. In addition to a deficiency of mystery, this picture is not helped by the cast, who plod through the proceedings with evident disinterest. DP. French and Spanish dialogue dubbed into English.

Eddie Constantine *Eddie* • Silvia Solar *Rosa* • Maria Silva *Wilma* • Jacinto San Emerito *Coll* • Elisa Montés *Esperanza* ■ *Dir* José Luis Monter • *Scr* Niels Larsen

As Long as They're Happy

★★ U

Comedy 1955 · UK · Colour · 90mins

This moderately amusing all-British comedy, with some music, was inspired by the 1950s craze for sob singer Johnny Ray. The plot has an American crying crooner (Jerry Wayne) causing havoc in an English family with whom he stays. Jack Buchanan plays the unamused head of the household and the father of three daughters (Janette Scott, Jean Carson and Susan Stephen) obsessed with the visitor. J Lee Thompson directs the large cast of familiar faces. RK

Jack Buchanan *John Bentley* • Janette Scott *Gwen* • Jean Carson *Pat* • Susan Stephen *Corinne* • Brenda de Banzie *Stella* • Jerry Wayne *Bobby Denver* • Diana Dors *Pearl* • Joan Sims *Linda* • Dora Bryan *Mavis* ■ *Dir* J Lee Thompson • *Scr* Alan Melville, from the play by Vernon Sylvaine

As Tears Go By

★★★ 18

Crime drama 1988 · HK · Colour · 95mins

Writer/director Wong Kar-Wai made his transition from scriptwriter to film-maker with this gritty and violent Hong Kong gangster drama. It's a love-versus-loyalty tale in which Andy Lau's low-level triad "big brother" is torn between his gang allegiance to his hot-tempered "little brother" Jacky Cheung and his blossoming romance with his gentle cousin Maggie Cheung. Encumbered slightly by its synthesiser-heavy soundtrack and poor quality film stock, this debut shows signs of what will become Wong's cinematic signature. Saturated reds and greens add rich, visual texture, while highly stylised set pieces enhance the conventional plot. SF. In Mandarin with English subtitles. Contains violence and swearing. DVD

Andy Lau *Wah* • Maggie Cheung *Ngor* • Jacky Cheung *Fly* • Alex Man *Tony* ■ *Dir/Scr* Wong Kar-Wai

As You Desire Me

★★★

Melodrama 1932 · US · BW · 69mins

It may be slow moving and a shade creaky today, but this Greta Garbo vehicle positively smoulders, and contains some of the most overt sensuality you're likely to see in a Hollywood movie of the period. It's a classy MGM production, with George Fitzmaurice directing and Melvyn Douglas and Erich von Stroheim as Garbo's co-stars. The scenes between the blonde, fashionably bobbed Garbo and the handsome Douglas have an unusually charged eroticism: can't be just acting, surely? TS

Greta Garbo *Zara* • Melvyn Douglas *Count Bruno Varelli* • Erich von Stroheim *Carl Salter* • Owen Moore *Tony* • Hedda Hopper *Madame Mantari* • Rafaela Ottiano *Lena* ■ *Dir* George Fitzmaurice • *Scr* Gene Markey, from the play by Luigi Pirandello

As You Like It

★★ U

Romantic comedy 1936 · UK · BW · 96mins

With her German accent and mispronunciations, Elisabeth Bergner is unintentionally hilarious as Rosalind in this lavish film version of Shakespeare's comedy, directed and produced by her husband Paul Czinner. Laurence Olivier speaks beautifully but seems awkward as Orlando in his first screen venture into Shakespeare. JM Barrie adds a whimsical edge to the adaptation. AE

Elisabeth Bergner *Rosalind* • Laurence Olivier *Orlando* • Sophie Stewart *Celia* • Leon Quartermaine *Jacques* • Henry Ainley *Exiled Duke* • Mackenzie Ward *Touchstone* • Felix Aylmer *Duke Frederick* • Richard Ainley *Sylvius* • Austin Trevor *Beau* • John Laurie *Oliver* ■ *Dir* Paul Czinner • *Scr* JM Barrie, Robert J Cullen, from the play by William Shakespeare

As You Like It

★ U

Romantic comedy 1992 · UK · Colour · 112mins

This ill-fated version of one of the Bard's finest comedies finds the forest of Arden transposed into a contemporary urban environment. Peopled by strays in cardboard boxes, the tale of Orlando's passion for the banished Rosalind misfires conceptually. The talents of Cyril Cusack, James Fox and Miriam Margolyes are wasted. LH

Emma Croft *Rosalind* • Andrew Tiernan *Orlando/Oliver* • James Fox *Jaques* • Griff Rhys Jones *Touchstone* • Cyril Cusack *Adam* • Miriam Margolyes *Audrey* • Don Henderson *The Dukes* • Celia Bannerman *Celia* • Ewen Bremner *Silvius* ■ *Dir* Christine Edzard • *Scr* from the play by William Shakespeare

As Young as You Feel

★★★ U

Comedy 1951 · US · BW · 73mins

This 20th Century-Fox comedy is still relevant today and provides a marvellous vehicle for Monty Woolley, here playing a 65-year-old print worker who refuses to go quietly when he is asked to retire. The acerbic tale is an early work by writer Paddy Chayefsky, who earned great acclaim in the golden years of TV drama and went on to win Oscars for *Marty*, *The Hospital* and *Network*. The supporting cast is particularly fine, most notably Thelma Ritter and Constance Bennett, but pay attention to that scene-stealing contract blonde – a certain Marilyn Monroe in an early role. TS DVD

Monty Woolley *John Hodges* • Thelma Ritter *Della Hodges* • David Wayne *Joe* • Jean Peters *Alice Hodges* • Constance Bennett *Lucille McKinley* • Marilyn Monroe *Harriet* ■ *Dir* Harmon Jones • *Scr* Lamar Trotti, from a story by Paddy Chayefsky

Asa Nu Maan Watna Da

★★ PG

Romantic drama 2004 · Ind · Colour · 179mins

What happens when a Punjabi emigrant family returns home and children born abroad have to adapt to social and cultural situations they've only experienced from a distance? Director Manmohan Singh initially explores these issues by contrasting attitudes in Canada and India. But once love blossoms between Arshvir Bajwa and Harbajan Mann, they merely provide the clichéd impetus for a sentimental melodrama. DP. In Punjabi and Hindi with some English subtitles.

Arshvir Bajwa • Harbajan Mann • Kirandeep Kimmi ■ *Dir/Scr* Manmohan Singh

The Ascent

★★★★ PG

Second World War drama 1976 · USSR · BW · 104mins

Filmed in harsh monochrome by Vladimir Chukhnov, this was Larissa Shepitko's fourth feature in a career than spanned 20 years; it was also the last she completed before her fatal car crash. It is clearly the work of an inspired film-maker, though, as she imbues this award-winning tale of desperate survival with a biblical spirit that further ennobles the deeds of the partisans who fought to liberate Belorussia. Refusing to toe the socialist realist line on the Second World War, Shepitko depicts such unpatriotic acts as cowardice and collaboration, as well as suggesting that the Russian climate was as dangerous an enemy as the Nazis. DP. A Russian language film.

Boris Plotnikov • Vladimir Gostukhin • Sergei Jakovlev • Anatoli Solinitzin ■ *Dir* Larissa Shepitko • *Scr* Yuri Klepikov, Larissa Shepitko, from a novel by Vassil Bykov • *Cinematographer* Vladimir Chukhnov

The Ascent

★★

Second World War adventure 1994 · US · Colour · 96mins

This offbeat adventure, set in Africa well away from the front line, centres on a PoW camp where the largely Italian inmates and their British guards get involved in a bizarre challenge to see who can climb a treacherous mountain peak nearby. Ben Cross and John DeVeillers fly the Union flag; Vincent Spano plays the PoW with more than just mountain climbing on his mind. The stunning locations and the oddness of the tale don't really compensate for the uneven script. JF. Contains violence and swearing.

Vincent Spano *Franco* • Ben Cross *Major Farrell* • Rachel Ward *Patricia* • Tony LoBianco *Aldo* • Mark Ingall *Sergeant Thomas* • John DeVeillers *Major Quinn* ■ *Dir* Donald Shebib • *Scr* David Wiltse

Ash Wednesday

★★★ 15

Drama 1973 · US · Colour · 94mins

To save her ailing marriage to Henry Fonda, Elizabeth Taylor decides to fly to Italy for a face-lift. Looking beautiful again, she has a fling with Euro-stud Helmut Berger. Sadly this isn't a comedy, but a heavy drama which shows the agonies of plastic surgery in unremitting detail before turning to the emotional pain of a splintering relationship. Playing 55, Taylor was a mere 40-year-old when she made the picture, and she looks utterly ravishing – and that's *before* the surgery. In that it looks at what it takes to be a movie star, this can be regarded as autobiographical. AT

Elizabeth Taylor *Barbara Sawyer* • Henry Fonda *Mark Sawyer* • Helmut Berger *Erich* • Keith Baxter *David* • Maurice Teynac *Dr Lambert* ■ *Dir* Larry Peerce • *Scr* Jean-Claude Tramont

Ash Wednesday

★★ 18

Crime drama 2002 · US · Colour · 94mins

Edward Burns produces, directs and stars in this routine, New York-set tale about Irish-American family ties. Elijah Wood plays a young man whose death has to be faked after he thwarts the attempted murder of his hoodlum brother (Burns) by a rival gang. Three years later, Wood "resurrects" himself in order to woo back his wife (Rosario Dawson). Overwrought and underwritten. DA. Contains swearing, violence. DVD

Edward Burns *Francis Sullivan* • Elijah Wood *Sean Sullivan* • Rosario Dawson *Grace Quinonez* • Oliver Platt *Moran* • Pat McNamara *Murph* • James Handy *Father Mahoney* • Michael Mulheren *Detective Pulaski* • Malachy McCourt *Whitey* • Julie Hale *Maggie Shea* ■ *Dir/Scr* Edward Burns

Ashanti

★★ 15

Adventure 1979 · Swi/US · Colour · 112mins

This overblown adventure stars Michael Caine and Beverly Johnson as married doctors, who are working for the World Health Organisation in a small West African village when Johnson is kidnapped by slave-trader Peter Ustinov for wealthy prince Omar Sharif. Caine (inanimate and inadequate) sets off to track her down – a journey as heavy-going as tap-dancing on sand thanks to Richard Fleischer's leisurely direction and Ustinov's lack of menace. TH. Contains swearing, violence. DVD

Michael Caine *Dr David Linderby* • Peter Ustinov *Suleiman* • Beverly Johnson *Dr Anansa Linderby* • Kabir Bedi *Malik* • Omar Sharif *Prince Hassan* • Rex Harrison *Brian Walker* • William Holden (2) *Jim Sandell* ■ *Dir* Richard Fleischer • *Scr* Stephen Geller, from the novel *Ebano* by Alberto Vasquez-Figueroa

Ashes and Diamonds

★★★★★ 12

Drama 1958 · Pol · BW · 99mins

This made an overnight star of Zbigniew Cybulski, who was hailed by some as the Polish James Dean. Set on the last day of the Second World War, the film follows an underground guerrilla as he plots to assassinate a communist leader whose views he despises, but whose humanity he admires. Cybulski is quite magnificent as the resistance fighter, whether debating where to draw the line between military and moral duty, romancing barmaid Ewa Krzyzanowska, or paying bitterly for his indecision. Demonstrating a mastery of location shooting, symbolism, characterisation and camera technique, this is Wajda's masterpiece. DP. In Polish with English subtitles.

Zbigniew Cybulski *Maciek* • Ewa Krzyzanowska *Krystyna* • Adam Pawlikowski *Andrzej* • Waclaw Zastrzezynski *Szczuka* • Bogumil Kobiela *Drewnowski* ■ *Dir* Andrzej Wajda • *Scr* Andrzej Wajda, Jerzy Andrzejewski, from the novel by Jerzy Andrzejewski • *Cinematographer* Jerzy Wojcik

Ashes of Time

★★★★

Period martial arts drama 1994 · HK/Tai · Colour · 100mins

Based on a cult novel and with A-list stars in its cast, this stylised swashbuckler should have been a huge commercial success. That it wasn't owes much to Wong Kar-Wai's refusal to tell the story in a linear manner, thus alienating the viewers he hadn't already confused. Yet the exploits of Leslie Cheung's band of assassins are elevated above standard martial arts fare by Wong's fragmentary exploration of time and memory, the mythical atmosphere generated by the desert locations, Christopher Doyle's exquisite lighting and Sammo Hung's kinetic fight sequences. DP. In Cantonese with English subtitles.

Leslie Cheung *Feng Ouyang* • Tony Leung Chiu-Wai [Tony Leung (2)] *Blind swordsman* • Tony Leung Kar-Fai [Tony Leung (1)] *Huang Yaoshi* • Brigitte Lin Ching Hsia [Brigitte Lin] *Murong Yin/Murong Yan* • Maggie Cheung *The woman* ■ *Dir* Wong Kar-Wai • *Scr* Wong Kar-Wai, from the novel *The Eagle-Shooting Heroes* by Jin Yong [Louis Cha]

Ashik Kerib

★★★★

Fantasy drama 1988 · USSR · Colour · 78mins

This was the last film completed by the extraordinarily talented Georgian film-maker Sergei Paradzhanov. Although actor Dodo Abashidze shares the directorial credit, the astonishing beauty and complexity of the imagery is so reminiscent of such earlier Paradjanov pictures as *The Colour of Pomegranates* that the film's authorship is never in doubt. Loosely based on a story by the Russian writer Mikhail Lermontov, the action follows a poor minstrel on his 1001-day exile from his true love. Cinematic poetry. DP. In Azerbaijani with Georgian voiceover and English subtitles.

Yuri Mgoyan *Ashik Kerib* • Veronika Metonidze • Levan Natroshvili • Sofiko Chiaureli • R Chkhlkvadze ■ *Dir* Dodo Abashidze, Sergei Paradjanov • *Scr* Giya Badridze, from the story *Ashik Kerib the Lovelorn Minstrel* by Mikhail Lermontov

Ask a Policeman ★★★ U

Comedy 1938 · UK · BW · 74mins

Will Hay had a thing about spooky crooks. Just as the villains in *Oh, Mr Porter!* exploited a local legend to keep snoopers at bay, so the smugglers in this corking comedy play on the myth of the headless horseman to go about their business undisturbed. The setting is a sleepy coastal berg where the police station is in danger of being closed down because Sergeant Dudfoot (Hay) claims there is no crime. Co-screenwriter Val Guest directed the shudderingly awful remake, *The Boys in Blue*, 45 years later. DP DVD

Will Hay *Sgt Dudfoot* • Graham Moffatt *Albert* • Moore Marriott *Harbottle* • Glennis Lorimer *Emily* • Peter Gawthorne *Chief Constable* • Charles Oliver *Squire* • Herbert Lomas *Coastguard* • Pat Aherne *Motorist* ■ *Dir* Marcel Varnel • *Scr* Marriott Edgar, Val Guest, from a story by Sidney Gilliat

Ask Any Girl ★★ U

Comedy 1959 · US · Colour · 97mins

This mediocre comedy has a top-notch cast, but George Wells's script is merely good-natured and, while it occasionally bubbles, it's still sparkling wine rather than champagne. Shirley MacLaine is wide-eyed and lovely as a waif with a glut of suitors, who are played with typical aplomb by David Niven, Gig Young and Rod Taylor. DP

David Niven *Miles Doughton* • Shirley MacLaine *Meg Wheeler* • Gig Young *Evan Doughton* • Rod Taylor *Ross Taford* • Jim Backus *Mr Maxwell* • Claire Kelly *Lisa* • Elisabeth Fraser *Jeannie Boyden* ■ *Dir* Charles Walters • *Scr* George Wells, from the novel by Winifred Wolfe

Asoka ★★★ 12

Epic historical drama
2001 · Ind · Colour · 169mins

Although its epic sweep contrasts sharply with the intense intimacy of *The Terrorist*, it's clear from the visual lyricism and symbolic preoccupation with water that this rousing historical drama was also directed by Santosh Sivan. His stylised use of close-ups, angles and cross-cutting lends an added personal touch to what is, essentially, a genre film, chronicling the life of the Mauryan emperor, who abandoned tyranny to embrace Buddhism. Shah Rukh Khan is dashing in the title role and Kareena Kapoor impressive as his wife. DP. In Hindi with English subtitles. DVD

Shah Rukh Khan *Asoka* • Kareena Kapoor *Kaurwaki* • Danny Denzongpa *Virat* • Rahul Dev *Bheema* ■ *Dir* Santosh Sivan • *Scr* Saket Chaudhary, Santosh Sivan

Aspen Extreme ★ 15

Drama 1993 · US · Colour · 113mins

It's rather apt that this movie is about skiing, because it really is downhill all the way. Quitting Detroit for a life on the piste, Peter Berg is quickly on the slide, while his buddy Paul Gross slaloms between Teri Polo and Finola Hughes. DP DVD

Paul Gross *TJ Burke* • Peter Berg *Dexter Rutecki* • Finola Hughes *Bryce Kellogg* • Teri Polo *Robin Hand* • William Russ *Dave Ritchie* • Trevor Eve *Karl Stall* • Martin Kemp *Franc Hauser* ■ *Dir/Scr* Patrick Hasburgh

Asphalt ★★★★

Silent drama 1928 · Ger · BW · 114mins

Making exceptional use of sequence montage, superimpositions, neon lighting and meticulously re-created interiors, Joe May brings a gritty realism to what is essentially a melodramatic tale of petty crime, seduction and misplaced loyalty. Betty Amann is beguiling as the jewel thief who uses her charms to silence eager policeman Gustav Fröhlich, whose slavish devotion causes him to kill her lover. Combining the visual dynamism of the "city symphony" with the dramatic authenticity of the "street film", this is an astute summation of the styles dominating German cinema at the end of the silent era. DP

Gustav Fröhlich *Police Constable Albert Holk* • Betty Amann *Else Kramer* • Albert Steinrück *Police Sergeant Holk* • Else Heller *Mrs Holk* • Hans Adalbert von Schlettow *Lagen* ■ *Dir* Joe May • *Scr* Fred Majo, Hans Szekely, Rolf E Vanloo • *Cinematographer* Günther Rittau

The Asphalt Jungle ★★★★★ PG

Crime thriller 1950 · US · BW · 107mins

Shot with an almost documentary realism, this exceptional *film noir* from director John Huston continues to influence heist movies today. It has everything you could ask of a thriller. There's a scintillating plot (co-scripted by Ben Maddow and Huston from WR Burnett's novel), in which the perfect plan unravels with compelling inevitability; a seminal performance from Oscar-nominated Sam Jaffe as a criminal mastermind; totally convincing ensemble playing from his bungling gang (including Sterling Hayden and Anthony Caruso); and superb support from Jean Hagen and Marilyn Monroe as molls. Add Miklos Rozsa's atmospheric score and Harold Rosson's gritty photography and you have a masterpiece. DP

Sterling Hayden *Dix Handley* • Louis Calhern *Alonzo D Emmerich* • Jean Hagen *Doll Conovan* • James Whitmore *Gus Ninissi* • Sam Jaffe *Doc Erwin Riedenschneider* • John McIntire *Police Commissioner Hardy* • Marc Lawrence (1) *Cobby* • Barry Kelley *Lieutenant Ditrich* • Anthony Caruso *Louis Ciavelli* • Marilyn Monroe *Angela Phinlay* ■ *Dir* John Huston • *Scr* Ben Maddow, John Huston, from the novel by WR Burnett

The Asphyx ★★★★ 15

Supernatural horror
1972 · UK · Colour · 82mins

This thoughtful and convincing British horror oddity explores aspects of immortality with a sci-fi spin. The title refers to a soul-snatching being from another dimension that approaches the body at the moment of death. Photographer Robert Stephens captures one such life form in the hope he can claim eternal life. Morbid, intriguing and acted with conviction, director Peter Newbrook's cerebral chiller is a wordy Gothic drama masquerading as a supernatural terroriser. AJ. Contains violence. DVD

Robert Stephens *Hugo Cunningham* • Robert Powell *Giles Cunningham* • Jane Lapotaire *Christina Cunningham* • Alex Scott (1) *President* • Ralph Arliss *Clive Cunningham* • Fiona Walker *Anna Cunningham* • Terry Scully *Pauper* ■ *Dir* Peter Newbrook • *Scr* Brian Comfort

The Assam Garden ★★ U

Drama 1985 · UK · Colour · 90mins

Deborah Kerr's first film since 1969 is a mild, inconsequential affair. Returning from Assam to England, Kerr tends her recently deceased husband's eastern garden as a way of cherishing his memory. This, and her friendship with neighbour Madhur Jaffrey, are the means by which she tries to heal her grief. Kerr is as delightful as ever, but the film – written by Elisabeth Bond – lacks real substance. LH

Deborah Kerr *Helen* • Madhur Jaffrey *Ruxmani Lal* • Alec McCowen *Mr Philpott* • Zia Mohyeddin *Mr Lal* • Anton Lesser *Mr Sutton* • Iain Cuthbertson *Arthur* • Tara Shaw *Sushi* ■ *Dir* Mary McMurray • *Scr* Elisabeth Bond

Assassin ★★

Spy drama 1973 · UK · Colour · 82mins

Without the extraneous style and a couple of the more extended scenes, this might have made a decent half-hour TV thriller. Instead, director Peter Crane piles on the flashy visuals in an attempt to turn a humdrum espionage caper into a meaningful tract on the state's dispassionate sanctioning of murder and the isolation of the professional killer. Amid the directorial pyrotechnics, however, Ian Hendry is highly effective. DP

Ian Hendry *Assassin* • Edward Judd *MI5 Control* • Frank Windsor *John Stacey* • Ray Brooks *Edward Craig* • John Hart Dyke *Janik* • Verna Harvey *Girl* • Mike Pratt *Matthew* ■ *Dir* Peter Crane • *Scr* Michael Sloan

The Assassin ★★ 18

Thriller 1993 · US · Colour · 103mins

Luc Besson's *Nikita*, starring the luminous Anne Parillaud, was a throbbing, stylish look at a convicted murderess who receives secret government training as a hired gun. Remade here with a plodding hand by John Badham and featuring an ill-at-ease Bridget Fonda, what was once witty, if somewhat vacuous, entertainment has been reduced to a series of one-dimensional thrills. There's a fine supporting cast, but this still ends up as a rather gutless piece. SH. Contains violence, swearing, sex scenes, nudity. DVD

Bridget Fonda *Maggie* • Gabriel Byrne *Bob* • Dermot Mulroney *J P* • Miguel Ferrer *Kaufman* • Anne Bancroft *Amanda* • Olivia D'Abo *Angela* • Richard Romanus *Fahd Bahktiar* • Harvey Keitel *Victor the cleaner* ■ *Dir* John Badham • *Scr* Robert Getchell, Alexandra Seros, from the film *Nikita* by Luc Besson

Assassin for Hire ★★

Crime drama 1951 · UK/US · BW · 66mins

A dependable supporting player, Sydney Tafler was always on the verge of the action as a sneaky crook or a disreputable nightclub owner. Here he has one of his rare opportunities in a leading role and he acquits himself very ably as a professional killer, under pressure from an enterprising detective. Director Michael McCarthy gets a surprising amount of suspense from the slightest of stories. DP

Sydney Tafler *Antonio Riccardi* • Ronald Howard *Inspector Carson* • John Hewer *Guiseppi Riccardi* • Kathryn Blake [Katharine Blake] *Maria Riccardi* • Gerald Case *Sergeant Scott* • Ian Wallace *Charlie* • Martin Benson *Catesby* ■ *Dir* Michael McCarthy • *Scr* Rex Rientis

Assassin of the Tsar ★★★ 15

Psychological drama
1991 · Rus/UK · Colour · 100mins

Malcolm McDowell stars as a psychiatric patient who believes he assassinated the Tsar and his family in 1918. From his hospital bed in present-day Moscow, McDowell is taken back to the past by his psychiatrist, Oleg Yankovsky (who also plays the Tsar), in an attempt to free him of his delusion. Shot in both English and Russian versions, its flaws are obvious. However, McDowell's portrait of schizophrenia is often disturbing, and the whole picture is a fascinating and gripping study of madness. TS. Russian dialogue dubbed into English.

Malcolm McDowell *Timofeev/Yurovsky* • Oleg Yankovsky *Dr Smirnov/Tsar Nicholas Ii* • Armen Dzhigarkhanyan *Alexander Egorovich* • Iurii Sherstnev *Kozlov* • Angela Ptashuk *Marina* • Viktor Seferov *Voikov* ■ *Dir* Karen Shakhnazarov • *Scr* Aleksandr Borodianskii, Karen Shakhnazarov

Assassination ★★ 15

Thriller 1986 · US · Colour · 84mins

Charles Bronson is the minder to the American president's wife (here played by Bronson's own wife, Jill Ireland) who goes on the run with her when killers threaten. It has its moments of tension but the relationship never achieves much credibility. Bronson dozes off in scene one and doesn't even begin to stir before the end. JM. Contains swearing and violence.

Charles Bronson *Jay Killian* • Jill Ireland *Lara Royce Craig* • Stephen Elliott *Fitzroy* • Jan Gan Boyd *Charlotte Chang* • Randy Brooks *Tyler Loudermilk* • Michael Ansara *Senator Hector Bunsen* • Erik Stern *Reno Bracken* ■ *Dir* Peter Hunt • *Scr* Richard Sale

The Assassination Bureau ★★★★

Period black comedy
1969 · UK · Colour · 111mins

This dry period comedy stars Diana Rigg as a journalist infiltrating a gang of professional killers whose members only accept contracts on those who "deserve" to die. Director Basil Dearden infuses the tale with joyous glee and no little character insight as Rigg persuades the gang's leader, Oliver Reed, to allow himself to become a target as a challenge to his professionalism. It's a clever twist in a madcap yarn by Jack London and Robert Fish, while Reed is wonderfully malevolent through his charm, while the quality cast gauges the light tone perfectly. TH

Oliver Reed *Ivan Dragomiloff* • Diana Rigg *Sonya Winter* • Telly Savalas *Lord Bostwick* • Curt Jurgens *General von Pinck* • Philippe Noiret *Lucoville* • Warren Mitchell *Weiss* • Beryl Reid *Madame Otero* • Clive Revill *Cesare Spado* ■ *Dir* Basil Dearden • *Scr* Michael Relph, from the novel *The Assassination Bureau Limited* by Jack London, Robert Fish

The Assassination of Richard Nixon ★★★ 15

Biographical drama
2004 · US · Colour · 95mins

Based on little-known but actual events of 1974, this stars Sean Penn as Samuel Bicke, an American whose grip on reality fails at the same time as his marriage. As both his personal life and fledgling business founder, Bicke channels his dissatisfaction into a plan to assassinate the president. The film features a strong performance from Penn, aided by Don Cheadle and Naomi Watts as the friend and estranged wife respectively. The film misses an opportunity to say something new about what drives disturbed individuals to such acts, but Penn still brings fascinating shades of light and dark to a striking story of American madness. KK. Contains swearing and violence.

Sean Penn *Samuel Bicke* • Naomi Watts *Marie Bicke* • Don Cheadle *Bonny Simmons* • Jack Thompson *Jack Jones* • Brad Henke *Martin Jones* • Michael Wincott *Julius Bicke* • Mykelti Williamson *Harold Mann* • April Grace *Mae Simmons* ■ *Dir* Nils Mueller • *Scr* Nils Mueller, Kevin Kennedy

The Assassination of Trotsky ★★ 15

Historical drama
1972 · Fr/It · Colour · 98mins

Despite being shot on authentic locations, Joseph Losey's botched film is often dull and fatally lacking in both historical perspective and on-screen drama. Richard Burton acts his socks off as Leon Trotsky, the Russian revolutionary who was gruesomely murdered on Stalin's orders in Mexico City in 1940.However, while Alain Delon has a certain menace as the assassin, he's never a flesh-and-blood character. The film was a flop everywhere. AT. Contains violent scenes. DVD

Richard Burton *Leon Trotsky* • Alain Delon *Frank Jacson* • Romy Schneider *Gita* • Valentina Cortese *Natasha* • Luigi Vannucchi *Ruiz* • Duilio Del Prete *Felipe* • Simone Valère *Mrs Rosmer* ■ *Dir* Joseph Losey • *Scr* Nicholas Mosley, Masolino D'Amico

Assassination Tango ★★ 15

Romantic thriller
2002 · US · Colour · 109mins

Robert Duvall allows a private passion to cloud his professional judgement with this Argentina-set thriller in this self-directed drama. Indeed, his portrayal of a hitman who is seduced by dancer Luciana Pedraza while on a mission to Buenos Aires ranks among the worst of an illustrious career, as there's no nobility or heart in the meticulous killer. Moreover, there's too little narrative justification (beside Duvall's genuine fascination with the tango) for stalling an already turgid thriller to put Pedraza through her paces. DP. Contains swearing and violence. DVD

Robert Duvall *John J Anderson* • Rubén Blades *Miguel* • Kathy Baker *Maggie* • Luciana Pedraza *Manuela* • Julio Oscar Mechoso *Orlando* • James Keane *Whitey* • Frank Gio *Frankie* • Katherine Micheaux Miller *Jenny* • Frank Cassavetes *Jo Jo* ■ *Dir/Scr* Robert Duvall

Assassins ★★★ 15

Action thriller 1995 · US · Colour · 127mins

This film should carry a warning: don't look too deeply for rhyme or reason or you'll end up with a nasty headache. Just ignore the holes in the plot and concentrate instead on the rivalry that develops between hitmen Sylvester Stallone and Antonio Banderas, especially when Stallone becomes enamoured of their target, hacker supreme Julianne Moore. Director Richard Donner lets Banderas get away with a lazy performance, but Stallone has rarely been so interesting. DP. Contains swearing, violence. DVD

Sylvester Stallone *Robert Rath* • Antonio Banderas *Miguel Bain* • Julianne Moore *Electra* • Anatoly Davydov *Nicolai* • Muse Watson *Ketcham* • Stephen Kahan [Steve Kahan] *Alan Branch* • Kelly Rowan *Jennifer* ■ *Dir* Richard Donner • *Scr* Andy Wachowski, Larry Wachowski, Brian Helgeland, from a story by Andy Wachowski, Larry Wachowski

Assault ★★ 18

Thriller 1970 · UK · Colour · 90mins

Made by *Carry On* producer Peter Rogers, this drama stars Suzy Kendall as an art teacher whose pupils are being targeted by a killer/rapist. Hoping to trap the murderer before he strikes again, she offers herself to the police as a decoy. Apart from its rather leery approach to the subject matter, this is a resolutely old-fashioned whodunnit, complete with a gallery of not-so-likely suspects, a series of mini-skirted would-be victims and a baffled cop played by Frank Finlay. AT

Suzy Kendall *Julie West* • Frank Finlay *Det Chief Supt John Velyan* • James Laurenson *Dr Gregory Lomax* • Lesley-Anne Down *Tessa Hurst* • Freddie Jones *Denning* • Tony Beckley *Leslie Sanford* • Dilys Hamlett *Mrs Sanford* ■ *Dir* Sidney Hayers • *Scr* John Kruse, from the novel *The Ravine* by Kendal Young

The Assault ★★★ PG

Drama 1986 · Neth · Colour · 120mins

Winner of the Oscar for best foreign film, this is a harrowing study of how a victim of the Nazi occupation of Holland is continually reminded of the horrific night when his entire family was arrested and executed in reprisal for the death of a collaborator. Derek De Lint conveys some of the survivor's pain and resilience, but the impact of this shocking incident is rather lost as the film comes up to date, with neither De Lint's encounters with others who were involved in the "assault" nor his moments of crushing guilt and depression having quite the same dramatic intensity. DP. In Dutch with English subtitles.

Derek De Lint *Anton Steenwijk* • Marc Van Uchelen *Anton as a boy* • Monique van de Ven *Truus Coster/Saskia De Graaff* • John Kraaykamp *Cor Takes* • Elly Weller *Mrs Beumer* • Ina Van Der Molen *Karin Korteweg* ■ *Dir* Fons Rademakers • *Scr* Gerard Soeteman, from the novel by Harry Mulisch

Assault on a Queen ★ U

Crime caper 1966 · US · Colour · 106mins

In *Ocean's 11*, Frank Sinatra and his cronies held up five casinos in Las Vegas. In this follow-up, Ol' Blue Eyes and even more cronies raise a U-boat from the ocean shallows to plunder the *Queen Mary* and its well-heeled passengers. It's heavy-handed in all departments, with leaden direction by Jack Donohue. AT

Frank Sinatra *Mark Brittain* • Virna Lisi *Rosa Lucchesi* • Tony Franciosa [Anthony Franciosa] *Vic Rossiter* • Richard Conte *Tony Moreno* • Alf Kjellin *Eric Lauffnauer* • Errol John *Linc Langley* ■ *Dir* Jack Donohue • *Scr* Rod Serling, from the novel by Jack Finney

Assault on Precinct 13 ★★★★ 18

Thriller 1976 · US · Colour · 87mins

Cult director John Carpenter's hybrid of *Rio Bravo* and *Night of the Living Dead* is a model of low-budget film-making and ranks as one of the best B-movies ever made in the urban horror/action genre. In this gripping thriller, a nearly abandoned police station in the worst neighbourhood in Los Angeles is placed under siege for harbouring the killer of a street gang's fearless leader. Paranoia abounds as Austin Stoker and his motley crew of quipping cops are attacked from all sides with no escape route. Carpenter also supplies a taut synthesiser score which adds untold atmosphere to this minor gem. AJ. Contains violence and swearing. DVD

Austin Stoker *Ethan Bishop* • Darwin Joston *Napoleon Wilson* • Laurie Zimmer *Leigh* • Martin West *Lawson* • Tony Burton *Wells* • Kim Richards *Kathy* ■ *Dir/Scr* John Carpenter

Assault on Precinct 13 ★★★ 15

Action thriller
2005 · US/Fr · Colour · 104mins

John Carpenter's cult classic – a simple urban western set in an isolated, sparsely manned Detroit police station under siege during its final night before closure – gets an exciting, contemporary re-working here. The relentless assailants want laid-back crime lord Laurence Fishburne, which forces the prisoners and cops inside into an uneasy alliance. Director Jean-François Richet cranks up the tension and the acting is enjoyable, too – despite some corny dialogue and clichéd characters – with Ethan Hawke's emotionally scarred police sergeant a particular standout. SF. Contains swearing, violence. DVD

Ethan Hawke *Sergeant Jake Roenick* • Laurence Fishburne *Marion Bishop* • John Leguizamo *Beck* • Maria Bello *Alex Sabian* • Jeffrey "Ja Rule" Atkins [Ja Rule] *Smiley* • Drea de Matteo *Iris Ferry* • Matt Craven *Capra* • Brian Dennehy *Jasper O'Shea* • Gabriel Byrne *Marcus Duvall* • Aisha Hinds *Anna* ■ *Dir* Jean-François Richet • *Scr* James DeMonaco, from the film by John Carpenter

The Assignment ★★ 18

Thriller 1997 · Can/US · Colour · 114mins

Director Christian Duguay dishes up a steady stream of graphic action in this thriller based on the story of real-life terrorist Carlos the Jackal. Aidan Quinn stars in a dual role, as the Jackal himself and an American naval officer with a remarkable resemblance to the wanted man. Donald Sutherland plays a CIA veteran obsessed with getting revenge for past humiliation, with Ben Kingsley as a Mossad agent eager to rid the world of the assassin. Despite the formulaic subject matter, this is well paced and moderately exciting fare. AJ. Contains nudity, swearing and violence. DVD

Aidan Quinn *Annibal Ramirez/Carlos* • Donald Sutherland *Jack Shaw/Henry Fields* • Ben Kingsley *Amos* • Claudia Ferri *Maura Ramirez* • Celine Bonnier *Carla* • Vlasta Vrana *KGB Head officer* • Liliana Komorowska *Agnieska* • Von Flores *Koj* ■ *Dir* Christian Duguay • *Scr* Dan Gordon, Sabi H Shabtai

Assignment K ★★ U

Spy drama 1968 · UK · Colour · 90mins

Director Val Guest is unable to bring to life this moribund espionage tale. Stephen Boyd gives a charmless performance as a spy working undercover as a toy manufacturer. Slowly he comes to realise that almost everyone he has trusted has deceived him. Camilla Sparv is adequate as his German girlfriend, but Michael Redgrave, as his loyal lieutenant, and Leo McKern, as his nemesis, contribute little. DP

Stephen Boyd *Philip Scott* • Camilla Sparv *Toni Peters* • Michael Redgrave *Harris* • Leo McKern *Smith* • Jeremy Kemp *Hal* • Robert Hoffmann *Paul Spiegler* • Jane Merrow *Martine* ■ *Dir* Val Guest • *Scr* Val Guest, Bill Strutton, Maurice Foster, from the novel *Department K* by Hartley Howard

Assignment – Paris ★★ U

Spy drama 1952 · US · BW · 84mins

This unremarkable Cold War thriller stars Dana Andrews as a reporter in the Paris office of the *New York Herald Tribune* who uncovers a conspiracy in Budapest. The communists throw him in jail and shoot him full of truth drugs; his editor (George Sanders) tries to forget that Andrews stole his girlfriend (Marta Toren) and fights for his release. Critics at the time thought the whole thing far-fetched; nowadays, it's just rather ho-hum. AT

Dana Andrews *Jimmy Race* • Marta Toren *Jeanne Moray* • George Sanders *Nick Strang* • Audrey Totter *Sandy Tate* • Sandro Giglio *Grischa* • Donald Randolph *Anton Borvitch* • Herbert Berghof *Andreas Ordy* ■ *Dir* Robert Parrish • *Scr* William Bowers, Paul Gallico, Jack Palmer White, from the story *Trial by Terror* by Paul Gallico, Pauline Gallico

Assignment Redhead ★

Crime drama 1956 · UK · BW · 80mins

Also known as *Million Dollar Manhunt*, this dismal thriller has all the hallmarks of a Butcher's production: shoddy script, cheap settings and a cast of has-beens and no-hopers. Ronald Adam can just about hold his head up as the crook intent on blagging $12 million worth of counterfeit Nazi cash. But Richard Denning as the agent on his tail and Carole Mathews as the singer who switches sides are just inept. DP

Richard Denning *Keen* • Carole Mathews *Hedy* • Ronald Adam *Scammel/Dumetrius* • Danny Green *Yottie* • Brian Worth *Ridgeway* • Jan Holden *Sally* ■ *Dir* Maclean Rogers • *Scr* Maclean Rogers, from the novel *Requiem for a Redhead* by Al Bocca

Assignment to Kill ★★

Crime drama 1968 · US · Colour · 99mins

International intrigue abounds in this tale of an insurance investigator on the trail of a dodgy European bigwig whose ships have a habit of going belly-up. The hero is played by Patrick O'Neal, while his prey is none other than a busking John Gielgud, whose lilting tones add a touch of class to the proceedings. Peter Van Eyck and Herbert Lom play heavies, Eric Portman is a corrupt civil servant, while Oscar Homolka pops up as an apoplectic Swiss policeman. AT

Patrick O'Neal *Richard Cutting* • Joan Hackett *Dominique Laurant* • John Gielgud *Curt Valayan* • Herbert Lom *Matt Wilson* • Eric Portman *Notary* • Peter Van Eyck *Walter Green* • Oscar Homolka *Inspector Ruff* ■ *Dir/Scr* Sheldon Reynolds

The Assisi Underground ★ PG

Second World War drama
1985 · It/US · Colour · 109mins

Underground is where this Second World War drama should have stayed. Its truth-based story of an Assisi-centred network, smuggling disguised Jewish refugees out of Italy via Franciscan monasteries, needed its own lifeline of credibility but didn't get it from a muddled script and banal direction. Ben Cross and James Mason are among those wasted in an important story that deserved better treatment. TH

Ben Cross *Padre Rufino* • James Mason *Bishop Nicolini* • Irene Papas *Mother Giuseppina* • Maximilian Schell *Colonel Mueller* • Karl-Heinz Hackl *Captain von Velden* ■ *Dir* Alexander Ramati • *Scr* Alexander Ramati, from his novel

The Associate ★★ PG

Comedy drama 1996 · US · Colour · 108mins

Whoopi Goldberg stars as a Wall Street analyst who can't move up the career ladder because she's a woman. Taking the rather radical action of setting up her own company with a fictitious male partner, matters are further complicated when her excuses for his absences run out and she actually has to produce the mystery man. Despite fun performances from Goldberg, Dianne Wiest and Bebe Neuwirth, there just aren't enough jokes. JB DVD

Whoopi Goldberg *Laurel* • Dianne Wiest *Sally* • Eli Wallach *Fallon* • Tim Daly [Timothy Daly] *Frank* • Bebe Neuwirth *Camille* • Austin Pendleton *Aesop* • Lainie Kazan *Cindy Mason* • George Martin (1) *Manchester* ■ *Dir* Donald Petrie • *Scr* Nick Thiel, from the film *L'Associé* by Jean-Claude Carrière and René Gainville, and the novel *El Socio* by Jenaro Prieto

Asterix and Cleopatra ★★★ U

Animated adventure
1968 · Fr/Bel · Colour · 72mins

Following on from *Asterix the Gaul*, this is the second animated feature culled from the classic comic books by René Goscinny and Albert Uderzo. Once again, the pair took dual directorial responsibility for this amusing (if racially suspect) odyssey, in which Asterix, Obelix, his pet pooch Dogmatix and the potion-brewing druid Getafix set out to cock a snook at Caesar by building a palace for the Queen of the Nile, whose retroussé nose is the talk

A

of the Roman Empire. DP. French dialogue dubbed into English. [video]

Dir René Goscinny, Albert Uderzo • *Scr* René Goscinny, Albert Uderzo, Pierre Tchernia, from the comic book by René Goscinny, Albert Uderzo

Asterix & Obelix: Mission Cleopatra ★★★ PG

Comedy fantasy adventure
2001 · Fr/Ger · Colour · 103mins

More in the spirit of Goscinny and Uderzo than Claude Zidi's Hollywoodised blockbuster *Asterix and Obelix Take on Caesar*, this is still nowhere near as satisfying as reading the original comic book. However, it's a vast improvement, as director Alain Chabat not only trusts his story, but also keeps a much tighter rein on Christian Clavier's exuberance and Gérard Depardieu's buffoonery. Monica Bellucci is perfectly cast as the Egyptian queen who demands that architect Jamel Debbouze build a golden palace within three months to win a bet with Caesar (Chabat). DP. In French with English subtitles. Contains some swearing. DVD

Gérard Depardieu *Obelix* • Christian Clavier *Asterix* • Jamel Debbouze *Numerobis* • Monica Bellucci *Cleopatra* • Alain Chabat *Julius Caesar* • Claude Rich *Panoramix* • Gérard Darmon *Amonbofis* ■ *Dir* Alain Chabat • *Scr* Alain Chabat, from the comic book by René Goscinny, Albert Uderzo

Asterix and Obelix Take On Caesar ★★ PG

Comedy fantasy adventure
1999 · Fr/Ger/It · Colour · 105mins

It may be one of the most expensive French movies ever made, but Claude Zidi's live-action romp has none of the wit or charm of the original comic books. With Christian Clavier and Gérard Depardieu well cast as the indomitable Gauls and Roberto Benigni milking every gag as a scheming centurion, the acting is suitably pantomimic. But the inability of Terry Jones (who penned the English language script and dubbed Depardieu) to duplicate René Goscinny's sublime linguistic games undermines the cast's efforts. DP. French dialogue dubbed into English. [video] DVD

Christian Clavier *Astérix* • Gérard Depardieu *Obélix* • Roberto Benigni *Detritus* • Marianne Sägebrecht *Bonnemine* • Gottfried John *César* • Laetitia Casta *Falbala* • Michel Galabru *Abaracourcix* • Claude Piéplu *Panoramix* ■ *Dir* Claude Zidi • *Scr* Claude Zidi, Gérard Lauzier, from the comic books by René Goscinny, Albert Uderzo

Asterix and the Big Fight ★★ U

Animated adventure
1989 · Fr/W Ger · Colour · 80mins

For fans of the Goscinny/Uderzo comic books, this is a bit of a letdown. Here, the wily Asterix tries to restore the memory of the village soothsayer so that his powers can be used in the fight against the Romans. The animation is rather stilted, and the British voices (Bill Oddie, Bernard Bresslaw, Ron Moody) are too well-known to let the characters speak for themselves. The puns and Latin gags are still great fun, however. TH. French dialogue dubbed into English. [video]

Bill Oddie *Asterix* • Bernard Bresslaw *Obelix* • Ron Moody *Prolix* • Brian Blessed *Caous* • Sheila Hancock *Impedimenta* • Andrew Sachs *Ardeco* ■ *Dir* Philippe Grimond • *Scr* George Roubicek, from the comic book by René Goscinny, Albert Uderzo

Asterix Conquers America ★★ U

Animated adventure
1994 · Ger · Colour · 81mins

Asterix's adventures are hardly the most politically correct at the best of times, but this adaptation is guilty of some unforgivable racist lapses. The story of Getafix's rescue from the New World is not the strongest in the series, though the anachronistic gags are as sharp as ever, while the familiar drawing style atones for the rather uninspired voiceovers. DP. German dialogue dubbed into English. [video]

John Rye *Narrator* • Craig Charles *Asterix* • Howard Lew Lewis *Obelix* • Henry McGee *Caesar* • Christopher Biggins *Lucullus* • Geoffrey Bayldon *Getafix* ■ *Dir* Gerhard Hahn • *Scr* Thomas Platt, Rhett Rooster, from an idea by Pierre Tchernia, Albert Uderzo, from the comic book *Asterix and the Great Crossing* by René Goscinny, Albert Uderzo

Asterix in Britain ★★★ U

Animated adventure
1986 · Fr · Colour · 75mins

By Jupiter! How superbus! In another animated movie to be lifted from the text and drawings of Goscinny and Uderzo's books, the pun-struck Gallic heroes come to the aid of a British village that's just been invaded by the Romans. The wily Asterix and the galumphing Obelix are on hand to satirise national stereotypes, and the puns are enough to make "wincemeat" of us all. TH. French dialogue dubbed into English. [video]

Jack Beaber *Asterix* • Bill Kearns [Billy Kearns] *Obelix* • Graham Bushnell *Anticlimax/Jolitorax* • Herbert Baskind *Totalapsus* • Jimmy Shuman *Chateaupetrus* • Ed Marcus *Stratocumulus* ■ *Dir* Pino Van Lamsweerde • *Scr* Pierre Tchernia, from the comic book by René Goscinny, Albert Uderzo

Asterix the Gaul ★★★ U

Animated adventure
1967 · Bel/Fr · Colour · 65mins

Almost a decade after the publication of René Goscinny and Albert Uderzo's first comic book, Asterix and his friends found their way on to the big screen. Made in Belgium, this is pretty much an introductory exercise, as the secret of Getafix's magic potion, the story behind Obelix's ludicrous strength and the reasons why Caesar's legions can't conquer a tiny Gaullish village are all explained. But there's also plenty of action as Asterix and his menhir-carrying chum set out to rescue their druid from an ambitious centurion. DP. French dialogue dubbed into English. [video]

Dir/Scr René Goscinny, Albert Uderzo

Asterix vs Caesar ★★★ U

Animated adventure
1985 · Fr · Colour · 73mins

Combining plotlines from *Asterix the Legionary* and *Asterix the Gladiator*, this big-screen adaptation of the bestselling adventures of the indomitable Gaul and his doltish sidekick, Obelix, follows on from *The 12 Tasks of Asterix*. The American dubbing grates horribly, but the puns are as deliciously bad as ever. The parodies of *Spartacus* and *Ben-Hur* should amuse, while aficionados might like to know that screenwriter Pierre Tchernia appears on p37 of Uderzo and Goscinny's original 1967 edition of *Legionary*. DP. French dialogue dubbed into English. [video]

Jack Bearber *Asterix* • Bill Kearns [Billy Kearns] *Obelix* • Allen Wenger *Caius Flavius* • Gordon Heath *Julius Caesar* ■ *Dir* Gaetan Brizzi, Paul Brizzi • *Scr* Pierre Tchernia, from the comic book by René Goscinny, Albert Uderzo

The Asthenic Syndrome ★★★★

Drama
1989 · USSR · Colour and BW · 153mins

Kira Muratova has made only eight features in her 30-year career, and this uncompromising study of the last days of the USSR shows why she had so much trouble with the Soviet censors and why she's ranked among the most important of all women film-makers. The winner of the Special Jury Prize at the Berlin film festival, the film suggests that Communist rule has subjected the entire population to asthenia, a condition that induces dejected passivity in times of stress. The pain of the opening monochrome sequence and the stark realism of the Moscow scenes make for most uncomfortable yet compelling viewing. DP. In Russian with English subtitles.

Sergei Popov *Nikolai* • Olga Antonova *Natascha* • Natalia Busko *Mascha, the brunette* • Galina Sakurdaeva *Mascha, the blonde* • Aleksandra Ovenskaia *Lehrerin* • Pavel Polischnuk • Natalia Rallewa ■ *Dir* Kira Muratova • *Scr* Kira Muratova, Sergei Popov, Aleksandr Chernitch, Vladimir Pankov

The Astonished Heart ★

Romantic drama
1949 · UK · BW · 87mins

Noël Coward stars a psychiatrist whose understanding wife (Celia Johnson) attempts to condone his adultery with her beautiful best friend (Margaret Leighton). A low point in the career of all three principals and co-director Terence Fisher, it sank into almost immediate obscurity. RK

Noël Coward *Christian Faber* • Celia Johnson *Barbara Faber* • Margaret Leighton *Leonora Vail* • Joyce Carey *Susan Birch* • Graham Payn *Tim Verney* • Amy Veness *Alice Smith* • Ralph Michael *Philip Lucas* • Michael Hordern *Ernest* ■ *Dir* Terence Fisher, Anthony Damborough • *Scr* Noël Coward, from his play

The Astounding She-Monster ★★

Science-fiction horror
1958 · US · BW · 59mins

A super-tall female alien in a skin-tight metallic spacesuit, spangled tights and high heels lands on Earth and uses her glow-in-the-dark touch to kill. A group of loyal citizens band together to fight the intergalactic menace in a prime example of ultra-cheap 1950s trash, which is so bad it's actually quite good fun. Pitiful special effects and deadly dull nocturnal strolls through the forest by the extraordinary-looking She-Monster (Shirley Kilpatrick) add to its camp charm. AJ

Robert Clarke *Dick Cutler* • Kenne Duncan *Nat Burdell* • Marilyn Harvey *Margaret Chaffee* • Jeanne Tatum *Esther Malone* • Shirley Kilpatrick *Monster* • Ewing Brown *Brad Conley* ■ *Dir* Ronnie Ashcroft • *Scr* Frank Hall

The Astronaut's Wife ★★ 18

Science-fiction psychological thriller
1999 · US · Colour · 109mins

One wonders what an actor with the impeccable taste of Johnny Depp was doing accepting the lead in Rand Ravich's directorial debut. Playing an astronaut who starts behaving oddly after an accident in space, Depp brings an undeserved degree of credibility to what is a derivative and unshocking sci-fi rehash of *Rosemary's Baby*. This is too serious for its own good, and no amount of inventive direction from Ravich can save it. AC. Contains violence, swearing and sex scenes. [video] DVD

Johnny Depp *Spencer Armacost* • Charlize Theron *Jillian Armacost* • Joe Morton *Sherman Reese* • Clea DuVall *Nan* • Samantha Eggar *Doctor* • Donna Murphy *Natalie Streck* • Nick Cassavetes *Alex Streck* • Gary Grubbs *NASA director* ■ *Dir/Scr* Rand Ravich

Asya's Happiness ★★★★★ PG

Drama 1967 · USSR · BW · 97mins

Suppressed by the Communist authorities because of the critical political opinions expressed by some of the male characters and not released abroad until the late 1980s, this film exemplifies why director Andrei Mikhalkov-Konchalovsky was one of the USSR's premier directors before decamping to Hollywood and taking on more commercial fare (as plain Andrei Konchalovsky). The magnificent Iya Savvina, supported by a largely non-professional and extraordinarily natural cast, stars in this account of life and hardships in a rural village. This absorbing and moving film is rich in detail, authentic atmosphere and honesty. RK. In Russian with English subtitles.

Iya Savvina *Asya Klyachinka* • Lyubov Sokolova • Alexander Surin • Gennady Yegorychev ■ *Dir* Andrei Mikhalkov-Konchalovsky [Andrei Konchalovsky] • *Scr* Ivan Petrov, Yuri Klepikov

Asylum ★★★ 15

Horror 1972 · UK · Colour · 88mins

This rippingly good terror anthology of *Psycho* author Robert Bloch's tales showcases reanimated, dismembered limbs, a magic suit, homicidal split personalities and tiny murdering robots. With an ingenious linking device – each story is a mental patient's case history – building to a *Grand Guignol* twist finale, the excellent cast wrings every ounce of horror from a clever script, while the underplayed black humour is a bonus. AJ. Contains violence. [video] DVD

Peter Cushing *Smith* • Britt Ekland *Lucy* • Herbert Lom *Byron* • Patrick Magee *Dr Rutherford* • Barry Morse *Bruno* • Barbara Parkins *Bonnie* • Robert Powell *Dr Martin* • Charlotte Rampling *Barbara* • Sylvia Syms *Ruth* • Richard Todd *Walter* ■ *Dir* Roy Ward Baker • *Scr* Robert Bloch, from his stories

At Close Range ★★★★ 15

Drama based on a true story
1985 · US · Colour · 110mins

This powerful drama about crime and misguided family loyalties features a magnificent performance from Sean Penn as the bored son who's lured into the world of gangsters by evil dad Christopher Walken. Downbeat and very tough, the grim tale is even more compelling and chilling for being true. Director James Foley's decision to shoot the movie with documentary-style realism is one of the movie's great strengths, as it gives the gripping chain of events a pervasive atmosphere of simmering violence that's tremendously effective. AJ. Contains swearing, violence. [video] DVD

Sean Penn *Brad Whitewood Jr* • Christopher Walken *Brad Whitewood Sr* • Mary Stuart Masterson *Terry* • Christopher Penn [Chris Penn] *Tommy Whitewood* • Millie Perkins *Julie Whitewood* • Eileen Ryan *Grandmother* • Kiefer Sutherland *Tim* ■ *Dir* James Foley • *Scr* Nicholas Kazan, from a story by Elliott Lewitt, Nicholas Kazan • *Cinematographer* Juan Ruiz-Anchia

...At First Sight ★★★

Romantic comedy
1995 · US · Colour · 90mins

Jonathan Silverman stars as a lovable schmuck who's dating the lovely Allison Smith. But his pal Dan Cortese bullies him into more adventurous romantic escapades. Like its main characters, however, it doesn't really go anywhere. The film features a hilarious cameo from voice actress Pamela Segall as a wallflower turned vamp. ST

Dan Cortese *Joey Fortone* • Jonathan Silverman *Lenny Kaminski* • Allison Smith *Rhonda Glick* • Monte Markham *Lester Glick* •

Kathleen Freeman *Grandma* • Susan Walters *Cindy One* • Pamela Segall *Tracy* ■ *Dir* Steven Pearl • *Scr* Ken Copel

At First Sight ★★★ 12

Drama 1998 · US · Colour · 123mins

Like *Awakenings*, this medical melodrama is also drawn from the casebook of Dr Oliver Sacks, but it's not so dramatically satisfying and is less well acted. However, the tale of courage is so remarkable that any filming of it would seem trite and sentimental. Val Kilmer's infuriatingly mannered performance doesn't help matters, but Kelly McGillis as his sister and Mira Sorvino as his lover give accompished performances that prevent the material from entering disease-of-the-week TV movie territory. No classic, but thoughtful and solidly crafted. DP. Contains swearing and brief nudity. DVD

Val Kilmer *Virgil Adamson* • Mira Sorvino *Amy Benic* • Kelly McGillis *Jennie Adamson* • Steven Weber *Duncan Allanbrook* • Bruce Davison *Dr Charles Aaron* • Nathan Lane *Phil Webster* • Ken Howard *Virgil's father* • Laura Kirk *Betsy Ernst* • Jack Dodick *Dr Goldman* • Oliver Sacks *Reporter* ■ *Dir* Irwin Winkler • *Scr* Steve Levitt, from the article *To See and Not See* from *An Anthropologist on Mars* by Oliver Sacks

At Five in the Afternoon ★★★★ U

Drama 2003 · Ir/Fr · Colour · 101mins

Although the focus of this incisive blend of social reality and romantic idealism is on the discrimination still facing women in post-Taliban Afghanistan, Iranian director Samira Makhmalbaf also highlights the extent to which everyone's beliefs and duties are determined by the politico-cultural agendas of the powers that be. The bleak landscape captured by Ebrahim Ghafori's camera reinforces the sense of despair that prompts Abdolgani Yousefrazi to keep his family constantly on the move around a combat-scarred Kabul. But the charmingly expressive Agheleh Rezaie's minor acts of defiance and outspoken self-confidence provide an optimistic challenge to the status quo. DP. In Farsi with English subtitles. DVD

Agheleh Rezaie *Noqreh* • Abdolgani Yousefrazi *Father* • Razi Mohebi *Poet* ■ *Dir* Samira Makhmalbaf • *Scr* Samira Makhmalbaf, Mohsen Makhmalbaf

At Gunpoint ★★ U

Western 1955 · US · Colour · 81mins

This is a very average Allied Artists western owing much to *High Noon* in its plotting. It stars a very glum Fred MacMurray, but the ever-glamorous Dorothy Malone (seemingly born to play frontierswomen) is the main attraction here, doing sterling work as Fred's wife. The whole benefits from being filmed in CinemaScope, but director Alfred Werker's pace is just too slow for comfort. TS

Fred MacMurray *Jack Wright* • Dorothy Malone *Martha Wright* • Walter Brennan *Doc Lacy* • Tommy Rettig *Billy* • John Qualen *Livingstone* • Irving Bacon *Ferguson* • Skip Homeier *Bob* • Jack Lambert *Kirk* ■ *Dir* Alfred Werker • *Scr* Daniel B Ullman

At Long Last Love ★★ U

Musical romance
1975 · US · Colour · 114mins

Despite predictions that this spoof on 1930s' musicals would become a cult classic to look back on with affection, it's embarrassing the way aspiration became affectation. Playboy Burt Reynolds, icy-blonde Cybill Shepherd, Broadway star Madeline Kahn and gambler Duilio Del Prete find contrivances to weave in and out of 16 Cole Porter songs, and get lost in the process. TH

Burt Reynolds *Michael Oliver Pritchard III* • Cybill Shepherd *Brooke Carter* • Madeline Kahn *Kitty O'Kelly* • Duilio Del Prete *Johnny Spanish* • Eileen Brennan *Elizabeth* • John Hillerman *Rodney James* • Mildred Natwick *Mabel Pritchard* • Quinn Redeker *Phillip* • M Emmet Walsh *Harold* ■ *Dir/Scr* Peter Bogdanovich • *Music* Cole Porter

At Play in the Fields of the Lord ★★ 15

Adventure drama
1991 · US · Colour · 185mins

Unless you're fascinated by the ecological issues raised, Hector Babenco's Amazonian rainforest saga is unlikely to sustain your interest throughout its mammoth running time. This tale of religious, emotional and physical conflict in one of the most beautiful vistas on Earth is sincere, and Aidan Quinn, Kathy Bates and Tom Berenger give committed performances. Alas, the unsympathetic characters, rambling plot and extreme length are hurdles Babenco is ultimately unable to overcome. JC

Tom Berenger *Lewis Moon* • John Lithgow *Leslie Huben* • Daryl Hannah *Andy Huben* • Aidan Quinn *Martin Quarrier* • Tom Waits *Wolf* • Kathy Bates *Hazel Quarrier* • Stenio Garcia *Boronai* ■ *Dir* Hector Babenco • *Scr* Jean-Claude Carrière, Hector Babenco, from the novel by Peter Matthiessen

At the Circus ★★★ U

Comedy 1939 · US · BW · 83mins

This picture marked the start of the Marx Brothers' fall from grace, as their humorous anarchy was severely restricted by MGM's big-studio regulations. Here Groucho plays a shyster lawyer who teams up with Harpo and Chico to save a circus from bankruptcy. There are some great moments but the exuberance has been toned down. The trio also seem reluctant to follow the plot, especially if it means being on the same bill as crooner Kenny Baker. TH DVD

Groucho Marx *Attorney Loophole* • Chico Marx *Antonio* • Harpo Marx *Punchy* • Kenny Baker (1) *Jeff Wilson* • Eve Arden *Peerless Pauline* • Margaret Dumont *Mrs Dukesbury* • Florence Rice *Julie Randall* • Nat Pendleton *Goliath* ■ *Dir* Edward Buzzell • *Scr* Irving Brecher

At the Earth's Core ★★ PG

Science-fiction adventure
1976 · UK · Colour · 86mins

Victorian explorer Doug McClure and fidgety scientist Peter Cushing encounter all manner of unconvincing monsters as they burrow through the earth with a giant boring device to the subterranean kingdom of Pellucidar. This childish and chintzy adaptation of an Edgar Rice Burroughs novel would be an even bigger patience-tester if not for sultry heroine Caroline Munro and the truly awful man-in-rubber-suit special effects, which will inspire hoots of laughter. AJ DVD

Doug McClure *David Innes* • Peter Cushing *Dr Abner Perry* • Caroline Munro *Dia* • Cy Grant *Ra* • Godfrey James *Ghak* • Sean Lynch *Hooja* ■ *Dir* Kevin Connor • *Scr* Milton Subotsky, from the novel by Edgar Rice Burroughs

At the Height of Summer ★★★ PG

Drama 1999 · Fr/Ger/Viet · Colour · 108mins

Vietnamese director Tran Anh Hung produces here another film of immense beauty and psychological significance. But it's also a tad convoluted and precious. There is such a focus on aquatic symbolism and the essence of ritual that it's easy to become distracted from the problems facing three Hanoi sisters. Both Le Khanh and Nguyen Nhu Quynh impress as wronged wives, but only Tran Nu Yen Khe's ambiguous relationship with her brother is untainted by sophisticated soap operatics. DP. In Vietnamese with English subtitles. DVD

Tran Nu Yen-Khe *Lien* • Nguyen Nhu Quynh *Suong* • Le Khanh *Khanh* • Ngo Quang Hai *Hai* ■ *Dir/Scr* Tran Anh Hung

At War with the Army ★★★ U

Comedy 1950 · US · BW · 91mins

The third film for comedy team Dean Martin and Jerry Lewis was a massive hit. It consolidated their screen images (Martin's the smoothie, Lewis is the nerd) and ensured their success throughout a generation.This is slapdash film-making, but also very funny, and a scene involving a soda machine is priceless. Dean croons three songs as he enjoins Jerry to help him out of female trouble, and Polly Bergen makes an attractive movie debut. TS DVD

Dean Martin *Sergeant Puccinelli* • Jerry Lewis *Private Korwin* • Mike Kellin *Sergeant McVey* • Jimmie Dundee *Eddie* • Dick Stabile *Pokey* • Tommy Farrell *Corporal Clark* • Frank Hyers *Corporal Shaughnessy* • Dan Dayton *Sergeant Miller* • Polly Bergen *Helen* ■ *Dir* Hal Walker • *Scr* Fred F Finklehoffe, from the play by James B Allardice

L'Atalante ★★★★★ PG

Romantic drama 1934 · Fr · BW · 85mins

Few films can claim to have inspired two revolutions. Jean Vigo's masterpiece not only established the visual style of 1930s poetic realism, but was also one of the key influences on the New Wave of the late 1950s. It's a simple, almost uneventful picture, chronicling barge captain Jean Dasté's first days of marriage to Dita Parlo. Yet it becomes a mesmerising personal vision thanks to Vigo's sophisticated blend of fairy-tale romance, documentary realism, surrealist fantasy, bawdy humour and song. Michel Simon's scene-stealing improvisation and the exceptional cinematography further enhance the pleasure to be derived from one of the most completely cinematic pictures ever made. DP. In French with English subtitles. DVD

Michel Simon *Père Jules* • Jean Dasté *Jean* • Dita Parlo *Juliette* • Gilles Margaritis *Pedlar* • Louis Lefebvre *Cabin boy* • Fanny Clar *Juliette's mother* • Raphael Diligent *Juliette's father* • Charles Goldblatt *Thief* • René Bleck *Best man* ■ *Dir* Jean Vigo • *Scr* Jean Vigo, Jean Guinée, Albert Riera • *Cinematographer* Boris Kaufman, Louis Berger, Jean-Paul Alphen

Atanarjuat: the Fast Runner ★★★★ 15

Drama 2001 · Can · Colour · 161mins

Set in the Canadian Arctic and based on ancient Inuit legend, the first film to be written in the Inuktitut language is a sublime cross between an anthropological study and a Jacobean tragedy. Exposing the threat posed to communal security by ambition and desire, Zacharias Kunuk's debut feature has an intimacy that belies its epic scope. After winning the heart of a woman betrothed to the son of an elder, Natar Ungalaaq earns the enmity of the man that erupts into violence. Compelling on both a dramatic and a documentary level, this is an exceptional achievement. DP. In Inuktitut with English subtitles. Contains violence, sex scenes and nudity. DVD

Natar Ungalaaq *Atanarjuat* • Sylvia Ivalu *Atuat* • Peter Henry Arnatsiaq *Oki* • Lucy Tulugarjuk *Puja* ■ *Dir* Zacharias Kunuk • *Scr* Paul Apak

Athena ★★ U

Musical 1954 · US · Colour · 95mins

An unusual idea is let down by a paper-thin plot in this musical starring Jane Powell and Debbie Reynolds as two of seven sisters who belong to a family of health and exercise fanatics. Crooner Vic Damone and cardboard cut-out Edmund Purdom are their suitors and Mr Universe-turned-movie-star Steve Reeves is on hand to support the theory about healthy living ensuring the body beautiful. Some pleasant singing livens up the routine proceedings. RK

Jane Powell *Athena* • Debbie Reynolds *Minerva* • Virginia Gibson *Niobe* • Nancy Kilgas *Aphrodite* • Dolores Starr *Calliope* • Jane Fischer *Medea* • Cecile Rogers *Ceres* • Edmund Purdom *Adam Calhorn Shaw* • Vic Damone *Johnny Nyle* • Louis Calhern *Grandpa Mulvain* • Steve Reeves *Ed Perkins* ■ *Dir* Richard Thorpe • *Scr* William Ludwig, Leonard Spigelgass

Atlantic Adventure ★★

Crime drama 1935 · US · BW · 68mins

From the days when reporters (rather than private detectives and spies) were heroic figures, comes this lively B-picture about a journalist involved in murderous intrigue and intriguing murder aboard an ocean liner. Lloyd Nolan and Nancy Carroll make the best of a not-so-bad job. TH

Nancy Carroll *Helen* • Lloyd Nolan *Dan* • Harry Langdon *Snapper* • Arthur Hohl *Frank* • Robert Middlemass *Van Dieman* • John Wray *Mitts* • EE Clive *McIntosh* • Dwight Frye *Spike* • Nana Bryant *Mrs Van Dieman* ■ *Dir* Albert S Rogell • *Scr* John T Neville, Nat Dorfman, from a story by Diana Bourbon

Atlantic City ★★★ U

Musical 1944 · US · BW · 87mins

A surprise offering from the poverty row studio Republic, this agreeable little musical chronicles the professional trials, personal tribulations and eventual triumphs of a young impresario (Brad Taylor) as he pursues his ambition to make Atlantic City into a world-class entertainment playground. The plus factors include the presence of Paul Whiteman and Louis Armstrong with their orchestras, some good musical numbers, and Constance Moore lending the turbulent romantic interest. RK

Brad Taylor [Stanley Brown] *Brad Taylor* • Constance Moore *Marilyn Whitaker* • Charley Grapewin *Jake Taylor* • Jerry Colonna *Professor* • Robert B Castaine *Carter Graham* • Adele Mara *Barmaid* • Louis Armstrong • Paul Whiteman • Dorothy Dandridge • Belle Baker ■ *Dir* Ray McCarey • *Scr* Doris Gilbert, Frank Gill Jr, George Carleton Brown, from a story by Arthur Caesar

Atlantic City, USA ★★★★★ 15

Crime drama
1980 · US/Can · Colour · 104mins

In this wonderfully beguiling and bizarre study of small-time losers from director Louis Malle, Burt Lancaster stars as a voyeuristic, over-the-hill hood reduced to running a gambling racket and living off fake memories of days with famous gangsters of yesteryear. Paradoxically, this role is one of Lancaster's best, and his performance is matched by that of Susan Sarandon as the woman with whom he becomes involved when a stash of drugs is stolen from the Mafia. Hard to define – it's neither a thriller nor a love story – this gangster movie displays abundant Gallic charm, while Sarandon is the perfect foil for Lancaster. TH. Contains violence, swearing and brief nudity. DVD

Burt Lancaster *Lou* • Susan Sarandon *Sally* • Michel Piccoli *Joseph* • Hollis McLaren *Chrissie* • Robert Joy *Dave* • Kate Reid *Grace*

• Moses Znaimer *Felix* • Al Waxman *Alfie* • Robert Goulet *Singer* ■ *Dir* Louis Malle • *Scr* John Guare

Atlantis ★★ U

Documentary 1991 · Fr · Colour · 74mins

After making *Nikita*, director Luc Besson returned to the ocean depths of *The Big Blue* for a stunningly shot but boring documentary on undersea life that proved he was no Jacques Cousteau. Concentration lapses are numerous for such a short film, barely released outside his native France. AJ. A French language film. [video] DVD

Dir Luc Besson

Atlantis, the Lost Continent ★★

Fantasy adventure
1960 · US · Colour · 90mins

Famed producer/director George Pal came unstuck with this silly fantasy after winning praise for his *The War of the Worlds* and *The Time Machine*. Anthony Hall is the young Greek sailor facing danger, animal men and atomic death rays in the final days of the fabled city before it slips into the deep, thanks to a volcanic eruption. Even the special effects are below sea level in this uneasy mix of comic-book science fiction and tacky sand-and-sandal epic. AJ

Anthony Hall [Sal Ponti] *Demetrios* • Joyce Taylor *Antillia* • John Dall *Zaren* • Bill Smith [William Smith] *Captain of the guard* • Frank De Kova *Sonoy* • Edward Platt *Azor* • Berry Kroeger *Surgeon* ■ *Dir* George Pal • *Scr* Daniel Mainwaring, from the play *Atlanta, a Story of Atlantis* by Gerald Hargreaves

Atlantis: the Lost Empire ★★★★ U

Animated fantasy adventure
2001 · US · Colour · 91mins

Taking its cue from Japanese *manga* and the current breed of adult-friendly animation, this visually delightful tale of explorers hunting for a mythical lost continent dispenses with Disney's traditional trademarks of cute animals and foot-tapping songs. Instead, it offers grown-up, multi-layered storytelling combined with a relentless pace. Exquisitely animated and voiced, the fantasy presents Atlantis as an earthly paradise, before the consequences of its characters' foibles and ambitions explode into a thrilling climax. A straight-to-video sequel, *Atlantis: Milo's Return*, followed in 2003. SF [video] DVD

Michael J Fox *Milo Thatch* • James Garner *Commander Rourke* • Cree Summer *Princess Kida* • Leonard Nimoy *King of Atlantis* • Don Novello *Vinny Santorini* • Claudia Christian *Helga Sinclair* • Jacqueline Obradors *Audrey Ramirez* • John Mahoney *Preston B Whitmore* • Corey Burton *Mole* • David Ogden Stiers *Fenton Q Harcourt* • Jim Varney *Cookie* ■ *Dir* Gary Trousdale, Kirk Wise • *Scr* Tab Murphy, from a story by Kirk Wise, Gary Trousdale, Joss Whedon, Bryce Zabel, Jackie Zabel, Tab Murphy

Atlas ★★ U

Fantasy adventure
1960 · US · Colour · 78mins

Muscles and baloney combine in this early outing from exploitation director Roger Corman, here trawling through Greek myths and dredging up risible rubbish about an Olympic champion (Michael Forest) who, despite being bribed by Praximedes (Frank Wolff), opts for democracy and fighting on behalf of the ordinary citizen. The solitary saving grace is that the film was shot in Greece. TH

Michael Forest *Atlas* • Barboura Morris *Candia* • Frank Wolff *Praximedes* • Walter Maslow *Garnis* • Christos Exarchos *Indros* • Andreas Philippides *Talectos* ■ *Dir* Roger Corman • *Scr* Charles Griffith

The Atomic Café ★★★

Satirical political documentary
1982 · US · Colour and BW · 92mins

This absorbing documentary, assembled from an amazing array of 1950s government and educational films, reveals how Americans were eased into the atomic era and the threat of possible nuclear annihilation. The film shows soldiers being subjected to A-bomb tests, while schoolchildren are taught how to "duck and cover" under their desks to avoid the harmful effects of fallout. The naive assumption that an atomic war would be survivable is one of the many shocking facts to emerge from this worthwhile nostalgia trip, which is at once scary and hilarious, informative and compelling. AJ

Dir Jayne Loader, Kevin Rafferty, Pierce Rafferty

The Atomic Kid ★★ U

Science-fiction comedy
1954 · US · BW · 85mins

Made at a time when nuclear power could be treated as a joke, this happy-go-lucky tosh has Mickey Rooney as a prospector who survives an atomic test in the desert and finds he's immune to radiation. His special powers come in handy when he helps the FBI catch a ring of communist spies. The story is by Blake Edwards, who went on to make such comic gems as *10*; this film, however, is more of a four. TH

Mickey Rooney *Blix Waterberry* • Robert Strauss *Stan Cooper* • Elaine Davis *Audrey Nelson* • Bill Goodwin *Dr Rodell* • Whit Bissell *Dr Edgar Pangborn* ■ *Dir* Leslie H Martinson • *Scr* Benedict Freedman, John Fenton Murray, from a story by Blake Edwards

The Atomic Submarine ★★ PG

Science-fiction drama
1960 · US · BW · 67mins

Endearing hokum about an underwater alien, with a nicely sustained tense atmosphere from director Spencer Gordon Bennet. But the real star of this B-movie is producer Alex Gordon, who assembled a memorable cast for movie buffs. The nominal star is Arthur Franz and in support are a veritable clutch of familiar faces, all past their sell-by date. TS [video]

Arthur Franz *Reef* • Dick Foran *Wendover* • Brett Halsey *Carl* • Tom Conway *Sir Ian Hunt* • Paul Dubov *Dave* • Bob Steele *Griff* • Victor Varconi *Kent* • Joi Lansing *Julie* ■ *Dir* Spencer G Bennet [Spencer Gordon Bennet] • *Scr* Orville H Hampton

Atomic Train ★★ PG

Disaster thriller 1999 · US · Colour · 115mins

There's plenty of disaster potential in having a locomotive hurtle towards Denver with a smuggled stash of Russian nuclear waste on board, but the combination of implausible plotting, inferior effects and plodding direction from Dick Lowry and David Jackson serves only to highlight the glaring silliness of the situation and this TV movie. DP [video] DVD

Rob Lowe *John Seger* • Kristin Davis *Megan Seger* • Esai Morales *Mac MacKenzie* • John Finn *Wally Phister* • Mena Suvari *Grace Seger* • Edward Herrmann *President* ■ *Dir* Dick Lowry, David Jackson • *Scr* D Brent Mote, Phil Penningroth, Rob Fresco, from a story by D Brent Mote, Jeff Fazio, Armand Speca, Phil Penningroth

Attack! ★★★★ PG

Second World War drama
1956 · US · BW · 103mins

Director Robert Aldrich didn't have much time for human aspirations, and never less so than in this US Army shocker about a cowardly captain (Eddie Albert) endangering the lives of his men during the Battle of the Bulge. As the heroic platoon leader, Jack Palance has never been better, and neither has Lee Marvin as the colonel presiding over the whole affair. In Aldrich's macho view, war is only hell because men make it so, but his true skill is to make these unattractive characters convincing and understandable. TH [video] DVD

Jack Palance *Lieutenant Costa* • Eddie Albert *Captain Cooney* • Lee Marvin *Colonel Bartlett* • Robert Strauss *Private Bernstein* • Richard Jaeckel *Private Snowden* • Buddy Ebsen *Sergeant Tolliver* • William Smithers *Lieutenant Woodruff* ■ *Dir* Robert Aldrich • *Scr* James Poe, from the play *The Fragile Fox* by Norman Brooks

Attack Force Z ★★ 15

Second World War drama
1981 · Aus/Tai · Colour · 89mins

John Phillip Law is the nominal star of this 1950s-style war yarn, now more notable for featuring an early performance from Mel Gibson, with able support from Sam Neill. A commando group is sent on an impossible mission to rescue the survivors of a plane wreck on a Japanese island. Some decent action scenes (filmed in Taiwan), typically dry humour and Law's trademark teak-forest performance keep the interest going, though the script quickly runs out of ideas. AT [video]

John Phillip Law *Lt JA Veitch* • Mel Gibson *Capt PG Kelly* • Sam Neill *Sgt DJ Costello* • Chris Haywood *Able Seaman AD Bird* • John Waters (3) *Sub Lt EP King* ■ *Dir* Tim Burstall • *Scr* Roger Marshall, Lee Robinson

Attack of the Crab Monsters ★★★

Science-fiction horror
1957 · US · BW · 62mins

Atomic testing on a remote Pacific island causes the crab population to mutate into giant monsters in one of cult director Roger Corman's earliest successes. The crustaceans look shoddy and laughable (you can often glimpse the stuntmen's feet under the costumes), but Charles Griffith's compact script successfully mines the concept for keen menace and gruesome shock. (The crabs decapitate victims and eat the heads in order to assimilate their brain power.) Lunatic but fast-moving fun. AJ

Richard Garland *Dale Drewer* • Pamela Duncan *Martha Hunter* • Russell Johnson *Hank Chapman* • Leslie Bradley *Dr Karl Weigand* • Mel Welles *Jules Deveroux* • Richard H Cutting *Dr James Carson* ■ *Dir* Roger Corman • *Scr* Charles Griffith

Attack of the 50 Foot Woman ★★

Cult science-fiction 1958 · US · BW · 65mins

Though it's no more than a barely competent example of low-budget 1950s sci-fi, this poverty row cheapie has come to be regarded as a legendary absurd classic. There's a strangely contemporary feminist slant to the tale, with Allison Hayes teaching her cheating husband a lesson after a bald alien turns her into a giantess, clothed in a bedsheet bikini. However, with the effects at their least special, Hayes's accelerating voluptuousness also exerts a curious fascination. AJ

Allison Hayes *Nancy Archer* • William Hudson *Harry Archer* • Roy Gordon *Dr Cushing* • Yvette Vickers *Honey Parker* • Ken Terrell *Jessup Stout* • George Douglas *Sheriff Dubbitt* ■ *Dir* Nathan Hertz [Nathan Juran] • *Scr* Mark Hanna

Attack of the 50 Ft Woman ★ 12

Science fiction 1993 · US · Colour · 89mins

A pointless revamp of the beloved 1958 cult classic that often looks cheesier than its inspiration. Daryl Hannah narrates and stars as the rich, unhappy wife, abused by both her unfaithful husband and her uncaring father, who takes revenge when she grows to monstrous proportions after being zapped by an alien ray. Christopher Guest directs half-heartedly, missing more satirical targets than he hits. AJ. Contains some swearing. [video]

Daryl Hannah *Nancy Archer* • Daniel Baldwin *Harry Archer* • William Windom *Hamilton Cobb* • Frances Fisher *Dr Cushing* • Cristi Conaway *Honey* • Paul Benedict *Dr Loeb* • O'Neal Compton *Sheriff Denby* • Victoria Haas *Deputy Charlie Spooner* ■ *Dir* Christopher Guest • *Scr* Joseph Dougherty, from the 1958 film

Attack of the Giant Leeches ★ PG

Horror 1960 · US · BW · 62mins

A small town in the swampy South is terrorised by bloodthirsty giant leeches (the stuntmen barely covered by their ill-fitting rubber suits) in this thankfully short cheapie produced by cult director Roger Corman. Uninspired trash with a lousy script and inept direction it may be, but starlet Yvette Vickers is good value. AJ DVD

Ken Clark *Steve Benton* • Yvette Vickers *Liz Walker* • Jan Shepard *Nan Greyson* • Michael Emmet *Cal Moulton* • Tyler McVey *Doc Greyson* • Bruno VeSota *Dave Walker* • Gene Roth *Sheriff Kovis* ■ *Dir* Bernard L Kowalski • *Scr* Leo Gordon

Attack of the Killer Tomatoes ★ PG

Horror comedy 1978 · US · Colour · 86mins

Behind an irresistible title lurks one of the worst movies ever made. Deliberately planned as a bad movie from the start, the fact that director John DeBello totally achieves his aim is the only good thing to say about this dire spoof, in which giant tomatoes rampage through San Diego to avenge fruit mistreatment. Intentionally awful special effects (the tomatoes are beach balls), ludicrous dialogue and low camp turn this parody of monster movies into a mind-numbing splatter bore. Still, it did spawn three sequels (including *Return of the Killer Tomatoes*, which starred George Clooney) and a television cartoon show. AJ [video] DVD

David Miller *Mason Dixon* • George Wilson *Jim Richardson* • Sharon Taylor *Lois Fairchild* • Jack Riley *Agricultural official* • Rock Peace *Wilbur Finletter* • Eric Christmas *Senator Polk* • Al Sklar *Ted Swan* ■ *Dir* John DeBello • *Scr* Costa Dillon, John DeBello, Steve Peace

Attack of the Puppet People ★★

Horror 1958 · US · BW · 78mins

Doll manufacturer John Hoyt gets lonely and starts reducing people to marionette size so they'll be his obedient "friends" in this routine riff on *The Incredible Shrinking Man* from veteran copycat exploitation director Bert I Gordon. John Agar is the rebel rocker who leads five other miniature companions on a mission to return to normal dimensions. Featuring better special effects than usual for Gordon and a nice tongue-in-cheek flavour. AJ

John Agar *Bob Westley* • John Hoyt *Mr Franz* • June Kenney *Sally Reynolds* • Michael Mark

A

Emil • Kenny Miller [Ken Miller] *Stan* ■ *Dir* Bert I Gordon • *Scr* George Worthing Yates, from a story by Bert I Gordon

Attack on the Iron Coast ★★ U

Second World War drama
1968 · US/UK · Colour · 89mins

As a cinema actor, Lloyd Bridges never really gained major star status, but his TV appearances, especially in the long-running series *Sea Hunt*, made his face familiar to millions. He is a useful presence in this generally uninvolving Second World War action adventure. The film was shot in England, and a supporting cast of British TV names such as Mark Eden and Andrew Keir does what is expected of it, but the overall style is curiously flat. TS

Lloyd Bridges *Major James Wilson* • Andrew Keir *Capt Owen Franklin* • Sue Lloyd *Sue Wilson* • Mark Eden *Lt Com Donald Kimberley* • Maurice Denham *Sir Frederick Grafton* • Glyn Owen *Lt Forrester* ■ *Dir* Paul Wendkos • *Scr* Herman Hoffman, from a story by John C Champion

The Attic: the Hiding of Anne Frank ★★★★ PG

Drama based on a true story
1988 · US/UK · Colour · 95mins

Like the room in question, this is near the top of the many film versions of the story of the Frank family, who were forced to hide from the Jew-hunting Gestapo. Told from an unusual perspective – that of Miep Gies – it relates how the courageous Dutch woman (played by the wonderful Mary Steenburgen) gave shelter to her employer Otto Frank (Paul Scofield) and his family, including his daughter Anne. A TV movie, directed by John Erman, it successfully conveys a sense of the claustrophobia of the situation and the courage of the family – refugees in their own country. TH

Mary Steenburgen *Miep Gies* • Paul Scofield *Otto Frank* • Lisa Jacobs *Anne Frank* • Eleanor Bron *Edith Frank* • Frances Cuka *Petronella van Daan* • Victor Spinetti *Herman van Daan* • Ian Sears *Peter van Daan* • Georgia Slowe *Margot Frank* • Jeffrey Robert *Albert Dussel* ■ *Dir* John Erman • *Scr* William Hanley, from the non-fiction book *Anne Frank Remembered* by Miep Gies, Allison Leslie Gold

Attraction ★★ 15

Thriller 2000 · US · Colour · 91mins

Matthew Settle stalks ex-girlfriend Gretchen Mol in a slow and baffling drama. It's unconvincing from the off, as Settles's increasingly obsessive behaviour provokes little more than a mild reprimand from Mol and best friend Tom Everett Scott. Samantha Mathis is likeable as an aspiring actress who gets involved with Settle, but her nude performance in an experimental play is little more than an excuse for writer/director Russell DeGrazier to provide titillation. JC DVD

Samantha Mathis *Corey* • Gretchen Mol *Liz* • Tom Everett Scott *Garrett* • Matthew Settle *Matthew* ■ *Dir/Scr* Russell DeGrazier

Au Hasard, Balthazar ★★★★★ PG

Drama 1966 · Fr/Swe · BW · 91mins

This extraordinary film by director Robert Bresson tells the story of a donkey named Balthazar, who is, at various times, an adored children's playmate, a circus performer and a harsh mill owner's slave. Finally, and fatefully, he carries smugglers' contraband over the mountains. The film is a religious parable, with the donkey – like Jesus – taking the sins of the world upon his back. It is also one of the great masterpieces of cinema: austere, warm, grim, surreal, shocking and heartbreaking. AT. In French with English subtitles. DVD

Anne Wiazemsky *Marie* • François Lafarge *Gérard* • Philippe Asselin *Marie's father* • Nathalie Joyaut *Marie's mother* • Walter Green *Jacques* • JC Guilbert [Jean-Claude Guilbert] *Arnold, the tramp* • Pierre Klossowski *Corn merchant* • Jean Rémignard *Notary* ■ *Dir/Scr* Robert Bresson

Au Revoir les Enfants ★★★★ PG

Second World War drama
1987 · Fr · Colour · 100mins

As a reminiscence of bigotries past, French director Louis Malle's autobiographical memoir has a discreet integrity rare among films dealing with anti-Semitism. A 12-year-old boy at a strict Carmelite convent school in 1944 wonders why a newcomer is treated so differently – bullied by other boys, shielded by teachers. The arrival of the Gestapo shows why – the boy is Jewish. It all works so extremely well because Malle never sentimentalises friendships or cruelty, and the result is a powerful tract in miniature. TH. In French with English subtitles.

Gaspard Manesse *Julien Quentin* • Raphael Fejtö *Jean Bonnet* • Francine Racette *Mme Quentin* • Stanislas Carré de Malberg *François Quentin* • Philippe Morier-Genoud *Father Jean* • François Berléand *Father Michel* ■ *Dir/Scr* Louis Malle

Audition ★★★★ 18

Psychological horror
1999 · Jpn/S Kor · Colour · 110mins

Containing scenes of surreal violence and excruciating torture that many will find difficult to watch, this controversial film from cult Japanese director Takashi Miike begins like a typical romantic comedy. A lonely Tokyo widower is persuaded to start looking for a new wife. Together with a producer friend, he holds a fake audition so he can screen a group of beautiful women – ostensibly for the part of a heroine in a new movie. But, when Ryo Ishibashi picks out ex-ballerina Eihi Shiina and tentatively begins to woo her, events take a shocking turn in a battle of the sexes that has caused worldwide controversy. With stunning imagery and a mounting sense of puzzled dread, this is a profoundly moving shocker. AJ. In Japanese with English subtitles. DVD

Ryo Ishibashi *Shigeharu Aoyama* • Eihi Shiina *Asami Yamazaki* • Tetsu Sawaki *Shigehiko Aoyama* • Jun Kunimura *Yasuhisa Yoshikawa* ■ *Dir* Takashi Miike • *Scr* Daisuke Tengan, from a novel by Ryu Murakami

The Audrey Hepburn Story ★★★ PG

Biographical drama
2000 · US · Colour · 128mins

In this TV-movie biopic, buxom teen movie star Jennifer Love Hewitt is neither gamine nor delicately classy enough to embody Hepburn, though she has a fair stab at the emotional points of the actress's life. Told in flashback from the set of *Breakfast at Tiffany's*, the film follows Audrey's experiences in wartime Holland and her early career, but while the tribute is an honourable one, there isn't enough drama to maintain interest until the end. JB DVD

Jennifer Love Hewitt *Audrey Hepburn* • Eric McCormack *Mel Ferrer* • Frances Fisher *Ella* • Keir Dullea *Joseph* • Gabriel Macht *William Holden* ■ *Dir* Steven Robman • *Scr* Marsha Norman

Audrey Rose ★★★ 15

Supernatural thriller
1977 · US · Colour · 108mins

Anthony Hopkins hams it up in this cash-in on the 1970s post-*Exorcist* interest in possession and the supernatural, with a tale about a young girl who may in fact be a reincarnation of Hopkins's deceased daughter. The cast (including Marsha Mason and John Beck as the girl's understandably concerned parents) is capable, but this is let down by the drawn-out plot and unlikely ending. JB DVD

Anthony Hopkins *Elliot Hoover* • Marsha Mason *Janice Templeton* • John Beck *Bill Templeton* • Susan Swift *Ivy Templeton/Audrey Rose* • Norman Lloyd *Dr Steven Lipscomb* ■ *Dir* Robert Wise • *Scr* Frank De Felitta, from his novel

Auggie Rose ★★★

Crime drama 2000 · US · Colour · 109mins

This drama has Jeff Goldblum giving a fun performance as an insurance salesman, bored with his dull life, who takes on the persona of an ex-con who dies in his arms. Goldblum is suitably manic as the man leading a double life, and there's good support from a strong cast. Sadly, towards the end huge plot holes and contrivances begin to emerge, but for the first half this is entertaining stuff. JB

Jeff Goldblum *John C Nolan* • Anne Heche *Lucy Brown* • Timothy Olyphant *Roy Mason* • Nancy Travis *Carol* • Richard T Jones *Officer Decker* • Joe Santos *Emanuel* • Kim Coates *Auggie Rose* ■ *Dir/Scr* Matthew Tabak

August ★★★ PG

Period drama 1995 · UK · Colour · 89mins

Chekhov's *Uncle Vanya* is relocated to 19th-century Wales in Anthony Hopkins's handsomely shot directorial debut. Although the new setting and a British cast that includes Leslie Phillips and Kate Burton (Richard's daughter) lend some appeal, the slow pacing and not terribly sympathetic characters will be a turn-off for some. Hopkins gives an energetic performance as the estate manager Ieuan/Vanya, whose unrequited feelings for Burton and frustration with his lot are fuelled by bouts of drinking. Probably best appreciated as a showcase for Hopkins's talent (he also composed the score). JC. Contains violence.

Anthony Hopkins *Ieuan Davies* • Kate Burton *Helen Blathwaite* • Leslie Phillips *Professor Alexander Blathwaite* • Gawn Grainger *Dr Michael Lloyd* • Rhian Morgan *Sian Blathwaite* • Hugh Lloyd *Thomas "Pocky" Prosser* • Rhoda Lewis *Mair Davies* • Menna Trussler *Gwen* ■ *Dir* Anthony Hopkins • *Scr* Julian Mitchell, from the play *Uncle Vanya* by Anton Chekhov, from the play *August* by Julian Mitchell • *Cinematographer* Robin Vidgeon

August in the Water ★★★

Fantasy 1995 · Jpn · Colour · 117mins

As Fukuoka city swelters in drought-inducing heat and its citizens fall prey to a mysterious epidemic, champion diver Rena Komine emerges from a coma and begins to experience visions of a rock face which resembles the meteorites that have recently been falling to earth. A hybrid of Leni Riefenstahl's *Olympia* and Andrei Tarkovsky's *Solaris*, Sogo Ishii's visually sumptuous sci-fi puzzle could all too easily be dismissed as mystical tosh. It's certainly leisurely and self-consciously obscure, but it's rather refreshing to watch something that makes you search for enlightenment. DP. A Japanese language film.

Shinsuke Aoki *Mao* • Rena Komine *Izumi* • Reiko Matsuo *Miki* • Masaaki Takarai *Ukiya* • Naho Toda *Yo* ■ *Dir/Scr* Sogo Ishii

Aunt Julia and the Scriptwriter ★★★ 15

Comedy 1990 · US · Colour · 102mins

Mario Vargas Llosa's novel is translated to the big screen by director Jon Amiel, while the action is transported from Peru to 1950s New Orleans. Barbara Hershey is the aunt of the title, Keanu Reeves plays her gullible nephew, and Peter Falk steals the show as the gruff, obsessive radio scriptwriter who has more going on than meets the eye. It's enjoyably quirky stuff, beautifully played by the impressive cast. JB DVD

Barbara Hershey *Aunt Julia* • Keanu Reeves *Martin Loader* • Peter Falk *Pedro Carmichael* • Bill McCutcheon *Puddler* • Patricia Clarkson *Aunt Olga* • Richard Portnow *Uncle Luke* • Dan Hedaya *Robert Quince* • Elizabeth McGovern *Elena Quince* • Hope Lange *Margaret Quince* ■ *Dir* Jon Amiel • *Scr* William Boyd, from the novel by Mario Vargas Llosa

Aunt Sally ★★ U

Musical comedy 1933 · UK · BW · 80mins

A vehicle for the irrepressible comedian and musical comedy star Cicely Courtneidge, this good-natured and thoroughly silly little British musical has her pretending to be a French nightclub star in order to get a job, only to find herself dealing with gangsters with a grudge against the club's owner (Sam Hardy). This is a romp for addicts of 1930s English nostalgia. RK

Cicely Courtneidge *Mademoiselle Zaza/Sally Bird* • Sam Hardy *Michael "King" Kelly* • Phyllis Clare *Queenie* • Billy Milton *Billy* • Hartley Power *"Gloves" Clark* • Ben Weldon *Casion* • Enrico Naldi *Little Joe* • Ann Hope *Joan* ■ *Dir* Tim Whelan • *Scr* Tim Whelan, Guy Bolton, AR Rawlinson

Auntie Lee's Meat Pies ★★

Horror comedy 1991 · US · Colour · 100mins

Satanist Karen Black fills her tasty meat pies with the flesh of men lured by her gorgeous nieces, all played by *Playboy* models, in this take on the *Sweeney Todd* story. Surprisingly low on titillation considering director Joseph F Robertson is famous for his porno movies (he used the alias Adele Robbins for those), it's laughably bad in the special effects department. AJ

Karen Black *Auntie Lee* • Pat Morita *Chief Koal* • Kristine Anne Rose *Fawn* • Michael Berryman *Larry* • Pat Paulsen *Minister* • Huntz Hall *Farmer* • Ava Fabian *Magnolia* • Teri Weigel *Coral* ■ *Dir* Joseph F Robertson • *Scr* Joseph F Robertson, Gerald M Steiner

Auntie Mame ★★★★

Comedy 1958 · US · Colour · 143mins

"Life's a banquet and most suckers are starving to death", quips Patrick Dennis's flamboyant aunt in this definitive film version of her fantastical life, following the successful stage show based on Dennis's book. Rosalind Russell is simply fabulous in the outrageous leading role, filling the screen with an ebullience equalled only by Robert Preston in director Morton Da Costa's other Warner Bros hit, *The Music Man*. Forget Beatrice Lillie (who played the role on stage in London) and all of those musical "Mames" – Russell *is* Auntie Mame. TS

Rosalind Russell *Mame Dennis* • Forrest Tucker *Beauregard Burnside* • Coral Browne *Vera Charles* • Roger Smith *Patrick Dennis* • Fred Clark *Mr Babcock* • Peggy Cass *Agnes Gooch* • Patric Knowles *Lindsay Woolsey* ■ *Dir* Morton Da Costa • *Scr* Betty Comden, Adolph Green, from the play by Jerome Lawrence, Robert E Lee, from the novel by Patrick Dennis

The Aurora Encounter ★★★ U

Science-fiction drama
1985 · US · Colour · 86mins

Good performances and some neat special effects lift this drama from being yet another run-of-the-mill alien-on-earth fantasy. It's the Old West at the end of the 19th century when a powerful but cute little alien turns up to give the locals a scare. Not exactly brain-straining stuff, but an entertaining watch for fantasy fans just the same. TS [video]

Jack Elam *Charlie* • Peter Brown *Sheriff* • Carol Bagdasarian *Alain* • Dottie West *Irene* • Will Mitchell *Ranger* • Charles B Pierce *Preacher* • Mickey Hays *Aurora spaceman* • Spanky McFarland *Governor* ■ *Dir* Jim McCullough Sr • *Scr* Jim McCullough Jr

Austin Powers: International Man of Mystery ★★★★ 15

Spy spoof 1997 · US · Colour · 90mins

This Swinging Sixties spy spoof is a fast, furious and fabulously funny ride that expertly mocks every groovy fad, psychedelic fashion and musical style of the period. Mike Myers is brilliant as the secret agent-cum-fashion photographer, cryogenically frozen so he can foil the world domination plans of his arch nemesis Dr Evil (Myers again) in the 1990s. Witty, sophisticated and hysterically stupid by turns, the side-splitting humour arises from clever culture-clash comedy, knockabout farce, Austin's catch phrases and countless references to 007, Matt Helm and *Our Man Flint*. AJ. Contains swearing and sexual references. [video] DVD

Mike Myers *Austin Powers/Dr Evil* • Elizabeth Hurley *Vanessa Kensington* • Michael York *Basil Exposition* • Mimi Rogers *Mrs Kensington* • Robert Wagner *Number Two* • Seth Green *Scott Evil* • Fabiana Udenio *Alotta Fagina* • Mindy Sterling *Frau Farbissina* • Burt Bacharach ■ *Dir* Jay Roach • *Scr* Mike Myers

Austin Powers: the Spy Who Shagged Me ★★★★ 12

Spy spoof 1999 · US · Colour · 91mins

If you liked the International Man of Mystery's first adventure, then you'll love this shagadelic sequel. Mike Myers goes back to the 1960s to reclaim his "mojo" which has been stolen by his nemesis Dr Evil (also played by Myers). While the star and his returning director, Jay Roach, revisit the same free-for-all secret agent spoofing of the original, they do it with just the right degree of retro style, knowing geniality and complete lack of taste and restraint. A lava lamp lampoon as stupid and (for Powers fans) as sophisticated as the first excursion. AJ. Contains sexual references. [video] DVD

Mike Myers *Austin Powers/Dr Evil/Fat Bastard* • Heather Graham *Felicity Shagwell* • Michael York *Basil Exposition* • Robert Wagner *Number Two* • Seth Green *Scott Evil* • Mindy Sterling *Frau Farbissina* • Rob Lowe *Young Number Two* • Gia Carides *Robin Swallows* • Verne Troyer *Mini-Me* • Elizabeth Hurley *Vanessa Kensington* • Kristen Johnston *Ivana Humpalot* • Burt Bacharach • Elvis Costello • Will Ferrell *Mustafa* ■ *Dir* Jay Roach • *Scr* Mike Myers, Michael McCullers, from characters created by Mike Myers

Austin Powers in Goldmember ★★★ 12

Spy spoof 2002 · US · Colour · 90mins

Co-writer, producer and star Mike Myers doesn't take many risks with this enjoyable third outing for the groovy secret agent and his nemesis Dr Evil, sticking to his tried and tested formula of cool catch phrases, bad-taste buffoonery and surreal slapstick. He perhaps overstretches himself this time, taking on the additional role of eponymous Dutch villain Goldmember, and there's a distinct feeling of *déjà vu* about his comic shtick. But despite the occasional lacklustre sequence, there are memorable contributions from the most colourful supporting cast of the series. JC [video] DVD

Mike Myers *Austin Powers/Dr Evil/Fat Bastard/Goldmember* • Michael Caine *Nigel Powers* • Beyoncé Knowles *Foxxy Cleopatra* • Seth Green *Scott Evil* • Michael York *Basil Exposition* • Robert Wagner *Number Two* • Mindy Sterling *Frau Farbissina* • Verne Troyer *Mini-Me* • Fred Savage *Number Three, "The Mole"* ■ *Dir* Jay Roach • *Scr* Mike Myers, Michael McCullers, from characters created by Mike Myers

Australia ★★ U

Romantic drama
1989 · Fr/Bel/Swi · Colour · 118mins

Set in southern Australia and the Belgian town of Verviers in the 1950s, this plodding drama of sheep farming and adultery instantly pulls the wool over our eyes, and is quite content to let it remain there. Director Jean-Jacques Andrien would have us believe that glossy visuals, authentic period trappings, a stately pace and the presence of such stars as Jeremy Irons and Fanny Ardant are compensation for the fact that virtually nothing happens. DP

Jeremy Irons *Edouard Pierson* • Fanny Ardant *Jeanne Gauthier* • Tcheky Karyo *Julien Pierson* • Agnes Soral *Agnès Decker* • Hélène Surgère *Madame Pierson* • Maxime Laloux *François Gauthier* • Patrick Bauchau *André Gauthier* ■ *Dir* Jean-Jacques Andrien • *Scr* Jean-Jacques Andrien, Jean Gruault, Jacques Audiard

Author! Author! ★★ PG

Comedy 1982 · US · Colour · 109mins

An ill-cast but effective Al Pacino is having a slew of domestic troubles as his new play opens on Broadway, and director Arthur Hiller has a tough time finding the requisite lightness of touch to make all the shenanigans convincing. There is, though, a sort of rough-edged charm to the piece, largely thanks to the blissful performances of clever Dyan Cannon and the sublime Tuesday Weld as the gals in Pacino's life, but the material involving the threesome's respective offspring is extraordinarily tasteless. TS [video] DVD

Al Pacino *Ivan Travalian* • Dyan Cannon *Alice Detroit* • Tuesday Weld *Gloria* • Alan King *Kreplich* • Bob Dishy *Finestein* • Bob Elliott *Patrick Dicker* • Eric Curry *Igor* • Elva Leff *Bonnie* ■ *Dir* Arthur Hiller • *Scr* Israel Horovitz

Auto Focus ★★★★ 18

Biographical drama
2002 · US · Colour · 101mins

This is one of Paul Schrader's most sustained and successful treatments of the dark side of sexuality. Based on the life of actor Bob Crane (star of the 1960s US sitcom *Hogan's Heroes*), it charts his descent into a libidinous hell as he becomes addicted to casual sex, videotaping an endless succession of meaningless encounters (aided by Willem Dafoe's noxious video technician). Greg Kinnear is excellent as the vacuous hedonist, and there's also a standout performance from Ron Leibman as the tender-hearted agent who watches with horror as his client's life implodes. Schrader doesn't spare us the numerous, often depressing sex acts, but in the end this is a moral and often funny tour de force. AS. Contains violence, swearing, sex scenes, drug abuse, nudity. [video] DVD

Greg Kinnear *Bob Crane* • Willem Dafoe *John Carpenter* • Rita Wilson *Anne Crane* • Maria Bello *Patricia Olsen Crane* • Ron Leibman *Lenny* • Bruce Solomon *Edward H Feldman, producer* • Michael Rodgers *Richard Dawson* • Kurt Fuller *Werner Klemperer/Col Klink* ■ *Dir* Paul Schrader • *Scr* Michael Gerbosi, from the non-fiction book *The Murder of Bob Crane* by Robert Graysmith

Autobiography of a Princess ★★★ PG

Drama 1975 · UK · Colour · 55mins

An early (and short) Merchant Ivory offering in their traditional reserved vein, scripted as ever by Ruth Prawer Jhabvala. James Mason and Madhur Jaffrey star as a former secretary to a maharajah and the maharajah's daughter who meet up in London. Through watching old home movies of India they share caustic reminiscences of their time there and of past relationships. An insubstantial but well-observed study of age. LH [video] DVD

James Mason *Cyril Sahib* • Madhur Jaffrey *The princess* • Keith Varnier *Delivery man* • Diane Fletcher *Seductress* • Timothy Bateson *Blackmailer* • Nazruh Rahman *Papa* ■ *Dir* James Ivory • *Scr* Ruth Prawer Jhabvala • *Producer* Ismail Merchant

The Autobiography of Miss Jane Pittman ★★★★★ 12

Drama 1974 · US · Colour · 97mins

This ambitious adaptation of Ernest J Gaines's novel won nine Emmy awards and is one of the finest TV movies ever made. As the 110-year-old African-American woman who experienced both the abolition of slavery at the end of the Civil War and the start of the civil rights movement in the 1960s, Cicely Tyson gives a towering performance. We see her progress from timid innocent to sassy senior citizen, no longer prepared to tolerate the injustices of a supposedly civilised society. Tracy Keenan Wynn's script is occasionally unfocused and overly reliant on journalist Michael Murphy to link the episodes, but, nonetheless, this informative work of fiction makes for compelling viewing. Released on video and DVD as *The White People's Fountain*. DP [video] DVD

Cicely Tyson *Jane Pittman* • Michael Murphy *Quentin Lerner* • Richard Dysart *Master Bryant* • Collin Wilcox-Horne [Collin Wilcox Paxton] *Mistress Bryant* • Thalmus Rasulala *Ned* • Dean Smith *Ned, aged 15* • Odetta *Big Laura* • Barbara Chaney *Amma Dean* ■ *Dir* John Korty • *Scr* Tracy Keenan Wynn, from the novel by Ernest J Gaines

Autobus ★★★★ 15

Thriller 1991 · Fr · Colour · 93mins

Presenting all-aboard thrills well before Sandra Bullock bought a ticket downtown, Eric Rochant's compelling drama might not be able to compete with *Speed's* high-octane stunts, but it more than compensates in terms of tension and performance. Yvan Attal is outstanding as the emotionally unstable man who hijacks a school bus in the hope of impressing girlfriend Charlotte Gainsbourg, veering between menace and confusion as he gets to know teacher Kristin Scott Thomas and the little charmers in her charge. Rochant makes the most of the cramped confines and perfectly judges the shifts in tone. DP. In French with English subtitles. [video]

Yvan Attal *Bruno* • Kristin Scott Thomas *Teacher* • Marc Berman *Driver* • Charlotte Gainsbourg *Juliette* • Renan Mazeas *Bruno's brother* • Francine Olivier *Bruno's mother* • Michèle Foucher *Juliette's mother* • Aline Still *Headmistress* • Daniel Milgram *Brigadier* ■ *Dir/Scr* Eric Rochant

Automatic ★★★ 15

Science-fiction action thriller
1994 · US · Colour · 86mins

In this sci-fi thriller, a cutting-edge electronics corporation tries to hush up a homicidal fault that develops within its top secret prototype, a cyborg bodyguard/servant called J269 (Oliver Gruner), by sending in a SWAT team to eliminate it. Unfortunately, a lowly secretary (Daphne Ashbrook) has witnessed the murderous glitch and will have to be erased, too. There's rarely a dull moment in this effective, well-mounted entertainment in the *Die Hard* mould. AJ. Contains swearing and violence. [video] DVD

Olivier Gruner *J269* • Daphne Ashbrook *Nora Rochester* • John Glover *Goddard Marx* • Jeff Kober *Major West* • Penny Johnson *Julia Rodriguez* • Marjean Holden *Epsilon leader* ■ *Dir* John Murlowski • *Scr* Susan Lambert, Patrick Highsmith

An Autumn Afternoon ★★★★★

Drama 1962 · Jpn · Colour · 112mins

Yasujiro Ozu, one of film's great artists, signed off with this typically gentle study of family obligation and the relentless advance of life. Making only his second film in colour, Ozu keeps his camera still and at its customarily low angle, giving us the freedom to explore the meticulously composed frame. It also allows us to concentrate on Chishu Ryu's touching performance as the widowed bookkeeper who reluctantly convinces his daughter (Shima Iwashita) that it's her duty to wed and leave him to the companionship of his drinking buddies. Suffused with genial humanity, this warm, wise tale is both pure cinema and a sheer delight. DP. In Japanese with English subtitles.

Chishu Ryu *Shuhei Hirayama* • Shima Iwashita *Michiko Hirayama* • Shinichiro Mikami *Kazuo Hirayama* • Keiji Sada *Koichi Hirayama* • Mariko Okada *Akiko Hirayama* • Nobuo Nakamura *Shuzo Kawai* • Kuniko Miyake *Nobuko Kawai* ■ *Dir* Yasujiro Ozu • *Scr* Yasujiro Ozu, Kogo Noda

The Autumn Heart ★★

Drama 1998 · US · Colour · 110mins

Tyne Daly is a school bus driver who, after suffering a heart attack asks her daughters to search out their estranged brother. The brother was taken by their father when he deserted the family 16 years earlier and the sisters discover that, while they have been on the breadline, their father has become extremely rich and their brother is living it up at Harvard. A working-class/middle-class culture clash ensues with warm and funny results. Nevertheless, this remains conventional. LH

Ally Sheedy *Deb* • Tyne Daly *Ann* • Davidlee Willson *Daniel* • Marceline Hugot *Donna* • Jack Davidson *Lee* • Marla Sucharetza *Diane* • Willy O'Donnell • Julian Sands ■ *Dir* Steven Maler • *Scr* Davidlee Willson

Autumn in New York ★ 15

Romantic drama
2000 · US · Colour · 101mins

Richard Gere and Winona Ryder are the incredibly unlikely couple in this unbelievable romance. He's the suave restaurateur who can have any babe he wants, she's the quirky hat designer half his age who also happens to be dying. The whole thing is given a slightly creepy twist when the audience learns that he actually once had a thing for her mother. Directed like a Dairy Milk advert by Joan Chen. JB [video] DVD

Richard Gere *Will Keane* • Winona Ryder *Charlotte Fielding* • Anthony LaPaglia *John* • Elaine Stritch *Dolly* • Vera Farmiga *Lisa* • Sherry Stringfield *Sarah* ■ *Dir* Joan Chen • *Scr* Allison Burnett

Autumn Leaves ★★★

Melodrama 1956 · US · BW · 108mins

In this dark melodrama, Joan Crawford marries her toyboy lover and then discovers that he's a little, shall we say, disturbed, if not totally deranged. Given an X certificate for its release in the UK, this features all the hallmarks of director Robert Aldrich: misogyny, misanthropy and murderous intent. Cliff Robertson puts in a distinguished performance as Crawford's dangerous other half, although his naturalistic acting style clashes somewhat with Crawford's all-stops-out performance. TS

Joan Crawford *Milly Wetherby* • Cliff Robertson *Burt Hanson* • Vera Miles *Virginia* • Lorne Greene *Mr Hanson* • Ruth Donnelly *Liz* • Shepperd Strudwick *Dr Couzzens* • Selmer Jackson *Mr Wetherby* • Maxine Cooper *Nurse Evans* ■ *Dir* Robert Aldrich • *Scr* Jack Jevne [Hugo Butler, Jean Rouverol], Robert Blees, Lewis Metzer

Autumn Marathon ★★★

Comedy 1979 · USSR · Colour · 92mins

Georgian director Georgi Danelia described this satire on Leningrad academe as a "sad comedy", because a reasonably decent cove manages to drive everyone to distraction through his inability to finish what he started. Only Norbert Kukhinke, the Danish professor with whom he goes jogging, has any sympathy for literary translator Oleg Basilashvili, whose innocent bungling and lapses of memory alienate both his wife, Natalia Gundareva, and mistress, Marina Neyelova. Wittily scripted by Alexander Volodin and played by Basilashvili with a finely judged blend of self-obsession, incompetence and pathos. DP. In Russian with English subtitles.

Oleg Basilashvili *Andrei* • Natalia Gundareva *Nina* • Marina Neyelova *Alla* • Yevgeny Leonov *Vasily* • Norbert Kukhinke ■ *Dir* Georgi Danelia • *Scr* Alexander Volodin

Autumn Moon ★★★★

Drama 1992 · HK/Jpn · Colour · 108mins

Set during the days when Hong Kong's post-colonial destiny had been determined but was still some time off, this is an elegant and intelligent exploration of the differences between two of Asia's most vibrant economies. Li Pui Wai is a teenager whose experience of first love eases the worry of her grandmother's illness, while Masatoshi Nagase, as the Japanese visitor she befriends, finds his past flirtations no longer satisfy him. Directed with delicious understatement by Clara Law from a subtle script, this is a thoughtful, intimate drama, made all the more intriguing by the fact that much of the dialogue is delivered in faltering English. DP. In Cantonese, Japanese and English with subtitles.

Masatoshi Nagase *Tokio* • Li Pui Wai *Wai* • Choi Siu Wan *Granny* • Maki Kiuchi *Miki* • Suen Ching Hung *Wai's boyfriend* • Sung Lap Yeung *Wai's father* • Tsang Yuet Guen *Wai's mother* • Chu Kit Ming *Wai's brother* ■ *Dir* Clara Law • *Scr* Ling Ching Fong

Autumn Sonata ★★★ 15

Drama 1978 · Swe/W Ger · Colour · 88mins

Originally intended to run for four hours, this harrowing film was the result of a difficult shoot, during which Ingmar and Ingrid Bergman frequently fell out and Ms Bergman had to resume treatment for the cancer that eventually killed her. This stifling study of resentment and regret is superbly played, particularly by Liv Ullmann, who can't forgive her musician mother for the childhood of neglect that she claims crippled her sister, Lena Nyman. Yet it was Ingrid who received the Oscar nomination, as, less deservingly, did Ingmar, for a script over-laden with theatrical speeches. DP. In Swedish with English subtitles. DVD

Ingrid Bergman *Charlotte* • Liv Ullmann *Eva* • Lena Nyman *Helena* • Halvar Bjork *Viktor* • Arne Bang-Hansen *Uncle Otto* • Gunnar Björnstrand *Paul* • Erland Josephson *Josef* • Georg Lokkeberg *Leonardo* • Linn Ullmann *Eva as a Child* ■ *Dir/Scr* Ingmar Bergman • *Producer* Lew Grade, Martin Starger

An Autumn Tale ★★★★ U

Romantic comedy drama
1998 · Fr · Colour · 106mins

Eric Rohmer is one of the few contemporary directors still interested in people. This is a typically intimate human drama, in which bookish Marie Rivière becomes overly involved with the lonely heart date (Alain Libolt) she has arranged for her wine-growing friend (Béatrice Romand). This deft, meticulously paced exploration of emotional confusion develops into a delightful comedy of errors, with Rohmer mirroring the plight of his middle-aged leads in the romantic tangles of teenager Alexia Portal. Drawing us inexorably into the lives of characters whose foibles are instantly recognisable, *An Autumn Tale* is a triumph of literate cinema. DP. In French with English subtitles.

Marie Rivière *Isabelle* • Béatrice Romand *Magali* • Alain Libolt *Gérard* • Didier Sandre *Etienne* • Alexia Portal *Rosine* • Stéphane Darmon *Léo* • Aurélia Alcaïs *Emilia* • Mathieu Davette *Grégoire* • Yves Alcaïs *Jean-Jacques* ■ *Dir/Scr* Eric Rohmer

Avalanche ★★ 15

Disaster movie 1978 · US · Colour · 86mins

Cult director Roger Corman produced this cut-rate disaster movie coasting on the 1970s' fascination with the genre. Rich developer Rock Hudson opens a ski resort during avalanche season and watches as the low-rent celebrities fall foul of the "six million tons of icy terror" promised in the ads. Poor effects match the acting in what was supposed to be Corman's ticket to mainstream respectability. Its lacklustre box-office performance sent him back to B-movie territory. AJ

Rock Hudson *David Shelby* • Mia Farrow *Caroline Brace* • Robert Foster *Nick Thorne* • Jeanette Nolan *Florence Shelby* • Rick Moses *Bruce Scott* • Steve Franken *Henry McDade* • Barry Primus *Mark Elliott* ■ *Dir* Corey Allen • *Scr* Corey Allen, Claude Pola

Avalanche ★★ 12

Thriller 1994 · US · Colour · 87mins

David Hasselhoff plays a jewel smuggler who bales out over Alaska after double-crossing his partners and triggers a massive avalanche. Saved by the holidaying Michael Gross and his two children, he then plots to dump his saviours. Hasselhoff is too much of a square-jawed hero to be bad, but Gross acquits himself well and director Paul Shapiro makes good use of the Canadian settings for this TV movie. JF. Contains some violence. DVD

David Hasselhoff *Snyder* • Michael Gross *Brian Kemp* • Deanna Milligan *Deirdre* • Myles Ferguson *Max* • Ben Cardinal *Hunter* • Don Davis [Don S Davis] *Whitney* • George Josef *Major* ■ *Dir* Paul Shapiro • *Scr* Tim Redman

Avalanche Express ★★ PG

Spy drama 1979 · Ire · Colour · 84mins

Ruthless CIA agent Lee Marvin uses defector Robert Shaw to entrap Soviet scientist Maximilian Schell in this ill-fated Cold War thriller. Set on a cross-border train impeded by blizzards, the film suffered its own tragedies when both Shaw and director Mark Robson died before production was completed. The repair job on what was left doesn't hide the joins, though the acting has an impressive energy. TH. Contains violence.

Robert Shaw *General Marenkov* • Lee Marvin *Colonel Harry Wargrave* • Linda Evans *Elsa Lang* • Maximilian Schell *Nikolai Bunin* • Mike Connors *Haller* • Joe Namath *Leroy* • Horst Buchholz *Scholten* • David Hess *Geiger* ■ *Dir* Mark Robson • *Scr* Abraham Polonsky, from the novel by Colin Forbes

Avalon ★★★ U

Epic drama 1990 · US · Colour · 122mins

Director Barry Levinson's lengthy family epic – a sort of *Godfather* without guns – is saved from schmaltz by a wonderfully assured and generous performance by Armin Mueller-Stahl. He plays the head of an immigrant clan who arrives in America on 4 July, 1914. Four generations of family loving and feuding follow, with the bulk of the film taking place just after the Second World War. While Joan Plowright and Elizabeth Perkins are featured, it's primarily a movie about men, though everyone is so talkily eloquent they eventually become tiresome. TH

Aidan Quinn *Jules Krichinsky* • Elizabeth Perkins *Ann Kaye* • Armin Mueller-Stahl *Sam Krichinsky* • Leo Fuchs *Hymie Krichinsky* • Eve Gordon *Dottie Kirk* • Lou Jacobi *Gabriel Krichinsky* • Joan Plowright *Eva Krichinsky* • Kevin Pollak *Izzy Krichinsky* • Elijah Wood *Michael Kaye* ■ *Dir/Scr* Barry Levinson

Avalon ★ 12

Futuristic thriller
2000 · Jpn/Pol/Fr · Colour, sepia · 102mins

Baffling in the extreme, there seems to be no rational explanation for the stylish events that unfold during this convoluted slice of futuristic role-playing. Set in a ruined, nameless metropolis, the story revolves around fearless loner Malgorzata Foremniak, who competes in the deadly and illegal virtual-reality war game Avalon. However, once this has been showcased in a magnificent opening sequence, the film loses its way. SF. In Polish with English subtitles. DVD

Malgorzata Foremniak *Ash* • Wladyslaw Kowalski *Game Master* • Jerzy Gudejko *Murphy* • Dariusz Biskupski *Bishop* • Bartek Swiderski *Stunner* • Katarzyna Bargielowska *Receptionist* ■ *Dir* Mamoru Oshii • *Scr* Kazunori Ito

Avanti! ★★★★★ 12

Romantic comedy
1972 · US · Colour · 138mins

This is perhaps Billy Wilder's most neglected masterpiece. It's a sublime romantic comedy which spins on one of Wilder's favourite themes: the confrontation between the brashness of America, where he worked, and the sophistication of Europe, where he was born. Jack Lemmon's harried business executive flies from Baltimore to Italy to collect his father's corpse. Juliet Mills arrives from England to pick up her mother's body, and before you can say "espresso", the odd couple are re-enacting their parents' affair. The picture is long (justifiably), impeccably plotted and brimming with marvellous characters – a desert island movie if ever there was one. AT. Contains swearing and brief nudity. DVD

Jack Lemmon *Wendell Armbruster* • Juliet Mills *Pamela Piggott* • Clive Revill *Carlo Carlucci* • Edward Andrews *JJ Blodgett* • Gianfranco Barra *Bruno* • Franco Angrisano *Arnold Trotta* • Pippo Franco *Mattarazzo* • Franco Acampora *Armando Trotta* ■ *Dir* Billy Wilder • *Scr* Billy Wilder, IAL Diamond, from the play by Samuel Taylor

The Avengers ★ 12

Action comedy thriller
1998 · US · Colour · 85mins

The cult 1960s TV series gets royally shafted by Hollywood in a stunningly designed blockbuster that's stunningly awful in every other department. Ralph Fiennes and Uma Thurman are miscast as John Steed and Emma Peel, here trying to stop villainous Sir August De Wynter (Sean Connery) holding the world's weather to ransom. Ruthlessly edited before release and packed with arch one-liners, bad puns and vulgar double entendres, this is misguided and misbegotten. AJ. Contains violence, swearing. DVD

Ralph Fiennes *John Steed* • Uma Thurman *Doctor Emma Peel* • Sean Connery *Sir August De Wynter* • Jim Broadbent *Mother* • Fiona Shaw *Father* • Eddie Izzard *Bailey* • Eileen Atkins *Alice* • Shaun Ryder *Donavan* • Patrick Macnee *Invisible Jones* ■ *Dir* Jeremiah Chechik • *Scr* Don MacPherson, from the TV series created by Sydney Newman • *Production Designer* Stuart Craig

Avenging Angel ★ 18

Crime drama 1985 · US · Colour · 93mins

Taking on the role played by Donna Wilkes in the original film, *Angel*, Betsy Russell here puts her streetwalking days behind her to search for the killers of the cop who saved her from prostitution. Little more than an excuse for some cheap sex and violence, this is only of interest to western fans curious to see what happened to Rory Calhoun. DP

Betsy Russell *Angel/Molly Stewart* • Rory Calhoun *Kit Carson* • Robert F Lyons *Detective Andrews* • Susan Tyrrell *Solly Mosler* • Ossie Davis *Captain Moradian* • Barry Pearl *Johnny Glitter* • Ross Hagen *Ray Mitchell* ■ *Dir* Robert Vincent O'Neil • *Scr* Robert Vincent O'Neil, Joseph M Cala

Avenging Angelo ★★ 15

Romantic comedy
2002 · US · Colour · 93mins

It's a shame that the late Anthony Quinn's final film was this patchy romantic comedy. Still he handles his fleeting role as a Mob boss with dignity, standing out in a sloppily acted film. Sylvester Stallone stars as a Mafia bodyguard who vows to protect Quinn's secret daughter Madeleine Stowe after the kingpin's murder. Stowe's contribution is little more than hysteria-prone eye candy, though Stallone demonstrating a softer side has its charm. Lame and slack. SF. Contains swearing, violence and sex scenes. DVD

Sylvester Stallone *Frankie Delano* • Madeleine Stowe *Jennifer Barrett Allieghieri* • Raoul Bova *Marcello/Gianni Carboni* • Anthony Quinn *Angelo Allieghieri* • Harry Van Gorkum *Kip Barrett* • Billy Gardell *Bruno* • George Touliatos *Lucio Malestesta* ■ *Dir* Martyn Burke • *Scr* Will Aldis [Will Porter], Steve Mackall

Avenging Force ★★ 18

Martial arts action thriller
1986 · US · Colour · 98mins

It's too bad that Steve James exits this movie halfway through. He is not only a much better actor than top-billed Michael Dudikoff, but he shows he had the stuff to be a big action star. Dudikoff plays a retired secret agent who lends his aspiring politician buddy (James) a hand when a neo-Nazi group makes him a target. The fight scenes are exciting, but the brutal violence leaves a bad impression. KB

Michael Dudikoff *Matt Hunter* • Steve James (1) *Larry Richards* • James Booth *Admiral Brown* • John P Ryan *Glastenbury* • Bill Wallace *Delaney* • Karl Johnson *Wallace* • Marc Alaimo *Lavall* • Allison Gereighty *Sarah Hunter* ■ *Dir* Sam Firstenberg • *Scr* James Booth

The Avenging Hand ★

Thriller 1936 · UK · BW · 66mins

Staying in a gloomy English hotel, Chicago gangster Noah Beery tracks down the killer of an old match-seller with the help of a hotel clerk and then disappears back to America. This

U = SUITABLE FOR ALL Uc = SUITABLE FOR ALL, ESPECIALLY FOR YOUNG CHILDREN (VIDEO ONLY) PG = PARENTAL GUIDANCE

somewhat confused thriller is feeble, forgettable and largely forgotten. RK

Noah Beery *Lee Barwell* • Kathleen Kelly *Gwen Taylor* • Louis Borell *Pierre Charrell* • James Harcourt *Sam Hupp* • Charles Oliver *Toni Visetti* • Reginald Long *Charles Mason* • Ben Welden *Slug Clarke* ■ *Dir* Victor Hanbury • *Scr* Akos Talney, Reginald Long

Aventure Malgache ★★★ PG

Second World War adventure
1944 · UK · BW · 29mins

The second of the two wartime shorts that Alfred Hitchcock made for the Ministry of Information was prompted by the feuding between the Free French who had worked on the first, *Bon Voyage*. Co-scripting with Angus MacPhail, "Hitch" introduced a note of levity that was unusual for propaganda films of the time to help encourage co-operation between partisans of all regional, personal and political persuasions. Yet the anecdote told by an exiled amateur actor about his Resistance activities against the Vichy regime on Madagascar didn't meet with the approval of Whitehall, and the film was never shown. DP. In French with English subtitles. [VIDEO]

Dir Alfred Hitchcock • *Scr* Angus MacPhail, Alfred Hitchcock

The Aviator ★★ PG

Period drama 1985 · US · Colour · 92mins

Christopher Reeve stars as a pilot haunted by the crash that killed his buddy, is ordered to fly rebellious Rosanna Arquette to college to avoid an adultery scandal. It's loathe at first sight, but their bickering ceases when they are forced down in a mountain wilderness. The need to survive brings about the sort of change of heart that only happens in thinly-plotted movies. Reeve and Arquette barely raise a spark. DP [VIDEO] DVD

Christopher Reeve *Edgar Anscombe* • Rosanna Arquette *Tillie Hansen* • Jack Warden *Moravia* • Sam Wanamaker *Bruno Hansen* • Scott Wilson *Jerry Stiller* • Tyne Daly *Evelyn Stiller* • Marcia Strassman *Rose Stiller* ■ *Dir* George Miller (1) • *Scr* Marc Norman, from the novel by Ernest K Gann

The Aviator ★★★ 12

Biographical drama
2004 · US/Ger · Colour · 163mins

If *The Aviator* lacks the punch of Martin Scorsese's earlier biopic *Raging Bull*, it's perhaps because Howard Hughes presents him with too much raw material. A millionaire at 18 (he inherited the Hughes Tool Company from his father), Hughes went on to become an aircraft designer and movie mogul. Hughes's childhood is dismissed in a brief prologue that sets up his obsession with cleanliness, then it's straight on to the beginning of his Hollywood career. The film is uneven, seemingly unsure of whether its protagonist is hero or villain, but Leonardo DiCaprio brings an impressive intensity to the role of Hughes. Cate Blanchett is a treat as Katharine Hepburn, but Kate Beckinsale is hopelessly miscast as Ava Gardner. BP [VIDEO] DVD

Leonardo DiCaprio *Howard Hughes* • Cate Blanchett *Katharine Hepburn* • Kate Beckinsale *Ava Gardner* • John C Reilly *Noah Dietrich* • Alec Baldwin *Juan Trippe* • Alan Alda *Senator Ralph Owen Brewster* • Ian Holm *Professor Fitz* • Danny Huston *Jack Frye* • Gwen Stefani *Jean Harlow* • Jude Law *Errol Flynn* ■ *Dir* Martin Scorsese • *Scr* John Logan

The Aviator's Wife ★★★★ PG

Comedy 1980 · Fr · Colour · 101mins

Eric Rohmer launched his *Comedies and Proverbs* series with this shrewd tale of tortured emotions, deceptive appearances and missed opportunities. Racked by the sight of girlfriend Marie Rivière leaving her apartment with pilot Mathieu Carrière, postal worker Philippe Marlaud begins to pursue his rival, enlisting the assistance of amused schoolgirl Anne-Laure Meury. Although Bernard Lutic's photography glories in the parks and backstreets of Paris, this is still a typically garrulous picture. Rohmer's sympathy for these lost souls makes everything most engaging. DP. In French with English subtitles. DVD

Philippe Marlaud *François* • Marie Rivière *Anne* • Anne-Laure Meury *Lucie* • Mathieu Carrière *Christian* • Philippe Caroit *Friend* • Coralie Clément *Colleague* • Lisa Heredia *Girlfriend* ■ *Dir/Scr* Eric Rohmer

L'Avventura ★★★★★ PG

Classic drama 1960 · It/Fr · BW · 136mins

Booed at Cannes (where it still won the Special Jury Prize) and branded immoral by the American National League of Decency, Michelangelo Antonioni's masterpiece is a mystery without a solution. Shot in real time, this adventure in cinematic technique is a brilliant and troubling study of alienation, privileged indolence and psychological sterility, in which the search for a missing woman gradually becomes irrelevant as her lover and best friend are drawn into an unsatisfying relationship of their own. Antonioni coaxes memorable performances from his cast, while he uses cinematographer Aldo Scavarda's exceptional views to reveal his characters' emotional states. DP. In Italian with English subtitles. [VIDEO]

Monica Vitti *Claudia* • Gabriele Ferzetti *Sandro* • Lea Massari *Anna* • Dominique Blanchar *Giulia* • James Addams *Carrado, her husband* • Renzo Ricci *Anna's father* • Esmeralda Ruspoli *Patrizia* • Lelio Luttazzi *Raimondo* ■ *Dir* Michelangelo Antonioni • *Scr* Michelangelo Antonioni, Elio Bartolini, Tonino Guerra, from a story by Michelangelo Antonioni

The Awakening ★ 15

Horror 1980 · UK/US · Colour · 95mins

This adaptation of a Bram Stoker novel is a dreadful plod. Surprising, given the cinematography's by the great Jack Cardiff and promising British director Mike Newell is behind the camera.The symbolism is heavy-handed, and Charlton Heston reads the script as if it were the Ten Commandments, forgetting Cecil B DeMille's 11th commandment: Thou Shalt Not Bore. AT [VIDEO]

Charlton Heston *Matthew Corbeck* • Susannah York *Jane Turner* • Jill Townsend *Anne Corbeck* • Stephanie Zimbalist *Margaret Corbeck* • Patrick Drury *Paul Whittier* • Nadim Sawalha *Dr El Sadek* • Miriam Margolyes *Kadira* ■ *Dir* Mike Newell • *Scr* Allan Scott, Chris Bryant, Clive Exton, from the novel *The Jewel of Seven Stars* by Bram Stoker

Awakening of the Beast ★★★ 18

Horror 1969 · Bra · Colour and BW · 92mins

With his top hat, cape and curling talons, Coffin Joe is a Latin horror legend. The alter ego of Brazilian actor/director José Mojica Marins, he's at both his most eccentric and socially conscious in this anti-drugs story, which so outraged the military government of the time that it was banned. Opening with a disturbing injection sequence, the tone shifts into pseudo-documentary mode as Marins outlines an LSD experiment he has conducted on a quartet of addicts, whose humiliations range from the blue to the bloody. What makes this film so effective, however, is cinematographer Giorgio Attili's ingenious use of disparate film stocks. DP. In Portuguese with English subtitles. DVD

José Mojica Marins *Coffin Joe* • Sergio Hingst *Dr Sergio* • Ozualdo Candeias • Andreia Bryan ■ *Dir/Scr* José Mojica Marins

Awakenings ★★★★ 15

Drama based on a true story
1990 · US · Colour · 115mins

Robert De Niro and Robin Williams star in this powerful dramatisation of neurologist Oliver Sacks's book, based on his real-life success in "awakening" patients who had been trapped in a comatose state for more than 30 years after contracting sleeping sickness in the 1920s. Williams shows his versatility by playing the shy scientist, though it was De Niro who got the Oscar nomination. Too upbeat for some tastes, Penny Marshall's film got mixed reviews on its release, but also earned an Oscar nomination for best picture. PF. Contains some swearing. [VIDEO] DVD

Robert De Niro *Leonard Lowe* • Robin Williams *Dr Malcolm Sayer* • Julie Kavner *Eleanor Costello* • Ruth Nelson *Mrs Lowe* • John Heard *Dr Kaufman* • Penelope Ann Miller *Paula* • Alice Drummond *Lucy* • Judith Malina *Rose* • Max von Sydow *Dr Peter Ingham* ■ *Dir* Penny Marshall • *Scr* Steven Zaillian, from the book by Oliver Sacks

Awara Paagal Deewana ★★★ 15

Comedy 2002 · Ind · Colour · 157mins

Action sequences inspired by *The Matrix* add a little midair panache to this frenetic crime caper. Gangster Om Puri sets things in motion by bequeathing a diamond stash to his children Rahul Dev and Preeti Jhangiani and her husband, Akshay Kumar, providing they take equal shares. However, the action only starts to hot up when the scene shifts to New York and the eccentric Paresh Rawal and his scheming son-in-law Aftab Shivdasani become embroiled in the dangerous game. DP. In Hindi with English subtitles. [VIDEO] DVD

Akshay Kumar *Guru Gulab Khatri* • Sunil Shetty *Yeda Anna* • Aftab Shivdasani *Dr Anmol Acharya* • Preeti Jhangiani *Preeti* • Amrita Arora *Mona* • Aarti Chhabria *Tina* • Paresh Rawal *Manilal* • Om Puri • Rahul Dev *Vikrant* ■ *Dir* Vikram Bhatt

Away All Boats ★★★ U

Second World War drama
1956 · US · Colour · 113mins

Today's cynicism would blow this gung-ho Second World War drama out of the water – which is what nearly happens to the wartime attack transport boat *Belinda*. Jeff Chandler is the inevitably unyielding captain who has to encourage a fighting spirit among his dispirited crew. It takes him all his time, and ours, though the action scenes pass the time spectacularly enough and there's a very young Clint Eastwood to be spotted. Otherwise, the flag-waving patriotism makes it an interesting curio from a bygone era. TH

Jeff Chandler *Captain Jebediah Hawks* • George Nader *Lieutenant MacDougall* • Lex Barker *Commander Quigley* • Julie Adams *Nadine MacDougall* • Keith Andes *Dr Bell* • Richard Boone *Lieutenant Fraser* • William Reynolds *Kruger* • Clint Eastwood ■ *Dir* Joseph Pevney • *Scr* Ted Sherdeman, from a novel by Kenneth M Dodson

The Awful Dr Orloff ★★ 15

Horror 1962 · Sp/Fr · BW · 82mins

Trash-meister Jesus Franco's incredible directing career took off with this graphic Spanish shocker (which credits the director as Norbert Moutier, one of many pseudonyms he has taken to avoid France's strict quota laws). Demented Howard Vernon kidnaps starlets to perform skin-graft operations on his disfigured daughter. Franco's early gore landmark is rather talky, but the expressionistic black-and-white photography still impresses. Four sequels followed. AJ. Contains violence and nudity. [VIDEO]

Howard Vernon *Dr Orloff* • Conrado San Martin *Inspector Tanner* • Diana Lorys *Wanda Bronsky* • Perla Cristal *Arne* • Maria Silva *Dany* • Ricardo Valle *Morpho* • Mara Lasso *Irma Gold* • Venancio Muro *Jean Rousseau* • Felix Dafauce *Inspector* ■ *Dir* Norbert Moutier [Jesus Franco] • *Scr* Jesus Franco, from the novel *Gritos en la Noche* by David Khune [Jesus Franco]

The Awful Truth ★★★★★ U

Classic screwball comedy
1937 · US · BW · 87mins

This is a wonderful example of Cary Grant at his screwball comic best, playing one half of a sniping, divorcing couple, who trade insults like gunfire and seek to spoil each other's future plans. Irene Dunne is the superb foil for Grant's laconic asides, and the two leads are assisted by a great supporting cast, which includes Ralph Bellamy and Cecil Cunningham. Leo McCarey's assured direction was rightly rewarded with an Oscar. Many stars, including Tom Hanks and Hugh Grant, have laid claim to Grant's mantle, but this movie illustrates once again that they are light years away from the man at his best. Remade in 1953 as *Let's Do It Again*. SH [VIDEO] DVD

Irene Dunne *Lucy Warriner* • Cary Grant *Jerry Warriner* • Ralph Bellamy *Daniel Leeson* • Alexander D'Arcy [Alex D'Arcy] *Armand Duvalle* • Cecil Cunningham *Aunt Patsy* • Molly Lamont *Barbara Vance* • Esther Dale *Mrs Leeson* • Joyce Compton *Dixie Belle Lee/ Toots Binswanger* ■ *Dir* Leo McCarey • *Scr* Viña Delmar [Vina Delmar], from the play by Arthur Richman

An Awfully Big Adventure ★★★ 15

Black comedy 1994 · UK · Colour · 107mins

Under-rated on its release, this watchable and entertaining adaptation of Beryl Bainbridge's jet-black comedy novel hits the right cynical notes. Focusing on the romantic intrigues involving the members of a British repertory theatre as they prepare to mount a production of *Peter Pan* in the late 1940s, the film has Hugh Grant cast against type as the egomaniacal director, while Alan Rickman's charismatic and stylish portrayal of the ageing matinée idol steals the handsomely mounted show. AJ. Contains swearing, brief nudity. [VIDEO]

Alan Rickman *PL O'Hara* • Hugh Grant *Meredith Potter* • Georgina Cates *Stella* • Alun Armstrong *Uncle Vernon* • Peter Firth *Bunny* • Prunella Scales *Rose* • Rita Tushingham *Aunt Lily* • Nicola Pagett *Dotty Blundell* ■ *Dir* Mike Newell • *Scr* Charles Wood, from the novel by Beryl Bainbridge

Ay, Carmela! ★★★ 15

War drama 1990 · Sp/It · Colour · 98mins

As a tragicomedy in the rose-tinted nostalgic style of the Oscar-winning *Belle Epoque*, this is a highly enjoyable and eventually moving story of a vaudevillian couple's contact with the opposing sides in the Spanish Civil War. As a political satire, it is markedly less successful, with both the Falangists and the Republicans being drawn as broad caricatures, while the pokes at military bureaucracy, cynical survivalism and the macho nature of Spanish society are as gentle as they are obvious. Nevertheless, director Carlos Saura re-creates the period admirably and coaxes fine performances from Andres Pajares and the astonishing Carmen Maura. DP. In Spanish with English subtitles. [VIDEO]

Carmen Maura *Carmela* • Andres Pajares *Paulino* • Gabino Diego *Gustavete* • Maurizzio De Razza *Lieutenant Ripamonte* • Miguel

Angel Rellan *Interrogating lieutenant* • Edward Zentara *Polish officer* • Mario DeCandia *Bruno* • José Sancho *Artillery captain* • Antonio Fuentes *Artillery subaltern* ■ *Dir* Carlos Saura • *Scr* Carlos Saura, Rafael Azcona, from the play by Jose Sanchis Sinistierra

BF's Daughter ★★

Political romantic drama
1948 · US · BW · 107mins

John P Marquand's novel was a serious study in social mores, but the film adaptation became little more than a vehicle for Barbara Stanwyck, who over-emotes as only she can as the rich man's daughter who destroys her weak liberal husband, Van Heflin. Director Robert Z Leonard's pacing is sluggish, yet Stanwyck fans won't want to miss this. TS

Barbara Stanwyck *"Polly" Fulton* • Van Heflin *Thomas W Brett* • Charles Coburn *BF Fulton* • Richard Hart *Robert S Tasmin III* • Keenan Wynn *Martin Delwyn Ainsley* • Margaret Lindsay *"Apples" Sandler* • Spring Byington *Gladys Fulton* ■ *Dir* Robert Z Leonard • *Scr* Luther Davis, from the novel by John P Marquand

BMX Bandits ★★ PG

Adventure 1983 · Aus · Colour · 86mins

This lively but very ordinary adventure story would probably be gathering dust by now if it weren't for the presence of a pre-stardom Nicole Kidman. She and her chums get mixed up with a gang of crooks who might have got away with it if it weren't for those darned BMX bikes. JF DVD

David Argue *Duane Whitey* • John Ley *"Moustache"* • Nicole Kidman *Judy* • James Lugton *Goose* • Bryan Marshall *The Boss* • Angelo D'Angelo *PJ* ■ *Dir* Brian Trenchard-Smith • *Scr* Patrick Edgeworth, from a screenplay (unproduced) by Russell Hagg

B Monkey ★★★ 18

Romantic thriller
1996 · UK/US · Colour · 88mins

Tired of her life of crime, sexy jewel thief Asia Argento decides to go straight. But as romance with schoolteacher Jared Harris beckons, can she really give up the guns, drugs and glamorous danger of London's underworld? Distinctly old-fashioned, this fast-moving thriller from director Michael Radford features well-drawn characters who help smooth over the bumpier plot jolts. Argento – in her English-language debut – glows with charisma. AJ. Contains swearing, violence, drug abuse and sex scenes.

Asia Argento *Beatrice (B. Monkey)* • Jared Harris *Alan* • Rupert Everett *Paul* • Jonathan Rhys Meyers *Bruno* • Tim Woodward *Frank* • Ian Hart *Steve* ■ *Dir* Michael Radford • *Scr* Chloe King, Michael Radford, Michael Thomas, from the novel by Andrew Davies

Baadasssss! ★★★★ 15

Drama based on a true story
2003 · US · Colour · 108mins

A thoroughly entertaining movie that crackles with raw energy, this offers a dramatised account of the making of Melvin Van Peebles's landmark 1971 blaxploitation picture *Sweet Sweetback's Baad Asssss Song*. Actor/director Mario Van Peebles plays his tenacious dad, who went to extraordinary lengths to get his self-starring tale about a street hustler-turned-revolutionary shot and into theatres. Chronicling the increasingly desperate events with a sharp and blackly comic touch, Mario delivers an enjoyably manic history lesson about the birth of black independent cinema, but what really gives the project its richness is his refusal to glamorise his cigar-chomping father. SF. Contains swearing and sex scenes.

Mario Van Peebles *Melvin Van Peebles* • Joy Bryant *Priscilla* • TK Carter *Bill Cosby* • Terry Crews *Big T* • Ossie Davis *Granddad* • David Alan Grier *Clyde Houston* • Nia Long *Sandra* • Paul Rodriguez *Jose Garcia* • Saul Rubinek *Howard "Howie" Kaufman* • Adam West *Bert* ■ *Dir* Mario Van Peebles • *Scr*Mario Van Peebles, Dennis Haggerty from the memoir *The Making of Sweet Sweetback's Baadassss Song* by Melvin Van Peebles

Baazigar ★★★ 15

Psychological drama
1993 · Ind · Colour · 173mins

Not since George Raft has a bad guy been able to trip the light fantastic as well as Shahrukh Khan. One of the most popular villains in recent Bollywood history, he turns in an impeccable performance of malevolent charm in this psychological masala from directing duo Abbas/Mustan. Equally impressive is Kajol, as the beauty who discovers that the supposedly deceased killer of her sister is alive, well and on her trail. DP. In Hindi with English subtitles.

Shahrukh Khan [Shah Rukh Khan] • Kajol • Shilpa Shetty • Dalip Tahil • Siddharth • Johnny Lever • Krish Malik • Anant ■ *Dir* Abbas, Mustan • *Scr* Robin Bhatt, Javed Sidique, Akash Khurana

Bab El-Oued City ★★★

Drama 1994 · Alg · Colour · 93mins

Although established as his country's leading film-maker, Merzak Allouache took a considerable risk in painting so graphic a portrait of Muslim Algeria. He not only suggests that the heroes of the 1988 protests were gangsters using religion as a pretext for their activities, but also reveals Algiers to be a city teaming with prostitutes and petty crooks for whom the teachings of the Koran mean next to nothing. DP. In Arabic with English subtitles.

Hassan Abdou *Boualem* • Nadia Kaci *Yamina* • Nadia Samir *Ouardya* • Mohamed Ourdache *Said* ■ *Dir/Scr* Merzak Allouache

The Babe ★★★ PG

Sports biography
1992 · US · Colour · 109mins

This was only released on video in the UK, perhaps because it was felt we would rather count sheep than watch baseball. It is, however, a character study of a flawed talent, baseball legend Babe Ruth, rather than a sports film centred on endless action. John Goodman perfectly captures the hero's enthusiasm, insecurity and weaknesses, and helps distract from the episodic nature of the film. JM

John Goodman *George Herman "Babe" Ruth* • Kelly McGillis *Claire Hodgeson-Ruth* • Trini Alvarado *Helen Woodford-Ruth* • Bruce Boxleitner *Jumpin' Joe Dugan* • Peter Donat *Harry Frazee* • James Cromwell *Brother Mathias* ■ *Dir* Arthur Hiller • *Scr* John Fusco

Babe ★★★★ U

Fantasy comedy 1995 · Aus · Colour · 88mins

This Australian family comedy came out of nowhere to enchant millions around the world. The "babe" of the title is an orphaned piglet adopted by a family of Border collies who learns how to handle sheep under the patient training of soft-hearted farmer James Cromwell. The mixture of live action and animatronics brings the animals magically to life (the film won an Oscar for visual effects). A delight from start to finish. JF DVD

James Cromwell *Farmer Arthur Hoggett* • Magda Szubanski *Esme Hoggett* • Christine Cavanaugh *Babe* • Miriam Margolyes *Fly* • Danny Mann *Ferdinand* • Hugo Weaving *Rex* • Miriam Flynn *Maa* • Roscoe Lee Browne *Narrator* ■ *Dir* Chris Noonan • *Scr* Chris Noonan, George Miller, from the novel *The Sheep-Pig* by Dick King-Smith

Babe: Pig in the City ★★★ U

Fantasy comedy adventure
1998 · US/Aus · Colour · 91mins

This rather disappointing sequel isn't anywhere near the equal of the endearing original. Here, Babe finds himself in constant danger when he travels to the city to earn money after Farmer Hoggett is injured. The action is taken at too frantic a pace to let the personalities come through, though the special-effects work with the animals is still quite wonderful and visually impressive. TH DVD

James Cromwell *Farmer Hoggett* • Magda Szubanski *Esme Hoggett* • Mickey Rooney *Fugly Floom* • Mary Stein *Landlady* • Julie Godfrey *Neighbour* • EG Daily [Elizabeth Daily] *Babe* • Glenne Headly *Zootie* • Steven Wright *Bob* • Miriam Margolyes *Fly* • Hugo Weaving *Rex* ■ *Dir* George Miller (2) • *Scr* George Miller, Judy Morris, Mark Lamprell, from characters created by Dick King-Smith • *Cinematographer* Andrew Lesnie

The Babe Ruth Story ★★ U

Sports biography 1948 · US · BW · 105mins

In the USA George "Babe" Ruth achieved heroic status for helping drag baseball back to respectability after the 1919 White Sox Scandal. Of the several biopics of the famous slugger, this was the first, the most sentimental and least accurate in the omission of his legendary drinking, womanising and gluttony. Bendix does a reasonable impersonation of the burly player, Claire Trevor is good, and there is intercut documentary footage of "Babe" in his heyday. BB

William Bendix *George Herman/Babe Ruth* • Claire Trevor *Claire Hodgson Ruth* • Charles Bickford *Brother Matthias* • Sam Levene *Phil Conrad* • William Frawley *Jack Dunn* ■ *Dir* Roy Del Ruth • *Scr* Bob Considine, George Callahan, from the non-fiction book *The Babe Ruth Story* by Babe Ruth as told to Bob Considine

Babes in Arms ★★★★ U

Musical 1939 · US · BW · 95mins

Not much of Rodgers and Hart's Broadway score was left in this MGM film version, but that didn't matter to audiences who turned out in force to watch Judy Garland and Mickey Rooney. They were brought together in the very first musical produced by genius Arthur Freed, whose later work would include such classics as *On the Town*. Rooney is magnificent, earning an Oscar nomination but losing to Robert Donat. He's a perfect foil for Garland, her wayward vulnerability contrasting with his brashness. Just sit back and enjoy their obvious pleasure in singing *Good Morning*. TS

Mickey Rooney *Mickey Moran* • Judy Garland *Patsy Barton* • Charles Winninger *Joe Moran* • Guy Kibbee *Judge Black* • June Preisser *Baby Rosalie Essex* • Grace Hayes *Florrie Moran* ■ *Dir* Busby Berkeley • *Scr* Jack McGowan, Kay Van Riper, from the musical by Richard Rodgers, Lorenz Hart

Babes in Toyland ★★★★ U

Musical fantasy 1934 · US · BW · 70mins

Fairy-tale whimsy with Laurel and Hardy! What could be better for children of all ages? Victor Herbert's light operetta was adapted – to the extent there's nothing left of the original – with Stan and Ollie as incompetent assistants to Santa Claus. They order 100 six-foot wooden soldiers instead of 600 foot-tall militants, but the combatants come in handy when miser Barnaby parts Tom-Tom from his beloved Bo-Peep and tries to take over nurseryland. Simple-minded joy. Released on video and DVD as *March of the Wooden Soldiers*. TH [video] DVD

Stan Laurel *Stanley Dum* • Oliver Hardy *Oliver Dee* • Charlotte Henry *Little Bo-Peep* • Felix Knight *Tom-Tom* • Henry Kleinbach [Henry Brandon] *Evil Silas Barnaby* • Florence Roberts *Widow Peep* • Ferdinand Munier *Santa Claus* ■ *Dir* Gus Meins, Charles Rogers • *Scr* Nick Grinde, Frank Butler, from the operetta *Babes in Toyland* by Victor Herbert, Glen MacDonough

Babes in Toyland ★★ U

Musical fantasy 1961 · US · Colour · 101mins

The second of three film adaptations of Victor Herbert's light opera, this earned a couple of Oscar nominations but it isn't a patch on the classic Laurel and Hardy version. Personally produced by Walt Disney, this was the studio's first live-action musical, but there's a distinct lack of magic. The special effects that allow Tommy Sands to lead an army of toy soldiers to rescue Annette Funicello from the grasp of evil Ray Bolger are clever enough, but Jack Donohue's direction is uninspired. DP [video]

Ray Bolger *Barnaby* • Tommy Sands *Tom Piper* • Annette Funicello *Mary Contrary* • Ed Wynn *Toymaker* • Tommy Kirk *Grumio* • Kevin Corcoran *Boy Blue* • Henry Calvin *Gonzorgo* ■ *Dir* Jack Donohue • *Scr* Ward Kimball, Joe Rinaldi, Lowell S Hawley, from the operetta by Victor Herbert, Glen MacDonough

Babes on Broadway ★★★ U

Musical 1941 · US · BW · 117mins

An appallingly contrived, sentimental mishmash created to suit the talents of its stars, but when those particular stars are the incomparable Judy Garland and the ineffable Mickey Rooney, frankly they could have dispensed with the plot entirely. As it is, the arch plot structure enables them to go though their paces – Rooney performs an amazing Carmen Miranda impression and Judy pretends to be Sarah Bernhardt. But be warned: the minstrel number seems incredibly tasteless today and there's an air of corny wartime patriotism. TS

Mickey Rooney *Tommy Williams* • Judy Garland *Penny Morris* • Fay Bainter *Miss Jones* • Virginia Weidler *Barbara Jo* • Ray McDonald *Ray Lambert* • Richard Quine *Morton "Hammy" Hammond* • Donald Meek *Mr Stone* • Alexander Woollcott ■ *Dir* Busby Berkeley • *Scr* Fred F Finklehoffe, Elaine Ryan, from a story by Fred F Finklehoffe

Babette's Feast ★★★★★ U

Period drama 1987 · Den · Colour · 103mins

This Danish film with a French star deservedly won the best foreign film Oscar and transcended the barriers of subtitles to capture the imagination of cinema-goers everywhere. Set in the 1870s, the story unfolds against the background of the grim Jutland peninsula, where two spinster sister (Bodil Kjer, Birgitte Federspiel), daughters of the former pastor, continue his work in leading the religious sect he founded. Into their lives comes Babette (Stéphane Audran), seeking refuge from war-torn Paris, who becomes their housekeeper. Her presence gradually effects changes in the austere community, culminating in a magnificent feast that she cooks 14 years later. Faithfully and brilliantly adapted by Gabriel Axel, this original and poignant tale is leavened with well-judged humour. RK. In Danish with English subtitles. [video] DVD

Stéphane Audran *Babette Hersant* • Jean-Philippe Lafont *Achille Papin* • Gudmar Wivesson *Young Lorenz Lowenhielm* • Jarl Kulle *Old Lorenz Lowenhielm* • Bibi Andersson *Swedish court lady-in-waiting* • Hanne Stensgaard *Young Philippa* ■ *Dir* Gabriel Axel • *Scr* Gabriel Axel, from a story by Isak Dinesen [Karen Blixen]

Babul ★★ U

Romantic drama 1950 · Ind · BW · 124mins

A huge hit at the Indian box office, this romance not only takes tragedy to new heights, but also comes pretty close to crossing the boundaries of credibility. It's intrigue all the way as the new village postman becomes the subject of a tug-of-war between his boss's daughter and the spoilt sibling of the local landowner. Dilip Kumar broke all sorts of cinematic conventions by jilting Nargis and opting for the resistible Munawar Sultana, but what they fail to comment on is the ludicrousness of the finale. DP. In Hindi with English subtitles. [video]

Dilip Kumar *Ashok* • Nargis *Bela* • Munawar Sultana *Usha* ■ *Dir* SU Sunny • *Scr* Azm Bazidpuri

The Baby ★★★

Horror 1973 · US · Colour · 85mins

Kept in nappies by his man-hating mother, taunted by his psycho sister and desired by a well-meaning social worker, life has been anything but easy for teenager David Manzy, and it's going to get worse. Director Ted Post makes a decent fist of this bizarre horror film and is rewarded with good performances from the likes of Ruth Roman, Marianna Hill and Anjanette Comer, though his use of actual footage depicting mentally disabled children is in very poor taste. DP

Ruth Roman *Mrs Wadsworth* • Anjanette Comer *Ann Gentry* • Marianna Hill *Germaine* • Suzanne Zenor *Alba* • Beatrice Manley Blau *Judith* • David Manzy *Baby* ■ *Dir* Ted Post • *Scr* Abe Polsky

The Baby and the Battleship ★★ U

Comedy 1956 · UK · Colour · 95mins

It was in Malta, when shooting this picture, that Bryan Forbes coined his nickname for Richard Attenborough. "Bunter" he called him and "Bunter" he remained, owing to Attenborough's addiction to chocolate. Nowadays that little piece of trivia is rather more significant than the movie, which is a juvenile comedy about an Italian baby smuggled aboard HMS *Gillingham* while the ship is docked in Naples. It's all too twee for words and the single joke is stretched almost beyond endurance. AT

John Mills *Puncher Roberts* • Richard Attenborough *Knocker White* • André Morrell *Marshal* • Bryan Forbes *Professor* • Michael Hordern *Captain* • Harold Siddons *Whiskers* • Clifford Mollison *Sails* • Lionel Jeffries *George* • Gordon Jackson *Harry* • Michael Howard *Joe* • Ernest Clark *Commander Digby* • Lisa Gastoni *Maria* ■ *Dir* Jay Lewis • *Scr* Jay Lewis, Gilbert Hackforth-Jones, from the novel by Anthony Thorne

Baby Boom ★★★ PG

Comedy 1987 · US · Colour · 105mins

Diane Keaton stars as a ruthless New York executive whose business ambitions falter when she's forced to foster a dead relative's baby girl. The men in her life – boss Sam Wanamaker and lover Harold Ramis – aren't sympathetic to her new working mother status, so she buys a money-pit mansion in the country and tries to make it on her own, with local veterinarian Sam Shepard popping in. With its mix of cuteness and acuteness, it's one of Keaton's more likeable films. TH. Contains some swearing and brief nudity. [video] DVD

Diane Keaton *JC Wiatt* • Harold Ramis *Steven Buchner* • Sam Wanamaker *Fritz Curtis* • Sam Shepard *Dr Jeff Cooper* • James Spader *Ken Arrenberg* • Pat Hingle *Hughes Larrabee* • Britt Leach *Vern Boone* • Kristina Kennedy *Elizabeth Wiatt* • Michelle Kennedy *Elizabeth Wiatt* • Kim Sebastian *Robin* ■ *Dir* Charles Shyer • *Scr* Nancy Meyers, Charles Shyer

Baby Boy ★★ 15

Drama 2001 · US · Colour · 124mins

Director John Singleton's companion piece to his career-making debut *Boyz N the Hood* falls way short of its predecessor's power, poignancy and perception. Set in South Central Los Angeles, the plot revolves around 20-year-old Tyrese Gibson who still lives at home with his mother and has fathered two children by different women. Little attempt is made to explore Gibson's psychological state, so fringe characters played by Omar Gooding and Ving Rhames prove far more interesting. DP [video] DVD

Tyrese Gibson *Jody* • Omar Gooding *Sweetpea* • AJ Johnson [Adrienne-Joi Johnson] *Juanita* • Taraji P Henson *Yvette* • Snoop Dogg *Rodney* • Tamara LaSeon Bass *Peanut* • Ving Rhames *Melvin* ■ *Dir/Scr* John Singleton

Baby Cart at the River Styx ★★★ 18

Period martial arts adventure
1972 · Jpn · Colour · 81mins

The second *Lone Wolf and Cub* movie earned notoriety in the 1980s when it was branded a video nasty. Tomisaburo Wakayama returns as the disgraced executioner who supplements his sword skills with the blades studding his baby son's pram. He's allowed a few moments to reflect on the pain of both losing his wife and being betrayed by his brethren, but his primary purpose is to shed blood, which he does with awesome power. Four more films followed in the series. DP. In Japanese with English subtitles. Contains violence, swearing, nudity. [video]

Tomisaburo Wakayama *Ogami Itto* • Akihiro Tomikawa *Daigoro* • Kayo Matsuo *Sayaka* ■ *Dir* Kenji Misumi • *Scr* Kazuo Koike, from a story by Kazuo Koike, Goseki Kojima

Baby Doll ★★★ PG

Melodrama 1956 · US · BW · 109mins

The film that scandalised America has been tamed by the passage of some four decades. It is hard to keep a smile off one's face at the thought of millions of respectable citizens being pinned back in their seats by the emotional G-force emanating from the screen and their own sense of delicious guilt. Yet Tennessee Williams's screenplay is not without its highlights, thanks to the skilled direction of his favourite film-maker, Elia Kazan, notably the scene on a swing in which Eli Wallach, in his film debut, seeks revenge on arsonist Karl Malden by seducing his bride. DP [video]

Karl Malden *Archie* • Carroll Baker *Baby Doll* • Eli Wallach *Silva Vacarro* • Mildred Dunnock *Aunt Rose Comfort* • Lonny Chapman *Rock* • Eades Hogue *Town Marshall* • Noah Williamson *Deputy* ■ *Dir* Elia Kazan • *Scr* Tennessee Williams, from his story

Baby Face ★★★

Drama 1933 · US · BW · 68mins

A tour-de-force performance from the incomparable Barbara Stanwyck enlivens this tale of a small-town girl who makes it to the mansion by using and abusing every gullible schmuck who crosses her silk-stockinged path. This is essentially a pretty ordinary movie – everything moves along predictably and the clichés have been shared out even-handedly – made extraordinary by its star who is in her sashaying, gimlet-eyed, "don't mess with me" prime. Keep an eye out for a youthful John Wayne, but everyone is acted off the screen by Stanwyck. SH

Barbara Stanwyck *Lily "Baby Face" Powers* • George Brent *Trenholm* • Donald Cook *Stevens* • Arthur Hohl *Sipple* • John Wayne *Jimmy McCoy* • Henry Kolker *Mr Carter* • Margaret Lindsay *Ann Carter* • Theresa Harris *Chico* ■ *Dir* Alfred E Green • *Scr* Gene Markey, Kathryn Scola, from a story by Mark Canfield [Darryl F Zanuck]

Baby Face Morgan ★★

Crime comedy 1942 · US · BW · 60mins

In this would-be gangster comedy the camerawork is so inept and the sets so obviously cheap that the very incompetence of the production makes for compulsive viewing. Richard Cromwell plays the title mobster's son who gets embroiled in an insurance scam. This is poor quality stuff, but it's enlivened by sterling work from a cast headed by B-movie girl Mary Carlisle and Robert Armstrong. TS

Mary Carlisle *Virginia Clark* • Richard Cromwell *"Baby Face" Morgan* • Robert Armstrong *"Doc" Rogers* • Chick Chandler *Oliver Harrison* • Charles Judels *"Deacon" Davis* • Warren Hymer *Wise Willie* ■ *Dir* Arthur Dreifuss • *Scr* Edward Dein, Jack Rubin, from a story by Oscar Brodney, Jack Rubin

Baby Face Nelson ★★★

Film noir crime drama
1957 · US · BW · 84mins

Casting Mickey Rooney, the baby face of all those cutesy MGM movies, was a wonderfully subversive idea, and Rooney turns in an energetic, scary and convincing performance as the principal psychotic of the 1930s. Falling in with Leo Gordon's gang, Rooney goes bonkers and goes on to become America's Public Enemy Number One. Carolyn Jones is the girlfriend who has to put up with his highly charged antics. What distinguishes this movie is its refusal to moralise: it's a slick, sick celebration of anti-social behaviour. AT

Mickey Rooney *Lester "Baby Face Nelson" Gillis* • Carolyn Jones *Sue* • Cedric Hardwicke *Doc Saunders* • Chris Dark [Christopher Dark] *Jerry* • Ted De Corsia *Rocco* • Emile Meyer *Mac* • Tony Caruso [Anthony Caruso] *Hamilton* • Leo Gordon *John Dillinger* • Dan Terranova *Miller* • Elisha Cook Jr *Van Meter* ■ *Dir* Don Siegel • *Scr* Irving Shulman, Geoffrey Homes [Daniel Mainwaring], from a story by Irving Shulman

Baby Geniuses ★ PG

Comedy fantasy adventure
1999 · US · Colour · 90mins

This rotten, infantile comedy marks a career low for Kathleen Turner. She plays a nasty children's magnate who is carrying out tests on a host of brainy litte nippers on the shaky premise that infants can actually converse in a secret language. However, she meets her match in twins, played irritatingly by triplets Leo, Myles and Gerry Fitzgerald. The artlessly staged slapstick will amuse only toddlers. JF [video] DVD

Kathleen Turner *Elena* • Christopher Lloyd *Heep* • Kim Cattrall *Robin* • Peter MacNicol *Dan* • Dom DeLuise *Lenny* • Ruby Dee *Margo* • Kyle Howard *Dickie* • Kaye Ballard *Mayor* ■ *Dir* Bob Clark • *Scr* Bob Clark, Greg Michael, from a story by Steven Paul, Francisca Matos, Robert Grasmere

Baby It's You ★★★ 15

Romantic comedy drama
1983 · US · Colour · 100mins

One of the earlier films from independent writer/director John Sayles, this slice-of-life drama, set in 1960s New Jersey, centres on the efforts of an Italian Catholic boy (Vincent Spano) to romance a middle-class Jewish girl (Rosanna Arquette). Sayles's talents weren't yet fully formed and the film rather runs out of steam in the later stages, but the attention to detail, plus some bursts of typically sharp Sayles dialogue are indicative of the movie mastery he would exhibit in later films. DA. Contains violence, swearing, sex scenes, drug abuse and nudity.

Rosanna Arquette *Jill Rosen* • Vincent Spano *"Sheikh" Capadilupo* • Joanna Merlin *Mrs Rosen* • Jack Davidson *Dr Rosen* • Nick Ferrari *Mr Capadilupo* • Dolores Messina *Mrs Capadilupo* • Robert Downey Jr *Stewart* • Matthew Modine *Steve* ■ *Dir* John Sayles • *Scr* John Sayles, from a story by Amy Robinson

The Baby Maker ★★ 18

Drama 1970 · US · Colour · 104mins

This early investigation into surrogate motherhood sees childless couple Sam Groom and Collin Wilcox-Horne hire hippy Barbara Hershey to have a child by the husband. An explosive situation – Hershey falls for the husband, while lover Scott Glenn gets jealous – is played for all it's worth, but the characters are so self-centred they cast no social shadows. What might have been a compelling comment on surrogacy is obscured by soapy lather. TH

Barbara Hershey *Tish Gray* • Collin Wilcox-Horne *Suzanne Wilcox* • Sam Groom *Jay Wilcox* • Scott Glenn *Ted Jacks* • Jeannie Berlin *Charlotte* • Lili Valenty *Mrs Culnick* ■ *Dir/Scr* James Bridges

The Baby of Macon ★★★ 18

Period drama 1993 · UK · Colour · 121mins

There's a certain irony in the fact that a film about the deceptiveness of appearance should itself glitter without ever being golden. Thanks to Sacha Vierny's sumptuous photography, this is a visual if disturbing delight, but director Peter Greenaway allows his twin penchants for thematic controversy and stylistic contrivance to run away with him. In deriding the faith and rituals of Christianity, he finds himself unable to resist the visual temptations offered by its art and architecture, while the theatricality of the action sits uncomfortably with Greenaway's highly cinematic style. DP. Contains violence and nudity.

Julia Ormond *Daughter* • Ralph Fiennes *Bishop's son* • Philip Stone *Bishop* • Jonathan Lacey *Cosimo Medici* • Don Henderson *Father Confessor* • Celia Gregory *Mother Superior* • Jeff Nuttall *Major Domo* ■ *Dir/Scr* Peter Greenaway

Baby on Board ★★ PG

Romantic comedy thriller
1993 · Can · Colour · 86mins

There are precious few cuddly moments in this thriller, as a posse of Brylcreemed mafiosos follow taxi driver Judge Reinhold and passengers Carol Kane and her young daughter. This is basically one very long and very predictable chase movie, in which squealing brakes and interior car shots dominate so exclusively that the entire cast could have shot this trouserless and we'd be none the wiser. SH

Judge Reinhold *Ernie* • Carol Kane *Maria* • Geza Kovacs *Carmine* • Alex Stapley *Angelica* • Conrad Bergschneider *Lorenzo* • Lou Pitoscias *Vincenzo* • Jason Blicker *Frankie* • Holly Stapley *Angelica* ■ *Dir* Francis A Schaeffer • *Scr* Damian Lee, James Shavick, from a story by Doug Moore

Baby: Secret of the Lost Legend ★★★ PG

Comedy adventure
1985 · US · Colour · 92mins

Disney's old-fashioned adventure fantasy is a pleasant enough tale about palaeontologist Sean Young and her sports writer husband William Katt discovering a brontosaurus family in Africa. Scientist Patrick McGoohan is the villain of the piece who wants the baby bronto brought back to civilisation. Veering from cute to violent, this reworked *Lost World* tale is too bland to properly satisfy. Yet kids will love the huggable Baby, for all its winsome plasticity. AJ DVD

William Katt *George Loomis* • Sean Young *Susan Matthews-Loomis* • Patrick McGoohan *Dr Erick Kiviat* • Julian Fellowes *Nigel Jenkins* • Kyalo Mativo *Cephu* • Hugh Quarshie *Kenge Obe* • Edward Hardwicke *Dr Pierre Dubois* ■ *Dir* BWL Norton [Bill L Norton] • *Scr* Clifford Green, Ellen Green

The Baby-Sitter's Club ★★★ U

Comedy drama 1995 · US · Colour · 90mins

Based on the popular Ann M Martin novels, this agreeable comedy drama directed by former *thirtysomething* star Melanie Mayron concerns a group of young girls dealing with parents and romance while earning extra money looking after children at a day camp. Sissy Spacek's daughter, Schuyler Fisk, appeared in her first starring role and, despite a nice performance, has done very little since. JB

Schuyler Fisk *Kristy* • Bre Blair *Stacey* • Rachael Leigh Cook *Mary Anne* • Larisa Oleynik *Dawn* • Tricia Joe *Claudia* • Stacey Linn Ramsower *Mallory* • Zelda Harris *Jessi* • Vanessa Zima *Rosie Wilder* • Bruce Davison *Watson* • Ellen Burstyn *Mrs Haberman* ■ *Dir* Melanie Mayron • *Scr* Dalene Young, from the novels by Ann M Martin

Baby, Take a Bow ★★ U

Crime drama 1934 · US · BW · 75mins

This was Shirley Temple's first starring vehicle after Fox signed her to a seven-year contract. She had her sixth birthday while making it and enchanted critics and audiences with her performance as the daughter of an ex-convict (James Dunn) who saves him from false accusations of theft. American women's groups winced at such a young child being seen mixed up with criminals. AE

Shirley Temple *Shirley Ellison* • James Dunn *Eddie Ellison* • Claire Trevor *Kay Ellison* • Alan Dinehart *Welch* • Ray Walker *Larry Scott* • Dorothy Libaire *Jane* ■ *Dir* Harry Lachman • *Scr* Philip Klein, Ee Paramore Jr, from the play *Square Crooks* by James P Judge

Baby the Rain Must Fall ★★★

Drama 1965 · US · BW · 98mins

The great Steve McQueen in one of his sombre roles, fresh out of jail and reunited with his wife, played by Lee Remick, and the daughter he has never seen. He has a nothing job by day but sings with a band at night, though any hopes he has of fame are dashed by his foster mother, a domineering woman who becomes the catalyst for later events. McQueen and Remick are both excellent, while Robert Mulligan's direction not only eschews any easy melodramatics, but also beautifully evokes the flatness and deadness of small-town Texas, all of which acts as a tinderbox for McQueen's pent-up emotions. AT

Lee Remick *Georgette Thomas* • Steve McQueen *Henry Thomas* • Don Murray *Slim* • Paul Fix *Judge Ewing* • Josephine Hutchinson *Mrs Ewing* • Ruth White *Miss Clara* • Charles Watts *Mr Tillman* • Carol Veazie *Mrs Tillman* • Estelle Hemsley *Catherine* ■ *Dir* Robert Mulligan • *Scr* Horton Foote

Babyfever ★★★

Comedy drama 1994 · US · Colour · 110mins

Constantly threatening to outstay its welcome, yet always managing to come up with another worthwhile line of inquiry, Henry Jaglom's typically talky treatise on babies was clearly inspired by the fact he had just fathered a second child with his wife, the film's star Victoria Foyt. As Gena, Foyt is so tormented by the ticking of her biological clock that she can barely make a rational choice between dull, worthy boyfriend Matt Salinger and her reckless ex, Eric Roberts. The verbosity of the baby-shower scene will alienate many, but some of the insights are disarmingly honest – if not particularly original. DP. Contains swearing.

Victoria Foyt *Gena* • Matt Salinger *James* • Dinah Lenney *Roz* • Eric Roberts *Anthony* • Frances Fisher *Rosie* • Elaine Kagan *Milly* • Zack Norman *Mark* ■ *Dir* Henry Jaglom • *Scr* Henry Jaglom, Victoria Foyt

Babylon ★★★

Drama 1980 · UK · Colour · 94mins

This ground-breaking British film about contemporary black life in London was not the first of its kind, but it was the first to give white audiences an insight into the significance of such things as "sound systems", the Stop-and-Search Law and Rastafarianism. The action revolves around young garage mechanic Blue, who is trying to take part in a sound-system contest while dealing with domestic, racial and cultural pressures. Natural performances and desolate locations give a vivid impression of south London life prior to the real-life riots, only a year ahead. DM. In English and Jamaican patois with subtitles.

Karl Howman *Ronnie* • Trevor Laird *"Beefy"* • Brian Bovell *"Spark"* • Victor Evans Romero *"Lover"* • David N Haynes *Errol* • Archie Pool *"Dreadhead"* • T Bone Wilson *Wesley* • Mel Smith *Alan* • Bill Moody *Man on balcony* ■ *Dir* Franco Rosso • *Scr* Martin Stellman, Franco Rosso

Babymother ★★ 15

Musical comedy drama
1998 · UK · Colour · 78mins

Writer/director Julian Henriques's feature debut has in its favour an undeniable energy and a gutsy performance from Anjela Lauren Smith, as the mother of two battling against the odds and the indifference of her partner to become a reggae singer. Yet too often the narrative is hijacked by musical interludes, and there's insufficient dramatic focus. DP. Contains swearing, some mild violence and a sex scene. DVD

Anjela Lauren Smith *Anita* • Caroline Chikezie *Sharon* • Jocelyn Esien *Yvette* • Wil Johnson *Byron* • Don Warrington *Luther* • Tameka Empson *Dionne* • Diane Bailey *Bee* • Vas Blackwood *Caesar* • Andrea Francis *Yvette's Sister* ■ *Dir* Julian Henriques • *Scr* Julian Henriques, Vivienne Howard

Baby's Day Out ★★★ PG

Comedy 1994 · US · Colour · 94mins

John Hughes (*Home Alone*) here comes up with another successful spin on the small-people-humiliating-adults theme, with a wee baby standing in for Macaulay Culkin. The little tot – the precious child of a wealthy family – is snatched by a bungling trio of kidnappers and proceeds to make their life hell. Wit and subtlety are hardly to the fore, but the action does rip along at a cracking pace, the comic set pieces are executed with precision, and Joe Mantegna, Joe Pantoliano and Brian Haley are good fun as the crooks. JF DVD

Joe Mantegna *Eddie Mauser* • Lara Flynn Boyle *Laraine Cotwell* • Joe Pantoliano *Norby LeBlaw* • Brian Haley *Veeko Riley* • Cynthia Nixon *Gilbertine* • Fred Dalton Thompson *FBI agent Grissom* ■ *Dir* Patrick Read Johnson • *Scr* John Hughes

The Babysitter ★ 18

Erotic thriller 1995 · US · Colour · 85mins

This litany of tired sex fantasies went straight to video, and we might never have heard of it at all had not Alicia Silverstone scored such a huge hit in the same year with *Clueless*. She has little to do here but look alluring as her employers and their neighbours contemplate soft-core encounters in a series of daydreams that only rarely rise above the squalid. DP. Contains violence, swearing, drug abuse, sex scenes and nudity.

Alicia Silverstone *Jennifer* • Jeremy London *Jack* • JT Walsh *Harry Tucker* • Lee Garlington *Dolly Tucker* • Nicky Katt *Mark* • Lois Chiles *Bernice Holsten* • George Segal *Bill Holsten* ■ *Dir* Guy Ferland • *Scr* Guy Ferland, from the short story by Robert Coover

The Bacchantes ★★

Drama 1960 · Fr/It · Colour · 100mins

Euripides receives the sword-and-sandal treatment in this rattling ancient adventure that, like so many of its ilk, is a little hit and myth. Akim Tamiroff, the selfless support in many a Hollywood picture, gets his moment in the sun as Tiresias, who predicts disaster when the people of Thebes abandon their faith in the city's god, Bacchus. Over-plotted, overplayed, and not over quickly enough. DP. In Italian with English subtitles.

Taina Elg *Dirce* • Pierre Brice *Dionysus* • Alessandra Panaro *Manto* • Alberto Lupo *Pentheus* • Akim Tamiroff *Tiresias* ■ *Dir* Giorgio Ferroni • *Scr* Giorgio Stegani, Giorgio Ferroni, from the play *The Bacchae* by Euripides

Bach and Broccoli ★★★ U

Comedy drama 1986 · Can · Colour · 95mins

A box-office sensation in its native Quebec, the *Tales for All* series of children's films won over 100 international awards. This third entry brought about a reunion between producer Rock Demers and André Melançon, who directed the first film in the series, *The Dog Who Stopped the War*. Mahée Paiement is hugely impressive as the 11-year-old orphan who arrives with her pet skunk, Bottine (or Broccoli), to disrupt the ordered life of her uncle, Raymond Legault. Maintaining a light touch, Melançon doesn't labour his life lessons. DP. French dialogue dubbed into English.

Mahée Paiement *Fanny* • Raymond Legault *Jonathan* • Harry Marciano *Sean* • Andrée Pelletier *Bernice* ■ *Dir* André Melançon • *Scr* Bernadette Renaud, André Melançon

The Bachelor ★★★

Romantic drama 1990 · It · Colour · 105mins

Roberto Faenza directs Keith Carradine, Miranda Richardson and Kristin Scott Thomas in a drama about loss and love, adapted from Arthur Schnitzler's novel. Carradine, a middle-class, middle-aged doctor who has never married, is devastated when his close sibling (Richardson) commits suicide. He subsequently embarks on a string of sexual liaisons with three women, one of whom is played by Richardson in a secondary role. This understated and atmospheric drama about midlife crisis and masculinity is a fine example of good European cinema – an all-too-rare occurrence in the age of the Europudding. LH

Keith Carradine *Dr Emil Grasler* • Miranda Richardson *Frederica/Widow* • Kristin Scott Thomas *Sabine* • Sarah-Jane Fenton *Katerina* • Max von Sydow *Von Schleheim* ■ *Dir* Roberto Faenza • *Scr* Enrico DeConcini, Roberto Faenza, Hugh Fleetwood (English language version), from the novel *Dr Grasler, Spa Physician* by Arthur Schnitzler • *Music* Ennio Morricone

B

The Bachelor ★★ 12

Romantic comedy
1999 · US · Colour · 97mins

This weak update of Buster Keaton's 1925 classic *Seven Chances* stars Chris O'Donnell as a young man who must get married by his 30th birthday (just 24 hours away) if he is to inherit $100 million from his deceased grandfather. His girlfriend (Renee Zellweger) has already given up on him, so he has to try all his ex-girlfriends. O'Donnell lacks the charisma and comic timing to hold this unfunny film together. JB [video] DVD

Chris O'Donnell *Jimmy Shannon* • Renee Zellweger *Anne* • Hal Holbrook *O'Dell* • James Cromwell *Priest* • Artie Lange *Marco* • Edward Asner *Gluckman* • Marley Shelton *Natalie* • Sarah Silverman *Carolyn* • Peter Ustinov *Grandad* • Mariah Carey *Ilana* • Brooke Shields *Buckley* ■ *Dir* Gary Sinyor • *Scr* Steve Cohen, from the film *Seven Chances* by Clyde Bruckman, Jean Havez, Joseph A Mitchell, from the play by Roi Cooper Megrue

The Bachelor and the Bobby-Soxer ★★★★ U

Comedy 1947 · US · BW · 90mins

Teenager Shirley Temple has a crush on womaniser Cary Grant (who wouldn't?), so her sister, judge Myrna Loy, orders Grant to wine and dine Temple until she grows sick of him. It's a thin premise for Grant's 50th movie (also known in the UK as *Bachelor Knight*), but sparkling playing and sheer starpower, not to mention Sidney Sheldon's Oscar-winning screenplay, turned this trifle into one of the top box-office hits of its day. Time hasn't dented its appeal. TS [video]

Cary Grant *Dick* • Myrna Loy *Margaret* • Shirley Temple *Susan* • Rudy Vallee *Tommy* • Ray Collins *Beemish* • Harry Davenport *Thaddeus* • Johnny Sands *Jerry* • Don Beddoe *Tony* • Lillian Randolph *Bessie* ■ *Dir* Irving Reis • *Scr* Sidney Sheldon

Bachelor Apartment ★★★

Drama 1931 · US · BW · 77mins

It's always interesting to see a Hollywood sex comedy from before when the puritanical Hays Code pooped the party. Here Lowell Sherman, who made a speciality of playing lecherous lovers, is the confirmed bachelor with three women on the go simultaneously. They are ladylike Irene Dunne (in one of her first films), vampish Mae Murray (in one of her last films) and innocent Claudia Dell. It's a trifle theatrical, but Sherman directs smoothly enough. RB

Lowell Sherman *Wayne Carter* • Irene Dunne *Helene Andrews* • Mae Murray *Agatha Carraway* • Ivan Lebedeff *Henri De Maneau* • Norman Kerry *Lee Graham* • Noel Francis *Janet* • Claudia Dell *Lita Andrews* ■ *Dir* Lowell Sherman • *Scr* John Howard Lawson, J Walter Ruben (adaptation and dialogue)

Bachelor Bait ★★

Romantic comedy 1934 · US · BW · 74mins

This mediocre little programme filler is of interest mainly as an early full-length feature directed by the great George Stevens. Stevens does well by this RKO comedy about a marriage bureau called Romance, Incorporated. It stars the amiable Stuart Erwin and the sexy Rochelle Hudson, and pert Pert Kelton scores as a gold-digger, but there's little else of real note. Stevens prefered to view the following year's *Alice Adams* as his directorial debut. TS

Stuart Erwin *Wilbur Fess* • Rochelle Hudson *Linda* • Pert Kelton *Allie Summers* • Skeets Gallagher [Richard "Skeets" Gallagher] *Van Dusen* • Berton Churchill *Big Barney* • Grady Sutton *Don Belden* • Clarence H Wilson [Clarence Wilson] *District Attorney* ■ *Dir* George Stevens • *Scr* Glenn Tryon, from a story by Edward Halperin, Victor Halperin

The Bachelor Father ★★★

Comedy 1931 · US · BW · 91mins

A rather nice vehicle for the venerable C Aubrey Smith, best known today as a crusty old actor in supporting roles embodying stiff-upper-lippery. Although Marion Davies and Ralph Forbes are billed above Sir C, this is his picture all the way. He plays the titular role of a man searching for his three grown-up children. Director Robert Z Leonard stands back and just lets the old ham get on with it. He does achieve some genuinely touching moments, but fails to completely disguise the film's theatrical origins. TS

Marion Davies *Tony Flagg* • Ralph Forbes *John Ashley* • C Aubrey Smith *Sir Basil Winterton* • Ray Milland *Geoffrey Trent* • Guinn "Big Boy" Williams *Dick Berney* • David Torrence *Doctor MacDonald* ■ *Dir* Robert Z Leonard • *Scr* Lawrence E Johnson, from the play by Edward Childs Carpenter

Bachelor Flat ★★★ U

Comedy 1961 · US · Colour · 91mins

Director Frank Tashlin scored cinematic bull's-eyes with his colourfully trenchant and hysterical satires, most famously *Son of Paleface* and *The Girl Can't Help It*. Here he cocks an anti-English snoot at California-style education, as girls run hot and cold through professor Terry-Thomas's beachside apartment. Terry-Thomas has had far better scripts than this to get his gapped teeth into; nevertheless he's compulsively watchable. TS

Tuesday Weld *Libby Bushmill* • Richard Beymer *Mike Pulaski* • Terry-Thomas *Professor Bruce Patterson* • Celeste Holm *Helen Bushmill* • Francesca Bellini *Gladys* • Howard McNear *Dr Bowman* • Ann Del Guercio *Liz* ■ *Dir* Frank Tashlin • *Scr* Frank Tashlin, Bud Grossman, from the play by Bud Grossman

Bachelor in Paradise ★★★

Comedy 1961 · US · Colour · 108mins

A typical relic of the Eisenhower era, this breezy satire on American lifestyle and morals stars Bob Hope as a famous travel-writer-cum-sociologist who, for tax reasons, adopts a phoney identity and settles down in a model housing development called "Paradise". The film's targets are marriage (Hope causes three divorces) and modern household gadgetry; the result is like a Jacques Tati version of *The Stepford Wives*. Hope quips his way through the jubilantly sexist material and cop-out ending. AT

Bob Hope *Adam J Niles* • Lana Turner *Rosemary Howard* • Janis Paige *Dolores Jynson* • Jim Hutton *Larry Delavane* • Paula Prentiss *Linda Delavane* • Don Porter *Thomas W Jynson* • Virginia Grey *Camille Quinlaw* ■ *Dir* Jack Arnold • *Scr* Valentine Davies, Hal Kanter, from a story by Vera Caspary

Bachelor Mother ★★★ U

Comedy 1939 · US · BW · 78mins

Although Ginger Rogers and David Niven are top-billed in this contrived but hugely enjoyable comedy, the real star is that cuddly curmudgeon Charles Coburn. As the department store tycoon who threatens to dismiss Rogers from the toy counter after she finds an abandoned baby, he times every disapproving look to perfection before melting like the big softy he was. Felix Jackson's story earned an Oscar nomination, but it's Norman Krasna's screenplay that merits the praise, along with the slick direction of Garson Kanin. DP [video]

Ginger Rogers *Polly Parrish* • David Niven *David Merlin* • Charles Coburn *JB Merlin* • Frank Albertson *Freddie Miller* • EE Clive *Butler* ■ *Dir* Garson Kanin • *Scr* Norman Krasna, from a story by Felix Jackson

Bachelor of Hearts ★★★ U

Romantic comedy
1958 · UK · Colour · 94mins

German actor Hardy Kruger stars in this rather charming romantic comedy, directed by the talented Wolf Rilla, and aided by a lovely performance from co-star Sylvia Syms. Today these gauche student antics look a little daft, but they are neatly depicted here by a pair of young screenwriters who have since become much more famous: Leslie Bricusse, distinguished co-writer of *Stop the World I Want to Get Off*, and Frederic Raphael, who collected an Oscar for *Darling*. TS

Hardy Kruger *Wolf* • Sylvia Syms *Ann* • Ronald Lewis *Hugo* • Jeremy Burnham *Adrian* • Peter Myers *Jeremy* • Philip Gilbert *Conrad* • Charles Kay *Tom* ■ *Dir* Wolf Rilla • *Scr* Leslie Bricusse, Frederic Raphael • *Cinematographer* Geoffrey Unsworth

The Bachelor Party ★★★★

Drama 1957 · US · BW · 94mins

Screenwriter Paddy Chayefsky's gift for realism-as-fable was never grittier than in this adaptation of his own TV play, in which a bawdy stag-night becomes an odyssey in which the American male's inherent fear of women is brilliantly explored – from porn movies to strip-show to hooker confrontation – all floated along on a river of alcohol. Nervous groom-to-be Philip Abbott is counterbalanced by Don Murray, the married man wondering if he did the right thing, while office bachelor Jack Warden presents a cheery persona to hide his own loneliness. As a companion piece to *Marty*, two years earlier, it has some profound things to say about the macho psyche. TH

Don Murray *Charlie Samson* • EG Marshall *Walter* • Jack Warden *Eddie* • Philip Abbott *Arnold* • Larry Blyden *Kenneth* • Patricia Smith *Helen Samson* • Carolyn Jones *Existentialist* • Nancy Marchand *Julie* • Karen Norris *Hostess* ■ *Dir* Delbert Mann • *Scr* Paddy Chayefsky, from his TV play

Bachelor Party ★★ 18

Comedy 1984 · US · Colour · 101mins

Chaos ensues as Tom Hanks's bachelor binge degenerates into a bawdy riot, in a plot similar to the formula used in *National Lampoon's Animal House* and *Porky's*. Neal Israel's bid to produce a riotous comedy doesn't really hit the mark and Hanks, already showing early promise, is the film's only redeeming feature. NF. Contains violence, swearing, sex scenes and nudity. [video] DVD

Tom Hanks *Rick Gassko* • Tawny Kitaen *Debbie Thompson* • Adrian Zmed *Jay O'Neill* • Robert Prescott *Cole Whittier* • George Grizzard *Mr Thompson* • Barbara Stuart *Mrs Thompson* • William Tepper *Dr Stan Gassko* ■ *Dir* Neal Israel • *Scr* Neal Israel, Pat Proft, from a story by Bob Israel

Back Door to Heaven ★★★

Crime drama 1939 · US · BW · 73mins

In its day, this grim 20th Century-Fox melodrama was much-discussed – it's a sort of *Cathy Come Home* about how the underprivileged drift into crime. A teacher awaits the return of former pupils, but one of them has ended up in reform school. Although the nominal star is sturdy Wallace Ford, the most interesting cast member is young Van Heflin as the errant student. Three movies after this one Van Heflin won an Oscar at MGM for *Johnny Eager*. TS

Aline MacMahon *Miss Williams* • Jimmy Lydon [James Lydon] *Frankie as a boy* • Anita Magee *Carol* • William Harrigan *Mr Rogers* • Jane Seymour (1) *Mrs Rogers* • Robert Wildhack *Rudolph Herzing* • Van Heflin *John Shelley as an adult* ■ *Dir* William K Howard • *Scr* William K Howard, John Bright, Robert Tasker

Back Door to Hell ★★

Second World War drama
1964 · US/Phil · BW · 69mins

The first of four films Jack Nicholson made with director Monte Hellman is a sparse war drama, shot in the Philippines at the same time as *Flight to Fury* and costing around $80,000. Nicholson plays one of three marines who reconnoitre a Japanese-held island ahead of the American invasion force. As far as Nicholson is concerned, the film allows us to see him learning as he goes along without giving any inkling that a major star was in the process of being born. AT

Jimmie Rodgers *Lieutenant Craig* • Jack Nicholson *Burnett* • John Hackett *Jersey* • Annabelle Huggins *Maria* • Conrad Maga *Paco* • Johnny Monteiro *Ramundo* • Joe Sison *Japanese captain* ■ *Dir* Monte Hellman • *Scr* Richard A Guttman, John Hackett, from a story by Richard A Guttman

Back from Eternity ★★★

Adventure drama 1956 · US · BW · 97mins

Director John Farrow waited 17 years to remake his movie *Five Came Back* and, if anything, the idea works even better the second time around. Rod Steiger and Robert Ryan star in this story of a plane that crash-lands in cannibal country, using every trick of the acting trade to up-stage each other. It's still an obvious situation, but the budget is better than it was for the 1939 original and the treatment more spectacular. TH

Robert Ryan *Bill* • Anita Ekberg *Rena* • Rod Steiger *Vasquel* • Phyllis Kirk *Louise* • Keith Andes *Joe* • Gene Barry *Ellis* • Fred Clark *Crimp* • Beulah Bondi *Martha* ■ *Dir* John Farrow • *Scr* Jonathan Latimer, from a story by Richard Carroll

Back in Action ★★ 18

Action thriller 1993 · Can · Colour · 79mins

When a nasty drug dealer guts his partner, cop Roddy Piper sets his sights on eliminating the gang. At the same time, cabbie Billy Blanks attempts to shelter his uncooperative sister from the same gang, who want her rubbed out because she witnessed the killing. An incredibly brutal film that boasts about one shoot-out or bone-breaking fight every ten minutes but, to its credit, it doesn't take itself too seriously. KB [video] DVD

"Rowdy" Roddy Piper [Roddy Piper] *Frank Rossi* • Billy Blanks *Billy* • Bobbie Phillips *Helen* • Kai Soremekun *Tara* ■ *Dir* Steve DiMarco • *Scr* Karl Schiffman

Back in the USSR ★ 15

Romantic thriller
1992 · US/Rus · Colour · 83mins

This uninspiring thriller propels Frank Whaley from support roles (where he should, quite frankly, have stayed) to lead protagonist as an American getting lost in the Russian underworld. Encountering the feisty Natalya Negoda, the two become romantically entwined. Far from generating excitement, their relationship makes the film about as unappealing as a piece of tripe. LH [video] DVD

Frank Whaley *Archer Sloan* • Natalya Negoda *Lena* • Roman Polanski *Kurilov* • Andrew Divoff *Dimitri* • Dey Young *Claudia* • Ravil Issyanov *Georgi* • Harry Ditson *Whittier* • Brian Blessed *Chazov* ■ *Dir* Deran Sarafian • *Scr* Lindsay Smith, from a story by Lindsay Smith, Ilmar Taska

Back of Beyond ★ 15

Romantic crime thriller
1995 · Aus · Colour · 81mins

This below-par Australian thriller was actually inspired by the Quentin Tarantino-scripted *True Romance*. Paul Mercurio reveals why we've heard so little of him since *Strictly Ballroom* with his unconvincing portrayal of a garage owner shaken by the motorcycle death of his sister, while a peroxided Colin Friels gives a risible rendition of paranoid villainy. DP

Paul Mercurio *Tom McGregor* • Colin Friels *Connor* • Dee Smart *Charlie* • John Polson *Nick* • Bob Maza *Gilbert* • Rebekah Elmaloglou *Susan McGregor* ■ *Dir* Michael Robertson • *Scr* Richard J Sawyer, Paul Leadon, AM Brooksbank, from a story by Richard J Sawyer, from a treatment by Michael Robertson

Back Roads ★★ 15

Comedy drama 1981 · US · Colour · 94mins

A big-hearted hooker in the Deep South falls in love with an unsuccessful boxer who is unable to pay for her services. Together they take to the road to seek better times. Starring Sally Fields and Tommy Lee Jones and directed by Martin Ritt, this cutesy road movie is a journey to nowhere: an unbelievable collection of outmoded clichés and a waste of its talented leads. RK

Sally Field *Amy Post* • Tommy Lee Jones *Elmore Pratt* • David Keith *Mason* • Miriam Colon *Angel* • Michael V Gazzo *Tazio* • Dan Shor *Spivey* • M Emmet Walsh *Arthur* ■ *Dir* Martin Ritt • *Scr* Gary DeVore

Back Room Boy ★★ U

Second World War comedy
1942 · UK · BW · 82mins

How many flag-waving British comedies during the Second World War rehashed the old "haunted house full of spies" plot? The year after Will Hay used the premise in *The Ghost of St Michael's*, his regular sidekicks Graham Moffatt and Moore Marriott cropped up in this inferior version set on an Orkney island lighthouse, tailored for the talents of Arthur Askey. The main problem is that the film hammers home every gag, with Askey particularly at fault. DP

Arthur Askey *Arthur Pilbeam* • Googie Withers *Bobbie* • Moore Marriott *Jerry* • Graham Moffatt *Albert* • Vera Frances *Jane* • Joyce Howard *Betty* ■ *Dir* Herbert Mason • *Scr* Val Guest, Marriott Edgar

Back Street ★★

Romantic melodrama
1932 · US · BW · 84mins

This tale of the self-sacrificing mistress of a married man, who comes to grief after over 20 years of "backstreet" fidelity, would be filmed twice more (in 1941 and 1961) to be wept over by successive generations. This first version, directed by John M Stahl, is the least successful, due to a stilted script and an even more stilted and unattractive performance from John Boles. Ladylike and long-suffering, the accomplished Irene Dunne radiates her usual sweetness. RK

Irene Dunne *Ray Schmidt* • John Boles *Walter Saxel* • June Clyde *Freda Schmidt* • George Meeker *Kurt Schendler* • ZaSu Pitts *Mrs Dole* • Shirley Grey *Francine* • Doris Lloyd *Mrs Saxel* ■ *Dir* John M Stahl • *Scr* Gladys Lehman, Lynn Starling, from the novel by Fannie Hurst

Back Street ★★★★

Romantic melodrama
1941 · US · BW · 88mins

This remake of the 1932 film of Fannie Hurst's tear-jerking bestseller about the long-standing mistress of a married man, whose understanding, discretion and fidelity lead only to heartbreak, stars the luminous Margaret Sullavan, who waits in vain for her wealthy banker lover, played by the smoothly sexy Charles Boyer. Both stars pull out all the stops in conveying their torment under the expert direction of Robert Stevenson and with a little help from an excellent supporting cast. An irresistible period romance, requiring a handy box of Kleenex for a totally enjoyable wallow. RK

Charles Boyer *Walter Saxel* • Margaret Sullavan *Ray Smith* • Richard Carlson *Curt Stanton* • Frank McHugh *Ed Porter* • Frank Jenks *Harry Niles* • Tim Holt *Richard Saxel* • Peggy Stewart *Freda Smith* • Samuel S Hinds *Felix Darren* ■ *Dir* Robert Stevenson • *Scr* Bruce Manning, Felix Jackson, from the novel by Fannie Hurst

Back Street ★★★★

Romantic melodrama
1961 · US · Colour · 105mins

The third and final version of the three-handkerchief weepie about a long-running and painful love affair between a married man and his mistress updates the story and gives it the full Ross Hunter treatment. This time the suffering pair are cast for glamour, with Susan Hayward languishing in luxury and sumptuous clothes by Jean Louis, and the glossily good-looking John Gavin playing the object of her tormented affections. David Miller directs efficiently, while Vera Miles supplies an entertaining turn as Gavin's alcoholic wife. Wildly enjoyable melodrama. RK

Susan Hayward *Rae Smith* • John Gavin *Paul Saxon* • Vera Miles *Liz Saxon* • Charles Drake *Curt Stanton* • Virginia Grey *Janie* • Reginald Gardiner *Dalian* • Tammy Marihugh *Caroline Saxon* • Robert Eyer *Paul Saxon Jr* ■ *Dir* David Miller • *Scr* Eleanore Griffin, William Ludwig, from the novel by Fannie Hurst

Back to Bataan ★★★ PG

Second World War drama
1945 · US · BW · 87mins

MGM scored a tremendous success with the then topical war film *Bataan* back in 1943, so it was a Hollywood inevitability that the Philippines would be revisited. However, instead of the searing campaign study that was expected, RKO plumped for a routine action film starring John Wayne. Still exciting for all that, the plot features a surprisingly subdued Duke as a colonel leading his unit of guerrillas in an undercover mission through the rather obvious studio foliage to victory. It's all expertly directed by former editor Edward Dmytryk. TS

John Wayne *Colonel Madden* • Anthony Quinn *Captain Andres Bonifacio* • Beulah Bondi *Miss Bertha Barnes* • Fely Franquelli *Dalisay Delgado* • Richard Loo *Major Hasko* • Philip Ahn *Colonel Kuroki* • "Ducky" Louie *Maximo* ■ *Dir* Edward Dmytryk • *Scr* Ben Barzman, Richard Landau, from a story by Aeneas MacKenzie, William Gordon

Back to God's Country ★★★

Adventure 1953 · US · Colour · 77mins

Rock Hudson makes a splendid job of starring in this rugged story set in the far Canadian north. Hudson is a sea captain, married to the rather colourless Marcia Henderson, who has to face up to the tough weather and an even tougher Steve Cochran. Hudson tackles his plight splendidly, or at least well enough to convince his bosses at Universal he was ready for promotion to A-features: next came *Taza, Son of Cochise*, then his star-making performance in *Magnificent Obsession*. TS

Rock Hudson *Peter Keith* • Marcia Henderson *Dolores Keith* • Steve Cochran *Paul Blake* • Hugh O'Brian *Frank Hudson* • Chubby Johnson *Billy Shorter* • Tudor Owen *Fitzsimmons* • John Cliff *Joe* ■ *Dir* Joseph Pevney • *Scr* Tom Reed, from the novel by James Oliver Curwood

Back to School ★★ 15

Comedy 1986 · US · Colour · 92mins

Co-written by Harold Ramis, of *Groundhog Day* fame, this ham-fisted comedy stars Rodney Dangerfield as a wealthy middle-aged man returns to college to prove there's life in the old dog yet. Dangerfield drives in every gag with the subtlety of a steam hammer. Keith Gordon and Robert Downey Jr try hard as Dangerfield's weedy son and his radical pal, but the standouts are English teacher Sally Kellerman and coach M Emmett Walsh. DP

Rodney Dangerfield *Thornton Melon* • Keith Gordon *Jason Melon* • Sally Kellerman *Diane Turner* • Burt Young *Lou* • Robert Downey Jr *Derek* • Paxton Whitehead *Philip Barbay* • Terry Farrell *Valerie Desmond* • M Emmet Walsh *Coach Turnbull* ■ *Dir* Alan Metter • *Scr* Steven Kampmann, Will Porter, Peter Torokvei, Harold Ramis, from a story by Rodney Dangerfield, Greg Fields, Dennis Snee

Back to the Beach ★★★ PG

Satirical comedy 1987 · US · Colour · 88mins

Twenty years after hanging up their swimsuits in the highly successful *Beach Party* movies, 1960s teen idols Annette Funicello and Frankie Avalon returned for more fun in the sun in this agreeably nostalgic surf down pop culture's trash-filled memory lane. Now married, and living in Ohio, the couple decide to visit their daughter in California. Little do they know she's living with a beach bum, and when Frankie's old flame Connie Stevens also turns up, more rifts occur in the perfect family unit. Cleverly sending up the entire beach genre and crammed with camp cameos, Frankie and Annette parody their own squeaky clean personas with glee. AJ

Frankie Avalon *The Big Kahuna* • Annette Funicello *Annette* • Connie Stevens *Connie* • Lori Loughlin *Sandi* • Tommy Hinkley *Michael* • Demian Slade *Bobby* • Pee-wee Herman [Paul Reubens] *Pee-wee Herman* • Don Adams *Harbor master* ■ *Dir* Lyndall Hobbs • *Scr* Peter Krikes, Steve Meerson, Christopher Thompson, from the story by James Komack, from characters created by Lou Rusoff

Back to the Future ★★★★★ PG

Comedy adventure
1985 · US · Colour · 111mins

This irresistible combination of dazzling effects and sly comedy propelled Michael J Fox to stardom and Robert Zemeckis to the front rank of Hollywood directors. Fox plays the student who travels back in time to the 1950s and acts as matchmaker for his future parents. It's beautifully played by the cast (honourable mentions to Christopher Lloyd, Lea Thompson and Crispin Glover), making the most of an ingenious script, which finds time to poke fun at 50s icons between the bouts of time travelling. Zemeckis's direction is adroit and he never lets the effects swamp the film. JF. Contains swearing. DVD

Michael J Fox *Marty McFly* • Christopher Lloyd *Dr Emmett Brown* • Lea Thompson *Lorraine Baines* • Crispin Glover *George McFly* • Thomas F Wilson *Biff Tannen* • Claudia Wells *Jennifer Parker* • Marc McClure *Dave McFly* • Wendie Jo Sperber *Linda McFly* ■ *Dir* Robert Zemeckis • *Scr* Robert Zemeckis, Bob Gale • *Special Effects* Kevin Pike

Back to the Future Part II ★★★ PG

Comedy adventure
1989 · US · Colour · 103mins

After the success of the first time-travelling caper a sequel was inevitable, although this time around director Robert Zemeckis is guilty of over-gilding the lily. Stars Michael J Fox and Christopher Lloyd return, along with Lea Thompson and Thomas F Wilson, but the script is too clever for its own good and the film gets bogged down by cramming in too many ideas and settings (past, future, alternative universes). The effects, however, are even better than in the first film. JF. Contains swearing, violence. DVD

Michael J Fox *Marty McFly/Marty McFly Jr/Marlene McFly* • Christopher Lloyd *Dr Emmett Brown* • Lea Thompson *Lorraine* • Thomas F Wilson *Biff Tannen/Griff Tannen* • Harry Waters Jr *Marvin Berry* • Charles Fleischer *Terry* • Elisabeth Shue *Jennifer* ■ *Dir* Robert Zemeckis • *Scr* Bob Gale, from a story by Bob Gale, Robert Zemeckis

Back to the Future Part III ★★★★ PG

Comedy adventure
1990 · US · Colour · 113mins

Director Robert Zemeckis's blockbusting trilogy went slightly off the rails with the second segment, but it got right back on track with the concluding instalment. The film is set predominantly in the Old West and, as before, the plot revolves around the need to tinker with time and the problem of how to power the trusty DeLorean car so that Fox can get back to the present. Bob Gale and Zemeckis have come up with an ingenious plot and a clutch of in-jokes, Michael J Fox is on cracking form and Christopher Lloyd's romance with Mary Steenburgen is surprisingly touching. JF. Contains swearing. DVD

Michael J Fox *Marty McFly/Seamus McFly* • Christopher Lloyd *"Doc" Emmett Brown* • Mary Steenburgen *Clara Clayton* • Thomas F Wilson *Buford "Mad Dog" Tannen/Biff Tannen* • Lea Thompson *Maggie McFly/Lorraine McFly* • Elisabeth Shue *Jennifer* • Richard Dysart *Barbed wire salesman* • Pat Buttram *Saloon old timer* • Harry Carey Jr *Saloon old timer* • Dub Taylor *Saloon old timer* ■ *Dir* Robert Zemeckis • *Scr* Bob Gale, from a story by Bob Gale, Robert Zemeckis

Backbeat ★★★ 15

Biographical drama
1993 · UK · Colour · 99mins

Iain Softley's account of the Fab Four's Hamburg days is rather like their music of the time: loud, raw and full of energy. It also betrays a lack of experience, leaving too much to enthusiasm. Focusing primarily on the relationship between John Lennon and "Fifth Beatle" Stuart Sutcliffe, it descends into tacky melodrama once Sutcliffe falls for photographer Astrid Kirchherr. Ian Hart is solid enough in another of his outings as Lennon (he played the Beatle in *The Hours and Times*), but Stephen Dorff and Sheryl Lee only occasionally convince as the star-crossed lovers. DP. Contains violence, swearing, drug abuse and nudity. DVD

Sheryl Lee *Astrid Kirchherr* • Stephen Dorff *Stuart Sutcliffe* • Ian Hart *John Lennon* • Gary Bakewell *Paul McCartney* • Chris O'Neill *George Harrison* • Scot Williams *Pete Best* • Kai Wiesinger *Klaus Voormann* • Jennifer Ehle *Cynthia Powell* ■ *Dir* Iain Softley • *Scr* Iain Softley, Michael Thomas, Stephen Ward

Backdraft ★★★★ 15

Action drama 1991 · US · Colour · 131mins

Director Ron Howard has become one of the most accomplished of Hollywood craftsmen, and this sturdy star-studded fare was deservedly a mainstream hit. Kurt Russell and William Baldwin are the two warring, firefighting brothers who have to cope with a rash of fires sparked by a seemingly deranged arsonist, whose lethal "backdrafts" are resulting in death and destruction. The plot is hardly original, but Howard marshals the sprawling elements with great finesse and the fire footage, if harrowing at times, is genuinely exhilarating. JF. Contains swearing, sex scenes and nudity. DVD

Kurt Russell *Stephen McCaffrey* • William Baldwin *Brian McCaffrey* • Robert De Niro *Donald Rimgale* • Jennifer Jason Leigh *Jennifer Vaitkus* • Scott Glenn *John Adcox* • Rebecca De Mornay *Helen McCaffrey* • Jason Gedrick *Tim Krizminski* • JT Walsh *Martin Swayzak* • Donald Sutherland *Ronald Bartel* ■ *Dir* Ron Howard • *Scr* Gregory Widen

U = SUITABLE FOR ALL Uc = SUITABLE FOR ALL, ESPECIALLY FOR YOUNG CHILDREN (VIDEO ONLY) PG = PARENTAL GUIDANCE

Backfire ★

Mystery 1950 · US · BW · 91mins

With Gordon MacRae and Virginia Mayo in the leads, this ought to be a musical. As an ex-soldier just released from hospital and his obliging nurse, they're clearly unsuited to serious detective work as they investigate the disappearance of Edmond O'Brien, a friend of MacRae's wanted for murder. Too many writers cooked up the convoluted story, with its excess of flashbacks, and Vincent Sherman's direction fails to liven the pace. AE

Virginia Mayo *Julie Benson* • Gordon MacRae *Bob Corey* • Edmond O'Brien *Steve Connolly* • Dane Clark *Ben Arno* • Viveca Lindfors *Lysa Randolph* • Ed Begley *Capt Garcia* ■ *Dir* Vincent Sherman • *Scr* Larry Marcus, Ivan Goff, Ben Roberts

Backfire ★★ 18

Mystery thriller
1987 · US/Can · Colour · 88mins

Occasionally, films get better performances than they deserve. Here it's Karen Allen and Keith Carradine who rise above the predictable plotting. Allen is pretty convincing, although her plan to bump off husband Jeff Fahey and share his loot with lover Dean Paul Martin is gruyère-like in its feasibility. Things perk up a bit when stranger Keith Carradine gives her a taste of her own hallucinogenic medicine, but the direction is too deliberate for any surprises. DP

Karen Allen *Mara* • Keith Carradine *Reed* • Jeff Fahey *Donnie* • Bernie Casey *Clint* • Dean Paul Martin *Jake* ■ *Dir* Gilbert Cates • *Scr* Larry Brand, Rebecca Reynolds

Background ★★

Drama 1953 · UK · BW · 82mins

This stiff little picture is supposed to be a grown-up drama about the need to adopt a responsible attitude to divorce. However, by overplaying the "for the sake of the children" angle and allowing Valerie Hobson and Philip Friend to bicker in clipped BBC accents, director Daniel Birt succeeds not in discussing a difficult subject in a meaningful way, but only in drawing unintentional laughs. DP

Valerie Hobson *Barbie Lomax* • Philip Friend *John Lomax* • Norman Wooland *Bill Ogden* • Janette Scott *Jess Lomax* • Mandy Miller *Linda Lomax* • Jeremy Spenser *Adrian Lomax* ■ *Dir* Daniel Birt • *Scr* Warren Chetham Strode, Don Sharp, from the play by Warren Chetham Strode

Background to Danger ★★★

Second World War spy drama
1943 · US · BW · 79mins

One of the few starring roles not turned down by Warner Bros contract artist George Raft (he allegedly said no to *The Maltese Falcon* and *Casablanca* among others), this is a rattling good action film, with smoothie Raft battling Nazis in a studio-bound Turkey (the *Casablanca* sets revamped?). Warner stalwarts and *Casablanca* veterans Sydney Greenstreet and Peter Lorre are on welcome stand-by, but Brenda Marshall (then married to actor William Holden) is unfortunately a rather glamour-less leading lady. TS

George Raft *Joe Barton* • Brenda Marshall *Tamara* • Sydney Greenstreet *Colonel Robinson* • Peter Lorre *Zaleshoff* • Osa Massen *Ana Remzi* • Turhan Bey *Hassan* • Willard Robertson *McNamara* ■ *Dir* Raoul Walsh • *Scr* WR Burnett, from the novel *Uncommon Danger* by Eric Ambler

Backlash ★★★

Western 1956 · US · Colour · 84mins

This is a bizarre western, with a superbly neurotic Richard Widmark as the gunfighter searching for gold and the sole survivor of a mining party that was massacred by Indians. Made by John Sturges just before his classic *Gunfight at the OK Corral*, this develops into a heavily symbolic Freudian story that has to be seen to be believed. AT

Richard Widmark *Jim Slater* • Donna Reed *Karyl Orton* • William Campbell *Johnny Cool* • John McIntire *Jim Bonniwell* • Barton MacLane *George Lake* • Edward Platt *Sheriff Marson* ■ *Dir* John Sturges • *Scr* Borden Chase, from a novel by Frank Gruber

Backlash ★★★

Road movie 1986 · Aus · Colour · 90mins

Produced, scripted and directed by documentarist Bill Bennett, this highly distinctive road movie builds up suspense through improvised dialogue, off-screen cries in the dead of night, and the disconcerting contrasts between the claustrophobic confines of a police car and the untamed vastness of the Australian outback. The performances are credible, and Bennett's use of locations is often inspired. DP. Contains violence, swearing and some nudity.

David Argue *Trevor Darling* • Gia Carides *Nikki Iceton* • Lydia Miller *Kath* • Brian Syron *Executioner* • Anne Smith *Mrs Smith* • Don Smith *Mr Smith* ■ *Dir/Scr* Bill Bennett

Backsliding ★★

Psychological thriller
1991 · Aus/UK · Colour · 88mins

This little-seen Australian thriller begins promisingly, only to descend rapidly and irreversibly into clichéd chaos. Director Simon Target handles the set pieces with confidence, but his grasp of character and atmosphere leaves a lot to be desired. Unfortunately, he's given little assistance from a cast headed by Tim Roth, as the drifter whose arrival at an outback gas plant sparks tension between born-again ex-convict Jim Holt and his holier-than-thou wife, Odile LeClezio. DP

Tim Roth *Tom Whitton* • Jim Holt *Jack Tyson* • Odile Le Clezio *Alison Tyson* • Ross McGregor *Pastor* ■ *Dir* Simon Target • *Scr* Simon Target, Ross Wilson

Backstreet Dreams ★★ 18

Drama 1990 · US · Colour · 95mins

Jason O'Malley has no one to blame but himself as he co-produced, wrote and stars in this self-indulgent, contrived tale. It mixes elements of crime and family dramas to no logical effect, and an interesting cast can do little but flounder. O'Malley plays a small-time crook with an autistic child who finds an unlikely friend in PhD psychology student Brooke Shields when his wife (Sherilyn Fenn) leaves him. JF. Contains violence, swearing and drug abuse.

Brooke Shields *Stephanie Bloom* • Jason O'Malley *Dean Costello* • Sherilyn Fenn *Lucy Costello* • Tony Fields *Manny Santana* • Burt Young *Luca Garibaldi* • Anthony Franciosa *Angelo Carnivale* ■ *Dir* Rupert Hitzig • *Scr* Jason O'Malley

Backtrack ★★★

Western 1969 · US · Colour · 95mins

This Wild West reworking of *The Three Musketeers* is an entertaining curiosity. Not only do cast members of hit TV series *The Virginian* and *Laredo* reprise their characters, but background scenes and out-takes from the shows are utilised by director Earl Bellamy. Fernando Lamas revels in his villainy, but he proves no match for Doug McClure as the cowhand who teams up with a trio of Texas Rangers while on a mission to Mexico. But maybe most intriguing is the inclusion of Hollywood sirens Ida Lupino and Rhonda Fleming. DP

Neville Brand *Reese* • James Drury *Ramrod* • Doug McClure *Trampas* • Peter Brown *Chad* • William Smith *Riley* • Philip Carey *Captain Parmalee* • Ida Lupino *Mama Dolores* • Rhonda Fleming *Carmelita Flanagan* • Fernando Lamas *Captain Estrada* • Royal Dano *Faraway* • LQ Jones *Belden* ■ *Dir* Earl Bellamy • *Scr* Borden Chase

Bad ★★★★ 18

Black comedy 1976 · US · Colour · 58mins

Camp icon Carroll Baker (*Baby Doll*) pulls out all the stops as a Queens housewife using her electrolysis business as a front for a freelance assassination operation. Very funny and very sick (the scene where a baby is thrown out of a window is justly infamous), director Jed Johnson's absurdist excursion into John Waters territory is a hugely satisfying satire on rotten 1970s society. Not for those of a nervous disposition. AJ

Carroll Baker *Mrs Aiken* • Perry King *LT* • Susan Tyrrell *Mary Aiken* • Stefania Casini *PG* • Cyrinda Foxe *RC* • Mary Boylan *Grandmother* • Brigid Polk *Estelle* ■ *Dir* Jed Johnson • *Scr* Pat Hackett, George Abagnalo

The Bad and the Beautiful ★★★★ PG

Drama 1952 · US · BW · 113mins

Riven by political investigation, competition from TV and the realisation that the Golden Age had passed, Hollywood produced a series of withering self-portraits in the early 1950s that revealed, beneath the tinsel, a sordidness worthy of Dorian Gray. Full of insider gags, Vincente Minnelli's fizzing melodrama touches more than a few raw nerves as it charts the decline and fall of a movie mogul (Kirk Douglas) through the eyes of a writer (Dick Powell), a director (Barry Sullivan) and an actress (Lana Turner). Allegedly an amalgam of David O Selznick and Val Lewton, the character of Jonathan Shields is made truly detestable by Douglas. DP

Kirk Douglas *Jonathan Shields* • Lana Turner *Georgia Lorrison* • Walter Pidgeon *Harry Pebbel* • Dick Powell *James Lee Bartlow* • Barry Sullivan *Fred Amiel* • Gloria Grahame *Rosemary Bartlow* • Vanessa Brown *Kay Amiel* ■ *Dir* Vincente Minnelli • *Scr* Charles Schnee, from a story by George Bradshaw

Bad Bascomb ★★ U

Western 1946 · US · BW · 110mins

MGM tried to perk up the career of ageing Wallace Beery by putting him opposite rising moppet Margaret O'Brien as well as teaming him again with character actress Marjorie Main. It's another case of Beery the badman being reformed – this time by O'Brien and Main as members of a Mormon wagon train. Produced to excessive length by the unfortunately named OO Dull, it has its sickly moments but the action pieces are well handled. AE

Wallace Beery *Zeb Bascomb* • Margaret O'Brien *Emmy* • Marjorie Main *Abbey Hanks* • J Carrol Naish *Bart Yancy* • Frances Rafferty *Dora* • Marshall Thompson *Jimmy Holden* • Russell Simpson *Elijah Walker* ■ *Dir* Sylvan Simon [S Sylvan Simon] • *Scr* William Lipman, Grant Carrett, from a story by DA Loxley

Bad Behaviour ★★★ 15

Comedy drama 1992 · UK · Colour · 99mins

This slightly eccentric comedy is in the new Mike Leigh school of movie-making; in other words, wry, improvised, rooted in social nuance and dependent on the audience's recognition of character types. Director Les Blair has fashioned an amusing look at the external stresses that can crack a seemingly idyllic partnership, with Stephen Rea and Sinead Cusack as the oddly cast but affecting pair. This bobs along pleasingly enough but with a curious lack of soul. SH. Contains drug abuse.

Stephen Rea *Gerry McAllister* • Sinead Cusack *Ellie McAllister* • Philip Jackson *Howard Spink* • Clare Higgins *Jessica Kennedy* • Phil Daniels *The Nunn Brothers* • Mary Jo Randle *Winifred Turner* • Saira Todd *Sophie Bevan* • Amanda Boxer *Linda Marks* ■ *Dir/Scr* Les Blair

Bad Blood ★★★★ 18

Crime drama based on a true story
1982 · UK/NZ · Colour · 109mins

This has been rightly hailed as a key release in New Zealand cinema – even if many of those involved are foreign imports. Based on a notorious murder case, it stars Australian Jack Thompson as a reclusive farmer who refuses to surrender his weapons to the authorities during the Second World War, leading to a violent manhunt. British director Mike Newell keeps the tension simmering, while managing to look sympathetically at the farmer's plight. Thompson is superb, but veteran New Zealand character actor Martyn Sanderson steals the show. JF

Jack Thompson *Stanley Graham* • Carol Burns *Dorothy Graham* • Denis Lill *Ted Best* • Donna Akersten *Doreen Bond* • Martyn Sanderson *Les North* • Marshall Napier *Trev Bond* ■ *Dir* Mike Newell • *Scr* Andrew Brown, from the book *Manhunt: The Story of Stanley Graham* by Howard Willis

Bad Boy Bubby ★★★ 18

Horror comedy
1993 · Aus/It · Colour · 109mins

This experimental attempt at the cinema of the grotesque will not be to everyone's taste. It's the grim and controversial story of an imprisoned, abused, childlike 35-year-old who has never encountered another human being other than his mother, and what happens when the outside world finally crashes in on his squalid existence. Using differing cinematic styles to relate each of Bubby's adventures, director Rolf De Heer lets the viewer feel some of Bubby's disorientation. Hugely effective at best, irritating and shocking at worst. AJ. Contains swearing and sex scenes.

Nicholas Hope *Bubby* • Claire Benito *Mom* • Ralph Cotterill *Pop* • Carmel Johnson *Angel* • Syd Brisbane *Yobbo* • Nikki Price *Screaming woman* • Norman Kaye *Scientist* • Paul Philpot *Paul* ■ *Dir/Scr* Rolf De Heer

Bad Boys ★★★ 18

Prison drama 1983 · US · Colour · 104mins

Sean Penn stars as a young street thug who tries to steal a pile of drugs from a rival gang, only for it all to go horribly wrong. Penn ends up serving time in the same correctional facility as the rival he tried to cheat. Littered with violence (a revenge rape, shootings, fights) and flashy direction from Rick Rosenthal (*Halloween II*), this can be hard to stomach, but does boast an early strong and neurotic performance from Penn. JB DVD

Sean Penn *Mick O'Brien* • Reni Santoni *Ramon Herrera* • Jim Moody *Gene Daniels* • Eric Gurry *Horowitz* • Esai Morales *Paco Moreno* • Ally Sheedy *JC Walenski* ■ *Dir* Richard L Rosenthal [Rick Rosenthal] • *Scr* Richard DiLello

Bad Boys ★★★★ 18

Action comedy thriller
1995 · US · Colour · 114mins

This is a perfect example of debuting director Michael Bay's slick abilities. In fact, this is probably one of the best buddy movies in years, with Bay's eye for cool ultra-violence enhanced by the inspired double-act of Will Smith and Martin Lawrence. The plot revolves around the audacious robbery of a huge cache of heroin. Enter our two heroes: Smith as the womanising bachelor and Lawrence as his married strait-laced partner, who are forced to swap lifestyles to fool the only witness to the crime (Téa Leoni). JF. Contains violence and swearing. DVD

Martin Lawrence *Marcus Burnett* • Will Smith *Mike Lowrey* • Téa Leoni *Julie Mott* • Tcheky Karyo *Fouchet* • Theresa Randle *Theresa Burnett* • Marg Helgenberger *Alison Sinclair* • Nestor Serrano *Detective Sanchez* ■ *Dir* Michael Bay • *Scr* Michael Barrie, Jim Mulholland, Doug Richardson, from a story by George Gallo

Bad Boys II ★★ 15

Action comedy thriller
2003 · US · Colour · 140mins

This overindulgent sequel reteams bickering cops Will Smith and Martin Lawrence and features high-gloss action and brutal bloodshed on a formidable scale. Add a hollow romantic subplot with Gabrielle Union and the banal premise of taking down a Cuban drugs lord, and this extends to a torturous length. By the end, you just want to escape from this smug, sadistic nonsense. JC. Contains violence and swearing. DVD

Martin Lawrence *Det Marcus Burnett* • Will Smith *Det Mike Lowrey* • Jordi Molla *Hector Juan Carlos "Johnny" Tapia* • Gabrielle Union *Sydney "Syd" Burnett* • Peter Stormare *Alexei* • Theresa Randle *Theresa Burnett* • Joe Pantoliano *Captain Howard* ■ *Dir* Michael Bay • *Scr* Ron Shelton, Jerry Stahl, from a story by Marianne Wibberley, Cormac Wibberley, Ron Shelton, from characters created by George Gallo

Bad Company ★★

Crime drama 1931 · US · BW · 73mins

Following their success in *Her Man* (1930), director Tay Garnett reunited Ricardo Cortez and Helen Twelvetrees for this hammy Mob melodrama, which survived initial hostility to become one of the genre's real curios. It was one of the first movies to portray organised crime as a family business. Although occasionally prone to excess, Twelvetrees still demonstrates considerable pluck as the bride discovering that both lawyer husband John Garrick and brother Frank Conroy are Cortez's lackeys. DP

Helen Twelvetrees *Helen King* • Ricardo Cortez *Goldie Gorio* • John Garrick *Steven Carlyle* • Paul Hurst *Butler* • Frank Conroy *Markham King* • Frank McHugh *Doc* ■ *Dir* Tay Garnett • *Scr* Tom Buckingham, Tay Garnett, from the novel *Put on the Spot* by Jack Lait

Bad Company ★★★★ 15

Western 1972 · US · Colour · 88mins

This oddball take on the American Civil War stars Jeff Bridges as the leader of runaways from conscription. He's joined by Barry Brown, and the crew become outlaws, drifting towards the Mississippi. As an evocation of past times, it's a remarkably successful venture for first-time director Robert Benton, a Robert Altman protégé who co-wrote *Bonnie and Clyde*. Woody Allen's one-time cinematographer, Gordon Willis, provides the autumnal mood that gives the idea an elegaic resonance. TH DVD

Jeff Bridges *Jake Rumsey* • Barry Brown *Drew Dixon* • Jim Davis *Marshal* • David Huddleston *Big Joe* • John Savage *Loney* • Jerry Houser *Arthur Simms* • Damon Cofer *Jim Bob Logan* • Joshua Hill Lewis *Boog Bookin* ■ *Dir* Robert Benton • *Scr* David Newman, Robert Benton

Bad Company ★★★ 18

Thriller 1994 · US · Colour · 86mins

Two of video's biggest draws, Lance Henriksen and Eric Roberts, team up for this novel spin on *The Hitcher*. Essentially a two-hander, Henriksen plays a salesman travelling cross-country in a state being stalked by the serial killer of the title. When he reluctantly hooks up with sinister hitch-hiker Roberts, it soon becomes apparent that both men have dark secrets to hide. Director Victor Salva edgily plays out the cat-and-mouse games between two dangerous men. JF. Contains violence, sex scenes, swearing and drug abuse.

Lance Henriksen *Jack Powell* • Eric Roberts *Adrian (Dusty)* • Brion James *Sheriff Gordon* • Sasha Jenson *Gerald* • Ana Gabriel *Dahlia* ■ *Dir/Scr* Victor Salva

Bad Company ★★ 15

Thriller 1995 · US · Colour · 103mins

On paper this sexy thriller must have looked foolproof, with the two charismatic leads, Laurence Fishburne and Ellen Barkin, capable of generating a fair amount of on-screen steam. However, the plodding direction and an unnecessarily convoluted script put paid to any high expectations. Fishburne plays the newest recruit to a shadowy organisation specialising in industrial espionage, who becomes romantically involved with one of his colleagues (Barkin). JF. Contains swearing, violence, sex scenes.

Ellen Barkin *Margaret Wells* • Laurence Fishburne *Nelson Crowe* • Frank Langella *Vic Grimes* • Spalding Gray *Walter Curl* • Michael Beach *Tod Stapp* • Gia Carides *Julie Ames* ■ *Dir* Damian Harris • *Scr* Ross Thomas

Bad Company ★★★ 12

Action comedy thriller
2002 · US · Colour · 111mins

This pedestrian take on the traditional buddy movie is a brash, self-satisfied tale, in which Anthony Hopkins's veteran CIA agent must transform unrefined motormouth Chris Rock into a believable replacement for his murdered agent twin brother. While there's no denying everything looks great, strip away the sleek veneer and what remains is a virtual A to Z of action comedy techniques and clichés. Chris Rock is implausible as he repeatedly slips out of character, but the one saving grace is Hopkins, whose dry wit and gentle dignity run rings around Rock's tiresome buffoonery. SF. Contains violence and swearing. DVD

Anthony Hopkins *Gaylord Oakes* • Chris Rock *Jake Hayes/Kevin Pope* • Gabriel Macht *Agent Seale* • Peter Stormare *Adrik Vas* • John Slattery *Roland Yates* • Garcelle Beauvais-Nilon *CNN reporter, Nicole* • Kerry Washington *Julie* • Matthew Marsh *Dragan Adjanic* ■ *Dir* Joel Schumacher • *Scr* Jason Richman, Michael Browning, from a story by Gary Goodman, David Himmelstein

Bad Day at Black Rock ★★★★★ PG

Drama 1955 · US · Colour · 78mins

An Oscar-nominated Spencer Tracy gives a masterclass in screen acting, playing the one-armed Second World War veteran who arrives in a small south-western town to present a Japanese farmer with his son's posthumous medal. However, the remote desert community harbours a dark secret that Robert Ryan and his fellow rednecks are prepared to do anything to protect. Director John Sturges and cinematographer William C Mellor achieve an atmosphere of deceptive calm that makes the wait for the surprisingly shocking showdown all the more tense. Ryan is on career-best form, while Ernest Borgnine and Lee Marvin are marvellously malevolent as racist heavies. DP

Spencer Tracy *John J Macreedy* • Robert Ryan *Reno Smith* • Anne Francis *Liz Wirth* • Dean Jagger *Tim Horn* • Walter Brennan *Doc Velie* • John Ericson *Pete Wirth* • Ernest Borgnine *Coley Trimble* • Lee Marvin *Hector David* ■ *Dir* John Sturges • *Scr* Millard Kaufman, from the story *Bad Day at Hondo* by Howard Breslin • *Cinematographer* William C Mellor

Bad Education ★★★ 15

Drama 2004 · Sp · Colour · 101mins

Rising film-maker Fele Martínez is approached by an old school pal (Gael García Bernal), who has a story entitled *The Visit*. The friend is revealed to be the director's boyhood love and elements of their story populate *The Visit*, including the abuse Bernal suffered at the hands of a priest. Martínez agrees to film the story with wannabe actor Bernal in the lead, but soon discovers that his leading man is living a shocking lie. Though Pedro Almodóvar skilfully manipulates his labyrinthine storyline, he overcomplicates this tribute to Hollywood melodrama with too many heavy-handed references. AJ. In Spanish with English subtitles. Contains swearing and drug abuse. DVD

Gael García Bernal *Ángel/Zahara/Juan* • Fele Martínez *Enrique Goded* • Daniel Giménez-Cacho [Daniel Gimenez Cacho] *Father Manolo* • Lluís Homar *Señor Berenguer* • Francisco Boira *Ignacio Rodriguez* • Javier Cámara *Paca* • Petra Martínez *Ignacio's mother* • Ignacio Pérez *Young Ignacio* • Raúl García Forneiro *Young Enrique* ■ *Dir/Scr* Pedro Almodóvar

Bad for Each Other ★

Drama 1954 · US · BW · 82mins

Doctor Charlton Heston returns from patching up wounded soldiers in Korea and must decide between a practice in the rich area of Pittsburgh or the nearby mining community. He chooses money and Lizabeth Scott until a catastrophe at the mine makes him rethink his priorities. Made before Heston acquired his epic-hero status, this moral medico-melo was panned by critics and was a major flop. AT

Charlton Heston *Dr Tom Owen* • Lizabeth Scott *Helen Curtis* • Dianne Foster *Joan Lasher* • Mildred Dunnock *Mrs Mary Owen* • Arthur Franz *Dr Jim Crowley* • Ray Collins *Dan Reasonover* ■ *Dir* Irving Rapper • *Scr* Irving Wallace, Horace McCoy, from the story *Scalpel* by Horace McCoy

Bad Girl ★★★ U

Melodrama 1931 · US · BW · 90mins

A misleading title for the account of a year in the life of a young working-class couple, from their meeting to their marriage and the birth of their first child. James Dunn is a hardworking lad from the tenements intent on bettering himself, Sally Eilers the girl he loves, and Minna Gombell her best friend and his verbal sparring partner. Frank Borzage brings realism and humour to this depiction of life in a more innocent era. RK

Sally Eilers *Dorothy Haley* • James Dunn *Eddie Collins* • Minna Gombell *Edna Driggs* • Frank Darien *Lathrop* • William Pawley *Jim Haley* ■ *Dir* Frank Borzage • *Scr* Edwin Burke, from the novel by Viña Delmar [Vina Delmar], Eugene Delmar, from the play by Viña Delmar [Vina Delmar], Brian Marlowe

Bad Girls ★★ 15

Western 1994 · US · Colour · 95mins

You can imagine the pitch: *Young Guns*, but with babes. It's actually not a bad idea and largely succeeds despite the weak script. The bad girls of the title are four prostitutes (Andie MacDowell, Madeleine Stowe, Drew Barrymore and Mary Stuart Masterson) who find a price on their heads when Stowe shoots a disagreeable client. Their spirited performances are enjoyable to watch, even if they fail to deliver the toughness promised by the title. JF. Contains violence, swearing and nudity. DVD

Madeleine Stowe *Cody Zamora* • Mary Stuart Masterson *Anita Crown* • Andie MacDowell *Eileen Spenser* • Drew Barrymore *Lilly Laronette* • James Russo *Kid Jarrett* • James LeGros *William Tucker* • Robert Loggia *Frank Jarrett* • Dermot Mulroney *Josh McCoy* ■ *Dir* Jonathan Kaplan • *Scr* Ken Friedman, Yolande Finch, from a story by Albert S Ruddy, Charles Finch, Gary Frederickson

Bad Guy ★★★ 18

Drama 2001 · S Kor · Colour · 102mins

Cult Korean director Kim Ki-Duk's stylised view of exploitation and crime on the backstreets of Seoul combines disconcerting realism with moments of grim humour and unexpected tenderness. Duped into prostitution by loan sharks, student Seo Won endures endless humiliation in a gaudy shop-front brothel, while mobster Cho Jae-Hyeon keeps tabs on her through a two-way mirror. It's a sordid neon-lit hell, but the evocative design and doughty performances enable romance and a semblance of redemption to seep through. DP. In Korean with English subtitles. DVD

Cho Jae-Hyeon *Han-gi* • Seo Won *Sun-hwa* • Kim Yoon-Tae *Jung-Tae* • Choi Duk-Mun *Hyun-Ja* ■ *Dir/Scr* Kim Ki-Duk

Bad Guys ★ PG

Comedy 1986 · US · Colour · 86mins

A dreadful attempt to cash-in on the popularity of wrestling, this has Adam Baldwin and Mike Jolly as a pair of bumbling policemen who turn to the ring when they lose their day jobs. However, their bid to become wrestling stars soon arouses emnity among the professional wrestling community. Bottom of the barrel. JF

Adam Baldwin *Skip Jackson* • Mike Jolly *Dave Atkins* • Michelle Nicastro *Janice Edwards* • Ruth Buzzi *Petal McGurk* • James Booth *Lord Percy* • Gene LeBell *Turk McGurk* ■ *Dir* Joel Silberg • *Scr* Brady W Setwater, Joe Gillis

Bad Influence ★ 18

Mystery thriller 1990 · US · Colour · 94mins

In this wildly implausible mystery thriller, a stranger (Rob Lowe) befriends a down-at-heel suit (James Spader) and is soon conducting a cat-and-mouse game of psychological manipulation. This soon disintegrates into pulp that wastes the talents of the gifted Spader. LH. Contains swearing, violence, sex scenes, nudity and drug abuse. DVD

Rob Lowe *Alex* • James Spader *Michael Boll* • Lisa Zane *Claire* • Christian Clemenson *Pismo Boll* • Kathleen Wilhoite *Leslie* • Tony Maggio *Patterson* • David Duchovny *Clubgoer* ■ *Dir* Curtis Hanson • *Scr* David Koepp

Bad Jim ★★★

Western 1989 · US · Colour · 90mins

An affectionate, cosily paced western that comes up with a different spin on the story of Billy the Kid. Now it's the late outlaw's horse that is the focus of attention, with the film tracing the stallion's adventures as it falls into the hands of a trio of cowboys. Clyde Ware's direction is perhaps too unhurried, but he is rewarded with some amiable performances from a line-up that is headed by James Brolin and Richard Roundtree and features Clark Gable's son, John Clark Gable, making his film debut. JF

James Brolin *BD Sweetman* • Richard Roundtree *July* • John Clark Gable *JT Coleman* • Harry Carey Jr *CJ Lee* • Ty Hardin *Tom Jefford* • Rory Calhoun *Sam Harper* • Pepe Serna *Virgilio* • Suzanne Wouk *Elizabeth* ■ *Dir/Scr* Clyde Ware

B

Bad Karma ★★

Psychological thriller
2001 · US · Colour · 89mins

British director John Hough is hamstrung by pedestrian plotting in this adaptation of Douglas Clegg's novel. The premise has mental patient Patsy Kensit go on a Lector-like spree as she assumes various guises to wreak revenge on Patrick Muldoon, the psychiatrist she believes to be the reincarnation of Jack the Ripper, who murdered her in a previous life. Played with little enthusiasm and directed with even less. DP

Patsy Kensit *Agnes Thatcher* • Patrick Muldoon *Dr Trey Campbell* • Amy Locane *Carly Campbell* • Damian Chapa *Mr Miller* ■ *Dir* John Hough • *Scr* from the novel by Douglas Clegg

Bad Lands ★★

Western 1939 · US · BW · 70mins

This has a stronger script than most B-pictures, being RKO's unacknowledged re-make in western dress of its 1934 desert war drama *The Lost Patrol*, which was powerfully directed by the great John Ford. Here the British soldiers of the original become a posse trapped in the desert by Apaches and picked off one by one. The lacklustre cast is headed by Robert Barrat and Noah Beery Jr. AE

Robert Barrat *Sheriff* • Noah Beery Jr *Chile Lyman* • Guinn Williams [Guinn "Big Boy" Williams] *Billy Sweet* • Douglas Walton *Mulford* • Andy Clyde *Cliff* • Addison Richards *Rayburn* • Robert Coote *Eaton* • Paul Hurst *Curley Tom* • Francis Ford *Garth* ■ *Dir* Lew Landers • *Scr* Clarence Upson Young

The Bad Liaisons ★★

Drama 1955 · Fr · BW · 90mins

Although he made several films, Alexandre Astruc is better known as the critic who devised the *caméra-stylo* concept that underlays auteur theory. Anouk Aimée is suitably enigmatic as she talks about the various men she has encountered since arriving in Paris with inspector Yves Robert, who is investigating her links with abortionist Claude Dauphin. With its voiceover narration and reliance on flashbacks, this once controversial drama now seems contrived. Astruc would later denounce the excessively stylised imagery. DP. A French language film.

Anouk Aimée *Catherine Racan* • Jean-Claude Pascal *Blaise Walter* • Claude Dauphin *Doctor Danieli* • Philippe Lemaire *Alain Bergere* • Yves Robert *Commissaire Forbin* ■ *Dir* Alexandre Astruc • *Scr* Alexandre Astruc, Roland Laudenbach, from the novel *Cette Sacrée Salade* by Cecil Saint-Laurent

Bad Lieutenant ★★★★ 18

Crime drama 1992 · US · Colour · 90mins

When director Abel Ferrara's films are good, they are exceptionally good, as proved by this highly controversial tale of a corrupt cop (Harvey Keitel) getting one last chance at redemption when he investigates the rape of a nun. The problem is that she has forgiven her attackers and therefore refuses to name them. This depiction of one man's vice-ridden hell is sexually explicit and brutally violent to an extreme degree, but the intention to shock audiences out of their complacency is Ferrara's point. Keitel gives one of the bravest performances of his career as the lapsed Catholic in serious debt and even worse moral and ethical chaos. AJ. Contains swearing, drug abuse and nudity. [VIDEO] DVD

Harvey Keitel *Lieutenant* • Victor Argo *Beat cop* • Paul Calderone [Paul Calderon] *Cop* • Leonard Thomas *Cop* • Robin Burrows *Ariane* • Frankie Thorn *Nun* • Victoria Bastel *Bowtay* ■ *Dir* Abel Ferrara • *Scr* Zoe Tamarlaine Lund, Abel Ferrara

The Bad Lord Byron ★★

Biographical drama 1949 · UK · BW · 84mins

Released at a time when hopes were high that British cinema would be able to compete with Hollywood, this historical fantasy was massacred by the critics. It hasn't really improved with age, although it provided Dennis Price with a useful run-through for the role of the equally caddish Louis Mazzini in the following year's classic *Kind Hearts and Coronets*. There is precious little biography on display, but the way the script whizzes you round the celebrities of the day is fun. DP

Dennis Price *Lord Byron* • Mai Zetterling *Teresa Guiccioli* • Joan Greenwood *Lady Caroline Lamb* • Linden Travers *Augusta Leigh* • Sonia Holm *Arabella Millbank* • Raymond Lovell *John Hobhouse* • Leslie Dwyer *Fletcher* ■ *Dir* David MacDonald • *Scr* Terence Young, Anthony Thorne, Peter Quennell, Lawrence Kitchen, Paul Holt

Bad Man of Brimstone ★★

Western 1938 · US · BW · 88mins

Ugly mug Wallace Beery stars in this western about a gunfighter redeemed when he meets his long-lost son, a boxer turned lawyer played by Dennis O'Keefe. (This was the first time O'Keefe used that name; up to this point, he was billed as Bud Flanagan.) It's the sort of morality tale that only MGM could make, with a message about the evil of violence and the importance of society that comes courtesy of a script co-written by future Bond scribe Richard Maibaum. AT

Wallace Beery *"Trigger" Bill* • Virginia Bruce *Loretta Douglas* • Dennis O'Keefe *Jeffrey Burton* • Joseph Calleia *Ben* • Lewis Stone *Mr Jack Douglas* • Guy Kibbee *"Eight Ball" Harrison* ■ *Dir* J Walter Reuben • *Scr* Cyril Hume, Richard Maibaum, from a story by J Walter Reuben, Maurice Rapf

Bad Manners ★★★ PG

Psychological drama
1998 · US · Colour · 60mins

Jonathan Kaufer was briefly regarded as a promising young talent around Hollywood in the 1980s but his career never seemed to get into gear. This caustic drama shows what we have been missing. A bitter take on academic and sexual jealousy, it finds David Strathairn and Bonnie Bedelia as married lecturers crossing psychological swords with the latter's former lover (Saul Rubinek) and his young girlfriend (Caroleen Feeney). It's a claustrophobic affair but beautifully played, written and directed. JF [VIDEO]

David Strathairn *Wes Westlund* • Bonnie Bedelia *Nancy Westlund* • Saul Rubinek *Matt Carroll* • Caroleen Feeney *Kim Matthews* • Julie Harris *Professor Harper* ■ *Dir* Jonathan Kaufer • *Scr* David Gilman, from his play *Ghost in the Machine*

Bad Man's River ★★ 12

Comedy western
1971 · Sp/It/Fr · Colour · 88mins

There's very little to raise the temperature in this comedy western about an attempt to blow up a Mexican arms arsenal for revolutionary reasons. The bizarre casting of Lee Van Cleef and James Mason as rivals for the affection of Gina Lollobrigida doesn't help this co-production, and neither does the freeze-frame trickery of director Gene Martin. TH [VIDEO] DVD

Lee Van Cleef *Roy King* • James Mason *Montero* • Gina Lollobrigida *Alicia* • Simon Andreu *Angel Sandos* • Diana Lorys *Dolores* • John Garko *Ed Pace* • Lone Ferk *Conchita* ■ *Dir* Gene Martin [Eugenio Martin] • *Scr* Gene Martin [Eugenio Martin], Philip Yordan

Bad Medicine ★★ 15

Comedy 1985 · US · Colour · 93mins

After hitting it big with *Police Academy* and *Cocoon*, Steve Guttenberg came a cropper with this dim comedy. He is the lazy student who winds up in a dodgy medical school in Latin America – run by Alan Arkin, complete with preposterous accent – only to discover a conscience. Director Harvey Miller serves up an unappealing menu of old medical jokes and toilet humour, and then gets all sentimental. JF [VIDEO]

Steve Guttenberg *Jeff Marx* • Alan Arkin *Dr Ramon Madera* • Julie Hagerty *Liz Parker* • Bill Macy *Dr Gerald Marx* • Curtis Armstrong *Dennis Gladstone* • Candy Milo *Maria Morales* ■ *Dir* Harvey Miller • *Scr* Harvey Miller, from the novel *Calling Dr Horowitz* by Steven Horowitz, Neil Offen

Bad Moon ★ 18

Horror thriller 1996 · US · Colour · 76mins

Michael Paré is mauled by a beast in Nepal and returns home to sister Mariel Hemmingway and her son, in the hope their love will stop him having to wear one of the most ill-fitting fur suits in cinematic history. It's up to the family dog to sniff out the truth – and plug the plot holes. AJ. Contains violence, nudity and sex scenes. [VIDEO]

Mariel Hemingway *Janet* • Michael Paré *Ted Harrison* • Mason Gamble *Brett* ■ *Dir* Eric Red • *Scr* Eric Red, from the novel *Thor* by Wayne Smith

The Bad News Bears ★★★ PG

Sports comedy 1976 · US · Colour · 97mins

Walter Matthau is on fine form in one of the first sports comedies to use the now familiar "underdogs taking on the big boys" scenario. He plays a boozy coach trying to lick a bunch of no-hoper Little League baseball misfits into shape, with a little help from star-pitcher Tatum O'Neal. It's the relationship between coach and team that pulls you in, while the child actors are more than a match for old pro Matthau – especially O'Neal, who has more screen presence than dad Ryan ever had. A small winner. JC [VIDEO]

Walter Matthau *Coach Morris Buttermaker* • Tatum O'Neal *Amanda Whurlizer* • Vic Morrow *Roy Turner* • Joyce Van Patten *Cleveland* • Ben Piazza *Councilman Whitewood* • Jackie Earle Haley *Kelly Leak* • Alfred W Lutter [Alfred Lutter] *Ogilvie* ■ *Dir* Michael Ritchie • *Scr* Bill Lancaster

The Bad News Bears Go to Japan ★

Sports comedy 1978 · US · Colour · 91mins

Aside from Tony Curtis's star turn as a greedy hustler who takes charge of the titular Little Leaguers, there's little to say about this lifeless, pointless second sequel. Curtis sees a lucrative dollar opportunity in a tour of Japan, which involves the kids taking on the National Champions. A dud. JC

Tony Curtis *Marvin Lazar* • Jackie Earle Haley *Kelly Leak* • Matthew Douglas Anton *ERW Tillyard III* • Erin Blunt *Ahmad Abdul Rahim* • George Gonzales *Miguel Agilar* • Brett Marx *Jimmy Feldman* • David Pollock *Rudy Stein* ■ *Dir* John Berry • *Scr* Bill Lancaster

The Bad News Bears in Breaking Training ★★

Sports comedy 1977 · US · Colour · 99mins

The plucky Junior League baseball team is preparing for a big game, with the reward being a trip to Japan. Jackie Earle Haley's reunion with her estranged father William Devane affords director Michael Pressman one of several opportunities to explore the problems of growing up, but only wiseacre pitcher Jimmy Baio emerges from the mediocre ensemble in this far-fetched sequel. DP

William Devane *Mike Leak* • Clifton James *Sy Orlansky* • Jackie Earle Haley *Kelly Leak* • Jimmy Baio *Carmen Ronzonni* • Chris Barnes *Tanner Boyle* • Erin Blunt *Ahmad Abdul Rahim* • Jaime Escobedo *Jose Agilar* • George Gonzales *Miguel Agilar* ■ *Dir* Michael Pressman • *Scr* Paul Brickman, from characters created by Bill Lancaster

Bad Santa ★★ 15

Crime black comedy
2003 · US/Ger · Colour · 91mins

Director Terry Zwigoff comes unstuck with this charmless black comedy about an alcoholic safe cracker. Billy Bob Thornton plays Willie T Stokes, who scopes out shopping malls to rob by posing as a holiday Father Christmas. As he and his "elf" sidekick (Tony Cox) attempt to perform the scam one last time, Thornton becomes involved with a Santa-loving barmaid (Lauren Graham) and a lonely overweight child (Brett Kelly). While the film thinks it's subversively critiquing Christmas sentimentality, the constant foul-mouthed shouting becomes dispiriting very early on. GM. Contains swearing, violence, sexual references.

Billy Bob Thornton *Willie T Stokes* • Tony Cox *Marcus* • Brett Kelly *The Kid* • Lauren Graham *Sue* • Lauren Tom *Lois* • Bernie Mac *Gin* • John Ritter *Bob Chipeska* ■ *Dir* Terry Zwigoff • *Scr* Glenn Ficarra, John Requa

The Bad Seed ★★★★

Psychological horror
1956 · US · BW · 128mins

This is an adaptation of playwright Maxwell Anderson's Broadway and West End success about an irredeemably evil eight-year-old child, played on stage and here on screen by the brilliant Patty McCormack. Also imported from the Broadway production are Nancy Kelly as the girl's mother, Eileen Heckart, as the mother of one of the girl's school friends, and a particularly effective Henry Jones as the venal caretaker. This is *Grand Guignol* stuff, really, but veteran Mervyn LeRoy directs effectively. TS

Nancy Kelly *Christine* • Patty McCormack *Rhoda* • Henry Jones *LeRoy* • Eileen Heckart *Mrs Daigle* • Evelyn Varden *Monica* • William Hopper *Kenneth* • Paul Fix *Bravo* • Jesse White *Emory* ■ *Dir* Mervyn LeRoy • *Scr* John Lee Mahin, from the play by Maxwell Anderson and the novel by William March

Bad Sister ★★ U

Drama 1931 · US · BW · 69mins

Extrovert and flirtatious small-town girl Sidney Fox falls for a big-city swindler Humphrey Bogart. The couple elopes, with unhappy consequences for her, but her actions lead to the happy union of her respectable rejected suitor Conrad Nagel and her demure sister Bette Davis. This flaccid drama, directed by Hobart Henley for Universal, is notable only as marking Davis's screen debut – though it gives little intimation of the fact that she wouldn't be playing the subsidiary good girl for long. RK

Conrad Nagel *Dr Dick Lindley* • Sidney Fox *Marianne* • Bette Davis *Laura* • ZaSu Pitts *Minnie* • Slim Summerville *Sam* • Charles Winninger *Mr Madison* • Emma Dunn *Mrs Madison* • Humphrey Bogart *Corliss* ■ *Dir* Hobart Henley • *Scr* Raymond L Schrock, Tom Reed, Edwin H Knopf, from the novel *The Flirt* by Booth Tarkington

The Bad Sleep Well ★★ PG

Crime drama 1960 · Jpn · BW · 127mins

In this drama about corporate corruption in postwar Japan, Toshiro Mifune lays down his samurai sword to play a housing company employee who marries the boss's daughter purely to expose his new father-in-law, whom he

B

believes was responsible for his own father's "suicide". Akira Kurosawa turns what should have been a taut thriller into a rather sombre exercise in morality, with Shakespearean themes of revenge and remorse. The film flopped in Japan (critiques of the economic recovery were rare) and led to the eventual collapse of the director's production company. AT. In Japanese with English subtitles.

Toshiro Mifune *Koichi Nishi* • Takeshi Kato *Itakura* • Masayuki Mori *Iwabuchi* • Takashi Shimura *Moriyama* • Akira Nishimura *Shirai* ■ *Dir* Akira Kurosawa • *Scr* Akira Kurosawa, Shinobu Hashimoto, Hideo Oguni, Ryuzo Kikushima, Eijiro Hisaita

Bad Taste ★★★★ 18

Horror comedy 1987 · NZ · Colour · 87mins

Director Peter Jackson began his career began with this cheerfully disgusting Kiwi sickie, made over a four-year period. Directed in chaotic fashion, with epic quantities of gore, flying viscera, macabre humour and wild special effects, Jackson's man-eating alien invasion film remained the bloody benchmark of sci-fi horror, though he topped it five years later with *Braindead*. The title says it all, so those of a sensitive disposition should steer clear. AJ DVD

Peter Jackson *Derek/Robert* • Mike Minett *Frank* • Peter O'Herne *Barry* • Terry Potter *Ozzy* • Craig Smith *Giles* • Doug Wren *Lord Crumb* ■ *Dir/Scr* Peter Jackson

Bad Timing ★★★★ 18

Drama 1980 · UK · Colour · 117mins

One to admire or abhor, director Nicolas Roeg's case history of a sexual obsession dazzles with flashbacks and disturbs with "What if?" sidetracks. Art Garfunkel is the psycho-psychiatrist involved with Theresa Russell in a sadistic affair, which starts with the girl's suicide attempt and ends with even nastier revelations about their relationship. Roeg piles on angst-ridden chic to the detriment of human values and sympathy, but, for what he achieves in complexity and conviction, it's well worth watching. TH. Contains swearing, sex scenes and nudity. DVD

Art Garfunkel *Dr Alex Linden* • Theresa Russell *Milena Flaherty* • Harvey Keitel *Inspector Netusil* • Denholm Elliott *Stefan Vognic* • Dana Gillespie *Amy* • Daniel Massey *Foppish man* ■ *Dir* Nicolas Roeg • *Scr* Yale Udoff

Badge 373 ★★ 15

Crime drama 1973 · US · Colour · 110mins

The real-life New York cop who inspired *The French Connection* was called Eddie Egan, and he served as this film's technical adviser. Presumably, then, he endorsed Robert Duvall's portrait of a bigoted, racist thug with a badge. Here Egan (renamed Ryan) is up against the Puerto Ricans and tends to shoot or punch first and ask questions later, if ever. AT

Robert Duvall *Eddie Ryan* • Verna Bloom *Maureen* • Henry Darrow *Sweet William* • Eddie Egan *Scanlon* • Felipe Luciano *Ruben* • Tina Cristiani *Mrs Caputo* ■ *Dir* Howard W Koch • *Scr* Pete Hamill

The Badlanders ★★★

Western 1958 · US · Colour · 83mins

A decent western, directed by the reliable Delmer Daves and starring Alan Ladd and Ernest Borgnine as ex-convicts who emerge from prison in Yuma with a plan to rob a gold mine. Since this involves blowing up a mountain and escaping with half a ton of rock, it takes some organising. The picture is actually less a western than a suspense thriller, with plenty of surprises, a thrilling chase through a carnival and some excellent performances, notably from Nehemiah Persoff as the gunpowder expert. AT

Alan Ladd *Peter Van Hock* • Ernest Borgnine *John McBain* • Katy Jurado *Anita* • Claire Kelly *Ada Winton* • Kent Smith *Cyril Lounsberry* • Nehemiah Persoff *Vincente* • Robert Emhardt *Sample* • Anthony Caruso *Comanche* • Adam Williams *Leslie* ■ *Dir* Delmer Daves • *Scr* Richard Collins, from the novel *The Asphalt Jungle* by WR Burnett

Badlands ★★★★ 18

Crime drama 1973 · US · Colour · 89mins

Reclusive director Terrence Malick's film about the infamous Charlie Starkweather murders in the 1950s is a moodily disturbing cult item. Martin Sheen plays the alienated killer on a psychopathic rampage through the American Midwest, accompanied by his loyal teenage girlfriend, Sissy Spacek. Both leads are highly effective as the apathetic and icy duo caught up in a series of horrific events that are dazzlingly and daringly depicted by Malick. Yet, it's the matter-of-fact dreamy approach, defying convention by leaving loose ends, that makes this a truly scary experience. AJ. Contains violence and swearing. DVD

Martin Sheen *Kit Carruthers* • Sissy Spacek *Holly* • Warren Oates *Father* • Ramon Bieri *Cato* • Alan Vint *Deputy* • Gary Littlejohn *Sheriff* • John Carter *Rich man* • Bryan Montgomery *Boy* • Gail Threlkeld *Girl* ■ *Dir/Scr* Terrence Malick

Badman's Territory ★★★ U

Western 1946 · US · BW · 97mins

An excellent Randolph Scott western, featuring such tried-and-tested supporting players as grizzled George "Gabby" Hayes and the great Chief Thundercloud. Rather like those Universal horror movies that gathered together Dracula, Frankenstein's monster and the Wolf Man, this RKO special has Jesse and Frank James, Sam Bass, Belle Starr and the Dalton gang as opponents to Scott, as he attempts to turn the Oklahoma territory into a full-grown state. Cleverly directed by Tim Whelan, who doesn't let the clutter of characters spoil the flow. TS

Randolph Scott *Mark Rowley* • Ann Richards *Henryette Alcott* • George "Gabby" Hayes *Coyote* • Steve Brodie *Bob Dalton* • Ray Collins *Colonel Farewell* • Lawrence Tierney *Jesse James* • Tom Tyler *Frank James* • Nestor Paiva *Sam Bass* • Isabel Jewell *Belle Starr* • William Moss *Bill Dalton* ■ *Dir* Tim Whelan • *Scr* Jack Natteford, Luci Ward, Clarence Upson Young, Bess Taffel

Bagdad Café ★★★★ PG

Comedy drama
1987 · W Ger · Colour · 87mins

Co-written and co-produced with his wife Eleanore and starring his regular favourite Marianne Sägebrecht, German director Percy Adlon's first American feature is a hypnotic blend of feminist fantasy and Capra-esque feel-good. Set in a run-down diner in the middle of the Arizona desert, the action centres on the impact Sägebrecht has on the claustrophobic local community, in particular on café boss CCH Pounder and an ageing hippy artist, played with an instinctive comic touch by Jack Palance. Although there are some shrewd asides on racial friction, this is still the kind of gentle comedy you can simply sink into your armchair and enjoy. DP. Contains swearing and nudity. DVD

Marianne Sägebrecht *Jasmin Münchgstettner* • CCH Pounder *Brenda* • Jack Palance *Rudi Cox* • Christine Kauffman *Debby* • Monica Calhoun *Phyllis* • Darron Flagg *Sal Junior* • George Aquilar *Cahuenga* • G Smokey Campbell *Sal* • Hans Stadlbauer *Münchgstettner* • Alan S Craig *Eric* ■ *Dir* Percy Adlon • *Scr* Percy Adlon, Eleonore Adlon

Bagh Bahadur ★★★

Drama 1989 · Ind · Colour · 91mins

Bengali poet Buddhadev Dasgupta gave up his job as an economics lecturer at Calcutta University to direct films, starting with realist studies of city life such as *Dooratwa*. However, this tragic tale, also known as *The Tiger Dancer*, is set in a small village and is closer in tone to a folk tale. Pavan Malhotra stars as a quarry worker who returns home to dance in a traditional festival and marry his sweetheart, only to lose both his place of honour and his girl when a circus troupe sets up camp nearby. He's upstaged by a beautiful caged leopard. DP. In Hindi with English subtitles.

Pavan Malhotra *Ghunuram* • Archana *Radha* • Vasudev Rao *Sibal* • Rajeshwari Roy Choudhury ■ *Dir/Scr* Buddhadev Dasgupta

Baghban ★★ PG

Musical romantic drama
2003 · Ind · Colour · 180mins

This Bollywood domestic drama stars Amitabh Bachchan and Hema Malini as the married couple who discover their four sons are too busy with their own concerns to care for them in old age. Salman Khan and Mahima Chaudhary lead the impressive supporting cast, but despite its well-intentioned attempt to bridge the age gap, this sentimental melodrama feels old-fashioned. DP. In Hindi with English subtitles. DVD

Amitabh Bachchan *Raj Malhotra* • Hema Malini *Pooja, his wife* • Salman Khan • Mahima Chaudhary • Sameer Soni • Divya Dutta • Paresh Rawal ■ *Dir* Ravi Chopra • *Scr* Shafiq Ansari, Satish Bhatnagar, Ram Govind, Achala Nagar • *Cinematographer* Barun Mukerji

Baiju Bawra ★★★ U

Epic romantic musical
1952 · Ind · BW · 154mins

Although set in the Mughal court, this melodrama owes about as much to historical fact as such western classical music biopics as *Song of Love*. Director Vijay Bhatt is primarily concerned with the clash of personalities between court composer Surendra and itinerant musician Bharat Bhushan, who go head to head in a tuneful showdown after the latter's father is murdered by palace guards. However, it was Ali Naushad who took most of the plaudits for the songs that made this a box-office hit and turned Meena Kumari into a major star after 12 years in Bollywood as Baby Meena. DP. In Hindi with English subtitles.

Meena Kumari *Gauri* • Bharat Bhushan *Baiju* • Surendra *Tansen* • Bipin Gupta *Akhbar* ■ *Dir* Vijay Bhatt • *Scr* RS Choudhury, Ramchandra Thakur

Baise-Moi ★★ 18

Erotic crime thriller
2000 · Fr · Colour · 73mins

This angry, aggressive film explores female empowerment in terms of an equal right to revel in guilt-free sex and perform random acts of violence. Karen Bach and Raffaëla Anderson embark on their spree partly as a reaction to Anderson's rape. But while co-directors Virginie Despentes and Coralie Trinh Thi employ a grungy style to deglamorise the duo's brutal amorality, they also refuse to examine their motives, with the result that their actions become gratuitous. DP. In French with English subtitles. DVD

Raffaëla Anderson *Manu* • Karen Bach *Nadine* • Delphine McCarty *Severine* • Lisa Marshall *Karla* • Estelle Isaac *Alice* • HPG [Hervé P Gustave] *Martin* ■ *Dir* Virginie Despentes, Coralie Trinh Thi • *Scr* Virginie Despentes, Coralie Trinh Thi, from the novel by Virginie Despentes

The Bait ★★★★ 15

Crime drama 1995 · Fr · Colour · 111mins

Shot in the same uncompromising manner as his policier *L.627*, Bertrand Tavernier's lowlife thriller is darker than the average *film noir* as both the crime and the violence are so chillingly pitiless. Driven by an ambition to open a chain of boutiques in the States, shopgirl-cum-model Marie Gillain agrees to distract her wealthy male contacts while they're burgled by boyfriend Olivier Sitruk and his doltish buddy Bruno Putzulu. The resolution is never in doubt, but the action remains engrossing as Tavernier, aided by a credible cast, strips the daydreams down to their seedy reality. DP. In French with English subtitles.

Marie Gillain *Nathalie* • Olivier Sitruk *Eric* • Bruno Putzulu *Bruno* • Richard Berry *Alain* • Philippe Duclos *Antoine* • Marie Ravel *Karine* • Clotilde Courau *Patricia* • Jean-Louis Richard *Restaurant owner* ■ *Dir* Bertrand Tavernier • *Scr* Colo Tavernier O'Hagan, Bertrand Tavernier, from a book by Morgan Sportes

The Baited Trap ★★★

Crime thriller 1959 · US · Colour · 86mins

This tense suspense film from writer/director Norman Panama – a man more usually known for his comedies – is a better movie than it ought to be thanks to an above-average cast. Lawyer Richard Widmark returns to his small home town of Tula to help villainous Lee J Cobb escape into Mexico. There he must deal with his father (Carl Benton Reid) and his ex-girlfriend (Tina Louise), who's now married to Widmark's brother. TH

Richard Widmark *Ralph Anderson* • Lee J Cobb *Victor Massonetti* • Earl Holliman *Tippy Anderson* • Tina Louise *Linda Anderson* • Carl Benton Reid *Sheriff Anderson* • Lorne Greene *Davis* ■ *Dir* Norman Panama • *Scr* Richard Alan Simmons, Norman Panama

Baker's Hawk ★★★

Western 1976 · US · Colour · 96mins

Clint Walker only enjoyed brief stardom, but this family western shows what a capable actor he could be. Here he plays the father of Lee H Montgomery, a young boy who helps recluse Burl Ives and his pet hawk escape from hooligans. It could be an episode of the TV series *Cheyenne*, which made Walker's name before that other Clint (Eastwood) moseyed along. However, Lyman D Dayton's direction gives the film a moral dimension that lifts it out of the ordinary. TH

Clint Walker *Dan Baker* • Burl Ives *Mr McGraw* • Diane Baker *Jenny Baker* • Lee H Montgomery [Lee Montgomery] *Billy Baker* • Alan Young *Mr Carson* • Taylor Lacher *Sweeney* ■ *Dir* Lyman D Dayton [Lyman Dayton] • *Scr* Dan Greer, Hal Harrison Jr, from the novel by Jack Bickham

The Baker's Wife ★★★★

Comedy 1938 · Fr · BW · 118mins

While Marcel Pagnol's style may be regarded as hopelessly old-fashioned by many post-New Wave critics, there's no escaping the wit and warmth of this tale of simple Provençal folk. Villagers have to band together to disrupt the romance between a shepherd (Charles Moulin) and a faithless wife (Ginette Leclerc) to encourage their cuckolded baker to make bread again. One of the screen's finest comic actors, Raimu is superb as the broken-hearted *boulanger*. But what makes the film so irresistible is Pagnol's attention to detail and mastery at creating the close-knit communal atmosphere. DP. In French with English subtitles.

Raimu *Aimable, the baker* • Ginette Leclerc *Aurelie, the baker's wife* • Charles Moulin *Dominique, the shepherd* • Robert Vattier *The*

U = SUITABLE FOR ALL Uc = SUITABLE FOR ALL, ESPECIALLY FOR YOUNG CHILDREN (VIDEO ONLY) PG = PARENTAL GUIDANCE

priest • Robert Bassac *The schoolteacher* ■ *Dir* Marcel Pagnol • *Scr* Marcel Pagnol, from the novel *Jean le Bleu* by Jean Giono

Le Bal ★★★ PG

Musical 1983 · Alg/Fr/It · Colour · 107mins

In addition to landing a best foreign film Oscar nomination, Ettore Scola won the best director prize at Berlin for this stylised adaptation of Jean-Claude Penchenat's experimental stage play. Original members of the Théâtre du Campagnol cast re-enact routines inspired by events in France from 1936 to the early 1980s. But while their expertise is undeniable and Vladimir Cosma's score cleverly plays on the popular tunes of the different periods, the action says more about Scola's ingenuity than the incidents on which it's supposed to be commenting. DP. A French language film.

Etienne Guichard *Provincial student* • Régis Bouquet *Ballroom owner* • Francesco de Rosa *Toni* • Nani Noël *Goodtime girl* • Liliane Delval *Girl with long hair* • Arnault Lecarpentier *Young printer* • Martine Chauvin *Flower girl* ■ *Dir* Ettore Scola • *Scr* Ettore Scola, Ruggero Maccari, Furio Scarpelli, Jean-Claude Penchenat, from the Théâtre du Campagnol stage production, from an original idea by Jean-Claude Penchenat

Balalaika ★ U

Musical 1939 · US · BW · 102mins

This monumentally boring and incredibly dull MGM adaptation of Eric Maschwitz's popular West End operetta, retains only the title song from the original and turns the Russian setting into something vaguely Ruritanian. Nelson Eddy and Ilona Massey (amazingly originally billed as "The New Dietrich") are the supremely uninteresting leads, and Reinhold Schunzel's direction is truly uninspired, if not actually incompetent. TS

Nelson Eddy *Prince Peter Karagin* • Ilona Massey *Lydia Pavlovna Marakova* • Charlie Ruggles [Charles Ruggles] *Private Nicki Popoff* • Frank Morgan *Ivan Danchenoff* • Lionel Atwill *Professor Marakov* • C Aubrey Smith *General Karagin* • Dalies Frantz *Dimitri Marakov* ■ *Dir* Reinhold Schünzel • *Scr* Leon Gordon, Charles Bennett, Jacques Deval, from the operetta by Eric Maschwitz, George Posford, Bernard Grun

La Balance ★★★★ 18

Crime thriller 1982 · Fr · Colour · 101mins

An American in Paris was responsible for this hard-as-nails thriller, which won several Césars including best picture, best actor and best actress. Stylishly exploiting the seedy streets of Belleville, Bob Swaim brings an unswerving authenticity to this tale of a pimp (Philippe Léotard) who agrees to inform on neighbourhood thug Maurice Ronet to prevent detective Richard Berry from harming the whore he adores. Although Swaim makes the most of the action sequences, the film's real strength lies in the conviction of the performances. Nathalie Baye's hardened hooker is a revelation. DP. In French with English subtitles. DVD

Nathalie Baye *Nicole* • Philippe Léotard *Dede* • Richard Berry *Inspector Paluzzi* • Christophe Malavoy *Tintin* • Jean-Paul Connart *The Belgian* • Bernard Freyd *The Captain* • Albert Dray *Carlini* • Florent Pagny *Simoni* • Maurice Ronet *Roger Massina* ■ *Dir/Scr* Bob Swaim

Balboa ★★ 15

Melodrama 1982 · US · Colour · 91mins

1980s glitz and big-business scheming are rather unoriginally rehashed in this disjointed pseudo-soap. Tony Curtis goes over the top as the villainous tycoon, while everyone around him is busy with sexual intrigue. The supporting cast includes Sonny Bono and a lost-looking Chuck Connors. While ludicrous, this still has moments of inane delight for those connoisseurs of the decade. TH

Tony Curtis *Ernie Stoddard* • Carol Lynley *Erin Blakely* • Jennifer Chase *Kathy Love* • Chuck Connors *Alabama Dern* • Lupita Ferrer *Rita Carlo* • Sonny Bono *Terry Carlo* • Catherine Campbell *Cindy Dern* • Steve Kanaly *Sam Cole* ■ *Dir* James Polakof • *Scr* James Polakof, Gail Willumsen, Nicki Lewis

The Balcony ★★★ 15

Drama fantasy 1963 · US · BW · 80mins

This is a fascinating film version of Jean Genet's controversial play set in a brothel. While the revolutionaries occupy the streets below, the brothel becomes the headquarters of the government, the state police, religion and the media. The brothel itself is designed like a film studio, with different sets, lighting and even back projection to add "reality" to the clients' sexual fantasies. Deeply allegorical, it captures the off-Broadway ambience of the period. AT. Contains swearing and sex scenes. DVD

Shelley Winters *Madame Irma* • Peter Falk *Police chief* • Lee Grant *Carmen* • Ruby Dee *Thief* • Peter Brocco *Judge* • Jeff Corey *Bishop* • Joyce Jameson *Penitent* • Arnette Jens *Horse* • Leonard Nimoy *Roger* ■ *Dir* Joseph Strick • *Scr* Ben Maddow, from the play by Jean Genet • *Music* Igor Stravinsky

Ball of Fire ★★★★ U

Comedy 1941 · US · BW · 106mins

A scintillating and hysterically funny update of *Snow White and the Seven Dwarfs*, featuring Barbara Stanwyck as Sugarpuss O'Shea, a moll on the run who falls in with a group of wacky academics working on a language dictionary. Gawky, lovable Gary Cooper is the professor quizzing fireball Babs (hence the title) about contemporary slang. Director Howard Hawks creates a minor comic masterpiece from the witty screenplay by Billy Wilder and Charles Brackett, and all the performances are spot-on. Hawks remade the film seven years later as *A Song Is Born*, with Danny Kaye. TS

Gary Cooper *Professor Bertram Potts* • Barbara Stanwyck *Sugarpuss O'Shea* • Oscar Homolka *Professor Gurkakoff* • Henry Travers *Professor Jerome* • SZ "Cuddles" Sakall [SZ Sakall] *Professor Magenbruch* • Tully Marshall *Professor Robinson* • Leonid Kinskey *Professor Quintana* ■ *Dir* Howard Hawks • *Scr* Charles Brackett, Billy Wilder, from the story *From A to Z* by Thomas Monroe, Billy Wilder

Ballad in Blue ★★ U

Drama 1964 · UK · BW · 88mins

Ray Charles's only major film is a well-intentioned though mawkish tale, in which the singer (playing himself) enriches the lives of a mother and her blind son. Charles is no actor and the rest of the cast seem to have picked up his slow, deliberate pace; but fans will not want to miss him singing a dozen numbers, including *Hit the Road, Jack* and *Busted*. DM

Ray Charles • Tom Bell *Steve Collins* • Mary Peach *Peggy Harrison* • Piers Bishop *David Harrison* • Dawn Addams *Gina Graham* • Betty McDowall *Helen Babbidge* • Lucy Appleby *Margaret Babbidge* • Joe Adams *Fred Parker* ■ *Dir* Paul Henreid • *Scr* Burton Wohl, from a story by Paul Henreid, Burton Wohl

Ballad of a Soldier ★★★★ U

War drama 1959 · USSR · BW · 87mins

The winner of the special jury prize at Cannes, Grigori Chukhrai's picaresque home-front drama is a classic example of the socialist-realist style films that dominated postwar Soviet cinema. As much a statement about the resilience of Stalin's citizenry as a pacifist tract, this is a surprisingly sentimental tale, in which the naive hero (Vladimir Ivashov) encounters a series of people as he travels to spend a four-day leave with his mother. Particularly striking is the contrast between the pitiable infidelity of a comrade's frightened wife and Ivashov's brief romance with peasant girl Shanna Prokhorenko. DP. In Russian with English subtitles.

Vladimir Ivashov *Alyosha* • Shanna Prokhorenko *Shura* • Antonina Maximova *Alyosha's mother* • Nikolai Kruchkov *General* ■ *Dir* Grigori Chukhrai • *Scr* Grigori Chukhrai, Valentin Yezhov

The Ballad of Cable Hogue ★★★★ PG

Comedy western 1970 · US · Colour · 116mins

This elegy for the Old West about an itinerant prospector who "found water where there wasn't" is a beautifully crafted and very funny film. Like director Sam Peckinpah's earlier and more explicitly violent *The Wild Bunch*, it leaves an audience with nostalgic pangs for a lifestyle that perhaps only existed in motion pictures. Tender and ironic by turns, it contains marvellous performances from a whimsical Jason Robards (arguably a career best) in the title role as Hogue and sexy Stella Stevens (definitely a career best) as the hooker who becomes his lady. TS. Contains swearing.

Jason Robards *Cable Hogue* • Stella Stevens *Hildy* • David Warner *Joshua* • Strother Martin *Bowen* • Slim Pickens *Ben* • LQ Jones *Taggart* • Peter Whitney *Cushing* ■ *Dir* Sam Peckinpah • *Scr* John Crawford, Edmund Penney

The Ballad of Gregorio Cortez ★★★ 15

Western based on a true story 1983 · US · Colour · 105mins

This unusual western is based on the true story of a Mexican cowhand, who was mistakenly arrested by Texas Rangers in 1901. He kills a sheriff in the struggle to escape and leads the posse after him on a merry dance. Shot in the locations where the real Cortez was actually imprisoned and tried, this saga of racial bigotry and language barriers gains drama by being told from multiple perspectives. Edward James Olmos makes a sympathetic Cortez, even if the film is a trifle worthy at times. AJ

Edward James Olmos *Gregorio Cortez* • James Gammon *Sheriff Frank Fly* • Tom Bower *Boone Choate* • Bruce McGill *Bill Blakely* • Brion James *Captain Rogers* • Alan Vint *Mike Trimmell* • Timothy Scott *Sheriff Morris* ■ *Dir* Robert M Young • *Scr* Victor Villasenor, Robert M Young, from the novel *With His Pistol in His Hands* by Americo Paredes

The Ballad of Josie ★★ U

Comedy western 1968 · US · Colour · 101mins

Bland is too strong a word for this tepid flick, which never really catches fire despite being directed by western ace Andrew V McLaglen. Doris Day is good, even though by this stage in her career she was becoming hard to cast, but the men are uninteresting – only Andy Devine brings a sense of authenticity to this western where the jeans look newly ironed and the faces are too well scrubbed. TS

Doris Day *Josie Minick* • Peter Graves (2) *Jason Meredith* • George Kennedy *Arch Ogden* • Andy Devine *Judge Tatum* • William Talman *Charlie Lord* • David Hartman *Fonse Pruitt* • Guy Raymond *Doc* ■ *Dir* Andrew V McLaglen • *Scr* Harold Swanton

The Ballad of Little Jo ★★★ 15

Western 1993 · US · Colour · 116mins

In director Maggie Greenwald's sobering, beautifully understated western, Suzy Amis gives a superb performance as the socialite driven into exile after a scandal, who is forced to pose as a man to survive in a wild frontier town. Greenwald makes some telling points about the chauvinistic attitudes prevalent in the Old West and creates a believable picture of the harshness of the life. JF. Contains violence, swearing, nudity.

Suzy Amis *Josephine Monaghan* • Bo Hopkins *Frank Badger* • Ian McKellen *Percy Corcoran* • David Chung *Tinman Wong* • Carrie Snodgress *Ruth Badger* • René Auberjonois *Streight Hollander* • Heather Graham *Mary Addie* • Sam Robards *Jasper Hill* • Tom Bower *Lyle* ■ *Dir/Scr* Maggie Greenwald

The Ballad of Lucy Whipple ★★★

Period drama 2001 · US · Colour

Glenn Close is typically effective in this TV movie as the New England widow who transports her young family to Gold Rush California, only for her eldest daughter to rebel and embark on a series of adventures of her own. Thus, it's teenager Jena Malone who carries the bulk of the action, as she learns about life from preacher Robert Pastorelli, cowboy Meat Loaf and sheriff Wilford Brimley. Thanks to the generosity of her co-stars, she handles the responsibility with aplomb. DP

Glenn Close *Arvella Whipple* • Jena Malone *Lucy "California" Whipple* • Bruce McGill *Jonas Scatter* • Meat Loaf *Aaron* • Chloe Webb *Sophie* • Dennis Christopher *Joshua "Carrots" Beale* ■ *Dir* Jeremy Paul Kagan • *Scr* Christopher Lofton, from the novel by Karen Cushman

The Ballad of Narayama ★★★

Drama 1958 · Jpn · Colour · 98mins

Kinuyo Tanaka gives a remarkable rendition of stoic resignation in this stylised adaptation of Shichiro Fukazawa's novels. Focusing on the custom of abandoning the elderly to die on a mountain top, Keisuke Kinoshita's heart-breaking drama is consciously played in a Kabuki manner against theatrical settings to remove any vestige of realism and thus increase the folkloric nature of a practice that will seem barbaric to most Western observers. DP. A Japanese language film.

Kinuyo Tanaka *Orin* • Teiji Takahashi *Tatsuhei* • Yuko Mochizuki *Tama-yan* • Danko Ichikawa *Kesakichi* • Keiko Ogasawara *Mutsu-yan* • Seiji Miyaguchi *Mata-yan* • Yunosuke Ito *Mata-yan's Son* • Ken Mitsuda *Teru-yan* ■ *Dir* Keisuke Kinoshita • *Scr* Keisuke Kinoshita, from the novels by Shichiro Fukazawa

The Ballad of Narayama ★★★★

Drama 1983 · Jpn · Colour · 130mins

A far cry from Keisuke Kinoshita's earlier adaptation, Shohei Imamura's Palme d'Or-winning reworking of Shichiro Fukazawa's novels dispassionately places humanity in the context of the natural world, with all its seemingly callous acts of survivalism. Thus, rape, infant mortality and death by burial are presented as nothing more sensational than scrabbling for subsistence in a famine. Stoically accepting the tradition of the elderly being left on a mountain top to ease the communal burden, Sumiko Sakamoto goes about settling her affairs with a calculation that contrasts with the brutality of the daily grind and the abjection of her final journey. DP. In Japanese with English subtitles.

Ken Ogata *Tatsuhei* • Sumiko Sakamoto *Orin-yan* • Tonpei Hidari *Risuke, "Smelly"* • Takejo Aki *Tama-yan* • Shoichi Ozawa *Shozo* • Mitsuaki Fukamizu *Tada-yan* • Seiji Kurasaki *Kesakichi* • Junko Takada *Matsu-yan* ■ *Dir* Shohei Imamura • *Scr* Shohei Imamura, from the novels by Shichiro Fukazawa

B

The Ballad of the Sad Café ★★ 15

Drama 1991 · US/UK · Colour · 100mins

A critical success but commercial flop on release, this sometimes brutal directorial debut by actor Simon Callow takes a bizarre but wonderfully written book by Carson McCullers and, by way of Edward Albee's stage version, gives it the enclosed, soundstage-on-a-shoestring-budget treatment. Its toe-curling pretentiousness knows no bounds, crowned by an execrable over-the-top performance by Vanessa Redgrave who attacks her role with full rolling-eyed abandon. SH DVD

Vanessa Redgrave *Miss Amelia Evans* • Keith Carradine *Marvin Macy* • Cork Hubbert *Cousin Lymon* • Rod Steiger *Reverend Willin* • Austin Pendleton *Lawyer Taylor* • Beth Dixon *Mary Hale* • Lanny Flaherty *Merlie Ryan* ■ *Dir* Simon Callow • *Scr* Michael Hirst, from the play by Edward Albee, from the novel by Carson McCullers

Ballistic: Ecks vs Sever ★ 15

Science-fiction action thriller
2002 · US · Colour · 87mins

This abysmal tale is too slow and unexciting to deserve its action thriller label. FBI man Antonio Banderas and his agent foe Lucy Liu make insipid leads as they unite to defeat a common enemy who's stolen a deadly, injectable micro-device. With its poorly executed fight scenes, clumsy camerawork and wooden support, this is a painful experience. SF. Contains violence. DVD

Antonio Banderas *Jeremiah Ecks* • Lucy Liu *Sever* • Gregg Henry *Robert Gant/Clark* • Ray Park *AJ Ross* • Talisa Soto *Vinn Gant/Rayne* • Miguel Sandoval *Julio Martin* ■ *Dir* Kaos [Wych Kaosayananda] • *Scr* Alan B McElroy

Balmaa ★★ PG

Drama 1993 · Ind · Colour · 132mins

There are dark undercurrents as Lawrence D'Souza's drama about an orphan who begins to have doubts about committing herself to marriage when her best friend is murdered shortly after setting up home with her seemingly charming husband. With Ayesha Jhulka impressive as the imperilled innocent and assured support from Saeed Jaffrey, this may have the plotline of a straight-to-video thriller, but the setting gives it a certain curio value. DP. In Hindi with English subtitles.

Avinash Wadhawan • Ayesha Jhulka • Saeed Jaffrey • Anjana Mumtaz • Shammi ■ *Dir* Lawrence D'Souza • *Scr* Talat Rekhi

The Baltimore Bullet ★★ 15

Comedy 1980 · US · Colour · 98mins

The Hustler for wimps, with James Coburn and protégé Bruce Boxleitner touring the pool halls of America and taking on the sharks. A big tournament lies ahead, for which Coburn needs a minimum stake of $20,000 if he is to take on the Deacon (Omar Sharif). Subplots about local gangsters and the drug trade juggle for screen time with the rather repetitive pool games, though the film just about gets by on the charm of its two stars. AT

James Coburn *Nick Casey* • Omar Sharif *Deacon* • Ronee Blakley *Carolina Red* • Bruce Boxleitner *Billie Joe Robbins* • Jack O'Halloran *Max* • Michael Lerner *Paulie* • Calvin Lockhart *Snow White* ■ *Dir* Robert Ellis Miller • *Scr* John Brascia, Robert Vincent O'Neill

Balto ★★★ U

Animated adventure
1995 · US/UK · Colour · 77mins

This well-crafted cartoon tells the story of an outcast sled dog who tries to save the children of the isolated Alaskan town of Nome during a diphtheria epidemic in 1925. Kevin Bacon's voice turns the wolf-dog crossbreed into a no-nonsense hero with a sense of duty that far outweighs the pride of his deadly rival, Steele, while Bob Hoskins's eccentric Russian goose provides the comedy. This is a touch darker than most animated features. A made-for-video sequel followed in 2001. DP DVD

Kevin Bacon *Balto* • Bob Hoskins *Boris* • Bridget Fonda *Jenna* • Jim Cummings *Steele* • Phil Collins *Muk/Luk* • Jack Angel *Nikki* ■ *Dir* Simon Wells • *Scr* Cliff Ruby, Elana Lesser, David Steven Cohen [David Cohen], Roger SH Schulman, from a story by Elana Lesser, Cliff Ruby

Balzac and the Little Chinese Seamstress ★★★ 12

Period comedy drama
2002 · Fr/Chi · Colour · 106mins

Dai Sijie makes his directorial debut with this self-consciously handsome adaptation of his autobiographical novel about life in rural China during the Cultural Revolution. Dai uses Western literature – read to seamstress Zhou Xun by exiled city-dwellers Chen Kun and Liu Ye – to comment on Beijing's current cautious acceptance of external influences. Ultimately sentimental and lacking in political rigour, this is still a lyrical and engaging study of clashing cultures. DP. In Mandarin with English subtitles. DVD

Zhou Xun *Little Chinese seamstress* • Liu Ye *Ma* • Chen Kun *Luo* • Wang Shuangbao *Village chief* • Cong Zhijun *Old tailor* • Wang Hongwei *Four Eyes* ■ *Dir* Dai Sijie • *Scr* Dai Sijie, Nadine Perront, from the novel *Balzac et la Petite Tailleuse Chinoise* by Dai Sijie

La Bamba ★★★ 15

Biographical drama
1987 · US · Colour · 104mins

Most pop biopics are tepid affairs, but the same cannot be said for director Luis Valdez's engrossing re-creation of Ritchie Valens's short life. Los Angeles band Los Lobos perform impassioned versions of the young man's songs, and their playing is mirrored by Lou Diamond Phillips's intense performance, which brings the 1950s rock 'n' roll star to life with a lot of vibrant detail while generally avoiding the usual clichés of the genre. As Ritchie's bad-boy half-brother, Esai Morales also contributes to the authenticity. JM. Contains swearing and some nudity. DVD

Lou Diamond Phillips *Ritchie Valens/Richard Valenzuela* • Esai Morales *Bob Morales* • Rosana De Soto *Connie Valenzuela* • Elizabeth Peña *Rosie Morales* • Danielle Von Zerneck *Donna Ludwig* • Joe Pantoliano *Bob Keene* ■ *Dir/Scr* Luis Valdez

Bambi ★★★★★ U

Animation 1942 · US · Colour · 66mins

The classic status of this Disney landmark is merely buffed up by time, as successive generations discover its peerless mix of ecological message and anthropomorphic fun. It traces the formative seasons of a deer – imbued with human characteristics, as are his companions Flower, the shy skunk, and Thumper, the exuberant rabbit – who learns the lessons of life in the forest. The death of his mother at the hands of a hunter ("Man" personified) remains one of cinema's most memorable, though it isn't actually shown. This still has plenty to tell children and strikes a deft artistic balance between naturalism and cartoonery. AC DVD

Bobby Stewart *Bambi* • Peter Behn *Thumper* • Stan Alexander *Flower* • Cammie King *Phylline* ■ *Dir* David D Hand [David Hand] • *Scr* Perce Pearce, Larry Morey, from a story by Felix Salten, from his novel

Le Bambole ★★★

Portmanteau comedy
1965 · Fr/It · Colour · 111mins

In Dino Risi's *The Telephone Call*, Nino Manfredi takes advantage of Virna Lisi's endless call to flirt with a neighbour, while in Franco Rossi's *The Soup*, Monica Vitti attempts to dispose of her husband. *Treatise on Eugenics* sees Elke Sommer search for the perfect Latin father for her baby, while *Monsignor Cupid* focuses on hotel receptionist Gina Lollobrigida's attempts to seduce the nephew of prelate Akim Tamiroff (Jean Sorel). Portmanteau pictures have always been hit-and-miss affairs. However, one expects slightly more, even in a vignette, from directors of the calibre of Luigi Comencini and Mauro Bolognini, who settle for mischief rather than meaning in their respective episodes. DP. An Italian language film.

Virna Lisi *Luisa, the wife* • Nino Manfredi *Giorgio, the husband* • Elke Sommer *Ulla* • Maurizio Arena *Massimo* • Monica Vitti *Giovanna* • John Karlsen *Alfonso, her husband* • Orazio Orlando *Richetto, her lover* • Gina Lollobrigida *Beatrice* • Akim Tamiroff *Monsignor Arendi* • Jean Sorel *Vincenzo* ■ *Dir* Dino Risi, Luigi Comencini, Franco Rossi, Mauro Bolognini • *Scr* Rodolfo Sonego, Tullio Pinelli (from a story by Luciano Salce, Steno, Luigi Magni), Leo Benvenuti (from a story by Piero De Bernardi, from the story *Il Decamerone* by Giovanni Boccaccio)

The Bamboo Blonde ★★ U

Second World War romance
1946 · US · BW · 67mins

Anthony Mann's tenth feature ranks among the least distinguished of his career. Shot quickly and cheaply for RKO, it wavers between being a wartime adventure, a romantic melodrama and a musical. Ultimately, it succeeds only in being a bore, despite Frances Langford's pretty crooning of some catchy ditties. Ralph Edwards is suitably seedy as the Manhattan nightclub boss who exploits Langford, but there's no chemistry among the leading players. DP

Frances Langford *Louise Anderson* • Ralph Edwards *Eddie Clark* • Russell Wade *Patrick Ransom Jr* • Iris Adrian *Montana* • Richard Martin (1) *Jim Wilson* • Jane Greer *Eileen Sawyer* ■ *Dir* Anthony Mann • *Scr* Olive Cooper, Lawrence Kimble, from the story *Chicago Lulu* by Wayne Whittaker

Bamboozled ★★★ 15

Satirical drama 2000 · US · Colour · 130mins

Spike Lee's dark, biting satire is both thought provoking and amusing. Damon Wayans plays the only black writer at a network TV station, who's dismayed at his employer's decision to dumb down in a bid to boost ratings. He wants to quit, but station boss Michael Rapaport won't let him. So Wayans decides to get himself fired by creating a programme so controversial that the station won't touch it – an old-style minstrel show, with blacks portrayed as grinning idiots who dwell in watermelon patches. The plan backfires when Rapaport loves the idea, and the show draws huge audiences. DA. Contains swearing. DVD

Damon Wayans *Pierre Delacroix* • Savion Glover *Manray/Mantan* • Jada Pinkett Smith *Sloan Hopkins* • Tommy Davidson *Womack/Sleep 'n' Eat* • Michael Rapaport *Dunwitty* • Thomas Jefferson Byrd *Honeycutt* • Paul Mooney *Junebug* ■ *Dir/Scr* Spike Lee

Banana Peel ★★★

Comedy 1964 · Fr/It · BW · 97mins

Although his father Max was renowned for sparkling sophistication in his films, Marcel Ophüls's debut feature owes more to the brash panache of Hollywood satirist Preston Sturges. Set among the idle rich of the French Riviera and its constant round of double-dealings, this has a couple of sharp swindlers trying to con a miserly millionaire. Revelling in the badinage, Jeanne Moreau and Jean-Paul Belmondo are ideally matched as they cross swords with the far from helpless Gert Fröbe. DP. In French with English subtitles.

Jeanne Moreau *Cathy* • Jean-Paul Belmondo *Michel* • Gert Fröbe *Lachard* • Claude Brasseur *Charlie* • Jean-Pierre Marielle *Reynaldo* • Alain Cuny *Bontemps* ■ *Dir* Marcel Ophüls • *Scr* Marcel Ophüls, Claude Sautet, Daniel Boulanger, from the novel *Nothing in Her Way* by Charles Williams

Banana Ridge ★★

Comedy 1941 · UK · BW · 87mins

Along with Ralph Lynn and Tom Walls, Robertson Hare was one of the stalwarts of the Aldwych farces in the 1920s. He reprises one of his stage roles in this creaky comedy by the great Ben Travers. Set on a Malaysian rubber plantation, the story of gold digging, guilty secrets and disputed paternity follows the farce formula to the last letter, but it lacks the pace and complexity essential for a first-class comedy. DP

Robertson Hare *Willoughby Pink* • Alfred Drayton *Mr Pound* • Isabel Jeans *Sue Long* • Nova Pilbeam *Cora Pound* • Adele Dixon *Mrs Pound* • Patrick Kinsella *Jones* • Valentine Dunn *Mrs Pink* ■ *Dir* Walter C Mycroft • *Scr* Lesley Storm, Walter C Mycroft, Ben Travers, from the play by Ben Travers

Bananas ★★★ 15

Comedy 1971 · US · Colour · 78mins

With a title that refers to both banana republics and the Marx Brothers film *Cocoanuts*, Woody Allen's second picture as director and star is one of his least convincing outings. Packed with nods to cinematic maestros such as Eisenstein, Chaplin, Buñuel and Bergman, it's the work of a comic delighting in his gags rather than a director in control of his material. A touch of political satire might have helped stem the endless flow of throwaway lines and surreal incidents, as well as giving the plot a little more focus. Inconsistent, but when it's funny, it's a riot. DP DVD

Woody Allen *Fielding Mellish* • Louise Lasser *Nancy* • Carlos Montalban *General Emilio M Vargas* • Natividad Abascal *Yolanda* • Jacobo Morales *Esposito* • Miguel Suarez [Miguel Angel Suarez] *Luis* • Sylvester Stallone *Subway thug* ■ *Dir* Woody Allen • *Scr* Woody Allen, Mickey Rose

Band of Angels ★★

Period drama 1957 · US · Colour · 114mins

After the death of her father, beautiful Southern belle Yvonne De Carlois discovers that her mother was a slave. As a result she's sold as a slave to millionaire Clark Gable, whose mistress she becomes. Directed by the veteran Raoul Walsh, who must have been forced into it, and with Sidney Poitier as a slave, this utter tosh strains credibility to the limits and has little to recommend it other than De Carlo's glamour. RK

Clark Gable *Hamish Bond* • Yvonne De Carlo *Amantha Starr* • Sidney Poitier *Rau-Ru* • Efrem Zimbalist Jr *Ethan Sears* • Rex Reason *Seth Parton* • Patric Knowles *Charles de Marigny* • Torin Thatcher *Captain Canavan* ■ *Dir* Raoul Walsh • *Scr* John Twist, Ivan Goff, Ben Roberts, from the novel by Robert Penn Warren

B

Band Waggon ★★★ U

Musical comedy 1939 · UK · BW · 85mins

The radio spin-off movie may be unheard of today, but they were all the rage in the 1930s. Although it only ran for some two years, *Band Waggon*, with its quirky characters and rapid-fire humour, was hugely popular. Here, the script restricts the fabled ad-libbing of Arthur Askey and Richard "Stinker" Murdoch, but it's still good fun as the pair stray from their famous flat in the eaves of Broadcasting House only to encounter spies in a haunted castle – a plot familiar to director Marcel Varnel from his time with Will Hay. DP

Arthur Askey *Big Hearted Arthur* • Richard Murdoch *Stinker* • Jack Hylton • Pat Kirkwood *Pat* • Moore Marriott *Jasper* • Peter Gawthorne *Claude Pilkington* • Wally Patch *Commissionaire* ■ *Dir* Marcel Varnel • *Scr* Marriott Edgar, Val Guest, from the radio series by Harry S Pepper, Gordon Crier, Vernon Harris

The Band Wagon ★★★★★ U

Classic musical 1953 · US · Colour · 107mins

This clever and witty backstage musical has Fred Astaire playing a Broadway star who's out of step with the very modern musical he has been hired to headline. It boasts brilliant direction from Vincente Minnelli and fabulous Technicolor production design, and to many marks the peak of Astaire's screen work. Astaire is stunning as he partners the gorgeous Cyd Charisse in *Dancing in the Dark* and the Mickey Spillane parody *The Girl Hunt* ballet superbly choreographed by Michael Kidd and Oliver Smith. As good as musicals get. TS [video] DVD

Fred Astaire *Tony Hunter* • Cyd Charisse *Gaby Berard* • Jack Buchanan *Jeffrey Cordova* • Oscar Levant *Lester Marton* • Nanette Fabray *Lily Marton* • James Mitchell *Paul Byrd* • Robert Gist *Hal Benton* • Ava Gardner *Movie star* ■ *Dir* Vincente Minnelli • *Scr* Betty Comden, Adolph Green • *Lyrics* Howard Dietz • *Music* Arthur Schwartz

Bande à Part ★★★★ PG

Crime drama 1964 · Fr · Colour · 95mins

A playful effort from Jean-Luc Godard in which his then wife, the radiant Anna Karina, teams up with a couple of petty crooks – Sami Frey and Claude Brasseur – in a hair-brained scheme to rob her aunt. In characteristic fashion, Godard drops the plot at every opportunity to indulge in homages to various Hollywood genres – the thriller, the musical and so on – and to allow his camera to idolise Karina's beauty. Some may find it irritating beyond endurance, but in its day its freshness was greeted like rain in a drought. Thirty years later, a certain Quentin Tarantino rediscovered the film and liked it so much he named his production company "A Band Apart". AT. A French language film. [video] DVD

Anna Karina *Odile* • Sami Frey *Franz* • Claude Brasseur *Arthur* • Louisa Colpeyn *Madame Victoria* • Danièle Girard *English teacher* • Chantal Darget *Arthur's aunt* • Ernest Menzer *Arthur's uncle* • Jean-Luc Godard *Narration* ■ *Dir* Jean-Luc Godard • *Scr* Jean-Luc Godard, from the novel *Fool's Gold (Pigeon Vole)* by Dolores Hitchens

Bandido ★★ U

Western 1956 · US · Colour · 91mins

This routine 1950s western adventure stars Robert Mitchum as an American soldier of fortune who joins forces with a rebel leader in a bid to intercept a shipment of arms during the Mexican Revolution. Mitchum is better than the script, but the film still offers action, sufficient intrigue and picturesque landscapes. You could do worse. PF

Robert Mitchum *Wilson* • Ursula Thiess *Lisa* • Gilbert Roland *Escobar* • Zachary Scott *Kennedy* • Rodolfo Acosta *Sebastian* • Henry Brandon *Gunther* • Douglas Fowley *McGee* • José I Torvay [José Torvay] *Gonzalez* • Victor Junco *Lorenzo* ■ *Dir* Richard Fleischer • *Scr* Earl Felton

Bandini ★★★★ U

Drama 1963 · Ind · BW · 145mins

Bimal Roy's final feature is regarded by many as his crowning achievement. The key lay in persuading Nutan out of her post-nuptial retirement to play the strictly raised, poetry-loving village girl, Kalyani. Her passion for a revolutionary, played by Ashok Kumar, leads first to her imprisonment for murder and then to her redemption through the love of a prison doctor (Dharmendra). The heartbreaking intensity of her performance is considerably enhanced by cinematographer Kamal Bose's authentic re-creation of 1930s Bengal and SD Burman's score, which provided legendary backing singer Gulzar with a memorable debut. DP. In Hindi with English subtitles. [video] DVD

Nutan *Kalyani* • Ashok Kumar *Bikash Ghosh* • Dharmendra *Devendra* ■ *Dir* Bimal Roy • *Scr* M Ghosh, Nabendu Ghosh

The Bandit of Sherwood Forest ★★ U

Swashbuckling adventure
1946 · US · Colour · 86mins

Cornel Wilde stars as Robin Hood's son, who tries to save the Magna Carta and Britain from the constitutional ravages of Henry Daniell's royal schemer, the wayward Regent. It's really just a western in weird costumes with added peasantry, shot on the Columbia backlot in bright-as-a-button Technicolor. Not a patch on Errol Flynn's classic *The Adventures of Robin Hood*, this is an enjoyable romp just the same. AT

Cornel Wilde *Robert of Nottingham* • Anita Louise *Lady Catherine Maitland* • Jill Esmond *Queen Mother* • Edgar Buchanan *Friar Tuck* • Henry Daniell *Regent* • George Macready *Fitz-Herbert* • Russell Hicks *Robin Hood* • John Abbott *Will Scarlet* • Ray Teal *Little John* ■ *Dir* George Sherman, Henry Levin • *Scr* Wilfred H Pettit, Melvyn Levy, from the novel *Son of Robin Hood* by Paul A Castleton

The Bandit of Zhobe ★★ U

Action adventure 1959 · UK · Colour · 81mins

Very silly Northwest Frontier romp, with Victor Mature in dark make-up as a fearsome but noble Indian leader whose family has been massacred by Brits. There ensues much pillage, a lot of smirking by Mature, romantic interest from forgotten starlet Anne Aubrey and some wince-inducing comic mugging from Anthony Newley. Quite a lot of money was thrown at it, but this remains a B-movie at heart. AT

Victor Mature *Kasim Khan* • Anne Aubrey *Zena Crowley* • Anthony Newley *Corporal Stokes* • Norman Wooland *Major Crowley* • Dermot Walsh *Captain Saunders* • Walter Gotell *Azhad* ■ *Dir* John Gilling • *Scr* John Gilling, from a story by Richard Maibaum

Bandit Queen ★★★★ 18

Biographical drama
1994 · Ind/UK · Colour · 114mins

Released to a storm of protest throughout the subcontinent and the displeasure of its subject, Phoolan Devi herself, this is a damning condemnation of both the caste system and the subservience of women in modern Indian society. Director Shekhar Kapur deserves great credit for depicting provocative events without the slightest hint of sensationalism, whether it is Devi's gang-rape at the hands of some Uttar Pradeshi bandits or her merciless revenge, which culminated in the Behmai massacre of 1981. Seema Biswas is superb as the folkloric figure who avoided capture for five years before surrendering in 1983. DP. In Hindi with English subtitles. [video]

Seema Biswas *Phoolan Devi* • Nirmal Pandey *Vikram Mallah* • Manoj Bajpai *Man Singh* • Rajesh Vivek *Mustaqim* • Raghuvir Yadav *Madho* • Govind Namdeo *Sriram* • Saurabh Shukla *Kailash* • Aditya Srivastava *Puttilal* ■ *Dir* Shekhar Kapur • *Scr* Mala Sen

Bandits ★★★ 12

Crime comedy drama
2001 · US · Colour · 117mins

Bruce Willis and Billy Bob Thornton star as charismatic bank robbers in this enjoyable (if utterly nonsensical) comedy drama from Barry Levinson. They earn the nickname of "sleepover bandits" because of their habit of casually kidnapping bank managers the night before a job. However, their modus operandi is complicated when they both fall for Cate Blanchett, whom they take along for the ride. The film is at its best when Willis and Thornton are exchanging witty banter. JB. Contains swearing, violence. [video] DVD

Bruce Willis *Joe Blake* • Billy Bob Thornton *Terry Collins* • Cate Blanchett *Kate Wheeler* • Troy Garity *Harvey Pollard* • Brian F O'Byrne *Darill Miller* • Stacey Travis *Cloe Miller* ■ *Dir* Barry Levinson • *Scr* Harley Peyton

The Bandits of Corsica ★ U

Adventure 1953 · US · BW · 80mins

The 1942 Douglas Fairbanks Jr swashbuckler *The Corsican Brothers* was only loosely based on the characters created by Alexandre Dumas, but this sequel is even further removed. Every expense seems to have been spared in the mounting of this clumping adventure, in which Richard Greene manages to give two poor performances. DP

Richard Greene *Mario/Carlos* • Paula Raymond *Christina* • Raymond Burr *Jonatto* • Dona Drake *Zelda* • Raymond Greenleaf *Paoli* • Lee Van Cleef *Nerva* • Frank Puglia *Riggio* ■ *Dir* Ray Nazarro • *Scr* Richard Schayer, from a story by Frank Burt

Bandits of Orgosolo ★★★★

Crime drama 1961 · It · BW · 98mins

Stripping neorealism to its bare essentials, this austere study of survival in rural Sardinia would be noteworthy if only for its influence on Pier Paolo Pasolini's *The Gospel According to St Matthew*. But ex-documentarist Vittorio De Seta's use of the unforgiving landscape and his non-professional cast is exemplary, appearing simply to observe life rather than fashion a drama. Peppeddu Cuccu is particularly impressive as the shepherd wrongfully accused of rustling, who takes to the hills rather than submit to justice. It's only a shame that De Seta opted to over-dub the local dialect to make it more accessible to urban audiences. DP. In Italian with English subtitles.

Michele Cossu *Michele* • Peppeddu Cuccu *Peppeddu* • Vittorina Pisano *Mintonia* ■ *Dir* Vittorio De Seta • *Scr* Vittorio De Seta, Vera Gherarducci

Bandolero! ★★ 15

Western 1968 · US · Colour · 101mins

This would-be rollicking adventure suffers from chronic miscasting. All-time good guys James Stewart and Dean Martin play outlaw brothers who hold a peculiarly accented Raquel Welch hostage after she loses her husband in a botched bank raid. The actual good guy, surprisingly, is George Kennedy, but he's no match for these particular baddies. This uneven mixture of contemporary violence and traditional western values is a mess, but not unenjoyable. TS [video] DVD

James Stewart *Mace Bishop* • Dean Martin *Dee Bishop* • Raquel Welch *Maria* • George Kennedy *Sheriff Johnson* • Andrew Prine *Roscoe Bookbinder* • Will Geer *Pop Chaney* • Clint Ritchie *Babe* • Denver Pyle *Muncie Carter* ■ *Dir* Andrew V McLaglen • *Scr* James Lee Barrett, from the unpublished story *Mace* by Stanley L Hough

Bandwagon ★★★

Musical comedy 1995 · US · Colour · 99mins

Richard Lester's seminal 1964 rock and road movie *A Hard Day's Night* influenced scores of music-orientated successors, including this amiable debut by writer/director John Schultz. His not so Fab Four are North Carolina working-class guys who optimistically hope that playing gigs will bring fame and easy fortune. They produce a single, tour with some success in the South, but find that life for aspirational 20-somethings can be tough. The leads synchronise the songs efficiently but their quirkiness may make some viewers happy to see the tour bus leave ahead of them. BB

Kevin Corrigan *Wynn Knapp* • Steve Parlavecchio *Eric Ellwood* • Lee Holmes *Tony Ridge* • Matthew Hennessey *Charlie Flagg* • Doug McMillan *Linus Tate* • Doug McCallie *Chester* ■ *Dir/Scr* John Schultz

Bang ★★★ 18

Drama 1995 · US · Colour · 94mins

Struggling Japanese-American actress Darling Narita steals an LA cop's uniform and motorcycle and finds that she is treated differently by everyone she meets. Her newly found status also enables her to take revenge on the producer who tried to molest her. Written and directed by London-born Ash (real name Ashley Baron Cohen), this ambitious US indie was made for just $20,000 with hand-held cameras and no permits. RT. Contains swearing, violence, sex scenes. [video]

Darling Narita *The girl* • Peter Greene *Adam* • Michael Newland *Officer Rattler* • David Allen Graf [David Alan Graf] *Peter Fawcette, the producer* • Everlast *Pimp* • Art Cruz *Juan* • Luis Guizar *Jezuz* ■ *Dir/Scr* Ash

Bang the Drum Slowly ★★★★

Period sports drama
1973 · US · Colour · 98mins

Director John Hancock's moving buddy drama is one of the best baseball movies ever made. Telling the engrossing tale of how New York pitcher Michael Moriarty helps his terminally ill catcher Robert De Niro through one more season, this 1950s-set heartbreaker resonates with emotional truths while evoking nostalgia for a more innocent era. It's superlatively performed by De Niro (then unknown) and Moriarty, with excellent support from Vincent Gardenia, as their manager. The underlying theme of people coming through for each other in times of dire trouble is expertly handled by Hancock from a first-class script by Mark Harris. AJ

Robert De Niro *Bruce Pearson* • Vincent Gardenia *Dutch Schnell* • Phil Foster *Joe Jaros* • Ann Wedgeworth *Katie* • Patrick McVey *Pearson's father* • Heather MacRae *Holly Wiggin* • Selma Diamond *Tootsie* ■ *Dir* John Hancock • *Scr* Mark Harris, from his novel

Bang! You're Dead ★★

Crime drama 1954 · UK · BW · 88mins

Simply because the plot revolves around a young boy finding a gun and accidentally killing a much detested local man, only for the victim's most outspoken detractor to be arrested for murder, this minor British crime drama has been compared to both 1949's *The Window* and 1952's *The Yellow Balloon*. Yet there's considerably less insight into the boy's guilt-stricken torment than in either of those films, with director Lance Comfort settling for a mildly suspenseful countdown to the predictable climax. DP

Jack Warner *Mr Bonsell* • Derek Farr *Detective Grey* • Veronica Hurst *Hilda* • Michael Medwin *Bob Carter* • Gordon Harker *Mr Hare* • Anthony Richmond *Cliff Bonsell* • Sean Barrett (1) *Willy* ■ *Dir* Lance Comfort • *Scr* Guy Elmes, Ernest Borneman

The Banger Sisters ★★★ 15

Comedy drama 2002 · US · Colour · 93mins

This is a likeable attempt to see what happens to groupies after the tours and tequila have dried up. Goldie Hawn stars as an over-the-hill rock chick travelling across the country to hook up with former partner-in-crime Susan Sarandon, now a model of suburban respectability. Once they meet, the life lessons are trotted out with predictable regularity and the writing fails to deliver on the promising premise. But Hawn and Sarandon are a winning pairing, and they're ably assisted by Geoffrey Rush. IF. Contains swearing, drug abuse, sex scenes. DVD

Goldie Hawn *Suzette* • Susan Sarandon *Lavinia "Vinnie" Kingsley* • Geoffrey Rush *Harry Plumber* • Erika Christensen *Hannah* • Eva Amurri *Ginger* • Robin Rhomas *Raymond* • Matthew Carey *Jules* ■ *Dir/Scr* Bob Dolman

Bangkok Dangerous ★★★ 18

Crime thriller 2000 · Thai · Colour · 105mins

Deaf-mute hitman Pavarit Mongkolpisit at first plays it all mean and moody as the archetypal loner, isolated by his profession and his inability to communicate. Then he meets unsuspecting pharmacy assistant Premsinee Ratanasopha and the possibility of a redemptive romance is introduced. However, debuting writers/directors Oxide and Danny Pang are too interested in atmospheric neon nightscapes and over-the-top pyrotechnics to develop the characters or their relationship, so the action proceeds in a depressingly familiar vein. DP. In Thai with English subtitles. Contains violence. DVD

Pavarit Mongkolpisit *Kong* • Premsinee Ratanasopha *Fon* • Patharawarin Timkul *Aom* ■ *Dir/Scr* Oxide Pang, Danny Pang

Banjo on My Knee ★★★

Musical drama 1936 · US · BW · 95mins

Here's feisty Barbara Stanwyck in one of her early tours de force. After being abandoned by new husband Joel McCrea, Stanwyck, as riverboat moll Pearl, takes over the whole show: she dances with Buddy Ebsen, sings with Tony Martin and even gets into a fight with Katherine DeMille, adopted daughter of the legendary Cecil B. John Cromwell's direction is perfunctory, but the supporting players (Walter Brennan, Helen Westley, Walter Catlett) are a joy, and the movie paved the way for Stanwyck's triumph the following year in *Stella Dallas*. TS

Barbara Stanwyck *Pearl* • Joel McCrea *Ernie Holley* • Helen Westley *Grandma* • Buddy Ebsen *Puddy* • Walter Brennan *Newt Holley* • Walter Catlett *Warfield Scott* • Tony Martin *Chick Bean* • Minna Gombell *Ruby* • Katherine DeMille *Leota Long* ■ *Dir* John Cromwell • *Scr* Nunnally Johnson, from the novel by Harry Hamilton

The Bank ★★★★

Thriller 2001 · Aus/It · Colour · 106mins

Enthralling both as a thriller and as a caustic portrait of corporate greed, writer/director Robert Connolly's superb debut delivers a crowd-pleasing comeuppance to an institution that people love to hate – the bank. David Wenham plays a brilliant Australian mathematician who is close to perfecting a computer programme that will be able to predict major stock market ups and downs. His employer (Anthony LaPaglia), the head of a big Australian bank, has other ideas. Wenham is excellent as a man coping with the conflict between his moral code and a desire to leave his mark on the world of mathematics, while LaPaglia offers up the most monstrous business executive since Michael Douglas's Gordon Gecko. JF

David Wenham *Jim Doyle* • Anthony LaPaglia *Simon O'Reilly* • Sibylla Budd *Michelle Roberts* • Mitchell Butel *Stephen* • Mandy McElhinney *Diane Davis* • Greg Stone *Vincent* ■ *Dir/Scr* Robert Connolly

The Bank Dick ★★★★★ U

Comedy 1940 · US · BW · 72mins

Scripted by WC Fields under the name of Mahatma Kane Jeeves, this is one of his finest comedies. Playing the wonderfully named Egbert Sousé, Fields growls and grumbles his way through some inspired routines as the indolent passer-by who is rewarded with the post of bank detective after inadvertently foiling a raid. Even though several gags are rehashed from his celebrated shorts, they are done to a crisp by Fields and a superb supporting cast, in which Cora Witherspoon, Una Merkel and Jessie Ralph are outstanding as the women who delight in pointing out the shortcomings he considers his assets. DP

WC Fields *Egbert Sousé* • Cora Witherspoon *Agatha Sousé* • Una Merkel *Myrtle Sousé* • Evelyn Del Rio *Elsie May Adele Brunch Souse* • Jessie Ralph *Mrs Hermisillo Brunch* • Franklin Pangborn *J Pinkerton Snoopington* • Shemp Howard *Joe Guelpe* • Richard Purcell [Dick Purcell] *Mackley Q Greene* • Grady Sutton *Og Oggilby* • Russell Hicks *J Frothingham Waterbury* • Pierre Watkin *Mr Skinner* ■ *Dir* Edward Cline • *Scr* Mahatma Kane Jeeves [WC Fields], Richard Carroll

Bank Holiday ★★★

Comedy drama 1938 · UK · BW · 86mins

While today it may look slightly laboured, in 1938 this neat comedy drama was acclaimed for its naturalism, restraint and shrewd characterisation. Following a group of day-trippers to Brighton, the film is smoothly directed by Carol Reed, who sustains interest in a variety of stock figures by flitting between them in the style of a soap opera instalment. Margaret Lockwood wins sympathy as a nurse who is distracted from a dirty weekend by her concern for a grieving widow, but the standout performances come from Kathleen Harrison as a prim Cockney wife and Wilfrid Lawson as a world-weary police sergeant. DP

John Lodge *Stephen Howard* • Margaret Lockwood *Catherine* • Hugh Williams *Geoffrey* • René Ray *Doreen* • Merle Tottenham *Milly* • Linden Travers *Ann Howard* • Wally Patch *Arthur* • Kathleen Harrison *May* • Garry Marsh *Manager* ■ *Dir* Carol Reed • *Scr* Rodney Ackland, Roger Burford, from a story by Hans Wilhelm, Rodney Ackland

The Bank Raiders ★ U

Crime thriller 1958 · UK · BW · 60mins

A dismal B-movie about a bank robber who spends his swag too quickly and attracts the rozzers, obliging him to turn kidnapper. Designed as something to have on the screen while the queue was being let in to the cinema, it's cheap and cheerless wallpaper. AT

Peter Reynolds *Terry* • Sandra Dorne *Della* • Sydney Tafler *Sholton* • Lloyd Lamble *Inspector Mason* • Rose Hill *Mrs Marling* • Arthur Mullard *Linders* ■ *Dir* Maxwell Munden • *Scr* Brandon Fleming

Bank Robber ★★★ 18

Crime comedy 1993 · US · Colour · 89mins

A modern-day version of the Robin Hood legend, with twists provided by the fact that this outlaw not only steals from the rich, but also gets shafted by the poor. Most of the action takes place in one room in writer/director Nick Mead's interesting mix of dark comedy, surreal action and extreme social significance. With the exception of a bland Patrick Dempsey, the cast rises to the offbeat occasion, providing exuberant fun and some seriously sexy moments. AJ

Patrick Dempsey *Billy* • Lisa Bonet *Priscilla* • Judge Reinhold *Officer Gross* • Forest Whitaker *Officer Battle* • Olivia D'Abo *Selina* • Mariska Hargitay *Marisa Benoit* • Joe Alaskey *2nd night clerk* ■ *Dir/Scr* Nick Mead

Bank Shot ★★ PG

Crime caper 1974 · US · Colour · 80mins

This bizarre outing for George C Scott is a far cry from his magnificent performance four years earlier in the Second World War biopic *Patton*. This feeble comedy caper too often stretches credibility as escaped convict Scott literally steals a bank by lifting it up and dragging it off. Although there are some neat gags and shrewd ideas, the result is all at sea. TH

George C Scott *Walter Ballantine* • Joanna Cassidy *El* • Sorrell Booke *Al G Karp* • G Wood *FBI Agent Andrew Constable* • Clifton James *Frank "Bulldog" Streiger* • Robert Balaban [Bob Balaban] *Victor Karp* ■ *Dir* Gower Champion • *Scr* Wendell Mayes, from the novel by Donald E Westlake

Banning ★★

Drama 1967 · US · Colour · 101mins

This golfing melodrama feels like 101 minutes spent in the deepest bunker with a snooker cue. Robert Wagner takes a job as a country club pro and becomes the focus of attention for a number of women, including the sophisticated Anjanette Cromer. He also finds himself up against old adversary Guy Stockwell for the huge cash prize in a special tournament. Ron Winston's saga feels like the failed pilot for a soap. DP

Robert Wagner *Mike Banning* • Anjanette Comer *Carol Lindquist* • Jill St John *Angela Barr* • Guy Stockwell *Jonathan Linus* • James Farentino *Chris Patton* • Susan Clark *Cynthia Linus* • Gene Hackman *Tommy Del Gaddo* ■ *Dir* Ron Winston • *Scr* James Lee, from a story by Hamilton Maule

BAPS ★ 15

Comedy 1997 · US · Colour · 88mins

This lame, ludicrous comedy stars Halle Berry and Natalie Desselle as a couple of garishly dressed Georgia homegirls who travel to LA to audition for a music video, but get caught up in a scam involving dying millionaire Martin Landau. The title stands for "Black American Princesses", and the idea seems to be some sort of African-American *Pygmalion*. But the result is insulting and unfunny. JC

Halle Berry *Nisi* • Martin Landau *Mr Blakemore* • Ian Richardson *Manley* • Natalie Desselle *Mickey* • Troy Beyer *Tracy* • Luigi Amodeo *Antonio* • Jonathan Fried *Isaac* • Pierre *Ali* • AJ Johnson [Anthony Johnson] *James* ■ *Dir* Robert Townsend • *Scr* Troy Beyer

Bar Girls ★ 18

Romantic comedy 1994 · US · Colour · 94mins

On its release, this was well received at various festivals, including Toronto and Berlin, but it must have been part of a very bad batch. The criticism that dares not speak its name has to say that if this was about eight heterosexuals in a bar – and not eight upfront lesbians – the movie probably would not have been considered for selection. This self-indulgent film fails to sufficiently flesh out either the characters or screenplay. SH

Nancy Allison Wolfe *Loretta* • Liza D'Agostino *Rachel* • Camila Griggs *JR* • Michael Harris (2) *Noah* • Justine Slater *Veronica* • Lisa Parker *Annie* • Pam Raines *Celia* ■ *Dir* Marita Giovanni • *Scr* Lauran Hoffman, from her play

Barabbas ★★★ PG

Epic biblical drama 1961 · It · Colour · 127mins

An impressive quasi-biblical epic, produced by Dino De Laurentiis on a grand scale and directed with a fine sense of period by Richard Fleischer. It's best remembered today, however, for the fact that the Crucifixion was photographed against an actual eclipse of the sun. Anthony Quinn does well in the title role as the murderer and thief pardoned in place of Christ, and the climactic arena sequences involving Jack Palance are splendid. However, it's overlong and dull, like the novel on which it is based. TS DVD

Anthony Quinn *Barabbas* • Silvana Mangano *Rachel* • Arthur Kennedy *Pontius Pilate* • Katy Jurado *Sara* • Harry Andrews *St Peter* • Vittorio Gassman *Sahak* • Jack Palance *Torvald* • Ernest Borgnine *Lucius* • Valentina Cortese *Julia* ■ *Dir* Richard Fleischer • *Scr* Christopher Fry, Ivo Perilli, Diego Fabbri, Nigel Balchin, from the novel by Par Lagerkvist

Baraka ★★ PG

Documentary 1992 · US · Colour · 92mins

Shot on Todd-AO 70mm stock, so that every image positively shimmers, Ron Fricke's heartfelt film is, sadly, a wasted opportunity. The ecological points he makes are blatant and laboured, while his over-reliance on snazzy editing and time-lapse photography draws too much attention to technique at the expense of the visual content. The contrasts between urban jungles and the areas of natural beauty they imperil do, occasionally, strike home, but, while it's easy to look at these often beautiful moving postcards, Fricke presents locations without identifying them, so most viewers will quickly find themselves lost and overwhelmed. DP

Dir Ron Fricke • *Music* Michael Stearns

Barb Wire ★ 18

Science-fiction adventure 1995 · US · Colour · 100mins

"Don't call me babe!" scowls Pamela Anderson, as she roves around Steel Harbor zapping agents of the Congressional Directorate. OK, providing you don't ask us to call this insulting reworking of *Casablanca* a film. Director David Hogan isn't interested in storytelling, which is just as well as he doesn't have much of a tale to tell. DP. Contains violence, swearing, nudity.

Pamela Anderson Lee [Pamela Anderson] *Barb Wire* • Temuera Morrison *Axel Rood* • Victoria Rowell *Cora D* • Jack Noseworthy *Charlie* • Xander Berkeley *Alexander Willis* • Steve Railsback *Colonel Pryzer* • Udo Kier *Curly* ■ *Dir* David Hogan • *Scr* Chuck Pfarrer, Ilene Chaiken, from the story by Ilene Chaiken

Barbara Taylor Bradford's Everything to Gain ★ 12

Mystery 1996 · US · Colour · 87mins

Sean Young stars in this TV movie as a woman who tries to rebuild her life after her husband and two children are murdered. Alone and depressed, she joins forces with gritty detective Jack Scalia to find the thugs responsible for the crime. Unless you're a rabid fan of Barbara Taylor Bradford, you have nothing to gain from this preposterous drivel. MC DVD

U = SUITABLE FOR ALL Uc = SUITABLE FOR ALL, ESPECIALLY FOR YOUNG CHILDREN (VIDEO ONLY) PG = PARENTAL GUIDANCE

Sean Young *Mallory Jordan* • Jack Scalia *Detective DeMarco* • Charles Shaughnessy *Andrew Keswick* • Joanna Miles *Jessica Jordan* • Samantha Eggar *Diana Keswick* ■ *Dir* Michael Miller (2) • *Scr* Cathleen Young, from the novel by Barbara Taylor Bradford

Barbarella ★★★ 15

Cult science-fiction fantasy
1967 · Fr/It · Colour · 93mins

The famed French comic strip comes to glorious psychedelic life in director Roger Vadim's 41st-century space opera. Once you get past Jane Fonda's infamous antigravity striptease, however, the script turns rather dull. The imaginative sets steal the whole show, as Fonda's nubile intergalactic bimbo experiences close encounters of the sexually bizarre kind. A pleasure machine, cannibalistic dolls and Anita Pallenberg's Black Queen help ease the verbal vacuum. AJ. Contains violence and sex scenes. [VIDEO] DVD

Jane Fonda *Barbarella* • John Phillip Law *Pygar* • Anita Pallenberg *Black Queen* • Milo O'Shea *Concierge/Durand-Durand* • David Hemmings *Dildano* • Marcel Marceau *Professor Ping* • Ugo Tognazzi *Mark Hand* • Claude Dauphin *President of Earth* ■ *Dir* Roger Vadim • *Scr* Terry Southern, Brian Degas, Claude Brulé, Jean-Claude Forest, Clement Biddle Wood, Tudor Gates, Vittorio Bonicelli, Roger Vadim, from the comic by Jean-Claude Forest • *Cinematographer* Claude Renoir

The Barbarian ★★★

Romance 1933 · US · BW · 82mins

Made when screen idol Ramon Novarro was nearing the end of the peak of his career and Myrna Loy was at the start of hers, this hot-blooded desert romance was of a kind leftover from the silent period, yet its sensibility remains far from old hat. When tourist Loy is cautioned by her uncle that she is hiring as a guide a man she knows nothing about, she replies, "But look at that profile!" Dashing Novarro sings *Love Songs of the Nile*, while sparkling Loy takes an on-screen bath and relishes the risqué pre-code dialogue. Viewed in the right spirit, this is great fun. TV

Ramon Novarro *Jamil* • Myrna Loy *Diana* • Reginald Denny *Gerald* • Louise Closser Hale *Powers* • C Aubrey Smith *Cecil* • Edward Arnold *Achmed* • Blanche Frederici *Mrs Hume* ■ *Dir* Sam Wood • *Scr* Anita Loos, Elmer Harris, from the story by Edgar Selwyn

The Barbarian and the Geisha ★ U

Historical drama
1958 · US · Colour · 100mins

Tough-guy director John Huston teamed up with John Wayne for the first and last time to make this historical drama about Townsend Harris, America's first consul to Japan. Wayne was attracted to the role because it got him out of westerns and showed America's historical influence over their wartime enemy. Wayne and Huston loathed each other from day one, however, and the movie was a disaster. AT [VIDEO]

John Wayne *Townsend Harris* • Eiko Ando *Okichi* • Sam Jaffe *Henry Heusken* • So Yamamura *Tamura* • Norman Thomson *Ship captain* • James Robbins *Lieutenant Fisher* • Morita *Prime minister* • Kodaya Ichikawa *Daimyo* ■ *Dir* John Huston • *Scr* Charles Grayson, from a story by Ellis St Joseph

The Barbarian Invasions ★★★★ 18

Comedy drama
2003 · Can/Fr · Colour · 95mins

In director Denys Arcand's follow-up to his acclaimed 1986 film *The Decline of the American Empire*, a womanising history professor who is dying of cancer reflects on his life. Old lovers and friends congregate to help Rémy Girard celebrate and analyse a life that has earned the disapproval of his son, financial whizzkid Stéphane Rousseau. While this reunites the characters of the earlier film, it does not depend on familiarity with them for its success in painting a picture that is by turns funny and poignant. BP. In French and English with subtitles. [VIDEO] DVD

Rémy Girard *Rémy* • Stéphane Rousseau *Sébastien* • Marie-Josée Croze *Nathalie* • Marina Hands *Gaëlle* • Dorothée Berryman *Louise* • Johanne-Marie Tremblay *Sister Constance* • Pierre Curzi *Pierre* • Yves Jacques *Claude* ■ *Dir/Scr* Denys Arcand

Barbarians at the Gate ★★★★ 15

Satirical drama based on a true story
1993 · US · Colour · 102mins

Based on Bryan Burrough and John Helyar's bestseller, this superior TV movie recounts one of the most vicious takeover deals in American business history. James Garner is admirable as the head of multinational power player RJR Nabisco, who tries to buy the company when he realises its smokeless cigarette project isn't going to catch light. Stealing the show, however, is Jonathan Pryce as the wheeler-dealer determined to block him. The script is razor-sharp and Glenn Jordan's direction red hot. DP. Contains swearing. [VIDEO]

James Garner *F Ross Johnson* • Jonathan Pryce *Henry Kravis* • Peter Riegert *Peter Cohen* • Joanna Cassidy *Linda Robinson* • Fred Dalton Thompson *Jim Robinson* • Leilani Ferrer *Laurie Johnson* • Matt Clark *Ed Horrigan* • Jeffrey DeMunn *John Greeniaus* ■ *Dir* Glenn Jordan • *Scr* Larry Gelbart, from the book *Barbarians at the Gate: the Fall of RJR Nabisco* by Bryan Burrough, John Helyar

Barbarosa ★★ PG

Western 1982 · US · Colour · 86mins

Country-and-western star Willie Nelson was chosen by director Fred Schepisi to be this film's western legend. But it doesn't work as well as intended, despite Nelson's endearing partnership with goofy farmboy Gary Busey, because the idea of an ageing outlaw forever on the lam is not only predictable but monotonous. TH [VIDEO]

Willie Nelson *Barbarosa* • Gary Busey *Karl* • Gilbert Roland *Don Braulio* • Isela Vega *Josephina* • Danny De La Paz *Eduardo* • Alma Martinez *Juanita* • George Voskovec *Herman Pahmeyer* • Sharon Compton *Hilda* ■ *Dir* Fred Schepisi • *Scr* William D Wittliff

Barbary Coast ★★★ PG

Period action drama 1935 · US · BW · 86mins

This rowdy action drama, directed by Howard Hawks, was scripted by Ben Hecht and Charles MacArthur, but Hawks rewrote the script and the pair wanted to have their names taken off the credits. Miriam Hopkins plays a gold-digger who arrives in San Francisco intending to marry a rich man but, when she discovers he's dead, she switches her affections to crime boss Edward G Robinson. Then Joel McCrea shows up and confuses the issue. Sharp performances make this an enjoyable romp. AT [VIDEO]

Miriam Hopkins *Mary Rutledge* • Edward G Robinson *Louis Chamalis* • Joel McCrea *James Carmichael* • Walter Brennan *Old Atrocity* • Frank Craven *Colonel Marcus* • Brian Donlevy *Knuckles* ■ *Dir* Howard Hawks • *Scr* Ben Hecht, Charles MacArthur

Barbary Coast Gent ★★ U

Western 1944 · US · BW · 86mins

The main attraction of this Gold Rush rough-and-tumble is Wallace Beery, starring as a San Francisco conman gloriously named Honest Plush Brannon, who is forced out of town after a shooting fracas with his enemy John Carradine. Waved goodbye to by his understanding girlfriend Binnie Barnes, he makes for Nevada and strikes gold, but that's not the end of the story. Directed by Roy Del Ruth, it features a cast of familiar character actors, and was produced appropriately by Orville Dull. RK

Wallace Beery *Honest Plush Brannon* • Binnie Barnes *Lil Damish* • John Carradine *Duke Cleat* • Bruce Kellogg *Bradford Bellamy III* • Frances Rafferty *Portia Adair* • Chill Wills *Sheriff Hightower* • Noah Beery Sr [Noah Beery] *Pete Hannibal* • Louise Beavers *Bedelia* ■ *Dir* Roy Del Ruth • *Scr* William R Lipman, Grant Garrett, Harry Ruskin

The Barber of Seville ★★★ U

Opera 1946 · It · BW · 96mins

Director Mario Costa will go down in film history as the man who discovered Gina Lollobrigida. Yet he also handled several operatic adaptations in the 1940s which, while not particularly inventive in visual terms, do adequate justice to both the music and its performance. American journalist Deems Taylor (who narrated Disney's *Fantasia*) reworked the libretto for the screen to enable Costa to place the emphasis firmly on Rossini's memorable score. As Figaro, the barber who matchmakes lovesick count Ferruccio Tagliavini and miser's ward Nelly Corradi, the flamboyant Tito Gobi is in fine fettle. DP. In Italian with English subtitles.

Ferruccio Tagliavini *Count Almaviva* • Tito Gobbi *Figaro* • Nelly Corradi *Rosina* • Vito de Tarranto *Don Bartolo* • Italo Tajo *Don Basilio* • Natalia Nicolini *Berta* • Nino Mazziotti *Fiorello* ■ *Dir* Mario Costa • *Scr* Deems Taylor, from the opera by Giacomo Rossini

The Barber of Siberia ★★ 12

Period drama 1999 · Rus · Colour · 169mins

Staged with a grandeur that undermines his trademark intimacy, Nikita Mikhalkov's Tsarist epic suffers from thematic imprecision, uncertainty of tone and excessive length. The lack of spark between American Julia Ormond and soldier Oleg Menshikov further strains the credibility of this long-cherished project, which inexplicably lurches from comedy to melodrama partway through. Thanks to Pavel Lebeshev's glorious photography, the evocation of the 1880s is impeccable. DP. In English and Russian with subtitles. [VIDEO] DVD

Julia Ormond *Jane Callahan* • Richard Harris *Douglas McCracken* • Oleg Menshikov *Andre Tolstoy* • Alexei Petrenko *General Radlov* • Alexander Yakovlev *Maximich* • Marat Bacharov *Polievsky* • Daniel Olbrychski *Kopnovsky* ■ *Dir* Nikita Mikhalkov • *Scr* Nikita Mikhalkov, Rustam Ibragimbekov, Rospo Pallenberg, from a story by Nikita Mikhalkov

The Barber Shop ★★★★ U

Comedy 1933 · US · BW · 20mins

WC Fields engages in surrealist experimentation in his last two-reeler for comic king Mack Sennett. A cello has a romance, a fat man is steamed skeletally thin and a dog develops a taste for severed ears as Fields reworks material that had served him since his vaudeville days. The plotline – about the bungled capture of a fleeing bank robber – is almost an irrelevance; the real interest lies in Fields as he absent-mindedly wields a razor and deals with the various eccentrics who enter his shop. Director Arthur Ripley is nominally in charge, but there's only one creative force at work here. DP [VIDEO] DVD

WC Fields *Cornelius O'Hare* ■ *Dir* Arthur Ripley • *Scr* WC Fields

Barbershop ★★★ 12

Comedy 2002 · US · Colour · 98mins

Ice Cube gives a self-assured performance here as the jaded owner of a Chicago hairdressing salon threatened with foreclosure. A warm, but far from tame, slice-of-life comedy, this follows the salon through what could be its last day, as barbers and their customers trade jokes and neighbourhood gossip and the boss struggles to come up with the cash. The message is short on subtlety, and a slapstick subplot about a stolen ATM is a needless distraction. However, the camaraderie and antagonistic banter of the workplace are well observed and brightly performed. JC. Contains violence and swearing. [VIDEO] DVD

Ice Cube *Calvin Palmer* • Anthony Anderson *JD* • Cedric the Entertainer *Eddie* • Sean Patrick Thomas *Jimmy* • Eve *Terri* • Troy Garity *Isaac Rosenberg* ■ *Dir* Tim Story • *Scr* Mark Brown, Don D Scott, Marshall Todd, from a story by Mark Brown

Barbershop 2: Back in Business ★★★ 12

Comedy 2004 · US · Colour · 101mins

Calvin (Ice Cube) discovers that his shop's future on Chicago's South Side is threatened when super-hairdressing salon Nappy Cutz is set to open across the street. This sequel is more character-driven than the original, with the ever-opinionated Cedric the Entertainer's backstory benefiting from the flashback treatment, while Queen Latifah joins the ranks of eccentrics and oddballs as the proprietress of the beauty shop next door. Director Kevin Rodney Sullivan has perhaps tried too hard to make it likeable, but that's not at all unwelcome. TH. Contains swearing. DVD

Ice Cube *Calvin Palmer* • Cedric the Entertainer *Eddie* • Sean Patrick Thomas *Jimmy* • Eve *Terri* • Troy Garity *Isaac Rosenberg* • Michael Ealy *Ricky Nash* • Leonard Earl Howze *Dinka* • Harry Lennix *Quentin Leroux* • Robert Wisdom *Alderman Brown* • Queen Latifah *Gina* ■ *Dir* Kevin Rodney Sullivan • *Scr* Don D Scott, from characters created by Mark Brown

Barcelona ★★★★ 12

Comedy drama 1994 · US · Colour · 96mins

Louche observation, tart dialogue and droll wit are director Whit Stillman's hallmarks, and they're all astutely called on in this sophisticated rumination on the sex and social lives of two American cousins living in the cosmopolitan Spanish city during the 1980s. Solemn salesman Taylor Nichols and loudmouth navy officer Christopher Eigeman clash with each other as much as the foreign culture, while roaming the Ramblas and seducing the senoritas in a spot-on view of the Eurotrash disco scene. AJ. Contains some violence, swearing, nudity and substance abuse. [VIDEO]

Taylor Nichols *Ted Boynton* • Christopher Eigeman [Chris Eigeman] *Fred Mason* • Tushka Bergen *Montserrat* • Mira Sorvino *Marta Ferrer* • Pep Munne *Ramon* • Hellena Schmied *Greta* • Nuria Badia *Aurora* • Thomas Gibson *Dickie Taylor* ■ *Dir/Scr* Whit Stillman

Barefoot Adventure ★★★

Documentary 1960 · US · Colour · 74mins

Filmed at some of the most famous beaches in Hawaii – including North Shore at Oahu and Point Surf at Makaha, where the waves are legendarily huge – Bruce Brown's third feature is the beneficiary of a lucky accident. As the original voice track had been lost, he wrote a completely new commentary that enabled him to reminisce about the US surfing scene in the 1960s, as well as comment on the action. With an evocative jazz score by Bud Shank and some stunning cinematography (shot from within a Plexiglass case), this is a wry, yet wistful memoir of a gloriously hedonistic lifestyle. DP DVD

Dir Bruce Brown

B

The Barefoot Contessa ★★★★ PG

Drama 1954 · US · Colour · 125mins

"The world's most beautiful animal," shrieked the ads for this mordant satire on the movie business, and, unsurprisingly, nobody disputed the fact, for "the animal" was none other than Ava Gardner in her prime, playing a character based on Rita Hayworth. Humphrey Bogart plays her cynical director: "I made her," he snarls, and you believe him. Director/writer Joe Mankiewicz had satirised Broadway in the multi-Oscar winning *All about Eve*, and this is similar, but far less theatrical. Edmond O'Brien collected an Oscar here as the sweaty publicist, and there's a star-making performance from Rossano Brazzi. TS DVD

Humphrey Bogart *Harry Dawes* • Ava Gardner *Maria Vargas* • Edmond O'Brien *Oscar Muldoon* • Marius Goring *Alberto Bravano* • Valentina Cortesa [Valentina Cortese] *Eleanora Torlato-Favrini* • Rossano Brazzi *Vincenzo Torlato-Favrini* • Elizabeth Sellars *Jerry* ■ *Dir/Scr* Joseph L Mankiewicz • *Cinematographer* Jack Cardiff

The Barefoot Executive ★★★ U

Comedy 1971 · US · Colour · 91mins

This Disney comedy may blunt some of its point with whimsy, but it's still an enjoyable spoof of the way TV companies chase ratings. Here, a chimpanzee is discovered to be an ace television programmer, leading to a battle between rival companies to sign up the simian marvel. Human lead Kurt Russell looks bewildered, but the chimp proves what the rest of us have always known about scheduling: it's all just monkey business. TH

Kurt Russell *Steven Post* • Joe Flynn *Francis X Wilbanks* • Harry Morgan *EJ Crampton* • Wally Cox *Mertons* • Heather North *Jennifer Scott* • Alan Hewitt *Farnsworth* • Hayden Rorke *Clifford* • John Ritter *Roger* ■ *Dir* Robert Butler • *Scr* Joseph L McEveety, from a story by Lila Garrett, Bernie Kahn, Stuart C Billett

Barefoot in the Park ★★★★ PG

Romantic comedy
1967 · US · Colour · 101mins

In this delightful comedy, adapted by Neil Simon from his hit Broadway show, Robert Redford (who appeared in the stage play) and Jane Fonda star as the young married couple attempting to achieve newly wedded bliss. Redford is a joy in a reasonably rare comic role, though Mildred Natwick almost steals the show as Fonda's mother. It's handled well by director Gene Saks, who maintains the humour and a lively pace until half an hour from the end. JB DVD

Robert Redford *Paul Bratter* • Jane Fonda *Corie Bratter* • Charles Boyer *Victor Velasco* • Mildred Natwick *Mrs Ethel Banks* • Herb Edelman *Telephone man* • James Stone *Delivery man* • Ted Hartley *Frank* ■ *Dir* Gene Saks • *Scr* Neil Simon, from his play

Barfly ★★ 18

Comedy drama 1987 · US · Colour · 95mins

Confirming the notion that there's no one more boring than a drunk, *Barfly* gives Mickey Rourke and Faye Dunaway the chance to slur their words and blur their meaning for 90-odd minutes. Written by Charles Bukowski from his own experiences propping up a bar in a dimly-lit dive in some lost zone of Los Angeles, the story puts the casualties of life who think they are poets or romantics, or both, on display. AT

Mickey Rourke *Henry Chinaski* • Faye Dunaway *Wanda Wilcox* • Alice Krige *Tully Sorenson* • Jack Nance *Detective* • JC Quinn *Jim* • Frank Stallone *Eddie* • Sandy Martin *Janice* • Roberta Bassin *Lilly* • Gloria LeRoy *Grandma Moses* • Joe Unger *Ben* ■ *Dir* Barbet Schroeder • *Scr* Charles Bukowski

The Bargee ★★ PG

Comedy 1964 · UK · Colour · 101mins

Having failed to make an international movie star out of Tony Hancock with *The Rebel*, Ray Galton and Alan Simpson tried to fashion a film comedy for their *Steptoe and Son* protégé Harry H Corbett. However, in spite of the presence of a number of comic luminaries, the result is disappointing. The poverty of the plot (in which Corbett's "Lothario of the Locks" is duped into matrimony) is nothing next to its intrinsic sexism. DP

Harry H Corbett *Hemel* • Hugh Griffith *Joe* • Eric Sykes *The mariner* • Ronnie Barker *Ronnie* • Julia Foster *Christine* • Miriam Karlin *Nellie* • Eric Barker *Foreman* • Derek Nimmo *Dr Scott* • Norman Bird *Waterways supervisor* • Richard Briers *Tomkins* ■ *Dir* Duncan Wood • *Scr* Ray Galton, Alan Simpson

The Barker ★★

Silent drama 1928 · US · BW · 86mins

Starring Milton Sills as a fairground barker, this movie captures the colourful milieu of the tent-show world and boasts a cast that includes silent stars Betty Compson and Dorothy Mackaill. With direction by George Fitzmaurice and superior photography from Lee Garmes, it promises good if modest entertainment. Unfortunately, however, it was made as a silent with some sound subsequently added. This is of such poor quality that it becomes a pain to watch the film. RK

Milton Sills *Nifty Miller* • Dorothy Mackaill *Lou* • Betty Compson *Carrie* • Douglas Fairbanks Jr *Chris Miller* • Sylvia Ashton *Ma Benson* • George Cooper *Hap Spissel* ■ *Dir* George Fitzmaurice • *Scr* Benjamin Glazer, Joseph Jackson, Herman J Mankiewicz (titles), from the play by Kenyon Nicholson

The Barkleys of Broadway ★★★ U

Musical 1949 · US · Colour · 104mins

This movie was originally intended as a vehicle for the successful *Easter Parade* team, but in fact resulted in the reteaming of Ginger Rogers and Fred Astaire after a ten-year break, with Rogers replacing an ailing Judy Garland. Fred is as chirpy and debonair as ever, but time hasn't been kind to Ginger, who has lost her freshness – and she's not helped by some of the hokey situations. Cherishable, but a bit disappointing. TS

Fred Astaire *Josh Barkley* • Ginger Rogers *Dinah Barkley* • Oscar Levant *Ezra Miller* • Billie Burke *Mrs Belney* ■ *Dir* Charles Walters • *Scr* Betty Comden, Adolph Green • *Choreography* Hermes Pan • *Music* Harry Warren • *Lyrics* Ira Gershwin

Barnabo of the Mountains ★★ 12

Drama 1994 · Fr/It/Swi · Colour · 124mins

This earnest blend of nature documentary and Christian allegory is so painfully slow that it quickly alienates even the most temperate viewer. Lingering over every glance and gesture, director Mario Brenta treats his non-professional cast like emotionless puppets, as he relates the story of the Dolomite mountain ranger whose refusal to kill either man or beast costs him the respect of locals plagued by smugglers. DP. In Italian with English subtitles.

Marco Pauletti *Barnabo* • Duilio Fontana *Berton* • Carlo Caserotti *Molo* • Antonio Vecellio *Marden* • Angelo Chiesura *Del Colle* • Alessandra Milan *Ines* • Elisa Gasperini *Grandmother* ■ *Dir* Mario Brenta • *Scr* Angelo Pasquini, Mario Brenta, Francesco Alberti, Enrico Soci, from a novel by Dino Buzzati

Barnacle Bill ★ U

Comedy 1957 · UK · BW · 85mins

The last of the Ealing comedies, this is a wearisome affair. There are echoes of *Kind Hearts and Coronets* (with Alec Guinness playing his ancestors in several contrived flashbacks), and the action brims over with eccentric characters who could be refugees from any of the film's more illustrious predecessors. An unfunny and slightly embarrassing bore. DP

Alec Guinness *Captain Ambrose/his ancestors* • Irene Browne *Mrs Barrington* • Percy Herbert *Tommy* • Harold Goodwin (2) *Duckworth* • Maurice Denham *Crowley* • Victor Maddern *Figg* • George Rose *Bullen* • Jackie Collins *June* • Warren Mitchell *Artie White* • Donald Pleasence *Teller* ■ *Dir* Charles Frend • *Scr* TEB Clarke

Barney's Great Adventure ★★★ U

Fantasy 1998 · US · Colour · 73mins

Television's popular purple dinosaur magically appears to teach three vacationing youngsters all about the worlds of the farmyard and the circus as they undertake a quest to find a nearly-hatched alien egg. Devoid of all the usual Hollywood special effects razzmatazz, but not so sugary sweet that it will cause tooth decay, this colourful, energetic and endurable nursery rhyme-style fantasy will have children hitting the rewind button from now until for ever. AJ DVD

George Hearn *Grandpa Greenfield* • Shirley Douglas *Grandma Greenfield* • Trevor Morgan *Cody Newton* • Kyla Pratt *Marcella* ■ *Dir* Steve Gomer • *Scr* Stephen White, from a story by Sheryl Leach, Dennis DeShazer, Stephen White, from characters created by Kathy Parker, Sheryl Leach, Dennis DeShazer

Barnum ★★★

Biographical drama
1986 · US/Can · Colour · 90mins

Burt Lancaster's past as a circus acrobat comes in handy for his role here as the charismatic 19th-century showman who coined the phrase "The Greatest Show on Earth". Among Barnum's discoveries were the "Smallest Man Alive", General Tom Thumb and the "Swedish Nightingale", Jenny Lind. Narrated in flashback by the ageing showman, this TV movie's plot leaves much to be desired, but, with Queen Victoria and Jumbo the Elephant having walk-on roles, there's plenty to enjoy. TH

Burt Lancaster *Phineas T Barnum* • Hanna Schygulla *Jenny Lind* • John Roney *Young Barnum* • Sandor Raski *Young Tom Thumb* • Patty Maloney *Older Tom Thumb* • Laura Press *Charity* • Kirsten Bishop *Nancy* • Lorena Gale *Joyce Heth* • Bronwen Mantel *Queen Victoria* ■ *Dir* Lee Philips • *Scr* Michael Norell, from a story by Michael Norell, Andy Siegel

Baron Blood ★★★ 15

Horror 1972 · It/W Ger · Colour · 93mins

One of the most richly visual and atmospheric works in the chill catalogue of Italian horror genius Mario Bava. Joseph Cotton plays the Austrian baron whose ancestral castle is being turned into a luxury hotel and also his moldy-faced reincarnation wanting to put his 16th-century torture chamber to good use again. Elke Sommer screams a lot as she and her lover Antonio Cantafora revive the warlock baron. Commendable for its taut chase scenes, grisly gore and eerie photography, Bava evokes a style and tone that was a deliberate throwback to his early 1960s successes. AJ. Italian dialogue dubbed into English.

Joseph Cotten *Alfred Becker/Otto von Kleist* • Elke Sommer *Eva Arnold* • Massimo Girotti *Uncle Karl Hummel* • Antonio Cantafora *Peter von Kleist* ■ *Dir* Mario Bava • *Scr* William A Bairn, Vincent Fotre, Willibald Eser, Mario Bava, from a story by Vincent Fotre

Baron Münchhausen ★★★ PG

Fantasy 1943 · Ger · Colour · 110mins

The eponymous Baron, described as "the greatest liar of all time", was a real-life character who lived in Germany and became an 18th-century folk hero with his outrageous stories. None of them were true; all of them were entertaining. He has formed the basis of three feature films. This first version, directed by the Hungarian Josef von Baky, is an extraordinary technical achievement. The film was commissioned by Joseph Goebbels to celebrate the 25th anniversary of the UFA studios in Berlin. AT. A German language film. DVD

Hans Albers *Baron Münchhausen* • Brigitte Horney *Catherine the Great* • Wilhelm Bendow *The Man in the Moon* • Michael Bohnen *Prince Karl of Brunswick* • Hans Brausewetter *Frederick von Hartenfeld* • Marina von Ditmar *Sophie von Riedesel* ■ *Dir* Josef von Baky • *Scr* Berthold Bürger [Erich Kästner]

Baron Munchhausen ★★★

Part-animated fantasy adventure
1961 · Cz · Colour · 81mins

Czech animator Karel Zeman tackled the fantastic adventures of the notorious mythomaniac by using puppets, cartoons, special effects and live action against painted backdrops. Zeman's inspiration sprang from the 1862 edition of Gottfried Burger's novel, with its drawings by Gustave Doré, and the turn of the century films of conjurer and cinema pioneer Georges Méliès. Yet, fascinating as it is visually, it is rather stilted and uninvolving. RB. A Czech language film.

Milos Kopecky *Baron Munchhausen* • Jana Brejchova *Bianca* • Rudolf Jelinek *Tonik* • Jan Werich *Captain of Dutch ship* • Rudolf Hrusinsky *Sultan* • Eduard Kohout *Commander of the fortress* • Karel Hoger *Cyrano de Bergerac* • Karel Effa *Officer of the guard* ■ *Dir* Karel Zeman • *Scr* Karel Zeman, Jiri Brdecka, Josef Kainar, from the novel *Baron Prásil* by Gottfried Burger and the illustrations by Gustave Doré

The Baron of Arizona ★★

Western 1950 · US · BW · 96mins

The second film of maverick writer/director Samuel Fuller, this low-budget, fact-based drama tells the story of a land office clerk in the 19th century who forges documents to prove himself the "Baron of Arizona". The forger is played rather ponderously by Vincent Price and the film becomes bogged down in detail. AE

Vincent Price *James Addison Reavis* • Ellen Drew *Sofia Peralta-Reavis* • Vladimir Sokoloff *Pepito* • Reed Hadley *Griff* • Robert Barrat *Judge Adams* • Robin Short *Lansing* • Tina Rome *Rita* ■ *Dir/Scr* Samuel Fuller

The Baroness and the Butler ★★

Romantic comedy 1938 · US · BW · 79mins

French beauty and future wife of Tyrone Power, Annabella, made an uncomfortable Hollywood debut in this whimsy as the wayward baroness daughter of the Hungarian prime minister. William Powell co-stars as the butler to the household who leaves his job to go into politics, becomes Leader of the Opposition, and returns to declare his love for the baroness. The script is silly and Annabella is deficient in both spoken English and light comedy, but this is partly redeemed by the always polished Powell and an A-list supporting cast. RK

William Powell *Johann Porok* • Annabella *Baroness Katrina Marissey* • Helen Westley *Countess Sandor* • Henry Stephenson *Count Albert Sandor* • Joseph Schildkraut *Baron Georg Marissey* • J Edward Bromberg *Zorda* ■ *Dir* Walter Lang • *Scr* Sam Hellman, Lamar Trotti, Kathryn Scola, from the play *Jean* by Ladislaus Bus-Fekete

Barquero ★★★ 15

Western 1970 · US · Colour · 104mins

A violent American western in the European style, and here that's a recommendation, especially since this is one of the few movies to give a decent co-starring role to the estimable Warren Oates. Here, a black-clad Oates is pitted mercilessly against Lee Van Cleef as the tenacious ferryman of the title. There's a moral of sorts amid all the slaughter, and it's interesting to see how veteran western director Gordon Douglas adapts himself to the new, freer style. TS. Contains violence and swearing.

Lee Van Cleef *Travis* • Warren Oates *Jake Remy* • Forrest Tucker *Mountain Phil* • Kerwin Mathews *Marquette* • Mariette Hartley *Anna* • Marie Gomez *Nola* • Brad Weston *Driver* • Craig Littler *Pitney* ■ *Dir* Gordon Douglas • *Scr* George Schenck, William Marks

The Barretts of Wimpole Street ★★★★ U

Biographical drama 1934 · US · BW · 109mins

One of the great triumphs of producer Irving G Thalberg's reign at MGM, this managed to be both intelligent in execution and a commercial success. As Elizabeth Barrett, Norma Shearer (Mrs Thalberg) is superb, but the real star is Charles Laughton as Elizabeth's tyrannical father, whose incestuous love for his daughter is hinted at but never addressed. In fact, he was only a year older than his "daughter" Shearer and two years younger than Fredric March, uncomfortably cast as poet Robert Browning. TS

Norma Shearer *Elizabeth Barrett* • Fredric March *Robert Browning* • Charles Laughton *Edward Moulton Barrett* • Maureen O'Sullivan *Henrietta Barrett* • Katharine Alexander [Katherine Alexander] *Arabel Barrett* • Ralph Forbes *Captain Surtees Cook* • Marion Clayton *Bella Hedley* • Una O'Connor *Wilson* ■ *Dir* Sidney Franklin • *Scr* Ernest Vajda, Claudine West, Donald Ogden Stewart, from the play by Rudolf Besier

The Barretts of Wimpole Street ★★ U

Period drama 1956 · UK · Colour · 105mins

This recounts the story of the love affair between the invalid poetess Elizabeth Barrett and Robert Browning, with whom she elopes to escape the rigid and frightening control of her father (John Gielgud). Sidney Franklin, who directed the 1934 Hollywood version, also directed this British remake. Although stylish and sober-minded, with a Freudian take on Barrett's relationship with his daughters (Virginia McKenna is featured as the other victim of his wrath), the film emerges as slow, heavy-handed and uninvolving. RK

Jennifer Jones *Elizabeth* • John Gielgud *Barrett* • Bill Travers *Robert Browning* • Virginia McKenna *Henrietta* • Susan Stephen *Bella* ■ *Dir* Sidney Franklin • *Scr* John Dighton, from the play by Rudolf Besier

Barricade ★★

Western 1950 · US · Colour · 75mins

This exercise in rough brutality features Raymond Massey as the owner of a mine in the middle of nowhere who slave-drives his labourers with sadistic cruelty, until nemesis arrives in the form of a fugitive from justice (Dane Clark). Both the screenplay and Peter Godfrey's direction are undistinguished, but as a merciless depiction of violence in a different era the movie has its moments. RK

Ruth Roman *Judith Burns* • Dane Clark *Bob Peters* • Raymond Massey *"Boss" Kruger* • Robert Douglas *Aubry Milburn* • Morgan Farley *Judge* • Walter Coy *Benson* • George Stern *Tippy* • Robert Griffin *Kirby* ■ *Dir* Peter Godfrey • *Scr* William Sackheim

Barry Lyndon ★★★★★ PG

Period drama 1975 · UK · Colour · 177mins

Stanley Kubrick provides this awesome work with an authentic 18th-century look and a unique atmosphere that totally convinces. It is the slow and utterly hypnotic tale of an Irish youth whose adventures and misfortunes take in the Seven Years' War, the gambling clubs of Europe and marriage into the English aristocracy. In Kubrick's scheme of things, character means less than context, so Ryan O'Neal may appear bloodless and Marisa Berenson wholly vacant, but this turns out to be a strength, not a weakness. There are fine turns by Leonard Rossiter, Hardy Kruger and, best of all, Leon Vitali as O'Neal's stepson. There is also a definitive climactic duel scene, a confiding narration by Michael Hordern and ravishing photography. AT. Contains some violence. DVD

Ryan O'Neal *Barry Lyndon* • Marisa Berenson *Lady Lyndon* • Patrick Magee *The Chevalier* • Hardy Kruger *Captain Potzdorf* • Steven Berkoff *Lord Ludd* • Gay Hamilton *Nora* • Leonard Rossiter *Captain Quin* • Godfrey Quigley *Captain Grogan* • Marie Kean *Barry's mother* ■ *Dir* Stanley Kubrick • *Scr* Stanley Kubrick, from the novel by William Makepeace Thackeray • *Cinematographer* John Alcott • *Art Director* Ken Adam

Barry McKenzie Holds His Own ★★ 18

Comedy adventure
1974 · Aus · Colour · 96mins

When Dame Edna is mistaken for the Queen, she and her nephew Barry are whisked off to Transylvania by Count Plasma. A lot of this sequel to *The Adventures of Barry McKenzie* is naff, lazily shot and rather boring. But when the actors get fired up and the Aussie slang starts flowing, it's splendidly vulgar and even subversive in its trouncing of racial stereotypes and political hypocrisy. AT

Barry Crocker *Barry McKenzie/Ken McKenzie* • Barry Humphries *Buck-toothed Englishman/ Edna Everage/Senator Douglas Manton/Dr Meyer de Lamphrey* • Donald Pleasence *Erich, Count Plasma* • Roy Kinnear *Bishop of Paris* • John Le Mesurier *English emigrant* • Tommy Trinder *Arthur McKenzie* • Dick Bentley *Colonel Lucas* ■ *Dir* Bruce Beresford • *Scr* Barry Humphries, Bruce Beresford, from the comic strip *The Wonderful World of Barry McKenzie* by Barry Humphries

Barsaat ★★★ U

Musical drama 1949 · Ind · BW · 157mins

The popular romantic team of Nargis and Raj Kapoor were reunited for this enduring Bollywood classic, which the latter also produced and directed. Defying her father's wishes, country girl Nargis's plans to elope with the wealthy Kapoor are thwarted when she's rescued from near-drowning by a fisherman (KN Singh), who claims her as his bride. The story may be packed with such melodramatic devices as class prejudice, spurned love and incredible coincidence, but there's also a level of social comment in Ramanand Sagar's screenplay, which is reinforced by the moody symbolism of Jal Mistry's photography. DP. In Hindi with English subtitles.

Raj Kapoor *Pran* • Nargis *Reshma* • Premnath *Gopal* • KN Singh *Fisherman* ■ *Dir* Raj Kapoor • *Scr* Ramanand Sagar

Bartleby ★★★

Drama 1971 · UK · Colour · 78mins

Herman Melville's short story makes for a unremittingly downbeat yet fascinating movie, mainly due to the riveting interplay between its two stars. John McEnery plays Bartleby, a reclusive, diffident accounts clerk who simply won't accept he has been fired by Paul Scofield. Instead, he carries on accounting until he achieves his ultimate aim, which is total exclusion from society – in other words, death. A mysterious, chilling allegory, this was a labour of love for all concerned. There was a remake in 1976 made by French actor/director Maurice Ronet. AT

Paul Scofield *The accountant* • John McEnery *Bartleby* • Thorley Walters *The colleague* • Colin Jeavons *Tucker* • Raymond Mason *Landlord* • Charles Kinross *Tenant* • Neville Barber *First client* ■ *Dir* Anthony Friedman • *Scr* Anthony Friedman, Rodney Carr-Smith, from the story *Bartleby the Scrivener* by Herman Melville

Bartleby ★★★ PG

Black comedy 2000 · US · Colour · 83mins

Written in 1853, Herman Melville's short story provided both a psychological and a satirical insight into urban alienation and the dehumanising effect of monotonous labour. But Jonathan Parker finds the material less cinematically malleable than it first appears. The soul-destroying setting is splendid, as is David Paymer's performance as the record office boss whose inadequacies are exposed by eccentric clerk Crispin Glover's refusal to follow orders or vacate the premises. However, too many minor figures border on caricature, while additions such as the fascistic fantasy sequence prove to be seriously miscalculated. DP

David Paymer *The Boss* • Crispin Glover *Bartleby* • Glenne Headly *Vivian* • Maury Chaykin *Ernie* • Joe Piscopo *Rocky* • Seymour Cassel *Frank Waxman* • Carrie Snodgress *Book publisher* • Dick Martin *The Mayor* ■ *Dir* Jonathan Parker • *Scr* Jonathan Parker, Catherine di Napoli, from the short story *Bartleby the Scrivener* by Herman Melville

Bartok the Magnificent ★★★ U

Animated adventure
1999 · US · Colour · 65mins

Reasoning that if Disney can spin off from their cartoon hits so can he, Don Bluth awards the voluble bat from *Anastasia* his chance to shine in this cheap and cheerful prequel. The voice talents are impeccable, enlivening an already noisy story, in which the critters abandon their con trickery to undertake a trio of impossible tasks in order to rescue the Tsarevich from the clutches of his evil tutor. DP

Hank Azaria *Bartok* • Kelsey Grammer *Zozi* • Andrea Martin *Baba Yaga* • Catherine O'Hara *Ludmilla* • Tim Curry *The Skull* • Jennifer Tilly *Piloff* ■ *Dir* Don Bluth, Gary Goldman • *Scr* Jay Lacopo

Barton Fink ★★★★ 15

Period drama 1991 · US · Colour · 111mins

This is the most brilliantly observed Hollywood put-down since *Day of the Locust*. Only the Coen brothers would dare to make such a vitriolic attack on the industry supporting them and actually get away with it. Part David Lynch, part Kafka and wholly demanding, this tale features John Turturro as the social realist playwright snapped up by 1940s Hollywood to script a Wallace Beery wrestling picture. But, even as his life collapses around him, and his next door neighbour (John Goodman) turns serial killer, he just can't sacrifice his ideals on the altar of commercialism. A gorgeously designed paranoid parable packed with sharp detail, great in-jokes and an Oscar-nominated performance by Michael Lerner as the studio mogul from hell. AJ. Contains violence and swearing. DVD

John Turturro *Barton Fink* • John Goodman *Charlie Meadows* • Judy Davis *Audrey Taylor* • Michael Lerner *Jack Lipnik* • John Mahoney *WP Mayhew* • Tony Shalhoub *Ben Geisler* • Jon Polito *Lou Breeze* • Steve Buscemi *Chet* ■ *Dir* Joel Coen • *Scr* Joel Coen, Ethan Coen

BASEketball ★★★ 15

Sports comedy 1998 · US · Colour · 103mins

Unfairly denied a British cinema release after a disastrous US run, this sports spoof from director David Zucker (who made *Airplane!*, and the first two *Naked Gun* movies) is wildly offensive fun. It stars *South Park* creators Trey Parker and Matt Stone, who play a pair of infantile slobs who invent a popular new game that combines the hoops of basketball with the runs of baseball – and a few sick twists of their own. There are more hits than misses in the slapstick gags and ultra-crude humour, but this is still ideal Friday night fodder. JC. Contains swearing. DVD

Trey Parker *Joseph Cooper* • Matt Stone *Doug Remer* • Robert Vaughn *Baxter Cain* • Ernest Borgnine *Theodore Denslow* • Dian Bachar *Kenny "Squeak" Scolari* • Yasmine Bleeth *Jenna Reed* • Jenny McCarthy *Yvette Denslow* ■ *Dir* David Zucker • *Scr* David Zucker, Robert LoCash, Jeff Wright, Lewis Friedman

Basic ★★ 15

Thriller 2003 · US/Ger/UK · Colour · 94mins

John McTiernan's risible attempt at a military thriller misfires on practically all levels. A platoon of US Army Rangers goes in to the Panamanian jungle on a routine training exercise, and only two come out alive. DEA agent John Travolta is brought in to investigate the killings – alongside inexperienced sidekick Connie Nielsen – and uncovers a nexus of corruption. As the incoherent plotting reveals a layer upon layer of deceit, it is difficult to care about anything as it is bound to be revealed as bogus. IF DVD

John Travolta *Tom Hardy* • Connie Nielsen *Lt Julia Osborne* • Samuel L Jackson *Sgt Nathan West* • Giovanni Ribisi *Levi Kendall* • Brian Van Holt *Raymond Dunbar* • Taye Diggs *Pike* • Tim Daly [Timothy Daly] *Col Bill Styles* ■ *Dir* John McTiernan • *Scr* James Vanderbilt

Basic Instinct ★★★ 18

Erotic thriller 1992 · US · Colour · 122mins

Director Paul Verhoeven's reputation is built on his wonderful lack of taste and restraint, and these "qualities" are fully to the fore in this controversial but massively successful thriller. Sharon Stone became a sex symbol of the 1990s for her cool portrayal of the predatory novelist who may or may not be a murderer, but who enjoys tormenting policeman Michael Douglas all the same. Writer Joe Eszterhas shamelessly reworks ideas and themes he had earlier exploited in films such as *Jagged Edge* and *Music Box*, but the sheer overheated nature of Verhoeven's direction makes this extremely watchable. JF. Contains swearing, violence, sex scenes and nudity. DVD

Michael Douglas *Detective Nick Curran* • Sharon Stone *Catherine Tramell* • George Dzundza *Gus* • Jeanne Tripplehorn *Dr Beth Garner* • Denis Arndt *Lieutenant Walker* • Leilani Sarelle *Roxy* ■ *Dir* Paul Verhoeven • *Scr* Joe Eszterhas

Basil ★★ 15

Period drama 1998 · US · Colour · 98mins

Writer/director Radha Bharadwaj here delivers a stiff costume drama, based on the novel by Wilkie Collins. Jared Leto is miscast as rich man's son Basil, who offends his father by marrying the mysterious Claire Forlani and befriending commoner Christian Slater. This being a tale of oppression, love and revenge, you'd expect some twists in the tale. However, Bharadwaj signposts each one so obviously that you know what the characters are up to almost before they do. JB. Contains some violence. DVD

Jared Leto *Basil* • Christian Slater *John Mannion* • Jack Wild *Peddler* • Claire Forlani *Julia Sherwin* • Derek Jacobi *Basil's father, Frederick* • David Ross *Mr Sherwin* • Crispin Bonham-Carter *Ralph* ■ *Dir* Radha Bharadwaj • *Scr* Radha Bharadwaj, from the novel *Basil: a Story of Modern Life* by Wilkie Collins

Basil the Great Mouse Detective ★★★ U

Animated adventure
1986 · US · Colour · 73mins

An attractive idea, but rather crudely done for Disney animation, this is about a young mouse devotee of Sherlock Holmes who helps to investigate the disappearance of a mouse toymaker and a plot against the Mouse Queen. It's notable for Vincent Price's wonderfully arch voiceover as the master scoundrel Professor Ratigan, proving that villains have all the best lines. TH DVD

Vincent Price *Professor Ratigan* • Barrie Ingham *Basil/Bartholomew* • Val Bettin *Dr David Q Dawson/Thug guard* • Diana Chesney *Mrs Judson* • Candy Candido *Fidget* • Susanne Pollatschek *Olivia Flaversham* • Eve Brenner *The Mouse Queen* ■ *Dir* Ron Clements, Dave Michener, John Musker, Burny Mattinson • *Scr* Eve Titus, Paul Galdone

Basket Case ★★★★ 18

Horror comedy 1982 · US · Colour · 85mins

This gore-drenched, gutter-trash classic is one of the key horror movies of the 1980s. It tells the bizarre story of the Bradley brothers – normal Duane (Kevin Van Hentenryck) and his hideously deformed Siamese twin Belial, whom he carries around in a wicker basket – and how they wreak revenge on the quack doctor who separated them years before. Graphic blood-letting is juxtaposed with comic relief, but lurking behind its cruel and crude façade is an accomplished shocker laced with great artistry and pathos. AJ DVD

Kevin Van Hentenryck *Duane Bradley* • Terri Susan Smith *Sharon* • Beverly Bonner *Casey* • Robert Vogel *Hotel manager* • Diana Browne *Dr Judith Kutter* • Lloyd Pace *Dr Harold Needleman* • Bill Freeman *Dr Julius Lifflander* • Joe Clarke *Brian "Mickey" O'Donovan* ■ *Dir/Scr* Frank Henenlotter

Basket Case 2 ★★ 18

Horror comedy 1990 · US · Colour · 86mins

The saga of Duane and Belial, his grotesque Siamese twin, continues as they both escape from hospital and media attention to hide out in a Staten Island shelter for freaks. Suffering from latex monster overkill and with too many references to Tod Browning's *Freaks* for comfort, director Frank Henenlotter's poor follow-up is nothing more than a cynical and calculated cash-in. AJ DVD

Kevin Van Hentenryck *Duane Bradley* • Annie Ross *Granny Ruth* • Kathryn Meisle *Marcie Elliott* • Heather Rattray *Susan* • Jason Evers *Lou the editor* • Ted Sorel *Phil* • Matt Mitler *Artie* ■ *Dir/Scr* Frank Henenlotter

Basket Case 3: the Progeny ★★★ 18

Horror comedy 1992 · US · Colour · 85mins

Director Frank Henenlotter's second sequel to his inspired original is a far less depressing experience than *Basket Case 2*. Dealing more in edgy cartoon craziness than gory splatter, the film follows the Bradley twins, Duane and Belial, as they accompany Granny Ruth to the redneck Deep South. It's when Belial's flesh-hungry offspring are stolen by the police department that Henenlotter's frenzied rubber romp takes off. AJ DVD

Kevin Van Hentenryck *Duane Bradley* • Annie Ross *Granny Ruth* • Dan Biggers *Uncle Hal* • Gil Roper *Sheriff Griffith* • James O'Doherty *Little Hal* ■ *Dir* Frank Henenlotter • *Scr* Frank Henenlotter, Robert Martin

The Basketball Diaries ★★ 18

Biographical drama
1995 · US · Colour · 97mins

This attempts to plumb the depths of adolescent despair but only betrays the pop-video limitations of debut director Scott Kalvert's imagination. Leonardo DiCaprio occasionally comes close to real pathos as the hoop dreamer wallowing in a mire of sex, drugs and squalor, though his misery is founded on cliché and there's no real torment in his pain. Best buddy Mark Wahlberg and desperate mum Lorraine Bracco are more persuasive. DP. Contains violence, swearing, drug abuse and nudity. DVD

Leonardo DiCaprio *Jim Carroll* • Bruno Kirby *Swifty* • Lorraine Bracco *Jim's mother* • Ernie Hudson *Reggie Porter* • Patrick McGaw *Neutron* • James Madio *Pedro* • Mark Wahlberg *Mickey* • Juliette Lewis *Diane Moody* ■ *Dir* Scott Kalvert • *Scr* Brian Goluboff, from the memoirs of Jim Carroll

The Basque Ball: Skin against Stone ★★★ 15

Political documentary
2003 · Sp · Colour · 110mins

The refusal of either the Spanish government or the Basque separatist group ETA to participate in this debate about the Basque country conflict clearly diminishes its focus. But such is the scope and balance of Julio Medem's documentary that the political and cultural complexities of the Euskal Herria region of France and Spain become readily apparent. If anything, the film has too many opinions from too many interested parties for non-specialists to follow the arguments, and Medem's clumsy method of introducing speakers in captioned batches hardly helps. But many human tragedies emerge from the confusion of racial intransigence and emotive intellectualising and it's impossible to remain unmoved. DP. In French, Spanish and Basque with subtitles. Contains violence. DVD

Dir Julio Medem • *Cinematographer* Javier Aguirre, Jon Elicegui, Ricardo de Gracia

Basquiat ★★★ 15

Biographical drama
1996 · US · Colour · 106mins

This is the story of artist Jean-Michel Basquiat (Jeffrey Wright) as told by his friend and contemporary, director Julian Schnabel. Basquiat went from being an angry graffiti artist to one of Andy Warhol's close circle before overdosing on heroin in the late 1980s. Schnabel's aim is to show how the man was uncomfortable being lionised by the bourgeoisie he so despised. But Basquiat comes off more as a tiresome antihero in this well-meaning biopic, which fails to reveal why he's more deserving of remembrance than any other Warhol satellite. AJ. Contains violence, swearing and drug abuse. DVD

Jeffrey Wright *Jean-Michel Basquiat* • Michael Wincott *René Ricard* • Benicio Del Toro *Benny Dalmau* • Claire Forlani *Gina Cardinale* • David Bowie *Andy Warhol* • Dennis Hopper *Bruno Bischofberger* • Gary Oldman *Albert Milo* • Christopher Walken *Interviewer* • Willem Dafoe *Electrician* • Parker Posey *Mary Boone* • Paul Bartel *Henry Geldzahler* • Courtney Love *Big Pink* • Tatum O'Neal *Cynthia Kruger* ■ *Dir* Julian Schnabel • *Scr* Julian Schnabel, from a story by Lech J Majewski, John Bowe

The Bat ★★ PG

Mystery thriller 1959 · US · BW · 79mins

Intrepid mystery writer Agnes Moorehead rents a country mansion for the summer, only to be terrorised by a mad hooded killer called "The Bat". Money is stolen, a real bat turns up and Vincent Price becomes the prime suspect in this creaky, improbable thriller. Sluggishly paced and old-fashioned in the extreme, it nevertheless has a comfortably nostalgic appeal. AJ DVD

Vincent Price *Dr Malcolm Wells* • Agnes Moorehead *Cornelia Van Gorder* • Gavin Gordon *Lieutenant Anderson* • John Sutton *Warner* • Lenita Lane *Lizzie Allen* • Elaine Edwards *Dale Bailey* ■ *Dir* Crane Wilbur • *Scr* Crane Wilbur, from the play by Mary Roberts Rinehart, Avery Hopwood, from their novel *The Circular Staircase*

BAT-21 ★★ 15

War drama 1988 · US · Colour · 100mins

Set during the Vietnam War, this drama stars Gene Hackman as an officer (codenamed BAT-21), who crashes behind enemy lines and is brought face to face with the human misery of the conflict. Hackman makes the career soldier a strongly believable character, while Danny Glover is excellent as as the helicopter pilot trying to track him down. However, the episodic nature of the tale never allows a sense of urgency to surface. TH. Contains violence and swearing.

Gene Hackman *Lt Col Iceal Hambleton* • Danny Glover *Captain Bartholomew Clark* • Jerry Reed *Colonel George Walker* • David Marshall Grant *Ross Carver* • Clayton Rohner *Sergeant Harley Rumbaugh* ■ *Dir* Peter Markle • *Scr* William C Anderson, George Gordon, from the novel by William C Anderson

The Bat Whispers ★★★ U

Mystery thriller 1930 · US · BW · 84mins

Roland West's talkie remake of his own 1926 silent film *The Bat* is by far the best movie adaptation of the stock spoof horror play set in a creepy mansion. It's also a superior chiller in its own right. Sure, it's a dusty antique, but the impressively surreal imagery is unusual for the period, making it well worth a look. Using remarkable special effects and miniature sets, the fluid camera darts about as much as the titular caped criminal for a fun combination of screams and laughs. AJ

Chester Morris *Detective Anderson* • Grayce Hampton *Cornelia Van Gorder* • Chance Ward *Police lieutenant* • Richard Tucker *Mr Bell* • Wilson Benge *The butler* • Maude Eburne *Lizzie Allen* ■ *Dir* Roland West • *Scr* Roland West, from the play *The Bat* by Mary Roberts Rinehart, Avery Hopwood, from their novel *The Circular Staircase*

Bataan ★★

Second World War drama
1943 · US · BW · 114mins

General MacArthur was forced to abandon the Philippines to the Japanese during the Second World War, and this scrappy piece of patriotic action re-creates one of the battles before the pull-out. Robert Taylor and Barry Nelson are among those caught in the jungled MGM backlot, exchanging bullets and sanctimonous dialogue. AT

Robert Taylor (1) *Sergeant Bill Dane* • George Murphy *Lieutenant Steve Bentley* • Thomas Mitchell *Corporal Jake Feingold* • Lloyd Nolan *Corporal Barney Todd/Danny Burns* • Lee Bowman *Captain Lassiter* ■ *Dir* Tay Garnett • *Scr* Robert D Andrews

La Bataille du Rail ★★★

Second World War drama
1946 · Fr · BW · 87mins

Director René Clément's directing debut is about the war waged by the French railway workers against their Nazi oppressors. Using a largely amateur cast of genuine railway personnel (an introduction and narration by Charles Boyer was added for foreign release), Clément depicts in great detail the various acts of sabotage and subtle route changes that were to cause havoc to the German supply lines. AT. In French with English subtitles.

Jean Daurand *Railroad worker* • Jacques Desagneaux *Maquis Chief* • Leroy *Station master* • Redon *Mechanic* • Pauléon *Station master at St André* • Charles Boyer *Narrator* ■ *Dir* René Clément • *Scr* Colette Audry, René Clément, Jean Daurand, from stories by Colette Audry

Bathing Beauty ★★★ U

Musical 1944 · US · Colour · 101mins

MGM contractee Esther Williams became a star overnight in this, the first of her many swimfests, and who could ever forget her as she steps on to the MGM diving board? Esther had a robust, sexy aura that director George Sidney knew exactly how to exploit, although this movie actually started life as a Red Skelton vehicle, one of those school romps about romance among the co-eds. The film's a little too long, but Esther's worth every single Technicolored frame. TS

Red Skelton *Steve Elliott* • Esther Williams *Caroline Brooks* • Basil Rathbone *George Adams* • Bill Goodwin *Willis Evans* • Ethel Smith *Organist* • Jean Porter *Jean Allenwood* • Carlos Ramírez *Carlos* • Donald Meek *Chester Klazenfrantz* ■ *Dir* George Sidney (2) • *Scr* Dorothy Kingsley, Allen Boretz, Frank Waldman, Joseph Schrank, from a story by Kenneth Earl, MM Musselman

Batman ★★★★ U

Action fantasy 1966 · US · Colour · 104mins

This is the movie spin-off from the hit TV series of the 1960s, with Adam West as the Caped Crusader and Burt Ward as the Boy Wonder. Lee Meriwether, the least well known of the three actresses who played Catwoman in the 1960s (the others were Julie Newmar and Eartha Kitt), takes on the role. Director Leslie H Martinson lets the pace slacken occasionally, but Lorenzo Semple Jr's script overflows with irresistable throwaway gags. DP DVD

Adam West *Batman/Bruce Wayne* • Burt Ward *Robin/Dick Grayson* • Lee Meriwether *Catwoman/Kitka* • Cesar Romero *Joker* • Burgess Meredith *Penguin* • Frank Gorshin *Riddler* • Alan Napier *Alfred* • Neil Hamilton *Commissioner Gordon* • Stafford Repp *Chief O'Hara* • Madge Blake *Aunt Harriet Cooper* ■ *Dir* Leslie H Martinson • *Scr* Lorenzo Semple Jr, from characters created by Bob Kane

Batman ★★★★★ 15

Action fantasy 1989 · US · Colour · 121mins

Only director Tim Burton could take the Caped Crusader into the darkest realms of comic-strip nightmare yet still manage to weave an arresting tale full of doomy Shakespearean irony. From the camera crawling around the Bat symbol under the opening credits to the *Hunchback of Notre Dame*-inspired finale, Burton captures the spirit of artist Bob Kane's creation to produce a sophisticated *film noir*. With Michael Keaton's brooding Batman/Bruce Wayne and Jack Nicholson's superlative Joker/Jack Napier on the knife-edge of good and evil, Burton cleverly places both tragic characters within the same psychotic bracket, making the film the *Blue Velvet* of superhero movies. RT. Contains violence and swearing. DVD

Michael Keaton *Batman/Bruce Wayne* • Jack Nicholson *Joker/Jack Napier* • Kim Basinger *Vicki Vale* • Robert Wuhl *Alexander Knox* • Pat Hingle *Commissioner Gordon* • Billy Dee Williams *Harvey Dent* • Michael Gough *Alfred* • Jack Palance *Carl Grissom* • Jerry Hall *Alicia* ■ *Dir* Tim Burton • *Scr* Sam Hamm, Warren Skaaren, from a story by Sam Hamm, from characters created by Bob Kane • *Production Designer* Anton Furst

Batman and Robin ★★ PG

Action fantasy 1997 · US · Colour · 119mins

With the *Batman* franchise looking decidedly tired, Caped Crusader Mark 3 was introduced in the shape of George Clooney in an attempt to pep up the flagging formula. The rugged former TV medic doesn't disgrace himself in this wild special-effects extravaganza that is as close to a cartoon adventure as director Joel Schumacher could get. This is still the least satisfying entry in the series. JF. Contains violence and swearing. DVD

Arnold Schwarzenegger *Mr Freeze/Dr Victor Fries* • George Clooney *Batman/Bruce Wayne* • Chris O'Donnell *Robin/Dick Grayson* • Uma Thurman *Poison Ivy/Pamela Isley* • Alicia Silverstone *Batgirl/Barbara Wilson* • Michael Gough *Alfred Pennyworth* ■ *Dir* Joel Schumacher • *Scr* Akiva Goldsman, from characters created by Bob Kane

Batman Begins ★★★★ 12A

Action fantasy 2005 · US · Colour · 139mins

Christopher Nolan this gloriously epic comic-book yarn starring Christian Bale, who imbues the Caped Crusader with beguiling dignity. Nolan offers a darker, more gripping psychological portrait of Bruce Wayne and his painful evolution into Batman. Bursts of adrenalin-pumping action relieve all the brooding, although the plot sometimes creaks under the strain of so much going on. It also lacks a truly terrifying villain, but a sterling cast stands persuasively for lofty ideals as a climate of fear threatens to bring down Gotham City. This swoops you up and doesn't let go till the end. SP. Contains violence.

Christian Bale *Bruce Wayne/Batman* • Michael Caine *Alfred Pennyworth* • Liam Neeson *Henri Ducard* • Katie Holmes *Rachel Dawes* • Gary Oldman *Detective Sergeant James Gordon* • Cillian Murphy *Dr Jonathan Crane/Scarecrow* • Tom Wilkinson *Carmine Falcone* • Rutger Hauer *Richard Earle* • Ken Watanabe *Ra's al Ghul* • Morgan Freeman *Lucius Fox* ■ *Dir* Christopher Nolan • *Scr* David S Goyer, Christopher Nolan, from a story by David S Goyer, from characters created by Bob Kane

Batman Forever ★★★★ PG

Action fantasy 1995 · US · Colour · 114mins

Although it performed well at the box office, the critics were less than convinced by the gloomy turn taken by *Batman Returns*. So, when Tim Burton said no to a third outing, Warners brought in the flamboyant Joel Schumacher. This entry is nowhere near as dark as its predecessors, even though the brooding Val Kilmer took over the Dark Knight's mantle from Michael Keaton. It's easily the funniest of the quartet to date, with the action hurtling along at a breakneck pace. Throw in stylish special effects from a team that includes the legendary John Dykstra and Oscar-nominated photography from Stephen Goldblatt, and you have a rousingly undemanding piece of popcorn fodder. DP. Contains violence. DVD

Val Kilmer *Batman/Bruce Wayne* • Tommy Lee Jones *Harvey Two-Face/Harvey Dent* • Jim Carrey *The Riddler/Edward Nygma* • Nicole Kidman *Dr Chase Meridian* • Christopher O'Donnell [Chris O'Donnell] *Robin/Dick Grayson* • Michael Gough *Alfred Pennyworth* • Pat Hingle *Commissioner James Gordon* • Debi Mazar *Spice* • Drew Barrymore *Sugar* ■ *Dir* Joel Schumacher • *Scr* Lee Batchler, Janet Scott Batchler, Akiva Goldsman, from a story by Lee Batchler, Janet Scott Batchler, from characters created by Bob Kane

Batman: Mask of the Phantasm ★★★★ PG

Animated action fantasy
1993 · US · Colour · 73mins

Released in cinemas after the TV animated series took off, this cartoon feature expertly captures the feel of the comics. The Phantasm is a formidable vigilante who painstakingly executes Gotham's most powerful criminals. After both the police and the underworld mistakenly hold the Dark Knight responsible, Batman must unmask the real culprit. Stylishly drawn and with a strong cast of voices including Stacy Keach and *Star Wars's* Mark Hamill, this is a spirited riposte to the live-action films. AJ DVD

Kevin Conroy *Batman/Bruce Wayne* • Dana Delany *Andrea Beaumont* • Hart Bochner *Councilman Arthur Reeves* • Stacy Keach *Phantasm/Carl Beaumont* • Abe Vigoda *Salvatore Valestra* • Dick Miller *Chuckie Sol* ■ *Dir* Eric Radomski, Bruce W Timm • *Scr* Alan Burnett, Paul Dini, Martin Pasko, Michael Reaves, from a story by Alan Burnett, from characters created by Bob Kane

Batman Returns ★★★★ 15

Action fantasy 1992 · US · Colour · 121mins

Director Tim Burton refused to lighten up for the second of the Batman movies and the result is another moody, gloomy and occasionally perverse portrait of the Dark Knight. The sets are stunning and, while action may not be Burton's strongest suit, there are still some dazzling set pieces and a range of new gadgets. The only real problem is that all the best lines are bagged by the villains – Danny DeVito's tragic Penguin, Michelle Pfeiffer in *that* suit as Catwoman. It's still impressive stuff. JF. Contains some violence. DVD

Michael Keaton *Batman/Bruce Wayne* • Danny DeVito *Oswald Cobblepot/The Penguin* • Michelle Pfeiffer *Catwoman/Selina Kyle* • Christopher Walken *Max Shreck* • Michael Gough *Alfred* • Michael Murphy *Mayor* ■ *Dir* Tim Burton • *Scr* Daniel Waters, from a story by Daniel Waters, Sam Hamm, from characters created by Bob Kane

Bats ★ 15

Horror 1999 · US · Colour · 87mins

Genetically enhanced killer bats are released upon an unsuspecting Texas town by a mad scientist. A perky zoologist, her cowardly sidekick and the town's sheriff fight desperately to fend off the flying monsters in this by-the-numbers monster movie, in which the lead characters never say or do anything of any interest. ST. Contains violence and swearing. DVD

Lou Diamond Phillips *Emmett Kimsey* • Dina Meyer *Dr Sheila Casper* • Bob Gunton *Dr Alexander McCabe* • Leon *Jimmy Sands* ■ *Dir* Louis Morneau • *Scr* John Logan

*batteries not included ★★★ PG

Science-fiction fantasy
1987 · US · Colour · 106mins

The presence of Hume Cronyn and Jessica Tandy makes this retread of *Cocoon* worth watching. They play residents of a doomed New York block of flats, who find the unlikeliest of allies in the shape of a friendly group of aliens. Director Matthew Robbins lets sentimentality run supreme, but Cronyn and Tandy rise above it all, and children and soft-hearted adults will be enchanted. JF DVD

Hume Cronyn *Frank Riley* • Jessica Tandy *Faye Riley* • Frank McRae *Harry Noble* • Elizabeth Peña *Marisa* • Michael Carmine *Carlos* • Dennis Boutsikaris *Mason* • Tom Aldredge *Sid* ■ *Dir* Matthew Robbins • *Scr* Brad Bird, Matthew Robbins, Brent Maddock, SS Wilson, from a story by Mick Garris, Steven Spielberg

The Battle ★★

Romantic drama
1934 · Fr /UK · Colour · 83mins

Directed with ponderous gravity by Nicholas Farkas, this was filmed simultaneously in French and English versions. Charles Boyer stars in both, as a Japanese nobleman who so fears for the fate of his country's navy in the imminent 1905 war with Russia that he offers his wife (Merle Oberon) to British officer John Loder, in the hope that he will share some military secrets. Boyer is clearly unhappy in Oriental make-up, but he gamely captures the proud sense of patriotism that inspires his dishonourable actions. DP

Charles Boyer *Marquis Yorisaka* • John Loder *Commander Fergan* • Merle Oberon *Marquise Yorisaka* • Betty Stockfeld *Betty Hockley* • Valery Inkijinoff *Hirata* • Miles Mander *Felze* • Henri Fabert *Admiral* ■ *Dir* Nicholas Farkas • *Scr* Nicholas Farkas, Bernard Zimmer, Robert Stevenson, from the novel *La Bataille* by Claude Farrère

The Battle at Apache Pass ★★★ U

Western 1952 · US · Colour · 85mins

Universal contract star Jeff Chandler created a tremendous impression as the native American chief Cochise in the remarkably liberal (for its time) *Broken Arrow*. Here he reprises the role in another sympathetic western, which deals primarily with Apache warrior Geronimo, played by native American actor Jay Silverheels. Intelligent writing and performances make up for the lack of political depth and there's a splendid staging of the battle. Western fans won't be disappointed. TS

Jeff Chandler *Cochise* • John Lund *Major Jim Colton* • Beverly Tyler *Mary Kearny* • Bruce Cowling *Neil Baylor* • Susan Cabot *Nono* • John Hudson (1) *Lieutenant George Bascom* • Jay Silverheels *Geronimo* ■ *Dir* George Sherman • *Scr* Gerald Drayson Adams

Battle at Bloody Beach ★★

Second World War drama
1961 · US · BW · 83mins

Audie Murphy, the most decorated American in the Second World War, is out of uniform in this Pacific adventure as he scours the Philippines for Dolores Michaels, the wife who disappeared when the Japanese interrupted their Manila honeymoon. Convinced he died in the invasion, she's become involved with resistance leader Alejandro Rey, who proceeds to enlist Murphy in his guerrilla rearguard. The jungle sequences are directed with gung-ho efficiency, but the romantic triangle is wearisome. DP

Audie Murphy *Craig Benson* • Gary Crosby *Marty Sackler* • Dolores Michaels *Ruth Benson* • Alejandro Rey *Julio Fontana* • Marjorie Stapp *Caroline Pelham* ■ *Dir* Herbert Coleman • *Scr* Richard Maibaum, Willard Willingham [William Willingham], from a story by Richard Maibaum

Battle beneath the Earth ★★ U

Science fiction action adventure
1968 · UK · Colour · 91mins

The Red Chinese have dug a series of tunnels beneath the United States. In go Chinese H-bombs and lasers, and in after them goes Kerwin Matthews, the Harrison Ford of British cinema back in the 1960s, to do a job even 007 might have found taxing. Everyone takes it very seriously and, as a result, it's hugely enjoyable rubbish. AT

Kerwin Mathews *Commander Jonathan Shaw* • Viviane Ventura *Tila Yung* • Robert Ayres *Admiral Felix Hillebrand* • Peter Arne *Arnold Kramer* • Al Mulock *Sergeant Marvin Mulberry* • Martin Benson *General Chan Lu* ■ *Dir* Montgomery Tully • *Scr* Lance Z Hargreaves

Battle beyond the Stars ★★★ PG

Science-fiction adventure
1980 · US · Colour · 98mins

This entertaining slice of hokum from Roger Corman production company is great B-movie fodder. Essentially it's *The Magnificent Seven* in space; Corman even manages to rope in one of the original cast, Robert Vaughn, to take his place alongside the likes of John Saxon (as the baddie), George Peppard and Richard Thomas from *The Waltons*. The knowing script is by John Sayles, now better known as the writer/director of such critically acclaimed films as *Passion Fish* and *Lone Star*. JF

Richard Thomas *Shad* • Robert Vaughn *Gelt* • John Saxon *Sador* • George Peppard *Cowboy* • Darlanne Fluegel *Nanelia* • Sybil Danning *St Exmin* • Sam Jaffe *Dr Hephaestus* • Morgan Woodward *Cayman* • Steve Davis *Quopeg* ■ *Dir* Jimmy T Murakami • *Scr* John Sayles, from a story by John Sayles, Ann Dyer

Battle beyond the Sun ★

Science fiction
1959 · USSR · Colour · 67mins

This version of the space race to Mars between the Russians and the Americans was constructed by cult director Roger Corman out of special effects and footage from an existing Russian sci-fi movie, *Nebo Sovyot*, combined with new footage. This includes the major highlight – a notoriously kitsch battle between a penis-shaped monster and a vagina-shaped alien. Otherwise it's a deadly dull combination of conflicting styles and hastily matched edits. AJ

Edd Perry [Ivan Pereverzev] *Kornev* • Andy Stewart [Aleksandr Shvorin] *Gordiyenko* • Kirk Barton [K Bartashevich] *Klark* • Gene Tonner [G Tonunts] *Verst* • Barry Chertok [V Chernyak] *Somov* ■ *Dir* Thomas Colchart [A Kozyr], M Karyukov • *Scr* M Karyukov, Nicholas Colbert [A Sazonov], Edwin Palmer [Yevgeny Pomeshchikov], Francis Ford Coppola (English version adaptation)

Battle Circus ★★

War drama 1953 · US · BW · 90mins

Humphrey Bogart coasts through this movie, playing the commanding officer of a US Army surgical unit during the Korean War, who falls in love with idealistic nurse June Allyson between dodging bullets and indulging in blokeish camaraderie. Released six months before the Korean war ended, this is clichéd and doesn't have much to say about the conflict. AT

Humphrey Bogart *Major Jeb Webbe* • June Allyson *Lt Ruth McCara* • Keenan Wynn *Sergeant Orvil Statt* • Robert Keith (1) *Lt Col Hillary Whalters* • William Campbell *Captain John Rustford* • Perry Sheehan *Lt Lawrence* • Patricia Tiernan *Lt Rose Ashland* ■ *Dir* Richard Brooks • *Scr* Richard Brooks, from a story by Allen Rivkin, Laura Kerr

B

Battle Cry ★★★★ PG

Second World War drama
1955 · US · Colour · 142mins

It may seem dated today, but this impressive Warner Bros drama based on Leon Uris's semi-fictional account of his own wartime experiences still packs a terrific emotional punch. It is exceptionally well cast, with a key star-making role for Tab Hunter, though top-billed Van Heflin has little to do but act gritty as the leader of "Huxley's Harlots". Watch out, too, for Justus E McQueen as LQ Jones, who took his professional name from the character he portrays here. There's also a rousing Oscar-nominated score by the great Max Steiner. TS DVD

Van Heflin *Major Huxley* • Aldo Ray *Andy* • Mona Freeman *Kathy* • Nancy Olson *Pat* • James Whitmore *Sergeant Mac* • Raymond Massey *General Snipes* • Tab Hunter *Danny* • Justus E McQueen [LQ Jones] *LQ Jones* ■ *Dir* Raoul Walsh • *Scr* Leon Uris, from his novel

Battle for the Planet of the Apes ★ PG

Science-fiction fantasy
1973 · US · Colour · 86mins

This is the fifth, final and least effective entry in the *Planet of the Apes* series. It's good apes versus guerrilla gorillas as our heroes attempt to restore racial harmony to Earth and make humans social equals. Spotting who's who under the hairy masks will while away the time as this threadbare monkey business wends its time-warp way back to the beginning of the original film. Endless action can't disguise the cheapness of the production or the lack of novelty and story values. AJ DVD

Roddy McDowall *Caesar* • Claude Akins *Aldo* • John Huston *Lawgiver* • Natalie Trundy *Lisa* • Severn Darden *Kolp* • Lew Ayres *Mandemus* • Paul Williams *Virgil* • Austin Stoker *MacDonald* • Noah Keen *Teacher* ■ *Dir* J Lee Thompson • *Scr* John William Corrington, Joyce Hooper Corrington, from a story by Paul Dehn, from characters created by Pierre Boulle

Battle Hymn ★★★ U

War drama based on a true story
1957 · US · Colour · 108mins

From the producer-director team of Ross Hunter and Douglas Sirk, responsible for glossy remakes of classic weepies such as *Imitation of Life* and *Magnificent Obsession*, comes this earnest biopic about Dean Hess. As a combat flyer he accidentally bombed a German orphanage in the Second World War; how, as a minister in the Korean war, Hess heroically atones for this mistake, forms the stuff of this starring vehicle for Rock Hudson. RK

Rock Hudson *Colonel Dean Hess* • Anna Kashfi *En Soon Yang* • Dan Duryea *Sgt Herman* • Don DeFore *Capt Skidmore* • Martha Hyer *Mary Hess* • Jock Mahoney *Major Moore* • Alan Hale Jr *Mess Sergeant* • James Edwards *Lt Maples* ■ *Dir* Douglas Sirk • *Scr* Charles Grayson , Vincent B Evans, from the memoirs of Colonel Dean Hess

Battle in Heaven ★★

Crime drama
2005 · Mex/Fr · Colour · 101mins

Mexican director Carlos Reygadas's deliberately slow-paced, fuzzy rumination on Catholic guilt begins and ends on explicit sexual imagery. When he and his wife botch a baby kidnapping for ransom, chauffeur Marco Hernández confesses responsibility for the infant's death to his boss's prostitute daughter (Anapola Mushkadiz). Both enigmatic and baffling, Reygadas's single-minded focus is on earthy emotions and bodily functions. AJ. In Spanish with English subtitles. Contains violence, nudity and sex scenes.

Marcos Hernández *Marcos* • Anapola Mushkadiz *Ana* • Berta Ruiz *Marcos's wife* ■ *Dir/Scr* Carlos Reygadas

The Battle of Algiers ★★★★★ 15

Political war drama
1965 · Alg/It · BW · 116mins

The winner of the Golden Lion at Venice and nominated for three Oscars, this stark and compelling drama about the rise of the Front de Libération Nationale in Algeria was banned by a French government still smarting from the recent loss of that country. Yet, one of the strengths of Gillo Pontecorvo's *cinéma-vérité* approach is its refusal to condemn or condone: French and Algerian rhetoric is given an equal airing. Depressingly, this compassionate masterpiece of political analysis still has much contemporary resonance, but it also has a vigour, a commitment and an intelligence that is absent from too much modern cinema. DP. In French and Arabic with English subtitles. Contains violence. DVD

Yacef Saadi *Saari Kader* • Jean Martin *Colonel Mathieu* • Brahim Haggiag *Ali la Pointe* • Tommaso Neri *Captain Dubois* • Michèle Kerbash [Samia Kerbash] *Fathia* ■ *Dir* Gillo Pontecorvo • *Scr* Franco Solinas, from a story by Franco Solinas, Gillo Pontecorvo

The Battle of Austerlitz ★★ U

Historical drama
1960 · Fr/It/Yug · Colour · 122mins

Watching international superstars re-enact Napoleon's greatest victory is a pleasant enough way of passing the time. But it's sad to realise that this rather tawdry epic is the penultimate feature of veteran French director Abel Gance. By 1960, Gance was still able to eke out a living from the cinema, having spent his early years virtually inventing it, and this is barely recognisable as the work of the director of the masterpiece *Napoléon*. TS. French and Italian dialogue dubbed into English.

Pierre Mondy *Napoleon Bonaparte* • Jean Mercure *Talleyrand* • Jack Palance *General Weirother* • Orson Welles *Robert Fulton* • Martine Carol *Josephine* • Leslie Caron *Mademoiselle de Vaudey* • Claudia Cardinale *Pauline* • Jean Marais *Carnot* ■ *Dir* Abel Gance • *Scr* Abel Gance, Roger Richebe

Battle of Britain ★★★ PG

Second World War epic
1969 · UK · Colour · 126mins

This worthy tribute to "the few" has spectacular air battles, a memorable re-creation of the Blitz and a terrific cast. It is interesting today to watch so many great names in the twilight of their careers: not just knights Ralph Richardson, Michael Redgrave and Laurence Olivier, but also Trevor Howard, Robert Shaw, Kenneth More and Curt Jurgens. Most of Sir William Walton's original score was dumped and replaced by Ron Goodwin's, but a tantalising fragment remains in the air battles. TS DVD

Laurence Olivier *Air Chief Marshal Sir Hugh Dowding* • Robert Shaw *Squadron Leader Skipper* • Christopher Plummer *Squadron Leader Colin Harvey* • Susannah York *Section Officer Maggie Harvey* • Ian McShane *Sergeant Pilot Andy* • Michael Caine *Squadron Leader Canfield* • Kenneth More *Group Captain Baker* • Trevor Howard *Air Vice-Marshal Keith Park* • Ralph Richardson *British Minister in Switzerland* • Curd Jürgens [Curt Jurgens] *Baron von Richter* • Michael Redgrave *Air Vice-Marshal Evill* ■ *Dir* Guy Hamilton • *Scr* James Kennaway, Wilfred Greatorex, from the book *The Narrow Margin* by Derek Wood, Derek Dempster

The Battle of El Alamein ★★ PG

Second World War drama
1968 · It/Fr · Colour · 101mins

This might have been an intriguing, alternative account of the battle that marked a turning point in the war in North Africa. Viewing the conflict from the Axis perspective, it reveals an uneasy alliance, in which the Italian Division Folgore ("Thunderbolt Division") is left high and dry by Rommel's grand design. As the rival field marshals, Robert Hossein and Michael Rennie (presented as the villain of the piece) are adequate, but this is something of a wasted opportunity. DP. Italian dialogue dubbed into English.

Michael Rennie *Field Marshal Montgomery* • Robert Hossein *Field Marshal Rommel* • George Hilton *Lieutenant Graham* • Ira Furstenberg [Ira von Fürstenberg] *Marta* • Enrico Maria Salerno *Captain Hubert* • Frederick Stafford *Lt Claudio Borri* ■ *Dir* Calvin Jackson Padget [Giorgio Ferroni] • *Scr* Ernesto Gastaldi

The Battle of Elderbush ★★★

Silent western 1914 · US · BW · 29mins

This very early western was the last two-reeler made by DW Griffith before embarking on America's first feature-length films. For this simple tale of Indians attacking a settlement, Griffith constructed a complete three-dimensional town in the San Fernando Valley. Brilliantly shot by Billy Bitzer, the short becomes more and more compelling towards its climax, as a baby whose parents have been killed escapes the shelter of her cabin and must be rescued by a posse. The baby, who was actually black and was selected by Griffith from a foundling home for her photogenic eyes, curiously grows up to be the white Blanche Sweet. RB

Mae Marsh *The waif* • Alfred Paget *Her uncle* • Charles H Mailes [Charles Hill Mailes] *The ranch owner* • Lillian Gish *Young wife* • Robert Harron *Young husband* • Kate Bruce *Settler* • W Chrystie Miller [Walter Miller] *Settler* • Blanche Sweet *Child* ■ *Dir/Scr* DW Griffith

The Battle of Mary Kay ★★★

Comedy drama based on a true story
2002 · Can/US · Colour · 100mins

Hard facts blur into camp kitsch in a madcap re-creation of the rivalry between cosmetics queen Mary Kay Ash and sassy wannabe Jinger Heath. Director Ed Gernon indulges in all manner of visual pyrotechnics, but his attention-seeking style too often distracts from the full-on performances of Shirley MacLaine and Parker Posey. They rip into their roles in this TV biopic with a bitchy glee that's fun to watch. DP

Shirley MacLaine *Mary Kay Ash* • Parker Posey *Jinger Heath* • Shannen Doherty *Lexi Wilcox* • Maggie Butterfield *Doris* • Terri Cherniak *Liz* ■ *Dir* Ed Gernon • *Scr* Patricia Resnick

The Battle of Midway ★★★★

Second World War documentary
1942 · US · Colour · 18mins

One of a striking series of Second World War documentaries made by the world's greatest film directors – this time John Ford, uncredited, for the US Navy. Ford did some of the camerawork himself and captured the searing, tragic sense of destruction in a battle that marked a turning point in the war against Japan. In the cutting rooms, aided by Robert Parrish and some familiar voices (you'll easily recognise Henry Fonda) Ford wove a structure around his material and, with his original 16mm Technicolor blown up to 35mm, made a superb propagandist tract. TS

Henry Fonda • Jane Darwell • Donald Crisp • Irving Pichel ■ *Dir* John Ford • *Cinematographer* John Ford • *Music* Alfred Newman • *Editor* Robert Parrish

Battle of Midway ★★★ PG

Second World War action drama
1976 · US · Colour · 131mins

Charlton Heston juts his jaw aggressively and Henry Fonda falters reflectively in this blockbuster drama about the events leading up to the decisive battle fought between the navies of the US and Japan during the Second World War. The techniques of the star-studded cast are blown away somewhat by the big guns of audio technology, though the din of the original ear-blasting Sensurround has been diminished to clarify the narrative. Star performers line up to do their bit for Uncle Sam, but can't prevent the movie overstaying its welcome. TH DVD

Charlton Heston *Capt Matt Garth* • Henry Fonda *Adm Chester W Nimitz* • James Coburn *Capt Vinton Maddox* • Glenn Ford *Rear Adm Raymond A Spruance* • Hal Holbrook *Cmdr Joseph Rochefort* • Toshiro Mifune *Adm Isoroku Yamamoto* • Robert Mitchum *Adm William F Halsey* • Cliff Robertson *Cmdr Carl Jessop* • Robert Wagner *Lt Cmdr Ernest L Blake* ■ *Dir* Jack Smight • *Scr* Donald S Sanford

The Battle of Neretva ★★ PG

Second World War adventure
1969 · Yug/US/It/W Ger · Colour · 126mins

A sluggish vanity project for the Yugoslavian dictator General Tito, who lavished US$12 million on the story of how the partisan army overthrew the Nazis and Italians in Western Bosnia. It's pitched as the Balkan equivalent to *The Longest Day* or *Battle of Britain*, with an all-star cast that includes Orson Welles, and the Russian Sergei Bondarchuk, who had made the nine-hour *War and Peace*. *The Battle for Neretva* originally ran at three hours long, but was later cut by an hour for international release. AT

Yul Brynner *Vlado* • Hardy Kruger *Colonel Kranzer* • Franco Nero *Captain Riva* • Sylva Koscina *Danica* • Orson Welles *Senator* • Curt Jurgens *General Löhring* • Anthony Dawson [Antonio Margheriti] *General Morelli* • Milena Dravic *Girl* • Sergei Bondarchuk *Artillery Man Martin* ■ *Dir* Veljko Bulajic • *Scr* Ugo Pirro, Ratko Durovic, Stevan Bulajic, Veljko Bulajic

The Battle of Russia ★★

Second World War documentary
1943 · US · BW · 80mins

Lt Col Frank Capra, Lt Col Anatole Litvak and other ranking Hollywood soldiers made this documentary, one of a series of seven designed to show Americans what the Second World War was all about. This one's about the ally Russia, from the time of Alexander Nevsky to the Nazi invasion. The vast amount of documentary footage is accompanied by soundtrack composer Dimitri Tiomkin's copious borrowings from Prokofiev, Tchaikovsky and Shostakovich. AT

Walter Huston *Narrator* • Anthony Veiller *Narrator* ■ *Dir* Frank Capra, Anatole Litvak • *Scr* Anatole Litvak

Battle of the Bulge ★★★★ PG

Second World War action drama
1965 · US · Colour · 149mins

This truly spectacular war epic is based on the last German offensive of the war, when thousands of tanks smashed their way through the snowy pine forests of the Ardennes. It's a study of resolve on both the American and the German sides; representing

U = SUITABLE FOR ALL   Uc = SUITABLE FOR ALL, ESPECIALLY FOR YOUNG CHILDREN (VIDEO ONLY)   PG = PARENTAL GUIDANCE

Uncle Sam are Robert Ryan and Dana Andrews, with Henry Fonda as the only man who sees the German tactic months before it happens. But the picture is dominated by Robert Shaw as the German colonel, a riveting portrait of military genius infested with paranoia. The climax is *High Noon* with tanks. AT [video] DVD

Henry Fonda *Lt Col Kiley* • Robert Shaw *Colonel Hessler* • Robert Ryan *General Grey* • Dana Andrews *Colonel Pritchard* • George Montgomery *Sergeant Duquesne* • Ty Hardin *Schumacher* • Pier Angeli *Louise* • Barbara Werle *Elena* • Charles Bronson *Wolenski* ■ *Dir* Ken Annakin • *Scr* Philip Yordan, Milton Sperling, John Melson

Battle of the Coral Sea ★★ PG

Second World War drama
1959 · US · BW · 82mins

This numbingly predictable war movie from director Paul Wendkos has a rather a misleading title, as much of the action takes place in a PoW camp. Cliff Robertson's submarine captain is one of the dullest heroes ever to turn the tables on his captors. There's plenty of square-jawed defiance, but not enough humanity to make us care whether he gets back to his commanders in time to report on Japanese shipping movements prior to the key 1942 battle. DP [video]

Cliff Robertson *Lieutenant Commander Jeff Conway* • Gia Scala *Karen Philips* • Teru Shimada *Commander Mori* • Patricia Cutts *Lieutenant Peg Whitcomb* • Rian Garrick *Al Schechter* • Gene Blakely *Lieutenant Len Ross* • LQ Jones *Yeoman Halliday* ■ *Dir* Paul Wendkos • *Scr* Stephen Kandel, Dan Ullman [Daniel B Ullman], from a story by Stephen Kandel

The Battle of the River Plate ★★★ U

Second World War adventure
1956 · UK · Colour · 118mins

Though this true-life Second World War adventure hardly rates alongside *A Matter of Life and Death* and *The Red Shoes* on the CV of the writing-producing-directing duo Michael Powell and Emeric Pressburger, it is a tale well told and features some impressive location work – not least at sea in the Mediterranean. Peter Finch pulls off a noble German officer (no mean feat in a British war film, even in the 1950s), captain of pocket battleship the *Graf Spee*, the pursuit of which forms the basis of the action. Despite a surfeit of naval detail, the climax in Montevideo makes it a worthwhile watch. AC [video] DVD

John Gregson *Captain Bell* • Anthony Quayle *Commodore Harwood* • Peter Finch *Captain Langsdorff* • Ian Hunter *Captain Woodhouse* • Jack Gwillim *Captain Barry* • Bernard Lee *Captain Dove* • Lionel Murton *Mike Fowler* • Anthony Bushell *Mr Millington-Drake* • Peter Illing *Dr Guani* • Michael Goodliffe *Captain McCall* • Patrick Macnee *Lt Cmdr Medley* • John Chandos *Dr Langmann* • Douglas Wilmer *M Desmoulins* ■ *Dir/Scr* Michael Powell, Emeric Pressburger

The Battle of the Sexes ★★★

Silent drama 1914 · US · BW · 50mins

Long thought lost, this is a five-reeler made by the great film pioneer DW Griffith, one of his amazing total of 495 movies. Like many of Griffith's morality playlets from this period, this drama of a father demanding that his daughter live a moral life to which he himself does not aspire may prove hard to watch today, but there is no denying the sheer creativity at work in the storytelling. Here are close-ups, here, too, a moving camera – tools of the trade we now take for granted. TS

Lillian Gish *Jane Andrews* • Owen Moore *Andrews, Frank* • Mary Alden *Mrs Frank Andrews* • Fay Tincher *Cleo* • Robert Harron *The son* • Donald Crisp • WE Lawrence ■ *Dir* DW Griffith • *Scr* by Daniel Carson Goodman

The Battle of the Sexes ★★★ U

Comedy 1960 · UK · BW · 80mins

This features one of the most underrated performances by Peter Sellers. He plays a Scottish accountant revenging himself on efficiency expert Constance Cummings, who wants his firm to get rid of old-fashioned impedimenta like him. There's an industrial message that's still relevant today, though director Charles Crichton never seems to be enough in control to make it matter. TH [video] DVD

Peter Sellers *Mr Martin* • Robert Morley *Robert MacPherson* • Constance Cummings *Angela Barrows* • Ernest Thesiger *Old MacPherson* • Jameson Clark *Andrew Darling* • Moultrie Kelsall *Graham* • Alex Mackenzie *Robertson* ■ *Dir* Charles Crichton • *Scr* Monja Danischewsky, from the short story *The Catbird Seat* by James Thurber

The Battle of the V1 ★★

Second World War drama
1958 · UK · BW · 104mins

Weakly cast and excessively long, this fitfully exciting melodrama stars Michael Rennie and David Knight as two Polish patriots who discover the latest Nazi secret weapon – the flying missiles or "doodlebugs" that were eventually unleashed on London. The low-budget production awkwardly mixes documentary footage from old enemy newsreels with standard underground heroics that were filmed in the Sussex countryside. AE

Michael Rennie *Stefan Nowak* • Patricia Medina *Zofia* • Milly Vitale *Anna* • David Knight *Tadek* • Esmond Knight *Stricker* • Christopher Lee *Brunner* ■ *Dir* Vernon Sewell • *Scr* Jack Hanley, Eryk Wlodek, from the novel *They Saved London* by Bernard Newman

The Battle of the Villa Fiorita ★★ U

Romance 1965 · UK/US · Colour · 111mins

Hankies out for this slick weepie. Shamelessly emulating the glossy soap-opera style of Douglas Sirk, writer/director Delmer Daves makes the most of the gorgeous Italian scenery, as runaway wife Maureen O'Hara and her composer lover Rossano Brazzi are dogged by the disapproval of her children. Brazzi is suavity personified, but O'Hara's flame-haired ebullience is disappointingly buried beneath an unexpected veneer of suffering. DP

Maureen O'Hara *Moira* • Rossano Brazzi *Lorenzo* • Richard Todd *Darrell* • Phyllis Calvert *Margot* • Martin Stephens *Michael* • Elizabeth Dear *Debby* • Olivia Hussey *Donna* • Maxine Audley *Charmian* • Ursula Jeans *Lady Anthea* ■ *Dir* Delmer Daves • *Scr* Delmer Daves, from the novel by Rumer Godden

Battle Royale ★★★★ 18

Futuristic action thriller
2000 · Jpn · Colour · 108mins

Much has been made of the violence in Kinji Fukasaku's dark satire of reality TV. The film depicts an annual competition of the future in which, as a lesson to unruly youth, a class of schoolchildren are taken to an island, equipped with various weapons and given just three days to reduce their number to the sole survivor who will then be allowed to rejoin society. This is a film of contrasting moods, with moments of bleak comedy and grotesque horror being interspersed with genuinely touching insights into teen trauma. It's occasionally ragged, but the characterisation is sharp – particularly "Beat" Takeshi as a world-weary former teacher who monitors the teenagers' "progress" – and the murderous set pieces are often inspired. DP. In Japanese with English subtitles. [video] DVD

"Beat" Takeshi [Takeshi Kitano] *Kitano* • Taro Yamamoto *Shogo Kawada, male student 5* • Masanobu Ando *Kazuo Kiriyama, male student 6* • Sosuke Takaoka *Hiroki Sugimura, male student 11* • Tatsuya Fujiwara *Shuya Nanahara, male student 15* • Hirohito Honda *Niida Yoriyuki, male student 16* • Eri Ishikawa *Yukie Utsumi, female student 2* ■ *Dir* Kinji Fukasaku • *Scr* Kenta Fukasaku, from a novel by Koshun Takami

Battle Royale 2: Requiem ★★ 18

Futuristic action thriller
2003 · Jpn · Colour · 132mins

Battle Royale director Kinji Fukasaku died shortly after beginning this inferior sequel. His son Kenta took over, and the resulting picture underplays the original's satirical elements in favour of awkward politics and clumsy moralising. Contest survivor-turned-terrorist leader Tatsuya Fujiwara publicly calls for violence against western tyranny. He and his supporters hole up on an island, and the government forcibly dispatches a student class to wipe them out. Far-fetched, tedious and disappointing. SF. In Japanese with English subtitles. Contains violence. [video] DVD

Tatsuya Fujiwara *Shuya Nanahara* • Ai Maeda *Shiori Kitano* • Shugo Oshinari *Takuma Aoi* • Ayana Sakai *Nao Asakura* • Haruka Suenaga *Haruka Kuze* • "Beat" Takeshi [Takeshi Kitano] *Kitano* ■ *Dir* Kenta Fukasaku, Kinji Fukasaku • *Scr* Kenta Fukasaku, Norio Kida

Battle Shock ★★

Psychological drama 1956 · US · BW · 88mins

Directed by the actor Paul Henreid – better known as the Resistance leader in *Casablanca* – this thriller, released in the States as *A Woman's Devotion*, finds artist Ralph Meeker and wife Janice Rule snarled up in a murder hunt while holidaying in Mexico. TH

Ralph Meeker *Trevor Stevenson* • Janice Rule *Stella Stevenson* • Paul Henreid *Captain Henrique Monteros* • Rosenda Monteros *Maria* • Fanny Schiller *Senora Reidl* • José Torvay *Gomez* • Yerye Beirute *Amigo Herrera* ■ *Dir* Paul Henreid • *Scr* Robert Hill

Battle Taxi ★ U

War drama 1955 · US · BW · 80mins

In this Korean war drama, Sterling Hayden plays the commander of a unit of rescue helicopters who's getting trouble from Arthur Franz, a former jet pilot who resents his present assignment and starts launching attacks in his unarmed chopper. Hayden was way too good an actor for this dime-budget stuff, which has precious little time for character development beyond the odd frown. AT

Sterling Hayden *Captain Russ Edwards* • Arthur Franz *Lieutenant Pete Stacy* • Marshall Thompson *2nd Lieutenant Tim Vernon* • Leo Needham *Staff Sergeant Slats Klein* • Jay Barney *Lt Col Stoneham* ■ *Dir* Herbert L Strock • *Scr* Malvin Wald, from a story by Art Arthur, Malvin Wald

Battlefield Earth ★ 12

Science-fiction action adventure
2000 · US · Colour · 112mins

This expensive stinker is very much a labour of love for its producer and star, John Travolta. In the year 3000, Earth is controlled by ten-foot-tall aliens from the planet Psychlo; the few remaining humans either hide out in the mountains or live and die as slaves. Barry Pepper dares to rebel against the invaders, bringing him into conflict with the fearsome chief of security, a dreadlocked Travolta. Unfeasibly banal. NS [video] DVD

John Travolta *Terl* • Barry Pepper *Jonnie Goodboy Tyler* • Forest Whitaker *Ker* • Kim Coates *Carlo* • Richard Tyson *Robert the Fox* • Sabine Karsenti *Chrissie* • Michael Byrne *Parson Staffer* ■ *Dir* Roger Christian • *Scr* Corey Mandell, JD Shapiro, from the novel by L Ron Hubbard

Battleground ★★★★ PG

Second World War drama
1949 · US · BW · 113mins

This grimy and authentic-looking study of wartime close combat comes from MGM, home of glamour and gloss. The studio supplied an all-star cast, and then proceeded to make the likes of Van Johnson, George Murphy and Ricardo Montalban virtually unrecognisable in combat duds as members of a US Army infantry unit trapped during the siege of Bastogne in 1944. Writer Robert Pirosh actually served at Bastogne, and his screenplay won an Oscar, as did Paul C Vogel's cinematography, though director William A Wellman lost out to Joseph L Mankiewicz. Even those who aren't fans of war movies might find much to appreciate in this one. TS [video] DVD

Van Johnson *Holley* • John Hodiak *Jarvess* • Ricardo Montalban *Roderigues* • George Murphy *Pop Stazak* • Marshall Thompson *Jim Layton* • Jerome Courtland *Abner Spudler* • Don Taylor *Standiferd* • Bruce Cowling *Wolowicz* • James Whitmore *Kinnie* ■ *Dir* William Wellman [William A Wellman] • *Scr* Robert Pirosh

The Battleship Potemkin ★★★★★ PG

Silent historical drama
1925 · USSR · BW · 65mins

Originally planned as a brief episode in an epic history of the 1905 Revolution, Sergei Eisenstein's classic remains one of the most influential films ever made. A masterpiece of editorial dexterity, it proved that symbolic imagery could have the same emotional and intellectual impact on an audience as a straightforward narrative. You don't need a working knowledge of Russian history, Marxist dialectic, Japanese pictographs or the techniques of "montage" to appreciate the power of the plate smashing that sparks the mutiny, the fog scene and the massacre on the Odessa Steps. Don't be put off by its highbrow reputation, this is essential cinema. DP [video] DVD

Mikhail Gomarov *Sailor* • Repnikova *Woman on the steps* • Aleksander Antonov *Vakulinchuk the sailor* • Grigori Aleksandrov *Chief Officer Gilyarovsky* • Vladimir Barsky *Captain Golikov* • Alexander Lyovshin *Petty officer* • Beatrice Vitoldi *Mother with baby carriage* • I Bobrov *Humiliated soldier* ■ *Dir* Sergei Eisenstein • *Scr* Sergei Eisenstein, Nina Agadzhanova-Shutko • *Cinematographer* Edouard Tissé

Battlestar Galactica ★★ PG

Science-fiction adventure
1978 · US · Colour · 119mins

This feature film spin-off consists of two episodes from the short-lived TV series, cloned from *Star Wars* and unsuccessfully sued for plagiarism by the makers of that blockbuster hit. Lorne Greene stars as the commander of a fleet of starships trying to return to Earth after it has virtually been wiped out by the Cylons, a robot race programmed to destroy mankind. The result is a tacky, juvenile and derivative space opera with a "gee whizz" aesthetic. AJ [video] DVD

Lorne Greene *Commander Adama* • Richard L Hatch [Richard Hatch] *Captain Apollo* • Dirk Benedict *Lieutenant Starbuck* • Maren Jensen *Athena* • Herb Jefferson Jr [Herbert Jefferson Jr] *Lieutenant Boomer* • Terry Carter *Colonel*

Tigh • Jane Seymour (2) *Serina* • Noah Hathaway *Boxey* ■ *Dir* Richard A Colla • *Scr* Glen A Larson

Battletruck ★★★ 15

Science fiction 1982 · US · Colour · 88mins

Lone warrior hero Michael Beck takes on bloodthirsty pirates and their super truck after 21st-century oil wars cause a fuel shortage. Further friction occurs when Annie McEnroe, the villain's daughter, is caught between the opposing camps. This may be a rather juvenile *Mad Max* clone, but director Harley Cokliss ensures that the subtle ecological messages don't get in the way of the fast-paced mayhem. AJ

Michael Beck *Hunter* • Annie McEnroe *Corlie* • James Wainwright *Straker* • John Ratzenberger *Rusty* • Randolph Powell *Judd* • Bruno Lawrence *Willie* • Diana Rowan *Charlene* • John Bach *Bone* ■ *Dir* Harley Cokliss • *Scr* Irving Austin, Harley Cokliss, John Beech

Battling Butler ★★★

Silent comedy 1926 · US · BW · 80mins

Although this was Buster Keaton's most profitable silent film (and one he once cited as his favourite), it is generally rated among his weaker ventures. The pioneering use of deep-focus photography gives it a certain historical value, but there is too little comic business to relish. Keaton plays a wealthy milksop who is sent into the woods to toughen up, only to be mistaken for a prizefighter by mountain girl Sally O'Neil. The duck shoot is ingeniously staged, and there are a couple of amusing training camp gags, but what lingers longest is the brutality of the final boxing bout. DP

Buster Keaton *Alfred Butler* • Sally O'Neil *Mountain girl* • Snitz Edwards *His valet* • Francis McDonald *Alfred "Battling Butler"* • Mary O'Brien *His wife* • Tom Wilson *The trainer* • Eddie Borden *His manager* • Walter James *The girl's father* ■ *Dir* Buster Keaton • *Scr* Paul Gerard Smith, Albert Boasberg, Charles Smith, Lex Neal, Ballard McDonald, from the play *Battling Butler* by Stanley Brightman, Austin Melford, Walter L Rosemont, Douglas Furber

The Bawdy Adventures of Tom Jones ★★ 15

Period musical romp
1976 · UK · Colour · 88mins

The success of Tony Richardson's film *Tom Jones* (1963), led to other Fielding adaptations. Desperation must have set in early, adding hopeful temptation to audiences with promises of Tom's bawdy behaviour. This was inspired by a stage musical, but only three songs intrude on the lacklustre events depicting his life and loves. Nicky Henson, as the rascally hero, heads a memorable cast who all sink without trace. BB

Nicky Henson *Tom Jones* • Trevor Howard *Squire Western* • Terry-Thomas *Mr Square* • Arthur Lowe *Dr Thwackum* • Georgia Brown *Jenny Jones/Mrs Waters* • Joan Collins *Black Bess* • Geraldine McEwan *Lady Bellaston* ■ *Dir* Cliff Owen • *Scr* Jeremy Lloyd, from the musical by Don MacPherson, Paul Holden, from the novel by Henry Fielding

Baxter ★★★

Drama 1973 · UK · Colour · 104mins

Actor-turned-director Lionel Jeffries never puts a foot wrong through the quagmire of clichés that can so often swamp stories of ill-adjusted youngsters. The 12-year-old hero (Scott Jacoby) is being treated for his lisp by speech therapist Patricia Neal, which seems to put him at odds with his friends and compounds the problem of his parents splitting up. The acting throughout lives up to the gravitas of the film's theme. TH

Patricia Neal *Dr Clemm* • Jean-Pierre Cassel *Roger Tunnell* • Britt Ekland *Chris Bentley* • Lynn Carlin *Mrs Baxter* • Scott Jacoby *Robert Baxter* • Sally Thomsett *Nemo* • Paul Eddington *Mr Rawling* • Paul Maxwell *Mr Baxter* • Ian Thomson *Dr Walsh* ■ *Dir* Lionel Jeffries • *Scr* Reginald Rose

Bay Boy ★★★ 15

Period drama 1984 · Can/Fr · Colour · 96mins

Kiefer Sutherland's first starring role was in this downbeat but interesting film from Canada. He plays a Nova Scotia lad destined for the priesthood who witnesses the murder of a Jewish couple and keeps quiet about it because he knows the killer, a cop who is the father of the girl he fancies. Set in 1937, Daniel Petrie's tale is semi-autobiographical and rather low-key; even so, Sutherland is appealing and his problems with his mother (Liv Ullmann) are often touching. AT. Contains swearing and nudity.

Liv Ullmann *Mrs Jennie Campbell* • Kiefer Sutherland *Donald Campbell* • Alan Scarfe *Sergeant Tom Coldwell* • Peter Donat *Mr Will Campbell* • Mathieu Carrière *Father Chaisson* • Chris Wiggins *Chief Charles McInnes* • Isabelle Mejias *Mary McNeil* • Leah Pinsent *Saxon Coldwell* • Stéphane Audran *Blanche* ■ *Dir/Scr* Daniel Petrie

Bay of Blood ★★★ 18

Horror 1971 · It · Colour · 80mins

Italian horror maestro Mario Bava's influential body count stalk-and-slash template opens with a classic double murder (copied exactly by *Friday the 13th Part 2*) and then hurtles on in scream-lined fashion to kill each of the 13 candidates in line to gain a vast fortune in cash and property. Unreeling like a macabre joke, the shock ending has to be seen to be believed in Bava's part Elizabethan tragedy, part Tex Avery cartoon, ultra-violent carnage spectacular. AJ. Italian dialogue dubbed into English. DVD

Claudine Auger *Renata* • Luigi Pistilli *Albert* • Claudio Volonté [Claudio Camaso] *Simon* • Anna Maria Rosati *Laura* ■ *Dir* Mario Bava • *Scr* Mario Bava, Joseph McLee, Filippo Ottoni, from a story by Franco Barberi, Dardano Sacchetti

The Bay of Saint Michel ★★

Adventure 1963 · UK · BW · 73mins

That marvellous French monument, Le Mont-Saint-Michel, with its broad sweep of sandy bay, makes a spectacular location for this unassuming little thriller about a commando unit that reforms after the Second World War and sets about finding some buried Nazi loot. American star Keenan Wynn is in charge of the operation, while Mai Zetterling, a Swedish actress who made many movies in Britain, plays a mystery Frenchwoman. AT

Keenan Wynn *Nick Rawlings* • Mai Zetterling *Helene Bretton* • Ronald Howard *Bill Webb* • Rona Anderson *Pru Lawson* • Trader Faulkner *Dave Newton* • Edward Underdown *Col Harvey* • Michael Peake *Capt Starkey* • Rudolph Offenbach *Father Laurent* ■ *Dir* John Ainsworth • *Scr* Christopher Davis

Bay of the Angels ★★★★

Drama 1963 · Fr · BW · 85mins

Jacques Demy's second feature is a *noir*-ish study of seduction and obsession. Yet Jean Rabier's modish monochrome photography and Michel Legrand's cascading score add romance to a tale of ruinous addiction that in less assured hands would have been unbearably melodramatic. As the woman who has abandoned her baby to prowl the tables of the Riviera, Jeanne Moreau vivaciously personifies the thrills and the perils of gambling, as she clings to timorous bank clerk Claude Mann during a typically brief winning streak. Demy's adroit attention to visual detail gives this neglected classic its class. DP. In French with English subtitles.

Jeanne Moreau *Jackie Demaistre* • Claude Mann *Jean Fournier* • Paul Guers *Caron* • Henri Nassiet *Jean's father* ■ *Dir/Scr* Jacques Demy

Baywatch the Movie: Forbidden Paradise ★★

Adventure drama 1995 · US · Colour · 90mins

David Hasselhoff and his sillicone-enchanced lifesavers swap the polluted shores of California for an undeserved Hawaiian break in the usual banal mix of soap, surf and sun. The regulars all get their own little subplots. But they are there basically to be photographed against the tourist delights of the islands and to be seen in something other than those familiar red cossies. JF

David Hasselhoff *Mitch* • David Charvet *Matt* • Pamela Anderson *CJ* • Alexandra Paul *Stephanie* • Yasmine Bleeth *Caroline* • Jaason Simmons *Logan* ■ *Dir* Douglas Schwartz

Be Cool ★★ 12A

Crime comedy 2005 · US · Colour · 119mins

This sequel to *Get Shorty* tries hard to emulate its hip, flip style, but it just can't carry it off. This time around, wise guy-turned-movie producer Chili Palmer (John Travolta) has tired of the film business and decides to try his luck with the music industry. However, he quickly discovers that making records can be even more dangerous than making movies. Travolta and Uma Thurman exude an easy-going charisma, but this is just not cool enough. JF. Contains violence, swearing.

John Travolta *Chili Palmer* • Uma Thurman *Edie Athens* • Vince Vaughn *Raji* • Harvey Keitel *Nick Carr* • The Rock *Elliot Wilhelm* • Cedric the Entertainer *Sin LaSalle* • André Benjamin *Dabu* • Danny DeVito *Martin Weir* • Steven Tyler ■ *Dir* F Gary Gray • *Scr* Peter Steinfeld, from the novel by Elmore Leonard

Be My Guest ★★★ U

Drama 1965 · UK · BW · 78mins

The second of two unassuming but spirited little pop musicals (the first was *Live It Up*) released during the British beat boom of the 1960s. David Hemmings is once again the star, this time playing a newspaper office boy, who tries to launch the "Brighton beat", but tangles with unscrupulous music industry bigwigs. The format and mood belong to the earlier rock 'n' roll era (Jerry Lee Lewis is one of the guest stars). But the snappy script is played with verve by all concerned, and the result is a very jolly piece of pop history. DM

David Hemmings *Dave* • Steven Marriott *Ricky* • John Pike *Phil* • Andrea Monet *Erica* • Ivor Salter *Herbert* • Anna King *Margaret* • Avril Angers *Mrs Pucil* ■ *Dir* Lance Comfort • *Scr* Lyn Fairhurst

Be My Star ★★★

Romantic comedy drama
2001 · Austria/Ger · Colour · 65mins

Writer/director Valeska Grisebach makes her feature debut with this brief, Berlin-based drama about adolescent angst that's packed with incident and some perceptive observations. Slyly playing on the chasm in maturity that exists between underage girls and barely legal boys, the relationship between 14-year-old Nicole Gläser and the seemingly cocky Christopher Schöps is littered with cosy clinches and juvenile squabbles that are both coarsely comic and achingly acute. DP. In German with English subtitles.

Nicole Gläser *Nicole* • Monique Gläser • Jeanine Gläser • Christopher Schöps *Christopher* • Marcel Eichelberger • Anika Jahn • Nicole Lehmann • Sebastian Rinka ■ *Dir/Scr* Valeska Grisebach

The Beach ★★★★ 15

Adventure thriller
2000 · US/UK · Colour · 114mins

This film from the *Trainspotting* team takes a tour round the mind of Leonardo DiCaprio, a young backpacker seeking adventure in Thailand who gets more than he bargained for when drug-crazed madman Robert Carlyle tells him the location of a secret beach. John Hodge's clever, witty script keeps the narrative firmly on track, while leaving director Danny Boyle ample room to luxuriate in the Orient's visual delights. DiCaprio gives a mature, multi-layered performance, and Virginie Ledoyen is a great find as the love interest. SR. Contains violence, swearing, drug abuse and nudity. DVD

Leonardo DiCaprio *Richard* • Tilda Swinton *Sal* • Virginie Ledoyen *Françoise* • Guillaume Canet *Etienne* • Robert Carlyle *Daffy* • Paterson Joseph *Keaty* • Lars Arentz Hansen *Bugs* • Daniel York *Hustler* ■ *Dir* Danny Boyle • *Scr* John Hodge, from the novel by Alex Garland

Beach Blanket Bingo ★★

Comedy 1965 · US · Colour · 100mins

A mindless, pointless title for a mindless, pointless movie, unless you happen to be a fan of American-International's stream of post-*Beach Party* teen films, many of which never played at cinemas in the UK. For those who care, this yet again features those oh-so-nice singing stars Frankie Avalon and Annette Funicello, and it's sad to see the great Buster Keaton paying the rent with a walk-on cameo. The music is utter drivel and the direction nonexistent, but it's an extraordinary time capsule to wonder at. TS

Frankie Avalon *Frankie* • Annette Funicello *Dee Dee* • Deborah Walley *Bonnie Graham* • Harvey Lembeck *Eric Von Zipper* • John Ashley *Steve Gordon* • Jody McCrea *Bonehead* • Linda Evans *Sugar Kane* • Don Rickles *Big Drop* • Paul Lynde *Bullets* • Buster Keaton ■ *Dir* William Asher • *Scr* Sher Townsend, Leo Townsend

Beach Party ★★★ U

Comedy 1963 · US · Colour · 97mins

The first, and best, of AIP's phenomenally successful surfin' series. These naive frolics proved to a British audience that America, post-Beatles, was positively archaic. Viewed charitably (is there any other way?), this teen-slanted Frankie Avalon/ Annette Funicello beach romp is not without charm, though the inclusion of grown-ups Bob Cummings and Dorothy Malone wastes two usually likeable screen performers in a subplot of astounding banality that looks as though it was filmed separately from the rest of the movie. TS

Bob Cummings [Robert Cummings] *Professor Sutwell* • Dorothy Malone *Marianne* • Frankie Avalon *Frankie* • Annette Funicello *Dolores* • Harvey Lembeck *Eric Von Zipper* • Jody McCrea *Deadhead* • John Ashley *Ken* • Morey Amsterdam *Cappy* • Eva Six *Ava* ■ *Dir* William Asher • *Scr* Lou Rusoff

Beach Red ★★★★ 12

Second World War drama
1967 · US · Colour · 99mins

Former beefcake star Cornel Wilde became a maverick director to reckon with in later life, producing self-starring vehicles, invariably also featuring his wife, Jean Wallace, as co-star. This ferocious Pacific war opus is one of his better efforts, an uncompromising movie with minimal narrative. The film's editing, by *Bullitt's* Frank P Keller, is stunning, and was rightly

U = SUITABLE FOR ALL Uc = SUITABLE FOR ALL, ESPECIALLY FOR YOUNG CHILDREN (VIDEO ONLY) PG = PARENTAL GUIDANCE

Oscar nominated, and the depiction of war's savagery is truly remarkable: no one who has seen this film will ever forget the shot of the soldier leaving his arm behind on the beach. TS. Contains violence and nudity. [video]

Cornel Wilde *Captain MacDonald* • Rip Torn *Sergeant Honeywell* • Dewey Stinger III *Mouse* • Patrick Wolfe *Cliff* • Burr DeBenning *Egan* • Jean Wallace *Julie MacDonald* • Linda Albertano *Girl in Baltimore* • Jan Garrison *Susie* • Gene Blakely *Goldberg* ■ *Dir* Cornel Wilde • *Scr* Clint Johnston, Donald A Peters, Jefferson Pascal, from the novel *Sunday Red Beach* by Peter Bowman

The Beachcomber ★★ U

Drama 1954 · UK · Colour · 78mins

W Somerset Maugham's story of the drunken derelict who is reformed by a prissy missionary had been filmed under its original title, *Vessel of Wrath*, in 1938 with Charles Laughton and Elsa Lanchester in the leads. Robert Newton seems so aware of the stature of Laughton's performance that he allows his own to lapse into a slurred variation on Long John Silver. Newton's blustering blows poor Glynis Johns and the rest of a decent cast off the screen. DP [video]

Robert Newton *Ted* • Glynis Johns *Martha* • Donald Sinden *Ewart Gray* • Paul Rogers *Owen* • Donald Pleasence *Tromp* • Walter Crisham *Vederala* • Michael Hordern *Headman* • Auric Lorand *Alfred* ■ *Dir* Muriel Box • *Scr* Sydney Box, from the story *Vessel of Wrath* by W Somerset Maugham

Beaches ★★★ 12

Drama 1988 · US · Colour · 118mins

This movie about a lifetime friendship between two women stars powerhouse Bette Midler and Barbara Hershey. They both make the most of their roles as two girls from different backgrounds who meet as 11-year-olds and remain friends over the years. Garry Marshall directs slickly and Hershey is very appealing as a poor little rich girl, but the movie belongs to the astonishing Midler, playing a brash, selfish singer. It's at its best when Midler gives free rein to her character rather than when it slips into schmaltz. SH. Contains swearing. [video] DVD

Bette Midler *CC Bloom* • Barbara Hershey *Hillary Whitney Essex* • John Heard *John Pierce* • Spalding Gray *Dr Richard Milstein* • Lainie Kazan *Leona Bloom* • James Read *Michael Essex* • Grace Johnston *Victoria Essex* ■ *Dir* Garry Marshall • *Scr* Mary Agnes Donoghue, from the novel by Iris Rainer Dart

Beachhead ★★

Second World War drama
1954 · US · Colour · 89mins

Tony Curtis served in the US Navy during the Second World War and saw action in the South Pacific; he was then stationed on Guam, where many Japanese were imprisoned. Perhaps that explains why he got rather emotionally involved in this otherwise unexceptional war movie, set in the Solomon Islands. Curtis is a marine who goes behind enemy lines on a spying mission, prior to a bombing raid on a Japanese base. AT

Tony Curtis *Burke* • Frank Lovejoy *Sergeant Fletcher* • Mary Murphy *Nina* • Eduard Franz *Bouchard* • Skip Homeier *Reynolds* • John Doucette *Major Scott* • Alan Wells *Biggerman* ■ *Dir* Stuart Heisler • *Scr* Richard Alan Simmons, from the novel *I've Got Mine* by Richard G Hubler

Bean ★★★★ PG

Comedy 1997 · UK · Colour · 85mins

This very enjoyable American outing for Rowan Atkinson's celebrated TV character has the bumbling Bean jetting off to the States to oversee the unveiling of the newly acquired Whistler's Mother. There are some familiar sketches, but the cohesive, engaging and fast-moving story is perfectly suited to Atkinson's singular style of physical comedy – his close encounter with "America's greatest painting" is an absolute riot. Peter MacNicol's anxiety-ridden American host is the perfect foil to Atkinson and Burt Reynolds is, well, Burt Reynolds in a general's uniform. The film was a massive international hit and deservedly so. JC [video] DVD

Rowan Atkinson *Mr Bean* • Peter MacNicol *David Langley* • Pamela Reed *Alison Langley* • Harris Yulin *George Grierson* • Burt Reynolds *General Newton* • Larry Drake *Elmer* • Chris Ellis *Detective Butler* • Johnny Galecki *Stingo Wheelie* ■ *Dir* Mel Smith • *Scr* Richard Curtis, Robin Driscoll, from the character created by Rowan Atkinson, Richard Curtis

The Beans of Egypt, Maine ★★★ 18

Drama 1994 · US · Colour · 95mins

This drama – co-produced for TV's *American Playhouse* – is based on the novel by Carolyn Chute and follows the life and loves of the Bean family, who live in the small town of Egypt. Focusing particularly on randy young Beal (Patrick McGaw) and his relationship with a feisty neighbour (Martha Plimpton, who narrates the tale), this doesn't quite capture the full depth of the novel, but features nice performances from Plimpton, Kelly Lynch and Rutger Hauer. Released on video in the UK under the title *Forbidden Choices*. JB [video]

Martha Plimpton *Earlene Pomerleau* • Kelly Lynch *Roberta Bean* • Rutger Hauer *Reuben Bean* • Patrick McGaw *Beal Bean* • Michael MacRae *Cole Deveraux* • Ariana Lamon-Anderson *Bonnie Loo* ■ *Dir* Jennifer Warren • *Scr* Bill Phillips, from the novel by Carolyn Chute

The Bear ★★★★ PG

Adventure 1988 · Fr · Colour · 89mins

A (tooth-)ripping yarn by director Jean-Jacques Annaud, this tells of the adventures of a small bear, befriended by a larger cousin who is a tempting target for a couple of trappers. It's filmed with enormous expertise and the eco-warrior case is put with great sympathy, but its anthropomorphism makes it seem like a glossy and more symbolic version of the Disney real-life stories that used to be all the rage in the 1960s. TH [video]

Jack Wallace *Bill* • Tcheky Karyo *Tom* • André Lacombe *Joseph, the dog handler* ■ *Dir* Jean-Jacques Annaud • *Scr* Gérard Brach, John Brownjohn, Alexander Whitelaw, from the novel *The Grizzly King* by James Oliver Curwood • *Cinematographer* Philippe Rousselot

Bear Island ★ PG

Action thriller
1979 · UK/Can · Colour · 102mins

Obviously unimpressed by Alistair MacLean's story of fascists bidding for world domination by means of meteorological mastery, director Don Sharp rejects plot in favour of a series of earnest conversations in ludicrous accents and a glut of action sequences which never threaten to set pulses racing. DP. Contains some swearing and violence. [video]

Donald Sutherland *Frank Lansing* • Vanessa Redgrave *Hedi Lindquist* • Richard Widmark *Otto Gerran* • Christopher Lee *Lechinski* • Barbara Parkins *Judith Ruben* • Lloyd Bridges *Smithy* • Lawrence Dane *Paul Hartman* • Patricia Collins *Inge Van Zipper* ■ *Dir* Don Sharp • *Scr* David Butler, Murray Smith, Don Sharp, from the novel by Alistair MacLean

The Bears and I ★★ U

Adventure 1974 · US · Colour · 88mins

In attempting to follow in his father John's footsteps, Patrick Wayne set himself a mission impossible. A decade after he appeared in the last in a series of westerns with the Duke himself, Patrick struck out on his own in this passable live-action adventure from Disney. Playing a Vietnam veteran who settles in a national park, he finds himself with the dual problem of preventing native American land from falling into the hands of racist rednecks and of raising a trio of mischievous bear cubs. DP

Patrick Wayne *Bob Leslie* • Chief Dan George *Chief A-Tas-Ka-Nay* • Andrew Duggan *Commissioner Gaines* • Michael Ansara *Oliver Red Fern* • Robert Pine *John McCarten* • Val DeVargas *Sam Eagle Speaker* ■ *Dir* Bernard McEveety • *Scr* John Whedon, from the novel by Robert Franklin Leslie

Beast Cops ★★★ 18

Action thriller 1998 · HK · Colour · 104mins

This violent cop thriller cleaned up at the Hong Kong Film Awards in 1999. Anthony Wong is the hard-nosed detective who is prepared to bend all sorts of laws in the constant battle with the Triads; Michael Wong is his more conventional superior, uneasy about his colleague's relationship with the criminal fraternity. It's a familiar enough story but the raw, unflinching direction by Gordon Chan and Dante Lam gives it a gritty ring of truth and the splashes of violence are unsettling. JF. In Cantonese and English with subtitles. [video] DVD

Michael Wong Man-Tak [Michael Wong] *Michael Cheung* • Anthony Wong Chau-Sang [Anthony Wong (1)] *Tung* • Kathy Chow Hoi-Mei *Yoyo* • Roy Cheung Yiu-Yeung [Roy Cheung] *Big Brother* • Sam Lee Chan-Sam [Sam Lee] *Lam* • Patrick Tam Yiu-Man *Ah Wah* ■ *Dir* Gordon Chan Ka-Seung [Gordon Chan], Dante Lam Chiu-yin • *Scr* Gordon Chan, Steve Chan Hing-kai

Beast from Haunted Cave ★★

Horror 1959 · US · BW · 67mins

Crooks hiding out in a ski resort get their comeuppance at the paws of a cave-dwelling snow beast. This is a painless, cost-conscious effort typical of producer Roger Corman, made by his company and filmed in Deadwood, South Dakota. Yet it is infused with flair and imagination by director Monte Hellman. Hellman later directed the cult westerns *Ride in the Whirlwind* (1965) and *The Shooting* (1967), and this unusual mobster versus monster melange shows his early promise. AJ

Michael Forest *Gill* • Sheila Carol *Gypsy* • Frank Wolff *Alex* • Richard Sinatra *Marty* • Wally Campo *Byron* • Linne Ahlstrand *Natalie* ■ *Dir* Monte Hellman • *Scr* Charles B Griffith

The Beast from 20,000 Fathoms ★★★★ PG

Science-fiction adventure
1953 · US · BW · 76mins

The first prehistoric-monster-on-the-rampage feature and arguably the best. It marked the solo debut of special effects genius Ray Harryhausen, who would refine his stop-motion puppetry in the Sinbad fantasies and *Jason and the Argonauts*. Freed from a prehistoric hibernation by an atomic blast at the North Pole, the monster tramples through New York and ends up taking a bite out of the Coney Island roller coaster. This was the *Jurassic Park* of its day and spawned countless imitations. AJ DVD

Paul Christian *Tom Nesbitt* • Paula Raymond *Lee Hunter* • Cecil Kellaway *Professor Elson* • Kenneth Tobey *Colonel Evans* • Jack Pennick *Jacob* • Donald Woods *Captain Jackson* • Lee Van Cleef *Corporal Stone* • Steve Brodie *Sergeant Loomis* ■ *Dir* Eugène Lourié • *Scr* Lou Morheim, Fred Freiberger, from the story *The Fog Horn* by Ray Bradbury

The Beast in the Cellar ★ 15

Horror 1970 · UK · Colour · mins

Two sinister sisters hide a dark secret in their basement in this ponderously talky horror tale. With the title revealing all, James Kelly has nowhere interesting to go and what little atmosphere he initially conjures up is soon dissipated in a pretty tedious, badly constructed and unsuspenseful affair. AJ. Contains violence. DVD

Beryl Reid *Ellie Ballantyne* • Flora Robson *Joyce Ballantyne* • Tessa Wyatt *Joanna Sutherland* • John Hamill *Corporal Alan Marlow* • TP McKenna *Superintendent Paddick* • David Dodimead *Dr Spencer* • Christopher Chittell *Baker* ■ *Dir/Scr* James Kelly

The Beast Must Die ★★ 15

Horror 1974 · UK · Colour · 87mins

A clumsily contrived variation on the old dark house whodunnit, in which one of the guests invited to eccentric Calvin Lockhart's hunting lodge is not merely a murderer but a werewolf to boot. Even with the lame "werewolf break" gimmick (the film suddenly stops and viewers are asked to guess the lurking lycanthrope's identity), it all boils down to the same horror clichés, with the wolf rather too obviously played by a dressed-up dog. Ever-reliable Peter Cushing turns in top work as a Nordic professor. AJ. Contains violence. [video] DVD

Calvin Lockhart *Tom Newcliffe* • Peter Cushing *Dr Christopher Lundgren* • Charles Gray *Bennington* • Anton Diffring *Pavel* • Marlene Clark *Caroline Newcliffe* • Ciaran Madden *Davina Gilmore* • Tom Chadbon *Paul Foote* • Michael Gambon *Jan Jarmokowski* ■ *Dir* Paul Annett • *Scr* Michael Winder, from the story *There Shall Be No Darkness* by James Blish

The Beast of Hollow Mountain ★★

Science-fiction western
1956 · US/Mex · Colour · 81mins

Based on a story by *King Kong* animator Willis O'Brien, this low-budget production could have done with his stop-motion skills. When the tyrannosaurus finally makes its long-awaited entrance in this cowboys versus prehistoric monster saga, its appearance is a disappointment. Shot in Mexico, this tells the tale of greedy land barons, with Guy Madison giving a plucky performance as a rancher and Patricia Medina making a decent heroine, but their efforts are overshadowed by the hokey effects. AJ

Guy Madison *Jimmy Ryan* • Patricia Medina *Sarita* • Eduardo Noriega (1) *Enrique Rios* • Carlos Rivas *Felipe Sanchez* ■ *Dir* Edward Nassour, Ismael Rodriguez • *Scr* Robert Hill, Jack DeWitt, from the story *Valley of the Mist* by Willis H O'Brien

The Beast of the City ★★★

Crime drama 1932 · US · BW · 86mins

In direct response to a request by President Herbert Hoover that the police be glorified on screen rather than gangsters, MGM turned out this crusading drama with Walter Huston well cast as the incorruptible police chief waging war on Jean Hersholt's big shot and his empire of crime. Jean Harlow puts in a torrid appearance as the gangster's moll who proves irresistible to Huston's younger brother, played by Wallace Ford. AE

Walter Huston *Jim Fitzpatrick* • Jean Harlow *Daisy* • Wallace Ford *Edward Fitzpatrick* • Jean Hersholt *Sam Belmonte* • Dorothy Peterson *Mary Fitzpatrick* • Tully Marshall *Michaels* • John Miljan *District attorney* • Emmett Corrigan *Chief of Police* • Sandy Roth *Mac* • Mickey Rooney *Mickey Fitzpatrick* ■ *Dir* Charles Brabin • *Scr* John Lee Mahin, from the story by WR Burnett

B

The Beast of War ★★★ 18

War drama 1988 · US · Colour · 109mins

Yet another movie to prove that war is hell. And yet, with its exotic locations and intense relationships, director Kevin Reynolds's carefully balanced drama brings its message home with a fierce urgency. Set in 1981 during the second year of the Soviet-Afghan war, the beast of the title is a Soviet tank that has helped raze a village to the ground and, becoming separated from its unit, is trapped in a mountainous dead-end by guerrillas bent on reprisals. Emotions within the tank are overheated, with paranoid commander George Dzundza at odds with crew member Jason Patric. TH. In English and Pashtu with subtitles. Contains violence and swearing. DVD

George Dzundza *Daskal* • Jason Patric *Koverchenko* • Steven Bauer *Taj* • Stephen Baldwin *Golikov* • Don Harvey *Kaminski* • Kabir Bedi *Akbar* • Erick Avari *Samad* ■ *Dir* Kevin Reynolds • *Scr* William Mastrosimone, from his play *Nanawatai*

The Beast with a Million Eyes ★★

Science fiction 1955 · US · BW · 79mins

Made for a paltry $23,000, this Roger Corman executive-produced allegory has been written off because of its peculiar premise and its bargain-basement effects. The prospect of watching birds and barnyard animals turning on humans at the behest of a malevolent alien force may, indeed, seem preposterous. As does the rationale that this evil entity can be tamed by folksy, American love. But the notion that we are being watched over by a potentially malicious presence is actually rather provocative. Flawed, but laudably unconventional. DP

Paul Birch *Allan Kelley* • Lorna Thayer *Carol Kelley* • Dona Cole *Sandy Kelley* • Dick Sargent *Deputy Larry Brewster* • Leonard Tarver *"Him"* • Chester Conklin *Old Man Webber* ■ *Dir* David Kramarsky • *Scr* Tom Filer

The Beast with Five Fingers ★★★★ 15

Horror 1946 · US · BW · 81mins

Peter Lorre acts deliciously deranged, as only he can, when the severed hand of a dead concert pianist returns from the grave to haunt his tortured soul. Or is he just imagining it? Lorre steals the show with a masterfully bravura performance in a superior slice of psychological horror, marshalling the sinister staples of mythic madness and macabre music into a satisfying scare-fest. Give a big hand to Robert Florey for his adept direction, and to the key special effect itself (which Luis Buñuel had a hand in), a marvellously nightmarish image. AJ

Robert Alda *Bruce Conrad* • Andrea King *Julie Holden* • Peter Lorre *Hilary Cummins* • Victor Francen *Francis Ingram* • J Carrol Naish *Ovidio Castanio* • Charles Dingle *Raymond Arlington* • John Alvin *Donald Arlington* • David Hoffman *Duprex* ■ *Dir* Robert Florey • *Scr* Curt Siodmak, from a story by William Fryer Harvey

The Beast Within ★★★

Psychological drama
1995 · Den · Colour · 79mins

This unstinting rite-of-passage picture established the Nimbus company, which transformed Danish cinema through its sponsorship of Dogme 95. Bemused by his mother's relationships with her husband, the vicar and his headmaster, Cyron Bjorn Melville seeks sinister solace in assuming the demonic personality secretly summoned in the woods by his mischievous friends. Carsten Rudolf's strikingly composed comedy benefits from exceptional support playing from Jens Okking and Soren Pilmark. DP. A Danish language film.

Cyron Bjorn Melville *Frederik* • Jens Okking *Otto Steppe* • Michelle Bjorn-Andersen *Marie Andersen* • Soren Pilmark *Vicar* ■ *Dir/Scr* Carsten Rudolf

The Beastmaster ★★★ 15

Fantasy action adventure
1982 · US · Colour · 113mins

A daft sword-and-sorcery fantasy adventure from director Don Coscarelli of *Phantasm* fame. Muscleman Marc Singer is Dar, a prehistoric Doctor Dolittle, who can telepathically talk to jungle animals and uses them to battle evil magician Maax (an over-the-top Rip Torn), the plunderer of his barbarian village. Lots of glitzy special effects, zombie guards in bondage gear and some amazing animal stunts spice up the proceedings. AJ. Contains violence and brief nudity. DVD

Marc Singer *Dar* • Tanya Roberts *Kiri* • Rip Torn *Maax* • John Amos *Seth* • Josh Milrad *Tal* • Rod Loomis *Zed* • Ten Hammer *Young Dar's father* • Ralph Strait *Sacco* • Billy Jacoby *Young Dar* ■ *Dir* Don Coscarelli • *Scr* Don Coscarelli, Paul Pepperman, from the novel by Andre Norton

Beastmaster 2: through the Portal of Time ★★★ PG

Fantasy action adventure
1991 · US · Colour · 102mins

This better-than-average sequel to *The Beastmaster* has benevolent barbarian Dar (Marc Singer) following evil ruler Arklon (Wings Hauser) through a time gate, opened by sorceress Sarah Douglas, to modern-day Los Angeles. Arklon wants the "neutron detonator" to secure world domination; Dar – aided by his trusty eagle, tiger and two ferrets – tries to stop him. It's a likeable, comic book fantasy tinged with light camp comedy. A second sequel (1995) was not up to the same standard. AJ

Marc Singer *Dar* • Wings Hauser *Arklon* • Sarah Douglas *Lyranna* • Kari Wuhrer *Jackie Trent* • James Avery *Captain Coberly* • Robert Fieldsteel *Bendowski* • Robert Z'Dar *Zavik* ■ *Dir* Sylvio Tabet • *Scr* Jim Wynorski, RJ Robertson, Sylvio Tabet, Ken Hauser, Doug Miles, from the story by Jim Wynorski, RJ Robertson, from the characters created by Paul Pepperman, Don Coscarelli, from the novel *The Beastmaster* by Andre Norton

The Beat Generation ★★

Psychological detective drama
1959 · US · BW · 94mins

This is one of those mesmerisingly bad productions with a sordid storyline and a compulsively watchable eclectic period cast. Here we've got tough detective Steve Cochran on the hunt for a sex killer, along the way meeting the likes of blonde sexpot Mamie Van Doren, sex kitten Fay Spain and sexy Maggie Hayes. Talented director Charles Haas makes the grim goings-on compulsive viewing, though without much conviction. TS

Steve Cochran *Dave Culloran* • Mamie Van Doren *Georgia Altera* • Ray Danton *Stan Hess* • Fay Spain *Francee Culloran* • Louis Armstrong • Maggie Hayes [Margaret Hayes] *Joyce Greenfield* • Jackie Coogan *Jake Baron* • Jim Mitchum [James Mitchum] *Art Jester* • Ray Anthony *Harry Altera* • Vampira *Poetess* • Charles Chaplin Jr *Lover Boy* ■ *Dir* Charles Haas • *Scr* Richard Matheson, Lewis Meltzer

Beat Girl ★★ 12

Drama 1960 · UK · BW · 88mins

Beatnik parties in backstreet sin cellars, nights in sleazy Soho strip joints, unsupervised drag racing – it's easy to see why this raucous juvenile-delinquency romp raised eyebrows and scared adults back in 1960. But the failed attempt to launch Adam Faith as yet another of Britain's answers to Elvis Presley is now a great pop history lesson in teenage attitudes and rock 'n' roll rebellion, complete with cool jive talk and swinging sounds from the John Barry Seven. AJ. Contains mild swearing and brief nudity.

David Farrar *Paul Linden* • Noelle Adam *Nichole* • Christopher Lee *Kenny* • Gillian Hills *Jennifer* • Adam Faith *Dave* • Shirley Anne Field *Dodo* • Peter McEnery *Tony* • Claire Gordon *Honey* • Oliver Reed *Plaid shirt* ■ *Dir* Edmond T Gréville • *Scr* Dail Ambler

Beat Street ★★ 15

Musical dance drama
1984 · US · Colour · 101mins

Although it trades in such 1980s phenomena as break-dancing, rapping and graffiti, this exploitative teen pic proves only that the "puttin' on a show" formula has changed little since the days of Judy Garland and Mickey Rooney. Director Stan Lathan doggedly attempts to depict the degradation in which many inner-city black Americans are forced to live. But DJ Guy Davis and spray-can artist Jon Chardiet are stereotypes and, while the latter's subway murder is effectively handled, the former's romance with student Rae Dawn Chong is unconvincing. DP

Rae Dawn Chong *Tracy* • Guy Davis *Kenny* • Jon Chardiet *Ramon* • Leon W Grant *Chollie* • Saundra Santiago *Carmen* • Robert Taylor (2) *Lee* • Lee Chamberlin *Alicia* • Mary Alice *Cora* ■ *Dir* Stan Lathan • *Scr* Andrew Davis, David Gilbert, Paul Golding, from a story by Steven Hager • *Music* Harry Belafonte, Arthur Baker

Beat the Devil ★★★ U

Comedy thriller 1953 · UK/It · BW · 89mins

This sophisticated international romp (co-scripted by Truman Capote and John Huston) must have been more fun to make than to watch. Nevertheless, the splendid cast ensures that the jokes play and the romance works. Peter Lorre and Humphrey Bogart work again here with Huston, with support from Jennifer Jones as the wife of oh-so-English Edward Underdown, and goonish gangsters Robert Morley and Ivor Barnard. Not terribly well appreciated in its day, this quirky one-off has achieved something of a cult status. TS DVD

Humphrey Bogart *Billy Dannreuther* • Jennifer Jones *Gwendolen Chelm* • Gina Lollobrigida *Maria Dannreuther* • Robert Morley *Petersen* • Peter Lorre *O'Hara* • Edward Underdown *Harry Chelm* • Ivor Barnard *Major Ross* • Bernard Lee *CID Inspector* ■ *Dir* John Huston • *Scr* John Huston, Truman Capote, from the novel by James Helvick

The Beating of the Butterfly's Wings ★★★

Romantic drama 2000 · Fr · Colour · 90mins

This delightful comedy takes place in Paris over 24 hours and is centred on the rippling effects of chaos theory. Audrey Tatou plays a shopgirl whose horoscope has predicted she's about to meet the love of her life. But events conspire to keep her away from Faudel until fate ensures that a group of seemingly unrelated people conspire to effect their meeting. It's as if the City of Light is coaxing each member of the charming ensemble to do their bit for romance. DP. In French with English subtitles.

Audrey Tautou *Irène* • Faudel *Younès* • Eric Savin *Richard* • Irène Ismailoff *Stéphanie* • Eric Feldman *Luc* ■ *Dir/Scr* Laurent Firode

Beatrice Cenci ★★★

Historical tragedy 1969 · It · Colour · 99mins

Italian director Lucio Fulci regarded this blend of costume melodrama and stylised horror as his finest film. Opening on the morning of the Cenci family's execution, the action is constructed from a series of flashbacks that slowly reveals the fate of the brutal patriarch, George Wilson. But while the torture scenes deter the squeamish, they serve to highlight the unswerving loyalty of Tomas Milian as he seeks to prevent the unworldly Adrienne Larussa from suffering the consequences of her justifiable act of revenge. In stark contrast stands the duplicity of the Catholic Church. DP. Italian dialogue dubbed into English.

Tomas Milian *Olimpio* • Adrienne Larussa *Beatrice Cenci* • Georges Wilson *Cenci* • Raymond Pellegrin *Cardinal Lanciani* • Ignazio Spalla *Catalano* ■ *Dir* Lucio Fulci • *Scr* Lucio Fulci, Roberto Gianviti, from the play *The Cenci* by Percy Bysshe Shelley

Beau Brummell ★★★ U

Historical drama
1954 · US · Colour · 111mins

Robert Morley had the distinction of playing the late-18th century's two unhappiest monarchs: Louis XVI of France (in *Marie Antoinette*, for which he earned an Oscar nomination) and George III in this over-inflated historical pageant. Stewart Granger cuts a dashing figure as the Regency fop, whose life, loves and dress sense set tongues wagging. Faced with the exuberance of Morley, Granger and Peter Ustinov (deliciously affected as the Prince of Wales), Elizabeth Taylor seems a little daunted. DP

Stewart Granger *Beau Brummell* • Elizabeth Taylor *Lady Patricia* • Peter Ustinov *Prince of Wales* • Robert Morley *King George III* • James Donald *Lord Edwin Mercer* • James Hayter *Mortimer* • Rosemary Harris *Mrs Fitzherbert* • Paul Rogers *William Pitt* ■ *Dir* Curtis Bernhardt • *Scr* Karl Tunberg, from the play by Clyde Fitch

Beau Geste ★★★★

Silent adventure 1926 · US · BW · 101mins

One of the most popular films of the silent era and still a ripping yarn, thanks to the irresistible appeal of PC Wren's story and the flamboyance of the performances. Ronald Colman, Ralph Forbes and Neil Hamilton are the three English brothers who join the Foreign Legion in search of a family heirloom, the Blue Water diamond. The story unfolds in a series of flashbacks and revelations – quite complex and innovative for the time – and director Herbert Brenon has the knack of combining epic tragedy with lightweight adventure. AT

Ronald Colman *Michael "Beau" Geste* • Neil Hamilton *Digby Geste* • Ralph Forbes *John Geste* • Alice Joyce *Lady Brandon* • Mary Brian *Isobel* • Noah Beery *Sgt Lejaune* • Norman Trevor *Maj de Beaujolais* • William Powell *Boldini* • Victor McLaglen *Hank* ■ *Dir* Herbert Brenon • *Scr* Paul Schofield, John Russell, from the novel by PC Wren

Beau Geste ★★★★★ PG

Classic adventure 1939 · US · BW · 108mins

The definitive version of PC Wren's *Boys' Own* classic saga of the Foreign Legion and the events surrounding Fort Zinderneuf. Gary Cooper makes a perfect Beau, while Ray Milland and Robert Preston are well cast as his brothers John and Digby. Also watch out for a very young Donald O'Connor as Beau as a boy. Discerning viewers (and silent movie fans) will spot that this is virtually a shot-for-shot remake of the Ronald Colman version, but a major plus here (apart from sound) is the casting of Brian Donlevy as the evil Sergeant Markoff, who garnered an Oscar nomination. The heroic and romantic attitudes on display may now seem out of date, but that's the fault of the times, not the story. TS

Gary Cooper *Beau Geste* • Ray Milland *John Geste* • Robert Preston *Digby Geste* • Brian Donlevy *Sgt Markoff* • Susan Hayward *Isobel*

Rivers • J Carrol Naish *Rasinoff* • Albert Dekker *Schwartz* • Broderick Crawford *Hank Miller* • Charles Barton *Buddy McMonigal* ■ *Dir* William A Wellman • *Scr* Robert Carson, from the novel by PC Wren

Beau Geste ★★

Adventure 1966 · US · Colour · 104mins

This is the third – and by far the least impressive – adaptation of PC Wren's foreign legion yarn. Guy Stockwell isn't in the same league as Ronald Colman and Gary Cooper, and only Telly Savalas as the sadistic sergeant major comes close to matching his predecessors. Writer/director Douglas Heyes takes several liberties with the original story, most notably reducing the three Geste brothers to two and changing their nationality from English to American. The action scenes are well handled, however, and Bud Thackery's colour photography of the desert is eye-catching. AT

Telly Savalas *Sergeant Major Dagineau* • Guy Stockwell *Beau* • Doug McClure *John* • Leslie Nielsen *Lieutenant De Ruse* • Robert Wolders *Fouchet* • David Mauro *Boldini* • Leo Gordon *Krauss* ■ *Dir* Douglas Heyes • *Scr* Douglas Heyes, from the novel by PC Wren

Beau Ideal ★★

Adventure 1931 · US · BW · 82mins

Beau Geste was such a huge success in 1926 that Paramount knocked out a quickie sequel, *Beau Sabreur*, two years later. This is the second sequel to the original film; Ralph Forbes returns as John Geste, as does original director Herbert Brenon. This time around, John meets up with his childhood buddy in the foreign legion. Loretta Young is the girl back in England who keeps their hearts fluttering and perpetuates their romantic rivalry. AT

Frank McCormack *Carl Neyer* • Ralph Forbes *John Geste* • Lester Vail *Otis Madison* • Otto Matieson *Jacob Levine* • Don Alvarado *Ramon Gonzales* • Bernard Siegel *Ivan Radinoff* • Irene Rich *Lady Brandon* • Myrtle Stedman *Mrs Frank Madison* • Loretta Young *Isobel Brandon* ■ *Dir* Herbert Brenon • *Scr* Elizabeth Meehan, from the novel by PC Wren

Beau James ★★★★

Biographical drama
1957 · US · Colour · 106mins

Bob Hope had been successful in a sentimental semi-comic role in *The Seven Little Foys*, and here he is reunited with the under-rated writer/director Melville Shavelson for this sparkling biopic of New York's flamboyant former mayor Jimmy Walker. Hope is superb, effortlessly capturing the cynicism and brashness of this son of the Roaring Twenties, and there's a fine support cast. Walter Winchell, the narrator of *The Untouchables* on TV, narrated the American version, with Alistair Cooke, his equivalent in Britain, lending an authenticity belied by the glamorised and inaccurate screen story. TS

Bob Hope *Jimmy Walker* • Vera Miles *Betty Compton* • Paul Douglas *Chris Nolan* • Alexis Smith *Allie Walker* • Darren McGavin *Charley Hand* • Joe Mantell *Bernie Williams* • Horace McMahon *Prosecutor* • Richard Shannon *Dick Jackson* ■ *Dir* Melville Shavelson • *Scr* Jack Rose, Melville Shavelson, from the book by Gene Fowler

Le Beau Mariage ★★★★ PG

Comedy drama 1982 · Fr · Colour · 95mins

Having impressed as an adolescent in *Claire's Knee*, Béatrice Romand is reunited with director Eric Rohmer for this bittersweet treatise on the clash between feminist and old-fashioned ideals, winning the Best Actress prize at Venice. The action flits between Paris and Le Mans as Romand's art student decides to quit the romantic rat race and find a husband. However, it soon becomes clear that lawyer André Dussolier is immune to her charms and humiliation is in the offing. Bristling with life, Rohmer's slyly witty film is as chatty and keenly observed as ever. DP. In French with English subtitles. [video] DVD

Béatrice Romand *Sabine* • André Dussollier *Edmond* • Arielle Dombasle *Clarisse* • Feodor Atkine *Simon* • Huguette Faget *Antique dealer* • Thamila Mezbah *Mother* • Sophie Renoir *Lise* ■ *Dir/Scr* Eric Rohmer

Beau Sabreur ★★★

Silent adventure 1928 · US · BW · 67mins

In this silent movie, Gary Cooper elegantly disports himself in the desert, as a French legionnaire who is sent to the Sahara to negotiate a treaty with an oil-rich sheik and falls in love with Evelyn Brent on the way. It followed *Beau Geste* (1926), and was meant to use up pieces of leftover location film from the first movie. Cooper went on to star in the sound version of *Beau Geste* in 1939. TH

Gary Cooper *Major Henri de Beaujolais* • Evelyn Brent *May Vanbrugh* • Noah Beery Sr [Noah Beery] *Sheikh El Hamel* • William Powell *Becque* • Mitchell Lewis *Suleiman the Strong* • Frank Reicher *Gen de Beaujolais* • Oscar Smith *Djikki* ■ *Dir* John Waters (1) • *Scr* Tom J Geraghty [Tom Geraghty] (story), Julian Johnson (titles), from the story by PC Wren

Le Beau Serge ★★★★ 12

Drama 1958 · Fr · BW · 94mins

Traditionally hailed as the first feature of the French New Wave, Claude Chabrol's inconsistent debut was made while he was still working as a film critic, with a small sum inherited by his wife. The picture's American title, *Bitter Reunion*, sums up the story, in which Jean-Claude Brialy returns home to find that his gifted childhood friend Gérard Blain has destroyed his life through drink. Shunning the directorial pyrotechnics associated with contemporaries such as Godard and Truffaut, Chabrol coaxes intelligent performances from his leads and makes effective use of Sardent, the town where he spent part of his own youth. DP. In French with English subtitles. [video]

Gérard Blain *Serge* • Jean-Claude Brialy *François Bayon* • Michèle Meritz *Yvonne* • Bernadette Lafont *Marie* • Edmond Beauchamp *Glomaud* • Claude Cerval *The curé* • André Dino *Michel, the doctor* ■ *Dir/Scr* Claude Chabrol

Beau Travail ★★★★ 15

Psychological drama
1999 · Fr · Colour · 89mins

Translating Herman Melville's *Billy Budd* from the 18th-century Royal Navy to the modern Foreign Legion, Claire Denis has produced a simmering study of petty tyranny, fatuous duty and homoerotic repression. Spurning the barked histrionics of American boot camp pictures, she uses stylised rhythms to convey the ennui endured by an isolated unit in Djibouti. As the sergeant seized by a pathological hatred of new recruit Grégoire Colin, Denis Lavant gives a remarkable, almost wordless performance that culminates in some astonishing disco gyrations. DP. In French with English subtitles. [video] DVD

Denis Lavant *Galoup* • Michel Subor *Commander* • Grégoire Colin *Sentain* • Richard Courcet *Legionnaire* ■ *Dir* Claire Denis • *Scr* Claire Denis, Jean-Pol Fargeau, from the novella *Billy Budd, Sailor* by Herman Melville

Beaumarchais l'Insolent ★★★ 15

Historical biographical drama
1996 · Fr · Colour · 96mins

Edouard Molinaro directs this breathless biopic of one of France's most dashing heroes, Beaumarchais. In chronicling the playwright's more picturesque activities, from law reform to arms dealing and espionage, fact and fantasy become entangled and there's barely room to mention his love life, let alone celebrate his literary achievement. However, Fabrice Luchini's vibrant performance ensures this isn't merely a series of elegant tableaux, while Molinaro evokes the theatrical milieu to give the action a true sense of pageant and place. DP. In French with English subtitles. [video]

Fabrice Luchini *Pierre-Augustin Caron de Beaumarchais* • Manuel Blanc *Gudin* • Sandrine Kiberlain *Marie-Thérèse* • Michel Serrault *Louis XV* • Jacques Weber *Duc de Chaulnes* • Michel Piccoli *Prince de Conti* • Jean-François Balmer *Sartine* ■ *Dir* Edouard Molinaro • *Scr* Edouard Molinaro, Jean-Claude Brisville, from a play by Sacha Guitry

La Beauté du Diable ★★★

Fantasy drama 1949 · Fr/It · BW · 95mins

René Clair is arguably the finest director of comic fantasy in screen history. Though he does not quite hit the heights here, this is still a sparkling version of the Faust legend. The picture uses stylised sets similar to those of pioneer film-maker Georges Méliès and poet-director Jean Cocteau to create a world touched more by magic than evil. Clair's cutest trick, however, is to have Michel Simon and Gérard Philipe swap places after the former sells his soul in return for the latter's devilish good looks. DP. In French with English subtitles.

Michel Simon *Old Mephistopheles/Faust* • Gérard Philipe *Young Faust/Mephistopheles* • Simone Valère *Princess* • Nicole Besnard *Marguerite* • Carlo Ninchi *Prince* • Paolo Stoppa *Prosecutor* ■ *Dir* René Clair • *Scr* René Clair, Armand Salacrou

The Beautician and the Beast ★★ PG

Romantic comedy
1997 · US · Colour · 102mins

Fran Drescher made her name as the "hostess with the mostest" in *This Is Spinal Tap*, and this was intended to kickstart her career on the big screen. It's actually not too bad, with Drescher playing the very "Noo Yawk" beautician who mistakenly winds up as governess to the family of the dictator (Timothy Dalton) of an Eastern European country and gradually melts his heart. JF. Contains sexual references. [video] DVD

Fran Drescher *Joy Miller* • Timothy Dalton *Boris Pochenko* • Ian McNeice *Grushinsky* • Patrick Malahide *Kleist* • Lisa Jakub *Katrina* • Michael Lerner *Jerry Miller* • Phyllis Newman *Judy Miller* • Adam LaVorgna *Karl* ■ *Dir* Ken Kwapis • *Scr* Todd Graff

Beautiful ★★

Comedy drama 2000 · US · Colour · 112mins

Actress Sally Field directs her debut feature which is yet another "tribute" to the beauty pageant. Minnie Driver stars as a girl obsessed with becoming Miss Illinois who is prepared to cheat fourfold to get there. Supported by the bizarrely unconditional love of best friend Joey Lauren Adams, Driver's supremacy is only threatened by exposure from TV news hack Leslie Stefanson. The problem is you care as little for Driver as you do for the principle of the pageant itself. LH

Minnie Driver *Mona* • Hallie Kate Eisenberg *Vanessa* • Joey Lauren Adams *Ruby* • Kathleen Turner *Verna Chickle* • Leslie Stefanson *Joyce Parkins* • Bridgette L Wilson [Bridgette Wilson] *Lorna Larkin, Miss Texas* • Kathleen Robertson *Wanda Love, Miss Tennessee* ■ *Dir* Sally Field • *Scr* Jon Bernstein

The Beautiful Blonde from Bashful Bend ★★★★

Comedy western 1949 · US · Colour · 76mins

Though one of Betty Grable's better vehicles, this burlesque western was considered to be one of the major catastrophes of 1949 – a setback for its talented writer/director Preston Sturges, who had acquired a reputation for churning out wacky and risqué comedies. Viewed today, however, this farce can be regarded as a comedy triumph for both star and director, fabulously photographed in that gloriously garish 1940s Technicolor. TS

Betty Grable *Freddie* • Cesar Romero *Blackie Jobero* • Rudy Vallee *Charles Hingleman* • Olga San Juan *Conchita* • Sterling Holloway *Basserman Boy* • Hugh Herbert *Doctor* • El Brendel *Mr Jorgenson* • Porter Hall *Judge O'Toole* ■ *Dir* Preston Sturges • *Scr* Preston Sturges, from a story by Earl Felton • *Cinematographer* Harry Jackson

Beautiful Boxer ★★★

Biographical action drama
2003 · Thai · Colour · 118mins

Nong Toom is one of the biggest names in muay thai (Thai boxing). However, this biopic of the transsexual kickboxer settles for a rags-to-riches approach that rarely allows us inside the mind of a gentle soul who took up a violent sport to help his troubled family. Former kickboxing champion Asanee Suwan plays Nong Toom and is suitably sweet as he struggles to reconcile his athletic prowess with a yearning to assume his true gender. While director Ekachai Uekrongtham stages the bouts with vigour, he rather tiptoes round Suwan's supposedly seismic identity crises. DP. In Thai and English with subtitles.

Asanee Suwan *Nong Toom* Parinya Chareonphol • Sorapong Chatree *Pi Chart* • Orn-anong Panyawong *Nong Toom's mother* • Kyoko Inoue *Kyoke Inoue* • Sitiporn Niyom *Nat* • Yuka Hyodo *Japanese fan* • Keagan Kang *Jack* • Nukkid Boonthong *Nong Toom's father* ■ *Dir* Ekachai Uekrongtham • *Scr* Ekachai Uekrongtham, Desmond Sim Kim Jin

Beautiful but Dangerous ★★ U

Comedy drama 1954 · US · BW · 88mins

Having bought RKO in 1948, Howard Hughes took a shine to Jean Simmons and imported her from England, casting her opposite Robert Mitchum in Otto Preminger's torrid *Angel Face*. Since the on-screen chemistry between the two stars was combustible, this second rendezvous was concocted; the mistake was to make it a comedy. Simmons plays an heiress with a guilt complex and Mitchum is the local doctor who rumbles her. Intended as a satire on small-town hypocrisy, it's stilted and slackly directed. AT

Robert Mitchum *Doc Sellars* • Jean Simmons *Corby Lane* • Arthur Hunnicutt *Otey* • Edgar Buchanan *Ad Meeker* • Wallace Ford *Joe* • Raymond Walburn *Judge Holbert* ■ *Dir* Lloyd Bacon • *Scr* DD Beauchamp, William Bowers, Richard Flournoy, from the story *Enough for Happiness* by DD Beauchamp

Beautiful but Dangerous ★★

Romantic drama
1955 · It/Fr · Colour · 102mins

This pallid period piece, shot in Italy (where it was known as *The World's Most Beautiful Woman*), was one of the last pictures made by Robert Z Leonard. Gina Lollobrigida plays Lina

Cavalieri, the 19th-century opera singer who finds love with Prince Sergei Bariatine (Vittorio Gassman), the Russian royal whom she had encountered many years before. A polished but plodding affair. DP. Italian dialogue dubbed into English.

Gina Lollobrigida *Lina Cavalieri* • Vittorio Gassman *Prince Sergei Bariatine* • Robert Alda *Doria* • Tamara Lees *Manolita* • Anne Vernon *Carmela* ■ *Dir* Robert Z Leonard • *Scr* Cesare Cavagna, Liana Ferri, Frank Gervasi, Mario Monicelli, Luciano Martino, Piero Pierotti, Franco Solinas, Giovanna Soria, from a story by Maleno Malenotti

The Beautiful Country ★★★

Drama 2004 · Nor/US · Colour · 136mins

Set in 1990, this lyrical, if slightly overlong, picaresque drama follows Damien Nguyen as he travels from a Far Eastern fishing village to America to find his Caucasian father. It's a harrowing adventure, but Norwegian director Hans Petter Moland finds exotic beauty and brutality alike in both the Eastern and North American settings and admirably resists sentimentality, though the relentless grimness may induce empathy fatigue. LF. In English, Vietnamese, Cantonese and Mandarin with subtitles.

Damien Nguyen *Binh* • Nick Nolte *Steve* • Tim Roth *Captain Oh* • Bai Ling *Ling* • Temuera Derek Morrison [Temuera Morrison] *Snakehead* • Tran Dang Qouc Thinh *Tam* • Chau Thi Kim Xuan *Mai* ■ *Dir* Hans Petter Moland • *Scr* Sabina Murray, Larry Gross, from a story by Lingard Jervey, from an idea by Terrence Malick

Beautiful Creatures ★★★ 18

Black comedy thriller
2000 · UK · Colour · 84mins

If you don't have a sensitive stomach when it comes to jet-black comedy involving sadomasochism, violence, drugs and corpses, this British gangster movie is certainly interesting. Rachel Weisz and Susan Lynch are two very different women brought together by violence, who then find themselves with a dead body on their hands. It's one of those films where everyone is trying to outwit and double-cross everyone else, but thanks to the stars' winning performances, this is a thoroughly enjoyable film. JB. Contains violence, swearing, drug abuse and sex scenes. [video] DVD

Rachel Weisz *Petula* • Susan Lynch *Dorothy* • Iain Glen *Tony* • Maurice Roëves *Ronnie McMinn* • Alex Norton *Detective Inspector George Hepburn* • Tom Mannion *Brian McMinn* ■ *Dir* Bill Eagles • *Scr* Simon Donald

Beautiful Dreamers ★★ 15

Period drama based on a true story
1990 · Can · Colour · 103mins

The under-rated Rip Torn gives a tour de force performance as legendary American poet Walt Whitman who, while visiting the London Asylum for the Insane in Ontario, encounters psychiatrist Dr Maurice Bucke (Colm Feore). The pair proceed to make waves with their revolutionary ideas on the treatment of mental illness. A little trite and predictable in places, this is more of a Disney-style history lesson than a dissection of Victorian attitudes towards madness. LH [video]

Colm Feore *Dr Maurice Bucke* • Rip Torn *Walt Whitman* • Wendel Meldrum *Jessie Bucke* • Sheila McCarthy *Molly Jessop* • Colin Fox *Rev Randolph Haines* • David Gardner *Dr Lett* ■ *Dir/Scr* John Kent Harrison

The Beautiful End of This World ★★

Thriller 1983 · W Ger · Colour · 90mins

For all their good intentions, films in the "Green Screen" tradition tend to approach their themes so earnestly that they often pay scant attention to the dramatic storylines that would make their propagandist message both more palatable and effective. This thriller, about a German chemical executive whose conscience is pricked while planning to build a chemical plant in the Australian wilds, is a sort of *Local Hero* without the laughs. Director Rainer Erler fails to capitalise on the local colour and lays on his ecological ideas with a trowel. DP. German dialogue dubbed into English.

Robert Atzorn *Dr Michael Brandt* • Claire Oberman *Elaine* • Götz George *Craig* • Judy Winter *Ursula* ■ *Dir/Scr* Rainer Erler

Beautiful Girls ★★★ 15

Comedy drama 1996 · US · Colour · 107mins

A starry cast illuminates this high-school reunion movie, though the end result is rather disappointingly low-key and lacking in sparkle. Timothy Hutton is the New York pianist at a crossroads in his life who returns to his small-town roots and is depressed to discover that his schoolmates are stuck in dead-end jobs. If director Ted Demme's situations are stereotypical, the film is made memorable by writer Scott Rosenberg's cutting dialogue and sharp-edged script. The bigger stars are upstaged by Natalie Portman as Hutton's intelligent and surprisingly mature teenage neighbour. LH. Contains violence, swearing, sexual references and drug abuse. [video] DVD

Matt Dillon *Tommy "Birdman" Rowland* • Timothy Hutton *Willie Conway* • Noah Emmerich *Michael "Mo" Morris* • Annabeth Gish *Tracy Stover* • Lauren Holly *Darian Smalls* • Rosie O'Donnell *Gina Barrisano* • Martha Plimpton *Jan* • Natalie Portman *Marty* • Michael Rapaport *Paul Kirkwood* • Mira Sorvino *Sharon Cassidy* • Uma Thurman *Andera* • David Arquette *Bobby Conway* ■ *Dir* Ted Demme • *Scr* Scott Rosenberg

Beautiful Joe ★★ 15

Romantic drama
2000 · UK/US · Colour · 93mins

Sharon Stone seizes the opportunity to shed her customary glamour in this rather old-fashioned entertainment. She plays a white-trash mom, who is pursued by gangsters after she steals a small fortune from Billy Connolly, an Irish florist who has been mistaken for a syndicate bigwig by crime boss Ian Holm. Shifting from Kentucky to Vegas, this caper comedy is short on laughs and even more bereft of originality. Stephen Metcalfe's direction is energetic, but uninspired. DP. Contains swearing and some violence and sex scenes. [video] DVD

Sharon Stone *Hush* • Billy Connolly *Joe* • Ian Holm *The geek* • Gil Bellows *Elton* • Jurnee Smollett *Vivien* ■ *Dir/Scr* Stephen Metcalfe

A Beautiful Mind ★★★ 12

Biographical drama
2001 · US · Colour · 129mins

The true story of maths genius John Forbes Nash Jr, who battled paranoid schizophrenia at the height of his academic success and eventually won the Nobel Prize, is tailor-made Oscar fare (it won four). It has the triumph-over-tragedy theme going for it, plus a powerhouse performance from Russell Crowe. Nash is presented as a difficult man with a complex psychological condition – reduced to a series of delusional episodes to furnish a thriller subplot – who has devoted his life to an almost insurmountably dry subject, namely advanced mathematics theory. Sadly, the film's overweening desire to be taken seriously gets in the way of the story. AC [video] DVD

Russell Crowe *John Forbes Nash Jr* • Ed Harris *William Parcher* • Jennifer Connelly *Alicia Larde Nash* • Paul Bettany *Charles Herman* • Adam Goldberg *Sol* • Judd Hirsch *Helinger* • Josh Lucas *Hansen* • Anthony Rapp *Bender* • Christopher Plummer *Dr Rosen* ■ *Dir* Ron Howard • *Scr* Akiva Goldsman, from the book *A Beautiful Mind: a Biography of John Forbes Nash Jr* by Sylvia Nasar

Beautiful People ★★★ 15

Comedy drama 1999 · UK · Colour · 103mins

Jasmin Dizdar's debut feature is a creditable achievement, especially bearing in mind it cost a mere £1.1 million. It includes snippets from an affair between a Tory MP's doctor daughter and an exiled war criminal, and follows a TV reporter filming a football hooligan's accidental transformation into a hero. These diverse plot strands ambitiously attempt to meld romance, black comedy and political critique. The ensemble cast brings commitment and wit to the proceedings, which, while rarely credible, are never dull. DP [video]

Rosalind Ayres *Nora Thornton* • Charlotte Coleman *Portia Thornton* • Edin Dzandzanovic *Pero Guzina* • Nicholas Farrell *Doctor Mouldy* • Siobhan Redmond ■ *Dir/Scr* Jasmin Dizdar

Beautiful Stranger ★

Crime drama 1954 · UK · BW · 89mins

Ginger Rogers, moving inexorably towards her sell-by date, stars in this thriller set on the French Riviera. She plays a woman who, let down by her wealthy and married racketeer lover Stanley Baker, contemplates killing herself but, instead, hooks up with Frenchman Jacques Bergerac and finds herself implicated in murder. Labyrinthine, depressing and unconvincing. RK

Ginger Rogers *Johnny Victor* • Herbert Lom *Emil Landosh* • Stanley Baker *Louis Galt* • Jacques Bergerac *Pierre Clement* • Margaret Rawlings *Marie Galt* • Eddie Byrne *Luigi* • Ferdy Mayne *Chief of Police* • Coral Browne *Helen* ■ *Dir* David Miller • *Scr* Robert Westerby, Carl Nystrom, from a story by Rip Van Ronkel, David Miller

The Beautiful Swindlers ★★

Portmanteau crime comedy
1964 · Fr/It/Jpn/Neth · BW · 90mins

Despite a promising premise, this is a pretty lame portmanteau picture. Things might have been better had Jean-Luc Godard decided not to withdraw his contribution and release it as the short, *Le Grand Escroc*. Yet, Claude Chabrol's *Paris*, in which a gullible hick buys the Eiffel Tower, has its amusing moments, while Hiromichi Horikawa's *Tokyo*, about a barmaid charged with murder after she attempts to pawn an old man's false teeth, smacks of life's grim desperation. Unlike the necklace at its core, Roman Polanski's *Amsterdam* is a gaudy bauble, while Ugo Gregoretti's *Naples* is a trivial anecdote about a double-dealing pimp. DP

Nicole Karen • Jan Tuelings • Gabriella Giorgelli • Jean-Pierre Cassel • Catherine Deneuve • Mie Hama ■ *Dir* Roman Polanski, Ugo Gregoretti, Claude Chabrol, Hiromichi Horikawa • *Scr* Roman Polanski, Gérard Brach

Beautiful Thing ★★★ 15

Drama 1995 · UK · Colour · 87mins

Two teenage neighbours on a London council estate discover they are gay in director Hettie MacDonald's urban fairy tale. How the boys deal with their sexual awakening is endearingly explored via a rough kitchen-sink backdrop, camp one-liners and a soundtrack leaning heavily on hits from Mama Cass. Newcomers Glen Berry and Scott Neal give purposely raw-edged performances to match their on-screen naivety, but it's Linda Henry who shines as the indomitable single mother. AJ. Contains violence, swearing and nudity. [video] DVD

Glen Berry *Jamie Gangel* • Linda Henry *Sandra Gangel* • Scott Neal *Ste Pearce* • Ben Daniels *Tony* • Tameka Empson *Leah* • Meera Syal *Miss Chauhan* ■ *Dir* Hettie MacDonald • *Scr* Jonathan Harvey, from his play

Beauty and the Beast ★

Period fantasy 1962 · US · Colour · 79mins

Duke Mark Damon, condemned by a curse to roam his castle by night as a growling beast, is set free by the love of Joyce Taylor and regains his handsome, human identity. This Technicolor travesty of the fairy tale is sub-standard in every department.. RK

Joyce Taylor *Lady Althea* • Mark Damon *Duke Eduardo* • Eduard Franz *Baron Orsini* • Michael Pate *Prince Bruno* • Merry Anders *Princess Sybil* • Dayton Lummis *Count Roderick* ■ *Dir* Edward L Cahn • *Scr* George Bruce, Orville H Hampton

Beauty and the Beast ★★ U

Fantasy 1987 · US · Colour · 89mins

In another reworking of the classic tale of the young woman taken hostage by a half-man, half-beast whom she eventually falls in love with, Rebecca De Mornay (*The Hand that Rocks the Cradle*) is bland as Beauty, while John Savage (*The Deer Hunter*) is gruffly enjoyable as the Beast. But they both flounder during the duff song and dance numbers in the middle. JB [video]

Rebecca De Mornay *Beauty* • John Savage *Beast/Prince* • Yossi Graber *Father* • Michael Schneider *Kuppel* • Carmela Marner *Bettina* • Ruth Harlap *Isabella* • Joseph Bee *Oliver* ■ *Dir* Eugene Marner • *Scr* Carole Lucia Satrina

Beauty and the Beast ★★★★★ U

Animated musical fantasy
1991 · US · Colour · 80mins

The first feature-length cartoon to be nominated for the best picture Oscar, this is one of the most ambitious films ever produced by Disney. Three and a half years in the making, the movie was one of the first animations to include computer-generated imagery, seen to best advantage during the ballroom and *Be Our Guest* sequences. With visuals based on such French artists as Fragonard and a storyline inspired by the famous fairy tale, the film also boasts the vocal talents of Angela Lansbury (who sings the Oscar-winning title song), Paige O'Hara and Robby Benson. DP [video] DVD

Paige O'Hara *Belle* • Robby Benson *Beast* • Rex Everhart *Maurice* • Richard White *Gaston* • Jesse Corti *Le Fou* • Angela Lansbury *Mrs Potts* • Jerry Orbach *Lumiere* • David Ogden Stiers *Cogsworth/Narrator* • Bradley Michael Pierce [Bradley Pierce] *Chip* ■ *Dir* Gary Trousdale, Kirk Wise • *Scr* Linda Woolverton, from a story by Brenda Chapman, Burny Mattinson, Brian Pimental, Joe Ranft, Kelly Asbury, Christopher Sanders, Kevin Harkey, Bruce Woodside, Tom Ellery, Robert Lence, from the fairy tale by Mme Leprince de Beaumont

Beauty and the Beast: the Enchanted Christmas ★★★ U

Animated fantasy 1997 · US · Colour · 67mins

This made-for-video sequel to the wonderful 1991 Disney animated musical fantasy finds Belle still a prisoner in the castle and attempting to convince the Beast to celebrate Christmas. While many of the cast return to lend their voices, this doesn't quite have the production values or charm of the original, but it should enchant young children if not their more fussy parents. Haley Joel Osment replaced Bradley Pierce as the voice of Chip, the little teacup. JB [video] DVD

Paige O'Hara *Belle* • Robby Benson *Beast* • Jerry Orbach *Lumiere* • David Ogden Stiers *Cogsworth* • Bernadette Peters *Angelique* •

Tim Curry *Forte* • Haley Joel Osment *Chip* • Paul Reubens *Fife* • Angela Lansbury *Mrs Potts* ■ *Dir* Andy Knight • *Scr* Flip Kobler, Cindy Marcus, Bill Motz, Bob Roth

Beauty for the Asking ★★

Drama 1939 · US · BW · 68mins

Leaving Lucille Ball's outstanding comic gifts on the back burner, RKO cast her to play straight in this plodding and uncertain tale of a beautician who, after being jilted by smooth Patric Knowles, comes up with a new face cream that makes millions. It's directed without distinction by Glenn Tryon, but there's some fun to be had from the backroom bitching in the cosmetics industry. RK

Lucille Ball *Jean Russell* • Patric Knowles *Denny Williams* • Donald Woods *Jeffrey Martin* • Frieda Inescort *Flora Barton* • Inez Courtney *Gwen Morrison* • Leona Maricle *Eva Harrington* • Frances Mercer *Patricia Wharton* • Whitney Bourne *Peggy Ponsby* ■ *Dir* Glenn Tryon • *Scr* Doris Anderson, Paul Jerrico

The Beauty Jungle ★★

Drama 1964 · UK · Colour · 114mins

Portraying the seedier side of beauty contests in the early 1960s, this is a bustling but predictable rise-and-fall story, in which Janette Scott discovers that fame sometimes doesn't even last 15 minutes. Charting her progress to the Miss Globe title, Val Guest's film unerringly descends upon the tawdry and the fake, whether exposing the cattiness behind the catwalk or the emptiness behind celebrity. Scott is suitably naive, while Ian Hendry and Edmund Purdom reek of insincerity as the men promising her stardom. DP

Ian Hendry *Don Mackenzie* • Janette Scott *Shirley* • Ronald Fraser *Walter* • Edmund Purdom *Carrick* • Jean Claudio *Armand* • Kay Walsh *Mrs Freeman* • Norman Bird *Freeman* • Janina Faye *Elaine* • Tommy Trinder *Charlie Dorton* • David Weston *Harry* ■ *Dir* Val Guest • *Scr* Robert Muller, Val Guest

Beauty Shop ★★ 12A

Comedy 2005 · US · Colour · 105mins

Barbershop 2's sassy hairdresser-next-door, Gina (Queen Latifah), gets her own movie in this companion piece to the male-focused comedy franchise. It's a sprightly, raucous affair in which Gina, now relocated to Atlanta, tells her flamboyant, condescending boss Kevin Bacon to stick his job and sets about establishing her own beauty shop. There are a fair few laugh-out-loud moments, but the film is too clichéd and sprawling. SF. Contains swearing, sexual references.

Queen Latifah *Gina Norris* • Alicia Silverstone *Lynn* • Andie MacDowell *Terri Green* • Alfre Woodard *Ms. Josephine* • Mena Suvari *Joanne Marcus* • Kevin Bacon *Jorge Christophe* • Djimon Hounsou *Joe* ■ *Dir* Bille Woodruff • *Scr* Kate Lanier, Norman Vance Jr, from a story by Elizabeth Hunter

Beavis and Butt-head Do America ★★★ 12

Animated comedy
1996 · US · Colour · 77mins

Moronic animated twosome Beavis and Butt-head (voiced by creator and director Mike Judge) star in this entertaining full-length feature that sees them uprooted from their couch in front of the TV. The exotic plot has the sniggering pair chased across the country after they become unwitting carriers of a lethal chemical weapon. Bruce Willis and Demi Moore score as the villains, while Robert Stack is spot on as the head of the FBI. JF. Contains a sex scene, brief nudity and some swearing. [video] DVD

Mike Judge *Beavis/Butt-head* • Cloris Leachman *Old woman on plane and bus* • Robert Stack *Agent Flemming* • Eric Bogosian *Ranger* • Richard Linklater *Tour bus driver* • Bruce Willis *Muddy Grimes* • Demi Moore *Dallas Grimes* ■ *Dir* Mike Judge • *Scr* Mike Judge, Joe Stillman

Bebe's Kids ★★★ PG

Animated musical comedy
1992 · US · Colour · 69mins

Based on the characters invented by comedian Robin Harris and scripted by Reginald Hudlin, this was the only animated feature released during the black cinema boom of the early 1990s. Some of the snipes at African-American and white culture are predictable, others are way off beam. Yet when they do hit the target, they are both sassy and funny. The gruff voice of baby Pee-Wee is provided by rap singer Tone Loc. DP [video]

Faizon Love *Robin Harris* • Vanessa Bell Calloway *Jamika* • Wayne Collins Jr *Leon* • Jonell Greene *LaShawn* • Marques Huston *Kahlil* • Tone Loc *Pee-Wee* • Myra J *Dorothea* • Nell Carter *Vivian* • Reynaldo Rey *Lush* ■ *Dir* Bruce Smith • *Scr* Reginald Hudlin, from characters created by Robin Harris

Because of Him ★★★ PG

Musical romance 1946 · US · BW · 83mins

Ten years after she arrived as a teenage singing star to save Universal studios from bankruptcy and two years before her retirement from the screen at the age of 27, Deanna Durbin starred in this "grown-up" version of her previous adolescent-dream-come-true movies. The plot has waitress Durbin determinedly seeking the help of famous actor Charles Laughton to establish her stage career and overcoming his resistance with her rendition of *Danny Boy*. Franchot Tone is the playwright who is initially immune to her charms. Director Richard Wallace exploits the sugar content of the formula. RK [video] DVD

Deanna Durbin *Kim Walker* • Franchot Tone *Paul Taylor* • Charles Laughton *Sheridan* • Helen Broderick *Nora* • Stanley Ridges *Charlie Gilbert* • Donald Meek *Martin* • Charles Halton *Mr Dunlap* ■ *Dir* Richard Wallace • *Scr* Edmund Beloin, fromthe story by Edmund Beloin, Sig Herzig

Because of Winn-Dixie ★★★ U

Comedy drama 2004 · US · Colour · 106mins

Wayne Wang directs this homespun fairy tale, brimming with old-fashioned values and charm. AnnaSophia Robb is delightful as a kind-hearted 10-year-old, who moves to a small Florida town with her single parent father and preacher, Jeff Daniels. Lonely and struggling to fit in, she adopts a stray dog that she names after the local supermarket. The leisurely adventures that follow have a whimsical, almost magical feel, as girl and pooch bring together the eclectic community. This may not appeal to everyone, with older youngsters perhaps finding its traditionalism a bit too twee. SF

AnnaSophia Robb *Opal* • Jeff Daniels *Preacher* • Cicely Tyson *Gloria Dump* • Eva Marie Saint *Miss Franny* • Dave Matthews *Otis* • Courtney Jines *Amanda Wilkinson* • Nick Price *Dunlap Dewberry* • Elle Fanning *Sweetie Pie Thomas* • Luke Benward *Stevie Dewberry* • BJ Hopper *Mr Alfred* ■ *Dir* Wayne Wang • *Scr* Joan Singleton, from the novel by Kate DiCamillo

Because They're Young ★★★

Drama 1960 · US · Colour · 98mins

This little Columbia teenage angst flick. was given street credibility by the starring presence of *American Bandstand* host Dick Clark, who unfortunately proved to be no thespian. At the helm was superior cult director Paul Wendkos, perhaps best-remembered for *Gidget* (1959). The student cast is a teen dream: here's Tuesday Weld and James Darren (who also recorded the theme song), plus *Cat Ballou*'s Michael Callan and *Blue Denim*'s Warren Berlinger. TS

Dick Clark *Neil* • Michael Callan *Griff* • Tuesday Weld *Anne* • Victoria Shaw *Joan* • Roberta Shore *Ricky* • Warren Berlinger *Buddy* • Doug McClure *Jim* • Linda Watkins *Frances McCalla* • Duane Eddy • The Rebels ■ *Dir* Paul Wendkos • *Scr* James Gunn, from the novel *Harrison High* by John Farris

Because You're Mine ★★ U

Musical comedy 1952 · US · Colour · 103mins

Amazingly selected as the 1953 Royal Command Film, this Mario Lanza vehicle is memorable today as the feeble follow-up to his biggest success, *The Great Caruso*. This is a thankless affair, with Lanza as an opera star conscripted into the army who falls for his sergeant's sister, less than winningly played by Broadway *Kismet* star Doretta Morrow. However, apart from the rich period Technicolor, there's little to sing about in this lacklustre MGM musical. TS

Mario Lanza *Renaldo Rossano* • Doretta Morrow *Bridget Batterson* • James Whitmore *Sgt Batterson* • Dean Miller *Ben Jones* • Paula Corday [Rita Corday] *Francesca Landers* • Jeff Donnell *Patty Ware* • Spring Byington *Mrs Montville* ■ *Dir* Alexander Hall • *Scr* Karl Tunberg, Leonard Spigelgass, from a story by Ruth Brooks Flippen, Sy Gomberg • *Music* Sammy Cahn

Becket ★★★★ PG

Historical drama
1964 · UK/US · Colour · 141mins

This is distinguished by overwhelmingly historic histrionics, with a double-whammy of charismatic performances by Richard Burton and Peter O'Toole. Edward Anhalt's Oscar-winning script from Jean Anouilh's stage play tells of the friendship, at the 12th century court, between Henry II (O'Toole) and Archbishop Becket (Burton) – here seen as friends from childhood. The insights into their power struggle are more modern than medieval, but they make for a wholly engrossing portrayal of the past. TH [video]

Richard Burton *Thomas Becket* • Peter O'Toole *King Henry II* • John Gielgud *King Louis VII of France* • Donald Wolfit *Bishop Folliot* • Martita Hunt *Queen Matilda* • Pamela Brown *Queen Eleanor* • Paolo Stoppa *Pope Alexander III* • Gino Cervi *Cardinal Zambelli* • Sian Phillips *Gwendolen* ■ *Dir* Peter Glenville • *Scr* Edward Anhalt, from the play *Becket, ou l'Honneur de Dieu* by Jean Anouilh • *Producer* Hal B Wallis • *Cinematographer* Geoffrey Unsworth • *Costume Designer* Margaret Furse

Becky Sharp ★★★★

Period drama 1935 · US · Colour · 84mins

Rouben Mamoulian's picture is notable as the first full-length feature in three-strip Technicolor. And what exquisite colour it is! The costumes are dazzling and are seen at their best in the ball scenes on the eve of Waterloo. Francis Edward Faragoh's script focuses on the famous central character from Thackeray's *Vanity Fair*, romping through her rise and fall in a breathtakingly audacious bowdlerisation and distortion of the original. An Oscar-nominated Miriam Hopkins makes a spirited if unsubtle and hoydenish Becky, while most of the supporting characters are reduced to fleeting cardboard cut-outs or caricatures. Never dull. RK

Miriam Hopkins *Becky Sharp* • Frances Dee *Amelia Sedley* • Cedric Hardwicke *Marquis of Steyne* • Billie Burke *Lady Bareacres* • Alison Skipworth *Miss Crawley* • Nigel Bruce *Joseph Sedley* ■ *Dir* Rouben Mamoulian • *Scr* Francis Edward Faragoh, from a play by Langdon Mitchell, from the novel *Vanity Fair* by William Makepeace Thackeray • *Cinematographer* Ray Rennahan

Becoming Colette ★★ 18

Biographical drama
1991 · Ger/UK/Fr · Colour · 96mins

A stilted account of the life and early career of the French author who wrote as Colette (Mathilda May), this details her transformation from a naive country girl to a Paris socialite, her disastrous marriage to Henri Gauthier-Villars (Klaus Maria Brandauer) and her sexual awakening. A rather superficial and empty period piece with indifferent performances from the lead actors, this proves director Danny Huston is no match for his father John. AJ [video]

Klaus Maria Brandauer *Henri Gauthier-Villars* • Mathilda May *Sidonie Gabrielle Colette* • Virginia Madsen *Polaire Sorel* • Paul Rhys *Chapo* • John Van Dreelen *Albert* • Jean-Pierre Aumont *Captain* • Lucienne Hamon *Sido* • Georg Tryphon *Creditor* ■ *Dir* Danny Huston • *Scr* Ruth Graham, Burt Weinshanker

Bed and Board ★★★ PG

Comedy drama 1970 · Fr · Colour · 93mins

Antoine Doinel, the hero of *The 400 Blows*, is now married to Claude Jade but still can't settle down. He has an affair with a Japanese girl and enters a ludicrous Zen period; after a variety of pointless jobs, he appears to mature by writing a novel and becoming a father. While *Bed and Board* is not in the same class as its gorgeous predecessor, *Stolen Kisses*, the gentle comedy and romance make for an utterly charming film, shot through with Truffaut's trademark optimism about human nature. AT. In French with English subtitles. [video] DVD

Jean-Pierre Léaud *Antoine Doinel* • Claude Jade *Christine Doinel* • Hiroko Berghauer *Kyoko* • Daniel Ceccaldi *Lucien Darbon* • Claire Duhamel *Madame Darbon* • Daniel Boulanger *Tenor* • Barbara Laage *Monique* ■ *Dir* François Truffaut • *Scr* François Truffaut, Claude de Givray, Bernard Revon

Bed & Breakfast ★★★ 15

Romantic comedy
1992 · US · Colour · 88mins

A modest yet entertaining comedy from *Reuben, Reuben* director Robert Ellis Miller, which contains a surprisingly good performance by Roger Moore. He stars as a conman whose arrival in a small New England community brings a sparkle to the lives of widow Colleen Dewhurst, her daughter Talia Shire and granddaughter Nina Siemaszko. Barely released in the cinema, this pleasantly unusual and self-effacing movie was the swan song of Dewhurst, who died of cancer in 1991. TH [video]

Roger Moore *Adam* • Talia Shire *Claire* • Colleen Dewhurst *Ruth* • Nina Siemaszko *Cassie* • Ford Rainey *Amos* • Stephen Root *Randolph* • Jamie Walters *Mitch* ■ *Dir* Robert Ellis Miller • *Scr* Cindy Myers

Bed of Roses ★★ PG

Romantic comedy drama
1995 · US · Colour · 84mins

Life isn't always rosy in this uncertain attempt to combine realism and romance. Christian Slater is a florist whose wife died giving birth. Grieving madly (and rather badly), he gradually falls for "suit" Mary Stuart Masterson. As their relationship develops, both attempt to heal past wounds. Well meaning, but this wilts rather than blooms. LH [video]

Christian Slater *Lewis* • Mary Stuart Masterson *Lisa* • Pamela Segall *Kim* • Josh Brolin *Danny* • Gina Torres *Francine* • Ally Walker *Wendy* ■ *Dir/Scr* Michael Goldenberg

The Bed Sitting Room ★★★

Comedy 1969 · UK · Colour · 91mins

One of comic genius Spike Milligan's two great West End hits, this antiwar play by Milligan and John Antrobus seemed ideal screen material. It's set

B

three years after the great nuclear holocaust and the cast gradually transmutes into various altered physical states (Arthur Lowe becomes a parrot). Ralph Richardson stars, joined by a cast full of priceless British eccentrics, including Milligan's *Goon Show* pal Harry Secombe, Peter Cook and Dudley Moore. Richard Lester is quite at home in this surreal world, but despite its undoubted originality, this fails to transfer successfully from stage to screen. Watch carefully for Marty Feldman in his movie debut. TS

Ralph Richardson *Lord Fortnum* • Rita Tushingham *Penelope* • Peter Cook *Inspector* • Dudley Moore *Sergeant* • Arthur Lowe *Father* • Roy Kinnear *Plastic Mac Man* • Mona Washbourne *Mother* • Michael Hordern *Captain Bules Martin* • Spike Milligan *Mate* • Harry Secombe *The Shelter Man* • Jimmy Edwards *Nigel* • Marty Feldman *Nurse Arthur* ■ *Dir* Richard Lester • *Scr* John Antrobus, from the play by Spike Milligan, John Antrobus

Bedazzled ★★★ PG

Comedy 1967 · UK · Colour · 103mins

From the days when London was swinging and Peter Cook and Dudley Moore were a partnership made in comedy heaven, this Faustian fantasy has Dud as a cook lusting after waitress Eleanor Bron and being granted seven wishes by Pete, as a drawlingly engaging Devil hungry for Dud's soul. A briefly clad, briefly glimpsed Raquel Welch is one of the Deadly Sins, while Barry Humphries turns in a typically hilarious performance as Envy. Director Stanley Donen settles for quirky comedy instead of razor-sharp satire, and his determinedly trendy direction means that the film ends up being as patchy as Raquel's outfit. TH DVD

Peter Cook *George Spiggot* • Dudley Moore *Stanley Moon* • Raquel Welch *Lillian Lust* • Eleanor Bron *Margaret* • Alba *Vanity* • Robert Russell *Anger* • Barry Humphries *Envy* • Parnell McGarry *Gluttony* • Daniele Noel *Avarice* • Howard Goorney *Sloth* ■ *Dir* Stanley Donen • *Scr* Peter Cook, Dudley Moore, from a story by Peter Cook • *Music* Dudley Moore

Bedazzled ★★★ 12

Comedy 2000 · US/Ger · Colour · 89mins

Liz Hurley is the Devil in disguise in this remake of the 1967 Dudley Moore/Peter Cook comedy. In a contemporary riff on the Faustian premise, Satan Hurley grants geeky Brendan Fraser seven wishes in exchange for his soul. Fraser uses these to try to attain the object of his affections, Frances O'Connor, while Hurley uses them to subvert his desires. Extremely funny in places, this is director Harold Ramis at his superficial best, providing instant, but forgettable, gratification. LH. Contains swearing and drug abuse. DVD

Brendan Fraser *Elliott Richards* • Elizabeth Hurley *The Devil* • Frances O'Connor *Alison Gardner/Nicole* • Miriam Shor *Carol/ Penthouse hostess* • Orlando Jones *Dan/ Esteban/Beach jock/Sportscaster/African party guest* • Paul Adelstein *Bob/Roberto/ Beach jock/Sportscaster/Lincoln aide* • Toby Huss *Jerry/Alejandro/Beach jock/ sportscaster/Lance* ■ *Dir* Harold Ramis • *Scr* Harold Ramis, Peter Tolan, Larry Gelbart, from the 1967 film

Bedelia ★★

Crime drama 1946 · UK · BW · 89mins

Made when Britain's glamorous and highly popular "wicked lady" Margaret Lockwood was at the peak of her stardom, the postwar public flocked to this tale of a classy married woman who, having poisoned three husbands, is planning to dispose of the present one (Ian Hunter). Lance Comfort directs this utter drivel, which offers a nice twist ending, photography by Frederick A Young and a giggly *frisson* for Lockwood fans. RK

Margaret Lockwood *Bedelia Carrington* • Ian Hunter *Charlie Carrington* • Barry K Barnes *Ben Chaney* • Anne Crawford *Ellen Walker* • Jill Esmond *Nurse Harris* • Barbara Blair *Sylvia Johnstone* ■ *Dir* Lance Comfort • *Scr* Vera Caspary, Herbert Victor, from the novel by Vera Caspary

Bedevilled ★

Crime drama 1955 · US · Colour · 85mins

Anne Baxter is wasted as a nightclub singer on the run who finds refuge in a church and the sensitive arms of priest-to-be Steve Forrest, who gives a terribly wooden performance. The production itself was bedevilled with so many problems that MGM chief Dore Schary fired director Mitchell Leisen towards the end of shooting and had John Sturges take over. AT

Anne Baxter *Monica Johnson* • Steve Forrest *Gregory Fitzgerald* • Victor Francen *Father Du Rocher* • Simone Renant *Francesca* • Maurice Teynac *Trevelle* • Robert Christopher *Tony Lugacetti* • Ina De La Hye *Mama Lugacetti* • Joseph Tomelty *Father Cunningham* ■ *Dir* Mitchell Leisen • *Scr* Jo Eisinger

The Bedford Incident ★★★★ PG

Adventure 1965 · UK · BW · 101mins

This superior Cold War sea drama-cum-chase movie, directed by Stanley Kubrick's one-time producer James B Harris, explores similar nuclear fears to Kubrick's *Dr Strangelove*, but in more sober fashion. Richard Widmark gives a notable performance as the captain of a nuclear-armed American naval destroyer, who has become overly zealous in his hunt for Russian subs. Sidney Poitier plays a journalist who comes along for the exciting ride. PF DVD

Richard Widmark *Captain Eric Finlander* • Sidney Poitier *Ben Munceford* • James MacArthur *Ensign Ralston* • Martin Balsam *Lieutenant Commander Chester Potter* • Wally Cox *Sonar operator* • Eric Portman *Commander Wolfgang Schrepke* • Michael Kane *Commander Allison* • Donald Sutherland *Pharmacist's mate* ■ *Dir* James B Harris • *Scr* James Poe, from the novel by Mark Rascovich

Bedknobs and Broomsticks ★★★ U

Musical fantasy 1971 · US · Colour · 133mins

This was a conscious effort on the part of Disney to repeat the success of *Mary Poppins*. Angela Lansbury is splendidly dotty as amateur witch Eglantine Price, but neither David Tomlinson nor the trio of cockney evacuees offer her much support. But then neither does the story, cobbled together from a couple of Mary Norton novels, in which the Nazi invasion of Britain is repelled by magic. The animated sequences are easily the highlights of the film, which is now available in full (for many years we had to make do with a 98-minute version). DP DVD

Angela Lansbury *Eglantine Price* • David Tomlinson *Emelius Browne* • Roddy McDowall *Mr Jelk* • Sam Jaffe *Bookman* • John Ericson *Colonel Heller* • Bruce Forsyth *Swinburne* • Reginald Owen *General Teagler* • Tessie O'Shea *Mrs Hobday* ■ *Dir* Robert Stevenson • *Scr* Bill Walsh, Don DaGradi, from the books *The Magic Bed-Knob* and *Bonfires and Broomsticks* by Mary Norton

Bedlam ★★★

Horror 1946 · US · BW · 79mins

Was there ever a star who played sadistic men with as much relish as Boris Karloff? He's given ample room to snarl here as an asylum boss in 18th-century London who interns an innocent woman to stop her from exposing his harsh rule. Intelligently written and acted, with its production design modelled on Hogarth's engravings, this atmospheric chiller is let down by Mark Robson's rather pedestrian direction. RS

Boris Karloff *Master Sims* • Anna Lee *Nell Bowen* • Billy House *Lord Mortimer* • Jason Robards [Jason Robards Sr] *Oliver Todd* • Richard Fraser *Hannay* • Glenn Vernon *The gilded boy* • Ian Wolfe *Sidney Long* • Leyland Hodgson *John Wilkes* ■ *Dir* Mark Robson • *Scr* Carlos Keith [Val Lewton], Mark Robson, from the engravings by William Hogarth • *Cinematographer* Nicholas Musuraca

The Bedroom Window ★★★ 15

Thriller 1987 · US · Colour · 108mins

Steve Guttenberg must have seen this thriller as a means of escaping being typecast in the zany *Police Academy* series. Unfortunately, for all his efforts, he comes off second best to his female co-stars, Elizabeth McGovern and Isabelle Huppert. Writer/director Curtis Hanson keeps this bright and entertaining, but he eventually runs into trouble when he tries to resolve the many intrigues and plot twists. TH. Contains swearing, sex scenes and brief nudity. DVD

Steve Guttenberg *Terry Lambert* • Elizabeth McGovern *Denise Connelly* • Isabelle Huppert *Sylvia Wentworth* • Paul Shenar *Collin Wentworth* • Carl Lumbly *Detective Quirke* • Wallace Shawn *Henderson's attorney* ■ *Dir* Curtis Hanson • *Scr* Curtis Hanson, from the novel *The Witnesses* by Anne Holden

Bedrooms and Hallways ★★★ 15

Romantic comedy
1998 · UK · Colour · 91mins

More commercial than her debut film *Go Fish*, Rose Troche's second feature is an intelligent and funny examination of 1990s sexuality. Kevin McKidd, a quiet homosexual, starts exploring his masculinity in an overly serious men's group. There McKidd meets James Purefoy and, embarking on a relationship with him, is distraught to discover Purefoy is the boyfriend of his first love and good friend Jennifer Ehle. Impressive in its open attitude, where the characters' sexual bent is not as important as their essential humanity, this is a funny and perceptive film. LH. Contains swearing, sexual scenes.

Kevin McKidd *Leo* • Jennifer Ehle *Sally* • Simon Callow *Keith* • Hugo Weaving *Jeremy* • Christopher Fulford *Adam* • Julie Graham *Angie* • Tom Hollander *Darren* • Harriet Walter *Sybil* • James Purefoy *Brendan* ■ *Dir* Rose Troche • *Scr* Robert Farrar

Bedside Manner ★★

Romantic comedy 1945 · US · BW · 78mins

Ruth Hussey stars as a doctor who, on her way to Chicago, stops off at the small-town surgery of her uncle Charles Ruggles to lend a helping hand. There, her brilliant treatment of every kind of complaint proves nothing short of miraculous, until the faked head injury of romantically smitten John Carroll confounds her. An idiotic screenplay, pedestrian direction and a less than glittering cast ensure that this remains firmly second rate. RK

John Carroll *Morgan Hale* • Ruth Hussey *Hedy Fredericks* • Charles Ruggles *Doc Fredericks* • Ann Rutherford *Lola* • Claudia Drake *Tanya* • Renee Godfrey *Stella* • Esther Dale *Gravitt* • Grant Mitchell *Mr Pope* ■ *Dir* Andrew L Stone • *Scr* Frederick Jackson, Malcolm Stuart Boylan, from the story by Robert Carson

Bedtime for Bonzo ★★ U

Comedy 1951 · US · BW · 83mins

Apart from the fact that this wretched farce starred an actor destined to be President of the United States, this nature-versus-nurture joke has little going for it. The story, which looks at how environment shapes personality, is about a chimpanzee being brought up as a human baby and the monkey business which ensues. It's an amiable idea, perhaps, but director Frederick De Cordova's cramped style of approach affords it little room for comic manouevre. TH

Ronald Reagan *Professor Peter Boyd* • Diana Lynn *Jane* • Walter Slezak *Professor Hans Neumann* • Lucille Barkley *Valerie Tillinghast* • Jesse White *Babcock* • Herbert Heyes *Dean Tillinghast* • Herb Vigran *Lt Daggett* ■ *Dir* Frederick De Cordova • *Scr* Val Burton, Lou Breslow, from a story by Raphael David Blau [Raphael Blau], Ted Berkman

Bedtime Story ★★★

Screwball comedy 1942 · US · BW · 84mins

Sparks fly when the starry actress wife (Loretta Young) of a theatre-obsessed playwright (Fredric March) insists on retiring from the stage. A rather over-extended one-joke situation is enlivened by sporadically successful attempts at screwball comedy, but eventually it wears a bit thin and the formidable March is somewhat unsympathetic. The ravishing Young holds it together, however, with the aid of an excellent supporting cast, notably the sublime Eve Arden, who assists March in one of his schemes to lure his wife back into his new play. RK

Fredric March *Lucius Drake* • Loretta Young *Jane Drake* • Robert Benchley *Eddie Turner* • Allyn Joslyn *William Dudley* • Eve Arden *Virginia Cole* • Helen Westley *Emma Harper* • Joyce Compton *Beulah* • Tim Ryan *Mac* ■ *Dir* Alexander Hall • *Scr* Richard Flournoy, from a story by Horace Jackson, Grant Garrett

Bedtime Story ★★★★ PG

Comedy 1964 · US · Colour · 98mins

Marlon Brando – the ultimate method actor – and David Niven – the ultimate exponent of relaxed, intuitive style – make for an unlikely double act, but the results are absolutely hilarious. They play two rival conmen on the French Riviera who try and trick TV soap star Shirley Jones out of her riches. Besides Niven's irresistible debonair charm, we have Brando's extraordinary catalogue of accents and disguises, notably his Ruritanian prince Ruprecht. It's marred by some phoney sets and back projection, but it deserves to be known in its own right rather than just as the basis for the Michael Caine/Steve Martin remake, *Dirty Rotten Scoundrels*. AT DVD

Marlon Brando *Freddy Benson* • David Niven *Lawrence Jameson* • Shirley Jones *Janet Walker* • Dody Goodman *Fanny Eubank* • Aram Stephan *Andre* • Parley Baer *Colonel Williams* • Marie Windsor *Mrs Sutton* • Rebecca Sand *Miss Trumble* ■ *Dir* Ralph Levy • *Scr* Stanley Shapiro, Paul Henning

The Bee Keeper ★★★ 18

Drama 1986 · Gr/Fr · Colour · 121mins

Marcello Mastroianni is an elderly schoolteacher, at the end of his life and his tether, who sets out to visit his beloved beehives, family and old friends before his intended suicide. Along the road he picks up a teenage hitch-hiker (Nadia Mourouzi) who may or may not revive him spiritually and sexually. This is a beautifully shot, but over-extended allegory, though Mastroianni delivers a detailed and very moving performance. AT. In Greek with English subtitles.

Marcello Mastroianni *Spyros* • Nadia Mourouzi *Girl* • Serge Reggiani *Sick man* • Jenny Roussea *Spyros's wife* • Dinos Iliopoulos *Spyros's friend* ■ *Dir* Theodoros Angelopoulos [Theo Angelopoulos] • *Scr* Thodorus Angelopoulos, Dimitris Nollas, Tonino Guerra • *Cinematographer* Yorgos Arvanitis

B

Beefcake ★★★ 18

Erotic drama documentary
1998 · Can/UK/Fr/It · Colour · 91mins

This is a worthy attempt at a documentary about American "male physique" photographer Bob Mizer. A surprising amount of Mizer's pictures and films have survived but, with the notable exception of Warhol superstar Joe Dallesandro, a Mizer model in 1967, those who worked in the semi-illicit world of nude photography tend not to have done. Much of Mizer's life is therefore reconstructed by actors. Director Thom Fitzgerald initially pretends, as did Mizer, that the blatantly homoerotic material is artistic and non-sexual. The truth emerges in a climactic court case (transcripts are used as dialogue) in which Mizer is accused of "pandering". DM [VIDEO] DVD

Daniel MacIvor *Bob Mizer* • Josh Peace *Neil O'Hara* • Carroll Godsman *Delia Mizer* • Jack Griffin Mazeika *Red* • Jonathan Torrens *David* • Joe Dallesandro • Jack LaLanne ■ *Dir* Thom Fitzgerald • *Scr* Thom Fitzgerald, from a non-fiction book by F Valentine Hooven III

Beer ★ 15

Comedy 1985 · US · Colour · 79mins

An old-fashioned and rather naive satire on the Madison Avenue advertising industry, which strains to be funny and credible but ends up being bland and unsubtle. Aggressive executive Loretta Swit comes up with an outrageous advertising campaign which upsets various minority groups due to the sleazy, sexist and camp approach taken by its alcoholic director, Rip Torn. AJ [VIDEO]

Loretta Swit *BD Tucker* • Rip Torn *Buzz Beckerman* • Kenneth Mars *AJ Norbecker* • David Alan Grier *Elliot Morrison* • William Russ *Merle Draggett* • Saul Stein *Frankie Falcone* • Peter Michael Goetz *Harley Feemer* • Dick Shawn *Talk show host* ■ *Dir* Patrick Kelly • *Scr* Allan Weisbecker

Bees in Paradise ★★

Musical comedy 1943 · UK · BW · 75mins

Co-scripted by director Val Guest and gagsmith Marriott Edgar, this is one of Arthur Askey's lesser-known vehicles. This may be because there's a sauciness to the dialogue and lyrics that makes it rather risqué for its time. As one of four pilots stranded on a South Sea island, Askey revels in the attentions of the local maidens, only to discover that it's traditional for husbands to commit suicide once the honeymoon is over. DP

Arthur Askey *Arthur Tucker* • Anne Shelton *Rouana* • Peter Graves (1) *Peter Lovell* • Max Bacon *Max Holer* • Jean Kent *Jani* • Ronald Shiner *Ronald Wild* • Antoinette Cellier *Queen* • Joy Shelton *Almura* ■ *Dir* Val Guest • *Scr* Val Guest, Marriott Edgar

Beethoven ★★★★ U

Comedy 1992 · US · Colour · 83mins

This is a cute family comedy about an adorable St Bernard dog named Beethoven and the effect he has on an American family. Charles Grodin (best known for his performance opposite Robert De Niro in *Midnight Run*) is the father who ends up with a puppy he doesn't want, which turns into a huge eating and slobbering machine. *The Flintstones* director Brian Levant keeps the comedy coming fast and furious so this never lapses into soppy territory, while Beethoven is gorgeous enough to soften even the hardest dog-hater's heart. Watch out for David Duchovny as the sleazy yuppie who reckons he's a coffee connoisseur. JB [VIDEO] DVD

Charles Grodin *George Newton* • Bonnie Hunt *Alice Newton* • Dean Jones *Dr Varnick* • Nicholle Tom *Ryce* • Christopher Castile *Ted* • Sarah Rose Karr *Emily* • Oliver Platt *Harvey* • Stanley Tucci *Vernon* • David Duchovny *Brad* • Patricia Heaton *Brie* ■ *Dir* Brian Levant • *Scr* Edmond Dantes [John Hughes], Amy Holden Jones

Beethoven's 2nd ★★★ U

Comedy 1993 · US · Colour · 84mins

With the paw prints of *One Hundred and One Dalmatians* all over it, this cosy sequel sees the Newton children trying to hide a litter of ultra-cute St Bernard puppies from their still dog-shy father, Charles Grodin. While all eyes will be on the four pups (who were played by over 100 pooches at various times), let's not forget the amiable performances of Grodin and Bonnie Hunt, and the Cruella-like villainy of scheming Debi Mazar, who dognaps Missy (Beethoven's beloved) to use as a pawn in her divorce. DP [VIDEO] DVD

Charles Grodin *George Newton* • Bonnie Hunt *Alice Newton* • Nicholle Tom *Ryce* • Christopher Castile *Ted* • Sarah Rose Karr *Emily* • Debi Mazar *Regina* • Chris Penn *Floyd* • Ashley Hamilton *Taylor* • Danny Masterson *Seth* ■ *Dir* Rod Daniel • *Scr* Len Blum, from characters created by Edmond Dantes [John Hughes], Amy Holden Jones

Beethoven's 3rd ★★ U

Comedy 2000 · US · Colour · 94mins

Charles Grodin hands the leash over to Judge Reinhold for the huggable St Bernard's next adventure. Realising that the disaster-laden trip to California is short on laughs, Reinhold overcompensates by playing each scene as if it were an amateur-dramatics pantomime. As Reinhold's wife, Julia Sweeney just about keeps her embarrassment at bay. DP [VIDEO] DVD

Judge Reinhold *Richard Newton* • Julia Sweeney *Beth Newton* • Joe Pichler *Brennan Newton* • Michaela Gallo *Sara Newton* • Mike Ciccolini *Tommy* • Jamie Marsh *Bill* • Frank Gorshin *Uncle Morrie* ■ *Dir* David M Evans [David Mickey Evans] • *Scr* Jeff Schechter, from characters created by Edmond Dantes [John Hughes], Amy Holden Jones

Beethoven's 4th ★★ U

Comedy 2001 · US · Colour · 89mins

With a "Prince and the Paw-per" scenario, this fourth adventure featuring the St Bernard with the kid-pleasing ability to emit slobber from one end and noxious gases from the other is an improvement on its predecessor. Clearly someone had told Judge Reinhold to go easy on the pantomimics and let the star do the work, as Beethoven becomes mixed up with a perfectly behaved pedigree pooch named Michelangelo. A fifth film followed in 2003. DP [VIDEO] DVD

Judge Reinhold *Richard Newton* • Julia Sweeney *Beth Newton* • Joe Pichler *Brennan Newton* • Michaela Gallo *Sara Newton* • Kaleigh Krish *Madison Sedgewick* • Matt McCoy *Reginald Sedgewick* • Veanne Cox *Martha Sedgewick* ■ *Dir* David Mickey Evans • *Scr* John Loy, from characters created by Edmond Dantes [John Hughes], Amy Holden Jones

Beetle Juice ★★★★ 15

Horror comedy 1988 · US · Colour · 88mins

This refreshingly flaky fantasy from director Tim Burton is a landmark supernatural comedy that ingeniously showcases monstrously zany special effects, demonic one-liners and offbeat performances. Michael Keaton is amazing as the unstable freelance exorcist called in to help recently deceased Geena Davis and Alec Baldwin rid their new home of human pests. Burton's marvellously imaginative view of the afterlife as a ghoulish extension of mundane earthbound problems is a visionary masterstroke crammed with wit and invention. AJ. Contains violence and swearing. [VIDEO] DVD

Michael Keaton *Betelgeuse* • Geena Davis *Barbara Maitland* • Alec Baldwin *Adam Maitland* • Catherine O'Hara *Delia Deetz* • Winona Ryder *Lydia Deetz* • Jeffrey Jones *Charles Deetz* • Robert Goulet *Maxie Dean* • Sylvia Sidney *Juno* ■ *Dir* Tim Burton • *Scr* Michael McDowell, Warren Skaaren, from a story by Michael McDowell, Larry Wilson • *Special Effects Supervisor* Chuck Gaspar • *Special Effects* Robert Short • *Visual Effects* Peter Kuran

Before and After ★★ 12

Drama 1996 · US · Colour · 103mins

Meryl Streep and Liam Neeson's lives are irrevocably changed when their son is accused of murdering his girlfriend in director Barbet Schroeder's unfocused pseudo-thriller. A turgid pace coupled with poor plotting stretches credibility to breaking point in a bland morality melodrama, notable only for Streep's fine, suitably distressed performance. AJ. Contains violence and swearing. [VIDEO]

Meryl Streep *Carolyn Ryan* • Liam Neeson *Ben Ryan* • Edward Furlong *Jacob Ryan* • Julia Weldon *Judith Ryan* • Alfred Molina *Panos Demeris* • Daniel Von Bargen *Fran Conklin* • John Heard *Wendell Bye* • Ann Magnuson *Terry Taverner* ■ *Dir* Barbet Schroeder • *Scr* Ted Tally, from the book by Rosellen Brown

Before I Hang ★★★

Horror 1940 · US · BW · 62mins

A short and sweet programme filler allowing Boris Karloff to veer superbly between brilliant scientist and rabid madman. This time he's dabbling in serums to combat old age and uses a criminal's blood for some behind bars experimentation after he's imprisoned for a "mercy killing". There's loads of fun psychobabble about medicine being for the good of mankind, but what it eventually turns into is another twist on the *Frankenstein* theme. Yet Karloff glues it all together as ever. AJ

Boris Karloff *Dr John Garth* • Evelyn Keyes *Martha Garth* • Bruce Bennett *Dr Paul Ames* • Edward Van Sloan *Dr Ralph Howard* • Ben Taggart *Warden Thompson* ■ *Dir* Nick Grinde • *Scr* Robert D Andrews

Before Night Falls ★★★★★ 15

Biographical drama
2000 · US · Colour · 127mins

Director Julian Schnabel's follow-up to *Basquiat* is another compelling portrait of a troubled artist, this time gay Cuban poet Reinaldo Arenas, brought to moving life by Spanish superstar Javier Bardem who won an Oscar nomination for his searing portrayal. From Arenas's birth in rural Cuba, 1943, to his Aids-related death in New York, 1990, Schnabel's polished, visually distinctive and confident biography covers the key episodes in the poet's traumatic life. An intelligent and affecting masterpiece that succinctly captures the spirit of Arenas himself. AJ. In English and Spanish with subtitles. [VIDEO] DVD

Javier Bardem *Reinaldo Arenas* • Olivier Martinez *Lázaro Gómez Carilles*, • Andrea Di Stefano *Pepe Malas* • Johnny Depp *Bon Bon/ Lieutenant Victor* • Sean Penn *Cuco Sánchez* • Michael Wincott *Herberto Zorilla Ochoa* ■ *Dir* Julian Schnabel • *Scr* Julian Schnabel, Cunningham O'Keefe, Lázaro Gómez Carilles, from the memoir *Antes que Anochezca* by Reinaldo Arenas • *Cinematographer* Xavier Perez Grobet, Guillermo Rosas

Before Sunrise ★★★★ 15

Romantic drama 1995 · US · Colour · 97mins

When American slacker Ethan Hawke meets French student Julie Delpy on a train to Vienna, the romantic sparks fly and they spend one eventful night together in this exhilarating drama. Announcing his presence as a major talent after grabbing attention with *Dazed and Confused*, director Richard Linklater's understated use of gorgeous Viennese backgrounds, coupled with a smart, funny and touching script, make this ultra-modern romance hip yet timeless. AJ. Contains swearing. [VIDEO] DVD

Ethan Hawke *Jesse* • Julie Delpy *Céline* • Andrea Eckert *Wife on train* • Hanno Poschl *Husband on train* • Karl Bruckschwaiger *Guy on bridge* • Tex Rubinowitz *Guy on bridge* • Erni Mangold *Palm reader* • Dominik Castell *Street poet* ■ *Dir* Richard Linklater • *Scr* Richard Linklater, Kim Krizan

Before Sunset ★★★ 15

Romantic drama 2004 · US · Colour · 76mins

Nine years after their brief encounter in Vienna in *Before Sunrise*, director Richard Linklater reunites his two lovers for a second tryst, this time in Paris. Meeting "by chance" in a city bookshop, the pair converse during a 70-minute stroll that plays out in real time. Ethan Hawke and Julie Delpy reprise their roles, and Linklater directs his often perceptive script with quiet style, but the characters are talky and at times pretentious. DA. Contains swearing and sexual references. DVD

Ethan Hawke *Jesse Wallace* • Julie Delpy *Céline* • Vernon Dobtcheff *Bookstore manager* • Louise Lemoine Torres *Journalist number one* • Rodolphe Pauly *Journalist number two* • Mariane Plasteig *Waitress* • Diabolo *Philippe* • Albert Delpy *Man at grill* • Marie Pillet *Woman in courtyard* ■ *Dir* Richard Linklater • *Scr* Richard Linklater, Julie Delpy, Ethan Hawke, from a story by Richard Linklater, Kim Krizan, from characters created by Richard Linklater, Kim Krizan

Before the Night ★★ 18

Erotic thriller 1995 · US · Colour · 93mins

Talk about keeping it in the family. Talia Shire makes her directorial debut with this instantly forgettable erotic thriller, but just to bolster her confidence ex-husband David Shire composed the score, while older brother Francis Ford Coppola and his mentor Roger Corman also helped out behind the scenes. Coppola regular Frederic Forrest even crops up as the father whose daughter may or may not have been murdered by A Martinez, the very man with whom lonely Ally Sheedy has a one-night stand. DP. Contains swearing, sex scenes and nudity [VIDEO]

Ally Sheedy *Michelle "Mickey" Sanderson* • A Martinez *Jack Gillman* • Frederic Forrest *Michael Joslyn* • Don Novello *Warren Miller* • Diane Salinger *Barbara Joslyn* ■ *Dir* Talia Shire • *Scr* Marty Casella

Before the Rain ★★★ 15

Portmanteau drama
1994 · Mac/UK/Fr · Colour · 108mins

Winner of the Golden Lion at Venice and nominated for the best foreign film Oscar, this was the first film produced in the newly formed Republic of Macedonia. Director Milcho Manchevski brings an imposing portentousness to this portmanteau picture, but too often he mistakes ponderousness for gravity. DP. In Macedonian, Albanian and English with subtitles. [VIDEO]

Josif Josifovski *Father Marko* • Rade Serbedzija *Aleksandar* • Grégoire Colin *Kiril* • Labina Mitevska *Zamira* • Boris Delcevski *Petre* • Dejan Velkov *Mate* • Kiril Ristoski *Father Damjan* • Mladen Krstevski *Trifun* • Dzemail Maksut *Kuzman* • Katrin Cartlidge *Anne* • Phyllida Law *Anne's mother* • Jay Villiers *Nick* ■ *Dir/Scr* Milcho Manchevski

Before the Revolution ★★★★ 15

Political drama 1964 · It · BW · 106mins

The second feature from Bernardo Bertolucci, director of *Last Tango in Paris* and *The Last Emperor*, tells of a young man whose involvement with radical politics and affair with an aunt is countered by his need to conform and settle down with a pretty girl. Bertolucci refined these themes over and over again, notably in his masterpiece *The Conformist* (1969). This is a fascinating apprentice effort, even if it is full of dated, gimmicky effects apparently borrowed from Jean-Luc Godard. AT. In Italian with English subtitles.

Adriana Asti *Gina* • Francesco Barilli *Fabrizio* • Morando Morandini *Cesare* • Allen Midgette *Agostino* • Cristina Pariset *Clelia* • Domenico Alpi *Fabrizio's father* ■ *Dir/Scr* Bernardo Bertolucci

Before Winter Comes ★★★

Drama 1968 · UK · Colour · 107mins

Instead of merrily fiddling on the roof, here's Topol cheerfully trifling with the truth. He plays a Russian deserter, masquerading as a Slav interpreter who speaks 13 languages, helping major David Niven run a displaced persons camp in Austria at the end of the Second World War. Both are in conflict over local girl Anna Karina, but J Lee Thompson's relaxed direction fails to generate sufficient tension. Niven's punctilious dignity is as memorable as ever, however. TH

David Niven *Major Giles Burnside* • Topol *Janovic* • Anna Karina *Maria Holz* • John Hurt *Lieutenant Francis Pilkington* • Anthony Quayle *Brigadier-General Bewley* • Ori Levy *Captain Kamenev* • John Collin *Sergeant Woody* • Karel Stepanek *Count Kerassy* ■ *Dir* J Lee Thompson • *Scr* Andrew Sinclair, from the story *The Interpreter* by Frederick L Keefe in *New Yorker*

Before Women Had Wings ★★★ 15

Drama 1997 · US · Colour · 88mins

Once you get past the naff title, there's actually some decent drama to be found in this TV movie "presented by" Oprah Winfrey. The film stars Oprah (of course) as the kindly woman who takes in the children of downtrodden mother Ellen Barkin. While Winfrey goes for melodrama, Barkin adds much needed class and grit and is backed up by nice performances from hot young actress Julia Stiles. DP DVD

Oprah Winfrey *Miss Zora* • Ellen Barkin *Glory Marie Jackson* • Tina Majorino *"Bird"* • Julia Stiles *Phoebe Jackson* • John Savage *Billy Jackson* • Burt Young *Mr Ippolito* • William Lee Scott *Hank* • Louis Crugnali *LJ Ippolito* • David Hart *Sheriff* ■ *Dir* Lloyd Kramer • *Scr* Connie May Fowler, from her novel

Before You Go ★★★ 15

Comedy drama 2002 · UK · Colour · 91mins

Bravura turns by Julie Walters, Joanne Whalley and Victoria Hamilton inject vivacity into this old-fashioned, fantasy-tinged tragicomedy. The trio play three sisters returning home for their formidable mother's funeral who each find their own way of coping with the loss. Troubled Whalley is haunted by visions of their mother's ghost, while health fanatic Walters sparkles in yet another eccentric role and Hamilton mops up the left over laughter as the stoned nymphomaniac. Tom Wilkinson and John Hannah do wonders to support the sardonic edge of this low-key melodrama. AJ DVD

Julie Walters *Teresa* • John Hannah *Mike* • Joanne Whalley *Mary* • Victoria Hamilton *Catherine* • Patricia Hodge *Violet Heaney* • Tom Wilkinson *Frank* • Hugh Ross *Mr Berry* ■ *Dir* Lewis Gilbert • *Scr* Shelagh Stephenson, from her play *The Memory of Water*

Beggars of Life ★★★

Drama 1928 · US · BW · 80mins

After killing her brutal stepfather, farm girl Louise Brooks, disguised as a boy, flees into hiding in company with youthful hobo Richard Arlen. Much of the action famously has them hopping freight trains and dossing down in a community of tramps, where Wallace Beery is top dog. Director William A Wellman, filming on location on railways and in the Californian desert, creates strong atmosphere and Brooks is beguiling, but the film is slow and sketchy after its explosive opening scenes. It was filmed as a silent movie, but some snatches of dialogue and a music track were added to qualify it, a little dubiously, as Paramount's first talkie feature. RK

Wallace Beery *Oklahoma Red* • Louise Brooks *Nancy* • Richard Arlen *Jim* • Edgar Blue Washington *Mose* • HA Morgan [Horace Morgan] *Skinny* • Andy Clark *Skelly* • Mike Donlin *Bill* ■ *Dir* William A Wellman • *Scr* Benjamin Glazer, Jim Tully, from the story by Jim Tully

The Beggar's Opera ★★★ U

Operetta 1953 · US · Colour · 94mins

What with Laurence Olivier launching into lilting vocals as highwayman MacHeath, and Dorothy Tutin in exasperated voice as Polly Peachum, this movie debut of radical stage producer Peter Brook had some distinguished credentials for success. But John Gay's satirical operetta comes across as stagey and stilted, despite music arranged by Sir Arthur Bliss and a script by playwrights Dennis Cannan and Christopher Fry. But it does have some visual and harmonious delights that make it an intriguing spectacle. TH DVD

Laurence Olivier *Capt MacHeath* • Stanley Holloway *Lockit* • George Devine *Peachum* • Mary Clare *Mrs Peachum* • Athene Seyler *Mrs Trapes* • Dorothy Tutin *Polly Peachum* • Daphne Anderson *Lucy Lockit* • Hugh Griffith *The Beggar* • Margot Grahame *The actress* ■ *Dir* Peter Brook • *Scr* Dennis Cannan, Christopher Fry, from the comic opera by John Gay • *Cinematographer* Guy Green

Beginner's Luck ★★ 15

Comedy 2001 · UK · Colour · 85mins

This comedy from first-time writer/directors Nick Cohen and James Callis is based on their own disastrous experiences with a fringe theatre group in the 1980s. The shambolic efforts of the Vagabond Theatre Company to stage an experimental version of *The Tempest* has Callis playing the troupe director who leads his thespians through a string of ill-conceived and poorly received performances. Sadly, an experienced cast can't rise above the banal script and clichéd direction. TH. Contains swearing. DVD

Julie Delpy *Anya* • Steven Berkoff *Bob* • Christopher Cazenove *Andrew Fontaine* • Fenella Fielding *Aunt Emily* • Jean Yves Bertolot *Javaad* • James Callis *Mark* • Nick Cohen *"Old luvvy"* ■ *Dir/Scr* Nick Cohen, James Callis

Beginning of the End ★

Science-fiction horror
1957 · US · BW · 72mins

An atomic radiation leak kills off scores of farmers in the Midwest and produces giant grasshoppers that march in formation on hapless Chicago, slaughtering everyone who stands in their way. Featuring performances from Peter Graves is the baffled boffin and Peggy Castle as a boggled journalist, this rubbishy horror is cheesy and hammy. AT

Peggie Castle *Audrey* • Peter Graves (2) *Ed Wainwright* • Morris Ankrum *General Hanson* • Richard Benedict *Corporal Mathias* • James Seay *Captain Barton* ■ *Dir* Bert I Gordon • *Scr* Fred Freiberger, Lester Gorn

The Beginning or the End ★★★ U

Second World War drama
1947 · US · BW · 111mins

MGM's dramatisation of America's development of the atom bomb is a portentous and turgid, yet absolutely fascinating, relic of the Cold War era. Hume Cronyn plays the scientist, J Robert Oppenheimer, while a cast of dozens play other real-life personages, including Einstein, Roosevelt and Harry Truman. The movie celebrates Yankee know-how, but also wonders if the invention might herald an apocalyptic dawn and wipe out humanity for good. There's a framing device about a time capsule to be opened in the year 2446 that's simply mind-boggling. AT

Brian Donlevy *Maj-Gen Leslie R Groves* • Robert Walker *Col Jeff Nixon* • Tom Drake *Matt Cochran* • Beverly Tyler *Ann Cochran* • Audrey Totter *Jean O'Leary* • Hume Cronyn *Dr J Robert Oppenheimer* • Hurd Hatfield *Dr John Wyatt* • Godfrey Tearle *President Roosevelt* • Ludwig Stossel *Dr Albert Einstein* • Art Baker *President Truman* ■ *Dir* Norman Taurog • *Scr* Frank Wead

The Beguiled ★★★ 15

Western drama 1971 · US · Colour · 99mins

An eccentric change of pace for Clint Eastwood and action director Don Siegel who successfully collaborated on *Dirty Harry*, this could be entitled "Sex and the Single Girls". For it is the frustrated sexuality of the young ladies in the Southern school run by Geraldine Page that leads to the downfall of Eastwood's wounded Unionist soldier, whom they nurse and protect. It might have played better as a languid black comedy – Siegel's camera is too energetic for its own good – but it's still effective. TH. Contains some nudity.

Clint Eastwood *John McBurney* • Geraldine Page *Martha Farnsworth* • Elizabeth Hartman *Edwina Dabney* • Jo Ann Harris *Carol* • Darleen Carr *Doris* • Mae Mercer *Hallie* • Pamelyn Ferdin *Amy* • Melody Thomas *Abigail* • Peggy Drier *Lizzie* ■ *Dir* Don Siegel • *Scr* John B Sherry, Grimes Grice, from the novel by Thomas Cullinan

Behind Convent Walls ★★ 18

Erotic drama 1977 · It · Colour · 90mins

Former animator Walerian Borowczyk descends into erotic parody for this loose adaptation of the Stendhal story *A Walk in Rome*. The film's initial concern is with the heinous practice of confining inconvenient heiresses to luxurious convent exile. However, the action soon shifts into a self-consciously shocking exposé of the repressed lusts of Ligia Branice (Borowczyk's wife) and her sisters, as smouldering confessor Mario Maranzana seeks to impose a stricter regime. Constroversial, and stuffed with ponderous satire and unsubtle phallic imagery. DP. In Italian with English subtitles.

Ligia Branice *Sister Clara* • Marina Pierro *Sister Veronica* • Gabriella Giacobbe *Abbess Flavia Orsini* • Loredana Martinez *Sister Martina* • Mario Maranzana *Father Confessor* ■ *Dir* Walerian Borowczyk • *Scr* Walerian Borowczyk, from the story *A Walk in Rome* by Stendhal

Behind Enemy Lines ★★ 12

Wartime action drama
2001 · US · Colour · 101mins

Owen Wilson plays a naval reconnaissance pilot who's shot down over Bosnia after inadvertently filming evidence of war crimes. Gene Hackman is the maverick admiral who battles Nato caution to find his flyboy before the pursuing Serbs do. Former commercials director John Moore proves a dab hand at the action stuff but, pyrotechnics aside, the rest of film is less enthralling. DA DVD

Owen Wilson *Lieutenant Chris Burnett* • Gene Hackman *Reigart* • Gabriel Macht *Stackhouse* • Charles Malik Whitfield *Rodway* • Joaquim de Almeida *Piquet* • David Keith *O'Malley* • Olek Krupa *Lokar* ■ *Dir* John Moore (3) • *Scr* David Veloz, Zak Penn, from a story by James Thomas, John Thomas

Behind the Forbidden City ★★★★ 15

Drama 1996 · Chi/Fr/Neth · Colour · 90mins

Announced as the first Chinese film to tackle homosexuality, this intense interrogation drama is also an allegory on the complex relationship between the people and the forces of law and order. Si Han uses flashbacked episodes from his life to force a sexually ambivalent cop, Hu Jun, to confront his own preferences. Set around the public toilets on the edge of Tiananmen Square, which gives the film its slang title, this controversial drama led to the confiscation of Zhang Yuan's passport and the formation of the Film Bureau to outlaw production of unapproved independent pictures. Released on DVD in the UK as *East Palace, West Palace*. DP. In Mandarin with English subtitles. DVD

Si Han *A-Lan* • Hu Jun *Shi Xiaohua* ■ *Dir* Zhang Yuan • *Scr* Yuan Zhang, Xiaobo Wang

Behind the Headlines ★★★

Drama 1937 · US · BW · 58mins

Having played Hildy Johnson on Broadway in the jewel of newsroom dramas, *The Front Page*, Lee Tracy was frequently cast as fast-talking, sharp-witted reporters on screen. This superior B-melodrama finds him playing just such a character. Good at getting scoops, Tracy finds his relationship with his reporter girlfriend (Diana Gibson) threatened by their rivalry, though circumstances eventually require him to rescue her from danger. Well directed by Richard Rosson, with good performances from the leads and a solid supporting cast. RK

Lee Tracy *Eddie Haines* • Diana Gibson *Mary Bradley* • Donald Meek *Potter* • Paul Guilfoyle (1) *Art Martin* • Philip Huston *Bennett* • Frank M Thomas *Naylor* ■ *Dir* Richard Rosson • *Scr* J Robert Bren, Edmund L Hartmann, from a story by Thomas Ahearn

Behind the Headlines ★★ U

Thriller 1956 · UK · BW · 67mins

This is elevated above the morass of British crime B-movies by a sure sense of newsroom atmosphere that owes more to Hollywood than Pinewood. This tale of showgirls, blackmail and murder presents an unromanticised view of journalism and there's a convincing seediness about the backstage milieu thanks to Geoffrey Faithfull's unfussy photography, but it lacks suspense and newsman Paul Carpenter is short on charisma. DP

Paul Carpenter *Paul Banner* • Adrienne Corri *Pam Barnes* • Hazel Court *Maxine* • Ewen Solon *Supt Faro* • Alfie Bass *Sammy* • Harry Fowler *Alfie* • Tom Gill *Creloch* ■ *Dir* Charles Saunders • *Scr* Allan MacKinnon, from the novel by Robert Chapman

Behind the Mask ★★

Medical drama 1958 · UK · Colour · 108mins

Much of this potboiling drama about feuding surgeons, put-upon housemen and devoted nurses is taken up with a dispute between Michael Redgrave and Niall MacGinnis over the management of their hospital. Director Brian Desmond Hurst seems unable to choose between realism and melodrama, leaving his actors unsure how to pitch their performances. DP

Michael Redgrave *Sir Arthur Benson Gray* • Tony Britton *Philip Selwood* • Carl Mohner *Dr*

Carl Romek • Niall MacGinnis *Neil Isherwood* • Vanessa Redgrave *Pamela Gray* • Ian Bannen *Alan Crabtree* • Brenda Bruce *Elizabeth Fallon* • Lionel Jeffries *Walter Froy* • Ann Firbank *Mrs Judson* ■ *Dir* Brian Desmond Hurst • *Scr* John Hunter, from the novel *The Pack* by John Rowan Wilson

Behind the Mask ★★ PG

Drama based on a true story
1999 · US · Colour · 90mins

Donald Sutherland plays a doctor who suffers a heart attack while running a facility for the disabled in this TV movie. When a mentally challenged janitor (Matthew Fox) saves his life, he becomes the doctor's surrogate son – much to the chagrin of Sutherland's own son, who has long felt neglected by his father. Fox and Sutherland deliver honest, powerful performances under Tom McLoughlin's steady direction. MC DVD

Donald Sutherland *Dr Bob Shushan* • Matthew Fox *James Jones* • Bradley Whitford *Brian Shushan* • Sheila Larken *Dana* • Lorena Gale *Mrs Flowers* • Currie Graham *Geller* • Mary McDonnell *Mary Shushan* ■ *Dir* Tom McLoughlin • *Scr* Gregory Goodell

Behind the Rising Sun ★★

Second World War drama
1943 · US · BW · 87mins

"Know your enemy" is the motto behind this propaganda exercise, which sets out to show how cruel and ruthless the Japanese are. The writer and director had already performed a similar job on the Germans with *Hitler's Children*. This time a Japanese diplomat's son (Tom Neal) is forced to join the army, where he sees the horrors of the inhuman soldiers for himself and falls in love with Margo (a Mexican actress playing Japanese), while his dad does the honourable thing and kills himself. AT

Margo *Tama* • Tom Neal *Taro* • J Carrol Naish *Publisher* • Robert Ryan *Lefty* • Gloria Holden *Sara* • Don Douglas *O'Hara* • George Givot *Boris* ■ *Dir* Edward Dmytryk • *Scr* Emmett Lavery Sr, from a book by James R Young [James Young]

Behind the Screen ★★★ U

Silent satire 1916 · US · BW · 20mins

At a time when movies had scarcely moved out of the freak-show stage, the novelty of Charlie Chaplin's sophisticated slapstick made a star of him. In this Biograph silent, he satisfied the public's curiosity about the new medium by taking us behind the scenes at a movie studio. Also known as *The Pride of Hollywood*, its story is simple – Charlie, in Little Tramp guise, sneaks into a studio where a film is being made, only to be pursued by the usual burly, wild-eyed nemesis of Eric Campbell. Several film personalities, such as producer Hal Roach, can be seen in passing and, although very dated, it is a fascinating glimpse of a bygone age and art. TH VIDEO DVD

Charles Chaplin *David, a stagehand* • Eric Campbell *Goliath, his boss* • Edna Purviance *Girl seeking film job* • Frank J Coleman *Assistant director* • Albert Austin *A stagehand* • Henry Bergman *Dramatic director* • Lloyd Bacon *Comedy director* ■ *Dir* Charles Chaplin • *Scr* Charles Chaplin

Behind the Sun ★★★ 12

Period drama
2001 · Bra/Swi/Fr · Colour · 88mins

This handsome tale of feuding families in the Brazilian badlands of the early 20th century brandishes its art house credentials like a badge of honour. Every composition devised by director Walter Salles and his *Central Station* cinematographer Walter Carvalho is painstakingly exquisite, as Rodrigo Santoro hits the road with circus performer Flavia Marco Antonio and tries to experience life before his destiny overtakes him. However, for all gushing pathos, there's no real thematic or emotional depth to the proceedings. DP. In Portuguese with English subtitles. VIDEO DVD

José Dumont *Father* • Rodrigo Santoro *Tonho* • Rita Assemany *Mother* • Luiz Carlos Vasoncelos *Salustiano* • Ravi Ramos Lacerda *Pacu* ■ *Dir* Walter Salles • *Scr* Walter Salles, Sergio Machado, Karim Ainouz, from the novel *Abril Despedaçado* by Ismail Kadaré

Behold a Pale Horse ★★★

Drama 1964 · US · BW · 119mins

As an exiled former Spanish Civil War guerrilla, Gregory Peck is drawn into a confrontation years later with brutal police chief Anthony Quinn, in a story based on a novel by Emeric Pressburger. Director Fred Zinnemann continues his *High Noon* tradition of combining moral dilemmas with violent action, and the film contains one of Peck's finest – and least heroic – performances. Omar Sharif is miscast as a young priest, however, spouting the message of virtue versus vengeance a little too blatantly. TH

Gregory Peck *Manuel Artiguez* • Anthony Quinn *Captain Vinolas* • Omar Sharif *Father Francisco* • Mildred Dunnock *Pilar* • Raymond Pellegrin *Carlos* • Paolo Stoppa *Pedro* • Daniela Rocca *Rosanna* • Christian Marquand *Lieutenant Zaganar* ■ *Dir* Fred Zinnemann • *Scr* JP Miller, from the novel *Killing a Mouse on Sunday* by Emeric Pressburger

Beijing Bastards ★★★

Musical drama
1993 · HK/Chi · Colour · 88mins

Director Zhang Yuan fell foul of the Chinese authorities with this film, which resulted in his blacklisting. This semi-documentary study of teenage delinquency focuses on the disillusion of post-Tiananmen Square youth with the party hierarchy and the social system it maintains, and features subversive pop icon Cui Jian. Zhang's aggressive direction adds to the pace and punch of the picture, but style too often counts for more than content, and his preoccupation with provocative images makes it hard to identify with the characters. DP. In Mandarin with English subtitles.

Wei Li *Karzi* • Cui Jian *Rock singer* ■ *Dir* Zhang Yuan • *Scr* Cui Jian, Tang Dalian, Zhang Yuan

Beijing Bicycle ★★★★ PG

Drama 2001 · Chi/Tai/Fr · Colour · 113mins

Wang Xiaoshuai explores the socio-psychological pressure of making one's mark in the world in this homage to the neorealist classic *Bicycle Thieves*. Cui Lin's progress as a pedal-bike courier is cut short when his only means of support is swiped. But Wang's portrayal of this event is less an attempt to elicit sympathy for him than the conscious establishment of a contrast to the need demonstrated by teenager Li Bin. He refuses to part with the bike he acquired at a flea market, as his status at school depends upon it. DP. In Mandarin with English subtitles. VIDEO DVD

Cui Lin *Guei* • Li Bin (2) *Jian* • Zhou Xun *Qin* • Gao Yuanyuan *Xiao* ■ *Dir* Wang Xiaoshuai • *Scr* Wang Xiaoshuai, Tang Danian, Peggy Chiao Hsiung-Ping, Hsu Hsiao-Ming

Being at Home with Claude ★★★ 18

Crime drama
1992 · Can · Colour and BW · 85mins

This stylised blend of romantic drama and mystery thriller makes the most of its claustrophobic setting to focus our attention on the motive for the crime committed in the arresting opening sequence. Cutting between a series of graphic black and white flashbacks and the intense interview between gay hustler Roy Dupuis and police inspector Jacques Godin, director Jean Beaudin reveals why Dupuis loved his partner to death – literally. Occasionally self-indulgent, this is still well staged and impeccably acted. DP. In French with English subtitles. VIDEO

Roy Dupuis *Yves* • Jacques Godin *Inspector* • Jean-François Pichette *Claude* • Gaston Lepage *Stenographer* • Hugo Dube *Policeman* • Johanne-Marie Tremblay *Inspector's wife* ■ *Dir* Jean Beaudin • *Scr* Jean Baudin, from the play by René-Daniel Dubois

Being Human ★★★ 15

Comedy drama
1994 · UK/US · Colour · 116mins

This unclassifiable picture very nearly spelt the end for director Bill Forsyth. Shelved after its disastrous US opening, the film re-emerged with an added narration by Theresa Russell that was supposed to tie together the five tales spanning 6,000 years. For all the ingenious interaction of recurrent themes and motifs, none of these understated stories is particularly memorable in itself, yet this is a thoughtful, if obscure, experiment, with Robin Williams endlessly inventive as a caveman, a Roman slave, a medieval wanderer, a 17th-century nobleman and a modern-day New Yorker. DP VIDEO

Robin Williams *Hector* • John Turturro *Lucinnius* • Kelly Hunter *Deidre* • Anna Galiena *Beatrice* • Vincent D'Onofrio *Priest* • Jonathan Hyde *Francisco* • Lizzy McInnerny *Ursula* • Hector Elizondo *Dom Paulo* • Ewan McGregor *Alvarez* • Helen Miller *Betsy* • Lindsay Crouse *Janet* • Lorraine Bracco *Anna* • William H Macy *Boris* • Theresa Russell *The Storyteller* ■ *Dir/Scr* Bill Forsyth • *Producer* David Puttnam, Robert F Colesberry

Being John Malkovich ★★★★★ 15

Fantasy comedy 1999 · US · Colour · 108mins

Spike Jonze's crazy, surreal comedy consistently dazzles while never losing its grip on unreality. The daringly original, metaphysical fantasy still finds time to ponder the human status quo, sexual gender and identity, as down-on-his-luck street puppeteer John Cusack takes a job at a strange Manhattan firm where a small door hidden behind a filing cabinet reveals a dark tunnel that leads into the head of movie star John Malkovich. When he tells co-worker Catherine Keener about his new-found celebrity joy ride, they form a business partnership that offers jaded New Yorkers the chance to be the actor for 15 minutes at $200 a time. Super-smart, hip and darkly subversive, Jonze's Kafkaesque mind trip is a real shock to the system. AJ Contains swearing and sex scenes. VIDEO DVD

John Cusack *Craig Schwartz* • Catherine Keener *Maxine* • Cameron Diaz *Lotte Schwartz* • John Malkovich *John Horatio Malkovich* • Orson Bean *Dr Lester* • Mary Kay Place *Floris* • Carlos Jacott *Larry the agent* • Charlie Sheen *Charlie* • Brad Pitt • Sean Penn ■ *Dir* Spike Jonze • *Scr* Charlie Kaufman

Being Julia ★★★ 12

Period comedy drama
2004 · Can/UK/Hun/US · Colour · 99mins

The glamour and superficiality surrounding the London theatre scene of the 1930s is stylishly brought to life by István Szabó. Annette Bening is the 40-something stage actress and society queen, who begins a turbulent affair with a gold-digging young American (Shaun Evans). Initially energised by their illicit meetings, the married diva is increasingly pained by Evans's playboy ways, particularly his relationship with a beautiful acting hopeful (Lucy Punch). This character-driven piece benefits from solid performances and a sharply amusing script, although Bening occasionally overplays her role. SF. Contains swearing. DVD

Annette Bening *Julia Lambert* • Jeremy Irons *Michael Gosselyn* • Bruce Greenwood *Lord Charles* • Miriam Margolyes *Dolly de Vries* • Juliet Stevenson *Evie* • Shaun Evans *Tom Fennel* • Lucy Punch *Avice Crichton* • Maury Chaykin *Walter Gibbs* • Sheila McCarthy *Grace Dexter* • Michael Gambon *Jimmie Langton* • Rita Tushingham *Aunt Carrie* ■ *Dir* István Szabó • *Scr* Ronald Harwood, from the novella *Theatre* by W Somerset Maugham

Being There ★★★★ 15

Satirical comedy
1979 · US · Colour · 123mins

Hal Ashby's satirical parable on the way the USA surrenders itself to homespun evangelicals gives Peter Sellers the role of a lifetime as the naive, illiterate gardener thrust into an outside world that takes his ignorance for philosophical depth. TV-nurtured, he comments to a seductive Shirley MacLaine that he likes watching and gives her entirely the wrong idea. Veteran Melvyn Douglas refuses to be upstaged by Sellers and thoroughly deserved his Oscar for best supporting actor. TH VIDEO DVD

Peter Sellers *Chance* • Shirley MacLaine *Eve Rand* • Melvyn Douglas *Benjamin Rand* • Jack Warden *President, "Bobby"* • Richard Dysart *Dr Robert Allenby* • Richard Basehart *Vladimir Skrapinov* • Ruth Attaway *Louise* • Dave Clennon [David Clennon] *Thomas Franklin* ■ *Dir* Hal Ashby • *Scr* Jerzy Kosinski, from his novel

Bela Lugosi Meets a Brooklyn Gorilla ★

Comedy horror 1952 · US · BW · 74mins

The last film Bela Lugosi made before he fell into the clutches of Ed Wood, this cheapie was produced (in just two weeks) to cash in the "success" of the Lon Chaney Jr vehicle, *Bride of the Gorilla*. Although Lugosi was the nominal star (and his mad scientist's simmering menace is the film's sole virtue), producer Jack Broder was much more interested in showcasing the negligible talents of his Martin and Lewis lookalikes, Duke Mitchell and Sammy Petrillo. DP

Bela Lugosi *Dr Zabor* • Duke Mitchell • Sammy Petrillo • Charlita *Nona* • Muriel Landers *Salome* • Al Kikume *Chief Rakos* ■ *Dir* William Beaudine • *Scr* Tim Ryan

Believe in Me ★★

Drama 1971 · US · Colour · 87mins

Michael Sarrazin is the New York hospital intern, Jacqueline Bisset his live-in partner; together they slip into the outer limits of drug addiction. Eventually, Bisset sees sense, leaving Sarrazin just as heroin looks like taking over from amphetamines. This is a stern health warning aimed at the audience of the time, who habitually turned up stoned to watch a movie. AT

Michael Sarrazin *Remy* • Jacqueline Bisset *Pamela* • Jon Cypher *Alan* • Allen Garfield *Stutter* • Kurt Dodenhoff *Matthew* • Marcia Jean Kurtz *ER nurse* • Kevin Conway *Clancy* • Roger Robinson *Angel* • Antonio Fargas *Boy* ■ *Dir* Stuart Hagmann • *Scr* Israel Horovitz

The Believer ★★★★ 15

Drama based on a true story
2001 · US · Colour · 98mins

Though controversial, screenwriter-turned-director Henry Bean's feature debut is no cheap-trick shocker. Instead, the story of Danny Balint, a young Jewish New Yorker who rejects his faith in favour of rabid fascism and a role as a neo-Nazi mouthpiece, makes its mark with rawness, intelligence and maturity. Devoid of sensationalism yet truly unnerving, the stomach-churning drama reinforces its grit with choppy camera work and grainy visuals. Ryan Gosling's enigmatic and blisteringly feral lead performance is perfectly judged. SF. Contains violence, swearing and sex scenes. DVD

Ryan Gosling *Danny Balint* • Summer Phoenix *Carla Moebius* • Glenn Fitzgerald *Drake* • Theresa Russell *Lina Moebius* • Billy Zane *Curtis Zampf* • Elizabeth Reaser *Miriam* ■ *Dir* Henry Bean • *Scr* Henry Bean, from a story by Henry Bean, Mark Jacobson

The Believers ★★★ 18

Horror 1987 · US · Colour · 109mins

John Schlesinger directs this tale of a voodoo cult holding Manhattan in a grip of terror, but clearly feels the material is beneath him and tries upgrading it to a *Rosemary's Baby*-style exercise in paranoia. Wrong choice. Despite the presence of the ever-dependable Martin Sheen, as a police psychiatrist trying to save his son from Satan, and a very polished style, this uninspired suspense tale is more depressing than chilling. AJ. Contains swearing and violence. DVD

Martin Sheen *Cal Jamison* • Helen Shaver *Jessica Halliday* • Harley Cross *Chris Jamison* • Robert Loggia *Lieutenant Sean McTaggert* • Elizabeth Wilson *Kate Maslow* • Harris Yulin *Donald Calder* • Lee Richardson *Dennis Maslow* • Richard Masur *Marty Wertheimer* ■ *Dir* John Schlesinger • *Scr* Mark Frost, from the novel *The Religion* by Nicholas Conde

Belizaire the Cajun ★★★

Historical drama
1985 · US · Colour · 101mins

This indie effort dramatises the persecution of French-speaking Cajuns by landowners and their henchmen in the 1850s. The main characters are Armand Assante as a Cajun herbalist, Gail Youngs as his former girlfriend and Will Patton as her common-law husband. All are happy to farm the land and keep themselves to themselves, but are inexorably caught up in the violence and necktie parties. The film was developed at Robert Redford's Sundance Institute with the active support of Robert Duvall, who makes a cameo appearance. AT. Contains violence, swearing.

Armand Assante *Belizaire Breaux* • Gail Youngs *Alida Thibodaux* • Michael Schoeffling *Hypolite Leger* • Stephen McHattie *James Willoughby* • Will Patton *Matthew Perry* • Nancy Barrett *Rebecca* • Robert Duvall *Preacher* ■ *Dir/Scr* Glen Pitre

Bell, Book and Candle ★★★ U

Comedy 1958 · US · Colour · 98mins

The fun side of *Rosemary's Baby* was a theatre hit for the elegant pairing of Rex Harrison and Lilli Palmer. James Stewart and Kim Novak are pleasant enough in this screen version, but they are left struggling in a lush but charmless adaptation sadly lacking the right witches' brew. Still, the Oscar-nominated art direction/set decoration is effective, there's a fine performance from Pyewacket the cat, and rival witches Hermione Gingold and Elsa Lanchester are good fun. TS DVD

James Stewart *Shepherd Henderson* • Kim Novak *Gillian Holroyd* • Jack Lemmon *Nicky Holroyd* • Ernie Kovacs *Sidney Redlitch* • Hermione Gingold *Mrs De Pass* • Elsa Lanchester *Queenie* ■ *Dir* Richard Quine • *Scr* Daniel Taradash, from the play by John Van Druten • *Art Director* Cary Odell • *Set Designer* Louis Diage

Bell-Bottom George ★★ U

Second World War comedy
1943 · UK · BW · 97mins

This wartime comedy is so full of tired plot that it could easily have been assembled after a recce of the cutting room floor. George Formby is rejected by the armed forces only to find himself in the thick of the action after he puts on a handy uniform. Like so many British flag-wavers, the storyline concerns a nest of Nazi spies. DP

George Formby *George* • Anne Firth *Pat* • Reginald Purdell *Birdie Edwards* • Peter Murray Hill *Shapley* • Charles Farrell *Jim Benson* • Eliot Makeham *Johnson* • Manning Whiley *Church* ■ *Dir* Marcel Varnel • *Scr* Peter Fraser, Edward Dryhurst, from a story by Richard Fisher, Peter Cresswell

A Bell for Adano ★★★

Second World War drama
1945 · US · BW · 103mins

The prolific director Henry King was always a safe pair of hands but rarely an inspired artist in a film career that spanned half a century, and this is a typical example of his work. No masterpiece, in other words, but still a gentle and engaging Second World War tale about a US Army unit that occupies an Italian town and wins over the locals by, among other things, providing them with a new bell after the old one had been melted down for the war effort. PF

Gene Tierney *Tina* • John Hodiak *Major Victor Joppolo* • William Bendix *Sgt Borth* • Glenn Langan *Lt Livingstone* • Richard Conte *Nicolo* • Stanley Prager *Sgt Trampani* • Henry Morgan [Harry Morgan] *Capt Purvis* ■ *Dir* Henry King • *Scr* Lamar Trotti, Norman Reilly Raine, from the novel by John Hersey

The Bell Jar ★★

Drama 1979 · US · Colour · 112mins

A disappointingly dull adaptation of Sylvia Plath's autobiographical novel, published pseudonymously in 1963 and then under her own name in 1966. The heroine, Esther Greenwood, lives with her widowed mother in comfortable, middle-class 1950s America before becoming a journalist in Boston. Bright and pretty, she's also self-absorbed, neurotic, sexually disturbed and suicidal. Greenwood/Plath is played by Marilyn Hassett, a briefly shining star of the 1970s. AT

Marilyn Hassett *Esther* • Julie Harris *Mrs Greenwood* • Anne Jackson *Dr Nolan* • Barbara Barrie *Jay Cee* • Robert Klein *Lenny* • Donna Mitchell *Joan* • Mary Louise Weller *Doreen* ■ *Dir* Larry Peerce • *Scr* Marjorie Kellogg, from the novel by Sylvia Plath

The Bell of Hell ★★★

Horror 1973 · Sp/Fr · Colour · 97mins

Right to the end of this bizarre revenge shocker, one is never sure what to believe. Is Renaud Verley as disturbed as aunt Viveca Lindfors claims, or is he just a practical joker? Spanish director Claudio Guerin Hill's stylish flair is diverting, often reminiscent of the Italian master, Mario Bava; but the relentless mystery is never quite as gripping nor as coherent as one would have liked. At the end of shooting, Hill died when he either fell or jumped from the bell-tower which features in the unfathomable denouement. DM. Spanish dialogue dubbed into English.

Renaud Verley *Juan* • Viveca Lindfors *Marta* • Alfredo Mayo *Pedro* • Maribel Martin *Esther* • Nuria Gimeno *Teresa* ■ *Dir* Claudio Guerin Hill • *Scr* Santiago Moncada

The Bellboy ★★★ U

Comedy 1960 · US · BW · 71mins

After 17 films with partner Dean Martin, and a further seven solo, Jerry Lewis persuaded Paramount to let him take on the directorial duties for the first time in one of his own films. Little more than a series of sketches set in the famous Fontainebleau Hotel in Miami, this very funny movie (which Lewis also produced and wrote) confirmed a clear directorial style, and proved Lewis well capable of continuing the tradition of American comedy auteurs. Unfortunately, his talent has only really been recognised in France; most British critics still loathe Lewis's humour. TS DVD

Jerry Lewis *Stanley* • Alex Gerry *Manager* • Bob Clayton *Bell Captain* • Herkie Styles *Bellboy* • Sonny Sands *Bellboy* • Eddie Shaeffer *Bellboy* • David Landfield *Bellboy* ■ *Dir/Scr* Jerry Lewis

Belle de Jour ★★★★★ 18

Psychological drama
1967 · Fr/It · Colour · 95mins

Luis Buñuel embarked on this picture convinced it would be his last. However, the receipt of the Golden Lion at Venice and universal critical acclaim persuaded him to undertake five further features, each one a masterpiece. Stunningly photographed by Sacha Vierny, this complex parable on social, sexual and emotional repression flits between dream and reality with such deft sleights of hand that we are never sure whether we are watching episodes from Catherine Deneuve's life or sharing her fantasies. Deneuve is utterly beguiling as the housewife who seeks escape in prostitution, but the director is the film's true star. DP. In French with English subtitles. Contains sex scenes, swearing, violence. DVD

Catherine Deneuve *Séverine Sérizy* • Jean Sorel *Pierre Sérizy* • Geneviève Page [Genevieve Page] *Mme Anaïs* • Michel Piccoli *Henri Husson* • Pierre Clémenti *Marcel* • Macha Méril *Renée Févret* • Francisco Rabal *Hyppolite* ■ *Dir* Luis Buñuel • *Scr* Luis Buñuel, Jean-Claude Carrière, from the novel by Joseph Kessel

Belle Epoque ★★★★ 15

Comedy drama
1992 · Sp/Por/Fr · Colour · 104mins

Winner of the best foreign language film Oscar, this charming picture recalls not only a key moment in Spanish history, at the dawning of the short-lived Republic, but also a golden age in film-making when romantic comedies were about innocence, discovery and love. Director Fernando Trueba claims his only mentor is Billy Wilder, but there is more than a touch of Buñuel about the opening sequences and the down-to-earth-with-a-bump finale. Although the romantic entanglements involving army deserter Jorge Sanz and the four bewitching sisters hold centre stage, the film is stolen by Fernando Fernán Gómez as their anarchist artist father. DP. In Spanish with English subtitles. Contains some swearing and sex scenes. DVD

Fernando Fernán Gómez *Manolo* • Jorge Sanz *Fernando* • Maribel Verdú *Rocio* • Ariadna Gil *Violeta* • Miriam Diaz-Aroca *Clara* • Penélope Cruz *Luz* • Mary Carmen Ramirez *Amalia, Manola's wife* • Gabino Diego *Juanito* ■ *Dir* Fernando Trueba • *Scr* Rafael Azcona, from a story by Rafael Azcona, José Luis García Sanchez , Fernando Trueba

La Belle Equipe ★★★★

Drama 1936 · Fr · BW · 101mins

Jean Renoir was originally to make this classic example of the poetic realist style that dominated French cinema under the Popular Front. However, Julien Duvivier makes a fine job of juggling the quirks and concerns of the five nobodies who decide to invest their lottery winnings in a rundown inn. Jean Gabin is outstanding, as cameraderie turns to contempt and the pals fall out over the renovation and the beguiling Viviane Romance. A revised ending is now generally shown, although the pessimistic version is perhaps more revealing about the fragility of happiness. DP. In French with English subtitles.

Jean Gabin *Jean, "Jeannot"* • Charles Vanel *Charles, "Charlot"* • Raymond Aimos *Raymond, "Tintin"* • Charles Dorat *Jacques* • Raphael Medina *Mario* • Micheline Cheirel *Huguette* • Viviane Romance *Gina* • Marcelle Géniat *The grandmother* • Raymond Cordy *Drunk* ■ *Dir* Julien Duvivier • *Scr* Charles Spaak, Julien Duvivier

La Belle et la Bête ★★★★★ PG

Fantasy 1946 · Fr · BW · 93mins

Although René Clément got a co-directing credit for his technical assistance, this adaptation of the timeless fairy tale is clearly the work of the poet-director Jean Cocteau. With interiors that owe much to the paintings of Doré and Vermeer, this visual feast is enhanced by the magical realism of Henri Alekan's photography, exquisite costumes and Georges Auric's audacious score. Josette Day is a delight as Beauty, while Jean Marais, in his dual role as the Beast and the Prince, manages to be truly touching beneath the superb make-up. DP. In French with English subtitles. DVD

Jean Marais *Avenant/The Beast/The Prince* • Josette Day *Beauty* • Marcel André *The Merchant* • Mila Parely *Adelaide* • Nane Germon *Felice* • Michel Auclair *Ludovic* ■ *Dir* Jean Cocteau, René Clément • *Scr* Jean Cocteau • *Costume Designer* Christian Bérard, Antonio Castillo, Marcel Escoffier

Une Belle Fille Comme Moi ★★ 15

Black comedy 1973 · Fr · Colour · 93mins

François Truffaut so misjudges the tone of this black comedy that brusque becomes strident and risqué becomes tasteless. He has Bernadette Lafont recall in flashback to sociologist André Dussolier the experiences that landed her in jail. Stuffing the action with in-jokes, autobiographical snippets and cinematic allusions, Truffaut succeeds only in making singer Guy Marchand, ratcatcher Charles Denner and lawyer Claude Brasseur seem as one-dimensional as the satire. DP. A French language film.

Bernadette Lafont *Camille Bliss* • Claude Brasseur *Monsieur Murène* • Charles Denner *Arthur* • Guy Marchand *Sam Golden* • André Dussollier *Stanislas Previne* • Philippe Léotard *Clovis Bliss* • Michel Delahaye *Marchal* ■ *Dir* François Truffaut • *Scr* François Truffaut, Jean-Loup Dabadie, from the novel *Such a Gorgeous Kid* by Henry Farrell

La Belle Noiseuse ★★★★★ 15

Drama 1991 · Fr · Colour · 228mins

In its full form (as opposed to the 125-minute *Divertimento*), this is a majestic study of art and the agonies of creation from one of the masters of the French New Wave, Jacques Rivette. The sophisticated seduction games played by artist Michel Piccoli as he sketches his new model Emmanuelle Béart make for fascinating viewing, but nothing is as compelling as the artist's hand at work. The sight of the drawing taking shape and the sound of the charcoal or nib scratching paper are hypnotic. A courageous, rewarding masterpiece. DP. In French with English subtitles. Contains nudity. DVD

Michel Piccoli *Frenhofer* • Jane Birkin *Liz* • Emmanuelle Béart *Marianne* • David Bursztein *Nicolas* • Marianne Denicourt *Julienne* • Gilles Arbona *Porbus* • Bernard Dufour *The painter* ■ *Dir* Jacques Rivette • *Scr* Pascal Bonitzar, Christine Laurent, from the story *Le Chef d'Oeuvre Inconnu* by Honoré de Balzac

B

The Belle of New York

★★★★ U

Musical 1952 · US · Colour · 80mins

Utterly charming , this MGM Technicolor musical stars the inimitable Fred Astaire, in an idle playboy role perfectly suited to his louche screen persona, and the often under-rated Vera-Ellen as the social worker he falls for. The film offers many delights along the way, notably Astaire's superb *I Wanna Be a Dancin' Man* number. Vera-Ellen dazzles in partnership (with vocals dubbed by an uncredited Anita Ellis), and unfairly neglected director Charles Walters turns this elderly Broadway show into a tiptop Metro musical. TS

Fred Astaire *Charlie Hill* • Vera-Ellen *Angela Bonfils* • Marjorie Main *Mrs Phineas Hill* • Keenan Wynn *Max Ferris* • Alice Pearce *Elsie Wilkins* • Clinton Sundberg *Gilfred Spivak* • Gale Robbins *Dixie McCoy* • Lisa Ferraday *Frenchie* ■ *Dir* Charles Walters • *Scr* Robert O'Brien, Irving Elinson, Chester Erskine (adaptation), from a play by Hugh Morton

Belle of the Nineties ★★★

Comedy 1934 · US · BW · 71mins

Following her smash-hits *She Done Him Wrong* and *I'm No Angel*, queen of the double entendre Mae West returned with more of the same in a lavish production under Leo McCarey's expert direction. The screenplay – originally entitled *It Ain't No Sin* until the Hays Office said no – was penned by the buxom star herself. It's no great shakes (St Louis saloon singer engages in two romances while fending off a third), but the innuendos flow, and Mae's musical numbers are backed up by Duke Ellington and his Orchestra. RK

Mae West *Ruby Carter* • Roger Pryor *Tiger Kid* • John Mack Brown [Johnny Mack Brown] *Brooks Claybourne* • John Miljan *Ace Lamont* • Katherine DeMille *Molly Brant* • James Donlan *Kirby* • Stuart Holmes *Dirk* ■ *Dir* Leo McCarey • *Scr* Mae West

Belle of the Yukon ★★

Musical western 1944 · US · Colour · 84mins

Set in the gold rush days, this stars Randolph Scott as a conman, so convincing that he is dubbed "Honest John" by the Klondike miners who entrust their gold dust to his safekeeping. Scott's plans are hindered by his romance with the Belle of the title, played by famous stripper Gypsy Rose Lee. Some nice comedy and lively performances contribute to the sporadic pleasures of an over complicated screenplay. RK

Randolph Scott *Honest John Calhoun* • Gypsy Rose Lee *Belle Devalle* • Dinah Shore *Lettie Candless* • Charles Winninger *Pop Candless* • Bob Burns *Sam Slade* • Florence Bates *Viola* • Guinn "Big Boy" Williams *Marshall Maitland* ■ *Dir* William A Seiter • *Scr* James Edward Grant, from a story by Houston Branch

Belle Starr ★★

Western 1941 · US · Colour · 87mins

The inexperience of the breathtakingly beautiful Gene Tierney, relatively early in her career, shows through in her unconvincing, one-note performance as a Missouri slave-owner determined to see off the Yankees. This shameless rewriting of history converts America's famous 19th-century female bandit into a Southern plantation owner, complete with loyal "mammy" (Louise Beavers) and a husband (Randolph Scott) who leads guerrilla actions against the North under Major Dana Andrews. Short on action and characterisation, with a weak script. RK

Randolph Scott *Sam Starr* • Gene Tierney *Belle Starr* • Dana Andrews *Major Thomas Crall* • John Shepperd [Shepperd Strudwick] *Ed Shirley* • Elizabeth Patterson *Sarah* • Chill Wills *Blue Duck* • Louise Beavers *Mammy Lou* • Olin Howlin *Jasper Tench* ■ *Dir* Irving Cummings • *Scr* Lamar Trotti, from a story by Niven Busch, Cameron Rogers

Belle Starr's Daughter

★★ U

Western 1948 · US · BW · 85mins

Seven years after the 1941 original, 20th Century-Fox made this lacklustre sequel. Ruth Roman, playing Belle's daughter, chases marshal George Montgomery who she thinks (wrongly, of course) shot and killed her mother. Not much more than an average co-feature, it's of interest today as one of the higher-budgeted westerns directed by Lesley Selander, who made almost 200 such films for the big screen. TS

George Montgomery *Tom Jackson* • Rod Cameron *Bob "Bittercreek" Yauntis* • Ruth Roman *Rose of Cimarron* • Wallace Ford *Bailey* • Charles Kemper *Gaffer* • William Phipps *Yuma* • Edith King *Mrs Allen* • Jack Lambert *Brone* • Isabel Jewell *Belle Starr* ■ *Dir* Lesley Selander • *Scr* WR Burnett

Les Belles de Nuit ★★★★

Fantasy drama 1952 · Fr · BW · 89mins

From René Clair, one of the great stylists of European cinema, comes this wistful, ironic and sexy fantasy about a shy young man who escapes his bleak life by dreaming of adventure and romantic encounters in different places at different historical periods. The star is the devastatingly handsome Gérard Philipe, one of France's great actors as well as the premier matinée idol of his generation. The main purveyors of feminine pulchritude are Gina Lollobrigida and Martine Carol. Philipe and Carol are marvellous together in this dreamlike film. RK. In French with English subtitles.

Gérard Philipe *Claude* • Gina Lollobrigida *Leila* • Magali Vendeuil *Suzanne* • Marilyn Buferd *Bonny* • Raymond Cordy *Gaston* • Martine Carol *Edmée* ■ *Dir/Scr* René Clair

The Belles of St Trinian's

★★★ U

Comedy 1954 · UK · BW · 86mins

Most people's memory of the *St Trinian's* films dates from their own youth, when the wonderful indiscipline of the tearaways and the debauched indifference of the staff had them longing for their own school to be run along similar lines. In 1954 nothing had ever been seen to compare with this anarchic adaptation of Ronald Searle's cartoons, which turned traditional ideas of female gentility on their heads. Alastair Sim's Miss Fritton and George Cole's Flash Harry became icons of British comic lore, but the real star of the film is Joyce Grenfell. Followed by *Blue Murder at St Trinian's*. DP

Alastair Sim *Millicent Fritton/Clarence Fritton* • Joyce Grenfell *Sergeant Ruby Gates* • George Cole *Flash Harry* • Vivienne Martin *Arabella* • Eric Pohlmann *Sultan of Makyad* • Lorna Henderson *Princess Fatima* • Hermione Baddeley *Miss Drownder* • Betty Ann Davies *Miss Waters* ■ *Dir* Frank Launder • *Scr* Frank Launder, Sidney Gilliat, Val Valentine, from the drawings by Ronald Searle

Belles on Their Toes ★★★ U

Comedy 1952 · US · Colour · 89mins

A delightful and equally popular sequel to *Cheaper by the Dozen*, with a lascivious Edward Arnold romancing newly widowed Myrna Loy but not wanting to take her extraordinarily large family with him to the altar. Jeanne Crain heads up the brood and Clifton Webb appears briefly, so don't blink in the finale. Loy battles hard on her own in this early feminist tract, backed by a typical 1950s cast. TS

Jeanne Crain *Ann Gilbreth* • Myrna Loy *Mrs Lillian Gilbreth* • Debra Paget *Martha* • Jeffrey Hunter *Dr Bob Grayson* • Edward Arnold *Sam Harper* • Hoagy Carmichael *Tom Bracken* • Barbara Bates *Ernestine* • Robert Arthur *Frank Gilbreth* ■ *Dir* Henry Levin • *Scr* Phoebe Ephron, Henry Ephron, from a novel by Frank B Gilbreth Jr, Ernestine Gilbreth Carey

Belleville Rendez-vous

★★★★ 12

Animated adventure
2003 · Fr/Can/Bel/UK · Colour/BW · 77mins

This animated adventure is a graphic delight and a triumph of invention. Effortlessly combining slapstick, character quirk and nostalgia, it follows a club-footed grandmother and her pudgy mutt across the Atlantic as they attempt to rescue the cyclist grandson who has been kidnapped from the Tour de France by two sinister gangsters. Splendid set pieces abound and, while there's the occasional longueur, the throwaway gags and passing homages give this ambitious entertainment a unique charm. DP. A French language film. DVD

Dir/Scr Sylvain Chomet

Bellissima ★★★ U

Drama 1951 · It · BW · 103mins

Italian aristocrat Luchino Visconti is best known for his sumptuous, operatic approach in films such as *Senso* and *The Leopard*. His early career, however, saw him as a pioneer of neorealism, focusing on the harsh reality of working-class life. In this, his third feature film, the powerful, uninhibited Anna Magnani plays a mother from the slums attempting to get her small daughter into a film at Rome's Cinecittà studios. The portrayal of life in the contrasting worlds of the tenements and the film studio is fascinating. RK. In Italian with English subtitles.

Anna Magnani *Maddalena Cecconi* • Walter Chiari *Alberto Annovazzi* • Tina Apicella *Maria Cecconi* • Gastone Renzelli *Spartaco Cecconi* ■ *Dir* Luchino Visconti • *Scr* Suso Cecchi D'Amico, Francesco Rosi, Luchino Visconti, from the story by Cesare Zavattini

Bellman & True ★★★ 15

Crime thriller 1987 · UK · Colour · 116mins

This low-budget British crime thriller proves that there's sentiment, if not honour, among thieves. Bernard Hill is the alcoholic computer ace, forever telling bedtime stories to his small stepson (Kieran O'Brien), who's leaned on by villains (Derek Newark, Richard Hope) to hack into a bank prior to a heist. Despite stereotypes – the sinisterly silken chief crook calls victims "Dear Heart" – this includes some great moments of tension, especially the tragicomic break-in. TH. Contains swearing, violence and sexual references. DVD

Bernard Hill *Hiller* • Derek Newark *Guv'nor* • Richard Hope *Salto* • Ken Bones *Gort* • Frances Tomelty *Anna* • Kieran O'Brien *Boy* • John Kavanagh *The Donkey* • Arthur Whybrow *The Peterman* ■ *Dir* Richard Loncraine • *Scr* Desmond Lowden, Richard Loncraine, Michael Wearing, from the novel by Desmond Lowden

Bells Are Ringing ★★★ U

Musical comedy 1960 · US · Colour · 125mins

Judy Holliday's Broadway performance was enshrined for ever when she repeated it in this sophisticated but lacklustre Vincente Minnelli musical. By the time this was made, MGM had lost its magic touch and it was a case of *The Party's Over* for its stylish brand of musical tonic. But there is still much pleasure to be had in watching the radiant Holliday in her last screen appearance before her tragically early death from cancer in 1965. TS

Judy Holliday *Ella Peterson* • Dean Martin *Jeffrey Moss* • Fred Clark *Larry Hastings* • Eddie Foy Jr *J Otto Prantz* • Jean Stapleton *Sue* • Ruth Storey *Gwynne* • Dort Clark *Inspector Barnes* • Frank Gorshin *Blake Barton* ■ *Dir* Vincente Minnelli • *Scr* Betty Comden, Adolph Green, from the musical play by Betty Comden, Adolph Green, Jule Styne

The Bells Go Down ★★ U

Comedy drama 1943 · UK · BW · 85mins

From wartime days, when British film-makers thought the lower orders all spoke cockney and made cups of tea in times of crisis, comes this uneasy Ealing chronicle of the work of a London firefighting unit, which still fascinates for its social documentation and class conflict. As a tribute to the Auxiliary Fire Service, it has an embarrassingly contrived plot, but comedian Tommy Trinder and James Mason still manage to convince by sheer force of personality. TH

Tommy Trinder *Tommy Turk* • James Mason *Ted Robbins* • Philip Friend *Bob* • Mervyn Johns *Sam* • Billy Hartnell [William Hartnell] *Bookes* • Finlay Currie *Dist Officer MacFarlane* • Philippa Hiatt *Nan* • Meriel Forbes *Susie* ■ *Dir* Basil Dearden • *Scr* Roger MacDougall, from the novel by Stephen Black

Bells of Rosarita ★★★

Western 1945 · US · BW · 68mins

According to this offbeat Roy Rogers picture, cowboy stars are just as resourceful in real life as they are up there on screen. Rogers is quietly making a western on location at a circus when he finds out the pretty owner (Dale Evans) is in danger of being cheated out of her property. Roy summons five of his fellow Republic stars to stage a benefit on her behalf and they end up corralling the bad guys. AE

Roy Rogers • George "Gabby" Hayes *Baggy Whittaker* • Dale Evans *Sue Farnum* • Adele Mara *Patty Phillips* • Wild Bill Elliott [Bill Elliott] • Allan "Rocky" Lane [Allan Lane] • Donald Barry • Robert Livingston • Sunset Carson ■ *Dir* Frank McDonald • *Scr* Jack Townley

Bells of San Angelo ★★ U

Western 1947 · US · Colour · 77mins

This was the Republic studio movie intended to toughen up the image of Roy Rogers, whose hand-tailored outfits had never previously shown any signs of dirt, and whose morals outweighed his screen presence. Here, villain John McGuire actually beats up our hero, and, at last, in the fight sequences there's a realistic feeling of characters being hurt. Rogers moves as comfortably in the action sequences as he does wielding a guitar. TS

Roy Rogers • Dale Evans *Lee Madison* • Andy Devine *Cookie* • John McGuire *Rex Gridley* • Olaf Hytten *Lionel Bates* ■ *Dir* William Witney • *Scr* Sloan Nibley

The Bells of St Mary's

★★★ U

Musical drama 1945 · US · BW · 125mins

A massively popular success in its day, this pairs Bing Crosby with Ingrid Bergman. Crosby reprises the role that won him an Oscar, that of wise and lovable Father O'Malley from *Going My Way*. Today, Crosby's priest seems rather insufferable as he helps Sister Ingrid fix up her rundown mission with a bit of song and a lot of charm. Crosby fans will brook no arguments, of course, but others may feel director Leo McCarey has his tongue well and truly in his cheek and only made this for the money. TS

Bing Crosby *Father O'Malley* • Ingrid Bergman *Sister Benedict* • Henry Travers *Mr Bogardus* • Joan Carroll *Patsy* • Martha Sleeper *Patsy's mother* • William Gargan *Joe Gallagher* • Ruth

Donnelly *Sister Michael* • Dickie Tyler *Eddie* ■ *Dir* Leo McCarey • *Scr* Dudley Nichols, from a story by Leo McCarey

B

Belly ★★ 18

Crime thriller 1998 · US · Colour · 95mins

This frenetic thriller, as directed by rap video film-maker Hype Williams, is all stuttering edits and flash visuals, as it tells of the decline and fall of two violent young black men (played by rap musicians Nas and DMX) in the last weeks of 1999. The film has dubious credentials, having been banned by an American cinema chain on the grounds that "it raises concerns about the film's overwhelmingly negative and violent depiction of African-Americans, as well as its potential to create disruptive situations in our theatres". TH. Contains swearing and violence.

Nas [Nasir Jones] *Sincere* • DMX [Earl Simmons] *Tommy Brown* • Taral Hicks *Kisha* • Tionne "T-Boz" Watkins *Tionne* • Method Man *Shameek* • Tyrin Turner *Big* • Hassan Johnson *Mark* • Power [Oliver "Power" Grant] *Knowledge* ■ *Dir* Hype Williams • *Scr* Hype Williams, from a story by Anthony Bodden, Nas [Nasir Jones]

The Belly of an Architect ★★★ 15

Psychological drama
1987 · It/UK · Colour · 113mins

This features Peter Greenaway's trademark strongly visual approach and multiple referencing to birth, death and the insubstantial human condition. Brian Dennehy stars as a self-obsessed American architect travelling to Italy to supervise an exhibition about an 18th-century French architect. His work is subverted by his preoccupation with his own stomach pains and with his wife Chloe Webb's attempts to conceive. This won't disappoint Greenaway fans, but others may prefer to avoid. LH

Brian Dennehy *Stourley Kracklite* • Chloe Webb *Louisa Kracklite* • Lambert Wilson *Caspasian Speckler* • Sergio Fantoni *Io Speckler* • Stefania Casini *Flavia Speckler* • Vanni Corbellini *Frederico* • Alfredo Varelli *Julio Ficcone* • Geoffrey Copleston *Caspetti* • Francesco Carnelutti *Pastarri* ■ *Dir/Scr* Peter Greenaway

Beloved ★★ 15

Period drama 1998 · US · Colour · 164mins

Despite a strong lead performance from Oprah Winfrey, this gets bogged down in a laborious attempt to make something worthy. Winfrey is the ex-slave who killed her own daughter to prevent her being taken into slavery, only to have a young, childlike woman (an overcooked performance from Thandie Newton) turn up on her doorstep years later who seems to have all the characteristics of the child she killed. JB. Contains violence, nudity.

Oprah Winfrey *Sethe* • Danny Glover *Paul D* • Thandie Newton *Beloved* • Kimberly Elise *Denver* • Beah Richards *Baby Suggs* • Lisa Gay Hamilton *Younger Sethe* • Albert Hall *Stamp Paid* ■ *Dir* Jonathan Demme • *Scr* Akosua Busia, Richard LaGravenese, Adam Brooks, from the novel by Toni Morrison

Beloved Enemy ★★★ U

Romantic drama 1936 · US · BW · 82mins

An odd subject for the movie debut of director HC ("Hank") Potter, the Yale Drama School graduate best remembered for comedies such as *Hellzapoppin'* and *Mr Blandings Builds His Dream House*. One of the few mainstream Hollywood movies to deal with the political upheaval in Ireland in the early part of this century, this features top-billed Merle Oberon falling for Irish rebel leader Brian Aherne. Though the title's of literary derivation, the plot clearly isn't. Nevertheless, it's intelligent and well-made. TS

Merle Oberon *Helen Drummond* • Brian Aherne *Dennis Riordan* • Karen Morley *Cathleen* • Theodore von Eltz *O'Brian* • Jerome Cowan *O'Rourke* • David Niven *Gerald Preston* • John Burton *Hall* ■ *Dir* HC Potter • *Scr* John Balderston, Rose Franken, William Brown Meloney, David Hart, from a story by John Balderston

Beloved/Friend ★★★

Drama 1998 · Sp · Colour · 91mins

Catalan director Ventura Pons is renowned for ensemble pieces in which emotions are revealed through earnest conversation. Such is the case here, as a group of friends fall out over the contents of a dying academic's will. Adapted from his own play by Josep M Benet I Jornet, the action retains a staginess that enhances the airless atmosphere of this enclosed world. However, it's the intensity of the performances that really gives the intricate drama its fascination. DP. In Catalan with English subtitles.

Josep Maria Pou [José Maria Pou] *Jaume Clara* • Rosa Maria Sarda *Fanny* • Mario Gas *Pere Roure* • David Selvas *David Vila* • Irene Montalà *Alba* ■ *Dir* Ventura Pons • *Scr* Josep M Benet I Jornet from his play *Testament*

Beloved Infidel ★★★

Romantic drama
1959 · US · Colour · 122mins

This screen version of Sheilah Graham's bestselling memoir is sunk by the staggering miscasting of Gregory Peck as F Scott Fitzgerald, though Deborah Kerr makes a brave stab at Graham. Director Henry King concentrates on the period feel, and the CinemaScope photography is stunning, but to no avail. Legend has it that Peck was annoyed that the first edit of the film favoured Kerr, and summoned brilliant film editor William Reynolds to see him. "Why do you think they pay me a fortune to do this?" demanded Peck. "I really can't imagine," replied Reynolds. TS

Gregory Peck *F Scott Fitzgerald* • Deborah Kerr *Sheilah Graham* • Eddie Albert *Carter* • Philip Ober *John Wheeler* • Herbert Rudley *Stan Harris* • John Sutton *Lord Donegal* • Karin Booth *Janet Pierce* • Ken Scott *Robinson* ■ *Dir* Henry King • *Scr* Sy Bartlett, from the book by Sheilah Graham, Gerold Frank • *Cinematographer* Leon Shamroy

Below ★★★ 15

Supernatural horror thriller
2002 · US · Colour · 100mins

A supernatural presence haunts an American submarine during the Second World War in director David Twohy's ghost tale. Or does it? After the USS *Tiger Shark* rescues three survivors from a torpedoed hospital ship, the low-key tension and claustrophobia mounts as the crew members attempt to conceal their dark, mutinous secrets against a psychologically intense backdrop. Twohy doesn't quite mine the creepy premise for all its macabre potential, but this will tingle undemanding spines. AJ. Contains violence, swearing. DVD

Matt Davis [Matthew Davis] *Ensign Douglas O'Dell* • Bruce Greenwood *Lt Brice* • Olivia Williams *Claire Paige* • Holt McCallany *Loomis* • Scott Foley *Coors* • Zach Galifianakis *Weird Wally* • Jason Flemyng *Stumbo* • Dexter Fletcher *Kingsley* ■ *Dir* David Twohy • *Scr* Lucas Sussman, Darren Aronofsky, David Twohy

The Belstone Fox ★★ PG

Drama 1973 · UK · Colour · 98mins

In this workmanlike adaptation of David Rook's novel, Eric Porter is the huntsman who adopts an abandoned fox cub and rears it with a litter of puppy hounds. When the hunting season starts, the fox reverts to its role as quarry and Porter lives to regret his moment of weakness. The film impresses more for its wildlife photography than for its dramatic interest. PF DVD

Eric Porter *Asher* • Rachel Roberts (1) *Cathie* • Jeremy Kemp *Kendrick* • Bill Travers *Tod* • Dennis Waterman *Stephen* ■ *Dir* James Hill • *Scr* James Hill, from the novel *Ballad of the Belstone Fox* by David Rook • *Cinematographer* John Wilcox, James Allen

Ben ★★

Horror 1972 · US · Colour · 94mins

This sequel to *Willard* is probably best known for its theme song (which was a hit for Michael Jackson), as few horror aficionados have much time for its unconvincing blend of gore and gushing sentimentality. Yet it's a polished piece of work, with Lee Harcourt Montgomery fine as the kid sheltering the rodent hordes, and Joseph Campanella business-like as the pursuing cop who discovers who is leading a pack of killer rats. DP

Lee Harcourt Montgomery [Lee Montgomery] *Danny Garrison* • Joseph Campanella *Cliff Kirtland* • Arthur O'Connell *Bill Hatfield* • Rosemary Murphy *Beth Garrison* • Meredith Baxter *Eve Garrison* • Kaz Garas *Joe Greer* • Paul Carr *Kelly* • Richard Van Fleet *Reade* ■ *Dir* Phil Karlson • *Scr* Gilbert A Ralston, from characters created by Stephen Gilbert [Gilbert A Ralston]

Ben-Hur ★★★★★ PG

Period epic 1959 · US · Colour · 213mins

Back in 1959, this epic was the most costly movie ever made. Many believe that it is not a match for the 1925 silent version, while it certainly lasts almost as long as the Roman Empire itself. Nor will it ever win any prizes for experimental film-making. But, never mind, enjoy Charlton Heston's chariot-driving, galley-rowing and toga-wearing, and, above all, feel the vital statistics. A thousand-strong force toiled for a year to construct the 18-acre chariot arena, which was eventually filled with 8,000 extras for the 20-minute race that forms the famous climax. The film, in all, used over 300 sets, 40,000 tons of sand (for the chariot track) and swept up a record 11 Oscars, a total that was equalled in 1998 by James Cameron's *Titanic* and in 2004 by Peter Jackson's *The Lord of the Rings: The Return of the King*. PF DVD

Charlton Heston *Judah Ben-Hur* • Stephen Boyd *Messala* • Haya Harareet *Esther* • Jack Hawkins *Quintus Arrius* • Hugh Griffith *Sheik Ilderim* • Martha Scott *Miriam* • Cathy O'Donnell *Tirzah* • Frank Thring *Pontius Pilate* • Sam Jaffe *Simonides* • Finlay Currie *Balthasar* ■ *Dir* William Wyler • *Scr* Karl Tunberg, from the novel by Lew Wallace • *Music* Miklos Rozsa • *Cinematographer* Robert L Surtees [Robert Surtees] • *Special Effects* A Arnold Gillespie, Robert MacDonald, Milo Lory • *Art Director* Edward Carfagno, William A Horning • *Costume Designer* Elizabeth Haffenden • *Editor* Ralph E Winters, John Dunning

Ben-Hur: a Tale of the Christ ★★★★★ PG

Silent period epic
1925 · US · BW and Colour · 142mins

A landmark movie in every respect, this story of the friendship and hatred between a Jew and a Roman allowed for plenty of moralising as well as rousing action scenes. Lew Wallace's novel – a Victorian potboiler – had been a Broadway hit and MGM almost broke the bank buying the rights. Filming was due to begin in Italy with George Walsh as Ben-Hur, under the direction of Charles Brabin. But the footage was so terrible MGM junked everything and fired Walsh. He was replaced by Ramon Novarro, and Fred Niblo took over as director. The footage was better, but filming the sea battle claimed the lives of at least three Italian extras. The result flabbergasted critics and audiences alike, but its final cost of $4 million was too much to see any profit. The occasional static, over-pious scenes are a small price to pay for so much stunning spectacle. AT

Ramon Novarro *Ben-Hur* • Francis X Bushman *Messala* • May McAvoy *Esther* • Betty Bronson *Mary* • Claire McDowell *Princess of Hur* • Kathleen Key *Tirzah* ■ *Dir* Fred Niblo • *Scr* Bess Meredyth, Carey Wilson, June Mathis, from the novel by Lew Wallace

A Bench in the Park ★★★

Romantic comedy
1998 · Sp · Colour · 82mins

Agusti Vila's first feature is a lightweight comedy of manners. Alex Brendemühl becomes convinced love can only come from chance encounters after his longtime girlfriend departs for London. He therefore decides to divide his afternoons between a park bench and a bar stool, and soon finds himself unable to choose between spiky drifter Victoria Freire and scholarly Mónica López. While happy to let his three protagonists prattle on, Vila can't resist employing a range of self-conscious camera movements, which neither capture the atmosphere of the scene nor the stunning Barcelona backdrops. DP. In Spanish with English subtitles.

Alex Brendemühl *Juan* • Victoria Freire *Alicia* • Mónica López *Ana* • Aitor Merino *Carlos* ■ *Dir/Scr* Agusti Vila

Bend It like Beckham ★★★ 12

Sports comedy drama
2001 · Ger/UK · Colour · 107mins

This feel-good teen-oriented comedy drama has two things going for it, besides its opportunistic title: it's set in the world of female football and against a background of intransigent first-generation Indian tradition in suburban Britain. Newcomer Parminder Nagra is skilled in both acting and ball-control as the teenager who "worships" at her shrine to England captain David Beckham, and culture clashes are played with knowing humour. But the predictability of the storyline and wooden co-star Keira Knightley let this down. AC. Contains swearing. DVD

Parminder Nagra *Jess Bhamra* • Keira Knightley *Jules* • Jonathan Rhys Meyers *Joe* • Anupam Kher *Mr Bhamra* • Archie Panjabi *Pinky Bhamra* • Juliet Stevenson *Paula* ■ *Dir* Gurinder Chadha • *Scr* Guljit Bindra, Gurinder Chadha, Paul Mayeda Berges

Bend of the River ★★★★ PG

Western 1952 · US · Colour · 90mins

This is a magnificent western, one of a superb postwar series of films starring James Stewart and directed by Anthony Mann. Here, Stewart is a wagon train scout trying to hide his past, pitted against former partner Arthur Kennedy in a story that takes on the dimensions of Greek tragedy. Watch, too, for an early star-making performance from Rock Hudson, who forms a bond with reformed outlaw Stewart. A satisfying work, with action sequences and performances that repay several viewings. TS DVD

James Stewart *Glyn McLyntock* • Arthur Kennedy *Cole Garett* • Rock Hudson *Trey Wilson* • Julia Adams [Julie Adams] *Laura Baile* • Lori Nelson *Marjie* • Stepin' Fetchit [Stepin Fetchit] *Adam* ■ *Dir* Anthony Mann • *Scr* Borden Chase, from the novel *Bend of the Snake* by Bill Gulick

B

Beneath Clouds ★★★

Drama 2002 · Aus · Colour · 88mins

Ivan Sen's haunting, award-winning debut feature film is an affecting racial drama that tells the story of young mixed-race teenager Dannielle Hall who sets off to the city to find her long-lost Irish father. On route, she hooks up with angry Aboriginal youth Damian Pitt who has escaped from prison in a bid to see his mother before she dies. The stark beauty of the rural landscape reflects the emotional desolation of the troubled teens and the end result is an uncomfortable portrait of race relations in Australia. JF

Dannielle Hall *Lena* • Damian Pitt *Vaughn* • Jenna Lee Connors *Ty* • Simon Swan *Jimmy* • Mundurra Weldon *Liam* • Judy Duncan *Jen* • Kevin Pitt *Smiley* • Arthur Dignam *Old man* ■ *Dir/Scr* Ivan Sen

Beneath the Planet of the Apes ★★★ 15

Science-fiction adventure 1969 · US · Colour · 90mins

The first sequel to the enormously successful *Planet of the Apes* is also the best. Less subtle and profound than its predecessor, it's still an exciting and colourful action adventure. This time out, astronaut James Franciscus and chimpanzee scientist Kim Hunter search for Charlton Heston (star of the first film) in the nuclear-devastated future, evading militaristic apes only to stumble upon an underground community of mutant, telepathic humans. The destruction of the world didn't stop three more progressively silly sequels, with *Escape from the Planet of the Apes* (1971) the next in the series. AJ. Contains violence. [VIDEO] DVD

James Franciscus *Brent* • Charlton Heston *Taylor* • Kim Hunter *Dr Zira* • Maurice Evans *Dr Zaius* • Linda Harrison *Nova* • Paul Richards (1) *Mendez* • Victor Buono *Fat man* • James Gregory *Ursus* • Roddy McDowall *Narrator* ■ *Dir* Ted Post • *Scr* Paul Dehn, from a story by Mort Abrahams, Paul Dehn, from characters created by Pierre Boulle

Beneath the 12-Mile Reef ★★ U

Adventure 1953 · US · Colour · 100mins

Having already shot the Crucifixion (*The Robe*) and Marilyn Monroe (*How to Marry a Millionaire*) in CinemaScope, 20th Century-Fox took its new wonder process underwater for this scuba-frolic. Robert Wagner cuts a dash as a sponge diver, Gilbert Roland is his dad, Terry Moore is the love interest, Richard Boone the heavy and an octopus shows up when the plot begins to leak. AT DVD

Robert Wagner *Tony Petrakis* • Gilbert Roland *Mike Petrakis* • J Carrol Naish *Soak* • Richard Boone *Thomas Rhys* • Harry Carey Jr *Griff Rhys* • Terry Moore *Gwyneth Rhys* • Peter Graves (2) *Arnold* • Angela Clarke *Mama* ■ *Dir* Robert D Webb • *Scr* Al Bezzerides

Beneath the Valley of the Ultra Vixens ★★★ 18

Cult sex comedy 1979 · US · Colour · 92mins

This quintessential sex comedy is Russ Meyer's last movie to date as director, and it's all here: comic violence, insatiable busty women, religion, necrophilia, impotent bumbling men, chainsaws and Martin Bormann. The plot revolves around stripper "Kitten" Natividad's attempts to steer her husband away from perversion, with Anne Marie and Uschi Digard along for the rollercoaster ride through Meyer's lusty small-town landscape. The director plays himself in this satirical semi-autobiography, which has a strong moral code at its soft-core centre. AJ [VIDEO]

Francesca "Kitten" Natividad [Kitten Natividad] *Lavonia/Lola Langusta* • Anne Marie *Eufaula Roop* • Ken Kerr *Lamar Shedd* • June Mack *"Junk-yard" Sal* • Uschi Digard *Supersoul* ■ *Dir* Russ Meyer • *Scr* Roger Ebert, Russ Meyer

Benefit of the Doubt ★★★ 18

Thriller 1993 · US/Ger · Colour · 87mins

This modest, occasionally gripping little thriller manages some neat variations on a familiar theme. An almost unrecognisable Amy Irving is the struggling single mum who is less than enamoured when she learns that her father (Donald Sutherland) is about to be released from prison, particularly because it was her testimony as a child that convicted him of the murder of her mother. The two leads, particularly the ambivalent Sutherland, are good, but the film is let down by a half-hearted climax. JF. Contains violence, swearing and nudity. [VIDEO]

Donald Sutherland *Frank Braswell* • Amy Irving *Karen Braswell* • Rider Strong *Pete Braswell* • Christopher McDonald *Dan* • Graham Greene (2) *Sheriff Calhoun* • Theodore Bikel *Gideon Lee* • Gisele Kovach *Susanna* • Ferdinand Mayne [Ferdy Mayne] *Mueller* • Julie Hasel *Young Karen* ■ *Dir* Jonathan Heap • *Scr* Christopher Keyser, Jeffrey Polman, Michael Lieber

Bengal Brigade ★★ U

Period adventure 1954 · US · Colour · 87mins

Straight after *Death of a Salesman* and *The Wild One*, director Laslo Benedek cranked out this North-West Frontier caper. Rock Hudson plays a British Army captain who is framed and court-martialled, and resigns his commission. He becomes a big-game hunter yet still manages to suss out rebel plans, win the girl and keep the British Raj running. AT

Rock Hudson *Jeff Claybourne* • Arlene Dahl *Vivian Morrow* • Ursula Thiess *Latah* • Torin Thatcher *Colonel Morrow* • Arnold Moss *Rajah Karam Jee* • Dan O'Herlihy *Captain Ronald Blaine* • Michael Ansara *Major Puran Singh* ■ *Dir* Laslo Benedek • *Scr* Richard Alan Simmons, from the novel by Hall Hunter

Bengazi ★★

Adventure 1955 · US · BW · 79mins

Richard Conte here makes the most of a script that seems content to rehash a job-lot of clichés and assorted dead ends. Recalling his peak of fame as a hard-nut gangster, Conte is energetically gritty playing an unsavoury character trying to unearth hidden gold in North Africa. Sadly, director John Brahm's laudable attempts at style are punctured by moments of unplanned hilarity. Mediocre. JM

Richard Conte *Gilmore* • Victor McLaglen *Donovan* • Richard Carlson *Levering* • Mala Powers *Aileen Donovan* • Richard Erdman *Selby* • Hillary Brooke *Nora* • Maury Hill *Peters* • Jay Novello *Basim* • Albert Carrier *MacMillan* ■ *Dir* John Brahm • *Scr* Endre Bohem, Louis Vittes, from a story by Jeff Bailey

Benjamin Smoke ★★★

Music documentary 1999 · US · Colour and BW · 80mins

Shot in glowing monochrome and pieced together in typically fragmentary fashion by Jem Cohen (in conjunction with Peter Sillen), this is a fond, if rarely profound memoir of Benjamin (Robert Curtis Dickerson), the gravel-voiced, cross-dressing frontman of the indie bands Opal Foxx Quartet and Smoke. With its distinctive use of instrumentation and its quirky lyrics, the music is provocatively non-mainstream, while Benjamin's anecdotes about life in Atlanta's Cabbagetown, his sexual odyssey and his imminent Aids-related death are as witty as they're moving. But Cohen fails to break down his subject's defences, and this portrait has more style than substance. DP

Dir Jem Cohen, Peter Sillen

Benji ★★★ Uc

Adventure 1974 · US · Colour · 85mins

So what if the production values are shoddy, the kids can't act and the plot was old hat when Rin Tin Tin was a pup. This is a cheer-to-the-rafters adventure, thanks to the exuberant ingenuity and adorably expressive face of a mongrel called Higgins. A veteran of TV's *Petticoat Junction*, the 18-year-old dog was brought out of retirement for this role of a lifetime, as the family pet who foils a kidnapping attempt. Benji pulls off a series of truly amazing tricks that won him the Georgie for the animal act of the year. A first sequel, *For the Love of Benji*, followed in 1977. DP [VIDEO]

Patsy Garrett *Mary* • Allen Fiuzat *Paul* • Cynthia Smith *Cindy* • Peter Breck *Dr Chapman* • Edgar Buchanan *Bill* ■ *Dir/Scr* Joe Camp

Benji the Hunted ★★ U

Adventure 1987 · US · Colour · 85mins

A litter of cuddly cougar cubs comes close to upstaging our cute hero in the fourth film in the Benji series. It was made seven years after *Oh, Heavenly Dog!*, but the passage of time did little to refresh director Joe Camp's imagination, as the plot is nothing more than a cross-breed between a Lassie movie and Disney adventures such as *The Incredible Journey*. However, with a shipwreck, a trek through the wilderness and a series of murderous attacks, it's packed with enough incident to retain the interest of children. Camp directed a further sequel, *Benji: Off the Leash*, 17 years later. DP [VIDEO] DVD

Red Steagall *Hunter* • Nancy Francis *Newscaster* • Frank Inn • Mike Francis *TV cameraman* ■ *Dir/Scr* Joe Camp

Benny and Joon ★★★ 15

Comedy drama 1993 · US · Colour · 94mins

You'll either find this so-so romantic fable a whimsical joy or annoyingly eccentric, as beguiling man-child Johnny Depp woos mentally unstable Mary Stuart Masterson, much to her brother Aidan Quinn's concern. It's one of those "lunatics are saner than the rest of us" polemics, admittedly heartfelt but, ultimately, too underwritten to put its message across properly. However, the performances do wonders in papering over the credibility gaps, and Depp's silent movie skills. AJ [VIDEO] DVD

Johnny Depp *Sam* • Mary Stuart Masterson *Joon Pearl* • Aidan Quinn *Benny Pearl* • Julianne Moore *Ruthie* • Oliver Platt *Eric* • CCH Pounder *Doctor Garvey* • Dan Hedaya *Thomas* • Joe Grifasi *Mike* • William H Macy *Randy Burch* ■ *Dir* Jeremiah Chechik • *Scr* Barry Berman, from a story by Barry Berman, Leslie McNeil

The Benny Goodman Story ★★ U

Musical biography 1955 · US · Colour · 116mins

Universal had a surprise smash hit with *The Glenn Miller Story* and this forlorn follow-up proved that lightning doesn't strike twice, despite the great Benny himself playing clarinet to Steve Allen's miming. TV chat show host Allen lacks both the screen charisma and acting experience to make this involving, even though he's surrounded by real-life musicians and has Donna Reed as co-star. Inexperienced director Valentine Davies can't manage the pace or the mood. TS

Steve Allen *Benny Goodman* • Donna Reed *Alice Hammond* • Berta Gersten *Mom Goodman* • Herbert Anderson *John Hammond* • Robert F Simon *Pop Goodman* • Sammy Davis Sr *Fletcher Henderson* • Dick Winslow *Gil Rodin* ■ *Dir/Scr* Valentine Davies

Benny's Video ★★★★ 18

Drama 1992 · Austria/Swi · Colour · 109mins

The desensitising nature of popular culture is a theme that recurs throughout most of Michael Haneke's films, but rarely has it been more chillingly debated than in this almost nonchalant study of dysfunction and death. Technically, the tactic of viewing the world through a camcorder lens may not be original. But the dispassionate way in which Arno Frisch – a spoiled but neglected teenager who subsists on violent movies – murders the stranger he has lured to the family home is as stupefyingly horrific as the callous passivity with which his parents learn of the crime. A subtly disturbing experience. DP. In German with English subtitles.

Arno Frisch *Benny* • Angela Winkler *Mother* • Ulrich Mühe *Father* • Ingrid Stassner *Young girl* ■ *Dir/Scr* Michael Haneke

Bent ★★ 18

Drama 1996 · UK/US/Jpn · Colour · 100mins

Lothaire Bluteau and Clive Owen star as fellow prisoners and lovers against the background of the appallingly cruel conditions of the Nazi concentration camps. Martin Sherman adapted his own West End play about Nazi homophobia and persecution, while theatre stalwart Sean Mathias directs. Mathias fails to give the film any emotional urgency, so it's the actors, including Ian McKellen, who have to carry the main burden. They stagger a bit, but provide the impetus the direction lacks. TH. Contains violence, swearing and sex scenes. [VIDEO] DVD

Lothaire Bluteau *Horst* • Clive Owen *Max* • Ian McKellen *Uncle Freddie* • Mick Jagger *Greta/George* • Brian Webber *Rudy* • Nikolaj Waldau [Nikolaj Coster-Waldau] *Wolf* • Jude Law *Stormtrooper* ■ *Dir* Sean Mathias • *Scr* Martin Sherman

Bent Keltoum ★★★

Drama 2001 · Tun/Fr/Bel · Colour · 116mins

Despite its surface superficiality, the story of a Swiss-based model who returns to her Saharan homeland to discover why she was abandoned for adoption has much to say about the social mores and grinding poverty that exist in northern Africa. Director Mehdi Charef takes a chance in allowing Cylia Malki to adopt such a superior attitude towards her compatriots, as her disregard for their basic amenities and traditional customs frequently appears supercilious. But the relentless depiction of deprivation and the humanity of the Maghreb locals Malki encounters, including eccentric aunt Baya Belal, root this in a reality beyond the travelogue visuals. DP. In French and Arabic with English subtitles.

Cylia Malki *Rallia* • Baya Belal *Nedjma* • Jean-Roger Milo *Djibril* • Deborah Lamy *Kaltoum* ■ *Dir/Scr* Mehdi Charef

Benzina ★★★ 15

Crime thriller 2001 · It · Colour · 85mins

Monica Stambrini's adaptation is more concerned with exposing intolerance within Italian society than with exploring the seemingly disparate personalities of mousy Regina Orioli and her mechanic lover Maya Sansa. The action opens with the accidental death of Orioli's disapproving mother and alternates between the couple's desire to dump the body and embark on a new life and their encounters on the road with a thuggish twosome, whose voyeuristic girlfriend films their increasingly hostile antics. It's packed with incident and ideas, but it's also decidedly inconsistent. DP. In Italian with English subtitles. Contains swearing and sex scenes. DVD

Maya Sansa *Stella* • Regina Orioli *Lenni* • Mariella Valentini *Lenni's mother* • Chiara Conti *Pippi* • Marco Quaglia *Sandro* • Pietro Ragusa *Filippo* • Luigi Maria Burruano *Padre Gabriele* ■ *Dir* Monica Lisa Stambrini • *Scr* Monica Stambrini, Elena Stancanelli, AnneRitte Ciccone, from the novel by Elena Stancanelli

Bequest to the Nation ★★

Historical drama
1972 · UK · Colour · 116mins

Though lofty in tone, playwright Terence Rattigan's acount of the relationship between Lord Nelson and Lady Hamilton reduces it to the Trafalgar hero's "little bit on the side". Fine performances by Peter Finch as Nelson and Glenda Jackson as Hamilton do little to animate the walking-waxworks style of what amounts to video history. TH

Glenda Jackson *Lady Emma Hamilton* • Peter Finch *Lord Horatio Nelson* • Michael Jayston *Captain Hardy* • Anthony Quayle *Lord Minto* • Margaret Leighton *Lady Frances Nelson* • Dominic Guard *Master George Matcham Jr* • Nigel Stock *George Matcham Sr* • Barbara Leigh-Hunt *Catherine "Catty" Matcham* ■ *Dir* James Cellan Jones • *Scr* Terence Rattigan, from his play

Berkeley Square ★★★★ U

Period romantic fantasy
1933 · US · BW · 89mins

Leslie Howard is so entranced by the early 18th-century diaries of his namesake ancestor that he takes on his identity and finds himself transported back to a periwigged past, where he consorts with the likes of Sir Joshua Reynolds. This quaint and delightful fantasy, ornamented with immaculate and sumptuous period detail, has Howard repeating the role he created on Broadway with all the polished elegance and poetic presence that made him a star of stage and screen. The accomplished direction is by Scottish-born Frank Lloyd. RK

Leslie Howard *Peter Standish* • Heather Angel *Helen Pettigrew* • Valerie Taylor *Kate Pettigrew* • Irene Browne *Lady Ann Pettigrew* • Beryl Mercer *Mrs Barwick* • Colin Keith-Johnston *Tom Pettigrew* • Alan Mowbray *Maj Clinton* • Lionel Belmore *Innkeeper* ■ *Dir* Frank Lloyd • *Scr* Sonya Levien, John L Balderston, from the play by John L Balderston

Berlin Alexanderplatz ★★★

Drama 1931 · Ger · BW · 90mins

With sound still in its infancy, it was the visual aspect of this adaptation of Alfred Döblin's sprawling novel that made the greatest impression, even though the author co-wrote the screenplay. Clearly influenced by the "city symphony" style so popular in the late silent era, director Phil Jutzi captures the sights and rhythms of Berlin with a vibrancy that stands in stark contrast to the grim Depression existence of reformed criminal Heinrich George, whose obsession with Margarete Schlegel prompts him to return to his wicked ways. Something of the book's scope would be restored in Rainer Werner Fassbinder's magisterial 13-part television version. DP. In German with English subtitles.

Heinrich George *Franz Bieberkopf* • Bernhard Minetti *Reinhold* • Margarete Schlegel *Mieze* • Albert Florath *Pums* • Paul Westermeier *Henschke* ■ *Dir* Phil Jutzi • *Scr* Alfred Döblin, Hans Wilhelm, from the novel by Alfred Döblin

Berlin Alexanderplatz ★★★★★

Drama 1980 · W Ger/It · Colour · 921mins

Originally screened as a 13-part TV series, this epic study of sexual obsession is far superior to Phil Jutzi's 1931 version, even though Alfred Döblin, who wrote the source novel, was among that film's scriptwriters. The book was Rainer Werner Fassbinder's lifelong inspiration and his fascination with its themes and central character, Franz Biberkopf, is evident from the deeply personal epilogue. As played by Günther Lamprecht, Biberkopf is the plaything of a callous society that would rather destroy him than allow him to thrive as an individual. A remarkable undertaking that has to be seen. DP. In German with English subtitles.

Hanna Schygulla *Eva* • Günther Lamprecht [Günter Lamprecht] *Franz Biberkopf* • Franz Buchrieser *Meck* • Gottfried John *Reinhold* • Barbara Sukowa *Mieze* • Peter Kolleck *Nachum* • Elisabeth Trissenaar *Lina* • Brigitte Mira *Frau Bast* • Hans Zander *Eliser* • Mechthild Grossmann *Paula* • Karin Baal *Minna* ■ *Dir* Rainer Werner Fassbinder • *Scr* Rainer Werner Fassbinder, from the novel by Alfred Doblin

Berlin Correspondent ★★ U

Second World War spy drama
1942 · US · BW · 69mins

This routine, low-budget wartime espionage drama is set in the days before Pearl Harbor, with Dana Andrews as an American radio journalist in Berlin whose broadcasts contain coded information about Nazi plans. He is rumbled by beautiful Virginia Gilmore who, naturally, is about to forsake her Nazi beliefs. AT

Virginia Gilmore *Karen Hauen* • Dana Andrews *Bill Roberts* • Mona Maris *Carla* • Martin Kosleck *Captain von Rau* • Sig Rumann [Sig Ruman] *Dr Dietrich* • Kurt Katch *Weiner* • Erwin Kalser *Mr Hauen* • Hans Schumm *Gunther* ■ *Dir* Eugene Forde • *Scr* Steve Fisher, Jack Andrews

Berlin Express ★★★

Spy thriller 1948 · US · BW · 86mins

The nondescript title hides a really tense suspense tale from talented cult director Jacques Tourneur, in his *film noir* period before he hit his swashbuckling stride with *The Flame and the Arrow* and *Anne of the Indies*. Paul Lukas plays the suave German democrat kidnapped by an underground group of Nazis opposed to the unification of their country. Merle Oberon and the impressive Robert Ryan star as the fellow travellers who become involved in the plot. The Nazis are strictly clichéd, but the view of postwar Germany rings very true and Tourneur keeps up the tension throughout. TS

Merle Oberon *Lucienne Mirbeau* • Robert Ryan *Robert Lindley* • Charles Korvin *Henri Perrot* • Paul Lukas *Dr Heinrich Bernhardt* • Robert Coote *James Sterling* ■ *Dir* Jacques Tourneur • *Scr* Harold Medford, from a story by Curt Siodmak

Berlin Jerusalem ★★★

Drama
1989 · Fr/Is/Neth/UK · Colour · 89mins

Israeli director Amos Gitai's film may be an uphill struggle for many viewers, but it's still a fascinating attempt to depict the lives and friendship of two little-known, real-life women in the 1920s and 1930s: the German poet Else Lasker-Schüler and the Russian revolutionary Tania Shochat. The ambition often outpaces the technique, but Gitai is helped by the sheer artistry of the great French cinematographer Henri Alekan. TS. In German and Hebrew with English subtitles.

Lisa Kreuzer *Else* • Rivka Neuman *Tania* • Markus Stockhausen *Ludwig* • Vernon Dobtcheff *Editor* • Veronica Lazare [Veronica Lazar] *Secretary* • Bernard Eisenschitz *Man in Berlin café* ■ *Dir* Amos Gitai • *Scr* Amos Gitai, Gudie Lawaetz

Berlin: Symphony of a Great City ★★★★★

Experimental silent documentary
1927 · Ger · BW · 77mins

As with so much in German silent cinema, this artistic masterpiece was conceived by the screenwriter Carl Mayer, who was to disassociate himself from the project when director Walter Ruttman opted for an abstract, rather than a sociological, approach. Applying still novel theories of montage to Karl Freund's vibrant imagery, Ruttman created a rhythmical portrait of the city, which seems to last a day, but was, in fact, the product of 18 months of candid photography. Dropping in on various workplaces and night spots, the film pulses with life and remains as inventive and viscerally thrilling as it must have seemed to audiences in 1927. DP

Dir Walter Ruttmann • *Scr* Walter Ruttmann, Karl Freund, from an idea by Carl Mayer

The Bermuda Mystery ★★

Crime mystery 1944 · US · BW · 65mins

This watchable little 1940s B-movie is the usual mixture of murder and money, featuring the rather too stolid Preston Foster in the lead and an interesting support cast. Ann Rutherford, perhaps best known as Polly Benedict in the Andy Hardy films, makes a charming leading lady, while the rather camp Charles Butterworth gives added value. TS

Preston Foster *Steve Carromond* • Ann Rutherford *Constance Martin* • Charles Butterworth *Dr Tilford* • Helene Reynolds *Angela* • Jean Howard *Mrs Tilford* • Richard Lane *Detective Donovan* • Roland Drew *Mr Best* ■ *Dir* Benjamin Stoloff [Ben Stoloff] • *Scr* W Scott Darling, from a story by John Larkin

Berserk ★★ 12

Mystery thriller 1967 · UK · Colour · 92mins

Here, in the twilight of her career, Joan Crawford stars in a tale about murderous goings-on in a circus, which is at least marginally better than her caveman fiasco *Trog*. She's backed up by some interesting faces but, sadly, it just isn't any good. It's a shame to watch an actress of Crawford's stature gawking at such explicit sadism, for many that is this tawdry flick's main appeal. TS

Joan Crawford *Monica Rivers* • Ty Hardin *Frank Hawkins* • Diana Dors *Matilda* • Michael Gough *Dorando* • Judy Geeson *Angela Rivers* • Robert Hardy *Det Supt Brooks* • Geoffrey Keen *Commissioner Dalby* ■ *Dir* Jim O'Connor • *Scr* Aben Kandel, Herman Cohen, from their story

Bert Rigby, You're a Fool ★★ 15

Musical comedy 1989 · US · Colour · 90mins

American director Carl Reiner was so impressed by Robert Lindsay in a West End show that he wrote this wish-fulfilling fable for him. He's a striking miner, whose impersonations of Gene Kelly and Fred Astaire take him to Hollywood stardom, and collisions with clichéd characters such as Anne Bancroft, portraying the frustrated wife of a film producer. It's like *Little Voice* with a social attitude. Songs by Cole Porter and Irving Berlin do their best to enliven the idea, but fail. TH

Robert Lindsay *Bert Rigby* • Anne Bancroft *Meredith Perlestein* • Corbin Bernsen *Jim Shirley* • Robbie Coltrane *Sid Trample* • Cathryn Bradshaw *Laurel Pennington* • Jackie Gayle *Il Perlestein* • Bruno Kirby *Kyle DeForest* • Liz Smith *Mrs Rigby* ■ *Dir/Scr* Carl Reiner

Besieged ★★ PG

Romantic drama 1998 · It · Colour · 93mins

Echoes of director Bernardo Bertolucci's previous work – notably *Last Tango in Paris* and *Tragedy of a Ridiculous Man* – abound here. Originally intended as a 60-minute TV drama, the tale of a timid pianist's obsession with his housekeeper is intriguing without ever being wholly engaging. Thandie Newton is solid enough as the medical student forced into service to make ends meet after fleeing a tyrannical African regime, but David Thewlis is wildly erratic as her besotted benefactor. A very minor work. DP. Contains brief nudity.

Thandie Newton *Shandurai* • David Thewlis *Jason Kinsky* • Claudio Santamaria *Agostino* • John C Ojwang *Singer* • Cyril Nri *Priest* • Massimo De Rossi *Patient* • Andrea Quercia *Child pianist* • Mario Mazzetti Di Pietralata *Piano buyer* ■ *Dir* Bernardo Bertolucci • *Scr* Clare Peploe, Bernardo Bertolucci, from a story by James Lasdun

The Bespoke Overcoat ★★★

Supernatural drama 1955 · UK · BW · 33mins

Jack Clayton's directorial debut was this atmospheric version of a ghost story by Gogol. It won many awards, including a 1956 Oscar for best short film. In this two-reeler, a poor clerk (Alfie Bass) working in a clothing factory is refused a coat by his bosses. A tailor friend agrees to make him one, but the clerk's death from freezing before it's finished leaves his ghost to seek retribution. Wolfgang Suschitzky's superb chiaroscuro camerawork helps belie the modest budget. BB

Alfie Bass *Fender* • David Kossoff *Morry* • Alan Tilvern *Ranting* • Alf Dean *Gravedigger* ■ *Dir* Jack Clayton • *Scr* Wolf Mankowitz, from the short story by Nikolai Gogol

Best ★★ 15

Sports biography
1999 · UK · Colour · 102mins

This is a shoddy biography of soccer genius George Best. Normally, it's the match scenes that let football films down: you either have actors who can't play, or players who can't act. Ironically, though, *Best*'s match scenes, a blend of grainy original footage and cleverly integrated re-creations, are one of its few plus points. The bulk of the film, however, focuses on George's downward spiral into alcoholism and unfulfilled potential. It's muddled in structure, melodramatic in direction and boringly repetitive. DA DVD

John Lynch *George Best* • Ian Bannen *Sir Matt Busby* • Jerome Flynn *Bobby Charlton* • Ian Hart *Nobby Stiles* • Patsy Kensit *Anna* • Cal MacAninch *Paddy Crerand* • Linus Roache *Denis Law* • Roger Daltrey *Rodney Marsh* ■ *Dir* Mary McGuckian • *Scr* Mary McGuckian, John Lynch, George Best (script consultant)

Best Boy ★★★★ 18

Documentary 1979 · US · Colour · 104mins

Disregarding the documentarist's supposed duty to remain impartial, Ira Wohl directly influences the action in this life-affirming Oscar winner, as he prizes his 52-year-old cousin, Philly, away from the parents who have devotedly cossetted him on account of his mental incapacity. Realising that they are ageing (indeed, the father is dying), Wohl attempts to prepare Philly for life on his own. Nonetheless, he remains sensitive to the fact that each small accomplishment is as much a source of regret as of pride for the selfless people witnessing their son's dependence on them diminishing.

Movingly inspirational. A sequel, *Best Man*, followed. DP

Dir/Scr Ira Wohl

The Best Day of My Life ★★★ 15

Drama 2002 · It/UK · Colour · 98mins

Cristina Comencini presents a decent family riven with good intentions and bad judgements in this emotionally dense drama. Matriarch Virna Lisi blames herself for the problems being experienced by wounded widow Margherita Buy, unhappily adulterous Sandra Ceccarelli and sexually confused Luigi Lo Cascio. By viewing the action partially from the perspective of Ceccarelli's daughters, Francesca Perini and Maria Luisa De Crescenzo, Comencini imparts a generational spin on the key questions. However, her dialogue is often so formal that it undermines the authenticity of the impressive performances. DP. In Italian with English subtitles. Contains swearing and sex scenes.

Virna Lisi *Irene* • Margherita Buy *Sara* • Sandra Ceccarelli *Rita* • Luigi Lo Cascio *Claudio* • Marco Baliani *Carlo* • Marco Quaglio *Luca* • Jean-Hugues Anglade *Davide* • Ricky Tognazzi *Sandro Berardi* • Francesca Perini *Silvia* • Maria Luisa De Crescenzo *Chiara* ■ *Dir* Cristina Comencini • *Scr* Cristina Comencini, Lucilla Schiaffino, Giulia Calenda, from a story by Cristina Comencini

Best Defense ★★ 18

Comedy 1984 · US · Colour · 90mins

This anti-establishment comedy was filmed as a Dudley Moore vehicle, but the result pleased nobody. After previews, the movie was recalled, rewritten and partially reshot, incorporating a very expensive Eddie Murphy, billed awkwardly as "Strategic guest star". It still doesn't work, but it's fascinating to see how Murphy was filmed without interfacing with the rest of the existing cast and action. The anti-Russian material is tasteless and the comedy unfunny, but Kate Capshaw and Helen Shaver make it watchable. TS. Contains swearing, sex scenes, brief nudity. DVD

Dudley Moore *Wylie Cooper* • Eddie Murphy *Landry* • Kate Capshaw *Laura* • George Dzundza *Loparino* • Helen Shaver *Claire Lewis* • Mark Arnott *Brank* • Peter Michael Goetz *Frank Joyner* ■ *Dir* Willard Huyck • *Scr* Gloria Katz, Willard Huyck, from the novel *Easy and Hard Ways Out* by Robert Grossbach

Best Foot Forward ★★★ U

Musical 1943 · US · Colour · 95mins

This early MGM Technicolor musical is a movie adaptation of a famous George Abbott Broadway show, and is notable for importing many of the Broadway cast to MGM. Although the feeble leading men didn't stay the course, Hollywood fell for peppy June Allyson and zesty Nancy Walker. The plot, originally purchased for Lana Turner, revolves around movie star Lucille Ball visiting a military academy. The glamorous Gloria DeHaven steals every scene in which she appears. Period nonsense, but watchable. TS

Lucille Ball • William Gaxton *Jack O'Riley* • Virginia Weidler *Helen Schlessenger* • Tommy Dix *Elwood* • Nancy Walker *Nancy* • Gloria DeHaven *Minerva* • Kenny Bowers *Dutch* • June Allyson *Ethel* ■ *Dir* Edward Buzzell • *Scr* Irving Brecher, Fred F Finklehoffe

Best Friends ★★★ PG

Comedy 1982 · US · Colour · 104mins

Before he became the director of such hits as *Rain Man* and *Disclosure*, Barry Levinson worked as a scriptwriter, often in collaboration with his first wife, Valerie Curtin. Proving that the couple who write together also fight together, this overexcitable comedy is a dramatic exaggeration of their real-life relationship. Burt Reynolds and Goldie Hawn are well-matched as the Hollywood scriptwriters and, once the bickering begins, they hurl their lines at each other with some enthusiasm, but this only partly atones for the fact that they are never very funny. DP

Burt Reynolds *Richard Babson* • Goldie Hawn *Paula McCullen* • Jessica Tandy *Eleanor McCullen* • Barnard Hughes *Tim McCullen* • Audra Lindley *Ann Babson* • Keenan Wynn *Tom Babson* • Ron Silver *Larry Weisman* • Carol Locatell *Nellie Ballou* ■ *Dir* Norman Jewison • *Scr* Valerie Curtin, Barry Levinson

The Best House in London ★★★

Period comedy 1968 · UK · Colour · 96mins

Scripted Denis Norden and directed with bawdy good humour by Philip Saville, this ranks among the most lavish soft-core comedies ever produced in Britain. The choicest moment involves George Saunders and John Cleese attempting to take tiffin under fire, but there's also much fun to be had in cameos from such celebrities as Willie Rushton and Clement Freud. Keeping the narrative's end up is David Hemmings, who enjoys a dual role as a mild-mannered PR man smitten with anti-smut campaigner Joanna Pettet and the opportunistic manager of a licensed brothel. DP

David Hemmings *Walter Leybourne/Benjamin Oakes* • Joanna Pettet *Josephine Pacefoot* • George Sanders *Sir Francis Leybourne* • Dany Robin *Babette* • Warren Mitchell *Count Pandolfo* • John Bird *Home secretary* • William Rushton *Sylvester Wall* • Bill Fraser *Inspector Macpherson* • Maurice Denham *Editor of "The Times"* • Martita Hunt *Headmistress* • Clement Freud *Mr Mason* ■ *Dir* Philip Saville • *Scr* Denis Norden

Best in Show ★★★★ 12

Satire 2000 · US · Colour · 86mins

After lampooning a heavy metal band in *This Is Spinal Tap* and amateur dramatics in *Waiting for Guffman*, "mockumentary" maestro Christopher Guest scores again with this howlingly funny look at dog owners. Guest co-writes, directs and acts in this sharp, but never malicious satire that follows a cross section of contestants preparing for a (fictitious) Philadelphia dog show. The impeccable ensemble improvises its way through an inspired series of keenly observed set pieces. This is laugh-out-loud comedy with pedigree and bite. DP. Contains some swearing. DVD

Christopher Guest *Harlan Pepper* • Eugene Levy *Gerry Fleck* • Catherine O'Hara *Cookie Fleck* • Michael McKean *Stefan Vanderhoof* • John Michael Higgins *Scott Donlan* • Fred Willard *Buck Laughlin* • Jennifer Coolidge *Sherri Ann Ward Cabot* • Jane Lynch *Christy Cummings* • Parker Posey *Meg Swan* • Michael Hitchcock *Hamilton Swan* • Bob Balaban *Dr Theodore W Millbank III* ■ *Dir* Christopher Guest • *Scr* Christopher Guest, Eugene Levy

Best Intentions ★★★★ PG

Drama 1992 · Swe · Colour · 173mins

Although a six-hour version was made for Swedish TV, director Bille August here settled on half that time to explore the tempestuous early relationship of Ingmar Bergman's parents. The great film-maker's script returns to the theme of troubled young love that informed so many of his early features, but there's also plenty of the spiritual and emotional angst that characterised much of his later work. The difficulties facing Samuel Froler and Pernilla August (Bille's wife) provide plenty of dramatic interest, especially when they come in the form of the disapproving father, magisterially played by Max von Sydow. This is the first of an autobiographical trilogy, that continues with *Sunday Children* and *Private Confessions*. DP. In Swedish with English subtitles.

Samuel Froler *Henrik Bergman* • Pernilla August *Anna Akerblom* • Max von Sydow *Johan Akerblom* • Ghita Norby *Karin Akerblom* • Mona Malm *Alma Bergman* • Lena Endre *Frida Strandberg* • Keve Hjelm *Fredrik Bergman* • Björn Kjellman *Ernst Akerblom* • Börje Ahlstedt *Carl Akerblom* ■ *Dir* Bille August • *Scr* Ingmar Bergman

Best Laid Plans ★★★ 15

Crime thriller 1999 · US · Colour · 89mins

Alessandro Nivola is called to Josh Brolin's house in the middle of the night where his friend confesses that he has been accused of raping a girl (Reese Witherspoon) he had picked up. To make matters worse, it turns out she is only 16 and Brolin has her tied up downstairs. All is not what it seems, however. Director Mike Barker creates a complex tale of robbery and deception, and displays a sympathetic eye for the small-town, blue-collar backdrop to the film. Although the tone is uneven, the performances are charismatic. JF. Contains violence, swearing and sex scenes. DVD

Alessandro Nivola *Nick* • Reese Witherspoon *Lissa* • Josh Brolin *Bryce* • Rocky Carroll *Bad ass dude* • Michael G Hagerty *Charlie* • Terrence Howard *Jimmy* • Jamie Marsh *Barry* ■ *Dir* Michael Barker [Mike Barker] • *Scr* Ted Griffin

The Best Little Whorehouse in Texas ★★★ 15

Musical comedy 1982 · US · Colour · 109mins

This lightweight version of the much grittier long-running Broadway musical stars Dolly Parton and Burt Reynolds, two performers noted for their sex appeal, but who fail to ignite the proper sparks here. Parton plays the madam of the Chicken Ranch brothel, who comes to blows with her sheriff lover (Reynolds) when TV evangelist Dom DeLuise tries to close the place down. Some great routines augmented with new songs keep everything on a lively and likeable keel. AJ

Burt Reynolds *Sheriff Dodd* • Dolly Parton *Miss Mona* • Dom DeLuise *Melvin* • Charles Durning *Governor* • Jim Nabors *Deputy Fred* • Robert Mandan *Senator Wingwood* • Lois Nettleton *Dulci Mae* ■ *Dir* Colin Higgins • *Scr* Larry L King, Peter Masterson, Colin Higgins, from the musical by Peter Masterson

The Best Man ★★★★

Political drama 1964 · US · BW · 101mins

Political satire is a tough subject to convey successfully in a movie, but director Franklin J Schaffner succeeded brilliantly with Gore Vidal's scabrous look at the underbelly of Washington. Not surprisingly a commercial failure, this brilliantly cast, superbly acted drama got lost on its release alongside the similar but more expensive *Advise and Consent* and *Dr Strangelove*, but this movie is almost their equal. Daring in its day – two political rivals have deep and dark secrets in their past – this is a mature and satisfying work, and contains an almost career-best performance from the great Henry Fonda. TS

Henry Fonda *William Russell* • Cliff Robertson *Joe Cantwell* • Edie Adams *Mabel Cantwell* • Margaret Leighton *Alice Russell* • Shelley Berman *Sheldon Bascomb* • Lee Tracy *Art Hockstader* • Ann Sothern *Mrs Gamadge* • Gene Raymond *Don Cantwell* • Kevin McCarthy *Dick Jensen* ■ *Dir* Franklin Schaffner [Franklin J Schaffner] • *Scr* Gore Vidal, from his play

The Best Man ★★★ PG

Period romantic drama
1998 · It · Colour · 100mins

Pupi Avati's melodrama is set on the last day of the 19th century and its resulting symbolism is heavy-handed. There's no faulting Pasquale Rachini's sumptuous photography or the lavish attention to period detail. But there's something damningly novelettish about Inès Sastre's attempt to circumvent her marriage to doddering tycoon Dario Cantarelli by addressing her vows to Diego Abatantuono, his dashingly mysterious best man. DP. In Italian with English subtitles.

Diego Abatantuono *Angelo Beliossi* • Inès Sastre *Francesca Babini* • Dario Cantarelli *Edgardo Osti* • Cinia Mascoli *Peppina Campeggi* • Valeria D'Obici *Olimpia Campeggi Babini* ■ *Dir/Scr* Pupi Avati

B

The Best Man ★★ 15

Comedy drama 1999 · US · Colour · 115mins

In this first feature from writer/director Malcolm D Lee (cousin of Spike), Taye Diggs discovers that his debut novel, as yet unpublished, has been leaked to his friends as they prepare to reunite for a wedding. Since the book is drawn from his own experiences, they're none too pleased with his representation of them. The great soundtrack features Stevie Wonder and Lauren Hill, but the dud script undermines the considerable talents of the stars. LH DVD

Nia Long *Jordan* • Taye Diggs *Harper* • Morris Chestnut *Lance* • Terrence Howard *Quentin* • Harold Perrineau Jr [Harold Perrineau] *Murch* • Sanaa Lathan *Robin* • Monica Calhoun *Mia* • Melissa De Sousa *Shelby* • Victoria Dillard *Anita* ■ *Dir/Scr* Malcolm D Lee

Best Men ★ 15

Crime comedy drama
1997 · US/UK · Colour · 86mins

Just released from prison, and on the way to his wedding with Drew Barrymore, Luke Wilson finds himself in trouble when one of the friends driving him to church makes an unscheduled stop to rob a bank. In predictable fashion, the bungled heist quickly escalates into a full-scale hostage situation. It's a ridiculous story, made worse by the clueless direction. AJ DVD

Drew Barrymore *Hope* • Dean Cain *Sergeant Buzz Thomas* • Andy Dick *Teddy Pollack* • Sean Patrick Flanery *Billy Phillips* • Mitchell Whitfield *Sol Jacobs* • Luke Wilson *Jesse Chandler* • Fred Ward *Sheriff Bud Phillips* ■ *Dir* Tamra Davis • *Scr* Art Edler Brown, Tracy Fraim

The Best of Benny Hill ★★★ PG

Comedy compilation
1974 · UK · Colour · 83mins

No matter where you stand on the content of Benny Hill's bawdy comedy, there's no escaping the fact that he was one of British television's biggest ever stars. Featuring such familiar characters as Fred Scuttle, this compilation comes from sketches that originally appeared in his Thames series between 1969 and 1972. Regulars such as Bob Todd, Jenny Lee Wright and Henry McGee do their usual selfless stooging, and there's the inevitable "Hill's Angels" chase to Boots Randolph's immortal *Yakety Sax* theme. DP DVD

Benny Hill *Benny Hill/Fred Scuttle/Mervyn Cruddy* • Bob Todd • Anne Irving • Bettine Le Beau • David Prowse [Dave Prowse] • Henry McGee • Nicholas Parsons • Patricia Hayes • Jenny Lee Wright ■ *Dir* John Robins • *Scr* Benny Hill

B

The Best of Enemies

★★★ PG

Second World War comedy drama
1961 · UK/It · BW · 99mins

As the rival commanders, David Niven and Alberto Sordi are given admirable support by such stalwarts as Michael Wilding, Harry Andrews and Bernard Cribbins. The great Nino Rota composed the score, while Fellini's regular cameraman Giuseppe Rotunno provides some stunning visuals. Yet, in spite of Guy Hamilton's steady direction and the odd amusing moment, this account of the misadventures of a British army unit in Abyssinia in the early 1940s never really gathers momentum. DP

David Niven *Major Richardson* • Alberto Sordi *Capt Blasi* • Michael Wilding *Lt Burke* • Amedeo Nazzari *Major Fornari* • Harry Andrews *Capt Rootes* • Noel Harrison *Lt Hilary* • David Opatoshu *Captain Bernasconi* • Aldo Giuffre *Sgt Todini* • Duncan Macrae *Sgt Trevethan* • Bernard Cribbins *Pvt Tanner* • Ronald Fraser *Cpl Prefect* ■ *Dir* Guy Hamilton • *Scr* Jack Pulman, Age Scarpelli [Agenore Incrocci and Furio Scarpelli] (adaptation), Suso Cecchi D'Amico (adaptation), from a story by Luciano Vincenzoni

The Best of Everything ★★

Romantic drama
1959 · US · Colour · 120mins

"We've proven romance is still the best of everything," croons Johnny Mathis over the titles, but this preposterous 20th Century-Fox tosh is not really a romance: it's a steamy melodrama about power and glamour in the New York publishing jungle. An ageing and predatory Joan Crawford chews the scenery with aplomb, making mincemeat of Fox's young contract players Hope Lange, Suzy Parker and Diane Baker, all of whom nowadays add to the period charm. TS

Joan Crawford *Amanda Farrow* • Hope Lange *Caroline Bender* • Stephen Boyd *Mike* • Louis Jourdan *David Savage* • Suzy Parker *Gregg* • Martha Hyer *Barbara* • Diane Baker *April* • Brian Aherne *Mr Shalimar* • Robert Evans *Dexter Key* • Brett Halsey *Eddie* ■ *Dir* Jean Negulesco • *Scr* Edith Sommer, Mann Rubin, from the novel by Rona Jaffe

Best of the Badmen ★★ U

Western 1951 · US · Colour · 83mins

A collection of noted western outlaws ride together in this innocuous RKO film. Robert Ryan is top billed as a former Confederate colonel pitted against a rather bland Robert Preston, while *Stagecoach* veteran Claire Trevor and Jack Buetel provide able support. Walter Brennan makes the most of his role as an ex-Quantrill's raider who wonders why there's now a price on his head for doing something which brought him glory in the Civil War. Too talky and not terribly interesting. TS

Robert Ryan *Jeff Clanton* • Claire Trevor *Lily* • Jack Buetel *Bob Younger* • Robert Preston *Matthew Fowler* • Walter Brennan *Doc Butcher* • Bruce Cabot *Cole Younger* • John Archer *Curley Ringo* • Lawrence Tierney *Jesse James* • Barton MacLane *Joad* ■ *Dir* William D Russell • *Scr* Robert Hardy Andrews, John Twist, from a story by Robert Hardy Andrews

Best of the Best ★★ 15

Martial arts sports drama
1989 · US · Colour · 93mins

The US karate team take on the Koreans in a slick "against the odds" martial arts drama that alternates between body blows and tugs on the heartstrings. Formulaic in the extreme, with nice fighter Eric Roberts given every possible reason to triumph (his son's in a coma after a traffic accident *and* he has a nasty shoulder injury), this compendium of clichés is undone by sentimentality and paper-thin characterisation. JC DVD

Eric Roberts *Alex Grady* • James Earl Jones *Coach Couzo* • Sally Kirkland *Catherine Wade* • Phillip Rhee *Tommy Lee* • Chris Penn *Travis Brickley* ■ *Dir* Robert Radler • *Scr* Paul Levine, from a story by Phillip Rhee, Paul Levine

Best of the Best II ★★ 18

Action thriller 1992 · US · Colour · 95mins

The original was a glossy, straight-to-video action tale that benefited from a surprisingly good cast. There's no James Earl Jones this time around, but Eric Roberts, Chris Penn and martial arts expert Phillip Rhee are reunited for another bout of mindless but entertaining biffing. Two more sequels followed. JF DVD

Eric Roberts *Alex Grady* • Phillip Rhee *Tommy Lee* • Edan Gross *Walter Grady* • Ralph Moeller *Brakus* • Chris Penn *Travis Brickley* • Sonny Landham *James* • Wayne Newton *Weldon* • Meg Foster *Sue* ■ *Dir* Robert Radler • *Scr* Max Strom, John Allen Nelson, from characters created by Paul Levine

The Best of Times ★★ 15

Comedy drama 1986 · US · Colour · 99mins

All-American whimsy, set in small-town California, where Robin Williams and Kurt Russell are two of life's failures. Williams is a banker, living in the shadow of a missed pass at a high school football game; Russell was the school's star quarterback, now also on the skids. When Williams decides the town needs a little encouragement, we're into a rehash of *It's a Wonderful Life*, except that the characters are one dimensional, there aren't any jokes, and the tone is glutinous. AT. Contains swearing.

Robin Williams *Jack Dundee* • Kurt Russell *Reno Hightower* • Pamela Reed *Gigi Hightower* • Holly Palance *Elly Dundee* • Donald Moffat *The Colonel* • Margaret Whitton *Darla* • M Emmet Walsh *Charlie* • Donovan Scott *Eddie* ■ *Dir* Roger Spottiswoode • *Scr* Ron Shelton

The Best of Youth ★★★★ 15

Epic drama 2003 · It · Colour · 373mins

Spanning nearly six hours of screen time, this compelling sibling saga charts the lives of two brothers from the summer of 1966 through to the present. Luigi Lo Cascio's politically active psychiatrist and Alessio Boni's duty-driven cop may share few scenes, but the unforced manner in which their lives interconnect not only reveals director Marco Tullio Giordana's narrative finesse, but also an intuitive understanding of both Italian history and the national temperament. However, the various domestic feuds, turbulent romances and personal tragedies ensure that this remains as much a human drama as an incisive portrait of a vibrant, but too often conflicted and corrupted society. A truly epic achievement. DP. In Italian with English subtitles.

Luigi Lo Cascio *Nicola Carati* • Alessio Boni *Matteo Carati* • Adriana Asti *Adriana Carati* • Sonia Bergamasco *Giulia Monfalco* • Maya Sansa *Mirella Utano* • Andrea Tidona *Angelo Carati* • Fabrizio Gifuni *Carlo Tommasi* • Valentina Carnelutti *Francesca Carati* ■ *Dir* Marco Tullio Giordana • *Scr* Sandro Petraglia, Stefano Rulli

The Best Pair of Legs in the Business ★

Comedy drama 1972 · UK · Colour · 87mins

Taking a break from the buses, Reg Varney finds himself at a holiday camp in this old-fashioned seaside comedy. Although he's the world's worst entertainer, our Reg is convinced that the big time is just a soft-shoe shuffle away. A trouper through and through, Varney always tries to make the most of even the lowest grade material, yet even he struggles to pep up this maudlin mess. DP. Contains swearing.

Reg Varney *"Sherry" Sheridan* • Diana Coupland *Mary Sheridan* • Jean Harvey (2) *Emma* • Lee Montague *Charlie* • David Lincoln *Ron* • George Sweeney *Dai* ■ *Dir* Christopher Hodson • *Scr* Kevin Laffan

Best Revenge ★★ 18

Thriller 1983 · Can · Colour · 91mins

John Heard can be electric in a part with some depth, but here he is saddled with a film that has none. Instead, he is required to wrestle with the obviously episodic story of a small-potatoes drugs runner who is arm-twisted into undertaking a larger errand when a friend is taken hostage. As he tries to bring unseemly quantities of cannabis from Morocco to America, all the regulation nastiness is given full rein. *Midnight Express* it ain't. JM

John Heard *Charlie Grainger* • Levon Helm *Bo* • Alberta Watson *Dinah* • Stephen McHattie *Brett Munro* • Moses Znaimer *Leo Ellis* • John Rhys-Davies *Mustapha* • Benjamin Gordon *Willy* ■ *Dir* John Trent • *Scr* David Rothberg, Rick Rosenthal, Logan N Danforth, from a story by David Rothberg

Best Seller ★★★★ 18

Thriller 1987 · US · Colour · 91mins

In between making his own quirky horror films, Larry Cohen turned his writing attention to the crime genre and the result was this ingenious, electric thriller. Brian Dennehy is the policeman turned writer who forms an uneasy alliance with hitman James Woods, who has promised to put him back on the bestseller lists. Cohen delivers a typically witty script and director John Flynn is a dab hand at the action set pieces. Woods mesmerises as the strangely likeable killer. JF. Contains some swearing and violence. DVD

Brian Dennehy *Dennis Meechum* • James Woods *Cleve* • Victoria Tennant *Roberta Gillian* • Allison Balson *Holly Meechum* • Paul Shenar *David Madlock* • George Coe *Graham* • Ann Pitoniak [Anne Pitoniak] *Mrs Foster* • Mary Carver *Cleve's mother* • Sully Boyar *Monks* ■ *Dir* John Flynn • *Scr* Larry Cohen

The Best Things in Life Are Free ★★★★ U

Musical biographical drama
1956 · US · Colour · 104mins

Director Michael Curtiz's stirring musical biopic is about the songwriting team of BG De Sylva, Ray Henderson and Lew Brown. It matters not a jot if you've never heard of them, since they're played with tremendous verve by Gordon MacRae, Dan Dailey and Ernest Borgnine. Sheree North simply sizzles in two superb dance routines, a vibrant (and definitive) *Birth of the Blues* with the great Jacques d'Amboise and a very snazzy *Black Bottom*. TS

Gordon MacRae *BG "Buddy" De Sylva* • Dan Dailey *Ray Henderson* • Ernest Borgnine *Lew Brown* • Sheree North *Kitty* • Tommy Noonan *Carl* • Murvyn Vye *Manny* • Phyllis Avery *Maggie Henderson* • Jacques d'Amboise *Speciality dancer* ■ *Dir* Michael Curtiz • *Scr* William Bowers, Phoebe Ephron, from a story by John O'Hara

The Best Years of Our Lives ★★★★★ U

Drama 1946 · US · BW · 170mins

Undoubtedly one of the finest and most satisfying achievements in American cinema, this Samuel Goldwyn production now tends, regrettably, to be overlooked by film scholars. Despite its length, it still retains its capacity to move an audience. The tale of three returning GIs adjusting to civilian life after the Second World War may have lost some relevance post-Vietnam, but there's no denying the magnificent craftsmanship as director William Wyler and photographer Gregg Toland (*Citizen Kane*) bring Robert E Sherwood's vivid screenplay to life. Stars Fredric March, Myrna Loy and Dana Andrews are at their postwar peaks here, but it is the performance of real-life wartime amputee Harold Russell that is most touching, and he rightly won two Academy Awards for his role (a special award for bringing hope to other veterans along with that of best supporting actor). Awarded six other Oscars, this movie is hard to overpraise. TS DVD

Myrna Loy *Milly Stephenson* • Fredric March *Al Stephenson* • Dana Andrews *Fred Derry* • Harold Russell *Homer Parrish* • Teresa Wright *Peggy Stephenson* • Virginia Mayo *Marie Derry* • Cathy O'Donnell *Wilma Cameron* • Hoagy Carmichael *Butch Engle* ■ *Dir* William Wyler • *Scr* Robert E Sherwood, from the blank verse novella *Glory for Me* by MacKinlay Kantor • *Cinematographer* Gregg Toland • *Editor* Daniel Mandell • *Music* Hugo Friedhofer

La Bête ★★★ 18

Erotic fantasy drama
1975 · Fr · Colour · 94mins

The perverse sexual content of this erotic fairy tale earned it a notoriety that detracted from its value as a savage social satire and a film of painterly beauty. Polish-born former animator Walerian Borowczyk errs on the wrong side of political correctness in contrasting the experiences of an 18th-century bride and an American heiress, both about to marry into the same aristocratic family. The bestial nature of some of the dream-diary sequences might cause offence, but there is a playfulness about the eccentric couplings. DP. In French with English subtitles. DVD

Sirpa Lane *Romilda de l'Espérance* • Lisbeth Hummel *Lucy Broadhurst* • Elizabeth Kaza [Elisabeth Kaza] *Virginia Broadhurst* • Pierre Benedetti *Mathurin de l'Espérance* • Guy Tréjan *Pierre, Marquis Pierre de l'Espérance* • Dalio [Marcel Dalio] *Duc Rommondelo de Balo* • Pascale Rivault *Clarisse de l'Espérance* ■ *Dir/Scr* Walerian Borowczyk

La Bête Humaine ★★★★★ PG

Crime drama 1938 · Fr · BW · 98mins

Zola's dark, fatalistic novel of the railway tracks was turned by Jean Renoir into one of the classics of pre-war French cinema. The incomparable Jean Gabin stars as the train driver who acquires a young mistress, and together they plot to murder her husband. Hollywood would use Zola's yarn as a template for many *films noirs* (*The Postman Always Rings Twice*, *Double Indemnity*) but Renoir's film is every inch their equal. It's a wonderful, painterly evocation of the railway and a poetic drama that just gets grimmer and grimmer. Fritz Lang remade it in Hollywood as *Human Desire* with Glenn Ford and Gloria Grahame, a dead ringer for this film's pathetic heroine, Simone Simon. AT. In French with English subtitles. DVD

Jean Gabin *Jacques Lantier* • Simone Simon *Séverine* • Fernand Ledoux *Roubaud, Séverine's husband* • Julien Carette *Pecqueux* • Blanchette Brunoy *Flore* • Jean Renoir *Cabuche, the poacher* • Gérard Landry *Dauvergne's son* • Jenny Hélia *Philomène* ■ *Dir* Jean Renoir • *Scr* Jean Renoir, from the novel by Emile Zola

Bethune: the Making of a Hero ★★★ 15

Biographical drama
1990 · Can/Fr/Chi · Colour · 111mins

Having already played controversial Canadian doctor Norman Bethune in Eric Till's 1977 biopic, Donald Sutherland returned to the role for this troubled co-production. He gives a warts-and-all portrayal of the surgeon whose detestation of fascism led him first to participate in the Spanish Civil

U = SUITABLE FOR ALL Uc = SUITABLE FOR ALL, ESPECIALLY FOR YOUNG CHILDREN (VIDEO ONLY) PG = PARENTAL GUIDANCE

War, and then to assist Mao Tse-tung on his famous Long March. Strikingly filmed by Mike Molloy and Raoul Coutard, the scenery makes an imposing impression. DP

Donald Sutherland *Dr Norman Bethune* • Helen Mirren *Frances Penny Bethune* • Helen Shaver *Ms Dowd* • Colm Feore *Chester Rice* • James Pax *Mr Tung* • Ronald Pickup *Alan Coleman* • Da Guo *Dr Chian* • Harrison Liu *Dr Fong* • Anouk Aimée *Marie-France Coudaire* ■ *Dir* Phillip Borsos • *Scr* Ted Allan

Betrayal ★★★★ 15

Romantic drama 1982 · UK · Colour · 91mins

This film version of Harold Pinter's 1978 play has Patricia Hodge married to Ben Kingsley but having an affair with Jeremy Irons. The story – a sort of sexual charade – starts at the end and works backwards, dealing with a sequence of betrayals between the three friends. Razor sharp in its depiction of a rather pretentious literary London, it includes an unforgettable scene in a restaurant when Kingsley goes ballistic. This was distinguished producer Sam Spiegel's final film. AT. Contains swearing.

Jeremy Irons *Jerry* • Ben Kingsley *Robert* • Patricia Hodge *Emma* • Avril Elgar *Mrs Banks* • Ray Marioni *Waiter* • Caspar Norman *Sam* ■ *Dir* David Jones (3) • *Scr* Harold Pinter, from his play

Betrayal from the East ★★

Second World War drama
1945 · US · BW · 82mins

Lee Tracy is enlisted by the Japanese in 1941 to spy for them. In particular they want the defence plans for the Panama Canal, which they apparently hope to destroy. But Tracy, though broke, isn't morally bankrupt, and intends to trick the Japanese with the help of double agent Nancy Kelly. This cheapo war drama isn't the expected flag waver. AT

Lee Tracy *Eddie* • Nancy Kelly *Peggy* • Richard Loo *Tanni* • Abner Biberman *Yamato* • Regis Toomey *Scott* • Philip Ahn *Kato* • Addison Richards *Capt Bates* • Bruce Edwards *Purdy* ■ *Dir* William Berke • *Scr* Kenneth Gamet, Aubrey Wisberg, from the book by Alan Hynd

Betrayed ★★★

Thriller 1944 · US · BW · 67mins

This effective, moody B-thriller was originally titled *When Strangers Marry* but was quickly changed to *Betrayed* when people expected a marital comedy. It stars Kim Hunter as the latest wife of Dean Jagger, whom she suspects may be a murderer. Hunter's fears are calmed by her former boyfriend Robert Mitchum, whose hulking, laconic presence dominates the picture. AT

Robert Mitchum *Fred* • Kim Hunter *Millie* • Dean Jagger *Paul* • Neil Hamilton *Blake* • Lou Lubin *Houser* • Milton Kibbee *Charlie* • Dewey Robinson *News stand man* • Claire Whitney *Middle-aged woman* ■ *Dir* William Castle • *Scr* Philip Yordan, Dennis J Cooper, from a story by George V Moscov

Betrayed ★★ U

Second World War spy drama
1954 · US · Colour · 108mins

Directed by Gottfried Reinhardt at MGM's British studios, this old-fashioned, plodding film about spies, Resistance workers and traitors is chiefly notable for marking the end of Clark Gable's 22-year tenure with the studio, before he went lucratively freelance for his remaining years. Co-starring with Victor Mature and Lana Turner, the ageing "King" of Hollywood was hardly challenged by this outmoded melodrama. RK

Clark Gable *Colonel Pieter Deventer* • Lana Turner *Carla Van Oven* • Victor Mature *"The Scarf"* • Louis Calhern *General Ten Eyck* • OE Hasse *Colonel Helmuth Dietrich* • Wilfrid Hyde White *General Charles Larraby* • Ian Carmichael *Captain Jackie Lawson* • Niall MacGinnis *"Blackie"* • Nora Swinburne *"The Scarf's" mother* • Roland Culver *General Warsleigh* ■ *Dir* Gottfried Reinhardt • *Scr* Ronald Millar, George Froeschel

Betrayed ★★★★ 18

Political thriller 1988 · US · Colour · 121mins

An intelligent and intriguing political thriller from director Costa-Gavras about an undercover FBI agent – played by the excellent Debra Winger – sent to investigate a Midwest farmer who's suspected of having links with a white supremacist organisation. Tom Berenger is suitably charming and chilling as Winger's prey, but Costa-Gavras gives the convoluted plot such a plethora of twists and turns that cohesive tension is ultimately lost. The performances and set pieces raise it up, but this film is simply too long. SH. Contains violence, swearing. DVD

Debra Winger *Cathy Weaver/Katie Phillips* • Tom Berenger *Gary Simmons* • John Heard *Michael Carnes* • Betsy Blair *Gladys Simmons* • John Mahoney *Shorty* • Ted Levine *Wes* • Jeffrey DeMunn *Flynn* • Albert Hall *Al Sanders* • David Clennon *Jack Carpenter* ■ *Dir* Costa-Gavras • *Scr* Joe Eszterhas

The Betsy ★★ 18

Drama 1978 · US · Colour · 120mins

It was said when this film was first released that it was too up-market to be a successful adaptation of a Harold Robbins novel. Well, if your idea of sophistication is the sight of Laurence Olivier bouncing around on a bed, then director Daniel Petrie's full-throttle tale of cars, lust and greed will be right up your street. Ageing 50 years over a series of flashbacks, Olivier acts up a storm, and is joined at the ham counter by Tommy Lee Jones and Lesley-Anne Down. DP. Contains swearing and nudity.

Laurence Olivier *Loren Hardeman Sr* • Robert Duvall *Loren Hardeman III* • Katharine Ross *Sally Hardeman* • Tommy Lee Jones *Angelo Perino* • Jane Alexander *Alicia Hardeman* • Lesley-Anne Down *Lady Bobby Ayres* • Joseph Wiseman *Jake Weinstein* • Kathleen Beller *Betsy Hardeman* ■ *Dir* Daniel Petrie • *Scr* Walter Bernstein, William Bast, from the novel by Harold Robbins

Betsy's Wedding ★★★ 15

Comedy 1990 · US · Colour · 90mins

A movie directed by Alan Alda always means a touch of Woody Allen meets vaudeville and that's the case with this tale of a group of eccentric New Yorkers all trying to get Betsy married off according to their own agendas. Molly Ringwald is neatly understated as the title gal who wishes to make an honest man of a nice boy who is neither Jewish like Ringwald's mom (an excellent Madeline Kahn) nor makes breakfast seem like a scene from *Tosca*, as does her Italian dad (Alda, at his best). The cast is faultless, right down to the minor roles. SH. Contains violence and swearing. DVD

Alan Alda *Eddie Hopper* • Madeline Kahn *Lola Hopper* • Molly Ringwald *Betsy Hopper* • Ally Sheedy *Connie Hopper* • Anthony LaPaglia *Stevie Dee* • Joe Pesci *Oscar Henner* • Catherine O'Hara *Gloria Henner* • Joey Bishop *Eddie's father* • Samuel L Jackson *Mickey, taxi dispatcher* ■ *Dir/Scr* Alan Alda

Better Late Than Never ★★ PG

Comedy 1983 · UK · Colour · 91mins

Great talent, shame about the script. David Niven and Art Carney are a couple of con-men competing for the affections of a ten-year-old heiress (Kimberley Partridge). Her grandmother (Maggie Smith) is a dithering amnesiac, so it's up to the girl to decide which one is her true grandfather. Writer/director Bryan Forbes is as flat-footed here as he was with *International Velvet*. TH

David Niven *Nick Cartland* • Art Carney *Charley Dunbar* • Maggie Smith *Anderson* • Kimberley Partridge *Bridget* • Catherine Hicks *Sable* • Lionel Jeffries *Hargreaves* • Melissa Prophet *Marlene* ■ *Dir/Scr* Bryan Forbes

Better Off Dead ★★ 15

Comedy 1985 · US · Colour · 92mins

John Cusack is suicidal after being dumped by his beautiful but shallow girlfriend (Amanda Wyss) – and that's just the start of his problems. Writer/director Savage Steve Holland surrounds the always engaging star with a variety of quirky neighbourhood characters and slapstick sight gags. This is pretty lightweight compared to such classier Cusack comedies as *The Sure Thing*. JC DVD

John Cusack *Lane Myer* • David Ogden Stiers *Al Myer* • Kim Darby *Jenny Myer* • Demian Slade *Johnny Gasparini* • Scooter Stevens *Badger Myer* • Diane Franklin *Monique Junet* ■ *Dir/Scr* Savage Steve Holland

Better than Sex ★★★

Romantic comedy drama
2000 · Aus/Fr/US · Colour · 84mins

As fashion designer Susie Porter and wildlife photographer David Wenham's one-night stand takes on increasing emotional significance, it's hard not to warm to their lusts and insecurities in Jonathan Teplitzky's debut feature. However, the tactic of having them describe their feelings in post-event interviews robs both their *Blind Date*-style confidences of any spontaneity and the relationship of its fumbling unpredictability. Porter copes better with the format than Wenham. Amiably raunchy. DP

David Wenham *Josh* • Susie Porter *Cin* • Catherine McClements *Sam* • Kris McQuade *Taxi driver* ■ *Dir/Scr* Jonathan Teplitzky

A Better Tomorrow ★★★★ 18

Action thriller 1986 · HK · Colour · 90mins

One of the defining films in Hong Kong action cinema, this not only made names out of director John Woo and star Chow Yun-Fat, but also exerted a considerable influence over one Quentin Tarantino. Chow takes his now familiar role as the lethal but honorable crook – in this case a counterfeiter – who, with his weary partner in crime (Ti Lung), attempts to go straight but is led back into a battle to the death with a ruthless gangster. The artfully choreographed scenes of slow-motion destruction more than compensate for the occasional lapses into clumsy sentimentality. This is available on video in both dubbed and subtitled versions, although the latter is unintentionally funny because of dubious translation. JF. A Cantonese language film. DVD

Chow Yun-Fat *Mark* • Ti Lung *Ho* • Leslie Cheung *Kit Sung* • Lee Waise *Shing* ■ *Dir/Scr* John Woo

A Better Tomorrow II ★★★ 18

Action thriller 1987 · HK · Colour · 94mins

Less a sequel than a remake, this nevertheless consolidated John Woo's reputation as the hippest of Hong Kong's action directors. Most of the stars of the original are back on board: Chow Yun-Fat this time plays the brother of the master counterfeiter of the first film, while Ti Lung and Leslie Cheung return as the two brothers from different sides of the law. The childish attempts at humour will leave western audiences embarrassed, but once again the set pieces are stunning. JF. In Cantonese with English subtitles.

Chow Yun-Fat *Ken* • Ti Lung *Ho* • Leslie Cheung *Kit* • Dean Shek *Lung* ■ *Dir* John Woo • *Scr* John Woo, Tsui Hark • *Producer* Tsui Hark

B

A Better Tomorrow III ★★ 18

Action thriller 1989 · HK · Colour · 106mins

John Woo jumped ship after the first two *Better Tomorrow* films, so producer Tsui Hark took over the directorial reins. This one is a prequel, although it bares only a passing resemblance to the first two. Chow Yun-Fat is back on board, although his co-star Tony Leung takes centre stage, as he attempts to bring his relatives out of South Vietnam as the communists move in. While this is not in the same league as the first two movies, Tsui Hark is no slouch when it comes to extravagant destruction. JF. In Cantonese with English subtitles.

Chow Yun-Fat *Cheung Chi-Keung (Mark)* • Anita Mui *Chow Ying-Kit (Kitty Chow)* • Tony Kar-Fai Leung [Tony Leung (1)] *Cheung Chi Mun (Mun)* • Saburo Tokito *Ho Cheung-Ching* • Cheng Wai Lan *Pat* • Shek Kin *Uncle* • Maggie Cheung *Ling* ■ *Dir* Tsui Hark • *Scr* Tai Fu-Ho, Leung Yiu-Ming

A Better Way to Die ★★ 18

Action thriller 2000 · US · Colour · 97mins

Scott Wiper is a minor-leaguer, but he still had sufficient clout to write, direct and co-star in this boorish road movie. He's certainly an imposing presence and stages some sequences with blustering bravura. But his talents do not lie in screenwriting. The dialogue consists solely of threats, curses and platitudes, while the story of a disillusioned cop who is mistaken for the quarry of a private eye, the FBI and the Chicago underworld is one long cliché. DP DVD

André Braugher *Cleveland* • Scott Wiper *Boomer* • Lou Diamond Phillips *Special Agent William Dexter* • Natasha Henstridge *Kelly* • Matt Gallani *Laslov* • Wayne Duvall *Rifkin* • Joe Pantoliano *Flash* ■ *Dir/Scr* Scott Wiper

Betty Blue ★★★★★ 18

Drama 1986 · Fr · Colour · 116mins

Blessed with a beautiful score by Gabriel Yared, this is the finest example of the type of French film known, rather snipingly, as *cinéma du look*. The usual accusation of all style and no content simply can't be aimed at Jean-Jacques Beineix's Oscar-nominated return to form after *Moon in the Gutter*. The tragic relationship of Betty and Zorg is as compelling as it is chic. Béatrice Dalle is unbelievably vibrant as the waitress living on the edge of her passions, but Jean-Hugues Anglade does manage to keep up as the would-be novelist coping with her exhilarating highs and destructive lows. DP. In French with English subtitles. Contains violence, swearing, sex scenes and nudity.

Béatrice Dalle *Betty* • Jean-Hugues Anglade *Zorg* • Consuelo de Haviland *Lisa* • Gérard Darmon *Eddy* • Clémentine Célarié *Annie* • Jacques Mathou *Bob* • Claude Confortes *Zorg's boss* ■ *Dir* Jean-Jacques Beineix • *Scr* Jean-Jacques Beineix, from the novel by Philippe Dijan

Betty Fisher and Other Stories ★★★ 15

Psychological crime thriller
2001 · Fr/Can · Colour · 98mins

Director Claude Miller's adaptation of a Ruth Rendell novel is an intriguing combination of psychological chic, lowlife graft and bourgeois irony. Unless you can accept a world, in which bestselling authors accept kidnap victims as substitutes for deceased sons, abusive mothers twist reality for their own devices and conmen are left mansions by erstwhile lovers, then you will spend the entire film looking for holes in its tortuous logic. But if you surrender to the spirited performances and Miller's arch manipulations, the kooky atmosphere and unlikely contrivances will keep you interested. DP. In French with English subtitles. Contains violence and swearing. DVD

Sandrine Kiberlain *Betty Fisher* • Nicole Garcia *Margot Fisher* • Mathilde Seigner *Carole Novacki* • Edouard Baer *Alex Basato* • Stéphane Freiss *Edouard* ■ *Dir* Claude Miller • *Scr* Claude Miller, from the novel *The Tree of Hands* by Ruth Rendell

The Betty Ford Story ★★★★

Biographical drama 1987 · US · Colour · 96mins

Gena Rowlands gives a stunning performance as the president's wife who battled an addiction to prescription drugs and alcohol in this powerful TV movie, based on Mrs Ford's autobiography. The story is told with candour and the film offers an intimate view of the emotional pain Ford and her family suffered because of her destructive behaviour. The drama is bolstered by strong acting from the supporting cast, especially Josef Sommer as Gerald Ford. MC

Gena Rowlands *Betty Ford* • Josef Sommer *President Gerald Ford* • Nan Woods *Susan Ford* • Concetta Tomei *Jan* • Jack Radar *First doctor* • Joan McMurtrey *Diane* • Kenneth Tigar *Dr Lukash* • Laura Leigh Hughes *Gayle Ford* ■ *Dir* David Greene • *Scr* Karen Hall, from the autobiography *The Times of My Life* by Betty Ford, Chris Chase

Between Friends ★★★ 15

Drama 1983 · US · Colour · 95mins

Forget the old hat story and enjoy watching two great stars strut their stuff as middle-aged divorcees from different backgrounds who meet by accident and help each other through their midlife crises. In a neat twist, Carol Burnett plays the object of all men's desire, while Elizabeth Taylor can't even get close to a boyfriend. The two leads give incandescent performances in this cable television movie, and are the sole reason for its success. AJ

Elizabeth Taylor *Deborah Shapiro* • Carol Burnett *Mary Catherine Castelli* • Barbara Bush [Barbara Tyson] *Francie Castelli* • Henry Ramer *Sam Tucker* • Bruce Gray *Malcolm Hollan* • Charles Shamata [Chuck Shamata] *Dr Seth Simpson* • Lally Cadeau *Lolly James* ■ *Dir* Lou Antonio • *Scr* Shelley List, Jonathan Estrin, from the novel *Nobody Makes Me Cry* by Shelley List

Between Heaven and Hell ★★

Second World War drama 1956 · US · Colour · 93mins

A routine 20th Century-Fox feature from Richard Fleischer, the skilled director of such classics as *The Vikings* and *Compulsion*. The plot favours the 1950s psychological approach, as rich southern recruit Robert Wagner suffers in combat under psychotic bully Broderick Crawford, but the structure is messy and confused, and Wagner's brilliantined hairstyle is well out of the Second World War period. TS

Robert Wagner *Sam Gifford* • Terry Moore *Jenny* • Broderick Crawford *Waco* • Buddy Ebsen *Willie* • Robert Keith (1) *Colonel Gozzens* • Brad Dexter *Joe Johnson* • Mark Damon *Terry* • Ken Clark *Morgan* ■ *Dir* Richard Fleischer • *Scr* Harry Brown, from the novel *The Day the Century Ended* by Francis Gwaltney

Between the Devil and the Deep Blue Sea ★★

Drama 1995 · Bel/Fr/UK · Colour · 92mins

Stephen Rea is an unlikely choice to play a Greek-Irish radio operator whose ship is stranded in Hong Kong when the company goes bust. While he's waiting to move on, he befriends a ten-year-old Chinese girl who cooks and cleans for him in order to care for her blind father. Made by a Belgian director, this anecdotal tale gets a mite pretentious when letters from Rea's girlfriend are heard over the soundtrack (read by Jane Birkin). AT

Stephen Rea *Nikos* • Chu Ling *Li* • Adrian Brine *Captain* • Maka Kotto *African sailor* • Mischa Aznavour *Young sailor* • Jane Birkin *Woman's voice* ■ *Dir* Marion Hänsel • *Scr* Marion Hänsel, Louis Grospierre, from a short story by Nikos Kavvadias

Between the Lines ★★★★ 15

Comedy 1977 · US · Colour · 101mins

A warm-hearted character comedy revolving around staff members of a Boston underground newspaper just before it's sold to a profit-minded publisher. The perceptive humour comes from the last bastion of 1960s political radicalism taking on corporate thinking, coupled with a brilliant ensemble cast milking every moment for wit and poignancy. Rock critic Jeff Goldblum's ad-libbed music lecture is a hoot, while photographer Lindsay Crouse's feminist rapport with stripper Marilu Henner is another highlight. Engrossing and believable. AJ

John Heard *Harry* • Bruno Kirby *David* • Lindsay Crouse *Abbie* • Gwen Welles *Laura* • Jeff Goldblum *Max* • Stephen Collins *Michael* • Jill Eikenberry *Lynn* • Michael J Pollard *Hawker* • Marilu Henner *Danielle* ■ *Dir* Joan Micklin Silver • *Scr* Fred Barron, from a story by Fred Barron, David Helpern

Between Two Women ★★★★

Drama 2000 · UK · Colour · 93mins

Classic British kitchen sink drama is given a refreshing contemporary spin in this powerful and passionate tale of suppressed sexuality. A poignant and sharply observant social commentary interlaced with the most tender romance, it superbly captures the inter-class friction of late 1950s Yorkshire. Barbara Marten delivers a tear-jerking performance as the working-class mother struggling with her feelings for middle-class schoolteacher Andrina Carroll. While the film throbs with emotional intensity, it's never gratuitous; instead, Woodcock relies on mood and perfectly captured facial expressions to build the tension to heart-rending levels. SF

Barbara Marten *Ellen* • Andrina Carroll *Kathy* • Andrew Dunn *Geoff* • Julia Deakin *Alice* • Edward Woodcock *Victor* • Frank Windsor *Mr Walker* • Eileen O'Brien *Mrs Walker* • Paul Shane *Mayor* ■ *Dir/Scr* Steven Woodcock

Between Two Worlds ★★★

Fantasy drama 1944 · US · BW · 111mins

This is a revamped and updated version of Sutton Vane's allegorical play *Outward Bound*, which was filmed in 1930. It has a shipload of "dead" Warner Bros contract players en route to the next world, some going on to Heaven and others to Hell. Rather turgid stuff, it has good performances from Isobel Elsom, as a dreadful snob, Edmund Gwenn, as the steward, and Sydney Greenstreet as God's great divider, which make it worth watching, while John Garfield overacts. RB

John Garfield *Tom Prior* • Paul Henreid *Henry* • Sydney Greenstreet *Thompson* • Eleanor Parker *Ann* • Edmund Gwenn *Scrubby* • George Tobias *Pete Musick* • George Coulouris *Lingley* • Faye Emerson *Maxine* ■ *Dir* Edward A Blatt • *Scr* Daniel Fuchs, from the play *Outward Bound* by Sutton Vane

The Beverly Hillbillies ★★ PG

Comedy 1993 · US · Colour · 89mins

Hollywood loves rehashing old TV shows into movies and this transfer of the 1960s show to the big screen seems just as pointless as the others of its ilk, despite Penelope Spheeris's direction, which tries hard to put a modern edge on nostalgia. The cast, including Dabney Coleman and Cloris Leachman, mainly mimics their predecessors. For fans of the TV show, the only highlight is a cameo from Buddy Ebsen, star of the original. AT DVD

Jim Varney *Jed Clampett* • Diedrich Bader *Jethro/Jethrine* • Erika Eleniak *Elly May* • Cloris Leachman *Granny* • Lily Tomlin *Miss Hathaway* • Dabney Coleman *Mr Drysdale* • Lea Thompson *Laura* • Rob Schneider *Tyler* • Dolly Parton • Buddy Ebsen *Barnaby Jones* • Zsa Zsa Gabor ■ *Dir* Penelope Spheeris • *Scr* Lawrence Konner, Mark Rosenthal, Jim Fisher, Jim Staahl, Rob Schneider, Alex Herschlag, from a story by Lawrence Konner, Mark Rosenthal, from the TV series by Paul Henning

Beverly Hills Brats ★★ 15

Comedy 1989 · US · Colour · 91mins

The Sheen clan (Martin stars, with son Ramon in the cast and daughter Janet as associate producer) often displays an earnestness in their work that too often gives way to pretentiousness. That's what happens here in a film that attempts to expose the self-obsession of privileged Californians and purports to be satire but soon becomes superficial. JM. Contains some swearing and nudity.

Martin Sheen *Jeffrey Miller* • Burt Young *Clive* • Terry Moore *Veronica Miller* • Peter Billingsley *Scooter Miller* • Ramon Sheen *Sterling Miller* • Cathy Podewell *Tiffany* ■ *Dir* Dimitri Sotirakis • *Scr* Linda Silverthorn, from a story by Terry Moore, Jerry Rivers

Beverly Hills Cop ★★★★ 15

Action comedy 1984 · US · Colour · 100mins

This was the blockbuster that propelled Eddie Murphy to superstardom at a time when his brash, confident swagger still appeared fresh and he hadn't descended into caricature. In the first and best of the trilogy, he stars as the Detroit street cop who causes a major upset in posh Beverly Hills when he turns up to investigate the murder of an old friend. Director Martin Brest orchestrates the senseless set pieces with slick precision and British actor Steven Berkoff takes the money and runs as the villain of the piece. JF. Contains violence and swearing. DVD

Eddie Murphy *Axel Foley* • Judge Reinhold *Detective Billy Rosewood* • Lisa Eilbacher *Jenny Summers* • Steven Berkoff *Victor Maitland* • John Ashton *Sergeant Taggart* • Ronny Cox *Lieutenant Bogomil* • James Russo *Mikey Tandino* • Jonathan Banks *Zack* • Bronson Pinchot *Serge* ■ *Dir* Martin Brest • *Scr* Daniel Petrie Jr, from a story by Daniel Petrie Jr, Danilo Bach

Beverly Hills Cop II ★★ 15

Action comedy 1987 · US · Colour · 98mins

Eddie Murphy is back and the set pieces are even more spectacular – shame they forgot about the script. This blockbusting sequel replays the plot of the original, but any wit goes largely by the wayside and Murphy's mugging becomes increasingly irritating. Jürgen Prochnow and Brigitte Nielsen ham it up as the obligatory foreign-accented baddies, but fail to make much impact, and Tony Scott's direction is flashy but superficial. JF. Contains swearing, violence. DVD

Eddie Murphy *Axel Foley* • Judge Reinhold *Billy Rosewood* • Jürgen Prochnow *Maxwell Dent* • Ronny Cox *Andrew Bogomil* • John Ashton *John Taggart* • Brigitte Nielsen *Karla Fry* • Allen Garfield *Harold Lutz* • Dean Stockwell *Charles "Chip" Cain* ■ *Dir* Tony Scott • *Scr* Larry Ferguson, Warren Skaaren, from a story by Eddie Murphy, Robert D Wachs, from characters created by Danilo Bach, Daniel Petrie Jr

Beverly Hills Cop III ★★ 15

Action comedy 1994 · US · Colour · 99mins

Eddie Murphy and Judge Reinhold go through their paces for a third time, beginning once again on Murphy's home turf in Detroit and moving to Beverly Hills and a theme park called Wonder World. John Landis, who also directed Murphy in *Trading Places* and *Coming to America*, does pull off the occasional visual joke. If Murphy looks bored by the whole thing, that fine character actor Hector Elizondo adds some genuine quirkiness. AT DVD

Eddie Murphy *Axel Foley* • Judge Reinhold *Billy Rosewood* • Hector Elizondo *Jon Flint* • Timothy Carhart *Ellis DeWald* • Stephen McHattie *Steve Fulbright* • Theresa Randle *Janice* • John Saxon *Orrin Sanderson* • Bronson Pinchot *Serge* ■ *Dir* John Landis • *Scr* Steven E de Souza, from characters created by Danilo Bach, Daniel Petrie Jr

Beverly Hills Ninja ★★★ 12

Martial arts comedy 1997 · US · Colour · 84mins

A box-office number one in the States, *Beverly Hills Ninja* comes from the producers of *Dumb and Dumber* and *Kingpin* and features one of the last performances of comic Chris Farley. An American baby washes up on the shores of Japan and is brought up by a clan of martial arts masters. Now Haru (Farley), a willing but clumsy pupil, must journey to the "Hills of Beverly" to rescue a beautiful American girl from yakuza counterfeiters. Slapstick fun for the undemanding. JF. Contains swearing, violence and sexual references. DVD

Chris Farley *Haru* • Nicollette Sheridan *Alison* • Robin Shou *Gobei* • Nathaniel Parker *Tanley* • Soon-Tek Oh [Soon-Teck Oh] *Sensei* • Keith Cooke Hirabayashi *Nobu* • Chris Rock *Joey* • François Chau *Izumo* • John Farley *Policeman* • Kevin Farley *Policeman* ■ *Dir* Dennis Dugan • *Scr* Mark Feldberg, Mitch Klebanoff

Beware, My Lovely ★★★

Drama 1952 · US · BW · 76mins

In this tense drama, vulnerable widow Ida Lupino hires craggy handyman Robert Ryan to help her prepare for Christmas, only to discover that he's a psychopath. Director Harry Horner creates such a claustrophobic atmosphere of pervasive nastiness that this film was rightly given an X certificate for its cinema release in Britain. Much disliked by the critics of the day, this is tough stuff, indeed. It was produced by Lupino's second husband, Collier Young. TS

Ida Lupino *Helen Gordon* • Robert Ryan *Howard Wilton* • Taylor Holmes *Mr Armstrong* • Barbara Whiting *Ruth Williams* • James Willmas *Mr Stevens* • OZ Whitehead *Mr Franks* ■ *Dir* Harry Horner • *Scr* Mel Dinelli, from his story and play *The Man*

Beware of a Holy Whore ★★★

Comedy 1970 · W Ger/It · Colour · 103mins

Inspired by Rainer Werner Fassbinder's own unhappy experience of shooting *Whity* in Spain, this is a real eye-opener for those who doggedly believe in cinema as a glamorous business. A brutally honest – if self-indulgent – auto-critique, this is as much about the frustration of failing to find a means of expression as the dangerous vanity of artists. Yet there is still much satirical fun to be had at the expense of director Lou Castel, his bolshy film crew and the preening star, played with conscious irony by Eddie Constantine. DP. In German with English subtitles.

Lou Castel *Jeff, the director* • Eddie Constantine *Eddie Constantine, lead actor* • Marquard Bohm *Ricky, lead actor* • Hanna Schygulla *Hanna, lead actress* • Rainer Werner Fassbinder *Sascha Berling, production manager* • Margarethe von Trotta *Babs, production secretary* ■ *Dir* Rainer Werner Fassbinder • *Scr* Rainer Werner Fassbinder

Beware of Pity ★★

Romantic drama 1946 · UK · BW · 102mins

Lilli Palmer is touchingly vulnerable as the disabled baroness whose happiness with army officer Albert Lieven is jeopardised when she discovers the real motive for his attentions. Having learnt his trade in the silent era, director Maurice Elvey can't resist overplaying the melodrama, but the cast keeps things on track. DP

Lilli Palmer *Baroness Edith* • Albert Lieven *Lt Anton Marek* • Cedric Hardwicke *Dr Albert Condor* • Gladys Cooper *Klara Condor* • Linden Travers *Ilona Domansky* • Ernest Thesiger *Baron Emil de Kekesfalva* • Peter Cotes *Cusma* • Freda Jackson *Gypsy* ■ *Dir* Maurice Elvey • *Scr* WP Lipscomb, from the novel by Stefan Zweig

Beware! The Blob ★ 15

Science-fiction horror
1971 · US · Colour · 86mins

Noteworthy only for being directed by Larry (*Dallas*) Hagman – it was re-released in the 1980s with the tag line "The film that JR shot!" – this pointless sequel to the 1958 classic rehashes virtually the same plot, but dumbs it down with amateurish special effects and strained acting. Godfrey Cambridge brings a globule of alien jelly back from the Arctic, which thaws out to become a homicidal protoplasm that increases its size by attacking partygoers and bowling alleys. AJ [video]

Robert Walker Jr *Bobby Hartford* • Gwynne Gilford *Lisa Clark* • Godfrey Cambridge *Chester* • Richard Stahl *Edward Fazio* • Richard Webb *Sheriff Jones* • Carol Lynley *Leslie* • Shelley Berman *Hairdresser* • Larry Hagman *Cop* ■ *Dir* Larry Hagman • *Scr* Anthony Harris, Jack Woods, from a story by Richard Clair, Anthony Harris

Bewitched ★★

Drama 1945 · US · BW · 65mins

Arch Oboler, a radio producer who turned to movies, is nowadays best known, if at all, for his ground-breaking 3-D feature *Bwana Devil*. This adaptation of his story *Alter Ego* was the first of a series of films that invariably featured bizarre or supernatural themes. Phyllis Thaxter plays a woman suffering from a dual personality disorder, an unusual subject for this period, but the sheer talkiness betrays the writer/director's background in radio. TS

Phyllis Thaxter *Joan Alris Ellis* • Edmund Gwenn *Dr Bergson* • Henry H Daniels Jr *Bob Arnold* • Addison Richards *John Ellis* • Kathleen Lockhart *Mrs Ellis* • Francis Pierlot *Dr George Wilton* ■ *Dir* Arch Oboler • *Scr* Arch Oboler, from his story *Alter Ego*

Beyond a Reasonable Doubt ★★★★ PG

Film noir 1956 · US · BW · 80mins

While perhaps overdependent on coincidence and contrivance, this deft thriller guards its secret right to the end and proved a fitting swan song to Fritz Lang's Hollywood career. Dana Andrews brings a chilling calculation to the role of a journalist whose crusade against circumstantial evidence results in a murder rap, while Joan Fontaine is the loyal fiancée who campaigns to prove his innocence. But it is Lang's teasing direction that keeps the viewer guessing as his camera alights on seemingly inconsequential details that are just as likely to be red herrings as vital clues. DP [video]

Dana Andrews *Tom Garrett* • Joan Fontaine *Susan Spencer* • Sidney Blackmer *Austin Spencer* • Philip Bourneuf *Roy Thompson* • Shepperd Strudwick *Wilson* • Arthur Franz *Bob Hale* • Edward Binns *Lt Kennedy* ■ *Dir* Fritz Lang • *Scr* Douglas Morrow

Beyond Bedlam ★ 18

Psychological thriller
1993 · UK · Colour · 85mins

Director Vadim Jean displays little talent in this convoluted, violent and ineffectual thriller. The cat-and-mouse tale involves a detective (Craig Fairbrass) who stumbles upon a scientist (Elizabeth Hurley) conducting gross experiments on serial killer Keith Allen. The B-list British cast doesn't bode well. LH [video] DVD

Craig Fairbrass *Terry Hamilton* • Elizabeth Hurley *Stephanie Lyell* • Keith Allen *Marc Gilmour* • Anita Dobson *Judith Hamilton* • Craig Kelly (2) *Matthew Hamilton* • Georgina Hale *Sister Romulus* • Jesse Birdsall *Scott* ■ *Dir* Vadim Jean • *Scr* Rob Walker, Vadim Jean, from the novel *Bedlam* by Harry Adam Knight

Beyond Borders ★★ 15

Wartime romantic drama
2003 · US/Ger · Colour · 121mins

Thanks to Phil Meheux's glossy photography, poverty and repression have rarely looked so picturesque as in this well-meaning, but naive melodrama. Clive Owen's militant maverick throws himself into aiding the destitute of Ethiopia, Cambodia and Chechnya, but succeeds only in alienating an audience whose credibility has already been strained by do-gooding socialite Angelina Jolie, who periodically abandons husband Linus Roche to lend Owen some moral and sexual support. DP. In English and Khmer with subtitles. Contains swearing and violence. [video] DVD

Angelina Jolie *Sarah Jordan* • Clive Owen *Nick Callahan* • Teri Polo *Charlotte Jordan* • Linus Roache *Henry Bauford* • Noah Emmerich *Elliott Hauser* • Yorick van Wageningen *Steiger* • Timothy West *Lawrence Bauford* ■ *Dir* Martin Campbell • *Scr* Caspian Tredwell-Owen

Beyond Evil ★ 15

Horror 1980 · US · Colour · 90mins

This is a stale and predictable exercise in outmoded exorcism material. Newlyweds John Saxon and Lynda Day George move to a tropical island, but a tenant of their idyllic home is a 100-year-old witch who soon possesses Day George with cheap special effects including badly animated green laser eyes. Capably acted, yet poorly scripted and bankrupt of any originality. AJ. Contains violence and nudity. [video] DVD

John Saxon *Larry* • Lynda Day George *Barbara* • Michael Dante *Del* • Mario Milano *Albanos* • Janice Lynde *Alma* • David Opatoshu *Dr Solomon* • Anne Marisse *Leia* • Zitto Kazann *Esteban* ■ *Dir* Herb Freed • *Scr* Herb Freed, David Baughn, Paul Ross

Beyond Mombasa ★★ U

Action adventure 1957 · US · Colour · 90mins

This safari adventure has Cornel Wilde's plans to mine uranium hampered by a leopard-worshipping tribe who have already flayed his brother alive. Wilde later directed and starred in *The Naked Prey*, one of the most distinctive African yarns ever made. However, this effort is content to roll out every cliché – from blowpipes and missionaries turned mad by malaria and greed, to the obligatory damsel in distress (played by Donna Reed). AT

Cornel Wilde *Matt Campbell* • Donna Reed *Ann Wilson* • Leo Genn *Ralph Hoyt* • Ron Randell *Elliott Hastings* • Christopher Lee *Gil Rossi* • Eddie Calvert *Trumpet player* • Dan Jackson *Ketimi* • MacDonald Parke *Tourist* ■ *Dir* George Marshall • *Scr* Richard English, Gene Levitt, from the story *The Mark of the Leopard* by James Eastwood

Beyond Rangoon ★★★★ 15

Drama 1995 · US · Colour · 99mins

John Boorman's powerful indictment of Burma's oppressive military regime stars Patricia Arquette as a naive American doctor who becomes embroiled in the country's problems. She finds herself drawn to the campaign of Aung San Suu Kyi, the democratic leader under house arrest. Filmed in neighbouring Malaysia, it follows *The Year of Living Dangerously* and *The Killing Fields* by using a westerner as its protagonist: "Some people have found that her grief is in some sense trivial against the horrors of a nation's bloodshed," said Boorman, "but my feeling was that this woman shares the audience's ignorance... she's drawn into it and learns about it as we do." AT [video]

Patricia Arquette *Laura Bowman* • U Aung Ko • Frances McDormand *Andy* • Spalding Gray *Jeremy Watt* • Tiara Jacquelina *Desk clerk* • Kuswadinath Bujang *Colonel* • Victor Slezak *Mr Scott* • Jit Murad *Sein Htoo* • Ye Myint *Zaw Win* • Adelle Lutz *Aung San Suu Kyi* ■ *Dir* John Boorman • *Scr* Alex Lasker, Bill Rubenstein

Beyond Reasonable Doubt ★★★ PG

Drama based on a true story
1980 · NZ · Colour · 103mins

David Hemmings gives his best performance since he became a Swinging Sixties' sensation, playing a malicious New Zealand cop planting evidence to put a noose around the neck of a feeble-minded farmer (John Hargreaves) accused of a husband-and-wife murder. The farmer went for two trials, was found guilty and then pardoned. John Laing directs without any sense of urgency, but the fact that it's a true story makes it memorable. TH. Contains some violence. [video]

David Hemmings *Inspector Hutton* • John Hargreaves *Arthur Allen Thomas* • Martyn Sanderson *Lem Demler* • Tony Barry *Detective John Hughes* • Grant Tilly *David Morris* • Diana Rowan *Vivien Thomas* ■ *Dir* John Laing • *Scr* David Yallop, from his non-fiction book

Beyond Silence ★★★ 12

Drama 1996 · Ger · Colour · 113mins

More interested in the problem of living with deaf people than with deafness itself, this is still an ambitious attempt to combine the problem picture and the tear-jerker, within the confines of the European art movie. Caroline Link makes evocative use of sound throughout as she shows how a young girl finds release in music from the routine of signing for her deaf-mute parents. Both Tatjana Trieb and Sylvie Testud excel as the maturing Lara, although the latter is forced to deal with a melodramatic plotline when she becomes torn between her father and her friends in Berlin. DP. In German with English subtitles. Contains a mild sex scene.

Sylvie Testud *Lara* • Tatjana Trieb *Lara as a child* • Howie Seago *Martin* • Emmanuelle Laborit *Kai* • Sibylle Canonica *Clarissa* • Matthias Habich *Gregor* • Alexandra Bolz *Marie* • Hansa Czypionka *Tom* ■ *Dir* Caroline Link • *Scr* Caroline Link, Beth Serlin

Beyond the Blue Horizon ★★★

Musical comedy 1942 · US · Colour · 76mins

Sporting her trademark sarong in yet another of her popular South Seas movies, Dorothy Lamour stars as an orphan who has grown up living native on a tropical isle with a tiger and a chimp for company. Richard Denning supplies the romance, while Lamour's discovery that she's a millionairess peps up the plot. Treated as the fantastical nonsense it is by director Alfred Santell, this is gloriously tongue-in-cheek, escapist fare. RK

Dorothy Lamour *Tama* • Richard Denning *Jakra* • Jack Haley *Squidge* • Walter Abel *Thornton* • Helen Gilbert *Carol* • Patricia Morison *Sylvia* • Frances Gifford *Charlotte* • Elizabeth Patterson *Mrs Daly* ■ *Dir* Alfred Santell • *Scr* Frank Butler, from a story by E Lloyd Sheldon, Jack DeWitt

Beyond the Call ★★★ 15

Drama 1996 · US · Colour · 96mins

In this moving TV movie, Sissy Spacek plays a housewife who becomes involved in a battle to save the life of David Strathairn, a former boyfriend and Vietnam veteran who is on death row after murdering a policeman. She learns that the tragedy was the result of post-traumatic shock syndrome, but her campaign puts her own marriage to Arliss Howard in jeopardy. The performances are first rate and the direction from Tony Bill is sympathetically understated. JF. Contains violence and swearing. DVD

Sissy Spacek *Pam O'Brien* • David Strathairn *Russell Gates* • Arliss Howard *Keith O'Brien* • Janet Wright *Fran* • Lindsay Murrell *Rebecca O'Brien* • Andrew Sardella *Mark O'Brien* ■ *Dir* Tony Bill • *Scr* Doug Magee

Beyond the Clouds ★★ 18

Portmanteau drama
1995 · It/Ger/Fr · Colour · 104mins

At the age of 82 and in poor health, Michelangelo Antonioni filmed this quartet of short stories, linked by John Malkovich as a film director looking for his next idea. At times the visuals betray the presence of a master film-maker, but otherwise this is a flimsy and rather sad enterprise. AT. In English, French and Italian with subtitles. Contains swearing, nudity. [video]

John Malkovich *The Director* • Sophie Marceau *Young woman* • Inés Sastre *Carmen* • Kim Rossi Stuart *Silvano* • Chiara Caselli *Olga* • Peter Weller *Husband* • Jean Reno *Carlo* • Fanny Ardant *Patricia* • Irène Jacob *Girl* • Vincent Perez *Boy* • Marcello Mastroianni *Maestro* • Jeanne Moreau *Woman* ■ *Dir* Michelangelo Antonioni • *Scr* Michelangelo Antonioni, Wim Wenders, Tonino Guerra, from the short story collection *That Bowling Alley on the River Tiber* by Michelangelo Antonioni

Beyond the Curtain ★ U

Thriller 1960 · UK · BW · 91mins

This shoddy propaganda piece is bargain-basement nonsense. It stars Richard Greene as a pilot who drops behind the Iron Curtain to prise air hostess Eva Bartok out of the clutches of the communists. Faced with a dismal script and locations that would shame poverty row, the unfortunate cast doesn't even try to convince. DP

Richard Greene *Captain Jim Kyle* • Eva Bartok *Karin von Seefeldt* • Marius Goring *Hans Koertner* • Lucie Mannheim *Frau von Seefeldt* • Andrée Melly *Linda* • George Mikell *Pieter* • John Welsh *Turner* • Dennis Shaw [Denis Shaw] *Krumm* ■ *Dir* Compton Bennett • *Scr* John Cresswell, Compton Bennett, from the novel *Thunder Above* by Charles F Blair

B

Beyond the Forest ★★

Melodrama 1949 · US · BW · 76mins

The great Bette Davis occasionally teetered on the edge of farce, only saved from producing a parody of herself by a strong directorial hand on the tiller. Sadly, King Vidor does not provide it here. Davis is the disenchanted wife of a hick doctor – a competent Joseph Cotten – stuck in a small town and soon embroiled in a murder puzzle. Vidor tries too hard and fails miserably to engender an atmosphere of tension and menace, while Davis at her most arch and uncontained is not a pretty sight. SH

Bette Davis *Rosa Moline* • Joseph Cotten *Dr Lewis Moline* • David Brian *Neil Latimer* • Ruth Roman *Carol* • Minor Watson *Moose* • Dona Drake *Jenny* • Regis Toomey *Sorren* • Sara Selby [Sarah Selby] *Mildred* ■ *Dir* King Vidor • *Scr* Lenore Coffee, from the novel by Stuart Engstrand

Beyond the Law ★★★ U

Detective drama 1968 · US · BW · 85mins

This abrasive second film from novelist-turned-director Norman Mailer shows the off-duty hours of three Manhattan cops. Mailer himself plays the senior detective, while his colleagues are all racist bigots who bend the rules in their quest for a collar. The style is *cinéma vérité* – the cameraman is noted documentarist DA Pennebaker – and the script consists of improvised dialogue made up on the spot. It's a grubby, shambolic movie with some terrible scenes, but there's also some powerful stuff here, most of it involving Rip Torn as a hippy accused of murder. AT

Rip Torn *Popcorn* • George Plimpton *Mayor* • Norman Mailer *Lieutenant Francis Xavier Pope* • Mickey Knox *Mickey Berk* • Buzz Farbar *Rocco Gibraltar* • Beverly Bentley *Mary Pope* • Mara Lynn *Ilse Fuchs* • Marcia Mason *Marcia Stillwell* ■ *Dir/Scr* Norman Mailer

Beyond the Mat ★★★★ 15

Sports documentary
1999 · US · Colour · 98mins

Barry W Blaustein, an ex-*Saturday Night Live* writer, makes his directorial debut with this behind-the-scenes look at the World Wrestling Federation. Highlighting the sport's meticulously choreographed showmanship, Blaustein focuses specifically on the way hard-nosed commercialism drives the stars to push themselves to the limits of physical endurance. However, while Terry Funk is seemingly content to wrestle on at the age of 53, the sport has clearly ruined the life of Jake "the Snake" Roberts, whose relationship with his daughter provides painful moments matched only by Mick Foley seeing the impact his fearless style has on his kids. Glib in places, but sympathetic. DP [video] DVD

Dir/Scr Barry W Blaustein • *Cinematographer* Michael Grady

Beyond the Poseidon Adventure ★★ 15

Disaster movie 1979 · US · Colour · 109mins

It's ironic that this sequel to the blockbuster that initiated the disaster movie cycle should effectively finish off the genre and the career of its king, Irwin Allen. Michael Caine, Sally Field and Karl Malden play the members of a salvage team who come to the rescue of the overturned *Poseidon* passenger liner and find themselves fighting off villainous Telly Savalas, who is after the ship's valuable secret cargo. Even the effects aren't up to much. JF [video]

Michael Caine *Captain Mike Turner* • Sally Field *Celeste Whitman* • Telly Savalas *Stefan Svevo* • Peter Boyle *Frank Mazzetti* • Jack Warden *Harold Meredith* • Shirley Knight *Hannah Meredith* • Shirley Jones *Gina Rowe* • Karl Malden *Wilbur Hubbard* • Veronica Hamel *Suzanne Constantine* • Slim Pickens *Tex* • Mark Harmon *Larry Simpson* ■ *Dir* Irwin Allen • *Scr* Nelson Gidding, from the novel by Paul Gallico

Beyond the River ★★

Drama 1956 · US · Colour · 88mins

The original American title, *The Bottom of the Bottle*, should alert you to the content of this maudlin adaptation of a Georges Simenon novel. The physically similar Van Johnson and Joseph Cotten are well cast as psychologically mismatched brothers, one an alcoholic fugitive, the other a respected attorney. Despite veteran director Henry Hathaway's expert handling, the story barely fills the CinemaScope screen; it would have worked better as a tight, black-and-white production. TS

Van Johnson *Donald Martin* • Joseph Cotten *PM* • Ruth Roman *Nora Martin* • Jack Carson *Hal Breckinridge* • Margaret Hayes *Lil Breckinridge* • Bruce Bennett *Brand* • Brad Dexter *Stanley Miller* • Peggy Knudsen *Ellen Miller* ■ *Dir* Henry Hathaway • *Scr* Sydney Boehm, from a novel by Georges Simenon

Beyond the Sea ★★★ 12

Musical biographical drama
2004 · UK/Ger · Colour · 113mins

This is very much a labour of love for Kevin Spacey, who, as well as taking the all-singing, all-dancing lead, co-wrote and directed this biopic of crooner Bobby Darin. Charting the singer's astonishing life from an illness-ridden childhood to his death at the tragically young age of 37, it takes in Darin's recording triumphs, marriage to Sandra Dee (Kate Bosworth) and success in Vegas and Hollywood. Spacey is outstanding as Darin, but the film's structure – a strange blend of flashbacks and fantasy – will prove too odd for some viewers. AS. Contains swearing. [video] DVD

Kevin Spacey *Bobby Darin* • Kate Bosworth *Sandra Dee* • John Goodman *Steve Blauner* • Bob Hoskins *Charlie Cassotto Maffia* • Brenda Blethyn *Polly Cassotto* • Greta Scacchi *Mary Duvan* • Caroline Aaron *Nina Cassotto Maffia* • Peter Cincotti *Dick Behrke* ■ *Dir* Kevin Spacey • *Scr* Lewis Colick, Kevin Spacey

Beyond the Stars ★★★ PG

Drama 1988 · Can/US · Colour · 87mins

A very young looking Christian Slater is the teenager who dreams of becoming an astronaut in this charming drama. His life changes for ever when he discovers that a reclusive neighbour (Martin Sheen) actually took part in a Moon landing, and the two form an uneasy friendship. Both Slater and Sheen are delightful in this enjoyable tale, and they are joined by an impressive cast, which includes F Murray Abraham, Robert Foxworth and a pre-*Basic Instinct* Sharon Stone. JB. Contains swearing. [video] DVD

Martin Sheen *Paul Andrews* • Christian Slater *Eric Mason* • Robert Foxworth *Richard Michaels* • Sharon Stone *Laurie McCall* • Olivia D'Abo *Mara Simons* • F Murray Abraham *Harry* ■ *Dir/Scr* David Saperstein

Beyond the Time Barrier ★★ U

Science fiction 1960 · US · BW · 75mins

Pilot Robert Clarke breaks the time barrier in an experimental hypersonic aircraft, crosses the fifth dimension, and finds himself on post-World War III Earth where the underground civilisation is menaced by mutants caused by "the cosmic nuclear plague of 1971". A flimsy fantasy from cult director Edgar G Ulmer, saddled with a dreadful script, amateur acting and a crudely expressed "ban the bomb" political message. AJ

Robert Clarke *Maj William Allison* • Darlene Tompkins *Trirene* • Arianne Arden *Markova* • Vladimir Sokoloff *The Supreme* ■ *Dir* Edgar G Ulmer • *Scr* Arthur C Pierce

Beyond the Valley of the Dolls ★★★★ 18

Cult satirical melodrama
1970 · US · Colour · 104mins

Dubbed "BVD" by die-hard trash lovers, soft-core porn king Russ Meyer's hilarious exposé of Hollywood sex, drugs and rock 'n' roll is platinum-plated cult camp. Telling the fabulous rags-to-bitches story of all-girl band the Carrie Nations as they scale the dizzy heights of rock-star fame and then crash-land into decadent sleaze, Meyer's pneumatic parody flashes between soap-opera morality, caricature deviance, flower-power lunacy and shock horror with such breathless audacity that you'll watch it in open-mouthed disbelief. AJ. Contains swearing, nudity. [video] DVD

Dolly Read *Kelly MacNamara* • Cynthia Myers *Casey Anderson* • Marcia McBroom *Pertonella Danforth* • John La Zar [John LaZar] *Z-Man* • Michael Blodgett *Lance Rocke* • David Gurian *Harris Allworth* • Edy Williams *Ashley St Ives* • Erica Gavin *Roxanne* • Charles Napier *Baxter Wolfe* ■ *Dir* Russ Meyer • *Scr* Roger Ebert

Beyond the Walls ★★ 18

Prison drama 1984 · Is · Colour · 98mins

An Israeli contender for the best foreign film Oscar, this is an overloud and hysterical prison drama. Though well intentioned it's over-directed, derivative and strident. The plot is naive: in a maximum security jail an Israeli criminal and an Arab terrorist team up to start a prison strike and stop the escalation of violence between inmates and guards. Director Uri Barbash's simplistic premise is that these Israeli-Arab prison relationships serve as a metaphor for the Middle East conflict. TS. In Hebrew with English subtitles. [video]

Arnon Zadok *Uri* • Muhamad Bakri *Issam* • Assi Dayan *Assaf* • Hilel Ne'eman *Hershko, the security officer* • Rami Danon *Fittusi* • Boaz Sharaabi *"The Nightingale"* • Adib Jahashan *Malid* • Roberto Polak *Yechiel* • Naffi Salach *Sanji* ■ *Dir* Uri Barbash, Arnon Zadok, Muhamad Bakri, Rudy Cohen • *Scr* Benny Barbash, Eran Preis, Uri Barbash

Beyond Therapy ★★★ 15

Comedy 1987 · US · Colour · 89mins

With his scattergun style, director Robert Altman tends to miss as many targets as he hits. So it proves in this weirdly wacky love story, in which bisexual Jeff Goldblum's relationship with neurotic Julie Hagerty is helped and hindered by their respective psychiatric agony aunts. Glenda Jackson intimidates everyone and there are some great one-liners, but this exercise in disconnected thinking might have worked better with a more coherent approach. TH [video]

Julie Hagerty *Prudence* • Jeff Goldblum *Bruce* • Glenda Jackson *Charlotte* • Tom Conti *Dr Stuart Framingham* • Christopher Guest *Bob* • Genevieve Page *Zizi* • Cris Campion *Andrew* • Sandrine Dumas *Cindy* ■ *Dir* Robert Altman • *Scr* Christopher Durang, Robert Altman, from the play by Christopher Durang

Beyond This Place ★★

Drama 1959 · UK · BW · 90mins

Cameraman-turned-director Jack Cardiff was still finding his feet with this, his second film. It's a rather turgid tale about a grown-up wartime evacuee who returns to England to clear his dad of murder. Anglophile Van Johnson is not an ideal lead, though he furrows his brow nicely, but there's a fine British supporting cast. The budget limitations are obvious, despite the presence of US import Vera Miles and a brief location shoot in Liverpool. TS

Van Johnson *Paul Mathry* • Vera Miles *Lena Anderson* • Emlyn Williams *Enoch Oswald* • Bernard Lee *Patrick Mathry* • Jean Kent *Louise Birt* • Leo McKern *McEvoy* • Rosalie Crutchley *Ella Mathry* • Vincent Winter *Paul, as a child* ■ *Dir* Jack Cardiff • *Scr* Kenneth Taylor, from a novel by AJ Cronin

Bhaji on the Beach ★★★ 15

Comedy drama 1993 · UK · Colour · 96mins

Gurinder Chadha's debut feature is an astute look at what it means to be Asian, female and British. Following a group of Brummies on a day trip to Blackpool, the film's great strength is the way it interweaves the different plot strands so that each one develops into a fascinating little story in its own right before being neatly brought together at the end. Chadha and scriptwriter Meera Syal were a touch overambitious in trying to tackle so many themes, but their insights are often provocative. DP. Contains violence and swearing. [video] DVD

Kim Vithana *Ginder* • Jimmi Harkishin *Ranjit* • Sarita Khajuria *Hashida* • Mo Sesay *Oliver* • Lalita Ahmed *Asha* • Shaheen Khan *Simi* • Zohra Segal *Pushpa* • Amer Chadha-Patel *Amrik* • Nisha Nayar [Nisha K Nayar] *Ladhu* ■ *Dir* Gurinder Chadha • *Scr* Meera Syal, from a story by Meera Syal, Gurinder Chadha

Bhoot ★★★ 15

Horror thriller 2003 · Ind · Colour · 110mins

Director Ram Gopal Varma scored a major box-office success by dispensing with any song 'n' dance routines and concentrating on the supernatural in this haunted house chiller. The central plot strand owes much to *The Exorcist*, but the emphasis is on atmosphere and the use of camera and soundtrack to generate suspense and shock. Urmila Matondkar impresses as the wife terrorised in a Mumbai apartment, with Nana Patekar's cop, Seema Biswas's maid and Rekha's medium offering scene-stealing support. The denouement is a disappointment, however. DP. In Hindi with English subtitles. [video] DVD

Ajay Devgan *Vishal* • Urmila Matondkar *Swati* • Rekha *Witch doctor* • Victor Banerjee *Dr Rajan* • Nana Patekar *Inspector Liyacat* • Tanuja *Mrs Khosla* • Seema Biswas *Maid* ■ *Dir* Ram Gopal Varma • *Scr* Lalit Marathe, Sameer Sharma

Bhowani Junction ★★

Period drama 1956 · US · Colour · 109mins

Director George Cukor's record with action was far from enviable when he set off for Pakistan to shoot this adaptation about inflamed political and romantic passions in the last days of the Raj. Yet the crowd scenes and the acts of Communist terror are the best parts of this rather turgid melodrama, in which Cukor fails to coax any kind of performance out of Ava Gardner. Stewart Granger and Bill Travers are scarcely more animated. DP

Ava Gardner *Victoria Jones* • Stewart Granger *Colonel Rodney Savage* • Bill Travers *Patrick Taylor* • Abraham Sofaer *Surabhai* • Francis Matthews *Ranjit Kasel* • Marne Maitland *Govindaswami* • Peter Illing *Ghanshyam* • Edward Chapman *Thomas Jones* ■ *Dir* George Cukor • *Scr* Sonya Levien, Ivan Moffat, from the novel by John Masters

The Bible...in the Beginning ★★ U

Biblical epic 1966 · US/It · Colour · 163mins

This is a reverential but onerous adaptation of the first 22 chapters of Genesis. Director John Huston makes a lovely job of the Creation, but the stellar casting too often works against the drama. George C Scott is imposing as Abraham, however, while Huston

B

himself makes a suitably humble Noah. Giuseppe Rotunno's photography is striking, but Toshiro Mayuzumi's Oscar-nominated score is somewhat overbearing. DP [VIDEO] DVD

Michael Parks *Adam* • Ulla Bergryd *Eve* • Richard Harris *Cain* • John Huston *Noah* • Stephen Boyd *Nimrod* • George C Scott *Abraham* • Ava Gardner *Sarah* • Peter O'Toole *Three Angels* • Franco Nero *Abel* ■ *Dir* John Huston • *Scr* Christopher Fry, Jonathan Griffin, Ivo Perilli, Vittorio Bonicelli

Bicentennial Man ★★ 12

Science-fiction comedy drama
1999 · US · Colour · 125mins

Based on the work of two of science fiction's literary giants, Isaac Asimov and Robert Silverberg, this could have become a poignant tale about what it means to be human. Unfortunately, Robin Williams plays for tears as the android butler assembled to serve one family over four generations. With marvellous effects and ideas scuppered by sentimentality, it's enough to make a mechanical man weep. TH. Contains swearing. [VIDEO] DVD

Robin Williams *Andrew* • Embeth Davidtz *Little Miss/Portia* • Sam Neill *Sir* • Oliver Platt *Rupert Burns* • Wendy Crewson *Ma'am* • Stephen Root *Dennis Mansky* ■ *Dir* Chris Columbus • *Scr* Nicholas Kazan, from a short story by Isaac Asimov and from the novel *The Positronic Man* by Isaac Asimov, Robert Silverberg

Les Biches ★★★★ 15

Erotic drama 1968 · Fr/It · Colour · 94mins

New Wave director Claude Chabrol entered a new phase – which would ultimately lead to such masterpieces as *Le Boucher* – with this cool study of a *ménage à trois* between rich lesbian Stéphane Audran, her penniless young plaything Jacqueline Sassard, and handsome architect Jean-Louis Trintignant. Set on the Riviera, the movie has a marvellously fluid style that matches the seesawing sexuality of the characters and builds towards a startling climax. AT. In French with English subtitles. [VIDEO] DVD

Jean-Louis Trintignant *Paul* • Jacqueline Sassard *Why* • Stéphane Audran *Frederique* • Nane Germon *Violetta* • Henri Attal *Robeque* • Dominique Zardi *Riais* • Claude Chabrol *Film-maker* ■ *Dir* Claude Chabrol • *Scr* Claude Chabrol, Paul Gégauff

Bicycle Thieves ★★★★★ U

Drama 1948 · It · BW · 84mins

Scripted by Cesare Zavattini and directed by Vittorio De Sica, this urban parable is the masterwork of the neorealist movement. Exploring the response of ordinary people to the socio-political changes sweeping postwar Italy, the film adopts a "flow of life" structure, comprising vignettes of differing emotional intensity as it follows Lamberto Maggiorani and his son, Enzo Staiola, around Rome in search of the stolen bicycle on which the family depends for its livelihood. Alternating travelling shots of poetic symbolism with stark close-ups of his non-professional leads, De Sica achieves an ironic humanism that can't fail to touch the heart. DP. In Italian with English subtitles. [VIDEO]

Lamberto Maggiorani *Antonio Ricci* • Lianella Carell *Maria Ricci* • Enzo Staiola *Bruno Ricci* • Elena Altieri *The Lady* • Vittorio Antonucci *The Thief* ■ *Dir* Vittorio De Sica • *Scr* Cesare Zavattini, Suso Cecchi D'Amico, Vittorio De Sica, Oreste Biancoli, Adolfo Franci, Gherardo Gherardi, Guerrier Gerardo, from a novel by Luigi Bartolini • *Cinematographer* Carlo Montuori

Bienvenido Mr Marshall ★★★★ U

Comedy 1953 · Sp · BW · 83mins

A prime example of Spanish neorealism, this gentle satire was mistakenly accused of being anti-American on its release. Cannes juror Edward G Robinson was particularly annoyed by the dream sequences that depict a spoof western, a Ku Klux Klan lynching and a House Un-American Activities Committee hearing. Yet, while director Luis Garcia Berlanga is swift to poke fun at US philanthropic pomposity, he saves most of his barbs for the residents of a small Castilian village (each one seemingly a national stereotype), whose greed at the prospect of receiving aid from the Marshall Plan only worsens their plight. DP. In Spanish with English subtitles.

Lolita Sevilla *Carmen Vargas* • Manolo Moran *Manolo* • Jose Isbert *Don Pablo, el alcalde* • Alberto Romea *Don Luis, el caballero* ■ *Dir* Luis G Berlanga [Luis Garcia Berlanga] • *Scr* JA Bardem [Juan Antonio Bardem], LG Berlanga [Luis Garcia Berlanga], Miguel Mihura, a story by JA Bardem [Juan Antonio Bardem], LG Berlanga [Luis Garcia Berlanga]

Big ★★★★ PG

Comedy 1988 · US · Colour · 99mins

Oscar-winner Tom Hanks only received a nomination for this, one of his finest performances to date. He plays a 12-year-old boy transplanted by a carnival wishing contraption into a man's body. Elizabeth Perkins also makes an impact as a co-worker who finds herself strangely attracted to Hanks's little big man. This may well be a formula fantasy movie, but Penny Marshall's polished direction combined with Hanks's gauche charm make it the best of the spate of body-swap movies that were turned out by Hollywood in the late 1980s. PF. Contains swearing. [VIDEO] DVD

Tom Hanks *Josh Baskin* • Elizabeth Perkins *Susan Lawrence* • Robert Loggia *"Mac" MacMillan* • John Heard *Paul Davenport* • Jared Rushton *Billy Kopeche* • David Moscow *Young Josh* • Jon Lovitz *Scotty Brennen* • Mercedes Ruehl *Mrs Baskin* • Josh Clark *Mr Baskin* ■ *Dir* Penny Marshall • *Scr* Gary Ross, Anne Spielberg

Big Bad Mama ★★★ 18

Crime drama 1974 · US · Colour · 84mins

Angie Dickinson comes on strong in a typical early-seventies B-movie from the Roger Corman production line, clearly based on *Bonnie and Clyde* and *Bloody Mama*. Dickinson plays a high-spirited widow in 1930s Texas who goes on a bank-robbing spree with her two nubile daughters when the Depression bites. Full of sex, violence, machine guns and banjo music, it's a rambunctious quickie effortlessly touching each exploitation base. *Star Trek*'s William Shatner turns up to romance Dickinson, and her eye-popping nude scenes have made this one a cult favourite. AJ [VIDEO] DVD

Angie Dickinson *Wilma McClatchie* • William Shatner *William J Baxter* • Tom Skerritt *Fred Diller* • Susan Sennett *Billy Jean McClatchie* • Robbie Lee *Polly McClatchie* • Noble Willingham *Barney* • Joan Prather *Jane Kingston* • Royal Dano *Reverend Johnson* • William O'Connell *Preacher* ■ *Dir* Steve Carver • *Scr* William Norton, Frances Doel

Big Bad Mama II ★★★ 18

Crime drama 1987 · US · Colour · 80mins

A cheap and cheerful follow-up – albeit 13 years later – to Roger Corman's cult gangster hit, with Angie Dickinson reviving her role as the gun-toting matriarch. In this adventure, she takes time off from her bank-robbing activities to do battle with slimy politician Bruce Glover, with journalist Robert Culp also on her trail. Although this lacks the knockabout charm and the eclectic casting of the original, director Jim Wynorski delivers a lightweight, knowing slice of exploitation. JF. Contains violence, swearing and nudity. [VIDEO]

Angie Dickinson *Wilma McClatchie* • Robert Culp *Daryl Pearson* • Danielle Brisebois *Billie Jean McClatchie* • Julie McCullough *Polly McClatchie* • Bruce Glover *Crawford* • Jeff Yagher *Jordan Crawford* ■ *Dir* Jim Wynorski • *Scr* RJ Robertson, Jim Wynorski

The Big Bang ★★★ 18

Documentary 1989 · US · Colour · 73mins

Among the most unconventional directors in modern American cinema, James Toback usually has something to say in his films. But here, he contented himself with a few appeals for cash to potential backers and leaves the serious talking to an eloquent and refreshingly candid cast in this compelling documentary on life, the universe and everything. An artist, an astronomer, a basketball player and a gangster are among those with an option to share. But the most poignant "talking head" is Barbara Traub, an Auschwitz survivor whose thoughts have much greater resonance than all the others, particularly those of successful film producer Don Simpson. DP. Contains swearing. [VIDEO]

Dir/Scr James Toback

The Big Bird Cage ★★ 18

Blaxploitation 1972 · US · Colour · 86mins

The sequel to *The Big Doll House* is more of the same – a blaxploitation mix of broad humour, random violence and dodgy politics. Anitra Ford is jailed in a bamboo sugar mill for knowing too much about a banana republic's revolutionary government and gets imprisoned in the titular torture device. Sid Haig, meanwhile, swoops in to rescue his girlfriend (Pam Grier) and incite a bloody insurrection. This is predictable escapist mayhem with the accent on laughs. AJ [VIDEO] DVD

Pam Grier *Blossom* • Anitra Ford *Terry* • Candice Roman *Carla* • Teda Bracci *Bull Jones* • Carol Speed *Mickie* • Karen McKevic *Karen* • Sid Haig *Django* ■ *Dir/Scr* Jack Hill

The Big Blockade ★★★ U

Second World War drama
1942 · UK · BW · 71mins

Initially conceived as a propaganda short for the Ministry of Information, this Ealing flagwaver sought to emphasise the importance of winning the economic war while Europe remained occupied. Adopting the docudramatic style that would be the prime legacy of British wartime cinema, Charles Frend expounds his message efficiently enough. However, Robert Morley and his fellow Nazis are embarrassing caricatures to set alongside the committed gravitas of Michael Redgrave's Russian and the dignified heroism of Michael Rennie and John Mills. DP [VIDEO]

Will Hay *Skipper, Royal Navy* • Bernard Miles *Mate, Royal Navy* • John Stuart *Naval officer, Royal Navy* • David Evans *David, Royal Air Force* • John Mills *Tom, Royal Air Force* • Michael Rennie *George, Royal Air Force* • Robert Morley *von Geiselbrecht* • Michael Wilding *Captain* • Thora Hird *Waitress* • Michael Redgrave *Russian* ■ *Dir* Charles Frend • *Scr* Angus MacPhail, Charles Frend

The Big Blue ★★★★ 15

Romantic adventure
1988 · US · BW and Colour · 114mins

Action director Luc Besson (*The Fifth Element*) pays homage to the ocean-exploring documentaries of Jacques Cousteau with this stunning, if long and slightly pretentious, underwater cult epic. The story – about two rival deep-sea divers (Besson regular Jean Reno and Jean-Marc Barr) who are crazy about dolphins – is a little shallow, and Rosanna Arquette's role, as a New York insurance investigator who meets Barr in Peru, does seem rather like an afterthought. But Reno mines great humour from his macho mother's boy role, Barr looks impossibly handsome, and the sensational ocean photography is absolutely magnificent. AJ [VIDEO] DVD

Rosanna Arquette *Joanna Cross* • Jean-Marc Barr *Jacques Mayol* • Jean Reno *Enzo Molinari* • Paul Shenar *Dr Laurence* • Sergio Castellitto *Novelli* • Jean Bouise *Uncle Louis* • Marc Duret *Roberto* • Griffin Dunne *Duffy* ■ *Dir* Luc Besson • *Scr* Luc Besson, Robert Garland, Marilyn Golding, Jacques Mayol, Marc Perrier, from a story by Luc Besson • *Cinematographer* Carlo Varini

The Big Boss ★★★ 18

Martial arts drama
1971 · HK · Colour · 94mins

Bruce Lee's Hong Kong film breakthrough may be a bit rough around the edges, but it remains an electrifying example of the martial arts master at work. The plot is fairly perfunctory: Lee is a young man who travels to Thailand, promising to keep out of trouble only to find himself caught up with a drugs ring. However, his graceful charisma shines throughout and director Lo Wei and fight co-ordinator Han Ying-Chieh (who also plays the villain of the piece) orchestrate some stunning set pieces. JF. A Cantonese language film. Contains violence. [VIDEO] DVD

Bruce Lee *Cheng Chao-An* • Maria Yi *Lin Hau-Mei* • James Tien *Hsu Chien* • Nora Miao *Prostitute* • Hang Ying-Chieh ■ *Dir/Scr* Lo Wei

The Big Bounce ★

Crime drama 1969 · US · Colour · 102mins

Ryan O'Neal makes his big screen debut as a cucumber picker who jumps in and out of bed with various women and ends up accused of murder. One of his dalliances (Leigh Taylor-Young) likes having sex in graveyards; another (Lee Grant) commits suicide. Made in 1969, this adaptation of an Elmore Leonard novel is one of those "youth movies" that's full of hippy characters, free sex, "daring" nudity and a general air of social rebellion. AT

Ryan O'Neal *Jack Ryan* • Leigh Taylor-Young *Nancy Barker* • Van Heflin *Sam Mirakian* • Lee Grant *Motel resident* • James Daly *Ray Richie* • Robert Webber *Bob Rogers* • Cindy Eilbacher *Cheryl* ■ *Dir* Alex March • *Scr* Robert Dozier, from a novel by Elmore Leonard

The Big Bounce ★★ 12

Crime comedy thriller
2004 · US · Colour · 84mins

Owen Wilson plays a laid-back petty thief whose roving eye gets him into serious trouble when he falls for the criminally-minded thrill-seeker Sara Foster. Despite being perfectly cast, Wilson struggles to carry the feature, never completely convincing with his easy charm. It's partly due to the weak script and unnecessarily convoluted plot, which twists and turns without any real explanation or character development to support it. Even the entertaining smart-talk rapidly degenerates into farce. SF DVD

Owen Wilson *Jack Ryan* • Morgan Freeman *Walter Crewes* • Gary Sinise *Ray Ritchie* • Sara Foster *Nancy Hayes* • Vinnie Jones *Lou Harris* • Charlie Sheen *Bob Rogers Jr* • Bebe Neuwirth *Alison Ritchie* • Harry Dean Stanton *Bob Rogers Sr* • Willie Nelson *Joe Lurie* • Andrew Wilson *Ned Coleman* ■ *Dir* George Armitage • *Scr* Sebastian Gutierrez, from the novel by Elmore Leonard

B

The Big Brawl ★★ 15

Martial arts comedy
1980 · US · Colour · 91mins

This was an early tilt at the American market from Jackie Chan – although he would have to wait for more than a decade before breaking through. Chan plays a martial arts star in 1930s America who decides to take part in a no-holds barred fighting competition, bringing him into conflict with local gangsters. Robert Clouse expertly stages the many fight sequences, although even then Chan was putting equal emphasis on comedy. The period trappings add a fresh flavour to the otherwise predictable plotting. JF

Jackie Chan *Jerry* • José Ferrer *Dominici* • Kristine DeBell *Nancy* • Mako *Herbert* • Ron Max *Leggetti* • David Sheiner *Morgan* • Rosalind Chao *Mae* • Lenny Montana *John* ■ *Dir* Robert Clouse • *Scr* Robert Clouse, from a story by Fred Weintraub, Robert Clouse

The Big Broadcast ★★★★

Musical comedy 1932 · US · BW · 83mins

Radio was huge in the 1930s and families listening in at home was starting to pose a threat to cinema, so Paramount cleverly exploited the trend by making this vehicle for radio stars on the big screen. The paper-thin plot has Stuart Erwin taking over a failing radio station run by George Burns and – guess what? – putting on an all-star show. So successful was this flick that three sort-of sequels followed, all successful. Somehow they lack the quaint and specific charm of the original, which even manages to bring some fresh cleverness to its familiar triangle subplot. TS

Bing Crosby *Bing Hornsby* • Stuart Erwin *Leslie McWhinney* • Leila Hyams *Anita Rogers* • Sharon Lynne *Mona* • George Burns *George* • Gracie Allen *Gracie* • George Barbier *Clapsaddle* • Ralph Robertson *Announcer* ■ *Dir* Frank Tuttle • *Scr* George Marion Jr, from the play *Wild Waves* by William Ford Manley

The Big Broadcast of 1936 ★★★ U

Musical comedy 1935 · US · BW · 94mins

In this second of Paramount's all-star collections of radio stars on the silver screen the linking plot seems strangely prophetic, as Gracie Allen's alleged uncle invents a device called television that can send pictures of artistes performing to anywhere in the world. Jack Oakie is the nominal star, as a radio station owner. But more importantly this is your opportunity to catch such major period names as Amos 'n' Andy (Freeman Gosden and Charles Correll, blackfaced), Ethel Merman, the great Bill Robinson and the Vienna Boys' Choir. TS

Jack Oakie *Spud* • George Burns *George* • Gracie Allen *Gracie* • Fayard Nicholas *Dash* • Harold Nicholas *Dot* • Akim Tamiroff *Boris* • Bing Crosby • Ethel Merman • Amos 'n' Andy • Bill Robinson ■ *Dir* Norman Taurog • *Scr* Walter DeLeon, Francis Martin, Ralph Spence

The Big Broadcast of 1937 ★★★ U

Musical comedy 1936 · US · BW · 104mins

The third of Paramount's showcases for big radio names ostensibly stars the great George Burns and Gracie Allen, but actually teams Gracie with the incorrigible Jack Benny, to great and hilarious effect. There is a plot of sorts involving Ray Milland and Shirley Ross going on the town. But, as ever, this is really just an excuse for some of the biggest stars of the day to strut their stuff – those on show include the volatile, big-mouthed Martha Raye, whose *Vote for Mr Rhythm* number is the film's highlight. TS

Jack Benny *Jack Carson* • George Burns *Mr Platt* • Gracie Allen *Mrs Platt* • Bob Burns *Bob Black* • Frank Forest *Frank Rossman* • Ray Milland *Bob Miller* • Shirley Ross *Gwen Holmes* • Martha Raye *Patsy* • Benny Goodman • Leopold Stokowski ■ *Dir* Mitchell Leisen • *Scr* Walter DeLeon, Francis Martin, from a story by Barry Trivers, Arthur Kober, Erwin Gelsey

The Big Broadcast of 1938 ★★ U

Musical comedy 1937 · US · BW · 90mins

The last and frankly weakest of Paramount's all-star series is missing George Burns and Gracie Allen, but benefits from starring the great WC Fields. Though nearly crippled by a dumb plot about racing ocean liners, the film does include a moment that bequeaths immortality upon it – a radio comic called Bob Hope, making his film debut, joins star Shirley Ross in a specially written bittersweet duet entitled *Thanks for the Memory*. The song rightfully won an Oscar and became Bob Hope's theme song. TS

WC Fields *T Frothingill Bellows/SB Bellows* • Martha Raye *Martha Bellows* • Dorothy Lamour *Dorothy Wyndham* • Shirley Ross *Cleo Fielding* • Russell Hicks *Capt Stafford* • Dorothy Howe *Joan Fielding* • Lionel Pape *Lord Droopy* • Bob Hope *Buzz Fielding* • Kirsten Flagstad ■ *Dir* Mitchell Leisen • *Scr* Walter DeLeon, Francis Martin, Ken Englund, Howard Lindsay, Russel Crouse, from a story by Frederick Hazlitt Brennan

Big Brown Eyes ★★★

Crime drama 1936 · US · BW · 76mins

This crime drama sought to emulate the success of *The Thin Man* in its teaming of Cary Grant and Joan Bennett, but it has rather more violence and action, including the accidental shooting of a baby. Grant is a little awkward as the two-fisted detective who finds his vaudeville past as a ventriloquist useful in a tight spot, but Bennett is on top form as the wisecracking hotel manicurist turned reporter, who helps him collar Walter Pidgeon's suave racketeer. AE

Cary Grant *Danny Barr* • Joan Bennett *Eve Fallon* • Walter Pidgeon *Richard Morey* • Lloyd Nolan *Russ Cortig* • Alan Baxter *Cary Butler* • Marjorie Gateson *Mrs Cole* • Isabel Jewell *Bessie Blair* • Douglas Fowley *Benny Bottle* ■ *Dir* Raoul Walsh • *Scr* Raoul Walsh, Bert Hanlon, from the short stories *Hahsit Babe* and *Big Brown Eyes* by James Edward Grant

Big Bully ★ PG

Comedy 1996 · US · Colour · 86mins

Chances are you've never heard of this awful comedy from horror specialist Steve Miner, and for good reason. The plot is unappealing (boy bullied at school grows up to be Rick Moranis and continues to be tormented by Tom Arnold), the black humour falls flat and the notion that Arnold can find renewed meaning in his life through thuggery is vaguely offensive. JC

Rick Moranis *David Leary* • Tom Arnold *Rosco Bigger (Fang)* • Julianne Phillips *Victoria* • Carol Kane *Faith* • Jeffrey Tambor *Art* • Curtis Armstrong *Clark* • Faith Prince *Betty* ■ *Dir* Steve Miner • *Scr* Mark Steven Johnson

The Big Bus ★★ PG

Disaster movie spoof
1976 · US · Colour · 84mins

In this intended parody of the 1970s disaster movie genre, the usual bunch of misfits climbs aboard the world's first nuclear-powered coach, travelling from New York to Denver. More like *The Big Blunderbuss* in its scattergun attack on its targets, the likes of Joseph Bologna, Stockard Channing, Lynn Redgrave and Ned Beatty make a lot of noise to occasionally pleasing comic effect. You have to admire their intentions, but most "serious" disaster movies of the period had slipped into unintentional self-parody by 1976. SR DVD

Joseph Bologna *Dan Torrance* • Stockard Channing *Kitty Baxter* • John Beck *Shoulders* • René Auberjonois *Father Kudos* • Ned Beatty *Shorty Scotty* • Bob Dishy *Dr Kurtz* • José Ferrer *Ironman* • Ruth Gordon *Old lady* • Harold Gould *Professor Baxter* • Larry Hagman *Parking lot doctor* • Sally Kellerman *Sybil Crane* ■ *Dir* James Frawley • *Scr* Fred Freeman, Lawrence J Cohen

Big Business ★★★★★ U

Silent comedy 1929 · US · BW · 18mins

Hailed by some critics as the greatest Laurel and Hardy comedy ever filmed, this has the dynamic duo fighting back in an orgy of reciprocal destruction. They're door-to-door salesmen selling Christmas trees in sunny California, up against their ever-wrathful stooge, James Finlayson – he of the pop-eyes and belligerent moustache – as a householder driven to take apart, bit by bit, their car, while they tear up his house and garden. Stan's crocodile tears win over the on-guard policeman, but Ollie's giveaway grin ruins any chance of a happy-ever-after finale. Even from them this is outstanding. TH DVD

Stan Laurel *Stan* • Oliver Hardy *Ollie* • James Finlayson *Homeowner* • Tiny Sandford *Policeman* • Lyle Tayo *Husbandless woman* • Retta Palmer *Neighbor* ■ *Dir* James W Horne • *Scr* Leo McCarey, HM Walker (titles)

Big Business ★★ PG

Comedy 1988 · US · Colour · 93mins

One of those frenetic double-role efforts, this strains the talents and energy levels of Bette Midler and Lily Tomlin to breaking point, along with the audience, who are asked to not so much suspend disbelief as leave their brains on the sideboard during viewing. This could have been enormous fun – a brace of old comedy pros playing two sets of identical twins juggled at birth and meeting years later in a posh New York hotel. But director Jim Abrahams jettisons coherent narrative in favour of giving his leads enough rope to hang themselves. SH DVD

Bette Midler *Sadie Shelton/Sadie Ratliff* • Lily Tomlin *Rose Shelton/Rose Ratliff* • Fred Ward *Roone Dimmick* • Edward Herrmann *Graham Sherbourne* • Michele Placido *Fabio Alberici* • Daniel Gerroll *Chuck* • Barry Primus *Michael* • Michael Gross *Dr Jay Marshall* • Deborah Rush *Binky Shelton* • Seth Green *Jason* ■ *Dir* Jim Abrahams • *Scr* Dori Pierson, Marc Rubel

The Big Caper ★★★

Crime thriller 1957 · US · BW · 84mins

Rory Calhoun is part of a motley gang of fruitcakes and no-hopers, who plan to be a million dollars richer by robbing a bank. Things don't quite go to plan, however. This dime-budget thriller is directed by Robert Stevens, who maintains the tension and evokes the small-town atmosphere rather well. AT

Rory Calhoun *Frank Harber* • Mary Costa *Kay* • James Gregory *Flood* • Robert Harris *Zimmer* • Corey Allen *Roy* • Roxanne Arlen *Doll* • Paul Picerni *Harry* • Pat McVey [Patrick McVey] *Sam Loxley* ■ *Dir* Robert Stevens • *Scr* Martin Berkeley, from a novel by Lionel White

The Big Chance ★★ U

Crime drama 1957 · UK · BW · 61mins

This is an efficient but hackneyed variation on the well-worn movie notion that crime must never pay. From the moment travel agent William Russell claps eyes on foxy socialite Adrienne Corri and decides to abandon his humdrum married existence for a life of South American excess, we know it will end in tears. Events move at such a pace that there's scarcely time to notice the poverty of the plot and the stiffness of the acting. DP

Adrienne Corri *Diana Maxwell* • William Russell *Bill Anderson* • Ian Colin *Adam Maxwell* • Penelope Bartley *Betty* • Ferdy Mayne *Alpherghis* • John Rae *Jarvis* • Douglas Ives *Stan Willett* ■ *Dir* Peter Graham Scott • *Scr* Peter Graham Scott, from the novel by Pamela Barrington

The Big Chill ★★★★ 15

Drama 1983 · US · Colour · 100mins

At one time a cult movie among 20-somethings, this chic comedy is now also known as the picture from which Kevin Costner had all his scenes cut. Smartly written by director Lawrence Kasdan and Barbara Benedek, the Oscar-nominated script clearly owes a debt to John Sayles's overlooked and superior reunion drama *The Return of the Secaucus Seven*. However, there are still plenty of original insights into both 1960s counterculture and the pretensions of the chattering classes. There's a dream cast, while the soundtrack is packed with the anthems of an age. Over clever, but very slick. DP. Contains swearing, drug abuse and brief nudity. DVD

Kevin Kline *Harold Cooper* • Glenn Close *Sarah Cooper* • William Hurt *Nick* • Jeff Goldblum *Michael* • Tom Berenger *Sam* • Meg Tilly *Chloe* • JoBeth Williams *Karen* • Mary Kay Place *Meg* • Don Galloway *Richard* ■ *Dir* Lawrence Kasdan • *Scr* Lawrence Kasdan, Barbara Benedek

The Big Circus ★★★ U

Adventure 1959 · US · Colour · 103mins

Cult favourite Joseph M Newman directs a fine, though slightly second-rung, cast, headed by world-weary Victor Mature and featuring such stars as Peter Lorre (as a neurotic clown) and Gilbert Roland (as the tightrope walker). Although clearly hindered by budget limitations, this is a worthy attempt to break new ground, and rejects the phoney romanticism of *The Greatest Show on Earth* to good effect. Though not the box-office hit it so desperately wanted to be, this remains a treat. TS

Victor Mature *Hank Whirling* • Red Buttons *Randy Sherman* • Rhonda Fleming *Helen Harrison* • Kathryn Grant *Jeannie Whirling* • Vincent Price *Hans Hagenfeld* • David Nelson *Tommy Gordon* • Gilbert Roland *Zach Colino* • Peter Lorre *Skeeter* ■ *Dir* Joseph M Newman • *Scr* Irwin Allen, Charles Bennett, Irving Wallace, from a story by Irwin Allen

Big City ★★

Drama 1937 · US · BW · 79mins

Rival New York cab companies are at loggerheads but you'd think that the Third World War had broken out, so overwrought is this movie. Cabs get smashed, faces get smashed, the unions march in and then bombs go off and the city teeters on anarchy. Spencer Tracy, as one of the cabbies, tries to stay calm, while his pregnant Russian immigrant wife, Luise Rainer, is accused of causing explosions. Just awful, but compulsive viewing. AT

Spencer Tracy *Joe Benton* • Luise Rainer *Anna Benton* • Charley Grapewin *Mayor* • Janet Beecher *Sophie Sloane* • Eddie Quillan *Mike Edwards* • Victor Varconi *Paul Roya* • Oscar O'Shea *John C Andrews* ■ *Dir* Frank Borzage • *Scr* Dore Schary, Hugo Butler, from a story by Norman Krasna

The Big City ★★★★ U

Drama 1963 · Ind · BW · 131mins

Satyajit Ray won the best director prize at Berlin for this, the first of his films with a contemporary setting. Although thematically related to the "salaryman" comedies of Yasujiro Ozu, the style remains that blend of elements from Jean Renoir and neorealism that characterised Ray's earliest work. Touching on the mores of Anglo-Indians, the film deals primarily with the social role of women, as it traces Madhabi Mukherjee's progress from traditional housewife to middle-class heroine. Minutely observed and flawlessly acted, this gently satirical study of the changing face of Calcutta was typical of Ray's wry approach to all things political. DP. In Bengali with English subtitles.

Madhabi Mukherjee *Arati* • Anil Chatterjee *Subrata Mazumdar* • Haradhan Bannerjee *Mukherjee* • Haren Chatterjee *Father* • Vicky Redwood *Edith Simmons* • Jaya Bhaduri [Jaya Bachchan] *Sister* ■ *Dir* Satyajit Ray • *Scr* Satyajit Ray, from novel Narendranath Mitra's *Abataranika*

The Big Clock ★★★

Film noir 1948 · US · BW · 95mins

An excellent second-eleven *film noir* with Charles Laughton as a publisher who murders his mistress and then gets one of his employees, crime editor Ray Milland, to investigate. What Laughton doesn't know is that Milland shared the same girlfriend, so lots of juicy complications ensue, especially as Milland hates Laughton for his oppressive business practices. With the huge office clock ticking away like a countdown to doom, and Laughton looking every ugly inch a caseload of neuroses, this is highly effective. AT

Ray Milland *George Stroud* • Charles Laughton *Earl Janoth* • Maureen O'Sullivan *Georgette Stroud* • George Macready *Steven Hagen* • Rita Johnson *Pauline York* • Elsa Lanchester *Louise Patterson* • Harold Vermilyea *Don Klausmeyer* • Dan Tobin *Ray Cordette* ■ *Dir* John Farrow • *Scr* Jonathan Latimer, from the novel by Kenneth Fearing

The Big Combo ★★★★ PG

Film noir 1955 · US · BW · 87mins

This is as tough and nasty as they come, and that's a recommendation! Cult director Joseph H Lewis trawls the mean streets as his lead character, cop Cornel Wilde, turns over the local rocks to see what slime crawls out from underneath. A co-feature on its original release, and barely noticed, this movie was accorded a reissue in repertory cinemas in the 1980s. A whole new audience responded to the amorality and the raw violence, delighting in the twisted viciousness of evil Richard Conte and positively revelling in the demise of Brian Donlevy. TS [video]

Cornel Wilde *Diamond* • Richard Conte *Brown* • Brian Donlevy *McClure* • Jean Wallace *Susan* • Robert Middleton *Peterson* • Lee Van Cleef *Fante* • Ted De Corsia *Bettini* • Helen Walker *Alicia* ■ *Dir* Joseph H Lewis • *Scr* Philip Yordan

The Big Country ★★★★★ PG

Western 1958 · US · Colour · 159mins

Unfairly neglected today, this major western is a film of truly epic dimensions. It tells the tale of a greenhorn sent to the wide-open spaces, a role to which co-producer and star Gregory Peck is particularly suited – he is one of the few actors whose innate pacificism rings true. Thanks to the combination of top director William Wyler and a superb cast that includes Jean Simmons, Charlton Heston and the Oscar-winning Burl Ives the film never palls, despite its length. It also features a great theme tune, a triumph for composer Jerome Moross. Though misused by a score of commercials, when heard in context, the music rightfully lifts this distinguished movie to the realm of screen classic. TS [video] DVD

Gregory Peck *James McKay* • Jean Simmons *Julie Maragon* • Carroll Baker *Patricia Terrill* • Charlton Heston *Steve Leech* • Burl Ives *Rufus Hannassey* • Charles Bickford *Major Henry Terrill* • Alfonso Bedoya *Ramon* • Chuck Connors *Buck Hannassey* ■ *Dir* William Wyler • *Scr* James R Webb, Robert Wilder, Sy Bartlett, Robert Wyler, from the novel by Donald Hamilton, adapted by Jessamyn West, Robert Wyler • *Cinematographer* Franz F Planer [Franz Planer]

The Big Cube ★

Drama 1969 · US/Mex · Colour · 98mins

This sad coda to the great Lana Turner's career came three years after her last glamorous Ross Hunter/ Universal production, *Madame X*. Co-stars George Chakiris, Richard Egan and Dan O'Herlihy – all well past their prime – lend this demented melodrama a camp attraction. But its sheer ineptitude, combined with Turner's ravaged looks and (to be kind) uncertain performance, make it hard to watch, let alone take seriously. TS

Lana Turner *Adriana Roman* • George Chakiris *Johnny Allen* • Richard Egan *Frederick Lansdale* • Dan O'Herlihy *Charles Winthrop* • Karin Mossberg *Lisa Winthrop* • Pamela Rodgers *Bibi* ■ *Dir* Tito Davison • *Scr* William Douglas Lansford, from a story by Tito Davison, Edmundo Baez

Big Daddy ★★★★ 12

Comedy 1999 · US · Colour · 89mins

This "adoption-by-proxy" comedy is a perfect example of how a sparkling central performance can make even the most crudely sentimental fluff hilariously palatable. Thanks to slacker superstar Adam Sandler and his infectious goofball sweetness, this film works like a charm, even though the story springs few surprises (lazy loafer takes his flatmate's love-child under his wing; they bond; and the parental challenges change him sufficiently to win the hand of Miss Right, Joey Lauren Adams). Yes, it's contrived, mawkish and manipulative, but director Dennis Dugan's effortless handling of the tale and Sandler's confident puppy-dog demeanour ensure that it delivers huge laughs. AJ. Contains swearing, sexual and drug references. [video] DVD

Adam Sandler *Sonny Koufax* • Joey Lauren Adams *Layla* • Jon Stewart *Kevin* • Cole Sprouse *Julian* • Dylan Sprouse *Julian* • Josh Mostel *Mr Brooks* • Leslie Mann *Corinne* • Allen Covert *Phil* • Rob Schneider *Delivery guy* • Kristy Swanson *Vanessa* • Joseph Bologna *Mr Koufax* • Steve Buscemi *Homeless guy* ■ *Dir* Dennis Dugan • *Scr* Steve Franks, Tim Herlihy, Adam Sandler, from a story by Steve Franks

Big Deal on Madonna Street ★★★★

Heist comedy 1958 · It · BW · 91mins

A smashing comedy, mainly a send-up of *Rififi*, about a band of incompetent layabouts and petty crooks who plan a major heist by breaking into an empty flat and drilling through to the bank vault next door. The plan goes slightly awry and leads to a hilarious twist in the tale. Made quickly and cheaply, it stars Marcello Mastroianni and Vittorio Gassman, the latter made up to hide his Latin lover image completely, and features an early performance by Claudia Cardinale. Louis Malle remade it in 1984 as *Crackers*; it was loosely remade again in 1995 as *Palookaville*. AT. An Italian language film.

Vittorio Gassman *Peppe* • Marcello Mastroianni *Tiberio* • Toto *Dante* • Renato Salvatori *Mario* • Carla Gravina *Nicoletta* • Claudia Cardinale *Carmelina* • Memmo Carotenuto *Cosimo* • Tiberio Murgia *Ferribotte* ■ *Dir* Mario Monicelli • *Scr* Mario Monicelli, Suso Cecchi D'Amico, Age Scarpelli [Agenore Incrocci and Furio Scarpelli]

The Big Doll House ★★ 18

Prison drama 1971 · US · Colour · 89mins

An early example of the women-in-prison picture, a 1970s genre that was generally regarded as too hot for UK audiences. In this one, the extremely popular Pam Grier and four other tough ladies generally do what is expected of them (fight, have showers, try to escape). Roger Corman protégé Jack Hill shot it cheaply in the Philippines, the location for many exploitation films of the period. Unwatchable trash or a cult classic, depending on your attitude. A quickie sequel, *The Big Bird Cage*, followed in 1972. DM [video] DVD

Judy Brown [Judith Brown] *Collier* • Roberta Collins *Alcott* • Pam Grier *Grear* • Brooke Mills *Harrad* • Pat Woodell *Bodine* • Sid Haig *Harry* • Christiane Schmidtmer *Miss Dietrich* ■ *Dir* Jack Hill • *Scr* Don Spencer

The Big Easy ★★★★ 15

Crime thriller 1986 · US · Colour · 96mins

After watching this sizzling crime thriller, you'll wonder why director Jim McBride and stars Dennis Quaid and Ellen Barkin failed to go on to take Hollywood by storm. Rather than the start of something big, this was the career peak of all three, but what heights they attained! Sparks fly from the moment cop Quaid and assistant district attorney Barkin come together to investigate a New Orleans Mob killing, but their conflicting moral codes threaten to take the heat out of their steamy affair. Ned Beatty and John Goodman provide gritty support, while McBride brings the unique quality of the city to throbbing life. DP. Contains violence, swearing and sex scenes. [video] DVD

Dennis Quaid *Remy McSwain* • Ellen Barkin *Anne Osborne* • Ned Beatty *Jack Kellom* • Ebbe Roe Smith *Detective Dodge* • John Goodman *Detective DeSoto* • Lisa Jane Persky *Detective McCabe* • Charles Ludlam *Lamar* • Thomas O'Brien *Bobby* ■ *Dir* Jim McBride • *Scr* Daniel Petrie Jr, Jack Baran

Big Eden ★★ PG

Romantic drama
2000 · US · Colour · 115mins

In the mythical Montana town of Big Eden, where all the local yokels are pro-gay, non-racist and open to suggestion, closeted New York artist Arye Gross arrives to look after his grandfather. But the accepting townsfolk guess his secret and force him to choose between a relationship with his hunky ex-school friend Tim DeKay and the American Indian general store owner Eric Schweig. Although an unbelievably saccharine cornball fantasy at times, very awkwardly scripted in some key scenes and laid on far too thick by director Thomas Bezucha, the crisp acting and well-meaning stance exerts a certain charm and warmth. AJ DVD

Arye Gross *Henry Hart* • Eric Schweig *Pike Dexter* • Tim DeKay *Dean Stewart* • Louise Fletcher *Grace Cornwell* • George Coe *Sam Hart* • Nan Martin *Widow Thayer* ■ *Dir/Scr* Thomas Bezucha

Big Fat Liar ★★ PG

Comedy 2002 · US/Ger · Colour · 84mins

This children's comedy starts well, but descends rather too readily into mean-spirited slapstick. Frankie Muniz plays a 14-year-old habitual liar who's understandably disbelieved by his mum and dad when he tells the far-fetched truth for once: that an unscrupulous Hollywood film producer (Paul Giamatti) has filched his latest tall tale, and is turning it into the summer's movie blockbuster. Determined to restore his rep, Muniz heads for Beverley Hills – cue lights, camera, traction as the pilfering producer gets his comeuppance. DA [video] DVD

Frankie Muniz *Jason Shepherd* • Paul Giamatti *Marty Wolf* • Amanda Bynes *Kaylee* • Amanda Detmer *Monty Kirkham* • Lee Majors *Vince* • Donald Faison [Donald Adeosun Faison] *Frank Jackson/Kenny Trooper* ■ *Dir* Shawn Levy • *Scr* Dan Schneider, from a story by Dan Schneider, Brian Robbins

Big Fella ★★ U

Musical drama 1937 · UK · BW · 73mins

Paul Robeson stars as an idle vagabond on the Marseille waterfront, known to all for his great singing voice. Hired to find a missing boy, he succeeds in his mission, but the child is a runaway who threatens him with accusations of kidnapping if he is returned to his family. This is unworthy of its star, but it does offer a few twists and turns, a couple of songs, and the pleasure of seeing the splendid Elisabeth Welch in her prime, as a singer in the café where Robeson and his charge take refuge. RK

Paul Robeson *Joe* • Elizabeth Welch [Elisabeth Welch] *Manda* • Roy Emerton *Spike* • James Hayter *Chuck* • Lawrence Brown *Corney* • Eldon Grant *Gerald Oliphant* ■ *Dir* J Elder Wills • *Scr* Ingram D'Abbes, Fenn Sherie, from the novel *Banjo* by Claude McKay

Big Fish ★★ PG

Fantasy drama 2003 · US · Colour · 119mins

Director Tim Burton returns to familiar territory here – a strange place somewhere between reality and fantasy, dream and nightmare. Albert Finney plays Edward Bloom, a travelling salesman whose apparent selfishness and ridiculous stories of his exploits have driven a wedge between him and son Billy Crudup. Called to his father's deathbed, Crudup is infuriated when his wife is regaled with tall tales featuring young Edward (Ewan McGregor). Intent on exposing his father, the disgruntled son sets out to learn the truth. This drifts colourfully along, but lacks edge. BP [video] DVD

Ewan McGregor *Young Edward Bloom* • Albert Finney *Edward Bloom* • Billy Crudup *Will Bloom* • Jessica Lange *Sandra Bloom* • Helena Bonham Carter *Jenny/The Witch* • Alison Lohman *Young Sandra* • Robert Guillaume *Dr Bennett* • Marion Cotillard *Josephine* ■ *Dir* Tim Burton • *Scr* John August, from the novel *Big Fish, a Story of Mythic Proportions* by Daniel Wallace

The Big Fisherman ★★ U

Biblical drama 1959 · US · Colour · 166mins

Howard Keel is competent enough as Simon Peter in this biblical saga, directed by Frank Borzage, an Oscar-winning veteran of the 1920s and 1930s. The film is handsomely mounted and photographed, as befits the epic genre, but it's still a plodding bore, the main excitement in which comes from a princess (Susan Kohner) out to kill Herod (Herbert Lom) and a prince (John Saxon) who is hopelessly in love with her. AJ

Howard Keel *Simon Peter* • Susan Kohner *Fara* • John Saxon *Voldi* • Martha Hyer *Herodias* • Herbert Lom *Herod Antipas* • Ray Stricklyn *Deran* ■ *Dir* Frank Borzage • *Scr* Howard Estabrook, Rowland V Lee, from a novel by Lloyd C Douglas

The Big Fix ★★★ 15

Comedy detective drama
1978 · US · Colour · 103mins

Richard Dreyfuss turned actor/producer for this off-the-wall private eye thriller that takes in the demise of 1960s radicalism, Latino tensions and what might be summed up as post-Watergate disenchantment. Dreyfuss plays the Jewish gumshoe Moses Wine, a former campus activist with an ex-wife, two kids and a heap of debt. Then the plot kicks in – something about dirty tricks during a political campaign – and quickly gets very complicated. Principally a character study, superbly portrayed by Dreyfuss, it flopped, putting paid to plans for a series based on the novels of Roger L Simon. AT [video]

Richard Dreyfuss *Moses Wine* • Susan Anspach *Lila* • Bonnie Bedelia *Suzanne* • John Lithgow *Sam Sebastian* • Ofelia Medina *Alora*

• Nicolas Coster *Spitzler* • F Murray Abraham *Eppis* • Fritz Weaver *Oscar Procari Sr* • Mandy Patinkin *Pool man* ■ *Dir* Jeremy Paul Kagan • *Scr* Roger L Simon, from his novel

B

The Big Gamble ★★ U

Adventure 1961 · US · Colour · 100mins

Stephen Boyd teamed up with Juliette Greco for this plodding adventure about truck drivers in equatorial Africa. Boyd and Greco start off in Dublin, where they raise the cash for their trip and, after a comic interlude with aunt Sybil Thorndike, head for the dark continent. Obviously inspired by Henri-Georges Clouzot's suspense classic *The Wages of Fear* and shot on location in the Ivory Coast, this must have been murder to make. Sadly, it delivers only modest thrills. AT

Stephen Boyd *Vic Brennan* • Juliette Greco *Marie Brennan* • David Wayne *Samuel Brennan* • Sybil Thorndike *Aunt Cathleen* • Gregory Ratoff *Daltenberg* • Harold Goldblatt *Father Frederick* • Philip O'Flynn *John Brennan* • Maureen O'Dea *Margaret Brennan* • Marie Kean *Cynthia* ■ *Dir* Richard Fleischer, Elmo Williams • *Scr* Irwin Shaw

The Big Green ★★ U

Sports comedy 1995 · US · Colour · 95mins

After the success of ice hockey movie *The Mighty Ducks* (which, with the help of likeable Emilio Estevez, spawned two sequels), it probably seemed a good idea to use the same ingredients (little team does good and the players learn more about themselves and each other in the process) for other sports. However, here the plot is rehashed for a movie about soccer, and Estevez is replaced by a man whose career is even further in the dumpster, Steve Guttenberg. JB DVD

Steve Guttenberg *Sheriff Tom Palmer* • Olivia D'Abo *Anna Montgomery* • Jay O Sanders *Jay Huffer* • John Terry *Edwin V Douglas* • Chauncey Leopardi *Evan Schiff* • Patrick Renna *Larry Musgrove* • Billy L Sullivan *Jeffrey Luttrell* • Yareli Arizmendi *Marbelly Morales* ■ *Dir/Scr* Holly Goldberg Sloan

A Big Hand for a Little Lady ★★★ U

Comedy western 1966 · US · Colour · 95mins

This amiable comedy western was originally devised as a 50-minute TV programme. Although there are a few visible stretch marks, screenwriter Sidney Carroll and director Fielder Cook have done a creditable job in filling it out to feature length. With echoes of both *The Sting* and *Maverick*, it is slickly played by Henry Fonda, Joanne Woodward, Jason Robards, Charles Bickford and Burgess Meredith. DP

Henry Fonda *Meredith* • Joanne Woodward *Mary* • Jason Robards *Henry Drummond* • Charles Bickford *Benson Tropp* • Burgess Meredith *Doc Scully* • Kevin McCarthy *Otto Habershaw* • Robert Middleton *Dennis Wilcox* • Paul Ford *Ballinger* ■ *Dir* Fielder Cook • *Scr* Sidney Carroll, from his teleplay *Big Deal at Laredo*

The Big Hangover ★★★ U

Comedy drama 1950 · US · BW · 82mins

An engaging comedy with Van Johnson working for a law firm and trying to conceal an allergy to alcohol brought on during the war when the cellar he was hiding in flooded with brandy. This is where Elizabeth Taylor comes in. She's the boss's daughter and an amateur shrink, who sets out to cure our hero of his allergy. There's also a subplot about Johnson deciding whether to become a rich man's brief or take up arms for the poor. You'd think that prissy old MGM would not wish to encourage boozing, though Taylor, in her first adult role, could probably persuade any man to overcome any phobia. AT

Van Johnson *David* • Elizabeth Taylor *Mary Belney* • Percy Waram *John Belney* • Fay Holden *Martha Belney* • Leon Ames *Carl Bellcap* • Edgar Buchanan *Uncle Fred Mahoney* • Selena Royle *Kate Mahoney* ■ *Dir/Scr* Norman Krasna

The Big Heat ★★★★ 15

Film noir 1953 · US · BW · 85mins

Glenn Ford crusades against Mob-led civic corruption and hunts for vengeance in this classic *film noir* from director Fritz Lang. Its most famous scene, when moll Gloria Grahame is scalded by hot coffee hurled by crook Lee Marvin, was trimmed by the censors before the movie could be released in Britain with an X certificate. Now fully restored, it's tame by today's standards, but still packs a punch. Ford is excellent as the cop with a mission – his character was based on the investigators during the televised 1950s Estes Kefauver Senate investigations – and Lang gives the vicious exposé a sleek and glossy surface. TS

Glenn Ford *Dave Bannion* • Gloria Grahame *Debby Marsh* • Jocelyn Brando *Katie Bannion* • Alexander Scourby *Mike Lagana* • Lee Marvin *Vince Stone* • Jeanette Nolan *Bertha Duncan* • Peter Whitney *Tierney* • Willis Bouchey *Lt Wilkes* ■ *Dir* Fritz Lang • *Scr* Sydney Boehm, from the serial in *The Saturday Evening Post* by William P McGivern • *Cinematographer* Charles B Lang [Charles Lang]

The Big Hit ★★ 18

Action thriller 1998 · US · Colour · 87mins

This tries very hard to be offbeat and quirky, but ends up as merely dumb and annoying. Mark Wahlberg does well as the girl-juggling assassin, though Lou Diamond Phillips overdoes his performance as Wahlberg's accomplice. Despite a dazzling pair of slam-bang action bookends from director Kirk Wong, this isn't clever, funny or engaging enough to be the exercise in killer cool it craves to be. JC. Contains violence, swearing and brief nudity. DVD

Mark Wahlberg *Melvin Smiley* • Lou Diamond Phillips *Cisco* • Christina Applegate *Pam Shulman* • Avery Brooks *Paris* • Bokeem Woodbine *Crunch* • Antonio Sabato Jr *Vince* • China Chow *Keiko Nishi* • Lainie Kazan *Jeanne Shulman* • Elliott Gould *Morton Shulman* • Sab Shimono *Jiro Nishi* ■ *Dir* Che-Kirk Wong [Kirk Wong] • *Scr* Ben Ramsey

The Big House ★★★★

Prison drama 1930 · US · BW · 84mins

This powerful exposé of conditions in a men's prison, prompted by newspaper headlines of rioting convicts, was such as a smash hit that it served as a template for dozens of pictures. Robert Montgomery is the new inmate, a well-bred weakling sentenced for manslaughter, who has to share a cell with Wallace Beery's tough gangster and Chester Morris's repentant forger. Co-written by a leading female screenwriter, Frances Marion, and directed by her husband, George Hill, the film vividly evokes the grimness of prison life, from overcrowded cells to a spell in solitary. The long take down the empty corridor of the solitary wing as the inmates call out to each other for company is unforgettable. AE

Chester Morris *John Morgan* • Wallace Beery *Butch Schmidt* • Lewis Stone *Warden James Adams* • Robert Montgomery *Kent Marlowe* • Leila Hyams *Ann Marlowe* • George F Marion *Pop Riker* • JC Nugent *Mr Marlowe* • Karl Dane *Olsen* ■ *Dir* George Hill • *Scr* Frances Marion, Joe Farnham, Martin Flavin • *Cinematographer* Harold Wenstrom

Big House, USA ★★★

Action crime drama 1955 · US · BW · 82mins

A tight, compressed thriller about a kidnapped boy, some buried ransom money and the heavies and psychos who break out of jail intending to dig it up. All the while, FBI man Reed Hadley lies in wait. A strong cast of B-movie regulars – Broderick Crawford, Charles Bronson and Ralph Meeker, as the kidnapper – contribute some agreeably cheesy characterisations. AT

Broderick Crawford *Rollo Lamar* • Ralph Meeker *Jerry Barker* • Reed Hadley *James Madden* • Randy Farr *Nurse Emily Evans* • William Talman *Machinegun Mason* • Lon Chaney Jr *Alamo Smith* • Charles Bronson *Benny Kelly* • Peter Votrian *Danny Lambert* ■ *Dir* Howard W Koch • *Scr* John C Higgins

Big Jack ★★

Black comedy western
1949 · US · BW · 84mins

Wallace Beery was another good-hearted rogue in his last picture, released shortly after his death at the age of 64. Marjorie Main played opposite him for the seventh time, as his wife, in this comedy western. Beery's Big Jack, the feared leader of outlaws in the early 19th century, befriends Richard Conte's young physician and offers a supply of bodies for his medical experiments. Sadly, the black humour isn't forceful enough to overcome the tedium. AE

Wallace Beery *Big Jack Horner* • Richard Conte *Dr Alexander Meade* • Marjorie Main *Flapjack Kate* • Edward Arnold *Mayor Mahoney* • Vanessa Brown *Patricia Mahoney* • Clinton Sundberg *C Patronius Smith* • Charles Dingle *Mathias Taylor* • Clem Bevans *Saltlick Joe* ■ *Dir* Richard Thorpe • *Scr* Gene Fowler, Marvin Borowsky, Osso Van Eyss, from a story by Robert Thoeren

Big Jake ★★ 15

Western 1971 · US · Colour · 109mins

It might just as well have been titled *Big John*, because that's all it is, really: close-ups of the grizzled John Wayne, in the twilight of his career, nostalgically paired (for the fifth and last time) with an elegantly ageing Maureen O'Hara. There's precious little plot, though, and George Sherman's direction is lazy and untidy. Still, William Clothier's outdoor photography is worth a look and Richard Boone makes a fine larger-than-life baddie. But the whole sad enterprise is altogether too routine, and the leads just look too old. TS DVD

John Wayne *Jacob McCandles* • Richard Boone *John Fain* • Maureen O'Hara *Martha McCandles* • Patrick Wayne *James McCandles* • Chris Mitchum [Christopher Mitchum] *Michael McCandles* • Bobby Vinton *Jeff McCandles* • Bruce Cabot *Sam Sharpnose* ■ *Dir* George Sherman • *Scr* Harry Julian Fink, Rita M Fink

Big Jim McLain ★ U

Spy drama 1952 · US · BW · 86mins

John Wayne produced and starred in this nasty piece of propaganda in which he and James Arness, as House Un-American Activities Committee investigators, rout out communist spies in Hawaii. The astonishingly crude script portrays communists as inadequate human beings who behave like gangsters and make stupid mistakes. If Wayne hoped to make the subject more palatable by dressing it up as standard action fare, he was to be disappointed. Movie-goers smelled a rat, and it performed poorly. AE

John Wayne *Big Jim McLain* • Nancy Olson *Nancy Vallon* • James Arness *Mal Baxter* • Alan Napier *Sturak* • Veda Ann Borg *Madge* • Gayne Whitman *Dr Gelster* • Hal Baylor *Poke* ■ *Dir* Edward Ludwig • *Scr* James Edward Grant, Richard English, Eric Taylor

The Big Job ★★★ U

Comedy 1965 · UK · BW · 84mins

Sidney James is the the leader of a gang of incompetent crooks who discover a police station has been built on the site where they stashed the loot from their last robbery. Partners-in-crime Sylvia Syms, Dick Emery and Lance Percival bungle his recovery plans with practised buffoonery, but they are often reduced to slapstick props. In contrast, Joan Sims's landlady, Jim Dale's goofy plod and Deryck Guyler's idle desk sergeant are much more fully developed comic creations. DP

Sidney James *George Brain* • Sylvia Syms *Myrtle Robbins* • Dick Emery *Fred "Booky" Binns* • Lance Percival *Tim "Dipper" Day* • Joan Sims *Mildred Gamely* • Jim Dale *Harold* • Edina Ronay *Sally Gamely* • Deryck Guyler *Police sergeant* ■ *Dir* Gerald Thomas • *Scr* Talbot Rothwell

The Big Kahuna ★★★ 15

Drama 1999 · US · Colour · 90mins

Kevin Spacey plays one of a trio of salesmen who have gathered at an anonymous hotel suite for a convention. Spacey, all hyperactive bluster, is determined to secure a major client – the Big Kahuna of the title. However, it's the new boy on the team, Peter Facinelli, who may hold the key to capturing the elusive prize. This claustrophobic drama struggles to shake-off its stage origins, but Spacey delivers a bravura performance and is more than matched by Danny DeVito's understated melancholy as his world-weary partner. JF. Contains swearing.

Kevin Spacey *Larry Mann* • Danny DeVito *Phil Cooper* • Peter Facinelli *Bob Walker* ■ *Dir* John Swanbeck • *Scr* Roger Rueff, from his play *Hospitality Suite*

The Big Knife ★★★★

Drama 1955 · US · BW · 113mins

An intelligent, haunting film full of wonderful performances, particularly from Jack Palance (never better) and Rod Steiger as, respectively, the movie star coming apart at the seams and the studio boss who wants to cover up the paranoia at any price. This is one of the more successful films that Hollywood has made about itself, blessed with a marvellously literate script from the play by Clifford Odets and able direction from Robert Aldrich. A great movie suffused with realistic tension and lacerating satire. SH

Jack Palance *Charles Castle* • Ida Lupino *Marion Castle* • Shelley Winters *Dixie Evans* • Wendell Corey *Smiley Coy* • Jean Hagen *Connie Bliss* • Rod Steiger *Stanley Hoff* ■ *Dir* Robert Aldrich • *Scr* James Poe, from the play by Clifford Odets

The Big Land ★★★ U

Western 1957 · US · Colour · 92mins

Called *Stampede* in the UK, this was one of star Alan Ladd's production ventures, made by his own company Jaguar. Ladd's wife and agent, former actress Sue Carol, often chose these projects, and cocooned her husband with quality factors. In this case he is reunited with Virginia Mayo and Gordon Douglas, his co-star and director respectively from *The Iron Mistress* (1952). Ladd is now sadly unfashionable and almost forgotten, but there was much more to him than *Shane*. Watch how effortlessly he turns this ordinary western into an impressive star vehicle. TS

Alan Ladd *Chad Morgan* • Virginia Mayo *Helen* • Edmond O'Brien *Jagger* • Anthony Caruso *Brog* • Julie Bishop *Kate Johnson* • John Qualen *Sven Johnson* • Don Castle *Draper* • David Ladd *David Johnson* ■ *Dir* Gordon Douglas • *Scr* David Dortort, Martin Rackin, from an adaptation by David Dortort of the novel *Buffalo Grass* by Frank Gruber

Big Leaguer ★★ U

Sports drama 1953 · US · BW · 53mins

Robert Aldrich made his directing debut with this baseball drama, shot in 16 days in the area of Florida that was to become Cape Canaveral. Edward G Robinson stars as real-life John B Lobert, who ran a training camp for the New York Giants' potential recruits. Vera-Ellen plays Robinson's niece, while Richard Jaeckel is among the young hopefuls. Most of the story is concerned with the kids' social background – rich and poor, cocky and shy, Cuban and American – and paints Robinson's character as one of the world's kindest people. AT

Edward G Robinson *John B "Hans" Lobert* • Vera-Ellen *Christy* • Jeff Richards *Adam Polachuk* • Richard Jaeckel *Bobby Bronson* • William Campbell *Julie Davis* • Carl Hubbell • Paul Langton *Brian McLennan* ■ *Dir* Robert Aldrich • *Scr* Herbert Baker, from a story by John McNulty, Louis Morheim

The Big Lebowski ★★★★ 18

Comedy 1997 · US/UK · Colour · 112mins

While not in the same class as the Coen Brothers' previous film, *Fargo*, this goofy tribute to Raymond Chandler and *film noir* still comes gift-wrapped with enough good lines, ingenious plot twists and eccentric characters to satisfy the siblings' dedicated army of fans. There are in fact two Lebowskis: one is Jeff Bridges, who calls himself "the Dude", an ageing hippy who becomes embroiled in the kidnapping of the other Lebowski's wife, aided and abetted by tenpin bowling chum John Goodman. What follows is an insane labyrinth of plot that encompasses the drug and porn underworlds, Busby Berkeley fantasies and bathtime with a savage marmot, sharply edited by the Coens (under the pseudonym of Roderick Jaynes). AT. Contains swearing, sexual references and some violence. [VIDEO] DVD

Jeff Bridges *Jeff "The Dude" Lebowski* • John Goodman *Walter Sobchak* • Julianne Moore *Maude Lebowski* • Steve Buscemi *Donny* • David Huddleston *The Big Lebowski* • Philip Seymour Hoffman *Brandt* • John Turturro *Jesus Quintana* • Tara Reid *Bunny Lebowski* ■ *Dir* Joel Coen • *Scr* Ethan Coen, Joel Coen • *Producer* Ethan Coen

The Big Lift ★★★ PG

Drama 1950 · US · BW · 119mins

The talented and tragic Montgomery Clift only completed 17 features, but each movie is of supreme interest. That's because Clift was the forerunner of today's naturalistic school of screen acting, predating Brando's film debut by a good couple of years. This is one of five films Clift made with a German or militarist theme – a propagandist piece celebrating the airlift from postwar Berlin. Paul Douglas plays the blustering mouthpiece for American policy, and Cornell Borchers charmingly smooches with Clift. TS DVD

Montgomery Clift *Danny MacCullough* • Paul Douglas *Hank* • Cornell Borchers *Frederica* • Bruni Lobel *Gerda* • OE Hasse *Stieber* ■ *Dir/Scr* George Seaton

The Big Man ★ 18

Sports drama 1990 · UK · Colour · 115mins

What a shame that Liam Neeson got his first starring role in this ham-fisted drama. He plays an unemployed Scottish miner who becomes a bare-knuckle fighter, a Spartacus for corrupt businessman Ian Bannen. Joanne Whalley-Kilmer, Hugh Grant and a not particularly comic Billy Connolly complete the interesting cast. The picture is irredeemably dull, and was a resounding flop that hastened the demise of the ailing Palace Pictures. AT. Contains violence, swearing. [VIDEO]

Liam Neeson *Danny Scoular* • Joanne Whalley-Kilmer [Joanne Whalley] *Beth Scoular* • Billy Connolly *Frankie* • Ian Bannen *Matt Mason* • Maurice Roëves *Cam Colvin* • Hugh Grant *Gordon* • Kenny Ireland *Tony* ■ *Dir* David Leland • *Scr* Don MacPherson, from the novel by William McIlvanney

Big Man on Campus ★★

Comedy 1989 · US · Colour · 102mins

Allan Katz, who also wrote the script, steals the show here mainly because, for all his grunts and rampaging, he never forgets to make his wild man character lovable. Mr Looga is a feral man discovered living secretly on a Californian university campus. Melora Hardin plays the student who volunteers to civilise him, investing her role with a refreshing sweetness. More pleasant than laugh-out-loud funny. KB

Allan Katz *Bob* • Corey Parker *Alex Kaminsky* • Cindy Williams *Diane Girard* • Melora Hardin *Cathy* • Tom Skerritt *Dr Webster* • Jessica Harper *Dr Fisk* • Gerrit Graham *Stanley Hoyle* ■ *Dir* Jeremy Paul Kagan • *Scr* Allan Katz

Big Meat Eater ★★★ 18

Musical science-fiction comedy
1982 · Can · Colour · 78mins

A maniac has killed the mayor of a Canadian small town, only for aliens to arrive and re-animate the corpse as their slave. This bizarre cult oddity combines cheap-and-cheerful special effects (the aliens are toy robots shot in extreme close-up) with songs such as *Baghdad Boogie* and *Chemical World*. Director Chris Windsor's quirky genre references and canny awareness of all things Rocky Horror make this a one-off that's worth catching. AJ [VIDEO]

George Dawson *Bob Sanderson* • Andrew Gillies *Jan Wczinski* • Big Miller [Clarence "Big" Miller] *Abdulla* • Stephen Dimopoulos *Joseph Wczinski* • Georgina Hegedos *Rosa Wczinski* • Ida Carnevali *Babushka* • Howard Taylor *Mayor Carmine Rigatoni* ■ *Dir* Chris Windsor • *Scr* Phil Savath, Laurence Keane, Chris Windsor

Big Momma's House ★★★ 12

Comedy 2000 · US/Ger · Colour · 94mins

Martin Lawrence plays an "underblubber" agent, trying to catch escaped bank robber Terrence Howard by posing as the 300lb southern momma of the villain's ex-girlfriend Nia Long. The comedy derives both from Lawrence's roly-poly impersonation and from his falling for the girl he's guarding. The humour is pretty obvious, but Lawrence works hard to give this one-joke film enough crowd-pleasing moments to justify the ticket price. DA [VIDEO] DVD

Martin Lawrence *Malcolm Turner* • Nia Long *Sherry* • Paul Giamatti *John* • Jascha Washington *Trent* • Terrence Howard *Lester* ■ *Dir* Raja Gosnell • *Scr* Darryl Quarles, Don Rhymer, from a story by Darryl Quarles

The Big Money ★★ U

Comedy 1956 · UK · Colour · 86mins

There are too many British comedies in which the talents of a superb cast are wasted by an inferior script. This offering is a case in point, though it does boast a decent story about a family of crack crooks whose eldest son couldn't pass a counterfeit note in a game of Monopoly. Ian Carmichael is perfectly cast in the lead, but director John Paddy Carstairs hammers every gag into place, and staying the course seems like a life sentence. DP

Ian Carmichael *Willie Frith* • Belinda Lee *Gloria* • Kathleen Harrison *Mrs Frith* • Robert Helpmann *The Reverend* • James Hayter *Mr Frith* • George Coulouris *The Colonel* • Jill Ireland *Doreen Frith* • Renee Houston *Bobby* • Leslie Phillips *Receptionist* ■ *Dir* John Paddy Carstairs • *Scr* John Baines

The Big Mouth ★

Comedy 1967 · US · Colour · 107mins

Comedian Jerry Lewis opens his mouth to the usual embarrassingly idiotic effect as a less-than-aggressive little guy who is the double of a gangster and becomes involved in a search for stolen diamonds. Directed, produced and co-written by Lewis, the film focuses almost continually on the star, which is a pity. Sadly, he does little here to convince non-devotees that he's a taste worth acquiring. TH

Jerry Lewis *Gerald Clamson* • Harold J Stone *Thor* • Susan Bay *Suzie Cartwright* • Buddy Lester *Studs* • Del Moore *Mr Hodges* • Paul Lambert *Moxie* • Leonard Stone *Fong* • Jeannine Riley *Bambi Berman* ■ *Dir* Jerry Lewis • *Scr* Jerry Lewis, Bill Richmond, from a story by Bill Richmond

Big News ★★★

Crime drama 1929 · US · BW · 75mins

This early talkie entry in the popular reporter-turned-detective cycle is directed with a good feel for authenticity by Gregory La Cava and is marked by some witty exchanges and a breezy leading performance from Robert Armstrong. He plays a reckless newspaper reporter with a taste for drinking in speakeasies, who courts trouble in his determination to nail a narcotics gang. Carole Lombard – not yet a star – demonstrates why she became one. RK

Robert Armstrong *Steve Banks* • Carole Lombard *Margaret Banks* • Tom Kennedy *Sgt Ryan* • Warner Richmond *Phelps* • Wade Boteler *O'Neil* • Sam Hardy *Joe Reno* • Louis Payne *Hensel* • James Donlan *Deke* • Cupid Ainsworth *Vera Wilson* • Lew Ayres *Copy Boy* ■ *Dir* Gregory La Cava • *Scr* Walter DeLeon, Jack Jungmeyer, from the play *For Two Cents* by George S Brooks

The Big Night ★★ U

Drama 1951 · US · BW · 73mins

When sports columnist Howard St John beats up widowed ex-boxer Preston Foster for no apparent reason, the victim's young son John Barrymore Jr goes on a night-long quest for the attacker through murky nightclubs, bars and hotels. Flashily directed (and co-written) by Joseph Losey, who offers a compendium of nightlife underbelly clichés, and featuring a 19-year-old lead in Barrymore Jr who lacks the weight of his famous father, this is nonetheless a vivid and quite enjoyable little movie. RK

John Barrymore Jr [John Drew Barrymore] *George La Main* • Preston Foster *Andy La Main* • Joan Lorring *Marion Rostina* • Howard St John *Al Judge* • Dorothy Comingore *Julie Rostina* • Philip Bourneuf *Dr Lloyd Cooper* • Howland Chamberlin *Flanagan* • Emil Meyer [Emile Meyer] *Packingpaugh* ■ *Dir* Joseph Losey • *Scr* Stanley Ellin, Joseph Losey, from the novel *Dreadful Summit* by Stanley Ellin

Big Night ★★★★ 15

Period comedy drama
1996 · US · Colour · 104mins

Actors Campbell Scott and Stanley Tucci impress as promising directors in this small-scale 1950s tale, a gastronomic dream for all lovers of fine Italian food that offers a crisp chianti of comedy as accompaniment. Brothers Tony Shalhoub and Tucci run a not particularly successful restaurant in New Jersey. Their constant bickering reaches a crescendo with the prospect that entertainer Louis Prima will come to dinner and help resurrect their failing business. Superb in support, Isabella Rossellini and Minnie Driver supply the love interest. LH. Contains swearing, sex scenes. [VIDEO]

Stanley Tucci *Secondo* • Tony Shalhoub *Primo* • Isabella Rossellini *Gabriella* • Ian Holm *Pascal* • Minnie Driver *Phyllis* • Marc Anthony *Cristiano* • Campbell Scott *Bob* ■ *Dir* Stanley Tucci, Campbell Scott • *Scr* Joseph Tropiano, Stanley Tucci

The Big Noise ★★★

Silent comedy 1928 · US · BW

Former vaudevillian, circus clown and Keystone Kop, Chester Conklin, a great comedy favourite of the silent era, stars in this efficiently made romp combining farce and satire. Sporting his trademark moustache, Conklin plays an ineffectual New York subway guard who accidentally falls on the track in front of an oncoming express. When a daily tabloid turns the incident into a heroic deed, he temporarily becomes a "big noise". It's a bit creaky now, but it has its moments for fans of the early comic style. RK

Chester Conklin *John Sloval* • Alice White *Sophie Sloval* • Bodil Rosing *Ma Sloval* • Sam Hardy *Philip Hurd* • Jack Egan *Bill Hedges* • Ned Sparks *William Howard* • David Torrence *Managing editor* ■ *Dir* Allan Dwan • *Scr* Thomas J Geraghty [Tom Geraghty], George Marion (titles), from a story by Ben Hecht

The Big Noise ★★ U

Comedy 1944 · US · BW · 73mins

Laurel and Hardy are on the skids in this incompetently staged story of two dumb-luck detectives, hired to guard an inventor's new bomb – the titular "Big Noise". Biggest laughs are in the performance of Jack Norton, whose "drunk" routine has its moments. The rest, though, has scarcely any. TH

Stan Laurel *Stan* • Oliver Hardy *Ollie* • Doris Merrick *Evelyn* • Arthur Space *Hartley* • Louis Arco *German officer* • Beal Wong *Japanese officer* • Veda Ann Borg *Mayme* • Bobby Blake [Robert Blake] *Egbert* • Jack Norton *Drunk* ■ *Dir* Mal St Clair [Malcolm St Clair] • *Scr* Scott Darling

The Big One ★★★★ PG

Satirical documentary
1997 · US/UK · Colour · 86mins

Documentary film-maker Michael Moore is something of a thorn in the side of politicians and big business in the United States. He's tackled General Motors, George W Bush and the gun industry, but here he turns the camera on his very own book tour for his bestseller *Downsize This!* with a mix of comedy, political commentary, observation, and his singular distrust of corporate America. It's a superbly realised, often funny and sometimes depressing documentary, but it's never boring. Indeed, it's worth it just to see Moore's suggestion that Nike should move their factory to Flint, or even his attempts to get past security guards to interview millionaire company chairmen. JB DVD

Michael Moore (2) *Narrator* ■ *Dir/Scr* Michael Moore (2) • *Cinematographer* Brian Danitz, Chris Smith

The Big Operator ★★★

Crime drama 1959 · US · BW · 90mins

It's small beer today, but in 1959 this was a real toughie, beginning with a man being chucked into a cement mixer. It stars Mickey Rooney as a sadistic racketeer who takes the fifth while under investigation by the Senate. Rooney had already essayed Baby Face Nelson, and here he creates another memorable and plausible psycho. Co-star Mamie Van Doren adds allure as the wife of Steve Cochran, whom Rooney has tortured, while Mel Tormé cruises along nicely until Mickey has him torched. AT

Mickey Rooney *Little Joe Braun* • Steve Cochran *Bill Gibson* • Mamie Van Doren *Mary Gibson* • Mel Tormé *Fred McAfee* • Ray Danton *Oscar Wetzel* • Jim Backus *Cliff Heldon* • Ray Anthony *Slim Clayburn* • Jackie

Coogan *Ed Brannell* • Charles Chaplin Jr *Bill Tragg* ■ *Dir* Charles Haas • *Scr* Robert Smith, Allen Rivkin, from a story by Paul Gallico

B

The Big Parade ★★★★★ U

Silent war drama
1925 · US · BW and Colour · 137mins

Rich industrialist's idle son John Gilbert enlists in the army when America enters the First World War and is sent to France. Billeted in a village, he meets and falls in love with French farm girl Renée Adorée before going to the front. A simple synopsis doesn't begin to convey the beauty of the love story, the poignancy of comradeship among men almost certainly facing death, or the authentic power and horror of the battle. Director King Vidor's approach to his subject, and his great artistry in executing it, has given us one of the great antiwar films – an unqualified masterpiece, enacted by a uniformly first-class cast. RK

John Gilbert (1) *James Apperson* • Renée Adorée *Mélisande* • Hobart Bosworth *Mr Apperson* • Claire McDowell *Mrs Apperson* • Claire Adams *Justyn Reed* • Robert Ober *Harry* • Tom O'Brien *Bull* • Karl Dane *Slim* • Rosita Marstini *French mother* ■ *Dir* King Vidor • *Scr* Henry Behn, Joseph Farnham (titles), from a story by Laurence Stallings • *Cinematographer* John Arnold, Henrik Sartov

The Big Parade ★★★★ U

Drama 1986 · Chi · Colour · 137mins

Thanks to the imposing finale, filmed with suitable pomp and scale by Zhang Yimou, this study of soldiers preparing for China's National Day parade was embraced by the authorities as a fitting tribute to the People's Liberation Army. Yet Chen Kaige was ordered to add this triumphant ending to lessen the impact of the gruelling training sequences, which were criticised for glorifying the achievements of the individual rather than extolling the virtues of communal endeavour. Chen's main aim is clearly a critique of the communist system, but this is also a powerful paean to the indomitability of the human spirit. DP. In Mandarin with English subtitles.

Wang Xueqi *Li Weicheng* • Sun Chun *Sun Fang* • Lu Lei *Jiang Junbiao* • Wu Ruofu *Lu Chun* • Guan Qiang *Liu Guoqiang* • Kang Hua *Hao Xiaoyuan* ■ *Dir* Chen Kaige • *Scr* Lili Gao

The Big Picture ★★★★ 15

Satire 1989 · US · Colour · 96mins

Three years before *The Player*, this criminally neglected satire hit the same Hollywood targets first. But what else would you expect from director Christopher Guest and his *This Is Spinal Tap* co-writer Michael McKean? Hilariously detailing just how much film student Kevin Bacon is willing to compromise his integrity to get his first feature made, Guest smartly dissects the movie industry with malicious glee, film buff in-jokes and gentle humour, while also providing a fascinating insight into its power plays and studio politics. The cast is uniformly excellent. AJ. Contains some swearing and nudity.

Kevin Bacon *Nick Chapman* • Emily Longstreth *Susan Rawlings* • JT Walsh *Allen Habel* • Jennifer Jason Leigh *Lydia Johnson* • Martin Short *Neil Sussman* • Michael McKean *Emmett Sumner* • Kim Miyori *Jenny Sumner* • Teri Hatcher *Gretchen* • John Cleese *Bartender* • Elliott Gould *Attorney* ■ *Dir* Christopher Guest • *Scr* Michael Varhol, Christopher Guest, Michael McKean, from a story by Michael Varhol, Christopher Guest

The Big Pond ★★★

Romantic musical 1930 · US · BW · 78mins

This vehicle for Maurice Chevalier is not in the same class as the previous year's hit *The Love Parade*, though he received a joint Oscar nomination for both films in 1929/1930. (This was the era of split-year Academy Awards.) The featherbrained screenplay, with additional dialogue from future master of satire Preston Sturges, has the star as a French tour guide in Venice falling for wealthy American tourist Claudette Colbert. Hobart Henley directs competently enough, and Chevalier, oozing his usual Gallic charm, sings a clutch of excellent songs. RK

Maurice Chevalier *Pierre Mirande* • Claudette Colbert *Barbara Billings* • George Barbier *Mr Billings* • Marion Ballou *Mrs Billings* • Elaine Koch *Jennie* • Nat Pendleton *Pat O'Day* • Frank Lyon *Ronnie* • Andrée Corday *Toinette* ■ *Dir* Hobart Henley • *Scr* Robert Presnell, Garrett Fort, Preston Sturges, from the play by George Middleton, AE Thomas

Big Red ★ U

Adventure 1962 · US · Colour · 85mins

This Disney wildlife adventure is about an Irish setter called Big Red and the young orphan boy who trains him. Their friendship is put to the test when old curmudgeon Walter Pidgeon decides to split them up. Romantic interest is provided by a female Irish setter, reinforcing the impression that the dogs are far more human than anything on two legs. Set in Quebec, this is a movie of unspeakable treacliness. AT

Walter Pidgeon *James Haggin* • Gilles Payant *René Dumont* • Emile Genest *Emile Fornet* • Janette Bertrand *Terese Fornet* • George Bouvier *Baggageman* • Doris Lussier *Farmer Mariot* • Roland Bedard *Conductor* ■ *Dir* Norman Tokar • *Scr* Louis Pelletier, from the novel by Jim Kjelgaard

The Big Red One ★★★★ 15

Second World War drama
1980 · US · Colour · 108mins

Samuel Fuller's skills had been blunted by working in American TV in the 1960s, but the director returned to form on the big screen with this graphic war movie, arguably one of his most accomplished features. An infantryman in the Second World War, Fuller drew on the brutalities that he had witnessed and recorded to produce a powerful and, at times, poetic tale of five soldiers who experience the shocking realities of combat. The squad is lead by Lee Marvin, a perfect choice as the tight-jawed, bullish, growling sergeant. The 2005 reconstructed version of the film contains 47 minutes of restored footage cut by the studio on its initial release and is as close to the late director's original vision. JM. Contains violence and swearing. DVD

Lee Marvin *Sergeant* • Mark Hamill *Griff* • Robert Carradine *Zab* • Bobby DiCicco *Vinci* • Kelly Ward *Johnson* • Siegfried Rauch *Schroeder* • Stéphane Audran *Walloon* • Serge Marquand *Rensonnet* • Charles Macaulay *General/Captain* ■ *Dir/Scr* Samuel Fuller

The Big Risk ★★★

Crime drama 1960 · Fr/It · BW · 111mins

This very early feature by Claude Sautet is clearly influenced as much by the gangster thrillers of Jean-Pierre Melville as Hollywood models. Lino Ventura plays a gangster hiding out in Nice with his two children. His former associates in Paris hire a hitman to kill him but the two men become friends. Ventura is a sort of French Bogart and carries a romantic sense of doomy heroism. As the killer who switches allegiances, Jean-Paul Belmondo is all youth and recklessness. AT. A French language film.

Lino Ventura *Abel Davos* • Sandra Milo *Liliane* • Jean-Paul Belmondo *Eric Stark* • Marcel Dalio *Arthur Gibelin* • Jacques Dacqmine *Blot* • Claude Cerval *Raoul Fargier* ■ *Dir* Claude Sautet • *Scr* José Giovanni, Claude Sautet, Pascal Jardin, from the novel *Classe Tous Risques* by José Giovanni

The Big Shot ★★★

Crime drama 1942 · US · BW · 81mins

This was one of the movies Humphrey Bogart made just before *Casablanca* that consolidated the cynical, hard-boiled, louche image he had established in 1941's *The Maltese Falcon* – and would endearingly perpetuate in those later great Howard Hawks and John Huston pictures. It comes as no surprise, then, to discover that this flick is little more than a standard Warner Bros potboiler, albeit with a slightly more clever exposition than most, with Bogie as a self-styled three-time loser framed after a heist. He virtually carries the movie single-handedly. TS

Humphrey Bogart *Duke Berne* • Irene Manning *Lorna Fleming* • Richard Travis *George Anderson* • Susan Peters *Ruth Carter* • Stanley Ridges *Martin Fleming* • Minor Watson *Warden Booth* • Chick Chandler *Dancer* ■ *Dir* Lewis Seiler • *Scr* Bertram Millhauser, Abem Finkel, Daniel Fuchs

Big Shot's Funeral ★★★ PG

Satirical comedy
2001 · Chi/HK · Colour · 96mins

In this over-striving satire, Ge You stars as a frustrated cinematographer, who is hired by Rosamund Kwan to make a documentary record of Hollywood honcho Donald Sutherland's bid to shoot a costume drama in the Forbidden City. There's a relaxed buddiness about the dispirited Sutherland's relationship with the chipper cameraman, but the humour becomes strained after Sutherland is fired and Ge misunderstands his joking invitation to arrange a "comedy funeral" for him. Fun, but hardly subtle. DP. In Mandarin and English with subtitles. DVD

Ge You *YoYo* • Rosamund Kwan *Lucy* • Donald Sutherland *Don Tyler* • Paul Mazursky *Tony* • Ying Da *Louis Wang* ■ *Dir* Feng Xiaogang • *Scr* Feng Xiaogang, Li Xiaoming, Shi Kang

The Big Show ★★★ U

Drama 1961 · US · Colour · 112mins

This lavish circus epic stars the fabulous Esther Williams, her MGM swimming pool days behind her and her Amazonian physique now deployed on the high wire. Esther is super to watch, as is the young star she has the hots for, Cliff Robertson. While it doesn't quite come off, the European circus background is enthralling. TS

Esther Williams *Hillary Allen* • Cliff Robertson *Josef Everard* • Nehemiah Persoff *Bruno Everard* • Robert Vaughn *Klaus Everard* • Margia Dean *Carlotta Martinez* • David Nelson *Eric Solden* • Carol Christensen *Garda Everard* ■ *Dir* James B Clark • *Scr* Ted Sherdeman

The Big Showdown ★★

Spaghetti western
1972 · It/W Ger/Fr · Colour · 94mins

Although he was Sergio Leone's assistant on both *The Good, the Bad and the Ugly* and *Once upon a Time in the West*, there's little of the great man's influence in Giancarlo Santi's directorial debut. However, he does manage to blur the moral lines between gunslingers Lee Van Cleef and Horst Frank, which leaves us unsure where to place our sympathies as they head for the inevitable shoot-out. The staging is hesitant, though, and composer Luis Enriquez Bacalov is no Ennio Morricone. DP. Italian dialogue dubbed into English.

Lee Van Cleef *Sheriff Clayton* • Bob Clark *Deputy* • Horst Frank *David Saxon* • Peter O'Brien (1) *Philipp Wermeer* • Sandra Cardini *Anita* • Dominique Darel *Elisabeth* ■ *Dir* Giancarlo Santi • *Scr* Ernesto Gastaldi

The Big Sky ★★★★ U

Western adventure 1952 · US · BW · 121mins

An eventful epic western, directed with great flair by maestro Howard Hawks, which could have been a great one with better casting. Kirk Douglas in the lead, good though he is, looks too urbane, not to mention intense, for this particular role, while his co-stars are not up to the splendour of Dudley Nichols's fine screenplay. There's a problem of taste, too – the finger amputation scene is played for laughs – but the film overall is so satisfying you'll forgive its faults. TS

Kirk Douglas *Jim Deakins* • Dewey Martin *Boone Caudill* • Arthur Hunnicutt *Zeb* • Elizabeth Threatt *Teal Eye* • Steven Geray *Jourdonnais* • Buddy Baer *Romaine* • Hank Worden *Poordevil* • Jim Davis *Streak* ■ *Dir* Howard Hawks • *Scr* Dudley Nichols, from the novel by AB Guthrie

The Big Sleep ★★★★★ PG

Classic detective drama
1946 · US · BW · 109mins

This ultra-witty romantic thriller from director Howard Hawks – the second screen pairing of real-life lovers Humphrey Bogart and Lauren Bacall – is one of the great pleasures of the silver screen. Its original release was delayed to give Hawks time to exploit and build up the Bogie-Bacall scenes, and as a result the movie sizzles with sexual chemistry as each exchange hides a censor-baiting double or triple entendre. The Raymond Chandler plot is notoriously confusing, and ultimately irrelevant, but the delights are many: Martha Vickers's sexy Carmen ("She tried to sit in my lap when I was standing up"), Dorothy Malone's bookshop flirt and Elisha Cook Jr's sad fall guy. The pace never lets up, and the result is a classic. TS DVD

Humphrey Bogart *Philip Marlowe* • Lauren Bacall *Vivian Rutledge* • John Ridgely *Eddie Mars* • Martha Vickers *Carmen Sternwood* • Dorothy Malone *Girl in bookshop* • Peggy Knudsen *Mona Mars* • Regis Toomey *Bernie Ohls* • Charles Waldron *General Sternwood* • Charles D Brown *Norris, the butler* • Bob Steele *Canino* • Elisha Cook Jr *Harry Jones* • Louis Jean Heydt *Joe Brody* • Sonia Darren *Agnes* ■ *Dir* Howard Hawks • *Scr* William Faulkner, Jules Furthman, Leigh Brackett, from the novel by Raymond Chandler • *Cinematographer* Sid Hickox • *Music* Max Steiner

The Big Sleep ★★ 15

Detective drama 1978 · UK · Colour · 95mins

Having given an excellent account of himself in *Farewell, My Lovely*, Robert Mitchum returned to the role of Philip Marlowe for this curious reworking of Raymond Chandler's hard-boiled novel. Shifted to 1970s London, the action loses nearly all of its *noirish* atmosphere and, although Michael Winner sticks closer to the book than the writers responsible for Howard Hawks's seminal 1946 version, he's not in the same class. DP DVD

Robert Mitchum *Philip Marlowe* • Sarah Miles *Charlotte Regan* • Richard Boone *Lash Canino* • Candy Clark *Camilla Sternwood* • Joan Collins *Agnes Lozelle* • Edward Fox *Joe Brody* • John Mills *Inspector Carson* • James Stewart *General Sternwood* • Oliver Reed *Eddie Mars* • Harry Andrews *Norris* ■ *Dir* Michael Winner • *Scr* Michael Winner, from the novel by Raymond Chandler

The Big Squeeze ★★

Crime comedy 1996 · US · Colour · 107mins

A lukewarm black comedy, with a hint of *noir* skullduggery thrown in for good measure. There's a couple of original twists offered – barmaid Lara Flynn Boyle schemes to con money out of her estranged, religious-nut husband rather than having him meet with an accident – and the quirky plotting separates it from more conventional "con" movies. Unfortunately, it's far less plausible than others of its ilk, and the casting is dubious, too. JC

Peter Dobson *Benny O'Malley* • Lara Flynn Boyle *Tanya Mulhill* • Luca Bercovici *Henry Mulhill* • Danny Nucci *Jesse* • Teresa DiSpina *Cece* • Sam Vlahos *Father Sanchez* • Valente Rodriguez *Father Arias* • Michael Chieffo *Inspector* ■ *Dir/Scr* Marcus DeLeon

The Big Stampede ★★ U

Western 1932 · US · BW · 51mins

The second of six B-westerns John Wayne dashed off for Warner Bros early in his career, its big studio pedigree puts this a cut above Wayne's subsequent poverty row efforts, and it has character actor Berton Churchill as New Mexico Governor Lew Wallace dispatching John Wayne's deputy sheriff to deal with cattle rustlers. AE [video]

John Wayne *John Steele* • Noah Beery *Sam Crew* • Mae Madison *Ginger Malloy* • Luis Alberni *Sonora Joe* • Berton Churchill *Gov Lew Wallace* • Paul Hurst *Arizona* • Sherwood Bailey *Pat Malloy* ■ *Dir* Tenny Wright • *Scr* Kurt Kempler, from a story by Marion Jackson

The Big Steal ★★★ PG

Film noir 1949 · US · BW · 71mins

Don Siegel's third feature is a thriller with more mirth than menace, and the sexual banter between Robert Mitchum and Jane Greer sometimes rivals that of Bogart and Bacall. The plot is simple – $300,000 of army payroll money has gone missing – and the extended chase throws up a great deal of subplots and shifty characters, notably Ramon Novarro as a lazy police chief. Real locations, rather than studio backdrops, are an asset, and Siegel never lets the pace sag or the shoestring budget show. AT [video]

Robert Mitchum *Lieutenant Duke Halliday* • Jane Greer *Joan Graham* • William Bendix *Captain Vincent Blake* • Patric Knowles *Jim Fiske* • Ramon Novarro *Colonel Ortega* • Don Alvarado *Lieutenant Ruiz* • John Qualen *Julius Seton* • Pasqual Garcia Peña *Manuel* ■ *Dir* Don Siegel • *Scr* Geoffrey Homes [Daniel Mainwaring], Gerald Drayson Adams, from the story *The Road to Carmichael's* by Richard Wormser

The Big Steal ★★★ 15

Comedy 1990 · Aus · Colour · 96mins

Fans of the 1986 Australian comedy *Malcolm* will enjoy this equally quirky offering from the husband-and-wife team of director Nadia Tass and writer/cameraman David Parker. This comedy of cars and romance stars Ben Mendelsohn (*The Year My Voice Broke*) as a shy teenager who craves a Jaguar so that he can woo a local beauty. When his dad gives him a battered old Nissan, our hero gets involved with shady car dealers and a 1973 Jag of dubious provenance. It's a slight but charming movie that takes its time to get on the road. AT [video]

Ben Mendelsohn *Danny Clark* • Claudia Karvan *Joanna Johnson* • Steve Bisley *Gordon Farkas* • Marshall Napier *Desmond Clark* • Damon Herriman *Mark Jorgensen* • Angelo D'Angelo *Vangeli Petrakis* • Tim Robertson *Desmond Johnson* • Maggie King *Edith Clark* • Sheryl Munks *Pam Schaeffer* ■ *Dir* Nadia Tass • *Scr* David Parker, Max Dunn

The Big Store ★★★★ U

Comedy 1941 · US · BW · 79mins

The last of five MGM comedies by the Marx Brothers, this has more plot than is usual for them. They play ramshackle detectives hired to guard a vast emporium in which customers take second place to the various under-the-counter shenanigans, in which the Brothers participate. As usual, Groucho woos massive Margaret Dumont, with insult amounting to injury but, more unusually, the romantic subplot is let loose, and allows Tony Martin to sing *Tenement Symphony*. Corny, but confident. TH [video] DVD

Groucho Marx *Wolf J Flywheel* • Chico Marx *Ravelli* • Harpo Marx *Wacky* • Tony Martin *Tommy Rogers* • Virginia Grey *Joan Sutton* • Margaret Dumont *Martha Phelps* • William Tannen (1) *Fred Sutton* ■ *Dir* Charles Reisner • *Scr* Sid Kuller, Hal Fimberg, Ray Golden, from a story by Nat Perrin

The Big Street ★★★

Comedy melodrama 1942 · US · BW · 88mins

Writer Damon Runyon produced this movie version of his own short story, *Little Pinks*, which has an oddly cast Henry Fonda playing the busboy with a crush on moll Lucille Ball. When Ball is injured by her sadistic boss, Fonda leaps at the chance to care for her and prove his devotion. It's sentimental stuff, but Runyon's unique streetwise dialogue and brilliantly sketched gallery of eccentric supporting characters make this a pleasure to watch. TS

Henry Fonda *Little Pinks* • Lucille Ball *Gloria* • Barton MacLane *Case Ables* • Eugene Pallette *Nicely Nicely Johnson* • Agnes Moorehead *Violette* • Sam Levene *Horsethief* • Ray Collins *Professor B* • Marion Martin *Mrs Venus* ■ *Dir* Irving Reis • *Scr* Leonard Spiegelglass, from the short story *Little Pinks* by Damon Runyon

The Big Swap ★★ 18

Erotic drama 1997 · UK · Colour · 116mins

An ambitious but ultimately doomed British look at modern sexual politics and relationships. The set-up is promising: a large group of 30-somethings, all of whom have partners, decide to spice up their lives by randomly swapping their respective boyfriends and girlfriends via the old car keys lottery. It's raunchy stuff, but the performances from the largely unknown cast fail to convince. JF. Contains swearing, sex scenes and some violence. [video] DVD

Antony Edridge *Jack* • Sorcha Brooks *Ellen* • Richard Cherry *Hal* • Julie-Ann Gillitt *Liz* • Kevin Howarth *Julian* • Alison Egan *Eve* • Mark Caven *Michael* • Clarke Hayes *Fi* • Jackie Sawiris *Sydney* • Thierry Harcourt *Tony* • Mark Adams *Sam* ■ *Dir/Scr* Niall Johnson

The Big TNT Show ★★★★

Music concert documentary 1966 · US · BW · 93mins

Shot in Electrovision on November 29, 1965 at the Moulin Rouge nightclub in Hollywood, this fabulous concert film delivers one legendary performance after another and captures the precise moment old school rock 'n' roll turned hippy. The happy-go-lucky atmosphere is infectious as the Byrds, Petula Clark, Bo Diddley, the Ronettes, the Lovin' Spoonful, Roger Miller and other contemporary acts sock out their hits and drive the crowd wild, with the orchestra swelling under Phil Spector's giant production. A superb pop time capsule and an ideal companion piece to the earlier (and very similar) *The TAMI Show*. AJ

Dir Larry Peerce • *Producer* Phil Spector

The Big Tease ★★ 15

Comedy 1999 · US/UK · Colour · 82mins

Gay Scottish crimper Craig Ferguson believes that, thanks to his talent with the curling tongs, he's been invited to Los Angeles to take part in an international hairdressing competition. His hopes are dashed, however, when he realises he's only been summoned to appear in the celebrity audience. Refusing to curl up and dye, he charms his way into the contest via hard-nosed Hollywood agent Frances Fisher, millionaire sponsor Charles Napier and the usual bunch of eccentrics. The result is an intermittently amusing affair. AJ. Contains swearing. [video] DVD

Craig Ferguson *Crawford Mackenzie* • Frances Fisher *Candace "Candy" Harper* • Mary McCormack *Monique Geingold* • Donal Logue *Eamonn McGarvey* • Larry Miller *Dunston Cactus, hotel manager* • Charles Napier *Senator Warren Crockett* • Michael Paul Chan *Clarence* • David Hasselhoff ■ *Dir* Kevin Allen • *Scr* Sacha Gervasi, Craig Ferguson

Big Time ★ PG

Music documentary 1988 · US · Colour · 92mins

Put together by singer/songwriter Tom Waits, his wife Kathleen Brennan and Levis 501 commercials director Chris Blum, this indulgent concert documentary was shot during the raspy lounge lizard's 1987 tour and contains all, or snatches of, 22 songs in his haphazard repertoire. The main focus of this vanity production – with Waits often in extreme close-up as he sings – are the three dull Island Records albums recorded prior to the tour. Anyone other than the ardent fan will find *Big Time* a hard time. AJ [video]

Dir Chris Blum • *Scr* Tom Waits, Kathleen Brennen, Chris Blum

The Big Tip Off ★

Crime drama 1955 · US · BW · 78mins

In one of Hollywood's first efforts to discredit its burgeoning rival, television, journalist Richard Conte is duped by gangster Bruce Bennett who diverts funds from a charity telethon into his own pocket. The telethon scam is only one of several strands in a baffling plot. The treatment is decidedly lacklustre, and the minor stars are generally a wan bunch. AT

Richard Conte *Johnny Denton* • Constance Smith *Penny Conroy* • Bruce Bennett *Bob Gilmore* • Cathy Downs *Sister Joan* • James Millican *Lt East* • Dick Benedict *First hood* • Sam Flint *Father Kearney* • Mary Carroll *Sister Superior* • George Sanders ■ *Dir* Frank McDonald • *Scr* Steve Fisher

Big Top Pee-wee ★★★ U

Comedy 1988 · US · Colour · 81mins

As a bizarre star, he blazed only briefly in this and *Pee-wee's Big Adventure* before his career was abruptly halted by ignominy. But Pee-wee Herman, alias Paul Reubens, and his childish eccentricity of manner and dress contrived an odd originality, at least in this account of his funny farm – a hot-dog tree is the least of it – into which Kris Kristofferson's circus is blown during a storm. The talking pig is amusingly oinkish, but for most of the time the film has all the eerie fascination of a freak show – with Pee-wee as the main exhibit. TH [video]

Pee-wee Herman [Paul Reubens] *Pee-wee Herman* • Penelope Ann Miller *Winnie* • Kris Kristofferson *Mace Montana* • Valeria Golino *Gina* • Wayne White *Vance the Pig* • Susan Tyrrell *Midge Montana* • Albert Henderson *Mr Ryan* • Jack Murdock *Otis* • Terrence V Mann [Terrence Mann] *Snowball the Clown* • Benicio Del Toro *Duke, the Dog-Faced Boy* ■ *Dir* Randal Kleiser • *Scr* Paul Reubens, George McGrath, from the character created by Paul Reubens

The Big Town ★★ 15

Drama 1987 · US · Colour · 105mins

Matt Dillon plays an extremely sulky would-be high-roller in this formulaic, sepia-toned, crap-shooting movie. Director Ben Bolt ladles on the fug and finger snappin' with a heavy-handed trowel, but this remains a fruitless, sterile exercise with deep pretentions to style but little discernible substance. That said, there are solid performances from the always interesting Tommy Lee Jones and the pouting Diane Lane, as a deeply unsavoury couple who inveigle Dillon into further naughty doings. SH. Contains some swearing. [video]

Matt Dillon *JC Cullen* • Diane Lane *Lorry Dane* • Tommy Lee Jones *George Cole* • Bruce Dern *Mr Edwards* • Lee Grant *Ferguson Edwards* • Tom Skerritt *Phil Carpenter* • Suzy Amis *Aggie Donaldson* • David Marshall Grant *Sonny Binkley* ■ *Dir* Ben Bolt • *Scr* Robert Roy Pool, from the novel *The Arm* by Clark Howard

The Big Trail ★★★★ U

Western 1930 · US · BW · 116mins

Fox made this truly epic western to celebrate the centenary of a famous pioneers' trek from Independence, Missouri. Under director Raoul Walsh, the cast and crew arduously re-created the highlights of that journey, lowering wagons and horses down cliff-faces, fighting heat, blizzards, raging rivers and Indians, giving the film an amazing documentary look. It was shot for both 70mm widescreen (the shortlived Fox Grandeur process) and for standard 35mm. A then unknown John Wayne took the lead: some of his lines are awkwardly spoken but he makes an authoritative figure of the wagon train scout. Unfairly, he took most of the flack for the film's failure, and was relegated to minor parts for a while. AE [video] DVD

John Wayne *Breck Coleman* • Marguerite Churchill *Ruth Cameron* • El Brendel *Gussie* • Tully Marshall *Zeke* • Tyrone Power [Tyrone Power Sr] *Red Flack* • David Rollins *Dave Cameron* • Ian Keith *Bill Thorpe* • Frederick Burton *Pa Bascom* • Russ Powell *Windy Bill* ■ *Dir* Raoul Walsh • *Scr* Jack Peabody, Marie Boyle, Florence Postal, Fred Sersen, from a story by Hal G Evarts, Raoul Walsh

The Big Trees ★★★ PG

Drama 1952 · US · Colour · 89mins

A saga about a forest of giant redwood trees that lumberjack Kirk Douglas wants to cut down, much to the horror of the local Quaker community. Cue drama and romance with a demure Quaker girl, played by Eve Miller. For Douglas, still chasing after real stardom, this low-budget movie was a way out of a stifling contract with Warner Bros: he did the picture for nothing and earned his independence. Filmed in Oregon, the picture is routinely exciting and delivers a powerful environmental message for the time. AT [video] DVD

Kirk Douglas *John Fallon* • Eve Miller *Alicia Chadwick* • Patrice Wymore *Daisy Fisher* • Edgar Buchanan *Yukon Burns* • John Archer *Frenchy Lecroix* • Alan Hale Jr *Tiny* ■ *Dir* Felix Feist • *Scr* John Twist, James R Webb, from a story by Kenneth Earl

Big Trouble ★★★ 15

Comedy 1985 · US · Colour · 89mins

An odd switch of tactics for the great improvisational director, John Cassavetes – a blandly contrived take-off of *Double Indemnity*, with insurance man Alan Arkin conniving with Beverly D'Angelo to take out a lethal kind of insurance policy on her husband Peter Falk. So far, so conventional. But there are enough off-the-wall surprises to raise it just above the average spoof thriller – one of which is that Arkin needs the money to send his trio of musical children to Yale. TH. Contains some violence and swearing. [video] DVD

Peter Falk *Steve Rickey* • Alan Arkin *Leonard Hoffman* • Beverly D'Angelo *Blanche Rickey* • Charles Durning *O'Mara* • Paul Dooley *Noozel* • Robert Stack *Winslow* • Valerie Curtin *Arlene Hoffman* • Richard Libertini *Dr Lopez* ■ *Dir* John Cassavetes • *Scr* Warren Bogle

Big Trouble ★★ 12

Crime comedy 2002 · US · Colour · 81mins

Barry Sonnenfeld's manic, Miami-based ensemble comedy faced post-September 11 release problems in the US, because of its climactic satirising

B

of poor airport security, which allows a nuclear bomb onto a plane. There's barely enough plot to cover the short running time of this crime farce, as chance, coincidence and an explosive suitcase bring together a dozen characters. Tim Allen and Rene Russo are the nominal stars, but this appealing partnership is hampered by puerile plotting and a surplus of over-acting supporting players. JC DVD

Tim Allen *Eliot Arnold* • Rene Russo *Anna Herk* • Stanley Tucci *Arthur Herk* • Tom Sizemore *Snake* • Johnny Knoxville *Eddie* • Dennis Farina *Henry* • Jack Kehler *Leonard* • Janeane Garofalo *Monica Romero* • Barry Sonnenfeld *Confused sports radio caller* ■ *Dir* Barry Sonnenfeld • *Scr* Robert Ramsey, Matthew Stone, from the novel by Dave Barry

Big Trouble in Little China ★★ 15

Action adventure 1986 · US · Colour · 95mins

Horror maestro John Carpenter is clearly in awe of Hong Kong movies, but this brave attempt to fuse martial arts action with a westernised adventure story sadly doesn't gel. Kurt Russell makes an amiably inept hero as the lorry driver who gets mixed up with ancient Chinese magic when he ventures beneath the streets of San Francisco. The fight scenes are surprisingly stodgy, however, and the special effects take over. JF DVD

Kurt Russell *Jack Burton* • Kim Cattrall *Gracie Law* • Dennis Dun *Wang Chi* • James Hong *Lo Pan* • Victor Wong (2) *Egg Shen* • Kate Burton *Margo* • Donald Li *Eddie Lee* • Carter Wong *Thunder* ■ *Dir* John Carpenter • *Scr* Gary Goldman, David Z Weinstein, WD Richter

Big Wednesday ★★★★ PG

Sports drama 1978 · US · Colour · 114mins

It's easy to dismiss this Malibu surfing saga as pretentious nonsense, with beach bums Jan-Michael Vincent, William Katt and Gary Busey forever seeking the great Californian wave that will give meaning to their lives. However, director John Milius – who went on to script *Apocalypse Now* – shows a personal commitment to all the mystical bonding. The result rises above the pseudo-intellectual twaddle to make a poignant statement about the lack of purpose in the 1960s, and the way Vietnam forced even infantile hunks such as these to take on responsibility. TH DVD

Jan-Michael Vincent *Matt Johnson* • William Katt *Jack Barlow* • Gary Busey *Leroy Smith* • Patti D'Arbanville *Sally Johnson* • Lee Purcell *Peggy Gordon* • Darrell Fetty *Jim "Waxer" King* • Sam Melville *"The Bear"* • Barbara Hale *Mrs Barlow* ■ *Dir* John Milius • *Scr* John Milius, Dennis Aaberg

The Big Wheel ★★ U

Sports drama 1949 · US · BW · 88mins

Tough guy Mickey Rooney gets back into the racing car seat again, this time to prove he's as good as his old man, who, of course, died on the track. Clichéd stuff, but done with confidence and bravura, though alas without much style. Rooney continues to amaze, giving real credence to the duffest dialogue and situations, but don't expect too much. TS DVD

Mickey Rooney *Billy Coy* • Thomas Mitchell *Red Stanley* • Michael O'Shea *Vic Sullivan* • Mary Hatcher *Louise Riley* • Spring Byington *Mary Coy* • Lina Romay *Dolores Raymond* • Steve Brodie *Happy* • Allen Jenkins *George* ■ *Dir* Edward Ludwig • *Scr* Robert Smith

The Bigamist ★★★ PG

Drama 1953 · US · BW · 79mins

This is a gritty but far-fetched tale, directed by and co-starring Ida Lupino, in which feckless travelling salesman Edmond O'Brien ends up with two wives – Lupino and the suffering Joan Fontaine. This is adult material and director Lupino really makes you believe in O'Brien's dilemma. It's an unusual and serious subject that is given a dramatic outing for a change. The only weakness is in the framing story, with lovable Edmund Gwenn as an investigator. TS DVD

Edmond O'Brien *Harry Graham* • Joan Fontaine *Eve Graham* • Ida Lupino *Phyllis Martin* • Edmund Gwenn *Mr Jordan* • Jane Darwell *Mrs Connelley* • Kenneth Tobey *Tom Morgan* • John Maxwell *Judge* ■ *Dir* Ida Lupino • *Scr* Collier Young, from a story by Larry Marcus, Lou Schor

Bigfoot and the Hendersons ★★ PG

Comedy 1987 · US · Colour · 106mins

This resembles a watered-down, terrestrial remake of *ET*, and is produced by Steven Spielberg's company Amblin Entertainment. A Seattle family adopts America's answer to the abominable snowman and suffers the ludicrous consequences, while trying to keep it a secret from the neighbours. It's cosier, cutesier and even more sentimental than the Spielberg norm and became a short-lived TV sitcom. AJ. Contains some strong language.

John Lithgow *George Henderson* • Melinda Dillon *Nancy Henderson* • Margaret Langrick *Sarah Henderson* • Joshua Rudoy *Ernie Henderson* • Kevin Peter Hall *Harry* • David Suchet *Jacques Lafleur* • Lainie Kazan *Irene Moffitt* • Don Ameche *Dr Wallace Wrightwood* • M Emmet Walsh *George Henderson Sr* ■ *Dir* William Dear • *Scr* William Dear, William E Martin, Ezra D Rappaport

A Bigger Splash ★★★ 15

Biographical documentary
1974 · UK · Colour · 98mins

Jack Hazan's documentary portrait of artist David Hockney admirably captures the visual style of the artist, without ever quite breaking through his defences. Touching on the closeness of his friendships and his penchant for revisiting favourite haunts, the action mostly concerns his relationship with his latest sitter, Peter Schlesinger. The film is less concerned with Hockney's methods than with the way in which he relates to his model and how he copes with the completion of his work. Precious, but illuminating. DP

Dir Jack Hazan • *Scr* Jack Hazan, David Mingay

Bigger than Life ★★★★ 12A

Psychological drama
1956 · US · Colour · 95mins

One of those legendary 1950s melodramas, this was treated as a routine release in America and Britain, but hailed as a major work of art by the French (notably Jean-Luc Godard and François Truffaut) because it is a film by Nicholas Ray, the director of *Rebel without a Cause* and *They Live by Night*. James Mason, in one of his best roles, is a mild-mannered teacher whose life is wrecked by his addiction to cortisone, which turns him into a monster. Made in CinemaScope and famous for its dramatic colour scheme (New York cabs are at their yellowest), it is a real humdinger. AT

James Mason *Ed Avery* • Barbara Rush *Lou* • Walter Matthau *Wally* • Robert Simon [Robert F Simon] *Dr Norton* • Christopher Olsen *Richie Avery* • Roland Winters *Dr Ruric h* • Rusty Lane *La Porte* ■ *Dir* Nicholas Ray • *Scr* Cyril Hume, Richard Maibaum, from the article *Ten Feet Tall* by Berton Roueche • *Cinematographer* Joseph MacDonald [Joe MacDonald]

The Biggest Bundle of Them All ★★

Crime comedy
1968 · US/It · Colour · 107mins

Robert Wagner kidnaps rival mobster Vittorio De Sica. When no one offers to pay the ransom, De Sica takes over the gang and proposes stealing $5 million of valuable platinum. The resulting caper is a little too frantic for its own good; however, Edward G Robinson is on excellent form as the mastermind who plans the heist, while Raquel Welch has a lot of fizz as Wagner's moll. AT

Vittorio De Sica *Cesare Celli* • Raquel Welch *Juliana* • Robert Wagner *Harry* • Godfrey Cambridge *Benny* • Edward G Robinson *Professor Samuels* • Davy Kaye *Davey* • Francesco Mule *Tozzi* • Victor Spinetti *Captain Giglio* ■ *Dir* Ken Annakin • *Scr* Sy Salkowitz, Josef Shaftel, Riccardo Aragno, from a story by Josef Shaftel

Biggie & Tupac ★★ 15

Documentary 2001 · US · Colour · 107mins

British documentary maker Nick Broomfield investigates the unsolved murders of US rap stars Tupac Shakur and Christopher Wallace (aka Biggie Smalls, The Notorious BIG), throwing up allegations of conspiracy, corruption and police complicity in the killings. With a sound unit strapped satchel-style across his chest, Broomfield comes across as a diligent scholar. Doggedly chasing his interview subjects, he's both relentless and meticulous in his approach, and for this he's rewarded with some fascinating, though sometimes questionable, testimonies. Broomfield's gaffes and preambles are included, as in his previous projects, but the assumed air of bumbling incompetence gives the film an inappropriate and unintentionally humorous touch, and weakens the power of his case. SF DVD

Dir Nick Broomfield • *Cinematographer* Joan Churchill

Biggles ★ PG

Science-fiction adventure
1986 · UK · Colour · 88mins

A hero to a generation of young readers, Captain WE Johns's immortal flying ace is made to look very foolish in this ghastly spoof, directed with a leaden touch by John Hough. Neil Dickson does his best to give Biggles his customary gung-ho cheeriness, but his efforts are shot to pieces by a shambles of a story in which burger-bar boss Alex Hyde-White is whisked from modern America back to the First World War to join his time-twin, the flying ace on a secret mission. However, the saddest aspect of this sorry episode is that it was Peter Cushing's final film. DP DVD

Neil Dickson *James "Biggles" Bigglesworth* • Alex Hyde-White *Jim Ferguson* • Fiona Hutchison *Debbie Stevens* • Peter Cushing *Colonel Raymond* • Marcus Gilbert *Eric von Stalhein* • William Hootkins *Chuck* • Michael Siberry *Algy* ■ *Dir* John Hough • *Scr* John Groves, Ken Walwin, from characters created by Captain WE Johns

Les Bijoutiers du Clair de Lune ★★ PG

Crime thriller 1957 · Fr/It · Colour · 87mins

The respective contours of the Spanish landscape and Brigitte Bardot are all that interest director Roger Vadim in this sordid little thriller. Beset by shooting difficulties, the tension between Bardot and Stephen Boyd is tangible, although it doesn't make them any more credible as a protective convent girl and the man who killed her uncle and seduced her aunt. Alida Valli fares better in the latter role. The sex scenes that were considered frisky in their day have now lost much of their oomph. DP. In French with English subtitles. DVD

Brigitte Bardot *Ursula* • Alida Valli *Aunt Florentine* • Stephen Boyd *Lambert* • Pepe Nieto [José Nieto] *Count Ribera* • Maruchi Fresno *Conchita* • Adriano Dominguez *Fernando* ■ *Dir* Roger Vadim • *Scr* Roger Vadim, Jacques Rémy, Peter Viertel, from the novel *The Midnight Jewellers* by Albert Vidalie

Bike Boy ★★★

Experimental satire
1967 · US · Colour · 96mins

An endlessly amusing Warhol specimen, this Factory model appeared shortly after the artist's big-screen triumph, *The Chelsea Girls*, and took its cue from that film's languid obsession with flagrantly uninhibited (and unhinged) characters who aren't the least bit camera-shy. It features none-hit-wonder Joe Spencer as an intrinsically uninteresting biker hunk who wanders in for a series of static episodes in which he is subjected to some of the more entertainingly impossible members of the Warhol set. The conspicuous editing, the playful tensions between artifice and naturalism and the camp appeal of people doing "being" make for a fluid, modern experience. AJ

Joe Spencer *Motorcyclist* • Viva *Girl on couch* • Brigid Polk *Woman with husband* • Ingrid Superstar *Girl in kitchen* • Vera Cruz *Other motorcyclist* • George Ann *Salesman* • Bruce Ann *Salesman* • Ed Hood *Florist* • Valerie Solanis ■ *Dir/Scr* Andy Warhol

Biker Boyz ★★ 12

Action drama 2003 · US · Colour · 106mins

This tepid drama is centred around underground motorcycle gangs burning rubber in the streets of California. After a full-throttle race opening, in which a spectacular crash leaves brash teen Derek Luke fatherless, the film decelerates into a standard tale of a talented racer desperate to prove himself the best of the best. Laurence Fishburne, as the veteran, undefeated "King of Cali", is a picture of virile coolness, though both he and a capable African-American cast are held back by their formulaic stock characters. JC. Contains violence and swearing. DVD

Laurence Fishburne *Smoke* • Derek Luke *Kid* • Orlando Jones *Soul Train* • Djimon Hounsou *Motherland* • Lisa Bonet *Queenie* • Brendan Fehr *Stuntman* • Larenz Tate *Wood* ■ *Dir* Reggie Rock Bythewood • *Scr* Craig Fernandez, Reggie Rock Bythewood, from the article in the *New Times* by Michael Gougis

Bikini Beach ★★★ U

Comedy 1964 · US · Colour · 99mins

The third in the fun-in-the-sun teen series features Frankie Avalon in two roles – his usual lovesick surfer lusting after Annette Funicello and a British pop idol named the Potato Bug with the same idea. There's the usual quota of beach frolics, disapproving adults, camp Hell's Angels and drag races, while fluffy pop ditties from the leads are complemented by appearances from Little Stevie Wonder, The Exciters and The Pyramids. This go-go delight is one of the best in the series, even though Avalon's English accent, Beatle wig and "yeah yeahs" strain the wafer-thin credibility further by teetering on the embarrassing. AJ

Frankie Avalon *Frankie/Potato Bug* • Annette Funicello *Dee Dee* • Martha Hyer *Vivien Clements* • Harvey Lembeck *Eric Von Zipper* • Don Rickles *Big Drag* • John Ashley *Johnny* • Little Stevie Wonder [Stevie Wonder] *Little Stevie Wonder* • Keenan Wynn *Harvey Huntington Honeywagon* • Boris Karloff *Art dealer* ■ *Dir* William Asher • *Scr* William Asher, Leo Townsend, Robert Dillon

B

Bill ★★★★ PG

Drama based on a true story
1981 · US · Colour · 91mins

Almost 60 years after making his showbiz debut, mini-dynamo Mickey Rooney turns in what many rate a career-best performance, playing a mentally retarded man who has to learn to survive on his own in New York City after spending almost half a century in institutions. The film teeters on the edge of over-sentimentality. But, thanks to the sheer class of Rooney's performance, it never quite topples over. Made for TV, *Bill* earned Rooney an Emmy. Had it been made for the cinema, it might well have earned him an Oscar. Dennis Quaid co-stars in this true story, which spawned a sequel, *Bill: On His Own*. DA

Mickey Rooney *Bill Sackter* • Dennis Quaid *Barry Morrow* • Largo Woodruff *Bev Morrow* • Harry Goz *Thomas Walz* • Anna Maria Horsford *Marge Keating* • Kathleen Maguire *Florence Archer* • Jenny Rebecca Dweir *Amy Hill* • Tony Turco *Dr Peters* ■ *Dir* Anthony Page • *Scr* Corey Blechman, from a story by Barry Morrow

Bill & Ted's Bogus Journey ★★★★ PG

Comedy 1991 · US · Colour · 89mins

Wayne's World heroes Wayne and Garth may have won at the box office, but Bill and Ted remain the original and best dudes. This time around the two airheads (played with enormous energy by Alex Winter and Keanu Reeves) are still trying to get their band together when they are murdered by their robotic doppelgängers, sent from the future by the evil Joss Ackland. This sequel lacks the inspired stupidity of the first, but it is still a hoot, especially the knowing nods to Ingmar Bergman's classic *The Seventh Seal* as the duo play battleships with the Reaper. Reeves and Winter are once again cheerfully inept, and director Peter Hewitt stages the spectacular set pieces with panache. JF. Contains swearing. DVD

Keanu Reeves *Ted/Evil Ted* • Alex Winter *Bill/Evil Bill* • George Carlin *Rufus* • Joss Ackland *De Nomolos* • Sarah Trigger *Joanna* • Annette Azcuy *Elizabeth* • Hal Landon Jr *Captain Logan* • William Sadler *Grim Reaper* ■ *Dir* Peter Hewitt • *Scr* Ed Solomon, Chris Matheson

Bill & Ted's Excellent Adventure ★★★★ PG

Comedy 1988 · US · Colour · 89mins

A nonstop giggle from start to finish, this beguiling grab-bag of time-travel clichés, hard-rock music and Valley-speaking cool dudes is a flawless, purpose-built junk movie. Director Stephen Herek's scattershot style perfectly complements the wayward cosmic capers, and Keanu Reeves (in his pre-sex symbol days) bravely takes on comedian Alex Winter in competing for the "Most Witlessly Appealing Airhead" crown. Reeves resembles a moronic puppet with loose strings ambling amiably through this happy-go-lucky voyage into the short circuits of history. Engaging to the max. AJ. Contains some swearing. DVD

Keanu Reeves *Ted "Theodore" Logan* • Alex Winter *Bill S Preston* • George Carlin *Rufus* • Terry Camilleri *Napoleon* • Dan Shor *Billy the Kid* • Tony Steedman *Socrates* • Rod Loomis *Sigmund Freud* • Al Leong *Genghis Khan* • Jane Wiedlin *Joan of Arc* ■ *Dir* Stephen Herek • *Scr* Chris Matheson, Ed Solomon

A Bill of Divorcement ★★★ U

Drama 1932 · US · BW · 68mins

More of interest for its place in cinema history than its dramatic content, this film features Katharine Hepburn's screen debut and introduced Hepburn to her favourite director, George Cukor, later responsible for such Hepburn delights as *The Philadelphia Story* and *Adam's Rib*. Star John Barrymore, though prone to ham, is extraordinarily moving as the former mental asylum inmate reunited with his family, including daughter Hepburn. Billie Burke is also effective as Barrymore's wife, but many of today's viewers may find both the acting style and proscenium-based direction very creaky. TS

John Barrymore *Hilary Fairfield* • Katharine Hepburn *Sydney Fairfield* • Billie Burke *Margaret Fairfield* • David Manners *Kit Humphrey* • Elizabeth Patterson *Aunt Hester* • Paul Cavanagh *Gray Meredith* • Henry Stephenson *Dr Alliot* ■ *Dir* George Cukor • *Scr* Howard Estabrook, Harry Wagstaff Gribble, from the play by Clemence Dane

A Bill of Divorcement ★★★ PG

Drama 1940 · US · BW · 74mins

Confined to an asylum for 20 years and unaware that his wife has divorced him and is to remarry, Adolphe Menjou suddenly regains sanity and unexpectedly returns to the family home, precipitating emotional havoc. The 1932 version marked the screen debut of Katharine Hepburn and was a box-office hit. This straight remake was unfavourably compared to the original but, sacrilegious as it might be to say this, stands up better for a modern audience. It creaks in the same places, but offers a stunning performance from Maureen O'Hara, while John Farrow directs with depth and sensitivity. RK

Maureen O'Hara *Sydney Fairfield* • Adolphe Menjou *Hilary Fairfield* • Fay Bainter *Margaret Fairfield* • Herbert Marshall *Gray Meredith* • Dame May Whitty *Hester Fairfield* • Patric Knowles *John Storm* • C Aubrey Smith *Dr Alliot* • Ernest Cossart *Dr Pumphrey* ■ *Dir* John Farrow • *Scr* Dalton Trumbo, from the play by Clemence Dane

Billabong Odyssey ★★ PG

Sports documentary
2003 · US/Brazil · Colour · 87mins

The pitch for this occasionally spectacular but ultimately disappointing documentary is certainly enticing. A group of the world's most advanced big-wave surfers embark on an 18-month project to find the biggest waves on the planet and to surf them. It brings to mind Bruce Brown's seminal surfing film *Endless Summer*, which perfectly captured both the questing character of the athletes and the sheer physical poetry of the sport at its best. Sadly, this mostly delivers the usual competition footage and none of the personal, meditative flavour or camaraderie of its superior predecessor. AS DVD

Dir Philip Boston

Billie ★★★ U

Musical comedy 1965 · US · Colour · 86mins

An Oscar-winner at 16 for her startling performance as the young Helen Keller in *The Miracle Worker* (1962), Patty Duke returned to the screen three years later to play a tomboy whose astonishing prowess at athletics humiliates her male team-mates, bruises her beau's ego and embarrasses her mayoral candidate father. Directed with a pleasingly light touch by Don Weis, this high-school comedy is both innocuous and entertaining. RK

Patty Duke *Billie Carol* • Jim Backus *Howard G Carol* • Jane Greer *Agnes Carol* • Warren Berlinger *Mike Benson* • Billy De Wolfe *Mayor Davis* • Charles Lane (2) *Coach Jones* • Dick Sargent *Matt Bullitt* • Susan Seaforth *Jean Matthews* • Ted Bessell *Bob Matthews* ■ *Dir* Don Weis • *Scr* Ronald Alexander, from the play *Time Out for Ginger* by Ronald Alexander

Billion Dollar Brain ★★ PG

Spy thriller 1967 · UK · Colour · 104mins

The third of the Harry Palmer pictures (after *The Ipcress File* and *Funeral in Berlin*) has a story that smacks of substandard Bond, as Michael Caine travels to Finland to infiltrate power-crazed Ed Begley's secret organisation and prevent him from taking over the world. Ken Russell was perhaps an unlikely choice as director, but his exuberance prevents the plot from lapsing into predictability. In 1995, Harry Palmer was brought out of retirement for *Bullet to Beijing* and *Midnight in St Petersburg*. DP

Michael Caine *Harry Palmer* • Karl Malden *Leo Newbigin* • Françoise Dorléac *Anya* • Oscar Homolka *Colonel Stok* • Ed Begley *General Midwinter* • Guy Doleman *Colonel Ross* • Vladek Sheybal *Dr Eiwort* • Milo Sperber *Basil* ■ *Dir* Ken Russell • *Scr* John McGrath, from the novel by Len Deighton

The Billion Dollar Hobo ★★

Comedy 1978 · US · Colour · 96mins

In this wish fulfilment fable, Tim Conway discovers he'll only inherit a vast fortune if he duplicates his benefactor's experiences during the Depression. Stuart E McGowan's film intends to be make satirical points about unemployment and its consequences, but the vagrant script (co-written by Conway) wanders away from dramatic issues. TH

Tim Conway *Vernon Praiseworthy* • Will Geer *Choo Choo Trayne* • Eric Weston *Steve* • Sydney Lassick *Mitchell* • John Myhers *Leonard Cox* • Frank Sivero *Ernie* • Sharon Weber *Jen* • Sheela Tessler *Rita* ■ *Dir* Stuart E McGowan • *Scr* Stuart E McGowan, Tim Conway, Roger Beatty

A Billion for Boris ★★ PG

Comedy 1984 · US · Colour · 90mins

This comedy has a great idea at its core, but it isn't followed through, and the whole thing ends up a bit of a mess. The story tells of a ten-year-old electronics expert who fixes a TV set so it can show the next day's programmes, much to the delight of his sister's boyfriend, who sees it as a great way of making money. What could have been an interesting piece of whimsy is given a heavy-handed treatment by director Alex Grasshoff and the cast, which includes Lee Grant. A missed opportunity. JB

Scott Tiler *Boris Harris* • Mary Tanner *Annabel Andrews* • Seth Green *Ape-Face* • Lee Grant *Sascha Harris* • Tim Kazurinsky *Bartholomew Bacon* ■ *Dir* Alex Grasshoff • *Scr* Sandy Gartin, from the novel by Mary Rodgers

Billy Bathgate ★★★ 15

Crime drama 1991 · US · Colour · 102mins

An only partially successful exercise in re-creating the world of the gangland vendetta from director Robert Benton, in which visual flair jostles uneasily for supremacy with a complicated narrative. Dustin Hoffman as infamous mobster Dutch Schultz gives one of his more over-egged performances, but Nicole Kidman is sterling in support as a society moll. The credentials of this mahogany-toned movie are pretty impressive – original novel by EL Doctorow, script by Tom Stoppard – and there is an obvious intelligence that shines through the many nasty killings on offer. SH. Contains violence, swearing and nudity. DVD

Dustin Hoffman *Dutch Schultz* • Nicole Kidman *Drew Preston* • Loren Dean *Billy Bathgate* • Bruce Willis *Bo Weinberg* • Steven Hill *Otto Berman* • Steve Buscemi *Irving* • Billy Jaye *Mickey* ■ *Dir* Robert Benton • *Scr* Tom Stoppard, from the novel by EL Doctorow • *Cinematographer* Nestor Almendros

Billy Budd ★★★ U

Adventure drama 1962 · UK · BW · 124mins

Although this allegory about good versus evil is more suited to declamatory opera than cinema, writer/director Peter Ustinov's adaptation of Herman Melville's novel about life aboard an 18th-century British warship has a cannonade of powerful performances, notably from Ustinov as the indecisive captain, Robert Ryan as the sadistic Master-at-Arms, and an Oscar-nominated Terence Stamp as the innocent Billy. The film backs off from the fable that Melville intended, but it's a rather plodding treatment compared with Benjamin Britten's intense opera version. TH

Terence Stamp *Billy Budd* • Peter Ustinov *Captain Edward Fairfax Vere* • Robert Ryan *Master-at-Arms John Claggart* • Melvyn Douglas *The Dansker* • Ronald Lewis *Jenkins* • David McCallum *Lt Wyatt* • John Neville *Lt John Ratcliffe* • Ray McAnally *O'Daniel* ■ *Dir* Peter Ustinov • *Scr* Peter Ustinov, DeWitt Bodeen, Robert Rossen, from the play by Louis O Coxe and Robert H Chapman, from the novel *Billy Budd, Foretopman* by Herman Melville

Billy Elliot ★★★★ 15

Drama 2000 · UK · Colour · 105mins

Stage director Stephen Daldry's debut feature is an amiable study of daring to be different in the face of intractable tradition. The decision to set the story of an 11-year-old north-easterner's bid to become a ballet dancer against the backdrop of the 1984 miners' strike has more emotional resonance than social relevance. But it's the heart, not the conscience, that Daldry is keenest to tweak, and he succeeds triumphantly, thanks largely to Jamie Bell's eager performance in the title role and the marvellous supporting turns from Gary Lewis as the lad's reactionary dad and Julie Walters as his chain-smoking dance instructor. DP. Contains swearing. DVD

Julie Walters *Mrs Wilkinson* • Gary Lewis *Dad* • Jamie Draven *Tony* • Jean Heywood *Grandmother* • Jamie Bell *Billy* • Stuart Wells *Michael* • Mike Elliot *George Watson* ■ *Dir* Stephen Daldry • *Scr* Lee Hall

Billy Galvin ★★★ PG

Drama 1986 · US · Colour · 90mins

This pleasingly gritty blue-collar drama is held together by a powerful performance from screen veteran Karl Malden. In a neat twist on a familiar story, he plays a stubborn construction worker who doesn't want his rebellious son Lenny Von Dohlen to join him on the scaffolding. John E Gray's direction is admirably low key. JF. Contains swearing.

Karl Malden *Jack Galvin* • Lenny Von Dohlen *Billy Galvin* • Joyce Van Patten *Mae* • Toni Kalem *Nora* • Keith Szarabajka *Donny* • Alan North *Georgie* • Paul Guilfoyle (2) *Nolan* • Barton Heyman *Kennedy* ■ *Dir/Scr* John E Gray [John Gray]

Billy Jack ★★★ 18

Action drama 1971 · US · Colour · 109mins

Directing himself (under the name of TC Frank), Tom Laughlin stars as a mixed-race Vietnam veteran who comes to the aid of a school that is being harassed by a group of racists. Following 1967's *Born Losers*, this is very much a family affair – co-star and co-scriptwriter Delores Taylor is Laughlin's wife – this achieved a surprisingly good return at the box office in spite of its humble origins and its apparent advocation of achieving peace through violence. The series continued with 1974's *The Trial of Billy Jack*. TH. Contains violence, swearing and nudity.

Tom Laughlin *Billy Jack* • Delores Taylor *Jean Roberts* • Clark Howat *Sheriff Cole* • Bert Freed *Posner* • David Roya *Bernard* • Julie Webb *Barbara* • Kenneth Tobey *Deputy* • Victor Izay *Doctor* ■ *Dir* TC Frank [Tom Laughlin] • *Scr* TC Frank [Tom Laughlin], Teresa Christina [Delores Taylor]

Billy Jack Goes to Washington ★

Drama 1977 · US · Colour · 155mins

The Billy Jack saga (introduced in *Born Losers* and continued through *Billy Jack* and *The Trial of Billy Jack*) reaches a humdrum conclusion in star/writer/director Tom Laughlin's disastrous vanity production. The mixed-race hapkido expert and former Green Beret hero takes his idealistic hippy causes to the White House and ends up fighting political corruption in this bland, out-of-step, Capra-esque retread. Preachy, incredibly naive and well past its sell-by date. AJ

Tom Laughlin *Billy Jack* • Delores Taylor *Jean Roberts* • EG Marshall *Senator Joseph Paine* • Teresa Laughlin *Staff worker* • Sam Wanamaker *Bailey* • Lucie Arnaz *Saunders McArthur* • Dick Gautier *Governor Hubert Hopper* ■ *Dir* TC Frank [Tom Laughlin] • *Scr* TC Frank [Tom Laughlin], Teresa Christina [Delores Taylor], from the film *Mr Smith Goes to Washington* by Sidney Buchman, from a novel by Lewis R Foster • *Producer* Frank Capra Jr

Billy Liar ★★★★★ PG

Comedy drama 1963 · UK · BW · 93mins

A hit on page and stage, Keith Waterhouse and Willis Hall's *Billy Liar* was brought to the screen by John Schlesinger as a faultless blend of social realism and satirical fantasy. Tom Courtenay is at his career best – so far – as the undertaker's assistant who escapes from his mundane existence into the neverland of Ambrosia, where he is supreme dictator. The performances are all first rate, notably Julie Christie and Helen Fraser as two of the three women in his life, Wilfred Pickles and Mona Washbourne as his long-suffering parents, and Leonard Rossiter as his humourless boss. DP DVD

Tom Courtenay *Billy Fisher* • Julie Christie *Liz* • Wilfred Pickles *Geoffrey Fisher* • Mona Washbourne *Alice Fisher* • Ethel Griffies *Florence, grandmother* • Finlay Currie *Duxbury* • Rodney Bewes *Arthur Crabtree* • Helen Fraser *Barbara* • Leonard Rossiter *Shadrack* ■ *Dir* John Schlesinger • *Scr* Keith Waterhouse, Willis Hall, from their play and the novel by Keith Waterhouse

Billy Madison ★★★ PG

Comedy 1995 · US · Colour · 85mins

Your enjoyment of this gimmicky comedy will depend on your feelings about the low-brow comedy of Adam Sandler. He plays an infantile loser who won't be given control of his father's business empire unless he agrees to repeat his school education in just 24 weeks. Exploiting the star's talent for slapstick stupidity, this has some entertaining moments as he clashes with junior classmates and falls for his pretty teacher (Bridgette Wilson). Not in the same league as *The Wedding Singer*, but enjoyably dumb fun for fans. JC DVD

Adam Sandler *Billy Madison* • Darren McGavin *Brian Madison* • Bridgette Wilson *Veronica* • Bradley Whitford *Eric Gordon* • Josh Mostel *Max Anderson* • Norm MacDonald *Frank* • Mark Beltzman *Jack* • Larry Hankin *Carl Alphonse* ■ *Dir* Tamra Davis • *Scr* Tim Herlihy, Adam Sandler

Billy Rose's Diamond Horseshoe ★★★ U

Musical 1945 · US · Colour · 100mins

Probably the best of the Betty Grable vehicles. For once, she had a decent director in George Seaton, who ensured that the garish 20th Century-Fox production was well appointed – check those wacky condiment costumes – and that the songs were well above the usual recycled standard of the period. (This is the film that introduced the endearing hit *The More I See You*.) Grable and co-star Dick Haymes are well supported by troupers Phil Silvers and Margaret Dumont, but the plot's as meagre as usual. TS

Betty Grable *Bonnie Collins* • Dick Haymes *Joe Davis Jr* • Phil Silvers *Blinky Walker* • William Gaxton *Joe Davis Sr* • Beatrice Kay *Claire Williams* • Margaret Dumont *Mrs Standish* • Roy Benson *Harper* • George Melford *Pop* • Hal K Dawson *Carter* ■ *Dir* George Seaton • *Scr* George Seaton, from a play by John Kenyon Nicholson • *Music* Alfred Newman, Charles Henderson • *Costume Designer* Kay Nelson, Rene Hubert, Sascha Brastoff, Bonnie Cashin

Billy the Kid ★★★★

Western 1930 · US · BW · 95mins

The first sound film about Billy the Kid tells a now familiar story of his friendship with a kindly British rancher and his relentless pursuit of the man's killers who have the law in their pocket. It shows its age at times, but director King Vidor presents the story in an austere, anti-romantic fashion, with a realistic regard for the effects of hunger and thirst on men under siege – and for the pain and finality of violent death, as when the previously comical Roscoe Ates is riddled with bullets in a valiant attempt to bring water to Billy and others. Johnny Mack Brown makes an excellent Kid, while Wallace Beery is restrained and believable as the fair-minded sheriff Pat Garrett. The film was shot with alternative endings, tragic and upbeat; it is the latter which is now usually shown. AE

John Mack Brown [Johnny Mack Brown] *Billy* • Wallace Beery *Barrett* • Kay Johnson *Claire* • Karl Dane *Swenson* • Wyndham Standing *Tunston* • Russell Simpson *McSween* • Blanche Frederici *Mrs McSween* ■ *Dir* King Vidor • *Scr* Wanda Tuchock, Laurence Stallings, Charles Macarthur, from the novel *The Saga of Billy the Kid* by Walter Noble Burns

Billy the Kid ★★★

Western 1941 · US · Colour · 94mins

The superb use of three-strip Technicolor doesn't altogether compensate for a certain dullness in this portrayal of the west's most famous outlaw, played by Robert Taylor dressed entirely in black. It's an image of the Kid that endured for another two decades as boys all over the world followed his black-clad comic-book adventures in the Thriller Picture Library. First-time feature director and former editor David Miller has the benefit of the MGM production process, but, despite Gene Fowler's literate and inventive screenplay, which makes Billy and his nemesis Pat Garrett (here renamed Jim Sherwood) childhood friends, fans of this oft-told tale may be disappointed. TS

Robert Taylor (1) *Billy Bonney* • Brian Donlevy *Jim Sherwood* • Ian Hunter *Eric Keating* • Mary Howard *Edith Keating* • Gene Lockhart *Dan Hickey* • Lon Chaney Jr *Spike Hudson* • Henry O'Neill *Tim Ward* • Guinn Williams [Guinn "Big Boy" Williams] *Ed Bronson* ■ *Dir* David Miller • *Scr* Gene Fowler, from a story by Howard Emmett Rogers, Bradbury Foote, suggested by the book *The Saga of Billy the Kid* by Walter Noble Burns

Billy the Kid Returns ★★ U

Western 1938 · US · BW · 55mins

This starring vehicle for Roy Rogers has him playing Billy the Kid. After the outlaw is killed by sheriff Pat Garrett (Wade Boteler), Roy Rogers uses his strong resemblance to Billy to carry on the good work of protecting homesteaders and merchants from the machinations of a local rancher. Seven songs are packed into the brief running time, delivered by Rogers and sidekick Smiley Burnette. Leading lady Lynne Roberts made six subsequent appearances opposite Rogers. AE

Roy Rogers *Billy the Kid* • Smiley Burnette *Frog* • Lynne Roberts *Ellen* • Morgan Wallace *Morganson* • Fred Kohler Sr [Fred Kohler] *Matson* • Wade Boteler *Garrett* • Edwin Stanley *Miller* ■ *Dir* Joseph Kane • *Scr* Jack Natteford

Billy the Kid vs Dracula ★★ PG

Horror western 1966 · US · Colour · 73mins

This example of high-camp fun bordered on exploitation and came at the end of William Beaudine's career. John Carradine stars as Dracula (a role he had last played 20 years before) who's way out west and lusting after the blood of a pretty ranch owner. Unluckily for the Count, her fiancé is the reformed outlaw Billy the Kid. Let battle commence in a cheap but not nasty B-picture. BB

Chuck Courtney *Billy the Kid* • John Carradine *Count Dracula* • Melinda Plowman *Betty Bentley* • Virginia Christine *Eva Oster* • Walter Janovitz *Franz Oster* ■ *Dir* William Beaudine • *Scr* Carl K Hittleman, from a story by Carl K Hittleman

Billy Two Hats ★★★

Western 1973 · UK/US · Colour · 99mins

An example of how Hollywood's elder statesmen (here Gregory Peck) tried to connect with the new "youth" audience of the 1970s by co-starring with fresh talent, in this case Desi Arnaz Jr, best known for being the son of Desi Arnaz and Lucille Ball. It's a western about a bungled robbery, filmed in Israel, which looks like Spain pretending to be New Mexico. It offers some decent action sequences and the novelty of the usually presidential Peck ostensibly playing a baddie. AT. Contains swearing.

Gregory Peck *Deans* • Desi Arnaz Jr *Billy* • Jack Warden *Gifford* • Sian Barbara Allen *Esther* • David Huddleston *Copeland* • John Pearce *Spencer* • Dawn Littlesky *Squaw* ■ *Dir* Ted Kotcheff • *Scr* Alan Sharp

Billy's Hollywood Screen Kiss ★★★ 15

Romantic comedy
1998 · US · Colour · 92mins

Director Tommy O'Haver's farce and furious gay comedy drama serves up some disarmingly honest truths about confused passion in a camp cascade of glossy style, glamorous drag queens and glorious vamping. As wannabe LA photographer Sean P Hayes shoots homoerotic portraits based on famous Hollywood kisses and falls in lust with one of his models, the sexually confused Brad Rowe. Although never quite scalpel-sharp or profound enough to put it in the *Priscilla, Queen of the Desert* category, O'Haver's classy confection is nevertheless an engaging enough diversion held together by Hayes's central turn. AJ. Contains swearing and sexual references.

Sean P Hayes [Sean Hayes] *Billy* • Brad Rowe *Gabriel* • Meredith Scott Lynn *Georgiana* • Richard Ganoung *Perry* • Armando Valdes-Kennedy *Fernando* • Paul Bartel *Rex Webster* • Matthew Ashford *Whitey* • Carmine Giovinazzo *Gundy* ■ *Dir/Scr* Tommy O'Haver

Biloxi Blues ★★★★ 15

Second World War comedy
1988 · US · Colour · 102mins

Playwright Neil Simon's semi-autobiographical trilogy began with *Brighton Beach Memoirs* (1986) and ended with *Broadway Bound* (1991), but this second instalment is the most entertaining of the three. Matthew Broderick plays Simon's altered ego Eugene Jerome, whose army boot camp training involves him in the lives of the various soldiers around him – from Christopher Walken's surprisingly desolate sergeant to Matt Mulhern's dumb-ox bully boy. Director Mike Nichols makes up for the lack of momentum with character-revealing conversation and the result is comic and poignant. TH DVD

Matthew Broderick *Eugene* • Christopher Walken *Sgt Toomey* • Matt Mulhern *Wykowski* • Corey Parker *Epstein* • Markus Flanagan *Selridge* • Casey Siemaszko *Carney* • Michael Dolan *Hennessey* • Penelope Ann Miller *Daisy* • Park Overall *Rowena* ■ *Dir* Mike Nichols • *Scr* Neil Simon, from his play

Bingo ★★ PG

Adventure 1991 · US · Colour · 86mins

This tale of a boy's tearful split from his faithful canine companion has enough sentiment to make you cringe. Every cliché in the "youngsters and pets" genre is played out from the moment Robert J Steinmiller Jr adopts a circus dog. Despite the earnest nature of the performances, this will stretch the patience of even the most soft-hearted viewer. SH. Contains swearing and violence. DVD

Cindy Williams *Natalie Devlin* • David Rasche *Hal Devlin* • Robert J Steinmiller Jr *Chuckie Devlin* • Kurt Fuller *Lennie* • Joe Guzaldo *Eli* • David French *Chickie Devlin* • Glenn Shadix *Duke* • Suzie Plakson *Ginger* ■ *Dir* Matthew Robbins • *Scr* Jim Strain, from the film *The Littlest Hobo* by Dorrell McGowan

The Bingo Long Travelling All-Stars and Motor Kings ★★★★ 15

Period sports comedy
1976 · US · Colour · 106mins

This sports comedy set in 1939 takes a less than serious look at the issue of racial prejudice. Billy Dee Williams and James Earl Jones are the stars of a black baseball team, who decide to set up their own club in defiance of Negro League manager Ted Ross. Needless to say the bosses don't like it and try to put the All-Stars out of business. In this crowd-pleasing mix of skill and farce, Richard Pryor almost steals the show with his attempts to crash the race barrier. TH

Billy Dee Williams *Bingo Long* • James Earl Jones *Leon* • Richard Pryor *Charlie Snow* • Rico Dawson *Willie Lee* • Sam "Birmingham" Briston *Louis* • Jophery Brown *Champ Chambers* • Leon Wagner *Fat Sam* • Tony Burton *Isaac* ■ *Dir* John Badham • *Scr* Hal Barwood, Matthew Robbins, from a novel by William Brashler

Bio-Dome ★ 12

Comedy 1996 · US · Colour · 93mins

Excruciatingly awful comedy about a couple of crude, lewd and generally nauseating brothers (Pauly Shore and Stephen Baldwin) who accidentally gatecrash a year-long science bio-dome experiment. Naturally, they trash the place. The brain-dead brothers' juvenile antics grate and the plotting is an insult. JC DVD

Pauly Shore *Bud Macintosh* • Stephen Baldwin *Doyle Johnson* • William Atherton *Dr Noah Faulkner* • Denise Dowse *Olivia Biggs* • Dara Tomanovich *Mimi Simkins* • Kevin West *TC Romulus* • Kylie Minogue *Petra Von Kant* • Joey Adams [Joey Lauren Adams] *Monique* • Patricia Hearst *Doyle's mother* • Roger Clinton *Professor Bloom* ■ *Dir* Jason Bloom • *Scr* Kip Koenig, Scott Marcano, from a story by Adam Leff, Mitchell Peck, Jason Blumenthal

Birch Interval ★★★★

Drama 1976 · US · Colour · 103mins

Not shown in British cinemas, this marvellous film is touching and sensitive in its telling of the story of a young American girl growing up in the midst of an Amish community. Finely directed by Delbert Mann, this features an exceptionally strong cast is headed by veterans Eddie Albert and Rip Torn, and marks a last return to film by blacklisted Oscar-winner Anne Revere. Little seen, this is a minor classic in search of recognition. TS

Eddie Albert *Pa Strawacher* • Rip Torn *Thomas* • Ann Wedgeworth *Marie* • Susan McClung *Jesse* • Brian Part *Samuel* • Jann Stanley *Esther* • Bill Lucking [William Lucking] *Charlie* • Anne Revere *Mrs Tanner* • Joanna Crawford *Lady on Bus* ■ *Dir* Delbert Mann • *Scr* Joanna Crawford, from her novel

Bird ★★★★ 15

Biographical drama
1988 · US · Colour · 154mins

Charlie Parker, the black American alto saxophonist who was the driving force behind the bebop jazz revolution, sacrificed his well-being, and that of his lover, to the tempting whirlwind of his music. As Parker, Forest Whitaker gives a pumping performance, with Diane Venora no second best as his lady, who goes from strutting dancer to empty soul. Director Clint Eastwood is perfectly in tune with his subject, giving the film a claustrophobic atmosphere as it portrays the anarchy of bebop. The innovative soundtrack, enhancing Parker's recordings using present-day musicians, is a perfect accompaniment. JM. Contains swearing. [VIDEO]

Forest Whitaker *Charlie "Yardbird" Parker* • Diane Venora *Chan Richardson* • Michael Zelniker *Red Rodney* • Samuel E Wright *Dizzy Gillespie* • Keith David *Buster Franklin* • Michael McGuire *Brewster* • James Handy *Esteves* • Damon Whitaker *Young Bird* ■ *Dir* Clint Eastwood • *Scr* Joel Oliansky

Bird of Paradise ★★★

Romantic adventure 1932 · US · BW · 81mins

Producer David O Selznick wheeled in the big guns at RKO for this romance about love across the racial divide on a Polynesian island, sending Joel McCrea, the luscious Dolores Del Rio and distinguished director King Vidor off to locations in Hawaii. Appalling weather plagued the shoot, but can't be blamed for the turgid and messy screenplay, which deadens the drama. The production values are first-rate, though, while the doom-laden tale, played with conviction by the subtle and beautiful Del Rio and the attractive McCrea, is undeniably atmospheric. RK

Dolores Del Rio *Luana* • Joel McCrea *Johnny Baker* • John Halliday *Mac* • Richard "Skeets" Gallagher *Chester* • Creighton Chaney [Lon Chaney Jr] *Thornton* • Bert Roach *Hector* • Napoleon Pukui *The King* • Sofia Ortega *Mahumahu* ■ *Dir* King Vidor • *Scr* Wells Root, Leonard Praskins, Wanda Tuchok, from a play by Richard Walton Tully

Bird of Paradise ★

Romantic adventure
1951 · US · Colour · 100mins

Bird of Paradise was originally filmed in black and white by RKO in 1932, with stellar leads, a top-class director and loads of authentic atmosphere. This pointless Technicolor remake from Fox has no merit, despite being written and directed by the usually reliable Delmer Daves. The over-lush visuals engulf the human drama, and much of the film descends into idiotic fake ritual. RK

Louis Jourdan *Andre Laurence* • Debra Paget *Kalua* • Jeff Chandler *Tenga* • Everett Sloane *The beachcomber* • Maurice Schwartz *The Kahuna* • Jack Elam *The trader* • Prince Leilani *Chief* • Otto Waldis *Skipper* ■ *Dir* Delmer Daves • *Scr* Delmer Daves, from a play by Richard Walton Tully

Bird on a Wire ★★★ 15

Comedy action thriller
1990 · US · Colour · 105mins

Mel Gibson plays a former small-time drugs runner who has been in hiding since turning state's evidence, but who ends up on the run with an old flame (Goldie Hawn) when his cover is broken. It's frothy nonsense for the most part, but expertly packaged by director John Badham. Hawn is an able if sometimes irritating foil, while David Carradine, Bill Duke (best known now as the director of films such as *Deep Cover* and *A Rage in Harlem*) and Stephen Tobolowsky are an entertaining trio of villains. JF. Contains swearing, violence. [VIDEO] DVD

Mel Gibson *Rick Jarmin* • Goldie Hawn *Marianne Graves* • David Carradine *Eugene Sorenson* • Bill Duke *Albert Diggs* • Stephen Tobolowsky *Joe Weyburn* • Joan Severance *Rachel Varney* • Harry Caesar *Marvin* • Jeff Corey *Lou Baird* ■ *Dir* John Badham • *Scr* David Seltzer, Louis Venosta, Eric Lerner, from a story by Louis Venosta, Eric Lerner

The Bird with the Crystal Plumage ★★★★ 18

Thriller 1969 · It/W Ger · Colour · 92mins

Who is the new Jack the Ripper holding Rome in a grip of terror? American author Tony Musante knows he's witnessed a vital clue to the chilling conundrum – but what is it exactly? Dario Argento's *giallo* trendsetter (*giallo*, or "yellow", being a term for all Italian thrillers more concerned with the modus operandi of the bloody murders than their whodunnit aspect) is a glossy and jagged mystery firmly entrenched in Hitchcockian paranoia. A seminal work, it shows Argento's visual flair for horrific set pieces and introduced the trademark themes he'd develop in such subsequent violent nightmares as *Suspiria* and *Opera*. AJ. Italian dialogue dubbed into English. [VIDEO] DVD

Tony Musante *Sam Dalmas* • Suzy Kendall *Julia* • Eva Renzi *Monica* • Enrico Maria Salerno *Morosini* • Mario Adorf *Berto* • Renato Romano *Dover* • Umberto Rano *Ranieri* ■ *Dir/Scr* Dario Argento • *Music* Ennio Morricone • *Cinematographer* Vittorio Storaro

The Birdcage ★★★ 15

Comedy 1996 · US · Colour · 114mins

The knives were out for this camp comedy from the start. Film snobs were convinced it would besmirch the memory of *La Cage aux Folles*, and the gay lobby denounced the making of such a cosy film in the Aids era. Yet, in the end, nearly everyone was pleasantly surprised by a picture that trivialised neither its source nor its sensitive issues. Robin Williams underplays sensibly, Nathan Lane almost matches the peerless Michel Serrault, and Gene Hackman shows again what a deft comic he can be. Less assured, however, is director Mike Nichols and writer Elaine May's clumsy political satire at the expense of the American right. DP. Contains swearing. [VIDEO] DVD

Robin Williams *Armand Goldman* • Gene Hackman *Senator Keeley* • Nathan Lane *Albert* • Dianne Wiest *Louise Keeley* • Dan Futterman *Val Goldman* • Calista Flockhart *Barbara Keeley* • Hank Azaria *Agador* • Christine Baranski *Katherine* ■ *Dir* Mike Nichols • *Scr* Elaine May, from the film *La Cage aux Folles* by Jean Poiret, Francis Veber, Edouard Molinaro, Marcello Danon, from the play *La Cage aux Folles* by Jean Poiret

Birdman of Alcatraz ★★★★ PG

Biographical drama 1962 · US · BW · 142mins

Real-life killer Robert Stroud was apparently quite unlike the tough, taciturn inmate portrayed by Burt Lancaster in director John Frankenheimer's thought-provoking study of one man's attempt to survive an unforgiving prison system. Stroud used his years in solitary confinement to become a world authority on ornithology, despite the cruel injustices meted out by the prison warden (convincingly played by Karl Malden). Lancaster was Oscar-nominated for a performance that is ranked by many to be one of the finest of his career, while Burnett Guffrey's claustrophobic black-and-white photography is mastery. DP [VIDEO] DVD

Burt Lancaster *Robert Stroud* • Karl Malden *Harvey Shoemaker* • Thelma Ritter *Elizabeth Stroud* • Betty Field *Stella Johnson* • Neville Brand *Bull Ransom* • Edmond O'Brien *Tom Gaddis* • Hugh Marlowe *Roy Comstock* • Telly Savalas *Feto Gomez* • Crahan Denton *Kramer* ■ *Dir* John Frankenheimer • *Scr* Guy Trosper, from the non-fiction book *Birdman of Alcatraz; the Story of Robert Stroud* by Thomas E Gaddis

The Birdmen ★★ PG

War drama based on a true story
1971 · US · Colour · 88mins

This workmanlike TV adventure opens with US officer Doug McClure landing in Norway to rescue atomic scientist René Auberjonois, before switching to the Alpine castle of Beckstadt after McClure and Auberjonois are captured. The need to build a glider to fly to freedom before the Nazis discover Auberjonois's true identity adds to the intrigue of the PoW sequences, and a solid supporting cast underpins the drama, although McClure's tendency to overact is a minus. DP [VIDEO]

Doug McClure *Major Harry Cook* • René Auberjonois *Halden Brevik/Olav Volda* • Richard Basehart *Schiller* • Chuck Connors *Colonel Morgan Crawford* • Max Baer Jr *Tanker* • Tom Skerritt *Orville "Fitz" Fitzgerald* ■ *Dir* Philip Leacock • *Scr* David Kidd

The Birds ★★★★★ 15

Classic horror 1963 · US · Colour · 113mins

A black comedy moonlighting as a genuinely unsettling, horrific allegory, this Hitchcock classic somehow strayed from favour for awhile. Yet in the realm of popular mythology, it is now rivalled only by *Psycho*. Set in the remote California coastal town of Bodega Bay, the story concerns a small group of unsatisfied creatures. Two women and a young girl are all fixed on one man (Rod Taylor), and when a fourth (Tippi Hedren) arrives from San Francisco with a certain determination in her heart, a menacing populace of birds descends on the town wreaking terror, right up until the film's inscrutable ending. AJ. Contains violence. [VIDEO] DVD

Rod Taylor *Mitch Brenner* • "Tippi" Hedren [Tippi Hedren] *Melanie Daniels* • Jessica Tandy *Lydia Brenner* • Suzanne Pleshette *Annie Hayworth* • Veronica Cartwright *Cathy Brenner* • Ethel Griffies *Mrs Bundy* • Charles McGraw *Sebastian Sholes* • Ruth McDevitt *Mrs MacGruder* ■ *Dir* Alfred Hitchcock • *Scr* Evan Hunter, from the short story by Daphne du Maurier

The Birds and the Bees ★★ U

Comedy 1956 · US · Colour · 94mins

Directed by Norman Taurog with Mitzi Gaynor, David Niven and George Gobel, this is a direct copy of Preston Sturges's *The Lady Eve*, the story of a father-daughter duo of cardsharps who fleece a gullible millionaire, which is a magic amalgam of satire, farce, slapstick and romance. While the original is now regarded as an enduring gem of screwball comedy, this Technicolor remake is only mildly amusing and short on charm. RK

George Gobel *George Hamilton* • Mitzi Gaynor *Jean Harris* • David Niven *Colonel Harris* • Reginald Gardiner *Gerald* • Fred Clark *Mr Hamilton* • Harry Bellaver *Marty Kennedy* • Hans Conried *Duc Jacques de Montaigne* • Margery Maude *Mrs Hamilton* ■ *Dir* Norman Taurog • *Scr* Sidney Sheldon, Preston Sturges, from a story by Monckton Hoffe

Birds Anonymous ★★★★ U

Animated comedy 1957 · US · Colour · 6mins

Fritz Freleng's distinguished career spanned the fledgeling Disney studios in the 1920s and his own DePatie–Freleng organisation of the 1960s and beyond, with a lengthy period at Warner Brothers in between (he was their longest serving director). At Warners, he developed into a master of timing, rivalling Avery in sharpness if not in wackiness. In this imaginative Tweety and Sylvester vehicle, Sylvester the cat is within inches of eating the sadistic canary when another feline interrupts him with an invitation to an AA-style meeting for canary addicts. This film received an Academy Award for Best Short Cartoon of its year (one of five Freleng received in his career). CLP [VIDEO]

Mel Blanc *Sylvester/Tweety* ■ *Dir* Friz Freleng • *Scr* Warren Foster • *Music* Milt Franklyn

The Birds, the Bees, and the Italians ★★

Comedy 1965 · Fr/It · BW · 115mins

Bursting with Italianate gusto, director Pietro Germi's film is one of the many compendium works from Italy with sex as the subject of their intentionally humorous tales. This contribution, in which Virna Lisi is the best-known name, offers three episodes dealing variously with a deceived husband, a henpecked husband and an underage girl who is the favoured bed-mate of most of the male population of her village. Efficient enough, it now seems rather dated and tedious, though American and British audiences found it hilarious in its day. RK. An Italian language film.

Virna Lisi *Milena Zulian* • Gastone Moschin *Osvaldo Bisigato* • Nora Ricci *Gilda Bisigato* • Alberto Lionello *Toni Gasparini* • Olga Villi *Ippolita Gasparini* • Franco Fabrizi *Lino Benedetti* • Beba Loncar *Noemi Castellan* • Gigi Ballista *Dr Giancinato Castellan* ■ *Dir* Pietro Germi • *Scr* Age Scarpelli [Agenore Incrocci and Furio Scarpelli], Luciano Vincenzoni, Pietro Germi, from a story by Age Scarpelli [Agenore Incrocci and Furio Scarpelli], Pietro Germi

Birdy ★★★★ 15

Drama 1984 · US · Colour · 115mins

This engrossing psychological drama features powerful performances from Matthew Modine and Nicolas Cage as two young friends since childhood who are scarred by the trauma of fighting in Vietnam. Director Alan Parker shows his versatility by adapting William Wharton's complex novel with sensitivity and skill, while Modine is exceptional as the boy who believes he's a bird. PF. Contains violence, swearing, sex scenes. [VIDEO] DVD

Matthew Modine *Birdy* • Nicolas Cage *Al Columbato* • John Harkins *Dr Weiss* • Sandy Baron *Mr Columbato* • Karen Young *Hannah Rourke* • Bruno Kirby *Renaldi* • Nancy Fish *Mrs Prevost* • George Buck *Birdy's father* • Dolores Sage *Birdy's mother* ■ *Dir* Alan Parker • *Scr* Sandy Kroopf, Jack Behr, from the novel by William Wharton

B

Birth ★★★★ 15

Mystery drama
2004 · US/Ger · Colour · 100mins

A ten-year-old boy claims to be the reincarnation of a woman's dead husband in director Jonathan Glazer's utterly captivating New York-set fairy tale. This gripping film considers the overriding power of love and how the strength of belief can lead individuals into moral minefields. Nicole Kidman astonishes anew with a performance of haunting intensity as the about-to-be-remarried widow whose life is turned upside down by Cameron Bright's intrusive pre-pubescent. This elegantly shot and sophisticated curiosity is intriguingly ambiguous, stark and elusive. AJ. Contains nudity and a sex scene. DVD

Nicole Kidman *Anna* • Cameron Bright *Sean* • Danny Huston *Joseph* • Lauren Bacall *Eleanor* • Alison Elliott (2) *Laura* • Arliss Howard *Bob* • Anne Heche *Clara* • Peter Stormare *Clifford* ■ *Dir* Jonathan Glazer • *Scr* Jean-Claude Carrière, Milo Addica, Jonathan Glazer

The Birth of a Nation ★★★★ 15

Silent historical epic
1915 · US · BW · 192mins

This colossal, majestic Civil War epic from pioneer director DW Griffith is one of the most successful films of all time. In terms of film history, the film was ground-breaking: a long and epic narrative telling a complex tale interweaving two families' fortunes, with dramatic reconstructions of key events including the assassination of Abraham Lincoln, not to mention accurate (and costly) re-creations of Civil War battlefields. But – and it's a very big "but" – the source material is fervently racist, and Griffith remains true to his source. It's hard to applaud a film where the Ku Klux Klan rides triumphantly to the rescue, and this, alas, undoes all the sterling work put in earlier and the wonderful performances. Griffith tried to make amends with *Intolerance*, but the damage was done. TS DVD

Lillian Gish *Elsie Stoneman* • Mae Marsh *Flora Cameron* • Henry B Walthall *Ben Cameron* • Miriam Cooper *Margaret Cameron* • Mary Alden *Lydia Brown* • Ralph Lewis *Hon Austin Stoneman* • George Siegmann *Silas Lynch* • Walter Long *Gus* • Jack Ford [John Ford] *Klansman* ■ *Dir* DW Griffith • *Scr* DW Griffith, Frank E Woods, from the novel and the play *The Clansman* and the novel *The Leopard's Spots* by Thomas Dixon Jr • *Cinematographer* Billy Bitzer

The Birth of the Blues ★★★ U

Musical 1941 · US · BW · 86mins

Bing Crosby, Brian Donlevy, Mary Martin and real-life trombonist Jack Teagarden head the line-up in this rather flimsy fiction about a pioneering group who progress from being street entertainers to taking New Orleans by storm as the original Dixieland jazz band. Plot and characterisation, however, are secondary to such great numbers as *St Louis Blues*, *Melancholy Baby* and the title number. A supposed history of the blues, it's a good-natured, well-directed film that will delight fans of the music. RK

Bing Crosby *Jeff Lambert* • Mary Martin *Betty Lou Cobb* • Brian Donlevy *Memphis* • Carolyn Lee *Aunt Phoebe* • Eddie "Rochester" Anderson *Louie* • Jack Teagarden *Pepper* • J Carrol Naish *Blackie* • Warren Hymer *Limpy* ■ *Dir* Victor Schertzinger • *Scr* Harry Tugend, Walter DeLeon, from a story by Harry Tugend

Birthday Girl ★★★ 15

Romantic comedy drama
2001 · UK/US · Colour · 89mins

Worth seeing for Nicole Kidman's downbeat and brave performance as a Russian mail-order bride, this blackly comic film suffers from a genre identity crisis. Ben Chaplin is the suburban bank clerk who summons Kidman to England via the internet. But once she's ensconced in his semi, Chaplin is disappointed with her lack of English and grunge style, but forgives her when she compensates with action in the bedroom. Then two men claiming to be Kidman's relatives arrive and soon all he holds dear is in danger. Well-meaning, but not quite funny – or hard – enough. LH. Contains swearing, sex scenes and some violence. DVD

Nicole Kidman *Sophia/"Nadia"* • Ben Chaplin *John Buckingham* • Vincent Cassel *Alexei* • Mathieu Kassovitz *Yuri* • Kate Evans *Clare* • Alexander Armstrong *Robert Moseley* • Sally Phillips *Karen* ■ *Dir* Jez Butterworth • *Scr* Jez Butterworth, Tom Butterworth

The Birthday Party ★★★ 15

Drama 1968 · UK · Colour and BW · 118mins

Directing his second film, William Friedkin opted for a safe and rather uncinematic approach to Harold Pinter's first full-length play. This is all about text and performance, and, compelling though the action is, it's clearly diminished by the loss of the immediacy you get in the theatre. Robert Shaw is too sturdy an actor to convince as the frightened mystery man hiding away in a seaside B&B. Veterans Sydney Tafler and Dandy Nichols are left to steal the show with performances that suggest both had been rather wasted during their earlier movie careers. DP DVD

Robert Shaw *Stanley Weber* • Patrick Magee *Shamus McCann* • Dandy Nichols *Meg Bowles* • Sydney Tafler *Nat Goldberg* • Moultrie Kelsall *Petey Bowles* ■ *Dir* William Friedkin • *Scr* Harold Pinter, from his play

The Birthday Present ★★ U

Drama 1957 · UK · BW · 99mins

Pat Jackson directs this doleful, overlong slice of surburban life, in which Tony Britton shows why he never made it as even a minor movie star, playing a toy salesman whose world falls apart when he is arrested for smuggling a wrist watch. Sylvia Syms, as the long-suffering wife who can take no more, deserves better than this. DP

Tony Britton *Simon Scott* • Sylvia Syms *Jean Scott* • Jack Watling *Bill Thompson* • Walter Fitzgerald *Sir John Dell* • Geoffrey Keen *Colonel Wilson* • Howard Marion-Crawford *George Bates* • John Welsh *Chief customs officer* • Lockwood West *Mr Barraclough* ■ *Dir* Pat Jackson • *Scr* Jack Whittingham

The Biscuit Eater ★★★ U

Adventure drama 1940 · US · BW · 80mins

Stuart Heisler, a former editor then assistant to John Ford, made his solo debut with this simple and deeply affecting story of two boys – one black, one white – who are given the runt of a litter of dogs and turn their aptly named Promise into a champion. There's a bitter twist when they are blackmailed into shaming the dog to run from the final show trial. Although Promise does return to the boys, animal lovers should be prepared for a tearful ending. Superbly shot on Georgia locations, this was the first of several socially committed films from a neglected director. BB

Billy Lee *Lonnie McNeil* • Cordell Hickman *Text* • Richard Lane *Harvey McNeil* • Lester Matthews *Mr Ames* • Helene Millard *Mrs McNeil* ■ *Dir* Stuart Heisler • *Scr* Stuart Anthony, Lillie Hayward, from the short story *The Biscuit Eater* by James Street in *The Saturday Evening Post*

The Biscuit Eater ★★ U

Adventure drama 1972 · US · Colour · 86mins

As the pals who overcome the racial prejudices of the adults around them to transform a wild hunting dog into a champion, Johnny Whitaker and George Spell avoid the winsome boyishness usually portrayed in Hollywood outdoor adventures. But director Vincent McEveety tub-thumps the liberal American values and allows sentiment to turn to mush in this sugar-coated Disney offering. DP

Earl Holliman *Harve McNeil* • Lew Ayres *Mr Ames* • Godfrey Cambridge *Willie Dorsey* • Patricia Crowley [Pat Crowley] *Mrs McNeil* • Beah Richards *Charity Tomlin* • Johnny Whitaker *Lonnie McNeil* • George Spell *Text Tomlin* • Clifton James *Mr Eben* ■ *Dir* Vincent McEveety • *Scr* Lawrence Edward Watkin, from the short story by James Street in *The Saturday Evening Post*

The Bishop's Wife ★★★ U

Fantasy comedy 1947 · US · BW · 105mins

Cary Grant stars as an angel who descends from heaven to put the marriage of irritable, materialistic bishop David Niven and Loretta Young in order, and to raise money for a new church. There were tensions on the set as Grant clashed with Young and director Henry Koster over the script, which Grant thought substandard. However, the playing from all three stars is enjoyable and the festive setting allows Grant to trim a Christmas tree with the flick of a finger. His best line, "The only people who grow old are people who were born old to begin with," might well have been his own epitaph. Remade in 1996 as *The Preacher's Wife*, starring Denzel Washington. DP DVD

Cary Grant *Dudley* • David Niven *Henry Brougham* • Loretta Young *Julia Brougham* • Monty Woolley *Professor Wutheridge* • James Gleason *Sylvester* • Gladys Cooper *Mrs Hamilton* • Elsa Lanchester *Matilda* ■ *Dir* Henry Koster • *Scr* Robert E Sherwood, Leonardo Bercovici, from the novel *In Barleyfields* by Robert Nathan

A Bit of Scarlet ★★★ 12

Documentary
1996 · UK · Colour and BW · 74mins

While not as good as its recent American counterpart *The Celluloid Closet*, this miscellany of gay and lesbian clips culled from British movies of the past 60 years has a fun time contrasting its stereotypical images with the supposed rules of the genre: all relationships must end with broken hearts; you will not be the main character; go to public school. The usual suspects are all here – *The Killing of Sister George*, *Victim*, Charles Hawtrey, *Carry On Spying* – and Ian McKellen narrates with ironic aplomb. AJ

Ian McKellen *Narrator* ■ *Dir* Andrea Weiss • *Scr* Andrea Weiss, Stuart Marshall

The Bit Player ★★★

Comedy 1973 · Fr · Colour · 96mins

Marcello Mastroianni stars as a bit-part actor, separated from his wife (Carla Gravina) and children, and living with his jealous mistress (Françoise Fabian). When she leaves him, he tries to go back to his wife, who is now carrying another man's child. Directed by Yves Robert, who undermines the sardonic comedy with a dollop of sentimentality, the film depends for its appeal on Mastroianni's entertaining, melancholy performance,and that of Jean Rochefort as his friend. RB. French dialogue dubbed into English.

Marcello Mastroianni *Nicolas* • Françoise Fabian *Peggy* • Jean Rochefort *Clement* • Carla Gravina *Elizabeth* ■ *Dir* Yves Robert • *Scr* Jean-Loup Dabadie, Yves Robert

The Bitch ★★★ 18

Erotic drama 1979 · UK · Colour · 88mins

This kitsch classic – a sequel to *The Stud* – follows the further adventures of promiscuous club owner Fontaine Khaled (Joan Collins), as she goes through a messy divorce and tries to get her London disco back in the celebrity limelight. Add a jewel robbery, handsome conmen, horse racing and glamorous parties, and you have the usual Jackie Collins cocktail of sexy sleaze and camp hysteria. Collins's demon diva performance led to *Dynasty* and her golden years as TV's supreme super-bitch. AJ DVD

Joan Collins *Fontaine Khaled* • Michael Coby *Nico Cantafora* • Kenneth Haigh *Arnold Rinstead* • Ian Hendry *Thrush Feather* • Carolyn Seymour *Polly* • Sue Lloyd *Vanessa* • Mark Burns *Leonard* • John Ratzenberger *Hal* ■ *Dir* Gerry O'Hara • *Scr* Gerry O'Hara, from the novel by Jackie Collins

Bite the Bullet ★★★ PG

Western adventure
1975 · US · Colour · 125mins

A gripping, allegorical drama about a 700-mile horse race from writer/director Richard Brooks. Entrants include Gene Hackman, James Coburn, Candice Bergen, Ben Johnson, Ian Bannen and Jan-Michael Vincent, pitting old-school values against the shallowness of capitalism. Filmed amid the stunning scenery of Nevada, Colorado and New Mexico, the picture is perhaps too long, with too many trough-stops for discourses about machismo and the motives of the competitors. But on the hoof it's an excellent adventure with a splendid cast and some spectacular turn-of-the-century settings. AT. Contains some swearing. DVD

Gene Hackman *Sam Clayton* • Candice Bergen *Miss Jones* • James Coburn *Luke Matthews* • Ben Johnson *Mister* • Jan-Michael Vincent *Carbo* • Ian Bannen *Norfolk* • Mario Arteaga *Mexican* ■ *Dir/Scr* Richard Brooks

Bitter Harvest ★★

Drama 1963 · UK · Colour · 100mins

As the young Welsh innocent who is abused by various London ne'er-do-wells, Janet Munro exhibits not only a touching vulnerability but also a credible inner reserve, which sustains her after she herself exploits a kindly barman (John Stride). Scripted by Ted Willis, this lacks the bite of contemporary examples of social realism, but it's solidly made. DP

Janet Munro *Jeannie Jones* • John Stride *Bob Williams* • Anne Cunningham *Ella* • Alan Badel *Karl Denny* • Vanda Godsell *Mrs Pitt* • Norman Bird *Mr Pitt* • Terence Alexander *Andy* • Richard Thorp *Rex* ■ *Dir* Peter Graham Scott • *Scr* Ted Willis, from the novel *The Street Has a Thousand Skies* by Patrick Hamilton

Bitter Harvest ★★ 18

Erotic crime thriller
1993 · US · Colour · 93mins

If you've ever wanted to watch beautiful women throwing themselves at Stephen Baldwin for no apparent reason, *Bitter Harvest* is for you. Baldwin plays Travis, a young man who has just inherited his father's house. And it's not a coincidence that, at the same time as he takes possession of the house, two attractive blondes start hanging around and trying to seduce him at every opportunity. ST

Patsy Kensit *Jolene* • Stephen Baldwin *Travis Graham* • Jennifer Rubin *Kelly Ann* • M Emmet Walsh *Sheriff Bob* • Adam Baldwin *Bobby* ■ *Dir* Duane Clark • *Scr* Randall Fontana

Bitter Moon ★★★ 18

Drama 1992 · Fr/UK · Colour · 133mins

Roman Polanski's slickly told psychological drama – set on board a

U = SUITABLE FOR ALL Uc = SUITABLE FOR ALL, ESPECIALLY FOR YOUNG CHILDREN (VIDEO ONLY) PG = PARENTAL GUIDANCE

liner – tries to make sexual sadism into a metaphor for human relationships. Innocents Hugh Grant and Kristin Scott Thomas become entangled in the fantasies of paralysed writer Peter Coyote and Emmanuelle Seigner (Polanski's wife). It should have been played as a Buñuel-esque comedy, but it's no laughing matter, and ponderous solemnity finally makes it seem like a psychiatric casebook of the kind only Polanski could love. TH. Contains violence, swearing, sex scenes, nudity. [video] DVD

Peter Coyote *Oscar* • Emmanuelle Seigner *Mimi* • Hugh Grant *Nigel Dobson* • Kristin Scott Thomas *Fiona Dobson* • Victor Bannerjee [Victor Banerjee] *Mr Singh* • Sophie Patel *Amrita* • Patrick Albenque *Steward* • Stockard Channing *Beverly* ■ *Dir* Roman Polanski • *Scr* Roman Polanski, Gérard Brach, John Brownjohn, from the novel *Lunes de Fiel* by Pascal Bruckner

Bitter Rice ★★★

Drama 1949 · It · BW · 107mins

This Italian film about a woman (Silvana Mangano) who comes from the city each year to labour in the rice fields of the Po valley and falls in love with a macho petty villain (Vittorio Gassman), who is planning to steal the crop, caused a sensation in its day. The reason was not, however, the Academy Award-nominated original story, but the presence of the then 19-year-old, voluptuous beauty Mangano, clad in skimpy shorts and emanating sexuality from every pore. The story is no longer original, but the steamy eroticism is intact. RK. In Italian with English subtitles.

Silvana Mangano *Silvana* • Doris Dowling *Francesca* • Vittorio Gassman *Walter* • Raf Vallone *Marco* • Checco Rissone *Aristide* • Nico Pepe *Beppe* • Adriana Sivieri *Celeste* • Lia Croelli *Amelia* ■ *Dir* Giuseppe De Santis • *Scr* Giuseppe De Santis, Carlo Lizzani, Gianni Puccini, from a story by Giuseppe De Santis, Carlo Lizzani

Bitter Springs ★★★ U

Period adventure
1950 · Aus/UK · BW · 88mins

Dismissed by many critics as a mere outback western, this is a typical Ealing attempt to humanise a pressing social problem. In this case, it's the relationship between Australia's white and Aboriginal populations. There is an adventure element to the clash over water rights between pioneer Chips Rafferty and tribesman Henry Murdoch. However, while the action is set in the early 20th century, it has an obvious contemporary resonance – right down to the uncomfortable truce. Tommy Trinder is the unlikely star. DP

Tommy Trinder *Tommy* • Chips Rafferty *Wally King* • Gordon Jackson *Mac* • Jean Blue *Ma King* • Charles "Bud" Tingwell [Charles Tingwell] *John King* • Nonnie Piper *Emma King* • Nicky Yardley *Charlie* • Michael Pate *Trooper* ■ *Dir* Ralph Smart • *Scr* WP Lipscomb, Monja Danischewsky, from a story by Ralph Smart • *Producer* Michael Balcon

Bitter Suite ★★

Romantic comedy
2000 · US/Ger · Colour · 91mins

Nastassja Kinski and Timothy Dalton don't have great track records when it comes to comedy, and this uninspired TV holiday romance doesn't improve the situation. It's loathe at first sight when Kinski's humourless scientist and Dalton's pernickety cook discover they've double booked a beach house. The direction is determinedly sunny, but there's a real desperation about some of the slapstick set pieces. DP. Contains swearing.

Nastassja Kinski *Julia* • Timothy Dalton *Matt* • Kevin Zegers *Thomas* • Cameron Finley *Max* • Billy Kay *Lewis* ■ *Dir* Sharon von Wietersheim • *Scr* Eric Tuchman

Bitter Sweet ★★

Operetta 1933 · UK · BW · 94mins

Produced, directed and partly written by Herbert Wilcox from Noël Coward's operetta, and starring his future wife Anna Neagle, this wistful period piece recounts the tale of a girl who elopes with her music teacher to 1870s Vienna. They live in happy poverty until tragedy strikes – but the movie's message is optimistically romantic. The Belgian actor Fernand Gravey, billed as "Graavey" for pronunciation reasons and later to make a Hollywood career as Gravet, made his English-speaking film debut as the lover. MGM remade it as a ludicrously sumptuous vehicle for Jeanette MacDonald and Nelson Eddy in 1940. RK

Anna Neagle *Sari Linden* • Fernand Graavey [Fernand Gravet] *Carl Linden* • Esme Percy *Hugh Devon* • Clifford Heatherley *Herr Schlick* • Ivy St Helier *Manon La Crevette* • Miles Mander *Captain August Lutte* • Pat Paterson *Dolly* ■ *Dir* Herbert Wilcox • *Scr* Herbert Wilcox, Lydia Hayward, Monckton Hoffe, from the operetta by Noël Coward

Bitter Sweet ★★★ U

Operetta 1940 · US · Colour · 93mins

One of the greatest of Noël Coward's scores, lavishly redone by MGM in the heart of their golden era. Deciding to photograph in sumptuous and expensive three-strip Technicolor was a clear indication of how highly studio boss Louis B Mayer prized his team of songbirds (not even Garbo rated colour), the legendary "Iron Butterfly" Jeanette MacDonald and her partner, the now-almost-unwatchable Nelson Eddy, but the songs are fabulous. TS

Jeanette MacDonald *Sarah Millick* • Nelson Eddy *Carl Linden* • George Sanders *Baron Von Tranisch* • Ian Hunter *Lord Shayne* • Felix Bressart *Max* • Edward Ashley *Harry Daventry* • Lynne Carver *Dolly* • Diana Lewis *Jane* ■ *Dir* WS Van Dyke II [WS Van Dyke] • *Scr* Lesser Samuels, from the operetta by Noël Coward

The Bitter Tea of General Yen ★★★★ PG

Drama 1933 · US · BW · 90mins

This genuinely exotic oddity is superbly performed by stars Barbara Stanwyck and the Swedish actor Nils Asther, and magnificently directed by a young Frank Capra. The first film ever to play the famous Radio City Music Hall, New York, this deeply sensuous movie was banned throughout the UK and the Commonwealth for dealing so blatantly with the then taboo subject of miscegenation. Stanwyck is magnificent, and the final close-up of her face deserves to be as well known in cinema annals as the similar shot of Garbo at the end of *Queen Christina*. Sensual and disturbing, this film is a revelation. TS [video]

Barbara Stanwyck *Megan Davis* • Nils Asther *General Yen* • Gavin Gordon *Dr Robert Strike* • Lucien Littlefield *Mr Jackson* • Toshia Mori *Mah-Li* • Richard Loo *Captain Li* • Clara Blandick *Mrs Jackson* • Walter Connolly *Jones* ■ *Dir* Frank Capra • *Scr* Edward Paramore, from the novel by Grace Zaring Stone • *Editor* Edward Curtiss

The Bitter Tears of Petra von Kant ★★★★ 15

Melodrama 1972 · W Ger · Colour · 118mins

Inspired by both his own experiences as a gay man and Joseph L Mankiewicz's *All about Eve*, this is Rainer Werner Fassbinder's tribute to the Hollywood "woman's picture". Petra von Kant (Margit Carstensen) is the fashion designer who embarks on a stormy lesbian affair with her model Hanna Schygulla. Fassbinder shows the classic relationship issues of dominance, submission and jealousy are just as prevalent in homosexual affairs as straight ones. The production is heavily stylised but such is the elegance of the gliding camerawork and the symbolic kitsch of the furnishings that the action never feels stagey. DP. In German with English subtitles. [video]

Margit Carstensen *Petra von Kant* • Hanna Schygulla *Karin Thimm* • Irm Hermann *Marlene* • Katrin Schaake *Sidonie von Grasenabb* • Eva Mattes *Gabriele von Kant* • Gisela Fackeldey *Valerie von Kant* ■ *Dir/Scr* Rainer Werner Fassbinder • *Cinematographer* Michael Ballhaus

Bitter Victory ★★★

Second World War drama
1957 · Fr/US · BW · 101mins

In this taut and fraught war drama, Richard Burton and Curt Jurgens lead an assault on Rommel's HQ. Jurgens cracks up under the strain, and tries to kill Burton. Everything stems from an affair Burton had with Jurgens's wife. The picture veers from realism to surrealism (Jurgens watching a scorpion crawling over Burton) and then to overblown melodrama. Jurgens is an impressive fraudulent hero and Burton comes across as a sort of TE Lawrence figure, the neurotic scholar-soldier. It was filmed in Libya and heavily cut for American release. AT

Richard Burton *Captain Leith* • Curt Jurgens *Major Brand* • Ruth Roman *Mrs Brand* • Raymond Pellegrin *Makron* • Anthony Bushell *General Paterson* • Alfred Burke *Lt Col Callander* • Christopher Lee *Sergeant Barney* ■ *Dir* Nicholas Ray • *Scr* Rene Hardy, Nicholas Ray, Gavin Lambert, from the novel by Rene Hardy

Bittersweet Love ★★

Drama 1976 · US · Colour · 90mins

Meredith Baxter and Scott Hylands fall in love. She becomes pregnant. Then they discover they're half-siblings as a result of the one-night stand of her mother (Lana Turner) and his father (Robert Lansing) who are married, respectively, to Robert Alda and Celeste Holm. Starting from a not uninteresting idea, this degenerates into an endless debate about whether Baxter should have an abortion. RK

Lana Turner *Claire* • Robert Lansing *Howard* • Celeste Holm *Marian* • Robert Alda *Ben* • Meredith Baxter Birney [Meredith Baxter] *Patricia* • Scott Hylands *Michael* • Gail Strickland *Roz* ■ *Dir* David Miller • *Scr* Adrian Morrall, DA Kellogg

Black ★★★★ 12

Drama 2004 · Ind · Colour · 124mins

Amitabh Bachchan plays the dedicated mentor who attempts to teach the blind and deaf Rani Mukherji. By encouraging, coaxing and even bullying the intelligent, determined girl, he succeeds, but Bachchan's own life begins to change when he is diagnosed with Alzheimer's disease. As he comes to rely on his former student, the pair form a deep bond. The camaraderie between the two central characters is convincing, and Sanjay Leela Bhansali's meticulously crafted film captures the determination of the human spirit with understated elegance. OA. In Hindi with English subtitles. DVD

Amitabh Bachchan *Debraj Sahai* • Rani Mukherjee [Rani Mukherji] *Michelle McNally* • Ayesha Kapoor *Young Michelle McNally* • Shernaz Patel *Catherine McNally* • Dhritiman Chaterji [Dhritiman Chatterjee] *Paul McNally* • Nandana Sen *Sara McNally* ■ *Dir* Sanjay Leela Bhansali • *Scr* Bhavani Iyer, Prakash Kapadia

The Black Abbot ★

Crime comedy thriller
1934 · UK · BW · 56mins

This low-budget programme filler hurtles through a pot-holed plot with little regard for character development or cinematic invention. Richard Cooper struggles to convince as the nobleman who proves more than a match for his kidnapper John Stuart. Director George A Cooper does little more than point the camera at the action, which is staged on as few sets as possible to keep the costs down. DP

John Stuart *Frank Brooks* • Judy Kelly *Sylvia Hillcrest* • Richard Cooper *Lord Jerry Pilkdown* • Ben Welden *Charlie Marsh* • Drusilla Wills *Mary Hillcrest* • Edgar Norfolk *Brian Heslewood* • Farren Souter *John Hillcrest* • Cyril Smith *Alf Higgins* • John Turnbull *Inspector Lockwood* ■ *Dir* George A Cooper • *Scr* H Fowler Mear, from the novel *The Grange Mystery* by Phillip Godfrey

Black and White ★★ 15

Police thriller 1998 · US · Colour · 93mins

Gina Gershon's hard-nosed amorality is the main reason for watching this otherwise routine police thriller. Bristling with attitude and allure, she's installed as the prime suspect for a string of low-life murders by Internal Affairs investigator Ron Silver. But her rookie partner and new lover, Rory Cochrane, is convinced that a tyre track at the scene of the latest slaying will lead elsewhere. DP DVD

Gina Gershon *Nora Hugosian* • Rory Cochrane *Chris O'Brien* • Ron Silver *Simon Herzel* • Alison Eastwood *Lynn Dombrowsky* • Ross Partridge *Michael Clemence* ■ *Dir* Yuri Zeltser • *Scr* Yuri Zeltser, Leon Zeltser

Black and White ★★★ 18

Drama 1999 · US · Colour · 95mins

A group of affluent white teens obsessed with hip-hop culture are at the heart of James Toback's provocative look at race relations in contemporary America. A web of tenuously connected storylines covers everything from blackmail to documentary film-making and there's an eclectic cast that includes Robert Downey Jr, Claudia Schiffer, boxer Mike Tyson, and Oliver "Power" Grant (from Wu-Tang Clan), as a thug trying to go legit as a rap music producer. The largely improvised script gives the film a raw energy at the expense of a cohesive narrative. Tyson, portraying himself, gives a performance that's funny and surprisingly wise. ST [video] DVD

Robert Downey Jr *Terry* • Brooke Shields *Sam* • Stacy Edwards *Sheila King* • Allan Houston *Dean* • Scott Caan *Scotty* • Gaby Hoffman [Gaby Hoffmann] *Raven* • Kidada Jones *Jesse* • Jared Leto *Casey* • Marla Maples *Muffy* • Power [Oliver "Power" Grant] *Rich Bower* • Claudia Schiffer *Greta* • Mike Tyson ■ *Dir/Scr* James Toback

Black and White ★★ 15

Historical drama
2002 · Aus/UK/Swe · Colour · 97mins

The trial of Max Stuart, the Aborigine accused of murdering a nine year-old girl in the South Australian resort of Ceduna in December 1958, proved a turning point in the career of newspaperman Rupert Murdoch. But, despite its care and muted sense of outrage, Craig Lahiff's re-creation never captures the significance of the case. Robert Carlyle lacks conviction as the Adelaide lawyer duelling with crown prosecutor Charles Dance, while Kerry Fox is wasted as his assistant. DP. Contains swearing, violence. [video] DVD

Robert Carlyle *David O'Sullivan* • Charles Dance *Roderic Chamberlain* • Kerry Fox *Helen Devaney* • Colin Friels *Father Tom Dixon* • Ben Mendelsohn *Rupert Murdoch* • David Ngoombujarra *Max Stuart* ■ *Dir* Craig Lahiff • *Scr* Louis Nowra

B

Black and White in Color ★★★

First World War satire
1976 · Fr/Iv C/Swi · Colour · 91mins

Set in a remote trading post in a French colony in West Africa on the outbreak of the First World War, this co-production deals with a group of French colonists, who mobilise the natives to attack a German fort. A rather specious satire on colonialism, it certainly has many amusing moments, but most of the humour is largely dependent on racist and sexist stereotypes. The debut feature of former TV-commercials director Jean-Jacques Annaud, it won the Oscar for the best foreign film in a bad year. RB. In French with English subtitles.

Jean Carmet *Sergeant Bosselet* • Jacques Dufilho *Paul Rechampot* • Catherine Rouvel *Marinette* • Jacques Spiesser *Hubert Fresnoy* • Dora Doll *Maryvonne* • Maurice Barrier *Caprice* • Claude Legros *Jacques Rechampot* • Jacques Monnet *Père Simon* ■ *Dir* Jean-Jacques Annaud • *Scr* Georges Conchon, Jean-Jacques Annaud

Black Angel ★★

Film noir 1946 · US · BW · 80mins

Dan Duryea stars in this darkish thriller as a songwriter whose wife is strangled, presenting him with any number of suspects. It turns out she had been blackmailing someone, and then... well, it gets a little too complicated for its own good. Duryea's profession as a tunesmith is merely an excuse to cram in some musical sequences with June Vincent, set mainly in Peter Lorre's nightclub. The film is anonymously directed by Roy William Neill, and Duryea doesn't really have leading man appeal. AT

Dan Duryea *Martin Blair* • June Vincent *Catherine* • Peter Lorre *Marko* • Broderick Crawford *Captain Flood* • Wallace Ford *Joe* • Hobart Cavanaugh *Jake* • Constance Dowling *Marvis Marlowe* • Freddie Steele *Lucky* ■ *Dir* Roy William Neill • *Scr* Roy Chanslor, from a novel by Cornell Woolrich

The Black Arrow ★★ U

Historical adventure 1948 · US · BW · 75mins

There's trouble brewing in Ye Olde House of York, as Louis Hayward discovers when he returns from the War of the Roses. Uncle George Macready has seized power, hacking off many heads in the process, including that of Hayward's father. Loosely based (they used the title) on Robert Louis Stevenson's novel, it's moderately entertaining, with Hayward looking fetching in shining armour, behaving with the utmost chivalry and cooing over demure Janet Blair. AT

Louis Hayward *Richard Shelton* • Janet Blair *Joanna Sedley* • George Macready *Sir Daniel Brackley* • Edgar Buchanan *Lawless* • Lowell Gilmore *Duke of Gloucester* • Russell Hicks *Sir Harry Shelton* ■ *Dir* Gordon Douglas • *Scr* Richard Schayer, David P Sheppard, Thomas Seller, from the novel by Robert Louis Stevenson

Black Bart ★★ U

Western 1948 · US · Colour · 80mins

Universal combines its exotic dancing cycle with a standard western plot and does little justice to two fascinating historical figures. Yvonne De Carlo is the legendary dancer Lola Montez who tries to reform Dan Duryea's robber, Black Bart. De Carlo looks great in Technicolor (and has two flamenco numbers) while Duryea exhibits roguish charm as the highwayman who in reality never met Montez. The script was recycled in 1967 for *The Ride to Hangman's Tree.* AE

Yvonne De Carlo *Lola Montez* • Dan Duryea *Charles E Boles/Black Bart* • Jeffrey Lynn *Lance Hardeen* • Percy Kilbride *Jersey Brady* • Lloyd Gough *Sheriff Gordon* ■ *Dir* George Sherman • *Scr* Luci Ward, Jack Natteford, William Bowers, from a story by Luci Ward, Jack Natteford

Black Beauty ★★ U

Drama 1933 · US · BW · 47mins

This version of Anna Sewell's famous horsey tale is a very average low-budgeter, competently directed by studio hack Phil Rosen, with former silent star Esther Ralston topping a largely forgettable cast. The horse sequences may look vaguely familiar, since they went into the studio stock library and used material featured in many other films of that time. TS

Esther Ralston *Leila Lambert* • Alexander Kirkland *Henry Cameron* • Hale Hamilton *Bledsoe* • Gavin Gordon *Captain Jordan* • Don Alvarado *Renaldo* • George Walsh *Junk man* ■ *Dir* Phil Rosen • *Scr* Charles Logue, from the novel by Anna Sewell

Black Beauty ★★ U

Drama 1946 · US · BW · 73mins

An early score from ace composer Dimitri Tiomkin, best known for *Giant* and *The Alamo*, distinguishes this pallid version of Anna Sewell's equine classic. Although this is set in England, none of the cast seriously modify their Yank accents. Ingénue Mona Freeman would appear in many horse operas later on, but is perhaps best remembered as Miriam Wilkins in the very 1940s trilogy *Dear Ruth*. A moderate low-budget film, drably directed by Polish expatriate Max Nosseck (*Dillinger*). TS

Mona Freeman *Anne Wendon* • Richard Denning *Bill Dixon* • Evelyn Ankers *Evelyn Carrington* • Charles Evans *Squire Wendon* • JM Kerrigan *John* • Moyna MacGill *Mrs Blake* • Terry Kilburn *Joe* • Tom Dillon [Thomas P Dillon] *Skinner* ■ *Dir* Max Nosseck • *Scr* Lillie Hayward, Agnes Christine Johnston, from the novel by Anna Sewell

Black Beauty ★★ PG

Drama
1971 · UK/W Ger/Sp · Colour · 101mins

This version of Anna Sewell's classic children's story doesn't really hit the mark, despite starring the winsome Mark Lester. Director James Hill obviously knows how to work with animals, having made both *Born Free* and *The Belstone Fox*, but his talent couldn't save this muddled and undistinguished Euro-pudding, produced at German and Spanish studios with a pan-European cast, but made in English. SG DVD

Mark Lester (2) *Joe* • Walter Slezak *Hackenschmidt* • Peter Lee Lawrence *Gervaise* • Ursula Glas *Marie* • Patrick Mower *Sam Greene* • John Nettleton *Sir William* • Maria Rohm *Anne* • Eddie Golden *Evans* ■ *Dir* James Hill • *Scr* Wolf Mankowitz, from the novel by Anna Sewell

Black Beauty ★★★ U

Drama 1994 · UK/US · Colour · 84mins

This glossy reworking of Anna Sewell's much-filmed classic marked the directorial debut of Caroline Thompson, a writer whose successes include *Edward Scissorhands* and *The Addams Family*. The horses look superb and Beauty even sounds convincing, thanks to Alan Cumming's clever voiceover. The largely British cast does its bit, too, with Sean Bean and David Thewlis revealing previously unsuspected soft centres, but the acting honours go to Peter Cook and Eleanor Bron, as Lord and Lady Wexmire. DP DVD

Sean Bean *Farmer Grey* • David Thewlis *Jerry Barker* • Jim Carter *John Manly* • Peter Davison *Squire Gordon* • Alun Armstrong *Reuben Smith* • John McEnery *Mr York* • Eleanor Bron *Lady Wexmire* • Peter Cook *Lord Wexmire* • Andrew Knott *Joe Green* • Alan Cumming *Voice of Black Beauty* ■ *Dir* Caroline Thompson • *Scr* Caroline Thompson, from the novel by Anna Sewell

Black Belt Jones ★★ 18

Martial arts crime thriller
1974 · US · Colour · 80mins

Having pulled off a major box office coup with *Enter the Dragon*, producers Fred Weintraub and Paul Heller were denied the services of their recently deceased star, Bruce Lee. So they turned to karate champion Jim Kelly for this rollicking (albeit overplotted) mixture of blaxploitation and kung fu. Kelly teams up with Scatman Crothers and his daughter (Gloria Hendry) to prevent property developer Malik Carter and mobster Andre Phillipe from taking over their rundown martial arts school. Robert Wall's fight sequences are slickly choreographed. A popular sequel followed in 1978. DP

Jim Kelly *Black Belt Jones* • Gloria Hendry *Sydney* • Scatman Crothers *Pop* • Alan Weeks *Tippy* • Eric Laneuville *Quincy* • Andre Philippe *Don Steffano* • Vincent Barbi *Big Tuna* • Nate Esformes *Roberts* ■ *Dir* Robert Clouse • *Scr* Oscar Williams, from a story by Alex Rose, Fred Weintraub • *Choreographer* Robert Wall

The Black Bird ★★★★

Silent crime drama 1926 · US · BW

In seedy Limehouse, a master criminal known as the Black Bird covers his crimes by assuming the identity of his disabled "twin" and uses a charity mission house as an elaborate front. Thanks to a brilliant performance by Lon Chaney, kept in a deliberate and darkly fantastic key by director Tod Browning, a preposterous premise is transformed into convincing entertainment. There's a nasty sting in the tall tale and the plot's essential irrationalities are masked by Browning's masterful direction, as he distracts viewer attention by remaining on the dangerous side of farce. An exaggerated vision of the shadowy underworld from two seminal masters of silent shock. AJ

Lon Chaney *The Blackbird/The Bishop of Limehouse* • Owen Moore *West End Bertie* • Renée Adorée *Fifi* • Doris Lloyd *Limehouse Polly* • Andy MacLennan *The Shadow* • William Weston *Red* • Eric Mayne *Sightseer* • Sidney Bracey *Bertie's No 1 Man* • Ernie S Adams *Bertie's No 2 Man* ■ *Dir* Tod Browning • *Scr* Waldemar Young, from the story *The Mockingbird* by Tod Browning

The Black Bird ★★

Detective spoof 1975 · US · Colour · 97mins

This send-up of *The Maltese Falcon* has Sam Spade Jr (George Segal) discovering the priceless statuette among his dad's old files. It's a nice idea, thoroughly botched – it simply isn't funny, tense or even nostalgic, despite appearances from the original's Lee Patrick and Elisha Cook Jr. There is, however, one clever in-joke. Anxious to raise some money for the falcon, Segal takes it to a pawnbroker named Kerkorian, who offers him a paltry $15. This is a reference to Kirk Kerkorian, who owned MGM at the time and sold off its most famous props. AT

George Segal *Sam Spade Jr* • Stéphane Audran *Anna Kemidov* • Lionel Stander *Gordon Andre Jackson Immerman* • Lee Patrick *Effie* • Elisha Cook Jr *Wilmer* • Felix Silla *Litvak* • Signe Hasso *Dr Crippen* • John Abbot *DuQuai* • Howard Jeffrey *Kerkorian* ■ *Dir* David Giler • *Scr* David Giler, from a story by Don M Mankiewicz, Gordon Cotler, from characters created by Dashiell Hammett

Black Caesar ★★★ 18

Blaxploitation crime drama
1973 · US · Colour · 89mins

Tried and tested gangster themes from *Little Caesar* and *Scarface* are updated using elements of the blaxploitation genre of the early 1970s in B-movie maestro Larry Cohen's funky inner-city thriller. Former American football star Fred Williamson gives one of his best performances as the shoeshine boy who rises through the mobster ranks to become Harlem's crime lord. Violent heroics clash with relative morality, but in its quieter moments this spirited action pic offers tender moments brimming with emotional truth. Williamson and Cohen returned for the sequel *Hell Up in Harlem*. AJ. Contains swearing, violence, nudity. DVD

Fred Williamson *Tommy Gibbs* • Phillip Roye *Joe Washington* • Gloria Hendry *Helen* • Julius W Harris [Julius Harris] *Mr Gibbs* • Val Avery *Cardoza* • Minnie Gentry *Mama Gibbs* • Art Lund *John McKinney* • D'Urville Martin *Reverend Rufus* ■ *Dir/Scr* Larry Cohen

The Black Castle ★★

Gothic horror 1952 · US · BW · 81mins

Swashbuckling adventurer Richard Greene believes that sinister Austrian count Stephen MacNally has captured and killed two of his friends in this half-hearted *Most Dangerous Game* rerun. So it's off to the count's sinister castle where he braves secret passageways, torture chambers, prowling leopards and a moat filled with alligators before falling in love with the count's unhappy wife (Rita Corday). Boris Karloff does little but stand around looking ominous as the imprisoned doctor in this tame, dull Gothic horror marking the feature debut of Nathan Juran. AJ

Richard Greene *Sir Ronald Burton/Richard Beckett* • Boris Karloff *Dr Meissen* • Stephen McNally *Count Karl von Bruno* • Rita Corday *Countess Elga von Bruno* • Lon Chaney Jr *Gargon* • Michael Pate *Count Ernst von Melcher* ■ *Dir* Nathan Juran • *Scr* Jerry Sackheim

The Black Cat ★★★★★ 15

Horror 1934 · US · BW · 62mins

One of the landmark horror films of the 1930s, this was the first feature to double bill Boris Karloff and Bela Lugosi, both of whom were given reverential sole surname billing on the credits. Karloff is the satanist playing chess with doctor Lugosi for innocent lives. More Aleister Crowley than the Edgar Allan Poe story it's actually based on, it's a triumph of bizarre Art Deco sets, innovative style, classical music and eerie tension. This timeless classic is superbly directed by Edgar G Ulmer before his career lurched into the quickie arena. Lugosi has never been so sympathetic or Karloff so evil and the heady finale is incredibly potent stuff for the era. AJ

Karloff [Boris Karloff] *Hjalmar Poelzig* • Bela Lugosi *Dr Vitus Verdegast* • David Manners *Peter Allison* • Jacqueline Wells [Julie Bishop] *Joan Allison* • Lucille Lund *Karen* • Egon Brecher *Majordomo* • Henry Armetta *Sergeant* • Albert Conti *Lieutenant* ■ *Dir* Edgar G Ulmer • *Scr* Edgar G Ulmer, Peter Ruric, from the story by Edgar Allan Poe • *Cinematographer* John J Mescall • *Art Director* Charles D Hall

The Black Cat ★★

Horror 1941 · US · BW · 70mins

It's sad to see such great horror icons as Bela Lugosi, Basil Rathbone and Gale Sondergaard in this unremarkable creepie which is based on a story by Edgar Allan Poe. Real-estate promoter Broderick Crawford and dizzy antiques collector Hugh Herbert gate-crash the reading of a will. To make up for the film's simple-mindedness, the old dark house atmosphere is elegantly photographed by Stanley Cortez. Alan Ladd makes a brief appearance. TH

Basil Rathbone *Hartley* • Hugh Herbert *Mr Penny* • Broderick Crawford *Hubert Smith* • Bela Lugosi *Eduardo* • Gale Sondergaard *Abigail Doone* • Anne Gwynne *Elaine Winslow*

• Gladys Cooper *Myrna Hartley* • Alan Ladd *Richard Hartley* ■ *Dir* Albert S Rogell • *Scr* Robert Lees, Fred Rinaldo, Eric Taylor, Robert Neville, from the story by Edgar Allan Poe

The Black Cat ★★ 18

Horror 1981 · It/UK · Colour · 88mins

This is a lopsided version of the classic Edgar Allan Poe tale, shot through with Italian director Lucio Fulci's trademark gore theatrics. Medium Patrick Magee tries to contact dead people via electrical equipment, American photographer Mimsy Farmer snaps murder victims, and Scotland Yard detective David Warbeck investigates local disappearances, all while supernatural forces are unleashed by a cat's death. The best thing about this oddly atmospheric chiller is the terrific score by Pino Donaggio. AJ [video] DVD

Patrick Magee *Robert Miles* • Mimsy Farmer *Jill Travers* • David Warbeck *Inspector Gorley* • Dagmar Lassander *Mrs Grayson* • Daniela Dorio *Maureen* ■ *Dir* Lucio Fulci • *Scr* Lucio Fulci, Biagio Proietti, from a story by Biagio Proietti, from a short story by Edgar Allan Poe

Black Cat, White Cat ★★★★ 15

Comedy drama
1998 · Fr/Ger/Ser · Colour · 123mins

Vowing to quit after the savage press reception for his Cannes Palme d'Or winner *Underground*, director Emir Kusturica returned with this riotous blend of crime, comedy and romance. Originally planned as a documentary about gypsy musicians, this is a scattershot affair, with offbeat hilarity competing with coarse slapstick. The network of fictional relationships between the various Romany families takes time to establish but, once all are assembled for a wedding, this gleeful romp goes into overdrive. Kusturica's celebration of gypsy culture is far from subtle but, thanks to exuberant storytelling and a magnificent non-professional cast, it is irresistible. DP. In Serbo-Croat, German and Romany with English subtitles. Contains swearing and drug abuse. [video]

Bajram Severdzan *Matko Destanov* • Srdjan Todorovic *Dadan Karambolo* • Florijan Ajdini *Zare Destanov* • Salija Ibraimova *Afrodita Karambolo, "Ladybird"* • Jasar Destani *Grga Veliki* • Sabri Sulejmani *Grga Pitic* ■ *Dir* Emir Kusturica • *Scr* Gordan Mihic, Emir Kusturica

The Black Cauldron ★★★ U

Animated adventure
1985 · US · Colour · 78mins

The most distinguished element of this Disney animation, from a Tolkien-like series by Lloyd Alexander, is the solemn intonation of narrator John Huston. Otherwise, it's standard stuff about likeable teenagers (of course!) trying to stop the Horned King from using a magic cauldron to raise an Army of the Dead. As swords-and-sorcery, it's potboiling stuff. TH [video] DVD

John Huston *Narrator* • Grant Bardsley *Taran* • Susan Sheridan *Princess Eilonwy* • Freddie Jones *Dallben* • Nigel Hawthorne *Fflewddur* • Arthur Malet *King Eidilleg* • John Byner *Gurgi/Doli* • John Hurt *Horned King* ■ *Dir* Ted Berman, Richard Rich • *Scr* David Jonas, Vance Gerry, Ted Berman, Richard Rich, Al Wilson, Roy Morita, Peter Young, Art Stevens, Joe Hale, from the book series *The Chronicles of Prydain* by Lloyd Alexander

Black Christmas ★★★★ 18

Horror 1974 · Can · Colour · 97mins

An under-rated horror that pre-dated the *Halloween* cycle and practically established the genre's hard-and-fast rules. A maniac is on the loose in a closed-for-Christmas girls' boarding school. Director Bob Clark's neat little chiller scores scares thanks to stylish visuals, fiendishly inventive slaughter and unexpected twists. Promoted at the time with the wicked tag line "If this picture doesn't make your skin crawl, it's on too tight!", the film also features above-average performances from Olivia Hussey and Margot Kidder. AJ. Contains swearing. [video] DVD

Olivia Hussey *Jess* • Keir Dullea *Peter* • Margot Kidder *Barb* • Andrea Martin *Phyl* • John Saxon *Lieutenant Fuller* • Marian Waldman *Mrs Mac* • Art Hindle *Chris* • Lynne Griffin *Clare Harrison* • James Edmond *Mr Harrison* ■ *Dir* Bob Clark • *Scr* Roy Moore

Black Dog ★★★ 12

Action road movie
1998 · US · Colour · 84mins

Movie-goers weren't quite ready for a *Dukes of Hazzard* revival, and, as a result, this similarly themed Patrick Swayze vehicle was waved into the straight-to-video lane in Britain. It's a shame, because this action drama is entertaining enough in a rough-hewn kind of way. Swayze is the ex-convict trucker caught up in a feud with a religious zealot (Meat Loaf) after he is duped into delivering a cargo of stolen weapons. It's not subtle, but the vehicular destruction will bring a nostalgic tear to the eyes of *Smokey and the Bandit* fans. JF. Contains some swearing and violence. [video]

Patrick Swayze *Jack Crews* • Randy Travis *Earl* • Meat Loaf *Red* • Gabriel Casseus *Sonny* • Brian Vincent *Wes* • Brenda Strong *Melanie* • Graham Beckel *Cutler* • Charles Dutton [Charles S Dutton] *Agent Ford* ■ *Dir* Kevin Hooks • *Scr* William Mickelberry, Dan Vining

Black Eagle ★★★ 15

Martial arts thriller
1988 · US · Colour · 89mins

Malta is the location for this Jean-Claude Van Damme martial arts thriller. Remember the Cold War? CIA and KGB agents hurtling around the globe in pursuit of top secret weapons? Well, there is nothing hush-hush about this action fest, in which the "Muscles from Brussels" plays a Soviet killing machine intent on seizing a laser device lost in a plane crash, before high-kicking hero Sho Kosugi can lay his mitts on it. Directed with maximum noise by Eric Karson. DP. Contains swearing, violence. [video] DVD

Sho Kosugi *Ken Tani* • Jean-Claude Van Damme *Andrei* • Doran Clark *Patricia Parker* • Vladimir Skomarovsky *Vladimir Klimenko* • Bruce French *Father Joseph Bedelia* • Dorota Puzio *Natasha* • William Bassett *Dean Rickert* ■ *Dir* Eric Karson • *Scr* AE Peters, Michael Gonzales, from a story by Shimon Arama

Black Eyes ★★

Drama 1939 · UK · BW · 75mins

Creaking more with each frame, this only passable melodrama concerns a father who is forced to lead a double life to prevent his proud daughter from discovering that, rather than being a high-flying tycoon, he is merely a waiter at a posh restaurant. Frank Capra told a similar story with considerably more charm in *Lady for a Day* and, try as he might, Otto Kruger is too stuffy to be sympathetic. DP

Otto Kruger *Petroff* • Mary Maguire *Tania* • Walter Rilla *Roudine* • John Wood *Karlo* • Marie Wright *Miss Brown* ■ *Dir* Herbert Brenon • *Scr* Dudley Leslie

The Black Fox ★★★

Documentary 1962 · US · BW · 89mins

The winner of the Oscar for best documentary feature, this is a fascinating exploration of the historical factors that led to the rise (and fall) of Adolf Hitler. Narrated by Marlene Dietrich (who refused Nazi overtures to make a triumphant return to the Fatherland), Louis Clyde Stoumen's film resorts to some overly familiar newsreel footage. But it also offers some perceptive insights into the general European situation and the nature of the German people, who so readily accepted a fascist dictatorship. Less successful are the references to Goethe's retelling of the medieval fable of *Reynard the Fox*. DP

Marlene Dietrich *Narrator* ■ *Dir* Louis Clyde Stoumen • *Scr* Louis Clyde Stouman

Black Fury ★★

Drama based on a true story
1935 · US · BW · 93mins

A committed social melodrama torn, as Warner Bros was wont to say, from the headlines, about a mine worker who falls victim to corrupt employers and racketeers. Paul Muni's presence guarantees some "serious" acting and serious make-up, but there are compensations, notably Michael Curtiz's characteristically pacy direction and an extraordinary full-scale underground mine built on the Warner Bros ranch. A box-office flop, it was banned in Pennsylvania where the main industry is coal mining. AT

Paul Muni *Joe Radek* • Karen Morley *Anna Novak* • William Gargan *Slim* • Barton MacLane *McGee* • John Qualen *Mike Shemanski* • J Carrol Naish *Steve Croner* • Vince Barnett *Kubanda* • Henry O'Neill *JW Hendricks* ■ *Dir* Michael Curtiz • *Scr* Abem Finkel, Carl Erickson, from the play *Bohunk* by Henry R Irving and the story *Jan Volkanik* by Judge MA Musmanno

Black Girl ★★★

Drama 1972 · US · Colour · 96mins

Lurking behind the catchpenny, blaxploitation title is a rather perceptive and thought-provoking study of foster parenting and the integration of children within a caring family unit. Louise Stubbs is the put-upon mother trying to cope with her two daughters and their new half-sister, who aspires to be a dancer and makes life intolerable in the process. Astutely directed by actor Ossie Davis, it has a ring of truth rarely achieved by other contemporary dramas commenting on the African-American experience. AJ

Brock Peters *Earl* • Leslie Uggams *Netta* • Claudia McNeil *Mu' Dear* • Louise Stubbs *Mama Rosie* • Gloria Edwards *Norma* • Loretta Greene *Ruth Ann* • Kent Martin *Herbert* • Peggy Pettit *Billie Jean* ■ *Dir* Ossie Davis • *Scr* JE Franklin, from his play

Black God, White Devil ★★★★

Drama 1964 · Bra · BW · 120mins

Glauber Rocha was one of the driving forces behind Brazilian *cinema nôvo*. Set in the 1940s and exhibiting both indigenous cultural and international filmic influences, this *sertao* western epitomises the movement's initial preoccupation with the politicisation of the peasantry. Alternately presented in long takes and montage sequences, the action follows Geraldo d'el Rey as he veers between bandit Othon Bastos and his sworn enemy Maurício de Valle. In so doing, Rocha illustrates how difficult it was for uneducated farmhands to know where to place allegiance in the struggle against the oppression of the pitiless landowners. De Valle would return in the sequel, *Antonio das Mortes* (1969). DP. In Portuguese with English subtitles.

Yona Magalhaes *Rosa* • Geraldo Del Rey *Manuel* • Othon Bastos *Sebastian* • Maurício de Valle *Antonio* • Lidio Silva *Corisco* • Sonia dos Humildes *Dada* ■ *Dir/Scr* Glauber Rocha

Black Gold ★★ U

Melodrama 1947 · US · Colour · 89mins

Named after the winner of the 1924 Kentucky Derby, this minor drama gave Anthony Quinn his first starring role as an illiterate Indian who becomes an oil tycoon and horse-racing enthusiast. Quinn's then-wife, Katherine DeMille, co-stars as the native American's well-educated spouse with "Ducky" Louie playing the Chinese boy they adopt. Harsh Cinecolor and a dreary plot emphasising tears and tolerance leaves Quinn's dynamic performance as the stand-out feature of the production. AE

Anthony Quinn *Charley Eagle* • Katherine DeMille *Sarah Eagle* • Elyse Knox *Ruth Frazer* • Kane Richmond *Stanley Lowell* • "Ducky" Louie *Davey* • Raymond Hatton *Bucky* • Thurston Hall *Colonel Caldwell* ■ *Dir* Phil Karlson • *Scr* Agnes Christine Johnston, from a story by Caryl Coleman

Black Gold ★★ U

Adventure 1963 · US · BW · 98mins

This Warner Bros drama is one of those curious pictures that was made in the interim between the decline of the B-movie and the advent of the teleplay. Philip Carey and James Best feature as buddies who go searching for oil in 1920s Oklahoma and fall out over Diane McBain. Claude Akins steals the show as a tycoon who lets the wildcatters take all the risks before staking his claim to their strike. Leslie H Martinson directs with efficiency, but little style. DP

Philip Carey *Frank McCandless* • Diane McBain *Ann Evans* • James Best *Jericho Larkin* • Fay Spain *Julie* • Claude Akins *Chick Carrington* • William Phipps *Albert Mailer* • Dub Taylor *Doc* ■ *Dir* Leslie H Martinson • *Scr* Bob Duncan, Wanda Duncan, from a story by Henry Whittington

The Black Hand ★★

Crime drama 1950 · US · BW · 90mins

A potentially fascinating study of the roots of the Mafia in turn-of-the-century New York is not helped by its odd casting and by the MGM studio gloss that makes this feature look artificial. Precisely why casting directors thought Gene Kelly should play the young Italian seeking to avenge his father's death is beyond comprehension. The Pittsburgh-Irish Kelly is quite wrong, and his earnest manner grates throughout. Richard Thorpe's not the director for this kind of material, either, and the whole seems a rare miscalculation, though Kelly devotees may find it interesting. TS

Gene Kelly *Johnny Columbo* • J Carrol Naish *Louis Lorelli* • Teresa Celli *Isabella Gomboli* • Marc Lawrence (1) *Caesar Xavier Serpi* • Frank Puglia *Carlo Sabballera* • Barry Kelley *Captain Thompson* • Mario Siletti *Benny Danetta* ■ *Dir* Richard Thorpe • *Scr* Luther Davis, from a story by Leo Townsend

Black Hawk Down ★★★ 15

War drama 2001 · US · Colour · 138mins

The fact that this noisy, gung-ho modern war movie is based on the disastrous 1993 "Battle of Mogadishu" in Somalia does not temper its flag-waving, pro-American militarism.The film's poster tagline "Leave no man behind" disguises what was a strategic American mess – in reality, 18 Americans were killed, as were hundreds of Somalis during a 15-hour firefight. It's sensitive, cool-headed and intelligent, but its call for "heroes" makes it little more than a recruitment film. AC. Contains violence and swearing. [video] DVD

Josh Hartnett *Ranger Staff Sgt Matt Eversmann* • Ewan McGregor *Ranger Spec Grimes* • Tom Sizemore *Ranger Lt Col Danny McKnight* • Eric Bana *Delta Sgt First Class "Hoot" Gibson* • William Fichtner *Delta Sgt First Class Jeff Sanderson* • Ewen Bremner *Specialist Shawn Nelson* • Sam Shepard *Maj Gen William F Garrison* • Jason Isaacs *Captain Mike Steele* • Orlando Bloom *Private First*

Class Todd Blackburn ■ Dir Ridley Scott • Scr Ken Nolan, Steve Zaillian, from a non-fiction book and articles by Mark Bowden

B

The Black Hole ★★★ PG

Science-fiction adventure
1979 · US · Colour · 97mins

It seems strange now, but there was a time in the 1970s when Disney seemed to have lost its magic touch, and this unwieldy sci-fi epic didn't really succeed in halting the decline of the period. It's actually not too bad, boasting some stunning special effects and an intriguing story about a disturbed scientist (Maximilian Schell) who is about to boldly go where no man has been before into a black hole in space. The cast is dependable, but it's a bit staid. JF DVD

Maximilian Schell *Dr Hans Reinhardt* • Anthony Perkins *Dr Alex Durant* • Robert Forster *Captain Dan Holland* • Joseph Bottoms *Lieutenant Charles Pizer* • Yvette Mimieux *Dr Kate McCrae* • Ernest Borgnine *Harry Booth* • Tommy McLoughlin *Captain STAR* ■ *Dir* Gary Nelson • *Scr* Jeb Rosebrook, Gerry Day, from a story by Bob Barbash, Richard Landau, Jeb Rosebrook • *Special Effects* Peter Ellenshaw, Art Cruickshank, Eustace Lycett, Danny Lee, Harrison Ellenshaw, Joe Hale

Black Horse Canyon ★★ U

Western 1954 · US · Colour · 81mins

Joel McCrea may be top billed in this fitfully entertaining Universal western, but his limelight is stolen by a superb wild stallion called Outlaw who won the 1955 Patsy Award of Excellence for animal actors. Here, Outlaw plays the horse that McCrea's co-stars Mari Blanchard and Mervyn Vye want to capture for breeding purposes – and that's about it as far as the plot is concerned. It's directed by Jesse Hibbs from a warm-hearted screenplay by the prolific Geoffrey Homes. TS

Joel McCrea *Del Rockwell* • Mari Blanchard *Aldia Spain* • Race Gentry *Ti* • Murvyn Vye *Jennings* • Irving Bacon *Doc* • Ewing Mitchell *Sheriff* • John Pickard *Duke* • Pilar Del Rey *Juanita* ■ *Dir* Jesse Hibbs • *Scr* Daniel Mainwaring, from the novel *The Wild Horse* by Les Savage Jr, adapted by David Lang

Black Jack ★★

Drama 1952 · US/Fr · BW · 101mins

Julien Duvivier was one of the finest exponents of the poetic realist style, which laid bare the soul of France in the 1930s. However, he never recovered his assured sense of atmosphere and place after a wartime sojourn in Hollywood. Co-scripted by Duvivier and his longtime collaborator Charles Spaak, this wearying tale of duplicity among the idle rich of the Riviera is never as frothy or intricate as the makers intend it to be. DP

George Sanders *Mike Alexander* • Patricia Roc *Ingrid* • Herbert Marshall *James* • Agnes Moorehead *Emily* • Marcel Dalio *Captain* ■ *Dir* Julien Duvivier • *Scr* Julien Duvivier, Charles Spaak

Black Jack ★★

Satirical comedy 1972 · US · Colour · 87mins

Produced by exploitation hive American International Pictures, this demented Cold War satire is a sort of poor man's *Dr Strangelove*. Georg Stanford Brown and Brandon de Wilde star as a couple of escaped peaceniks who hijack a B-52 so they can drop an atom bomb on Fort Knox. William T Naud wrote, directed, produced and edited this scattershot portrait of a nation torn apart by Vietnam fallout. However, its main significance is that it marked the last appearance of 30-year-old de Wilde, who never really capitalised on the Oscar nomination he received for the classic western, *Shane*. DP

Georg Stanford Brown *Lynch* • Brandon de Wilde *Josh* • Keenan Wynn *General Harry Gobohare* • Tim O'Connor *Senator Bob Recker* • Dick Gautier *Diver* • Robert Lansing *Major Reason* • Larry Hovis *Captain Breen* • Bernie Kopell *Penrat* ■ *Dir* William T Naud • *Scr* Dick Gautier, William T Naud, from a story by Peter Marshall, Dick Gautier, William T Naud

Black Jack ★★★ U

Adventure 1979 · UK · Colour · 109mins

This family film evokes the atmosphere of its setting brilliantly, but a real star might have made it more coherent. Burt Lancaster wanted to play the hero, but director Ken Loach's aversion to stars meant that French actor Jean Franval took the role of the 18th-century rogue. His escape from hanging – by lodging a bullet in his throat – leads to adventures with young Stephen Hirst and Louise Cooper. TH

Jean Franval *Black Jack* • Stephen Hirst *Tolly* • Andrew Bennet *Hatch* • Louise Cooper *Belle* • Packie Byrne *Dr Carmody* • John Young *Dr Hunter* • Russell Waters *Dr Jones* • Pat Wallis *Mrs Gorgandy* • William Moore *Mr Carter* ■ *Dir* Kenneth Loach [Ken Loach] • *Scr* Kenneth Loach, from the novel by Leon Garfield

Black Joy ★★

Comedy 1977 · UK · Colour · 97mins

Although Anthony Simmons's film tries to say something significant about the experience of being black in Brixton in the mid-1970s, he and co-writer Jamal Ali fail to achieve a consistent tone, as they veer between back-street realism and front-line comedy. There are a few rough-hewn gems hidden in the dialogue, but the acting is as variable as the writing, with only Norman Beaton (as a wily waster) and Trevor Thomas (as the young Guyanan he dupes) convincing throughout. DP. Contains swearing and sex scenes.

Norman Beaton *Dave King* • Trevor Thomas *Benjamin Jones* • Floella Benjamin *Miriam* • Dawn Hope *Saffra* • Oscar James *Jomo* • Paul Medford *Devon* • Shango Baku *Raastaman* ■ *Dir* Anthony Simmons • *Scr* Anthony Simmons, Jamal Ali, from the play *Dark Days and Light Nights* by Jamal Ali

The Black Knight ★★★ U

Historical drama
1954 · UK/US · Colour · 86mins

An under-rated Alan Ladd vehicle, released a year after his leading role in the classic western *Shane*. Skilled director Tay Garnett brings a fair amount of boisterous charm to this not-to-be-taken-seriously studio-bound Arthurian romp. The 1950s' Technicolor is absolutely splendid and the supporting cast of British stalwarts, such as Peter Cushing and Harry Andrews, is a joy to behold. A better script wouldn't really have helped – and doesn't really matter. TS

Alan Ladd *John* • Patricia Medina *Linet* • André Morell *Sir Ontzlake* • Harry Andrews *Earl of Yeonil* • Peter Cushing *Sir Palamides* • Anthony Bushell *King Arthur* • Laurence Naismith *Major Domo* • Patrick Troughton *King Mark* ■ *Dir* Tay Garnett • *Scr* Alec Coppel

Black Knight ★★ PG

Comedy 2001 · US · Colour · 91mins

This struggles to turn a loose version of Mark Twain's *A Connecticut Yankee in King Arthur's Court* into a suitable vehicle for comic Martin Lawrence, whose inconsistent performance doesn't help the cause. Lawrence plays an underachieving employee at on-the-skids theme park Medieval World. After falling into a moat, he is magically zapped back to a 14th-century England, that he initially fails to comprehend because "they're all such good actors". Director Gil Junger seems unable to control Lawrence's tedious cheeky-chappy persona and leaves little room for laughs, action or other characters. TH DVD

Martin Lawrence *Jamal Walker* • Marsha Thomason *Victoria* • Tom Wilkinson *Sir Knolte* • Vincent Regan *Sir Percival* • Kevin Conway *King Leo* • Jeannette Weegar *Princess Regina* ■ *Dir* Gil Junger • *Scr* Darryl J Quarles, Peter Gaulke, Gerry Swallow

The Black Legion ★★★

Crime drama 1937 · US · BW · 83mins

A young Humphrey Bogart stars as a devoted family man and factory worker who becomes hopelessly and tragically embroiled with a Ku Klux Klan-style secret society, which is dedicated to "cleansing" America of so-called foreigners. Straight from the heart of Warner Bros' social conscience cycle, the drama is grim and the moral message against intolerance strong. Basically a B-picture, it's elevated by its subject and some compelling supporting performances. RK

Humphrey Bogart *Frank Taylor* • Dick Foran *Ed Jackson* • Erin O'Brien-Moore *Ruth Taylor* • Ann Sheridan *Betty Grogan* • Robert Barrat *Brown* • Helen Flint *Pearl Davis* • Joseph Sawyer [Joe Sawyer] *Cliff Moore* • Addison Richards *Prosecuting Attorney* ■ *Dir* Archie Mayo • *Scr* Abem Finkel, William Wister Haines, from a story by Robert Lord

Black like Me ★★

Biographical drama 1964 · US · BW · 107mins

This relates the real-life experiences of white writer John Howard Griffin, who decided to pose as a black man in the South. The consequences of this and the racial discrimination that he suffers are wholly predictable. James Whitmore and the supporting cast, most notably Clifton James and Roscoe Lee Browne, try to make a slack script taut but, despite good intentions, this never convinces other than as a piece of 1960s anti-racist propaganda. TH

James Whitmore *John Finley Horton* • Clifton James *Eli Carr* • Lenka Peterson *Lucy Horton* • Roscoe Lee Browne *Christopher* • Sorrell Booke *Doctor Jackson* ■ *Dir* Carl Lerner • *Scr* Gerda Lerner, Carl Lerner, from the book by John Howard Griffin

Black Magic ★★

Swashbuckling drama
1949 · US · BW · 105mins

Orson Welles's hobby was conjuring, but no sleight of hand can disguise the ramshackle nature of this swashbuckler, one of those low-grade acting jobs he took to raise funds to make his Shakespearian films, *Macbeth* and *Othello*. He plays a notorious court magician around the time of the French Revolution, who becomes part of a plot to switch Marie Antoinette for a servant girl (both played by Nancy Guild). Ponderous rubbish, though Welles manages to be a compelling ham. TH

Orson Welles *Cagliostro* • Nancy Guild *Marie Antoinette/Lorenza* • Akim Tamiroff *Gitano* • Frank Latimore *Gilbert* • Valentina Cortesa [Valentina Cortese] *Zoraida* • Margot Grahame *Madame Dubarry* • Stephen Bekassy *DeMontagne* • Berry Kroeger *Alexandre Dumas Sr* • Gregory Gaye *Chambord* • Raymond Burr *Alexandre Dumas Jr* ■ *Dir* Gregory Ratoff • *Scr* Charles Bennett, from the novel *Joseph Balsamo* by Alexandre Dumas

Black Mama, White Mama ★★ 18

Blaxploitation action adventure
1972 · US · Colour · 81mins

The Defiant Ones changes sex and gets the blaxploitation treatment in hack Filipino director Eddie Romero's trashy action filler. Hooker Pam Grier and guerrilla fighter Margaret Markov are the chicks in chains who escape from a prison and flee disguised as nuns. This was the movie (amazingly from a story co-written by future director Jonathan Demme) that apparently convinced future black superstar Grier to become a full-time actress – so it wasn't a complete waste of everyone's time. AJ. Contains violence, swearing, nudity. DVD

Pam Grier *Lee Daniels* • Margaret Markov *Karen Brent* • Sid Haig *Ruben* • Lynn Borden *Densmore* • Zaldy Zshornack *Ernesto* • Laurie Burton *Logan* ■ *Dir* Eddie Romero • *Scr* HR Christian, from a story by Joseph Viola, Jonathan Demme

The Black Marble ★★★ 15

Romantic comedy
1980 · US · Colour · 105mins

Dognapping would hardly seem to be the stuff of riveting drama. Yet this cop thriller, taken from Joseph Wambaugh's bestseller, is a thoughtful look at the human side of police work. Transferred from the homicide department after a gruelling child murder case, burnt-out Robert Foxworth teams up with Paula Prentiss to investigate animal burglary. Strong acting takes up the trivial slack. AJ

Robert Foxworth *Sgt Valnikov* • Paula Prentiss *Sgt Natalie Zimmerman* • James Woods *Fiddler* • Harry Dean Stanton *Philo* • Barbara Babcock *Madeline Whitfield* • John Hancock *Clarence Cromwell* • Raleigh Bond *Capt Hooker* • Judy Landers *Pattie Mae* • Pat Corley *Itchy Mitch* ■ *Dir* Harold Becker • *Scr* Joseph Wambaugh, from his novel

Black Mask ★★★★ 18

Martial arts action thriller
1996 · HK · Colour · 83mins

This was the film that introduced UK audiences to Hong Kong action star Jet Li. The deliriously bonkers plot has Li as a former member of an elite group of assassins who, after radical nerve surgery, feel neither pain nor emotion. He escapes to take up a new life – as a librarian! – but is forced back into action. Director Daniel Lee takes the action sequences to mind-boggling new extremes with some jaw-dropping ultra-violence, while Li gets to showcase his dazzling physical talents. The star didn't return for the dismal 2001 sequel directed by Tsui Hark. JF. Cantonese dialogue dubbed into English. Contains violence, swearing and sex scenes. DVD

Jet Li *Tsui* • Lau Ching Wan *Shi* • Karen Mok *Tracy* • Françoise Yip *Yu Lan* • Patrick Lung-Kang *Commander Hung* ■ *Dir* Daniel Lee • *Scr* Hark Tsui, Hui Kuan, Teddy Chen, Joe Ma

Black Moon ★★★

Fantasy drama 1974 · Fr · Colour · 100mins

Beautifully photographed by Sven Nykvist, Louis Malle's first film in English is a weird, futuristic fantasy set in a countryside where symbols abound. Not all of this enigmatic movie comes off, but Malle's Wonderland is full of surprising things, including talking rats, unicorns and ex-Andy Warhol hunk Joe Dalessandro. Cathryn Harrison, Rex's granddaughter, is adequate as the Alice figure; the title refers to the time of chaos that preludes some cataclysmic change. RB

Cathryn Harrison *Lily* • Thérèse Giehse *The old lady* • Alexandra Stewart *Sister* • Joe Dallesandro *Brother* ■ *Dir* Louis Malle • *Scr* Louis Malle, Ghislain Uhry, Joyce Buñuel

Black Moon Rising ★★ 18

Action thriller 1985 · US · Colour · 94mins

Director Harley Cokliss plays too safe, here sticking to a standard action-thriller format. Similarly, there are solid but not outstanding performances from the cast, with the exception of the ever-excellent Tommy Lee Jones. Linda Hamilton and Robert Vaughn provide able support, but even they are not at their best. Co-written by John

Carpenter from his own story, it could have been so much better with him as director. NF. Contains violence, swearing and nudity.

Tommy Lee Jones *Quint* • Linda Hamilton *Nina* • Robert Vaughn *Ryland* • Richard Jaeckel *Earl Windom* • Lee Ving *Marvin Ringer* • Bubba Smith *Johnson* • Dan Shor *Billy Lyons* • William Sanderson *Tyke Thayden* • Keenan Wynn *Iron John* • Nick Cassavetes *Luis* ■ *Dir* Harley Cokliss • *Scr* John Carpenter, Desmond Nakano, William Gray, from a story by John Carpenter

Black Narcissus ★★★★★ U

Classic drama 1946 · UK · Colour · 100mins

Winner of Oscars for art design and cinematography, Michael Powell and Emeric Pressburger's adaptation of Rumer Godden's simmering novel is one of the most striking examples of studio-controlled artifice in film history. Jack Cardiff's lush colour images not only enhance the beauty of the stylised Himalayan scenery, but also bring a certain grandeur to the melodramatic events at a remote mountain mission, where the visit of English agent David Farrar is causing passions to run dangerously out of control. Kathleen Byron's eye-rolling jealousy awakens the occasionally sleepy plot and her scene with Deborah Kerr on the bell-tower is a true classic. DP DVD

Deborah Kerr *Sister Clodagh* • Sabu *Dilip Rai* • David Farrar *Mr Dean* • Flora Robson *Sister Philippa* • Esmond Knight *General* • Jean Simmons *Kanchi* • Kathleen Byron *Sister Ruth* • Jenny Laird *Blanche, Sister Honey* ■ *Dir* Michael Powell, Emeric Pressburger • *Scr* Michael Powell, Emeric Pressburger, from the novel by Rumer Godden • *Cinematographer* Jack Cardiff • *Art Director* Alfred Junge

The Black Orchid ★★ U

Drama 1959 · US · BW · 98mins

Hollywood, on the whole, gave the luscious Sophia Loren a raw deal, leaving her native Italy to provide worthy vehicles for her talent. Without her, and Anthony Quinn's excellent co-starring performance, this New York-based saga about a widower (Quinn) fighting his children's opposition to his marrying a gangster's widow (Loren) would hardly be worth staying in for. Nonetheless, the Italian star won the acting award at the Venice Film Festival for her sterling efforts. RK

Sophia Loren *Rose Bianco* • Anthony Quinn *Frank Valente* • Ina Balin *Mary Valente* • Mark Richman [Peter Mark Richman] *Noble* • Jimmy Baird *Ralphie Bianco* • Virginia Vincent *Alma Gallo* • Naomi Stevens *Guilia Gallo* • Frank Puglia *Henry Gallo* ■ *Dir* Martin Ritt • *Scr* Joseph Stefano

Black Orpheus ★★★ PG

Romance 1958 · Fr/Br/It · Colour · 102mins

Winner of the Oscar for best foreign film and the Palme d'Or at Cannes, this transposition of the myth of Orpheus and the Underworld to Rio de Janeiro at Carnival time is a riot of exotic colour and dynamic movement. Yet there's also an overweening sentimentality about trolleybus conductor Breno Mello's doomed affair with Marpessa Dawn, and director Marcel Camus is guilty of a certain naiveté in his political symbolism and of failing to compensate for the limitations of his inexperienced cast. Yet, this remains a visually exhilarating and – thanks largely to a superb score – vibrant experience. DP. In Portuguese with English subtitles.

Breno Mello *Orpheus* • Marpessa Dawn *Eurydice* • Lourdes de Oliveria *Mira* • Lea Garcia *Serafina* • Ademar da Silva *Death* • Alexandro Constantino *Hermes* • Waldetar de Souza *Chico* ■ *Dir* Marcel Camus • *Scr* Jacques Viot, Marcel Camus, from the play *Orfeu da Conceicao* by Vinicius DeMoraes • *Cinematographer* Jean Bourgoin • *Music* Antonio Carlos Jobim, Luiz Bonfa

The Black Pirate ★★★★ PG

Silent swashbuckling adventure
1926 · US · Colour · 97mins

Hailed as the first full-length feature to be made in two-tone Technicolor, this was one of the most spectacular swashbucklers undertaken by Douglas Fairbanks (who also took a story credit as Elton Thomas). It was a stormy production, with co-star Donald Crisp being ousted from the director's chair in favour of the more malleable Albert Parker. Yet what emerged was a ripsnorting adventure, in which the aristocratic Fairbanks joins a pirate band to avenge the death of his father. The knife-blade descent down a billowing sail thrilled audiences of the day. DP

Douglas Fairbanks *The Black Pirate* • Billie Dove *The Princess* • Anders Randolf *Pirate leader* • Donald Crisp *McTavish* • Tempe Pigott *Duenna* • Sam De Grasse *Pirate* • Charlie Stevens [Charles Stevens] *Powder man* • Charles Belcher *Chief passenger* ■ *Dir* Albert Parker • *Scr* Lotta Woods, Jack Cunningham, from a story by Elton Thomas [Douglas Fairbanks]

Black Point ★★ 15

Crime drama 2001 · Can · Colour · 102mins

As an ex-soldier trying to restart his life in the Pacific Northwest, David Caruso is easy prey for *femme fatale* Susan Haskell in this predictable TV crime drama. Thomas Ian Griffith (who also co-scripted) plays the abusive husband whose stolen Mob money is in Haskell's sights. This is *film noir* by numbers. DP. Contains violence and swearing. DVD

David Caruso *John Hawkins* • Susan Haskell *Natalie Travis* • Thomas Ian Griffith *Gus Travis* • Miguel Sandoval *Malcolm* • Gordon Tootoosis *Standing Bear* ■ *Dir* David Mackay • *Scr* Greg Mellot, Thomas Ian Griffith

Black Rain ★★★★ PG

Drama 1988 · Jpn · BW · 122mins

From its devastating re-creation of the atomic bombing of Hiroshima, this intense and affecting drama exercises the fiercest of grips. Set mainly five years on from the blast, the story focuses on a woman whose marriage prospects have been dashed because the male population of her country village fear she contracted radiation sickness. Yoshiko Tanaka gives an exceptional performance, as does Keisuke Ishida as the tormented stonemason with whom she strikes up an uneasy relationship. However, the powerful insights into the social and psychological aftermath of the bomb make this very much director Shohei Imamura's film. DP. In Japanese with English subtitles.

Yoshiko Tanaka *Yasuko* • Kazuo Kitamura *Shigematsu Shizuma* • Etsuko Ichihara *Shigeko Shizuma* • Shoichi Ozawa *Shokichi* ■ *Dir* Shohei Imamura • *Scr* Shohei Imamura,Toshiro Ishido, from the novel by Masuji Ibuse

Black Rain ★★★ 18

Thriller 1989 · US · Colour · 120mins

This tense, glossy and violent film stars Michael Douglas and Andy Garcia as New York cops on assignment in Japan where yakuza gangsters wield swords and where Kate Capshaw hangs out in a nightclub à la Marlene Dietrich. This being a Ridley Scott film, the atmosphere is so hyped up that the picture threatens to burst an artery. Jan De Bont's photography delights in the neon-lit locations and makes the city of Osaka look like a vision of hell, but beneath all this is a very conventional cop thriller. AT. Contains violence, swearing. DVD

Michael Douglas *Nick Conklin* • Andy Garcia *Charlie Vincent* • Ken Takakura *Masahiro Matsumoto* • Kate Capshaw *Joyce Kingsley* • Yusaku Matsuda *Sato* • Tomisaburo Wakayama *Sugai* • Shigeru Koyama *Ohashi* • John Spencer *Oliver* ■ *Dir* Ridley Scott • *Scr* Craig Bolotin, Warren Lewis

Black Rainbow ★★★★ 15

Supernatural thriller
1989 · UK · Colour · 98mins

Achieving a ring of truth very few fantasies spire to, Mike Hodges's most personal movie is an intriguing psychic thriller containing numerous eerie surprises. One of the main shocks is Rosanna Arquette, in her finest role to date, as the Doris Stokes-type medium who can plug into the link between this world and the spiritual one – the "black rainbow" of the title. And when she successfully predicts a murder, the unusual scene is set for a clairvoyant cat-and-mouse chase through previously uncharted suspense territory. AJ. Contains swearing and brief nudity. DVD

Rosanna Arquette *Martha Travis* • Jason Robards *Walter Travis* • Tom Hulce *Gary Wallace* • Mark Joy *Lloyd Harley* • Ron Rosenthal *Detective Irving Weinberg* • John Bennes *Ted Silas* • Linda Pierce *Mary Kuron* • Olek Krupa *Tom Kuron* ■ *Dir/Scr* Mike Hodges

The Black Rider ★★ U

Crime caper 1954 · UK · BW · 66mins

This amiable low-budget crime caper also takes the idea of using spooks to cover a smuggling operation and adds a dash of *Famous Five* exuberance to create a formula familiar to fans of the cartoon series *Scooby Doo*. The plot zips along like one of the motorbikes owned by the club members who expose the villains with the help of a crusading journalist. Director Wolf Rilla was the author of a manual called *A-Z of Making Movies*, and this is very much film-making by the book, but it's a pleasing time-passer. DP

Jimmy Hanley *Jerry Marsh* • Rona Anderson *Mary* • Leslie Dwyer *Robert* • Beatrice Varley *Mrs Marsh* • Lionel Jeffries *Brennan* • Valerie Hanson *Karen* • Vincent Ball *Ted Lintott* ■ *Dir* Wolf Rilla • *Scr* AR Rawlinson

Black Robe ★★★ 15

Historical drama
1991 · Can/Aus · Colour · 96mins

Adapted by Brian Moore from his own novel, this saga about the clash between native Americans and Jesuits in the 17th century invites comparison with *The Mission* as well as *Dances with Wolves*. Directed by Bruce Beresford amid stunning forest scenery in Quebec, it's an austere, small-scale epic that turns on the sexuality of the Indians and the morality of organised, colonialist religion. It's a dark, intense piece, powerfully acted by Lothaire Bluteau (*Jesus of Montreal*) as the head priest, and Sandrine Holt as the chief's daughter who falls in love with a Frenchman. AT. In English and French with subtitles.

Lothaire Bluteau *Father Laforgue* • Aden Young *Daniel* • Sandrine Holt *Annuka* • August Schellenberg *Chomina* • Tantoo Cardinal *Chomina's wife* • Billy Two Rivers *Ougebmat* • Lawrence Bayne *Neehatin* • Harrison Liu *Awondoie* • Wesley Cote *Oujita* ■ *Dir* Bruce Beresford • *Scr* Brian Moore, from his novel

The Black Room ★★★

Horror 1935 · US · BW · 68mins

Boris Karloff plays 19th-century twins in a standard Gothic melodrama in which an evil brother murders the good one and impersonates him until an ancient family curse comes true. Generally effective, with the "black room" debauchery, sadism and torture implied rather than shown, it's primarily a showcase for Karloff to display his acting range between "hateful" and "sympathetic". He does it brilliantly. AJ

Boris Karloff *Baron Gregor de Berghman/ Anton de Berghman* • Marian Marsh *Thea Hassel* • Robert Allen *Lt Albert Lussan* • Thurston Hall *Col Hassel* • Katherine DeMille *Mashka* • John Buckler *Beran* • Henry Kolker *Baron de Berghman* ■ *Dir* Roy William Neill • *Scr* Arthur Strawn, Henry Myers, from a story by Arthur Strawn

The Black Rose ★★ U

Romantic adventure
1950 · UK · Colour · 120mins

Filmed in England and North Africa, this sweeping yarn set in the 13th century stars Tyrone Power as the bastard son of a Saxon nobleman who travels from England to the Far East. On the way to Cathay, he rescues a blonde slave girl (the diminutive French actress Cécile Aubry) and confronts a Mongolian warlord (Orson Welles, hamming it up behind heavy Oriental make-up). The film looks good, but most of the dialogue is so bad it's painful to listen to. RB

Tyrone Power *Walter of Gurnie* • Orson Welles *Bayan* • Cécile Aubry *Maryam* • Jack Hawkins *Tristram* • Michael Rennie *King Edward* • Finlay Currie *Alfgar* • Herbert Lom *Anthemus* • Mary Clare *Countess of Lessford* ■ *Dir* Henry Hathaway • *Scr* Talbot Jennings, from the novel by Thomas B Costain

Black Sabbath ★★★★

Portmanteau horror
1963 · US/Fr/It · BW · 95mins

This chillingly effective portmanteau piece is from the Italian master of horror and suspense, Mario Bava. Veteran Boris Karloff, acting as master of ceremonies, introduces three classic tales. In the first a woman steals a ring from a corpse only to be haunted by her spirit. In the second a prostitute is terrified by a phantom telephone caller and lastly Karloff himself turns in one of his creepiest performances as a vampire cursed to chew only upon his own family. Pictorially stunning, this also has a script of above average intelligence for a horror movie. Bava imbues every scene with darkly imposing atmosphere and conjures up some truly terrifying set pieces. Two versions of the film exist – in Italian and English – with slight variations. RS. Some dialogue dubbed into English.

Jacqueline Pierreux [Jacqueline Soussard] *Helen Corey* • Milli Monti *Maid* • Michèle Mercier *Rosy* • Lidia Alfonsi *Mary* • Gustavo de Nardo *Frank* • Boris Karloff *Gorka* • Mark Damon *Vladimir D'Urfe* • Susy Anderson *Sdenka* ■ *Dir* Mario Bava • *Scr* Marcello Fondato, Alberto Bevilacqua, Mario Bava • *Cinematographer* Ubaldo Terzano

The Black Scorpion ★★★

Science-fiction drama
1957 · US · BW · 87mins

The slumber of giant scorpions is disturbed by volcanic activity in director Edward Ludwig's low-budget sci-fi drama. The leader of the angry arachnids takes one look at the desert and heads straight for Mexico City and a showdown with a cast headed by B-movie regulars Richard Denning and Mara Corday. Special effects come courtesy of Willis O'Brien, who helped give life to King Kong. The film's climax, in the Mexico City stadium, is wonderfully schlocky. AT

Richard Denning *Henry Scott* • Mara Corday *Teresa* • Carlos Rivas *Arturo Ramos* • Mario Navarro *Juanito* • Carlos Muzquiz *Doctor Velasco* • Pasqual Garcia Peña *Jose de la Cruz* ■ *Dir* Edward Ludwig • *Scr* David Duncan, Robert Blees, from a story by Paul Yawitz

B

Black Sheep ★★

Crime drama 1935 · US · BW · 70mins

Returning to Hollywood after a brief sojourn in Britain, veteran director Allan Dwan resumed his career with this shipboard melodrama. Edmund Lowe stars as the transatlantic gambler who prevents Tom Brown from the taking the rap for a jewel robbery – without letting the boy know he's really his father. While never riveting, Lowe and Trevor are admirable, and Adrienne Ames is thoroughly hissable as a scheming vamp. DP

Edmund Lowe *John Francis Dugan* • Claire Trevor *Janette Foster* • Tom Brown *Fred Curtis* • Eugene Pallette *Col Upton Calhoun Belcher* • Adrienne Ames *Mrs Millicent Caldwell Bath* ■ *Dir* Allan Dwan • *Scr* Allen Rivkin, from the story *Baa Baa Black Sheep* by Allan Dwan

Black Sheep ★★ 12

Comedy 1996 · US · Colour · 82mins

Wayne's World director Penelope Spheeris continues her erratic career with this mindless vehicle for double act Chris Farley and David Spade. Farley is the overweight, accident-prone brother of would-be State Governor Tim Matheson. To get Farley out of the way the caustic Spade is enlisted to "baby-sit", and everything that the large one comes into contact with is flattened or destroyed. There's chemistry between Farley and Spade, but the jokes are uninspired. JC DVD

Chris Farley *Mike Donnelly* • David Spade *Steve Dodds* • Tim Matheson *Al Donnelly* • Christine Ebersole *Governor Tracy* • Gary Busey *Drake Sabitch* • Grant Heslov *Robbie Mieghem* • Timothy Carhart *Roger Kovary* • Bruce McGill *Neuschwender* • "Gypsy" Spheeris *Pocket pool lady* • Kevin P Farley [Kevin Farley] *Bouncer* • John Farley *Bouncer* ■ *Dir* Penelope Spheeris • *Scr* Fred Wolf

The Black Sheep of Whitehall ★★★★ U

Comedy 1941 · UK · BW · 73mins

Co-directing, as well as starring, Will Hay is at his blithering best as the incompetent principal of a correspondence college. He stumbles across a dastardly plot involving Nazi Felix Aylmer masquerading as a famous economist so that he and treacherous journalist Basil Sydney can disrupt a vital trade pact between Britain and South America. Adopting a series of hilariously transparent disguises, Hay and sole pupil John Mills finally capture the villains in a corking chase sequence, with Hay (dressed as a nurse) being dragged along in a Bath chair. This wonderful wartime comedy is the neglected classic in the Hay canon. DP

Will Hay *Professor Davis* • John Mills *Bobby* • Basil Sydney *Costello* • Henry Hewitt *Professor Davys* • Felix Aylmer *Crabtree* • Frank Cellier *Innsbach* • Joss Ambler *Sir John* • Frank Allenby *Onslow* ■ *Dir* Will Hay, Basil Dearden • *Scr* Angus MacPhail, John Dighton

The Black Shield of Falworth ★★ U

Swashbuckling adventure
1954 · US · Colour · 98mins

Janet Leigh and Tony Curtis made six films together during their marriage, and here the glam couple cavort across Ye Merrie Olde Englande (or the Universal backlot) to save Henry IV from a fate worse than a Kenneth Branagh remake. This swashbuckler features suave Herbert Marshall, decent swordfights, early CinemaScope photography and some wonderful Brooklyn accents. AT

Tony Curtis *Myles Falworth* • Janet Leigh *Lady Anne* • David Farrar *Earl of Alban* • Barbara Rush *Meg Falworth* • Herbert Marshall *Earl of Mackworth* • Torin Thatcher *Sir James* • Dan O'Herlihy *Prince Hal* • Rhys Williams *Diccon Bowman* • Ian Keith *King Henry IV* ■ *Dir* Rudolph Maté • *Scr* Oscar Brodney, from the novel *Men of Iron* by Howard Pyle

The Black Sleep ★

Horror thriller 1956 · US · BW · 82mins

In order to cure his wife's catalepsy, mad doctor Basil Rathbone performs surgery on innocent victims to unlock the secrets of the brain. His failed lobotomy experiments eventually escape their cellar prison and rebel against him. Aside from the unique spectacle of seeing such horror heavies as Rathbone, Bela Lugosi, Lon Chaney Jr, John Carradine, Tor Johnson and Akim Tamiroff, this wasted opportunity is barely watchable. AJ

Basil Rathbone *Sir Joel Cadman* • Akim Tamiroff *Odo* • Lon Chaney Jr *Mungo* • John Carradine *Borg* • Bela Lugosi *Casimir* • Herbert Rudley *Dr Gordon Ramsay* • Patricia Blake *Laurie* • Tor Johnson *Curry* ■ *Dir* Reginald Le Borg • *Scr* John C Higgins

Black Spurs ★★ U

Western 1965 · US · Colour · 81mins

A routine western with Rory Calhoun as a bounty hunter buying up a nice little town and turning it into his own fiefdom. However, when the local sheriff is tarred and feathered, Calhoun starts to rethink his anti-social behaviour. Not much more here than you'll find in an average episode of *Gunsmoke*, though the film does include a musical interlude. AT

Rory Calhoun *Santee* • Terry Moore *Anna* • Linda Darnell *Sadie* • Scott Brady *Tanner* • Lon Chaney Jr *Kile* • Bruce Cabot *Henderson* • Richard Arlen *Pete* • Patricia Owens *Clare Grubbs* • James Best *Sheriff Elkins* ■ *Dir* RG Springsteen • *Scr* Steve Fisher

The Black Stallion ★★★★★ U

Adventure 1979 · US · Colour · 112mins

Adapted by Melissa Mathison (who wrote the script for *ET*), Jeanne Rosenberg and William Witliff, this is among the most magical children's films ever made. Making his debut as director, Carroll Ballard blends stunning visuals with a heart-warming story in which a small boy trains the horse he rescued from a shipwreck. The storm and the desert island scenes are breathtaking, and, if the training and racing sequences have all been done before, they have an energy and an eye-catching splendour that more than compensate. Mickey Rooney earned an Oscar nomination as a has-been trainer, but the true stars are 11-year-old Kelly Reno and the horse Cass-ole. DP DVD

Mickey Rooney *Henry Dailey* • Kelly Reno *Alec Ramsey* • Teri Garr *Alec's mother* • Clarence Muse *Snoe* • Hoyt Axton *Alec's father* • Michael Higgins *Jim Neville* • Ed McNamara *Jake* • Doghmi Larbi *Arab* ■ *Dir* Carroll Ballard • *Scr* Melissa Mathison, Jeanne Rosenberg, William Witliff, from the novel by Walter Farley • *Executive Producer* Francis Ford Coppola • *Cinematographer* Caleb Deschanel • *Editor* Robert Dalva

The Black Stallion Returns ★★ U

Adventure 1983 · US · Colour · 98mins

Having edited Carroll Ballard's original film, Robert Dalva made his directorial debut with this substandard sequel, which is short on both fantasy and charm. Although the action is handsomely photographed by Carlo Di Palma and Caleb Deschanel, too few risks are taken with the storyline, which again sees Kelly Reno and his superb horse overcome all manner of trials to reunite in time for a big race. DP DVD

Hoyt Axton *Narrator* • Kelly Reno *Alec Ramsay* • Vincent Spano *Raj* • Allen Goorwitz [Allen Garfield] *Kurr* • Woody Strode *Meslar* • Ferdy Mayne *Abu Ben Ishak* • Jodi Thelen *Tabari* • Teri Garr *Alec's mother* ■ *Dir* Robert Dalva • *Scr* Richard Kletter, Jerome Kass, from the novel by Walter Farley • *Executive Producer* Francis Ford Coppola

Black Sunday ★★★★ 15

Crime thriller 1976 · US · Colour · 137mins

John Frankenheimer is on top form with this thriller based on the novel by Thomas Harris, author of *The Silence of the Lambs*, about terrorists planning to cause mayhem at a Super Bowl football game. Maniacs on both sides of the law (Robert Shaw and Bruce Dern) explain their motives, but it's the violent action that makes the film so fraught and yet so exciting. The clash between police helicopters and a hijacked blimp is the highlight of the outstanding set pieces. TH. Contains swearing and violence.

Robert Shaw *Major Kabakov* • Bruce Dern *Michael Lander* • Marthe Keller *Dahlia Iyad* • Fritz Weaver *Corley* • Steven Keats *Robert Moshevsky* • Bekim Fehmiu *Fasil* • Michael V Gazzo *Muzi* • William Daniels *Pugh* • Tom McFadden *Farley* ■ *Dir* John Frankenheimer • *Scr* Ernest Lehman, Kenneth Ross, Ivan Moffat, from the novel by Thomas Harris

The Black Swan ★★★★

Swashbuckling adventure
1942 · US · Colour · 81mins

The kind of movie they used to make before they stopped making them like that any more, this is a rip-roaring tale of swashbuckling, buccaneering and damsel-wooing, starring Tyrone Power. Power plays a reformed sea wolf, whose former partner in piracy (Laird Cregar) is made governor of Jamaica. They join forces to rid the neighbourhood of assorted rogues and one-eyed knaves. Much swordplay – plus intermittent courtship of Maureen O'Hara by Power – ensues, all captured by Oscar-winning colour cinematography. Vintage stuff. PF

Tyrone Power *James Waring* • Maureen O'Hara *Margaret Denby* • Laird Cregar *Captain Henry Morgan* • Thomas Mitchell *Tommy Blue* • George Sanders *Captain Billy Leech* • Anthony Quinn *Wogan* • George Zucco *Lord Denby* • Edward Ashley *Roger Ingram* ■ *Dir* Henry King • *Scr* Ben Hecht, Seton I Miller, from the novel by Rafael Sabatini • *Cinematographer* Leon Shamroy

The Black Tent ★★ U

Second World War drama
1956 · UK · Colour · 92mins

Brian Desmond Hurst directs this contrived drama in which wounded officer Anthony Steel joins with Bedouin sheikh André Morell to confound the Nazis. The romance with Anna-Maria Sandri sits awkwardly alongside the action, while Donald Sinden's clipped bravado as Steel's brother occasionally borders on the comic. The script by Robin Maugham and Bryan Forbes is undistinguished. DP

Anthony Steel *David Holland* • Donald Sinden *Charles Holland* • Anna-Maria Sandri *Mabrouka* • André Morell *Sheikh Salem* • Ralph Truman *Croft* • Donald Pleasence *Ali* • Anthony Bushell *Baring* • Michael Craig *Faris* • Anton Diffring *German officer* • Frederick Jaeger *German officer* ■ *Dir* Brian Desmond Hurst • *Scr* Robin Maugham, Bryan Forbes

The Black Torment ★★ 15

Gothic horror 1964 · UK · Colour · 82mins

This barnstorming period horror is no longer the marrow-chiller it once was. Nevertheless, it has a literate script and still delivers some mild shocks as it wheels out a time-honoured tale of suicide, gloomy castles, ghosts and mad relatives locked in the attic. It's directed by Robert Hartford-Davis, an unsung hero of British horror, and actors John Turner and Heather Sears work miracles in making this Gothic melodrama believable. AJ

John Turner *Sir Richard Fordyke* • Heather Sears *Lady Elizabeth* • Ann Lynn *Diane* • Peter Arne *Seymour* • Raymond Huntley *Colonel Wentworth* • Annette Whiteley *Mary* • Norman Bird *Harris* • Roger Croucher *Apprentice* • Joseph Tomelty *Sir Giles* • Patrick Troughton *Ostler* • Edina Ronay *Lucy Judd* ■ *Dir* Robert Hartford-Davis • *Scr* Donald Ford, Derek Ford

The Black Tulip ★★

Historical adventure
1963 · Fr · Colour · 110mins

French superstar Alain Delon stars in this Alexandre Dumas tale about the exploits of *La Tulipe Noire*, a sort of Robin Hood figure of 18th-century France. He also has a twin brother, so it's as much a dual role as a duelling one. Virna Lisi makes a glamorous heroine, and Akim Tamiroff hams away as the local big *fromage*. It's slackly directed by Christian-Jaque, who shows none of the style that won him the best director award at Cannes for the swashbuckler *Fanfan la Tulipe*. AT. French dialogue dubbed into English.

Alain Delon *Guillaume de Saint-Preux/Julien de Saint-Preux* • Virna Lisi *Caroline* • Dawn Addams *Marquise de Vigogne* • Francis Blanche *Plantin* • Akim Tamiroff *Marquis de Vigogne* • Robert Manuel *Prince Alexander de Grassilach* ■ *Dir* Christian-Jaque • *Scr* Henri Jeanson, from the novel *La Tulipe Noire* by Alexandre Dumas

A Black Veil for Lisa ★

Crime thriller
1969 · It/W Ger · Colour · 87mins

One of John Mills's lowest career points, this is a Euro-pudding cop thriller that dredges up every cliché of the British B-movie, relocates them to Hamburg and adds some nudity and violence. Mills is a detective more concerned with the infidelities of his wife (Luciana Paluzzi) than solving the various high-profile drug trafficking cases on his desk. This hardly passes muster in any department. AT. Some dialogue dubbed into English.

John Mills *Bulon* • Luciana Paluzzi *Lisa* • Robert Hoffmann *Max* • Renata Kasche *Marianne* • Tullio Altamura *Ostermeyer* • Carlo Hintermann *Mansfeld* • Enzo Fiermonte *Siegert* • Loris Bazzocchi *Kruger* ■ *Dir* Massimo Dallamano • *Scr* Giuseppe Belli, Vittoriano Petrilli, Massimo Dallamano, Audrey Nohra, from a story by Giuseppe Belli

The Black Watch ★★ U

Adventure 1929 · US · BW · 9mins

Just before the Fox company took up talking pictures, John Ford had directed a visually striking and fast-paced adventure story starring Victor McLaglen as a British army officer in India who feigns desertion to win the affection of Myrna Loy's goddess of the tribes and thus avert a rebellion. Then one of the supporting players, Lumsden Hare, was engaged to add talking sequences, mainly love scenes between McLaglen and Loy, which held up the picture and had audiences laughing at the stilted dialogue. AE

Victor McLaglen *Capt Donald Gordon King* • Myrna Loy *Yasmini* • David Rollins *Lt Malcolm King* • Lumsden Hare *Colonel of the Black Watch* • Roy D'Arcy *Rewa Ghunga* • Mitchell Lewis *Mohammed Khan* • Cyril Chadwick *Maj Twynes* • David Torrence *Field Marshall* ■ *Dir* John Ford • *Scr* John Stone, James Kevin McGuinness, from the novel *King of the Khyber Rifles* by Talbot Mundy

Black Widow ★★

Murder mystery 1954 · US · Colour · 94mins

A starry cast, a decent build-up of tension and a surprise denouement overcome a slow start and a superficial screenplay in this moderately enjoyable murder mystery. Van Heflin is the producer suspected of killing a young

Broadway hopeful, and Ginger Rogers his poisonous leading lady; the glamorous Gene Tierney plays another stage star, while George Raft is the purposeful investigating detective. RK

Ginger Rogers *Lottie* • Van Heflin *Peter* • Gene Tierney *Iris* • George Raft *Detective Bruce* • Peggy Ann Garner *Nancy Ordway* • Reginald Gardiner *Brian* • Virginia Leith *Claire Amberly* • Otto Kruger *Ling* ■ *Dir* Nunnally Johnson • *Scr* Nunnally Johnson, from the novel by Patrick Quentin [Hugh Wheeler]

Black Widow ★★★ 15

Thriller 1987 · US · Colour · 97mins

It's not quite in the same league as his dense psychological dramas from the early 1970s, but this intriguing thriller marked a return to form for Bob Rafelson. Theresa Russell is the black widow of the title, who specialises in bumping off wealthy millionaires, among them Dennis Hopper and Nicol Williamson. Debra Winger is the uptight FBI agent who sets out to bring her to justice. The cat-and-mouse games played by Winger and Russell crackle with tension and there is a lovely twist at the end. JF. Contains violence, swearing, nudity. [video] DVD

Debra Winger *Alexandra Barnes* • Theresa Russell *Catharine* • Sami Frey *Paul Nuytten* • Dennis Hopper *Ben Dumers* • Nicol Williamson *William Macauley* • Terry O'Quinn *Bruce* • James Hong *Shin* • Diane Ladd *Etta* ■ *Dir* Bob Rafelson • *Scr* Ronald Bass

The Black Windmill ★★

Spy thriller 1974 · UK · Colour · 106mins

A disappointing thriller from *Dirty Harry* director Don Siegel, with Michael Caine as an agent whose son is kidnapped by a mysterious military organisation, which demands diamonds in return for his release. The plot is over-thickened with cat-and-mouse sequences and Siegel's acclaimed naturalistic style is intrusive here, but the performances are fine. DP. Contains swearing.

Michael Caine *Major John Tarrant* • Joseph O'Conor *Sir Edward Julyan* • Donald Pleasence *Cedric Harper* • John Vernon *McKee* • Janet Suzman *Alex Tarrant* • Delphine Seyrig *Ceil Burrows* • Joss Ackland *Chief Superintendent Wray* • Clive Revill *Alf Chestermann* ■ *Dir* Don Siegel • *Scr* Leigh Vance, from the novel *Seven Days to a Killing* by Clive Egleton

Black Zoo ★★★

Horror 1963 · US · Colour · 88mins

Michael Gough stars in this gleefully eccentric, but decidedly macabre chiller. Throwing restraint to the winds, Gough indulges himself as the owner of a private zoo whose obsession with big cats has brought nothing but misery to his wife, Jeanne Cooper, and his mute son, Rod Lauren. The sequence in which Gough plays the organ for his brood encapsulates the picture's camp tone, but there are moments of genuine unease as the furtive animal-worshipping cultist disposes of those opposed to his twisted schemes. DP

Michael Gough *Michael Conrad* • Jeanne Cooper *Edna Conrad* • Rod Lauren *Carl* • Virginia Grey *Jenny* • Jerome Cowan *Jeffrey Stengle* • Elisha Cook Jr *Joe* ■ *Dir* Robert Gordon • *Scr* Herman Cohen, Aben Kandel

Blackball ★ 15

Comedy 2003 · UK · Colour · 92mins

This charmless comedy is rooted in the same kind of so-called humour that one hoped had died out in the 1970s with the likes of *On the Buses*. Paul Kaye plays an obnoxious bad boy of bowls who's blackballed by his stuffy club, then reluctantly re-instated to take on the visiting Aussie champions. Despite a likeable cast, the laughs are way off-target. DA [video] DVD

Paul Kaye *Cliff Starkey* • James Cromwell *Ray Speight* • Alice Evans *Kerry Speight* • Bernard Cribbins *Mutley* • Johnny Vegas *Trevor* • Vince Vaughn *Rick Schwartz* • Imelda Staunton *Bridget* • James Fleet *Alan the Pipe* • David Ryall *Giles Wilton* • Ian McNeice *Hugh the Sideburns* • Kenneth Cranham *Chairman Collins* ■ *Dir* Mel Smith • *Scr* Tim Firth

Blackbeard the Pirate ★★ U

Swashbuckling adventure
1952 · US · Colour · 94mins

RKO producer Val Lewton had, at one time, planned this swashbuckler as a vehicle for Boris Karloff, and, in view of the outlandish performance by Robert Newton, one can only lament the fact that he didn't take the starring role. Newton throws in every cliché ever used by a pantomime pirate and occasionally comes close to making this vigorous adventure almost unwatchable. Fortunately, director Raoul Walsh's sure handling of the action sequences and a good supporting cast keep it afloat. DP

Robert Newton *Blackbeard* • Linda Darnell *Edwina* • William Bendix *Worley* • Keith Andes *Maynard* • Torin Thatcher *Sir Henry Morgan* • Irene Ryan *Alvina* • Alan Mowbray *Noll* ■ *Dir* Raoul Walsh • *Scr* Alan LeMay, from a story by DeVallon Scott

Blackbeard's Ghost ★★★ U

Comedy 1967 · US · Colour · 102mins

This Disney caper is overlong and short on inspiration, but it does have a lively lead in the incomparable Peter Ustinov as the buccaneer condemned to wander in limbo until he performs a good deed. Poaching the picture from him, however, is Elsa Lanchester, as one of the old dears he must save from gambling gangsters. It's corny and over the top, but entertaining nonetheless. DP [video] DVD

Peter Ustinov *Captain Blackbeard* • Dean Jones *Steve Walker* • Suzanne Pleshette *Jo Anne Baker* • Elsa Lanchester *Emily Stowecroft* • Joby Baker *Silky Seymour* • Elliott Reid *TV commentator* • Richard Deacon *Dean Wheaton* • Norman Grabowski *Virgil* ■ *Dir* Robert Stevenson • *Scr* Bill Walsh, Don DaGradi, from the novel by Ben Stahl

The Blackboard Jungle ★★★ 12

Drama 1955 · US · BW · 96mins

A teenage angst picture, following hot on the heels of James Dean's *Rebel without a Cause*, with Glenn Ford as the gauche schoolteacher who wonders why his class beat him up and "don't wanna loin nuthin'". Anne Francis offers him a shoulder to cry on, while American parents everywhere sobbed in sympathy. Filmed in sombre black and white, director Richard Brooks's film rams home his message without much subtlety. It has a footnote in history for introducing rock music to mainstream cinema, courtesy of Bill Haley's *Rock around the Clock* which is played over the credit titles. AT [video]

Glenn Ford *Richard Dadier* • Anne Francis *Anne Dadier* • Louis Calhern *Jim Murdock* • Margaret Hayes *Lois Judby Hammond* • John Hoyt *Mr Warneke* • Richard Kiley *Joshua Y Edwards* • Emile Meyer *Mr Halloran* • Warner Anderson *Dr Bradley* ■ *Dir* Richard Brooks • *Scr* Richard Brooks, from the novel by Evan Hunter • *Cinematographer* Russell Harlan

Blackboards ★★★★ PG

Political drama
2000 · Iran/It/Jpn · Colour · 81mins

In stark contrast to the easy urban charm of *The Apple*, Samira Makhmalbaf's second feature is a bleakly neorealistic account of life in Iran's hostile borderlands. Examining the value of education to the dispossessed Kurds whose sole concern is survival, it boldly blends hard-hitting drama with comic diversion and towering vistas with moments of acute intimacy. Said Mohamadi and Bahman Ghobadi admirably convey a sense of dignity and desperation as the peripatetic teachers touting for work. This is both courageous and compelling. DP. In Kurdish with English subtitles. [video] DVD

Said Mohamadi *Said, teacher* • Behnaz Jafari *Halaleh, young woman* • Bahman Ghobadi *Reeboir, teacher* • Mohamad Karim Rahmati *Father* • Rafat Moradi *Ribvar* ■ *Dir* Samira Makhmalbaf • *Scr* Samira Makhmalbaf, Mohsen Makhmalbaf

Blackmail ★★★ PG

Thriller 1929 · UK · BW · 81mins

Alfred Hitchcock's first talking picture was also the earliest in which he used a famous landmark to stage the finale. The visuals are eerily expressionistic, the trick photography in the British Museum sequence is first class and the recurrence of the word "knife" on the soundtrack is amusingly ghoulish. But the restrictions placed on film-makers by primitive sound recording techniques render the action and the acting fatally stilted. There is a predominantly silent version of this film, which is infinitely better. Although most film histories claim this to be the first British talkie, the honour actually goes to Arthur Maude's *The Clue of the New Pin*. DP [video]

Anny Ondra *Alice White* • John Longden *Frank Webber* • Donald Calthrop *Tracy* • Sara Allgood *Mrs White* • Charles Paton *Mr White* • Cyril Ritchard *Artist* • Harvey Braban *Inspector* • Phyllis Monkman *Gossip* • Hannah Jones *Landlady* ■ *Dir* Alfred Hitchcock • *Scr* Alfred Hitchcock, Benn W Levy, Charles Bennett, Michael Powell (uncredited), from the play *Blackmail* by Charles Bennett • *Cinematographer* Jack Cox

Blackmail ★★★

Prison drama 1939 · US · BW · 80mins

Edward G Robinson fights fires on Oklahoma's oil fields but serves time on a chain-gang for a crime he did not commit, and is then blackmailed by Gene Lockhart. MGM was trying to splice two genres here – the social drama, such as *I Am a Fugitive from a Chain Gang*, and the sexy melodrama. It works, sort of, mainly due to the powerful performances of Robinson and Lockhart, as well as some well-handled scenes of burned-out oil-rigs and burned-out convicts. AT

Edward G Robinson *John R Ingram* • Ruth Hussey *Helen Ingram* • Gene Lockhart *William Ramey* • Bobs Watson *Hank Ingram* • Guinn Williams [Guinn "Big Boy" Williams] *Moose McCarthy* • John Wray *Diggs* • Arthur Hohl *Rawlins* • Esther Dale *Sarah* • Charles Middleton *First deputy* ■ *Dir* HC Potter • *Scr* David Hertz, William Ludwig, Brown Holmes, Nathalie Buchnall, from a story by Endre Bohem, Dorothy Yost

Blackout ★★

Thriller 1950 · UK · BW · 73mins

Directed by Robert S Baker, this is a fanciful projects, about a blind man (Maxwell Reed) who recovers his sight in time to tackle a counterfeiting ring led by supposed air-crash victim Kynaston Reeves. Written by future horror director John Gilling, this is a by-the-numbers thriller, although the photography is seedily atmospheric. DP

Maxwell Reed *Chris Pelley* • Dinah Sheridan *Patricia Dale* • Eric Pohlmann *Otto* • Patric Doonan *Chalky* • Michael Brennan *Mickey* • Michael Evans (1) *Sinclair* • Annette Simmonds *Lila Drew* • Campbell Singer *Inspector* ■ *Dir* Robert S Baker • *Scr* Robert S Baker, John Gilling • *Cinematographer* Monty Berman

The Blackout ★★ 18

Thriller 1997 · US/Fr · Colour · 94mins

Abel Ferrara uses a rather blunt scalpel to expose the living hell of Hollywood stardom in another of his typically unrestrained rants. Matty (played with autobiographical candour by Matthew Modine) is a high-living movie celebrity who can't curtail his booze and drug lifestyle despite increasing blackouts. Did he commit murder during one such bout of unconsciousness? Sleazy nightclub owner Dennis Hopper helps him sift through the truth. AJ. Contains swearing, violence, drug abuse and sex scenes. [video] DVD

Matthew Modine *Matty* • Claudia Schiffer *Susan* • Béatrice Dalle *Annie 1* • Sarah Lassez *Annie 2* • Dennis Hopper *Mickey Wayne* • Steven Bauer *Mickey's studio actor* ■ *Dir* Abel Ferrara • *Scr* Abel Ferrara, Marla Hanson, Christ Zois

Blackrock ★★★

Drama 1997 · Aus · Colour · 100mins

Based on a true event, this compulsive Aussie drama deals with various personal and social issues, although there's an element of exploitation alongside the high-mindedness. Young Laurence Breuls throws a party for his surfing pal Simon Lyndon. Matters get desperately out of hand when several of the boys drunkenly rape a teenage girl, who is found dead the following day. Stargazers should watch out for Heath Ledger in a small part. BB

Laurence Breuls *Jared Kirby* • Linda Cropper *Diane Kirby* • Simon Lyndon *Ricko* • Chris Haywood *Det Sgt Wilansky* • Rebecca Smart *Cherie* • Essie Davis *Det Gilhooley* • Heath Ledger *Toby* ■ *Dir* Steven Vidler • *Scr* Nick Enright

The Blackwater Lightship ★★★

Drama 2004 · US · Colour · 110mins

This is a moving study of an Irish family's reunion in the face of tragedy, adapted by Shane Connaughton from Colm Toibin's Booker-shortlisted novel. Although the dramatic impetus in this TV movie is provided by Keith McErlean's return to his coastal home to endure the final stages of Aids, the focus falls mainly on the strained relationships between his sister (Gina McKee), his mother (Dianne Wiest) and his grandmother (Angela Lansbury). The performances are understandably intense, but director John Erman imbues proceedings with an over-stylised air that reduces the story's emotional impact. DP

Angela Lansbury *Dora* • Keith McErlean *Declan* • Gina McKee *Helen* • Dianne Wiest *Lily* ■ *Dir* John Erman • *Scr* Shane Connaughton, from the novel by Colm Toibin

Blackwater Trail ★★★ 18

Thriller 1995 · Aus · Colour · 95mins

Judd Nelson hasn't enjoyed much success since the heyday of the Brat Pack in the 1980s. This Australian thriller provides him with one of his strongest roles as a writer who returns to his home town for the funeral of an old friend, a policeman who had been involved in the case of a serial killer. The imported star is well supported by a galaxy of familiar Aussie soap stars. Although the plotting is contrived, director Ian Barry delivers some genuinely scary jolts. JF. Contains violence and some swearing. [video]

Judd Nelson *Matt Curran* • Dee Smart *Cathy* • Peter Phelps *Dr Frank Jamison* • Mark Lee *Chris* • Brett Climo *Father Michael* • Rowena Wallace *Beth* • Gabrielle Fitzpatrick *Sandra* ■ *Dir* Ian Barry • *Scr* Andrew Russell

B

Blacula ★★★ 15

Blaxploitation horror
1972 · US · Colour · 89mins

This is one of the better novelty blaxploitation horror romps, despite its eventual turn toward predictable genre conventions in the last half. Noted Shakespearean actor William Marshall stars as an African prince turned into a vampire by Count Dracula, who arrives in contemporary Los Angeles and starts cleaning up the ghetto by putting the bite on drug dealers, pimps and homosexuals. Thalmus Rasulala is the nemesis who finally stakes him out. The tongue-in-cheek humour makes this undemanding fun. AJ. Contains swearing, sexual references.

William Marshall (2) *Blacula* • Vonetta McGee *Tina* • Denise Nicholas *Michelle* • Thalmus Rasulala *Gordon Thomas* • Gordon Pinsent *Lieutenant Peters* • Charles McCauley *Dracula* • Emily Yancy *Nancy* • Lance Taylor Sr *Swenson* ■ *Dir* William Crain • *Scr* Joan Torres, Raymond Koenig

Blade ★★★ 18

Fantasy action adventure
1998 · US · Colour · 115mins

Wesley Snipes plays the half-mortal, half-vampire who hunts down creatures of the night in this flashy action adventure based on the popular comic. Aided by gruff-and-tough Kris Kristofferson, he sets out to thwart the evil schemes of fellow vampire Stephen Dorff, whose plans include running a nightclub that will supply humans for his fiendish pals to feed on. This is daft stuff indeed, but Snipes looks great in leather, it's snappily paced and the performances are perfectly tongue in cheek. JB. Contains swearing, violence. DVD

Wesley Snipes *Blade* • Stephen Dorff *Frost* • Kris Kristofferson *Whistler* • Kevin Patrick Walls *Krieger* • N'Bushe Wright *Karen* • Donal Logue *Quinn* • Arly Jover *Mercury* • Udo Kier *Dragonetti* • Traci Lords *Raquel* ■ *Dir* Stephen Norrington • *Scr* David S Goyer, from characters created for Marvel Comics by Marv Wolfman, Gene Colan

Blade II ★★★ 18

Fantasy action adventure
2002 · US/Ger · Colour · 112mins

Mexican genre maestro Guillermo del Toro directs the next episode in the Daywalker chronicles, based on the character from cult Marvel comic *Tomb of Dracula*. Pitching the moody half-vampire/half-human Blade (Wesley Snipes) as a sort of nocturnal James Bond with gadgets and gimmicks galore, the film's unrelenting action never flags. This time Blade reluctantly joins forces with vampire overlord Damaskinos (Thomas Kretschmann) to wipe out a new breed of super-vampires. It looks fabulous, but has zero character substance and isn't remotely scary. AJ DVD

Wesley Snipes *Blade* • Kris Kristofferson *Whistler* • Ron Perlman *Reinhardt* • Leonor Varela *Nyssa* • Norman Reedus *Scud* • Thomas Kretschmann *Damaskinos* • Luke Goss *Nomak* ■ *Dir* Guillermo del Toro • *Scr* David S Goyer, from the character created by Marv Wolfman, Gene Colan

Blade: Trinity ★ 15

Fantasy action adventure
2004 · US · Colour · 108mins

Franchise fatigue shows in all areas of this third Blade outing, directed by series writer David S Goyer. The plot is an incoherent mess, with Wesley Snipes's half-vampire vigilante teaming up with Ryan Reynolds and Jessica Biel to take on a vampire leader Parker Posey. Compared to the previous instalments, the horror is negligible and the action scenes tepid and repetitive. Add that to the sloppy direction and the disjointed script, and this is just plain inept. AJ. Contains violence and swearing. DVD

Wesley Snipes *Blade* • Kris Kristofferson *Abraham Whistler* • Jessica Biel *Abigail Whistler* • Ryan Reynolds *Hannibal King* • Parker Posey *Danica Talos* • Dominic Purcell *Dracula "Drake"* • Triple H [Paul Michael Levesque] *Jarko Grimwood* • Natasha Lyonne *Sommerfield* ■ *Dir* David S Goyer • *Scr* David S Goyer, from characters created by Marv Wolfman, Gene Colan

Blade Runner ★★★★★ 15

Futuristic science-fiction thriller
1982 · US · Colour · 111mins

A super Philip K Dick story, about superdick Harrison Ford battling rebellious replicants, translates here into a violent eye-popper, based in a futuristic American Chinatown, which set the acid rain/neon-drenched metropolis design standard for 1980s' sci-fi. As influential as *2001: a Space Odyssey* and *Star Wars*, and as thought provoking as the Kubrick classic, Ridley Scott's atmospheric downer is a compelling *noir* thriller pleading for harmony between man and machine. Rutger Hauer is exceptional as the blond humanoid who, like the others, has been implanted with memories of a nonexistent youth. The Director's Cut, which drops Ford's voiceover, actually adds more depth to the 1982 original, so the full masterpiece can shine through. AJ. Contains violence, swearing and brief nudity. DVD

Harrison Ford *Rick Deckard* • Rutger Hauer *Roy Batty* • Sean Young *Rachael* • Edward James Olmos *Gaff* • M Emmet Walsh *Bryant* • Daryl Hannah *Pris* • William Sanderson *Sebastian* • Brion James *Leon* ■ *Dir* Ridley Scott • *Scr* Hampton Fancher, David Peoples, from the story *Do Androids Dream of Electric Sheep?* by Philip K Dick • *Cinematographer* Jordan Cronenweth • *Music* Vangelis • *Production Design* Lawrence G Paull • *Special Effects* Douglas Trumbull

The Blair Witch Project ★★★★ 15

Supernatural horror
1998 · US · Colour and BW · 77mins

Made on a shoestring ($40,000), this no-frills, no-stars, no-effects horror yarn was released amid expectations that might have been hard to live up to had the film not been so different and so simple. Through arch use of the internet and word-of-mouth, it became a box-office sensation. A campfire ghost story in which three students go into the Maryland woods to film their own search for a mythical monster, the film's rough, video-diary edge and shaky point-of-view camerawork – while demanding on the eye – take the viewer right into the unfolding story. Scary without being explicit, it is a 1990s cinematic landmark, and best judged away from the hype. A disgraceful sequel, *Book of Shadows: Blair Witch 2*, followed in 2000. AC. Contains swearing. DVD

Heather Donahue • Michael Williams • Joshua Leonard • Bob Griffith *Interviewee* • Jim King *Interviewee* • Sandra Sanchez *Interviewee* • Ed Swanson *Interviewee* ■ *Dir* Daniel Myrick, Eduardo Sanchez • *Scr* Eduardo Sanchez, Daniel Myrick

Blame It on Rio ★★ 15

Comedy 1984 · US · Colour · 97mins

Michael Caine and Joseph Bologna may give decent enough performances as best friends on a spree in Rio, but the romance that develops between Caine and Bologna's teenage daughter (Michelle Johnson) is just too leery for comfort. The holiday atmosphere is well evoked, but the bad taste from director Stanley Donen is an unpleasant surprise. TH. Contains swearing and nudity. DVD

Michael Caine *Matthew Hollis* • Joseph Bologna *Victor Lyons* • Valerie Harper *Karen Hollis* • Michelle Johnson *Jennifer Lyons* • Demi Moore *Nicole Hollis* • José Lewgoy *Eduardo Marques* • Lupe Gigliotti *Signora Botega* • Michael Menaugh *Peter* ■ *Dir* Stanley Donen • *Scr* Charlie Peters, Larry Gelbart, from the film *Un Moment d'Egarement* by Claude Berri

Blame It on the Bellboy ★★★ 12

Comedy 1992 · UK · Colour · 75mins

A bellboy (Bronson Pinchot in a wonderfully farcical turn) is responsible for a series of mistaken identity mix-ups at a Venice hotel in this daft but fun slapstick-style comedy. Dudley Moore, Bryan Brown and Patsy Kensit are among the people getting confused in an intermittently hilarious tale that which owes much of its charm to the supporting performances from Richard Griffiths, Penelope Wilton and the always reliable Alison Steadman. JB. Contains swearing. DVD

Dudley Moore *Melvyn Orton* • Bryan Brown *Charlton Black/Mike Lawton* • Richard Griffiths *Maurice Horton* • Patsy Kensit *Caroline Wright* • Andreas Katsulas *Scarpa* • Alison Steadman *Rosemary Horton* • Penelope Wilton *Patricia Fulford* • Bronson Pinchot *Bellboy* • Jim Carter *Rossi* ■ *Dir/Scr* Mark Herman

Blame It on the Night ★★ PG

Drama 1984 · US · Colour · 84mins

Of most note since the screenplay is based on an original story by director Gene Taft and rock legend Mick Jagger, this shoddy, misbegotten family drama also showcases rock stars Billy Preston and Merry Clayton. Nick Mancuso plays an ageing rock star trying to buy the affections of his illegitimate son and one can only suppose that the plot has resonance for Mr Jagger, because there's little here for any audience. Tatty and ludicrous. TS

Nick Mancuso *Chris Dalton* • Byron Thames *Job Dalton* • Leslie Ackerman *Shelly* • Dick Bakalyan [Richard Bakalyan] *Manzini* • Leeyan Granger *Melanie* • Rex Ludwick *Animal* • Michael Wilding Jr *Terry* • Merry Clayton • Billy Preston ■ *Dir* Gene Taft • *Scr* Len Jenkin, from a story by Gene Taft, Mick Jagger

Blanche ★★★★ PG

Period drama 1971 · Fr · Colour · 89mins

Fairy tale, morality play and wry political allegory, Walerian Borowczyk's remarkable period drama is as visually alluring as it's tantalisingly ambiguous. Set in the castle of Michel Simon's 13th-century French baron, it considers such diverse themes as allegiance and honour, passion and possession, pride and folly, as his son, Lawrence Trimble, attempts to protect his stepmother's purity from the lustful advances of king Georges Wilson and his page, Jacques Perrin. Simon is gloriously grotesque as the slavering vassal, while Ligia Branice's porcelain stillness demurely conveys Borowczyk's vision of sacrificial perfection. DP. In French with English subtitles.

Ligia Branice *Blanche* • Lawrence Trimble *Nicolas* • Georges Wilson *The King* • Michel Simon *The Baron* • Jacques Perrin *Bartolomeo* • Denise Péronne *Lady Harcourt* ■ *Dir* Walerian Borowczyk • *Scr* Walerian Borowczyk, from the novel *Mazepa* by Juliusz Slowacki

Blanche Fury ★★★★ PG

Melodrama 1948 · UK · Colour · 90mins

This dark, brooding tale about inheritance and forbidden passion is set in a rambling English country home and stars an impressive Stewart Granger as a maverick estate manager. Granger is pitted against the best that British melodrama had to offer at the time, including Valerie Hobson in the title role, Maurice Denham and Michael Gough. This also benefits from an excellent screenplay and some taut direction from Marc Allégret, but it's the distinctive atmosphere that lingers in the memory. SH

Valerie Hobson *Blanche Fury* • Stewart Granger *Philip Thorn* • Walter Fitzgerald *Simon Fury* • Michael Gough *Lawrence Fury* • Maurice Denham *Major Frazer* • Sybilla Binder *Louisa* • Edward Lexy *Colonel Jenkins* • Allan Jeayes *Wetherby* ■ *Dir* Marc Allégret • *Scr* Audrey Erskine Lindop, Hugh Mills, Cecil McGivern, from the novel by Joseph Shearing • *Cinematographer* Guy Green, Geoffrey Unsworth

Blank Check ★★ PG

Comedy 1994 · US · Colour · 93mins

Clearly hoping to cash in on the success of *Home Alone*, Disney seemingly produced this kiddie comedy with nothing but the urgency of the release date in mind. The story of how pre-teen Brian Bonsall forges a cheque, sets himself up in the lap of luxury and then defends his patch is patently ludicrous – but with a little more imagination it might have made an entertaining romp. DP DVD

Brian Bonsall *Preston Waters* • Karen Duffy *Shay Stanley* • James Rebhorn *Fred Waters* • Jayne Atkinson *Sandra Waters* • Michael Faustino *Ralph Waters* • Chris Demetral *Damian Waters* • Miguel Ferrer *Quigley* • Michael Lerner *Biderman* ■ *Dir* Rupert Wainwright • *Scr* Blake Snyder, Colby Carr

Blankman ★★★ 12

Comedy 1994 · US · Colour · 91mins

Nerdy inventor Damon Wayans creates a bulletproof fabric, fashions a ridiculous superhero costume from it and becomes an inept crimefighter battling ghetto gangsters in this above-average comedy. Despite having no superpowers and with only his daft inventions and luck on his side, Wayans sets out to beat underworld kingpin Jon Polito and get the girl – TV news reporter Robin Givens. AJ

Damon Wayans *Darryl Walker/Young Kevin Walker* • David Alan Grier *Kevin Walker* • Robin Givens *Kimberly Jonz* • Christopher Lawford *Mayor Marvin Harris* • Lynne Thigpen *Grandma Walker* • Jon Polito *Michael "The Suit" Minelli* • Nicky Corello *Sammy the Blade* • Jason Alexander *Mr Stone* • Michael Wayans *Young Darryl* • Greg Kinnear *Talk show host* • Arsenio Hall ■ *Dir* Mike Binder • *Scr* JF Lawton, Damon Wayans, from a story by Damon Wayans

Blast from the Past ★★★ 12

Comedy 1998 · US · Colour · 98mins

Convinced that an atomic bomb is about to drop on 1960s America, married couple Sissy Spacek and Christopher Walken seal themselves in a fallout shelter for 35 years. What will their naive son Brendan Fraser make of the cynical 1990s when he's sent out into the world for the first time, enlisting the aid of streetwise Alicia Silverstone in his quest for supplies? Though the tone is sweet, the gags fail to bite in this somewhat laboured "culture clash" romantic comedy, but Fraser's goofy charm is winning. AJ. Contains swearing. DVD

Brendan Fraser *Adam* • Christopher Walken *Calvin* • Sissy Spacek *Helen* • Alicia Silverstone *Eve* • Dave Foley *Troy* • Joey Slotnick *Soda jerk* • Rex Linn *Dave* ■ *Dir* Hugh Wilson • *Scr* Bill Kelly, Hugh Wilson, from a story by Bill Kelly

Blaze ★★★ 15

Biographical drama
1989 · US · Colour · 112mins

The story of the passionate love affair between feisty Louisiana governor Earl Long and infamous New Orleans stripper Blaze Starr in the straight-laced 1950s is sanitised in director

Ron Shelton's sometimes insightful look into the dangerous and volatile mix of sex and politics. Paul Newman has fun moments as the uninhibited maverick who advocated black voting rights and Lolita Davidovich gives a memorable performance as the well-endowed hillbilly burlesque queen. While the combination of truth and comedy doesn't quite work, the two stars deliver a fair account of the tabloid scandal, and the real Blaze appears as backstage stripper Lily in a tiny cameo. AJ. Contains swearing and nudity. DVD

Paul Newman *Earl Kemp Long* • Lolita Davidovich *Fannie Belle Fleming/Blaze Starr* • Jerry Hardin *Thibodeaux* • Gailard Sartain *LaGrange* • Jeffrey DeMunn *Tuck* • Garland Bunting *Doc Ferriday* • Richard Jenkins *Times-Picayune Reporter* • Brandon Smith *Arvin Deeter* ■ *Dir* Ron Shelton • *Scr* Ron Shelton, from the autobiography *Blaze Starr: My Life as Told to Huey Perry* by Blaze Starr, Huey Perry

Blaze of Noon ★★

Adventure drama 1947 · US · BW · 90mins

William Holden, returning to civvy street and Paramount studios after four years of active service, stars in this tale of stunt-circus flying brothers who switch to the commercial world of airmail delivery. Set in the 1920s and adapted from a novel by Ernest K Gann, it was directed by John Farrow for maximum excitement in the air – it collapses on the ground thanks to the turgidly scripted, drawn-out relationship between Holden and Anne Baxter. RK

Anne Baxter *Lucille Stewart* • William Holden (2) *Colin McDonald* • William Bendix *Porkie* • Sonny Tufts *Roland McDonald* • Sterling Hayden *Tad McDonald* • Howard Da Silva *Gafferty* • Johnny Sands *Keith McDonald* • Jean Wallace *Poppy* • Edith King *Mrs Murphy* ■ *Dir* John Farrow • *Scr* Frank Wead, Arthur Sheekman, from the novel by Ernest K Gann

Blazing Saddles ★★★★ 15

Spoof western 1974 · US · Colour · 88mins

Mel Brooks's all-singing, all-belching western spoof remains one of his finest creations. Cleavon Little is the railway worker who is appointed the first black sheriff to a hell-raising western town; Gene Wilder is the drunken gunman who helps him out. The two stars are great, but there are even better performances from Madeline Kahn (sending up Marlene Dietrich) and the crazed Harvey Korman. There's not a lot of subtlety, but loads of slapstick, and even more jokes about bodily functions. JF. Contains swearing. DVD

Cleavon Little *Bart* • Gene Wilder *Jim, the Waco Kid* • Slim Pickens *Taggart* • Harvey Korman *Hedley Lamarr* • Madeline Kahn *Lili Von Shtupp* • Mel Brooks *Governor Lepetomane/Indian chief* • David Huddleston *Olson Johnson* • Liam Dunn *Rev Johnson* • Alex Karras *Mongo* ■ *Dir* Mel Brooks • *Scr* Mel Brooks, Norman Steinberg, Andrew Bergman, Richard Pryor, Alan Uger, from a story by Andrew Bergman

Bleak Moments ★★★★ PG

Drama 1971 · UK · Colour · 106mins

Written and directed by Mike Leigh and produced and edited by Leslie Blair, this may be the work of two dedicated realists, but it isn't quite the depressing prospect suggested by the title. However, it is an unflinching look at the everyday difficulties facing people leading quietly extraordinary lives. Among them is Anne Raitt, who struggles to communicate with those she knows, from her mentally disabled sister and her daydreaming office-mate to the hippy in her garage and her kindly teacher boyfriend. Everyone remembers the Chinese meal, but it's the aggregate of little episodes that makes this so moving. DP DVD

Anne Raitt *Sylvia* • Sarah Stephenson *Hilda* • Eric Allan *Peter* • Joolia Cappleman *Pat* • Mike Bradwell *Norman* • Liz Smith *Pat's mother* ■ *Dir/Scr* Mike Leigh

Bleeder ★★★ 18

Drama 1999 · Den · Colour · 93mins

Questioning the truism that movies are responsible for violence in society, and containing one of the most sadistic modes of execution ever witnessed on screen, this has much in common with Nicolas Winding Refn's debut feature, *Pusher*. However, while Kim Bodnia's abusive relationship with pregnant girlfriend Rikke Louise Andersson is sickening in the extreme, there's a hint of optimism in video geek Mads Mikkelsen's timid regard for waitress Liv Corfixen. Flawed but provocative. DP. In Danish with English subtitles. Contains violence. DVD

Kim Bodnia *Leo* • Mads Mikkelsen *Lenny* • Rikke Louise Andersson *Louise* • Liv Corfixen *Lea* • Levino Jensen *Louis* • Zlatko Buric *Kitjo* • Claus Fluggare *Joe* ■ *Dir/Scr* Nicolas Winding Refn

Bless the Beasts and Children ★★

Drama 1971 · US · Colour · 101mins

An environmental fable about six adolescent boys, all from broken families, who rescue a herd of buffalo destined for the slaughterhouse. Since this is a movie from Stanley Kramer, purveyor of such big message pictures as *On the Beach* and *Guess Who's Coming to Dinner*, the story is milked for every drop of meaning, symbolism and Biblical parallel. Years ahead of the eco-movement, the film draws one's admiration and sympathy. A pity it's so heavy-handed and contrived. AT

Bill Mumy *Teft* • Barry Robins *Cotton* • Miles Chapin *Shecker* • Darel Glaser *Goodenow* • Bob Kramer *Lally I* • Marc Vahanian *Lally II* • Elaine Devry *Cotton's mother* • Jesse White *Shecker's father* ■ *Dir* Stanley Kramer • *Scr* Mac Benoff, from a novel by Glendon Swarthout

Bless the Child ★★ 15

Supernatural thriller
2000 · US/Ger · Colour · 107mins

One minute Kim Basinger's winning an Oscar for *LA Confidential*, the next she's starring in this below-average supernatural yarn. Basinger plays a nurse who rears her drug-addicted sister's baby as her own, until the sister turns up with a creepy new husband (Rufus Sewell) and demands the return of the youngster, who's started to manifest all sorts of magical powers. Basinger teams up with an FBI officer (Jimmy Smits) to track the child down. Utter nonsense, but entertaining in a daft sort of way. JB. Contains some swearing and violence. DVD

Kim Basinger *Maggie O'Connor* • Jimmy Smits *John Travis* • Rufus Sewell *Eric Stark* • Ian Holm *Reverend Grissom* • Angela Bettis *Jenna* • Holliston Coleman *Cody* • Christina Ricci *Cheri* ■ *Dir* Chuck Russell • *Scr* Tom Rickman, Clifford Green, Ellen Green, from a novel by Cathy Cash Spellman

Bless This House ★★ U

Comedy 1972 · UK · Colour · 85mins

In the 1970s, there was a misguided belief among British film-makers that successful sitcoms could be transferred to the big screen. The majority proved to be huge disappointments, and this was no exception, although it did have one saving grace: the incomparable Sidney James. He is the grouchy father, married to Diana Coupland, who is trying to come to grips with his teenage children and his neighbours (Terry Scott and June Whitfield). There are more laughs in the naff 1970s fashions than in the script. JF DVD

Sidney James *Sid Abbot* • Diana Coupland *Jean Abbot* • Sally Geeson *Sally Abbot* • Terry Scott *Ronald Baines* • June Whitfield *Vera Baines* • Peter Butterworth *Trevor Lewis* • Robin Askwith *Mike Abbot* • Bill Maynard *Oldham* • Wendy Richard *Carol* ■ *Dir* Gerald Thomas • *Scr* Dave Freeman

Blessed Event ★★★

Comedy drama 1932 · US · BW · 82mins

Band singer Dick Powell, who would go on to have a successful career in both musicals and tough-guy roles, made his screen debut in this version of a hit Broadway play set in the worlds of newspapers and showbiz. However, the movie belongs to its star, Lee Tracy, in the role of a newspaperman. Aided by dialogue that snaps, crackles and pops, he gives the performance of his career as a ruthless gossip columnist tangling with colleagues, crooners and chorus girls – though Ned Sparks, as a misogynistic journalist, gives him a run for his money. Amusing, authentic and entertaining. RK

Lee Tracy *Alvin Roberts* • Mary Brian *Gladys Price* • Allen Jenkins *Frankie Wells* • Ruth Donnelly *Miss Stevens* • Ned Sparks *George Moxley* • Dick Powell *Bunny Harmon* ■ *Dir* Roy Del Ruth • *Scr* Howard J Green, from the play by Manuel Seff, Forrest Wilson

Blessed Stranger: after Flight 111 ★★

Drama 2000 · Can · Colour · 92mins

In September 1998, Swissair Flight 111 crashed into the Atlantic Ocean off Nova Scotia, killing all 229 people on board. This TV movie centres on two strangers bound together by the tragedy. Kate Nelligan is typically assured as a mother hoping to find evidence that her teenage daughter somehow survived the tragedy. Hugh Thompson offers solid support as a fisherman still traumatised by his failure to rescue anyone from the sea following the crash. DP

Kate Nelligan *Kate O'Rourke* • Hugh Thompson *Everett Barkhouse* • Stacy Smith *Sandy Martel* • Janet Kidder *Cheryl Barkhouse* • Peter MacNeill *Earl Barkhouse* ■ *Dir* David Wellington • *Scr* Michael Amo

Blind Adventure ★★ U

Spy comedy drama 1933 · US · BW · 62mins

Robert Armstrong is the American in London who gets mixed up with a bunch of criminal rogues that includes charming burglar Roland Young. Helen Mack is the heroine of this routine film, which adopts a comic tone but is defeated by a tediously muddled plot. The surprise is that it was written by Ruth Rose and directed by her husband Ernest B Schoedsack, in the same year she co-wrote and he co-directed *King Kong*. RK

Robert Armstrong *Richard Bruce* • Helen Mack *Rose Thorne* • Roland Young *Holmes, the burglar* • Ralph Bellamy *Jim Steele* • John Miljan *Regan* • Laura Hope Crews *Lady Rockingham* ■ *Dir* Ernest B Schoedsack • *Scr* Ruth Rose, Robert Benchley (additional dialogue)

Blind Alley ★★★

Crime thriller 1939 · US · BW · 69mins

Remade in 1948 with William Holden as *The Dark Past*, this adaptation of James Warwick's play keeps the original Broadway title. Chester Morris, two years before he took on the role of "Boston Blackie", is interestingly cast as a thug who holds a psychologist prisoner, getting himself analysed in the process. (This was one of the first films to offer a Freudian explanation for a character's behaviour.) Likeable Ralph Bellamy is extremely sympathetic as the shrink hostage. TS

Chester Morris *Hal Wilson* • Ralph Bellamy *Dr Shelby* • Ann Dvorak *Mary* • Joan Perry *Linda Curtis* • Melville Cooper *George Curtis* • Rose Stradner *Doris Shelby* • John Eldredge *Dick Holbrook* • Ann Doran *Agnes* • Marc Lawrence (1) *Buck* ■ *Dir* Charles Vidor • *Scr* Phillip MacDonald, Michael Blankfort, Albert Duffy, from the play by James Warwick

Blind Alley ★★★ 18

Thriller 1984 · US · Colour · 87mins

The start of Larry Cohen's film plays a similar tune to the 1985 Harrison Ford hit *Witness*, in that it has a young boy witnessing a murder. The similarities end there, though, and what follows is a smart romantic thriller whose different plot strands come together neatly at the climax. Anne Carlisle plays the boy's mother, while Brad Rijn plays the Mafia hitman with whom she becomes involved. NF

Anne Carlisle *Sally* • Brad Rijn *Johnny Ross* • John Woehrle *Fred* • Matthew Stockley *Matthew* • Stephen Lack *Lt Burns* • Ann Magnuson *Maida* • Zachary Hains *Maletti* • Otto von Wernherr *Private eye* ■ *Dir/Scr* Larry Cohen

Blind Chance ★★★ 18

Drama 1987 · Pol · Colour · 113mins

The basic premise of this politically loaded drama is essentially sound. Boguslaw Linda runs for a train and three potential fates ensue: the first sees him become a Communist aparatchik; the next reveals him dabbling in underground protest and religion; while the third shows him pursuing an apolitical medical career. However, the rigidity of the structure prevents director Krzysztof Kieslowski from exploring his themes in any depth. Indeed, he recognised the flaws while editing and always deemed the film a failure. Yet its historical context and its anticipation of the ideas considered in *The Double Life of Véronique* and *Three Colours Red* enhance its significance. DP. In Polish with English subtitles. Contains swearing, sex scenes, nudity. DVD

Boguslaw Linda *Witek* • Tadeusz Lomnicki *Werner* • Zbigniew Zapasiewicz *Adam* • Marzena Trybala *Werka* • Jacek Borkowski *Marek* • Monika Gozdzik *Olga* • Zygmunt Hübner *Dzirkan* ■ *Dir/Scr* Krzysztof Kieslowski

Blind Date ★★★

Crime drama 1959 · UK · BW · 94mins

This usually overlooked entry in the Joseph Losey canon is actually quite a daring and sophisticated investigation into British attitudes towards sex, class and the establishment in the late 1950s. Adapted from Leigh Howard's novel, the story is pretty unremarkable, but Losey's assured handling of character and location forces you to share the plight of Dutch painter Hardy Kruger, as he becomes embroiled in a political scandal after the mistress he shares with the French ambassador in London is murdered. Stanley Baker investigates with quiet efficiency. DP

Hardy Kruger *Jan van Rooyen* • Stanley Baker *Inspector Morgan* • Micheline Presle *Jacqueline Cousteau* • Robert Flemyng *Sir Brian Lewis* • Gordon Jackson *Police sergeant* • John Van Eyssen *Westover* ■ *Dir* Joseph Losey • *Scr* Ben Barzman, Millard Lampell, from the novel by Leigh Howard

Blind Date ★ 18

Crime thriller 1984 · US · Colour · 99mins

Blind Joseph Bottoms is able to see again after doctor Keir Dullea fits him up with a computer implant. But what's the link between him and a mad serial killer? You won't care in this Greece-set slasher that's so high on tortuous logic and so low on conviction that only the scriptwriters could swallow it. Writer/director Nico Mastorakis gets it wrong in every area, especially the inane dialogue. AJ

Joseph Bottoms *Jonathon Ratcliffe* • Kirstie Alley *Claire Simpson* • James Daughton *Dave* • Lana Clarkson *Rachel* • Keir Dullea *Dr Steiger* • Charles Nicklin *Robert* • Marina Sirtis *Hooker* ■ *Dir* Nico Mastorakis • *Scr* Nico Mastorakis, Fred C Perry

Blind Date ★★ 15

Comedy 1987 · US · Colour · 91mins

When Bruce Willis's feature debut was released, it was mauled by the critics and some predicted he would join the many TV stars who had attempted to cross over into Hollywood and failed. The film's box-office success and the subsequent career of the former *Moonlighting* actor have proved the critics wrong, but this would-be comedy hasn't improved with age. Willis is fixed up with the blind date from hell in the shape of Kim Basinger. The two leads are likeable enough, but Blake Edwards's direction is crass and chaotic. JF. Contains violence, swearing and drug abuse. DVD

Bruce Willis *Walter Davis* • Kim Basinger *Nadia Gates* • John Larroquette *David Bedford* • William Daniels *Judge Harold Bedford* • George Coe *Harry Gruen* • Mark Blum *Denny Gordon* • Phil Hartman *Ted Davis* ■ *Dir* Blake Edwards • *Scr* Dale Launer

Blind Flight ★★★★ 15

Drama based on a true story
2003 · UK/Ger/Ire · Colour · 92mins

This powerful drama recounts the true story of hostages Brian Keenan and John McCarthy and their years of captivity in Lebanon. Following their release, both men published books on their ordeal as well as helping to shape the screenplay for writer/director John Furse's feature debut. Ian Hart (as Keenan) and Linus Roache (as McCarthy) bring the experiences of these two very different men vividly to life, as their resolve is tested by the indignities, hardships and horrors of a life of incarceration. But what is surprising is the understanding extended to the kidnappers ("We all have our reasons," says McCarthy), that serves only to enhance the unfolding human drama. TH. Contains violence and swearing. DVD

Ian Hart *Brian Keenan* • Linus Roache *John McCarthy* • Bassem Breish *Joker* • Ziad Lahoud *Said* • Mohamad Chamas *Abed* ■ *Dir* John Furse • *Scr* Brian Keenan, John McCarthy, John Furse

Blind Fury ★★★ 18

Action thriller 1990 · US · Colour · 82mins

Two years after he hit the big time with the fabulous *Dead Calm*, Australian director Phillip Noyce made this nifty martial arts saga, in which blind Vietnam veteran Rutger Hauer rescues his buddy's son from evil gangsters and then hits the road, bonding with the boy while fending off the bad guys at every available opportunity. It's a gimmicky, but above-average, action adventure (based on the hugely popular Japanese *Zatoichi* film series). AJ. Contains violence, swearing.

Rutger Hauer *Nick Parker* • Terrance O'Quinn [Terry O'Quinn] *Frank Devereaux* • Brandon Call *Billy Devereaux* • Lisa Blount *Annie Winchester* • Randall "Tex" Cobb *Slag* • Noble Willingham *MacCready* • Meg Foster *Lynn Devereaux* • Sho Kosugi *Assassin* ■ *Dir* Phillip Noyce • *Scr* Charles Robert Carner

The Blind Goddess ★★

Drama 1948 · UK · BW · 87mins

Nobody can do decent coves caught in a dilemma quite like Michael Denison and he's perfectly cast again in this screen version of Patrick Hastings's hit stage play as a secretary who shops his embezzling boss. But, unfortunately, this reunion with director Harold French (after the same year's *My Brother Jonathan*) suffers from some uncertain handling, with the courtroom scenes in particular sapped of the suspense that made them so compelling in the theatre. DP

Eric Portman *Sir John Dearing* • Anne Crawford *Lady Brasted* • Hugh Williams *Lord Brasted* • Michael Denison *Derek Waterhouse* • Nora Swinburne *Lady Dearing* • Claire Bloom *Mary Dearing* • Raymond Lovell *Mr Mainwaring* • Frank Cellier *Judge* • Maurice Denham *Butler* ■ *Dir* Harold French • *Scr* Muriel Box, Sydney Box, from the play by Patrick Hastings

Blind Husbands ★★★★

Silent melodrama 1919 · US · BW · 129mins

After the First World War, when Erich von Stroheim's "Horrible Hun" roles were no longer in demand, he persuaded Universal to let him direct this cynical, witty and erotic drama set in the Alps. Stroheim also wrote the script, designed the sets and played the lead role of the dashing Lieutenant von Steuben, who seduces a bored American wife on holiday. With its careful attention to detail in the decor and costumes, and the acute psychological observation of the characters, Stroheim's debut movie prefigured his later, more mature work. The picture was a commercial and critical success; it was also the only one of his films to be released without considerable studio interference. RB

Sam De Grasse *Dr Robert Armstrong* • Francelia Billington *Margaret Armstrong* • Erich von Stroheim *Lieutenant von Steuben* • TH Gibson-Gowland [Gibson Gowland] *Sepp* • Fay Holderness *Vamp waitress* • Ruby Kendrick *"A Village Blossom"* ■ *Dir* Erich von Stroheim • *Scr* Erich von Stroheim, Lillian Ducey (titles), from the story *The Pinnacle* by Erich von Stroheim • *Cinematographer* Ben Reynolds

Blind Shaft ★★★★ 15

Drama 2003 · Ger/HK · Colour · 88mins

Li Yang's debut feature relates a tale that's as bleak as its northern Chinese setting. By merely implying the desperation of the men drawn to the region's poorly regulated coal mines, Li condemns the society that allows such poverty to exist. Yet neither does he condone the iniquitous racket run by Wang Shuangbao and Li Yixiang, who persuade strangers to pose as their relatives to secure employment and then kill them in faked accidents in order to blackmail the pit owners into paying illicit compensation. Nor does he melodramatise the encounter with teenager, Wang Baoqiang, that seals their fate. DP. In Mandarin with English subtitles. Contains swearing and sex scenes. DVD

Li Yixiang *Song Jinming* • Wang Shuangbao *Tang Zhaoyang* • Wang Baoqiang *Yuan Fengming* ■ *Dir* Li Yang • *Scr* Li Yang, from the novel *Shenmu [Sacred Wood]* by Liu Qingbang

Blind Spot: Hitler's Secretary ★★★ PG

Documentary 2002 · Austria · Colour · 87mins

Shortly before her death in 2002, and after 50 years of silence, Traudl Junge, who worked as one of Adolf Hitler's secretaries, finally told her story to André Heller and Othmar Schmiderer. Sadly the resulting film doesn't do justice to the often fascinating intimate detail of daily life with one of history's most monstrous men. While there is an affecting poignancy to Junge's inability to forgive herself for things over which she had no control, the film-makers' decision to include no archive material and to simply present a "talking head" leaves the frustrating impression that there is still plenty of raw material for an excellent documentary. AS. In German with English subtitles. DVD

Dir/Scr André Heller, Othmar Schmiderer

Blind Terror ★★ 15

Thriller 1971 · UK · Colour · 83mins

Blind Mia Farrow splashes mud on a young drifter's cowboy boots while travelling to her uncle's isolated mansion. In revenge, he slaughters her entire family and relentlessly pursues her around the old dark house. Written by Brian Clemens (*The Avengers*) on what must clearly have been an off-day, Richard Fleischer's cumbersome chiller has minimal shocks and suspense. Farrow tries her best to convince, but the half-baked premise is too full of ridiculous red herrings to be even remotely believable. AJ

Mia Farrow *Sarah* • Robin Bailey *George Rexton* • Dorothy Alison *Betty Rexton* • Norman Eshley *Steve Reding* • Diane Grayson *Sandy Rexton* • Paul Nicholas *Jacko* • Christopher Matthews *Frost* • Brian Rawlinson *Barker* • Michael Elphick *Gypsy Tom* ■ *Dir* Richard Fleischer • *Scr* Brian Clemens

Blind Vision ★★

Thriller 1992 · US · Colour · 90mins

Attempting to recapture the eerie voyeurism present in many of Hitchcock's best films, this is about a man who becomes a murder suspect when the boyfriend of the woman he is spying on ends up dead. The voyeur is played by Lenny Von Dohlen and the object of his desire is Deborah Shelton. Most eyes will, however, be on the supporting cast. Standard thriller fare. AT. Contains swearing, violence, sex scenes and brief nudity.

Lenny Von Dohlen *William Dalton* • Deborah Shelton *Leanne Dunaway* • Ned Beatty *Sergeant Dave Logan* • Robert Vaughn *Mr X* • Louise Fletcher *Virginia Taylor* • Stoney Jackson *Tony Davis* • Catherine McGoohan *Gloria Byers* ■ *Dir* Shuki Levy • *Scr* Shuki Levy, Winston Rickard

Blindfold ★★★ U

Comedy mystery
1966 · US · Colour · 101mins

Had Philip Dunne resisted the temptation to parody Hitchcock, this might have been a first-rate thriller. The levity undercuts the tension that develops as society psychiatrist Rock Hudson begins to realise that Alejandro Rey (the patient he's been seeing in such secrecy that he's blindfolded to and from their consultations) is actually in grave danger. The romance with Rey's sister Claudia Cardinale and some uncomfortable slapstick prevent the action from being genuinely nail-biting. DP

Rock Hudson *Dr Bartholomew Snow* • Claudia Cardinale *Victoria Vail/Vicky Vincenti* • Jack Warden *General Pratt* • Guy Stockwell *Fitzpatrick* • Brad Dexter *Harrigan* • Anne Seymour *Smitty* • Alejandro Rey *Arthur Vincenti* • Hari Rhodes *Captain Davis* ■ *Dir* Philip Dunne • *Scr* Philip Dunne, WH Menger, from the novel by Lucille Fletcher

Blink ★★★ 18

Thriller 1994 · US · Colour · 101mins

The concept is not new – blind woman in peril fights back – but, thanks to a winning, sassy performance from Madeleine Stowe, this rises above the routine. Stowe is a folk fiddle player recovering from an operation that will eventually allow her to see again. For the time being, she gets fleeting moments of vision and during one of these periods she catches sight of a murderer, thereby putting her own life in danger. Aidan Quinn is the sceptical policeman assigned to watch over her. Director Michael Apted competently cranks up the tension, and Stowe's faltering flashes of sight are brilliantly realised. JF. Contains violence, swearing and nudity. DVD

Madeleine Stowe *Emma Brody* • Aidan Quinn *Detective John Hallstrom* • James Remar *Thomas Ridgely* • Peter Friedman *Doctor Ryan Pierce* • Bruce A Young *Lieutenant Mitchell* • Laurie Metcalf *Candice* • Matt Roth *Crowe* • Paul Dillon *Neal Booker* ■ *Dir* Michael Apted • *Scr* Dana Stevens

Blinky Bill ★★★ Uc

Animated adventure
1992 · Aus · Colour · 93mins

Yoram Gross pioneered cartoons with an ecological theme in a series of films about Dot and her animal friends, and his message found its biggest audience in this loose adaptation of Dorothy Wall's 1930s story collection, which has become a cultural (and consumer) phenomenon. Once again the main theme is the threat posed to wildlife by "progress", as a baby koala learns to fend for himself after he's separated from his mother. The animation isn't particularly sophisticated, but the ideas certainly are. DP DVD

Dir Yoram Gross • *Scr* Yoram Gross, Leonard Lee

Bliss ★★★★ 18

Black comedy 1985 · Aus · Colour · 107mins

A movie of great charm and style, this concentrates on the hoary old "cheating death and rediscovering life" chestnut, but gives it some fresh and funny topspin. The performances, particularly from frenzied Barry Otto as a hapless advertising executive, are universally excellent, but it is Ray Lawrence's adroit and deft direction that turns a simple and oft-told tale – about a man who dramatically changes his life after a heart attack – into a miniature comic tour de force. SH. Contains swearing.

Barry Otto *Harry Joy* • Lynette Curran *Bettina Joy* • Helen Jones *Honey Barbara* • Miles Buchanan *David Joy* • Gia Carides *Lucy Joy* • Tim Robertson *Alex Duval* • Jeff Truman *Joel* • Bryan Marshall *Adrian* • Jon Ewing *Aldo* ■ *Dir* Ray Lawrence • *Scr* Ray Lawrence, Peter Carey, from the novel by Peter Carey

Bliss ★★ 18

Erotic drama 1997 · US · Colour · 99mins

Despite the high production values, a quality cast and a wordy script, this is not that different from many formulaic erotic thrillers. Craig Sheffer and Sheryl Lee star as a young, newly married couple whose sex life is proving to be a damp squib. In desperation they turn to therapist Terence Stamp, who introduces them to a new world of sexual experience. Stamp steals the show from the unconvincing leads, while the soft-focus photography undermines the worthy intentions of writer/director Lance Young. JF. Contains swearing and sex scenes.

Terence Stamp *Baltazar Vincenza* • Craig Sheffer *Joseph* • Sheryl Lee *Maria* • Spalding Gray *Alfred* • Casey Siemaszko *Tanner* • Ken Camroux *Hank* • Pamela Perry *Dottie* • Blu Mankuma *Nick* ■ *Dir/Scr* Lance Young

The Bliss of Mrs Blossom ★★

Comedy 1968 · UK · Colour · 93mins

Shirley MacLaine stars in this otherwise all-British comedy, written by Alec Coppel and Denis Norden and directed by Joseph McGrath. She plays the wife of a brassière manufacturer (Richard Attenborough), who manages to conceal her lover (James Booth), one of her husband's employees, in the attic for three years before her husband tumbles to the situation. A kind of screwball farce, it is played with evident gusto by MacLaine and a cast that features Freddie Jones, Patricia Routledge, Bob Monkhouse and William Rushton, who, defying the total absurdity of the situation, manage to ellicit some laughs. RK

Shirley MacLaine *Harriet Blossom* • Richard Attenborough *Robert Blossom* • James Booth *Ambrose Tuttle* • Freddie Jones *Detective Sergeant Dylan* • William Rushton *Dylan's assistant* • Bob Monkhouse *Dr Taylor* • Patricia Routledge *Miss Reece* • John Bluthal *Judge* • Barry Humphries *Mr Wainwright, art dealer* • Clive Dunn *Man* • John Cleese *Clerk* ■ *Dir* Joseph McGrath • *Scr* Alec Coppel, Denis Norden, from the story by Josef Shaftel, from the play *A Bird in the Nest* by Alec Coppel

Blithe Spirit ★★★★ U

Comedy fantasy 1945 · UK · Colour · 91mins

In this polished adaptation of Noël Coward's comedy, widower Rex Harrison is happily remarried to Constance Cummings and visited by the ghost of his first wife, Kay Hammond. The architect of this event is a dotty old medium, played by the unforgettable Margaret Rutherford. David Lean directed – Coward was away in America and the great British director was worried he was the wrong man for the job. According to Kevin Brownlow's monumental biography of Lean, Coward attended the first preview and was distinctly unimpressed. The critics lapped it up, though, and the dainty special effects won an Oscar. AT [video] DVD

Rex Harrison *Charles Condomine* • Constance Cummings *Ruth Condomine* • Kay Hammond *Elvira* • Margaret Rutherford *Madame Arcati* • Hugh Wakefield *Dr Bradman* • Joyce Carey *Mrs Bradman* • Jacqueline Clark *Edith* ■ *Dir* David Lean • *Scr* Anthony Havelock-Allan, David Lean, Ronald Neame, from the play by Noël Coward • *Cinematographer* Ronald Neame • *Special Effects* Thomas Howard

The Blob ★★★ 15

Science-fiction drama
1958 · US · Colour · 82mins

Steve McQueen got his first starring role in this musty delight about a giant red alien jelly terrorising small-town America and absorbing the population. A quintessential 1950s classic (which spawned a successful 1988 remake), the gaudy colours, self-mocking tone and the neat title creature add up to loads of unsettling fun. The scene where the outer space ooze invades a local cinema has become one of science-fiction cinema's key images. AJ. Contains some violence. [video] DVD

Steven McQueen [Steve McQueen] *Steve* • Aneta Corseaut *Judy* • Earl Rowe *Police lieutenant* • Olin Howlin *Old man* • Steven Chase [Stephen Chase (1)] *Doctor* • John Benson *Sergeant Jim Bert* • Vince Barbi *George* • Tom Ogen • Julie Cousins • Ralph Roseman ■ *Dir* Irvin S Yeaworth Jr • *Scr* Irvin S Yeaworth Jr, Theodore Simonson, Ruth Phillips, from an idea by Irvine H Millgate

The Blob ★★★★ 18

Science fiction 1988 · US · Colour · 90mins

The Space Sponge returns in a super remake of the cult monster movie from sci-fi's golden era. As with John Carpenter and his remake of *The Thing*, director Chuck Russell (*The Mask*) gets his revamp exactly right. By re-interpreting all the potent moments from the Steve McQueen original in today's sophisticated special-effects terms, and updating the plot to include contemporary mores and political issues, Russell creates a breakneck monster-on-the-loose crowd-pleaser with a fun nostalgic pulse. AJ [video]

Shawnee Smith *Meg Penny* • Donovan Leitch *Paul Taylor* • Kevin Dillon *Brian Flagg* • Ricky Paull Goldin *Scott Jeskey* • Billy Beck *Can man* • Jeffrey DeMunn *Sheriff Herb Geller* • Candy Clark *Fran Hewitt* • Beau Billingslea *Moss Woolsey* ■ *Dir* Chuck Russell • *Scr* Chuck Russell, Frank Darabont

Block Busters ★★ U

Comedy 1944 · US · BW · 60mins

Before the East Side Kids became the Bowery Boys, there was a pleasing rough edge to their comedy, and here a new French kid on the block proves to be the very model of international camaraderie as he helps the boys win their local baseball game. Symbolic, you betcha! Back in the dark days of the Second World War, this was a lesson in how to be good neighbours for all audiences. TH

Leo Gorcey *Muggs* • Huntz Hall *Glimpy* • Gabriel Dell *Skinny* • Billy Benedict *Butch* • Jimmy Strand *Danny* • Bill Chaney *Tobey* • Minerva Urecal *Amelia* • Roberta Smith *Jinx* • Noah Beery Sr [Noah Beery] *Judge* • Harry Langdon *Higgins* ■ *Dir* Wallace Fox • *Scr* Houston Branch

Blockade ★★

War drama 1938 · US · BW · 85mins

The Spanish Civil War was a crusade for many Hollywood liberals and one might have expected a screenwriter such as John Howard Lawson, later one of the original Hollywood Ten, to have produced something less lily-livered than this. The picture tells us that war is wrong and nothing else. Henry Fonda and Madeleine Carroll are mixed up in it – he's a peasant, she's one of dozens of spies – but the story is hopelessly muddled. AT

Henry Fonda *Marco* • Madeleine Carroll *Norma* • Leo Carrillo *Luis* • John Halliday *Andre* • Vladimir Sokoloff *Basil* • Robert Warwick *General Vallejo* ■ *Dir* William Dieterle • *Scr* John Howard Lawson

Blockheads ★★★★ U

Classic comedy 1938 · US · BW · 56mins

Stan Laurel, left to guard a trench in 1917, is discovered two decades later with a pile of empty bean cans, still on guard. Ollie takes the trench hero home, where they become involved in a farcical situation with jealous big-game hunter Billy Gilbert. One to relish for its innuendos and sight gags, John G Blystone's remake of the short *Unaccustomed as We Are* is one of Laurel and Hardy's more appealing comedies. TH [video] DVD

Stan Laurel *Stan* • Oliver Hardy *Ollie* • Billy Gilbert *Mr Gilbert* • Patricia Ellis *Mrs Gilbert* • Minna Gombell *Mrs Hardy* • James Finlayson *Mr Finn* ■ *Dir* John G Blystone • *Scr* Felix Adler, Arnold Belgard, Harry Langdon, James Parrott, Charles Rogers

The Blockhouse ★★★

Second World War drama
1973 · UK · Colour · 103mins

An almost unseen Peter Sellers movie, this features the star in a rare straight role. In wartime Germany, slave workers from all over Europe are used to build German coastal fortifications while the Allies bombard the sites. Several workers take refuge in a network of underground tunnels and are subsequently sealed in. Although the bunkers contain ample supplies, the workers undergo a tortuous time in their subterranean prison. This grim movie based on real-life events (two men were discovered in 1951, having been trapped for six years in a similar situation). This difficult film sat on the shelf for several years, before surfacing briefly in 1978. DF

Peter Sellers *Rouquet* • Charles Aznavour *Visconti* • Per Oscarsson *Lund* • Peter Vaughan *Aufret* • Jeremy Kemp *Grabinski* • Leon Lissek *Kozhek* • Nicholas Jones *Kramer* • Alfred Lynch *Larshen* ■ *Dir* Clive Rees • *Scr* John Gould, Clive Rees, from the novel *Le Blockhaus* by Jean Paul Clebert

Blond Cheat ★ U

Comedy 1938 · US · BW · 62mins

Intended as a farce with an English slant, this miserable offering from RKO and director Joseph Santley needed five writers to dream up the tale of a British millionaire (Cecil Kellaway) who offers to finance a new show for an actress (Joan Fontaine, before her career took off with *Rebecca*) on condition she breaks up the romance between his daughter (Lilian Bond) and a smooth socialite (Derrick DeMarney). There is little to recommend it. RK

Joan Fontaine *Julie Evans* • Derrick DeMarney *Michael Ashburn* • Cecil Cunningham *Genevieve Trent* • Lillian Bond *Roberta Trent* • Robert Coote *Gilbert Potts* • Olaf Hytten *Paul Douglas* • Gerald Hamer *Waiter* • Cecil Kellaway *Rufus Trent* ■ *Dir* Joseph Santley • *Scr* Charles Kaufman, Paul Yawitz, Viola Brothers Shore, Harry Segall, from a story by Aladar Lazlo

Blonde Bombshell ★★★★

Comedy 1933 · US · BW · 90mins

A chance to see Jean Harlow in the movie that originally opened as *Bombshell*. It's a perceptive yet affectionate satire on Hollywood itself, with the peroxide sex symbol playing movie sexpot Lola Burns, desperate for a life away from the cameras. It's quite a wacky farce with some biting observations, and Harlow really proves her worth, keeping sentimentality at bay while revealing a warm yet snappy comedic style that would serve her well in her next film, the all-star classic *Dinner at Eight*. This movie is directed by one of Hollywood's most under-rated craftsmen, Victor Fleming of *Gone with the Wind* and *The Wizard of Oz* fame, who squeezes every inch of mileage out of a plot one suspects he understood very well. TS

Jean Harlow *Lola* • Lee Tracy *Space* • Frank Morgan *Pops* • Franchot Tone *Gifford Middleton* • Pat O'Brien *Brogan* • Una Merkel *Mae* • Ted Healy *Junior* • Ivan Lebedeff *Marquis* • Mary Forbes *Mrs Middleton* • C Aubrey Smith *Mr Middleton* ■ *Dir* Victor Fleming • *Scr* Jules Furthman, John Lee Mahin, from the play by Caroline Francke, Mack Crane

Blonde Crazy ★★★

Crime comedy drama
1931 · US · BW · 78mins

Fast-talking James Cagney's follow-up to his smash hits *Public Enemy* and *Smart Money* was this nifty little melodrama, shown in the UK as *Larceny Lane*. Here, he's a conman and she's his business partner/girlfriend who marries a relative newcomer to Hollywood, a startlingly young looking Ray Milland. The pace never lets up, and the success of this movie forced boss Jack Warner to up Cagney's salary to a richly deserved $1,000 per week after the star threatened to go elsewhere. TS

James Cagney *Bert Harris* • Joan Blondell *Ann Roberts* • Louis Calhern *Dapper Dan Barker* • Noel Francis *Helen Wilson* • Raymond Milland [Ray Milland] *Joe Reynolds* • Guy Kibbee *Rupert Johnson* • Polly Walters *Peggy* • Charles Lane (2) *Four-eyes, desk clerk* ■ *Dir* Roy Del Ruth • *Scr* Kubec Glasmon, John Bright

Blonde Fever ★★

Comedy drama 1944 · US · BW · 60mins

Based on Ferenc Molnar's play *Delila*, this familiar tale of a married man falling for the charms of a gold-digger needed a Lubitsch but instead got the uninspired direction of Richard Whorf. It remains watchable due to the MGM production gloss, Gloria Grahame, in her screen debut as the scheming waitress, and a beautiful performance by veteran Mary Astor, as the wife. TV

Philip Dorn *Peter Donay* • Mary Astor *Delilah Donay* • Felix Bressart *Johnny* • Gloria Grahame *Sally Murfin* ■ *Dir* Richard Whorf • *Scr* Patricia Coleman, from the play *Delila* by Ferenc Molnar

B

Blonde Fist ★ 15

Comedy drama 1991 · UK · Colour · 98mins

Real-life brother and sister Frank and Margi Clarke fail to live up to early promise as, respectively, writer/director and star of this lumbering *Film on Four* about a working-class woman with a mess of a life but a socking right hook, inherited from her bare-knuckle boxing dad. One to duck. PF. Contains violence and swearing. [video]

Margi Clarke *Ronnie O'Dowd* • Carroll Baker *Lovelle Summers* • Ken Hutchison *John O'Dowd* • Sharon Power *Mary* • Angela Clarke *Brenda Doyle* • Lewis Bester *Young Tony* • Gary Mavers *Tony Bone* • Jeff Weatherford *Dan* ■ *Dir/Scr* Frank Clarke

A Blonde in Love ★★★★ 15

Romantic comedy 1965 · Cz · BW · 88mins

Combining sly situation comedy with charming observation, Milos Forman's second feature thoroughly merited its Oscar nomination – all the more so considering the inexperienced cast improvised much of its dialogue. Hana Brejchova is superb as the small-town factory girl whose earnest (and one-sided) pursuit of pianist Vladimir Pucholt comes to a head when she follows him to his parents' house in Prague. Full of the affectionate irony that characterises Forman's early studies of naive youth, this is also a subtly acerbic social satire. DP. In Czech with English subtitles. [video]

Hana Brejchova *Andula* • Vladimir Pucholt *Milda* • Vladimir Mensik *Vacovsky* • Milada Jezkova *Milda's mother* • Josef Sebanek *Milda's father* • Ivan Kheil *Manas* • Jiri Hruby *Burda* • Marie Salacova *Marie* ■ *Dir* Milos Forman • *Scr* Milos Forman, Jaroslav Papousek, Ivan Passer

Blonde Venus ★★★★★ PG

Drama 1932 · US · BW · 93mins

The fifth of director Josef von Sternberg's collaborations with Marlene Dietrich is unfortunately only ever wheeled out for teasing snatches of its dazzling club scene involving Dietrich and a gorilla suit, when in fact the film offers many more riches. The story, with Dietrich's medically dependant husband Herbert Marshall unsettled by his wife's friendly, financial connection to tycoon Cary Grant is, as ever with Sternberg, merely a departure point for more important matters. You'll not see many films superior to this in their use of visual detail, tempo, humour and double-edged significance. Art as entertainment, from the original "all is not what it seems" director. DO [video]

Marlene Dietrich *Helen Faraday/Helen Jones* • Herbert Marshall *Edward Faraday* • Cary Grant *Nick Townsend* • Dickie Moore *Johnny Faraday* • Gene Morgan *Ben Smith* • Rita La Roy *"Taxi Belle" Hooper* • Robert Emmett O'Connor *Dan O'Connor* • Sidney Toler *Detective Wilson* • Morgan Wallace *Doctor Pierce* • Hattie McDaniel *Cora, Helen's maid* • Francis Sayles *Charlie Blaine* ■ *Dir* Josef von Sternberg • *Scr* SK Lauren, Jules Furthman, from a story by Jules Furthman, Josef von Sternberg • *Cinematographer* Bert Glennon • *Costume Designer* Travis Banton

Blondes Have More Guns ★★ 18

Detective spoof 1995 · US · Colour · 89mins

Trash specialist Troma attempts a *Naked Gun*-style parody in this scattershot collection of crass puns and crude sight gags. However, if you're in the right mood, this could just be the formula to have you helpless with infantile laughter. *Basic*

Instinct is the prime target, although *Indecent Proposal* and *The Crying Game* don't escape, as cop Michael McGaharn strives to track down a *femme fatale* with a serial addiction to chainsaw slaughter. Subtlety is not the name of the game here. DP

Michael McGaharn *Harry Bates* • Elizabeth Key *Montana Beaver-Shotz* • Richard Neil *Dick Smoker* • Gloria Lusiak *Dakota Beaver* • André Brazeau *Captain Hook* • Brian A York *The Doctor* ■ *Dir* George Merriweather • *Scr* George Merriweather, Dan Goodman, Mary Guthrie

Blondie! ★★★ U

Comedy 1938 · US · BW · 69mins

This was the first in the long-running series of films – 28 episodes over 12 years – about the chaotic household of Blondie and Dagwood Bumstead, based on the strip cartoon by Chic Young. In this introduction to the family, Dagwood loses his job; his attempts to keep this a secret cause Blondie to suspect him of infidelity. Penny Singleton's delightfully dippy housewife makes an amusing mate for the bumbling Arthur Lake, while the audience of the time could readily identify with the family's dilemmas. TH

Penny Singleton *Blondie Bumstead* • Arthur Lake *Dagwood Bumstead* • Larry Simms *Baby Dumpling* • Gene Lockhart *CP Hazlip* • Jonathan Hale *JC Dithers* • Gordon Oliver *Chester Franey* • Danny Mummert *Alvin* • Kathleen Lockhart *Blondie's mother, Mrs Miller* • Ann Doran *Elsie Hazlip* • Dorothy Moore *Dorothy* • Fay Helm *Mrs Fuddle* • Irving Bacon *Mailman* ■ *Dir* Frank R Strayer • *Scr* Richard Flournoy, from the comic strip by Chic Young

Blondie of the Follies ★★★

Musical comedy 1932 · US · BW · 91mins

The plotline of this musical comedy must have titillated those in the know at the time. Scorned by nice young Robert Montgomery, Marion Davies becomes the kept plaything of older man Douglass Dumbrille. Davies was the mistress of newspaper magnate William Randolph Hearst, whose Cosmopolitan film company funded this opus. Parallels aside, this is a likeable romp, which really centres on Davies and Billie Dove vying for Montgomery's affections. TS

Marion Davies *Blondie McClune* • Robert Montgomery *Larry Belmont* • Billie Dove *Lottie Callahan* • Jimmy Durante *Jimmy* • James Gleason *Pa McClune* • ZaSu Pitts *Gertie* • Sidney Toler *Pete* • Douglass Dumbrille *Murchenson* ■ *Dir* Edmund Goulding • *Scr* Frances Mario, Anita Loos

Blood Alley ★★ U

Adventure 1955 · US · Colour · 110mins

The first film to be made by John Wayne's production company, Batjac, this began shooting with Robert Mitchum playing the American seafarer who leads 180 villagers in an escape from Communist China to Hong Kong. Mitchum and director William A Wellman clashed and Wayne was obliged to fire Mitchum. When Gregory Peck and Humphrey Bogart's demands for high fees were turned down, Wayne himself stepped in as Mitchum's replacement. The result is a typical piece of Yellow Peril propaganda, sluggish and predictable. AT

John Wayne *Wilder* • Lauren Bacall *Cathy* • Paul Fix *Mr Tso* • Joy Kim *Susu* • Berry Kroeger *Old Feng* • Mike Mazurki *Big Han* • Anita Ekberg *Wei Long* • Henry Nakamura *Tak* • WT Chang *Mr Han* ■ *Dir* William Wellman [William A Wellman] • *Scr* AS Fleischmann, from his novel

Blood and Black Lace ★★★★★ 18

Crime thriller
1964 · Fr/It/W Ger · Colour · 84mins

Director Mario Bava's grisly fever dream is an elegantly mounted, visually stunning and erotically charged catalogue of homicidal cruelty. The models at Eva Bartok's fashion house are violently murdered by a sadistic masked assailant, for a diary containing incriminating scandal in an ahead-of-its time psycho-chiller that has influenced everyone from Martin Scorsese to Dario Argento. A spectacular study in voyeuristic delirium and shadowy atmospheric terror, Bava's seminal blueprint for all the spaghetti thrillers of the 1970s is a *Grand Guignol* masterpiece. AJ. Italian dialogue dubbed into English.

Eva Bartok *Cristina* • Cameron Mitchell *Max Martan* • Thomas Reiner *Inspector Silvester* • Arianna Gorini *Nicole* • Mary Arden *Peggy* • Franco Ressel *Marquis Richard Morell* ■ *Dir* Mario Bava • *Scr* Marcel Fondat [Marcel Fondat], Joe Barilla, Mario Bava

Blood and Roses ★★★

Horror 1960 · Fr/It · Colour · 84mins

Brigitte Bardot's Svengali, Roger Vadim, updated Sheridan Le Fanu's Gothic horror story, *Carmilla*, setting it among Rome's idle rich. His then wife, Annette Stroyberg, is Carmilla who believes she is possessed by the spirit of a vampire and attacks her cousin Mel Ferrer's fiancée Elsa Martinelli. Although the film was a commercial failure, only fleetingly released in the UK, cameraman Claude Renoir creates elegant images of women gliding around house and garden. The highlight in a pared-down, uneventful storyline is the striking dream sequence, which utilised new optical technology. DM

Mel Ferrer *Leopoldo De Karnstein* • Elsa Martinelli *Georgia Monteverdi* • Annette Vadim *Carmilla von Karnstein* • Jacques-René Chauffard *Dr Verari* • Marc Allégret *Judge Monteverdi* ■ *Dir* Roger Vadim • *Scr* Roger Vadim, Roger Vailland, Claude Brulé, Claude Martin, Peter Viertel, from the story *Carmilla* by J Sheridan Le Fanu

Blood and Sand ★★★ U

Silent epic 1922 · US · Tinted · 79mins

Hot on the heels of the previous year's *Four Horsemen of the Apocalypse* and *The Sheik* came this third smash hit for superstar Rudolph Valentino. This time, the Latin lover plays a matador led into temptation by a decadent vamp (Nita Naldi). Almost gored to death in the bull ring, he recovers through the tender loving care of his wife (Lila Lee). Fred Niblo's film defies modern criticism, so far are we from its exaggerated histrionics and early techniques. However, it's clear why Valentino's potent presence captured the female hearts of a generation. RK DVD

Rudolph Valentino *Juan Gallardo* • Lila Lee *Carmen* • Rosa Rosanova *Senora Augustias* • George Periolat *Marquise de Guevera* • Nita Naldi *Doña Sol* • Walter Long *Plumitas* • Rosita Marstini *El Carnacione* ■ *Dir* Fred Niblo • *Scr* June Mathis, from the play *Blood and Sand* by Tom Cushing, from the novel *Sangre y Arena* by Vicente Blasco Ibanez

Blood and Sand ★★★★ PG

Drama 1941 · US · Colour · 119mins

This expensively mounted 20th Century-Fox treatment of the famous novel about a young matador is as sexy as 1940s censorship would allow. Rita Hayworth, in a star-making performance, taunts unlikely bullfighter Tyrone Power, who is handsome but miscast. The pace is slow and the attitudes astoundingly naive, but there is a fine lushness and a wonderful symbolic use of Technicolor that gives the film a rare distinction, and the sheer soppiness of the whole enterprise is breathtakingly endearing. TS

Tyrone Power *Juan Gallardo* • Linda Darnell *Carmen Espinosa* • Rita Hayworth *Dona Sol des Muire* • Anthony Quinn *Manolo de Palma* • Alla Nazimova *Senora Augustias* • J Carrol Naish *Garabato* • John Carradine *Nacional* • Laird Cregar *Natalio Curro* • Lynn Bari *Encarnacion* ■ *Dir* Rouben Mamoulian • *Scr* Jo Swerling , from the novel *Sangre y Arena* by Vincente Blasco Ibanez • *Choreographer* Budd Boetticher

Blood and Sand ★★ 18

Drama 1989 · Sp/US · Colour · 96mins

Sharon Stone stars in the third – and weakest – screen version of Vicente Blasco Ibanez's novel. Christopher Rydell is happily married to Ana Torrent and nurses a burning ambition to become a famous toreador. A rehearsal with a dangerous bull the night before a big fight backfires, and it is left to Stone to show him the ropes. Rydell falls in love with her, causing his career and marriage to go down the pan. Lacking the gusto of a real bullfight, this Spanish drama is a piece of Euro-pudding nonsense. LH

Christopher Rydell *Juan Gallardo* • Sharon Stone *Doña Sol* • Ana Torrent *Carmen* • Antonio Flores *Chiripa* • Simon Andreu *Juan's uncle* • Albert Vidal ■ *Dir* Javier Elorrieta • *Scr* Rafael Azcona, Ricardo Franco, Thomas Fucci, from the novel *Sangre y Arena* by Vicente Blasco Ibanez

Blood and Wine ★★★ 15

Crime thriller
1996 · US/UK/Fr · Colour · 96mins

Paired for the first time, Jack Nicholson and Michael Caine are supremely sleazy as a couple of businessmen/thieves who steal a costly necklace from one of wine dealer Nicholson's affluent Florida clients. It's a delicious double act: Nicholson is, well, Nicholson, and Caine, with dyed black hair and an alarming cough, creates his vilest villain since *Mona Lisa*. Stephen Dorff and Jennifer Lopez offer sexy support , while director Bob Rafelson stylishly juggles the complexities of characters and plot. JC. Contains swearing and violence.

Jack Nicholson *Alex Gates* • Stephen Dorff *Jason* • Jennifer Lopez *Gabriela* • Judy Davis *Suzanne Gates* • Michael Caine *Victor Spansky* • Harold Perrineau Jr [Harold Perrineau] *Henry* • Robyn Peterson *Dina* • Mike Starr *Mike* • John Seitz *Frank* ■ *Dir* Bob Rafelson • *Scr* Nick Villiers, Alison Cross, from a story by Bob Rafelson, Nick Villiers

Blood Beach ★★

Horror 1981 · US · Colour · 89mins

What's sucking sun-worshippers and concerned locals under the sand on a south California beach? Nothing more than a stock papier-mâché monster in this workmanlike update of a formula 1950s B-movie. A little atmosphere is created when heroine Mariana Hill finds the creature's lair by accident, but elsewhere director Jeffrey Bloom's first foray into the horror genre is familiar territory. AJ

David Huffman *Harry Caulder* • Mariana Hill [Marianna Hill] *Catherine* • John Saxon *Captain Pearson* • Otis Young *Lieutenant Piantadosi* • Stefan Gierasch *Dr Dimitrios* • Burt Young *Sergeant Royko* • Darrell Fetty *Hoagy* ■ *Dir* Jeffrey Bloom • *Scr* Jeffrey Bloom, from a story by Steven Nalevansky, Jeffrey Bloom

The Blood Beast Terror ★

Horror 1967 · UK · Colour · 87mins

Peter Cushing considered this clumsy chiller the worst picture he ever made. In many respects he was right. He's the policeman investigating vampiristic murders carried out by a giant death's-head moth masquerading as the "daughter" of a renowned Victorian entomologist. It must have seemed a good idea at the time. AJ

Peter Cushing *Inspector Quennell* • Robert Flemyng *Professor Mallinger* • Wanda Ventham *Clare Mallinger* • Vanessa Howard *Meg Quennell* • Roy Hudd *Morgue attendant* • David Griffin *William* • Kevin Stoney *Grainger* • Glynn Edwards *Sergeant Allan* ■ *Dir* Vernon Sewell • *Scr* Peter Bryan

The Blood Demon ★★★

Horror 1967 · W Ger · Colour · 80mins

Without so much as two original ideas to rub together, veteran director Harald Reinl still manages to create a remarkably atmospheric and enjoyable piece of Gothic horror. It inspired many similar films in Germany and became a minor cult worldwide. Wicked Count Christopher Lee is executed for his crimes, but is revived as in *Dracula – Prince of Darkness* and tries to kill Lex Barker with an Edgar Allan Poe-like pendulum. Another victim is Reinl's wife, Karin Dor (they worked together regularly). DM. German dialogue dubbed into English.

Christopher Lee *Count Regula* • Lex Barker *Roger Montelis* • Karin Dor *Lilian von Brandt* • Carl Lange *Anatole* ■ *Dir* Harald Reinl • *Scr* Manfred R Köhler, from the story *The Pit and the Pendulum* by Edgar Allan Poe

Blood Feast ★ 18

Horror 1963 · US · Colour · 66mins

Although it virtually invented the splatter genre, the first in director Herschell Gordon Lewis's infamous gore trilogy (*Two Thousand Maniacs!* and *Color Me Blood Red* being the other two) is one of the sickest, stupidest and most inept exploitation movies ever made. Mal Arnold kills young women in brutal fashion so body parts can be used in an ancient Egyptian ritual. The fake, hokey, yet powerfully gruesome mutilations are relieved by Lewis's hopelessly amateur directing and the consummate bad acting. He directed a belated sequel in 2002. AJ DVD

Thomas Wood [William Kerwin] *Pete Thornton* • Mal Arnold *Fuad Ramses* • Connie Mason *Suzette* • Scott H Hall *Police captain* • Lyn Bolton *Mrs Fremont* • Toni Calvert *Trudy* ■ *Dir* Herschell G Lewis [Herschell Gordon Lewis] • *Scr* Allison Louise Downe

Blood Feud ★

Drama 1979 · It · Colour · 112mins

In the mid-1970s, Italian director Lina Wertmuller became a sensation in America, mainly because *Seven Beauties* (1976) made her the first woman ever to be nominated for a best director Oscar. After that, Wertmuller cashed in on her fame by making increasingly pretentious films with increasingly long titles. So there you have it. Set in Sicily at the birth of fascism, it has Marcello Mastroianni and Sophia Loren making their umpteenth film together and probably regretting every second of it. AT. Italian dialogue dubbed into English.

Sophia Loren *Titina Paterno* • Marcello Mastroianni *Spallone* • Giancarlo Giannini *Nick* • Turi Ferro *Baron* ■ *Dir/Scr* Lina Wertmuller

Blood for Dracula ★★★ 18

Horror 1974 · It · Colour · 98mins

In contrast to this film's Andy Warhol-produced companion piece, *Flesh for Frankenstein* in 3-D, The Factory's in-house director Paul Morrissey here accents wit over gore in a clever twist on the vampire myth. Udo Kier is tragicomic as the anaemic Transylvanian Count looking for "wirgin" blood in an Italian household of females. Trouble is, sexy handyman Joe Dallesandro keeps deflowering his prospective prey. Heavy bloodshed is lightened by the consistently humorous tone of the tale. Directors Vittorio De Sica and Roman Polanski put in telling cameos in this funny fang farce. AJ

Joe Dallesandro *Mario* • Udo Kier *Dracula* • Vittorio De Sica *Marquis* • Maxime McKendry *Marquisa* • Arno Juerging *Anton* • Milena Vukotic *Esmeralda* • Dominique Darel *Saphiria* • Stefania Casini *Rubinia* • Roman Polanski • Vittorio De Sica ■ *Dir/Scr* Paul Morrissey • *Producer* Carlo Ponti, Andy Warhol

Blood from the Mummy's Tomb ★★★ 15

Horror 1971 · UK · Colour · 93mins

Statuesque Valerie Leon is possessed by the spirit of an ancient Egyptian queen in this cult Hammer horror based on Bram Stoker's *The Jewel of Seven Stars*. With hardly a bandage in sight, director Seth Holt tried to radically rethink the mummy genre, and largely succeeded in creating a fascinating fantasy with a uniquely menacing atmosphere dripping in delicious irony. Sadly, Holt died during shooting; Hammer boss Michael Carreras took over and the film is not as interesting as it should have been. AJ DVD

Andrew Keir *Professor Fuchs* • Valerie Leon *Margaret/Tera* • James Villiers *Corbeck* • Hugh Burden *Dandridge* • George Coulouris *Berigan* • Mark Edwards *Tod Browning* • Rosalie Crutchley *Helen Dickerson* • Aubrey Morris *Dr Putnum* • David Markham *Dr Burgess* ■ *Dir* Seth Holt, Michael Carreras • *Scr* Christopher Wicking, from the novel *The Jewel of Seven Stars* by Bram Stoker

Blood, Guts, Bullets & Octane ★★ 15

Action comedy 1997 · US · Colour · 86mins

This quirky thriller is about two motor-mouthed used car salesmen who get embroiled in a bizarre plot to smuggle rare blood supplies across the Mexican/American border. The film starts strongly, with some super-fast one-take talk scenes that are neatly scripted and cleverly acted. Once the plot kicks in, though, it is marked by the irritating and wilful quirkiness that mars so many independent movies. DA. Contains swearing, violence.

Mike Maas *Victor Drub* • Nick Fenske *Mechanic* • Mark Priolo *Frank Priolo* • Joe Carnahan *Sid French* • Andrew Fowler *Mike Carbuyer* • Gloria Gomez *Julie Carbuyer* • Dan Leis *Bob Melba* • Josephine Arreola *Elda* ■ *Dir/Scr* Joe Carnahan

Blood In Blood Out ★★ 18

Drama 1992 · US · Colour · 172mins

Co-written by poet Jimmy Santiago Baca, this is based on his real-life experiences. Director Taylor Hackford blunts his treatise on the cultural ties that bind through excessive length and off-putting violence. Three Chicano cousins take the viewer on a gruelling journey through the Latino experience, as they go from the gang-run streets of East LA to the brutal confines of San Quentin prison. The unknown leads turn in strong performances and Hackford intermittently packs the sermonising saga with a powerfully emotional punch. AJ

Damian Chapa *Miklo* • Jesse Borrego *Cruz* • Benjamin Bratt *Paco* • Enrique J Castillo [Enrique Castillo] *Montana* • Victor Rivers *Magic Mike* • Delroy Lindo *Bonafide* • Tom Towles *Red Ryder* • Carlos Carrasco *Popeye* ■ *Dir* Taylor Hackford • *Scr* Jimmy Santiago Baca, Jeremy Iacone, Floyd Mutrux, from a story by Ross Thomas

Blood Money ★★ 18

Martial arts western
1974 · It/HK/Sp · Colour · 95mins

This is an unappetising mix of spaghetti western and chop-socky action movie. Lee Van Cleef snarls in the accustomed manner as a bounty hunter seeking four women who have the clues to buried treasure tattooed on their bodies. Italian director Antonio Margheriti (billed under the pseudonym Anthony M Dawson) struggles to sustain the blistering pace expected of a martial arts movie. The brutality of the fight sequences are definitely not for the faint-hearted. DP

Lee Van Cleef *Dakota* • Lo Lieh *Wang Ho Kiang* • Karen Yeh *Yeh Ling Chih/Lia Hua* • Julian Ugarte *Deacon Yancy Hobbitt* • Goyo Peralta *Indio* • Al Tung *Wang* ■ *Dir* Anthony M Dawson [Antonio Margheriti] • *Scr* Barth Jules Sussman

Blood Money ★★★

Crime thriller 1980 · Aus · Colour · 63mins

Bryan Brown never quite gets the proper credit for performances such as this one. He's a former international criminal who returns Down Under to try to redeem his name and die with dignity. But even such a simple endeavour causes problems, both legal and emotional. Christopher Fitchett directs, Chrissie James is the girl who's unconvinced by the crook's best endeavours, while John Flaus is the man who believes him – but doesn't care. This is short but poignant. TH

John Flaus *Pete Shields* • Bryan Brown *Brian Shields* • Chrissie James *Jeannie Shields* • Peter Stratford *Curtis* • Peter Curtain *Dan* • Sue Jones *Doctor* • John Proper *Jack* ■ *Dir* Christopher Fitchett • *Scr* Christopher Fitchett, John Ruane, Ellery Ryan

Blood Oath ★★★★ 15

Courtroom drama
1990 · Aus · Colour · 103mins

Before he took to commercials as a car tout, Bryan Brown was a considerable lean and leathery presence in Australian movies, notably in this courtroom drama in which he's the Aussie officer prosecuting an Oxford-educated Japanese commander (George Takei) for war crimes. His task is complicated by Americans wanting a "not guilty" verdict for reasons of political expediency. Brown's role is based on the experiences of the father of co-scriptwriter Brian A Williams, and Brown brings a sardonic edge to the search for motives. TH. Contains violence and swearing.

Bryan Brown *Captain Robert Cooper* • George Takei *Vice-Admiral Baron Takahashi* • Terry O'Quinn *Major Tom Beckett* • John Bach *Major Frank Roberts* • Toshi Shioya *Lieutenant Hideo Tanaka* • John Clarke (2) *Mike Sheedy* • Deborah Unger [Deborah Kara Unger] *Sister Carol Littell* • Jason Donovan *Private Talbot* • Russell Crowe *Lieutenant Jack Corbett* ■ *Dir* Stephen Wallace • *Scr* Denis Whitburn, Brian A Williams

The Blood of a Poet ★★★ PG

Experimental drama 1930 · Fr · BW · 49mins

Jean Cocteau's first film – made when he was 41, his fame already established as a writer, poet and artist – follows the dream-like encounters and observations of a young poet as he views the world on the other side of a mirror. Highly experimental and devoid of any conventional narrative, the film offers a series of arresting images (executions, hermaphrodites, opium smokers), and exerted a strong influence on the American avant-garde. The surreal symbolism is inaccessible to the majority of viewers, however, who are more likely to appreciate Cocteau's ravishing *La Belle et la Bête*, made 16 years later. RK. In French with English subtitles.

Lee Miller *The statue* • Pauline Carton *Child's tutor* • Odette Talazac • Enrico Rivero *The poet* • Jean Desbordes *The friend in Louis XV costume* • Fernand Dichamps • Lucien Jager • Féral Benga *The black angel* • Barbette *Spectator in lodge* • Jean Cocteau *Narrator* ■ *Dir/Scr* Jean Cocteau • *Cinematographer* Georges Périnal

Blood of Dracula ★★ PG

Horror 1957 · US · BW · 69mins

A routine 1950s' "schlock 'n' roller", this is great drive-in movie trash. As is so often the case in these morality-tinged horrors, carnal thoughts equal out-of-control monsterhood, as staid college girl Sandra Harrison turns tramp vamp when hypnotised by a magic amulet owned by her evil chemistry teacher. The solemn intensity Harrison brings to her ludicrous tight-sweater role is a joy to behold. A scream, but not quite in the way anyone intended. AJ DVD

Sandra Harrison *Nancy Perkins* • Louise Lewis (1) *Miss Branding* • Gail Ganley *Myra* • Jerry Blaine *Tab* • Heather Ames *Nola* • Malcolm Atterbury *Lieutenant Dunlap* • Mary Adams *Mrs Thorndyke* • Thomas B Henry [Thomas Browne Henry] *Mr Perkins* • Don Devlin *Eddie* ■ *Dir* Herbert L Strock • *Scr* Ralph Thornton

Blood of Dracula's Castle ★

Gothic horror 1967 · US · Colour · 84mins

This dreadful attempt by exploitation maverick Al Adamson to update the Dracula myth finds high-class vampires Alex D'Arcy and Paula Raymond living in a castle in modern California. A half-wit hunchback keeps the cellar stocked with nubile victims, who are drained of blood for gruesome cocktail hours. An S&M-tinged tacky terror. AJ

John Carradine *George* • Paula Raymond *Countess Townsend* • Alex D'Arcy *Count Townsend* • Robert Dix *Johnny* • Gene O'Shane *Glen Cannon* • Barbara Bishop *Liz* ■ *Dir* Al Adamson • *Scr* Rex Carlton

The Blood of Fu Manchu ★★ 15

Horror
1968 · US/UK/Sp/W Ger · Colour · 89mins

Actually more like a western, thanks to its Brazilian setting and bandit subplot, the fourth outing for Christopher Lee as Sax Rohmer's insidious Oriental is cheaply made horror exotica. Lee's stiff performance doesn't help the daft story, as Fu Manchu endows ten gorgeous girls with the "kiss of death" via an Inca poison deadly only to the male and programmes them to kill any influential power-broker who touches their passionate lips. AJ. Contains violence and swearing. DVD

Christopher Lee *Fu Manchu* • Götz George *Carl Janson* • Richard Greene *Nayland Smith* • Howard Marion-Crawford *Dr Petrie* • Tsai Chin *Lin Tang* • Maria Rohm *Ursula* • Shirley Eaton *Black Widow* ■ *Dir* Jess Franco [Jesus Franco] • *Scr* Harry Alan Towers

The Blood of Others ★★ 15

Second World War drama
1984 · Can/Fr · Colour · 263mins

Adapted from the novel by Simone De Beauvoir, and with additional dialogue by the Irish-Canadian author Brian Moore, this wartime drama efficiently captures the claustrophobic paranoia of Occupied Paris, without ever involving us in the fate of its protagonists. Torn between her loyalty to imprisoned Resistance fighter Michael Ontkean and a love of luxury that draws her towards pro-Nazi businessman Sam Neill, Jodie Foster gives one of her least credible performances. DP

Jodie Foster *Hélène* • Michael Ontkean *Jean Blomart* • Sam Neill *Bergman* • Lambert Wilson *Paul* • Stéphane Audran *Gigi* • Jean-Pierre Aumont *André Blomart* • Micheline Presle *Denise* ■ *Dir* Claude Chabrol • *Scr* Brian Moore, from the novel *Le Sang des Autres* by Simone de Beauvoir

Blood of the Vampire ★★

Horror 1958 · UK · Colour · 85mins

Universal nabbed Hammer's gore theatrics along with their resident scriptwriter, Jimmy Sangster, in the effort to beat the House of Horror at its own game. The result is enjoyable hokum with, for the era, some edgily gruesome torture chamber scenes . Thespian legend Donald Wolfit goes predictably over the top as Doctor Callistratus, who needs blood to stay alive and uses victims from his insane asylum for the grisly transfusion purpose. Hammer heroine Barbara Shelley adds the glamour, while Victor Maddern wears the daftest make-up imaginable as the scarred servant of the mad doctor. AJ

Donald Wolfit *Dr Callistratus* • Vincent Ball *Dr John Pierre* • Barbara Shelley *Madeleine* • Victor Maddern *Carl* • William Devlin *Kurt Urah* • Andrew Faulds *Wetzler* • Hal Osmond *Sneak thief* • Bernard Bresslaw *Sneak thief* • John Le Mesurier *Chief Justice* ■ *Dir* Henry Cass • *Scr* Jimmy Sangster

Blood of the Virgins ★★

Erotic horror 1967 · Arg · Colour · 72mins

Best known for the ingeniously eccentric chiller *The Curious Dr Humpp*, Emilio Vieyra confirmed his genius for overcoming budgetary constraints while making this, Argentina's first vampire movie. In order to disguise the fact he didn't have any footage of flying bats, he smothered shots of seagulls with red tint in the hope that the atmospheric shock would prevent people from looking too closely. Certainly, the first audiences would have had a distraction, as Vierya hired Susana Beltrán to wander up and down the cinema aisles in a nightdress flashing her gore-soaked fangs. DP. In Spanish with English subtitles.

Ricardo Bauleo • Gloria Prat • Rolo Puente • Susana Beltran ■ *Dir/Scr* Emilio Vieyra

Blood on My Hands ★★

Crime drama 1948 · US · BW · 77mins

This downbeat melodrama was star Burt Lancaster's first stab at being involved in production through the company named after his wife, Norma Productions. Set in a Hollywood studio re-creation of postwar London, it stars Lancaster as the violent war veteran who accidentally kills a man in a pub and goes on the run. He's blackmailed by a witness (played with exaggerated relish by Robert Newton) and befriended by a nurse (Joan Fontaine in her most sensitive mode). Despite some visual flair from Norman Foster's direction and Russell Metty's photography, plus one of Miklos Rozsa's best scores, this is mostly tedious and unbelievable. AE

Joan Fontaine *Jane Wharton* • Burt Lancaster *Bill Saunders* • Robert Newton *Harry Carter* • Lewis L Russell *Tom Widgery* • Aminta Dyne *Landlady* • Grizelda Hervey *Mrs Paton* • Jay Novello *Sea captain* • Colin Keith-Johnston *Judge* ■ *Dir* Norman Foster • *Scr* Leonardo Bercovici, Walter Bernstein, Hugh Gray, Ben Maddow, from the novel *Kiss the Blood off My Hands* by Gerald Butler

Blood on Satan's Claw ★★★ 18

Horror 1970 · UK · Colour · 92mins

Devil-worshipping children in 17th-century England cause havoc for their village in this super-stylish supernatural shocker with a strong period flavour. While this is more sensational, violent and crude than its obvious model *Witchfinder General*,

Piers Haggard's tense direction keeps the cauldron of fiendish orgies, demonic tortures and Linda Hayden's sultry turn as the devil's advocate bubbling at an even terror temperature until the satanic slow-motion climax. Vintage British horror at its lip-smacking best. AJ DVD

Patrick Wymark *Judge* • Linda Hayden *Angel* • Barry Andrews *Ralph* • Michele Dotrice *Margaret* • Wendy Padbury *Cathy* • Anthony Ainley *Reverend Fallowfield* • Charlotte Mitchell *Ellen* • Tamara Ustinov *Rosalind* ■ *Dir* Piers Haggard • *Scr* Robert Wynne

Blood on the Moon ★★★ U

Western 1948 · US · BW · 87mins

If there's such a thing as "western *noir*", then this is it, as director Robert Wise and distinguished photographer Nicholas Musuraca team up again (following 1944's *The Curse of the Cat People*) for this psychological take on the genre. Robert Mitchum brings some weighty experience to his role as a drifter forced to turn against his one-time mentor (an oily Robert Preston before his Broadway stardom). The mood is satisfyingly dark. TS

Robert Mitchum *Jim Garry* • Barbara Bel Geddes *Amy Lufton* • Robert Preston *Tate Riling* • Walter Brennan *Kris Barden* • Phyllis Thaxter *Carol Lufton* • Frank Faylen *Jake Pindalest* • Tom Tully *John Lufton* ■ *Dir* Robert Wise • *Scr* Willie Hayward, from the novel *Gunman's Chance* by Luke Short, adapted by Harold Shumate

Blood on the Sun ★★★ PG

Period drama 1945 · US · BW · 93mins

The Cagney brothers chose a formidable subject for their second independent production, with Bill producing and Jimmy starring as an aggressive editor of an American newspaper in Tokyo, who daringly publishes the Japanese Master Plan for world domination. This doesn't go down too well with Colonel Tojo, nor did the film with the public when it was released. As scripted by blacklisted left-wing Hollywood Ten veteran Lester Cole, the movie packs a powerhouse message, appropriate in its day and still worth heeding. But the propaganda content overwhelms the drama and, despite the valiant efforts of Cagney, Sylvia Sidney and Robert Armstrong, the melodrama doesn't really catch fire. TS DVD

James Cagney *Nick Condon* • Sylvia Sidney *Iris Hilliard* • Wallace Ford *Ollie Miller* • Rosemary DeCamp *Edith Miller* • Robert Armstrong *Colonel Tojo* • John Emery *Premier Tanaka* • Leonard Strong *Hijikata* • Frank Puglia *Prince Tatsugi* • John Halloran *Captain Oshima* ■ *Dir* Frank Lloyd • *Scr* Lester Cole, from a story by Garrett Fort

Blood Orange ★★

Crime drama 1953 · UK · BW · 80mins

Made for Hammer's B-movie outlet, Exclusive, this is an unremarkable offering from director Terence Fisher, who went on to make some of the studio's best horrors. Jan Read's tepid story about a retired FBI agent who gets involved with jewel thieves following the murder of model Delphi Lawrence gives him little to work with. The real problem, however, is Tom Conway's lacklustre performance. DP

Tom Conway *Conway* • Mila Parely *Helen Pascall* • Naomi Chance *Gina* • Eric Pohlmann *Mercedes* • Andrew Osborn *Captain Simpson* • Richard Wattis *Macleod* • Margaret Halstan *Lady Marchant* • Eileen Way *Fernande* • Delphi Lawrence *Chelsea* ■ *Dir* Terence Fisher • *Scr* Jan Read

The Blood Oranges ★

Erotic drama 1997 · US · Colour · 93mins

Unintentionally hilarious, this is another peepshow masquerading as a profound statement from Philip Haas. Sheryl Lee and Charles Dance are holidaying hippies who tempt another couple into a sexual foursome. Overlong, self-indulgent and completely unconvincing, this dippy nonsense gives art movies a bad name. AJ

Charles Dance *Cyril* • Sheryl Lee *Fiona* • Laila Robins *Catherine* • Colin Lane *Hugh* • Rachael Bella *Meredith* • Aida Lopez *Rosella* ■ *Dir* Philip Haas • *Scr* Philip Haas, Belinda Haas, from the novel by John Hawkes

Blood Red ★ 15

Period action drama
1988 · US · Colour · 87mins

Immigrant Sicilian grape farmers try to stop tycoon Dennis Hopper from building a railroad through the Napa Valley wine country of the late 19th century in this weak action adventure. It's interesting for two reasons: future superstar Julia Roberts makes her screen debut; and it's the only film she's made with her brother Eric (she plays his sister). The over-ripe script quickly withers on the vine. AJ

Eric Roberts *Marco Collogero* • Giancarlo Giannini *Sebastian Collogero* • Dennis Hopper *William Bradford Berrigan* • Burt Young *Andrews* • Carlin Glynn *Miss Jeffreys* • Lara Harris *Angelica* • Francesca De Sapio *Rosa Collogero* • Julia Roberts *Maria Collogero* • Michael Madsen *Enzio* • Elias Koteas *Silvio* ■ *Dir* Peter Masterson • *Scr* Ron Cutler

Blood Relatives ★★★ 18

Crime drama 1977 · Can/Fr · Colour · 90mins

Adapted from an Ed McBain novel, this is directed by the French master Claude Chabrol with a sharp eye for the middle-class hypocrisies of a Canadian community. Donald Sutherland is the detective investigating the assault and murder of a young Montreal girl, with accusations and confessions flying thick and fast, though it's only in the film's final section that there's any real tension. The rest of the drama is – astonishingly for Chabrol – actually a little wooden and flat. TH. Contains violence and swearing. DVD

Donald Sutherland *Steve Carella* • Aude Landry *Patricia Lowery* • Lisa Langlois *Muriel* • Laurent Malet *Andy Lowery* • Stéphane Audran *Mrs Lowery* • Donald Pleasence *Doniac* • David Hemmings *Jack Armstrong* • Walter Massey *Mr Lowery* ■ *Dir* Claude Chabrol • *Scr* Claude Chabrol, Sydney Banks, from the novel by Evan Hunter [Ed McBain]

Blood Simple ★★★★ 18

Thriller 1983 · US · Colour · 94mins

A jealous Texas husband hires a sleazy private eye to murder his adulterous wife and her lover in the Coen Brothers' feature debut. Blending elements of James M Cain, *film noir*, Hitchcock thrillers and contemporary horror movies, this dark morality tale deviates imaginatively from the 1940s' murder mysteries it evokes. The acting is first rate (the long road to Frances McDormand's Oscar for *Fargo* started here) and the atmosphere appropriately brooding. The Coens' use of light and space is impressive, and the innovative camera work to increase the suspense is breathtaking. A modern classic. AJ. Contains sex scenes, violence, swearing. DVD

John Getz *Ray* • Frances McDormand *Abby* • Dan Hedaya *Julian Marty* • M Emmet Walsh *Visser* • Samm-Art Williams *Maurice* • Deborah Neumann *Debra* • Raquel Gavia *Landlady* • Van Brooks *Man from Lubbock* ■ *Dir* Joel Coen • *Scr* Ethan Coen, Joel Coen • *Cinematographer* Barry Sonnenfeld

Blood Surf ★ 18

Science-fiction horror
2000 · US/S Afr · Colour · 84mins

James Hickox can usually be relied on to deliver the gory goods in endearing exploitation packages. But his talents desert him in this dire *Lake Placid* knock-off concerning a TV film crew travelling to a tropical island to document surfers who end up battling a giant crocodile. A *Jaws*-like subplot about crusty sea captain Duncan Regehr who sees the croc as his own personal nemesis fills out the threadbare story. This comes complete with variable special effects, rubber reptiles, elongated sex scenes and a barely-there script. AJ DVD

Dax Miller *Bog* • Matt Borlenghi *Zach Jardine* • Joel West *Jeremy* • Kate Fischer *Cecily* • Duncan Regehr *John Dirks* • Taryn Reif *Arly* ■ *Dir* James DR Hickox [James Hickox] • *Scr* Sam Bernard, Robert L Levy

Blood Wedding ★★★★ U

Dance drama 1981 · Sp · Colour · 67mins

Setting the minimalist tone that persisted through *Carmen* and *El Amor Brujo*, the first of Carlos Saura's "flamenco trilogy" is an exhilarating blend of passionate choreography and rhythmic camerawork. By setting the action on a bare stage with the minimum of props, Saura focuses our attention on the intricacy and symbolism of the dance. As well as designing the flamboyant routines, Antonio Gades stars as one of the troupe rehearsing a musical version of the celebrated play by Federico Garcia Lorca, in which a jilted husband pursues the wife who abandoned him at the altar. DP. In Spanish with English subtitles.

Antonio Gades *Leonardo* • Cristina Hoyos *Bride* • Juan Antonio Jimenez *Groom* • Pilar Cardenas *Mother* • Carmen Villena *Wife* • Pepe Blanco *Wedding guest* • Lario Diaz *Wedding guest* • Enrique Esteve *Wedding guest* ■ *Dir* Carlos Saura • *Scr* Carlos Saura, from a play by Federico Garcia Lorca • *Choreographer* Antonio Gades • *Cinematographer* Teo Escamilla

Blood Work ★★ 15

Murder mystery thriller
2002 · US · Colour · 105mins

This is one of director Clint Eastwood's depressingly average efforts. Eastwood also stars as an FBI agent who leaves the agency after a heart attack. While recovering from a transplant, he is brought out of retirement for one last case – the twist is that the victim was his organ donor. Apart from that, it's a routine thriller with an unconvincing romance thrown in. Eastwood's stodgy direction doesn't help. StH DVD

Clint Eastwood *Terry McCaleb* • Jeff Daniels *Buddy Noone* • Anjelica Huston *Dr Bonnie Fox* • Wanda De Jesús *Graciela Rivers* • Tina Lifford *Jaye Winston* • Paul Rodriguez *Det Ronaldo Arrango* • Dylan Walsh *Det John Waller* • Mason Lucero *Raymond* ■ *Dir* Clint Eastwood • *Scr* Brian Helgeland, from the novel by Michael Connelly

Bloodbath at the House of Death ★ 18

Horror comedy 1983 · UK · Colour · 91mins

Lampoons of everything from *Carrie* and *ET* to *Star Wars* and *Friday the 13th* are dragged screaming through this painfully thin comedy starring Kenny Everett and Pamela Stephenson as paranormal researchers investigating Vincent Price's devil-worshipping cult at Headstone Manor. Nothing more than an excuse for Everett and his chums to indulge in low-grade lavatorial humour. AJ

Kenny Everett *Dr Lucas Mandeville* • Pamela Stephenson *Dr Barbara Coyle* • Vincent Price *Sinister man* • Gareth Hunt *Elliot Broome* • Don Warrington *Stephen Wilson* • John Fortune *John Harrison* • Sheila Steafel *Sheila Finch* • John Stephen Hill *Henry Noland* • Cleo Rocos *Deborah Kedding* • Barry Cryer *Police inspector* • Ray Cameron *Policeman* ■ *Dir* Ray Cameron • *Scr* Ray Cameron, Barry Cryer

Bloodbrothers ★★

Drama 1978 · US · Colour · 116mins

Richard Gere is surprisingly good in the unlikely role of an aspiring social worker in this familiar tale of conflict in an Italian-American family. Gere wants to work with children but Dad (Tony LoBianco) wants him to stay in the macho world of construction. Unfortunately, any insights are diverted by way of narrative short cuts, though it's interesting to see how good Gere was before he became a big name. TH

Paul Sorvino *Chubby DeCoco* • Tony LoBianco *Tommy DeCoco* • Richard Gere *Stony DeCoco* • Lelia Goldoni *Marie* • Yvonne Wilder *Phyllis* • Kenneth McMillan *Banion* • Floyd Levine *Doctor Harris* • Marilu Henner *Annette* ■ *Dir* Robert Mulligan • *Scr* Walter Newman, from the novel by Richard Price

Bloodfist ★ 18

Martial arts action drama
1989 · US · Colour · 82mins

Three times world kickboxing champion Don "The Dragon" Wilson plays it safe in his first major role cast as – yes, you've guessed it – a kickboxer who travels from Los Angeles to Manila to avenge the death of his brother by competing in a fight tournament. Director Terence H Winkless offers nothing new to the martial arts genre, serving up uninspired fight sequences with the stunt guys missing each other's jaws by miles. Although Wilson demonstrates little screen presence, he went on to star in all seven of the *Bloodfist* sequels. RS DVD

Don "The Dragon" Wilson *Jake Raye* • Joe Mari Avellana *Kwong* • Michael Shaner *Baby Davies* • Riley Bowman *Nancy* • Rob Kaman *Raton* • Billy Blanks *Black Rose* • Kris Aguilar *Chin Woo* • Vic Diaz *Detective* ■ *Dir* Terence H Winkless • *Scr* Robert King

Bloodhounds of Broadway ★★★ U

Musical 1952 · US · Colour · 89mins

This enjoyable 20th Century-Fox musical gives the marvellous Mitzi Gaynor the chance to sing such super numbers as *I Wish I Knew*, in a whirl of Damon Runyon-inspired nonsense. Gaynor's co-star is Scott Brady, and watch out for a typecast Charles Buchinski (later Charles Bronson). This was remade in 1989 with an all-star cast, but that film only received a limited release. This version is both breezier and bawdier, and much closer to Runyon in spirit. TS

Mitzi Gaynor *Emily Ann Stackerlee* • Scott Brady *Numbers Foster* • Mitzi Green *Tessie Sammis* • Marguerite Chapman *Yvonne* • Michael O'Shea *Inspector McNamara* • Wally Vernon *Poorly Sammis* • Henry Slate *Dave the Dude* • George E Stone *Ropes McGonigle* ■ *Dir* Harmon Jones • *Scr* Sy Gomberg, from the short stories by Damon Runyon

Bloodhounds of Broadway ★★ PG

Comedy drama 1989 · US · Colour · 83mins

Not to be confused with the (better) 1952 musical of the same name, this is an adaptation of a collection of short stories by Damon Runyon. Set in New York on New Year's Eve, 1928, it traces the ins and outs of a group of Mafia gangsters and their molls. Madonna, Jennifer Grey, Matt Dillon, Randy Quaid and Rutger Hauer star, but even their combined efforts fail to make Howard Brookner's film anything more than a lacklustre amalgam of tales and cabaret. LH

Madonna *Hortense Hathaway* • Randy Quaid *Feet Samuels* • Matt Dillon *Regret* • Josef Sommer *Waldo Winchester* • Jennifer Grey *Lovey Lou* • Tony Longo *Crunch Sweeney* • Rutger Hauer *The Brain* • Stephen McHattie *Red Henry* • Steve Buscemi *Whining Willie* •

Tony Azito *Waiter* ■ *Dir* Howard Brookner • *Scr* Howard Brookner, Colman deKay, from the short stories by Damon Runyon

Bloodline ★★ 18

Mystery melodrama
1979 · US/W Ger · Colour · 111mins

An anaemic script pumps little in the way of drama into this tedious thriller, adapted from Sidney Sheldon's novel. Audrey Hepburn is the heiress to a pharmaceutical conglomerate, who takes control of the company only to find that she's in fear for her life. James Mason, Ben Gazzara and Omar Sharif try for some smoothly silken menace, but it comes across as hair-shirt denim. Ennio Morricone's music is probably best appreciated without the accompanying dialogue. TH [VIDEO]

Audrey Hepburn *Elizabeth Roffe* • Ben Gazzara *Rhys Williams* • James Mason *Sir Alec Nichols* • Claudia Mori *Donatella* • Irene Papas *Simonetta Palazzi* • Michelle Phillips *Vivian Nichols* • Maurice Ronet *Charles Martin* • Romy Schneider *Helene Martin* • Omar Sharif *Ivo Palazzi* • Beatrice Straight *Kate Erling* ■ *Dir* Terence Young • *Scr* Laird Koenig, from the novel by Sidney Sheldon

Bloodsport ★★ 18

Martial arts action drama
1987 · US · Colour · 88mins

This is the movie that consolidated Jean-Claude Van Damme's standing in the martial arts film world. Loosely based on a true story, it stars Van Damme as the first western fighter to enter a lethal martial arts tournament in Hong Kong. The always frightening Bolo Yeung is the man standing in his way. The Belgian star unsurprisingly merits even fewer acting plaudits than usual, but director Newt Arnold wisely concentrates on the violent bouts. JF. Contains violence, swearing and nudity. [VIDEO] DVD

Jean-Claude Van Damme *Frank Dux* • Donald Gibb *Ray Jackson* • Leah Ayres *Janice* • Norman Burton *Helmer* • Forest Whitaker *Rawlins* • Roy Chiao *Senzo "Tiger" Tanaka* • Philip Chan *Captain Chen* ■ *Dir* Newt Arnold • *Scr* Sheldon Lettich, Christopher Cosby, Mel Friedman, from a story by Sheldon Lettich

Bloodsport II: The Next Kumite ★★ 18

Martial arts action
1996 · US · Colour · 82mins

The original *Bloodsport* catapulted Jean-Claude Van Damme to stardom, but the sequel didn't do the same for fellow biffer Daniel Bernhardt. He plays a gentleman thief who ends up in a Thai jail and discovers that his only passport out is to fight in the legendary *kumite*, a last-man-standing martial arts championship. There's plenty of bone-crunching action, but the plotting and acting is strictly average. A further, bottom-of-the-barrel sequel followed in 1997. JF [VIDEO] DVD

Daniel Bernhardt *Alex* • Pat Morita *Leung* • Donald Gibb *Tiny* • Lori Lynn Dickerson *Janine* • Philip Tan *John* • James Hong *Sun* • Nick Hill *Sergio* • Ron Hall *Cliff* ■ *Dir* Alan Mehrez • *Scr* Jeff Schechter

Bloody Angels ★★★ 18

Crime thriller 1998 · Nor/UK · Colour · 98mins

An Oslo detective travels to a snowbound backwater to investigate a killing in this dour thriller. With his flash Jag and open contempt for the hicks, Reidar Sorensen's big city cop has little hope of identifying the masked vigilantes who drowned a local lad suspected of the rape and murder of a mentally handicapped girl. He has even less chance of halting the cycle of violence that leads to the brutal victimisation of the dead man's angelic younger brother. Ingmar Bergman meets David Lynch in an austere whodunnit where everyone is corrupted. NS. In Norwegian with English subtitles.

Reidar Sorensen *Nicholas Ramm* • Jon Oigarden *Baste Hartmann* • Gaute Skjegstad *Niklas Hartmann* • Trond Hovik *Holger* • Stig Henrik Hoff *Dwayne Karlson* • Laila Goody *Victoria* • Simon Norrthon *Cato* • Kjersti Holmen *Andrea Hartmann* ■ *Dir* Karin Julsrud • *Scr* Kjetil Indregard

The Bloody Brood ★

Crime drama 1959 · Can · BW · 69mins

Peter Falk would undoubtedly prefer to forget his early appearance in this cheap Canadian crime melodrama. He's the only member of the cast to have become well known, and he's the only reason for watching it. In fact, he's quite effective in a ridiculous part, giving a cold, emotionless performance as the psychopathic gangleader who feeds a youngster a deadly hamburger containing ground-up glass. The dead man's brother seeks revenge by infiltrating the film's bizarre world of beatniks and weirdos. AE

Peter Falk *Nico* • Jack Betts *Cliff* • Ronald Hartman *Francis* • Barbara Lord *Ellie* • Robert Christie *Detective McLeod* • William Brydon *Studs* • George Sperdakos *Ricky* • Ron Taylor (1) *Dave* ■ *Dir* Julian Roffman • *Scr* Elwood Ullman, Ben Kerner, from a story by Anne Howard Bailey

The Bloody Judge ★★ 18

Horror
1969 · It/UK/Sp/W Ger · Colour · 89mins

Christopher Lee says his portrayal of the depraved 17th century Lord Chief Justice Judge Jeffreys, who cruelly condemned women as witches to further his political and sexual needs, is one of his best performances. Shame it's wasted in this cheap *Witchfinder General* imitation from Spanish hack Jess Franco. The plot revolves around Maria Rohm romancing the son of the Earl of Wessex, and submitting to the judge's perversions in order to save her rebel lover from the death sentence. Badly structured, often boring. AJ [VIDEO] DVD

Christopher Lee *Lord George Jeffreys* • Leo Genn *Earl of Wessex* • Maria Schell *Mother Rosa* • Maria Rohm *Mary Gray* • Margaret Lee *Alicia Gray* ■ *Dir* Jess Franco [Jesus Franco] • *Scr* Enrico Colombo, Jess Franco [Jesus Franco]

Bloody Mama ★★★ 18

Period crime drama
1970 · US · Colour · 89mins

Shelley Winters is the quintessential Ma Barker in cult director Roger Corman's gangster movie about her infamous bank-robbing brood who terrorised the Depression-hit Midwest during the 1930s. A satisfyingly sleazy salute to Middle American family values – the family that slays together, stays together – Corman's supposedly true crime saga is a riotous stew of sentimental blood-bonding and perverse bloody violence. In one of his earliest appearances, Robert De Niro is electrifying as the drug-addicted son. AJ [VIDEO]

Shelley Winters *Kat "Ma" Barker* • Pat Hingle *Sam Pendlebury* • Don Stroud *Herman Barker* • Diane Varsi *Mona Gibson* • Bruce Dern *Kevin Kirkman* • Clint Kimbrough *Arthur Barker* • Robert Walden *Fred Barker* • Robert De Niro *Lloyd Barker* • Alex Nicol *George Barker* ■ *Dir* Roger Corman • *Scr* Robert Thom, from a story by Robert Thom, Don Peters

Bloody Sunday ★★★★ 15

Historical drama
2001 · Ire/UK · Colour · 105mins

Based on Don Mullan's acclaimed book, this is an unblinking account of the events of 30 January 1972 that resulted in 13 civilians being killed by members of the Parachute Regiment while on a protest march through the city of Londonderry. Employing a gritty, *vérité* filming style that is complemented by superb editing, writer/director Paul Greengrass not only captures the tension between the sectarian communities and the British forces, but also conveys the shattered hopes of the civil rights movement and the march organisers, including MP Ivan Cooper (played with solemn dignity by James Nesbitt). This is a powerful and provocative testament. DP [VIDEO] DVD

James Nesbitt *Ivan Cooper* • Tim Pigott-Smith *Maj Gen Ford* • Nicholas Farrell *Brigadier Patrick MacLellan* • Gerard McSorley *Chief Supt Lagan* • Kathy Keira Clarke *Frances* • Allan Gildea *Kevin McCorry* • Gerard Crossan *Eamonn McCann* • Mary Moulds *Bernadette Devlin* ■ *Dir* Paul Greengrass • *Scr* Paul Greengrass, from the non-fiction book *Eyewitness Bloody Sunday* by Don Mullan

bl,.m ★★

Drama 2003 · Ire · Colour · 111mins

This brave attempt to film James Joyce's masterpiece fails to find the audiovisual equivalent of the dexterous stream of consciousness that dazzled and scandalised readers in the 1920s. Moreover, neither Stephen Rea nor Hugh O'Conor comes close to capturing the personalities of wittily bitter cuckold Leopold Bloom and self-absorbed poet Stephen Dedalus. Angeline Ball more successfully conveys Molly Bloom's intense sensuality, but her performance is never convincingly incorporated into the fragmented structure. Most disappointing of all, however, is director Sean Walsh's handling of the novel's most important character, Dublin on 16 June 1904. DP

Stephen Rea *Leopold Bloom* • Angeline Ball *Molly Bloom* • Hugh O'Conor *Stephen Dedalus* • Patrick Bergin *The Citizen* • Alan Devlin *Simon Dedalus* • Phelim Drew *Martin Cunningham* ■ *Dir* Sean Walsh • *Scr* Sean Walsh, from the novel *Ulysses* by James Joyce

Bloomfield ★ PG

Sports drama 1969 · UK/Is · Colour · 91mins

Richard Harris made a disastrous directorial debut with this blend of soccer and sentiment. He also stars as the Israeli footballer who, though well past his sell-by date, goes a game too far because he's been offered a car to fix the result. The soccer sequences are poorly staged, while the vistas that accompany ten-year-old Yossi Yadin on his trek to Jaffa to see his hero are achingly dull. DP [VIDEO]

Richard Harris *Eitan* • Romy Schneider *Nira* • Kim Burfield *Nimrod* • Maurice Kaufmann *Yasha* • Yossi Yadin *Weiner* • Shraga Friedman *Chairman* • Aviva Marks *Teddy* ■ *Dir* Richard Harris • *Scr* Wolf Mankowitz, from a story by Joseph Gross

Blossom Time ★★ U

Musical romance 1934 · UK · BW · 91mins

Fans of Richard Tauber, once the world's most popular Viennese tenor, will enjoy this period romance with music set in the Hapsburg capital of the 1820s. Tauber plays a composer who not only gracefully concedes defeat when the girl he loves falls for a titled Royal dragoon of the Archduchess's regiment, but also persuades the Archduchess to give his rival permission to marry a commoner. Old-fashioned, formulaic and slow, but undeniably charming. RK

Richard Tauber *Schubert* • Jane Baxter *Vicki* • Carl Esmond *Rudi* • Athene Seyler *Archduchess* • Paul Graetz *Wimpassinger* • Charles Carson *Lafont* • Marguerite Allan *Baroness* • Edward Chapman *Meyerhoffer* ■ *Dir* Paul L Stein • *Scr* Roger Burford, GH Clutsam, John Drinkwater

Blossoms in the Dust ★★★

Biographical drama
1941 · US · Colour · 100mins

All the MGM gloss in the world can't hide the fact that this is a tear-jerker of the first order, but director Mervyn LeRoy and stars Greer Garson and Walter Pidgeon embrace the subject head on, and knowingly create a fine biopic, enhanced by Oscar-winning interior decoration and some first-rate Technicolor. This is the tale of Edna Gladney, who started the Texas Children's Home and Aid Society of Fort Worth, caring for orphans and strays. Nobody could be better equipped to play her than Oscar-nominated Garson, but despite the film's undoubted worthiness, Garson's stubborn refusal to age alongside the narrative reduces the drama to bathos. TS

Greer Garson *Edna Gladney* • Walter Pidgeon *Sam Gladney* • Felix Bressart *Dr Max Breslar* • Marsha Hunt *Charlotte* • Fay Holden *Mrs Kahly* • Samuel S Hinds *Mr Kahly* • Kathleen Howard *Mrs Keats* • George Lessey *Mr Keats* ■ *Dir* Mervyn LeRoy • *Scr* Anita Loos, from a story by Ralph Wheelwright • *Cinematographer* Karl Freund, W Howard Greene • *Set Designer* Cedric Gibbons, Urie McCleary, Edwin B Willis

Blow ★★★ 18

Biographical drama
2001 · US · Colour · 118mins

The rise and fall of the 1970s' biggest cocaine importer, George Jung, is charted in Ted Demme's vivid biopic. Johnny Depp lends an affable charm to his portrayal of the naive entrepreneur who gets in way over his head. There's also a clutch of fine characterisations from the likes of Paul Reubens as a camp hairdresser cum dealer, and Ray Liotta and Rachel Griffiths as Jung's parents. Aside from a certain predictability in Jung's slippery slope, the film's weakness lies in the unbalanced pacing and direction. The period details are outstanding though, with particular praise reserved for Depp's spectacular range of bad-hair days. JC [VIDEO] DVD

Johnny Depp *George Jung* • Penélope Cruz *Mirtha* • Franka Potente *Barbara* • Rachel Griffiths *Ermine Jung* • Paul Reubens *Derek Foreal* • Jordi Mollà *Diego Delgado* • Ray Liotta *Fred Jung* ■ *Dir* Ted Demme • *Scr* David McKenna, Nick Cassavetes

Blow Dry ★★ 15

Comedy drama
2000 · UK/Ger/US · Colour · 86mins

The glitz and glamour of the British hairdressing championships form the backdrop to this bittersweet comedy drama. It's set in a sleepy Yorkshire town, where ex-champion barber Alan Rickman faces stiff competition from favourite Bill Nighy. Sadly, it's a bit of a mess – a subplot involving Natasha Richardson as Rickman's cancer-afflicted estranged wife – jars with some farcical stylist skulduggery. There are some affecting moments, but the laughs are few. JC. Contains swearing, nudity. [VIDEO] DVD

Alan Rickman *Phil Allen* • Natasha Richardson *Shelley* • Rachel Griffiths *Sandra* • Rachael Leigh Cook *Christina* • Josh Hartnett *Brian* • Bill Nighy *Ray Robertson* • Warren Clarke *Tony* • Rosemary Harris *Daisy* • Hugh Bonneville *Louis* ■ *Dir* Paddy Breathnach • *Scr* Simon Beaufoy

Blow Out ★★★★ 18

Thriller 1981 · US · Colour · 107mins

Long before *Pulp Fiction*, John Travolta's best role was in Brian De Palma's audio version of Michelangelo Antonioni's *Blowup*, laced with the director's usual quota of Hitchcockian black humour and startling suspense. Travolta is marvellous as the cheesy horror flick sound-effects man who

B

accidentally tapes events leading to the drowning of a presidential candidate. Nothing is what it seems in a paranoid mystery deliciously overflowing with De Palma's trademark high style right up until the knockout ending. AJ. Contains violence, swearing, nudity. DVD

John Travolta *Jack Terry* • Nancy Allen *Sally Badina* • John Lithgow *Burke* • Dennis Franz *Manny Karp* • John Aquino *Detective Mackey* • Peter Boyden *Sam* • Curt May *Donahue* • John McMartin *Lawrence Henry* • Deborah Everton *Hooker* ■ *Dir/Scr* Brian De Palma

Blowback ★★ 18

Science-fiction crime thriller
1999 · US · Colour · 87mins

In this preposterous but mildly enjoyable thriller, James Remar's serial killer is secretly saved from execution by a shady government group that wants him as an assassin. Mario Van Peebles does his usual humourless work as the cop who becomes certain that his apparently dead adversary is disposing of the jury who sent him to the gas chamber. It all makes little sense, but Remar makes a decent villain and director Mark L Lester manages some serviceable suspense. JC. Contains swearing, violence, sex scenes and nudity. DVD

James Remar *John Matthew Whitman/Schmidt* • Mario Van Peebles *Don Morrell* • Gladys Jimenez *Charlotte Hart-Morrell* • Sharisse Baker *Monica Ricci* • David Groh *Captain Barnett* ■ *Dir* Mark L Lester • *Scr* Randall Frakes, Jeffrey Goldenberg, Bob Held

Blowing Wild ★★★

Adventure 1953 · US · BW · 89mins

"Marina mine..." belted out Frankie Laine over the opening titles of this 1930s-set oil-rig melodrama (and so secured himself a substantial hit). Marina is played by Barbara Stanwyck. She's married to tycoon Anthony Quinn, but has the hots for former lover Gary Cooper, a wildcatter from her past who turns up in her life just when he shouldn't. Director Hugo Fregonese makes the most of the Mexican locations, even though he seems incapable of reining in his stars, who emote at full throttle. TS

Barbara Stanwyck *Marina Conway* • Gary Cooper *Jeff Dawson* • Ruth Roman *Sal* • Anthony Quinn *Paco Conway* • Ward Bond *Dutch Peterson* • Juan Garcia *El Gavilan* • Ian MacDonald *Jackson* ■ *Dir* Hugo Fregonese • *Scr* Phillip Yordan

Blown Away ★★ 15

Thriller 1994 · US · Colour and BW · 115mins

Jeff Bridges stars as a bomb disposal expert and Tommy Lee Jones is his former colleague who wants Bridges blown away in this bungled hi-tech thriller. The film aims to deliver a tense sequence every 15 minutes or so, while Bridges and Jones, two of the best around, can make nothing of the thinly written, often tasteless, material. Lloyd Bridges and Forest Whitaker are completely wasted. AT. Contains brief nudity, violence, swearing. DVD

Jeff Bridges *Jimmy Dove* • Tommy Lee Jones *Ryan Gaerity* • Suzy Amis *Kate* • Lloyd Bridges *Max O'Bannon* • Forest Whitaker *Anthony Franklin* • Stephi Lineburg *Lizzy* • John Finn *Captain Roarke* • Caitlin Clarke *Rita* • Chris De Oni *Cortez* ■ *Dir* Stephen Hopkins • *Scr* Joe Batteer, John Rice, from a story by John Rice, Joe Batteer, M Jay Roach [Jay Roach]

Blowup ★★★ 15

Mystery drama
1966 · UK/It · Colour · 106mins

One of the true tests of a great work of art is its ability to transcend time. Film can have the shortest shelf life of any art form, and Michelangelo Antonioni's first English language feature is a case in point. Hailed in its day as a work of genius, an intriguing, if self-indulgent, challenge to the idea that the camera never lies, this might-be murder mystery is now often dismissed as ostentatious and exploitative. Sarah Miles walked out during production, leaving Vanessa Redgrave to strip off, look gawky and fidget while David Hemmings puts on a jazz record. If you can ignore the pretensions, this does contain fleeting moments of brilliance. DP. Contains swearing and nudity. DVD

Vanessa Redgrave *Jane* • Sarah Miles *Patricia* • David Hemmings *Thomas* • John Castle *Patricia's artist husband* • Jane Birkin *Teenager* • Gillian Hills *Teenager* • Peter Bowles *Ron* • Verushka [Veruschka Von Lehndorff] *Model* ■ *Dir* Michelangelo Antonioni • *Scr* Michelangelo Antonioni, Tonino Guerra, Edward Bond, from the short story *Final del Juego* by Julio Cortázar • *Cinematographer* Carlo di Palma [Carlo Di Palma]

Blue ★★

Western 1968 · US · Colour · 112mins

Strikingly photographed by Stanley Cortez, this is an otherwise undistinguished western from Silvio Narizzano. As the adopted son of Mexican bandit Ricardo Montalban, Terence Stamp rescues respectable Karl Malden and his daughter Joanna Pettet only to learn the hard facts of life in the Old West. Archly acted and heavy-handed in its symbolism, this is a long haul for little reward. DP

Terence Stamp *Blue/Azul* • Joanna Pettet *Joanne Morton* • Karl Malden *Doc Morton* • Ricardo Montalban *Ortega* • Anthony Costello *Jess Parker* • Joe De Santis *Carlos* • James Westerfield *Abe Parker* • Stathis Giallelis *Manuel* • Sally Kirkland *Sara Lambert* • Peggy Lipton *Laurie Kramer* ■ *Dir* Silvio Narizzano • *Scr* Meade Roberts, Ronald M Cohen, from the story by Ronald M Cohen

Blue ★★★★ 15

Experimental 1993 · UK · Colour · 75mins

Derek Jarman's work has been overpraised by critics desperate for an original voice in British cinema, but there is no doubting the courage and sincerity of this deeply moving swansong. The screen remains a shimmering shade of blue for the entire film, while Nigel Terry, John Quentin, Tilda Swinton and the director himself read extracts from Jarman's diary and other writings to the accompaniment of Simon Fisher Turner's imaginative score. The meditations might meander now and then, but there is no self-pity or bitterness in his comments on Aids, the loss of his friends, his own blindness and the inevitability of death. DP. Contains swearing.

Derek Jarman • John Quentin • Nigel Terry • Tilda Swinton ■ *Dir/Scr* Derek Jarman • *Music* Simon Fisher Turner

The Blue Angel ★★★★ PG

Drama 1930 · Ger · BW · 106mins

Contrary to popular myth, 28-year-old Marlene Dietrich had already appeared in almost 20 (admittedly minor) films in her native Germany when Josef von Sternberg cast her as Lola, the sensual cabaret singer who enslaves, humiliates and finally destroys middle-aged professor Emil Jannings. The film did, however, bring about the famous von Sternberg/Dietrich Hollywood collaboration. Jannings, making his first talking picture, has some wonderful moments in an uneven performance. But it was the cruel and seductive Dietrich, in top hat and black stockings, perched on a bar stool and huskily singing *Falling in Love Again*, that became one of the cinema's great iconic images. RK. In German with English subtitles. DVD

Emil Jannings *Professor Immanuel Rath* • Marlene Dietrich *Lola Frohlich* • Kurt Gerron *Kiepert, a magician* • Rosa Valette *Guste Kiepert, his wife* • Hans Albers *Mazeppa* • Eduard Von Winterstein *School principal* • Reinhold Bernt *The clown* • Hans Roth *Beadle* ■ *Dir* Josef von Sternberg • *Scr* Carl Zuckmayer, Karl Vollmöller, Robert Liebmann, from the novel *Professor Unrat* by Heinrich Mann • *Music* Friedrich Holländer

The Blue Angel ★

Drama 1959 · US · Colour · 107mins

A seriously misguided attempt by 20th Century-Fox to remake Josef von Sternberg's thirites German classic, about a cabaret singer who destroys the middle-aged professor obsessionally in love with her. Placed in a modern setting and filmed in CinemaScope, this is truly awful, losing the atmosphere, resonance and credibility of the original. Curt Jurgens and May Britt are the unfortunate substitutes for Emil Jannings and Marlene Dietrich. RK

Curt Jurgens *Professor Immanuel Rath* • May Britt *Lola-Lola* • Theodore Bikel *Klepert* • John Banner *Principal Harter* • Fabrizio Mioni *Rolf* • Ludwig Stossel *Professor Braun* • Wolfe Barzell *Clown* • Ina Anders *Gussie* ■ *Dir* Edward Dmytryk • *Scr* Nigel Balchin, from the film by Carl Zuckmeyer, Karl Vollmöller, Robert Liebmann, from the novel *Professor Unrat* by Heinrich Mann

The Blue Bird ★★★ U

Fantasy 1940 · US · Colour · 82mins

Twentieth Century-Fox's answer to MGM's *The Wizard of Oz* was this lavish version of the Maurice Maeterlinck play about a woodcutter's daughter, played by Shirley Temple, seeking the blue bird of happiness. Enjoy the fantastic settings and the fine Technicolor, for the characters never come to life and the handling is too literal. This was Temple's first box-office flop and her career never really recovered. Gale Sondergaard, though, is splendid, playing the treacherous family cat. AE

Shirley Temple *Mytyl* • Spring Byington *Mummy Tyl* • Nigel Bruce *Mr Luxury* • Gale Sondergaard *Tylette* • Eddie Collins *Tylo, the dog* • Edwin Maxwell *Oak* • Thurston Hall *Father Time* ■ *Dir* Walter Lang • *Scr* Ernest Pascal, Walter Bullock, from the play *L'Oiseau Bleu* by Maurice Maeterlinck

The Blue Bird ★★ U

Fantasy 1976 · US/USSR · Colour · 97mins

Patsy Kensit is in the glittering company of Liz Taylor, Ava Gardner and Jane Fonda in this retelling of the Maeterlinck theatrical fairy tale. Two children, Kensit and her brother Todd Lookinland, set out on a journey to find the blue bird of happiness accompanied by the human manifestations of, among others, a dog, a cat, a loaf of bread and fire. Despite the stellar cast, this first US/Soviet co-production is a turgid affair and is doubtful entertainment, even for the children it's aimed at. LH

Elizabeth Taylor *Mother/Light/Maternal Love/Witch* • Jane Fonda *Night* • Cicely Tyson *Cat* • Ava Gardner *Luxury* • Patsy Kensit *Mytyl* • Todd Lookinland *Tyltyl* • Mona Washbourne *Grandmother* • George Cole *Dog* • Robert Morley *Father Time* • Harry Andrews *Oak* ■ *Dir* George Cukor • *Scr* Hugh Whitemore, Alfred Hayes, Alexei Kapler, from the play *L'Oiseau Bleu* by Maurice Maeterlinck

Blue Black Permanent ★★★★ PG

Drama 1992 · UK · Colour · 85mins

A stunning feature debut from Margaret Tait, who also wrote the script. We watch, moved, as Scottish photographer Celia Imrie tells her boyfriend Jack Shepherd the heartrending story of her mother's death when she was a child, coming to realise as she does so just how much the event has shaped her life. Superbly performed, this is an unusual and thought-provoking drama about coping with loss and the guilt that comes with it, filled with unusual imagery that punctuates each emotion. While it doesn't always work, this is nonetheless an interesting film full of emotion and meaning. JB

Celia Imrie *Barbara Thorburn* • Jack Shepherd *Philip Lomax* • Gerda Stevenson *Greta Thorburn* • James Fleet *Jim Thorburn* • Sean Scanlan *Andrew Cunningham* • Hilary Maclean *Wendy* • Walter Leask *Sam Kelday* • Sheana Marr *Mrs Kemp* • Eoin MacDonald *Dan of Fea* ■ *Dir/Scr* Margaret Tait

Blue Blood ★ 18

Psychological thriller
1973 · UK · Colour · 78mins

It's hard to describe just how abysmal this reworking of *The Servant* really is. It is directed with revolting enthusiasm by Andrew Sinclair, who, unsurprisingly, has not been entrusted with many features since. As the vicious butler intent on destabilising his weak-kneed aristocratic employer (Derek Jacobi), Oliver Reed gesticulates and rolls his eyes. Dire. DP

Oliver Reed *Tom* • Derek Jacobi *Gregory* • Fiona Lewis *Lily* • Anna Gael *Carlotta* • Meg Wynn Owen *Beate Krug* • John Rainer *Clurman* • Richard Davies *Jones* • Gwyneth Owen *Agnes* ■ *Dir* Andrew Sinclair • *Scr* Andrew Sinclair, from the novel *The Carry-Cot* by Alexander Thynne

Blue Canadian Rockies ★★ U

Western 1952 · US · Sepia · 57mins

This Saturday morning fare is only for die-hard fans of the immensely popular singing cowboy Gene Autry. This programmer is a typical vehicle, with Autry's regular sidekick Pat Buttram also along for the ride. The real co-star, though, is Champion, who went on to become the only cowboy horse to have his own TV series. TS

Gene Autry • Pat Buttram *"Rawhide" Buttram* • Gail Davis *Sandra Higbee* • Carolina Cotton • Ross Ford *Todd Markley* ■ *Dir* George Archainbaud • *Scr* Gerald Geraghty

Blue Car ★★★ 15

Drama 2001 · US · Colour · 87mins

Familiar themes such as adolescent angst, domestic dysfunction and betrayed trust are given a new lease in Karen Moncrieff's affecting debut. Desperate to find a father figure to compensate for the neglect of her overworked mother and the stress of coping with a disturbed sister, teenager Agnes Bruckner's growing dependence on teacher David Strathairn reaches a predictable climax when he persuades her to enter a poetry contest in faraway Florida. But such is the fragility of Bruckner's performance and the tact with which Moncrieff approaches her problems and aspirations that it's impossible not to become involved. DP

David Strathairn *Auster* • Agnes Bruckner *Meg* • Margaret Colin *Diane* • Regan Arnold *Lily* • Frances Fisher *Delia* • AJ Buckley *Pat* ■ *Dir/Scr* Karen Moncrieff

Blue Chips ★★★ 15

Sports drama 1994 · US · Colour · 103mins

Ron Shelton is probably the finest writer of sports movies Hollywood has produced. Although not up there with *Bull Durham*, this is still a perceptive take on the machinations of the American sporting industry. This time the target is basketball, with an excellent Nick Nolte as the honourable college coach under pressure to succumb to the dodgy practices of his

B

peers by secretly paying for young stars to join his team. Director William Friedkin, better known for his action thrillers, films the basketball set pieces with his usual aplomb. DP. Contains swearing. [VIDEO]

Nick Nolte *Pete Bell* • Mary McDonnell *Jenny* • JT Walsh *Happy* • Ed O'Neill *Ed* • Alfre Woodard *Lavada McRae* • Bob Cousy *Vic* • Shaquille O'Neal *Neon* • Louis Gossett Jr *Father Dawkins* ■ *Dir* William Friedkin • *Scr* Ron Shelton

Blue City ★★ 18

Thriller 1986 · US · Colour · 79mins

Though the sublime Ry Cooder supplies part of the soundtrack, this is an overwrought, largely forgettable, crime drama, in which Judd Nelson attempts to discover the truth behind the death of his father. Nelson and Ally Sheedy, who starred together the year before in *The Breakfast Club*, look out of their depth while the other familiar faces in the cast are wasted. Only the reliable Paul Winfield emerges from this mess with reputation intact. JF. Contains swearing and violence. [VIDEO]

Judd Nelson *Billy Turner* • Ally Sheedy *Annie Rayford* • David Caruso *Joey Rayford* • Paul Winfield *Luther Reynolds* • Scott Wilson *Perry Kerch* • Anita Morris *Malvina Kerch* • Luis Contreras *Lieutenant Ortiz* • Julie Carmen *Debbie Torez* ■ *Dir* Michelle Manning • *Scr* Lukas Heller, Walter Hill, from the novel by Ross MacDonald

Blue Collar ★★★★ 18

Drama 1978 · US · Colour · 108mins

After writing the scripts for *Taxi Driver* and an early version of *Close Encounters of the Third Kind*, Paul Schrader made his directorial debut with *Blue Collar*, a rare Hollywood feature in that it deals with America's industrial relations in a factory, more the province of British realist pictures of the 1960s. It's the grinding boredom of the production line that interests Schrader and how his three workers – Richard Pryor, Harvey Keitel, Yaphet Kotto – plan to break free of it by robbing their union. It's tough, convincing and littered with ripe language, capturing the atmosphere of the streets and domestic lives with the same sort of pulse as *Taxi Driver*. AT. Contains swearing, drug abuse and brief nudity. [VIDEO]

Richard Pryor *Zeke Brown* • Harvey Keitel *Jerry Bartowski* • Yaphet Kotto *Smokey* • Ed Begley Jr *Bobby Joe* • Harry Bellaver *Eddie Johnson* • George Memmoli *Jenkins* • Lucy Saroyan *Arlene Bartowski* ■ *Dir* Paul Schrader • *Scr* Paul Schrader, Leonard Schrader, from source material by Sydney A Glass

Blue Crush ★★★ 12

Romantic sports drama
2002 · US · Colour · 99mins

Unlike the usual babes-in-bikinis epics, this looks at the reality behind an adrenalin-fuelled life on the ocean wave. The film centres on three girls (Kate Bosworth, Michelle Rodriguez and Sanoe Lake) who work at a luxury Hawaiian resort in order to support their surf addiction. Bosworth is the favourite to win the upcoming tournament and turn pro, but she has distractions: a kid sister to look after and a budding romance with a visiting American football player. Director John Stockwell provides the exciting wave action, and brilliantly shot it is, too. TH. Contains swearing and sexual references. [VIDEO] DVD

Kate Bosworth *Anne Marie* • Matthew Davis *Matt* • Michelle Rodriguez *Eden* • Sanoe Lake *Lena* • Mika Boorem *Penny* • Chris Taloa *Drew* • Kala Alexander *Kala* • Ruben Tejada *JJ* ■ *Dir* John Stockwell • *Scr* Lizzy Weiss, from her story, from the article *Surf Girls of Maui* by Susan Orlean

The Blue Dahlia ★★★★

Film noir 1946 · US · BW · 100mins

This terrifically taut thriller was written for the screen from his own original story by the great Raymond Chandler, with lines and whole scenes as hard-boiled and witty as in the better known *films noirs*, *The Big Sleep* or *Double Indemnity*. Steely-eyed, super-cool Alan Ladd returns from the war to find his wife Doris Dowling cheating and then dead, with himself as the chief murder suspect. He meets sultry Veronica Lake, and their scenes together simply sizzle. Under George Marshall's expert direction, the fight sequences are unusually realistic and brutal. TS

Alan Ladd *Johnny Morrison* • Veronica Lake *Joyce Harwood* • William Bendix *Buzz Wanchek* • Howard Da Silva *Eddie Harwood* • Doris Dowling *Helen Morrison* • Tom Powers *Captain Hendrickson* • Hugh Beaumont *George Copeland* • Howard Freeman *Corelli* ■ *Dir* George Marshall • *Scr* Raymond Chandler, from his story • *Music* Victor Young • *Cinematographer* Lionel Lindon

Blue Denim ★★★

Drama 1959 · US · BW · 89mins

Considered shocking in its day, Philip Dunne's drama stands in stark contrast to the more frivolous teen pictures produced in the late 1950s. There's an undeniable sweetness about the way alienated high school kids Brandon de Wilde and Carol Lynley fall in love, which makes their need to visit an abortionist all the more distressing. However, this being Hollywood under the Production Code, what would have been the inevitable conclusion in life is hijacked by moral rectitude. Both principals, however, are outstanding. DP

Carol Lynley *Janet Willard* • Brandon de Wilde *Arthur Bartley* • Macdonald Carey *Maj Malcolm Bartley, Ret* • Marsha Hunt *Jessie Bartley* • Warren Berlinger *Ernie* • Buck Class *Axel Sorenson* • Nina Shipman *Lillian Bartley* ■ *Dir* Philip Dunne • *Scr* Edith Sommer, Philip Dunne, from the play by James Leo Herlihy, William Noble

The Blue Gardenia ★★★

Film noir 1953 · US · BW · 90mins

Director Fritz Lang, one of the great expressionists and innovators of cinema (*Metropolis*, *M*) fled the Nazis in 1936 and made a second career in Hollywood. Reined in by studio executives who tampered with his vision, he nonetheless established himself as a master of *film noir*. This modest offering stars Anne Baxter who, duped into drunkenness by baddie Raymond Burr, comes to in his apartment, finds him dead and flees the scene. Co-star Richard Conte is a powerful newspaper columnist who invites the unknown killer to surrender. The plot and the denouement are incredible, but it's made with Langian flair. Entertaining. RK

Anne Baxter *Norah Larkin* • Richard Conte *Casey Mayo* • Ann Sothern *Crystal Carpenter* • Raymond Burr *Harry Prebble* • Jeff Donnell *Sally Ellis* • Richard Erdman *Al* • George Reeves *Police Captain Haynes* • Ruth Storey *Rose Miller* • Nat King Cole ■ *Dir* Fritz Lang • *Scr* Charles Hoffman, from the story *Gardenia* by Vera Caspary

Blue Gate Crossing ★★★ 12A

Romantic comedy drama
2001 · Tai/Fr · Colour · 82mins

Having focused on a woman who discovers that her heart's desire is gay in his debut feature, *Lonely Hearts Club*, Taiwanese director Yee Chih-Yen here transfers the scenario to a Taipei high school. This time it's swimming star Chen Bo-Lin who realises that the boyish Guey Lun-Mei would rather be canoodling with her best friend, Liang Shu-Hui – a situation made all the more awkward as Guey was supposed to be interceding with Chen on Liang's behalf. The easy byplay between Chen and Guey is delightful, but the sweet story lacks originality. DP. In Mandarin with English subtitles.

Chen Bo-Lin *Zhang Shihao* • Guey Lun-Mei *Meng Kerou* • Liang Shu-Hui *Lin Yuezhen* • Joanna Chou *Mrs Meng* ■ *Dir/Scr* Yee Chih-Yen

Blue Hawaii ★★★ PG

Musical comedy drama
1961 · US · Colour · 96mins

Though one of Elvis Presley's biggest successes, this movie was directly responsible for turning him from the new James Dean into the king of pap. Confronted with the huge box office grosses, Elvis's controllers – venal manager Colonel Tom Parker and film producer Hal Wallis – decided that every movie their boy made from then on would be the same mix of girls, songs and exotic locations. Thirty films later, they'd sacrificed both their audience and Presley's screen credibility. For all that, this is colourful, amiable fluff. TS [VIDEO] DVD

Elvis Presley *Chad Gates* • Joan Blackman *Maile Duval* • Nancy Walters *Abigail Prentace* • Roland Winters *Fred Gates* • Angela Lansbury *Sarah Lee Gates* • John Archer *Jack Kelman* • Howard McNear *Mr Chapman* • Flora Hayes *Mrs Manaka* ■ *Dir* Norman Taurog • *Scr* Hal Kanter, from a story by Allan Weiss • *Cinematographer* Charles Lang Jr [Charles Lang]

Blue Heat ★★★ 15

Police action drama
1990 · US · Colour · 101mins

Brian Dennehy looks fearsome enough to go off like a one-man firework display, but also kindly enough to play Santa Claus down at your local store. This odd ability is put to good use in this action drama, in which Dennehy co-stars with Joe Pantoliano, Jeff Fahey and Bill Paxton as members of an elite unit working for the Los Angeles police. Striving to be a political allegory, the story works better as a tale of Dennehy and his unit against the drugs barons, even when the action sequences fall flat. JM. Contains swearing, violence, drug abuse. [VIDEO]

Brian Dennehy *Frank Daly* • Joe Pantoliano *Wayne Gross* • Jeff Fahey *Ricky Rodriguez* • Bill Paxton *Howard "Hojo" Jones* • Michael C Gwynne *Anthony Reece* • Henry Stolow *Stant* • Guy Boyd *RJ Norringer* • Henry Darrow *Captain Joe Torres* • Deborra-Lee Furness *Linda Daly* ■ *Dir* John Mackenzie • *Scr* Jere Cunningham, Thomas Lee Wright, George Armitage, from a story by Jere Cunningham

Blue Ice ★★ 15

Thriller 1992 · US/UK · Colour · 100mins

Michael Caine stars in this thriller featuring a central character who resembles a warmed-up version of *The Ipcress File's* Harry Palmer (Caine, naturally), a performance from Sean Young that is all mannerism and no depth, and direction from Russell Mulcahy that is all gloss and no suspense. Still, at least a London of dark encounters and ne'er-do-wells looks properly seedy. JM. Contains swearing, violence and nudity. [VIDEO]

Michael Caine *Harry Anders* • Sean Young *Stacy Mansdorf* • Ian Holm *Sir Hector* • Bobby Short *Buddy* • Alun Armstrong *Det Sgt Osgood* • Sam Kelly *George* • Jack Shepherd *Stevens* • Philip Davis *Westy* ■ *Dir* Russell Mulcahy • *Scr* Ron Hutchinson, from the character created by Ted Allbeury

The Blue Iguana ★ 15

Crime comedy 1988 · US · Colour · 86mins

An off-target attempt to satirise gumshoe pictures, B-movies and *film noir*, this is directed by John Lafia, who displays no grasp of basic comic timing. The story concerns a hopeless bounty hunter who heads south of the border to retrieve $20 million in drug money. JM. Contains violence, swearing, drug abuse. [VIDEO]

Dylan McDermott *Vince Holloway* • Jessica Harper *Cora* • James Russo *Reno* • Pamela Gidley *Dakota* • Yano Anaya *Yano* • Flea *Floyd* ■ *Dir/Scr* John Lafia

Blue in the Face ★★★ 15

Comedy drama 1995 · US · Colour · 79mins

A funny thing happened after director Wayne Wang and novelist Paul Auster completed *Smoke*, their excellent look at Brooklyn life as distilled through Harvey Keitel's cigar shop. The actors had had such a good time making it, they didn't want to go home, and Wang and Auster had the set for another week. Hence this bookend featuring mainly improvised scenes on the power of the weed, mixed in with video documentary footage. Self-indulgent at times, and distinctly different from the original, but in its own small way equally as entertaining. AJ. Contains swearing and nudity. [VIDEO] DVD

Harvey Keitel *Auggie Wren* • Michael J Fox *Peter* • Roseanne Barr *Dot* • Mel Gorham *Violet* • Lily Tomlin *Derelict* • Madonna *Singing telegram girl* • Jim Jarmusch • Lou Reed • Jared Harris *Jimmy Rose* ■ *Dir/Scr* Wayne Wang, Paul Auster

Blue Jean Cop ★★★ 18

Action crime thriller
1988 · US · Colour · 92mins

Forget the implausibilities in the dumb plot of this *Lethal Weapon* copy and marvel at how director James Glickenhaus choreographs the truly spectacular stuntwork. With highlights such as undercover cop Sam Elliott swinging off 42nd Street cinema balconies like an urban Tarzan and the frenetic Coney Island roller-coaster chase, this kinetic sleaze-fest delivers the action goods. AJ. Contains violence and swearing. [VIDEO]

Peter Weller *Roland Dalton* • Sam Elliott *Richie Marks* • Richard Brooks *Michael Jones* • Jude Ciccolella *Patrick O'Leary* • Tom Waites [Thomas G Waites] *Officer Kelly* • George Loros *Officer Varelli* • Daryl Edwards *Dr Watson* • Antonio Fargas *Nicky Carr* ■ *Dir/Scr* James Glickenhaus

Blue Juice ★★ 15

Comedy drama 1995 · UK · Colour · 94mins

What's this? A British movie about surfing! Since it's set on the rocky, chilly beaches of Cornwall, it's no wonder you see little of the sport itself. Instead, director Carl Prechezer focuses on the less interesting dilemma facing surfer Sean Pertwee. Terrified of turning 30, he must choose between his woman (Catherine Zeta-Jones) and the waves. One look at the weather throughout this contrived melodrama and there's no contest. Watch for Ewan McGregor's drug-popping psycho. AJ. [VIDEO] DVD

Sean Pertwee *JC* • Catherine Zeta-Jones *Chloe* • Ewan McGregor *Dean Raymond* • Steven Mackintosh *Josh Tambini* • Peter Gunn *Terry Colcott* • Heathcote Williams *Shaper* • Colette Brown *Junior* • Michelle Chadwick *Sarah* • Keith Allen *Mike* ■ *Dir* Carl Prechezer • *Scr* Peter Salmi, Carl Prechezer, from an idea by Peter Salmi, Carl Prechezer, Tim Veglio

The Blue Kite ★★★★ 12

Drama 1992 · HK/Chi · Colour · 134mins

Banned by the Chinese authorities, this is a rich and courageous study of the impact that the policies pursued by the Communist Party between 1949 and 1967 had on ordinary people. Based on director Tian Zhuangzhuang's memories and the stories told to him by family and friends, this tough film combines strident criticisms of Mao's regime with moments of great personal drama as careers, romances, friendships and rivalries are affected by momentous political and historical events. DP. In Mandarin with English subtitles.

Yi Tian *Tietou as an infant* • Zhang Wenyao *Tietou as a child* • Chen Xiaoman *Tietou as a teenager* • Lu Liping *Mum (Chen Shujuan)* • Pu Quanxin *Dad (Lin Shaolong)* • Guo Baochang *Stepfather (Lao Wu)* ■ *Dir* Tian Zhuangzhuang • *Scr* Xiao Mao

The Blue Knight ★★★

Police drama 1973 · US · Colour · 102mins

This police drama was originally made for American television, ran at nearly four hours and was shown on four consecutive nights. After it won several awards, it was cut by two-thirds and released in cinemas in Britain. Based on the bestselling book by former cop Joseph Wambaugh, it's set among the drug dealers and low-lifes of Los Angeles, but concentrates on the character of weary, craggy patrolman William Holden, who is obsessed with finding the killer of a prostitute. AT

William Holden (2) *"Bumper" Morgan* • Lee Remick *Cassie* • Joe Santos *Sergeant Cruze* • Eileen Brennan *Glenda* • Emile Meyer *Bartender* • Sam Elliott *Homicide detective* • Ernest Esparza III *Rudy Garcia* • Anne Archer *Call-girl* • Vic Tayback *Retired cop* ■ *Dir* Robert Butler • *Scr* E Jack Neuman, from the novel by Joseph Wambaugh

The Blue Lagoon ★★★

Romantic adventure
1949 · UK · Colour · 103mins

An immensely popular and very likeable British version of the sexy little tale by Henry Devere Stacpoole about two children marooned on a desert island paradise, growing up to discover sex and their attraction to each other. The book had to be slightly modified to meet the needs of the censor (a problem not encountered by the ludicrous 1980 remake with Brooke Shields). Here the castaways are played with great charm by Donald Houston and lovely Jean Simmons. TS

Jean Simmons *Emmeline Foster* • Susan Stranks *Emmeline as child* • Donald Houston *Michael Reynolds* • Peter Jones *Michael as child* • Noel Purcell *Paddy Button* • James Hayter *Dr Murdoch* • Cyril Cusack *James Carter* • Nora Nicholson *Mrs Stannard* ■ *Dir* Frank Launder • *Scr* Frank Launder, John Baines, Michael Hogan, from the novel by Henry de Vere Stacpoole • *Cinematographer* Geoffrey Unsworth

The Blue Lagoon ★★ 15

Romantic adventure
1980 · US · Colour · 100mins

This is a remake of the 1949 British film, in which two children were shipwrecked on a deserted island. In this update, teenage self-discovery and love ensue as Brooke Shields and co-star Christopher Atkins grow up isolated from the world. It's beautifully shot and there's much nudity and suggested sex, but it's all very, very silly, as the lovebirds conform to traditional marriage-and-baby values. Don't waste your time with the 1991 sequel, *Return to the Blue Lagoon*. LH. Contains sex scenes, nudity. DVD

Brooke Shields *Emmeline* • Christopher Atkins *Richard* • Leo McKern *Paddy Button* • William Daniels *Arthur Lestrange* • Elva Josephson *Young Emmeline* • Glenn Kohan *Young Richard* • Alan Hopgood *Captain* • Gus Mercurio *Officer* ■ *Dir* Randal Kleiser • *Scr* Douglas Day Stewart, from the novel by Henry de Vere Stacpoole

The Blue Lamp ★★★★ PG

Crime drama 1949 · UK · BW · 80mins

Jack Warner rose from the dead to star in TV's *Dixon of Dock Green* after his character was bumped off by petty crook Dirk Bogarde in this crime classic. Produced by Michael Balcon and scripted by TEB Clarke (a former policeman who penned many an Ealing comedy), the film yet again revealed the influence of the documentary on postwar British cinema, with its realistic depiction of the austere times that pushed some people to crime. Jimmy Hanley is a touch lightweight, but the rest of director Basil Dearden's cast is outstanding. DP DVD

Jack Warner *PC George Dixon* • Jimmy Hanley *PC Andy Mitchell* • Dirk Bogarde *Tom Riley* • Robert Flemyng *Sergeant Roberts* • Gladys Henson *Mrs Dixon* • Bernard Lee *Inspector Cherry* • Peggy Evans *Diana Lewis* • Patric Doonan *Spud* • Bruce Seton *Constable Campbell* • Dora Bryan *Maisie* ■ *Dir* Basil Dearden • *Scr* TEB Clarke

The Blue Light ★★★★

Drama 1932 · Ger · BW · 77mins

The mountain film was hugely popular with German audiences in the 1930s. Having starred in four features for the master of the genre, Dr Arnold Fanck, Leni Riefenstahl made her directorial debut with this tale of a Dolomite villager who is denounced as a witch for her ability to climb the unscaleable Mount Cristallo. As the maiden who plunges to her death after her lover removes the peak's magic crystals, Riefenstahl does a steady job. However, it's the stylised beauty of her direction that takes this simple moral fable on to a higher plane and landed her the post of Hitler's film-maker. DP. An Italian/German language film.

Leni Riefenstahl *Junta* • Mattias Weimann *Vigo* • Max Holzboer *Innkeeper* • Beni Führer *Tonio* • Franz Maldacea *Guzzi* • Martha Mair *Lucia* ■ *Dir* Leni Riefenstahl • *Scr* Leni Riefenstahl, Béla Balázs • *Cinematographer* Hans Schneeberger

The Blue Max ★★★★ PG

First World War drama
1966 · UK/US · Colour · 137mins

A film about the short lives and lengthy lusts of German First World War fighter aces – it sounds luridly sensational, but action director John Guillermin makes it a rare treat of aerial excitement. George Peppard is the reckless high-flier who endangers his comrades and beds Ursula Andress, wife of commander James Mason. The love story is unconvincingly staged and compares badly with the camaraderie of men under stress. But the superb in-flight photography reveals the grit as well as the glamour of their manic escapades. TH DVD

George Peppard *Bruno Stachel* • James Mason *Count von Klugermann* • Ursula Andress *Countess Kaeti* • Jeremy Kemp *Willi von Klugermann* • Karl Michael Vogler *Heidemann* • Anton Diffring *Holbach* • Harry Towb *Kettering* • Peter Woodthorpe *Rupp* • Derek Newark *Ziegel* ■ *Dir* John Guillermin • *Scr* David Pursall, Jack Seddon, Gerald Hanley, Ben Barzman, Basilio Franchina, from the novel *The Blue Max* by Jack D Hunter • *Cinematographer* Douglas Slocombe

Blue Monkey ★★★

Horror thriller 1987 · US · Colour · 98mins

Silly, scary and lots of fun, director William Fruet's throwback to 1950s monster movies offers knowing chuckles and disturbing horror in roughly equal proportion. A gardener cuts himself on an exotic plant and promptly vomits up a larva, and steroids turn the insect into a giant mutant bug. Camp dialogue ("We still have a few bugs to iron out"), cardboard creatures and gleeful schlock combine to make this an enjoyably slime-encrusted B-movie. AJ

Steve Railsback *Detective Jim Bishop* • Gwynyth Walsh *Dr Rachel Carson* • Susan Anspach *Dr Judith Glass* • John Vernon *Roger Levering* • Joe Flaherty *George Baker* • Robin Duke *Sandra Baker* • Don Lake *Elliot Jacobs* • Sandy Webster *Fred Adams* ■ *Dir* William Fruet • *Scr* George Goldsmith

Blue Murder at St Trinian's ★★★ U

Comedy 1957 · UK · BW · 82mins

While hugely enjoyable, the second of Frank Launder and Sidney Gilliat's adaptations of Ronald Searle's popular cartoons is something of a disappointment after the riotous success of *The Belles of St Trinian's*. The main problem is that there's only a fleeting glimpse of Alastair Sim as Miss Fritton, but the plot – about a tour of Europe and some stolen gems – is also somewhat under par. However, the flirting between coach company owner Terry-Thomas and undercover cop Joyce Grenfell is a comic delight. Followed by *The Pure Hell of St Trinian's*. DP

Joyce Grenfell *Sergeant Gates* • Terry-Thomas *Romney Carlton-Ricketts* • George Cole *Flash Harry* • Alastair Sim *Miss Amelia Fritton* • Sabrina (1) *Virginia* • Lionel Jeffries *Joe Mangan* • Lloyd Lamble *Superintendent* • Raymond Rollett *Chief Constable* ■ *Dir* Frank Launder • *Scr* Sidney Gilliat, Frank Launder, Val Valentine, from the drawings by Ronald Searle

The Blue Parrot ★★

Crime drama 1953 · UK · BW · 71mins

This features an unoriginal plot and a title that recalls the Graham Greene-inspired thriller *The Green Cockatoo*. The budget was tight and the story, about an American cop who solves a case and falls for a pretty English girl while on secondment to Scotland Yard, is hardly riveting stuff. Dermot Walsh does his best with lacklustre material, and John Le Mesurier turns up in a supporting slot, but there's little else to recommend it. DP

Dermot Walsh *Bob Herrick* • Jacqueline Hill *Maureen* • Ballard Berkeley *Supt Chester* • Ferdy Mayne *Stevens* • Valerie White *Eva West* • John Le Mesurier *Henry Carson* • Richard Pearson *Quinney* • June Ashley *Gloria* ■ *Dir* John Harlow • *Scr* Alan Mackinnon, from the story *Gunman* by Percy Hoskins

The Blue Peter ★★★ U

Comedy drama 1955 · UK · Colour · 94mins

Group 3 was a government-backed British film production company set up to make low-budget projects utilising new talent. This adventure romp was co-written by talented director Don Sharp and directed by equally talented writer Wolf Rilla. It brought Irish hunk Kieron Moore back from Hollywood to play a Korean War veteran teaching Aberdovey students at an outdoor camp. The youngsters include Anthony Newley and Harry Fowler. TS

Kieron Moore *Mike Merriworth* • Greta Gynt *Mary Griffith* • Sarah Lawson *Gwyneth Thomas* • Mervyn Johns *Captain Snow* • John Charlesworth *Andrew Griffin* • Harry Fowler *Charlie Barton* • Mary Kerridge *Mrs Snow* • Ram Gopal *Dr Tigara* • Russell Napier *Raymond Curtiss* • Anthony Newley *Sparrow* • Vincent Ball *Digger* ■ *Dir* Wolf Rilla • *Scr* Don Sharp, John Pudney

Blue Scar ★★★ U

Drama 1947 · UK · BW · 102mins

A year after her outstanding documentary study of postwar Plymouth, *The Way We Live*, Jill Craigie made her fiction debut with this openly political drama. Craigie and producer William MacQuitty raised the budget themselves and shot much of the action in a converted cinema in South Wales. The director later dismissed the tale of mining engineer Emrys Jones's visit to London as "amateurish". The acting of the largely nonprofessional cast is certainly stilted, but this is still a bold attempt to present a truthful portrait. DP

Emrys Jones *Tom Thomas* • Gwyneth Vaughan *Olwen Williams* • Rachel Thomas *Gweneth Williams* • Anthony Pendrell [Tony Pendrell] *Alfred Collins* • Prysor Williams *Ted Williams* • Madoline Thomas *Granny* • Jack James *Dai Morgan* • Kenneth Griffith *Thomas Williams* ■ *Dir/Scr* Jill Craigie

Blue Skies ★★★ U

Musical 1946 · US · Colour · 106mins

When dancer Paul Draper turned out to be unsuitable, Paramount called up the great Fred Astaire to replace him opposite crooner Bing Crosby in this garishly Technicolored Irving Berlin songfest. Thank goodness. Beside the divine Astaire, Crosby looks clumsy as they declare that they're *A Couple of Song and Dance Men*. The undoubted highlight is Astaire's classic solo dance routine during *Puttin' On the Ritz*. The girls are weak, the comedy's patchy, the plot's paper-thin, but who cares when Astaire's on screen dancing to Berlin? TS

Fred Astaire *Jed Potter* • Bing Crosby *Johnny Adams* • Joan Caulfield *Mary O'Hara* • Billy De Wolfe *Tony* • Olga San Juan *Nita Nova* • Mikhail Rasmuny *François* • Carol Andrews *Dolly* • Dorothy Barrett *Showgirl* • Robert Benchley *Businessman* ■ *Dir* Stuart Heisler • *Scr* Arthur Sheekman, from an idea by Irving Berlin

Blue Sky ★★★★ 15

Drama 1991 · US · Colour · 96mins

This fragmented yet compelling drama is distinguished by Jessica Lange's merciless, Oscar-winning performance as a wife who's a walking nervous breakdown. Tommy Lee Jones matches her every spasm as her US Army husband, an atomic scientist facing the risk of meltdown in both his work and his marriage when Lange sets her sights on commanding officer Powers Boothe. Set in the early 1960s, director Tony Richardson's final film uses the couple's personal crises to echo the nation's nuclear dilemma. TH. Contains violence, swearing and nudity. DVD

Jessica Lange *Carly Marshall* • Tommy Lee Jones *Hank Marshall* • Powers Boothe *Vince Johnson* • Carrie Snodgress *Vera Johnson* • Amy Locane *Alex Marshall* • Chris O'Donnell *Glenn Johnson* • Mitchell Ryan *Ray Stevens* ■ *Dir* Tony Richardson • *Scr* Rama Laurie Stagner, Arlene Sarner, Jerry Leichtling, from a story by Arlene Stagner

Blue Steel ★★ U

Western 1934 · US · BW · 54mins

A programme filler made for Monogram Studios, this stars John Wayne before he had managed to break free from such routine fare. There's not a lot to commend here: George "Gabby" Hayes makes a watchable tobacco-chewing sheriff and Yakima Canutt, a mainstay of this series, appears as the quaintly monikered Polka Dot Bandit. The plot's that old chestnut about the marshal disguising himself to nail the baddies, and there's little artistry in Robert N Bradbury's perfunctory direction. TS DVD

John Wayne *John Beaumont* • Eleanor Hunt *Betty Mason* • George "Gabby" Hayes *Sheriff Jake* • Ed Peil Sr [Edward Peil Sr] *Melgrove* • Yakima Canutt *Danti, The Polka Dot Bandit* • George Cleveland *Hank* • George Nash *Bridegroom* ■ *Dir/Scr* Robert N Bradbury

Blue Steel ★★★★ 18

Thriller 1990 · US · Colour · 97mins

Made a year before the male-dominated *Point Break*, this intelligent, provocative thriller from director Kathryn Bigelow stars Jamie Lee Curtis as the rookie police officer who tries to prevent an armed robbery in a supermarket. Ron Silver is the

U = SUITABLE FOR ALL Uc = SUITABLE FOR ALL, ESPECIALLY FOR YOUNG CHILDREN (VIDEO ONLY) PG = PARENTAL GUIDANCE

businessman and firearms nut who picks up the robber's gun and embarks on a chilling game of cat and mouse with her. Curtis is outstanding as the harassed officer and Silver is genuinely creepy. Bigelow skilfully defines the almost fetishistic attraction of weaponry, and stages some exhilarating action set pieces. JF. Contains violence, swearing and sex scenes. [video] DVD

Jamie Lee Curtis *Megan Turner* • Ron Silver *Eugene Hunt* • Clancy Brown *Nick Mann* • Elizabeth Peña *Tracy Perez* • Louise Fletcher *Shirley Turner* • Philip Bosco *Frank Turner* • Kevin Dunn *Assistant Chief Stanley Hoyt* • Tom Sizemore *Wool cap* ■ *Dir* Kathryn Bigelow • *Scr* Kathryn Bigelow, Eric Red

Blue Streak ★★★ 12

Crime comedy 1999 · US · Colour · 90mins

Emerging from prison, thief Martin Lawrence is horrified to find that the construction site where he hid a stolen jewel is now a police station. Joining the boys in blue, his "wrong side of the law" approach to crime-solving yields some extraordinary results. Unlike so many action comedies, Les Mayfield's film boasts an intricate and cleverly structured plot, though the tension is undermined by Lawrence's wild overacting. Unashamedly lowbrow entertainment, but great fun nonetheless. SR. Contains swearing and violence. [video] DVD

Martin Lawrence *Miles Logan* • Luke Wilson *Carlson* • Peter Greene *Deacon* • Dave Chappelle *Tulley* • Nicole Ari Parker *Melissa Green* • Graham Beckel *Rizzo* • Robert Miranda *Glenfiddish* • Olek Krupa *LaFleur* ■ *Dir* Les Mayfield • *Scr* Michael Berry, John Blumenthal, Steve Carpenter [Stephen Carpenter]

Blue Suede Shoes ★★

Music documentary
1980 · UK · Colour · 95mins

Some critics will tell you that the truest form of documentary is one in which the director resists the temptation either to participate or impose an editorial slant. However, the simple recording of events without any spin invariably makes for very dull viewing. This is a film brimming with personalities as director Curtis Clark poses the question, "Why do these people dress in long outmoded threads and hurl themselves around to music the devil no longer seems to have a use for?" Shot with all the vibrance of a Pat Boone B-side. DP

Dir Curtis Clark

Blue Sunshine ★★★★ 18

Horror thriller 1976 · US · Colour · 94mins

One of the best shockers produced in the 1970s, director Jeff Leiberman's cult classic is a psychedelic chiller of the highest order. Intriguing pulp fiction invades subversive David Cronenberg territory as the ten-year-delayed after-effects of an LSD derivative result in a group of former Stanford University students to losing their hair, then their cool, before turning into crazed, vicious killers. Directed with economic flair and sly black humour, this drug-culture allegory sizzles with invention and frenetical horror. AJ [video] DVD

Zalman King *Jerry Zipkin* • Deborah Winters *Alicia Sweeney* • Mark Goddard *Edward Flemming* • Robert Walden *David Blume* • Charles Siebert *Detective Clay* • Ann Cooper *Wendy Flemming* • Ray Young *Wayne Mulligan* • Brion James *Tony* ■ *Dir/Scr* Jeff Lieberman

Blue Thunder ★★★ 15

Action thriller 1983 · US · Colour · 105mins

Directed by John Badham, this is a *Boys' Own*-style action drama involving a super-helicopter, complete with hi-tech surveillance gadgets and mega-weapons. It's flown by LA cop Roy Scheider, who learns that his bitter enemy Malcolm McDowell plans to sabotage the machine. This slick if somewhat predictable adventure was spun off into a TV series starring James Farentino and *Wayne's World*'s Dana Carvey. JB. Contains violence, swearing and nudity. [video] DVD

Roy Scheider *Frank Murphy* • Malcolm McDowell *Colonel Cochrane* • Candy Clark *Kate* • Warren Oates *Captain Braddock* • Daniel Stern *Lymangood* • Paul Roebling *Icelan* • David Sheiner *Fletcher* • Ed Bernard *Sergeant Short* ■ *Dir* John Badham • *Scr* Dan O'Bannon, Don Jakoby

Blue Tiger ★★★ 18

Action crime thriller
1994 · US · Colour · 84mins

Japanese gangsters were briefly in vogue in the mid-1990s, mainly on the back of *Rising Sun*. This, along with *American Yakuza*, is the pick of the straight-to-video bunch, thanks to a charismatic turn from Virginia Madsen in the lead role. She plays a mother who, after her son is killed during a gun battle, goes gunning for the yakuza. Director Norbeto Barba keeps the foot firmly on the accelerator and serves up some slick scenes of ultra-violence. JF [video] DVD

Virginia Madsen *Gina Hayes* • Toru Nakamura *Seiji* • Dean Hallo *Henry Soames* • Ryo Ishibashi *Gan* • Sal Lopez *Luis* • Yuji Okumoto *Sakagami* • Harry Dean Stanton *Smith* • Brenda Varda *Emily* ■ *Dir* Norberto Barba • *Scr* Joel Soisson, from a story by Taka Ichise

Blue Valley Songbird ★★ PG

Musical drama 1999 · US · Colour · 91mins

Dolly Parton's spirited performance here is undermined by the formulaic melodramatics of this mediocre TV movie. Director Richard A Colla overplays the comparisons between the abuse inflicted on the teenage country singer by her father and the control freakery of her boyfriend-cum-manager, John Terry, whose fear that he will be dumped if Dolly finds fame is preventing her shot at the big time. Parton handles the songs with expected aplomb, but all else fails to convince. DP [video] DVD

Dolly Parton *Leanna Taylor* • John Terry *Hank* • Billy Dean *Bobby* • Kimberley Kates *Thelma Russell* ■ *Dir* Richard A Colla • *Scr* Ken Carter, Annette Haywood-Carter

The Blue Veil ★★★★

Romantic drama 1951 · US · BW · 108mins

Already an Oscar-winner for *Johnny Belinda* and a best actress nominee for *The Yearling*, Jane Wyman arrived at RKO on loan from Warner Bros. She picked up another nomination and delivered a massive profit for the small and often troubled studio. Wyman plays a a woman who devotes her life to caring for the children of others and winning their devotion, only to descend into lonely poverty. The star's convincing and dignified portrayal, together with an exceptional set of supporting performances from Joan Blondell (also Oscar-nominated), Charles Laughton, Agnes Moorehead and 13-year-old Natalie Wood, makes for a thoroughly satisfying, high-class tear-jerker. RK

Jane Wyman *Louise Mason* • Charles Laughton *Fred K Begley* • Joan Blondell *Annie Rawlins* • Richard Carlson *Gerald Kean* • Agnes Moorehead *Mrs Palfrey* • Don Taylor *Dr Robert Palfrey* • Audrey Totter *Helen Williams* • Cyril Cusack *Frank Hutchins* • Natalie Wood *Stephanie Rawlins* ■ *Dir* Curtis Bernhardt • *Scr* Norman Corwin, from a story by François Campaux

Blue Velvet ★★★★★ 18

Cult mystery thriller
1986 · US · Colour · 115mins

This is the most complete of David Lynch's films, made before his disturbing black vision of small-town American life veered into self-parody. The dark tone is set from the opening sequence, which starts with white picket fences and cheery firemen but ends with a man suffering a stroke in his garden while insect life seethes beneath the lawn. Lynch regular Kyle MacLachlan is the young innocent who gets sucked into the bizarre sadomasochistic relationship between nightclub singer Isabella Rossellini and monstrous local crime boss Dennis Hopper (who resurrected his career with his crazed portrait of evil). Listening to Roy Orbison's *In Dreams* will never be the same again. JF. Contains violence, swearing, drug abuse, sex scenes, nudity. [video] DVD

Kyle MacLachlan *Jeffrey Beaumont* • Isabella Rossellini *Dorothy Vallens* • Dennis Hopper *Frank Booth* • Laura Dern *Sandy Williams* • Hope Lange *Mrs Williams* • Dean Stockwell *Ben* • George Dickerson *Detective Williams* • Brad Dourif *Raymond* • Jack Nance *Paul* ■ *Dir/Scr* David Lynch • *Cinematographer* Frederick Elmes • *Music* Angelo Badalamenti

The Blue Villa ★★★

Drama 1994 · Bel/Fr/Swi · Colour · 100mins

More than 30 years after electrifying world cinema with his screenplay for *Last Year at Marienbad*, Alain Robbe-Grillet was still playing intellectual games with structure and perception. Shuffling dreams, memory and reality, Robbe-Grillet and co-director Dimitri de Clercq ally us with a Greek policeman, as he tries to decide whether a sailor (who could be a ghost) was responsible for the murder of the daughter of a screenwriter – or whether she is still alive and a resident of the local brothel. The control is as admirable as it's arch. DP. In French with English subtitles.

Fred Ward *Frank* • Arielle Dombasle *Sarah-la-Blonde* • Charles Tordjman *Edouard Nordmann* • Sandrine Le Berre *Santa* • Dimitri Poulikakos *Thieu* • Christian Maillet *The Father* • Muriel Jacobs *Kim* ■ *Dir/Scr* Alain Robbe-Grillet, Dimitri de Clercq

Blue Water, White Death ★★★ U

Documentary 1971 · US · Colour · 98mins

Four years before *Jaws* made seaside swimming seem a hazardous occupation for tourists, director Peter Gimbel mined the same deep-water fears in this outstanding documentary. Using the device of divers searching for the hunting grounds of the great white shark, Gimbel's cameras get unflinchingly up close and dangerously personal with the ocean's eating machines. Yet the film manages to avoid the clichés that have become the norm since the success of Steven Spielberg's shocker. Fans of wildlife programmes will love it. AJ

Dir Peter Gimbel, James Lipscomb • *Scr* Peter Gimbel

Bluebeard ★★★

Horror 1944 · US · BW · 71mins

It wasn't often that poverty row studio PRC (Producers Releasing Corporation) came up with a film worth watching, but it did give the highly talented director Edgar G Ulmer some artistic freedom. Here he coaxes a beautifully restrained performance from the flamboyant character actor John Carradine, in one of his few starring roles, as the artist and puppeteer in 19th-century Paris who has an irresistible urge to murder his models. With production values that transcend the low budget, this is a small miracle of polished film-making. AE

John Carradine *Gaston* • Jean Parker *Lucille* • Nils Asther *Insp Lefevre* • Ludwig Stossel *Lamarte* • George Pembroke *Insp Renard* • Teala Loring *Francine* • Sonia Sorel *Renee* • Iris Adrian *Mimi* ■ *Dir* Edgar G Ulmer • *Scr* Pierre Gendron, from a screenplay (unproduced) by Arnold Phillips, Werner H Furst

Bluebeard ★★★

Drama drama 1962 · Fr/It · Colour · 115mins

Claude Chabrol gave Charles Denner his first leading film role in this true story of Landru, a man who charmed a number of unsuspecting women and then murdered them. The magnetic Denner, with bald dome, bushy eyebrows and black beard, was an ideal interpreter of Chabrol's characteristic acid wit. But the screenplay by novelist Françoise Sagan lacks the sympathy or depth that Charlie Chaplin brought to the same subject in *Monsieur Verdoux* (1947). However, the photography, the sets, and the bevy of beautiful actresses are pleasing to the eye. RB. French dialogue dubbed into English.

Michèle Morgan *Celestine Buisson* • Danielle Darrieux *Berthe Heon* • Charles Denner *Henri-Désire Landru* • Hildegarde Knef [Hildegarde Neff] *Madame Ixe* • Juliette Mayniel *Anna Colomb* • Stéphane Audran *Fernande Segret* • Mary Marquet *Madame Guillin* ■ *Dir* Claude Chabrol • *Scr* Françoise Sagan, Claude Chabrol • *Cinematographer* Jean Rabier • *Costume Designer* Maurice Albray

Bluebeard ★

Crime thriller
1972 · It/Fr/W Ger · Colour · 123mins

This take on the infamous serial killer is likely to offend almost everyone. The execution is so ham-fisted, and the murders so exploitative, that the film is oddly repugnant. Richard Burton apparently took the role because he fancied a trip to Budapest, while his female victims are encouraged to strip and camp it up before they meet their untimely ends. AT

Richard Burton *Baron Von Sepper* • Raquel Welch *Magdalena* • Joey Heatherton *Anne* • Virna Lisi *Elga* • Nathalie Delon *Erika* • Marilu Tolo *Brigitte* • Karin Schubert *Greta* • Agostina Belli *Caroline* ■ *Dir* Edward Dmytryk • *Scr* Ennio Di Concini, Edward Dmytryk, Maria Pia Fusco, from a story by Ennio Di Concini, Edward Dmytryk, Maria Pia Fusco

Bluebeard's Eighth Wife ★★

Screwball comedy 1938 · US · BW · 84mins

An impoverished daughter of the French nobility becomes the eighth wife of a millionaire who finds he has finally met his match. Marking the first screenplay collaboration of Charles Brackett and Billy Wilder, and directed by Ernst Lubitsch, this romantic comedy promises much but, alas, delivers little. After the delightful opening sequence, in which the stars "meet cute" in a store's pyjama department, the famous "Lubitsch touch" disappears and gives way to increasing tedium. RK

Claudette Colbert *Nicole de Loiselle* • Gary Cooper *Michael Brandon* • Edward Everett Horton *de Loiselle* • David Niven *Albert De Regnier* • Elizabeth Patterson *Aunt Hedwige* • Herman Bing *Monsieur Pepinard* • Charles Halton *Monsieur de la Coste* • Barlowe Borland *Uncle Fernandel* • Warren Hymer *Kid Mulligan* • Franklin Pangborn *Assistant hotel manager* ■ *Dir* Ernst Lubitsch • *Scr* Charles Brackett, Billy Wilder, from the translation by Charlton Andrews of the play *La Huitième Femme de Barbe-Bleu* by Alfred Savoir

Blueberry ★★★ 15

Western adventure
2004 · Fr/UK/Mex · Colour · 124mins

Jan Kounen allows his technology to get the better of him in this accomplished, but inconsistent adaptation of Jean "Moebius" Giraud's cult comic books. Too much time is spent in the morphed mind of Cajun sheriff Vincent Cassel, as he strives to settle an old score with Michael Madsen, the hissable adventurer who caused the death of Cassel's first love and now seeks the secret of some sacred mountains. The supporting cast ably captures the spirit of the Old West, but the visuals swamp the slender storyline. DP. In French, English, German and Spanish with subtitles. Contains nudity.

Vincent Cassel *Mike S Blueberry* • Juliette Lewis *Maria Sullivan* • Michael Madsen *Wally Blount* • Temuera Morrison *Runi* • Djimon Hounsou *Woodhead* • Colm Meaney *Jimmy McClure* • Tcheky Karyo *The Uncle* • Ernest Borgnine *Rolling Star* • Nichole Hiltz *Lola* • Eddie Izzard *Prosit* ■ *Dir* Jan Kounen • *Scr* Gérard Brach, Matt Alexander, Jan Kounen, from the comic book series by Jean "Moebius" Giraud, Jean-Michel Charlier

Blueberry Hill ★★ 15

Drama 1988 · US · Colour · 88mins

Though set in the mid-1950s, this dysfunctional-family drama is far less rock 'n' roll than the time-frame and Fats Domino-derived title might suggest. Carrie Snodgress plays an overwound mum and Jennifer Rubin is the daughter who discovers the twin secrets about her dad's death and her inheritance of his honkytonk piano-playing skills. DA

Carrie Snodgress *Becca Dane* • Margaret Avery (2) *Hattie Cale* • Jennifer Rubin *Ellie Dane* • Matt Lattanzi *Denny Logan* • Tommy Swerdlow *Ray Porter* ■ *Dir* Strathford Hamilton • *Scr* Lonon F Smith

Blueberry Hill ★★★

Drama 1989 · Bel · Colour · 90mins

Awash with nostalgia, yet never guilty of descending into mawkishness, this admirable rite-of-passage picture from Belgian director Robbe de Hert expertly evokes an era and its attitudes. Accompanied by the throbbing of 1950s jukebox hits, this semi-autobiographical tale touches on everything from teenage rebellion and first love to authoritarianism and Catholic hypocrisy. Michael Pas is hugely impressive as the bright kid who would rather hang around a nightclub than pore over his books. Charming, with backbone. DP. In Flemish with English subtitles.

Michael Pas *Robin De Hert* • Babette Van Veen *Cathy* • Hilde Heijnen *Jeanine* • Frank Aendenboom *Verbist* • Myriam Mézières *Suzanne Claessens* • Ronny Coutteure *Valère* ■ *Dir* Robbe de Hert • *Scr* Robbe de Hert, Noel Degeling, Walter Van Den Broeck

The Blues Brothers ★★★★ 15

Musical comedy 1980 · US · Colour · 127mins

This wonderful sprawling mess of a movie remains one of the best musical comedies of modern times. John Belushi and Dan Aykroyd are the criminally minded brothers on a mission from God, who resurrect their old rhythm-and-blues band to raise money for their old orphanage. The skimpiest of plots provides the excuse for a string of rousing musical numbers and cameo appearances from music legends such as Ray Charles, Aretha Franklin and Cab Calloway. When the music runs out, director John Landis stages a ludicrously spectacular car chase involving the massed forces of law and order, a rabid country-and-western band and neo-Nazis. JF. Contains swearing. DVD

John Belushi *"Joliet" Jake Blues* • Dan Aykroyd *Elwood Blues* • Kathleen Freeman *Sister Mary Stigmata* • James Brown (2) *Reverend Cleophus James* • Cab Calloway *Curtis* • Carrie Fisher *Mystery woman* • Ray Charles *Ray* • Aretha Franklin *Soul food café owner* • John Candy *Burton Mercer* • Henry Gibson *Nazi leader* • Steven Spielberg *Cook county clerk* • Twiggy *Chic lady* • Paul Reubens *Waiter* ■ *Dir* John Landis • *Scr* John Landis, Dan Aykroyd

Blues Brothers 2000 ★★★ PG

Musical comedy 1998 · US · Colour · 118mins

It took 18 years for actor Dan Aykroyd and director John Landis to "get the band back together". Although viewers will miss the marvellous slapstick slobbishness of the late John Belushi, this sequel is still a lot of fun. The wafer-thin plot has Elwood Blues (Aykroyd) hooking up with the band's former musicians. But the movie's *raison d'être* is the irresistible R 'n' B numbers performed by Aykroyd, his co-star John Goodman and dynamic performers such as Aretha Franklin, BB King and James Brown. It's definitely worth catching if you can forgive Landis's self-indulgent touches. JC. Contains swearing, violence. DVD

Dan Aykroyd *Elwood Blues* • John Goodman *Mighty Mack McTeer* • Joe Morton *Cabel Chamberlain* • J Evan Bonifant *Buster* • Aretha Franklin *Mrs Murphy* • James Brown (2) *Reverend Cleophus James* • BB King *Malvern Gasperon* • Steve Cropper *Steve "The Colonel" Cropper* • Donald Dunn *Donald "Duck" Dunn* ■ *Dir* John Landis • *Scr* John Landis, Dan Aykroyd, from their film *The Blues Brothers*

Blues in the Night ★★

Musical drama 1941 · US · BW · 87mins

A tough, interesting Warner Bros drama, purporting to deal honestly with the life of itinerant jazz musicians, with murky direction by Anatole Litvak. The film almost works, but the pivotal role of a musician bent on self-destruction is played by the bland, amorphous Richard Whorf who would swiftly switch to directing at MGM. The support, though, is excellent, and includes a young, acting Elia Kazan playing (or miming) the clarinet. But, despite the gritty look and those wonderful much-copied Warner Bros montages, the film never quite hangs together. TS

Priscilla Lane *Ginger* • Betty Field *Kay Grant* • Richard Whorf *Jigger Pine* • Lloyd Nolan *Del Davis* • Jack Carson *Leo Powell* • Wally Ford [Wallace Ford] *Brad Ames* • Elia Kazan *Nickie Haroyan* ■ *Dir* Anatole Litvak • *Scr* Robert Rossen, from the play by Edwin Gilbert

Blume in Love ★★★★ 15

Comedy drama 1973 · US · Colour · 110mins

One of the best sex comedies from the fast-and-loose 1970s, with a wonderfully warm performance from George Segal as a lawyer whose harassed humour endears us to his infidelities. His wife (Susan Anspach), alas, feels differently, throwing him out on his ear to repent at leisure and ponder passions past. Writer/director Paul Mazursky – who made *Bob & Carol & Ted & Alice* four years earlier – indulges his usual predilection for lengthy exposition, while the Italian locations add more travelogue gloss than emotional point. Segal's characterisation makes it all worthwhile, however. TH

George Segal *Blume* • Susan Anspach *Nina Blume* • Kris Kristofferson *Elmo* • Marsha Mason *Arlene* • Shelley Winters *Mrs Cramer* • Donald F Muhich *Analyst* • Paul Mazursky *Blume's partner* ■ *Dir/Scr* Paul Mazursky

Boardwalk ★★

Drama 1979 · US · Colour · 100mins

American theatre luminaries Lee Strasberg and Ruth Gordon star as a happily married Jewish couple approaching their golden wedding anniversary whose lives – and those of their friends – are blighted by the disintegration of their Brooklyn neighbourhood. Steven Verona's depressing and ineptly-made film offers no insight into the problems it exaggeratedly depicts. RK

Ruth Gordon *Becky Rosen* • Lee Strasberg *David Rosen* • Janet Leigh *Florence* • Joe Silver *Leo Rosen* • Eli Mintz *Mr Friedman* • Eddie Barth *Eli Rosen* • Merwin Goldsmith *Charlie* • Michael Ayr *Peter* ■ *Dir* Stephen Verona • *Scr* Stephen Verona, Leigh Chapman

Boat Trip ★ 15

Comedy
2002 · US/Ger · Colour and BW · 90mins

Cuba Gooding Jr stars in this limp comedy about two straight men who wind up on an all-gay ocean cruise. The film-makers also contrive to get the bikini-clad lovelies of a Swedish tanning team on board. The humour is as subtle as high explosive and about as funny, though Roger Moore's cameo as an ageing queen produces one or two amusing lines. DA. Contains swearing. DVD

Cuba Gooding Jr *Jerry* • Horatio Sanz *Nick* • Roger Moore *Lloyd* • Roselyn Sanchez *Gabriella* • Vivica A Fox *Felicia* • Lin Shaye *Sonya* • Victoria Silvstedt *Inga* • Bob Gunton *Captain* • Richard Roundtree *Malcolm* ■ *Dir* Mort Nathan • *Scr* Mort Nathan, William Bigelow, Brian Pollack, Mert Rich

The Boatniks ★★ U

Comedy adventure
1970 · US · Colour · 99mins

Rocking the boat with his outrageous mugging, Phil Silvers eventually capsizes this unremarkable Disney comedy. As a smart-talking, but decidedly minor league, jewel thief, he fails to outwit the equally gormless Robert Morse, who, up to that point, had been carving his little niche as the worst-ever coastguard in the history of California. A much firmer hand was needed on the tiller than that applied by director Norman Tokar, but there are a couple of neat set pieces. DP

Robert Morse *Ensign Thomas Garland* • Stefanie Powers *Kate Fairchild* • Phil Silvers *Harry* • Norman Fell *Max* • Mickey Shaughnessy *Charlie* • Don Ameche *Commander Taylor* • Wally Cox *Jason Bennett* ■ *Dir* Norman Tokar • *Scr* Arthur Julian, from a story by Marty Roth

Bob & Carol & Ted & Alice ★★★ 15

Comedy 1969 · US · Colour · 100mins

This slice of flower-power permissiveness alarmed some at the time because of promised revelations, but disappointed others because romance got in the way. Natalie Wood, Robert Culp, Elliott Gould and Dyan Cannon make up the two Californian couples who go in for group therapy and confessing to extramarital sex. The result is too many words and too little action courtesy of director Paul Mazursky. There's an intimidating sentimentality, too, but the film was still an important landmark in its day. TH. Contains swearing, drug abuse and nudity.

Natalie Wood *Carol* • Robert Culp *Bob* • Elliott Gould *Ted* • Dyan Cannon *Alice* • Horst Ebersberg *Horst* • Lee Bergere *Emelio* • Donald F Muhich *Psychiatrist* • Noble Lee Holderread Jr *Sean* • KT Stevens *Phyllis* ■ *Dir* Paul Mazursky • *Scr* Paul Mazursky, Larry Tucker • *Cinematographer* Charles Lang

Bob Le Flambeur ★★★★ PG

Crime comedy drama 1955 · Fr · BW · 97mins

This little-known classic counts as one of Jean-Pierre Melville's very best. It's a bizarre heist movie that spins on a delicious irony: Bob plans to rob the casino at Deauville but wins the money at the tables. There are tragic overtones, but this is still an absurdist comedy with bags of atmosphere, romance, jazz music, pretentious dialogue, great locations and a wonderfully brooding performance from Roger Duchesne. AT. In French with English subtitles. DVD

Isabelle Corey *Anne* • Roger Duchesne *Robert "Bob" Montagné* • Daniel Cauchy *Paolo* • Guy Decomble *Inspector Ledru* • André Garret *Roger* • Claude Cerval *Jean* • Gérard Buhr *Marc* • Howard Vernon *McKimmie* ■ *Dir* Jean-Pierre Melville • *Scr* Jean-Pierre Melville, Auguste Le Breton

The Bob Mathias Story ★ U

Biographical sports drama
1954 · US · BW · 70mins

Although his achievement of becoming the first decathlete to retain his Olympic title was laudable, Bob Mathias is hopelessly miscast in this sanctimonious biopic. Neither he nor his wife Melba have the charisma to overcome either their dramatic inexperience or the platitudes in the gushingly patriotic screenplay. DP

Bob Mathias • Ward Bond *Coach Jackson* • Melba Mathias • Paul Bryar *Andrews* • Ann Doran *Mrs Mathias* • Howard Petrie *Dr Mathias* • Diane Jergens *Pat Mathias* ■ *Dir* Francis D Lyon • *Scr* Richard Collins

Bob Roberts ★★★★ 15

Spoof political documentary
1992 · US · Colour · 99mins

1992 was the year of Tim Robbins. Not only did he star in Robert Altman's savage Hollywood satire *The Player* but he also starred in, wrote and directed this hilarious pseudo-documentary about a folk-singing right-wing politician running for the US Senate. Taking its style from *This Is Spinal Tap* with a deliberate on-screen homage to the Bob Dylan tour movie *Don't Look Back*, *Bob Roberts* is both witty and wickedly pointed, if a shade smug at times. Immaculately cast, with telling performances from Alan Rickman, Gore Vidal and John Cusack, the film was a substantial achievement for its young *auteur*. TS. Contains swearing

Tim Robbins *Bob Roberts* • Giancarlo Esposito *Bugs Raplin* • Ray Wise *Chet MacGregor* • Rebecca Jenkins *Delores Perrigrew* • Harry Lennix *Franklin Dockett* • John Ottavino *Clark Anderson* • Robert Stanton *Bart Macklerooney* • Alan Rickman *Lukas Hart III* • Gore Vidal *Senator Brickley Paiste* • James Spader *Chuck Marlin* • Helen Hunt *Rose Pondell* • Susan Sarandon *Tawna Titan* • John Cusack *TV host* ■ *Dir/Scr* Tim Robbins

Bob, Son of Battle ★★ U

Drama 1947 · US · Colour · 103mins

Clean-cut Lon McCallister is in love with his dog, in a movie directed by Louis King. Peggy Ann Garner is sweet, Edmund Gwenn watchable as ever and the scenery attractive, but, unless you particularly enjoy boy-and-dog movies, you may want to give it a miss. TS

Edmund Gwenn *Adam McAdam* • Lon McCallister *David McAdam* • Peggy Ann Garner *Maggie Moore* • Reginald Owen *James Moore* • Charles Irwin *Long Kirby* • Dave Thursby *Samuel Thornton* • John Rogers *Mackenzie* ■ *Dir* Louis King • *Scr* Jerome Cady, from the novel by Alfred Ollivant

Bobbikins ★ U

Fantasy comedy 1959 · UK · BW · 89mins

Even die-hard Max Bygraves fans will be hard pressed to squeeze much enjoyment out of this cinematic lemon. Impoverished entertainer Bygraves becomes rich after his 14-month-old baby begins picking up financial titbits from his park bench conversations with Chancellor Charles Carson. Preposterous. DP

Max Bygraves *Benjamin Barnaby* • Shirley Jones *Betty Barnaby* • Steven Stacker *Bobbikins* • Billie Whitelaw *Lydia* • Barbara Shelley *Valerie* • Colin Gordon *Dr Phillips* •

Charles Tingwell *Luke* • Lionel Jeffries *Gregory Mason* • Charles Carson *Sir Jason Crandall* ■ *Dir* Robert Day • *Scr* Oscar Brodney

Bobby ★★★ PG

Musical romance
1973 · Ind · Colour · 160mins

Movie references abound in this colourful masala, which is not only packed with memorable songs, but also manages to tack a happy ending on to the *Romeo and Juliet* story. Director Raj Kapoor is in playful mood throughout, making many of the love scenes between his son Rishi and Dimple Kapadia mirror classic moments from his own on-screen teaming with 1950s superstar Nargis. DP. In Hindi with English subtitles.

Rishi Kapoor *Raj Nath* • Dimple Kapadia *Bobby* • Pran *Rishi's father* • Premnath *Bobby's father* • Prem Chopra ■ *Dir* Raj Kapoor • *Scr* KA Abbas, VP Sathe

Bobby Deerfield ★★★ PG

Romantic drama
1977 · US · Colour · 118mins

A self-consciously arty (and often just plain dumb) yet strangely compelling melodrama, with Al Pacino as a Formula One racing driver who falls in love with a terminally ill Italian beauty, played by Marthe Keller. Thanks to Pacino's addiction to speed, there's a death sentence hanging over both of them, making this a peculiarly morbid experience. It's worth watching for the quality of Pacino's performance and director Sydney Pollack's assured coverage of the races and use of Florence locations. AT

Al Pacino *Bobby Deerfield* • Marthe Keller *Lillian Morelli* • Anny Duperey *Lydia* • Walter McGinn *Leonard* • Romolo Valli *Uncle Luigi* • Stephan Meldegg *Karl Holtzmann* • Jaime Sanchez *Delvecchio* ■ *Dir* Sydney Pollack • *Scr* Alvin Sargent, from the novel *Heaven Has No Favorites* by Erich Maria Remarque

Bobby Jones: Stroke of Genius ★★ PG

Sports biography
2004 · US · Colour · 123mins

Rowdy Herrington stages some credible golfing sequences in this hagiographic memoir, but he fails to distinguish between the events that made up perpetual amateur Bobby Jones's unrivalled Grand Slam success. Consequently, aficionados will be left frustrated, while casual viewers will be dissuaded by the sanctimonious dismissal of professionalism. Jim Caviezel mistakes sincerity for charisma in the title role and is gloriously upstaged by Jeremy Northam as Jones's chief rival, Walter Hagen. DP DVD

Jim Caviezel *Bobby Jones* • Claire Forlani *Mary Jones* • Jeremy Northam *Walter Hagen* • Connie Ray *Clara Jones* • Brett Rice *Big Bob* • Malcolm McDowell *OB Keeler* ■ *Dir* Rowdy Herrington • *Scr* Rowdy Herrington, Tony DePaul, Bill Pryor, from a story by Rowdy Herrington, Kim Dawson

The Bobo ★★

Comedy 1967 · UK · Colour · 103mins

Director Robert Parrish is both talented and under-rated, but you'd never guess it from his mishandling of this bizarre Peter Sellers vehicle. This was one of a string of ill-chosen projects that tarnished Sellers's reputation before he returned to the Clouseau role in the mid-1970s. Here he plays an unsuccessful matador who has to seduce Barcelona's most desirable lady in order to get a booking as a singer. It's not very funny, but the locations are gorgeous, and the sublime Hattie Jacques is a treat. TS

Peter Sellers *Juan Bautista* • Britt Ekland *Olimpia Segura* • Rossano Brazzi *Carlos Matabosch* • Adolfo Celi *Francisco Carbonell* • Hattie Jacques *Trinity Martinez* • Alfredo Lettieri [Al Lettieri] *Eugenio* • Kenneth Griffith *Gamazo* • Marne Maitland *Castillo* ■ *Dir* Robert Parrish • *Scr* David R Schwartz, from his play

Bob's Weekend ★★ 15

Comedy 1996 · UK · Colour · 89mins

In first-time director Jevon O'Neill's amicable but underwritten odd-couple comedy, Bruce Jones plays a Manchester security guard who's fired from his job and cuckolded by his wife Anna Jaskolka. He heads for Blackpool determined to throw himself off the pier, but a chance encounter with perky psychology student Charlotte Jones affords him a new take on life. Their unlikely friendship is engagingly played. DP. Contains violence and swearing. DVD

Bruce Jones *Bob* • Charlotte Jones (2) *Angela* • Anna Jaskolka *Brenda* • Brian Glover *The Boss* • Ricky Tomlinson *Jack* ■ *Dir* Jevon O'Neill • *Scr* Jevon O'Neill, Jayson Rothwell

Boccaccio '70 ★★

Portmanteau comedy drama
1961 · It/Fr · Colour · 149mins

A compendium of three separate stories, each with a major director wasting his gifts on a contemporary *Decameron* that focuses on women in relation to different aspects of sex. Fellini directs Anita Ekberg as a billboard model taking a swipe at puritanism; Visconti's segment has Romy Schneider playing a wife who takes unexpected action on learning that her husband frequents brothels; Sophia Loren auctions herself as a raffle prize under Vittorio De Sica's guidance. The film veers between the vulgar, the boring and the intermittently amusing; only Loren's episode manages to be poignant. RK. In Italian with English subtitles.

Anita Ekberg *Anita* • Peppino De Filippo *Dr Antonio Mazzuolo* • Romy Schneider *Pupe* • Tomas Milian *The count* • Romolo Valli *The lawyer* • Sophia Loren *Zoe* • Luigi Giuliani *Gaetano* • Alfio Vita *The sexton* • Giacomo Furia • Alberto Sorrentino • Marisa Solinas *Luciana* • Germano Giglioli *Renzo* ■ *Dir* Federico Fellini, Vittorio De Sica, Luchino Visconti, Mario Monicelli • *Scr* Federico Fellini, Ennio Flaiano, Tullio Pinelli, Suso Cecchi D'Amico, Luchino Visconti, Cesare Zavattini, Giovanni Arpino, Italo Calvino, Mario Monicello

Bodies, Rest and Motion ★★★ 15

Drama 1993 · US · Colour · 90mins

An average "20-something" tale, similar to Cameron Crowe's *Singles* (but without the cool Seattle soundtrack). Phoebe Cates, Bridget Fonda, Tim Roth and Eric Stoltz bum around Arizona musing about life, love and shallow relationships that no one will particularly care about except them. A disappointment from director Michael Steinberg, who previously made the moving and meaningful drama *The Waterdance* with Neal Jimenez, which also starred Stoltz. JB. Contains swearing.

Phoebe Cates *Carol* • Bridget Fonda *Beth* • Tim Roth *Nick* • Eric Stoltz *Sid* • Alicia Witt *Elizabeth* • Sandra Lafferty *Yard-sale lady* • Sidney Dawson *TV customer* • Jon Proudstar *Station attendant* ■ *Dir* Michael Steinberg • *Scr* Roger Hedden, from his play

The Body ★★ 12

Religious thriller
2000 · US/Ger/Is · Colour · 104mins

A sliver of originality is rapidly buried beneath the rubble in this torpid thriller from first-time director Jonas McCord. When archaeologist Olivia Williams discovers what appears to be the body of Jesus Christ in the back streets of Jerusalem, Vatican troubleshooter Antonio Banderas is sent to refute the claim that the Resurrection is a myth. Unfortunately, this adaptation lacks both depth and pace, and compounds matters by trivialising the region's political complexities and abandoning any form of intellectual discussion for a tacky romance and a crude action finale. DP DVD

Antonio Banderas *Father Matt Gutierrez* • Olivia Williams *Sharon Golban* • Derek Jacobi *Dr Pierre Lavelle* • John Wood *Cardinal Pesci* • Jason Flemyng *Father Walter Winstead* • John Shrapnel *Moshe Cohen* ■ *Dir* Jonas McCord • *Scr* Jonas McCord, from the novel by Richard Ben Sapir

Body and Soul ★★

First World War spy drama
1931 · US · BW · 81mins

The principal interest today of this apparently lost First World War flying-and-spying drama is the brief appearance of Humphrey Bogart. He plays an American flyer in France who dies trying to shoot down a German observation balloon. After Bogie's demise, Charles Farrell falls for his dead pal's widow Elissa Landi, who comes under suspicion of being a spy. The arrival of Myrna Loy, also claiming to have been Bogart's dame, complicates matters. AE

Charles Farrell *Maj Andrews* • Elissa Landi *Carla* • Humphrey Bogart *Jim Watson* • Myrna Loy *Alice Lester* • Donald Dillaway *Tap Johnson* • Crawford Kent [Crauford Kent] *Major Burke* • Pat Somerset *Major Knowles* • Ian MacLaren *Gen Trofford Jones* ■ *Dir* Alfred Santell • *Scr* Jules Furthman, from the play *Squadrons* by AE Thomas and the story *Big Eyes and Little Mouth* by Elliot White Springs

Body and Soul ★★★★★ PG

Sports drama 1947 · US · BW · 100mins

The greatest boxing movie of all time, *Raging Bull* and *Champion* notwithstanding. James Wong Howe's in-the-ring photography set landmark standards, as he dispensed with tripods and roller skated with a hand-held camera. Robert Parrish's Oscar-winning editing (with Francis D Lyon) prefigured his directing career, as did Robert Aldrich's assistant direction. John Garfield is superb as the champ with an uncertain sense of ethics, and Lilli Palmer simply mouthwatering as his doll. There's a tautness in Robert Rossen's direction that he would recapture 14 years later in his equally masterly *The Hustler*. TS

John Garfield *Charley Davis* • Lilli Palmer *Peg Born* • Hazel Brooks *Alice* • Anne Revere *Anna Davis* • William Conrad *Quinn* • Joseph Pevney *Shorty Polaski* • Canada Lee *Ben Chaplin* • Lloyd Goff *Roberts* ■ *Dir* Robert Rossen • *Scr* Abraham Polonsky

Body and Soul ★★ 18

Sports drama 1981 · US · Colour · 93mins

This pallid remake of the powerful 1947 John Garfield boxing classic is remarkable for all the wrong reasons. Hidden away near the bottom of the cast list are two of the most charismatic figures in popular culture: Muhammad Ali, playing himself in a brief cameo; and Rat Packer Peter Lawford, here cast, oddly enough, as a gangster. FL

Leon Isaac Kennedy *Leon Johnson* • Jayne Kennedy *Julie Winters* • Michael V Gazzo *Frankie* • Peter Lawford *Big Man* • Perry Lang *Charles Golphin* • Kim Hamilton *Mrs Johnson* • Muhammad Ali ■ *Dir* George Bowers • *Scr* Leon Isaac Kennedy

Body Armor ★★

Action thriller 1996 · US · Colour · 90mins

The above average cinematography of this made-for-video thriller can't improve the substandard action sequences. Matt McColm plays an arrogant hero, muttering profanities under his breath as he smugly takes on an evil chemist (a bored Ron Perlman) after he's hired by his ex-girlfriend. The extremely silly ending does, however, almost make it worth sitting through. KB

Matt McColm *Ken Conway* • Annabel Schofield *Marisa* • Carol Alt *Agent Monica McBride* • Morgan Brittany *Sloane Matthews* • John Rhys-Davies *Rasheed* • Ron Perlman *Dr Ramsey Krago* ■ *Dir* Jack Gill • *Scr* Stuart Beattie, Andrea Buck, Jack Gill, Duncan McLachlan, from a story by Paul Steven • *Cinematographer* Robert Hays

Body Chemistry ★★ 18

Erotic thriller 1990 · US · Colour · 80mins

An early entry in the erotic thriller stakes, and one which, like *Indecent Behaviour* and *Animal Instincts*, developed into a profitable video franchise. In this one, Lisa Pescia plays a doctor who gets mixed up in sexual mind games with one of her colleagues, video stalwart Marc Singer. It's the usual mix of sub-*noir* thrills and soft-core bonking, but it looks pretty enough. JF

Marc Singer *Dr Tom Redding* • Mary Crosby *Marlee* • Lisa Pescia *Dr Claire Archer* • David Kagen *Freddie* • H Bradley Barneson *Jason* • Doreen Alderman *Kim* • Lauren Tuerk *Wendy* • Joseph Campanella *Doctor Pritchard* ■ *Dir* Kristine Peterson • *Scr* Jackson Barr

Body Chemistry 2: Voice of a Stranger ★★ 18

Erotic thriller 1992 · US · Colour · 80mins

Lisa Pescia returns for another slice of sexy shenanigans from this profitable erotic thriller franchise. This time around, bad doctor Claire Archer has assumed a new identity as a radio therapist. Two further sequels followed. JF

Gregory Harrison *Dan* • Lisa Pescia *Dr Claire Archer* • Robin Riker *Brenda* • Morton Downey Jr *Big Chuck* • Clint Howard *Larabee* • John Landis *Dr Edwards* ■ *Dir* Adam Simon • *Scr* Jackson Barr, Christopher Wooden

Body Count ★★ 18

Crime drama 1997 · US/UK · Colour · 80mins

After the massive success of the first series of *NYPD Blue*, its star David Caruso seemed destined for bigger things. So far his big screen career hasn't gone quite to plan, though this is one of his better efforts. He's part of a bickering gang of robbers who, having just pulled off a multi-million dollar art heist, must now get to Miami to cash in their haul. While the performances can't be faulted, this is lower-league Tarantino. JF. Contains swearing, drug abuse and violence. DVD

David Caruso *Hobbs* • Linda Fiorentino *Natalie* • John Leguizamo *Chino* • Ving Rhames *Pike* • Donnie Wahlberg *Booker* • Forest Whitaker *Crane* • Michael Corrigan *Security officer no 1* • Michael Hunter *Security officer no 2* ■ *Dir* Robert Patton-Spruill • *Scr* Theodore Witcher

The Body Disappears ★★ U

Fantasy comedy 1941 · US · BW · 72mins

Warner Bros sought to cash in on Universal's continuing *Invisible Man* series with this comedy. Edward Everett Horton proves what a practised farceur he was as the dotty scientist who views comatose playboy Jeffrey Lynn as the ideal cadaver for his resurrection serum. However, the concoction renders Lynn invisible, prompting the "fun" to start. DP

Jeffrey Lynn *Peter DeHaven III* • Jane Wyman *Joan Shotesbury* • Edward Everett Horton *Prof Shotesbury* • Herbert Anderson *George "Doc" Appleby* • Marguerite Chapman *Christine Lunceford* ■ *Dir* D Ross Lederman • *Scr* Scott Darling, Erna Lazarus

B

Body Double ★★★★ 18

Erotic thriller 1984 · US · Colour · 109mins

No one is better at apeing Alfred Hitchcock than director Brian De Palma. In this engrossingly sly shocker, he combines the master's predilection for kinky storytelling with his own engaging high style and taste for designer violence. Little does B-movie horror actor Craig Wasson know when he spies on Deborah Shelton undressing in her Hollywood home that it will lead him to witnessing murder. Tense, deliciously sleazy and blackly comic – and sporting a gorgeous Pino Donaggio score – De Palma's *Rear Window* update is his most outrageous and voyeuristic film to date. AJ. Contains violence, swearing, sex scenes and nudity. DVD

Craig Wasson *Jake Scully* • Melanie Griffith *Holly Body* • Gregg Henry *Sam Bouchard* • Deborah Shelton *Gloria Revelle* • Guy Boyd *Jim McClean* • Dennis Franz *Rubin* • David Haskell *Drama teacher* • Rebecca Stanley *Kimberly* ■ *Dir* Brian De Palma • *Scr* Brian De Palma, Robert Avrech, from a story by Brian De Palma

Body Heat ★★★★ 18

Thriller 1981 · US · Colour · 108mins

Lawrence Kasdan's dazzling directorial debut packs a steamy punch. William Hurt plays the small-town lawyer who falls for *femme fatale* Kathleen Turner only to find himself ensnared in a tortuous plot to murder her wealthy husband (Richard Crenna). Kasdan respectfully tips his hat to classics such as *Double Indemnity*, but the intricate plotting and sly humour ensure that his film stands in its own right. The performances are first rate, too: Turner positively sizzles, while Hurt is excellent as the ordinary Joe getting increasingly out of his depth. There's also a creepy cameo from Mickey Rourke and a jolly supporting role for the then unknown Ted Danson. JF. Contains violence, swearing, sex scenes and nudity. DVD

William Hurt *Ned Racine* • Kathleen Turner *Matty Walker* • Richard Crenna *Edmund Walker* • Ted Danson *Peter Lowenstein* • JA Preston *Oscar Grace* • Mickey Rourke *Teddy Lewis* • Kim Zimmer *Mary Ann* • Jane Hallaren *Stella* • Lanna Sanders *Roz Kraft* ■ *Dir/Scr* Lawrence Kasdan

Body Melt ★★ 18

Horror comedy 1993 · Aus · Colour · 79mins

Inhabitants of a suburban Melbourne cul-de-sac become unwitting guinea pigs for a new body enhancement drug in this splatter satire from Australian director Philip Brophy. Exploding genitalia, kangaroo cannibalism and placentas taking on lives of their own are a few of the over-the-top gross-outs in this corrosive stomach-churner. Hysterical acting and pointless horror homages lessen the confrontational nature of Brophy's *Knots Landing* in Hell. AJ DVD

Gerard Kennedy *Det Sam Phillips* • Andrew Daddo *Johnno* • Ian Smith *Dr Carrera* • Vincent Gil *Pud* • Regina Gaigalas *Shaan* ■ *Dir* Philip Brophy • *Scr* Philip Brophy, Rod Bishop

Body of Evidence ★★★ 18

Erotic thriller 1992 · US · Colour · 96mins

With this erotic thriller, director Uli Edel attempted to out-steam the same year's *Basic Instinct*, but, although it makes for rather hokey fun, it lacks the outrageous flair of Paul Verhoeven's notorious hit. Madonna is the *femme fatale* accused of killing her elderly millionaire boyfriend; Willem Dafoe is the lawyer who gets seduced into a dangerous affair with his client. The story is absolute rot, and it's more interesting to guess how much of the erotic footage survived the snip. The distinguished supporting cast adds some class to the proceedings. JF. Contains swearing, violence, sex scenes and nudity. DVD

Madonna *Rebecca Carlson* • Willem Dafoe *Frank Dulaney* • Joe Mantegna *Robert Garrett* • Anne Archer *Joanne Braslow* • Julianne Moore *Sharon Dulaney* • Stan Shaw *Charles Biggs* • Jürgen Prochnow *Dr Alan Paley* ■ *Dir* Uli Edel • *Scr* Brad Mirman

Body of Influence ★★

Erotic thriller 1993 · US · Colour · 92mins

Soft-core king Gregory Hippolyte is reunited once again with Shannon Whirry (*Animal Instincts*) in this steamy tale of sexy shenanigans on the psychiatrist's couch. She's the sultry *femme fatale* claiming to be suffering from amnesia who gets her hooks into gullible psychiatrist Nick Cassavetes. Don't expect the thriller elements to tax the brain. A lazy sequel followed. JF. Contains nudity, sexual situations and some swearing.

Nick Cassavetes *Dr Jonathon Brooks* • Shannon Whirry *Laura/Lana* • Sandahl Bergman *Clarissa* • Don Swayze *Biker* • Anna Karin *Beth* • Diana Barton *Jennifer* • Richard Roundtree *Harry Reams* ■ *Dir* Gregory Hippolyte • *Scr* David Schreiber

Body Parts ★★★ 18

Horror thriller 1991 · US · Colour · 84mins

From the writers of novels that inspired the film classics *Diabolique* and *Vertigo* comes this not-so-classic sci-fi horror, blending hi-tech surgery with low-grade shocks. After a car accident, prison psychiatrist Jeff Fahey has the arm of an executed killer grafted on to his shoulder, which develops a murderous life of its own. Then he meets other recipients of the psycho's body parts suffering similar symptoms. Eric Red directs all this sinister lunacy with a sure hand – but is it his own? An outrageously ghoulish thriller if you can keep a straight face. AJ. Contains swearing and violence.

Jeff Fahey *Bill Chrushank* • Lindsay Duncan *Dr Webb* • Kim Delaney *Karen Chrushank* • Brad Dourif *Remo Lacey* • Zakes Mokae *Detective Sawchuk* • Peter Murnik *Mark Draper* • Paul Ben-Victor *Ray Kolberg* • John Walsh *Charlie Fletcher* ■ *Dir* Eric Red • *Scr* Eric Red, Norman Snider, from a story by Patrica Herskovic, Joyce Taylor, from the novel *Choice Cuts* by Thomas Narcejac, Pierre Boileau

Body Shot ★★ 18

Erotic crime thriller
1994 · US · Colour · 93mins

Not many people would root for a member of the paparazzi, but at least the unlikely hero lends a novel twist to an otherwise by-the-numbers thriller. A blond Robert Patrick plays a sleazy snapper who is obsessed with reclusive rock superstar Michelle Johnson. Things go pear-shaped when he ends up framed for her murder. The plot stretches credibility to the limit, but the dependable cast makes it just about bearable. JF DVD

Robert Patrick *Mickey Dane* • Michelle Johnson *Danielle Wilde/Chelsea* • Ray Wise *Dwight Frye* • Jonathan Banks *Simon Deverau/Blake Donner* • Kim Miyori *Christine Wyler* • Peter Koch *Elmer Hatch* • William Steis *Curt Lomann* ■ *Dir* Dimitri Logothetis • *Scr* Robert Ian Strauss

Body Shots ★★★ 18

Drama 1999 · US · Colour · 99mins

Michael Cristofer directs this debate-sparking study of 20-something morality. It looks like we've a long night ahead of us as eight near-identical Los Angelenos go through their pre-club rituals. However, when wannabe actress Tara Reid accuses pro-footballer Jerry O'Connell of date rape, the fun stops and sides are taken. Snappily shot in hip image bites by Rodrigo Garcia and astutely structured by writer David McKenna (*American History X*), this breaks no new ground but still manages to tease, amuse and provoke. DP

Sean Patrick Flanery *Rick Hamilton* • Jerry O'Connell *Michael Penorisi* • Amanda Peet *Jane Bannister* • Tara Reid *Sara Olswang* • Ron Livingston *Trent Barber* • Emily Procter *Whitney Bryant* • Brad Rowe *Shawn Denigan* • Sybil Temchen *Emma Cooper* ■ *Dir* Michael Cristofer • *Scr* David McKenna

The Body Snatcher ★★★★★ PG

Horror 1945 · US · BW · 78mins

Producer Val Lewton's magnificent version of Robert Louis Stevenson's Burke and Hare-like corpse-stealing short story is a horror masterpiece. Striking attention to historical authenticity and a magnificently evil performance from Boris Karloff as the vile cab driver supplying cadavers to desperate anatomist Henry Daniell, make for a grippingly literate and macabre shocker. Sinister support from Bela Lugosi and imaginative direction from Robert Wise give the tale a restrained ominousness and unseen terror until the justifiably famous hallucination climax. AJ

Boris Karloff *John Gray* • Bela Lugosi *Joseph* • Henry Daniell *Dr MacFarlane* • Edith Atwater *Meg Camden* • Russell Wade *Donald Fettes* • Rita Corday *Mrs Marsh* • Sharyn Moffett *Georgina Marsh* • Donna Lee *Street singer* ■ *Dir* Robert Wise • *Scr* Carlos Keith [Val Lewton], Philip MacDonald, from a short story by Robert Louis Stevenson

Body Snatchers ★★★★ 15

Science-fiction horror
1993 · US · Colour · 83mins

Those interstellar pods capable of duplicating humans return for a third sinister attempt on mankind's individual identities in director Abel Ferrara's masterly reinterpretation of the classic Jack Finney terror tale. On an empathic par with the 1956 original chiller *Invasion of the Body Snatchers*, Ferrara's keen contemporary eye, controlled vision and heartless shock tactics make the underlying message seem as pertinent and vital as ever. Meg Tilly and Gabrielle Anwar make indelible impressions as they take on the horrifying enemy infiltrating their military home base. AJ. Contains violence, swearing, nudity. DVD

Terry Kinney *Steve Malone* • Meg Tilly *Carole Malone* • Gabrielle Anwar *Marty Malone* • Forest Whitaker *Doctor Collins* • Reilly Murphy *Andy Malone* • Billy Wirth *Tim Young* • Christine Elise *Jenn Platt* • R Lee Ermey *General Platt* ■ *Dir* Abel Ferrara • *Scr* Stuart Gordon, Dennis Paoli, Nicholas St John, from a story by Larry Cohen, Raymond Cistheri, from the novel *The Body Snatchers* by Jack Finney

The Body Stealers ★ PG

Science-fiction adventure
1969 · US/UK · Colour · 86mins

Parachutists pass through a red mist and disappear into thin air. And before long you will, too! There is little point in sticking around to find out it's alien Maurice Evans putting sky divers in suspended animation and substituting duplicates. Talky, laughably low-budget and hopelessly inept. AJ DVD

George Sanders *General Armstrong* • Maurice Evans *Dr Matthews* • Patrick Allen *Bob Megan* • Neil Connery *Jim Radford* • Hilary Dwyer *Julie Slade* • Robert Flemyng *WC Baldwin* • Lorna Wilde *Lorna* • Allan Cuthbertson *Hindesmith* ■ *Dir* Gerry Levy • *Scr* Mike St Clair, Peter Marcus

Bodyguard ★★★

Crime thriller 1948 · US · BW · 62mins

Lawrence Tierney plays a cop in this efficient thriller from director Richard Fleischer. However, soon after quitting the police force to watch over wealthy widow Elisabeth Risdon, Tierney becomes the prime suspect in a murder case. With Philip Reed and Steve Brodie providing hissable support, and Priscilla Lane giving a nicely weighted performance as Tierney's fiancée, this admirably demonstrates why so many lament the passing of the B-movie. DP

Lawrence Tierney *Mike Carter* • Priscilla Lane *Doris Brewster* • Philip Reed *Freddie Dysen* • June Clayworth *Connie* • Elisabeth Risdon *Gene Dysen* • Steve Brodie *Fenton* ■ *Dir* Richard Fleischer • *Scr* Harry Essex, Fred Niblo Jr, from a story by George W George, from a story by Robert B Altman [Robert Altman]

The Bodyguard ★★★ 15

Romantic thriller
1992 · US · Colour · 123mins

Kevin Costner and Whitney Houston fall in love, she trilling all the while, amid a highly charged atmosphere of jealousy and death threats in this entertaining load of old baloney. Director Mick Jackson created a wildly successful film, much to several critics' snooty chagrin, by teaming two megastars and adding a daft but jaunty script, loud rock soundtrack and a few well-staged exciting moments. Costner is a trifle stern, but Houston makes a very creditable acting debut. SH. Contains violence, swearing and a sex scene. DVD

Kevin Costner *Frank Farmer* • Whitney Houston *Rachel Marron* • Gary Kemp *Sy Spector* • Bill Cobbs *Devaney* • Ralph Waite *Herb Farmer* • Tomas Arana *Portman* • Michele Lamar Richards *Nicki* • Mike Starr *Tony* ■ *Dir* Mick Jackson • *Scr* Lawrence Kasdan, from his story

Bodysong ★★★★ 18

Experimental documentary
2002 · UK · Colour and BW · 78mins

American poet Walt Whitman encouraged us to *Sing the Body Electric*, and director Simon Pummell has done just that with this bold and experimental documentary. Laying out his themes of birth, growth, sex, violence, death and dreams as a laudatory hymn to human existence, the film occasionally backs off from the truly shocking – such as the casual slaughter of the Vietnam War – but does capture the sudden appalled awareness of a new-born child, rudely awakened from the womb's comfortable environs. Radiohead's Jonny Greenwood has boosted some remarkable archive images with his music and, while there seem to be some strange blanks in the film's understanding of the human condition, this is put together with a wit and craft that defy expectations. TH DVD

Dir/Scr Simon Pummell • *Music* Jonny Greenwood • *Editor* Daniel Goddard

Bodywork ★ 18

Thriller 1999 · UK · Colour · 89mins

This undistinguished addition to the recent British gangster film cycle was perhaps fortunate to avoid the ignominy of going straight to video. Hans Matheson buys a "luxury" motor from a couple of very dodgy second-hand car dealers, but the clapped-out car turns out to have a corpse in the boot. The tone is uneven and so is the acting, while the plot is so convolutedly daft that you'll rapidly lose interest. DA. Contains violence, swearing

Hans Matheson *Virgil Guppy* • Charlotte Coleman *Tiffany Shades* • Peter Ferdinando *Alex Gordon* • Beth Winslet *Fiona Money* • Lynda Bellingham *Poppy Fields* • Clive Russell *Billy Hunch* • Michael Attwell *David Leer* ■ *Dir/Scr* Gareth Rhys Jones

B

Boeing Boeing ★★★

Romantic comedy
1965 · US · Colour · 102mins

Marc Camoletti's hit play achieved astoundingly long theatrical runs throughout the world, so a screen version of this latter-day Feydeauesque farce was an inevitability. With a genuinely funny plot about a casanova of the airlines skewed by modern technology, this is beautifully cast by skilled producer Hal Wallis and features two great comedians – the incorrigibly brash Tony Curtis and a disciplined and subdued Jerry Lewis – who work together impeccably. TS

Jerry Lewis *Robert Reed* • Tony Curtis *Bernard Lawrence* • Dany Saval *Jacqueline Grieux* • Christiane Schmidtmer *Lise Bruner* • Suzanna Leigh *Vicky Hawkins* • Thelma Ritter *Bertha* • Lomax Study *Pierre* • Françoise Ruggieri *Taxi driver* ■ *Dir* John Rich • *Scr* Edward Anholt, from the play by Marc Camoletti • *Cinematographer* Lucien Ballard

Boesman & Lena ★★ 15

Period drama
2000 · Fr/S Afr · Colour and BW · 84mins

Danny Glover stars as the alcoholic outsider forced to reappraise his relationship with both his wife and the unjust world, after his shanty-town home is demolished. Despite some probing camerawork and the inclusion of a couple of flashbacks to show Glover and Angela Bassett in happier times, veteran director John Berry singularly fails to prise this adaptation away from its proscenium confines. Verbose and mannered. DP. Contains swearing. DVD

Danny Glover *Boesman* • Angela Bassett *Lena* • Willie Jonah *Old African* ■ *Dir* John Berry • *Scr* John Berry, from a play by Athol Fugard

The Bofors Gun ★

Drama 1968 · UK · Colour · 105mins

The setting for this drama of violent personal conflict is a British army camp in Germany; the year is 1954. David Warner plays an indecisive corporal in charge of a guard detail, while Nicol Williamson is the abrasive, self-despising Irish gunner under his command. Too talkative and claustrophobic by half, this unremittingly downbeat study of futility, weakness and hatred takes an inordinate time to reach its very predictable conclusion. AE

Nicol Williamson *O'Rourke* • Ian Holm *Flynn* • David Warner *Evans* • Richard O'Callaghan *Rowe* • Barry Jackson *Shone* • Donald Gee *Crawley* • John Thaw *Featherstone* • Peter Vaughan *Sergeant Walker* ■ *Dir* Jack Gold • *Scr* John McGrath, from his play *Events While Guarding the Bofors Gun*

Bogus ★★ PG

Fantasy comedy 1996 · US · Colour · 106mins

Moonstruck director Norman Jewison has Whoopi Goldberg and Gérard Depardieu at his disposal for this fantasy comedy, as well as *Sixth Sense* star Haley Joel Osment, and all he produces is sentimental codswallop. Admittedly, the clichéd story doesn't give him much to aim at. The recently orphaned Osment is sent to live with his child-loathing aunt (Goldberg) and develops a relationship with an imaginary friend called Bogus (Depardieu) in order to survive the ordeal. Trite stuff. LH [video]

Whoopi Goldberg *Harriet Franklin* • Gerard Depardieu [Gérard Depardieu] *Bogus* • Haley Joel Osment *Albert* • Andrea Martin *Penny* • Nancy Travis *Lorraine* • Denis Mercier *M Antoine* • Ute Lemper *Babette* • Sheryl Lee Ralph *Ruth Clark* ■ *Dir* Norman Jewison • *Scr* Alvin Sargent, from a story by Jeff Rothberg, Francis X McCarthy

Bogus Bandits ★★ U

Comedy opera 1933 · US · BW · 88mins

A very dubious outing for Laurel and Hardy, this has the glorious boobies playing second fiddle to a *Desert Song*-style operetta. Dennis King is a dashing brigand in 18th-century Italy, wooing Thelma Todd, the neglected wife of lord James Finlayson. Stan and Ollie are vagrants trying to earn a living as bandits. There are some wonderful music-hall moments, but they can't shine through the clichéd blackout of a ridiculous plot. TH [video]

Stan Laurel *Stanlio* • Oliver Hardy *Olio* • Dennis King *Fra Diavolo/Marquis de San Marco* • Thelma Todd *Lady Pamela* • James Finlayson *Lord Rocberg* • Lucille Browne *Zerlina* • Arthur Pierson *Lorenzo* • Henry Armetta *Matteo* ■ *Dir* Charles Rogers, Hal Roach • *Scr* Jeanie Macpherson, from the opera *Fra Diavolo* by Daniel F Auber

Bogwoman ★★★ 15

Drama 1997 · Ire · Colour · 77mins

This is a provocative study of how 1960s Northern Irish politics impacted on people's everyday lives. Rachel Dowling gives a mettlesome performance as the single mother who crosses the border to settle in Derry's Bogside and, having married, comes to realise she's capable of more than just slaving for her chauvinistic husband (Peter Mullan). Tom Collins's film is given added resonance by the fact that it ends on the eve of the Troubles. DP. Contains swearing. [video]

Rachel Dowling [Rachael Dowling] *Maureen* • Sean McGinley *Mr D* • Peter Mullan *Barry* • Noelle Brown *Mrs D* ■ *Dir/Scr* Tom Collins

La Bohème ★★ U

Silent romantic drama
1926 · US · BW · 106mins

A characteristically soulful and touching Lillian Gish and an athletically exuberant and sincere John Gilbert are the lovers doomed to be parted by death in this silent enactment of the story familiar to those who know Puccini's popular opera. Director King Vidor expertly steers the changes of mood from the boisterous to the tragic in the Latin quarter of Paris. Despite its virtues, however, its style is too outmoded to hold much appeal for audiences now. RK

Lillian Gish *Mimi* • John Gilbert (1) *Rodolphe* • Renée Adorée *Musette* • George Hassell *Schaunard* • Roy D'Arcy *Vicomte Paul* • Edward Everett Horton *Colline* • Karl Dane *Benoit* • Mathilde Comont *Madame Benoit* ■ *Dir* King Vidor • *Scr* Ray Doyle, Harry Behn, Fred De Gresac, William Conselman (titles), Ruth Cummings (titles), from the novel *Scènes de La Vie de Bohème (The Latin Quarter)* by Henri Murger

The Bohemian Girl ★★ U

Comedy 1936 · US · BW · 67mins

Not even the great Laurel and Hardy can lift the spirits of this damp adaptation of the operetta by Michael Balfe, about gypsies who, in revenge, kidnap a nobleman's daughter and bring her up as one of their own. Stan and Ollie are snatch-purses, not that it matters much. Their gags disappear in the banal and confused plot and they look as embarrassed as audiences feel. This was the last film of their regular co-star Thelma Todd, who died of carbon monoxide poisoning just after this film was completed. TH [video]

Stan Laurel *Stan* • Oliver Hardy *Ollie* • Thelma Todd *Gypsy Queen's daughter* • Antonio Moreno *Devilshoof* • Jacqueline Wells [Julie Bishop] *Arline* • Mae Busch *Mrs Hardy* • James Finlayson *Captain Finn* ■ *Dir* James W Horne, Charles Rogers • *Scr* Alfred Bunn, from the opera by Michael Balfe

Boiler Room ★★★★ 15

Drama 2000 · US · Colour · 114mins

This amorality tale of financial swizz-kids focuses on young chancer Giovanni Ribisi who joins an "off-Broadway" brokerage firm that offers sky-high paycheques to successful agents. Fuelled by equal measures of drink, drugs, adrenalin and testosterone, the young fiends of the firm's high-pressure "boiler room" are an obnoxious bunch. Writer/director Ben Younger worked in a real-life "boiler room" to research the film, and the result is a dynamite debut. There's great acting, too, from Ribisi, Vin Diesel and Ben Affleck, cameoing as the firm's Mr Motivator. DA [video] DVD

Giovanni Ribisi *Seth Davis* • Nia Long *Abby Halperin* • Vin Diesel *Chris* • Ben Affleck *Jim Young* • Tom Everett Scott *Michael* • Ron Rifkin *Marty Davis* • Nicky Katt *Greg* • Bill Sage *Agent Drew* ■ *Dir/Scr* Ben Younger

Boiling Point ★★★★ 18

Thriller 1990 · Jpn · Colour · 92mins

Takeshi "Beat" Kitano followed up his excellent directorial debut, *Violent Cop*, with this equally assured mix of abrasive action and earthy humour. Set again in the sinister world of the yakuza, the film focuses on the efforts of daydreaming greenhorn Masahiko Ono to protect his boss after he lands him in a gangster's bad books. As the manic former hood Ono hires to save the day, Takahito Iguchi gives a performance as hilarious as it is disturbing. This is essentially a samurai tale given an urban twist, and Kitano makes the city of Okinawa look a particularly forbidding place. Brutal, perhaps, but great fun, too. DP. In Japanese with English subtitles. Contains violence, nudity. [video] DVD

Masahiko Ono *Masaki* • Yuriko Ishida *Sayaka* • Takahito Iguchi *Takashi* • Minoru Iizuka *Kazuo* • Makoto Ashikawa *Akira* • Hitoshi Ozawa *Kanai* • Hisashi Igawa *Otomo, gang boss* ■ *Dir/Scr* Takeshi Kitano

Boiling Point ★★★★ 15

Thriller 1993 · US · Colour · 88mins

On its cinema release, this was promoted as a straightforward action thriller, but it's far more intelligent than that. Wesley Snipes plays a treasury agent who hits the vengeance trail when his partner is killed during an undercover operation that goes wrong. Dennis Hopper and Viggo Mortensen are his targets, who are also trying to keep one step ahead of the Mob. While there are some excellent action set pieces, director James B Harris is more interested in exploring the relationships between the hunters and the hunted, and delivers a melancholic tale of crime and punishment. JF. Contains swearing and violence. [video] DVD

Wesley Snipes *Jimmy Mercer* • Dennis Hopper *Red* • Lolita Davidovich *Vikki* • Viggo Mortensen *Ronnie* • Valerie Perrine *Mona* • Seymour Cassel *Leach* • Jonathan Banks *Max* • Christine Elise *Carol* • Tony LoBianco *Dio* • James Tolkan *Levitt* ■ *Dir* James B Harris • *Scr* James B Harris, from the novel *Money Men* by Gerald Petievich

El Bola ★★★ 15

Drama 2000 · Sp · Colour · 83mins

Made with the assistance of Unicef, this is an important film that focuses on a still largely taboo topic. Juan José Ballesta excels as the timorously rebellious 12-year-old who lives in dread of his short-fused father, Mañuel Marón, and envies the normality of buddy Pablo Galan's home life. Playing on the deceptiveness of social appearances (Marón is a respected shopkeeper, while Galan's dad, played by Alberto Gimenez, is a tattoo artist), first-time director Achero Mañas explores the contentious issue of domestic violence with great sensitivity, while also highlighting the difficulties in bringing such abuse to the attention of the authorities. DP. In Spanish with English subtitles. DVD

Juan José Ballesta *Pablo* • Pablo Galán *Alfredo* • Alberto Jimenez *José* • Mañuel Morón *Mariano* ■ *Dir/Scr* Achero Mañas

The Bold and the Brave ★★

Second World War drama
1956 · US · BW · 87mins

If you can stand Mickey Rooney at full throttle, you may warm to this Second World War drama set on the front line in Italy. Rooney, as the soldier who wins a fortune in a marathon crap game, is contrasted with sensitive infantryman Wendell Corey, who fears he may have turned yellow, and Don Taylor, as the puritanical sergeant involved with Nicole Maurey, a local girl who hasn't been as good as she should have been. The film plays down the heroics and doesn't run to major battle scenes. AE

Wendell Corey *Fairchild* • Mickey Rooney *Dooley* • Don Taylor *Preacher* • Nicole Maurey *Fiamma* • John Smith *Smith* • Race Gentry *Hendricks* • Ralph Votrian *Wilbur* ■ *Dir* Lewis R Foster • *Scr* Robert Lewin

Bolero ★★★

Romantic drama 1934 · US · BW · 82mins

A romantic drama with a good script, expertly directed by Wesley Ruggles, has stars George Raft and Carole Lombard as a dancing duo competing for attention with the hypnotic spell of Ravel's *Bolero*. He opens a smart nightclub in Paris, she goes off to marry a wealthy man, but they're reunited unexpectedly after the First World War, dancing to the aforementioned number as a lead-up to a dramatic climax. RK

George Raft *Raoul DeBaere* • Carole Lombard *Helen Hathaway* • Sally Rand *Arnette* • Frances Drake *Leona* • William Frawley *Mike DeBaere* • Ray Milland *Lord Robert Coray* • Gloria Shea *Lucy* • Gertrude Michael *Lady D'Argon* ■ *Dir* Wesley Ruggles • *Scr* Carey Wilson Kubec Glasmon, Horace Jackson (adaptation), from an idea by Ruth Ridenour • *Music* Ralph Rainger, Maurice Ravel

Bolero ★ 18

Period erotic drama
1984 · US · Colour · 100mins

One of the funniest bad movies ever made. Virginal heiress Bo Derek goes to the Sahara desert and Spain in search of pure sexual ecstasy, and ends up making love with a sheik and a bullfighter. Set in the 1920s for no apparent reason, director John Derek's anti-erotic valentine to his wife is packed with hilariously awful encounters that are further undermined by insipid dialogue. AJ [video]

Bo Derek *Ayre McGillvary* • George Kennedy *Cotton* • Andrea Occhipinti *Angel Contreras* • Ana Obregon *Catalina* • Greg Bensen *Sheik* • Olivia D'Abo *Paloma* • Ian Cochrane *Robert Stewart* ■ *Dir/Scr* John Derek

Bolivia ★★★

Drama 2001 · Arg · BW · 75mins

Israel Adrián Caetano adopts a monochrome approach for this study of exiles trying to find their niche in a largely hostile environment. Julián Apezteguia's handheld camera restlessly accumulates details of the forthright and more subtly pernicious prejudice faced by Bolivian cook Freddy Flores and Paraguayan waitress Rosa Sánchez in Enrique Liporace's Buenos Aires eaterie. It's an all-too-familiar story, yet Caetano allows the migrants the occasional small pleasure away from the cruel ironies of the daily grind. Short, sharp and depressingly convincing. DP. In Spanish with English subtitles.

Freddy Flores *Freddy* • Rosa Sánchez *Rosa* • Oscar Bertea *Osa* • Enrique Liporace *Enrique Galmes* • Marcelo Videla *Marcelo* ■ *Dir* Israel Adrián Caetano • *Scr* Israel Adrián Caetano, from a story by Romina Lafranchini

B

Bollywood Calling ★★★ 15

Satirical comedy
2000 · Ind · Colour · 101mins

Following the acute social criticism of his pioneering Indian independent film *Hyderabad Blues*, director Nagesh Kukunoor disappointingly settles for easy targets in this patchy satire on the chaos that is the subcontinent's movie capital. The incomparable Om Puri stars as gregarious producer Subra. His brainchild is to import washed-up Hollywood action man Pat Cusick to play the long-lost American brother of ageing superstar Navin Nischol in a corny melodrama called *Maut*. Puri is excellent, Cusick a revelation, but this fast and furious farce lacks finesse. DP. In English and Hindi with English subtitles. DVD

Om Puri *Subramaniam, "Subra"* • Pat Cusick *Pat Stormare* • Navin Nischol *Manu Kapoor* ■ *Dir/Scr* Nagesh Kukunoor

Bollywood/Hollywood ★★★ 12

Musical comedy romance
2002 · Can · Colour · 105mins

This culture-clash satire is a breezy parody of Bollywood conventions from Deepa Mehta. The movie spoofs are shrewd and the byplay between wealthy Indian-Canadian Rahul Khanna and Lisa Ray – the supposedly Spanish escort he hires to pose as his fiancé in order to assuage his fussing family – has an old-fashioned screwball energy. The supporting turns are equally worthy, but Sandeep Chowta's musical numbers are disappointingly average. DP. In English and Hindi with subtitles. DVD

Rahul Khanna *Rahul Seth* • Lisa Ray *Sue "Sunita" Singh* • Moushumi Chatterjee *Mummy Ji/Ruby Seth* • Dina Pathak *Grandma Ji* • Kalbhushan Kharbanda *Mr Singh* • Ranjit Chowdhry *Rocky* • Jessica Paré *Kimberly* ■ *Dir/Scr* Deepa Mehta

Bollywood Queen ★★ PG

Musical romantic drama
2002 · UK · Colour · 85mins

Jeremy Wooding makes a shaky feature debut with this unpersuasive mix of Bollywood masala and backstreet realism. Essentially a Romeo-and-Juliet story with a dash of culture-clash controversy tossed in, the romance between East End Indian Preeya Kalidas and country boy James McAvoy feels as contrived as the song-and-dance routines, which are staged without the stylised exuberance that makes Bollywood musicals so unique. DP. In English and Hindi with subtitles. DVD

Preeya Kalidas *Geena* • James McAvoy *Jay* • Ciaran McMenamin *Dean* • Ray Panthaki *Anil* • Ian McShane *Frank* • Kat Bhathena *Anjali* ■ *Dir* Jeremy Wooding • *Scr* Neil Spencer, Jeremy Wooding

Bolwieser ★★★

Drama 1977 · W Ger · Colour · 201mins

This bitter study of marital discord, social rigidity and incipient fascism was edited down from a two-part television film. Kurt Raab cuts a pathetically dignified figure as the genial stationmaster who is twice cuckolded by wife Elisabeth Trissenaar, whose desire for freedom ultimately results in her husband's imprisonment. In exploring the dispiriting notion that love has no place in the law, director Rainer Werner Fassbinder was also keen to show that, even in a supposedly patriarchal society, the female is the deadlier of the species. The result is subtlety symbolic, yet uncompromisingly bleak. DP. In German with English subtitles.

Kurt Raab *Bolwieser* • Elisabeth Trissenaar *Frau Hanni* • Gustl Bayrhammer *Hanni's father* • Bernhard Helfrich *Merkl* • Udo Kier *Schaffthaler* • Volker Spengler *Mangst* ■ *Dir* Rainer Werner Fassbinder • *Scr* Rainer Werner Fassbinder, from the novel by Oskar Maria Graf

Bombardier ★★

Second World War adventure
1943 · US · BW · 98mins

An airborne propaganda picture, this follows a bomber crew on a mission to Japan. At times the picture has all the excitement of a technical manual – no switch, no scanner, no nut and bolt is ignored by the script. Released after Japan's attack on Pearl Harbor – though production started before – the story is filled with vengeance and the Japanese are, of course, depicted as perpetrators of hideous cruelty, and lacking in military know-how. Routine, but lifted by a decent cast. AT

Pat O'Brien *Major Chick Davis* • Randolph Scott *Captain Buck Oliver* • Anne Shirley *Burt Hughes* • Eddie Albert *Tom Hughes* • Robert Ryan *Joe Connors* • Walter Reed *Jim Carter* • Barton MacLane *Sergeant Dixon* ■ *Dir* Richard Wallace • *Scr* John Twist, from a story by John Twist, Martin Rackin

Bombay ★★★ 12

Drama 1995 · Ind · Colour · 135mins

Shot in southern India and recalling the civil unrest that occurred in Bombay in the early 1990s, this film achieved several things. It confirmed the reputation of Mani Rathnam as one of the most uncompromising contemporary Indian directors, while also sealing the celebrity of now red-hot composer AR Rahman. But, more importantly, this story of a couple's search for their missing children proved that masala musicals could be suitable vehicles for social comment. Indeed, the film was so effective that it was banned, yet its sheer polish made it a box-office smash. DP. In Tamil and Hindi with English subtitles.

Tinnu Anand • Manisha Koirala • Nazar • Arvind Swamy ■ *Dir/Scr* Mani Rathnam

Bombay Boys ★★★

Drama 1998 · Ind · Colour · 105mins

This modern Indian drama takes an uncompromising look at the seedier side of Bombay and the influence returning prodigals have upon it. New Yorker Naveen Andrews arrives with ambitions of Bollywood stardom; gay musician Alexander Gifford leaves London looking for love, while Aussie Rahul Bose is in search of his brother. Director Kaizad Gustad sets out to shock and succeeds triumphantly. DP. Contains sex scenes and nudity.

Naveen Andrews *Krishna Sahni* • Rahul Bose *Ricardo Fernandez* • Alexander Gifford *Xerxes Mistry* • Naseeruddin Shah *Don Mastana* • Roshan Seth *Pesi* ■ *Dir/Scr* Kaizad Gustad

Bombay Talkie ★★ PG

Romantic drama
1970 · Ind · Colour · 105mins

There's a hollow ring to this Merchant/Ivory tale of the doomed romance between a self-centred western novelist and an image-conscious Bollywood star. The opening parody of masala musicals creates something of a false impression; this is a melodrama of the old school, in which Jennifer Kendal toys in a callously destructive manner with the affections of Shashi Kapoor. A mediocre outing at best. DP DVD

Shashi Kapoor *Vikram* • Jennifer Kendal *Lucia Lane* • Zia Mohyeddin *Hari* • Aparna Sen *Mala* • Utpal Dutt *Bose* • Nadira *Anjana Devi* • Pincho Kapoor *Swamiji* ■ *Dir* James Ivory • *Scr* Ruth Prawer Jhabvala, James Ivory, from a story by Ruth Prawer Jhabvala • *Producer* Ismail Merchant

The Bomber Boys ★★

Crime adventure 1995 · US · Colour · 87mins

A slight but amusing children's film, of interest to grown-ups thanks to the surprising quality of its cast. Martin Sheen, Rod Steiger, Joe Mantegna and *Star Trek: Voyager* star Kate Mulgrew lend their talents to this tale of a group of young boys who discover an old atomic bomb and use it to get the President to cancel school. All the adults spend their time bumbling around and this results in a few laughs in this kids' caper flick. JB

Martin Sheen *Jeff Snyder* • Joe Mantegna *Joey Franelli* • Joanna Pacula *Brenda Franelli* • Joe Piscopo *Mr Wareman* • Rod Steiger *The President* • Ryan Thomas Johnson *The Slug* • Joshua Schaefer *Mickey Boyle* • Michael Bower *Frank Pescoe* • Kate Mulgrew *Mrs Pesco* ■ *Dir/Scr* Charles Gale

Bombers B-52 ★★ U

Drama 1957 · US · Colour · 106mins

Released in this country under the title *No Sleep till Dawn*, this is a clumsy melodrama directed with little sense of either drama or irony by Gordon Douglas. Karl Malden might not have had the greatest range in Hollywood, but he could fret like few others. Here he gets the chance to work himself into a right old lather as he considers a move into civvy street, as well as daughter Natalie Wood's romance with flashy flyboy Efrem Zimbalist Jr. DP

Natalie Wood *Lois Brennan* • Karl Malden *Sergeant Chuck Brennan* • Marsha Hunt *Edith Brennan* • Efrem Zimbalist Jr *Colonel Jim Herlihy* • Don Kelly [Don O'Kelly] *Sergeant Darren McKind* ■ *Dir* Gordon Douglas • *Scr* Irving Wallace, from a story by Sam Rolfe • *Cinematographer* William Clothier

Bomber's Moon ★★ U

Second World War drama
1943 · US · BW · 69mins

American pilot George Montgomery is shot down over Germany and thrown into a POW camp. As luck would have it, he shares his cell with a female Russian doctor, played by Annabella, the French actress best known for marrying Tyrone Power. Breaking out of the camp, Montgomery, Annabella and Kent Taylor head for England, dodging the enemy and generally behaving heroicall. No great shakes. AT

George Montgomery *Captain Jeff Dakin* • Annabella *Lt Alexandra Zoreich* • Kent Taylor *Captain Paul Husnik* • Walter Kingsford *Friedrich Mueller* • Martin Kosleck *Major von Streicher* • Dennis Hoey *Major von Grunow* • Robert Barrat *Ernst* • Kenneth Brown *Karl* ■ *Dir* Charles Fuhr [Edward Ludwig], Harold Schuster • *Scr* Kenneth Gamet, Aubrey Wisberg, from a story by Leonard Lee

Bombón – El Perro ★★★★ 15

Drama 2004 · Arg/Sp · Colour · 98mins

Argentine director Carlos Sorin's award-winning film is an understated, intensely human depiction of life's little miracles. Sorin unfolds a quiet fable about an unemployed garage mechanic's depressed existence changing for the better when he is given a dog in return for a favour. But this dog is not any old pet – it's a game-hound of noble pedigree and a potential dog-show winner. Newcomer Juan Villegas (a car-park attendant in real life) gives a remarkable and totally unaffected performance as an individual making the best of the harsh realities he's been dealt. How his canine-career dream transforms into an attainable goal is utterly believable and yet still quite magical. AJ. In Spanish with English subtitles. Contains swearing.

Juan Villegas *Juan "Coco" Villegas* • Walter Donado • Pascual Condito *Pascual* • Mariela Diaz *Coco's daughter* • Rosa Valsecchi *Susana* ■ *Dir* Carlos Sorin • *Scr* Carlos Sorin, Santiago Calori, Salvador Roselli, from an idea by Carlos Sorin

Bon Voyage ★★★ U

Spy drama 1944 · UK · BW · 25mins

Returning from Hollywood at the behest of the Ministry of Information, Alfred Hitchcock commanded a weekly rate of just £10 for this propaganda boost for the French Resistance. It also served to advocate general vigilance, as a superbly controlled flashback sequence reveals to doltish RAF pilot John Blythe the tell-tale signs he missed as he was escorted back from a PoW camp by a Gestapo agent masquerading as a Pole. With its shocking dénouement, this provocative short was atmospherically shot by the exiled Günther Krampf, who'd also filmed such key expressionist silents as *Pandora's Box*. DP. In French with English subtitles.

John Blythe *John Dougall* ■ *Dir* Alfred Hitchcock • *Scr* JOC Orton, Angus MacPhail, from an idea by Arthur Calder-Marshall

Bon Voyage! ★★★ U

Comedy 1962 · US · Colour · 126mins

There have been plenty of movies about Americans in Paris, but rarely one as bland as this family film from Disney. The family in question, headed by Fred MacMurray and Jane Wyman, have a series of comic misadventures you can see coming a mile off, while the open-mouthed awe with which they greet all things European is that of the simple-minded for the sophisticated. That said, the various twists and turns have a rather endearing innocence, and the costumes were nominated for an Academy Award. TH

Fred MacMurray *Harry Willard* • Jane Wyman *Katie Willard* • Michael Callan *Nick O'Mara* • Deborah Walley *Amy Willard* • Jessie Royce Landis *La Countessa* • Tommy Kirk *Elliott Willard* • Georgette Anys *Madame Clebert* ■ *Dir* James Neilson • *Scr* Bill Walsh, from the novel by Marrijane Hayes, Joseph Hayes • *Costume Designer* Bill Thomas

Bon Voyage ★★★★ 12

Second World War black comedy
2003 · Fr · Colour · 110mins

Impeccably mounted and played with relish by a stellar cast, this is an unashamedly old-fashioned entertainment that oozes class. Director Jean-Paul Rappeneau ably combines romance, suspense and dark comedy as Isabelle Adjani's scheming screen star exploits both lustful government minister Gérard Depardieu and aspiring author Grégori Derangère to cover up a Parisian killing. Beneath all the surface sophistication, Rappeneau also explores some of the deeper issues concerning the move to Vichy control. DP. In French with English subtitles. Contains violence. DVD

Isabelle Adjani *Viviane Denvert* • Gérard Depardieu *Minister Jean-Etienne Beaufort* • Virginie Ledoyen *Camille* • Yvan Attal *Raoul* • Grégori Derangère *Frédéric Auger* • Peter Coyote *Alex Winkler* • Jean-Marc Stehlé *Professor Kopolski* • Aurore Clément *Jacqueline de Lusse* ■ *Dir* Jean-Paul Rappeneau • *Scr* Jean-Paul Rappeneau, Patrick Modiano, Gilles Marchand, Jérôme Tonnerre, Julian Rappeneau

Bon Voyage, Charlie Brown ★★★ U

Animation 1980 · US · Colour · 72mins

Inspired by Charles Schulz's long-running *Peanuts* comic strip, this animated feature proves the gently sardonic tone that hooked millions is present and correct by appending the bracketed rider *(And Don't Come Back)* to the title. Heading to Europe for an exchange visit, the worldly-wise toddlers find themselves living it up in a French château at the expense of a mysterious patron. There are some nice cultural asides, but what makes this so enjoyable is the trademark philosophising – plus, of course, Snoopy who, after years of practice against the garage door, finally gets to play at Wimbledon. DP

Dir Bill Melendez • *Scr* Charles M Schulz, from his comic strip *Peanuts*

El Bonaerense ★★★ 15

Police drama
2002 · Arg/Neth/Fr/Chil · Colour · 94mins

Exposés of police corruption are nothing new, but this cynical, realist insight into the prejudice and ineptitude of the Buenos Aires force also considers the extent to which these problems are exacerbated by under-funding. Locksmith-turned-rookie Jorge Román is forced to begin again after events conspire against him. But he wrecks a potentially redemptive relationship with police academy lecturer Mimí Ardú before using the pernicious skills he's learned on the job to extricate himself from his plight. DP. In Spanish with English subtitles. Contains swearing, violence and sex scenes. DVD

Jorge Román *Zapa/Enrique Orlando Mendoza* • Darío Levy *Deputy Inspector Gallo* • Mimí Ardú *Mabel* • Hugo Anganuzzi *Polaco* • Victor Hugo Carrizo *Inspector Molinari* • Graciana Chironi *Graciana, Zapa's mother* ■ *Dir/Scr* Pablo Trapero

Bond Street ★★

Portmanteau drama
1948 · UK · BW · 109mins

Clearly inspired by *Tales of Manhattan*, in which dozens of guest stars helped director Julien Duvivier tell the life story of a tail coat, this portmanteau drama, set around the preparations for a wedding, works best when it's funny and drags when it's not. The stars of the show are undoubtedly Kathleen Harrison as a chirpy seamstress and Roland Young as the befuddled father of the bride. Kenneth Griffith is suitably hissable as disabled Patricia Plunkett's ne'er-do-well spouse, but Derek Farr is embarrassingly unconvincing as a twitchy killer. DP

Jean Kent *Ricki Merritt* • Roland Young *George Chester-Barrett* • Kathleen Harrison *Mrs Brawn* • Derek Farr *Joe Marsh* • Hazel Court *Julia Chester-Barrett* • Ronald Howard *Steve Winter* • Paula Valenska *Elsa* • Patricia Plunkett *Mary* ■ *Dir* Gordon Parry • *Scr* Anatole de Grunwald, Terence Rattigan, Rodney Ackland, from an idea by JG Brown

Bone ★

Horror 1972 · US · Colour · 91mins

Also known as *Housewife* and *Beverly Hills Nightmare*, this piece of schlock was released in Britain in 1979 as *Dial Rat for Terror*. Yaphet Kotto stars, along with a lot of cockroaches, a dead rat in a swimming pool and a Beverly Hills couple going bananas. There's an allegory about wealth and white privilege lurking among the wooden performances and silly shock effects. AT. Contains violence, swearing, sex scenes and nudity.

Yaphet Kotto *Bone* • Andrew Duggan *Bill* • Joyce Van Patten *Bernadette* • Jeannie Berlin *Girl* ■ *Dir/Scr* Larry Cohen

The Bone Collector ★★★ 15

Crime thriller 1999 · US · Colour · 113mins

A run-of-the-mill story is turned into an above-average thriller, thanks to impressive central performances from Denzel Washington and Angelina Jolie as two very different cops who team up to track down a serial killer. Washington plays a decorated police officer now confined to his bed, virtually paralysed following an accident on the job. Jolie's the young rookie who's brought in to explore the deepest, darkest areas of Manhattan under his instruction as they follow the trail of a sadistic murderer. This benefits from Phillip Noyce's fast-paced direction. JB. Contains violence and swearing. DVD

Denzel Washington *Lincoln Rhyme* • Angelina Jolie *Amelia Donaghy* • Queen Latifah *Thelma* • Michael Rooker *Captain Howard Cheney* • Mike McGlone *Detective Kenny Solomon* • Luis Guzman *Eddie Ortiz* • Leland Orser *Richard Thompson* • John Benjamin Hickey *Dr Barry Lehman* • Ed O'Neill *Detective Paulie Sellitto* ■ *Dir* Phillip Noyce • *Scr* Jeremy Iacone, from the novel by Jeffery Deaver

Bone Daddy ★★★ 18

Horror thriller 1998 · US · Colour · 87mins

Ex-medical examiner Rutger Hauer writes a fictional bestseller about a serial killer, who then gets up to his old tricks again in this above-average horror thriller. Hauer is put back on the case when bones – removed from the still-living body of his literary agent – begin arriving at police headquarters. The suspects mount up with little sense of suspense or hope of a satisfying resolution, but Hauer acquits himself well in a role tailor-made for his talents. AJ. Contains violence and some swearing. DVD

Rutger Hauer *William Palmer* • Barbara Williams (2) *Sharon Hewlett* • RH Thomson *Marshall Stone* • Joseph Kell *Peter Palmer* • Robin Gammell *Cobb* • Blu Mankuma *Trent* ■ *Dir* Mario Azzopardi • *Scr* Thomas Szollosi

Bones ★★ 18

Black comedy horror
2001 · US · Colour · 92mins

US rapper Snoop Dogg struts his stuff as a re-animated avenger in this blaxploitation-style supernatural horror. The star cuts a classy figure as a murdered neighbourhood kingpin who comes back from the dead to get even with his killers. However, aside from the schlock elements, there's little to hold the attention, since the tale lacks atmosphere, the visual effects are substandard and the performances cartoonish. SF DVD

Snoop Dogg *Jimmy Bones* • Pam Grier *Pearl* • Michael T Weiss *Lupovich* • Clifton Powell *Jeremiah Peet* • Ricky Harris *Eddie Mack* • Bianca Lawson *Cynthia* • Khalil Kain *Patrick* ■ *Dir* Ernest Dickerson [Ernest R Dickerson] • *Scr* Adam Simon, Tim Metcalfe

The Bonfire of the Vanities ★★★ 15

Drama 1990 · US · Colour · 120mins

Brian De Palma's adaptation of Tom Wolfe's scathing attack on the yuppie lifestyles of the Wall Street rich and Park Avenue famous is, admittedly, a flawed satire (the casting of Tom Hanks and Melanie Griffith didn't help). Nonetheless, it's hardly the irredeemably awful disaster most critics led you to believe. Even a lesser De Palma picture is a whole lot more interesting than many A-list directors' good ones. Purely from a technical standpoint, it's brilliant – the opening four-minute continuous shot, for example – and, with hindsight, its subtle entertainment values now shine through. AJ. Contains violence, sex scenes, swearing, nudity. DVD

Tom Hanks *Sherman McCoy* • Bruce Willis *Peter Fallow* • Melanie Griffith *Maria Ruskin* • Kim Cattrall *Judy McCoy* • Saul Rubinek *Jed Kramer* • Morgan Freeman *Judge White* • F Murray Abraham *Abe Weiss* • John Hancock *Reverend Bacon* • Kevin Dunn *Tom Killian* ■ *Dir* Brian De Palma • *Scr* Michael Cristofer, from the novel by Tom Wolfe • *Cinematographer* Vilmos Zsigmond

Le Bonheur ★★★★

Romantic drama 1965 · Fr · Colour · 79mins

The under-rated Agnès Varda here produced one of new French cinema's most controversial films. Few could find fault with her elliptical narrative, elegant compositions and psychological use of colour. But debates raged over her motive for having an adulterous carpenter settle down happily with his mistress and children after his wife drowns herself, rather than accept a suggested *ménage à trois*. Irrespective of the film's mischievous morality, the romantic imagery and Mozart score provide an ironic contrast to the contentious sexual politics, which were given an added *je ne sais quoi* by the fact that Jean-Claude Drouot's screen kin were played by his own family. DP. In French with English subtitles.

Jean-Claude Drouot *François* • Claire Drouot *Thérèse* • Sandrine Drouot *Gisou* • Olivier Drouot *Pierrot* • Marie-France Boyer *Emilie* ■ *Dir/Scr* Agnès Varda

Le Bonheur Est dans le Pré ★★★ 15

Comedy 1995 · Fr · Colour · 101mins

Etienne Chatiliez is no stranger to the themes of belonging and dislocation. But here he seems less interested in astute social observations than in relating the simple story of toilet king Michel Serrault, who seizes the opportunity presented by a case of mistaken identity to abandon his workshy employees and grasping wife, Sabine Azéma, to enjoy a rural idyll with Carmen Maura. Although an amiable picture, this lacks both the satirical edge of Chatiliez's *Life Is a Long Quiet River* and the black comedy of his *Tatie Danielle*. DP. In French with English subtitles. Contains some swearing, sexual references. DVD

Michel Serrault *Francis Bergeaud* • Eddy Mitchell *Gérard* • Sabine Azéma *Nicole Bergeaud* • Carmen Maura *Dolores Thivart* • François Morel *Pouillaud* • Eric Cantona *Lionel* ■ *Dir* Etienne Chatiliez • *Scr* Florence Quentin

Bonjour Tristesse ★★★ PG

Drama 1958 · US · BW and Colour · 89mins

Otto Preminger's Riviera-set romantic drama stars David Niven as the widower whose affair with Deborah Kerr is subverted by his daughter, Jean Seberg. Loosely based on the novel by Françoise Sagan, it's fluffy stuff, enjoyable for Niven's deft playing and for Seberg, whose radiant performance caused a stir not unlike the one caused by Audrey Hepburn in *Roman Holiday*. The film was a huge hit in France, and Seberg became an overnight cult sensation. TH

Deborah Kerr *Anne Larsen* • David Niven *Raymond* • Jean Seberg *Cecile* • Mylène Demongeot *Elsa Mackenbourg* • Geoffrey Horne *Philippe* • Juliette Greco *Nightclub singer* • Walter Chiari *Pablo* ■ *Dir* Otto Preminger • *Scr* Arthur Laurents, from the novel by Françoise Sagan

Bonne Chance ★★★★

Comedy 1935 · Fr · Colour · 78mins

Establishing the mischievous style that was to become his trademark, this sprightly comedy (which was once believed lost) also marked the beginning of Sacha Guitry's ten-film collaboration with Jacqueline Delubac. As the struggling artist and ingénue who split the cost of a lottery ticket and risk the ire of her soldier boyfriend by spending their winnings on a luxury holiday, they make a splendid team and are much better suited than Ginger Rogers and Ronald Colman in the 1940 remake, *Lucky Partners*. DP. In French with English subtitles.

Sacha Guitry *Claude* • Jacqueline Delubac *Marie* • André Numès *Prosper* • Robert Darthez *Gastion Lepeltier* • Pauline Carton *Mother* ■ *Dir/Scr* Sacha Guitry

La Bonne Soupe ★★★

Romantic comedy drama
1963 · Fr/It · BW · 96mins

Round up a dozen stars of the past, present and future, and jolly them through their paces in a film version of a successful boulevard comedy. It's like Shaftesbury Avenue some 40 years ago as an ageing woman recalls her life, her loves, her highs, her lows. In this roundabout story Marie Bell (played as a girl by Annie Girardot) is seduced, marries for money and ends up as a classy call girl. The cream of French cinema strut their stuff as they join the merry-go-round. BB. In French with English subtitles.

Annie Girardot *Marie-Paule, young* • Marie Bell *Marie-Paule, older* • Gérard Blain *Painter* • Bernard Blier *Monsieur Joseph* • Jean-Claude Brialy *Jacquot* • Sacha Distel *Roger* • Franchot Tone *Montasi Jr* ■ *Dir* Robert Thomas • *Scr* Robert Thomas, from the play by Félicien Marceau

Les Bonnes Femmes ★★★★

Drama 1960 · Fr/It · BW · 98mins

Meeting no great critical acclaim on its first release, this is now rated one of Claude Chabrol's early masterpieces and a major film of the French New Wave. The "good girls" of the title are four young Parisian women, who make up for the ennui of their working life in an electrical goods shop by regularly hitting the town in search of glamour and romance. Chabrol's mixture of documentary-style realism, slice-of-life drama and black humour combines with stunning black-and-white photography and fine performances to impressive effect. PF. In French with English subtitles.

Bernadette Lafont *Jane* • Lucile Saint-Simon *Rita* • Clothilde Joano *Jacqueline* • Stéphane Audran *Ginette* • Mario David *André Lapierre* • Claude Berri *André* • Claude Chabrol ■ *Dir* Claude Chabrol • *Scr* Paul Gégauff, Claude Chabrol • *Cinematographer* Henri Decaë

Bonnie and Clyde ★★★★★ 18

Crime drama 1967 · US · Colour · 106mins

"They're young! They're in love! And they kill people!" When this stylish and uncompromising gangster picture was released, graphic screen violence was very rare, and this influential film was misread by some American critics, who dismissed it as a gimmicky, gory crime thriller. However, it proved to be the box-office hit of the year, and scooped ten Oscar nominations. Faye Dunaway and Warren Beatty excel as the gun-toting criminals who roamed the American Midwest during the Depression, while David Newman and Robert Benton's sizzling script (originally offered to both François Truffaut and Jean-Luc Godard) and Arthur Penn's bravura direction are as fresh as ever. DP. Contains violence. DVD

Warren Beatty *Clyde Barrow* • Faye Dunaway *Bonnie Parker* • Michael J Pollard *CW Moss* • Gene Hackman *Buck Barrow* • Estelle Parsons *Blanche* • Denver Pyle *Frank Hamer* • Dub Taylor *Ivan Moss* • Evans Evans *Velma Davis* • Gene Wilder *Eugene Grizzard* ■ *Dir* Arthur Penn • *Scr* David Newman, Robert Benton, Robert Towne (uncredited) • *Cinematographer* Burnett Guffey • *Costume Designer* Theadora Van Runkle

B

The Bonnie Parker Story ★★

Crime drama 1958 · US · BW · 75mins

Dorothy Provine stars as half of the infamous 1930s' duo, Bonnie and Clyde, in this fictionalised account of their partnership. After her husband is sent to prison for 175 years, Bonnie Parker waits at tables and hangs out with undesirables, eventually teaming up with ruffian Guy Darrow (renamed as Clyde Barrow's family was still alive when the film was made) for a "lonesome ride on a one-way ticket". This low-budget effort bravely steers away from glamorising the couple's murderous antics. AT

Dorothy Provine *Bonnie Parker* • Jack Hogan *Guy Darrow* • Richard Bakalyan *Duke Jefferson* • Joe Turkel *Chuck Darrow* • William Stevens *Paul* • Ken Lynch *Manager of restaurant* • Douglas Kennedy *Tom Steel* • Patt Huston *Chuck's girl* • Joel Colin *Bobby* ■ *Dir* William Witney • *Scr* Stanley Shpetner

Bonnie Prince Charlie ★ [U]

Historical drama
1948 · UK · Colour · 139mins

This shoddy costume drama must rank as one of the worst films ever made in this country. It contains some quite dreadful dialogue delivered in atrocious accents by an all-star cast led by a hopelessly miscast David Niven. The studio sets look home-made, but they are nowhere near as embarrassing as the twee, cliché-ridden score. DP

David Niven *Bonnie Prince Charlie* • Margaret Leighton *Flora MacDonald* • Judy Campbell *Clementine Walkinshaw* • Jack Hawkins *Lord George Murray* • Morland Graham *Donald* • Finlay Currie *Marquis of Tullibardine* • Elwyn Brook-Jones *Duke of Cumberland* • John Laurie *Blind Jamie* ■ *Dir* Anthony Kimmins • *Scr* Clemence Dane

Bonnie Scotland ★★★★ [U]

Comedy 1935 · US · BW · 76mins

An overcomplicated plot – and some comedy routines from previous movies – can't prevent this from being one of the most delightful comedies from the "golden period" of the Laurel and Hardy series of laughter-makers. It includes a litter-picking exercise by the twosome that becomes a soft-shoe shuffle, which is a classic of fanciful timing. Stan and Ollie go to Scotland to claim Stan's inheritance, which turns out to be bagpipes and a snuff box, and from there they are unwittingly recruited to the British Army in India. There's the added bonus of the pop-eyed, moustachioed James Finlayson, as a dastardly sergeant major, making up for the wan love interest provided by June Lang. TH [video]

Stan Laurel *Stanley McLaurel* • Oliver Hardy *Ollie* • Anne Grey *Lady Violet Ormsby* • David Torrence *Mr Miggs* • June Lang *Lorna McLaurel* • William Janney *Alan Douglas* • James Mack *Butler* • James Finlayson *Sergeant Major* ■ *Dir* James W Horne • *Scr* Frank Butler, Jefferson Moffitt

Boo, Zino and the Snurks ★★ [U]

Animated fantasy
2004 · Ger/Sp/UK · Colour · 87mins

The first computer-generated movie produced in Germany features Boo and Zino, a pair of furry creatures who present their own TV series on Gaya. They hurtle into action – in the company of their co-stars, Princess Alanta and a trio of reprehensible Snurks – when a scheming professor, who's jealous of their success, steals the precious stone that gives their world its energy. Director Lenard Fritz Krawinkel relentlessly sustains the adventure's breakneck pace, but the principal characters could have been more appealing. DP [video] DVD

Alan Mariot *Boo* • Glenn Wrage *Zino* • Patrick Stewart *Albert Drollinger* • Emily Watson *Alanta* • John Schwab *Zeck* • John Guerrasio *Galger* • Red Pepper *Bramph* • Lorelei King *Susi/Female Gayan* ■ *Dir* Lenard Fritz Krawinkel • *Scr* Bob Shaw, Donald McEnery, Jan Berger

Booby Trap ★

Crime thriller 1957 · UK · BW · 72mins

A dire British B-feature, barely seen when it first came out. Absent-minded boffin Tony Quinn invents an explosive fountain pen, timed to go off on the first stroke of Big Ben. The pen falls into the hands of drug peddler Sydney Tafler who, as it happens, hides his wares in fountain pens. The build-up is feeble and none of the characters engage one's interest. AE

Sydney Tafler *Hunter* • Patti Morgan *Jackie* • Tony Quinn *Professor Hasdane* • John Watson *Major Cunliffe* • Jacques Cey *Bentley* • Richard Shaw *Richards* • Harry Fowler *Sammy* ■ *Dir* Henry Cass • *Scr* Peter Bryan, Bill Luckwell, from a novel by Peter Bryan

Boogeyman ★★ [15]

Horror thriller 2005 · US · Colour · 85mins

This may be sloppily written, nonsensical and unconvincing, but it still manages a few shivers and jolts, thanks to director Stephen T Kay's well-oiled if clichéd style. Barry Watson returns to his childhood home to confront his greatest fear, the monster that he believes dwells in his bedroom closet and that snatched his father when he was eight years old. There are gaping plot holes, but also enough cheap thrills to paper over them. AJ [video] DVD

Barry Watson *Tim* • Emily Deschanel *Kate* • Skye McCole Bartusiak *Franny* • Tory Mussett *Jessica* • Andrew Glover *Boogeyman* • Lucy Lawless *Tim's mother* • Charles Mesure *Tim's father* ■ *Dir* Stephen T Kay [Stephen Kay] • *Scr* Eric Kripke, Juliet Snowdon, Stiles White, from a story by Eric Kripke

The Boogie Man Will Get You ★★★

Comedy horror 1942 · US · BW · 66mins

Here's a fun cast in a lively programme filler that cheered up many a wartime audience. Boris Karloff plays a demented (what else?) scientist who attempts to turn salesmen into supermen in a crazy plot, which also involves the wonderful Peter Lorre. Larry Parks is the juvenile lead, with Jeff Donnell aboard to add romantic interest. Lew Landers successfully juggles the lunatic elements of plot and action. TS

Boris Karloff *Professor Nathaniel Billings* • Peter Lorre *Dr Lorentz* • Maxie Rosenbloom *Maxie* • Larry Parks *Bill Leyden* • Jeff Donnell *Winnie Leyden* • Maude Eburne *Amelia Jones* • Don Beddoe *J Gilbert Brampton* • George McKay *Ebenezer* • Frank Puglia *Silvio Baciagalupi* ■ *Dir* Lew Landers • *Scr* Edwin Blum, Paul Gangelin (adaptation), from a story by Hal Fimberg, Robert E Hunt

Boogie Nights ★★★★★ [18]

Drama 1997 · US · Colour · 149mins

Pornography, drugs and disco are the driving forces of director Paul Thomas Anderson's potent parable of the partying 1970s. Spanning the height of the disco era, this rags-to-bitches allegory is a visually stunning and poignant exploration of the adult entertainment industry. Charting the rise, fall and rise again of bus boy-turned-porn star Mark Wahlberg, Anderson's surreal take on the American Dream is as startling as it is highly entertaining. Burt Reynolds was Oscar nominated for his brilliant turn as sleaze-movie producer Jack Horner, the patriarch of an extended family of life's flotsam and jetsam. Scintillating support is provided by Heather Graham as Rollergirl, and Julianne Moore (also Oscar-nominated) as leading lady Amber Waves. The breathtaking opening Steadicam shot is justifiably famous. AJ. Contains violence, swearing, sex scenes, drug abuse and nudity. [video] DVD

Mark Wahlberg *Eddie Adams/Dirk Diggler* • Burt Reynolds *Jack Horner* • Julianne Moore *Amber Waves* • John C Reilly *Reed Rothchild* • Melora Walters *Jessie St Vincent* • Robert Ridgely *The Colonel James* • Don Cheadle *Buck Swope* • Heather Graham *Rollergirl* • William H Macy *Little Bill* ■ *Dir/Scr* Paul Thomas Anderson

The Book of Life ★★★★

Satirical black comedy
1998 · Fr/US · Colour · 63mins

Director Hal Hartley is never dull but he remains an acquired taste. Taking the millennium as potentially apocalyptic, Hartley films a discussion between Satan (Thomas Jay Ryan), Jesus (Martin Donovan) and Magdalena (PJ Harvey) on New Year's Eve, 1999, about the survival of the human race. This is a fascinating black comedy, in which we have Christ and his girl Friday wandering round JFK airport lamenting mortals and Satan getting drunk in a hotel bar. Bizarre, and yet at times brilliant. LH

Martin Donovan (2) *Jesus Christ* • PJ Harvey *Magdalena* • Thomas Jay Ryan *Satan* • David Simonds *Dave* • Miho Nikaido *Edie* • DJ Mendel *Lawyer* ■ *Dir/Scr* Hal Hartley

Book of Numbers ★★★ [15]

Blaxploitation period drama
1972 · US · Colour · 81mins

Directed by its star, Raymond St Jacques, this is a rare blaxploitation venture into period drama. St Jacques joins with fellow city slacker Philip Thomas in an attempt to beat the Depression by setting up a numbers racket in a small Arkansas town. But can our roguish duo overcome the threat posed by racist gangster Gilbert Greene? Although budgetary constraints leave it looking a little ragged around the edges, this is a mostly entertaining caper movie. DP. Contains swearing and violence. [video]

Raymond St Jacques *Blueboy Harris* • Freda Payne *Kelly Simms* • Philip Thomas [Philip Michael Thomas] *Dave Greene* • Hope Clarke *Pigmeat Goins* • Willie Washington Jr *Makepeace Johnson* • Doug Finell *Eggy* • Sterling St Jacques *Kid Flick* ■ *Dir* Raymond St Jacques • *Scr* Larry Spiegel, from the novel by Robert Deane Pharr

Book of Shadows: Blair Witch 2 ★ [15]

Supernatural horror
2000 · US · Colour · 86mins

First of all, there is no mention of a book of any sort in this sequel to the phenomenally successful *The Blair Witch Project*. Second, there are hardly any scares, either. The story begins as a group of misfits interested in the original film sign up for a tour of Burkittsville, where the first movie was set. Whether you love or hate the original, there's no denying that it was an innovative idea, brilliantly marketed, which fired many an evening's conversation. The only thing people will say after seeing this sequel is "Can I have my money back?" JB. Contains violence and swearing. [video] DVD

Kim Director *Kim* • Jeffrey Donovan *Jeff* • Erica Leerhsen *Erica* • Tristen Skyler *Tristen* • Stephen Barker Turner *Stephen* ■ *Dir* Joe Berlinger • *Scr* Dick Beebe, Joe Berlinger

Boom ★★

Drama 1968 · UK/US · Colour · 112mins

A piece of preening self-indulgence by Richard Burton and Elizabeth Taylor at a time when the two stars thought they could be forgiven anything. An adaptation by Tennessee Williams of his play *The Milk Train Doesn't Stop Here Anymore*, it clashes symbols with its study of life among the idle rich. Taylor is a six-times married virago, while Burton is a freeloading poet. Noël Coward gives it all some semblance of life as Flora's confidant – but can't make up for the film's deficiencies. TH

Elizabeth Taylor *Flora Goforth* • Richard Burton *Chris Flanders* • Noël Coward *Witch of Capri* • Joanna Shimkus *Blackie* • Michael Dunn *Rudy* • Romolo Valli *Dr Luilo* • Veronica Wells *Simonetta* • Fernando Piazza *Giulio* • Howard Taylor *Journalist* ■ *Dir* Joseph Losey • *Scr* Tennessee Williams, from his play *The Milk Train Doesn't Stop Here Anymore*

Boom Town ★★★★

Adventure drama 1940 · US · BW · 118mins

After the huge success of *San Francisco* and *Test Pilot*, Clark Gable and Spencer Tracy were reunited for another sprawling adventure, this time about two pioneers in the oil business. Although there were reports of behind-the-scenes tensions, the two stars give memorably larger-than-life performances and the female leads, Claudette Colbert and Hedy Lamarr, are on equally good form. Director Jack Conway stages some stunning set pieces (notably a burning oil field) and keeps the action roaring along. JF

Clark Gable *Big John McMasters* • Spencer Tracy *Square John Sand* • Claudette Colbert *Betsy Bartlett* • Hedy Lamarr *Karen Vanmeer* • Frank Morgan *Luther Aldrich* • Lionel Atwill *Harry Compton* • Chill Wills *Harmony Jones* ■ *Dir* Jack Conway • *Scr* John Lee Mahin, from a story by James Edward Grant

Boomerang! ★★★★

Crime drama 1947 · US · BW · 85mins

A riveting 20th Century-Fox social thriller from a period in which *film noir* style and location shooting were combined in the safe hands of *March of Time* producer Louis de Rochemont. Quintessential 1940s icon Dana Andrews heads a fine cast that includes then stage actors Arthur Kennedy, Lee J Cobb and Sam Levene, who flourish under New Yorker Elia Kazan's direction. This was Kazan's third feature film, having just completed *A Streetcar Named Desire* on Broadway. If the denouement seems contrived, remember this is based on a true story. TS

Dana Andrews *Henry L Harvey* • Jane Wyatt *Mrs Harvey* • Lee J Cobb *Chief Robinson* • Cara Williams *Irene Nelson* • Arthur Kennedy *John Waldron* • Sam Levene *Woods* • Taylor Holmes *Wade* • Robert Keith (1) *McCreery* ■ *Dir* Elia Kazan • *Scr* Richard Murphy, from the *Reader's Digest* article *The Perfect Case* by Anthony Abbott

Boomerang ★★★

Thriller 1976 · Fr · Colour · 100mins

Co-written and produced by Alain Delon with pulp novelist José Giovanni, who also directed, this under-rated film offers a shrewd mix of social comment and human drama. Although it adopts a preachy tone in its discussion of drug culture, the story of a businessman's determination to help his son following the murder of a cop – even though it will mean the exposure of his own criminal past – is told crisply and convincingly. Yet it's the solid acting that gives the action its authenticity. DP. French dialogue dubbed into English.

Alain Delon *Jacques* • Charles Vanel *Lawyer* • Carla Gravina *Wife* • Louis Julien *Eddy* • Dora Doll *Mother* • Suzanne Flon *Widow* ■ *Dir* José Giovanni • *Scr* Alain Delon, José Giovanni

Boomerang ★★★ 15

Comedy 1992 · US · Colour · 111mins

After a few years in the wilderness following flops such as *The Golden Child* and *Harlem Nights*, Eddie Murphy returned with this amiable if slightly overlong comedy from *House Party* director Reginald Hudlin. Murphy is on form as the womaniser who gets his comeuppance when he tries his smooth-talking ways on canny Robin Givens, who turns the tables when she treats him as a sex object. However, it is the supporting performances from Grace Jones and Eartha Kitt that really give the film a buzz. JB. Contains sex scenes, nudity, swearing. DVD

Eddie Murphy *Marcus Graham* • Robin Givens *Jacqueline* • Halle Berry *Angela* • David Alan Grier *Gerard* • Martin Lawrence *Tyler* • Grace Jones *Strangé* • Geoffrey Holder *Nelson* • Eartha Kitt *Lady Eloise* • Chris Rock *Bony T* • Lela Rochon *Christie* ■ *Dir* Reginald Hudlin • *Scr* Barry W Blaustein, David Sheffield, from a story by Eddie Murphy

The Boondock Saints ★ 18

Crime thriller
1999 · Can/US · Colour and BW · 103mins

This dated, annoyingly stylised crime thriller presents one of Willem Dafoe's most embarrassing screen performances. Sean Patrick Flanery and Norman Reedus are the "saints" of the title, a couple of working class lads from Boston's Irish community who embark on a bloody vigilante rampage against Mafia types. Dafoe is the gay FBI agent who begins to develop a grudging admiration for the young killers. JF DVD

Willem Dafoe *Paul Smecker* • Sean Patrick Flanery *Connor MacManus* • Norman Reedus *Murphy MacManus* • David Della Rocco *Rocco* • Billy Connolly *Il Duce* ■ *Dir/Scr* Troy Duffy

The Boost ★★★ 18

Drama 1988 · US · Colour · 90mins

Better known for the rumours behind the scenes than for the action in front of the camera (during the filming stars Sean Young and James Woods allegedly had an affair that ended rather bitterly in lawsuits), this overlooked drama from director Harold Becker has moments of insight in between the screaming matches. The film catalogues a couple's descent into drug addiction. Although more time is spent banging home the anti-drug message than on developing character, both Woods and Young give gutsy enough performances to lift the film above the dismal. JB. Contains violence, swearing, sex scenes, drug abuse and nudity. DVD

James Woods *Lenny Brown* • Sean Young *Linda Brown* • John Kapelos *Joel* • Steven Hill *Max Sherman* • Kelle Kerr *Rochelle* • John Rothman *Ned Leavis* • Amanda Blake *Barbara* • Grace Zabriskie *Sheryl* • Marc Poppel *Mark* ■ *Dir* Harold Becker • *Scr* Darryl Ponicsan, from the novel *Ludes* by Benjamin Stein

Das Boot ★★★ 12

Second World War action drama
1981 · W Ger · Colour · 199mins

This sprawling U-boat epic is based on actual incidents during the 1941 battle for the North Atlantic. Submarine warfare offers film-makers little in the way of variation, and the action inevitably alternates between tense periods of silent stalking and frantic moments of engagement (brilliantly captured by Jost Vacano's darting camera). Director Wolfgang Petersen adopts an understandably anti-Nazi tone and depicts the crew as courageous conscripts serving a cause to which they are not wholeheartedly committed. However, his preoccupation with the terrors of their claustrophobic existence means that, apart from steely captain Jürgen Prochnow, few of the characters come alive. DP. A German language film. Contains some violence and swearing. DVD

Jürgen Prochnow *Captain* • Herbert Grönemeyer *Lieutenant Werner/Correspondent* • Klaus Wennemann *Chief Engineer* • Hubertus Bengsch *First Lieutenant/Number One* • Martin Semmelrogge *Second Lieutenant* • Bernd Tauber *Chief Quartermaster* • Erwin Leder *Johann* ■ *Dir* Wolfgang Petersen • *Scr* Wolfgang Petersen, from the novel *Das Boot* by Lothar-Guenther Buchheim

Boot Hill ★★ PG

Spaghetti western 1969 · It · Colour · 91mins

As the vogue for spaghetti westerns began to wane, Italian actors Mario Girotti and Carlo Pedersoli created a sub-genre based on the new-found traditions, effectively imitating the imitators. They gave themselves the American-sounding names of Terence Hill and Bud Spencer respectively, and became immensely popular (and rich) primarily for a series of films featuring "Trinity" or "Nobody" in the titles. This movie pre-dates those, and non-fans will find the inept dubbing and poor story structure irritating. TS. Italian dialogue dubbed into English. Contains violence.

Bud Spencer *Hutch Bessy* • Woody Strode *Thomas* • Edward Ciannelli [Eduardo Ciannelli] *Boone* • Terence Hill *Cat Stevens* ■ *Dir/Scr* Giuseppe Colizzi

Bootmen ★★★ 15

Dance drama
2000 · Aus/US · Colour · 88mins

Set in the rundown Australian town of Newcastle, this working-class fantasy traces the origins of the Tap Dogs and Steel City dance troupes. Defying his homophobic father, Adam Garcia attempts to stage a benefit for his jobless buddies. But with most of the blokes obsessed with sporting muscle and amber nectar, getting a crew together proves an uphill battle. With too much time spent on sub-plots, Dein Perry skimps on the industrial dance sequences, which is frustrating, as they have a real kinetic kick. DP Contains swearing, violence.. DVD

Adam Garcia *Sean* • Sophie Lee *Linda* • Sam Worthington *Mitchell* • William Zappa *Walter* • Richard Carter *Gary* • Susie Porter *Sara* • Anthony Hayes *Huey* ■ *Dir* Dein Perry • *Scr* Steve Worland, from a story by Hilary Linstead, Dein Perry, Steve Worland

Boots! Boots! ★★ U

Musical 1934 · UK · BW · 87mins

Now here's a collector's item. If you ignore a 1915 film called *By the Shortest of Heads*, in which he appeared when he was only 11, George Formby made his proper screen debut in this cheap hotel comedy. It's not hard to spot that much of the action was filmed in a single room above a Manchester garage, but what is of more interest is the fact that George's co-star is Beryl, the domineering wife who exerted such a firm grip on his career that she tried to prevent him from kissing any of his later heroines. Hopelessly dated, but a must for fans. DP

George Formby *John Willie* • Beryl Formby *Beryl* • Arthur Kingsley *Manager* • Tonie Forde *Chambermaid* • Lilian Keyes *Lady Royston* • Donald Reid *Sir Alfred Royston* • Betty Driver *Betty* ■ *Dir* Bert Tracy • *Scr* George Formby, Arthur Mertz

Boots Malone ★★ U

Sports drama 1951 · US · BW · 103mins

Although William Holden had already made *Sunset Boulevard* and *Born Yesterday*, Paramount still loaned him out for rubbish like this family movie. It's an awfully sentimental tale, set at a racing stables where Johnny Stewart is a rich kid who loves horses. Holden is a jockey's agent who hasn't won a race in years but who thinks "The Kid" might change his luck. Veteran director William Dieterle had the chore of calling the shots, and he relies heavily on Holden's innate charm. AT

William Holden (2) *Boots Malone* • Johnny Stewart *"The Kid"* • Stanley Clements *Stash Clements* • Basil Ruysdael *Preacher Cole* • Carl Benton Reid *John Williams* • Ralph Dumke *Beckett* • Ed Begley *Howard Whitehead* • Hugh Sanders *Matson* ■ *Dir* William Dieterle • *Scr* Milton Holmes, Harold Buchman (uncredited)

Booty Call ★★ 18

Comedy 1997 · US · Colour · 75mins

Jamie Foxx and Tommy Davidson are absolutely determined to score with their girls before the night's out. But as they search for contraceptives, Vivica A Fox and Tamala Jones refuse to give in that easily in this lame battle-of-the-sexes comedy aimed squarely below the belt. If you find testicular surgery, baby urine and butt-sniffing remotely funny, then this deliberately raw gross-out will be just your *National Lampoon*-style cup of tea. AJ. Contains swearing.

Jamie Foxx *Bunz* • Tommy Davidson *Rushon* • Tamala Jones *Nikki* • Vivica A Fox *Lysterine* • Scott LaRose *Singh* • Ric Young *Mr Chiu* • Art Malik *Akmed* ■ *Dir* Jeff Pollack • *Scr* Takashi Bufford, Bootsie

Bopha! ★★★ 15

Political drama 1993 · US · Colour · 113mins

Morgan Freeman made his directorial debut with this powerful study of apartheid, which presented South Africa from the viewpoint of the black population rather than white liberals. As the police sergeant torn between the comforts his career provides and the inescapable consequences of prejudice, Danny Glover gives one of his finest performances. Alfre Woodard is also impressive as his wife, while Maynard Eziashi shows great promise as the son whose support for active protest turns the family's world upside down. Malcolm McDowell keeps on just the right side of caricature as a sadistic Special Branch officer. DP. Contains violence, swearing. DVD

Danny Glover *Micah Mangena* • Malcolm McDowell *De Villiers* • Alfre Woodard *Rosie Mangena* • Marius Weyers *Van Tonder* • Maynard Eziashi *Zweli Mangena* • Malick Bowens *Pule Rampa* ■ *Dir* Morgan Freeman • *Scr* Brian Bird, John T Wierick, from the play by Percy Mtwa

The Border ★★ 18

Drama 1981 · US · Colour · 103mins

It's good cop Jack Nicholson versus bad cop Harvey Keitel on the Tex-Mex border of El Paso, trying to stop "wetbacks" illegally entering America. Well-meaning Nicholson pities the poor immigrants and takes on the corrupt Keitel's smuggling operations in this bland and simplistic human rights drama. Naturally, Nicholson is good as the cop with a crisis of conscience. However, it's a surprisingly limp look at what still remains a hot issue. The ending was changed to make Nicholson's character more heroic. AJ

Jack Nicholson *Charlie Smith* • Harvey Keitel *Cat* • Valerie Perrine *Marcy Smith* • Warren Oates *Red* • Elpidia Carrillo *Maria* • Shannon Wilcox *Savannah* • Manuel Viescas *Juan* • Jeff Morris *JJ* ■ *Dir* Tony Richardson • *Scr* Deric Washburn, Walon Green, David Freeman

Border Incident ★★★

Film noir 1949 · US · BW · 95mins

This is one of Hollywood's early attempts to tackle the thorny topic of illegal immigration across the Mexican/American border, though the so-called "wetbacks" play second fiddle to a routine plot about racketeering. It was one of several *film noir*-style thrillers from director Anthony Mann, and is an intelligent picture that belies its low budget. Top-billed Ricardo Montalban gives a fine performance. AT

Ricardo Montalban *Pablo Rodriguez* • George Murphy *Jack Bearnes* • Howard Da Silva *Owen Parkson* • James Mitchell *Juan Garcia* • Arnold Moss *Zopilote* • Alfonso Bedoya *Cuchillo* • Teresa Celli *Maria* ■ *Dir* Anthony Mann • *Scr* John C Higgins, from a story by John C Higgins, George Zuckerman

Border Radio ★

Musical drama 1987 · US · BW · 87mins

Allison Anders made her name as a director with the excellent *Gas, Food, Lodging*, but judging by the standard of this, her debut film, she was lucky to get a second chance behind the camera. This road movie should have been parked on the hard shoulder and leftthere. DP. Contains swearing.

Chris D *Jeff* • Luana Anders *Lu* • John Doe *Dean* • Chris Shearer *Chris* • Dave Alvin *Dave* • Iris Berry *Scenester* • Texacala Jones *Babysitter* • Devon Anders *Devon* • Chuck Shepard *Expatriot* • Craig Stark *Thugs* ■ *Dir/Scr* Allison Anders, Dean Lent, Kurt Voss

Border River ★★★

Western 1954 · US · Colour · 80mins

It's often forgotten how effective Joel McCrea was in westerns and he turns in another display of muscular decency in this efficient American Civil War tale from director George Sherman. Refusing to admit the cause is lost, McCrea's Confederate major heads across the Rio Grande with $2 million in stolen Union gold to buy weapons from duplicitous Mexican general, Pedro Armendáriz. Insufficiently intense to qualify as a psychological western, this is still superior to the average genre fare. RT

Joel McCrea *Clete Mattson* • Yvonne De Carlo *Carmelita Caris* • Pedro Armendáriz *General Calleja* • Howard Petrie *Newlund* • Ivan Triesault *Baron Von Hollden* ■ *Dir* George Sherman • *Scr* William Sackheim, Louis Stevens, from a story by Louis Stevens

Border Shootout ★★

Western 1990 · US · Colour · 110mins

You don't expect a western from big-city writer Elmore Leonard (*Get Shorty*). But the plot, adapted from his novel, is the best thing in this morality tale, about townsfolk who elect an unworldly farmer as deputy sheriff to ageing lawman Glenn Ford so that they can go vigilante lynching. There's an intriguing set-up, but the production is as simple-minded as the deputy and even Ford is subdued. TH. Contains mild swearing.

Glenn Ford *Sheriff Danahar* • Cody Glenn *Kirby Frye* • Charlene Tilton *Edith Hanasain* • Jeff Kaake *Phil Sundeen* • Danny Nelson *Harold Mendez* • Michael Ansara *Chuluka* • Sergio Calderone [Sergio Calderon] *Juaquin* ■ *Dir* Chris McIntyre • *Scr* Chris McIntyre, from the novel *The Law at Randado* by Elmore Leonard

Borderline ★★ 15

Crime drama 1980 · US · Colour · 98mins

In this lacklustre thriller, Charles Bronson stars as a patrolman on the US-Mexican border out to thwart those who make a profit out of illegal immigrants. Ed Harris, in his first major role, is outstanding as the chief baddie, but Bronson can't smuggle an expression of any kind onto that Mount Rushmore face of his. Director Jerrold Freedman tries valiantly to squeeze fresh blood from the script's collection of clichés. TH DVD

Charles Bronson *Jeb Maynard* • Bruno Kirby *Jimmy Fante* • Bert Remsen *Carl Richards* •

Michael Lerner *Henry Lydell* • Kenneth McMillan *Malcolm Wallace* • Ed Harris *Hotchkiss* • Karmin Murcelo *Elena Morales* • Enrique Castillo *Arturo* ■ *Dir* Jerrold Freedman • *Scr* Steve Kline, Jerrold Freedman

B

Borderline ★★

Drama 1994 · Gr/Ger/UK · Colour · 85mins

This is a complex drama about the corrupting influences of city life and how little we ultimately know about the people closest to us. Co-written and directed by Panos Karkanevatos, the film focuses on two brothers from a remote mining village who are parted when the older of the two fakes his own death only to be found later, alive and well, by his police officer sibling. For all its pretensions, this is a rather inconsequential picture. DP. In Greek with English subtitles.

Aris Lebassopoulos *Yannis Markou* • Stavros Zalmas *Stelios* • Christos Kalavrouzos *Father* • Yannis Bofilios • Efi Drossou • Dinos Karydis • Maria Kiriaki • Patis Koutsaftis ■ *Dir* Panos Karkanevatos • *Scr* Panos Karkanevatos, Yannis Xanthopoulos

Bordertown ★★★

Crime drama 1935 · US · BW · 90mins

This super-pacey melodrama from Warner Bros stars Paul Muni as a disbarred lawyer who heads south to the US-Mexico border in search of work. There he finds sex in the form of playgirl Margaret Lindsay and hotblood Bette Davis. Davis's role, which culminates in a tremendous trial sequence, is quite sympathetic, since her lust for Muni is presented as entirely understandable because she's married to the gross Eugene Pallette. Daring then, and still stirring now, despite Muni's hamminess, it's essentially a love-triangle drama with social pretensions. TS

Paul Muni *Johnny Ramirez* • Bette Davis *Marie Roark* • Margaret Lindsay *Dale Elwell* • Eugene Pallette *Charlie Roark* • Soledad Jiminez *Mrs Ramirez* • Robert Barrat *Padre* • Gavin Gordon *Brook Mandillo* ■ *Dir* Archie Mayo • *Scr* Laird Doyle, Wallace Smith, from the novel by Carroll Graham

Bordertown Cafe ★★★

Comedy drama 1991 · Can · Colour · 101mins

A wry, warm-hearted Canadian comedy drama that takes an affectionate look at the relationship between a divorced woman and her troubled adolescent son. Susan Hogan is a larger-than-life owner of a café, something of an embarrassment to her teenage offspring who longs for a normal existence. There are shades of *Bagdad Café* in the rich mix of eccentric characters, but director Norma Bailey also succeeds in making some telling points about the generation gap. JF. Contains swearing.

Susan Hogan *Marlene* • Janet Wright *Maxime* • Lora Schroeder *Linda* • Gordon Michael Woolvett • Sean McCann • Nicholas Campbell ■ *Dir* Norma Bailey • *Scr* Kelly Rebar

Bored Olives ★★

Comedy drama
2000 · Aus/Jpn · Colour · 78mins

Everyone's trying a bit too hard in this Australian indie comedy set in a pizza delivery shop. Screenwriter Stephen Davis has packed the plot with caricatures, which Belinda Chayko directs with humdrum efficiency. So we never get to care whether manageress Hayley McElhinney can cope with either her duties or wayward boyfriend Sullivan Stapleton; or whether Brendan Cowell and Kellie Jones take the big step from buddies to lovers. DP

Sullivan Stapleton *Dom* • Ryan Johnson *Misha* • Kellie Jones *Erin* • Brendan Cowell *Robert* ■ *Dir* Belinda Chayko • *Scr* Stephen Davis

Born Again ★ PG

Biographical drama
1978 · US · Colour · 104mins

A weird, inferior appendage to the Watergate scandal, this chronicles the rise of White House employee Charles Colson, who served time in prison for his involvement in the affair and became a born-again Christian. Former blues singer (and born-again) Christian Dean Jones plays Colson. The cringe factor is high. AT

Dean Jones *Charles Colson* • Anne Francis *Patty Colson* • Jay Robinson *David Shapiro* • Dana Andrews *Tom Phillips* • Raymond St Jacques *Jimmy Newsom* • George Brent *Judge Gerhard Gesell* • Harry Spillman *President Richard M Nixon* • Peter Jurasik *Henry Kissinger* • Richard Caine *HR Haldeman* ■ *Dir* Irving Rapper • *Scr* Walter Bloch

Born Free ★★★★ U

Wildlife adventure based on a true story
1966 · US · Colour · 91mins

Beautifully shot and sensitively staged by director James Hill, this charming adaptation of Joy Adamson's bestseller is one of the great animal films. It goes without saying that all eyes will be on Elsa the lioness whenever she is on the screen, with her reluctance to take the first steps back into the wild bringing a lump to every throat. But the human performances are also first rate, with Virginia McKenna and Bill Travers bringing real warmth to their roles, while Geoffrey Keen excels as the kindly commissioner who persuades them to part with their pet. *Living Free* continued the Adamsons' story. DP DVD

Virginia McKenna *Joy Adamson* • Bill Travers *George Adamson* • Geoffrey Keen *Kendall* • Peter Luckoye *Nuru* • Omar Chambati *Makkede* • Bill Godden *Sam* • Bryan Epsom *Baker* • Robert Cheetham *Ken* ■ *Dir* James Hill • *Scr* Gerald LC Copley [Lester Cole], from the books by Joy Adamson • *Cinematographer* Ken Talbot

Born in East LA 

Comedy drama 1987 · US · Colour · 80mins

Based on Cheech Marin's parody of Bruce Springsteen's rock anthem *Born in the USA*, this weak-kneed effort lacks the wit of the Marin recording and cannot even muster a fraction of the Boss's own power. This tale of a third-generation Hispanic American who is wrongly deported to Tijuana starts by taking a handful of amiable pot shots, but eventually allows itself to be smothered by blandness. Nonetheless Marin, who writes, directs and stars in the film, supplies a comfortable comic presence. JM. Contains swearing.

Cheech Marin [Richard "Cheech" Marin] *Rudy Robles* • Daniel Stern *Jimmy* • Paul Rodriguez *Javier* • Kamala Lopez [Kamala Dawson] *Dolores* • Jan-Michael Vincent *McCalister* • Lupe Ontiveros *Rudy's mother* • Urbanie Lucero *Rudy's sister* • Chastity Ayala *Rudy's niece* ■ *Dir/Scr* Richard Marin [Richard "Cheech" Marin]

Born in Flames ★★★ 15

Drama 1983 · US · Colour · 79mins

In a futuristic New York, ten years after a peaceful revolution has made all men equal, three feminists from different backgrounds (the army, radio and performance arts) join together to fight for the rights of women irrespective of their race or sexual preference. A classic women's rights movie that utilises an in-your-face, *cinéma vérité* style, poignant arguments and razor-sharp humour to put across the hopeful fantasy of liberation against oppression. Among the cast is future director Kathryn (*Strange Days*) Bigelow. AJ

Honey • Adele Bertei *Isabel* • Jeanne Satterfield *Adelaide* • Flo Kennedy *Zella* • Pat Murphy *Newspaper editor* • Kathryn Bigelow *Newspaper editor* • Becky Johnston *Newspaper editor* • Hillary Hurst *Leader of women's army* ■ *Dir* Lizzie Borden • *Scr* Hisa Tayo, from a story by Lizzie Borden

Born Into Brothels: Calcutta's Red Light Kids ★★★

Documentary 2003 · US · Colour · 85mins

New York-based photojournalist Zana Briski began photographing Calcutta's red-light district in 1998. But, on discovering that the prostitutes' children had an instinctive gift for capturing telling images, she began to teach them how to record the world around them and devoted herself to both their perspectives and their potential. Yet, while the visual aspects of this Oscar-winning documentary are powerful and striking, Briski and co-director Ross Kauffman try to include too many desperately sad stories, with the result that we don't get as full an insight into the kids' daily lives or their hopes and fears for the future as we might. Conversely, the loose structure allows the youngsters' personalities to shine through, and this remains a poignant study of how hope is crushed by reality in the world's poorest communities. DP. An English/Bengali language film. Contains swearing.

Dir Ross Kauffman, Zana Briski

Born Losers 

Crime drama 1967 · US · Colour · 106mins

Don't be fooled by the credits for director TC Frank, screenwriter E James Lloyd and producer Donald Henderson – they are all pseudonyms for Tom Laughlin, the rough-and-ready auteur who also starred in this bruising encounter between a mixed-race ex-Green Beret and a sadistic biker gang. Nowadays it's hard to fathom why this crude exploitation flick was one of the 1960s highest grossers. But the rescue of Elizabeth James was attended by such sickening violence that audiences were shocked to the edge of their seats. Laughlin would revive the character for three disappointing sequels, beginning with *Billy Jack* in 1971. DP

Tom Laughlin *Billy Jack* • Elizabeth James *Vicky Barrington* • Jane Russell *Mrs Shorn* • Jeremy Slate *Danny Carmody* • William Wellman Jr *Child* • Robert Tessier *Cue Ball* • Jeff Cooper *Gangrene* • Edwin Cook *Crabs* ■ *Dir* TC Frank [Tom Laughlin] • *Scr* E James Lloyd [Tom Laughlin]

Born of Fire ★★★

Supernatural horror
1987 · UK · Colour · 84mins

British concert flautist Peter Firth heads to Turkey for a musical duel with a supernatural magician in a puzzling and hallucinatory mystical adventure about the power of religion. Heavy symbolism and paradoxical events are the mainstay of this beautifully photographed cautionary tale, which also finds astronomer Suzan Crowley mating with a deformed dwarf and giving birth to an insect. Vagueness has never been given a more esoteric or disturbing sheen. AJ

Peter Firth *Paul Bergson* • Suzan Crowley *Woman astronomer* • Oh-Tee *Master Musician* • Nabil Shaban *Silent One* • Stefan Kalipha *Bilal* ■ *Dir* Jamil Dehlavi • *Scr* Raficq Abdulla • *Cinematographer* Bruce McGowan

Born on the Fourth of July ★★★★★ 18

Biographical drama
1989 · US · Colour · 138mins

The second film in director Oliver Stone's Vietnam trilogy is a masterpiece, on a much broader canvas than its predecessor *Platoon*. It stars Tom Cruise as Ron Kovic, who enlists in the marines because he loves his country. Then he is hideously wounded, endures the rat-infested hell of a veterans' hospital and comes home to find the Stars and Stripes being burned in the streets. He drops out in Mexico, then returns to America to conduct an antiwar campaign from his wheelchair. Stone had won the director's Oscar for *Platoon* and he won it again for his work here. Sadly, Cruise had to settle for a nomination, but his transformation from golden boy to embittered paraplegic is utterly convincing. AT. Contains violence, sex scenes, swearing, nudity. DVD

Tom Cruise *Ron Kovic* • Kyra Sedgwick *Donna* • Raymond J Barry *Mr Kovic* • Caroline Kava *Mrs Kovic* • Willem Dafoe *Charlie* • Josh Evans *Tommy Kovic* • Jamie Talisman *Jimmy Kovic* • Tom Berenger *Recruiting sergeant* • Oliver Stone *News reporter* ■ *Dir* Oliver Stone • *Scr* Oliver Stone, Ron Kovic, from Ron Kovic's autobiography

Born Reckless ★★

Crime drama 1930 · US · BW · 73mins

A Little Italy gangster, arrested for robbery, is given the opportunity to serve his country rather than serve a prison sentence. He accepts and becomes a hero on the battlefield but, home again, he's drawn back into the underworld and gets involved in bootlegging. This suffers from a miscast Edmund Lowe and an inept screenplay. However, it's also an early example of John Ford's work before he became the premier director of westerns, and, as such, is of some cinematic interest. RK

Edmund Lowe *Louis Beretti* • Catherine Dale Owen *Joan Sheldon* • Lee Tracy *Bill O'Brien* • Marguerite Churchill *Rosa Beretti* • Warren Hymer *Big Shot* • William Harrigan *Good News Brophy* • Frank Albertson *Frank Sheldon* • Eddie Gribbon *Bugs* ■ *Dir* John Ford • *Scr* Dudley Nichols, from the novel *Louis Beretti* by Donald Henderson Clarke

Born Reckless ★

Crime drama 1937 · US · BW · 60mins

Racing driver Brian Donlevy becomes a cabbie, but finds the cab company under threat from ruthless racketeer Barton MacLane who wants to own it and turns nasty when he's thwarted. Donlevy joins forces with MacLane's moll (Rochelle Hudson) to collect evidence that will put the heavy behind bars. Directed by Malcolm St Clair, this crime drama is so pointless and feeble that it caused the *New York Times* critic to dismiss it as "a little cinematic starveling". RK

Rochelle Hudson *Sybil Roberts* • Brian Donlevy *Bob "Hurry" Kane* • Barton MacLane *Jim Barnes* • Robert Kent *Les Martin* • Harry Carey *Dad Martin* • Pauline Moore *Dorothy Collins* • Chick Chandler *Windy Bowman* • William Pawley *Mac* ■ *Dir* Malcolm St Clair • *Scr* John Patrick, Robert Ellis, Helen Logan, from a story by Jack Andrews

Born Reckless ★

Musical drama 1959 · US · BW · 79mins

The same title was used for an early John Ford failure about bootlegging, and again in 1937 for a programme-filler about taxi wars. This time around, it's used for a feeble musical with a western theme. The almost non-existent plot has luckless rodeo cowboy Jeff Richards taking to the road with his old-timer pal Arthur Hunnicutt and sexy blonde trick rider Mamie Van Doren. RK

Mamie Van Doren *Jackie Adams* • Jeff Richards *Kelly Cobb* • Arthur Hunnicutt *Cool Man* • Carol Ohmart *Liz* • Tom Duggan *Wilson* • Tex Williams • Don "Red" Barry [Donald Barry] *Oakie* • Nacho Galindo *Papa Gomez* ■ *Dir* Howard W Koch • *Scr* Richard Landau, from a story by Aubrey Schenck, Richard Landau

B

Born Romantic ★★★ 15

Romantic comedy
2000 · UK · Colour · 92mins

Writer/director David Kane returns to the territory of his debut feature *This Year's Love* with this enjoyable London-based romantic comedy. The setting is a salsa club, where 30-somethings Jane Horrocks, Olivia Williams and Catherine McCormack interact with Craig Ferguson, Jimi Mistry and David Morrissey. Cabbie Adrian Lester provides transport and some much-needed advice to these romantic no-hopers. There's whimsical humour rather than belly laughs, and good performances, but it's all a little over familiar. JB [video] DVD

Craig Ferguson *Frankie* • Ian Hart *Second cab driver* • Jane Horrocks *Mo* • Adrian Lester *Jimmy* • Catherine McCormack *Jocelyn* • Jimi Mistry *Eddie* • David Morrissey *Fergus* • Olivia Williams *Eleanor* ■ *Dir/Scr* David Kane

Born to Be Bad ★★ PG

Drama 1950 · US · BW · 89mins

Unfortunately for RKO, Joan Fontaine was put on this earth to be timid and twee on screen, if not in real life, and acting bad did not come easily. She fails to convince in this flat drama, playing an ambitious, callous woman who arrives in San Francisco determined to have it all her own way. Robert Ryan and Zachary Scott look unconvinced as the men caught up in her wiles. DP [video] DVD

Joan Fontaine *Christabel Caine* • Robert Ryan *Nick Bradley* • Zachary Scott *Curtis Carey* • Joan Leslie *Donna Foster* • Mel Ferrer *Gobby* • Harold Vermilyea *John Caine* • Virginia Farmer *Aunt Clara* ■ *Dir* Nicholas Ray • *Scr* Edith Sommer, Robert Soderberg, George Oppenheimer, Charles Schnee (adaptation), from the novel *All Kneeling* by Anne Parrish

Born to Be Wild ★★ U

Adventure 1995 · US · Colour · 94mins

Only the youngest viewers will fail to spot that animal star Katie is nothing more than a fur-covered collection of gears and wires in this simian reworking of *Free Willy*. It's a shame, as the story of a lonely kid who befriends a three-year-old gorilla in a behavioural study lab is actually quite entertaining, at least until it reaches the ponderous courtroom sequences. Wil Horneff interacts well with the animatronic ape, while Peter Boyle comes up with some deliciously hammed-up villainy. DP [video]

Wil Horneff *Rick Heller* • Helen Shaver *Margaret Heller* • John C McGinley *Max Carr* • Peter Boyle *Gus Charnley* • Jean Marie Barnwell *Lacey Carr* • Marvin J McIntyre *Bob the paramedic* • Gregory Itzin *Walter Mallinson* ■ *Dir* John Gray • *Scr* Paul Young, John Bunzel, from a story by Paul Young

Born to Boogie ★★★

Music documentary
1972 · UK · Colour · 75mins

Glam rock fans won't be able to resist this invaluable record of Marc Bolan and T Rex's concert at the Empire Pool, Wembley, on 18 March 1972. All the classic tracks are trotted out with pouting proficiency. There are also a couple of studio treats, as Elton John and director Ringo Starr jam along on versions of *Tutti-Frutti* and *Children of the Revolution*. Some may find the surreal interludes a touch self-indulgent, but they're hugely revealing of Bolan's view of both himself and his art. A memorable snapshot of the glam rock era in all its gaudy glory. DP [video] DVD

Dir Ringo Starr

Born to Dance ★★★ U

Musical 1936 · US · BW · 105mins

A vintage MGM musical, in which a young and lovable James Stewart croons (in his own inimitable voice) to Eleanor Powell – she of the mesmerising tap shoes. Stewart is especially amiable, but there's also talented support from loose-limbed Buddy Ebsen and lovely Virginia Bruce, and the fine Cole Porter score includes the classic *I've Got You under My Skin*. Those glossy MGM production values give a rare sheen to the proceedings and the black and white is positively luminous, making you care less about the extremely silly plot. TS

Eleanor Powell *Nora Paige* • James Stewart *Ted Barker* • Virginia Bruce *Lucy James* • Una Merkel *Jenny Saks* • Sid Silvers *Gunny Saks* • Frances Langford *Peppy Turner* • Raymond Walburn *Captain Dingby* • Alan Dinehart *McKay* ■ *Dir* Roy Del Ruth • *Scr* Jack McGowan, Sid Silvers, from a story by Jack McGowan, Sid Silvers, BG DeSylva • *Cinematographer* Ray June

Born to Ride ★★ PG

Second World War action adventure
1991 · US · Colour · 85mins

Mechanic John Stamos joins the army to help phase in the use of motorbikes, but he only succeeds in upsetting those in command. To make matters worse, both he and his superior (John Stockwell) fall for the commanding officer's daughter (Teri Polo). Stamos can't handle himself or his bike in this rather unappealing mix of romance and wartime adventure. TH. Contains swearing. [video]

John Stamos *Grady* • John Stockwell *Hassler* • Teri Polo *Beryl Ann* • Thom Mathews *Willis* • Dean Yacalis *Tony* • Salvator Xuereb *Levon* • Justin Lazard *Brooks* • Keith Cooke *Broadwater* ■ *Dir* Graham Baker • *Scr* Janice Hickey, Michael Patridge

Born to Win ★★ 15

Black comedy 1971 · US · Colour · 85mins

Robert De Niro appeared in more than ten movies before his real breakthrough parts in *Mean Streets* and *The Godfather Part II*. One of his early films, directed by Czech émigré Ivan Passer, this deals lightly with the New York drug scene. George Segal is the shaggy-haired ex-crimper who needs $100 a day to pay for his heroin habit, but can't even seem to rob a diner successfully. De Niro shows little star potential. AT DVD

George Segal *Jay Jay* • Karen Black *Parm* • Jay Fletcher *Billy Dynamite* • Hector Elizondo *The Geek* • Marcia Jean Kurtz *Marlene* • Robert De Niro *Danny* • Paula Prentiss *Veronica* • Sylvia Syms *Cashier* ■ *Dir* Ivan Passer • *Scr* David Scott Milton, Ivan Passer

Born Yesterday ★★★★★ U

Comedy 1950 · US · BW · 98mins

This is a wonderfully funny look at Washington corruption and the age-old battle between the sexes. As Billie Dawn, mistress to Broderick Crawford's junk trader-made-good, Judy Holliday affects a voice that could curdle cream and a persona that will melt your heart. It's a measure of her performance that she beat both Bette Davis (for *All About Eve*) and Gloria Swanson (for *Sunset Boulevard*) to the best actress Oscar. Garson Kanin's dialogue is acid on toast, and director George Cukor cleverly knows when to let the action play in splendid long takes; the gin rummy scene is cinematic perfection. As the nice guy, William Holden demonstrates the subtle charm that would make him a movie legend. TS [video] DVD

Judy Holliday *Billie Dawn* • Broderick Crawford *Harry Brock* • William Holden (2) *Paul Verrall* • Howard St John *Jim Devery* • Frank Otto *Eddie* • Larry Oliver *Norval Hedges* • Barbara Brown *Mrs Hedges* • Grandon Rhodes *Sanborn* ■ *Dir* George Cukor • *Scr* Albert Mannheimer, from the play by Garson Kanin • *Cinematographer* Joseph Walker

Born Yesterday ★★★ PG

Comedy 1993 · US · Colour · 96mins

If you can put George Cukor's original Oscar-winning charmer to the back of your mind, this makes for an amiable, easy-going journey. Melanie Griffith takes the Judy Holliday role of the sassy, deceptively smart girlfriend of rich businessman John Goodman. He wants her smartened up for Washington, so he hires jaded journalist Don Johnson. Johnson looks uncomfortable with light comedy, while Griffith lacks Holliday's razor-sharp comic timing. However, John Goodman is, as always, a delight. JF. Contains violence and swearing. [video]

Melanie Griffith *Billie Dawn* • John Goodman *Harry Brock* • Don Johnson *Paul Verrall* • Edward Herrmann *Ed Devery* • Max Perlich *JJ* • Michael Ensign *Philippe* • Benjamin C Bradlee *Secretary Duffee* ■ *Dir* Luis Mandoki • *Scr* Douglas McGrath, from the play by Garson Kanin

The Borrower ★★★ 18

Science-fiction horror thriller
1989 · US · Colour · 87mins

John McNaughton's follow-up to the hugely controversial *Henry: Portrait of a Serial Killer* finds him in more straightforward sci-fi horror territory. The story tracks an alien creature with a penchant for ripping the heads off unsuspecting humans and plonking them on his own neck. Rae Dawn Chong and Don Gordon are the puzzled detectives on its trail. McNaughton has some fun playing around with genre conventions and it offers enough scares to keep horror fans happy. JF. Contains swearing and sexual situations. [video]

Rae Dawn Chong *Diana Pierce* • Don Gordon *Charles Krieger* • Antonio Fargas *Julius Caesar Roosevelt* • Tom Towles *Bob Laney* • Neil Giuntoli *Scully* • Pam Gordon *Connie* • Mädchen Amick *Megan* • Larry Pennell *Captain Scarcelli* ■ *Dir* John McNaughton • *Scr* Sam Egan [Mason Nage], Richard Fire, from a story by Sam Egan [Mason Nage]

The Borrowers ★★★ U

Fantasy adventure
1997 · UK · Colour · 83mins

Mary Norton's charming children's stories about a diminutive family (the "Borrowers" of the title) are here turned into a delightful family film. Jim Broadbent is the head of the tiny brood while John Goodman is the unscrupulous full-sized lawyer who intends to demolish their home. Peter Hewitt directs this fun children's adventure, which features a host of British comedy talent, but it's the clever special effects that steal the show. JB [video] DVD

John Goodman *Ocious P Potter* • Jim Broadbent *Pod Clock* • Mark Williams *Exterminator Jeff* • Celia Imrie *Homily Clock* • Hugh Laurie *Officer Steady* • Ruby Wax *Town hall clerk* • Bradley Pierce *Pete Lender* • Flora Newbigin *Arietty Clock* ■ *Dir* Peter Hewitt • *Scr* Gavin Scott, John Kamps, from the novels by Mary Norton • *Special Effects* Digby Milner, Lyn Nicholson, Peter Chiang, Tim Field

Borsalino ★★★★ 15

Crime thriller 1970 · Fr/It · Colour · 119mins

Jean-Paul Belmondo and Alain Delon are in top serio-comic form as two small-time hoodlums breaking into the Marseille criminal underworld of the 1930s. The superb period detailing and Claude Bolling's hum-along score are additional delights in Jacques Deray's bloody gangster pastiche, which liberally borrows ideas from the work of Howard Hawks and Jean-Pierre Melville, among others. It's *The Public Enemy*, Gallic-style, with engaging tongue-in-cheek wit and a cheeky comic-strip atmosphere. AJ. In French with English subtitles. [video]

Jean-Paul Belmondo *Capella* • Alain Delon *Siffredi* • Michel Bouquet *Rinaldi* • Catherine Rouvel *Lola* • Françoise Christophe *Mme Escarguel* • Corinne Marchand *Mme Rinaldi* ■ *Dir* Jacques Deray • *Scr* Jean-Claude Carrière, Claude Sautet, Jacques Deray, Jean Cau, from the book *Bandits à Marseille* by Eugène Soccomare

Borsalino and Co ★★

Thriller 1974 · Fr/It/W Ger · Colour · 110mins

Gangster Alain Delon fights heroin addiction and his mob enemies for control of the criminal underworld in 1930s Marseille in a hackneyed rehash of the far superior *Borsalino*. While clearly taking pointers from *French Connection II*, it fails to do anything interesting with them. Despite the sleazy dockside glamour setting, director Jacques Deray's lazy sequel is for Delon completists only. AJ. French dialogue dubbed into English.

Alain Delon *Roch Siffredi* • Riccardo Cucciolla *Volpone* • Reinhardt Kolldehoff [Reinhard Kolldehoff] *Sam* • Lionel Vitrant *Lionel* • Catherine Rouvel *Lola* • Daniel Ivernel *Fanti* ■ *Dir* Jacques Deray • *Scr* Jacques Deray, Pascal Jardin

Le Bossu ★★ PG

Swashbuckling adventure
1959 · Fr/It · Colour · 101mins

This French swashbuckler stars Jean Marais as an adventurer who cares for a small girl when her nobleman father is murdered. As the dashing hero, Marais avenges his friend's death by infiltrating the enemy camp disguised as a hunchback. It's all a bit *Three Musketeers* – not surprising, since director André Hunebelle had already adapted the Dumas classic in 1953, while Marais played D'Artagnan in *Le Masque de Fer* (1962). AT. French dialogue dubbed into English. DVD

Jean Marais *Chevalier de Legardère* • André Bourvil [Bourvil] *Passepoil* • Sabina Selman [Sabina Sesselman] *Aurore de Nevers, Isabelle de Caylus* • Hubert Noël *Duc de Nevers* • François Chaumette *Gonzague* • Jean Le Poulain *Monsieur de Peyrolles* • Paulette Dubost *Dame Marthe* ■ *Dir* André Hunebelle • *Scr* Jean Halain, Pierre Foucaud, from the novel by Paul Féval

Le Bossu ★★★ 15

Swashbuckling adventure
1997 · Fr/It/Ger · Colour · 123mins

This most recent version of Paul Féval's classic adventure feels more like a serial than a seamless narrative. That said, this pacey and polished picture is never anything less than sabre-rattling entertainment. Although not known for action heroics, Daniel Auteuil emerges from this rousing romp with flying colours, as he hones his fencing skills and assumes the disguise of a hunchback to avenge the murder of Vincent Perez by scheming financier Fabrice Luchini. Director Philippe de Broca is a master swashbuckler, but his handling of Auteuil's romance with Marie Gillain is less assured. DP. In French with English subtitles. Contains some violence and swearing. [video] DVD

Daniel Auteuil *Lagardère/The Hunchback (Le Bossu)* • Fabrice Luchini *Gonzague* • Vincent Perez *Duc de Nevers* • Marie Gillain *Aurore* • Yann Colette *Peyrolles* • Jean-François Stévenin *Cocardasse* • Didier Pain *Passepoil* • Charles Nelson [Charlie Nelson] *Aesop* • Philippe Noiret *Philippe d'Orléans* ■ *Dir* Philippe de Broca • *Scr* Philippe de Broca, Jean Cosmos, Jérôme Tonnerre, from the novel by Paul Féval

B

Boston Kickout ★★★ 18

Black comedy 1995 · UK · Colour · 100mins

Youthful exuberance and an affectionate eye for suburban life help paper over the technical deficiencies of this oddball black comedy. John Simm plays a confused teen desperate to get out of his dead-end life, as his friends drift improbably into crime. It's a bit erratic but there are some nice lines, plus a memorably psychotic turn from Marc Warren (*The Vice, Game On*). JF. Contains swearing, violence and sex scenes. DVD

John Simm *Phil* • Emer McCourt *Shona* • Andrew Lincoln *Ted* • Nathan Valente *Matt* • Richard Hanson *Steve* • Marc Warren *Robert* • Derek Martin *Ray* ■ *Dir* Paul Hills • *Scr* Paul Hills, Diane Whitley, Roberto Troni, from a story by Paul Hills

The Boston Strangler ★★★★ 18

Biographical crime drama
1968 · US · Colour · 109mins

This is a suspenseful and often disturbing re-creation of the crimes, capture and psychoanalysis of Albert DeSalvo (played here by Tony Curtis), who confessed to being the notorious Boston Strangler, the killer of 13 women in the early 1960s. Director Richard Fleischer deftly captures the pensive atmosphere of a frightened city with a stark, documentary-style approach that makes good use of split-screen sequences. As an all-star line-up of lawmen tightens the net around the elusive maniac, Curtis proves beyond doubt he could act with a nuanced performance of considerable depth and power. AJ. Contains violence and nudity. DVD

Tony Curtis *Albert DeSalvo* • Henry Fonda *John S Bottomly* • George Kennedy *Phil Di Natale* • Mike Kellin *Julian Soshnick* • Hurd Hatfield *Terence Huntley* • Murray Hamilton *Frank McAfee* • Jeff Corey *John Asgeirsson* • Sally Kellerman *Dianne Cluny* ■ *Dir* Richard Fleischer • *Scr* Edward Anhalt, from the book by Gerold Frank • *Cinematographer* Richard H Kline

The Bostonians ★★ PG

Period drama 1984 · UK · Colour · 116mins

This Merchant Ivory production is adapted by Ruth Prawer Jhabvala from the Henry James novel. Vanessa Redgrave stars as the Bostonian suffragette who gets involved with a faith healer's daughter, while Christopher Reeve appears out of his depth as the cousin who falls for the girl. James is notoriously difficult to convey on film and this moves at a snail's pace. As a result, it's a tad dull, despite the loving attention paid to period detail. LH DVD

Christopher Reeve *Basil Ransome* • Vanessa Redgrave *Olive Chancellor* • Madeleine Potter *Verena Tarrant* • Jessica Tandy *Miss Birdseye* • Nancy Marchand *Mrs Burrage* • Wesley Addy *Dr Tarrant* • Barbara Bryne *Mrs Tarrant* • Linda Hunt *Dr Prance* ■ *Dir* James Ivory • *Scr* Ruth Prawer Jhabvala, from the novel by Henry James

Botany Bay ★★★

Adventure 1952 · US · Colour · 93mins

Alan Ladd is a medical student unjustly transported to Australia, and James Mason is the sadistic captain of the prison ship that takes him there. While Ladd and Mason square up to each other, Patricia Medina sets both their hearts fluttering. In the end, after some flogging, snogging and an outbreak of plague, they all arrive Down Under, where a tribe of savage Aborigines sort out the unresolved plotlines. Clark Gable and Charles Laughton put gloss on the dross. AT

Alan Ladd *Hugh Tallant* • James Mason *Capt Paul Gilbert* • Patricia Medina *Sally Munroe* • Cedric Hardwicke *Governor Phillips* • Murray Matheson *Rev Thynne* • Malcolm Lee Beggs *Nick Sabb* • Jonathan Harris *Tom Oakley* • Dorothy Patten *Mrs Nellie Garth* ■ *Dir* John Farrow • *Scr* Jonathan Latimer, from the novel by Charles Nordhoff , James Norman Hall

Bottle Rocket ★★★ 15

Comedy crime drama
1996 · US · Colour · 87mins

This agreeably eccentric comedy crime tells the story of a dopey trio (Luke and Owen Wilson, Robert Musgrave) who bewilderingly think they are cut out for a life in crime. Debuting Wes Anderson observes their bungling antics and personality disorders with obvious affection, while continually taking the episodic tale in unexpected directions. The leads deliver expertly judged performances and there's a nice cameo from James Caan. JF. Contains violence, swearing, a sex scene and brief nudity. DVD

Luke Wilson *Anthony Adams* • Robert Musgrave *Bob Mapplethorpe* • Owen C Wilson [Owen Wilson] *Dignan* • Lumi Cavazos *Inez* • James Caan *Mr Henry* • Andrew Wilson *Future Man* • Ned Dowd *Dr Nichols* • Shea Fowler *Grace* ■ *Dir* Wes Anderson • *Scr* Owen C Wilson, Wes Anderson

Bottoms Up ★★ U

Comedy 1959 · UK · BW · 88mins

Frank Muir, Denis Norden and Michael Pertwee collaborated on the script for this school-based comedy, which sought to cash in on the successful Jimmy Edwards *Whack-O!* TV series. Leslie Howard's brother Arthur again plays stooge to Jimmy's cane-wielding headmaster, as he tries to raise the profile of his academy by passing off his bookie's son as eastern royalty. The strong supporting cast makes a solid contribution to an otherwise hit-and-miss comedy. DP

Jimmy Edwards *Professor Jim Edwards* • Arthur Howard (2) *Oliver Pettigrew* • Martita Hunt *Lady Gore-Willoughby* • Sydney Tafler *Sid Biggs* • Raymond Huntley *Garrick Jones* • Reginald Beckwith *Bishop Wendover* • Vanda Hudson *Matron* • Richard Briers *Colbourne* • Melvyn Hayes *Cecil Biggs* ■ *Dir* Mario Zampi • *Scr* Michael Pertwee, with additional dialogue by Frank Muir, Denis Norden

Le Boucher ★★★★ 15

Psychological drama
1969 · Fr/It · Colour · 88mins

One of Claude Chabrol's most accomplished and celebrated films has the director returning to the provincial world of his first film *Le Beau Serge* a decade later. Chabrol's then wife, Stéphane Audran plays a village schoolteacher who gradually comes to realise that her new friend, a shy butcher (Jean Yanne), is the sex murderer the police are searching for. With certain nods to Chabrol's idol Alfred Hitchcock, the film is much more than a thriller – it's a sympathetic psychological study of sexual frustration. The two leads are superb, and the film is brilliantly shot by Jean Rabier, Chabrol's usual cinematographer. RB. In French with English subtitles. DVD

Stéphane Audran *Hélène* • Jean Yanne *Popaul* • Antonio Passalia *Angelo* • Mario Beccaria *Léon Hamel* • Pasquale Ferone *Père Cahrpy* • Roger Rudel *Police Inspector Grumbach* ■ *Dir/Scr* Claude Chabrol

Boudu, Saved from Drowning ★★★★ PG

Comedy 1932 · Fr · BW · 80mins

Jean Renoir's classic farce-cum-satire of bourgeois ways will seem familiar to anyone who has seen *Down and Out in Beverly Hills* – Hollywood's 1986 remake. Boudu, a particularly smelly and ill-natured tramp, is saved from suicide in the Seine by a nice, middle-class chap, who invites Boudu into his home. Once installed, the tramp shows his gratitude by wreaking havoc on the household. It's a neat idea, executed to fine comic effect by a master film-maker. PF. In French with English subtitles. DVD

Michel Simon *Boudu* • Charles Grandval *Monsieur Lestingois* • Marcella Hainia *Madame Lestingois* • Sévérine Lerczynska *Anne-Marie* • Jean Dasté *Student* • Max Dalban *Godin* • Jean Gehret *Vigour* • Jacques Becker *Poet on bench* ■ *Dir* Jean Renoir • *Scr* Jean Renoir, from the play by René Fauchois

The Boulangère de Monceau ★★★

Romantic drama 1962 · Fr · BW · 26mins

Rohmer worked as an influential critic and director for 12 years before announcing his "Six Moral Tales" – a series of similarly themed works of which this elegant short was the first. He promised that each story would deal "less with what people do, than with what is going on in their mind while they are doing it". The sextet view relationships from the male perspective – in this case a vague young man (Barbet Schroeder) who approaches one girl, then a second arranging a meeting with both on the same day. The series, with its intellectual intimacy, unifying structure and cool detachment, established his international reputation. BB. In French with English subtitles.

Barbet Schroeder • Claudine Soubrier • Michèle Girardon • Bertrand Tavernier • Fred Junck • Michel Mardore ■ *Dir/Scr* Eric Rohmer

Boulevard ★★ 18

Crime drama 1994 · US · Colour · 95mins

Despite a better-than-average cast, this still lands on the wrong side of the exploitation/gritty drama divide. Kari Wuhrer plays a young victim of domestic violence who heads to the city and drifts into the seamier side of life, despite the best attentions of prostitute Rae Dawn Chong. Lou Diamond Phillips is way over the top as a vicious pimp; Lance Henriksen also pops up as a tough but fair cop. Director Penelope Buitenhuis has a good eye for the mean streets, but loses the fight against the sleazier elements of the story. JF

Rae Dawn Chong *Ola* • Kari Wuhrer *Jennefer* • Joel Bissonnette *J-Rod* • Lance Henriksen *McClaren* • Lou Diamond Phillips *Hassan* • Judith Scott *Sheila* ■ *Dir* Penelope Buitenhuis • *Scr* Rae Dawn Chong

Boulevard Nights ★★ 18

Drama 1979 · US · Colour · 97mins

Despite wearing its social conscience blatantly on its sleeve, this story of two Mexican Americans in downtown Los Angeles is ultimately rather a bore. Danny De La Paz is compelling enough as the Chicano trying to extricate his brother Richard Yniguez from the clutches of the local gang and there's lots of hard-breathing atmosphere and rebel-with-a-cause angst. But director Michael Pressman never manages to raise much impetus or interest. TH

Richard Yniguez *Raymond Avila* • Danny De La Paz *Chuco Avila* • Marta DuBois *"Shady" Landeros* • James Victor *Gil Moreno* • Betty Carvalho *Mrs Avila* • Carmen Zapata *Mrs Landeros* • Gary Cervantes *"Big Happy"* • Victor Millan *Mr Landeros* ■ *Dir* Michael Pressman • *Scr* Desmond Nakano

Boulevard of Broken Dreams ★★

Drama 1988 · Aus · Colour · 95mins

Pino Amenta, best known for directing episodes of TV series such as *The Sullivans, The Flying Doctors* and cult hit *Farscape*, here directs a mediocre drama about a successful screenwriter (John Waters) who realises he has lost his soul and abandoned the dreams he had earlier in his career. This covers no new ground. JB

John Waters (3) *Tom Garfield* • Penelope Stewart *Helen Garfield* • Kim Gyngell *Ian McKenzie* • Nicki Paull *Suzy Daniels* • Andrew McFarlane *Jonathan Lovell* • Kevin Miles *Geoff Bormann* • Ross Thompson *Cameron Wright* ■ *Dir* Pino Amenta • *Scr* Frank Howson

Bounce ★★ 12

Romantic drama
2000 · US · Colour · 101mins

Ben Affleck is the brash advertising guy who gives up his seat on a plane to a man who wants to get home to his wife – only to hear the next morning that the plane crashed, killing all on board. Racked with guilt, Affleck takes refuge in the bottle and later seeks out the man's widow (Gwyneth Paltrow). Paltrow is moving as the bereaved young wife, while Affleck is well cast as the arrogant young lothario whose life almost falls apart, but this is slow in places and overly sentimental in others. JB. Contains swearing. DVD

Ben Affleck *Buddy Amaral* • Gwyneth Paltrow *Abby Janello* • Joe Morton *Jim Weller* • Natasha Henstridge *Mimi* • Tony Goldwyn *Greg Janello* • Johnny Galecki *Seth* • Alex D Linz *Scott Janello* ■ *Dir/Scr* Don Roos

Bound ★★★★ 18

Crime thriller 1996 · US · Colour · 104mins

This original and intensely black comedy thriller from Larry and Andy Wachowski stars Jennifer Tilly and Gina Gershon as lesbian lovers who, following a series of steamy liaisons, hatch a plan to steal a fortune from the Mob. Tilly and Gershon form a convincing *Thelma and Louise*-style team, who take their punches like men, while Joe Pantoliano, as Tilly's crooked boyfriend, is an able foil to their conniving. Visually dynamic and strong on gallows humour, this is further proof that the Wachowski brothers' subsequent success with *The Matrix* wasn't merely a flash in the pan. LH. Contains violence, swearing, sex scenes and nudity. DVD

Jennifer Tilly *Violet* • Gina Gershon *Corky* • Joe Pantoliano *Caesar* • John P Ryan *Mickey Malnato* • Christopher Meloni *Johnny Marconi* • Richard C Sarafian *Gino Marzzone* • Barry Kivel *Shelly* • Mary Mara *Bartender* ■ *Dir/Scr* Larry Wachowski, Andy Wachowski

Bound and Gagged: a Love Story ★★★ 18

Black comedy 1992 · US · Colour · 89mins

More a road movie than the love story the title suggests, this focuses on Ginger Lynn Allen, who escapes her thuggish husband by beginning an affair with another woman. However, this romance takes on a bizarre turn when her lover kidnaps her after Allen refuses to divorce her husband, and takes her on on a journey through the badlands of Minnesota. Strange and often funny stuff, capably directed, and featuring two strong lead performances from Allen and Elizabeth Saltarrelli. JB

Ginger Lynn Allen *Leslie* • Karen Black *Carla* • Chris Denton *Cliff* • Elizabeth Saltarrelli *Elizabeth* • Mary Ella Ross *Lida* • Chris Mulkey *Steve* ■ *Dir/Scr* Daniel B Appleby

Bound for Glory ★★★★ PG

Biographical drama
1976 · US · Colour · 142mins

This is a moving account of the folk singer Woody Guthrie, a real-life rebel who travelled through the Dust Bowl during the Depression years, singing and whingeing as he went along. David Carradine, who provides his own vocals, makes a credible Guthrie, while

U = SUITABLE FOR ALL Uc = SUITABLE FOR ALL, ESPECIALLY FOR YOUNG CHILDREN (VIDEO ONLY) PG = PARENTAL GUIDANCE

director Hal Ashby creates many a vivid composition lit by flashes of real insight. Guthrie influenced many of today's balladeers; watching this, it's not hard to see why. TH [video] DVD

David Carradine *Woody Guthrie* • Ronny Cox *Ozark Bule* • Melinda Dillon *Mary Guthrie* • Gail Strickland *Pauline* • John Lehne *Locke* • Ji-Tu Cumbuka *Slim Snedeger* • Randy Quaid *Luther Johnson* • Elizabeth Macey *Liz Johnson* ■ *Dir* Hal Ashby • *Scr* Robert Getchell, from Woody Guthrie's autobiography

Boundaries of the Heart ★★

Romantic drama
1988 · Aus · Colour · 105mins

This movie takes the small-town theme and runs with it to exhaustion point. Wendy Hughes is good as a manipulative man-eater, but John Hargreaves is a shade too vacuous in the chief supporting role. There is much rumour-mongering and townsfolk muttering behind their hands, which gives the movie an enclosed, claustrophic feel, but the story goes nowhere. SH. Contains some swearing.

Wendy Hughes *Stella Marsden* • John Hargreaves *Andy Ford* • Norman Kaye *WH (Billy) Marsden* • Michael Siberry *Arthur Pearson* • Julie Nihill *June Thompson* • Max Cullen *Blanco White* • John Clayton *Riley* • Vivienne Garrett *Freda* • Beverley Shaw *Millie* ■ *Dir* Lex Marinos • *Scr* Peter Yeldham

The Bounty ★★★★ 15

Historical drama
1984 · UK · Colour · 127mins

Unlike the Charles Laughton/Clark Gable and Trevor Howard/Marlon Brando versions of *The Mutiny on the Bounty*, this sticks closely to historical fact. Consequently, Lieutenant – as he was at the time of the mutiny – William Bligh emerges as a gentleman bound by duty and loyalty who expected nothing less of his crew, while Fletcher Christian comes across as a man driven by heartfelt but half-digested notions of liberty and romance. Mel Gibson, despite his efforts, is acted off the screen by the magnificent Anthony Hopkins, who holds together this intelligent film. DP [video] DVD

Mel Gibson *Fletcher Christian* • Anthony Hopkins *Lieutenant William Bligh* • Laurence Olivier *Admiral Hood* • Edward Fox *Captain Greetham* • Daniel Day-Lewis *John Fryer* • Bernard Hill *Cole* • John Sessions *Smith* • Philip Davis *Young* • Liam Neeson *Churchill* ■ *Dir* Roger Donaldson • *Scr* Robert Bolt, from the non-fiction book *Captain Bligh and Mr Christian* by Richard Hough

The Bounty Hunter ★★★ PG

Western 1954 · US · Colour · 75mins

A straightforward yet satisfying Randolph Scott western, in which the stone-faced one sets out after three marauding bank robbers, all of whom are in disguise as respectable townsfolk. These Andre De Toth directed horse operas were screened as co-features, often with a minor musical or thick-ear thriller (this one partnered the original *Dragnet* on its release), and provided satisfactory, value-for-money programming. TS [video]

Randolph Scott *Jim Kipp* • Dolores Dorn *Julie Spencer* • Marie Windsor *Alice* • Howard Petrie *Sheriff Brand* • Harry Antrim *Dr Spencer* • Robert Keys *George Williams* • Ernest Borgnine *Rachin* • Dub Taylor *Danvers* ■ *Dir* Andre De Toth • *Scr* Winston Miller, from a story by Winston Miller, Finlay McDermid

The Bounty Killer ★★

Western 1965 · US · Colour · 92mins

This B-western has Dan Duryea as an easterner who, by accident, becomes a vicious bounty hunter out west and only meets his match when a young bounty hunter (played by Duryea's son, Peter) appears to settle the score. The director, former stuntman Spencer G Bennet, was a veteran of sagebrush operas and serials such as *Superman* and *Batman and Robin*. For this effort, one of his last films, he gathered a nostalgic supporting cast. AT

Dan Duryea *Willie Duggan* • Audrey Dalton *Carole Ridgeway* • Fuzzy Knight *Luther* • Rod Cameron *Johnny Liam* • Richard Arlen *Ridgeway* • Buster Crabbe [Larry "Buster" Crabbe] *Mike Clayman* • Johnny Mack Brown *Sheriff Green* • Bob Steele *Red* ■ *Dir* Spencer G Bennet [Spencer Gordon Bennet] • *Scr* R Alexander, Leo Gordon

The Bourne Identity ★★★ 12

Spy action thriller
2002 · US/Cz Rep · Colour · 113mins

In this all-action espionage thriller, Matt Damon plays a man dragged out of the Mediterranean, barely alive and suffering from amnesia. The only clue to his identity is in a device found under his skin that contains the address of a Swiss bank. On his way to Zurich, Damon is chased by cops, shot at by assassins but, with no knowledge of who he is, has no idea why. The problem – and it's one that undermines the film despite some decent action heroics – is that we know precisely who Damon is (a top CIA assassin). We also know who the bad guys are and what they're up to, so any tension is lost. StH. Contains violence and swearing. [video] DVD

Matt Damon *Jason Bourne* • Franka Potente *Marie Kreutz* • Chris Cooper *Ted Conklin* • Clive Owen *The Professor* • Brian Cox *Ward Abbott* • Adewale Akinnuoye-Agbaje *Nykwana Wombosi* ■ *Dir* Doug Liman • *Scr* Tony Gilroy, William Blake Herron, from the novel by Robert Ludlum

The Bourne Supremacy ★★★★ 12

Spy action thriller
2004 · US/Ger · Colour · 104mins

British film-maker Paul Greengrass takes over the directing duties from Doug Liman for this sequel to *The Bourne Identity* and improves on the original. Two years after ex-CIA operative Matt Damon apparently escaped the attentions of his spymasters, a corrupt Russian businessman frames him for a double assassination, which drags Damon back into the murky world of international espionage. Greengrass uses his drama documentary background to good effect, delivering consistently exciting action without ever pushing the bounds of credibility. Damon impresses in a role that goes against his wholesome image, moving slickly and almost silently through the film like a small, angry black hole. AS. Contains violence, swearing. [video] DVD

Matt Damon *Jason Bourne* • Franka Potente *Marie Kreutz* • Brian Cox *Ward Abbott* • Julia Stiles *Nicolette* • Karl Urban *Kirill* • Gabriel Mann *Zorn* • Joan Allen *Agent Pamela Landy* • Marton Csokas *Jarda* • Tom Gallop *Tom Cronin* ■ *Dir* Paul Greengrass • *Scr* Tony Gilroy, from the novel by Robert Ludlum

The Bowery ★★★

Drama 1933 · US · BW · 94mins

Lovable Wallace Beery and child star Jackie Cooper had a huge public and critical success in *The Champ* (1931), and here they're reunited in a film based on some romantic legends of old New York. Tough guy George Raft is Steve Brodie, who (in)famously jumped off the Brooklyn Bridge in 1886 (an incident shown to dramatic effect here), while Beery plays his sparring partner in this fast-paced Raoul Walsh production, complete with colourful Bowery language and even more colourful Bowery characters. TS

Wallace Beery *Chuck Connors* • George Raft *Steve Brodie* • Jackie Cooper *Swipes McGurk* • Fay Wray *Lucy Calhoun* • Pert Kelton *Trixie Odbray* • George Walsh *John L Sullivan* • Oscar Apfel *Mr Herman* ■ *Dir* Raoul Walsh • *Scr* Howard Estabrook, James Gleason, from the novel *Chuck Connors* by Michael L Simmons, Bessie Ruth Solomon

The Bowery Boys Meet the Monsters ★★★

Comedy horror 1954 · US · BW · 65mins

In 1946 surviving members of the Dead End Kids, who'd come to prominence in films such as in *Angels with Dirty Faces*, became the Bowery Boys to conveyor-belt feed the nation's adolescents with juvenile slapstick comedies of which this was the most commercially successful. A monster spoof, in the vein of those perpetrated by Abbott and Costello, this has the Boys running foul of a family that makes the Addams clan look like something out of Enid Blyton. Although not particularly funny, it's directed by Edward Bernds at such a pace that boredom doesn't get a look in. RS

Leo Gorcey *Slip* • Huntz Hall *Sach* • Bernard Gorcey *Louie* • Lloyd Corrigan *Anton* • Ellen Corby *Amelia* • John Dehner *Derek* • Laura Mason *Francine* ■ *Dir* Edward Bernds • *Scr* Elwood Ullman, Edward Bernds

Bowery Champs ★★★

Comedy 1944 · US · BW · 61mins

This is one of the more amusing entries in the *East Side Kids* series, thanks to a super in-joke that has former *Dead End Kid* Bobby Jordan playing himself. The running gag is threaded throughout this daft tale of Muggs (Leo Gorcey) getting himself involved – yet again – in a murder hunt. Journeyman director William Beaudine keeps the pace up; he became a regular for the *Bowery Boys* series that subsequently grew out of this picture. TS

Leo Gorcey *Muggs* • Huntz Hall *Glimpy* • Billy Benedict *Skinny* • Jimmy Strand *Danny* • Bobby Jordan *Kid* • Bud Gorman *Shorty* • Anne Sterling *Jane* • Gabriel Dell *Jim* ■ *Dir* William Beaudine • *Scr* Earle Snell

Bowfinger ★★★★ 12

Comedy 1999 · US · Colour · 92mins

A bang-on-target satire of low-budget Hollywood film-making featuring Steve Martin's best comic performance since *Dirty Rotten Scoundrels*. He's an ambitious but financially challenged director who can't get A-list action star Eddie Murphy for his new sci-fi project. So he follows the actor around, setting up various silly scenarios and filming Murphy's shocked reactions. Martin – who also wrote the hilarious screenplay – is immensely engaging, and there's sparkling support from Murphy (in dual roles) and Heather Graham, as a talentless actress who's quite happy to sleep her way to a larger role. JC. Contains some swearing. [video] DVD

Steve Martin *Bowfinger* • Eddie Murphy *Kit Ramsey/Jeff Ramsey* • Heather Graham *Daisy* • Christine Baranski *Carol* • Jamie Kennedy *Dave* • Barry Newman *Kit's agent* • Adam Alexi-Malle *Afrim* • Terence Stamp *Terry Stricter* • Robert Downey Jr *Jerry Renfro* ■ *Dir* Frank Oz • *Scr* Steve Martin

Bowling for Columbine ★★★★★ 15

Documentary
2002 · US/Can/Ger · Colour · 114mins

In his 1989 debut *Roger & Me*, "people's film-maker" Michael Moore went after the CEO of General Motors. Here, his quest is much broader: what actually causes America's alarming gun-related annual death toll? Whether opening a bank account that comes with a free rifle or harassing retail giant K-Mart to persuade them to stop selling the type of bullets used at the 1999 Columbine school massacre, Moore leaves no stone unturned, addressing issues such as foreign policy, race, welfare and the post-11 September climate of fear. Shifting with surprising ease between humour and pathos, this is an important, outspoken film, if not an easy one to watch. Moore's confrontation with National Rifle Association president Charlton Heston proves especially uncomfortable, but, at a time when Moore could be branded "unpatriotic" for his views, here is a rousing film that urges you think about what patriotism really means. AC [video] DVD

Dir/Scr Michael Moore (2)

Box of Moonlight ★★★★ 15

Comedy 1996 · US · Colour · 106mins

Electrical engineer John Turturro lives by the clock, plays by the book and is as boring as hell, until the day he hears what his co-workers truly think of him and decides to go back to the lake where he spent his childhood. There he meets Sam Rockwell, a free spirit who lives in a dilapidated trailer and steals garden gnomes for a living. How his new companion's chaotic existence changes Turturro's attitudes is highly engaging, very affecting and always amusing. Beautifully shot and scripted, with director Tom DiCillo supplying a weird, yet welcome, atmosphere, this allegorical fairy tale is a box of sheer delights. AJ. Contains swearing, sexual references, violence. [video]

John Turturro *Al Fountain* • Sam Rockwell *Bucky, "Kid"* • Catherine Keener *Floatie Dupre* • Lisa Blount *Purlene Dupre* • Annie Corley *Deb Fountain* • Rica Martens *Doris* • Ray Aranha *Soapy* • Alexander Goodwin *Bobby Fountain* ■ *Dir/Scr* Tom DiCillo

Boxcar Bertha ★★★ 18

Biographical crime drama
1972 · US · Colour · 88mins

Director Martin Scorsese broke into the big time with this Roger Corman-produced bloodfest that clearly signalled he was a major film-maker in waiting. Based on the autobiography of Bertha Thompson, this is a good girl-gone-bad picture, with Barbara Hershey as the farmer's daughter driven to crime by misfortune and an uncaring system. There's the occasional bravura shot and some coal-black humour, but essentially Scorsese is bound too tightly by Corman's usual exploitation formula to have space for such luxuries as character development. Negligible in itself, but fascinating in its context. DP. Contains swearing, violence and nudity. [video] DVD

Barbara Hershey *Boxcar Bertha* • David Carradine *Big Bill Shelley* • Barry Primus *Rake Brown* • Bernie Casey *Von Morton* • John Carradine *H Buckram Sartoris* • Victor Argo *One of the McIvers* • David R Osterhout *One of the McIvers* • Michael Powell *Chicken Holleman* • Emeric Pressburger *Graham Pratt* ■ *Dir* Martin Scorsese • *Scr* Joyce H Corrington, John William Corrington, from characters in *Sister of the Road, the Autobiography of Boxcar Bertha Thompson* by Bertha Thompson, Dr Ben L Reitman

The Boxer ★★★ 15

Political drama
1997 · Ire/UK/US · Colour · 108mins

A knock-out performance by Daniel Day-Lewis embellishes this otherwise under-nourished tale that seems at times to be a polemic for the Irish Republican cause. He plays an IRA prisoner who returns to his former profession of boxing and establishes a gym, giving delinquents the chance to pummel their way to a better life. Directed and co-written by Jim Sheridan, it feels as sweatily authentic as the inside of a boxing glove, but the flatness of the narrative makes it seem rather dull. TH. Contains swearing and some violence. [video] DVD

Daniel Day-Lewis *Danny Flynn* • Emily Watson *Maggie* • Brian Cox *Joe Hamill* • Ken Stott *Ike Weir* • Gerard McSorley *Harry* • Eleanor Methven *Patsy* • Ciaran Fitzgerald *Liam* • David McBlain *Sean* ■ *Dir* Jim Sheridan • *Scr* Jim Sheridan, Terry George

B

Boxing Helena ★★ 18

Erotic thriller 1993 · US · Colour · 100mins

Infamous for provoking a feminist controversy and a lawsuit (Kim Basinger was sued for backing out of the lead role), the directorial debut of Jennifer Lynch is a fudged allegorical fantasy about aberrant human behaviour and sexual complexes. Sick surgeon Julian Sands falls in love with Sherilyn Fenn and, after she has a car accident, removes her legs and arms to keep her captive on a pedestal. By turns macabre and silly. AJ

Julian Sands *Dr Nick Cavanaugh* • Sherilyn Fenn *Helena* • Bill Paxton *Ray O'Malley* • Kurtwood Smith *Dr Alan Harrison* • Art Garfunkel *Dr Lawrence Augustine* • Betsy Clark *Anne Garrett* • Nicolette Scorsese *Fantasy lover/Nurse* • Meg Register *Marion Cavanaugh* ■ *Dir* Jennifer Lynch [Jennifer Chambers Lynch] • *Scr* Jennifer Chambers Lynch, from the story by Philippe Caland

A Boy, a Girl and a Bike ★★

Comedy drama 1949 · UK · BW · 91mins

A minor, good-natured British comedy romance that follows the adventures and love affairs of a Yorkshire cycling club. Future Avenger Honor Blackman is the girl whose affections are vied for by humble Patrick Holt and rich boy John McCallum, while Anthony Newley and Diana Dors play other members of the group. The cosy enterprise demonstrates why, with certain superior exceptions, the public preferred American films. RK

John McCallum *David Howarth* • Honor Blackman *Susie Bates* • Patrick Holt *Sam Walters* • Diana Dors *Ada Foster* • Maurice Denham *Bill Martin* • Leslie Dwyer *Steve Hall* • Anthony Newley *Charlie Ritchie* • Megs Jenkins *Nan Ritchie* • Thora Hird *Mrs Bates* ■ *Dir* Ralph Smart • *Scr* Ted Willis, from a story by Ralph Keene, John Sommerfield

A Boy and His Dog ★★★★ 15

Science-fiction black comedy 1975 · US · Colour · 86mins

Featuring a very early screen appearance by Don Johnson, this film remains one of his best. He's actually not particularly brilliant in it as he is upstaged by his canine co-star, but this offbeat sci-fi black comedy has deservedly become a cult favourite. Set in a post-apocalyptic world, the story follows the adventures of Johnson and his super intelligent dog when they get mixed up with a strange subterranean community, unable to reproduce sexually. Director LQ Jones (best known as a western character actor) works wonders with a tiny budget and maintains a pleasingly black tone throughout. JF DVD

Don Johnson *Vic* • Susanne Benton *Quilla June* • Jason Robards Jr [Jason Robards] *Mr Craddock* • Alvy Moore *Dr Moore* • Helene Winston *Mez* • Charles McGraw *Preacher* • Hal Baylor *Michael* • Ron Feinberg *Fellini* • Mike Rupert *Gary* ■ *Dir* LQ Jones • *Scr* LQ Jones, from the novella by Harlan Ellison

A Boy Called Hate ★★★ 15

Road movie 1995 · US · Colour · 93mins

Scott Caan makes his film debut alongside his more famous dad, James, in this intriguing road movie. Caan Jr plays a delinquent teenager who comes to the aid of would-be rape victim Missy Crider and ends up on the run from both the law and the girl's guardian. First-time director Mitch Marcus coaxes intense performances out of his two young leads, while Caan Sr and Elliott Gould add class and experience to the proceedings. JF. Contains swearing, violence and sex scenes.

Scott Caan *Steve "Hate" Bason* • Missy Crider *Cindy* • James Caan *Jim* • Elliott Gould *Richard* • Adam Beach *Billy Little Plume* ■ *Dir/Scr* Mitch Marcus

The Boy David Story ★★ PG

Documentary 2002 · UK · Colour · 99mins

This condensed update of journalist Desmond Wilcox's award-winning TV series about Scottish surgeon Ian Jackson's bid to reconstruct the disease-disfigured face of abandoned Peruvian baby David Lopez is a remarkable account of courage, compassion and medical ingenuity – as well as a scathing exposé of the bureaucratic iniquities inherent in the US immigration system. Having endured around 100 operations, David's determination to make his mark as an artist is truly inspirational, but Dougray Scott's narration is needlessly florid, and Christopher Gunning's score is riddled with pan pipe clichés. DP

Dougray Scott *Narrator* ■ *Dir* Alex McCall • *Scr* Desmond Wilcox, Alex McCall

Boy, Did I Get a Wrong Number ★ U

Comedy 1966 · US · Colour · 98mins

Not even an ageing Bob Hope can save this cheapskate, dumbed-down comedy, in which he plays an estate agent who becomes involved with sexy starlet Elke Sommer after she runs away from the set of her latest film. It's hard to believe that director George Marshall is the same man who directed such classics as *The Blue Dahlia* and *Destry Rides Again*. TH

Bob Hope *Tom Meade* • Elke Sommer *Didi* • Phyllis Diller *Lily* • Cesare Danova *Pepe* • Marjorie Lord *Martha Meade* • Kelly Thordsen *Schwartz* • Benny Baker *Regan* • Terry Burnham *Doris Meade* ■ *Dir* George Marshall • *Scr* Burt Syler, Albert E Lewin, George Kennett, from a story by George Beck

Boy Eats Girl ★★★

Horror comedy 2005 · Ire · Colour

Director Stephen Bradley's witty Irish zombie comedy has lovelorn David Leon accidentally hanging himself after spying Samantha Mumba supposedly making out with another schoolmate. He is brought back to life by his mother using an ancient voodoo ritual and infects the class bully, unleashing a horde of ravenous undead. But will he ever have the guts (or anybody else's) to tell Mumba his true feelings? Drawing good-natured strength from deliberate tongue-in-cheek cheesiness and B-movie cheapness, Bradley artfully builds to moments of pure horror hilarity. AJ

Samantha Mumba *Jessica* • David Leon *Nathan* • Deirdre O'Kane *Grace* • Mark Huberman *Samson* • Tadhg Murphy *Diggs* • Denis Conway *Craig* • Bryan Murray *Mr Frears* ■ *Dir* Stephen Bradley • *Scr* Derek Landy

The Boy Friend ★★★ U

Musical comedy 1971 · UK · Colour · 104mins

Indebted to the Warner Bros classic *42nd Street*, this is an energetic and invigorating adaptation of Sandy Wilson's stage success, in which the members of a provincial rep company discover their true selves in the process of putting on a show. A warm-hearted tribute to master choreographer Busby Berkeley, the film unsurprisingly lacks his inspiration. Yet Ken Russell makes a fair fist of the song and dance numbers, while Twiggy is ideally cast as the willing gofer who gets the chance to become a star when the lead (an uncredited Glenda Jackson) injures an ankle. DP

Twiggy *Polly Browne* • Christopher Gable *Tony Brockhurst* • Barbara Windsor *Hortense* • Moyra Fraser *Mme Dubonnet* • Bryan Pringle *Percy Parkhill* • Max Adrian *Max* • Catherine Willmer *Lady Brockhurst* • Vladek Sheybal *De Thrill* • Tommy Tune *Tommy* ■ *Dir* Ken Russell • *Scr* Ken Russell, from a play by Sandy Wilson

The Boy from Mercury ★★★★ PG

Drama 1996 · UK/Fr/Ire · Colour · 83mins

Martin Duffy made his debut as a writer/director with this semi-autobiographical tale set at the dawn of the space age. Paying homage to both 1950s sci-fi and 1960s kitchen sink drama, Duffy not only gets the fashions and furnishings right, but also re-creates the cinematic look of the period thanks to Seamus Deasy's ingeniously faded photography. James Hickey is magnificent as the eight-year-old who compensates for the loss of his dad by adopting Flash Gordon as his hero and claiming interstellar ancestry. Sean O'Flanagain is equally engaging as his bullied, cowboy-crazy pal, while there are expert cameos from Rita Tushingham and Tom Courtenay. All in all, a gem. DP

James Hickey *Harry* • Tom Courtenay *Uncle Tony* • Rita Tushingham *Harry's mother* • Hugh O'Conor *Paul* • Joanne Gerard *Sarah, Paul's girlfriend* • Sean O'Flanagain *Sean McCarthy* ■ *Dir/Scr* Martin Duffy

The Boy from Oklahoma ★★★ U

Western 1954 · US · Colour · 88mins

This pleasant film stars Roy Rogers Jr as a law student who becomes the peace-loving sheriff of Bluerock. Rogers Jr didn't have what it took to become a star, but a minor cowboy player in this movie did become one of America's most famous chat-show hosts: watch out for Merv Griffin in his early incarnation as an actor. TS

Will Rogers Jr *Tom Brewster* • Nancy Olson *Katie Brannigan* • Lon Chaney Jr *Crazy Charlie* • Anthony Caruso *Barney Turlock* • Wallace Ford *Wally Higgins* • Clem Bevans *Pop Pruty* • Merv Griffin *Steve* • Louis Jean Heydt *Paul Evans* ■ *Dir* Michael Curtiz • *Scr* Frank Davis, Winston Miller, from a story by Michael Fessier in *The Saturday Evening Post*

The Boy in Blue ★★ 15

Biographical sports drama 1986 · Can · Colour · 93mins

This Canadian curio is not the most compelling picture Nicolas Cage has ever been in. But a screen biography of Ned Hanlan, the Ontario-based ne'er-do-well who held the world speed sculling title towards the end of the last century, was never likely to be. Cage deserves some credit for involving us in Hanlan's struggles, but it's mostly dispiriting stuff and the rowing scenes are largely devoid of energy and tension. DP. Contains swearing and nudity.

Nicolas Cage *Ned* • Christopher Plummer *Knox* • Cynthia Dale *Margaret* • David Naughton *Bill* • Sean Sullivan *Walter* • Melody Anderson *Dulcie* • Walter Massey *Mayor* ■ *Dir* Charles Jarrott • *Scr* Douglas Bowie, from an original idea by John Trent

The Boy in the Plastic Bubble ★★★ 12

Drama based on a true story 1976 · US · Colour · 93mins

This teleplay became part of another true-life tragedy when John Travolta's lover, Diana Hyland, who won an Emmy for her portrayal of his mother, died of cancer within a year of its release. The role of a teenager born with an acute immunity deficiency was a risk for Travolta, who was then cutting a dash in the sitcom *Welcome Back, Kotter*. But his combination of courage and vulnerability does him credit, while Randal Kleiser avoids undue schmaltz in depicting his relationship with neighbour Glynnis O'Connor. The film was spoofed in 2001's *Bubble Boy*. DP DVD

John Travolta *Tod Lubitch* • Glynnis O'Connor *Gina Biggs* • Robert Reed *Johnny Lubitch* • Diana Hyland *Mickey Lubitch* • Karen Morrow *Martha Biggs* • Ralph Bellamy *Dr Ernest Gunther* ■ *Dir* Randal Kleiser • *Scr* Douglas Day Stewart, from a story by Douglas Day Stewart, Joe Morgenstern

Boy Meets Girl ★★★

Screwball comedy 1938 · US · BW · 87mins

When you see the picture, you'll discover that the title isn't as corny at as it sounds, but ironic. For this is a frenetic screwball comedy with James Cagney and Pat O'Brien as screenwriters who take the strut out of an arrogant star (Dick Foran) by casting him opposite a scene-stealing infant. As always, Cagney's presence is highly combustible, even having exchanged a machine gun for a typewriter, and the direction by Lloyd Bacon (of *42nd Street* fame) is suitably breezy. Real-life radio announcer Ronald Reagan is played by... Ronald Reagan. AT

James Cagney *Robert Law* • Pat O'Brien *J Carlyle Benson* • Marie Wilson *Susie* • Ralph Bellamy *E Elliott Friday* • Dick Foran *Larry Toms* • Frank McHugh *Rosetti* • Bruce Lester *Rodney Bevan* • Ronald Reagan *Announcer* ■ *Dir* Lloyd Bacon • *Scr* Samuel Spewack, Bella Spewack, from their Broadway play

A Boy Named Charlie Brown ★★★ U

Animated musical comedy 1969 · US · Colour · 79mins

The first of four feature-length films starring Charles M Schulz's much-loved *Peanuts* gang finds the eternal no-hoper Charlie Brown filled with anxiety as he prepares for a national spelling competition and the opening day of baseball season. Director Bill Melendez, a veteran of the Disney and Warner Bros animation studios and countless animated commercials, puts his expertise to charming and imaginative effect, though the gentle antics and excruciatingly twee songs – Oscar-nominated at the time – have dated badly. AME

Peter Robbins *Charlie Brown* • Pamelyn Ferdin *Lucy Van Pelt* • Glenn Gilger *Linus Van Pelt* • Andy Pforsich *Schroeder* • Sally Dryer *Patty* • Anne Altieri *Violet* • Erin Sullivan *Sally* • Linda Mendelson *Frieda* ■ *Dir* Bill Melendez • *Scr* Charles M Shulz, from his comic strip *Peanuts*

Boy on a Dolphin ★ U

Adventure 1957 · US · Colour · 106mins

A dreary mismatch of the voluptuous Sophia Loren, in her first film for a Hollywood studio, with the ageing Alan Ladd, a last-minute replacement for Robert Mitchum. She's a Greek sponge diver, he's an American archaeologist, and the slight but protracted story is about the raising of a priceless statue from the bed of the Aegean. Loren towered over Ladd, so the island where filming took place was riddled with trenches to even up their heights. AE

Alan Ladd *Dr James Calder* • Sophia Loren *Phaedra* • Clifton Webb *Victor Parmalee* • Jorge Mistral *Rhif* • Laurence Naismith *Dr Hawkins* • Alexis Minotis *Government Man* • Piero Giagnoni *Niko* ■ *Dir* Jean Negulesco • *Scr* Ivan Moffat, Dwight Taylor, from the novel by David Divine

Boy Slaves ★★★

Drama 1938 · US · BW · 66mins

This drama about forced labour on the turpentine farms of the South during the Depression has the excellent Anne Shirley as a victim trapped by the system. In a largely unknown cast, teen-gang leader James McCallion and runaway Roger Daniel are standouts. This is harrowing stuff, melodramatic and preachy by turns, but credit should go to producer/director PJ Wolfson for managing to get it made at all. TS

Anne Shirley *Annie* • Roger Daniel *Jesse* • James McCallion *Tim* • Alan Baxter *Graff* • Johnny Fitzgerald *Knuckles* • Walter Ward *Miser* • Charles Powers *Lollie* • Walter Tetley *Pee Wee* ■ *Dir* PJ Wolfson • *Scr* Albert Bein, Ben Orkow, from a story by Albert Bein

The Boy Who Caught a Crook ★★U

Crime adventure 1961 · US · BW · 72mins

Having debuted in *A Dog's Best Friend*, Roger Mobley was joined by another canine companion in his second feature. He's also accompanied by a genial hobo, which is just as well as the excitable newsboy spends much of the action being menaced by a villain desperate to recover a briefcase containing $100,000 in stolen loot. With some 50 B-movies to his credit, director Edward L Cahn knows exactly which buttons to push. DP

Wanda Hendrix *Laura* • Roger Mobley *Kid* • Don Beddoe *Colonel* • Richard Crane *Connors* • Johnny Seven *Rocky Kent* • Robert J Stevenson *Sergeant* • William Walker *Keeper* • Henry Hunter *Flannigan* ■ *Dir* Edward L Cahn • *Scr* Nathan Juran

The Boy Who Could Fly ★★★PG

Fantasy drama 1986 · US · Colour · 103mins

With a touch more imagination and a little less saccharin, this could have been one of the best family films of the 1980s, but writer/director Nick Castle couldn't resist the flights of fancy that hijack the action. It's a touching tale about an autistic boy, whose attempts to fly from the roof of his house attract the attention of a girl who has moved to the neighbourhood after her father's suicide. Jay Underwood and Lucy Deakins are splendid as the teenage friends, while Bonnie Bedelia and Colleen Dewhurst provide sympathetic support. DP [video]

Lucy Deakins *Milly Michaelson* • Jay Underwood *Eric Gibb* • Bonnie Bedelia *Charlene Michaelson* • Fred Savage *Louis Michaelson* • Colleen Dewhurst *Mrs Sherman* • Fred Gwynne *Uncle Hugo* • Mindy Cohen *Geneva* • Janet MacLachlan *Mrs D'Gregario* ■ *Dir/Scr* Nick Castle

The Boy Who Cried Bitch ★★★

Psychological drama
1991 · US · Colour · 101mins

Disturbed adolescent Harley Cross is expelled from prep school, and ends up in a psychiatric hospital where he threatens his room-mate, torches the hallway and has convulsions in the classroom. Eventually his mother brings him home, where he leads his brothers astray and threatens her with a gun. Argentine director Juan José Campanella builds up an all-too believable scenario in his desire to show what Charles Manson, and other similar mass murderers, were probably like as children. AJ

Harley Cross *Dan Love* • Karen Young *Candice Love* • Jesse Bradford *Mike Love* • JD Daniels *Nick Love* • Gene Canfield *Jim Cutler* • Moira Kelly *Jessica* • Adrien Brody *Eddy* • Dennis Boutsikaris *Orin Fell* ■ *Dir* Juan José Campanella • *Scr* Catherine May Levin

The Boy Who Had Everything ★18

Drama 1984 · Aus · Colour · 90mins

Chariots of Fire meets *Oedipus Rex* in this inconsequential tale of overachieving college student Jason Connery. He's caught between his mother (Diane Cilento, his real mother), a blonde girlfriend and loyalty to a private school where sadistic humiliation rites are the norm, despite his athletic ability. Awkwardly acted and preciously directed, Stephen Wallace's old-fashioned melodrama has little to say about relationships and growing up. AJ [video]

Jason Connery *John* • Diane Cilento *Mother* • Laura Williams *Robin* • Lewis Fitz-Gerald *Vandervelt* • Ian Gilmour *Pollock* • Nique Needles *Cummerford* • Michael Gow *Kaplin* ■ *Dir/Scr* Stephen Wallace

The Boy Who Stole a Million ★U

Comedy 1960 · UK · BW · 84mins

Co-written by director Charles Crichton and one-time documentarist John Eldridge, the story of a Spanish boy who steals from a bank to help his impoverished family is supposed to be gnawingly realistic. However, not even the drab photography or the run-down locations can increase the authenticity of the protracted pursuit by some sniffy bank officials and a gang of sneaky criminals. A cloying and unconvincing disappointment. DP

Virgilio Texera [Virgilio Teixeira] *Miguel* • Maurice Reyna *Paco* • Marianne Benet *Maria* • Harold Kasket *Luis* • George Coulouris *Bank manager* • Bill Nagy *Police chief* • Warren Mitchell *Pedro* • Tutte Lemkow *Mateo* ■ *Dir* Charles Crichton • *Scr* Charles Crichton, John Eldridge, from a story by Neils West Larsen, Antonio de Leon

The Boy Who Turned Yellow ★★

Science-fiction fantasy
1972 · UK · Colour · 55mins

It is a film-making tragedy that, after 1960's *Peeping Tom*, director Michael Powell's reputation took a nose dive. This peculiar little film, which was the final teaming of Powell with longtime collaborator Emeric Pressburger, sadly did nothing to resurrect his career. Here, schoolboy Mark Dightman takes a trip to the Tower of London and loses his pet mouse. Sent home from school later for falling asleep in a class on electricity, he dreams (or does he?) that the people on the tube and in the street have turned yellow. LH

Mark Dightman *John* • Robert Eddison *Nick* • Helen Weir *Mrs Saunders* • Brian Worth *Mr Saunders* • Esmond Knight *Doctor* • Laurence Carter *Schoolteacher* • Patrick McAlinney *Supreme Beefeater* ■ *Dir* Michael Powell • *Scr* Emeric Pressburger

The Boy with Green Hair ★★★U

Fantasy drama 1948 · US · Colour · 82mins

One of the last pictures studio chief Dore Schary made at RKO, this somewhat clumsy mix of whimsy and allegory marked the Hollywood feature debut of director Joseph Losey. Howard Hughes ordered wholesale changes to the film when he bought the studio, but the tolerance theme that he detested so much remained largely intact. Dean Stockwell does well as the orphan whose hair changes colour, and there's some expert support. Most notable, however, are the splendid against-type performances of Robert Ryan and Pat O'Brien. DP

Robert Ryan *Dr Evans* • Dean Stockwell *Peter* • Pat O'Brien *Gramp* • Barbara Hale *Miss Brand* • Richard Lyon *Michael* • Walter Catlett *"The King"* • Samuel S Hinds *Dr Knudson* • Regis Toomey *Mr Davis* ■ *Dir* Joseph Losey • *Scr* Ben Barzman, Alfred Lewis Levitt, from a story by Betsy Beaton

Boycott ★★★★PG

Historical drama
2001 · US · Colour and BW · 108mins

Biopics by American cable network HBO are generally of a high standard and this is no exception, re-creating with intelligence and clarity the 1955 boycott of Alabama buses by its segregated black population. An excellent Jeffrey Wright is perfectly cast as Martin Luther King, whose fearless and committed involvement – in the face of death threats and police corruption – was crucial in the development of the modern civil rights movement. Time and place are wonderfully evoked and the variety of film stocks and cinematic techniques used, including direct addresses to camera by Alabama citizens, heightens, rather than deflects, the drama. A stirring movie that never strays into sentimentality. JC [video] DVD

Jeffrey Wright *Martin Luther King Jr* • Terrence Howard *Ralph Abernathy* • CCH Pounder *Jo Ann Robinson* • Carmen Ejogo *Coretta King* • Reg E Cathey *ED Nixon* ■ *Dir* Clark Johnson • *Scr* Herman Daniel Farrell Iii, Timothy J Sexton, from the non-fiction book *Daybreak of Freedom* by Stewart Burns

The Boyfriend School ★★15

Romantic comedy
1990 · US · Colour · 97mins

Steve Guttenberg is a cartoonist with Hodgkin's disease whose recent dose of chemotherapy has left him bald, bloated and with little hope of finding a girlfriend. So his sister (Shelley Long) decides to help by transforming him into a grizzled Kiwi biker. Soon Guttenberg is being pursued by Jami Gertz, a girl attracted to the wrong sort of guy. Clumsy. Released on video in the UK under the title *Don't Tell Her It's Me*. DF [video]

Shelley Long *Lizzie Potts* • Steve Guttenberg *Gus Kubicek* • Jami Gertz *Emily Pear* • Kyle MacLachlan *Trout* • Kevin Scannell *Mitchell Potts* • Mädchen Amick *Mandy* ■ *Dir* Malcolm Mowbray • *Scr* Sarah Bird, from her novel

Boyfriends ★★★18

Drama 1996 · UK · Colour · 81mins

Co-directors Neil Hunter and Tom Hunsinger's promising feature debut shows consummate skill in getting under the skin of homosexual neuroses, as it follows the exploits of three troubled gay couples on a country weekend. A shining example of British low-budget film-making, this accurately scrutinises gay sex and love in the 1990s. AJ. Contains swearing, sex scenes, nudity. [video] DVD

James Dreyfus *Paul* • Mark Sands *Ben* • Andrew Ableson *Owen* • Michael Urwin *Matt* • David Coffey *Will* • Darren Petrucci *Adam* • Michael McGrath *James* • Russell Higgs *Mark* ■ *Dir/Scr* Neil Hunter, Tom Hunsinger

The Boys ★★

Courtroom drama 1961 · UK · BW · 123mins

This badly dated courtroom drama from Sidney J Furie proves that some things never change – Jess Conrad, Dudley Sutton and their pals are suspected of murder simply because they're young and rebellious. The film becomes both patronising and predictable as canny lawyer Richard Todd champions the lads' cause, but the strong cast redeems the movie. DP

Richard Todd *Victor Webster* • Robert Morley *Lewis Montgomery* • Felix Aylmer *Judge* • Dudley Sutton *Stan Coulter* • Ronald Lacey *Billy Herne* • Tony Garnett *Ginger Thompson* • Jess Conrad *Barney Lee* • Wilfred Bramble [Wilfrid Brambell] *Robert Brewer* • Wensley Pithey *Mr Coulter* ■ *Dir* Sidney J Furie • *Scr* Stuart Douglas

The Boys ★★★PG

Black comedy 1991 · US · Colour · 90mins

Based on the careers of William Link and Richard Levinson, this is a film *à clef*, in other words a biopic with the names changed to allow a little dramatic latitude. Link and Levinson were the writing duo behind such TV hits as *Columbo* and *Murder, She Wrote*, until the latter died from cancer contracted from inhaling the former's cigarette smoke. Written by Link, the film is directed without mawkishness by Glenn Jordan. It's the inspired teaming of James Woods and John Lithgow, however, that lifts this TV movie a notch above the pack. DP [video]

James Woods *Walter Farmer* • John Lithgow *Artie Margulies* • Joanna Gleason *Marie Margulies* • Eve Gordon *Amanda Freeman* • Alan Rosenberg *Psychiatrist* • Rosemary Dunsmore *Helene Farmer* ■ *Dir* Glenn Jordan • *Scr* William Link

Boys ★★15

Romantic drama 1995 · US · Colour · 82mins

A flimsy but watchable teen drama with Lukas Haas as the boarding school boy whose friends discover sexy and mysterious Winona Ryder unconscious in a field. He decides to smuggle her back to his dormitory. Unfortunately, the unravelling secrets of her past aren't quite as thrilling as one would hope for. But both Haas and Ryder give good turns, and there are nice supporting performances from John C Reilly, Skeet Ulrich and Chris Cooper. JB. Contains some swearing, drug use, and mild violence and sexual references. [video] DVD

Winona Ryder *Patty Vare* • Lukas Haas *John Baker Jr* • Skeet Ulrich *Bud Valentine* • John C Reilly *Officer Kellogg Curry* • Bill Sage *Officer Bill Martone* • Matt Malloy *Bartender* • Wiley Wiggins *John Phillips* • Russell Young *John Van Slieder* • Marty McDonough *Teacher* • Charlie Hofheimer *John Cooke* • James LeGros *Fenton Ray* • Chris Cooper *Mr John Baker* ■ *Dir* Stacy Cochran • *Scr* Stacy Cochran, from the short story *Twenty Minutes* by James Salter

The Boys ★★★★18

Drama 1998 · Aus/UK · Colour · 81mins

This Australian-set drama is the bleak, disorientating flipside to *Neighbours*. David Wenham, just released from prison, returns to his suburban home, where he immediately begins to torment girlfriend Toni Collette, his sleazy weak-willed brothers, their girlfriends and even his long-suffering mother. Although confined largely to one set, director Rowan Woods sustains an almost suffocating air of menace, which is further heightened by dislocating flash-forwards to an unknown future crime. An almost unrecognisable Collette demonstrates once again her range, but the real star here is Wenham, who delivers frighteningly believable portrait of a monstrous sociopath. JF. Contains violence and swearing. [video] DVD

David Wenham *Brett Sprague* • Toni Collette *Michelle* • Lynette Curran *Sandra Sprague* • John Polson *Glenn Sprague* • Jeanette Cronin *Jackie* • Anthony Hayes *Stevie Sprague* • Anna Lise *Nola* • Pete Smith *George "Abo"* ■ *Dir* Rowan Woods • *Scr* Stephen Sewell, from the play by Gordon Graham

Boys and Girls ★12

Romantic comedy
2000 · US · Colour · 89mins

A miscast Claire Forlani (who's far too pretty to be this insecure) forms a close friendship with Freddie Prinze Jr (who's far too handsome to be a nerd), taking the entire movie to reach the obvious amorous conclusion. This patchwork quilt of clichés from other smarter, sassier movies, is not aided by the clumsy episodic structure and grating, one-dimensional characters. Even the pop soundtrack fails to sparkle. JC DVD

Freddie Prinze Jr *Ryan* • Claire Forlani *Jennifer* • Jason Biggs *Hunter* • Heather Donahue *Megan* • Amanda Detmer *Amy* • Alyson Hannigan *Betty* ■ *Dir* Robert Iscove • *Scr* The Drews [Andrew Lowery, Andrew Miller]

B

The Boys Club ★★★ 15

Thriller 1996 · Can · Colour · 87mins

This disturbing crime drama also offers a well-deserved lead role for Chris Penn. He plays a mysterious stranger with a bullet in his leg who is found sheltering in a deserted shack used by three disaffected teenagers. Penn claims to be a cop on the run from corrupt colleagues and the three boys immediately warm to his bluff charm and macho wisdom. But is he who he says he is? It's a dark coming-of-age fable, and all the more chilling for it. As good as Penn is, he is actually eclipsed by the talented young supporting cast. JF

Chris Penn *Luke* • Dominic Zamprogna *Kyle* • Stuart Stone *Brad* • Devon Sawa *Eric* • Amy Stewart *Megan* • Jarred Blancard *Jake* • Nicholas Campbell *Kyle's dad* ■ *Dir* John Fawcett • *Scr* Peter Wellington, from a story by Doug Smith

Boys Don't Cry ★★★ 18

Drama based on a true story 1999 · US · Colour · 113mins

The tragic true-life case history of Teena Brandon, a young girl from Nebraska who disguised herself as a man and was brutally raped and murdered in 1993, is compassionately brought to the screen by writer/director Kimberly Peirce. While Oscar-winner Hilary Swank gives a remarkable performance as the hero(ine), there's an exploitative sordidness to the enterprise that limits our sympathy. Not since *The Accused* has rape been shown so savagely on screen – though that's hardly a recommendation. NS DVD

Hilary Swank *Teena Brandon/Brandon Teena* • Peter Sarsgaard *John* • Chloë Sevigny *Lana* • Brendan Sexton III *Tom* • Alison Folland *Kate* • Alicia Goranson *Candace* • Matt McGrath *Lonny* • Rob Campbell *Brian* ■ *Dir* Kimberly Peirce • *Scr* Kimberly Peirce, Andy Bienen

The Boys from Brazil ★★★ 18

Thriller 1978 · US · Colour · 118mins

Ira Levin's ingenious novel about the cloning of Hitler's body tissue, producing identical little boys who would revive the Third Reich, is given the epic treatment by director Franklin J Schaffner. Masterminding the genetic engineering is the infamous Dr Mengele, played by Gregory Peck in a convincing departure from his usual good-guy roles. James Mason is his accomplice and Laurence Olivier is the Nazi hunter modelled on Simon Wiesenthal who tracks them down. More plausible now than it was in the late 1970s and still an accomplished, globe-trotting thriller. AT. Contains violence. DVD

Gregory Peck *Dr Josef Mengele* • Laurence Olivier *Ezra Lieberman* • James Mason *Eduard Seibert* • Lilli Palmer *Esther Lieberman* • Uta Hagen *Frieda Maloney* • Rosemary Harris *Herta Doring* • Jeremy Black *Bobby/Jack/Erich/Simon* • Steve Guttenberg *Barry Kohler* • John Rubinstein *David Bennett* • Michael Gough *Mr Harrington* • Bruno Ganz *Professor Bruckner* • Denholm Elliott *Sidney Beynon* • Prunella Scales *Mrs Harrington* ■ *Dir* Franklin J Schaffner • *Scr* Heywood Gould, from the novel by Ira Levin

The Boys from Syracuse ★★★ U

Musical comedy 1940 · US · BW · 73mins

Undercast (and in desperate need of colour), this jolly romp is the film of Rodgers and Hart's Broadway hit, itself based on Shakespeare's *Comedy of Errors*. Only Martha Raye and Joe Penner seem to capture the requisite Broadway brashness, and a wan Allan Jones in the lead looks uncomfortable and strained. Period comedians Charles Butterworth and Eric Blore have a camp old time mining the gags. TS

Allan Jones *Antipholus of Ephesus/Antipholus of Syracuse* • Martha Raye *Luce* • Joe Penner *Dromio of Ephesus/Dromio of Syracuse* • Rosemary Lane *Phyllis* • Charles Butterworth *Duke of Ephesus* • Irene Hervey *Adriana* • Alan Mowbray *Angelo* • Eric Blore *Pinch* • Samuel S Hinds *Aegon* ■ *Dir* Edward Sutherland [A Edward Sutherland] • *Scr* Leonard Spigelgass, Charles Grayson, from the play by George Abbott, with music and lyrics by Richard Rodgers, Lorenz Hart, from the play *Comedy of Errors* by William Shakespeare

The Boys in Blue ★ PG

Comedy 1983 · UK · Colour · 93mins

This is a serious contender for the unwanted title of worst British film ever made. Over 40 years after he helped adapt Sidney Gilliat's story for the Will Hay vehicle *Ask a Policeman*, director Val Guest returned to the scene of the crime for this shudderingly awful remake, with TV comedy duo Tommy Cannon and Bobby Ball as the bumpkin bobbies whose station is reprieved when a gang of villains moves into their manor. DP DVD

Bobby Ball *Police Constable Bobby Ball* • Tommy Cannon *Sergeant Tommy Cannon* • Suzanne Danielle *Kim* • Roy Kinnear *Hector Lloyd* • Eric Sykes *Chief Constable* • Jack Douglas *Chief Superintendent* • Edward Judd *Hilling* • Jon Pertwee *Coastguard* • Arthur English *Farmer* ■ *Dir* Val Guest • *Scr* Val Guest, from Sidney Gilliat's story for the film *Ask a Policeman*

Boys in Brown ★★★

Crime drama 1949 · UK · BW · 85mins

Former variety comedian Jack Warner brings quiet conviction to one of the avuncular roles that brought him film fame in the 1940s. This time he's the governor of a boys' reformatory who does his best to convert his charges to the straight and narrow. Based on a play by Reginald Beckwith, this is a taut tale with a gallery of fine players including Richard Attenborough, Barbara Murray and Thora Hird. The most unregenerate of the delinquents is played by Dirk Bogarde, who was to menace Warner again when he shot dead PC Dixon (Warner) in the classic thriller *The Blue Lamp*. TV

Jack Warner *Governor* • Richard Attenborough *Jackie Knowles* • Dirk Bogarde *Alfie Rawlins* • Jimmy Hanley *Bill Foster* • Barbara Murray *Kitty Hurst* • Patrick Holt *Tigson* • Andrew Crawford *Casey* • Thora Hird *Mrs Knowles* ■ *Dir* Montgomery Tully • *Scr* Montgomery Tully, from a play by Reginald Beckwith

The Boys in Company C ★★★

War drama 1978 · US/HK · Colour · 125mins

A Vietnam war drama financed in Hong Kong and designed as a quickie to cash in on the then-imminent release of *Apocalypse Now*. Following a bunch of raw recruits played by a largely unknown cast, the movie explores the ideas and moral terrain later refined by *Platoon*. But this tour of duty ends surprisingly with a soccer match between GIs and a Vietnamese team, effectively reducing the war to an absurdist symbol. AT

Stan Shaw *Tyrone Washington* • Andrew Stevens *Billy Ray Pike* • James Canning *Alvin Foster* • Michael Lembeck *Vinnie Fazio* • Craig Wasson *Dave Bisbee* • Scott Hylands *Captain Collins* • James Whitmore Jr *Lieutenant Archer* • Noble Willingham *Sergeant Curry* • Lee Ermey [R Lee Ermey] *Sergeant Loyce* ■ *Dir* Sidney J Furie • *Scr* Rick Natkin, Sidney J Furie

The Boys in the Band ★★★ 15

Comedy drama 1970 · US · Colour · 114mins

The first and most famous Hollywood film on the subject of male homosexuality, director William Friedkin's stagey version of the off-Broadway hit captures early glimmers of gay liberation while dealing with the self-hating, straight-acting and overly camp stereotypes of the era. Eight gay men gather for a Manhattan birthday party and a heterosexual visitor from the host's past turns up, adding vicious bitchiness to the awkward proceedings. It's all very dated, but some of the lines are still hilarious, while Leonard Frey's performance as the Jewish birthday boy is a kitsch classic. AJ

Kenneth Nelson *Michael* • Leonard Frey *Harold* • Frederick Combs *Donald* • Cliff Gorman *Emory* • Reuben Greene *Bernard* • Robert La Tourneaux *Cowboy* • Laurence Luckinbill *Hank* • Keith Prentice *Larry* • Peter White *Alan* ■ *Dir* William Friedkin • *Scr* Mart Crowley, from his play

The Boys Next Door ★★ 18

Crime drama 1985 · US · Colour · 86mins

Penelope Spheeris, best known for *Wayne's World*, directs this tough, grim drama about two 18-year-olds (played by Maxwell Caulfield and Charlie Sheen) who embark on a series of brutal murders for no apparent reason. Although a sometimes shocking look at teen violence, the film eventually seems too slick for its own good, and any message Spheeris may have been trying to get across is lost in a cacophony of flashiness and moody glares from the two leads. JB

Maxwell Caulfield *Roy Alston* • Charlie Sheen *Bo Richards* • Christopher McDonald *Woods* • Hank Garrett *Detective Ed Hanley* • Patti D'Arbanville *Angie* ■ *Dir* Penelope Spheeris • *Scr* Glen Morgan, James Wong

Boys' Night Out ★★

Comedy 1962 · US · Colour · 115mins

A bachelor and his three married friends decide to rent an apartment with a dishy blonde inside and use it, and her, for a week each. What they don't know is that the lady of the night is actually a sociology student doing her thesis on the American male, and she is singularly inimpressed with the men's ability to sustain a playboy lifestyle. This may be revealing of early 1960s sexual mores but falls absolutely flat as a comedy. Once Oscar Homolka appears as a sociologist spouting theories, it becomes singularly embarrassing. AT

Kim Novak *Cathy* • James Garner *Fred Williams* • Tony Randall *George Drayton* • Howard Duff *Doug Jackson* • Janet Blair *Marge Drayton* • Patti Page *Joanne McIllenny* • Jessie Royce Landis *Ethel Williams* • Oscar Homolka *D Prokosch* ■ *Dir* Michael Gordon • *Scr* Ira Wallach, Marion Hargrove (adaptation), from a story by Marvin Worth, Arne Sultan

The Boys of Paul Street ★★★ U

Comedy drama 1968 · US/Hun · Colour · 104mins

Previously filmed in Hollywood by Frank Borzage as *No Greater Glory* in 1934, this Oscar-nominated adaptation by Zoltan Fabri of Ferenc Molnar's autobiographical novel returned to its original Budapest locations. Although intended as an allegory on the futility of war, the feud between two rival gangs over an unclaimed patch of land also has a Party angle, as it's the benevolent forces of authority that eventually claim the lot for building work. The film still has the freshness that typified most Eastern European cinema in the mid-1960s. DP. A Hungarian/English language film.

Anthony Kemp *Nemecsek* • William Burleigh *Boka* • Julien Holdaway *Feriats* • Peter Delmar *Older Pasztor* • Andras Avar *Szabo* • Mari Torocsik *Nemecsek's mother* • Sandor Pecsi *Professor Racz* ■ *Dir* Zoltan Fabri • *Scr* Zoltan Fabri, Endre Bohém, from the novel *A Pal Utcai Fiuk* by Ferenc Molnar

Boys of the City ★★

Crime comedy 1940 · US · BW · 68mins

The first in the series featuring the East Side Kids, after they were the Dead End Kids and before they were the Bowery Boys, was typical of the films of the streetwise gang – whatever they were called. The crude farce (also known as *The Ghost Creeps*) has the lads, headed by Leo Gorcey and Bobby Jordan, sent to the country where they get involved with murder in a haunted house. The director Joseph H Lewis went on to make *film noir* classics such as 1949's *Gun Crazy*. RB

Bobby Jordan *Danny* • Leo Gorcey *Muggs* • Dave O'Brien *Knuckles Dolan* • George Humbert *Tony* • Hally Chester [Hal E Chester] *Boy* • Sunshine Morrison ["Sunshine Sammy" Morrison] *Morrison Scruno* ■ *Dir* Joseph H Lewis • *Scr* William Lively, from his story

Boys on the Beach ★★ 15

Comedy drama 1998 · Fr · Colour · 86mins

Djamel Bensalah's feature debut bursts with energy and flirts with realism, but has little sense of restraint or quality control. Arriving in Biarritz having won a video competition, a mixed race quartet of Parisian suburbanites discover there's more to life than gawping at babes. The film offers little beneath its surface nihilism, although Jamel Debbouze impresses as the only lad to learn from his experiences. DP. In French with English subtitles.

Jamel Debbouze *Youssef* • Julien Courbey *Mike* • Lorant Deutsch *Christophe* • Stéphane Soo Mongo *Stéphane* • Olivia Bonamy *Lydie* • Mariù Roversi *Christelle* • Julia Vaidis Bogard *Lea* ■ *Dir/Scr* Djamel Bensalah

Boys on the Side ★★★★ 15

Drama 1995 · US/Fr · Colour · 112mins

Starting out as a comfortable *Thelma and Louise* retread before settling down into harder-edged *Fried Green Tomatoes at the Whistle Stop Cafe* territory, director Herbert Ross's emotional rollercoaster ride has three crackerjack central performances oiling its unconventional fugitive tale. Lesbian Whoopi Goldberg, HIV-positive Mary-Louise Parker and pregnant Drew Barrymore head for California, but find themselves grounded in Arizona when Parker falls ill. It's a tender drama that's smart, sassy and really quite special, and when Roy Orbison's *You Got It* strikes up there won't be a dry eye in the house. AJ. Contains violence, swearing and brief nudity.

Whoopi Goldberg *Jane DeLuca* • Mary-Louise Parker *Robin Nickerson* • Drew Barrymore *Holly* • Matthew McConaughey *Abe Lincoln* • James Remar *Alex* • Billy Wirth *Nick* • Anita Gillette *Elaine* • Dennis Boutsikaris *Massarelli* • Estelle Parsons *Louise* • Amy Aquino *Anna* ■ *Dir* Herbert Ross • *Scr* Don Roos

Boys Town ★★★

Biographical drama 1938 · US · Sepia · 92mins

In this incredibly corny and manipulative tear-jerker Spencer Tracy plays Father Flanagan, a Nebraskan priest who wants to set up a sanctuary for society's lost causes, while Mickey Rooney is one of the juvenile delinquents he tries to save. When the picture opened, the real Father Flanagan complained about the studio gloss and how that had affected donations since people assumed his refuge was rolling in money. Mayer went on the radio saying, "Boys Town does need your money, so keep it coming, Americans!" Tracy won his second consecutive Oscar for this film and dedicated it to Flanagan. AT

Spencer Tracy *Father Edward Flanagan* • Mickey Rooney *Whitey Marsh* • Henry Hull *Dave Morris* • Leslie Fenton *Dan Farrow* • Addison Richards *Judge* • Edward Norris *Joe Marsh* • Gene Reynolds *Tony Ponessa* • Minor Watson *Bishop* ■ *Dir* Norman Taurog • *Scr* John Meehan, Dore Schary, from a story by Dore Schary, Eleanore Griffin

Boys Will Be Boys ★★★ U

Comedy 1935 · UK · BW · 72mins

Although Will Hay had included the "Fourth Form at St Michael's" sketch in his music-hall act since the early 1920s, this was the first time he donned the familiar mortar board, gown and pince-nez on the screen. He plays Dr Alec Smart, whose rogue's progress takes him from a prison classroom to the headmaster's study of that school for crooks, Narkover. The script is based on characters invented by JB Morton for the legendary "Beachcomber" newspaper column, and Hay retains the blend of bluster and dishonesty that makes his films irresistible. DP [video] DVD

Will Hay *Dr Alec Smart* • Gordon Harker *Faker Brown* • Claude Dampier *Theo P Finch* • Jimmy Hanley *Cyril Brown* • Davy Burnaby *Colonel Crableigh* • Norma Varden *Lady Korking* • Charles Farrell *Louis Brown* • Percy Walsh *Governor* ■ *Dir* William Beaudine • *Scr* Will Hay, Robert Edmunds, from the characters created by JB Morton

Boyz N the Hood ★★★★★ 15

Drama 1991 · US · Colour · 111mins

Alongside Quentin Tarantino's *Reservoir Dogs*, this was the most astonishing and hard-hitting directorial debut of the 1990s. John Singleton was a mere 23 when he wrote and directed this powerhouse picture about growing up black in inner-city America. Rougher and readier than Spike Lee on the same subject, Singleton largely avoids sermonising to present a brutally candid view of the realities of LA street life. Cuba Gooding Jr and co-stars Morris Chestnut and Ice Cube impress as the friends for whom the future looks uncertain (if not downright unlikely), while Larry (now Laurence) Fishburne is outstanding as Gooding's disciplinarian father. DP. Contains violence and swearing. [video] DVD

Larry Fishburne [Laurence Fishburne] *Furious Styles* • Ice Cube *Doughboy Baker* • Cuba Gooding Jr *Tre Styles* • Nia Long *Brandi* • Morris Chestnut *Ricky Baker* • Tyra Ferrell *Mrs Baker* • Angela Bassett *Reva Styles* • Redge Green *Chris* ■ *Dir/Scr* John Singleton

Braddock: Missing in Action III ★ 18

Action thriller 1988 · US · Colour · 98mins

Dispatching Colonel James Braddock to 1980s Vietnam to find both the wife he believed dead and the son he never knew he had, this is a sequel too far for Chuck Norris and his director brother Aaron. Not only is this gung-ho actioner morally dubious, but it's also exceedingly dull. DP [video]

Chuck Norris *Colonel James Braddock* • Roland Harrah III *Van Tan Cang* • Aki Aleong *General Quoc* • Miki Kim *Lin Tang Cang* • Yehuda Efroni *Reverend Polanski* • Ron Barker *Mik* ■ *Dir* Aaron Norris • *Scr* James Bruner, Chuck Norris, from the character created by Arthur Silver, Larry Levinson, Steve Bing

The Brady Bunch Movie ★★★ 12

Comedy 1995 · US · Colour · 84mins

In the 1990s, Hollywood studios desperately ransacked their old TV archives for cinema remakes, with very mixed results. This one is probably the most innovative of the lot, even if it doesn't always work. If anyone can't remember, the Brady bunch were a cute-as-pie American family suffering the mildest of 1970s domestic discord every week. And in this remake, the same applies, except that everyone else is now living in the 1990s. A cue, then, for loads of postmodernist laughs, expertly served up by a cast headed by Shelley Long and Gary Cole. JF. Contains some swearing. [video] DVD

Shelley Long *Carol Brady* • Gary Cole *Mike Brady* • Michael McKean *Mr Dittmeyer* • Christine Taylor *Marcia Brady* • Christopher Daniel Barnes *Greg Brady* • Jennifer Elise Cox *Jan Brady* • Paul Sutera *Peter Brady* • Olivia Hack *Cindy Brady* • Jesse Lee *Bobby Brady* • Henriette Mantel *Alice* ■ *Dir* Betty Thomas • *Scr* Laurice Elehwany, Rick Copp, Bonnie Turner, Terry Turner, from characters created by Sherwood Schwartz

The Brain ★★★ 12

Science fiction
1962 · W Ger/UK · BW · 83mins

Hammer Horror veteran Freddie Francis does a decent job directing this version of Curt Siodmak's *Donovan's Brain*. Peter Van Eyck is the scientist controlled by the power-crazed organ of a sadistic tycoon kept alive after a plane crash. More of a mystery than an all-stops-out horror, the moody tale has some eerie moments and is efficiently involving. A competent cast, including producer Raymond Stross's wife Anne Heywood, injects new life into a familiar story. AJ [video]

Anne Heywood *Anna* • Peter Van Eyck *Doctor Peter Corrie* • Cecil Parker *Stevenson* • Bernard Lee *Frank Shears* • Ellen Schwiers *Ella* • Maxine Audley *Marion* • Jeremy Spenser *Martin* • Ann Sears *Secretary* ■ *Dir* Freddie Francis • *Scr* Robert Stewart, Phil Macki, from the novel *Donovan's Brain* by Curt Siodmak

The Brain ★ PG

Comedy caper
1969 · Fr/US/It · Colour · 95mins

Despite sterling work by David Niven as a master criminal, this frenetic French comedy needs a brain transplant in the script department. Put in charge of security for the transportation of NATO's military funds – which he intends to snatch – Niven finds himself competing for the loot with two French rogues (Jean-Paul Belmondo and Bourvil) as well as with the Mafia. A mess, which not even Niven can save. TH. French dialogue dubbed into English. [video]

David Niven *The Brain* • Jean-Paul Belmondo *Arthur* • Bourvil *Anatole* • Eli Wallach *Scannapieco* • Silvia Monti *Sofia* • Fernand Valois *Bruno* • Raymond Gerome *Le Commanissaire* • Jacques Balutin *Pochet* ■ *Dir* Gérard Oury • *Scr* Gérard Oury, Marcel Julian, Daniele Thompson

Brain Damage ★★★★ 18

Horror comedy 1988 · US · Colour · 85mins

This outrageously gory and excessively violent fable is infused with the junk culture and trash aesthetic of cult director Frank Henenlotter's demented imagination. *The Muppet Show* meets *The Tingler* in this spaced-out gore joke about Elmer, the all-singing, all-dancing alien parasite, who injects a euphoric hallucinogenic fluid into his host, Rick Herbst, in return for donors it can suck brains from. The more Herbst gets addicted to Elmer's secretion, the more dangerous the risks he's prepared to take to satisfy his vicious pet's bloodlust. Quirky, inventive and completely offensive – some death scenes deliberately use pornographic imagery – this is a wickedly humorous slice of warped genius. AJ [video]

Rick Herbst *Brian* • Gordon MacDonald *Mike* • Jennifer Lowry *Barbara* • Theo Barnes *Morris Ackerman* • Lucille Saint-Peter *Martha Ackerman* • Vicki Darnell *Blonde in Hell Club* • Joe Gonzales *Guy in shower* • Bradlee Rhodes *Night watchman* • Don Henenlotter *Policeman* ■ *Dir/Scr* Frank Henenlotter

Brain Dead ★★★ 15

Psychological horror
1990 · US · Colour · 80mins

Neurologist Bill Pullman is blackmailed by business friend Bill Paxton into studying the case history of paranoid accountant-turned-serial killer Bud Cort in order to unlock the secrets in his mind. After brain surgery and shock therapy, however, Cort switches personalities with Pullman, turning director Adam Simon's enjoyably quirky *Twilight Zone* update into a crazed splatter romp. Dreams within dreams, nightmare flashbacks and terrifying visions keep the pace lively and interesting even if it is hard to follow exactly what's going on. AJ [video]

Bill Pullman *Rex Martin* • Bill Paxton *Jim Reston* • Bud Cort *Jack Halsey* • Patricia Charbonneau *Dana Martin* • Nicholas Pryor *Conklin/Ramsen* • George Kennedy *Vance* • Brian Brophy *Ellis* ■ *Dir* Adam Simon • *Scr* Charles Beaumont, Adam Simon, from a story by Charles Beaumont

Brain Donors ★ PG

Comedy 1992 · US · Colour · 76mins

Director Dennis Dugan's flat farce has the occasional flash of high-energy outrageousness, but little else to commend it. Shyster lawyer John Turturro and his two wacky assistants, Bob Nelson and Mel Smith, take over rich widow Nancy Marchand's ballet company, with suitably dire consequences. Dugan's laboured burlesque throws every tired gag into the frantic action hoping it hits the fan – sorry, screen. AJ [video]

John Turturro *Roland T Flakfizer* • Bob Nelson *Jacques* • Mel Smith *Rocco Melonchek* • Nancy Marchand *Lillian Oglethorpe* • John Savident *Lazlo* • George De La Pena *"The Great" Volare* • Spike Alexander *Alan* • Juli Donald *Lisa* • Teri Copley *Blonde* ■ *Dir* Dennis Dugan • *Scr* Pat Proft

The Brain Eaters ★★ PG

Science-fiction adventure
1958 · US · BW · 60mins

An uncredited adaptation of Robert Heinlein's landmark alien invasion novel *The Puppet Masters*, this routine B-movie exemplifies the atomic-era paranoia genre. Despite the laughable, hairy, neck-burrowing parasites and the stock scientist-versus-the-military scenario, director Bruno VeSota creates an imaginatively bleak atmosphere through tilted camera angles and crisp photography. Though no great shakes, this sci-fi adventure is only an hour long and *Star Trek* fanatics can see Leonard Nimoy in an early role. AJ [video] DVD

Edwin Nelson *Dr Kettering* • Joanna Lee *Alice* • Jody Fair *Elaine* • Alan Frost *Glenn* • Jack Hill *Senator Powers* • David Hughes (2) *Dr Wyler* • Robert Ball *Dan Walker* • Greigh Phillips *Sheriff* • Orville Sherman *Cameron* • Leonard Nimoy *Protector* ■ *Dir* Bruno VeSota • *Scr* Gordon Urquhart

The Brain from Planet Arous ★★ PG

Science fiction 1958 · US · BW · 70mins

An all-time camp schlock classic, with bad-movie icon John Agar an absolute hoot as the nuclear physicist possessed by a floating alien brain called Gor, in its first step towards Earth domination. Soon Agar is sporting silver contact lenses and setting model planes on fire with a glance, while his pet dog is taken over by Gor's rival for the final axe battle. Unsurprisingly, director Nathan Hertz changed his name to Nathan Juran later the same year. AJ [video] DVD

John Agar *Steve* • Joyce Meadows *Sally Fallon* • Robert Fuller *Dan* • Thomas Browne Henry *John Fallon* • Henry Travis *Colonel Grogley* • Ken Terrell *Colonel* • Tim Graham *Sheriff Paine* • E Leslie Thomas *General Brown* • Bill Giorgio *Russian* ■ *Dir* Nathan Hertz [Nathan Juran] • *Scr* Ray Buffum

The Brain Machine ★★ U

Crime thriller 1954 · UK · BW · 79mins

This British B-movie begins, promisingly, in sci-fi mode but soon lapses into routine thrillerdom. The machine of the title, known as an "electroencephalograph", is attached to an accident victim who may also be a psychopath. Despite its cheap production values and leaden acting, the picture has a trashy energy that can be enjoyed if you disengage your own brain. AT [video]

Patrick Barr *Dr Geoffrey Allen* • Elizabeth Allan *Dr Philippa Roberts* • Maxwell Reed *Frank Smith* • Russell Napier *Inspector Durham* • Gibb McLaughlin *Spencer Simon* • Edwin Richfield *Ryan* • Neil Hallett *Sergeant John Harris* • Vanda Godsell *Mae* • Bill Nagy *Charlie* ■ *Dir/Scr* Ken Hughes

Brain Smasher... a Love Story ★★ PG

Comedy action adventure
1993 · US · Colour · 84mins

In straight-to-video director Albert Pyun's mildly amusing action comedy, bouncer Andrew Dice Clay joins supermodel Teri Hatcher and her botanist sister to stop a sacred mystical lotus flower, which holds the key to unlimited power over matter, from falling into the hands of a suave band of Chinese ninja monks. Although described as Rambo, Superman and the Terminator all rolled into one, wild comedian Clay prefers one-liners to kick-boxing. AJ [video]

Andrew Dice Clay *Ed Malloy* • Teri Hatcher *Samantha Crain* • Deborah Van Valkenburgh • Yuji Okamoto • Brion James • Tim Thomerson • Charles Rocket ■ *Dir/Scr* Albert Pyun

The Brain That Wouldn't Die ★★

Horror thriller 1959 · US · BW · 81mins

After decapitating his fiancée Virginia Leith in a car crash, demented surgeon Jason Evers decides to transplant her still living head onto the body of a facially scarred stripper. But Leith wants to die and telepathically manipulates the giant pinhead mutant locked up in Evers's cupboard to go on the rampage. This rock-bottom fantasy exploitation pic reaches high levels of engaging absurdity through poverty-row production values and ludicrous, blood-soaked action. This appalling cheapie has nonetheless become a brainless cult classic. AJ

Jason Evers *Dr Bill Cortner* • Leslie Daniel *Kurt* • Paula Maurice *B-Girl* • Virginia Leith *Jan Compton* • Adele Lamont *Doris* • Bruce Brighton *Doctor* • Lola Mason *Donna Williams* • Audrey Devereau *Jeannie* ■ *Dir* Joseph Green • *Scr* Joseph Green, from a story by Rex Carlton, Joseph Green

Braindead ★★★★★ 18

Comedy horror 1992 · NZ · Colour · 99mins

New Zealand director Peter Jackson's horrendously funny gross-out shocker is a brilliant black comedy and the ultimate gore movie. Timothy Balme's mother gets bitten by a Sumatran "rat monkey" carrying a living-dead virus and turns into a rabid zombie with terrible table manners. Cue zombie sex, kung fu priests, reanimated spinal columns and half-eaten craniums, all building towards a final, gore-drenched massacre. Jackson's outrageously sick groundbreaker is a virtuoso *Grand Guignol* masterpiece. AJ. Contains sex scenes, violence, swearing. DVD

Timothy Balme *Lionel* • Diana Peñalver *Paquita* • Liz Moody *Mum* • Ian Watkin *Uncle Les* • Brenda Kendall *Nurse McTavish* • Stuart Devenie *Father McGruder* • Jed Brophy *Void* • Elizabeth Brimilcombe *Zombie mum* • Peter Jackson *Undertaker's assistant* ■ *Dir* Peter Jackson • *Scr* Peter Jackson, Stephen Sinclair, Francis Walsh

The Brainiacs.com ★★

Comedy 2000 · US · Colour · 94mins

This far-fetched comedy from director Blair Treu stars Michael Angarano as an entrepreneurial youngster who hatches an internet scam to help his widower father (Kevin Kilner), who's neglecting his family to run a struggling toy company. Dom DeLuise is good value as Kilner's grasping bank manager, but this is for unfussy children only. DP

Michael Angarano *Matt Tyler* • Kevin Kilner *David Tyler* • Kevin Jamal Woods *Danny* • Vanessa Zima *Kelly Tyler* • David Bickford *Walter* • Allen Lulu *Miles* • Florence Stanley *Grandma Tyler* • Dom DeLuise *Ivan Lucre* ■ *Dir* Blair Treu • *Scr* Jeff Phillips, from a story by Roger Mende, Kathleen Lohr, Jeff Phillips

Brainscan ★★★ 15

Science-fiction horror
1994 · Can/US/UK · Colour · 90mins

Misfit loner Edward Furlong sends off for the virtual reality game *Brainscan*, advertised as the ultimate in terror, only to wake up with memory loss and a severed foot in the refrigerator. Frank Langella is the cop on his trail. But will he believe the murder is really the work of the Trickster, a vile demon who represents the dark side of anybody playing the game? Despite some inferior special effects, this bleak and intense chiller effectively uses the virtual reality hook. AJ DVD

Edward Furlong *Michael Brower* • Frank Langella *Detective Hayden* • T Rider-Smith *Trickster* • Amy Hargreaves *Kimberly* • Jamie Marsh *Kyle* • Victor Ertmanis *Martin* • David Hemblen *Dr Fromberg* • Vlasta Vrana *Frank* ■ *Dir* John Flynn • *Scr* Andrew Kevin Walker, from a story by Brian Owens

Brainstorm ★★

Crime thriller 1965 · US · BW · 114mins

A 1960s directorial effort from portly actor William Conrad, who is best remembered as television cop Frank Cannon. Here Jeffrey Hunter plots to kill Dana Andrews, not because Andrews's acting is extremely dull and boring, but because Hunter's in love with the latter's wife, the beautiful Anne Francis. Meanwhile, wise Viveca Lindfors counsels from the wings. Hunter acquits himself well, but the film would have worked better with some judicious editing. TS

Jeff Hunter [Jeffrey Hunter] *James Grayam* • Anne Francis *Lorrie Benson* • Dana Andrews *Cort Benson* • Viveca Lindfors *Dr Elizabeth Larstadt* ■ *Dir* William Conrad • *Scr* Mann Rubin, from a story by Larry Marcus

Brainstorm ★★★★ 15

Science-fiction thriller
1983 · US · Colour · 101mins

In films today, such as *The Lawnmower Man* and *Strange Days*, it's called virtual reality. But when *2001: a Space Odyssey* special effects genius Douglas Trumbull directed this film (which turned out to be Natalie Wood's last), he termed it "telepathic engineering". Louise Fletcher (giving a standout performance) and Christopher Walken invent a headset enabling the wearer to experience the sensory recordings of others. Although flawed and naive, Trumbull's metaphysical odyssey is a technically dazzling triumph. AJ

Christopher Walken *Michael Brace* • Natalie Wood *Karen Brace* • Cliff Robertson *Alex Terson* • Louise Fletcher *Lillian Reynolds* • Donald Hotton *Landon Marks* • Joe Dorsey *Hal Abramson* • Darrell Larson *Security technician* ■ *Dir* Douglas Trumbull • *Scr* Robert Statzel, Phillip Frank Messina, from a story by Bruce Joel Rubin

Brainwaves ★★ 18

Science-fiction thriller
1982 · US · Colour · 76mins

This suffers from a low budget and some clumsy writing and direction. Suzanna Love plays a woman who regains consciousness after a coma only to discover that, thanks to some ground-breaking surgery, she has inherited the brainwaves of a murdered woman. There are some nifty moments but the main point of interest is the eclectic casting – as well as Vera Miles and Keir Dullea there is Tony Curtis in a ripe cameo as an improbable brain surgeon. JF

Keir Dullea *Julian Bedford* • Suzanna Love *Kaylie Bedford* • Vera Miles *Marian* • Percy Rodrigues *Dr Robinson* • Tony Curtis *Dr Clavius* • Paul Wilson [Paul Willson] *Dr Schroder* • Ryan Seitz *Danny Bedford* • Nicholas Love *Willy Meiser* ■ *Dir* Ulli Lommel • *Scr* Ulli Lommel, Suzanna Love

Bram Stoker's Dracula ★★★★ 18

Horror 1992 · US · Colour · 121mins

Eerie, romantic and operatic, this exquisitely mounted revamp of the undead legend is a supreme artistic achievement. Francis Ford Coppola's film is grandiose in visual approach and uses every cinematic trick – from the basic atmospheric lighting of the silent era to today's more sophisticated techniques – to accentuate the poetic sensuality of Stoker's chiller rather than the more exploitative blood-sucking elements. Keanu Reeves's acting may not be to everyone's taste, but, as the tired count who has overdosed on immortality, Gary Oldman's towering performance holds centre stage and burns itself into the memory. AJ. Contains violence, nudity. DVD

Gary Oldman *Dracula* • Winona Ryder *Mina Murray/Elisabeta* • Anthony Hopkins *Professor Abraham Van Helsing* • Keanu Reeves *Jonathan Harker* • Richard E Grant *Doctor Jack Seward* • Cary Elwes *Lord Arthur Holmwood* • Bill Campbell *Quincey P Morris* • Sadie Frost *Lucy Westenra* • Tom Waits *RM Renfield* ■ *Dir* Francis Ford Coppola • *Scr* James V Hart, from the novel by Bram Stoker • *Cinematographer* Michael Ballhaus

Bram Stoker's Legend of the Mummy ★★ 18

Horror 1998 · US · Colour · 96mins

A familiar cocktail of ancient curses and dusty bandages from B-movie veteran Jeffrey Obrow. When her father incurs the wrath of the reanimated Queen Tera, Amy Locane enlists the aid of retired tomb raider Louis Gossett Jr to return the Egyptian ruler to eternal rest. This blunt-edged chiller features the least believable mummy make-up in horror history. AJ. Contains swearing and nudity. DVD

Louis Gossett Jr *Corbeck* • Amy Locane *Margaret Trelawny* • Eric Lutes *Robert Wyatt* • Mark Lindsay Chapman *Daw* • Lloyd Bochner *Abel Trelawny* • Mary Jo Catlett *Mrs Grant* • Aubrey Morris *Dr Winchester* • Laura Otis *Lily* ■ *Dir* Jeffrey Obrow • *Scr* Jeffrey Obrow, Lars Hauglie, John Penney, from the novel *The Jewel of the Seven Stars* by Bram Stoker

Bram Stoker's Shadowbuilder ★ 18

Horror 1997 · US/Can · Colour · 96mins

A demon tries to open the gates of hell by sacrificing an innocent child during a solar eclipse. A renegade, chain-smoking priest must stop the ancient prophecy coming true in a silly, sexed-up shocker that has more to do with Jackie Collins than Bram Stoker. This is a death, darkness and blasphemy-fuelled wash-out. AJ. Contains some swearing, violence and nudity. DVD

Kevin Zegers *Chris Hatcher* • Tony Todd *Evert Covey* • Michael Rooker *Father Vassey* ■ *Dir* Jamie Dixon • *Scr* Michael Stokes, from the short story by Bram Stoker

The Bramble Bush ★★

Drama 1960 · US · Colour · 93mins

Richard Burton is ill at ease here as a New England doctor who returns to his Cape Cod home town and falls in love with his dying friend's wife. Adapted from a bestseller by Charles Mergendahl, it's a soap opera lacking in strong characters and situations, though corruption and adultery figure as prominently as ever. Barbara Rush and the great Jack Carson are suitably angst-ridden for the material, but Burton looks all at sea. TH

Richard Burton *Guy Montford* • Barbara Rush *Mar McFie* • Jack Carson *Bert Mosley* • Angie Dickinson *Fran* • James Dunn *Stew Schaeffer* • Henry Jones *Parker Welk* • Tom Drake *Larry McFie* • Frank Conroy *Dr Kelsey* ■ *Dir* Daniel Petrie • *Scr* Milton Sperling, Philip Yordan, from the novel by Charles Mergendahl

Branches of the Tree ★★

Drama 1990 · Fr/Ind · Colour · 120mins

Satyajit Ray's penultimate film as a director is anything but the work of a master. Mostly set in a single room, the film explores the relationship between a wealthy man who has a heart attack and his four sons, one of whom is mentally disturbed. As the declamatory speeches become longer and more turgid, each brother rejects his upbringing and the values of a bygone era. The overwrought acting is certainly off-putting, but it's Ray's theatrical staging that is so dismaying. DP. In Hindi with English subtitles.

Ajit Bannerjee *Ananda Majumdar* • Haradhan Bannerjee *Probodh* • Soumitra Chatterjee *Prashanto* • Dipankar Dey • Ranjit Mullick • Lily Chakravarty • Mamata Shankar ■ *Dir/Scr* Satyajit Ray • *Co-Producer* Gérard Depardieu

Branded ★★★

Western 1950 · US · Colour · 94mins

More psychological than most westerns – and the better for it – this lavish Paramount picture stars Alan Ladd as the gunman who is persuaded to impersonate the long-lost son of wealthy rancher Charles Bickford. Predictably, Ladd becomes sick of the deception when he comes under the warm and loving embrace of a family that includes Mona Freeman as the beautiful daughter. Putting director Rudolph Maté, previously an outstanding cinematographer, with one of Hollywood's finest practising cameramen, Charles Lang, results in a visually arresting western in glorious Technicolor, and Ladd shows what an under-rated actor he was. AE

Alan Ladd *Choya* • Mona Freeman *Ruth Lavery* • Charles Bickford *Mr Lavery* • Robert Keith (1) *Leffingwell* • Joseph Calleia *Rubriz* • Peter Hansen [Peter Hanson] *Tonio* • Selena Royle *Mrs Lavery* • Milburn Stone *Dawson* • Tom Tully *Ransome* ■ *Dir* Rudolph Maté • *Scr* Sydney Boehm, Cyril Hume, from the novel by Evan Evans

Branded to Kill ★★★★ 18

Thriller 1967 · Jpn · Colour · 87mins

Filming the year after the surreal crime comedy *Tokyo Drifter* and the uncompromising political drama *Elegy to Violence*, director Seijun Suzuki outdid himself with this astonishing blend of yakuza movie, *film noir* and *nouvelle vague*. The picture starts off in classic crime mode, with a ruthless hitman goaded by a *femme fatale* into a confrontation with his deadliest rival. As our hero begins to lose his grip, however, the tone changes completely and we are bombarded with a dizzying array of cinematic tricks. A puzzle that resists an easy solution, the film represents a controversial peak for the director's style. DP. In Japanese with English subtitles. Contains violence and nudity. DVD

Jo Shishido *Goro Hanada* • Mariko Ogawa *Mami Hanada* • Koji Nanbara *Number One Killer* • Mari Annu *Nakajo Misako* ■ *Dir* Seijun Suzuki • *Scr* Hachiro Guryu

Brandy for the Parson ★★ U

Comedy 1951 · UK · BW · 78mins

This comedy has a distinctly Ealing feel and a touch of realism about it. Director John Eldridge makes leisurely use of the coastal locations as holidaymakers James Donald and Jean Lodge become entangled with genial smuggler Kenneth More. A few more comic set pieces wouldn't have gone amiss, but this is still an amiable entertainment. DP

Kenneth More *Tony Rackman* • James Donald *Bill Harper* • Jean Lodge *Petronella Brand* • Frederick Piper *Customs Inspector* • Charles Hawtrey *George Crumb* • Michael Trubshawe *Redworth* • Alfie Bass *Dallyn* • Wilfred Caithness *Mr Minch* ■ *Dir* John Eldridge • *Scr* John Dighton, Walter Meade, from the novel by Geoffrey Household

Brannigan ★★★ 15

Crime drama 1975 · UK · Colour · 108mins

Richard Attenborough plays the Scotland Yard police officer whose job it is to make sure visiting American cop John Wayne plays things by the book. It's essentially a western transported to London, with red double-deckers instead of stagecoaches and hangovers from swinging London. It is also a blatant rip-off of Clint Eastwood's *Coogan's Bluff* and *Dirty Harry*, which Wayne bitterly regretted turning down after seeing the film. AT. Contains violence, swearing. DVD

John Wayne *Jim Brannigan* • Richard Attenborough *Commander Swann* • Judy Geeson *Jennifer Thatcher* • Mel Ferrer *Mel Fields* • John Vernon *Larkin* • Daniel Pilon *Gorman* • Del Henney *Drexel* • John Stride *Traven* • Lesley-Anne Down *Luana* • Barry Dennen *Julian* ■ *Dir* Douglas Hickox • *Scr* Christopher Trumbo, Michael Butler, William P McGivern, William Norton, from a story by Christopher Trumbo, Michael Butler

Branwen ★★ 15

Political drama 1994 · UK · Colour · 101mins

Director Ceri Sherlock never comes close to convincing us that the hostility felt by the Welsh towards the English is on a par with the sentiments harboured by Irish Republicans. But where the film really falls flat is by pitting Branwen and her Northern Irish husband against her adopted soldier brother, who has just been wounded in Bosnia. This is unbalanced by its political indignation and undone by its ludicrous plot contrivances. DP. In Welsh, Gaelic and English with subtitles.

Morfudd Hughes *Branwen Roberts* • Richard Lynch *Kevin McCarthy* • Jo Roberts *Llion Roberts* • Robert Gwyn Davies *Mathonwy Roberts* ■ *Dir* Ceri Sherlock • *Scr* Gareth Miles, Angela Graham, Ceri Sherlock, from a play by Gareth Miles

The Brass Bottle ★★

Comedy 1964 · US · Colour · 89mins

Tony Randall never seems to get a chance to show off his comedic talents, though this witless farce – adapted from F Anstey's perennial bestseller – tries to do so. Randall is a naive architect who opens an antique brass bottle and releases a genie that makes threats and offers to grant wishes. There's good back-up from Burl Ives and Barbara Eden (from the TV series *I Dream of Jeannie*). But the material is too thin to stretch very far and it soon splits disastrously. TH

Tony Randall *Harold Ventimore* • Burl Ives *Fakrash* • Barbara Eden *Sylvia* • Edward Andrews *Professor Kenton* • Ann Doran *Martha Kenton* • Kamala Devi *Tezra* • Lulu Porter *Belly dancer* • Philip Ober *William Beevor* ■ *Dir* Harry Keller • *Scr* Oscar Brodney, from the novel by F Anstey

The Brass Legend ★★★

Western 1956 · US · BW · 79mins

An impressive B-western with Raymond Burr as the psychotic killer captured by Arizona lawman Hugh O'Brian, who then has to deal with various factions within the town and keep Burr from escaping. Critics at the time admired the showdown between the two antagonists, which was filmed like a medieval joust with the two men facing each other down on charging horses. However, the whole movie has an admirable tension and a neatly dovetailed gallery of characters. AT

Hugh O'Brian *Sheriff Wade Adams* • Nancy Gates *Linda* • Raymond Burr *Tris Hatten* • Reba Tassell *Millie* • Donald MacDonald *Clay* • Robert Burton *Gipson* • Eddie Firestone *Shorty* • Willard Sage *Tatum* ■ *Dir* Gerd Oswald • *Scr* Don Martin, from a story by George Zuckerman, Jess Arnold

The Brass Monkey ★★

Comedy thriller 1948 · UK · BW · 81mins

This is a bizarre combination of a Saki-esque parable and a vehicle for radio talent scout Carroll Levis. Here he's pitted against an evil connoisseur bent on obtaining the titular Buddhist artefact. This was the penultimate film (not released until 1951) of tragic Hollywood actress Carole Landis, who committed suicide after breaking up with the married Rex Harrison. TS

Carole Landis *Kay Sheldon* • Carroll Levis • Herbert Lom *Peter Hobart* • Avril Angers • Ernest Thesiger *Ryder-Harris* • Henry Edwards *Inspector Miller* • Edward Underdown *Max Taylor* ■ *Dir* Thornton Freeland • *Scr* Alec Coppel, Thornton Freeland, C Denis Freeman, from the story by Alec Coppel

Brass Target ★★ 15

Thriller 1978 · US · Colour · 106mins

Thick layers of plot make for a very thin enterprise in a film that lacks any central focus point. It's the kind of picture that is so mesmerised by the detail of its basic idea – what if General Patton was killed just after the war in the course of his investigation into a gold bullion heist? – that it allows class performers to wander in and out of the story, spouting slabs of dialogue rather than developing their roles. Sophia Loren is the prime victim. JM. Contains violence, swearing. [video]

Sophia Loren *Mara* • John Cassavetes *Major Joe De Lucca* • George Kennedy *Gen George S Patton Jr* • Robert Vaughn *Colonel Donald Rogers* • Patrick McGoohan *Colonel Mike McCauley* • Bruce Davison *Colonel Robert Dawson* • Edward Herrmann *Colonel Walter Gilchrist* • Max von Sydow *Shelley/Webber* • Ed Bishop *Colonel Stewart* ■ *Dir* John Hough • *Scr* Alvin Boretz, from the novel *The Algonquin Project* by Frederick Nolan

Brassed Off ★★★★ 15

Drama 1996 · UK/US · Colour · 103mins

There's a certain Ealing-like quality in the way the mining town of Grimley rallies around the colliery's brass band as it progresses to the national finals amid talk of pit closures and redundancies. But there's no coy comedy here – the humour is acerbic and near the knuckle. Also missing is the Capra-esque last act in which the everyday folk triumph over adversity. Instead, there's only the promise of more struggle and the grim realisation that a way of life has gone for ever. But the edgy pace Mark Herman brings to the drama and his presentation of the musical sequences can't be faulted, and he draws remarkable performances from a strong cast. DP. Contains swearing. [video] DVD

Pete Postlethwaite *Danny* • Tara FitzGerald *Gloria* • Ewan McGregor *Andy* • Stephen Tompkinson *Phil* • Jim Carter *Harry* • Ken Colley [Kenneth Colley] *Greasley* • Peter Gunn *Simmo* • Mary Healey *Ida* • Melanie Hill *Sandra* • Philip Jackson *Jim* • Sue Johnston *Vera* ■ *Dir/Scr* Mark Herman

The Bravados ★★ PG

Western 1958 · US · Colour · 93mins

Gregory Peck tracks down a gang he thinks raped and murdered his wife. What is intended here is a parable about revenge that shows Peck descending into madness and seeking religious salvation at the end. It's a good story, but the treatment needs far more emotional conviction than either Peck or director Henry King give it. Joan Collins co-stars in an under-written role. AT [video] DVD

Gregory Peck *Jim Douglas* • Joan Collins *Josefa Velarde* • Stephen Boyd *Bill Zachary* • Albert Salmi *Ed Taylor* • Henry Silva *Lujan* • Kathleen Gallant *Emma* • Barry Coe *Tom* • Lee Van Cleef *Alfonso Parral* ■ *Dir* Henry King • *Scr* Philip Yordan, from the novel by Frank O'Rourke

The Brave ★★ 15

Drama 1997 · US · Colour · 118mins

Johnny Depp's eclectic career has seen collaborations with a host of deeply idiosyncratic directors, from Jim Jarmusch and Tim Burton to Roman Polanski and Emir Kusturica. His own directing debut, however, displays little of their flair. It's a muddled and pretentious affair about a native American (played by Depp) who agrees to star in a real-life snuff film in order to provide for his family. Marlon Brando co-stars in a movie that premiered at the 1997 Cannes Film Festival. RT DVD

Johnny Depp *Raphael* • Marlon Brando *McCarthy* • Marshall Bell *Larry* • Elpidia Carrillo *Rita* • Clarence Williams III *Father Stratton* • Frederic Forrest *Lou Sr* • Max Perlich *Lou Jr* ■ *Dir* Johnny Depp • *Scr* Paul McCudden, Johnny Depp, DP Depp, from the novel by Gregory McDonald

The Brave Bulls ★★

Drama 1951 · US · BW · 112mins

This is a fraught exploration of the psychology of a bullfighter (Mel Ferrer), whose fear before a fight intensifies after his girlfriend (Czech actress Miroslava) dies in a car crash. Co-star Anthony Quinn, who plays Ferrer's personal manager, claims the film as one of his personal favourites but blamed its lack of commercial success on the studio, which dumped it when director Robert Rossen was named a communist in the McCarthy hearings. As a result of being made by a "Red", the film never found a large following, but it's pretty average stuff. AT

Mel Ferrer *Luis Bello* • Miroslava *Linda de Calderon* • Anthony Quinn *Raul Fuentes* • Eugene Iglesias *Pepe Bello* • José Torvay *Eladio Gomez* • Charlita *Raquelita* • Jose Luis Vasquez *Yank Delgado* • Alfonso Alvirez *Loco Ruiz* ■ *Dir* Robert Rossen • *Scr* John Bright, from a novel by Tom Lea

The Brave Don't Cry ★★

Disaster drama 1952 · UK · BW · 89mins

In this downbeat reconstruction of a true-life Scottish mining disaster, Philip Leacock admirably captures the stoicism of the hundred or so men trapped in a suffocating chamber following a landslide. However, he is less successful in eliciting credible performances from the non-professionals who make up the villagers. DP

John Gregson *John Cameron* • Meg Buchanan *Margaret Wishart* • John Rae *Donald Sloan* • Fulton Mackay *Dan Wishart* • Andrew Keir *Charlie Ross* • Wendy Noel *Jean Knox* • Russell Walters *Hughie Aitken* • Jameson Clark *Dr Andrew Keir* ■ *Dir* Philip Leacock • *Scr* Montagu Slater

The Brave Little Toaster ★★★★ U

Animated adventure
1987 · US · Colour · 90mins

A good number of ex-Disney personnel were involved in crafting this imaginative, unofficial remake of Disney favourite *The Incredible Journey*, substituting household appliances for the animals in the classic Disney house style. And, knowing a good thing when it sees it, Disney snapped the film up for release on its video label in America. The songs are a bit of a letdown, but the sharp humour and heart-warming sentiments make it marvellous fun for all the family. AJ [video] DVD

Jon Lovitz *Radio* • Tim Stack [Timothy Stack] *Lampy* • Timothy E Day *Blanky* • Thurl Ravenscroft *Kirby* • Deanna Oliver *Toaster* • Phil Hartman *Air conditioner/hanging lamp* • Joe Ranft *Elmo St Peters* ■ *Dir* Jerry Rees • *Scr* Jerry Rees, Joe Ranft, from a story by Jerry Rees, Joe Ranft, Brian McEntee, from the novella by Thomas M Disch

The Brave One ★★★ U

Drama 1956 · US · Colour · 94mins

Owing to the anti-communist blacklist that operated in Hollywood throughout the 1950s, Dalton Trumbo had to wait until 1975 to collect the best story Oscar he won (under the pseudonym of Robert Rich) for this charming tale of childlike innocence and loyalty. Transposing events that occurred in Barcelona in the mid-1930s to Mexico allows the screenplay to concentrate on the peasant sensibility of Michel Ray, the farm boy who doggedly follows his pet bull all the way to the Plaza de Mexico. Director Irving Rapper handles the melodrama touchingly. DP

Michel Ray *Leonardo* • Rodolfo Hoyos *Rafael Rosillo* • Elsa Cardenas *Maria* • Carlos Navarro *Don Alejandro* • Joi Lansing *Marion Randall* • George Trevino *Salvador* • Carlos Fernandez *Manuel* ■ *Dir* Irving Rapper • *Scr* Harry Franklin, Merrill G White, from a story by Robert Rich [Dalton Trumbo]

Braveheart ★★★★ 15

Historical drama
1995 · US · Colour · 179mins

Mel Gibson directs this 13th-century saga of Scottish revolt against English tyranny with a claymore-like flourish, defying the criticism that there are moments as bogus as plastic haggis. Gibson's rebel leader and rabble-rouser William Wallace is an intrepid champion from the mould of Hollywood heroes, made believable by the grace of the star. However, Patrick McGoohan as the villainous King Edward "Longshanks" is a jeering, sneering cliché too far. As director, Gibson's control over thousands of extras in the swift succession of gruesome hand-to-hand battles is effective, but when the action moves in for the emotional kill, the film loses credibility. Yet this Oscar-winner for best picture succeeds in bringing to life the reality of Scottish patriotism and brilliantly captures the spirit of a revolution. TH. Contains violence, swearing and some nudity. [video] DVD

Mel Gibson *William Wallace* • Sophie Marceau *Princess Isabelle* • Patrick McGoohan *"Longshanks", King Edward I* • Catherine McCormack *Murron* • Brendan Gleeson *Hamish* • James Cosmo *Campbell* • David O'Hara *Stephen* • Angus MacFadyen *Robert the Bruce* • Ian Bannen *Leper* ■ *Dir* Mel Gibson • *Scr* Randall Wallace

Brazil ★★★ U

Musical comedy 1944 · US · BW · 91mins

A Brazilian composer (Tito Guizar) takes exception to an uncomplimentary book called *Why Marry a Latin?* and sets out to put the record straight with its attractive American author (Virginia Bruce). A big-budget musical from a little studio (Republic), Joseph Santley's film doesn't set the world on fire, but it is pleasing and lively. RK

Virginia Bruce *Nicky Henderson* • Tito Guizar *Miguel "Mike" Soares* • Edward Everett Horton *Everett St John Everett* • Robert Livingston *Rod Walker* • Richard Lane *Edward Graham* • Roy Rogers • Aurora Miranda *Speciality dancer* ■ *Dir* Joseph Santley • *Scr* Frank Gill Jr, Laura Kerr, from a story by Richard English

Brazil ★★★★★ 15

Science-fiction fantasy
1985 · US/UK · Colour · 137mins

In this extraordinary vision of a futuristic bureaucratic hell from director Terry Gilliam, Jonathan Pryce stars as the Orwellian hero, a permanently harassed clerk at the all-seeing Department of Information Retrieval. Pryce is only kept sane by his vivid daydreams, which see him as a heroic flying warrior coming to the aid of a beautiful woman (Kim Greist). As unpredictable as Gilliam's Monty Python animations, this daring and dazzling take on *1984* creates a weird world inhabited by an assortment of crazy characters, including Robert De Niro as an SAS-style repairman. The movie's sledgehammer conclusion gave studio executives sleepless nights. JC [video] DVD

Jonathan Pryce *Sam Lowry* • Robert De Niro *Archibald "Harry" Tuttle* • Katherine Helmond *Mrs Ida Lowry* • Ian Holm *Mr Kurtzmann* • Bob Hoskins *Spoor* • Michael Palin *Jack Lint* • Ian Richardson *Mr Warrenn* • Peter Vaughan *Mr Eugene Helpmann* • Kim Greist *Jill Layton* • Jim Broadbent *Dr Jaffe* ■ *Dir* Terry Gilliam • *Scr* Terry Gilliam, Tom Stoppard

Breach of Trust ★★ PG

Drama 1999 · US · Colour · 85mins

Derry-born Roma Downey must have needed the patience of a saint to cope with the melodramatic demands made on her in this tear-jerking TV movie. Also known as *A Secret Life*, it's the kind of film they'd once have made with, say, Jane Wyman as the wife who discovers her husband has a mistress after he's been left comatose in a plane crash and Margaret O'Brien as the love child from that illicit union. Downey and Kristina Malota do well enough in the roles, but this is pretty heavy going. DP [video] DVD

Roma Downey *Cassie Whitman* • William Russ *Mark Whitman* • Kristina Malota *Erica* ■ *Dir* Larry Peerce

Bread and Roses ★★★ 15

Political drama
2000 · UK/Ger · Colour · 105mins

Ken Loach seems to be British cinema's sole surviving social conscience. It's disappointing, therefore, that amid such political apathy he should decamp to Los Angeles for this naively over-simplified account of a janitorial workforce's struggle for representation. It's a laudable project, but the mainly non-professional cast seems uncomfortable with his improvisational style. However, the debuting Pilar Padilla embodies Loachian zeal as she unites with Adrien Brody's rabble-rouser to expose indifference and corruption. Made with additional funding from Spain, France and Italy. DP. Mainly in Spanish with English subtitles. Contains swearing. DVD

Pilar Padilla *Maya* • Adrien Brody *Sam* • Elpidia Carrillo *Rosa* • Jack McGee *Bert* • Frankie Davila *Luis* ■ *Dir* Ken Loach • *Scr* Paul Laverty

Bread and Tulips ★★★ 12A

Romantic comedy
2000 · It · Colour · 116mins

Directed with humour and humanity by Silvio Soldini, this is a delightful midlife rebellion comedy, set against the glorious vistas of Venice. Accidentally abandoned by her lowbrow family on a cut-price coach tour, Licia Maglietta decides to treat herself to an adventure and finds professional fulfilment in an elderly anarchist's flower ship and unexpected romance with Icelandic waiter Bruno Ganz. The all-round geniality is reinforced by the amiably bungling performance of Giuseppe Battiston, as the inept plumber/private eye hired by Maglietta's desperate husband (Antonio Catania) to track her down. DP. In Italian with English subtitles.

Licia Maglietta *Rosalba Barletta* • Bruno Ganz *Fernando Girasoli* • Marina Massironi *Grazia* • Giuseppe Battiston *Constantino* • Felice Andreasi *Fermo* • Antonio Catania *Mimmo Barletta* ■ *Dir* Silvio Soldini • *Scr* Doriana Leondeff, Silvio Soldini

Bread, Love and Dreams ★★★

Comedy 1953 · It · BW · 97mins

Dated now, this is a typically frothy Italian comedy of the postawar years, set in a mountain village and dominated by of Gina Lollobrigida. "La Lollo" plays the wild beauty lustily in love with a young policeman. She also catches the eye of Vittorio De Sica, playing the newly arrived police chief, who locks her up in his jail. Village elders and the priest frown at the sexual intrigue. A huge hit in Italy and released widely abroad, it led to a quickie sequel, *Bread, Love and Jealousy*, which reunited the cast and director. AT. An Italian language film.

Vittorio De Sica *The marshal* • Gina Lollobrigida *The girl/"Frisky"* • Marisa Merlini *The midwife/"Annarella"* • Roberto Risso *The carabiniere/"Stelluti"* • Virgilio Riento *Priest "/Dom Emidio"* • Maria Pia Casilio *Priest's niece/"Paoletta"* • Memmo Carotenuto *Another carabiniere* • Tina Pica *Housekeeper/ "Caramel"* ■ *Dir* Luigi Comencini • *Scr* Ettore Margadonna [Ettore Maria Margadonna], Luigi Comencini, from a story by Ettore Margadonna [Ettore Maria Margadonna]

The Break ★★ 12

Mystery thriller 1962 · UK · BW · 100mins

Lance Comfort directs this plodding whodunnit, in which a detective, a novelist, a fleeing crook and his sister stumble upon dark deeds on a Devon farm. Tony Britton does his best in the lead, but the mystery isn't likely to put too much strain on your little grey cells. DP

Tony Britton *Greg Parker* • William Lucas *Jacko Thomas* • Eddie Byrne *Judd Tredegar* • Robert Urquhart *Pearson* • Sonia Dresdel *Sarah* • Edwin Richfield *Moses* • Gene Anderson *Jean Tredegar* ■ *Dir* Lance Comfort • *Scr* Pip Baker, Jane Baker

Break in the Circle ★★ U

Adventure drama 1955 · UK · BW · 90mins

Adventurer Forrest Tucker is hired by wealthy foreign baron Marius Goring to smuggle a Polish scientist out of East Germany. However, he is nabbed in Hamburg by the gang who are holding the boffin captive. The glamorous Eva Bartok comes to his rescue, but things are not what they seem. Written and directed by Val Guest, this is an efficient and energetic British thriller, not without the odd moment of humour, but it's of only passing interest now. RK

Forrest Tucker *Skip Morgan* • Eva Bartok *Lisa* • Marius Goring *Baron Keller* • Eric Pohlmann *Emile* • Guy Middleton *Hobart* • Arnold Marlé *Kudnic* • Fred Johnson *Farquarson* • Reginald Beckwith *Dusty* ■ *Dir* Val Guest • *Scr* Val Guest, from the novel by Philip Lorraine

Break of Dawn ★★★★

Biographical drama
1988 · US · Colour · 105mins

A strong, affecting TV biopic that tells the story of a courageous, unsung Los Angeles folk hero. Pedro J Gonzalez, played by Mexican actor/singer Oscar Chavez, was the city's first Hispanic radio host who, instead of opting to play a few mariachi songs and recommending taco outlets, tried to rouse his compatriots into nonviolent political action. Through the use of an intelligent script, a merciful lack of clichés and Chavez's fine performance, we come to understand the man and the hornet's nest he stirred up. SH. In English and Spanish with subtitles.

Oscar Chavez *Pedro J Gonzalez* • Maria Rojo *Maria Gonzalez* • Tony Plana *Gene Rodriguez* • Pepe Serna *Hector Gonzalez* • Peter Henry Schroeder *Kyle Mitchell* • Socorro Valdez *Matilde Gonzalez* • Kamala Lopez [Kamala Dawson] *Linda Galvan* ■ *Dir/Scr* Isaac Artenstein

Break of Hearts ★★★ U

Romantic drama 1935 · US · BW · 77mins

This is one of a string of RKO features that lead to cinema exhibitors listing Katharine Hepburn as box-office poison. She plays a struggling young composer in Greenwich Village who falls for a famous international conductor, played by French heart-throb Charles Boyer. They both suffer unmercifully and he becomes a lush. Of course, she nurses him. Taken in the right spirit, on a wet matinée afternoon, this tosh has pleasure to offer, but the story is so familiar that there are no real surprises in store. TS

Katharine Hepburn *Constance Roberti* • Charles Boyer *Fritz Roberti* • John Beal *Johnny* • Jean Hersholt *Talma* • Sam Hardy *Marx* • Inez Courtney *Miss Wilson* • Helene Millard *Sylvia* ■ *Dir* Philip Moeller • *Scr* Sarah Y Mason, Anthony Veiller, Victor Heerman, from a story by Lester Cohen

Break Up ★ 18

Crime thriller 1998 · US · Colour · 96mins

Bridget Fonda is the battered wife – deaf thanks to one of her husband's beatings – who is suspected of his murder when a charred body is found in his burnt-out car. Kiefer Sutherland and Steven Weber are the cops who only discover clues when the plot has slowed to the point of stagnation, while Penelope Ann Miller and Tippi Hedren are among the cast wondering what they did to deserve a daft film like this. JB

Bridget Fonda *Jimmy Dade* • Kiefer Sutherland *John Box* • Hart Bochner *Frankie Dade* • Steven Weber *Ramsey* • Penelope Ann Miller *Grace* • Tippi Hedren *Mom* ■ *Dir* Paul Marcus • *Scr* Anne Amanda Opotowsky

Breakdance ★★ PG

Musical drama 1984 · US · Colour · 82mins

Adolfo "Shabba-Doo" Quinones and Michael "Boogaloo Shrimp" Chambers teach white waitress Lucinda Dickey their moves so that she can win a dance contest in a film that was rush-released to cash in on the short-lived breakdance craze. Great street choreography comes a poor second to the yawn-inducing, youth-versus-establishment plot with *Flashdance* trappings. Still, this dance culture is where hip-hop and rap found their acceptable public face. AJ DVD

Lucinda Dickey *Kelly* • Adolfo "Shabba-Doo" Quinones *Ozone* • Michael "Boogaloo Shrimp" Chambers [Michael Chambers (1)] *Turbo* • Phineas Newborn III *Adam* • Christopher McDonald *James* ■ *Dir* Joel Silberg • *Scr* Allen DeBevoise, from a story by Allen DeBevoise, Charles Parker

Breakdance 2 – Electric Boogaloo ★★ PG

Musical drama 1984 · US · Colour · 89mins

This super-quick sequel finds the same lead characters using their dance talents once more to save their rundown community centre. Adolfo "Shabba-Doo" Quinones and Michael "Boogaloo Shrimp" Chambers put on a show to raise cash and halt the urban developers who want to turn the centre into a shopping mall. A standard-issue follow-up with stereotypical humour undercutting its happy-go-lucky breeziness. AJ DVD

Lucinda Dickey *Kelly* • Adolfo "Shabba-Doo" Quinones *Ozone* • Susie Bono *Rhonda* • Harry Caesar *Byron Smith* • Jo De Winter *Mrs Bennett* • John Christy Ewing *Mr Bennett* • Michael "Boogaloo Shrimp" Chambers [Michael Chambers (1)] *Turbo* ■ *Dir* Sam Firstenberg • *Scr* Jan Ventura, Julie Reichert, from the characters created by Charles Parker, Allen DeBevoise

Breakdown ★★★★ 15

Thriller 1997 · US · Colour · 89mins

Director Jonathan Mostow twists the knife with a certain taut flair in this gripping thriller, in which Kurt Russell and Kathleen Quinlan play a city couple moving west, whose car breaks down in the middle of nowhere. Trucker J T Walsh gives Quinlan a lift to the nearest phone, but when she subsequently vanishes he denies ever seeing her. This is enjoyably old-fashioned, with Russell giving an engaging performance. The resolution isn't as clever as you might think, but you'll be too busy chewing your cuticles to really care. JC. Contains swearing and violence. DVD

Kurt Russell *Jeff Taylor* • JT Walsh *Red Barr* • Kathleen Quinlan *Amy Taylor* • MC Gainey *Earl* • Jack Noseworthy *Billy* • Rex Linn *Sheriff Boyd* • Ritch Brinkley *Al* • Moira Harris *Arleen* ■ *Dir* Jonathan Mostow • *Scr* Sam Montgomery, Jonathan Mostow, from a story by Jonathan Mostow

Breaker Morant ★★★★ PG

War drama based on a true story
1979 · Aus · Colour · 102mins

Director Bruce Beresford has never quite matched the impact he made with this true story of three soldiers (led by Edward Woodward) fighting the Boers, who are court-martialled by the British in need of scapegoats for war crimes. What Beresford sometimes lacks in subtlety, he makes up for in an impassioned sense of injustice and he draws powerful performances from Woodward, reluctant counsel Jack Thompson and Bryan Brown. JF DVD

Edward Woodward *Lt Harry Harbord "Breaker" Morant* • Jack Thompson *Major JF Thomas* • John Waters (3) *Captain Alfred Taylor* • Bryan Brown *Lt Peter Handcock* • Charles Tingwell *Lt Col Denny* • Terence Donovan *Captain Simon Hunt* • Vincent Ball *Colonel Ian "Johnny" Hamilton* • Chris Haywood *Corporal Sharp* ■ *Dir* Bruce Beresford • *Scr* Jonathan Hardy, David Stevens, Bruce Beresford, from the play by Kenneth Ross and the book *The Breaker* by Kit Denton

Breakfast at Tiffany's ★★★★★ PG

Romantic drama
1961 · US · Colour · 114mins

Audrey Hepburn's Holly Golightly has passed, happily, into cinematic folklore. Director Blake Edwards's hymn to New York high style and high living, with its charming heroine and those wonderful Johnny Mercer *Moon River* lyrics, has hardly dated since its release. Originally a creation of writer Truman Capote, Holly, as written for the screen by George Axelrod and portrayed by Hepburn, is quite enchanting, even though period censorship makes it rather unclear what she actually does for a living. Despite the presence of handsome George Peppard and Patricia Neal, this is Hepburn's movie, her black dress and long cigarette holder ready to start a fashion revolution. Only Mickey Rooney's phoney caricature of a Japanese gent seems out of kilter in what is otherwise a thoroughly entertaining and wonderfully escapist movie. TS DVD

Audrey Hepburn *Holly Golightly* • George Peppard *Paul Varjak* • Patricia Neal *"2-E"* • Buddy Ebsen *Doc Golightly* • Martin Balsam *OJ Berman* • Mickey Rooney *Mr Yunioshi* • Vilallonga [José-Luis De Villalonga] *Jose* • Dorothy Whitney *Mag Wildwood* • John McGiver *Tiffany's clerk* ■ *Dir* Blake Edwards • *Scr* George Axelrod, from the novella by Truman Capote • *Cinematographer* Franz Planer • *Music* Henry Mancini

The Breakfast Club ★★★★ 15

Drama 1985 · US · Colour · 92mins

One of the high-water marks of the 1980s teenpic, John Hughes's Saturday detention drama has lost some of its freshness in the face of time and endless inferior imitations. Yet this chat-fest still rings true often enough to be relevant to both overgrown teenagers and the disgruntled kids of today. Brat Packers Emilio Estevez, Judd Nelson and Ally Sheedy are joined by teen favourite of the time, Molly Ringwald, and the underestimated Anthony Michael Hall for this mix of justified grievances, self-pitying whinges and hard-hitting home truths. The cast breathes life into their essentially clichéd characters. DP. Contains swearing and drug abuse.

Emilio Estevez *Andrew Clark* • Molly Ringwald *Claire Standish* • Paul Gleason *Richard Vernon* • Anthony Michael Hall *Brian Johnson* • John Kapelos *Carl* • Judd Nelson *John Bender* • Ally Sheedy *Allison Reynolds* • Perry Crawford *Allison's father* • John Hughes *Brian's father* ■ *Dir/Scr* John Hughes

Breakfast for Two ★★★ U

Screwball comedy 1937 · US · BW · 67mins

This little known screwball comedy gives Barbara Stanwyck and Herbert Marshall plenty of opportunities to strike sparks off each other. She's a Texan heiress and he's a playboy, who prefers the bottle to facing up to his responsibilities as heir to a shipping line. Stanwyck buys the company as part of her plan to reform and marry him. Running at barely over an hour, the picture has bags of energy and a strong supporting cast. AT

Barbara Stanwyck *Valentine Ransome* • Herbert Marshall *Jonathan Blair* • Glenda Farrell *Carol Wallace* • Eric Blore *Butch* • Etienne Girardot *Meggs* • Donald Meek

B

Justice of the peace ■ *Dir* Alfred Santell • *Scr* Charles Kaufman, Paul Yawitz, Viola Brothers Shore

Breakfast of Champions ★ 15

Black comedy 1999 · US · Colour · 105mins

As the richest man in a small town, Bruce Willis is having an existential crisis in this tedious adaptation of the Kurt Vonnegut Jr novel. He spends most of the movie contemplating ending it all and, after enduring two hours of this mess, you might too. An able cast is hindered by an incoherent script and uncertain direction. ST [VIDEO]

Bruce Willis *Dwayne Hoover* • Albert Finney *Kilgore Trout* • Barbara Hershey *Celia Hoover* • Nick Nolte *Harry Le Sabre* • Glenne Headly *Francine Pefko* • Lukas Haas *Bunny Hoover* • Omar Epps *Wayne Hoobler* • Buck Henry *Fred T Barry* ■ *Dir* Alan Rudolph • *Scr* Alan Rudolph, from the novel by Kurt Vonnegut Jr

Breakheart Pass ★★ PG

Western murder mystery
1976 · US · Colour · 93mins

This Alistair MacLean caper has Charles Bronson on the trail of gun-runners and running into a murder mystery. And, if that wasn't enough, the plot is thickened by an outbreak of diphtheria. There are more red herrings than a chef could wave a skillet at, for this is really Agatha Christie in western garb, complete with a wonderful old steam train that steals every scene in which it appears. AT [VIDEO] DVD

Charles Bronson *John Deakin* • Ben Johnson *Nathan Pearce* • Richard Crenna *Richard Fairchild* • Jill Ireland *Marcia Scoville* • Charles Durning *Frank O'Brien* • Ed Lauter *Major Claremont* • David Huddleston *Dr Molyneux* • Roy Jenson *Banlon* ■ *Dir* Tom Gries • *Scr* Alistair MacLean, from his novel

Breakin' All the Rules ★★★ 12

Romantic comedy
2004 · US · Colour · 81mins

Oscar-winner Jamie Foxx stars in this boisterous exploration of modern romance. Sharply scripted by director Daniel Taplitz, it sees Foxx go from heartbroken to sizzling when he writes a bestselling break-up guide for men after being dumped by his fiancée. Though the screwball events that follow as he tries to help others practice what he preaches verge on TV sitcom territory, they're no less enjoyable, benefiting from perky performances and spot-on delivery. SF. Contains swearing and sexual references. DVD

Jamie Foxx *Quincy Watson* • Gabrielle Union *Nicky Callas* • Morris Chestnut *Evan Fields* • Peter MacNicol *Phillip Gascon* • Jennifer Esposito *Rita Monroe* • Bianca Lawson *Helen Sharp* • Jill Ritchie *Amy* ■ *Dir/Scr* Daniel Taplitz

Breaking Away ★★★★ PG

Comedy drama 1979 · US · Colour · 96mins

Director Peter Yates's delightfully unpredictable comedy uses a local bicycle race to uncover the sexual, class and economic tensions within an all-American community. The Oscar-winning script by Steve Tesich has a wry wit and great sensitivity. The performances are marvellous, especially from Dennis Quaid and, more particularly, Dennis Christopher, who plays a character so enamoured of the Italian cycling team that he speaks with an Italian accent, bursts into Verdi arias and re-names his cat Fellini. Costing a mere $2.4 million to make, it was destined to be dumped by the studio, but became a huge box-office success, initiating the scores of brat-pack, rite-of-passage pictures of the 1980s. AT. Contains swearing. [VIDEO]

Dennis Christopher *Dave Stohler* • Dennis Quaid *Mike* • Daniel Stern *Cyril* • Jackie Earle Haley *Moocher* • Barbara Barrie *Mrs Stohler* • Paul Dooley *Mr Stohler* • Robyn Douglass *Katherine* • Hart Bochner *Rod* • Amy Wright *Nancy* ■ *Dir* Peter Yates • *Scr* Steve Tesich

Breaking Glass ★★ 15

Musical drama 1980 · UK · Colour · 99mins

Singer Hazel O'Connor claws her way into the charts, with help from spiv promoter Phil Daniels, only to find the glitter of fame tarnished. Efficiently directed by Brian Gibson, this hopelessly dated musical is completely formulaic, yet intriguing from a New Wave nostalgia perspective. O'Connor, who wrote all the songs, hit the Top Ten with *Eighth Day* before fading into obscurity. The "life imitating art" subtext adds another level of interest to what is basically a chronicle of music-biz clichés. AJ [VIDEO]

Phil Daniels *Danny Price* • Hazel O'Connor *Kate Crawley* • Jon Finch *Bob Woods* • Jonathan Pryce *Ken* • Peter-Hugo Daly *Mick Leaf* • Mark Wingett *Tony* • Paul McCartney • Rod Stewart ■ *Dir/Scr* Brian Gibson

Breaking In ★★★ 15

Comedy 1989 · US · Colour · 90mins

This proved to be an over-optimistic title for Scottish director Bill Forsyth, who was making his second attempt at a Hollywood breakthrough after the British success of *Gregory's Girl* and *Local Hero*. Burt Reynolds, as an ageing burglar teaching his skills to a younger man (Casey Siemaszko), suits the humorous style, but John Sayles's script stresses mildness at the expense of momentum. The resulting shaggy-dog story possesses a measure of charm, but more bite would have helped. TH. Contains swearing. [VIDEO] DVD

Burt Reynolds *Ernie Mullins* • Casey Siemaszko *Mike Lefebb* • Sheila Kelley *Carrie* • Lorraine Toussaint *Delphine* • Albert Salmi *Johnny Scat* • Harry Carey [Harry Carey Jr] *Shoes* • Maury Chaykin *Tucci* • Stephen Tobolowsky *District attorney* ■ *Dir* Bill Forsyth • *Scr* John Sayles

The Breaking Point ★★★

Drama 1950 · US · BW · 97mins

Ernest Hemingway's short novel, *To Have and Have Not*, became a classic movie in 1944, starring Humphrey Bogart and Lauren Bacall. This version, directed by Michael Curtiz, co-stars John Garfield and Patricia Neal. Hawks's version at least used Hemingway's title. This movie doesn't even bother to do that, replacing the tale of wartime gun-running with one of peacetime smuggling, but retaining its core relationship about an unlucky guy, a bunch of hoodlums and a girl in the middle. It's efficient, if forgettable. AT

John Garfield *Harry Morgan* • Patricia Neal *Leona Charles* • Phyllis Thaxter *Lucy Morgan* • Juano Hernandez *Wesley Park* • Wallace Ford *Duncan* • Edmond Ryan [Edmon Ryan] *Rogers* • Ralph Dumke *Hannagan* • Guy Thomajan *Danny* • William Campbell *Concho* ■ *Dir* Michael Curtiz • *Scr* Ranald MacDougall, from the novel *To Have and Have Not* by Ernest Hemingway

The Breaking Point ★ U

Crime thriller 1961 · UK · BW · 58mins

If stars were awarded for plot contrivance, this low-budget thriller would be well into double figures. There's a bank note printer with a gambling debt, revolutionaries with a counterfeiting plan, an armed robbery, a bomb, a touch of adultery and a speeding plane finale. All of this is crammed into under an hour of screen time, with not one character ringing true nor one fragment of the storyline seeming the least bit credible. DP

Peter Reynolds *Eric Winlatter* • Dermot Walsh *Robert Wade* • Joanna Dunham *Cherry Winlatter* • Lisa Gastoni *Eva* • Brian Cobby *Peter de Savory* • Jack Allen *Ernest Winlatter* ■ *Dir* Lance Comfort • *Scr* Peter Lambert, from a novel by Laurence Meynell

Breaking Point ★

Crime drama 1976 · Can · Colour · 91mins

Bo Svenson, a sort of expressionless forerunner of fellow Swede Dolph Lundgren, takes the stand against the Mafia and is set up with another identity by decent cop Robert Culp. But the Mafia soon sniff Svenson out and threaten his family and then we're into *Death Wish* vigilante land. AT

Bo Svenson *Michael McBain* • Robert Culp *Frank Sirrianni* • John Colicos *Vincent Karbone* • Belinda Montgomery [Belinda J Montgomery] *Diana McBain* • Stephen Young *Peter Stratis* • Linda Sorenson *Helen McBain* ■ *Dir* Bob Clark • *Scr* Roger Swaybill, Stanley Mann, from a story by Roger Swaybill

Breaking the Rules ★

Road movie comedy drama
1992 · US · Colour · 100mins

Since his promising starring debut in Francis Ford Coppola's *The Outsiders*, C Thomas Howell has appeared to harbour a career death wish, appearing in increasingly bad movies. He hit the jackpot with this misconceived disease-of-the-week pic about a leukaemia sufferer (Jason Bateman) who takes his two best mates (Howell and Jonathan Silverman) on a van trip to California so he can appear on TV's *Jeopardy* before croaking. Appalling. RS

Jason Bateman *Phil Stepler* • C Thomas Howell *Gene Michaels* • Jonathan Silverman *Rob Konigsberg* • Annie Potts *Mary Klingsmith* • Kent Bateman *Mr Stepler* • Shawn Phelan *Young Phil* • Jackey Vinson *Young Gene* ■ *Dir* Neal Israel • *Scr* Paul Shapiro

Breaking the Waves ★★★★★ 18

Drama 1996 · Den/Swe/Fr · Colour · 152mins

A staggeringly honest performance from newcomer Emily Watson coupled with a wrenching central theme – the meaning of true love – illuminate this extraordinarily moving testament to the human spirit, which marked the English-language debut of Danish director Lars von Trier. Set in a remote Scottish village, and shot in pseudo home-video style to keep the profound events real and exposed, it tells the heartbreaking story of a devoutly religious and simple-minded woman who sacrifices everything for the man she adores. An often uncompromising and uncomfortable saga of faith, hope and charity; keep the hankies close by for the unforgettable climax. AJ. Contains violence, swearing, sex scenes and nudity. [VIDEO] DVD

Emily Watson *Bess* • Stellan Skarsgård *Jan* • Katrin Cartlidge *Dodo* • Jean-Marc Barr *Terry* • Udo Kier *Man on the trawler* • Adrian Rawlins *Doctor Richardson* • Jonathan Hackett *The minister* • Sandra Voe *Bess's mother* ■ *Dir* Lars von Trier • *Scr* Lars Von Trier, Peter Asmussen

Breaking Up ★ 15

Romantic drama 1996 · US · Colour · 85mins

The talented Russell Crowe and Salma Hayek are both completely wasted in this low-budget, endlessly drawn-out explanation of a marriage. Scriptwriter Michael Cristofer clearly had a great deal of emotional baggage to sort through; perhaps he should've kept it to himself. LH. Contains swearing, sex scenes and nudity. [VIDEO]

Russell Crowe *Steve* • Salma Hayek *Monica* • Abraham Alvarez *Minister* ■ *Dir* Robert Greenwald • *Scr* Michael Cristofer

Breakout ★★★ 15

Action adventure 1975 · US · Colour · 92mins

In this off-target thriller, adventurer Charles Bronson rescues Robert Duvall from the Mexican prison he's been languishing in since being framed by father-in-law John Huston. The film starts rather slowly, but the tension builds as Duvall seeks revenge. Jill Ireland is third-billed as Duvall's yearning spouse. Huston is nearly as villainous as he was in *Chinatown*, though the best work in the movie comes from Randy Quaid, Sheree North and Alejandro Rey in supporting roles. TH DVD

Charles Bronson *Nick Colton* • Robert Duvall *Ray Wagner* • Jill Ireland *Ann Wagner* • John Huston *Harris Wagner* • Randy Quaid *Hawk Hawkins* • Sheree North *Myrna* • Alejandro Rey *Sanchez* • Paul Mantee *Cable* ■ *Dir* Tom Gries • *Scr* Howard B Kreitsek, Marc Norman, Elliott Baker, from a novel by Warren Hinckle, William Turner, Eliot Asinof

Breakthrough ★★

Second World War drama
1950 · US · BW · 90mins

This tale of an infantry platoon's progress through Europe following the Normandy landings has been wholly sanitised by the screenwriters. From David Brian's blokish captain down, each man is a caricature, but none more so than John Agar's green lieutenant, who turns out to be a natural born warrior. Director Lewis Seiler might have been advised to keep inserting archival footage, as in the boot-camp segment, but he lets his cast banter inanely. DP

David Brian *Captain Hale* • John Agar *Lieutenant Joe Mallory* • Frank Lovejoy *Sergeant Bell* • William Campbell *Dominick* • Paul Picerni *Private Ed Rojeck* • Greg McClure *Private Frank Finlay* ■ *Dir* Lewis Seiler • *Scr* Bernard Girard, Ted Sherdeman, from a story by Joseph I Breen Jr [Joseph Breen]

Breakthrough ★ 15

Second World War drama
1978 · W Ger · Colour · 92mins

A sorry sequel to Sam Peckinpah's classic war drama *Cross of Iron*, this tawdry affair has Richard Burton as Sergeant Steiner, the role so magnificently created by James Coburn in the original, and features a totally wasted all-star support cast. Burton doesn't seem interested in making his character believable, and it's hard to disguise the lack of both production values and a decent script. TS [VIDEO]

Richard Burton *Sergeant Steiner* • Rod Steiger *General Webster* • Robert Mitchum *Colonel Rogers* • Curt Jurgens *General Hoffmann* • Helmut Griem *Major Stransky* • Michael Parks *Sergeant Anderson* • Klaus Loewitsch [Klaus Löwitsch] *Corporal Krueger* • Veronique Vendell *Yvette* ■ *Dir* Andrew V McLaglen • *Scr* Tony Williamson

Breast Men ★★★ 18

Black comedy 1997 · US · Colour · 91mins

Lawrence O'Neil's witheringly cynical direction offers up a mordant picture of beauty-obsessed America in this racy and frequently hilarious history of the fake boob industry. David Schwimmer and Chris Cooper star as the pioneering surgeons who make a fortune through their silicone implants in the drug-fuelled 1970s, only to fall out. Schwimmer relishes his first major chance to drop his lovable *Friends* persona, and he receives first-class support from a talented cast. JF. Contains nudity, swearing. [VIDEO] DVD

David Schwimmer *Dr Christopher Saunders/ Kevin Saunders* • Chris Cooper *Dr William Larson* • Emily Procter *Laura Pierson* • Matt Frewer *Gerald* • Terry O'Quinn *Hersch Lawyer* • Kathleen Wilhoite *Tammi-Jean Lindsey* • John

Stockwell *Robert Renaud* • Louise Fletcher *Mrs Saunders* • Lyle Lovett *Research scientist* ■ *Dir* Lawrence O'Neil • *Scr* John Stockwell

B

A Breath of Scandal ★★

Romance 1960 · US · Colour · 97mins

The costumes are nice, the colour's lovely and Sophia Loren looks gorgeous. But there's little ace director Michael Curtiz can do to make this somewhat misguided version of Molnar's hoary old play sparkle, especially when wooden John Gavin is cast as the light in Loren's eye. Still, Maurice Chevalier and Isabel Jeans delight both eye and ear and Angela Lansbury plays Loren's lying arch rival, so there's some pleasure to be had among the tedium. TS

Sophia Loren *Princess Olympia* • John Gavin *Charlie Foster* • Maurice Chevalier *Prince Philip* • Isabel Jeans *Princess Eugenie* • Angela Lansbury *Countess Lina* • Tullio Carminati *Albert* • Roberto Risso *Aide* • Carlo Hintermann *Prince Ruprecht* • Milly Vitale *Can-can girl* ■ *Dir* Michael Curtiz • *Scr* Walter Bernstein, Ring Lardner Jr, Sidney Howard, from the play *Olympia* by Ferenc Molnar

Breathless ★★★ 18

Crime drama 1983 · US · Colour · 95mins

A remake of Jean-Luc Godard's 1959 classic *A Bout de Souffle*, this suffers greatly in comparison. But judged on its own merits, it's a fair attempt at an on-the-run-style drama. Driving a stolen car, Richard Gere kills a cop and then heads into the arms of Valerie Kaprisky, a French student with whom he's had a brief affair. As the police close in, director Jim McBride (*The Big Easy*) seems most interested in getting both his actors to display as much flesh as possible. It's stylish but shallow, and Gere fits his superficial role like a glove. JB. Contains violence, swearing and nudity. DVD

Richard Gere *Jesse Lujack* • Valérie Kaprisky *Monica* • Art Metrano *Birnbaum* • John P Ryan *Lieutenant Parmental* • William Tepper *Paul* • Robert Dunn (1) *Sergeant Enright* • Garry Goodrew *Berutti* • Lisa Persky [Lisa Jane Persky] *Salesgirl* ■ *Dir* Jim McBride • *Scr* Jim McBride, LM "Kit" Carson, from the film *A Bout de Souffle* by Jean-Luc Godard, from a story by François Truffaut

The Breed ★★★ 18

Futuristic action horror
2001 · US · Colour · 87mins

Adrian Paul has a nice line in deadpan humour as a Polish bloodsucker teaming-up with vampire-hating cop Bokeem Woodbine in this slickly enjoyable futuristic thriller. Director Michael Oblowitz adds an impressive surface sheen to a fast-paced effort, shot in moody Budapest locations. Beneath the novelty window-dressing, it's merely a standard, formulaic buddy movie, but there are a few noteworthy narrative touches, and this is a more entertaining package than the straight-to-video tag suggests. JC DVD

Adrian Paul *Aaron Gray* • Bokeem Woodbine *Steve Grant* • Bai Ling *Lucy Westenra* • Peter Halasz *Cross* ■ *Dir* Michael Oblowitz • *Scr* Ruth C Fletcher, Christos N Gage

A Breed Apart ★★ 15

Drama 1984 · US · Colour · 91mins

Rutger Hauer plays a damaged and eccentric Vietnam veteran who's chosen to live as a recluse on a remote island. There he turns into a bird fancier and is pitted against Powers Booth, who has been hired by a rich egg collector to steal from Rutger's nest of eagles. Add to this unlikely scenario Kathleen Turner, who initiates an improbable love triangle, and you have a picture as risible as the moment when Hauer rides his white steed across the island, dressed as a pirate and carrying a crossbow. LH. Contains violence, swearing.

Rutger Hauer *Jim Malden* • Kathleen Turner *Stella Clayton* • Powers Boothe *Michael Walker* • Donald Pleasence *Whittier* • Jayne Bentzen *Amy Rollings* • Adam Fenwick *Adam Clayton* • John Dennis Johnston *Peyton* • Brion James *Miller* ■ *Dir* Philippe Mora • *Scr* Paul Wheeler • *Music* Maurice Gibb

Breezy ★★★

Drama 1973 · US · Colour · 107mins

In 1973, this gentle, middle-age romance marked a real departure for Clint Eastwood as director, though he stopped short of taking the main role himself. Instead the craggy and irresistibly charming William Holden plays the cynical divorcee who becomes infatuated with a young girl named Breezy, the sort of hippy who says, "I love being horizontal." There are vague echoes of the heyday of Ernst Lubitsch, Leo McCarey and Billy Wilder, along with some echoes of Eastwood's private life (he tested Sondra Locke for the part but gave it to the younger Kay Lenz). AT

William Holden (2) *Frank Harmon* • Kay Lenz *Breezy* • Roger C Carmel *Bob Henderson* • Marj Dusay *Betty Tobin* • Joan Hotchkis *Paula Harmon* • Jamie Smith-Jackson *Marcy* ■ *Dir* Clint Eastwood • *Scr* Jo Heims

Brenda Starr ★★ PG

Fantasy adventure
1989 · US · Colour · 98mins

This cheap and cheerful comic-strip adaptation is let down by a plastic performance from Brooke Shields in the title role. She is the annoyingly intrepid ace reporter on the trail of a mad inventor and pursued by a posse of rival journalists and baddies. The latter are the most fun, while Timothy Dalton is the romantic interest. There are some camp moments, but it's not really trashy enough to be truly enjoyable. JF DVD

Brooke Shields *Brenda Starr* • Timothy Dalton *Basil St John* • Tony Peck *Mike Randall* • Diana Scarwid *Libby "Lips" Lipscomb* • Nestor Serrano *José, seaplane pilot* • Jeffrey Tambor *Vladimir* • June Gable *Luba* • Charles Durning *Francis I Livright, editor* ■ *Dir* Robert Ellis Miller • *Scr* Noreen Stone, James David Buchanan, Delia Ephron, from a story by Noreen Stone, James David Buchanan, from the comic strip by Dale Messick

Brennus – Enemy of Rome ★ U

Historical adventure
1963 · It · Colour · 90mins

Anyone who has seen the engaging Australian spoof *Hercules Returns* won't be able to keep a straight face through this sort of costume epic. That said, the vast majority of them were beyond parody anyway, and this ludicrous tale of marauding Gauls and brave Romans is no exception. The inevitable dubbing will have you in fits, as will the desperately straight-faced performances of the international cast. JF. Italian dubbed into English.

Gordon Mitchell (1) *Brennus* • Ursula Davis *Nisia* • Massimo Serato *Camillus* • Erno Crisa *Vatinius* ■ *Dir* Giacomo Gentilomo • *Scr* De Riso Scolaro, Arpad De Riso

Brewster McCloud ★★ 15

Comedy 1970 · US · Colour · 105mins

Robert Altman had just made *MASH* and was deluged by offers from the major studios. He chose to make this eccentric movie with Bud Cort as a modern-day Icarus, who kits himself out with wings and wants to fly in the Houston Astrodome. Altman probably felt he had a giant symbol on his hands – an allegory for freedom. In fact, he simply had a Disney-ish story without the layers of syrup. Making things even wackier is Shelley Duvall in her first film role. AT. Contains swearing and nudity.

Bud Cort *Brewster McCloud* • Sally Kellerman *Louise* • Michael Murphy *Frank Shaft* • William Windom *Sheriff Weeks* • Shelley Duvall *Suzanne* • René Auberjonois *Lecturer* • Stacy Keach *Abraham Wright* • John Schuck *Policeman Johnson* ■ *Dir* Robert Altman • *Scr* Doran William Cannon

Brewster's Millions ★★ U

Comedy 1945 · US · BW · 79mins

The idea of a young man who must spend a million to inherit many times that amount is one of the most popular comedy plots, with film versions dating back almost to the dawn of cinema. This time Dennis O'Keefe is the guy who finds it harder to spend his loot than he expects. Although only sporadically amusing, this fast-paced farce is still probably the funniest take on the tale. SR

Dennis O'Keefe *Monty Brewster* • Helen Walker *Peggy Gray* • Eddie "Rochester" Anderson *Jackson* • June Havoc *Trixie Summers* • Gail Patrick *Barbara Drew* • Mischa Auer *Michael Michaelovich* ■ *Dir* Allan Dwan • *Scr* Sig Herzig, Charles Rogers, Wilkie Mahoney, from the novel by George Barr McCutcheon, from the play by Winchell Smith, Byron Ongley

Brewster's Millions ★★ PG

Comedy 1985 · US · Colour · 96mins

Director Walter Hill and comedy are always an uneasy combination, and this hackneyed, overlong tale glaringly proves the point. Add the manic, rolling-eyed Richard Pryor, and you have a major disappointment that fell flat even when it was made. This was the seventh time the story had been filmed – man left millions in will but first has to spend large amount in 30 days – which should have sounded a note of caution all round, but didn't. As usual, Pryor overacts wildly. SH. Contains some swearing. DVD

Richard Pryor *Montgomery Brewster* • John Candy *Spike Nolan* • Lonette McKee *Angela Drake* • Stephen Collins *Warren Cox* • Jerry Orbach *Charley Pegler* • Pat Hingle *Edward Roundfield* • Tovah Feldshuh *Marilyn* • Hume Cronyn *Rupert Horn* • Rick Moranis *Morty King* • Reni Santoni *Vin Rapelito* ■ *Dir* Walter Hill • *Scr* Herschel Weingrod, Timothy Harris, from the novel by George Barr McCutcheon

Brian's Song ★★★★ PG

Sports drama based on a true story
1971 · US · Colour · 74mins

This tragic true story brought a new respectability to that despised genre, the TV movie, proving that real quality was possible. James Caan finally achieved stardom (his next role would be Sonny in *The Godfather*) as Brian Piccolo, a Chicago Bears football star dying of cancer. This moving story was based on the real-life account entitled *I Am Third* written by Piccolo's friend Gale Sayers, here played by Billy Dee Williams. Under-rated director Buzz Kulik (*Warning Shot*) displays a remarkable sensitivity, and Michel Legrand's score is wonderful. Remade in 2001, also as a TV movie. TS

James Caan *Brian Piccolo* • Billy Dee Williams *Gale Sayers* • Jack Warden *Coach George Halas* • Shelley Fabares *Joy Piccolo* • Judy Pace *Linda Sayers* • Bernie Casey *JC Caroline* • David Huddleston *Ed McCaskey* • Ron Feinberg *Doug Atkins* ■ *Dir* Buzz Kulik • *Scr* William E Blinn, from the book *I Am Third* by Gale Sayers with Al Silverman • *Music* Michel Legrand

The Bribe ★★★

Crime drama 1949 · US · BW · 97mins

This was as close as that home of gloss, MGM, got to making a genuine *film noir*. Federal agent Robert Taylor heads south of the border to encounter a cleverly cast assortment of genre clichés, including ailing crook John Hodiak and sultry singer Ava Gardner. Villains Charles Laughton and Vincent Price are both seemingly well out of directorial control, which is perhaps not surprising as the movie was started by arch stylist Vincente Minnelli and finished by the credited director Robert Z Leonard. The Steve Martin vehicle *Dead Men Don't Wear Plaid* included great chunks of this movie to great effect. TS

Robert Taylor (1) *Rigby* • Ava Gardner *Elizabeth Hintten* • Charles Laughton *JJ Bealler* • Vincent Price *Carwood* • John Hodiak *Tug Hintten* • Samuel S Hinds *Dr Warren* • John Hoyt *Gibbs* • Tito Renaldo *Emilio Gomez* • Martin Garralaga *Pablo Gomez* ■ *Dir* Robert Z Leonard • *Scr* Marguerite Roberts, from the short story by Frederick Nebel

The Bridal Path ★★ U

Comedy 1959 · UK · Colour · 95mins

Frank Launder and Sidney Gilliat's powers were clearly on the wane when they made this slipshod romantic comedy. Bill Travers presents only a slight variation on his performance in the same team's earlier film, *Geordie*, as a tetchy Scottish giant whose doltish unwillingness to come to terms with modern life precipitates what is intended to be rib-tickling confusion. Hamming gleefully, George Cole and Gordon Jackson only emphasise Travers's one-dimensional acting. DP

Bill Travers *Ewan McEwan* • Alex Mackenzie *Finlay* • Eric Woodburn *Archie* • Jack Lambert *Hector* • John Rae *Angus* • Roddy McMillan *Murdo* • Jefferson Clifford *Wallace* • Nell Ballantyne *Jessie* • George Cole *Sergeant Bruce* • Fiona Clyne *Katie* • Gordon Jackson *Constable Alec* ■ *Dir* Frank Launder • *Scr* Frank Launder, Geoffrey Willans, Nigel Tranter, from the novel by Nigel Tranter

The Bride ★★ 15

Gothic horror drama
1985 · US · Colour · 114mins

This is one of the more unnecessary versions of Mary Shelley's man-makes-monster story. A bizarre cast has Sting as Baron Frankenstein, bringing Jennifer Beals to life (now *that* takes some doing!) under the watchful gaze of monster number one Clancy Brown, whose touching scenes with the late David Rappaport effortlessly steal the movie. Michael Seymour's production design is lush and impressive, as is Maurice Jarre's score, but this one is a nonstarter. TS

Sting *Baron Frankenstein* • Jennifer Beals *Eva* • Anthony Higgins *Clerval* • Clancy Brown *Viktor* • David Rappaport *Rinaldo* • Geraldine Page *Mrs Baumann* • Alexei Sayle *Magar* • Phil Daniels *Bela* • Veruschka [Veruschka Von Lehndorff] *Countess* • Quentin Crisp *Dr Zalhus* ■ *Dir* Franc Roddam • *Scr* Lloyd Fonvielle, from characters created by Mary Shelley • *Music* Maurice Jarre • *Editor* Michael Ellis • *Production Designer* Michael Seymour

Bride & Prejudice ★★★ 12

Romantic comedy
2004 · UK/Ger · Colour · 106mins

Jane Austen's classic story is transposed to India and given a Bollywood makeover here by director Gurinder Chadha. Aishwarya Rai takes the Elizabeth Bennet role as Lalita, one of four eligible daughters from a good family. She meets handsome but haughty American Will Darcy (Martin Henderson) at a wedding, and soon the sparks are flying and saris whirling for cast-of-hundreds musical numbers. The script nimbly pulls off the location and time shift of Austen's tale, but there's a fatal lack of chemistry between the two leads and the stretches between the singing occasionally fall flat. LF DVD

Aishwarya Rai *Lalita Bakshi* • Martin Henderson *Will Darcy* • Naveen Andrews *Balraj*

B

Bingley • Indira Varma *Kiran Bingley* • Namrata Shirodkar *Jaya Bakshi* • Peeya Rai Chodhuri *Lucky Bakshi* • Meghnaa *Maya Bakshi* • Nadira Babbar *Mrs Bakshi* • Anupam Kher *Mr Bakshi* • Daniel Gillies *Johnny Wickham* • Nitin Ganatra [Nitin Chandra Ganatra] *Mr Kholi* ■ *Dir* Gurinder Chadha • *Scr* Gurinder Chadha, Paul Mayeda Berges, from the novel *Pride and Prejudice* by Jane Austen

The Bride and the Beast ★ PG

Psychological horror 1958 · US · BW · 73mins

What else could this painfully cheap *King Kong* variant be but junk, when its author is Ed Wood Jr, the world's worst director? On their wedding night, Charlotte Austin is curiously attracted to hubby Lance Fuller's pet ape. Under hypnosis, she learns that in a previous incarnation she was queen of the gorillas. So it's off on an African safari (cue endless stock footage) to meet her hairy destiny. Laughably inept and for Wood completists only. AJ

Charlotte Austin *Laura* • Lance Fuller *Dan* • Johnny Roth *Taro* • Steve Calvert *Beast* • William Justine *Dr Reiner* • Jeanne Gerson *Marka* • Gil Frye *Captain Cameron* ■ *Dir* Adrian Weiss • *Scr* Edward D Wood Jr, from a story by Adrian Weiss

Bride by Mistake ★★

Comedy 1944 · US · BW · 81mins

Lovely Laraine Day nearly achieved stardom in the mid-1940s, having built up a following as Mary Lamont in MGM's popular *Dr Kildare* series. Eventually she secured leads in major movies, playing opposite Gary Cooper in *The Story of Dr Wassell* and Cary Grant in *Mr Lucky*. This film followed those two major roles, but did little for her career. A minor feature that showcased her charms, it led to co-starring roles supporting Lana Turner and John Wayne. TS

Alan Marshal *Tony Travis* • Laraine Day *Norah Hunter* • Marsha Hunt *Sylvia* • Allyn Joslyn *Phil Vernon* • Edgar Buchanan *Connors* • Michael St Angel *Corey* • Marc Cramer *Ross* • William Post Jr *Donald* • Bruce Edwards *Chaplain* ■ *Dir* Richard Wallace • *Scr* Phoebe Ephron, Henry Ephron, from a story by Norman Krasna

The Bride Came COD ★★★ U

Comedy 1941 · US · BW · 91mins

The unlikely comic pairing of movie greats James Cagney and Bette Davis may seem a mite arch, but they seem to enjoy each other's company. The plot is a heavily diluted comic caper about mistaken identities and runaway brides – he's a flier, she's an heiress and, for some obscure reason, they spend a lot of time together marooned in a desert ghost town. Cagney manages to give Davis a pretty good run for her money and is better at the farcical moments, especially as most of the jokes involve Davis losing her dignity. Still, Davis was a born trouper, and rises above this nonsense with style and grace. TS

James Cagney *Steve Collins* • Bette Davis *Joan Winfield* • Stuart Erwin *Tommy Keenan* • Jack Carson *Allen Brice* • George Tobias *Peewee* • Eugene Pallette *Lucius K Winfield* • Harry Davenport *Pop Tolliver* • William Frawley *Sheriff McGee* ■ *Dir* William Keighley • *Scr* Julius J Epstein, Philip G Epstein, from a story by Kenneth Earl, MM Musselman

The Bride Comes Home ★★★ U

Comedy 1935 · US · BW · 82mins

Having chalked up a success by pairing Claudette Colbert and newcomer Fred MacMurray in the romantic comedy *The Gilded Lily* (1935), Paramount recycled the formula – same stars, same director (Wesley Ruggles) and the same screenwriter (Claude Binyon). Once again the delightful Colbert is in a tug of war between two suitors. She's now an impoverished but feisty heiress involved in a magazine-publishing venture with mega-rich and sweet-natured Robert Young. MacMurray is Young's ill-tempered, and poor, sidekick. No prizes for guessing which man she chooses in the end. RK

Claudette Colbert *Jeanette Desmereau* • Fred MacMurray *Cyrus Anderson* • Robert Young (1) *Jack Bristow* • William Collier Sr *Alfred Desmereau* • Donald Meek *The judge* • Richard Carle *Frank* • Johnny Arthur *Otto* ■ *Dir* Wesley Ruggles • *Scr* Claude Binyon, from a story by Elizabeth Sanxay Holding

Bride for Sale ★★★

Romantic comedy 1949 · US · BW · 87mins

Although her career would extend another two decades, this was the last comedy made by the sparkling Claudette Colbert. It's slight stuff – she's torn between sturdy George Brent and cheerful Robert Young – made watchable by its attractive stars. Colbert's next role was to have been Margo Channing in *All about Eve*, but she injured her back. TS

Claudette Colbert *Nora Shelly* • Robert Young (1) *Steve Adams* • George Brent *Paul Martin* • Max Baer *Litka* • Gus Schilling *Timothy* • Charles Arnt *Dobbs* • Mary Bear *Miss Stone* • Ann Tyrrell *Miss Swanson* ■ *Dir* William D Russell • *Scr* Bruce Manning, Islin Auster, from a story by Joseph Fields

The Bride Is Too Beautiful ★★ PG

Romantic comedy 1956 · Fr · BW · 93mins

This Brigitte Bardot vehicle was made when the "sex kitten" could break your heart with a look. Also featuring Louis Jourdan, the film has Bardot as a girl from the sticks who becomes a top model after she is spotted by the publishers of a Paris magazine. Micheline Presle brings class to the silly proceedings in a lightweight offering. Released on video and DVD as *Her Bridal Night*. TS. French dialogue dubbed into English. DVD

Brigitte Bardot *Chouchou* • Micheline Presle *Judith* • Louis Jourdan *Michel* • Marcel Amont *Tom* • Jean-François Calvé *Patrice* • Roger Dumas *Marc* • Madeleine Lambert *Aunt Agnès* • Marcelle Arnold *Madame Victoire* ■ *Dir* Pierre Gaspard-Huit • *Scr* Philippe Agostini, Odette Joyeux, Juliette Saint-Giniez, from a story by Odette Joyeux

Bride of Chucky ★★★ 18

Horror spoof 1998 · US · Colour · 85mins

This fourth encounter with devilish doll Chucky is the most entertaining of the *Child's Play* series, thanks to Ronny Yu's colourful direction, a wickedly humorous tone and the irresistible presence of Jennifer Tilly. There's more laughter than slaughter as Chucky and new dolly girl Tiffany plot to escape their diminutive frames. Although the story is lightweight, the witty references to horror classics of past and present and the hilarious interplay between the rubber lovers resurrect this series from its movie grave. JC. Contains swearing, violence. DVD

Jennifer Tilly *Tiffany* • Brad Dourif *Chucky* • Katherine Heigl *Jade* • Nick Stabile *Jesse* • Alexis Arquette *Damien Baylock* • Gordon Michael Woolvett *David* • John Ritter *Chief Warren Kincaid* • Lawrence Dane *Lieutenant Preston* ■ *Dir* Ronny Yu • *Scr* Don Mancini

Bride of Frankenstein ★★★★★ PG

Classic horror 1935 · US · BW · 74mins

James Whale's extravagantly produced sequel to his own *Frankenstein* still ranks as one of horrordom's greatest achievements. From his wittily eccentric direction and Elsa Lanchester's electric hairdo, to Ernest Thesiger's ingenious portrayal of the perverse Dr Pretorius and Boris Karloff's alternately poignant and pushy monster, it's a class act from amazing start to religious-slanted finish. They don't get any better than this and some scenes – the unveiling of the bride to the sound of wedding bells, the miniature people in bell jars – are classics. *Son of Frankenstein* followed in 1939. AJ DVD

Boris Karloff *Monster* • Colin Clive *Henry Frankenstein* • Valerie Hobson *Elizabeth* • Ernest Thesiger *Doctor Pretorius* • Elsa Lanchester *Mary Wollstonecraft Shelley/Monster's mate* • Gavin Gordon *Lord Byron* • Douglas Walton *Percy Bysshe Shelley* • Una O'Connor *Minnie* ■ *Dir* James Whale • *Scr* William Hurlbut, John Balderston [John L Balderston], Tom Reed (uncredited), from the novel *Frankenstein; or, the Modern Prometheus* by Mary Wollstonecraft Shelley • *Cinematographer* John J Mescall • *Art Director* Charles D Hall • *Special Effects* John P Fulton • *Make-up* Jack Pierce

Bride of Re-Animator ★★ 18

Horror comedy 1991 · US · Colour · 92mins

Nowhere near as impactful, witty or fresh as the original HP Lovecraft-based cult movie *Re-Animator*, director Brian Yuzna's gloriously gory sequel (he produced the first outing) sadly ventures more into standard Frankenstein territory. Jeffrey Combs is good value as the mad doctor with the luminous green serum that revives dead tissue to create a living woman out of assorted body parts. Gruesomely over-the-top; followed by a second sequel, *Beyond Re-Animator* (2003). AJ. Contains violence and swearing. DVD

Jeffrey Combs *Herbert West* • Bruce Abbott *Dan Cain* • Claude Earl Jones *Lieutenant Leslie Chapham* • Fabiana Udenio *Francesca Danelli* • David Gale *Doctor Carl Hill* • Kathleen Kinmont *Gloria – The Bride* ■ *Dir* Brian Yuzna • *Scr* Woody Keith, Rick Fry, from a story by Brian Yuzna, Woody Keith, Rick Fry, from the story *Herbert West – the Re-Animator* by HP Lovecraft

Bride of the Monster ★ PG

Horror 1955 · US · BW · 68mins

Many will know about this movie purely because Tim Burton expertly re-created key scenes in his superb *Ed Wood* biopic. The movie itself is pure torture to watch, but has to be seen to be believed. Bela Lugosi, in his only true starring role in an Ed Wood exploiter, is a fugitive Russian scientist trying to create a race of super-beings in his swamp-based hideout. The whole sorry affair comes complete with light-bulb special effects and the infamous pit fight between Lugosi and a lifeless rubber octopus stolen from a John Wayne movie. AJ

Bela Lugosi *Dr Eric Vornoff* • Tor Johnson *Lobo* • Tony McCoy *Lieutenant Dick Craig* • Loretta King *Janet Lawton* • Harvey B Dunn *Captain Robbins* • George Becwar *Professor Strowski* • Paul Marco *Kelton* • Don Nagel *Martin* ■ *Dir* Edward D Wood Jr • *Scr* Edward D Wood Jr, Alex Gordon

Bride of the Wind ★

Biographical drama 2001 · US/UK/Ger · Colour · 99mins

Bruce Beresford's bio pic of Alma Mahler, wife of Gustav Mahler is a sorry affair (or should we say – full of sorry affairs). Alma (Sarah Wynter) bed-hops through the Viennese rich and famous. First she meets and seduces Mahler (Jonathan Pryce). Then the hussy is repeatedly unfaithful to him – blaming his passion for music as her just cause. Dire performances and a dry script don't improve matters much either. To be avoided. LH

Sarah Wynter *Alma Mahler* • Jonathan Pryce *Gustav Mahler* • Vincent Perez *Oskar Kokoschka* • Simon Verhoeven *Walter Gropius* • Gregor Seberg *Franz Werfel* • Dagmar Schwarz *Anna Moll* • Wolfgang Hubsch *Karl Moll* • August Schmolzer *Gustav Klimt* ■ *Dir* Bruce Beresford • *Scr* Marilyn Levy

Bride of Vengeance ★

Drama 1949 · US · BW · 92mins

The Borgias get up to all sorts of shady dealings in Renaissance Italy, especially Lucretia, who is sent out to kill a man, but falls in love with him. This was a disaster for all concerned – director Michael Keisen loathed the script, and Ray Milland refused to appear in it and was suspended by the studio. So bad were the reviews, and so thin was the box office, that Paramount sacked its contract star, Paulette Goddard. AT

Paulette Goddard *Lucretia Borgia* • John Lund *Alfonso D'Este* • Macdonald Carey *Cesare Borgia* • Albert Dekker *Vanetti* • John Sutton *Bisceglie* • Raymond Burr *Michelotto* • Charles Dayton *Bastino* • Donald Randolph *Tiziano* • Billy Gilbert *Beppo* ■ *Dir* Mitchell Leisen • *Scr* Cyril Hume, Michael Hogan, Clemence Dane, from a story by Michael Hogan

The Bride Walks Out ★★

Comedy 1936 · US · BW · 80mins

A Barbara Stanwyck vehicle in which the star demonstrated that, without a strong director and clever script, comedy was not her forte. She tries hard as a model who becomes a housewife, but the material defeats her. Yet, there's still pleasure to be had in watching a cast that includes such super character players as Ned Sparks and Hattie McDaniel. TS

Barbara Stanwyck *Carolyn Martin* • Gene Raymond *Michael Martin* • Robert Young (1) *Hugh McKenzie* • Ned Sparks *Paul Dodson* • Helen Broderick *Mattie Dodson* • Willie Best *Smokie* • Robert Warwick *Mr McKenzie* • Billy Gilbert *Donovan* • Hattie McDaniels [Hattie McDaniel] *Maime* ■ *Dir* Leigh Jason • *Scr* PJ Wolfson, Philip G Epstein, Edmund Joseph (uncredited), from a story by Howard Emmett Rogers

The Bride with White Hair ★★★★ 18

Martial arts fantasy romance
1993 · HK · Colour · 88mins

The extraordinary Hong Kong movie that created a massive fan base for Ronny Yu (later to make *Bride of Chucky* and *The 51st State*), this is an intoxicating fantasy. Brigitte Lin's wolf-raised killing machine and Leslie Cheung's warrior fall in love and face the wrath of Lin's evil, dual-sexed Siamese twin fiancée. No, really. Much of the huge budget went on the amazing sets, which complement Yu's phenomenal eye for composition, dazzling fight choreography, stunning photography and artistic bloodletting. The occasionally confusing story is really one big pantomime, yet this doesn't lessen the film's poetic potency. It was followed by a sequel produced by Yu. JC. In Cantonese with English subtitles. DVD

Leslie Cheung *Zhou Yihang* • Brigitte Lin *Lian Nichang* • Ng Chun-yu [Francis Ng] *Ji Wu Shang, Siamese male twin* • Elaine Lui *Ji Wu Shang, Siamese female twin* ■ *Dir* Ronny Yu • *Scr* Lam Kei Tou, Tseng Pik Yin, David Wu, Ronny Yu

The Bride Wore Black ★★★★

Mystery 1967 · Fr/It · Colour · 107mins

In adapting Cornell Woolrich's novel and hiring Bernard Herrmann for the score, François Truffaut paid his most conscious tribute to Alfred Hitchcock. Jeanne Moreau gives a chameleon-like performance as the widow seeking retribution from the quintet who accidentally killed her husband on their wedding day. Each of them is an archetype of male boorishness, yet their deaths invoke a mixture of emotions and calculated flashbacks revealing the extent of Moreau's loss temper the callousness of her crimes. DP. In French with English subtitles.

Jeanne Moreau *Julie Kohler* • Jean-Claude Brialy *Corey* • Michel Bouquet *Coral* • Charles Denner *Fergus* • Claude Rich *Bliss* • Daniel Boulanger *Holmes/Delvaux* • Michael Lonsdale [Michel Lonsdale] *Rene Morane* • Serge Rousseau *David* ■ *Dir* François Truffaut • *Scr* François Truffaut, Jean-Louis Richard, from the novel by William Irish [Cornell Woolrich] • *Cinematographer* Raoul Coutard

The Bride Wore Boots ★★

Comedy 1946 · US · BW · 86mins

This comedy of marital disharmony has Barbara Stanwyck detesting her husband Robert Cummings's interest in the Civil War and Cummings detesting her love of horses. There's a divorce, a horse that's in love with Cummings and a championship steeplechase. And that's about it, really, with both stars making the most of their modest material, especially Cummins. A very young Natalie Wood plays one of two precocious by-products of the marriage. AT

Barbara Stanwyck *Sally Warren* • Robert Cummings *Jeff Warren* • Diana Lynn *Mary Lou Medford* • Patric Knowles *Lance Gale* • Peggy Wood *Grace Apley* • Robert Benchley *Tod Warren* • Willie Best *Joe* • Natalie Wood *Carol Warren* ■ *Dir* Irving Pichel • *Scr* Dwight Michael Wiley, from a story by Dwight Michael Wiley, from a play by Harry Segall

The Bride Wore Red ★★★ U

Drama 1937 · US · BW · 103mins

A fairly typical, though slightly more eccentric than most, Joan Crawford vehicle. The star plays a cabaret singer who gets to travel to the obviously studio-bound and back-projected Austrian Tyrol and can't choose between handsome and dashing playboy Robert Young or handsome and dashing postman Franchot Tone. Not, of course, that it matters one jot in this entertaining tosh. This tale was directed by the only woman director in mainstream Hollywood at the time, Dorothy Arzner; it's just a shame that she wasn't more talented. TS

Joan Crawford *Anni* • Franchot Tone *Giulio* • Robert Young (1) *Rudi Pal* • Billie Burke *Contessa di Milano* • Reginald Owen *Admiral Monti* • Lynne Carver *Magdalena Monti* • George Zucco *Count Armalia* • Mary Phillips [Mary Philips] *Maria* ■ *Dir* Dorothy Arzner • *Scr* Tess Slesinger, Bradbury Foote, from the play *The Girl from Trieste* by Ferenc Molnar

The Brides of Dracula ★★★★

Horror 1960 · UK · Colour · 85mins

While Christopher Lee worried about typecasting, Hammer went ahead anyway with this sequel (in name only) to its huge 1958 hit *Dracula*. Anaemic David Peel as Baron Meinster is a poor substitute for Lee's more full-blooded undead Count, but that's the only point of contention in a classic Terence Fisher-directed shocker. The marvellous atmosphere drips with a lingering Gothic ghoulishness, the sexuality is remarkably upfront for its time, and the climax set in the shadow of a moonlit windmill is the stuff of fairy-tale nightmare. AJ

Peter Cushing *Dr Van Helsing* • Martita Hunt *Baroness Meinster* • Yvonne Monlaur *Marianne* • Freda Jackson *Greta* • David Peel *Baron Meinster* • Miles Malleson *Dr Tobler* • Henry Oscar *Herr Lang* • Mona Washbourne *Frau Lang* ■ *Dir* Terence Fisher • *Scr* Jimmy Sangster, Peter Bryan, Edward Percy, from characters created by Bram Stoker

The Brides of Fu Manchu ★★ U

Crime drama 1966 · UK · Colour · 90mins

The second outing for Christopher Lee as Sax Rohmer's mastermind (after *The Face of Fu Manchu*) was the first step down the slippery slope of inadequate stories and deteriorating quality for the series. In this bid for world domination, Fu Manchu kidnaps the daughters of 12 international diplomats to cause political chaos. Don Sharp's direction rarely lives up to his surname, although Lee's performance is as entertaining as always. *The Vengeance of Fu Manchu* followed in 1967. AJ DVD

Christopher Lee *Fu Manchu* • Douglas Wilmer *Nayland Smith* • Marie Versini *Marie Lentz* • Heinz Drache *Franz Baumer* • Howard Marion-Crawford *Dr Petrie* • Kenneth Fortescue *Sergeant Spier* • Joseph Furst *Otto Lentz* • Carole Gray *Michele* ■ *Dir* Don Sharp • *Scr* Peter Welbeck [Harry Alan Towers], from characters created by Sax Rohmer

The Bridesmaid ★★★ 15

Psychological thriller
2004 · Fr/Ger · Colour · 110mins

Director Claude Chabrol returns to the work of crime novelist Ruth Rendell for this sinister thriller. Sales rep Benoît Magimel loses his grip on reality after falling for Laura Smet (sadly lacking sufficient "femme fatale" quality) after being struck by her similarity to a garden statue that his mother Aurore Clément had given to her lover Bernard Le Coq. Chabrol is still a master at dissecting bourgeois manners and creating slow-burning suspense, but while he generates a typically unnerving atmosphere here, the storyline is short on surprises. DP. In French with English subtitles. Contains sex scenes.

Benoît Magimel *Philippe Tardieu* • Laura Smet *Senta* • Aurore Clément *Christine Tardieu* • Bernard Le Coq *Gérard* • Solène Bouton *Sophie* • Anna Mihalcea *Patricia* • Michel Duchaussoy *The tramp* • Suzanne Flon *Madame Crespin* ■ *Dir* Claude Chabrol • *Scr* Claude Chabrol, Pierre Leccia, from the novel by Ruth Rendell

The Bridge ★★★★

Second World War drama
1959 · W Ger · BW · 106mins

Although many German features in the 1950s tackled the aftermath of the Second World War (the so-called "rubble films"), few dealt with the conflict itself. Actor Bernhard Wicki made his debut as writer/director with this docudramatic reconstruction of an actual incident involving seven teenage recruits who were ordered to defend a strategically irrelevant bridge in the last days of the American advance. Rarely has the rigidity of Nazi discipline or the futility of war been as powerfully exposed as in this Oscar-nominated drama, which is not only forcibly directed, but also impeccably played by its suitably inexperienced cast. DP. In German with English subtitles.

Volker Bohnet *Hans Scholten* • Fritz Wepper *Albert Mutz* • Michael Hinz *Walter Forst* • Frank Glaubrecht *Jurgen Borchert* • Karl Michael Balzer *Karl Horber* • Volker Lechtenbrink *Klaus Hager* • Gunther Hoffmann *Sigi Bernhard* ■ *Dir* Bernhard Wicki • *Scr* Michael Mansfeld, Karl-Wilhelm Vivier, from the novel *Die Brucke* by Manfred Gregor

The Bridge ★★ 15

Period drama 1990 · UK · Colour · 97mins

A heritage cast-off from the Merchant Ivory school, this genteel British period piece lacks both subtlety and dynamism. The brilliant Saskia Reeves is underused as a bored wife who falls head over heels for a young artist (David O'Hara) while on holiday with her children. Even with the acting clout of Joss Ackland, Geraldine James and Rosemary Harris behind him, director Sydney Macartney simply doesn't have the artistry of James Ivory. LH

Saskia Reeves *Isobel Hetherington* • David O'Hara *Philip Wilson Steer* • Joss Ackland *Smithson* • Rosemary Harris *Aunt Jude* • Anthony Higgins *Reginald Hetherington* • Geraldine James *Mrs Todd* • Tabitha Allen *Emma Hetherington* • Dominique Rossi *Mary* ■ *Dir* Sydney Macartney • *Scr* Adrian Hodges, from the novel by Maggie Hemingway

The Bridge ★★★

Drama 1999 · Fr · Colour · 88mins

Screenwriter François Dupeyron, who directed Gérard Depardieu in *A Strange Place to Meet*, again explores the randomness of attraction in this measured drama, which the actor co-directed with Frédéric Auburtin. In a bid to reinforce his themes, Depardieu archly cast his off-screen lover, Carole Bouquet, as the perfect wife who has an affair with Charles Berling, an engineer working on the same bridge as her husband. The film is truthful but slightly lacking in dramatic impetus. DP. In French with English subtitles.

Gérard Depardieu *Georges* • Carole Bouquet *Mina* • Charles Berling *Matthias* • Stanislas Crevillen *Tommy* • Dominique Reymond *Claire Daboval* • Mélanie Laurent *Lisbeth* • Michèle Goddet ■ *Dir* Gérard Depardieu, Frédéric Auburtin • *Scr* François Dupeyron, from a novel by Alain LeBlanc

The Bridge at Remagen ★★★ PG

Second World War drama
1969 · US · Colour · 112mins

A great performance by George Segal, as a die-hard platoon leader, lifts this "war is hell" saga out of the ordinary. Filming in Czechoslovakia and interrupted by the actual Russian invasion, big-budget director John Guillermin was clearly trying to achieve something different by adding sober measures of cynical disenchantment to the conventional Second World War melodramatic mix. Epic explosions and razzle-dazzle camerawork ultimately win out over any such grandiose "thinking action man" ideas, however. An A for effort, though. AJ DVD

George Segal *Lieutenant Phil Hartman* • Robert Vaughn *Major Paul Kreuger* • Ben Gazzara *Sergeant Angelo* • Bradford Dillman *Major Barnes* • EG Marshall *Brig Gen Shinner* • Peter Van Eyck *General von Brock* • Matt Clark *Colonel Jellicoe* • Fritz Ford *Colonel Dent* ■ *Dir* John Guillermin • *Scr* Richard Yates, William Roberts, Ray Rigby, from a story by Roger Hirson [Roger O Hirson], from the novel by Kenneth William Hechler

Bridge of Dragons ★★ 18

Action thriller 1999 · US · Colour · 87mins

Dolph Lundgren remains a popular draw in videoland and this won't disappoint his fans. Set in a post-apocalyptic future, it stars Lundgren as a programmed killing machine – an always helpful plot device since it explains the wooden acting. When he comes to the rescue of a princess, he incurs the wrath of evil warlord Cary-Hiroyuki Tagawa. While this offers plenty of high-quality biffing and loud explosions, it's the charismatic Tagawa who steals the show. JF DVD

Dolph Lundgren *Warchyld* • Cary-Hiroyuki Tagawa *Ruecheng* • Rachel Shane [Valerie Chow] *Halo* ■ *Dir* Isaac Florentine • *Scr* Carlton Holder

The Bridge on the River Kwai ★★★★★ PG

Second World War drama
1957 · UK · Colour · 155mins

Few Second World War films are as enduring – or whistleable – as director David Lean's multi-Oscar-winning examination of the stiff upper lip. Alec Guinness plays Colonel Nicholson, the epitome of British dignity and resolve who, after brutal treatment at the hands of his Japanese captors in Burma, leads his men in the building of a strategically vital railway bridge for the enemy, as an exercise in keeping up their – and his – morale. This is interesting enough, but the ironies of war are further pointed up by the subplot in which wily American escapee William Holden is dispatched back into the jungle to blow up said bridge. The central performances are first rate, including Sessue Hayakawa as the Japanese commander, but most notably Guinness, who imbues Nicholson with a brand of pride, patriotism and courage that speak of another age. AC DVD

William Holden (2) *Shears* • Alec Guinness *Colonel Nicholson* • Jack Hawkins *Major Warden* • Sessue Hayakawa *Colonel Saito* • James Donald *Major Clipton* • Geoffrey Horne *Lieutenant Joyce* • André Morell *Colonel Green* • Peter Williams *Captain Reeves* • John Boxer *Major Hughes* ■ *Dir* David Lean • *Scr* Pierre Boulle (front for Carl Foreman, Michael Wilson), from the novel by Pierre Boulle • *Music* Malcolm Arnold • *Editor* Peter Taylor

Bridge to the Sun ★★ U

Second World War biographical drama
1961 · US/Fr · BW · 112mins

In a major change of pace from her infamous role in *Baby Doll*, Carroll Baker stars as an American girl who marries Japanese diplomat James Shigeta and accompanies him to Japan in time for Pearl Harbor. Needless to say, the couple endure social, cultural and emotional difficulties as well as wartime hardships, and suffer a tragedy at the war's end. Based on an autobiography by Gwen Terasaki, the subject itself is fascinating and the locations are visually interesting, but, although proficient, the film remains surprisingly dull and uninvolving. RK

Carroll Baker *Gwen Terasaki* • James Shigeta *Hidenari Terasaki* • James Yagi *Hara* • Tetsuro Tamba *Jiro* • Sean Garrison *Fred Tyson* • Ruth Masters *Aunt Peggy* ■ *Dir* Etienne Périer • *Scr* Charles Kaufman, from the autobiography by Gwen Terasaki

A Bridge Too Far ★★★ 15

Second World War drama
1977 · UK · Colour · 168mins

Richard Attenborough's epic retelling of one of the Second World War's biggest debacles is impressive enough, with its eye-catching list of stars, fabulous parachute-drop sequences and superb Panavision photography from Geoffrey Unsworth. But the depressing nature of this story of human suffering and sacrifice makes for grim, unedifying viewing, no matter how cleverly writer William Goldman has created drama from the event. Only Sean Connery and Edward Fox really shine in an all-star cast, though Hardy Kruger and Maximilian Schell emerge with credibility as Germans. TS. Contains violence and swearing. DVD

Dirk Bogarde *Lt Gen Frederick Browning* • James Caan *Staff Sergeant Eddie Dohun* • Michael Caine *Lt Col Joe Vandeleur* • Sean Connery *Maj Gen Robert Urquhart* • Edward Fox *Lt Gen Brian Horrocks* • Elliott Gould *Colonel Bobby Stout* • Gene Hackman *Maj Gen Stanislaw Sosabowski* • Anthony Hopkins *Lt Col John Frost* • Hardy Kruger *Maj Gen Ludwig* • Laurence Olivier *Dr Spaander* • Ryan O'Neal *Brig Gen James M Gavin* • Robert Redford *Major Julian Cook* • Maximilian Schell *Lt Gen Bittrich* ■ *Dir* Richard Attenborough • *Scr* William Goldman, from the book by Cornelius Ryan

B

The Bridges at Toko-Ri ★★★★ U

War drama 1954 · US · Colour · 98mins

This glossy, star-laden Korean War movie that manages to be both superbly entertaining and extremely moving, thanks to solid direction from the under-rated Mark Robson. The source material is from the prolific writer James A Michener, and his view of the futility of the war in Korea is given expert emphasis by the fine performances of William Holden as a reserve officer recalled to service and Fredric March as a gruff admiral. Grace Kelly is simply luminous as Holden's navy wife. The movie won an Oscar for its special effects. TS [video] DVD

William Holden (2) *Lieutenant Harry Brubaker* • Fredric March *Rear Admiral George Tarrant* • Grace Kelly *Nancy Brubaker* • Mickey Rooney *Mike Forney* • Robert Strauss *Beer Barrel* • Charles McGraw *Commander Wayne Lee* • Keiko Awaji *Kimiko* • Earl Holliman *Nestor Gamidge* • Richard Shannon *Lieutenant Olds* ■ *Dir* Mark Robson • *Scr* Valentine Davies, from a novel by James A Michener

The Bridges of Madison County ★★★★ 12

Romantic drama
1995 · US · Colour · 129mins

Clint Eastwood directs and stars in this romantic drama based on Robert James Waller's bestseller. He plays a photographer drawn into an intense love affair with rancher's wife Meryl Streep when he arrives in Iowa to take pictures of Madison County's covered bridges. Told in flashback after Streep's death, when her grown-up children discover a diary and realise how deeply affected their mother was by the experience. Eastwood's moving film avoids easy sentimentality in favour of a more complex exploration of family responsibility, marital fidelity and self denial. Very few film adaptations outshine the book they are based on, but this is a rare exception. TH. Contains swearing. [video] DVD

Clint Eastwood *Robert Kincaid* • Meryl Streep *Francesca Johnson* • Annie Corley *Carolyn Johnson* • Victor Slezak *Michael Johnson* • Jim Haynie *Richard* • Sarah Kathryn Schmitt *Young Carolyn* • Christopher Kroon *Young Michael* • Phyllis Lyons *Betty* ■ *Dir* Clint Eastwood • *Scr* Richard LaGravenese, from the novel by Robert James Waller

Bridget Jones: the Edge of Reason ★★★ 15

Romantic comedy
2004 · UK/US/Fr/Ire · Colour · 103mins

This occasionally tiresome sequel has the gormless but lovable Bridget (Renée Zellweger) no longer single, having hooked the dishy but taciturn lawyer Colin Firth. It's not long, however, before they're squabbling over such foibles as Firth's habit of folding his boxer shorts before going to bed, so Bridget heads off to Thailand to compile a travel programme with handsome cad Hugh Grant. The characterisations are once more excellent, so it's unfortunate that the scriptwriters felt it necessary to revisit jokes from the original. BP. Contains swearing, sex scenes. [video] DVD

Renée Zellweger [Renee Zellweger] *Bridget Jones* • Hugh Grant *Daniel Cleaver* • Colin Firth *Mark Darcy* • Jim Broadbent *Bridget's dad* • Gemma Jones *Bridget's mum* • Jacinda Barrett *Rebecca* • Sally Phillips *Shazzer* • Shirley Henderson *Jude* • James Callis *Tom* • Jessica Stevenson *Magda* • Neil Pearson *Richard Finch* ■ *Dir* Beeban Kidron • *Scr* Helen Fielding, Andrew Davies, Richard Curtis, Adam Brooks, from the novel by Helen Fielding

Bridget Jones's Diary ★★★★★ 15

Romantic comedy
2001 · UK/US · Colour · 92mins

So well adapted by Richard Curtis that it appeals to both sexes, the film is actually far better than the book. Star Renee Zellweger, as the 1990s heroine, is far more endearing than the book's Bridget. Then one cannot imagine Helen Fielding ever having the luxury of suitor super duo Hugh Grant and Colin Firth, who both surpass expectations. What we have here is the best in British romantic comedy, well directed by newcomer Sharon Maguire, well acted by an ensemble of stellar cast and very, very funny indeed. Daft, delicious, decidedly dippy and quite brilliant. LH. Contains swearing [video] DVD

Renée Zellweger [Renee Zellweger] *Bridget Jones* • Colin Firth *Mark Darcy* • Hugh Grant *Daniel Cleaver* • Jim Broadbent *Bridget's dad* • Gemma Jones *Bridget's mum* • Sally Phillips *Sharon* • Shirley Henderson *Jude* • James Callis *Tom* • Embeth Davidtz *Natasha* • Celia Imrie *Una Alconbury* • Honor Blackman *Penny Husbands-Bosworth* ■ *Dir* Sharon Maguire • *Scr* Helen Fielding, Andrew Davies, Richard Curtis, from the novel by Helen Fielding

Brief Encounter ★★★★★ PG

Classic romantic drama
1945 · UK · BW · 82mins

Co-adapted by Noël Coward from his own one-act play *Still Life*, this is one of the finest films ever made in Britain. What makes the illicit love between doctor Trevor Howard and housewife Celia Johnson so memorable is their sheer ordinariness – they really could be anybody sat in the dark or in the comfort of their armchair. Romancing to the strains of Rachmaninov's *Second Piano Concerto*, the leads are outstanding, but credit should also go to the forgotten Cyril Raymond, whose decent dullness as Johnson's husband makes those stolen Thursdays seem so special. DP [video] DVD

Celia Johnson *Laura Jesson* • Trevor Howard *Dr Alec Harvey* • Cyril Raymond *Fred Jesson* • Stanley Holloway *Albert Godby* • Joyce Carey *Myrtle Bagot* • Everley Gregg *Dolly Messiter* • Margaret Barton *Beryl Waters* • Dennis Harkin *Stanley* • Irene Handl *Organist* ■ *Dir* David Lean • *Scr* Noël Coward, David Lean, Anthony Havelock-Allan, Ronald Neame, from the play *Still Life* by Noël Coward • *Cinematographer* Robert Krasker

Brief Encounter ★★ PG

Drama 1974 · UK/US · Colour · 99mins

Richard Burton and Sophia Loren step uncomfortably into Trevor Howard and Celia Johnson's shoes as the married strangers drifting into a poignant affair. There's no denying the bittersweet source material still packs an emotional punch even in this lavish treatment. But the ever-gorgeous Loren, as an Italian housewife who married into the English middle class, barely convinces. AJ [video]

Richard Burton *Alec Harvey* • Sophia Loren *Anna Jesson* • Jack Hedley *Graham Jesson* • Rosemary Leach *Mrs Gaines* • John Le Mesurier *Stephen* • Gwen Cherrell *Dolly* • Jumoke Debayo *Mrs Harris* • Madeline Hinde *Grace* ■ *Dir* Alan Bridges • *Scr* John Bowne, from the play *Still Life* by Noël Coward

A Brief History of Time ★★★

Documentary 1992 · US/UK · Colour · 80mins

Using computers and synthesizers to circumvent the devastating effects of amyotrophic lateral sclerosis, Stephen Hawking succeeded in transforming our notions about the formation of the universe and, through his bestseller *A Brief History of Time*, became the world's most famous theoretical physicist. Steering scrupulously clear of Hawking's then-complex love life, innovative documentarist Errol Morris delves into his past to discover a rebellious student whose mental faculties sharpened as his physical condition deteriorated. With stylised graphics illuminating the theories, and Philip Glass's score imbuing them with a suitable sense of awesomeness, this is a fascinating study. DP

Dir Errol Morris • *Scr* Stephen Hawking, from his book

Brigadoon ★★★★ U

Musical romantic fantasy
1954 · US · Colour · 103mins

This beguiling MGM version of Alan J Lerner and Frederick Loewe's magical stage musical about a Scottish village that comes to life every hundred years is an overlooked and often derided movie in director Vincente Minnelli's canon: time has proved there's no reason for such harsh judgement. It boasts a wonderful score and magnificent arrangements, plus an imaginative studio set, while the use of early CinemaScope enhances the brilliant lateral stage choreography. Yet the real heart of the film lies in the casting. The great Gene Kelly could not be bettered as the American in love in a faraway time and a foreign clime. His duet with Cyd Charisse – *The Heather on the Hill* – is enchanting and, as Kelly's buddy-in-booze, Van Johnson positively shines. TS [video] DVD

Gene Kelly *Tommy Albright* • Van Johnson *Jeff Douglas* • Cyd Charisse *Fiona Campbell* • Elaine Stewart *Jane Ashton* • Barry Jones *Mr Lundie* • Hugh Laing *Harry Beaton* • Albert Sharpe *Andrew Campbell* • Virginia Bosler *Jean Campbell* ■ *Dir* Vincente Minnelli • *Scr* Alan Jay Lerner, from the musical by Alan Jay Lerner, Frederick Loewe • *Choreographer* Gene Kelly • *Art Director* Cedric Gibbon, Preston Ames • *Set Designer* Edwin B Willis, Keogh Gleason • *Costume Designer* Irene

Brigham Young ★★

Historical drama 1940 · US · BW · 112mins

It was jolly difficult to tell the true story of the Mormon trek westward when the censor forbade polygamy on the screen. Director Henry Hathaway gets around this by ignoring the facts and concentrating instead on such eye-catching events as an impressive locust attack on the Mormons' first spring crop. Tyrone Power and Linda Darnell are top billed, but the title role is played by Dean Jagger with his customary sense of rugged integrity and conviction. TS

Tyrone Power *Jonathan Kent* • Linda Darnell *Zina Webb* • Dean Jagger *Brigham Young* • Brian Donlevy *Angus Duncan* • Jane Darwell *Eliza Kent* • John Carradine *Porter Rockwell* • Mary Astor *Mary Ann Young* • Vincent Price *Joseph Smith* • Jean Rogers *Clara Young* ■ *Dir* Henry Hathaway • *Scr* Lamar Trotti, from the story by Louis Bromfield

Bright Angel ★★ 15

Road movie 1990 · US · Colour · 89mins

A heavenly cast are rather lost at sea in this over-stylised thriller. Dermot Mulroney plays a Montana boy inveigled by runaway hippy Lili Taylor to go to Wyoming and find a man who will spring her brother from jail. A pair of innocents, their road trip places them up to their necks in unpleasant but interesting characters. A depressing examination of Midwest life, drifters and "Generation X". LH [video]

Dermot Mulroney *George Russell* • Lili Taylor *Lucy* • Sam Shepard *Jack Russell* • Valerie Perrine *Aileen Russell* • Burt Young *Art Falcone* • Bill Pullman *Bob* • Benjamin Bratt *Claude* • Mary Kay Place *Judy* • Delroy Lindo *Harley* ■ *Dir* Michael Fields • *Scr* Richard Ford

Bright Eyes ★★

Comedy 1934 · US · BW · 84mins

A must for Shirley Temple fans (but others beware) as here, at six years' old, she performs her most famous song, *On the Good Ship Lollipop*. In the last of some ten 1934 screen appearances, the hard-working moppet is the daughter of a maid killed in a road accident. Her mother's employers grudgingly look after Temple to keep in with a rich relative (Charles Sellon) who dotes on her. In memorable contrast to Hollywood's favourite moppet is Jane Withers in her first substantial role as a spoiled and sadistic brat. Two years older than Temple, she went on to become a child star in her own right. AE

Shirley Temple *Shirley Blake* • James Dunn *Loop Merritt* • Jane Darwell *Mrs Higgins* • Judith Allen *Adele Martin* • Lois Wilson *Mary Blake* • Charles Sellon *Uncle Ned Smith* • Walter Johnson *Thomas, the chauffeur* • Jane Withers *Joy Smythe* ■ *Dir* David Butler • *Scr* William Conselman, Edwin Burke, David Butler

Bright Leaf ★★

Drama 1950 · US · BW · 110mins

After appearing together in *The Fountainhead*, Gary Cooper and Patricia Neal were reunited for this turgid melodrama about rival tobacco barons. In the middle of a run of mundane movies and not in the best of health, Cooper gives a lazy performance that stands in stark contrast to Donald Crisp and Neal, who both overact wildly as the father and daughter who seek to ruin him. Director Michael Curtiz could scarcely coax better out of Lauren Bacall, but there's always Karl Freund's lush photography to help pass the time. DP

Gary Cooper *Brant Royle* • Lauren Bacall *Sonia Kovac* • Patricia Neal *Margaret Jane Singleton* • Jack Carson *Chris Malley* • Donald Crisp *Major James Singleton* • Gladys George *Rose* • Elizabeth Patterson *Tabitha Jackson* ■ *Dir* Michael Curtiz • *Scr* Ranald MacDougall, from the novel by Foster Fitz-Simons

Bright Leaves ★★★★ PG

Documentary
2003 · US/UK · Colour · 107mins

Ross McElwee's reputation for personal documentaries with a deceptively wider perspective is reinforced with this investigation into his North Carolina family's role in the corporatisation of the tobacco business. Seeking to establish whether the character played by Gary Cooper in Michael Curtiz's 1950 melodrama *Bright Leaf* was based on his great-grandfather, McElwee winds up considering everything from cinematic license to the capricious nature of history and public health. Dotting his treatise with archive material and home movies, he avoids the temptation to preach by approaching his subject with wry, self-deprecating sagacity and the result is disarmingly charming. DP

Dir/Scr Ross McElwee

Bright Lights, Big City ★★ 18

Drama 1988 · US · Colour · 102mins

The archetypal 1980s movie, this has oodles of RayBans, credit cards, minimalist furniture, naked ambition and enough South American nose candy to make antihero Michael J Fox's coffee table look like Mount Kilimanjaro. At the time, though, it all creaked and groaned, largely due to Fox's inability to portray the complexities of an aspiring young New York novelist on the skids. Phoebe Cates turns in a pleasing performance as Fox's disillusioned wife, but Fox and his grungy chum Kiefer Sutherland are wholly unsympathetic. SH. Contains swearing and drug abuse. [video] DVD

Michael J Fox *Jamie Conway* • Kiefer Sutherland *Tad Allagash* • Phoebe Cates *Amanda* • Swoosie Kurtz *Megan* • Frances Sternhagen *Clara Tillinghast* • Tracy Pollan *Vicky* • John Houseman *Mr Vogel* • Charlie Schlatter *Michael* • Jason Robards *Alex Hardy* • Dianne Wiest *Mother* ■ *Dir* James Bridges • *Scr* Jay McInerney, from his novel

Bright Road ★★★ U

Drama 1953 · US · BW · 68mins

A modest second feature, this is about a pupil (Philip Hepburn) in an all-black school, emotionally troubled as a result of racism and a depressed home life, who overcomes his difficulties with the dedicated help of sympathetic teacher Dorothy Dandridge. It's a worthy, well-acted effort with some touching moments, but it's hampered by a screenplay that pulls its punches and deprives itself of dramatic opportunities. RK

Dorothy Dandridge *Jane Richards* • Philip Hepburn *CT Young* • Harry Belafonte *School principal* • Barbara Ann Sanders *Tanya* • Robert Horton *Dr Mitchell* • Maidie Norman *Tanya's mother* • Renee Beard *Booker T Jones* ■ *Dir* Gerald Mayer • *Scr* Emmett Lavery, from the short story *See How They Run* by Mary Elizabeth Vroman

Bright Victory ★★★

Drama 1951 · US · BW · 97mins

Blinded in the war, soldier Arthur Kennedy faces another kind of battle as he attempts to adjust to his disability, first in hospital, then back home, where his girlfriend Julia Adams is waiting for him. Further emotional complications arise through his relationship with Peggy Dow he meets while in hospital. A moving, if sentimental drama, this is lent added interest by its insight into the rehabilitation methods for the blind. Kennedy gives a superbly convincing performance that earned him a deserved Oscar nomination. RK

Arthur Kennedy *Larry Nevins* • Peggy Dow *Judy Greene* • Julia Adams [Julie Adams] *Chris Paterson* • James Edwards *Joe Morgan* • Will Geer *Mr Nevins* • Minor Watson *Mr Paterson* • Jim Backus *Bill Grayson* • Joan Banks *Janet Grayson* • Rock Hudson *Cpl John Flagg* ■ *Dir* Mark Robson • *Scr* Robert Buckner, from the novel *Lights Out* by Bayard Kendrick

Bright Young Things ★★★ 15

Period comedy drama
2003 · UK · Colour · 101mins

Stephen Fry's adaptation of Evelyn Waugh's classic novel *Vile Bodies* is a solid enough directorial debut. The tale of inter-war youthful plutocrats engaging in endless partying and occasional spasms of self-loathing has been semi-faithfully transferred to the screen. Stephen Campbell Moore stars as a frustrated writer who sets out to marry his girlfriend Emily Mortimer, but it's Fenella Woolgar who really shines as a ditzy socialite. Some of Waugh's finely wrought style evaporates in the transfer and the film drags occasionally as a result, despite a solid supporting cast and a glittering collection of cameos. AS. Contains drug abuse. DVD

Stephen Campbell Moore *Adam Fenwick-Symes* • Emily Mortimer *Nina Blount* • Fenella Woolgar *Agatha Runcible* • James McAvoy *Lord Simon Balcairn* • Michael Sheen *Miles* • David Tennant *Ginger* • Guy Henry *Archie* • Dan Aykroyd *Lord Monomark* • Jim Broadbent *Drunken Major* • Simon Callow *King of Anatolia* • Stockard Channing *Mrs Melrose Ape* • Julia McKenzie *Lottie Crump* • Sir John Mills [John Mills] *Gentleman at party* • Peter O'Toole *Colonel Blount* • Harriet Walter *Lady Metroland* • Bill Paterson *Sir James Brown* • Margaret Tyzack *Lady Throbbing* • Stephen Fry *Chauffeur* ■ *Dir* Stephen Fry • *Scr* Stephen Fry, from the novel *Vile Bodies* by Evelyn Waugh

A Brighter Summer Day ★★★★★

Drama 1991 · Tai · Colour · 185mins

Rather overshadowed by his better-known and much-lauded compatriot Hou Hsiao-Hsien on the international stage, director Edward Yang is still a remarkable film-maker in his own right. Sharing many of the themes of Hou's *A City of Sadness* (which Yang produced), this sprawling, stately epic presents a compelling portrait of growing up in a young nation that was itself struggling to find its identity after the break with China. Three years in the making, it was inspired by a true event encapsulated in the Taiwanese title that translates as *Incident of a Juvenile Murder on Ku Ling Street*. The gang war is less interesting than the social comment, but this is undoubtedly the work of a master. DP. In Mandarin with English subtitles.

Zhen Zhang *Xiao S'ir (Zhang Zhen)* • Lisa Yang *Ming (Liu Zhiming)* • Zhang Guozhu *Zhang Ju (Father)* • Elaine Jin *Mrs Zhang (Mother)* • Wang Juan *Juan (Eldest sister)* • Zhang Han *Lao Er (Elder brother)* • Jiang Xiuqiong *Qiong (Middle sister)* • Lai Fanyun *Yun (Youngest sister)* ■ *Dir* Edward Yang • *Scr* Edward Yang, Yan Hongya, Yang Shunqing, Lai Mingtang

Brighton Beach Memoirs ★★★ 15

Comedy drama 1986 · US · Colour · 104mins

Neil Simon is an expert at angst-ridden autobiography and loves to mine the seam of Jewish family life. Nobody does this particular brand of head-banging better, and this slice of strudel boasts a lovely, acerbic portrayal from Jonathan Silverman as Simon's adolescent doppelgänger, Eugene Jerome. However, Simon has fails to open out his stage play enough for the film to breathe. SH

Jonathan Silverman *Eugene* • Blythe Danner *Kate* • Bob Dishy *Jack* • Brian Drillinger *Stanley* • Stacey Glick *Laurie* • Judith Ivey *Blanche* • Lisa Waltz *Nora* ■ *Dir* Gene Saks • *Scr* Neil Simon, from his play

Brighton Rock ★★★★ PG

Crime drama 1947 · UK · BW · 88mins

This is one of the most sinister crime films ever made in Britain and, but for several cuts by the censor, it would also have been one of the most shocking. However, Graham Greene, scripting from his own novel (not in collaboration with Terence Rattigan, as many sources state), also drew some of the film's teeth by allowing gullible waitress Carol Marsh the faint hope that her malicious husband might love her after all. Richard Attenborough turns in the best performance of his career. DP DVD

Richard Attenborough *Pinkie Brown* • Hermione Baddeley *Ida Arnold* • William Hartnell *Dallow* • Carol Marsh *Rose* • Nigel Stock *Cubitt* • Wylie Watson *Spicer* • Harcourt Williams *Prewitt* • Alan Wheatley *Fred Hale/ Kolley Kibber* ■ *Dir* John Boulting • *Scr* Graham Greene, from his novel

The Brighton Strangler ★★★

Thriller 1945 · US · BW · 67mins

Set in Britain during the Second World War, but filmed (extremely quickly and cheaply) in Hollywood, this intriguing little programme filler was directed by Max Nosseck, whose bizarre career ranges from directing Buster Keaton in French, through a notable Yiddish-language feature, *Overture to Glory*, to the 1950s nudist comedy, *Garden of Eden*. This stars a rather wooden John Loder, who appears on stage as "the Brighton Strangler", and, after a blow to the head, begins to live out his stage role in real life. Cleverly done, and really quite eerie. TS

John Loder *Reginald/Edward* • June Duprez *April* • Michael St Angel *Bob* • Miles Mander *Allison* • Rose Hobart *Dorothy* • Gilbert Emery *Dr Manby* • Rex Evans *Shelton* • Matthew Boulton *Inspector Graham* ■ *Dir* Max Nosseck • *Scr* Arnold Phillips, Max Nosseck

Brilliant Lies ★★

Courtroom drama
1996 · Aus · Colour · 93mins

Gia Carides plays an embittered employee who accuses her boss Anthony LaPaglia of sexual harassment and unfair dismissal. The two take their case to court, inveigling the support of others along the way, and gradually the truth comes out. This is mildly engaging, but the problem is that both principles appear conniving and unsympathetic. LH

Gia Carides *Susy Connor* • Anthony LaPaglia *Gary Fitzgerald* • Zoe Carides *Katy Connor* • Ray Barrett *Brian Connor* • Michael Veitch *Paul Connor* • Catherine Wilkin *Marion Lee* • Neil Melville *Vince Williams* • Jennifer Jarman Walker *Ruth Miller* ■ *Dir* Richard Franklin • *Scr* Richard Franklin, Peter Fitzpatrick, from the play by David Williamson

Brimstone and Treacle ★★★ 18

Black comedy thriller
1982 · UK · Colour · 83mins

The movie version of Dennis Potter's controversial television play (taped by the BBC, but then promptly banned) emerges as an uneven and theatrical thriller with dark religious underpinnings. Demonic Sting is the cunning stranger who worms his way into the household of an atheist hymn composer (Denholm Elliot), his devout wife (Joan Plowright) and their comatose daughter (Suzanna Hamilton) for nefarious reasons. It's persuasively performed and typical Potter – by turns unpleasant and thought-provoking – but director Richard Loncraine goes for mood and atmosphere above any sense of logic or reality. AT DVD

Sting *Martin Taylor* • Denholm Elliott *Thomas Bates* • Joan Plowright *Norma Bates* • Suzanna Hamilton *Patricia Bates* • Mary McLeod *Valerie Holdsworth* • Benjamin Whitrow *Businessman* ■ *Dir* Richard Loncraine • *Scr* Dennis Potter

Bring It On ★★ 12

Comedy 2000 · US · Colour · 94mins

Kirsten Dunst swaps the cut-throat world of beauty pageants (*Drop Dead Gorgeous*) for the equally competitive arena of high-school cheerleading. Dunst takes over as leader of a crack San Diego high-school squad whose prowess is in stark contrast to the shambolic football team they support. Things don't go smoothly. Peyton Reed's rah!-rah!-rah! chronicle lacks a satirical edge. The 2004 sequel went straight to video. TH DVD

Kirsten Dunst *Torrance Shipman* • Eliza Dushku *Missy Pantone* • Jesse Bradford *Cliff Pantone* • Gabrielle Union *Isis* • Sherry Hursey *Christine Shipman* • Holmes Osborne *Bruce Shipman* ■ *Dir* Peyton Reed • *Scr* Jessica Bendinger

Bring Me the Head of Alfredo Garcia ★★★★ 18

Crime drama 1974 · US · Colour · 107mins

Sam Peckinpah's enormous talent was on the wane when he made this gruesome Mexican crime drama. But if you can bear to look beneath its gory exterior as piano player Warren Oates becomes caught up with bounty hunters pursuing *that* head for a wealthy landowner, there are still enough moments when Peckinpah's greatness shines through. Excitingly told, this is like *The Wild Bunch*, but even wilder. TH. Contains swearing, violence and nudity. DVD

Warren Oates *Bennie* • Isela Vega *Elita* • Gig Young *Quill* • Robert Webber *Sappensly* • Helmut Dantine *Max* • Emilio Fernandez *El Jefe* • Kris Kristofferson *Paco* • Chano Urueta *One-armed bartender* ■ *Dir* Sam Peckinpah • *Scr* Sam Peckinpah, Gordon Dawson, from a story by Frank Kowalski

Bring Me the Head of Mavis Davis ★ 15

Comedy 1997 · UK · Colour · 95mins

Rik Mayall plays a record producer who realises that his pride and joy, singer Jane Horrocks, is worth more to him dead than alive. So he hires a hitman to do the dirty deed. Mayall's shouting and Horrocks's shrieking are almost unbearable, and there are some pretty unpleasant gags to boot. Not even an actor as accomplished as Danny Aiello can enliven the clumsy script and naff scenario. LH. Contains swearing and violence. DVD

Rik Mayall *Marty Starr* • Jane Horrocks *Marla Dorland* • Danny Aiello *Rathbone* • Ronald Pickup *Percy Stone* • Philip Martin Brown *Inspector Furse* • Ross Boatman *Rock star* • Paul Shearer *Presenter 1980* • Stuart Bunce *Aspirant* ■ *Dir* John Henderson • *Scr* Craig Strachan, from an idea by Joanne Reay

Bring on the Girls ★★

Romantic musical comedy
1945 · US · Colour · 91mins

Millionaire Eddie Bracken joins the navy hoping that, as a humble sailor, he'll find a girl who'll love him for himself. Around such thin stuff is woven a feeble assembly-line musical comedy which, under Sidney Lanfield's dull direction, wastes the considerable talents of Bracken, star of such gems as *Hail the Conquering Hero*. Sonny Tufts plays Bracken's buddy; Veronica Lake and Marjorie Reynolds are the girls they hitch up with. RK

Veronica Lake *Teddy Collins* • Sonny Tufts *Phil North* • Eddie Bracken *J Newport Bates* • Marjorie Reynolds *Sue Thomas* • Grant Mitchell *Uncle Ralph* • Johnny Coy *Benny Lowe* • Peter Whitney *Swede* ■ *Dir* Sidney Lanfield • *Scr* Karl Turnberg, Darrell Ware, from a story by Pierre Wolff

Bring On the Night ★★ 15

Music documentary
1985 · UK · Colour · 96mins

As the brains behind TV's seminal *7 Up* series, Michael Apted is no stranger to documentary. But he fails to prevent this behind-the-scenes account of Sting's *Dream of the Blue Turtles* tour from becoming a pretentious, self-glorifying vehicle for the one-time Police frontman. While it's fascinating to watch him rehearsing his new band in a palatial French mansion, the talking-head pieces (whether discussions of music or more serious issues) are less than inspiring. The songs, however, with their jazz-rock feel, are superb. DP DVD

Dir Michael Apted

Bring Your Smile Along ★★★

Musical comedy 1955 · US · Colour · 83mins

The dynamic singer Frankie Laine made five musicals for producer Jonie Taps in the 1950s and this is the best, brightened by the assured comic touch of writer/director Blake Edwards, making his directorial debut. The plot, which has a timid schoolmarm venturing to the big city and writing the lyrics for a string of hit songs recorded by Laine, is an amusing trifle, filling the spaces between Frankie's electrifying musical renditions. TV

Frankie Laine *Jerry Dennis* • Keefe Brasselle *Martin Adams* • Constance Towers *Nancy Willows* • Lucy Marlow *Marge Stevenson* •

William Leslie *David Parker* • Mario Siletti *Ricardo* • Ruth Warren *Landlady* • Jack Albertson *Jenson* ■ *Dir* Blake Edwards • *Scr* Blake Edwards, from a story by Blake Edwards, from a story by Richard Quine

Bringing Down the House ★ 12

Comedy 2003 · US · Colour · 100mins

Steve Martin stars in this unfunny, sentimental mush as an uptight lawyer whose perfectly ordered life is turned upside down by an escaped black female convict (Queen Latifah) who's determined to have him prove her innocence. Martin and Latifah's chemistry feels forced, and many will detect racism and homophobia in the film's crass manipulation of stereotypes. AS [VIDEO] DVD

Steve Martin *Peter Sanderson* • Queen Latifah *Charlene Morton* • Eugene Levy *Howie Rottman* • Joan Plowright *Mrs Arness* • Jean Smart *Kate* • Kimberly J Brown *Sarah Sanderson* • Angus T Jones *Georgey Sanderson* • Betty White *Mrs Kline* ■ *Dir* Adam Shankman • *Scr* Jason Filardi

Bringing out the Dead ★★★ 18

Drama 1999 · US · Colour · 115mins

Martin Scorsese lends his customary intensity and visual razzle-dazzle to this 72-hour insight into the exhausting lives of New York paramedics. The director reunites with his *Taxi Driver* collaborator Paul Schrader to conjure up a powerful, blackly comic and often hallucinatory portrait, with Nicolas Cage perfectly cast as crumbling protagonist Frank Pierce. However, the other performances are so unhinged (mad medics Tom Sizemore and Ving Rhames especially), and the episodic encounters so overwrought, that the drama never really grabs as it should. JC [VIDEO] DVD

Nicolas Cage *Frank Pierce* • Patricia Arquette *Mary Burke* • John Goodman *Larry* • Ving Rhames *Marcus* • Tom Sizemore *Tom Wolls* • Marc Anthony *Noel* • Mary Beth Hurt *Nurse Constance* • Martin Scorsese *Dispatcher* ■ *Dir* Martin Scorsese • *Scr* Paul Schrader, from the novel by Joe Connelly

Bringing Up Baby ★★★★★ U

Classic screwball comedy
1938 · US · BW · 102mins

How sublime can movies get? This is perfectly cast (Katharine Hepburn in a celebrated screwball role), brilliantly written by Hagar Wilde and Dudley Nichols and fabulously well directed by Howard Hawks. It's a genuinely funny original that repays repeated viewings, especially to marvel at the variety of subtle expressions on the face of Cary Grant, who gives one of the most wonderful comic performances ever to grace the silver screen. Regarded as too wacky by half when it was released, this shimmering dissection of the male-female relationship is now regarded as a classic. By the way, "Baby" is a pet leopard. TS [VIDEO] DVD

Katharine Hepburn *Susan Vance* • Cary Grant *Dr David Huxley* • Charlie Ruggles [Charles Ruggles] *Major Horace Applegate* • Walter Catlett *Constable Slocum* • Barry Fitzgerald *Mr Gogarty* • May Robson *Mrs Carleton Random, Aunt Elizabeth* • Fritz Feld *Dr Fritz Lehmann* • Leona Roberts *Mrs Hannah Gogarty* • George Irving *Mr Alexander Peabody* • Tala Birell *Mrs Lehmann* • Virginia Walker *Alice Swallow* ■ *Dir* Howard Hawks • *Scr* Dudley Nichols, Hagar Wilde, from a short story by Hagar Wilde in *Collier's* • *Cinematographer* Russell Metty • *Art Director* Van Nest Polglase

The Brink's Job ★★★ PG

Crime comedy 1978 · US · Colour · 98mins

William Friedkin directs this wild, but often hugely entertaining heist comedy. Re-creating what was then dubbed "the crime of the century", it stars Peter Falk as the leader of a gang of amateur crooks who knock over a Boston security firm to the tune of nearly $3 million. The art direction team notched up an Oscar nomination for their stylish period designs, but it's the cast that catches the eye, with Warren Oates a standout as Falk's doltish sidekick. DP [VIDEO]

Peter Falk *Tony Pino* • Peter Boyle *Joe McGinnis* • [Allen Garfield] *Vinnie Costa* • Warren Oates *Specs O'Keefe* • Gena Rowlands *Mary Pino* • Paul Sorvino *Jazz Maffie* • Sheldon Leonard *J Edgar Hoover* • Gerard Murphy *Sandy Richardson* ■ *Dir* William Friedkin • *Scr* Walon Green, from the book *Big Stick Up at Brink's* by Noel Behn • *Art Director* Dean Tavoularis, Angelo Graham • *Set Designer* George R Nelson, Bruce Kay

Britannia Hospital ★★★ 15

Black comedy 1982 · UK · Colour · 111mins

Director Lindsay Anderson's top-heavy symbolism all but crushes the satirical life out of this attempt to lampoon the state of the nation, with a run-down hospital expecting a royal visit to celebrate its 500th anniversary used as a metaphor for Britain's moral decay. Media hacks, strike-bent workers, bureaucratic chaos and sinister laboratory experiments are Anderson's targets, although the burlesque humour makes it seem closer to "Carry On Casualty". Malcolm McDowell stars in a film saved by some of Britain's finest character actors. TH. Contains violence, swearing, nudity. [VIDEO] DVD

Leonard Rossiter *Potter* • Graham Crowden *Millar* • Malcolm McDowell *Mike* • Joan Plowright *Phyllis* • Marsha A Hunt *Amanda* • Frank Grimes *Fred* • Jill Bennett *MacMillan* • Robin Askwith • Peter Jeffrey • Fulton Mackay • John Moffatt • Dandy Nichols • Alan Bates ■ *Dir* Lindsay Anderson • *Scr* David Sherwin

Britannia Mews ★★★

Drama 1949 · UK · BW · 91mins

Twentieth Century-Fox made this interesting version of part of Margery Sharp's excellent but dour novel about Victorian class relationships to use up part of their frozen UK assets. It's a striking and original film, though undermined by the bizarre casting of the usually dependable Dana Andrews in a dual role as Maureen O'Hara's two husbands, in one of which he is rather weirdly revoiced. Nevertheless, O'Hara is striking as ever and the British contingent makes this sordid opus compulsively watchable. TS

Maureen O'Hara *Adelaide Culver* • Dana Andrews *Gilbert Lauderdale/Henry Lambert* • Sybil Thorndike *Mrs Mounsey* • June Allen *Adelaide as a child* • Anthony Tancred *Treff Culver* • Anthony Lamb *Treff as a child* • Wilfrid Hyde White *Mr Culver* • Fay Compton *Mrs Culver* ■ *Dir* Jean Negulesco • *Scr* Ring Lardner Jr, from the novel by Margery Sharp

Britannic ★★★ 15

First World War drama
2000 · US · Colour · 93mins

The appeal of this TV movie is its cheeky attempt to rip off James Cameron's 1997 blockbuster – but on a fraction of its budget. True, the *Titanic's* sister ship, the *Britannic*, was also sunk (in November 1916), but whether the hospital ship was torpedoed because of espionage activities is one of the weaker points of the movie. Actually the special effects aren't bad, but the inevitable romance unnecessarily pads out the final voyage. DM [VIDEO] DVD

Edward Atterton *Reynolds* • Amanda Ryan *Vera Campbell* • Jacqueline Bisset *Lady Lewis* • Ben Daniels *First Officer Townsend* • John Rhys-Davies *Captain Barrett* • Bruce Payne *Dr Baker* ■ *Dir* Brian Trenchard-Smith • *Scr* Kim Smith, Brett Thompson, Dennis A Pratt, Brian Trenchard-Smith

British Agent ★★★ U

Historical spy adventure
1934 · US · BW · 79mins

This historical drama dares to show ungentlemanly conduct on the part of the British Government, which is here shown trying to stop the Bolsheviks making peace with Germany in 1917. Leslie Howard stars as Britain's unofficial representative, who is readily betrayed when he becomes a political embarrassment to his country. Luckily, he has more on his mind than politics after meeting the delectable Kay Francis, who is – as she puts it – a woman first and a Russian agent second. Laird Doyle's screenplay is often tiresome, but director Michael Curtiz brings his usual pace and visual flair to the proceedings. AE

Leslie Howard *Stephen Locke* • Kay Francis *Elena Moura* • William Gargan *Bob Medill* • Phillip Reed [Philip Reed] *Gaston LeFarge* • Irving Pichel *Sergei Pavlov* • Ivan Simpson *Evans Poohbah* • Halliwell Hobbes *Sir Walter Carrister* • J Carroll Naish [J Carrol Naish] *Commissioner for War Trotsky* • Walter Byron *Stanley* • Cesar Romero *Tito Del Val* ■ *Dir* Michael Curtiz • *Scr* Laird Doyle, Roland Pertwee, from the novel by RH Bruce Lockhart

Broadcast News ★★★★ 15

Comedy drama 1987 · US · Colour · 126mins

The self-serving natures of three Washington-based TV journalists form the focus of James L Brooks's sweet-and-sour comedy of superegos pursuing serious news, but ending up with spurious glamour. Undervalued William Hurt, as a newscaster who can bring phoney tears to his eyes, is one corner of a romantic triangle; the underused Albert Brooks, as a seasoned investigator, is another. But it's Holly Hunter, as the hard-nosed producer and object of their attentions (long before her Oscar-winning role in *The Piano*) who really provokes the sorrow and the pity of lives at the mercy of their careers. TH. Contains swearing and brief nudity. [VIDEO] DVD

William Hurt *Tom Grunick* • Albert Brooks *Aaron Altman* • Holly Hunter *Jane Craig* • Jack Nicholson *Bill Rorich, news anchor* • Lois Chiles *Jennifer Mack* • Joan Cusack *Blair Litton* • Peter Hackes *Paul Moore* • Christian Clemenson *Bobby* ■ *Dir/Scr* James L Brooks

Broadway ★★★

Musical crime drama
1929 · US · BW and Colour · 105mins

One of the most eye-catching of the early sound musicals, boasting elaborate settings for its production numbers. It also has an entertainingly suspenseful plot, in which a dancer Glenn Tryon becomes unwittingly caught up in a murder. Robert Ellis is an effective villain, while Evelyn Brent scores as a chorus girl. Director Paul Fejos devised a versatile and high-speed crane specially for the film, and the climactic nightclub sequence is photographed in "natural" colour. RK

Glenn Tryon *Roy Lane* • Evelyn Brent *Pearl* • Merna Kennedy *Billie Moore* • Thomas E Jackson *Dan McCorn* • Robert Ellis *Steve Crandall* • Otis Harlan *"Porky" Thompson* • Paul Porcasi *Nick Verdis* • Marion Lord *Lil Rice* ■ *Dir* Paul Fejos • *Scr* Edward T Lowe Jr, Charles Furthman, from the play by Philip Dunning, George Abbott • *Cinematographer* Hal Mohr • *Choreographer* Maurice L Kusell

Broadway ★★★

Musical crime drama
1942 · US · BW · 91mins

George Raft stars in this remake of the 1929 musical, which was taken, in turn, from a 1927 Broadway hit. This version is a crime melodrama with a decent helping of snappy songs, some dance and the neat twist of having Raft play himself. As he reminisces about the Roaring Twenties, when bootleggers and mobsters were part of the New York showbiz scene, his memories fold into flashback to tell a tale of backstage murder in which he once found himself involved. Broderick Crawford is excellent as the villain of the piece, Janet Blair is Raft's girlfriend and dance partner, and Pat O'Brien plays a detective. RK

George Raft • Pat O'Brien *Dan McCorn* • Janet Blair *Billie* • Broderick Crawford *Steve Crandall* • Marjorie Rambeau *Lili* • Anne Gwynne *Pearl* • SZ Sakall *Nick* • Edward S Brophy [Edward Brophy] *Porky* ■ *Dir* William A Seiter • *Scr* Felix Jackson, John Bright, from the play by Philip Dunning, George Abbott

Broadway Bill ★★★ U

Drama 1934 · US · BW · 102mins

The title is the name of the racehorse bought by businessman Warner Baxter, who gives up everything to run the horse. Baxter's sister-in-law Myrna Loy believes in him, so therefore we all should. A Frank Capra movie, this is simply brimming over with nice people and good intentions – you may find a little of it goes a long way, but then you'd be being churlish. Capra remade it in 1950 as *Riding High* with Bing Crosby (who, unlike Warner Baxter, actually liked horses). TS [VIDEO]

Warner Baxter *Dan Brooks* • Myrna Loy *Alice Higgins* • Walter Connolly *JL Higgins* • Raymond Walburn *Colonel Pettigrew* • Clarence Muse *Whitey* • Helen Vinson *Margaret Brooks* • Douglas Dumbrille [Douglass Dumbrille] *Eddie Morgan* • Lynne Overman *Happy McGuire* • Lucille Ball ■ *Dir* Frank Capra • *Scr* Robert Riskin, from a story by Mark Hellinger

Broadway Bound ★★★ PG

Comedy drama 1991 · US · Colour · 89mins

Has any modern playwright made as many dramatic mountains out of his life's domestic molehills as Neil Simon? Made as a TV movie but shown in cinemas in Britain, this is the final segment – its predecessors were *Brighton Beach Memoirs* and *Biloxi Blues* – of an autobiographical trilogy. Here, Simon's alter ego Eugene (Corey Parker) makes it to the big time with his brother Stan (Jonathan Silverman). The strong cast skilfully puts acting flesh on skeletal memory, but the material is thin. TH [VIDEO]

Anne Bancroft *Kate Jerome* • Hume Cronyn *Ben* • Corey Parker *Eugene Morris Jerome* • Jonathan Silverman *Stan Jerome* • Jerry Orbach *Jack Jerome* • Michele Lee *Blanche* • Marilyn Cooper *Mrs Pitkin* • Pat McCormick *Announcer* ■ *Dir* Paul Bogart • *Scr* Neil Simon, from his play

Broadway Danny Rose ★★★★ PG

Comedy 1984 · US · BW · 80mins

Romping gleefully rather than analysing deeply, Woody Allen as director, writer and star brings his own light touch to every frame of this film. Putting egotistical, arty Manhattan on hold, and cutting down on his verbal wit to boot, Allen rings the changes not only by taking us to the swamps of New Jersey but also by squeezing humour primarily from situation and character rather than dialogue. Allen the director keeps the caper aspect on a beautifully tight leash at all times and, as the star, he fairly sparkles with eccentricity as a small-fry showbiz agent, while Mia Farrow is amusingly, nasally blunt as a gangster's moll with daft hair. JM [VIDEO] DVD

Woody Allen *Danny Rose* • Mia Farrow *Tina Vitale* • Nick Apollo Forte *Lou Canova* • Craig Vandenburgh *Ray Webb* • Herb Reynolds *Barney Dunn* • Paul Greco *Vito Rispoli* • Frank Renzulli *Joe Rispoli* • Edwin Bordo *Johnny Rispoli* ■ *Dir/Scr* Woody Allen

Broadway Limited ★★ U

Comedy 1941 · US · BW · 75mins

This is named after a Chicago to New York express train and concerns showbiz shenanigans. Here they're provided by Leonid Kinskey's wily Russian film producer, Marjorie Woodworth as his hot young film star, ZaSu Pitts as the president of her fan club, and Patsy Kelly as her loyal secretary. Victor McLaglen appears as the railroad engineer who finds a baby for the star as a publicity stunt, and Dennis O'Keefe plays her true love. AE

Victor McLaglen *Mike* • Marjorie Woodworth *April* • Patsy Kelly *Patsy* • Dennis O'Keefe *Dr Harvey North* • ZaSu Pitts *Myra* • Leonid Kinskey *Ivan* ■ *Dir* Gordon Douglas • *Scr* Rian James

The Broadway Melody ★★★

Musical comedy 1929 · US · BW · 102mins

The first Hollywood musical, and the prototype for the backstage musical romance that grew, flourished and evolved to become a unique cinematic art form for some three decades. Bessie Love and Anita Page star as a vaudeville sister act, vying for the attentions of dancer Charles King. The drama is woven around a marvellous musical score that includes the enduring title number, as well as the even more ageless *Give My Regards to Broadway*. The movie was voted best picture at the 1928/1929 Oscar ceremony – only the second – with nominations for director Harry Beaumont and Love. Stylistically dated, but there is still much to enjoy. RK

Anita Page *Queenie* • Bessie Love *Hank* • Charles King (1) *Eddie* • Jed Prouty *Uncle Jed* • Kenneth Thomson *Jock Warriner* • Edward Dillon *Stage manager* • Mary Doran *Blonde* • JE Beck *Bebe Hatrick* • Marshall Ruth *Stew* ■ *Dir* Harry Beaumont • *Scr* James Gleason, Norman Houston, Sarah Y Mason, from a story by Edmund Goulding • *Art Director* Cedric Gibbons

Broadway Melody of 1936 ★★★★ U

Musical comedy 1935 · US · BW · 100mins

A terrific, warm and wonderful MGM follow-up to its smash hit *The Broadway Melody*, this has a fabulous Arthur Freed and Nacio Herb Brown score, which includes most of those songs that you probably heard for the first time in *Singin' in the Rain*. Eleanor Powell is devastating as a dancer, and she is well backed by Jack Benny as a theatre columnist and handsome hero Robert Taylor. Powell taps up a storm, and her *I've Got a Feeling You're Fooling* picked up the dance direction Oscar for choreographer Dave Gould. Swell stuff. TS

Jack Benny *Bert Keeler* • Eleanor Powell *Irene Foster* • Robert Taylor (1) *Bob Gordon* • Una Merkel *Kitty Corbett* • Sid Silvers *Snoop* • Buddy Ebsen *Ted* • June Knight *Lillian Brent* • Vilma Ebsen *Sally* ■ *Dir* Roy Del Ruth • *Scr* Jack McGowan, Sid Silvers, Harry Cohn, from a story by Moss Hart • *Choreographer* Dave Gould • *Music Director* Alfred Newman

Broadway Melody of 1938 ★★★ U

Musical comedy 1937 · US · BW · 105mins

For connoisseurs, this contains some knockout routines from that fabulous tap dancer Eleanor Powell. On the singing side, there's Sophie Tucker putting her all into *Your Broadway and My Broadway*, but for fans of Judy Garland, it has something unforgettable – the song *Dear Mr Gable*. It was originally written to be performed at a birthday party on the MGM lot, sung by the young Garland to the tune of the standard *You Made Me Love You*, with additional lyrics by Roger Edens. When studio boss Louis B Mayer heard it, he ordered it to be filmed for posterity. TS [video]

Robert Taylor (1) *Steve Raleigh* • Eleanor Powell *Sally Lee* • George Murphy *Sonny Ledford* • Binnie Barnes *Caroline Whipple* • Buddy Ebsen *Peter Trot* • Sophie Tucker *Alice Clayton* • Judy Garland *Betty Clayton* ■ *Dir* Roy Del Ruth • *Scr* Jack McGowan, from a story by Jack McGowan, Sid Silvers • *Music Director* George Stoll

Broadway Melody of 1940 ★★★★★ U

Musical 1940 · US · BW · 101mins

The fourth and last of MGM's great *Broadway Melody* series is perfection in rhythm. Fred Astaire and George Murphy play sparring dance partners, though together they perform terrifically; the seemingly effortless sophistication of *Please Don't Monkey with Broadway* is utterly beguiling. The movie's undoubted highlight is Astaire sublimely performing a tap with toothy Eleanor Powell to Cole's *Begin the Beguine* on a glossy, highly polished black-and-white set. As Frank Sinatra said in *That's Entertainment!*: "You can wait around and hope, but you'll never see its like again." TS

Fred Astaire *Johnny Brett* • Eleanor Powell *Clara Bennett* • George Murphy *King Shaw* • Frank Morgan *Bob Casey* • Ian Hunter *Bert C Matthews* • Florence Rice *Amy Blake* • Lynne Carver *Emmy Lou Lee* • Ann Morriss *Pearl* ■ *Dir* Norman Taurog • *Scr* Leon Gordon, George Oppenheimer, from a story by Jack McGowan, Dore Schary • *Music Director* Alfred Newman

Broadway Rhythm ★★ U

Musical 1944 · US · Colour · 114mins

George Murphy stars as a Broadway producer beset by various problems in mounting his extravagant new revue-style show. And that's about the size of it. This is excessively lengthy, devoid of any appreciable narrative and directed without flair by Roy del Ruth. What it does offer is an excuse to parade a string of talented performers. RK

George Murphy *Johnnie Demming* • Ginny Simms *Helen Hoyt* • Charles Winninger *Sam Demming* • Gloria DeHaven *Patsy Demming* • Nancy Walker *Trixie Simpson* • Ben Blue *Felix Gross* • Lena Horne *Fernway De La Fer* • Eddie "Rochester" Anderson *Eddie* ■ *Dir* Roy Del Ruth • *Scr* Dorothy Kingsley, Harry Clark, from a story by Jack McGowan, from the musical *Very Warm for May* by Jerome Kern, Oscar Hammerstein II

Broadway Serenade ★★

Musical 1939 · US · BW · 113mins

Marital problems inevitably arise between a songwriter husband (Lew Ayres) and his singer wife (Jeanette MacDonald) when she soars to stardom and he doesn't. MacDonald, minus Nelson Eddy, doesn't fare too well in this opulent but otherwise leaden offering. A lumbering production in which even a grand finale choreographed by Busby Berkeley goes horribly wrong. RK

Jeanette MacDonald *Mary Hale* • Lew Ayres *James Geoffrey Seymour* • Ian Hunter *Larry Bryant* • Frank Morgan *Cornelius Collier Jr* • Wally Vernon *Joey, the Jinx* • Rita Johnson *Judy Tyrrell* • Virginia Grey *Pearl* ■ *Dir* Robert Z Leonard • *Scr* Charles Lederer, from a story by Lew Lipton, from John Taintor Foote, Hans Kräly

Broadway through a Keyhole ★★★★

Musical 1933 · US · BW · 92mins

Famous New York gossip columnist Walter Winchell wrote the story, using himself and his broadcasts on the Broadway and gangland scenes as a framework for the plot. The story is simple: mobster Paul Kelly falls for decent Constance Cummings and gets her a job in Texas Guinan's nightclub, where the shows are directed by volatile Gregory Ratoff. Grateful Cummings tries to stay loyal, but falls in love with crooner Russ Columbo. Directed with style and pace by Lowell Sherman, this is a sharp peep into a 1930s New York where showbiz and the mob overlap. Sophisticated, unusual and vastly entertaining. RK

Constance Cummings *Joan Whelan* • Russ Columbo *Clark Brian* • Paul Kelly (1) *Hank Rocci* • Blossom Seeley *Sybil Smith* • Gregory Ratoff *Max Mefooski* • Texas Guinan *Tex Kaley* • Hugh O'Connell *Chuck Haskins* ■ *Dir* Lowell Sherman • *Scr* Gene Towne, C Graham Baker, from a story by Walter Winchell • *Music Director* Alfred Newman

Broadway to Hollywood ★★★

Musical 1933 · US · BW and Colour · 87mins

This chronicles the struggles of a showbusiness family across three generations, with Eddie Quillan ending up as a Hollywood star almost half a century after his grandparents (Frank Morgan and the gutsy Alice Brady) started out on the hard road of vaudeville. This is a sentimental but lively look at a vanished era. Featuring a 13-year-old Mickey Rooney, it marks the screen debut of Nelson Eddy and includes appearances by Jackie Cooper and Jimmy Durante. RK

Alice Brady *Lulu Hackett* • Frank Morgan *Ted Hackett* • Madge Evans *Anne Ainslee* • Russell Hardie *Ted Hackett Jr* • Jackie Cooper *Ted Hackett Jr as a child* • Eddie Quillan *Ted the Third* • Mickey Rooney *Ted the Third as a child* • Tad Alexander *David* • Jimmy Durante *Hollywood character* • Nelson Eddy *John Sylvester* ■ *Dir* Willard Mack • *Scr* Willard Mack, Edgar Allan Woolf

Brokedown Palace ★★ 12

Prison drama 1999 · US · Colour · 96mins

If it weren't for sterling performances from Claire Danes and Kate Beckinsale, this would be yet another turgid rehash of the plot in which nice American kids get burnt by Bangkok drug laws. Slammed in a *Tenko*-style women's prison (whose most bizarre inmate is a cockney-accented Amanda de Cadenet), they pin their hopes on renegade lawyer Bill Pullman. The film, subsequently cold-shouldered by both stars, is formulaic, predictable and dull. LH. Contains swearing. [video] DVD

Claire Danes *Alice Marano* • Bill Pullman *Henry "Yank Hank" Greene* • Kate Beckinsale *Darlene Davis* • Lou Diamond Phillips *Roy Knox* • Jacqueline Kim *Yon Greene* • Daniel Lapaine *Skip Kahn, "Nick Parks"* • Tom Amandes *Doug Davis* ■ *Dir* Jonathan Kaplan • *Scr* David Arata, from a story by Adam Fields, David Arata

Broken Arrow ★★★★ PG

Western 1950 · US · Colour · 88mins

Director Delmer Daves's massively influential western was among the first to tell the native American side of the story. James Stewart heads the cast as a war-weary scout who falls, controversially, for Apache maiden Debra Paget during his mission to negotiate a truce, while Jeff Chandler became an international star following his performance here as Cochise, a role he was to reprise twice. The screenplay credited to Michael Blankfort was nominated for an Oscar, but was actually written by blacklisted author Albert Maltz. TS [video] DVD

James Stewart *Tom Jeffords* • Jeff Chandler *Cochise* • Debra Paget *Sonseeahray* • Basil Ruysdael *General Howard* • Will Geer *Ben Slade* • Joyce MacKenzie *Terry* • Arthur Hunnicutt *Duffield* • Raymond Bramley *Colonel Bernall* • Jay Silverheels *Goklia* ■ *Dir* Delmer Daves • *Scr* Michael Blankfort (front for Albert Maltz), from the novel *Blood Brother* by Elliott Arnold

Broken Arrow ★★★ 15

Action thriller 1996 · US · Colour · 103mins

For his second Hollywood film after the Jean-Claude Van Damme vehicle *Hard Target*, hyper-kinetic Hong Kong director John Woo teams up with reinvented hard man John Travolta for a tepid techno-thriller. Despite rattling along at a breakneck pace, this is a cliché-ridden tale, but Travolta charismatically milks his new-found icon status as an amoral stealth-bomber pilot. Christian Slater is an able good guy, pursuing his manic adversary across the desert into ever more ludicrous action set pieces, while Samantha Mathis is refreshingly capable as Slater's sidekick. AJ. Contains violence, swearing. [video] DVD

John Travolta *Vic Deakins* • Christian Slater *Riley Hale* • Samantha Mathis *Terry Carmichael* • Delroy Lindo *Colonel Max Wilkins* • Bob Gunton *Pritchett* • Frank Whaley *Giles Prentice* • Howie Long *Kelly* • Vondie Curtis-Hall *Lt Col Sam Rhodes* • Jack Thompson *Chairman, Joint Chiefs of Staff* ■ *Dir* John Woo • *Scr* Graham Yost

Broken Blossoms ★★★★ PG

Silent drama
1919 · US · BW and Tinted · 94mins

Set in London's Limehouse, this melodrama is the last of director DW Griffith's undisputed masterpieces. Shot in just 18 days, the story of brutalised waif Lillian Gish's chaste relationship with noble Chinese merchant Richard Barthelmess was Griffith's most expensive film to date. It marked both his earliest experiment with tinted film stock and his first exclusive use of studio sets. The atmosphere of misty dilapidation was achieved by cinematographer Billy Bitzer and effects expert Hendrik Sartov, but it's the way in which Griffith exploits his seedy setting to enhance the ethereality of the romance between the girl and the merchant that makes the film so memorable. DP [video] DVD

Lillian Gish *Lucy* • Donald Crisp *"Battling" Burrows* • Arthur Howard (1) *Burrows's manager* • Richard Barthelmess *Cheng Huan* • Edward Peil [Edward Peil Sr] *Evil Eye* • Norman Selby *A prizefighter* • George Beranger *The Spying One* • Ernest Butterworth ■ *Dir* DW Griffith • *Scr* DW Griffith, from the short story *The Chink and the Child* by Thomas Burke from the collection *Limehouse Nights*

Broken Blossoms ★★

Drama 1936 · UK · BW · 88mins

Five years after directing his last feature, DW Griffith – the father of narrative film – was invited by Twickenham Studios to remake his 1919 classic about doomed love in London's Limehouse. When he dropped out, Emlyn Williams hurriedly produced a script based on the Griffith original, and German exile John Brahm was hired to direct. The result is better than might be expected, with Brahm emulating the visual delicacy of the silent version. However, the dialogue is excruciating in places, Dolly Haas is no Lillian Gish, and Williams can't match Richard Barthelmess. DP

Dolly Haas *Lucy Burrows* • Emlyn Williams *Chen* • Arthur Margetson *Battling Burrows* • Gibb McLaughlin *Evil Eye* • Donald Calthrop *Old Chinaman* • Ernest Sefton *Manager* • Jerry Verno *Bert* • Bertha Belmore *Daisy* • Ernest Jay *Alf* ■ *Dir* John Brahm • *Scr* Emlyn Williams, from the story *The Chink and the Child* by Thomas Burke, from the 1919 film • *Cinematographer* Curt Courant

Broken English ★★

Romantic drama 1981 · US · Colour · 93mins

This is a well-meaning but overly emphatic treatise on interracial marriage. Moving between Senegal, Tunisia and France, the action centres on Beverly Ross's relationship with black African Jacques Martial and the response of her family and friends. The attitudes are predictable, but there's a touching togetherness about the way the couple confront their detractors. However, the main point of interest here is the sole screen appearance of Oona Chaplin, who defied her playwright father, Eugene O'Neill, to marry Charlie Chaplin in 1943, despite an age gap of 36 years. DP

Beverly Ross *Sarah* • Jacques Martial *Maas* • Greta Rannigen *Leslie* • Mansour Sy *Cheekh* • Oona Chaplin *Sarah's mother* • Frankie Stein *Cecile* • Sandy Whitelaw *Arms dealer* • Serge Rynecki *Jacques* ■ *Dir/Scr* Michie Gleason

Broken English ★★★ 18

Romantic drama 1996 · NZ · Colour · 88mins

Having scored an international hit with *Once Were Warriors*, producer Robin Scholes returned to similar territory with this Auckland-based variation on the *Romeo and Juliet* story. Debutant director Gregor Nicholas lacks Lee Tamahori's flair, however, and his insights into the need for racial tolerance in a melting-pot society are frequently overstated in a bid to provoke. Moreover, the glossy visuals often detract from the authenticity of this otherwise downbeat drama. DP. An English/Maori/Serbo-Croat language film. Contains swearing, sex scenes and some violence. [VIDEO]

Aleksandra Vujcic *Nina* • Julian Arahanga *Eddie* • Rade Serbedzija *Ivan* • Marton Csokas *Darko* • Madeline McNamara *Mira* • Elizabeth Mavric *Vanya* • Zhao Jing *Clara* • Li Yang *Wu* ■ *Dir* Gregor Nicholas • *Scr* Gregor Nicholas, Johanna Pigott, Jim Salter

Broken Harvest ★★

Historical epic
1994 · Ire · Colour and BW · 101mins

The period immediately following the Irish civil war has been relatively neglected by film-makers. However, Maurice O'Callaghan's study of the tensions that remained after independence admirably captures the atmosphere of retrenchment and remembrance that characterised the early De Valera years. Yet there's a predictability about the storyline, in which two men refuse to call a ceasefire in the feud that began decades before over a woman. DP

Colin Lane *Arthur O'Leary* • Niall O'Brien *Josie McCarthy* • Marian Quinn *Catherine O'Leary* • Darren McHugh *Jimmy O'Leary* • Joy Florish *Mary Finnegan* • Joe Jeffers *Willie Hogan* ■ *Dir* Maurice O'Callaghan • *Scr* Maurice O'Callaghan, Kate O'Callaghan, from the story *The Shilling* by Maurice O'Callaghan

The Broken Hearts Club: a Romantic Comedy ★★★ 15

Comedy drama 2000 · US · Colour · 91mins

Simmering with bitchy insults, lustful laments and slyly understated truths, this gay ensemble comedy resembles *Swingers* in a *Diner* in search of *Sex in the City*. But who says you have to be original to be amusing? Every one of Timothy Olyphant's team-mates on John Mahoney's softball team flirts with stereotype. Yet they all emerge as credible characters, whether they're flightily gay, podgily insecure or posturingly macho. Writer/director Greg Berlanti judges the mix of camp quippery, Hollywood affectation and romantic pathos to a nicety. DP. Contains swearing, drug abuse and sex scenes. [VIDEO] DVD

Timothy Olyphant *Dennis* • Andrew Keegan *Kevin* • John Mahoney *Jack* • Dean Cain *Cole* • Matt McGrath *Howie* • Zach Braff *Benji* • Ben Weber *Patrick* • Billy Porter *Taylor* • Justin Theroux *Marshall* • Mary McCormack *Anne* ■ *Dir/Scr* Greg Berlanti

Broken Journey ★★ U

Melodrama 1948 · UK · BW · 85mins

A plane full of mismatched characters comes down in the Alps. Guess what happens next? Watching painfully earnest tales like this makes you wonder why anyone bothers with disaster movies, and why it took so long for *Airplane!* to come along and mock them. Director Ken Annakin, on his third picture, has little idea how to freshen up the stock situations, while there are few hidden depths in the overfamiliar characters. DP [VIDEO]

Phyllis Calvert *Mary Johnstone* • Margot Grahame *Joanna Dane* • James Donald *Bill Haverton* • Francis L Sullivan *Anton Perami* • Raymond Huntley *Edward Marshall* • Derek Bond *Richard Faber* • Guy Rolfe *Captain Fox* • Sonia Holm *Anne Stevens* ■ *Dir* Ken Annakin • *Scr* Robert Westerby

Broken Lance ★★★★ U

Western 1954 · US · Colour · 92mins

This splendid western stars a magnificently grizzled Spencer Tracy in the role he was born to play – King Lear. Even though the daughters have become sons, this is the (uncredited) westernisation of Shakespeare's tragedy about the royal patriarch and his disparate family. Still, despite the claims for Akira Kurosawa's *Ran*, this is the definitive screen version of the Bard's celebrated work, and the western setting provides a dimension of grandeur: it's no accident, surely, that this was one of the first subjects used to show off the then new CinemaScope process. TS [VIDEO] DVD

Spencer Tracy *Matt Devereaux* • Robert Wagner *Joe Devereaux* • Jean Peters *Barbara* • Richard Widmark *Ben* • Katy Jurado *Senora Devereaux* • Hugh O'Brian *Mike Devereaux* • Eduard Franz *Two Moons* • Earl Holliman *Denny Devereaux* • EG Marshall *Governor* ■ *Dir* Edward Dmytryk • *Scr* Richard Murphy, from a story by Philip Yordan

The Broken Land ★★

Western 1962 · US · Colour · 59mins

A B-western about a tyrannical sheriff who winds up committing rape, murder and sundry other offences while trying to wipe out anyone who can speak against him. Kent Taylor plays the vile man, Diana Darrin is his main accuser, and Jody McCrea (Joel's son) plays the good guy, who looks like dead meat from the start. Some reviewers at the time felt the script was written by a 1960s shrink, since it's full of gestalt stuff about violent impulses and guilt. Now, though, the movie is likely to be viewed solely for an early appearance by Jack Nicholson. AT

Kent Taylor *Jim Kogan* • Diana Darrin *Marva Aikens* • Jody McCrea *Deputy Ed Flynn* • Robert Sampson *Gabe Dunson* • Jack Nicholson *Will Broicous* • Gary Sneed *Billy Bell* • Don Orlando ■ *Dir* John A Bushelman • *Scr* Edward J Lakso, Dixie McCoy

Broken Lizard's Club Dread ★★ 15

Comedy horror 2004 · US · Colour · 113mins

Unlike comedy group Broken Lizard's limp *Super Troopers*, this feature has an obvious plot (albeit derivative) and a relatively coherent structure, even if it's not sure what genre it wants to be. It's a schlocky horror comedy, in which a machete-wielding psycho picks off the incompetent staff at the booze-soaked party resort of Coconut Pete's Pleasure Island. The group blends juvenile, goofball laughs with extreme gore, and it won't have much appeal beyond its target teen audience. SF. Contains swearing, violence. [VIDEO] DVD

Bill Paxton *Coconut Pete* • Jay Chandrasekhar *Putnam Livingston* • Kevin Heffernan *Lars* • Steve Lemme *Juan Castillo* • Paul Soter *Dave* • Erik Stolhanske *Sam* • Brittany Daniel *Jenny* • MC Gainey *Hank* • Jordan Ladd *Penelope* ■ *Dir* Jay Chandrasekhar • *Scr* Broken Lizard [Jay Chandrasekhar, Kevin Heffernan, Steve Lemme, Paul Soter, Erik Stolhanske]

Broken Vessels ★★★ 18

Medical drama 1998 · US · Colour · 90mins

Here's some advice. If you're ever taken ill in the States, get yourself to hospital. Do not, under any circumstances, call the paramedics. In Martin Scorsese's *Bringing Out the Dead*, a strung-out Nicolas Cage hallucinated his way through his own personal heart of darkness. Now Todd Field and Jason London do likewise in an edgy little indie drama. Despite the low-tech, almost documentary style this remains unfocused and disjointed. DA

Todd Field *Jimmy Warzniak* • Jason London *Tom Meyer* • Roxana Zal *Elizabeth* • Susan Traylor *Susy* • James Hong *Mr Chen* ■ *Dir* Scott Ziehl • *Scr* Scott Ziehl, David Baer, John McMahon

Broken Wings ★★★ 15

Drama 2002 · Is · Colour · 80mins

A fascinating portrait of getting by in a patriarchal society emerges in Nir Bergman's debut feature, as middle-class Israeli 40-something Orli Zilberschatz-Banay struggles to raise four children following the demise of her husband. Yet the burden of the daily routine largely falls on her teenage daughter, Maya Maron, who jeopardises her chances of a singing career to atone for the guilt she feels over her father's death. Episodes involving the younger siblings are less well realised, but the insights into grieving and coping are sensitive and sensible. DP. In Hebrew with English subtitles. DVD

Orli Banay-Zilverschatz *Dafna Ulman* • Maya Maron *Maya Ulman* • Nitai Gvirtz *Yair Ulman* • Vladimir Freedman [Vladimir Friedman] *Dr Valentin Goldman* • Mooki Niv [Danny Niv] *Yoram* ■ *Dir/Scr* Nir Bergman

Bronco Billy ★★★ PG

Comedy western
1980 · US · Colour · 111mins

Director Clint Eastwood also takes the starring role as a shoe sales clerk who dreams of becoming a cowboy in this small-scale charmer. Eastwood assembles a bunch of other no-hopers and oddballs, among them Sondra Locke, who launch a Wild West show. Eastwood deftly plays with his image as a solitary man of action, the loner who resents company but gets it all the same. He is a sure judge of tone, and there's sufficient edge and wit to keep bathos at bay. AT. Contains some swearing. [VIDEO]

Clint Eastwood *"Bronco Billy" McCoy* • Sondra Locke *Antoinette Lily* • Geoffrey Lewis *John Arlington* • Scatman Crothers *"Doc" Lynch* • Bill McKinney *"Lefty" LeBow* • Sam Bottoms *Leonard James* • Dan Vadis *Chief Big Eagle* • Sierra Pecheur *Lorraine Running Water* ■ *Dir* Clint Eastwood • *Scr* Dennis Hackin

Bronco Bullfrog ★★★ 12

Drama 1970 · UK · BW · 112mins

This product of the British social realist school was much admired in its day with director Barney Platts-Mills being favourably compared to Ken Loach. Made on a shoestring in London's East End with a cast of non-professionals, the film shows how Del, a 17-year-old in a dead-end job, is lured into crime by a borstal boy nicknamed Bronco Bullfrog. Although rough around the edges and containing some weak supporting performances, the depiction of the restless, day-to-day existence of ordinary youngsters was arguably the most authentic to date. DM DVD

Del Walker *Del Quant* • Anne Gooding *Irene Richardson* • Sam Shepherd *Jo Saville/Bronco Bullfrog* • Roy Haywood *Roy* • Freda Shepherd *Mrs Richardson* • Dick Philpott *Del's father* • Chris Shepherd *Chris* ■ *Dir/Scr* Barney Platts-Mills

Bronco Buster ★★ U

Western 1952 · US · Colour · 80mins

Standard rodeo spills and thrills come from this tale of a promising young rider, played by Scott Brady, who is groomed for stardom by John Lund's champ. Brady's success goes to his head and he becomes obnoxious, even attempting to take Lund's girl (Joyce Holden) away from him. Several rodeo stars are featured, and director Budd Boetticher makes the most of the film's limited potential. AE

John Lund *Tom Moody* • Scott Brady *Bart Eaton* • Joyce Holden *Judy Bream* • Chill Wills *Dan Bream* • Don Haggerty *Dobie* • Dan Poore *Elliott* • Casey Tibbs *Rodeo rider* ■ *Dir* Budd Boetticher • *Scr* Horace McCoy, Lillie Hayward, from a story by Peter B Kyne

The Brontë Sisters ★★

Biographical drama
1979 · Fr · Colour · 115mins

The major – indeed, the only – interest in this alternative take on the literary sisters is provided by the casting of three of France's most talented actresses: the Isabelles Adjani and Huppert, and Marie-France Pisier. Director André Téchiné (who also co-wrote the script) seems to have a misplaced vision of the claustrophobic life lived by the famous family in their remote Yorkshire parsonage and, in concentrating on the tortured life of the sisters' doomed brother Branwell (Pascal Greggory) and their relationship with him, detracts from the carefully constructed period atmosphere. RB. In French with English subtitles.

Isabelle Adjani *Emily* • Marie-France Pisier *Charlotte* • Isabelle Huppert *Anne* • Pascal Greggory *Branwell* • Patrick Magee *Father* • Hélène Surgère *Mrs Robinson* • Roland Bertin *Nicholls* ■ *Dir* André Téchiné • *Scr* Pascal Bonitzer, André Téchiné, Jean Gruault

A Bronx Tale ★★★★ 18

Crime drama 1993 · US · Colour · 116mins

This is an intelligent portrait of a time (the 1960s) and place (New York's Little Italy) that eschews some of the more extravagant sweeps of Martin Scorsese, probably cinema's most famous chronicler of Italian-American life. Goodness is a hard quality to depict without sentimentality, yet Robert De Niro manages to convey it well, as a bus driver whose impressionable young son (Lillo Brancato) is attracted to a sharp-dressing local gangster (played by Chazz Palminteri). De Niro's sense of place and pace (this was his directorial debut) and screenwriter Palminteri's autobiographical insights into the neighbourhood make this a compelling picture. DP. Contains swearing, violence. [VIDEO] DVD

Robert De Niro *Lorenzo Anello* • Chazz Palminteri *Sonny* • Lillo Brancato *Calogero Anello, aged 17* • Francis Capra *Calogero Anello, aged nine* • Taral Hicks *Jane* • Katherine Narducci *Rosina Anello* • Clem Caserta *Jimmy Whispers* • Alfred Sauchelli Jr *Bobby Bars* • Joe Pesci *Carmine* ■ *Dir* Robert De Niro • *Scr* Chazz Palminteri, from his play

The Brood ★★★★ 18

Horror 1979 · Can · Colour · 88mins

Oliver Reed, a doctor experimenting with the new science of psychoplasmics, persuades Samantha Eggar to "shape her rage" and give birth to deformed children with killer instincts in another of director David Cronenberg's disturbing shockers. An intriguing metaphor for both unexplained bodily changes and the mental abuse some parents heap on

B

their offspring, this genuinely creepy and upsetting stomach churner is a modern horror classic. Eggar's performance gives a poignant emotional depth to Cronenberg's complex chiller. AJ DVD

Oliver Reed *Dr Hal Raglan* • Samantha Eggar *Nola Carveth* • Art Hindle *Frank Carveth* • Cindy Hinds *Candice Carveth* • Nuala Fitzgerald *Julianna Kelly* • Henry Beckman *Barton Kelly* • Susan Hogan *Ruth Mayer* • Michael McGhee *Inspector Mrazek* ■ *Dir/Scr* David Cronenberg

Brother ★★★★ 18

Crime drama 1997 · Rus · Colour · 95mins

A controversial hit in Russia, Alexei Balabanov's unflinchingly naturalistic *noir* equates democratic St Petersburg with the Chicago of the 1920s. Crime is as unavoidable as American consumerism, rabid nationalism, urban decay and dehumanising poverty, so ex-soldier Sergei Bodrov Jr has little option but to emulate his assassin brother, Viktor Sukhorukov, to survive. It's a perilous existence, though the wages of sin afford him the chance to rescue tram driver Svetlana Pismichenko from her abusive marriage and indulge his passion for pop heroes Nautilus. Grimly impressive. A sequel followed in 2000. DP. In Russian with English subtitles. DVD

Sergei Bodrov Jr *Danila Bragov* • Viktor Sukhorukov *Viktor Bragov* • Svetlana Pismichenko *Sveta* ■ *Dir/Scr* Alexei Balabanov

Brother ★★★ 18

Crime drama
2000 · Jpn/UK/US/Fr · Col · 108m

Takeshi Kitano attempts to reach a wider audience with this typically deadpan tale of a yakuza, set – for the first time – in the US. It's essentially a greatest bits movie, enticing the uninitiated while providing knowing winks to aficionados, as Kitano's gangster flees a Tokyo turf war only to precipitate an equally bloody showdown in Los Angeles. Exploring cultural contrasts, the criminal code and notions of brotherhood, this is polished and perceptive. DP. In English and Japanese with subtitles. Contains violence, swearing, brief nudity. DVD

"Beat" Takeshi [Takeshi Kitano] *Yamamoto* • Omar Epps *Denny* • Claude Maki *Ken* • Masaya Kato *Shirase* • Susumu Terajima *Kato* ■ *Dir/Scr* Takeshi Kitano

Brother Bear ★★★ U

Animated fantasy adventure
2003 · US · Colour · 81mins

This Disney film is an old-fashioned morality tale with solid messages of love, trust and loyalty. A flighty young native American man, Kenai, learns his life lessons the hard way after the Great Spirits turn him into a bear. It's a movie with considerable charm, beautifully animated, and the characters are well developed, helped by excellent voice talent. Phil Collins's uncharacteristically restrained songs further emphasise the comedy and emotion. SF DVD

Joaquin Phoenix *Kenai* • Jeremy Suarez *Koda* • Rick Moranis *Rutt* • Dave Thomas *Tuke* • DB Sweeney *Sitka* • Jason Raize *Denahi* • Joan Copeland *Tanana* ■ *Dir* Aaron Blaise, Robert Walker • *Scr* Steve Bencich, Lorne Cameron, Ron J Friedman, David Hoselton, Tab Murphy

The Brother from Another Planet ★★★ 15

Science-fiction satire
1984 · US · Colour · 108mins

A beguiling and thoughtful example of science fiction as social satire from independent writer/director John Sayles, the best purveyor of refreshingly new gritty comedies in the business. As the mute ET wandering Harlem streets in a daze, whose "magical touch" enables him to mend any household object, Joe Morton gives a tour de force performance. However, Sayles mainly uses his alien hero's inability to speak as an object lesson in human behaviour. AJ. Contains violence, swearing and drug abuse.

Joe Morton *The Brother* • Daryl Edwards *Fly* • Steve James (1) *Odell* • Leonard Jackson *Smokey* • Bill Cobbs *Walter* • Maggie Renzi *Noreen* • Tom Wright *Sam* • Ren Woods *Bernice* ■ *Dir/Scr* John Sayles

Brother John ★★

Fantasy drama 1970 · US · Colour · 95mins

The title role is so admirably suited to the saintly-looking Sidney Poitier, it's almost a cliché in itself. A black man returns to his Alabama home town to see if racial tensions have eased over the years. It turns out he's an angel who's recording it all for the heavenly host. As a fantasy it's pleasant enough, but James Goldstone's film could have been been much more searching in its implications. TH

Sidney Poitier *John Kane* • Will Geer *Doc Thomas* • Bradford Dillman *Lloyd Thomas* • Beverly Todd *Louisa MacGill* • Ramon Bieri *Orly Ball* • Warren J Kemmerling [Warren Kemmerling] *George* ■ *Dir* James Goldstone • *Scr* Ernest Kinoy

Brother Orchid ★★★

Crime spoof 1940 · US · BW · 87mins

There is always a down side to Warner Bros gangster pictures – a rather out-of-place moral dimension, meant to counterbalance the fast-living world of guys and molls. The down side here, after the pleasure of watching Edward G Robinson and Humphrey Bogart as partners who fall out, is having to watch Robinson transform himself into a pious friar. The two stars are on good form as they run rival protection rackets and rub out the lesser names on the cast list. Ann Sothern adds a lot of humour as Robinson's girl, while Lloyd Bacon directs with machine-gun speed. AT

Edward G Robinson *Little John Sarto* • Humphrey Bogart *Jack Buck* • Ann Sothern *Flo Addams* • Donald Crisp *Brother Superior* • Ralph Bellamy *Clarence Fletcher* • Allen Jenkins *Willie the Knife* • Charles D Brown *Brother Wren* • Cecil Kellaway *Brother Goodwin* • Morgan Conway *Philadelphia Powell* ■ *Dir* Lloyd Bacon • *Scr* Earl Baldwin, from the *Collier's Magazine* article by Richard Connell

Brother Sun, Sister Moon ★ PG

Biographical religious drama
1972 · It/UK · Colour · 115mins

Avoid this insipid rendering of the early life of St Francis of Assisi. As seen by Franco Zeffirelli, Francesco di Bernadone was a prototype hippy with flowers in his hair who approved of free love (the only sort he could afford) and social equality. To play him, Zeffirelli first fancied the young Al Pacino, but the studio said "Who?". So Graham Faulkner, another unknown, was hired. AT DVD

Graham Faulkner *Francesco* • Judi Bowker *Clare* • Leigh Lawson *Bernardo* • Kenneth Cranham *Paolo* • Lee Montague *Pietro di Bernardone* • Valentina Cortese *Pica di Bernardone* • Alec Guinness *Pope Innocent III* ■ *Dir* Franco Zeffirelli • *Scr* Suso Cecchi D'Amico, Kenneth Ross, Lina Wertmuller, Franco Zeffirelli

The Brotherhood ★★

Crime drama 1968 · US · Colour · 96mins

Made before *The Godfather* revealed how fascinating and complex a subject the Mafia could be, this is a straightforward tale of generational conflict within the criminal "family". Kirk Douglas (who also produced) stars as the traditionalist at odds with his younger brother (Alex Cord), although the real drama arises when each has to carry out the role of executioner. There are the usual strong performances to be found in a Martin Ritt film, but it suffers as a result of failing to synthesise the good and bad aspects of Douglas's character. AE

Kirk Douglas *Frank Ginetta* • Alex Cord *Vince Ginetta* • Irene Papas *Ida Ginetta* • Luther Adler *Dominick Bertolo* • Susan Strasberg *Emma Ginetta* • Murray Hamilton *Jim Egan* ■ *Dir* Martin Ritt • *Scr* Lewis John Carlino

Brotherhood ★★★ 15

Epic war drama
2004 · S Kor · Colour · 148mins

A phenomenal success in its native South Korea, this reworks Steven Spielberg's *Saving Private Ryan* for the Korean War. When bothers Jin-tae (Jang Dong-gun) and Jin-seok (Won Bin) are drafted into the army to fight the Communist invaders, Jin-tae transforms himself into a one-man killing machine after learning that winning the medal of honour will spare his brother from frontline duty. While throwing gore and severed limbs around the screen with terrifying abandon, there is also plenty of scope for maudlin melodrama. Kang Je-gyu avoids the usual anti-North propaganda and looks at both the North and the South's far from glorious war records. JR. In Korean with English subtitles. Contains violence and swearing.

Jang Dong-gun *Jin-tae* • Wong Bin *Jin-seok* • Lee Eun-joo *Young-shin* • Gong Hyung-jin *Young-man* • Lee Young-ran *Mother* ■ *Dir* Kang Je-gyu • *Scr* Kang Je-gyu , Kim Sang-don, Han Ji-hoon

Brotherhood of Justice ★★ 15

Action drama 1986 · US · Colour · 93mins

Proving that everyone has to start somewhere, this high-school version of *Death Wish* finds a young Keanu Reeves, in one of his early roles, deciding to fight back against rising crime at school and in the city. However, it's not long before the junior vigilantes get out of control. This made-for-TV crime drama also provides early roles for such luminaries as Kiefer Sutherland and Billy Zane, so it's not without curiosity value – but it has little else to offer. JF DVD

Keanu Reeves *Derek* • Lori Loughlin *Christie* • Kiefer Sutherland *Victor* • Joe Spano *Bob Grootemat* • Darren Dalton *Scottie* • Evan Mirand *Mule* • Billy Zane *Les* ■ *Dir* Charles Braverman • *Scr* Noah Jubelirer, Jeffrey Bloom, from a story by Noah Jubelirer

Brotherhood of Satan ★★★ 18

Horror 1970 · US · Colour · 88mins

Strother Martin heads a Californian devil cult kidnapping local children for soul transference purposes. This eerie witchcraft extravaganza packs an unsettling punch because of its ordinary setting and the imaginative and versatile use of its low-budget trappings. It's a great example of what can be achieved with very little, enhanced by uniformly good acting, classy direction by Bernard McEveety and clever small-scale special effects (for example, the kids' toys being enlarged to life-size) make this an unpretentious winner. AJ

Strother Martin *Don Duncan* • LQ Jones *Sheriff* • Charles Bateman *Ben* • Anna Capri [Ahna Capri] *Nicky* • Charles Robinson *Priest* • Alvy Moore *Tobey* ■ *Dir* Bernard McEveety • *Scr* William Welch, from an idea by Sean MacGregor

Brotherhood of the Wolf ★★★ 15

Period action fantasy
2001 · Fr · Colour · 139mins

Blending historical fact with hysterical fiction, this flamboyant fantasy attempts to give substance to France's own Loch Ness Monster legend – the fabled Beast of Gévaudan that killed more than a hundred women and children between 1764 and 1767. Taking this still unexplained visceral mystery as his inspiration, Christophe Gans details how forward-thinking naturalist Samuel Le Bihan and his Iroquois blood brother Mark Dacascos are sent by King Louis XV to destroy the mythical creature. A visual tour de force, but essentially hollow. AJ. In French with English subtitles. DVD

Samuel Le Bihan *Grégoire de Fronsac* • Vincent Cassel *Jean-François de Morangias* • Emilie Dequenne *Marianne de Morangias* • Monica Bellucci *Sylvia* • Jérémie Rénier *Thomas d'Apcher* • Mark Dacascos *Mani* • Jean Yanne *Count de Morangias* ■ *Dir* Christophe Gans • *Scr* Stéphane Cabel, Christophe Gans, from a treatment by Stéphane Cabel

The Brothers ★★ PG

Drama 1947 · UK · BW · 87mins

Cecil B DeMille's one-time assistant David MacDonald returned to his native Scotland for this tempestuous melodrama. While Stephen Dade's images of Skye are highly evocative, there's little passion in the romance between Patricia Roc and Andrew Crawford, even though she's the housekeeper of his deadliest rival (Finlay Currie). Part of the problem is the straightlaced nature of postwar British cinema, which kept emotions firmly in check. DP

Patricia Roc *Mary* • Will Fyffe *Aeneas McGrath* • Maxwell Reed *Fergus Macrae* • Finlay Currie *Hector Macrae* • Duncan Macrae *John Macrae* • John Laurie *Dugald* • Andrew Crawford *Willie McFarish* • James Woodburn *Priest* ■ *Dir* David MacDonald • *Scr* Muriel Box, Sydney Box, Paul Vincent Carroll, David MacDonald, from a novel by L AG Strong

Brothers ★★

Prison drama based on a true story
1977 · US · Colour · 105mins

Films *à clef* are supposed to be fictionalised versions of real people's lives. However, screenwriters Edward and Mildred Lewis haven't bothered to rework too many of the events in this misguided drama inspired by the relationship between black activist Angela Davis and San Quentin inmate George Jackson, whose brother and a judge were killed during an attempted breakout from the Marin County Courthouse. What makes this angry film so resistible, however, is the racial stereotyping. DP

Bernie Casey *David Thomas* • Vonetta McGee *Paula Jones* • Ron O'Neal *Walter Nance* • Renny Roker *Lewis* • Stu Gilliam *Robinson* • John Lehne *McGee* ■ *Dir* Arthur Barron • *Scr* Edward Lewis, Mildred Lewis

Brothers ★ 18

Comedy drama 1999 · UK · Colour · 94mins

Debut director Martin Dunkerton proves that sheer enthusiasm does not a good movie make. This tale of lads abroad puking, farting and drinking would offend even the most loyal reader of *Loaded*. Badly acted, poorly realised, terribly written and filled with boring shots of Grecian scenery, this is truly one of the worst films ever made. JB DVD

Justin Brett *Matt "Mystic Matey" Davidson* • Daren Jacobs *Chris "Beercan" Sullivan* • Daniel Fredenburgh *Julian "The King"*

U = SUITABLE FOR ALL Uc = SUITABLE FOR ALL, ESPECIALLY FOR YOUNG CHILDREN (VIDEO ONLY) PG = PARENTAL GUIDANCE

Davidson • Rebecca Cardinale *Anna Stefanos* ■ *Dir* Martin Dunkerton • *Scr* Martin Dunkerton, Nick Valentine

The Brothers ★★★ 15

Comedy drama 2001 · US · Colour · 98mins

This sharply written film spurns cinema's usual African-American stereotypes and focuses on the universal themes of romantic commitment and the bonds of friendship. Four well-to-do young black men have to reassess their lives, loves and loyalties when one of their lifelong friends suddenly announces that he's getting married, despite having once sworn to remain single for ever. In the characters' familiar fears of commitment, there are sharp echoes of real life. DA VIDEO DVD

Morris Chestnut *Jackson Smith* • DL Hughley *Derrick West* • Bill Bellamy *Brian Palmer* • Shemar Moore *Terry White* • Tamala Tones *Sheila West* ■ *Dir/Scr* Gary Hardwick

Brothers ★★★ 15

Drama
2004 · Den/UK/Swe/Nor · Colour · 117mins

When the helicopter carrying army major Ulrich Thomsen is shot down in Afghanistan, his family back home in Copenhagen is told he is missing, presumed dead. The tragedy forges a bond between his wife Connie Nielsen and wayward brother Nikolaj Lie Kaas that develops into sexual attraction. But then it transpires Michael is alive and recovering from his brutal treatment at the hands of the Taliban. The film's handheld cinematography lends immediacy while some finely observed touches freshen up the potentially overwrought plot. LF. In Danish with English subtitles. Contains swearing and violence.

Connie Nielsen *Sarah* • Ulrich Thomsen *Michael* • Nikolaj Lie Kaas *Jannik* • Bent Mejding *Henning* • Solbjorg Hojfeldt *Else* • Paw Henriksen *Niels Peter, "NP"* • Laura Bro *Ditte* ■ *Dir* Susanne Bier • *Scr* Thomas Anders Jensen from a story by Thomas Anders Jensen, Susanne Bier

Brothers and Relations ★★★

Drama 1988 · Viet · BW

Few films had been made in Vietnam before the civil war, when the majority of those produced were amateurish propaganda efforts. However, once the dust settled, indigenous directors took a more reflective look at the conflict and its impact. Set in the mid-1970s, there is poignancy in the tale of a wounded veteran who is forced to seek work and restore his self-esteem in Hanoi after he returns home to discover that his family has leased out his room presuming him dead. DP. In Vietnamese with English subtitles.

Dang Viet Bao • Bui Bai Binh • Ngoc Bich • Ngoc Thu ■ *Dir* Tran Vu, Nguyen Huu Luyen • *Scr* Thu Huong Duong

The Brothers and Sisters of the Toda Family ★★★★

Drama 1941 · Jpn · BW · 105mins

Yasujiro Ozu only completed two features during the war and both this domestic drama and *There Was a Father* avoided any overt avowal of national-policy tendencies. The action revolves around the abnegation of familial duty by widow Fumiko Katsuragi's wealthy children and the sacrifices made by her youngest offspring, Shin Saburi and Mieko Takamine. Some critics have accused Ozu of propagandising by part-setting the action in Manchuria. But he was more likely exploiting the current vogue for "city films", which denounced bourgeois decadence and stressed the importance of youth in rethinking tradition. DP

Mieko Takamine *Setsuko, Toda's youngest daughter* • Shin Saburi *Shojiro, Toda's second son* • Hideo Fujino *Shintaro Toda* • Fumiko Katsuragi *Toda's wife* • Mitsuko Yoshikawa *Chizuru, Toda's eldest daughter* • Masao Hayama *Ryokichi* • Tatsuo Saito *Shinichiro, Toda's eldest son* • Yoshiko Tsubouchi *Ayako, Toda's second daughter* • Chishu Ryu *Inoue, a friend* ■ *Dir* Yasujiro Ozu • *Scr* Yasujiro Ozu, Tadao Ikeda

Brothers in Arms ★★ 18

Action crime thriller
1988 · US · Colour · 87mins

In a crude cross between *The Texas Chain Saw Massacre* and *Deliverance*, brothers Todd Allen and Charles Grant find themselves crossing swords with a family of barmy backswoodmen who don't take kindly to strangers. Apart from Michelle Pfeiffer's sister Dedee and *The X Files* regular Mitch Pileggi, the cast is largely undistinguished. There is precious little suspense and even less imagination shown in the monotonous blood-letting. JF VIDEO

Todd Allen *Joey* • Charles Grant *Dallas* • Dedee Pfeiffer *Stevie* • Jack Starrett *Father* • Mitch Pileggi *Caleb* • Dan Bell *Aaron* ■ *Dir* George Jay Bloom III • *Scr* Steve Fisher

Brothers in Arms ★★★

Political thriller 1990 · Fr · Colour · 122mins

This is an interesting political thriller about terrorism and underworld crime on the mean streets of Paris. Added interest comes from the odd-couple pairing of a Jewish vice squad agent and an Arab undercover man on an assignment to hunt for the supplier of a killer drug. The unlikely partnership is put under even more strain when the cop's ex-wife falls in love with his partner. PF. A French language film.

Richard Berry *Karim Hamida* • Patrick Bruel *Simon Atlan* • Corinne Dacla *Lisa* • Bruno Cremer *Joulin* • Said Amadis *Ali Radjani* ■ *Dir* Alexandre Arcady • *Scr* Daniel St-Hamont [Daniel Saint-Hamont], Benedicte Kermadec, Pierre Aknine

Brothers in Law ★★★★ U

Comedy 1956 · UK · BW · 90mins

The Boulting brothers' delightfully witty follow-up to their smash hit *Private's Progress* features many of the same cast. Its source novel is by Henry Cecil, himself a distinguished QC, and hopefully quite unlike the absent-minded QC played by Miles Malleson to whom our hero Ian Carmichael is apprenticed. Carmichael is surrounded here by a cast of accomplished character actors, including the splendid Terry-Thomas and the redoubtable Richard Attenborough as a smarmy fellow barrister. This is still very funny and relevant today. TS VIDEO

Richard Attenborough *Henry Marshall* • Ian Carmichael *Roger Thursby* • Terry-Thomas *Alfred Green* • Jill Adams *Sally Smith* • Miles Malleson *Kendall Grimes* • Eric Barker *Alec Blair* • Irene Handl *Mrs Potter* • John Le Mesurier *Judge Ryman* • Raymond Huntley *Tatlock* • Nicholas Parsons *Charles Poole* ■ *Dir* Roy Boulting • *Scr* Roy Boulting, Frank Harvey, Jeffrey Dell, from the novel by Henry Cecil

Brothers in Trouble ★★★ 15

Drama 1995 · UK · Colour · 97mins

Director Udayan Prasad betrays his inexperience with narrative in this well-meaning, but rather contrived drama about illegal immigrants living in 1960s Britain. While making atmospheric use of the cramped house in which the 18 illegals live, Prasad also draws fine performances from Pavan Malhotra, Angeline Ball and the leading Indian star Om Puri. But the story begins to disintegrate when the script abandons telling observation in favour of sensationalist melodrama. Flawed, but worthwhile. DP. Contains swearing, a sex scene and nudity. VIDEO

Om Puri *Hussein Shah* • Angeline Ball *Mary* • Pavan Malhotra *Amir* • Ahsen Bhatti *Irshad* • Bhasker *Gholam* • Pravesh Kumar *Sakib* • Lesley Clare O'Neill *Prostitute* • Kulvinder Ghir *Agent* • Badi Uzzaman *Old Ram* ■ *Dir* Udayan Prasad • *Scr* Robert Buckler, from the novel *Return Journey* by Abdullah Hussein

The Brothers Karamazov ★★★

Drama 1958 · US · Colour · 145mins

Most famous in its day for the fact that Marilyn Monroe wanted to play Grushenka – or so she breathily gasped to an assembled press – this rather stodgy but undeniably well-made MGM epic could well have benefited from such courageous casting, for, excellent though Maria Schell is, she just isn't Monroe. Nevertheless, the brothers themselves are superb, with Yul Brynner a dashing Dmitri, Richard Basehart as Ivan, and William Shatner, in his debut, as the young Alexey. Although long, this is accessible, capturing the essence of Dostoyevsky without losing substance or tone. TS

Yul Brynner *Dmitri Karamazov* • Maria Schell *Grushenka* • Claire Bloom *Katya* • Lee J Cobb *Fyodor Karamazov* • Richard Basehart *Ivan Karamazov* • Albert Salmi *Smerdyakov* • William Shatner *Alexey Karamazov* • Judith Evelyn *Madame Anna Hohlakov* • Edgar Stehli *Grigory* ■ *Dir* Richard Brooks • *Scr* Richard Brooks, from the novel by Fyodor Dostoyevsky, adapted by Julius J Epstein, Philip G Epstein

The Brothers McMullen ★★★ 15

Comedy drama 1995 · US · Colour · 94mins

Edward Burns starred as handsome soldier Reiben in *Saving Private Ryan*, but he's better known as a noted director of quirky independent movies. He made his directorial debut with this endearing look at the mixed up romantic lives of three Irish Catholic brothers who share the family home in New York following their widowed mother's return to Ireland. Dealing with unusually heavyweight topics for a comedy drama, such as religious ethics and sexual morality, the literate and amusing script keeps things bubbling along nicely. AJ VIDEO DVD

Edward Burns *Barry* • Mike McGlone *Patrick* • Jack Mulcahy *Jack* • Shari Albert *Susan* • Maxine Bahns *Audry* • Catharine Bolz *Mrs McMullen* ■ *Dir/Scr* Edward Burns

The Brothers Rico ★★★

Crime drama 1957 · US · BW · 91mins

As *film noir* disappeared in the late 1950s, this crude example of the genre emerged. Richard Conte is the gangster turned successful businessman whose younger brothers have been earmarked for assassination by the mob. The *noir* element is provided by Conte's meaningless quest and the disorderly world around him, but director Phil Karlson piles on enough violence to flatten the subtleties of French writer Georges Simenon's original story. TH

Richard Conte *Eddie Rico* • Dianne Foster *Alice Rico* • Kathryn Grant *Norah* • Larry Gates *Sid Kubik* • James Darren *Johnny Rico* • Argentina Brunetti *Mrs Rico* • Lamont Johnson *Peter Malaks* • Harry Bellaver *Mike Lamotta* ■ *Dir* Phil Karlson • *Scr* Lewis Meltzer, Ben Perry, from the novella *Les Frères Rico* by Georges Simenon

The Brown Bunny ★★★

Erotic road movie drama
2003 · US/Jap/Fr · Colour · 90mins

Famously reviled by many critics when it premiered at the Cannes film festival, but also championed by a passionate few, this erotic drama is both a tone poem about lost love and a singularly uneventful road movie where nothing much happens until the notorious, supposedly for-real oral-sex scene at the end. For most of the running time, writer/editor/director/star Vincent Gallo drives across the US, starring moodily into a lens and meeting a variety of women who instantly fall in love with his motorbiking hero. Enjoyment is aided by a high tolerance for Gordon Lightfoot songs and slow, unbroken and quite beautiful shots of scenery. Watch and judge for yourself. LF

Vincent Gallo *Bud Clay* • Chloë Sevigny *Daisy* • Cheryl Tiegs *Lilly* • Elizabeth Blake *Rose* • Anna Vareschi *Violet* ■ *Dir/Scr* Vincent Gallo

Brown Sugar ★★★ 12

Romantic comedy drama
2002 · US · Colour · 104mins

Director and co-writer Rick Famuyiwa's follow up to *The Wood* treads a similar path to that pleasant drama – the onset of commitment prompting romantic reassessment – but doubles as a love letter to hip hop. Lifelong friends Sanaa Lathan and Taye Diggs are both involved in the music industry and both are concerned with keeping the music real while remaining oblivious to the true nature of their feelings for one another. The assured performances and witty script mean that you really warm to these characters. RT VIDEO DVD

Taye Diggs *Dre* • Sanaa Lathan *Sidney* • Mos Def *Chris* • Nicole Ari Parker *Reese* • Boris Kodjoe *Kelby* • Queen Latifah *Francine* ■ *Dir* Rick Famuyiwa • *Scr* Michael Elliot, Rick Famuyiwa, from a story by Michael Elliot

The Browning Version ★★★★ U

Drama 1951 · UK · BW · 89mins

Infinitely superior to Mike Figgis's 1994 remake, this is another expert collaboration between writer Terence Rattigan and director Anthony Asquith. What makes this version of Rattigan's hit play so memorable is the mesmerising performance of Michael Redgrave as the classics teacher whose life is as redundant as his subject. The supporting cast is also first rate, with Jean Kent chillingly heartless as Redgrave's adulterous wife and Nigel Patrick suitably cocky as the man who cuckolds him. The shabby gentility of the school is neatly captured and the merciless revelation of each new woe is, thanks to Redgrave's dignified self-pity, agonising to watch. Only the optimistic conclusion fails to ring true. DP VIDEO

Michael Redgrave *Andrew Crocker-Harris* • Jean Kent *Millie Crocker-Harris* • Nigel Patrick *Frank Hunter* • Wilfrid Hyde White *Frobisher* • Brian Smith (1) *Taplow* • Bill Travers *Fletcher* • Ronald Howard *Gilbert* • Paul Medland *Wilson* ■ *Dir* Anthony Asquith • *Scr* Terence Rattigan, from his play • *Art Director* Carmen Dillon

The Browning Version ★★★ 15

Drama 1994 · UK · Colour · 93mins

The last film that Mike Figgis made prior to achieving long-overdue international recognition with *Leaving Las Vegas*, this version of Terence Rattigan's play is a polished, if slightly old-fashioned piece of work. However, it doesn't bear comparison with Anthony Asquith's 1951 adaptation, with Albert Finney giving a less finely shaded performance than Michael Redgrave in the role of the timid, under-appreciated schoolmaster. A curious choice for its director, perhaps, but still an affecting tale. DP. Contains violence, swearing and brief nudity. VIDEO

Albert Finney *Andrew Crocker-Harris* • Greta Scacchi *Laura Crocker-Harris* • Matthew Modine *Frank Hunter* • Julian Sands *Tom*

Gilbert • Michael Gambon *Dr Frobisher* • Ben Silverstone *Taplow* • Maryam D'Abo *Diana Rafferty* • James Sturgess *Bryant* ■ *Dir* Mike Figgis • *Scr* Ronald Harwood, from the play by Terence Rattigan

B

Brown's Requiem ★★ 18

Crime drama 1998 · US · Colour · 100mins

This competent adaptation of James Ellroy's first novel suffers from unavoidable comparisons with the superb film version of the author's *LA Confidential*. Michael Rooker has the appropriately intimidating frame and throaty voice for Fritz Brown, a low-rent, ex-alcoholic private investigator assigned to keeping an eye on a young girl who's involved with a local heavy. Although director/screenwriter Jason Freeland creates a convincing shady milieu, the flawed characters and cynical voiceover are pretty run of the mill. JC DVD

Michael Rooker *Fritz Brown* • Selma Blair *Jane Baker* • Jack Conley *Richard Ralston* • Harold Gould *Solly K* • Tobin Bell *Stan the Man* • Brad Dourif *Edwards* • Brion James *Cathcart* ■ *Dir* Jason Freeland • *Scr* Jason Freeland, from the novel by James Ellroy

Brubaker ★★★★ 15

Prison drama 1980 · US · Colour · 124mins

Robert Redford is in reformist mode here, determined to combat brutality and corruption in a state prison farm. Director Stuart Rosenberg piles on the agony with sequences of bleak action, while the acting – especially from Jane Alexander and Yaphet Kotto – is formidable enough to take on all that social responsibility. A touch downbeat, and at times ponderous and sanctimonious, this prison drama still sends out an ominous message to those who care about what society does with its misfits. TH. Contains violence and swearing. DVD

Robert Redford *Henry Brubaker* • Yaphet Kotto *Richard "Dickie" Coombes* • Jane Alexander *Lillian Gray* • Murray Hamilton *Deach* • David Keith *Larry Lee Bullen* • Morgan Freeman *Walter* • Matt Clark *Purcell* • Tim McIntire *Huey Rauch* • Richard Ward *Abraham* ■ *Dir* Stuart Rosenberg • *Scr* WD Richter, from the story by WD Richter, Arthur Ross, from a book by Thomas O Murton, Joe Hyams

The Bruce ★ 15

Historical adventure
1996 · UK · Colour · 106mins

This is a ramshackle historical drama about Robert the Bruce, the Scots hero who, according to legend, was inspired by the persistence of a stranded spider to renew his bid to expel the English from Scotland. Less low-budget than no-budget, the film was largely funded by public subscriptions. One has to admire the bravehearts who at least got *The Bruce* made. Unfortunately, one can't much admire the film itself. DA

Sandy Welch *Robert the Bruce* • Brian Blessed *King Edward* • Michael van Wijk *De Bohun* • Oliver Reed *Bishop Wisharton* ■ *Dir* Bob Carruthers • *Scr* Bob Carruthers, Michael Leighton

Bruce Almighty ★★★ 12

Comedy fantasy 2003 · US · Colour · 96mins

When professionally wacky TV news reporter Jim Carrey is passed over for promotion, he vents his anger live on air, is sacked and curses God for doing a lousy job. Rising to the bait, the Almighty – a coolly majestic Morgan Freeman – gives the sceptical Carrey the chance to see if he can do any better. He does what you might expect: enlarges girlfriend Jennifer Aniston's boobs, performs a Red Sea-style parting of his tomato soup and pulls the Moon out of its usual orbit to create a romantic moment. A neat premise and plenty of laughs, but hardly memorable. BP DVD

Jim Carrey *Bruce Nolan* • Morgan Freeman *God* • Jennifer Aniston *Grace Connelly* • Philip Baker Hall *Jack Keller* • Catherine Bell *Susan Ortega* • Lisa Ann Walter *Debbie* ■ *Dir* Tom Shadyac • *Scr* Steve Koren, Mark O'Keefe, Steve Oedekerk, from a story by Steve Koren, Mark O'Keefe

Brushfire! ★★

Action adventure 1962 · US · BW · 80mins

This modest work was the only film made by Jack Warner Jr (as co-writer, producer and director). The son of Jack L Warner, of Warner Bros fame, he once said of his father, "If his brothers hadn't hired him he'd have been out of work." This second feature relies on an exclamation mark to suggest drama and excitement, neither of which it delivers. Its a conventional story of two planters in South East Asia, who are kidnapped by rebels for a ransom, and the efforts of a group of fellow westerners to free them. BB

John Ireland *Jeff Saygure* • Everett Sloane *Chevern McCase* • Jo Morrow *Easter Banford* • Al Avalon *Tony Banford* • Carl Esmond *Martin* ■ *Dir* Jack Warner Jr • *Scr* Irwin R Blacker, Jack Warner Jr, from a story by Irwin R Blacker

The Brutal Truth ★★ 18

Drama 1999 · US · Colour · 85mins

In this well-meaning but contrived and confused ensemble piece, Christina Applegate plays a young woman who organises a college reunion for her old chums at her isolated farm. When an unexpected turn of events leaves them stranded at the house, her friends try to piece together the whys and wherefores. The eclectic cast – Applegate excepted – seem about as confused as most viewers about what is actually going on and the clumsy pacing does little to help. JF

Christina Applegate *Emily* • Justin Lazard *T J* • Johnathon Schaech *James* • Moon Zappa *Alex* • Molly Ringwald *Penelope* ■ *Dir* Cameron Thor • *Scr* Tim Puntillo

Brute Force ★★★★

Prison drama 1947 · US · BW · 94mins

This is one of the great prison dramas, tough even by today's standards, and a film whose parallels to the Nazi concentration camps would have been obvious to the audience of the time. Hume Cronyn is a sadistic prison warden whose staff systematically brutalise their captives; Burt Lancaster, in his second picture, leads the prisoners in a *Spartacus*-style revolt. Apart from the flashbacks showing prisoners with their wives and girlfriends, the whole movie is a masterpiece of escalating violence. It's a disturbing, powerful picture, handled in an urgent, documentary style by Jules Dassin. AT

Burt Lancaster *Joe Collins* • Hume Cronyn *Capt Munsey* • Charles Bickford *Gallagher* • Whit Bissell *Tom Lister* • Sam Levene *Louie* • John Hoyt *Spencer* • Yvonne De Carlo *Gina* • Ann Blyth *Ruth* • Ella Raines *Cora* • Anita Colby *Flossie* ■ *Dir* Jules Dassin • *Scr* Richard Brooks, from a story by Robert Patterson • *Cinematographer* William Daniels [William H Daniels]

El Bruto ★★★

Drama 1952 · Mex · BW · 82mins

This simmering drama is among director Luis Buñuel's more interesting failures. Although he clearly has little sympathy with the worker who becomes a boss's lackey, Buñuel clearly demonstrates the desperate domestic situation that would compel a man to betray his class. Shot in a mere 18 days, the film looks rough, but this only reinforces the atmosphere of life around Mexico City's abattoirs. Katy Jurado is superb, as always, but Pedro Armendáriz – Mexico's greatest actor – seems more interested in preserving his macho image than giving a germane performance. DP. In Spanish with English subtitles.

Pedro Armendáriz *Pedro, El Bruto* • Katy Jurado *Paloma* • Rosita Arenas *Meche* • Andres Soler *Andres Cabrera* • Beatriz Ramos *Doña Marta* • Paco Martinez *Don Pepe* ■ *Dir* Luis Buñuel • *Scr* Luis Buñuel, Luis Alcoriza

The Brylcreem Boys ★★★ 15

Second World War comedy drama
1996 · UK · Colour · 101mins

Loosely based on actual events, the film is set in the Republic of Ireland which, as a neutral country during the Second World War, was committed to interning both German and Allied personnel – in the same camp. Canadian flier Bill Campbell and German air ace Angus MacFadyen are the two newest internees who come to blows over both the conflict and a local farm girl. There are some pleasing supporting turns – in particular Gabriel Byrne – while director/co-writer Terence Ryan affably melds together the comic, romantic and dramatic elements. JF. Contains swearing, violence. DVD

Bill Campbell *Myles Keogh* • William McNamara *Sam Gunn* • Angus MacFadyen *Rudolph Von Stegenbek* • John Gordon-Sinclair *Richard Lewis* • Oliver Tobias *Hans Jorg Wolff* • Jean Butler *Mattie Guerin* • Joe McGann *Captain Deegan* • Hal Fowler *Bunty Winthrop* • Gabriel Byrne *Commandant O'Brien* ■ *Dir* Terence Ryan • *Scr* Terence Ryan, Jamie Brown, Susan Morrall

Bubba Ho-tep ★★★ 15

Black comedy horror
2002 · US · Colour · 88mins

This irreverent, B-movie-style horror comedy offers an alternative version of what became of Elvis Presley. In an astonishingly spot-on performance, Bruce Campbell plays the king of rock 'n' roll, now an elderly unknown living in an East Texas rest home. When fellow pensioners start inexplicably dying, Campbell teams up with a black resident (Ossie Davis), who believes he's President Kennedy, to solve the mystery. Crudely hilarious, this no-frills frolic combines below-the-belt geriatric wit with Three Stooges-type slapstick. The climax, however, is disappointing. SF. Contains swearing, violence and sexual references. DVD

Bruce Campbell *Elvis* • Ossie Davis *Jack* • Ella Joyce *The nurse* • Heidi Marnhout *Callie* • Bob Ivy *Bubba Ho-tep* • Edith Jefferson *Elderly woman* ■ *Dir* Don Coscarelli • *Scr* Don Coscarelli, from the short story by Joe R Lansdale

The Bubble ★★

Science-fiction drama
1966 · US · Colour · 93mins

Arch Oboler is the man who brought us the first ever 3-D movie, *Bwana Devil* in 1952. While Hollywood lost interest in the costly process, Oboler persisted and finally perfected Space-Vision (his own 3-D system) and released *The Bubble*. Ironically this overly talky movie about three people trapped in a town populated by mindless zombies and surrounded by an energy shield hardly merited or benefited from 3-D exposure. Perhaps more imagination should have been invested in the plot and characterisations rather than in the technical angle. RS

Michael Cole *Mark* • Deborah Walley *Catherine* • Johnny Desmond *Tony* • Kassid McMahon ■ *Dir/Scr* Arch Oboler

Bubble Boy ★★ 12

Comedy 2001 · US · Colour · 80mins

In this wildly uneven comedy, Jake Gyllenhaal plays a young man with immune deficiencies who is forced by his worried mum (Swoosie Kurtz) to live his life in a bubble. However, when he falls for the girl next door (Marley Shelton), who is about to marry a sleazy musician, the boy and his bubble set off cross-country to reclaim his true love. It's deeply politically incorrect – in the US, the Immune Deficiency Foundation called for a boycott – but it has its moments and is enthusiastically played. JF DVD

Jake Gyllenhaal *Jimmy Livingston* • Swoosie Kurtz *Mrs Livingston* • Marley Shelton *Chloe* • Danny Trejo *Slim* • John Carroll Lynch *Mr Livingston* ■ *Dir* Blair Hayes • *Scr* Cinco Paul, Ken Daurio

The Buccaneer ★★ U

Swashbuckling adventure
1938 · US · BW · 125mins

Cecil B DeMille's lavish juggernaut of a swashbuckler is set during the British-American war of 1812-15, but rather lacks the lightness and humour the genre needs. Fredric March plays the pirate Jean Lafitte, who sides with President Andrew Jackson and runs the British out of New Orleans. The leading lady is Franciska Gaal, a Hungarian discovery of DeMille's who subsequently went home and vanished without a trace. Anthony Quinn, DeMille's son-in-law at the time, plays one of March's henchman. In 1958 Quinn remade the film, as his sole directorial effort. AT

Fredric March *Jean Lafitte* • Franciska Gaal *Gretchen* • Akim Tamiroff *Dominique You* • Margot Grahame *Annette* • Walter Brennan *Ezra Peavey* • Ian Keith *Crawford* • Spring Byington *Dolly Madison* • Douglass Dumbrille *Governor Claiborne* • Hugh Sothern *Andrew Jackson* • Anthony Quinn *Beluche* ■ *Dir* Cecil B DeMille • *Scr* Edwin Justus Mayer, Harold Lamb, C Gardner Sullivan, Jeanie Macpherson, from the book *Lafitte the Pirate* by Lyle Saxon

The Buccaneer ★★★ U

Swashbuckling adventure
1958 · US · Colour · 118mins

This is actor Anthony Quinn's only film as director and while it's a little long and drawn out, the Technicolor is splendid and it boasts quite a cast. This time a bewigged Yul Brynner is the dashing Lafitte and his women are Claire Bloom and Inger Stevens, while Charlton Heston appears as General Andrew Jackson. The most impressive sequence is a well-mounted but studio-bound Battle of New Orleans. The anti-British sentiments might put off some viewers, but for students of American history and for fans of a Hollywood in decline this is worth a look. TS

Yul Brynner *Jean Lafitte* • Charlton Heston *General Andrew Jackson* • Claire Bloom *Bonnie Brown* • Charles Boyer *Dominique You* • Inger Stevens *Annette Claiborne* • Henry Hull *Ezra Peavey* • EG Marshall *Governor Claiborne* • Lorne Greene *Mercier* ■ *Dir* Anthony Quinn • *Scr* Jesse L Lasky Jr, Bernice Mosk, from the 1938 film, from the book *Lafitte the Pirate* by Lyle Saxon

Buchanan Rides Alone ★★★ U

Western 1958 · US · Colour · 79mins

One of the colourful B westerns co-produced by star Randolph Scott and Harry Joe Brown for their Ranown independent production company, and directed by the talented Budd Boetticher. This is an unusual entry in the cycle, since it's based on a novel in a cowboy series (the "Buchanan" books by Jonas Ward) and features a rather more cheerful, humorous hero than usually portrayed by the craggy, taciturn Scott. The myriad plot convolutions are mightily effective, too, but there are no standouts in the rather feeble supporting cast. TS

Randolph Scott *Buchanan* • Craig Stevens *Abe Carbo* • Barry Kelley *Lou Agry* • Tol Avery

Simon Agry • Peter Whitney *Amos Agry* • Manuel Rojas *Juan* • LQ Jones *Pecos Bill* • Robert Anderson (2) *Waldo Peek* ■ *Dir* Budd Boetticher • *Scr* Charles Lang, from the novel *The Name's Buchanan* by Jonas Ward

La Bûche ★★★ 15

Comedy drama 1999 · Fr · Colour · 107mins

Screenwriter Danièle Thompson's directorial debut is the kind of women's picture Hollywood can't do any more without submerging it in life-affirming sentiment. There will be clichéd characters in any ensemble piece, but rarely will they be as well played as they are here. Everyone impresses, from Charlotte Gainsbourg's lonely career girl and Emmanuelle Béart's jilted model housewife to their pregnant singer sister Sabine Azéma and her indecisive married lover, Jean-Pierre Darroussin. Though the episodes seem mundane, they vibrate with wit and warmth. DP. In French with English subtitles. Contains swearing and sex scenes.

Sabine Azéma *Louba* • Emmanuelle Béart *Sonia* • Charlotte Gainsbourg *Milla* • Claude Rich *Stanislas* • Françoise Fabian *Yvette* • Christopher Thompson *Joseph* • Jean-Pierre Darroussin *Gilbert* • Isabelle Carré *Annabelle* ■ *Dir* Danièle Thompson • *Scr* Danièle Thompson, Christopher Thompson

Buck and the Preacher ★★★ PG

Western 1972 · US · Colour · 98mins

Sidney Poitier's first film as director is a lively reworking of a *Wagon Train* idea, with Poitier as leader of a group of slaves, newly freed after the American Civil War, making their way through the wilderness despite harassment by white nightriders trying to take them back to the plantations. A mainly black cast notably avoids "hush-mah-mouth" clichés, while Harry Belafonte gives real edge to his con-man preacher whose slickness turns eventually to integrity. TH. Contains swearing. [VIDEO] DVD

Sidney Poitier *Buck* • Harry Belafonte *Preacher* • Ruby Dee *Ruth* • Cameron Mitchell *Deshay* • Denny Miller *Floyd* • Nita Talbot *Madame Esther* • John Kelly (3) *Sheriff* • Tony Brubaker *Headman* • James McEachin *Kingston* ■ *Dir* Sidney Poitier • *Scr* Ernest Kinoy, from a story by Ernest Kinoy, Drake Walker

Buck Benny Rides Again ★★★ U

Comedy 1940 · US · BW · 84mins

A knockabout throwback to the golden age of American radio, this spin-off from Jack Benny's beloved programme is a gleeful mishmash of in-jokes, inspired lunacy and silly situations. Determined to impress aspiring singer Ellen Drew, Benny convinces her he's a rodeo-rouser and then has to live up to his boasts when they meet up on a dude ranch. Sprightly entertainment, even during the occasionally intrusive musical numbers. DP

Jack Benny • Ellen Drew *Joan Cameron* • Eddie "Rochester" Anderson *Rochester* • Phil Harris *Phil* • Dennis Day *Dennis* • Virginia Dale *Virginia* • Ward Bond *Outlaw* • Morris Ankrum *Outlaw* ■ *Dir* Mark Sandrich • *Scr* William Morrow, Edmund Beloin, from the short story *Woman Handled* by Arthur Stringer, adapted by Zion Myers

Buck Privates ★★★ U

Comedy 1941 · US · BW · 80mins

A decade after they first joined forces as a vaudeville act, Abbott and Costello went stellar with this, their second film. It's hard to see why the picture grossed over $10 million at the US box office – a phenomenal sum for the times – though it's amusing enough. Here Bud and Lou are drafted by accident and find themselves having to adjudicate in a military *ménage à trois* between Alan Curtis, Lee Bowman and Jane Frazee. The Andrews Sisters sing some top-notch tunes, including the Oscar-nominated *Boogie Woogie Bugle Boy from Company B*. DP [VIDEO]

Bud Abbott *Slicker Smith* • Lou Costello *Herbie Brown* • Lee Bowman *Randolph Parker III* • Alan Curtis *Bob Martin* • Jane Frazee *Judy Gray* • Laverne Andrews • Maxene Andrews • Patty Andrews ■ *Dir* Arthur Lubin • *Scr* Arthur T Horman, John Grant

Buck Privates Come Home ★ U

Comedy 1947 · US · BW · 77mins

After the huge success of Abbott and Costello's second feature, a sequel was inevitable. But Bud and Lou had packed 18 movies into the six years that separated the two films, and it's all too obvious to see how thinly the material has been spread. The story sees the boys having to baby-sit a French orphan who has been smuggled home by their army buddy. Time weighs heavily. DP

Bud Abbott *Cpl Slicker Smith* • Lou Costello *Herbie Brown* • Tom Brown *Bill Gregory* • Joan Fulton *Sylvia Hunter* • Nat Pendleton *Sgt Collins* • Don Beddoe *Mr Roberts* • Don Porter *Captain* ■ *Dir* Charles Barton • *Scr* John Grant, Frederic I Rinaldo, Robert Lees, from a story by Richard Macauley, Bradford Ropes

Buck Rogers in the 25th Century ★★ 15

Science-fiction adventure
1979 · US · Colour · 88mins

Only American television could lavishly update a 1930s' film serial and make it more trivial and corny than the original. Even funnier, in the post-*Star Wars* glow of space warriors, cute cyborgs and colourful spectacle, is the fact that people actually paid money to see this TV pilot in the cinema. Hunky Gil Gerard jockeys his way through the good versus evil pastiche, with added comedy relief, and the whole thing remains strictly kids' stuff. AJ [VIDEO]

Gil Gerard *"Buck" Rogers* • Pamela Hensley *Princess Ardala* • Erin Gray *Colonel Wilma Deering* • Henry Silva *Kane* • Tim O'Connor *Dr Huer* • Felix Silla *Twiki* • Mel Blanc *Twiki* • Joseph Wiseman *Draco* ■ *Dir* Daniel Haller • *Scr* Glen A Larson, Leslie Stevens, from characters created by Robert C Dille

A Bucket of Blood ★★★ 15

Horror comedy 1959 · US · BW · 64mins

Essential Roger Corman. Hopeless as a horror film, but priceless as a hip black comedy, this beatnik variation on *House of Wax* has coffee-bar worker Walter Paisley (wonderfully played by Corman regular Dick Miller) hailed as a cool "art" genius when he turns dead bodies into sculpture. Filmed in five days, Corman's cult sickie-quickie is a brilliant satire on the whole Beat Generation scene. Corman remade it in 1995 as *Dark Secrets*. AJ [VIDEO] DVD

Dick Miller *Walter Paisley* • Barboura Morris *Carla* • Antony Carbone *Leonard* • Julian Burton *Brock* • Ed Nelson *Art Lacroix* • John Brinkley *Will* • John Shaner *Oscar* ■ *Dir* Roger Corman • *Scr* Charles B Griffith

Buddy ★★★ U

Biographical drama
1997 · US · Colour · 83mins

This sweet but unassuming film stars Rene Russo as Trudy Lintz, a woman in the 1920s who became known for the collection of animals she looked after at her Long Island home. Director Caroline Thompson focuses on Lintz's attempts to raise Buddy, a baby gorilla whom she treats as her own child. Robbie Coltrane plays Lintz's husband and fellow Scot Alan Cumming also appears. JB [VIDEO] DVD

Rene Russo *Trudy Lintz* • Robbie Coltrane *Dr Lintz* • Alan Cumming *Dick* • Irma P Hall *Emma* • Paul Reubens *Professor Spatz* • John Aylward *Mr Bowman* • Mimi Kennedy *Mrs Bowman* ■ *Dir* Caroline Thompson • *Scr* Caroline Thompson, from a story by William Joyce, Caroline Thompson, from the book *Animals Are My Hobby* by Gertrude Davies Lintz

Buddy Boy ★★ 18

Psychological thriller
1999 · US · Colour · 105mins

The repressed mummy's boy meets the guilt-ridden voyeur in this self-consciously cultish thriller. Director Mark D Hanlon shovels in an excess of religious iconography and laboured macabre comedy to set the tone. Aidan Gillen plays the loner who finds release from the demands of his bedridden stepmother in the arms of Emmanuelle Seigner, but it's Susan Tyrrell who dominates the unlikely proceedings with her grotesque display of alcoholic tyranny. DP. Contains violence, swearing and drug abuse.

Aidan Gillen *Francis* • Emmanuelle Seigner *Gloria* • Susan Tyrrell *Sal* • Mark Boone Junior *Vic* • Harry Groener *Father Gillespie* • Hector Elias *Mr Salcedo* • Richard Assad *Haroonian* ■ *Dir/Scr* Mark D Hanlon

Buddy Buddy ★★ 15

Comedy 1981 · US · Colour · 91mins

Ever since their first film together Jack Lemmon and Walter Matthau have been the odd couple of the movies, as inseparable as Laurel and Hardy. But this farce marks the low point in their chalk-and-cheese collaboration, with slapstick usurping the biting wit of previous productions. Matthau is a hitman who's hampered in his job by a suicide-bent Lemmon. Adapted from the funnier French comedy, *A Pain in the A...!*, its jokes are ill-timed and the mutual admiration society of its two stars becomes tedious. TH [VIDEO]

Jack Lemmon *Victor Clooney* • Walter Matthau *Trabucco* • Paula Prentiss *Celia Clooney* • Klaus Kinski *Dr Zuckerbrot* • Dana Elcar *Captain Hubris* • Miles Chapin *Eddie the bellhop* • Michael Ensign *Assistant manager* • Joan Shawlee *Receptionist* ■ *Dir* Billy Wilder • *Scr* Billy Wilder, IAL Diamond, from the story and play *A Pain in the A ...* by Francis Veber

The Buddy Holly Story ★★★★ PG

Biographical drama
1978 · US · Colour · 108mins

A stunningly well-made biopic of the legendary rock 'n' roller, who met his tragically premature end in a plane crash in 1959. Gary Busey has never matched the marvellous Oscar-nominated performance he gives here, contenting himself instead with a rogues' gallery of roles as cops and psychos ever since. Director Steve Rash has likewise never managed to recapture the verve he conjures up here. The movie is made doubly enjoyable by the knowledge that Busey and the movie's Crickets actually do their own singing and playing, generating their own very palpable raw energy in the process. TS [VIDEO] DVD

Gary Busey *Buddy Holly* • Don Stroud *Jesse Clarence* • Charles Martin Smith *Ray Bob Simmons* • William Jordan *Riley Randolph* • Maria Richwine *Maria Elena Santiago* • Conrad Janis *Ross Turner* • Albert Popwell *Eddie Foster* • Amy Johnston *Cindy Lou* ■ *Dir* Steve Rash • *Scr* Robert Gittler, from a story by Alan Swyer, from the biography *Buddy Holly His Life and Music* by John Coldrosen

The Buddy System ★★ PG

Romantic comedy drama
1984 · US · Colour · 105mins

From the doldrums of Richard Dreyfuss's movie career comes this pale imitation of *The Goodbye Girl*. This time round he is a frustrated writer, forced to take a security job at the local school where he pals up with single mom Susan Sarandon's precocious 11-year-old son. You'd think that such a cast would be box-office gold, but the pair fail to sizzle. FL [VIDEO]

Richard Dreyfuss *Joe* • Susan Sarandon *Emily* • Nancy Allen *Carrie* • Jean Stapleton *Mrs Price* • Wil Wheaton *Tim* • Edward Winter *Jim Parks* • Keene Curtis *Dr Knitz* ■ *Dir* Glenn Jordan • *Scr* Mary Agnes Donoghue

Buddy's Song ★★ PG

Drama 1990 · UK · Colour · 102mins

Nigel Hinton has done his popular teen novel a major disservice with his clumsy adaptation that fails to convince. Roger Daltrey gives a knowing and willing performance as Chesney Hawkes's teddy boy dad, but Sharon Duce and Michael Elphick settle for caricatures. DP. Contains swearing and brief nudity. [VIDEO]

Roger Daltrey *Terry Clark* • Chesney Hawkes *Buddy* • Sharon Duce *Carol* • Michael Elphick *Des King* • Douglas Hodge *Bobby Rosen* • Paul McKenzie *Julius* • Lee Ross *Jason* • Nick Moran *Mike* ■ *Dir* Claude Whatham • *Scr* Nigel Hinton, from his novel

Buena Vista Social Club ★★★★ U

Music documentary
1998 · Ger · Colour · 100mins

This charming documentary from director Wim Wenders follows in the footsteps of the album by legendary guitarist Ry Cooder, capturing the rhythm and blues of a group of elderly Cuban musicians – the oldest over 90. Their music had largely been forgotten (some of the musicians featured had long been in retirement), but now it can be heard by a world that had consigned them to a bygone age. The visual style sometimes detracts from the lyrical substance – the camera circles the soloists to an irritating degree – but, despite that, this is still one of the best music documentaries ever made and a compelling testament to the strength of the human spirit. TH. In English and Spanish with English subtitles. [VIDEO] DVD

Dir Wim Wenders

Buffalo Bill ★★★ U

Western 1944 · US · Colour · 86mins

You won't learn much about the real William Frederick Cody from this conventional and sentimental western, with a stalwart, though rather dull, Joel McCrea in the lead. Still, redhead Maureen O'Hara and the striking locations were made for Fox Technicolor – though these days you have to take Anthony Quinn and Linda Darnell made-up as Cheyenne Indians with a pinch of salt. Director William A Wellman keeps the film moving. TS DVD

Joel McCrea *Buffalo Bill* • Maureen O'Hara *Louisa Cody* • Linda Darnell *Dawn Starlight* • Thomas Mitchell *Ned Buntline* • Edgar Buchanan *Sergeant Chips* • Anthony Quinn *Yellow Hand* • Moroni Olsen *Senator Frederici* • Frank Fenton *Murdo Carvell* ■ *Dir* William A Wellman • *Scr* Aeneas MacKenzie, Clements Ripley, Cecile Kramer, from a story by Frank Winch • *Cinematographer* Leon Shamroy

Buffalo Bill and the Indians, or Sitting Bull's History Lesson ★★ PG

Western 1976 · US · Colour · 118mins

Like so many of Robert Altman's pictures, this is a glorious, infuriating mess, a whirl of half-baked ideas, missed opportunities and startling moments. Paul Newman plays Buffalo Bill with golden locks and a twinkle in his eye, a phoney and a showman, who hires Sitting Bull for his travelling Wild West show. Co-stars drift in and out of a picture driven solely by Altman's unfocused vision of a people on the edge of extinction and a country in turmoil. AT DVD

Paul Newman *Buffalo Bill* • Joel Grey *Nate Salsbury* • Burt Lancaster *Ned Buntline* • Kevin McCarthy *Major John Burke* • Harvey Keitel *Ed Goodman* • Allan Nicholls *Prentiss Ingraham* • Geraldine Chaplin *Annie Oakley* • John Considine *Frank Butler* • Frank Kaquitts *Sitting Bull* ■ *Dir* Robert Altman • *Scr* Alan Rudolph, Robert Altman, from the play *Indians* by Arthur Kopit

Buffalo '66 ★★★★ 15

Drama 1998 · Can/US · Colour · 109mins

Touted by actor/director Vincent Gallo as a self-styled masterpiece, this searing view of disillusionment is indeed as arrogantly conceited as the man himself. But his grimy, ironic look at uncaring family life, and the emotional pain it causes, is also an amazing slice of neo-existentialism that takes some breathtaking risks. Gallo plays the born loser desperate for a lucky break, who unknowingly finds one when he kidnaps Christina Ricci to play his wife during an overdue family visit. Sharp dialogue and unusual flashbacks lead to an uplifting pay-off that is well worth the wait. This is a minor gem. AJ. Contains swearing, violence, nudity. DVD

Vincent Gallo *Billy Brown* • Christina Ricci *Layla* • Ben Gazzara *Jimmy Brown* • Mickey Rourke *The Bookie* • Rosanna Arquette *Wendy Balsam* • Jan-Michael Vincent *Sonny* • Anjelica Huston *Janet "Jan" Brown* ■ *Dir* Vincent Gallo • *Scr* Vincent Gallo, Alison Bagnall, from a story by Vincent Gallo • *Music* Vincent Gallo

Buffalo Soldiers ★★★ 15

Western drama 1997 · US · Colour · 90mins

Based on actual events, this quality TV movie is well worth a look. In post-Civil War New Mexico, an all-black cavalry troop under the leadership of a fearless ex-slave (Danny Glover) pursues an Apache warrior through the territory. The tight-knit group must also suffer the endless degradation heaped upon them by white officers in the segregated army. Glover gives an excellent performance, and the action is handled efficiently by ex-*Hill Street Blues* veteran Charles Haid. MC. Contains violence.

Danny Glover *Sergeant Wyatt* • Bob Gunton *Colonel Grierson* • Carl Lumbly *Horse* • Glynn Turman *Sergeant Joshua "Joju" Judges Ruth* • Mykelti Williamson *Corporal William Christy* • Lamont Bentley *Corporal Sea* • Tom Bower *General Pike* • Timothy Busfield *Major Robert Carr* ■ *Dir* Charles Haid • *Scr* Frank Military, Susan Rhinehart, from a story by Jonathan Klein, Frank Military

Buffalo Soldiers ★★★★ 15

Black comedy drama
2001 · UK/Ger/US · Colour · 94mins

You know you're in satirical territory when a stoned US soldier stationed in Germany watches live news footage of the Berlin Wall coming down and asks: "Where's Berlin?". Gregor Jordan's self-consciously hip adaptation of Robert O'Connor's novel presents the US military – as embodied by Joaquin Phoenix's charismatic wheeler-dealer – as bored and morally bankrupt. But the film makes the serious point that warriors in peacetime will go looking for conflict. Given the post "9/11", post-Iraq War climate, this entertaining and nihilistic black comedy now carries a greater political significance than ever could have been intended. AC. Contains swearing, violence and drug abuse. DVD

Joaquin Phoenix *Ray Elwood* • Ed Harris *Col Wallace Berman* • Scott Glenn *Sgt Robert Lee* • Anna Paquin *Robyn Lee* • Elizabeth McGovern *Mrs Berman* • Dean Stockwell *Gen Lancaster* • Leon Robinson [Leon] *Stoney* ■ *Dir* Gregor Jordan • *Scr* Gregor Jordan, Eric Axel Weiss, Nora Maccoby, from the novel by Robert O'Connor

Buffet Froid ★★★ 15

Black comedy 1979 · Fr · Colour · 89mins

Not since *The Treasure of the Sierra Madre* has a son directed his father with such a mischievous sense of respect as in this savage black comedy. As the inspector drawn into a series of bizarre murders, Bernard Blier is given full rein by his son, Bertrand, who also coaxes a full-throttled display of blue collar boorishness from Gérard Depardieu as the casual killer caught up in the crimes of serial maniac Jean Carmet. For all its exuberance, though, the film does occasionally feel like a smorgasboard of leftovers from Buñuel and other absurdists. DP. In French with English subtitles. DVD

Gérard Depardieu *Alphonse Tram* • Bernard Blier *Inspector Morvandieu* • Jean Carmet *Murderer* • Genevieve Page *Widow* • Denise Gence *Hostess* • Carole Bouquet *Young girl* • Michel Serrault *Man in subway* ■ *Dir/Scr* Bertrand Blier

Buffy the Vampire Slayer ★★★ 15

Comedy horror 1992 · US · Colour · 81mins

Clueless meets *Dracula* in this engagingly silly, yet knowing, horror comedy that deserves cult status. Kristy Swanson is cheerfully dim-witted as LA teenager Buffy, who's surprised to discover that she is actually the only person who can save the city from suave Rutger Hauer and his fellow vampires. Director Fran Rubel Kuzui rightly plays it like a comic strip and draws perfectly judged performances from an eclectic cast that also includes teen heart-throb Luke Perry, Donald Sutherland, an unrecognisable Paul Reubens (Pee-wee Herman) and an uncredited appearance from Ben Affleck. Fun, but fans of the TV series will be disappointed. JF DVD

Kristy Swanson *Buffy* • Donald Sutherland *Merrick* • Paul Reubens *Amilyn* • Rutger Hauer *Lothos* • Luke Perry *Pike* • Michele Abrams *Jennifer* • Hilary Swank *Kimberly* • Paris Vaughn *Nicole* • David Arquette *Benny* ■ *Dir* Fran Rubel Kuzui • *Scr* Joss Whedon

Bug ★★ 15

Horror 1975 · US · Colour · 95mins

The last film produced by William Castle, the king of gimmick cinema (*The Tingler, Macabre*), is one of his better efforts. An earthquake unleashes a swarm of fire-making insects and scientist Bradford Dillman mates them with the common cockroach in order to communicate with them. The initial nature-revenge plot tends to get lost once the routine mad-doctor thread takes over, but zestful direction and tongue-in-cheek acting eke out some decent thrills and chills from the implausible tale. AJ

Bradford Dillman *James Parmiter* • Joanna Miles *Carrie Parmiter* • Richard Gilliland *Metbaum* • Jamie Smith-Jackson *Norma Tacker* • Alan Fudge *Mark Ross* • Jesse Vint *Tom Tacker* • Brenden Dillon *Charlie* ■ *Dir* Jeannot Szwarc • *Scr* Thomas Page, William Castle, from the novel *The Hephaestus Plague* by Thomas Page

Bugles in the Afternoon ★★ U

Western 1952 · US · Colour · 84mins

A disappointing, would-be stirring Warner Bros western, adapted from an excellent novel by Ernest Haycox, but seriously hampered by poor casting. The urbane Ray Milland looks uncomfortable out west and fails to convince as a disgraced coward. He's not helped by a sub-par supporting cast and a totally inadequate leading lady in Helena Carter. Nevertheless, the exterior Technicolor location photography is impressive, and the action scenes are well staged, within obvious budgetary limitations. TS

Ray Milland *Kern Shafter* • Helena Carter *Josephine Russell* • Hugh Marlowe *Captain Edward Garnett* • Forrest Tucker *Private Donovan* • Barton MacLane *Captain Myles Moylan* • George Reeves *Lieutenant Smith* • James Millican *Sergeant Hines* ■ *Dir* Roy Rowland • *Scr* Geoffrey Homes [Daniel Mainwaring], Harry Brown, from a novel by Ernest Haycox • *Music* Dmitri Tiomkin • *Cinematographer* Wilfrid M Cline

Bugs Bunny 1001 Rabbit Tales ★★★

Animation compilation
1982 · US · Colour · 90mins

This slickly assembled compilation film was produced by Friz Freleng, the genius behind many of the most popular Warner Bros cartoon characters and a pioneer of the crash-bang style of animation known as "socko". Voiced, as ever, by the legendary Mel Blanc, Bugs Bunny and Daffy Duck here find themselves reliving some classic capers as they try to sell books to some highly resistant customers. As you would expect, the quality is inconsistent, but there are some cracking slapstick gags and lots of cringe-worthy puns. DP

Mel Blanc ■ *Dir* David Detiege, Art Davis, Bill Perez, Friz Freleng • *Scr* John Dunn, David Detiege, Friz Freleng

The Bugs Bunny/Road Runner Movie ★★★★ U

Animation compilation
1979 · US · Colour · 93mins

Not really a film in the true sense of the word, this is essentially the best of Bugs tenuously linked by the presence of the much-loved rabbit. But as it brings together some of the most memorable shorts devised by animation legend Chuck Jones, who's complaining? Along with Bugs, his long-suffering adversaries Daffy Duck and Porky Pig get plenty of screen time, while Wile E Coyote gets to suffer endless humiliation at the hands of his nemesis, Road Runner. JF

Mel Blanc ■ *Dir* Chuck Jones, Phil Monroe • *Scr* Chuck Jones, Michael Maltese

A Bug's Life ★★★★ U

Animated adventure
1998 · US · Colour · 93mins

Director John Lasseter's follow-up to the ground-breaking *Toy Story* may have less beguiling characters than Woody and Buzz Lightyear, but the computer-animated effects are if anything even more wondrous. In an ant colony, clumsy worker Flik (voiced by Dave Foley) accidentally destroys the grain that's regularly offered to appease a band of hostile grasshoppers led by the bullying Hopper (a superb characterisation by Kevin Spacey). As the ants struggle to find twice as much grain, Flik employs a flea circus of colourful eccentrics to do battle with the grasshoppers. The result is a witty variation on *The Seven Samurai*. TH DVD

Dave Foley *Flik* • Kevin Spacey *Hopper* • Julia Louis-Dreyfus *Princess Atta* • Hayden Panettiere *Princess Dot* • Phyllis Diller *Queen* • Richard Kind *Molt* • David Hyde Pierce *Slim* • Denis Leary *Francis* • Jonathan Harris *Manny* • Madeline Kahn *Gypsy* • Bonnie Hunt *Rosie* • Mike McShane [Micheal McShane] *Tuck/Roll* • Roddy McDowall *Mr Soil* ■ *Dir* John Lasseter • *Scr* Andrew Stanton, Donald Mcenery, Bob Shaw, from the story *The Ant and the Grasshopper* by Aesop

Bugsy ★★★★ 18

Crime drama 1991 · US · Colour · 130mins

While avoiding the usual gangster film clichés, director Barry Levinson also insists that Warren Beatty does more than coast through the movie on matinée idol looks and easy charm. Beatty is charismatically dangerous as gangster Benjamin "Bugsy" Siegel, switching unnervingly from flirtation to rage, even if his on-screen romance with Annette Bening never really catches fire (unlike their off-screen relationship, which led to marriage and parenthood). This double Oscar winner (for costume and art direction) is strong on pumping narrative and strewn with memorable scenes and distinctive criminals. JM. Contains violence and swearing. DVD

Warren Beatty *Benjamin "Bugsy" Siegel* • Annette Bening *Virginia Hill* • Harvey Keitel *Mickey Cohen* • Ben Kingsley *Meyer Lansky* • Elliott Gould *Harry Greenberg* • Joe Mantegna *George Raft* • Richard Sarafian [Richard C Sarafian] *Jack Dragna* • Bebe Neuwirth *Countess Di Frasso* ■ *Dir* Barry Levinson • *Scr* James Toback, from the book *We Only Kill Each Other: the Life and Bad Times of Bugsy Siegel* by Dean Jennings • *Art Director* Dennis Gassner • *Set Designer* Nancy Haigh • *Costume Designer* Albert Wolsky

Bugsy Malone ★★★★ U

Spoof crime musical
1976 · UK · Colour · 89mins

Alan Parker's debut feature, following a number of social-realist scripts for the BBC, was a deliberate attempt to get attention. And, by casting children as American gangsters whose Tommy guns fire gunk, Parker achieved his ambition: the movie was the toast of the Cannes film festival and a flamboyant career was under way. Using techniques borrowed from old Hollywood movies, as well as the polish that he learned from his many TV commercials, Parker creates a vibrant pastiche that hovers just on the brink of cuteness. The children – most notably Jodie Foster – have an edge to their performances that cuts through sentiment . AT DVD

Scott Baio *Bugsy Malone* • Jodie Foster *Tallulah* • Florrie Dugger *Blousey* • John Cassisi *Fat Sam* • Martin Lev *Dandy Dan* • Paul Murphy *Leroy* • "Humpty" Albin Jenkins *Fizzy* • Davidson Knight *Cagey Joe* ■ *Dir/Scr* Alan Parker • *Music/lyrics* Paul Williams

Build My Gallows High ★★★★★ PG

Classic film noir 1947 · US · BW · 92mins

This classic 1940s *film noir* – better known in America as *Out of the Past* – contains a memorably languid performance by Robert Mitchum as the hard-boiled former private eye who falls for the woman (Jane Greer) he's been hired to track by gangster Kirk Douglas. Unfairly under-rated for many years, this is in fact a stylish, atmospheric, highly watchable and strongly recommended masterpiece from genre expert Jacques Tourneur. Remade in 1984 as the inferior *Against All Odds* (with Jeff Bridges and Rachel Ward). PF

Robert Mitchum *Jeff Bailey/Jeff Markham* • Jane Greer *Kathie Moffat* • Kirk Douglas *Whit Sterling* • Rhonda Fleming *Meta Carson* • Richard Webb *Jim* • Steve Brodie *Jack Fisher* • Virginia Huston *Ann Miller* • Paul Valentine *Joe Stefanos* ■ *Dir* Jacques Tourneur • *Scr* Geoffrey Homes [Daniel Mainwaring], from his novel • *Cinematographer* Nicholas Musuraca

Bukowski: Born into This ★★★★

Biographical documentary
2003 · US · Colour · 130mins

Venerated by some, but castigated by others as a hell-raising misanthrope, the poet and novelist Charles

Bukowski was undoubtedly one of American literature's roughest diamonds. Utilising interview footage shot by Taylor Hackford and Barbet Schroeder (who directed the disappointing biopic, *Barfly*), John Dullaghan's documentary traces Bukowski's journey from his strict childhood to unexpected cult celebrity. The film is at its best when recalling the decades of dead-end jobs and the endless rejection letters for his stories and verse – although the more colourful anecdotes surround the substance abuse and sexual excesses that attended his success in the 1960s. Bukowski unsurprisingly emerges as quite a character, but it's the gritty power and gnarled tenderness of his writing that comes across most forcibly. DP

Dir John Dullaghan (2) • *Scr* Victor Livingston

Bull Durham ★★★★ 18

Comedy drama 1988 · US · Colour · 103mins

Director Ron Shelton has proved something of a specialist with baseball movies, having also brought *Cobb* to the big screen, in which Tommy Lee Jones thunders magnificently as the twisted sports star. In this winning drama, Shelton's detailed love of the sport never becomes the usual tired tale of the heart. Instead it propels what is a smart and witty character piece – an electric love story between Susan Sarandon and Tim Robbins, with Kevin Costner brooding convincingly in the wings. All three actors make the picture sizzle. JM. Contains swearing, nudity. DVD

Kevin Costner *Crash Davis* • Susan Sarandon *Annie Savoy* • Tim Robbins *Ebby Calvin "Nuke" LaLoosh* • Trey Wilson *Joe "Skip" Riggins* • Robert Wuhl *Larry Hockett* • William O'Leary *Jimmy* • David Neidorf *Bobby* • Danny Gans *Deke* ■ *Dir/Scr* Ron Shelton

The Bulldog Breed ★★ PG

Comedy 1960 · UK · BW · 93mins

There is no doubt where the fun lies in this merely adequate comedy – it's in the brief sight of hopefuls Michael Caine and Oliver Reed playing second fiddle to Norman Wisdom. Norman is not at his best as the fumbling shop assistant whose career in the navy culminates in an ill-fated moonshot. The script does him few favours, restricting the opportunities for sentimental slapstick in order to accommodate the surplus plot. Dependable stooges do all that is expected. DP DVD

Norman Wisdom *Norman Puckle* • Ian Hunter *Admiral Sir Bryanston Blyth* • David Lodge *CPO Knowles* • Robert Urquhart *Commander Clayton* • Edward Chapman *Mr Philpots* • John Le Mesurier *Prosecuting counsel* • Michael Caine *Sailor* • Oliver Reed ■ *Dir* Robert Asher • *Scr* Jack Davies, Henry Blyth, Norman Wisdom

Bulldog Drummond ★★★

Detective mystery adventure
1929 · US · BW · 90mins

Suave Ronald Colman's first talkie revealed to movie-goers the dulcet tones and perfect enunciation that would become a model for all future screen matinée idols. As the ex-army adventure hero of a series of popular novels by HC "Sapper" McNeile, Colman is splendidly cast. He provides a Drummond that others found impossible to better, while Claud Allister is the definitive Algy, Drummond's constant companion. This is an exceptionally well-mounted early talkie with much of value, though its creakiness can sometimes make it difficult to view. TS

Ronald Colman *Bulldog Drummond* • Joan Bennett *Phyllis Benton* • Lilyan Tashman *Erma Peterson* • Montagu Love *Carl Peterson* • Lawrence Grant *Doctor Lakington* • Wilson Benge *Danny* • Claud Allister *Algy Longworth* ■ *Dir* F Richard Jones • *Scr* Wallace Smith, Sidney Howard, from the play by HC "Sapper" McNeile

Bulldog Drummond Comes Back ★★ U

Detective mystery adventure
1937 · US · BW · 58mins

It may seem an ignominious end for one of the greatest American actors of his day to guest in a B-movie series. But John Barrymore seems to enjoy himself in this film, one of his three outings for Paramount as Scotland Yard hotshot Colonel Nielson. He certainly upstages John Howard, whose Drummond seems a very dull dog by comparison. The story turns around the kidnapping of Louise Campbell by J Carrol Naish, who leaves clues to lure the detecting duo into a trap. DP

John Barrymore *Colonel Nielson* • John Howard (1) *Capt Hugh "Bulldog" Drummond* • Louise Campbell *Phyllis Clavering* • Reginald Denny *Algy Longworth* • EE Clive *Tenny* • J Carrol Naish *Mikhail Valdin* ■ *Dir* Louis King • *Scr* Edward T Lowe, from the novel *The Female of the Species* by HC "Sapper" McNeile

Bulldog Drummond Escapes ★★ U

Detective mystery adventure
1937 · US · BW · 64mins

Ray Milland is somewhat miscast in the first of Paramount's low-budget adaptations from the casebook of Bulldog Drummond. Drummond's bid to deliver helpless heiress Heather Angel from the clutches of an avaricious admirer never gathers any momentum as too much time is spent introducing his devoted sidekicks, Reginald Denny, EE Clive and Scotland Yard supremo Guy Standing. DP

Ray Milland *Captain Hugh "Bulldog" Drummond* • Sir Guy Standing [Guy Standing] *Inspector Nielson* • Heather Angel *Phyllis Clavering* • Reginald Denny *Algy Langworth* • Porter Hall *Norman Merridew* • Fay Holden *Natalie* • EE Clive *Tenny* ■ *Dir* James Hogan • *Scr* Edward T Lowe, from the play *Bulldog Drummond Again* by HC "Sapper" McNeile, Gerard Fairlie

Bulldog Drummond in Africa ★★ U

Detective mystery adventure
1938 · US · BW · 58mins

John Howard returns as the dapper troubleshooter in a pretty shoddy affair, with stock footage and unconvincing sets standing in for master criminal J Carrol Naish's jungle lair. Typically, Naish revels in his villainy as he readies Scotland Yard inspector HB Warner for some long-overdue revenge. However, he counted without Howard's rescue party, in which fiancée Heather Angel seems to be along for the ride only so that she can be imperilled by various beasts, natives and henchmen. DP

John Howard (1) *Captain Hugh "Bulldog" Drummond* • Heather Angel *Phyllis Clavering* • HB Warner *Colonel Nielson* • J Carrol Naish *Richard Lane/Charles Mega* • Reginald Denny *Algy Longworth* • EE Clive *Tenny* • Anthony Quinn *Deane Fordine* ■ *Dir* Louis King • *Scr* Garnett Weston, from the novel *Challenge* by HC "Sapper" McNeile

Bulldog Drummond Strikes Back ★★★

Detective mystery adventure
1934 · US · BW · 83mins

Ronald Colman in his rarely seen second outing as super-sleuth and 007 precursor Bulldog Drummond. Colman is suave, fearless and witty, while co-star Loretta Young is there to look pretty and to be kidnapped more than once. Roy Del Ruth, best known for his breezy musicals, directs with dollar efficiency to disguise the dime budget. AT

Ronald Colman *Captain Hugh Drummond* • Loretta Young *Lola Field* • C Aubrey Smith *Inspector Nielsen* • Charles Butterworth *Algy Longworth* • Una Merkel *Gwen* • Warner Oland *Prince Achmed* • George Regas *Singh* • Mischa Auer *Hassan* ■ *Dir* Roy Del Ruth • *Scr* Nunnally Johnson, Henry Lehrman, from the novel by HC "Sapper" McNeile

Bulldog Drummond Strikes Back ★

Detective mystery adventure
1947 · US · BW · 64mins

One of the 20-odd movies to feature the James Bond forerunner Bulldog Drummond, created by HC "Sapper" McNeile as a post-First World War clubland hero whose daring exploits sold in their millions. Kicked off in 1929 with Ronald Colman, the series quickly went down-market as various British and American studios bought and sold the franchise. This dismal entry stars Ron Randell, an Australian actor who played Drummond twice. AT

Ron Randell *Bulldog Drummond* • Gloria Henry *Ellen Curtiss* • Pat O'Moore [Patrick O'Moore] *Algy Longworth* • Anabel Shaw *Ellen Curtiss #2* • Holmes Herbert *Inspector McIver* • Wilton Graff *Cedric Mason* • Matthew Boulton *William Cosgrove* • Terry Kilburn *Seymour* ■ *Dir* Frank McDonald • *Scr* Edward Anhalt, Edna Anhalt, from the novel by HC "Sapper" McNeile

Bulldog Drummond's Bride ★★ PG

Detective mystery adventure
1939 · US · BW · 56mins

Paramount wound down its undistinguished crime series with this routine adaptation. Yet again, the sole reason for watching is the malevolent ingenuity of the villain – in this case the lugubrious Eduardo Ciannelli's master of disguise. Director James Hogan packs plenty into the budget running time, but much of it feels like padding, particularly where John Howard's wedding to Heather Angel is concerned. DP

John Howard (1) *Captain Hugh C Drummond* • Heather Angel *Phyllis Clavering* • HB Warner *Colonel Nielson* • Reginald Denny *Algy Longworth* • EE Clive *Tenny* • Elizabeth Patterson *Aunt Blanche* • Eduardo Ciannelli *Henri Armides* ■ *Dir* James Hogan • *Scr* Stuart Palmer, Garnett Weston, from the short story *Bulldog Drummond and the Oriental Mind* by HC "Sapper" McNeile

Bulldog Drummond's Peril ★★ U

Detective mystery adventure
1938 · US · BW · 66mins

In the last of John Barrymore's guest appearances as Colonel Nielson, he effortlessly outshines the nominal star, John Howard, despite being marginalised for much of the picture. This has Drummond forced once more to postpone his wedding to Phyllis Clavering (again played by Louise Campbell) as he pursues a gang that has purloined some synthetic diamonds. Porter Hall chews the scenery as the villain. DP

John Barrymore *Colonel Nielson* • John Howard (1) *Captain Hugh "Bulldog" Drummond* • Louise Campbell *Phyllis Clavering* • Reginald Denny *Algy Longworth* • EE Clive *Tenny* • Porter Hall *Dr Max Botulian* • Elizabeth Patterson *Aunt Blanche* ■ *Dir* James Hogan • *Scr* Stuart Palmer, from the novel *The Third Round* by HC "Sapper" McNeile

Bulldog Drummond's Revenge ★★ U

Detective mystery adventure
1937 · US · BW · 55mins

Director Louis King was more of a western specialist than a master of suspense. Consequently, there's a fatal slackness about this adaptation of HC "Sapper" McNeile's novel, which is itself a pretty routine espionage yarn. John Howard this time locks horns with master thief Frank Puglia, who absconds with a consignment of explosive material. But Howard's lack of charisma means that he's easily overshadowed by John Barrymore as Nielson. DP

John Barrymore *Colonel Nielson* • John Howard (1) *Captain Hugh "Bulldog" Drummond* • Louise Campbell *Phyllis Clavering* • Reginald Denny *Algy Longworth* • EE Clive *Tenny* • Frank Puglia *Draven Nogais* ■ *Dir* Louis King • *Scr* Edward T Lowe, from the novel *The Return of Bulldog Drummond* by HC "Sapper" McNeile

Bulldog Jack ★★★ U

Detective comedy adventure
1934 · UK · BW · 69mins

British comedies have rarely travelled well across the Atlantic, but none has been so mistreated as this Gaumont spoof on the Bulldog Drummond myth, which was shown in the States as a straight thriller with all the gags removed! In his only screen teaming with his brother Claude, Jack Hulbert is all jutting chin and silly expressions as he pursues villainous Ralph Richardson and rescues 1930s scream queen Fay Wray. DP

Fay Wray *Ann Manders* • Jack Hulbert *Jack Pennington* • Claude Hulbert *Algy Longworth* • Ralph Richardson *Morelle* • Paul Graetz *Salvini* • Gibb McLaughlin *Denny* • Atholl Fleming *Bulldog Drummond* ■ *Dir* Walter Forde • *Scr* HC "Sapper" McNeile, Gerard Fairlie, JOC Orton, Sidney Gilliat, from an idea by Jack Hulbert, from a character created by HC "Sapper" McNeile

Bullet ★ 18

Crime drama 1995 · US · Colour · 90mins

The first few moments of Mickey Rourke (in his late 30s) acting and dressing like a gang-banger must be some of the most unintentionally hilarious footage ever shot for a motion picture. Unfortunately, the laughs soon evaporate when he starts to mutter in his infamous style and his performance is enough to bury any other good impressions that this snail-paced movie could have generated. KB. Contains swearing, sex scenes and violence. DVD

Mickey Rourke *Butch "Bullet" Stein* • Tupac Shakur *Tank* • Ted Levine *Louis* • Donnie Wahlberg *Big Balls* • John Enos III [John Enos] *Lester* • Adrien Brody *Ruby* • Jerry Grayson *Sol Stein* ■ *Dir* Julien Temple • *Scr* Bruce Rubinstein, Sir Eddie Cook

Bullet Boy ★★★ 15

Crime drama 2004 · UK · Colour · 89mins

The rise of inner-city gun crime is at the heart of this low-budget British film, set and filmed around Hackney, east London, near the area nicknamed "Murder Mile". A minor street fracas spirals into tragedy and caught up in the ensuing tit-for-tat carnage are teenager Ricky (Ashley Walters), freshly released from youth custody, and, most shockingly, his 12-year-old brother. Walters – better known as So Solid Crew member Asher D – is joined by many first-time actors in this rough and ready film that is still convincing enough in its depiction of corrupted innocence. DA. Contains swearing, violence and sex scenes.

Ashley Walters *Ricky* • Luke Fraser *Curtis* • Leon Black *Wisdom* • Clare Perkins *Beverley* • Sharea-Mounira Samuels *Shea* • Curtis Walker

Leon • Rio Tison *Rio* • Clark Lawson *Godfrey* ■ *Dir* Saul Dibb • *Scr* Saul Dibb, Catherine R Johnson

Bullet for a Badman ★★★ PG

Western 1964 · US · Colour · 76mins

This is a rare decent role for Audie Murphy, and the baby-faced war hero rises to the occasion, making one regret that he had so few opportunities to fulfil his potential. This RG Springsteen western has Murphy vying with baddie Darren McGavin for Ruta Lee, as he heads a posse escorting McGavin back to town for justice. Photographed by the great Joe Biroc and featuring a marvellous supporting cast of familiar faces, this is a pleasure to watch. TS

Audie Murphy *Logan Keliher* • Darren McGavin *Sam Ward* • Ruta Lee *Lottie* • Beverley Owen *Susan* • Skip Homeier *Pink* • George Tobias *Diggs* • Alan Hale Jr *Leach* • Berkeley Harris *Jeff* ■ *Dir* RG Springsteen • *Scr* Mary Willingham, Willard Willingham, from the novel by Marvin H Albert

A Bullet for Joey ★★

Spy crime drama 1955 · US · BW · 86mins

A disappointing reunion of Edward G Robinson and George Raft, this economically made crime melodrama revolves about a communist spy's use of an exiled gangster to kidnap an atomic scientist. Raft plays the gangster, while Robinson is the police inspector who uncovers the scheme. The two stars' climactic encounter on a boat takes far too long to materialise and feebly suggests that even mobsters are patriots when it comes to the Red menace. AE

Edward G Robinson *Inspector Raoul Leduc* • George Raft *Joe Victor* • Audrey Totter *Joyce Geary* • George Dolenz *Carl Macklin* • Peter Hanson *Fred* • Peter Van Eyck *Eric Hartman* ■ *Dir* Lewis Allen • *Scr* Geoffrey Homes [Daniel Mainwaring], AI Bezzerides, from a story by James Benson Nablo

A Bullet for Sandoval ★★

Spaghetti western
1970 · It/Sp · Colour · 91mins

Well, the climax is good: a battle between four desperate gringos and hundreds of Mexican soldiers, all crowded into a bullring where they blast each other to pieces. It's the sort of deadly, crimson-coloured ballet that Sergio Leone made famous, and one which Julio Buchs stages with just as much arty brio. Until then, though, it's the usual overcooked spaghetti, with Ernest Borgnine wading through a botched revenge plot. AT. Italian dialogue dubbed into English.

Ernest Borgnine *Don Pedro Sandoval* • George Hilton *Warner* • Alberto de Mendoza *Lucky boy* • Leo Anchoriz *Padre* • Antonio Pica *Sam* • José Manuel Martin *Cross-eyed man* • Manuel de Blas *Jose* • Manuel Miranda *Francisco* ■ *Dir* Julio Buchs • *Scr* Ugo Guerra, Jose Luis Martinez Molla, Federico De Urrutia, Julio Buchs, from a story by Jose Luis Martinez Molla, Federico De Urrutia

A Bullet for the General ★★★ 18

Spaghetti western
1966 · It · Colour · 112mins

Think spaghetti western and Sergio Leone will always spring to mind. Other directors who toyed with the form are generally overlooked, including Italian Damiano Damiani, whose film is a very decent stab at the genre. Capably instilling the violence with intelligent, probing moral concern, Damiani also casts Gian Maria Volonté and Klaus Kinski, both of whom star alongside Clint Eastwood in *For a Few Dollars More*. There is a creative tension throughout between introspection and exuberance. JM. Italian dialogue dubbed into English. DVD

Gian Maria Volonté *El Chuncho* • Klaus Kinski *Santo* • Lou Castel *Bill Tate* • Jaime Fernandez *General Elias* • Andrea Checchi *Don Felipe* • Spartaco Conversi *Cirillo* • Joaquin Parra *Picaro* • José Manuel Martin *Raimundo* ■ *Dir* Damiano Damiani • *Scr* Salvatore Laurani, Franco Solinas

Bullet in the Head ★★★ 18

Crime drama 1990 · HK · Colour · 125mins

One of the more personal films in John Woo's canon and one which combines the highly stylised themes and motifs of his gangster films with a grittier than usual edge. Tony Leung, Jacky Cheung and Lee Waise play a trio of Hong Kong chums who see the chance to make a fortune in 1960s Vietnam, but find their friendship pushed to the limit by the war. It's not without its flaws, but bravura direction from Woo carries the day and it provides a fascinating view of a conflict usually seen from a western perspective. JF. In Cantonese with English subtitles. Contains violence and swearing. DVD

Tony Chiu-Wai Leung [Tony Leung (2)] *Ben* • Jacky Cheung *Frank* • Lee Waise *Paul* • Simon Yam *Luke* • Fennie Yeun *Jane* ■ *Dir* John Woo • *Scr* John Woo, Patrick Leung, Janet Chung

A Bullet Is Waiting ★ U

Crime drama 1954 · US · Colour · 81mins

The audience is waiting, too – for something, *anything* to happen. The film starts with a plane crash that strands Stephen McNally's sheriff at a sheep ranch with his captive (Rory Calhoun), an alleged murderer. It becomes bogged down in endless talk as lonely shepherdess Jean Simmons takes a shine to Calhoun. AE

Jean Simmons *Cally Canham* • Rory Calhoun *Ed Stone* • Stephen McNally *Sheriff Munson* • Brian Aherne *David Canham* ■ *Dir* John Farrow • *Scr* Thames Williamson, Casey Robinson, from a story by Thames Williamson

Bullet to Beijing ★★ 15

Spy thriller
1995 · UK/Can/Rus · Colour · 100mins

Thirty years after the film of Len Deighton's novel *The Ipcress File*, Michael Caine resurrects his British spy Harry Palmer. In this very average affort, Harry Palmer is in Russia, working with former KGB agents to prevent North Korea from using biological weapons. Michael Gambon plays a Russian magnate and there's the casting in-joke of Jason Connery as a Russian agent, while Sue Lloyd makes a welcome appearance, reprising her role of Jean from *The Ipcress File*. Caine and Connery made a second Palmer movie, *Midnight in St Petersburg*, back to back with this one. AT. Contains violence, swearing and brief nudity.

Michael Caine *Harry Palmer* • Jason Connery *Nikolai* • Mia Sara *Natasha* • Michael Sarrazin *Craig* • Michael Gambon *Alexei* • John Dunn-Hill *Louis* • Burt Kwouk *Kim Soo* • Sue Lloyd *Jean* ■ *Dir* George Mihalka • *Scr* Peter Welbeck [Harry Alan Towers], from the novel by Len Deighton

Bulletproof ★ 15

Action adventure 1987 · US · Colour · 90mins

Gary Busey stars in this preposterous action film that gives new meaning to the word derivative. He plays the indestructible Frank "Bulletproof" McBain, lured out of retirement to retrieve a secret weapon. Steve Carver fills the screen with enough comic-book characters to keep Marvel in business for years. RS DVD

Gary Busey *Frank McBain* • Darlanne Fluegel *Lieutenant Devon Shepard* • Henry Silva *Colonel Kartiff* • Thalmus Rasulala *Billy Dunbar* • LQ Jones *Sergeant O'Rourke* • Rene Enriquez *General Brogado* ■ *Dir* Steve Carver • *Scr* TL Lankford, Steve Carver, from a story by Fred Olen Ray, TL Lankford

Bulletproof ★ 18

Action comedy 1996 · US · Colour · 80mins

Director Ernest Dickerson (a brilliant cinematographer on Spike Lee's earlier movies) delivers some slick shoot-outs in this buddy movie, but everything else here is all wrong. Undercover cop Damon Wayans and drug dealer Adam Sandler are utterly unappealing as ex-friends forced to team up against crime lord James Caan. The performances are annoying, the tasteless jokes are lame and the violence is plain nasty. JC. Contains swearing, violence, nudity. DVD

Adam Sandler *Moses* • Damon Wayans *Keats* • James Caan *Frank Colton* • Jeep Swenson *Bledsoe* • James Farentino *Captain Jensen* • Kristen Wilson *Traci* • Larry McCoy *Detective Sulliman* • Allen Covert *Detective Jones* ■ *Dir* Ernest R Dickerson • *Scr* Lewis Colick, Joe Gayton, from a story by Joe Gayton

Bulletproof Monk ★ 12

Fantasy action adventure
2002 · US · Colour · 99mins

This fantasy produced by John Woo is based on a late 1990s cult comic book. The plot concerns an ancient life-prolonging Tibetan scroll that's protected by nameless monk Chow Yun-Fat and his pickpocket disciple Seann William Scott, who are pursued by former Nazi officer Karl Roden. Combining daft fortune-cookie philosophy and overdone stunts, this cheesy misadventure soon collapses. AJ. In English and Tibetan with subtitles. DVD

Chow Yun-Fat *Monk with No Name* • Seann William Scott *Kar* • Jaime King *Jade/Bad Girl* • Karel Roden *Struker* • Victoria Smurfit *Nina* • Marcus Jean Pirae *Mr Funktastic* • Mako *Mr Kojima* ■ *Dir* Paul Hunter • *Scr* Ethan Reiff, Cyrus Voris, from the Flypaper Press comic book

Bullets or Ballots ★★★ PG

Crime drama 1936 · US · BW · 78mins

A taut and tough crime drama, with Edward G Robinson as a New York City cop who infiltrates the rackets run by Barton MacLane. Warner Bros churned this type of film out by the yard in the 1930s, claiming they were good for the nation's morals, but the casts and the straightforward style makes them seem rather special nowadays. This one co-stars feisty Joan Blondell and Humphrey Bogart, who has a great showdown with Robinson and the director is William Keighley, a second-string contract director who usually got the job done well and on time. AT

Edward G Robinson *Johnny Blake* • Joan Blondell *Lee Morgan* • Barton MacLane *Al Kruger* • Humphrey Bogart *Nick "Bugs" Fenner* • Frank McHugh *Herman* • Joseph King (1) *Captain Dan McLaren* • Richard Purcell [Dick Purcell] *Ed Driscoll* ■ *Dir* William Keighley • *Scr* Seton I Miller, from a story by Martin Mooney

Bullets over Broadway ★★★★ 15

Period crime comedy
1994 · US · Colour · 95mins

Woody Allen celebrates the heyday of New York's theatreland, but remains behind the camera, allowing his typically excellent ensemble cast to shine. As the earnest playwright making his Broadway debut, John Cusack rather fumbles some classic Woodyisms. Dianne Wiest thoroughly deserved her best supporting actress Oscar, but Chazz Palminteri is, perhaps, even more remarkable. Providing teasing insights into how Allen views his own body of work, this is essentially a debate about whether the artist's duty is to retain his own integrity or pander to popular taste. It's also darn good entertainment. DP. Contains swearing. DVD

John Cusack *David Shayne* • Chazz Palminteri *Cheech* • Dianne Wiest *Helen Sinclair* • Jennifer Tilly *Olive Neal* • Jim Broadbent *Warner Purcell* • Jack Warden *Julian Marx* • Joe Viterelli *Nick Valenti* • Rob Reiner *Sheldon Flender* • Mary-Louise Parker *Ellen* • Harvey Fierstein *Sid Loomis* ■ *Dir* Woody Allen • *Scr* Woody Allen, Douglas McGrath

The Bullfighter and the Lady ★★★

Drama 1951 · US · BW · 87mins

Director Budd Boetticher and his co-writer Ray Nazarro were Oscar-nominated for the story, but the story's the least of it. For the love of pretty senorita Joy Page, clean-cut, all-American guy Robert Stack goes to Mexico to become a bullfighter, ending up a hero in the final fade. On this flimsy and unconvincing premise, Boetticher builds a colourful and absorbing account of the training and art of the matador. Filming on location, he captures all the excitement of this bloody sport. RK

Robert Stack *Chuck Regan* • Joy Page *Anita de la Vega* • Gilbert Roland *Manolo Estrada* • Virginia Grey *Lisbeth Flood* • John Hubbard *Barney Flood* • Katy Jurado *Chelo Estrada* • Antonio Gomez ■ *Dir* Budd Boetticher • *Scr* James Edward Grant, from a story by Budd Boetticher, Ray Nazarro

The Bullfighters ★ PG

Comedy 1945 · US · BW · 60mins

Laurel and Hardy's final Hollywood film was, as Stan said later, "a vast disappointment". Not only were their usual hairstyles changed and slicked down, but the studio (20th Century-Fox) only allowed a brief snatch of their "cuckoo theme" in the music. The studio really had it in for them. TH

Stanley Laurel [Stan Laurel] *Stan* • Oliver Hardy *Ollie* • Margo Woods *Tangerine* • Richard Lane *Hot Shot Coleman* • Carol Andrews *Hattie Blake* ■ *Dir* Malcolm St Clair • *Scr* W Scott Darling

Bullitt ★★★★ 15

Crime thriller 1968 · US · Colour · 108mins

Steve McQueen did better work in his tragically shortened career, but this is one of the films that helped make him a screen icon. He's at his deadpan best as the maverick cop who's assigned to protect a key government witness against a crime syndicate. Director Peter Yates gives it more, in terms of urban reality, than the predictable script deserves, while Frank P Keller won an Oscar for editing the famous San Francisco hill-bouncing car chase, but it's always McQueen's movie. TH. Contains some violence and swearing. DVD

Steve McQueen *Bullitt* • Robert Vaughn *Chalmers* • Jacqueline Bisset *Cathy* • Don Gordon *Delgetti* • Robert Duvall *Weissberg* • Simon Oakland *Captain Bennett* • Norman Fell *Baker* • Georg Stanford Brown *Dr Willard* ■ *Dir* Peter Yates • *Scr* Alan R Trustman, Harry Kleiner, from the novel *Mute Witness* by Robert L Pike

Bullseye! ★ 15

Comedy thriller 1990 · US · Colour · 88mins

A hideously unfunny comedy of errors from Michael Winner that must rank as a career low for nearly all involved. Poor old Michael Caine and Roger Moore play conmen who set out to steal gems from under the noses of their lookalikes. Neither seems comfortable for a second, while the glamorous locations and the glut of cameos can't plug the gaps in an awful script. DP

Michael Caine *Sidney Lipton/Dr Daniel Hicklar* • Roger Moore *Gerald Bradley-Smith/Sir John Bavistock* • Sally Kirkland *Willie Metcalfe* • Deborah Barrymore *Flo Fleming* • Lee Patterson *Darrell Hyde* • Mark Burns *Nigel Holden* • Derren Nesbitt *Insp Grosse* ■ *Dir* Michael Winner • *Scr* Leslie Bricusse, Laurence Marks, Maurice Gran, from a story by Leslie Bricusse, Michael Winner, Nick Mead

Bullshot ★ [PG]

Spoof adventure 1983 · UK · Colour · 88mins

A risible spoof of the Bulldog Drummond stories, this stars Alan Shearman, Ron House and Diz White, who wrote the screenplay and the stage play on which it is based. Shearman plays the fearless "Bullshot" Crummond with all the subtlety of a salesman on commission. But he has left himself with little option as every pun and sight gag in this atrocious tale, of German cads pursuing a top secret formula, demands to be rammed home with steam-hammer finesse. Billy Connolly, Mel Smith and Nicholas Lyndhurst are among the celebrities whose cameos can't help the cause. DP. Contains violence and mild swearing. [video]

Alan Shearman *"Bullshot" Crummond* • Diz White *Rosemary Fenton* • Ron House *Count Otto von Bruno* • Frances Tomelty *Fraulein Lenya Von Bruno* • Ron Pember *Dobbs* • Mel Smith *Crouch* • Michael Aldridge *Rupert Fenton* • Billy Connolly *Hawkeye McGillicuddy* • Nicholas Lyndhurst *Nobby Clark* ■ *Dir* Dick Clement • *Scr* Ron House, Alan Shearman, Diz White, from their play

Bullwhip ★★★ [U]

Western 1958 · US · Colour · 80mins

Rhonda Fleming plays a part-Cheyenne Indian with money-making ambitions in the fur trade who wields a bullwhip to get her way. When she requires a spouse in order to inherit property, she makes a deal with condemned cowboy Guy Madison. Loosely based on Shakespeare's *The Taming of the Shrew*, this unusual and rarely seen B-western was written by genre veteran Adele Buffington, and while the over-the-top comedy elements are a little hard to take, it's decently acted and photographed in attractive Technicolor by John J Martin. RK

Guy Madison *Steve* • Rhonda Fleming *Cheyenne* • James Griffith *Karp* • Don Beddoe *Judge* • Peter Adams (1) *Parnell* • Dan Sheridan *Podo* ■ *Dir* Harmon Jones • *Scr* Adele Buffington

Bully ★★★★ [18]

Drama based on a true story
2001 · US/Fr · Colour · 107mins

Stylistically echoing his brutal yet dazzling debut feature *kids*, director Larry Clark here unleashes a superbly shot drama that's not so much entertainment as a stomach-churning life-lesson. Based on the true story of a sadistic Florida teenager who was hideously murdered by the friends he victimised, the film presents a terrifying snapshot of alienated young America. An ultra-realistic portrayal of morally corrupt youth, illuminated by startling performances from the largely unknown cast, it turns from powerful social commentary into an authentic horror movie as the nerve-shredding events unfold. SF [video] [DVD]

Brad Renfro *Mario "Marty" Puccio* • Rachel Miner *Lisa Connelly* • Nick Stahl *Bobby Kent* • Bijou Phillips *Alice "Ali" Willis* • Michael Pitt *Donny Semenec* • Kelli Garner *Heather Swallers* ■ *Dir* Larry Clark • *Scr* Zachary Long, Roger Pullis, from the book *Bully: a True Story of High School Revenge* by Jim Schutze

Bulworth ★★★★ [18]

Political comedy drama
1998 · US · Colour · 103mins

Warren Beatty's astonishingly fearless political satire is one of the boldest studio films to come out of Hollywood in years. Beatty, who writes and directs, also stars as a disillusioned liberal senator who takes out a contract on his own life, giving him three days to start saying what he really believes. Just when you think Beatty won't dare to be more radical than his acidic (and very funny) swipes at just about everybody, he re-invents himself as a street-wise urban rapper. Sharper and riskier than the more conventional political satires such as *Bob Roberts* or *Primary Colors*, the film succeeds as both a startlingly original comedy and a fang-baring assault on the American political system. JC. Contains drug abuse, coarse language and sexual references. [video] [DVD]

Warren Beatty *Jay Bulworth* • Halle Berry *Nina* • Paul Sorvino *Graham Crockett* • Christine Baranski *Constance Bulworth* • Kimberly Deauna Adams *Denisha* • Vinny Argiro *Debate director* • Sean Astin *Gary* • Kirk Baltz *Debate producer* ■ *Dir* Warren Beatty • *Scr* Warren Beatty, Jeremy Pikser, from a story by Warren Beatty

Bunco Squad ★★

Crime drama 1950 · US · BW · 67mins

This is the penultimate movie of B-feature director Herbert I Leeds (dead a year later at the age of 42) who was taking a break from *Cisco Kid* and *Mr Moto* programme fillers. Likeable Robert Sterling foils a plot involving phoney psychics cheating Elisabeth Risdon, conned into parting with $2 million at a fake seance. TS

Robert Sterling *Steve* • Joan Dixon *Grace* • Ricardo Cortez *Anthony Wells* • Douglas Fowley *McManus* • Elisabeth Risdon *Jessica Royce* • Marguerite Churchill *Barbara* • John Kellogg *Reed* • Bernadene Hayes *Liane* ■ *Dir* Herbert I Leeds • *Scr* George Callahan, from a story by Reginald Taviner

Bundle of Joy ★★ [U]

Musical comedy 1956 · US · Colour · 98mins

This perfectly preserved slice of pop culture from a bygone era is a starring vehicle for "America's Sweethearts", Eddie Fisher, king of the pre-rock 'n' roll pop charts, and his new bride Debbie Reynolds. It's a remake of the popular Ginger Rogers movie *Bachelor Mother* with music added, but Fisher is no film star and the movie remains a silly, laboured farce. TS

Debbie Reynolds *Polly Parrish* • Eddie Fisher *Dan Merlin* • Adolphe Menjou *JB Merlin* • Tommy Noonan *Freddie Miller* • Nita Talbot *Mary* • Una Merkel *Mrs Dugan* • Melville Cooper *Adams* • Bill Goodwin *Mr Creely* ■ *Dir* Norman Taurog • *Scr* Norman Krasna, Robert Carson, Arthur Sheekman, from a story by Felix Jackson

Bundy ★★ [18]

Biographical crime drama
2002 · UK/US · Colour · 95mins

This biopic of notorious serial killer Ted Bundy (he was the first multiple murderer to whom the term was applied, having bludgeoned, raped and mutilated a large number of women in the 1970s) never really attempts to find a motive for his actions. Instead, director Matthew Bright concentrates on re-creating his sadistic attacks in as much unpleasant detail as possible. Michael Reilly Burke is plausible as the suave psychopath, but the screenplay engages in unwarranted speculation about what Bundy did with his victims as well as delivering a leering, gratuitous final scene. AS [video] [DVD]

Michael Reilly Burke *Ted Bundy* • Boti Ann Bliss *Lee* • Steffani Brass *Julie* • Marina Black *Kate* • Wayne Morse *Bob* • Renee Madison Cole *Cutler* ■ *Dir* Matthew Bright • *Scr* Stephen Johnston, Matthew Bright

The Bunker ★★★ [15]

Second World War horror
2001 · UK · Colour · 87mins

Director Rob Green's feature debut relies on the shadowy and the unseen for its terror charge. A platoon of German soldiers hide from advancing US forces in a deserted bunker, but their safe haven is built over the site of a frenzied medieval massacre and soon the soldiers start witnessing mysterious occurrences. Expertly making the most of one prime location and cranking up the atmospherics to suspenseful breaking points, Green's modest miniature is an effective haunted house of shell-shocked horror. AJ. Contains violence. [DVD]

Jason Flemyng *Cpl Baumann* • Charley Boorman *Pte First Class Franke* • Jack Davenport *Lance Cpl Ebert* • Andrew Lee-Potts *Pte Neumann* • Christopher Fairbank *Sgt Heydrich* • Nicholas Hamnett *Pte Engels* ■ *Dir* Rob Green • *Scr* Clive Dawson

Bunny Lake Is Missing ★★★

Mystery drama 1965 · US · BW · 107mins

Laurence Olivier (as a leaden-paced, raincoated British copper) and Noël Coward may have regarded this as a bit of slumming, judging by the way they camp it up. However, director Otto Preminger uses their archness to consolidate the nightmarish quality of this story about American Carol Lynley's illegitimate little girl being absent without mum's leave. Keir Dullea demonstrates that, even prior to *2001: a Space Odyssey*, he was an unconventional actor, and his performance reflects the illusory atmosphere of the movie. TH

Laurence Olivier *Newhouse* • Carol Lynley *Ann* • Keir Dullea *Steven* • Noël Coward *Wilson* • Martita Hunt *Ada Ford* • Anna Massey *Elvira* • Clive Revill *Andrews* • Finlay Currie *Doll maker* • Richard Wattis *Shipping Clerk* ■ *Dir* Otto Preminger • *Scr* John Mortimer, Penelope Mortimer, from the novel by Evelyn Piper

Bunny O'Hare ★

Crime comedy 1971 · US · Colour · 92mins

In her golden years, veteran diva Bette Davis took on practically any role to prove she was still alive and a viable actress. But nothing can really explain why she sank as low as this dreadful gimmick flick, where she's a bored grandmother in hippy gear and a long blonde wig, who decides to rob banks with ageing partner-in-crime Ernest Borgnine. Appalling. AJ

Bette Davis *Bunny O'Hare* • Ernest Borgnine *Bill Green* • Jack Cassidy *Detective Greeley* • Joan Delaney *RJ Hart* • Jay Robinson *Banker* • Reva Rose *Lulu* ■ *Dir* Gerd Oswald • *Scr* Stanley Z Cherry, Coslough Johnson, from a story by Stanley Z Cherry

Bunty Aur Babli ★★ [PG]

Romantic adventure
2005 · Ind · Colour · 169mins

Abhishek Bachchan and Rani Mukherji star in this tale of criminal lovers who become folk heroes and terrorise a series of cities. Because this is Bollywood, director Shaad Ali Sehgal replaces violence with a steady supply of gags and a crisp script. The film has an air of romanticism, but when tough cop Amitabh Bachchan (Abhishek's real-life father) enters the fray, determined to hunt down the dastardly duo, this rapidly descends into melodrama. OA. In Hindi with English subtitles.

Amitabh Bachchan *Dashrath Singh* • Abhishek Bachchan *Bunty* • Rani Mukherji *Babli* ■ *Dir* Shaad Ali Sehgal [Shaad Ali] • *Scr* Jaideep Sahni

Buona Sera, Mrs Campbell ★★★

Comedy drama 1968 · It · Colour · 111mins

Gina Lollobrigida looks a treat in director Melvin Frank's rather tasteless comedy drama about an Italian single mother whose promiscuous wartime past comes back to haunt her. There's earnest support from Phil Silvers, Telly Savalas and suave Peter Lawford as the three American airmen who each believe they fathered Lollobrigida's child 20 years ago, and who have been paying child support ever since. If you're a fan of 1960s farces and find comedy of the opening-and-shutting-door variety funny, this glossy romp may well pass muster. TS

Gina Lollobrigida *Carla* • Telly Savalas *Walter Braddock* • Shelley Winters *Shirley Newman* • Phil Silvers *Phil Newman* • Peter Lawford *Justin Young* • Lee Grant *Fritzie Braddock* • Janet Margolin *Gia* • Marian Moses *Lauren Young* ■ *Dir* Melvin Frank • *Scr* Melvin Frank, Sheldon Keller, Denis Norden

The 'Burbs ★★★★ [PG]

Comedy 1989 · US · Colour · 96mins

When the Klopeks move into a run-down house in an otherwise spick-and-span suburb, Tom Hanks – playing a one-man neighbourhood watch scheme – starts to fret. Just what are the Klopeks up to, digging in the garden and making all those clanking noises at night? This light-hearted and very funny comedy is an askew parable about small-town America, with Hanks as the ultimate conformist surrounded by weirdos. Bruce Dern and Carrie Fisher offer fine support to the affable Hanks. Director Joe Dante excels at this sort of thing and this is a constantly intriguing picture. AT. Contains swearing and violence. [video] [DVD]

Tom Hanks *Ray Peterson* • Bruce Dern *Mark Rumsfield* • Carrie Fisher *Carol Peterson* • Rick Ducommun *Art Weingartner* • Corey Feldman *Ricky Butler* • Henry Gibson *Dr Werner Klopek* • Brother Theodore *Uncle Reuben Klopek* • Courtney Gains *Hans Klopek* ■ *Dir* Joe Dante • *Scr* Dana Olsen

Burden of Dreams ★★★★

Documentary 1982 · US · Colour · 94mins

A remarkable documentary by Les Blank about the appalling slog involved in making Werner Herzog's *Fitzcarraldo*. In telling the story of an opera lover (Klaus Kinski) who hauls a ship through the South American jungle to bring music to the natives, the visionary German director embarked upon an overtaxing labour of love that frayed tempers and stirred skirmishes with the locals. Rarely have the rigours of location filming been so dramatically and painstakingly chronicled. TH

Dir Les Blank • *Scr* Michael Goodwin

Bureau of Missing Persons ★★★

Comedy thriller 1933 · US · BW · 73mins

A pacey action movie from Warner Bros, which is, in effect, a selection of different overlapping stories, tightly held together by the direction of Roy Del Ruth. The central tale features Bette Davis, who may or may not have killed her husband, and tough-talking cop Pat O'Brien, who has to sort out the mystery. There's much pleasure to be had from watching Warners' hard-boiled rep company goes through their paces, but none of them can surpass Davis. TS

Bette Davis *Norma Phillips* • Lewis Stone *Captain Webb* • Pat O'Brien *Butch Saunders* • Glenda Farrell *Belle* • Allen Jenkins *Joe Musik* • Ruth Donnelly *Pete* • Hugh Herbert *Slade* • Alan Dinehart *Therme Roberts* ■ *Dir* Roy Del Ruth • *Scr* Robert Presnell, from the book *Missing Men* by John H Ayres, Carol Bird

B

The Burglar ★★★

Film noir 1956 · US · BW · 90mins

This little gem is the real thing, a sordid little flick with great style, directed with panache by cult favourite Paul Wendkos, who latterly has made some of the hardest edged TV movies. The cast is well worth tuning in for: Dan Duryea (the Richard Widmark of the Bs) is the disturbed titular crook, while Jayne Mansfield, early in her career, and seldom better, and *The Big Sleep's* Martha Vickers provide terrific female support. Bleak and bizarre. TS

Dan Duryea *Nat Harbin* • Jayne Mansfield *Gladden* • Martha Vickers *Della* • Peter Capell *Baylock* • Mickey Shaughnessy *Dohmer* • Wendell Phillips *Police captain* • Phoebe Mackay *Sister Sara* ■ *Dir* Paul Wendkos • *Scr* David Goodis, from his novel

Burglar ★★ 15

Comedy thriller 1987 · US · Colour · 97mins

Whoopi Goldberg stars in this disappointing mix of humour and action, and even the added talents of Bob "Bobcat" Goldthwait and John Goodman have little impact on the comedy. Goldberg is the burglar of the title who witnesses a murder and then finds herself suspected of the crime, but even the actress's comic timing and acting talents can't keep you from guessing what will happen before her character does. JB. Contains violence, swearing.

Whoopi Goldberg *Bernice Rhodenbarr* • Bob Goldthwait [Bobcat Goldthwait] *Carl Hefler* • GW Bailey *Ray Kirschman* • Lesley Ann Warren *Dr Cynthia Sheldrake* • James Handy *Carson Verrill* • Anne De Salvo *Detective Todras* • John Goodman *Detective Nyswander* ■ *Dir* Hugh Wilson • *Scr* Joseph Loeb III, Matthew Weisman, Hugh Wilson, from the books by Lawrence Block

The Burglars ★★ 18

Crime drama 1971 · Fr/It · Colour · 109mins

The worldwide success of *The Sicilian Clan* meant that French director Henri Verneuil could call on an international cast and a high-powered location shoot for his next movie. Jean-Paul Belmondo and Omar Sharif co-star in this colourful remake of the 1956 *noir* thriller, *The Burglar*, this time shot in Greece and containing some of the most irritating dubbing you're ever likely to hear in a film of such pedigree. TS. French dialogue dubbed into English.

Jean-Paul Belmondo *Azad* • Omar Sharif *Abel Zacharia* • Dyan Cannon *Lena* • Robert Hossein *Ralph* • Nicole Calfan *Hélène* • Renato Salvatori *Renzi* • José-Luis De Villalonga *Tasco* • Myriam Colombi *Mme Tasco* • Raoul Delfosse *Caretaker* • Steve Eckardt *Malloch* ■ *Dir* Henri Verneuil • *Scr* Henri Verneuil, Vahe Katcha, from the film an novel *The Burglar* by David Goodis

Buried Alive ★ 18

Horror 1990 · US · Colour · 86mins

This is a shoddy rehash of Edgar Allan Poe (misspelt Allen in the credits!) plonked down in South Africa and directed by one-time porn film-maker Gerard Kikoine. Robert Vaughn runs the Ravenscroft Institute, populated by shady students and eccentric teachers (including grey-wigged Donald Pleasence), where Poe's psychological horrors are made stupidly literal. John Carradine's appearance as a walled-up victim was his last and saddest. AJ. Contains swearing and violence.

Robert Vaughn *Dr Gary* • Donald Pleasence *Dr Schaeffer* • Karen Witter *Janet* • John Carradine *Jacob* • Nia Long *Fingers* • Ginger Lynn Allen *Debbie* • Bill Butler *Tim* • Janine Denison *Shiro* ■ *Dir* Gérard Kikoine • *Scr* Jake Clesi, Stuart Lee, from stories by Peter Welbeck [Harry Alan Towers], Edgar Allan Poe

Buried Alive ★★★ 15

Thriller 1990 · US · Colour · 89mins

This superior TV-movie thriller stars Tim Matheson as a businessman who survives not only poisoning but also burial by his adulterous wife. Matheson does well as the unsuspecting husband and Jennifer Jason Leigh is equally as good as his scheming spouse. This was well enough received to spawn a sequel called, rather unoriginally, *Buried Alive II*. PF. Contains violence, swearing. DVD

Tim Matheson *Clint Goodman* • Jennifer Jason Leigh *Joanna Goodman* • William Atherton *Cortland Van Owen* • Hoyt Axton *Sheriff Sam Eberly* ■ *Dir* Frank Darabont • *Scr* Mark Patrick Carducci

Buried Loot ★★

Crime 1934 · US · BW · 18mins

This two-reeler initiated MGM's *Crime Does Not Pay* series, which ran to 48 titles over 12 years, giving movie houses quality shorts and enabling the studio to try out new talent. Here the recently signed 23-year-old Robert Taylor was given the principal role of the thief who hides his loot, aiming to recover it after serving time in prison. What with a jailbreak, plastic surgery and a twist ending, it packed a full B-feature plot into 18 minutes. Taylor soon became a star, while later *Crime Does Not Pay* entries became informative exposés of rackets that were fooling the public. AE

Robert Taylor (1) *Al Douglas* • Robert Livingston ■ *Dir* George B Seitz • *Scr* George B Seitz, from a story by Marty Brooks

Burke and Wills ★★★

Biographical drama 1985 · Aus · Colour · 140mins

Robert Burke and William Wills, who with two others were the first explorers to cross Australia from south to north, are here played with lantern-jawed determination and righteous zeal by Jack Thompson and Nigel Havers. The same team of explorers were spoofed by another version of the tale, *Wills and Burke*, released at roughly the same time but with a very different take on the tale. Indeed, even here there are certain grandiose moments that border on parody and so nudge the film towards unintended hilarity. Otherwise the extended scenes of bravery and endurance have an authentic period atmosphere and psychological resonance. JM. Contains some violence and swearing.

Jack Thompson *Robert O'Hara Burke* • Nigel Havers *William John Wills* • Greta Scacchi *Julia Matthews* • Matthew Fargher *John King* • Ralph Cotterill *Charley Gray* • Drew Forsythe *William Brahe* ■ *Dir* Graeme Clifford • *Scr* Michael Thomas

The Burmese Harp ★★★★

War drama 1956 · Jpn · BW · 116mins

Adapted from Michio Takeyama's novel by director Kon Ichikawa's wife, Natto Wada, this lyrical epic is among the most moving acts of atonement made by the postwar Japanese film industry. Yet the decision of a young musician (Shoji Yasui) to renounce his homeland and remain in Burma as a Buddhist monk is less an indictment of militarism and more a cry of anguish on behalf of all those who suffered during the Second World War. Ichikawa occasionally allows sincerity to lapse into sentimentality, but he clearly felt deeply about the story, which he remade (less memorably) in 1985. DP. In Japanese with English subtitles.

Rentaro Mikuni *Captain Inouye* • Shoji Yasui *Private Yasuhiko* • Tatsuya Mihashi *Defence Commander* • Tanie Kitabayashi *Old woman* • Yunosuke Ito *Village head* ■ *Dir* Kon Ichikawa • *Scr* Natto Wada, from the novel by Michio Takeyama

The Burmese Harp ★★★

War drama 1985 · Jpn · Colour · 132mins

Strikingly filmed in colour by Setsuo Kobayashi, Kon Ichikawa's remake of his 1956 classic lacks the original's contemporary resonance. This time, in seeking to expose the fanaticism and brutality of the militarist tendency, Ichikawa overdoes the humanist earnestness that inspires a soldier musician to remain in Burma after the Imperial Army's retreat and join the Buddhist monks in burying the dead. This moving film would, perhaps, have been more effective had it not been quite so deliberate. DP. A Japanese language film.

Koji Ishizaka *Captain Inoue* • Kiichi Nakai *Private Mizushima* • Takuzo Kawatani *Sgt Ito* • Atsushi Watanabe *PteKobayashi* • Fujio Tokita *Old man* • Tanie Kitabayashi *Old woman* • Bunta Sugawara *Commander of Sankaku Mountain Platoon* ■ *Dir* Kon Ichikawa • *Scr* Natto Wada, from the novel by Michio Takeyama

Burn! ★★★★

Period drama 1970 · It/Fr · Colour · 112mins

Even at the height of his stardom, Marlon Brando was prepared to take chances by accepting challenging roles. In this attack on colonial manipulation – a period swashbuckler with attitude – he plays a cynical British secret agent who ignites a Caribbean island revolution against the ruling Portuguese using slave labour on a sugar-cane plantation. It's clumsily handled at times by director Gillo Pontecorvo, but it still has scenes of enormous visual power. Brando is magnificent. TH

Marlon Brando *Sir William Walker* • Evaristo Marquez *Jose Dolores* • Renato Salvatori *Teddy Sanchez* • Norman Hill *Shelton* • Tom Lyons *General Prada* • Wanani *Guarina* • Joseph Persuad *Juanito* • Giampiero Albertini *Henry* ■ *Dir* Gillo Pontecorvo • *Scr* Franco Solinas, Giorgio Arlorio, from a story by Gillo Pontecorvo, Franco Solinas, Giorgio Arlorio • *Cinematographer* Marcello Gatti

Burn Hollywood Burn ★ 15

Satirical comedy 1997 · US · Colour · 81mins

In this monumentally awful celebrity-packed Hollywood "mockumentary", Eric Idle plays Allan Smithee, the joke being that this is the pseudonym used by directors who don't want to have their real name credited on a movie. Sylvester Stallone, Jackie Chan and Whoopi Goldberg look embarrassed playing themselves, which is unsurprising given that the Joe Eszterhas script makes his *Showgirls* work read like Shakespeare. Unsubtle, unfunny and an unbelievable waste of time. JC. Contains swearing.

Ryan O'Neal *James Edmunds* • Coolio *Dion Brothers* • Chuck D *Leon Brothers* • Eric Idle *Alan Smithee* • Leslie Stefanson *Michelle Rafferty* • Sandra Bernhard *Ann Glover* • Cherie Lunghi *Myrna Smithee* • Harvey Weinstein *Sam Rizzo* • Naomi Campbell *Attendant no 2* • Sylvester Stallone • Whoopi Goldberg • Jackie Chan • Robert Evans • Joe Eszterhas ■ *Dir* Alan Smithee [Arthur Hiller] • *Scr* Joe Eszterhas

The Burning ★ 18

Horror 1981 · US · Colour · 87mins

A highly derivative *Friday the 13th* clone that found itself on the infamous video nasty list that caused a furore in the early 1980s. A horribly-burned summer camp caretaker returns with scissors and shears to take bloody vengeance on the promiscuous teens responsible for the joke-gone-wrong that caused his fiery scars. Inept direction by Tony Maylam and a predictable script cause boredom to set in very early on. AJ DVD

Brian Matthews *Todd* • Leah Ayres *Michelle* • Brian Backer *Alfred* • Larry Joshua *Glazer* • Jason Alexander *Dave* • Ned Eisenberg *Eddy* • Fisher Stevens *Woodstock* • Holly Hunter *Sophie* ■ *Dir* Tony Maylam • *Scr* Peter Lawrence, Bob Weinstein, from a story by Harvey Weinstein, Tony Maylam, Brad Grey

The Burning Bed ★★★★ 15

Drama based on a true story 1984 · US · Colour · 91mins

Farrah Fawcett left her blonde bimbo *Charlie's Angels* image behind for ever with this superb performance as a battered wife who takes revenge on her husband by setting him on fire while he is sleeping. Based on a true story, this Emmy-nominated drama from Robert Greenwald – who also made the neglected *Sweet Hearts Dance* and the hilariously abysmal *Xanadu* – is carefully and sensitively handled, and never lapses into melodrama. Thought provoking, moving and exceptionally well played. JB

Farrah Fawcett *Francine Hughes* • Paul Le Mat *Mickey Hughes* • Richard Masur *Aryon Greydanus* • Grace Zabriskie *Flossie Hughes* • Penelope Milford *Gaby* • Christa Denton *Christy, aged 12* • James Callahan *Berlin Hughes* • Gary Grubbs *District Attorney* ■ *Dir* Robert Greenwald • *Scr* Rose Leiman Goldemberg, from a book by Faith McNulty

The Burning Hills ★★ PG

Western 1956 · US · Colour · 88mins

This minor western has Tab Hunter setting out on a vengeance trail and finding Natalie Wood as a Mexican/American who nurses him when he's shot. Casting these two young and pretty things to star in a western was unusual in those days, a studio ploy to lure teenagers away from their dance halls and TV sets. Hunter proves himself a rather anaemic hero, though his popularity later gained him his own TV show. AT

Tab Hunter *Trace Jordan* • Natalie Wood *Maria Colton* • Skip Homeier *Jack Sutton* • Eduard Franz *Jacob Lantz* • Earl Holliman *Mort Bayliss* • Claude Akins *Ben Hindeman* • Ray Teal *Joe Sutton* ■ *Dir* Stuart Heisler • *Scr* Irving Wallace, from the novel by Louis L'Amour

Burning Memory ★★★

War drama 1988 · Is · Colour · 93mins

This harrowing Israeli feature was based on debutant director Yossi Somer's experiences as a paramedic during the war with the Lebanon. Somer depicts Israel as a nation fraught with internal strife, which is only kept in check by the need to unite in the face of a common enemy. But, as one would expect from a film that went through three editors, the action is too often disjointed. Nevertheless, there is an affecting performance from Danny Roth as the shellshocked soldier, who knows he must return to the front as soon as he is cured. DP. In Hebrew with English subtitles.

Danny Roth *Gary* • Shmuel Edelman *Tzvika* • Pauli Reshef *Alex* • Etti Ankri *Ruth* • Alon Oliarchick *Rubi* • Yossef El-Dror *Avram* • Reuven Dayan *Nissim* • Yahli Bergman *Ronen* • Koby Hagoel *Tzukerman* • Avi Gilor *Amos* ■ *Dir* Yossi Somer • *Scr* Ami Amir, Yossi Somer

The Burning Season ★★★★ 15

Drama based on a true story 1994 · US · Colour · 117mins

In one of his last roles before his tragically early death, Raul Julia is both committed and convincing as Chico Mendes, the Brazilian union leader who was assassinated in 1990. Superbly scripted, and directed with power by John Frankenheimer, this superior TV movie never allows its passionate support for Mendes and his cause (the preservation of the Amazon rainforests) to deteriorate into either hagiography or melodrama. Green film-making at its best. DP. Contains swearing and violence.

Raul Julia *Chico Mendes* • Kamala Dawson *Ilzamar* • Edward James Olmos *Wilson Pinhairo* • Sonia Braga *Regina De Carvaiho* • Esai Morales *Jair* • Carmen Argenziano *Allredo Sezero* • Enrigue Novi *Nilo Sergio* • Jorge Zepeda *Thomas Sanjos* • Nigel Havers *Steven Kaye* ■ *Dir* John Frankenheimer • *Scr* Michael Tolkin, Ron Hutchinson, William Mastrosimone, from the novel by Andrew Revkin

Burning Secret ★★★ PG

Period drama
1988 · US/UK/W Ger · Colour · 103mins

Director Andrew Birkin here shows the sure grasp of child psychology that made his later adaptation of Ian McEwan's *The Cement Garden* so engrossing. This is a thoughtful child's-eye view of the charged relationship that develops between an asthmatic boy's mother (Faye Dunaway) and a rakish Austrian baron (Klaus Maria Brandauer) during the youth's treatment at a mountain spa town after the First World War. Young David Eberts responds well to Birkin's sensitive direction and, if the pace occasionally slackens, there is always the consolation of the beauties of Prague (standing in for Vienna). DP

Faye Dunaway *Sonya Tuchman* • Klaus Maria Brandauer *Baron Alexander Maria von Hauenschild* • David Eberts *Edmund Tuchman* • Ian Richardson *Father* • Martin Obernigg *Concierge* • John Nettleton *Dr Weiss* • Vaclav Stekl *Asst concierge* ■ *Dir* Andrew Birkin • *Scr* Andrew Birkin, from the short story *Brennendes Geheimnis* by Stefan Zweig

Burnt Barns ★★

Drama 1973 · Fr · Colour · 95mins

A dead woman is discovered on a farm, and suspicion falls on the son of Simone Signoret, a widowed matriarch who rules her family with a rod of iron. Alain Delon plays the local magistrate, who uncovers the sort of familial resentment that can only be put down to peasant tradition and in-breeding. The presence of Signoret and Delon made Jean Chapot's sombre film a sure-fire hit in France, although it's really rather ordinary. AT. French dialogue dubbed into English.

Alain Delon *Larcher* • Simone Signoret *Rose* • Paul Crauchet *Pierre* • Catherine Allégret *Françoise* • Bernard Le Coq *Paul* • Miou-Miou *Monique* • Pierre Rousseau *Louis* • Renato Salvatori *Patron* ■ *Dir* Jean Chapot • *Scr* Sebastian Roulet, Frantz-Andre Burget

Burnt by the Sun ★★★★★ 15

Period drama
1995 · Rus/Fr · Colour · 129mins

This period drama from director Nikita Mikhalkov plunges into the heart of darkness that was Stalin's Russia in the mid-1930s. Mikhalkov also stars as a complacent military hero of the Soviet Revolution, whose country house is visited unexpectedly by his young wife's former childhood sweetheart. Against the backdrop of a lazy summer's day, the truth behind Stalin's rule and the reason for the visit become apparent. Winner of the Oscar for best foreign film, this masterpiece of visual audacity – the vast balloon displaying an image of Stalin is a highlight – depicts, with vivid candour, a nation's paranoia grievously turned in upon itself. TH. In Russian with English subtitles. Contains violence, swearing, sex scenes and nudity. DVD

Nikita Mikhalkov *Sergei Petrovich Kotov* • Oleg Menshikov *Dmitrii* • Ingeborga Dapkunaite *Marusia Kotov* • Nadia Mikhalkova *Nadia* • André Umansky *Philippe* • Vyacheslav Tikhonov *Vsevolod Konstantinovich* • Svetlana Kriuchkova *Mokhova* ■ *Dir* Nikita Mikhalkov • *Scr* Nikita Mikhalkov, Rustam Ibragimbekov, from a story by Nikita Mikhalkov • *Cinematographer* Vilen Kaliuta

Burnt Offerings ★ 15

Horror 1976 · US · Colour · 110mins

In this chiller, Karen Black, Oliver Reed and family take a house for the summer. The fact that the house is owned by that old fruitcake Burgess Meredith should have told them at the start that things will soon get very bumpy in the night. Too long and not at all scary. AT DVD

Karen Black *Marian* • Oliver Reed *Ben* • Burgess Meredith *Brother* • Eileen Heckart *Roz* • Lee Montgomery *David* • Dub Taylor *Walker* • Bette Davis *Aunt Elizabeth* ■ *Dir* Dan Curtis • *Scr* William F Nolan, Dan Curtis, from the novel by Robert Marasco

Bury Me an Angel ★★

Action drama 1972 · US · Colour · 86mins

Dixie Peabody (who disappeared not long after this movie) plays a female biker who hits the road to find and kill the guy who blew off her brother's head with a shotgun. With a woman as writer/director, it isn't surprising the movie takes time to focus on Peabody and her sometimes interesting interactions with other characters. Sadly, the material between is slow, with not much action and not much sex, making it far from the "howling hellcat humping a hot steel hog on a roaring rampage of revenge" that the original ads promised. KB

Dixie Peabody *Dag* • Terry Mace *Jonsie* • Clyde Ventura *Bernie* • Stephen Whittaker (1) *Killer* • Maureen Math • Joanne Moore Jordan • Marie Denn • Dennis Peabody ■ *Dir/Scr* Barbara Peeters

Bus 174 ★★★★ 15

Crime documentary
2002 · Bra · Colour and BW · 131mins

An outstanding example of the crusading documentary, this account of the tragic life and times of Rio street kid Sandro do Nascimento lays bare the inhumanity, incompetence and indifference that allow so many born into poverty to sink into depravity. On 12 June 2000, Sandro hijacked a bus and held the occupants hostage for more than four hours. The stand-off was broadcast live to the nation and José Padilha and co-director Felipe Lacerda make compelling use of the contemporary TV footage. They also reveal his traumatic childhood and interview friends, SWAT officers and surviving hostages. The violent denouement is perhaps over-dramatised, but, by then, the film-makers' points about Sandro, urban decay and the class divide in Brazilian society have been more than well made. DP. In Portuguese with English subtitles. Contains swearing and violence. DVD

Dir José Padilha, Felipe Lacerda

Bus Riley's Back in Town ★★★

Drama 1965 · US · Colour · 93mins

Michael Parks shuffles and mumbles his way through this small-town melodrama. He plays a former sailor twice jilted by the voluptuous Ann-Margret, who has married a sugar daddy but still fancies Parks. He is something of a weakness but this is a quiet, understated study of frustrated ambition. The original author, noted playwright William Inge, demanded his real name be removed from the credits and the movie bombed. AT

Ann-Margret *Laurel* • Michael Parks *Bus Riley* • Janet Margolin *Judy* • Brad Dexter *Slocum* • Jocelyn Brando *Mrs Riley* • Larry Storch *Howie* • Crahan Denton *Spencer* ■ *Dir* Harvey Hart • *Scr* Walter Gage [William Inge]

Bus Stop ★★★★ U

Comedy 1956 · US · Colour · 90mins

This was the film that proved Marilyn Monroe was a considerable screen actress, and capable of much, much more than her sexpot image indicated. Whether Monroe's performance is a result of director Joshua Logan's patience or Lee and Paula Strasberg's legendary coaching is irrelevant: she is superb as the down-at-heel saloon chanteuse whom young cowboy Don Murray (impressive in his film debut) decides to marry. Based on William Inge's stage play, this is a movie that rewards – especially memorable is Monroe's delivery of an off-kilter *That Old Black Magic* in an outfit that leaves little to the imagination. TS DVD

Marilyn Monroe *Cherie* • Don Murray *Bo* • Arthur O'Connell *Virgil* • Betty Field *Grace* • Eileen Heckart *Vera* • Robert Bray *Carl* • Hope Lange *Elma* • Hans Conried *Life • photographer* • Casey Adams [Max Showalter] *Life • reporter* ■ *Dir* Joshua Logan • *Scr* George Axelrod, from the play by William Inge

Bush Christmas ★★★ U

Adventure 1947 · Aus/UK · BW · 61mins

The first film made for J Arthur Rank's Children's Cinema Club, this adventure was beautifully photographed in the sultry Blue Mountains of New South Wales with an all-Australian cast and crew. Chips Rafferty, at the time the only world-famous Australian actor, heads the cast in the tale of a group of children who trek through the bush in order to catch the rustlers who have stolen their father's horses. The film doesn't talk down to its youthful audience and is fine family fare. TV

Chips Rafferty *Long Bill* • John Fernside *Jim* • Stan Tolhurst *Blue* • Pat Penny *Father* • Thelma Grigg *Mother* • Clyde Combo *Old Jack* • John McCallum *Narrator* • Helen Grieve *Helen* ■ *Dir/Scr* Ralph Smart • *Cinematographer* George Heath

Bush Christmas ★★★

Adventure 1983 · Aus · Colour · 91mins

A remake of the 1947 original, this amiable outdoor adventure is of primary interest for marking the screen debut of Nicole Kidman. Along with brother Mark Spain, English cousin James Wingrove and Aboriginal stablehand Manalpuy, she spends much of the film pursuing roguish horse thieves John Ewart and John Howard. Directed with a kid-friendly mix of humour and action by Henri Safran and splendidly shot by Malcolm Richards and Ross Berryman, this is family fare of a high order. DP

Nicole Kidman *Helen* • Mark Spain *John* • James Wingrove *Michael* • Manalpuy • John Ewart *Bill* • John Howard (2) *Sly* • Vineta O'Malley *Kate Thompson* • Peter Sumner *Ben Thompson* ■ *Dir* Henri Safran • *Scr* Ted Roberts, from the film by Ralph Smart

The Bushido Blade ★★ 15

Period action drama
1981 · US/UK · Colour · 90mins

Despite its handsome trappings, this is an unremarkable historical adventure. In his last film, Richard Boone is typically gruff as the American commander who leads an expedition to 19th-century Japan to recover a ceremonial sword that has been stolen by those opposed to the forces of westernisation. The narrative is too episodic to engross, but Toshiro Mifune lends a little class in the role he would reprise in a spin-off mini-series. DP

Richard Boone *Matthew Perry* • Sonny Chiba *Prince Edo* • Frank Converse *Captain Hawk* • Laura Gemser *Edo's cousin* • James Earl Jones *Harpooner* • Mako *Friend* • Toshiro Mifune *Shogun's commander* ■ *Dir* Tom Kotani • *Scr* William Overgard

Bushwhacked ★ PG

Comedy 1995 · US · Colour · 86mins

This calamitous comedy might appeal to those youngsters who thought that Daniel Stern being pummelled in *Home Alone* was hilariously funny. Here, Stern is a doltish delivery man who poses as a scout leader while trying to beat a murder rap. Unsubtle slapstick. DP. Contains swearing. DVD

Daniel Stern *Max Grabelski* • Jon Polito *Agent Palmer* • Brad Sullivan *Jack Erickson* • Ann Dowd *Mrs Patterson* • Anthony Heald *Bragdon* • Tom Wood *Agent McMurrey* ■ *Dir* Greg Beeman • *Scr* John Jordan, Danny Byers, Tommy Swerdlow, Michael Goldberg, from a story by John Jordan, Danny Byers

A Business Affair ★★ 15

Romantic comedy
1993 · Fr/UK/Ger/Sp · Colour · 97mins

It's hard to believe the combined talents of Christopher Walken and Jonathan Pryce could make such a lacklustre film. Pryce plays a novelist whose writer's block is seriously aggravated when his wife Carole Bouquet achieves sudden success as a novelist. To make matters worse, she elopes with her husband's literary agent (Walken). Charlotte Brandstrom's film is simply too fluffy for its heavyweight cast. LH

Christopher Walken *Vanni Corso* • Carole Bouquet *Kate Swallow* • Jonathan Pryce *Alec Bolton* • Sheila Hancock *Judith* • Anna Manahan *Bianca* • Fernando Guillen-Cuervo *Angel* • Tom Wilkinson *Bob* ■ *Dir* Charlotte Brandstrom • *Scr* William Stadiem, from a story by Charlotte Brandstrom, William Stadiem, from the books *Tears Before Bedtime* and *Weep No More* by Barbara Skelton

Business as Usual ★★ 15

Drama 1987 · UK · Colour · 85mins

Lezli-An Barrett's debut feature has a tendency towards the didactic. Glenda Jackson, in her pre-Labour MP days, plays a Liverpool boutique manager who becomes a supporter of workers' rights when she's sacked by her boss for complaining about the sexual harassment of an employee. Very 1980s and anti-Thatcher in its approach, the film is watchable thanks to the conviction of the cast, but not helped by the heavy-handed treatment of the subject matter. LH

Glenda Jackson *Babs Flynn* • John Thaw *Kieran Flynn* • Cathy Tyson *Josie Patterson* • Mark McGann *Stevie Flynn* • Eamon Boland *Mr Barry* • James Hazeldine *Mark* • Buki Armstrong *Paula Douglas* • Stephen McGann *Terry Flynn* ■ *Dir/Scr* Lezli-An Barrett

Business Is Business ★★★ 18

Comedy drama 1971 · Neth · Colour · 88mins

The huge success of this spicy comedy drama in Holland allowed first-time feature director Paul Verhoeven to helm his international breakthrough hit *Turkish Delight*. Based on a booklet of anecdotes about prostitutes working in Amsterdam's red light district, it follows the risqué adventures of Ronnie Bierman and Sylvia de Leur as they ply their trade, specialising in deviant sex for mainly upper-class clients, avoiding trouble with pimps in the process. Engrossing and highly entertaining. AJ. Dutch dialogue dubbed into English. DVD

Ronnie Bierman *Blonde Greet* • Sylvia de Leur *Nel* • Piet Romer *Piet* • Bernhard Droog ■ *Dir* Paul Verhoeven • *Scr* Gerard Soeteman, from a book by Albert Mol

The Business of Strangers ★★★ 15

Drama 2001 · US · Colour · 80mins

Patrick Stettner's debut feature begins with a confidence that makes its descent into melodrama all the more disappointing. Sassy assistant Julia Stiles incessantly scrutinises the vulnerability beneath Stockard Channing's crisp professional demeanour, but her irresponsible duplicity, and the brutal treatment of smarmy headhunter Frederick Waller, upsets the delicate balance of this dark satire. Channing's multilayered performance proves that she's still one of the most under-rated actresses around. DP. Contains swearing, sex scenes. DVD

Stockard Channing *Julie Styron* • Julia Stiles *Paula Murphy* • Frederick Weller *Nick Harris* • Mary Testa *Receptionist* • Jack Hallett *Mr Fostwick* ■ *Dir/Scr* Patrick Stettner

Busman's Honeymoon ★★

Crime thriller 1940 · UK · BW · 98mins

Lord Peter Wimsey gets married and vows to drop all his detective work until a corpse appears in his honeymoon hideaway in Devon. It's based on the novel by Dorothy L Sayers and you can almost hear the stage boards creaking. However, Robert Montgomery and Constance Cummings, while the clear camerawork is by Freddie Young, who later won Oscars for *Lawrence of Arabia* and *Doctor Zhivago*. AT

Robert Montgomery *Lord Peter Wimsey* • Constance Cummings *Harriet Vane* • Leslie Banks *Inspector Kirk* • Seymour Hicks *Bunter* • Robert Newton *Frank Crutchley* • Googie Withers *Polly* • Frank Pettingell *Puffett* • Joan Kemp-Welch *Aggie Twitterton* ■ *Dir* Arthur B Woods • *Scr* Monckton Hoffe, Angus MacPhail, Harold Goldman, from the novel by Dorothy L Sayers

Buster ★★★ 15

Biographical crime drama
1988 · UK · Colour · 98mins

Phil Collins takes on his first lead movie role, playing Buster Edwards, one of the gang involved in the Great Train Robbery. Julie Walters plays his wife and they make the most of their roles as loveably cheeky Cockney sparrers chirruping away in Acapulco after fleeing London. *EastEnders*-style clichés fall as thick and fast as the pair's "aitches", and, while Collins does his best, it's Walters who scores as a woman missing the comforts of home. Too squeaky clean to be believable, this is a fairy-tale view of law-breaking. TH. Contains swearing, violence, nudity. DVD

Phil Collins *Buster Edwards* • Julie Walters *June Edwards* • Larry Lamb *Bruce Reynolds* • Stephanie Lawrence *Franny Reynolds* • Ellen Beaven *Nicky Edwards* • Michael Attwell *Harry* • Ralph Brown *Ronnie* • Christopher Ellison *George* • Sheila Hancock *Mrs Rothery* ■ *Dir* David Green • *Scr* Colin Shindler

Buster and Billie ★★★ 18

Period drama 1974 · US · Colour · 95mins

Rural Georgia in 1948, where local boys loaf about eying the girls and wonder how far they will go in a sexual relationship. The exception is Joan Goodfellow who lives in squalor on the other side of the tracks and entertains the boys at the drop of a hat. When Jan-Michael Vincent abandons his childhood sweetheart for her, things come to a head. The movie should have been a potboiler but it's a bit too well behaved, too self-consciously "literate" and too preoccupied with period trappings to be more than just absorbing. AT

Jan-Michael Vincent *Buster Lane* • Joan Goodfellow *Billie* • Pamela Sue Martin *Margie Hooks* • Clifton James *Jake* • Robert Englund *Whitey* • Jessie Lee Fulton *Mrs Lane* • JB Joiner *Mr Lane* • Dell C Payne *Warren* ■ *Dir* Daniel Petrie • *Scr* Ron Turbeville, from a story by Ron Baron, Ron Turbeville

The Buster Keaton Story ★ U

Biographical comedy drama
1957 · US · BW · 91mins

Blockbuster novelist Sidney Sheldon was responsible (as co-writer, co-producer and director) for this insult to the comic genius of the Great Stone Face. Even though Keaton himself supervised the re-created moments of peerless slapstick, he was so furious at the flagrant fictions littering the script that he almost walked out of the Hollywood premiere in disgust. Tacky and inaccurate. DP

Donald O'Connor *Buster Keaton* • Ann Blyth *Gloria* • Rhonda Fleming *Peggy Courtney* • Peter Lorre *Kurt Bergner* • Larry Keating *Larry Winters* • Richard Anderson *Tom McAffee* • Dave Willock *Joe Keaton* • Claire Carleton *Myrna Keaton* • Jackie Coogan *Elmer Case* • Cecil B DeMille ■ *Dir* Sidney Sheldon • *Scr* Sidney Sheldon, Robert Smith

Buster's World ★★★

Comedy drama 1984 · Den · Colour · 77mins

This charming rite-of-passage picture is considerably more personal than Bille August's more internationally acclaimed study of childhood, *Pelle the Conqueror*. Mads Bugge Andersen gives a wonderfully eccentric performance as the daydreaming pre-teen who uses his grandfather's magic kit not only to ward off the bullies who threaten his crippled sister, but also to further his chances with the poor little rich girl he meets at the fair. Clearly influenced by the likes of *Kes*, this is an astute blend of pathos and comedy. DP. In Danish with English subtitles.

Mads Bugge Andersen *Buster* • Katerina Stenbeck *Buster's sister* • Peter Schrøder *Father* • Kirsten Rolffes *Joanna's mother* • Berthe Qvistgaard *Mrs Larsen* • Buster Larsen *Shopkeeper* • Signe Dahl Madsen *Joanna* • Katja Miehe-Renard *Mother* ■ *Dir* Bille August • *Scr* Bjarne Reuther, from his novel

Bustin' Loose ★★★ 15

Comedy 1981 · US · Colour · 88mins

Richard Pryor wrote and co-produced this story of an ex-convict shepherding teacher Cicely Tyson and her class of maladjusted children to a rural retreat, revealing that sentiment was as much his line as deadpan wisecracks. The film took two years to complete, because it was interrupted by Pryor's near-fatal drug-related accident, and, as a result, theatre director Oz Scott, in his film debut, was left with insurmountable discrepancies in continuity. Despite a queasy mix of pratfalls and pathos, Pryor still comes across as hugely likeable. TH. Contains swearing and violence.

Richard Pryor *Joe Braxton* • Cicely Tyson *Vivian Perry* • Alphonso Alexander *Martin* • Kia Cooper *Samantha* • Edwin Deleon *Ernesto* • Jimmy Hughes *Harold* • Edwin Kinter *Anthony* ■ *Dir* Oz Scott • *Scr* Roger L Simon, Lonne Elder III, from a story by Richard Pryor

Busting ★★ 18

Crime drama 1974 · US · Colour · 87mins

An early attempt to show the Los Angeles police as corrupt, bureaucratic and just like any other government department. While Elliott Gould and Robert Blake are the vice detectives forced to crack down on minor drug dealers, top managers are taking payoffs from high ranking mobsters. Peter Hyams's direction bustles farcically to make its case that the LAPD is lapdog to the Syndicate, but it's too raucous to make the point at all coherently. TH

Elliott Gould *Michael Keneely* • Robert Blake *Patrick Farrell* • Allen Garfield *Carl Rizzo* • William Sylvester *Mr Weldman* • Logan Ramsey *Dr Berman* • Richard X Slattery *Desk sergeant* • John Lawrence *Sergeant Kenfick* ■ *Dir/Scr* Peter Hyams

The Busy Body ★★★

Black comedy 1967 · US · Colour · 101mins

This is a black comedy about Mafia folk and is based on the novel by Donald E Westlake, author of *Point Blank*. Sid Caesar is the Mafia employee suspected of stealing a bundle, Robert Ryan, always a joy to watch, is the *numero uno* mobster and there's rich support from Anne Baxter and Richard Pryor in his screen debut. Sloppy in places, this is nonetheless a delightful tongue-in-cheek piece for connoisseurs of the crime movie. AT

Sid Caesar *George Norton* • Robert Ryan *Charley Barker* • Anne Baxter *Margo Foster* • Kay Medford *Ma Norton* • Jan Murray *Murray Foster* • Richard Pryor *Whittaker* • Arlene Golonka *Bobbi Brody* • Dom DeLuise *Kurt Brock* ■ *Dir* William Castle • *Scr* Ben Starr, from the novel by Donald E Westlake

But I'm a Cheerleader ★★ 15

Satire 1999 · US · Colour · 88mins

This sugar-coated satire sacrifices the important points it makes regarding homophobia and prejudice for the sake of an easy gag. Teenager Natasha Lyonne is suspected of being a lesbian by her friends and family, so she's shipped off to a rehabilitation camp that promises to "cure" her sexual preference. But there she meets the sexy Clea DuVall. Lyonne is good value and drag artist RuPaul is fun as the butch camp counsellor whose job it is to straighten the kids out. However, the initial spoofing of gay culture soon loses its edge. AJ DVD

Natasha Lyonne *Megan Bloomfield* • Clea DuVall *Graham Eaton* • RuPaul Charles [RuPaul] *Mike* • Eddie Cibrian *Rock* • Bud Cort *Peter* • Melanie Lynskey *Hilary* • Mink Stole *Nancy Bloomfield* • Cathy Moriarty *Mary Brown* • Julie Delpy *Lipstick lesbian* ■ *Dir* Jamie Babbit • *Scr* Brian Wayne Peterson, from a story by Jamie Babbit

But Not for Me ★★★ U

Romantic comedy 1959 · US · BW · 104mins

Here Clark Gable stars as a fading theatre producer who almost succumbs to the charms and devotion of his new secretary (Carroll Baker). A pleasingly suitable vehicle for its ageing star, the film lacks effervescence, but Walter Lang directs with polish, while Lilli Palmer is ideal as the woman who boxes more to Gable's weight. RK

Clark Gable *Russell Ward* • Carroll Baker *Eleanor Brown* • Lilli Palmer *Kathryn Ward* • Lee J Cobb *Jeremiah MacDonald* • Barry Coe *Gordon Reynolds* • Thomas Gomez *Demetrios Bacos* • Charles Lane (2) *Atwood* • Wendell Holmes *Montgomery* ■ *Dir* Walter Lang • *Scr* John Michael Hayes, from the play *Accent on Youth* by Samson Raphaelson

Butch and Sundance: the Early Days ★★★ PG

Comedy western
1979 · US · Colour · 106mins

Completely inconsequential when measured against its phenomenally successful progenitor, this fictional version of the early outlaw careers of Butch Cassidy and the Sundance Kid is still an enjoyable romp. William Katt and Tom Berenger emit oodles of charm as the cowboy heroes' younger selves, and director Richard Lester laces the ambitious material with the same wit and irony he brought to *The Three Musketeers*. AJ

William Katt *Sundance Kid* • Tom Berenger *Butch Cassidy* • Jeff Corey *Sheriff Ray Bledsoe* • John Schuck *Harvey Logan* • Michael C Gwynne *Mike Cassidy* • Peter Weller *Joe LeFors* • Brian Dennehy *OC Hanks* • Chris Lloyd [Christopher Lloyd] *Bill Carver* ■ *Dir* Richard Lester • *Scr* Allan Burns

Butch Cassidy and the Sundance Kid ★★★★★ PG

Western comedy drama
1969 · US · Colour · 105mins

This freewheeling adventure was made in a vintage year for the western, with *The Wild Bunch* and *True Grit* joining it among the releases, and in many ways it's the western's answer to *Bonnie and Clyde*. George Roy Hill's film was one of the biggest box-office hits in the genre's history. Some of the credit must go to the Oscar-winning trio of William Goldman, Conrad Hall and Burt Bacharach for the witty script, luminous photography and jaunty score respectively. But the true charm of this ever-popular picture lies in the exhilarating performances of Paul Newman and Robert Redford, who turn the ruthless desperados of fact into lovable rogues and, ultimately, tragic heroes. DP. Contains violence. DVD

Paul Newman *Butch Cassidy* • Robert Redford *Sundance Kid* • Katharine Ross *Etta Place* • Strother Martin *Percy Garris* • Henry Jones *Bike salesman* • Jeff Corey *Sheriff Bledsoe* • George Furth *Woodcock* • Cloris Leachman *Agnes* • Ted Cassidy *Harvey Logan* ■ *Dir* George Roy Hill • *Scr* William Goldman

The Butcher Boy ★★★★

Silent comedy 1917 · US · BW · 30mins

Although the career of silent film comedian Roscoe "Fatty" Arbuckle was to end in scandal, this shows just how deft and delicate he could be in fast-moving farce. It's a simple-minded tale of love among the meat-hooks, the first of the Comique films he signed up for with Paramount's Joseph Schenck. The occasional vulgarity of his Keystone movies was left behind and, generously, he gave a first chance to one of his vaudeville friends whose routine with a coin and molasses in the film almost upstaged "Fatty" himself. The friend? Buster Keaton, who supported Arbuckle after scandal had ruined his career. TH

Roscoe "Fatty" Arbuckle *Butcher boy* • Buster Keaton *Customer* • Al St John *Rival* • Josephine Stevens *Proprietor's daughter/Pupil at girls' boarding school* ■ *Dir* Roscoe "Fatty" Arbuckle • *Scr* Roscoe "Fatty" Arbuckle, from a story by Joe Roach [Joseph Anthony Roach]

The Butcher Boy ★★★★ 15

Black comedy drama
1997 · Ire/US · Colour · 105mins

Novelist Patrick McCabe's portrait of small-town Irish life in the 1960s is viewed through dark-tinted glasses in this shocking, often surreal adaptation by Neil Jordan. Armed only with comics, movies and visions of the Virgin Mary (Sinead O'Connor), Eamonn Owens excels as the breezy teenager whose grip on reality begins to loosen as he returns from a pitiless Catholic remand home to witness the descent of father Stephen Rea into alcoholism and mother Aisling O'Sullivan into madness. DP. Contains swearing, violence and sexual references.

Stephen Rea *Da Brady* • Fiona Shaw *Mrs Nugent* • Eamonn Owens *Francie Brady* • Ian Hart *Uncle Alo* • Aisling O'Sullivan *Ma Brady* • Sinead O'Connor *Our Lady/Colleen* • Ardal O'Hanlon *Mr Purcell* • Milo O'Shea *Father Sullivan* ■ *Dir* Neil Jordan • *Scr* Neil Jordan, Patrick McCabe, from the novel by Patrick McCabe

B

The Butcher's Wife ★★★ 15

Romantic comedy
1991 · US · Colour · 104mins

In this quirky but quiet romantic comedy, Demi Moore plays a blonde psychic who cheerfully tries to sort out the lives of her lonely neighbours in New York, who include besotted Jeff Daniels, Mary Steenburgen and Frances McDormand. Director Terry Hughes succeeds in conjuring up a bittersweet, magical atmosphere which is rarely cloying, and he is well served by a talented cast. JF. Contains some swearing. VIDEO DVD

Demi Moore *Marina* • Jeff Daniels *Alex* • George Dzundza *Leo* • Mary Steenburgen *Stella* • Frances McDormand *Grace* • Margaret Colin *Robyn* • Max Perlich *Eugene* • Miriam Margolyes *Gina* ■ *Dir* Terry Hughes • *Scr* Ezra Litwak, Marjorie Schwartz

Butley ★★★ 15

Drama 1973 · UK · Colour · 123mins

A tour de force for Alan Bates in a filmed play – made for the American Film Theatre – of Simon Gray's drama about an academic whose wit and know-all attitude lacerates those around him. In the end, though, his self-destructiveness hurts no one but himself. Playwright Harold Pinter directs with a laconic style that has little to do with cinema. TH DVD

Alan Bates *Ben Butley* • Jessica Tandy *Edna Shaft* • Richard O'Callaghan *Joey Keyston* • Susan Engel *Anne Butley* • Michael Byrne *Reg Nuttall* • Georgina Hale *Miss Heasman* ■ *Dir* Harold Pinter • *Scr* Simon Gray, from his play

The Butter Cream Gang ★★

Drama 1991 · US · Colour · 93mins

The titular gang consists of four boys, so full of sunshine and charity that their home town of Upbridge just adores them. But when one of them moves to Chicago, the Windy City proves to be a bad influence and, instead of helping old ladies up the stairs, he'd rather push them down. When he goes back to Upbridge and forms a new gang of yobs, the three he left behind take action. Despite being moral and upright, the tale itself is very mediocre. AT

Jason Johnson *Scott* • Michael D Weatherred *Pete* • Brandon Blaser *Eldon* • Jason Glenn *Larry* • Michael Scott *Reverend Wilde/Coach* • Stephanie Dees *Margaret* ■ *Dir* Bruce Neibaur • *Scr* Forrest S Baker III

Butterbox Babies ★★★ 15

Drama based on a true story
1995 · Can · Colour · 94mins

A well-made and interesting TV drama based on the true story of Lila and William Young, who ran a maternity home and adoption service in Nova Scotia during the Depression. Portrayed as a haven for unmarried mothers to be, it was actually a front for illegal adoptions, and many of the babies died in mysterious circumstances and were buried in boxes from the local creamery in the garden of the home. Stars Susan Clark, Peter MacNeill and Michael Riley manage to portray events with the minimum of hysteria, never lapsing into melodrama. JB VIDEO DVD

Susan Clark *Lila Young* • Peter MacNeill *William Young* • Catherine Fitch *Iris* • Michael Riley *Russell Cameron* • Shannon Lawson *Nurse Ann O'Dwyer* • Nicholas Campbell *Clayton Oliver* • Corinne Conley *Mrs Chadway* • Cedric Smith *Dr Frank Davis* ■ *Dir* Don McBrearty • *Scr* Raymond Storey, from the book by Bette Cahill

The Buttercup Chain ★

Drama 1970 · UK · Colour · 94mins

Filled with the psycho-sexual babble of the Swinging Sixties, this awful movie has Hywel Bennett as the founder member of a group of four inseparable friends who swap partners, generally relate to each other and are clearly destined for an unhappy ending. Bennett is sullen throughout while Jane Asher and Leigh Taylor-Young model some short skirts as the story flits around Europe. AT

Hywel Bennett *France* • Leigh Taylor-Young *Manny* • Jane Asher *Margaret* • Sven-Bertil Taube *Fred* • Clive Revill *George* • Roy Dotrice *Martin Carr-Gibbons* • Michael Elphick *Chauffeur* ■ *Dir* Robert Ellis Miller • *Scr* Peter Draper, from a novel by Janice Elliott

Butterfield 8 ★★★ 15

Drama 1960 · US · Colour · 108mins

Elizabeth Taylor's Oscar-winning performance as an up-market whore with a heart is the chief interest of this otherwise weak and dated drama. The film's attitude to sex was controversial on its release in 1960, but it is tepid stuff today. Eddie Fisher, Taylor's husband at the time, fails to convince as the call girl's long-time friend, while Laurence Harvey looks uncomfortable as the married man with whom she has a passionate affair. PF VIDEO

Elizabeth Taylor *Gloria Wandrous* • Laurence Harvey *Weston Liggett* • Eddie Fisher *Steve Carpenter* • Dina Merrill *Emily Liggett* • Mildred Dunnock *Mrs Wandrous* • Betty Field *Mrs Fanny Thurber* • Jeffrey Lynn *Bingham Smith* ■ *Dir* Daniel Mann • *Scr* Charles Schnee, John Michael Hayes, from the novel by John O'Hara

Butterflies Are Free ★★ PG

Drama 1972 · US · Colour · 104mins

Eileen Heckart won a best supporting actress Oscar for her role as blind Edward Albert's possessive mother, trying to protect her son from the advances of free spirit Goldie Hawn. Unfortunately, this often laughably corny product of the flower power era hasn't dated well, but it may offer some nostalgic pleasure for those old enough to remember. AT. Contains some swearing. VIDEO

Goldie Hawn *Jill* • Edward Albert *Don Baker* • Eileen Heckart *Mrs Baker* • Michael Glasser *Ralph* • Mike Warren [Michael Warren] *Roy* ■ *Dir* Milton Katselas • *Scr* Leonard Gershe, from his play

Butterfly ★★ 18

Drama 1982 · US · Colour · 103mins

James M Cain's tough and complex crime novel about silver mines, incest and murder becomes a patience-testing sexploitation thriller thanks to Matt Cimber's soft-focus direction and a mind-numbing, Lolita-style performance from low-rent starlet Pia Zadora. Stacy Keach plays Zadora's long-lost father who succumbs to her feminine wiles and ore-stripping scam. Orson Welles cameos as a lecherous judge, while Ennio Morricone supplies the music. Too awful to be taken seriously, yet too camp to miss. AJ VIDEO

Stacy Keach *Jeff Tyler* • Pia Zadora *Kady* • Orson Welles *Judge Rauch* • Lois Nettleton *Belle Morgan* • Edward Albert *Wash Gillespie* • James Franciscus *Moke Blue* • Stuart Whitman *Rev Rivers* • Ed McMahon *Mr Gillespie* ■ *Dir* Matt Cimber • *Scr* Matt Cimber, John Goff, from the novel by James M Cain

The Butterfly Effect ★★★ 15

Comedy 1995 · Sp/Fr/UK · Colour · 108mins

Using chaos theory as the pretext for setting in motion a domino run of coincidences and catastrophes, this cleverly constructed comedy touches on everything from machismo and European unity to incest and *Star Trek*. Director Fernando Colomo expertly picks his way through the maze of tangled relationships that forms after Coque Malla's mother sends him to London to learn about life. Debunking cultural stereotypes at every plot turn, the film even has sufficient courage of its comic convictions to attempt an audacious socio-political finale. DP. In Spanish with English subtitles.

Maria Barranco *Olivia* • Coque Malla *Luis* • Rosa Maria Sarda *Noelia* • James Fleet *Oswald* • Peter Sullivan *Duncan* • Cécile Pallas *Chantal* • José Maria Pou *Rafa* • John Faal *Nick* ■ *Dir* Fernando Colomo • *Scr* Joaquín Oristrell, Fernando Colomo

The Butterfly Effect ★★★ 15

Supernatural thriller
2003 · US/Can · Colour · 108mins

Ashton Kutcher stars in this ambitious film based on the idea of chaos theory, which speculates that the smallest of events can have the hugest of consequences. Kutcher plays a troubled college student who discovers he has the ability to go back in time and re-write the past. Touching on provocative themes such as child abuse, disability and terminal illness, J Mackye Gruber and Eric Bress have created a powerful and disturbing tale. It's spoilt by a rushed and overly simplistic conclusion, but both Kutcher and Eric Stoltz deliver strong performances. SF. Contains swearing and violence. DVD

Ashton Kutcher *Evan Treborn* • Amy Smart *Kayleigh Miller* • Eric Stoltz *George Miller* • William Lee Scott *Tommy Miller* • Elden Henson *Lenny Kagan* • Ethan Suplee *Thumper* • Melora Walters *Andrea Treborn* • Callum Keith Rennie *Jason Treborn* ■ *Dir/Scr* Eric Bress, J Mackye Gruber

Butterfly Kiss ★★ 18

Drama 1994 · UK · Colour and BW · 87mins

Thelma and Louise meets *The Silence of the Lambs* in this weird British road movie that stars Amanda Plummer as a lesbian serial killer and Saskia Reeves as her willing associate. It's narrated by Reeves, who plays the extremely dense shop assistant picked up by punkette Plummer at a service station. Instead of being shockingly original, it's merely drab and depressing. AT. Contains violence, swearing, sex scenes and nudity. VIDEO

Amanda Plummer *Eunice* • Saskia Reeves *Miriam* • Ricky Tomlinson *Robert* • Des McAleer *Eric* • Paul Bown *Gary* • Freda Dowie *Elsie* • Fine Time Fontayne *Tony* ■ *Dir* Michael Winterbottom • *Scr* Frank Cottrell Boyce, from an idea by Frank Cottrell Boyce, Michael Winterbottom

Butterfly Man ★★ 15

Romantic drama
2002 · UK/Thai · Colour · 91mins

A laudable motive and some glorious scenery are not enough to distract from the clichés and caricatures that blight this mediocre exposé of the seedy underside of Thai tourism. The drama gets off to a shaky start with British backpacker Stuart Laing's contrived Bangkok break-up with sulky girlfriend Kirsty Mitchell. Things improve marginally when Laing embarks on a romance with Thai masseuse Napakpapha Nakprasitte, but the action lurches back to lumpen melodrama when penury drives him into the clutches of a gang of human traffickers. DP VIDEO DVD

Stuart Laing *Adam* • Napakpapha "Mamee" Nakprasitte *Em* • Francis Magee *Joey* • Gavan O'Herlihy *Bill Kincaid* • Vasa Vatcharayon *Noi* • Abigail Good *No Name* • Kirsty Mitchell *Kate* ■ *Dir/Scr* Kaprice Kea

The Butterfly Murders ★★★

Martial arts mystery horror
1979 · HK · Colour · 88mins

Tsui Hark made his directorial debut with this eerie hybrid of the horror and swordplay genres. Edgar Allan Poe's *The Masque of the Red Death* is the clear inspiration for this elaborate tale of killer butterflies, hidden identities and fantastical contraptions. By reinforcing the claustrophobic atmosphere of the labyrinthine castle setting, Fan Jinyu's photography makes the explosive action all the more dynamic and ethereal as warrior/scholar Liu Zhaoming seeks to eradicate the lepidopteran peril. DP. In Cantonese with English subtitles.

Liu Zhaoming *Fang Hongye* • Michelle Mee *Green Shadow* • Huang Shutang *Tian Feng* • Zhang Guozhu *Shen Qing* • Chen Qiqi *Lady Shen* • Wang Jiang *Li "The Thousand Hands"* • Gao Ziong *Guo "The Magic Fire"* • Xu Xiaoling *Ah Zhi* • Xia Jiangli *Number 10 of the Red Flags* ■ *Dir* Tsui Hark • *Scr* Lin Fan

Butterfly's Tongue ★★★ 15

Period drama 1999 · Sp · Colour · 95mins

Lushly photographed and indulgently nostalgic, José Luis Cuerda's pre-Spanish Civil War drama has an anecdotal structure and a surface charm that barely suggest the political torrent raging beneath. However, such a disarmingly genial approach suits Cuerda's intention of exploring the cruel irrationality and agonising consequences of dogmatic strife. As the maverick schoolteacher, Fernando Fernán Gómez exudes the wisdom and humanity that charms young Manuel Lozano, an adorable yet potentially dangerous bundle of curiosity. DP. In Spanish with English subtitles. Contains a sex scene.

Fernando Fernán Gómez *Don Gregorio* • Manuel Lozano *Moncho* • Uxía Blanco *Rosa* ■ *Dir* José Luis Cuerda • *Scr* Rafael Azcona, from a stories by Manuel Riva

Buttoners ★★★★

Portmanteau drama
1997 · Cz Rep · Colour · 108mins

Although this ingeniously structured portmanteau picture often recalls the surrealist antics of Luis Buñuel, Petr Zelenka's astute mix of satire, science fiction and historical supposition owes more to the eccentric strain of Czech comedy that also inspires the likes of Jan Svankmajer. Starting with the atomic assault on Hiroshima, Zelenka relates six stories which gradually link together to form a mischievous thesis on the role of chance, coincidence, fate and forgiveness in everyday life. This is a gleefully quirky and superbly controlled film. DP. In Czech with English subtitles.

Pavel Zajicek *Radio 1 moderator* • Jan Haubert *Guest* • Seisuke Tsukahara *Japanese man with spectacles* • Frantisek Cerny *Franta, taxi driver* • Vladimir Dlouhy *Psychiatrist* • Jiri Kodet *Honza, host* • Rudolf Hrusinsky Jr *Unsuccessful man* • Mariana Stojlovova *Girl at seance* ■ *Dir/Scr* Petr Zelenka

Buy & Cell ★★ 15

Comedy 1988 · US · Colour · 92mins

Filmed at the height of Wall Street's insider trading crisis, this slight comedy stars Robert Carradine as the naive stockbroker taking the rap for his crooked boss with Malcolm McDowell as the disreputable prison warden. Although the latter has his moments, a good idea has been frittered away by a lacklustre script. Consequently, the satire is slapdash and the inmates are uninspired stereotypes. DP. Contains swearing. VIDEO

Malcolm McDowell *Warden Tennant* • Robert Carradine *Herbie Altman* • Michael Winslow *Sly* • Randall "Tex" Cobb *Wolf* • Ben Vereen *Shaka* • Lise Cutter *Dr Ellen Scott* ■ *Dir* Robert Boris • *Scr* Neal Israel, Larry Siegel

Buying the Cow ★ 15

Romantic comedy
2000 · US · Colour · 84mins

A decent 30-something cast is laid low in this head-on collision between a romantic comedy and a gross-out farce. Given two months by longtime girlfriend Bridgette Wilson to rid himself of his "why buy the cow when you can get the milk for free" mentality, slacker Jerry O'Connell goes on a bender with buddies Ryan Reynolds and Bill Bellamy. Puerile, offensive and unfunny. DP DVD

Jerry O'Connell *David Collins* • Bridgette L Wilson [Bridgette Wilson] *Sarah* • Ryan Reynolds *Mike* • Bill Bellamy *Jonesy* • Alyssa Milano *Amy* • Jon Tenney *Andrew Hahn* • Annabeth Gish *Nicole* ■ *Dir* Walt Becker • *Scr* Walt Becker, Peter Nelson

Bwana Devil ★

Action adventure 1952 · US · Colour · 79mins

The film that launched the 3-D craze of the 1950s with its slogan "A lion in your lap! A lover in your arms!" did record business as a novelty attraction. However, writer/producer/ director Arch Oboler's film was so flat dramatically that it saddled the stereoscopic process with the reputation of being all gimmick. The substandard colour certainly didn't help, either. AE

Robert Stack *Bob Hayward* • Barbara Britton *Alice Hayward* • Nigel Bruce *Dr Angus Ross* • Ramsay Hill *Maj Parkhurst* • Paul McVey *Commissioner* • Hope Miller *Portuguese girl* ■ *Dir/Scr* Arch Oboler

By Candlelight ★★★

Romantic comedy 1934 · US · BW · 70mins

During a European train journey, a nobleman's manservant (Paul Lukas) is mistaken for his employer (Nils Asther) by a lovely woman (Elissa Landi) and he does nothing to disillusion her. In due course, the nobleman turns up and is taken for his servant. Universal Studios' James Whale, the star director of its famous horror cycle, trespasses here on territory more generally associated with Paramount and Ernst Lubitsch. While not quite up to the rival studio's standard of sophisticated romantic comedies peopled by aristocrats, this is a more than respectably assembled film, well directed and well acted, particularly by Lukas. RK

Elissa Landi *Marie* • Paul Lukas *Josef* • Nils Asther *Count von Bommer* • Dorothy Revier *Countess von Rischenheim* • Lawrence Grant *Count von Rischenheim* • Esther Ralston *Baroness von Ballin* • Warburton Gamble *Baron von Ballin* • Lois January *Ann* ■ *Dir* James Whale • *Scr* Hans Kräly, F Hugh Herbert, Karen De Wolf, Ruth Cummings, from the play *Candlelight* by Siegfried Geyer

By Love Possessed ★★★★

Romantic drama
1961 · US · Colour · 115mins

Meriting four stars for excess rather than consistent quality, this heavenly example of the sleazy, lurid and luxurious finds the gorgeous Lana Turner saddled with an impotent husband (Jason Robards) and an opulent wardrobe of designer gowns. So she drowns her sorrows in drink, riding and the willing arms of Efrem Zimbalist Jr. Her lover's father-in-law (Thomas Mitchell) is an embezzler, while his son (George Hamilton) is up on a rape charge. And that's just for starters! The only normal person in director John Sturges's cast of characters is Barbara Bel Geddes as Zimbalist's estranged wife. RK

Lana Turner *Marjorie Penrose* • Efrem Zimbalist Jr *Arthur Winner* • Jason Robards Jr [Jason Robards] *Julius Penrose* • George Hamilton *Warren Winner* • Susan Kohner *Helen Detweiler* • Barbara Bel Geddes *Clarissa Winner* • Thomas Mitchell *Noah Tuttle* • Everett Sloane *Reggie* • Yvonne Craig *Veronica Kovacs* • Carroll O'Connor *Bernie Breck* ■ *Dir* John Sturges • *Scr* John Dennis [Charles Schnee], Isobel Lennart, William Roberts, Ketti Frings, from the novel *By Love Possessed* by James Gould Cozzens • *Costume Designer* Bill Thomas

By the Law ★★★★

Silent drama 1926 · USSR · BW · 83mins

This Alaskan-based drama remains the least expensive feature ever produced in Russia. Working on a single set erected in the studio courtyard, Lev Kuleshov choreographed each expression and gesture to attain maximum dramatic effect and intensity of performance. The director's wife, Alexandra Khokhlova, excels as the gold prospector's wife who insists that avaricious Irishman Sergei Komarov is tried according to the law for the murder of his companions. A masterly experiment in silent stylisation. DP

Alexandra Khokhlova *Edith* • Sergei Komarov *Hans* • Vladimir Fogel *Michael* ■ *Dir* Lev Kuleshov • *Scr* Lev Kuleshov, Viktor Shklovsky, from the story *The Unexpected* by Jack London

By the Light of the Silvery Moon ★★★ U

Musical comedy 1953 · US · Colour · 101mins

Following the success of *On Moonlight Bay*, Warners Bros brought back its top songbird, the fabulous Doris Day (her hair a slightly blonder shade), and her sweetheart Gordon MacRae for this sequel in which they cope with life in the 1920s. The Technicolor styling is superb, the treatment of the old songs enchanting and veterans Ames and, particularly, Mary Wickes as the maid are fun to watch. But it's the combination of Day and MacRae that is irresistible, a couple who manage to convey the pleasure of their work to an audience. TS

Doris Day *Marjorie Winfield* • Gordon MacRae *William Sherman* • Leon Ames *George Winfield* • Rosemary DeCamp *Mrs Winfield* • Billy Gray *Wesley* • Mary Wickes *Stella* • Russell Arms *Chester Finley* • Maria Palmer *Miss LaRue* ■ *Dir* David Butler • *Scr* Robert O'Brien, Irving Elinson, from the *Penrod*,*stories by Booth Tarkington*

By the Sword ★★ 15

Sports drama
1992 · US · Colour and BW · 87mins

This made-for-TV fencing movie has two teachers clashing on the honourable way of fighting: F Murray Abraham is the mysterious elderly pupil who turns up at the school run by undefeated Olympic champion Eric Roberts and the two are soon locked in a personal battle. The plotting is confused and Roberts is over the top. JF. Contains swearing.

F Murray Abraham *Max Suba* • Eric Roberts *Alexander Villard* • Mia Sara *Erin Clavelli* • Christopher Rydell *Jimmy Trebor* • Elaine Kagan *Rachel* • Brett Cullen *Danny Gallagher* • Doug Wert *Hobbs* • Stoney Jackson *Johnson* • Caroline Barclay *Tatiana* ■ *Dir* Jeremy Kagan [Jeremy Paul Kagan] • *Scr* John McDonald, James Donadio

Bye Bye Birdie ★★★★ U

Musical comedy 1963 · US · Colour · 110mins

A wonderfully energetic and colourful adaptation of the smash Broadway hit, satirising the traumatic induction of one Elvis Presley into the US Army. Named Conrad Birdie here (a reference to contemporary rock 'n' roll star Conway Twitty), this focuses on the legendary rocker bestowing "one last kiss" on a small-town girl – a gimmick started by the star's promoter, played by Dick Van Dyke re-creating his Broadway role. It's splendid stuff and, although the satire has dated, the sheer exuberance of veteran director George Sidney's guiding hand endures, as does the talent of vivacious Ann-Margret. There are lots of laughs along the way, especially from stage star Paul Lynde. Remade (badly) for television in 1995. TS

Janet Leigh *Rosie DeLeon* • Dick Van Dyke *Albert Peterson* • Ann-Margret *Kim McAfee* • Maureen Stapleton *Mama* • Bobby Rydell *Hugo Peabody* • Jesse Pearson *Conrad Birdie* • Ed Sullivan • Paul Lynde *Mr McAfee* ■ *Dir* George Sidney (2) • *Scr* Irving Brecher, from the musical comedy by Michael Stewart, with music and lyrics by Charles Strouse, Lee Adams

Bye Bye Blues ★★★ PG

Romantic drama
1989 · Can · Colour · 116mins

Post-Second World War cinema was so intent on telling tales of male heroism or sympathising with the problems of returning veterans that it completely ignored the dilemmas facing women who had spread their wings while their men were away fighting. Based on the experiences of director Anne Wheeler's own mother, this tear-jerker shows just how much of an upheaval the war was for women. Helped by a nostalgic dance band soundtrack, this is warm, wise and beautifully acted. DP. Contains brief nudity.

Rebecca Jenkins *Daisy Cooper* • Luke Reilly *Max Gramley* • Michael Ontkean *Teddy Cooper* • Stuart Margolin *Slim Godfrey* • Wayne Robson *Pete* • Robyn Stevan *Frances Cooper* • Leon Pownall *Bernie Blitzer* • Sheila Moore *Doreen Cooper* ■ *Dir/Scr* Anne Wheeler

Bye Bye Braverman ★★★★

Comedy drama 1968 · US · Colour · 94mins

This wickedly acerbic midlife crisis comedy anticipates *The Big Chill* in plot and theme, as a group of New York intellectuals mourn a deceased childhood friend and reflect on the state of their own lives on the way to his funeral. Brilliantly acted by a cast headed by George Segal and *Dr No*'s Joseph Wiseman, with comedian Alan King superb as a rabbi, this deserves to be better known, though its mordant theme almost certainly restricted its initial theatrical release. Director Sidney Lumet is not usually recognised for lightness of touch, but acquits himself extremely well here. TS

George Segal *Morroe Rieff* • Jack Warden *Barnet Weiner* • Joseph Wiseman *Felix Ottensteen* • Sorrell Booke *Holly Levine* • Jessica Walter *Inez Braverman* • Phyllis Newman *Myra Mandelbaum* • Zohra Lampert *Etta Rieff* • Godfrey Cambridge *Taxicab driver* • Alan King *Rabbi* ■ *Dir* Sidney Lumet • *Scr* Herbert Sargent, from the novel *To an Early Grave* by Wallace Markfield

Bye Bye Brazil ★★★

Adventure drama
1979 · Bra/Fr · Colour · 100mins

It's hard to imagine a more flamboyant picture with such a downbeat message. Traipsing through northern Brazil, magician Jose Wilker, dancer Betty Faria and strongman Fabio Junior become increasingly despondent. Not only has their brand of live entertainment gone out of fashion, they are also appalled at how traditional lifestyles have been corroded by the incursion of social and consumerist "progress". Making telling use of colour and the Amazonian landscapes, this is a lively and poignant film. DP. In Portuguese with English subtitles.

Betty Faria *Salome* • José Wilker *Lorde Cigano* • Fabio Junior *Cico* • Zaira Zambelli *Dasdo* • Principe Nabor *Swallow* ■ *Dir/Scr* Carlos Diegues

Bye Bye Love ★★ 12

Comedy 1995 · US · Colour · 101mins

Some ghastly slapstick and several clumsy social situations ruin any chance this smarmy comedy has of success. The premise of showing how three divorced fathers cope with life after marriage is essentially a sound one, but not only is the screenplay littered with lines begging to be cut, but director Sam Weisman also has a forte for playing each scene at precisely the wrong pace. Matthew Modine escapes relatively unscathed, but Randy Quaid comes off badly during his encounter with daunting date Janeane Garofalo. DP. Contains some swearing and sexual references.

Matthew Modine *Dave* • Randy Quaid *Vic* • Paul Reiser *Donny* • Janeane Garofalo *Lucille* • Amy Brenneman *Susan* • Eliza Dushku *Emma* • Ed Flanders *Walter* • Maria Pitillo *Kim* • Lindsay Crouse *Grace* • Rob Reiner *Dr Townsend* ■ *Dir* Sam Weisman • *Scr* Gary David Goldberg, Brad Hall

Bye Bye Monkey ★★★

Black comedy drama
1978 · It/Fr · Colour · 114mins

Euro director Marco Ferreri, who had an international hit with *La Grande Bouffe*, made this fable in New York with rising star Gérard Depardieu and old master Marcello Mastroianni. Depardieu keeps a pet chimpanzee and is an electrician in a radical theatre where he's raped; Mastroianni is an asthmatic eccentric who lives in a rat-infested hovel and is on the verge of suicide. Praised at Cannes but barely released, this follows the descent of man from ape to human, from tenderness into barbarism among the rotting skyscrapers of Manhattan. Mastroianni rated his performance among his best. AT. Contains violence, nudity, sexual situations and swearing.

Gérard Depardieu *Gérard Lafayette* • Marcello Mastroianni *Luigi Nocello* • James Coco *Andreas Flaxman* • Gail Lawrence *Angelica* • Geraldine Fitzgerald *Toland* • Avon Long *Miko* ■ *Dir* Marco Ferreri • *Scr* Marco Ferreri, Gérard Brach, Rafael Azcona

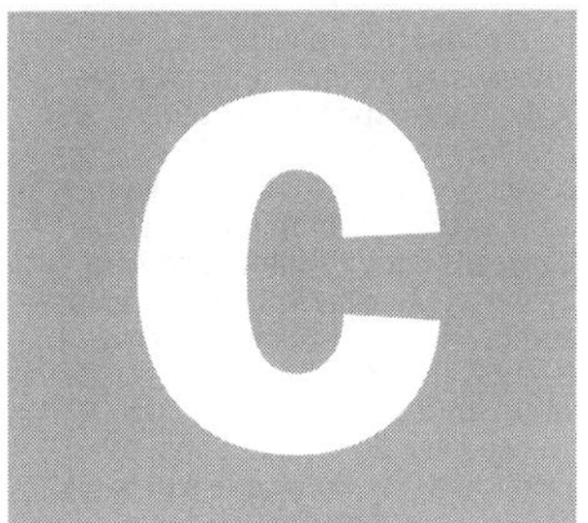

CB4 ★★★ 18

Satire 1993 · US · Colour · 84mins

Although this comedy lacks cohesion and feels like a series of loosely-linked sketches, it takes several well-aimed pot shots at both gangsta rap and the culture that engendered it. Surprisingly, considering it was directed by a woman, it somewhat ducks the issue of sexism, but Chris Rock and his rappers clearly have a ball. DP. Contains swearing, sex scenes and drug abuse, nudity. [VIDEO]

Chris Rock *Albert* • Allen Payne *Euripides* • Deezer D *Otis* • Chris Elliott *A White* • Phil Hartman *Virgil Robinson* • Charlie Murphy *Gusto* • Ice-T • Ice Cube • Flavor Flav • Shaquille O'Neal ■ *Dir* Tamra Davis • *Scr* Chris Rock, Nelson George, Robert LoCash, from a story by Chris Rock, Nelson George

CIA – Codename Alexa ★★ 18

Action thriller 1992 · US · Colour · 94mins

This is a by-the-numbers affair which grafts some sci-fi elements on to a fairly standard action plot. Kathleen Kinmont is the terrorist courted by moody CIA agent Lorenzo Lamas, who wants her to betray crime boss Alex Cord. Director Joseph Merhi makes sure all the ingredients for a straight-to-video success are present and correct, though mainstream film fans won't be impressed. JF [VIDEO] DVD

Lorenzo Lamas *Mark Graver* • Kathleen Kinmont *Alexa* • Alex Cord *Victor Mahler* • OJ Simpson *Nick Murphy* ■ *Dir* Joseph Merhi • *Scr* John Weidner, Ken Lamplugh

Ca Commence Aujourd'hui ★★★★ 12

Drama 1999 · Fr · Colour · 118mins

The winner of the international critics prize at Berlin, this film recalls the fluid starkness of Bertrand Tavernier's police thriller *L.627*, as the camera restlessly prowls headmaster Philippe Torreton's school to witness how his staff make light of financial constraints to fascinate and protect their pupils. Whether challenging an abusive "uncle", encouraging youngsters or lambasting the mayor, Torreton is outstanding in his energy and insight. Apart from the disappointingly cosy and optimistic conclusion, this is social drama at its best. DP. In French with English subtitles. [VIDEO]

Philippe Torreton *Daniel Lefebvre* • Maria Pitarresi *Valéria* • Nadia Kaci *Samia Damouni* • Véronique Ataly *Madame Liénard* ■ *Dir* Bertrand Tavernier • *Scr* Dominique Sampiero, Tiffany Tavernier, Bertrand Tavernier

Cabaret ★★★★★ 15

Musical drama 1972 · US · Colour · 118mins

This is a tremendously effective and affecting adult musical version of writer Christopher Isherwood's Berlin memoirs. The tale is transformed here through the Oscar-winning magic of director Bob Fosse (replacing first choice Gene Kelly) and star Liza Minnelli into a lasting screen classic, sparing no punches as it depicts the rise of Hitler and the spread of anti-Semitism through the twilight world of the Berlin cabaret. As the emcee of the Kit-Kat club, Joel Grey positively exudes decadence, and also collected one of the movie's eight Oscars. Fosse achieves several compelling cinematic moments, notably a chilling crescendo of emotion as a young Nazi sings Kander and Ebb's hymn-like *Tomorrow Belongs to Me*. If brash Minnelli seems a mite too talented for the Sally Bowles character, it really doesn't matter: she is, quite simply, magnificent in this role. TS [VIDEO] DVD

Liza Minnelli *Sally Bowles* • Joel Grey *Master of Ceremonies* • Michael York *Brian Roberts* • Helmut Griem *Maximilian von Heune* • Fritz Wepper *Fritz Wendel* • Marisa Berenson *Natalia Landauer* ■ *Dir* Bob Fosse • *Scr* Jay Presson Allen, from the musical by Joe Masteroff, from the play *I Am a Camera* by John Van Druten, from the short story collection *Goodbye to Berlin* by Christopher Isherwood • *Choreography* Bob Fosse • *Cinematographer* Geoffrey Unsworth • *Music* Ralph Burnes • *Editor* David Bretherton • *Art Director* Rolf Zehetbauer, Jurgen Kiebach

Cabaret Balkan ★★★ 18

Black comedy drama
1998 · Gr/Mac/Yug · Colour · 98mins

Darkly comic, this is a sobering portrait of a population perched on a powder keg. Expertly interweaving the various vignettes that invariably start with a minor indiscretion and escalate into an act of pitiless violence, this is a highly cinematic experience that is both intellectually and emotionally exhausting. Each superbly played character is deftly sketched, each incident provides a chilling insight into how civil war, corruption and propaganda could turn a civilised city like Belgrade into a simmering cauldron of hatred and fear. Made with additional funding from France, Germany and Turkey. DP. In Serbo-Croat with English subtitles. [VIDEO]

Miki Manojlovic *Michael, the homecoming man* • Sergej Trifunovic *Young man chewing gum who takes the bus hostage* • Mirjana Jokovic *Ana, the flirt on the bus* • Lazar Ristovski *The boxer who takes the train* • Mira Banjac *Bosnia-Serb mother* • Ivan Bekjarev *Man on the bus who thinks he's tough* • Aleksandar Bercek *Dimitri, the crippled ex-cop from the local café* • Vojislav Brajovic *Topi, the ex-student revolutionary trafficker* ■ *Dir* Goran Paskaljevic • *Scr* Goran Paskaljevic, Zoran Andric, Filip David, from the play *Bure Baruta* by Dejan Dukovski

Cabeza de Vaca ★★

Historical epic 1990 · Mex · Colour · 111mins

With the exception of Werner Herzog's *Aguirre, Wrath of God*, films about the Spanish conquest of the New World have been hugely disappointing. This one recounts the extraordinary story of Alvar Nuñez Cabeza de Vaca, a 16th-century soldier who was shipwrecked off the coast of what is now Florida. Following a series of miraculous cures, he is hailed as a messiah by the local tribes. Nicolas Echevarria's epic makes some telling points but is too slow to fire the imagination. DP. In Spanish with English subtitles.

Juan Diego • Daniel Gimenez Cacho • Roberto Sosa • Jose Flores ■ *Dir* Nicolas Echevarria • *Scr* Nicolas Echevarria, Guillermo Sheridan, from the autobiography *Shipwrecks* by Alvar Nuñez Cabeza de Vaca

Cabin Boy ★★ 12

Comedy 1994 · US · Colour · 76mins

This "fish out of water" comedy gets low marks for originality but succeeds in raising the odd laugh. Chris Elliott (*Groundhog Day*) plays Nathanial Mayweather, a spoilt brat who mistakes a fishing boat for a luxury cruise liner and gets a lesson in life from the salty crew. Elliott is fine in the lead role, and watch for some interesting cameos. JF. Contains swearing. [VIDEO]

Chris Elliott *Nathanial Mayweather* • Ritch Brinkley *Captain Greybar* • James Gammon *Paps* • Brian Doyle-Murray *Skunk* • Brion James *Big Teddy* ■ *Dir* Adam Resnick • *Scr* Adam Resnick, from a story by Adam Resnick, Chris Elliott

Cabin by the Lake ★★★

Black comedy thriller
2000 · US · Colour · 91mins

Director Po Chih Leong imbues this TV movie with a deeply disturbing atmosphere and no little suspense. Judd Nelson impresses as the screenwriter who draws inspiration from kidnapping and killing young women, whom he then buries in his underwater garden of remembrance. However, his last victim, Hedy Burress, proves a more than capable adversary. With its eerily ingenious photography and agonisingly measured pace, this might just change your views on teleplays. Director and star reunited for a sequel the following year. DP

Judd Nelson *Stanley Caldwell* • Hedy Burress *Mallory McCall* • Michael Weatherly *Boone Preston* • Susan Gibney *Regan Kendrick* • Bernie Coulson *Duncan* ■ *Dir* Po Chih Leong • *Scr* C David Stephens

Cabin Fever ★★ 15

Horror thriller 2002 · US · Colour · 88mins

Five college friends are struck down at their forest cabin retreat by a deadly flesh-eating virus in Eli Roth's cultish, gory exploitation flick. Designed as an all-out gratuitous splatter-fest in the video nasty tradition, this delights in delivering toe-curling shocks. Roth's direction is assured, but it's hard to know if this is a parody or a straight horror, or a mixture of both. AJ. Contains violence, swearing. [VIDEO] DVD

Rider Strong *Paul* • Cerina Vincent *Marcy* • James DeBello *Bert* • Jordan Ladd *Karen* • Joey Kern *Jeff* • Arie Verveen *Hermit* • Eli Roth *Justin* ■ *Dir* Eli Roth • *Scr* Eli Roth, Randy Pearlstein, from a story by Eli Roth

Cabin in the Cotton ★★ U

Drama 1932 · US · BW · 79mins

Caught between loyalty to his own people – poor tenant farmers – and the friendship of his plantation-owner boss, sharecropper Richard Barthelmess faces further problems when he betrays his sweetheart (Dorothy Jordan) by succumbing to the shameless advances of the boss's predatory daughter (Bette Davis). The dramatic tension is dissipated by a poor script, a lifeless and confused-looking Barthelmess, and run-of-the-mill direction by Michael Curtiz. RK

Richard Barthelmess *Marvin* • Dorothy Jordan *Betty* • Bette Davis *Madge* • Berton Churchill *Lane Norwood* • Walter Percival *Cleve Clinton* • William LeMaire *Jake Fisher* ■ *Dir* Michael Curtiz • *Scr* Paul Green, from the novel by Harry Harrison Kroll

Cabin in the Sky ★★★★ U

Musical 1943 · US · BW · 94mins

An all-black fable about heaven and hell fighting for one man's soul. Sounds patronising, doesn't it? Well, this little gem is one of the cinema's great surprises: a stunning directorial debut from Broadway import Vincente Minnelli, featuring a sublime score performed by such fabulous artistes as Lena Horne, Ethel Waters, Louis Armstrong and the Duke Ellington Orchestra. The film's theatrical origins are terrifically subsumed in Minnelli's clever and stylish direction, and Eddie "Rochester" Anderson's performance in the pivotal role of Joe is a revelation. Viewed today, the black stereotypes on display here may be deemed offensive. TS [VIDEO]

Ethel Waters *Petunia Jackson* • Eddie "Rochester" Anderson *Little Joe Jackson* • Lena Horne *Georgia Brown* • Louis Armstrong *Trumpeter* • Rex Ingram (2) *Lucius/Lucifer Jr* • Kenneth Spencer *Rev Green/The General* • John "Bubbles" Sublett *Domino Johnson* ■ *Dir* Vincente Minnelli • *Scr* Joseph Schrank, from the musical play by Lynn Root • *Music Director* George Stoll

The Cabinet of Caligari ★★

Horror 1962 · US · BW · 102mins

Horror clichés abound in this pseudo-Freudian nonsense, as a young woman's car breaks down near a mansion and she is held prisoner by its sinister owner, played with exuberant vigour by Dan O'Herlihy. There are moments of well-handled delirium and suspense featuring scenes of murder and voyeurism, but mostly it's a bore. RS

Glynis Johns *Jane Lindstrom* • Dan O'Herlihy *Paul/Caligari* • Richard Davalos *Mark* • Lawrence Dobkin *David* • Constance Ford *Christine* ■ *Dir* Roger Kay • *Scr* Robert Bloch

The Cabinet of Dr Caligari ★★★★★ U

Silent horror 1919 · Ger · BW · 51mins

Like Sergei Eisenstein's *Battleship Potemkin*, this venerable silent classic changed the way movies were made and appreciated. Adapting techniques from the German theatrical style known as expressionism, it explores the world and mind of a psychotic fairground showman who hypnotises a sleepwalker to commit a murder for him. However, the sleepwalker abducts the intended victim instead. The use of lopsided sets, odd camera angles and general weirdness caused a sensation at the time, and still look amazing. However, modern audiences may find the exaggerated acting and stilted movements of the characters dated and rather laughable. AT [VIDEO] DVD

Werner Krauss *Dr Caligari* • Conrad Veidt *Cesare* • Friedrich Feher *Francis* • Lil Dagover *Jane* • Hans von Twardowski *Alan* • Rudolf Lettinger *Dr Olson* • Rudoph Klein-Rogge *A criminal* ■ *Dir* Robert Wiene • *Scr* Carl Mayer, Hans Janowitz, from the film *Das Kabinett des Dr Caligari* by Robert Wiene • *Cinematographer* John L Russell

Cabiria ★★★★

Silent epic 1914 · It · BW · 210mins

The international success of this Italian spectacle, the longest and most expensive motion picture made up to that date, allowed DW Griffith to gain support for his large-scale projects. The film, which took an unprecedented six months to shoot in studios and locations in Sicily, the Alps and Tunisia, follows the adventures of Cabiria, a kidnapped girl, and Maciste, her giant slave companion, during the Second Punic War. Giovanni Pastrone directed, but the lion's share of the credit went to Gabriele D'Annunzio, although the latter's contribution was limited to the intertitles. RB

Italia Almirante Manzini *Sophonisba* • Vitale de Stefano *Massinissa* • Bartolomeo Pagano *Maciste* • Lidia Quaranta *Cabiria* • Umberto Mozzato *Fulvio Axilla* • Enrico Gemelli *Archimedes* • Ignazio Lupi *Arbace* ■ *Dir* Piero Fosco [Giovanni Pastrone] • *Scr* Giovanni Pastrone

The Cable Guy ★★★ 12

Satirical comedy 1996 · US · Colour · 91mins

Jim Carrey was afforded the opportunity to do something different in this jet-black satire on the power of television, and he responds with a performance that brings a dark edge to his wacky persona. Carrey is on top form as a manic cable television technician who takes a special interest in customer Matthew Broderick. Psycho stalker Carrey starts invading every aspect of Broderick's life, with both hilarious and sobering results. Ben Stiller's film may suffer from dull patches, but it's much better than you've heard it is. AJ. Contains violence and swearing. [VHS] DVD

Jim Carrey *Chip Douglas* • Matthew Broderick *Steven Kovacs* • Leslie Mann *Robin* • Jack Black *Rick* • George Segal *Steven's father* • Diane Baker *Steven's mother* • Ben Stiller *Sam Sweet* • Eric Roberts • Janeane Garofalo *Waitress* ■ *Dir* Ben Stiller • *Scr* Lou Holtz Jr

C

Caboblanco ★★ 18

Adventure 1980 · US · Colour · 91mins

Everybody comes to Giff's, the seedy bar run by Giff Hoyt (Charles Bronson), a tough guy with a past who has washed up in Peru. There's Jason Robards as an ex-Nazi gangster, Fernando Rey as a corrupt police chief, and Dominique Sanda as a mystery woman looking for her lover and $22 million in treasure. With its tongue only half inside its cheek, this yarn never quite gets going, though the exotic setting helps create an agreeably torpid atmosphere. AT [VHS] DVD

Charles Bronson *Giff Hoyt* • Dominique Sanda *Marie Claire Allesandri* • Fernando Rey *Terredo* • Jason Robards *Gunther Beckdorff* • Simon MacCorkindale *Lewis Clarkson* • Camilla Sparv *Hera* • Clifton James *Lorrimer* • Gilbert Roland *Dr Ramirez* ■ *Dir* J Lee Thompson • *Scr* Milton Gelman, Mort Fine [Morton S Fine]

Cactus ★★★ PG

Drama 1986 · Aus · Colour · 91mins

Isabelle Huppert, on holiday Down Under, has a car crash and loses sight in one eye. Doctors recommend she has the eye removed to prevent sympathetic blindness in the other. Her choice is complicated when she falls in love with a blind man and contemplates total blindness. A painful topic is handled with naturalism and insight in a drama that weaves in and out of Huppert's life and the lives of her family and friends. LH [VHS]

Isabelle Huppert *Colo* • Robert Menzies *Robert* • Norman Kaye *Tom* • Monica Maughan *Bea* • Banduk Marika *Banduk* • Sheila Florance *Martha* ■ *Dir/Scr* Paul Cox

Cactus Flower ★★★ PG

Comedy 1969 · US · Colour · 99mins

Goldie Hawn won a best supporting actress Oscar for converting her lovable *Laugh-In* bimbo into a believable screen persona as dentist Walter Matthau's young girlfriend. Matthau deflects Hawn's talk of marriage by presenting his receptionist Ingrid Bergman (in one of several screen comebacks) as his wife. Hawn is enchanting and Matthau is always watchable, but the material is wafer thin, and Bergman seems ill at ease in this glossy adaptation. TS [VHS] DVD

Walter Matthau *Julian Winston* • Ingrid Bergman *Stephanie Dickinson* • Goldie Hawn *Toni Simmons* • Jack Weston *Harvey Greenfield* • Rick Lenz *Igor Sullivan* • Vito Scotti *Senor Sanchez* • Irene Hervey *Mrs Durant* ■ *Dir* Gene Saks • *Scr* IAL Diamond, from the play by Abe Burrows, from the French play by Barillet & Gredy

Cactus Jack ★★ PG

Comedy western 1979 · US · Colour · 85mins

This attempt at spoofing old westerns stars Arnold Schwarzenegger and Kirk Douglas in what sounds like a comic meeting of the two chins. Made before anyone had the wit to relaunch Arnie as a pneumatic self-parody, this is an example of crass comic mistiming in the extreme. At least Ann-Margret looks as striking as ever. JM [VHS]

Kirk Douglas *Cactus Jack* • Ann-Margret *Charming Jones* • Arnold Schwarzenegger *Handsome Stranger* • Paul Lynde *Nervous Elk* • Foster Brooks *Bank clerk* • Ruth Buzzi *Damsel in distress* • Jack Elam *Avery Simpson* • Strother Martin *Parody Jones* ■ *Dir* Hal Needham • *Scr* Robert G Kane

Caddie ★★

Drama 1976 · Aus · Colour · 106mins

A worthy drama from Down Under about a woman who is forced to make radical changes to her lifestyle when she leaves her cheating husband. Helen Morse gives a dignified performance as the woman trying to make her own way in the very macho world of Australia between the wars, and Jack Thompson is as reliable as ever. Donald Crombie's direction, however, is uninspired. JF

Helen Morse *Caddie* • Takis Emmanuel *Peter* • Jack Thompson *Ted* • Jacki Weaver *Josie* • Melissa Jaffer *Leslie* • Ron Blanchard *Bill* • Deborah Kounnas *Ann Marsh aged 2* ■ *Dir* Donald Crombie • *Scr* Joan Long, from the autobiography by "Carrie"

The Caddy ★★ U

Comedy 1953 · US · BW · 95mins

Relying on the popularity and appeal of Dean Martin and Jerry Lewis, this hotch-potch of a comedy is chiefly memorable for spawning the Oscar-nominated smash hit, *That's Amore*. The unfocused screenplay has Lewis caddying for Martin, with predictably chaotic consequences. Donna Reed and Barbara Bates are the boys' girls, and golfers Sam Snead and Ben Hogan put in appearances. RK

Jerry Lewis *Harvey Miller* • Dean Martin *Joe Anthony* • Donna Reed *Kathy Taylor* • Barbara Bates *Lisa* • Joseph Calleia *Papa Anthony* • Clinton Sundberg *Charles* • Howard Smith *Golf official* • Marshall Thompson *Bruce Reeber* ■ *Dir* Norman Taurog • *Scr* Danny Arnold

Caddyshack ★★★ 15

Comedy 1980 · US · Colour · 93mins

This wonderfully crass comedy from director Harold Ramis breezes along in a cheerfully tasteless manner. Loud-mouth millionaire Rodney Dangerfield gets up snobbish Ted Knight's nose when he attempts to take over the golf club, setting the scene for a climactic contest on the links. There's an annoying subplot about caddies, and Chevy Chase is given little to do as the louche golf professional. Bill Murray nearly steals the show as a psychopathic groundsman continuing a running battle with the club's resident gophers. JF. Contains violence, sex scenes, swearing, nudity. [VHS] DVD

Chevy Chase *Ty Webb* • Rodney Dangerfield *Al Czervik* • Ted Knight *Judge Smails* • Michael O'Keefe *Danny Noonan* • Bill Murray *Carl Spackler* • Sarah Holcomb *Maggie O'Hooligan* • Scott Colomby *Tony D'Annunzio* • Cindy Morgan *Lacey Underall* ■ *Dir* Harold Ramis • *Scr* Brian Doyle-Murray, Harold Ramis, Douglas Kenney

Caddyshack II ★ 15

Comedy 1988 · US · Colour · 93mins

The first *Caddyshack* may have been funny, but take away some of the talent from the original – Bill Murray, Rodney Dangerfield, director Harold Ramis – and you're left with this mess. Instead you have Jackie Mason as a self-made millionaire who decides to take revenge when he's refused membership to an up-market country club. Meanwhile, Chevy Chase reprises his role of spaced-out golfer to little effect, while Dan Aykroyd runs around aimlessly. JB. Contains swearing. [VHS]

Jackie Mason *Jack Hartounian* • Robert Stack *Chandler Young* • Dina Merrill *Cynthia Young* • Dyan Cannon *Elizabeth Pearce* • Jonathan Silverman *Harry* • Randy Quaid *Peter Blunt* • Chevy Chase *Ty Webb* • Dan Aykroyd *Captain Tom Everett* ■ *Dir* Allan Arkush • *Scr* Harold Ramis, Peter Torokvei

Cadillac Man ★★★ 15

Comedy drama 1990 · US · Colour · 93mins

After his success with *Good Morning, Vietnam*, Robin Williams was still having difficulty finding another star vehicle equal to his talents when he accepted the lead in this comedy from Roger Donaldson. The role of the sleazy car salesman having an incredibly bad day was not Williams's best career choice, but luckily his comedic skills give the film the life it needs. Also on hand to keep things going are Tim Robbins, playing a gun-toting husband who holds up the car lot, and, in smaller roles, Annabella Sciorra and Lori Petty. JB. Contains swearing, violence, nudity. [VHS] DVD

Robin Williams *Joey O'Brien* • Tim Robbins *Larry* • Pamela Reed *Tina O'Brien* • Fran Drescher *Joy Munchack* • Zack Norman *Harry Munchack* • Annabella Sciorra *Donna* • Lori Petty *Lila* • Paul Guilfoyle (2) *Little Jack Turgeon* • Bill Nelson *Big Jack Turgeon* ■ *Dir* Roger Donaldson • *Scr* Ken Friedman

Cadillac Ranch ★★ 15

Comedy 1996 · US · Colour · 98mins

Three sisters hit the road with some stolen loot in a muddled journey made palatable by likeable performances from Suzy Amis, Renee Humphrey and Caroleen Feeney. Lisa Gottlieb's *Thelma and Louise*-style movie has plenty going on – and that's the problem. Female bonding, a hint of idealised romance, reminiscences about their criminal dad and a killer on their trail make this a recipe with too many ingredients. JC. Contains swearing, violence, nudity. [VHS]

Christopher Lloyd *Wood Grimes* • Suzy Amis *CJ Crowley* • Caroleen Feeney *Frances Crowley* • Renee Humphrey *Mary Katherine Crowley* • Jim Metzler *Travis Crowley* ■ *Dir* Lisa Gottlieb • *Scr* Jennifer Cecil

Caesar and Cleopatra ★★ U

Historical drama 1945 · UK · Colour · 122mins

Legend has it that Hungarian producer Gabriel Pascal managed to convince George Bernard Shaw he was the only person who could do justice to the great man's plays. Unfortunately, Pascal wasn't content to be merely producer here: he also directed, with astounding ineptitude.There's no denying the Technicolor is splendid, but, despite the spirited efforts of Claude Rains and Vivien Leigh as the titular couple, there's no sexual chemistry at all. TS [VHS] DVD

Vivien Leigh *Cleopatra* • Claude Rains *Caesar* • Stewart Granger *Apollodorus* • Flora Robson *Ftatateeta* • Francis L Sullivan *Pothinus* • Basil Sydney *Rufio* • Cecil Parker *Britannus* • Raymond Lovell *Lucius Septimius* • Anthony Eustrel *Achillas* • Ernest Thesiger *Theodotus* • Anthony Harvey *Ptolemy* ■ *Dir* Gabriel Pascal • *Scr* George Bernard Shaw, Majorie Deans, from the play by George Bernard Shaw

Cafe Flesh ★★ 18

Cult erotic drama 1982 · US · Colour · 69mins

Although only a classy porn movie with artistic pretensions, Stephen Sayadian's cult classic (directed under his pseudonym Rinse Dream) is extraordinarily prophetic when viewed in an Aids-related context. Well-made and acted for a picture that features only one heavy-duty porn queen (Michelle Bauer, aka Pia Snow), initial intrigue in the plot soon wears off as genre clichés take over. AJ [VHS]

Andrew Nichols [Andy Nichols] *Max Melodramatic* • Paul McGibboney *Nick* • Pia Snow [Michelle Bauer] *Lana* • Marie Sharp *Angel* • Dondi Bastone *Spike* ■ *Dir* Rinse Dream [Stephen Sayadian] • *Scr* Rinse Dream [Stephen Sayadian], Herbert W Day [Jerry Stahl], FX Pope [Stephen Sayadian] • *Cinematographer* FX Pope [Stephen Sayadian]

Café Lumière ★★★★ U

Drama 2003 · Jpn/Tai · Colour · 103mins

This exquisite drama was made to commemorate the centenary of the birth of director Yasujiro Ozu. Hou Hsiao-Hsien not only replicates the style of the Japanese auteur, he also captures the essence of Ozu's deceptive simplicity. At the heart of the story is the delightful relationship between writer Yo Hitoto and train buff Tadanobu Asano. So it comes as a surprise to learn that she is pregnant by the Taiwanese boyfriend she has no desire to marry. Hou recalls Ozu's preoccupation with the urban landscape, but he also explores his key themes, including the tension between parents and children and the absence of effective communication in the modern world. DP. In Japanese with English subtitles.

Yo Hitoto *Yoko Inoue* • Tadanobu Asano *Hajime Takeuchi* • Masato Hagiwara *Seiji* • Kimiko Yo *Yoko's stepmother* • Nenji Kobayashi *Yoko's father* ■ *Dir* Hou Hsiao-Hsien • *Scr* Hou Hsiao-Hsien, Chu Tien-wen

Café Metropole ★★★

Romantic comedy 1937 · US · BW · 83mins

A complicated plot involving the suave, less than honest, proprietor of a Paris restaurant, a penniless Ivy Leaguer who gets into trouble over a hefty gambling debt to the aforesaid gentleman, an American heiress whom the handsome gambler courts in the guise of Russian royalty, and a refugee waiter who is the real prince, makes for a jolly romp. Tyrone Power and Loretta Young are as gorgeous a romantic duo as one could wish for, and are surrounded by a first-class supporting cast, all of whom bring the requisite light touch to a pleasingly amiable and sophisticated script. RK

Loretta Young *Laura Ridgeway* • Tyrone Power *Alexis Paneiev/Alexander Brown* • Adolphe Menjou *Monsieur Victor Lobard* • Gregory Ratoff *Paul* • Charles Winninger *Joseph Ridgeway* • Helen Westley *Margaret Ridgeway* ■ *Dir* Edward H Griffith • *Scr* Jacques Deval, from a story by Gregory Ratoff

Cage ★★★ 18

Action drama 1989 · US · Colour · 96mins

Incredible Hulk star Lou Ferrigno gives his best performance in this violent movie. He and Reb Brown play Vietnam veterans who run a Los Angeles bar in an area where fixed, no-holds-barred fights are the latest illegal money-spinner. Ferrigno is conned into entering the bare-knuckle "cage" and putting his life on the line for Chinatown mobsters. Sleazy, obnoxiously racist and nasty it may be, but Lang Elliott's carnage caper delivers the goods in bloody excitement. A less successful sequel followed in 1994. AJ [VHS]

Lou Ferrigno *Billy Thomas* • Reb Brown *Scott Monroe* • Michael Dante *Tony Baccola* • Al Leong *Tiger Joe* • Mike Moroff *Mario* • James Shigeta *Tim Lum Yin* • Marilyn Tokuda *Morgan Garrett* • Branscombe Richmond *Diablo* ■ *Dir* Lang Elliott • *Scr* Hugh Kelley

La Cage aux Folles ★★★★ 15

Comedy 1978 · Fr/It · Colour · 87mins

One of the most successful foreign films ever released, this frilly farce led to two sequels, a Broadway hit musical and a Hollywood remake starring Robin Williams (1996's *The Birdcage*). It's the remarkably inoffensive and non-threatening tale of what happens when the gay owners of a St Tropez transvestite club meet the straight parents of the daughter their heterosexual son (don't ask!) wants to marry. Cue much mistaken identity humour, mainly revolving around the exaggerated effeminacy of brilliant Michel Serrault as the highly strung drag diva. AJ. In French with English subtitles. [VHS] DVD

Michel Serrault *Albin, "Zaza"* • Ugo Tognazzi *Renato* • Michel Galabru *Charrier* • Claire Maurier *Simone* • Remi Laurent *Laurent* • Benny Luke *Jacob* • Carmen Scarpitta *Madame Charrier* • Luisa Maneri *Andrea* ■ *Dir* Edouard Molinaro • *Scr* Marcello Danon, Edouard Molinaro, Francis Veber, Jean Poiret, from the play by Jean Poiret

La Cage aux Folles II ★★ 12

Comedy 1980 · Fr/It · Colour · 95mins

Michel Serrault and Ugo Tognazzi return as the bickering lovers in this so-so sequel to the 1978 camp classic. Complete with spies, corpses and secret microfilms, the espionage elements of the plot get in the way of the much more amusing character farce. However, director Edouard Molinaro makes the most of the unlikely situations, especially when Serrault has to pretend to be Tognazzi's bride to fool the latter's ultra-conservative mother. DP. In French with English subtitles. DVD

Michel Serrault *Albin, "Zaza"* • Ugo Tognazzi *Renato* • Marcel Bozzuffi *Broca* • Paola Borboni *Signora Baldi* • Giovanni Vettorazzo *Milan* • Glauco Onorato *Luigi* • Roberto Bisacco *Ralph* • Benny Luke *Jacob* • Michel Galabru *Charrier* ■ *Dir* Edouard Molinaro • *Scr* Jean Poiret, Francis Veber, Marcello Danon, from characters created by Jean Poiret

La Cage aux Folles III: "Elles" Se Marient ★ 15

Comedy 1985 · Fr/It · Colour · 87mins

The second sequel to the popular French farce *La Cage aux Folles* finds drag queen nightclub owner Michel Serrault forced to sire a child so he can inherit a fortune. His partner Ugo Tognazzi)can only stand back and watch the shrieking and high camp tantrums that this outrageous ultimatum precipitates. It's all too strident, loud and silly. AJ. In French with English subtitles.

Michel Serrault *Albin, "Zaza"* • Ugo Tognazzi *Renato* • Michel Galabru *Charrier* • Benny Luke *Jacob* • Stéphane Audran *Matrimonia* • Antonella Interlenghi *Cindy* ■ *Dir* Georges Lautner • *Scr* Philippe Nicaud, Christine Carère, Marcello Danon, Jacques Audiard, Michel Audiard, Georges Lautner, Gérard Lamballe, from a story by Philippe Nicaud, Christine Carère, Marcello Danon, from characters created by Jean Poiret

Cage of Gold ★★

Crime drama 1950 · UK · BW · 83mins

An overwrought melodrama from director Basil Dearden, with David Farrar cast somewhat against type as an RAF rogue who, having cheated on Jean Simmons with French singer Madeleine Lebeau during the war, deserts the pregnant Simmons shortly after their marriage in order to smuggle jewels for Paris club owner Herbert Lom. There are simply too many underdrawn characters flitting in and out of the increasingly preposterous plot for comfort or comprehension. DP

Jean Simmons *Judith Moray* • David Farrar *Bill Brennan* • James Donald *Alan Keane* • Herbert Lom *Rahman* • Madeleine Lebeau *Marie* • Maria Mauban *Antoinette* • Bernard Lee *Inspector Grey* ■ *Dir* Basil Dearden • *Scr* Jack Whittingham, Paul Stein, from a story by Jack Whittingham

A Cage of Nightingales ★★★ U

Musical drama 1945 · Fr · BW · 88mins

A young working man (Noël-Noël) writes a novel about his life, which includes a spell in a reformatory. His past is revealed to his girlfriend (Micheline Francey) when she reads the book; we see the tale unfold in flashback as she does so. A neat blend of past and present, this modest film from Jean Dréville is a truthful, sober and understanding picture of juvenile delinquency, offering excellent performances and a positive message. It was Oscar-nominated for Best Original Story, losing out, not surprisingly, to *Miracle on 34th Street*. RK. In French with English subtitles.

Noël-Noël *Clément* • Micheline Francey *Martine* • George Biscot *Raymond* • René Génin *Maxence* • René Blancard *Rachin* • Marguerite Ducouret *Mme Martine* ■ *Dir* Jean Dréville • *Scr* Noël-Noël, René Wheeler, Georges Chaperot

Caged ★★★

Melodrama 1950 · US · BW · 91mins

A typical Warner Bros prison melodrama, only this time it's a women's prison. So instead of James Cagney, there's an unglamorous Eleanor Parker as the innocent victim who grows tougher after exposure to the brutality of life on the inside. There's an interesting censor-circumventing prison matron who clearly displays lesbian tendencies, played convincingly by Hope Emerson. It's a slow, absorbing work, and its very drabness renders it rather tedious for viewers. Watch it for the under-rated Parker, a terrific actress who was never really given her due. TS

Eleanor Parker *Marie Allen* • Agnes Moorehead *Ruth Benton* • Ellen Corby *Emma* • Hope Emerson *Evelyn Harper* • Betty Garde *Kitty Stark* • Jan Sterling *Smoochie* • Lee Patrick *Elvira Powell* • Jane Darwell *Isolation Matron* • Sheila Stevens *Helen* ■ *Dir* John Cromwell • *Scr* Virginia Kellogg, Bernard C Schoenfeld

Caged Heat ★★★ 18

Drama 1974 · US · Colour · 73mins

Jonathan Demme's debut as writer/director bears all the hallmarks of his mentor, exploitation maestro Roger Corman, who was making this kind of "babes-behind-bars" flick back in the late 1950s. Horror icon Barbara Steele returns to the screen after a five-year absence to play the sadistic wheelchair-bound governor, a role that had been written specially for her. There's plenty of humour to leaven the story of naive Juanita Brown's struggle against the system, but the biggest laughs come from the tremendous 1970s outfits. DP. Contains violence, swearing and nudity.

Juanita Brown *Maggie* • Roberta Collins *Belle Tyson* • Erica Gavin *Jacqueline Wilson* • Barbara Steele *Mcqueen* • Ella Reid *Pandora Williams* ■ *Dir/Scr* Jonathan Demme

Cagney & Lacey ★★★★ 15

Police drama 1981 · US · Colour · 91mins

The pilot of the hugely popular TV series about two lady cops, here played by Tyne Daly (who continued her role in the series) and Loretta Swit of TV's *M*A*S*H* (who was replaced by Meg Foster and, subsequently, Sharon Gless). As many fans will remember, the series got a bit ropey in later years, but this pilot is a reminder of how great *Cagney & Lacey* was in the beginning. Daly looks youthful (well, it was 1981) and Swit is suitably tough-as-nails as her partner. One can only assume Gless was brought in to be a younger, more glamorous version of Chris Cagney when the producers realised the series would run for almost a decade. JB

Loretta Swit *Christine Cagney* • Tyne Daly *Mary Beth Lacey* • Al Waxman *Detective Samuels* • Joan Copeland *Mrs Friedlander* • Ronald Hunter *Harvey* ■ *Dir* Ted Post • *Scr* Barbara Avedon

Cahill, United States Marshal ★★★ 15

Western 1973 · US · Colour · 97mins

Director Andrew V McLaglen could always be depended upon to hammer out gruff, good-looking westerns from the most unpromising material. Here he saddles up John Wayne for a parable on the extent to which modern youth had been corrupted while America was away solving the problems of the world. As a political statement, it's reactionary and naive, but it passes muster as a late Wayne western, with the Duke looking every day of his 66 years as the absentee father out to teach villainous George Kennedy a lesson for enticing his teenage sons into crime. DP. Contains violence. DVD

John Wayne *JD Cahill* • George Kennedy *Abe Fraser* • Gary Grimes *Danny Cahill* • Neville Brand *Lightfoot* • Clay O'Brien *Billy Joe Cahill* • Marie Windsor *Mrs Green* • Morgan Paull *Struther* • Dan Vadis *Brownie* • Royal Dano *MacDonald* • Scott Walker *Ben Tildy* ■ *Dir* Andrew V McLaglen • *Scr* Harry Julian Fink, Rita M Fink, from a story by Barney Slater

Cain and Mabel ★★ U

Musical comedy 1936 · US · BW · 90mins

The penultimate movie of talented star Marion Davies, best known today for being the mistress and protégée of newspaper magnate William Randolph Hearst. It's an unfortunate way to remember the delightful actress, here woefully miscast as a Broadway star pretending to romance a boxer for publicity. Since the heavyweight is played by Clark Gable, Davies has trouble holding the screen. There's a clever cast, some witty dialogue and a production number of such unremitting vulgarity that it almost takes the breath away. TS

Marion Davies *Mabel O'Dare* • Clark Gable *Larry Cain* • Allen Jenkins *Dodo* • Roscoe Karns *Aloysius K Reilly* • Walter Catlett *Jake Sherman* • David Carlyle [Robert Paige] *Ronny Cauldwell* • Hobart Cavanaugh *Milo* ■ *Dir* Lloyd Bacon • *Scr* Laird Doyle, Earl Baldwin (uncredited), from a story by HC Witwer

The Caine Mutiny ★★★ U

Drama 1954 · US · Colour · 119mins

This rather dourly scripted adaptation of Herman Wouk's Pulitzer Prize-winning novel veers between the best high drama and plodding, explanatory narrative. A sterling cast (José Ferrer, Fred MacMurray, Van Johnson) brings the court-martial scenes vividly to life, but the film is let down considerably by lengthy speeches of unremitting moral rectitude. Humphrey Bogart's snivelling Captain Queeg lacks much of the actor's former screen punch and, with hindsight, one can see the sad spectre of a sick man nearing the end of his career. This could have been a classic but ended up an also-ran. SH DVD

Humphrey Bogart *Captain Queeg* • José Ferrer *Lt Barney Greenwald* • Van Johnson *Lt Steve Maryk* • Fred MacMurray *Lt Tom Keefer* • Robert Francis *Ensign Willie Keith* • Tom Tully *Captain DeVriess* • EG Marshall *Lt Cmdr Challee* • Lee Marvin *Meatball* ■ *Dir* Edward Dmytryk • *Scr* Stanley Roberts, from the novel and play by Herman Wouk • *Music* Max Steiner

Cairo ★

Crime drama 1962 · US/UK · BW · 90mins

A sand-blown remake of just about every caper movie ever made – *The Asphalt Jungle, Rififi*, you name it. George Sanders plays a master thief who decides to steal Tutankhamen's jewels from the Cairo museum, so he forms a gang of rogues to execute his plan. Directed by Wolf Rilla, this is a real letdown with some very listless patches of narrative. TH

George Sanders *Major Pickering* • Richard Johnson *Ali* • Faten Hamama *Amina* • John Meillon *Willy* • Ahmed Mazhar *Kerim* • Eric Pohlmann *Nicodemos* • Walter Rilla *Kuchuk* • Salah Nazmi *Commandant* ■ *Dir* Wolf Rilla • *Scr* Joan Scott, from the novel *The Asphalt Jungle* by WR Burnett

Cairo Road ★★ U

Crime drama 1950 · UK · BW · 86mins

A British B-movie about drug smuggling, with Eric Portman as an Egyptian detective and Laurence Harvey as his ambitious assistant. While Portman rather overplays his part, Harvey is fascinating to watch as a scene-stealing star on the rise. Despite some location sequences (a rarity for a low budget production), the action is fairly slow and routine. AT

Eric Portman *Colonel Youssef Bey* • Laurence Harvey *Lieutenant Mourad* • Maria Mauban *Marie* • Anna Michelis *Camelia* • Harold Lang *Humble* • Coco Aslan *Lombardi* ■ *Dir* David MacDonald • *Scr* Robert Westerby

Cairo Station ★★★★

Drama 1958 · Egy · BW · 86mins

Brimming with life and adroitly balancing harsh reality with glimmers of optimism, this drama established Egyptian director Youssef Chahine on the international stage. He also plays the key role of the disabled news vendor whose obsession with soft drinks seller Hind Rustum (herself besotted with porter Farid Shawqi) precipitates a tragic accident. Exploring the impact of western ideas on cultural and religious tradition, as well as the dire poverty in which many of the station workers exist, Chahine exploits his location to suggest a state in flux. DP. In Arabic with English subtitles.

Youssef Chahine *Kenaoui* • Hind Rostom *Hanouma* • Farid Shawqi *Abou Serib* ■ *Dir* Youssef Chahine • *Scr* Abdel Hay Adib

Cal ★★★★ 15

Romantic thriller 1984 · UK · Colour · 98mins

Pat O'Connor made his feature debut with this adaptation by Bernard MacLaverty of his own novel. At times treading a mite too carefully along the sectarian divide, this is nevertheless a credible and often compelling look at how the Troubles intrude upon what should be the events of everyday life. There's a genuine warmth in the relationship between widow Helen Mirren (who won Best Actress at Cannes) and John Lynch, the getaway driver on the IRA mission that resulted in the death of her RUC husband. But the tension amid which their romance blossoms is also well conveyed by O'Connor and his impressive supporting cast. DP

Helen Mirren *Marcella* • John Lynch *Cal* • Donal McCann *Shamie* • John Kavanagh *Skeffington* • Ray McAnally *Cyril Dunlop* • Stevan Rimkus *Crilly* ■ *Dir* Pat O'Connor • *Scr* Bernard MacLaverty, from his novel

Calamity Jane ★★★★★ U

Musical comedy western
1953 · US · Colour · 96mins

The opening of this wonderful musical is pure pleasure, as Doris Day rides the Deadwood stage across the screen and into our hearts. This isn't the real Wild West, of course, but Warner Bros's Technicolor riposte to MGM's *Annie Get Your Gun*: the studio even poached the same leading man, Howard Keel, who is excellent here as Wild Bill Hickok. The specially commissioned score is a treat, but the strength of the movie is Day giving a marvellous musical comedy performance in her finest role, creating a warm, robust yet tender character; just marvel at her timing in *Just Blew In from the Windy City*, while *Secret Love*, recorded by Day in just one take, won the best song Oscar and is beautifully staged by choreographer Jack Donohue. TS DVD

Doris Day *Calamity Jane* • Howard Keel *Wild Bill Hickok* • Allyn McLerie [Allyn Ann McLerie] *Katie Brown* • Philip Carey *Lt Gilmartin* • Dick Wesson *Francis Fryer* • Paul Harvey *Henry Miller* • Chubby Johnson *Rattlesnake* • Gale Robbins *Adelaide Adams* ■ *Dir* David Butler • *Scr* James O'Hanlon • *Music* Sammy Fain, Paul Francis Webster

Calamity Jane and Sam Bass ★★ U

Western 1949 · US · Colour · 85mins

Martha Jane Burke, Calamity Jane of western lore, was played by Jean Arthur for Cecil B DeMille in *The Plainsman* (1936), and would soon be immortalised by a ripsnortin' Doris Day in the Warner Bros musical. But here she's incarnated by exotic Yvonne De Carlo in a routine western that plays fast and loose with the facts. Former radio star Howard Duff is cast as Calamity's romantic interest, outlaw Sam Bass, whose character is whitewashed beyond all recognition. TS

Yvonne De Carlo *Calamity Jane* • Howard Duff *Sam Bass* • Dorothy Hart *Katharine Egan* • Willard Parker *Sheriff Will Egan* • Norman Lloyd *Jim Murphy* • Lloyd Bridges *Joel Collins* • Marc Lawrence (1) *Dean* ■ *Dir* George Sherman • *Scr* Maurice Geraghty, Melvin Levy, from a story by George Sherman

The Calcium Kid ★ 15

Sports comedy
2003 · UK/Fr/US · Colour · 84mins

Orlando Bloom plays a milkman-turned-boxer in this dire comedy. The daft premise has Bloom so fond of the white stuff he delivers that his bones have become rock hard as a result. When Bloom accidentally KOs Britain's top challenger in a sparring match, he becomes the next in line for a shot at the world title. DA. Contains swearing. DVD

Orlando Bloom *Jimmy Connelly* • Omid Djalili *Herbie Bush* • Rafe Spall *Stan* • Tamer Hassan *Pete Wright* • Michael Peña [Michael Pena] *Jose Mendez* • Michael Lerner *Artie Cohen* • Billie Piper *Angel* ■ *Dir* Alex De Rakoff • *Scr* Alex De Rakoff, Raymond Friel, Derek Boyle

Calculated Risk ★

Crime drama 1963 · UK · BW · 71mins

The only thing of interest about this tatty little drama is a cameo from Warren Mitchell as a dodgy market trader who sells William Lucas the explosives he needs for his bank job. The story isn't a bad one – about a gang that comes across an unexploded Second World War bomb while tunnelling into a vault – but Norman Harrison directs with no sense of suspense. DP. Contains swearing.

John Rutland *Kip* • William Lucas *Steve* • Dilys Watling *Julie* • Warren Mitchell *Simmie* • Shay Gorman *Dodo* • Terence Cooper *Nodge* ■ *Dir* Norman Harrison • *Scr* Edwin Richfield

Calcutta ★★★

Thriller 1947 · US · BW · 83mins

Clean-cut, good-looking Alan Ladd and pug-faced William Bendix, his frequent on-screen partner, trawl the threatening back alleys, colourful bazaars and sleazy hotels of India's teeming city (built on the Paramount backlot). There Ladd's search for whoever killed his friend gets them entangled with the underworld and its questionable inhabitants. The result is an old-fashioned, low-budget formula thriller, but one that makes for easy and entertaining viewing. RK

Alan Ladd *Neale Gordon* • William Bendix *Pedro Blake* • Gail Russell *Virginia Moore* • June Duprez *Marina* • Lowell Gilmore *Eric Lasser* • Edith King *Mrs Smith* • Paul Singh *Malik* • Gavin Muir *Kendricks* ■ *Dir* John Farrow • *Scr* Seton I Miller

The Calendar ★★

Drama 1948 · UK · BW · 79mins

British cinema was heavily dependent on the mysteries of Edgar Wallace in the early talkie era. Few of these creaky thrillers were ever remade, until someone at Gainsborough Productions felt the need to bring this veritable stage warhorse under starter's orders for a second time. It's all clipped accents and impossibly earnest hamming from the off, as trainer Greta Gynt tries to prove that owner John McCallum didn't throw a race to improve the odds of his horse at a later Ascot meeting. DP

Greta Gynt *Wenda* • John McCallum *Garry* • Raymond Lovell *Willie* • Sonia Holm *Mollie* • Leslie Dwyer *Hillcott* • Charles Victor *John Dory* • Felix Aylmer *Lord Forlingham* • Diana Dors *Hawkins* ■ *Dir* Arthur Crabtree • *Scr* Geoffrey Kerr, from the play by Edgar Wallace

Calendar ★★★

Drama
1993 · Can/Arm · BW and Colour · 75mins

This fascinating treatise on communication, appreciation and the limits of the static image co-stars Armenian-Canadian director Atom Egoyan and real-life partner Arsinée Khanjian as a couple who drift apart during a visit to Armenia to photograph churches for a calendar. As one would expect of this most inventive of film-makers, Egoyan isn't content simply to tell his story through flashbacks, but uses video footage to recall the breakdown of his relationship and lush colour film to show how his life since then has been dominated by disappointing dinner dates and painful memories. Personal it may be, but it's also compelling viewing. DP

Arsinée Khanjian *Translator* • Ashot Adamian *Driver* • Atom Egoyan *Photographer* ■ *Dir/Scr* Atom Egoyan

Calendar Girl ★★ 15

Comedy drama 1993 · US · Colour · 87mins

A surprisingly understated big-screen appearance from Jason Priestley, making the most of his *Beverly Hills 90210* fame. Set in the early 1960s, the story follows the adventures of a trio of teenagers who leave their small town to go to Hollywood to meet their idol Marilyn Monroe. Although it's marred by some *Animal House*-style slapstick, it remains an affectionate coming-of-age comedy. JF. Contains swearing, drug abuse and nudity.

Jason Priestley *Roy Darpinian* • Gabriel Olds *Ned Bleuer* • Jerry O'Connell *Scott "The Dood" Foreman* • Joe Pantoliano *Uncle Harvey Darpinian* • Kurt Fuller *Arturo Gallo* • Stephen Tobolowsky *Antonio Gallo* ■ *Dir* John Whitesell • *Scr* Paul W Shapiro

Calendar Girls ★★★★ 12

Comedy drama based on a true story
2003 · UK/US · Colour · 103mins

Often compared to *The Full Monty*, Nigel Cole's film is actually less broad in its comedy and much gentler in tone. It is the very genteel nature of the North Yorkshire Women's Institute milieu that provides the film with its "high concept" (middle-aged women strip for charity). While the pivotal shooting of the calendar itself provides comic gold (during which the spare-part husbands gather in the pub like expectant fathers – a lovely touch), there is a moving, fallible humanity to the performances that keeps the whole thing this side of farce. Julie Walters, Helen Mirren and Linda Bassett shine from a spotless cast of "ladies of a certain age". AC DVD

Helen Mirren *Chris* • Julie Walters *Annie* • Penelope Wilton *Ruth* • Annette Crosbie *Jessie* • Celia Imrie *Celia* • Linda Bassett *Cora* • Georgie Glen *Kathy* • Angela Curran *May* • Rosalind March *Trudy* • Ciaran Hinds *Rod* • John Alderton *John* • Philip Glenister *Lawrence* • John-Paul MacLeod *Jem* • Geraldine James *Marie* • John Fortune *Frank* ■ *Dir* Nigel Cole • *Scr* Juliette Towhidi, Tim Firth

California ★★

Western 1946 · US · Colour · 98mins

A routine Gold Rush western, with Ray Milland drinking too much and Barbara Stanwyck shuffling stacked decks as the woman with a history. Directed by John Farrow in his customary no-nonsense manner, it breezes along nicely without seeming to get anywhere. Paramount lavished bright-as-a-button Technicolor on it, as well as a couple of songs mimed by Stanwyck and a good supporting cast. AT

Ray Milland *Jonathan Trumbo* • Barbara Stanwyck *Lily Bishop* • Barry Fitzgerald *Michael Fabian* • George Coulouris *Pharoah Coffin* • Albert Dekker *Mr Pike* • Anthony Quinn *Don Luis* ■ *Dir* John Farrow • *Scr* Frank Butler, Theodore Strauss, from the story by Boris Ingster

The California Dolls ★★ 18

Comedy drama 1981 · US · Colour · 108mins

Although this dismal final effort from Robert Aldrich purports to be about women's wrestling, it's actually a shameless plug for MGM's Grand Hotel in Reno, Nevada, the glitzy casino where much of the action takes place. What the picture needed was a light satirical touch, not Aldrich's heavy-handed approach which tends to leer when it should laugh. Even so, Peter Falk as the girls' manager and Burt Young as the shady promoter are in their seedy element and provide the few moments of interest. AT

Peter Falk *Harry* • Vicki Frederick *Iris* • Laurene Landon *Molly* • Burt Young *Eddie Cisco* • Tracy Reed *Diane* • Ursaline Bryant-King *June* • Richard Jaeckel *Reno Referee* ■ *Dir* Robert Aldrich • *Scr* Mel Frohman

California Dreaming ★★

Romantic comedy drama
1979 · US · Colour · 92mins

This rather sour drama seeks to deglamorise the myth of happy people surfing through sun-dappled waters in the spirit of counterculture harmony. Arriving from the Midwest with a nerdy eagerness that's every bit as resistible as the beach bums' arrogance, Dennis Christopher approaches a credible sense of betrayal on discovering his idols have clay feet. However, there's a smug "told you so-ness" about the screenplay. DP

Glynnis O'Connor *Corky* • Seymour Cassel *Duke* • Dorothy Tristan *Fay* • Dennis Christopher *T T* • John Calvin *Rick* • Tanya Roberts *Stephanie* ■ *Dir* John Hancock • *Scr* Ned Wynn

California Man ★★ PG

Comedy fantasy 1992 · US · Colour · 88mins

This was a belated attempt to cash in on *Bill and Ted*-style comic capers, although by now Californian teen speak was becoming more irritating than funny. Sean Astin and Pauly Shore play the two nerdish teenagers who dig up a deep-frozen caveman (Brendan Fraser) and educate him in the ways of adolescent etiquette. Fraser makes for a pleasingly gormless hunk and there are some amusing moments, but this lacks the winning stupidity of Bill and Ted's two adventures. Released in the USA as *Encino Man*. JF. Contains drug abuse. DVD

Sean Astin *Dave Morgan* • Brendan Fraser *Link* • Pauly Shore *Stoney Brown* • Megan Ward *Robyn Sweeney* • Robin Tunney *Ella* • Michael DeLuise *Matt* • Patrick Van Horn *Phil* • Dalton James *Will* • Richard Masur *Mr Morgan* • Rose McGowan *Nora* ■ *Dir* Les Mayfield • *Scr* Shawn Schepps, from a story by Shawn Schepps, George Zaloom

California Split ★★★

Comedy 1974 · US · Colour · 108mins

Robert Altman's off-the-wall insight into macho men is too wordy, but still has enough gambling action to hold the attention while leads Elliott Gould and George Segal drink themselves through casino-surfing romps. As the girls sidelined by the men's fixation with the tables, Ann Prentis and Gwen Welles give as bad as they get – Altman's women characters are always real people, not ciphers – but it's really the disintegration of the buddies' friendship that forms the core of a movie that is more rewarding than its initial scenes suggest. TH

George Segal *Bill Denny* • Elliott Gould *Charlie Walters* • Ann Prentiss *Barbara Miller* • Gwen Welles *Susan Peters* • Edward Walsh *Lew* • Joseph Walsh *Sparkie* • Jay Fletcher *Robber* ■ *Dir* Robert Altman • *Scr* Joseph Walsh

California Straight Ahead ★★★ U

Action adventure 1937 · US · BW · 68mins

This vintage chase movie – a kind of Depression-era precursor to *The Cannonball Run* – is made extremely watchable by the casting of John Wayne, trapped in a career no man's land in the years between *The Big Trail* and *Stagecoach*. Ignore the shaky back projection and enjoy the sight of Big John playing one of a pair of truckers engaged in dangerous rivalry. Director Arthur Lubin keeps it all going at a rate of knots and the result is great fun. TS

John Wayne *Biff Smith* • Louise Latimer *Mary Porter* • Robert McWade *Corrigan* • Theodore von Eltz *James Gifford* • Tully Marshall *Harrison* • Emerson Treacy *Charlie Porter* ■ *Dir* Arthur Lubin • *Scr* Scott Darling, from a story by Herman Boxer

California Suite ★★★★ 15

Comedy 1978 · US · Colour · 98mins

Neil Simon is at his most rapier-witted with this adaptation of his hit Broadway comedy, a classy confection of oddball vignettes set in the up-market Beverly Hills Hotel. The cast is a superior blend of seasoned comic performers and acting heavyweights, all having a ball with Simon's quick-fire one-liners. The standout turns are from Walter Matthau and Elaine May, and from Maggie Smith, who deservedly won the best supporting actress Oscar for her performance as, coincidentally, an actress preparing for the Academy Awards. There is substance to counteract the froth, particularly in Jane Fonda's moving performance. SH. Contains swearing. DVD

Alan Alda *Bill Warren* • Michael Caine *Sidney Cochran* • Bill Cosby *Dr Willis Panama* • Jane Fonda *Hannah Warren* • Walter Matthau *Marvin Michaels* • Elaine May *Millie Michaels* • Richard Pryor *Dr Chauncey Gump* • Maggie Smith *Diana Barrie* ■ *Dir* Herbert Ross • *Scr* Neil Simon, from his play

Caligula ★ 18

Historical drama
1979 · US/It · Colour · 98mins

This purports to be a biographical drama about the infamous Roman emperor, but it's nothing more than toga-dropping soft porn celebrating the most basic of human instincts. Malcolm McDowell glares balefully as the lustful, unhinged emperor, embarking on an increasingly sadistic road to destruction. Italian director Tinto Brass couldn't quite plumb the depths demanded, so extra scenes of titillation were allegedly added. A milestone of smut and hugely controversial in its day. TH. Contains violence, sex scenes and nudity.

Malcolm McDowell *Caligula* • Theresa Ann Savoy [Teresa Ann Savoy] *Drusilla* • Peter O'Toole *Tiberius* • John Gielgud *Nerva* • Helen Mirren *Caesonia* ■ *Dir* Tinto Brass • *Scr* Gore Vidal

Call Him Savage ★★★

Romantic comedy
1975 · Fr · Colour · 107mins

There's much to enjoy in this screwball comedy that trades heavily on the appeal of its French megastars, Catherine Deneuve and Yves Montand. The story kicks off in South America where Deneuve walks out on her fiancé and into the arms of next door neighbour Montand, who is himself on the run from his wife. Together they sail to the South Seas. AT. In French with English subtitles.

Catherine Deneuve *Nelly* • Yves Montand *Martin* • Luigi Vannucchi *Vittorio* • Tony Roberts *Alex* • Dana Wynter *Wife* ■ *Dir* Jean-Paul Rappeneau • *Scr* Jean-Paul Rappeneau, Elizabeth Rappeneau, Jean-Loup Dabadie

Call Me ★★ 18

Thriller 1988 · US · Colour · 90mins

Patricia Charbonneau is the New York journalist who gets all excited when she gets an obscene phone call, thinking it's from her boyfriend. Things change, however, when she learns that the guy at the other end is a cold-blooded killer. There are more holes than in a piece of Swiss cheese, and Charbonneau is stuck with a character who is so naive you can't believe she has survived in the big city this long, let alone land her own newspaper column. JB

Patricia Charbonneau *Anna* • Patti D'Arbanville *Cori* • Boyd Gaines *Bill* • Stephen McHattie *Jellybean* • John Seitz *Pressure* • David Strathairn *Sam* • Ernest Abuba *Boss* • Steve Buscemi *Switchblade* ■ *Dir* Sollace Mitchell • *Scr* Karyn Kay, from a story by Sollace Mitchell, Karyn Kay

Call Me Bwana ★★★ U

Comedy adventure
1963 · US /UK · Colour · 93mins

Viewed as outrageously patronising nowadays, this comedy stars Bob Hope as a bogus, bumbling explorer who helps CIA agent Edie Adams find an American space capsule lost in deepest, darkest Africa. Anita Ekberg and Lionel Jeffries play the enemy spies trying to thwart the mission. Despite its political incorrectness, this isn't bad considering the rubbish Hope was churning out at the time. The film was produced by the James Bond team of Albert R Broccoli and Harry Saltzman, who gave it a plug in *From Russia with Love*. TH

Bob Hope *Matt Merriwether* • Anita Ekberg *Luba* • Edie Adams *Frederica Larsen* • Lionel Jeffries *Dr Ezra Mungo* • Arnold Palmer ■ *Dir* Gordon Douglas • *Scr* Nate Monaster, Johanna Harwood • *Producer* Harry Saltzman

Call Me Claus ★★★ PG

Seasonal comedy 2001 · US · Colour · 86mins

Nigel Hawthorne tries to convince Whoopi Goldberg that she should take over the reindeer reins as Santa Claus for the next 200 years. This TV vehicle for Goldberg's grouchy, sharp-tongued schtick has her playing a home shopping channel producer who discovers a money magnet in Hawthorne, whose jolly, sincere demeanour charms the viewers. The stars acquit themselves well enough and despite some manipulative moments, there's an amusing sideline in Christmas cynicism. JC DVD

Whoopi Goldberg *Lucy Cullins* • Nigel Hawthorne *Nick* • Brian Stokes Mitchell *Cameron* • Victor Garber *Taylor* • Taylor Negron *Ralph* ■ *Dir* Peter Werner • *Scr* Sara Bernstein, Gregory Bernstein, Brian Bird, from a story by Paul Mooney • *Music* Garth Brooks

Call Me Madam ★★★★ U

Musical comedy 1953 · US · Colour · 114mins

After 644 performances as "the hostess with the mostest" in Irving Berlin's hit Broadway show, Ethel Merman repeated her tour de force for the rest of the world's benefit. Acting and singing up a storm with her foghorn voice, whirlwind energy and larger-than-life personality, Merman dominates this lively, lavish movie. Yet she doesn't quite outdo the scintillating dancing of Donald O'Connor and Vera-Ellen; nor does she upstage the suave George Sanders, who steals Merman's heart and has his own musical number. RK

Ethel Merman *Mrs Sally Adams* • Donald O'Connor *Kenneth* • Vera-Ellen *Princess Maria* • George Sanders *Cosmo Constantine* • Billy De Wolfe *Pemberton Maxwell* • Walter Slezak *Tantinnin* ■ *Dir* Walter Lang • *Scr* Arthur Sheekman, from the musical by Howard Lindsay, Russel Crouse • *Music* Irving Berlin • *Choreographer* Robert Alton

Call Me Mister ★★★ U

Musical 1951 · US · Colour · 95mins

A long-running Broadway revue that 20th Century-Fox brought to the screen as a Betty Grable/Dan Dailey vehicle. It's pleasant enough and the dance routines are choreographed by the great Busby Berkeley, though he's well past his prime. The supporting cast is a veritable roster of rising stars, including Dale Robertson, Jeffrey Hunter and Richard Boone. The plot deteriorates into a "putting on a show in an army camp" piece of nothingness, but Grable is attractive and Dailey is, as ever, outstanding. TS

Betty Grable *Kay Hudson* • Dan Dailey *Shep Dooley* • Danny Thomas *Stanley* • Dale Robertson *Captain Johnny Comstock* • Benay Venuta *Billie Barton* • Richard Boone *Mess Sergeant* ■ *Dir* Lloyd Bacon • *Scr* Albert E Lewin, Burt Styler, from the musical by Harold J Rome, Arnold M Auerbach

Call Northside 777 ★★★★

Crime drama based on a true story
1948 · US · BW · 110mins

James Stewart doesn't always convince as the investigating reporter trying to clear Richard Conte of a murder he didn't commit, but the growing sense of injustice carries you along in director Henry Hathaway's crime drama based on a real-life story. With producer Louis de Rochemont, Hathaway had forged a new style of gritty movie-making that reconstructed true stories with a realism and attention to the details of police procedure that made them seem more like documentaries than thrillers. The technique soon became clichéd, but this still works as a crusading piece of film-making. DP

James Stewart *McNeal* • Richard Conte *Frank Wiecek* • Lee J Cobb *Brian Kelly* • Helen Walker *Laura McNeal* • Betty Garde *Wanda Skutnik* • Kasia Orzazewski *Tillie Wiecek* ■ *Dir* Henry Hathaway • *Scr* Jerome Cady, Jay Dratler, from articles by James P McGuire in the *Chicago Times* adapted by Leonard Hoffman, Quentin Reynolds • *Music* Alfred Newman

The Call of the Wild ★★★

Adventure 1935 · US · BW · 93mins

While not exactly true to Jack London's source novel, this is still an enjoyable romantic adventure. It was during the making of this movie that Clark Gable had a brief affair with his co-star, the lovely Loretta Young, resulting in an illegitimate daughter who for years didn't know who her father was. The movie is tremendous fun, with a great sense of pace. Despite being filmed high on Washington State's Mount Baker, the snowbound locations still look suspiciously like the 20th Century-Fox backlot. TS

Clark Gable *Jack Thornton* • Loretta Young *Claire Blake* • Jack Oakie *Shorty Hoolihan* • Frank Conroy *John Blake* • Reginald Owen *Smith* • Sidney Toler *Groggin* ■ *Dir* William Wellman [William A Wellman] • *Scr* Gene Fowler, Leonard Praskins, from the novel by Jack London

Call of the Wild ★ PG

Adventure 1972 · UK · Colour · 100mins

This version of the yarn about the Yukon gold rush stars a husky dog and Charlton Heston, who, in his memoirs, considers it "the worst movie I ever made". Heston blames the mess on a British producer and the fact that finance came from Germany, France, Italy and Spain. "It was a United Nations of a movie," he wrote, "using actors according to nationality rather than ability." AT DVD

Charlton Heston *John Thornton* • Michèle Mercier *Calliope Laurent* • Raimund Harmstorf *Pete* ■ *Dir* Ken Annakin • *Scr* Peter Wellbeck [Harry Alan Towers], Wyn Wells, Peter Yeldman, from the novel by Jack London

The Call of the Wild ★★★ 12

Adventure 1996 · Can · Colour · 86mins

Yet another version of this story about the dog with the heart of an ox. Richard Dreyfuss is the narrator upon whom director Peter Svatek relies to bring London's richly evocative words to the screen and get into the mind of its canine legend, Buck. The actors, headed by Rutger Hauer as John Thornton, are not so well-served, though the famous sled-race scene is as heartstopping as ever. FL DVD

Rutger Hauer *John Thornton* • Luc Morissette *Perrault* • Richard Dreyfuss *Buck/Narrator* • Charles Powell *Hal* • Robert Pierre Cote *François* • Burke Lawrence *Charles* ■ *Dir* Peter Svatek • *Scr* Graham Ludlow, from the novel by Jack London

Call Out the Marines ★★ U

Musical spy comedy 1941 · US · BW · 67mins

Victor McLaglen and Edmund Lowe were one of the screen's great comic partnerships, co-starring as the roistering Captain Flagg and Sergeant Quirt in the 1926 silent war classic *What Price Glory?* and continuing in a popular series of boisterous follow-ups. By the time they made this semi-musical spy story, however, they were both well past their sell-by date. Here the duo vie for the love of nightclub hostess Binnie Barnes. TS

Victor McLaglen *Jimmy McGinnis* • Edmund Lowe *Harry Curtis* • Binnie Barnes *Vi Hall* • Paul Kelly (1) *Jim Blake* • Robert Smith *Billy Harrison* • Dorothy Lovett *Mitzi* • Franklin Pangborn *Wilbur* • Corinna Mura *Rita* ■ *Dir/Scr* Frank Ryan, William Hamilton

Callan ★★★ 15

Spy drama 1974 · UK · Colour · 101mins

In 1967, James Mitchell turned his novel *A Red File for Callan* into an *Armchair Theatre* production called *A Magnum for Schneider*. This movie expands that play to feature-length status to cash in on the success of the popular TV series. The film is disappointingly slow off the mark, but thanks to Don Sharp's slick direction, the pace eventually begins to pick up, with Edward Woodward excelling as the ex-agent whose ruthless professionalism belies a highly developed conscience. DP

Edward Woodward *Callan* • Eric Porter *Hunter* • Carl Mohner *Schneider* • Catherine Schell *Jenny* • Peter Egan *Meres* • Russell Hunter *Lonely* • Kenneth Griffith *Waterman* • Dave Prowse *Arthur* • Don Henderson *George* ■ *Dir* Don Sharp • *Scr* James Mitchell, from his TVplay *A Magnum for Schneider*, from his novel *A Red File for Callan*

Callas Forever ★★ 15

Fantasy music drama
2002 · It/UK/Fr/Rom/Sp · Colour · 108mins

In the 1970s, Franco Zeffirelli tried to persuade the Greek diva Maria Callas to lip-sync her way through movie versions of her operatic triumphs. Ultimately, she declined. But the veteran director was clearly so tantalised by the concept that he used it as the premise of this unpersuasive fantasy. Jeremy Irons plays a gay, ponytailed impresario who attempts to rescue the ailing career of Callas (Fanny Ardant) by staging a glossy rendition of Bizet's *Carmen*. The arias have passion and panache, while Ardant captures something of the insecurity that beset Callas. However, the remainder is rather precious and old-fashioned. DP. Contains swearing.

Fanny Ardant *Maria Callas* • Jeremy Irons *Larry Kelly* • Joan Plowright *Sarah Keller* • Jay Rodan *Michael* • Gabriel Garko *Marco* • Manuel de Blas *Esteban Gomez* ■ *Dir* Franco Zeffirelli • *Scr* Martin Sherman, Franco Zeffirelli

Callaway Went Thataway ★★★ U

Comedy western 1951 · US · BW · 81mins

When the old movies of forgotten western star "Smoky" Callaway – whereabouts unknown – enjoy a resurgence of popularity on TV, publicists Fred MacMurray and Dorothy McGuire hire a dim-witted lookalike to impersonate him in personal appearances. In due course, the genuine article – now a washed-up drunk – materialises. Howard Keel plays both roles, though he's better as the fake "Smoky" than the real one. RK

Fred MacMurray *Mike Frye* • Dorothy McGuire *Deborah Patterson* • Howard Keel *"Stretch" Barnes/"Smoky" Callaway* • Jesse White *George Markham* • Fay Roope *Tom Lorrison* • Natalie Schafer *Martha Lorrison* • Clark Gable • Elizabeth Taylor • Esther Williams ■ *Dir/Scr* Norman Panama, Melvin Frank

Calle Mayor ★★★

Comedy drama 1956 · Sp/Fr · BW · 94mins

Things do not go according to plan when virile young Jose Suarez accepts a bet from his friends to court plain spinster Betsy Blair. Also known as *Main Street* and *The Love Maker*, this is one of the films that put the dissident Spanish film-maker Juan Antonio Bardem on the international map. Skilfully capturing the stifling atmosphere of Franco's Spain (indeed, Bardem was arrested and jailed while filming it), it is not uninteresting. RK. Spanish dialogue dubbed into English.

Betsy Blair *Isabelle* • José Suarez *Juan* • Yves Massard *Jean* • Dora Doll *Antonia* • Lila Kedrova *Mme Pepita* • René Blancard ■ *Dir/Scr* Juan Antonio Bardem

The Caller ★ 18

Drama 1987 · US · Colour · 92mins

This is a curious two-hander – which premiered at Cannes and was hardly seen again – in which Malcolm McDowell mysteriously shows up at Madolyn Smith's remote log cabin. As a TV play, this might have worked; as a movie, though, it never stood a chance. AT

Malcolm McDowell *The caller* • Madolyn Smith *The girl* ■ *Dir* Arthur Allan Seidelman • *Scr* Michael Sloan

C

Calling Bulldog Drummond ★★ U

Detective mystery adventure
1951 · UK · BW · 79mins

Bulldog Drummond had last been seen doing B-feature duties in a Hollywood series at Fox when MGM claimed him for this more substantial one-off picture, filmed at its British studios. Walter Pidgeon plays the sleuth who helps Scotland Yard nail a gang of thieves by going undercover, while the strong supporting cast includes Margaret Leighton as his police assistant. Freddie Young's photography lends some class. AE

Walter Pidgeon *Hugh Drummond* • Margaret Leighton *Sergeant Helen Smith* • Robert Beatty *"Guns"* • David Tomlinson *Algy Longworth* • Peggy Evans *Molly* • Charles Victor *Inspector McIver* ■ *Dir* Victor Saville • *Scr* Gerard Fairlie, Howard Emmett Rogers, Arthur Wimperis, from the story by Gerard Fairlie, from characters created by HC "Sapper" McNeile

Calling Dr Death ★★

Mystery 1943 · US · BW · 62mins

Universal launched its short-lived B series based on the cult radio show, *Inner Sanctum*, (which was itself derived from a collection of pulp thrillers) with this taut, but ultimately unsurprising mystery. It's narrated (somewhat intrusively) by Lon Chaney Jr, who also stars as a neurologist who is haunted by the impression he may have murdered unfaithful wife, Ramsay Ames, during one of his increasingly recurrent blackouts. Inspector J Carrol Naish also has him down as No 1 suspect, but Edward Dein's screenplay allows the doubts to linger for as long as possible. More than anything, it's a fascinating clash of acting styles. DP

Lon Chaney [Lon Chaney Jr] *Doctor Mark Steele* • Patricia Morison *Stella Madden* • J Carrol Naish *Inspector Gregg* • David Bruce *Robert Duval* • Ramsay Ames *Maria Steele* • Fay Helm *Mrs Duval* • Holmes Herbert *Bryant, butler* ■ *Dir* Reginald LeBorg [Reginald Le Borg] • *Scr* Edward Dein, from the radio series *Inner Sanctum Mysteries*

Calling Dr Gillespie ★★★

Medical drama 1942 · US · BW · 83mins

With the departure of Dr Kildare from Blair General, the focus of attention in MGM's popular medical series shifted on to the crotchety Dr Gillespie. Disguising his soft centre beneath a thick crust as usual, Lionel Barrymore rose to the challenge and carried the franchise for a further six cases. Here he puts his new Dutch assistant Philip Dorn through his paces, although the central plot strand involves the demented attempts of Phil Brown to dispatch the senior surgeon. Efficiently combining mystery with melodrama, director Harold S Bucquet also finds time to squeeze in a walk-on for a young Ava Gardner. DP

Lionel Barrymore *Dr Leonard Gillespie* • Philip Dorn *Dr John Hunter Gerniede* • Donna Reed *Marcia Bradburn* • Phil Brown *Roy Todwell* • Nat Pendleton *Joe Wayman* • Alma Kruger *Molly Byrd* • Ava Gardner *Student at Miss Hope's* ■ *Dir* Harold S Bucquet • *Scr* Willis Goldbeck, Harry Ruskin, Lawrence P Bachmann, from a story by Kubec Glasmon, from characters created by Max Brand

Calling Dr Kildare ★★

Medical drama 1939 · US · BW · 86mins

The second in MGM's hospital series (after 1938's *Young Dr Kildare*) finds the Blair General intern (Lew Ayres) packed off by crusty but kind-hearted Dr Gillespie (Lionel Barrymore) to a humble neighbourhood clinic for a lesson in life. This is well-made, pleasant and sanitised stuff, despite the intrusion of the criminal underworld and Lana Turner as a wounded gunman's glamorous sister. The movie cemented the formula and popularity of the series. *The Secret of Dr Kildare* followed later the same year. RK

Lew Ayres *Dr James Kildare* • Lionel Barrymore *Dr Leonard Gillespie* • Laraine Day *Mary Lamont* • Nat Pendleton *Joe Wayman* • Lana Turner *Rosalie* • Samuel S Hinds *Dr Stephen Kildare* • Walter Kingsford *Dr Walter Carew* • Alma Kruger *Molly Byrd* ■ *Dir* Harold S Bucquet • *Scr* Harry Ruskin, Willis Goldbeck, from a story by Max Brand

Caltiki, the Immortal Monster ★★

Science-fiction horror 1959 · It · BW · 76mins

Future horror maestro Mario Bava directed 70 per cent of this endearing Italian-style mixture of *The Quatermass Experiment* and *The Blob* when director Riccardo Freda walked off the film and left his cinematographer in confused charge. Yet this purported Mayan legend, about a radioactive monster unleashed when explorers defile its holy lair, nevertheless demonstrates how inventively Bava's technical genius overcame the micro-budgets he was to suffer throughout his long and illustrious career. AJ

John Merivale *Dr John Fielding* • Didi Sullivan [Didi Perego] *Ellen Fielding* • Gerard Herter *Max Gunther* • Daniela Rocca *Linda* ■ *Dir* Robert Hampton [Riccardo Freda] • *Scr* Filippo Sanjust

Calypso Joe ★★ U

Musical romance 1957 · US · BW · 75mins

Made by Allied Artists (formerly "Poverty Row" studio Monogram) to cash in on the short-lived calypso craze, this stars one-time Duke Ellington vocalist Herb Jeffries, who had a movie career in the 1930s as the cowboy hero of a series of all-black westerns. His leading lady is sultry Angie Dickinson, and there are some wonderful numbers featuring such genuine Jamaican calypso stars as Lord Flea and the Duke of Iron. TS

Herb Jeffries *Joe* • Angie Dickinson *Julie* • Edward Kemmer *Lee Darling* • Stephen Bekassy *Rico Vargas* • Laurie Mitchell *Leah* • Claudia Drake *Astra Vargas* ■ *Dir* Edward Dein • *Scr* Edward Dein, Mildred Dein

Camelot ★★★★ U

Period musical romance
1967 · US · Colour · 175mins

Despite Joshua Logan's stodgy staging, this sumptuous screen version of the Arthurian musical by Lerner and Loewe still pierces the heart in *Excalibur* fashion. Vanessa Redgrave as Guenevere convincingly enthrals King Arthur (Richard Harris), Lancelot (Franco Nero) and us. The stars may not be exactly tuneful, but they compensate for that with their dramatic and moving interpretation of the glorious songs. TH [video] DVD

Richard Harris *King Arthur* • Vanessa Redgrave *Queen Guenevere* • Franco Nero *Lancelot Du Lac* • David Hemmings *Mordred* • Lionel Jeffries *King Pellinore* • Laurence Naismith *Merlyn* • Pierre Olaf *Dap* • Estelle Winwood *Lady Clarinda* ■ *Dir* Joshua Logan • *Scr* Alan J Lerner, from the musical by Alan J Lerner, Frederick Loewe, from the novel *The Once and Future King* by TH White

The Camels Are Coming ★★ U

Comedy 1934 · UK · BW · 71mins

Directed by American Tim Whelan, this was hardly a feather in producer Michael Balcon's cap. But comedies of this kind went down a treat with audiences in the 1930s and it was their success that later enabled Balcon to make the Gainsborough costume dramas and Ealing comedies. Star Jack Hulbert teamed with Guy Bolton and WP Lipscomb on the script, and he and Anna Lee make a pleasing partnership as they unmask desert drug smugglers. DP [video]

Jack Hulbert *Jack Campbell* • Anna Lee *Anita Rodgers* • Hartley Power *Nicholas* • Harold Huth *Dr Zhiga* • Allan Jeayes *Sheikh* • Peter Gawthorne *Colonel Fairley* ■ *Dir* Tim Whelan • *Scr* Guy Bolton, Jack Hulbert, WP Lipscomb, from a story by Tim Whelan, Russell Medcraft

Camera Buff ★★★★ 12

Drama 1979 · Pol · Colour · 107mins

Despite being one of the key titles in the Cinema of Moral Anxiety that helped shape Poland's fate in the Solidarity era, this scathing satire is Krzysztof Kieslowski's most accessible and amusing feature. Exploring both the addictive nature of film-making and the way in which visual imagery can be corrupted by its context, the story of Jerzy Stuhr's journey from home-movie novice to factory PR lackey and prize-winning auteur is related in a deceptively light tone that belies the intensity of Kieslowski's detestation of censorship and state control. Stuhr is typically excellent, although Malgorzata Zabkowska and Stefan Czyzewski also impress as his alienated wife and hectoring boss. DP. In Polish with English subtitles. DVD

Jerzy Stuhr *Filip Mosz* • Malgorzata Zabkowska *Irka Mosz* • Ewa Pokas *Anna Wlodarczyk* • Stefan Czyzewski *Director* • Jerzy Nowak *Osuch* • Tadeusz Bradecki *Witek* ■ *Dir/Scr* Krzysztof Kieslowski

The Cameraman ★★★★★

Silent comedy 1928 · US · BW · 67mins

This is a superb example of Buster Keaton's comic genius. He's a street photographer who wants to become a newsreel cameraman to get close to Marceline Day with whom he's fallen in love. The film was remade for comedian Red Skelton as *Watch the Birdie* in 1950, but that went nowhere compared with the original. In one bit of knockabout Keaton hitches a ride on a fire engine to get a scoop, only to find it's returning from the fire. TH

Buster Keaton *Luke Shannon/Buster* • Marceline Day *Sally Richards* • Harold Goodwin (1) *Harold Stagg* • Sidney Bracy [Sidney Bracey] *Edward J Blake, boss of film office* • Harry Gribbon *Hennessey the cop* • Edward Brophy *Fat man in bathhouse* • William Irving *Photographer* • Vernon Dent *Man in tight bathing suit* ■ *Dir* Edward Sedgwick • *Scr* Clyde Bruckman, Lew Lipton, Richard Schayer, Joe W Farnham [Joseph Farnham]

Cameron's Closet ★ 18

Supernatural horror
1988 · UK · Colour · 83mins

This indigestible slice of 1980s horror pulp centres on a boy whose telekinetic powers conjure up a red-eyed monster that resides in his closet. The result is an odd mix of mawkish family drama and graphic gore; 1950s star Tab Hunter has the right idea when he exits this dull affair early on. When it arrives, the Carlo Rambaldi-designed creature wouldn't terrify a Muppets fan. RS [video]

Cotter Smith *Sam Talliaferro* • Mel Harris *Nora Haley* • Scott Curtis *Cameron Lansing* • Chuck McCann *Ben Majors* • Leigh McCloskey *Det Pete Groom* • Tab Hunter *Owen Lansing* ■ *Dir* Armand Mastroianni • *Scr* Gary Brandner

Camila ★★★ 15

Period drama 1984 · Arg · Colour · 107mins

Such was the contemporary resonance of this true-life period drama that director Maria Luisa Bemberg was denied permission to film it for many years. Those pillars of Argentine society – the church, the state and the family – come in for pitiless barrage as Buenos Aires socialite Susu Pecoraro and Jesuit priest Imanol Arias briefly defy the conventions extant under the brutal de Rosas dictatorship to set up housekeeping in a country village. DP. In Spanish with English subtitles.

Susu Pecoraro *Camila O'Gorman* • Imanol Arias *Father Ladislao Gutierrez* • Héctor Alterio *Adolfo O'Gorman* • Elena Tasisto *Dona Joaquina O'Gorman* • Carlos Munoz *Monsignor Elortondo* ■ *Dir* Maria Luisa Bemberg • *Scr* Maria Luisa Bemberg, Beda Docampo Feijo, Juan Batista Stagnaro

Camilla ★★★ 12

Drama 1993 · Can/UK · Colour · 94mins

It's impossible to watch this variation on the road movie theme without getting a lump in your throat. In her final role, Jessica Tandy gives a performance of regal impudence that helps elevate a rather undistinguished film to something worth cherishing. The scenes she shares with husband of 51 years Hume Cronyn are exquisitely poignant, but they're over far too soon as Tandy and new-found buddy Bridget Fonda leave in pursuit of the latter's musical dream. DP. Contains some swearing. [video]

Bridget Fonda *Freda Lopez* • Jessica Tandy *Camilla Cara* • Elias Koteas *Vincent Lopez* • Maury Chaykin *Harold Cara* • Graham Greene (2) *Hunt Weller* • Hume Cronyn *Ewald* • Ranjit Chowdhry *Kapur* • George Harris (2) *Jerry* ■ *Dir* Deepa Mehta • *Scr* Paul Quarrington

Camille ★★

Silent romantic drama
1921 · US · BW · 72mins

The great Russian actress Alla Nazimova stars as Marguerite in an updated version of Alexandre Dumas's frequently filmed novel which, unaccountably and unacceptably, removes Armand from the famous deathbed finale, leaving the consumptive heroine to expire in the company of her servants. The bob-haired star displays her considerable range of emotions to the full, and is well-partnered by an elegant, handsome and suitably restrained Rudolph Valentino. RK

Alla Nazimova *Camille/Marguerite Gautier* • Rudolph Valentino *Armand Duval* • Arthur Hoyt *Count de Varville* • Zeffie Tillbury *Prudence* • Rex Cherryman *Gaston* • Edward Connelly *Duke* ■ *Dir* Ray C Smallwood • *Scr* June Mathis, from the novel *La Dame aux Camélias* by Alexandre Dumas fils

Camille

Silent romantic drama 1927 · US · BW

Yet another in the string of silent adaptations of Dumas's famous novel, starring one of America's queens of the silent screen, Norma Talmadge, as the ill-fated Marguerite and a bland Gilbert Roland as her lover, Armand. This is, sadly, a lost film and is on the American Film Institute's "most wanted" list. However, along with previous attempts, it has been overshadowed by MGM's deathless sound version, made ten years later with Greta Garbo and Robert Taylor. RK

Norma Talmadge *Camille/Marguerite* • Gilbert Roland *Armand* • Lilyan Tashman *Olympe* • Maurice Costello *Monsieur Duval* • Harvey Clark *The Baron* • Alec B Francis *The Duke* ■ *Dir* Fred Niblo • *Scr* Olga Printzlau, Chandler Sprague, Fred De Gresac, from the novel *La Dame aux Camélias* by Alexandre Dumas fils

Camille ★★★★ PG

Romantic drama 1937 · US · BW · 104mins

Greta Garbo never won an Oscar for a specific role (she received a special one in 1954), but the New York film critics did give her their best actress gong for what is now one of her most famous performances, as the doomed heroine in George Cukor's sumptuous film of the younger Alexandre Dumas's classic play and novel. She certainly pulls out all the stops, whether expressing her love for young Armand (Robert Taylor), modelling a glamorous wardrobe, or finally breathing her last in one of cinema's most celebrated death scenes. Cukor handles the whole thing with confidence, but it is Garbo's movie all the way. PF

Greta Garbo *Marguerite* • Robert Taylor (1) *Armand* • Lionel Barrymore *Monsieur Duval* • Elizabeth Allan *Nichette* • Jessie Ralph *Nanine* • Henry Daniell *Baron De Varville* • Lenore Ulric *Olympe* • Laura Hope Crews *Prudence* • Rex O'Malley *Gaston* • Russell Hardie *Gustave* ■ *Dir* George Cukor • *Scr* Zoe Akins, Frances Marion, James Hilton, from the novel *La Dame aux Camélias* by Alexandre Dumas fils • *Costume Designer* Adrian

Camille Claudel ★★★ PG

Biographical drama
1988 · Fr · Colour · 167mins

It is fascinating to discover that Rodin's mistress Camille Claudel was a talented sculptress, and agonising to watch her sublimation beneath Rodin, who used her talent to further his own. Isabelle Adjani and Gérard Depardieu are well cast in this re-creation of the Rodin/Claudel relationship, which, in typical French style, makes the journey through the emotional maelstrom akin to walking barefoot over broken glass. Adjani was nominated for an Oscar, and her descent into self-destruction is moving. LH. In French with English subtitles.

Isabelle Adjani *Camille Claudel* • Gérard Depardieu *Auguste Rodin* • Laurent Crevill *Paul Claudel* • Alain Cuny *Mr Claudel* • Madeleine Robinson *Madame Claudel* • Katrine Boorman *Jessie* ■ *Dir* Bruno Nuytten • *Scr* Marilyn Goldin, from a biography by Reine-Marie Paris, Bruno Nuytten

Camorra ★★ 18

Crime thriller 1985 · It · Colour · 89mins

Lina Wertmuller's muddle of Mob thriller and moral melodrama is further evidence of the controversial director's fall from critical grace. Here, she adopts a neo-tabloid manner that has little to do with the harsh realism to which the action aspires. There's no doubting the sincerity of the maternal indignation that prompts Angela Molina – a former prostitute who runs a hostel with loyal friend Daniel Ezralow – to take on the drug pushers polluting her Neopolitan neighbourhood. But Wertmuller fails to keep the lid on proceedings after Molina is assaulted and a serial killer begins bumping off the dealers. DP

Angela Molina *Annunziata* • Francisco Rabal *Guaglione* • Harvey Keitel *Frankie Acquasanta* • Daniel Ezralow *Antonio* • Paolo Bonacelli *Tango* • Isa Danieli *Carmela* ■ *Dir* Lina Wertmuller • *Scr* Elvio Porta, Lina Wertmuller

Camouflage ★★★

Comedy satire 1977 · Pol · Colour · 100mins

Made by Krzysztof Zanussi and considered by many to be a landmark of Polish cinema, this intelligent and subtly understated film explores the themes of bureaucratic pettiness and the crushing of idealism. Using a summer seminar for linguistic students, held at a palatial country estate as his fulcrum, Zanussi addresses the concerns of the generation gap through a youthful protagonist, liberal professor Piotr Garlicki, who confronts the collective cynicism of the status quo, and an older colleague (Zbigniew Zapasiewicz). RB. A Polish language film.

Piotr Garlicki *Jaroslaw Kruszynski* • Zbigniew Zapasiewicz *Jakub Szelestowski* • Christine Paul-Podlasky *Mary* • Mariusz Dmochowski *Vice-rector* ■ *Dir/Scr* Krzysztof Zanussi

Camp ★★★ 12

Musical comedy drama
2003 · US · Colour · 105mins

Think *Fame* in a summer camp for teenage Broadway hopefuls and that's actor/writer Todd Graff's sweet, feel-good directorial debut in a nutshell. Despite a variable tone, this sparkling celebration of musical theatre lives up to its title. Fame-hungry types gather at Camp Ovation to rehearse four shows every two weeks for the locals. Talented (and straight) new student Daniel Letterle becomes everyone's lust object as he engineers a benefit finale written by Broadway-has-been-turned-counselor Don Dixon. Graff handles complex issues of teen sexuality in totally un-clichéd ways, while the unknown cast captures such emotional growing pains without losing any entertainment value in a treat for all theatre geeks. AJ DVD

Daniel Letterle *Vlad* • Joanna Chilcoat *Ellen* • Robin de Jesus *Michael* • Don Dixon *Bert Hanley* • Steven Cutts *Shaun* • Vince Rimoldi *Spitzer* • Tiffany Taylor *Jenna* • Sasha Allen *Dee* • Alana Allen *Jill* • Anna Kendrick *Fritzi* • Stephen Sondheim ■ *Dir/Scr* Todd Graff

Camp Nowhere ★ PG

Comedy 1994 · US · Colour · 91mins

Every conceivable stereotype of American teenagehood is on display in this woefully unfunny slice of wish fulfilment, as a bunch of spoilt nerds set up their own summer camp with unemployed drama teacher Christopher Lloyd in nominal charge. DP DVD

Jonathan Jackson *Morris "Mud" Himmel* • Christopher Lloyd *Dennis Van Welker* • Andrew Keegan *Zack Dell* • Marne Patterson *Trish Prescott* • Melody Kay *Gaby Nowicki* • Raymond Baker [Ray Baker] *Norris Prescott* • Kate Mulgrew *Rachel Prescott* • M Emmet Walsh *TR Polk* • Burgess Meredith *Feln* ■ *Dir* Jonathan Prince • *Scr* Andrew Kurtzman, Eliot Wald

The Camp on Blood Island ★★★

Second World War drama
1958 · UK · BW · 82mins

The Hammer House of Horror took a rest from gothic gore to take a grim look at the real-life horrors of the Second World War. A sensation in its day, Hammer faced condemnation on all fronts for daring to tell the moving tale of British PoWs fearing a massacre if their cruel captors learn that the war has ended. Based on a true story, Hammer didn't flinch from the subject's pathos or its sadistic shock value. A sequel, *The Secret of Blood Island*, followed in 1965. AJ

Carl Mohner *Piet Van Elst* • André Morell *Colonel Lambert* • Edward Underdown *Dawes* • Walter Fitzgerald *Beattie* • Barbara Shelley *Kate* ■ *Dir* Val Guest • *Scr* Jon Manchip White, Val Guest, from a story by Jon Manchip White

Campbell's Kingdom ★★ U

Adventure 1957 · UK · Colour · 97mins

Dirk Bogarde dons some checked shirts and sets out to prove that he can stand up to mean Stanley Baker, who is out to swipe his land, in this unconvincing adventure set in Canada. There is some stunning location photography and a reliable British supporting cast, but director Ralph Thomas looks a little out of his depth in this genre. JF

Dirk Bogarde *Bruce Campbell* • Stanley Baker *Owen Morgan* • Michael Craig *Boy Bladen* • Barbara Murray *Jean Lucas* • James Robertson-Justice *James Macdonald* • Athene Seyler *Miss Abigail* • John Laurie *Mac* • Sidney James *Driver* ■ *Dir* Ralph Thomas • *Scr* Robin Estridge, from the novel by Hammond Innes

Can-Can ★★ U

Musical 1960 · US · Colour · 124mins

When Soviet premier Khrushchev visited Hollywood, he was taken on to the set of this 20th Century-Fox musical and shown the can-can number being filmed. He commented: "The face of humanity is more beautiful than its backside." A very poor PR result, but then Fox did sometimes lack taste when it came to musicals. Although based on Cole Porter's Broadway hit, set in turn-of-the-century Paris, this movie manages to lose some of Porter's best material, notably the brilliant lyric to *Can-Can* itself, and remains resolutely anachronistic. TS

Frank Sinatra *François Durnais* • Shirley MacLaine *Simone Pistache* • Maurice Chevalier *Paul Barrière* • Louis Jourdan *Philippe Forrestier* • Juliet Prowse *Claudine* • Marcel Dalio *Head waiter* ■ *Dir* Walter Lang • *Scr* Dorothy Kingsley, Charles Lederer, from the musical by Abe Burrows, Cole Porter

Can Heironymus Merkin Ever Forget Mercy Humppe and Find True Happiness? ★★

Musical comedy 1969 · UK · Colour · 117mins

Anthony Newley's sprawling musical fantasy, a Fellini-esque hotch-potch of dream-like sequences and irreverent whimsy, is a film that could only have been made in the 1960s. Heironymous Merkin sits on a beach surrounded by the flotsam and jetsam of his life, including a film biography which he projects to his family. We learn his story from the vignettes contained in the film-within-the-film. Meanwhile, back in the present, the film company expresses its concern that his movie still has no ending. Joan Collins, Newley's wife at the time, shows off her assets, and there's a rare feature film appearance from Bruce Forsyth. DF

Anthony Newley *Heironymus Merkin* • Joan Collins *Polyester Poontang* • Milton Berle *Good Time Eddie Filth* • George Jessel *The Presence* • Stubby Kaye *Fat Writer* • Bruce Forsyth *Uncle Limelight* • Patricia Hayes *Grandma* • Victor Spinetti *Sharpnose* ■ *Dir* Anthony Newley • *Scr* Herman Raucher, Anthony Newley

Can She Bake a Cherry Pie? ★★★★ 15

Comedy 1983 · US · Colour · 90mins

Maverick director Henry Jaglom continues on his own sweet way with this entrancing tale of opposites attracting. Mostly improvising their lines, the leads are simply superb. When she's not belting out blues numbers, kooky Karen Black frets over her divorce and the impossibility of finding romance the second time around. Meanwhile, fussy, balding Michael Emil declaims at great length about anything and everything. Teetering on the brink of self-indulgence, this meticulously-paced picture allows us to get to know the characters, whose eccentricities and opinions inexorably reel us in. DP

Karen Black *Zee* • Michael Emil *Eli* • Michael Margotta *Larry* • Frances Fisher *Louise* • Martin Harvey Friedberg *Mort* ■ *Dir/Scr* Henry Jaglom

Can You Keep It Up for a Week? ★★ 18

Sex comedy 1974 · UK · Colour · 93mins

This is one of the better-known British sex comedies of the 1970s. The flesh count is high, but there are also some giggles along the way as Jeremy Bulloch tries to resist temptation and hang on to a job for a week so that his girlfriend will marry him. DP. Contains sex scenes, nudity.

Jeremy Bulloch *Gil* • Neil Hallett *Gerry Grimwood* • Jill Damas *Annette* • Joy Harrington *Mrs Grimwood* ■ *Dir* Jim Atkinson • *Scr* Robin Gough

Can't Hardly Wait ★ 12

Romantic comedy
1998 · US · Colour · 96mins

Flat characters are stuck in underdeveloped situations in first-time directors Deborah Kaplan and Harry Elfont's attempt to recapture the mood of a John Hughes 1980s teen comedy. Set around a post-graduation party where couples meet, get drunk, indulge in bonding and gross slapstick, every stereotypical situation is pulled out of the old-hat formula plot. AJ. Contains swearing and sexual references. DVD

Jennifer Love Hewitt *Amanda Beckett* • Ethan Embry *Preston Meyers* • Charlie Korsmo *William Lichter* • Lauren Ambrose *Denise Fleming* • Peter Facinelli *Mike Dexter* • Melissa Joan Hart *Yearbook girl* ■ *Dir/Scr* Harry Elfont, Deborah Kaplan

Canadian Bacon ★★ PG

Satirical comedy 1995 · US · Colour · 90mins

Director Michael Moore had impressed both with his satirical documentary *Roger & Me* and his small-screen series *TV Nation*, but he came a cropper with his feature debut. Reversing the old *The Mouse That Roared* idea, the story has US President Alan Alda declaring war on Canada to boost his popularity rating. There should have been some incisive cross-border comedy, but Moore too often goes for easy laughs and settles for national stereotypes instead of fully rounded characters. DP. Contains swearing. DVD

Alan Alda *President* • John Candy *Bud B Boomer* • Rhea Perlman *Deputy Honey* • Kevin Pollak *Stuart Smiley* • Rip Torn *General Dick Panzer* • Kevin J O'Connor *Roy Boy* • Bill Nunn *Kabral* • Steven Wright *Niagara Mountie* • James Belushi *Charles Jackal* ■ *Dir/Scr* Michael Moore (2)

Canadian Pacific ★★ U

Western 1949 · US · Colour · 94mins

Randolph Scott drives the railroad through the Rocky mountains, fighting off Indians and trappers every inch of the way. Shot on authentic locations, this Fox effort can't quite match the scale and pomposity of *Union Pacific*, which Cecil B DeMille made ten years earlier. As the heroic railroad surveyor, Scott underplays everything, despite juggling two women – Nancy Olsen and doctor Jane Wyatt – and dodging various explosions. AT

Randolph Scott *Tom Andrews* • Jane Wyatt *Dr Edith Cabot* • J Carrol Naish *Dynamite Dawson* • Victor Jory *Dirk Rourke* • Nancy Olson *Cecille Gautier* • Robert Barrat *Cornelius Van Horne* ■ *Dir* Edwin L Marin • *Scr* Jack DeWitt, Kenneth Gamet, from a story by Jack DeWitt

The Canadians ★★ U

Western 1961 · US · Colour · 85mins

Following the Battle of the Little Bighorn, 6,000 Sioux Indians flee to Canada. They live in peace until some cowboys from Montana cross the border looking for stolen horses. Canadian Mountie Robert Ryan, standing up for Sioux rights, bars their path. Some lovely location photography barely compensates for the solemn, self-righteous tone of this early "New Age" western, which follows the Canadian line that everything bad starts below the 49th parallel. AT

Robert Ryan *Inspector Gannon* • John Dehner *Frank Boone* • Torin Thatcher *Master Sgt McGregor* • Burt Metcalfe *Constable Springer* • John Sutton *Supt Walker* • Jack Creley *Greer* ■ *Dir/Scr* Burt Kennedy

The Canary Murder Case ★★★

Detective mystery 1929 · US · BW · 80mins

This first of 15 films from SS Van Dine's novels featuring sophisticated sleuth Philo Vance has William Powell in the role (which he would play four times). It made a welcome change from the gallery of rogues for which the actor was becoming known and paved the way for his famously urbane detective, Nick Charles, in the *Thin Man* series. The "canary" of this case is Louise Brooks, an alluring beauty not above a bit of blackmail. Shot as a silent by Malcom St Clair, it was reworked by Frank Tuttle as a talkie before its release. RK

William Powell *Philo Vance* • Louise Brooks *Margaret O'Dell* • James Hall *Jimmy Spotswoode* • Jean Arthur *Alice LaFosse* • Gustav von Seyffertitz *Dr Ambrose Linquist* • Charles Lane (1) *Charles Sportswoode* ■ *Dir* Malcolm St Clair, Frank Tuttle • *Scr* Florence Ryerson, Albert S LeVino, Herman J Mankiewicz, from a novel by SS Van Dine

Cancel My Reservation ★ U

Comedy western 1972 · US · Colour · 86mins

This incompetent farce from Bob Hope – one of the last he made – reprises so many themes from his earlier movies it feels like a remake. Hope does his cowardly lion routine as a TV talk show host who becomes entangled with murder and Eva Marie Saint while vacationing in Arizona. TH

Bob Hope *Dan Bartlett* • Eva Marie Saint *Sheila Bartlett* • Ralph Bellamy *John Ed* • Forrest Tucker *Reese* • Anne Archer *Crazy* • Keenan Wynn *Sheriff Riley* ■ *Dir* Paul Bogart • *Scr* Arthur Marx, Robert Fisher, from the novel *The Broken Gun* by Louis L'Amour

The Candidate ★★★★ PG

Political drama 1972 · US · Colour · 105mins

Robert Redford's engaging performance breathes fresh life into the all-power-corrupts theme. He stars as an idealistic lawyer who succumbs to mass-merchandising politics when he sets out to be a senator. With a campaign engineered by party managers Peter Boyle and Allen Garfield, he ends up alienating his wife Karen Carlson and compromising his principles. Director Michael Ritchie gives a documentary-like credibility to the piece. TH

Robert Redford *Bill McKay* • Peter Boyle *Marvin Lucas* • Don Porter *Senator "Crocker" Jarmon* • Allen Garfield *Howard Klein* • Karen Carlson *Nancy McKay* • Quinn Redeker *Rich Jenkin* • Michael Lerner *Paul Corliss* • Melvyn Douglas *John J McKay* ■ *Dir* Michael Ritchie • *Scr* Jeremy Larner

Candlelight in Algeria ★★ U

Second World War spy drama
1943 · UK · BW · 85mins

Throughout the Second World War, Allied intelligence chiefs were worried that the image of the doltish Nazi depicted in films might make people underestimate the Germans as an enemy. Certainly, the officers on parade in this tepid potboiler pose few problems for James Mason as he attempts to steal the film that will betray the location of a top secret meeting. Director George King misses out on suspense and authenticity. DP

James Mason *Alan Thurston* • Carla Lehmann *Susan Foster* • Walter Rilla *Dr Muller* • Raymond Lovell *Von Alven* • Enid Stamp-Taylor *Maritza* • Pamela Stirling *Yvette* ■ *Dir* George King • *Scr* Brock Williams, Katherine Strueby, from a story by Dorothy Hope

Candleshoe ★★★ U

Comedy 1977 · UK/US · Colour · 96mins

In her fifth outing for Disney, Jodie Foster is in fine fettle as a tomboy turning the tables on bungling crook Leo McKern. The star of the show is David Niven, who is clearly having a ball beneath his various disguises, but there's also solid support from Helen Hayes as the owner of a stately children's hostel that will be closed down unless some buried treasure is unearthed. Solid entertainment, with a good story and fine acting. DP

Jodie Foster *Casey Brown* • Helen Hayes *Lady St Edmund* • David Niven *Priory* • Leo McKern *Harry Bundage* • Veronica Quilligan *Cluny* ■ *Dir* Norman Tokar • *Scr* David Swift, Rosemary Anne Sisson, from the novel *Christmas at Candleshoe* by Michael Innes

Candy ★

Comedy 1968 · US/It/Fr · Colour · 124mins

This is a sex farce of mind-boggling ineptitude. The impressive roster of co-stars were each paid $50,000 for a week's work, though it's such a shambolic, episodic mess that the movie seems a monument to the arrogance and indifference of stars tanked up on drugs, booze and undiluted ego. Marlon Brando, a close friend of director Christian Marquand and the film's prime mover, plays an Indian guru addicted to sex. It is the actor's all-time career low, though Richard Burton's Dylan Thomas take-off rivals it for sheer laziness. AT

Ewa Aulin *Candy* • Charles Aznavour *The hunchback* • Marlon Brando *Grindl* • Richard Burton *McPhisto* • James Coburn *Dr Krankeit* • John Huston *Dr Dunlap* • Walter Matthau *General Smight* • Ringo Starr *Emmanuel* • John Astin *Daddy, Uncle Jack* • Anita Pallenberg *Nurse Bullock* ■ *Dir* Christian Marquand • *Scr* Buck Henry, from the novel by Terry Southern

The Candy Man ★

Crime thriller 1969 · US · Colour · 97mins

This deservedly obscure kidnapping drama shot on location in Mexico City stars George Sanders as a British drug pusher who decides to branch out by abducting the daughter of an American film star. Sanders's tired performance is typical of the boredom that drove him to suicide three years later; in contrast, Leslie Parrish over-emotes as the frantic mother. AE

George Sanders *Sidney Carter* • Leslie Parrish *Julia Evans* • Manolo Fabregas *Lieutenant Garcia* • Gina Ronan *Greta Hansen* • Carlos Cortez *Rick Pierce* • Pedro Galvan *Roger West* ■ *Dir* Herbert J Leder • *Scr* Herbert J Leder, from a story by Francis Swann

Candy Mountain ★★★ 15

Road movie 1987 · US · Colour · 91mins

Ambitious musician Kevin J O'Connor pretends to know a legendary guitar-maker named Elmore Silk (Harris Yulin) in order to get a job with rocker David Johansen's band. When his bluff is finally called, he attempts to track Silk down via encounters with friends, lovers and relatives. The result is a quirky, if downbeat road movie that's more a celebration of the marginal than a straight story with a cohesive narrative. In a difficult role that requires him to put across a despairing ordinariness, O'Connor sustains the interest right up to the honest and uplifting pay-off. AJ

Kevin J O'Connor *Julius Book* • Harris Yulin *Elmore Silk* • Tom Waits *Al Silk* • Bulle Ogier *Cornelia* • Roberts Blossom *Archie* • Leon Redbone *Huey* • Dr John *Henry* • Rita MacNeil *Winnie* • Joe Strummer *Mario* • Laurie Metcalf *Alice* • David Johansen *Keith* ■ *Dir* Robert Frank, Rudy Wurlitzer • *Scr* Rudy Wurlitzer

Candyman ★★★★ 18

Horror 1992 · US · Colour · 94mins

Horror maestro Clive Barker's short story *The Forbidden* is the inspiration for director Bernard Rose's electrifying shocker in which student Virginia Madsen, researching urban legends in Chicago, uncovers a hook-handed mythical killer who then catapults her into the chilling realms of dread and destiny. Intelligent, gripping and refreshingly gimmick-free, this adult-orientated study in psychological fear is a breath of fresh scare. Madsen is terrific, giving a well-shaded performance as the emotionally abandoned heroine, and Rose's bold direction milks every terrifying moment of this compelling and atmospheric movie. AJ. Contains violence, swearing and nudity. DVD

Virginia Madsen *Helen Lyle* • Tony Todd *Candyman* • Xander Berkeley *Trevor Lyle* • Kasi Lemmons *Bernadette Walsh* • Vanessa Williams *Anne-Marie McCoy* • DeJuan Guy *Jake* • Marianna Eliott *Clara* • Ted Raimi *Billy* • Ria Pavia *Monica* • Mark Daniels *Student* ■ *Dir* Bernard Rose • *Scr* Bernard Rose, from the short story *The Forbidden* by Clive Barker

Candyman: Day of the Dead ★ 18

Horror 1999 · US · Colour · 89mins

In this dreadful made-for-video sequel, Tony Todd returns to little effect as the hook-handed bogeyman who tries to frame his artist descendent (Donna D'Errico) for the nasty murders of her best friends so she'll join him as a spectral legend and ease his netherworld loneliness. Overdoing the gore to a laughable degree, this remains yawningly predictable and unrelentingly stupid. AJ DVD

Tony Todd *Candyman/Daniel Robitaille* • Donna D'Errico *Caroline McKeever* • Wade Andrew Williams *Detective Samuel Kraft* • Nick Corri *David de la Paz* • Alexia Robinson *Tamara* ■ *Dir* Turi Meyer • *Scr* Al Septien, Turi Meyer, from the character created by Clive Barker

Candyman: Farewell to the Flesh ★★ 18

Horror 1995 · US · Colour · 90mins

Director Bill Condon shows little of the flair or fluency he would bring to his Oscar-winning *Gods and Monsters* in this long-winded and utterly conventional sequel to a marvellous original. Tony Todd returns as the hook-handed slave spirit, this time terrorising New Orleans during Mardi Gras. Not even the colourful carnival backdrop makes up for the predictable plot. AJ. Contains violence, swearing and brief nudity. DVD

Tony Todd *Candyman/Daniel Robitaille* • Kelly Rowan *Annie Tarrant* • Timothy Carhart *Paul McKeever* • Veronica Cartwright *Octavia Tarrant* • William O'Leary *Ethan Tarrant* • Fay Hauser *Pam Carver* • Bill Nunn *Reverend Ellis* ■ *Dir* Bill Condon • *Scr* Rand Ravich, Mark Kruger, from a story by Clive Barker

Cane Toads – an Unnatural History ★★★ PG

Cult documentary
1987 · Aus · Colour · 46mins

Those who believe nature is rendered safe by the urbane explanations of David Attenborough might well be checking behind the sofa or under the bed after this rude shock. It's a wonderfully dotty history lesson about the wholesale import of cane toads into Australia in 1935 to annihilate the cane beetle, showing how the utter uselessness of the attempt bordered on the surreal. Not only were they unfit for the job, but the grubby beasts devoured everything in sight except for their appointed targets. They were also so highly sexed they were incessantly breeding and were quite happy to cosy up to some mud in the absence of anything more animate. JM

Dir/Scr Mark T Lewis

Cannery Row ★★★ 15

Drama 1982 · US · Colour · 115mins

Raquel Welch was originally cast in David S Ward's over-reverential production of two John Steinbeck novels, but was fired midway through filming. It's a pity, as her buxom sexuality might have roused this story of waterfront bums from its languor. Ward wrote *The Sting*, but his screenplay here lacks that movie's zip and suffers from an episodic narrative. Debra Winger takes on the Welch role of a hooker who yearns for Nick Nolte, excellent as a baseball star turned marine biologist. TH

Nick Nolte *Doc* • Debra Winger *Suzy* • Audra Lindley *Fauna* • Frank McRae *Hazel* • M Emmet Walsh *Mack* • Tom Mahoney *Hughie* • John Malloy *Jones* • James Keane *Eddie* • John Huston *Narrator* ■ *Dir* David S Ward • *Scr* David S Ward, from the novels *Cannery Row* and *Sweet Thursday* by John Steinbeck

Cannibal Ferox ★★ 18

Horror 1981 · It · Colour · 83mins

One of the more reprehensible *Cannibal Holocaust* rip-offs, this maintains a pro-ecological stance while indulging in gratuitous blood-letting. It is surprisingly well made, but is heavy going, gruesome without being entertaining, and the script is rubbish. A group of young researchers and an obnoxious drug dealer (horror star John Morghen) find cannibals in Colombia. The original version featured genuine animal slaughter, removed before the BBFC cut a further six seconds, then passed the film in 2000. DM. Italian dialogue dubbed into English. DVD

John Morghen [Giovanni Lombardo Radice] *Mike Logan* • Lorraine de Selle *Gloria Davis* • Bryan Redford [Danilo Mattei] *Rudy Davis* • Zora Kerowa [Zora Kerova] *Pat* • Richard Bolla [Robert Kerman] *Lieutenant Rizzo* ■ *Dir/Scr* Umberto Lenzi

Cannibal Girls ★

Comedy horror 1973 · Can · Colour · 83mins

Before making the grade in Hollywood, Ivan Reitman churned out this dismal horror spoof featuring improvised patter by Second City TV alumni Eugene Levy and Andrea Martin. The couple play a musician and his girlfriend who breakdown in the Canadian backwoods where they encounter a trio of *femme fatales* with a penchant for flesh. Failing to deliver either laughs or shivers, this micro-budgeted effort was originally promoted with a buzzer to warn of impending nastiness and a chime to signal when to open one's eyes again. The gimmick was the best part of the movie. AJ

Eugene Levy *Clifford Sturges* • Andrea Martin *Gloria Wellaby* • Ronald Ulrich *Reverend Alex St John* • Randall Carpenter *Anthea* • Bonnie Neilson *Clarissa* • Mira Pawluk *Leona* ■ *Dir* Ivan Reitman • *Scr* Robert Sandler

Cannibal Holocaust ★★★ 18

Horror 1979 · It · Colour · 86mins

One of the titles most often quoted during the British "video nasties" scandal of the early 1980s, this gruesome offering is probably the finest of that bad bunch, and certainly the best of the cannibal genre. A New York professor (Robert Kerman alias porn actor Richard Bolla) goes to the Amazon jungle in search of a missing documentary film crew and finds horrifying evidence of their fate. Although the script is banal, director Ruggero Deodato makes the hunt for the film-makers exciting. As for the special effects, newspapers perpetuated the myth the murders enacted were genuine, well into the 1990s. The film was not legally available in Britain until 2001 when it was passed (with 5 minutes 44 seconds of cuts). DM. Italian dialogue dubbed into English. [video] DVD

Robert Kerman *Professor Harold Monroe* • Francesca Ciardi *Faye Daniels* • Perry Pirkanen *Jack Anders* • Luca Barbareschi *Mark Tommaso* ■ *Dir* Ruggero Deodato • *Scr* Gianfranco Clerici, from his story

Cannibal! the Musical ★★★ 18

Spoof musical comedy
1993 · US · Colour · 97mins

Only the creators of *South Park*, Trey Parker and Matt Stone, could have come up with this an "all singing, all dancing, all flesh-eating" gore flick that's a weird, wonderfully awful mix of western spoof, *Scream*-style horror and cod Hollywood musical. This satire features the sole survivor of an ill-fated mining expedition who tells how his taste for gold was replaced by one for human flesh while singing of gay love, horses and snowmen. AJ. Contains violence. [video]

Juan Schwartz [Trey Parker] *Alferd Packer* • Ian Hardin *Shannon Bell* • Matthew Stone [Matt Stone] *James Humphrey* • Jon Hegel *Israel Swan* • Jason McHugh *Frank Miller* • Dian Buchar *George Noon* ■ *Dir/Scr* Trey Parker

Cannibal Women in the Avocado Jungle of Death ★ 12

Comedy adventure
1989 · US · Colour · 85mins

Can any film with a title this great be any good? "No" is the short answer, as far as this deadpan feminist send-up is concerned. Tough anthropologist Shannon Tweed is sent by the CIA on an expedition into the Californian wilderness to locate a legendary tribe of man-eating cannibal babes. The safari is a mix of stupid sex farce and talky rhetoric on women's issues. AJ. Contains some nudity, swearing and violence. [video]

Shannon Tweed *Dr Margo Hunt* • Adrienne Barbeau *Dr Kurtz* • Bill Maher *Jim* • Karen Mistal *Bunny* • Brett Stimely *Jean-Pierre* ■ *Dir/Scr* JF Lawton

Cannon for Cordoba ★★★ 12

Western 1970 · US · Colour · 99mins

The Wild Bunch it ain't, but this western adventure is still an entertaining affair. George Peppard is a suitably heroic lead, playing an American soldier battling Mexican bandits in the early 20th century, and there's enough action to satisfy fans. The director is Paul Wendkos, an experienced Hollywood hand who since the 1970s has concentrated mainly on made-for-TV movies. JF. Contains swearing and violence. [video]

George Peppard *Captain Rod Douglas* • Giovanna Ralli *Leonora Cristobal* • Raf Vallone *Cordoba* • Pete Duel *Andy Rice* • Don Gordon *Sergeant Jackson Harkness* ■ *Dir* Paul Wendkos • *Scr* Stephen Kandel

Cannonball ★★ 12

Adventure thriller
1976 · HK/US · Colour · 90mins

This is nothing more than a poor retread of director Paul Bartel's wilder and wittier *Death Race 2000*, with all the expensive futuristic trappings removed and loads more epic car crashes added. David Carradine is "Cannonball" Buckman, who signs up for the illegal Trans-American Grand Prix cross-country car race between Los Angeles and New York, where no rules apply and underhand sabotage is *de rigueur*. Great stunts, shame about the formula-one plot. AJ DVD

David Carradine *Coy "Cannonball" Buckman* • Bill McKinney *Cade Redman* • Veronica Hamel *Linda* • Gerrit Graham *Perman Waters* • Robert Carradine *Jim Crandell* • Belinda Balaski *Maryann* • Martin Scorsese *Mafioso* • Roger Corman • Sylvester Stallone • Joe Dante ■ *Dir* Paul Bartel • *Scr* Paul Bartel, Donald C Simpson

Cannonball Fever ★ PG

Comedy 1989 · US · Colour · 91mins

Depressingly, this is one of the most expensive movies ever filmed in Canada. It's impossible to see where all the money went, for this third instalment in the *Cannonball Run* series is so bad it's embarrassing. This time a bunch of minor celebrities find themselves behind the wheels after the original racers are jailed by sheriff Peter Boyle. DP. [video]

John Candy *Charlie Cronyn* • Donna Dixon *Tiffany* • Matt Frewer *Alec* • Joe Flaherty *Vic* • Tim Matheson *Jack* • Mimi Kuzyk *Heather* • Melody Anderson *Lee* • Shari Belafonte *Margaret* • Peter Boyle *Chief Spiro T Edsel* • Lee Van Cleef *Grandfather* ■ *Dir* Jim Drake • *Scr* Michael Short

The Cannonball Run ★★ PG

Action comedy 1981 · US · Colour · 91mins

This big-budget take on the illegal coast-to-coast car race movie was made at the height of Burt Reynolds's stardom and Roger Moore's tenure as James Bond. Not surprisingly it was a global smash, but as entertainment it leaves a lot to be desired. There's not nearly enough pile-ups and too many duff jokes from a cameo-studded cast, who act as if they're starring in each other's home movies. RS [video] DVD

Burt Reynolds *JJ McClure* • Roger Moore *Seymour* • Farrah Fawcett *Pamela* • Dom DeLuise *Victor* • Dean Martin *Jamie Blake* • Sammy Davis Jr *Fenderbaum* • Jack Elam *Doctor* • Adrienne Barbeau *Marcie* • Terry Bradshaw *Terry* • Jackie Chan *First Subaru driver* • Jamie Farr *Sheik* • Peter Fonda *Chief biker* • Bianca Jagger *Sheik's sister* ■ *Dir* Hal Needham • *Scr* Brock Yates

Cannonball Run II ★ PG

Action comedy 1983 · US · Colour · 103mins

One of the worst films ever made starring a plethora of old has-beens who try in vain to recapture the whimsical success of *The Cannonball Run*. This purports to be an all-action comedy, but should be approached with extreme caution. SH. Contains some coarse language. [video]

Burt Reynolds *JJ McClure* • Dom DeLuise *Victor* • Dean Martin *Jamie Blake* • Sammy Davis Jr *Fenderbaum* • Jamie Farr *Sheik* • Telly Savalas *Hymie* • Shirley MacLaine *Veronica* • Jackie Chan *Jackie* • Frank Sinatra ■ *Dir* Hal Needham • *Scr* Hal Needham, Albert S Ruddy, Harvey Miller, from characters created by Brock Yates

Can't Buy Me Love ★★ 15

Comedy 1987 · US · Colour · 92mins

Fed up with his nerdy reputation at high school, Patrick Dempsey pays sexpot senior Amanda Peterson a hard-earned $1,000 to pose as his girlfriend for a month. The image-building works fine until she blows the gaff. A very predictable boy meets, hires and loses girl saga, this is given far too sentimental a spin to work well as romantic comedy. AJ. Contains swearing. [video] DVD

Patrick Dempsey *Ronald Miller* • Amanda Peterson *Cindy Mancini* • Courtney Gains *Kenneth Wurman* • Tina Caspary *Barbara* • Seth Green *Chuckie Miller* • Dennis Dugan *David Miller* ■ *Dir* Steve Rash • *Scr* Michael Swerdlick

Can't Help Singing ★★ U

Musical western 1944 · US · Colour · 86mins

An apt title indeed for this Deanna Durbin vehicle, and her devotees will doubtless embrace this western, vaguely influenced by the Broadway success of *Oklahoma!* Non-Durbin fans, however, will struggle with the dumb plot (Deanna heads west to marry, then changes her mind), uncharismatic leading man Robert Paige and director Frank Ryan's non-existent grasp of simple film narrative. TS [video] DVD

Deanna Durbin *Caroline* • Robert Paige *Lawlor* • Akim Tamiroff *Gregory* • David Bruce *Latham* • Leonid Kinskey *Koppa* • Ray Collins *Senator Frost* • June Vincent *Miss MacLean* • Andrew Tombes *Sad Sam* ■ *Dir* Frank Ryan • *Scr* Lewis R Foster, Frank Ryan, from the novel *Girl of the Overland Trail* by Curtis B Warshawsky, Samuel J Warshawsky

Can't Stop the Music ★★★ PG

Musical 1980 · US · Colour · 117mins

Aspiring songwriter Steve Guttenberg and girlfriend Valerie Perrine scour Greenwich Village looking for singers to do justice to his music in this heavily fictionalised account of how disco sensation the Village People rose to fame. All references to the group's gay genesis were placed on the periphery for commercial safety, although much fun can be had spotting the deliberate clues planted by director Nancy Walker. Reviled at the time for being dishonest, coy and late, from a distance this camp catastrophe is great fun and sums up the entire hedonistic era. AJ [video]

Valerie Perrine *Samantha Simpson* • Bruce Jenner *Ron White* • Steve Guttenberg *Jack Morell* • Paul Sand *Steve Waits* • Tammy Grimes *Sydney Channing* • June Havoc *Helen Morell* • Barbara Rush *Norma White* • Ray Simpson *Ray, policeman* • David Hodo *David, construction worker* • Felipe Rose *Felipe, Indian* • Randy Jones *Randy, cowboy* • Glenn Hughes *Glenn, leatherman* • Alexander Briley *Alexander, GI* ■ *Dir* Nancy Walker • *Scr* Bronte Woodard, Allan Carr

A Canterbury Tale ★★★★ U

Second World War drama
1944 · UK · BW · 119mins

Michael Powell and Emeric Pressburger's re-think of Chaucer is the most peculiar piece of wartime propaganda ever devised. Two army sergeants (one British, one American) and a girl arrive at a Kentish village which is within praying distance of Canterbury. There, girls who fraternise with servicemen are having glue poured into their hair as punishment. While it's hard to convey the film's eerie shifts of mood, it impresses as a study of a community resistant to change. This far-sighted film was dismissed at the time but is a lyrical celebration of a disappearing England. AT [video] DVD

Eric Portman *Thomas Colpepper* • Sheila Sim *Alison Smith* • John Sweet *Bob Johnson* • Dennis Price *Peter Gibbs* • Charles Hawtrey *Thomas Duckett* • Hay Petrie *Woodcock* ■ *Dir/Scr* Michael Powell, Emeric Pressburger

The Canterbury Tales ★★★

Historical comedy drama
1971 · It/Fr · Colour · 104mins

Coming between *The Decameron* and *Arabian Nights* in Pier Paolo Pasolini's classic tales trilogy, this adaptation of Chaucer's masterpiece outraged the purists with its bawdy bowdlerisation. Reinforcing his status as auteur, Pasolini also guests as the poet accompanying the party of pilgrims, who relieve the tedium of their journey to Beckett's shrine with a variety of tales. Glorying in the filth and vulgarity of medieval life and the grotesqueness of the characters, this is a film teeming with life and insight. DP. An English/Italian language film.

Pier Paolo Pasolini *Geoffrey Chaucer* • Tom Baker *Jenkin* • Laura Betti *Wife of Bath* • JP Van Dyne *Cook* • Derek Deadman *Pardoner* • George Bethell Datch *Host of the Tabard* ■ *Dir* Pier Paolo Pasolini • *Scr* Pier Paolo Pasolini, from the stories by Geoffrey Chaucer

The Canterville Ghost ★★★

Supernatural comedy
1944 · US · BW · 95mins

An enjoyable MGM version of Oscar Wilde's story, with the wonderfully irascible Charles Laughton in the title role as the spirit who can only free himself from eternally roaming by performing one good deed. Made in the heat of wartime, this has dated owing to its emphasis on harmonising Anglo-American relationships. However, a super cast including talented moppet Margaret O'Brien, amiable Robert Young and suave Peter Lawford handle the stilted sentiments with aplomb. TS

Charles Laughton *Sir Simon De Canterville/ The Ghost* • Robert Young (1) *Cuffy Williams* • Margaret O'Brien *Lady Jessica De Canterville* • William Gargan *Sergeant Benson* • Reginald Owen *Lord Canterville* • Peter Lawford *Anthony De Canterville* ■ *Dir* Jules Dassin • *Scr* Edwin Harvey Blum, from the story by Oscar Wilde

Canticle of the Stones ★★★

Documentary drama
1990 · Bel/UK/Ger · Colour · 110mins

Following the acclaimed *Wedding in Galilee*, Michel Khleifi attempted to meld drama with archive footage in this study of life in Gaza between the riots of the 1960s and the Intifada. The documentary material is particularly provocative, as various Palestinians recall the fighting that reduced their settlements to rubble and decimated a generation of their youth. The fictional segments, however, involving reunited lovers Bushra Karaman and Makram Khouri, are awash with pompous pronouncements which trivialise the genuine tragedy of this troubled region. DP. In Arabic with English subtitles.

Bushra Karaman • Makram Khouri ■ *Dir* Michel Khleifi

Canyon Passage ★★★★ U

Western 1946 · US · Colour · 91mins

This routine story of harsh frontier life was one of the first mature postwar westerns. Director Jacques Tourneur makes wonderful use of the Oregon locations and lifts the material by his thoughtful staging of everything from a cabin-raising ceremony for a newly married couple to the saloon fight between hero Dana Andrews and heavy Ward Bond. Alas, Britain's Patricia Roc – making her bid for Hollywood fame – is no match for the fiery Susan Hayward. AE

Dana Andrews *Logan Stuart* • Brian Donlevy *George Camrose* • Susan Hayward *Lucy Overmire* • Patricia Roc *Caroline Marsh* • Ward Bond *Honey Bragg* • Andy Devine *Ben Dance* ■ *Dir* Jacques Tourneur • *Scr* Ernest Pascal, from the novel by Ernest Haycox

Cape Fear ★★★★ 15

Classic thriller 1962 · US · BW · 101mins

This is a gripping and tension-laden thriller about embittered ex-con Robert Mitchum terrorising the frightened family of the meek lawyer (Gregory Peck) who put him in prison. Great shocks increase the climactic suspense, with Mitchum giving a portrayal of villainy that's unforgettably vicious and sadistic. Director J Lee Thompson's skilful use of light and shadow enhances the uncomfortable mood, while Bernard Herrmann's score counterpoints the growing dread with deft precision. AJ [video] DVD

Gregory Peck *Sam Bowden* • Robert Mitchum *Max Cady* • Polly Bergen *Peggy Bowden* • Lori Martin *Nancy Bowden* • Martin Balsam *Mark Dutton* • Jack Kruschen *Dave Grafton* • Telly

Savalas *Charles Sievers* ■ *Dir* J Lee Thompson • *Scr* James R Webb, from the novel *The Executioners* by John D MacDonald • *Cinematographer* Sam Leavitt

Cape Fear ★★★★ 18

Thriller 1991 · US · Colour · 122mins

Martin Scorsese has flirted with Hollywood in the past, but this remake of the 1962 classic is an unashamed bid for the mainstream. Robert De Niro takes the Robert Mitchum role, playing a psychotic ex-convict who torments his former attorney Nick Nolte. De Niro is way over the top as the Bible-babbling psychopath, but where Scorsese scores is in his portrayal of Nolte and his family (Jessica Lange, Juliette Lewis). In the original they were the embodiment of apple-pie American values, but here they are falling apart at the seams. Scorsese brings a dazzling array of cinematic techniques to the party and only loses his way in a crowd-pleasing but ludicrous finale. JF. Contains swearing, violence. DVD

Robert De Niro *Max Cady* • Nick Nolte *Sam Bowden* • Jessica Lange *Leigh Bowden* • Juliette Lewis *Danielle Bowden* • Joe Don Baker *Claude Kersek* • Robert Mitchum *Lieutenant Elgart* • Gregory Peck *Lee Heller* • Martin Balsam *Judge* • Illeana Douglas *Lori Davis* ■ *Dir* Martin Scorsese • *Scr* Wesley Strick, from the 1962 film, from the novel *The Executioners* by John D MacDonald • *Cinematographer* Freddie Francis

Capone ★★★ 18

Biographical crime drama
1975 · US · Colour · 97mins

Ben Gazzara gained 20 pounds by eating spaghetti for the title role in this slick exploitation biography of Al Capone. Showing the rise of the iron-hearted, death-dealing kingpin of Chicago's machine-gun mobs in the Roaring Twenties, his fall at the hands of the tax men and descent into syphilitic madness, director Steve Carver emphasises fast-paced action, copious blood-letting and speakeasy atmospheres above the true facts. Sylvester Stallone plays Frank "The Enforcer" Nitti, Capone's treacherous lieutenant. AJ

Ben Gazzara *Al Capone* • Susan Blakely *Iris Crawford* • Harry Guardino *Johnny Torrio* • John Cassavetes *Frankie Yale* • Sylvester Stallone *Frank Nitti* ■ *Dir* Steve Carver • *Scr* Howard Browne

Cappuccino ★★★

Comedy 1989 · Aus · Colour · 86mins

As with most cappuccinos, this Australian film is all froth and precious little substance. Yet there is something about this portrait of Sydney theatreland that keeps you going to the bitter end. It's certainly not the script, which lurches from chic café chit-chat to broad comedy, and from crime to frantic chase sequences with little cohesion. What saves this lukewarm offering are the performances, with Rowena Wallace as a stage star who wants to direct and viciously ambitious Cristina Parker the standouts. TH. Contains swearing.

John Clayton *Max* • Rowena Wallace *Anna French* • Jeanie Drynan *Maggie Spencer* • Barry Quin *Larry* • Cristina Parker *Celia* • Ritchie Singer *Bollinger* • Simon Mathew *Nigel* ■ *Dir* Anthony Bowman [Antony J Bowman] • *Scr* Anthony Bowman

Caprice ★★★ U

Comedy thriller 1967 · US · Colour · 97mins

The later movies of Doris Day now look like period artefacts; in this confection, co-produced by her then-husband Martin Melcher, she plays an agent working for an international cosmetics company. Director Frank Tashlin shows his usual deft hand with a daft plot and is skilled in getting the most out of Leon Shamroy's cinematography, despite Day's apparent insistence that her close-ups were filmed through multilayered gauze. Day's co-star is a quaintly cast Richard Harris, whose own insistence on wearing blue eye shadow effectively sabotages his right to be taken seriously. TS

Doris Day *Patricia Foster* • Richard Harris *Christopher White* • Ray Walston *Stuart Clancy* • Jack Kruschen *Matthew Cutter* • Edward Mulhare *Sir Jason Fox* • Lilia Skala *Madame Piasco* • Michael J Pollard *Barney* ■ *Dir* Frank Tashlin • *Scr* Jay Jayson, Frank Tashlin, from a story by Martin Hale

Capricious Summer ★★★★★

Period comedy drama
1968 · Cz · Colour · 78mins

It's not often that you come across a method director, but Jiří Menzel learned to walk the tightrope for his role as an itinerant showman in this enchanting period comedy drama. He also manages to slip a little subversive allegory into the story of a trio of friends whose tranquil existence is shaken by the appearance of Menzel's stunning wife, Jana Drchalova. Perfectly capturing the ambience of provincial life, the film's real strength is the impeccable performances of swimming pool boss Rudolf Hrusinsky, indolent mayor Vlastimil Brodsky and priest Frantisek Rehak. DP. In Czech with English subtitles.

Rudolf Hrusinsky *Dura* • Vlastimil Brodsky *Major Hugo* • Mila Myslikova *Durova* • Frantisek Rehak *Abbé Roch* • Jana Drchalova *Anna* • Jiří Menzel *Arnostek* ■ *Dir* Jiří Menzel • *Scr* Jiří Menzel, from a novel by Vladislav Vancura, Vaclau Nyult

Capricorn One ★★★★ PG

Thriller 1978 · US · Colour · 118mins

Did the Americans really land on the Moon, or did they fake it in a TV studio? That's the premise of this ingenious thriller, in which three men are bound for Mars until there's a technical hitch on the launch pad. The astronauts end up faking the mission to save face but their space capsule (which went without them) burns up on re-entry. Problem one: three embarrassingly alive astronauts. Problem two: their distraught families. Problem three: Elliott Gould as a nosey reporter. Directed by Peter Hyams with real flair, this is hugely enjoyable with a gripping finale. AT DVD

Elliott Gould *Robert Caulfield* • James Brolin *Charles Brubaker* • Sam Waterston *Peter Willis* • Brenda Vaccaro *Kay Brubaker* • OJ Simpson *John Walker* • Hal Holbrook *Dr James Kelloway* • Karen Black *Judy Drinkwater* • Telly Savalas *Albain* ■ *Dir/Scr* Peter Hyams

The Captain ★★★

Period drama 1960 · Fr/It · Colour · 115mins

While it is hard to fault the period trappings and sense of time and place created by director André Hunebelle, this is a pale imitation of the kind of rousing swashbuckler that came from the pen of Alexandre Dumas. Set in 17th-century France, it concerns the plot of Marie de Medicis to murder her son, Louis XIII. Jean Marais is more statuesque than ever as a loyal courtier, and not even the attentions of Elsa Martinelli can rouse him from his lethargy. DP. French dialogue dubbed into English.

Jean Marais *François de Capestang* • Elsa Martinelli *Gisele d'Angoulême* • Bourvil *Cogolin* • Arnoldo Foà *Concini* • Pierrette Bruno *Giuseppa* • Christian Fourçade *Louis XIII* ■ *Dir* André Hunebelle • *Scr* Jean Halain, André Hunebelle, Pierre Foucard, from the novel by Michel Zevaco

Captain America ★★ PG

Action adventure 1990 · US · Colour · 93mins

This is another botched attempt to revive the popular American cartoon character, with Matt Salinger battling the evil Red Skull. Albert Pyun is a competent director of sci-fi and martial arts action movies, but this tough, brooding comic-book fantasy suffers in comparison to other big-budget superhero adventures, and Salinger lacks charisma as the hero. JF. Contains violence.

Matt Salinger *Steve Rogers/Captain America* • Ned Beatty *Sam Kolawetz* • Scott Paulin *Red Skull* • Ronny Cox *President Tom Kimball* • Darren McGavin *General Fleming* • Melinda Dillon *Mrs Rogers* ■ *Dir* Albert Pyun • *Scr* Stephen Tolkin

Captain Apache ★★★ 12

Western 1971 · US/Sp · Colour · 89mins

One of a series of ferociously violent westerns produced by a group of left-leaning American expatriates who fetched up in Spain in the late 1960s and early 1970s. Director Alexander Singer once made the now forgotten mini-masterpiece, *A Cold Wind in August*, but he seems less happy here. Nevertheless, there's some real tension generated amid the excellent use of the landscape, while English character actor Percy Herbert holds his own against such western stalwarts as Stuart Whitman and Lee Van Cleef. TS. Contains swearing. DVD

Lee Van Cleef *Captain Apache* • Carroll Baker *Maude* • Stuart Whitman *Griffin* • Percy Herbert *Moon* • Elisa Montés *Rosita* • Tony Vogel *Snake* • Charles Stalnaker *O'Rourke* • Charlie Bravo *Sanchez* ■ *Dir* Alexander Singer • *Scr* Milton Sperling, Philip Yordan, from the novel by SE Whitman

Captain Blood ★★★★ PG

Swashbuckling adventure
1935 · US · BW · 94mins

"Come, feel the wind that fills the sails that carry us all to freedom!" Errol Flynn, a last-minute substitute for asthma sufferer Robert Donat, stars as Peter Blood, doctor-turned-pirate, in Michael Curtiz's marvellous adventure. Today, it's a little long and creaks in places, and Flynn was never much of an actor, but the camera (and the ladies) loved his devil-may-care arrogance, and *Captain Blood* remains important as the first leading role of one of the greatest of all movie legends. TS

Errol Flynn *Captain Blood* • Olivia de Havilland *Arabella Bishop* • Lionel Atwill *Colonel Bishop* • Basil Rathbone *Captain Levasseur* • Ross Alexander (1) *Jeremy Pitt* • Guy Kibbee *Hagthorpe* ■ *Dir* Michael Curtiz • *Scr* Casey Robinson, from the novel by Rafael Sabatini

Captain Boycott ★★★

Historical drama 1947 · UK · BW · 92mins

This "serious comedy" from the team of Frank Launder and Sidney Gilliat is about absentee British landowners in Ireland and their rebellious Irish workers. Set in the 1880s, it stars Stewart Granger and Kathleen Ryan, with Cecil Parker as the unpleasant Boycott, whose name entered the language after a failed attempt to collect the rent by force. Lavishly made, it falls uneasily between historical adventure and political lampoon. AT

Stewart Granger *Hugh Davin* • Kathleen Ryan *Anne Killain* • Cecil Parker *Captain Boycott* • Robert Donat *Charles Stewart Parnell* • Mervyn Johns *Watty Connell* • Alastair Sim *Father McKeogh* • Niall MacGinnis *Mark Killain* • Maurice Denham *Lt Col Strickland* ■ *Dir* Frank Launder • *Scr* Frank Launder, Wolfgang Wilhelm, from the novel by Philip Rooney

Captain Carey, USA ★★

Spy drama 1950 · US · BW · 82mins

Alan Ladd is the US army captain sent to an Italian town to root out Nazi collaborators who betrayed his compatriots during the Second World War. A promising premise, but the plot is a mass of confusion that defeats director Mitchell Leisen and leaves the viewer feeling as numb as Ladd looks. The only real success is the Oscar-winning song *Mona Lisa*, which sold a million copies for Nat King Cole. RK

Alan Ladd *Webster Carey* • Wanda Hendrix *Giula* • Celia Lovsky *Contessa Francesca De Cresci* • Angela Clarke *Serafina* • Richard Avonde *Count Carlo De Cresci* • Joseph Calleia *Dr Lunati* ■ *Dir* Mitchell Leisen • *Scr* Robert Thoeren, from the novel *After Midnight* by Martha Albrand

Captain Corelli's Mandolin ★★ 15

Second World War romantic drama
2001 · US/Fr/UK · Colour · 123mins

Louis de Bernière's surprise bestseller about a Nazi- and Italian-occupied Greek island during the Second World War was so much more than the picture-postcard love story depicted here. Director John Madden and cinematographer John Toll certainly fashion a sumptuous holiday brochure out of Cephalonia, while a sanitised version of the multilayered book plays out like a carnival of dodgy accents. Nicolas Cage's mandolin-plucking Italian is a cartoon, and over-rated Penélope Cruz plays doctor's daughter Pelagia as Spanish-Greek. AC. Contains violence, swearing. DVD

Nicolas Cage *Captain Antonio Corelli* • Penélope Cruz *Pelagia* • John Hurt *Dr Iannis* • Christian Bale *Mandras* • David Morrissey *Captain Gunther Weber* • Irene Papas *Drosoula* ■ *Dir* John Madden • *Scr* Shawn Slovo, from the novel by Louis de Bernières • *Cinematographer* John Toll

Captain Eddie ★★★ U

Biographical drama 1945 · US · BW · 107mins

The life and times of Eddie Rickenbacker, the First World War flying ace and racing driver, are re-created in this lavish biopic. The focal point is the time when he crashed his plane and nearly drowned in the middle of the Pacific, an event which makes his whole life pass in front of him – and us. Fred MacMurray handles the part with his customary charm; you really believe he's a hero who can handle everything with a shrug and a grin. The film is episodic and not without its dull stretches, but it's still a genuine slice of Americana. AT

Fred MacMurray *Eddie Rickenbacker* • Lloyd Nolan *Lieutenant Whittaker* • Charles Bickford *William Rickenbacker* • Thomas Mitchell *Ike Howard* • Lynn Bari *Adelaide Frost* • Mary Phillips [Mary Philips] *Elsie Rickenbacker* • Richard Conte *Bartek* ■ *Dir* Lloyd Bacon • *Scr* John Tucker Battle

Captain from Castile ★★★

Adventure 1947 · US · Colour · 139mins

An expansive and sumptuous 20th Century-Fox epic, set around the 16th-century conquest of Mexico by Cortez (one of Cesar Romero's best performances) and distinguished by one of the finest musical scores in Hollywood history. Today's audiences may be less tolerant of its length, and a miscast Tyrone Power grows ever more wooden as the tortuous tale of revenge and greed unfurls. Despite its shortcomings, though, this is diverting and colourful entertainment. TS

Tyrone Power *Pedro De Vargas* • Jean Peters *Catana Perez* • Cesar Romero *Hernando Cortez* • Lee J Cobb *Juan Garcia* • John Sutton *Diego De Silva* • Antonio Moreno *Don Francisco* ■ *Dir* Henry King • *Scr* Lamar Trotti, from the novel by Samuel Shellabarger

The Captain Hates the Sea ★★★

Comedy 1934 · US · BW · 84mins

Comedy tends to date more than any other genre, but there's still enjoyment to be had from this slightly wacky film based around the captain of an ocean liner, played by Walter Connolly. An episodic plot about some of the passengers includes an appearance by John Gilbert – ex-silent star, close companion of Garbo and notorious alcoholic – as a man trying to give up the bottle. Unusually for the time, the film was shot on location, and director Lewis Milestone keeps a tight rein on the various plot strands. SG

Victor McLaglen *Schulte* • Helen Vinson *Janet Grayson* • John Gilbert (1) *Steve Bramley* • Alison Skipworth *Mrs Magruder* • Wynne Gibson *Mrs Jeddock* • Walter Connolly *Captain Helquist* ■ *Dir* Lewis Milestone • *Scr* Wallace Smith

Captain Horatio Hornblower RN ★★★ U

Swashbuckling adventure
1951 · UK · Colour · 116mins

Based on three CS Forester stories about the scourge of Napoleon's navy, this sprawling, handsome, but flat feature suffers from too many shifts of emphasis between action adventure and psychological study. Gregory Peck (in a role originally meant for Errol Flynn) plays Hornblower as a high-principled stuffed shirt and thus confounds director Raoul Walsh's efforts to inject some pace. What should have been stirring stuff spends too much time becalmed. DP

Gregory Peck *Captain Horatio Hornblower* • Virginia Mayo *Lady Barbara Wellesley* • Robert Beatty *Lieutenant William Bush* • James Robertson-Justice *Quist* • Terence Morgan *Lieutenant Gerard* • Stanley Baker *Mr Harrison* • Christopher Lee *Captain* ■ *Dir* Raoul Walsh • *Scr* Ivan Goff, Ben Roberts, Aeneas MacKenzie, from the novels by CS Forester

Captain Hurricane ★★ U

Drama 1935 · US · BW · 71mins

Deprived of action (apart from a climactic sea blaze) and saddled with dull minor characters, director John S Robertson soon found himself becalmed with this RKO seafaring adaptation. But James Barton gives a good account of himself in his first talkie as the weather-beaten sailor whose retirement plans are shattered by the need to return to sea to pay his mortgage. DP

James Barton *Zenas Henry* • Helen Westley *Abbie* • Helen Mack *Matie* • Gene Lockhart *Capt Jeremiah* • Douglas Walton *Jimmy* • Henry Travers *Capt Ben* • Otto Hoffman *Silas Coffin* ■ *Dir* John S Robertson • *Scr* Joseph Lovett, from the novel *The Taming of Zenas Henry* by Sara Ware Bassett

Captain Jack ★★★ PG

Comedy adventure
1998 · UK · Colour · 96mins

A slight but genial seafaring adventure, with Bob Hoskins playing the good captain of the title. Tiring of endless pleasure cruises, Jack decides to re-create the journey of an 18th-century whaler, Captain Scoresby, who sailed from Whitby to the Arctic. He assembles a disparate crew of loners and losers and together they set off on the adventure of a lifetime. Jack Rosenthal's script lacks the sharpness of his best TV work, but the scenery is nice, the performances adept and the direction from Robert Young refreshingly uncynical. JF. Contains mild swearing. [VIDEO] DVD

Bob Hoskins *Captain Jack* • Anna Massey *Phoebe* • Gemma Jones *Eunice* • David Troughton *Emmett* • Peter McDonald *Andy* • Sadie Frost *Tessa* • Maureen Lipman *Miss Barbara Bostock* • Patrick Malahide *Mr Lancing* ■ *Dir* Robert Young (2) • *Scr* Jack Rosenthal, from articles by Nick Davies

Captain January ★★★ U

Musical drama 1936 · US · BW · 72mins

This perky Shirley Temple vehicle casts her as a little girl rescued from a shipwreck that claims the life of her parents. Adopted by Guy Kibbee's kindly lighthouse keeper, she runs into trouble when the local truant officer (Sara Haden) decides to dispatch her to boarding school. The highlight is Temple and Buddy Ebsen singing and dancing *At the Codfish Ball* to Jack Donahue's choreography. This was one of four 1936 releases that maintained Temple as the biggest box-office draw in America for the second year running. AE DVD

Shirley Temple *Star* • Guy Kibbee *Captain January* • Slim Summerville *Captain Nazro* • June Lang *Mary Marshall* • Buddy Ebsen *Paul Roberts* • Sara Haden *Agatha Morgan* • Jane Darwell *Eliza Croft* ■ *Dir* David Butler • *Scr* Sam Hellman, Gladys Lehman, Harry Tugend, from a story by Laura E Richards

Captain Kidd ★★★ U

Swashbuckling adventure
1945 · US · BW · 88mins

Charles Laughton, his triumph as Captain Bligh in *Mutiny on the Bounty* behind him, takes to the high seas again in this period swashbuckler. The star is in barnstorming, picture-stealing form as the devious and bloodthirsty pirate, while his larger-than-life posturings are both fearful and funny. Gilbert Roland and John Carradine make fine henchman, Randolph Scott is the hero, while Barbara Britton is the film's fleeting gesture towards romance. RK [VIDEO] DVD

Charles Laughton *Captain William Kidd* • Randolph Scott *Adam Mercy* • Barbara Britton *Lady Anne* • Reginald Owen *Cary Shadwell* • John Carradine *Orange Povey* • Gilbert Roland *Jose Lorenzo* • John Qualen *Bert Blivens* ■ *Dir* Rowland V Lee • *Scr* Norman Reilly Raine, from a story by Robert H Lee

Captain Kidd and the Slave Girl ★★ U

Period adventure 1954 · US · Colour · 84mins

A second-league but reasonably entertaining swashbuckler-cum-romance in which a wicked earl uses a beautiful young woman as bait to discover the whereabouts of Captain Kidd's treasure. Trouble is the pirate and the lady fall in love. No big star names here, but Anthony Dexter, who looks more like a nerdy executive than a famous pirate, and the younger, less famous Gabor sister, Eva, are fine. RK

Anthony Dexter *Captain Kidd* • Eva Gabor *Slave girl* • Alan Hale Jr ■ *Dir* Lew Landers • *Scr* Jack Pollexfen, Aubrey Wisberg

Captain Kronos: Vampire Hunter ★★★ 15

Horror 1972 · UK · Colour · 87mins

In a bid to revitalise the genre during the 1970s, Hammer gave writer/director Brian Clemens, the brains behind *The Avengers*, carte blanche to bring new blood to the vampire myth. The result is a bright and breezy blend of horror, comedy, swashbuckler and Italian western that follows Horst Janson as he tracks down aristocratic bloodsuckers, with a little help from hunchback professor John Carson and exotic gypsy dancer Caroline Munro. A fun fear-frolic that became an instant Hammer cult. AJ [VIDEO] DVD

Horst Janson *Captain Kronos* • John Carson *Dr Marcus* • John Cater *Professor Grost* • Shane Briant *Paul Durward* • Caroline Munro *Carla* • Ian Hendry *Kerro* • Wanda Ventham *Lady Durward* ■ *Dir/Scr* Brian Clemens

Captain Lightfoot ★★ U

Period adventure 1955 · US · Colour · 94mins

Rock Hudson stars as a 19th-century Irish rebel who joins an outfit led by Jeff Morrow to fight against the English. Morrow is wounded and leaves the heroics to Hudson, who, between battles, romances the boss's daughter (Barbara Rush). Authentic locations do little to rescue this dreary and basically uneventful adventure story, produced by Ross Hunter and directed by Douglas Sirk. RK

Rock Hudson *Michael Martin* • Barbara Rush *Aga Doherty* • Jeff Morrow *John Doherty (Captain Thunderbolt)* • Kathleen Ryan *Lady Anne More* • Finlay Currie *Callahan* ■ *Dir* Douglas Sirk • *Scr* WR Burnett, Oscar Brodney, from a story by WR Burnett

Captain Nemo and the Underwater City ★ U

Fantasy adventure
1969 · UK · Colour · 105mins

Did anyone have faith in this project? Robert Ryan as Nemo looks as if experiencing the "bends" would be preferable to participating in the picture, which has barely adequate effects and a shoddy script made up of borrowed ideas. DP

Robert Ryan *Captain Nemo* • Chuck Connors *Senator Robert Fraser* • Nanette Newman *Helena* • John Turner *Joab* • Luciana Paluzzi *Mala* • Bill Fraser *Barnaby* • Kenneth Connor *Swallow* • Allan Cuthbertson *Lomax* • Christopher Hartstone *Philip* ■ *Dir* James Hill • *Scr* Jane Baker, R Wright Campbell, from characters created by Jules Verne

Captain Newman, MD ★★★

Comedy drama 1963 · US · Colour · 126mins

Gregory Peck is the military hospital psychiatrist dealing with three cases involving guilt. Corporal Bobby Darin believes himself to be a coward; colonel Eddie Albert feels responsible for the deaths of his men in combat; while Robert Duvall hates himself for hiding out in Nazi territory. The actors are good, and it's entertaining up to a point, but suffers from its uncomfortable mix of drama, sentimentality and comedy. RK

Gregory Peck *Capt Josiah J Newman* • Tony Curtis *Corp Jackson Laibowitz* • Angie Dickinson *Lieut Francie Corum* • Bobby Darin *Corporal Jim Tompkins* • Eddie Albert *Col Norval Algate Bliss* • Bethel Leslie *Mrs Paul Cabot Winston* • Larry Storch *Corporal Gavoni* • Jane Withers *Lieut Grace Blodgett* • Robert Duvall *Capt Paul Cabot Winston* ■ *Dir* David Miller • *Scr* Richard L Breen, Phoebe Ephron, Henry Ephron, from a novel by Leo Rosten

Captain Ron ★★ PG

Comedy 1992 · US · Colour · 95mins

There's not much worth noting in this Disney attempt at maritime comedy, in which Kurt Russell dons an eye-patch and something that looks like a bikini. When businessman Martin Short and his wife Mary Kay Place set sail with their sassy kids, they hire Russell for his supposed sailing expertise. Although the film contains some hilarious moments, they are too few and far between. TH. Contains some coarse language. [VIDEO] DVD

Kurt Russell *Captain Ron* • Martin Short *Martin Harvey* • Mary Kay Place *Katherine Harvey* • Benjamin Salisbury *Benjamin Harvey* • Meadow Sisto *Caroline Harvey* • Emmanuel Logrono *General Armando* • Jorge Luis Ramos *General's translator* • JA Preston *Magistrate* ■ *Dir* Thom Eberhardt • *Scr* Thom Eberhardt, John Dwyer, from a story by John Dwyer

Captain Scarlett ★★ U

Period action adventure
1953 · US · Colour · 72mins

The Mexican locations and supporting cast are a major stumbling block for this would-be swashbuckler that is actually set in post-Napoleonic France. Director Thomas Carr seems as indifferent to the location as he is to the pacing and content of the narrative. Mercifully, Richard Greene is on noble form, as he returns from war to find his estates misappropriated by scheming duke Manolo Fabregas and princess Leonora Amar in the clutches of count Eduardo Noriega. DP [VIDEO]

Richard Greene *Captain Scarlett* • Leonora Amar *Princess Maria* • Nedrick Young *Pierre DuCloux* • Manolo Fabregas *Duke of Corlaine* • Eduardo Noriega (1) *Count Villiers* • Isobel del Puerto *Josephine* • Carlos Muzquiz *Etienne Dumas* • George Trevino *Friar* ■ *Dir* Thomas Carr • *Scr* Howard Dimsdale

Captain Sindbad ★★★ PG

Fantasy adventure
1963 · US/W Ger · Colour · 81mins

With ingenious effects and vigorously directed by Byron Haskin, this is a hugely enjoyable Arabian Nights adventure, despite its dark undertones. Gnarled Mexican veteran Pedro Armendáriz steals the show as the villainous sultan whose indefatigability depends on his heart remaining outside his body! But American lug Guy Williams makes a serviceable hero as he delivers the inanimate Heidi Brühl from Armendáriz's castle. DP [VIDEO]

Guy Williams *Capt Sindbad* • Heidi Brühl *Princess Jana* • Pedro Armendáriz *El Kerim* • Abraham Sofaer *Galgo* • Bernie Hamilton *Quinius* • Helmut Schneider *Bendar* ■ *Dir* Byron Haskin • *Scr* Samuel B West [Ian McLellan Hunter], Harry Relis [Guy Endore], from a story by Samuel B West [Ian McLellan Hunter]

Captains Courageous ★★★ U

Adventure 1937 · US · BW · 111mins

Spencer Tracy landed an Oscar for the unlikely role of a Portuguese fisherman with a penchant for sea shanties in MGM's big-budget rendering of Rudyard Kipling's adventure tale. A pampered young toff (Freddie Bartholomew) falls off a liner and is scooped from the briny by a fishing crew, who teach him the basics of life. A box-office hit at the time, it now shows its age, while Tracy's Portuguese lilt takes a while to get used to. But the sum of the parts remains wholesome family entertainment. PF [VIDEO]

Spencer Tracy *Manuel* • Freddie Bartholomew *Harvey* • Lionel Barrymore *Disko* • Melvyn Douglas *Mr Cheyne* • Mickey Rooney *Dan* • Charley Grapewin *Uncle Salters* • John Carradine *"Long Jack"* • Oscar O'Shea *Cushman* ■ *Dir* Victor Fleming • *Scr* John Lee Mahin, Marc Connelly, Dale Van Every, from the novel by Rudyard Kipling

Captains of April ★★★

Historical drama
2000 · Fr/Por/It · Colour · 124mins

Maria de Medeiros directs this accomplished and ambitious drama set against the overthrow of the fascist dicatorship in 1975. Naively exuberant in its revolutionary zeal and occasionally cumbersome in its structure, the story of the army captains who bungled their way towards democracy is, nevertheless, imbued with a genuine longing for the period's misplaced innocence and political passion. De Medeiros draws a bemusedly determined performance from Stefano Accorsi as the rookie rebel and handles the crowd scenes with considerable aplomb. DP. In Portuguese with English subtitles.

Stefano Accorsi *Maia* • Maria de Medeiros *Antonia* • Joaquim de Almeida *Gervasio* • Frédéric Pierrot *Manuel* • Fele Martínez *Lobao* ■ *Dir* Maria de Medeiros • *Scr* Eve Deboise, Maria de Medeiros

Captains of the Clouds

★★★ U

Second World War drama
1942 · US · Colour · 113mins

Happy to support the war effort, Warner Bros recruited some of their finest, led by James Cagney, to join the Royal Canadian Air Force and fight the Germans. Despite Cagney's initial cockiness (irritating to Canadians who knew there was more at stake than American machismo), the result was this patriotic propaganda piece, directed with his usual efficiency by Michael Curtiz. TH

James Cagney *Brian MacLean* • Dennis Morgan *Johnny Dutton* • Brenda Marshall *Emily Foster* • Alan Hale *Tiny Murphy* • George Tobias *Blimp Lebec* • Reginald Gardiner *Scrounger Harris* • Reginald Denny *Commanding officer* ■ *Dir* Michael Curtiz • *Scr* Arthur T Horman, Richard Macaulay, Norman Reilly Raine, from a story by Arthur T Horman, Roland Gillette

The Captain's Paradise

★★★ U

Comedy 1953 · UK · BW · 85mins

Alec Coppel received an Oscar nomination for the original story of this self-satisfied comedy, in which bigamy is laughed off as the ideal solution to the sociosexual vacillation of an outwardly charming sea captain. Called upon to do little more than vegetate in Gibraltar and tango around Tangier, Alec Guinness cruises through this lightweight picture, which charts an even more predictable course than the ferry he commands. Yvonne De Carlo confuses noise with exoticism, but Celia Johnson is splendid as the mouse wife. DP DVD

Alec Guinness *Captain Henry St James* • Yvonne De Carlo *Nita* • Celia Johnson *Maud* • Charles Goldner *Chief Officer Ricco* • Miles Malleson *Lawrence St James* • Bill Fraser *Absalom* • Tutte Lemkow *Principal dancer* ■ *Dir* Anthony Kimmins • *Scr* Alec Coppel, Nicholas Phipps, from a story by Alec Coppel

The Captain's Table

★★ U

Comedy 1958 · UK · Colour · 86mins

Richard Gordon's *Doctor* series had been the mainstay of the Rank Organisation in the 1950s. This adaptation of another Gordon novel was obviously something of a gratuity for services rendered, as almost every scene seems like an out-take from *Doctor at Sea*. At the helm is John Gregson as a bluff sea cove whose colourful cargo-ship banter is hardly suitable for the passengers of the luxury liner he now commands. The class clash throws up the usual cosy gags. DP

John Gregson *Captain Ebbs* • Peggy Cummins *Mrs Judd* • Donald Sinden *Shawe-Wilson* • Nadia Gray *Mrs Porteous* • Maurice Denham *Major Broster* • Reginald Beckwith *Burtweed* • Bill Kerr *Bill Coke* • Joan Sims *Maude Pritchett* ■ *Dir* Jack Lee • *Scr* John Whiting, Bryan Forbes, Nicholas Phipps, from the novel by Richard Gordon

Captive

★★★ 18

Thriller 1986 · UK/Fr · Colour · 94mins

Wealthy heiress Irina Brook is kidnapped, brainwashed and eventually re-educated by terrorists to recognise the hollowness of her existence in a vague approximation of the Patty Hearst story. Multilayered in thematic structure (as one would expect from writer/director Paul Mayersberg, who wrote the screenplay for Nicolas Roeg's *The Man Who Fell to Earth*), this is a constantly intriguing, if overly intellectual polemic on privilege and self-discovery. AJ

Irina Brook *Rowena Le Vay* • Oliver Reed *Gregory Le Vay* • Xavier Deluc *D* • Corinne Dacla *Bryony* • Hiro Arai *Hiro* • Nick Reding *Leo* • Annie Leon *Pine* ■ *Dir/Scr* Paul Mayersberg

The Captive

★★★ 15

Drama 2000 · Fr/Bel · Colour · 112mins

All film-maker Chantal Akerman's trademarks are contained in this rigidly controlled adaptation of Marcel Proust's short story *La Prisonnière*. However, these trademarks – the long takes and impeccable compositions, the fascination with corridors and journeys, and the justifiable anger at cinema's continuing fixation with objectifying women – all serve to distance us from the disturbing storyline. This is often intriguing, but the solemnity of the staging makes it's difficult to engage with either the impassive Sylvie Testud or Stanislas Merhar, the jealous suitor who hires her best friend, Olivia Bonamy, to spy on her. DP. In French with English subtitles. DVD

Stanislas Merhar *Simon* • Sylvie Testud *Ariane* • Olivia Bonamy *Andrée* • Liliane Rovère *Françoise* • Françoise Bertin *The grandmother* • Aurore Clément *Léa* ■ *Dir* Chantal Akerman • *Scr* Chantal Akerman, Eric de Kuyper, from the novel *La Prisonnière* by Marcel Proust

The Captive City

★★★

Crime drama 1952 · US · BW · 91mins

This exposé of organised crime is seen through the eyes of small-town newspaper editor John Forsythe. Using the documentary approach, director Robert Wise creates an authentic atmosphere of corruption. The story is framed in flashback during Forsythe's journey to Washington where he testifies to the Senate Crime Investigating Committee headed by Senator Kefauver (who makes a cameo appearance). Estes Kefauver was a feared figure in Hollywood, having criticised the studios' glamorising of crime. AT

John Forsythe *Jim Austin* • Joan Camden *Marge Austin* • Harold J Kennedy *Don Carey* • Ray Teal *Chief Gillette* • Marjorie Crossland *Mrs Sirak* • Victor Sutherland *Murray Sirak* ■ *Dir* Robert Wise • *Scr* Karl Kamb, Alvin M Josephy Jr, from a story by Alvin M Josephy Jr

Captive City

★★

Second World War drama
1962 · It · BW · 91mins

The city? Athens. The period? The dog days of the Second World War. The exact location? A hotel where a disparate group of actors are in search of work and offshore payments. This Euro-pudding of a movie was cobbled together by three writers and put into the hands of former actor and dancer-turned-director, Joseph Anthony. A formulaic piece about British forces defending an arms cache, it depicts the characters behaving well, interestingly or badly according to star status and ability. BB

David Niven *Major Peter Whitfield* • Lea Massari *Lelia* • Ben Gazzara *Capt George Stubbs* • Daniela Rocca *Doushka* • Martin Balsam *Feinberg* • Michael Craig *Captain Elliot* ■ *Dir* Joseph Anthony • *Scr* Guy Elmes, Marc Brandel, Eric Bercovici, from the novel *Captive City* by John Appleby,

The Captive Heart

★★★★ PG

Second World War drama
1946 · UK · BW · 94mins

British cinema produced many fine prisoner-of-war movies, but this, made within a year of the liberation of the camps, is the best. Perhaps the most notable thing about the production is the almost documentary-like re-creation of the boredom, frustration and claustrophobia of stalag life. Basil Dearden's meticulous direction keeps melodrama at bay, but the real power of the piece comes from the performance of Michael Redgrave, who is superb as the frightened Czech whose deceptions arouse the suspicions of friend and foe alike. DP

Michael Redgrave *Captain Karel Hasek* • Rachel Kempson *Celia Mitchell* • Frederick Leister *Mr Mowbray* • Mervyn Johns *Private Evans* • Rachel Thomas *Mrs Evans* • Jack Warner *Corporal Horsfall* • Gladys Henson *Mrs Horsfall* • Gordon Jackson *Lieutenant Lennox* ■ *Dir* Basil Dearden • *Scr* Angus MacPhail, Guy Morgan, from a story by Patrick Kirwan

Captive Hearts

★ 15

Drama 1988 · US · Colour · 96mins

An American serviceman, imprisoned by the Japanese during the Second World War, falls for a local girl in this lame drama, co-written by star Noriyuki "Pat" Morita (*The Karate Kid*). The script's weak plea for universal tolerance and world unity reduces proceedings to the level of a cartoon. So wooden you can almost hear the entire cast creak. JM

Chris Makepeace *Robert* • Noriyuki "Pat" Morita [Pat Morita] *Fukushima* • Michael Sarrazin *McManus* • Mari Sato *Miyoko* • Seth Sakai *Takayama* ■ *Dir* Paul Almond • *Scr* Noriyuki "Pat" Morita, John A Kuri, from a screenplay (unproduced) by Sargon Tamimi

A Captive in the Land

★★

Action drama
1991 · USSR/US · Colour · 96mins

The concept is familiar – a mismatched duo must bury their differences to survive in a hostile environment – but the striking locations raise it above the norm. Sam Waterston is the American pilot who forms an unlikely alliance with Russian flyer Alexander Potapov when the two become stranded in the Arctic wastes. This two-hander recycles more than a couple of well-worn clichés, but director John Berry skilfully evokes the desolation of their predicament. JF

Sam Waterston *Royce* • Alexander Potapov *Averyanov* ■ *Dir* John Berry • *Scr* Lee Gold, from a novel by James Aldridge

Captive of the Desert

★★★★ PG

Biographical drama
1990 · Fr · Colour · 101mins

Anyone seduced by the beauties of the desert while watching *The English Patient* should give this remarkable true-life tale a try. Although hardly saying a word, Sandrine Bonnaire gives a powerful performance portraying the story of Françoise Claustre, the Frenchwoman who was kidnapped as a political protest by a tribe of nomadic rebels in Chad in 1975. Director Raymond Depardon captures Bonnaire's shift from desperation to acclimatisation with great subtlety, while he records the daily rituals of the desert people with a respectful curiosity that makes the mundane seem fascinating. DP. In French with English subtitles.

Sandrine Bonnaire *Frenchwoman* • Dobi Kor • Fadi Taha • Dobi Wachink • Badei Barka • Atchi Wahi-li • Daki Kor • Isai Kor • Brahim Barka ■ *Dir/Scr* Raymond Depardon

Captive Rage

★★ 18

Action adventure 1988 · US · Colour · 87mins

Oliver Reed plays a South American despot whose son is thrown in jail by Robert Vaughn of America's Drug Enforcement Agency. Mucho miffed by this, Reed retaliates big time by hijacking a plane of lissome young gringos – including Vaughn's daughter. The hostages are then routinely abused, tortured and fed to Reed's pet piranhas. Not subtle. AT

Oliver Reed *General Belmondo* • Robert Vaughn *Eduard Delacorte* • Claudia Udy *Chiga* • Deon Stewardson *Carlos Belmondo* ■ *Dir* Cedric Sundstrom • *Scr* Rick Marx, Cedric Sundstrom, Peter Welbeck [Harry Alan Towers]

Captives

★★★ 15

Drama 1994 · UK · Colour · 95mins

In this drama made by the BBC and given a limited cinema release, Julia Ormond stars as a dentist with marital problems who takes work in a high security prison where she falls for a dangerous criminal, played by Tim Roth. From this decidedly offbeat premise emerges a strange love story and suspense thriller, tightly directed by Angela Pope and sharply written by Frank Deasy. AT. Contains violence, swearing and sex scenes.

Tim Roth *Philip Chaney* • Julia Ormond *Rachel Clifford* • Keith Allen *Lenny* • Siobhan Redmond *Sue* • Peter Capaldi *Simon* • Colin Salmon *Towler* • Richard Hawley *Sexton* • Annette Badland *Maggie* • Jeff Nuttall *Harold* • Kenneth Cope *Dr Hockley* • Mark Strong *Kenny* ■ *Dir* Angela Pope • *Scr* Frank Deasy

The Capture

★★★

Drama 1950 · US · BW · 90mins

A nifty little flashback movie from the pen of Niven Busch, who was also responsible for that bubbling cauldron of overwrought emotion *Duel in the Sun*. Busch's then-wife, Teresa Wright, gives a typically adroit performance as the widow involved with oil executive Lew Ayres, blissfully unaware that he killed her husband during an investigation of a payroll robbery. The script is occasionally overcooked, but the leads and the ever-sinister Victor Jory are eminently watchable. DP

Lew Ayres *Vanner* • Teresa Wright *Ellen* • Victor Jory *Father Gomez* • Jacqueline White *Luanda* • Jimmy Hunt *Mike* • Barry Kelley *Mahoney* • Duncan Renaldo *Carlos* • William Bakewell *Tobin* • Edwin Rand *Tevlin* ■ *Dir* John Sturges • *Scr* Niven Busch

Captured

★★★ 18

Psychological thriller
1998 · US · Colour · 91mins

Car thief Andrew Divoff makes a second stab at stealing the flashy motor of stressed-out developer Nick Mancuso, falling foul of a sneaky new security system. Essentially, this is a dogless variation on Stephen King's *Cujo*, with the car-caged Divoff taunted and tortured by his unbalanced captor in a number of sadistic ways, ranging from loud music to wire cutters. Although hampered by limited locations (mainly a small garage), bland direction and crazed overacting from Mancuso, this does maintain interest and provokes some interesting ideas, albeit in a deranged fashion. JC DVD

Nick Mancuso *Holden Downs* • Andrew Divoff *Robert Breed* • Michael Mahonen *Joey Breed* • Linda Hoffman *Faye Downs* • Seth Peterson *Buddy* ■ *Dir/Scr* Peter Liapis

Capturing the Friedmans

★★★★ 15

Documentary 2003 · US · Colour · 103mins

Director Andrew Jarecki refuses to adjudicate whether the story of a retired Long Island teacher's arrest for paedophilia is a suburban scandal or a hysterical conspiracy. Accused of assaulting boys attending lessons in the family basement, Arnold Friedman's fall from grace represented a domestic tragedy for his unforgiving wife, Elaine, and his largely supportive sons, David, Seth and Jesse (who was also jailed on child abuse charges). Comprising the Friedmans' own revealing home movies, interviews and news footage, this compelling film raises disturbing questions about the law's attitude to those accused of sex crimes. DP DVD

Dir Andrew Jarecki • *Editor* Richard Hankin • *Music* Andrea Morricone

The Car ★★★

Horror 1977 · US · Colour · 98mins

This schlock horror about a demonic killer car is not particularly original, but is nonetheless surprisingly effective. What success it does achieve is largely owing to its excellent use of night shooting and a superb dramatic use of sound from dubbing editor John Stacy. The cast is interesting, but the star is really the car. TS

James Brolin *Deputy Sheriff Wade Parent* • Kathleen Lloyd *Lauren* • John Marley *Sheriff Everett Peck* • RG Armstrong *Amos* • John Rubinstein *John Morris* • Elizabeth Thompson *Margie* ■ *Dir* Elliot Silverstein • *Scr* Dennis Shryack, Michael Butler, Lane Slate, from a story by Dennis Shryack

Car 54 Where Are You? ★★ 15

Comedy 1991 · US · Colour · 84mins

Yet another Hollywood movie with its origins in a TV sitcom. Devised originally by Nat Hiken, creator of the *Sergeant Bilko* TV series, the show teamed Joe E Ross and Fred Gwynne as the doltish cops who brought chaos to New York's 53rd Precinct. David Johansen and John C McGinley step into their uniforms for this drab reworking, which sees the officers trying to protect Mafia informer Jeremy Piven. It's easy to see why this went unreleased for three years. DP. Contains violence. [VIDEO]

David Johansen *Officer Gunther Toody* • John C McGinley *Officer Francis Muldoon* • Fran Drescher *Velma Velour* • Nipsey Russell *Captain Dave Anderson* • Rosie O'Donnell *Lucille Toody* • Daniel Baldwin *Don Motti* • Jeremy Piven *Herbert Hortz* • Al Lewis *Patrolman Leo Schnauzer* ■ *Dir* Bill Fishman • *Scr* Eric Tarloff, Ebbe Roe Smith, Peter McCarthy, Peter Crabbe, from a story by Nat Hiken, from the TV series by Eric Tarloff

Car of Dreams ★★ U

Musical comedy 1935 · UK · BW · 72mins

The British film industry has never been renowned for its musicals, but this romantic frippery is made more palatable by the sight of John Mills doing a spot of crooning and hoofing. Mills plays the son of a musical instrument tycoon, who poses as a chauffeur to win the heart of factory girl Grete Mosheim. The songs are pretty dire, but the presence of J Robertson Hare more than compensates. DP

John Mills *Robert Miller* • Mark Lester (1) *Miller Sr* • Norah Howard *Anne Fisher* • J Robertson Hare [Robertson Hare] *Henry Butterworth* • Grete Mosheim *Vera Hart* • Margaret Withers *Mrs Hart* ■ *Dir* Graham Cutts, Austin Melford • *Scr* C Stafford Dickens, R Benson, from a story by Austin Melford

Car Trouble ★ 15

Comedy 1985 · UK · Colour · 89mins

This tale of an adulterous wife who steals her husband's beloved Jaguar and proceeds to get stuck, literally, in flagrante with an obsequious car dealer would barely have provided enough sniggers for a sitcom. But director David Green strings it out to an excruciating length that taxes even Julie Walters's ingenuity. DP [VIDEO] DVD

Julie Walters *Jacqueline Spong* • Ian Charleson *Gerald Spong* • Stratford Johns *Reg Sampson* • Vincenzo Ricotta *Kevin* • Hazel O'Connor *Maureen* ■ *Dir* David Green • *Scr* James Whaley, AJ Tipping

Car Wash ★★★★ PG

Comedy 1976 · US · Colour · 92mins

A great little movie, made for small change and all the bacon butties the crew could eat, which deservedly erupted into a major hit. The premise is simple, but bursting with energy and high octane joy. A bevy of finger snappin', jive talkin' car wash attendants josh and joke their way through 24 hours in their downmarket establishment's precarious life. A largely unknown cast, a barely known director and one run-down location all add up to a minor movie classic. SH. Contains swearing. [VIDEO] DVD

Franklyn Ajaye *TC* • Sully Boyar *Mr B* • Richard Brestoff *Irwin* • George Carlin *Taxi driver* • Professor Irwin Corey *Mad Bomber* • Bill Duke *Duane* • Antonio Fargas *Lindy* • Richard Pryor *Daddy Rich* ■ *Dir* Michael Schultz • *Scr* Joel Schumacher

Les Carabiniers ★★★

War drama 1963 · Fr/It · BW · 79mins

Jean-Luc Godard's bleak semi-documentary follows two uncouth peasant boys who sign up for war, commit terrible crimes and are stunned when they are not regarded as heroes. The movie adopts a casual approach to violence that is reflected in the attitudes of its main characters. Critical reaction was so hostile that the film was initially withdrawn, while modern audiences may be confused by Godard's cultural teasing. That said, it remains a provocative study of war. AT. In French with English subtitles.

Marino Mase *Ulysses* • Albert Juross *Michel-Ange* • Genevieve Galéa *Vênus* • Catherine Ribeiro *Cléopâtre* • Gérard Poirot *1st Carabinier* • Jean Brassat *2nd Carabinier* • Alvaro Gheri *3rd Carabinier* • Barbet Schroeder *Car salesman* ■ *Dir* Jean-Luc Godard • *Scr* Jean-Luc Godard, Jean Gruault, Roberto Rossellini, from the play *I Carabinieri* by Benjamino Joppolo, adapted by Jacques Audiberti

Carandiru ★★★★ 15

Prison drama
2003 · Bra/US · Colour · 139mins

Hector Babenco's harrowing true story of conditions inside Carandiru, the biggest prison in South America, leaves you scorched and exhausted. The jail's brutality and squalor is introduced through the eyes of a new doctor (Luiz Carlos Vasconcelos), brought in to help control an escalating Aids epidemic. Despite the depravity, he finds solidarity and a lust for life among the inmates, who divulge their stories to him. This sprawling film uses at least a thousand extras in its second-half riot scenes and, while Babenco's control over everything might not be altogether firm, his device of letting inhabitants explain themselves to camera is highly effective. TH. In Portugese with English subtitles. Contains swearing, violence and drug abuse. DVD

Luiz Carlos Vasconcelos *Doctor* • Milton Goncalves *Chico* • Ivan de Almeida *Ebony* • Ailton Graca *Highness* • Maria Luisa Mendonca *Dalva* • Aida Leiner *Rosirene* ■ *Dir* Hector Babenco • *Scr* Victor Navas, Hector Babenco, Fernando Bonassi, from the novel *Estação Carandiru* by Drauzio Varella

Caravaggio ★★★★ 18

Biographical drama
1986 · UK · Colour · 88mins

With Nigel Terry excelling in the lead, this portrait of the artist as a gay man is Derek Jarman's most accessible, revealing and beautiful work. Jarman frees himself from the constraints of the traditional biopic by slotting anachronistic details into a *mise en scène* that is almost mannerist in its solemn grandeur. He investigates not only the painter's relationships with male model Sean Bean and his mistress, Tilda Swinton, but also the source of his inspiration. And, since this is a study of a visual medium, he forces us to seek significance in gestures, silences and exquisitely reproduced tableaux. DP. Contains violence, swearing and nudity. [VIDEO]

Nigel Terry *Caravaggio* • Sean Bean *Ranuccio Thomasoni* • Tilda Swinton *Lena* • Garry Cooper *Davide* • Spencer Leigh *Jerusaleme* • Nigel Davenport *Giustiniani* • Robbie Coltrane *Scipione Borghese* • Michael Gough *Cardinal Del Monte* ■ *Dir/Scr* Derek Jarman • *Cinematographer* Gabriel Beristain

Caravan ★★

Musical drama 1934 · US/Fr · BW · 98mins

This was filmed in both French and American versions, both starring Charles Boyer and directed by Erik Charell. A young Hungarian countess (Loretta Young/Annabella) inherits a large estate, conditional on getting married. Ignoring the suggestion of the local baron (C Aubrey Smith/Jules Racourt) that his son, whom she has never met, would make a suitable husband, she marries gypsy musician Boyer. Then the baron's son (Phillips Holmes/Pierre Brasseur) appears on the scene. Although eye-catchingly filmed, with leading ladies to match, this whimsical, operetta-style movie is long and largely tedious, not helped by Boyer hamming it up. RK

Charles Boyer *Lazi* • Annabella *Princess Wilma (French version)* • Loretta Young *Countess Wilma (US version)* • Pierre Brasseur *Lieutenant of Tokay (French version)* • Phillips Holmes *Lieutenant von Tokay (US version)* • Conchita Montenegro *Tinka (French version)* • Jean Parker *Tinka (US version)* • Marcel Vallée *Innkeeper (French version)* • Noah Beery *Innkeeper (US version)* • Jules Racourt *Baron de Tokay (French version)* • C Aubrey Smith *Baron von Tokay (US version)* ■ *Dir* Erik Charell • *Scr* (French version) Samson Raphaelson, Robert Liebmann, Arthur Ripley; (Us verison) Hans Kraly, Raymond Van Sickel, Erik Charell; from the short story *Gypsy Melody* by Melchior Lengyel

Caravan ★★★

Period romantic drama
1946 · UK · BW · 122mins

Set in 19th century Spain, this period melodrama from Gainsborough Studios was a huge hit in 1946, with Stewart Granger's derring-do just the thing to take cinema audiences' minds off postwar rationing. Granger plays an impoverished writer who dallies with Jean Kent's gypsy dancer, but his heart is really set on Anne Crawford's lady of the manor. Meanwhile Dennis Price oozes caddishness from every pore as his deadly rival. Overdressed, overheated and deliriously silly. AT

Stewart Granger *Richard* • Anne Crawford *Oriana* • Jean Kent *Rosal* • Dennis Price *Francis* • Robert Helpmann *Wycroft* • Gerard Heinz *Don Carlos* • Arthur Goullet *Suiza* • John Salew *Diego* ■ *Dir* Arthur Crabtree • *Scr* Roland Pertwee, from the novel by Lady Eleanor Smith

Caravan to Vaccares ★★ 15

Action adventure
1974 · UK/Fr · Colour · 93mins

Caravan to vacuity, more like, in this implausible adaptation of a far-fetched Alistair MacLean novel in which boorish American David Birney and seductress Charlotte Rampling team up to try to smuggle Hungarian scientist Michael Bryant from Provence to New York. The lush Camargue locations and co-star Michel Lonsdale's ironic asides are two meagre reasons to watch. TH [VIDEO]

Charlotte Rampling *Lila* • David Birney *Neil Bowman* • Michael Lonsdale [Michel Lonsdale] *Duc de Croytor* • Marcel Bozzuffi *Henri Czerda* • Michael Bryant *Stefan Zuger* ■ *Dir* Geoffrey Reeve • *Scr* Paul Wheeler, from the novel by Alistair MacLean

Caravans ★★

Adventure 1978 · US/Iran · Colour · 123mins

A year before he was deposed by the Ayatollahs, the Shah of Iran financed this flabby epic, based on James Michener's novel. Set in 1948, this is the tale of American beauty Jennifer O'Neill who runs off with desert chieftain Anthony Quinn. It offers some breathtaking (not to mention unfamiliar) scenery, beautifully shot by British maestro Douglas Slocombe, while Quinn adds another nationality to his ethnic bag of tricks. AT

Anthony Quinn *Zulfigar* • Michael Sarrazin *Mark Miller* • Jennifer O'Neill *Ellen Jasper* • Christopher Lee *Sardar Khan* • Joseph Cotten *Crandall* • Behrooz Vosoughi *Nazrullah* ■ *Dir* James Fargo • *Scr* Nancy Voyles Crawford, Thomas A McMahon, Lorraine Williams, from the novel by James Michener

Carbine Williams ★★

Biographical drama 1952 · US · BW · 91mins

James Stewart stars as Marsh Williams, the inventor of the M-1 carbine, a weapon that revolutionised modern warfare. One interesting feature of this rather dour story, directed by Richard Thorpe in a pedestrian manner, was that Williams did his work on the rifle while in prison for bootlegging. RB

James Stewart *Marsh Williams* • Jean Hagen *Maggie Williams* • Wendell Corey *Capt HT Peoples* • Carl Benton Reid *Claude Williams* • Paul Stewart *"Dutch" Kruger* • Otto Hulett *Mobley* • Rhys Williams *Redwick Karson* • Herbert Heyes *Lionel Daniels* ■ *Dir* Richard Thorpe • *Scr* Art Cohn

Carbon Copy ★ 15

Comedy drama 1981 · US · Colour · 87mins

This tepid race satire drives its point home with sledgehammer subtlety. The usually dependable George Segal is wasted here as a successful business executive whose life falls apart following the sudden arrival of the son he never knew he had. Shock, horror – the boy (Denzel Washington) is black! Heavy-going for all concerned. DF [VIDEO]

George Segal *Walter Whitney* • Susan Saint James *Vivian Whitney* • Jack Warden *Nelson Longhurst* • Denzel Washington *Roger Porter* • Dick Martin *Victor Bard* • Paul Winfield *Bob Garvey* • Vicky Dawson *Mary Ann* ■ *Dir* Michael Schultz • *Scr* Stanley Shapiro

The Card ★★★ U

Comedy drama 1952 · UK · BW · 87mins

Adapted from Arnold Bennett's 1911 novel, this is a stylish, if rather empty, rags to riches story set in the author's beloved Five Towns. Eric Ambler's script is full of smart situations and witty lines, but Alec Guinness is hardly stretched as the laundress's son who achieves wealth and respectability through his machiavellian schemes. There is admirable support from Glynis Johns and Valerie Hobson as the women in his life, but the film suffers from the attempt to cast it in the Ealing comedy mould. DP [VIDEO]

Alec Guinness *Edward Henry "Denry" Machin* • Glynis Johns *Ruth Earp* • Valerie Hobson *Countess of Chell* • Petula Clark *Nellie Cotterill* • Edward Chapman *Mr Duncalf* • Joan Hickson *Mrs Codleyn* • Michael Hordern *Bank manager* ■ *Dir* Ronald Neame • *Scr* Eric Ambler, from the novel by Arnold Bennett

The Card Player ★★ 15

Crime thriller 2004 · It · Colour · 99mins

In this lethargic whodunnit, a psychopath challenges Roman policewoman Stefania Rocca to games of Internet poker for the lives of abducted women. If she loses, the screaming victims are murdered live on webcam. Can Rocca and Irish cop Liam Cunningham uncover the weird clues to the cyber assassin's identity?

C

Sporting little of director Dario Argento's signature flair or flamboyant style, this is a dreary-looking and bloodless bust. AJ. In English and Italian with subtitles. Contains swearing and violence. DVD

Stefania Rocca *Anna Mari* • Liam Cunningham *John Brennan* • Silvio Muccino *Remo* • Adalberto Maria Merli *Chief of Police* • Claudio Santamaria *Carlo Sturni* • Fiore Argento *Lucia* ■ *Dir* Dario Argento • *Scr* Dario Argento, Franco Ferrini

Cardboard Cavalier ★★ U

Period comedy 1949 · UK · BW · 99mins

Popular music hall duo Sid Field and Jerry Desmonde team up for this eager period comedy that, in spite of some spirited playing, soon outstays its welcome. Set during the Cromwellian Commonwealth, the story, in which Field's barrow boy carries secret messages for Desmonde's Royalist spy, has all the appearances of being a flag-waver left over from the war, with puritanism continuously being equated with fascism. Field's high-camp style is an acquired taste. DP

Sid Field *Sidcup Buttermeadow* • Margaret Lockwood *Nell Gwynne* • Jerry Desmonde *Lovelace* • Jack McNaughton *Uriah Croup* • Alfie Dean *Murdercasket* • Brian Worth *Tom Pride* • Irene Handl *Lady Agnes* ■ *Dir* Walter Forde • *Scr* Noel Langley

The Cardinal ★★★

Epic drama 1963 · US · Colour · 175mins

This is an earnest though rather long adaptation of one of those American doorstop novels about faith, produced on a vast transworld scale by director Otto Preminger. Despite its sweep, scale and obvious intelligence, however, this failed to make a dent in both screen history and the box office. The blame lies in the serious miscasting of Tom Tryon in the pivotal title role, as he lacks both range and sympathy. But Preminger surrounds him with a strong supporting cast, while the Technicolor photography is impressive. TS

Tom Tryon *Stephen Fermoyle* • John Huston *Cardinal Glennon* • Raf Vallone *Cardinal Quarenghi* • Romy Schneider *Annemarie* • Carol Lynley *Mona/Regina Fermoyle* • Dorothy Gish *Celia Fermoyle* • Burgess Meredith *Father Ned Halley* • Ossie Davis *Father Gillis* • Cecil Kellaway *Monsignor Monaghan* ■ *Dir* Otto Preminger • *Scr* Robert Dozier, from the novel by Henry Morton Robinson • *Cinematographer* Leon Shamroy

Cardinal Richelieu ★★★ U

Biographical drama 1935 · US · BW · 82mins

This diverting biopic stars George Arliss as Louis XIII's first minister, whose plans to unify France earned him the enmity of the disaffected nobility and the king's womenfolk. Director Rowland V Lee has a tenuous grasp of the period atmosphere, but this scarcely matters as the historical facts are little more than an excuse for a series of melodramatic intrigues from which Arliss emerges triumphant like some scarlet-caped crusader. DP

George Arliss *Cardinal Richelieu* • Maureen O'Sullivan *Lenore* • Edward Arnold *Louis XIII* • Cesar Romero *Andre de Pons* • Douglass Dumbrille *Baradas* • Francis Lister *Gaston* • Halliwell Hobbes *Father Joseph* ■ *Dir* Rowland V Lee • *Scr* Maude Howell, Cameron Rogers, WP Lipscomb, from the play *Richelieu* by Sir Edward Bulwer-Lytton [Edward George Bulwer-Lytton]

The Care Bears Movie ★★ U

Animated adventure
1985 · Can · Colour · 75mins

Only teen bands have shorter life cycles than children's television characters, so it will be interesting to see how a generation reared on the Teletubbies reacts to their 1980s equivalents. Although 1960s luminaries Carole King and John Sebastian supply some tunes, there's not much in this for adults, and the animation is tame. The film struck a chord with kids, spawning two sequels and a TV series. JF DVD

Mickey Rooney *Mr Cherrywood* • Jackie Burroughs *The Spirit* • Harry Dean Stanton *Lion* • Sunny Besen Thrasher *Jason* • Georgia Engel *Love-a-Lot* ■ *Dir* Arna Selzick • *Scr* Peter Sauder

Career ★★★

Drama 1959 · US · BW · 106mins

Anthony Franciosa is excellent in this screen version of James Lee's Broadway play about an aspiring actor waiting for his big break in New York. Directed by Joseph Anthony with an A-list cast – Shirley MacLaine as Franciosa's alcoholic wife, Dean Martin as a stage director, Carolyn Jones as a talent scout – the movie is too long and a little plodding. However, it is gritty and authentic, and earned cinematographer Joseph LaShelle an Oscar nomination. RK

Anthony Franciosa *Sam Lawson* • Dean Martin *Maury Novak* • Shirley MacLaine *Sharon Kensington* • Carolyn Jones *Shirley Drake* • Joan Blackman *Barbara* • Robert Middleton *Robert Kensington* • Donna Douglas *Marjorie Burke* • Frank McHugh *Charlie* ■ *Dir* Joseph Anthony • *Scr* James Lee, from his play

Career Girls ★★★★ 15

Comedy drama 1997 · UK · Colour · 83mins

Mike Leigh isn't cinema's foremost realist, but he's definitely its most perceptive people-watcher. The deceptively simple characters he favours reveal hidden depths that make them utterly fascinating. Here, arrogantly affected Katrin Cartlidge and twitchily timid Lynda Steadman are pretty resistible during the flashbacks to their college days. But they capture our sympathies during a series of low-key misadventures with three old friends and a detestable newcomer. With its tentatively optimistic ending, this may be a small, rather safe film, yet it's also funny, touching and plausible. DP. Contains swearing and a sex scene. DVD

Katrin Cartlidge *Hannah Mills* • Lynda Steadman *Annie* • Kate Byers *Claire* • Mark Benton *Richard "Ricky" Burton* • Andy Serkis *Mr Evans* • Joe Tucker *Adrian Spinks* • Margo Stanley *Ricky's Nan* • Michael Healy *Lecturer* ■ *Dir/Scr* Mike Leigh

Career Opportunities ★★ 15

Comedy 1991 · US · Colour · 79mins

Written by teen chronicler John Hughes, this unexciting story has Frank Whaley as a young, incompetent conman hired as night watchman at a department store. On his first night on the job, he finds town beauty Jennifer Connelly asleep in a changing room and thwarts some would-be thieves. It might have worked with a touch of fantasy, but the straightforward treatment means Bryan Gordon's bland comedy is never elevated above the routine. TH

Frank Whaley *Jim Dodge* • Jennifer Connelly *Josie McClellan* • Dermot Mulroney *Nestor Pyle* • Kieran Mulroney *Gil Kinney* • John M Jackson *Bud Dodge* • Jenny O'Hara *Dotty Dodge* • Barry Corbin *Officer Don* • John Candy *Store manager* ■ *Dir* Bryan Gordon • *Scr* John Hughes

Carefree ★★ U

Musical comedy 1938 · US · BW · 79mins

One of the weakest of the Astaire/Rogers features, but there's still plenty to enjoy in this rather silly musical comedy. Fred looks uneasy as a psychiatrist trying to find a cure for best pal Ralph Bellamy's dippy, wedding-shy fiancée (played by Ginger), and she looks mortified at having to endure hypnotic mischief sequences. The highlight is Fred's exquisite golfing routine to the title song. SH

Fred Astaire *Tony Flagg* • Ginger Rogers *Amanda Cooper* • Ralph Bellamy *Stephen Arden* • Luella Gear *Aunt Cora* • Jack Carson *Connors* • Walter Kingsford *Dr Powers* • Kay Sutton *Miss Adams* ■ *Dir* Mark Sandrich • *Scr* Ernest Pagano, Allan Scott, from a story by Dudley Nichols, Hagar Wilde, Marian Ainslee, Guy Endore • *Music* Irving Berlin

Careful ★★★★

Black comedy drama
1992 · Can · Colour · 100mins

Director Guy Maddin is something of a cult figure in Canadian cinema and this costume curio is one of his most ambitious and enjoyable projects. Shot to look like a 1920s melodrama – complete with stylised silent acting, dialogue captions and whole scenes tinted in atmospheric colours – it tells of the secret passions that lurk behind the respectable façade of the Bavarian town of Tolzbad, which is in such peril from avalanches that everyone talks in whispers or in specially soundproofed rooms to prevent disaster. DP. Contains sex scenes and nudity.

Kyle McCulloch *Grigorss* • Gosia Dobrowolska *Zenaida* • Sarah Neville *Klara* • Brent Neale *Johann* • Paul Cox *Count Knotgers* • Victor Cowie *Herr Trotta* ■ *Dir* Guy Maddin • *Scr* Guy Maddin, George Toles

Careful, He Might Hear You ★★★★ PG

Drama 1983 · Aus · Colour · 112mins

In adapting Sumner Locke Elliott's novel for the screen, Carl Schultz has been careful to ensure that much of the action is seen from orphan Nicholas Gledhill's perspective as his aunts struggle for custody. Yet he also emphasises several adult themes, among them Australia's relationship with the "mother country", the impact of the Depression on all strata of society, and the role of women in a repressive patriarchy. John Stoddart's sets and John Seale's photography give the film a nostalgic glow. DP

Wendy Hughes *Vanessa* • Robyn Nevin *Lila* • Nicholas Gledhill *PS* • John Hargreaves *Logan* • Geraldine Turner *Vere* • Isabelle Anderson *Agnes* • Peter Whitford *George* • Colleen Clifford *Ettie* • Julie Nihill *Diana* ■ *Dir* Carl Schultz • *Scr* Michael Jenkins, from the novel by Sumner Locke Elliott

Careful, Soft Shoulder ★★★★ U

Second World War comedy drama
1942 · US · BW · 69mins

An engaging and intelligently subversive movie from director Oliver HP Garrett, who co-scripted *Duel in the Sun* with David O Selznick. Virginia Bruce stars as a world-weary social butterfly who casually mentions at a cocktail party that she fancies spying for the Nazis. Aubrey Mather takes her up on it. Told primarily in flashback by Bruce, whom Garrett interestingly makes sympathetic, this is a classy film with a witty central performance. It's all the more remarkable when one considers the majority of gung-ho dross on offer at the time. SH

Virginia Bruce *Connie Mathers* • James Ellison *Thomas Aldrich* • Aubrey Mather *Mr Fortune* • Sheila Ryan *Agatha Mathers* • Ralph Byrd *Elliot Salmon* • Sigurd Tor *Milo* • Charles Tannen *Joe* ■ *Dir/Scr* Oliver HP Garrett

The Careless Years ★★

Drama 1957 · US · BW · 72mins

Arthur Hiller waited five years to follow up this uneasy feature debut, but he later hit the box-office and Oscar jackpot with *Love Story*. Here the romance is less sugary and tells of high school girl Natalie Trundy who falls in love with handsome fellow student Dean Stockwell. The trouble is, her parents are rich and his are poor, and both sides disapprove. The youngsters elope and head for Mexico but happiness eludes them. BB

Dean Stockwell *Jerry Vernon* • Natalie Trundy *Emily Meredith* • John Larch *Sam Vernon* • Barbara Billingsley *Helen Meredith* • John Stephenson *Charles Meredith* • Maureen Cassidy *Harriet* ■ *Dir* Arthur Hiller • *Scr* Edward Lewis, front for John Howard Lawson, Mitch Lindemann

The Caretaker ★★★ PG

Drama 1963 · UK · BW · 100mins

One of Harold Pinter's most famous plays – a study in sinister pauses and comic shifts of emphasis – is wonderfully given over to its fine cast of actors. Alan Bates and Robert Shaw play two brothers who give shelter to Donald Pleasence, a scruffy tramp forever on his way to Sidcup. Either a doomy allegory or a realistic drama with menaces, it's directed without fuss by Clive Donner. A memorable piece of theatre, if not particularly effective as cinema. TH DVD

Donald Pleasence *Davies* • Alan Bates *Mick* • Robert Shaw *Aston* ■ *Dir* Clive Donner • *Scr* Harold Pinter, from his play

The Caretakers ★

Melodrama 1963 · US · BW · 97mins

Considering its subject matter and setting (a mental hospital), producer/director Hall Bartlett's incident-packed melodrama is almost insulting in its lack of seriousness, accuracy or insight. However, it's the kind of awful film which, viewed decades later, entertains for all the wrong reasons – notably Joan Crawford as a senior psychiatric nurse, locked in disagreement with medic Robert Stack's compassionate approach to the disturbed inmates. Hysterical, in every sense of the word. RK

Robert Stack *Dr Donovan MacLeod* • Polly Bergen *Lorna Melford* • Joan Crawford *Lucretia Terry* • Janis Paige *Marion* • Herbert Marshall *Dr Jubal Harrington* • Robert Vaughn *Jim Melford* ■ *Dir* Hall Bartlett • *Scr* Henry F Greenberg, from a story by Hall Bartlett, Jerry Paris and a novel by Dariel Telfer

The Carey Treatment ★★ 15

Murder mystery 1972 · US · Colour · 96mins

A bizarre murder mystery involving a *Coma*-style hospital racket in body parts, with James Coburn failing to convince as the Californian pathologist trying to disentangle a colleague from a murder frame-up. It's directed by Blake Edwards, who is better known for *The Pink Panther* comedies, and he is clearly not at home with this sort of drama. As the body count rises, this veers towards self parody. TH. Contains some swearing.

James Coburn *Peter Carey* • Jennifer O'Neill *Georgia Hightower* • Pat Hingle *Captain Pearson* • Skye Aubrey *Angela Holder* • Elizabeth Allen *Evelyn Randall* • John Fink *Murphy* • Dan O'Herlihy *JD Randall* ■ *Dir* Blake Edwards • *Scr* James P Bonner, from the novel *A Case of Need* by Jeffrey Hudson

The Cariboo Trail ★★ U

Western adventure
1950 · US · Colour · 79mins

A moderately interesting Randolph Scott vehicle, produced by western veteran Nat Holt. Victor Jory is Scott's usual snarling foe, but the real interest lies in the use of primitive two-strip Cinecolor. The implacable Randy is eminently watchable, but the plot and direction are resolutely routine. TS

Randolph Scott *Jim Redfern* • George "Gabby" Hayes *Grizzly* • Bill Williams *Mike*

Evans • Karin Booth *Frances* • Victor Jory *Frank Walsh* • Douglas Kennedy *Murphy* • Jim Davis *Miller* • Dale Robertson *Will Gray* ■ *Dir* Edwin L Marin • *Scr* Frank Gruber, from a story by John Rhodes Sturdy

Carla's Song ★★★ 15

Drama 1996 · UK/Ger/Sp · Colour · 119mins

Robert Carlyle stars in this sombre story of love among the revolutionaries from director Ken Loach. Carlyle is the Glasgow bus driver who falls in love with exotic Oyanka Cabezas, a refugee from war-torn Nicaragua. He insists they go there so that she can confront her demons, only for him to learn just what she's had to suffer. The story runs out of steam once the action moves from Scotland, but Loach is a persuasive propagandist and Carlyle has enormous charm. TH. In English and Spanish with subtitles. Contains violence and swearing. DVD

Robert Carlyle *George* • Oyanka Cabezas *Carla* • Scott Glenn *Bradley* • Salvador Espinoza *Rafael* • Louise Goodall *Maureen* • Richard Loza *Antonio* • Gary Lewis *Sammy* • Subash Singh Pall *Victor* • Stewart Preston *McGurk* ■ *Dir* Ken Loach • *Scr* Paul Laverty

Carlito's Way ★★★★ 18

Crime drama 1993 · US · Colour · 138mins

Ten years after *Scarface*, Al Pacino and director Brian De Palma reunited for another crime-doesn't-pay drama. Pacino plays Puerto Rican hoodlum Carlito Brigante, sprung from jail by his lawyer Sean Penn and determined to go straight. But Penn, who fancies himself as a gangster, scoffs at the idea, and when Pacino meets up with his old acquaintances, he's soon back in trouble. Combined with regular scriptwriter David Koepp's smart and funny script, De Palma's visual flair comes into its own in the seedy milieu of New York's clubs and backstreet dives. The set pieces are among the most thrilling De Palma has ever filmed, while Pacino's restrained performance allows plenty of scope for the supporting cast to chew the scenery. AT. Contains violence, swearing, sex scenes, drug abuse and nudity. DVD

Al Pacino *Carlito Brigante* • Sean Penn *Dave Kleinfeld* • Penelope Ann Miller *Gail* • John Leguizamo *Benny Blanco* • Ingrid Rogers *Steffie* • Luis Guzman *Pachanga* • James Rebhorn *Norwalk* • Viggo Mortensen *Lalin* ■ *Dir* Brian De Palma • *Scr* David Koepp, from the novels *Carlito's Way* and *After Hours* by Edwin Torres

Carlton-Browne of the FO ★★ U

Satire 1958 · UK · BW · 86mins

Slightly silly Boulting Brothers farce, with a talented cast, led by Terry-Thomas and Peter Sellers, put to disappointing use by a rather bizarre script about the world's worst diplomat dispatched to a faraway but suddenly mineral-rich British colony. His mission is to save the day for Blighty, but he blunders instead. PF DVD

Terry-Thomas *Cadogen de Vere Carlton-Browne* • Peter Sellers *Prime Minister Amphibulos* • Ian Bannen *Young king* • Thorley Walters *Colonel Bellingham* • Raymond Huntley *Foreign Office minister* • John Le Mesurier *Grand Duke* • Luciana Paluzzi *Princess Ilyena* ■ *Dir/Scr* Roy Boulting, Jeffrey Dell

Carmen ★★★★ U

Silent drama 1915 · US · BW · 62mins

One of the great Cecil B DeMille's biggest early hits, this was one of the movies actually responsible for popularising cinema itself. Unfairly vilified later for his naive and expansive film spectacles, DeMille was one of the film industry's pioneers, and the first to exploit the climate of the Californian orange grove known as Hollywood. As producer, he also pioneered the multiple picture contract; starring here, in the first movie of a three-picture deal, is Metropolitan Opera soprano Geraldine Farrar. She is superb, but co-star Wallace Reid's career ended tragically, both life and stardom eroded by drug abuse. TS

Geraldine Ferrar *Carmen* • Wallace Reid *Don José* ■ *Dir* Cecil B DeMille • *Scr* William C DeMille, from the novel by Prosper Mérimée and the opera by Georges Bizet

Carmen ★★★★ PG

Dance drama 1983 · Sp · Colour · 97mins

Coming between *Blood Wedding* and *El Amor Brujo*, this is the best-known segment of Carlos Saura's "flamenco trilogy". Bringing a new zest to the old cliché that life imitates art, Saura cross-cuts between rehearsals and performance as Antonio Gades becomes fatally bewitched with tempestuous co-star Laura Del Sol. As Teo Escamilla's camera is choreographed as meticulously as the dancers, the action is at once joyous and tragic; while the blend of folk music and opera manages to both send up and celebrate Bizet's famous score. With its exemplary editing, this passionate picture is both kinetic and cinematic. DP. In Spanish with English subtitles. DVD

Antonio Gades *Antonio* • Laura Del Sol *Carmen* • Paco de Lucia *Paco* • Cristina Hoyos *Cristina* • Juan Antonio Jimenez *Juan* • Sebastian Moreno *Escamillo* • Jose Yepes *Pepe Giron* • Pepa Flores ■ *Dir* Carlos Saura • *Scr* Carlos Saura, Antonio Gades, from the novel by Prosper Mérimée and the opera by Georges Bizet • *Cinematographer* Teo Escamila • *Editor* Pedro del Rey

Carmen 

Opera 1984 · Fr/It · Colour · 148mins

Georges Bizet's adaptation of Prosper Mérimée's novel is here cloaked in realism by Italian director Francesco Rosi. There's nothing stylised about the Andalusian settings in which the fiercely independent Julia Migenes-Johnson exploits her relationship with besotted soldier Placido Domingo. Poverty gnaws at the bones of everyone who works in the hellish cigarette factory, yet cinematographer Pasqualino De Santis's control of colour is so inspired that he make the run-down buildings seem the perfect place for passion. A treat for both eye and ear. DP. In French with English subtitles. DVD

Julia Migenes-Johnson *Carmen* • Placido Domingo *Don José* • Ruggero Raimondi *Escamillo* • Faith Esham *Micaëla* • Jean-Philippe Lafont *Dancaïre* • Gérard Garino *Remendado* • Lilian Watson *Frasquita* ■ *Dir* Francesco Rosi • *Scr* Francesco Rosi, Tonino Guerra, from the novel by Prosper Mérimée and the opera by Georges Bizet

Carmen ★★★ 15

Romantic drama 2003 · Sp/UK/It · Colour · 119mins

Vincente Aranda returns to Mérimée's original story for this account of the doomed romance between a tempestuous beauty and a lovesick soldier. Paz Vega smoulders in the title role, but Leonardo Sbaraglia struggles to convey reckless. Similarly, Aranda's storytelling is not always as crisp as cinematographer Paco Femenía's evocation of 1830s Andalucia. Handsomely staged, but short on real passion. DP. In Spanish with English subtitles.

Paz Vega *Carmen* • Leonardo Sbaraglia *José Lizarrabengoa* • Jay Benedict *Prospero* • Antonio Dechent *Tuerto* • Joan Crosas *Dancaire* • Joe Mackay *Teniente* • Josep Linuesa [José Linuesa] *Lucas* ■ *Dir* Vicente Aranda • *Scr* Joaquín Jordá, Vicente Aranda, from the novel by Prosper Mérimée

Carmen Jones ★★★★ U

Musical melodrama
1954 · US · Colour · 103mins

This is 20th Century-Fox's all-black version of Bizet's opera *Carmen*, based on the Oscar Hammerstein II Broadway triumph. As the ultimate *femme fatale* Carmen Jones, Dorothy Dandridge sizzles on screen, although her singing voice was dubbed by the then unknown Marilyn Horne. LeVern Hutcherson sings for handsome Harry Belafonte, but the rest of the cast largely sings for itself. The music has an enjoyable Hollywood zest and *Carmen* fans will warm to the wit of this interpretation. TS DVD

Dorothy Dandridge *Carmen* • Harry Belafonte *Joe* • Olga James *Cindy Lou* • Pearl Bailey *Frankie* • Diahann Carroll *Myrt* • Roy Glenn *Rum* • Nick Stewart *Dink* • Joe Adams *Husky* • Brock Peters *Sergeant Brown* • Sandy Lewis *T-Bone* ■ *Dir* Otto Preminger • *Scr* Harry Kleiner, from the musical by Oscar Hammerstein II

Carmen Miranda: Bananas Is My Business ★★★★

Documentary
1994 · US/Bra · Colour · 92mins

Born Maria do Carmo Miranda da Cunha near Lisbon in Portugal, Carmen Miranda became an international symbol of Brazilian pizzazz, and her sudden death at 46 was the cause of national mourning. A star of Brazilian films and Broadway before she conquered Hollywood, Miranda was unquestionably wasted by producers who thought that all she had to offer was a genius for mangling the English language and an exoticism that could brighten up an ordinary musical with a few colourful routines. As this revealing documentary tribute proves, she was capable of much more. DP. In Portuguese and English with subtitles.

Cynthia Adler *Luella Hopper* • Erick Barreto *Carmen Miranda (fantasy sequences)* • Leticia Monte *Carmen Miranda (as a teenager)* • Helena Solberg *Narrator* ■ *Dir* Helena Solberg

Carnages ★★ 15

Drama
2002 · Fr/Bel/Sp/Swi · Colour · 127mins

Acclaimed shorts director Delphine Gleize's feature debut seeks to link several tenuously connected stories only to end up shortchanging them all. The unifying factor is a bull that gores matador Julien Lescarret before being slaughtered and having its carcass dispatched into the orbit of, among others, struggling Italian actress Chiara Mastroianni, guilt-ridden Spaniard Angela Molina, adulterous French scientist Jacques Gamblin and hyper-imaginative child Raphaëlle Molinier. DP. In French and Spanish with English subtitles. Contains swearing, violence and sex scenes. DVD

Chiara Mastroianni *Carlotta* • Angela Molina *Alice* • Lio *Betty* • Lucia Sanchez *Jeanne* • Esther Gorintin *Rosy* • Maryline Even *Lucy* • Clovis Cornillac *Alexis* • Jacques Gamblin *Jacques* ■ *Dir/Scr* Delphine Gleize

Carnal Knowledge ★★★★ 18

Drama 1971 · US · Colour · 93mins

This 1970s drama featured one of the roles which brought Jack Nicholson to international attention and was a precursor to the emerging debate into the price the sexual revolution had on personal relationships. Mike Nichols directs a tale of two old college chums traversing life with some incisive flair, and Ann-Margret is especially fine as a vulnerable partner eager to salvage honesty from the emotional debris. If Nicholson is a touch too vulpine and slavering (at times he teeters on the edge of caricature), the film admirably retains its edge and pace. SH. Contains swearing. DVD

Jack Nicholson *Jonathan* • Arthur Garfunkel [Art Garfunkel] *Sandy* • Ann-Margret *Bobbie* • Candice Bergen *Susan* • Rita Moreno *Louise* • Cynthia O'Neal *Cindy* • Carol Kane *Jennifer* ■ *Dir* Mike Nichols • *Scr* Jules Feiffer

Carnegie Hall ★★★ U

Musical 1947 · US · BW · 144mins

That venerable New York institution is presented here in an over-stuffed, overlong pudding of a picture that has the sublime merit of featuring many of the greatest classical performers of its day, including Leopold Stokowski, Jascha Heifetz, Artur Rubinstein, Lily Pons and Rise Stevens. Big bandsters Harry James and Vaughn Monroe provide some populist appeal, but the music is somewhat dissipated by the thin plot, which sees Marsha Hunt trying to get her offspring onto the concert stage. It is the most upmarket movie that cult B-movie director Edgar G Ulmer ever made. TS

Marsha Hunt *Nora Ryan* • William Prince *Tony Salerno Jr* • Frank McHugh *John Donovan* • Martha O'Driscoll *Ruth Haines* • Hans Jaray *Tony Salerno Sr* • Joseph Buloff *Anton Tribik* • Olin Downes • Emile Boreo *Henry* • Alfonso D'Artega *Tchaikovsky* ■ *Dir* Edgar G Ulmer • *Scr* Karl Kamb, from a story by Seena Owen

Un Carnet de Bal ★★★★

Portmanteau drama 1937 · Fr · BW · 129mins

Boasting an exceptional cast and Maurice Jaubert's haunting melody, *Valse Grise*, this episodic drama won the Coupe Mussolini at Venice and earned its director, Julien Duvivier, an invitation to Hollywood. Marie Bell holds centre stage as a widow who decides to trace the men with whom she danced at her first ball. Naturally, the majority have strayed from the straight and narrow, giving each encounter its socio-symbolic tone. There's also plenty of humour and an affecting finale in this old-fashioned showcase to treasure. DP. In French with English subtitles.

Harry Baur *Alain Regnault* • Marie Bell *Christine Surgère* • Pierre Blanchar *Thierry* • Fernandel *Fabien Coutissol* • Jeanne Fusier-Gir *Newspaper vendor* • Louis Jouvet *Pierre Verdier/Jo* • Milly Mathis *Cécile* • Raimu *François Patusset* • Françoise Rosay *Mme Audié* • Pierre Richard-Willm *Eric Irvin* • Sylvie *Thierry's mistress* ■ *Dir* Julien Duvivier • *Scr* Julien Duvivier, Jean Sarment, Pierre Wolff, Yves Mirande, Bernard Zimmer, Henri Jeanson

Carnival ★★

Romantic melodrama
1946 · UK · BW · 93mins

Ballet dancer Sally Gray falls in love with sculptor Michael Wilding, but refuses to compromise her honour by living with him. When he leaves her, she makes the unhappy mistake of marrying Cornish farmer Bernard Miles. This drama is a relentlessly morose and uninteresting film with a melodramatically tragic ending. RK

Michael Wilding *Maurice Avery* • Stanley Holloway *Charlie Raeburn* • Bernard Miles *Trewhella* • Jean Kent *Irene Dale* • Catherine Lacey *Florrie Raeburn* • Hazel Court *May Raeburn* ■ *Dir* Stanley Haynes • *Scr* Eric Maschwitz, Stanley Haynes, Peter Ustinov, Guy Green, from a story by Compton Mackenzie

Carnival in Flanders ★★★ 12

Period comedy 1935 · Fr/Ger · BW · 109mins

Directed and co-written by Jacques Feyder, this witty and sophisticated farce is set in 17th-century Flanders, wonderfully conjured up by Lazare Meerson's terrific sets and costumes. The accomplished Françoise Rosay stars as the wife of a mayor whose small town is invaded by Spanish troops. The men take fright and go into hiding; the women enjoy the attentions of the occupiers. Although not nearly as daring as it seemed in the 1930s, the film remains a charming romp. RK. In French with English subtitles. DVD

Françoise Rosay *Madame Burgomaster* • Jean Murat *The Duke* • André Alerme *Burgomaster* • Louis Jouvet *The Priest* • Lynne Clévers *Fishmonger's wife* • Micheline Cheirel *Siska* ■ *Dir* Jacques Feyder • *Scr* Bernard Zimmer, Charles Spaak, Jacques Feyder, from a story by Charles Spaak

C

Carnival of Souls ★★★★ 15

Horror 1962 · US · BW · 74mins

A young church organist finds herself in a strange limbo, haunted by spectral ghouls, in the creepy cult classic that director George A Romero credits as being his major inspiration for *Night of the Living Dead*. Representing the ultimate triumph of talent over budget, Herk Harvey's sole film as director is a crude but compelling chiller evoking a genuinely eerie atmosphere. Harvey also plays the lead phantom pursuing the heroine, played by the excellent Candace Hilligoss. AJ DVD

Candace Hilligoss *Mary Henry* • Herk Harvey *The Man* • Frances Feist *Landlady* • Sidney Berger *John Linden* • Art Ellison *Minister* ■ *Dir* Herk Harvey • *Scr* John Clifford, from a story by John Clifford, Herk Harvey

Carnival of Souls ★★★ 18

Horror 1999 · US · Colour · 83mins

The black-and-white 1962 original remains a genuinely creepy tale of possession – fertile material for modern horror maestro Wes Craven. Sadly, though, he only served as executive producer on this slick update. Bobbie Phillips plays a young woman who is haunted by visions of her hated stepfather (comic actor Larry Miller in a surprisingly creepy performance), who she insists is trying to kill her. Problem is, the police insist he is already dead! Director Adam Grossman piles on some jolting shocks, but never manages to re-create the haunting melancholy of Herk Harvey's cult classic. JF DVD

Bobbie Phillips *Alex* • Larry Miller *Louis* • Shawnee Smith *Sandra* ■ *Dir/Scr* Adam Grossman

Carnival Story ★★

Drama 1954 · US · Colour · 94mins

Anne Baxter stars as a German girl seeking refuge from unhappiness by joining a carnival. She falls prey to a lustful cad (Steve Cochran), marries the troupe's high-diver (Lyle Bettger) and... well, see for yourself. This is tacky, but the erotic and suspenseful big-top atmosphere exerts its usual fascination. RK

Anne Baxter *Willie* • Steve Cochran *Joe Hammond* • Lyle Bettger *Frank Colloni* • George Nader *Vines* • Jay C Flippen *Charley* • Helene Stanley *Peggy* • Adi Berber *Groppo* ■ *Dir* Kurt Neumann • *Scr* Hans Jacoby, Kurt Neumann, from the story by Marcel Klauber, CB Williams

Carnosaur ★★

Science-fiction horror 1993 · US · Colour · 82mins

Executive producer Roger Corman's cheap answer to *Jurassic Park* finds evil scientist Diane Ladd developing a virus in chicken eggs that makes women give birth to savage dinosaurs. It's ably directed by Adam Simon, and delivers the copious blood and gore the child-friendly Steven Spielberg blockbuster couldn't. However, the dreadful model monsters, dodgy animatronics and overly talky script quickly and rightly made this extinct. AJ

Diane Ladd *Dr Jane Tiptree* • Raphael Sbarge *"Doc" Smith* • Jennifer Runyon *Thrush* • Harrison Page *Sheriff* • Clint Howard *Trucker* ■ *Dir* Adam Simon • *Scr* Adam Simon, from a novel by Harry Adam Knight

Carny ★★★★ 18

Drama 1980 · US · Colour · 102mins

Set behind the scenes of a travelling carnival, this very dark tale stars Robbie Robertson (formerly of rock group The Band) as a conman and fixer, Gary Busey as an insane dimwit, and Jodie Foster as the teenage runaway who comes between them. The setting, complete with authentic sideshows and genuine freaks, gives an added creepiness to the proceedings, and, although director Robert Kaylor tries to concentrate on buddy bonding and life on the road, it's the strangeness of it all that leaves the biggest impression. Unusual, but also unmissable. JB. Contains swearing.

Jodie Foster *Donna* • Gary Busey *Frankie Chipman* • Robbie Robertson *Patch Beaudry* • Meg Foster *Gerta* • Kenneth McMillan *Heavy St John* • Elisha Cook [Elisha Cook Jr] *"On Your Mark"* • Tim Thomerson *Doubles* • Theodore Wilson [Teddy Wilson] *Nails* • John Lehne *Skeet* ■ *Dir* Robert Kaylor • *Scr* Thomas Baum, from a story by Phoebe Taylor, Robert Kaylor, Robbie Robertson

Caroline? ★★★★

Mystery drama 1990 · US · Colour · 100mins

Here's a made-for-TV movie that's way above average, transferring an old Hollywood standby plot to the glossy world of "movie of the week". Stephanie Zimbalist returns to claim her inheritance after her family thought she was dead. Of course, Anastasia-like, they don't think she's who she says she is. This won Emmy Awards for outstanding drama and the direction of Joseph Sargent. TS

Stephanie Zimbalist *Caroline* • Pamela Reed *Grace Carmichael* • George Grizzard *Paul Carmichael* • Shawn Phelan *Winston Carmichael* • Jenny Jacobs *Heidi Carmichael* • Patricia Neal *Mrs Trollope* • Dorothy McGuire *Mrs Adkin* ■ *Dir* Joseph Sargent • *Scr* Michael de Guzman, from the novel *Father's Arcane Daughter* by EL Konigsburg

Carousel ★★★★ U

Musical 1956 · US · Colour · 123mins

This is a marvellous screen version of what is arguably Rodgers and Hammerstein's finest Broadway show, immaculately cast and filmed in part on glorious Maine locations. Some may find this tale of a reprobate's return to Earth to look out for his daughter arch in the extreme, but it is a tribute to the superb score and sensitive handling of the material that the film is moving. Gordon MacRae and Shirley Jones have the roles of their lives, though they're done no favours by the static direction. TS DVD

Gordon MacRae *Billy Bigelow* • Shirley Jones *Julie* • Cameron Mitchell *Jigger* • Barbara Ruick *Carrie* • Claramae Turner *Cousin Nettie* • Robert Rounseville *Mr Snow* • Gene Lockhart *Starkeeper* • Audrey Christie *Mrs Mullin* ■ *Dir* Henry King • *Scr* Phoebe Ephron, Henry Ephron, from the musical by Richard Rodgers, Oscar Hammerstein II, Benjamin F Glazer, Ferenc Molnar

The Carpetbaggers ★★★★

Drama 1964 · US · Colour · 143mins

With the lustre of age, nostalgia for its stars and that vanished art of storytelling know-how, this trashy tale has now acquired a certain fascination. Based on the Harold Robbins potboiler, it sprawls across nearly three hours and as many decades, focusing on the life and loves of tycoon George Peppard. Alan Ladd, as a cowboy star, makes his final screen appearance and Hollywood sexpot Carroll Baker drapes herself over both of them. It's lumpen, lavish and lascivious, a gripping cocktail of melodrama and moralising. AT

George Peppard *Jonas Cord Jr* • Alan Ladd *Nevada Smith* • Carroll Baker *Rina* • Bob Cummings [Robert Cummings] *Dan Pierce* • Martha Hyer *Jennie Denton* • Elizabeth Ashley *Monica Winthrop* • Martin Balsam *Bernard B Norman* • Lew Ayres *McAllister* • Tom Tully *Amos Winthrop* ■ *Dir* Edward Dmytryk • *Scr* John Michael Hayes, from the novel by Harold Robbins

Carpool ★★ PG

Comedy 1996 · US · Colour · 85mins

The ex-Mr Roseanne Barr, Tom Arnold, won the "Razzie" award for worst actor for his performance in this annoying chase movie. Ironically, though, he's the only reason for watching it. His affably juvenile persona can be grating at times, but it suits his role here as a bumbling crook holding a carload of kids hostage. Filmed in Vancouver (standing in for Seattle), this runs out of gas way before the end. RS. Contains swearing, sexual references.

Tom Arnold *Franklin Laszlo* • David Paymer *Daniel Miller* • Rhea Perlman *Martha* • Rod Steiger *Mr Hammerman* • Kim Coates *Detective Erdman* • Rachael Leigh Cook *Kayla* ■ *Dir* Arthur Hiller • *Scr* Don Rhymer

Carrie ★★★ U

Romantic melodrama
1952 · US · BW · 116mins

This full-blown romance from the great William Wyler stars Jennifer Jones stars as the small-town girl who gets seduced into a life of crime and passion in early 20th century Chicago, while Laurence Olivier is in fine form as the married man who whisks her off her feet. Based on the Theodore Dreiser novel, the story veers between agony and ecstasy in the way that only a Hollywood melodrama can. It may not be vintage Wyler, but the pairing of Jones and Olivier is electric. RT DVD

Jennifer Jones *Carrie Meeber* • Laurence Olivier *George Hurstwood* • Miriam Hopkins *Julia Hurstwood* • Eddie Albert *Charlie Drouet* • Basil Ruysdael *Mr Fitzgerald* • Ray Teal *Allan* • Barry Kelley *Slawson* ■ *Dir* William Wyler • *Scr* Ruth Goetz, Augustus Goetz, from the novel *Sister Carrie* by Theodore Dreiser

Carrie ★★★★★ 18

Horror 1976 · US · Colour · 93mins

Brian De Palma's modern Gothic fairy tale, based on Stephen King's bestseller, offers a tense and lyrical web of emotions. Sissy Spacek is heartbreaking as the telekinetic Cinderella turning her school prom into a bloody massacre after a macabre joke is played on her by vicious teens (including John Travolta). Piper Laurie as Spacek's religious fanatic mother is equally striking and her symbolic "crucifixion" is a thrilling highlight in an unforgettable package of pop psychology and psychic phenomena. Despite a much-copied plot and even more copied shock climax, De Palma's best movie remains a transfixing experience. A belated, very inferior sequel of sorts, *The Rage: Carrie 2*, followed in 1999. AJ. Contains violence, swearing, nudity. DVD

Sissy Spacek *Carrie White* • Piper Laurie *Margaret White* • Amy Irving *Sue Snell* • William Katt *Tommy Ross* • John Travolta *Billy Nolan* • Nancy Allen *Chris Hargenson* • Betty Buckley *Miss Collins* • Priscilla Pointer *Mrs Snell* ■ *Dir* Brian De Palma • *Scr* Lawrence D Cohen, from the novel by Stephen King

La Carrière de Suzanne ★★★★ PG

Drama 1963 · Fr · BW · 52mins

The second of Eric Rohmer's "Six Moral Tales" is a witty, wise and wonderfully-told story about the gulf in emotional maturity that exists between young men and women. The men behaving badly here are a medical student whose worthless friendship with his lothario buddy costs him not only his meagre supply of cash, but also his chance of romance with Suzanne, the interpreter who at first tolerates and then repudiates their childish games. No one films Paris better than Rohmer, and he coaxes such naturalistic performances from his young cast that you part from them only with the greatest reluctance. DP. In French with English subtitles.

Catherine Sée *Suzanne* • Philippe Beuzen *Bertrand* • Christian Charrière *Guillaume* • Diane Wilkinson *Sophie* • Jean-Claude Biette *Jean-Louis* ■ *Dir/Scr* Eric Rohmer

Carriers ★★

Thriller 1998 · US · Colour · 92mins

Compared with a big budget project such as *Outbreak*, this is more like a mild bout of flu. It shares the same basic plotline of the Dustin Hoffman vehicle – a race against the clock to track down a lethal virus that could result in widespread deaths – but the execution is hindered by the small-screen frame and the casting. TV-movie regulars Judith Light, as the military medic, and Pamela Reed, as a campaigning journalist, are the stars, but neither is believable. RT

Judith Light *Major Carmen Travis* • Pamela Reed *Holly Parker* • Bill Nunn *Captain Arends* • Philip Bosco *Colonel Bailey* • Nicholas Pryor *Frank Sanborn* ■ *Dir* Alan Metzger • *Scr* Joyce Heft Brotman, from the novel by Patrick Lynch

Carrington ★★★★ 18

Biographical drama
1995 · UK · Colour · 117mins

The extraordinary romance between androgynous painter Dora Carrington and homosexual writer Lytton Strachey is captivatingly portrayed by Emma Thompson and Jonathan Pryce in the directing debut of Christopher Hampton, writer of *Dangerous Liaisons*. Few love stories have been so intense or unusual as this account of the non-sexual relationship between the Bloomsbury group twosome, who shared their nonconformist alliance with Carrington's husband and Strachey's occasional boyfriends. Hampton's fascinating account is beautifully crafted, wittily scripted and intelligently realised, with Pryce giving the performance of a lifetime. Costume drama is rarely this compelling or moving. AJ DVD

Emma Thompson *Carrington* • Jonathan Pryce *Lytton Strachey* • Steven Waddington *Ralph Partridge* • Samuel West *Gerald Brenan* • Rufus Sewell *Mark Gertler* • Penelope Wilton *Lady Ottoline Morrell* • Janet McTeer *Vanessa Bell* • Peter Blythe *Phillip Morrell* • Jeremy Northam *Beacus Penrose* • Alex Kingston *Frances Partridge* ■ *Dir* Christopher Hampton • *Scr* Christopher Hampton, from the book *Lytton Strachey* by Michael Holroyd

Carrington VC ★★★ PG

Courtroom drama 1954 · UK · BW · 101mins

David Niven had no formal acting training, but he was capable of giving performances of both subtlety and power. Unfortunately, producers typecast him in debonair roles and only rarely gave him the chance to tackle more demanding characters. Here he shows the depth of his instinctive talent as a war hero driven to theft by delays in repayments of his expenses. Niven's shifts between despair, dignity and determination are masterly, and he is well supported by Margaret Leighton as his shrewish wife. DP

David Niven *Major Carrington VC* • Margaret Leighton *Valerie Carrington* • Noelle Middleton *Captain Alison Graham* • Allan Cuthbertson *Lt Col Henniker* • Victor Maddern *Owen* • Raymond Francis *Maj Jim Mitchell* • Geoffrey Keen *President of the Court* • Laurence Naismith *Major Panton* • Clive Morton *Lt Col Huxford* • Maurice Denham *Lt Col Reeve* ■ *Dir* Anthony Asquith • *Scr* John Hunter, from a play by Dorothy Christie, Campbell Christie

Carry Me Back ★★★

Black comedy 1982 · NZ · Colour · 102mins

Consistently contrived and shamelessly sexist, this corpse-carting comedy makes *Weekend at Bernie's* look like a sensitive study in bereavement. Yet, the story of a couple of New Zealand brothers who have to smuggle their dead dad back to the farm to secure their inheritance is so stuffed with slapstick calamities and eccentric characters that it's hard to stay mad at it for long. Grant Tilly and Kelly Johnson make suitably doltish hicks and Dorothy McKegg steals the show as the no-nonsense aunt. DP

Grant Tilly *Arthur Donovan* • Kelly Johnson *Jimmy Donovan* • Dorothy McKegg *Aunty Bird* • Derek Hardwick *TK Donovan* • Joanne Mildenhall *Girl* ■ *Dir* John Reid • *Scr* Keith Aberdein, Derek Morton

Carry On Abroad ★★ PG

Comedy 1972 · UK · Colour · 85mins

This disappointing outing is every bit as jerry-built as the Elsbels Palace Hotel itself. With a stingy quota of jokes, the team's holiday to Spain rapidly descends into innuendo and second-rate slapstick. There are one or two neat observations on the British abroad, but there is too little for the regulars to do, and it's a sad series swan song for the inimitable Charles Hawtrey. DP DVD

Sidney James *Vic Flange* • Kenneth Williams *Stuart Farquhar* • Charles Hawtrey *Tuttle* • Peter Butterworth *Pepe* • Joan Sims *Cora Flange* • Kenneth Connor *Stanley Blunt* • Jimmy Logan *Bert Conway* • Barbara Windsor *Sadie* • June Whitfield *Evelyn Blunt* • Hattie Jacques *Floella* • Bernard Bresslaw *Brother Bernard* • Jack Douglas *Harry* • Patsy Rowlands *Miss Dobbs* ■ *Dir* Gerald Thomas • *Scr* Talbot Rothwell

Carry On Admiral ★★ U

Comedy 1957 · UK · BW · 78mins

Not one of the *Carry Ons*, but an unremarkable screen adaptation of an almost forgotten stage farce. Also known as *The Ship Was Loaded*, this comedy of errors has more in common with radio hit *The Navy Lark* than its saucier namesakes. David Tomlinson and Brian Reece goof gamely as the civil servant and the sailor whose identities get muddled, but it's AE Matthews (at the ripe old age of 87) who steals the show. DP

David Tomlinson *Tom Baker* • Peggy Cummins *Susan Lashwood* • Brian Reece *Peter Fraser* • Eunice Gayson *Jane Godfrey* • AE Matthews *Admiral Godfrey* • Joan Sims *Mary* ■ *Dir* Val Guest • *Scr* Val Guest, from the play *Off the Record* by Ian Hay, Stephen King-Hall

Carry On Again Doctor ★★★★ PG

Comedy 1969 · UK · Colour · 85mins

The 18th *Carry On* is easily the funniest of the medical capers. Rejoicing under the glorious name of Dr Nookey, Jim Dale holds centre stage with some aplomb, most notably matching Sid James gag for gag during the wonderfully sleazy Beatific Island scenes. Charles Hawtrey also has one of his better outings, hissing bitterly as the covetous Dr Stoppidge who is forced to resort to drag in order to discover the secret of Dale's revolutionary slimming tonic. As usual, Talbot Rothwell litters his script with wincingly witty one-liners. DP DVD

Kenneth Williams *Frederick Carver* • Jim Dale *Dr James Nookey* • Sidney James *Gladstone Screwer* • Charles Hawtrey *Dr Ernest Stoppidge* • Joan Sims *Ellen Moore* • Hattie Jacques *Matron* • Barbara Windsor *Goldie Locks* • Patsy Rowlands *Miss Fosdick* ■ *Dir* Gerald Thomas • *Scr* Talbot Rothwell

Carry On at Your Convenience ★★ PG

Comedy 1971 · UK · Colour · 86mins

Among the weakest of the *Carry Ons*, this is toilet humour in every sense of the phrase. Plumbing the depths of his imagination, screenwriter Talbot Rothwell throws up a spoof on "everybody out" trade unionism that is hardly flush with originality. To relieve the comic drought, he packs bosses and workers alike into a charabanc for a works outing that has all the appearance of a desperate time-filler. Sid James and Hattie Jacques have the best scenes, but the remaining regulars deserve better. DP DVD

Sidney James *Sid Plummer* • Kenneth Williams *WC Boggs* • Charles Hawtrey *Charles Coote* • Joan Sims *Chloe Moore* • Hattie Jacques *Beattie Plummer* • Bernard Bresslaw *Bernie Hulke* • Patsy Rowlands *Miss Withering* • Bill Maynard *Fred Moore* ■ *Dir* Gerald Thomas • *Scr* Talbot Rothwell

Carry On Behind ★★ PG

Comedy 1975 · UK · Colour · 86mins

This caravan version of *Carry On Camping* marked the beginning of the end for the classic comedy series, with neither Sid James nor scriptwriter Talbot Rothwell on board. Regulars Bernard Bresslaw, Kenneth Connor and Joan Sims are unfortunately restricted to supporting roles in this woeful effort from writer Dave Freeman, a series newcomer, which attempts to combine caravan-holiday capers and archaeological high jinks. The only fragments of fun come from Kenneth Williams and Elke Sommer as relic hunters on a dig. DP DVD

Elke Sommer *Professor Anna Vrooshka* • Kenneth Williams *Professor Roland Crump* • Joan Sims *Daphne Barnes* • Bernard Bresslaw *Arthur Upmore* • Jack Douglas *Ernie Bragg* • Windsor Davies *Fred Ramsden* • Kenneth Connor *Major Leep* • Liz Fraser *Sylvia Ramsden* • Peter Butterworth *Barnes* ■ *Dir* Gerald Thomas • *Scr* Dave Freeman

Carry On Cabby ★★★ PG

Comedy 1963 · UK · BW · 87mins

The best of the black-and-white *Carry Ons* began life as a script by the then little known Talbot Rothwell entitled *Call Me a Cab*. Having just parted company with regular scriptwriter Norman Hudis, producer Peter Rogers brought Rothwell into the fold and he went on to pen the next 19 films in the series. Pitting Sid James against the long-suffering Hattie Jacques, the battle between Speedee Taxis and Glamcabs is packed with hilarious incidents and cracking performances, not least from Kenneth Connor and Esma Cannon as the respective loyal lieutenants and Charles Hawtrey as the hapless Pint-Pot. DP DVD

Sidney James *Charlie* • Hattie Jacques *Peggy* • Kenneth Connor *Ted* • Charles Hawtrey *Pint-Pot* • Esma Cannon *Flo* • Liz Fraser *Sally* • Bill Owen *Smiley* • Milo O'Shea *Len* • Jim Dale *Small man* • Amanda Barrie *Anthea* ■ *Dir* Gerald Thomas • *Scr* Talbot Rothwell, from a story by Sidney Green [SC Green], Richard Hills [RM Hills]

Carry On Camping ★★★ PG

Comedy 1969 · UK · Colour · 85mins

The 17th outing is one of the liveliest *Carry Ons*, with the cast making light of the fact that they were shooting in freezing temperatures in fields that were so muddy they were sprayed green to give the impression of high summer. Yet again, the big slapstick finale is a disappointment after all the wonderful double entendre incidents, but there is the compensation of Sid James as a hippy, while Peter Butterworth has his finest hour as the miserly site owner. DP DVD

Sidney James *Sid Boggle* • Kenneth Williams *Dr Soper* • Joan Sims *Joan Fussey* • Charles Hawtrey *Charlie Muggins* • Bernard Bresslaw *Bernie Lugg* • Terry Scott *Peter Potter* • Barbara Windsor *Babs* • Hattie Jacques *Miss Haggerd* • Peter Butterworth *Joshua Fiddler* ■ *Dir* Gerald Thomas • *Scr* Talbot Rothwell

Carry On Cleo ★★★★ PG

Comedy 1964 · UK · Colour · 87mins

Mercilessly mocking Elizabeth Taylor's disastrous *Cleopatra*, this corking ancient history lesson sees the *Carry On* team at the peak of their powers. The puns have never been better ("infamy, infamy, they've all got it in for me!") and the sets are positively luxuriant (and very familiar!). Amanda Barrie is exquisitely dippy in the title role, and Kenneth Connor and Jim Dale do well as the Britons in the imperial guard. But topping them all are Sid James's lecherous Mark Antony and Kenneth Williams's snivelling Caesar. DP DVD

Sidney James *Mark Antony* • Kenneth Williams *Julius Caesar* • Kenneth Connor *Hengist Pod* • Charles Hawtrey *Seneca* • Joan Sims *Calpurnia* • Jim Dale *Horsa* • Amanda Barrie *Cleo* • Julie Stevens *Gloria* • Sheila Hancock *Senna Pod* • Warren Mitchell *Spencius* ■ *Dir* Gerald Thomas • *Scr* Talbot Rothwell

Carry On Columbus ★ PG

Comedy 1992 · UK · Colour · 87mins

Oh dear. With many of the original *Carry On* regulars no longer with us or (sensibly) otherwise engaged, it was left to more contemporary comedians to put the final nail in the *Carry On* coffin with a cacophony of puerile jokes and general atrociousness. This mainly fails because the *Carry On* films are, like many other historic things, probably best remembered rather than re-created. JB

Jim Dale *Christopher Columbus* • Peter Richardson *Bart* • Alexei Sayle *Achmed* • Sara Crowe *Fatima* • Julian Clary *Diego* • Bernard Cribbins *Mordecai Mendoza* • Richard Wilson *Don Felipe* • Keith Allen *Pepi* • Nigel Planer *Wazir* • Rik Mayall *Sultan* • Tony Slattery *Baba* • Maureen Lipman *Countess Esme* • Jon Pertwee *Duke of Costa Brava* • Leslie Phillips *King Ferdinand* • June Whitfield *Queen Isabella* • Martin Clunes *Martin* ■ *Dir* Gerald Thomas • *Scr* Dave Freeman

Carry On Constable ★★★ U

Comedy 1960 · UK · BW · 82mins

The fourth in the *Carry On* series is the first to feature the excellent Sid James, who stars as the sergeant detailed to wet nurse rookies Kenneth Williams, Leslie Phillips, Charles Hawtrey and Kenneth Connor. Having studied the policeman's lot at Slough, screenwriter Norman Hudis confessed he could find nothing funny about pounding the beat, but he still turned in a chucklesome script. The bungling bobbies have their moments, but their thunder is stolen by seasoned supports Joan Hickson, Irene Handl and Esma Cannon, inevitably playing their usual eccentrics. DP DVD

Sidney James *Sergeant Frank Wilkins* • Kenneth Williams *Constable Benson* • Hattie Jacques *Sergeant Laura Moon* • Eric Barker *Inspector Mills* • Kenneth Connor *Constable Charlie Constable* • Charles Hawtrey *Special Constable Gorse* • Leslie Phillips *Constable Potter* • Joan Sims *Policewoman Gloria Passworthy* ■ *Dir* Gerald Thomas • *Scr* Norman Hudis, from an idea by Brock Williams

Carry On Cowboy ★★★ PG

Comedy 1965 · UK · Colour · 90mins

When Marshall P Knutt (Jim Dale) rides into Stodge City, Judge Burke (Kenneth Williams) is convinced that he is the lawman who will rid him of the Rumpo Kid (Sid James) and his band of desperadoes. But to a sanitary engineer like Knutt, cleaning up the town has a totally different meaning. Shot in the untamed wilds of Pinewood Studios, the 11th *Carry On* finds the team in mid-season form. All the regulars impress, but Charles Hawtrey steals the picture as the firewater-swilling Chief Big Heap. DP DVD

Sidney James *Rumpo Kid* • Kenneth Williams *Judge Burke* • Jim Dale *Marshall P Knutt* • Charles Hawtrey *Chief Big Heap* • Joan Sims *Belle* • Angela Douglas *Annie Oakley* • Bernard Bresslaw *Little Heap* • Peter Butterworth *Doc* • Jon Pertwee *Sheriff Earp* ■ *Dir* Gerald Thomas • *Scr* Talbot Rothwell

Carry On Cruising ★★★ U

Comedy 1962 · UK · Colour · 85mins

The first in colour and the last *Carry On* written by Norman Hudis, this is the most charming film in the series. Set aboard the SS *Happy Wanderer*, it charts the course of captain Sid James's tenth anniversary cruise, during which the members of his new crew seek to find their sea legs. Kenneth Connor enjoys one of his best outings as the nervous ship's doctor and Lance Percival has fun as the cook-it-and-see chef. DP DVD

Sidney James *Captain Crowther* • Kenneth Williams *Leonard Marjoribanks* • Kenneth Connor *Arthur Binn* • Liz Fraser *Gladys Trimble* • Dilys Laye *Flo Castle* • Lance Percival *Wilfred Haines* ■ *Dir* Gerald Thomas • *Scr* Norman Hudis, from a story by Eric Barker

Carry On Dick ★★★ PG

Comedy 1974 · UK · Colour · 86mins

Packed with more than the usual amount of smutty innuendo, this spoof on period adventures does not live up to the team's previous best. It is chiefly memorable for being Sid James's 19th and last *Carry On*. He plays feared highwayman Dick Turpin, who masquerades as country vicar the Reverend Flasher. Also leading a double life, Barbara Windsor gives one of her best performances of the series as Turpin's sidekick. DP DVD

Sidney James *Dick Turpin/Reverend Flasher* • Barbara Windsor *Harriet/Harry* • Kenneth Williams *Captain Desmond Fancey* • Hattie Jacques *Martha Hoggett* • Bernard Bresslaw *Sir Roger Daley* • Joan Sims *Madame Desiree* • Kenneth Connor *Constable* • Peter Butterworth *Tom "Doc" Scholl* • Jack Douglas *Sergeant Jock Strapp* ■ *Dir* Gerald Thomas • *Scr* Talbot Rothwell, from a treatment by Lawrie Wyman, George Evans

Carry On Doctor ★★★ PG

Comedy 1968 · UK · Colour · 90mins

After seven consecutive spoofs of other movies, the *Carry On* crew returned to the world of work for this lively comedy that virtually takes up from where *Carry On Nurse* left off. The timing of another hospital picture couldn't have been better for Sid James, who was genuinely bedridden for much of the production. Consequently, most of the workload falls upon Kenneth Williams as a sneering consultant, Jim Dale as the clumsy Dr Kilmore, and Frankie Howerd, making an impressive series debut as a faith healer. DP DVD

Frankie Howerd *Francis Bigger* • Sidney James *Charlie Roper* • Kenneth Williams *Dr Tinkle* • Charles Hawtrey *Mr Barron* • Jim Dale *Dr Kilmore* • Barbara Windsor *Sandra May* • Joan Sims *Chloe Gibson* • Hattie Jacques *Matron* • Bernard Bresslaw *Ken Biddle* • Peter Butterworth *Mr Smith* ■ *Dir* Gerald Thomas • *Scr* Talbot Rothwell

Carry On – Don't Lose Your Head ★★★★ PG

Comedy 1966 · UK · Colour · 86mins

Originally not intended to be a *Carry On*, this turns out to be one of the jewels of the series. Hilariously spoofing *The Scarlet Pimpernel*, Talbot Rothwell's script is stuffed with comic incidents and names ranging from Sir Rodney Ffing to the Duc de Pommfrit. Sid James is superb, whether camping it up as a society fop or cutting a dash as the Black Fingernail, while Kenneth Williams's Citizen Camembert is great as "the big cheese" of the French Revolution. DP [video] DVD

Sidney James *Sir Rodney Ffing/The Black Fingernail* • Kenneth Williams *Citizen Camembert* • Jim Dale *Lord Darcy* • Charles Hawtrey *Duc de Pommfrit* • Joan Sims *Desirée Dubarry* • Peter Butterworth *Citizen Bidet* ■ *Dir* Gerald Thomas • *Scr* Talbot Rothwell

Carry On Emmannuelle ★ 15

Comedy 1978 · UK · Colour · 84mins

Spoofing the series of erotic movies starring Sylvia Kristel, this was the last *Carry On* made during the series' golden age. Sadly, it's the weakest of the lot. Lance Peters's script is a gag-free zone that is utterly dependent on smutty innuendo and severely taxes the talents of the few regulars on duty. An embarrassment. DP. Contains some swearing, sex scenes and brief nudity. [video] DVD

Suzanne Danielle *Emmannuelle Prevert* • Kenneth Williams *Emile Prevert* • Kenneth Connor *Leyland* • Jack Douglas *Lyons* • Joan Sims *Mrs Dangle* • Peter Butterworth *Richmond* • Beryl Reid *Mrs Valentine* ■ *Dir* Gerald Thomas • *Scr* Lance Peters

Carry On England ★ PG

Comedy 1976 · UK · Colour · 84mins

The real secret of the *Carry Ons* success was in the scriptwriting, which provided the actors with an endless supply of stinging ammunition. This woeful effort by Jack Seddon and David Pursall (about a Battle of Britain anti-aircraft battery) leaves what is essentially a B-team with nothing to fire but blanks. DP [video] DVD

Kenneth Connor *Captain S Melly* • Windsor Davies *Sergeant Major "Tiger" Bloomer* • Patrick Mower *Sergeant Len Able* • Judy Geeson *Sergeant Tilly Willing* • Jack Douglas *Bombardier Ready* • Melvyn Hayes *Gunner Shorthouse* • Joan Sims *Private Sharpe* • Peter Jones *Brigadier* • Peter Butterworth *Major Carstairs* ■ *Dir* Gerald Thomas • *Scr* David Pursall, Jack Seddon

Carry On Follow That Camel ★★ PG

Comedy 1967 · UK · Colour · 90mins

Originally released under the title *Follow That Camel*, this disappointing spoof on *Beau Geste* was only later added to the *Carry On* series and it sits uncomfortably alongside the rest. Although many of the regular team are on duty, the presence of Phil Silvers overbalances the story. There are comic oases along the way, however, with the Mustapha Leek joke being the most memorable. DP [video] DVD

Phil Silvers *Sergeant Nocker* • Jim Dale *Bertram Oliphant West* • Peter Butterworth *Simpson* • Charles Hawtrey *Captain Le Pice* • Kenneth Williams *Commandant Burger* • Anita Harris *Corktip* • Joan Sims *Zigzig* • Bernard Bresslaw *Abdul* • Angela Douglas *Lady Jane Ponsonby* • John Bluthal *Corporal Clotski* ■ *Dir* Gerald Thomas • *Scr* Talbot Rothwell

Carry On Girls ★★ PG

Comedy 1973 · UK · Colour · 84mins

When councillor Sidney Fiddler (Sid James) decides that a beauty contest is the only way to put the sleepy seaside resort of Fircombe on the map, the local feminists are soon up in arms. The least focused of the *Carry On* series, this combines the gentle social satire of an Ealing comedy with the sniggering sauciness of a Donald McGill postcard. It's not one of Talbot Rothwell's best scripts, but there are some splendid supporting performances. DP [video] DVD

Sidney James *Sidney Fiddler* • Joan Sims *Connie Philpotts* • Kenneth Connor *Frederick Bumble* • Barbara Windsor *Hope Springs* • Bernard Bresslaw *Peter Potter* • June Whitfield *Augusta Prodworthy* • Peter Butterworth *Admiral* • Jack Douglas *William* • Patsy Rowlands *Mildred Bumble* • Joan Hickson *Mrs Dukes* • Wendy Richard *Ida Downs* ■ *Dir* Gerald Thomas • *Scr* Talbot Rothwell

Carry On Henry ★★★ PG

Comedy 1971 · UK · Colour · 86mins

This raucous history lesson is something of an on-off affair. For once, Talbot Rothwell's script isn't as sharp as an executioner's axe, but there are still plenty of wicked one-liners and savage parodies. Sid James makes a suitably merry monarch, while Joan Sims gives her best performance of the series as his garlic-gobbling queen. Exceptional support is provided by Kenneth Williams and Charles Hawtrey as the wonderfully named Sir Roger de Lodgerley. DP [video] DVD

Sidney James *Henry VIII* • Kenneth Williams *Thomas Cromwell* • Charles Hawtrey *Sir Roger de Loggerley* • Joan Sims *Queen Marie* • Terry Scott *Cardinal Wolsey* • Barbara Windsor *Bettina* • Kenneth Connor *Lord Hampton of Wick* • Bill Maynard *Fawkes* ■ *Dir* Gerald Thomas • *Scr* Talbot Rothwell

Carry On Jack ★★ PG

Comedy 1963 · UK · Colour · 87mins

The innuendos continue as the *Carry On* crew takes to the seas in the first of the historical costume parodies tackled by the team. Alas, some of the regulars are missing, making it one of the less memorable productions in the series. Bernard Cribbins in the lead role doesn't carry the same clout as Sid James, but director Gerald Thomas keeps the fun shipshape and Bristol fashion. NF [video] DVD

Bernard Cribbins *Albert Poop-Decker* • Kenneth Williams *Captain Fearless* • Juliet Mills *Sally* • Charles Hawtrey *Walter* • Donald Houston *Howett* • Percy Herbert *Angel* ■ *Dir* Gerald Thomas • *Scr* Talbot Rothwell

Carry On Loving ★★ PG

Comedy 1970 · UK · Colour · 86mins

Containing more double entendres than an exhibition of smutty postcards, Talbot Rothwell's script for this patchy effort spends too much time in the company of Terry Scott and the other clients of the Wedded Bliss Marriage Bureau. Consequently, we get not enough of the bureau's proprietors: Hattie Jacques and Sid James, amorous spinster Joan Sims and marriage guidance counsellor Kenneth Williams. The sound you can hear during the slapstick wedding finale is barrels being scraped. DP [video] DVD

Sidney James *Sidney Bliss* • Kenneth Williams *Percival Snooper* • Charles Hawtrey *James Bedsop* • Joan Sims *Esme Crowfoot* • Hattie Jacques *Sophie* • Terry Scott *Terence Philpot* • Bernard Bresslaw *Gripper Burke* • Patsy Rowlands *Miss Dempsey* • Joan Hickson *Mrs Grubb* • Bill Maynard *Mr Dreery* ■ *Dir* Gerald Thomas • *Scr* Talbot Rothwell

Carry On Matron ★★★ PG

Comedy 1972 · UK · Colour · 85mins

Subtitled *From Here to Maternity*, the fourth *Carry On* to be set in a hospital is the last in the series that manages to be consistently funny throughout. The regulars are all present, with Hattie Jacques in the title role as the object of consultant Kenneth Williams's confused affections, while crooked Sid James leads a raid on the clinic where they work to steal contraceptive pills. Amid the innuendo, cross-dressing and crude slapstick, there are lovely cameos from Kenneth Connor and Joan Sims. DP [video] DVD

Sidney James *Sid Carter* • Kenneth Williams *Sir Bernard Cutting* • Charles Hawtrey *Dr Francis Goode* • Joan Sims *Mrs Tidey* • Hattie Jacques *Matron* • Bernard Bresslaw *Ernie* • Kenneth Cope *Cyril Carter* • Terry Scott *Dr Prodd* • Barbara Windsor *Nurse Susan Ball* • Kenneth Connor *Mr Tidey* • Bill Maynard *Freddy* • Patsy Rowlands *Evelyn Banks* ■ *Dir* Gerald Thomas • *Scr* Talbot Rothwell

Carry On Nurse ★★★ PG

Comedy 1959 · UK · BW · 82mins

The second film in the *Carry On* series overdoses on bedpan, large needle and inedible food gags, but, as most of them are funny, no one will mind in the slightest. Hattie Jacques is superb as the bullying matron whose clipped supervision of nurses Shirley Eaton and Joan Sims prompts Kenneth Connor, Leslie Phillips and Kenneth Williams to give her a taste of her own medicine, while Wilfrid Hyde White has fun as a lecherous colonel in a private ward. DP [video] DVD

Kenneth Connor *Bernie Bishop* • Charles Hawtrey *Mr Hinton* • Hattie Jacques *Matron* • Shirley Eaton *Dorothy Denton* • Wilfrid Hyde White *Colonel* • Bill Owen *Percy Hickson* • Leslie Phillips *Jack Bell* • Joan Sims *Stella Dawson* • Kenneth Williams *Oliver Reckitt* • Terence Longdon [Terence Longden] *Ted York* ■ *Dir* Gerald Thomas • *Scr* Norman Hudis, from the play *Ring for Catty* by Patrick Cargill, Jack Searle

Carry On Regardless ★★★ PG

Comedy 1960 · UK · BW · 86mins

The fifth *Carry On* is unique in that it does not have a single storyline, but consists of a loose collection of sketches linked by the "Helping Hands" employment agency, run by Sid James to tackle the oddest of jobs. The assignments vary in comic value, but the ones in which Joan Sims gets hammered at a snooty wine tasting and Kenneth Williams baby-sits a chimpanzee stand out. The inimitable Esma Cannon simpers and sniggers superbly as Sid's assistant, but Charles Hawtrey and Kenneth Connor have little to do. DP [video] DVD

Sidney James *Bert Handy* • Kenneth Connor *Sam Twist* • Kenneth Williams *Francis Courtenay* • Charles Hawtrey *Gabriel Dimple* • Joan Sims *Lily Duveen* • Liz Fraser *Delia King* • Bill Owen *Mike Weston* • Hattie Jacques *Frosty-faced Sister* • Terence Longdon [Terence Longden] *Montgomery Infield-Hopping* • Joan Hickson *Matron* • Esma Cannon *Miss Cooling* ■ *Dir* Gerald Thomas • *Scr* Norman Hudis

Carry On Screaming ★★★★ PG

Comedy 1966 · UK · Colour · 92mins

This is one of the finest entries in Britain's most popular comedy series. Mocking that other bastion of British cinema in the 1960s, the Hammer horror film, Talbot Rothwell's script positively bristles with classic one-liners, the most memorable being Kenneth Williams's gleeful "Frying tonight!" as he sinks into a bubbling cauldron. In his only *Carry On*, Harry H Corbett is superb as the Holmesian detective and Fenella Fielding revels in her role as a vampish vampire, but the picture belongs to Williams as the undead Dr Watt, an amalgam of every mad scientist who ever set foot in a lab. DP [video] DVD

Kenneth Williams *Dr Watt* • Harry H Corbett *Detective Sergeant Bung* • Fenella Fielding *Valeria* • Jim Dale *Albert Potter* • Charles Hawtrey *Dan Dann* • Joan Sims *Emily Bung* • Bernard Bresslaw *Sockett* • Jon Pertwee *Dr Fettle* ■ *Dir* Gerald Thomas • *Scr* Talbot Rothwell

Carry On Sergeant ★★★ U

Comedy 1958 · UK · BW · 80mins

This is the first of a phenomenon. Like many of the early outings, it centres on an occupation at the heart of British life and is, therefore, closer to Ealing whimsy than the raucous fun of the later *Carry Ons*. William Hartnell (who became a household name as the first Doctor Who) stars as the sergeant determined to make soldiers out of his final batch of national service conscripts. Alongside Bob Monkhouse, a handful of regulars are on duty, with Kenneth Connor splendid as a weedy hypochondriac, Kenneth Williams as a smarmy know-all, and Charles Hawtrey as the wonderfully named Private Golightly. DP [video] DVD

William Hartnell *Sergeant Grimshawe* • Bob Monkhouse *Charlie Sage* • Shirley Eaton *Mary* • Eric Barker *Captain Potts* • Dora Bryan *Nora* • Bill Owen *Corporal Copping* • Charles Hawtrey *Peter Golightly* • Kenneth Connor *Horace Strong* • Kenneth Williams *James Bailey* • Hattie Jacques *Captain Clark* ■ *Dir* Gerald Thomas • *Scr* Norman Hudis, from the novel *The Bull Boys* by RF Delderfield

Carry On Spying ★★★ U

Spy spoof 1964 · UK · BW · 83mins

Mercilessly ribbing the Bond movies and Graham Greene's espionage entertainments, the ninth *Carry On* saw Barbara Windsor make her series debut as the most resourceful of a hamstrung quartet of agents sent to Vienna to recover a secret formula. The Casbah scenes rather slow things down, but the action picks up pace in STENCH's underground HQ (a wonderfully observed 007 send-up). Bernard Cribbins, Charles Hawtrey and Kenneth Williams are on form as Babs's weak-kneed accomplices and there are splendid turns from Jim Dale and Eric Barker. DP [video] DVD

Kenneth Williams *Desmond Simpkins* • Barbara Windsor *Daphne Honeybutt* • Bernard Cribbins *Harold Crump* • Charles Hawtrey *Charlie Bind* • Eric Barker *Chief* • Dilys Laye *Lila* • Jim Dale *Carstairs* ■ *Dir* Gerald Thomas • *Scr* Talbot Rothwell, Sid Colin

Carry On Teacher ★★★ U

Comedy 1959 · UK · BW · 82mins

The third in the *Carry On* series is a gentle comedy about the concerted efforts of both the pupils and staff of Maudlin Street School to dissuade headmaster Ted Ray from accepting a post elsewhere. The pranks are Bash Street Kids' calibre and raise few laughs, but the staff-room infighting is good value, with drama teacher Kenneth Williams and educational psychologist Leslie Phillips squabbling with maths teacher Hattie Jacques over corporal punishment, and gym mistress Joan Sims feuding with school assessor Rosalind Knight over weedy Kenneth Connor. DP [video] DVD

Ted Ray *William Wakefield* • Kenneth Connor *Gregory Adams* • Charles Hawtrey *Michael Bean* • Leslie Phillips *Alistair Grigg* • Joan Sims *Sarah Allcock* • Kenneth Williams *Edwin Milton* • Hattie Jacques *Grace Short* • Rosalind Knight *Felicity Wheeler* ■ *Dir* Gerald Thomas • *Scr* Norman Hudis

Carry On Up the Jungle ★★★ PG

Comedy 1970 · UK · Colour · 86mins

One of the weaker of the genre spoofs, but there's still much to raise a titter as Frankie Howerd and Kenneth Connor lead an expedition to Africa (Pinewood sets at their most gloriously economical) in order to find the Oozalum bird. Along for the ride are Joan Sims in search of her long-lost son and Sid James seeking a rumble in the jungle. The reception committee includes Terry Scott as an infantile Tarzan and Charles Hawtrey as the Great Tonka, a tribal chief with a guilty secret. DP DVD

Frankie Howerd *Professor Inigo Tinkle* • Sidney James *Bill Boosey* • Charles Hawtrey *Tonka/Walter* • Joan Sims *Lady Evelyn Bagley* • Terry Scott *Jungle Boy* • Kenneth Connor *Claude Chumley* • Bernard Bresslaw *Upsidasi* ■ *Dir* Gerald Thomas • *Scr* Talbot Rothwell

Carry On Up the Khyber ★★★★ PG

Comedy 1968 · UK · Colour · 85mins

Only the *Carry Ons* could get away with using a wooden gate in Snowdonia as the farthest flung outpost of the British Empire! Originally to be called *Carry On the Regiment*, this is rightly regarded as one of the best in the series. Affectionately mocking Hollywood's Raj adventures, Talbot Rothwell's script is stuffed with ludicrous names, classic one-liners and memorable moments, none better than the dinner under fire. Kenneth Williams is superb as the Khasi of Kalabar, but it's Sid James and Joan Sims who steal the show as the Ruff-Diamonds. DP DVD

Sidney James *Sir Sidney Ruff-Diamond* • Kenneth Williams *Khasi of Kalabar* • Charles Hawtrey *Private James Widdle* • Roy Castle *Captain Keene* • Joan Sims *Lady Ruff-Diamond* • Bernard Bresslaw *Bungdit Din* • Terry Scott *Sergeant Major MacNutt* ■ *Dir* Gerald Thomas • *Scr* Talbot Rothwell

The Cars That Ate Paris ★★★★ 15

Black comedy 1974 · Aus · Colour · 83mins

Peter Weir achieved a career high as the Oscar-nominated director of *The Truman Show*. His directorial debut, however, could not be more different from films such as *Picnic at Hanging Rock* and *Witness*, with which he made his reputation. It's a darkly comic tale of a small Australian town that feeds on passing travellers for their car parts; Terry Camilleri is the newcomer who decides to fight back. Rough edges notwithstanding, it's a sharp, vaguely unsettling affair and fortunately free of some of the portentous imagery that occasionally mars Weir's later work. JF. Contains swearing. DVD

Terry Camilleri *Arthur* • John Meillon *Mayor* • Melissa Jaffa *Beth* • Kevin Miles *Dr Midland* • Max Gillies *Metcalfe* • Peter Armstrong *Gorman* ■ *Dir* Peter Weir • *Scr* Peter Weir, Keith Gow, Piers Davies

Carson City ★★★ U

Western 1952 · US · Colour · 86mins

Randolph Scott stars as a railway foreman in director Andre De Toth's roistering western, leading the fight against villain Raymond Massey and his gang of bandits. De Toth had a good rapport with Scott, and this is one of the best of their several westerns together. It's also notable for being one of the first movies filmed in Warnercolor, Warner Bros's short-lived rival to Technicolor. TS

Randolph Scott *Jeff Kincaid* • Lucille Norman *Susan Mitchell* • Raymond Massey *Big Jack Davis* • Richard Webb *Alan Kincaid* • James Millican *Jim Squires* • Larry Keating *William Sharon* • Don Beddoe *Zeke Mitchell* ■ *Dir* Andre De Toth • *Scr* Sloan Nibley, Winston Miller, from a story by Sloan Nibley

Carthage in Flames ★ PG

Historical adventure
1960 · It/Fr · Colour · 106mins

Rome puts Carthage to the torch and the natives run hither and thither, sorting out their petty romantic problems while the rival navies meet on the high seas. The actors, meanwhile, mouth Italian, having been badly dubbed into American. Italian epics are an acquired taste, and there isn't much to recommend this one. Carthage burns prettily, however, and former British beauty queen Anne Heywood swans around in some fetching Punic tunics. AT. Italian dialogue dubbed into English.

Anne Heywood *Fulvia* • José Sáurez *Hiram* • Pierre Brasseur *Sidone* • Ilaria Occhini *Ophir* • Daniel Gélin *Phegor* ■ *Dir* Carmine Gallone • *Scr* Ennio De Concini, Duccio Tessari, Carmine Gallone, William De Lane Lea, from the novel *Cartagine in fiamme* by Emilio Salgari

Cartouche ★★ U

Swashbuckling adventure
1954 · It/US · BW · 73mins

It's pre-Revolutionary France and Richard Basehart is in exile, trying to prove he didn't murder a prince while evading the various titled gents who want revenge. Basehart joins a troupe of travelling players and romances Patricia Roc; elsewhere, Akim Tamiroff can be found hamming away under a mountain of make-up. AT

Richard Basehart *Jacques de Maudy* • Patricia Roc *Donna Violante* • Massimo Serato *Vaubranche* • Akim Tamiroff *Marchese di Salpiere* ■ *Dir* Steve Sekely, Gianni Vernuccio • *Scr* Louis Stevens, from a story by Tullio Pinelli, Gian Paolo Callegari

Cartouche ★★★ 15

Swashbuckling comedy adventure
1961 · Fr/It · Colour · 110mins

Cartouche was a Gallic cousin of Robin Hood and he makes an irresistible hero, especially when played by Jean-Paul Belmondo with dashing charm. No true swashbuckler would be complete without an utterly unscrupulous enemy and a beautiful heroine. This one is blessed with Philippe Lemaire as the slimy Chief of Police, and Claudia Cardinale as the newest addition to Belmondo's band of robbers. DP. French dialogue dubbed into English.

Jean-Paul Belmondo *Cartouche* • Claudia Cardinale *Vénus* • Odile Versois *Isabelle de Ferrussac* • Philippe Lemaire *de Ferrussac* • Marcel Dalio *Malichot* • Noël Roquevert *Recruiting sergeant* • Jess Hahn *La Douceur* ■ *Dir* Philippe de Broca • *Scr* Philippe De Broca, Charles Spaak, Daniel Boulanger

Carve Her Name with Pride ★★★★ PG

Second World War spy drama
1958 · UK · BW · 113mins

Made by the same team of director Lewis Gilbert and co-writer Vernon Harris that had previously brought us the Douglas Bader biopic *Reach for the Sky*, this is another well-crafted biographical film inspired by real-life heroism beyond the call of duty in the Second World War. Virginia McKenna gives an understated performance as Violette Szabo, a glamorous woman who, after her French officer husband was killed in action, became a British spy on the continent. PF DVD

Virginia McKenna *Violette Szabo* • Paul Scofield *Tony Fraser* • Jack Warner *Mr Bushell* • Denise Grey *Mrs Bushell* • Alain Saury *Etienne Szabo* • Maurice Ronet *Jacques* • Bill Owen *NCO Instructor* • Billie Whitelaw *Winnie* • Michael Caine ■ *Dir* Lewis Gilbert • *Scr* Vernon Harris, Lewis Gilbert, from the novel by RJ Minney

Casa de los Babys ★★

Drama 2003 · US · Colour · 95mins

Although he's capable of profound socio-political insight, writer-director John Sayles is also occasionally prone to unsubtle soap-boxing and this self-conscious – not to say cliché-ridden – study of six women awaiting to adopt in an unnamed South American country is one of his least persuasive efforts. Only Susan Lynch's Irish exile avoids broad-brush caricature and, thus, manages to express some genuine emotion. Other characters are merely cyphers for Sayles's opinions on religion, US imperialism and the state of modern womanhood. DP. In English and Spanish with subtitles.

Maggie Gyllenhaal *Jennifer* • Marcia Gay Harden *Nan* • Daryl Hannah *Skipper* • Susan Lynch *Eileen* • Mary Steenburgen *Gayle* • Lili Taylor *Leslie* • Rita Moreno *Señora Muñoz* • Vanessa Martinez *Asuncion* ■ *Dir/Scr* John Sayles

Casablanca ★★★★★ U

Classic romantic drama
1942 · US · BW · 98mins

This is one of those films, like *Citizen Kane* and *Gone with the Wind*, that exists outside of conventional criticism. Though dissected to within an inch of its life by scholars, the reason *Casablanca* endures is that it's a timeless love story wrapped inside a gripping wartime thriller, written with such wit and meaning it's still quoted (and misquoted) decades later. Humphrey Bogart gives a career best performance as Rick, the cynical, seemingly apolitical expat nightclub owner who becomes embroiled in the hunt for Paul Henreid's resistance leader by the SS. Henreid fetches up with Rick's old flame, the luminous Ingrid Bergman, and two exit visas wind up in the piano. Memorable support comes from Peter Lorre, Conrad Veidt and Claude Rains, and Max Steiner's score is superb, but the final credit must go to director Michael Curtiz, who pieces it all together with verve, symbolism and torrid emotion. AC DVD

Humphrey Bogart *Rick Blaine* • Ingrid Bergman *Ilsa Lund* • Paul Henreid *Victor Lazlo* • Claude Rains *Louis Renault* • Conrad Veidt *Major Strasser* • Sydney Greenstreet *Ferrari* • Peter Lorre *Ugarte* • SZ Sakall *Carl* • Madeleine Lebeau *Yvonne* • Dooley Wilson *Sam* ■ *Dir* Michael Curtiz • *Scr* Julius J Epstein, Philip G Epstein, Howard Koch, from the unproduced play *Everybody Comes to Rick's* by Murray Burnett, Joan Alison • *Producer* Hal B Wallis • *Cinematographer* Arthur Edeson • *Music* Max Steiner

Casanova ★★★★

Silent drama
1927 · Fr · BW and Tinted · 132mins

Here's a rare treat: the life of the great Italian seducer, made in France but directed by and starring Russians. This jewel of the French silent cinema arrived to some controversy in Paris when it premiered in a censored version in 1931. Finished in 1927, the same year as Abel Gance's mighty *Napoléon*, it stars the great Russian émigré Ivan Mosjoukine, who makes a bold, if temperamental Casanova. This treasure is a fitting reminder of the glory of silent cinema. TS

Ivan Mosjoukine *Casanova* • Diana Karenne *Maria Mari* • Suzanne Bianchetti *Catherine II* • Jenny Jugo *Therese* • Rina De Liguro *Corticelli* • Nina Kochitz *Countess Vorontzoff* • Olga Day *Baroness Stanhope* ■ *Dir* Alexandre Volkoff • *Scr* Norbert Falk, Ivan Mosjoukine, Alexandre Volkoff

Casanova ★★★ 18

Biographical historical drama
1976 · It · Colour · 147mins

Federico Fellini variously considered this sprawling period fantasy to be the worst film he ever made and his "most complete, expressive and courageous" vision. The answer lies somewhere in between. Private distractions, labour disputes and a tense shoot, in which the director's relationship with Donald Sutherland deteriorated daily, hardly facilitated creative endeavour. Yet it was Fellini's determination to undermine accepted notions of romantic love and depict the legendary lothario as a pompous, decadent sex machine that rendered the action so cold and detached. DP DVD

Donald Sutherland *Giacomo Casanova* • Tina Aumont *Henriette* • Cicely Browne *Madame D'Urfe* • Carmen Scarpitta *Madame Charpillon* • Clara Algranti *Marcolina* • Margareth Clementi *Sister Maddalena* • Olimpia Carlisi *Isabella* ■ *Dir* Federico Fellini • *Scr* Federico Fellini, Bernardino Zapponi, from the autobiography *Histoire de Ma Vie* by Giacomo Casanova de Seingalt • *Music* Nino Rota • *Costume Designer* Danilo Donati

Casanova '70 ★★★

Comedy 1965 · Fr/It · Colour · 112mins

Six writers contributed to the Oscar-nominated screenplay for this smug sex comedy from Mario Monicelli, which aimed to satirise the effect of female emancipation on the modern male. Marcello Mastroianni, on the other hand, signed up to play the NATO official who discovers he can only rise to the occasion in moments of peril in a bid to debunk the tired image of the Latin lover. Neither director nor star totally succeeded in their intentions, but Marcello exhibits all his Fellini-esque foibles, while Virni Lisi is quite enchanting. DP. In Italian with English subtitles.

Marcello Mastroianni *Major Andrea Rossi-Colombetti* • Virna Lisi *Gigliola* • Michèle Mercier *Noelle* • Marisa Mell *Thelma* • Marco Ferreri *Count Ferreri* • Bernard Blier *Commissioner* ■ *Dir* Mario Monicelli • *Scr* Furio Scarpelli, Agenore Incrocci, Suso Cecchi D'Amico, Mario Monicelli, from a story by Tonino Guerra, Giorgio Salvioni

Casanova & Co ★

Comedy
1976 · Austria/It/Fr/W Ger · Colour · 101mins

Tony Curtis's Casanova conceals his impotence by hiring a man of prodigious sexual appetite who also happens to be his exact double. Released soon after Fellini's sumptuous take on the notorious womaniser, this is really just a soft-core skin flick featuring an army of semi-naked women. AT

Tony Curtis *Giacomo Casanova/Giacomino* • Marisa Berenson *Calipha of Shiraz* • Hugh Griffith *Caliph of Shiraz* • Marisa Mell *Duchess Francesca* • Britt Ekland *Countess Trivulzi* ■ *Dir* François Legrand [Franz Antel] • *Scr* Joshua Sinclair, Tom Priman

Casanova Brown ★★

Comedy 1944 · US · BW · 91mins

About to marry for the second time, Gary Cooper learns that his ex-wife Teresa Wright has given birth to his child and is about to have it adopted. Horrified, he spirits the baby away and hides out in a downmarket hotel. Sam Wood's film is not a fraught drama, but a rather undernourished comedy that raises no more than the occasional smile. RK

Gary Cooper *Casanova "Cas" Q Brown* • Teresa Wright *Isabel Drury* • Frank Morgan *JJ Ferris* • Anita Louise *Madge Ferris* • Edmund Breon *Mr Drury* • Patricia Collinge *Mrs Drury* • Jill Esmond *Dr Martha Zernerke* ■ *Dir* Sam Wood • *Scr* Nunnally Johnson, Joe St Armand, from the play *The Little Accident* by Floyd Dell, Thomas Mitchell, and the novel *An Unmarried Father* by Floyd Dell

Casanova's Big Night ★★★ U

Musical comedy 1954 · US · Colour · 82mins

Bob Hope's self-created screen image always cast him as a *faux-naïf* – leching yet never leched after. It's interesting, then, to find him playing a Casanova substitute, perpetually mistaken for Vincent Price's genuine womaniser. The film is beautifully designed, and Paramount's Technicolor Venice capably stands in for the real thing. With Basil Rathbone as a suave arch villain, this is one of Hope's better comic vehicles. TS

Bob Hope *Pippo Popolino* • Joan Fontaine *Francesca Bruni* • Basil Rathbone *Lucio* • Raymond Burr *Bragadin* • Audrey Dalton *Elena* • Vincent Price *Casanova* • John Carradine *Minister Foressi* • Lon Chaney Jr *Emo* ■ *Dir* Norman Z McLeod • *Scr* Hal Kanter, Edmund Hartmann [Edmund L Hartmann], from a story by Aubrey Wisberg

Casbah ★★★★

Musical drama 1948 · US · BW · 93mins

Crooner Tony Martin steps into the shoes of Charles Boyer in this thoroughly entertaining remake of *Algiers*, which was itself a reworking of the classic *Pepe le Moko*. This is enthrallingly romantic or excruciatingly corny, depending on your point of view, but there's no denying the pleasure afforded by Harold Arlen and Leo Robin's musical numbers. Peter Lorre gives arguably his best Hollywood performance, there's the sultry allure of Yvonne De Carlo, and watch very closely for the briefest glimpse of a young Eartha Kitt. TS

Yvonne De Carlo *Inez* • Tony Martin *Pépé le Moko* • Peter Lorre *Slimane* • Marta Toren *Gaby* • Hugo Haas *Omar* • Thomas Gomez *Louvain* • Douglas Dick *Carlo* • Eartha Kitt ■ *Dir* John Berry • *Scr* L Bus-Fekete, Arnold Manoff, from a story by Erik Charell, from the novel *Pépé le Moko* by Detective Roger D'Ashelbe [Henri La Barthe]

A Case for PC 49 ★

Crime drama 1950 · UK · BW · 78mins

Unfortunately, every expense was spared in relating this tale of models, millionaires and murder. Hardly fitting treatment for Brian Reece, British crime fiction's first uniformed hero, who solved over a hundred cases on the airwaves between 1947 and 1953. Such was his popularity that he starred in the *Eagle* comic and in his own board game, *Burglars*. However, thanks to director Francis Searle, he never appeared on screen again. DP

Brian Reece *Archibald Berkeley-Willoughby* • Joy Shelton *Joan Carr* • Christine Norden *Della Dainton* • Leslie Bradley *Victor Palantine* • Gordon McLeod *Inspector Wilson* • Campbell Singer *Sergeant Wright* • Jack Stewart *Cutler* • Michael Balfour *Chubby Price* ■ *Dir* Francis Searle • *Scr* Alan Stranks, Vernon Harris, from their radio series

The Case of Dr Laurent ★★★

Drama 1957 · Fr · Colour · 111mins

An intense yet sensitive performance from Jean Gabin holds together this medical melodrama from writer/director Jean-Paul Le Chanois. Quitting his Parisian practice for a rural village, Gabin tries to win the locals round to his ideas on natural childbirth. With opposition to the doctor's theories duly provided, the action could easily have lapsed into a typical "tradition vs progress" tirade. Thanks to Henri Alekan's evocative photography and Joseph Kosma's delicate soundtrack, however, the story has stealthily captured the imagination by the time Nicole Courcel has her baby. The birth was actually shown on screen and became a source of some controversy. DP. In French with English subtitles.

Jean Gabin *Dr Laurent* • Nicole Courcel *Francine* • Sylvia Monfort *Catherine Loubet* • Arius *Dr Bastide* • Daxely *Simonet the baker* • Michel Barbey *André Loubet* • Yvonne Gamy *Midwife* ■ *Dir* Jean-Paul Le Chanois • *Scr* Jean-Paul Le Chanois, Rene Barjavel

A Case of Honor ★★ 15

Action adventure
1988 · Phil · Colour · 88mins

Timothy Bottoms stars in this unsubtle Vietnam War action adventure. Bottoms booms out his dialogue with more competence than conviction as he joins his fellow PoWs in an audacious escape bid after a decade's illegal detention. Veteran Filipino director Eddie Romero rams the pieces into place as the group liberates some hookers before attempting to fix an abandoned US helicopter, while Russian and Vietnamese patrols close in. Romero's a great old pro, but this is strictly routine. DP

Timothy Bottoms *Sergeant Joseph "Hard" Case* • John Phillip Law *Captain Roger L'Barnes* • Candy Raymond *Charlene "Charlie" Delibes* • Nick Nicholson *Pops* ■ *Dir* Eddie Romero • *Scr* John Trayne

The Case of Lena Smith ★★★

Silent romantic drama
1929 · US · BW · 68mins

While on holiday in Vienna, naive and pretty peasant girl Esther Ralston falls in love with army officer James Hall and marries him. Back at his family manse, Ralston is tyrannised by her father-in-law Gustave von Seyffertitz and pilloried by society because of her lowly origins. A silent melodrama of quality but unrelieved gloom, this is a searing attack on the evils of pre-1914 class prejudice in Europe. Director Josef von Sternberg's feeling for Vienna permeates the film and gives it an authentic feel. RK

Esther Ralston *Lena Smith* • James Hall *Franz Hofrat* • Gustav von Seyffertitz *Herr Hofrat* • Emily Fitzroy *Frau Hofrat* • Fred Kohler *Stefan* ■ *Dir* Josef von Sternberg • *Scr* Jules Furthman, Julian Johnson (titles), from a story by Samuel Ornitz

The Case of the Black Cat ★★★

Mystery 1936 · US · BW · 66mins

The debonair, wise-cracking Warren William was replaced by Ricardo Cortez for this entry in the Perry Mason series, in which the puzzling death of a bedridden millionaire sets off a chain of killings. Directed by William McGann, this is one of the better Mason movies, even though Cortez is a poor actor and Della Street (June Travis) is reduced to a bit part. AJ

Ricardo Cortez *Perry Mason* • June Travis *Della Street* • Jane Bryan *Wilma Laxter* • Craig Reynolds *Frank Oafley* • Carlyle Moore Jr *Douglas Keene* • Gordon Elliott [Bill Elliott] *Sam Laxter* ■ *Dir* William McGann • *Scr* F Hugh Herbert, from the story *The Case of the Caretaker's Cat* by Erle Stanley Gardner

The Case of the Black Parrot ★★

Mystery 1941 · US · BW · 59mins

Noel Smith's suspense-free thriller has intrepid reporter William Lundigan charging around a transatlantic liner in search of the diamonds stolen by a criminal during a fake submarine alert. With a couple of murders thrown in to reduce still further the list of suspects, it wouldn't take Nancy Drew to identify the culprit. DP

William Lundigan *Jim Moore* • Eddie Foy Jr *Tripod* • Maris Wrixon *Sandy Vantine* • Paul Cavanagh *Max Armand* • Luli Deste *Madame de Charriere* • Cyril Thornton *Rogers* ■ *Dir* Noel M Smith • *Scr* Robert E Kent, from the play *In the Next Room* by Eleanor Belmont, Harriet Ford, from the novel *Mystery of the Boule Cabinet* by Burton E Stevenson

The Case of the Howling Dog ★★

Mystery 1934 · US · BW · 75mins

A year after Erle Stanley Gardner created him, Perry Mason made his screen debut in this teasing murder mystery. Although Warren William had just finished playing another detective, Philo Vance, his portrayal of the ingenious attorney owed more to William Powell's soused sleuth, Nick Charles, in cult hit *The Thin Man*. Alan Crosland keeps the clues close to his chest and shifts suspicion between Mary Astor and her fellow suspects with some skill. DP

Warren William *Perry Mason* • Mary Astor *Bessie Foley* • Helen Trenholme *Della Street* • Allen Jenkins *Sgt Holcomb* • Grant Mitchell *Claude Drumm* ■ *Dir* Alan Crosland • *Scr* Ben Markson, from a novel by Erle Stanley Gardner

The Case of the Lucky Legs ★★

Mystery 1935 · US · BW · 78mins

The law and Perry Mason are on the trail of a crooked sponsor of "best legs" contests. When he is found murdered, however, the hunt becomes one for his killer. Warren William, the best of the actors to play Erle Stanley Gardner's lawyer/sleuth, stars in this entry, with Genevieve Tobin providing a vivacious Della Street. Alas, the script is so relentlessly jokey as to bury any possibility of excitement or interest in the over-complicated mystery. RK

Warren William *Perry Mason* • Genevieve Tobin *Della Street* • Patricia Ellis *Margie Clune* • Lyle Talbot *Dr Doray* • Allen Jenkins *Spudsy* • Barton MacLane *Bissonette* • Peggy Shannon *Thelma Bell* ■ *Dir* Archie Mayo • *Scr* Brown Holmes, Ben Markson, Jerome Chodorov, from a novel by Erle Stanley Gardner

The Case of the Mukkinese Battle Horn ★★★ U

Spoof mystery 1955 · UK · BW · 28mins

Dick Emery stands in for Harry Secombe in this pseudo-Goons picture. The theft of the eponymous instrument is of virtually no significance other than to give Peter Sellers the opportunity to play three characters. Spike Milligan also gets to reprise his beloved character, Eccles. The opening pastiche and the door-knocking sequence are the highlights. DP

Peter Sellers *Narrator/Superintendent Quilt/Assistant Commissioner Sir Jervis Fruit/Henry Crun* • Spike Milligan *Sgt Brown/J Smith/Minnie Bannister/Catchpole Burkington* • Dick Emery *Mr Nodule/Mr Crimp/Maurice Ponke/Maxie/Wormscrew* ■ *Dir* Joseph Sterling • *Scr* Harry Booth, Spike Milligan, Peter Sellers, Larry Stephens, from a story by Larry Stephens

The Case of the Stuttering Bishop ★★ U

Mystery 1937 · US · BW · 71mins

Lacking the enlivening presence of Warren William, the first and best of the Perry Masons, this run-of-the-mill episode stars Donald Woods as the investigative lawyer and Ann Dvorak as Della Street. The plot finds Mason having to determine whether the granddaughter of a millionaire is the genuine article or an impostor. The uninspiring action culminates in the courtroom. RK

Donald Woods *Perry Mason* • Ann Dvorak *Della Street* • Anne Nagel *Janice Alma Brownley* • Linda Perry *Janice Seaton* • Craig Reynolds *Gordon Bixter* ■ *Dir* William Clemens • *Scr* Don Ryan, Kenneth Gamet, from the novel by Erle Stanley Gardner

The Case of the Velvet Claws ★★★

Mystery 1936 · US · BW · 64mins

One of the better entries in the Perry Mason series, featuring the urbane Warren William as Erle Stanley Gardner's lawyer/sleuth, which finds him actually married to his loyal secretary Della Street, played this time around by Claire Dodd. The honeymoon, however, is delayed when Mason is forced at gunpoint to take on a blackmail case. Moderately sinister and quite amusing. RK

Warren William *Perry Mason* • Claire Dodd *Della Street* • Winifred Shaw *Eva Belter* • Gordon Elliott [Bill Elliott] *Carl Griffin* • Joseph King (1) *George C Belter* • Eddie Acuff *Spudsy* ■ *Dir* William Clemens • *Scr* Tom Reed, from a story by Erle Stanley Gardner

Casey's Shadow ★★★ PG

Drama 1978 · US · Colour · 92mins

A charming portrayal by Walter Matthau carries this fairly insubstantial family drama. Overlong (though trimmed considerably for its UK release) and relentlessly soft-hearted, it nevertheless offers the welcome sparring of horse-trainer Matthau with horse-breeder Alexis Smith. The action is in the firm but sensitive hands of *Hud* director Martin Ritt, who knows just how much rope to hand out. TS. Contains some swearing.

Walter Matthau *Lloyd Bourdelle* • Alexis Smith *Sarah Blue* • Robert Webber *Mike Marsh* • Murray Hamilton *Tom Patterson* • Andrew A Rubin [Andrew Rubin] *Buddy Bourdelle* ■ *Dir* Martin Ritt • *Scr* Carol Sobieski, from the short story *Ruidoso* by John McPhee

Cash McCall ★★ U

Romantic comedy
1960 · US · Colour · 101mins

Warner Bros was enjoying commercial success at the time with glossy adaptations of popular novels, but this film version of the bestseller by *Executive Suite* writer Cameron Hawley suffered from poor development on its way to the screen. Despite a good cast headed by James Garner – terrific as the title tycoon – and a radiant Natalie Wood in her first adult role, the end result is too superficial. TS

James Garner *Cash McCall* • Natalie Wood *Lory Austen* • Nina Foch *Maude Kennard* • Dean Jagger *Grant Austen* • EG Marshall *Winston Conway* • Henry Jones *Gil Clark* • Otto Kruger *Will Atherson* ■ *Dir* Joseph Pevney • *Scr* Lenore Coffee, Marion Hargrove, from the novel by Cameron Hawley

Cash on Demand ★★★★ U

Crime thriller 1961 · UK · BW · 88mins

One of the best British second features ever made, this is a tense thriller, which hooks the viewer from the beginning, then springs surprises right until the end. The life of truculent bank manager Peter Cushing (in one of his least-known but most complex roles) is changed when he is visited by "insurance investigator" André Morell. Director Quentin Lawrence, whose TV credits include *Coronation Street* and *The Avengers*, controls the suspense with such skill that it's a surprise his movie career didn't take off. DM

Peter Cushing *Fordyce* • André Morell *Hepburn* • Richard Vernon *Pearson* • Norman Bird *Sanderson* • Kevin Stoney *Detective Inspector Mason* • Barry Lowe *Peter Harvill* ■ *Dir* Quentin Lawrence • *Scr* David T Chantler, Lewis Greifer, from the teleplay *The Gold Inside* by Jacques Gillies

Casino ★★★★ 18

Crime drama 1995 · US · Colour · 170mins

GoodFellas goes to Las Vegas in Martin Scorsese's under-rated tale of power, money and depravity. Robert De Niro plays a master bookie turned big-shot casino manager whose head for business deserts him when he marries ex-hooker Sharon Stone. But it's when Joe Pesci, De Niro's boyhood acquaintance, arrives in town with an ambitious agenda of his own that things take a further downward spiral. Written by Nicholas Pileggi, an Oscar nominee for *GoodFellas*, *Casino* goes for absorbing realism, intriguing subplots and expertly drawn characters, while Stone is a revelation in her demanding role. AJ. Contains violence, swearing, sex scenes, drug abuse and nudity. DVD

Robert De Niro *Sam "Ace" Rothstein* • Sharon Stone *Ginger McKenna* • Joe Pesci *Nicky Santoro* • James Woods *Lester Diamond* • Don Rickles *Billy Sherbert* • Alan King *Andy Stone* • Kevin Pollak *Phillip Green* ■ *Dir* Martin Scorsese • *Scr* Nicholas Pileggi, Martin Scorsese, from the novel by Nicholas Pileggi

The Casino Murder Case ★★

Detective mystery 1935 · US · BW · 82mins

Several actors played SS Van Dine's popular sleuth Philo Vance. The first, and best, was William Powell, who made four films in the series; by 1935, Warren William and Basil Rathbone had each had an outing. This information is more interesting than the seventh film, which stars a miscast Paul Lukas on the trail of a mad poisoner who succeeds in killing three members of a bizarre family before Vance solves the case. RK

Paul Lukas *Philo Vance* • Rosalind Russell *Doris* • Alison Skipworth *Mrs Llewellyn* • Donald Cook *Lynn* • Arthur Byron *Kincaid* • Ted Healy *Sgt Heath* ■ *Dir* Edwin L Marin • *Scr* Florence Ryerson, Edgar Allan Woolf, from a novel by SS Van Dine

Casino Royale ★★★ PG

Spy spoof 1967 · UK · Colour · 125mins

It is perhaps wise not to think of this unwieldy spy caper as a James Bond movie at all. Though nominally based on Ian Fleming's first 007 novel (originally a 1954 TV show starring Barry Nelson), it is in actual fact a spoof, in which David Niven's retired Bond rounds up assorted 007 agents to avenge the death of "M" (John Huston). A surfeit of screenwriters and directors lends the whole a chaotic, disjointed air, but there is much fun to be had along the way. AC [VIDEO] DVD

David Niven *Sir James Bond* • Peter Sellers *Evelyn Tremble* • Ursula Andress *Vesper Lynd* • Orson Welles *Le Chiffre* • Joanna Pettet *Mata Bond* • Woody Allen *Jimmy Bond, Dr Noah* • Deborah Kerr *Agent Mimi, Lady Fiona McTarry* • William Holden (2) *Ransome* • Charles Boyer *Le Grand* • John Huston *McTarry* • Jean-Paul Belmondo *French legionnaire* • George Raft • Barbara Bouchet *Moneypenny* • Peter O'Toole *Scotch piper* • Geoffrey Bayldon *"Q"* • Ronnie Corbett *Polo* • Bernard Cribbins *Taxi driver* • Jacqueline Bisset *Miss Goodthighs* • Derek Nimmo *Hadley* ■ *Dir* John Huston, Ken Hughes, Val Guest, Robert Parrish, Joe McGrath [Joseph McGrath] • *Scr* Wolf Mankowitz, John Law, Michael Sayers (with uncredited contributions from Billy Wilder, Val Guest, Joseph Heller, Ben Hecht, Terry Southern), from the novel by Ian Fleming

Casper ★★★★ PG

Supernatural comedy drama
1995 · US · Colour · 95mins

With comic books and cartoon series full of muscle-bound superheroes vying for big-screen superstardom, it's nice to see a gentler character making such an impact in his first film outing. Here, Casper the Friendly Ghost is doing his bit to make Whipstaff Manor a homelier place for lonely Christina Ricci to live in, but it's his ghoulish uncles Stretch, Stinkie and Fatso who scare up all the fun in this enchanting family comedy. Cathy Moriarty's hissable villainy nearly steals the show. DP. Contains swearing. [VIDEO] DVD

Christina Ricci *Kat Harvey* • Bill Pullman *Dr James Harvey* • Cathy Moriarty *Carrigan Crittenden* • Eric Idle *Dibs* • Malachi Pearson *Casper* • Joe Nipote *Stretch* • Joe Alaskey *Stinkie* • Brad Garrett *Fatso* • Clint Eastwood • Mel Gibson ■ *Dir* Brad Silberling • *Scr* Sherri Stoner, Deanna Oliver, from a story by Joseph Oriolo, Seymour Reit, from characters created by Joseph Oriolo • *Special Effects* Michael Lantieri

Casper: a Spirited Beginning ★★ U

Supernatural comedy
1997 · US · Colour · 91mins

The friendly ghost does a runner from the ghost training centre and makes friends with a bullied young boy (Brendon Ryan Barrett) in this charmless straight-to-video sequel. Steve Guttenberg stars as the boy's workaholic building contractor dad who pays him little attention, and Lori Loughlin is Barrett's teacher who's trying to stop Guttenberg demolishing a local mansion to make way for a mini-mall. A cheesy concoction, clumsily mixing ghoulish humour and children's angst. JC [VIDEO] DVD

Brendon Ryan Barrett *Chris Carson* • Steve Guttenberg *Tim Carson* • James Earl Jones *Kibosh* • Pauly Shore *Snivel* • Michael McKean *Bill Case* • Rodney Dangerfield *Mayor Johnny Hunt* • James Ward *Stretch* • Bill Farmer *Stinkie* • Jeff Harnell *Fatso* • Jeremy Foley *Casper* ■ *Dir* Sean McNamara • *Scr* Jymn Magon, Thomas Hart, from the comic book *Harvey Comics' Casper the Friendly Ghost* by Joseph Oriolo,

Casper Meets Wendy ★ U

Supernatural comedy
1998 · US · Colour · 90mins

Teri Garr, Cathy Moriarty and Shelley Duvall reach career lowpoints as a trio of witches hiding away at a summer resort in a straight-to-video release that makes *Home Alone* look like an exercise in subtlety. Their niece Wendy (the helium-voiced Hilary Duff) is being sought by arched-eyebrow pantomime warlock George Hamilton. Unbearably manic. JC [VIDEO] DVD

Hilary Duff *Wendy* • Jeremy Foley *Casper* • Shelley Duvall *Gabby* • Teri Garr *Fanny* • Cathy Moriarty *Geri* • George Hamilton *Desmond Spellman* ■ *Dir* Sean McNamara • *Scr* Jymn Magon, Rob Kerchner, from characters created by Joseph Oriolo

Casque d'Or ★★★★

Drama 1952 · Fr · BW · 97mins

Based on an actual *crime passionnel*, this is one of the jewels of that much-maligned strain of literate French film-making, cynically dubbed, by François Truffaut, the "tradition of quality". In re-creating the underworld Paris of the Impressionists, director Jacques Becker creates a vibrant world of amiable rogues and sensual delight. Radiant at its centre is Simone Signoret, whose golden beauty prompts the tragic rivalry between naive carpenter Serge Reggiani and calculating gangster Claude Dauphin. DP. A French language film.

Simone Signoret *Marie* • Serge Reggiani *Manda* • Claude Dauphin *Felix Leca* • Raymond Bussières *Raymond* • William Sabatier *Roland* • Gaston Modot *Danard* • Loleh Bellon *Billy* • Claude Castaing *Fredo* ■ *Dir* Jacques Becker, Jacques Becker • *Scr* Jacques Companeez

Cass Timberlane ★★★★

Romantic drama 1947 · US · BW · 118mins

Cass Timberlane (Spencer Tracy) is a highly respected judge in a small Minneapolis town, beloved of the country club set but living alone since the death of his wife. When he falls passionately in love with a beautiful girl from the "wrong" side of town (Lana Turner), a series of shock waves, professional and personal, are unleashed. A good, old-fashioned drama that reveals Turner's often overlooked and mismanaged talent and offers Tracy at his magnificently nuanced best. Zachary Scott's womanising lawyer and Mary Astor's society bitch add extra bite. RK

Spencer Tracy *Cass Timberlane* • Lana Turner *Virginia Marshland* • Zachary Scott *Brad Criley* • Tom Drake *Jamie Wargate* • Mary Astor *Queenie Havock* • Albert Dekker *Boone Havock* ■ *Dir* George Sidney (2) • *Scr* Donald Ogden Stewart, Sonya Levien, from the novel by Sinclair Lewis

Cassandra ★★★ 18

Supernatural thriller
1987 · Aus · Colour · 89mins

This interesting little movie from Australia belts along effectively enough, featuring Tessa Humphries as a young woman who discovers that her brother has been jailed for causing their mother's death. As if this isn't enough of a shock, her brother has escaped from prison. The jolts are expertly placed, the cast is nicely twitchy and, despite the fact that Humphries shows an uncommon stoicism, this film is intriguing stuff. SH. Contains violence and nudity. [VIDEO]

Tessa Humphries *Cassandra* • Shane Briant *Steven Roberts* • Briony Behets *Helen Roberts* • Susan Barling *Libby* ■ *Dir* Colin Eggleston • *Scr* Colin Eggleston, John Ruane, Chris Fichett

The Cassandra Crossing ★ PG

Disaster thriller
1976 · UK/It/W Ger · Colour · 123mins

A terrorist has passed on a deadly plague to the passengers of a luxury express train, which has to be rerouted across a rickety bridge to a deserted concentration camp in order to prevent a worldwide epidemic. Burt Lancaster has the right idea when he suggests blowing the train to smithereens – ideally with the film inside. DP [VIDEO]

Richard Harris *Dr Jonathan Chamberlain* • Sophia Loren *Jennifer Rispoli Chamberlain* • Burt Lancaster *Col Stephen Mackenzie* • Ava Gardner *Nicole Dressler* • Martin Sheen *Robby Navarro* • Ingrid Thulin *Dr Elena Stradner* • Lee Strasberg *Herman Kaplan* • John Phillip Law *Major Stack* • Ann Turkel *Susan* • OJ Simpson *Father Haley* ■ *Dir* George Pan Cosmatos • *Scr* Tom Mankiewicz, Robert Katz, George Pan Cosmatos, from a story by Robert Katz, George Pan Cosmatos

Casshern ★★★ 15

Science-fiction action fantasy
2004 · Jpn · Colour · 141mins

This Japanese action fantasy is set in a not-too-distant future where a race of super robots is trying to take over the world. Into this mayhem comes the heroic but troubled Casshern, who has been made similarly invincible by his dear old scientist dad's plundered technology. Though hampered by a fiendishly complicated plot, *Casshern* is ravishing to look at and sets a new standard for the melding of live action, digital effects and animation. Don't worry about the story, just allow the heady mix of futuristic landscapes and gizmo-laden creatures to wash over you. LF. In Japanese with English subtitles. Contains violence. DVD

Yusuke Iseya *Casshern/Tetsuya Azuma* • Kumiko Aso *Luna Kozuki* • Toshiaki Karasawa *Burai* • Akira Terao *Prof Kotaro Azuma* • Kanako Higuchi *Midori Azuma* • Fumiyo Kohinata *Dr Kozuki* • Hiroyuki Miyasako *Akubon* • Mayumi Sada *Sagray* ■ *Dir* Kazuaki Kiriya • *Scr* Kazuaki Kiriya, Shotaro Suga, Dai Sato, from the animated TV series *Shinzo ningen Casshern* by Tatsuo Yoshida

Cast a Dark Shadow ★★★

Drama thriller 1957 · UK · BW · 82mins

After murdering his wife Mona Washbourne for her money, Dirk Bogarde marries canny Margaret Lockwood who proves less easy to dispose of. When he meets Kay Walsh, however, murder is back on the agenda. A modest but entertaining melodrama, directed by Lewis Gilbert with a stylish and proficient cast. Lockwood, who would return to the screen only once more two decades later, is particularly effective. RK

Dirk Bogarde *Edward Bare* • Mona Washbourne *Monica Bare* • Margaret Lockwood *Freda Jeffries* • Kay Walsh *Charlotte Young* • Kathleen Harrison *Emmie* ■ *Dir* Lewis Gilbert • *Scr* John Cresswell, from the play *Murder Mistaken* by Janet Green

Cast a Giant Shadow ★★★ PG

War drama 1966 · US · Colour · 132mins

This expensive epic tells one of the great stories of the early days in Israel's struggle for independence. The role of American-born colonel David "Mickey" Marcus is ruggedly incarnated by Kirk Douglas, apt casting for the orthodox Jew, born Issur Danielovitch. Marcus's story is impressive enough without the array of guest stars writer/director Melville Shavelson assembled in a distracting attempt to ensure box office respectability. For an absolutely hilarious account of the filming, read Shavelson's own book, *How to Make a Jewish Movie*. TS [VIDEO] DVD

Kirk Douglas *Colonel David "Mickey" Marcus* • Senta Berger *Magda Simon* • Angie Dickinson *Emma Marcus* • Gary Merrill *Pentagon Chief of Staff* • Haym Topol [Topol] *Abou Ibn Kader* • Frank Sinatra *Vince* • Yul Brynner *Asher Gonen* • John Wayne *General Mike Randolph* ■ *Dir* Melville Shavelson • *Scr* Melville Shavelson, from a biography by Ted Berkman

Cast a Long Shadow ★★ U

Western drama 1959 · US · Colour · 82mins

It's illegitimacy that casts the long shadow here, turning Audie Murphy's cowpoke into an embittered, hard-drinking, gambling drifter. Then he inherits the estate of a wealthy rancher who may have been his father, whereupon he becomes an intolerant trail boss during an arduous cattle drive. The script sorts him out in due course, but leaves some irritating loose ends. AE

Audie Murphy *Matt Brown* • Terry Moore *Janet Calvert* • John Dehner *Chip Donohue* • James Best *Sam Mullen* • Rita Lynn *Hortensia* • Denver Pyle *Harrison* ■ *Dir* Thomas Carr • *Scr* Martin G Goldsmith, John McGreevey, from a novel by Wayne D Overholser, from a story by Martin G Goldsmith

Cast Away ★★★ 12

Adventure drama
2000 · US · Colour · 137mins

Proving, to an extent, that the old ideas are often the best ones, Tom Hanks plays a Robinson Crusoe for the 21st century in this near one-man-show adventure from his *Forrest Gump* director, Robert Zemeckis. Alone on screen for most of the film's duration, Hanks's plight makes for riveting viewing as he struggles to keep body and soul together. It's only when he arrives home to a woolly, unsatisfying conclusion that the film unravels. AC. Contains swearing. [VIDEO] DVD

Tom Hanks *Chuck Noland* • Helen Hunt *Kelly Frears* • Nick Searcy *Stan* • Lari White *Bettina Peterson* ■ *Dir* Robert Zemeckis • *Scr* William Broyles Jr • *Cinematographer* Don Burgess

Castaway ★★ 15

Drama based on a true story
1986 · UK · Colour · 112mins

This is Nicolas Roeg's version of the real-life experiences of Lucy Irvine, who replied to a newspaper advert from Gerald Kingsland for a woman to join him for a year on a desert island. Both Amanda Donohoe and Oliver Reed cope well with their roles as the castaway and the sex-mad, middle-aged man who is her companion, but in the end you can't help feeling the nudity is only there to spice up a tale of two selfish people who probably deserved each other. JB. Contains swearing, sex scenes and nudity. [VIDEO]

Oliver Reed *Gerald Kingsland* • Amanda Donohoe *Lucy Irvine* • Georgina Hale *Sister St Margaret* • Frances Barber *Sister St Winifred* ■ *Dir* Nicolas Roeg • *Scr* Allan Scott, from the books *Castaway* by Lucy Irvine and *The Islander* by Gerald Kingsland

The Castaway Cowboy ★★★ U

Western 1974 · US · Colour · 87mins

The ever-amiable James Garner is the best thing in this Disney family movie about the first big cattle ranch to be set up in the Hawaiian islands. Garner plays a Texan cowboy who helps pretty widow Vera Miles convert her land from potatoes to beef. Robert Culp is a shady operator and Garner's romantic rival, and there are various natives on hand to cause trouble. AT DVD

James Garner *Lincoln Costain* • Vera Miles *Henrietta MacAvoy* • Robert Culp *Bryson* • Eric Shea *Booton MacAvoy* • Elizabeth Smith *Liliha* • Manu Tupou *Kimo* • Gregory Sierra *Marrujo* • Nephi Hannermann *Malakoma* ■ *Dir* Vincent McEveety • *Scr* Don Tait, from a story by Don Tait, Richard Bluel, Hugh Benson

The Castilian ★★ U

Historical adventure
1963 · US/Sp · Colour · 129mins

This uninvolving costume epic concerns the 10th-century legend of Fernan Gonzales, who tried to free Spain from the Moors. First, though, he has to unite Spain, despite fierce opposition from Broderick Crawford. This is one of a clutch of second-rate pictures Crawford made between *Highway Patrol* and *The Private Files of J Edgar Hoover*. JG

Cesar Romero *Jeronimo* • Frankie Avalon *Jerifan* • Broderick Crawford *Don Sancho* • Alida Valli *Queen Teresa* • Spartaco Santoni *Fernan Gonzales* • Teresa Velazquez *Sancha* • Fernando Rey *Ramiro II, King of Leon* • George Rigaud [Georges Rigaud] *Saint Milan* ■ *Dir* Javier Seto • *Scr* Paulino Rodrigo Diaz, Javier Seto, Luis de los Arcos, Sidney Pink, from the epic poem by Fernan Gonzales

The Castle ★★★★ 15

Comedy 1997 · Aus · Colour · 81mins

This utterly splendid Aussie comedy didn't make a big impact in the UK, but don't let that deter you – although it flags a little at the end it remains one of the funniest films of the decade. Former soap stars Michael Caton (*The Sullivans*) and Anne Tenney (*A Country Practice*) are the engagingly dim heads of the Kerrigan family who are delighted with their dream home, which borders the runway of Melbourne's airport. When the airport authority decides to compulsorily purchase their property to make way for expansion, the bumbling Kerrigans go into battle against the authorities. JF. Contains swearing. DVD

Michael Caton *Darryl Kerrigan* • Anne Tenney *Sal Kerrigan* • Stephen Curry *Dale Kerrigan* • Anthony Simcoe *Steve Kerrigan* • Sophie Lee *Tracey Kerrigan* • Wayne Hope *Wayne Kerrigan* ■ *Dir* Rob Sitch • *Scr* Rob Sitch, Santo Cilauro, Tom Gleisner, Jane Kennedy

Castle Keep ★★★ 15

Second World War drama
1969 · US · Colour · 102mins

Sydney Pollack's fourth film as director is strange indeed: a heavily allegorical Second World War drama about a squad of American soldiers who defend a Belgian castle, its impotent count and art treasures from the approaching Germans. Often pretentious, often startling and rooted in symbol and unreality, it's as if maverick director Sam Fuller had remade *Last Year at Marienbad*. AT. Contains swearing. DVD

Burt Lancaster *Major Abraham Falconer* • Peter Falk *Sergeant Orlando Rossi* • Patrick O'Neal *Captain Lionel Beckman* • Jean-Pierre Aumont *Henri Tixier, Comte De Maldorais* • Bruce Dern *Lieutenant Billy Byron Bix* ■ *Dir* Sydney Pollack • *Scr* Daniel Taradash, David Rayfiel, from the novel by William Eastlake

The Castle of Cagliostro ★★★★ PG

Animated mystery adventure
1979 · Jpn · Colour · 100mins

Master thief Lupin infiltrates an impenetrable stronghold with more hidden tricks, traps and secrets than a Magic Circle convention in this outstanding action *animé*. Directed with cinematic style and pace by Japanese pioneer Hayao Miyakazi, this combines the neat gadgetry and death-defying confrontations of James Bond with the comic irreverence of silent slapstick. The simplistic character animation doesn't detract from an elaborate, entertaining story and even those normally disconcerted by the genre's philosophising will enjoy Lupin's clear-cut mission to get the girl, beat the bad guy and take the treasure. JC. Japanese dialogue dubbed into English. DVD

Dir Hayao Miyakazi • *Scr* Hayao Miyakazi, Haruya Yamazaki, from a story by Monkey Punch • *Animator* Yasuo Otsuka

Castle of Evil ★

Horror 1966 · US · Colour · 80mins

Relatives of a dead, mad scientist gather in his creepy castle for the reading of the will, only to be systematically murdered by a robot fashioned in the image of the deceased. The result is a ridiculously bad mixture of Agatha Christie and schlock horror, featuring 1940s sex goddess Virginia Mayo as the madman's ex-mistress. A free funeral was promised if you died of fright while watching this amateur exploiter, though one is more likely to die laughing. AJ

Scott Brady *Matt Granger* • Virginia Mayo *Sable* • Lisa Gaye *Carol Harris* • David Brian *Robert Hawley* • Hugh Marlowe *Dr Corozal* • William Thourlby *The robot* • Shelley Morrison *Lupe Tekal d'Esperanza* ■ *Dir* Francis D Lyon • *Scr* Charles A Wallace

The Castle of Fu Manchu ★ PG

Horror
1968 · W Ger/Sp/It/UK · Colour · 88mins

The appalling final entry in the series featuring Sax Rohmer's Oriental arch-villain has Christopher Lee once more plotting world domination on a shoestring budget. Director Jess Franco is currently being lauded in some cineaste circles as an unsung demented genius. Judge for yourself with this atrocious turkey. AJ DVD

Christopher Lee *Fu Manchu* • Richard Greene *Nayland Smith* • Howard Marion-Crawford *Dr Petrie* • Tsai Chin *Lin Tang* • Günther Stoll *Curt* ■ *Dir* Jess Franco [Jesus Franco] • *Scr* Harry Alan Towers

Castle on the Hudson ★★★

Prison drama 1940 · US · BW · 74mins

The castle in question is Sing Sing penitentiary, where John Garfield is serving a long stretch for robbery. Girlfriend Ann Sheridan campaigns for his release; when she's injured in a car crash, the prison warden (Pat O'Brien, who else?) goes soft and lets Garfield out. Despite this B-movie's relatively short running time, it still manages to veer off into a typical Warner Bros exposé of political expediency. It's breathless and dated, though Garfield's strengths as an actor still shine through. AT

John Garfield *Tommy Gordon* • Ann Sheridan *Kay* • Pat O'Brien *Warden Long* • Burgess Meredith *Steven Rockford* • Henry O'Neill *District Attorney* • Jerome Cowan *Ed Crowley* • Guinn "Big Boy" Williams *Mike Cagle* ■ *Dir* Anatole Litvak • *Scr* Seton I Miller, Brown Holmes, Courtenay Terrett [Courtney Terrett], from the book *20,000 Years in Sing Sing* by Lewis E Lawes

Casual Sex? ★★★ 18

Comedy 1988 · US · Colour · 83mins

This talky but likeable post-Aids comedy might equally have been called *Sex and the Single Girl*. The setting is an up-market health centre, where Lea Thompson and Victoria Jackson hope to bump into a hunky, healthy guy. While they're at it, they reflect on the new sexual realities of the late 1980s. Comedian Andrew Dice Clay shows that he can be more than just an offensive stand-up with an amusing cameo as a New Jersey male with an attitude problem. PF

Lea Thompson *Stacy* • Victoria Jackson *Melissa* • Stephen Shellen *Nick* • Jerry Levine *Jamie* • Andrew Dice Clay *Vinny* • Mary Gross *Ilene* ■ *Dir* Genevieve Robert • *Scr* Wendy Goldman, Judy Toll, from their play

Casualties ★★★ 18

Psychological thriller
1997 · US · Colour · 82mins

After supporting roles in Hollywood movies such as *Disclosure* and *White Squall*, UK actress Caroline Goodall gets top billing in her own right in this creepy American indie chiller. She plays the abused wife of cop Jon Gries who strikes up a friendship with seemingly nice Mark Harmon, a fellow student in her cookery class. However, it quickly becomes apparent that her idealised "new man" is more than a couple of eggs short of an omelette. Alex Graves's direction is appreciably claustrophobic and he elicits strong performances from his two leads. JF

Mark Harmon *Tommy Nance* • Caroline Goodall *Annie Summers* • Jon Gries [Jonathan Gries] *Bill Summers* • Michael Beach *Clark* • John Diehl *Polito* ■ *Dir* Alex Graves • *Scr* Gary Preisler, Alex Graves

Casualties of War ★★★★ 18

War drama 1989 · US · Colour · 108mins

This disturbing and provocative Vietnam War tale has at its centre the fact-based story of a Vietnamese woman who is kidnapped and brutally raped by four GIs. While battle-scarred Sean Penn leads the assault, new recruit Michael J Fox stands back but doesn't help her. The film's compassion for the woman hits us directly, as does the way director Brian De Palma sets up the episode by showing the brutalisation of Penn and his colleagues in the preceding scenes. Filmed with all of the director's technical bravura, it heads towards an epilogue that reaches an emotional precipice and then leaps confidently over it. AT. Contains violence, swearing, sex scenes and nudity. DVD

Michael J Fox *Eriksson* • Sean Penn *Sergeant Tony Meserve* • Don Harvey *Corporal Thomas E Clark* • John C Reilly *Herbert Hatcher* • John Leguizamo *Diaz* • Thuy Thu Le *Oahn* • Erik King *Sergeant Frank Brown* • Jack Gwaltney *Rowan* • Ving Rhames *Lieutenant Reilly* ■ *Dir* Brian De Palma • *Scr* David Rabe, from the book by Daniel Lang

Cat and Mouse ★★★

Drama 1958 · UK · BW · 79mins

This claustrophobic thriller denies documentary director Paul Rotha the chance to demonstrate his facility with realism. Yet he still generates a fair amount of suspense as Ann Sears finds herself caught between an American army deserter and the villains searching for the diamonds stolen by her recently executed father. With Hilton Edwards and Lee Paterson imposing as her pursuers, this is superior to the majority of British B-movies made at the time. DP

Lee Patterson *Rod Fenner* • Ann Sears *Ann Coltby* • Hilton Edwards *Mr Scruby* • Victor Maddern *Superintendent Harding* • George Rose *Dealer* ■ *Dir* Paul Rotha • *Scr* Paul Rotha, from the novel *Cat and Mouse* by Michael Halliday

The Cat and the Canary ★★★★

Silent mystery 1927 · US · BW · 82mins

Paul Leni was the first of the great expressionist German directors to go to Hollywood, and he made his US debut with this silent mystery that was a strong influence on subsequent horror movies. Moodily shot, this classic "old dark house" picture is played mostly for laughs. The canary is a wealthy old man and the cat, or rather cats, are those who gather at midnight 20 years after his death to hear a reading of the will. It was remade with Bob Hope in 1939, and again in 1979. Leni died of blood poisoning in 1929, aged 44. RB

Laura La Plante *Annabelle West* • Creighton Hale *Paul Jones* • Forrest Stanley *Charles Wilder* • Tully Marshall *Roger Crosby* • Gertrude Astor *Cecily Young* • Arthur Edmund Carewe *Harry Blythe* • Flora Finch *Susan Sillsby* ■ *Dir* Paul Leni • *Scr* Robert F Hill, Alfred A Cohn, from the play by John Willard

The Cat and the Canary ★★★★ PG

Mystery comedy 1939 · US · BW · 73mins

Unfairly neglected today, this also suffered on release from the fact that 1939 was the *annus mirabilis* of Hollywood's Golden Era. This is the definitive haunted-house movie, much copied, never bettered, in which Bob Hope cements his screen image: at once cowardly, lecherous, vulnerable and attractive. Lovely Paulette Goddard makes a fine foil for Hope; so successful were they together that they were immediately re-teamed in *The Ghost Breakers*, with which this film is often confused. This is a remake of an equally good silent version, and was itself remade by porn king Radley Metzger in 1979. TS DVD

Bob Hope *Wally Campbell* • Paulette Goddard *Joyce Norman* • John Beal *Fred Blythe* • Douglass Montgomery *Charlie Wilder* • Gale Sondergaard *Miss Lu* • George Zucco *Lawyer Crosby* • Elizabeth Patterson *Aunt Susan* ■ *Dir* Elliott Nugent • *Scr* Walter DeLeon, Lynn Starling, from the play by John Willard

The Cat and the Canary ★★ 15

Murder mystery 1979 · UK · Colour · 93mins

This remake is not a patch on either Paul Leni's silent original or Bob Hope's cornball reworking. An all-star British cast works hard to raise both laughs and the hairs on the back of your neck, but only succeeds in being annoying. Radley Metzger's tepid direction almost completely misses the eerie atmosphere and the grisly graveyard humour that made John Willard's play such a natural for the screen. DP DVD

Honor Blackman *Susan Sillsby* • Edward Fox *Hendricks* • Michael Callan *Paul Jones* • Wendy Hiller *Allison Crosby* • Olivia Hussey *Cicily Young* • Beatrix Lehmann *Mrs Pleasant* • Carol Lynley *Annabelle West* • Daniel Massey *Harry Blythe* • Peter McEnery *Charlie Wilder* • Wilfrid Hyde White *Cyrus West* ■ *Dir* Radley Metzger • *Scr* Radley Metzger, from the play by John Willard

The Cat and the Fiddle
★★★ U

Romantic musical
1934 · US · BW and Colour · 88mins

This witty film stars the actress who was undoubtedly queen of movie operetta, "iron butterfly" Jeanette MacDonald. She's paired here with silent screen idol Ramon Novarro, whose matinée good looks and singing voice endured in talkies until his notorious private life led to a severe fall-off in screen popularity. This is good fun, with a sparkling script and the bonus of a last reel in early three-strip Technicolor. TS

Ramon Novarro *Victor* • Jeanette MacDonald *Shirley* • Frank Morgan *Daudet* • Charles Butterworth *Charles* • Jean Hersholt *Professor* ■ *Dir* William K Howard • *Scr* Bella Spewack, Sam Spewack, from the musical by Jerome Kern, Otto Harbach

Cat Ballou
★★★★ PG

Comedy western 1965 · US · Colour · 92mins

In this very entertaining comedy western, Jane Fonda's schoolteacher hires a gunman to avenge her murdered father. The man she hires is Kid Shelleen, a long-haired, buckskinned gunfighter played by Lee Marvin, who wakes up sozzled and gets worse by the minute. Even his horse is a drunkard, leaning against a barn for support. This showpiece role won an Oscar for Marvin, who also plays straight man to himself as Shelleen's psychotic brother, a killer with a silver nose. Nat King Cole and Stubby Kaye string along for a singalong in what is a very amiable affair. AT [VIDEO] DVD

Jane Fonda *Cat Ballou* • Lee Marvin *Kid Shelleen/Tim Strawn* • Michael Callan *Clay Boone* • Dwayne Hickman *Jed* • Tom Nardini *Jackson Two-Bears* • John Marley *Frankie Ballou* • Reginald Denny *Sir Harry Percival* • Arthur Hunnicutt *Butch Cassidy* ■ *Dir* Elliot Silverstein • *Scr* Frank Pierson, Walter Newman, from the novel by Roy Chanslor

Cat Chaser
★★ 18

Thriller 1989 · US · Colour · 86mins

This tough political thriller, adapted from the Elmore Leonard novel, is a disappointment. Peter Weller is the ex-soldier who gets lured into an affair and dangerous intrigue with former flame Kelly McGillis, now the wife of a particularly nasty Latin American policeman. Weller is fine as the tormented hero, but McGillis is an unconvincing *femme fatale*. JF. Contains swearing, violence, sex scenes and nudity. [VIDEO] DVD

Peter Weller *George Moran* • Kelly McGillis *Mary de Boya* • Charles Durning *Jiggs Scully* • Frederic Forrest *Nolan Tyner* • Tomas Milian *Andres de Boya* ■ *Dir* Abel Ferrara • *Scr* Elmore Leonard, James Borrelli, Alan Sharp, from the novel by Elmore Leonard

The Cat Concerto
★★★★★

Animated musical comedy
1947 · US · Colour · 8mins

This classic Tom and Jerry cartoon makes wonderful slapstick comedy around Liszt's *Second Hungarian Rhapsody* as Tom the cat's initially pompous, concert-hall rendition of the piece is reduced to rubble by Jerry the mouse, who is disturbed while sleeping in Tom's piano. During production, a mix-up at the Technicolor labs caused a similar Warner Bros cartoon, *Rhapsody Rabbit* (1946), to be delivered to MGM by mistake. MGM then rushed production of their film in order to submit it for that spring's Oscar nominations, later winning the award. A deserved gain for William Hanna and Joseph Barbera, as this is arguably their finest cartoon. CLP

Dir William Hanna, Joseph Barbera • *Animator* Kenneth Muse, Ed Barge, Irv Spence, Bob Gentle • *Music* Scott Bradley

The Cat from Outer Space
★★ U

Comedy 1978 · US · Colour · 94mins

Harmless Disney matinée fodder, with alien feline "Jake" grounded on Earth and in need of human dexterity to repair its disabled spacecraft. Startling similarities to *ET* add an unforeseen layer of entertainment value to a bland package that could have done with a bit of Spielberg magic. A pretty uninspired juvenile romp. AJ [VIDEO]

Ken Berry *Dr Frank Wilson* • Sandy Duncan *Dr Liz Bartlett* • Harry Morgan *General Stilton* • Roddy McDowall *Stallwood* • McLean Stevenson *Dr Carl Link* • Jesse White *Earnest Ernie* • Alan Young *Dr Wenger* ■ *Dir* Norman Tokar • *Scr* Ted Key

The Cat Gang
★★ U

Crime drama 1959 · UK · BW · 50mins

Based on a story by George Ewart Evans, this featurette might have kept kids amused in the late 1950s. However, the demands of young audiences have changed dramatically since those more innocent times, and a tale of smuggling devoid of special effects will now have few takers. That said, their parents will no doubt be fascinated to see a youthful Francesca Annis among the gang assisting a grumpy customs officer in the recovery of some valuable contraband. DP

Francesca Annis *Sylvia* • John Pike *John* • Jeremy Bullock [Jeremy Bulloch] *Bill* • John Gabriel *Mason* • John Stacy *Dodds* • Paddy Joyce *Banks* ■ *Dir* Darrell Catling • *Scr* John Eldridge, from a story by G Ewart Evans [George Ewart Evans]

Cat on a Hot Tin Roof
★★★★ 15

Drama 1958 · US · Colour · 103mins

This is Tennessee Williams at his most overheated, with familial strife in the Deep South coming atmospherically alive in all its steamy, fly-blown glory. Elizabeth Taylor overdoes the Southern accent, though Paul Newman is splendid as the sullen but only upright member of a thoroughly dislikeable clan. The surprise plus is Burl Ives as the dying patriarch Big Daddy. One of the sounder screen adaptations of the playwright's work, even if the play's references to the homosexuality of Newman's character were watered down for the film. SH. Contains some sexual references. [VIDEO] DVD

Elizabeth Taylor *Maggie Pollitt* • Paul Newman *Brick Pollitt* • Burl Ives *Big Daddy Pollitt* • Jack Carson *Gooper Pollitt* • Judith Anderson *Big Mama Pollitt* • Madeleine Sherwood *Mae Pollitt* • Larry Gates *Dr Baugh* • Vaughn Taylor *Deacon Davis* ■ *Dir* Richard Brooks • *Scr* Richard Brooks, James Poe, from the play by Tennessee Williams

Cat o'Nine Tails
★★★ 18

Thriller 1971 · Fr/It/W Ger · Colour · 107mins

Blind Karl Malden and journalist James Franciscus unravel a mystery combining industrial espionage, homosexuality and genetic dementia in director Dario Argento's visually creative study in psycho terror. Thrilling subjective camerawork masks the maniac's identity in a triumph of style over content that marks the beginning of the director's obsession with eyes and blades. The train platform murder and the skylight finale are textbook examples of what Argento calls "violence as art". AJ. Some dialogue dubbed into English. [VIDEO] DVD

Karl Malden *Franco Arno* • James Franciscus *Carlo Giordani* • Catherine Spaak *Anna Terzi* • Cinzia De Carolis *Lori* • Carlo Alighiero *Dr Calabresi* • Vittorio Congia *Righetto* • Aldo Reggiani *Dr Casoni* ■ *Dir* Dario Argento • *Scr* Dario Argento, from a story by Luigi Collo, Dardano Sacchetti, Dario Argento • *Cinematographer* Erico Menczer

Cat People
★★★★ PG

Psychological horror 1942 · US · BW · 72mins

Produced by Val Lewton and directed by the great Jacques Tourneur, this was one of the first Hollywood horrors to play on the audience's fears rather than expose them to ghouls and monsters. Simone Simon makes one of cinema's most sensual menaces as the sketch artist who turns into a panther as a result of an ancient Serbian curse. Apart from Simon, the acting's pretty ropey, but the film is packed with eerie moments. DP [VIDEO]

Simone Simon *Irena Dubrovna* • Tom Conway *Dr Judd* • Jane Randolph *Alice Moore* • Jack Holt *Commodore* • Kent Smith *Oliver Reed* • Alan Napier *Carver* • Elizabeth Dunne *Miss Plunkett* • Elizabeth Russell *The cat woman* • Mary Halsey *Blondie* ■ *Dir* Jacques Tourneur • *Scr* DeWitt Bodeen • *Cinematographer* Nicholas Musuraca

Cat People
★★★ 18

Horror 1982 · US · Colour · 112mins

Paul Schrader's stylish remake of producer Val Lewton's horror classic features a well-cast Nastassja Kinski as one of the last survivors of a race of beings who transform into felines in the heat of passion. Malcolm McDowell is her kinky brother and John Heard the zookeeper unaware that not all of the animals are behind bars. Driven by nudity, gore and sensuality, Schrader's emotionally cold fantasy begins well, but degenerates into a surrealistic, gruesome mess. AJ. Contains violence, swearing, sex scenes and nudity. [VIDEO] DVD

Nastassia Kinski [Nastassja Kinski] *Irena Gallier* • Malcolm McDowell *Paul Gallier* • John Heard *Oliver Yates* • Annette O'Toole *Alice Perrin* • Ruby Dee *Female* • Ed Begley Jr *Joe Creigh* ■ *Dir* Paul Schrader • *Scr* Alan Ormsby, from the film by DeWitt Bodeen • *Music* Giorgio Moroder

The Cat Returns
★★ U

Animated fantasy
2002 · Jpn/US · Colour · 75mins

Made by the same studio that gave us *Spirited Away*, Hiroyuki Morita's film just isn't on a par with its enchanting, Oscar-winning stablemate. This tells the tale of teenager Haru, who's invited to visit the Kingdom of Cats after saving the life of a moggie prince. But then the king decides that Haru should marry his son and never return to the human world. The unfolding storyline is disappointingly simple, while the visuals rarely impress. SF. Japanese dialogue dubbed into English.

Anne Hathaway *Haru* • Cary Elwes *Baron* • Peter Boyle *Muta* • Elliott Gould *Toto* • Andrew Bevis *Prince Lune* • Tim Curry *Cat King* • Judy Greer *Yuki* • Kristen Bell *Hiromi* • René Auberjonois *Natori* ■ *Dir* Hiroyuki Morita • *Scr* Reiko Yoshida, Cindy Davis Hewitt (English version), Donald H Hewitt (English version), from the comic book *Baron the Cat Baron* by Aoi Hiragi

Cat-women of the Moon
★ U

Science-fiction adventure
1953 · US · BW · 62mins

"You've Never Seen Anything Like It" screamed the posters for this delightfully abysmal camp classic. Astronaut Sonny Tufts leads an expedition to the dark side of the moon and discovers a bevy of telepathic feline beauties out to steal his spaceship and invade Earth. With a set left over from a submarine movie, cat-women dancers in black wigs and leotards, toy zap guns, a tacky giant spider and the wooden Tufts making the absolute least of his screen time, this is lunar lunacy. AJ [VIDEO]

Sonny Tufts *Grainger* • Victor Jory *Kip* • Marie Windsor *Helen* • William Phipps *Doug* • Douglas Fowley *Walter* • Carol Brewster *Alpha* • Suzanne Alexander *Zeta* ■ *Dir* Arthur Hilton • *Scr* Roy Hamilton, from a story by Al Zimbalist, Jack Rabin

C

Catacombs
★ 18

Horror 1988 · US · Colour · 84mins

This is yet another instalment in the otherwise unconnected *Curse* series, also known as *Curse IV: The Ultimate Sacrifice*. A new father superior (Jeremy West), a young monk losing his faith (Timothy Van Patten) and a visiting Catholic schoolteacher (Laura Schaefer) join forces to fight a revived medieval demon. Ho-hum horror featuring limited special effects. AJ [VIDEO]

Timothy Van Patten *Father John Durham* • Ian Abercrombie *Father Orsini* • Jeremy West *Father Marinus* • Laura Schaefer *Elizabeth Magrino* ■ *Dir* David Schmoeller • *Scr* Giovanni Dimarco, R Barker Price

The Catamount Killing
★★★

Crime drama
1974 · W Ger/US · Colour · 97mins

Coming between those landmarks in Polish cinema, *Illumination* and *Camouflage*, this English language crime drama may seem something of an aberration on the part of Krzysztof Zanussi. Yet, as banker Horst Buchholz and his lover Ann Wedgeworth flee with the proceeds of their heist, it becomes clear the director's recurrent themes of moral decline and the disintegration of meaningful relationships are both present and correct. DP

Horst Buchholz *Mark Kalvin* • Ann Wedgeworth *Kit Loring* • Chip Taylor *Ken Travers* • Louise Clark *Iris Loring* • Patricia Joyce *Alice Craig* ■ *Dir* Krzysztof Zanussi • *Scr* Julien More, Sheila More, from the novel *I'd Rather Stay Poor* by James Hadley Chase

Catch Me a Spy
★★

Spy thriller 1971 · UK · Colour · 94mins

This lame spy thriller about missing secret files has a sometimes clever and witty script by the ace TV team of Dick Clement and Ian La Frenais. However, it's rather let down by Clement's uncertain direction, while Kirk Douglas's peculiar intensity isn't best suited to a comedy. Trevor Howard and Tom Courtenay seem more at home with the spy spoof material, though. AT

Kirk Douglas *Andrej* • Marlène Jobert *Fabienne* • Trevor Howard *Sir Trevor Dawson* • Tom Courtenay *Baxter Clarke* • Patrick Mower *John Fenton* • Bernadette Lafont *Simone* • Bernard Blier *Webb* ■ *Dir* Dick Clement • *Scr* Dick Clement, Ian La Frenais, from the novel by George Marton, Tibor Meray

Catch Me If You Can
★★★★ 12

Biographical comedy drama
2002 · US · Colour · 134mins

Director Steven Spielberg backtracks to the 1960s for this stylish slice of entertainment. Leonardo DiCaprio exudes movie-star charisma as Frank Abagnale Jr who, while still a teenager, charmed and cheated his way across America, posing as an airline pilot, doctor and lawyer in order to cash forged cheques. Tom Hanks turns in an unshowy supporting performance as Carl Hanratty, the dogged FBI agent who obsessively pursued the larcenous young man. Sentimentality is allowed to intrude with the depiction of Abagnale's family life, but not into Christopher Walken's superb turn as the conman's father. Despite these momentary dips, the deft blend of comedy and suspense, great period detail and sheer directorial class ensures that this is one of Spielberg's most purely enjoyable movies. IF DVD

Leonardo DiCaprio *Frank William Abagnale Jr/ Frank Taylor/Frank Conners/Barry Allen* • Tom Hanks *Carl Hanratty* • Christopher Walken *Frank William Abagnale Sr* • Martin Sheen *Roger Strong* • Nathalie Baye *Paula Abagnale* • Amy Adams *Brenda Strong* • James Brolin *Jack Barnes* • Brian Howe *Tom Fox* • Frank W Abagnale *French policeman* • Jennifer Garner *Cheryl Ann* ■ *Dir* Steven Spielberg • *Scr* Jeff Nathanson, from the autobiography *Catch Me If You Can: the Amazing True Story of the Most Extraordinary Liar in the History of Fun and Profit* by Frank Abagnale Jr, Stan Redding

Catch My Soul ★

Musical 1973 · US · Colour · 95mins

Lance LeGault, the demonic leader of a desert-based religious commune, manipulates black preacher Richie Havens into murdering his white hippy wife Season Hubley in a fit of jealous rage. This updated musical version of Shakespeare's *Othello* is to be avoided by all but the most dedicated fans of 1970s rock operas. Boring when it doesn't infuriate. RK

Richie Havens *Othello* • Lance LeGault *Iago* • Season Hubley *Desdemona* • Tony Joe White *Cassio* • Susan Tyrrell *Emilia* ■ *Dir* Patrick McGoohan • *Scr* Jack Good, from the play *Othello* by William Shakespeare • *Music* Tony Joe White

Catch That Kid ★★★ PG

Action adventure 2004 · US · Colour · 87mins

Its "crime pays" message may be dubious for a family film, but this fast-paced *Mission: Impossible*-style action adventure is still imaginative, exciting and wonderfully entertaining. Kristen Stewart plays a young girl who teams up with two male friends to carry out a hi-tech bank heist to get the cash to pay for a costly operation for her paralysed father. Though the plot's far-fetched, it's well-executed, skilfully balancing intelligence, suspense and humour. The acting, too, is highly engaging. SF DVD

Kristen Stewart *Maddy* • Corbin Bleu *Austin* • Max Thieriot *Gus* • Jennifer Beals *Molly* • Sam Robards *Tom* • John Carroll Lynch *Mr Hartman* • James Le Gros [James LeGros] *Ferrell* • Michael Des Barres *Brisbane* • Stark Sands *Brad* ■ *Dir* Bart Freundlich • *Scr* Michael Brandt, Derek Haas, from the film *Klatretosen* by Nikolaj Arcel, Hans Fabian Wullenweber, Erlend Loe

Catch-22 ★★★ 15

War satire 1970 · US · Colour · 116mins

Alan Arkin is splendid as Captain Yossarian, the innocent abroad at a US Air Force base in the Mediterranean, in this war satire based on Joseph Heller's bestseller. It's more violent burlesque than tragi-farce, but it certainly draws attention to its hero's "no win situation" as he struggles to cope with sham, hypocrisy and the deaths of too many comrades. Mike Nichols's direction of Buck Henry's script is an organisational tour de force, though the episodic structure requires concentration and the black comedy seems, at times, a bit laboured. TH. Contains violence, swearing and brief nudity. DVD

Alan Arkin *Capt Yossarian* • Martin Balsam *Col Cathcart* • Richard Benjamin *Major Danby* • Art Garfunkel *Capt Nately* • Jack Gilford *Doc Daneeka* • Buck Henry *Lt Col Korn* • Bob Newhart *Major Major* • Anthony Perkins *Chaplain Tappman* • Paula Prentiss *Nurse Duckett* • Martin Sheen *Lt Dobbs* • Jon Voight *Milo Minderbinder* • Orson Welles *Gen Dreedle* • Bob Balaban *Capt Orr* • Charles Grodin *Aarfy Aardvark* • Austin Pendleton *Col Moodus* ■ *Dir* Mike Nichols • *Scr* Buck Henry, from the novel by Joseph Heller

Catch Us If You Can ★★ PG

Musical 1965 · UK · BW · 87mins

Despite a run of jolly, sunny-sounding pop hits, the Dave Clark Five chose former documentarist John Boorman to direct this starkly black-and-white and unexpectedly bleak first feature. It's no *A Hard Day's Night*, but it paved the way for Boorman to make the massively influential *Point Blank*. Clark and the lads are singularly charmless and unskilled at thesping, but Barbara Ferris does a nice turn as a model on the lam. TS

Dave Clark *Steve* • Lenny Davidson *Lenny* • Rick Huxley *Rick* • Mike Smith *Mike* • Denis Payton *Denis* • Barbara Ferris *Dinah* • David Lodge *Louis* • Robin Bailey *Guy* ■ *Dir* John Boorman • *Scr* Peter Nichols

Catchfire ★★★ 15

Thriller 1989 · US · Colour · 98mins

Disowned by director Dennis Hopper (hence the Alan Smithee directorial credit), this remains an oddly watchable mess. Hopper also stars as the Mafia hitman who is ordered to assassinate a witness to a gangland killing (Jodie Foster), only to fall in love with his victim. It's an offbeat combination of black comedy and gangster thriller, but the tone is uneven. However, Hopper and Foster spark off each other nicely, while a starry supporting cast keeps you hooked. JF. Contains violence, sex scenes, swearing, nudity. DVD

Jodie Foster *Anne Benton* • Dennis Hopper *Milo* • Dean Stockwell *John Luponi* • Vincent Price *Lino Avoca* • John Turturro *Pinella* • Joe Pesci *Leo Carelli* • Fred Ward *Pauling* • Charlie Sheen *Bob* ■ *Dir* Alan Smithee [Dennis Hopper] • *Scr* Rachel Kronstadt-Mann, Ann Louise Bardach, Stephen L Cotler, Lanny Cotler, from a story by Rachel Kronstadt-Mann

The Catered Affair ★★★ U

Comedy 1956 · US · BW · 93mins

Bette Davis is miscast as a downtrodden Bronx taxi driver's wife, but she used to glory in shedding the glamour now and then. A passably fine script from Gore Vidal and a good supporting cast (including Ernest Borgnine and Debbie Reynolds) made this a major hit in its day, though it's a B-league effort compared to the rest of Davis's cinematic work. SH

Bette Davis *Mrs Tom Hurley* • Ernest Borgnine *Tom Hurley* • Debbie Reynolds *Jane Hurley* • Barry Fitzgerald *Uncle Jack Conlon* • Rod Taylor *Ralph Halloran* • Robert Simon [Robert F Simon] *Mr Halloran* • Madge Kennedy *Mrs Halloran* ■ *Dir* Richard Brooks • *Scr* Gore Vidal, from the TV play by Paddy Chayefsky

Catholic Boys ★★★ 15

Comedy 1985 · US · Colour · 99mins

Angst, guilt and raging hormones combine to provide a fresh, affecting glimpse of life behind the steel doors of a Catholic boys' school – its regime is so strict that it makes the institutions envisioned by Dickens look positively luxurious. There are a clutch of strong performances, most notably from Andrew McCarthy and Kevin Dillon, while Donald Sutherland is at his brooding best as chief monk and administrator of major whackings. In his feature film debut, director Michael Dinner deals intelligently with a well-worn theme and injects some subtle nuances. SH. Contains swearing.

Andrew McCarthy *Michael Dunn* • Kevin Dillon *Rooney* • Donald Sutherland *Brother Thadeus* • John Heard *Brother Timothy* • Mary Stuart Masterson *Danni* • Kate Reid *Grandma* • Wallace Shawn *Father Abruzzi* • Philip Bosco *Brother Paul* • Patrick Dempsey *Corbet* ■ *Dir* Michael Dinner • *Scr* Charles Purpura

Cathy's Child ★★★ PG

Drama based on a true story
1979 · Aus · Colour · 84mins

Inspired by actual events, this provocative assault on the relevance of patriarchal jurisdiction to the modern state is also a rare tale of tabloid heroism, as a Sydney newspaper champions the cause of a young mother whose estranged husband has spirited their daughter away to Greece. With a style redolent of kitchen sink realism, the film marked something of a departure for Donald Crombie after a couple of period pictures. However, he strikes the right tone of protest throughout. DP

Michele Fawdon *Cathy Baikis* • Alan Cassell *Dick Wordley* • Bryan Brown *Paul Nicholson* • Arthur Dignam *Minister* • Willie Fennel *Australian Consul* • Bob Hughes *Solicitor* ■ *Dir* Donald Crombie • *Scr* Ken Quinnell, from a non-fiction book by Dick Wordley

Catlow ★★ PG

Western 1971 · Sp · Colour · 92mins

Yul Brynner takes the title role, a cattle rustler caught between marshal Richard Crenna, who wants to lock him up, and bounty hunter Leonard Nimoy, who wants him dead. It's an unpretentious effort that veers more towards knockabout comedy than spaghetti-style ketchup. Silent movie aficionados will relish the brief appearance by Bessie Love. AT

Yul Brynner *Catlow* • Richard Crenna *Cowan* • Leonard Nimoy *Miller* • Daliah Lavi *Rosita* • Jo Ann Pflug *Christina* • Jeff Corey *Merridew* • Michael Delano *Rio* • Julian Mateos *Recalde* • Bessie Love *Mrs Frost* ■ *Dir* Sam Wanamaker • *Scr* Scot Finch [Scott Finch], JJ Griffith, from the novel by Louis L'Amour

Cats & Dogs ★★ PG

Part-animated fantasy comedy
2001 · US/Aus · Colour · 87mins

This kiddy-oriented comedy adventure mixes live action, animatronics and computer-generated animation to create a covert struggle for world domination between cats and dogs. It's a nice concept but messy execution and a weak script serve to undermine any potential charm. The problem lies in the uneasy switch from real animal actors – the cute central beagle Lou (voiced by Tobey Maguire), various innocent looking kitties – to all-too-obvious puppets. AC DVD

Jeff Goldblum *Professor Brody* • Elizabeth Perkins *Mrs Brody* • Miriam Margolyes *Sophie* • Alexander Pollack [Alexander Pollock] *Scott Brody* • Tobey Maguire *Lou* • Alec Baldwin *Butch* • Sean Hayes *Mr Tinkles* • Susan Sarandon *Ivy* • Joe Pantoliano *Peek* • Charlton Heston *The Mastiff* ■ *Dir* Lawrence Guterman • *Scr* John Requa, Glenn Ficarra

Cats Don't Dance ★★ U

Animated musical comedy
1998 · US · Colour · 71mins

This overly ambitious animated musical is set in late-1930s Hollywood. Danny (voiced by Scott Bakula) is a Gene Kelly-type small-town feline who discovers that animals are relegated to the background, while the humans hog the movie limelight. Interestingly, Kelly himself acted as consultant for the film's sprightly dance choreography, which deserves praise for its energy and originality. Unfortunately, the characters are rather dull and Randy Newman contributes some disappointing tunes. JC

Scott Bakula *Danny* • Jasmine Guy *Sawyer* • Natalie Cole *Sawyer* • Ashley Peldon *Darla Dimple* • Lindsay Rideway *Darla Dimple* • Kathy Najimy *Tillie* • John Rhys-Davies *Woolie* • George Kennedy *LB Mammoth* • René Auberjonois *Flanigan* • Hal Holbrook *Cranston* ■ *Dir* Mark Dindal • *Scr* Roberts Gannaway [Robert Gannaway], Cliff Ruby, Elana Lesser, Theresa Pettengill, from a story by Rick Schneider, Robert Lence, Mark Dindal, Brian McEntee, David Womersley, Kelvin Yasuda

Cat's Eye ★★★ 15

Horror 1984 · US · Colour · 90mins

A generally entertaining trilogy of terror tales from the ubiquitous Stephen King, the Big Mac of horror literature. James Woods tries an unorthodox method of quitting smoking, *Airplane!'s* Robert Hays is forced into a deadly bet and Drew Barrymore comes under attack from a rather unappetising gnome-like monster in a swift-paced anthology that works more often than not because of strong casting and a refreshingly throwaway tone. AJ. Contains violence, swearing. DVD

Drew Barrymore *Girl* • James Woods *Morrison* • Alan King *Dr Donatti* • Kenneth McMillan *Cressner* • Robert Hays *Norris* • Candy Clark *Sally Ann* • James Naughton *Hugh* • Tony Munafo *Junk* ■ *Dir* Lewis Teague • *Scr* Stephen King, from his short stories *Quitters Inc*, *The Ledge* and *The General*

The Cat's Meow ★★★ 12

Period comedy drama
2001 · Ger/UK/US · Colour · 109mins

Peter Bogdanovich investigates the mysterious demise of Thomas Ince, the Hollywood pioneer whose trip aboard tycoon William Randolph Hearst's yacht dominated the front pages of November 1924. The approach is more Agatha Christie than *Citizen Kane*, with teleplay plastic visuals depicting an all-star cast bandying bon mots in stitch-perfect costumes. Yet, for all its shallowness, this is still entertaining. DP DVD

Kirsten Dunst *Marion Davies* • Edward Herrmann *William Randolph Hearst* • Eddie Izzard *Charlie Chaplin* • Cary Elwes *Thomas Ince* • Joanna Lumley *Elinor Glyn* • Jennifer Tilly *Louella Parsons* ■ *Dir* Peter Bogdanovich • *Scr* Steven Peros, from the play by Steven Peros

The Cat's Paw ★★★ U

Comedy 1934 · US · BW · 101mins

Harold Lloyd, the silent comedian archivists usually overlook, stars in a comedy that shows off little of his acutely timed talents. He plays Ezekiel Cobb, a missionary's son raised in China who arrives in America to find himself up to his spectacles in corrupt politicians. From the man who used cliffhanger comedy so brilliantly in *Safety Last*, this film comes as something of a disappointment. TH

Harold Lloyd *Ezekiel Cobb* • Una Merkel *Petunia Pratt* • George Barbier *Jake Mayo* • Nat Pendleton *Strozzi* • Grace Bradley *Dolores Dace* • Alan Dinehart *Mayor Morgan* • Grant Mitchell *"Silk Hat" McGee* ■ *Dir* Sam Taylor • *Scr* Sam Taylor, from a story by Clarence Budington Kelland

Cattle Annie and Little Britches ★★★

Western 1980 · US · Colour · 97mins

In this cheerful family western, never released in Britain, Diane Lane and Amanda Plummer play a pair of teenage girls intent on joining Burt Lancaster's gang of bank robbers, while Rod Steiger is the lawman determined to bring them all to justice. The scenes where he discusses changing times with Lancaster are the most memorable moments in Lamont Johnson's film, which manages to be quite enjoyable despite an irritating banjo-strumming soundtrack. TH

Burt Lancaster *Bill Doolin* • John Savage *Bittercreek Newcomb* • Rod Steiger *Tilghman* • Diane Lane *Jenny/Little Britches* • Amanda Plummer *Annie/Cattle Annie* • Scott Glenn *Bill Dalton* ■ *Dir* Lamont Johnson • *Scr* David Eyre, Robert Ward, from a story and novel by Robert Ward

C

Cattle Drive ★★★ U

Western 1951 · US · Colour · 77mins

Dean Stockwell, better known to today's audiences for TV's *Quantum Leap*, had a major career as a child star. In this Universal western, he plays a spoiled rich brat growing up out west alongside grizzled trail boss Joel McCrea, learning the cowboy ropes from the likes of veterans Chill Wills and Bob Steele. Kurt Neumann directs with warmth and understanding, and the Technicolor photography of the Death Valley locations is superb. TS

Joel McCrea *Dan Mathews* • Dean Stockwell *Chester Graham Jr* • Chill Wills *Dallas* • Leon Ames *Mr Graham* • Henry Brandon *Jim Currie* • Howard Petrie *Cap* • Bob Steele *Careless* • Griff Barnett *Conductor O'Hara* ■ *Dir* Kurt Neumann • *Scr* Jack Natteford, Lillie Hayward • *Cinematographer* Maury Gertsman

Cattle Empire ★★ U

Western 1958 · US · Colour · 82mins

Little more than a B-feature, this routine western dates from the twilight of veteran Joel McCrea's career, a period when his name could only guarantee co-feature status. McCrea lends real authority to the tale, but classic western fans will shy away from this Charles Marquis Warren confection, as he brings all the TV production values that enabled him to produce such long-running series as *Gunsmoke* and *Rawhide* quickly and economically. TS

Joel McCrea *John Cord* • Gloria Talbott *Sandy* • Don Haggerty *Ralph Hamilton* • Phyllis Coates *Janice Hamilton* • Bing Russell *Douglas Hamilton* • Paul Brinegar *Tom Jeffrey* • Hal K Dawson *George Jeffrey* • Duane Grey *Aruzza* ■ *Dir* Charles Marquis Warren • *Scr* Eric Norden, Endre Bohem, from a story by Daniel B Ullman

Cattle King ★★ U

Western 1963 · US · Colour · 89mins

Robert Taylor drifts through this B-western, which tells an all-too-familiar story of Wyoming settlers who want to fence in their land and evil ranchers who think their cows should roam free. Guns come out, cattle stampede, and the dispute goes all the way to the president. AT

Robert Taylor (1) *Sam Brassfield* • Joan Caulfield *Sharleen Travers* • Robert Loggia *Johnny Quatro* • Robert Middleton *Clay Mathews* • Malcolm Atterbury *Clevenger* ■ *Dir* Tay Garnett • *Scr* Thomas Thompson

Cattle Queen of Montana ★★★ PG

Western 1954 · US · Colour · 84mins

One of two low-budget westerns made by Barbara Stanwyck – the other was 1956's *The Maverick Queen* – before she found her glorious late-career stride with such titles as *Forty Guns* and TV's *The Big Valley*. Aided by thoughtful direction from the prolific and talented Allan Dwan, this movie now has great curiosity value, in that the leading man is former US president Ronald Reagan, a bland performer when pitted against screen villains Gene Evans and Jack Elam. The location scenery is very attractive, the action sequences well-staged, and Stanwyck as tough as ever. TS [video]

Barbara Stanwyck *Sierra Nevada Jones* • Ronald Reagan *Farrell* • Gene Evans *Tom McCord* • Lance Fuller *Colorados* • Anthony Caruso *Natchakoa* • Jack Elam *Yost* • Yvette Dugay *Starfire* • Morris Ankrum *Jl "Pop" Jones* • Chubby Johnson *Nat* ■ *Dir* Allan Dwan • *Scr* Robert Blees, Howard Estabrook, from a story by Thomas Blackburn

Catwoman ★★ 12

Fantasy action adventure
2004 · US/Aus · Colour · 99mins

Director Pitof's lame fantasy action adventure is a spin-off from the *Batman* franchise in name only. Halle Berry gives an uneven performance as scatty artist Patience Philips, who's revived by a mystical cat after being murdered to become the eponymous superheroine. Using her new-found skills, Berry sets about uncovering a plot to flood the world with a toxic face cream, a scheme fronted by the excellent Sharon Stone. A romantic subplot involving sexy policeman Benjamin Bratt serves only to muddy the main story, while the special effects are poor. KK. Contains violence and sexual references. [video] DVD

Halle Berry *Patience Phillips/Catwoman* • Benjamin Bratt *Tom Lone* • Lambert Wilson *George Hedare* • Frances Conroy *Ophelia Powers* • Sharon Stone *Laurel Hedare* • Alex Borstein *Sally* • John Cassini *Graphologist* ■ *Dir* Pitof • *Scr* John Brancato, Michael Ferris, John Rogers, from a story by Theresa Rebeck, Michael Ferris, John Brancato, from the character created by Bob Kane

Caught ★★ U

Romantic melodrama
1949 · US · BW · 84mins

In this trite soap opera, the attractive wife (Barbara Bel Geddes) of a neurotic and unpleasant millionaire (Robert Ryan) falls in love with an idealistic doctor (James Mason). The only surprise in this romantic melodrama is that it is directed by the distinguished Max Ophüls, whose expertise and commitment bring some texture and gloss to the dour proceedings. The film marked Mason's Hollywood debut. RK [video]

James Mason *Larry Quinada* • Barbara Bel Geddes *Leonora Eames* • Robert Ryan *Smith Ohlrig* • Ruth Brady *Maxine* • Curt Bois *Franzi* • Frank Ferguson *Dr Hoffman* • Natalie Schafer *Dorothy Dale* • Art Smith *Psychiatrist* • Sonia Darrin *Miss Chambers* ■ *Dir* Max Ophüls • *Scr* Arthur Laurents, from the novel *Wild Calendar* by Libbie Bloch

Caught ★★★ 18

Drama 1996 · US · Colour · 105mins

A menacing adult drama bolstered by fine performances. Edward James Olmos plays a New Jersey fish merchant who takes drifter Arie Verveen under his wing, only for the kid to strike up a steamy affair with his wife (Maria Conchita Alonso). Trouble brews when the couple's shifty son (Steven Schub) returns home unexpectedly and smells something fishy. It all ends in tears. DA [video]

Edward James Olmos *Joe* • Maria Conchita Alonso *Betty* • Arie Verveen *Nick* • Steven Schub *Danny* • Bitty Schram *Amy* ■ *Dir* Robert M Young • *Scr* Edward Pomerantz

Caught in the Act ★★★ PG

Comedy 1996 · UK · Colour · 92mins

Such is the dominance of American films in Britain that dozens of UK films go unreleased each year. This gentle comedy is a case in point. Sara Crowe turns in an endearing performance as the aspiring diva, who teams up with Annette Badland and Nadia Sawalha in a bid to win a talent contest organised by the man of her dreams. With knowing support from Leslie Phillips and a pleasing sense of small-town Norfolk life, this is no blockbuster, but it's fun all the same. RT [video]

Sara Crowe *Lucinda* • Annette Badland *Katherine* • Leslie Phillips *Sydney Fisher* • Paul Shelley *Neville Goodenough* • Guy Henry *Algie* ■ *Dir* Mark Greenstreet • *Scr* Mark Greenstreet, Caroline Hill

Cauldron of Blood ★ 15

Horror 1967 · US/Sp · Colour · 94mins

Boris Karloff plays a blind sculptor using real human bones in his statues, courtesy of his psychopathic spouse, who kills people and dumps them in an acid bath in the basement. Filmed in 1967 but not released until 1971, two years after the star's death, this co-production offers grisly tedium and few chills. RS. Spanish dialogue dubbed into English. [video]

Jean-Pierre Aumont *Claude Marchand* • Boris Karloff *Franz Badulescu* • Viveca Lindfors *Tania Badulescu* • Jacqui Speed *Pilar* • Rosenda Monteros *Valerie* • Ruben Rojo *Lover* ■ *Dir* Edward Mann [Santos Alcocer] • *Scr* John Melson, Jose Luis Bayonas, Edward Mann, from a story by Edward Mann

Cause for Alarm ★★★

Film noir 1951 · US · BW · 73mins

This *film noir* has a blacker shade than usual, as finger-fluttering, saucer-eyed Loretta Young tries to retrieve a letter sent by her bedridden husband before his death that blames her for his demise. Director Tay Garnett may have been an MGM hack, but, despite some risibly optimistic touches, his craftsmanship is very evident. TH

Loretta Young *Ellen Jones* • Barry Sullivan *George Z Jones* • Bruce Cowling *Dr Grahame* • Margalo Gillmore *Mrs Edwards* • Bradley Mora *Billy* • Irving Bacon *Carston* • Georgia Backus *Mrs Warren* • Don Haggerty *Russell* ■ *Dir* Tay Garnett • *Scr* Tom Lewis, Mel Dinelli, from a story by Larry Marcus

Cavalcade ★★★ U

Historical drama 1933 · US · BW · 111mins

Noël Coward uses a well-to-do family as a microcosm in this look at British life down the years, from the Boer War to the Great Depression. Critics at the time loved this rather sanctimonious jaunt through history. Seen from the vantage point of post-Second World War egalitarianism, however, it all appears quaint and riddled with accepted class differences. While Coward, via director Frank Lloyd, pulls out all the stops, a modern audience will remain resolutely dry-eyed. SH

Diana Wynyard *Jane Marryot* • Clive Brook *Robert Marryot* • Herbert Mundin *Alfred Bridges* • Una O'Connor *Ellen Bridges* • Ursula Jeans *Fanny Bridges* • Beryl Mercer *Cook* ■ *Dir* Frank Lloyd • *Scr* Reginald Berkeley, from the play by Noël Coward

Cavalry Scout ★★ U

Western 1951 · US · Colour · 77mins

This minor western, photographed in the elementary Cinecolor process, centres around the efforts of an army scout (granite-faced Rod Cameron) to prevent stolen Gatling guns from falling into the hands of hostile Indians. Audrey Long is the trader whose wagons are being surreptitiously used to transport weapons by villain James Millican. AE

Rod Cameron *Kirby Frye* • Audrey Long *Claire* • Jim Davis *Lt Spaulding* • James Millican *Martin Gavin* • James Arness *Barth* • John Doucette *Varney* • William Phillips [William "Bill" Phillips] *Sgt Wilkins* • Stephen Chase (1) *Col Drumm* • Rory Mallinson *Corporal* ■ *Dir* Lesley Selander • *Scr* Dan Ullman [Daniel B Ullman], Thomas Blackburn

Cave of Outlaws ★★ U

Western 1951 · US · Colour · 75mins

Long before William Castle hit his stride as the maker of gimmick horror films and producer of the classic *Rosemary's Baby*, he cut his teeth directing B-features, invariably minor swashbucklers or routine westerns. This example of his work is a western whose only distinction is in its location usage of New Mexico's Carlsbad Caverns where the climactic shoot-out takes place. The Technicolor is rich, but Alexis Smith is wasted and MacDonald Carey is far too bland. TS

Macdonald Carey *Pete Carver* • Alexis Smith *Liz Trent* • Edgar Buchanan *Dobbs* • Victor Jory *Ben Cross* • Hugh O'Brian *Garth* ■ *Dir* William Castle • *Scr* Elizabeth Wilson

Caveman ★★★ PG

Comedy adventure
1981 · US · Colour · 87mins

Ringo Starr is perfectly cast as a hapless cave-dweller in an endearingly stupid prehistoric romp that introduced a couple of future stars to the world. The former Beatle is a caveman drummed out of his tribe for making eyes at the chief's woman (played by his real-life wife Barbara Bach). So he teams up with fellow misfits Shelley Long and Dennis Quaid to advance man's evolution. The result is dumb slapstick fun. JF [video] DVD

Ringo Starr *Atouk* • Dennis Quaid *Lar* • Shelley Long *Tala* • Barbara Bach *Lana* • John Matuszak *Tonda* • Avery Schreiber *Ock* • Jack Gilford *Gog* • Cork Hubbert *Ta* ■ *Dir* Carl Gottlieb • *Scr* Carl Gottlieb, Rudy DeLuca

Cecil B Demented ★★★ 18

Satirical comedy 2000 · US · Colour · 84mins

This is a maliciously witty, if disjointed, Hollywood satire from John Waters. Stephen Dorff plays the lunatic film-maker of the title, who kidnaps pampered, petulant star Melanie Griffith and forces her into headlining his underground art film, which uses the "ultimate reality" of real people and real terror. Waters's Tinseltown put-down sends up everything from industry protocol and recent hits to porno movies and celebrity gossip. The problem is that the movie revels in its plethora of in-jokes at the expense of entertaining its audience. AJ [video] DVD

Stephen Dorff *Cecil B Demented* • Melanie Griffith *Honey Whitlock* • Alicia Witt *Cherish* • Adrian Grenier *Lyle* • Larry Gilliard Jr *Lewis* • Maggie Gyllenhaal *Raven* • Jack Noseworthy *Rodney* • Mike Shannon [Michael Shannon] *Petie* ■ *Dir/Scr* John Waters (2)

Ceiling Zero ★★★

Adventure 1935 · US · BW · 95mins

Director and erstwhile pilot Howard Hawks proved the ideal guiding hand for this version of flying expert and author Frank "Spig" Wead's Broadway play. Though most of the activity takes place on the ground in the office of a commercial airline, the incidents and tensions never let up. However, despite a terrific performance from James Cagney as the daredevil pilot and knockout verbal sparring with Pat O'Brien, the movie creaks a bit today, with phoney back projection sky sequences and poor model shots. TS

James Cagney *Dizzy Davis* • Pat O'Brien *Jack Lee* • June Travis *Tommy Thomas* • Stuart Erwin *Texas Clark* • Henry Wadsworth *Tay Lawson* • Isabel Jewell *Lou Clark* • Barton MacLane *Al Stone* ■ *Dir* Howard Hawks • *Scr* Frank Wead, from his play

Celà S'Appelle l'Aurore ★★

Drama 1956 · Fr/It · BW · 102mins

Luis Buñuel adapted an Emmanuel Roblès novel for his first film in Europe after 23 years of exile, setting it in Corsica and casting the implacable and uncharismatic Georges Marchal as a doctor who falls in love with widow Lucia Bosé in his wife's absence. Essentially a melodrama whose level is raised by the director's unmistakable social consciousness, the film is solidly assembled, but minor. RB. A French language film.

Georges Marchal *Doctor Valerio* • Lucia Bosé *Clara* • Gianni Esposito *Sandro* • Julien Bertheau *Fasaro* • Nelly Borgeaud *Angela* •

Jean-Jacques Delbo *Gorzone* ■ *Dir* Luis Buñuel • *Scr* Jean Ferry, Luis Buñuel, from a novel by Emmanuel Roblès

Celebrity ★★★ 15

Comedy drama 1998 · US · BW · 113mins

After having his private life splashed all over the tabloids, writer/director Woody Allen uses his own cameras to probe the nature of celebrity. Kenneth Branagh steps up to play the Allen-esque "Ordinary Joe" who finds himself mixing with supermodels (Charlize Theron), spoiled stars (Leonardo DiCaprio) and oversexed actresses (Melanie Griffith), while his ex-wife (Judy Davis) tries to find her own identity as a TV presenter. While not vintage Allen, this amusement has some choice moments and some fun tongue-in-cheek performances. JB. Contains drug use, sexual references and swearing. DVD

Hank Azaria *David* • Kenneth Branagh *Lee Simon* • Joe Mantegna *Tony Gardella* • Judy Davis *Robin Simon* • Winona Ryder *Nola* • Leonardo DiCaprio *Brandon Darrow* • Famke Janssen *Bonnie* • Melanie Griffith *Nicole Oliver* • Charlize Theron *Supermodel* • Bebe Neuwirth *Hooker* ■ *Dir/Scr* Woody Allen

Celia ★★

Crime drama 1949 · UK · BW · 66mins

Not much more than an hour in length, this small-scale, low-budget and largely forgotten British thriller may be wildly old-fashioned, but it's perfectly competent, whimsical and not without a certain degree of charm and humour. Directed by Francis Searle and based on a BBC radio serial, it concerns actress Hy Hazell who, short of money, does a stint as a private detective. Disguised as her aunt, she foils a murderous scheme. RK

Hy Hazell *Celia* • Bruce Lister [Bruce Lester] *Larry Peters* • John Bailey *Lester Martin* • James Raglan *Inspector Parker* • Elsie Wagstaffe *Aunt Nora* ■ *Dir* Francis Searle • *Scr* Francis Searle, AR Rawlinson, Edward J Mason, from a radio serial by Edward J Mason

Celia ★★★★ 15

Drama 1988 · Aus · Colour · 98mins

The innocence and dark horrors of childhood have rarely been better portrayed than in this bewitching, often disturbing Australian drama. Set in a dull suburban Melbourne of the 1950s, Ann Turner's striking directorial debut focuses on a nine-year-old girl (a startlingly good performance by Rebecca Smart), whose confusion and resentment over adult behaviour sees her slip into a fantasy world, with tragic consequences. Turner beautifully captures the stuffy conservatism of the period, as well as the sheer wonder of growing up in what is, to a young child, a very strange world. JF

Rebecca Smart *Celia Carmichael* • Nicholas Eadie *Ray Carmichael* • Mary-Anne Fahey *Pat Carmichael* • Margaret Ricketts *Granny* • Victoria Longley *Alice Tanner* • Alexander Hutchinson *Steve Tanner* ■ *Dir/Scr* Ann Turner

Celine and Julie Go Boating ★★★★★

Experimental supernatural drama
1974 · Fr · Colour · 193mins

Inspired by two Henry James stories and intended as a homage to Lewis Carroll and Jean Cocteau, this astonishing film alludes to so many different writers, artists and film-makers that it's impossible to begin listing them. Constantly blurring the line between fantasy and reality, Jacques Rivette dazzles us with his inventiveness as magician Juliet Berto takes librarian Dominique Labourier on a series of adventures around a mysterious town house, inhabited by the equally fantastic Bulle Ogier and Marie-France Pisier. DP. In French with English subtitles.

Juliet Berto *Celine* • Dominique Labourier *Julie* • Bulle Ogier *Camille* • Marie-France Pisier *Sophie* • Barbet Schroeder *Olivier* • Philippe Clevenot *Guilou* • Nathalie Asnar *Madlyn* • Marie-Therese Saussure *Poupie* ■ *Dir* Jacques Rivette • *Scr* Eduardo de Gregorio, Juliet Berto, Dominique Labourier, Bulle Ogier, Marie-France Pisier, Jacques Rivette, from stories by Henry James

The Cell ★★★ 18

Psychological horror thriller
2000 · US/Ger · Colour · 104mins

Music-video maestro Tarsem Singh makes a visually audacious debut with this sci-fi hybrid. Psychotherapist Jennifer Lopez employs cutting-edge brain-jaunting technology to enter the subconscious of comatose serial killer Vincent D'Onofrio and help rescue his latest victim. Singh reinforces his credentials as a magpie imagist, employing a veritable barrage of digital trickery to conjure up the nightmarish mindscape of a psychopath. While his grasp of plotting and pacing is less assured, this remains an often dazzling showcase for his imagination. DP. Contains violence, swearing, sex scenes and nudity. DVD

Jennifer Lopez *Catherine Deane* • Vince Vaughn *Agent Peter Novak* • Vincent D'Onofrio *Carl Stargher* • Marianne Jean-Baptiste *Dr Miriam Kent* ■ *Dir* Tarsem Singh • *Scr* Mark Protosevich

Cellular ★★ 15

Action thriller
2004 · US/Ger · Colour · 90mins

This blackly comic action thriller is never quite as tense as it should be. The opening scenes are gripping, with science teacher and mother Kim Basinger the victim of a brutal kidnapping. Young slacker Chris Evans races to save her after she randomly calls his mobile using the remains of a shattered phone. However, Basinger's chief abductor, Jason Statham, is too weak a villain for us to ever believe she's in real jeopardy. The film becomes increasingly preposterous, but there's enough to enjoy, not least the solid turns from the cast. SF. Contains violence, swearing. DVD

Kim Basinger *Jessica Martin* • Chris Evans *Ryan* • William H Macy *Mooney* • Eric Christian Olsen *Chad* • Jessica Biel *Chloe* • Jason Statham *Ethan* • Brendan Kelly *Mad Dog* • Richard Burgi *Craig Martin* ■ *Dir* David R Ellis • *Scr* Chris Morgan, from a story by Larry Cohen

The Celluloid Closet ★★★★★ 15

Documentary
1995 · US · Colour and BW · 101mins

How gays and lesbians have fared on the big screen is the subject of this hilarious and poignant documentary. Narrated by Lily Tomlin and featuring candid interviews with Gore Vidal, Susan Sarandon and Shirley MacLaine, to name just a few, this is both a history of homosexual images and a damning indictment of the cavalier way Hollywood has shaped views on sexuality. But mostly it's a feast for cinephiles with over a hundred clips from early Thomas Edison shorts to *Philadelphia*, assembled with wit, care and precision to illustrate a spicy and thought-provoking study. AJ

Lily Tomlin *Narrator* ■ *Dir* Rob Epstein, Jeffrey Friedman • *Scr* Armistead Maupin, from a story by Rob Epstein [Robert Epstein], Jeffrey Friedman, Sharon Wood, Vito Russo

Celtic Pride ★★★ 12

Sports comedy 1996 · US · Colour · 86mins

This sports comedy stars Daniel Stern and Dan Aykroyd as die-hard fans of the Boston Celtics basketball team. Starting out with some fairly astute knocks at the superstitions that fans have about their teams, director Tom DeCerchio becomes a bit heavy-handed once Stern and Aykroyd have kidnapped the arrogant star of their arch-rivals (played by Daman Wayans). The three leads make it a watchable, if not rib-tickling, experience. JF. Contains swearing. DVD

Damon Wayans *Lewis Scott* • Daniel Stern *Mike O'Hara* • Dan Aykroyd *Jimmy Flaherty* • Gail O'Grady *Carol* • Adam Hendershott *Tommy* • Paul Guilfoyle (2) *Kevin O'Grady* ■ *Dir* Tom DeCerchio • *Scr* Judd Apatow, from a story by Colin Quinn, Judd Apatow

Celui Qui Doit Mourir ★★

Political religious drama
1957 · Fr/It · BW · 126mins

The radical Jules Dassin directs this sturdy version of the Nikos Kazantzakis novel, filmed on the island of Crete in visually arresting black-and-white CinemaScope. It tells of Greek villagers, under Turkish rule in 1921, who are rehearsing a Passion Play. Nearby compatriots plead for help when attacked by Turks but are refused, until the player Christ intervenes. Though well meaning, this is probably too wordy and pretentious for modern audiences. BB. In French with English subtitles.

Jean Servais *Fotis, the Pope* • Carl Mohner *Lukas* • Grégoire Aslan *Agha* • Gert Froebe [Gert Fröbe] *Patriarchéas, lord of the village* • Teddy Bilis *Hadji Nikolis, the schoolteacher* ■ *Dir* Jules Dassin • *Scr* Ben Barzman, Jules Dassin, André Obey, from the novel *Le Christ Recrucifié* by Nikos Kazantzakis • *Cinematographer* Jacques Natteau

The Cement Garden ★★★★ 18

Drama 1992 · Ger/Fr /UK · Colour · 100mins

One of the few films based on Ian McEwan's psychologically complex novels that actually works, largely due to some outstanding acting and a script from director Andrew Birkin that sticks close to its source material. This disturbing story, adapted from McEwan's first novel, is about children and their reactions to death and loss, and it refuses to conform to any cosy notion of grief. As such, with its central theme about sexual desire and incest, it occasionally makes uncomfortable, intellectually challenging viewing. SH. Contains swearing, a sex scene and nudity. DVD

Andrew Robertson *Jack* • Charlotte Gainsbourg *Julie* • Sinead Cusack *Mother* • Alice Coulthard *Sue* • Ned Birkin *Tom* • Hanns Zischler *Father* • Jochen Horst *Derek* ■ *Dir* Andrew Birkin • *Scr* Andrew Birkin, from the novel by Ian McEwan

The Cemetery Club ★★★ 15

Comedy drama 1993 · US · Colour · 106mins

Former actor Bill Duke directs this gentle comedy drama, which scores highly by having three fine actresses – two of them Oscar-winners – top the bill. Ellen Burstyn, Diane Ladd and Olympia Dukakis play Pittsburgh widows who meet up, chat and help each other cope with their problems. At times, however, Duke's film looks like the pilot for a TV series, while some viewers may feel it betrays its stage origins. AT. Contains swearing. DVD

Ellen Burstyn *Esther Moskowitz* • Olympia Dukakis *Doris Silverman* • Diane Ladd *Lucille Rubin* • Danny Aiello *Ben Katz* • Christina Ricci *Jessica* • Bernie Casey *John* • Wallace Shawn *Larry* ■ *Dir* Bill Duke • *Scr* Ivan Menchell, from the play by Ivan Menchell

Cemetery Man ★★★★ 18

Horror 1994 · It/Fr · Colour · 98mins

This highly acclaimed Italian horror masterpiece dwells on the more metaphysical elements of the genre. Graveyard undertaker Rupert Everett is seduced by zombie Anna Falchi and embarks on a crusade against the living. Beautifully directed by Michele Soavi with wit, style and emotional substance, Everett gives a bravura central performance in a unique original bursting with both gore and brains. Soavi's sophisticated shocker is a mordant delight. AJ. Italian dialogue dubbed into English.

Rupert Everett *Francesco Dellamorte* • François Hadji-Lazaro *Gnaghi* • Anna Falchi *She* • Stefano Masciarelli *Mayor* • Mickey Knox *Marshall Straniero* ■ *Dir* Michele Soavi • *Scr* Gianni Romoli, from the novel *Dellamorte Dellamore* by Tiziano Sclavi

Les Cent et Une Nuits ★★★

Romantic comedy documentary
1995 · Fr/UK · Colour · 125mins

Produced to celebrate the centenary of cinema, Agnès Varda's quirky history of the medium demonstrates that her approach to the moving image is just as lively as it was when she launched the *nouvelle vague* with the short *La Pointe Courte* in 1954. The veritable who's who of international stars proves the esteem in which she's held. She even ropes in Michel Piccoli to play Simon Cinéma, the archivist who guides student Julie Gayet through his collection of clips and memorabilia. Highly personal, entirely accessible and most enjoyable. DP. In French with English subtitles.

Michel Piccoli *Simon Cinéma* • Marcello Mastroianni *The Italian friend* • Henri Garcin *Firmin, the butler* • Julie Gayet *Camille* • Mathieu Demy *Mica* • Emmanuel Salinger *Vincent* ■ *Dir/Scr* Agnès Varda

Centennial Summer ★★★ U

Period musical 1946 · US · Colour · 102mins

A nostalgic period musical from Fox, set in Philadelphia in 1876, where the Great Exposition is a cause for excitement. The film stars Jeanne Crain and Linda Darnell as sisters whose relationship suffers when they both take a fancy to dashing Frenchman Cornel Wilde. Veterans Dorothy Gish (sister of Lillian and a one-time silent star) and Walter Brennan play the girls' parents, but the real star of Otto Preminger's undemanding trifle is the music, composed by Jerome Kern shortly before his death. RK

Jeanne Crain *Julia* • Cornel Wilde *Philippe Lascalles* • Linda Darnell *Edith Rogers* • William Eythe *Benjamin Franklin Phelps* • Walter Brennan *Jesse Rogers* • Constance Bennett *Zenia Lascalles* • Dorothy Gish *Harriet Rogers* ■ *Dir* Otto Preminger • *Scr* Michael Kanin, from the novel by Albert E Idell

The Center of the World ★★ 18

Erotic drama 2001 · US · Colour · 84mins

It's a sad fact that the naturalism and intimacy of the digital video format encourages directors to focus on "breaking down the barriers" at the expense of actual storytelling. Wayne Wang's disappointing character study is a case in point: it's an inert, lifeless exploration of the Las Vegas weekend shared by rich but lonely computer mogul Peter Sarsgaard and the uninhibited stripper Molly Parker he pays to "entertain" him. Despite the film's candour, the attempt at psychological depth feels as fake and contrived as Vegas itself. JC DVD

Peter Sarsgaard *Richard Longman* • Molly Parker *Florence* • Mel Gorham *Roxanne* • Jason McCabe *Calacanis* • Carla Gugino *Jerri*

• Balthazar Getty *Brian Pivano* • Pat Morita *Taxi driver* ■ *Dir* Wayne Wang • *Scr* Ellen Benjamin Wong [Wayne Wang, Paul Auster, Siri Hustvedt], from a story by Wayne Wang, Miranda July, Paul Auster, Siri Hustvedt

Center Stage ★ 12

Drama 2000 · US · Colour · 110mins

Idealistic Amanda Schull gets accepted into a top New York ballet school, finds it tougher than expected, and becomes romantic focus for resident hunk Ethan Stiefel and boring but true Sascha Radetsky. The tedious sub-*Fame* proceedings aren't helped by a teeth-grindingly bad script, wooden performances and hilarious dance numbers. JB [video] DVD

Amanda Schull *Jody* • Zoe Saldana [Zoë Saldana] *Eva* • Susan May Pratt *Maureen* • Peter Gallagher *Jonathan* • Donna Murphy *Juliette* • Debra Monk *Nancy* • Ethan Stiefel *Cooper* • Sascha Radetsky *Charlie* ■ *Dir* Nicholas Hytner • *Scr* Carol Heikkinen • *Cinematographer* Geoffrey Simpson

Central Airport ★ U

Adventure 1933 · US · BW · 74mins

This tedious airborne romance finds pilot Richard Barthelmess jilted by parachutist Sally Eilers when she marries his brother Tom Brown instead. This never gets off the ground. Blame the script, not to mention the papier-mâché planes. AT

Richard Barthelmess *Jim* • Tom Brown *Neil* • Sally Eilers *Jill* • Grant Mitchell *Mr Blaine* • James Murray *Eddie* ■ *Dir* William A Wellman • *Scr* Rian James, from a story by Jack Moffitt, James Seymour

Central Station ★★★★ 15

Drama
1998 · Bra/Fr/Sp/Jpn · Colour · 105mins

This captivating Brazilian road movie picked up awards all around the world, as well as a deserved Oscar nomination for 69-year-old actress Fernanda Montenegro. Initially shown as selfish and uncaring, her character's gradual softening as she accompanies young Vinicius de Oliveira on a quest to find his dad makes for compelling viewing. Director Walter Salles's filming of their journey of discovery stunningly captures an unglamorous land, seen from the perspective of two travellers whose final destination is far from certain. JC. In Portuguese with English subtitles. Contains some swearing. [video] DVD

Fernanda Montenegro *Dora* • Marilia Pêra *Irene* • Vinicius de Oliveira *Josue* • Sôia Lira *Ana* • Othon Bastos *César* ■ *Dir* Walter Salles • *Scr* João Emanuel Carneiro, Marcos Bernstein, from an idea by Walter Salles

Century ★★★ 15

Period drama 1993 · UK · Colour · 107mins

Stephen Poliakoff takes an absorbing look at a frantic culture in the midst of technological advancement and uncertainty about the future. Clive Owen is the hot-headed medical researcher on the loose in late-Victorian London who exposes the dubious practices of eminent professor Charles Dance. Robert Stephens steals the sumptuously mounted show as Owen's eccentric Romanian father and brings a welcome touch of humour to what many will find a rather arch conceit. AJ. Contains some nudity. [video]

Charles Dance *Professor Mandry* • Clive Owen *Paul Reisner* • Miranda Richardson *Clara* • Robert Stephens *Mr Reisner* • Joan Hickson *Mrs Whiteweather* • Lena Headey *Miriam* ■ *Dir/Scr* Stephen Poliakoff

La Cérémonie ★★★★ 15

Thriller 1995 · Fr · Colour · 107mins

Two of France's greatest current female stars, Sandrine Bonnaire and Isabelle Huppert, help make director Claude Chabrol's adaptation of British thriller writer Ruth Rendell's novel *A Judgement in Stone* an authentically chilling account of the way the French middle class brings ruin upon itself. Bonnaire is the new housekeeper, hired by a sweet-natured but condescending Breton family, whose relationship with envious postmistress Huppert results in a shocking finale. TH. In French with English subtitles. Contains violence and swearing. [video]

Sandrine Bonnaire *Sophie* • Isabelle Huppert *Jeanne* • Jacqueline Bisset *Catherine* • Jean-Pierre Cassel *Georges* • Virginie Ledoyen *Melinda* ■ *Dir* Claude Chabrol • *Scr* Claude Chabrol, Caroline Eliacheff, from the novel *A Judgement in Stone* by Ruth Rendell

The Ceremony ★★

Crime drama 1963 · US/Sp · BW · 107mins

Few actors were as chilling as Laurence Harvey, who also directed and produced this oddity in Spain. Harvey plays a bank robber, sentenced to death, whose 11th-hour escape is arranged by his brother disguised as a priest. Sarah Miles is the girl in the middle. This is a half-baked religious allegory, with every scene screaming "I am an Art Movie". The result barely works as an oddball thriller. AT

Laurence Harvey *Sean McKenna* • Sarah Miles *Catherine* • Robert Walker Jr *Dominic* • John Ireland *Prison Warden* ■ *Dir* Laurence Harvey • *Scr* Ben Barzman, Alun Falconer, Laurence Harvey

Certain Fury ★★ 18

Action crime drama
1985 · US · Colour · 82mins

It's not often you get to watch two Oscar-winners making total prats of themselves, so sit back and enjoy this risible rubbish from director Stephen Gyllenhaal. Tatum O'Neal and Irene Cara play two fugitives, handcuffed together and on the run after a violent court breakout. Any chance of exploring racial tensions between the women is sacrificed on the altar of a fast-moving plot. RS [video]

Tatum O'Neal *Scarlet* • Irene Cara *Tracy* • Nicholas Campbell *Sniffer* • George Murdock *Lieutenant Speier* • Moses Gunn *Doctor Freeman* • Peter Fonda *Rodney* • Rodney Gage *Superman* ■ *Dir* Stephen Gyllenhaal • *Scr* Michael Jacobs

A Certain Smile ★★

Romantic drama
1958 · US · Colour · 104mins

Directed by Jean Negulesco with an eye for the visual possibilities of Paris and the French Riviera, this adaptation of Françoise Sagan's precocious bestseller is an otherwise limp and lacklustre affair. Christine Carere plays a student who gets involved with the middle-aged Rossano Brazzi before returning to the more suitable Bradford Dillman; Joan Fontaine co-stars as Brazzi's betrayed wife. Johnny Mathis's performance of the title song is all that's noteworthy. RK

Rossano Brazzi *Luc* • Joan Fontaine *Françoise Ferrand* • Christine Carere *Dominique Vallon* • Bradford Dillman *Bertrand* • Eduard Franz *M Vallon* ■ *Dir* Jean Negulesco • *Scr* Frances Goodrich, Albert Hackett, from the novel by Françoise Sagan

Cervantes ★★

Historical drama
1968 · Fr/It/Sp · Colour · 111mins

Horst Buchholz takes the title role in this dismal European co-production, which doesn't seem to bear much relation to the life of the famous Spanish writer. While on a secret mission from the Pope, Buchholz gets waylaid in a series of adventures involving the likes of Gina Lollobrigida, José Ferrer and Louis Jourdan. JF

Horst Buchholz *Miguel de Cervantes* • Gina Lollobrigida *Giulia* • José Ferrer *Hassan Bey* • Louis Jourdan *Cardinal Acquaviva* • Fernando Rey *King Philip II of Spain* ■ *Dir* Vincent Sherman • *Scr* David Karp, Enrique Llovet, Enrico Bomba, from the book by Bruno Frank

César ★★★★

Drama 1936 · Fr · BW · 125mins

The third and final film in writer Marcel Pagnol's sublime trilogy, which began with *Marius* in 1931 and continued with *Fanny* in 1932, is the only one of the three directed by Pagnol himself. It is 20 years later, and Marius (Pierre Fresnay) is working in a garage in Toulon. Fanny (Orane Demazis) tells her son Césariot (André Fouché) that Marius is his real father; with help from his grandfather, César (Raimu), the lovers are reunited. If Pagnol's direction is less expert than that of his predecessors, it's still a satisfying end to his humorous, sympathetic and acute portrait of Marseille life. RK. In French with English subtitles.

Raimu *César* • Orane Demazis *Fanny* • Pierre Fresnay *Marius* • Fernand Charpin *Panisse* • Milly Mathis *Aunt Claudine* • André Fouché *Césariot* • Maupi *Chauffeur* ■ *Dir/Scr* Marcel Pagnol

César and Rosalie ★★★

Comedy 1972 · Fr · Colour · 105mins

Claude Sautet is a keen observer of the mores and susceptibilities of middle-aged, middle-class France, as this deft study of personal freedom and the pain involved in securing it proves. There's nothing particularly new about the romantic triangle formed by single mother Romy Schneider, wealthy lover Yves Montand and her old flame, Sami Frey. But thanks to a thoughtful script and plausible performances, this is a civilised, witty and ultimately moving drama. DP. A French language film.

Yves Montand *César* • Romy Schneider *Rosalie* • Sami Frey *David* • Umberto Orsini *Antoine* ■ *Dir* Claude Sautet • *Scr* Claude Sautet, Jean-Loup Dabadie

C'est la Vie ★★★★ 12

Period drama 1990 · Fr · Colour · 96mins

Set in the seaside resort of La Baule in 1958, this charming evocation of childhood summers concludes Diane Kurys's autobiographical trilogy, which began with *Diabolo Menthe* and continued with *Entre Nous*. Each little moment of mischief, amusement and affection is as fresh and colourful as a holiday snap, thus making the sudden intrusion of real life seem all the more shocking and sad. Julie Bataille and Candice Lefranc are splendid as the sisters by the sea, whether fooling with their cousins, teasing their nanny or responding with dismay to the news that their parents, Nathalie Baye and Richard Berry, are splitting up. DP. In French with English subtitles. Contains brief nudity.

Nathalie Baye *Lena* • Richard Berry *Michel* • Zabou *Bella Mandel* • Jean-Pierre Bacri *Léon Mandel* • Julie Bataille *Frédérique* • Candice Lefranc *Sophie* ■ *Dir* Diane Kurys • *Scr* Diane Kurys, Alain Le Henry

Cha-Cha-Cha ★★★

Romantic comedy
1998 · Sp · Colour · 109mins

Four of Spain's hottest young stars headline this 1990s variation on the *Pygmalion* theme. However, it's Eduardo Noriega who shines brightest as the doltish 20-something who is given a total personality makeover by Madrid advertising executive Ana Alvarez. This is so he can lure her dance instructor friend (Maria Adanez) away from Jorge Sanz, the chauvinistic hunk she's lusted after since a drunken one-night stand. Antonio del Real's vibrant comedy entertains throughout but leaves little lasting impression. DP. In Spanish with English subtitles.

Eduardo Noriega (2) *Antonio* • Ana Alvarez *Lucia* • Maria Adanez *Maria* • Jorge Sanz *Pablo* ■ *Dir* Antonio del Real • *Scr* Antonio del Real, Fernando Leon, Carlos Asorey Brey

Chachi 420 ★★★ PG

Comedy drama 1997 · Ind · Colour · 158mins

Mrs Doubtfire gets the Bollywood treatment in this highly entertaining comedy drama from actor/director Kamal Haasan. Forced to pose as a nanny to secure access to his daughter, divorced choreographer Haasan attempts to win back the affection of his ex-wife, Tabu, only to find himself fighting off the attentions of her tycoon father, Amrish Puri. Although the excellent Om Puri provides a little villainy, this is much more innocent than Robin Williams's blockbuster Hollywood version. DP. In Hindi with English subtitles. [video]

Kamal Haasan *Jayaprakash* • Amrish Puri *Seth Durga* • Tabu *Jhanki* • Om Puri *Bhanwari* ■ *Dir* Kamal Haasan

Chad Hanna ★★★ U

Period romantic drama
1940 · US · Colour · 88mins

Director Henry King displays a strong eye for Americana, and his film is full of offbeat episodes and oddball characters. The trouble is that nothing substantial ever really happens. Henry Fonda is well-cast as the country boy who becomes so infatuated with Dorothy Lamour's bareback rider that he joins the travelling circus where she performs. Wonderful Technicolor and a marvellous feeling for life on the road in upstate 1840s New York are the main assets here. AE

Henry Fonda *Chad Hanna* • Dorothy Lamour *Albany Yates* • Linda Darnell *Caroline* • Guy Kibbee *Huguenine* • Jane Darwell *Mrs Huguenine* • John Carradine *Bisbee* • Ted North *Fred Shepley* ■ *Dir* Henry King • *Scr* Nunnally Johnson, from the story *Red Wheels Rolling* by Walter D Edmonds

The Chain ★★ PG

Comedy 1984 · UK · Colour · 92mins

Two giants of British television, writer Jack Rosenthal and director Jack Gold, use the *La Ronde* style of storytelling to depict that most British of institutions: the housing chain. However, despite the presence of Denis Lawson, Nigel Hawthorne, Billie Whitelaw, Warren Mitchell and Leo McKern, the jokes fall flat. SR [video]

Denis Lawson *Keith* • Maurice Denham *Grandpa* • Nigel Hawthorne *Mr Thorn* • Billie Whitelaw *Mrs Andreos* • Judy Parfitt *Deidre* • Leo McKern *Thomas* • Bernard Hill *Nick* • Warren Mitchell *Bamber* • Anna Massey *Betty* • David Troughton *Dudley* • Phyllis Logan *Alison* ■ *Dir* Jack Gold • *Scr* Jack Rosenthal

Chain Lightning ★★ U

Second World War drama
1950 · US · BW · 94mins

This B-movie casts Humphrey Bogart as a fighter pilot, morbidly droning on about causing the death of his buddy (Richard Whorf) while testing an experimental safety device in a new-fangled jet. The clichés are thick on the ground, but Bogart has a face you have to look at. AT

Humphrey Bogart *Matt Brennan* • Eleanor Parker *Jo Holloway* • Raymond Massey *Leland Willis* • Richard Whorf *Carl Troxall* • James Brown (1) *Major Hinkle* ■ *Dir* Stuart Heisler • *Scr* Liam O'Brien, Vincent Evans, from a story by J Redmond Prior [Lester Cole]

Chain of Command ★★ 15

Action adventure
2000 · Fr/US · Colour · 91mins

This TV movie has lofty ambitions, but it doesn't have the effects budget that might have made up for the deficiencies in plotting and characterisation. Unwilling to serve President Roy Scheider on account of his womanising, Patrick Muldoon's Secret Service agent is assigned to "football" duty – the name for the case containing the nuclear button. When both the president and the case are targeted by terrorists, Muldoon must reassess his patriotism. DP

Roy Scheider *President* • Patrick Muldoon *Mike Connelly* • Maria Conchita Alonso *Vice-president Valdez* • Ric Young *Fung* ■ *Dir* John Terlesky • *Scr* Roger Wade

Chain of Desire ★ 18

Romantic drama
1992 · US · Colour · 102mins

An impressive cast – *The Last Seduction*'s Linda Fiorentino, Malcolm McDowell and *Crash* star Elias Koteas – can't conceal the lack of story or meaning in this film, which sets out to be some sort of Aids morality tale, but ends up as a series of tedious sexual encounters between a collection of pompous, unlikeable New Yorkers. Embarrassingly awful. JB

Malcolm McDowell *Hubert Bailey* • Linda Fiorentino *Alma D'Angeli* • Grace Zabriskie *Linda Baily* • Elias Koteas *Jesus* • Seymour Cassel *Mel* ■ *Dir/Scr* Temistocles Lopez

The Chain Reaction ★★★ 15

Thriller 1980 · Aus · Colour · 88mins

Boasting chase sequences by *Mad Max*'s George Miller, this chunk of Australian exploitation knocks spots off similar big-budget Hollywood offerings. Director Ian Barry's smart use of both camera and sound effects transforms many of the action set pieces. Unfortunately, there's a wasteful predictability about Steve Bisley and Arna Maria Winchester's bid to expose a leak at a nuclear plant. DP

Steve Bisley *Larry Stillson* • Arna-Maria Winchester *Carmel Stillson* • Ross Thompson *Heinrich Schmidt* • Ralph Cotterill *Grey* • Hugh Keays-Byrne *Eagle* ■ *Dir/Scr* Ian Barry

Chain Reaction ★★★ 12

Action thriller 1996 · US · Colour · 102mins

Keanu Reeves as a scientist seeking to make cheap power out of water is a little hard to take. But after he and fellow researcher Rachel Weisz go on the run from mysterious saboteurs after cracking the formula, director Andrew Davis's muddled suspense tale finally takes flight. With an unfocused script that's hazy on explanations, the film survives thanks to the pell-mell action that papers over the weak links in the convoluted plot. AJ. Contains violence, swearing. DVD

Keanu Reeves *Eddie Kasalivich* • Morgan Freeman *Paul Shannon* • Rachel Weisz *Lily Sinclair* • Fred Ward *FBI Agent Ford* • Kevin Dunn *FBI Agent Doyle* • Brian Cox *Lyman Earl Collier* • Joanna Cassidy *Maggie McDermott* • Chelcie Ross *Ed Rafferty* ■ *Dir* Andrew Davis • *Scr* JF Lawton, Michael Bortman, from a story by Josh Friedman, Arne L Schmidt, Rick Seaman

Chaindance ★★

Prison drama 1991 · US · Colour · 109mins

Michael Ironside plays a convict roped into a radical rehabilitation programme in which prisoners are used to help at a hospital for the physically handicapped. With Brad Dourif as his reluctant patient and Rae Dawn Chong as a sympathetic social worker, the casting can't be faulted, but the over-earnest script makes the plot difficult to swallow. JF. Contains swearing, violence and brief nudity.

Michael Ironside *JT Blake* • Rae Dawn Chong *Ilene* • Brad Dourif *Johnny Reynolds* • Bruce Glover *Casey* ■ *Dir* Allan A Goldstein • *Scr* Michael Ironside, Alan Aylward

Chained ★★★

Romantic drama 1934 · US · BW · 75mins

In this handsome romantic drama, Joan Crawford has to choose between shipping magnate Otto Kruger and playboy Clark Gable. The problem is, Crawford has already married Kruger and has several ocean liners in her name. What does Gable have that the older man doesn't? This sort of thing was a breeze for Gable and Crawford, in their fifth film together. Smartly written and stylishly directed, Clarence Brown's film motors along on star power and Crawford's show-stopping costumes. AT

Joan Crawford *Diane Lovering* • Clark Gable *Mike Bradley* • Otto Kruger *Richard Field* • Stuart Erwin *Johnny* • Una O'Connor *Amy* • Marjorie Gateson *Mrs Field* • Theresa Maxwell Conover *Secretary* • Lee Phelps *Bartender* ■ *Dir* Clarence Brown • *Scr* John Lee Mahin, from a story by Edgar Selwyn

Chained Heat ★★★ 18

Drama 1983 · US/W Ger · Colour · 93mins

This lip-smackingly good women-in-prison saga finds *Exorcist* star Linda Blair learning the cell block ropes the hard way via degenerate guards, domineering inmates and the usual lesbian quota. Bolstered by a great B-movie cast, this sequel to *The Concrete Jungle* (1982) might arguably be the ultimate jail-and-jiggle trash-fest. John Vernon is an absolute hoot as the sleazy warden who videotapes desperate lags in his office hot-tub while feeding them cocaine. *Chained Heat II* followed in 1993 starring Brigitte Nielsen. AJ. Contains swearing, sex scenes and violence.

Linda Blair *Carol* • John Vernon *Warden Backman* • Sybil Danning *Ericka* • Tamara Dobson *Duchess* • Stella Stevens *Captain Taylor* • Sharon Hughes *Val* • Henry Silva *Lester* • Edy Williams ■ *Dir* Paul Nicholas • *Scr* Vincent Mongol, Paul Nicholas

Chains of Gold ★★ 15

Crime drama 1989 · US · Colour · 91mins

One of the low points of John Travolta's wilderness years, this weak crime drama was sold to cable TV after failing to secure a theatrical release. Travolta actually turns in a reasonable performance as a social worker who goes undercover to find a kid who's been abducted by a vicious drug gang. But the script (which Travolta had a go at polishing) veers wildly between the nasty and the sentimental. DP. Contains swearing, violence and drug abuse. DVD

John Travolta *Scott Barnes* • Marilu Henner *Jackie* • Joey Lawrence *Tommy Burke* • Bernie Casey *Sergeant Palco* • Ramon Franco *James* • Hector Elizondo *Lieutenant Ortega* • Benjamin Bratt *Carlos* • Conchata Ferrell *Martha* ■ *Dir* Rod Holcomb • *Scr* John Petz, Linda Favila, Anson Downes, John Travolta

The Chairman ★★★

Spy thriller 1969 · UK · Colour · 101mins

J Lee Thompson's effective thriller uses the old comic-strip chestnut of a microchip in Gregory Peck's skull that's either a transmitter or a bomb detonator, depending upon the success of his assignment in Red China to track down a miraculous crop-growing formula. Laboured dashes of political sermonising aside, the *Mission Impossible*-style story is laced with enough outrageous twists and persistent suspense to grab full attention and deliver a gripping climax. AJ

Gregory Peck *John Hathaway* • Anne Heywood *Kay Hanna* • Arthur Hill *Shelby* • Alan Dobie *Benson* • Conrad Yama *Chairman* • Zienia Merton *Ting Ling* • Ori Levy *Shertov* ■ *Dir* J Lee Thompson • *Scr* Ben Maddow, from the novel by Jay Richard Kennedy

Chairman of the Board ★★

Comedy 1998 · US · Colour · 95mins

Scott "Carrot Top" Thompson is something of a cult figure Stateside, but is virtually unheard of over here. He mines the same sort of manic hysteria put to much more profitable use by Jim Carrey and, like the latter, you'll either love him or loathe him. Alex Zamm's comedy finds him becoming the unlikely head of a giant corporation, much to the displeasure of Larry Miller (excellent as usual) and Raquel Welch. It's relentlessly juvenile, frequently tasteless – and perfect for undemanding teenagers. JF

Carrot Top *Edison* • Courtney Thorne-Smith *Natalie* • Larry Miller *Bradford* • Jack Warden *Armand* • Estelle Harris *Ms Krubavitch* • Raquel Welch *Grace Kosik* • M Emmet Walsh *Freemont* • Little Richard ■ *Dir* Alex Zamm • *Scr* Alex Zamm, Turi Meyer, Al Septien, from a story by Turi Meyer, Al Septien

Chal Mere Bhai ★★ 15

Romantic comedy
2000 · Ind · Colour · 134mins

Comedy specialist David Dhawan surprised many of his fans with this unconvincing switch to romantic melodrama. The story focuses on two brothers – the business-like Sanjay Dutt and the gadabout Salman Khan – who both fall for the same girl, Karishma Kapoor. With the action sequences and several musical numbers feeling tacked on rather than integral to the proceedings, this is a disappointingly flat concoction. DP. In Hindi with English subtitles. DVD

Sanjay Dutt *Vicky Oberoi* • Salman Khan *Prem Oberoi* • Karishma Kapoor *Sapna* • Dilip Tahil [Dalip Tahil] *Balraj Oberoi* • Sushma Seth *Grandmother* ■ *Dir* David Dhawan • *Scr* Ikram Akhtar, Yunus Sajawal

The Chalk Garden ★★★ U

Melodrama 1964 · UK · Colour · 106mins

Director Ronald Neame has made little effort to hide the stage origins of Enid Bagnold's play in this adaptation. It's not merely a case of filmed theatre, however, as John Michael Hayes's screenplay shifts the emphasis away from Edith Evans's dotty grandmother and Deborah Kerr's mysterious governess, placing it instead on the precocious teenager played with typical bravado by Hayley Mills. With father John offering neat support as the family butler, this is a rather talkative acting showcase, while the Oscar-nominated Evans steals the limelight from the hesitant Kerr. DP

Deborah Kerr *Madrigal* • Hayley Mills *Laurel* • John Mills *Maitland* • Edith Evans *Mrs St Maugham* • Felix Aylmer *Judge McWhirrey* • Elizabeth Sellars *Olivia* • Lally Bowers *Anna* ■ *Dir* Ronald Neame • *Scr* John Michael Hayes, from the play by Enid Bagnold

The Challenge ★★★ PG

Adventure 1938 · UK · BW · 73mins

A remarkable mountaineering film about the scaling of the Matterhorn by Edward Whymper, here played by Robert Douglas. The film was co-directed by the great climber and film-maker Luis Trenker, who also made a simultaneous German version called *Der Berg Ruft*. It may seem a little creaky today, but there's genuine tension in the Alpine sequences and a sense of joy and achievement that is quite rare in cinema. TS

Robert Douglas *Edward Whymper* • Luis Trenker *Jean-Antoine Carrel* • Mary Clare *Carrel's mother* • Fred Groves *Favre* • Frank Birch *Rev Charles Hudson* • Joan Gardner *Felicitas* • Geoffrey Wardwell *Lord Francis Douglas* ■ *Dir* Milton Rosmer, Luis Trenker • *Scr* Patrick Kirwan, Milton Rosmer, from a story by Emeric Pressburger

The Challenge ★★

Crime drama 1960 · UK · BW · 95mins

Sometimes films are so mesmerisingly bad that they offer a diverse selection of delights to the viewer, though not all are intentional. This is one such movie, amazingly pairing Hollywood sexpot Jayne Mansfield and British classical actor Anthony Quayle in a crime thriller of murky intent and ludicrous result. Mansfield makes the least convincing criminal mastermind you'll ever clap eyes on, but Quayle is smitten with her all the same, and goes to jail to ensure the police don't capture the loot from a heist. TS

Jayne Mansfield *Billy Lacrosse* • Anthony Quayle *Jim Maxton* • Carl Mohner *Kristy* • Peter Reynolds *Buddy* ■ *Dir* John Gilling • *Scr* John Gilling, from his story

The Challenge ★★ 18

Thriller 1982 · US · Colour · 109mins

American boxer Scott Glenn helps Japanese descendants of revered samurai warriors reclaim their ancient heirlooms in this strange martial arts drama, co-written by John Sayles and directed by John Frankenheimer with little of his renowned flair. The basic thrust of the piece sets honourable traditions against venal westernised capitalism. The film is full of great kung fu fighting and Sayles's trademark ironies, but it's far too slow for a thriller. AJ

Scott Glenn *Rick* • Toshiro Mifune *Yoshida* • Donna Kei Benz *Akiko* • Atsuo Nakamura *Hideo* • Miiko Taka *Keiko* ■ *Dir* John Frankenheimer • *Scr* John Sayles, Richard Maxwell, Ivan Moffatt

A Challenge for Robin Hood ★★ U

Adventure 1967 · UK · Colour · 95mins

Although it will always be best known for its horrors, Hammer had something of a reputation for swashbuckling in the 1960s. Sadly, this adventure isn't half as much fun as Hammer's earlier Robin Hood outings. Barrie Ingham dons the Lincoln green to take on John Arnatt, here promoted to Sheriff of Nottingham after several seasons playing his scheming deputy in the 1950s TV series. The action is staged with little imagination, but compensation comes in the ample form of James Hayter's Friar Tuck. DP

Barrie Ingham *Robin* • James Hayter *Friar Tuck* • Leon Greene *Little John* • Peter Blythe *Roger de Courtenay* • Gay Hamilton *Maid Marian* • Jenny Till *Lady Marian* • John Arnatt *Sheriff of Nottingham* ■ *Dir* CM Pennington-Richards • *Scr* Peter Bryan

Challenge to Be Free ★★ U

Adventure 1972 · US · Colour · 83mins

Released four years after it was completed, and also shown as *Mad Trapper of the Yukon*, this was the last of the nearly 50 features directed by Tay Garnett (although he did get a little assistance from experienced action specialist Ford Beebe). The Hollywood veteran also takes a cameo role as the lawman in hot pursuit of fur trapper Mike Mazurki across Alaska. This is family entertainment of the tepid, worthy kind. DP

Mike Mazurki *Trapper* • Jimmy Kane *Old Tracks* • Fritz Ford *Sergeant* • Tay Garnett *Marshall McGee* • John McIntire *Narrator* ■ *Dir* Tay Garnett, Ford Beebe • *Scr* Chuck D Keen, Anne Bosworth, Tay Garnett

Challenge to Lassie ★★★ U

Drama 1949 · US · Colour · 75mins

This is a major character role for this best-loved pooch, as the famed collie retreats to late-19th-century Edinburgh from the great American outdoors to play a faithful dog who keeps returning to a churchyard where her master is buried. Sound familiar? It's Disney's 1960 film *Greyfriars Bobby*, which was an uncredited remake of this 1949 MGM film. Lassie is utterly splendid in the lead, and the late 1940s Technicolor is ravishing. TS

Edmund Gwenn *John Traill* • Donald Crisp *"Jock" Gray* • Geraldine Brooks *Susan Brown* • Reginald Owen *Sergeant Davie* • Alan Webb *James Brown* • Ross Ford *William Traill* ■ *Dir* Richard Thorpe • *Scr* William Ludwig, from the novel *Greyfriars Bobby* by Eleanor Atkinson

La Chamade ★★

Romantic drama
1968 · Fr/It · Colour · 95mins

Apart from the mesmerising *Thérèse* (1986), director Alain Cavalier's sparse output lacks real distinction. He was fortunate in attracting Catherine Deneuve, fresh from her triumph in *Belle de Jour*, for this version of a novel by Françoise Sagan. It has the elegant star as the lover of a wealthy man who leaves him for a summer romance, only to discover that she was happier before. BB. In French with English subtitles.

Catherine Deneuve *Lucile* • Michel Piccoli *Charles* • Roger Van Hool *Antoine* • Irène Tunc *Diane* • Jacques Sereys *Johnny* • Philippine Pascal *Claire* ■ *Dir* Alain Cavalier • *Scr* Françoise Sagan, Alain Cavalier, from a novel by Françoise Sagan

The Chamber ★★ 15

Mystery thriller 1996 · US · Colour · 107mins

Gene Hackman gives a sensational performance in a bleak, static potboiler, based on the John Grisham bestseller. Hackman is the Ku Klux Klansman held responsible for racial murders in 1967, with 28 days left before his execution. Grandson Chris O'Donnell grudgingly defends the white supremacist he hates. Director James Foley tries hard to make us care about the colourless characters, but interest remains low throughout the very draggy proceedings. AJ. Contains swearing, violence. [video] DVD

Chris O'Donnell *Adam Hall* • Gene Hackman *Sam Cayhall* • Faye Dunaway *Lee Bowen* • Robert Prosky *E Garner Goodman* • Raymond J Barry *Rollie Wedge* • Bo Jackson *Sergeant Packer* • Lela Rochon *Nora Stark* • Josef Sommer *Phelps Bowen* ■ *Dir* James Foley • *Scr* William Goldman, Chris Reese, from the novel by John Grisham

Chamber of Horrors ★★★★

Period horror 1966 · US · Colour · 97mins

Demented killer Patrick O'Neal chops off his own manacled hand to escape the hangman and terrorise 19th-century Baltimore in a great neglected shocker. Originally made as a TV series pilot, featuring Cesare Danova and Wilfrid Hyde White as crime-solving wax museum owners but considered too lurid to air, director Hy Averback's nifty nightmare had gimmicks added for its cinema audience, with "Horror Horn" and "Fear Flasher" warnings of when to close your eyes to the terror. A textbook example of classic 1960s American horror. AJ

Patrick O'Neal *Jason Cravette* • Cesare Danova *Anthony Draco* • Wilfrid Hyde White *Harold Blount* • Laura Devon *Marie Champlain* • Patrice Wymore *Vivian* • Suzy Parker *Barbara Dixon* • Tun Tun *Señor Pepe de Reyes* • Tony Curtis *Mr Julian* ■ *Dir* Hy Averback • *Scr* Stephen Kandel, from a story by Stephen Kandel, Ray Russell

The Chambermaid on the Titanic ★★★

Period romantic drama
1997 · Sp/Fr/It · Colour · 98mins

Set in the days when feature films were in their infancy, this dissertation on the art of storytelling is an unusually muted offering from the flamboyant Spanish director, Bigas Luna. Exploring the nature of truth and fiction, the tale of impoverished worker Olivier Martinez's nocturnal meeting with *Titanic* chambermaid Aitana Sanchez-Gijon is soon whipped up by constant retelling into an erotic epic that earns him the chance for theatrical fame. An intoxicating and atmospheric fantasy. DP. In French and English with subtitles.

Olivier Martinez *Horty* • Romane Bohringer *Zoe* • Aitana Sanchez-Gijon *Marie* • Didier Bezace *Simeon* • Aldo Maccione *Zeppe* • Jean-Marie Juan *Pascal* • Arno Chevrier *Al* • Marianne Groves *Bathilde* ■ *Dir* Bigas Luna • *Scr* Bigas Luna, Jean-Louis Benoit, Cuca Canals, from the novel *La Femme de Chambre du Titanic* by Didier Decoin

Chameleon Street ★★★★

Biographical comedy drama
1989 · US · Colour · 98mins

This is a riveting, true-life account of the life of William Douglas Street, a black man from Detroit who imitated a *Time* reporter, an exchange student, a lawyer and a surgeon – without any qualifications whatsoever. Written, directed and starring Wendell B Harris Jr, this biographical comedy drama won raves on the festival circuit, but received only a nominal release in the United States. A "lost" film that deserves to be found. TH

Wendell B Harris Jr *William Douglas Street* • Angela Leslie *Gabrielle* • Amina Fakir *Tatiana* • Paula McGee • Mano Breckenridge *Neelish Ratnayaka* • Richard David Kiley Jr *Dr Hand* ■ *Dir/Scr* Wendell B Harris Jr

The Champ ★★★★

Melodrama 1931 · US · BW · 86mins

In this classic weepie, a divorced, washed-up boxer (Wallace Beery) turns his back on drinking and gambling and goes into training for a return to the ring, accompanied by his adoring son (Jackie Cooper). MGM was a dab hand at tear-jerkers such as this, though the film's success owes much to Beery's performance and even more to young Cooper, who is disarmingly natural and precociously gifted. A massive hit in its day, it won Oscars for Beery and the story, and nominations for best picture and for its director, King Vidor. RK

Wallace Beery *Champ* • Jackie Cooper *Dink* • Irene Rich *Linda* • Roscoe Ates *Sponge* • Edward Brophy *Tim* • Hale Hamilton *Tony* • Jesse Scott *Jonah* ■ *Dir* King Vidor • *Scr* Leonard Praskins, from a story by Frances Marion

The Champ ★★★ PG

Sports drama 1979 · US · Colour · 117mins

Director Franco Zeffirelli made his Hollywood debut with this rather routine remake. Jon Voight takes on the washed-up prizefighter role made famous by Wallace Beery, while Ricky Schroder, as the son Voight is determined to make a splashy comeback for, wrings the emotions so effectively he must have shares in Kleenex. Ex-wife Faye Dunaway returns to undermine Voight and son's growing understanding, yet even her unconvincing performance can't sabotage the weepie finale. AJ [video]

Jon Voight *Billy Flynn* • Faye Dunaway *Annie* • Ricky Schroder [Rick Schroder] *TJ Flynn* • Jack Warden *Jackie* • Arthur Hill *Mike* • Strother Martin *Riley* • Joan Blondell *Dolly Kenyon* ■ *Dir* Franco Zeffirelli • *Scr* Walter Newman, from a story by Frances Marion

Champagne ★★★

Silent comedy 1928 · UK · BW · 86mins

Alfred Hitchcock abhorred his final silent, which stars Betty Balfour. Her descent into poverty is all part of a ruse by her millionaire father, Gordon Harker, to ensure that fiancé Jean Bradin isn't a gold-digger. The looming presence of Ferdinand von Alten provides a wisp of mystery, but the emphasis is firmly on frivolity. Minor fare maybe, but the use of subjective camera and expressionist fantasy is fascinating. DP

Betty Balfour *Betty* • Jean Bradin *The boy* • Gordon Harker *The father* • Ferdinand von Alten *The cosmopolitan* • Theo von Alten *The man* • Clifford Heatherley *The manager* • Jack Trevor *The officer* ■ *Dir* Alfred Hitchcock • *Scr* Alfred Hitchcock, Eliot Stannard, from an original story by Walter C Mycroft

Champagne Charlie ★★★ PG

Comedy drama 1944 · UK · BW · 186mins

This period romp from Ealing Studios gave the great Tommy Trinder one of his best screen roles. As music-hall star George Leybourne, he is engaged in a contest with bellicose Stanley Holloway to secure "the most popular drinking song of the era" – the era in question being the 1860s, beautifully re-created and superbly photographed by Wilkie Cooper. Director Alberto Cavalcanti obviously loves the Victorian music hall and has a fine eye for period detail. The film is well cast, with Betty Warren and Jean Kent as the leading ladies. TS [video] DVD

Tommy Trinder *George Leybourne* • Stanley Holloway *The Great Vance* • Betty Warren *Bessie Bellwood* • Jean Kent *Dolly Bellwood* • Austin Trevor *The Duke* • Peter De Greeff *Lord Petersfield* • Leslie Clarke *Fred Saunders* • Eddie Phillips *Tom Sayers* ■ *Dir* Alberto Cavalcanti • *Scr* Austin Melford, Angus MacPhail, John Dighton

Champagne for Caesar ★★★ U

Satire 1950 · US · BW · 99mins

One of the very earliest satires on the media, this little-known film is still topical in these days of million-pound quiz shows. Ronald Colman, in one of his last roles, is the unemployed mastermind who applies for a job at a soap company only to be snubbed by boss Vincent Price. In revenge, he enters a radio quiz show and proceeds to win a fortune, much to the chagrin of venal sponsor Price. Celeste Holm then poses as a nurse to try to sabotage Colman's winning run. Not quite as sharp or as funny as it might have been a decade later but nevertheless remarkably watchable. TS

Ronald Colman *Beauregard Bottomley* • Celeste Holm *Flame O'Neil* • Vincent Price *Burnbridge Waters* • Barbara Britton *Gwenn Bottomley* • Art Linkletter *Happy Hogan* ■ *Dir* Richard Whorf • *Scr* Hans Jacoby, Fred Brady Black

The Champagne Murders ★

Crime mystery 1966 · Fr · Colour · 98mins

A husband and wife (Anthony Perkins, Yvonne Furneaux), helped by Stéphane Audran, embark on an elaborate plan to convince playboy Maurice Ronet that he is a murderer. A deeply mediocre and offensive film from Claude Chabrol, going through career doldrums before rescuing his reputation with the stifling mastery of *The Butcher* three years later. A corked grotesquerie. RB. French dialogue dubbed into English.

Anthony Perkins *Christopher Balling* • Maurice Ronet *Paul Wagner* • Stéphane Audran *Jacqueline* • Yvonne Furneaux *Christine Balling* • Suzanne Lloyd *Evelyn Wharton* • Catherine Sola *Denise* ■ *Dir* Claude Chabrol • *Scr* Claude Brule, Derek Prouse, from a story by William Benjamin, Paul Gegauff

Champion ★★★★ PG

Drama 1949 · US · BW · 98mins

Kirk Douglas here gives one of the definitive performances of his career as ruthless boxer Midge Kelly, who will stop at almost nothing to become a success. Douglas betrays his disabled brother (Arthur Kennedy), his watchful manager (Paul Stewart) and the women in his life (Marilyn Maxwell and Ruth Roman among them) right up until his fist-breaking comeuppance. It's a punishment producer Stanley Kramer must have wished he could have inflicted upon Douglas in real life after the star had a nose job halfway through production, meaning nobody could lay a glove on him. TH [video]

Kirk Douglas *Midge Kelly* • Marilyn Maxwell *Grace Diamond* • Arthur Kennedy *Connie Kelly* • Paul Stewart *Tommy Haley* • Ruth Roman *Emma Bryce* • Lola Albright *Mrs Harris* ■ *Dir* Mark Robson • *Scr* Carl Foreman, from a story by Ring Lardner

Champions ★★★ PG

Biographical drama
1983 · UK · Colour · 109mins

Having always looked a bit on the wasted side, John Hurt was the perfect choice to play Bob Champion in this true story of a jockey who overcame cancer, an injured horse and the rest of the field to make a heroic comeback and win the Grand National. The film lacks psychological depth and risks going too far in avoiding the temptation of portraying Champion as a saint. Yet, this tear-jerking tale certainly holds the attention. PF. Contains swearing. [video]

John Hurt *Bob Champion* • Edward Woodward *Josh Gifford* • Ben Johnson *Burly Cocks* • Jan Francis *Jo Beswick* • Peter Barkworth *Nick Embiricos* • Ann Bell *Valda Embiricos* • Judy Parfitt *Dr Merrow* • Alison Steadman *Mary Hussey* • Kirstie Alley *Barbara* • Michael Byrne *Richard Hussey* ■ *Dir* John Irvin • *Scr* Evan Jones, from the book *Champion's Story* by Bob Champion, Jonathan Powell

Chan Is Missing ★★★ 15

Comedy 1982 · US · BW · 76mins

Debunking Charlie Chan stereotypes and faintly echoing *The Third Man*, this gently pulsating study of life in San Francisco's Chinatown was filmed for a mere $22,000. The search for "Chan", who owes cabbies Wood Moy and Marc Hayashi a small fortune, almost becomes an irrelevance as director Wayne Wang guides us through a community that is not only isolated from the rest of the country, but is also divided within itself by homeland political rivalries and cross-generational attitudes. Comic and intriguing, this was one of the first films to show what the American indie sector was capable of. DP

Wood Moy *Jo* • Marc Hayashi *Steve* • Laureen Chew *Amy* • Jud Y Nihei *Lawyer* • Peter Wang *Henry the cook* • Presco Tabios *Presco* • Frankie Alarcon *Frankie* ■ *Dir* Wayne Wang • *Scr* Wayne Wang, Isaac Cronin, Terrel Seltzer

Chance ★ 18

Crime drama 1990 · US · Colour · 81mins

Renegade cop Lawrence-Hilton Jacobs, who looks like a frightened animal staring into approaching headlights, becomes a kind of "Mild Harry" when his friend Dan Haggerty unwittingly repossesses a car holding diamonds from a recent robbery. There's so little story, the film frequently plays scenes unedited for time. KB [video]

Lawrence-Hilton Jacobs *Detective Jon Chance* • Dan Haggerty *Zach, the repo man* • Roger Rodd *Kingsley* • Addison Randall • Charlie Ganis *Alvin* • Pamela Dixon ■ *Dir* Charles T Kanganis, Addison Randall • *Scr* Joe Hart, Addison Randall, Lawrence-Hilton Jacobs

Chance of a Lifetime ★★ U

Comedy drama 1950 · UK · BW · 92mins

Played with conviction by a solid ensemble cast, this is a nostalgic look back to the days when people still believed in the co-operation of capital and labour. Regarded by some as a flight of fancy even on its original release, the story of a striking workforce that takes control of its factory seems more naive than ever. But there's more than a hint of truth behind many of the political platitudes and the finale has a pleasingly Capra-esque ring to it. DP

Basil Radford *Dickinson* • Niall MacGinnis *Baxter* • Bernard Miles *Stevens* • Julien Mitchell *Morris* • Kenneth More *Adam* • Geoffrey Keen *Bolger* • Josephine Wilson *Miss Cooper* • Patrick Troughton *Kettle* • Hattie Jacques *Alice* ■ *Dir* Bernard Miles, Alan Osbiston • *Scr* Bernard Miles, Walter Greenwood

Chance or Coincidence ★★★★ PG

Romantic drama
1999 · Fr/Can · Colour · 116mins

A young widow on a global odyssey to all the sights her dead son would have loved to visit – polar bears in the Arctic, the divers of Acapulco, a Montreal hockey game – is the thrust of director Claude Lelouch's touching rumination on the vital role that chance and coincidence play in life. Yet it's only when her camcorder is stolen, and the sentimental images it contains strike a chord with its buyer, that Lelouch's unique romance begins to take flight. Superbly acted by Alessandra Martines, this is one of those movies where it's impossible to guess what's going to happen next. AJ. In French with English subtitles. Contains some coarse language.

Alessandra Martines *Myriam Lini* • Pierre Arditi *Pierre Turi* • Marc Hollogne *Marc Deschamps* • Laurent Hilaire *Laurent* • Véronique Moreau *Catherine Desvilles* • Patrick Labbé *Michel Bonhomme* • Geoffrey Holder *Gerry* • Luigi Bonino *Mauro Lini* ■ *Dir/Scr* Claude Lelouch

Chances Are ★★★ PG

Romantic comedy
1989 · US · Colour · 103mins

The principle of reincarnation has provided fascinating material for film-makers over the years. While this slightly sexy romantic comedy visits the same territory as 1941's *Here Comes Mr Jordan*, it doesn't reach that film's high plateau. Here, a dead husband returns to Earth in a new body, but with a partial memory of his previous life, and falls for the daughter he never knew he had. Cybill Shepherd, Robert Downey Jr and Ryan O'Neal give the idea their best shot, but Emile Ardolino's direction misses the target. TH. Contains some swearing. DVD

Cybill Shepherd *Corinne Jeffries* • Robert Downey Jr *Alex Finch* • Ryan O'Neal *Philip Train* • Mary Stuart Masterson *Miranda Jeffries* • Christopher McDonald *Louie Jeffries* • Josef Sommer *Judge Fenwick* ■ *Dir* Emile Ardolino • *Scr* Perry Howze, Randy Howze

Chandu the Magician ★★★ U

Thriller 1932 · US · BW · 72mins

As played by Gayne Whitman in the 1931 children's radio serial, Chandu was a figure of mystery and magic. The casting of the urbane Edmund Lowe, therefore, somewhat hamstrung this serial-like adventure, especially as his unassuming presence was utterly swamped by the scene-stealing excesses of Bela Lugosi as his Egyptian nemesis. A breakneck tale of stolen death-rays and cliffhanging perils with stunning sets and effects, the film suffers nevertheless from the uncertainty of tone that hailed from the directorial pairing of William Cameron Menzies and Marcel Varnel. DP

Edmund Lowe *Chandu* • Irene Ware *Princess Nadji* • Bela Lugosi *Roxor* • Herbert Mundin *Albert Miggles* • Henry B Walthall *Robert Regent* ■ *Dir* Marcel Varnel, William C Menzies [William Cameron Menzies] • *Scr* Barry Connors, Philip Klein, from the radio series by Harry A Earnshaw, Vera M Oldham, RR Morgan

Chanel Solitaire ★★ 15

Biographical drama
1981 · UK/Fr · Colour · 106mins

Rutger Hauer made his English language debut in this disappointing fantasy on the early life of Coco Chanel. Crediting her with little inspiration, Julian More's screenplay suggests she rose from rags to riches simply by recognising the moment and exploiting everyone she knew. However, Marie-France Pisier suggests something of the sorrowful isolation of an icon whose affairs were all doomed to failure. DP

Marie-France Pisier *Gabrielle "Coco" Chanel* • Timothy Dalton *Boy Capel* • Rutger Hauer *Etienne de Balsan* • Karen Black *Emilienne D'Alençon* • Catherine Allégret ■ *Dir* George Kaczender • *Scr* Julian More, from a novel by Claude Delay

Chang ★★★★

Silent documentary drama
1927 · US · BW · 69mins

Jungle fever had infected film-makers Merian C Cooper and Ernest B Schoedsack, even before they made *King Kong* in 1933, as this plot-driven silent docudrama shows. Set in the jungles of Siam (now Thailand), it's the story of the farmer Kru and his family, fighting for survival amid the indifferent forces of nature and rampaging wild animals, including a herd of elephants ("Chang" is the Thai word for elephant). A blend of dramatic re-creations, invented narrative (bizarrely, the title cards even give Bimbo the monkey a couple of lines of dialogue) and astonishing documentary footage, this is a marvellous record of a vanishing way of life and an incredible piece of cinema history. TH

Dir/Scr Merian C Cooper, Ernest B Schoedsack

Change of Habit ★ PG

Musical comedy drama
1969 · US · Colour · 88mins

A change of pace and style for Elvis Presley, here playing a doctor working in an ghetto whose three new helpers, unbeknown to him, are novice nuns. The talented Mary Tyler Moore co-stars, though she looks distinctly uncomfortable. Presley's film career was in free fall by this time, and the scripts and situations were becoming increasingly desperate. DF DVD

Elvis Presley *Dr John Carpenter* • Mary Tyler Moore *Sister Michelle* • Barbara McNair *Sister Irene* • Jane Elliot *Sister Barbara* • Leora Dana *Mother Joseph* • Edward Asner *Lieutenant Moretti* • Robert Emhardt *The banker* ■ *Dir* William Graham [William A Graham] • *Scr* James Lee, SS Schweitzer, Eric Bercovici, from a story by Richard Morris, John Joseph

Change of Heart ★★ U

Romantic drama 1934 · US · BW · 77mins

The once magical and sure-fire box-office pairing of Janet Gaynor and Charles Farrell had lost its sheen by 1934 and this innocuous little offering couldn't arrest the decline. Here, the duo are joined by Ginger Rogers and James Dunn to make up a quartet of West Coast college graduates who head off to seek their fortunes in New York City. Gaynor wants to write, Farrell plans to become a lawyer and Dunn a radio crooner, while Rogers pursues stage stardom. Their ups and downs and various romances make for a mildly entertaining movie. RK

Janet Gaynor *Catherine Furness* • Charles Farrell *Chris Thring* • James Dunn *Mack McGowan* • Ginger Rogers *Madge Rountree* • Nick Foran *Nick* • Beryl Mercer *Harriet Hawkins* • Gustav von Seyffertitz *Dr Nathan Kurtzman* • Shirley Temple *Shirley* • Jane Darwell *Mrs McGowan* ■ *Dir* John G Blystone • *Scr* Sonya Levien, James Gleason, from the novel *Manhattan Love Story* by Kathleen Norris

Change of Heart ★★★ U

Musical 1943 · US · BW · 88mins

Songwriter John Carroll, burnt out and devoid of inspiration, teams up with Midwest girl Susan Hayward who obligingly ghosts his songs for him. A slender hook on which to hang a host of musical numbers and speciality acts, but this production, directed by Albert S Rogell for Poverty Row studio Republic, does just that. Wisecracking Eve Arden is on hand in a supporting role, Dorothy Dandridge performs, while Count Basie appears with his orchestra. A modest, cheerfully amusing musical romance. RK

John Carroll *Rick Farrell* • Susan Hayward *Jill Wright* • Gail Patrick *Toni Jarrett* • Eve Arden *Belinda Wright* • Melville Cooper *Bradley Cole* • Walter Catlett *J MacClellan Davis* • Mary Treen *Janie* • Tom Kennedy *Westinghouse* • Dorothy Dandridge ■ *Dir* Albert S Rogell • *Scr* Frank Gill Jr

A Change of Seasons ★★★ 15

Romantic drama 1980 · US · Colour · 97mins

When college professor Anthony Hopkins has an affair with student Bo Derek, his wife Shirley MacLaine retaliates by taking Michael Brandon to bed. In *Bob & Carol & Ted & Alice* fashion, they all take a holiday at a Vermont skiing resort just to show how broad-minded they are. Unfortunately, the leads are let down by a lacklustre script, co-written by *Love Story's* Erich Segal, and the film rapidly runs out of steam. It's only the chirpiness of MacLaine and the professionalism of the actors that hold our interest. TH. Contains swearing and nudity.

Shirley MacLaine *Karen Evans* • Anthony Hopkins *Adam Evans* • Bo Derek *Lindsey Rutledge* • Michael Brandon *Pete Lachapelle* • Mary Beth Hurt *Kasey Evans* • Ed Winter [Edward Winter] *Steven Rutledge* • Paul Regina *Paul DiLisi* ■ *Dir* Richard Lang • *Scr* Erich Segal, Fred Segal, Ronni Kern, from a story by Martin Ransohoff, Erich Segal

The Changeling ★★★ 15

Supernatural thriller
1980 · Can · Colour · 102mins

In this satisfying twist on the haunted house movie, George C Scott plays a recently widowed composer who moves into an old house in Seattle (really Vancouver) run by the local historic society. Before long, the house starts croaking, juddering and generally behaving badly. With the help of local historian Trish Van Devere (Scott's then-wife), a century-old murder is discovered; the shocks are neatly handled by Hungarian-born director Peter Medak, who sensibly refuses to let the special effects get the upper hand. AT DVD

George C Scott *John Russell* • Trish Van Devere *Claire Norman* • Melvyn Douglas *Senator Joseph Carmichael* • Jean Marsh *Mrs Joanna Russell* • Barry Morse *Dr Pemberton* • Bernard Behrens *Robert Lingstrom* ■ *Dir* Peter Medak • *Scr* William Gray, Diana Maddox, from a story by Russell Hunter

Changing Habits ★★

Romantic comedy drama
1997 · US · Colour · 95mins

Moira Kelly stars as a troubled young woman unable to have relationships with men thanks to her difficult upbringing with alcoholic father Christopher Lloyd. Retreating to a convent, Kelly begins a mural in the basement with materials shoplifted from her local art supplier (Dylan Walsh). A charming film from director Lynn Roth, with performances from the leads that compensate for the psychological baggage. LH

Moira Kelly *Soosh Teagarden* • Christopher Lloyd *Theo Teagarden* • Dylan Walsh *Felix Shepherd* • Shelley Duvall *Sister Agatha* • Bob Gunton *Bishop Creighton* • Eileen Brennan *Mother Superior* • Teri Garr *Connie* ■ *Dir* Lynn Roth • *Scr* Scott Davis Jones

Changing Lanes ★★★★ 15

Drama 2002 · US · Colour · 94mins

This offbeat drama charts the escalating urban warfare between self-absorbed attorney Ben Affleck and recovering alcoholic Samuel L Jackson following a minor road accident that causes both to miss important appointments. As they struggle to right their desperate situations, they are drawn into an increasingly vindictive battle of wills. Their duelling remains gripping throughout, with the deftly structured script and emotionally rich performances lending the slim premise unexpected weight. Director Roger Michell also encourages exceptional work from Toni Collette and Sydney Pollack. JC. Contains violence and swearing. DVD

Ben Affleck *Gavin Banek* • Samuel L Jackson *Doyle Gipson* • Toni Collette *Michelle* • Sydney Pollack *Delano* • William Hurt *Doyle's sponsor* • Amanda Peet *Cynthia Banek* • Kim Staunton *Valerie Gipson* • Richard Jenkins *Walter Arnell* ■ *Dir* Roger Michell • *Scr* Chap Taylor, Michael Tolkin, from a story by Chap Taylor

Un Chant d'Amour ★★★★ 18

Silent erotic drama 1950 · Fr · BW · 25mins

Jean Genet's only film is a silent ciné-poem containing many of the French novelist and playwright's themes and obsessions. Ex-thief Genet started writing in prison, and the setting of men alone in cells is a milieu he knew at first hand. Although the graphic scenes of masturbation and homosexual sex make this an intensely physical film, its lyrical evocation of passion and love raises it above the category of gay porn. RB DVD

Dir/Scr Jean Genet

The Chant of Jimmie Blacksmith ★★★★ 18

Drama 1978 · Aus · Colour · 112mins

Not so much a chant by the half-Aborigine, played with conviction by Tommy Lewis, as a war cry of ferocious rebellion. The poignancy in one of director Fred Schepisi's most powerful movies is that Jimmie really believes he's a stakeholder in the new federation of Australian States announced at the turn of the century. The tragedy is that, discovering he's still of Aborigine, and therefore inferior, status in white eyes, he goes on a murderous rampage. TH. Contains violence and swearing.

Tommy Lewis *Jimmie* • Freddy Reynolds *Mort* • Ray Barrett *Farrell* • Jack Thompson *Reverend Neville* • Angela Punch [Angela Punch McGregor] *Gilda Marshall* • Steve Dodds *Uncle Tabidgi* • Julie Dawson *Mrs Neville* ■ *Dir* Fred Schepisi • *Scr* Fred Schepisi, from the novel by Thomas Keneally

Chaos ★★★★ 15

Crime thriller 1999 · Jpn · Colour · 103mins

Dazzlingly deceitful and ingeniously intricate, Hideo Nakata's kidnap thriller consistently defies expectations as it shifts perspectives and time frames to compelling effect. Miki Nakatani's disappearance after a lunch date with wealthy husband Ken Mitsuishi comes out of the blue, but it's nothing compared to the twists and double-crosses that follow the ransom demand delivered by Masato Hagiwara. The labyrinthine plot wilfully confuses, but set pieces keep the nerves on edge until the audacious climax. DP. In Japanese with English subtitles. Contains swearing. DVD

Masato Hagiwara *Goro Kuroda* • Miki Nakatani *Satomi Tsushima* • Ken Mitsuishi *Takayuki Komiyama* • Jun Kunimura *Detective Hamaguchi* ■ *Dir* Hideo Nakata • *Scr* Hisashi Saito, from a novel by Shogo Utano

Chaplin ★★★ 15

Biographical drama
1992 · UK/US · Colour and BW · 138mins

This epic about the early part of Charlie Chaplin's life from co-producer/director Richard Attenborough is, for the most part, entertaining and intelligent, with Oscar-nominated Robert Downey Jr superb in the title role. The opening sequences are genuinely affecting, with Geraldine Chaplin playing Chaplin's mother (and her own grandmother), a music-hall singer who ended her days in an asylum. Yet, overall, the depiction of early Hollywood is too rose-tinted and the true tragic tale of a misunderstood comic genius is reduced to a series of star-studded vignettes. TS. Contains swearing and brief nudity. [video] DVD

Robert Downey Jr *Charlie Chaplin* • Geraldine Chaplin *Hannah Chaplin* • Paul Rhys *Sydney Chaplin* • John Thaw *Fred Karno* • Moira Kelly *Hetty Kelly/Oona O'Neill* • Anthony Hopkins *George Hayden* • Dan Aykroyd *Mack Sennett* • Marisa Tomei *Mabel Normand* • Penelope Ann Miller *Edna Purviance* • Kevin Kline *Douglas Fairbanks* • Milla Jovovich *Mildred Harris* • Kevin Dunn *J Edgar Hoover* • Diane Lane *Paulette Goddard* • James Woods *Lawyer Scott* • David Duchovny *Rollie Totheroh* ■ *Dir* Richard Attenborough • *Scr* William Boyd, Bryan Forbes, William Goldman, from a story by Diana Hawkins, the biography *Chaplin: His Life And Art* by David Robinson and the autobiography by Charles Chaplin

The Chapman Report ★★

Drama 1962 · US · Colour · 149mins

For "Chapman", read "Kinsey" in this glossy examination of four Los Angeles women with psychosexual difficulties: a bored housewife (the normally ebullient Shelley Winters); a nymphomaniac (the usually ice-cold Claire Bloom); a frigid widow (sexy Jane Fonda); and a romantic adulteress (coy Glynis Johns). George Cukor was the undisputed expert at handling actresses, but the distinguished veteran cannot dispel the impression that this is no more than a sleazy exploitation of early 1960s permissiveness. RK

Efrem Zimbalist Jr *Paul Radford* • Shelley Winters *Sarah Garnell* • Jane Fonda *Kathleen Barclay* • Claire Bloom *Naomi Shields* • Glynis Johns *Teresa Harnish* • Andrew Duggan *Dr George Chapman* ■ *Dir* George Cukor • *Scr* Wyatt Cooper, Don M Mankiewicz, from the novel by Irving Wallace

Chappaqua ★★ 15

Experimental biographical drama
1966 · US · Colour · 78mins

Forty years after his optical process enhanced Fritz Lang's *Metropolis*, Eugene Shuftan suffered the indignity of being fired from this trippy reverie by director/star Conrad Rooks. His replacement, Robert Frank, managed to produce some suitably hallucinatory cold turkey effects. Alas, nothing could save this autobiographical ramble, in which Rooks offers up blurred memories and confused visions of reality to the Parisian doctor (Jean-Louis Barrault) assigned to release him from his heroin addiction. DP [video]

Conrad Rooks *Russel Harwick* • Jean-Louis Barrault *Doctor Benoit* • William S Burroughs *Opium Jones* • Allen Ginsberg *Messiah* • Ravi Shankar *Sun god* • Paula Pritchett *Water woman* ■ *Dir/Scr* Conrad Rooks

Chapter Two ★★ PG

Comedy drama 1979 · US · Colour · 121mins

Novelist James Caan suffers guilt over remarrying after the death of his first wife; his anxieties cause problems in his second marriage. Adapted by Neil Simon from his semi-autobiographical Broadway play, the movie is heavy on wisecracks which defuse the potentially serious subject matter. Unfortunately, it's also heavy on talky and rather tedious argument. Caan is good, though, and Oscar-nominated Marsha Mason (the second Mrs Simon) is terrific. RK [video]

James Caan *George Schneider* • Marsha Mason *Jennie MacLaine* • Joseph Bologna *Leo Schneider* • Valerie Harper *Faye Medwick* • Alan Fudge *Lee Michaels* • Judy Farrell *Gwen Michaels* ■ *Dir* Robert Moore • *Scr* Neil Simon, from his play

Character ★★★★ 15

Period drama 1997 · Neth · Colour · 119mins

Adapted from Ferdinand Bordewijk's novel, a recognised classic of modern Dutch literature, Mike van Diem's Oscar-winning debut is demanding but hugely rewarding. Set in 1920s Rotterdam, it tells the story of a merciless bailiff (the ferociously austere Jan Decleir) and his twisted relationship with his illegitimate son (Fedja Van Huet). Victor Löw contributes a wonderfully eccentric performance, while the handsomely dour photography complements the stylised art direction. DP. In Dutch with English subtitles. Contains violence, some swearing and brief nudity. [video]

Jan Decleir *Dreverhaven* • Fedja Van Huet *Jacob Katadreuffe* • Betty Schuurman *Joba Katadreuffe* • Tamar van den Dop *Lorna Te George* • Victor Löw *De Gankelaar* ■ *Dir* Mike van Diem • *Scr* Mike van Diem, Laurens Geels, Ruud van Megen, from the novel *Karakter* by Ferdinand Bordewijk • *Cinematographer* Rogier Stoffers • *Art Director* Jelier & Schief

Charade ★★★★★ PG

Romantic comedy thriller
1963 · US · Colour · 108mins

An absolutely wonderful comedy thriller from director Stanley Donen that nearly out-Hitchcocks Hitchcock. With a MacGuffin so clever you'll never guess, and a dream cast of Cary Grant and Audrey Hepburn on ravishing Parisian locations, what more could you possibly want in the way of movie entertainment? There's a clever plot that never lets up, a wondrously romantic score (by Henry Mancini), star-making turns from Walter Matthau and James Coburn, and set pieces that deserve classic status: Grant taking a shower fully-clothed; Audrey and Cary falling in love on a Paris river boat; and a one-handed villain in a roof-top cliffhanger. TS [video] DVD

Cary Grant *Peter Joshua* • Audrey Hepburn *Regina "Reggie" Lampert* • Walter Matthau *Hamilton Bartholomew* • James Coburn *Tex Panthollow* • George Kennedy *Herman Scobie* • Ned Glass *Leopold Gideon* • Jacques Marin *Inspector Edouard Grandpierre* ■ *Dir* Stanley Donen • *Scr* Peter Stone, from the story *The Unsuspecting Wife* by Peter Stone, Marc Behm • *Costume Designer* Givenchy

The Charge at Feather River ★★★ U

Western 1953 · US · Colour · 95mins

A group of reprobates are rounded up and sent into Injun territory to rescue two white women in this marvellous western that anticipates the plot of *The Searchers*. Unfortunately, it is seriously marred by the miscasting of handsome Guy Madison in the lead. It was originally shown in 3-D, which explains why objects keep crashing towards the camera. Even without its gimmick, this is a well-written and well-directed movie. TS

Guy Madison *Miles Archer* • Frank Lovejoy *Sergeant Baker* • Helen Westcott *Ann McKeever* • Vera Miles *Jennie McKeever* • Dick Wesson *Cullen* ■ *Dir* Gordon Douglas • *Scr* James R Webb

Charge of the Lancers ★ U

Period spy drama 1954 · US · Colour · 73mins

Paulette Goddard was an intelligent and vivacious actress whose cinema career had virtually come to an end by 1954. Reduced to starring in one of the cheap potboilers churned out by the Sam Katzman unit at Columbia, she plays a gypsy who falls for a French captain (Jean-Pierre Aumont) and helps the English capture the Russian naval base at Sebastopol. AE

Paulette Goddard *Tanya* • Jean-Pierre Aumont *Captain Eric Evoir* • Richard Stapley *Major Bruce Lindsey* • Karin Booth *Maria Sand* ■ *Dir* William Castle • *Scr* Robert E Kent

The Charge of the Light Brigade ★★★★ PG

Historical war drama
1936 · US · BW · 115mins

This splendid early Errol Flynn vehicle bears little relation to historical fact, but who cares? This wonderful swashbuckler is set largely in India, but fetches up in the Crimea in time for a stunningly spectacular charge, punctuated with on-screen quotes from Tennyson. The great Michael Curtiz directs, with Olivia de Havilland returning as Flynn's love interest a year after their screen partnership began with *Captain Blood*. The magnificent score was Max Steiner's first for Warner Bros, and it provides the perfect accompaniment to this thunderingly good movie. TS [video]

Errol Flynn *Maj Geoffrey Vickers* • Olivia de Havilland *Elsa Campbell* • Patric Knowles *Capt Perry Vickers* • Henry Stephenson *Sir Charles Macefield* • Nigel Bruce *Sir Benjamin Warrenton* • Donald Crisp *Col Campbell* • David Niven *Capt James Randall* • C Henry Gordon *Surat Khan* • Spring Byington *Lady Octavia Warrenton* ■ *Dir* Michael Curtiz • *Scr* Michel Jacoby, Rowland Leigh, from a story by Michel Jacoby, inspired by the poem by Alfred Lord Tennyson

The Charge of the Light Brigade ★★★★★ PG

Historical war drama
1968 · UK · Colour · 130mins

The charge of 1854, immortalised by Tennyson, is etched deep in our national psyche as a blunder of heroic proportions. Tony Richardson's film of the event was a failure on release, despite its *Sergeant Pepper*-like marketing. But it's a great, unsung masterpiece, filled with extraordinary set pieces and chillingly funny performances. It is a blistering satire on England and those bickering, blithering aristocratic idiots who paid for their commissions and then picnicked as their men were mown down by Russian cannons. Richardson and his writer Charles Wood are less concerned with the "reason why" than with social context, a theme mirrored by Richard Williams's witty cartoon sequences. And the charge itself, brilliantly edited by Kevin Brownlow and Hugh Raggett, evokes the terrible carnage as pure chaos. AT [video] DVD

Trevor Howard *Lord Cardigan* • Vanessa Redgrave *Clarissa Codrington* • David Hemmings *Captain Nolan* • John Gielgud *Lord Raglan* • Harry Andrews *Lord Lucan* • Jill Bennett *Mrs Duberly* • Peter Bowles *Paymaster Duberly* • Mark Burns *Captain Morris* • Corin Redgrave *Featherstonhaugh* • Rachel Kempson *Mrs Codrington* ■ *Dir* Tony Richardson • *Scr* Charles Wood • *Cinematographer* David Watkin

Chariots of Fire ★★★★★ U

Sports drama 1981 · UK · Colour · 118mins

Unfairly dismissed by some as an empty exercise in cheap schmaltz, this has an old-fashioned innocence that celebrates the human spirit with a lot of careful detail. It's a powerful tale of two British athletes – one a contemplative Scottish missionary, the other an anxious Jewish student – aiming for glory in the 1924 Olympics, and it contains a compelling study of their characters and those of their competitors. Their experiences are drawn in thoughtfully by Hugh Hudson's direction and Colin Welland's Oscar-winning script. JM [video] DVD

Ben Cross *Harold Abrahams* • Ian Charleson *Eric Liddell* • Nigel Havers *Lord Andrew Lindsay* • Nicholas Farrell *Aubrey Montague* • Ian Holm *Sam Mussabini* • John Gielgud *Master of Trinity* • Lindsay Anderson *Master of Caius* • Nigel Davenport *Lord Birkenhead* • Cheryl Campbell *Jennie Liddell* • Alice Krige *Sybil Gordon* • Dennis Christopher *Charles Paddock* • Brad Davis *Jackson Scholz* • Patrick Magee *Lord Cadogan* • Richard Griffiths *Head Porter, Caius College* • Ruby Wax *Bunty* ■ *Dir* Hugh Hudson • *Scr* Colin Welland • *Cinematographer* David Watkin • *Editor* Terry Rawlings • *Music* Vangelis • *Costume Designer* Milena Canonero

Charley and the Angel ★★ U

Fantasy comedy 1973 · US · Colour · 90mins

This tolerable piece of family fare mismatches plot devices from *It's a Wonderful Life* and Dickens's *A Christmas Carol*. Although Fred MacMurray does a nice line in hangdog expressions, he lacks the look of tousled desperation that made James Stewart's performance in Capra's original so heartrending, while Harry Morgan comes a long way behind Henry Travers in the role of the angel coaxing his charge into reassessing his contribution to life. DP [video]

Fred MacMurray *Charley Appleby* • Cloris Leachman *Nettie Appleby* • Harry Morgan *Angel* • Kurt Russell *Ray Ferris* • Kathleen Cody *Leonora Appleby* ■ *Dir* Vincent McEveety • *Scr* Roswell Rogers, from the novel *The Golden Evenings of Summer* by Will Stanton

Charley Moon ★★★ U

Musical drama 1956 · UK · Colour · 90mins

This distinctly downbeat showbiz melodrama was co-written (with John Cresswell) by Leslie Bricusse, who went on to notch up ten Oscar nominations as a composer and songwriter. Here he paints a particularly lurid picture of life in the music halls, as Max Bygraves takes no prisoners on his way to the top before conscience finally triumphs over ambition. Offering fewer insights into the loneliness of the long-distance performer than, say, John Osborne's *The Entertainer*, the film nevertheless has a ring of authenticity. DP

Max Bygraves *Charley Moon* • Dennis Price *Harold Armytage* • Michael Medwin *Alf Higgins* • Florence Desmond *Mary Minton* • Shirley Eaton *Angel Dream* • Patricia Driscoll *Rose* ■ *Dir* Guy Hamilton • *Scr* Leslie Bricusse, John Cresswell, from the novel by Reginald Arkell

C

Charley Varrick ★★★★

Crime drama 1973 · US · Colour · 110mins

Walter Matthau stars as a small-time crook who lands himself in hot water when he mistakenly steals a small fortune belonging to the Mafia. hitman Joe Don Baker is soon on his trail, but the cunning Matthau has a few tricks up his sleeve. Don Siegel directs the clever, exciting script with verve, and also contributes a brief cameo as a table-tennis player. Unlike other crime thrillers of the period, this still seems fresh and invigorating. SR

Walter Matthau *Charley Varrick* • Joe Don Baker *Molly* • Felicia Farr *Sybil Fort* • Andy Robinson [Andrew Robinson] *Harman Sullivan* • Sheree North *Jewell Everett* • John Vernon *Maynard Boyle* • Jacqueline Scott *Nadine Varrick* ■ *Dir* Don Siegel • *Scr* Howard Rodman, Dean Riesner, from the novel *The Looters* by John Reese

Charley's Aunt ★★★ U

Comedy 1930 · US · BW · 90mins

Having previously been filmed silently in 1925, this was the first sound adaptation of Brandon Thomas's theatrical warhorse. Updating the action from 1895, Canadian veteran Al Christie uses all the experience gained from churning out countless slapstick shorts to input as much physical business as possible into Charlie Ruggles's impersonation of the spinster from Brazil, when he's pressed into posing as a chaperon to Oxford undergraduates Hugh Williams and Rodney McLennon and their visiting belles. However, the play's cheeky wit survives intact, as the action descends into broad farce as Ruggles is pursued by a pair of ageing admirers and Williams's real aunt. DP

Charlie Ruggles [Charles Ruggles] *Lord Babberly* • June Collyer *Amy Spettigue* • Hugh Williams *Charlie Wykeham* • Doris Lloyd *Donna D'Alvadores* • Halliwell Hobbes *Stephen Spettigue* • Flora Le Breton *Ela Delahay* • Rodney McLennon *Jack Chesney* • Flora Sheffield *Kitty Verdun* • Phillips Smalley *Sir Francis Chesney* • Wilson Benge *Brassett* ■ *Dir* Al Christie • *Scr* F McGrew Willis, from the story and play by Brandon Thomas

Charley's Aunt ★★★ U

Comedy 1941 · US · BW · 81mins

Brandon Thomas's memorable creation is this time immortalised by the great Jack Benny, who always seemed strangely at home in drag. True, he's a little long in the tooth as an Oxford student, and, if it all seems a mite familiar, that's probably because this is one of several film versions. There's a super pace to this one, though, and a fabulous supporting cast, headed by the oh-so-elegant Kay Francis and a very young and lovely Anne Baxter. TS

Jack Benny *Babbs* • Kay Francis *Donna Lucia* • James Ellison *Jack Chesney* • Anne Baxter *Amy Spettigue* • Edmund Gwenn *Stephen Spettigue* • Reginald Owen *Redcliff* • Laird Cregar *Sir Francis Chesney* ■ *Dir* Archie Mayo • *Scr* George Seaton, from the play by Brandon Thomas

Charley's (Big Hearted) Aunt ★★ U

Comedy 1940 · UK · BW · 75mins

Brandon Thomas's classic farce first saw the light of day on stage in 1892, an era when well-behaved young ladies required a chaperone while on a date. Hence the plot, in which an Oxford University student masquerades as the aunt of one of his friends in order to fulfil the function – providing the most famous and enduring of drag roles. Although British to the core, the oft-filmed tale has fared best in American hands, with Jack Benny the best "aunt". This is generally lacklustre, with English comedian Arthur Askey taking a no more than adequate stab at the role. RK

Arthur Askey *Arthur Linden-Jones* • Richard Murdoch *Stinker Burton* • Graham Moffatt *Albert Brown* • Moore Marriott *Jerry* • JH Roberts *Dean Bowgate* • Felix Aylmer *Henry Crawley, the proctor* ■ *Dir* Walter Forde • *Scr* Marriott Edgar, Ralph Smart, JOC Orton

Charlie ★★ 18

Biographical crime drama
2003 · UK · Colour · 90mins

One-time Bros sensation Luke Goss takes on the role of Charlie Richardson, the gang boss who terrorised London south of the river during the 1960s. This bloody, brutal biopic has a banged-up Richardson reminiscing, in flashback, about the days when pliers, planks and electrodes were the tools of his trade. Malcolm Needs's film is a mishmash of styles and morally questionable, but it's slickly made. DA DVD

Luke Goss *Charlie Richardson* • Steven Berkoff *Charlie Richardson Sr* • Leslie Grantham *Richard Waldeck* • Anita Dobson *Mrs Richardson Sr* • Nicole Sherwin *Jean Le Grange* • Marius Weyers *General Van den Bergh* • Douglas McFerran *Richard Aubury* • Antony Carrick *Judge Lawton* • Langley Kirkwood *Eddy Richardson* ■ *Dir/Scr* Malcolm Needs

Charlie Bubbles ★★★

Drama 1967 · UK · Colour · 89mins

Albert Finney, an archetypally sixites British screen icon, directed this contemporary romantic drama, as well as playing the title role. Charlie is a northern working-class lad made good – a popular theme of the time. A successful novelist, he's fed up with glitzy metropolitan values and decides to go in search of his roots. Rich in resonances of the era. RK

Albert Finney *Charlie Bubbles* • Colin Blakely *Smokey Pickles* • Billie Whitelaw *Lottie Bubbles* • Liza Minnelli *Eliza* • Timothy Garland *Jack Bubbles* • Richard Pearson *Accountant* ■ *Dir* Albert Finney • *Scr* Shelagh Delaney

Charlie Chan and the Curse of the Dragon Queen ★★ PG

Detective comedy
1981 · US · Colour · 91mins

This comedy is best viewed today as the film that introduced Michelle Pfeiffer to international audiences. It's an ill-advised attempt to resuscitate author Earl Derr Bigger's wily, politically incorrect Oriental detective, listlessly played by Peter Ustinov. Brian Keith, Lee Grant and Rachel Roberts throw away their dignity for the cash, but Richard Hatch, as Chan's half-Jewish, half-Chinese grandson, has some amusing moments. TS

Peter Ustinov *Charlie Chan* • Angie Dickinson *Dragon Queen* • Lee Grant *Mrs Lupowitz* • Richard Hatch *Lee Chan Jr* • Brian Keith *Police Chief* • Roddy McDowall *Gillespie* • Rachel Roberts (1) *Mrs Dangers* • Michelle Pfeiffer *Cordelia* • Paul Ryan *Masten* ■ *Dir* Clive Donner • *Scr* Stan Burns, David Axelrod, from a story by Jerry Sherlock, from characters created by Earl Derr Biggers

Charlie Chan at Monte Carlo ★★

Mystery 1937 · US · BW · 71mins

This proved to be the Swedish-born Warner Oland's final outing as Earl Derr Biggers's Chinese detective. The storyline offers plenty of twists and turns, but Eugene Forde takes the action at such a clip that it's never easy to remember who's deceiving who and which of the various characters assembled at a Monte Carlo hotel has been in contact with Sidney Blackmer's stolenbonds. Moderate fare. DP

Warner Oland *Charlie Chan* • Keye Luke *Lee Chan* • Virginia Field *Evelyn Grey* • Sidney Blackmer *Karnoff* • Harold Huber *French police inspector* • Kay Linaker *Joan Karnoff* ■ *Dir* Eugene Forde • *Scr* Charles Belden, Jerry Cady, from a story by Robert Ellis, Helen Logan, from characters created by Earl Derr Biggers

Charlie Chan at the Circus ★★★

Mystery 1936 · US · BW · 71mins

Warner Oland's 11th outing as Earl Derr Biggers's Oriental detective was directed by Harry Lachman. Set to investigate the murder of circus owner Paul Stanton, Oland uncovers a conspiracy involving blackmail, forged documents and a gorilla suit. However, there's also time for Number One Son Keye Luke to provide some comic relief, as his agrizoophobia ruins a hot date. Midget siblings George and Olive Brasno come close to stealing the show, but there's stiff competition from fellow suspects Francis Ford (brother of director John Ford) and J Carrol Naish, who played Chan on TV in the 1950s. DP

Warner Oland *Charlie Chan* • Keye Luke *Lee Chan* • George Brasno *Tim* • Olive Brasno *Tiny* • Francis Ford *John Gaines* • Maxine Reiner *Marie Norman* ■ *Dir* Harry Lachman • *Scr* Robert Ellis, Helen Logan, from characters created by Earl Derr Biggers

Charlie Chan at the Olympics ★★ U

Mystery 1937 · US · BW · 71mins

As if the presence of Hitler wasn't enough to blight the 1936 Berlin Games, the activities of a nest of spies nearly prevent Keye Luke from taking his place on the US swimming team. He's kidnapped when Warner Oland gets too close to discovering who is after the plans for a top secret autopilot mechanism. But the villains had not taken into consideration the debut appearance of Number Two Son (Layne Tom Jr), or Chan's unlikely alliance with the Nazi police. DP

Warner Oland *Charlie Chan* • Katherine DeMille *Yvonne Roland* • Pauline Moore *Betty Adams* • Allan Lane *Richard Masters* • Keye Luke *Lee Chan* • C Henry Gordon *Arthur Hughes* • John Eldredge *Cartwright* • Layne Tom Jr *Charlie Chan Jr* • Jonathan Hale *Hopkins* ■ *Dir* H Bruce Humberstone • *Scr* Robert Ellis, Helen Logan, from a story by Paul Burger, Earl Derr Biggers

Charlie Chan at the Opera ★★★

Mystery 1936 · US · BW · 64mins

The famously inscrutable Chinese shamus, exquisitely played by Warner Oland, tackles an elaborate mystery in a prime puzzler from the solidly entertaining series. Boris Karloff plays the amnesiac baritone who escapes from a mental asylum and is blamed for the murder of his wife and her lover during a performance of *Carnival* (a fake opera composed especially for the film by Oscar Levant). Karloff's singing voice may be dubbed, but his presence adds a formidable *frisson* to the usual suspenseful scenario. AJ

Warner Oland *Charlie Chan* • Boris Karloff *Gravelle* • Keye Luke *Lee Chan* • Charlotte Henry *Mlle Kitty* • Margaret Irving *Mme Lilli Rochelle* • Thomas Beck *Phil Childers* • Gregory Gaye *Enrico Barelli* ■ *Dir* H Bruce Humberstone • *Scr* Scott Darling, Charles Belden, from a story by Bess Meredyth, from characters created by Earl Derr Biggers

Charlie Chan at Treasure Island ★★

Mystery 1939 · US · BW · 73mins

Treasure Island was the name of a popular fairground attraction in San Francisco, which is the only reason for the title of this entry in the long-running series. Sidney Toler is Chan, upset by a friend's suicide and looking into the activities of racketeering astrologers as a result. Regular Chan director Norman Foster keeps the story moving along pre-ordained lines. AT

Sidney Toler *Charlie Chan* • Cesar Romero *Fred Rhadini* • Pauline Moore *Eve Cairo* • Victor Sen Yung *James Chan* • Douglas Fowley *Peter Lewis* • June Gale *Myra Rhadini* • Douglass Dumbrille *Thomas Gregory* ■ *Dir* Norman Foster • *Scr* John Larkin, from characters created by Earl Derr Biggers

Charlie Chan in Egypt ★★★

Mystery 1935 · US · BW · 73mins

This was the first of nine cases penned by Robert Ellis and Helen Logan, and it's easily one of the most exciting. At his inscrutable best, Warner Oland is called in by the managers of a French museum to investigate the rash of murders that follows the opening of a high priest's tomb. Young Rita Hayworth makes in her fourth credited appearance, still being billed as Rita Cansino. DP

Warner Oland *Charlie Chan* • Pat Paterson *Carol Arnold* • Thomas Beck *Tom Evans* • Rita Cansino [Rita Hayworth] *Nayda* • Jameson Thomas *Dr Anton Racine* • Frank Conroy *Professor John Thurston* ■ *Dir* Louis King • *Scr* Robert Ellis, Helen Logan, from characters created by Earl Derr Biggers

Charlie Chan in London ★★★ U

Mystery 1934 · US · BW · 78mins

Even though this was Swedish-born Warner Oland's sixth outing as Earl Derr Biggers's Oriental detective, this is only our second chance to see him in action as, sadly, *Charlie Chan Carries On*, *Charlie Chan's Chance*, *Charlie Chan's Courage* and *Charlie Chan's Greatest Case* have all perished. A teasing mystery and a superb supporting cast make this one of the most enjoyable entries in the series, as Chan investigates a murder among the hunting, shooting and fishing set. DP DVD

Warner Oland *Charlie Chan* • Drue Leyton *Pamela Gray* • Douglas Walton *Paul Gray* • Alan Mowbray *Geoffrey Richmond* • Mona Barrie *Lady Mary Bristol* • Ray Milland *Neil Howard* • EE Clive *Detective Sergeant Thacker* • Madge Bellamy *Becky Fothergill* ■ *Dir* Eugene Forde • *Scr* Philip MacDonald, from characters created by Earl Derr Biggers

Charlie Chan in Paris ★★ U

Mystery 1935 · US · BW · 71mins

Produced by Sol M Wurtzel, who later supervised 20th Century-Fox's other Oriental sleuth series, Mr Moto, the seventh case featuring Warner Oland is notable primarily for the introduction of Keye Luke as Lee Chan ("Number One Son"). Together they make short work of a gang of counterfeiters plaguing the City of Light with a batch of forged bonds. Toss in a little blackmail and murder and you have a briskly directed, sturdy thriller. DP

Warner Oland *Charlie Chan* • Mary Brian *Yvette Lamartine* • Thomas Beck *Victor Descartes* • Erik Rhodes *Max Corday* • Keye Luke *Lee Chan* • Perry Ivins *Bedell* ■ *Dir* Lewis Seiler • *Scr* Edward T Lowe, Stuart Anthony, from a story by Philip MacDonald, from characters created by Earl Derr Biggers

Charlie Chan in Reno ★★★

Mystery 1939 · US · BW · 70mins

Having handled several entries in Peter Lorre's Mr Moto series, director Norman Foster switched Oriental detectives for this brisk Fox programme filler. It was back projection all the way, as Sidney Toler (making only his second appearance as Earl Derr Biggers's sleuth) leaves Honolulu,

 U = SUITABLE FOR ALL Uc = SUITABLE FOR ALL, ESPECIALLY FOR YOUNG CHILDREN (VIDEO ONLY) PG = PARENTAL GUIDANCE

in the company of "Number Two Son" Victor Sen Yung, to investigate why Hawaiian neighbour Pauline Moore is being framed for murder. DP

Sidney Toler *Charlie Chan* • Ricardo Cortez *Dr Ainsley* • Phyllis Brooks *Vivian Wells* • Slim Summerville *Sheriff Fletcher* • Kane Richmond *Curtis Whitman* • Victor Sen Yung *James Chan* • Pauline Moore *Mary Whitman* ■ *Dir* Norman Foster • *Scr* Frances Hyland, Albert Ray, Robert E Kent, from the story *Death Makes a Decree* by Philip Wylie and characters created by Earl Derr Biggers

Charlie Chan in Rio ★★

Mystery 1941 · US · BW · 61mins

Charlie Chan goes to Brazil for Sidney Toler's tenth outing in this long-running B-movie franchise. Director Harry Lachman exploits his exotic location to provide a lively musical background to this tale of double murder. Yet, in spite of featuring some of the series' most ingenious clues and, most unusually, a brief burst of Mandarin (complete with subtitles), this is one of the least satisfying Chan mysteries. DP

Sidney Toler *Charlie Chan* • Mary Beth Hughes *Joan Reynolds* • Cobina Wright Jr *Grace Ellis* • Ted North *Carlos Dantas* • Victor Jory *Alfredo Marina* • Harold Huber *Chief Souto* • Victor Sen Yung *Jimmy Chan* ■ *Dir* Harry Lachman • *Scr* Samuel G Engel, Lester Ziffren, from characters created by Earl Derr Biggers

Charlie Chan in Shanghai ★★ U

Mystery 1935 · US · BW · 70mins

Swedish actor Warner Oland makes his ninth screen appearance as fabled Oriental sleuth Charlie Chan in this vintage tale of intrigue and murder. The suave Chinese detective is back on his home turf here, investigating an international opium ring. However, this is more of a children's picture than a smoky, sinister excursion, with "Number One Son" (Keye Luke) taking up a lot of screen time. AT

Warner Oland *Charlie Chan* • Irene Hervey *Diana Woodland* • Charles Locher [Jon Hall] *Philip Nash* • Russell Hicks *James Andrews* • Keye Luke *Lee Chan* • Halliwell Hobbes *Chief of Police* ■ *Dir* James Stone • *Scr* Edward T Lowe, Gerald Fairlie, from characters created by Earl Derr Biggers

Charlie Chan in The Chinese Cat ★★ PG

Mystery 1944 · US · BW · 62mins

The second and best of director Phil Rosen's six Charlie Chan pictures has more than a whiff of *The Maltese Falcon* about it, as the key to the case lies in a prized statue. Aided again by "Number Three Son", Benson Fong, Sidney Toler uncovers the dealings of a diamond smuggling racket, whose ringleader should be readily apparent, despite the deliberately obfuscating pace. However, the involvement of a gloved criminologist and a pair of identical twins residing in a fun-house at the end of a pier gives the story a twist. DP DVD

Sidney Toler *Charlie Chan* • Joan Woodbury *Leah Manning* • Mantan Moreland *Birmingham Brown* • Benson Fong *Tommy Chan* • Ian Keith *Dr Paul Recknik* • Cy Kendall *Webster Deacon* • Weldon Heyburn *Harvey Dennis* ■ *Dir* Phil Rosen • *Scr* George Callahan, from characters created by Earl Derr Biggers

Charlie Chan in the Secret Service ★★ U

Mystery 1944 · US · BW · 61mins

Two years after 20th Century-Fox dropped its option on Earl Derr Bigger's crime series, Sidney Toler acquired the rights and continued his stint in the title role at B-movie outfit Monogram Pictures. Having quit Honolulu, Chan enlists as a government agent to track down torpedo plans stolen from a murdered inventor. Much of the action takes place within the victim's Washington home, but the gallery of sinister suspects enables Russian-born director Phil Rosen to sustain pace and interest. DP DVD

Sidney Toler *Charlie Chan* • Gwen Kenyon *Inez Arranto* • Mantan Moreland *Birmingham Brown* • Arthur Loft *Jones* • Marianne Quon *Iris Chan* • Lelah Tyler *Mrs Winters* • Benson Fong *Tommy Chan* ■ *Dir* Phil Rosen • *Scr* George Callahan, from characters created by Earl Derr Biggers

Charlie Chan on Broadway ★★★

Mystery 1937 · US · BW · 68mins

An impressive cast was assembled for this above-average entry in the series. But was it newspaper tycoon J Edward Bromberg, ace reporter Donald Woods, nightclub boss Douglas Fowley or mobster Leon Ames who was responsible for the murder of the showgirl whose missing diary contains incriminating gangland details? One thing's for sure: "Number One Son" Keye Luke isn't the guilty party, but it still takes all of Warner Oland's ingenuity to convince the cops. DP

Warner Oland *Charlie Chan* • Keye Luke *Lee Chan* • Joan Marsh *Joan Wendall* • J Edward Bromberg *Murdock* • Douglas Fowley *John Burke* • Harold Huber *Insp Nelson* • Donald Woods *Speed Patten* ■ *Dir* Eugene Forde • *Scr* Charles Belden, Jerry Cady [Jerome Cady], from a story by Art Arthur, Robert Ellis, Helen Logan, from characters created by Earl Derr Biggers

Charlie Strapp and Froggy Ball ★★

Animated adventure
1991 · Swe · Colour · 83mins

Swedish children have been following the adventures of these cute critters through comics, records, plays and radio shows since the 1940s. In this story, chirpy cricket Charlie and his croaking sidekick Froggy attempt to protect their woodland habitat from careless visitors and ruthless developers. For all their well-meaning eco-advocacy, cartoon features such as *Once upon a Forest* and *Ferngully: the Last Rainforest* have not proved popular with younger viewers and this flatly animated tale will do little to reverse the trend. DP. Swedish dialogue dubbed into English.

Dir Jan Gissberg • *Scr* Thomas Funck

Charlie: the Life and Art of Charles Chaplin ★★★★ PG

Documentary
2003 · US · BW and Colour · 126mins

This is, without question, the most comprehensive documentary study of cinema's first superstar. Directed and scripted by critic Richard Schickel and narrated with enthusiasm by Sydney Pollack, it makes impeccable use of stills, newsreels, home movies and Chaplin's canon from *Kid Auto Races at Venice* (1914), for which he devised his famous Tramp character. But it's the quality of the talking-head contributions that makes this so compelling, with the memories of such co-stars as Norman Lloyd and Claire Bloom complementing the assessments of Richard Attenborough, Marcel Marceau, Milos Forman, Martin Scorsese and Woody Allen (who isn't always complimentary). DP

Sydney Pollack *Narrator* ■ *Dir/Scr* Richard Schickel

Charlie, the Lonesome Cougar ★★ U

Adventure 1967 · US · Colour · 86mins

One of the last of the Disney studio's *True Life Adventures*, in which trick photography and cutesy narration makes wild animals seem almost human in their responses and social behaviour. Uncle Walt entertained a whole generation of young moviegoers with the series until genuine nature documentaries on TV revealed how bogus the films were. In this effort, a cougar is reared from a cub by a forester in a lumber camp in Washington State. AT VIDEO

Ron Brown *Jess Bradley* • Brian Russell *Potlatch* • Linda Wallace *Jess's fiancée* • Jim Wilson (1) *Farmer* • Clifford Peterson *Mill manager* • Lewis Sample *Chief engineer* ■ *Dir* Winston Hibler • *Scr* Jack Speirs, from a story by Jack Speirs, Winston Hibler

Charlie's Angels ★★ 15

Action comedy adventure
2000 · US/Ger · Colour · 94mins

This take on one of the most popular TV shows of the 1970s is a gossamer-thin, pop culture patchwork. With its reheated plot, trashy single-entendre humour and ho-hum thrills, this rickety chick flick charmlessly sashays its bland way from one kitsch set piece to the next. Star and co-producer Drew Barrymore is part of the vampy super agent trio, alongside Cameron Diaz and Lucy Liu, hired to find a kidnapped software genius. Thank heavens for Bill Murray, whose presence rescues the whole thing from total doom. AJ. Contains swearing, violence. VIDEO DVD

Cameron Diaz *Natalie* • Drew Barrymore *Dylan* • Lucy Liu *Alex* • Bill Murray *Bosley* • Sam Rockwell *Eric Knox* • Tim Curry *Roger Corwin* • Kelly Lynch *Vivian Wood* • Crispin Glover *Thin Man* • John Forsythe *Charlie Townsend* • Matt LeBlanc *Jason* ■ *Dir* McG [Joseph McGinty Nichol] • *Scr* Ryan Rowe, Ed Solomon, John August, from the TV series created by Ben Roberts, Ivan Goff

Charlie's Angels: Full Throttle ★ 12

Action comedy adventure
2003 · US · Colour · 101mins

No amount of special effects, irritating cameos and tedious skits can disguise the fact that this sequel is celluloid trash. Cameron Diaz, Drew Barrymore and Lucy Liu are all very cute as they reprise their special agent roles – this time hunting two stolen rings encrypted with the true identities of incognito federal witnesses – but their endless costume changes and innuendo-riddled dialogue need a plot to support them. Only "fallen" Angel Demi Moore and returning villain Crispin Glover have any screen presence, but their inadequately scripted roles are ineffective. SF VIDEO DVD

Cameron Diaz *Natalie Cook* • Drew Barrymore *Dylan Sanders* • Lucy Liu *Alex Munday* • Bernie Mac *Jimmy Bosley* • Crispin Glover *The Thin Man* • Justin Theroux *Seamus O'Grady* • Robert Patrick *Ray Carter* • Demi Moore *Madison Lee* • John Forsythe *Charlie Townsend* • Shia LaBeouf *Max* • Matt LeBlanc *Jason Gibbons* • John Cleese *Mr Munday* ■ *Dir* McG [Joseph McGinty Nichol] • *Scr* John August, Cormac Wibberley, Marianne Wibberley, from a story by John August, from the TV series created by Ben Roberts, Ivan Goff

Charlie's Ghost Story ★★ PG

Supernatural comedy drama
1994 · US · Colour · 85mins

Trenton Knight is the misunderstood son of Anthony Edwards, an archaeologist more comfortable with ancient artefacts than parenting. When Edwards discovers the remains of the Spanish explorer Coronado, his ghost (Cheech Marin) starts doling out fatherly advice to Knight while ensuring his bones get properly buried. Occasionally funny. AJ VIDEO

Anthony Edwards *Dave* • Cheech Marin [Richard "Cheech" Marin] *Coronado* • Linda Fiorentino *Marta* • Trenton Knight *Charlie* • Charles Rocket *Van Leer* • JT Walsh *Darryl* • Daphne Zuniga *Penni* ■ *Dir* Anthony Edwards • *Scr* Lance W Dreesen, Clint Hutchison, from a short story by Mark Twain

C

Charlotte Gray ★★ 15

Second World War romantic drama
2001 · UK/Aus/Ger · Colour · 116mins

Cate Blanchett stars as the eponymous wartime agent, a Scots woman who parachutes into occupied France in pursuit of her missing lover, pilot Rupert Penry-Jones. On the ground she meets up with Resistance contact Billy Crudup and joins his unit on sabotage missions. The problem with this rather unconvincing portrait of wartime derring-do is that Blanchett appears to be merely along for the ride, and her performance is let down by the unlikely story. TH. Contains some violence, swearing and sex scenes. VIDEO DVD

Cate Blanchett *Charlotte Gray* • Billy Crudup *Julien Levade* • Michael Gambon *Levade* • Rupert Penry-Jones *Peter Gregory* • Anton Lesser *Renech* • James Fleet *Richard Cannerley* ■ *Dir* Gillian Armstrong • *Scr* Jeremy Brock, from the novel by Sebastian Faulks

Charlotte's Web ★★★ U

Animated musical
1973 · US · Colour · 94mins

Fans of such farmyard fables as *Babe* will love this charming animated adaptation of EB White's children's classic, one of the few features produced by celebrated cartoon team Hanna-Barbera. The critters are brought to life by some superb voiceovers as Charlotte the spider (Debbie Reynolds) joins with Templeton the rat (Paul Lynde) to save petrified porker Wilbur (Henry Gibson). The animation isn't up to Disney standard, and the Sherman brothers' songs are rather hit and miss, but it's pleasing all the same. DP VIDEO DVD

Debbie Reynolds *Charlotte* • Paul Lynde *Templeton* • Henry Gibson *Wilbur* • Rex Allen *Narrator* • Martha Scott *Mrs Arable* • Dave Madden *Old sheep* • Danny Bonaduce *Avery* • Don Messick *Geoffrey* • Herb Vigran *Lurvy* • Agnes Moorehead *The goose* ■ *Dir* Charles A Nichols, Iwao Takamoto • *Scr* Earl Hamner Jr, from the novel by EB White

Charly ★★★★ PG

Drama 1968 · US · Colour · 99mins

Cliff Robertson found himself cast as heroic types after he played the young John F Kennedy in *PT 109*, but the most rewarding role of his career came with this Oscar-winning portrayal of a mentally disabled man whose life is transformed by a brain operation. The scenes between Robertson and Claire Bloom are touching, and Algernon the mouse is unforgettable, so director Ralph Nelson can be forgiven for playing down some of the fascinating possibilities raised by Stirling Silliphant's script. DP VIDEO DVD

Cliff Robertson *Charly Gordon* • Claire Bloom *Alice Kinian* • Leon Janney *Dr Richard Nemur* • Lilia Skala *Dr Anna Straus* • Dick Van Patten *Bert* • William Dwyer *Joey* ■ *Dir* Ralph Nelson • *Scr* Stirling Silliphant, from the short story and novel *Flowers for Algernon* by Daniel Keyes

Charro! ★ U

Western 1969 · US · Colour · 92mins

By this stage in his career, Elvis Presley must have been desperate to get away from the fluffy nonsense of his musicals, but he should have chosen a far more convincing alternative than this bungled, "serious" western. The King struggles with his role as a supposedly hard-bitten gunfighter who fights to clear his name when he is set up by his old partners in crime, and the rest of the cast is not convincing either. JF

Elvis Presley *Jess Wade* • Ina Balin *Tracy* • Barbara Werle *Sara Ramsey* • Lynn Kellogg *Marcie* • Victor French *Vince* • Solomon Sturges *Billy Roy* • James Sikking [James B Sikking] *Gunner* ■ *Dir* Charles Marquis Warren • *Scr* Charles Marquis Warren, from a story by Frederic Louis Fox

Charulata ★★★★ U

Period drama 1964 · Ind · BW · 118mins

This beautifully observed study of 19th-century domestic habits, also known as *The Lonely Wife*, won Satyajit Ray the best director prize at the Berlin Film Festival. Never has his debt to the great French film-maker Jean Renoir been more apparent than in this gently ironic tale. Mocking both male authority and the gentility of Victorian society, it also boasts a superb performance by Madhabi Mukherjee as the neglected Calcuttan wife who sees an affair with her husband's cousin as a way of boosting both her self-esteem and her writing ambitions. DP. In Bengali with English subtitles.

Madhabi Mukherjee *Charulata* • Sailen Mukherjee *Bhupati Dutta* • Soumitra Chatterjee *Amal* • Shyamal Ghosal *Umapada* • Gitali Roy ■ *Dir* Satyajit Ray • *Scr* Satyajit Ray, from the story *Nastaneer* by Rabindranath Tagore

The Chase ★★★★

Film noir 1946 · US · BW · 85mins

Pretentious, bizarre and fascinating, this rarely shown psychological thriller stars Robert Cummings as the shell-shocked ex-soldier who becomes chauffeur to Steve Cochran's wealthy and sadistic gangster – a man whose favourite hobby is outrunning trains at level crossings. Michele Morgan plays his dissatisfied wife, while Peter Lorre is his bodyguard. Cleverly written by Philip Yordan from a novel by the outstanding crime writer Cornell Woolrich, with moody photography by Franz Planer, the result is a most dream-like *films noir*. AE

Robert Cummings *Chuck* • Michèle Morgan *Lorna* • Peter Lorre *Gino* • Steve Cochran *Roman* • Lloyd Corrigan *Johnson* • Jack Holt *Davidson* ■ *Dir* Arthur Ripley • *Scr* Philip Yordan, from the novel *The Black Path of Fear* by Cornell Woodrich

The Chase ★★★★ 15

Drama 1966 · US · Colour · 127mins

Before he directed *Bonnie and Clyde*, Arthur Penn made this impressively cast and wondrously overcooked drama about a Texan sheriff who protects an escaped convict against a town that has run out of control. Marlon Brando has immense stature as the sheriff, while Robert Redford is perfect as the angelic convict he protects. In one sense, Lillian Hellman's script is like an updated western; in another, it evokes the madness and violence that gripped America in the aftermath of the Kennedy assassination. Although Penn virtually disowned the picture after producer Sam Spiegel had it re-edited, it remains a disturbing evocation of that traumatic era. AT DVD

Marlon Brando *Sheriff Calder* • Jane Fonda *Anna Reeves* • Robert Redford *Bubber Reeves* • EG Marshall *Val Rogers* • Angie Dickinson *Ruby Calder* • Janice Rule *Emily Stewart* • Miriam Hopkins *Mrs Reeves* • Robert Duvall *Edwin Stewart* • James Fox *Jake Rogers* ■ *Dir* Arthur Penn • *Scr* Lillian Hellman, from the novel and play by Horton Foote

The Chase ★★★ 15

Action adventure 1994 · US · Colour · 84mins

Charlie Sheen stars as the lovable con who kidnaps millionaire's daughter Kristy Swanson, prompting a massive manhunt and a media frenzy. The two leads are seriously lightweight, but still spark off each other nicely, although the best performances come from supporting players Ray Wise and punk idol Henry Rollins, cast against type as a psychopathic policeman. Dumb but amiable. JF. Contains violence and swearing.

Charlie Sheen *Jack Hammond* • Kristy Swanson *Natalie Voss* • Henry Rollins *Officer Dobbs* • Josh Mostel *Officer Figus* • Wayne Grace *Chief Boyle* • Rocky Carroll *Byron Wilder* ■ *Dir/Scr* Adam Rifkin

Chase a Crooked Shadow ★★★ U

Mystery thriller 1957 · UK · BW · 83mins

Coming off the back of *The Dam Busters*, *1984* and *Around the World in 80 Days*, director Michael Anderson was destined for a disappointment, but it is to his credit that this ludicrously contrived thriller not only holds the attention, but also actually manages to induce a short intake of breath at the totally unexpected denouement. Anne Baxter gives her one of her best performances as a recuperating neurotic who is convinced long-lost brother Richard Todd is after her diamonds. DP

Richard Todd *Ward* • Anne Baxter *Kimberley* • Herbert Lom *Vargas* • Alexander Knox *Chandler Brisson* • Faith Brook *Mrs Whitman* • Alan Tilvern *Carlos* ■ *Dir* Michael Anderson • *Scr* David D Osborn, Charles Sinclair

Chasers ★★ 15

Comedy 1994 · US · Colour · 101mins

Dennis Hopper, once the notorious film maverick, must have been keen to show that he could direct a movie with mainstream appeal. Here he certainly succeeds, but the result is a bland comedy, indistinguishable from all the other high concept projects that roll off the Hollywood production line. Tom Berenger and William McNamara are the bickering navy military policemen who are called in to transport a troublesome sailor to jail. It's amiable enough, but lacks a quirky edge. JF. Contains swearing and nudity.

Tom Berenger *Rock Reilly* • William McNamara *Eddie Devane* • Erika Eleniak *Toni Johnson* • Crispin Glover *Howard Finster* • Dean Stockwell *Salesman Stig* • Gary Busey *Sergeant Vince Banger* • Seymour Cassel *Master Chief Bogg* ■ *Dir* Dennis Hopper • *Scr* Joe Batteer, John Rice, Dan Gilroy, from a story by Joe Batteer, John Rice

Chasing Amy ★★★★ 18

Romantic comedy
1996 · US · Colour · 108mins

Writer/director Kevin Smith comes up trumps with this cool, hilarious and sexy romantic comedy. New Jersey comic-book writer Ben Affleck falls for pal Joey Lauren Adams, despite the fact she's a lesbian. In addition to the chemistry between the two leads, it has an insightful and even heartbreaking script from Smith, hilarious support from Jason Lee as Affleck's sceptical pal, plus Jason Mewes and the director himself returning as regular characters Jay and Silent Bob. One of the hippest love stories of the 1990s. JB. Contains swearing and nudity. DVD

Ben Affleck *Holden* • Joey Lauren Adams *Alyssa* • Jason Lee *Banky* • Dwight Ewell *Hooper* • Jason Mewes *Jay* • Ethan Suplee *Fan* • Scott Mosier *Collector* • Casey Affleck *Little kid* • Guinevere Turner *Singer* • Matt Damon *Executive* • Kevin Smith (2) *Silent Bob* ■ *Dir/Scr* Kevin Smith (2)

Chasing Dreams ★★

Melodrama 1982 · Can · Colour · 94mins

Yet another dull story about a young lad's dream of playing college baseball is notable only for an early appearance from Kevin Costner. The actor would return to the subject nine years later in *Field of Dreams* – thankfully, to much greater effect. NF

David G Brown *Gavin Thompson* • John Fife *Parks* • Jim Shane *Mr Thompson* • Matthew Clark *Ben* • Kevin Costner *Ed* ■ *Dir* Sean Roche, Therese Conte • *Scr* David G Brown

Chasing Liberty ★★ 12

Romantic comedy
2004 · US/UK · Colour · 106mins

When the daughter of the US president and a Secret Service agent flee from protocol across Europe, you keep hoping for a bit of action to liven things up in what is essentially a tedious travelogue. Mandy Moore stars as the White House "princess" who makes a dash for it and ends up on the back of a Vespa driven by Matthew Goode. Sadly, there's only weak chemistry between the pair. TH. Contains swearing. DVD

Mandy Moore *Anna Foster* • Matthew Goode *Ben Calder* • Jeremy Piven *Agent Alan Weiss* • Annabella Sciorra *Agent Cynthia Morales* • Caroline Goodall *First Lady Michelle Foster* • Mark Harmon *President James Foster* ■ *Dir* Andy Cadiff • *Scr* Derek Guiley, David Schneiderman

Chasing the Deer ★★★ PG

Historical drama 1994 · UK · Colour · 90mins

Director Graham Holloway works wonders with a tiny budget for this Scottish labour of love, a gritty period piece about the events leading up to the ill-fated Battle of Culloden. The story focuses on a proud Highland family who unwittingly get drawn into – and are divided by – the Jacobite rebellion against the hated English. Money considerations means it doesn't have the epic sweep that is needed, but the talented cast make up for any budget deficiencies. JF

Brian Blessed *Major Elliot* • Iain Cuthbertson *Tullibardine* • Matthew Zajac *Alistair Campbell* • Fish *Angus Cameron* • Brian Donald *Old Campbell* • Sandy Welch *Old Cameron* • Peter Gordon *McKinnon* • Carolyn Konrad *Morag* ■ *Dir* Graham Holloway • *Scr* Jerome Vincent, Bob Carruthers, Steve Gillham, from an idea by Michele Ayson

Chastity ★★

Drama 1969 · US · Colour · 83mins

In an effort to change their hippy image and be more credible to the Woodstock generation, pop sensations Sonny and Cher produced this banal road movie. Written and scored by Sonny Bono, the film casts Cher as a teenage hitch-hiker who gets involved in a robbery on the way to Mexico and discusses world problems while encountering prostitution and lesbianism. The fiasco may have ruined them financially, but the couple still named their daughter after it. AJ

Cher *Chastity* • Barbara London *Diana Midnight* • Stephen Whittaker (1) *Eddie* • Tom Nolan *Tommy* • Danny Zapien *Cab driver* • Elmer Valentine *1st truck driver* • Burke Rhind *Salesman* • Richard Armstrong *Husband* ■ *Dir* Alessio DePaola • *Scr* Sonny Bono

Le Château de Ma Mère ★★★★ U

Drama 1990 · Fr · Colour · 94mins

Surpassing *La Gloire de Mon Père*, this is as delightful a film as you could wish to see. The characters are old friends by now and in comparison with the boorish game hunting of the original, the encounter with a family of fraudulent Bohemians and the duel with a grouchy watchman and his dog make for much more compelling viewing. Jean Rochefort is superb as the sham pseud and Robert Alazraki's photography of Provence is sublime. Yves Robert directs with a leisure that suggests long, hot summer days, while the ending is sure to bring a lump to your throat. DP. In French with English subtitles. DVD

Philippe Caubère *Joseph Pagnol* • Nathalie Roussel *Augustine Pagnol* • Didier Pain *Uncle Jules* • Thérèse Liotard *Aunt Rose* • Julien Ciamaca *Marcel* • Victorien Delamere *Paul* ■ *Dir* Yves Robert • *Scr* Jérôme Tonnerre, Yves Robert, from the story by Marcel Pagnol

Chato's Land ★★ 18

Western 1971 · UK · Colour · 95mins

A trashily enjoyable western, flashily directed on a tiny budget by Michael Winner, with Charles Bronson as the hero, slowly picking off the posse that is chasing him. Bronson is his usual craggy, monosyllabic self, while Jack Palance and James Whitmore complete a formidable trio. AT DVD

Charles Bronson *Pardon Chato* • Jack Palance *Quincey Whitmore* • Richard Basehart *Nye Buell* • James Whitmore *Joshua Everette* • Simon Oakland *Jubal Hooker* • Ralph Waite *Elias Hooker* • Victor French *Martin Hall* ■ *Dir* Michael Winner • *Scr* Gerald Wilson

Chattahoochee ★★ 15

Biographical drama
1989 · US · Colour · 92mins

Korean War veteran Emmett Foley (Gary Oldman) returns to his Southern home as a hero, goes on a shooting spree and ends up in a brutal insane asylum. The portrayal of his attempts to expose the nightmarish conditions in the 1950s psychiatric facility owe as much to Hammer horror as documentary-style realism in director Mick Jackson's grim drama, which is straight-jacketed by mental illness clichés. AJ

Gary Oldman *Emmett Foley* • Dennis Hopper *Walker Benson* • Frances McDormand *Mae Foley* • Pamela Reed *Earlene* • Ned Beatty *Doctor Harwood* • M Emmet Walsh *Morris* • William De Acutis *Missy* • Lee Wilkof *Vernon* ■ *Dir* Mick Jackson • *Scr* James Hicks

Chattanooga Choo Choo ★★ PG

Comedy 1984 · US · Colour · 97mins

One of the many films which rely on the plot device of a conditional will. Here George Kennedy will only inherit his father's fortune if he can restore the famous Chattanooga express and get it to run to New York on time. Real-life gridiron star Joe Namath makes one of his rare big-screen appearances, and the cast also features Barbara Eden, the genie from TV's *I Dream of Jeannie*. DF

Barbara Eden *Maggie* • George Kennedy *Bert* • Melissa Sue Anderson *Jenny* • Joe Namath *Newt* • Bridget Hanley *Estelle* • Christopher McDonald *Paul* ■ *Dir* Bruce Bilson • *Scr* Robert Mundy, Stephen Phillip Smith

Chatterbox ★★ U

Drama 1936 · US · BW · 68mins

A wholesome country girl from Vermont (Anne Shirley) has acting ambitions and makes for New York, where she gets her big break on Broadway in a play called *Virtue's Reward*. Things don't go quite to plan, however, leaving her to seek solace in the loving arms of a somewhat wooden Phillips Holmes. George Nichols Jr's direction is competent, but the end result is vapid and uninspiring. RK

Anne Shirley *Jenny Yates* • Phillips Holmes *Philip Greene Jr* • Edward Ellis *Uriah Lowell* • Erik Rhodes *Archie Fisher* • Margaret Hamilton

Emily Tipton • Lucille Ball *Lillian Temple* ■ *Dir* George Nichols Jr • *Scr* Sam Mintz, from a play by David Carb

Chatterbox ★ U

Comedy 1943 · US · BW · 76mins

There's much excitement when a popular radio personality (Joe E Brown) is signed to appear in a film. However, when he falls off a horse and is saved by his female co-star (Judy Canova), his image is badly dented. Needless to say, it's redeemed by the final fade. Joseph Santley directs this dismally unfunny display of ham acting by the two unattractive leads. RK

Joe E Brown *Rex Vane* • Judy Canova *Judy Boggs* • John Hubbard *Sebastian Smart* • Rosemary Lane *Carol Forest* • Chester Clute *Wilfred Peckinpaugh* • Emmett Vogan *Roger Grant* ■ *Dir* Joseph Santley • *Scr* George Carleton Brown, Frank Gill Jr

Che! ★★ 15

Biographical drama
1969 · US · Colour · 91mins

Hollywood's take on the Cuban revolution, with Omar Sharif as Che Guevara and Jack Palance as Fidel Castro. Sharif looks oddly convincing – just like the poster every middle-class Marxist had over his bed – and the movie certainly celebrates Che's status as a revolutionary martyr and Robin Hood figure. As Castro, though, Palance is a rascal and a drunkard, a caricature of the man every patriotic American loves to hate. Richard Fleischer directs efficiently, but this is not remotely believable. AT [video]

Omar Sharif *Che Guevara* • Jack Palance *Fidel Castro* • Cesare Danova *Ramon Valdez* • Robert Loggia *Faustino Morales* • Woody Strode *Guillermo* • Barbara Luna *Anita Marquez* ■ *Dir* Richard Fleischer • *Scr* Michael Wilson, Sy Bartlett, from a story by David Karp, Sy Bartlett

The Cheap Detective ★★★

Detective parody 1978 · US · Colour · 92mins

This Neil Simon-scripted spoof of Humphrey Bogart's classic *film noir* movies is directed by Robert Moore and has Peter Falk donning the raincoat as Lou Peckinpaugh. As an idea, it quickly loses steam and one is left idly checking off the *Casablanca* references like a shopping list. Scatman Crothers is Tinker, asked to play *Jeepers Creepers* again, while Louise Fletcher and Fernando Lamas fill the shoes of Ingrid Bergman and Paul Henreid. Fun for buffs, but a mite too detailed for the ordinary viewer. AT

Peter Falk *Lou Peckinpaugh* • Ann-Margret *Jezebel Dezire* • Eileen Brennan *Betty DeBoop* • Sid Caesar *Ezra Dezire* • Stockard Channing *Bess* • James Coco *Marcel* • Dom DeLuise *Pepe Damascus* • Louise Fletcher *Marlene DuChard* • John Houseman *Jasper Blubber* • Madeline Kahn *Mrs Montenegro* • Fernando Lamas *Paul DuChard* • Marsha Mason *Georgia Merkle* • Phil Silvers *Hoppy* • Nicol Williamson *Colonel Schlussel* • Scatman Crothers *Tinker* ■ *Dir* Robert Moore • *Scr* Neil Simon

Cheaper by the Dozen ★★★ U

Period comedy 1950 · US · Colour · 85mins

The success of *Meet Me in St Louis* and *Life with Father* led to a postwar hunger for turn-of-the-century nostalgia, and no studio managed to so regularly recapture those halcyon days as 20th Century-Fox, whose backlot was turned permanently into a standing period set. Here the Gilbreth family of 12 children, headed by the ineffable Clifton Webb and the incandescent Myrna Loy, raise a ruckus and proved so popular that a follow-up (*Belles on Their Toes*) was immediately ordered. TS

Clifton Webb *Frank Bunker Gilbreth* • Jeanne Crain *Ann Gilbreth* • Myrna Loy *Mrs Lillian Gilbreth* • Betty Lynn *Libby Lancaster* • Edgar Buchanan *Dr Burton* • Barbara Bates *Ernestine* • Mildred Natwick *Mrs Mebane* • Sara Allgood *Mrs Monahan* ■ *Dir* Walter Lang • *Scr* Lamar Trotti, from the novel by Frank B Gilbreth Jr, Ernestine Gilbreth Carey

Cheaper by the Dozen ★★ PG

Comedy 2003 · US · Colour · 94mins

This is basically an over-extended sitcom that owes little allegiance to the original book or the delightful 1950 comedy starring Clifton Webb and Myrna Loy. Here the weight of the humour is on Steve Martin, who plays father of 12 children. When his author wife Bonnie Hunt is called away for a book launch, he has to cope with his unruly offspring. TH [video] DVD

Steve Martin *Tom Baker* • Bonnie Hunt *Kate Baker* • Piper Perabo *Nora Baker* • Tom Welling *Charlie Baker* • Hilary Duff *Lorraine Baker* • Kevin G Schmidt *Henry Baker* • Alyson Stoner *Sarah Baker* • Jacob Smith *Jake Baker* • Liliana Mumy *Jessica Baker* • Morgan York *Kim Baker* • Forrest Landis *Mark Baker* ■ *Dir* Shawn Levy • *Scr* Sam Harper, Joel Cohen, Alec Sokolow, from a story by Craig Titley, from the novel by Frank Bunker Gilbreth Jr [Frank B Gilbreth Jr], Ernestine Gilbreth Carey

The Cheat ★★★

Silent melodrama 1915 · US · BW · 55mins

Directed by Cecil B DeMille, this melodrama caused a huge scandal in its day. Though its great age has blurred its quality and dramatic impact, it is interesting as an early example of lurid trash presented as high art. The plot concerns a society woman (Fannie Ward) who loses money that isn't hers on the stock market and borrows from a wealthy Oriental (Sessue Hayakawa) to pay her debts. When she refuses him her favours, he exacts a sadistic punishment, branding her as if she were cattle. Hayakawa was later Oscar-nominated for his performance in *The Bridge on the River Kwai*. RK

Fannie Ward *Edith Hardy* • James Neill *Jones* • Utaka Abe *Tori's valet* • Dana Ong *District attorney* • Hazel Childers *Mrs Reynolds* • Judge Arthur H William *Courtroom judge* • Sessue Hayakawa *Haka Arakau* • Jack Dean *Dick Hardy* ■ *Dir* Cecil B DeMille • *Scr* Hector Turnbull, Jeanie MacPherson

The Cheaters ★★★ U

Comedy 1945 · US · BW · 90mins

Billie Burke is the dizzy, spendthrift wife of a put-upon financier Eugene Pallette and soon their family of wealthy, upper-class eccentrics faces ruin. A solution presents itself when a rich uncle leaves his fortune to an actress (Ona Munson) he never met. After a plethora of plot complications, the situation is sorted out with the help of an attractive, down-on-his-luck actor (Joseph Schildkraut giving an outstanding performance). Directed at an appropriate pace by Joseph Kane, the result is an enjoyable melange of comedy and sentimentality. RK

Joseph Schildkraut *Mr M* • Billie Burke *Mrs Pidgeon* • Eugene Pallette *Mr Pidgeon* • Ona Munson *Florrie* • Raymond Walburn *Willie* • Anne Gillis [Ann Gillis] *Angela* • Ruth Terry *Therese* • Robert Livingston *Stephen Bates* ■ *Dir* Joseph Kane • *Scr* Frances Hyland, from a story by Frances Hyland, Albert Ray

Check and Double Check ★★

Comedy 1930 · US · BW · 77mins

Hollywood's stereotyping of Mantan Moreland and Stepin Fetchit as scaredy cats was iniquitous enough, but Amos and Andy were white men Freeman Gosden and Charles Correll in blackface make-up. Consequently, it's almost impossible to watch this haunted house comedy without shuddering for all the wrong reasons. Back in the early 1930s, the proprietors of the Harlem Fresh Air Taxicab Company were among US radio's biggest stars. But the physical reality of their racial deception is embarrassing to behold. DP

Freeman F Gosden *Amos* • Charles J Correll *Andy* • Sue Carol *Jean Blair* • Charles Norton *Richard Williams* • Ralf Harolde *Ralph Crawford* • Edward Martindel *John Blair* ■ *Dir* Melville Brown [Melville W Brown] • *Scr* J Walter Ruben, from a story by Bert Kalmar, Harry Ruby

The Check Is in the Mail ★★ 15

Comedy 1986 · US · Colour · 79mins

In what was his first starring role, Brian Dennehy plays a California pharmacist, an upstanding citizen married to the lovely Anne Archer. Everything goes pear-shaped when he accumulates massive gambling debts, so he reverts to a less materialistic age by ripping out the utilities, drawing water from a newly-dug well and growing his own food. Director Joan Darling cut her teeth on American TV sitcoms, and this might have been better had it been cut down to 30 minutes. AT [video]

Brian Dennehy *Richard Jackson* • Anne Archer *Peggy Jackson* • Hallie Todd *Robin Jackson* • Chris Hebert *Danny Jackson* • Michael Bowen *Gary Jackson* • Nita Talbot *Mrs Rappaport* ■ *Dir* Joan Darling • *Scr* Robert Kaufman

Checkers ★★ U

Sports comedy 1937 · US · BW · 78mins

Modest, cutesy, but enjoyably event-filled rural comedy-cum-domestic drama involving the conventional devices of the genre (money problems down on the farm, a flint-hearted bank manager etc). The plot concerns a horse who breaks his leg, but is saved by surgery and goes on to run the movie's climactic big race to the relief of his desperate owner Stuart Erwin and the delight of his niece Jane Withers. RK

Jane Withers *Checkers/Judy* • Stuart Erwin *Edgar Connell* • Una Merkel *Mamie Appleby* • Marvin Stephens *Jimmy Somers* • Andrew Tombes *Tobias Williams* ■ *Dir* H Bruce Humberstone • *Scr* Lynn Root, Frank Fenton, Robert Chapin, Karen De Wolf

Checking Out ★ 15

Black comedy 1988 · UK · Colour · 90mins

Barely released to cinemas, this was another nail in the coffin of George Harrison's already troubled HandMade Films. Jeff Daniels stars as an advertising executive who becomes deeply neurotic after his colleague dies of a heart attack. His odyssey isn't worth the journey. AT. Contains swearing and nudity. [video]

Jeff Daniels *Ray Macklin* • Melanie Mayron *Jenny Macklin* • Michael Tucker *Harry Lardner* • Kathleen York *Diana* • Ann Magnuson *Connie Hagen* • Allan Havey *Pat Hagen* • Jo Harvey Allen *Barbara* • Ian Wolfe *Mr D'Amato* ■ *Dir* David Leland • *Scr* Joe Eszterhas

Checkpoint ★★ U

Action adventure 1956 · UK · Colour · 85mins

Although they promise fast-paced action, fiction films about motor racing rarely get out of first gear. At least here there is the compensation of some nifty auto action to pep up an otherwise pedestrian tale of industrial espionage, in which Stanley Baker tries to poach top secret car designs. DP

Anthony Steel *Bill Fraser* • Odile Versois *Francesca* • Stanley Baker *O'Donovan* • James Robertson-Justice *Warren Ingram* • Maurice Denham *Ted Thornhill* • Michael Medwin *Ginger* • Paul Muller *Petersen* ■ *Dir* Ralph Thomas • *Scr* Robin Estridge

Checkpoint ★★★

Drama 1987 · US · Colour · 91mins

Set in the twilight days of the Carter presidency, this claustrophobic drama explores in microcosm the tensions that arose during the Iran hostage crisis. Written, produced, edited and directed by Parviz Sayyad, it suggests the freeze in US-Iranian relations was not solely the fault of the fundamentalist regime that overthrew the Shah. All shades of political opinion are expressed as Canadian border authorities detain a busload of students after they discover eight Iranians onboard. DP

Mary Apick *Firouzeh* • Houshang Touzie *Kazem* • Peter Spreague *Mike* • Mark Nichols *Bob* • Buck Kartalian *Frank* • Michael Zand *Farhad* • Mayeva Martin *Kate* • Ali Poutash *Hatam* ■ *Dir/Scr* Parviz Sayyad

C

Checkpoint ★★★★

War drama 1998 · Rus · Colour · 91mins

Following Sergei Bodrov's *Prisoner of the Mountains* into a Caucusus region that may or may not be Chechnya, Alexandr Rogozhkin's frontline drama is a tense and often bitterly humorous reminder of the futility of war. Fighting a campaign they care little about, an unruly Russian unit is dispatched to an isolated checkpoint as punishment for the needless death of a Muslim mother in a nearby village. Charting the troopers' uneasy accord with the locals, after they become the target of a woodland sniper, this dour battle of attrition benefits considerably from both the relentlessly bleak imagery and the naturalistic ensemble playing. DP. A Russian language film.

Andrei Krasko *Iliych* • Aleksander Ivanov *Boeing* • Zoya Buryak *Detective* • Aleksei Buldakov *General* • Roman Romantsov *Bones* ■ *Dir/Scr* Aleksandr Rogozhkin

Cheech and Chong's Next Movie ★★ 18

Comedy 1980 · US · Colour · 90mins

Tommy Chong made his directorial debut (he would go on to direct three more of the Cheech and Chong series) in this hit-and-miss follow-up to *Up in Smoke*, a massive cult hit around the world. The plotting this time around is even more episodic than before, but the subject matter and humour still seemed fresh and anarchic at the time. The result drifts along in an amiable, if hazy fashion. JF [video] DVD

Richard "Cheech" Marin *Cheech* • Thomas Chong [Tommy Chong] *Chong* • Evelyn Guerrero *Donna* • Betty Kennedy *Candy* • Sy Kramer *Mr Neatnik* • Rikki Marin *Gloria* • Michael Winslow *Welfare comedian* • Paul Reubens *Pee-wee Herman/Desk clerk* ■ *Dir* Thomas Chong [Tommy Chong] • *Scr* Thomas Chong, Richard "Cheech" Marin

Cheech and Chong's Nice Dreams ★★ 18

Comedy 1981 · US · Colour · 83mins

Number three in the series, and if you didn't appreciate the joke by now, you were never going to be won over. Stacy Keach returns from the original, Paul "Pee-Wee Herman" Reuben pops up, while the sharp-eyed will spot an early film appearance by Sandra Bernhard. There's even room for a cameo from 1960s drug icon Timothy Leary, playing himself. Otherwise it's the usual sloppy mix of dope chat and slapstick from the two stars, "Cheech" Marin and Tommy Chong. JF [video]

Tommy Chong *Chong* • Richard "Cheech" Marin *Cheech* • Stacy Keach *The Sarge* • Evelyn Guerrero *Donna* • Paul Reubens *Howie Hamburger* • Michael Masters *Willard "Animal" Bad* • Sandra Bernhard *Angie* ■ *Dir* Thomas Chong [Tommy Chong] • *Scr* Thomas Chong, Richard "Cheech" Marin

Cheech & Chong's Still Smokin' ★ 18

Comedy 1983 · US · Colour · 86mins

As the medical authorities continue to tell us, smoking too much marijuana can be bad for your health. Sadly, the same applies to Cheech and Chong movies. While the duo can't be blamed for wanting to visit a cannabis mecca like Amsterdam, the resulting film is the weakest in the series: a lazy mixture of rambling sketches and concert footage. JF DVD

Richard "Cheech" Marin *Cheech* • Thomas Chong [Tommy Chong] *Chong* • Carol Van Herwijnen *Hotel Manager* • Shireen Strooker *Assistant manager* ■ *Dir* Thomas Chong [Tommy Chong] • *Scr* Thomas Chong, Richard "Cheech" Marin

Cheech & Chong's The Corsican Brothers ★ 15

Comedy 1984 · US · Colour · 86mins

The stoner duo obviously enjoyed romping around in period dress in *Yellowbeard*, judging by this unwise departure from their successful dopehead formula. Loosely based on the classic novel by Alexandre Dumas, with the duo mugging their way through a variety of increasingly unfunny roles, this is a dreadful comic caper. JF. Contains violence, swearing. DVD

Richard "Cheech" Marin *Luis (Corsican brother)* • Thomas Chong [Tommy Chong] *Lucien (Corsican brother)* • Roy Dotrice *The Evil Fuckaire/Ye Olde Jailer* • Shelby Fiddis *1st Princess* • Rikki Marin *2nd Princess* ■ *Dir* Thomas Chong [Tommy Chong] • *Scr* Richard "Cheech" Marin, Thomas Chong

Cheech & Chong's Up in Smoke ★★★ 18

Cult comedy 1978 · US · Colour · 81mins

A good decade before the phrase was even coined, Richard "Cheech" Marin and Tommy Chong came up with what for some remains the ultimate "slacker" movie. Cheech and Chong originally existed on albums only, but they made a surprisingly successful transition to the big screen; the duo made six movies together, all essential viewing for students around the world. The first (and best) of all their films finds the genially stoned pair looking to find the best grass in town. Stacy Keach is the deranged cop on their trail, while the car made of cannabis is a hoot. JF DVD

Richard "Cheech" Marin *Pedro* • Thomas Chong [Tommy Chong] *Man* • Stacy Keach *Sergeant Stedenko* • Tom Skerritt *Strawberry* • Strother Martin *Arnold Stoner* ■ *Dir* Lou Adler • *Scr* Thomas Chong [Tommy Chong], Richard "Cheech" Marin

Cheer Boys Cheer ★★★ U

Comedy 1939 · UK · BW · 83mins

A pleasing British comedy about two warring breweries: one mechanised, the other traditional. CV France runs the good ale plant and makes the better brew; bullying Edmund Gwenn manages the other. In a subplot not a million miles from *Romeo and Juliet*, their offspring – lovely Nova Pilbeam (France's daughter) and dapper Peter Coke (Gwenn's son) – fall in love. TS

Nova Pilbeam *Margaret Greenleaf* • Edmund Gwenn *Edward Ironside* • Jimmy O'Dea *Matt Boyle* • Moore Marriott *Geordie* • Graham Moffatt *Albert* • CV France *Tom Greenleaf* • Peter Coke *John Ironside* • Alexander Knox *Saunders* ■ *Dir* Walter Forde • *Scr* Roger MacDougall, Allan Mackinnon, from a story by Ian Dalrymple, Donald Bull

Cheer Up! ★★ U

Musical 1936 · UK · BW · 68mins

The celebrated music hall and screen comedian Stanley Lupino (father of actress/director Ida) stars as a struggling writer/composer trying to get his show put on. While seeking backing from a millionaire, he is mistaken for one himself, saves a young actress (Sally Gray) from an unwelcome admirer and is plunged into a series of complications. This low-budget musical comedy is simplistic and coarse-grained. RK

Stanley Lupino *Tom Denham* • Sally Gray • Roddy Hughes *Dick Dirk* • Gerald Barry *John Harman* • Kenneth Kove *Wilfred Harman* • Wyn Weaver *Mr Carter* • Marjorie Chard *Mrs Carter* ■ *Dir* Leo Mittler • *Scr* Michael Barringer, from a story by Stanley Lupino

Cheers for Miss Bishop ★★★ U

Drama 1941 · US · BW · 94mins

After 50 years as a dedicated schoolteacher, Miss Bishop (Martha Scott) relives her life in flashback at a banquet in her honour. As the tale of her life unfolds, we learn why this attractive woman never married. Directed by Tay Garnett, this poignant weepie co-stars William Gargan as the grocer who carries a hopeless torch for the teacher, while Donald Douglas and Sidney Blackmer play the two men she loved and lost. RK

Martha Scott *Ella Bishop* • William Gargan *Sam Peters* • Edmund Gwenn *Corcoran* • Sterling Holloway *Chris Jensen* • Sidney Blackmer *John Stevens* • Mary Anderson *Amy Saunders* ■ *Dir* Tay Garnett • *Scr* Stephen Vincent Benet, Adelaide Heilbron, Sheridan Gibney, from the novel *Miss Bishop* by Bess Streeter Aldrich

Cheetah ★★★ U

Adventure 1989 · US · Colour · 80mins

Disney decamped to Kenya for what amounts to a children's version of *Born Free*. It's an amiable adventure about two Californian youngsters teaming up with a Masai boy to raise an orphaned cheetah cub, but there are few surprises in the storyline. Where the film does pick up points, however, is in the splendid photography of the Kenyan bush, the fascinating glimpses of the Masai lifestyle and the unsentimental way in which the harsh realities of nature are explained. DP DVD

Keith Coogan *Ted Johnson* • Lucy Deakins *Susan Johnson* • Collin Mothupi *Morogo* • Timothy Landfield *Earl Johnson* • Breon Gorman *Jean Johnson* • Ka Vundla *Kipoin* ■ *Dir* Jeff Blyth • *Scr* Erik Tarloff, John Cotter, Griff Du Rhone, from the book *The Cheetahs* by Alan Caillou • *Cinematographer* Thomas Burstyn

The Chelsea Girls ★★★★

Classic experimental movie
1967 · US · BW and Colour · 210mins

This was the first Andy Warhol film to emerge from the underground and play at art houses. The original version comprised two films projected side by side, with a combined running time of three-and-a-half hours. The version premiered in London in 1968, which still turns up occasionally, is one film lasting two hours. It consists of 12 virtually unedited takes in which such Warhol regulars as Nico, Ingrid Superstar and International Velvet improvise dialogue in rooms at New York's Chelsea Hotel. Many are boring or inaudible, but some of them are real shockers – like the "confession" scene in which "Pope" Ondine becomes genuinely violent. DM

Ondine *"Pope"* • Angelica "Pepper" Davis • Ingrid Superstar • Albert René Ricard *Albert René Ricard* • Mary Might [Mary Woronov] *Hanoi Hanna* • International Velvet [Susan Bottomly] • Brigid Polk • Ed Hood *Ed* • Patrick Flemming • Edie Sedgwick *Edie* • Arthur Loeb • Nico ■ *Dir* Andy Warhol • *Scr* Andy Warhol, Ronald Tavel • *Music* The Velvet Underground

Cherish ★★★

Romantic comedy thriller
2002 · US · Colour · 102mins

This blend of character study and beat-the-clock thriller is a three-act affair, with the opening revealing awkward animator Robin Tunney's lack of social graces, while the finale follows her search for the assailant whose bungled attempt at kidnapping gets her arrested for killing a cop. The central segment, however, is by far the most intriguing, as Tunney develops an edgy relationship with Tim Blake Nelson, her electronic-tagging supervisor. The 1980s pop soundtrack is splendid and the performances are engaging, but the narrative loses its way. DP

Robin Tunney *Zoe* • Tim Blake Nelson *Daly* • Brad Hunt *DJ* • Liz Phair *Brynn* • Jason Priestley *Andrew* • Lindsay Crouse *Therapist* ■ *Dir/Scr* Finn Taylor

Cherokee Strip ★★

Western 1940 · US · BW · 84mins

Richard Dix was no stranger to the Wild West, having earned an Oscar nomination for his role in the 1931 version of *Cimarron*, but he's rather looking his age in this unremarkable story about a square-jawed marshal taking on a gang of desperados. Lesley Selander, best known for his collaborations with Tim Holt and William "Hopalong Cassidy" Boyd, directs with undue fuss. DP

Richard Dix *Dave Morrell* • Florence Rice *Kate Cross* • Victor Jory *Coy Barrett* • Andy Clyde *Tex Crawford* • George E Stone *Abe Gabbert* • Morris Ankrum *Hawk* ■ *Dir* Lesley Selander • *Scr* Norman Houston, Bernard McConville, from a story by Bernard McConville

Cherry Falls ★★★ 18

Horror thriller 1999 · US · Colour · 87mins

A masked maniac is killing only the virgins among the local high-school teens in *Romper Stomper* director Geoffrey Wright's sprightly shocker. Cleverly toying with genre conventions, Wright's unpretentious psycho chiller reverses the "have sex and die" theme of the late 1970s, as the rush to get deflowered at a student organised orgy has the parents' blessing. The brisk script sparkles with quirky characters, off-kilter situations and crisp campus dialogue. AJ. Contains violence, swearing and brief nudity. DVD

Brittany Murphy *Jody Marken* • Michael Biehn *Sheriff Brent Marken* • Gabriel Mann *Kenny Ascott* • Jesse Bradford *Rod Harper* • Jay Mohr *Leonard Marliston* • Douglas Spain *Mark* • Keram Malicki-Sanchez *Timmy* • Natalie Ramsey *Sandy* • Candy Clark *Marge Marken* ■ *Dir* Geoffrey Wright • *Scr* Ken Selden

Cherry, Harry & Raquel ★★★ 18

Sex drama 1969 · US · Colour · 72mins

A seminal trip down mammary lane for Russ Meyer, the "King Leer" of the American soft-core sexploitation industry. The plot has something to do with corrupt sheriff Harry (Charles Napier, a Meyer favourite) trying to keep the lid on his marijuana-smuggling scam when threatened with exposure. Punctuating the flimsy story are sharply-edited bedroom scenes showing Harry, nurse Cherry and mob mistress Raquel in all manner of sexual situations. Witty and compact, this was co-scripted by famed author Tom Wolfe under the pseudonym Thomas J McGowan. AJ. Contains swearing, sexual situations and some violence. DVD

Larissa Ely *Raquel* • Linda Ashton *Cherry* • Charles Napier *Harry* • Bert Santos *Enrique* • Franklin H Bolger [Franklin Bolger] *Mr Franklin* • Astrid Lillimor [Uschi Digard] *Soul* • Michele Grand *Millie* • John Milo *Apache* • Robert Aiken *Tom* • Russ Meyer ■ *Dir* Russ Meyer • *Scr* Russ Meyer, Thomas J McGowan [Tom Wolfe], from a story by Russ Meyer • *Producer* Russ Meyer

The Cherry Orchard ★★★ PG

Drama 1998 · Gr/Cyp/Fr · Colour · 141mins

Anton Chekhov called his play a comedy, but there's nothing comic about this version from Greek director Michael Cacoyannis, which places the emphasis squarely on melancholy. Charlotte Rampling leaves an unhappy affair in Paris for a family estate inhabited by dissolute relatives. There, the only way to stave off bankruptcy is to have the orchard chopped down to make way for money-making new houses. Alan Bates plays Rampling's indecisive brother, Frances de la Tour is a deliciously mad governness, and it all looks stunning. The satire is missing, however, and the film is dour to the point of being lugubrious. TH

Charlotte Rampling *Lyubov Andreyevna (Ranevskaya)* • Alan Bates *Gaev (Leonid Andreyevich)* • Katrin Cartlidge *Varya (Varvara Mihailovna)* • Owen Teale *Lopahin (Yermolai Alexeyevich)* • Frances de la Tour *Charlotta* ■ *Dir* Michael Cacoyannis • *Scr* Michael Cacoyannis, from the play by Anton Chekhov

Cherry 2000 ★★ 15

Science-fiction thriller
1988 · US · Colour · 94mins

Melanie Griffith's career has certainly had its ups and downs, and this falls firmly into the latter category. Set in the year 2017 when sexual partners have been replaced by robot playmates, it follows the travails of David Andrews, who heads off into the desert for spare parts with expert scavenger Griffith when his mechanical dream girl breaks down. Some nice effects can't hide the B-movie performances. JB. Contains violence, swearing, sex scenes.

Melanie Griffith *E Johnson* • David Andrews *Sam Treadwell* • Ben Johnson *Six Finger Jake* • Tim Thomerson *Lester* • Brion James *Stacy* • Pamela Gidley *Cherry 2000* • Harry Carey Jr *Snappy Tom* • Cameron Milzer *Ginger* ■ *Dir* Steve De Jarnatt • *Scr* Michael Almereyda, from a story by Lloyd Fonvielle

Chess Fever ★★★ U

Silent comedy 1925 · USSR · BW · 27mins

Co-directed by Nikolai Shpikovsky, this was the first film by the celebrated Soviet director Vsevolod Pudovkin to secure a release. Attending an international tournament in Moscow, chess master José Capablanca had no idea he was being filmed for a comedy constructed by Pudovkin's teacher and the godfather of montage, Lev Kuleshov. However, there he is playing an unknowing part in reconciling chess fanatic Vladimir Fogel and fiancée Anna Zemtsova following a wedding day mix-up. This is a fond tribute to an inspirational mentor. DP

Vladimir Fogel *The Hero* • Anna Zemtsova *The Heroine* • José R Capablanca *Chess champion* ■ *Dir* Vsevolod I Pudovkin, Nikolai Shpikovsky • *Scr* Nikolai Shpikovsky

The Chess Player ★★★★ U

Silent period drama
1927 · Fr · BW and Tinted · 135mins

Although it boasts sumptuous production values, what most impresses about this period drama is the way in which director Raymond Bernard subtly uses silent imagery to convey exactly what all the characters are feeling. Hiding in a chess-playing automaton to avoid capture, Pierre Blanchar is surprisingly expressive as the Polish rebel who is delivered into the court of Catherine II (Marcelle Charles-Dullin). Banned by the Nazis in 1940, this exquisite film was restored 50 years later by archivist Kevin

Brownlow from prints found in four different countries. DP

Edith Jehanne *Sophie Novinska* • Pierre Blanchar *Boleslas Vorowski* • Pierre Batcheff *Prince Serge Oblomoff* • Charles Dullin *Baron von Kempelen* • Marcelle Charles-Dullin *Catherine II* ■ *Dir* Raymond Bernard • *Scr* Raymond Bernard, Jean-José Frappa, from the novel *Le Joueur d'Échecs* by Henri Dupuy-Mazuel

The Chess Players ★★★★ PG

Historical drama
1977 · Ind · Colour · 115mins

Largely dismissed for its precise symbolism and deliberate pacing, this is one of Satyajit Ray's most undervalued features. Exquisitely re-creating the opulence of Lucknow on the eve of the Indian Mutiny, this historical satire exposes both the ruthless ambition of the imperialists and the indolence of the local rulers. As the chess-playing noblemen who are as uninterested in their families as they are in affairs of state, Sanjeev Kumar and Saeed Jaffrey are deftly comic in their inability to equate their game with the power struggle going on around them. DP. In Hindi and English with subtitles.

Sanjeev Kumar *Mirza* • Saeed Jaffrey *Mir* • Amjad Khan *Wajid Ali Shah* • Richard Attenborough *General Outram* • Shabana Azmi *Mirza's wife* • Farida Jalal *Mir's wife* ■ *Dir* Satyajit Ray • *Scr* Satyajit Ray, from a story by Munshi Premchand

Le Cheval d'Orgeuil ★★★

Period drama 1980 · Fr · Colour · 118mins

Claude Chabrol, no stranger to the provinces, adopts an almost anthropological stance in chronicling the lives of a Breton family in the years preceding the Great War. Yet while he faithfully records the costumes and customs of the indomitable people celebrated in Pierre-Jakez Helias's book, he dilutes their socio-political problems by romanticising their poverty. DP. In French with English subtitles.

Jacques Dufilho *Alain Le Goff* • Bernadette Le Saché *Anne-Marie Le Goff* • François Cluzet *Pierre-Alain Le Goff* • Ronan Hubert *Pierre-Jacques aged 7* • Arnel Hubert *Pierre-Jacques aged 17* ■ *Dir* Claude Chabrol • *Scr* Claude Chabrol, Daniel Boulanger, from the novel by Pierre-Jakez Helias

Cheyenne Autumn ★★★★ U

Epic western 1964 · US · Colour · 124mins

The last western made by the great John Ford is effectively an apology for the many wrongs done by Hollywood to the American Indian. It maintains tremendous dignity in those sections actually dealing with the tragic resettlement of the Cheyenne by the US government, but it is undermined by a tasteless would-be comic central section set in Dodge City. Still, here's Ford's beloved Monument Valley and a distinguished cast headed by the under-rated Richard Widmark in a story of genuine epic scale. TS

Richard Widmark *Captain Thomas Archer* • Carroll Baker *Deborah Wright* • Karl Malden *Captain Oscar Wessels* • James Stewart *Wyatt Earp* • Edward G Robinson *Secretary of the Interior* • Sal Mineo *Red Shirt* • Dolores Del Rio *Spanish Woman* • Ricardo Montalban *Little Wolf* • Gilbert Roland *Dull Knife* • Arthur Kennedy *Doc Holliday* • John Carradine *Major Jeff Blair* ■ *Dir* John Ford • *Scr* James R Webb, from the novel by Mari Sandoz

The Cheyenne Social Club ★★★

Comedy western
1970 · US · Colour · 101mins

Gene Kelly was severely under-rated as a director in his post-MGM period, but his dry and lascivious wit was given full rein in several adult movies, notably *A Guide for the Married Man* and this tame western about a couple of cowboys who inherit a brothel. Since the pair are amiable James Stewart and Henry Fonda, pals since the early 1930s, there's a great deal of affectionate by-play between them. The photography (by western veteran William Clothier) looks good, but some may be deterred by Kelly's rather smutty treatment of the subject matter. TS. Contains swearing, nudity.

James Stewart *John O'Hanlan* • Henry Fonda *Harley Sullivan* • Shirley Jones *Jenny* • Sue Ane Langdon *Opal Ann* • Elaine Devry *Pauline* • Robert Middleton *Barman* • Arch Johnson *Marshal Anderson* • Dabbs Greer *Willowby* ■ *Dir* Gene Kelly • *Scr* James Lee Barrett

Cheyenne Warrior ★★★

Western drama 1994 · US · Colour · 86mins

A pregnant widow and a badly wounded Cheyenne brave team up to survive after a Civil War massacre in a commendable western with an exceptional script. Kelly Preston isn't up to the acting demands made of her by director Mark Griffiths, but Pato Hoffman plays his native American role with a winning conviction well beyond the call of duty in this Roger Corman production. It's when the couple fall in love, and the differences in their respective cultures come into play, that this surprising sleeper takes flight towards a satisfying conclusion. AJ

Kelly Preston *Rebecca Carver* • Pato Hoffmann *Hawk* • Bo Hopkins *Andrews* • Rick Dean *Kearney* • Clint Howard *Otto Nielsen* ■ *Dir* Mark Griffiths • *Scr* Michael B Druxman

Chicago ★★★★ 12

Musical comedy drama
2002 · US/Ger · Colour · 108mins

Renée Zellweger plays Roxie Hart, the ambitious newcomer who dreams of singing and dancing in one of the city's jazz clubs, and Catherine Zeta-Jones is Velma, the established performer. After the shootings of a lover and a faithless husband, they end up in prison, where they find that the publicity surrounding a capital murder case can be a boon to a career in showbusiness. Director Rob Marshall licks the problem of how to film a musical that was presented as vaudeville on stage by re-creating the musical numbers as fantasies in Roxie's head. He loses none of the energy of the stage version nor its dark subtext on the corrupting nature of stardom. Zellweger is perfect casting, while Zeta-Jones sings and high-kicks as if born on Broadway. BP. Contains violence, sexual references. DVD

Catherine Zeta-Jones *Velma Kelly* • Renée Zellweger [Renee Zellweger] *Roxie Hart* • Richard Gere *Billy Flynn* • Queen Latifah *Matron "Mama" Morton* • Christine Baranski *Mary Sunshine* • John C Reilly *Amos Hart* • Taye Diggs *The Band Leader* • Dominic West *Fred Casely* • Lucy Liu *Go-to-Hell Kitty* • Colm Feore *Martin Harrison* ■ *Dir* Rob Marshall • *Scr* Bill Condon, from the musical by Fred Ebb, John Kander, Bob Fosse, from the play by Maurine Dallas Watkins [Maurine Watkins] • *Cinematographer* Dion Beebe • *Production Designer* John Myhre • *Costume Designer* Colleen Atwood • *Editor* Martin Walsh

Chicago Cab ★★★

Drama 1998 · US · Colour · 89mins

Cameos from Gillian Anderson, Julianne Moore and John Cusack are what will draw most viewers to this overlooked day-in-the-life drama. But it'll be Paul Dillon's performance you'll remember: he adroitly captures the range of emotions that a taxi driver experiences on the streets of an often soulless city, as he picks up such diverse passengers as zealous church-goers, a rape victim, smug businessmen, wasted party animals and a pregnant couple in a hurry. He's abetted by an assured sense of location from married directors Mary Cybulski and John Tintori. DP. Contains swearing, drug abuse and a sex scene.

Paul Dillon *Cab driver* • Gillian Anderson *Southside girl* • John Cusack *Scary man* • Moira Harris *Religious mother* • Michael Ironside *Al* • Laurie Metcalf *Ad executive* • Julianne Moore *Distraught woman* • Kevin J O'Connor *Southside guy* • John C Reilly *Steve* ■ *Dir* Mary Cybulski, John Tintori • *Scr* Will Kern, from his play *Hellcab*

Chicago Confidential ★★★

Crime drama 1957 · US · BW · 73mins

In one of those gangster exposés that flourished in the late 1950s, the sincere and honest leader of a trade union is framed for murder by a gambling syndicate that wants to take over his organisation. Brian Keith, Beverly Garland and Elisha Cook Jr manage to hold the interest, while cowboy actor Dick Foran gets down from his horse to play the victimised union leader. It all feels rather predictable now, though. TH

Brian Keith *Jim Fremont* • Beverly Garland *Laura* • Dick Foran *Blane* • Beverly Tyler *Sylvia* • Elisha Cook Jr *Candymouth* • Paul Langton *Jake Parker* • Tony George *Duncan* ■ *Dir* Sidney Salkow • *Scr* Raymond T Marcus [Bernard Gordon], from the story by Hugh King (uncredited) and the book by Jack Lait, Lee Mortimer

Chicago Joe and the Showgirl ★★ 18

Wartime drama based on a true story
1989 · UK · Colour · 98mins

Bernard Rose, who made the Beethoven biopic *Immortal Beloved*, had previously cast his directorial eye over another true story with this tale of an English showgirl (Emily Lloyd, daft and annoying) and an American GI (Kiefer Sutherland, over the top) who become lovers in wartime England and go on a crime and murder spree. However, because no one knows to this day why the pair actually committed the crimes, Rose and his scriptwriter David Yallop have to resort to clichés. JB. Contains swearing.

Kiefer Sutherland *Karl Hulten/"Ricky Allen"* • Emily Lloyd *Elizabeth Maud Jones/"Georgina Grayson"* • Patsy Kensit *Joyce Cook* • Keith Allen *Lenny Bexley* • Liz Fraser *Mrs Evans* ■ *Dir* Bernard Rose • *Scr* David Yallop

The Chicken Chronicles ★★ 18

Comedy 1977 · US · Colour · 90mins

Not a particular highpoint for Phil Silvers in the twilight of his career, though he still comes off best from this cheap teen comedy. Silvers aside, this is notable only for providing a very early film role for Steve Guttenberg, who plays a randy and confused adolescent trying to make sense of his life. It's amusing, but tame compared to the likes of *American Pie*. JF

Phil Silvers *Max Ober* • Ed Lauter *Mr Nastase* • Steve Guttenberg *David Kessler* • Lisa Reeves *Margaret Shaffer* • Meredith Baer *Tracy* • Branscombe Richmond *Mark* • Will Seltzer *Weinstein* ■ *Dir* Francis Simon • *Scr* Paul Diamond, from his novel

Chicken Every Sunday ★★

Comedy 1948 · US · BW · 94mins

A down-home slice of mom's apple pie served over the white picket fence with a side order of regulation family values. Dan Dailey stars as the husband who thinks he can reject honest hard work in favour of ill-judged scheming. As he is taught his life's lesson very slowly, we are left to wonder what a nice all-American "gal" like Celeste Holm is doing with him in the first place. Very dated. SH

Dan Dailey *Jim Hefferen* • Celeste Holm *Emily Hefferen* • Colleen Townsend *Rosemary Hefferen* • Alan Young *Geoffrey Lawson* • Natalie Wood *Ruth* ■ *Dir* George Seaton • *Scr* George Seaton, Valentine Davies, from the play by Julius J Epstein, Philip G Epstein, from a novel by Rosemary Taylor

Chicken Ranch ★★★★ 15

Documentary 1983 · UK/US · Colour · 74mins

This sharp, engaging *cinéma vérité* film from Nick Broomfield and Sandi Sissel looks at society's outsiders with warmth and sympathy. The Chicken Ranch of the title is a legalised brothel in Nevada where the prostitutes live in rundown trailers, waiting for the next planeload of sex tourists to land on the spread's own airstrip. Although the life looks monotonous and depressing, Broomfield and Sissel capture humorous moments, not least in the ongoing battle between sullen sex worker Connie and her boss, the Chicken Ranch's sleazy owner Walter. Other characters include chirpie Mandy, anxious JJ and damaged Claudia, but the film doesn't judge the women or their clients. LF DVD

Dir Nick Broomfield, Sandi Sissel

Chicken Run ★★★★ U

Animated comedy adventure
2000 · US/UK · Colour · 80mins

This feathered pastiche of such PoW classics as *The Great Escape* and *Stalag 17* is an awesome achievement by consummate film-makers Aardman Animation. Rocky (voiced by Mel Gibson), a "lone free ranger" rooster, promises to help the hens in Mr and Mrs Tweedy's high-security egg farm find a way to freedom. The nods to classic film moments are funny and plentiful, the largely British voice cast lends moments of humour and pathos, and the set pieces are exhilarating in their ingenuity and comic élan. DP DVD

Mel Gibson *Rocky* • Julia Sawalha *Ginger* • Imelda Staunton *Bunty* • Jane Horrocks *Babs* • Miranda Richardson *Mrs Tweedy* • Phil Daniels *Fetcher* • Timothy Spall *Nick* ■ *Dir* Nick Park, Peter Lord • *Scr* Karey Kirkpatrick, Jack Rosenthal, from a story by Nick Park, Peter Lord

Chicken Tikka Masala ★★ 15

Romantic comedy
2005 · UK · Colour · 95mins

Sally Bankes's brassy turn isn't enough to save this mediocre comedy, made on a shoestring by first-time director Harmage Singh Kalirai. Chris Bisson plays a young Indian groom-to-be who can't bring himself to tell his parents he's gay and very much in love with Peter Ash. To make matters even more unlikely, misunderstandings lead his family to believe that Bisson is in a relationship with his landlady (Bankes). Contrived and sluggishly paced. DP. Contains swearing.

Chris Bisson *Jimi* • Peter Ash *Jack* • Saeed Jaffrey *Mr CP Chopra* • Sally Bankes *Vanessa* • Zohra Segal *Grandmother* • Jamila Massey *Mrs Asha Chopra* • Jinder Mahal *Simran* • Sushil Chudasama *Ravi Chopra* ■ *Dir* Harmage Singh Kalirai • *Scr* Roopesh Parekh, from an idea by Sanjay Tandon, Rony Ghosh

Chief Crazy Horse ★★

Biographical western
1955 · US · Colour · 86mins

Victor Mature is improbably cast as the great leader of the Sioux nation, but newcomers Ray Danton and Keith Larsen are on hand to add dignity, and veteran John Lund looks good in a cavalry outfit. There's no real thought or style on show here, and the target audience seems to have been a very young one. TS

Victor Mature *Crazy Horse* • Suzan Ball *Black Shawl* • John Lund *Major Twist* • Ray Danton

Little Big Man • Keith Larsen *Flying Hawk* • Paul Guilfoyle (1) *Worm* • David Janssen *Lieutenant Cartwright* • Robert Warwick *Spotted Tail* ■ *Dir* George Sherman • *Scr* Franklin Coen, Gerald Drayson Adams, from a story by Gerald Drayson Adams

C

Un Chien Andalou ★★★★★ 15

Silent experimental classic
1928 · Fr · BW · 15mins

How best to recommend a film that runs for less than 20 minutes, with no discernible plot, and that opens with one of cinema's most abidingly shocking sequences? The term "surreal" is nowadays used as a critical cover-all, but in this case, director Luis Buñuel and co-writer Salvador Dali were writing the book, and this is still regarded, rightly, as a cinematic landmark. Search for deeper meaning with due care and attention, or simply sit back and enjoy the abandon with which this juxtaposes ideas and images, sometimes jarringly, occasionally as visual rhymes, such as the cloud slicing across the moon that becomes a razor blade swiped across a woman's eyeball (still the film's greatest coup). AC DVD

Pierre Batcheff *Young man* • Simone Mareuil *Girl* • Luis Buñuel *Man with razor* • Salvador Dali *Marist priest* • Jaime Miravilles *Seminarist* ■ *Dir* Luis Buñuel • *Scr* Luis Buñuel, Salvador Dali

La Chienne ★★★★

Romantic drama 1931 · Fr · BW · 100mins

Unhappily married cashier and part-time artist Michel Simon becomes infatuated with prostitute Janie Marèze, and is callously exploited by her and her violent pimp Georges Flament. This moral fable, in which Simon inexorably slips down the criminal scale towards murder, was filmed by Jean Renoir on the streets of Montmartre – an influential break from the usual studio sets – and still makes for compelling viewing. Simon gives a superbly expressive performance; the film was remade in Hollywood by Fritz Lang as *Scarlet Street*. AT. In French with English subtitles.

Michel Simon *Maurice* • Janie Marèze *Lulu* • Georges Flament *André* ■ *Dir* Jean Renoir • *Scr* Jean Renoir, André Girard, from a novel by Georges de la Fouchardière

Les Chiens ★★★ 15

Psychological thriller
1978 · Fr · Colour · 99mins

Alain Jessua directs this brave and intriguing movie, a severe portrait of life in an impersonal environment depicted as a microcosm of a fascist state. In a town surrounded by mountains, a young doctor sets up practice and finds that he is treating a number of severe wounds. When the town's mayor is murdered he and his girlfriend try to escape the inhabitants, who have trained vicious dogs to subdue guest workers. While at times confusing and not an easy watch, this is still original and thought provoking. BB. In French with English subtitles.

Gérard Depardieu *Morel* • Victor Lanoux *Dr Henri Féret* • Nicole Calfan *Elisabeth Barrault* • Pierre Vernier *Gauthier* • Fanny Ardant *Nurse* ■ *Dir* Alain Jessua • *Scr* André Ruellan, Alain Jessua

Le Chignon d'Olga ★★★★ 15

Comedy drama
2002 · Fr/Bel · Colour · 92mins

Jérôme Bonnell's debut feature combines the idealism of youth with mundane reality without romanticising or demeaning either. The story charts teenager Hubert Benhamdine's growing obsession with glamorous bookshop assistant Delphine Rollin, which serves as an emotional buffer to the harsher reality of the recent death of his mother that has also had a traumatic effect on his father (Serge Riaboukine) and sister (Florence Loiret Caille). It's a literate, compassionate study of how to survive both the extraordinary and the everyday. DP. In French with English subtitles. DVD

Hubert Benhamdine *Julien* • Nathalie Boutefeu *Alice* • Serge Riabouklne *Gilles* • Florence Loiret Caille *Emma* • Antoine Goldet *Basile* • Delphine Rollin *Olga* • Valérie Stroh *Nicole* ■ *Dir/Scr* Jérôme Bonnell

Chihwaseon (Drunk on Women and Poetry) ★★★★ 15

Biographical drama
2002 · S Kor · Colour · 116mins

Im Kwon-taek shared the Director's prize at Cannes for this stately study of Jang Seung-up, the self-taught peasant who became Oh-won, the most important Korean artist of the late-19th century. Choi Min-sik gives a burly performance as the bibulous, womanising non-conformist who embraced external influences, supported the outlawed reform party, loved a persecuted Catholic and defied dignitaries and monarchs alike. Handsomely mounted and packed with incident and transient characters, this is complex and compelling. But the real fascination lies in watching Oh-won's breathtaking imagery take shape on the fragile roll paper, particularly when the black outlines are emblazoned with dramatic colour. DP. In Korean with English subtitles. DVD

Choi Min-sik *Jang Seung-up, Oh-won* • You Ho-jeong *Mae-hyang* • Ahn Sung-kee *Kim Byung-moon* • Kim Yeo-jin *Jin-hong* • Son Ye-jin *So-woon* ■ *Dir* Im Kwon-taek • *Scr* Kim Young-oak, Im Kwon-taek

Child in the House ★★★ U

Drama 1956 · UK · BW · 87mins

With her mother in hospital and her father (Stanley Baker) on the run, 11-year-old Mandy Miller is sent to live with her sniffy aunt Phyllis Calvert and rigid uncle Eric Portman. Her presence has an unexpected effect on all concerned. A modest British-made drama, co-directed by Cy Endfield (*Zulu*) and jam-packed with such stalwarts of the acting profession as Dora Bryan, Joan Hickson and Alfie Bass. Good for a tear or two. RK

Phyllis Calvert *Evelyn Acheson* • Eric Portman *Henry Acheson* • Stanley Baker *Stephen Lorimer* • Mandy Miller *Elizabeth Lorimer* • Dora Bryan *Cassie* • Joan Hickson *Cook* • Victor Maddern *Bert* • Alfie Bass *Ticket collector* ■ *Dir* C Raker Endfield [Cy Endfield], Charles de Lautour • *Scr* C Raker Endfield [Cy Endfield], from the novel by Janet McNeill

A Child Is Waiting ★★★

Drama 1962 · US · BW · 104mins

After John Cassavetes had shot this drama, producer Stanley Kramer fired him and edited it himself, turning what was reputedly a rather tough movie into a sentimental one that tub-thumps its message about the care of an autistic child, played by Bruce Ritchey. Burt Lancaster and Judy Garland star as the child's psychologists, and Gena Rowlands (Cassavetes's wife) and Steven Hill play his parents. Often powerful and always well acted, it was filmed in 1962 but went unreleased in Britain until 1966. AT

Burt Lancaster *Dr Matthew Clark* • Judy Garland *Jean Hansen* • Gena Rowlands *Sophie Widdicombe* • Steven Hill *Ted Widdicombe* • Bruce Ritchey *Reuben Widdicombe* • Gloria McGehee *Mattie* • Paul Stewart *Goodman* ■ *Dir* John Cassavetes • *Scr* Abby Mann, from his story

Child of Divorce ★★★

Drama 1946 · US · BW · 62mins

This is a poignant B-movie, given strength and focus by Sharyn Moffet's performance as a little girl whose parents separate. It is the feature debut of Richard Fleischer, who went on to direct such fine films as *Compulsion* and *10 Rillington Place*. Only an hour long, this is a good deal more touching than many a bigger film on the subject. TS

Sharyn Moffett *Bobby* • Regis Toomey *Ray* • Madge Meredith *Joan* • Walter Reed *Michael* • Una O'Connor *Nora* • Doris Merrick *Louise* ■ *Dir* Richard O Fleischer [Richard Fleischer] • *Scr* Lillie Hayward, from the play *Wednesday's Child* by Leopold Atlas

The Children ★★

Drama 1990 · UK/W Ger · Colour · 91mins

Previously filmed in 1929 as *The Marriage Playground*, Edith Wharton's novel is here respectfully adapted by playwright Timberlake Wertenbaker. Director Tony Palmer assembles an accomplished supporting cast around Ben Kingsley, who gives a typically sensitive performance as the Europe-based engineer whose plans to marry widow Kim Novak are waylaid by his growing obsession with Siri Neal. Though pictorially resplendent and played with precision, the film is technically naive and dramatically unsatisfying. DP

Ben Kingsley *Martin Boyne* • Kim Novak *Rose Sellars* • Geraldine Chaplin *Joyce Wheater* • Joe Don Baker *Cliff Wheater* • Siri Neal *Judith* • Britt Ekland *Lady Wrench* • Donald Sinden *Lord Wrench* • Karen Black *Sybil Lullmer* • Rupert Graves *Gerald Omerod* • Rosemary Leach *Miss Scope* • Terence Rigby *Duke of Mendip* • Robert Stephens *Dobree* ■ *Dir* Tony Palmer • *Scr* Timberlake Wertenbaker, from the novel by Edith Wharton

The Children Are Watching Us ★★★★

Drama 1943 · It · BW · 85mins

Somewhat overshadowed by the masterpieces that followed, this updating of Cesare Giulio Viola's novel, *Pricò*, marked director Vittorio De Sica and screenwriter Cesare Zavattini's first excursion into the territory that would, ultimately, be called neorealism. Although it never consistently avoids sentiment, the authentic approach to the disintegrating family's domestic plight is handled with surprising sensitivity, considering the maudlin tone of De Sica's earlier melodramas. His unpatronising direction of young Luciano De Ambrosis, as the toddler embroiled in bourgeois businessman Emilio Cigoli and adulterous Isa Pola's marital strife, is particularly impressive. DP. In Italian with English subtitles.

Luciano De Ambrosis *Pricò* • Isa Pola *Ines, his mother* • Emilio Cigoli *Andrea, his father* • Adriano Rimoldi *Roberto* • Giovanna Cigoli *Agnese* ■ *Dir* Vittorio De Sica • *Scr* Vittorio De Sica, Adolfo Franci, Gherarado Gherhardi, Margherita Maglione, Cesare Giulio Viola, Cesare Zavattini, from the novel *Pricò* by Cesare Giulio Viola

Children Galore ★★ U

Comedy 1954 · UK · BW · 60mins

In launching the famous Hammer horror cycle, Terence Fisher secured his place in history. However, this early comedy did nothing for his reputation even though, with its quaint country setting, it has a vaguely Ealing feel. By deciding to build a cottage for the family with the most grandchildren, squire Peter Evan Thomas sends the village of Tussock into turmoil, with neighbours jeopardising decades of friendship as the search for cute kids intensifies. DP

Eddie Byrne *Zacky Jones* • Marjorie Rhodes *Ada Jones* • June Thorburn *Milly Ark* • Peter Evan Thomas *Lord Redscarfe* • Marjorie Hume *Lady Redscarfe* • Lucy Griffiths *Miss Prescott* ■ *Dir* Terence Fisher • *Scr* John Bonnet, Emery Bonnet, Peter Plaskett

Children of a Lesser God ★★★★ 15

Romantic drama
1986 · US · Colour · 114mins

This adaptation of Mark Medoff's poignant play, about a woman for whom life's challenge is the fact she cannot hear, picks up even more resonance in its understanding of the casual hurts we inflict upon the hearing-impaired. William Hurt is subtly complex as the speech therapist attracted to his pupil, but it's the first-time performance by deaf actress Marlee Matlin that brilliantly articulates both a character and a condition. She deservedly won an Oscar for her powerful portrayal. TH. Contains swearing and nudity. DVD

William Hurt *James Leeds* • Marlee Matlin *Sarah Norman* • Piper Laurie *Mrs Norman* • Philip Bosco *Dr Curtis Franklin* • Allison Gompf *Lydia* • John F Cleary *Johnny* • Philip Holmes *Glen* • Georgia Ann Cline *Cheryl* • William D Byrd *Danny* • Frank Carter Jr *Tony* • John Limnidis *William* • Bob Hiltermann *Orin* ■ *Dir* Randa Haines • *Scr* Hesper Anderson, Mark Medoff, from the play by Mark Medoff

Children of Chance ★★

Drama 1949 · UK · BW · 100mins

Set, and shot, on the isle of Ischia, this turgid melodrama stars the lovely Patricia Medina in a tale of a racketeer's ill-gotten gains being put to good use by a priest to fund an orphanage. Well intentioned, but a long way from the neorealist roots of director Luigi Zampa. TS

Patricia Medina *Agostina* • Manning Whiley *Don Andrea* • Yvonne Mitchell *Australia* • Barbara Everest *Francesca* • Eliot Makeham *Vicar* • George Woodbridge *Butcher* • Frank Tickle *Mayor* • Eric Pohlmann *Sergeant* ■ *Dir* Luigi Zampa • *Scr* Piero Tellini, Michael Medwin, from a story by Piero Tellini

Children of Hannibal ★★★

Crime comedy 1998 · It · Colour · 89mins

Italian comedy doesn't always travel well, but this unconventional buddy movie has much to recommend it. Trading off their physical dissimilarity, unemployed Silvio Orlando and disillusioned executive Diego Abatantuono make an inspired team as they head to the photogenic southern region of Puglia with the proceeds of a bank robbery. In between experiments with camera speeds, framing techniques and transitional devices, director Davide Ferrario slips some gentle social comment into the engaging comedy. DP. An Italian language film.

Diego Abatantuono *Tommaso* • Silvio Orlando *Domenico* • Valentina Cervi *Rita* • Ugo Conti *Ermes* • Flavio Insinna *Orfeo* ■ *Dir* Davide Ferrario • *Scr* Diego Abatantuono, Davide Ferrario, from a story by Diego Abatantuono, Davide Ferrario, Sergio Rubini

The Children of Heaven ★★★★

Comedy drama 1997 · Iran · Colour · 88mins

This delightful comedy from Majid Majidi, a key member of the younger generation of Iranian film-makers, proved something of a favourite on the festival circuit. Like *The White Balloon* and *The Apple*, it confirms the Iranian industry's genius for movies about children, with Mohammad Amir Naji and Mir Farrokh Hashemian wondrously natural as the impoverished siblings who try to disguise the loss of the latter's shoes by sharing a pair for school. This enchants as much as it entertains. DP. A Farsi language film.

Mohammad Amir Naji *Ali* • Mir Farrokh Hashemian *Zahra* • Bahareh Seddiqi • Nasifeh Jafar Mohammadi *Roya* • Fereshte Sarabandi *Ali's mother* • Kamal Mirkarimi *Principal* • Bezhad Rafi'im *Coach* ■ *Dir/Scr* Majid Majidi

The Children of Sanchez ★

Drama 1978 · US/Mex · Colour · 126mins

This is a miserably dull drama about a poor Mexican trying to keep his small army of offspring from starving. Anthony Quinn is as professional as ever, but the real interest lies in the role of Grandma, played by Dolores Del Rio. Trivia gatherers may like to know that she was silent movie star Ramon Navarro's second cousin, and that she retired shortly afterwards. FL

Anthony Quinn *Jesus Sanchez* • Lupita Ferrer *Consuelo* • Dolores Del Rio *Grandma* • Stathis Giallelis *Roberto* • Lucia Mendez *Marta* • Duncan Quinn *Manuel* • Katy Jurado *Chata* • Carmen Montejo *Aunt Guadalupe* ■ *Dir* Hall Bartlett • *Scr* Cesare Zavattini, Hall Bartlett, from the novel by Oscar Lewis

Children of the Corn ★ 18

Horror 1984 · US · Colour · 93mins

Adapted from a short story in Stephen King's *Night Shift* anthology, this is a lame horror yarn padded to feature length with tepid special effects and ludicrous dialogue. Travellers Peter Horton and Linda Hamilton narrowly avoid being sacrificed to the "Corn God" in a rural Nebraska community, held in a grip of pagan terror by a 12-year-old preacher. Once past the atmospheric opening sequence – kids slaughtering their parents in a café – it's downhill all the way for this tacky nightmare. AJ [video] DVD

Peter Horton *Dr Burt Stanton* • Linda Hamilton *Vicky Baxter* • John Franklin *Isaac* • Courtney Gains *Malachai* • RG Armstrong *Diehl* • Robby Kiger *Job* • Annemarie McEvoy *Sarah* • John Philbin *Amos* • Julie Maddalena *Rachel* ■ *Dir* Fritz Kiersch • *Scr* George Goldsmith, from the short story by Stephen King

Children of the Corn II: the Final Sacrifice ★★ 18

Horror 1993 · US · Colour · 89mins

Tabloid journalists gather in Gatlin, Nebraska, to unravel the cause of the original massacre just as "He who walks behind the Rows" returns to manipulate the community's children into murdering again. Director David F Price's modestly mounted but efficient slice of horror is a quantum leap over the first film in terms of acting quality, homicidal set pieces and effective shock tactics. The endless nosebleed is a highlight. AJ [video] DVD

Terence Knox *John Garrett* • Paul Scherrer *Danny Garrett* • Ryan Bollman *Micah Balding* • Christie Clark *Lacey Hellerstar* • Rosalind Allen *Angela Casual* ■ *Dir* David F Price • *Scr* Al Katz, Gilbert Adler, from the short story *Children of the Corn* by Stephen King

Children of the Corn III: Urban Harvest ★★★ 18

Horror 1995 · US · Colour · 88mins

A refugee from the original corn cult of killer kids devises a plan to take their doctrine of dread to Chicago before going global. The enterprising second sequel to the Stephen King-based tale of terror is easily the best of the series, because director James Hickox (brother of horror veteran Anthony) knows how to use his low budget without sacrificing credibility or top-notch scares. After this high point, three more dismal sequels followed. AJ [video] DVD

Ron Melendez *Joshua* • Jim Metzler *William Porter* • Daniel Cerny *Eli* • Nancy Grahn *Alice* • Michael Ensign *Father Frank* ■ *Dir* James DR Hickox [James Hickox] • *Scr* Dode B Levenson, from the short story *Children of the Corn* by Stephen King

Children of the Damned ★★

Science-fiction thriller
1964 · UK · BW · 80mins

In this less-than-thrilling sequel to *Village of the Damned*, six children of assorted nationalities with deadly extra-sensory powers escape from their respective London embassies. The alien kids demonstrate their lethal gifts against the armed forces who are trying to destroy them in the name of world security. However, despite a literate script and thoughtful direction by Anton M Leader, the film quickly runs out of steam. AJ

Ian Hendry *Colonel Tom Lewellin* • Alan Badel *Dr David Neville* • Barbara Ferris *Susan Eliot* • Alfred Burke *Colin Webster* • Sheila Allen *Diana Looran* • Clive Powell *Paul* ■ *Dir* Anton M Leader • *Scr* John Briley, from the novel *The Midwich Cuckoos* by John Wyndham

The Children of the Marshland ★★★★ PG

Period comedy drama
1998 · Fr · Colour · 110mins

Fans of such art house classics as *Jean de Florette* will warm to this gentle portrait of rural France in the early 1930s. A sort of Gallic *Last of the Summer Wine*, Jean Becker's comedy disappointingly skirts around its darker themes. However, there's plenty of nostalgic pleasure to be had from the adventures of shell-shocked soldier Jacques Gamblin, disgruntled peasant Jacques Villeret, world-weary millionaire Michel Serrault and timid bachelor André Dussollier. Complete with a cameo from Eric Cantona, this may be lightweight and sentimental, but it's also undeniably cinematic. DP. In French with English subtitles. [video]

Jacques Villeret *Riton* • Jacques Gamblin *Garris* • André Dussollier *Amedée* • Michel Serrault *Pépé* • Isabelle Carré *Marie* • Eric Cantona *Jo Sardi* • Suzanne Flon *Old Cri Cri* ■ *Dir* Jean Becker • *Scr* Sébastien Japrisot, from the novel *Les Enfants du Marais* by Georges Montforez

Children of the Revolution ★★★★

Political comedy drama
1996 · Aus · Colour · 102mins

This classy black comedy from Australia boasts the combined talents of Judy Davis, Sam Neill, Rachel Griffiths and Geoffrey Rush. Joan (Davis) is a die-hard Stalinist living in 1940s Oz. After writing weekly letters to the great man, she ends up at the 1952 Party Congress and subsequently beds him. Their son (Richard Roxburgh) grows up to become a political agitator who brings the Australian government into a state of crisis. Director Peter Duncan deftly mixes newsreel footage, montage sequences and musical comedy, with hysterical results. LH

Judy Davis *Joan Fraser* • Sam Neill *Nine* • Richard Roxburgh *Joe* • Rachel Griffiths *Anna* • F Murray Abraham *Stalin* • Russell Kiefel *Barry* • John Gaden *Dr Wilf Wilke* • Geoffrey Rush *Zachary Welch* ■ *Dir/Scr* Peter Duncan

The Children of Theatre Street ★★★ U

Documentary
1977 · US/USSR · Colour · 92mins

It needed to be a special assignment to lure the former Grace Kelly out of cinematic retirement, and Robert Dornhelm and Earle Mack's fly-on-the-wall study of the Kirov Ballet School is exactly that. While recalling such great names of the past as Nijinsky, Pavlova, Nureyev and Baryshnikov, this Oscar-nominated documentary is also keen to concentrate on the stars of tomorrow as it follows three aspiring students through their stringent training. The reverential enthusiasm of Princess Grace's narration should fire the imagination of younger viewers, especially those already hooked on ballet's romantic elegance. DP. In English and Russian with subtitles.

Princess Grace of Monaco [Grace Kelly] *Narrator* ■ *Dir* Robert Dornhelm, Earle Mack • *Scr* Beth Gutcheon (uncredited)

The Children's Hour ★★★ 12

Drama 1961 · US · BW · 103mins

Retitled *The Loudest Whisper* in the UK, this screen remake of the notorious Lillian Hellman play is emphatically not for youngsters. Director William Wyler had filmed it before as *These Three* back in 1936 and, despite being shorn of its overt lesbian theme, the earlier version has considerably more power than this rather quiet and bloodless drama. Perhaps a few years on from 1961 the lesbian elements could have been properly dealt with, but here their muting harms the movie and both Audrey Hepburn and Shirley MacLaine fail to convince. James Garner, though, is very impressive, particularly in his weeping scene: many actors could not have done as well. TS DVD

Audrey Hepburn *Karen Wright* • Shirley MacLaine *Martha Dobie* • James Garner *Dr Joe Cardin* • Miriam Hopkins *Lily Mortar* • Fay Bainter *Amelia Tilford* • Karen Balkin *Mary Tilford* • Veronica Cartwright *Rosalie* ■ *Dir* William Wyler • *Scr* John Michael Hayes, from the play by Lillian Hellman

The Children's Midsummer Night's Dream ★★★ U

Comedy drama fantasy
2001 · UK · Colour · 113mins

Opening in a charming puppet theatre and performed among quaintly contrived woodland nooks, Christine Edzard's ambitious take on Shakespeare is the best school production you're ever likely to see. But, as a feature film, it lacks the immediacy that might have made it magical. The main problem is that the youngsters rarely seem comfortable with the poetry, their "recital by rote" style exposed by luminaries such as Derek Jacobi, who provide the voices of the marionettes. Yet its honesty and homely ingenuity render this an impossible film to dislike. DP [video]

Derek Jacobi • Frances Barber ■ *Dir* Christine Edzard • *Scr* from the play *A Midsummer Night's Dream* by William Shakespeare

Child's Play ★★★ U

Satirical comedy 1954 · UK · BW · 68mins

In this energetic film, which plays upon the 1950s' anxiety regarding nuclear science, the son of a scientist working at an atomic research plant invents radioactive popcorn. Margaret Thompson directs this quaintly backward look at the nuclear age, while Mona Washbourne heads a cast of otherwise unfamiliar names. Don Sharp, who wrote the original story, had a prolific career as director, screenwriter and occasional producer. RK

Mona Washbourne *Miss Goslett* • Peter Martyn *PC Parker* • Dorothy Alison *Margery Chappell* • Ingeborg Wells *Lea Blotz* • Carl Jaffe *Carl Blotz* • Ballard Berkeley *Dr Nightingale* • Joan Young *Mrs Chizzler* ■ *Dir* Margaret Thompson • *Scr* Peter Blackmore, from a story by Don Sharp

Child's Play ★★

Drama 1972 · US · Colour · 99mins

This melodramatic nonsense from Sidney Lumet is set in a Roman Catholic boarding school for boys, where hateful teacher James Mason is being victimised and discredited by fellow master Robert Preston. Despite having a mother dying of cancer and a stockpile of pornographic pin-ups, Mason becomes an almost heroic figure when set against the bluff and blustering Preston. The latter won his role after Marlon Brando turned it down. TH

James Mason *Jerome Malley* • Robert Preston *Joseph Dobbs* • Beau Bridges *Paul Reis* • Ronald Weyand *Father Mozian* • Charles White *Father Griffin* • David Rounds *Father Penny* • Kate Harrington *Mrs Carter* • Jamie Alexander *Sheppard* ■ *Dir* Sidney Lumet • *Scr* Leon Prochnik, from the play by Robert Marasco

Child's Play ★★★ 15

Horror 1988 · US · Colour · 83mins

Six-year old Alex Vincent's must-have "Good Guy" doll, Chucky, is possessed by the soul of dead serial killer Brad Dourif and goes on a wisecracking murder spree to get revenge on the cop (Chris Sarandon) who put him away. A steady stream of standard scares is dragged from a thinly-stretched, formula slasher plot, thanks to panache beyond the call of duty from director Tom Holland. Novelty value and great special effects made this dummy run a big hit. AJ [video] DVD

Catherine Hicks *Karen Barclay* • Chris Sarandon *Mike Norris* • Alex Vincent *Andy Barclay* • Brad Dourif *Charles Lee Ray* • Dinah Manoff *Maggie Peterson* • Tommy Swerdlow *Jack Santos* • Jack Colvin *Dr Ardmore* • Neil Giuntoli *Eddie Caputo* ■ *Dir* Tom Holland • *Scr* Don Mancini, Tom Holland, John Lafia, from a story by Don Mancini

Child's Play 2 ★★ 15

Horror 1990 · US · Colour · 80mins

Chucky, the living "Good Guy" doll, returns to continue stalking his former owner (Alex Vincent) and terrorise his new foster parents (Jenny Agutter and Gerrit Graham). Still nobody believes the kid's possessed Action Man story – until two seconds before they're brutally murdered, of course – resulting in a predictable, mean-spirited rehash of the original concept. A few neat touches lighten the load. AJ [video]

Alex Vincent *Andy Barclay* • Jenny Agutter *Joanne Simpson* • Gerrit Graham *Phil Simpson* • Christine Elise *Kyle* • Brad Dourif *Chucky* • Grace Zabriskie *Grace Poole* ■ *Dir* John Lafia • *Scr* Don Mancini

Child's Play 3 ★ 18

Horror 1991 · US · Colour · 85mins

Brought back to life when the "Good Guy" doll assembly line is reactivated, Chucky – the plastic Terminator – traces his former owner (Justin Whalin, taking over from moppet Alex Vincent) to military school and starts decimating the student body. Bottom-of-the-barrel, slice-and-dice nonsense. This entry in the series is now infamous for being cited in the tabloid frenzy surrounding the Jamie Bulger murder case in Britain. *Bride of Chucky*, followed in 1998. AJ [video]

Justin Whalin *Andy Barclay* • Perrey Reeves *DeSilva* • Jeremy Sylvers *Tyler* • Travis Fine *Shelton* • Dean Jacobson *Whitehurst* • Brad Dourif *Chucky* • Peter Haskell *Sullivan* ■ *Dir* Jack Bender • *Scr* Don Mancini

Chill Factor ★★ 15

Comedy action thriller
1999 · US · Colour · 97mins

Just three years after winning an Oscar for *Jerry Maguire*, Cuba Gooding Jr turned up in this bad rip-off of *Speed*. Diner employee Skeet Ulrich hijacks the truck of ice cream delivery driver Gooding Jr in order to transport a secret chemical weapon that will annihilate everything for miles around if its temperature rises above 50 degrees. Both stars are totally wasted in this routine thriller. ST [video] DVD

Cuba Gooding Jr *Arlo* • Skeet Ulrich *Tim Mason* • Peter Firth *Captain Andrew Brynner* • David Paymer *Doctor Richard Long* • Hudson Leick *Vaughn* ■ *Dir* Hugh Johnson • *Scr* Drew Gitlin, Mike Cheda

Chiller ★★★ 15

Horror 1985 · US · Colour · 87mins

In this better-than-average TV movie from *Scream* director Wes Craven, Michael Beck is thawed out after being cryogenically frozen for ten years. Alas, a machine malfunction during his hibernation causes him to lose his soul and start acting in strange ways as he climbs the corporate ladder. A slim idea is elaborately carried off by Craven, who keeps the suspense mounting and makes great use of first-class make-up effects. AJ

Michael Beck *Miles Creighton* • Beatrice Straight *Marion Creighton* • Paul Sorvino *Rev Penny* • Jill Schoelen *Stacey* • Dick O'Neill *Clarence Beeson* • Laura Johnson *Leigh* ■ *Dir* Wes Craven • *Scr* JD Feigelson

Chilly Scenes of Winter ★★★

Drama 1979 · US · Colour · 98mins

Originally released as *Head over Heels*, this was something of a disappointment after Joan Micklin Silver's earlier directorial efforts, including *Hester Street* and *Between the Lines*. As a take on modern American love, it has a ring of authenticity. In its keenness to avoid any kind of romantic cliché, however, the story ends up having too little heart, and we're left with John Heard's memories of an idyllic past and his increasingly irritating entreaties to Mary Beth Hurt to give it another try. DP

John Heard *Charles* • Mary Beth Hurt *Laura* • Peter Riegert *Sam* • Kenneth McMillan *Pete* • Gloria Grahame *Clara* • Nora Heflin *Betty* • Jerry Hardin *Patterson* • Tarah Nutter *Susan* • Griffin Dunne *Dr Mark* ■ *Dir* Joan Micklin Silver • *Scr* Joan Micklin Silver, from the novel *Head over Heels* by Ann Beattie

The Chiltern Hundreds ★★★ U

Comedy 1949 · UK · BW · 84mins

Although John Paddy Carstairs directed several Norman Wisdom vehicles, this wry political satire is his most accomplished picture. Adapted by William Douglas Home from his own play, the film takes its title from the nominal office MPs take when they wish to resign. Recalling the gentle class comedies produced by Ealing, the election battle between an earl's socialist son (David Tomlinson) and his true blue butler (Cecil Parker) is full of sly observations. DP

Cecil Parker *Benjamin Beecham* • AE Matthews *Lord Lister* • David Tomlinson *Tony, Viscount Pym* • Lana Morris *Bessie Sykes* • Marjorie Fielding *Lady Lister* • Joyce Carey *Lady Caroline* • Tom Macauley *Jack Cleghorn* ■ *Dir* John Paddy Carstairs • *Scr* William Douglas Home, Patrick Kirwan, from the play by William Douglas Home

Chimes at Midnight ★★★ U

Historical comedy drama
1966 · Swi/Sp · BW · 115mins

Drawing his material from five Shakespeare plays, as well as Raphael Holinshed's chronicles, writer/producer/director Orson Welles focuses on Falstaff's relationship with Prince Hal, later Henry V (Keith Baxter), who eventually deserts his rambunctious friend and mentor for kingly responsibility. This is a typical Wellesian venture, years in the making owing to its maker's characteristic difficulties with funding. The result is a technically uneven film that alternately irritates and dazzles. RK

Orson Welles *Falstaff* • Keith Baxter *Prince Hal, later King Henry V* • John Gielgud *Henry IV* • Margaret Rutherford *Mistress Quickly* • Jeanne Moreau *Doll Tearsheet* • Norman Rodway *Henry Percy, "Hotspur"* • Marina Vlady *Kate Percy* • Fernando Rey *Worcester* • Ralph Richardson *Narrator* ■ *Dir* Orson Welles • *Scr* Orson Welles, from *The Chronicles of England* by Raphael Holinshed, from the plays by William Shakespeare

China ★★

Second World War drama
1943 · US · BW · 78mins

An American trader, in China to make money, changes his priorities after the bombing of Pearl Harbor and joins a band of Chinese guerrillas. Directed by John Farrow, an expert manipulator of emotions, and starring Alan Ladd as the grimly determined hero who manages to blow up the Japanese forces almost singlehandedly, this patriotic wartime flag-waver feels laughably dated now. RK

Loretta Young *Carolyn Grant* • Alan Ladd *Mr Jones* • William Bendix *Johnny Sparrow* • Philip Ahn *Lin Cho* • Iris Wong *Kwan Su* • Victor Sen Yung *Lin Wei* • Marianne Quon *Tan Ying* • Jessie Tai Sing *Student* ■ *Dir* John Farrow • *Scr* Frank Butler, from the play *Fourth Brother* by Archibald Forbes

China Clipper ★★ U

Drama 1936 · US · BW · 89mins

Former pilot Pat O'Brien sacrifices friends and marriage for an obsession to start a trans-Pacific airline, flying from America to China. The now defunct Pan Am gets a big screen credit for assistance, with the picture clearly intended as an advert for them, and the script is by Frank "Spig" Wead, an aviation hero later played by John Wayne in *The Wings of Eagles*. The wonky flying scenes and dime-novel melodramas on the ground don't help, though. AT

Pat O'Brien *Dave Logan* • Beverly Roberts *Jean Logan* • Ross Alexander (1) *Tom Collins* • Humphrey Bogart *Hap Stuart* • Marie Wilson *Sunny Avery* • Henry B Walthall *Dad Brunn* ■ *Dir* Raymond Enright [Ray Enright] • *Scr* Frank Wead

China Corsair ★★ U

Adventure 1951 · US · BW · 67mins

A bargain basement adventure in which various shady characters are after priceless antiques on an island off the coast of China. Our hero is Jon Hall, while Lisa Ferraday is the pretty heroine engaged to rascally Ron Randell, who uses her to get the jewels. Watch out for an early appearance from Ernest Borgnine. AT

Jon Hall *McMillen* • Lisa Ferraday *Tamara* • Ron Randell *Paul Lowell* • Douglas Kennedy *Frenchie* • Ernest Borgnine *Hu Chang* • John Dehner *Pedro* • Marya Marco *Lotus* ■ *Dir* Ray Nazarro • *Scr* Harold R Greene

China Cry ★★★

Historical drama
1990 · Tai/US · Colour · 101mins

China's cultural upheaval in the 1950s meant no culture and a great deal of repression. This devotedly earnest retelling of a true story shows how a privileged girl witnessed some of Chairman Mao's atrocities before she escaped to Hong Kong, moving from there to the United States, where she has now settled. Julia Nickson-Soul portrays the girl as more than just a passive spectator, but the film remains too aloof from a nation's anguish for it to be anything more than just a harrowing tale that's moderately well-told. TH. Contains violence.

Julia Nickson-Soul *Sung Neng Yee* • Russell Wong *Lam Cheng Shen* • James Shigeta *Dr Sung* • France Nuyen *Mrs Sung* • Philip Tan *Colonel Cheng* • Elizabeth Sung *Interrogator* • Bennett Ohta *Labour camp doctor* • Daphne Cheung *Chung Shing* ■ *Dir* James F Collier • *Scr* James F Collier, from the book by Nora Lam [Sung Neng Yee], Irene Burke

China Doll ★★

Second World War romance
1958 · US · BW · 99mins

This out-and-out tearjerker marked the return of director Frank Borzage, Hollywood's most dedicated sentimentalist, after ten years in the McCarthyite wilderness. Alas, this tale of an American air force officer in China who marries his housekeeper is so overlaid with sugary sentimentality that it felt dated even in the 1950s. Worth a look, though, for fans of its male star, Victor Mature. RK

Victor Mature *Cliff Brandon* • Li Li Hua *Shu-Jen* • Ward Bond *Father Cairns* • Bob Mathias *Phil Gates* • Johnny Desmond *Steve Hill* • Elaine Curtis *Alice Nichols* ■ *Dir* Frank Borzage • *Scr* Kitty Buhler, from the story *China Doll* by James Benson Nablo, Thomas F Kelly and the story *Time Is a Memory* by Kitty Buhler

China Gate ★★★

War drama 1957 · US · BW · 90mins

American soldier Gene Barry hooks up with his estranged Eurasian wife Angie Dickinson, a political activist, to lead a guerrilla assault on a Chinese ammunition dump in French-controlled Vietnam. The marital war between the couple, caught in a love-hate relationship, parallels the battle against the Reds in this tough-minded movie, produced, written and directed by Samuel Fuller. Lee Van Cleef plays the communist leader, and Nat King Cole does a good job as a veteran GI. He also croons the title song. RK

Gene Barry *Brock* • Angie Dickinson *Lucky Legs* • Nat King Cole *Goldie* • Paul Dubov *Captain Caumont* • Lee Van Cleef *Major Cham* • George Givot *Corporal Pigalle* • Gerald Milton *Private Andreades* ■ *Dir/Scr* Samuel Fuller

China Girl ★★

Second World War drama
1942 · US · BW · 95mins

American news cameraman George Montgomery, in Mandalay just before the attack on Pearl Harbor and carrying secret military information, is pursued by two traitorous army personnel (Victor McLaglen, Lynn Bari) in the pay of the Japanese. Then he falls in love with a beautiful, American-educated Chinese girl (Gene Tierney). Director Henry Hathaway injects as much tension as possible into this melodrama, helped by some good action sequences. RK

Gene Tierney *Miss Young* • George Montgomery *Johnny Williams* • Lynn Bari *Captain Fifi* • Victor McLaglen *Major Bull Weed* • Alan Baxter *Chinese boy* • Sig Ruman *Jarubi* • Myron McCormick *Shorty* • Bobby Blake [Robert Blake] *Chinese boy* ■ *Dir* Henry Hathaway • *Scr* Ben Hecht, from a story by Melville Crossman [Darryl F Zanuck]

China Girl ★★★ 18

Romantic drama 1987 · US · Colour · 86mins

This is Abel Ferrara's stylised reworking of *Romeo and Juliet*. Even when he's misfiring, Ferrara can never be accused of being dull, and he makes superb use here of both Little Italy and Chinatown as Richard Panebianco and Sari Chang find love across the criminal codes. Only marginally less energetic than Baz Luhrmann's high-voltage version, the film echoes the key theme of *The Godfather*: that, in ignoring family tradition, the younger generation risks losing everything. The cast buckles under Ferrara's ambitious demands.DP

Richard Panebianco *Tony* • Sari Chang *Tye* • James Russo *Alby* • David Caruso *Mercury* ■ *Dir* Abel Ferrara • *Scr* Nicholas St John

China Moon ★★★ 18

Romantic thriller 1994 · US · Colour · 95mins

Fine acting and a surprising climactic revelation are the main virtues of this *film noir* from John Bailey, whose brilliant work as cinematographer includes *Cat People*, *Silverado*, *Mishima* and *As Good As It Gets*. The typical genre storyline sees detective Ed Harris and abused wife Madeleine Stowe succumb to passion in Florida, but although the main plot adds nothing new, there are enough original touches and tasty performances to sustain interest. JC DVD

Ed Harris *Kyle Bodine* • Madeleine Stowe *Rachel Munro* • Charles Dance *Rupert Munro* • Patricia Healy *Adele* • Benicio Del Toro *Lamar Dickey* • Tim Powell *Fraker* ■ *Dir* John Bailey • *Scr* Roy Carlson

China 9, Liberty 37 ★★★

Spaghetti western 1978 · It · Colour · 98mins

Director Monte Hellman's unusual mix of Sergio Leone and Sam Peckinpah (who has a bit part) is very interesting indeed. Gunslinger Fabio Testi is released from jail on condition he shoots rancher Warren Oates, enabling corrupt railroad barons to seize his land, However, once he meets Oates and falls for his sexually frustrated wife (Jenny Agutter), he finds the task difficult to accomplish. Gritty, violent and erotic, with a great score by Pino Donaggio. AJ. Some dialogue dubbed into English.

Warren Oates *Matthew* • Fabio Testi *Clayton* • Jenny Agutter *Catherine* • Sam Peckinpah *Wilbur Olsen* • Isabel Mestres *Barbara* ■ *Dir* Monte Hellman • *Scr* Gerald F Harvey, Douglas Venturelli

China O'Brien ★★ 18

Martial arts action thriller
1988 · US · Colour · 85mins

The breakthrough role – well, for the video market at least – for martial arts star Cynthia Rothrock, who provides a welcome antidote to the macho heroics of Chuck Norris et al. Here she plays a police officer who turns in her badge when she uses her martial arts skills to kill a villain in self-defence. But when she returns to her home town, her lethal abilities are once again called into use. A sequel followed. JF. Contains violence, swearing.

Cynthia Rothrock *China O'Brien* • Richard Norton *Matt* • Keith Cooke *Dakota* • Patrick Adamson *Lickner* • David Blackwell *Sheriff O'Brien* • Nijel *Jonsey* • Steven Kerby *Summers* • Robert Tiller *Owens* ■ *Dir* Robert Clouse • *Scr* Robert Clouse, from the story by Sandra Weintraub

China Seas ★★★★

Romantic adventure 1935 · US · BW · 86mins

The plot's tosh, the setting preposterous and the crew rip-roaring in this expensive MGM action melodrama. But who cares when the cast is solid gold? Clark Gable's the captain, sailing south to Singapore; Wallace Beery's a mutinous pirate; Rosalind Russell's the captain's aristocratic former mistress; and, best of all, Jean Harlow is the blonde floozy and another of Gable's ex-lovers. Splendidly directed by the under-rated Tay Garnett, this is a major treat. TS

Clark Gable *Captain Alan Gaskell* • Jean Harlow *China Doll "Dolly Portland"* • Wallace Beery *Jamesy MacArdle* • Lewis Stone *Tom Davids* • Rosalind Russell *Sybil Barclay* • Dudley Digges *Dawson* • C Aubrey Smith *Sir Guy Wilmerding* • Robert Benchley *Charlie McCaleb* ■ *Dir* Tay Garnett • *Scr* Jules Furthman, James Kevin McGuinness, from the novel by Crosbie Garstin

China Sky ★★

Second World War drama
1945 · US · BW · 78mins

RKO planned this adaptation of a novel by the once popular Pearl S Buck as a major starring vehicle for Claudette Colbert. But she took one look at the script and turned it down, leaving Ruth Warrick, Randolph Scott and Ellen Drew to co-star in what is a rather mundane romantic melodrama. Scott and Warrick play American doctors in a remote Chinese village threatened by Japanese forces; Drew is Scott's jealous viper of a wife, while Anthony Quinn is the local guerrilla leader. RK

Randolph Scott *Thompson* • Ruth Warrick *Sara* • Ellen Drew *Louise* • Anthony Quinn *Chen Ta* • Carol Thurston *Siu Mei* • Richard Loo *Col Yasuda* • "Ducky" Louie *"Little Goat"* • Philip Ahn *Dr Kim* ■ *Dir* Ray Enright • *Scr* Brenda Weisberg, Joseph Hoffmann, from the novel by Pearl S Buck

The China Syndrome ★★★★ PG

Drama 1979 · US · Colour · 116mins

A genuinely chilling "what if..." thriller in which savvy foreman Jack Lemmon just prevents an atomic meltdown at a nuclear power station. The government tries to hush it up, but TV newswoman Jane Fonda (in one of her best performances) and radical cameraman Michael Douglas (who also produced) probe for the truth in a solidly exciting movie still packed with political relevance. The cautionary conclusions were given a great deal of credence by life imitating art when the Three Mile Island near-tragedy occurred a few weeks after the movie opened. Note the complete lack of background music – Douglas felt music would trivialise the events. AJ [video] DVD

Jane Fonda *Kimberly Wells* • Jack Lemmon *Jack Godell* • Michael Douglas *Richard Adams* • Scott Brady *Herman De Young* • James Hampton *Bill Gibson* • Peter Donat *Don Jacovich* • Wilford Brimley *Ted Spindler* ■ *Dir* James Bridges • *Scr* Mike Gray, TS Cook, James Bridges

Chinatown ★★★★★ 15

Thriller 1974 · US · Colour · 125mins

Jack Nicholson here gives his best ever performance, playing a private eye called Jake Gittes, who pokes his nose rather too deeply into the lives of Faye Dunaway and her father, John Huston, a corrupt Los Angeles tycoon. Writer Robert Towne planned a trilogy about LA, and this first part, set in the 1930s, deals with the city's water supply and how that source of life leads to death and profit. The script is brilliantly organised, though the ending was changed when Roman Polanski arrived as director: Towne's story never got to Chinatown; Polanski insisted the climax was set there. The result was acrimony behind the scenes and genius on the screen in a masterpiece that repays any number of viewings. Nicholson reprised his role in the distinctly less successful *The Two Jakes*. AT. Contains violence and swearing. [video] DVD

Jack Nicholson *JJ Gittes* • Faye Dunaway *Evelyn Mulwray* • John Huston *Noah Cross* • Perry Lopez *Escobar* • John Hillerman *Yelburton* • Darrell Zwerling *Hollis Mulwray* • Diane Ladd *Ida Sessions* • Roy Jenson *Mulvihill* • Roman Polanski *Man with knife* ■ *Dir* Roman Polanski • *Scr* Robert Towne • *Cinematographer* John A Alonzo • *Music* Jerry Goldsmith • *Art Director* Richard Sylbert, W Stewart Campbell • *Editor* Sam O'Steen • *Costume Designer* Anthea Sylbert

Chinese Box ★★★★

Romantic drama
1997 · Jpn/Fr/US · Colour · 109mins

The brilliant Wayne Wang directs Jeremy Irons and Gong Li in a drama based around Hong Kong's return to China in 1997. Irons is a disgruntled journalist who discovers he has six months to live. Does he return to Britain or remain in Hong Kong, where he's fallen for bar girl Li (in her first English-speaking role)? As New Years Eve approaches, there's a strange ambiguity about what the future holds. The allegory is clear: Irons represents the dying colonial past, while Li's boss (Michael Hui) is the future. Fascinating, and full of minute nuances. LH. In English and Mandarin with subtitles.

Gong Li *Vivian* • Jeremy Irons *John* • Rubén Blades *Jim* • Maggie Cheung *Jean* • Michael Hui *Chang* • Jared Harris ■ *Dir* Wayne Wang • *Scr* Jean-Claude Carrière, Larry Gross, from a story by Paul Theroux, Wayne Wang, Jean-Claude Carrière

Chinese Boxes ★★★ 15

Crime thriller
1984 · W Ger/UK · Colour · 83mins

Will Patton (*No Way Out, The Postman*) plays an American in West Berlin who lands in a world of trouble when the daughter of a US diplomat winds up dead in his bathroom. Robbie Coltrane and Gottfried John, who would both turn up a decade later in Pierce Brosnan's 007 debut *GoldenEye*, are just two of the shady characters Patton encounters in a complex thriller from former *Time Out* critic Christopher Petit that owes a considerable debt to the work of Wim Wenders. RT [video]

Will Patton *Lang Marsh* • Gottfried John *Zwemmer* • Adelheid Arndt *Sarah* • Robbie Coltrane *Harwood* • Beate Jensen *Donna* • Susanne Meierhofer *Eva* • Jonathan Kinsler *Alan* ■ *Dir* Christopher Petit • *Scr* LM Kit Carson, Christopher Petit

The Chinese Connection ★★

Thriller 1988 · Fr · Colour · 85mins

France's colonial past provides the background for this thriller, set in the oriental quarter of Paris. Robin Renucci teams up with Marguerite Tran, the orphan he rescued during the fall of Saigon in 1975, to investigate a series of murders he's convinced stem from a feud between Chinese and Vietnamese gangsters. Solidly rooted in its environment, yet short on surprises, this holds the attention without being truly memorable. DP. French dialogue dubbed into English.

Robin Renucci *Mathieu* • Marguerite Tran *Jay* • Michel Piccoli *Batz* • Denys Hawthorne *Jason Hunt* • Luong Ham Chau *Sang* • Antoine Duléry *Bastien* • Claude Faraldo *Rinaldi* • JC Quinn *Mayotte* • Don Henderson *Malcolm* ■ *Dir* Denys Granier-Deferre • *Scr* Denys Granier-Deferre, Yves Stavrides

A Chinese Ghost Story ★★★★ 15

Martial arts horror
1987 · HK · Colour · 91mins

This marvellous example of the ghost genre popular in Hong Kong and most Asian areas is a real treat that combines excellent martial art sequences with lavish fantasy scenes and slapstick. (The merging of comedy and horror, a relative rarity in the west, has long been a staple of this market.) The story concerns a tax collector who falls in love with a ghost and is drawn into a battle for her soul. But the plot is secondary to the haunting visuals and set pieces that make it a classic of its type. DF. In Cantonese with English subtitles. [video] DVD

Leslie Cheung *Ning Tsai-Shen* • Wang Zuxian *Nieh Hsiao-Tsing* • Wu Ma *Yen Che-Hsia* ■ *Dir* Ching Siu-Tung • *Scr* Ruan Jizhi

A Chinese Ghost Story II ★★ 12

Martial arts horror
1990 · HK · Colour · 97mins

Leslie Cheung returns, this time as a scholar, rather than the first film's tax collector, in a bristling sequel that is more of a monster movie than its fantastical predecessor. The story sticks closely to the winning "haunted house" formula of the original, and among the many terrors our heroes confront are a rapidly defrosting zombie and a vicious centipede. There's the odd moment of quiet comedy, but the mysticism of the first film is much missed. DP. In Cantonese with English subtitles. Contains some moderate violence. [video]

Leslie Cheung *Ling Choi Sin* • Jacky Cheung *Chi Chau, "Autumn"* • Michelle Reis *Yuet Chi, "Moon"* • Joey Wong *Ching Fung, "Windy"* • Wu Ma *Yin Chek Hsia, swordsman* ■ *Dir* Ching Siu-Tung • *Scr* Tai-Mok Lau, Kei-To Lam, Yiu-Ming Leung

Chinese Odyssey 2002 ★★★ U

Period romantic comedy
2002 · HK/Jpn/Chi · Colour · 86mins

Lampooning everything from Peking Opera and Communist propaganda to chop socky and blaxploitation, Jeff Lau's scattershot period comedy is a breathless assault on social, sexual and cinematic stereotypes. The focus falls on hectoring Tony Leung and his restaurateur sister Vicky Zhao Wei and their encounters with cross-dressing princess Faye Wong and her fashion-conscious emperor brother, Chang Chen. The plot, however, is rarely as important as the plethora of in-jokes and when the gags run dry, Lau struggles to sustain the momentum. But there's still much to enjoy in the bouyant performances and glorious photography. DP. In Mandarin with English subtitles. DVD

Tony Leung (2) *Li Yilong* • Faye Wong *Princess Wushuang* • Vicky Zhao Wei [Zhao Wei] *Phoenix* • Chang Chen *Emperor Zheng De* ■ *Dir* Jeff Lau • *Scr* Ji An [Jeff Lau] • *Cinematographer* Ngor Chi Kwan

Chinese Roulette ★★★ 15

Drama 1976 · W Ger · Colour · 82mins

Icy in its satire, this is a cruelly manipulative and boldly unrealistic dissection of bourgeois foibles. Alexander Allerson and Margit Carstensen are tricked by their disabled daughter, Andrea Schober, into spending a weekend in the country with their respective lovers. Inevitably, this world of cheap deceptions and stylised poses is shattered as psychic shots give way to lethal lead during the eponymous truth game. Rainer Werner Fassbinder uses a roaming camera and reflective surfaces to expose their coldheartedness; alas, his cynical detachment leaves us appalled but unmoved. DP. In German with English subtitles. Contains some swearing and sex scenes. [video]

Margit Carstensen *Ariane* • Ulli Lommel *Kolbe* • Anna Karina *Irene* • Alexander Allerson *Gerhard* • Andrea Schober *Angela* • Macha Méril *Traunitz* • Brigitte Mira *Kast* ■ *Dir/Scr* Rainer Werner Fassbinder • *Cinematographer* Michael Ballhaus

La Chinoise ★★★★ PG

Experimental political drama
1967 · Fr · Colour · 95mins

Marking Jean-Luc Godard's passage from mainstream maverick to militant outsider, this diatribe on Maoism and the possibility of western revolution was also his first collaboration with Jean-Pierre Gorin, with whom he would work until 1972 within the Dziga Vertov co-operative. With the ever-engaging Jean-Pierre Léaud leading a discussion as naive as it's impassioned, the film was accused of trivialising socialism, particularly through Godard's use of agitprop slogans, calligraphic gimmicks and poster imagery. Beneath the surface superficiality and glib wit, however, this was a radical and prescient political statement that represented a determined break from the tyranny of screen narrative. DP. In French with English subtitles. DVD

Anne Wiazemsky *Véronique* • Jean-Pierre Léaud *Guillaume* • Michel Semeniako *Henri* • Lex de Bruijn *Kirilov* • Juliet Berto *Yvonne* ■ *Dir/Scr* Jean-Luc Godard

Chisum ★★ PG

Western 1970 · US · Colour · 106mins

This John Wayne movie, handsomely photographed by western veteran William H Clothier, uses a fictional variation on the Lincoln County cattle war to tell the tale of the man who first hired Billy the Kid. The Duke is well served by director Andrew V McLaglen (son of Victor), Forrest Tucker makes an imposing villain, and the Dominic Frontiere score is above average, but the plot rambles. TS [video] DVD

John Wayne *John Chisum* • Forrest Tucker *Lawrence Murphy* • Christopher George *Dan Nodeen* • Ben Johnson *James Pepper* • Glenn Corbett *Pat Garrett* • Bruce Cabot *Sheriff Brady* • Richard Jaeckel *Jess Evans* ■ *Dir* Andrew V McLaglen • *Scr* Andrew J Fenady

Chitty Chitty Bang Bang ★★★ U

Musical fantasy 1968 · UK · Colour · 136mins

Producer Albert R "Cubby" Broccoli gave this children's story from the pen of Bond author Ian Fleming the big-budget treatment, and it nearly worked. With the combined talents of the teams behind *Mary Poppins* and the Bond movies, this musical about a flying Edwardian motorcar should have been a box-office blockbuster. The fact that it wasn't is a mystery, given the expertise on board. It's probably too long but, if you're looking for something entertaining for younger children, look no further. AT [video] DVD

Dick Van Dyke *Caractacus Potts* • Sally Ann Howes *Truly Scrumptious* • Lionel Jeffries *Grandpa Potts* • Gert Frobe [Gert Fröbe] *Baron Bomburst* • Anna Quayle *Baroness Bomburst* • Benny Hill *Toymaker* • James Robertson-Justice *Lord Scrumptious* ■ *Dir* Ken Hughes • *Scr* Roald Dahl, Richard Maibaum, Ken Hughes, from the novel by Ian Fleming

Le Choc ★★★

Thriller 1982 · Fr · Colour · 100mins

The hardships of a professional killer when he decides to retire are well known, but none more so than those suffered by Alain Delon when he decides to rest his trigger finger. His boss wants him to keep working, while Catherine Deneuve offers sympathetic compensation. Directed with some style by Robin Davis from a bestselling novel, it's a romantic thriller of dubious ethics but great pace. TH. French dialogue dubbed into English.

Alain Delon *Martin Terrier* • Catherine Deneuve *Claire* • Philippe Léotard *Felix* • Etienne Chicot *Michel* • Stéphane Audran *Mme Faulques* • François Perrot *Cox* ■ *Dir* Robin Davis • *Scr* Alain Delon, Robin Davis, Claude Veillot, Dominique Robelet, from the novel *La Position du Tireur Couché* by Jean-Patrick Manchette

Chocolat ★★★★ PG

Drama 1988 · Fr · Colour · 99mins

Set in the Cameroons, *Chocolat* is both a highly intelligent political allegory and a sensitive study of adult interaction and emotion, seen through the eyes of a child. In her directorial debut, Claire Denis makes exceptional use of the parched landscape and the isolation of district governor François Cluzet's quarters to intensify the relationship between his young daughter and a black servant. In this environment, the arrival of a party of plane crash survivors seems an even more portentous intrusion. Isaach de Bankolé is supremely dignified as the misused houseboy, while Cécile Ducasse is impish and vulnerable as his devoted little friend. DP. In French with English subtitles.

Isaach de Bankole *Protée* • Giulia Boschi *Aimée* • François Cluzet *Marc* • Jean-Claude Adelin *Luc* • Laurent Arnal *Machinard* • Kenneth Cranham *Boothby* • Jacques Denis *Delpich* • Cécile Ducasse *France as a child* • Mireille Perrier *France* ■ *Dir* Claire Denis • *Scr* Claire Denis, Jean-Pol Fargeau

Chocolat ★★★★ 12

Romantic comedy drama
2000 · UK/US · Colour · 116mins

Director Lasse Hallström follows up *The Cider House Rules* with this delightful fable, adapted from the novel by Joanne Harris. Set in the late 1950s, the film stars Juliette Binoche as a rootless mother who appears overnight in a small French village and brazenly opens a chocolate shop – during Lent. Staunch Catholic mayor Alfred Molina disapproves of her lifestyle and fears the challenge to his authority, but Binoche's confections are soon raising spirits (and more) particularly among the local wives. The arrival of handsome river gypsy Johnny Depp further inflames passions. A truly delicious experience. LH. Contains swearing. DVD

Juliette Binoche *Vianne Rocher* • Lena Olin *Josephine Muscat* • Johnny Depp *Roux* • Judi Dench *Armande Voizin* • Alfred Molina *Comte de Reynaud* • Peter Stormare *Serge Muscat* • Carrie-Anne Moss *Caroline Clairmont* • Leslie Caron *Madame Audel* ■ *Dir* Lasse Hallström • *Scr* Robert Nelson Jacobs, from the novel by Joanne Harris • *Cinematographer* Roger Pratt • *Production Designer* David Gropman • *Costume Designer* Renee Ehrlich Kalfus

The Chocolate Soldier ★★★ U

Musical comedy 1941 · US · BW · 101mins

Not the Oscar Straus operetta from which it takes its title (and retains some of its songs), but Ferenc Molnar's famous play *The Guardsman*, (filmed in 1931) rejigged as a musical. Nelson Eddy is the husband whose insane jealousy leads him to disguise himself and court his wife to test her fidelity; then up-and-coming opera soprano Risë Stevens co-stars. The story now creaks with age, but Eddy's masquerade as an over-the-top Cossack officer is wonderful. RK

Nelson Eddy *Karl Lang/Vassily Vassilievitch* • Risë Stevens *Maria Lanyi* • Nigel Bruce *Bernard Fischer* • Florence Bates *Mme Helene Pugsy* • Nydia Westman *Liesel "Maid"* ■ *Dir* Roy Del Ruth • *Scr* Leonard Lee, Keith Winter, Ernest Vajda, Claudine West, from the play *Testör/The Guardsman* by Ferenc Molnar

The Chocolate War ★★★ 15

Drama 1988 · US · Colour · 99mins

Actor Keith Gordon made a creditable debut as writer/director with this brooding study of peer pressure gone mad. As the new boy who refuses the tradition of selling chocolates to boost school funds, Ilan Mitchell-Smith gives a stubborn rather than stoic performance, better at standing up to tyrannical headmaster John Glover than he is at resisting the ruthlessly persuasive methods of the Vigils, a senior elite charged with upholding Catholic principles. Making its points without undue insistence, this is as polished as it's provocative. DP

John Glover *Brother Leon* • Ilan Mitchell-Smith *Jerry* • Wallace Langham [Wally Ward] *Archie* • Doug Hutchison *Obie* • Adam Baldwin *Carter* • Brent Fraser *Emille* • Bud Cort *Brother Jacques* ■ *Dir* Keith Gordon • *Scr* Keith Gordon, from the novel by Robert Cormier

Choice of Arms ★★★★

Crime drama 1981 · Fr · Colour · 135mins

Having moved on from the thuggish persona that helped establish his credentials, Gérard Depardieu was reluctant to commit to Alain Corneau's *policier*. However, he gives an imposing performance as an escapee on the run who, along with Michel Galabru, seeks sanctuary on the stud farm of retired gangster Yves Montand. Although the action is often ferocious, Corneau deglamorises the violence by emphasising its finality. Though uncompromisingly staged and bleak in both tone and theme, this is superbly acted and touchingly concluded. DP. In French with English subtitles.

Yves Montand *Noel* • Gérard Depardieu *Mickey* • Catherine Deneuve *Nicole* • Michel Galabru *Bonnardot* • Gérard Lanvin *Sarlat* • Marc Chapiteau *Savin* • Pierre Forget *Serge* • Christian Marquand *Jean* ■ *Dir* Alain Corneau • *Scr* Alain Corneau, Michel Grisolia

The Choirboys ★ 18

Black comedy drama
1977 · US · Colour · 119mins

This confused cop movie shows an LAPD squad's on- and off-duty behaviour. Supposedly a raunchy comedy, it's directed by Robert Aldrich with all the subtlety of a rampaging rhino, and the result is a catalogue of bigoted attitudes that dismally fails to amuse. Joseph Wambaugh, who wrote the book on which this is based, successfully took legal action to have his name removed from the credits. AT. Contains violence, swearing, sex scenes, drug abuse and nudity.

Charles Durning *"Spermwhale" Whalen* • Louis Gossett Jr *Calvin Motts* • Perry King *Baxter Slate* • Clyde Kusatsu *Francis Tanaguchi* • Stephen Macht *Spencer Van Moot* • Tim McIntire *Roscoe Rules* • Randy Quaid *Dean Proust* • Don Stroud *Sam Lyles* • James Woods *Harold Bloomguard* • Burt Young *Sergeant Dominic Scuzzi* • Robert Webber *Deputy Chief Riggs* ■ *Dir* Robert Aldrich • *Scr* Christopher Knopf

Chokher Bali ★★★ PG

Drama 2003 · Ind · Colour · 123mins

This is an intense and meticulously made melodrama about a liberated widow (played by Aishwarya Rai), who becomes a companion to the mother of the man who once spurned her, and then proceeds to drive a wedge between him and his wife (Raima Sen). The atmosphere of Bengal prior to the 1905 partition is ably conveyed, but Ghosh's realist approach does not gel with the superstar aura of Bollywood icon Rai, who comes across a touch too modern. DP. In Bengali with English subtitles. DVD

Lily Chakraborty [Lily Chakravarty] *Rajlakshmi* • Prosenjit Chatterjee *Mahendra* • Tota Raychowdhury *Behari* • Aishwarya Rai *Binodini* • Raima Sen *Ashalata* ■ *Dir* Rituparno Ghosh • *Scr* Rituparno Ghosh, from the novel by Rabindranath Tagore

CHOMPS ★★ PG

Comedy 1979 · US · Colour · 86mins

Based on a story by Joseph Barbera (of Hanna-Barbera cartoon fame), this film falls between two stools. It's a bit gritty for younger children and too simplistic for the pre-teens, so its mix of crime and comedy won't find many takers. The title refers to the Canine Home Protection System designed in the shape of a robotic dog by inventor Wesley Eure in a bid to save Conrad Bain's security company. The slapstick has the feel you'd expect of the man who'd helped create Tom and Jerry. DP. Contains some swearing.

Wesley Eure *Brian Foster* • Valerie Bertinelli *Casey Norton* • Conrad Bain *Ralph Norton* • Chuck McCann *Brooks* • Red Buttons *Bracken* • Larry Bishop *Ken Sharp* • Hermione Baddeley *Mrs Flower* ■ *Dir* Don Chaffey • *Scr* Dick Robbins, Duane Poole, Joseph Barbera, from a story by Joseph Barbera

Choose Me ★★★★ 15

Romantic comedy drama
1984 · US · Colour · 102mins

A languid psychological mosaic from writer/director Alan Rudolph, whose films resemble a slowed-down version of his mentor, Robert Altman's. In the neon-lit bar that is the focal point of this romantic comedy drama, the main characters are the bar's owner (Lesley Ann Warren) and a radio agony aunt (Geneviève Bujold). Both offer sex, but are frustrated until newcomer Mickey (Keith Carradine) becomes the man in their lives. Alan Rudolph's work is an acquired taste; once acquired, though, it's addictive. TH DVD

Geneviève Bujold *Dr Nancy Love* • Keith Carradine *Mickey* • Lesley Ann Warren *Eve* • Patrick Bauchau *Zack Antoine* • Rae Dawn Chong *Pearl Antoine* • John Larroquette *Billy Ace* ■ *Dir/Scr* Alan Rudolph

Chop Suey ★★

Documentary
2000 · US · Colour and BW · 98mins

Having garnered an Oscar nomination for *Let's Get Lost*, photographer Bruce Weber ends a decade's sabbatical from cinema with this unfocused, if fittingly compulsive, treatise on obsession. It's a dazzling scrapbook of changing visual styles, but in allowing his fascination with dullard hunk Peter Johnson to seep into the foreground, Weber disappointingly marginalises such intriguing characters as Robert Mitchum, lesbian jazz legend Frances Faye and *Vogue* editor Diana Vreeland. Very much a vanity project. DP

Dir Bruce Weber

Chopper ★★★★★ 18

Biographical drama
2000 · Aus · Colour · 90mins

An extraordinary movie about an extraordinary man, *Chopper* is the boldest Australian film in decades. Downbeat, gritty and ultra-violent, the sensational feature debut of rock-video director Andrew Dominik is a long, sharp shock to the system. Featuring a show-stopping central performance from Aussie stand-up comic Eric Bana, this totally unclassifiable biography of notorious criminal Mark "Chopper" Read mixes startling facts from his numerous bestsellers (one was titled *How to Shoot Friends and Influence People*) with large doses of pulp fiction regarding the supposed 19 murders he committed. Using a wild array of stylistic tricks, Dominik's fascinating, funny and frightening look at Read's playful sadism is a masterpiece of innovation. AJ DVD

Eric Bana *Mark "Chopper" Brandon Read* • Simon Lyndon *Jimmy Loughnan* • David Field *Keithy George* • Dan Wyllie *Bluey* • Bill Young *Detective Downey* • Vince Colosimo *Neville Bartos* • Kenny Graham *Keith Read* ■ *Dir* Andrew Dominik • *Scr* Andrew Dominik, from the books (including *Chopper: From the Inside*) by Mark Brandon Read

Chopper Chicks in Zombietown ★ 15

Comedy horror 1990 · US · Colour · 85mins

At no-budget film empire Troma, a film's title is usually more important than the content. This is no exception. On paper it sounds suitably wacky: an all-girl biker gang ride into a small town and face their toughest test when they confront a population of zombies. However, the direction is inept, the script and performances are awful, and it scores pretty low in the all important bad-taste stakes as well. JF DVD

Jamie Rose *Dede* • Catherine Carlen *Rox* • Kristina Loggia *Jojo* • Martha Quinn *Mae Clutter* • Don Calfa *Ralph Willum* • Lycia Naff *TC* ■ *Dir/Scr* Dan Hoskins

Chori Chori ★★★★ U

Comedy 1956 · Ind · BW · 122mins

Having been the mainstay of RK Films for eight years, the most popular romantic teaming in the history of Indian cinema parted company after this reworking of the Frank Capra classic *It Happened One Night*. As the heiress who defies her father and elopes to marry a heel, Nargis is suitably haughty, but it's only when she meets up with journalist Raj Kapoor that the picture catches light. A treat for fans and a fascinating insight into remakes, Bollywood style. DP. A Hindi language film.

Nargis *Baby* • Raj Kapoor *Suman* • Master Bhagwan • Johnny Walker • Mukri ■ *Dir* Anant Thakur • *Scr* Aga Jani Kashmiri

The Chorus ★★★ 12A

Drama 2004 · Fr/Swi/Ger · Colour · 96mins

Jean Dréville's 1947 film *A Cage of Nightingales* provides the inspiration for this debut feature from writer/director Christophe Barratier. The story unfolds in flashback after a celebrated conductor returns to his native France and meets up with a friend who attended the same tough boarding school. The friend has brought with him the diary of Clément Mathieu, a teacher who managed to reach his delinquent charges through music, forming them into a choir and bringing out their natural gifts. Barratier's film contains every cliché in the book and is grossly sentimental, but it's rescued from mawkishness by the depth and charm of the characters and performances. BP. In French with English subtitles.

Gérard Jugnot *Clément Mathieu* • François Berléand *Rachin* • Kad Merad *Chabert* • Jean-Paul Bonnaire *Father Maxence* • Marie Bunel *Violette Morhange* • Paul Chariéas *Manager* • Carole Weiss *The countess* • Philippe du Janerand *Monsieur Langlois* ■ *Dir* Christophe Barratier • *Scr* Christophe Barratier, Philippe Lopes Curval, from the film *A Cage of Nightingales [La Cage aux Rossignols,] by Noël-Noël, René Wheeler, Georges Chaperot* • *Music* Bruno Coulais

A Chorus Line ★★★ PG

Musical 1985 · US · Colour · 117mins

The highly successful Broadway show was so relentlessly theatrical that it was generally considered impossible to film. The strength of the show remains, but, by incorporating flashbacks and, crucially, substituting songs and choreography, the original is undermined, not enhanced. Nevertheless, there is much of merit, especially Alyson Reed, touching as key dancer Cassie, and ex-*Dallas* regular Audrey Landers, who does well by one of the great show stoppers. Michael Douglas puts in a sharp performance as the show's producer. TS. Contains swearing. DVD

Michael Douglas *Zach* • Alyson Reed *Cassie* • Terrence Mann *Larry* • Michael Blevins *Mark* • Yamil Borges *Morales* • Vicki Frederick *Sheila* • Audrey Landers *Val* • Jan Gan Boyd *Connie* • Sharon Brown *Kim* • Gregg Burge *Richie* • Cameron English *Paul* • Nicole Fosse *Kristine* ■ *Dir* Richard Attenborough • *Scr* Arnold Schulman, from the musical by Michael Bennett, Nicholas Dante, James Kirkwood

A Chorus of Disapproval
★ PG

Comedy 1988 · UK · Colour · 95mins

If you want to remove the comedy, pithy insights, energy and spirit from the work of stage maestro Alan Ayckbourn, your first choice of director should be Michael Winner. The idea of Winner employing his customary sledgehammer to Ayckbourn's subtle drama is surreal in the extreme. And, as expected, the director lumbers his way through a text from which odd moments of social satire escape untouched, but more by good luck than design. JM. Contains swearing.

Anthony Hopkins *Dafydd Ap Llewellyn* • Jeremy Irons *Guy Jones* • Richard Briers *Ted Washbrook* • Gareth Hunt *Ian Hubbard* • Patsy Kensit *Linda Washbrook* • Alexandra Pigg *Bridget Baines* • Prunella Scales *Hannah Ap Llewellyn* • Jenny Seagrove *Fay Hubbard* • Lionel Jeffries *Jarvis Huntley-Pike* • Sylvia Syms *Rebecca Huntley-Pike* ■ *Dir* Michael Winner • *Scr* Alan Ayckbourn, Michael Winner, from the play by Alan Ayckbourn

The Chosen
★★★ PG

Drama 1981 · US · Colour · 103mins

Mannered or magnificent? Rod Steiger's performance as a Hassidic rabbi dominates the film, for good or bad. His son (Robby Benson) is venturing out of his restrictively religious range by becoming friends with the son of a Zionist professor (Maximilian Schell). Set in New York at the time of of the founding of Palestine, director Jeremy Paul Kagan conjures the time's fervent atmosphere, but it's Steiger's risk-all exhibition you'll remember. TH

Maximilian Schell *Professor David Malter* • Rod Steiger *Reb Saunders* • Robby Benson *Danny Saunders* • Barry Miller *Reuven Malter* ■ *Dir* Jeremy Paul Kagan • *Scr* Edwin Gordon, from the novel by Chaim Potok

Chosen Survivors
★★

Science fiction
1974 · US/Mex · Colour · 98mins

Jackie Cooper and Bradford Dillman are among a group of specially selected citizens who are carted off to a deep underground bunker to test individual reactions to probable nuclear war. Unfortunately a horde of killer vampire bats are locked in with them, and it's supper time. Sutton Roley's ecological revenge thriller is clearly inspired by Hitchcock's *The Birds* and the bat effects are wholly convincing, but his protagonists are obvious clichés and the direction has a TV-movie feel and ambition about it. RB

Jackie Cooper *Raymond Couzins* • Alex Cord *Steven Mayes* • Richard Jaeckel *Gordon Ellis* • Bradford Dillman *Peter Macomber* • Pedro Armendáriz Jr *Luis Cabral* • Diana Muldaur *Alana Fitzgerald* ■ *Dir* Sutton Roley • *Scr* HB Cross, Joe Reb Moffley, from a story by HB Cross

Christ Stopped at Eboli
★★★★ PG

Drama 1979 · It/Fr/W Ger · Colour · 213mins

Francesco Rosi's adaptation of Carlo Levi's memoir divided critics between those who felt it sentimentalised his opposition to the fascist regime, and those who reckoned the director's almost neorealist use of everyday characters and the rural landscape helped the film capture the spirit of its source. Surprisingly, for such a literate work, Rosi doesn't delve too deeply into the causes of Italy's lurch to the right. Thanks to a monumental performance from Gian Maria Volonté, however, he does succeed in conveying both the writer's fears for his country and his unswerving faith in the decency of its population. DP. In Italian with English subtitles.

Gian Maria Volonté *Carlo Levi* • Paolo Bonacelli *Don Luigi Magalone* • Alain Cuny *Baron Rotundo* • Lea Massari *Luisa Levi* • Irene Papas *Giulia* • François Simon *Don Traiella* ■ *Dir* Francesco Rosi • *Scr* Francesco Rosi, Tonino Guerra, Raffaele La Capria, from the memoirs *Cristo Si é Fermato a Eboli* by Carlo Levi

The Christian Licorice Store
★★★

Drama 1971 · US · Colour · 84mins

When did you last see a movie about a tennis champion who sells out to commercialism that boasts an acting role for Jean Renoir, one of the world's greatest directors? Add to this appearances by cult director Monte Hellman (*Two-Lane Blacktop*) and silent star Gilbert Roland, and you have a feast for buffs and a very arty, wacky piece of 1970s indulgence. The tennis player who "goes Hollywood" is played by Beau Bridges, while Bond girl Maud Adams is the photographer who covers his life story. AT

Beau Bridges *Franklin Cane* • Maud Adams *Cynthia Vicstrom* • Gilbert Roland *Jonathan Carruthers* • Allan Arbus *Monroe* • Anne Randall *Texas girl* • Monte Hellman *Joseph* • Jean Renoir ■ *Dir* James Frawley • *Scr* Floyd Mutrux

Christiane F
★★★★ 18

Drama 1981 · W Ger · Colour · 120mins

Sending moral campaigners scrambling for their soapboxes and critics reaching for superlatives, this graphic depiction of the miseries of drug addiction is strewn with powerful images and provocative insights. Based on a bestselling book written by two reporters from *Der Stern*, the film traces one 13-year-old girl's descent into heroin dependency and prostitution. Natja Brunckhorst and Thomas Haustein give agonisingly authentic performances, but director Uli Edel occasionally over-indulges himself, notably at the David Bowie concert. Sketchy in its sociology, but undeniably powerful. DP. In German with English subtitles. DVD

Natja Brunckhorst *Christiane F* • Thomas Haustein *Detlef* • Jens Kuphal *Axel* • Jan Georg Effler *Bernd* • Christiane Reichelt *Babsi* • Daniela Jaeger *Kessi* • Kerstin Richter *Stella* • David Bowie ■ *Dir* Ulrich Edel [Uli Edel] • *Scr* Herman Weigel, from a non-fiction book by Kai Hermann, Horst Rieck

Christie Malry's Own Double-Entry
★★ 18

Black comedy
2000 · UK/Neth/Lux · Colour · 91mins

Shirley Anne Field and Kate Ashfield impress as the dying mother and unsuspecting girlfriend of book-keeper Nick Moran. His twisted world view prompts him to commit increasingly deadly acts of subversion, which he tallies in a ledger detailing his notional fortune. However, the asides on the lethargy and cynicism of the modern world are lost within the flashy visuals and the parallel storyline that features the 15th-century mathematician Pacioli, who first recorded the double-entry method. DP. Contains swearing, sex scenes. DVD

Nick Moran *Christie Malry* • Neil Stuke *Headlam* • Kate Ashfield *Carol* • Mattia Sbragia *Leonardo da Vinci* • Marcello Mazzarella *Luca Pacioli* • Salvatore Lazzaro *Giacomo* • Sergio Albelli *Duke Ludovici* • Shirley Anne Field *Mary, Christie's mother* • Peter Sullivan *Wagner* ■ *Dir* Paul Tickell • *Scr* Simon Bent, from the novel by BS Johnson

Christine
★★★ 18

Horror 1983 · US · Colour · 105mins

Adapted from the novel by Stephen King, this killer car chiller is the ultimate in auto eroticism. The idea that a 1958 Plymouth Fury can turn into a jealous mistress is a cracker and, through his ingenious use of close-ups and seductive angles, director John Carpenter turns Christine into the sassiest thing on four wheels. He also gets a likeable performance out of Keith Gordon as the geek who becomes a dude the moment he inserts the key in the ignition. But it's overlong and more effective as a dark comedy than a horror. DP. Contains violence and swearing. DVD

Keith Gordon *Arnie Cunningham* • John Stockwell *Dennis Guilder* • Alexandra Paul *Leigh Cabot* • Robert Prosky *Will Darnell* • Harry Dean Stanton *Rudolph Junkins* • Christine Belford *Regina Cunningham* ■ *Dir* John Carpenter • *Scr* Bill Phillips, from the novel by Stephen King

A Christmas Carol
★★★ U

Seasonal drama 1938 · US · BW · 69mins

Few would dispute the fact that Alastair Sim is the finest screen Scrooge (in 1951's *Scrooge*), but Lionel Barrymore would have given him a hard act to follow. Sadly, disability forced him to withdraw from this typically polished MGM version of Charles Dickens's yuletide favourite. Reginald Owen is a good substitute, however, impressing particularly during the visitations of Marley and the other Christmas ghosts. DP

Reginald Owen *Ebenezer Scrooge* • Gene Lockhart *Bob Cratchit* • Kathleen Lockhart *Mrs Cratchit* • Terry Kilburn *Tiny Tim* • Barry Mackay *Fred* • Lynne Carver *Bess* ■ *Dir* Edwin L Marin • *Scr* Hugo Butler, from the story by Charles Dickens

A Christmas Carol
★★ U

Animated drama 1997 · US · Colour · 66mins

It's hard to arrive at a new approach to Charles Dickens's beloved yuletide tale. This isn't even the first animated adaptation, but it's certainly one of the most sentimental versions (courtesy of its ghastly songs), with the inspirational message of goodwill to all being given a determinedly contemporary consumerist feel. With a graphic style as flat and perfunctory as a TV cartoon, it's left to the vocal talents to enliven the action. Tim Curry gives a good account of himself as the miserly Scrooge, while Whoopi Goldberg and Edward Asner make imposing spirits. DP

Tim Curry *Ebeneezer Scrooge* • Whoopi Goldberg *Spirit of Christmas Present* • Michael York *Bob Cratchit* • Edward Asner *Marley* • Frank Welker *Debit* • Kath Soucie *Mrs Cratchit* ■ *Dir* Stan Phillips • *Scr* Jymn Magon, from the story by Charles Dickens

A Christmas Carol
★★★ PG

Seasonal drama 1999 · US · Colour · 89mins

As Ebenezer Scrooge, Patrick Stewart proves himself worthy company for Alastair Sim, Albert Finney and George C Scott. This TV movie is not the most lavish or inventive adaptation of Charles Dickens's most-filmed tale, but Joel Grey and Desmond Barrit acquit themselves well as two of the spirits whose midnight promptings transform Stewart from a penny-pinching curmudgeon into a joyous reveller. There's even a nod towards modernity with the casting of Richard E Grant and Saskia Reeves as the Cratchits. Stewart holds the piece together with a subtle performance. DP

Patrick Stewart *Mr Ebenezer Scrooge* • Richard E Grant *Bob Cratchit* • Joel Grey *The Ghost of Christmas Past* • Ian McNeice *Mr Albert Fezziwig* • Saskia Reeves *Mrs Cratchit* • Desmond Barrit *The Ghost of Christmas Present* • Bernard Lloyd *Jacob Marley* ■ *Dir* David Jones (3) • *Scr* Peter Barnes, from the story by Charles Dickens

Christmas Carol: the Movie
★ U

Part-animated seasonal drama
2001 · UK/Ger · Colour · 77mins

Charles Dickens's classic ghost story suffers the indignity of being turned into a sentimental and unimaginatively drawn cartoon. Director Jimmy T Murakami ruins the classic tale by adding tangential storylines, presumably to appeal to a more juvenile audience. The whole is framed by a live-action scene depicting Dickens (Simon Callow) arriving in Boston to read his story to an assembled audience. AJ DVD

Simon Callow *Scrooge/Charles Dickens* • Kate Winslet *Belle* • Nicolas Cage *Jacob Marley* • Jane Horrocks *Ghost of Christmas Past* • Michael Gambon *Ghost of Christmas Present* • Rhys Ifans *Bob Cratchit* • Juliet Stevenson *Mrs Cratchit/Mother Gimlet* • Robert Llewellyn *Old Joe* ■ *Dir* Jimmy T Murakami • *Scr* Piet Kroon, Robert Llewellyn, from the story *A Christmas Carol* by Charles Dickens

Christmas Eve
★★

Comedy drama 1947 · US · BW · 90mins

This sentimental comedy drama boasts an impressive cast but little else of note and basically consists of three interwoven stories, which culminate on Christmas Eve. They involve the three adopted sons of elderly Ann Harding who needs their help to escape the clutches of an avaricious nephew. The lost sons are a rodeo rider (Randolph Scott), an apparent criminal (George Raft) and a playboy (George Brent), but the movie was obviously constructed around these actors, leaving poor Harding rather unsatisfactorily cast as the spinster. BB

George Raft *Mario Torio* • George Brent *Michael Brooks* • Randolph Scott *Jonathan* • Joan Blondell *Ann Nelson* • Virginia Field *Claire* • Dolores Moran *Jean* • Ann Harding *"Aunt "Matilda" Reid* • Reginald Denny *Phillip Hastings* • Douglass Dumbrille *Doctor Bunyan* ■ *Dir* Edwin L Marin • *Scr* Laurence Stallings, from a stories by Laurence Stallings, from a stories by Richard H Landau, from a stories by Robert B Altman [Robert Altman, uncredited]

Christmas Holiday
★★★ PG

Film noir 1944 · US · BW · 88mins

With that frothy title and a cast teaming Gene Kelly and Deanna Durbin, you could well expect a musical. However, this melodrama treads on the wilder shores of *film noir* in the hands of expert director Robert Siodmak and screenwriter Herman J Mankiewicz. A miscast Kelly never really convinces as a returned murderer, but Durbin is excellent in her only non-frivolous role. TS DVD

Deanna Durbin *Jackie Lamont/Abigail Martin Manette* • Gene Kelly *Robert Manette* • Richard Whorf *Simon Fenimore* • Dean Harens *Lt Charles Mason* • Gladys George *Valerie De Merode* • Gale Sondergaard *Mrs Manette* • David Bruce *Lt Gerald Tyler* • Minor Watson *Townsend* ■ *Dir* Robert Siodmak • *Scr* Herman J Mankiewicz, from the novel by W Somerset Maugham

Christmas in Connecticut
★★★

Comedy 1945 · US · BW · 101mins

A corny little piece, but enjoyable nonetheless. Barbara Stanwyck almost convinces as the oh-so-chic journalist whose column extols the virtues of home cooking and country living. As a promotional stunt, she is forced to look after a navy hero (Dennis Morgan) for Christmas – except, of course, she lives in the city, can't cook and has to rent a cottage in Connecticut. The idea is sound enough, but it becomes awfully sentimental under Peter Godfrey's uninspired direction. TS

Barbara Stanwyck *Elizabeth Lane* • Dennis Morgan *Jefferson Jones* • Sydney Greenstreet

Alexander Yardley • Reginald Gardiner *John Sloan* • SZ Sakall *Felix Bassenak* • Robert Shayne *Dudley Beecham* • Una O'Connor *Norah* • Frank Jenks *Sinkewicz* • Joyce Compton *Mary Lee* ■ *Dir* Peter Godfrey • *Scr* Lionel Houser, Adele Comandini, from the story by Aileen Hamilton

C

Christmas in July ★★★ U

Comedy 1940 · US · BW · 67mins

Dick Powell stars as a young clerk who, mistakenly believing he's won $25,000 in a slogan-writing competition, goes on a manic spending spree. The second film from the uniquely inventive Preston Sturges is not in the same class as his first, *The Great McGinty*, or such subsequent classics as *The Lady Eve* and *Sullivan's Travels*. But it's beautifully played and peppered with brilliantly observed comedy cameos from a memorable supporting cast. RK

Dick Powell *Jimmy MacDonald* • Ellen Drew *Betty Casey* • Raymond Walburn *Mr Maxford* • Alexander Carr *Mr Schindel* • William Demarest *Mr Bildocker* • Ernest Truex *Mr Baxter* • Franklin Pangborn *Announcer* ■ *Dir/Scr* Preston Sturges

Christmas Present ★★★

Black comedy 1986 · It · Colour · 101mins

Pupi Avati directs this decidedly non-festive offering with a dark side. As the inveterate gambler who is lured into a card-playing Christmas by four people he considers to be his friends, Carlo Delle Piane gives a performance as subtle as a sharp's bluff. It's almost like watching a subtitled David Mamet play as the group round the table begin playing on each other's fears, while trying to hide their own weaknesses. *Christmas Rematch* followed in 2004. DP. In Italian with English subtitles.

Carlo Delle Piane *Santelia* • Diego Abatantuono *Franco* • Gianni Cavina *Ugo* • Alessandro Haber *Lele* • George Eastman *Stefano* ■ *Dir/Scr* Pupi Avati

A Christmas Romance ★★ U

Romantic comedy
1994 · US/Can · Colour · 91mins

A schmaltzy modern TV-movie spin on the Scrooge theme starring Olivia Newton-John. She plays a struggling single mother who receives a most unwelcome Christmas present: an eviction notice delivered by hard-hearted bank executive Gregory Harrison. However, he's trapped by a sudden snowstorm and gradually unfrozen by Newton-John and her young daughters. Heart-warming stuff, even if director Sheldon Larry puts in too much sugar. JF DVD

Olivia Newton-John *Julia Stonecypher* • Gregory Harrison *Brian Harding* • Chloe Lattanzi *Deenie Stonecypher* • Stephanie Sawyer *Emily Rose Stonecypher* ■ *Dir* Sheldon Larry • *Scr* Darrah Cloud, from the novel by Maggie Davis

A Christmas Story ★★★★ PG

Comedy 1983 · US · Colour · 89mins

A much under-rated look at what it's like to be an avaricious child with Christmas approaching, this witty, insightful, hugely enjoyable movie is riven with glorious home truths and a merciful lack of saccharin surrounding a topic that generally reduces directors to lachrymose morons. Even more surprising is that it comes from Bob Clark, director of the smutty teen comedy *Porky's*. Peter Billingsley plays Ralphie, and his quest for juvenile justice and a Red Ryder BB gun is an enormous joy. The follow-up, *It Runs in the Family* (1994), was a disappointment. SH

Melinda Dillon *Mrs Parker* • Darren McGavin *Mr Parker* • Peter Billingsley *Ralphie* • Ian Petrella *Randy* • Scott Schwartz *Flick* • RD Robb *Schwartz* • Tedde Moore *Miss Shields* ■ *Dir* Bob Clark • *Scr* Jean Shepherd, Leigh Brown, Bob Clark, from the novel *In God We Trust, All Others Pay Cash* by Jean Shepherd

The Christmas Tree ★★ U

Drama 1969 · Fr/It · Colour · 107mins

This marks a departure for Bond director Terence Young, who also scripted this heartfelt tale about a father's determination to make his son's last days as enjoyable as possible. Stricken with leukemia, Brook Fuller is presented with gifts as different as a tractor and wolves stolen from a zoo, as William Holden and his old army pal Bourvil pander to his every whim. Nicely photographed by Henri Alekan, but Georges Auric's score reinforces the film's gushing sentimentality. DP

William Holden (2) *Laurent* • Virna Lisi *Catherine* • Bourvil *Verdun* • Brook Fuller *Pascal* • Madeleine Damien *Marinette* • Friedrich Ledebur *Vernet* ■ *Dir/Scr* Terence Young

Christmas with the Kranks ★ PG

Seasonal comedy 2004 · US · Colour · 98mins

This soulless tale raises so few laughs, it barely justifies its comedy label. Tim Allen and Jamie Lee Curtis play the Kranks, a Chicago couple who incur the wrath of their local community when they decide to forgo Christmas and its associated trappings in favour of a luxury cruise. Poorly scripted and lazily directed, the film celebrates herd mentality and excessive consumerism. SF

Tim Allen *Luther Krank* • Jamie Lee Curtis *Nora Krank* • Dan Aykroyd *Vic Frohmeyer* • Erik Per Sullivan *Spike Frohmeyer* • Cheech Marin [Richard "Cheech" Marin] *Officer Salino* • Jake Busey *Officer Treen* • M Emmet Walsh *Walt Scheel* • Elizabeth Franz *Bev Scheel* ■ *Dir* Joe Roth • *Scr* Chris Columbus, from the novel *Skipping Christmas* by John Grisham

Christopher Columbus ★ U

Historical biography
1949 · UK · Colour · 105mins

If you thought Gérard Depardieu missed the mark in Ridley Scott's *1492: Conquest of Paradise*, wait till you set eyes on this turkey. Fredric March looks noble and the 1940s Technicolor is fabulous. Alas, the pace is nonexistent and the action is little more than a series of wax tableaux sporting familiar faces. TS

Fredric March *Christopher Columbus* • Florence Eldridge *Queen Isabella* • Francis L Sullivan *Francisco de Bobadilla* • Kathleen Ryan *Beatriz* • Derek Bond *Diego de Arana* • Nora Swinburne *Juana de Torres* • Abraham Sofaer *Luis de Santangel* • Linden Travers *Beatriz de Peraza* ■ *Dir* David MacDonald • *Scr* Sydney Box, Muriel Box, Cyril Roberts

Christopher Columbus: the Discovery ★ PG

Historical adventure
1992 · US · Colour · 120mins

This is not so much a milestone to mark the 500th anniversary of the discovery of America as a millstone round the neck of nearly everyone connected with it. George Corraface, as Columbus, bores for Spain and Rachel Ward's accent as Queen Isabella is almost as bizarre as Tom Selleck's wig. Marlon Brando, as Torquemada, resembles a tethered balloon. TH. Contains violence.

George Corraface [Georges Corraface] *Christopher Columbus* • Marlon Brando *Torquemada* • Tom Selleck *King Ferdinand* • Rachel Ward *Queen Isabella* • Robert Davi *Martin Pinzon* • Catherine Zeta-Jones *Beatriz* • Oliver Cotton *Harana* • Benicio Del Toro *Alvaro* • Mathieu Carrière *King John* ■ *Dir* John Glen • *Scr* John Briley, Cary Bates, Mario Puzo, from a story by Mario Puzo

Christopher Strong ★★★

Romantic melodrama
1933 · US · BW · 77mins

Katharine Hepburn's sturdy performance and an abundance of intriguing ideas go some way to compensate for Dorothy Arzner's uneven direction of this romantic drama. Extremely advanced for its years, the film examines female independence and society's demands on women through the story of gutsy flier Hepburn and her affair with a married politician. JM

Katharine Hepburn *Lady Cynthia Darrington* • Colin Clive *Christopher Strong* • Billie Burke *Elaine Strong* • Helen Chandler *Monica Strong* ■ *Dir* Dorothy Arzner • *Scr* Zor Akins, from the novel by Gilbert Frankau

Chronicle of a Death Foretold ★★★★ 15

Drama 1987 · It/Fr · Colour · 105mins

Sumptuously photographed by Pasqualino De Santis, this is a mesmerising (if occasionally sluggish) adaptation of Gabriel Garcia Marquez's novel of family honour, revenge and murder in a small Colombian town. Managing to create tension within a foregone conclusion, director Francesco Rosi deftly intercuts between flashbacks and reminiscences, as doctor Gian Maria Volonté attempts to uncover the facts behind a 20-year-old crime. While Rupert Everett is overly languid as the wealthy suitor who abandons deflowered bride Ornella Muti, the other members of the cast provide the ring of authenticity you'd expect from Italy's finest latter-day realist. DP. In Spanish with English subtitles.

Rupert Everett *Bayardo San Roman* • Ornella Muti *Angela Vicario* • Gian Maria Volonté *Cristo Bedoia* • Irene Papas *Angela's mother* ■ *Dir* Francesco Rosi • *Scr* Francesco Rosi, Tonino Guerra, from the novel by Gabriel Garcia Marquez

Chronicle of a Love ★★★ PG

Drama 1950 · It · BW · 97mins

Departing from the neorealism of his postwar documentaries, Michelangelo Antonioni made his feature debut with this atypically conventional tale of suspicion and snobbery, adultery and guilt. Clearly, though, he is already employing those trademark long takes and making symbolic use of the physical environment to explore the recurrent themes of urban alienation, social displacement and the impermanence of relationships. Yet this reliance on inanimates for psychological revelation somewhat devalues the contribution of the cast. DP. An Italian language film.

Lucia Bosé *Paola* • Massimo Girotti *Guido* • Ferdinando Sarmi *Fontana* • Gino Rossi *Carloni* • Marika Rowsky *Joy* • Rosi Mirafiore *Barmaid* • Rubi d'Alma ■ *Dir* Michelangelo Antonioni • *Scr* Michelangelo Antonioni, Danièle D'Anza, Silvio Giovaninetti, Francesco Maselli, Piero Tellini

Chronicle of Anna Magdalena Bach ★★★

Experimental biographical drama
1968 · W Ger/It · BW · 93mins

Avant-garde director Jean-Marie Straub's second feature views the life and times of Johann Sebastian Bach through the eyes of his second wife. Convincing in both its historical accuracy and musical authenticity, this is an almost documentary account of instrumentalists at work during the 18th century, with Gustav Leonhardt playing Bach in both senses of the word. RB. In German with English subtitles.

Gustav Leonhardt *Johann Sebastian Bach* • Christiane Lang *Anna Magdalena Bach* • Paolo Carlini *Hölzel* • Ernst Castelli *Steger* • Hans-Peter Boye *Born* • Joachim Wolf *Rector* ■ *Dir* Jean-Marie Straub • *Scr* Jean-Marie Straub, Danièle Huillet • *Cinematographer* Ugo Piccone

Chronicle of the Burning Years ★★★★

Political drama 1975 · Alg · Colour · 177mins

Throughout the period covered in this epic account of Algerian history (1939-54), the indigenous film industry was dominated by so-called "cinema mudjahad", or "freedom fighter cinema". It's ironic, therefore, that Mohammed Lakhdar-Hamina's film should belong to the tradition that succeeded it: "cinema djidid", or "new cinema". Couching a family drama in terms of a Hollywood melodrama and employing a diversity of symbolic character types, the film shows how the attempt to suppress cultural as well as political aspirations resulted in the politicisation of ordinary people and the FLN revolt against the colonial government. DP. An Arabic language film.

Yorgo Voyagis *Achmed* • Mohammed Lakhdar-Hamina *Milhoud* • Cheik Nourredine *Friend* ■ *Dir* Mohammed Lakhdar-Hamina • *Scr* Mohammed Lakhdar-Hamina, Rachid Boujedra

The Chronicles of Riddick ★★ 15

Science-fiction thriller
2004 · US · Colour · 114mins

A sci-fi movie with a tremendous sense of scale and visual splendour, this is ambitious but disappointing. David Twohy takes his monosyllabic anti-hero from *Pitch Black* and thrusts him into an imaginative universe full of sleek spacecraft and war-ravaged cities. Vin Diesel grunts his way through endless fights with bounty hunters, prison guards and an army of religious supermen. Unfortunately, Twohy forgets to provide a compelling story, and it all comes across as an overblown and pompous space opera. GM. Contains violence. DVD

Vin Diesel *Riddick* • Thandie Newton *Dame Vaako* • Karl Urban *Vaako* • Colm Feore *Lord Marshal* • Linus Roache *Purifier* • Keith David *Imam* • Yorick van Wageningen *The Guv* • Alexa Davalos *Kyra* • Nick Chinlund *Toombs* • Judi Dench *Aereon* ■ *Dir* David Twohy • *Scr* David Twohy, from the character created by Jim Wheat, Ken Wheat

Chu Chin Chow ★★★ U

Musical fantasy 1934 · UK · BW · 103mins

This legendary and massively popular British stage musical by Oscar Asche, replete with its unimaginative Frederick Norton score, finally reached the screen with all its faults revealed. Nevertheless, George Robey's performance as Ali Baba is forever enshrined here, and there's some interesting period casting, with Anna May Wong as Zahrat the slave girl and villain Fritz Kortner as boss of the 40 thieves. The uninspired choreography is by ballet great Anton Dolin. TS

George Robey *Ali Baba* • Fritz Kortner *Abu Hassan* • Anna May Wong *Zahrat* • John Garrick *Nur-al-din* • Pearl Argyle *Marjanah* • Dennis Hoey *Rakham* ■ *Dir* Walter Forde • *Scr* Sidney Gilliat, L DuGarde Peach, Edward Knoblock, from the musical by Oscar Asche, Frederic Norton

Chu Chu and the Philly Flash ★

Romantic comedy
1981 · US · Colour · 100mins

Silly title, silly film. This marks a career low for wonderful comedian Carol Burnett and co-star Alan Arkin. The story concerns Flash (Arkin), a former baseball player now dabbling in petty crime who finds a briefcase containing stolen documents. Far from comic. DF

Alan Arkin *Flash* • Carol Burnett *Emily* • Jack Warden *Commander* • Danny Aiello *Johnson* • Adam Arkin *Charlie* • Danny Glover *Morgan* • Sid Haig *Vince* ■ *Dir* David Lowell Rich • *Scr* Barbara Dana, from a story by Henry Barrow

Chubasco ★★

Drama 1967 · US · Colour · 99mins

Produced by William Conrad, better known as TV detective Frank Cannon, this is an occasionally interesting melodrama based around the California fishing industry. Christopher Jones (*Ryan's Daughter*) and Susan Strasberg, who were married in real-life at the time, play lovers whose relationship is threatened by her father (Richard Egan). RT

Richard Egan *Sebastian* • Christopher Jones *Chubasco* • Susan Strasberg *Bunny* • Ann Sothern *Angela* • Simon Oakland *Laurindo* • Audrey Totter *Theresa* • Preston Foster *Nick* • Peter Whitney *Matt* ■ *Dir/Scr* Allen H Miner

Chubby Down Under and Other Sticky Regions ★★ 18

Comedy 1998 · UK · Colour · 81mins

Roy "Chubby" Brown made his name as a blue comic, but is known to millions not through TV – he's far too rude and politically incorrect for that – but through his bestselling videos. This is actually his second theatrical release: unlike the sci-fi romp *UFO*, however, this is essentially a big-budget version of his stage show. Guaranteed to offend virtually everybody, there are no half measures with Brown's brand of filthy humour. JF. Contains swearing, coarse language and sexual references. [VIDEO]

Roy "Chubby" Brown ■ *Dir* Tom Poole • *Scr* Roy "Chubby" Brown

Chuck & Buck ★★★★ 15

Comedy drama 2000 · US · Colour · 95mins

Essentially a film about stalking, this excellent independent feature confounds expectations by opting for the creepy and the quirky. This surprise tack keeps the viewer intrigued and allows sympathy for both stalked and stalker, and it's rounded off with a delicious twist in the tale. Chris Weitz and Mike White are former schoolfriends who've drifted apart, but remain bonded by a single act of homosexual dabbling. When the childlike White's mum dies, he renews contact with Weitz, but the latter has a new life with fiancée Beth Colt. It's nicely scripted, skilfully directed, beautifully acted and, considering its subject matter, surprisingly warm and likeable. DA [VIDEO] DVD

Mike White *Buck O'Brien* • Chris Weitz *Charlie "Chuck" Sitter* • Lupe Ontiveros *Beverly* • Beth Colt *Carlyn* • Paul Weitz *Sam* • Maya Rudolph *Jamila* ■ *Dir* Miguel Arteta • *Scr* Mike White

CHUD ★ 18

Horror 1984 · US · Colour · 83mins

Thanks to toxic waste dumped in the Manhattan sewage system, tramps and derelicts have mutated into "Cannibalistic Humanoid Underground Dwellers". That's according to this lamentable urban horror movie, which is neither gory nor exciting enough to merit much attention. Ridiculous monsters and unappealing main characters only add insult to injury in this crass exploiter. AJ [VIDEO]

John Heard *George Cooper* • Kim Greist *Lauren Daniels* • Daniel Stern *The Reverend* • Christopher Curry *Captain Bosch* • George Martin (1) *Wilson* • John Ramsey *Commissioner* ■ *Dir* Douglas Cheek • *Scr* Parnell Hall

CHUD II: Bud the Chud ★ 15

Horror comedy 1989 · US · Colour · 84mins

Sequel in name only to the 1984 turkey, which sees a bunch of teenagers steal a corpse from a government research facility, only for it to turn cannibalistic and run amok in a small town. One look at the script, no doubt, prompted director David Irving to play this for broad laughs, but nobody saw the joke. RS [VIDEO]

Brian Robbins *Steve* • Bill Calvert *Kevin* • Tricia Leigh Fisher *Katie* • Gerrit Graham *Bud the Chud* • Robert Vaughn *Masters* ■ *Dir* David Irving • *Scr* M Kane Jeeves [Ed Naha]

Chuka ★★

Western 1967 · US · Colour · 105mins

John Mills has left the employ of Queen Victoria's Fifth Lancers and now commands a fort besieged by excited Arapaho Indians. Inside the stockade are a number of thugs, among them Chuka (Rod Taylor), a gunfighter who used to be friendly with the Indians and is now even more friendly with Luciana Paluzzi. Things pick up a bit when the Arapaho arrive. AT

Rod Taylor *Chuka* • Ernest Borgnine *Sergeant Otto Hansbach* • John Mills *Colonel Stuart Valois* • Luciana Paluzzi *Veronica Kleitz* • James Whitmore *Trent* • Angela Dorian [Victoria Vetri] *Helena Chavez* • Louis Hayward *Major Benson* ■ *Dir* Gordon Douglas • *Scr* Richard Jessup, from a novel by Richard Jessup

A Chump at Oxford ★★★ U

Comedy 1940 · US · BW · 62mins

Rewarded for foiling a bank robbery, Laurel and Hardy find themselves among the "dreaming spires" in this agreeable comedy. While the film reunites the boys with fabled producer Hal Roach, it also saddles them with third-rate director Alfred Goulding, who allows this loose collection of gags to ramble. Beside such stale situations as settling into the dean's lodgings, there are some classic moments, including the trek around the "haunted maze", Stan's glorious transformation into college hero Lord Paddington, and Ollie's demotion to the role of butler. Watch for Peter Cushing as one of the students. DP [VIDEO]

Stan Laurel *Stan* • Oliver Hardy *Ollie* • James Finlayson *Baldy Vandevere* • Peter Cushing *Jones* ■ *Dir* Alfred Goulding • *Scr* Felix Adler, Harry Langdon, Charles Rogers

Chung King Express ★★★★ 12

Romantic comedy
1994 · HK · Colour · 101mins

A film that Quentin Tarantino declared to be a masterpiece, and he's not far wrong, for director Wong Kar-Wai's exceptional control over the two disparate storylines is awe-inspiring. The first, shorter episode concerns a jilted cop's encounter with a blonde-wigged heroin trafficker, while the second focuses on a waitress's preoccupation with another cop, who doesn't appreciate her passion until it's too late. Established stars Tony Leung and Brigitte Lin are upstaged somewhat by newcomers Takeshi Kaneshiro and Faye Wong, but the performances as a whole are a joy. DP. In Cantonese and Mandarin with English subtitles. [VIDEO] DVD

Qingxia Lin [Brigitte Lin] *The drug dealer* • Takeshi Kaneshiro *He Qiwu, Cop 223* • Tony Chiu-Wai Leung [Tony Leung (2)] *Cop 663* • Faye Wong *Faye* • Valerie Chow *Air hostess* ■ *Dir/Scr* Wong Kar-Wai

Chunky Monkey ★★ 15

Black comedy 2001 · UK · Colour · 88mins

British writer/director Greg Cruttwell's low-budget black comedy debut is as intriguing as it is daft. A cross between a stage play and an offbeat sitcom, it's so outlandish that it keeps you hooked just to see where all the idiocy is leading. David Threlfall plays a psychopathic loner who's in the midst of clearing up his flat after committing a murder, getting it ready for an appointment with a Julie Andrews lookalike and a tub of Chunky Monkey ice cream. However, his work is disturbed by a succession of bizarre visitors. SF. Contains violence, swearing and sexual references.

David Threlfall *Donald* • Alison Steadman *Beryl* • Nicola Stapleton *Mandy* • David Schofield *Frank* • Colin McFarlane *Trevor* • Danny Nussbaum *Nuggett* ■ *Dir/Scr* Greg Cruttwell

The Church ★★★ 18

Horror 1988 · It · Colour · 97mins

Originally slated to complete Dario Argento's *Demons* trilogy, this Gothic horror was turned over to Michele Soavi. Opening with a medieval witch-hunt which results in a cathedral being built on the mass grave of some suspected Satanists, the story jumps forward in time to show bibliophile Tomas Arana and caretaker's daughter Asia Argento investigating the fiendish mechanical devices the architect installed to prevent malevolent spirits escaping into the world. Soavi's film is ingeniously designed, but the intriguing concept is wasted. DP. An Italian language film. [VIDEO]

Asia Argento *Lotte* • Thomas Arana [Tomas Arana] *Evald* • Feodor Chaliapin [Feodor Chaliapin Jr] *Bishop* • Hugh Quarshie *Father Gus* • Barbara Cupisti *Lisa* ■ *Dir* Michele Soavi • *Scr* Dario Argento, Franco Ferrini, Michele Soavi, from a story by Dario Argento, Franco Ferrini

Churchill: the Hollywood Years ★★ 15

Comedy 2004 · UK/Ire · Colour · 80mins

Peter Richardson's blunt satire on Hollywood's habit of rewriting history stars Christian Slater as the "real" Winston Churchill, a gung-ho American GI, and Neve Campbell as a spirited Princess Elizabeth, heir to the British throne. The Anglo-American twosome team up to foil a dastardly plot by Hitler (Antony Sher) to topple the monarchy. It's an amusingly bizarre notion, but Richardson's film fails to deliver on the promise of its premise, despite game performances. DA. Contains swearing. [VIDEO] DVD

Christian Slater *Winston Churchill* • Neve Campbell *Princess Elizabeth* • Antony Sher *Adolf Hitler* • Jessica Oyelowo *Princess Margaret* • Mackenzie Crook *Jim Charoo* • Miranda Richardson *Eva Braun* • Leslie Phillips *Lord W'ruff* • Rik Mayall *Baxter* • Bob Mortimer *Potter* • Vic Reeves *Bendle* • Harry Enfield *King George V* ■ *Dir* Peter Richardson • *Scr* Peter Richardson, Peter Richens

Ciao, Federico! ★★★★ 15

Documentary 1970 · US/It · Colour · 57mins

One critic said Fellini's films ceased to be art when Fellini himself became a work of art. That self-aggrandisement is evident in this documentary about the Italian maestro, caught while directing his exotic Roman tale, *Satyricon*. The great man proves to be impossible to interview: an evasive, chronic liar and sly keeper of his own image. But he's such a marvellous raconteur, you can't help loving him and admiring Gideon Bachmann for colluding so graciously. AT [VIDEO]

Dir Gideon Bachmann

Ciao! Manhattan ★★★ 18

Drama 1973 · US · Colour and BW · 91mins

It's somehow fitting that this patchwork portrait of model-actress Edie Sedgwick has been cobbled together from such sharply contrasting footage. One of the many who found her 15 minutes of fame with Andy Warhol, she exudes elfin charm in Chuck Wein's 1967 monochrome study. But by the time David Weisman and John Palmer caught up with the 28 year-old at her parents California home three years later, it was clear that this drug-addled, silicon-implanted Barbie was not long for this world. DP [VIDEO]

Edie Sedgwick *Susan* • Wesley Hayes *Butch* • Isabel Jewell *Mummy* • Paul America *Paul* • Viva *Fashion editor* • Roger Vadim *Dr Braun* • Christian Marquand *Entrepreneur* ■ *Dir/Scr* John Palmer, David Weisman

El Cid ★★★★★ U

Epic historical adventure
1961 · US/It · Colour · 171mins

The epic was in danger of losing its audience when this lavish account of the career of Spanish patriot Rodrigo Diaz de Bivar was first released. It gave Charlton Heston the chance to carry the weight of a nation on his shoulders again, as he takes on the occupying Moors. Director Anthony Mann avoids a mere history lesson, effectively handling the court intrigue and the feud between Heston and estranged wife Sophia Loren. But it's the astonishing action sequences produced by Yakima Canutt's second-unit crew that give the picture its Super Technirama impact. With outstanding supporting performances, a literate script and a superlative, Oscar-nominated score by Miklos Rozsa, this is 1960s Hollywood at its spectacular best. DP [VIDEO] DVD

Charlton Heston *Rodrigo Diaz de Bivar/El Cid* • Sophia Loren *Chimene* • John Fraser *King Alfonso* • Raf Vallone *Count Ordonez* • Genevieve Page *Queen Urraca* • Gary Raymond *King Sancho* • Herbert Lom *Ben Yussuf* • Massimo Serato *Fanez* • Douglas Wilmer *Moutamin* • Frank Thring *Al Kadir* • Hurd Hatfield *Count Arias* • Ralph Truman *King Ferdinand* • Andrew Cruickshank *Count Gomez* • Michael Hordern *Don Diego* ■ *Dir* Anthony Mann • *Scr* Philip Yordan, Fredric M Frank, Ben Barzman (uncredited), from a story by Fredric M Frank • *Music* Miklos Rozsa • *Cinematographer* Robert Krasker

The Cider House Rules ★★★★★ 12

Drama 1999 · US · Colour · 120mins

The third John Irving novel to reach the screen (after *The World According to Garp* and *The Hotel New Hampshire*), this is a rich, evocative period piece that makes the most of its New England locations. Tobey Maguire plays Homer Wells, a foundling who, having spent all his young life at an orphanage run by Michael Caine's kindly abortionist, decides to seek new pastures. Alas, he finds the codes he lives by of little use in the real world. Although drastically slimmed down from Irving's original (Homer's 15-year odyssey is reduced to a mere 15 months), Lasse Hallström's film has a simple integrity that fills every frame, while Caine won an Oscar for his performance as the ether-addicted Dr Larch. NS DVD

Tobey Maguire *Homer Wells* • Charlize Theron *Candy Kendall* • Delroy Lindo *Arthur Rose* • Paul Rudd *Wally Worthington* • Michael Caine *Dr Wilbur Larch* • Jane Alexander *Nurse Edna* • Kathy Baker *Nurse Angela* • Kate Nelligan *Olive Worthington* ■ *Dir* Lasse Hallström • *Scr* John Irving, from his novel

Il Cielo è Sempre Più Blu ★★★ 15

Drama 1995 · It · Colour · 109mins

With over 130 speaking parts and 30 different storylines, there's little wonder Antonello Grimaldi's ambitious film was dubbed "a Roman *Short Cuts*". Yet the roving style of Robert Altman is not the only influence on a picture that most vividly recalls the portmanteau compilations of short stories that were so popular in the 1960s. The action is naturally fragmented and some characters pass us by before we've even noticed them. There are neat vignettes, however, featuring Dario and Asia Argento, Margherita Buy (as a vindictive traffic warden) and Enrico Lo Verso as a lovesick postman. DP. In Italian with English subtitles. Contains violence, swearing and sex scenes.

Asia Argento *Teenage cousin* • Luca Barbareschi *Shyster* • Margherita Buy *Traffic warden* • Roberto Citran *Businessman* • Enrico Lo Verso *Postman* • Ivano Marescotti *Jogger* • Dario Argento *Man confessing to Franciscan monk* • Silvio Orlando *Mechanic* ■ *Dir* Antonello Grimaldi • *Scr* Daniele Cesarano, Paolo Marchesini

La Cienaga ★★★ 18

Comedy drama
2001 · Arg/Sp/US · Colour · 99mins

Former documentary director Lucrecia Martel makes an impressive feature film debut with this dark domestic melodrama set in the stifling provincial backwoods of northern Argentina. Events tumble out of control after wealthy drunk Graciela Borges has an accident during a stagnant pool party. Middle-class Borges's recovery brings her into contact with down-at-heel suburban cousin Mercedes Morán and her unruly family. Martel draws painfully persuasive performances from her ensemble cast. DP. In Spanish with English subtitles.

Mercedes Morán *Tali* • Graciela Borges *Mecha* • Martin Adjemian *Gregorio* • Diego Baenas *Joaquin* • Sofia Bertolotto *Momi* ■ *Dir/Scr* Lucrecia Martel

Cimarron ★★★★

Epic western 1931 · US · BW · 131mins

Richard Dix, newspaper owner and maverick campaigner for human rights, is also a restless wanderer who disappears for long periods, leaving his indomitable wife Irene Dunne to carry on the paper and the fight for justice. This sprawling epic cost RKO the unprecedented sum of $1,433,000. The studio was rewarded with Oscars for best picture – the only western to get the award until *Dances with Wolves* six decades later – art direction and screenplay. A little dated now, but otherwise excellent. RK

Richard Dix *Yancey Cravat* • Irene Dunne *Sabra Cravat* • Estelle Taylor *Dixie Lee* • Nance O'Neil *Felice Venable* • William Collier Jr *The Kid* ■ *Dir* Wesley Ruggles • *Scr* Howard Estabrook, from the novel by Edna Ferber • *Cinematographer* Edward Cronjager • *Art Director* Max Ree

Cimarron ★★ U

Epic western 1960 · US · Colour · 147mins

This remake of the classic 1931 version of Edna Ferber's novel about the Oklahoma Land Rush, is, sadly, a misfire. It's the very least of director Anthony Mann's works, marred by MGM's insistence on studio filming when locations were imperative, and by a hopelessly inept and miscast Maria Schell in the key role. Glenn Ford delivers a strong performance, but the film remains little more than an insubstantial melodrama. TS

Glenn Ford *Yancey Cravet* • Maria Schell *Sabra Cravet* • Anne Baxter *Dixie Lee* • Arthur O'Connell *Tom Wyatt* • Russ Tamblyn *Cherokee Kid* • Mercedes McCambridge *Sarah Wyatt* ■ *Dir* Anthony Mann • *Scr* Arnold Schulman, from the novel by Edna Ferber

The Cimarron Kid ★★★ U

Western 1951 · US · Colour · 83mins

The Dalton gang rides again in a serviceable western that, unusually, has Audie Murphy in the role of outlaw. Released on parole, he hides out with Noah Beery Jr and his gang after being falsely accused of a train heist. But, while the prospect of a new life with Beverly Tyler is enticing, Murphy is determined to take on one last job before he hangs up his guns. Better known for his psychological westerns, Budd Boetticher handles this programme filler with intelligent efficiency, drawing a thoughtful performance from Murphy. DP

Audie Murphy *Cimarron Kid* • Yvette Dugay *Rose of Cimarron* • Beverly Tyler *Carrie Roberts* • John Hudson (1) *Dynamite Dick* • James Best *Bitter Creek* • Leif Erickson *Marshal Sutton* • Noah Beery [Noah Beery Jr] *Bob Dalton* ■ *Dir* Budd Boetticher • *Scr* Louis Stevens, from a story by Louis Stevens, Kay Lenard

The Cincinnati Kid ★★★ PG

Drama 1965 · US · Colour · 97mins

Intended as a *Hustler* for poker players, this started out with Steve McQueen as the young hotshot and Spencer Tracy as his older, poker-faced adversary. Sam Peckinpah was the director and Paddy Chayefsky the screenwriter. Tracy was the first to go, being replaced by Edward G Robinson. Six days into shooting, Peckinpah was fired because he was working too slowly, though the press was told he shot a nude scene which wasn't in the script. Enter new writers and a new director, Norman Jewison. The result, considering the production's chequered history, is not at all bad. AT

Steve McQueen *Cincinnati Kid* • Edward G Robinson *Lancey Howard* • Ann-Margret *Melba* • Karl Malden *Shooter* • Tuesday Weld *Christian* • Joan Blondell *Lady Fingers* • Rip Torn *Slade* • Jack Weston *Pig* ■ *Dir* Norman Jewison • *Scr* Ring Lardner Jr, Terry Southern, from the novel by Richard Jessup

Cinderella ★★★★ U

Animated romance
1950 · US · Colour · 74mins

Industrial-strength Disney animation, with all the coy clichés of Charles Perrault's story reinforced, though not the sexual ones. There are some delightful singing mice, a sadistically erotic stepmother and a languidly cruel cat called Lucifer, voiced by June Foray. The songs are what give it an extra dimension, though: the Oscar-nominated *Bibbidi-Bobbidi-Boo*, sung by Verna Felton, and the winsome *A Dream Is a Wish Your Heart Makes*, performed by Ilene Woods. TH

Ilene Woods *Cinderella* • William Phipps *Prince Charming* • Eleanor Audley *Stepmother* • Verna Felton *Fairy Godmother* • James MacDonald *Jacques/Gus-Gus* • Rhoda Williams *Anastasia* ■ *Dir* Wilfred Jackson, Hamilton Luske, Clyde Geronimi • *Scr* William Peet, Ted Sears, Homer Brightman, Kenneth Anderson, Erdman Penner, Winston Hibler, Harry Reeves, Joe Rinaldi, from the story *Cinderella* by Charles Perrault

Cinderella II: Dreams Come True ★★ U

Animated romance
2002 · US · Colour · 70mins

Disney's made-for-video sequel to the 1950 classic takes over where its predecessor finished, with Cinders finding it hard adjusting to her new life as a princess. The main pleasure, as before, comes from lovable mice Gus and Jaq, who write a storybook that creates the film's three short segments. Ultimately, despite a couple of cute moments, the ordinary animation and terrible tunes suggest that Disney should have quit at the original fairy tale ending. JC DVD

Jennifer Hale *Cinderella* • Tress MacNeille *Anastasia* • Rob Paulsen *Jaq/Baker/Sir Hugh* • Corey Burton *Gus* • Russi Taylor *Fairy Godmother/Mary Mouse/Beatrice/Daphne/Drizella* • Holland Taylor *Prudence* ■ *Dir* John Kafka • *Scr* Tom Rogers, Jill E Blotevogel, Jule Selbo

Cinderella Jones ★★ U

Musical comedy 1946 · US · BW · 83mins

Amiable but dated Warner Bros fable, shot during the war but held back so long that all wartime references had to be removed and some rather bland linking material filmed especially. The director of this trifle is, surprisingly, the great choreographer Busby Berkeley, making a return to the studio whose coffers he once helped fill with his splendidly outré dance creations. This is altogether a more modest piece. TS

Joan Leslie *Judy Jones* • Robert Alda *Tommy Coles* • SZ Sakall *Gabriel Popik* • Edward Everett Horton *Keating* • Julie Bishop *Camille* • William Prince *Bart Williams* • Charles Dingle *Minland* • Ruth Donnelly *Cora Elliott* ■ *Dir* Busby Berkeley • *Scr* Charles Hoffman, from a story by Philip Wylie

Cinderella Liberty ★★★ 15

Drama 1973 · US · Colour · 111mins

Macho James Caan becomes hooked on Marsha Mason and the result is a blatantly manipulative urban fairy tale. The setting up of the schmaltzy floodgates is intriguing enough as Caan, a sailor in Seattle on the night-pass that gives its name to the movie, plays pool with hustling hooker Mason, with her body as his prize. After that, it becomes soggy with sentiment, though director Mark Rydell gives the ending a satisfyingly ironic twist. TH. Contains swearing, brief nudity.

James Caan *John Baggs* • Marsha Mason *Maggie* • Kirk Calloway *Doug* • Eli Wallach *Lynn Forshay* • Allyn Ann McLerie *Miss Watkins* • Burt Young *Master-at-arms* • Bruno Kirby Jr [Bruno Kirby] *Alcott* • Dabney Coleman *Executive officer* ■ *Dir* Mark Rydell • *Scr* Darryl Ponicsan, from the novel by Darryl Ponicsan

Cinderella Man ★★★★

Biographical sports drama
2005 · US · Colour · 144mins

This boxing picture may echo the basic plot of *Rocky* – a no-hoper unexpectedly gets the chance to fight for the heavyweight championship of the world – but has the added impact of being a true story, set during the Great Depression of the 1930s. Jim Braddock (Russell Crowe) had been a decent boxer who is reduced to labouring in the docks to feed his family. A comeback fight is the beginning of his journey towards a title clash with Max Baer (played here by Craig Bierko), a giant who had killed two previous opponents. Crowe is perfect casting as a pugilist who does not know when he is beat, and the film not only captures the mood of the times, but also the power, majesty and sheer brutality of the sport more effectively than virtually any other boxing film. BP

Russell Crowe *Jim Braddock* • Renée Zellweger [Renee Zellweger] *Mae Braddock* • Paul Giamatti *Joe Gould* • Craig Bierko *Max Baer* • Bruce McGill • Paddy Considine *Mike Wilson* ■ *Dir* Ron Howard • *Scr* Cliff Hollingsworth, Akiva Goldsman, from a story by Cliff Hollingsworth

A Cinderella Story ★★ PG

Romantic comedy
2004 · US · Colour · 91mins

Orphaned student Hilary Duff is smitten by an anonymous, online sweet-talker (Chad Michael Murray, a modern-day Prince Charming wooing via cyberspace), who's a dreamy diversion from the cruel demands of her self-obsessed stepmother (Jennifer Coolidge) and spiteful stepsisters. Duff and Murray make a cute but not particularly charismatic couple. Unfortunately their performances are undermined by corny dialogue and a hackneyed plotline that updates the original story too literally. SF DVD

Hilary Duff *Sam Montgomery* • Jennifer Coolidge *Fiona* • Chad Michael Murray *Austin Ames* • Dan Byrd *Carter* • Regina King *Rhonda* • Julie Gonzalo *Shelby* • Lin Shaye *Mrs Wells* • Madeline Zima *Brianna* ■ *Dir* Mark Rosman • *Scr* Leigh Dunlap

Cinderfella ★★★ U

Comedy 1960 · US · Colour · 84mins

This amiable retelling stars Jerry Lewis as the put-upon stepson and winsome Anna Maria Alberghetti as a demure "Princess Charming". As producer, Lewis affords himself some notable set pieces, especially the entrance at the ball, zigzagging down a seemingly endless stairway to Count Basie's beat. Non-Lewis fans may find the ballads and interminable goofing tiresome. TS DVD

Jerry Lewis *Fella* • Judith Anderson *Wicked stepmother* • Ed Wynn *Fairy godfather* • Anna Maria Alberghetti *Princess Charmein* • Henry Silva *Maximilian* • Robert Hutton *Rupert* • Count Basie ■ *Dir/Scr* Frank Tashlin

Cinema Paradiso ★★★★★ PG

Drama 1988 · It/Fr · Colour · 117mins

Winner of the Oscar for best foreign language film, this is both an unashamedly sentimental rite of passage picture and a charming reminder of the lost art of cinema-going. The undoubted stars are projectionist Philippe Noiret and his adorable young assistant, Salvatore Cascio. Yet it's the patrons of the village cinema in Sicily who give the film its irresistible flavour, entering into the spirit of each and every movie. The 1994 director's cut contains 32 minutes that were removed from Giuseppe Tornatore's original following a lukewarm domestic response, making it even more of a wonderfully nostalgic experience. DP. In Italian and French with English subtitles. Contains swearing and nudity. DVD

Philippe Noiret *Alfredo* • Jacques Perrin *Salvatore as an adult* • Salvatore Cascio *Toto (Salvatore as a child)* • Marco Leonardi *Salvatore as a teenager* • Agnese Nano *Elena* ■ *Dir* Giuseppe Tornatore • *Scr* Giuseppe Tornatore, Vanna Paoli

Cinéma Vérité: Defining the Moment ★★★★

Documentary
1999 · Can · BW and Colour · 110mins

Having dissected the significance of Noam Chomsky in a previous film, Peter Wintonick explores the genesis of another cultural phenomenon, the fly-on-the-wall documentary, in this assuredly self-referential study of a style that has influenced everything from reality TV to *The Blair Witch Project*. It's loaded with clips from such seminal Direct Cinema classics as *Primary* and *Don't Look Back* and interviews with key practitioners such as Michel Brault, Richard Leacock, Frederick Wiseman and Jean Rouch. But, equally impressively, it makes both social and technical information accessible, while also challenging the viewer's conception of how they watch moving images. DP. In English and French with subtitles.

Dir Peter Wintonick • *Scr* Kirwan Cox

Cinemania ★★★ 12A

Documentary
2002 · US/Ger · Colour · 83mins

Nothing takes precedence over sitting in the dark and gazing at a flickering screen where the five New York buffs depicted in Angela Christlieb and Stephen Kijack's disconcerting study of cinephilia are concerned. Mostly dependent on welfare and isolated from society at large, their lives revolve around movies to the extent that they timetable screenings months in advance. These curious characters are all models of obsessiveness: if Harvey Schwartz's encyclopedic knowledge of running times doesn't have you vowing to rethink your passion for film, 60-something Roberta Hill's pugnacious attitude to ticket stubs certainly will. DP

Dir Angela Christlieb, Stephen Kijak

The Circle ★★★★ PG

Drama 2000 · Iran/It/Swi · Colour · 90mins

Iranian director Jafar Panahi's award-winning movie highlights such contentious issues as divorce, abortion and prostitution to demonstrate the universal discrimination against women in modern Iranian society. An almost Hitchcockian tension develops as eight women suffer male oppression in everyday scenarios ranging from childbirth to buying a bus ticket, all in the space of 24 hours. The raw, hand-held camerawork captures the backstreet ambience of durability and despair. But it's the courageous naturalism of the non-professional cast that provides the drama with its poignancy and power. DP. In Farsi with English subtitles. [video] DVD

Fereshteh Sadr Orafai *Pari* • Maryiam Palvin Almani *Arezou* • Nargess Mamizadeh *Nargess* • Solmaz Gohlami *Solmaz* ■ *Dir* Jafar Panahi • *Scr* Kambuzia Partovi, from an idea by Jafar Panahi

Circle of Danger ★★★ U

Drama 1950 · UK · BW · 82mins

The clever plot here has Ray Milland investigating the death of his commando brother in the Second World War, only to find that things aren't quite what they seem to be. Despite the talented Jacques Tourneur in the director's chair and Alfred Hitchcock collaborator Joan Harrison as co-producer, the movie isn't quite what it seems to be either. Still, Tourneur does what he can with all those red herrings and makes the whole watchable enough. TS

Ray Milland *Clay Douglas* • Patricia Roc *Elspeth Graham* • Marius Goring *Sholto Lewis* • Hugh Sinclair *Hamish McArran* • Naunton Wayne *Reggie Sinclair* • Dora Bryan *Bubbles* ■ *Dir* Jacques Tourneur • *Scr* Philip MacDonald, from his novel *White Heather*

Circle of Deceit ★★

Drama 1981 · Fr/W Ger · Colour · 108mins

West German journalist Bruno Ganz, beset by marital woes, is on assignment in the Lebanon with his photographer Jerzy Skolimowski. Once there, he gets caught up in events – among them an affair with Hanna Schygulla – that compromise both his professional and personal integrity. A sobering but somewhat confused film from Germany's Volker Schlöndorff, this mix of the personal and the political is uneasy, and is compounded by a hero whose inadequacy and self-preoccupation render him deeply tiresome. RB. A German language film.

Bruno Ganz *Georg Laschen* • Hanna Schygulla *Arianna Nassar* • Jerzy Skolimowski *Hoffmann* • Gila Von Weitershausen *Greta Laschen* • Jean Carmet *Rudnik* ■ *Dir* Volker Schlöndorff • *Scr* Volker Schlöndorff, Jean-Claude Carrière, Margarethe von Trotta, Kai Hermann, from the novel *Die Fälschung* by Nicolas Born

Circle of Deception ★★★

Second World War drama
1960 · UK · BW · 99mins

During the Second World War, a nervy and sensitive Canadian officer (Bradford Dillman) is made a fall guy by British intelligence, who drop him in Normandy with false information, confident he'll be captured by the Germans and crack under pressure. Well-directed by Jack Lee, with convincing performances from Dillman and a host of first-class English stage and TV actors, this is a decent espionage drama. RK

Suzy Parker *Lucy Bowen* • Bradford Dillman *Paul Raine* • Harry Andrews *Captain Rawson* • Paul Rogers *Major Spence* • John Welsh *Major Taylor* • Robert Stephens *Captain Stein* ■ *Dir* Jack Lee • *Scr* Nigel Balchin, Robert Musel, from the story *Small Back Room in St Marylebone* by Alec Waugh in *Esquire* magazine

Circle of Friends ★★★★ 15

Romantic drama
1995 · US/Ire · Colour · 98mins

As feature debuts go, they don't come much better than Minnie Driver's. She not only holds together this amiable adaptation of Maeve Binchy's novel, but she positively lights up the screen as Benny, the country girl who has to abandon her Dublin education (and rugby star Chris O'Donnell) to work in the family shop and fight off the unwanted attentions of the wonderfully smarmy Alan Cumming. Colin Firth is overly mannered as the Protestant landlord, and Pat O'Connor slips in too many emerald vistas, but the story is told with wit and charm. DP. Contains swearing and sex scenes. [video] DVD

Chris O'Donnell *Jack* • Minnie Driver *Benny* • Geraldine O'Rawe *Eve* • Saffron Burrows *Nan* • Alan Cumming *Sean* • Colin Firth *Simon Westward* • Aidan Gillen *Aidan* • Mick Lally *Dan Hogan* • Ciaran Hinds *Professor Flynn* ■ *Dir* Pat O'Connor • *Scr* Andrew Davies, from the novel by Maeve Binchy

Circle of Passion ★★★

Romantic drama
1996 · US/UK · Colour · 94mins

Writer/director Charles Finch takes a leading role as an unhappily married banker who has a fling with hat-maker Sandrine Bonnaire during a business trip to Paris. He has to decide where to hang *his* hat when he falls in love with her. Jane March plays the banker's less than amorous other half, and the emotion of her performance is a revelation after her rather flat performances in such films as *The Lover* and *The Color of Night*. DA. In English and French with subtitles.

Sandrine Bonnaire *Katherine Beaufort* • Jane March *Amanda Murray* • James Fox *Arthur Trevane* • Charles Finch *Thomas Murray* • Jean Rochefort *Gerard Panier* • Julian Sands *Roderick* ■ *Dir/Scr* Charles Finch

Circle of Two ★

Drama 1980 · Can · Colour · 108mins

Sixteen-year-old student Tatum O'Neal goes to see a porno movie. Who should she spot in the audience but a haggard-looking Richard Burton! What follows is an inordinate amount of slush, with Burton urging O'Neal to become a writer and she urging him to resume his career as an artist. Burton received $750,000 for the role and delivered a bored performance that was hardly worth a single cent. AT

Richard Burton *Ashley St Clair* • Tatum O'Neal *Sarah Norton* • Nuala Fitzgerald *Claudia Aldrich* • Robin Gammell *Mr Norton* • Patricia Collins *Mrs Norton* • Donann Cavin *Smitty* • Michael Wincott *Paul* • Kate Reid *Dr Emily Reid* ■ *Dir* Jules Dassin • *Scr* Thomas Hedley, from the story *A Lesson in Love* by Marie Terese Baird

Circuitry Man ★★ 15

Science-fiction thriller
1990 · US · Colour · 88mins

This is a futuristic patchwork made up of snippets from a range of sci-fi films, most notably *Blade Runner*, *Logan's Run* and *Mad Max*. More time spent at the typewriter and a little less playing with special effects might have resulted in a better and certainly more coherent movie. As it is, Dana Wheeler-Nicholson's flight from the villainous Lu Leonard, carrying a case full of pleasure-inducing computer chips, is little more than a string of clichés and pompous pronouncements. Followed by a sequel, *Plughead Rewired: Circuitry Man II*. DP. Contains swearing and violence. [video]

Jim Metzler *Danner* • Dana Wheeler-Nicholson *Lori* • Lu Leonard *Juice* • Vernon Wells *Plughead* • Barbara Alyn Woods *Yoyo* • Dennis Christopher *Leech* ■ *Dir* Steven Lovy • *Scr* Steven Lovy, Robert Lovy

Circumstantial Evidence ★★★

Crime drama 1945 · US · BW · 67mins

A neat and unpretentious little 20th Century-Fox second feature about the fallibility of memory, in particular that of alleged eyewitnesses in a murder trial. The witnesses here see, or think they see, Michael O'Shea kill a grocer with whom he is fighting, resulting in his being accused of murder and subsequently convicted. That fine actor Lloyd Nolan brings his *Michael Shayne, Private Detective* persona to bear on this thoughtful plot, but O'Shea is a rather bland lead. Nevertheless, John Larkin's direction is assured, and the moral uncertainties. TS

Michael O'Shea *Joe Reynolds* • Lloyd Nolan *Sam Lord* • Trudy Marshall *Agnes Hannon* • Billy Cummings *Pat Reynolds* • Ruth Ford *Mrs Simms* • Reed Hadley *Prosecutor* • Roy Roberts *Marty Hannon* • Scotty Beckett *Freddy Hanlon* • Byron Foulger *Bolger* ■ *Dir* John Larkin • *Scr* Robert Metzler, Samuel Ornitz, from a story by Nat Ferber, Sam Duncan

The Circus ★★★★ U

Silent comedy 1928 · US · BW · 71mins

Charles Chaplin's theme of despondent love all but ovewhelms the brilliant slapstick set pieces (a chase through a hall of mirrors, being trapped in a lion's cage) when the Tramp, on the run from the police, joins the circus and falls for a bare-back rider (Merna Kennedy). Chaplin got a special award for acting, writing, directing and producing the film, but the best moments are the least self-conscious and hark back to his music hall origins (walking a tightrope with falling trousers and a clinging monkey, for example). Not the best Chaplin, but still pretty sensational. TH [video] DVD

Charlie Chaplin [Charles Chaplin] *Tramp* • Allan Garcia *Circus proprietor* • Merna Kennedy *Girl* • Harry Crocker *Rex* • George Davis *Magician* • Stanley J Stanford [Tiny Sanford] *Head property man* • Henry Bergman *Old clown* ■ *Dir/Scr* Charles Chaplin

Circus ★ 18

Comedy thriller
1999 · UK/US · Colour · 91mins

Set in Brighton, this clueless crime comedy in the Tarantino mould features a collection of unappealing crooks who repeatedly stab each other in the back and a ludicrous story that makes no sense. Bad casting abounds: John Hannah is far too wimpy to convince as a tough, wily killer, while comedian Brian Conley is embarrassing as the least menacing crime lord in movie history. JC [video] DVD

John Hannah *Leo Garfield* • Famke Janssen *Lily Garfield* • Peter Stormare *Julius Harvey* • Eddie Izzard *Troy Cabrara* • Fred Ward *Elmo Somerset* • Brian Conley *Bruno Maitland* • "Tiny" Lister Jr [Tom "Tiny" Lister Jr] *George "Moose" Marley* ■ *Dir* Rob Walker • *Scr* David Logan

Circus Boys ★★★★ PG

Drama 1989 · Jpn · BW · 101mins

One of the finest films to come out of Japan in years, this provides conclusive proof that cinema is much the poorer for the passing of black-and-white film. Yuichi Nagata's imagery has an austerity and clarity that few cinematographers could surpass, whether it's capturing the action in the big top, the disappointments behind the scenes or the deceptions of life on the open road. Director Kaizo Hayashi is similarly in total control of his art, conveying the passage of time with subtle symbolism and drawing a superb performance out of Hiroshi Mikami as the trapeze artist who turns to petty crime after a fall. DP. In Japanese with English subtitles. [video]

Hiroshi Mikami *Jinta* • Moe Kamura *Omocha* • Xia Jian *Wataru* • Michiru Akiyoshi *Maria* • Yuki Asayama *Sayoko* • Sanshi Katsura *Samejima* ■ *Dir/Scr* Kaizo Hayashi

Circus Friends ★★ U

Drama 1956 · UK · BW · 64mins

Although it doesn't add up to much today, this little picture deserves its place in British screen history as the first project brought to completion by producer Peter Rogers and director Gerald Thomas, the godfathers of the *Carry On* series. There's a sentimental charm to this rural tale in which Alan Coleshill and Carol White rescue their pet pony from farmer Meredith Edwards after their penurious father, John Horsley, sells it to help pay his circus bills. DP

Alan Coleshill *Nicky* • Carol White *Nan* • David Tilley *Martin* • Pat Belcher *Beryl* • Meredith Edwards *Farmer Beasley* • John Horsley *Bert Marlow* • Sam Kydd *George* ■ *Dir* Gerald Thomas • *Scr* Peter Rogers

Circus of Fear ★★

Horror thriller 1967 · UK · Colour · 90mins

Christopher Lee wears a black woolly hood for nearly all of his scenes in this lame whodunnit, based on the 1928 Edgar Wallace mystery *Again the Three Just Men*. He's the facially scarred lion tamer in Barberini's Circus, and one of the many suspects in a murder case investigated by Scotland Yard's Leo Genn. John Moxey's disappointing direction accents the cops-and-robbers elements over any marginal terror, but the stalwart efforts of the cast act as a safety net for the shaky plot. AJ

Christopher Lee *Gregor* • Leo Genn *Inspector Elliott* • Anthony Newlands *Barberini* • Heinz Drache *Carl* • Eddi Arent *Eddie* • Klaus Kinski *Manfred* • Margaret Lee *Gina* • Suzy Kendall *Natasha* ■ *Dir* John Moxey [John Llewellyn Moxey] • *Scr* Peter Welbeck [Harry Alan Towers], from a story by Edgar Wallace

Circus of Horrors ★★★ 15

Horror thriller 1960 · UK · Colour · 87mins

Definitely a film to make your flesh creep, this nifty British horror is more in keeping with the gimmicky style of Roger Corman or William Castle than your average Hammer. Anton Diffring is perfectly cast as an incompetent plastic surgeon who takes refuge under Donald Pleasence's big top after the knife slips once too often. Director Sidney Hayers makes superb use of the circus locale, dreaming up wonderfully grotesque ways of bumping off the outcasts that Diffring has remodelled when they try to escape his barbarous regime. DP [video]

Anton Diffring *Dr Schuler* • Erika Remberg *Elissa* • Yvonne Monlaur *Nicole* • Donald Pleasence *Vanet* • Jane Hylton *Angela* • Kenneth Griffith *Martin* • Conrad Phillips *Inspector Ames* • Jack Gwillim *Superintendent Andrews* ■ *Dir* Sidney Hayers • *Scr* George Baxt • *Cinematographer* Douglas Slocombe

C

The Cisco Kid ★★

Western 1931 · US · BW · 60mins

The huge success of the early talkie *In Old Arizona* (1929) prompted the Fox company to produce this lightweight follow-up with Warner Baxter and Edmund Lowe repeating their roles. Baxter's suave Mexican bandit robs a bank to save the ranch of a widow with young children and is again pursued by Lowe's Irish-American lawman. Mobile camerawork and a short running time aid this sentimental tale in which Baxter sacrifices his freedom over concern for the welfare of a small girl. The actor reprised the role in 1939's *The Return of the Cisco Kid*. AE

Warner Baxter *The Cisco Kid* • Edmund Lowe *Sgt Patrick "Mickey" Dunn* • Conchita Montenegro *Carmencita* • Nora Lane *Sally Benton* ■ *Dir* Irving Cummings • *Scr* Al Cohn, from the character created by O Henry in his short story *Caballero's Way* in *Everybody's Magazine* (July 1907)

The Cisco Kid and the Lady ★★★ U

Western 1939 · US · BW · 73mins

A deeply charming if fluffily slight outing for Cesar Romero as the Cisco Kid. The plot is a curious combination of boggling complexity and wafer-thin skimming: gold prospecting, abandoned babies, murder, weddings and funerals are all thrown helter-skelter into the tale and regurgitated as a delightful madcap romp. The supporting cast includes a veritable mishmash of the good Robert Barrat, the profoundly average Ward Bond and the simply dreadful George Montgomery. Overall good fun. SH

Cesar Romero *Cisco Kid* • Marjorie Weaver *Julie Lawson* • Chris-Pin Martin *Gordito* • George Montgomery *Tommy Bates* • Robert Barrat *Jim Harbison* • Virginia Field *Billie Graham* • Harry Green *Teasdale* • Ward Bond *Walton* ■ *Dir* Herbert I Leeds • *Scr* Frances Hyland, from a story by Stanley Rauh, from characters created by O Henry

Cisco Pike ★★★

Crime drama 1971 · US · Colour · 94mins

In order to create a sense of the emptiness at the centre of 1970s pop and drug culture, writer/director Bill L Norton decided here to dispense with any plot, with the result that his evocation of Los Angeles occasionally borders on the flabby. The film is awash with anti-establishment attitudes and creates an atmosphere that is still affecting, despite Norton's penchant for distracting showy touches. Kris Kristofferson, as the has-been rock star, and Gene Hackman, as the corrupt cop, supply plenty of electricity. JM. Contains swearing.

Kris Kristofferson *Cisco Pike* • Gene Hackman *Holland* • Karen Black *Sue* • Harry Dean Stanton *Jesse* • Viva *Merna* • Joy Bang *Lynn* • Roscoe Lee Browne *Music store owner* • Antonio Fargas *Buffalo* ■ *Dir/Scr* Bill L Norton

The Citadel ★★★★

Drama 1938 · US/UK · BW · 112mins

An idealistic young doctor (Robert Donat) battling the slum conditions of a Welsh mining village marries the local schoolteacher (Rosalind Russell) and moves to London, where he is corrupted by the moneyed ease of a society practice. Adapted from AJ Cronin's bestseller, this solid MGM drama makes for thoroughly satisfactory viewing. Donat is perfectly cast, as are Ralph Richardson as his friend and Cecil Parker as a bungling surgeon. Impeccably directed by King Vidor, the picture was voted the year's best by the New York Film Critics. RK

Robert Donat *Andrew Manson* • Rosalind Russell *Christine Manson* • Ralph Richardson *Denny* • Rex Harrison *Dr Lawford* • Emlyn Williams *Owen* • Francis L Sullivan *Ben Chenkin* • Mary Clare *Mrs Orlando* • Cecil Parker *Charles Every* ■ *Dir* King Vidor • *Scr* Ian Dalrymple, Elizabeth Hill, Frank Wead, from the novel by AJ Cronin

The Citadel ★★★ PG

Comedy drama 1989 · Alg · Colour · 98mins

Algerian director Mohamed Chouikh seeks to expose the iniquities of polygamy by presenting us with a stark portrait of life within a strict Muslim community. However, while he elicits sympathy for Khaled Barkat, the orphan adopted by decadent merchant Djillali Ain-Tedeles, and for the trio of wives the latter exploits, Chouikh fails to weave the characters into a satisfying dramatic whole. DP. In Arabic with English subtitles.

Khaled Barkat *Kaddour* • Djillali Ain-Tedeles *Sidi* • Fettouma Ousliha *Helima* • Momo *Aissa* • Fatima Belhadj *Nedjama* ■ *Dir/Scr* Mohamed Chouikh

Citizen Kane ★★★★★ U

Classic drama 1941 · US · BW · 114mins

Acclaimed by critics and film-makers alike, *Citizen Kane* has topped *Sight and Sound*'s decennial "all-time top ten" since 1962. Not bad for the feature film debut of a 25-year-old, whose experience lay in theatre and radio (most of the actors in *Kane* were colleagues from his Mercury Theatre company), and who claimed his sole preparation was to watch John Ford's *Stagecoach* 40 times. Unhindered by preconceptions, he proceeded to experiment with sound, camera angles and movement, and deep focus in a way few had even conceived of. Aided by cinematographer Gregg Toland, he brought visual drama to every shot, brilliantly disguising the picture's shoestring budget (it required a record 116 sets). In addition, Welles also turned in a magnificent performance as Charles Foster Kane, the press baron whose torrid life was so similar to that of William Randolph Hearst that the latter broke the film at the box office through negative publicity. Utterly unmissable. DP [video] DVD

Orson Welles *Charles Foster Kane* • Joseph Cotten *Jedediah Leland/Man in projection room* • Dorothy Comingore *Susan Alexander Kane* • Agnes Moorehead *Mary, Kane's mother* • Ruth Warrick *Emily Monroe Norton Kane* • Ray Collins *Jim W Gettys* • Erskine Sanford *Herbert Carter/Man in projection room* • Everett Sloane *Mr Bernstein* • William Alland *Jerry Thompson/Narrator of "News on the March"* • Paul Stewart *Raymond, head butler* • George Coulouris *Walter Parks Thatcher* • Fortunio Bonanova *Matiste* • Gus Schilling *John, head waiter/Man in projection room* ■ *Dir* Orson Welles • *Scr* Herman J Mankiewicz, Orson Welles • *Music* Bernard Herrmann • *Editor* Robert Wise • *Art Director* Van Nest Polglase, Perry Ferguson • *Special Effects* Vernon L Walker

Citizen Ruth ★★★

Black comedy 1996 · US · Colour · 105mins

Laura Dern carries this issue-based film singlehandedly as Ruth Stoops: a homeless, pregnant drug-abuser who, while sniffing patio sealant, triggers a violent debate between pro-lifers and abortion rights campaigners. The range of characters includes Swoosie Kurtz, her lesbian lover Kelly Preston, Burt Reynolds's pro-lifer and Tippi Hedren's pro-choice harpy. Clearly demonstrating the insanity that surrounds this issue in the US, director Alexander Payne manages to satirise as well as explain. LH

Laura Dern *Ruth Stoops* • Swoosie Kurtz *Diane Sieglar* • Kurtwood Smith *Norm Stoney* • Mary Kay Place *Gail Stoney* • Kelly Preston *Rachel* • MC Gainey *Harlan* • Kenneth Mars *Dr Charlie Rollins* • Tippi Hedren *Jessica Weiss* • Burt Reynolds *Blaine Gibbons* • Diane Ladd *Ruth's mother* ■ *Dir* Alexander Payne • *Scr* Alexander Payne, Jim Taylor

Citizen Verdict ★★ 15

Drama 2003 · UK/Ger/US · Colour · 93mins

Sliding that extra rung down the reality TV ladder, this imaginative piece of entertainment examines the sanctioning of the trial-by-television of US murder suspects, whose guilt or innocence is then decided by viewer vote. Chat-show host Jerry Springer plays the programme's originator, with Armand Assante as the defence lawyer initially seduced by its big bucks. Assante is as solid as usual, and Springer is fine when not asked to exceed his modest acting talents. DA DVD

Armand Assante *Sam Patterson* • Jerry Springer *Marty Rockman* • Roy Scheider *Governor Bull Tyler* • Justine Mitchell *Jessica Landers* • Raffaello Degruttola *Ricky Carr* • Dorette Potgieter *Carlene Osway* • Clive Scott *Judge Halvern* • Lynn Blades *Tawny Scott* ■ *Dir* Philippe Martinez • *Scr* Tony Clarke, Frank Rehwaldt, Kristina Hamilton, Philippe Martinez

Citizen X ★★★ 18

Thriller based on a true story
1995 · US/Hun · Colour · 98mins

The true story of the Soviet Union's most famous serial killer makes absorbing viewing. Former schoolteacher Chikatilo (Jeffrey DeMunn) murdered and mutilated 52 children over an eight-year period, yet managed to evade capture because of government corruption, ineffectual police procedures and the fact that the authorities couldn't admit to such western depravity polluting their culture. Stephen Rea is subtly convincing as the forensic expert who doggedly pursued the killer, while Donald Sutherland deservedly won numerous awards as the military man who finally backed his hunches. AJ. Contains violence and swearing. [video]

Stephen Rea *Detective Viktor Burakov* • Donald Sutherland *Colonel Fetisov* • Max von Sydow *Dr Aleksandr Bukhanovsky* • Jeffrey DeMunn *Andre Chikatilo* • John Wood *Gorbunov* • Joss Ackland *Bondarchuk* ■ *Dir* Chris Gerolmo • *Scr* Chris Gerolmo, from the non-fiction book *The Killer Department* by Robert Cullen

Citizens Band ★★★★

Comedy 1977 · US · Colour · 95mins

A highly amusing and raunchy comedy about CB radio enthusiasts (remember that craze?) in a small midwestern town, eavesdropping on one another with hilarious results. An excellent script, on-the-button performances from Paul Le Mat and Candy Clark, and a great soundtrack featuring Richie Havens and Joe Cocker brighten this charming slab of suburban American graffiti. An early effort from Jonathan Demme that more than hints at the excellence to come. AJ

Paul Le Mat *Blaine Lovejoy, Spider* • Candy Clark *Pam, Electra* • Ann Wedgeworth *Joyce Rissley, Dallas Angel* • Marcia Rodd *Connie Rissley, Portland Angel* • Charles Napier *Harold Rissley, Chrome Angel* • Roberts Blossom *Papa Thermodyne* • Bruce McGill *Dean Lovejoy, Blood* ■ *Dir* Jonathan Demme • *Scr* Paul Brickman

The City ★★★★ U

Documentary 1939 · US · BW · 43mins

Highly stylised in content, this ambitious, worthy and ultimately mesmerising socio-documentary was funded by the American Institute of Planners for the Roosevelt administration. Purporting to present the growth of an idealised city of the future and accompanied by an impressive Aaron Copland score, this 43-minute slice of social film-making by documentarists Ralph Steiner and Willard van Dyke today resembles extreme left-wing propaganda; indeed, it comes as no surprise to discover that Morris Carnovsky and writers Lewis Mumford and Pare Lorentz were subsequently blacklisted. TS

Morris Carnovsky *Narrator* ■ *Dir* Ralph Steiner, Willard van Dyke • *Scr* Lewis Mumford, Pare Lorentz

City across the River ★★★

Drama 1949 · US · BW · 90mins

The exploits of a teenage gang in New York, focusing in particular on one member (Peter Fernandez) and demonstrating how a petty criminal, driven by circumstance, can become a killer. Directed by Maxwell Shane in tough, semi-documentary style, the movie grips with its pace and its graphic depiction of the harsh conditions of tenement life. A very young Tony Curtis appears as a gang member. RK

Stephen McNally *Stan Albert* • Thelma Ritter *Mrs Cusack* • Peter Fernandez *Frank Cusack* • Luis Van Rooten *Joe Cusack* • Jeff Corey *Lt Macon* • Anthony Curtis [Tony Curtis] *Mitch* ■ *Dir* Maxwell Shane • *Scr* Dennis Cooper, Irving Schulman, Maxwell Shane, from the novel *The Amboy Dukes* by Irving Schulman

The City and the Dogs ★★★★

Drama 1985 · Peru · Colour · 133mins

Even though this was the novel that brought Mario Vargas Llosa to international attention, Francisco Lombardi, Peru's best-known film-maker, stripped the original non-linear story down to its bare essentials for this abrasive screen adaptation. Using the corruption and tyranny that existed within the country's military academies as a metaphor for the decay blighting Peruvian society as a whole, Lombardi occasionally errs on the side of sensationalism. Otherwise, though, he relates with persuasive realism the case of senior cadet Juan Manuel Ochoa, who kills a fellow clique member to cover up the exploitative activities tolerated by his superiors. DP. In Spanish with English subtitles.

Pablo Serra *Poet* • Gustavo Bueno *Lieutenant Gamboa* • Juan Manuel Ochoa *Jaguar* • Luis Alvarez *Colonel* • Eduardo Adrianzen *Slave* ■ *Dir* Francisco José Lombardi • *Scr* Jose Watanabe, from the novel *The City and the Dogs* by Mario Vargas Llosa

City beneath the Sea ★★★ U

Adventure 1953 · US · Colour · 86mins

One of those highly Technicolored Universal programme co-features that we all took for granted when they appeared in double bills, which are now a positive joy. This is an underwater adventure romp with Robert Ryan and Anthony Quinn snarling at each other over hidden treasure. Love interest is provided by Mala Powers and Suzan Ball, Lucille Ball's cousin, who would continue to act after her leg was amputated due to cancer, and who died tragically young in 1955. TS

Robert Ryan *Brad Carlton* • Mala Powers *Terry* • Anthony Quinn *Tony Bartlett* • Suzan Ball *Venita* • George Mathews *Captain Meade* • Karel Stepanek *Dwight Trevor* • Lalo Rios *Calypso* • Woody Strode *Djion* ■ *Dir* Budd Boetticher • *Scr* Jack Harvey, Ramon Romero, from the story *Port Royal – Ghost City beneath the Sea* by Harry E Riesberg

City beneath the Sea ★★ U

Science-fiction adventure
1971 · US · Colour · 89mins

Irwin Allen, Mr Disaster Movie himself, took a dive in this pilot for a TV series that was never made. It's easy to see why, as each crisis facing the vast submerged 21st-century metropolis of Pacifica had been done better in previous Allen shows. Asteroids on a collision course, sea monsters, internal dissension and bullion robberies are piled on in the desperate effort to build excitement. Wooden and waterlogged. AJ [VIDEO]

Stuart Whitman *Admiral Michael Matthews* • Robert Wagner *Brett Matthews* • Rosemary Forsyth *Lia Holmes* • Robert Colbert *Commander Woody Patterson* • Susana Miranda *Elena* • Burr DeBenning *Dr Aguila* • Richard Basehart *President* • Joseph Cotten *Dr Ziegler* ■ *Dir* Irwin Allen • *Scr* John Meredyth Lucas, from a story by Irwin Allen

City by the Sea ★★★ 18

Police drama based on a true story
2002 · US · Colour · 104mins

This performance-driven action drama is a poignant and powerful reflection on human weakness and the potential agonies of emotional attachment. Robert De Niro plays a respected New York City homicide detective who is torn between familial and professional notions of duty when a drug dealer's murder is attributed to his estranged son (James Franco). Swapping his characteristic swagger for a shuffling, tortured vulnerability, De Niro delivers a fine, heart-rending performance, and benefits from some weighty support. SF. Contains violence, swearing, drug abuse and sex scenes. [VIDEO] DVD

Robert De Niro *Lt Vincent LaMarca* • Frances McDormand *Michelle* • James Franco *Joey LaMarca* • Eliza Dushku *Gina* • William Forsythe *Spyder* • George Dzundza *Reg Duffy* • Patti LuPone *Maggie* • Anson Mount *Dave Simon* ■ *Dir* Michael Caton-Jones • *Scr* Ken Hixon, from the article *Mark of a Murderer* by Michael McAlary

City for Conquest ★★★★ PG

Melodrama 1940 · US · BW · 94mins

Director Anatole Litvak tells a tough tale as truck driver-turned-prize fighter James Cagney tries to protect his sensitive composer brother, superbly played by Arthur Kennedy in his adult movie debut. Check out future director Elia Kazan, here playing a hood, and watch Ann Sheridan interact with a young Anthony Quinn. A slightly sententious heaviness looms over the enterprise. TS [VIDEO]

James Cagney *Danny Kenny* • Ann Sheridan *Peggy Nash* • Frank Craven *"Old Timer"* • Donald Crisp *Scotty McPherson* • Arthur Kennedy *Eddie Kenny* • Elia Kazan *"Googi"* • Anthony Quinn *Murray Burns* ■ *Dir* Anatole Litvak • *Scr* John Wexley, from the novel by Aben Kandel

The City Girl ★★ 18

Drama 1984 · US · Colour · 81mins

The drama in Martha Coolidge's follow-up to *Valley Girl* derives from the opposing forces that pull struggling photographer Laura Harrington apart at the seams. Trying to assert her independence, she dumps her long-time partner to play the field. Things backfire badly when a pimp she is secretly snapping scares the living daylights out of her by trashing her apartment. Harrington impresses in this tale of a modern woman trying to survive in the big wide world. FL [VIDEO]

Laura Harrington *Anne* • Joe Mastroianni *Joey* • Carole McGill *Gracie* • Peter Riegert *Tim* • James Carrington *Steve* • Lawrence Phillips *The stripper* • Geraldine Baron *Monica* ■ *Dir* Martha Coolidge • *Scr* Judith Thompson, Leonard-John Gates, from a story by Martha Coolidge, John MacDonald

City Hall ★★★★ 15

Political drama 1996 · US · Colour · 106mins

This is reminiscent of one of those Warner Bros gangster films of the 1930s, but director Harold Becker's update is even more violent and exciting. Al Pacino is the New York mayor, rabble-rousing as he plots a path to the White House, but finding himself thwarted in his political ambition when a child is killed in the crossfire between a cop and a drug dealer. His naive deputy, John Cusack, investigates the crime with the help of attorney Bridget Fonda, only to find the perpetrators are uncomfortably close to home. Not particularly original, but superbly acted and entertaining. TH. Contains violence, swearing. [VIDEO] DVD

Al Pacino *Mayor John Pappas* • John Cusack *Kevin Calhoun* • Bridget Fonda *Marybeth Cogan* • Danny Aiello *Frank Anselmo* • Martin Landau *Judge Walter Stern* • David Paymer *Abe Goodman* • Tony Franciosa [Anthony Franciosa] *Paul Zapatti* • Lindsay Duncan *Sydney Pappas* ■ *Dir* Harold Becker • *Scr* Ken Lipper, Paul Schrader, Nicholas Pileggi, Bo Goldman

City Heat ★★★ 15

Comedy thriller 1984 · US · Colour · 93mins

Clint Eastwood and Burt Reynolds were dream casting, but this got off to a bad start. Originally called *Kansas City Jazz*, it had been written by Blake Edwards, who was also to direct. But Eastwood and Edwards disliked each other from the first, so Edwards left and Richard Benjamin took over. Despite the on-set problems, the movie is a nostalgic sprint through Prohibition-era Kansas City, with Eastwood as a cop and Reynolds as a private eye, who team up and clear the town of gangsters. AT. Contains swearing and violence. [VIDEO]

Clint Eastwood *Lieutenant Speer* • Burt Reynolds *Mike Murphy* • Jane Alexander *Addy* • Madeline Kahn *Caroline Howley* • Rip Torn *Primo Pitt* • Irene Cara *Ginny Lee* • Richard Roundtree *Dehl Swift* • Tony LoBianco *Leon Coll* ■ *Dir* Richard Benjamin • *Scr* Sam O Brown [Blake Edwards], Joseph C Stinson, from a story by Sam O Brown [Blake Edwards]

The City Is Dark ★★★

Film noir 1954 · US · BW · 73mins

Ex-con Gene Nelson on parole in Los Angeles attempts to go straight with the support of his wife Phyllis Kirk, but soon finds himself up against hostile forces. Nelson, better known for dancing up a storm in such musicals as *Lullaby of Broadway* and *Oklahoma!*, is excellent; so is Sterling Hayden as a vengeful and sadistic cop. Solid and pacey, Andre De Toth's movie takes a gritty look at police methods, the criminal world and the difficulties crooks face when they try to escape their former lives. RK

Sterling Hayden *Detective Sergeant Sims* • Gene Nelson *Steve Lacey* • Phyllis Kirk *Ellen* • Ted De Corsia *"Doc" Penny* • Charles Buchinsky [Charles Bronson] *Ben Hastings* • Jay Novello *Dr Otto Hessler* • James Bell *Daniel O'Keefe* ■ *Dir* Andre De Toth • *Scr* Crane Wilbur, Bernard Gordon, Richard Wormser, from the story *Criminals Mark* by John Hawkins, Ward Hawkins

City Lights ★★★★★ U

Silent comedy romance
1931 · US · BW · 82mins

A consummate storyteller, Charles Chaplin could reduce his audience to fits of laughter and, without warning, plunge them to the depths of pathos. With this masterpiece, telling the story of a tramp and the blind flower girl (Virginia Cherrill) he falls in love with, Chaplin went against the incoming tide of talking pictures by using only music, sound effects, subtitles and his own inestimable pantomime skills. He told Sam Goldwyn: "If it's a failure, I believe it will strike a deeper blow than anything else that has ever happened to me in this life." It was, in fact, a resounding success. TH [VIDEO] DVD

Charlie Chaplin [Charles Chaplin] *Tramp* • Virginia Cherrill *Blind girl* • Florence Lee *Her grandmother* • Harry Myers *Eccentric millionaire* • Allan Garcia *His butler* • Jean Harlow *Guest* ■ *Dir/Scr* Charles Chaplin • *Music* Charles Chaplin

City Limits ★★ 15

Science-fiction action adventure
1985 · US · Colour · 81mins

Set in a futuristic world where most adults have been eradicated by plague, this post-apocalyptic action adventure depicts a Los Angeles divided between two motorbike gangs. Orphaned John Stockwell comes to town to join one, only to uncover a plot to take control of the city by the sinister Sunya Corporation, whose chief is none other than Robby Benson! RT [VIDEO]

Darrell Larson *Mick* • John Stockwell *Lee* • Kim Cattrall *Wickings* • Rae Dawn Chong *Yogi* • John Diehl *Whitey* • Danny De La Paz *Ray* • James Earl Jones *Albert* ■ *Dir* Aaron Lipstadt • *Scr* Don Opper, from a story by James Reigle, Aaron Lipstadt

City of Angels ★★★ 12

Romantic fantasy drama
1998 · US · Colour · 109mins

A semi-remake of Wim Wenders's classic *Wings of Desire*, this Hollywood version has Nicolas Cage as an angel inhabiting Los Angeles who falls for heart surgeon Meg Ryan (yes, really). Will he give up his otherworldly delights so he can "fall" to earth and be with her? Will she realise he's not quite like other guys? And will they both drown in the slushy sentimentality of it all? Happily, not quite, thanks to a well-chosen soundtrack (Sarah McLachlan, Goo Goo Dolls, Alanis Morissette) and a winning – and moving – performance from Cage that will melt the hearts of his female fans. JB [VIDEO] DVD

Nicolas Cage *Seth* • Meg Ryan *Dr Maggie Rice* • Dennis Franz *Nathaniel Messinger* • André Braugher *Cassiel* • Colm Feore *Jordan* ■ *Dir* Brad Silberling • *Scr* Dana Stevens

City of Fear ★★

Drama 1959 · US · BW · 74mins

Following their collaboration on *Murder by Contract*, action man Vince Edwards and director Irving Lerner reteamed for this tense little thriller that boasts photography by Lucien Ballard and a score by Jerry Goldsmith. It follows Edwards as he tries to get rid of a canister that he thinks contains heroin, but is, in fact, loaded with a radioactive material. Edwards isn't the most gifted of actors, but it's not bad. DP

Vince Edwards *Vince Ryker* • Lyle Talbot *Chief Jensen* • John Archer *Lieutenant Mark Richards* • Steven Ritch *Dr Wallace* • Patricia Blair *June* • Joe Mell *Crown* ■ *Dir* Irving Lerner • *Scr* Steven Ritch, Robert Dillon

City of Fear ★

Spy drama 1965 · UK · BW · 75mins

Terry Moore, better known these days for her string of front-page love affairs and her secret marriage to Howard Hughes, stars in this low-budget spy picture, in which she goes behind the Iron Curtain to help refugees escape from Hungary. Moore's uninterest, the by-the-numbers plot, Peter Bezencenet's lumpen direction and Paul Maxwell's shocking performance as a reporter. DP

Terry Moore *Suzan* • Albert Lieven *Paul* • Marisa Mell *Ilona* • Paul Maxwell *Mike Foster* • Pinkas Braun *Ferenc* • Maria Takacs *Marika* ■ *Dir* Peter Bezencenet • *Scr* Peter Welbeck [Harry Alan Towers], Max Bourne

City of Ghosts ★★★ 15

Thriller 2002 · US · Colour · 111mins

Matt Dillon's directorial debut plays like a dark love letter to Cambodia. In this slow-burning thriller, the actor also takes the lead as a conman who flees the US for Cambodia following an insurance scam. Here, passionately detailed visuals present a snapshot of an alien culture, populated by quirky characters who add colour to Dillon's hunt for his shadowy associate James Caan. Though these fleeting figures need more explanation, particularly love interest Natascha McElhone, they provide a surrealistic touch that lifts the tale's overall bleakness. The picture lacks the complexity and pacing to really grip, but it's still an admirable effort. SF. Contains swearing, violence, sex scenes and drug abuse. [VIDEO] DVD

Matt Dillon *Jimmy Cremmins* • James Caan *Marvin* • Natascha McElhone *Sophie* • Gérard Depardieu *Emile* • Sereyvuth Kem *Sok* • Stellan Skarsgård *Kaspar* • Rose Byrne *Sabrina* • Shawn Andrews *Robbie* • Chalee Sankhavesa *Sideth* ■ *Dir* Matt Dillon • *Scr* Matt Dillon, Barry Gifford

City of God ★★★★★ 18

Crime thriller
2002 · Bra/Ger/Fr · Colour · 124mins

Inspired by Paulo Lins's fact-based novel, this three-act chronicle of gangland rivalry on the streets of Rio de Janeiro resists the temptation to glamorise crime, as so many New York Mob movies have done. Yet director Fernando Meirelles's audacious visual style may disconcert those expecting a neorealistic approach to the story of a teenage hoodlum's rise and fall. Comparisons with *GoodFellas* are certainly valid, as the often explosive and meticulously designed action spans the late 1960s to the early 1980s. But the no-holds-barred authenticity of the non-professional juvenile cast and Meirelles's edgy social commitment make it a wholly unique experience. DP. In Portuguese with English subtitles. Contains violence, swearing, sex scenes, drug abuse and nudity. [VIDEO] DVD

Alexandre Rodrigues *Buscapé, "Rocket"* • Leandro Firmino da Hora *Zé Pequeño, "Li'l Ze"* • Phellipe Haagensen *Bené, "Beny"* • Douglas Silva *Dadinho, "Li'l Dice"* • Jonathan Haagensen *Cabeleira, "Shaggy"* • Matheus Nachtergaele *Sandro Cenoura, "Carrot"* ■ *Dir* Fernando Meirelles • *Scr* Braulio Mantovani, from the novel by Paulo Lins

City of Hope ★★★★★ 15

Drama 1991 · US · Colour · 124mins

The title is ironic to the point of sarcasm, but that's just what you expect from director John Sayles, the greatest of Hollywood independents. This hugely impressive film brilliantly portrays the conflicts and corruption inherent within a New Jersey community as fault-lines upon which the community is built. It's how these seeming abstractions affect people's lives that concerns Sayles and, while there's no central star to light up the dark places, the cast's ensemble acting is vivid enough for an epic that winds down to a desperately bleak finale. TH. Contains violence, swearing and drug abuse. [VIDEO]

Vincent Spano *Nick Rinaldi* • Joe Morton *Wynn* • Tony LoBianco *Joe Rinaldi* • Barbara Williams (2) *Angela* • Stephen Mendillo *Yoyo* • Chris Cooper *Riggs* • Charlie Yanko *Stavros* • Jace Alexander *Bobby* • Angela Bassett *Reesha* ■ *Dir/Scr* John Sayles

City of Industry ★★ 18

Crime thriller 1996 · US · Colour · 92mins

This dour revenge thriller stars Harvey Keitel as a crook tracking down an associate who got greedy after a lucrative robbery. The solid, if unexceptional performances from Keitel and Stephen Dorff (as the unscrupulous scumbag he pursues), combined with John Irvin's no-frills direction and a by-the-numbers plot lend this the appearance of a tough TV movie. JC. Contains swearing, violence. [VIDEO] DVD

Harvey Keitel *Roy Egan* • Stephen Dorff *Skip Kovich* • Timothy Hutton *Lee Egan* • Famke Janssen *Rachel Montana* • Wade Dominguez

Jorge Montana • Michael Jai White *Odell Williams* • Elliott Gould *Gangster* ■ *Dir* John Irvin • *Scr* Ken Solarz

City of Joy ★★★ 15

Drama 1992 · Fr/UK · Colour · 129mins

A much derided movie on its release, Roland Joffé's overlong and occasionally muddled tale of life in a Calcutta slum actually has much to recommend it. Patrick Swayze turns in a credible performance as the dedicated if emotionally constipated doctor, and Pauline Collins is far from clichéd as the gutsy, confrontational nurse. Joffé brings the abject squalor of the overpopulated alleys to vibrant, atmospheric life, and all concerned give it their best shot. SH. Contains violence and swearing.

Patrick Swayze *Max Lowe* • Pauline Collins *Joan Bethel* • Om Puri *Hasari Pal* • Shabana Azmi *Kamla Pal* • Art Malik *Ashoka* • Ayesha Dharker [Ayesha Dharkar] *Amrita Pal* • Santu Chowdhury *Shambu Pal* • Imran Badsah Khan *Manooj Pal* ■ *Dir* Roland Joffé • *Scr* Mark Medoff, from the novel by Dominique LaPierre

The City of Lost Children ★★★★ 15

Fantasy adventure
1995 · Fr/Sp/Ger · Colour · 107mins

Ron Perlman stars in this sinister fantasy adventure from French directors Jean-Pierre Jeunet and Marc Caro who, with their extraordinary *Delicatessen*, set new standards for dark fables. From its nightmare opening to the climactic battle, this surreal tale is an astonishing eye-opener as carnival strongman One (Perlman) leads the fight against the evil Krank (Daniel Emilfork), who steals children's dreams. If you think films can do nothing new, prepare to be surprised. Also available in a dubbed version. TH. In French with English subtitles. DVD

Ron Perlman *One* • Daniel Emilfork *Krank* • Judith Vittet *Miette* • Dominique Pinon *Clones/Diver/Stocle* • Jean-Claude Dreyfus *Marcello, the flea tamer* • Mireille Mossé *Mademoiselle Bismuth* ■ *Dir* Marc Caro, Jean-Pierre Jeunet • *Scr* Gilles Adrien, Jean-Pierre Jeunet, Marc Caro, Guillaume Laurant

The City of No Limits ★★★ 12A

Thriller 2002 · Sp/Arg · Colour · 120mins

An old man's regrets and his family's guilty secrets intersect in Antonio Hernández's intriguing study of loyalty, memory and the consequences of momentous actions. Leonardo Sbaraglia avoids his romantic responsibilities towards both Argentinian girlfriend Leticia Bredice and sister-in-law Ana Fernández by embarking on a mission to lay Fernando Fernán Gómez's Civil War ghosts. Sbaraglia's search for a potentially mythical comrade-in-arms runs into occasional dead-ends, but Hernández recovers the emotional momentum to deliver a potent finale. DP. In French and Spanish with English subtitles.

Leonardo Sbaraglia *Victor* • Fernando Fernán Gómez *Max* • Geraldine Chaplin *Marie* • Ana Fernández *Carmen* • Adriana Ozores *Pilar* • Leticia Bredice *Eileen* • Roberto Alvarez *Luis* ■ *Dir* Antonio Hernández • *Scr* Enrique Brasó, Antonio Hernández

A City of Sadness ★★★★ 12

Drama 1989 · Tai · Colour · 151mins

The winner of the Golden Lion at Venice, this epic of intimate details puts a human face on the momentous events that buffeted Taiwan between the Japanese surrender in 1945 and the arrival of Chiang Kai-Shek's Nationalists four years later. There's a sense of microcosm about the deteriorating widower's household, with one son working as a translator during the occupation, another a deaf mute fighting for independence, the third a petty gangster and the fourth a soldier presumed killed in action. Hou Hsiao-Hsien's subtle compositions and meticulous pacing draw the viewer into the heart of the drama. DP. In Mandarin and Hokkien with English subtitles.

Tony Chiu-Wai Leung [Tony Leung (2)] *Lin Wen-Ching* • Xin Shufen *Hinomi* • Chen Sown-Yung *Lin Wen-Heung* • Kao Jai *Lin Wen-Leung* • Li Tianlu *Lin Ah-Lu* • Wu Yi-Fang *Hinoe* ■ *Dir* Hou Hsiao-Hsien • *Scr* Wu Nien-Jen, Chu Tien-Wen

The City of the Dead ★★★ 15

Horror 1960 · UK · BW · 76mins

Also known as *Horror Hotel*, this cheap and chilling supernatural thriller reeks of atmospheric horror and benefits enormously from its stagebound sets and black-and-white photography. A young history student goes to a remote Massachusetts village to research black magic and falls prey to a reincarnated witch burned at the stake 250 years earlier. Professor Christopher Lee is part of the modern coven holding the hamlet in a grip of sacrificial terror. AJ DVD

Christopher Lee *Professor Driscoll* • Venetia Stevenson *Nan Barlow* • Patricia Jessel *Elizabeth Selwyn/Mrs Newless* • Betta St John *Patricia Russell* • Valentine Dyall *Jethrow Keane* • Dennis Lotis *Richard Barlow* • Norman Macowan *Reverend Russell* • Ann Beach *Lottie* ■ *Dir* John Moxey [John Llewellyn Moxey] • *Scr* George Baxt, from a story by Milton Subotsky

City of Women ★★★★ 18

Fantasy drama 1980 · It/Fr · Colour · 139mins

Intended as Federico Fellini's contribution to a collaboration with Ingmar Bergman entitled *Love Duet* and briefly touted as a Dustin Hoffman vehicle, this is a sexual variation on the Scrooge theme. Marcello Mastroianni returns as Fellini's alter ego to embark on a revelatory journey through a gynocentric hell. There's little wonder feminist commentators decried the picture, but this phantasmagoria of flesh also contains priceless moments of parody, autobiography and satire. DP. In Italian with English subtitles.

Marcello Mastroianni *Snaporaz* • Anna Prucnal *Elena* • Bernice Stegers *Woman on train* • Jole Silvani *Motorcyclist* • Donatella Damiani *Feminist on roller skates* • Ettore Manni *Dr Katzone* ■ *Dir* Federico Fellini • *Scr* Federico Fellini, Bernardino Zapponi, Brunello Rondi

City on Fire ★★

Disaster movie 1979 · Can · Colour · 105mins

Leslie Nielsen plays it straight in this disaster movie, so it does at least provide some unintentional giggles. For the most part, it's minor league stuff, with a collection of vaguely familiar TV faces along with such movie legends as Henry Fonda and Ava Gardner almost being burned to a cinder after gasoline seeps into the city's sewer system. JF

Barry Newman *Frank Whitman* • Susan Clark *Diana Brockhurst-Lautrec* • Shelley Winters *Nurse Andrea Harper* • Leslie Nielsen *Mayor William Dudley* • James Franciscus *Jimbo* • Ava Gardner *Maggie Grayson* • Henry Fonda *Fire chief* ■ *Dir* Alvin Rakoff • *Scr* Jack Hill, David P Lewis, Celine La Freniere

City on Fire ★★★★ 18

Action thriller 1987 · HK · Colour · 100mins

In this violent Hong Kong thriller, the inspiration for Quentin Tarantino's *Reservoir Dogs*, Oriental superstar Chow Yun-Fat stars as an undercover cop who works his way into a gang planning a jewel heist. When it all goes wrong, the gang returns to its warehouse rendezvous, where the recriminations begin. Director Ringo Lam accelerates the violence with skill, though it lacks the poignancy that Tarantino was to inject into his ground-breaking crime drama. TH. In Cantonese with English subtitles. Contains violence, nudity. DVD

Chow Yun-Fat *Ko Chow* • Lee Sau Yin [Danny Lee] *Ah Foo* • Sun Yueh *Inspector Lau* • Carrie Ng *Hung* ■ *Dir* Ringo Lam • *Scr* Tommy Sham, from a story by Ringo Lam

City Slickers ★★★★ 15

Comedy western
1991 · US · Colour · 109mins

Billy Crystal and chums Daniel Stern and Bruno Kirby are the city folk who get the chance to play at *Rawhide* in a winning comedy blockbuster. Seeking to stave off middle age, the trio join a motley group who have volunteered to drive cattle across the range under the eye of irascible old cowboy Jack Palance. Despite some sentimental moments, this is an engaging, expertly played piece which gently pokes fun at both middle-aged angst and the Wild West. Palance won a best supporting actor Oscar for his performance, while director Ron Underwood proves to be as adept with the gags as he is with the large-scale set pieces. JF. Contains swearing. DVD

Billy Crystal *Mitch Robbins* • Daniel Stern *Phil Berquist* • Bruno Kirby *Ed Furillo* • Patricia Wettig *Barbara Robbins* • Helen Slater *Bonnie Rayburn* • Jack Palance *Curly* • Noble Willingham *Clay Stone* • Tracey Walter *Cookie* ■ *Dir* Ron Underwood • *Scr* Lowell Ganz, Babaloo Mandel, from a story by Billy Crystal

City Slickers II: the Legend of Curly's Gold ★★ 12

Comedy western
1994 · US · Colour · 110mins

Producers always rush out sequels to sleepers (or surprise box-office hits), hoping to cash in while the audience is still in the right mood. Unfortunately, sleepers are by definition films no one initially had much confidence in, and film-makers often struggle to repeat the inexplicably successful formula. This is a case in point. Jack Palance briefly reprises his Oscar-winning role, but a hit comedy needs more than cameos, cattle and scenery. DP. Contains some swearing.

Billy Crystal *Mitch Robbins* • Daniel Stern *Phil Berquist* • Jon Lovitz *Glen Robbins* • Jack Palance *Duke/Curly Washburn* • Patricia Wettig *Barbara Robbins* • Pruitt Taylor Vince *Bud* • Bill McKinney *Matt* • Lindsay Crystal *Holly Robbins* • Beth Grant *Lois* ■ *Dir* Paul Weiland • *Scr* Billy Crystal, Lowell Ganz, Babaloo Mandel

City Streets ★★★

Crime melodrama 1931 · US · BW · 73mins

The story of mobster's daughter Sylvia Sidney, jailed for a crime she didn't commit, and her romance with carnival worker Gary Cooper, who finds himself in trouble as a result of their involvement. One of the key offerings of its period, the film introduced Sylvia Sidney, the brilliantly understated stage actress with the born-to-suffer face, and made her an instant star at Paramount. Although this gangster melodrama seems very dated now, the stars and Rouben Mamoulian's innovative, atmospheric direction provide much to enjoy. RK

Gary Cooper *The Kid* • Sylvia Sidney *Nan Cooley* • Paul Lukas *Big Fellow Maskal* • Guy Kibbee *Pop Cooley* • William Boyd (1) *McCoy* • Wynne Gibson *Agnes* • Betty Sinclair *Pansy* • Stanley Fields *Blackie* ■ *Dir* Rouben Mamoulian • *Scr* Max Marcin, Oliver HP Garrett, from a story by Dashiell Hammett

City That Never Sleeps ★★

Detective drama 1953 · US · BW · 90mins

Chicago cop Gig Young plans to quit the force, and his wife, for nightclub dancer Mala Powers. To finance his desertion, he accepts an offer from crooked lawyer Edward Arnold to escort gangster William Talman to safety. A moderately entertaining crime entry that gives an authentic picture of night-time police work in Chicago. RK

Gig Young *Johnny Kelly* • Mala Powers *Sally Connors* • William Talman *Hayes Stewart* • Edward Arnold *Penrod Biddel* • Chill Wills *Joe Chicago* • Marie Windsor *Lydia Biddel* • Paula Raymond *Kathy Kelly* • Otto Hulett *Sgt John Kelly Sr* ■ *Dir* John H Auer • *Scr* Steve Fisher

City under the Sea ★★★ U

Science-fiction adventure
1965 · UK/US · Colour · 83mins

Tenuously based on Edgar Allan Poe, with Jules Verne being the main uncredited inspiration, this fanciful mix of comedy adventure and submarine suspense was director Jacques Tourneur's final feature. Vincent Price enjoyably camps it up as the immortal underwater leader of a Cornish contingent of smugglers-turned-gillmen, and the whole subterranean soufflé is highly watchable even if, sadly, it does slide from the poetic to the pathetic. AJ

Vincent Price *Captain, Sir Hugh Tregathion* • David Tomlinson *Harold Tiffin-Jones* • Tab Hunter *Ben Harris* • Susan Hart *Jill Tregellis* • John Le Mesurier *Rev Jonathan Ives* • Henry Oscar *Mumford* • Derek Newark *Dan* ■ *Dir* Jacques Tourneur • *Scr* Charles Bennett, Louis M Heyward, from the poems *The Doomed City (City in the Sea)/A Descent into the Maelstrom* by Edgar Allan Poe

A Civil Action ★★★ 15

Courtroom drama based on a true story
1998 · US · Colour · 110mins

John Travolta stars as an ambulance chasing attorney who takes on potentially lucrative cases so he can settle out of court and collect his cut. Writer/director Steven Zaillan's film isn't entirely credible, even if the events did actually happen. Travolta's metamorphosis from cynical manipulator to self-destructive righter of wrongs is hard to swallow, and even harder to empathise with. Classy performances all round, though, with a brilliant turn from Robert Duvall. JC. Contains swearing.

John Travolta *Jan Schlichtmann* • Robert Duvall *Jerome Facher* • Tony Shalhoub *Kevin Conway* • William H Macy *James Gordon* • Zeljko Ivanek *Bill Crowley* • Bruce Norris *William Cheeseman* • John Lithgow *Judge Skinner* • Kathleen Quinlan *Anne Anderson* • James Gandolfini *Al Love* • Stephen Fry *Pinder* • Dan Hedaya *John Riley* • Sydney Pollack *Al Eustis* • Kathy Bates *Judge* ■ *Dir* Steven Zaillian • *Scr* Steven Zaillian, from the novel by Jonathan Harr

Civilization ★★★

Silent drama 1916 · US · BW · 102mins

Widely considered to be both the father of the western and the founder of the studio system, Thomas Ince was a major player in Hollywood. But his celluloid reputation rests on this pacifist tract – although it's now believed such directors as Raymond West and Reginald Barker actually called the shots. Produced during the First World War, it is set in the kingdom of Wredpryd and has the spirit of Christ possessing a militaristic inventor who persuades the king to terminate a conflict after a tour of the battlefield. Though now deemed naive, it is nonetheless a valuable record of early movie allegory. DP

Herschel Mayall *The King of Wredpryd* • Lola May *Queen Eugenie* • Howard Hickman *Count Ferdinand* • Enid Markey *Katheryn Haldemann*

• George Fisher (1) *The Christus* ■ *Dir* Thomas Harper Ince [Thomas Ince], Raymond B West, Reginald Barker • *Scr* C Gardner Sullivan

The Claim ★★★★ 15

Period drama
2000 · UK/Can/Fr · Colour · 115mins

This ambitious drama, inspired by *The Mayor of Casterbridge* and set in a gold-rush town, boasts some superb performances. Peter Mullan sells his wife and baby daughter to a gold prospector in return for the claim to a gold mine. Years later, he has built the town of Kingdom Come and enjoys a relationship with a brothel owner (Milla Jovovich), but the past returns to haunt him in the form of his dying wife (Nastassja Kinski) and grown daughter (Sarah Polley). This is beautifully filmed by cinematographer Alwin Kuchler and, despite some underdeveloped characters, is an often haunting tale. JB. Contains violence, swearing and nudity. VIDEO DVD

Peter Mullan *Daniel Dillon* • Milla Jovovich *Lucia* • Wes Bentley *Dalglish* • Nastassja Kinski *Elena Dillon* • Sarah Polley *Hope Dillon* • Shirley Henderson *Annie* ■ *Dir* Michael Winterbottom • *Scr* Frank Cottrell Boyce, from the novel *The Mayor of Casterbridge* by Thomas Hardy • *Cinematographer* Alwin Kuchler • *Music* Michael Nyman

Claire Dolan ★★★ 18

Drama 1998 · US/Fr · Colour · 95mins

Lodge H Kerrigan's debut study of a haunted schizophrenic is a visually ambitious and boldly ambiguous film about a prostitute who seeks to start a new life away from her chillingly vicious pimp. Approaching her duties with a clinicial detachment, Claire is played with an authentic mixture of suppressed loathing, quiet self-worth and sheer terror by the excellent Katrin Cartlidge, whose determination to escape on her own terms underscores her emotional reserve. DP

Katrin Cartlidge *Claire Dolan* • Vincent D'Onofrio *Elton Garrett* • Colm Meaney *Roland Cain* • Patrick Husted *George* ■ *Dir/Scr* Lodge H Kerrigan

Claire of the Moon ★ 18

Drama 1992 · US · Colour · 103mins

At an all-female writer's retreat in Oregon, strait-laced psychologist Karen Trumbo finds herself sexually attracted to her fun-loving roommate, Trisha Todd. But will either overcome their insecurities and accept their true feelings? Full of tedious talk, lesbian stereotypes and stilted acting, this amateurish gay love story is pure soap opera. AJ VIDEO DVD

Trisha Todd *Claire Jabrowski* • Karen Trumbo *Dr Noel Benedict* • Craig Damen *Brian* • Faith McDevitt *Maggie* • Sheila Dickenson *BJ* • Caren Graham *Tara* • Melissa Mitchell *Adrienne* ■ *Dir/Scr* Nicole Conn

Claire's Knee ★★★★ PG

Comedy 1970 · Fr · Colour · 101mins

The fifth of Eric Rohmer's "Six Moral Tales", this is a hypnotic study of temptation, sumptuously shot by Nestor Almendros in the shimmering Annecy sunshine. Although events unfold from the viewpoint of diplomat Jean-Claude Brialy, the attention, as so often in Rohmer's films, is focused firmly on the emotions of young women, in this case, of the sisters (Laurence De Monaghan and Béatrice Romand) he has been encouraged to flirt with in a bid to experience passion before his wedding. Entertaining and provocative. DP. In French with English subtitles. VIDEO DVD

Jean-Claude Brialy *Jérôme* • Aurora Cornu *Aurora* • Béatrice Romand *Laura* • Laurence De Monaghan *Claire* • Michèle Montel *Madame Walter* • Gérard Falconetti *Gilles* ■ *Dir/Scr* Eric Rohmer • *Producer* Barbet Schroeder, Pierre Cottrell

The Clairvoyant ★★★

Drama 1934 · UK · BW · 80mins

Claude Rains was the villain or victim of many a Hollywood melodrama. This underused British actor gets a crack at the lead in this creaky drama from director Maurice Elvey, in which he peddles fake predictions at a music hall until he suddenly starts hitting nails on the head. Rains is impressive throughout, whether faking on the stage, pleading to be taken seriously or explaining his friendship with Jane Baxter to wife Fay Wray. TS

Claude Rains *Maximus* • Fay Wray *Rene* • Jane Baxter *Christine* • Mary Clare *Mother* • Ben Field *Simon* • Athole Stewart *Lord Southwood* • Felix Aylmer *Counsel* • Donald Calthrop *Derelict* ■ *Dir* Maurice Elvey • *Scr* Charles Bennett, Bryan Edgar Wallace, from the novel by Ernst Lothar

Clambake ★ U

Musical 1967 · US · Colour · 95mins

Elvis Presley's 25th film – a reworking of *The Prince and the Pauper* – looks like it cost next to nothing, and probably did. It features a perfunctory performance from the King, who has less screen time than his co-star Will Hutchins. The colour is garish, the back projection looks phoney and the songs are below par. TS VIDEO DVD

Elvis Presley *Scott Heyward* • Shelley Fabares *Dianne Carter* • Will Hutchins *Tom Wilson* • Bill Bixby *James Jamison III* • Gary Merrill *Sam Burton* • James Gregory *Duster Heyward* • Amanda Harley *Ellie* • Suzie Kaye *Sally* ■ *Dir* Arthur Nadel • *Scr* Arthur Browne Jr

Le Clan ★★ 15

Drama 2004 · Fr/Swi · Colour · 89mins

This offers an often visually striking but relentlessly grim look at masculinity through the story of three young brothers living in Annecy in France after the death of their mother. It's effectively a three-parter, following small-time drug dealer Nicolas Cazalé's feud with a drugs gang, his attempts to rope older brother and ex-con Stéphane Rideau into his plans for revenge, and the affair between youngest brother Thomas Dumerchez and one of Cazalé's male friends. The camera lingers lovingly on male flesh, but the result is neither lyrical nor provocative. LF. In French with English subtitles. Contains swearing, sexual references and nudity.

Nicolas Cazalé *Marc* • Stéphane Rideau *Christophe* • Thomas Dumerchez *Olivier* • Salim Kechiouche *Hicham* • Bruno Lochet *Father* • Jackie Berroyer *Robert* • Vincent Martinez *Teacher* • Aure Atika *Emilie* ■ *Dir* Gaël Morel • *Scr* Gaël Morel, Christophe Honoré

The Clan of the Cave Bear ★★ 15

Fantasy drama 1986 · US · Colour · 93mins

Daryl Hannah is the strange blond prehistoric human who is taken in by a gang of grunting Neanderthals and proceeds to make her own small contribution to the evolution of the species. This boasts a script by acclaimed film-maker John Sayles, but in the end it falls into the worthy but dull category. JF. Contains violence and nudity. VIDEO DVD

Daryl Hannah *Ayla* • Pamela Reed *Iza* • James Remar *Creb* • Thomas G Waites *Broud* • John Doolittle *Brun* • Curtis Armstrong *Goov* • Martin Doyle *Grod* • Adel C Hammoud *Vorn* ■ *Dir* Michael Chapman • *Scr* John Sayles, from the novel by Jean M Auel

Clancy Street Boys ★★ U

Comedy 1943 · US · BW · 65mins

This *East Side Kids* romp was originally filmed as *Grand Street Boys*. Leo Gorcey (as Muggs McGinnis, not yet the *Bowery Boys* wiseguy Slip Mahoney) gets the whole gang to pretend to be his relatives in order to fool uncle Noah Beery Sr. Connoisseurs of famous faces in drag should note the bizarre rig-out here of pawky Huntz Hall, essaying a very funny routine as a female sibling. TS

Leo Gorcey *Muggs* • Huntz Hall *Glimpy* • Bobby Jordan *Danny* • Bennie Bartlett *Bennie* • Noah Beery Sr [Noah Beery] *Pete* • Amelita Ward *Judy* • Rick Vallin *George* • Martha Wentworth *Mrs McGinnis* • J Farrell MacDonald *Flanagan* ■ *Dir* William Beaudine • *Scr* Harvey Gates

The Clandestine Marriage ★★ 15

Period comedy drama
1999 · UK · Colour · 87mins

Though gamely directed by Christopher Miles, this 18th-century period piece is a mismatched mating of British talents. Nigel Hawthorne heads the cast as a drunken lord trying to get his family entwined with the nouveau riche, while Joan Collins puts her best bosoms forward as a domineering snob. Alas, they can't convince us there's much wit in the piece. The film's walking waxworks look is impeccable, but it doesn't make us care about the mercenary characters. TH. Contains sex scenes. VIDEO

Nigel Hawthorne *Lord Ogleby* • Joan Collins *Mrs Heidelberg* • Timothy Spall *Sterling* • Tom Hollander *Sir John Ogleby* • Paul Nicholls *Lovewell* • Natasha Little *Fanny* • Cyril Shaps *Canton* ■ *Dir* Christopher Miles • *Scr* Trevor Bentham, from the play by George Coleman the Elder, David Garrick

Clara's Heart ★★★ 15

Melodrama 1988 · US · Colour · 108mins

Jamaican resort-hotel maid Clara (Whoopi Goldberg) gives comfort and wise counsel to a grieving couple (Kathleen Quinlan and Michael Ontkean) on vacation after the death of their baby. They then take her back with them to Baltimore to run their lives and that of their "rich kid" son (Neil Patrick Harris). Unashamedly old-fashioned and sentimental, this is a manipulative weepie-cum-feel good movie, expertly assembled by director Robert Mulligan. RK VIDEO

Whoopi Goldberg *Clara Mayfield* • Michael Ontkean *Bill Hart* • Kathleen Quinlan *Leona Hart* • Neil Patrick Harris *David Hart* • Spalding Gray *Dr Peter Epstein* • Beverly Todd *Dora* • Hattie Winston *Blanche Loudon* ■ *Dir* Robert Mulligan • *Scr* Mark Medoff, from the novel by Joseph Olshan • *Cinematographer* Freddie Francis • *Music* Dave Grusin

Clarence, the Cross-Eyed Lion ★★★ U

Adventure 1965 · US · Colour · 87mins

This pilot for the TV series *Daktari* is entertaining, but only hints at the superb blend of comedy and adventure that made the show such a big hit in the 1960s. Marshall Thompson and Cheryl Miller play the heads of an Animal Behaviour Centre deep in the African jungle, going on to become TV regulars. Here, though, they are upstaged – not only by the wonderful Clarence, but also by movie veterans Richard Haydn and Betsy Drake. DP VIDEO

Marshall Thompson *Dr Marsh Tracy* • Betsy Drake *Julie Harper* • Cheryl Miller *Paula* • Richard Haydn *Rupert Rowbotham* • Alan Caillou *Carter* • Rockne Tarkington *Juma* ■ *Dir* Andrew Marton • *Scr* Alan Caillou, from a story by Art Arthur, Marshall Thompson

Clash by Night ★★★

Melodrama 1952 · US · BW · 104mins

Tough Barbara Stanwyck returns to her seaside home town; she marries straight Paul Douglas, but hankers after smooth projectionist Robert Ryan. The top-billed stars are of secondary interest today, however, as this movie features an early appearance by Marilyn Monroe, giving an intelligent and astoundingly sexy performance. What is surprising is that this inexpensive RKO melodrama is from revered émigré director Fritz Lang, who fails to disguise the inherent dullness of the material. TS

Barbara Stanwyck *Mae Doyle* • Paul Douglas *Jerry D'Amato* • Robert Ryan *Earl Pfeiffer* • Marilyn Monroe *Peggy* • J Carrol Naish *Uncle Vince* • Keith Andes *Joe Doyle* ■ *Dir* Fritz Lang • *Scr* Alfred Hayes, David Dortort, from the play by Clifford Odets

Clash by Night ★

Crime drama 1963 · UK · BW · 75mins

This British crime drama was released in the US as *Escape by Night* to avoid confusion with the 1952 Fritz Lang melodrama of the same name. The only interesting thing about this bargain-basement tale of escaped prisoners is the sight of Peter Sallis gleefully torching a barn that has already been doused in paraffin. DP

Terence Longden *Martin Lord* • Jennifer Jayne *Nita Lord* • Harry Fowler *Doug Roberts* • Peter Sallis *Victor Lush* • Alan Wheatley *Ronald Grey-Simmons* • Vanda Godsell *Mrs Grey-Simmons* ■ *Dir* Montgomery Tully • *Scr* Maurice J Wilson, Montgomery Tully, from the novel by Rupert Croft-Brooke

Clash of the Titans ★★★ 15

Fantasy adventure
1981 · US/UK · Colour · 117mins

A stodgy re-run of *Jason and the Argonauts*, with Perseus, Andromeda and assorted giant livestock going through their mythological paces. Harry Hamlin and Judi Bowker make anaemic heroes, Ray Harryhausen's stop-motion special effects are wobblesome and Laurence Olivier overacts as Zeus. While fans of the genre may still find things to enjoy, professors of architecture will note that the ancient theatre used in the picture is of late-Roman design and, therefore, out of date by several centuries. AT VIDEO

Laurence Olivier *Zeus* • Harry Hamlin *Perseus* • Claire Bloom *Hera* • Maggie Smith *Thetis* • Ursula Andress *Aphrodite* • Judi Bowker *Andromeda* • Jack Gwillim *Poseidon* • Susan Fleetwood *Athena* • Pat Roach *Hephaestus* • Burgess Meredith *Ammon* • Sian Phillips *Cassiopeia* • Tim Pigott-Smith *Thallo* ■ *Dir* Desmond Davis • *Scr* Beverley Cross

Class ★★ 15

Comedy drama 1983 · US · Colour · 94mins

A typical sexual rites-of-passage movie, overlaid with dubious 1980s concerns about making money and wearing the right designer clothes. There is something queasily tacky about Jacqueline Bisset debagging her son's school friend in a glass-sided lift, and the rest of this distinctly self-satisfied movie is full of the kind of personal selfishness that takes you back to the decade of materialism. SH. Contains violence and swearing. VIDEO DVD

Rob Lowe *Skip* • Andrew McCarthy *Jonathan* • Jacqueline Bisset *Ellen* • Cliff Robertson *Mr Burroughs* • Stuart Margolin *Balaban* • John Cusack *Roscoe* ■ *Dir* Lewis John Carlino • *Scr* Jim Kouf, David Greenwalt

Class Act ★★ 15

Comedy 1992 · US · Colour · 93mins

There's trouble in the high school classroom when a tough street hood and an intellectual nerd swap identities. That's the premise behind this blunt comedy vehicle, built around the talents of one-time rap sensations Kid 'n' Play (Christopher Reid and Christopher Martin). The stars' winning personalities just about make this bearable, despite the fact that the film suffers from in-joke fatigue. AJ

Christopher Reid *Duncan Pinderhughes* • Christopher Martin *Blade* • Andre Rosey Brown *Jail guard* • Meshach Taylor *Duncan's dad* • Mariann Aalda *Duncan's mum* ■ *Dir* Randall Miller • *Scr* John Semper, Cynthia Freidlob, from a story by Michael Swerdlick, Wayne Rice, Richard Brenne

Class Action ★★★ 15

Courtroom drama
1991 · US · Colour · 104mins

Gene Hackman and Mary Elizabeth Mastrantonio play dad-and-daughter lawyers in this powerful courtroom drama from British director Michael Apted. Hackman is the concerned, scruffy liberal, while Mastrantonio is the thrusting achiever, with ambition and power suits hiding an essential decency. Unfortunately, the whiff of contrivance takes the edge off several scenes, as the lawyers' personal antipathy invades their working lives, but otherwise this is classy stuff that showcases two actors on top form. JM. Contains swearing. DVD

Gene Hackman *Jedediah Tucker Ward* • Mary Elizabeth Mastrantonio *Maggie Ward* • Joanna Merlin *Estelle Ward* • Colin Friels *Michael Grazier* • Jonathan Silverman *Brian* • Donald Moffat *Quinn* • Laurence Fishburne *Nick Holbrook* • Jan Rubes *Pavel* • Matt Clark *Judge Symes* ■ *Dir* Michael Apted • *Scr* Carolyn Shelby, Christopher Ames, Samantha Shad

Class of '44 ★★ 15

Drama 1973 · US · Colour · 95mins

It's graduation time at a Brooklyn high school, and three close friends must part; Oliver Conant goes off to war, while Jerry Houser and Gary Grimes enrol in college. This is a recycled version of Robert Mulligan's hugely successful *Summer of '42*, using the same screenwriter, characters and lead actors. Made with evocative attention to period detail and trading on the charm of Grimes and his co-stars, it's OK, but not more. RK

Gary Grimes *Hermie* • Jerry Houser *Oscy* • Oliver Conant *Benjie* • William Atherton *Fraternity President* • Sam Bottoms *Marty* • Deborah Winters *Julie* • Joe Ponazecki *Professor* • Murray Westgate *Principal* ■ *Dir* Paul Bogart • *Scr* Herman Raucher

Class of 1984 ★★ 18

Drama 1982 · Can · Colour · 93mins

This ultra-violent, ultra-cynical thriller built up something of a cult following: it spawned two equally nasty sequels, and continues to inspire bigger-budgeted imitators (*The Principal, The Substitute*). Perry King stars as the dedicated teacher who takes the law into his own hands to wrest control of his school back from psycho Timothy Van Patten and his chums, who are terrorising students and staff alike. Director Mark L Lester stages the set pieces with ruthless efficiency. JF

Perry King *Andy Norris* • Timothy Van Patten *Peter Stegman* • Merrie Lynn Ross *Diane Norris* • Roddy McDowall *Terry Corrigan* • Al Waxman *Detective Stawiski* • Lisa Langlois *Patsy* • Michael J Fox *Arthur* ■ *Dir* Mark L Lester • *Scr* John Saxton, Mark L Lester, from a story by Tom Holland

Class of 1999 ★★ 18

Science fiction 1990 · US · Colour · 91mins

This sequel to *Class of 1984* – directed, like the original, by Mark L Lester – presents the high school of the future as a violent battleground. It's so bad the teachers have been replaced by robots who can supposedly handle the psychopathic kids. Brutal and camp at the same time, this futuristic tale fails because Lester thinks he can insert some sort of message into the mayhem. A further sequel followed. JB DVD

Malcolm McDowell *Dr Miles Langford* • Bradley Gregg *Cody Culp* • John P Ryan *Mr Hardin* • Pam Grier *Ms Connors* • Stacy Keach *Dr Bob Forrest* • Traci Lin [Traci Lind] *Christine Langford* ■ *Dir* Mark L Lester • *Scr* C Courtney Joyner, from a story by Mark L Lester

The Class of Miss MacMichael ★★★ 15

Comedy drama 1978 · UK · Colour · 94mins

This chalkface bungle features two watchable, hyperactive performances by Glenda Jackson and Oliver Reed. At a special needs school, he's the headmaster who's a brute to the kids but a charmer with the parents, while she's a dedicated teacher whose caring integrity manages to break through student hostility. There's more sexual permissiveness unleashed here than in other teenage dramas of the time but, when Jackson and Reed are absent, this doesn't make it any more watchable. TH. Contains some swearing and violence.

Glenda Jackson *Conor MacMichael* • Oliver Reed *Terence Sutton* • Michael Murphy *Martin* • Rosalind Cash *Una Ferrar* • John Standing *Fairbrother* • Riba Akabusi *Gaylord* • Phil Daniels *Stewart* • Patrick Murray *Boysie* • Sylvia O'Donnell *Marie* • Sharon Fussey *Belinda* ■ *Dir* Silvio Narizzano • *Scr* Judd Bernard, from the novel by Sandy Hutson

Class of Nuke 'em High ★ 18

Science-fiction horror
1986 · US · Colour · 81mins

This typically bargain-basement production from Troma, the no-frills company who brought us the cult-ish *Toxic Avenger* movies, follows a bunch of high school kids who suffer radiation mutation from a local nuclear plant. It's awfully acted, insanely scripted and cluelessly directed. Two sequels followed. JC

Janelle Brady *Chrissy* • Gilbert Brenton *Warren* • Robert Prichard *Spike* • RL Ryan *Mr Paley* • James Nugent Vernon *Eddie* • Brad Dunker *Gonzo* • Gary Schneider *Pete* ■ *Dir* Richard W Haines, Samuel Weil [Lloyd Kaufman] • *Scr* Richard W Haines, Mark Rudnitsky, Samuel Weil [Lloyd Kaufman], Stuart Strutin, from a story by Richard W Haines

Class of '61 ★★★ PG

Period war drama 1993 · US · Colour · 90mins

Executive produced by Steven Spielberg and strikingly photographed by double Oscar-winner Janusz Kaminski, this strongly cast American Civil War tale of broken hearts and divided loyalties attempts lofty themes, but can't escape its melodramatic constraints. Joshua Lucas, Clive Owen and Dan Futterman play the West Point graduates forced into enmity with the outbreak of hostilities, with Sophie Ward as the sister of Unionist Owen who captures the heart of Confederate Futterman. An imposing, if prosaic, TV drama. DP

Clive Owen *Devin O'Neil* • Dan Futterman *Shelby Peyton* • Joshua Lucas [Josh Lucas] *George Armstrong Custer* • Sophie Ward *Shannen O'Neil* • Laura Linney *Lily Magraw* ■ *Dir* Gregory Hoblit • *Scr* Jonas McCord

La Classe de Neige ★★★ 15

Psychological thriller
1998 · Fr · Colour · 97mins

This potentially gripping drama suffers from indifferent handling, despite a heroic performance from Clément Van Den Bergh as the anxiety-ridden outsider at a school ski camp. Director Claude Miller makes effective use of the wintry light and the stunning snowscapes, which help get across the central theme of imagination and reality becoming dangerously intertwined. But Miller can't disguise the gaping holes in the screenplay, even if atmosphere and perception clearly matter more than tangible facts. DP. In French with English subtitles. .

Clément Van Den Bergh *Nicolas* • Lokman Nalcakan *Hodkann* • François Roy *The father* • Yves Verhoeven *Patrick* • Emmanuelle Bercot *Miss Grimm* ■ *Dir* Claude Miller • *Scr* Claude Miller, Emmanuel Carrère, from a novel by Emmanuel Carrère • *Cinematographer* Guillaume Schiffman

Claudelle Inglish ★

Drama 1961 · US · BW · 96mins

Diane McBain stars as a farm girl who goes to the bad with a succession of young men in this totally unengaging and unattractive melodrama. The supporting cast is uninspiring, while director Gordon Douglas can do nothing to disguise producer Leonard Freeman's inept screenplay. RK

Diane McBain *Claudelle Inglish* • Arthur Kennedy *Clyde Inglish* • Will Hutchins *Dennis Peasley* • Constance Ford *Jessie Inglish* • Claude Akins *ST Crawford* • Frank Overton *Harley Peasley* • Chad Everett *Linn Varner* ■ *Dir* Gordon Douglas • *Scr* Leonard Freeman, from the novel by Erskine Caldwell

Claudia ★★★★

Comedy drama 1943 · US · BW · 91mins

An enchanting film debut for Dorothy McGuire, who played the title role in Rose Franken's popular play on Broadway. Her performance as a young woman coming to terms with married life is the highlight of a film that's unusually frank for its time about domestic issues. Robert Young is perfectly cast as McGuire's husband and Ina Claire does well as her ailing mother. A less effective but equally well-acted sequel, *Claudia and David*, was released three years later. TS

Dorothy McGuire *Claudia* • Robert Young (1) *David Naughton* • Ina Claire *Mrs Brown* • Reginald Gardiner *Jerry Seymour* • Olga Baclanova *Madame Daruska* • Jean Howard *Julie* ■ *Dir* Edmund Goulding • *Scr* Morrie Ryskind, from the play by Rose Franken

Claudia and David ★★★

Comedy drama 1946 · US · BW · 77mins

The follow-up to 1943's charming *Claudia*, continuing the ever-so-slight tale of the titular couple as they have a son and discover what really matters in life. Keeping sentiment at bay, Dorothy McGuire and her under-rated screen partner Robert Young turn in suitably enthusiastic performances. Effortlessly directed by talented Walter Lang, this lacks the then-daring plotline of its predecessor, but is engaging nevertheless. TS

Dorothy McGuire *Claudia* • Robert Young (1) *David* • Mary Astor *Elizabeth Van Doren* • John Sutton *Phil Dexter* • Gail Patrick *Julia Naughton* • Rose Hobart *Edith Dexter* • Harry Davenport *Dr Harry* • Florence Bates *Nancy Riddle* ■ *Dir* Walter Lang • *Scr* Rose Franken, William Brown Meloney, from the story by Rose Franken

Claudine ★★★

Drama 1974 · US · Colour · 92mins

The trials and tribulations of a single black mother, attempting to rear six children in an urban environment, and her relationship with her refuse collector boyfriend. Well directed by John Berry, this engaging drama is beautifully played by Diahann Carroll (who was nominated for a best actress Oscar), James Earl Jones and an excellent cast of youngsters. Devoid of the usual dose of drugs and crime, the film points up the problems of the working-class black community. RK

Diahann Carroll *Claudine* • James Earl Jones *Roop* • Lawrence Hilton-Jacobs *Charles* • Tamu *Charlene* • David Kruger *Paul* • Yvette Curtis *Patrice* • Eric Jones *Francis* • Socorro Stephens *Lurlene* • Adam Wade *Owen* ■ *Dir* John Berry • *Scr* Tina Pine [Tina Rome], Lester Pine

The Clay Bird ★★★ PG

Period political drama
2002 · Fr/Ban · Colour · 98mins

Despite lacking the budget to fully re-create the tide of social unrest that swept through East Pakistan in the late 1960s, director Tareque Masud nevertheless succeeds in conveying the tensions and prejudices that led to the foundation of an independent Bangladesh by focusing on the trials of one divided family. Homeopath Jayanto Chattopadhyay's rigid adherence to traditional Muslim beliefs may seem overly melodramatic, while his son Nuril Islam Bablu's contrasting school experiences smack of contrivance. But the discussion of how unthinking religious belief and political commitment can provoke violent extremism remains valid. DP. In Bengali with English subtitles.

Nuril Islam Bablu *Anu* • Russell Farazi *Rokon* • Jayanto Chattopadhyay *Kazi* • Rokeya Prachy *Ayesha* • Soaeb Islam *Milon* ■ *Dir* Tareque Masud • *Scr* Tareque Masud, Catherine Masud

The Clay Pigeon ★★★

Thriller 1949 · US · BW · 63mins

This bracingly efficient thriller from stalwart director Richard Fleischer stars Bill Williams as the amnesiac sailor who wakes from a coma to find himself accused of informing on his comrades in a Japanese PoW camp. With a taut screenplay from *High Noon* writer Carl Foreman, and crisp photography from Robert De Grasse, Williams's gradual enlightenment is made more gripping by the knowledge that it was based on an actual incident in southern California. DP

Bill Williams *Jim Fletcher* • Barbara Hale *Martha Gregory* • Richard Quine *Ted Niles* • Richard Loo *Ken Tokoyama* • Frank Fenton *Lt Cmdr Prentice* • Martha Hyer *Miss Harwick* ■ *Dir* Richard O Fleischer [Richard Fleischer] • *Scr* Carl Foreman, from his story

Clay Pigeons ★★★ 15

Black comedy 1998 · US · Colour · 103mins

Joaquin Phoenix, Janeane Garofalo and Vince Vaughn embark on an entertaining and harrowing road trip in director David Dobkin's psychological comedy about double-double-cross and serial killing in Montana. Phoenix is a young man with a past who is befriended by a serial killer – and every woman he introduces to him seems to wind up dead. Bringing a satirical edge to the weather-beaten sleazy crime genre, this features a great Golden Oldie soundtrack. AJ. Contains violence, swearing, sex scenes, drug abuse and nudity. DVD

Joaquin Phoenix *Clay* • Vince Vaughn *Lester* • Janeane Garofalo *Agent Shelby* • Gregory Sporleder *Earl* • Georgina Cates *Amanda* • Scott Wilson *Sheriff Mooney* ■ *Dir* David Dobkin • *Scr* Matthew Healy • *Cinematographer* Eric Edwards

Clean ★★★★ 15

Drama 2004 · Fr/UK/Can · Colour · 110mins

This moving and elegiac overview of the present and possible future of a drug-addled former rock celebrity (played by Maggie Cheung) is beautifully paced with brilliant perfomances. After the death of her equally addicted rock-singer husband, Cheung sets out to find a better, cleaner life that will include her son (James Dennis). Now in the custody of her husband's parents (Nick Nolte and

Martha Henry) in Canada, the child barely knows his mother and what he does know, he hates. Shot in a confident and unhurried style, this is a mature piece of work from director Olivier Assayas. KK. In English, French and Cantonese with subtitles. Contains swearing and drug abuse.

Maggie Cheung *Emily Wang* • Nick Nolte *Albrecht Hauser* • Béatrice Dalle *Elena* • Jeanne Balibar *Irene Paolini* • Don McKellar *Vernon* • Martha Henry *Rosemary Hauser* • James Johnston *Lee* • James Dennis *Jay* ■ *Dir/Scr* Olivier Assayas

Clean and Sober ★★★ 15

Drama 1988 · US · Colour · 118mins

Although he made his name as a comic, Michael Keaton has always impressed in dramatic roles, particularly those with a darker tinge. This was his first real foray into straight territory, and he delivers a mesmerising performance as a cynical, bitter drug addict in rehab who slowly learns to face up to his responsibilities. There is able support from Kathy Baker and Morgan Freeman and, although the direction from *Moonlighting* creator Glenn Gordon Caron is too small-scale, there's no denying the film's power. JF [VIDEO]

Michael Keaton *Daryl Poynter* • Kathy Baker *Charlie Standers* • Morgan Freeman *Craig* • M Emmet Walsh *Richard Dirks* • Luca Bercovici *Lenny* • Tate Donovan *Donald Towle* • Henry Judd Baker *Xavier* • Claudia Christian *Iris* ■ *Dir* Glenn Gordon Caron • *Scr* Tod Carroll

Clean, Shaven ★★★★

Crime drama 1993 · US · Colour · 79mins

A schizophrenic searches for his daughter and falls under suspicion of being a child serial killer in director Lodge H Kerrigan's highly disturbing low-budget independent production. Peter Greene gives a haunting performance as the mentally disabled individual who hears voices and self-mutilates himself, while Kerrigan coldly points the finger at an uncaring society in this plea for tolerance. Not an easy film to watch, but undeniably powerful. AJ. Contains violence, swearing, sex scenes and nudity.

Peter Greene *Peter Winter* • Molly Castelloe *Melinda Frayne* • Megan Owen *Mrs Winter* • Jennifer MacDonald *Nicole Frayne* ■ *Dir/Scr* Lodge H Kerrigan

Clean Slate ★★★★ 12

Drama 1981 · Fr · Colour · 128mins

In transferring Jim Thompson's novel *Pop. 1280* from the American Deep South to equatorial Africa in 1938, Bertrand Tavernier passes comment on imperialism, appeasement and the corrupting nature of power, as well as exploring the psychology of a weak man pushed to his limits. For all the script's dark deliberations, however, the film's bite is provided by Philippe Noiret's dissemblingly shambolic performance as the scorned cop who abuses his position to cover up a murderous vendetta against everyone who's slighted him. DP. In French with English subtitles. [VIDEO]

Philippe Noiret *Lucien Cordier* • Isabelle Huppert *Rose* • Jean-Pierre Marielle *Le Peron/His brother* • Stéphane Audran *Huguette Cordier* • Eddy Mitchell *Nono* • Guy Marchand *Chavasson* ■ *Dir* Bertrand Tavernier • *Scr* Jean Aurenche, Bertrand Tavernier

Clean Slate ★★★ 12

Comedy 1994 · US · Colour · 102mins

Wayne's World star Dana Carvey plays a detective with a rare form of amnesia in this mildly amusing comedy. Every morning he wakes up with his memory wiped completely clean of the previous day's events – a particularly unfortunate occurrence seeing he's the key witness in a Mob trial. Chuckles may be thin on the ground during Carvey's constant manic memory refreshment, but the endearingly dotty premise proves compelling. AJ [VIDEO] DVD

Dana Carvey *Maurice Pogue* • Valeria Golino *Sarah/Beth* • James Earl Jones *Dolby* • Kevin Pollak *Rosenheim* • Michael Gambon *Cornell* • Michael Murphy *Dr Doover* • Jayne Brook *Paula* • Vyto Ruginis *Hendrix* • Olivia D'Abo *Judy* ■ *Dir* Mick Jackson • *Scr* Robert King

Clear and Present Danger ★★★ 12

Political thriller 1994 · US · Colour · 135mins

It's no wonder that three first-rank screenwriters were hired to adapt this sequel to *Patriot Games*, as there is so much plot in Tom Clancy's original novel that it's a minor miracle they squeezed it all into 135 minutes. It takes the picture some time to gather momentum, but, once the links between the Colombian drugs barons and some top US officials are established, it's action all the way, with Harrison Ford on commanding form for his second outing as CIA troubleshooter Jack Ryan. Ben Affleck took over the role in 2002 for *The Sum of All Fears*. DP. Contains some violence and swearing. [VIDEO] DVD

Harrison Ford *Jack Ryan* • Willem Dafoe *Clark* • Anne Archer *Cathy Ryan* • Joaquim de Almeida *Felix Cortez* • Henry Czerny *Robert Ritter* • Harris Yulin *James Cutter* • Donald Moffat *President Bennett* • Miguel Sandoval *Ernesto Escobedo* ■ *Dir* Phillip Noyce • *Scr* Donald Stewart, Steven Zaillian, John Milius, from the novel by Tom Clancy

Clearcut ★★★ 18

Fantasy thriller 1992 · Can · Colour · 97mins

Since *Dances with Wolves*, Graham Greene has been steadily building up an impressive body of work. As the volatile member of a band of Canadian Indians battling to keep a lumber company off their land, Greene gives a quietly imposing performance that suggests a deep commitment to the cause at issue. The film's subplot, about the corruption of the judicial system, is also handled with restraint, making the sudden outburst of violence even more shocking. DP. Contains violence and swearing. [VIDEO]

Ron Lea *Peter Maguire* • Graham Greene (2) *Arthur* • Rebecca Jenkins *Female reporter* • Michael Hogan (3) *Bud Rickets* • Floyd Red Crow Westerman *Wilf Redwing* • Tia Smith *Polly* ■ *Dir* Richard Bugajski [Ryszard Bugajski] • *Scr* Rob Forsyth, from the novel *A Dream Like Mine* by MT Kelly

The Clearing ★★★ 12

Thriller 2004 · US · Colour · 90mins

A mature Robert Redford is joined in this intriguing, understated kidnap drama by Helen Mirren and Willem Dafoe. Redford plays a used-car magnate who is kidnapped by Dafoe. The relationship between Redford and Dafoe is marked by subtle shifts in power and knowledge, and is central to the story. However, the suffering of those at home is given equal weight, as wife Mirren muses on marriage and Redford's infidelity. The acting is solid, as are the production values, but this doesn't quite fulfil its initial promise. LB [VIDEO] DVD

Robert Redford *Wayne Hayes* • Helen Mirren *Eileen Hayes* • Willem Dafoe *Arnold Mack* • Alessandro Nivola *Tim Hayes* • Matt Craven *Agent Ray Fuller* • Melissa Sagemiller *Jill Hayes* • Wendy Crewson *Louise Miller* • Larry Pine *Tom Finch* • Diana Scarwid *Eva Finch* ■ *Dir* Pieter Jan Brugge • *Scr* Justin Haythe, from a story by Pieter Jan Brugge, Justin Haythe

Cleo from 5 to 7 ★★★★★

Drama 1961 · Fr · Colour and BW · 93mins

This remarkable feature typifies all that was good in French film-making during its celebrated New Wave. Writer/director Agnès Varda (one of the unsung stalwarts of the period) constantly introduces the unexpected into both the central story and its many diversions, cinematographer Jean Rabier's images of Paris are uncomplicated, and the performances are cleverly stylised. Beneath her cool exterior, Corinne Marchand as Cleo manages to convey a range of emotions, whether worrying about her medical tests, chatting with strangers or singing with Michel Legrand. DP. In French with English subtitles.

Corinne Marchand *Cleo* • Antoine Bourseiller *Antoine* • Dorothée Blanck *Dorothee* • Michel Legrand *Bob, the pianist* • Dominique Davray *Angele* • José-Luis De Villalonga *The Lover* • Jean-Claude Brialy *Actor in comedy film* • Anna Karina *Actor in comedy film* • Eddie Constantine *Actor in comedy film* • Sami Frey *Actor in comedy film* • Danièle Delorme *Actor in comedy film* • Jean-Luc Godard *Actor in comedy film* • Yves Robert *Actor in comedy film* ■ *Dir/Scr* Agnès Varda

Cleopatra ★★★

Historical drama 1934 · US · BW · 99mins

Cecil B DeMille's film about Caesar, Anthony and Cleopatra isn't really a historical epic at all; it's a 1930s sex comedy about two guys and a gal who also happen to rule the world. DeMille can't quite jump the major hurdle – that Cleopatra never two-timed Caesar – and thus ends up with two separate stories, but the movie has real charm, if little substance. Colbert is sexy, but both Warren William and Henry Wilcoxon are lummoxes. AT

Claudette Colbert *Cleopatra* • Warren William *Julius Caesar* • Henry Wilcoxon *Marc Anthony* • Gertrude Michael *Calpurnia* • Joseph Schildkraut *Herod* • Ian Keith *Octavian* • C Aubrey Smith *Enobarbus* • Ian MacLaren *Cassius* • Arthur Hohl *Brutus* ■ *Dir* Cecil B DeMille • *Scr* Waldemar Young, Vincent Lawrence, Bartlett McCormick

Cleopatra ★★★ PG

Historical drama
1963 · US · Colour · 248mins

Taking inflation into account, *Cleopatra* remains the most expensive film ever made: around $40m at the time, roughly $250m in today's money. So why did it cost so much? Well, starting production in wintry England with Peter Finch, Stephen Boyd and director Rouben Mamoulian didn't help matters. Cranking up again in Rome – this time with Joseph L Mankiewicz shooting by day and writing by night – Elizabeth Taylor's frequent illnesses gave the accountants nightmares, even if her on-set romance with Richard Burton was a publicist's dream. The spectacle is the thing, yet the film does succeed in making some sense of a moment in history. AT [VIDEO] DVD

Elizabeth Taylor *Cleopatra* • Richard Burton *Mark Antony* • Rex Harrison *Julius Caesar* • Pamela Brown *High priestess* • George Cole *Flavius* • Hume Cronyn *Sosigenes* • Cesare Danova *Apollodorus* • Kenneth Haigh *Brutus* • Andrew Keir *Agrippa* • Martin Landau *Rufio* • Roddy McDowall *Octavian* ■ *Dir* Joseph L Mankiewicz • *Scr* Joseph L Mankiewicz, Ranald MacDougall, Sidney Buchman, from the works of Plutarch, Suetonius and Appian, and the novel *The Life and Times of Cleopatra* by Carlo Mario Franzero • *Costume Designer* Irene Sharaff, Vittorio Nino Novarese, Renie • *Cinematographer* Leon Shamroy • *Production Designer* John De Cuir • *Special Effects* Emil Kosa

Cleopatra Jones ★★ 15

Blaxploitation action drama
1973 · US · Colour · 84mins

After napalming opium fields in Turkey, statuesque narcotics agent Tamara Dobson returns to LA to confront Shelley Winters, lesbian queen of the drug underworld. Jack Starrett handles the action well, though clumsy martial arts and comic book theatrics conspire against his vigorous direction. Yet the meld of funky exuberance, urban angst and camp performances make this a heady, bad-ass cocktail. AJ [VIDEO] DVD

Tamara Dobson *Cleopatra Jones* • Bernie Casey *Reuben* • Brenda Sykes *Tiffany* • Antonio Fargas *Doodlebug* • Bill McKinney *Officer Purdy* • Dan Frazer *Detective Crawford* • Stafford Morgan *Sergeant Kert* • Shelley Winters *Mommy* ■ *Dir* Jack Starrett • *Scr* Max Julien, from a story by Max Julien, Sheldon Keller

Cleopatra Jones and the Casino of Gold ★★ 15

Blaxploitation action drama
1975 · US/HK · Colour · 92mins

Super-foxy Tamara Dobson is sent to Hong Kong to free two CIA agents caught in the Chinatown underworld clutches of the evil Dragon Lady (Stella Stevens). The result is more glossy high camp and low-grade action, with the statuesque Dobson piling on the silver eye shadow and changing into increasingly outlandish outfits. Slick and outrageous fun. AJ [VIDEO] DVD

Tamara Dobson *Cleopatra Jones* • Stella Stevens *Dragon Lady* • Tanny *Mi Ling* • Norman Fell *Stanley Nagel* • Albert Popwell *Matthew Johnson* • Caro Kenyatta *Melvin* ■ *Dir* Chuck Bail • *Scr* William Tennant, from characters created by Max Julien

Clerks ★★★★ 18

Comedy 1994 · US · BW · 88mins

Director Kevin Smith's prize-winning debut feature is a micro-budget marvel that focuses on a day in the life of a New Jersey convenience store. The double act of Brian O'Halloran and Jeff Anderson amuses, charms and offends as they lounge around discussing sex, videos, food prices, sex, *Star Wars* and sex. Their counterculture diatribes are by turn screamingly funny and wincingly accurate, although those of a sensitive nature should be warned. Smith's direction is as delightful as it is often unreliable. AJ [VIDEO]

Brian O'Halloran *Dante Hicks* • Jeff Anderson *Randal* • Marilyn Ghigliotti *Veronica* • Lisa Spoonauer *Caitlin* • Jason Mewes *Jay* • Kevin Smith (2) *Silent Bob* ■ *Dir/Scr* Kevin Smith (2)

The Client ★★★★ 15

Thriller 1994 · US · Colour · 115mins

Lawyer Susan Sarandon takes on the case of her career when young Brad Renfro, who has inadvertently witnessed a mob-related suicide, asks her to represent him. She soon finds herself up against the full might of the legal establishment led by ambitious federal attorney Tommy Lee Jones while at the same time trying to protect her youthful client from vengeful Mafia hitman Anthony LaPaglia. Director Joel Schumacher isn't noted for his subtlety, but he makes a pretty good go of producing a believable relationship between the stubborn but lonely Sarandon and the rebellious Renfro. JF. Contains violence, swearing. [VIDEO] DVD

Susan Sarandon *Reggie Love* • Tommy Lee Jones *Roy Foltrigg* • Mary-Louise Parker *Dianne Sway* • Anthony LaPaglia *Barry Muldano* • JT Walsh *McThune* • Anthony Edwards *Clint Von Hooser* • Brad Renfro *Mark Sway* • Will Patton *Sergeant Hardy* ■ *Dir* Joel Schumacher • *Scr* Akiva Goldsman, Robert Getchell, from the novel by John Grisham

Cliffhanger ★★★★ 15

Action thriller
1993 · US/Neth · Colour · 106mins

High adventure and vertigo blend with blood and bullets to make this tension-packed tall tale a spectacular avalanche of escapism. Sylvester Stallone is the rock-climbing "Rocky" clone who loses his nerve during the opening peak rescue and must find it again when a gang of desperate criminals crash-lands during a blizzard on his mountain manor. Nail-biting stunts and photography that's close to the edge are the true stars of this alpine *Die Hard*, directed with breathless energy by Renny Harlin. AJ. Contains swearing, violence. DVD

Sylvester Stallone *Gabe Walker* • John Lithgow *Qualen* • Michael Rooker *Hal Tucker* • Janine Turner *Jessie Deighan* • Rex Linn *Travers* • Caroline Goodall *Kristel* • Leon *Kynette* • Craig Fairbrass *Delmar* • Paul Winfield *Walter Wright* ■ *Dir* Renny Harlin • *Scr* Michael France, Sylvester Stallone, from a story by Michael France, from an idea by John Long • *Cinematographer* Alex Thomson, Adam Dale

Clifford's Really Big Movie ★★ U

Animated adventure
2004 · US · Colour · 74mins

Clifford the Big Red Dog gets his own big-screen adventure in this spin-off from the children's cartoon series, based on the books by Norman Bridwell. It sees the inexplicably humongous canine (voiced by the late John Ritter) and his regular-sized pals T-Bone and Cleo run away from home to join a floundering troupe of carnival animals. With its unsophisticated plot and flat, simplistic animation, this is an undemanding film that will appeal only to little ones. SF

John Ritter *Clifford* • Wayne Brady *Shackelford* • Grey DeLisle *Emily Elizabeth* • Jenna Elfman *Dorothy* • John Goodman *George Wolfsbottom* • Jess Harnell *Dirk* • Kel Mitchell *T-Bone* • Judge Reinhold *Larry* ■ *Dir* Robert C Ramirez • *Scr* Robert C Ramirez, Rhett Reese, from characters created by Norman Bridwell

Climbing High ★★ U

Comedy 1938 · UK · BW · 78mins

Although he won an Oscar for *Oliver!*, musicals weren't really Carol Reed's forte. However, he was fortunate to produce anything at all on this occasion, bearing in mind the tensions behind the scenes. Imported to play a bogus male model, American star Kent Taylor quit because of a delayed start, while Jessie Matthews disliked so many of the songs that they were dropped. It speaks volumes for Reed that the end result is not only watchable but rather entertaining, thanks, primarily, to Taylor's replacement, Michael Redgrave. DP

Jessie Matthews *Diana* • Michael Redgrave *Nicky Brooke* • Noel Madison *Gibson* • Alastair Sim *Max* • Margaret Vyner *Lady Constance* • Mary Clare *Lady Emily* • Francis L Sullivan *Madman* • Enid Stamp-Taylor *Winnie* ■ *Dir* Carol Reed • *Scr* Stephen Clarkson, from a story by Lesser Samuels, Marion Dix

The Clinic ★★★ 18

Comedy drama 1982 · Aus · Colour · 88mins

On paper, this tale of life at a VD clinic sounds like a raucous sex romp, but it's actually an affectionate and good-natured comedy drama about the disparate people and cases that pass through an under-pressure inner-city clinic in pre-Aids Australia. It's a tad preachy and rather televisual in look, but Chris Haywood shines among a solid ensemble cast. JF

Chris Haywood *Dr Eric Linden* • Simon Burke *Paul Armstrong* • Gerda Nicolson *Linda* • Rona McLeod *Dr Carol Young* • Suzanne Roylance *Pattie* • Veronica Lang *Nancy* • Pat Evison *Alda* • Max Bruch *Hassad* • Gabrielle Hartley *Gillian* ■ *Dir* David Stevens • *Scr* Greg Millin

Clive of India ★★★

Biographical drama 1935 · US · BW · 95mins

A very famous film of its day, this expensively produced but drearily directed epic offered the perfect role to the immaculately-spoken Ronald Colman: Robert Clive, one of Britain's great folk heroes. Colman is marvellous in the role, securing India for Britain at the cost of his own personal happiness, and it really doesn't matter at all that the real Clive lived a completely different life. Loretta Young looks lovely, and watch the battle scenes carefully: they all take place at night to save on budget. TS

Ronald Colman *Robert Clive* • Loretta Young *Margaret Maskelyne Clive* • Colin Clive *Captain Johnstone* • Francis Lister *Edmund Maskelyne* • Vernon Downing *Stringer* • Peter Shaw (1) *Miller* • Neville Clark *Vincent* • Ian Wolfe *Kent* ■ *Dir* Richard Boleslawski • *Scr* WP Lipscomb, RJ Minney, from their play *Clive*

Cloak and Dagger ★★★ PG

Spy thriller 1946 · US · BW · 106mins

Director Fritz Lang here turns a run-of-the-mill Second World War espionage tale into a gripping thriller that drips with nail-biting tension and brilliantly evokes the bleak atmosphere of the time. Gary Cooper plays the American nuclear research scientist who is sent to learn the secrets of Germany's atomic bomb programme. In hiding with the Resistance in war-torn, Nazi-occupied Italy, he is put in the care of violently anti-Fascist and embittered Lilli Palmer. Cooper is fine, and Palmer, making her American film debut, looks beautiful and shows an admirable grasp of a complex character. RK

Gary Cooper *Professor Alvah Jesper* • Lilli Palmer *Gina* • Robert Alda *Pinkie* • Vladimir Sokoloff *Dr Polda* • J Edward Bromberg *Trenk* • Marjorie Hoshelle *Ann Dawson* • Charles Marsh *Erich* ■ *Dir* Fritz Lang • *Scr* Albert Maltz, Ring Lardner Jr, from a story by Boris Ingster, John Larkin, from a non-fiction book by Corey Ford, Alastair MacBain

Cloak and Dagger ★★★ PG

Adventure thriller 1984 · US · Colour · 96mins

ET star Henry Thomas witnesses enemy agents trying to steal government secrets in director Richard Franklin's contrived update of the 1949 suspense classic, *The Window*. No one believes him apart from the evil spies themselves, so he goes on the run helped by imaginary superhero playmate Jack Flack (Dabney Coleman, who also plays the boy's father). Franklin lurches from tongue-in-cheek humour to exciting espionage, but undercuts any palpable menace by unsuccessfully shuffling the two tones together. AJ

Henry Thomas *Davey Osborne* • Dabney Coleman *Jack Flack/Hal Osborne* • Michael Murphy *Rice* • Christina Nigra *Kim Gardener* • John McIntire *George MacCready* • Jeanette Nolan *Eunice MacCready* ■ *Dir* Richard Franklin • *Scr* Tom Holland

Cloak without Dagger ★★ U

Mystery 1955 · UK · BW · 68mins

Had this British B-movie been possessed of a sense of humour, it might have invited comparison with those breezy spy romps churned out by Hollywood a decade earlier. However, director Joseph Sterling spurns the screwball possibilities in the relationship between agent Philip Friend and ditzy girlfriend Mary Mackenzie, who reunite years after her meddling caused him to bungle a Second World War mission. DP

Philip Friend *Felix Gratton* • Mary Mackenzie *Kyra Gabaine* • Leslie Dwyer *Fred Borcombe* • Allan Cuthbertson *Colonel Packham* • John G Heller *Peppi Gilroudian* ■ *Dir* Joseph Sterling • *Scr* AR Rawlinson

Clochemerle ★★★

Comedy 1948 · Fr · Colour · 94mins

Considered indelicate in some quarters on its release, this quaintly bawdy adaptation of Gabriel Chevallier's novel provides a priceless memoir of provincial France in the 1940s. At issue is whether mayor Jean Brochard has the right to install a new *vespasienne* (or open-air urinal) in the centre of his Beaujolais village. Gently lampooning the national character, as the dispute leads to the exposure of supposedly respectable citizens and the arrival of the army, director Pierre Chenal refrains from re-opening wartime wounds and, thus, dilutes the political satire. But this knowingly played romp remains an amusing example of the snowball farce. DP. In French with English subtitles.

Christian Argentin • Roland Armontel *Tafardel* • Max Dalban *Arthur Torbayon* • Paul Demange *Toumignon* • Jacqueline Dor *Rose Bivaque* • Maximilienne *Justine Putet* • Simone Michels *Judith Toumignon* • Christiane Muller *Adele Torbayon* • Jean Brochard *Mayor* ■ *Dir* Pierre Chenal • *Scr* Pierre Laroche, Gabriel Chevallier

The Clock ★★★★ U

Romantic drama 1945 · US · BW · 91mins

A charming MGM romance, containing a beguiling performance from the great Judy Garland, looking radiant and near her professional peak. She and soldier Robert Walker enjoy a brief encounter in New York, and director Vincente Minnelli cleverly makes the city the third character in the movie. There are also some minor players worthy of note: a drunken Keenan Wynn, a sympathetic James Gleason and a speechless Marshall Thompson. TS

Judy Garland *Alice Mayberry* • Robert Walker *Corporal Joe Allen* • James Gleason *Al Henry* • Keenan Wynn *Drunk* • Marshall Thompson *Bill* • Lucile Gleason *Mrs Al Henry* ■ *Dir* Vincente Minnelli • *Scr* Robert Nathan, Joseph Schrank, from a story by Paul Gallico, Pauline Gallico

Clockers ★★★ 18

Crime thriller 1995 · US · Colour · 123mins

Spike Lee's urban drama has cop Harvey Keitel investigating a killing. Low-level drug-dealer Mekhi Phifer is the prime suspect, though Phifer's brother Isaiah Washington has confessed to the crime. Not Lee's best work – some critics were distinctly cool about the stark imagery and idiosyncratic cinematography – but for once, at least, the director lets the story deliver the message, instead of imposing it from above. TH. Contains violence and swearing. DVD

Harvey Keitel *Rocco Klein* • John Turturro *Larry Mazilli* • Delroy Lindo *Rodney* • Mekhi Phifer *Strike* • Isaiah Washington *Victor* • Keith David *Andre the Giant* • Pee Wee Love *Tyrone* • Regina Taylor *Iris Jeeter* • Tom Byrd [Thomas Jefferson Byrd] *Errol Barnes* ■ *Dir* Spike Lee • *Scr* Richard Price, Spike Lee, from the novel by Richard Price

Clockstoppers ★★ PG

Science-fiction comedy adventure
2002 · US · Colour · 90mins

This adventure produced by the children's TV channel Nickelodeon shouldn't have made it past the small screen. Teenager Jesse Bradford discovers a watch among his father's possessions which can stop time, while the wearer can move around in space, as if invisible. However, Bradford doesn't do anything naught or novel with it. Instead he impresses the new girl at school (Paula Garcés), gives some bullies a lesson they'll never forget and helps a friend win a contest. StH DVD

Jesse Bradford *Zak Gibbs* • Paula Garcés *Francesca* • French Stewart *Dr Earl Dopler* • Michael Biehn *Gates* • Robin Thomas *Dr Gibbs* • Julia Sweeney *Jenny Gibbs* • Garikayi Mutambirwa *Meeker* ■ *Dir* Jonathan Frakes • *Scr* Rob Hedden, J David Stem, David N Weiss, from a story by Rob Hedden, Andy Hedden, J David Stem, David N Weiss

Clockwatchers ★★ 15

Comedy drama 1997 · US · Colour · 92mins

In seeking to capture the ennui of office life, director Jill Sprecher succeeds all too well with a film as repetitive and monotonous as its subject. There is much potential in this cast, but they're merely required to do the dramatic equivalent of licking envelopes. As the quartet of temps whose friendship is tested by an outbreak of petty pilfering, they each have moments of inspiration. For the most part, however, they seem subdued by the banality of the script and the slow pace. DP DVD

Toni Collette *Iris* • Parker Posey *Margaret* • Lisa Kudrow *Paula* • Alanna Ubach *Jane* • Helen FitzGerald *Cleo* • Stanley DeSantis *Art* • Jamie Kennedy *Eddie* ■ *Dir* Jill Sprecher • *Scr* Jill Sprecher, Karen Sprecher

Clockwise ★★★ PG

Comedy 1986 · UK · Colour · 91mins

John Cleese stars as a headmaster with a mania for punctuality who has to travel to Norwich for a conference. Unfortunately, he boards the wrong train, resulting in an increasingly frenzied cross-country dash with a schoolgirl and a former girlfriend in tow. Cleese finds it difficult to be unfunny, but the picture, written by Michael Frayn, is less a narrative than a series of sketches. Still, entertaining fare. JF. Contains swearing. DVD

John Cleese *Brian Stimpson* • Alison Steadman *Gwenda Stimpson* • Penelope Wilton *Pat* • Stephen Moore *Mr Jolly* • Sharon Maiden *Laura* • Constance Chapman *Mrs Wheel* • Joan Hickson *Mrs Trellis* • Ann Way *Mrs Way* • Pat Keen *Mrs Wisely* • Geoffrey Hutchings *Mr Wisely* ■ *Dir* Christopher Morahan • *Scr* Michael Frayn

Clockwork Mice ★★★ 15

Drama 1994 · UK · Colour · 94mins

Director Vadim Jean skirts the harsher side of life in a special needs school to concentrate on the unlikely friendship between unruly Ruaidhri Conroy and Ian Hart, the novice teacher convinced he can make a difference. The staffroom romance makes for a pleasing diversion and there are expert cameos from John Alderton and James Bolam. With its heart a little too determinedly on its sleeve, this is still an involving, amusing and, ultimately, rather sad film. DP. Contains swearing, brief nudity. DVD

Ian Hart *Steve Drake* • Ruaidhri Conroy *Conrad James* • Catherine Russell *Polly* • Art Malik *Laney* • Claire Skinner *Fairy* • Nigel Planer *Parkey* • John Alderton *Swaney* • James Bolam *Wackey* • Lilly Edwards *Mrs Charlton* • Robin Soans *Millwright* ■ *Dir* Vadim Jean • *Scr* Rod Woodruff

A Clockwork Orange ★★★ 18

Futuristic drama
1971 · UK · Colour · 130mins

Unseen between 1974 (when Stanley Kubrick himself quietly withdrew it) and 2000 (after his death), it is little wonder that an inflated degree of mythology surrounds this notorious futuristic drama. Dramatised from the 1962 Anthony Burgess novella about anarchic yobs ("droogs") in a dystopian future, it was shocking then and it's shocking today, particularly the scenes of rape and sadistic "ultraviolence" in the first half. Burgess and Kubrick may have been making intellectual points about the state and free will but the film is not quite the masterpiece that unattainability has bestowed on it. Fascinating and prescient, yes, and its moral ambiguity is brave, but only really essential viewing for cineastes and film students. AC. Contains violence, swearing, sex scenes and nudity. [video] DVD

Malcolm McDowell *Alex* • Patrick Magee *Mr Alexander* • Michael Bates *Chief Guard* • Warren Clarke *Dim* • John Clive *Stage Actor* • Adrienne Corri *Mrs Alexander* • Carl Duering *Dr Brodsky* • Paul Farrell *Tramp* • Miriam Karlin *Cat Lady* • Aubrey Morris *Deltoid* • Steven Berkoff *Constable* • David Prowse [Dave Prowse] *Julian* ■ *Dir* Stanley Kubrick • *Scr* Stanley Kubrick, from the novel by Anthony Burgess • *Cinematographer* John Alcott • *Editor* Bill Butler • *Production Designer* John Barry (2) • *Music* Walter Carlos

Close Encounters of the Third Kind ★★★★★ PG

Science-fiction drama
1977 · US · Colour · 126mins

Steven Spielberg's brilliantly realised suburban sci-fi saga reverses years of flying saucer attacks with the notion that visitors from outer space might just be friendly. Richard Dreyfuss strikes the perfect note of child-like inquisitiveness as the man "chosen" to make contact with alien lifeforms, despite obstruction by family and government. Spielberg confirms his genius at painting a convincing picture of mundane domestic life, subsequently shattered by extraordinary events (notably the terrifying kidnap of a young boy and Dreyfuss's slide into apparent insanity). The special effects are spectacular, John Williams's score is emotional charged, and it's impossible not to get caught up in the protracted climax. AC. [video] DVD

Richard Dreyfuss *Roy Neary* • François Truffaut *Claude Lacombe* • Teri Garr *Ronnie Neary* • Melinda Dillon *Jillian Guiler* • Bob Balaban *David Laughlin* • J Patrick McNamara *Project leader* • Warren Kemmerling *Wild Bill* • Roberts Blossom *Farmer* ■ *Dir/Scr* Steven Spielberg • *Cinematographer* Vilmos Zsigmond • *Music* John Williams • *Production Designer* Joe Alves • *Art Director* Dan Lomino • *Set Designer* Phil Abramson • *Special Effects* Douglas Trumbull, Roy Arbogast, Gregory Jein, Matthew Yuricich, Richard Yuricich

Close My Eyes ★★★ 18

Drama 1991 · UK · Colour · 104mins

In this overwrought and claustrophobic drama, Saskia Reeves and Clive Owen star as siblings who become a little too close for comfort. Stephen Poliakoff, as both writer and director, handles the controversial subject matter with sensitivity and he is rewarded with two heart-rendingly intense performances from his leads. However, the best playing comes from Alan Rickman as Reeves's husband, who delivers a witty yet melancholic performance. JF. Contains swearing, sex scenes and nudity. [video] DVD

Alan Rickman *Sinclair Bryant* • Clive Owen *Richard Gillespie* • Saskia Reeves *Natalie Gillespie* • Karl Johnson *Colin* • Lesley Sharp *Jessica* ■ *Dir/Scr* Stephen Poliakoff

Close to My Heart ★★★

Drama 1951 · US · BW · 90mins

The beautiful Gene Tierney and the dependable Ray Milland star as a couple in the process of adopting a baby from an orphanage, run by Fay Bainter. When they discover that the baby's father was a murderer, they nevertheless proceed with the adoption. Written and directed by William Keighley, this is a serviceable tale that combines drama with soap opera sentimentality and suggests environment is ultimately more important than heredity. RK

Ray Milland *Brad Sheridan* • Gene Tierney *Midge Sheridan* • Fay Bainter *Mrs Morrow* • Howard St John *EO Frost* • Mary Beth Hughes *Arlene* • Ann Morrison *Mrs Barker* • James Seay *Heilner* ■ *Dir* William Keighley • *Scr* James R Webb, from his story *A Baby for Midge* • *Cinematographer* Robert Burks • *Music* Max Steiner

Close-Up ★★★★ U

Experimental documentary drama
1989 · Iran · Colour · 93mins

Dazzling in its simple ingenuity, this fantasy on a true story is widely regarded as Abbas Kiarostami's masterpiece. The premise sounds complicated, with the action constantly cross-cutting between Hossain Sabzian's trial for impersonating celebrated Iranian director Mohsen Makhmalbaf, and reconstructions of the way in which he duped a family into believing their son was to star in one of his films. However, such is Kiarostami's mastery of his material and his delicious sense of mischief in exploring the contrasts between art and life that everything slots into place with awesome precision. DP. In Farsi with English subtitles. [video]

Hossain Sabzian • Mohsen Makhmalbaf • Abolfazl Ahankhah *Father* • Mehrdad Ahankhah *Son* • Manoochehr Ahankhah *Son* • Mahrokh Ahankhah *Daughter* • Nayer Mohseni Zonoozi *Daughter* • Abbas Kiarostami ■ *Dir/Scr* Abbas Kiarostami

Closely Observed Trains ★★★★ 15

Second World War comedy drama
1966 · Cz · BW · 88mins

One of the key pictures of the Czech New Wave of the mid-1960s, this is a superbly controlled piece of cinema that deserved its Oscar for best foreign language film. Set during the Nazi occupation, the film follows the bungled efforts of a bashful young apprentice railway guard to lose his virginity, seduce the stationmaster's wife and commit suicide. After a variety of misadventures, he meets a beautiful resistance fighter who finally offers him the chance to prove himself. Employing a complex, episodic structure, Jirí Menzel – making his feature debut – seamlessly dovetails satire, romance, heroism and the horror of war to devastating tragicomic effect. DP. In Czech with English subtitles. [video] DVD

Vaclav Neckar *Milos Hrma* • Jitka Bendova *Masa* • Vladimir Valenta *Stationmaster* • Josef Somr *Hubicka* • Libuse Havelkova *Stationmaster's wife* ■ *Dir* Jirí Menzel • *Scr* Jirí Menzel, Bohumil Hrabal

The Closer ★★

Psychological drama
1990 · US · Colour · 87mins

Slow and ponderous drama about the head of a real estate development firm (Danny Aiello) who is looking to retire and find a replacement. Rather than promote an executive, he decides to look for a salesman like himself to take over the company. Aiello is fine, but the character he plays is so unlikeable that this flip side of the Willy Loman story isn't much fun. ST

Danny Aiello *Chester Grant* • Michael Paré *Larry Freede* • Joe Cortese *John Mogen* • Justine Bateman *Jessica Grant* • Tim Quill *Chet Grant* • Rick Aiello *Billy Grant* • Diane Baker *Beatrice Grant* ■ *Dir* Dimitri Logothetis • *Scr* Robert Keats, Louis LaRusso Ii, from the play *The Wheelbarrow Closers* by Louis LaRusso II

Closer ★★★ 15

Drama 2004 · US · Colour · 99mins

Adapted by Patrick Marber from his own achingly modish hit play, this follows a quartet of London urbanites (played by Julia Roberts, Jude Law, Natalie Portman and Clive Owen) as their love lives intertwine and they – either deliberately or accidentally – inflict emotional damage on each other. The performances are as warm as the deliberately stagey dialogue will allow, with Owen the standout as aggressive consultant Larry, while Mike Nichols's superficial but elegant direction and Stephen Goldblatt's glossy cinematography give the story a sheen of sophistication. The decision not to open out the play for the screen leaves the film feeling oppressive, but it's an intelligent piece. AS. Contains swearing and sexual references. [video] DVD

Julia Roberts *Anna* • Jude Law *Dan* • Natalie Portman *Alice* • Clive Owen *Larry* ■ *Dir* Mike Nichols • *Scr* Patrick Marber, from his play

The Closer You Get ★★★ 12

Comedy 2000 · Ire/UK · Colour · 88mins

Uberto Pasolini, producer of *The Full Monty*, strays into *Waking Ned* territory with this ribald piece of Oirish whimsy. Screenwriter William Ivory has concocted an amiable fable about the sexual frustrations of a small Donegal community, which would rather resort to Florida beach babes and Spanish trawlermen than see beneath the workaday façade of their neighbours. Ian Hart excels as the crotch-obsessed butcher, while Ewan Stewart impresses as a virginal mammy's boy. DP [video] DVD

Ian Hart *Kieran* • Sean McGinley *Ian* • Niamh Cusack *Kate* • Ruth McCabe *Mary* • Ewan Stewart *Pat* • Sean McDonagh *Sean* ■ *Dir* Aileen Ritchie • *Scr* William Ivory, from a story by Herbie Wave

The Closet ★★★ 15

Comedy 2001 · Fr · Colour · 81mins

Almost a quarter century after he co-wrote *La Cage aux Folles*, writer/director Francis Veber has slightly altered his views on society's attitude to homosexuality – then he targeted bigotry, now it's the new political correctness in France. With its mix of high camp and mocking machismo, this is a resolutely unreconstructed farce. Daniel Auteuil pretends to be gay in order to avoid redundancy from Jean Rochefort's condom company, and Thierry Lhermitte's mischievous executive dupes the boorish Gérard Depardieu into befriending him to save his own skin. DP. In French with English subtitles. [video] DVD

Daniel Auteuil *François Pignon* • Gérard Depardieu *Félix Santini* • Thierry Lhermitte *Guillaume* • Michèle Laroque *Mademoiselle Bertrand* • Jean Rochefort *Kopel, company director* • Alexandra Vandernoot *Christine* ■ *Dir/Scr* Francis Veber

Closet Land ★★★

Political drama 1991 · US · Colour · 95mins

Co-executive produced by Ron Howard, with guidance from Amnesty International, this intense drama stars Alan Rickman as an interrogator-cum-torturer and Madeleine Stowe as his victim, an author of children's stories who is accused of subversion. Using a single set – a gleaming, hi-tech interrogation chamber – the drama is heavily allegorical: there are no names, no countries, just a universal symbol of oppression and a nod or two towards Franz Kafka. The sense of claustrophobia is overwhelming, and so are the performances, but Radha Bharadwaj's direction is perhaps better than her script. AT. Contains swearing.

Madeleine Stowe *Woman* • Alan Rickman *Man* ■ *Dir/Scr* Radha Bharadwaj

The Cloud Capped Star ★★★★ PG

Drama 1960 · Ind · BW · 121mins

Director Ritwik Ghatak combines social realism with stylised expressionism in this audacious melodrama, which also manages to evoke Bengali myth and the "selfless sister" pictures of the great Japanese director, Kenji Mizoguchi. Sacrificing her health and happiness to fulfil the ambitions of her siblings, Supriya Choudhury gives a performance of affecting determination and dignity. DP. In Bengali with English subtitles. [video] DVD

Supriya Choudhury *Nita* • Anil Chatterjee *Shankar* • Bijon Bhattacharya *Father* • Guita De *Mother* • Dwiju Bhawal *Montu, younger brother* • Niranjan Roy *Sanat* ■ *Dir* Ritwik Ghatak • *Scr* Ritwik Ghatak, from a story by Shaktipaka Rajguru

Cloud Cuckoo Land ★★ 12A

Drama 2004 · UK · Colour · 94mins

With few companies willing to back a project co-scripted by and starring an actor with cerebral palsy, the sheer fact that this inspirational drama was made at all is its crowning achievement. Steve Varden turns in a spirited performance as the 20-something who heads for the Lake District in a bid to establish his independence on learning that his beloved grandfather (Derek Jacobi) has cancer. However, the search for the wreckage of a valuable Second World War plane is not without its melodramatic moments, and Varden's romance with waitress Boo Pearce doesn't always ring true. DP

Steve Varden *Sandy Kenyon* • Derek Jacobi *Victor Kenyon* • Boo Pearce *Lucy* • Kriss Dosanjh *Vijay* • Billy Fane *Trevor* • Jane Wall *Jasmine* • Fuman Dar *Surgeon* • Sarah Beauvoisin *Irene* ■ *Dir* Matt Dickinson • *Scr* Matt Dickinson, Steve Varden

Cloud Dancer ★★

Drama 1979 · US · Colour · 91mins

Flying ace David Carradine thrills the crowd with his daredevil antics, but seems to have little time for his friends and family – until he helps drug-addicted pilot Joseph Bottoms kick his habit. Meanwhile, on the ground, Jennifer O'Neill fears for his safety. What he doesn't know is that she's just had his baby. Good aerial stunt work almost makes this bland melodrama worth watching. AJ

David Carradine *Bradley Randolph* • Jennifer O'Neill *Helen St Clair* • Joseph Bottoms *Tom Loomis* • Albert Salmi *Ozzie Randolph* • Salome Jens *Jean Randolph* • Arnette Jens Zerbe [Arnette Jens] *Edith Randolph* ■ *Dir* Barry Brown • *Scr* William Goodhart, from a story by William Goodhart, Barry Brown, Daniel Tamkus

Cloudburst ★★

Thriller 1951 · UK · BW · 83mins

The dynamic American stage and screen actor Robert Preston, yet to find stardom, is at the centre of this British-made thriller, directed by Francis Searle and co-starring Elizabeth Sellars. Preston is a code-cracking expert at the Foreign Office who uses the skills and contacts he accrued during the war to track down the hit-and-run criminals who killed his wife. The plot may strain credibility a little, but this bleak and violent potboiler is nevertheless quite involving. RK

Robert Preston *John Graham* • Elizabeth Sellars *Carol Graham* • Colin Tapley *Inspector Davis* • Sheila Burrell *Lorna* • Harold Lang *Mickie* • Mary Germaine *Peggy* ■ *Dir* Francis Searle • *Scr* Francis Searle, Leo Marks, from the play by Leo Marks

C

The Clouded Yellow ★★★ U

Crime drama 1950 · UK · BW · 111mins

This competent thriller has disgraced spy Trevor Howard involved with Jean Simmons and a case of murder after he becomes curator of a butterfly collection. As the cops close in, the couple head for a boat to Mexico with special agent Kenneth More in hot pursuit. The plot has too few tricks up its sleeve to engross, but director Ralph Thomas teases it out effectively by making good use of such images as the unnerving display cabinets and the Liverpool waterfront. DP

Jean Simmons *Sophie Malraux* • Trevor Howard *David Somers* • Sonia Dresdel *Jess Fenton* • Barry Jones *Nicholas Fenton* • Maxwell Reed *Nick* • Kenneth More *Willy* • André Morell *Chubb* ■ *Dir* Ralph Thomas • *Scr* Eric Ambler, from a story by Janet Green • *Cinematographer* Geoffrey Unsworth

The Clown ★★

Drama 1952 · US · BW · 92mins

Red Skelton is now a forgotten clown, and this reworking of *The Champ* shows us why. He plays an alcoholic old vaudevillian, idolised by his son (Tim Considine), who dreams of making a comeback on television. Alas, he's flawed, and floored, by his own weak character. Some moments suggest what Skelton was capable of, but there aren't enough to rescue director Robert Z Leonard's mawkish melodrama from bathos. TH

Red Skelton *Dodo Delwyn* • Tim Considine *Dink Delwyn* • Jane Greer *Paula Henderson* • Loring Smith *Goldie* • Fay Roope *Dr Strauss* • Philip Ober *Ralph Z Henderson* • Walter Reed *Joe Hoagley* ■ *Dir* Robert Z Leonard • *Scr* Martin Rackin, from a story by Frances Marion, Leonard Praskins

Clownhouse ★★ 15

Horror 1988 · US · Colour · 78mins

If viewers can somehow distance themselves from the behind-the-scenes scandal surrounding this movie (director Victor Salva molested one of his child actors), they will discover a genuinely spooky exercise in horror. In this incredibly atmospheric chiller, three escaped lunatics disguise themselves as clowns and terrorise three young brothers left home alone. The stalking sequences are nail-biting, though the lack of action makes things a little tedious. KB

Nathan Forrest Winters *Casey* • Brian McHugh *Geoffrey* • Sam Rockwell *Randy* • Tree *Evil Cheezo* ■ *Dir/Scr* Victor Salva

The Clowns ★★★★

Documentary
1970 · It/Fr/W Ger · Colour · 92mins

Italy's great ringmaster of the cinema returns to the source of his inspiration – the circus – and skilfully absorbs it into his own personal vision. Remembering the Rimini of his childhood when the circus came to town, Federico Fellini has stated: "My films owe an enormous amount to the circus. For me the clowns were always a traumatic visual experience, ambassadors of a vocation of a showman." Here, the maestro not only reveals their comedic craft by watching and talking to exponents of the profession. He also sends up the documentary-making process itself. RB. In Italian with English subtitles.

Dir Federico Fellini • *Scr* Federico Fellini, Bernardino Zapponi • *Music* Nino Rota

The Club ★★★ 18

Drama 1980 · Aus · Colour · 93mins

A bracing look behind the scenes at the personal and power politics involved in the running of an Australian Rules football club. It is based on an equally rumbustious stage play from David Williamson, who also wrote *Don's Party* – an earlier Australian film hit made by the same director, Bruce Beresford. This may not be as polished a film as Beresford's later success *Driving Miss Daisy*, but it makes up for what it might lack in finesse with rude energy and muscular acting. PF. Contains swearing and brief nudity.

Jack Thompson *Laurie Holden* • Graham Kennedy *Ted Parker* • Frank Wilson *Jock Riley* • Harold Hopkins *Danny Rowe* • John Howard (2) *Geoff Hayward* ■ *Dir* Bruce Beresford • *Scr* David Williamson, from his play

Club de Femmes ★★★★ 12

Comedy drama 1936 · Fr · BW · 95mins

This recently rediscovered melodrama is an enticing mix of social comment, sexual suggestion and screwball comedy. Gliding his camera around the mod-con hostel, with its swimming pool and gleaming sub-Deco furnishings, direcor Jacques Deval showcases the exuberance and beauty of youth, without neglecting either the doubts and desires simmering beneath the antiseptic veneer or the implicit chauvinism of the unseen male world outside. Danielle Darrieux shines as a boy-mad dancer, but Betty Stockfeld's corrupted innocent, Josette Day's blonde bombshell and Else Argal's tormented lesbian also impress. DP. In French with English subtitles.

Danielle Darrieux *Claire Derouve* • Betty Stockfield *Greta Kremmer* • Else Argal *Alice Hermin* • Raymond Galle *Robert* • Eve Francis *Mme Fargeton* • Josette Day *Juliette* ■ *Dir/Scr* Jacques Deval

Club le Monde ★★★ 18

Comedy drama 2001 · UK · Colour · 78mins

Director Simon Rumley's take on club culture works only fitfully, with its blend of drama and offbeat comedy. Subplots involving a conflicted bouncer, two underage toffs and a gossipy, coke-sniffing duo who refuse to leave the ladies' loo end up proving more diverting than the central plot strand involving Alison McKenzie and Brad Gorton's broken romance. However, the film does re-create the atmosphere of a club night successfully, while giving the episodes an "overheard" feel that's totally in keeping with the setting. DP DVD

Danny Nussbaum *Mr Sunglasses* • Emma Pike *Yas* • Tania Emery *Kelly* • Lee Oakes *Chas* • Emma Handy *Ra* • Tom Connolly *Anthony* • Tom Halstead *Patrick* • Daniel Ainsleigh *Steve* ■ *Dir/Scr* Simon Rumley

Club Paradise ★★ 15

Comedy 1986 · US · Colour · 91mins

Harold Ramis has matured into a fine comedy director – *Groundhog Day*, *Multiplicity* – but during the 1980s he specialised in crass efforts such as this early Robin Williams vehicle. Williams plays the host of a run-down Caribbean resort who has to cope with noisy American tourists and a brewing rebellion. The cast is eclectic, but the gags are about as sparse as the hotel's "luxury" facilities. JF. Contains swearing and drug abuse.

Robin Williams *Jack Moniker* • Peter O'Toole *Governor Anthony Croyden Hayes* • Rick Moranis *Barry Nye* • Jimmy Cliff *Ernest Reed* • Twiggy *Phillipa Lloyd* • Adolph Caesar *Prime Minister Solomon Gundy* • Eugene Levy *Barry Steinberg* • Joanna Cassidy *Terry Hamlin* ■ *Dir* Harold Ramis • *Scr* Harold Ramis, Brian Doyle-Murray, from a story by Ed Roboto, Tom Leopold, Chris Miller, David Standish

Clubbed to Death ★★ 18

Romantic drama
1996 · Fr/Por/Neth · Colour · 84mins

This strange, dark and narrative-less film from director Yolande Zauberman stars Elodie Bouchez as a girl who falls asleep on a bus and awakes to find herself on the outskirts of Paris. Stumbling around, she ends up in a nightclub where she encounters Roschdy Zem. Few words are spoken in this pop video-style foray into Parisian rave culture. LH. In French with English subtitles. Contains drug abuse, swearing, violence.

Elodie Bouchez *Lola Monnet* • Roschdy Zem *Emir Areski* • Béatrice Dalle *Saida* • Richard Courcet *Ismael* ■ *Dir* Yolande Zauberman • *Scr* Yolande Zauberman, Noémie Lvovsky, Emmanuel Salinger, D Belloc

Clue ★★ PG

Comedy 1985 · US · Colour · 92mins

Based on the board game Clue (known as Cluedo in the UK), this is a perfect example of a gimmick movie. The plot (an amalgam of various Agatha Christie clichés) involves a number of guests invited to dinner at a spooky mansion, where they endure a murderous evening. Scripted and written by British sitcom stalwart Jonathan Lynn in his first Hollywood venture, this is a broad, somewhat camp comedy. It was originally released with three different endings, though there was only one version in the UK. DF DVD

Tim Curry *Wadsworth* • Madeline Kahn *Mrs White* • Christopher Lloyd *Professor Plum* • Eileen Brennan *Mrs Peacock* • Michael McKean *Mr Green* • Martin Mull *Colonel Mustard* • Lesley Ann Warren *Miss Scarlett* ■ *Dir* Jonathan Lynn • *Scr* Jonathan Lynn, from the board game devised by Anthony E Pratt

Clueless ★★★★ 12

Romantic comedy
1995 · US · Colour · 93mins

Would you believe a loose adaptation of Jane Austen's *Emma* plonked down squarely in *Beverly Hills 90210*? Well, that's the idea behind this screamingly funny satire-cum-parody, which perfectly captures the inanities of contemporary teen America. Alicia Silverstone is a delight as Cher, the chic but dippy blonde who's devoted to improving the love lives of her Rodeo Drive-shopping high-school girlfriends, even though she can't sort out her own. Her lawyer father Dan Hedaya and intellectual stepbrother Paul Rudd look on in total bemusement. Director Amy Heckerling's smart satire sharpens its comedic scalpel on the manners and mores of self-centred fashion victims. AJ. Contains some swearing. DVD

Alicia Silverstone *Cher* • Stacey Dash *Dionne* • Paul Rudd *Josh* • Brittany Murphy *Tai* • Donald Adeosun Faison *Murray* • Elisa Donovan *Amber* • Wallace Shawn *Mr Hall* • Twink Caplan *Miss Geist* • Dan Hedaya *Mel* ■ *Dir* Amy Heckerling • *Scr* Amy Heckerling, from the novel *Emma* by Jane Austen

Cluny Brown ★★★

Romantic comedy 1946 · US · BW · 100mins

No longer quite what *Variety* called a "smasheroo", this somewhat outmoded satirical soufflé on British upper-class mores is nonetheless diverting. A comedy romance from director Ernst Lubitsch, whose famous "touch" is still very much in evidence, it stars Jennifer Jones as a lady plumber doubling up as a maid for an English family who are all vague to the point of imbecility. Charles Boyer is a Czech writer who arrives in the household having fled the Nazis. RK

Jennifer Jones *Cluny Brown* • Charles Boyer *Adam Belinski* • Peter Lawford *Andrew Carmel* • Helen Walker *Betty Cream* • Reginald Gardiner *Hilary Ames* • Reginald Owen *Sir Henry Carmel* • C Aubrey Smith *Col Duff-Graham* ■ *Dir* Ernst Lubitsch • *Scr* Samuel Hoffenstein, Elizabeth Reinhardt, from the novel by Margery Sharp

Coach Carter ★★★ 12A

Sports drama based on a true story
2005 · US · Colour · 136mins

Samuel L Jackson's barnstorming performance is the main reason to catch this solidly entertaining "true story". He plays a high-school basketball coach who took the unheard of step of benching his players and jeopardising their shot at the state title when he discovered they were failing academically. This, needless to say, didn't sit at all well with the students, who would rather be on the court than in the classroom. Clichéd it may be, but the movie is involving and well acted enough for us to forgive the fact that we've seen all this many times before. AS. Contains swearing and sexual references.

Samuel L Jackson *Coach Ken Carter* • Robert Ri'chard *Damien Carter* • Rob Brown *Kenyon Stone* • Ashanti *Kyra* • Debbi Morgan *Tonya Carter* • Rick Gonzalez *Timo Cruz* • Antwon Tanner *Worm* • Nana Gbewonyo *Junior Battle* • Channing Tatum *Jason Lyle* • Denise Dowse *Principal Garrison* ■ *Dir* Thomas Carter • *Scr* Mark Schwahn, John Gatins

Coal Miner's Daughter ★★★★ PG

Biographical drama
1980 · US · Colour · 119mins

Sissy Spacek won a best actress Oscar for her heartfelt portrayal of country singer Loretta Lynn in this movie biopic from British director Michael Apted. Based on Lynn's autobiography, the film charts the singer's life from poverty in deepest Kentucky to her becoming the queen of country music. It's a fascinating, no-holds-barred adaptation that includes Loretta's battle with drugs, her rocky marriage and the death of friend Patsy Cline. JB. Contains swearing and violence. DVD

Sissy Spacek *Loretta Lynn* • Tommy Lee Jones *Doolittle Lynn* • Levon Helm *Ted Webb* • Phyllis Boyens *Clara Webb* • William Sanderson *Lee Dollarhide* • Beverly D'Angelo *Patsy Cline* ■ *Dir* Michael Apted • *Scr* Tom Rickman, from the autobiography by Loretta Lynn, George Vescey

Coast to Coast ★★

Comedy 1980 · US · Colour · 94mins

Ever since *It Happened One Night* swept the Oscars in 1934, the runaway odd couple has been a comic staple in Hollywood. Here Dyan Cannon plays the screwball "fugitive" hitting the road to escape a conniving husband. But Cannon never really sparks with Robert Blake as the trucker who agrees to take her coast to coast in a bid to shake the brutal debt collector on his own tail. It's efficient entertainment, but the direction lacks energy and guile. DP

Dyan Cannon *Madie Levrington* • Robert Blake *Charlie Callahan* • Quinn Redeker *Benjamin Levrington* • Michael Lerner *Dr Froll* • Maxine Stuart *Sam Klinger* ■ *Dir* Joseph Sargent • *Scr* Stanley Weiser

Cobb ★★★★ 18

Biographical sports drama
1994 · US · Colour and BW · 122mins

This portrait of the sports hero as warped monster gives Tommy Lee Jones the chance to deliver a grandstand performance as Ty Cobb, the real-life baseball ace known as the "Georgia Peach". Soured by a lifetime of bigotry and bullying, Cobb is seen trying to camouflage past sins as he dictates his autobiography to a sports writer (Robert Wuhl). Director Ron Shelton, whose *Bull Durham* and *White Men Can't Jump* were jokey tales of disillusionment set in the sporting world, here redefines the life of an idol with honest savagery. TH. Contains violence, swearing and nudity.

Tommy Lee Jones *Ty Cobb* • Robert Wuhl *Al Stump* • Lolita Davidovich *Ramona* • Ned Bellamy *Ray* • Scott Burkholder *Jimmy* • Allan Malamud *Mud* ■ *Dir* Ron Shelton • *Scr* Ron Shelton, from the biography by Al Stump

Cobra ★★ 18

Detective action thriller
1986 · US · Colour · 83mins

"Crime is the disease and I'm the cure," claims cop Sylvester Stallone in a practically plotless mêlée of shooting and stabbing. The film tries to be Stallone's *Dirty Harry*, so it's unfortunate his idea of characterisation is mirror shades and a penchant for chewing matches. The relentless sequences of murder and mayhem are competently filmed by director George Pan Cosmatos. JC. Contains violence and some swearing. [VIDEO] DVD

Sylvester Stallone *Marion "Cobra" Cobretti* • Brigitte Nielsen *Ingrid* • Reni Santoni *Gonzales* • Andrew Robinson *Detective Monte* • Lee Garlington *Nancy Stalk* ■ *Dir* George Pan Cosmatos • *Scr* Sylvester Stallone, from the novel *Fair Game* by Paula Gosling

Cobra Verde ★★ PG

Drama 1988 · W Ger · Colour · 99mins

Although again depicting the exploits of an obsessive outsider in an inhospitable environment, this is the least cohesive of the epic collaborations between Klaus Kinski and Werner Herzog. Filmed under typically arduous conditions in Ghana, the action follows the fortunes of an exiled Brazilian bandit whose attempts to revive the slave trade are dashed by the insane ruler of Dahomey. As ever, Herzog succeeds in anthropologically dissecting the civilisation under his gaze, but his take on the evils of colonialism and the majesty of Africa is uninspired. DP. In German with English subtitles. [VIDEO] DVD

Klaus Kinski *Francisco Manoel da Silva* • Taparica *King Ampaw* • José Lewgoy *Don Octavio Coutinho* • Salvatore Basile *Captain Fraternidade* • Bossa Ahadee *Kwame II of Nsein* ■ *Dir* Werner Herzog • *Scr* Werner Herzog, from the novel *The Viceroy of Ouidah* by Bruce Chatwin

Cobra Woman ★★

Fantasy adventure
1944 · US · Colour · 70mins

High camp thrills aplenty in this richly dumb jungle melodrama about a bride-to-be kidnapped and taken to a mysterious island. There she discovers her evil twin sister is high priestess of a cobra-worshipping cult. Maria Montez is something of a cult figure today, and her performance here as the dual protagonists is considered a career best. Alas, Robert Siodmak directs this bunkum with too straight a face. RS

Maria Montez *Tollea/Naja* • Jon Hall *Ramu* • Sabu *Kado* • Lon Chaney Jr *Hava* • Edgar Barrier *Martok* • Mary Nash *Queen* • Lois Collier *Veeda* • Samuel S Hinds *Father Paul* • Moroni Olsen *MacDonald* ■ *Dir* Robert Siodmak • *Scr* Gene Lewis, Richard Brooks, from a story by W Scott Darling

The Cobweb ★★★★

Drama 1955 · US · Colour · 123mins

It's literally curtains for credibility as this wondrous tosh, one of the last of Hollywood's postwar psychiatric cycle, concerns the choosing of new drapes for the library of a psychiatric clinic, which causes as many problems for the staff as it does for the patients. The adaptation of William Gibson's novel becomes too wordy, but when you have the benefit of stars such as Richard Widmark, Lauren Bacall, Gloria Grahame, Lillian Gish and Charles Boyer, who cares? TH

Richard Widmark *Dr Stewart McIver* • Lauren Bacall *Meg Faversen Rinehart* • Charles Boyer *Dr Douglas N Devanal* • Gloria Grahame *Karen McIver* • Lillian Gish *Victoria Inch* • John Kerr *Steven W Holte* • Susan Strasberg *Sue Brett* ■ *Dir* Vincente Minnelli • *Scr* John Paxton, from the novel by William Gibson

The Coca-Cola Kid ★★★ 15

Comedy 1985 · Aus · Colour · 94mins

The political and sexual themes that Serbian director Dusan Makavejev explored in his earlier works are only quaintly challenging in this fizzy, offbeat comedy about corporate ideals. Eric Roberts is the Coca-Cola go-getter sent to Australia to test the market, where he comes into oddly engaging conflict with a wacky soft drinks manufacturer (Bill Kerr). The result is a laid-back, culture-clash whimsy full of incidental pleasures, the main one being Greta Scacchi burning up the screen as a sexy secretary. AJ [VIDEO]

Eric Roberts *Becker* • Greta Scacchi *Terri* • Bill Kerr *T George McDowell* • Max Gilles *Frank* • Kris McQuade *Juliana* • Tony Barry *Bushman* • Chris Haywood *Kim* ■ *Dir* Dusan Makavejev • *Scr* Frank Moorhouse, from his short stories

The Cocaine Fiends ★★

Drama 1935 · US · BW · 65mins

One of several lurid melodramas masquerading as public service films, this fell foul of many American censorship boards in its day and was unreleased in the UK until the 1970s, when it became a late-night attraction, usually paired with the better-known *Reefer Madness*. The contrived "thriller" plot, which begins with innocent Jane (Lois January) meeting dope peddler Nick (Noel Madison) and ends in kidnapping and suicide, all but renders the anti-drug message null and void. As with *Reefer Madness*, the chief appeal today is the tawdry over-emphasis: cocaine dependency is signified by dark circles under the victims' eyes. Short enough to be an offbeat amusement. DM

Lois January *Jane Bradford/Lil* • Noel Madison *Nick* • Sheila Mannors [Sheila Bromley] *Fanny* • Dean Benton *Eddie Bradford* ■ *Dir* William A O'Connor [William O'Connor]

The Cock-Eyed World ★★★

Comedy musical 1929 · US · BW · 115mins

This early talkie from Raoul Walsh – who went on to be one of the best directors of such gangster movies as *White Heat* – is a rollicking adventure comedy about the further exploits of Sergeants Flagg and Quirt (Victor McLaglen and Edmund Lowe), the heroes of *What Price Glory?* (1926). Always trying to one-up each other, they unite with their fists in adversity. It holds the interest, though the narrative technique looks dated. TH

Victor McLaglen *Sgt Flagg* • Edmund Lowe *Sgt Harry Quirt* • Lili Damita *Elenita* • Lelia Karnelly *Olga* • Bobby Burns *Connors* • Jean Bary *Fanny* ■ *Dir* Raoul Walsh • *Scr* Raoul Walsh, William K Wells, from a play by Maxwell Anderson, Laurence Stallings

The Cockettes ★★★ 15

Documentary 2001 · US · Colour · 99mins

Formed by George Harris (aka Hibiscus) in late-1960s San Francisco, the Cockettes were a street theatre drag troupe who became counterculture icons thanks to such anarchic revues as *Gone with the Showboat to Oklahoma* and low-budget movies such as *Tricia's Wedding*. But after a disastrous 1971 off-Broadway debut the much-changed line-up parted company and few members managed to live happily ever after. Drawing on the archives of ex-Cockette Martin Worman and including interviews with John Waters and Alice Cooper, this is an affectionate memoir of a time when peace, love and being fabulous were all that mattered. DP DVD

Dir Bill Weber, David Weissman

The Cockeyed Cowboys of Calico County ★★

Comedy western 1970 · US · Colour · 99mins

Developed to exploit the likeability of Dan Blocker (Hoss in the long-running western series *Bonanza*), this TV movie was impressive enough to be given a theatrical release. Blocker plays the local blacksmith of a western town who decides to move on when his bride-to-be jilts him. The townsfolk, reluctant to let him go, try to hitch him up with someone else. A so-so script is enlivened by a first-rate cast. DF

Dan Blocker *Charley* • Nanette Fabray *Sadie* • Jim Backus *Staunch* • Wally Cox *Mr Bester* • Jack Elam *Kittrick* • Henry Jones *Hanson* • Stubby Kaye *Bartender* • Mickey Rooney *Indian Tom* • Noah Beery [Noah Beery Jr] *Eddie* • Jack Cassidy *Roger Hand* ■ *Dir* Tony Leader • *Scr* Ranald MacDougall

The Cockleshell Heroes ★★★★ U

Second World War drama
1955 · UK · Colour · 93mins

Crisply directed by José Ferrer, this tremendously exciting war film sees Royal Marines go on a secret mission to destroy enemy shipping. Ferrer also leads the fine cast and commands the nighttime raid on the Bordeaux docks. Ferrer and Trevor Howard strike well against each other as the unorthodox major and resentful captain, and the training scenes are imaginative and effective. The movie was a big hit at the time, and was reissued as the top half of a double bill with the multi-Oscar-winning *From Here to Eternity*; this necessitated the optical adjustment of the latter into a widescreen format so that it wouldn't look too shabby alongside this film! TS [VIDEO] DVD

José Ferrer *Major Stringer* • Trevor Howard *Captain Thompson* • Victor Maddern *Sergeant Craig* • Anthony Newley *Clarke* • David Lodge *Ruddock* • Peter Arne *Stevens* • Percy Herbert *Loman* • Graham Stewart *Booth* ■ *Dir* José Ferrer • *Scr* Bryan Forbes, Richard Maibaum, from a story by George Kent

Cocktail ★★ 15

Romantic drama 1988 · US · Colour · 99mins

Having turned fighter pilots and pool players into sex objects, Tom Cruise did the same service for bartenders, learning the meaning of life by mixing drinks under the tutelage of Martini-mentor Bryan Brown. Cruise's technique is impressive; but then along comes Elisabeth Shue, who makes him re-assess his lifestyle. Perhaps the best one can say for this bland concoction mixed by agents and the studio executives is that every bartender in Hollywood wants to be Tom Cruise, and that suffices as an ironic subtext. AT. Contains swearing and nudity. [VIDEO] DVD

Tom Cruise *Brian Flanagan* • Bryan Brown *Doug Coughlin* • Elisabeth Shue *Jordan Mooney* • Lisa Banes *Bonnie* • Laurence Luckinbill *Mr Mooney* • Kelly Lynch *Kerry Coughlin* • Gina Gershon *Coral* • Ron Dean *Uncle Pat* ■ *Dir* Roger Donaldson • *Scr* Heywood Gould, from his novel

The Cocoanuts ★★★ U

Comedy 1929 · US · BW · 89mins

With an energy that bursts through any attempts at sophistication, this is the first film the Marx brothers made for Paramount. It's adapted – though you'd scarcely know it – from their Broadway stage hit, written by George S Kaufman and Irving Berlin. Groucho is the seedy manager of a Florida hotel, which has hot and cold running Harpo and Chico, besides jewel thieves and the matronly Margaret Dumont, a monument Groucho is always trying to climb or put down. Dated it may be, but still lots of fun. TH [VIDEO]

Groucho Marx *Hammer* • Harpo Marx *Harpo* • Chico Marx *Chico* • Zeppo Marx *Jamison* • Mary Eaton *Polly* • Oscar Shaw *Bob* • Katherine Francis *Penelope* • Margaret Dumont *Mrs Potter* ■ *Dir* Robert Florey, Joseph Santley • *Scr* Morris Ryskind, from the play by George S Kaufman, Irving Berlin

C

Cocoon ★★★★ PG

Science-fiction fantasy
1985 · US · Colour · 112mins

Director Ron Howard hit the big time with this blockbuster about pensioners finding a new lease of life after stumbling across aliens on a rescue mission from another planet. What saves it from a complete wallow in sentimentality is the sharp and sassy playing of a distinguished cast of Hollywood legends – Oscar-winning Don Ameche, Wilford Brimley, real-life husband and wife Jessica Tandy and Hume Cronyn – all of whom easily steal the show from the bland Steve Guttenberg and Tahnee Welch. Howard handles the human drama and sci-fi with equal aplomb. JF. Contains swearing and brief nudity. [VIDEO] DVD

Steve Guttenberg *Jack Bonner* • Brian Dennehy *Walter* • Don Ameche *Art Selwyn* • Wilford Brimley *Ben Luckett* • Hume Cronyn *Joe Finley* • Jack Gilford *Bernie Lefkowitz* • Maureen Stapleton *Mary Luckett* • Jessica Tandy *Alma Finley* • Gwen Verdon *Bess McCarthy* • Herta Ware *Rose Lefkowitz* • Tahnee Welch *Kitty* • Barret Oliver *David* ■ *Dir* Ron Howard • *Scr* Tom Benedek, from a story by David Saperstein

Cocoon: the Return ★★ PG

Science-fiction fantasy
1988 · US · Colour · 114mins

Straining far too hard to recapture the touching whimsy of Ron Howard's original film, director Daniel Petrie has succeeded only in producing a mawkish melodrama. Although the ever-dapper Don Ameche reprises his Oscar-winning role, there is much less of a spring in his step, and fellow old folks Wilford Brimley and Hume Cronyn are clearly equally uncomfortable with the glum script. The performances remain endearing, however. DP. Contains swearing. [VIDEO]

Don Ameche *Art Selwyn* • Hume Cronyn *Joe Finley* • Wilford Brimley *Ben Luckett* • Courteney Cox *Sara* • Jack Gilford *Bernie Lefkowitz* • Steve Guttenberg *Jack Bonner* • Maureen Stapleton *Mary Luckett* • Elaine Stritch *Ruby* • Jessica Tandy *Alma Finley* • Gwen Verdon *Bess McCarthy* ■ *Dir* Daniel Petrie • *Scr* Stephen McPherson, from a story by Stephen McPherson, Elizabeth Bradley, from characters created by David Saperstein

Code 46 ★★ 15

Futuristic romantic drama
2003 · UK/US · Colour · 89mins

In a gloomy future in which human cloning and genetic manipulation, Tim Robbins is a fraud investigator who's sent to Shanghai to find the source of some counterfeit travel documents. There, he is mysteriously drawn to Samantha Morton, who is also his chief suspect. Despite the intriguing premise, the film is rather tedious, the storyline plodding and obscure, and matters are not helped by the limited budget. The film is partly salvaged by a terrific performance from Samantha Morton, but Robbins lacks spark. DA. Contains sex scenes and nudity. DVD

Tim Robbins *William Geld* • Samantha Morton *Maria* • Jeanne Balibar *Sylvie Geld* • Om Puri *Backland* • Essie Davis *Doctor* ■ *Dir* Michael Winterbottom • *Scr* Frank Cottrell Boyce

Code Name: Emerald ★★ PG

Second World War thriller
1985 · US · Colour · 91mins

This is a polished piece of film-making. So polished, in fact, that any trace of originality or enterprise has been scrupulously wiped away. Surely the only excuse for making a Second World War espionage adventure in 1985 was to divulge the secrets of some hitherto hush-hush true-life operation. Not, as here, to take elements from any number of wartime thrillers and form them into yet another collage of double agents, decent Nazis and Gestapo sadists. DP. Contains swearing.

Ed Harris *Gus Lang* • Max von Sydow *Jurgen Brausch* • Horst Buchholz *Walter Hoffman* • Helmut Berger *Ernst Ritter* • Cyrielle Claire *Claire Jouvet* • Eric Stoltz *Andy Wheeler* • Patrick Stewart *Colonel Peters* • Graham Crowden *Sir Geoffrey Macklin* ■ *Dir* Jonathan Sanger • *Scr* Ronald Bass, from his novel *The Emerald Illusion*

Code of Silence ★★ 18

Action thriller 1985 · US · Colour · 96mins

Even with the rather wooden Chuck Norris in the lead, director Andrew Davis still manages to generate a fair bit of mindless excitement here. Norris is the maverick cop who gets caught up in a drug war. To make matters worse, he is not popular among his cop colleagues, supposedly because he breaks rank, but probably because they find him incredibly boring. Nevertheless, there are some great action set pieces. JF. Contains violence and swearing.

Chuck Norris *Eddie Cusack* • Henry Silva *Luis Comacho* • Bert Remsen *Commander Kates* • Mike Genovese *Tony Luna* • Nathan Davis *Felix Scalese* • Ralph Foody *Cragie* ■ *Dir* Andrew Davis • *Scr* Michael Butler, Dennis Shryack, Mike Gray, from a story by Michael Butler, Dennis Shyrack

Code Unknown ★★★★ 15

Drama 2000 · Fr/Ger/Rom · Colour · 112mins

Opening with an audacious nine-minute tracking shot, Michael Haneke returns to the territory of *71 Fragments of a Chronology of Chance* (1994) to accuse us of becoming both desensitied to both the world around us and lazy in our film watching. Set in a microcosmic Paris, the various stories involving a Romanian refugee, a teenage runaway, an abused African liberal and a disillusioned actress are interwoven with a facility that demonstrates a total mastery of both sound and image. If some of the political theorising is somewhat naive and the direction is occasionally manipulative, the acting, particularly from Juliette Binoche, is superb. DP. In French, Malinke, Romanian, German, English and Arabic with English subtitles. DVD

Juliette Binoche *Anne* • Thierry Neuvic *Georges* • Sepp Bierbichler *The farmer* • Alexandre Hamidi *Jean* ■ *Dir/Scr* Michael Haneke

Codename Wildgeese ★★ 15

Action adventure
1984 · UK/It · Colour · 88mins

This ridiculous commando movie bears absolutely no relation to the Richard Burton/Roger Moore action classic, *The Wild Geese*. What we get instead is a very sullen Lewis Collins leading a motley crew of mercenaries in a fight against an opium warlord in South East Asia. Plenty of explosions and car chases ensue, plus a fair quota of brutality. RS

Lewis Collins *Wesley* • Lee Van Cleef *China* • Ernest Borgnine *Fletcher* • Klaus Kinski *Charlton* • Manfred Lehmann *Klein* • Mimsy Farmer *Kathy* • Thomas Danneberg *Arbib* • Frank Glaubrecht *Stone* • Wolfgang Pampel *Baldwin* ■ *Dir* Anthony Dawson [Antonio Margheriti] • *Scr* Michael Lester

Un Coeur en Hiver ★★★★ 15

Drama 1992 · Fr · Colour · 100mins

Few film-makers are capable of producing such incisive studies of intimate relationships as Claude Sautet, yet it was only with this intense picture that he first received the international acclaim he so richly deserved. This subtle and superbly crafted film is so naturalistic and touches on so many raw emotional nerves that, at times, it is almost unbearable to watch. Daniel Auteuil and Emmanuelle Béart are exceptional as the violin-maker and the musician whose fated attraction intrudes calamitously upon a world of order and beauty. DP. In French with English subtitles. DVD

Daniel Auteuil *Stéphane* • Emmanuelle Béart *Camille* • André Dussollier *Maxime* • Elisabeth Bourgine *Hélène* • Brigitte Catillon *Régine* ■ *Dir* Claude Sautet • *Scr* Claude Sautet, Jacques Fieschi, Jérôme Tonnerre

Coffee and Cigarettes ★★ 15

Comedy 2003 · US · BW · 92mins

Jim Jarmusch's movie consists of 11 vignettes featuring a cast of famous actors and musicians chatting over the two titular vices, seeing what sparks might fly from the unusual pairings. Shot starkly in black and white (repeatedly using the same three or four angles) there's a nagging sense of *déjà vu*. With the exception of Cate Blanchett's double act playing against herself, there's rarely a moment to get the heart pumping. However, the wittiest episode features Steve Coogan and Alfred Molina, while the ever-reliable Bill Murray has a surreal encounter with hip-hop giants GZA and RZA. Punctuated by sporadic moments of pleasure, the film leaves you slightly irritated and in need of something more substantial. GM DVD

Roberto Benigni *Roberto* • Steven Wright *Steven* • Joie Lee *Good Twin* • Cinqué Lee *Evil Twin/Kitchen guy* • Steve Buscemi *Waiter* • Iggy Pop *Iggy* • Tom Waits *Tom* • Joe Rigano *Joe* • Vinny Vella *Vinny* • Vinny Vella Jr *Vinny Jr* • Renee French *Renee* • EJ Rodriguez *Waiter* • Alex Descas *Alex* • Isaach de Bankole *Isaach* • Cate Blanchett *Cate/Shelly* • Mike Hogan *Waiter* • Jack White (3) *Jack* • Meg White *Meg* • Alfred Molina *Alfred* • Steve Coogan *Steve* • Katy Hansz *Katy* • GZA • RZA • Bill Murray • Bill Rice *Bill* • Taylor Mead *Taylor* ■ *Dir/Scr* Jim Jarmusch

Coffy ★★★ 18

Blaxploitation action drama
1973 · US · Colour · 86mins

Nurse Pam Grier masquerades as a junkie to infiltrate a drug cartel and take revenge on the Mob who turned her little sister into an addict. Jack Hill's extremely violent, blaxploitation classic made the halter-topped, Capri-panted Grier, in her first leading role, queen of the genre, while plenty of nudity and nasty blood-letting keep the action bubbling along. Thanks to strong roles like this, and acting smarts to match, Grier became a cult star. AJ DVD

Pam Grier *Coffy* • Booker Bradshaw *Brunswick* • Robert DoQui *King George* • William Elliott *Carter* • Allan Arbus *Vitroni* • Sid Haig *Omar* • Barry Cahill *McHenry* ■ *Dir/Scr* Jack Hill

Cohen and Tate ★★ 18

Crime thriller 1988 · US · Colour · 82mins

Scoring a cult hit with *The Hitcher*, writer/director Eric Red sticks with the road movie format for this low-budget thriller about a boy who witnesses a gangland murder and gets kidnapped by a pair of hitmen, played by Roy Scheider and Adam Baldwin. High on humour and muscular doses of violence, the action is clumsily confined to the interior of a car, lending it a theatrical style. RS

Roy Scheider *Cohen* • Adam Baldwin *Tate* • Harley Cross *Travis Knight* • Cooper Huckabee *Jeff Knight* • Suzanne Savoy *Martha Knight* ■ *Dir/Scr* Eric Red

Cold Blood ★★ 18

Action thriller 1975 · W Ger · Colour · 75mins

Rutger Hauer made this obscure German thriller shortly before he began the collaboration with Paul Verhoeven that would transform his career. Still only a fledgeling star, he relies on moody macho rather than character depth to see him through a bruising encounter that, for all its nastiness, has few surprises to offer. Hooking up with innocent Vera Tschechowa after swindling his employers, Hauer has to draw on all his ingenuity when they are taken hostage. DP. German dialogue dubbed into English.

Rutger Hauer *Blondi* • Vera Tschechowa *Corinna* • Horst Frank *Chef* • Walter Richter *Arthur* • Günther Stoll *Stasi* • Erich Kleiber *Arzt* • Anna-Maria Asmus *Arztfrau* ■ *Dir* Ralf Gregan • *Scr* Günter Vaessen

Cold Comfort ★★★ U

Thriller 1989 · Can · Colour · 88mins

There are echoes of Stephen King's *Misery* in this chilling tale, but who's going to hear them out in the Canadian wilderness? A classic example of why you should never accept lifts from strangers, the story turns on the relationship that develops between teenager Margaret Langrick and the travelling salesman her father brings home as her birthday present. Maury Chaykin is splendidly malevolent as the deranged dad, while Paul Gross gives an astute performance as the lamb brought to the slaughter. Vic Sarin directs with a sure hand, leaving events tantalisingly open-ended. DP. Contains swearing and nudity.

Maury Chaykin *Floyd* • Paul Gross *Stephan* • Margaret Langrick *Dolores* ■ *Dir* Victor Sarin [Vic Sarin] • *Scr* Richard Beattie, L Elliott Simms, from a play by James Garrard

Cold Creek Manor ★ 15

Thriller 2003 · US/UK · Colour · 113mins

Absolutely ludicrous from hokey start to senseless finish, the only shock in this ersatz haunted house thriller is that Mike Figgis considered it worth directing. City slickers Dennis Quaid and Sharon Stone move to a dilapidated country mansion where they face sinister threats from former owner and ex-con Stephen Dorff who wants to keep a dark family secret buried there. AJ. Contains swearing and some violence. DVD

Dennis Quaid *Cooper Tilson* • Sharon Stone *Leah Tilson* • Stephen Dorff *Dale Massie* • Juliette Lewis *Ruby* • Kristen Stewart *Kristen Tilson* • Ryan Wilson *Jesse Tilson* • Dana Eskelson *Sheriff Ferguson* • Christopher Plummer *Mr Massie* ■ *Dir* Mike Figgis • *Scr* Richard Jefferies

Cold Dog Soup ★★ 15

Comedy 1989 · US · Colour · 84mins

A sexually inexperienced young innocent, promised a close encounter by a tempting young lass if he agrees to bury her mother's dog, meets a disturbed cab driver who demands they form a team and sell the dog. Equally inexperienced (and it shows) is director Alan Metter, who has a clutch of good ideas about surreal black comedy, but seems unable to produce the right tone to put them across to his audience. Randy Quaid, as the cabbie, squeezes some milage from one-note psychosis. JM

Randy Quaid *Jack Cloud* • Frank Whaley *Michael Latchmer* • Christine Harnos *Sarah Hughes* • Sheree North *Mrs Hughes* • Nancy Kwan *Mme Chang* • Seymour Cassel *JoJo* ■ *Dir* Alan Metter • *Scr* Thomas Pope from a novel by Stephen Dobyns

Cold Feet ★★ 15

Comedy 1989 · US · Colour · 88mins

This bizarre tale of western eccentrics has a brilliant but undisciplined cast who wander off into method acting overdrive because there is no firm hand on the directorial tiller. Based on a script by Jim Harrison and the terribly hip Thomas McGuane and featuring a narrative that doesn't so much rove as list from side to side, this is a small cult hit which charmed some on its release while massively infuriating others. SH. Contains violence and swearing.

Keith Carradine *Monte* • Sally Kirkland *Maureen* • Tom Waits *Kenny* • Bill Pullman *Buck* • Rip Torn *Sheriff* • Kathleen York *Laura* • Jeff Bridges *Bartender* ■ *Dir* Robert Dornhelm • *Scr* Thomas McGuane, Jim Harrison

Cold Fever ★★★★ 15

Drama
1994 · Ice/Ger/Swi/US · Colour · 81mins

Considering its size, the Icelandic film industry produces films of a remarkably high quality, and Fridrik Thor Fridriksson's road movie is a case in point. In his bid to perform a traditional burial service for his geologist parents who died in Iceland seven years earlier, Japanese businessman Masatoshi Nagase encounters all manner of eccentric locals who make his odyssey a truly memorable experience. Fridriksson makes magnificent use of the island's snowy wastes and distinctive settlements, and only the contrived appearances of American "tourists" Lili Taylor and Fisher Stevens jar. DP. In Japanese and Icelandic with English subtitles. DVD

Masatoshi Nagase *Atsushi Hirata* • Lili Taylor *Jill* • Fisher Stevens *Jack* • Gisli Halldorsson *Siggi* • Laura Hughes [Laura Leigh Hughes] *Laura* • Seijun Suzuki *Hirata's grandfather* • Hiromasa Shimada *Suzuki* • Mayayuki Sasaki *Higashino* ■ *Dir* Fridrik Thor Fridriksson • *Scr* Jim Stark, Fridrik Thor Fridriksson

Cold Front ★★★ 15

Spy thriller 1989 · US/Can · Colour · 89mins

A sturdy crime thriller which makes up for what it lacks in originality with two strong performances from Martin Sheen and Michael Ontkean (still best known as the sheriff in television's *Twin Peaks*). The pair play a US Drug Enforcement Agency officer and a plain-clothes Canadian Mountie respectively, who find themselves reluctantly teamed together when they get dragged into the world of espionage. It's simple, undemanding stuff, and the violent mayhem is ably held together by director Paul Bnarbic. JF. Contains swearing. DVD

Martin Sheen *John Hyde* • Michael Ontkean *Derek MacKenzie* • Kim Coates *Mantha* • Beverly D'Angelo *Amanda* • Yvan Ponton *Inspector Duchesne* ■ *Dir* Paul Bnarbic • *Scr* Sean Allan, Stefan Arngrim

Cold Heaven ★★★ 15

Psychological thriller
1992 · US · Colour · 102mins

Barely released to cinemas because the financing company ran into problems, this Nicolas Roeg mystery drama stars his wife, Theresa Russell, as a doctor's wife who starts an affair with another doctor only to discover her husband has been killed in a boating accident. What a coincidence! But then things start to get decidedly weird. Based on a novel by Brian

Moore, the picture never quite delivers the zingers it promises but the Mexican locations are splendid, and Russell is alluring. AT

Theresa Russell *Marie Davenport* • Mark Harmon *Alex Davenport* • James Russo *Daniel Corvin* • Will Patton *Father Niles* • Richard Bradford *Monsignor Cassidy* • Talia Shire *Sister Martha* • Julie Carmen *Anna Corvin* ■ *Dir* Nicolas Roeg • *Scr* Allan Scott, from the novel by Brian Moore

Cold Justice ★ 15

Crime drama 1991 · UK · Colour · 101mins

Imagine an episode of *Cheers* with all the humour taken out. Then blame Dennis Waterman, who co-wrote, produced and stars as "priest" Father Jim, bringing further misery to a group of barflies in this ill-conceived drama. While their lives are falling apart, Father Jim is busy scamming them out of their money, inadvertently ripping off a local gangster in the process. Overlong and depressing. RT

Roger Daltrey *Keith Gibson* • Dennis Waterman *Father Jim* • Ralph Foody *Ernie* • Ron Dean *Stan Lubinski* • Penelope Milford *Eileen* • Bert Rosario *Paquito* • Bridget O'Connell *Debbie* ■ *Dir* Terry Green • *Scr* Terry Green, Trevor Preston, Dennis Waterman

Cold Light of Day ★★ 18

Biographical horror drama
1990 · UK · Colour · 76mins

Some of the facts in the case of mass murderer Dennis Nilsen are presented with grubby realism in this British counterpart to *Henry: Portrait of a Serial Killer*. The shoestring budget presumably accounts for a minimum of camera set-ups and poor sound, and the overall effect is so grim the film was barely released. Intercutting the 15 murders with the interrogation of the suspect is an old-fashioned device, but Bob Flag is horribly plausible as the milquetoast maniac. DM

Bob Flag *Jordan March* • Geoffrey Greenhill *Inspector Simmons* • Martin Byrne-Quinn *Joe* • Andrew Edmans *Stephen* • Bill Merrow *Albert Green* ■ *Dir/Scr* Fhiona Louise

Cold Mountain ★★★ 15

Wartime romantic drama
2003 · US/UK/Rom/It · Colour · 147mins

The dream pairing of Jude Law and Nicole Kidman here delivers less on screen than it must have promised on paper. But it's not entirely the fault of the two leads, as Charles Frazier's award-winning novel dictates that they are kept apart for long stretches of this US Civil War drama. Law and Kidman play southern sweethearts who become separated when he heads off to fight for the Confederacy. The film then follows both his odyssey back from the front, with all the people and perils he encounters en route, and her struggle to survive on the mountain of the title. Along the way, Kidman is helped out by a drifter, played rather over-tetchily by Renée Zellweger. Director Anthony Minghella's film is beautifully shot by John Seale and has some great moments, but these are too few and far between. DA DVD

Jude Law *WP Inman* • Nicole Kidman *Ada Monroe* • Renée Zellweger [Renee Zellweger] *Ruby Thewes* • Donald Sutherland *Reverend Monroe* • Ray Winstone *Teague* • Brendan Gleeson *Stobrod Thewes* • Philip Seymour Hoffman *Reverend Veasey* • Natalie Portman *Sara* • Kathy Baker *Sally Swanger* • James Gammon *Esco Swanger* • Giovanni Ribisi *Junior* ■ *Dir* Anthony Minghella • *Scr* Anthony Minghella, from the novel by Charles Frazier

Cold River ★★ PG

Adventure 1982 · US · Colour · 90mins

This outdoor adventure will probably find its biggest audience among younger viewers. Suzanne Weber and Pat Petersen are forced to fend for themselves after their father succumbs to a heart attack in the sub-zero temperatures of the Adirondack Mountains. Cinematographer Bill Godsey supplies some spectacular views, but Fred G Sullivan's direction is a bit rough-and-ready. DP

Suzanne Weber *Lizzy Allison* • Pat Petersen *Tim Hood* • Richard Jaeckel *Mike Allison* • Robert Earl Jones *The Trapper* ■ *Dir* Fred G Sullivan • *Scr* Fred G Sullivan, from the novel *Winterkill* by William Judson

Cold Steel ★★ 18

Action drama 1987 · US · Colour · 86mins

An interesting cast of disparate acting talent isn't enough to save this standard action film from director Dorothy Ann Puzo, daughter of *Godfather* novelist Mario Puzo. Brad Davis is utterly wasted as an LA cop out to avenge the murder of his father. Lower down the billing is 1980s pop icon Adam Ant, who turns in a decent performance. Clichés abound, while car chases happen for the sheer sake of it. Worth catching only if you're curious to see a pre-*Basic Instinct* Sharon Stone. RS

Brad Davis *Johnny Modine* • Sharon Stone *Kathy* • Adam Ant *Mick* • Jonathan Banks *Iceman* • Jay Acovone *Cookie* • Eddie Egan *Lieutenant Hill* • Sy Richardson *Rashid* ■ *Dir* Dorothy Ann Puzo • *Scr* Michael Sonye, Moe Quigley, from a story by Lisa M Hansen, Dorothy Ann Puzo, Michael Sonye

The Cold Summer of 1953 ★★★

Political drama
1987 · USSR · Colour · 102mins

The films of Andrei Tarkovsky, John Ford and Akira Kurosawa provide the visual and thematic inspiration for this "Steppes western", which was one of the first *perestroika* features to criticise the gulag system openly. The Stalinist legacy is also called into question as a gang of criminals, released in the amnesty following his death, lay siege to a small Siberian town, which is delivered from its tyranny by escaped political prisoners Valeri Priyemykhov and Anatoli Papanov. Forcefully establishing the desolation of the landscape, director Alexandr Proshkin stages the violent action with a detachment. DP. In Russian with English subtitles.

Valeri Priyemykhov *Kopalich* • Anatoli Papanov *Luzga* • Zoya Buryak • Viktor Stepanov ■ *Dir* Alexandr Proshkin • *Scr* Edgar Dubrovski

Cold Sweat ★★ 15

Action thriller 1971 · Fr/It · Colour · 89mins

Stone-faced Charles Bronson takes time off from his busy urban vigilante schedule to head for the French Riviera, only to be forced into drug smuggling by crime boss James Mason. James Bond director Terence Young's overly familiar revenge tale relies on turgid violence and Bronson's laid-back, tough-guy persona. AJ. Contains some swearing, violence, sex scenes, nudity.

Charles Bronson *Joe Martin* • Liv Ullmann *Fabienne Martin* • James Mason *Ross* • Jill Ireland *Moira* • Michel Constantin *Whitey* ■ *Dir* Terence Young • *Scr* Shimon Wincelberg, Albert Simonin, from the novel *Ride the Nightmare* by Richard Matheson

Cold Sweat ★★ 18

Supernatural thriller
1993 · US · Colour · 92mins

A sex-and-slaying opus that has all the expected soft-core excesses of a Shannon Tweed vehicle. Naughty and naked as ever, Tweed plays the last target of hitman Ben Cross, who is planning to quit, having accidentally killed the innocent victim now haunting him. The ghostly subplot and the graveyard humour make it marginally more engaging than the average erotic thriller. DP. Contains swearing, sex scenes, violence and nudity. DVD

Ben Cross *Mark Cahill* • Adam Baldwin *Mitch* • Shannon Tweed *Beth* • Dave Thomas *Larry* • Henry Czerny *Sean* • Maria Del Mar *Joanne* • Lenore Zann *Ghost* ■ *Dir* Gail Harvey • *Scr* Richard Beattie

Cold Turkey ★★

Satire 1969 · US · Colour · 101mins

A comedy about a town in Iowa whose population goes "cold turkey" when a tobacco company offers them $25 million to stop smoking for a month. The film marked the directing debut of comedy producer Norman Lear and very much reflects the time in which it was made. Dick Van Dyke plays the local priest; veteran comic Edward Everett Horton plays the cigarette tycoon; while stand-up comic Bob Newhart is the public relations whizzkid who dreams up the idea. AT

Dick Van Dyke *Rev Clayton Brooks* • Bob Newhart *Merwin Wren* • Vincent Gardenia *Mayor Wrappler* • Pippa Scott *Natalie Brooks* • Tom Poston *Edgar Stopworth* • Edward Everett Horton *Hiram C Grayson* • Jean Stapleton *Mrs Wrappler* • Barbara Cason *Letitia Hornsby* ■ *Dir* Norman Lear • *Scr* Norman Lear, from a story by Norman Lear, William Price Fox Jr, from the novel *I'm Giving Them Up for Good* by Margaret Rau, Neil Rau

A Cold Wind in August ★★★

Melodrama 1961 · US · BW · 79mins

During an oppressively hot New York summer, a janitor's 17-year-old son (Scott Marlowe) is sent to fix the air conditioning of a much-married stripper (Lola Albright). The encounter leads to an affair and the shattering of the boy's illusions. A real shocker in its day, this tale of an older woman with a past seducing an innocent youngster still holds up thanks to Albright's superb performance and the all-round competence of first-time director Alexander Singer. RK

Lola Albright *Iris Hartford* • Scott Marlowe *Vito Perugino* • Herschel Bernardi *Juley Franz* • Joe De Santis *Papa Perugino* • Clarke Gordon *Harry* • Janet Brandt *Shirley* ■ *Dir* Alexander Singer • *Scr* Burton Wohl, from his novel

Coldblooded ★★ 18

Black comedy crime drama
1995 · US · Colour · 89mins

Jason Priestley is cast here as a nerdy Mafia bookie who gets promoted by his boss Robert Loggia to the rank of *Pulp Fiction*-style assassin, only to discover he has a natural talent for killing. This potentially novel spoof of hitman movies is smothered under a welter of unfunny gags and Priestley's charmless performance, though Michael J Fox, who co-produced the film, turns in an amusing cameo. RS. Contains violence and swearing.

Jason Priestley *Cosmo* • Kimberly Williams *Jasmine* • Peter Riegert *Steve* • Robert Loggia *Gordon* • Janeane Garofalo *Honey* • Josh Charles *Randy* • Michael J Fox *Tim Alexander* ■ *Dir/Scr* M Wallace Wolodarsky [Wallace Wolodarsky]

The Colditz Story ★★★★ U

Second World War drama
1954 · UK · BW · 93mins

One of seemingly dozens of PoW dramas made in the mid-1950s, this is set in the infamous German fortress of the title. The story about the daring escapes undertaken by Allied prisoners has little time for the psychology of imprisonment, but the action is still well-played – tense at times, music-hall jolly at others. John Mills plays Pat Reid, on whose first-hand account the film is based, and Eric Portman, Ian Carmichael, Lionel Jeffries and Bryan Forbes are the other inmates of heroic hue. AT DVD

John Mills *Pat Reid* • Eric Portman *Colonel Richmond* • Christopher Rhodes *Mac* • Lionel Jeffries *Harry* • Bryan Forbes *Jimmy* • Ian Carmichael *Robin* • Richard Wattis *Richard* ■ *Dir* Guy Hamilton • *Scr* Guy Hamilton, Ivan Foxwell, from the non-fiction book by PR Reid

C

Collateral ★★★★ 15

Action crime thriller
2004 · US · Colour · 114mins

Tom Cruise stars as a cold-blooded hitman in this effective, edgy thriller from director Michael Mann. After hijacking a taxi and its driver, Cruise embarks on a series of ruthlessly efficient assassinations across night-time LA while the hapless cabbie (Jamie Foxx) tries to work out ways to escape. Cruise is well cast against type and is surprisingly effective as the killer, but it's Michael Mann's astonishing style that really marks the film out. Shot on a mixture of film and digital video, the night-time lights of LA look alternately moody, surreal and dangerous. AS. Contains swearing and violence. DVD

Tom Cruise *Vincent* • Jamie Foxx *Max Durocher* • Jada Pinkett Smith *Annie* • Mark Ruffalo *Fanning* • Peter Berg *Richard Weidner* • Bruce McGill *Pedrosa* • Irma P Hall *Ida* • Barry Shabaka Henley [Barry "Shabaka" Henley] *Daniel* • Javier Bardem *Felix* ■ *Dir* Michael Mann • *Scr* Stuart Beattie

Collateral Damage ★★ 15

Action thriller 2001 · US · Colour · 104mins

Arnold Schwarzenegger plays a vengeful firefighter hunting the Colombian terrorists who've blown up an embassy building, killing his wife and child. The film's start and finish have plenty of bang for your buck but the flabby middle section sees Schwarzenegger's one-man army collecting a woman and child to protect which muddles both the action and the revenge theme. DA. Contains swearing and violence. DVD

Arnold Schwarzenegger *Gordy Brewer* • Elias Koteas *Agent Brandt* • Francesca Neri *Selena Perrini* • Cliff Curtis *Claudio, "El Lobo" Perrini* • John Leguizamo *Felix* • John Turturro *Sean Armstrong* ■ *Dir* Andrew Davis • *Scr* David Griffiths, Peter Griffiths, from a story by David Griffiths, Peter Griffiths, Ronald Roose

La Collectionneuse ★★★★ 15

Drama 1967 · Fr · Colour · 82mins

The third of Eric Rohmer's "Six Moral Tales", and the first of feature length. Winner of the special jury prize at Berlin, it tells of the summer encounter between sexually liberated teenager Haydée Politoff, antique dealer Patrick Bauchau and his friend Daniel Pommereulle. Attracted and unnerved by Politoff's amorous exploits, they attempt to reform her without becoming part of her collection of lovers. As you would expect of Rohmer, there is plenty of amusing and insightful chat, as his young cast flirt and succumb, resist and reproach. DP. In French with English subtitles.

Patrick Bauchau *Adrien* • Haydée Politoff *Haydée* • Daniel Pommereulle *Daniel* • Seymour Hertzberg [Eugene Archer] *Sam* • Mijanou Bardot *Carole* • Annik Morice *Carole's friend* ■ *Dir* Eric Rohmer • *Scr* Eric Rohmer, Patrick Bauchau, Haydée Politoff, Daniel Pommereulle

The Collector ★★★★ 15

Thriller 1965 · US/UK · Colour · 114mins

A genuinely disturbing chunk of *Grand Guignol* about a maladjusted, butterfly-collecting young man who kidnaps an art student and keeps her in his cellar. Based on an equally disturbing and complex novel by John Fowles, this was in its day a fashionable shocker and X-certificated. Now it comes across as a fascinating period piece, featuring two quintessential 1960s stars in possibly their best roles – painfully handsome Terence Stamp as the collector, and beautiful auburn-haired Samantha Eggar as the victim of his attentions. Kenneth More was also cast as Eggar's older lover, but his whole role was removed in the final edit. TS. Contains some violence.

Terence Stamp *Freddie Clegg* • Samantha Eggar *Miranda Grey* • Mona Washbourne *Aunt Annie* • Maurice Dallimore *Neighbour* • William Beckley *Crutchley* • Gordon Barclay *Clerk* ■ *Dir* William Wyler • *Scr* Stanley Mann, John Kohn, from the novel by John Fowles

Colleen ★★

Musical comedy 1936 · US · BW · 90mins

When eccentric millionaire Hugh Herbert puts gold-digger Joan Blondell in charge of his dress shop, his family is outraged. Complications ensue when his nephew, Dick Powell, brings Ruby Keeler in to take over. A feeble script and forgettable score make this a disappointing final outing for Powell and Keeler, paired for the sixth and last time in a Warner Bros musical. RK

Dick Powell *Donald Ames III* • Ruby Keeler *Colleen* • Jack Oakie *Joe Cork* • Joan Blondell *Minnie Hawkins* • Hugh Herbert *Cedric Ames* • Louise Fazenda *Alicia Ames* • Paul Draper *Paul* • Luis Alberni *Carlo* ■ *Dir* Alfred E Green • *Scr* Peter Milne, Frederick Hugh Herbert [F Hugh Herbert], Sig Herzig, from a story by Robert Lord • *Music Director* Leo Forbstein [Leo F Forbstein]

College ★★★★★ U

Silent romantic comedy
1927 · US · BW · 66mins

Buster Keaton's running, jumping but rarely standing-still film is a story about his going to college and trying to transcend athletically his bookworm exterior to win the heart of student Anne Cornwall. She's surrounded by admiring jocks, but he's determined to flatten them in a decathlon of sports, though he gets it all wrong – knocking down hurdles, or being thrown by the hammer instead of the other way around. There's one spectacular sequence in which he apes a soda-jerk to disastrous effect, and the final pole-vault to rescue the girl is balletically brilliant. TH DVD

Buster Keaton *Ronald* • Ann Cornwall *Mary Haines, the girl* • Flora Bramley *Mary's friend* • Harold Goodwin (1) *Jeff Brown, a rival* • Grant Withers *Jeff's friend* • Buddy Mason *Jeff's friend* • Snitz Edwards *Dean Edwards* ■ *Dir* James W Horne • *Scr* Carl Harbaugh, Bryan Foy

College Swing ★★

Musical 1938 · US · BW · 82mins

Despite having three writers on the movie, including an uncredited Preston Sturges, and Raoul Walsh as director, this is little more than an excuse for a variety show. The silly plot, such as it is, has bird-brained Gracie Allen inheriting a college and hiring vaudevillians as professors. Allen does a few turns with husband George Burns, Martha Raye yells a number of songs, Bob Hope cracks corny jokes and Betty Grable shakes her legs. Mildly entertaining. RB

George Burns *George Jonas* • Gracie Allen *Gracie Alden* • Martha Raye *Mabel* • Bob Hope *Bud Brady* • Edward Everett Horton *Hubert Dash* • Florence George *Ginna Ashburn* • Ben Blue *Ben Volt* • Betty Grable *Betty* • Jackie Coogan *Jackie* • John Payne *Martin Bates* ■ *Dir* Raoul Walsh • *Scr* Walter DeLeon, Francis Martin, from a story by Ted Lesser

Collision Course ★★ 18

Comedy 1987 · US · Colour · 96mins

This thoroughly unremarkable variation on the Arnold Schwarzenegger vehicle *Red Heat* was shelved for three years after it was made, because of the lawsuit that followed the bankruptcy of its production company, DEG. It wasn't until 1992 that it was released on video in the US – something of an embarrassment for Jay Leno, who had just assumed the host's chair of that famous US chatfest *The Tonight Show*. As the detective teamed with visiting Japanese inspector Pat Morita, Leno reveals why this is his sole starring role to date. A disappointment. DP

Noriyuki "Pat" Morita [Pat Morita] *Investigator Fujitsuka Natsuo* • Jay Leno *Detective Tony Costas* • Ernie Hudson *Shortcut* • Chris Sarandon *Philip Madras* • John Hancock *Lieutenant Ryerson* • Tom Noonan *Scully* • Al Waxman *Dingman* ■ *Dir* Lewis Teague • *Scr* Frank Darius Namei, Robert Resnikoff

Le Colonel Chabert ★★★ 12

Historical drama 1994 · Fr · Colour · 106mins

Cinematographer Yves Angelo made his directorial debut with this handsome adaptation of one of the novels making up Balzac's *Comédie Humaine*. Gérard Depardieu is typically bullish as the Napoleonic veteran returning ten years after his supposed death to discover his wife (Fanny Ardant) has remarried, taking his fortune with her. The war scenes are magnificent, the intrigue compelling and the sense of period faultless. However, Angelo occasionally gets so carried away by the grandeur and gravitas of the production that the pace drops to a crawl. DP. In French with English subtitles.

Gérard Depardieu *Chabert* • Fanny Ardant *Countess Ferraud* • Fabrice Luchini *Derville* • André Dussollier *Count Ferraud* • Daniel Prévost *Boucard* • Olivier Saladin *Huré* ■ *Dir* Yves Angelo • *Scr* Jean Cosmos, Yves Angelo, Véronique Legrange, from the novel by Honoré de Balzac

Colonel Effingham's Raid ★★★ U

Comedy 1945 · US · BW · 70mins

Bluff Charles Coburn's 1943 supporting Oscar for *The More the Merrier* helped elevate him to lead status, and here he's well cast in this minor 20th Century-Fox rustic comedy drama about a returning army officer fighting a one-man battle to preserve his southern town's heritage. Coburn himself was from Savannah, Georgia, despite his gentrified British appearance, and well understood this particular character. He seldom played leads again, but was Oscar-nominated and top-billed for his subsequent movie, *The Green Years*. TS

Charles Coburn *Colonel Effingham* • Joan Bennett *Ella Sue Dozier* • William Eythe *Al* • Allyn Joslyn *Earl Hoats* • Elizabeth Patterson *Emma* ■ *Dir* Irving Pichel • *Scr* Kathryn Scola, from the novel by Barry Fleming

Colonel March Investigates ★★

Crime mystery 1953 · UK · BW · 70mins

Boris Karloff runs a Scotland Yard division called the "Department of Queer Complaints", wears an eye-patch and carries a swordstick. These three short stories proving his investigative brilliance were actually glued together from Karloff's British TV show, *Colonel March of Scotland Yard*. Threadbare production values don't help this effort from Cy Endfield. AT

Boris Karloff *Colonel March* • Ewan Roberts *Inspector Ames* • Richard Wattis *Cabot* • John Hewer *John Parrish* • Sheila Burrell *Joan Forsythe* • Joan Sims *Marjorie Dawson* ■ *Dir* Cyril Endfield [Cy Endfield] • *Scr* Leo Davis, from the TV series by Carter Dickson

Colonel Redl ★★★★ 15

Period drama
1984 · Hun/W Ger/Austria · Colour · 143mins

This is a compelling study of the decaying Austro-Hungarian empire and the social, racial and political tensions that eventually undermined it. Klaus Maria Brandauer excels as the railwayman's son whose casual facility for deceit and obsessive devotion to honour enable him to rise through the ranks of the Imperial Army until both his background and his bisexuality become an embarrassment to the establishment. Armin Mueller-Stahl's ruthless Franz Ferdinand is equally impressive, but it's the chilling way director István Szabó charts the complex web of events that makes this sumptuous picture so memorable. DP. In German with English subtitles. Contains some violence, swearing, sex scenes and nudity.

Klaus Maria Brandauer *Alfred Redl* • Hans Christian Blech *Colonel von Roden* • Armin Mueller-Stahl *Archduke Franz Ferdinand* • Gudrun Landgrebe *Katalin Kubinyi* • Jan Niklas *Christoph Kubinyi* ■ *Dir* István Szabó • *Scr* István Szabó, Peter Dobai, from the play *A Patriot for Me* by John Osborne

Color Me Blood Red ★★ 18

Horror 1965 · US · Colour · 79mins

This is a surprisingly restrained schlocker, with Don Joseph (aka Gordon Oas-Heim) playing an egomaniacal artist who kills to maintain the stocks of red "paint" that have helped establish his reputation with the pretentious critic who had previously spurned him. Mostly acting with his eyes on stalks, Joseph conveys tortured self-delusion rather well. But the remainder of the cast are less effective. DP DVD

Don Joseph [Gordon Oas-Heim] *Adam Sorg* • Candi Conder *April* • Elyn Warner *Gigi* • Scott H Hall *Farnsworth* • Jerome Eden *Rolf* ■ *Dir/Scr* Herschell G Lewis [Herschell Gordon Lewis]

Color Me Dead ★★

Crime thriller 1969 · Aus · Colour · 97mins

An Australian movie that should be blushing with shame at its audacity in pinching its plot from *DOA* , the classic *film noir* from 1949, without identifying itself as a remake. An accountant is given a very slow-acting poison and tries to find out who has killed him, in advance of his death. TH

Tom Tryon *Frank Bigelow* • Carolyn Jones *Paula Gibson* • Rick Jason *Bradley Taylor* • Patricia Connolly *Marla Rukubian* • Tony Ward *Halliday* ■ *Dir* Eddie Davis • *Scr* Russell Rouse, Clarence Greene

Color of a Brisk and Leaping Day ★★★

Period drama 1996 · US · BW · 85mins

Fight your way through the title and you will find an American indie production about a man who wants to rebuild and reopen the railroad that once ran through Yosemite national park. This majestic wilderness was made world famous by Ansel Adams's photographs; Christopher Münch's film mirrors Adams's imagery while the Chinese-American hero, played by Peter Alexander, sets about realising his obsession. Like the story itself the movie is a labour of love, set in the 1940s, incorporating archive footage and full of remarkable detail. AT

Peter Alexander *John Lee* • Jeri Arredondo *Nancy* • Henry Gibson *Robinson* • Michael Stipe *Skeeter* • David Chung *Mr Lee* • Diana Larkin *Wendy* ■ *Dir/Scr* Christopher Münch • *Cinematographer* Rob Sweeney

The Color of Destiny ★★★

Political drama 1986 · Bra · Colour · 104mins

Although this hard-hitting resistance drama is set in Rio, the focal point is actually Chile under the Pinochet dictatorship. Teenager Guilherme Fontes barely remembers the torture and murder of his brother, but he struggles to justify his obsession with girls and art once his cousin, Julia Lemmertz, persuades him to join a demonstration outside the Chilean embassy and reawakens his commitment to overthrowing the tyrannical regime. Fontes gives a thoughtful performance DP. In Portuguese with English subtitles.

Guilherme Fontes *Paulo* • Norma Bengell *Laura* • Franklin Caicedo *Victor* • Julia Lemmertz *Patricia* • Andrea Beltrao *Helena* ■ *Dir* Jorge Duran • *Scr* Jorge Duran, Nelson Natotti, Jose Joffily, from a story by Jorge Duran

The Color of Love: Jacey's Story ★★★

Drama 2000 · US · Colour

Gena Rowlands is in imposing form in this heartwarming drama. She avoids sentimentality, as she struggles to raise the granddaughter she only discovered she had on learning of her own daughter's death. With Lou Gossett Jr equally impressive as Penny Bae Bridges's paternal grandfather, this TV movie makes some telling points about racial harmony, without straining for effect. DP

Gena Rowlands *Georgia Porter* • Louis Gossett Jr *Lou* • Penny Fuller *Madeleine Porter* • Stella Parton *Ellen Fuller* • Penny Bae Bridges *Jacey* ■ *Dir* Sheldon Larry • *Scr* Nancy Silvers

The Color of Money ★★★★ 15

Drama 1986 · US · Colour · 114mins

Paul Newman reprises the role of "Fast Eddie" Felson, the pool shark he played in 1961's *The Hustler*, and deservedly won the best actor Oscar. This time around, the ageing Felson takes on pushy pupil Vincent (Tom Cruise) and both learn a trick or two as Felson prepares his prodigy for a national tournament in Atlantic City. The confrontational climax never quite convinces, but Richard Price's knockout script is one to treasure and director Martin Scorsese brings his trademark visual style to bear on the production. Oscar-nominated Mary Elizabeth Mastrantonio puts in an accomplished performance as the naive Cruise's knowing girlfriend. TH. Contains violence, swearing and nudity. DVD

Paul Newman *"Fast Eddie" Felson* • Tom Cruise *Vincent Lauria* • Mary Elizabeth Mastrantonio *Carmen* • Helen Shaver *Janelle* • John Turturro *Julian* • Forest Whitaker *Amos* ■ *Dir* Martin Scorsese • *Scr* Richard Price, from the novel by Walter Tevis

Color of Night ★ 18

Erotic thriller 1994 · US · Colour · 134mins

Richard Rush was once a half-decent film-maker but he came a cropper with this atrocity, which became notorious after some full-frontal shots of Bruce Willis were snipped by the censors. So even though we don't get the Full Brucey, we do get a lousy whodunnit, in which every member of a therapy group goes out of their way to prove they're madder than the rest. This is so awful it can't be missed. DP. Contains swearing, violence, sex scenes and nudity. DVD

Bruce Willis *Dr Bill Capa* • Jane March *Rose* • Rubén Blades *Martinez* • Lesley Ann Warren *Sondra* • Scott Bakula *Dr Bob Moore* • Brad Dourif *Clark* • Lance Henriksen *Buck* • Kevin J

O'Connor *Casey* • Andrew Lowery *Dale* ■ *Dir* Richard Rush • *Scr* Matthew Chapman, Billy Ray, from a story by Billy Ray

The Color of Paradise ★★★★ PG

Drama 1999 · Iran · Colour · 86mins

Majid Majidi's follow-up to his Oscar-nominated delight, *The Children of Heaven*, combines a fairy-tale atmosphere with sensual imagery to produce a gentle parable on the dangers of social ambition and spiritual hypocrisy. There's a *Kikujiro* feel to the relationship between miner Hossein Mahjub and his eight-year-old son, Mohsen Ramezani, as the rascally widower comes to reappraise his priorities after a prestigious betrothal falls through. But leaving a deeper impression is Majidi's depiction of the blind boy's sensitivity to both his family (particularly his beloved grandmother) and the natural world around him. Simple but cinematic, moving and inspiring. DP. In Farsi with English subtitles.

Hossein Mahjub *Hashem, the father* • Mohsen Ramezani *Mohammad* • Salime Feizi *Grandmother* ■ *Dir/Scr* Majid Majidi

The Color Purple ★★★★ 15

Period drama 1985 · US · Colour · 147mins

On this film's release, it was fashionable to castigate director Steven Spielberg for his somewhat glossy, sugar-coated version of Alice Walker's celebrated Pulitzer Prize-winning novel about a young black woman's struggle for self and racial identity. Yet this is actually an impressive, dignified attempt to turn a radical and often difficult novel into mainstream entertainment with a message. Whoopi Goldberg is wonderful in the lead, Danny Glover and Margaret Avery are sublime, and watch out for Oprah Winfrey playing *very* out of character. SH. Contains violence and swearing. DVD

Whoopi Goldberg *Celie* • Danny Glover *Albert Johnson* • Margaret Avery (2) *Shug Avery* • Oprah Winfrey *Sofia* • Willard Pugh *Harpo* • Akosua Busia *Nettie* • Desreta Jackson *Young Celie* • Adolph Caesar *Old Mister* • Rae Dawn Chong *Squeak* ■ *Dir* Steven Spielberg • *Scr* Menno Meyjes, from the novel by Alice Walker

Colorado Territory ★★★

Western 1949 · US · BW · 94mins

An exciting westernised remake of the Humphrey Bogart classic *High Sierra*, with an identical plot and the same director in Raoul Walsh. Walsh manages to create a superbly sweaty atmosphere, with Joel McCrea this time as the outlaw on the run, hiding out in the desert. The themes are adult and the tension is beautifully sustained; indeed, structurally, this version is better than its famous predecessor. TS

Joel McCrea *Wes McQueen* • Virginia Mayo *Colorado Carson* • Dorothy Malone *Julie Ann* • Henry Hull *Winslow* • John Archer *Reno Blake* • James Mitchell *Duke Harris* • Morris Ankrum *US marshal* • Basil Ruysdael *Dave Rickard* • Frank Puglia *Brother Tomas* ■ *Dir* Raoul Walsh • *Scr* John Twist, Edmund H North, from the novel *High Sierra* by WR Burnett

Colors ★★★ 18

Crime drama 1988 · US · Colour · 126mins

With *Dragnet*-style gravity, this movie informs us of the 600 gangs, the 70,000 gang members and the 400 gang-related murders in LA County each year. Then cops Robert Duvall and Sean Penn take to the streets to apprehend the troublesome youths. Directed by Dennis Hopper with some urgency, the picture is tense and unpleasant, with sympathy for both sides of the war. Duvall and Penn make a fine combination of old sage and high-octane rookie, but this is so grim it's hard to enjoy. AT. Contains violence and swearing. DVD

Sean Penn *Danny McGavin* • Robert Duvall *Bob Hodges* • Maria Conchita Alonso *Louisa Gomez* • Randy Brooks *Ron Delaney* • Don Cheadle *Rocket* ■ *Dir* Dennis Hopper • *Scr* Michael Schiffer, from a story by Michael Schiffer, Richard DiLello

The Colossus of New York ★

Science-fiction horror
1958 · US · BW · 71mins

When Otto Kruger stays late at the lab to transplant his brother's brain into a robot, he ends up with a combination of Frankenstein's monster and *The Wrong Trousers*. The big lad is soon biting chunks out of the Big Apple. The dialogue and effects are wretched, Kruger and Ross Martin are lifeless, and the direction is more leaden than the creature's footwear. DP

Ross Martin *Dr Jeremy Spensser* • Mala Powers *Anne Spensser* • Charles Herbert *Billy Spensser* • John Baragrey *Dr Henry Spensser* • Otto Kruger *Dr William Spensser* • Robert Hutton *Professor John Carrington* • Ed Wolff *Colossus* ■ *Dir* Eugène Lourié • *Scr* Thelma Schnee, from a story by Willis Goldbeck

The Colossus of Rhodes ★★★

Period adventure
1961 · It/Fr/Sp · Colour · 127mins

Before he went on to make spaghetti westerns with such fierce artistry, and after several credits as screenwriter on historical epics, Sergio Leone made this spectacular adventure, his official debut as a director. Rory Calhoun stars as Athenian soldier Dario, who joins a slave uprising against oppressive ruler King Xerxes. There are some explicit torture and battle scenes, and touches of Leone irony to lighten the rather lumpen load. TH

Rory Calhoun *Dario* • Lea Massari *Diala* • Georges Marchal *Peliocles* • Conrado San Martin *Thar* • Angel Aranda *Koros* • Mabel Karr *Mirte* ■ *Dir* Sergio Leone • *Scr* Ennio De Concini, Sergio Leone, Cesare Seccia, Luciano Martino, Duccio Tessari, Age Gavioli, Carlo Gualtieri, Luciano Chittarini

Colossus: the Forbin Project ★★★

Science-fiction thriller
1969 · US · Colour · 99mins

The years have been kind to Joseph Sargent's thinking man's sci-fi entry, which imagines a time when one super computer has total control over all western defence systems. When it decides to link terminals with its Soviet counterpart in a bid for world domination, its human masters discover they can't switch the damn thing off. Cleverly playing up the thriller aspects of the story and cannily making the computer the film's central character, this is a well-acted and utterly persuasive shocker. RS

Eric Braeden *Dr Charles Forbin* • Susan Clark *Dr Cleo Markham* • Gordon Pinsent *The President* • William Schallert *Grauber* • Leonid Rostoff *1st Chairman* • Georg Stanford Brown *Fisher* • Tom Basham *Harrison* ■ *Dir* Joseph Sargent • *Scr* James Bridges, from the novel *Colossus* by DF Jones

The Colour of Lies ★★★★ 15

Thriller 1999 · Fr · Colour · 112mins

Couching the old-fashioned whodunnit in a deliciously modern form, Claude Chabrol brings an acute sense of character and place to this teasing mystery. Cameraman Eduardo Serra's views of Brittany are expertly alternated with tight close-ups, as police inspector Valéria Bruni-Tedeschi investigates the rape and murder of a ten-year-old girl. Jacques Gamblin's performance as the brooding artist – and prime suspect – is balanced neatly by his breezy nursing wife Sandrine Bonnaire, while the petty preoccupations of the locals are slyly contrasted with the opinions of media luvvie Antoine de Caunes. DP. In French with English subtitles.

Sandrine Bonnaire *Viviane Sterne* • Jacques Gamblin *René Sterne* • Antoine de Caunes *Germain-Roland Desmot* • Valéria Bruni-Tedeschi *Frederique Lesage* • Bulle Ogier *Yvelyne Bordier* ■ *Dir* Claude Chabrol • *Scr* Claude Chabrol, Odile Barski

The Colour of Pomegranates ★★★★★ U

Biographical drama
1969 · USSR · Colour · 69mins

Ostensibly this is a fantasy on the life of the 18th-century Armenian poet Arutiun Sayadin, the carpet weaver's apprentice who rose to become first the court minstrel Sayat Nova ("the king of song"), and then an archbishop. Yet the sumptuous tableaux devised by director Sergei Paradjanov are only vaguely concerned with the depiction of actual events. Instead, they are a breathtaking amalgam of subversive symbols drawn from both religious iconography and nationalist folklore. Much of the meaning will be indecipherable to those without specialist knowledge, but you can still surrender yourself to the rhythm and beauty of this remarkable film, made in 1969 but not seen in the West until 1977. DP. In Armenian with English subtitles.

Sofiko Chiaureli *Young Poet/Poet's Love/Nun/Angel/Mime* • V Galestyan *Poet in the Cloister* • M Aleksanian *Poet as a Child* • G Gegechkori *Poet–as an Old Man* ■ *Dir/Scr* Sergei Paradjanov

Colt .45 ★★★ U

Western 1950 · US · Colour · 72mins

One of the most successful westerns in a great year for the genre (*Wagon Master*, *The Gunfighter* and *Broken Arrow* were also produced in 1950). Here craggy Randolph Scott is a gun salesman whose deadly wares are stolen by Zachary Scott and used in a series of hold-ups. Apart from a romantic interlude with Ruth Roman that's totally unconvincing, it's a fast-moving, though conventional, western that benefits from the use of 1950s Technicolor and the iconic charm of Randolph Scott, an often undervalued tall guy in the saddle. TS

Randolph Scott *Steve Farrell* • Ruth Roman *Beth Donovan* • Zachary Scott *Jason Brett* • Lloyd Bridges *Paul Donovan* • Alan Hale *Sheriff Harris* • Ian MacDonald *Miller* • Chief Thundercloud *Walking Bear* ■ *Dir* Edwin L Marin • *Scr* Thomas Blackburn, from his story

Column South ★★★ U

Western 1953 · US · Colour · 84mins

A beautifully photographed Universal western in which fresh-faced former war hero Audie Murphy plays a cavalry officer sympathetic to the Indians, perceptively pointing out that helping the dispossessed native Americans would ultimately strengthen the Union. Don't worry, the politics don't get in the way of the well-staged action sequences. Director Frederick De Cordova was destined for a long and distinguished career in American television, most notably as producer of *The Johnny Carson Show*. TS

Audie Murphy *Lieutenant Jed Sayre* • Joan Evans *March Whitlock* • Robert Sterling *Captain Lee Whitlock* • Ray Collins *Brig Gen Storey* • Dennis Weaver *Menguito* ■ *Dir* Frederick De Cordova • *Scr* William Sackheim • *Cinematographer* Charles P Boyle

Coma ★★★★ 15

Thriller 1977 · US · Colour · 108mins

Doctor Geneviève Bujold and sinister surgeon Richard Widmark clash memorably in this taut medical thriller, faithfully adapted from Robin Cook's bestseller by doctor-turned-novelist Michael Crichton. The *ER*/*Jurassic Park* creator also directs and expertly turns the suspense screws in the gripping way that has become his trademark. Crichton's assured sense of creepy paranoia gives an extra disturbing edge to the hospital horrors. AJ. Contains violence, swearing and brief nudity.

Geneviève Bujold *Dr Susan Wheeler* • Michael Douglas *Dr Mark Bellows* • Elizabeth Ashley *Mrs Emerson* • Rip Torn *Dr George* • Richard Widmark *Dr George A Harris* • Lois Chiles *Nancy Greenly* • Harry Rhodes [Hari Rhodes] *Dr Morelind* • Tom Selleck *Sean Murphy* ■ *Dir* Michael Crichton • *Scr* Michael Crichton, from the novel by Robin Cook

Comanche ★★ U

Western 1956 · US · Colour · 87mins

This very routine western, allegedly based on fact, is made interesting by the fact that it introduced glamorous South American star Linda Cristal (who would go on to *The Alamo* and *Two Rode Together*) to an English-speaking audience. In the lead is the past-his-prime Dana Andrews, grim-faced and having trouble with his lines. TS

Dana Andrews *Read* • Kent Smith *Quanah Parker* • Linda Cristal *Margarita* • Nestor Paiva *Puffer* • Henry Brandon *Black Cloud* • John Litel *General Miles* • Reed Sherman *French* • Stacy Harris *Downey* • Lowell Gilmore *Ward* ■ *Dir* George Sherman • *Scr* Carl Krueger

Comanche Station ★★★★ PG

Western 1960 · US · Colour · 70mins

this final film in the series of Ranown westerns from director Budd Boetticher and co-producer/star Randolph Scott is a fine meditation on ageing. It's a companion piece thematically to John Ford's *The Searchers*, but arguably bleaker and more realistic – this austere work strips the genre to its bare essentials. Supporting the craggy Scott is the well-cast Claude Akins as a flamboyant bounty hunter, and their final confrontation is especially effective. Particularly notable is Burt Kennedy's screenplay, which utilises the western's emotive iconography brilliantly. TS

Randolph Scott *Jefferson Cody* • Nancy Gates *Mrs Lowe* • Claude Akins *Ben Lane* • Skip Homeier *Frank* • Richard Rust *Dobie* • Rand Brooks *Station man* • Dyke Johnson *Mr Lowe* ■ *Dir* Budd Boetticher • *Scr* Burt Kennedy

Comanche Territory ★★ U

Western 1950 · US · Colour · 75mins

American folk legend Jim Bowie (he of the knife fame) has been portrayed several times on the movie screen, perhaps most notably by Richard Widmark in *The Alamo* and Alan Ladd in *The Iron Mistress* . This, alas, is one of the more lacklustre versions of Bowie's exploits. Macdonald Carey fails to convey any sense of destiny as he tries to stop lovely Maureen O'Hara and her evil brother Charles Drake from mining on Indian territory. TS

Maureen O'Hara *Katie* • Macdonald Carey *James Bowie* • Will Geer *Dan'l Seeger* • Charles Drake *Stacey Howard* • Pedro De Cordoba *Quisima* • Ian MacDonald *Walsh* • Rick Vallin *Pakanah* • Parley Baer *Boozer* ■ *Dir* George Sherman • *Scr* Oscar Brodney, Lewis Meltzer, from a story by Lewis Meltzer

The Comancheros ★★★★ PG

Western 1961 · US · Colour · 102mins

A marvellous swan song for *Casablanca* director Michael Curtiz, who died after completing this film. Indeed, much of this handsome western was actually directed by star John Wayne, in tandem with second unit director Cliff Lyons. The scale is substantial, and Curtiz fills the screen with rip-roaring action. The score is one of Elmer Bernstein's best and most elegiac, and there's a terrific star-building performance from Lee Marvin. A big hit in its day, this is the sort of sprawling horse opera that died, alas, with its star. TS [video] DVD

John Wayne *Captain Jake Cutter* • Stuart Whitman *Paul Regret* • Ina Balin *Pilar* • Nehemiah Persoff *Graile* • Lee Marvin *Tully Crow* • Michael Ansara *Amelung* • Patrick Wayne *Tobe* • Bruce Cabot *Major Henry* • Henry Daniell *Gireaux* ■ *Dir* Michael Curtiz • *Scr* James Edward Grant, Clair Huffaker, from the novel by Paul I Wellman • *Cinematographer* William Clothier

Comandante ★★★ PG

Documentary 2002 · US/Sp · Colour · 95mins

Writer/director Oliver Stone makes an accomplished documentary debut with this portrait of Cuban revolutionary leader Fidel Castro. Given three days access, Stone peppers the ever-alert 75-year-old with questions about everything from the Bay of Pigs affair and the subsequent Missile Crisis to Ché Guevara and the Soviet alliance, and is only obviously sidestepped on such topics as his love life, religion, homosexuality and Cuba's role in Vietnam. The mix of archive footage and scenes of Castro touring Havana suggest his undiminished popularity, but Stone clearly isn't wholly convinced of the extent or permanence of his achievement. DP. In Spanish and English with subtitles. DVD

Dir Oliver Stone • *Scr* from an idea by José Ibañez, Alvaro Longoria

Combination Platter ★★★

Comedy drama 1993 · US · Colour · 84mins

This directorial debut from 23-year-old Tony Chan is a quiet little film about a Chinese restaurant in Queens, NY, that successfully exposes the culture clash between the Chinese owners and their American clients. The film centres on Jeff Lau, an illegal immigrant seeking to remain in the US via marriage. Aided by his pal Kenneth Lu, he starts dating Colleen O'Brien, who's oblivious to his mercenary intentions. Remarkably good considering its $250,000 budget. LH

Jeff Lau *Robert* • Colleen O'Brien *Claire* • Lester "Chit-Man" Chan *Sam* • Colin Mitchell *Benny* • Kenneth Lu *Andy* • Thomas K Hsiung *Mr Lee* ■ *Dir* Tony Chan • *Scr* Tony Chan, Edwin Baker

Come and Get It ★★ PG

Period drama 1936 · US · BW · 95mins

This is the story of humble young lumberjack Edward Arnold who becomes a wealthy and powerful tycoon. Sacrificing the woman he loves (Frances Farmer) to ambition along the way, he has to face the bitter disillusion of old age. Adapted from Edna Ferber's novel and co-directed by heavyweights William Wyler and Howard Hawks, this is a curate's egg of a period piece, while the film, beautifully mounted, runs out of steam halfway through. RK [video]

Edward Arnold *Barney Glasgow* • Joel McCrea *Richard Glasgow* • Frances Farmer *Lotta Morgan/Lotta Bostrom* • Walter Brennan *Swan Bostrom* • Andrea Leeds *Evvie Glasgow* • Frank Shields (1) *Tony Schwerke* ■ *Dir* Howard Hawks, William Wyler • *Scr* Jules Furthman, Jane Murfin, from the novel by Edna Ferber

Come and See ★★★ 15

Epic drama
1985 · USSR · Colour and BW · 142mins

Set in Byelorussia in 1943, this worthy picture traces the harrowing experiences which turn green teenager Alexei Kravchenko into a hardened resistance fighter. Elem Klimov employs glossy colour images to create striking set pieces, skilfully staged to shock. However, the whole film suffers from a severe case of "Schindler Syndrome": the depiction of indefensible events to ensure the viewer unquestioningly accepts the director's vision. DP. In Russian with English subtitles.

Alexei Kravchenko *Florya* • Olga Mironova *Glasha* • Liubomiras Laucevicius • Vladas Bagdonas ■ *Dir* Elem Klimov • *Scr* Elem Klimov, Ales Adamovich, from *The Khatyn Story* and *A Punitive Squad* by Ales Adamovich

Come Back, Little Sheba ★★★★ PG

Drama 1952 · US · BW · 91mins

Sheba is a little pooch and surrogate child that's gone missing; Shirley Booth is its owner desperate for its return. Her husband, meanwhile, a failed doctor, is so provoked by the cavortings of two virile student lodgers that he hits the bottle after a year on the wagon. Based on a Broadway hit, this is a classic slice of Americana, oscillating between comedy and tragedy and performed by actors who squeeze the text until not a drop of drama remains on the page. The show-stopper, though, is Booth, who won an Oscar for her screen debut. AT DVD

Burt Lancaster *Doc Delaney* • Shirley Booth *Lola Delaney* • Terry Moore *Marie Buckholder* • Richard Jaeckel *Turk Fisher* • Philip Ober *Ed Anderson* • Lisa Golm *Mrs Goffman* • Walter Kelley *Bruce* ■ *Dir* Daniel Mann • *Scr* Ketti Frings, from the play by William Inge

Come Back to the Five and Dime, Jimmy Dean, Jimmy Dean ★★★★ 15

Drama 1982 · US · Colour · 109mins

Robert Altman drops his usual scattergun approach to direct a wholly focused adaptation of Ed Graczyk's play about a group of women who gather to commemorate the death of their beloved Jimmy Dean. Sandy Dennis, Cher and Karen Black are among the beautiful losers who are now slightly older and bitchier than they were when they originally formed the fan club. Altman brilliantly conveys their changes of mood via a wall mirror in what is altogether one of the better variations on a stage theme. TH [video]

Sandy Dennis *Mona* • Cher *Sissy* • Karen Black *Joanne* • Sudie Bond *Juanita* • Marta Heflin *Edna Louise* • Kathy Bates *Stella May* • Mark Patton *Joe Qualley* ■ *Dir* Robert Altman • *Scr* Ed Graczyk, from his play

Come Blow Your Horn ★★

Comedy 1963 · US · Colour · 111mins

The first of playwright Neil Simon's Broadway comedy successes to be filmed, this is not quite as funny on screen as it thinks it is. There's sterling work from Frank Sinatra as an unrepentant Jewish bachelor, but the problem lies in the over-acting of Lee J Cobb and the great Yiddish comedian Molly Picon as Frankie's parents. It's one of those incredibly glossy 1960s productions from Paramount, and was Oscar-nominated for colour art direction, but all the dressing can't hide the lightweight, moralistic trifle that lies underneath. TS

Frank Sinatra *Alan Baker* • Lee J Cobb *Mr Baker* • Molly Picon *Mrs Baker* • Barbara Rush *Connie* • Jill St John *Peggy* • Tony Bill *Buddy Baker* • Dan Blocker *Mr Eckman* • Phyllis McGuire *Mrs Eckman* • Dean Martin *Bum* ■ *Dir* Bud Yorkin • *Scr* Norman Lear, from the play by Neil Simon • *Art Director* Hal Pereira, Roland Anderson

Come Fill the Cup ★★★

Drama 1951 · US · BW · 110mins

A reporter loses his job as a result of his drinking problem but rehabilitates himself with the help of a reformed alcoholic friend and goes on to give similar assistance to his boss's son. Although this descends into the maudlin and improbable somewhere along the way, a strong cast and Gordon Douglas's gritty direction make for an attention-holding melodrama that also involves gangster elements. The always mesmerising James Cagney stars as the reporter, with James Gleason, Raymond Massey and an Oscar-nominated Gig Young. RK

James Cagney *Lew Marsh* • Phyllis Thaxter *Paula Copeland* • Raymond Massey *John Ives* • James Gleason *Charley Dolan* • Gig Young *Boyd Copeland* • Selena Royle *Dolly Copeland* ■ *Dir* Gordon Douglas • *Scr* Ivan Goff, Ben Roberts, from the novel by Harlan Ware

Come Fly with Me ★★ U

Comedy 1962 · US/UK · Colour · 108mins

The romantic adventures and entanglements of three air hostesses (Dolores Hart, Pamela Tiffin, Lois Nettleton) make up this empty flimflam, more interesting as a glossy travelogue than a romantic comedy. Henry Levin directs the proceedings, with Karl Malden, Hugh O'Brian and the dishy German actor Karlheinz Böhm playing the male leads. The plotless waffle never becomes airborne, however. RK

Dolores Hart *Donna Stuart* • Hugh O'Brian *First Officer Ray Winsley* • Karl Boehm [Karlheinz Böhm] *Baron Franz von Elzingen* • Karl Malden *Walter Lucas* • Pamela Tiffin *Carol Brewster* • Lois Nettleton *Hilda "Bergie" Bergstrom* • Dawn Addams *Katie* • Richard Wattis *Oliver Garson* • Lois Maxwell *Gwen* ■ *Dir* Henry Levin • *Scr* William Roberts, from his story, from the novel *Girl on a Wing* by Bernard Glemser

Come Live with Me ★★★

Romantic comedy 1941 · US · BW · 86mins

Hedy Lamarr is the émigré who poor, starving writer James Stewart marries so she won't be thrown out of the country in this finely-mounted and intelligently-made MGM movie from Hollywood's golden era. Watch it for its star power alone, and marvel at how convincing and likeable the two leads are, as director Clarence Brown skilfully creates an atmosphere that allows you to care deeply about Lamarr's plight. The playing is exemplary, the mood sublime; this movie deserves to be better known. TS

James Stewart *Bill Smith* • Hedy Lamarr *Johnny Jones* • Ian Hunter *Barton Kendrick* • Verree Teasdale *Diana Kendrick* • Donald Meek *Joe Darsie* • Barton MacLane *Barney Grogan* • Edward Ashley *Arnold Stafford* ■ *Dir* Clarence Brown • *Scr* Patterson McNutt, from a story by Virginia Van Upp

Come Next Spring ★★★ U

Drama 1956 · US · Colour · 87mins

Long-absent Arkansas farmer Steve Cochran, cured of his drinking problems and restlessness, returns home to his understandably wary wife Ann Sheridan, his daughter Sherry Jackson (who lost the power of speech during one of his drinking bouts) and the son born after his departure. How he regains the love and respect of his family and the community forms the stuff of this rural tale. Directed by RG Springsteen, it's a whole lot better than it sounds. RK [video]

Ann Sheridan *Bess Ballot* • Steve Cochran *Matt Ballot* • Walter Brennan *Jeff Storys* • Sherry Jackson *Annie* • Richard Eyer *Abraham* • Edgar Buchanan *Mr Canary* • Sonny Tufts *Leroy Hytower* ■ *Dir* RG Springsteen • *Scr* Montgomery Pittman

The Come On ★★

Romantic thriller 1956 · US · BW · 83mins

Anne Baxter, looking great but struggling against the odds with an unconvincing script and Russell Birdwell's uncertain direction, is the star of this less than compelling melodrama. She plays an unhappily married woman who tries to persuade honest fisherman Sterling Hayden to kill her husband after he falls for her on a Mexican beach. Although he refuses, the involvement leads to further plot complications. RK

Anne Baxter *Rita Kendrick* • Sterling Hayden *Dave Arnold* • John Hoyt *Harley Kendrick* • Jesse White *JJ McGonigle* • Wally Cassell *Tony Margoli* • Alex Gerry *Chalmers* • Tyler McVey *Hogan* • Theodore Newton *Captain Getz* ■ *Dir* Russell Birdwell • *Scr* Warren Douglas, Whitman Chambers, from a novel by Whitman Chambers

Come On George ★★★ U

Comedy 1939 · UK · BW · 85mins

The remarkable thing about George Formby's film career is that he managed to make around 20 features, used a similar storyline in every single one, and nobody minded! He always played an eager beaver whom everyone thought was a dead loss apart from the girl whose smile inspired him to become a world-beater. Here, the object of his affections is Pat Kirkwood, and the sphere in which he gets to prove his unsuspected prowess is horse racing. DP [video]

George Formby *George* • Pat Kirkwood *Ann Johnson* • Joss Ambler *Sir Charles Bailey* • Meriel Forbes *Monica Bailey* • Cyril Raymond *Jimmy Taylor* • George "Gabby" Hayes *Bannerman* ■ *Dir* Anthony Kimmins • *Scr* Anthony Kimmins, Leslie Arliss, Val Valentine

Come On, Get Happy ★★

Biographical musical drama
1999 · US · Colour · 95mins

A cross between TV series *The Brady Bunch* and *The Monkees*, *The Partridge Family* was artificially assembled from casting calls and the show went on to enjoy massive success in the early-1970s, spawning hit singles and launching the pop career of David Cassidy. While everything appeared sweetness and light on screen, things were very different away from the cameras, especially for Danny Bonaduce, who produced and narrates this tacky TV movie. For fans only. DP

Eve Gordon *Shirley Jones/Shirley Partridge* • Rodney Scott *David Cassidy/Keith Partridge* • Kathy Wagner *Susan Dey/Laurie Partridge* • Shawn Pyfrom *Danny Bonaduce/Danny Partridge* ■ *Dir* David Burton Morris • *Scr* Jon S Denny, Jacqueline Feather, David Seidler

Come Out Fighting ★★

Comedy 1945 · US · BW · 62mins

This was the last of producer Sam Katzman's 22 *East Side Kids* B-movies; after this entry, star Leo Gorcey turned them into the *Bowery Boys*, under which moniker they made another 48 pictures. Considering the paltry plot – a police commissioner wants his nerdish son toughened up by the kids – you can see why Gorcey chose to rethink his position. The pace never lets up under veteran William "One Shot" Beaudine's direction, but the clowning is non-existent. TS

Leo Gorcey *Muggs* • Huntz Hall *Glimpy* • Billy Benedict *Skinny* • Gabriel Dell *Pete* • June Carlson *Jane* • Amelita Ward *Rita* • Addison Richards *Mr Mitchell* • George Meeker *Henley* ■ *Dir* William Beaudine • *Scr* Earl Snell

C

Come Play with Me ★ 18

Sex comedy 1977 · UK · Colour · 90mins

This atrocious sex comedy is one of the worst ever made, but was hyped to incredible box-office success by its producer and adult magazine publisher, David Sullivan. The plot – forgers take refuge on a health farm – marks time for a crude song-and-dance routine and turns by several well-known British character actors. However, the sex scenes, clearly added later, feature fleeting appearances by Sullivan's protegée, Mary Millington, then known as "Britain's Linda Lovelace". DM [video] DVD

Irene Handl *Lady Bovington* • Alfie Bass *Kelly* • George Harrison Marks *Clapworthy* • Ronald Fraser *Slasher* • Mary Millington *Sue* • Tommy Godfrey *Blitt* • Cardew Robinson *McIvor* • Toni Harrison Marks *Miss Dingle* ■ *Dir/Scr* George Harrison Marks

Come See the Paradise ★★★ 15

Period drama 1990 · US · Colour · 132mins

Never comfortable with the period or its implications, writer/director Alan Parker has an uphill struggle on his hands with this story about the treatment of America's Japanese population during the Second World War. However, his depiction of the romance between Dennis Quaid and Tamlyn Tomita is successful, although he doesn't always manage to keep Quaid's exuberant style in check. DP. Contains violence, swearing and nudity. [video]

Dennis Quaid *Jack McGurn* • Tamlyn Tomita *Lily Kawamura* • Sab Shimono *Mr Kawamura* • Shizuko Hoshi *Mrs Kawamura* • Stan Egi *Charlie Kawamura* • Ronald Yamamoto *Harry Kawamura* • Akemi Nishino *Dulcie Kawamura* ■ *Dir/Scr* Alan Parker

Come September ★★★

Romantic comedy 1961 · US · Colour · 113mins

When wealthy American businessman Rock Hudson visits his Italian villa in July, instead of September as usual, he discovers it is being run as a hotel in his absence. His major-domo (Walter Slezak), glamorous Gina Lollobrigida and young marrieds Bobby Darin and Sandra Dee (just married in real life, too) become involved in the comic confusions that follow. Directed with appropriate insouciance by Robert Mulligan and played with easy charm by Hudson, this amusing movie is typical of the style of early 1960s Hollywood. RK

Rock Hudson *Robert Talbot* • Gina Lollobrigida *Lisa Fellini* • Sandra Dee *Sandy* • Bobby Darin *Tony* • Walter Slezak *Maurice* • Rossana Rory *Anna* ■ *Dir* Robert Mulligan • *Scr* Stanley Shapiro, Maurice Richlin

Come to the Stable ★★★ U

Comedy drama 1949 · US · BW · 94mins

Unless you have an aversion to nun movies, there's a great deal of pleasure to be had from watching Loretta Young and Celeste Holm as they arrive in the New England town of Bethlehem and set about their charitable work, initially aided by Elsa Lanchester as a bohemian artist. (All three actresses were Oscar-nominated for their work in this film.) Director Henry Koster handles the tale well, keeping it warm without lapsing into schmaltz. TS

Loretta Young *Sister Margaret* • Celeste Holm *Sister Scolastica* • Hugh Marlowe *Robert Mason* • Elsa Lanchester *Miss Potts* • Thomas Gomez *Luigi Rossi* • Dorothy Patrick *Kitty* • Basil Ruysdael *Bishop* • Dooley Wilson *Anthony James* ■ *Dir* Henry Koster • *Scr* Oscar Millard, Sally Benson, from a story by Clare Boothe Luce

The Comeback ★ 18

Horror 1977 · UK · Colour · 96mins

1970s crooner Jack Jones starring in a horror movie? That's about the scariest thing in this far-fetched gothic tale about an American singer recording a new album in an isolated English country manor full of dead bodies, including his ex-wife's. Director Pete Walker's heavy-handed crossbreed of rock and horror draws on numerous genre clichés, but offers up no decent chills of its own. RS. Contains violence, swearing. [video] DVD

Jack Jones (2) *Nick Cooper* • Pamela Stephenson *Linda Everett* • David Doyle *Webster Jones* • Bill Owen *Mr B* • Sheila Keith *Mrs B* • Holly Palance *Gail Cooper* ■ *Dir* Pete Walker • *Scr* Murray Smith

The Comeback Trail ★★

Comedy 1972 · US · Colour · 76mins

A sad end to the career of Buster Crabbe, one of cinema's great action men and the US Olympic swimming star who delighted audiences as Flash Gordon and Buck Rogers. Here he plays an ageing B-movie actor coerced by a porno producer to appear in his latest movie. The movie was virtually completed in 1971 (the year Crabbe broke the world 400-metre freestyle record for the over-sixties), but it did not appear until 1982. Trivia fans might like to know that Hugh Hefner and veteran comic Henry Youngman appear as themselves. DF

Chuck McCann *Enrico Kodac* • Buster Crabbe [Larry "Buster" Crabbe] *Duke Montana* • Robert Staats *E Eddie Eastman* • Ina Balin *Julie Thomas* ■ *Dir* Harry Hurwitz • *Scr* Harry Hurwitz, from a story by Roy Frumkes, Robert J Winston, Harry Hurwitz

The Comedians ★★★ PG

Drama 1967 · Fr/US · Colour · 146mins

What a temptation it must have been for Elizabeth Taylor and Richard Burton to star in this Graham Greene adaptation of his own novel about the despairing turmoil of life in Haiti under the tyrannical Papa Doc Duvalier – a duet for two dramatic hands. Peter Glenville's leaden direction, however, generates little heat as Taylor, playing the wife of ambassador Peter Ustinov, has an affair with hotel owner Burton. Alec Guinness, as an arms dealer, makes the most profound contribution to an all-star cast. TH [video]

Richard Burton *Brown* • Alec Guinness *Major Jones* • Elizabeth Taylor *Martha Pineda* • Peter Ustinov *Ambassador Pineda* • Paul Ford *Mr Smith* • Lillian Gish *Mrs Smith* • Georg Stanford Brown *Henri Philipot* • James Earl Jones *Dr Magiot* ■ *Dir* Peter Glenville • *Scr* Graham Greene, from his novel

Comédie de l'Innocence ★★★ PG

Drama 2000 · Fr · Colour · 98mins

This story of bourgeois Parisian mother Isabelle Huppert who indulges her son in his claim that he belongs to another woman sets an ominous tone that recalls the sub-Hitchcock style of French master Claude Chabrol. In fact, this is the handiwork of the ever-perplexing director Raúl Ruiz, who mischievously underpins the mystery with larger questions of identity and individuality to create an unsettling domestic drama in which the actions of the characters are sometimes not only illogical but also plainly unfathomable. DP. In French with English subtitles. [video] DVD

Isabelle Huppert *Ariane d'Orville* • Jeanne Balibar *Isabella Stirner* • Charles Berling *Serge* • Edith Scob *Laurence* • Nils Hugon *Camille d'Orville* ■ *Dir* Raoul Ruiz [Raúl Ruiz] • *Scr* Françoise Dumas, Raoul Ruiz [Raúl Ruiz], from the novel *Il Figlio di Due Madri* by Massimo Bontempelli

The Comedy Man ★★★ 15

Comedy drama 1964 · UK · BW · 87mins

A struggling middle-aged rep actor, dreaming of the big break, finds fortune through a TV commercial, but walks away from the high life to pursue his career. Written by Peter Yeldham with a nice balance between irony and drama, and directed by Alvin Rakoff with an accurate eye for the dingy environments and brave bonhomie of unemployed actors, this modest British film boasts a superior cast. RK [video]

Kenneth More *Chick Byrd* • Cecil Parker *Rutherford* • Dennis Price *Tommy Morris* • Billie Whitelaw *Judy* • Norman Rossington *Theodore* • Angela Douglas *Fay* • Frank Finlay *Prout* • Edmund Purdom *Julian* ■ *Dir* Alvin Rakoff • *Scr* Peter Yeldham, from the novel by Douglas Hayes

The Comedy of Terrors ★★ 15

Horror comedy 1964 · US · Colour · 79mins

Undertakers Vincent Price and Peter Lorre (in one of his last films) drum up business by murdering potential customers in a lesser effort from Jacques Tourneur, director of such classics as *Cat People* and *Curse of the Demon*. Boris Karloff and Basil Rathbone complete a fearsome foursome who try hard to extract every ounce of humour from the regrettably dull script. A marginally interesting failure. AJ. Contains violence. [video]

Vincent Price *Waldo Trumbull* • Peter Lorre *Felix Gillie* • Boris Karloff *Amos Hinchley* • Basil Rathbone *John F Black* • Joe E Brown *Cemetery keeper* • Joyce Jameson *Amaryllis Trumbull* • Beverly Powers *Mrs Phipps* ■ *Dir* Jacques Tourneur • *Scr* Richard Matheson

Comes a Horseman ★★ 15

Western 1978 · US · Colour · 113mins

Montana has never looked more beautiful than in this interesting but mightily flawed attempt at a Fordian western from Alan J Pakula. Despite some valiant performances from Jane Fonda as a hard-bitten ranch boss and Jason Robards as a land-grabbing cattle baron, the movie ultimately plods through its paces. SH [video] DVD

James Caan *Frank Athearn* • Jane Fonda *Ella Connors* • Jason Robards *Jacob "JW" Ewing* • George Grizzard *Neil Atkinson* • Richard Farnsworth *Dodger* • Jim Davis *Julie Blocker* • Mark Harmon *Billy Joe Meynert* ■ *Dir* Alan J Pakula • *Scr* Dennis Lynton Clark • *Cinematographer* Gordon Willis

Comfort and Joy ★★★★ PG

Comedy 1984 · UK · Colour · 100mins

We're in the eccentric territory of a Bill Forsyth movie when a Glaswegian radio station holds a pin-up contest, even though listeners cannot see the contestants. The story, which is full of such felicities, involves local disc jockey Bill Paterson who has been abandoned by his partner Eleanor David. His redemption comes about when he finds he's mediating in an ice-cream war between two branches of the "Scotia Nostra". Forsyth's film works well as an urban fairy tale and contains a few quirky surprises. TH [video]

Bill Paterson *Alan "Dickie" Bird* • Eleanor David *Maddy* • CP Grogan [Clare Grogan] *Charlotte* • Alex Norton *Trevor* • Patrick Malahide *Colin* • Rikki Fulton *Hilary* • Roberto Bernardi *Mr McCool* • George Rossi *Bruno* • Peter Rossi *Paolo* ■ *Dir/Scr* Bill Forsyth

The Comfort of Strangers ★★ 18

Drama 1991 · It/UK · Colour · 100mins

The novels of Ian McEwan have proved irresistible to film-makers, but so far few have transferred to the screen with any degree of success. This brooding drama – about a couple (Rupert Everett and Natasha Richardson) drawn into Christopher Walken's sinister trap – lacks both the elegance and the bite of McEwan's prose. Paul Schrader is one of American cinema's most literate directors, but his over-deliberate approach means this cat-and-mouse tale drips with pretension. DP [video] DVD

Christopher Walken *Robert* • Natasha Richardson *Mary* • Rupert Everett *Colin* • Helen Mirren *Caroline* • Manfredi Aliquo *Concierge* ■ *Dir* Paul Schrader • *Scr* Harold Pinter, from the novel by Ian McEwan

The Comic ★★★★

Comedy drama 1969 · US · Colour · 95mins

An under-rated, little-seen tragicomedy about a silent film comic, magnificently played by Dick Van Dyke, who uses people and abuses himself in his struggle to get to the top. Written and directed by Carl Reiner (*All of Me, Oh, God!*), its Hollywood insights are many and brutal, while the acting is exceptional – Mickey Rooney is a standout. It only goes to show that comedy is no laughing matter. TH

Dick Van Dyke *Billy Bright* • Michele Lee *Mary Gibson* • Mickey Rooney *Cockeye* • Cornel Wilde *Frank Powers* • Nina Wayne *Sybil* • Pert Kelton *Mama* • Steve Allen • Barbara Heller *Ginger* • Ed Peck *Edwin C Englehardt* ■ *Dir* Carl Reiner • *Scr* Carl Reiner, Aaron Ruben

Comic Book Confidential ★★★ 15

Documentary 1988 · Can · Colour · 84mins

It's hard to know how to approach this documentary tracing the history of American comics from the 1940s onwards. The discussion by the country's leading cartoonists (including Marvel Comics' Stan Lee and the amazing Robert Crumb) of how the style and content of their work has changed is fascinating, and the comic books themselves are so irresistible that you find yourself longing to read them from cover to cover. But director Ron Mann presents his material in such a sloppy way that the energy and invention of the illustrations are frittered away. DP [video]

Dir/Scr Ron Mann

Comin' at Ya ★★★

Spaghetti western 1981 · It/Sp/US · Colour · 101mins

This daft, low-budget spaghetti western was shot in a new 3-D process and was such a success in the United States in 1981 that most Hollywood studios rushed 3-D films into production. However, the craze was as short-lived as it had been in the 1950s. The revenge plot – outlaw Tony Anthony goes in search of kidnapped bride Victoria Abril – is of no interest, so avoid the movie if it's a "flat" version. The 3-D, however, is impressive: the flaming arrows and the pitchfork really do make you wince. DM

Tony Anthony *HH Hart* • Gene Quintano *Pike* • Victoria Abril *Abilene* • Ricardo Palacios *Polk* ■ *Dir* Ferdinando Baldi • *Scr* Lloyd Battista, Wolf Lowenthal, Gene Quintano, from a story by Tony Petitto

Coming Home ★★★★ 18

Drama 1978 · US · Colour · 122mins

High-powered, Oscar-winning performances by Jon Voight and Jane Fonda are the big attraction of this post-Vietnam melodrama. The film is set on the home front, and centres on the romance between an embittered paraplegic and a Marine captain's wife, working as a volunteer in a veteran's hospital. Bruce Dern is also top-notch as Fonda's husband. The screenplay – based on a story commissioned by Fonda, a highly vocal Vietnam War activist – skirts close to sentimentality, if not soap opera at points. But it too won an Oscar, and only a hard heart would remain unmoved. PF. Contains swearing and sex scenes. DVD

Jane Fonda *Sally Hyde* • Jon Voight *Luke Martin* • Bruce Dern *Captain Bob Hyde* • Robert Ginty *Sergeant Dink Mobley* • Penelope Milford *Viola Munson* • Robert Carradine *Billy Munson* • Charles Cyphers *Pee Wee* ■ *Dir* Hal Ashby • *Scr* Waldo Salt, Robert C Jones, from a story by Nancy Dowd

C

Coming to America ★★★ 15

Romantic comedy
1988 · US · Colour · 111mins

Eddie Murphy teams up once again with his *Trading Places* director John Landis for a comedy that at least requires him to do more than just chuckle. Murphy is the pampered African prince who rebels against his father (James Earl Jones) and comes to America, with sidekick Arsenio Hall in tow, to find a wife. Landis aims for a 1930s-style feel but the script isn't as clever as it thinks it is, so it's left to Murphy to carry the picture. JF. Contains swearing and nudity. DVD

Eddie Murphy *Prince Akeem/Clarence/Saul/Randy Watson* • Arsenio Hall *Semmi/Morris/Extremely ugly girl/Reverend Brown* • James Earl Jones *King Jaffe Joffer* • Shari Headley *Lisa McDowell* • Madge Sinclair *Queen Aoleon* • Calvin Lockhart *Colonel Izzi* • John Amos *Cleo McDowell* • Allison Dean *Patrice McDowell* • Eriq La Salle *Darryl Jenks* • Don Ameche *Mortimer Duke* • Ralph Bellamy *Randolph Duke* ■ *Dir* John Landis • *Scr* David Sheffield, Barry W Blaustein, from a story by Eddie Murphy

The Command ★★★ U

Western 1954 · US · Colour · 93mins

This now-forgotten western was important in its day for being the first Warner Bros film to be made in CinemaScope. It was also filmed, though never released, in 3-D, Warners understandably hedging their bets against the future. Because two versions were filmed simultaneously, involving twice as much work for a single fee, the cast is relatively undistinguished. The action sequences, when they arrive, are undeniably spectacular. TS

Guy Madison *Capt MacClaw* • Joan Weldon *Martha* • James Whitmore *Sergeant Elliot* • Carl Benton Reid *Colonel Janeway* • Harvey Lembeck *Gottschalk* • Ray Teal *Dr Trent* • Bob Nichols *O'Hirons* • Don Shelton *Major Gibbs* ■ *Dir* David Butler • *Scr* Russell Hughes, Samuel Fuller, from the novel *Rear Guard* by James Warner Bellah

Command Decision ★★★★ U

Second World War drama
1948 · US · BW · 111mins

Should the commander of American bomber squadrons in Britain send his crews deeper into Germany to try to destroy a factory making long-range aircraft, knowing full well that such forays are effectively suicide missions? The unlikely bearer of this harrowing moral dilemma is Clark Gable, brilliantly anguished in a role given added resonance as a result of his own wartime flying experience on bombing missions. Under-rated director Sam Wood makes you forget that this was once a major Broadway theatrical hit, and a terrific cast gives Gable superb back-up. TS

Clark Gable *Brig Gen KC "Casey" Dennis* • Walter Pidgeon *Major Gen Roland G Kane* • Van Johnson *Tech Sgt Immanuel T Evans* • Brian Donlevy *Brig Gen Clifton L Garnet* • Charles Bickford *Elmer Brockhurst* • John Hodiak *Col Edward R Martin* • Edward Arnold *Congressman Arthur Malcolm* • Cameron Mitchell *Lt Ansel Goldberg* ■ *Dir* Sam Wood • *Scr* William R Laidlaw, George Froeschel, from the play by William Wister Haines

Command Performance ★ U

Musical 1937 · UK · BW · 83mins

This is another of the feeble vehicles that attempted to make a film star out of Arthur Tracy, popular on radio as "The Street Singer". Here he plays an entertainer who, suffering from stage fright, takes up with a band of nomads and falls in love with a gypsy girl. An unconvincing tale, awash with sentimentality and treacly ballads, its sole point of interest is the presence of Lilli Palmer and Finlay Currie. RK

Arthur Tracy *Street Singer* • Lilli Palmer *Susan* • Mark Daly *Joe* • Rae Collett *Betty* • Finlay Currie *Manager* • Jack Melford *Reporter* • Stafford Hilliard *Sam* • Julian Vedey *Toni* ■ *Dir* Sinclair Hill • *Scr* George Pearson, Michael Hankinson, Sinclair Hill, from the play by C Stafford Dickens

Commandments ★★ 15

Comedy drama 1996 · US · Colour · 84mins

Losing his wife, his house and his job in a series of disasters, Aidan Quinn decides to test God by systematically breaking every one of his Ten Commandments, in the hope of receiving some sort of sign as to The Lord's plan. Perhaps commandment number 11 should be "Thou Shalt Not Waste Good Actors On Material Like This." JB. Contains swearing, sexual references and some violence.

Aidan Quinn *Seth Warner* • Courteney Cox *Rachel Luce* • Anthony LaPaglia *Harry Luce* • Shirl Bernheim *Sylvia* • Peter Jacobson *Banker* • Patrick Garner *Banker* • Marcia DeBonis *Receptionist* • Amy Sedaris *Scholar* ■ *Dir/Scr* Daniel Taplitz

Commando ★★★ 18

Action adventure 1985 · US · Colour · 85mins

Arnold Schwarzenegger gets the good-guy role here, in his first movie after finding cult success with *The Terminator*. Although he still looks a little awkward with dialogue, he makes for a spectacularly destructive hero, playing a former commando called back into action when his daughter is kidnapped by an old adversary. Dan Hedaya is an engaging chief villain, and there's a spirited turn from Rae Dawn Chong as Arnie's unwilling partner. Mark L Lester is a no-frills director, but his set pieces pack an explosive punch. JF. Contains swearing and violence. DVD

Arnold Schwarzenegger *Colonel John Matrix* • Rae Dawn Chong *Cindy* • Dan Hedaya *General Arius* • Vernon Wells *Bennett* • James Olson *General Kirby* • David Patrick Kelly *Sully* • Alyssa Milano *Jenny* • Bill Duke *Cooke* ■ *Dir* Mark L Lester • *Scr* Steven E de Souza, from a story by Joseph Loeb III, Matthew Weisman, Steven E de Souza

The Commandos Strike at Dawn ★★

Second World War drama
1942 · US · BW · 99mins

Paul Muni plays a Norwegian fisherman fighting Nazi tyranny alongside a team of British commandos. When his daughter is held hostage by the Nazis he escapes to England and leads a sabotage mission to Norway. Based on a yarn by *Hornblower* writer CS Forester and adapted by Irwin Shaw, it's a bit plodding for a flagwaver, getting bogged down with romance supplied by Anna Lee, but boasts an interesting cast. AT

Paul Muni *Erik Toreson* • Anna Lee *Judith Bowen* • Lillian Gish *Mrs Bergesen* • Sir Cedric Hardwicke [Cedric Hardwicke] *Admiral Bowen* • Robert Coote *Robert Bowen* • Ray Collins *Bergesen* ■ *Dir* John Farrow • *Scr* Irwin Shaw, from a story by CS Forester

La Commare Secca ★★

Crime drama 1962 · It · BW · 91mins

Bernardo Bertolucci's first feature was based on a five-page outline by Pier Paolo Pasolini, whom the young man had assisted on *Accattone* the previous year. But Bertolucci had less interest in the Roman proletariat than Pasolini, and the film, which follows an investigation into the murder of a prostitute seen from different perspectives, is merely an interesting cinematic exercise. RB. In Italian with English subtitles.

Francesco Ruiu *Luciano Maialetti, "Canticchia"* • Giancarlo De Rosa *Nino* • Vincenzo Ciccora *Mayor* • Alvaro D'Ercole *Francolicchio* • Romano Labate *Pipito* ■ *Dir* Bernardo Bertolucci • *Scr* Bernardo Bertolucci, Sergio Citti, Pier Paolo Pasolini, from a story by Pier Paolo Pasolini

Comment J'ai Tué Mon Père ★★★ 15

Psychological drama
2001 · Fr/Sp · Colour · 94mins

This is a simmering, but largely superficial, study of bourgeois manners. Charles Berling is suitably uptight as the successful Parisian physician whose confidence is dented by the return of his father, Michel Bouquet, who abandoned the family years before to tend the sick in the Third World. Director Anne Fontaine captures the mix of envy, respect and animosity that fuels the relationship. But she leaves Berling's wife, Natacha Régnier, on the periphery, when her hesitant reaction might have provided an emotional counterbalance to the psychological posturing. DP. In French with English subtitles. DVD

Michel Bouquet *Maurice* • Charles Berling *Jean-Luc* • Natacha Régnier *Isa* • Stéphane Guillon *Patrick* • Amira Casar *Myriem* • Hubert Koundé *Jean-Toussaint* ■ *Dir* Anne Fontaine • *Scr* Jacques Fieschi, Anne Fontaine

The Commissar ★★★★ PG

Drama 1967 · USSR · BW · 108mins

The winner of the Silver Bear at Berlin, 20 years after it was banned by the Kremlin, this allegory on the birth of the Soviet state is also one of the few films of the Communist era to deal with anti-Semitism and revolutionary womanhood. Consciously evoking the visual style of the great silent montagists, the story of Red Army commissar Nonna Mordyukova's stay with an impoverished Jewish family during the last days of her pregnancy overflows with a tolerance and humanity utterly at odds with the Civil War raging outside. Director Alexander Askoldov's courageous stance meant he never worked again. DP. In Russian with English subtitles.

Nonna Mordyukova *Clavdia Vavilova* • Rolan Bykov *Yefim* • Raisa Niedashkovskaya *Maria* • Vasily Shukshin *Commander* • Tina Nedashkovskaya • Pavlik Levin • Ludmilla Volinskaya ■ *Dir/Scr* Alexander Askoldov

The Commitments ★★★★ 15

Musical drama 1991 · UK · Colour · 112mins

The soundtrack album sold like hot cakes, it walked away with Bafta awards for best film, best direction and best adapted screenplay, and it should have made bigger stars of several of its cast. Alan Parker's first feature on this side of the Atlantic since *Pink Floyd – the Wall* nearly a decade earlier, this was also the film that brought the work of future Booker Prize-winning author Roddy Doyle to the attention of the chattering classes. Laced with Irish charm and blessed with some superb music sung with passion by Andrew Strong, Bronagh Gallagher, Angeline Ball and Maria Doyle, it's also very funny. DP. Contains swearing. DVD

Robert Arkins *Jimmy Rabbitte* • Michael Aherne *Steven Clifford* • Angeline Ball *Imelda Quirke* • Maria Doyle [Maria Doyle Kennedy] *Natalie Murphy* • Dave Finnegan *Mickah Wallace* • Bronagh Gallagher *Bernie McGloughlin* • Felim Gormley *Dean Fay* • Glen Hansard *Outspan Foster* • Dick Massey *Billy Mooney* • Johnny Murphy *Joey "The Lips" Fagan* • Kenneth McCluskey *Derek Scully* • Andrew Strong *Deco Cuffe* ■ *Dir* Alan Parker • *Scr* Dick Clement, Ian La Frenais, Roddy Doyle, from the novel by Roddy Doyle

Committed ★★ 15

Romantic comedy
2000 · US · Colour · 93mins

In Lisa Krueger's spectacularly miscalculated treatise on marital fidelity, Heather Graham is woefully miscast as the New Yorker who takes her wedding vows so seriously that when her husband (Luke Wilson) abandons her to pursue his photographic career, she crosses the States to win him back. The trip here is an excuse to pack the action with quirky characters in the hope that no one notices the fact the story is going nowhere. DP. Contains swearing. DVD

Heather Graham *Joline* • Casey Affleck *Jay* • Luke Wilson *Carl* • Goran Visnjic *Neil* • Patricia Velasquez *Carmen* • Alfonso Arau *Grampy* • Mark Ruffalo *T-Bo* ■ *Dir/Scr* Lisa Krueger

Common-Law Cabin ★★★ 18

Cult crime melodrama
1967 · US · Colour · 69mins

One of sexploitation director Russ Meyer's early breast-obsessed, mock morality melodramas that put him on the cult map. Using his familiar theme of sexually frustrated men and top-heavy women flung together in a weird setting and succumbing to temptation before paying the price for their illicit lust, this is the most existential item Meyer ever made. Stripper Babette Bardot (no relation) plays the "housekeeper" of a dilapidated inn where customers "relax". AJ. Contains violence, swearing and nudity. DVD

Ken Swofford *Barney Rickert* • Alaina Capri *Shelia Ross* • Jack Moran *Dewey Hoople* • Adele Rein *Coral Hoople* • Andrew Hagara *Laurence Talbot III* • Franklin Bolger *Cracker* • Babette Bardot *Babette* • John Furlong *Dr Martin Ross* ■ *Dir* Russ Meyer • *Scr* Jack Moran

A Common Thread ★★★★ 12A

Drama 2004 · Fr · Colour · 87mins

Eléanore Faucher's debut feature offers a sensitive insight into the art of being a woman. Pregnant Angoulême teenager Lola Naymark and Ariane Ascaride, grieving for the loss of her son, seem to have nothing in common. But as they embroider fabric for a Parisian fashion house, they discover shared hopes and fears that surmount their generational differences. The intense silences allow Faucher and cinematographer Pierre Cottereau to concentrate on the intricate handicraft that is as mesmerising as the contrasts between Naymark's bubbly country girl and the ever-excellent Ascaride's world-weary loner. DP. In French with English subtitles.

Lola Naymark *Claire* • Ariane Ascaride *Madame Mélikian* • Thomas Laroppe *Guillaume* • Jacky Berroyer [Jackie Berroyer] *M Lescuyer* • Marie Félix *Lucile* • Anne Canovas *Madame Lescuyer* ■ *Dir* Eléanore Faucher • *Scr* Eléanore Faucher, Gaëlle Macé

C

Common Threads: Stories from the Quilt ★★★★

Documentary 1989 · US · Colour · 75mins

An Oscar-winning documentary, narrated by Dustin Hoffman, highlighting the heartache and sorrow behind many of the embroidered panels that made up the Aids quilt laid out on the Mall in Washington DC at the height of the tragic epidemic. The personal stories of loss are often unbearably moving and have a sizeable emotional impact as key social issues are raised and ill-informed perceptions are quashed. An important film in increasing awareness of a medical condition wrongly thought at the time to be just a gay problem. AJ

Dustin Hoffman *Narrator* ■ *Dir* Robert Epstein [Rob Epstein], Jeffrey Friedman • *Scr* Jeffrey Friedman, Robert Epstein

The Common Touch ★★★ U

Drama 1941 · UK · BW · 111mins

This London drama builds on the themes of poverty and deprivation explored in John Baxter's 1933 directorial debut, *Doss House*. The action follows teenage tycoon Geoffrey Hibbert, as he disguises himself as a derelict to discover the dark schemes being hatched by his company's ambitious managing director, Raymond Lovell. Seeking to expose the iniquities of slum housing and the corruption of big business may seem an odd topic for a wartime film, but it typifies Baxter's uncompromisingly socialist approach to cinema. DP

Greta Gynt *Sylvia Meadows* • Geoffrey Hibbert *Peter Henderson* • Joyce Howard *Mary Weatherby* • Harry Welchman *Porter, Lincoln's Inn* • Edward Rigby *Tich* • Raymond Lovell *Cartwright* ■ *Dir* John Baxter • *Scr* Barbara K Emary, Geoffrey Orme, from a novel by Herbert Ayres

Communion ★★ 15

Science-fiction thriller
1989 · US · Colour · 104mins

Was author Whitley Strieber abducted by aliens as outlined in his bestselling book *Communion*? Or was his close encounter and subsequent medical probing just a bizarre hallucination, or even a cynical marketing ploy? You really won't be any the wiser after watching this ponderous and pompous quasi-documentary, despite an enormous amount of conviction from Christopher Walken as the traumatised novelist. AJ. Contains violence and swearing. [VIDEO] DVD

Christopher Walken *Whitley Strieber* • Lindsay Crouse *Anne Strieber* • Joel Carlson *Andrew Strieber* • Frances Sternhagen *Dr Janet Duffy* • Andreas Katsulas *Alex* • Terri Hanauer *Sara* • Basil Hoffman *Dr Friedman* • John Dennis Johnston *Fireman* • Dee Dee Rescher *Mrs Greenberg* ■ *Dir* Philippe Mora • *Scr* Whitley Strieber, from his book

Company ★★★ 15

Crime drama 2001 · Ind · Colour · 155mins

Director Ram Gopal Varma takes a sturdy approach in this uncompromising exposé of how criminal gangs have taken control of every aspect of Indian life – from politics and commerce, to the running of Bollywood itself. A dangerous thing to do for Varma when the tentacles of crime do indeed extend into the fabric of Indian cinema. But, with Ajay Devgan and Vivek Oberoi flexing their muscles as the mortal foes and Mohan Lal impressing as a crusading police inspector, this makes for revealing and riveting viewing. DP. A Hindi language film. [VIDEO] DVD

Ajay Devgan *Malik* • Vivek Oberoi *Chandu* • Mohan Lal *Srinivasan* • Manisha Koirala *Saroja* • Antara Mali *Kannu* ■ *Dir* Ram Gopal Varma • *Scr* Jaideep Sahni

The Company ★★★★ 12

Drama 2003 · US/Ger/UK · Colour · 107mins

Director Robert Altman's latest look at a microcosmic community is more an interested glance than his usual penetrating glare. Yet it's still another seductive spellbinder, with Altman expertly choreographing his film to match the concepts of Chicago's Joffrey Ballet. This jettisons soap-opera histrionics for revealing glimpses of the sheer craft and commitment involved. It focuses on the progress of a promising ingénue (Neve Campbell) from chorus line to featured ballerina, under the watchful eye of mercurial company director Malcolm McDowell. Best known as queen of the *Scream* films, Campbell acquits herself surprisingly well. AJ DVD

Neve Campbell *Ry* • Malcolm McDowell *Alberto Antonelli* • James Franco *Josh* • Barbara Robertson *Harriet* • William Dick *Edouard* • Susie Cusack *Susie* • Marilyn Dodds Frank *Ry's mother* • John Lordan *Ry's father* ■ *Dir* Robert Altman • *Scr* Barbara Turner, from a story by Neve Campbell, Barbara Turner

Company Business ★★ 15

Comedy thriller 1991 · US · Colour · 94mins

While this is a competent enough spy caper, it went straight to video in the UK. Gene Hackman plays a former CIA agent who is drawn back into the world of espionage for a spy swap involving Russian agent Mikhail Baryshnikov. Hackman more than covers for any deficiencies in the acting department from his co-star, however, it lacks the verve and imagination that writer/director Nicholas Meyer usually brings to his work. JF. Contains some violence and swearing. [VIDEO] DVD

Gene Hackman *Sam Boyd* • Mikhail Baryshnikov *Pyiotr Grushenko* • Kurtwood Smith *Elliot Jaffe* • Terry O'Quinn *Colonel Grissom* • Daniel Von Bargen *Mike Flinn* ■ *Dir/Scr* Nicholas Meyer

Company Limited ★★★★ U

Drama 1971 · Ind · BW · 113mins

Although he had a huge following abroad, the Bengali director Satyajit Ray was often accused by Indian critics of ignoring the subcontinent's myriad of social and political problems. This mild attack on the educated middle classes is the kind of film Frank Capra might have made, had he allowed his head to rule his heart. As the sales manager prepared to brook a little corruption to secure privilege, Barun Chanda is quite superb. Subtle, satirical and sharp as a tack. DP. In Bengali with English subtitles.

Barun Chanda *Shyamal Chatterjee* • Sharmila Tagore *Tutul* • Parumita Chowdhary *Shyamal's sister-in-law* • Harindranath Chattopadhyay *Sir Baren* ■ *Dir* Satyajit Ray • *Scr* Satyajit Ray, from the novel *Seemabaddha* by Sankar

Company Man ★ 15

Comedy 2000 · US · Colour · 82mins

This film has a really impressive cast, and one can only assume that co-writer/co-director/star Douglas McGrath (who has appeared in several Woody Allen movies) convinced his players that he really was Woody Allen and that he was remaking *Bananas*. Instead, this comedy – about a teacher in the 1960s who becomes a spy and gets involved in a plot to overthrow Castro – is a mess. JB [VIDEO] DVD

Sigourney Weaver *Daisy Quimp* • Douglas McGrath *Allen Quimp* • John Turturro *Crocker Johnson* • Anthony LaPaglia *Fidel Castro* • Ryan Phillippe *Rudolph Petrov* • Denis Leary *Fry* • Woody Allen *Lowther* • Alan Cumming *General Batista* ■ *Dir/Scr* Peter Askin, Douglas McGrath

Company of Killers ★★

Crime thriller 1970 · US · Colour · 86mins

Veterans Van Johnson and Ray Milland find themselves on opposite sides of the law in this thriller. Professional killer John Saxon loses the confidence of his boss and attracts the attention of police chief Johnson following a spell in hospital. Ordered to carry out a hit for businessman Milland, Saxon runs into a police trap. This police drama aims to deliver gritty realism, but falls back on clichés. RT

Van Johnson *Sam Cahill* • Ray Milland *George DeSalles* • John Saxon *Dave Poohler* • Brian Kelly (1) *Nick Andros* • Fritz Weaver *John Shankalien* • Clu Gulager *Frank Quinn* ■ *Dir* Jerry Thorpe • *Scr* E Jack Neuman

The Company of Strangers ★★★★ PG

Drama 1990 · Can · Colour · 100mins

The sisterhood of women is lovingly proclaimed by this Canadian movie in which non-actors play themselves in a fictitious situation: in this case, seven elderly women who are stranded in a remote farmhouse when their touring bus breaks down. Each woman's story illuminates the experience of being female and being human as the group waits to be picked up. Paced by director Cynthia Scott with patient care, it has a rare distinction – it actually likes people. TH [VIDEO]

Alice Diabo *Alice* • Constance Garneau *Constance* • Winifred Holden *Winnie* • Cissy Meddings *Cissy* • Mary Meigs *Mary* • Catherine Roche *Catherine* • Michelle Sweeney *Michelle* • Beth Webber *Beth* ■ *Dir* Cynthia Scott • *Scr* Gloria Demmers, Cynthia Scott, David Wilson, Sally Bochner

The Company of Wolves ★★★ 18

Supernatural fantasy
1984 · UK · Colour · 91mins

Dark variations on the *Little Red Riding Hood* theme are adeptly explored by director Neil Jordan, co-writing with Angela Carter, in this arresting visual treat that at times resembles a pretentious Hammer horror. Dreams within dreams build up a psychological fright mosaic, as young Sarah Patterson goes through the broad spectrum of emotions generally known as adolescence. Angela Lansbury is in super-eccentric form as an archetypal granny. Overall, a fine exercise in art design, lyrical mood and sinister allegory. AJ. Contains violence. [VIDEO]

Angela Lansbury *Grandmother* • David Warner *Father* • Sarah Patterson *Rosaleen* • Stephen Rea *Young groom* • Graham Crowden *Old priest* • Shane Johnstone *Amorous boy* • Brian Glover *Boy's father* • Susan Porrett *Boy's mother* ■ *Dir* Neil Jordan • *Scr* Angela Carter, Neil Jordan, from the short stories by Angela Carter • *Cinematographer* Bryan Loftus • *Art Director* Anton Furst

The Company She Keeps ★★★

Drama 1950 · US · BW · 82mins

Notable for the screen debut of Jeff Bridges as a babe in arms, this is a suitably jaunty tale of an ex-con, played with convincing guile by Jane Greer, who dearly wishes to go straight but is not helped to that end when she falls for her parole officer's boyfriend. Greer is excellent, as is Dennis O'Keefe, and the two interact with just the right pinch of spice. A movie with a sizeable amount of charm inserted into its rather lame script. SH

Lizabeth Scott *Joan* • Jane Greer *Diane* • Dennis O'Keefe *Larry* • Fay Baker *Tilly* • John Hoyt *Judge Kendall* • James Bell *Mr Neeley* • Don Beddoe *Jamieson* • Bert Freed *Smitty* ■ *Dir* John Cromwell • *Scr* Ketti Frings

Les Compères ★★★★

Comedy drama 1983 · Fr · Colour · 92mins

Slickly scripted according to the rhythms of French stage farce, this was the second of three collaborations between director Francis Veber and actors Pierre Richard and Gérard Depardieu. As the journalist tricked into believing he is the father of teenage runaway Stephane Bierry, Depardieu essentially plays stooge to the manic-depressive Richard, who has been told the same fib by ex-girlfriend Anny Duperey. Less sentimental and more authentic than the Hollywood remake, *Fathers' Day*. DP. In French with English subtitles.

Pierre Richard *François Pignon* • Gérard Depardieu *Jean Lucas* • Anny Duperey *Christine Martin* • Michel Aumont *Paul Martin* • Stephane Bierry *Tristan Martin* • Roland Blanche *Jeannot* ■ *Dir/Scr* Francis Veber

The Competition ★★ 15

Romantic drama
1980 · US · Colour · 120mins

Does any actor visibly try harder than Richard Dreyfuss? In this romantic drama he plays a concert pianist, a sort of Richard Clayderman with pretensions, who duels over the ivories with a clearly besotted Amy Irving. Written and directed by Joel Oliansky, this is a clunky effort. AT. Contains swearing. [VIDEO]

Richard Dreyfuss *Paul Dietrich* • Amy Irving *Heidi Schoonover* • Lee Remick *Greta Vandemann* • Sam Wanamaker *Erskine* • Joseph Cali *Jerry DiSalvo* • Ty Henderson *Michael Humphries* ■ *Dir* Joel Oliansky • *Scr* Joel Oliansky, from a story by William Sackheim, Joel Oliansky

The Compleat Beatles ★★★ PG

Music documentary
1982 · US · Colour and BW · 115mins

Beatles fans are not fond of this patchy US documentary about the Fab Four, but there is still much to interest the casual viewer. Director Patrick Montgomery does a thorough job with the early years and has tracked down Allan Williams ("the man who sold the Beatles") and Tony Sheridan (who used the Beatles as a backing band) among others. The film was made without the co-operation of the Beatles and their wives. DM [VIDEO]

Malcolm McDowell *Narrator* ■ *Dir* Patrick Montgomery • *Scr* David Silver

Complex of Fear ★★★ 18

Thriller 1993 · US · Colour · 90mins

Chelsea Field lives in a creepy apartment block and feels threatened in this nifty little TV chiller, which focuses on a residential complex plagued by a series of vicious rapes. Field is a potential victim, Hart Bochner a resident rookie cop and the ever-reliable Joe Don Baker the investigating detective. The plotting is a mite predictable, but director Brian Grant still summons up an air of claustrophobic suspense. JF. Contains violence and swearing. [VIDEO] DVD

Hart Bochner *Ray Dolan* • Chelsea Field *Michelle Dolan* • Joe Don Baker *Detective Frank Farrel* • Brett Cullen *Ed Wylie* • Farrah Forke *Vicki* • Ashley Gardner *Doreen Wylie* • Jordan Williams *Lee Harrison* ■ *Dir* Brian Grant • *Scr* Dyanne Asimow, Matt Dorff

Complicity ★ 18

Thriller 1999 · UK · Colour · 95mins

You'd be better off going back to Iain Banks's original novel than waste your time with this unsatisfactory adaptation. Jonny Lee Miller stars as Banks's journalist antihero Cameron and, despite support from Brian Cox and Bill Paterson, he's endlessly bland. Director Gavin Millar seems all at sea with this Scotland-based tale, which involves sex, drugs and murderous atrocities. LH DVD

Jonny Lee Miller *Cameron* • Keeley Hawes *Yvonne* • Brian Cox *Detective Chief Inspector McDunn* • Paul Higgins *Andy Gould* • Jason Hetherington *William* • Rachael Stirling *Claire Gould* • Bill Paterson *Wallace Byatt* ■ *Dir* Gavin Millar • *Scr* Brian Elsley, from the novel by Iain Banks

C

Compromising Positions ★ 15

Comedy thriller 1985 · US · Colour · 94mins

Thelma and Louise star Susan Sarandon does her best with one of her few ropey roles in this uneven farce, about a woman who starts investigating the death of her dentist only to get caught up in a world of ex-mistresses and pornography. It's silly in the extreme, and Sarandon and her co-stars (Raul Julia, Joe Mantegna, Edward Herrmann) look distinctly uncomfortable. JB

Susan Sarandon *Judith Singer* • Raul Julia *Lieutenant David Suarez* • Edward Herrmann *Bob Singer* • Judith Ivey *Nancy Miller* • Mary Beth Hurt *Peg Tuccio* • Joe Mantegna *Bruce Fleckstein* • Anne De Salvo *Phyllis Fleckstein* ■ *Dir* Frank Perry • *Scr* Susan Isaacs, from a novel by Susan Isaacs

Compulsion ★★★★

Crime drama 1959 · US · BW · 103mins

Bradford Dillman and Dean Stockwell, two wealthy, homosexual college students, murder a boy in cold blood to prove that the perfect crime is possible. Adapted from Meyer Levin's book and brilliantly directed by Richard Fleischer in semi-documentary style, this is a thinly veiled account of the notorious 1924 Leopold and Loeb case. Dillman's sneering psychopath is superb, as is Stockwell's more human, less confident Steiner, while Orson Welles's defending counsel, modelled on the famous Clarence Darrow who saved Leopold and Loeb from the chair, is a tour de force. RK

Orson Welles *Jonathan Wilk* • Dean Stockwell *Judd Steiner* • Bradford Dillman *Artie Straus* • EG Marshall *Horn* • Diane Varsi *Ruth Evans* • Martin Milner *Sid* • Richard Anderson *Max* ■ *Dir* Richard Fleischer • *Scr* Richard Murphy, from the novel by Meyer Levin

The Computer Wore Tennis Shoes ★★ U

Comedy 1969 · US · Colour · 86mins

What might have been a nifty idea for a half-hour TV show is stretched to breaking point in this Disney comedy. Kurt Russell stars as the teenager who becomes a genius after a computer downloads its memory system into his brain. Suddenly, our hero is winning game shows and taking on Cesar Romero's stupendously inept crime ring. It's as engaging as it is predictable, although we could have done without the inevitable comic car chase. Russell returned for a follow-up film, *Now You See Him, Now You Don't* in 1972. DP DVD

Cesar Romero *AJ Arno* • Kurt Russell *Dexter* • Joe Flynn *Dean Higgins* • William Schallert *Professor Quigley* • Alan Hewitt *Dean Collingsgood* • Richard Bakalyan *Chillie Walsh* ■ *Dir* Robert Butler • *Scr* Joseph L McEveety

Comrade X ★★★ U

Romantic comedy 1940 · US · BW · 89mins

Hedy Lamarr was seldom more glamorous than as the Russian tram-driver who falls for hunky American journalist Clark Gable. You might expect more than just froth from master director King Vidor, but he was shrewd enough to know what wartime audiences wanted, and just let his two great stars get on with it. TS

Clark Gable *McKinley B Thompson* • Hedy Lamarr *Theodora* • Oscar Homolka *Vasiliev* • Felix Bressart *Vanya* • Eve Arden *Jane Wilson* • Sig Rumann [Sig Ruman] *Emil Von Hofer* • Natasha Lytess *Olga* • Vladimir Sokoloff *Michael Bastakoff* ■ *Dir* King Vidor • *Scr* Ben Hecht, Charles Lederer, from a story by Walter Reisch

Comrades: a Lanternist's Account of the Tolpuddle Martyrs and What Became of Them ★★★★ PG

Historical drama
1986 · UK · Colour · 174mins

Bill Douglas struggled to finance this epic tribute to those pioneer trades unionists. Although set in Dorset in the 1830s, the story of the farm labourers who were deported to Australia for protesting against their harsh conditions and meagre wages had a contemporary resonance as, 150 years later, the Thatcher government sought to break union power. However, while Douglas is keen to highlight the continued existence of exploitation and social hypocrisy, the superb performances keep it rooted in its period. DP

Robin Soans *George Loveless* • William Gaminara *James Loveless* • Stephen Bateman *Old Tom Stanfield* • Philip Davis *Young Stanfield* • Keith Allen *James Hammett* • Alex Norton *Lanternist* • James Fox *Norfolk* • Michael Hordern *Mr Pitt* • Vanessa Redgrave *Mrs Carlyle* ■ *Dir/Scr* Bill Douglas

La Comunidad ★★★ 15

Comedy thriller 2000 · Sp · Colour · 108mins

Alex de la Iglesia is in Chabrol territory with this mischievously macabre thriller. Carmen Maura throws herself into the role of an estate agent who discovers a lottery win stashed in a Madrid tenement, only to realise that the other occupants have no intention of letting her take it. From the feline credits to the high-rise finale, the pace is unrelenting as Maura fends off the attentions of murderous neighbours. Excess wins out over invention before the end, but the sheer bravura of the exercise sweeps you along. DP. In Spanish with English subtitles. Contains violence and swearing.

Carmen Maura *Julia* • Eduardo Antuña *Charly* • Jesús Bonilla *Ricardo* • Paca Gabaldón *Hortensia* • Sancho Gracia *Castro* • Emilio Gutiérrez Caba *Emilio* • Terele Pávez *Ramona* ■ *Dir* Alex de la Iglesia • *Scr* Jorge Guerricaechevarría, Alex de la Iglesia

Con Air ★★★★ 18

Action thriller 1997 · US · Colour · 110mins

This is a top-notch thrill-athon, with Nicolas Cage as an ex-marine jailed for a murder he committed in self-defence, whose release is interrupted when his flight home is hijacked by a bunch of America's most dangerous felons. Cage's impossibly cool macho posturing is irresistible, as is John Malkovich's tongue-in-cheek turn as a super criminal. John Cusack and Ving Rhames lend snappy support, while Steve Buscemi steals nearly every scene he is in with an inspired pastiche of Hannibal Lecter. Armed with an entertaining script by Scott Rosenberg, director Simon West delivers a dynamic debut that's nearly impossible to dislike. JC. Contains violence and swearing. DVD

Nicolas Cage *Cameron Poe* • John Cusack *Vince Larkin* • John Malkovich *Cyrus "the Virus" Grissom* • Steve Buscemi *Garland Greene* • Ving Rhames *Diamond Dog* • Colm Meaney *Duncan Malloy* • Rachel Ticotin *Sally Bishop* • Nick Chinlund *Billy Bedlam* ■ *Dir* Simon West • *Scr* Scott Rosenberg

The Con Artists ★ PG

Comedy 1976 · It · Colour · 89mins

Versatile director Sergio Corbucci turns his attention to crime with this clumsily plotted caper, but he lacks the lightness of touch to bring much life to this bovine variation on *The Sting*. Always prone to overplaying comedy, Anthony Quinn milks every gag as an escaped convict. DP. Italian dialogue dubbed into English.

Anthony Quinn *Philippe Bang* • Adriano Celentano *Felix* • Capucine *Belle Duke* • Corinne Cléry *Charlotte* ■ *Dir* Sergio Corbucci • *Scr* Arnold Maury, Max D'Rita

Conan the Barbarian ★★★ 15

Fantasy action adventure
1982 · US · Colour · 125mins

Arnold Schwarzenegger took a musclebound step closer to superstardom with this entertaining sword-and-scocery epic. Director/co-writer Milius quotes Nietzsche and ladles on the fantasy atmosphere with a Wagnerian flourish as Arnie's Nordic superman ventures forth to avenge his parents' death at the hands of James Earl Jones's warlord. He's aided in his quest by thief Sandahl Bergman and would-be comic sidekick Gerry Lopez. It's all too humourless for its own good, but looks fabulous. TH. Contains violence, swearing, nudity. DVD

Arnold Schwarzenegger *Conan* • James Earl Jones *Thulsa Doom* • Max von Sydow *King Osric* • Sandahl Bergman *Valeria* • Ben Davidson *Rexor* • Cassandra Gaviola *Witch* • Gerry Lopez *Subotai* • Mako *Wizard* ■ *Dir* John Milius • *Scr* John Milius, Oliver Stone, from characters created by Robert E Howard

Conan the Destroyer ★★ 15

Fantasy action adventure
1984 · US · Colour · 96mins

Arnold Schwarzenegger returns to his breakthrough role as the mythical hero but the kitsch magic of the John Milius original is missing this time around. However, the requisite number of ugly villains, beautiful temptresses and doe-eyed heroines are present and correct, Schwarzenegger doesn't have to do too much acting and director Richard Fleischer keeps the often violent action flowing smoothly. Look out for Grace Jones as a lethal warrior. JF. Contains violence. DVD

Arnold Schwarzenegger *Conan* • Grace Jones *Zula* • Wilt Chamberlain *Bombaara* • Mako *Akjiro, the "Wizard"* • Tracey Walter *Malak* • Sarah Douglas *Queen Taramis* • Olivia D'Abo *Princess Jehnna* ■ *Dir* Richard Fleischer • *Scr* Stanley Mann, from a story by Roy Thomas, Gerry Conway, from characters created by Robert E Howard

The Concert for Bangladesh ★★★ U

Concert documentary
1972 · US · Colour · 94mins

An unfussy documentary of one of the major media events of 1971: the twin benefit concerts held at Madison Square Garden for the starving refugee children of Bangladesh organized by George Harrison and noted sitar player Ravi Shankar. Press conferences and rehearsals are intercut with performances by Harrison (singing Beatles classics and solo hits), Shankar, Ringo Starr, Billy Preston, Leon Russell and Eric Clapton. The highlight is Bob Dylan, then making his first public appearance in two years, singing *Blowin' in the Wind* and *Just Like a Woman*. AJ

Dir Saul Swimmer • *Producer* George Harrison, Allen Klein

Concert for George ★★★★ PG

Concert movie
2003 · UK/US · Colour · 104mins

Staged at the Royal Albert Hall on 29 November 2002 – exactly a year after George Harrison's death – and unfussily filmed by David Leland and Chris Menges using over a dozen cameras, this celebration of Harrison's music proves that the "quiet Beatle" was a consummate songwriter in his own right. Surviving Beatles Ringo Starr and Paul McCartney (whose ukulele introduction to *Something* is a genuinely fond showstopper), Travelling Wilburys Jeff Lynne and Tom Petty, and key musical collaborators Eric Clapton and Ravi Shankar join Harrison's son Dhani in an all-star update of the first rock aid gig, *The Concert for Bangladesh*. DP DVD

Dir David Leland • *Cinematographer* Chris Menges

The Concrete Jungle ★★ 18

Drama 1982 · US · Colour · 99mins

Credulous Tracy Bregman realises she's trusted her love-rat boyfriend (Peter Brown) too much after he has her busted for drug smuggling. Tom DeSimone's idea of original film-making is to put warden Jill St John in spectacles to prove how neurotic she is. Barbara Luna, however, is a standout as a hard-bitten veteran of the cell regime. TH

Jill St John *Warden Fletcher* • Tracy Bregman *Elizabeth Demming* • Barbara Luna *Cat* • June Barrett *Icy* • Peter Brown *Danny* • Aimee Eccles *Spider* • Sondra Currie *Katherine* ■ *Dir* Tom DeSimone • *Scr* Alan J Adler

Condemned ★★ U

Drama 1929 · US · BW · 82mins

Oscar history was made within the Best Actor category of 1930. Ronald Colman, George Arliss and Maurice Chevalier all received two separate nominations, but only Arliss emerged triumphant. Colman is great fun in *Bulldog Drummond*, but it's harder to fathom why he was nominated for this creaky early talkie about a prisoner who falls in love with the warden's wife (Ann Harding). Directed by Wesley Ruggles, it's a clumsy mix of action adventure, drippy romance and an exposé of the iniquities of the infamous Devil's Island. DP

Ronald Colman *Michel Oban* • Ann Harding *Mme Vidal* • Dudley Digges *Warden Jean Vidal* • Louis Wolheim *Jacques Duval* • William Elmer *Pierre* • William Vaughn *Vidal's orderly* ■ *Dir* Wesley Ruggles • *Scr* Sidney Howard

The Condemned of Altona ★★

Drama 1962 · Fr/It · BW · 113mins

Director Vittorio De Sica and screenwriter Cesare Zavattini were responsible for some of the masterworks of Italian neorealism. But they singularly failed with this forbidding melodrama about the effects of war guilt on one Hamburg family. The action crackles with an anti-German feeling that ruinously undermines the case made against the Gerlachs in particular and the nation in general. DP. An Italian language film.

Sophia Loren *Johanna* • Maximilian Schell *Franz* • Fredric March *Gerlach* • Robert Wagner *Werner* • Françoise Prévost *Leni* ■ *Dir* Vittorio De Sica • *Scr* Abby Mann, Cesare Zavattini, from the play *Les Séquestrés d'Altona* by Jean-Paul Sartre

Condemned Women ★★★

Prison drama 1938 · US · BW · 76mins

A 1930s version of *Prisoner: Cell Block H*, minus the cardboard sets but heavy on the melodrama. There's no messing with these ladies of the slammer as they fight, eat, fight, sleep and fight again all the way to lights out, with surly Sally Eilers striking up a less than wholesome relationship with prison psychiatrist Louis Hayward. Nothing overly subtle here, but there are some cracking performances. SH

Sally Eilers *Linda Wilson* • Louis Hayward *Phillip Duncan* • Anne Shirley *Millie Anson* • Esther Dale *Matron Glover* • Lee Patrick *Big Annie* ■ *Dir* Lew Landers • *Scr* Lionel Houser

El Condor ★★

Western 1970 · US · Colour · 101mins

Director John Guillermin came unstuck with this western about a pair of mercenaries raiding a Mexican fort for its gold. The Spanish-shot movie contains none of the tongue-in-cheek humour that's often the salvation of the European western. As the protagonists, Lee Van Cleef and Jim Brown look good, but the constant brutality and slow pace make this very hard to enjoy. TS. Contains violence, swearing and nudity.

Lee Van Cleef *Jaroo* • Jim Brown *Luke* • Patrick O'Neal *Chavez* • Mariana Hill [Marianna Hill] *Claudine* • Iron Eyes Cody *Santana* • Imogen Hassall *Dolores* • Elisha Cook Jr *Old convict* • Gustavo Rojo *Colonel Aguinaldo* ■ *Dir* John Guillermin • *Scr* Larry Cohen, Steven W Carabatsos

Condorman ★ U

Comedy 1981 · US · Colour · 86mins

Disney, for all its ability to create animated magic, regularly churned out live-action pictures that would embarrass a camcorder enthusiast. This is worse than most. Michael Crawford stars in this dismal comic-book comedy, but surely both he and Oliver Reed (as the KGB agent trying to stop cartoonist Crawford rescuing spy Barbara Carrera) could have found something better to do? DP [video]

Michael Crawford *Woody* • Oliver Reed *Krokov* • Barbara Carrera *Natalia* • James Hampton *Harry* • Jean-Pierre Kalfon *Morovich* • Dana Elcar *Russ* • Vernon Dobtcheff *Russian agent* ■ *Dir* Charles Jarrott • *Scr* Marc Stirdivant, Glen Caron, Mickey Rose, from the novel *The Game of X* by Robert Sheckley

Conduct Unbecoming ★★ PG

Drama 1975 · UK · Colour · 102mins

Trevor Howard and Richard Attenborough almost redeem this dull, studio-bound drama set at the height of the British Raj. As the widow of the regimental hero, Susannah York accuses a newly arrived lieutenant of assaulting her, leading to his court martial, a lot of twitching moustaches and an exposure of Victorian moral hypocrisy. AT [video]

Michael York *Second Lieutenant Arthur Drake* • Richard Attenborough *Major Lionel Roach* • Trevor Howard *Colonel Benjamin Strang* • Stacy Keach *Captain Rupert Harper* • Christopher Plummer *Major Alastair Wimbourne* • Susannah York *Mrs Marjorie Scarlett* ■ *Dir* Michael Anderson • *Scr* Robert Enders, from the play by Barry England

The Conductor ★★★★

Musical drama 1980 · Pol · Colour · 110mins

After decades spent in the United States, a famous classical maestro (John Gielgud) returns to his birthplace in Poland as a guest conductor with the provincial town's struggling orchestra. Although in frail health and nearing the end of his life, he is able to inject new life into the musicians. Made by the great Andrzej Wajda, this poignant film is redolent with atmosphere and tension, but disappointingly hints at deeper significance without conveying much. Gielgud, however, is absolutely superb, despite being dubbed into Polish. RK. In Polish with English subtitles.

John Gielgud *John Lasocki* • Krystyna Janda *Marta* • Andrzej Seweryn *Adam Pietryk* ■ *Dir* Andrzej Wajda • *Scr* Andrzej Kijowski

Cone of Silence ★★★★

Drama 1960 · UK · BW · 76mins

An expertly made, taut British movie from *Scott of the Antarctic* director and former Hitchcock editor Charles Frend. It contains some fine heart-stopping moments, while Peter Cushing, George Sanders and character actor Bernard Lee give superb performances. Some of the technical details and hardware have inevitably dated in this aeronautical drama, but the striking black-and-white compositions and the beautifully paced editing by Max Benedict remain very impressive. TS

Michael Craig *Captain Hugh Dallas* • Peter Cushing *Captain Clive Judd* • Bernard Lee *Captain George Gort* • Elizabeth Seal *Charlotte Gort* • George Sanders *Sir Arnold Hobbes* • André Morell *Captain Edward Manningham* • Gordon Jackson *Captain Bateson* ■ *Dir* Charles Frend • *Scr* Robert Westerby, from the novel by David Beaty • *Cinematographer* Arthur Grant

Coneheads ★★ PG

Comedy 1993 · US · Colour · 86mins

The American satirical series *Saturday Night Live* has spawned some blockbuster movies – *The Blues Brothers* and *Wayne's World*, for instance – but this Dan Aykroyd creation sank without trace. Aykroyd is reunited with old TV colleagues Jane Curtin and Laraine Newman for this dismal comedy about a family of aliens trying to get to grips with life on Earth, but the characters are long past their sell-by date. JF. Contains some swearing and sex scenes. [video] DVD

Dan Aykroyd *Beldar* • Jane Curtin *Prymaat* • Michael McKean *Seedling* • Michelle Burke *Connie* • David Spade *Turnbull* • Chris Farley *Ronnie* • Jason Alexander *Larry Farber* • Lisa Jane Persky *Lisa Farber* • Sinbad *Otto* • Jon Lovitz *Dr Rudolf* • Phil Hartman *Marlax* • Laraine Newman *Laarta* • Ellen DeGeneres *Coach* ■ *Dir* Steve Barron • *Scr* Tom Davis, Dan Aykroyd, Bonnie Turner, Terry Turner

Coney Island ★★★ U

Musical comedy 1943 · US · Colour · 96mins

Here's Betty Grable at the peak of her wartime career, singing period songs like *Put Your Arms around Me, Honey* in gloriously garish, 20th Century-Fox Technicolor. It's a piece of tosh about saloon-keeper George Montgomery wanting to turn her into a big star, despite rival hotelier Cesar Romero, who wants her for himself. Familiar stuff, but vastly entertaining in its unsophisticated, mindless way. TS [video]

Betty Grable *Kate Farley* • George Montgomery *Eddie Johnson* • Cesar Romero *Joe Rocco* • Charles Winninger *Finnigan* • Phil Silvers *Frankie* ■ *Dir* Walter Lang • *Scr* George Seaton

Confession ★★★★

Melodrama 1937 · US · BW · 88mins

A splendid melodrama, told in flashback, starring the elegant Kay Francis as a singer who kills her seducer, pianist Basil Rathbone. (He'd taken a shine to her daughter, the swine!) This is a stunner, with design and camerawork very reminiscent of a classy German feature (it's based on a 1935 Pola Negri vehicle), while émigré director Joe May pulls out all the stops and weaves a wonderfully flamboyant Hollywood tapestry. TS

Kay Francis *Vera* • Ian Hunter *Leonide Kilrow* • Basil Rathbone *Michael Michailow* • Jane Bryan *Lisa* • Donald Crisp *Presiding judge* • Mary Maguire *Hildegard* • Dorothy Peterson *Mrs Koslov* ■ *Dir* Joe May • *Scr* Julius J Epstein, Margaret LaVino, Stanley Logan, from the film *Mazurka* by Hans Hameau • *Cinematographer* Sid Hickox • *Art Director* Anton Grot

Confession ★★ PG

Crime thriller 1955 · UK · BW · 86mins

The confidentiality of the confessional is a well-worn movie theme; here Ken Hughes finds nothing new to say about the subject: a priest hears a voice confess to murder and then finds his world collapsing around him as his vow of silence prevents him from passing on the information that will nail the killer. The film gives viewers a rare chance to see Charlie Chaplin's son, Sydney, in a leading role. DP [video]

Sydney Chaplin *Mike Nelson* • Audrey Dalton *Louise* • John Bentley *Inspector Kessler* • Peter Hammond *Alan* • John Welsh *Father Neil* • Jefferson Clifford *Pop* • Patrick Allen *Corey* • Pat McGrath *Williams* ■ *Dir* Ken Hughes • *Scr* Ken Hughes, from a play by Don Martin

The Confession ★★★

Political drama
1970 · Fr/It · Colour · 139mins

This *film à clef* is a thinly disguised account of the 1951 show trial in which Czech foreign minister Artur London and 13 other party officials were charged by the Communist regime with being American-backed, pro-Zionist spies. Clearly intent on demonstrating (after his right-wing exposé, *Z*) that extremism knows no boundaries, Costa-Gavras presents a grinding insight into Stalinist brutality. However, this works better as a portrait of a man under pressure than as a political argument. DP. In French with English subtitles.

Yves Montand *"Gerard"/Artur London* • Simone Signoret *Lise* • Gabriele Ferzetti *Kohoutek* • Michel Vitold *Smola* • Jean Bouise *Man in factory* • Laszlo Szabo *Secret policeman* ■ *Dir* Costa-Gavras • *Scr* Jorge Semprun, from the non-fiction book *L'Aveu* by Lise London, Artur London

The Confessional ★★★★ 15

Thriller
1995 · Can/UK/Fr · Colour and BW · 96mins

The filming in the 1950s of Hitchcock's *I Confess*, the Quebec-based thriller about the sanctity of a priest's confessional, provides the background to this intricate story of an adopted brother seeking his real father. It marks the film directorial debut of Robert Lepage, a noted Canadian theatre director whose style is as compelling as it is sumptuous. The story seesaws between 1989, and the hunt for paternal identity, and 1952, when Hitchcock (played by Ron Burrage) arrives in Quebec and blames his assistant (Kristin Scott Thomas) for letting the Catholic Church make too many cuts in his film. Too tricksy, but worth seeing for its display of dazzling, if complicated, talent at work. TH. In English and French with subtitles. [video]

Lothaire Bluteau *Pierre Lamontagne* • Patrick Goyette *Marc Lamontagne* • Jean-Louis Millette *Raymond Massicotte* • Kristin Scott Thomas *Hitchcock's secretary* • Ron Burrage *Alfred Hitchcock* • Richard Fréchette *André* • François Papineau *Lamontagne* • Anne-Marie Cadieux *Manon* ■ *Dir/Scr* Robert Lepage

Confessions from a Holiday Camp ★ 18

Sex comedy 1977 · UK · Colour · 84mins

The *Confessions* films relied on a blend of saucy humour and "What the Butler Saw"-style smut. This was the fourth and last of these cheap comedies, with Robin Askwith as an over-sexed entertainments officer at a camp run by an ex-prison officer. DP. Contains swearing, nudity. [video] DVD

Robin Askwith *Timothy Lea* • Anthony Booth *Sidney Noggett* • Doris Hare *Mum* • Bill Maynard *Dad* • Sheila White *Rosie* • Colin Crompton *Roughage* • Liz Frazer *Mrs Whitemonk* • Linda Hayden *Brigitte* ■ *Dir* Norman Cohen • *Scr* Christopher Wood, from a novel by Timothy Lea [Christopher Wood]

Confessions of a Dangerous Mind ★★★★ 15

Biographical comedy drama
2002 · US/Ger/UK · Colour · 108mins

For his remarkably accomplished debut behind the camera, George Clooney tackles the unreliable memoirs of Chuck Barris, the host and creator of influential US TV shows *The Dating Game* and *The Gong Show*, who also claims to have killed 33 people as a hitman for the CIA. Charlie Kaufman contributes a sharp, deadpan script, while the film's gleefully erratic tone and style fluctuates between gaudy 1960s psychedelia and muted Cold War grit, enriched by Clooney's fluency with a camera. Sam Rockwell is believable and entertaining as Barris, and Drew Barrymore is on good form as his girlfriend. JC. Contains sex scenes, violence, swearing. [video] DVD

Sam Rockwell *Chuck Barris* • Drew Barrymore *Penny Pacino* • George Clooney *Jim Byrd* • Julia Roberts *Patricia Watson* • Rutger Hauer *Keeler* • Maggie Gyllenhaal *Debbie* • Kristen Wilson *Loretta* • Jennifer Hall *Georgia* ■ *Dir* George Clooney • *Scr* Charlie Kaufman, from the autobiography *Confessions of a Dangerous Mind: an Unauthorized Autobiography* by Chuck Barris

Confessions of a Driving Instructor ★ 18

Sex comedy 1976 · UK · Colour · 85mins

The third in the series of smutty comedies based on the novels of Timothy Lea is something of an embarrassment for all concerned. The mix of *doubles entendres* and soft-core gropings can only be described as abysmal. Robin Askwith mugs like a trouper, but it's sad that accomplished comedy actresses Irene Handl and Liz Fraser signed up for this rubbish. DP. Contains swearing, nudity. [video] DVD

Robin Askwith *Timothy Lea* • Anthony Booth *Sidney Noggett* • Windsor Davies *Mr Truscott* • Sheila White *Rosie* • Doris Hare *Mum* • Bill Maynard *Dad* • Liz Fraser *Mrs Chalmers* • Irene Handl *Miss Slenderparts* • George Layton *Tony Bender* ■ *Dir* Norman Cohen • *Scr* Christopher Wood, from a novel by Timothy Lea [Christopher Wood]

Confessions of a Hit Man ★★ 15

Crime drama 1994 · US · Colour · 92mins

Ambitious but ultimately dreary take on the lot of a hired assassin. James Remar is the killer who, on what could be his last assignment, tries to make peace with his victims' loved ones and others who have crossed his path over the years. Remar does well in a weightier role than he usually gets, but it is far too talky and the existential air fails to convince. JF. Contains swearing and violence. [video]

James Remar *Bruno Sarrano* • Michael Wright *Charley* • Emily Longstreth *Corine* ■ *Dir* Larry Leahy • *Scr* Tony Cinciripini, Larry Leahy

Confessions of a Nazi Spy ★★★ U

Spy drama 1939 · US · BW · 110mins

Warner Bros declared war on Germany long before America itself and this documentary-style spy drama, showing G-men searching out Nazis rallying undercover in America, is one of its most blatant pieces of propaganda. Paul Lukas and Edward G Robinson blend into the woodwork well enough, but there's a whole casting directory of scar-faced villains to make you wonder how they ever got through immigration. What was topical for the time has inevitably dated, but director Anatole Litvak can still chill us with his depiction of the crawling swastika. TH

Edward G Robinson *Ed Renard* • Francis Lederer *Schneider* • George Sanders *Schlager* • Paul Lukas *Dr Kassel* • Henry O'Neill *DA Kellogg* • Lya Lys *Erika Wolff* • Grace Stafford *Mrs Schneider* ■ *Dir* Anatole Litvak • *Scr* Milton Krims, John Wexley, from a story by Milton Krims, John Wexley, from the article *Storm over America* by Leon G Turrou

C

Confessions of a Pop Performer ★ 18

Sex comedy 1975 · UK · Colour · 86mins

Robin Askwith abandons his window-cleaning round to help organise a tour for a band of no-hopers and finds himself knee-deep in groupies (the finale at the Palladium has to be seen to be believed). Askwith struggles with a dismal script and comes off much better than Tony Blair's father-in-law, Anthony Booth. Among the other familiar faces are Doris Hare and Bob Todd. DP. Contains swearing, sex scenes, nudity. DVD

Robin Askwith *Timothy Lea* • Anthony Booth *Sidney Noggett* • Bill Maynard *Mr Lea* • Doris Hare *Mrs Lea* • Sheila White *Rosie* • Bob Todd *Mr Barnwell* • Jill Gascoine *Mrs Barnwell* • Peter Cleall *Nutter Normington* ■ *Dir* Norman Cohen • *Scr* Christopher Wood, from a novel by Timothy Lea [Christopher Wood]

Confessions of a Serial Killer ★★★★ 15

Crime drama 1987 · US · Colour · 95mins

Savage yet brilliant, this minor masterpiece will inevitably be compared to the similar *Henry: Portrait of a Serial Killer*, made around the same time. In police custody, serial killer Daniel Ray Hawkins (extremely well-played by Robert A Burns) begins a series of confessions about his life and crimes. The flaw in this narrative device (we know Hawkins will eventually be caught) is outweighed by the movie's virtues, which include gritty location shooting that lends an authenticity to the proceedings. KB DVD

Robert A Burns *Daniel Ray Hawkins* • Dennis Hill *Moon Lawton* • Berkley Garrett *Sheriff Will Gaines* • Sidney Brammer *Molly* • DeeDee Norton *Monica* ■ *Dir/Scr* Mark Blair

Confessions of a Teenage Drama Queen ★★★ PG

Comedy 2004 · US/Ger · Colour · 85mins

Lindsay Lohan plays a popular New York teenager, who is transferred to a suburban New Jersey school where bitchy Megan Fox rules the roost. Instant rivals, the pair set out to snatch the lead role in a musical version of *Pygmalion* and light up the life of rock star Adam Garcia. Candyfloss colours and some animation give proceedings a little extra sparkle, which helps when the film takes itself too seriously. Lohan emerges as a real contender for grown-up stardom, while Carol Kane lends wonderfully eccentric support. TH DVD

Lindsay Lohan *Lola Cep* • Adam Garcia *Stu Wolff* • Glenne Headly *Karen Cep* • Alison Pill *Ella Gerard* • Carol Kane *Miss Baggoli* • Eli Marienthal *Sam* • Megan Fox *Carla Santini* • Sheila McCarthy *Mrs Gerard* ■ *Dir* Sara Sugarman • *Scr* Gail Parent, from the novel by Dyan Sheldon

Confessions of a Trickbaby ★★ 18

Black comedy thriller
1999 · US/Fr/Can · Colour · 93mins

The second film (after *Freeway*) in Matthew Bright's proposed trilogy of radically reworked fairy tales is so over-the-top, it's halfway down the other side. In this outrageous spin on *Hansel and Gretel*, Natasha Lyonne and Maria Celedonio play damaged teens who break out of detention and strike out on a murderous road trip to Mexico for a climactic confrontation with transvestite nun Vincent Gallo. Directed in the style of the sexploitation films it spoofs, this could earn cult status with those who appreciate its tongue-in-cheek extravagance. DA DVD

Natasha Lyonne *White Girl (Crystal)* • Maria Celedonio *Angela (Cyclona)* • Vincent Gallo *Sister Gomez* ■ *Dir/Scr* Matthew Bright

Confessions of a Window Cleaner ★ 18

Sex comedy 1974 · UK · Colour · 90mins

The first of the four saucy comedies adapted from the bestselling novels of Timothy Lea. In addition to introducing us to Robin Askwith and his shiftless brother-in-law (played by Tony Blair's father-in-law, Anthony Booth), the film also wastes some of Britain's finest comic talent, who vainly try to wring a laugh out of the smutty situations and limp jokes. DP. Contains swearing, sex scenes and nudity. DVD

Robin Askwith *Timothy Lea* • Anthony Booth *Sidney Noggett* • Sheila White *Rosie Noggett* • Dandy Nichols *Mrs Lea* • Bill Maynard *Mr Lea* • Linda Hayden *Elizabeth Radlett* • John Le Mesurier *Inspector Radlett* • Joan Hickson *Mrs Radlett* ■ *Dir* Val Guest • *Scr* Christopher Wood, Val Guest, from a novel by Timothy Lea [Christopher Wood]

Confessions of an Opium Eater ★★★

Melodrama 1962 · US · BW · 79mins

For years, Albert Zugsmith's deliriously sensational melodrama, with its scenes of slave trafficking and opium smoking, thrilled America's "midnight matinée" crowd. In Britain it was available only in an excessively censored version called *Evils of Chinatown*. Neither version bears any relation to Thomas De Quincey's memoir, except that the hero (Vincent Price) is described as a descendant of the author. Price is a seaman, who lands in San Francisco and helps rescue abducted women. There is a lot of dross to endure, but the weird atmosphere is often startling and Price's narration is also notable. DM

Vincent Price *De Quincey* • Linda Ho *Ruby Low* • Philip Ahn *Ching Foon* • Richard Loo *George Wah* • June Kim *Lotus* ■ *Dir* Albert Zugsmith • *Scr* Robert Hill, Seton I Miller, from the story *Confessions of an English Opium-eater* by Thomas De Quincey

Confidence ★★★★ U

Drama 1979 · Hun · Colour · 117mins

Although the underlying theme of this intense drama is the mutual confidence civilisation needs to survive, István Szabó is, for once, less concerned with the momentous events of history than the simple interaction of individuals. Forced to pose as a married couple during the Nazi occupation of Budapest, Ildiko Bansagi and Peter Andorai progress from fear and superstition to implicit trust and passion as they realise their interdependence. It's the claustrophobic exchanges that give it a power and truth that owes as much to Szabó and cinematographer Lajos Koltai as to the superlative leads. DP. In Hungarian with English subtitles.

Ildiko Bansagi *Kata* • Peter Andorai *Janos* • O Gombik *Old woman* • Karoly Csaki *Old man* ■ *Dir* István Szabó • *Scr* István Szabó, from a story by Erika Szanto, István Szábo

Confidence ★★★ 15

Crime thriller 2002 · US/Ger · Colour · 93mins

James Foley's twisty-turny thriller is enjoyable without ever being completely compelling. Grifter Edward Burns is co-opted by eccentric crime boss Dustin Hoffman into scamming a banker through a complex scheme involving corporate loans, wire transfers and offshore accounts. Burns gives an appealing turn and the film is packaged as a stylish *film noir*. But what makes this merely good rather than great is its inability to make its characters come off as real human beings rather than cyphers designed to ignite plot fireworks. IF DVD

Edward Burns *Jake Vig* • Rachel Weisz *Lily* • Andy Garcia *Gunther Butan* • Dustin Hoffman *Winston King* • Paul Giamatti *Gordo* • Donal Logue *Whitworth* • Luis Guzmán [Luis Guzman] *Omar Manzano* • Brian Van Holt *Miles* ■ *Dir* James Foley • *Scr* Doug Jung

Confidences Trop Intimes ★★★★ 15

Comedy drama 2004 · Fr · Colour · 99mins

Diametric opposites forge an unlikely link in Patrice Leconte's subtle and literate comedy of sexual manners. Initially, there's a gulf between Fabrice Luchini's fastidious tax lawyer and the mysterious Sandrine Bonnaire, who mistakes his office for that of her new psychiatrist. But as Bonnaire continues to seek him out to impart her sensual despair, Luchini gradually comes to appreciate that his entire existence is based upon a misconception of his true self. The consultations are occasionally racy, as Bonnaire explores the reasons for her deteriorating marriage to impotent Gilbert Melki. But, it's enchantment rather than lust that inspires Luchini's devotion and so his deceit never seems sinister. DP. In French with English subtitles. Contains swearing and sexual references. DVD

Fabrice Luchini *William Faber* • Sandrine Bonnaire *Anna Delambre* • Michel Duchaussoy *Dr Monnier* • Anne Brochet *Jeanne* • Gilbert Melki *Marc* • Laurent Gamelon *Luc* • Hélène Surgère *Madame Mulon* ■ *Dir* Patrice Leconte • *Scr* Jérôme Tonnerre, Patrice Leconte

Confidential ★★★

Crime drama 1935 · US · BW · 67mins

This fast-moving gangster movie dates from the period when prolific director Edward L Cahn was still making half-decent films. It stars Donald Cook as a G man who infiltrates the Mob and falls for sexy Evalyn Knapp while tangling with nasty sadist J Carrol Naish. It moves along at a fine rate as a good programme-filler should, and doesn't outstay its welcome. TS

Donald Cook *Dave Elliot* • Evalyn Knapp *Maxine* • Warren Hymer *Midget* • J Carrol Naish *Lefty* • Herbert Rawlinson *JW Keaton* • Theodore von Eltz *Walsh* • Morgan Wallace *Van Cleve* ■ *Dir* Edward L Cahn • *Scr* Weilyn Totman, Olive Cooper, from a story by John Rathmell, Scott Darling

Confidential ★ 18

Crime drama 1986 · Can · Colour · 87mins

No one has a good word to say about this Canadian thriller, and we're not about to buck the trend. Shooting with a minuscule budget and on a tight schedule, Bruce Pittman has come up with a *film noir* homage that looks as if it was made with next to nothing in next to no time. DP. Contains violence, swearing, nudity.

Neil Munro *Hugh Jameson* • August Schellenberg *Charles Ripley* • Chapelle Jaffe *Amelia* • Tom Butler *Edmund Eislin* • Antony Parr *Rufus* • Doris Petrie *Mrs McAlister* ■ *Dir/Scr* Bruce Pittman

Confidential Agent ★★

Thriller 1945 · US · BW · 117mins

A Warner Bros version of a novel by Graham Greene about a former Spanish musician who gives up his career to fight the Fascists and goes to Britain to stop the English selling coal to Franco's troops. Charles Boyer makes an engaging hero, but the Hollywood England takes some swallowing. Villains Peter Lorre and Katina Paxinou do their best to stop Boyer, but Lauren Bacall fails to convince as a British coal baron's daughter. This movie isn't uneventful, just uninvolving. TS

Charles Boyer *Denard* • Lauren Bacall *Rose Cullen* • Victor Francen *Licata* • Wanda Hendrix *Else* • George Coulouris *Captain Currie* • Peter Lorre *Contreras* • Katina Paxinou *Mrs Melandey* • John Warburton *Neil Forbes* ■ *Dir* Herman Shumlin • *Scr* Robert Buckner, from the novel by Graham Greene

Confidential Report ★★ PG

Film noir 1955 · Sp/Swi · BW · 93mins

Also known as *Mr Arkadin*, this fascinating picture is a fearful mess that betrays, all too clearly, the financial and production problems with which Orson Welles had to contend. As in *Citizen Kane*, the subject is a mysterious, all-powerful man, but this time around the approach is one of self-parody and self-indulgence. Welles filmed it in his beloved place of exile, Spain, with a fancy cast and fanciful camera angles. AT DVD

Orson Welles *Gregory Arkadin* • Robert Arden *Guy Van Stratten* • Paola Mori *Raina Arkadin* • Michael Redgrave *Burgomil Trebitsch* • Patricia Medina *Mily* • Akim Tamiroff *Jakob Zouk* • Mischa Auer *Professor* • Katina Paxinou *Sophie* ■ *Dir* Orson Welles • *Scr* Orson Welles, from his novel

Confidentially Connie ★★ U

Comedy 1953 · US · BW · 71mins

Unsuitable for vegetarians, this vapid comedy involves a professor of poetry (Van Johnson, if you can believe it) who is so underpaid he can't afford to buy meat for his pregnant wife (Janet Leigh). Gene Lockhart is the hungry dean who dines out on teachers angling for promotion, while Louis Calhern steals the picture as the flamboyant Texas rancher who puts steak back on the table. AE

Van Johnson *Joe Bedloe* • Janet Leigh *Connie Bedloe* • Louis Calhern *Opie Bedloe* • Walter Slezak *Emil Spangenberg* • Gene Lockhart *Dean Magruder* • Hayden Rorke *Simmons* • Robert Burton *Dr Willis Shoop* ■ *Dir* Edward Buzzell • *Scr* Max Shulman, from a story by Herman Wouk, Max Shulman

Confidentially Yours ★★★

Comedy mystery thriller
1983 · Fr · BW · 111mins

As he did with *Shoot the Pianist* and *The Bride Wore Black*, François Truffaut took an American pulp novel as the basis for this rather self-regarding, mildly amusing comedy thriller. Shot in black and white by Nestor Almendros in an attempt to capture the style of the 1940s *film noir*, it tells of real estate agent Jean-Louis Trintignant who, accused of the murder of his wife and her lover, goes into hiding while his secretary Fanny Ardant tries to prove his innocence. RB. In French with English subtitles.

Fanny Ardant *Barbara Becker* • Jean-Louis Trintignant *Julien Vercel* • Philippe Laudenbach *M Clement* • Caroline Sihol *Marie-Christine Vercel* • Xavier Saint-Macary *Bertrand Fabre* • Jean-Pierre Kalfon *Massoulier* ■ *Dir* François Truffaut • *Scr* François Truffaut, Suzanne Schiffman, Jean Aurel, from the novel *The Long Saturday Night* by Charles Williams

C

Confirm or Deny ★★★

Second World War drama
1941 · US · BW · 73mins

A top-flight cast who know their way around a Second World War spy thriller and a decent script (from a story co-written by Samuel Fuller) make this a cut above the ordinary blitzkrieg saga. The Ministry of Disinformation plotline gets a trifle convoluted in the middle, but the movie is saved from disappearing under its own self-importance by the effective playing of Don Ameche and Joan Bennett. TS

Don Ameche *Mitch* • Joan Bennett *Jennifer Carson* • Roddy McDowall *Albert Perkins* • John Loder *Captain Channing* • Raymond Walburn *H Cyrus Sturtevant* • Arthur Shields *Jeff* • Eric Blore *Mr Hobbs* • Helene Reynolds *Dorothy* • Claude Allister [Claud Allister] *Williams* ■ *Dir* Archie Mayo • *Scr* Jo Swerling, from a story by Henry Wales, Samuel Fuller

Conflagration ★★★★

Tragedy 1958 · Jpn · BW · 96mins

Adapted from Yukio Mishima's novel, *The Temple of the Golden Pavilion*, which was itself based on actual events, Kon Ichikawa's painstaking study of disillusion and misguided devotion has often been accused of being a clinical enterprise, obsessed with textured imagery and surface symbolism. However, Raizo Ichikawa poignantly conveys the pain experienced by the student priest, whose dismay at what he sees as the desecration of his temple prompts him to preserve its beauty and integrity by destroying it. DP. In Japanese with English subtitles.

Raizo Ichikawa *Mizoguchi* • Tatsuya Nakadai • Ganjiro Nakamura *Tayama* • Yoko Uraji • Michiyo Aratama • Tamao Nakamura ■ *Dir* Kon Ichikawa • *Scr* Natto Wada, Keiji Hasebe, Kon Ichikawa, from the novel *The Temple of the Golden Pavillion* by Yukio Mishima • *Cinematographer* Kazuo Miyagawa

Conflict ★★★ PG

Thriller 1945 · US · BW · 81mins

From a great period in *film noir*, this is a slightly substandard Warner Bros melodrama, despite a story co-written by Robert Siodmak (*Phantom Lady*, *The Killers*). It is held together by Humphrey Bogart, who occasionally looks as though he'd rather be somewhere else, even when he's plotting to do away with his wife in order to marry her sister. The censor was pretty tough in those days, but the mood's still dark and tense, even if the conclusion is obvious. TS [video]

Humphrey Bogart *Richard Mason* • Alexis Smith *Evelyn Turner* • Sydney Greenstreet *Dr Mark Hamilton* • Rose Hobart *Katherine Mason* • Charles Drake *Professor Norman Holdsworth* • Grant Mitchell *Dr Grant* • Patrick O'Moore *Detective Lieutenant Egan* • Ann Shoemaker *Nora Grant* • Frank Wilcox *Robert Freston* ■ *Dir* Curtis Bernhardt • *Scr* Arthur T Horman, Dwight Taylor, from a story by Robert Siodmak, Alfred Neumann

Conflict of Wings ★★ U

Comedy 1953 · UK · Colour · 85mins

The borrowings come thick and fast in this sentimental rural drama. The most obvious source is the wartime allegory *Tawny Pipit*, with more than a hint of *The Titfield Thunderbolt* and *Passport to Pimlico*. But, while it never lives up to its illustrious ancestry, this is still a pleasing little picture, with the Norfolk Broads looking lovely in Arthur Grant and Martin Curtis's washed-out colour photography. The folklore behind the tale is charming, there are a couple of tear-jerking moments and a rousing rally-round finale. DP

John Gregson *Bill Morris* • Muriel Pavlow *Sally* • Kieron Moore *Squadron Leader Parsons* • Niall MacGinnis *Harry Tilney* • Harry Fowler *Buster* • Guy Middleton *Adjutant* • Sheila Sweet *Fanny Bates* • Campbell Singer *Flight Sergeant Campbell* ■ *Dir* John Eldridge • *Scr* Don Sharp, John Pudney, from the novel by Don Sharp

The Conformist ★★★★★ 18

Drama 1969 · It/Fr/W Ger · Colour · 113mins

A masterful blend of Freud and Fascism, Bernardo Bertolucci's adaptation examines the link between sexual and political repression in order to assess the impact of Italy's authoritarian past on its deeply divided present. Aided by Vittorio Storaro's luscious cinematography, Bertolucci perfectly captures the false sense of well-being exuded by Mussolini's regime. Jean-Louis Trintignant is superb as the conformist of the title, a victim of child abuse who has grown up with a desperate desire to belong. Trintignant is ably supported by Stefania Sandrelli and Dominique Sanda in this disturbing, visually imposing and influential movie. DP. In Italian with English subtitles. Contains violence, swearing and nudity.

Jean-Louis Trintignant *Marcello Clerici* • Stefania Sandrelli *Giulia* • Gastone Moschin *Manganiello* • Enzo Tarascio *Quadri* • Pierre Clémenti *Lino Semirama* • Dominique Sanda *Anna Quadri* • Christian Alegny *Raoul* ■ *Dir* Bernardo Bertolucci • *Scr* Bernardo Bertolucci, from a novel by Alberto Moravia

Congo ★ 12

Adventure 1995 · US · Colour · 103mins

The plot here, combining a lost civilisation, a highly intelligent gorilla and venal scientists after diamonds for a laser gun, is a lacklustre *Boys' Own* no-brainer, and the movie scrapes the bottom of the fantasy barrel dire acting and clichéd special effects. AJ. Contains swearing. [video]

Dylan Walsh *Peter Elliot* • Laura Linney *Dr Karen Ross* • Ernie Hudson *Monroe Kelly* • Tim Curry *Herkermer Homolka* • Grant Heslov *Richard* • Joe Don Baker *RB Travis* • Mary Ellen Trainor *Moira* • Stuart Pankin *Boyd* ■ *Dir* Frank Marshall • *Scr* John Patrick Shanley, from the novel by Michael Crichton

Congo Crossing ★★

Crime drama 1956 · US · Colour · 85mins

This is set in an obscure jungle backwater in central Africa where outlaws congregate, safe from arrest. Into this tropical enclave of vice comes Virginia Mayo, on the run from a murder rap, and hero George Nader, who works for the Belgian government and is surveying the land to confirm whether it falls within the jurisdiction of the colonial government. Filmed in the crocodile-infested wilds of the Universal backlot, it serves up honest hokum and a lot of neat safari outfits. AT

Virginia Mayo *Louise Whitman* • George Nader *David Carr* • Peter Lorre *Colonel Arragas* • Michael Pate *Bart O'Connell* • Rex Ingram (2) *Dr Gorman* • Tonio Selwart *Carl Rittner* • Kathryn Givney *Amelia Abbott* • Tudor Owen *Emile Zorfus* • Raymond Bailey *Peter Mannering* ■ *Dir* Joseph Pevney • *Scr* Richard Alan Simmons, from a story by Houston Branch

Congress Dances ★★★

Musical 1931 · Ger · BW · 92mins

In Vienna for the 1814 Congress, Tsar Alexander of Russia (Willy Fritsch) falls for a shop assistant (Lillian Harvey) rather than the countess (Lil Dagover) put his way by the devious Prince Metternich (Conrad Veidt). Delicately directed by Erik Charell from a soufflé-light script, this early German musical largely ignores the political implications of the setting. Filmed in three different versions – English, French and German, with Henri Garat replacing Fritsch for the French market – its charm has faded with time, though its lightweight approach and opulent settings proved hugely influential throughout the decade. RK

Lillian Harvey [Lilian Harvey] *Christel Weinzinger* • Conrad Veidt *Prince Metternich* • Lil Dagover *The Countess* • Willy Fritsch *Tsar Alexander of Russia/Uralsky* • Gibb McLaughlin *Bibikoff, the Czar's adjutant* • Reginald Purdell *Pepi, his secretary* ■ *Dir* Erik Charell • *Scr* Norman Falk, Robert Liebmann

A Connecticut Yankee ★★★

Comedy 1931 · US · BW · 95mins

Will Rogers stars as a man who dreams that he is back in the middle ages, where he brings his foreign influence to bear on the manners and morals of King Arthur's court. Mark Twain's classic satirical fantasy had been the basis of a 1921 silent, and would resurface in 1949 as a Bing Crosby musical. This version, directed by David Butler with Maureen O'Sullivan, Myrna Loy, Frank Albertson and William Farnum in support, is witty and agreeable, yet somewhat dated. RK

Will Rogers *Hank* • William Farnum *King Arthur* • Myrna Loy *Queen Morgan Le Fay* • Maureen O'Sullivan *Alisande* • Frank Albertson *Clarence* • Mitchell Harris *Merlin* ■ *Dir* David Butler • *Scr* William Conselman, Owen Davis, from the novel *A Connecticut Yankee in King Arthur's Court* by Mark Twain

A Connecticut Yankee in King Arthur's Court ★★★ U

Musical 1949 · US · Colour · 102mins

Bing Crosby stars in this musical adaptation of Mark Twain's fantasy about a 20th-century American who dreams himself back to medieval times. Arriving at Camelot, he is regarded as something of a wizard at King Arthur's court. The film substitutes broad comedy for wit, and the musical numbers – with the exception of *Busy Doing Nothing* – are pretty forgettable. The Technicolor production is eye-catchingly lavish, though, as is romantic interest Rhonda Fleming. Crosby is in good voice, while Tay Garnett directs with spirit. RK [video]

Bing Crosby *Hank Martin* • William Bendix *Sir Sagramore* • Rhonda Fleming *Sandy* • Cedric Hardwicke *King Arthur* • Murvyn Vye *Merlin* • Henry Wilcoxon *Sir Lancelot* • Richard Webb *Sir Galahad* ■ *Dir* Tay Garnett • *Scr* Edmund Beloin, from the novel by Mark Twain

Connecting Rooms ★★

Romantic drama
1969 · UK · Colour · 103mins

This slightly bonkers drama has schoolteacher Michael Redgrave on the run from child abuse charges and near to suicide. Then there's a female cellist (Bette Davis) who claims to be a solo artist but is in fact a street busker. Together they share rooms in a shabby Bayswater B&B run by Kay Walsh. It's all very 1930s, except for the "Swinging London" appendages of pop stars and an air of kookiness. AT

Bette Davis *Wanda Fleming* • Michael Redgrave *James Wallraven* • Alexis Kanner *Mickey* • Kay Walsh *Mrs Brent* • Gabrielle Drake *Jean* ■ *Dir* Franklin Gollings • *Scr* Franklin Gollings, from the play *The Cellist* by Marion Hart

The Connection ★★★

Drama 1961 · US · BW · 111mins

The debut feature of the influential alternative film-maker Shirley Clarke is shot in documentary style, largely within the confines of one room, and framed as a film-within-a-film. This early example of independent film-making charts a day in the life of a group of Manhattan junkies as they sit around, waiting for their fix. Matter-of-fact, gritty stuff with excellent acting from unknowns; though there are no narrative frills, the movie is not without incident, some of it quite shocking. RK

William Redfield *Jim Dunn* • Warren Finnerty *Leach* • Garry Goodrow *Ernie* • Jerome Raphel *Solly* • James Anderson (2) *Sam* • Carl Lee *Cowboy* • Barbara Winchester *Sister Salvation* • Roscoe Lee Browne *JJ Burden* ■ *Dir* Shirley Clarke • *Scr* Jack Gelber, from his play

Connie and Carla ★★ 12

Comedy 2004 · US · Colour · 93mins

Writer Nia Vardalos's insipid follow up to 2002's surprise hit *My Big Fat Greek Wedding* has her and Toni Collette playing wannabe singers who decide to disguise themselves as performers in a West Hollywood drag club after accidentally witnessing a Mob murder. Weakly plotted gender-confusion comedy follows as Connie (Vardalos) falls for a drag queen's straight brother (a charm-free David Duchovny) who doesn't realise that she's a woman. Woefully underwritten and lacking fizz. AS [video] DVD

Nia Vardalos *Connie* • Toni Collette *Carla* • David Duchovny *Jeff* • Stephen Spinella *Robert/"Peaches"* • Alec Mapa *Lee/"N'Cream"* • Christopher Logan *Brian/"Brianna"* • Robert Kaiser *Paul* • Ian Gomez *Stanley* • Debbie Reynolds ■ *Dir* Michael Lembeck • *Scr* Nia Vardalos

The Conqueror ★★★ PG

Historical adventure
1956 · US · Colour · 106mins

This splendid hokum is rendered ludicrous today by the casting of John Wayne as Genghis Khan, but it doesn't deserve its reputation as one of the worst movies ever made. Splendidly directed by Dick Powell, it is best viewed dubbed into any foreign language as the dialogue is silly beyond belief. Susan Hayward is Wayne's woman, and their exchanges show what canny casting this was. TS DVD

John Wayne *Temujin* • Susan Hayward *Bortai* • Pedro Armendáriz *Jamuga* • Agnes Moorehead *Hunlun* • Thomas Gomez *Wang Kahn* • John Hoyt *Shaman* • William Conrad *Kasar* • Ted De Corsia *Kumlek* • Lee Van Cleef *Chepei* ■ *Dir* Dick Powell • *Scr* Oscar Millard

Conquest ★★★★ U

Historical romantic drama
1937 · US · BW · 115mins

"Sire, you stand in the sun." says Greta Garbo's Marie to Charles Boyer's Napoleon, perhaps aware for once of finding herself playing opposite a suitably talented co-star. Garbo, as you would expect, is simply superb as Bonaparte's Polish mistress, and the Great Lover himself makes an endearingly vulnerable Napoleon in this finely mounted MGM production. Clarence Brown – surely a film craftsman who deserves more appreciation – shows why he was Garbo's favourite director, enhancing her striking features and presenting her as a warm and tender woman fit for the Emperor of France. TS

Greta Garbo *Marie Walewska* • Charles Boyer *Napoleon* • Reginald Owen *Talleyrand* • Alan Marshal *Captain D'Ornano* • Henry Stephenson *Count Walewska* • Leif Erikson *Paul Lachinski* • Dame May Whitty *Laetitia Bonaparte* • C Henry Gordon *Prince Poniatowski* • Maria Ouspenskaya *Countess Pelagia* ■ *Dir* Clarence Brown • *Scr* Samuel Hoffenstein, Salka Viertel, SN Behrman, from a play by Helen Jerome, from the novel *Pani Walewska* by Waclaw Gasiorowski

The Conquest of Everest ★★★★ U

Documentary 1953 · UK · Colour · 74mins

Ever since Herbert G Ponting recorded Captain Scott's ill-fated bid to reach the South Pole, the movie camera has been accompanying heroic ventures. Shot in even more arduous conditions,

C

this is a remarkable account of the expedition that saw Edmund Hillary and Sherpa Tensing become the first to reach the peak of the world's highest mountain. It's a pity the camera couldn't make the final ascent, but the various stages of the climb, with their attendant difficulties and dangers, make gripping viewing thanks to some inspired editing, Louis MacNeice's literate commentary and Arthur Benjamin's rousing score. DP

Meredith Edwards *Narrator* ■ *Dir* George Lowe • *Scr* Louis MacNeice • *Editor* Adrian de Potier

Conquest of Space ★★★ U

Science-fiction drama
1955 · US · Colour · 77mins

Paramount slashed the budget and added soap-opera bubbles to George Pal's sequel to *Destination Moon*. With the accent more on science than on fiction, this aims to offer an accurate reflection of what a trip to Mars would be like technically, and how it would affect the crew psychologically. Despite an out-of-sync religious tone, the reverential approach still evokes a sense of wonder. AJ

Walter Brooke *Samuel Merritt* • Eric Fleming *Barney Merritt* • Mickey Shaughnessy *Mahoney* • Phil Foster *Siegle* • William Redfield *Cooper* • William Hopper *Fenton* • Ross Martin *Fodor* ■ *Dir* Byron Haskin • *Scr* Philip Yordan, Barre Lyndon, George Worthingtonyates, from the book *The Mars Project* by Chesley Bonestell, Willy Ley

Conquest of the Air ★★ U

Documentary drama
1936 · UK/US · BW · 70mins

This was to be the first instalment of an ambitious trilogy on the development of land, sea and air transport planned by producer Alexander Korda as part of his assault on the American market. However, this untidy collage of history lesson and dramatic reconstruction was an age in production and looked no better in the screening room. Zoltan Korda shared the directorial credit with several others, which can't have helped. DP

Frederick Culley *Roger Bacon* • Franklin Dyall *Jerome de Ascoli* • Alan Wheatley *Borelli* • Hay Petrie *Tiberius Cavallo* • John Abbott *Derozier* • Laurence Olivier *Vincent Lunardi* • Bryan Powley *Sir George Cayley* • Henry Victor *Otto Lilienthal* • John Trumbull *Von Zeppelin* ■ *Dir* Zoltan Korda, Alexander Esway, Alexander Shaw, John Monk Saunders • *Scr* Hugh Gray, Peter Bezencenet, from stories by John Monk Saunders, Antoine de St Exupery

Conquest of the Planet of the Apes ★★★ 15

Science-fiction adventure
1972 · US · Colour · 86mins

The fourth film in the sci-fi saga illustrates how the ape revolt happened in the first place. Caesar, played by series regular Roddy McDowall, gains the power of speech, forms enslaved fellow simians into guerrilla groups and leads them against the evil human race. Gritty direction from J Lee Thompson and plenty of fun philosophising, complete with intriguing moral lessons and neat ape/man role reversals. *Battle for the Planet of the Apes* (1973) concluded the series. AJ. Contains violence. DVD

Roddy McDowall *Caesar* • Don Murray *Breck* • Ricardo Montalban *Armando* • Natalie Trundy *Lisa* • Hari Rhodes *MacDonald* • Severn Darden *Kolp* • Lou Wagner *Busboy* • John Randolph *Commission chairman* ■ *Dir* J Lee Thompson • *Scr* Paul Dehn, from characters created by Pierre Boulle

Conquest of the South Pole ★★★ 12

Drama 1989 · UK · Colour · 95mins

Manfred Karge's allegorical fantasy was a huge hit for the Traverse Theatre in Edinburgh, so it's fitting that the film version should be shot in and around the now-defunct docks of the Scottish capital. Though hampered by an ultra-low budget, debutant director Gilles MacKinnon exploits the visual potential of this story of a group of unemployed youths who ward off despair by re-creating Amundsen's journey to the South Pole in their own back yard. Screenwriter Gareth Wardell deftly embroils us in the characters' lunatic quest. NS

Stevan Rimkus *Sloopianek* • Ewen Bremner *Penguin* • Leonard O'Malley *Butcher* • Laura Girling *Louise* • Gordon Cameron *Brown* • Alastair Galbraith *Frankieboy* • Julie-Kate Oliver *Rosie* ■ *Dir* Gillies MacKinnon • *Scr* Gareth Wardell, from the play by Manfred Karge

Conrack ★★

Biographical drama
1974 · US · Colour · 106mins

Jon Voight stars as liberal teacher Pat Conroy, who fetches up on one of South Carolina's barrier islands with a class of kids who can't read or write. Martin Ritt's movie is often sentimental and hectoring, ramming home the contrast between Voight's comfy, secure rebellion against the Vietnam War and the utter destitution and backwardness of his pupils. The film oozes sincerity yet somehow seems totally phoney. AT

Jon Voight *Pat Conroy* • Paul Winfield *Mad Billy* • Madge Sinclair *Mrs Scott* • Tina Andrews *Mary* • Antonio Fargas *Quickfellow* • Ruth Attaway *Edna* • James O'Rear *Little Man* • Hume Cronyn *Skeffington* ■ *Dir* Martin Ritt • *Scr* Irving Ravetch, Harriet Frank Jr, from the book *The Water Is Wide* by Pat Conroy

Consenting Adults ★★★ 15

Psychological thriller
1992 · US · Colour · 94mins

Kevin Kline and Mary Elizabeth Mastrantonio are the ordinary husband and wife whose lives are turned upside down when a couple-from-hell move in next door. Extremely plodding action from *All the President's Men* director Alan J Pakula and a rather wooden Kline slow things down somewhat, but the day is saved by a mesmerising performance from Kevin Spacey as the creepy neighbour. JB. Contains violence, swearing and nudity.

Kevin Kline *Richard Parker* • Mary Elizabeth Mastrantonio *Priscilla Parker* • Kevin Spacey *Eddy Otis* • Rebecca Miller *Kay Otis* • Forest Whitaker *David Duttonville* • EG Marshall *George Gordon* ■ *Dir* Alan J Pakula • *Scr* Matthew Chapman

The Consequences of Love ★★★★ 15

Crime drama 2004 · It · Colour · 104mins

Paulo Sorrentino's meticulous drama stars Toni Servillo as a secretive businessman who has been living for eight years in a quiet Swiss hotel near the Italian border. His routine consists of weekly trips to the local bank, the occasional card game and a regular heroin fix. But Servillo's growing affection for barmaid Olivia Magnani causes him to cross the mobsters who exiled him from his family following a financial indiscretion. There is little action here, but it still generates great suspense, thanks to impeccable performances and the work of cinematographer Luca Bigazzi, whose use of the hotel's sterile environment makes Servillo's plight all the more intriguing. DP. In Italian with English subtitles. Contains swearing and drug abuse.

Toni Servillo *Titta Di Girolamo* • Olivia Magnani *Sofia* • Adriano Giannini *Valerio* • Angela Goodwin *Isabella* • Raffaele Pisu *Carlo* • Enzo Vitagliano *Pippo D'Anto* • Vittorio Di Prima *Nitto Lo Riccio* ■ *Dir/Scr* Paolo Sorrentino

Consolation Marriage ★★★

Comedy drama 1931 · US · BW · 82mins

Irene Dunne and Pat O'Brien, both on the rebound, meet and marry for solace and companionship. They carve out a decent life for themselves and have a child, but their equilibrium is threatened when their former flames (Lester Vail and Myrna Loy) re-appear. This was one of the first of the "woman's weepie" roles that Dunne was to make her own, though director Paul H Sloane offers a satisfying measure of charm and humour to balance the sentimentality. RK

Irene Dunne *Mary Brown Porter* • Pat O'Brien *Steve Porter* • John Halliday *Jeff* • Myrna Loy *Elaine Brandon* • Lester Vail *Aubrey* • Matt Moore *Colonel* • Pauline Stevens *Baby* ■ *Dir* Paul Sloane [Paul H Sloane] • *Scr* Humphrey Pearson, from a story by William Cunningham

Conspiracy ★★★ 15

Second World War historical drama
2001 · US/UK · Colour · 95mins

This admirably dispassionate cable TV movie exposes the cold calculation that went into the planning of the Final Solution. Based on minutes from a meeting chaired by SS security chief Reinhard Heydrich, it's an open indictment of the sheer evil that underpinned the Nazi regime. But while every effort has been made to avoid caricature, the performances do occasionally seem mannered. The distinction is best seen in the contrast between Kenneth Branagh's charismatic Heydrich and Stanley Tucci's display of ruthless vanity as Eichmann. DP DVD

Stanley Tucci *Adolf Eichmann* • Kenneth Branagh *Reinhard Heydrich* • Colin Firth *Dr Wilhelm Stuckart* • Barnaby Kay *SS Major Rudolph Lange* • Ben Daniels *Dr Josef Buhler* • David Threlfall *Dr Wilhelm Kritzinger* • Jonathan Coy *Dr Erich Neumann* • Brendan Coyle *SS General Heinrich Muller* • Ian McNeice *Gerhard Klopfer* • Owen Teale *Dr Roland Freisler* ■ *Dir* Frank Pierson • *Scr* Loring Mandel

Conspiracy in Teheran ★ U

Spy drama 1947 · UK · BW · 87mins

In this shambolic British thriller it is 1943 and plans are afoot for the Allied invasion of Europe. Churchill, Stalin and Roosevelt meet in the Iranian capital to agree strategy. Journalist Derek Farr discovers a conspiracy. Farr is as bland as ever and takes an age to put together pieces larger than a three-year-old's jigsaw puzzle. DP

Derek Farr *Pemberton Grant* • Marta Labarr *Natalie Trubetzin* • Manning Whiley *Paul Sherek* • John Slater *Major Sobieski* • John Warwick *Major McIntyre* • Pamela Stirling *Hali* ■ *Dir* William Freshman • *Scr* Akos Tolnay, William Freshman

Conspiracy of Hearts ★★★★ U

Second World War drama
1960 · UK · BW · 112mins

This moving and under-rated tale about nuns helping Jewish children escape the Nazis in war-torn Italy was made with sincerity and feeling by Ralph Thomas. The movie boasts an immensely talented cast, headed by the luminous Lilli Palmer as the Mother Superior, with Sylvia Syms and Yvonne Mitchell as caring nuns and David Kossoff as a rabbi. This thoughtful casting lends the film resonance, and it's far better than its potentially mawkish plot combination of children and nuns would suggest. TS

Lilli Palmer *Mother Katherine* • Sylvia Syms *Sister Mitya* • Ronald Lewis *Major Spoletti* • Albert Lieven *Colonel Horsten* • Yvonne Mitchell *Sister Gerta* • Peter Arne *Lt Schmidt* • Nora Swinburne *Sister Tia* • Michael Goodliffe *Fr Desmaines* • David Kossoff *Rabbi* ■ *Dir* Ralph Thomas • *Scr* Robert Presnell Jr, from material by Dale Pitt (front for Adrian Scott)

A Conspiracy of Love ★★ U

Drama 1987 · US · Colour · 89mins

This dates from the "cute kiddie" period of Drew Barrymore's career, before rehab and her re-invention as a teen sexpot. She acquits herself well in this solid but formulaic TV weepie, which details an "only in America" custody battle involving Barrymore and her grandfather, played by veteran Robert Young. JF DVD

Robert Young (1) *Grandpa Joe* • Drew Barrymore *Jody Wykowski* • Elizabeth Wilson *Lillie Wykowski* • Mitchell Laurance *Jack* • John Fujioka *Mr Nakamura* • Alan Fawcett *Joe Wykowski* • Glynnis O'Connor *Marcia* ■ *Dir* Noel Black • *Scr* Barry Morrow

Conspiracy Theory ★★★ 15

Romantic comedy thriller
1997 · US · Colour · 129mins

Mel Gibson plays a neurotic New York cabbie consumed by wild conspiracy theories in director Richard Donner's uneven thriller. It's the newsletter Gibson produces that intensifies interest in him from ominous parties such as creepy Patrick Stewart, who may work for the CIA. But that's only the half of it, because when he turns to Justice Department attorney Julia Roberts for help, the *Manchurian Candidate*-like plot kicks off. Gibson and Roberts make an engaging team, but the uneasy combination of light laughs and unsavoury darkness conspires against it. AJ. Contains violence and swearing. DVD

Mel Gibson *Jerry Fletcher* • Julia Roberts *Alice Sutton* • Patrick Stewart *Dr Jonas* • Cylk Cozart *Agent Lowry* • Stephen Kahan [Steve Kahan] *Wilson* • Terry Alexander *Flip* • Alex McArthur *Cynic* ■ *Dir* Richard Donner • *Scr* Brian Helgeland

Conspirator ★ U

Spy drama 1949 · UK · BW · 86mins

A dire, anti-communist tract that fitted in with Hollywood's postwar paranoia but is transposed to Britain where Guards Officer Robert Taylor seems to be passing military secrets to the Russians. He's also married to Elizabeth Taylor, which makes matters even worse, because he's ordered to kill her; if he doesn't, he has to kill himself. Mr Taylor gives his usual impersonation of a plank of wood, while the young Miss Taylor looks gorgeous but seems lost. AT

Robert Taylor (1) *Maj Michael Curragh* • Elizabeth Taylor *Melinda Greyton* • Robert Flemyng *Capt Hugh Ladholme* • Harold Warrender *Col Hammerbrook* • Honor Blackman *Joyce* • Marjorie Fielding *Aunt Jessica* • Thora Hird *Broaders* • Wilfrid Hyde White *Lord Pennistone* ■ *Dir* Victor Saville • *Scr* Sally Benson, Gerard Fairlie, from a novel by Humphrey Slater

The Conspirators ★★

Spy drama 1944 · US · BW · 101mins

Is this an unofficial sequel to *Casablanca*? Resistance fighter Paul Henreid is finally in Lisbon after escaping from Holland, hunted by the Nazis but finding shelter with Sydney Greenstreet, Peter Lorre and exotic Hedy Lamarr who are all resistance underground members. The cast are like the furniture in your grandmother's living room – familiar, snug, a bit moth-eaten. But they more than compensate for the formulaic plotting and the patriotic slogans that pass for a script, and for the unusually lethargic direction by Jean Negulesco. AT

Hedy Lamarr *Irene* • Paul Henreid *Vincent* • Sydney Greenstreet *Quintanilla* • Peter Lorre *Bernazsky* • Victor Francen *Von Mohr* • Joseph Calleia *Capt Pereira* • Carol Thurston *Rosa* • Vladimir Sokoloff *Miguel* • George Macready *The Con Man* ■ *Dir* Jean Negulesco • *Scr* Vladimir Pozner, Leo Rosten, from a novel by Frederic Prokosch

Conspirators of Pleasure ★★★★ 18

Experimental fantasy comedy
1996 · Cz Rep/Swi/UK · Colour · 82mins

Focusing on the antics of some lonely Prague neighbours, Jan Svankmajer's dark satire explores everything from de Sade and Freud to the nature of political freedom, the influence of the media and the possibility of happiness in a world primed to prevent it. From the man making papier-mâché chickens out of porn mags and umbrellas to the woman with a bagful of breadcrumbs, the gallery of eccentrics is both sinister and sympathetic; the performances are all the more remarkable considering each fantasy is acted out in silence. DP. Contains nudity and violence. [video]

Petr Meissel *Mr Peony* • Gabriela Wilhelmova *Mrs Loubalova* • Barbara Hrzanova *Mrs Malkova the postmistress* • Anna Wetlinska *Mrs Beltinska the newscaster* • Jiri Labus *Mr Kula the news vendor* • Pavel Novy *Mr Beltinska the police commissioner* ■ *Dir/Scr* Jan Svankmajer

Constance ★★★★ 15

Drama 1984 · NZ · Colour · 98mins

The debuting Donogh Rees is outstanding in this inspired exploration of the relationship between the Hollywood "woman's picture" and real life in 1940s Auckland. Tempering the nostalgia evoked by his knowing visuals, director Bruce Morrison makes Rees's disastrous attempt to behave like a movie heroine truly excruciating. Although the dialogue is occasionally too self-conscious, the references to the films of Garbo, Dietrich, Davis and Crawford are splendidly staged, making their ironic commentary on the hapless Constance's existence all the more prescient. DP [video]

Donogh Rees *Constance Elsworthy* • Shane Briant *Simon Malyon* • Judie Douglass *Sylvia Elsworthy* • Martin Vaughan *Alexander Elsworthy* • Donald MacDonald *John Munroe* • Mark Wignall *Richard Lewis* • Graham Harvey *Errol Barr* ■ *Dir* Bruce Morrison • *Scr* Jonathan Hardy, Bruce Morrison

The Constant Factor ★★

Drama 1980 · Pol · Colour · 90mins

Physicist, multi-linguist and serious film-maker Krzysztof Zanussi often deals with complex themes but sometimes fails to engage audiences in his cinema of ideas and argument. Not least here because of a distinct lack of activity in the actual shooting. This film obviously resonated in contemporary Poland in its dissection of a society where corruption in the work place contradicted the equality promised by a Communist regime. Tadeusz Bradecki finds his ambitions frustrated as much by bureaucracy as his own inadequacies. There's sympathetic observation of his relationship with his mother and his everyday life, but time and history all seem rather remote. BB. In Polish with English subtitles.

Tadeusz Bradecki *Witold* • Zofia Mrozowska *Witold's mother* • Malgorzata Zajaczkowska *Grazyna* • Cezary Morawski *Stefan* ■ *Dir/Scr* Krzysztof Zanussi

The Constant Husband ★★★★ U

Comedy 1955 · UK · Colour · 88mins

Rex Harrison is superbly cast as an amnesiac philanderer in this jolly romp from British film-makers Frank Launder and Sidney Gilliat. Giving Harrison a run for his money are Kay Kendall (whom he later married), Margaret Leighton and French actress Nicole Maurey. The 1950s Technicolor photography gives the film a very pleasant period sheen, while the witty screenplay by Gilliat and Val Valentine ensures this comedy is a delight. TS

Rex Harrison *Charles Hathaway* • Margaret Leighton *Miss Chesterman* • Kay Kendall *Monica* • Cecil Parker *Llewellyn* • Nicole Maurey *Lola* • George Cole *Luigi Sopranelli* • Raymond Huntley *JF Hassett* ■ *Dir* Sidney Gilliat • *Scr* Sidney Gilliat, Val Valentine • *Cinematographer* Ted Scaife

The Constant Nymph ★

Silent drama 1928 · UK · BW · 110mins

This British-made silent version of a bestselling 1920s novel and a hit West End play is the first of three screen adaptations. It's by far the least successful, despite the presence of matinée idol Ivor Novello in the starring role as a composer inadvertently breaking the heart of a schoolgirl (Mabel Poulton), who remains in love with him into her adulthood. Over-long and under-characterised. RK

Mary Clare *Linda Sanger* • Ivor Novello *Lewis Dodd* • Mabel Poulton *Tessa Sanger* • Benita Hume *Antonia Sanger* • Dorothy Boyd *Pauline Sanger* ■ *Dir* Adrian Brunel • *Scr* Margaret Kennedy, Basil Dean, Alma Reville, from the play by Margaret Kennedy, Basil Dean, from the novel by Margaret Kennedy

The Constant Nymph ★★★

Drama 1933 · UK · BW · 97mins

After the ineptitude of the 1928 silent version of the hit play by Basil Dean and Margaret Kennedy (based on her popular novel), eminent theatre director Dean made this first sound version, starring Brian Aherne as the composer struggling for inspiration and Victoria Hopper as the young girl whose constant love provides it, only for events to end in tragedy. A fragile piece, somewhat sedately played, it's probably too delicate for present-day audiences, but remains a stylish and poignant offering. RK

Victoria Hopper *Tess Sanger* • Brian Aherne *Lewis Dodd* • Leonora Corbett *Florence* • Lyn Harding *Albert Sanger* • Mary Clare *Linda Sanger* • Jane Baxter *Antonia Sanger* ■ *Dir* Basil Dean • *Scr* Margaret Kennedy, Basil Dean, Dorothy Farnum, from the play by Margaret Kennedy, Basil Dean, from the novel by Margaret Kennedy • *Producer* Michael Balcon

The Constant Nymph ★★★

Drama 1943 · US · BW · 111mins

Already filmed twice in Britain, this Warner Bros version is sensitively directed, for maximum emotional impact, by Edmund Goulding. Charles Boyer stars as the composer loved by schoolgirl Joan Fontaine (Oscar-nominated), whose constancy accompanies her into adulthood. Interminably slow to get going, it nevertheless succeeds in tugging the heartstrings and it boasts a terrific supporting cast. RK

Charles Boyer *Lewis Dodd* • Joan Fontaine *Tessa Sanger* • Alexis Smith *Florence Creighton* • Charles Coburn *Charles Creighton* • Brenda Marshall *Toni Sanger* • Dame May Whitty *Lady Longborough* • Peter Lorre *Bercovi, Fritz* • Joyce Reynolds *Paula Sanger* ■ *Dir* Edmund Goulding • *Scr* Kathryn Scola, from the play by Margaret Kennedy, Basil Dean, from the novel by Margaret Kennedy

Constantine ★★★ 15

Supernatural action fantasy
2005 · Ger/US/Aus · Colour · 115mins

This diluted but visually arresting comic book adaptation stars Keanu Reeves as the chain-smoking John Constantine, a cancer-ridden exorcist who's condemned to save souls and take on all manner of vile demons on Earth. Rachel Weisz co-stars as a police detective who teams up with Constantine after her apparently loony twin sister (also played by Weisz) takes a swan dive off a high ledge. The script feels like little more than sticky tape holding together the visual effects, but they're very impressive effects indeed. LF [video] DVD

Keanu Reeves *John Constantine* • Rachel Weisz *Angela Dodson/Isabel Dodson* • Shia LaBeouf *Chas* • Tilda Swinton *Gabriel* • Pruitt Taylor Vince *Father Hennessy* • Djimon Hounsou *Midnite* • Gavin Rossdale *Balthazar* • Peter Stormare *Satan* ■ *Dir* Francis Lawrence • *Scr* Kevin Brodbin, Frank Cappello, from a story by Kevin Brodbin, from the comic book *Hellblazer* by Jamie Delano, Garth Ennis, from the character created by Alan Moore in *Swamp Thing*

Constantine and the Cross ★★★

Historical drama 1961 · It · Colour · 116mins

Cornel Wilde, suitably strong, serious and spiritual, stars as the crusading warrior-protector of persecuted Christians, who rose to become Emperor of the Holy Roman Empire. This Italian-made historical epic is packed with the obligatory ingredients of the genre, including political intrigue, romance, and much blood-letting, with no punches pulled in scenes of battle, torture and Christians being thrown to the lions. Christine Kaufmann (a future Mrs Tony Curtis) is a doomed Christian maid, and there's a standout performance from Massimo Serato as a scheming politico. RK. Italian dialogue dubbed into English.

Cornel Wilde *Constantine* • Christine Kaufmann *Livia* • Belinda Lee *Fausta* • Elisa Cegani *Helena* • Massimo Serato *Maxentius* • Fausto Tozzi *Hadrian* ■ *Dir* Lionello De Felice • *Scr* Ennio De Concini, Ernesto Guida, Lionello De Felice, Diego Fabbri, Fulvio Palmieri, Franco Rossetti, Guglielmo Santangelo

Consuming Passions ★★ 15

Comedy 1988 · UK/US · Colour · 94mins

Based on a play by Michael Palin and Terry Jones, of Monty Python fame, Giles Foster's comedy is not exactly a masterpiece. A floundering chocolate factory has its fortunes improve dramatically when three workers are accidentally knocked into a mixing vat. Suddenly the nation starts clamouring for their "special" chocolate with its mystery ingredient. Vanessa Redgrave delivers a strange performance as a litigating widow, while Jonathan Pryce seems to have developed an obsession with the word "yah". LH [video]

Vanessa Redgrave *Mrs Garza* • Jonathan Pryce *Mr Farris* • Tyler Butterworth *Ian Littleton* • Freddie Jones *Graham Chumley* • Sammi Davis *Felicity* • Prunella Scales *Ethel* • Thora Hird *Mrs Gordon* • William Rushton *Big Teddy* ■ *Dir* Giles Foster • *Scr* Paul D Zimmerman, Andrew Davies, from the play *Secrets* by Michael Palin, Terry Jones

Contact ★★★ PG

Science-fiction drama
1997 · US · Colour · 143mins

A rather over-zealous take on new age spirituality mars this otherwise impressive adaption of Carl Sagan's bestselling novel. Jodie Foster stars as the dedicated astronomer who receives a message from extraterrestrials explaining how humble humans can build a spacecraft and go to meet them. Matthew McConaughey is the religious adviser battling for her soul, while Tom Skerritt and James Woods portray sceptical presidential aides. The digital effects are stunning, and director Robert Zemeckis is at home with the action sequences; if only he had stuck to the sci-fi. JF [video] DVD

Jodie Foster *Dr Eleanor "Ellie" Arroway* • Matthew McConaughey *Palmer Joss* • Tom Skerritt *Dr David Drumlin* • Angela Bassett *Rachel Constantine* • John Hurt *SR Hadden* • David Morse *Theodore "Ted" Arroway* • Rob Lowe *Richard Rank* • William Fichtner *Kent* • James Woods *Michael Kitz* ■ *Dir* Robert Zemeckis • *Scr* James V Hart, Michael Goldenberg, from a story by Ann Druyan, Carl Sagan, from the novel by Carl Sagan

Contagion ★ 15

Science-fiction thriller
2000 · UK/US/Ger · Colour · 93mins

Germ unit security guard Peter Weller becomes the carrier of a fast-acting virus that kills anyone he touches within minutes. Scientist William Hurt is immune to the strain and he's sent to track him down with the help of Natascha McElhone. Anthony Hickox directs with his usual aplomb but is let down by a contrived, barely convincing script and Weller's absolutely terrible performance. AJ [video] DVD

William Hurt *David Whitman* • Peter Weller *Joseph Müller* • Natascha McElhone *Holly Anderson* • Katja Woywood *Karin Schiffer* • Michael Brandon *Wyles* • Christopher Cazenove *President of Clarion* • Geraldine McEwan *Lilian Rodgers* ■ *Dir* Anthony Hickox • *Scr* John Penney

The Contender ★★★ 15

Political drama
2000 · US/Fr · Colour · 121mins

Former film critic Rod Lurie makes an assured second feature (his debut was 1999's *Deterrence*) with this streetwise insight into both the predatory nature of Washington power-broking and the increasingly base motives of contemporary journalism. In a part written especially for her, Joan Allen gives an Oscar-nominated performance as the senator selected by popular president Jeff Bridges (also nominated) to succeed his recently deceased vice-president. DP [video] DVD

Gary Oldman *Shelly Runyon* • Joan Allen *Laine Hanson* • Jeff Bridges *President Jackson Evans* • Christian Slater *Reginald Webster* • William Petersen [William L Petersen] *Jack Hathaway* • Saul Rubinek *Jerry Toliver* • Sam Elliott *Kermit Newman* • Philip Baker Hall *Oscar Billings* ■ *Dir/Scr* Rod Lurie

Continental Divide ★★★ PG

Romantic comedy
1981 · US · Colour · 98mins

Although John Belushi will probably be only remembered for his gross clowning in the likes of *National Lampoon's Animal House* and *The Blues Brothers*, this under-rated romantic comedy demonstrated that he clearly possessed subtler gifts than that. In a not entirely successful attempt to re-create the golden age of Tracy and Hepburn, Belushi plays a slobbish, urbanised journalist who falls in and out of love with nature scientist Blair Brown. The leads work surprisingly well together and, although the pacing and tone is a little uneasy, the film is eminently watchable. JF [video]

John Belushi *Ernie Souchak* • Blair Brown *Nell Porter* • Allen Garfield *Howard* • Carlin Glynn *Sylvia* • Tony Ganios *Possum* • Val Avery *Yablonowitz* • Bill Henderson *Train conductor* • Liam Russell *Deke* ■ *Dir* Michael Apted • *Scr* Lawrence Kasdan

C

Contraband ★★★ U

Second World War spy thriller
1940 · UK · BW · 91mins

Directed by Michael Powell from a story by Emeric Pressburger, this is a neat wartime espionage thriller that depicts a London crawling with spies, rather in the manner of Alfred Hitchcock's *Sabotage* and *The Man Who Knew Too Much*. Powell makes brilliant use of the blackouts and includes one cheeky sequence when hundreds of unwanted plaster casts of Neville Chamberlain get shot to pieces. This would have been Deborah Kerr's first feature film, but all her scenes were left on the cutting-room floor. AT

Conrad Veidt *Captain Andersen* • Valerie Hobson *Mrs Sorensen* • Hay Petrie *Axel Skold/Erik Skold* • Esmond Knight *Mr Pidgeon* • Raymond Lovell *Van Dyne* ■ *Dir* Michael Powell • *Scr* Michael Powell, Brock Williams, from a story by Emeric Pressburger

Contraband Spain ★★ U

Mystery 1955 · UK · Colour · 82mins

Richard Greene headlines this mediocre thriller as an American agent intent on rounding up a gang of smugglers operating out of Barcelona. Clearly aiming for a Graham Greene sort of entertainment, writer/director Lawrence Huntington is hampered more by the paucity of his imagination than the meagreness of his resources. The acting is disappointing considering the calibre of the cast. DP

Richard Greene *Lee Scott* • Anouk Aimée *Elena Vargas* • Michael Denison *Ricky Metcalfe* • José Nieto *Pierre* • John Warwick *Bryan* • Philip Saville *Martin Scott* • Alfonso Estella *Marcos* • GH Mulcaster *Colonel Ingleby* ■ *Dir/Scr* Lawrence Huntington

The Contract ★★★

Drama 1980 · Pol · Colour · 111mins

A Warsaw doctor arranges the civil marriage of his son (Tadeusz Lomnicki) but his young wife refuses to go through with the subsequent church service. Nevertheless, her father-in-law goes ahead with the wedding reception, where sex, alcohol and family divisions crash the party. This is film-maker Krzysztof Zanussi at his most straightforward, making an ironic, sometimes funny film that examines a wealthy strata of Polish society on the brink of its collapse. Interesting and entertaining, it features a standout performance by Leslie Caron as a kleptomaniac ballerina. RB. In Polish, French, English, German and Swedish with subtitles.

Maja Komorowska *Dorota* • Tadeusz Lomnicki *Adam* • Magda Jaroszowna *Lilka* • Krzysztof Kolberger *Piotr* • Nina Andrycz *Olga* • Zofia Mrozowska *Maria* • Beata Tyszkiewicz *Nina* • Janusz Gajos *Boleslaw* • Leslie Caron *Penelope Wilson* ■ *Dir/Scr* Krzysztof Zanussi

Control Room ★★★★ 15

Documentary 2004 · US · Colour · 86mins

With documentaries such as *Outfoxed: Rupert Murdoch's War on Journalism* and *Orwell Rolls in His Grave* questioning the impartiality of the US media, Jehane Noujaim's portrait of Arabic TV network Al Jazeera at the outset of the US-led coalition's invasion of Iraq provides a fascinating counterbalance in the ongoing debate about the forces shaping the world's news agenda. Having outlined the station's commitment to democracy and its links with the BBC's disbanded Arab World Service, Noujaim casts a gently satirical eye over the contrasting operational tactics of Qatar-based producer Sameer Khader and US Marine Lt Josh Rushing, the press officer at the US military command post, CentCom. DP. In Arabic and English with subtitles. DVD

Dir Jehane Noujaim • *Cinematographer* Jehane Noujaim, Hani Salama

The Convent ★★

Mystery drama
1995 · Fr/Por · Colour · 90mins

The legend of Faust is cloaked in the conventions of the Gothic novel in this intriguing, if baffling curio from Portuguese maestro Manoel de Oliveira. Strewing the action with casual literary references, the veteran director prompts us to muse on the nature of good and evil as he lures us into the cavernous convent of Arrabida. John Malkovich is the scholar seeking to prove that Shakespeare was a Hispanic Jew, but for once he is outshone by Luis Miguel Cintra as the sinister guardian who tempts the professor with intellectual immortality in order to seduce his wife (Catherine Deneuve). DP. In English, French and Portuguese with subtitles.

Catherine Deneuve *Helene* • John Malkovich *Michael Padovic* • Luis Miguel Cintra *Baltar* • Leonor Silveira *Piedade* • Duarte D'Almeida *Baltazar* • Heloisa Miranda *Berta* ■ *Dir* Manoel de Oliveira • *Scr* Manoel de Oliveira, from an idea by Agustina Bessa-Luis

The Conversation ★★★★★ 15

Psychological thriller
1974 · US · Colour · 108mins

A small masterpiece from Francis Ford Coppola, who is superbly served by Gene Hackman playing a lonely surveillance expert tracking the movements and voices of Frederic Forrest and Cindy Williams, only to find that marital infidelity could be part of a murder plot. Coppola tweaks the idea to surreal effect, while editor Walter Murch orchestrates eavesdropping into a uniquely baffling wall of sound. Made two years after Coppola's *The Godfather*, this haunting thriller skilfully taps into post-Watergate paranoia resulting in an intensely fascinating study of a perpetrator turned victim of the surveillance society. TH. Contains violence and brief nudity. DVD

Gene Hackman *Harry Caul* • John Cazale *Stan* • Allen Garfield *"Bernie" Moran* • Frederic Forrest *Mark* • Cindy Williams *Ann* • Michael Higgins *Paul* • Elizabeth MacRae *Meredith* • Teri Garr *Amy* • Harrison Ford *Martin Stett* • Mark Wheeler *Receptionist* • Robert Shields *Mime* • Robert Duvall *The Director* ■ *Dir/Scr* Francis Ford Coppola • *Sound* Walter Murch, Arthur Rochester

Conversation Piece ★★★ 18

Drama 1974 · It/Fr · Colour · 116mins

Luchino Visconti, having suffered a major stroke that confined him to a wheelchair, concocted this story about an ageing, homosexual professor who lives surrounded by art and books. Cut off from the real world, he finds his ivory tower invaded when a countess and her jet-setting brood rent the apartment upstairs. Visconti's usual themes – the collision of cultures, the clash between old and new, the imminence of death – are covered in opulent fashion. AT. Contains swearing, sex scenes. DVD

Burt Lancaster *Professor* • Helmut Berger *Konrad Hubel* • Claudia Marsani *Lietta Brumonti* • Silvana Mangano *Bianca Brumonti* • Stefano Patrizi *Stefano* • Elvira Cortese *Erminia* • Claudia Cardinale *Professor's wife* ■ *Dir* Luchino Visconti • *Scr* Suso Cecchi D'Amico, Luchino Visconti, from a story by Enrico Medioli

Convict 99 ★★ U

Comedy 1938 · UK · BW · 84mins

Who else but Will Hay could apply for the headship of a school only to find himself appointed a prison governor and then get mistaken for the most dangerous inmate? Sadly, the film loses its way once Hay assumes power and introduces a regime so liberal that the lags take over. The great man is somewhat below par in this muddled and overlong comedy. DP DVD

Will Hay *Benjamin Twist* • Moore Marriott *Jerry the Mole* • Graham Moffatt *Albert* • Googie Withers *Lottie* • Garry Marsh *Johnson* • Peter Gawthorne *Sir Cyril Wagstaffe* • Basil Radford *Governor* ■ *Dir* Marcel Varnel • *Scr* Marriott Edgar, Val Guest, Jack Davies, Ralph Smart, from a story by Cyril Campion

Convicted ★★

Prison drama 1950 · US · BW · 90mins

Jailed for manslaughter after killing a man in a bar-room brawl, Glenn Ford becomes romantically entangled with Dorothy Malone, the daughter of governor Broderick Crawford. Ford's situation worsens, however, when he sees convict Millard Mitchell kill another inmate. Although strongly cast, well played and competently directed by Henry Levin, this prison melodrama is so monumentally routine that it quickly becomes predictable. RK

Glenn Ford *Joe Hufford* • Broderick Crawford *George Knowland* • Millard Mitchell *Malloby* • Dorothy Malone *Kay Knowland* • Carl Benton Reid *Capt Douglas* • Frank Faylen *Ponti* ■ *Dir* Henry Levin • *Scr* William Bowers, Fred Niblo Jr, Seton I Miller, from the play *The Criminal Code* by Martin Flavin

Convicts ★★★

Period drama 1991 · US · Colour · 92mins

There's a major theme here – the dying days of the Old South – but it's compressed by playwright/screenwriter Horton Foote into almost allegorical terms. Robert Duvall acts his socks off as the senile plantation owner who fights in the Civil War and then hires black convicts to work the place, thus preserving slavery. It's this shadowy history that is recalled by Lukas Haas in the film's rather peculiar dramatic structure. Duvall's portrayal of senility makes the film worth seeing. AT

Robert Duvall *Soll Gautier* • Lukas Haas *Horace Robedaux* • Starletta DuPois *Martha Johnson* • James Earl Jones *Ben Johnson* • Carlin Glynn *Asa* • Gary Swanson *Billy* • Mel Winkler *Jackson* ■ *Dir* Peter Masterson • *Scr* Horton Foote, from a play by Horton Foote

Convicts Four ★★

Prison drama 1962 · US · BW · 105mins

Also known as *Reprieve*, this dour prison drama takes a turn for the better when a convict is granted a stay of execution and takes up painting, a pastime which changes his uncaring character and leads to his eventual rehabilitation. Millard Kaufman's film is well-meaning and sincere, while Ben Gazzara, Vincent Price and Rod Stieger deliver strong performances. After a while, though, it becomes a bit dull. TH

Ben Gazzara *John Resko* • Stuart Whitman *Principal Keeper* • Ray Walston *Iggy* • Vincent Price *Carl Carmer* • Rod Steiger *Tiptoes* • Broderick Crawford *Warden* • Dodie Stevens *Resko's sister* • Sammy Davis Jr *Wino* ■ *Dir* Millard Kaufman • *Scr* Millard Kaufman, from the non-fiction book *Reprieve* by John Resko

Convoy ★★★ PG

Second World War drama
1940 · UK · BW · 85mins

A convoy of ships, led by captain Clive Brook, is intercepted in the North Sea by a German battleship. Its firepower destroys Brook's cruiser and kills the first officer (John Clements), who had been the lover of the skipper's wife. A taut, realistic and emotionally involving British flag-waver, well directed by the highly regarded Pen Tennyson, tragically killed in 1941 before he could fulfil his potential. RK

Clive Brook *Captain Armitage* • John Clements *Lieutenant Crawford* • Edward Chapman *Captain Eckersley* • Judy Campbell *Lucy Armitage* • Edward Rigby *Mr Mathews* • Charles Williams *Shorty Howard* • Allan Jeayes *Commander Blount* • John Laurie *Gates* • Stewart Granger *Sutton* • Michael Wilding *Dot* • Penelope Dudley Ward *Mabel* ■ *Dir* Pen Tennyson • *Scr* Pen Tennyson, Patrick Kirwan

Convoy ★★★ 12

Comedy adventure
1978 · US · Colour · 106mins

This film remains the epitome of trucking movies. Kris Kristofferson is the heroic driver who thumbs his nose at authority and collects a disparate group of truckers in an epic journey across the US, which sees him cross the roadblocks of sheriff Ernest Borgnine. It's pretty lightweight fare for director Sam Peckinpah, but he builds an unstoppable momentum that makes you forget the weak performances. The appalling title song, which is actually the source of the movie, was a massive hit at the time. JF. Contains swearing. DVD

Kris Kristofferson *Martin Penwald, "Rubber Duck"* • Ali MacGraw *Melissa* • Ernest Borgnine *Lyle Wallace, "Dirty"* • Burt Young *Bobby, "Pig Pen"* • Madge Sinclair *"Widow Woman"* • Franklyn Ajaye *"Spider Mike"* • Brian Davies *Chuck Arnoldi* • Seymour Cassel *Governor Gerry Haskins* ■ *Dir* Sam Peckinpah • *Scr* BWL Norton, from the song by CW McCall

Les Convoyeurs Attendent ★★★★ 15

Comedy drama
1999 · Bel/Fr/Swi · BW · 89mins

Having impressed as the serial killer in *Man Bites Dog*, Benoît Poelvoorde surpasses himself in this bizarre black comedy from Belgium. As the ambulance-chasing photojournalist bullying his son to break the world door-opening record in order to win a car in a millennial contest, he combines tough love, class consciousness and repressed self-loathing to create a truly unique character whose muddled motives almost excuse his eccentric excesses. An astute mix of melodrama and macabre humour. DP. In French with English subtitles.

Benoît Poelvoorde *Roger* • Morgane Simon *Luise* • Bouli Lanners *Coach* • Dominique Baeyens *Mother* • Philippe Grand'Henry *Felix* • Jean-François Devigne *Michel* • Lisa LaCroix *Jocelyne* ■ *Dir* Benoît Mariage • *Scr* Benôt Mariage, Emmanuelle Bada, Jean-Luc Seigle • *Cinematographer* Philippe Guilbert

Coogan's Bluff ★★★ 15

Crime drama 1968 · US · Colour · 90mins

Clint Eastwood still wore a cowboy hat in his first attempt to move from the western landscape into the contemporary urban setting, but under Don Siegel's taut direction he carried off the switch successfully. In many ways the forerunner of Dirty Harry, Eastwood's laconic Arizona sheriff tracking down a murderer in Manhattan was his first character to get upset by big city sleaze and escalating crime. This stylish and gritty crime drama set the seal on Eastwood's screen persona for decades to come. AJ. Contains violence, swearing. DVD

Clint Eastwood *Walt Coogan* • Lee J Cobb *Sheriff McElroy* • Susan Clark *Julie* • Tisha Sterling *Linny Raven* • Don Stroud *Ringerman* • Betty Field *Mrs Ringerman* • Tom Tully *Sheriff McCrea* • Melodie Johnson *Millie* ■ *Dir* Don Siegel • *Scr* Herman Miller, Dean Reisner, Howard Rodman, from a story by Herman Miller

The Cook, the Thief, His Wife and Her Lover ★★★★ 18

Black comedy drama
1989 · UK/Fr · Colour · 118mins

Avant-garde director Peter Greenaway's most accessible film to date is a truly elegant, shocking and transfixing experience. A Jacobean drama in contemporary clothing, this savage indictment of greed, power and control in today's wannabe society finds Helen Mirren memorably strutting her stuff in another risky, and risqué, performance, while manic Michael Gambon portrays evil personified. Memorably scored by Michael Nyman, Greenaway's stunning "designer dream" is sick, sexy and rude in about equal provocative proportions and totally unforgettable. AJ. Contains violence, swearing, sex scenes and nudity. [VIDEO] DVD

Richard Bohringer *Richard Borst, the Cook* • Michael Gambon *Albert Spica, the Thief* • Helen Mirren *Georgina Spica, the Wife* • Alan Howard *Michael, the Lover* • Tim Roth *Mitchel* • Gary Olsen *Spangler* • Liz Smith *Grace* • Alex Kingston *Adele* • Ian Dury *Terry Fitch* ■ *Dir/Scr* Peter Greenaway • *Cinematographer* Sacha Vierny • *Costume Designer* Jean-Paul Gaultier

Cookie ★★ 15

Crime comedy 1989 · US · Colour · 89mins

Emily Lloyd is the mobster's daughter trying to keep dad out of trouble in this uneven comedy. Unfortunately, despite the talents on board, director Susan Seidelman has still manages to make a bland, unfunny mess of a movie whose behind-the-scenes stories (Peter Falk allegedly slapped Lloyd, who annoyed him, during a scene when he was supposed to fake it) are much more interesting than what's going on in front of the camera. JB. Contains violence and swearing. [VIDEO]

Peter Falk *Dominick "Dino" Capisco* • Dianne Wiest *Lenore* • Emily Lloyd *Carmella "Cookie" Voltecki* • Michael V Gazzo *Carmine Taratino* • Brenda Vaccaro *Bunny* • Adrian Pasdar *Vito* • Lionel Stander *Enzo Della Testa* • Jerry Lewis *Arnold Ross* ■ *Dir* Susan Seidelman • *Scr* Nora Ephron, Alice Arlen

Cookie's Fortune ★★★ 12

Comedy drama 1999 · US · Colour · 112mins

Director Robert Altman has a bizarre collection of hits and misses in his *oeuvre*, and this falls somewhere in the middle. This ensemble piece finds Glenn Close and Julianne Moore hamming it up as two sisters trying to cover up the "disgraceful" suicide of ageing relative Cookie, while simultaneously attempting to inherit her worldly goods. Cookie's more worthy heirs, rebel Liv Tyler and long standing handyman Charles S Dutton, cotton on to their shenanigans. LH. Contains some sex scenes. [VIDEO] DVD

Glenn Close *Camille* • Julianne Moore *Cora Duvall* • Liv Tyler *Emma Duvall* • Chris O'Donnell *Jason Brown* • Charles S Dutton *Willis Richland* • Patricia Neal *Jewel Mae "Cookie" Orcutt* • Ned Beatty *Lester Boyle* ■ *Dir* Robert Altman • *Scr* Anne Rapp

Cool and Crazy ★★★★ 15

Music documentary
2000 · Nor/Swe/Fin · Colour · 100mins

The prospect of spending 105 minutes in the company of a Norwegian male voice choir may not sound that inviting, but Knut Erik Jensen's documentary portrait of the Berlevåg choristers is a delight. The members of the choir reside in a remote fishing town that's been badly hit by recession, and their music and cheerful camaraderie play an important part in sustaining morale. Whether depicting the choir rehearsing outdoors in the face of a blizzard or excitedly making their way to the Russian city of Murmansk for a recital, the film conveys the warmth of community that insulates these gloriously eccentric characters from their icy surroundings. Irrepressible and enthusiastic, each chorister has a story to tell and their testimony is invariably moving, amusing or astute. A little gem. DP. In Norwegian with English subtitles. [VIDEO] DVD

Dir Knut Erik Jensen • *Cinematographer* Svein Krøvel, Aslaug Holm

The Cool and the Crazy ★★★ 12

Drama 1958 · US · BW · 77mins

Take a walk on the jive side with this cheap and cheerful juvenile delinquent classic starring James Dean wannabe Scott Marlowe. It's all here: seedy pushers, flaming car crashes, wild ones "hooked on smoke", service station hold-ups and rebels without a cause resorting to violence to feed their addictions. Originally banned in Britain, this high school dope exposé is remarkably well acted, fast paced and realistic. AJ DVD

Scott Marlowe *Bennie Saul* • Gigi Perreau *Amy* • Dick Bakalyan [Richard Bakalyan] *Jackie Barzan* • Dick Jones [Dickie Jones] *Stu Summerville* • Shelby Storck *Lt Sloan* ■ *Dir* William Witney • *Scr* Richard C Sarafian

Cool as Ice ★★ PG

Drama 1991 · US · Colour · 87mins

Just what is it that makes singers think they can act? Here rapper Vanilla Ice (remember him?) proves that he hasn't mastered the thespian art, as he tries and fails to translate his musical persona to the screen. Ice rides into town with his posse like *The Wild One*, and he's soon romancing the kind of girl whose daddy wouldn't approve of anyone. Still, the music's catchy. JB. Contains swearing. [VIDEO]

Vanilla Ice *Johnny Van Owen* • Kristin Minter *Kathy* • Michael Gross *Gordon Winslow* • Sydney Lassick *Roscoe McCallister* • Dody Goodman *Mae McCallister* • Naomi Campbell *Singer at first club* • Candy Clark *Grace Winslow* ■ *Dir* David Kellogg • *Scr* David Stenn

Cool Blue ★ 15

Romantic comedy
1988 · US · Colour · 86mins

An early film role for Woody Harrelson, better known at the time for playing dumb barman Woody Boyd in the long-running sitcom *Cheers*. Here he plays an aspiring painter who loves, then loses a girl (Ely Pouget). A straight-to-video cheapie, notable only for featuring an uncredited cameo from Sean Penn. FL [VIDEO]

Woody Harrelson *Dustin* • Ely Pouget *Christiane* • Gloria LeRoy *Ida* • Hank Azaria *Buzz* • Sean Penn *Phil the plumber* ■ *Dir/Scr* Richard Shepard, Mark Mullin

A Cool, Dry Place ★★★ 15

Drama 1998 · US · Colour · 94mins

Not many people saw this vastly underrated drama about a single father who puts his career as a high-powered lawyer on hold to raise his five-year-old son in a small town. Vince Vaughn is awe-inspiring in the lead, and the rest of the cast, which includes Joey Lauren Adams as his new girlfriend and Monica Potter as his ex-wife, is also terrific. This may not be as showy as some dramas, but it has heart. ST [VIDEO]

Vince Vaughn *Russell Durrell* • Monica Potter *Kate* • Joey Lauren Adams *Beth* • Devon Sawa *Noah* ■ *Dir* John N Smith • *Scr* Matthew McDuffie, from the novel *Dance Real Slow* by Michael Grant Jaffe

Cool Hand Luke ★★★★ 15

Prison drama 1967 · US · Colour · 121mins

Chiming perfectly with the "Summer of Love" in which it was released, this subtle blend of acknowledging the needs of the individual and respecting a freedom of spirit was one of the key American films of the 1960s. It's basically an old-fashioned chain-gang movie, told in stunning Technicolor. Paul Newman is superb, and both the prologue and the egg-eating scene have become screen classics. The religious symbolism does get a little tiresome, but the movie is clearly the career high point of director Stuart Rosenberg. An immense pleasure to watch, and a real credit to Jack Lemmon's production company. TS. Contains violence, swearing, sex scenes and nudity. [VIDEO] DVD

Paul Newman *Luke Jackson* • George Kennedy *Dragline* • JD Cannon *Society Red* • Lou Antonio *Koko* • Robert Drivas *Loudmouth Steve* • Strother Martin *Captain* • Jo Van Fleet *Arletta* • Clifton James *Carr* • Dennis Hopper *Babalugats* ■ *Dir* Stuart Rosenberg • *Scr* Donn Pearce, Frank R Pierson, from a novel by Donn Pearce • *Cinematographer* Conrad Hall

The Cool Ones ★★ U

Musical comedy 1967 · US · Colour · 95mins

If you can endure its antiquated humour, this pop musical, one of several directed by former actor Gene Nelson, has some delights. The plot hasn't dated at all: fading pop singer Gil Peterson and go-go dancer Debbie Watson are persuaded by publicist Roddy McDowall to pretend to be a romantic item. Toni Basil's choreography is "fab", and tone deaf housewife Mrs Miller, who had a flash-in-the-pan pop career, murders Doris Day's hit *It's Magic*. Frivolous, and 20 minutes too long. DM

Roddy McDowall *Tony* • Debbie Watson *Hallie* • Gil Peterson *Cliff* • Robert Coote *Stan* • Phil Harris *MacElwaine* • Nita Talbot *Dee Dee* • Mrs Elva Miller *Mrs Miller* • Glen Campbell *Patrick* • Teri Garr *Hallie's friend* ■ *Dir* Gene Nelson • *Scr* Robert Kaufman, Gene Nelson, from a story by Joyce Geller

Cool Runnings ★★★★ PG

Sports comedy based on a true story
1993 · US · Colour · 94mins

If someone had invented the story of a Jamaican bobsleigh team entering the Olympics, they'd have been laughed out of the room. But, as the story is true and Disney knows how to produce feel-good material better than most, what results is a hugely entertaining comedy guaranteed to have you cheering on the underdogs. Admittedly, it's a little predictable at times, but the eager performances of John Candy and his Olympic hopefuls carry the day. DP [VIDEO] DVD

Leon *Derice Bannock* • Doug E Doug *Sanka Coffie* • Rawle D Lewis *Junior Bevil* • Malik Yoba *Yul Brenner* • John Candy *Irving Blitzer* • Raymond J Barry *Kurt Hemphill* • Peter Outerbridge *Josef Grool* • Paul Coeur *Roger* ■ *Dir* Jon Turteltaub • *Scr* Michael Goldberg, Tommy Swerdlow, Lynn Siefert, from a story by Lynn Siefert, Michael Ritchie

The Cool Surface ★★★ 18

Thriller 1993 · US · Colour · 88mins

This erotic thriller enjoyed a successful life on video, particularly when it was discovered that Teri Hatcher, the star of TV's *The New Adventures of Superman*, takes her clothes off. That said, this is a stylish, classy and faintly disturbing drama. Robert Patrick is the shy writer who finds reality and fiction becoming dangerously mixed when he gets involved with his beautiful neighbour (Hatcher). JF [VIDEO]

Robert Patrick *Jarvis Scott* • Teri Hatcher *Dani Payson* • Matt McCoy *Chazz Stone* • Ian Buchanan *Terrence* ■ *Dir/Scr* Erik Anjou

The Cool World ★★★★

Drama 1963 · US · BW · 105mins

A semi-underground movie and a near-classic, *The Cool World* depicts the lives of street gangs in the black ghetto of Harlem. Director Shirley Clarke had been born into affluent Park Avenue society and seemed destined to be a choreographer before she started making movies. Her first feature, *The Connection*, dealt frankly with heroin addiction, and this, her second, has the same documentary style and poetic rawness. Using non-professional actors, it shows life as it is lived (and lost) on the streets, with jazz and compassion but without condescension. It became an international art house hit. AT

Hampton Clanton *Duke* • Carl Lee *Priest* • Yolanda Rodriguez *Luanee* • Clarence Williams III *Blood* • Marilyn Cox *Miss Dewpoint* • Georgia Burke *Grandma* • Gloria Foster *Mrs Custis* • Bostic Felton *Rod* ■ *Dir* Shirley Clarke • *Scr* Shirley Clarke, Carl Lee, from the play by Robert Rossen, Warren Miller, from the novel by Warren Miller

Cool World ★★ 15

Part-animated comedy fantasy
1992 · US · Colour · 97mins

Gabriel Byrne is the creator of the comic *Cool World*, who discovers that his fictional creation – *femme fatale* Holli Would (voiced by Kim Basinger) – actually exists.She wants to be real; all that stands in her way is Brad Pitt, the human detective of the cartoon world. Although director Ralph Bakshi has come up with some stunning animated characters, they are not always seamlessly integrated with their live-action counterparts, and the cast hardly looks comfortable with the confusing, unfunny script. JF. Contains some violence and swearing. [VIDEO] DVD

Kim Basinger *Holli Would* • Gabriel Byrne *Jack Deebs* • Brad Pitt *Detective Frank Harris* • Michele Abrams *Jennifer Malley* • Janni Brenn-Lowen *Mom Harris* • William Frankfather *Cop* • Greg Collins *Cop* • Murray Podwal *Store patron* ■ *Dir* Ralph Bakshi • *Scr* Mark Victor, Michael Grais, Larry Gross, from a story by Ralph Bakshi, Frank Mancuso Jr • *Animation* Bruce Woodside

The Cooler ★★★★ 15

Romantic drama 2002 · US · Colour · 97mins

Is luck a product of fate or psychology? That's the question posed by director Wayne Kramer's wonderfully quirky film in which unlucky William H Macy is employed by casino manager Alec Baldwin (deservedly Oscar-nominated) to make high rollers to lose, simply by his presence. But when he falls in love with waitress Maria Bello, Macy's "cooling" abilities subside. By turn a tender love story about two lost souls finding their perfect match, a lament for the fading glamour of Rat Pack-era Las Vegas and a vaguely mystical parable about chance and destiny, this sexually frank tale is consistently smart, amusing and intriguing. AJ. Contains violence, swearing and sex scenes. [VIDEO] DVD

William H Macy *Bernie Lootz* • Maria Bello *Natalie Belisario* • Alec Baldwin *Shelly Kaplow* • Shawn Hatosy *Mikey* • Ron Livingston *Larry Sokolov* • Paul Sorvino *Buddy Stafford* • Estella Warren *Charlene* • Arthur J Nascarella [Arthur Nascarella] *Nicky "Fingers" Bonnatto* ■ *Dir* Wayne Kramer • *Scr* Frank Hannah, Wayne Kramer

A Cooler Climate ★★★ 15

Drama 1999 · US · Colour · 95mins

Revelling in the opportunity to demonstrate their contrasting acting styles, Sally Field and Judy Davis each earned an Emmy nomination for their work in Susan Seidelman's assertive TV adaptation of Zena Collier's bestseller. Guilty about the affair that ended her 26-year marriage, Field accepts a housekeeping post in a Maine sea town and soon seeks solace from Davis's fastidious snootiness in the arms of artist Winston Rekert. Seidelman refuses to succumb to touchy-feely platitudes and keeps the tone bullish, while steering her eager divas away from overt scene-stealing. DP [VIDEO]

Judy Davis *Paula* • Sally Field *Iris* • Winston Rekert *Jack* • Jerry Wasserman *Leo* • Carly Pope *Beth* ■ *Dir* Susan Seidelman • *Scr* Marsha Norman, from the novel by Zena Collier

Cooperstown ★★★★

Sports drama 1993 · US · Colour · 100mins

Even if your usual reaction to the word "sport" is to reach for the remote, think twice with this superior TV movie. You don't need to know much about baseball to enjoy the performances of Alan Arkin and Graham Greene in this wisecracking comedy drama about memory, friendship and regret. Having never forgiven recently deceased catcher Greene for the play that cost their team a big game, Arkin's forgotten pitcher sets out for the Cooperstown Hall of Fame to set the record straight. Beautifully written by playwright Lee Blessing, the banter between Arkin and Greene is as sharp as it's priceless. DP

Alan Arkin *Harry Willette* • Ed Begley Jr *Dave Cormeer* • Josh Charles *Jody* • Paul Dooley *Sid Wiggins* • Graham Greene (2) *Raymond Maracle* • Charles Haid *Little Eddie McVee* ■ *Dir* Charles Haid • *Scr* Lee Blessing

Le Cop ★★★★ 18

Comedy 1985 · Fr · Colour · 102mins

The wonderful Philippe Noiret is the French equivalent to Walter Matthau or an over-lunched great dane. Here he stars as a Parisian cop who lives with a tart in Montmartre, bets on the gee-gees, readily accepts bribes and buys lavish meals with the ill-gotten gains. More smalltime crook than cop, in fact, especially when he inducts his straightlaced rookie partner Thierry Lhermitte into the joys of crime. Noiret makes this skate along the moral edge, a balancing act to marvel at. AT. In French with English subtitles.

Philippe Noiret *René* • Thierry Lhermitte *François* • Régine *Simone* • Grace De Capitani *Natacha* • Julien Guiomar *Bloret* • Pierre Frag *Pierrot* • Claude Brosset *Inspector Vidal* • Albert Simono *Inspector LeBlanc* ■ *Dir* Claude Zidi • *Scr* Claude Zidi, Didier Kaminka

Cop ★★★★ 18

Crime thriller 1988 · US · Colour · 105mins

James Woods gives a dazzling, dangerous performance here and lifts what could have been merely another variation on the *Dirty Harry* theme into a different league altogether. Woods plays an obsessive homicide detective, bordering on the psychotic, who becomes convinced there is a serial killer on the loose in Los Angeles. The only common link appears to be feminist book shop manager Lesley Ann Warren. Director James B Harris fails to capture the twisted sickness of James Ellroy's source novel, but more than compensates by cranking up the tension. JF. Contains swearing, violence and sex scenes.

James Woods *Lloyd Hopkins* • Lesley Ann Warren *Kathleen McCarthy* • Charles Durning *Dutch Pelz* • Charles Haid *Whitey Haines* • Raymond J Barry *Fred Gaffney* • Randi Brooks *Joanie Pratt* • Steven Lambert *Bobby Franco* • Christopher Wynne *Jack Gibbs* ■ *Dir* James B Harris • *Scr* James B Harris, from the novel *Blood on the Moon* by James Ellroy

Le Cop II ★★★ 15

Comedy drama 1989 · Fr · Colour · 102mins

Claude Zidi's *Le Cop* was a huge hit in France and nabbed the nation's top film award, the César. A sequel was therefore inevitable, requiring Philippe Noiret and Thierry Lhermitte to reprise their roles as the dirty cop and his idealistic young apprentice. The story revolves around the latter's decision to go straight – an appalling prospect for his partner, who takes bribes and drugs race horses. Once again the low-life of Paris is beautifully observed. In 2003, Zidi made a belated second sequel, *Part-Time Cop*. AT. In French with English subtitles.

Philippe Noiret *René* • Thierry Lhermitte *François* • Guy Marchand *Felix Brisson* • Line Renaud *Simone* • Grace De Capitani *Natacha* • Michel Aumont *Commissioner Bloret* • Jean-Pierre Castaldi *Guy Portal* • Jean-Claude Brialy *Banker* ■ *Dir* Claude Zidi • *Scr* Claude Zidi, Simon Michael, Didier Kaminka

Cop and a Half ★ PG

Comedy thriller 1993 · US · Colour · 88mins

This feeble comedy thriller is the perfect yardstick for measuring just how far Burt Reynolds had fallen from grace since his peak in the 1970s. It wastes the talents of a star normally at ease with such frivolity, and the efforts of the rest of the cast are sunk by a heavy script and ponderous direction from former *Happy Days* star Henry Winkler. JM. Contains swearing and violence. DVD

Burt Reynolds *Nick McKenna* • Norman D Golden II *Devon Butler* • Ruby Dee *Rachel* • Holland Taylor *Captain Rubio* • Ray Sharkey *Fountain* • Sammy Hernandez *Raymond* • Frank Sivero *Chu* • Rocky Giordani *Quintero* ■ *Dir* Henry Winkler • *Scr* Arne Olsen

Cop au Vin ★★★★ 15

Drama 1984 · Fr · Colour · 104mins

There's usually a slap-up meal in every Chabrol movie, so how typical of him to name one after a cornerstone of French cuisine, *Poulet au Vinaigre*, but the English title is even wittier. The story involves a contentious property deal, a clutch of corpses, a postman and his crippled mother, played by Stéphane Audran. Yet the movie is dominated by Jean Poiret, who is an out-of-town detective with a nose for a suspect and the stomach for a big dinner. As ever, the combination of Chabrol's mordant tone and a certain technical flair produces a delectable dish. A sequel, *Inspector Lavardin* followed in 1986, with Poiret reprising his role. AT. In French with English subtitles.

Jean Poiret *Inspector Lavardin* • Stéphane Audran *Mme Cuno* • Michel Bouquet *Hubert Lavoisier* • Jean Topart *Philippe Morasseau* • Lucas Belvaux *Louis Cuno* • Pauline Lafont *Henriette Uriel* ■ *Dir* Claude Chabrol • *Scr* Dominique Roulet, Claude Chabrol, from the novel *Une Mort en Trop* by Dominique Roulet

Cop Land ★★★★ 18

Police drama 1997 · US · Colour · 110mins

This is a real change of pace for Sylvester Stallone, in a touching role as an out-of-shape New Jersey cop with a hearing disability and no self-esteem, who uncovers police corruption among his friends. Stallone gives it his all (including a dramatic weight gain for the role) and is easily the match of the terrific cast, which includes Robert De Niro, Harvey Keitel and a really nasty Ray Loitta. Writer/director James Mangold's urban western succumbs to a few clumsy contrivances, but the quality of acting and a riveting climax are recommendation enough. JC. Contains swearing, violence, nudity. DVD

Sylvester Stallone *Sheriff Freddy Heflin* • Robert De Niro *Moe Tilden* • Harvey Keitel *Ray Donlan* • Ray Liotta *Gary Figgis* • Peter Berg *Joey Randone* • Janeane Garofalo *Deputy Cindy Betts* • Robert Patrick *Jack Rucker* • Michael Rapaport *Murray Babitch* • Annabella Sciorra *Liz Randone* • Cathy Moriarty *Rose Donlan* ■ *Dir/Scr* James Mangold

Copacabana ★ U

Musical comedy 1947 · US · BW · 91mins

A staggeringly unscintillating pairing of two stars whose careers were all behind them: the great Groucho Marx and Carmen Miranda, who has difficulty accommodating her usual headgear on this cheapie's pathetic budget. Unless you're a fan of the stars, this turkey's a non-starter. TS

Groucho Marx *Lionel Q Devereaux* • Carmen Miranda *Carmen Novarro/Fifi* • Steve Cochran *Steve Hunt* • Gloria Jean *Anne* • Ralph Sanford *Liggett* • Andy Russell ■ *Dir* Alfred E Green • *Scr* Laslo Vadnay, Alan Boretz, Howard Harris, Sydney P Zelinka, from a story by Laslo Vadnay

Copper Canyon ★★★

Western 1950 · US · Colour · 83mins

1940s beauty Hedy Lamarr had just made something of a comeback in the blockbuster *Samson and Delilah* when Paramount put her in this intriguing western, set just after the Civil War and directed by John Farrow. Beautiful colour photography by Oscar-winning Charles Lang enhances the action, while Ray Milland is well cast as a Confederate officer working undercover to foil crooks out to exploit festering north-south antagonisms. TV

Ray Milland *Johnny Carter* • Hedy Lamarr *Lisa Roselle* • Macdonald Carey *Lane Travis* • Mona Freeman *Caroline Desmond* • Harry Carey Jr *Lt Ord* • Frank Faylen *Mullins* ■ *Dir* John Farrow • *Scr* Jonathan Latimer, from a story by Richard English

Cops and Robbers ★★★

Crime drama 1973 · US · Colour · 88mins

This rattling crime caper is taken at such a lick by director Aram Avakian that you don't notice the inconsistencies and contrivances in the plot. Cliff Gorman and Joseph Bologna give winning performances as a couple of New York cops who use a parade for returning astronauts as cover for an audacious Wall Street raid. The frantic action is given extra zip by the splendid score, composed by Michel Legrand with a little help from Ennio Morricone. DP

Cliff Gorman *Tom* • Joseph Bologna *Joe* • Dick Ward [Richard Ward] *Paul Jones* • Shepperd Strudwick *Eastpoole* • Ellen Holly *Mrs Wells* • John Ryan [John P Ryan] *Patsy O'Neill* • Nino Ruggeri *Mr Joe* ■ *Dir* Aram Avakian • *Scr* Donald E Westlake, from his novel

Cops and Robbersons ★★ PG

Comedy 1994 · US · Colour · 88mins

Jack Palance is the grouchy cop on surveillance duty, who is forced to move in with dysfunctional suburbanites the Robbersons, headed up by TV cop-show fan Chevy Chase. Chase, in amiable buffoon mode, makes a nice foil for Palance and there are creditable supporting turns from Robert Davi and Dianne Wiest, but director Michael Ritchie's heart doesn't appear to be in it. JF

Chevy Chase *Norman Robberson* • Jack Palance *Jack Stone* • Dianne Wiest *Helen Robberson* • Robert Davi *Osborn* • David Barry Gray *Tony Moore* • Jason James Richter *Kevin Robberson* • Fay Masterson *Cindy Robberson* ■ *Dir* Michael Ritchie • *Scr* Bernie Somers

Copycat ★★★★ 18

Thriller 1995 · US · Colour · 122mins

In this inventive, stylish and gripping thriller, tough detective Holly Hunter teams up with agoraphobic criminal psychologist Sigourney Weaver in the hunt for a serial killer duplicating the crimes of his most notorious predecessors. Thanks to the unbearable suspense created by Jon Amiel's imaginative direction – the bathroom-set climax is a crackerjack shocker – the super-smart script and the confident performances of the two stellar leads, this mimic murder mystery is one of the best crafted chillers of the 1990s. AJ. Contains swearing and violence DVD

Sigourney Weaver *Helen Hudson* • Holly Hunter *MJ Monahan* • Dermot Mulroney *Ruben Goetz* • William McNamara *Peter Foley* • Harry Connick Jr *Daryll Lee Cullum* • Will Patton *Nicoletti* • John Rothman *Andy* • Shannon O'Hurley *Susan Schiffer* ■ *Dir* Jon Amiel • *Scr* Ann Biderman, David Madsen

Coquette ★★★

Melodrama 1929 · US · BW · 75mins

Back in the silent era, Mary Pickford's little-girl mannerisms earned her the title of "The World's Sweetheart". This was her first talkie, in which she plays a Southern belle whose flirtation with handsome beau Johnny Mack Brown gets her into big trouble. Pickford won an Oscar for the film, though it was really in recognition of her previous work; the public weren't quite ready to see her as a Deep South damsel. TH

Mary Pickford *Norma Besant* • Johnny Mack Brown *Michael Jeffery* • Matt Moore *Stanley Wentworth* • John St Polis *Dr John Besant* ■ *Dir* Sam Taylor • *Scr* Sam Taylor, John Grey, Allen McNeil, from the play by George Abbott, Anne P Bridges

The Core ★★★ 12

Science-fiction action thriller 2002 · US/UK · Colour · 129mins

Having exhausted the more traditional threats to human existence, the Hollywood disaster movie now moves on to positively esoteric cataclysms: in this case the Earth's core ceasing to rotate. While international landmarks explode and surface-dwellers face terminal sunburn, a secret team of top scientists builds a burrowing machine designed to penetrate the core and set it spinning again. This is by-the-numbers movie-making, but it has enough excitingly staged set pieces to offset the daft plot. AS DVD

Aaron Eckhart *Dr Josh Keyes* • Hilary Swank *Major Rebecca "Beck" Childs* • Delroy Lindo *Dr Ed "Braz" Brazzelton* • Stanley Tucci *Dr Conrad Zimsky* • DJ Qualls *Taz "Rat" Finch* • Richard Jenkins *Gen Thomas Purcell* • Tcheky Karyo *Dr Serge Leveque* • Bruce Greenwood *Commander Robert Iverson* • Alfre Woodard *Talma "Stick" Stickley* ■ *Dir* Jon Amiel • *Scr* Cooper Layne, John Rogers

Corky ★ U

Drama 1972 · US · Colour · 88mins

Robert Blake, a grease monkey from the Deep South who is more in love with his car than his long-suffering wife (Charlotte Rampling), becomes insanely jealous when she gets a job. There's a fight here and a car chase there, but no. Bruce Geller was so incensed at the way his central character was treated that he had his screenwriting credit removed, though he was still billed as producer. FL

Robert Blake *Corky* • Charlotte Rampling *Corky's wife* • Patrick O'Neal *Randy* • Christopher Connelly *Billy* • Pamela Payton-Wright *Rhonda* • Ben Johnson *Boland* • Laurence Luckinbill *Wayne* • Paul Stevens *Tobin Hayes* ■ *Dir* Leonard Horn • *Scr* Eugene Price, Bruce Geller (uncredited)

Corky Romano ★ 12

Comedy 2001 · US · Colour · 82mins

In this is a lazy, lame Mob comedy, Chris Kattan plays the forgotten son of Mob boss Peter Falk, who is asked to infiltrate the FBI to retrieve some damning evidence against the family. Despite his persistent bungling he soon becomes regarded as a super-agent and finds his loyalties divided. Kattan mugs his way through the feeble slapstick set pieces and the talented supporting cast tries not to look embarrassed. JF DVD

Chris Kattan *Corky Romano* • Vinessa Shaw *Agent Kate Russo* • Peter Falk *Pops* • Peter Berg *Paulie* • Chris Penn *Peter* • Fred Ward

Leo Corrigan • Richard Roundtree *Howard Schuster* ■ *Dir* Rob Pritts • *Scr* David Garrett, Jason Ward

The Corn Is Green ★★★

Period drama 1945 · US · BW · 113mins

Bette Davis stars as legendary spinster schoolteacher Lilly Moffat in a very Warner Bros version of Emlyn Williams's distinguished play. Unfortunately, this film seriously betrays its theatrical origins, not just in its hokey plot about Davis trying to send her star pupil (John Dall, far too callow) to Oxford, but also in its relentlessly phoney Hollywood studio/Welsh village setting. Nevertheless, Davis is mighty fine and the supporting cast is excellent, particularly Nigel Bruce as the local squire. TS

Bette Davis *Lilly Moffat* • John Dall *Morgan Evans* • Joan Lorring *Bessie Watty* • Nigel Bruce *Squire* • Rhys Williams *Mr Jones* • Rosalind Ivan *Mrs Watty* • Mildred Dunnock *Miss Ronberry* • Arthur Shields *Will Davis* ■ *Dir* Irving Rapper • *Scr* Casey Robinson, Frank Cavett, from the play by Emlyn Williams

Cornered ★★★ U

Crime drama 1945 · US · BW · 62mins

This is a pleasant little toughie, not quite a thriller and a shade too bright for a *film noir*, and directed with consummate skill by Edward Dmytryk. Powell here continued to erase all memories of his Busby Berkeley days at Warners as he delivers a high-octane performance, chasing down his wife's murderer in Second World War Argentina, in a Buenos Aires peopled with veteran character actors. The women are a shade uninteresting, but Powell's tough demeanour more than compensates. TS

Dick Powell *Gerard* • Walter Slezak *Incza* • Micheline Cheirel *Madame Jarnac* • Nina Vale *Senora Camargo* • Edgar Barrier *DuBois* • Morris Carnovsky *Santana* • Steven Geray *Senor Camargo* • Jack La Rue [Jack LaRue] *Diego* ■ *Dir* Edward Dmytryk • *Scr* John Paxton, from a story by John Wexley, from a title by Ben Hecht

The Corporation ★★★★ PG

Documentary 2003 · Can · Colour · 144mins

Mark Achbar and Jennifer Abbott's epic documentary tackles everything from the constitutional protection afforded American companies to the bullying tactics of multinationals and the nag factor built into children's television advertising. The anti-capitalist agenda is readily evident, but with executives from the likes of Shell and Goodyear so willing to shoot themselves in the foot, the eloquence of the likes of Noam Chomsky, Naomi Klein and Michael Moore is almost redundant. The corruption, exploitation and eco-ignorance of big business has never been so damningly exposed. DP DVD

Dir Mark Achbar, Jennifer Abbott • *Scr* Joel Bakan, Harold Crooks (narration), Mark Achbar (narration), from the non-fiction book *The Corporation: the Pathological Pursuit of Profit and Power* by Joel Bakan

The Corpse ★★★★

Horror 1969 · UK · Colour · 93mins

In this effectively spooky thriller, a tyrannical stockbroker (Michael Gough at his beastliest) torments his wife and daughter to such a degree that they decide to murder him. Those who have seen *Les Diaboliques* will recognise the remainder of the plot. Writer Olaf Pooley (who also plays a nosey neighbour) does not play fair when it comes to the explanation, but director Viktors Ritelis wrings such tension out of every shocking development that one is prepared to forgive the underhandedness. DM

Michael Gough *Walter Eastwood* • Yvonne Mitchell *Edith Eastwood* • Sharon Gurney *Jane Eastwood* • Simon Gough *Rupert Eastwood* • Olaf Pooley *Reid* • David Butler *Gregson* • Mary Hignett *Mrs Roberts* ■ *Dir* Viktors Ritelis • *Scr* Olaf Pooley

Corridors of Blood ★★★ 15

Horror drama 1962 · UK · BW · 82mins

Surgeon Boris Karloff is forced to sign false death certificates when he gets involved with two loathsome grave-robbers (Christopher Lee and Francis de Wolff) during his work on an experimental anaesthetic. Boasting beautiful black-and-white photography, this 19th-century-set tale has a great combination of gas-lit melodrama, pseudo-historic science and body-snatcher gruesomeness. This marked the first time Karloff and Lee worked together. AJ

Boris Karloff *Dr Bolton* • Betta St John *Susan* • Christopher Lee *Resurrection Joe* • Finlay Currie *Supt Matheson* • Adrienne Corri *Rachel* ■ *Dir* Robert Day • *Scr* Jean Scott Rogers • *Cinematographer* Geoffrey Faithfull

Corrina, Corrina ★★★ U

Romantic drama
1994 · US · Colour · 110mins

Ray Liotta here provides the lone parental contrivance that enables housekeeper Whoopi Goldberg to get to grips with Tina Majorino, a sad little seven-year-old who has stopped speaking since the death of her mother. Goldberg and Majorino make one of the most appealing double acts of recent years. As the action is set in 1959, there are also some barbed comments about interracial love and the obstacles facing educated black women. DP DVD

Whoopi Goldberg *Corrina Washington* • Ray Liotta *Manny Singer* • Tina Majorino *Molly Singer* • Wendy Crewson *Jenny Davis* • Larry Miller *Sid* • Erica Yohn *Grandma Eva* • Jenifer Lewis *Jevina* • Joan Cusack *Jonesy* • Harold Sylvester *Frank* • Don Ameche *Grandpa Harry* ■ *Dir/Scr* Jessie Nelson

The Corrupt Ones ★★★

Thriller 1966 · Fr/It/W Ger · Colour · 92mins

This old-fashioned quest adventure is so sexist and racially dismissive that it wouldn't pass muster today. But, back in the mid-1960s, two-fisted mavericks were all the rage and Robert Stack's gung-ho photographer does form an accidental link between Allan Quartermain and Indiana Jones, having been presented with an ancient Chinese medallion containing clues to the location of an emperor's treasure trove. Elke Sommer has less to do as his pouting sidekick, but the action is pacy and slickly staged. DP

Robert Stack *Cliff Wilder* • Elke Sommer *Lily Mancini* • Nancy Kwan *Tina* • Christian Marquand *Joey Brandon* • Maurizio Arena *Danny Mancini* ■ *Dir* James Hill • *Scr* Brian Clemens

Corruption ★★★

Horror 1968 · UK · Colour · 90mins

Unanimously slated by the press as cheap and nasty when it was first shown, this horrific thriller is actually a minor masterpiece of *Grand Guignol* and under-rated director Robert Hartford-Davis's best film by far. It stars Peter Cushing as a surgeon, who goes to desperate lengths to get the pituitary glands he needs to restore fiancée Sue Lloyd's disfigured face. Cushing and Lloyd both throw themselves into their roles with gusto and are aided by a fast-moving script. Released in other countries as *Laser Killer*, though with more graphic material, the final scene remains one of the most demented ever filmed. DM

Peter Cushing *Sir John Rowan* • Sue Lloyd *Lynn Nolan* • Trevor Trevarthen *Steve Harris* • Kate O'Mara *Val Nolan* • David Lodge *Groper* • Anthony Booth *Mike Orme* ■ *Dir* Robert Hartford-Davis • *Scr* Donald Ford, Derek Ford

The Corruptor ★★ 18

Action crime thriller
1999 · US · Colour · 105mins

With muscle man Mark Wahlberg and cool Hong Kong star Chow Yun-Fat on board, you'd expect this tale of police corruption, Chinese gangs and murder in New York's Chinatown to be action-packed. Instead, this is a surprisingly plodding and confusing thriller that's low on interesting set pieces. James Foley's direction is uninspired and, while both stars have charisma to spare, they're bogged down by the unnecessarily convoluted plot. JB. Contains violence.

Chow Yun-Fat *Nick Chen* • Mark Wahlberg *Danny Wallace* • Ric Young *Henry Lee* • Paul Ben-Victor *Schabacker* • Andrew Pang *Willy Ung* • Byron Mann *Bobby Vu* • Elizabeth Lindsey *Louise Deng* • Brian Cox *Sean Wallace* ■ *Dir* James Foley • *Scr* Robert Pucci

The Corsican Brothers ★★★ U

Swashbuckling adventure
1941 · US · BW · 95mins

Douglas Fairbanks Jr summons up some of the swashbuckling bravado associated with his father in this adaptation of the Alexandre Dumas story. Fairbanks gets the dual role of separated Siamese twins, Mario and Lucien – one rich, the other poor – who reunite to seek out those who killed their relatives. It dawdles in places, Akim Tamiroff is more laughable than villainous and it lacks a proper heroine. Yet Fairbanks is worth watching, if only for his imitation of his father's mannerisms. AT

Douglas Fairbanks Jr *Mario Franchi/Lucien Franchi* • Ruth Warrick *Isabelle* • Akim Tamiroff *Colorra* • HB Warner *Dr Paoli* • Henry Wilcoxon *Count Franchi* • J Carrol Naish *Lorenzo* ■ *Dir* Gregory Ratoff • *Scr* George Bruce, from the novel by Alexandre Dumas

Corvette K-225 ★★ U

Second World War drama
1943 · US · BW · 98mins

This wartime flag-waver is an unabashed tribute to the crews of the Corvettes, the nimble craft that escorted freighters across the Atlantic, taking on the U-boats that preyed on them. Randolph Scott is the skipper who falls in love with Ella Raines, whose brother is on Scott's ship and whose other brother has already been killed in action. Below decks, Robert Mitchum takes a minor role in one of the 18 movies he made in 1943. AT

Randolph Scott *Lt Cmdr MacClain* • James Brown (1) *Paul Cartwright* • Ella Raines *Joyce Cartwright* • Barry Fitzgerald *Stooky O'Meara* • Andy Devine *Walsh* • Walter Sande *Evans* • Richard Lane *Admiral* • James Flavin *Gardner* • Robert Mitchum *Shepard* ■ *Dir* Richard Rosson • *Scr* John Rhodes Sturdy

Corvette Summer ★★★

Comedy adventure drama
1978 · US · Colour · 104mins

The directing debut of Matthew Robbins is a youth movie very much in the mould of *American Graffiti*. Mark Hamill, then fresh from the original *Star Wars*, stars as a young man who spends most of his time fondling, stroking and polishing the love of his life: a restored and customised Chevrolet Corvette. When the car is stolen, Hamill goes looking for it with the help of trainee prostitute Annie Potts. Robbins's directing career proved to be fairly undistinguished after this promising first feature. AT

Mark Hamill *Kent Dantley* • Annie Potts *Vanessa* • Eugene Roche *Ed McGrath* • Kim Milford *Wayne Lowry* • Richard McKenzie *Principal* • William Bryant *Police PR* • Philip Bruns *Gil* ■ *Dir* Matthew Robbins • *Scr* Hal Barwood, Matthew Robbins

Cosh Boy ★★★

Crime drama 1952 · UK · BW · 72mins

Packed with incidents that scandalised middle-class moralists, Lewis Gilbert's film claimed to be a realistic portrait of juvenile delinquency. It may have seemed daring at the time, but today this overwrought study of alienation and rebellion looks tame and stands only as a testament to an innocent age when people were more easily shocked. James Kenney seems the most gentle thug ever to terrorise the streets of London, but Joan Collins comes closer to life as the nice girl doomed to a life of misery. DP

James Kenney *Roy Walsh* • Joan Collins *Rene Collins* • Betty Ann Davies *Elsie Walsh* • Robert Ayres *Bob Stevens* • Hermione Baddeley *Mrs Collins* • Hermione Gingold *Queenie* • Nancy Roberts *Gran Walsh* • Stanley Escane *Pete* ■ *Dir* Lewis Gilbert • *Scr* Lewis Gilbert, Vernon Harris, from the play *Master Crook* by Bruce Walker

Cosi ★★★

Comedy 1996 · Aus · Colour · 100mins

Slacker Ben Mendelsohn takes a job as dramatic director at an asylum in this typically broad Australian comedy. One of the inmates is obsessed with staging the Mozart opera *Cosi Fan Tutte*, which Mendelsohn directs against all the odds and the wishes of the asylum's administrators. Mark Joffe's film is quite funny most of the way through, but it veers into cheap sentimentality towards the end. ST. Contains swearing.

Ben Mendelsohn *Lewis* • Barry Otto *Roy* • Toni Collette *Julie* • Aden Young *Nick* • Rachel Griffiths *Lucy* • Pamela Rabe *Ruth* • Colin Friels *Errol* ■ *Dir* Mark Joffe • *Scr* Louis Nowra, from his play

The Cosmic Man ★ U

Science fiction 1959 · US · BW · 69mins

John Carradine is the mysterious creature from another planet who arrives on Earth in a huge weightless globe. His presence unleashes a debate between the military authorities who want to blow him up, and the scientific establishment who want to keep him alive. This dismal science-fiction programme-filler is mercifully short in length and equally short of action and ideas. RK

Bruce Bennett *Dr Karl Sorenson* • John Carradine *Cosmic man* • Angela Greene *Kathy Grant* • Paul Langton *Colonel Mathews* • Scotty Morrow *Ken Grant* • Lyn Osborn *Sergeant Gray* • Walter Maslow *Dr Richie* ■ *Dir* Herbert Greene • *Scr* Arthur C Pierce

The Cossacks ★ U

Historical drama
1959 · It/Fr · Colour · 113mins

Edmund Purdom was a sort of downmarket Tony Curtis who went to Hollywood before eventually settling for Italian rubbish like this and a British TV series called *Sword of Freedom*. Purdom kept a straight face for this costume epic set in Imperial Russia, despite moments that surpass Monty Python for silliness. AT. Italian dialogue dubbed into English.

Edmund Purdom *Shamil* • John Drew Barrymore *Giamal* • Georgia Moll [Giorgia Moll] *Tatiana* • Pierre Brice *Boris* • Elena Zareschi *Patimat* ■ *Dir* Giorgio Rivalta, Victor Tourjansky • *Scr* Victor Tourjansky

Cottage to Let ★★★ U

Second World War thriller
1941 · UK · BW · 86mins

The American release title *Bombsight Stolen* is a clue to what Alfred Hitchcock would call the MacGuffin (or plot device) that drives this lively wartime propaganda piece from director Anthony Asquith. The story of a Nazi kidnap plot set in the wilds of Scotland is pretty much par for the course, but what sets this picture apart is the truly extraordinary cast. Michael Wilding and John Mills have to settle for supporting roles behind Leslie Banks and Alastair Sim, but stealing everyone's thunder is debutant George Cole (a protégé of Sim's) as the cockney evacuee who becomes a hero. DP

Leslie Banks *John Barrington* • Alastair Sim *Charles Dimble* • John Mills *Lieutenant George Perrey* • Jeanne de Casalis *Mrs Barrington* • Carla Lehmann *Helen Barrington* • George Cole *Ronald Mittsby* • Michael Wilding *Alan Trentley* ■ *Dir* Anthony Asquith • *Scr* Anatole de Grunwald, JOC Orton, from the play by Geoffrey Kerr

The Cotton Club ★★★ 15

Period drama 1984 · US · Colour · 123mins

Richard Gere gets a chance to reveal his cornet-playing abilities in this tale of music and the Mob in toe-tappin' 1920s Harlem. Sadly, Gere's musical talents far outshine his performance, which seems almost trance-like in places. The blame must lie with director Francis Coppola, who, in expending his energy on visual clout and showbiz set pieces (some of which are fabulous), under-directs his actors and forgets about the plot. Nevertheless, Bob Hoskins as the club owner and Fred Gwynne as his henchman certainly make their mark, while the Duke Ellington soundtrack is sheer bliss. JM. Contains violence, swearing and nudity. DVD

Richard Gere *Dixie Dwyer* • Gregory Hines *Sandman Williams* • Diane Lane *Vera Cicero* • Bob Hoskins *Owney Madden* • Lonette McKee *Lila Rose Oliver* • James Remar *Dutch Schultz* • Nicolas Cage *Vincent Dwyer* • Allen Garfield *Abbadabba Berman* • Fred Gwynne *Frenchy Demange* • Gwen Verdon *Tish Dwyer* • Larry Fishburne [Laurence Fishburne] *Bumpy Rhodes* ■ *Dir* Francis Coppola [Francis Ford Coppola] • *Scr* William Kennedy, Francis Ford Coppola, from a story by William Kennedy, Francis Ford Coppola, Mario Puzo, from a pictorial history by James Haskins

Cotton Comes to Harlem ★★★★

Crime comedy thriller
1970 · US · Colour · 96mins

Although a respected actor and civil rights activist, Ossie Davis put much more than his reputation on the line when he directed this abrasive crime comedy on the streets of Harlem. Residents and militant campaigners alike were appalled that he should choose to further the cause with such a seemingly flippant picture. But the script gives Raymond St Jacques plenty of scope to make social statements as he and Godfrey Cambridge investigate preacher Calvin Lockhart's dodgy pan-African association. A sequel, *Come Back Charleston Blue*, followed this huge commercial success. DP

Godfrey Cambridge *Gravedigger Jones* • Raymond St Jacques *Coffin Ed Johnson* • Calvin Lockhart *Rev Deke O'Malley* • Judy Pace *Iris* • Redd Foxx *Uncle Bud* • Cleavon Little *Lo Boy* ■ *Dir* Ossie Davis • *Scr* Ossie Davis, Arnold Perl, from a novel by Chester Himes

Cotton Mary ★★ 15

Period drama 1999 · UK · Colour · 118mins

This handsomely mounted study of the socio-racial rifts that divided India in the years after Independence proves once again that, while Ismail Merchant is a producer of exemplary taste, his approach to direction stifles potentially interesting ideas with ponderous performances and rarified aestheticism. Co-director Madhur Jaffrey's snobbish Anglo-Indian nurse overwhelms a drama already awash with unsympathetic characters, notably depressed Greta Scacchi and James Wilby as her adulterous husband. DP

Greta Scacchi *Lily MacIntosh* • Madhur Jaffrey *Cotton Mary* • James Wilby *John MacIntosh* • Sarah Badel *Mrs Evans* • Riju Bajaj *Mugs* • Gerson Da Cunha *Doctor Correa* • Joanna David *Mrs Smythe* • Neena Gupta *Blossom* ■ *Dir* Ismail Merchant, Madhur Jaffrey • *Scr* Alexandra Viets

Cotton Queen ★★ U

Comedy 1937 · UK · BW · 84mins

Long regarded as a mere journeyman, German-born director Bernard Vorhaus has enjoyed something of a renaissance of late. This was the last film he made in this country before relocating to Hollywood, although it's hard to see why the studio executives would have been impressed by this underfunded production, a creaky comedy in which mill owner's daughter Mary Lawson goes snooping in a rival's factory and falls for his son. DP

Will Fyffe *Bob Todcastle* • Stanley Holloway *Sam Owen* • Mary Lawson *Joan* • Helen Haye *Margaret Owen* • Jimmy Hanley *Johnny Owen* • Gibson Gowland *Jailor* ■ *Dir* Bernard Vorhaus • *Scr* Louis Golding, Scott Pembroke, from a story by Syd Courtnenay, Barry Peake

The Couch Trip ★★★ 15

Comedy 1988 · US · Colour · 93mins

In this often too slack offering, director Michael Ritchie is thankfully well served by the infectious comic nonsense of Dan Aykroyd, as a mental patient who carries out a nifty scam and becomes a celebrity therapist in LA. It is Aykroyd's wild, high-flying invention that turns this skinny offering into a one-man party at which the star has the most fun. Even Walter Matthau, typically lugubrious and crusty, is dull by comparison. JM. Contains swearing. DVD

Dan Aykroyd *John W Burns Jr* • Walter Matthau *Donald Becker* • Charles Grodin *Dr George Maitlin* • Donna Dixon *Dr Laura Rollins* • Richard Romanus *Harvey Michaels* • Mary Gross *Vera Maitlin* • David Clennon *Dr Lawrence Baird* • Arye Gross *Perry Kovin* • Chevy Chase *Condom father* ■ *Dir* Michael Ritchie • *Scr* Steven Kampmann, Will Porter, Sean Stein, from a novel by Ken Kolb

Counsellor-at-Law ★★★

Drama 1933 · US · BW · 77mins

Adapted by Elmer Rice from his own successful Broadway play, and impeccably directed by William Wyler, the movie details the professional and personal crises that beset a brilliant, self-made Jewish lawyer (John Barrymore) whose future is affected by the surfacing of a past indiscretion. Barrymore gives a compelling performance, with excellent support from Doris Kenyon as his unsympathetic gentile wife and Bebe Daniels as the secretary who loves him. Solid, substantial drama. RK

John Barrymore *George Simon* • Bebe Daniels *Regina Gordon* • Doris Kenyon *Cora Simon* • Onslow Stevens *John P Tedesco* • Isabel Jewell *Bessie Green* • Melvyn Douglas *Roy Darwin* • Thelma Todd *Lillian La Rue* • Marvin Kline *Weinberg* • John Qualen *Breitstein* ■ *Dir* William Wyler • *Scr* Elmer Rice, from his play

Count Dracula ★★ 12

Horror
1970 · Sp/It/W Ger/UK · Colour · 96mins

Fed up by Hammer playing fast and loose with the famous vampire figure, Christopher Lee joined forces with Spanish schlock-meister Jesus Franco to make the one of the most faithful adaptations of Bram Stoker's 1897 novel. The end result falls way short of those good intentions thanks to the low budget, numerous script inconsistencies, camera shadows in full view and Franco's usual deadly direction. AJ. Contains some violence.

Christopher Lee *Dracula* • Herbert Lom *Van Helsing* • Klaus Kinski *Renfield* • Soledad Miranda *Lucy Westenra* • Maria Rohm *Mina Harker* • Fred Williams *Jonathan Harker* • Jack Taylor *Quincy Morris* • Paul Muller *Dr Seward* ■ *Dir* Jesus Franco • *Scr* Jesus Franco, August Finochi, Harry Alan Towers, Carlo Fadda, Milo G Cuccia, Dietmar Behnke, from the novel *Dracula* by Bram Stoker

Count Five and Die ★★★

Second World War spy drama
1957 · UK · BW · 91mins

When plans to peddle false information to the Nazis about the whereabouts of the forthcoming D-Day invasion begin to come unstuck, British intelligence officer Nigel Patrick is made alert to the possibility of their being a traitor in his team. The obvious suspect is glamorous new radio operator Annemarie Düringer, with whom Patrick's second-in-command (Jeffrey Hunter) is in love. Though covering familiar territory that's well past its sell-by date, this is still suspenseful and entertaining. RK

Jeffrey Hunter *Ranson* • Nigel Patrick *Howard* • Anne-Marie Düringer [Annemarie Düringer] *Rolande* • David Kossoff *Mulder* • Claude Kingston *Willem* • Philip Bond *Piet* • Rolf Lefebvre *Faber* • Larry Burns *Martins* • Arthur Gross *Jan* ■ *Dir* Victor Vicas • *Scr* Jack Seddon, David Pursall

The Count of Monte Cristo ★★★★

Period adventure 1934 · US · BW · 113mins

Although written for Fredric March, who pulled out ahead of filming, Robert Donat stamped his mark as the Napoleonic sailor who is framed and imprisoned in the appalling Chateau d'If, supposedly to languish there for the rest of his days. However, he uses his time wisely, coolly plotting to escape and wreak his revenge on those who betrayed him. This handsomely mounted swashbuckler is the best of the adaptations of Alexandre Dumas's celebrated tale and showcases Donat at his charming, romantic best. AT

Robert Donat *Edmond Dantès* • Elissa Landi *Mercedes* • Louis Calhern *Raymond de Villefort Jr* • Sidney Blackmer *Mondego* • Raymond Walburn *Danglars* • OP Heggie *Abbé Faria* • William Farnum *Captain Leclere* ■ *Dir* Rowland V Lee • *Scr* Philip Dunne, Dan Totheroh, Rowland V Lee, from the novel by Alexandre Dumas

The Count of Monte Cristo ★★★ U

Period adventure 1974 · UK · Colour · 98mins

Richard Chamberlain is a sturdy Edmond Dantes in this lavish adaptation of the classic Alexandre Dumas tale about the disguised nobleman who exacts revenge on those who had him imprisoned. Director David Greene struggles with the more static jail sequences, but once the action switches to Paris he makes the most of the plush settings and the period costumes to bring the picture to life. Louis Jourdan does well as De Villefort, but nearly spoiling everything is Tony Curtis who confuses behaving like a star with acting. DP

Richard Chamberlain *Edmond Dantes* • Tony Curtis *Mondego* • Trevor Howard *Abbé Faria* • Louis Jourdan *De Villefort* • Donald Pleasence *Danglars* • Kate Nelligan *Mercedes* ■ *Dir* David Greene • *Scr* Sidney Carroll, from the novel by Alexandre Dumas

The Count of Monte Cristo ★★★ PG

Period adventure
2001 · US/UK/Ire · Colour · 125mins

Kevin Reynolds's stylistic excesses are mostly absent here, to the benefit of this old-fashioned, handsomely mounted version of the enduring adventure. Jim Caviezel plays Edmond Dantès, who, through his own youthful naivety and the devious scheming of his best friend Fernand Mondego (Guy Pearce), is thrown into a desolate island prison. But after 13 years of incarceration, he escapes, adopts a dashing new identity and proceeds to exact his revenge. Caviezel is both credible and sympathetic, while Pearce's sneering rogue avoids falling into caricature. JC DVD

Jim Caviezel *Edmond Dantès* • Guy Pearce *Fernand Mondego* • Richard Harris *Abbé Faria* • James Frain *Villefort* • Dagmara Dominczyk *Mercedes Iguanada* • Michael Wincott *Dorleac* • Luis Guzman *Jacopo* • Helen McCrory *Valentina Villefort* ■ *Dir* Kevin Reynolds • *Scr* Jay Wolpert, from the novel by Alexandre Dumas

The Count of the Old Town ★★★

Comedy 1935 · Swe · BW · 84mins

This film marked Ingrid Bergman's screen debut, although she is pretty much a peripheral character in a freewheeling tour around Stockholm's bohemian quarter. Valdemar Dahlquist topped the bill as the leader of a group of amiable wastrels. Playing a maid in one of their watering holes, Bergman also has some love scenes with Edvin Adolphson, but contemporary critics paid more attention to her puppy fat than her acting. DP. In Swedish with English subtitles.

Valdemar Dahlquist *The Count* • Sigurd Wallen *The Gherkin* • Eric Abrahamsson *Borstis* • Weyler Hildebrand *Detective Goransson* • Artur Cederborgh *Engstrom* • Ingrid Bergman *Elsa Edlund* ■ *Dir* Edvin Adolphson, Sigurd Wallen • *Scr* Arthur Natorp, Siegfried Fischer

Count the Hours ★★

Crime drama 1953 · US · BW · 76mins

When an itinerant farm worker is sentenced to death for murder, his wife and a lawyer, who shows more than a passing interest in her, battle to prove his innocence and bring the true culprit to book. MacDonald Carey, Teresa Wright, John Craven and Dolores Moran (as Carey's rich fiancée) star in an efficient directorial exercise for Don Siegel, who maintains the tension in what is essentially no more than a so-so programme-filler. RK

Macdonald Carey *Doug Madison* • Teresa Wright *Ellen Braden* • John Craven *George Braden* • Dolores Moran *Paula Mitchener* • Edgar Barrier *Gillespie* • Jack Elam *Max Verne* ■ *Dir* Don Siegel • *Scr* Doane R Hoag, Karen De Wolf, from a story by Doane R Hoag

Count Three and Pray ★★★

Drama 1955 · US · Colour · 102mins

This grim, bucolic period drama marked the screen debut of Broadway and TV actress Joanne Woodward, soon-to-be Mrs Paul Newman, as a tough-minded orphan gal caught up in the mayhem caused by new preacher in town Van Heflin, a pastor with a past. Notable today for its early use of CinemaScope, the movie benefits from fine acting from Heflin and Woodward, and a noteworthy typecast villain in Raymond Burr. TS

Van Heflin *Luke Fargo* • Joanne Woodward *Lissy* • Phil Carey [Philip Carey] *Albert Loomis* • Raymond Burr *Yancey Huggins* • Allison Hayes *Georgina Decrais* • Myron Healey *Floyd Miller* ■ *Dir* George Sherman • *Scr* Herb Meadow

Count Your Blessings ★★ U

Comedy 1959 · US · Colour · 102mins

As fatuous as its title, this soft-focus MGM confection has one of those plots that everyone hates: a loathsome child brings together an estranged couple, in this case hard-working Deborah Kerr and perpetually wooden Rossano Brazzi. Jean Negulesco directs this soggy romance, which not even Maurice Chevalier can help. TS

Deborah Kerr *Grace Allingham* • Rossano Brazzi *Charles-Edouard de Valhubert* • Maurice Chevalier *Duc de St Cloud* • Martin Stephens *Sigismond* • Tom Helmore *Hugh Palgrave* ■ *Dir* Jean Negulesco • *Scr* Karl Tunberg, from the novel *The Blessing* by Nancy Mitford

Countdown ★★★★ U

Drama 1968 · US · Colour · 97mins

A fascinating early work from Robert Altman about the planning of a mission to the Moon and its effect on the lives of those involved. There are early signs of what would become Altman trademarks (the large cast; the cool, documentary air) and he coaxes fine, naturalistic performances from James Caan and Robert Duvall as the two astronauts, only one of whom will go on the mission. JF [video]

James Caan *Lee Stegler* • Joanna Moore *Mickey Stegler* • Robert Duvall *Chiz* • Barbara Baxley *Jean* • Charles Aidman *Gus* • Steve Ihnat *Ross* • Michael Murphy *Rick* ■ *Dir* Robert Altman • *Scr* Loring Mandel, from the novel *The Pilgram Project* by Hank Searls

Countdown ★★ 18

Action thriller 1996 · US · Colour · 86mins

A cheap and not particularly cheerful spin on the barmy bomber theme popularised by *Speed*. An almost unrecognisable Lori Petty is the hard-nosed FBI agent on the trail of someone who seems intent on blowing up university lecturers. Director Keoni Waxman fails to hide the deficiencies in both plot and budget. JF [video]

Lori Petty *Sara Davis* • Jason London *Chris Murdoch* • James LeGros *Lieutenant* ■ *Dir/Scr* Keoni Waxman

Counter-Attack ★★★

Second World War drama
1945 · US · BW · 90mins

This worthy piece of pro-Soviet propaganda was one of the productions used to denounce screenwriter John Howard Lawson during Hollywood's postwar communist witch-hunt. It's hardly the most subtle of stories, yet it effectively conveys the bitter enmity that existed between Marxists and Nazis. It also serves as an involving psychological thriller, with Russians Paul Muni and Marguerite Chapman battling for the upper hand with seven enemy soldiers in a besieged factory cellar. DP

Paul Muni *Alexei Kulkov* • Marguerite Chapman *Lisa Elenko* • Larry Parks *Kirichenko* • Harro Meller *Ernemann* • Roman Bohnen *Kostyuk* • George Macready *Colonel Semenov* ■ *Dir* Zoltan Korda • *Scr* John Howard Lawson, from the play by Janet Stevenson, Philip Stevenson, from the play *Pobyeda* by Ilya Vershinin, Mikhail Ruderman

Counterblast ★★

Thriller 1948 · UK · BW · 99mins

Among the first films to consider Nazi experiments into germ warfare, this brisk British thriller boasts the interesting premise of turning a wanted war criminal into an accidental hero. Having killed an Australian doctor to escape a death camp, Mervyn Johns arrives in England to develop a lethal serum. However, a fondness for lab assistant Nova Pilbeam and the growing suspicions of scientist Robert Beatty cause him to rethink his tactics. This was an ambitious picture for its time. DP

Robert Beatty *Dr Rankin* • Mervyn Johns *Dr Bruckner* • Nova Pilbeam *Tracy Shaw* • Margaretta Scott *Sister Johnson* • Sybilla Binder *Martha* ■ *Dir* Paul L Stein • *Scr* Jack Whittingham, from a story by Guy Morgan

The Counterfeit Killer ★★ PG

Crime drama 1968 · US · Colour · 89mins

Joseph Leytes adapted this serviceable crime thriller from his own *The Faceless Man*, a 1966 episode of Chrysler Theatre TV dramas. Its main appeal lies in the casting, as it provides meaty roles for such character stalwarts as Jack Weston (playing a conniving fence) and Joseph Wiseman (a ruthless gang boss). But *Hawaii Five-O* fans will be tuning in to see future star Jack Lord play the government gunman who is ordered to go undercover to crack a counterfeit ring. DP [video]

Jack Lord *Don Owens* • Shirley Knight *Angie Peterson* • Jack Weston *Randolph Riker* • Charles Drake *Dolan* • Joseph Wiseman *Rajeski* • Don Hanmer *O'Hara* ■ *Dir* Josef Leytes [Joseph Leytes] • *Scr* Steven Bochco, Harold Clements [Harold Clemens], from TV play *The Faceless Man* by Joseph Leytes

The Counterfeit Traitor ★★★

Second World War spy drama
1962 · US · Colour · 140mins

Adapted from Alexander Klein's book about the true-life exploits of a Swedish undercover agent, this is a slickly-made espionage story, but with too few moments of nail-biting tension to justify its excessive running time. As the oil importer posing as a Nazi sympathiser, William Holden hurtles across northern Europe with some conviction, and is well supported in his endeavours by the likes of Lilli Palmer, Eva Dahlbeck and Klaus Kinski. But while writer/director George Seaton keeps the dialogue terse and credible, he too often dawdles when the action demands a bit of dash. DP

William Holden (2) *Eric Erickson* • Lilli Palmer *Marianne Mollendorf* • Hugh Griffith *Collins* • Ernst Schröder *Baron Von Oldenbourg* • Eva Dahlbeck *Ingrid Erickson* • Ulf Palme *Max Gumpel* • Carl Raddatz *Otto Holtz* ■ *Dir* George Seaton • *Scr* George Seaton, from a book by Alexander Klein

The Counterfeiters ★★

Crime thriller 1948 · US · BW · 73mins

Sam Newfield was such a prolific B-movie director that he occasionally used the pseudonyms Sherman Scott or Peter Stewart to cover up just how many sub-standard programme fillers he actually churned out. This "Peter Stewart" effort is slightly above his usual average, and he might have been better advised to release it under his own name. Playing against type, John Sutton is the Scotland Yard flatfoot on the trail of Hugh Beaumont's funny money gang. DP

John Sutton *Jeff MacAllister* • Doris Merrick *Margo* • Hugh Beaumont *Philip Drake* • Lon Chaney Jr *Louie* • George O'Hanlon *Frankie* • Douglas Blackley *Tony* • Herbert Rawlinson *Norman Talbott* ■ *Dir* Peter Stewart [Sam Newfield] • *Scr* Fred Myton, Barbara Worth, from a story by Maurice H Conn

Counterpoint ★★

Second World War drama
1967 · US · Colour · 106mins

Charlton Heston plays an American conductor who, along with his 70-strong orchestra, is captured by the Germans in Belgium during the Battle of the Bulge. Nazi general Maximilian Schell has orders to shoot all prisoners, but will spare the lives of the musicians if they play a concert. The Los Angeles Philharmonic Orchestra pulls out all the stops for the musical extracts, which are by far the most convincing moments in an otherwise implausible story. TH. Contains some swearing.

Charlton Heston *Lionel Evans* • Maximilian Schell *General Schiller* • Kathryn Hays *Annabelle Rice* • Leslie Nielsen *Victor Rice* • Anton Diffring *Colonel Arndt* • Linden Chiles *Lieutenant Long* ■ *Dir* Ralph Nelson • *Scr* Joel Oliansky, James Lee, from the novel *The General* by Alan Sillitoe

Counterspy ★★ U

Comedy thriller 1953 · UK · BW · 68mins

Typical "quota quickie" about a ring of spies who use an innocuous nursing home as their hideout. Some topicality is given to the otherwise threadbare plot – the spies are after plans for jet engines, and there's a chase through one of London's newest tourist attractions, the Festival Gardens on London's South Bank. AT

Dermot Walsh *Manning* • Hazel Court *Clare Manning* • Hermione Baddeley *Del Mar* • Alexander Gauge *Smith* • James Vivian *Larry* • Archie Duncan *Jim* • Frederick Schrecker *Plattnauer* • Hugh Latimer *Barlow* • Bill Travers *Rex* • Beryl Baxter *Girl* ■ *Dir* Vernon Sewell • *Scr* Gary Elmes, Michael Lefevre

Countess Dracula ★★★ 18

Horror 1970 · UK · Colour · 89mins

In order to masquerade as her own daughter, an ageing countess begins bathing in the blood of virgins to restore her youth. Ingrid Pitt, the first lady of British horror movies, excels in this colourful hokum based on the legend of notorious Hungarian countess Elizabeth Bathory. The film atones for its lack of terror with a brittle atmosphere of decay. DP. Contains violence, nudity. [video] DVD

Ingrid Pitt *Countess Elisabeth Nadasdy* • Nigel Green *Captain Dobi* • Sandor Eles *Imre Toth* • Maurice Denham *Master Fabio* • Lesley-Anne Down *Ilona* • Patience Collier *Julia* ■ *Dir* Peter Sasdy • *Scr* Jeremy Paul, from a story by Alexander Paal, Peter Sasdy, Gabriel Ronay

A Countess from Hong Kong ★★

Romantic comedy
1967 · UK · Colour · 122mins

Director Charles Chaplin sadly disappointed fans eagerly awaiting his first film in ten years, completely misjudging Sophia Loren and Marlon Brando in this clumsy romantic comedy. The result is hugely embarrassing, with Brando surly instead of suave as the diplomat who finds Russian émigrée aristocrat Loren stowed away in his cabin.TH

Marlon Brando *Ogden Mears* • Sophia Loren *Natascha* • Sydney Chaplin *Harvey Crothers* • Tippi Hedren *Martha* • Patrick Cargill *Hudson* • Margaret Rutherford *Miss Gaulswallow* • Michael Medwin *John Felix* • Oliver Johnston *Clark* ■ *Dir/Scr* Charles Chaplin

The Countess of Monte Cristo ★★

Musical 1948 · US · BW · 79mins

This marks the last screen appearance of Norwegian Olympic ice-skating champion Sonja Henie, who made several successful films in the late 1930s and early 1940s when her competitive days were over. Not one of her better movies, the one-joke plot has Henie and Olga San Juan as Norwegian barmaids posing as a countess and her maid at a luxury hotel. RK

Sonja Henie *Karen Kirsten* • Olga San Juan *Jenny Johnsen* • Michael Kirby *Paul von Cram* • Dorothy Hart *Peg Manning* • Arthur Treacher *Managing director* ■ *Dir* Frederick De Cordova • *Scr* William Bowers, from the film by Walter Reisch

Country ★★★ PG

Drama 1984 · US · Colour · 105mins

Iowa farmers Jessica Lange and Sam Shepard survive a twister, but face foreclosure and bankruptcy when the US government demands the full and immediate return on a huge loan. Very much a personal project for Lange, this social drama may beat its "big message" drum a little too loudly, but it also provides a convincing portrait of how harsh country life can be. It was the second on-screen pairing (after *Frances*) of real-life partners Shepard and Lange, the latter winning an Oscar nomination for her down-to-earth performance. AT [video]

Jessica Lange *Jewell Ivy* • Sam Shepard *Gil Ivy* • Wilford Brimley *Otis* • Matt Clark *Tom McMullen* • Therese Graham *Marlene Ivy* • Levi L Knebel *Carlisle Ivy* • Jim Haynie *Arlon Brewer* • Sandra Seacat *Louise Brewer* ■ *Dir* Richard Pearce • *Scr* William D Wittliff

The Country Bears ★★ PG

Musical comedy 2002 · US · Colour · 84mins

Christopher Walken's performance as a vengeful banker saves the day in this lacklustre family comedy. Based on a Disney theme park attraction, it's a simplistic morality tale about love, loyalty and friendship. The stars are the washed-out country-and-western bear group of the title (actually actors in unconvincing fuzzy suits). When a deliciously theatrical Walken threatens to repossess their Country Bear Hall, the quarrelling performers are persuaded to reform by an ardent young fan (another ursine critter, voiced by Haley Joel Osment). While there are plenty of toe-tapping tunes (and some cameos), it lacks the magic to really charm. SF [video] DVD

Haley Joel Osment *Beary* • Christopher Walken *Reed Thimple* • Stephen Tobolowsky *Norbert Barrington* • Daryl "Chill" Mitchell [Daryl Mitchell] *Officer Hamm* • MC Gainey *Roadie* • Diedrich Bader *Ted Bedderhead/ Officer Cheats* • Megan Fay *Mrs Barrington* • Eli Marienthal *Dex Barrington* • Candy Ford *Trixie St Clair* • James Gammon *Big Al* ■ *Dir* Peter Hastings • *Scr* Mark Perez, based on Walt Disney's Country Bear Jamboree

Country Dance ★★★

Drama 1970 · UK · Colour · 112mins

Peter O'Toole is ideally cast as Sir Charles Henry Arbuthnot Pinkerton Ferguson, a dipsomaniac Scots aristocrat who once canoodled with his sister in the barn and has been besotted by her ever since. But the sister, Susannah York, is now married to Michael Craig. Incest as a theme has always been a risky business and this accordingly bombed at the box office, perhaps because this title – it was originally *Brotherly Love* – threatened clogs and bagpipes. AT

Peter O'Toole *Sir Charles Henry Arbuthnot Pinkerton Ferguson* • Susannah York *Hilary Dow* • Michael Craig *Douglas Dow* • Harry Andrews *Brigadier Crieff* • Cyril Cusack *Dr Maitland* • Judy Cornwell *Rosie* • Brian Blessed *Jock Baird* • Robert Urquhart *Auctioneer* ■ *Dir* J Lee Thompson • *Scr* James Kennaway

The Country Doctor ★★

Drama 1936 · US · BW · 93mins

Jean Hersholt, who arguably played more doctors than any other Hollywood actor, is his usual solid, sympathetic self in this backwoods drama set in Canada, which involves a diphtheria outbreak, the fight to build a hospital and the birth of quintuplets to one of the doctor's patients. Inspired by the famous Dionne quintuplets, this version features real newsreel footage and the quins themselves playing their fictional counterparts. Folksy, worthy and old-fashioned. RK

Jean Hersholt *Dr John Luke* • June Lang *Mary MacKenzie* • George "Slim" Summerville [Slim Summerville] *Constable Jim Ogden* • Michael Whalen *Tony Luke* • Dorothy Peterson *Nurse Katherine Kennedy* • Robert Barrat *MacKenzie* • Jane Darwell *Mrs Graham* ■ *Dir* Henry King • *Scr* Sonya Levien, from a story by Charles E Blake

C

The Country Girl ★★★ PG

Drama 1954 · US · BW · 99mins

Grace Kelly won a Best Actress Oscar for putting on glasses and looking after alcoholic hubby Bing Crosby in this version of Clifford Odets's turgid play, which also won director George Seaton an Academy Award for his screenplay. William Holden plays the theatre director who becomes embroiled with Kelly. With hindsight, and the demise of all three principles, the film has an extra piquancy, provided the viewer knows that in real life Kelly was romantically involved with both Crosby and Holden. Many felt the Oscar should have gone to Judy Garland for *A Star Is Born*. According to Groucho Marx, it was "the greatest robbery since Brink's". TS DVD

Bing Crosby *Frank Elgin* • Grace Kelly *Georgie Elgin* • William Holden (2) *Bernie Dodd* • Anthony Ross *Phil Cook* • Gene Reynolds *Larry* • Eddie Ryder *Ed* ■ *Dir* George Seaton • *Scr* George Seaton, from the play by Clifford Odets

The Country Girls ★★★ PG

Period drama 1983 · UK · Colour · 102mins

Most rite of passage pictures focus on teenage lads, so it makes a refreshing change to follow a couple of girls discovering the pleasures and pitfalls of life. Adapted from the novel by Edna O'Brien, this engaging account of growing up in 1950s Ireland takes us along the familiar route from convent school to the big city. However, director Desmond Davis succeeds in presenting each act of rebellion and stolen moment of innocent passion as something exhilaratingly new. DP

Sam Neill *Mr Gentleman* • Maeve Germaine *Kate* • Jill Doyle *Baba Brennan* • Britta Smith *Lil* • John Olohan *Hickey* • Patricia Martin *Martha* • Des Nealon *Mr Brennan* • John Kavanagh *James* ■ *Dir* Desmond Davis • *Scr* Edna O'Brien, from the novel by Edna O'Brien

Country Life ★★★★ 12

Period drama 1994 · Aus · Colour · 112mins

This drawn-out but absorbing take on Chekhov's *Uncle Vanya* was adapted by Michael Blakemore and transplanted to post-First World War Australia. A failed writer (Blakemore himself) returns to a New South Wales sheep farm with new wife Greta Scacchi, who becomes the object of desire of drunken doctor Sam Neill and nervy landowner John Hargreaves. Neatly capturing the inherent comedy in people's everyday successes and failures, the film's vein of melancholy sets off that humour to real effect. TH

Sam Neill *Dr Max Askey* • Greta Scacchi *Deborah Voysey* • Kerry Fox *Sally Voysey* • John Hargreaves *Jack Dickens* • Michael Blakemore *Alexander Voysey* • Googie Withers *Hannah* • Patricia Kennedy *Maud Dickens* ■ *Dir* Michael Blakemore • *Scr* Michael Blakemore, from the play *Uncle Vanya* by Anton Chekhov

County Hospital ★★ U

Comedy 1932 · US · BW · 18mins

Who else but Stan Laurel would visit someone in traction and offer them hard-boiled eggs and nuts? Unfortunately, that's about as funny as this two-reeler gets. There are a couple of good moments as Ollie's plastered leg heads ceilingward. But once they head home, the action lapses back to the earliest days of silent slapstick as Stan careers through the streets causing all manner of chaos. Adding insult to unoriginality, director James Parrott stages the entire episode against a barely disguised back projection. Proof that even geniuses can have an off day. DP DVD

Stan Laurel *Stan* • Oliver Hardy *Ollie* • William Austin *Englishman* • Baldwin Cooke *Orderly* • Billy Gilbert *Doctor* • Belle Hare *Nurse* • Frank Holliday *Hospital visitor* • Lilyan Irene *Nurse* ■ *Dir* James Parrott • *Scr* HM Walker

Coupe de Ville ★★★ 15

Comedy drama 1990 · US · Colour · 97mins

This is funny, endearing and very unlike director Joe Roth's earlier films. Three estranged brothers are ordered by their father, Alan Arkin, to drive across America with a car for their mother's 50th birthday. Cue much argument and a particularly memorable scene where they all dispute the significance of hit song *Louie, Louie*. With decent comic gags throughout, this is slight but entertaining. LH

Patrick Dempsey *Bobby Libner* • Arye Gross *Buddy Libner* • Daniel Stern *Marvin Libner* • Annabeth Gish *Tammy* • Rita Taggart *Betty Libner* • Joseph Bologna *Uncle Phil* • Alan Arkin *Fred Libner* • James Gammon *Doc Sturgeon* ■ *Dir* Joe Roth • *Scr* Mike Binder

Courage Mountain ★★ U

Adventure drama
1989 · US/Fr · Colour · 94mins

Continuing Johanna Sypri's much-loved story about a joy-bringing Swiss mountain girl, this lovingly staged but impossibly contrived adventure will doubtless appeal to adolescent females. Juliette Caton leads her classmates to safety across the Alps when the First World War encroaches on their patch. Charlie Sheen gives a mortified performance as Peter the goatherd. DP

Juliette Caton *Heidi* • Charlie Sheen *Peter* • Leslie Caron *Jane Hillary* • Yorgo Voyagis *Signor Bonelli* • Laura Betti *Signora Bonelli* • Jan Rubes *Grandfather* • Joanna Clarke *Ursula* • Nicola Stapleton *Ilsa* ■ *Dir* Christopher Leitch • *Scr* Weaver Webb, from a story by Fred Brogger, Mark Brogger, from characters created by Johanna Spyri

Courage of Black Beauty ★ U

Drama 1957 · US · Colour · 79mins

In this belated attempt by independent producer Edward L Alperson to follow up his 1946 production of *Black Beauty*, the English setting of Anna Sewell's original novel is dropped in favour of California. Otherwise, though, it's the same old tale, and a big yawn, deficient in almost every area. AE

John Crawford *Bobby Adams* • Mimi Gibson *Lily Rowden* • John Bryant *Sam Adams* • Diane Brewster *Ann Rowden* • J Pat O'Malley *Mike Green* • Russell Johnson *Ben Farraday* ■ *Dir* Harold Shuster • *Scr* Steve Fisher, from the novel *Black Beauty* by Anna Sewell

Courage of Lassie ★★★ U

Second World War drama
1946 · US · Colour · 92mins

The title of this moving tale of wartime doggie heroism is misleading, as Lassie actually plays a collie called Bill. Humans on board include the lovely young Elizabeth Taylor (from *Lassie Come Home*) and the always likeable Frank Morgan. Tom Drake is also effective as the "boy next door", but the real star – apart from the mutt – is the sumptuous Technicolor. TS

Elizabeth Taylor *Kathie Merrick* • Frank Morgan *Harry MacBain* • Tom Drake *Sgt Smitty* • Selena Royle *Mrs Merrick* • Harry Davenport *Judge Payson* • George Cleveland *Old man* ■ *Dir* Fred M Wilcox • *Scr* Lionel Houser

Courage under Fire ★★★ 15

War drama 1996 · US · Colour · 111mins

This is a big, self-important Gulf War movie that looks good, sounds noble but rings rather hollow. Meg Ryan is a pilot due to get a posthumous medal for bravery, but has there been a cover-up of the real events? This is a *Rashomon* for the 1990s, with war hero Denzel Washington searching for the truth. The subject matter, strong performances and stylish direction from Edward Zwick combine to make the movie seem more incisive than it really is. AT. Contains violence and swearing. DVD

Denzel Washington *Nat Serling* • Meg Ryan *Karen Walden* • Lou Diamond Phillips *Monfriez* • Michael Moriarty *General Hershberg* • Matt Damon *Ilario* • Bronson Pinchot *Bruno* • Seth Gilliam *Altameyer* • Regina Taylor *Meredith Serling* • Scott Glenn *Tony Gartner* ■ *Dir* Edward Zwick • *Scr* Patrick Sheane Duncan

The Courier ★★ 15

Detective thriller
1987 · UK/Ire · Colour · 81mins

An Irish thriller with nothing to do with the Troubles? That in itself is something of a rarity. Alas, that's the only whiff of originality in this story of a motorbike messenger (Padraig O'Loingsigh) who becomes embroiled in a drugs ring. Gabriel Byrne is the chief villain, while Ian Bannen and some other distinguished Irish actors also put in appearances. Elvis Costello wrote the score under his real name, Declan McManus. TH

Gabriel Byrne *Val* • Ian Bannen *McGuigan* • Cait O'Riordan *Colette* • Kevin Doyle *Joe* • Padraig O'Loingsigh *Mark* • Mary Ryan *Carol* • Patrick Bergin *Christy* ■ *Dir* Joe Lee, Frank Deasy • *Scr* Frank Deasy

Cours du Soir ★★★ U

Comedy 1967 · Fr · Colour · 27mins

Taking the form of an evening class and shot on the set of *Playtime*, this may not be Jacques Tati's most innovative film, but it provides an invaluable record of the vaudeville sketches with which he made his name. Starting with a demonstration of smoking styles, Tati trots out his famous tennis, fishing and horse-riding techniques, as well as a brief reprise of his beloved postman routine. But you only have to look at how badly his besuited students cope with the simple slapstick task of tripping on a step to realise how deceptively easy Tati makes each mime appear. DP. In French with English subtitles.

Jacques Tati ■ *Dir* Nicolas Ribowski • *Scr* Jacques Tati

The Court Jester ★★★★ U

Comedy 1956 · US · Colour · 96mins

This medieval spoof, produced, written and directed by the formidable team of Norman Panama and Melvin Frank, gave Danny Kaye one of his finest roles, as the meek and mild valet who saves a kingdom from its tyrannical ruler. Basil Rathbone cuts an elegant figure of villainy, while Glynis Johns, Cecil Parker and Angela Lansbury get almost as many laughs as Kaye by playing it straight. It's as much horseplay as swordplay and, altogether, a witty delight. TH

Danny Kaye *Hawkins* • Glynis Johns *Maid Jean* • Basil Rathbone *Sir Ravenhurst* • Angela Lansbury *Princess Gwendolyn* • Cecil Parker *King Roderick* • Mildred Natwick *Griselda* • Robert Middleton *Sir Griswold* ■ *Dir/Scr* Norman Panama, Melvin Frank

The Court-Martial of Billy Mitchell ★★★★ U

Courtroom drama based on a true story
1955 · US · Colour · 100mins

This true-life courtroom drama is given enormous impact by director Otto Preminger and his Oscar-nominated writers, Milton Sperling and Emmet Lavery. The film is based on events in 1925, when US Army general Mitchell (played by Gary Cooper) dared to question bureaucracy and argue for a separate Air Force. He also predicted that America and Japan would one day go to war, years before Pearl Harbour. Cooper's languid sincerity makes its mark, but it's Rod Steiger as a venomous prosecutor who gets all the best lines. TH

Gary Cooper *General Billy Mitchell* • Rod Steiger *Major Allan Guillion* • Charles Bickford *General Guthrie* • Ralph Bellamy *Congressman Frank Reid* • Elizabeth Montgomery *Margaret Lansdowne* • Jack Lord *Commander Zachary Lansdowne* • Peter Graves (2) *Captain Elliott* • Darren McGavin *Russ Peters* ■ *Dir* Otto Preminger • *Scr* Milton Sperling, Emmet Lavery, from their story

The Court-Martial of Jackie Robinson ★★★★

Drama based on a true story
1990 · US · Colour · 93mins

This TV movie about Jackie Robinson, who went on to become the first black player in big-time baseball and a full-blown national hero, homes in on an incident early in his life when he endured bigotry as a GI. André Braugher supplies ample energy as Robinson while Bruce Dern stands out in an impressive supporting cast that also includes Ruby Dee, who played Robinson's wife in 1950's *The Jackie Robinson Story*, and who returns here as his mum. Director Larry Peerce cleverly avoids any self-conscious analysing of issues, thereby maintaining the power of the piece. JM

André Braugher *Jackie Robinson* • Ruby Dee *Mallie Robinson* • Stan Shaw *Joe Louis* • Daniel Stern *William Cline* • Bruce Dern *Ed Higgins* • Kasi Lemmons *Rachel Isum Robinson* ■ *Dir* Larry Peerce • *Scr* L Travis Clark, Steve Duncan, Clayton Frohman, Dennis Lynton Clark, from a story by Dennis Lynton Clark

The Courtneys of Curzon Street ★★★ U

Period drama 1947 · UK · BW · 120mins

Although it now seems twee, it's easy to see why this class-divide drama would have been so popular in postwar Britain. With an egalitarian theme and plenty of period gaiety to distract from the austerity of the time, this box-office smash perfectly demonstrates director Herbert Wilcox's ability to gauge public taste. However, Wilcox's master stroke was the teaming of his wife Anna Neagle and Michael Wilding. This was the second of their six collaborations, with Wilding's aristocrat shocking Victorian society by falling for Neagle's spirited maid. DP

Anna Neagle *Catherine O'Hallaron* • Michael Wilding *Sir Edward Courtney* • Gladys Young *Lady Courtney* • Michael Medwin *Edward Courtney* • Coral Browne *Valerie* • Daphne Slater *Cynthia* • Jack Watling *Teddy Courtney* ■ *Dir* Herbert Wilcox • *Scr* Nicholas Phipps, from a story by Florence Tranter

The Courtship of Andy Hardy ★★ U

Comedy drama 1942 · US · BW · 94mins

The Andy Hardy series clocked up a dozen episodes with this offering which gave all-American families role models and reassurance while father was away fighting the war. In this story, Judge Hardy (Lewis Stone, as usual) uses his son Mickey Rooney to help a married couple reconcile themselves to their tearaway daughter. Oh, and Andy gets caught stealing a car. Life is so complicated in sunny Carvel. AT

Mickey Rooney *Andy Hardy* • Lewis Stone *Judge James K Hardy* • Donna Reed *Melodie Nesbitt* • Fay Holden *Mrs Emily Hardy* • Cecilia Parker *Marian Hardy* • Ann Rutherford *Polly Benedict* • William Lundigan *Jeff Willis* • Sara Haden *Aunt Milly* ■ *Dir* George B Seitz • *Scr* Agnes Christine Johnston, from characters created by Aurania Rouverol

The Courtship of Eddie's Father ★★★★ U

Comedy drama 1963 · US · Colour · 118mins

This absolutely charming and unfairly neglected film is directed by Vincente Minnelli, beautifully filmed by veteran cinematographer Milton Krasner, and features a simply swell performance from the excellent Glenn Ford. Ronny Howard (now better known as director Ron Howard) keeps sentimentality at bay as the six-year-old Eddie, as do the dynamic Stella Stevens and Shirley Jones; there's also a terrific cameo from Dick Van Dyke's under-rated brother, Jerry. This is a warm-hearted treat, far superior to the TV series that followed. TS

Glenn Ford *Tom Corbett* • Ronny Howard [Ron Howard] *Eddie Corbett* • Shirley Jones *Elizabeth Marten* • Dina Merrill *Rita Behrens* • Stella Stevens *Dollye Daly* • Robert E Sherwood *Mrs Livingston* • Jerry Van Dyke *Norman Jones* ■ *Dir* Vincente Minnelli • *Scr* John Gay, from a novel by Mark Toby

Cousin Bette ★★★ 15

Period drama
1997 · US/UK · Colour · 104mins

This version of Balzac's novel has Jessica Lange in the title role, plotting revenge on her family who have virtually abandoned her while lavishing everything on her cousin. While its story of social upheaval is mirrored by the political chaos of mid-19th-century France, the picture suffers rather from international casting and other compromises brought on by trans-Atlantic financing. But Lange gives a wonderful portrait of malice, while Elisabeth Shue has fun as a flirtatious stage actress. AT. Contains nudity, sex scenes, swearing, violence.

Jessica Lange *Bette Fisher* • Elisabeth Shue *Jenny Cadine* • Geraldine Chaplin *Adeline Hulot* • Bob Hoskins *Mayor Cesar Crevel* • Hugh Laurie *Baron Hector Hulot* • Laura Fraser *Mariette* • Toby Stephens *Victorin Hulot* • Kelly Macdonald *Hortense Hulot* ■ *Dir* Des McAnuff • *Scr* Lynn Siefert, Susan Tarr, from the novel by Honoré de Balzac

Cousin Bobby ★★★ PG

Documentary 1992 · US · Colour · 70mins

Jonathan Demme directs this absolutely fascinating documentary about his cousin Robert Castle, an Episcopalian priest in Harlem. The Oscar-winning director follows the outspoken radical activist as he goes about his daily ministering and builds up a riveting portrait of the man, his life and the dedicated work he does among his adoring flock. The use of race riot footage is heavy-handed, but otherwise this is a nicely crafted valentine from one proud relative to another. AJ

Dir Jonathan Demme

Cousin, Cousine ★★★ 12

Comedy 1975 · Fr · Colour · 91mins

The problem with accessible art-house movies is that they often feel empty. That's certainly the case in this gentle satire on middle-class mores, which was so successful in the States that it was remade as *Cousins*. Fondly mocking the morality of his characters, Jean-Charles Tacchella refuses to rip into them as Buñuel would have done, choosing instead to make the romance between wronged wife Marie-Christine Barrault (who was Oscar-nominated for her performance) and Victor Lanoux seem rather sweet. DP. In French with English subtitles.

Marie-Christine Barrault *Marthe* • Victor Lanoux *Ludovic* • Marie-France Pisier *Karine* • Guy Marchand *Pascal* • Ginette Garcin *Biju* • Sybil Maas *Diane* • Jean Herbert *Sacy* ■ *Dir* Jean-Charles Tacchella • *Scr* Jean-Charles Tacchella, Danièle Thompson

Les Cousins ★★★★ 12

Drama 1959 · Fr · BW · 104mins

Winner of the Golden Bear at the 1959 Berlin Film Festival, this is an intriguing variation on the "town mouse and country mouse" theme which cynically asserts that just desserts are simply pie in the sky. Gérard Blain skilfully charts the descent from wide-eyed wonder to self-pitying despair as the student from the sticks who slaves at the Sorbonne, only to fail his exams and lose his girlfriend to his indolent but ultimately successful cousin (Jean-Claude Brialy). Parisian Claude Chabrol presents his home town with evident enthusiasm, though the scenes of student excess have dated badly. DP. In French with English subtitles.

Gérard Blain *Charles* • Jean-Claude Brialy *Paul* • Juliette Mayniel *Florence* • Claude Cerval *Clovis* • Genevieve Cluny *Genevieve* • Michèle Meritz *Yvonne* • Corrado Guarducci *Italian Count* • Guy Decomble *Librarian* ■ *Dir* Claude Chabrol • *Scr* Claude Chabrol, Paul Gegauff

Cousins 

Romantic comedy
1989 · US · Colour · 108mins

A remake of the French film *Cousin, Cousine*, this is a glossy romance featuring Isabella Rossellini and Ted Danson as relatives-by-marriage who find themselves falling in love during a succession of family gatherings. He's married to ice-cold Sean Young, who in turn is having an affair with Rossellini's hubby, William Petersen. Danson gives one of his most likeable movie performances, while Young manages to steal the show by playing the role of bitchy cheating wife to the max. Intermittently funny, but still a slight disappointment. JB DVD

Ted Danson *Larry Kozinski* • Isabella Rossellini *Maria Hardy* • Sean Young *Tish Kozinski* • William L Petersen *Tom Hardy* • Lloyd Bridges *Vince Kozinski* • Norma Aleandro *Edie Costello* • Keith Coogan *Mitch Kozinski* ■ *Dir* Joel Schumacher • *Scr* Stephen Metcalfe, from the film *Cousin, Cousine* by Jean-Charles Tacchella, Danièle Thompson

A Covenant with Death ★★

Courtroom drama 1967 · US · Colour · 96mins

A potentially interesting and original idea (an innocent man convicted of murder kills the hangman, and is then found not guilty of the first offence) is poorly handled by director Lamont Johnson, who ironically became regarded as a promising feature director on the strength of this film. Former television star George Maharis (*Route 66*) simply can't convey the moral quandary and angst the role demands, but there is a marvellous supporting cast, plus Gene Hackman in an early feature film role. TS.

George Maharis *Ben Lewis* • Laura Devon *Rosemary* • Katy Jurado *Eulalia* • Earl Holliman *Bryan Talbot* • Arthur O'Connell *Judge Hochstadter* • Sidney Blackmer *Colonel Oates* • Gene Hackman *Harmsworth* • John Anderson *Dietrich* ■ *Dir* Lamont Johnson • *Scr* Larry B Marcus, Saul Levitt, from a novel by Stephen Becker

Cover Girl ★★★★ U

Musical romantic comedy
1944 · US · Colour · 102mins

Not just a Technicolor treat featuring a ravishing Rita Hayworth and a score by Jerome Kern that includes *Long Ago and Far Away*, this was a milestone in the history of the glossy film musical. Columbia borrowed the young Gene Kelly from MGM and gave him free rein with his own sections of the movie. Kelly flexed his cinematic muscles here, knocking down soundstage walls to create a continuous street scene for himself, Hayworth and Phil Silvers to dance through without any need for cuts, and using trick photography to dance with himself in the "alter ego" routine. It's a little dated, a little overlong and a little corny, but a treat nonetheless. TS DVD

Rita Hayworth *Rusty Parker/Maribelle Hicks* • Gene Kelly *Danny McGuire* • Phil Silvers *Genius* • Lee Bowman *Noel Wheaton* • Jinx Falkenburg *Jinx* • Leslie Brooks *Maurine Martin* • Eve Arden *Cornelia Jackson* • Otto Kruger *John Coudair* • Jess Barker *John Coudair as a young man* • Anita Colby *Anita* ■ *Dir* Charles Vidor • *Scr* Virginia Van Upp, Marion Parsonnet, Paul Gangelin, from a story by Erwin Gelsey • *Cinematographer* Rudolph Maté, Allen M Davey • *Music Director* MW Stoloff [Morris Stoloff] • *Orchestration* Carmen Dragon • *Art Director* Lionel Banks, Gary Odell • *Set Designer* Fay Babcock

Cover Girl Killer 

Crime drama 1959 · UK · BW · 61mins

Apart from a handful of low-budget movies, writer/director Terry Bishop spent much of his career in TV, which would appear to have been the British cinema's loss if this clipped little thriller is anything to go by. The dialogue does strike a false note every now and then, but Bishop succeeds in re-creating a world of tawdry glamour that is a far cry from the glitz of today's supermodels as a serial killer targets a magazine's pin-ups. DP

Harry H Corbett *The man* • Felicity Young *June Rawson* • Spencer Teakle *John Mason* • Victor Brooks *Inspector Brunner* • Tony Doonan *Sergeant* • Bernadette Milnes *Gloria* • Christina Gregg *Joy* • Charles Lloyd Pack *Captain Adams* ■ *Dir/Scr* Terry Bishop

Cover-Up ★★ 18

Action thriller 1991 · US/Is · Colour · 87mins

Dolph Lundgren plays a journalist assigned to cover a raid on a military base in Israel. What could have been an engaging thriller spends too much time catching up with Lundgren's previous acquaintances, and things get bogged down quickly. Louis Gossett Jr is on hand to inject some urgency, but it's too little, too late. ST

Dolph Lundgren *Mike Anderson* • Louis Gossett Jr *Jackson* • John Finn *Colonel Jeff Cooper* • Lisa Berkley *Susan Clifford* ■ *Dir* Manny Coto • *Scr* William Tannen

The Covered Wagon ★★★★★

Silent western 1923 · US · BW · 98mins

Shot on a lavish scale in Utah and Nevada, this was the first truly epic western and one of the biggest-grossing silent movies ever made. It also created the imprint for countless movies and TV series with its story of pioneers facing redskins and ruffians on the wagon trail westwards. Directed by James Cruze – with, it's said, John Ford as his assistant – the film's many highlights include a buffalo hunt and a dramatic river crossing, though the vapid romance between J Warren Kerrigan and Lois Wilson tends to diminish the storyline. With terrific camerawork from Karl Brown, it set the standard for all future westerns. TH

Lois Wilson *Molly Wingate* • J Warren Kerrigan *Will Banion* • Ernest Torrence *Jackson* • Charles Ogle *Mr Wingate* • Ethel Wales *Mrs Wingate* • Alan Hale *Sam Woodhull* • Tully Marshall *Bridger* • Guy Oliver *Kit Carson* ■ *Dir* James Cruze • *Scr* Jack Cunningham

The Cow ★★★★

Drama 1969 · Iran · BW · 104mins

Dariush Mehrjui's hugely influential drama has the duel distinction of having been both part-funded (and then banned) by the Shah of Iran and the primary reason why the Ayatollah Khomeini allowed film-making after the Islamic Revolution. For all its dense symbolism, the plotline couldn't be simpler, as villager Ezzatollah Entezami feels the unexpected death of his cherished cow – the only one in the village – so personally that he gradually becomes convinced that he himself is a cow. This astute insight into rural poverty and the superstition and paranoia of village life has lost none of its power. DP. In Farsi with English subtitles.

Ezzatolah Entezami *Masht Hassan* • Mahmoud Dowlatabadi • Parviz Fanizadeh • Jamshid Mashayekhi *Abbas* • Ali Nassirian *Islam* • Esmat Safavi ■ *Dir* Dariush Mehrjui • *Scr* Dariush Mehrjui, from a play by Gholam-Hossein Saedi

The Cow and the President ★★★ PG

Comedy 2000 · Fr · Colour · 92mins

Inspired by a photograph of Bill Clinton and a Thanksgiving turkey, yet also recalling the 1951 Paul Gallico adaptation, *Never Take No for an Answer*, this is a charming example of the old movie adage that children invariably know better than grown-ups. Having both lost their mothers at birth, eight-year-old Mehdi Ortelsberg and a calf called Maéva strike up an unlikely friendship that looks set to be terminated by a BSE scare. Director Philippe Muyl challenges society's increasingly callous treatment of animals, yet avoids sentimentality in having the boy appeal to Paris for a reprieve. Nicely done. DP. In French with English subtitles.

Bernard Yerles *Romain* • Florence Pernel *Sarah* • Mehdi Ortelsberg *Lucas* • Christian Bujeau *Jean-René* • Bernard Bloch *Bichon* ■ *Dir/Scr* Philippe Muyl

Cowboy ★★★ U

Western 1958 · US · Colour · 91mins

This grim and gripping western reunited the star and director from the previous year's *3:10 to Yuma*, taciturn Glenn Ford and talented Delmer Daves. It's the story of a young tenderfoot (the excellent Jack Lemmon) and his relationship with tough trail boss Ford. The atmosphere is thoroughly authentic – listen to Ford's acute description of the intelligence of a cowboy's horse – and the Technicolor photography is particularly sharp. Accompanying the men is Marlon Brando's then wife, sultry Anna Kashfi. TS DVD

Glenn Ford *Tom Reece* • Jack Lemmon *Frank Harris* • Anna Kashfi *Maria Vidal* • Brian Donlevy *Doc Bender* • Dick York *Charlie* • Victor Manuel Mendoza *Mendoza* • Richard Jaeckel *Paul Curtis* ■ *Dir* Delmer Daves • *Scr* Edmund H North, from the non-fiction book *My Reminiscences as a Cowboy* by Frank Harris • *Cinematographer* Charles Lawton Jr

The Cowboy and the Lady ★★★ U

Comedy 1938 · US · BW · 87mins

This film started life as what today would be called a high-concept idea, with producer Samuel Goldwyn teaming up former mountain cowboy of few words Gary Cooper and aristocratic Merle Oberon. So far, so good, but what about a plot? The slight story Goldwyn came up with is actually encapsulated by the catchpenny title, but to compensate he had the good sense to hire some of the period's cleverest writers. The screen never ignites, but Merle and Coop make a handsome couple. TS

Gary Cooper *Stretch* • Merle Oberon *Mary Smith* • Patsy Kelly *Katie Callahan* • Walter Brennan *Sugar* • Fuzzy Knight *Buzz* • Mabel Todd *Elly* • Henry Kolker *Mr Smith* • Harry Davenport *Uncle Hannibal Smith* • Emma Dunn *Ma Hawkins* ■ *Dir* HC Potter • *Scr* SN Behrman, Sonya Levien, from a story by Leo McCarey, Frank R Adams

Cowboy Bebop: the Movie ★★ 12

Animated action fantasy
2001 · Jpn · Colour · 110mins

This flatly drawn and tediously plotted futuristic thriller is a spin-off from a supposedly popular TV cartoon. A small group of bounty hunters is trying to thwart a dastardly bio-terrorism plot. Despite a late 21st-century setting, this has an odd, out-of-date look, seemingly influenced by gritty Hollywood cop movies. Forsaking the computer-generated trimmings that often visually enliven the genre, neither the irritating characters nor the pedestrian pacing will appeal to anyone other than devoted *animé* fans. JC. In Japanese with English subtitles. Contains violence. DVD

Koichi Yamadera *Spike Spiegel* • Unsho Ishizuka *Jet Black* • Megumi Hayashibara *Faye Valentine* • Aoi Tada *Ed* • Yasuku Yara *Hoffman* ■ *Dir* Shinichiro Watanabe • *Scr* Keiko Nobumoto, from a story by Hajime Yatate

The Cowboy Way ★★ 12

Comedy western
1994 · US · Colour · 102mins

Woody Harrelson, with a gleeful disregard for restraint, whoops and hollers his way through the picture, as he and rodeo partner Kiefer Sutherland stalk the Big Apple in search of their Mexican buddy's kidnapped daughter. In Harrelson's defence, he does at least try to make something out of Bill Wittliff's hugely derivative script. There's also a neat turn from Ernie Hudson as a cowboy crazy cop, but as a whole it's all rather coarse and clumsy. DP. Contains swearing.

Woody Harrelson *Pepper* • Kiefer Sutherland *Sonny* • Dylan McDermott *Stark* • Ernie Hudson *Officer Sam Shaw* • Cara Buono *Teresa* • Marg Helgenberger *Margarette* ■ *Dir* Gregg Champion • *Scr* Bill Wittliff, from a story by Bill Wittliff, Rob Thomson

The Cowboys ★★ PG

Western 1972 · US · Colour · 121mins

John Wayne hires a group of schoolboys to help him on a cattle drive in this morose, awkwardly paced and overlong would-be epic western. In truth, this rite-of-passage saga just doesn't work, owing to a cumbersome structure and a rather nauseating pro-violence, revenge-is-good message. On the plus side, Bruce Dern and Slim Pickens are good to watch, and Roscoe Lee Browne and Colleen Dewhurst add dignity. TS DVD

John Wayne *Wil Andersen* • Roscoe Lee Browne *Jebediah Nightlinger* • Bruce Dern *Long Hair* • Colleen Dewhurst *Kate* • Slim Pickens *Anse* • Lonny Chapman *Preacher* ■ *Dir* Mark Rydell • *Scr* Irving Ravetch, Harriet Frank Jr, William Dale Jennings, from the novel by William Dale Jennings

Coyote ★★

Experimental erotic drama
1992 · Can · Colour · 95mins

Marking the debut of Mitsou, the controversial pop singer who took Canada by storm, this is a love story that ends up being consumed more by pretension than passion. Director Richard Ciupka manages some striking shots of a rundown suburb, but he is less successful in making us care what happens between aspiring film-maker Patrick Labbé and Mitsou, a waif whose troubled childhood continues to haunt her. Mitsou looks great in what is essentially a glorified video. DP. Contains violence, swearing, sex scenes and nudity.

Mitsou *Louise Coyote* • Patrick Labbé *Chomi* • Thierry Magnier • Claude Legault • Francois Massicotte ■ *Dir* Richard Ciupka • *Scr* Michel Michaud, Richard Sadler, Louise Anne Bouchard, Richard Ciupka

Coyote Ugly ★★ 12

Romantic comedy drama
2000 · US · Colour · 96mins

Think *Flashdance* meets *Cocktail* and you'll have a good idea what this flashy Jerry Bruckheimer production is all about. Cute girl Piper Perabo leaves her toll-booth-worker dad (John Goodman) and the safety of the New Jersey suburbs for the bright lights of New York City to pursue her dream of being a songwriter. In the meantime she lands a job at a notorious bar, Coyote Ugly (inspired by a real-life NYC watering hole). A glossy, pop-music-filled piece of fluff. JB DVD

Piper Perabo *Violet Sanford* • Adam Garcia *Kevin O'Donnell* • John Goodman *Bill* • Maria Bello *Lil* • Izabella Miko *Cammie* • Tyra Banks *Zoe* ■ *Dir* David McNally • *Scr* Gina Wendkos

Crack House ★★ 18

Crime drama 1989 · US · Colour · 86mins

In 50 years, this movie will be rediscovered and appreciated in the same way that *Reefer Madness* is now. Like that camp classic, this movie is an anti-drug pamphlet dressed up in exploitation clothing, though it's considerably more violent and sexually explicit. Drugs lord Jim Brown has everyone in his LA neighborhood on drugs except for one teenage Hispanic couple. Funny at times, this needs time to reach its full laugh potential. KB

Jim Brown *Steadman* • Richard Roundtree *Lieutenant Johnson* • Anthony Geary *Dockett* • Angel Tompkins *Mother* • Cheryl Kay *Melissa* • Gregg Gomez Thomsen *Rick Morales* ■ *Dir* Michael Fischa • *Scr* Blake Schaeffer, from a story by Jack Silverman

A Crack in the Floor ★ 18

Horror 2000 · US · Colour · 89mins

A group of dope-smoking, sex mad city kids go on a camping trip, find an old cabin in the woods they think is uninhabited and spend the rest of movie running from a psycho-killer. Co-director Corby Timbrook does nothing to elevate his mediocre bloodbath above the rest of the standard hack-and-thwack pack. This is one slasher terminally unbalanced by far more narrative flaws than usual even for this genre. AJ DVD

Mario Lopez *Lehman* • Gary Busey *Tyler Trout* • Bo Hopkins *Sheriff Talmidge* • Rance Howard *Floyd Fryed* • Tracy Scoggins *Jeremiah's mother* • Justine Priestley *Kate* • Daisy McCrackin *Heidi* • Bentley Mitchum *Johnny* ■ *Dir* Corby Timbrook, Sean Stanek • *Scr* Sean Stanek

Crack in the Mirror ★★★

Crime drama 1960 · US · BW · 96mins

A working-class woman of a certain age (Juliette Greco) murders her construction worker husband (Orson Welles) with the help of her virile young lover (Bradford Dillman). The couple are brought to trial, where she is defended by an ambitious young lawyer (Dillman again), who is having an affair with the wife (Greco) of the young man's elderly counsel (Welles). An ingenious idea, directed with pace and style by Richard Fleischer, and with excellent performance from the dual role-playing principals. The message is simplistic and obvious, however, and all six characters are cold, heartless and unsympathetic. RK

Orson Welles *Hagolin/Lamoriciere* • Juliette Greco *Exponine/Florence* • Bradford Dillman *Larnier/Claud* • Alexander Knox *President* • Catherine Lacey *Mother Superior* • William Lucas *Kerstner* • Maurice Teynac *Doctor* ■ *Dir* Richard Fleischer • *Scr* Mark Canfield [Darryl F Zanuck], from the novel *Drama in the Mirror* by Marcel Haedrich

Crack in the World ★★ U

Science-fiction thriller
1964 · US · Colour · 95mins

Scientists attempt to harness the inner energy of the earth and get it all wrong in this moderate sci-fi thriller. Director Andrew Marton knows how to milk this kind of thing, and no one looks more worried about the end of the world than tight-lipped Dana Andrews. The effects just about pass muster, though they may look familiar to fans of other movies in the genre. TS

Dana Andrews *Dr Stephen Sorensen* • Janette Scott *Mrs Maggie Sorensen* • Kieron Moore *Ted Rampion* • Alexander Knox *Sir Charles Eggerston* • Peter Damon *Masefield* • Gary Lasdun *Markov* ■ *Dir* Andrew Marton • *Scr* Jon Manchip White, Julian Halevy [Julian Zimet], from a story by Jon Manchip White

Crack-Up ★★ U

Spy drama 1936 · US · BW · 70mins

A very routine programme-filler, made far livelier than it has any right to be by the solid acting of an adept supporting cast. Brian Donlevy is a test pilot bribed to steal the design plans of a revolutionary new war plane. Peter Lorre, always watchable even in below-par formula espionage material like this, is the airport's dumb, bugle-blowing mascot who's really a double agent with his bug-eyes on the same blueprints. AJ

Peter Lorre *Colonel Gimpy* • Brian Donlevy *Ace Martin* • Helen Wood *Ruth Franklin* • Ralph Morgan *John Fleming* • Thomas Beck *Joe Randall* • Kay Linaker *Mrs Fleming* • Lester Matthews *Sidney Grant* ■ *Dir* Malcolm St Clair • *Scr* Charles Kenyon, Sam Mintz, from a story by John Goodrich

Crack-Up ★★

Thriller 1946 · US · BW · 93mins

In this dark thriller, Pat O'Brien plays an art lecturer and curator who suffers, or appears to suffer, a nervous breakdown when an international consortium of villains reckons he's too close to exposing a forgery racket. This is an unusual role for O'Brien who stars alongside Claire Trevor, as his loyal girlfriend, and classy Herbert Marshall as a Scotland Yard investigator posing as an art expert. Directed with real flair by Irving Reis, the movie gets off to a terrific start but promises more than it delivers. RK

Pat O'Brien *George Steele* • Claire Trevor *Terry* • Herbert Marshall *Traybin* • Ray Collins *Dr Lowell* • Wallace Ford *Cochrane* • Dean Harens *Reynolds* • Damian O'Flynn *Stevenson* • Erskine Sanford *Barton* • Mary Ware *Mary* ■ *Dir* Irving Reis • *Scr* John Paxton, Ben Bengal, Ray Spencer, from the short story *Madman's Holiday* by Fredric Brown

The Cracker Factory ★★★★

Drama 1979 · US/UK · Colour · 100mins

Natalie Wood excels in this made-for-TV movie, imbuing this distinguished drama with both class and dignity as a depressed suburban housewife committed to care after a failed suicide bid. There's a marvellous supporting cast on hand in this prestige production: watch for Vivian Blaine, who played Adelaide in the screen version of *Guys and Dolls*, plus Juliet Mills and a pre-*Cheers* appearance from Shelley Long. The men are negligible, but doctor Perry King is suitably sympathetic. TS

Natalie Wood *Cassie Barrett* • Perry King *Dr Edwin Alexander* • Peter Haskell *Charlie Barrett* • Shelley Long *Clara* • Vivian Blaine *Helen* • Marian Mercer *Eleanor* • Juliet Mills *Tinkerbell* • John Harkins *Father Dunhill* ■ *Dir* Burt Brinckerhoff • *Scr* Richard A Shapiro, from the novel by Joyce Rebeta-Burditt

Crackerjack ★★ U

Comedy drama 1938 · UK · BW · 76mins

Tom Walls, well-loved star of the Aldwych farces during the 1920s, here plays burglar Jack Drake, a sort of "Robbing Hood" who lifts from the rich to help the poor. His success makes other local crooks jealous, and thereby hangs this awfully thin tale, enlivened only by the youthful presence of the lovely Lilli Palmer as co-star. It takes a long time to get up to speed, and today seems very dated indeed. TS

Tom Walls *Jack Drake* • Lilli Palmer *Baroness von Haltse* • Noel Madison *Sculpie* • Edmond Breon [Edmund Breon] *Tony Davenport* • Leon M Lion *Hambro Golding* • Charles Heslop *Burge* • Ethel Griffies *Annie* • HG Stoker *Inspector Benting* ■ *Dir* Albert de Courville • *Scr* AR Rawlinson, Michael Pertwee, Basil Mason, from a novel by WB Ferguson

Crackers ★★ 15

Comedy 1984 · US · Colour · 87mins

Directed by Louis Malle, this offbeat American comedy caper is actually a remake of the 1956 Italian movie, *Big Deal on Madonna Street*. Donald Sutherland is an unemployed security guard who plots to crack the safe in Jack Warden's San Francisco pawn shop with his group of misfits. Like the plot itself, this is a botched job, neither as funny nor as tense as intended. That said, it is full of whimsy and weird performances, and features Sean Penn in an early role. AT

Donald Sutherland *Weslake* • Jack Warden *Garvey* • Sean Penn *Dillard* • Wallace Shawn *Turtle* • Larry Riley *Boardwalk* • Trinidad Silva *Ramon* • Christine Baranski *Maxine* ■ *Dir* Louis Malle • *Scr* Jeffrey Fiskin, from the film *Big Deal on Madonna Street* by Suso Cecchi D'Amico, Mario Monicelli, Agenore Incrocci, Furio Scarpelli

The Cracksman ★★ U

Crime comedy 1963 · UK · Colour · 107mins

This is far and away Charlie Drake's finest hour on the big screen. Sadly, that's not saying much. He also co-scripted this average crime comedy, in which he plays a locksmith whose devotion to duty lands him in jail. A muddle of slapstick and pathos, the film is ridiculously overlong and needlessly opulent. DP

Charlie Drake *Ernest Wright* • George Sanders *The Guv'nor* • Dennis Price *Grantley* • Nyree Dawn Porter *Muriel* • Eddie Byrne *Domino* • Finlay Currie *Feathers* • Percy Herbert *Nosher* ■ *Dir* Peter Graham Scott • *Scr* Lew Schwartz, Mike Watts, Charlie Drake

Cradle of Fear ★★★ 18

Portmanteau horror
2001 · UK · Colour · 119mins

Drenched in blood and bad taste, this chronicles the crimes of a cannibalistic hypnotist and his lugubrious henchman. Shot on high-resolution video against the backdrop of some quintessentially British locations, this gore quartet revels in its scabrous portrait of a decadent society in which no depravity is deemed excessive and no one is immune from an obsession with self-gratification. Harking back to the innocent days of the video nasty, without ever quite over-stepping the bounds of decency, this is still definitely not for the squeamish or the humourless. DP DVD

Dani Filth *The man* • Eileen Daly *Natalie* • Emily Bouffante *Melissa* • Stuart Laing *Richard* • David McEwen *Kemper* • Louie Brownsell *Nick* • Emma Rice *Emma* • Edmund Dehn *Detective Neilson* ■ *Dir/Scr* Alex Chandon

Cradle 2 the Grave ★★★ 15

Martial arts crime thriller
2003 · US · Colour · 97mins

Romeo Must Die duo Jet Li and rapper DMX here reunite with director Andrzej Bartkowiak for another frenetic slice of cultural fusion. An unpretentious action thriller combining eastern martial arts with western urban grit, this plays with the clichés of the buddy movie. DMX's streetwise entrepreneur is forced into an uneasy alliance with Taiwanese intelligence agent Li after his young daughter is kidnapped by Li's former partner (Mark Dacascos). This is witty, with the stereotypes inverted, and the action sequences are imaginative. SF. Contains violence, swearing and sex scenes. [VIDEO] DVD

Jet Li *Su* • DMX X *Tony Fait* • Anthony Anderson *Tommy* • Kelly Hu *Sona* • Tom Arnold *Archie* • Mark Dacascos *Ling* • Gabrielle Union *Daria* ■ *Dir* Andrzej Bartkowiak • *Scr* John O'Brien, Channing Gibson, from a story by John O'Brien

Cradle Will Rock ★★★ 15

Political drama based on a true story
1999 · US · Colour · 128mins

Set during the anti-communist witch-hunts of the 1930s, this dense and rather gruelling political drama focuses on the efforts of a bunch of New York theatre folk, including Orson Welles, to stage a left-wing play. When the powers that be block the project, all involved decide the show must go on. Tim Robbins marshals the material with skill, convincingly evoking the vibrancy of both place and period. Yet he over-eggs the pudding by cramming in too many intertwined storylines. DA [VIDEO] DVD

Hank Azaria *Marc Blitzstein* • Rubén Blades *Diego Rivera* • Joan Cusack *Hazel Huffman* • John Cusack *Nelson Rockefeller* • Cary Elwes *John Houseman* • Philip Baker Hall *Gray Mathers* • Cherry Jones *Hallie Flanagan* • Angus MacFadyen *Orson Welles* • Bill Murray *Tommy Crickshaw* • Vanessa Redgrave *Countess LaGrange* • Susan Sarandon *Margherita Sarfatti* • John Turturro *Aldo Silvano* • Emily Watson *Olive Stanton* ■ *Dir/Scr* Tim Robbins

The Craft ★★★ 15

Supernatural horror thriller
1996 · US · Colour · 100mins

A quartet of wannabe witches find that sorcery is a real help when it comes to relationship problems and dealing with their various physical and emotional worries. Until one of them seeks real power, that is. This engaging teen version of *The Witches of Eastwick* skilfully mixes a brew of plausible characters, neat visual effects and a few genuinely creepy moments. The attractive cast of stars-to-be (including *Scream*'s Neve Campbell and Skeet Ulrich) coupled with the film's glossy visual style lift this above your average genre fare, as does a smarter-than-expected script. JC [VIDEO] DVD

Robin Tunney *Sarah* • Fairuza Balk *Nancy* • Neve Campbell *Bonnie* • Rachel True *Rochelle* • Skeet Ulrich *Chris* • Christine Taylor *Laura Lizzie* • Breckin Meyer *Mitt* • Nathaniel Marston *Trey* • Cliff De Young *Mr Bailey* ■ *Dir* Andrew Fleming • *Scr* Peter Filardi, Andrew Fleming, from a story by Peter Filardi

The Craic ★★★ 15

Comedy 1999 · Aus · Colour · 85mins

Stand-up comic Jimeoin McKeown stars as a Belfast shirker, who has to flee with his mate Alan McKee after they fall foul of IRA leader Robert Morgan. Things get no better in Sydney, where his appearance on a TV dating game results in immigration officials, secret service agents and Morgan pursuing him through the outback. The winning personality of the star and the perfect pitch and pace of Ted Emery's direction ensured its place among the biggest box-office hits in Australian cinema history. DP. Contains swearing. [VIDEO]

Jimeoin [Jimeoin McKeown] *Fergus* • Alan McKee *Wesley* • Robert Morgan *Colin* • Jane Hall *Alice* • Kate Gorman *Margo* ■ *Dir* Ted Emery • *Scr* Jimeoin [Jimeoin McKeown]

Craig's Wife ★★

Drama 1936 · US · BW · 74mins

This was the movie that turned actress Rosalind Russell into a fully fledged box-office name: a turgid tale about a housewife who cares more for material things than for her husband. Overrated cult director Dorothy Arzner, a former editor and scriptwriter, tries to add hidden depths to the source material, an intractable play by Grace Kelly's uncle, George. TS

Rosalind Russell *Harriet Craig* • John Boles *Walter Craig* • Billie Burke *Mrs Frazier* • Jane Darwell *Mrs Harold* • Dorothy Wilson *Ethel Landreth* • Alma Kruger *Miss Austen* ■ *Dir* Dorothy Arzner • *Scr* Mary C McCall Jr, from the play by George Kelly

The Cranes Are Flying ★★★★ U

Romantic drama 1957 · USSR · BW · 91mins

One of the first Soviet films made after a political "thaw" which seemed to herald a new artistic freedom in the country's cinema, this prize-winning love story, directed by Mikhail Kalatozov, concerns a young hospital worker (Tatyana Samoilova) who contracts a loveless marriage following reports that her soldier fiancé has been killed. An unpretentious and poetic movie about love and the Second World War that benefits from some majestic camerawork and a sensitive performance by Samoilova. The film received the Palme d'Or at Cannes in 1958. RB

Tatyana Samoilova *Veronica* • Alexei Batalov *Boris* • Vasili Merkuriev *Byodor Ivanovich* • Aleksandr Shvorin *Mark* • S Kharitonova *Irina* ■ *Dir* Mikhail Kalatozov • *Scr* Victor Rosov, from a play by Victor Rosov • *Cinematographer* Sergei Urusevsky

Crash! ★

Horror 1977 · US · Colour · 89mins

An early low-budget wreck from director Charles Band, the king of 1970s schlock and future video horror maverick. Sue Lyon brings home a supernatural relic whose spirit possesses anything with wheels, including the family auto. When her crippled husband (José Ferrer) tries to kill her, the demonic vehicle tries to kill him in return. A strange mix of infidelity, sorcery and garage mechanics, this mediocre effort would be funny were it not so confusing. AJ

José Ferrer *Marc Denne* • John Carradine *Dr Edwards* • Sue Lyon *Kim Denne* • John Ericson *Greg* • Leslie Parrish *Kathy* ■ *Dir* Charles Band • *Scr* Marc Marais

Crash ★★★★★ 18

Drama 1996 · Can · Colour · 96mins

How the giving and receiving of love, and the sexual act that usually communicates those primal feelings, will evolve in our increasingly technological world, is at the core of this controversial masterpiece from director David Cronenberg. Based on JG Ballard's cult novel, this uncompromising film is set among a group of urban sophisticates so morally exhausted that they need to invent perversions to keep what sensuality they have left alive. Car accidents become sado-masochistic turn-ons and bodily injury becomes a metaphor for how we must reshape our eroded humanity to exist in the hi-tech future. In no way pornographic or exploitative, and containing the most astonishing performance from Deborah Kara Unger, Cronenberg's daring, intellectual wake-up call is potent food for thought and a landmark 1990s fantasy. AJ. Contains swearing, sex scenes, nudity, violence. [VIDEO] DVD

James Spader *James Ballard* • Holly Hunter *Dr Helen Remington* • Elias Koteas *Vaughan* • Deborah Kara Unger *Catherine Ballard* • Rosanna Arquette *Gabrielle* • Peter MacNeil [Peter MacNeill] *Colin Seagrave* ■ *Dir* David Cronenberg • *Scr* David Cronenberg, from the novel by JG Ballard

Crash ★★★★ 15

Drama 2004 · US · Colour · 112mins

A cross-section of Los Angeles residents interact in unpredictable ways in debuting director Paul Haggis's interwoven urban drama. The characters – the corrupt cop (Matt Dillon), the highly-strung wife (Thandie Newton), the sharp detective (Don Cheadle) among them – are fully developed, connected to each other by their very personalities as well as their proximity. Haggis's film offers innovative surprises while remaining dramatically accessible, as events, both kind and cruel, occur that even the most practiced moviegoer cannot foresee. Cinematic, entertaining and edifying. KK. Contains swearing and violence.

Sandra Bullock *Jean* • Don Cheadle *Graham Walters* • Matt Dillon *Officer Ryan* • Jennifer Esposito *Ria* • William Fichtner *Flanagan* • Brendan Fraser *Rick* • Terrence Howard *Cameron* • Chris "Ludacris" Bridges *Anthony* • Thandie Newton *Christine* • Ryan Phillippe *Officer Hanson* ■ *Dir* Paul Haggis • *Scr* Paul Haggis, Bobby Moresco, from a story by Paul Haggis

Crash Dive ★★ U

Second World War adventure
1943 · US · Colour · 101mins

It seems there was nothing more important over at 20th Century-Fox post-Pearl Harbor than whether handsome Tyrone Power or rugged Dana Andrews would land up with pretty Anne Baxter. But stick with this (it's dull in patches) to witness Hollywood propaganda at its most blatant. The special effects won an Oscar (Fred Sersen for visuals, Roger Heman for sound). TS DVD

Tyrone Power USMCR [Tyrone Power] *Lt Ward Stewart* • Anne Baxter *Jean Hewlett* • Dana Andrews *Lt Comm Dewey Connors* • James Gleason *McDonnell* • Dame May Whitty *Grandmother* ■ *Dir* Archie Mayo • *Scr* Jo Swerling, from a story by WR Burnett

Crash Landing ★ U

Disaster drama 1958 · US · BW · 76mins

This low-budget drama about a passenger airplane that develops engine trouble mid-Atlantic and is forced to ditch in the ocean has troubles of its own holding the audience's attention. There is the usual varied assortment of characters, with flashbacks to their lives on terra firma merely dissipating any tension that might have been built up. Gary Merrill is the captain, while Nancy Davis plays his wife; she quit acting after this film to concentrate on life as Mrs Ronald Reagan. AE

Gary Merrill *Steve Williams* • Nancy Reagan [Nancy Davis] *Helen Williams* • Irene Hervey *Bernice Willouby* • Roger Smith *John Smithback* • Bek Nelson *Nancy Arthur* • Jewell Lain *Ann Thatcher* • Sheridan Comerate *Howard Whitney* • Richard Newton *Jed Sutton* ■ *Dir* Fred F Sears • *Scr* Fred Freiberger

Crashout ★★★ 15

Crime drama 1955 · US · BW · 84mins

This tough crime drama follows six escaped convicts as they spend three days holed up in a cave before going after buried loot. The usual fall-outs and double crosses steadily reduce their number, but telling characterisations and clever plot developments maintain the interest. All credit to the usually undistinguished director and co-writer, Lewis R Foster, who has the benefit of some terrific black-and-white photography by Russell Metty. AE [VIDEO]

William Bendix *Van Duff* • Arthur Kennedy *Joe Quinn* • Luther Adler *Pete Mendoza* • William Talman *Swanee Remsen* • Gene Evans *Monk Collins* • Marshall Thompson *Billy Lang* • Beverly Michaels *Alice Mosher* • Gloria Talbott *Girl on train* ■ *Dir* Lewis R Foster • *Scr* Lewis R Foster, Hal E Chester

The Crater Lake Monster ★

Science fiction 1977 · US · Colour · 85mins

This account of a meteorite thawing a frozen dinosaur egg at the bottom of a lake is so slow and shoddy, it makes some of the worst 1950s monster movies look like masterpieces. It's more concerned with two cretins who live around the lake, getting into endless inane bouts of comic chatter and slapstick situations. KB

Richard Cardella *Sherriff Steve Hanson* • Glen Roberts *Arnie Chabot* • Mark Siegel *Mitch Kowalski* • Kacey Cobb *Susan Patterson* ■ *Dir* William R Stromberg • *Scr* William R Stromberg, Richard Cardella

The Crawling Hand ★★★

Horror 1963 · US · BW · 88mins

The dismembered hand of an alien-possessed astronaut lands on a beach in California, where a student finds it and discovers its evil, strangulating powers. Herbert L Strock's skilful direction, and a game cast rising to the illogical occasion, make this a delightfully schlocky exploitation film that successfully goes for the jugular with effective shock cuts and a demented drive. AJ

Peter Breck *Steve Curan* • Kent Taylor *Doc Weitzberg* • Rod Lauren *Paul Lawrence* • Sirry Steffen *Marta Farnstrom* • Alan Hale [Alan Hale Jr] *Sheriff* • Arline Judge *Mrs Hotchkiss* ■ *Dir* Herbert L Strock • *Scr* Herbert L Strock, William Idelson, from a story by Robert Young, Joseph Cranston

Craze ★

Horror 1973 · UK · Colour · 95mins

Jack Palance gives his eye-rolling all as a mad antique collector who plans to increase his wealth by sacrificing London dolly birds to his favourite African idol. Trashy, endless rubbish from producer Herman Cohen, with an amazingly eclectic cast, this infernal nonsense even defeats veteran horror director Freddie Francis. A waste of everyone's time. AJ

Jack Palance *Neal Mottram* • Diana Dors *Dolly Newman* • Julie Ege *Helena* • Edith Evans *Aunt Louise* • Trevor Howard *Superintendent Bellamy* • Suzy Kendall *Sally* • Michael Jayston *Detective Sergeant Wall* • Hugh Griffith *Solicitor* ■ *Dir* Freddie Francis • *Scr* Aben Kandel, Herman Cohen, from the novel *Infernal Idol* by Henry Seymour

The Crazies ★★★ 18

Science-fiction horror
1973 · US · Colour · 102mins

This is a commendable, if unsuccessful, attempt by director George A Romero to repeat the success of his revolutionary horror classic *Night of the Living Dead*. Here, panic and paranoia prevail when an army plane carrying a biochemical virus crashes in Pennsylvania and turns the locals into killers. Shifting points of view keep involvement to a minimum and greatly undercut the suspense, despite the sudden acts of shocking violence and some effective gore moments. AJ. Contains violence and swearing. DVD

Lane Carroll *Judy* • WG McMillan [Will MacMillan] *David* • Harold Wayne Jones *Clank* • Lloyd Hollar *Col Pockem* • Richard Liberty *Artie* • Lynn Lowry *Kathie* • Richard France *Dr Watts* ■ *Dir* George A Romero • *Scr* George A Romero, from a story by Paul McCollough

C

crazy/beautiful ★★★ 12

Romantic drama 2001 · US · Colour · 94mins

Director John Stockwell's sexy teen drama is predictable from beginning to end, but fortunately the journey is made bearable by the refreshing charm of Kirsten Dunst who illuminates even the most witless lines of dialogue. She plays a spoilt little rich girl who's constantly getting into drink and drug trouble. Deprived Hispanic Jay Hernandez, on the other hand, is a model student who takes his career goals seriously. They fall in love and wreak havoc on each other's differing lives, but at least the story is free of the usual clichés and manages to tread the fine line between moralising and being hip. AJ DVD

Kirsten Dunst *Nicole Oakley* • Jay Hernandez *Carlos Nunez* • Bruce Davison *Tom Oakley* • Herman Osorio *Luis* • Miguel Castro *Eddie* • Tommy De La Cruz *Victor* ■ *Dir* John Stockwell • *Scr* Phil Hay, Matt Manfredi

Crazy from the Heart ★★★★ PG

Romantic comedy
1991 · US · Colour · 90mins

The consistently under-rated Christine Lahti gives a glorious performance as a schoolteacher who falls for janitor Rubén Blades, causing all sorts of ructions in her small town. Lahti's real-life husband Thomas Schlamme directs with a sure, delicate touch that lifts this potentially ordinary story, revealing considerable character insight. The pace is nigh on perfect, the leading actors are believable and the charge generated between them keeps the audience guessing to the very end. SH. Contains swearing.

Christine Lahti *Charlotte Bain* • Rubén Blades *Ernesto Ontiveros* • William Russ *Coach Dewey Whitcomb* • Louise Latham *Mae Esther Bain* • Tommy Muñiz *Tomas Ontiveros* • Mary Kay Place *Merrilee Payton* • Robyn Lively *Franny Payton* ■ *Dir* Thomas Schlamme • *Scr* Linda Voorhees

Crazy in Alabama ★★★ 12

Comedy drama 1999 · US · Colour · 108mins

Antonio Banderas makes an accomplished directorial debut with an engaging mix of quirky comedy and civil rights drama that gives his partner, Melanie Griffith, her best role in years. While downtrodden housewife Lucille (Griffith) heads for Hollywood with her husband's head in a hatbox, her young nephew Peejoe (Lucas Black) becomes a key witness in the murder of a black protester. Robert Wagner and Rod Steiger shine in supporting roles. NS DVD

Melanie Griffith *Lucille* • David Morse *Dove* • Lucas Black *Peejoe* • Cathy Moriarty *Earlene* • Meat Loaf Aday [Meat Loaf] *Sheriff John Doggett* • Rod Steiger *Judge Mead* • Robert Wagner *Harry Hall* • Elizabeth Perkins *Joan Blake* ■ *Dir* Antonio Banderas • *Scr* Mark Childress, from his novel

Crazy in Love ★★★★ PG

Romantic drama 1992 · US · Colour · 89mins

Here's one for those who usually give TV movies a miss. Director Martha Coolidge conjures up a winning drama in which she gets the balance between comedy and sentiment just about right. This is the sort of frothy romance Hollywood made to order before someone mislaid the formula. Holly Hunter and her one-time flatmate Frances McDormand give lovely performances as two island dwellers trapped by convention and insecurity. Yet the film belongs to Gena Rowlands who makes acting look easy. DP

Holly Hunter *Georgie Symonds* • Gena Rowlands *Honora* • Frances McDormand *Clare* • Bill Pullman *Nick Symonds* • Julian Sands *Mark Constable* • Herta Ware *Pem* • Joanne Baron *Mona Tuchman* • Diane Robin *Jean Snizort* ■ *Dir* Martha Coolidge • *Scr* Gerald Ayres, from the novel by Luanne Rice

Crazy Mama ★★★

Crime road movie 1975 · US · Colour · 79mins

This rough-hewn road movie from director Jonathan Demme tracks three generations of women, plus their partners, on a lunatic trans-American crime spree. Cloris Leachman, Ann Sothern, Jim Backus and Stuart Whitman head the eclectic cast of an upbeat celebration of 1950s Americana that stems from Demme's so-called "exploitation" period. Worth seeing as an indication of where a top talent learns his trade. DA

Cloris Leachman *Melba* • Stuart Whitman *Jim Bob* • Ann Sothern *Sheba* • Jim Backus *Mr Albertson* • Donny Most *Shawn* • Linda Purl *Cheryl* • Bryan England *Snake* • Dennis Quaid ■ *Dir* Jonathan Demme • *Scr* Robert Thom, from a story by Frances Doel

Crazy Moon ★★★★ 15

Comedy drama 1986 · Can · Colour · 85mins

This comic tale originally went by the rather hideous name of *Huggers*, but don't let either title put you off: this sweet, if somewhat clichéd romance has a lot to recommend it. Kiefer Sutherland is moving as the wealthy high-school outsider who falls for a deaf girl (Vanessa Vaughan) and encounters opposition from family and peers. Judging from Allan Eastman's film, Sutherland has clearly inherited a considerable amount of talent from his father, Donald – though in subsequent movies it was not always so evident. JB DVD

Kiefer Sutherland *Brooks* • Peter Spence *Cleveland* • Vanessa Vaughan *Anne* • Ken Pogue *Alec* • Eve Napier *Mimi* • Harry Hill *Dr Bruno* ■ *Dir* Allan Eastman • *Scr* Tom Berry, Stefan Wodoslawsky

Crazy People ★ 15

Comedy 1990 · US · Colour · 87mins

An embarrassingly bungled comedy which started life with the best of intentions (to satirise the glossy excesses of the advertising industry) but which slipped heavily on its own banana skin. Dudley Moore, is the ad man who is thrown into a luxury sanatorium after he launches a campaign of slogans which tell the truth. So ineptly handled that it veers on the offensive. SH. Contains swearing. DVD

Dudley Moore *Emory Leeson* • Daryl Hannah *Kathy Burgess* • Paul Reiser *Stephen Bachman* • JT Walsh *Charles F Drucker* • Bill Smitrovich *Bruce* • Alan North *Judge* • David Paymer *George* • Mercedes Ruehl *Dr Liz Baylor* ■ *Dir* Tony Bill • *Scr* Mitch Markowitz

The Crazy World of Laurel and Hardy ★★★ U

Compilation 1964 · US · BW · 81mins

Robert Youngson was the master of the comedy compilation and his tributes to Stan and Ollie are vastly superior to this so-so selection from producer Jay Ward. While it's possible to overlook the slapdash treatment of their slapstick silents and the haphazard ordering of the talkie clips, it's hard to forgive the fact that the gags have been so pared down that all that remains is a fistful of punchlines. The boys are always welcome, but Garry Moore's smart-aleck commentary is an unwanted intrusion. DP

Stan Laurel *Stan* • Oliver Hardy *Ollie* • James Finlayson • Jean Harlow • Garry Moore *Narrator* ■ *Dir* Garry Moore • *Scr* Bill Scott

Creator ★★ 15

Romantic comedy drama
1985 · US · Colour · 103mins

This jumbled comedy drama involves a Nobel Prize-winning scientist turned college professor who tries to resurrect his long-dead wife via cloning. Peter O'Toole brings his customary God-like grandeur to the lead role, complemented by a young, amiable supporting cast. The film's chief handicap is an excess of soap opera-style plot strands. JC DVD

Peter O'Toole *Dr Harry Wolper* • Mariel Hemingway *Meli* • Vincent Spano *Boris* • Virginia Madsen *Barbara Spencer* • David Ogden Stiers *Sid Kuhlenbeck* • John Dehner *Paul* • Karen Kopins *Lucy Wolper* • Kenneth Tigar *Pavlo* ■ *Dir* Ivan Passer • *Scr* Jeremy Leven, from his novel

Creature from the Black Lagoon ★★★★ PG

Horror 1954 · US · BW · 75mins

It's horribly dated, the acting's lousy, the 3-D effects are worthless and the monster is a man in a rubber suit. Yet this remains one of the all-time classic monster movies. The by-the-numbers plot – explorers encounter a half-man, half-fish that has the hots for Julia Adams – is enlivened by director Jack Arnold's atmospheric use of the Florida Everglades locations and a sympathetic portrait of the "Gill-Man". (Champion swimmer Ricou Browning was picked for the role because he could hold his breath for four minutes at a time.) The underwater sequences are particularly memorable, while the scene where Adams swims alone with the creature watching from below plays upon all our fears of what may lurk beneath the sea. Avoid the two turgid sequels that followed: *Revenge of the Creature* (1955) and *The Creature Walks among Us* (1956). RS DVD

Richard Carlson *David Reed* • Julia Adams [Julie Adams] *Kay Lawrence* • Richard Denning *Mark Williams* • Antonio Moreno *Carl Maia* • Nestor Paiva *Lucas* • Whit Bissell *Edwin Thompson* • Ben Chapman *Gill-Man* • Ricou Browning *Gill-Man (underwater sequences only)* ■ *Dir* Jack Arnold • *Scr* Harry Essex, Arthur Ross, from a story by Maurice Zimm

The Creature Walks among Us ★★

Horror 1956 · US · BW · 78mins

The third and final outing for *The Creature from the Black Lagoon* (after 1955's *Revenge of the Creature*). Captured in the Everglades by scientists Jeff Morrow and Rex Reason, the famous Gillman is mutated so he can live on land. Blamed for a crime he didn't commit, the transformed semi-human (Don Megowan) breaks out of his cage to bring his tormentors to justice while falling under the spell of Leigh Snowden's sexy charms. Directed as just another conventional monster movie, this is a disappointment. AJ

Jeff Morrow *Dr William Barton* • Rex Reason *Dr Thomas Morgan* • Leigh Snowden *Marcia Barton* • Gregg Palmer *Jed Grant* • Maurice Manson *Dr Borg* • Don Megowan *Creature (on land)* ■ *Dir* John Sherwood • *Scr* Arthur Ross

Creature with the Atom Brain ★

Science-fiction crime horror
1955 · US · BW · 69mins

"He comes from beyond the grave!" hailed the poster, and you'll feel like crawling into one after watching this laboured hokum. Here a suitably bonkers Richard Denning uses atomic energy to create zombie-like robots as instruments of his tortured revenge. Curt Siodmak, who wrote the classic *I Walked with a Zombie* in 1943, really seems to be slumming it here. RS

Richard Denning *Dr Chet Walker* • Angela Stevens *Joyce Walker* • S John Launer *Captain Dave Harris* • Michael Granger *Frank Buchanan* • Gregory Gaye *Professor Steigg* ■ *Dir* Edward L Cahn • *Scr* Curt Siodmak

Les Créatures ★★★★

Drama
1966 · Fr/Swe · Colour and BW · 91mins

Agnès Varda's most avant-garde film begins with an inverted *hommage* to the scene in Robert Bresson's *Pickpocket*, as items are slipped into pockets rather as ideas unwittingly pop into heads. Following a car crash, as a result of which hard-boiled novelist Michel Piccoli is scarred and wife Catherine Deneuve is left mute, the action switches to the island of Noirmoutier, where Piccoli finds inspiration for his latest book by walking among the eccentric inhabitants. With copious shots of sea crabs, a sequence involving a talking rabbit and a human chess game, this is an often surreal experience. But its optimistic conclusion shifts it back from fairy tale into something approaching life. DP. In French with English subtitles.

Catherine Deneuve *Mylène* • Michel Piccoli *Edgar* • Eva Dahlbeck *Michèle Quellec* • Jacques Charrier *René de Montyon* • Nino Castelnuovo *Jean Modet* • Ursula Kubler *Vamp* ■ *Dir/Scr* Agnès Varda

Creatures the World Forgot ★★ 18

Horror 1971 · UK · Colour · 91mins

Hammer's fourth exotic excursion back to One Million Years BC skips monster dinosaurs and special effects to concentrate on sexy cavewomen. Buxom Julie Ege is the daughter of a tribal chief given to the leader of a rival clan, in a thin story that's just an excuse for the former Miss Norway to slip into a revealing wardrobe of leather bikinis and skimpy furs. Some may find this enough, though director Don Chaffey does try hard to keep his Jurassic lark on the side of seriousness. AJ. Contains nudity.

Julie Ege *Nala* • Brian O'Shaughnessy *Mak* • Tony Bonner *Toomak* • Robert John *Rool* • Marcia Fox *Dumb girl* • Rosalie Crutchley *Old crone* • Don Leonard *Old leader* ■ *Dir* Don Chaffey • *Scr* Michael Carreras

Creep ★★★ 18

Horror thriller
2004 · UK/Ger · Colour · 81mins

Christopher Smith's debut feature is an entertaining ghost-train ride through subterranean hazards. A late journey on the London Underground turns into a nightmare for Franka Potente when she falls asleep on a platform and finds herself trapped underground. An attempted rape sends her further into the dank, dark tunnels where something even more dangerous lurks. Tautly directed by Smith and well-anchored by a barnstorming turn from Potente, this often brutal tale creeps you out with sudden shocks, eerie atmospherics and gory thrills. AJ. Contains violence. DVD

Franka Potente *Kate* • Sean Harris *Craig* • Vas Blackwood *George* • Ken Campbell *Arthur* •

Jeremy Sheffield *Guy* • Paul Rattray *Jimmy* • Kelly Scott *Mandy* • Debora Weston *Mya* • Emily Gilchrist *Karen* ■ *Dir/Scr* Christopher Smith

The Creeping Flesh ★★★ 15

Horror 1972 · UK · Colour · 88mins

Scientist Peter Cushing discovers a giant skeleton in Borneo, which grows flesh when touched by water, in this over-complicated Victorian morality fable given a classy Hammer-style sheen by director Freddie Francis. Don't try to make sense of it: just enjoy the gloomily disturbing dark tone and some neat shocks provided by the prehistoric perambulating bones. Co-star Christopher Lee is bloodcurdling as an envious brother, while Cushing's sympathetic performance ranks with his best screen work. AJ [video] DVD

Christopher Lee *James Hildern* • Peter Cushing *Emmanuel Hildern* • Lorna Heilbron *Penelope* • George Benson *Waterlow* • Kenneth J Warren *Lenny* • Duncan Lamont *Inspector* • Harry Locke *Barman* • Hedger Wallace *Dr Perry* • Michael Ripper *Carter* ■ *Dir* Freddie Francis • *Scr* Peter Spenceley, Jonathon Rumbold

Creepozoids ★ 18

Horror 1987 · US · Colour · 68mins

Prolific hack director David DeCouteau strikes again with this substandard *Alien* copy set in post-nuclear 1998. Five army deserters shelter from acid rain in an abandoned laboratory where they are terrorised by bad muppet mutants including a shockingly awful giant rat and a baby monster. A vapid groan-inducer. AJ [video] DVD

Linnea Quigley *Bianca* • Ken Abraham *Butch* • Michael Aranda *Jesse* • Richard Hawkins *Jake* • Kim McKamy *Kate* ■ *Dir* David DeCoteau • *Scr* David DeCoteau, Burford Hauser

Creepshow ★★★ 15

Horror 1982 · US · Colour · 115mins

Night of the Living Dead director George A Romero and top terror writer Stephen King neatly capture the ironic spirit of those forbidden 1950s horror comics in a lively anthology of ghoulishly funny fear tales. Zombie fathers, green space fungus, caged ancient creatures and the walking dead adroitly come alive from the pages of a comic book thrown away by a concerned parent. Stylishly scary stuff. AJ. Contains swearing violence. [video]

Hal Holbrook *Henry* • Adrienne Barbeau *Wilma* • Fritz Weaver *Dexter* • Leslie Nielsen *Richard* • EG Marshall *Upson* • Ed Harris *Hank* • Ted Danson *Harry* • Stephen King *Jordy* ■ *Dir* George A Romero • *Scr* Stephen King

Creepshow 2 ★ 18

Horror 1987 · US · Colour · 85mins

Penny-dreadful in every respect, this three-part anthology is one of the worst vehicles off the Stephen King production line. A comic-crazed kid opens the latest issue of *Creepshow* and delves into tales concerning a murderous cigar store Indian, a killer oil slick and a zombie hitch-hiker. This slapdash dud is devoid of any imagination. AJ [video] DVD

Tom Savini *The Creep* • Domenick John *Boy Billy* • Dan Kamin *Old Chief Wood'nhead* • George Kennedy *Ray Spruce* • Dorothy Lamour *Martha Spruce* • Frank S Salsedo [Frank Salsedo] *Ben Whitemoon* • Paul Satterfield *Deke* ■ *Dir* Michael Gornick • *Scr* George A Romero, from stories by Stephen King

Cremaster 4 ★★ 12A

Experimental fantasy
1994 · US/UK/Fr · Colour · 42mins

American artist Matthew Barney here turns cinema into art with this first instalment in his ambitious five-part film project, the *Cremaster* cycle. Curiously beginning with *Cremaster 4* (episodes 1,5,2 and 3 follow respectively), this dreamy slice of abstract weirdness is simultaneously beguiling and bewildering. Everything unfolds so differently to conventional film-making that Barney immediately captures attention with a series of bizarre, dialogue-free scenarios that loosely centre around the Isle of Man TT races and Manx folklore. Yet unlike later parts of the cycle, the repetitive nature of these scenes and their languorous pace makes it hard to maintain this initial fascination. Visually, the film is remarkable. SF

Matthew Barney *Loughton candidate* • Dave Molyneux *Ascending hack, Team Molyneux* • Graham Molyneux *Ascending hack, Team Molyneux* • Steve Sinnot *Descending hack, Team Sinnot* • Karl Sinnot *Descending hack, Team Sinnot* • Sharon Marvel *Loughton faerie* ■ *Dir/Scr* Matthew Barney

Cremaster 1 ★★★ PG

Experimental musical
1995 · US · Colour · 41mins

Artist Matthew Barney's second instalment in his five-part *Cremaster* cycle is a cool and refined lesson in abstract image making, and is easier to fathom than its predecessor, *Cremaster 4*. Though the film's dialogue-free surrealism is still entirely bizarre, the symbolism is clearer, based on obvious themes of female fertility and reproduction. Mixing a retro vibe with sci-fi-style sterility, Barney uses two Goodyear airships floating above an American football stadium as the centrepiece to his celluloid art. Inside the craft, immaculately groomed air stewardesses flaunt their elegance, while on the pitch below dazzlingly dressed women perform synchronised dance routines à la Busby Berkeley. Hypnotically compelling. SF

Marti Domination *Goodyear* • Gemma Bourdon Smith *Goodyear hostess in Green Lounge* • Kathleen Crepeau *Goodyear hostess in Green Lounge* • Nina Kotov *Goodyear hostess in Green Lounge* • Jessica Sherwood *Goodyear hostess in Green Lounge* • Tanyth Berkeley *Goodyear hostess in Red Lounge* • Miranda Brooks *Goodyear hostess in Red Lounge* • Kari McKahan *Goodyear hostess in Red Lounge* • Catherine Mulchahy *Goodyear hostess in Red Lounge* ■ *Dir/Scr* Matthew Barney

Cremaster 5 ★★★ 12A

Experimental opera
1997 · US · Colour · 54mins

There's actually something of a conventional storyline in the third of artist Matthew Barney's sumptuous *Cremaster* cycle instalments. But the film offers far too much dazzling exotica to be concerned with such commonplace triviality. Ursula Andress plays the Queen of Chain, who sings mournful arias to her dead magician lover (Barney) in an alternate 19th-century Budapest, while flashbacks reveal his fate and a weird giant (Barney again) trots about in the waters of the city's famous Gellert Baths. Richly brought to life, with beautiful attention to detail, this is a baroque, colour-saturated marvel that luxuriates in warmth and passion. SF

Ursula Andress *Queen of Chain* • Matthew Barney *Diva/Giant/Magician* • Joanne Rha *Queen's Usher/Fudor Sprite* • Susan Rha *Queen's Usher/Fudor Sprite* ■ *Dir/Scr* Matthew Barney

Cremaster 2 ★★★ 18

Experimental drama
1999 · US · Colour · 79mins

The biological and reproductive themes that snake through American artist Matthew Barney's five-part cycle go from implicit to explicit in this, the penultimate instalment. An eccentric and challenging mishmash of surreal imagery and outright weirdness, the film artistically re-interprets the life of murderer Gary Gilmore, who received the death penalty for his crimes in 1977. The film mixes the polished sophistication of *Cremaster 1* with the grimy, incessant vulgarity of thrash metal music and the mystery of Houdini (played by Norman Mailer). Like the rest of the cycle, it's highly imaginative and visually astonishing, but this is also the most forceful and confrontational of the five films. SF

Norman Mailer *Harry Houdini* • Matthew Barney *Gary Gilmore* • Anonymous *Baby Fay La Foe* • Lauren Pine *Bessie Gilmore* • Scott Ewalt *Frank Gilmore* • Patty Griffin *Nicole Baker* • Michael Thomson *Max Jensen* ■ *Dir/Scr* Matthew Barney

Cremaster 3 ★★★★ 15

Experimental fantasy
2002 · US · Colour · 179mins

US artist Matthew Barney concludes his epic five-part film project with this sumptuous visual feast. An exotic and immaculately constructed celluloid experience, it's the most accessible of his so-called *Cremaster* cycle – an ambitious and provocative attempt to create pure cinematic art, which began with *Cremaster 4* back in 1994, and continued its wayward journey in episodes *1, 5, 2* respectively. Though all the films lack traditional narrative structures, *3* uses the imposing New York landmarks the Chrysler Building and the Guggenheim Museum as a centrepiece for a dream-like episode involving Masonic ritual, Celtic mythology, a demolition derby and the artist's signature molten Vaseline. The dazzling imagery may be practically impossible to decipher, but Barney's ability to turn abstract ideas into animated tableaux still makes his work spellbinding viewing. SF DVD

Richard Serra *Hiram Abiff* • Matthew Barney *Entered Apprentice* • Aimee Mullins *Entered Novitiate/Oonagh MacCumhail* • Paul Brady *Cloud Club maitre d'* • Terry Gillespie *Cloud Club barman* ■ *Dir/Scr* Matthew Barney • *Cinematographer* Peter Strietmann

The Cremator ★★★★

Black comedy drama 1968 · Cz · BW · 99mins

A prime example of Czech Gothic, this is not only a chilling study of psychological collapse, but also a disturbing insight into the seductive power of totalitarianism. As the Nazi-era undertaker who becomes convinced that he can save humanity by fire, Rudolf Hrusinsky gives a performance that irresistibly recalls Peter Lorre at his most pathetically unhinged. His distorted expressions are emphasised by Juraj Herz's insistent use of close-ups, notably during the scenes at the fairground waxworks and in the pristine bathroom, where he tries to lure his wife, Vlasta Chramostova, into a noose. DP. In Czech with English subtitles.

Vlasta Chramostova *Lakmé* • Rudolf Hrusinsky *Kopfrkingl* • Jirí Menzel *Dvorzak* • Ilja Prachar *Walter Reineke* ■ *Dir* Juraj Herz • *Scr* Juraj Herz, Ladislav Fuks, from the novel by Ladislav Fuks

Crescendo ★★★

Horror 1970 · UK · Colour · 95mins

This "mini-Hitchcock" thriller from Hammer Films borrows as much from *Psycho* as it does from the studio's own series of early 1960s whodunnits (*Paranoiac*, for example). Touted as a new departure for the "House of Horror", this demented tale of dead composers, lunatic twins and drug-addicted cripples merely adds sex and discreet nudity to the tried-and-tested shocker formula. If you can swallow Stefanie Powers as a PhD music student, this one's for you. AJ

Stefanie Powers *Susan* • James Olson *Georges* • Margaretta Scott *Danielle* • Jane Lapotaire *Lillianne* • Joss Ackland *Carter* • Kirsten Betts *Catherine* ■ *Dir* Alan Gibson • *Scr* Jimmy Sangster, Alfred Shaughnessy

Le Cri du Coeur ★★★

Drama
1994 · Fr/Burkina Faso · Colour · 86mins

Burkina Faso's Idrissa Ouedraogo is among the best known sub-Saharan film-makers, with *Yaaba* and *Tilä* garnering international acclaim. His seventh feature follows 11-year-old Moctar and his mother as they leave their village in Mali to join his father in Paris, where he has recently bought a garage. However, hopes that Moctar will one day study medicine are jeopardised after he suffers a series of nightmares about a wild hyena. Measured, thoughtful and earnestly played, this is not Ouedraogo's best work, but the insights into the lives of Africans in urban exile are fascinating. DP. In French with English subtitles.

Richard Bohringer *Paulo* • Said Diarra *Moctar* • Félicité Wouassi *Saffi* • Alex Descas *Ibrahim Sow* • Clémentine Célarié *Deborah* ■ *Dir* Idrissa Ouedraogo • *Scr* Idrissa Ouedraogo, Robert Gardner, Jacques Akchoti

Le Cri du Hibou ★★★★ 15

Black comedy thriller
1987 · Fr/It · Colour · 104mins

Patricia Highsmith's novel has been transposed from the USA to France, where Christophe Malavoy has left Paris, and his psychologically abusive wife, for Vichy. In the middle of a screaming-match divorce, he obsessively watches the beautiful Mathilda May, who responds by neglecting her dreary fiancé. When he disappears, the death-obsessed Malavoy becomes a suspect. Typically, Claude Chabrol is less concerned with narrative than with his characters and clinically dissecting the French middle classes. Elegantly acted by Malavoy, this is also notable for winning Mathilda May a César as most promising young actress. BB. In French with English subtitles. [video]

Christophe Malavoy *Robert* • Mathilda May *Juliette* • Virginie Thévenet *Veronique* • Jacques Penot *Patrick* • Jean-Pierre Kalfon *Commissioner* ■ *Dir* Claude Chabrol • *Scr* Odile Barski, Claude Chabrol, from the novel *The Cry of the Owl* by Patricia Highsmith

Cría Cuervos ★★★

Drama 1975 · Sp · Colour · 109mins

Although it became something of a totem of post-Franco optimism, this elliptical chronicle of a young woman's tormented inner life is really about the passivity of a population disenfranchised by fascism and the guilt it would have to endure before Spain's painful memories could be assuaged. As the child who believes she has power over death after witnessing the demise of her father, Ana Torrent superbly conveys that mix of terror and innocence that is unique to childhood. However, Carlos Saura muddles matters by having Geraldine Chaplin play both Ana's mother and Ana as an adult. DP. In Spanish with English subtitles.

Geraldine Chaplin *Ana as an adult/Maria* • Ana Torrent *Ana* • Conchita Perez *Irene* • Maite Sanchez *Juana* • Monica Randall *Paulina* ■ *Dir/Scr* Carlos Saura

Cries and Whispers ★★★★★ 18

Drama 1972 · Swe · Colour · 87mins

Focusing on the failure of love and the agony of loss, this is one of Ingmar Bergman's finest achievements. Combining memories, fantasies and moments of intense family drama, this harrowing study of pain, passion, sisterhood and death brought Bergman a hat-trick of Oscar nominations, although it was Sven Nykvist who won the award for his luscious cinematography. However, it's the stunning art direction of Marik Vos that provides this disturbing chamber drama with its unforgettable manor house setting and its mesmerising red colour scheme. Harriet Andersson, Ingrid Thulin and Liv Ullmann dominate proceedings as the well-heeled sisters, but Kari Sylwan is every bit as impressive as the peasant maid. DP. In Swedish with English subtitles. Contains emotional scenes of death and self-mutilation. DVD

Ingrid Thulin *Karin* • Liv Ullmann *Maria* • Harriet Andersson *Agnes* • Kari Sylwan *Anna* • Erland Josephson *Doctor* • George Arlin *Karin's husband* • Henning Moritzen *Joakin* ■ *Dir/Scr* Ingmar Bergman

Crime and Passion ★

Comedy drama
1976 · US/W Ger · Colour · 92mins

Shady investment banker Omar Sharif convinces his mistress/secretary Karen Black to marry tycoon Bernhard Wicki, to whom he's heavily in debt. Sharif and Black do their utmost to make the daft plot of this slight comedy drama fly, but it's an uphill battle, especially as they have no really suspenseful or amusing moments to back them up. AJ

Omar Sharif *Andre* • Karen Black *Susan* • Joseph Bottoms *Larry* • Bernhard Wicki *Rolf* ■ *Dir* Ivan Passer • *Scr* Jesse Lasky Jr, Pat Silver, from the novel *An Ace Up Your Sleeve* by James Hadley Chase

Crime and Punishment ★★★★

Crime drama 1935 · Fr · BW · 110mins

Pierre Blanchar walked away with the best actor prize at Venice for his portrayal of Raskolnikov, the angst-ridden student whose killing of a pawnbroker brings the relentless police inspector Porphyre (Harry Baur) down on his head. Blanchar is matched all the way by the brilliant Baur, but this is as much a triumph of art direction as it is of acting, with the doom-laden sets superbly capturing the poverty and despair that make Raskolnikov the most sympathetic of murderers. DP. In French with English subtitles.

Harry Baur *Porphyre* • Pierre Blanchar *Raskolnikov* • Madeleine Ozeray *Sonia* • Marcelle Géniat *Madame Raskolnikov* • Lucienne Lemarchand *Dounia* • Alexandre Rignault *Raxoumikhine* • Magdelaine Berubet *Aliona* ■ *Dir* Pierre Chenal • *Scr* Marcel Ayme, Pierre Chenal, Christian Stengal, Wladimir Strijewski, from the novel by Feodor Dostoyevsky • *Art Director* Eugène Lourié

Crime and Punishment ★★★★

Crime drama 1935 · US · BW · 87mins

An atypical Josef von Sternberg to be sure, but no less fascinating for that. Made on a relatively low budget at Columbia, this dark, semi-expressionist version of the Dostoyevsky classic is pared to the bone with an austerity and religious purity not unlike the works of Carl Dreyer and Robert Bresson. Peter Lorre, in a rare leading role and appearing unusually beautiful, is subtly compelling as the university graduate struggling to overcome his spiritual arrogance, while Edward Arnold is well cast as the resolute inspector who pokes and prods at Lorre's guilt. The pawnbroker murdered by Lorre is played by celebrated theatre actress Mrs Patrick Campbell in one of her rare film roles. Overall a very fine achievement. TS

Peter Lorre *Roderick Raskolnikov* • Edward Arnold *Inspector Porfiry* • Marian Marsh *Sonya* • Tala Birell *Antonya "Toni" Raskolnikov* • Elisabeth Risdon *Mrs Raskolnikov* • Robert Allen *Dmitri* • Douglass Dumbrille *Grilov* • Mrs Patrick Campbell *Pawnbroker* ■ *Dir* Josef von Sternberg • *Scr* SK Lauren, Joseph Anthony, from the novel by Feodor Dostoyevsky

Crime and Punishment ★★★

Crime drama 1983 · Fin · Colour · 93mins

This was the remarkably assured feature debut of Finnish director Aki Kaurismäki. He has made something of a speciality of updating literary classics, but this reworking of Dostoyevsky's harrowing novel is perhaps his most audacious. Markku Toikka stars as Rahikainen, a suitably dissolute-looking latter-day Raskolnikov, whose descent into crime is laid firmly at the door of 1980s Finnish society. DP. In Finnish with English subtitles.

Markku Toikka *Rahikainen* • Aino Seppo • Esko Nikkari • Hannu Lauri • Olli Tuominem ■ *Dir* Aki Kaurismäki • *Scr* Aki Kaurismäki, Paul Pentti, from the novel by Feodor Dostoyevsky

Crime + Punishment in Suburbia ★★ 15

Drama 2000 · US · Colour · 94mins

With its designer nihilism and new-wave gimmickry, director Rob Schmidt's reworking of Dostoyevsky is the darkest of the recent spate of teens-meet-classics pictures. But this dour diatribe has little else to recommend it. Abandoned by her mother Ellen Barkin and abused by her stepfather Michael Ironside, high-school student Monica Keena is driven to bloody revenge. Self-consciously directed by Schmidt, this essay in grunge-spattered melancholy lacks both suburban authenticity and genuine insight. DP DVD

Monica Keena *Roseanne Skolnik* • Vincent Kartheiser *Vincent* • Jeffrey Wright *Chris* • James DeBello *Jimmy* • Michael Ironside *Fred Skolnik* • Ellen Barkin *Maggie Skolnik* ■ *Dir* Rob Schmidt • *Scr* Larry Gross

Crime and Punishment, USA ★★★

Crime drama 1959 · US · BW · 80mins

A genuine curio from American independent director Denis Sanders, who won an Oscar for his brilliant short *A Time Out of War* and is now best remembered for his superb but atypical rockumentary, *Elvis: That's the Way It Is*. This update of Dostoyevsky's novel stars a debuting George Hamilton as the young law student involved in murder, and he gives an impressive performance that is totally at odds with his later "celebrity" status. TS

George Hamilton *Robert* • Mary Murphy *Sally* • Frank Silvera *Lt AD Porter* • Marian Seldes *Debbie Cole* • John Harding *Swanson* • Wayne Heffley *Rafe* • Toni Merrill *Mrs Cole* • Lew Brown (2) *Samuels* ■ *Dir* Denis Sanders • *Scr* Walter Newman, from the novel by Feodor Dostoyevsky

Le Crime de Monsieur Lange ★★★★ PG

Black comedy 1935 · Fr · BW · 80mins

This black comedy belongs to the optimistic phase of French film-making in the 1930s known as "poetic realism". Reflecting director Jean Renoir's enthusiasm for the new government of the left-wing Popular Front, it shows how the workers successfully take over a pulp publishing house on the reported death of its exploitative owner. Jules Berry, as the brutal boss, and René Lefèvre, as the writer whose "Arizona Jim" westerns revive the company's fortunes, are exceptional. However, the film's greatness rests on Renoir's masterly use of deep focus photography, which brings vibrant life to every corner of the magnificent studio set. DP. In French with English subtitles. DVD

René Lefèvre *Lange* • Jules Berry *Batala* • Florelle *Valentine* • Nadia Sibirskaia *Estelle* • Sylvia Bataille *Edith* • Henri Guisol *Meunier* • Maurice Baquet *Charles* • Marcel Levesque *Concierge* ■ *Dir* Jean Renoir • *Scr* Jacques Prévert, Jean Renoir, Jean Castanier, from a story by Jean Castanier • *Cinematographer* Jean Bachelet

Crime Doctor ★★

Horror mystery 1943 · US · BW · 65mins

Based on Max Marcin's popular radio series, this launched a ten-film franchise that was very much in the Columbia tradition of briskly buzzing B-movies. Warner Baxter takes the title role as the former gangster whose bout of amnesia prompts him to embark on a new life as a psychiatrist specialising in the criminal mind. An encounter with his old comrades dominates the opener, but, increasingly, his expertise, rather than his past, became the key to cases involving ghosts, twins, typhoid, dreams, art dealers and arsonists, as well as a good mixture of adroit and doltish cops. DP

Warner Baxter *Robert Ordway/Phil Morgan* • Margaret Lindsay *Grace Fielding* • John Litel *Emilio Caspari* • Ray Collins *Dr John Carey* • Harold Huber *Joe Dylan* • Don Costello (1) *Nick Ferris* • Leon Ames *Captain William Wheeler* • Constance Worth *Betty* ■ *Dir* Michael Gordon • *Scr* Graham Baker, Louis Lantz, Jerome Odlum, from the radio series by Max Marcin

Crime in the Streets ★★★★

Crime drama 1956 · US · BW · 90mins

A terrific early Don Siegel movie, a quintessential 1950s teen angst flick that contains the trademark intensity of writer Reginald Rose. Like Rose's *12 Angry Men*, released the following year, this film started life as a television play in the heyday of US TV drama. John Cassavetes may seem a little old for the teenage lead (he played the role on TV), but Sal Mineo and future director Mark Rydell are superb as his grisly sidekicks. These juvenile delinquents may try your patience as people, but they certainly demand attention in this razor-sharp depiction of street violence. TS

James Whitmore *Ben Wagner* • John Cassavetes *Frankie Dane* • Sal Mineo *Baby Gioia* • Mark Rydell *Lou Macklin* • Denise Alexander *Maria Gioia* • Malcolm Atterbury *Mr McAllister* • Peter Votrian *Richie Dane* • Virginia Gregg *Mrs Dane* ■ *Dir* Don Siegel • *Scr* Reginald Rose, from his TV play

Crime of Passion ★★★★

Film noir 1957 · US · BW · 85mins

In a role tailor-made for her, Barbara Stanwyck stars as the wife of decent cop Sterling Hayden. Ruthlessly ambitious for her husband, she sleeps with about-to-retire police chief Raymond Burr. When he names somebody else as his successor, however, the enraged Stanwyck pulls a gun on him. A skilful suspense drama in the *film noir* mould, this is well directed by Gerd Oswald and played for all its worth by both the principals and the supporting cast, which includes Royal Dano as Hayden's work rival and Fay Wray as Burr's ailing wife. RK

Barbara Stanwyck *Kathy Ferguson* • Sterling Hayden *Bill Doyle* • Raymond Burr *Inspector Tony Pope* • Fay Wray *Alice Pope* • Royal Dano *Captain Alidos* • Virginia Grey *Sara* ■ *Dir* Gerd Oswald • *Scr* Jo Eisinger

Crime of the Century ★★★★ 15

Drama based on a true story
1996 · US · Colour · 110mins

This interesting if rather downbeat movie focuses on the 1932 Lindbergh baby kidnapping and the German immigrant, Bruno Richard Hauptmann, who was arrested for the crime. Based on Ludovic Kennedy's book, the film stars *The Crying Game's* Stephen Rea as the unfortunate Hauptmann, while Isabella Rossellini plays Hauptmann's wife Anna, who stood by him when he was accused of the crime that shocked America and for which the authorities desperately needed a culprit. Gripping stuff, but don't expect all the ends to be tied up by the final credits. JB

Stephen Rea *Bruno Richard Hauptmann* • Isabella Rossellini *Anna Hauptmann* • JT Walsh *Colonel Norman Schwarzkopf Sr* • Michael Moriarty *Governor Harold Hoffman* • Allen Garfield *Lieutenant James Finn* ■ *Dir* Mark Rydell • *Scr* William Nicholson, from the non-fiction book *The Airman and the Carpenter* by Ludovic Kennedy

Crime on the Hill ★★

Crime drama 1933 · UK · BW · 68mins

When a member of the landed gentry is murdered, his estate is expected to go to his niece Sally Blane. But then Phyllis Dare reveals that she and the victim were secretly married. Local vicar Lewis Casson and his friend, doctor Nigel Playfair, decide to investigate further, with the finger of suspicion pointing at Blane's fiancé Anthony Bushell. A creaky, sub-Agatha Christie murder mystery. RK

Sally Blane *Sylvia Kennett* • Nigel Playfair *Dr Moody* • Lewis Casson *Rev Michael Gray* • Anthony Bushell *Tony Fields* • Phyllis Dare *Claire Winslow* • Judy Kelly *Alice Green* ■ *Dir* Bernard Vorhaus • *Scr* Michael Hankinson, Vera Allinson, EM Delafield, Bernard Vorhaus, from a play by Jack de Leon, Jack Celestin

Crime Spree ★★★ 15

Crime comedy
2002 · Can/US/UK · Colour · 95mins

Gérard Depardieu and ageing pop idol Johnny Hallyday star as the leaders of a crew of bumbling French crooks who are sent to Chicago to carry out a major jewellery heist, only to accidentally rob Mafia boss Harvey Keitel. While the film is predictable and derivative, it still works well, thanks in part to the actors' strong chemistry. The bawdy slapstick in the first half is particularly hilarious, although the humour occasionally sits uneasily with the violence. SF. In French and English with subtitles. Contains swearing, sex scenes violence. DVD

Gérard Depardieu *Daniel Foray* • Harvey Keitel *Frankie Zammeti* • Johnny Hallyday *Marcel Burot* • Renaud *Zero* • Richard Bohringer *Laurant Bastaldi* • Saïd Taghmaoui *Sami Zerhouni* • Albert Dray *Raymond Gayet* • Stéphane Freiss *Julien Labesse* ■ *Dir/Scr* Brad Mirman

Crime Story ★★★ 18

Martial arts action thriller
1993 · HK · Colour · 102mins

Although Jackie Chan's new Hollywood fans know him chiefly for such light-hearted romps as *Rush Hour*, when he was in Hong Kong he didn't shy away from harder-edged material. This is a prime example: an action-packed thriller, based loosely on the real-life epidemic of kidnapping that once plagued the former colony. Chan, playing a copy hunting for a missing business man, comes up trumps in some dazzling martial arts action, less fancy but more realistic than some of his later films. JF. In Cantonese with English subtitles. DVD

Jackie Chan *Inspector Eddie Chan* • Kent Cheng *Inspector Hung* • Lo Ka-Ying *Wong Yat-*

Fei ■ *Dir* Kirk Wong • *Scr* Cheun Tin-nam, Chan Man-keung, Cheung Tsi-sing, Chan Tak-sam

Crime without Passion ★★★

Crime drama 1934 · US · BW · 67mins

So successful was the writing partnership of Ben Hecht and Charles MacArthur – the creators of *The Front Page* – that Paramount gave them carte blanche to produce, direct and write this tale about a celebrated lawyer who murders his mistress when he falls for another woman. There's a nice twist in store, though, and a silky smooth Claude Rains unravels most effectively. It's smart, gripping and doesn't hang about. AT

Claude Rains *Lee Gentry* • Margo *Carmen Brown* • Whitney Bourne *Katy Costello* • Stanley Ridges *Eddie White* • Paula Trueman *Buster Malloy* • Leslie Adams *O'Brien* • Greta Granstedt *Della* • Esther Dale *Miss Keeley* ■ *Dir/Scr* Ben Hecht, Charles MacArthur

El Crimen del Padre Amaro ★★★ 15

Religious drama
2002 · Mex/Sp/Arg/Fr · Colour · 113mins

This tale of a young Catholic priest led into temptation during his new countryside posting has photogenic appeal, if limited depth, thanks to its soap-opera level script. Gael García Bernal has narrow scope for characterisation as the lustful priest, but the powerful finale does reveal a tougher side to his amiable personality. Although Bernal's union with attractive churchgoer Ana Claudia Talancón is the film's primary concern, the eccentric supporting characters and the exposé of political corruption within the town are what really fuel the story. Overall, the film lacks the cinematic skill required to justify its rather generous nomination for best foreign film. JC. In Spanish with English subtitles. [VIDEO] DVD

Gael García Bernal *Father Amaro* • Sancho Gracia *Father Benito* • Ana Claudia Talancón *Amelia* • Angélica Aragón *Sanjuanera* • Luisa Huertas *Dionisia* • Damián Alcázar *Father Natalio* • Ernesto Gómez Cruz *Bishop* • Pedro Armendáriz [Pedro Armendáriz Jr] *Municipal president* ■ *Dir* Carlos Carrera • *Scr* Vicente Leñero, from the novel by Eça de Queirós • *Cinematographer* Guillermo Granillo

Crimes and Misdemeanors ★★★★★ 15

Comedy drama 1989 · US · Colour · 99mins

Woody Allen is the finest practitioner of screen comedy since the collapse of the studio system. He is also more than capable of tackling weightier topics in the manner of his idol, Ingmar Bergman. In one of his most ambitious films, Allen combines his archetypal wisecracking style with his more serious moral preoccupations, and the result is a compelling piece of cinema that is as troubling as it is hilarious. The excellent Martin Landau plays an eye surgeon whose lover (Anjelica Huston) threatens to expose his private and professional indiscretions to his loyal wife (Claire Bloom). Allen, as a documentary film-maker, is also at war with himself, although he has a convenient scapegoat for his failures in his brother-in-law (Alan Alda), a TV sitcom director with a gleeful lack of taste and a talent for seducing women. This is a challenging and sophisticated picture that few other American directors could have carried off with such aplomb. DP. Contains some swearing. [VIDEO] DVD

Martin Landau *Judah Rosenthal* • Mia Farrow *Halley Reed* • Alan Alda *Lester* • Woody Allen *Clifford Stern* • Anjelica Huston *Dolores Paley* • Claire Bloom *Miriam Rosenthal* • Joanna Gleason *Wendy Stern* • Sam Waterston *Ben* ■ *Dir/Scr* Woody Allen

Crimes at the Dark House ★★★

Crime melodrama 1939 · UK · BW · 69mins

Tod Slaughter was one of the first cult stars of British cinema. Even at the height of his popularity, his rolling-eye acting style was the last thing in prime ham, yet the barnstorming melodramas in which he appeared make for marvellous entertainment and deserve their place in the hallowed halls of turkeydom. Who cares if this reworking of Wilkie Collins's classic *The Woman in White* creaks so loudly you can scarcely hear the dialogue? It's a rattling good yarn, played with amateur theatrical gusto. DP

Tod Slaughter *Sir Percival Glyde* • Hilary Eaves *Marian Fairlie* • Sylvia Marriott *Laura Fairlie* • Hay Petrie *Dr Fosco* • Geoffrey Wardwell *Paul Hartwright* • David Horne *Mr Fairlie* • Margaret Yarde *Mrs Bullen* ■ *Dir* George King • *Scr* Edward Dryhurst, Frederick Hayward, HF Maltby, from the novel *The Woman in White* by Wilkie Collins

Crimes of Passion ★★ 18

Erotic drama 1984 · US · Colour · 102mins

Ken Russell deserves some credit for attempting this pitch-black satire on sexual fantasy, puritanism and hypocrisy, but his execution leaves much to be desired. The nonchalant naturalism of Kathleen Turner's daytime existence and the lurid sensationalism of her nightly excursions as a hooker work quite well. But there is nothing erotic about her encounters with naive client John Laughlin or unnerving about her brushes with Anthony Perkins's preacher. DP. Contains violence, swearing, sex scenes, nudity. [VIDEO]

Kathleen Turner *Joanna Crane/China Blue* • Anthony Perkins *Reverend Peter Shayne* • John Laughlin *Bobby Grady* • Annie Potts *Amy Grady* • Bruce Davison *Donny Hopper* • Norman Burton *Lou Bateman* • James Crittenden *Tom Marshall* • Peggy Feury *Adrian* ■ *Dir* Ken Russell • *Scr* Barry Sandler

The Crimes of Stephen Hawke ★★★

Period melodrama 1936 · UK · BW · 69mins

Tod Slaughter throws himself with gusto into a gloriously over-the-top performance as a monstrous Regency supervillain, rolling the worst of Jack the Ripper, Frankenstein's monster and Jekyll and Hyde into one. Outwardly a kind-at-heart moneylender, he has, in fact, gained his wealth by murder, viciously snapping the spines of his victims. The only outlet for his humanity is his adopted daughter. A joyously hammy melodrama. PF

Tod Slaughter *Stephen Hawke* • Marjorie Taylor *Julia Hawke* • Eric Portman *Matthew Trimble* • Gerald Barry *Miles Archer* • Ben Soutten *Nathaniel* • DJ Williams *Joshua Trimble* • Charles Penrose *Sir Franklyn* • Norman Pierce *Landlord* ■ *Dir* George King • *Scr* HF Maltby, from a story by Jack Celestin

Crimes of the Future ★★

Science-fiction horror
1970 · Can · BW · 63mins

Canadian cult director David Cronenberg's second underground feature – a companion piece to his debut *Stereo* (1969) – deals with deadly cosmetics wiping out the female race, and how the male population sublimate their sexual desires by becoming paedophiles. All the diverse themes Cronenberg subsequently expands on in his later works are here in seminal form, but the film is rather pretentious, eccentric and over-stylised. AJ

Ronald Mlodzik *Adrian Tripod* • Jon Lidolt • Tania Zolty • Jack Messinger • William Haslam ■ *Dir/Scr* David Cronenberg

Crimes of the Heart ★★★★ 15

Comedy drama 1986 · US · Colour · 100mins

Beth Henley, adapting her own Pulitzer Prize-winning play, serves up three meaty parts for a trio of Hollywood's leading actresses – Jessica Lange, Diane Keaton and Sissy Spacek – and they certainly make the most of it. The story is pretty slight – three sisters are reunited after one of them is released from prison – and the stage origins are very apparent. However, all three actresses deliver stunning performances (though Spacek was the only one of the trio to receive an Oscar nomination), and the result is a warm, rewarding tragicomedy. JF. Contains swearing. [VIDEO] DVD

Diane Keaton *Lenny Magrath* • Jessica Lange *Meg Magrath* • Sissy Spacek *Babe Magrath* • Sam Shepard *Doc Porter* • Tess Harper *Chick Boyle* • David Carpenter *Barnette Lloyd* • Hurd Hatfield *Old Grandaddy* • Beeson Carroll *Zackery Botrelle* ■ *Dir* Bruce Beresford • *Scr* Beth Henley, from her play

Crimewave ★★★ PG

Crime comedy 1985 · US · Colour · 82mins

Opening with a car filled with nuns speeding through Detroit and ending with an extended chase sequence, this never slows down enough in between to pick up our interest, even though it wants to take us for a ride. It's a slapstick attempt at *film noir* by director Sam Raimi, who also co-wrote the script with Joel and Ethan Coen. The end result, however, is too simplistic, and its story of a security-systems installer caught between a couple of hitmen is rather patronising. There are some splendidly eccentric moments but it's all an in-joke that excludes the rest of us. TH [VIDEO]

Louise Lasser *Helene Trend* • Reed Birney *Vic Ajax* • Paul L Smith [Paul Smith] *Faron Crush* • Brion James *Arthur Coddish* • Sheree J Wilson *Nancy* • Edward R Pressman *Ernest Trend* • Bruce Campbell *Renaldo "The Heel"* • Antonio Fargas *Blind man* • Wiley Harker *Governor* ■ *Dir* Sam Raimi • *Scr* Joel Coen, Ethan Coen, Sam Raimi

The Criminal ★★★ PG

Prison drama 1960 · UK · BW · 93mins

A steely crime thriller, scripted by Alun Owen from a story by Jimmy Sangster, that unflinchingly explores the cut-throat nature of urban crime and the cold realities of prison life. Stanley Baker is outstanding as the tough villain whose contempt for authority of any sort makes him a target for both monstrous prison officer Patrick Magee and racketeer Sam Wanamaker after he refuses to disclose the whereabouts of the loot snatched during a racecourse heist. Director Joseph Losey punctuates the simmering tension with eruptions of violence that still shock today. DP [VIDEO]

Stanley Baker *Johnny Bannion* • Sam Wanamaker *Mike Carter* • Grégoire Aslan *Frank Saffron* • Margit Saad *Suzanne* • Jill Bennett *Maggie* • Rupert Davies *Mr Edwards* • Patrick Magee *Chief Warder Barrows* ■ *Dir* Joseph Losey • *Scr* Alun Owen, from a story by Jimmy Sangster

The Criminal ★★★ 15

Mystery drama
1999 · UK/US · Colour · 95mins

The opening sequence, in which J (as opposed to Kafka's equally victimized K) is lured into a one-night stand, is quite mesmerising. Yet from the moment he wakes to find himself up to his neck in conspiracy, the action follows an all-too-familiar route to its convoluted conclusion. Steven Mackintosh admirably conveys the everyman's terror at finding his head above the parapet. The best moments, however, are provided by cops Bernard Hill and Holly Aird. DP [VIDEO] DVD

Steven Mackintosh *"J" Jasper Rawlins* • Eddie Izzard *Peter Hume* • Natasha Little *Sarah Maitland* • Yvan Attal *Mason* • Holly Aird *Detective Sergeant Rebecca White* • Andrew Tiernan *Harris* • Justin Shevlin *Barker* • Barry Stearn *Noble* • Bernard Hill *Inspector Walker* ■ *Dir/Scr* Julian Simpson

Criminal ★★★ 15

Crime drama 2004 · US · Colour · 83mins

Steven Soderbergh's long-time collaborator Gregory Jacobs makes his directorial debut with this worthy remake of the Argentine crime drama *Nine Queens*. A twisting tale of two small-time con artists who stumble upon the scam of a lifetime, it's slick and stylish entertainment. In an enjoyably sleazy turn, John C Reilly plays unscrupulous mentor to Diego Luna's inexperienced grifter. With its crisp dialogue and subtle performances, this caper is smoothly seductive, but it falters in its over-reliance on coincidence. SF. Contains swearing. DVD

John C Reilly *Richard Gaddis* • Diego Luna *Rodrigo* • Maggie Gyllenhaal *Valerie* • Peter Mullan *William Hannigan* • Jonathan Tucker *Michael* • Enrico Colantoni *Bookish man* • Zitto Kazann *Ochoa* ■ *Dir* Gregory Jacobs • *Scr* Gregory Jacobs, Sam Lowry [Steven Soderbergh], from the film *Nine Queens* by Fabian Bielinsky

The Criminal Code ★★★

Prison drama 1930 · US · BW · 98mins

This was the film that elevated Boris Karloff to stardom and led to his portrayal of Frankenstein's monster. He'd played Ned Galloway on stage and the role was enlarged for this movie. Master draughtsman director Howard Hawks doesn't allow the theatrical origins to show, although the tragic ending has disappeared as Karloff now snarls: "That kid don't take no rap from me." Cell life is well evoked, and the film convinces as long as you believe warden Walter Huston would hire his daughter's lover, trusted convict Phillips Holmes, to be his personal driver! Stylistically, though, it creaks in places. TS

Walter Huston *Warden Brady* • Phillips Holmes *Robert Graham* • Constance Cummings *Mary Brady* • Boris Karloff *Ned Galloway* • Mary Doran *Gertrude Williams* • DeWitt Jennings *Gleason* • John Sheehan *McManus* • Otto Hoffman *Fales* ■ *Dir* Howard Hawks • *Scr* Fred Niblo Jr, Seton I Miller, from the play by Martin Flavin

Criminal Court ★★

Crime drama 1946 · US · BW · 62mins

Tom Conway is a defence lawyer with political ambitions, and nightclub singer Martha O'Driscoll is his fiancée. Conway, however, has accidentally killed someone, and O'Driscoll is blamed for it because she found the body. Conway defends her in court, finds time to get married *and* elected as district attorney. All this in about an hour's running time – and there's still time for a few songs! AT

Tom Conway *Steve Barnes* • Martha O'Driscoll *Georgia Gale* • June Clayworth *Joan Mason* • Robert Armstrong *Vic Wright* • Addison Richards *District Attorney Gordon* • Pat Gleason *Joe West* • Steve Brodie *Frankie* ■ *Dir* Robert Wise • *Scr* Lawrence Kimble, from a story by Earl Felton

Criminal Law ★★ 18

Thriller 1988 · US · Colour · 109mins

British actor Gary Oldman's first major Hollywood movie sees him in one of his oh-so-rare good guy roles. He's a defence attorney who gets suspected rapist/murderer Kevin Bacon off, only to later discover that's he's guilty. Despite director Martin Campbell's efficiency at creating tension, this starts off as fairly implausible and gets sillier as it goes on. JC

Gary Oldman *Ben Chase* • Kevin Bacon *Martin Thiel* • Tess Harper *Detective Stillwell* • Karen Young *Ellen Faulkner* • Joe Don Baker *Detective Mesel* • Ron Lea *Gary Hull* • Karen Woolridge *Claudia Curwen* ■ *Dir* Martin Campbell • *Scr* Mark Kasdan

C

Criminal Lawyer ★★★

Crime drama 1937 · US · BW · 71mins

Lee Tracy stars as a lawyer whose successful ascent up the power ladder comes to a halt when he confesses to his criminal associations. He brings gangland supremo Eduardo Ciannelli down with him, winning the heart of Margot Grahame in the process. Christy Cabanne directs this programme-filler from RKO, drawing first-class performances from his cast – in particular Tracy – to make for a tight and absorbing addition to the popular legal-political genre. RK

Lee Tracy *Brandon* • Margot Grahame *Madge Carter* • Eduardo Ciannelli *Larkin* • Erik Rhodes *Bandini* • Betty Lawford *Molly Walker* • Frank M Thomas *William Walker* • Wilfred Lucas *Brandon's assistant* ■ *Dir* Christy Cabanne • *Scr* GV Atwater, Thomas Lennon, from a story by Louis Stevens

The Criminal Life of Archibaldo de la Cruz ★★★

Crime black comedy
1955 · Mex · BW · 72mins

This was Luis Buñuel's response to his first return to Europe in almost a decade. His target was the kind of seemingly solid citizen who maintains the iniquitous status quo while proclaiming moral superiority. Buñuel shoots away his pedestal by portraying him as an inhibited transvestite whose childhood experience of death inspires a spree of fetishistic murder attempts. Employing a naturalism that makes Ernesto Alonso's imagined crimes all the more grotesquely amusing, this is an audacious but flawed black comedy. DP. In Spanish with English subtitles.

Miroslava *Lavinia* • Ernesto Alonso *Archibaldo de la Cruz* • Rita Macedo *Patricia Terrazas* • Ariadna Welter *Carlota* • Rodolfo Landa *Alejandro Rivas* • Andrea Palma *Senor Cervantes, mother of Carlota* ■ *Dir* Luis Buñuel • *Scr* Luis Buñuel, Eduardo Ugarte, from a novel by Rodolfo Usigli

Criminal Lovers ★★★ 18

Crime drama 1999 · Fr/Jap · Colour · 91mins

Juxtaposing tabloid and traditional terrors, writer/director François Ozon attempts to turn a fairy tale into an urban myth in this stylish and highly manipulative melodrama. He can't be faulted for the ambition of his conceit but, despite the often unbearable suspense, the disparate elements fail to gel. The action moves from the grimy reality of the school showers, where Natacha Régnier and Jérémie Rénier kill the youngster she claims raped her, to the storybook realm of the forest, where they bury the body. Then, in a nod to the tale of Hansel and Gretel, they encounter sinister woodsman, Miki Manojlovic, who imprisons them in his cellar. Ambitious and stylish. DP. In French with English subtitles. DVD

Natacha Régnier *Alice* • Jérémie Rénier *Luc* • Miki Manojlovic *The woodsman* • Salim Kechiouche *Saïd* • Yasmine Belmadi *Karim* ■ *Dir/Scr* François Ozon

The Criminal Mind ★★ 15

Action crime drama
1995 · US · Colour · 92mins

Up-and-coming DA Frank Rossi discovers one day that he's the younger brother to Mob boss Ben Cross. They were separated after the murders of their parents: Rossi grew up as a sheltered young man, while Cross was forced to work his way up through the ranks of the Mafia that killed his father. The result is a film so bad that you may find yourself engrossed before you realise it. ST

Ben Cross *Carlo Augustine* • Frank Rossi *Nick August* • Tahnee Welch *Gabrielle* • Lance Henriksen *Winslow* ■ *Dir* Joseph Vittorie • *Scr* Sam A Scribner

Crimson Gold ★★★★ 12

Drama 2003 · Iran · Colour · 92mins

Recalling Rainer Werner Fassbinder's *Why Does Herr R Run Amok?* in its meticulous accumulation of seemingly minor incident, this riveting and often amusing drama also reveals the shifting social attitudes that are slowly taking hold in modern Tehran. Flashing back from a jewellery store robbery, the action focuses on the unlikely events and chance encounters that prompt mild-mannered pizza delivery man Hossain Emadeddin to snap. This is a potent, poignant and soberingly credible piece of cinema. DP. In Farsi with English subtitles. DVD

Hossain Emadeddin *Hussein* • Pourang Nakhael *Pourang* • Azita Rayeji *The Bride* • Sheisi *Ali Kamyar* • Shahram Vaziri *Jeweller* ■ *Dir* Jafar Panahi • *Scr* Abbas Kiarostami

The Crimson Curtain ★★★★

Period romance 1952 · Fr · BW · 43mins

Novelist and film critic Alexandre Astruc, renowned for coining the phrase *camera-stylo*, wrote that cinema should be "a means of writing as supple and as subtle as that of written language". Practising what he preaches in this, his debut film as a director, he unfolds the tale of a young officer's illicit, silent and nocturnal affair with the daughter of the household where he's billeted. Stylish and unusual, the narrative takes the place of the dialogue, with the camera and mute presence of the actors conveying the drama. This jewel of a short feature, which demonstrates that, for movies, less can sometimes be more, stars Jean-Claude Pascal and the ravishingly lovely Anouk Aimée. RB. With English narration.

Jean-Claude Pascal *The officer* • Anouk Aimée *Albertine* • Madeleine Garcia *Her mother* • Jim Gérald *Her father* ■ *Dir* Alexandre Astruc • *Scr* Alexandre Astruc, from the short story *Le Rideau Cramoisi* by Barbey d'Aurevilly

The Crimson Kimono ★★★

Crime drama 1959 · US · BW · 81mins

An oddly poignant excursion into maverick American independent director Sam Fuller's underworld. Two detectives in the Little Tokyo district of Los Angeles fall for the same woman who's involved in their investigation into a stripper's murder. Characters range from the hard-boiled to the plain mushy, but Fuller's energetic methods stir up a sympathy not normally present in his other movies. This may be low-key and sometimes banal, but it's still a stylish movie that could not have been tailored by anyone else. TH

Victoria Shaw *Christine Downs* • Glenn Corbett *Detective Sergeant Charlie Bancroft* • James Shigeta *Detective Joe Kojaku* • Anna Lee *Mac* ■ *Dir/Scr* Samuel Fuller

The Crimson Pirate ★★★★ U

Swashbuckling adventure
1952 · US · Colour · 104mins

This is a gorgeous swashbuckler, with Burt Lancaster and his diminutive former circus colleague Nick Cravat swinging through the rigging with sharpened blades clamped between their perfect teeth. Encouraged by the success of *The Flame and the Arrow*, Lancaster and his partner Harold Hecht persuaded Warner Bros to agree to a big budget, and shooting got under way on European locations without a finished script. Most of the praise goes to Lancaster, who designed the terrific action sequences and puts in a mesmerising star turn. AT

Burt Lancaster *Vallo* • Nick Cravat *Ojo* • Eva Bartok *Consuelo* • Torin Thatcher *Humble Bellows* • James Hayter *Prudence* • Leslie Bradley *Baron Gruda* • Margot Grahame *Bianca* • Christopher Lee *Attache* ■ *Dir* Robert Siodmak • *Scr* Roland Kibbee

The Crimson Rivers ★★ 15

Crime thriller 2000 · Fr · Colour · 101mins

Mathieu Kassovitz's fourth feature is the first based on borrowed material and this lack of personal input proves fatal. The influence of *Se7en* is almost overwhelming, both in the tone of the grisly serial crimes and in the teaming of Jean Reno and Vincent Cassel as a veteran-rookie duo. Cinematographer Thierry Arbogast's filming of the Alpine locations is suitably spectacular, but neither the detectives nor their suspects at a sinisterly enclosed university have any depth. Surprisingly, a sequel followed in 2004. DP. In French with English subtitles. Contains violence and swearing. DVD

Jean Reno *Commissaire Pierre Niémans* • Vincent Cassel *Max Kerkerian* • Nadia Farès *Fanny Fereira* • Jean-Pierre Cassel *Dr Bernard Chernezé* • Karim Belkhadra *Capt Dahmane* ■ *Dir* Mathieu Kassovitz • *Scr* Mathieu Kassovitz, Jean-Christophe Grangé, from a novel by Jean-Christophe Grangé

Crimson Tide ★★★★ 15

Action thriller 1995 · US · Colour · 116mins

An American nuclear submarine is ordered to make a pre-emptive strike on Russian rebels who have taken over a missile base, then receives a second, incomplete, radio message suggesting it holds off the attack. Captain Gene Hackman is determined to use his nuclear capability, whatever the consequences. However, his mutinous executive officer (Denzel Washington) stands between him and the horribly alluring Doomsday button. Propelled at full throttle by fast pacing and a palpable friction between the two leads, this riveting thriller is further fuelled by a slick score from Hans Zimmer. AT . Contains violence and swearing. DVD

Denzel Washington *Lt Cdr Ron Hunter* • Gene Hackman *Capt Ramsey* • George Dzundza *Cob* • Viggo Mortensen *Lt Peter Ince* • Matt Craven *Lt Roy Zimmer* • James Gandolfini *Lt Bobby Dougherty* • Rocky Carroll *Lt Darik Westergaurd* ■ *Dir* Tony Scott • *Scr* Michael Schiffer, from a story by Michael Schiffer, Richard P Henrick

La Crise ★★★★ 15

Comedy 1992 · Fr · Colour · 91mins

Awarded a César for its screenplay, Coline Serreau's study of social exclusion continues her search to find genuine emotion beneath the masculine veneer of invulnerability. Sacked for being too good at his job and shocked by the infidelity of both his wife and his mother, bourgeois Parisian Vincent Lindon finds his glib idealism repeatedly shattered by the realities of modern life. Solace comes via an unlikely friendship with orphan Patrick Timsit. A dark satire with a distinctly Voltairean morality about it, the film's exposure of class snobbery and liberal hypocrisy eventually gives way to sentimentality, but the performances are first-rate. DP. In French with English subtitles.

Vincent Lindon *Victor* • Patrick Timsit *Michou* • Zabou *Isabelle* • Maria Pacôme *Victor's mother* • Yves Robert *Victor's father* • Annick Alane *Mamie* • Valerie Alane *Thérèse* • Gilles Privat *Laurent* ■ *Dir/Scr* Coline Serreau

Crisis ★★★

Silent drama 1928 · Ger · BW · 98mins

Exploring the ennui of bourgeois marriage and the scandalous temptations of the Berlin underground, this least known of GW Pabst's silent classics is both a compelling human drama and an invaluable record of socio-cultural life in Weimar Germany. Its depiction of decadence now seems rather quaint, but there's a sting in the tail, as bored housewife Brigitte Helm agrees to remarry Gustav Diessl, the stuffed shirt of a lawyer whose neglect drove her to dalliance and divorce. DP

Gustav Diessl *Thomas Beck* • Brigitte Helm *Irene* • Hertha von Walther *Liana* • Jack Trevor *Walter Frank* • Nico Turoff *Sam Taylor* ■ *Dir* GW Pabst • *Scr* Adolf Lantz, Ladislaus Vajda, Helen Gosewisch, from an idea by Fritz Schulz

Crisis ★★★ 12

Melodrama 1945 · Swe · BW · 88mins

Ingmar Bergman's directorial debut is overbalanced by the importation of a character from one of his own plays. Played by Stig Olin, the city cad shifts the focus away from country teenager Inga Landgré, who leaves foster mother Dagny Lind to work in birth mother Marianne Löfgren's beauty salon. Consequently, her seduction comes to matter less than his suicide, thus rendering her return to boy-next-door Allan Bohlin something of an anticlimax. However, there are nascent flashes of trademark Bergman, notably in his use of mirrors, dreams and expressionist symbolism. DP. In Swedish with English subtitles. DVD

Inga Landgré *Nelly* • Stig Olin *Jack* • Dagny Lind *Ingeborg* • Marianne Löfgren *Jenny* • Allan Bohlin *Ulf* ■ *Dir* Ingmar Bergman • *Scr* Ingmar Bergman, from the radio play *Moderhjertet/Mother Heart* by Leck Fischer

Crisis ★★

Melodrama 1950 · US · BW · 95mins

Cary Grant, the smooth embodiment of American decency in scores of Hollywood productions, strolls through this misfiring melodrama as a brain surgeon forced to perform a dangerous operation on a South American dictator. Ideas concerning repression and freedom are rather too obviously put forward in Richard Brooks's flawed directorial debut. JM

Cary Grant *Dr Eugene Norland Ferguson* • José Ferrer *Raoul Farrago* • Paula Raymond *Helen Ferguson* • Signe Hasso *Senora Isabel Farrago* • Ramon Novarro *Colonel Adragon* • Gilbert Roland *Gonzales* ■ *Dir* Richard Brooks • *Scr* Richard Brooks, from the story *The Doubters* by George Tabori

Criss Cross ★★★★

Film noir 1949 · US · BW · 87mins

This classic *film noir* stars Burt Lancaster as a decent armoured car guard who starts courting his ex-wife, Yvonne De Carlo, now engaged to rich mafioso Dan Duryea. Lancaster is trapped into robbing his own firm, leading to much double-crossing and murder. Having all the *noir* trappings one needs – fateful flashbacks, a drab urban setting, doom-laden Miklos Rozsa music – this also contains a lot of sexual energy, a thrillingly shot robbery and Tony Curtis, making a brief appearance as a pretty gigolo who dances with De Carlo. Steven Soderbergh remade this in 1995 as *The Underneath*. AT

Burt Lancaster *Steve Thompson* • Yvonne De Carlo *Anna* • Dan Duryea *Slim* • Stephen McNally *Ramirez* • Richard Long *Slade Thompson* • James Curtis [Tony Curtis] *Gigolo* ■ *Dir* Robert Siodmak • *Scr* Daniel Fuchs, from the novel by Don Tracy

CrissCross ★★ 15

Drama 1992 · US · Colour · 96mins

After all the acclaim for *A World Apart*, Chris Menges came horribly unstuck with this, his second stab at directing. While he admirably captures the sights and sounds of Key West in the late 1960s, he fails to inject any life into an all-too-predictable tale of a waitress who turns to stripping to support her son after they're abandoned by her Vietnam-scarred husband. Goldie Hawn is hopelessly miscast as the downtrodden mother. DP. Contains violence, swearing and nudity. [video]

Goldie Hawn *Tracy Cross* • Arliss Howard *Joe* • James Gammon *Emmett* • David Arnott *Chris Cross* • Keith Carradine *John Cross* • JC Quinn *Jetty* • Steve Buscemi *Louis* • Paul Calderon *Blacky* ■ *Dir* Chris Menges • *Scr* Scott Sommer, from his novella

Critical Care ★★★ 15

Medical drama 1997 · US · Colour · 102mins

A comedy drama about medical ethics, directed by Sidney Lumet and starring James Spader, Kyra Sedgwick and *Prime Suspect*'s Helen Mirren. Spader is on top form as a young resident doctor, supervising a man on life support and attempting to assist his two daughters, who fundamentally disagree on the choice of treatment. Kyra Sedgwick wants to pull the plug; Margo Martindale wants to maintain a state of vegetative survival as long as possible. The hospital, meanwhile, is content to keep the patient alive as long as his insurance money swells their coffers. LH DVD

James Spader *Dr Werner Ernst* • Kyra Sedgwick *Felicia Potter* • Helen Mirren *Stella* • Anne Bancroft *Nun* • Albert Brooks *Dr Butz* • Margo Martindale *Connie Potter* • Wallace Shawn *Furnaceman* ■ *Dir* Sidney Lumet • *Scr* Steven S Schwartz, from the novel by Richard Dooling

Critical Condition ★ 15

Comedy 1987 · US · Colour · 93mins

Director Michael Apted must have been having a bad day when he agreed to direct this unamusing star vehicle for Richard Pryor. Pryor, an influential comedian during the 1970s and early 1980s, plays a hustler who feigns insanity to stay out of prison and, after a series of ludicrous misadventures, ends up running the mental institution into which he has been committed. Yes, it's that ridiculous. JB. Contains swearing. [video] DVD

Richard Pryor *Eddie* • Joe Mantegna *Chambers* • Rubén Blades *Louis* • Rachel Ticotin *Rachel* • Bob Dishy *Dr Foster* • Sylvia Miles *Maggie* • Joe Dallesandro *Stucky* • Randall "Tex" Cobb *Box* ■ *Dir* Michael Apted • *Scr* Denis Hamill, John Hamill, from a story by Alan Swyer

Critic's Choice ★★★

Comedy 1963 · US · Colour · 99mins

This started life as a Broadway in-joke as to whether theatre critic Walter Kerr should review his wife Jean's play, but became diluted en route to the movies and fetched up as a vehicle for Bob Hope and Lucille Ball. It's not very funny, though director Don Weis paints a sharp picture of the waspish New York theatre milieu. Nice turns, too, from Marilyn Maxwell and Rip Torn. TS

Bob Hope *Parker Ballantine* • Lucille Ball *Angela Ballantine* • Marilyn Maxwell *Ivy London* • Rip Torn *Dion Kapakos* • Jessie Royce Landis *Charlotte Orr* • John Dehner *SP Champlain* ■ *Dir* Don Weis • *Scr* Jack Sher, from the play by Ira Levin

Critters ★★★ 15

Horror comedy 1986 · US · Colour · 82mins

Stephen Herek directs a cheeky smash-and-grab raid on *Gremlins* and comes up with a crude but entertaining horror comedy. The "critters" of the title are a race of nasty hedgehog-like alien creatures who invade a small American town and proceed to wreak havoc until two intergalactic bounty hunters arrive to save the day. The cast remains stoically straight-faced, the creatures nab the best lines (in subtitles), and Herek keeps his tongue stuck firmly in his cheek. JF. Contains violence, swearing. [video] DVD

Dee Wallace Stone *Helen Brown* • M Emmet Walsh *Harv* • Billy Green Bush *Jay Brown* • Scott Grimes *Brad Brown* • Nadine Van Der Velde *April Brown* • Don Opper *Charlie McFadden* • Terrence Mann *Johnny Steele* • Billy Zane *Steve Elliot* ■ *Dir* Stephen Herek • *Scr* Stephen Herek, Dominic Muir

Critters 2: the Main Course ★★ 15

Horror comedy 1988 · US · Colour · 82mins

Critters was cheap but hugely entertaining junk food. Quite how it manage to spawn so many sequels beggars belief, but this at least sticks pretty close to the original and manages to hold on to much of the cast. Scott Grimes is once again pressed into action when he discovers that two of the evil space scum have survived and are now a family. Director Mick Garris adeptly mixes the gags with the gore, but it doesn't quite satisfy the appetite as much as the first course. JF [video] DVD

Scott Grimes *Brad Brown* • Liane Curtis *Megan Morgan* • Don Opper *Charlie McFadden* • Barry Corbin *Harv* • Tom Hodges *Wesley* • Sam Anderson *Mr Morgan* • Lindsay Parker *Cindy Morgan* • Terrence Mann *Ug* ■ *Dir* Mick Garris • *Scr* DT Twohy [David Twohy], Mick Garris

Critters 3 ★★ 15

Horror comedy 1991 · US · Colour · 81mins

This largely forgotten entry in a largely forgettable B-movie franchise has received a new lease of life thanks to the presence of one Leonardo DiCaprio in the cast. He reveals little star potential in this cheap and cheerful caper, which finds the man-eating space critters terrorising the city for the first time and laying siege to a tenement building. JF. Contains violence and swearing. [video] DVD

Aimee Brooks *Annie* • John Calvin *Clifford* • Katherine Cortez *Marcia* • Leonardo DiCaprio *Josh* • Geoffrey Blake *Frank* • Don Opper *Charlie McFadden* ■ *Dir* Kristine Peterson • *Scr* David J Schow

Critters 4 ★★ 15

Horror comedy 1992 · US · Colour · 90mins

The *Critters* series has provided a few skeletons in the cupboard for now famous stars. This features Angela Bassett, later to find fame and acclaim in the Tina Turner biopic *What's Love Got to Do with It*. It's set in outer space, allowing for some gags at the expense of slightly bigger budget sci-fi fare. JF. Contains swearing and violence. [video] DVD

Don Keith Opper [Don Opper] *Charlie McFadden* • Angela Bassett *Fran* • Brad Dourif *Al Bert* • Paul Whitthorne *Ethan* • Terrence Mann *Ug/Counselor Tetra* ■ *Dir* Rupert Harvey • *Scr* Joseph Lyle, David J Schow

Crocodile ★ 15

Horror adventure 2000 · US · Colour · 90mins

Has the director of *The Texas Chain Saw Massacre* really been reduced to ripping off mediocre monster movies? Sadly, Tobe Hooper is at the helm of this stalk 'n' scoff farrago, in which a stereotypical gaggle of college kids are preyed upon by a fiend who has more in common with a junior art-class project than a cutting-edge special effect. Guaranteed to make you shriek with laughter, rather than terror, this is an appalling fate for a once-promising talent. DP DVD

Mark McLaughlin *Brady* • Caitlin Martin *Claire* • Chris Solari *Duncan* • Julie Mintz *Annabelle* • Sommer Knight *Sunny* ■ *Dir* Tobe Hooper • *Scr* Jace Anderson, Adam Gierasch, Michael D Weiss

"Crocodile" Dundee ★★★★ 15

Comedy adventure 1986 · Aus/US · Colour · 92mins

The first, and best, of the tales about the Australian outback's living legend, who can wrestle crocodiles with bare hands and subdue ladies with naked charisma. Paul Hogan took his lager-commercial he-man into the big time, and the big city, and the result is as agreeable as if it were Tarzan coping in a concrete jungle. Director Peter Faiman's languid pace gives us time to appreciate this particular Wizard from Oz as he survives sophisticates' taunts and outwits street villains. A pity Hogan couldn't keep the momentum going for later movies, but for this, he created a totally likeable superhero. TH. Contains swearing. [video] DVD

Paul Hogan *Michael J "Crocodile" Dundee* • Linda Kozlowski *Sue Charlton* • John Meillon *Walter Reilly* • David Gulpilil *Neville Bell* • Mark Blum *Richard Mason* • Michael Lombard *Sam Charlton* • Ritchie Singer *Con* ■ *Dir* Peter Faiman • *Scr* Paul Hogan, Ken Shadie, John Cornell, from a story by Paul Hogan

"Crocodile" Dundee II ★★★ PG

Comedy adventure 1988 · US/Aus · Colour · 111mins

Having scored a massive box-office hit with the first movie, Paul Hogan could be forgiven for reprising the role of Mick "Crocodile" Dundee. Less excusable, however, is the misguided attempt to blend the inspired comedy of the original with the kind of rescue adventure that was old hat in the long-gone days of the film serial. But Hogan is as amiable as before and there are funny moments, mostly in the attitudes of the Aborigines and bushwhackers towards the city slickers who have kidnapped Linda Kozlowski. JM. Contains violence, swearing. [video] DVD

Paul Hogan *Michael J "Crocodile" Dundee* • Linda Kozlowski *Sue Charlton* • John Meillon *Walter Reilly* • Hechter Ubarry *Rico* • Juan Fernandez *Miguel* • Ernie Dingo *Charlie* • Charles Dutton [Charles S Dutton] *Leroy Brown* • Mark Blum *Richard Mason* • Steve Rackman *Donk* • Gerry Skilton *Nugget* • Gus Mercurio *Frank* ■ *Dir* John Cornell • *Scr* Paul Hogan, Brett Hogan, from characters created by Paul Hogan

Crocodile Dundee in Los Angeles ★ PG

Comedy adventure 2001 · US/Aus · Colour · 91mins

Quite what drove Paramount Studios to bankroll a third instalment in the "Crocodile" Dundee franchise will be beyond anyone unlucky enough to sit through it. Characteristics that once seemed charming in star Paul Hogan are now as weathered as his face. The story concerns a Hollywood backlot art heist uncovered by Dundee. The direction borders on the soporific and, at 62, Hogan seems to know he is too old for this schtick. AC [video] DVD

Paul Hogan *Michael J "Crocodile" Dundee* • Linda Kozlowski *Sue Charleton* • Jere Burns *Arnan Rothman* • Jonathan Banks *Milos Drubnik* • Alec Wilson *Jacko* • Serge Cockburn *Mikey Dundee* • Gerry Skilton *Nugget O'Cass* ■ *Dir* Simon Wincer • *Scr* Matthew Berry, Eric Abrams, from characters created by Paul Hogan

The Crocodile Hunter: Collision Course ★★★ PG

Comedy adventure 2002 · Aus/US · Colour · 85mins

This good-natured romp starring eccentric Australian wildlife expert Steve Irwin is something of an oddity – a combination of documentary-style close encounters with various outback inhabitants and a lightweight thriller plot about the race to retrieve a fallen satellite gizmo. The so-called storyline – incorporating one-dimensional CIA agents and an aggressive female cattle rancher – is so slight it barely exists, but Irwin's enthusiastic and fearless one-on-one duels with deadly snakes, spiders and, of course, crocodiles (punctuated by educational addresses to the audience) are a scream. JC [video] DVD

Steve Irwin • Terri Irwin • Magda Szubanski *Brozzie Drewitt* • David Wenham *Sam Flynn* • Lachy Hulme *Agent Robert Wheeler* • Aden Young *Ron Buckwhiler* • Kenneth Ransom *Agent Vaughan Archer* • Kate Beahan *Jo Buckley* ■ *Dir* John Stainton • *Scr* Holly Goldberg Sloan, from a story by John Stainton

Cromwell ★★★★ PG

Historical drama 1970 · UK · Colour · 133mins

Richard Harris's warts-and-all Oliver Cromwell and Alec Guinness's unyielding Charles I make this a historical double act well worth catching. They bring past politics to vivid life and put pay to the idea that right and grace were on the side of royalist Cavaliers as opposed to the Puritan Roundheads. The usually undervalued writer/director Ken Hughes was given an enormous budget for a British film at the time, and the result is a long-winded but compulsive epic with some mighty battles mightily well-staged. TH [video] DVD

Richard Harris *Oliver Cromwell* • Alec Guinness *King Charles I* • Robert Morley *Earl of Manchester* • Dorothy Tutin *Queen Henrietta Maria* • Frank Finlay *John Carter* • Timothy Dalton *Prince Rupert* • Patrick Wymark *Earl of Strafford* • Patrick Magee *Hugh Peters* • Nigel Stock *Sir Edward Hyde* ■ *Dir* Ken Hughes • *Scr* Ken Hughes, Ronald Harwood • *Cinematographer* Geoffrey Unsworth • *Costume Designer* Vittorio Nino Novarese

Cronos ★★★★ 18

Horror 1992 · Mex · Colour · 88mins

A compelling, complex and wonderfully atmospheric film from Mexican director Guillermo del Toro. Although thematically profound, stately in pace and largely devoid of the kind of blood-letting beloved of schlock fans, this is still a highly effective chiller. Federico Luppi is superb as the antiques dealer who becomes enslaved by the Cronos device, a mysterious mechanical insect that forces its victims into acts of vampirism. DP. In English and Spanish with subtitles. Contains violence and swearing. [video] DVD

Federico Luppi *Jesus Gris* • Ron Perlman *Angel de la Guardia* • Claudio Brook *Dieter de la Guardia* • Margarita Isabel *Mercedes Gris* ■ *Dir/Scr* Guillermo del Toro

Crooked Hearts ★★★ 15

Drama 1991 · US · Colour · 107mins

This thoughtful low-budget movie disappeared swiftly on release but was revived some time later when word got around that it is rather good. Peter Coyote is solid in a pivotal role as an unfaithful patriarch causing ripples in the family pond. There are many strands to this intelligent, well paced film that evolve delicately on screen, aided by strong performances from Jennifer Jason Leigh and Vincent D'Onofrio. SH. Contains swearing, sex scenes and nudity.

C

Peter Berg *Tom* • Vincent Phillip D'Onofrio [Vincent D'Onofrio] *Charley* • Jennifer Jason Leigh *Marriet* • Noah Wyle *Ask* • Peter Coyote *Edward* • Cindy Pickett *Jill* • Juliette Lewis *Cassie* ■ *Dir* Michael Bortman • *Scr* Michael Bortman, from the novel by Robert Boswell

The Crooked Road ★★

Thriller 1964 · UK/Yug · BW · 94mins

This thriller is a story of Balkan intrigue starring Robert Ryan as a US reporter investigating a corrupt dictator. Stewart Granger plays the dictator, the Duke of Orgagna, with his tongue in his cheek, but the sad script, derived from a Morris West novel, lets the cast down badly. It was filmed in Yugoslavia, which President Tito was then promoting as the next Almeria. AT

Robert Ryan *Richard Ashley* • Stewart Granger *Duke of Orgagna* • Nadia Gray *Cosima* • Marius Goring *Harlequin* • George Coulouris *Carlos* • Catherine Woodville *Elena* • Robert Rietty *Police chief* ■ *Dir* Don Chaffey • *Scr* Jay Garrison, Don Chaffey, from the novel *The Big Story* by Morris L West

The Crooked Sky ★★ U

Crime thriller 1957 · US · BW · 76mins

This crime quickie is notable primarily because it was scripted by Norman Hudis, who went on to become a key scribe in both the *Carry On* and *Man from UNCLE* series. American actor Wayne Morris plays a detective flown over to help Scotland Yard smash an international counterfeit ring. Morris turns in a no-nonsense performance, but is easily upstaged by that master of menace, Anton Diffring. DP

Wayne Morris *Mike Conklin* • Karin Booth *Sandra Hastings* • Anton Diffring *Fraser* • Bruce Seton *Mac* • Sheldon Lawrence *Bill* • Collette Barthrop *Penny* • Frank Hawkins *Robson* • Murray Kash *Lewis* ■ *Dir* Henry Cass • *Scr* Norman Hudis, from a story by Lance Z Hargreaves, Maclean Rogers

Crooklyn ★★★ 12

Comedy drama 1994 · US · Colour · 109mins

An African-American family living in 1970s Brooklyn struggles to recover from the racial turmoil of the 1960s in Spike Lee's semi-autobiographical tale, inspired by his youth. Alfre Woodard and Delroy Lindo are excellent as the middle-class Carmichaels, whose household is a reflection of the outside tensions tearing at the fabric of society. Not as confrontational as Lee's other films, *Crooklyn* still suffers slightly from the director's choppy narrative style. That said, this is a sure and mature work. AJ

Alfre Woodard *Carolyn Carmichael* • Delroy Lindo *Woody Carmichael* • David Patrick Kelly *Tony Eyes* • Zelda Harris *Troy Carmichael* • Spike Lee *Snuffy* • Vondie Curtis-Hall *Uncle Brown* ■ *Dir* Spike Lee • *Scr* from a story by Joie Susannah Lee, Spike Lee, Joie Susannah Lee, Cinqué Lee

Crooks and Coronets ★★ U

Comedy crime thriller
1969 · UK · Colour · 104mins

An old-style English caper comedy, with the likes of Edith Evans, Hattie Jacques and Harry H Corbett improbably joined by Hollywood heavies Telly Savalas and Warren Oates. This strange casting gives the film a certain interest, not to mention eccentricity, as the cast are involved in a plot to rob a British stately home of its silver and art treasures. Dame Edith owns the stately pile and does her doddery old dowager act to perfection, but the overall tone is far too frantic and full of those terribly dated, Swinging Sixties fads and fashions. AT

Telly Savalas *Herbie Hassler* • Edith Evans *Lady Sophie Fitzmore* • Warren Oates *Marty Miller* • Cesar Romero *Nick Marco* • Harry H Corbett *Frank Finley* • Nicky Henson *Lord Fitzmore* • Hattie Jacques *Mabel* • Arthur Mullard *Perce* ■ *Dir/Scr* Jim O'Connolly

Crooks Anonymous ★★ U

Comedy 1962 · UK · BW · 83mins

Playing a stripper was hardly the most auspicious start to Julie Christie's career, but she manages to cover herself in some glory in this amiable if unremarkable comedy. It's an amusing but limited idea: what else would the members of a villains' self-help group do but put their individual expertise to collective misuse? Stanley Baxter and Leslie Phillips run through their usual tricks, while Wilfrid Hyde White, James Robertson-Justice and Robertson Hare steal scenes at will. DP

Leslie Phillips *Dandy Forsdyke* • Stanley Baxter *RS Widdowes* • Wilfrid Hyde White *Montague* • Julie Christie *Babette* • James Robertson-Justice *Sir Harvey Russelrod* • Michael Medwin *Ronnie* • Pauline Jameson *Prunella* • Robertson Hare *Grimsdale* ■ *Dir* Ken Annakin • *Scr* Jack Davies, Henry Blyth

Crooks in Cloisters ★★★ U

Comedy 1963 · UK · Colour · 93mins

Anything but a pseudo-*Carry On*, this cosy comedy is much more a product of the post-Ealing school and a close relation of bungled crime comedies such as *Too Many Crooks*. The emphasis is firmly on character as Ronald Fraser and his gang lie low in a monastery to throw the cops off their trail. Bernard Cribbins is in fine fettle as one of Fraser's gormless colleagues and Barbara Windsor is funnier than the *Carry Ons* ever allowed her to be. DP

Ronald Fraser *Walt* • Barbara Windsor *Bikini* • Grégoire Aslan *Lorenzo* • Bernard Cribbins *Squirts* • Davy Kaye *Specs* • Melvyn Hayes *Willy* • Wilfrid Brambell *Phineas* • Joseph O'Connor *Father Septimus* • Corin Redgrave *Brother Lucius* • Francesca Annis *June* ■ *Dir* Jeremy Summers • *Scr* TJ Morrison, Mike Watts, from a story by Mike Watts

Crooks' Tour ★★ U

Spy comedy 1940 · UK · BW · 81mins

Basil Radford and Naunton Wayne reprise the Charters and Caldicott characters first seen in Alfred Hitchcock's *The Lady Vanishes* in this slight comic flagwaver, adapted from a radio serial produced by that film's screenwriters, Frank Launder and Sidney Gilliat. Once again it's espionage all the way for the cricket-mad duo, who this time around are mistaken for Nazi spies in Baghdad. Director John Baxter maintains a jaunty pace throughout. DP

Basil Radford *Charters* • Naunton Wayne *Caldicott* • Greta Gynt *La Palermo* • Abraham Sofaer *Ali* • Charles Oliver *Sheik* • Gordon McLeod *Rossenger* ■ *Dir* John Baxter • *Scr* John Watt, Max Kester

Cross Creek ★★ U

Biographical drama
1983 · US · Colour · 115mins

Beautifully filmed by John A Alonzo, this autobiographical drama suggests how Marjorie Kinnan Rawlings might have got the inspiration for her sentimental classic, *The Yearling*. Yet in devoting so much of his energy to capturing the atmosphere of the Florida backwoods in the late 1920s, director Martin Ritt leaves little room for anything other than loosely connected vignettes. As the would-be author who leaves New York to learn her craft, Mary Steenburgen is passively doe-eyed, and not even her encounters with bullish Rip Torn shake her serenity. DP

Mary Steenburgen *Marjorie Kinnan Rawlings* • Rip Torn *Marsh Turner* • Peter Coyote *Norton Baskin* • Dana Hill *Ellie Turner* • Alfre Woodard *Geechee* • Malcolm McDowell *Maxwell Perkins* ■ *Dir* Martin Ritt • *Scr* Dalene Young, from the memoirs by Marjorie Kinnan Rawlings

Cross My Heart ★★★ 18

Comedy 1987 · US · Colour · 86mins

This thoroughly amiable and underrated romantic comedy makes up for what it lacks in wit with charming central performances. Intended as a vehicle for Martin Short, the picture is stolen out from under him by Annette O'Toole, who surely deserves to be a bigger star than she is. Barriers and pretences predictably come tumbling down as newly sacked Short and single mum O'Toole stumble through a date, while the contrived ending is a disappointing fudge. DP

Martin Short *David* • Annette O'Toole *Kathy* • Paul Reiser *Bruce* • Joanna Kerns *Nancy* • Jessica Puscas *Jessica* • Lee Arenberg *Parking attendant* ■ *Dir* Armyan Bernstein • *Scr* Armyan Bernstein, Gail Parent

Cross My Heart ★★★★ PG

Comedy drama 1990 · Fr · Colour · 104mins

Sylvain Copans is hugely impressive as the 12-year-old whose friends rally round to keep his mother's death a secret so that the authorities can't pack him off to an orphanage. The ingenious methods to which they resort to deflect suspicion have both an innocence and a black comedic edge that makes this such a treat for both the young and those who might have forgotten how troubling and invigorating childhood can be. Charming. DP. In French with English subtitles.

Sylvain Copans *Martin* • Nicolas Parodi *Jérôme* • Cécilia Rouaud *Marianne* • Delphine Gouttman *Hélène* • Olivier Montiège *Antoine* • Lucie Blossier *Claire* • Kaldi El Hadj *Dédé* ■ *Dir/Scr* Jacques Fansten

Cross of Iron ★★★★ 18

Second World War drama
1977 · UK/W Ger · Colour · 126mins

Director Sam Peckinpah switches from westerns such as *The Wild Bunch* to another kind of savagery – Germans in retreat on the Russian Front during the Second World War – and makes this as graphic an antiwar film as anything since *All Quiet on the Western Front*. James Coburn is the disillusioned sergeant, sickened by slaughter and the double dealings of officers such as Maximilian Schell. This exercise in macho ideals is bloody action, elegantly choreographed to chilling effect. Forget the dire 1978 sequel, *Breakthrough*. TH. Contains violence, swearing and sex scenes. DVD

James Coburn *Steiner* • Maximilian Schell *Stransky* • James Mason *Brandt* • David Warner *Kiesel* • Klaus Lowitsch [Klaus Löwitsch] *Kruger* • Vadim Glowna *Kern* • Roger Fritz *Triebig* ■ *Dir* Sam Peckinpah • *Scr* Herbert Asmodi, Julius J Epstein, from the book by Willi Heinrich

The Cross of Lorraine ★★★

Second World War drama
1943 · US · BW · 90mins

This sincere and well-made wartime tribute to the French Resistance tells the story of a group of PoWs held in a Nazi concentration camp. Yet, despite MGM's top-notch production values and a fine cast, it is difficult to accept the likes of Gene Kelly, Cedric Hardwicke and Peter Lorre in such a grim drama; only dashing Jean-Pierre Aumont and nasty Hume Cronyn really convince. As a piece of propaganda, though, the movie did its job well. TS

Jean-Pierre Aumont *Paul* • Gene Kelly *Victor* • Sir Cedric Hardwicke [Cedric Hardwicke] *Father Sebastian* • Richard Whorf *François* • Joseph Calleia *Rodriguez* • Peter Lorre *Sergeant Berger* • Hume Cronyn *Duval* • Billy Roy *Louis* ■ *Dir* Tay Garnett • *Scr* Michael Kanin, Ring Lardner Jr, Alexander Esway, Robert D Andrews, from a story by Lilo Damert, Robert Aisner, from the book *A Thousand Shall Fall* by Hans Habe

Crossed Swords ★★ U

Swashbuckling adventure
1954 · It/US · Colour · 83mins

One of the films Errol Flynn made in Europe during his flight from debts and marriage in America. A dyspeptic-looking Flynn strutting his stuff in a tinpot dukedom called Sidonia, which has decreed bachelorhood to be illegal. Of the dozens of women on offer it's Gina Lollobrigida, playing the duke's daughter, who lays down the law at Flynn's feet, threatening to put an end to his "wandering". Ace British cameraman Jack Cardiff shot it during an extended period in Italy. AT

Errol Flynn *Renzo* • Gina Lollobrigida *Francesca* • Cesare Danova *Raniero* • Nadia Gray *Fulvia* • Paola Mori *Tomasina* • Roldano Lupi *Pavoncello* • Alberto Rabagliati *Gennarelli* • Silvio Bagolini *Buio* ■ *Dir* Milton Krims, Vittorio Vassarotti • *Scr* Milton Krims

Crossfire ★★★★ PG

Film noir 1947 · US · BW · 82mins

This terrific thriller tells the story of four GIs, just back from the Second World War, who become involved in a murder. The original novel made the victim a homosexual, but in the movie he's a Jew – at the time, not only a safer choice as far as censorship was concerned, but also more resonant in the aftermath of the war and considering Hollywood's own racial mix. Directed by Edward Dmytryk and produced by Adrian Scott (both of whom were later blacklisted in the Communist witch-hunt), it's an impressive and gripping film, superbly performed. AT

Robert Young (1) *Finlay* • Robert Mitchum *Keeley* • Robert Ryan *Montgomery* • Gloria Grahame *Ginny* • George Cooper *Mitchell* • Steve Brodie *Floyd* • William Phipps *Leroy* • Sam Levene *Joseph Samuels* • Paul Kelly (1) *Man* • Jacqueline White *Mary Mitchell* ■ *Dir* Edward Dmytryk • *Scr* John Paxton, from the novel *The Brick Foxhole* by Richard Brooks

Crossfire ★★

Drama based on a true story
1989 · Is · Colour · 90mins

Having made his name as a documentary director, Gideon Ganani turned to two of Israel's most accomplished film-makers to help with his feature debut: producer Marek Rosenbaum and screenwriter Benny Barbash. Unfortunately, this promising trio came up with a film that, while benefiting from Ganani's location expertise, betrays his inexperience as a storyteller. Set in Tel Aviv and based on actual events, this Romeo and Juliet story makes a plea for greater understanding between the country's Arab and Jewish populations. The end result, though, is heavy going. DP. In Hebrew with English subtitles.

Dan Turgeman *George Chury* • Sharon Brandon-Hacohen *Miriam Ziedman* • Daniel Friedman *Israel* • Milad Matar *Pierre* • Peter Sinai *Shraga* ■ *Dir* Gideon Ganani • *Scr* Benny Barbash, from a story by Gideon Ganani, Hanan Peled

The Crossing ★★★

Historical war drama
2000 · US · Colour · 90mins

This made-for-TV account of the Continental Army's conflict-turning clash at Trenton, New Jersey, with Britain's feared Hessian mercenaries is unswervingly patriotic. Jeff Daniels is clearly conscious of the historical significance of the crossing of the Delaware River and brings a suitably heroic gravitas to the part of George Washington. However, while accepting director Robert Harmon's decision to employ graphic battlefield violence, one has to question the need to demonise the enemy. DP

Jeff Daniels *George Washington* • Sebastian Roché *Glover* • Roger Rees *Mercer* • Steven McCarthy *Alexander Hamilton* • John Henry Canavan *Knox* ■ *Dir* Robert Harmon • *Scr* Howard Fast, from his novel

Crossing Delancey ★★★★ PG

Romantic comedy
1988 · US · Colour · 92mins

Adapted by Susan Sandler from her own play, this charismatic comedy about 30-something New Yorkers proves that love is not only blind, but also has a poor sense of smell. Peter Riegert makes the unlikeliest romantic hero as the pickle maker who tries to convince pretentious bookseller Amy Irving that they are made for one another, in spite of her interest in hack novelist Jeroen Krabbé. Lovingly capturing the sights and sounds of the Jewish neighbourhood situated south of Delancey Street, director Joan Micklin Silver never allows emotion to descend into sentiment. DP

Amy Irving *Isabelle Grossman* • Peter Riegert *Sam Posner* • Jeroen Krabbé *Anton Maes* • Reizl Bozyk *Bubbie Kantor* • Sylvia Miles *Hannah Mandelbaum* ■ *Dir* Joan Micklin Silver • *Scr* Susan Sandler, from her play

The Crossing Guard ★★★★ 15

Drama 1995 · US · Colour · 106mins

This forceful drama, written and directed by Sean Penn, features Jack Nicholson as the father of a drink-driving victim who vows to kill the man responsible (David Morse). What follows is not a plot-heavy revenge thriller, but a poignant and believable study of a tragedy that has sucked the life out of its tormented protagonists. A slow-burning pace, fine performances and an intelligent script make this drama feel painfully real. Most of all, we genuinely care about the outcome. JC. Contains violence, swearing, a sex scene and nudity. DVD

Jack Nicholson *Freddy Gale* • David Morse *John Booth* • Anjelica Huston *Mary* • Robin Wright [Robin Wright Penn] *JoJo* • Piper Laurie *Helen Booth* • Priscilla Barnes *Verna* • Robbie Robertson *Roger* ■ *Dir/Scr* Sean Penn

Crossover Dreams ★★

Musical drama 1985 · US · Colour · 86mins

With the resurgent popularity of salsa, you might think a movie on the subject would be a good idea. Here's a film that will soon disabuse you of that notion. Rubén Blades stars as the Latino expert whose career appears on the ascendant. Yet his cockiness costs him the friends he needs when his latest record fails. Despite a great soundtrack, Leon Ichaso's effort is formulaic and trite. Blades has charisma and presence, though. LH

Rubén Blades *Rudy Veloz* • Shawn Elliot [Shawn Elliott] *Orlando* • Tom Signorelli *Lou Rose* • Elizabeth Peña *Liz Garcia* • Frank Robles *Ray Soto* • Joel Diamond *Neil Silver* • Virgilio Marti *Cheo Babalu* • Amanda Barber *Radio DJ* ■ *Dir* Leon Ichaso • *Scr* Leon Ichaso, Manuel Arce, Rubén Blades, from a story by Kenny Vance, Leon Ichaso, Manuel Arce

Crossplot ★★

Spy drama 1969 · UK · Colour · 96mins

Roger Moore wasn't James Bond when he made this, just a TV star with some time to kill between *The Saint* and *The Persuaders*. Set in swinging London, the plot has Moore as an advertising executive looking for the ideal girl for a campaign, who just happens to be mixed up with a sinister political organisation. *Variety* rightly condemned the film's listlessness, though they lacked prescience by saying "Moore is not wholly convincing as a man of action." Tell that to M. AT

Roger Moore *Gary Fenn* • Martha Hyer *Jo Grinling* • Claudie Lange *Marla Kogash* • Alexis Kanner *Tarquin* • Francis Matthews *Ruddock* • Bernard Lee *Chilmore* ■ *Dir* Alvin Rakoff • *Scr* Leigh Vance, John Kruse, from a story by Leigh Vance

Crossroads ★★

Mystery 1942 · US · BW · 83mins

William Powell stars as an amnesiac diplomat in Paris who becomes the target of blackmailers. He is then accused of being a wanted criminal in court and, because of his amnesia, cannot prove otherwise. Filmed on a studio backlot version of Paris, its chief virtues are in the cast: Hedy Lamarr as Powell's wife, Basil Rathbone as his blackmailer and Claire Trevor as a nightclub singer. AT

William Powell *David Talbot* • Hedy Lamarr *Lucienne Talbot* • Claire Trevor *Michelle Allaine* • Basil Rathbone *Henri Sarrow* • Felix Bressart *Dr Andre Tessier* • Margaret Wycherly *Mme Pelletier* • Reginald Owen *Concierge* ■ *Dir* Jack Conway • *Scr* Gus Trosper

Crossroads ★★ 15

Road movie 1986 · US · Colour · 94mins

Based on the myth that blues legend Robert Johnson sold his soul to the Devil, this is essentially a musical version of *The Karate Kid*. Joe Seneca plays as an old compadre of Johnson's who persuades the young guitarist to take him home to Mississippi. Only Seneca's yarns and Ry Cooder's lazy score make the trek tolerable, though it's infinitely more entertaining than the ludicrous finale, in which Macchio trades riffs with Frank Zappa's old axeman, Steve Vai. DP

Ralph Macchio *Eugene Martone* • Joe Seneca *Willie Brown* • Jami Gertz *Frances* • Robert Judd *Scratch* • Joe Morton *Scratch's assistant* • Steve Vai *Jack Butler* • Dennis Lipscomb *Lloyd* ■ *Dir* Walter Hill • *Scr* John Fusco

Crossroads ★★★ PG

Romantic comedy drama
2002 · US · Colour · 91mins

Despite its naive, picture-postcard view of America, this showcase for teen singing sensation Britney Spears is hard to dislike. Simplistic in the extreme but not without charm, the film sees Spears and childhood friends Zoë Saldana and Taryn Manning on a road trip of discovery. If you can cope with the high cheese factor, director Tamra Davis's rose-tinted movie is a mildly engaging journey through adolescent problem-page dilemmas, with natural, pleasing performances from Britney Spears and the girls, supported by experienced elders Dan Aykroyd and Kim Cattrall. JC DVD

Britney Spears *Lucy* • Anson Mount *Ben* • Zoë Saldana *Kit* • Taryn Manning *Mimi* • Kim Cattrall *Caroline* • Dan Aykroyd *Pete* • Justin Long *Henry* ■ *Dir* Tamra Davis • *Scr* Shonda Rhimes

Crossworlds ★★★ 15

Science-fiction adventure
1996 · US · Colour · 87mins

Cheap and cliché-ridden it may be, but this *Stargate* meets *Star Wars* hybrid is an enjoyably unpretentious fantasy romp. All-American Josh Charles learns from a mysterious stranger that the crystal around his neck is the key to a trans-dimensional portal where time and space have no meaning. In this crossworld, he teams up with Ben Kenobi clone Rutger Hauer in a battle for survival against megalomaniac Stuart Wilson. If you can get over the slow start, this will be an entertaining experience. AJ. Contains violence and some swearing. DVD

Rutger Hauer *A T* • Josh Charles *Joe Talbot* • Stuart Wilson (1) *Ferris* • Andrea Roth *Laura* • Perry Anzilotti *Rebo* ■ *Dir* Krishna Rao • *Scr* Krishna Rao, Raman Rao

Crouching Tiger, Hidden Dragon ★★★★★ 12

Period action romance
2000 · US/Chi/Tai · Colour · 115mins

Exhibiting cinematic influences ranging from John Ford and Akira Kurosawa to *The Matrix*, Ang Lee's handsome epic puts the art back into martial arts. Those familiar with the works of King Hu and Tsui Hark will revel in the unhurried way he reworks the conventions of the swordplay genre to explore the perennial themes of love and loyalty, duty and sacrifice. But Lee also combines brilliant stunt work with special effects to create such memorable sequences as the rooftop pursuit and the treetop battle. Chow Yun-Fat and Michelle Yeoh excel as the warriors seeking the stolen sword of Green Destiny, but the most electrifying performance is Zhang Ziyi's teenage thief. DP. In Mandarin with English subtitles. DVD

Chow Yun-Fat *Li Mu Bai* • Michelle Yeoh *Yu Shu Lien* • Zhang Ziyi *Jen* • Chang Chen *Lo* • Cheng Pei Pei *Jade Fox* ■ *Dir* Ang Lee • *Scr* James Schamus, Wang Hui-Ling, Tsai Kuo-Jung, from the novel by Wang Du Lu • *Cinematographer* Peter Pau • *Choreographer* Yuen Woo-Ping

Croupier ★★ 15

Thriller 1998 · Fr/Ger/UK · Colour · 90mins

This account of double-dealing in a London casino is fascinating in its detail, but the improbable romantic backdrop given to the story by scriptwriter Paul Mayersberg does director Mike Hodges no favours. Clive Owen plays a croupier-turned-writer who is prompted by his buccaneering father (Nicholas Ball) to return to the tables. Owen's poker-faced acting doesn't involve us, while the story strands never properly intertwine. TH. Contains violence, swearing, sex scenes and nudity. DVD

Clive Owen *Jack Manfred* • Alex Kingston *Jani de Villiers* • Kate Hardie *Bella* • Nicholas Ball *Jack Manfred Sr* • Gina McKee *Marion Neil* ■ *Dir* Mike Hodges • *Scr* Paul Mayersberg

The Crow ★★★★ 18

Action fantasy 1994 · US · Colour · 101mins

A dark, surreal version of James O'Barr's 1980s cult comic book. Brandon Lee (son of Bruce) plays a rock musician returning from the grave to take revenge on the notorious street gang who murdered him and his fiancée. It's a stunningly designed fantasy with *Grand Guignol* gloominess at a jolting premium. The comic-book origins may be too obvious at times, but the dynamic action scenes and the bravura kinetic style of director Alex Proyas mean it always grips and thoroughly entertains. This dark fable about life after death was given a poignant spin when Lee was tragically killed during an on-set stunt accident. AJ. Contains violence, swearing, drug abuse and brief nudity. DVD

Brandon Lee *Eric Draven* • Michael Wincott *Top Dollar* • Rochelle Davis *Sarah* • Ernie Hudson *Albrecht* • David Patrick Kelly *T Bird* • Angel David *Skank* ■ *Dir* Alex Proyas • *Scr* David J Schow, John Shirley, from the comic book by James O'Barr • *Cinematographer* Dariusz Wolski • *Art Director* Simon Murton

The Crow: City of Angels ★ 18

Supernatural action fantasy
1996 · US · Colour · 90mins

Vincent Perez replaces the late Brandon Lee as a murder victim resurrected from the dead to confront his killers in this shameless rehash of the original. Lacking the tragic resonance and strong performances of its Hammer-styled predecessor, director Tim Pope's sequel plays like an extended pop video and quickly becomes a rock-blasting, S&M-posturing endurance test. Ponderous, dull and mechanical, the only thing worth crowing about here is Iggy Pop's feisty performance. AJ. Contains sex scenes, swearing, violence. DVD

Vincent Perez *Ashe* • Mia Kirshner *Sarah* • Richard Brooks *Judah* • Iggy Pop *Curve* • Thuy Trang *Kali* • Ian Dury *Noah* • Thomas Jane *Nemo* • Vincent Castellanos *Spider Monkey* ■ *Dir* Tim Pope • *Scr* David S Goyer, from the comic book by James O'Barr

The Crowd ★★★★★

Silent drama 1928 · US · BW · 104mins

In this powerful silent drama from director King Vidor, James Murray gives a superlative performance as an idealistic young man trapped in a dead-end job whose ambitions are dogged by tragedy. Such was the film's influence that its depiction of regimented office life and the palliative power of mass laughter were later referenced by such eminent directors as Billy Wilder and Preston Sturges. Murray was plucked from a crowd of extras to star in the film. Sadly, he was unable to cope with celebrity and died in his mid-30s after falling into the Hudson River. Vidor continued the story in 1934's *Our Daily Bread*. AE

Eleanor Boardman *Mary* • James Murray *John* • Bert Roach *Bert* • Estelle Clark *Jane* • Daniel G Tomlinson *Jim* • Dell Henderson *Dick* ■ *Dir* King Vidor • *Scr* King Vidor, John VA Weaver, Harry Behn, Joe Farnham [Joseph Farnham] (titles), from a story by King Vidor • *Cinematographer* Henry Sharp

The Crowd Roars ★★★

Drama 1932 · US · BW · 84mins

This dated motor-racing melodrama is redeemed by a knock-out performance from a cocky James Cagney, acting away on all cylinders despite the rather obvious back projection and model shots. The film has all the fast-paced style Warner Bros fans expect, speedy dialogue and a batch of regulars in the cast. However, it's a far cry from Howard Hawks's best work and those studio racetrack shots really let it down. The same shots were used in the 1939 remake, *Indianapolis Speedway*. TS

James Cagney *Joe Greer* • Joan Blondell *Anne* • Eric Linden *Eddie Greer* • Ann Dvorak *Lee* • Guy Kibbee *Dad Greer* • Frank McHugh *Spud Connors* • Regis Toomey *Dick Wilbur* • William Arnold *Bill Arnold* ■ *Dir* Howard Hawks • *Scr* John Bright, Niven Busch, Kubec Glasmon

The Crowd Roars ★★

Sports drama 1938 · US · BW · 90mins

Robert Taylor plays a boxer who is soured on life after he accidentally kills an opponent. Becoming a pawn of Edward Arnold's racketeer, he falls in love with the man's daughter (Maureen O'Sullivan). Frank Morgan does one of his tipsy turns as Taylor's alcoholic father, while Richard Thorpe directs competently. Alas, the film lacks any real punch. Mickey Rooney starred in a 1947 remake, *Killer McCoy*. AE

Robert Taylor (1) *Tommy McCoy* • Edward Arnold *Jim Cain* • Frank Morgan *Brian McCoy* • Maureen O'Sullivan *Sheila Carson* • William Gargan *Johnny Martin* • Lionel Stander *"Happy" Lane* • Jane Wyman *Vivian* • Nat

Pendleton *"Pug" Walsh* ■ *Dir* Richard Thorpe • *Scr* Thomas Lennon, George Bruce, George Oppenheimer, from a story by George Bruce

The Crowded Sky ★★★

Drama 1960 · US · Colour · 105mins

Progenitor of the group jeopardy movie, with a pre-*Airport* collection of second-string movie stars slightly past their prime, this typically glossy Warner Bros melodrama has a look that virtually enshrines its year. The plot is satisfyingly and classically simple – an airliner and a navy jet are on a collision couse – and the whole is skilfully directed by craftsman Joseph Pevney. A camp treat, maybe, but a treat nonetheless. TS

Dana Andrews *Dick Barnett* • Rhonda Fleming *Cheryl Heath* • Efrem Zimbalist Jr *Dale Heath* • John Kerr *Mike* • Anne Francis *Kitty Foster* • Keenan Wynn *Nick Hyland* • Troy Donahue *McVey* • Patsy Kelly *Gertrude* ■ *Dir* Joseph Pevney • *Scr* Charles Schnee, from the novel by Hank Searls

Crows and Sparrows ★★★★

Political drama 1949 · Chi · BW · 113mins

Already established as one of China's finest film-makers with *Spring River Flows East* (1947), Zheng Junli had to change his political tune for a paean to Maoist ideology that confirmed his status within the communist film industry. There are similarities in this tale of tenement folk to Jean Renoir's Popular Front picture, *Le Crime de Monsieur Lange*, as various residents struggle to stay the right side of their avaricious landlord while also trying to pick a path through the minefield of political affiliations. DP. In Mandarin with English subtitles.

Zhao Dan *Little Broadcast* • Wu Yin *Mrs Xiao* • Wei Heling *Mr Kong* • Sun Daolin *Teacher Hua* • Shangguan Yunzhu *Mrs Hua* • Li Tianji *Mr Hou* ■ *Dir* Zheng Junli • *Scr* Baichen Chen, Lingu Wang, Tao Xu, Dan Zhao, Junli Zheng, Fu Shen

The Crucible ★★★★ 12

Period drama 1996 · US · Colour · 118mins

Arthur Miller's emotionally raw play about suspected witchcraft in 17th-century Massachusetts – a veiled attack on the McCarthy-inspired communist witch-hunts of the 1950s – is here brilliantly brought to the screen by director Nicholas Hytner. Hytner brilliantly captures both a believable period flavour and the stifling atmosphere of fear and suspicion in Salem. Daniel Day-Lewis is characteristically intense as the married man caught in the middle, but the real fireworks come from Winona Ryder, as the wicked young girl whose manipulative behaviour is the story's catalyst, and Paul Scofield's commanding presence as the trial's judge. Absolutely electrifying. JC. Contains violence, nudity. DVD

Daniel Day-Lewis *John Proctor* • Winona Ryder *Abigail Williams* • Paul Scofield *Judge Danforth* • Joan Allen *Elizabeth Proctor* • Bruce Davison *Reverend Parris* • Rob Campbell *Reverend Hale* • Jeffrey Jones *Thomas Putnam* • Peter Vaughan *Giles Corey* ■ *Dir* Nicholas Hytner • *Scr* Arthur Miller, from his play

Crucible of Terror ★ 18

Horror 1971 · UK · Colour · 85mins

Former Radio One disc jockey Mike Raven turned actor to appear in this kooky *House of Wax* variant. He shouldn't have given up his day job! Woodenly playing an insane sculptor, Raven covers the dead bodies of his murder victims in bronze after being possessed by an evil spirit. Longer on talk than terror, with stilted direction and ridiculous dialogue. AJ. Contains violence and nudity.

Mike Raven *Victor Clare* • Mary Maude *Millie* • James Bolam *John Davies* • Ronald Lacey *Michael* • Betty Alberge *Dorothy* • John Arnatt *Bill* • Beth Morris *Jane Clare* ■ *Dir* Ted Hooker • *Scr* Ted Hooker, Tom Parkinson

The Crucified Lovers ★★★★

Romantic period drama
1954 · Jpn · BW · 101mins

Originally written as a piece for marionettes by the 16th-century playwright Monzaemon Chikamatsu and subsequently adapted for the kabuki stage, this tale of doomed defiance has been filmed with a painterly yet wholly cinematic realism by the master Japanese director, Kenji Mizoguchi. Subtly depicting passion without any physical contact between merchant's wife Kyoko Kagawa and besotted clerk Kazuo Hasegawa, he retains the human element of the story in spite of his unceasing attention to period detail. He also makes expert use of the landscape (sublimely photographed by Kazuo Miyagawa) to contrast their innocent devotion with the brutality of shogunate society. DP. In Japanese with English subtitles.

Kazuo Hasegawa *Mohei* • Kyoko Kagawa *Osan* • Eitaro Shindo *Ishun* • Sakae Ozawa [Eitaro Ozawa] *Sukeemon* • Yoko Minamida *Otama* • Haruo Tanaka *Doki* • Chieko Naniwa *Oko* • Ichiro Sugai *Genbee* ■ *Dir* Kenji Mizoguchi • *Scr* Yoshikata Yoda, Matsutaro Kawaguchi, from the play *The Legend of the Grand Scroll Makers* by Monzaemon Chikamatsu

Cruel Intentions ★★★ 15

Drama 1999 · US · Colour · 93mins

Dangerous Liaisons for the under-20s is the basic premise of this sexed-up, revved-up teen picture. Sarah Michelle Gellar and Ryan Phillippe star as the contemporary Merteuil and Valmont, machinating round New York and laying their bet as to whether or not Phillippe can bed Reese Witherspoon. You can understand why director Roger Kumble saw the classic novel as an apt metaphor for teenage sexuality and exploration, but with the depth gone, this is simply an entertaining romp. LH. Contains swearing, sex scenes, drug abuse. DVD

Sarah Michelle Gellar *Kathryn Merteuil* • Ryan Phillippe *Sebastian Valmont* • Reese Witherspoon *Annette Hargrove* • Selma Blair *Cecile Caldwell* • Louise Fletcher *Helen Rosemond* • Joshua Jackson *Blaine Tuttle* ■ *Dir* Roger Kumble • *Scr* Roger Kumble, from the novel *Les Liasions Dangereuses* by Choderlos de Laclos

Cruel Intentions 2 ★★ 15

Drama 2000 · US · Colour · 83mins

Following the success of *Cruel Intentions*, Roger Kumble signed to direct a TV series entitled *Manchester Prep*. However, the show was cancelled before its first two episodes were even aired. So Kumble has stitched them together to make this shamelessly steamy prequel to his teenpic reworking of *Dangerous Liaisons*, in which a feckless playboy has to choose between true love and impressing his cynical stepsister. It atones in nastiness for what it lacks in star wattage. A second, straight-to-video sequel followed in 2004. DP. Contains swearing, nudity. DVD

Robin Dunne *Sebastian Valmont* • Amy Adams *Kathryn Merteuil* • Sarah Thompson *Danielle Sherman* • Keri Lynn Pratt *Cherie* • Barry Flatman *Sherman* • Mimi Rogers *Tiffany Merteuil-Valmont* ■ *Dir* Roger Kumble • *Scr* Roger Kumble, from characters created by Roger Kumble, from the novel *Les Liasions Dangereuses* by Choderlos de Laclos

The Cruel Sea ★★★★ PG

Second World War drama
1953 · UK · BW · 120mins

Charles Frend's *San Demetrio London* was one of the finest naval combat films made anywhere during the Second World War. Here, Frend's insight into the conditions endured and the emotions experienced by embattled sailors of all ranks is very much to the fore in a stirring adaptation (by Eric Ambler) of Nicholas Monsarrat's bestselling novel. Produced by Leslie Norman (father of Barry), this is a prime example of the docudramatic style that, spurning the gung-ho heroics of Hollywood, characterised the best British war films. DP DVD

Jack Hawkins *Ericson* • Donald Sinden *Lockhart* • John Stratton *Ferraby* • Denholm Elliott *Morrell* • Stanley Baker *Bennett* • Virginia McKenna *Julie Hallam* • Glyn Houston *Phillips* • Alec McCowen *Tonbridge* ■ *Dir* Charles Frend • *Scr* Eric Ambler, from the novel by Nicholas Monsarrat

The Cruise ★★★

Documentary 1998 · US · BW · 76mins

For all its technical limitations, this is a quizzically admiring and highly entertaining portrait of New York tour guide and street poet, Timothy "Speed" Levitch. Vivacious, brash and disarmingly persuasive, Levitch has an opinion on everything and is never shy to express it – at length. However, while director Bennett Miller is always prepared to let this nonconformist motormouth go into overdrive, he leaves unanswered too many questions about his background and his impact on the people he encounters. He also wastes the chance to explore Levitch's stomping ground in grainy video monochrome by resorting too often to tight close-up. DP

Dir Bennett Miller

Cruising ★★ 18

Detective thriller
1980 · US · Colour · 100mins

William Friedkin's typically intense thriller finds Al Pacino overacting alarmingly as the New York cop who enters the gay, sado-masochistic underworld in order to track down a psychopath. It pushes to the limit what is acceptable in a mainstream studio picture but, while the savagery of the murders and the explicitness of the sexual practices on display are initially unsettling, they soon become numbing. AT. Contains violence, swearing, sex scenes, drug abuse and nudity.

Al Pacino *Steve Burns* • Paul Sorvino *Captain Edelson* • Karen Allen *Nancy* • Richard Cox *Stuart Richards* • Don Scardino *Ted Bailey* ■ *Dir* William Friedkin • *Scr* William Friedkin, from a novel by Gerald Walker

Crumb ★★★★ 18

Documentary 1995 · US · Colour · 120mins

Robert Crumb became a hero of the American underground in the mid-1960s for such cartoon strips as *Fritz the Cat* and *Keep on Truckin'*. Yet, as Terry Zwigoff's documentary opens, the cult cartoonist was packing his bags to settle in France and abandon not just a legion of fans, but also the various feminist groups who denounced him for the sexism of his work and the chauvinism of his private life. This is anything but hagiography, with Crumb coming across as a highly resistible character, while his brothers Charles and Maxon prove every bit as fascinating. This is an often shocking, sometimes horrifying portrait of an artist and his world. DP DVD

Dir Terry Zwigoff

The Crusades ★★

Historical drama 1935 · US · BW · 123mins

Another episode in *The History of the World* by Cecil B DeMille. This time Cecil tackles the Crusades, following Richard I and the Christians as they set forth from Europe to attack Saladin's Muslim hordes. Loretta Young is Richard's lady love, whom he agrees to marry in exchange for food and horses; he absents himself from their wedding, sending his sword in his place. This was a box-office disaster, though the siege of Jerusalem is as juicy as one expects from this legendary director. AT

Loretta Young *Berengaria* • Henry Wilcoxon *Richard* • Ian Keith *Saladin* • Katherine DeMille *Alice* • C Aubrey Smith *The Hermit* • Joseph Schildkraut *Conrad of Montferrat* ■ *Dir* Cecil B DeMille • *Scr* Harold Lamb, Waldemar Young, Dudley Nichols, from the non-fiction book *The Crusade: Iron Men and Saints* by Harold Lamb

Crush ★★★ 18

Drama 1992 · NZ · Colour · 92mins

Alison Maclean makes an arresting feature debut with this dark treatise on sexual ambiguity, power games and identity crises. The mercenary Marcia Gay Harden exploits literary critic Donogh Rees's incapacity to move in on author William Zappa and his impressionable daughter, Caitlin Bossley. The bubbling mud of New Zealand's top tourist site Rotorua symbolises the seething emotions underlying the increasingly sinister events, while Harden's ruthless opportunism represents the threat of American cultural imperialism. This erotic psychological thriller eventually boils over into melodrama. DP

Marcia Gay Harden *Lane* • Donogh Rees *Christina* • Caitlin Bossley *Angela* • William Zappa *Colin* • Pete Smith *Horse* • Jon Brazier *Arthur* ■ *Dir* Alison Maclean • *Scr* Alison Maclean, Anne Kennedy

The Crush ★★★ 15

Thriller 1993 · US · Colour · 85mins

Fatal Attraction meets *Lolita* in this derivative thriller. Alicia Silverstone, making her film debut, is the precocious 14-year-old whose flirtation with Cary Elwes's journalist becomes a campaign of terror when he rejects her overtures in favour of a grown-up woman. There's some nastily unnerving fun, while Silverstone's psychotic performance displays star quality. AME. Contains violence, swearing, sex scenes, nudity.

Cary Elwes *Nick Eliot* • Alicia Silverstone *Darian* • Jennifer Rubin *Amy* • Kurtwood Smith *Cliff Forrester* • Gwynyth Walsh *Liv Forrester* ■ *Dir/Scr* Alan Shapiro

Crush ★★ 15

Romantic comedy drama
2001 · UK/Ger/US · Colour · 107mins

The plot centres on three 40-something single women – Andie MacDowell's way-too-glamorous headmistress, Anna Chancellor's swearing doctor and Imelda Staunton's frumpy policewoman – who meet to drink and commiserate with each other over their love lives. When MacDowell embarks on an affair with a 25-year-old former pupil (Kenny Doughty), the bonds of friendship begin to unravel. This is sabotaged by weak characterisation and an uneasy mix of comedy and tragedy. AC. Contains swearing and sex scenes. DVD

Andie MacDowell *Kate* • Imelda Staunton *Janine* • Anna Chancellor *Molly* • Kenny Doughty *Jed* • Bill Paterson *Rev Gerald Farquhar Marsden* ■ *Dir/Scr* John McKay

Crush Proof ★★★ 18

Drama 1998 · UK/Ire/Ger · Colour · 93mins

A million miles from the cosy Barrytown backstreets of Roddy Doyle, director Paul Tickell's bruising Dublin-set debut is an inner-city western, complete with horses, posses and mobile phones. No sooner out of jail than straight back into trouble, Darren Healy gives a defiant performance as the teenage outlaw to whom life keeps happening with a vengeance. Although reasons for his plight are touched upon, this is anything but a message movie. Instead, it's a frenetic frontier tale, with the unexpectedly quiet passages being every bit as effective as the shocking set pieces. DP. Contains violence, swearing, sex scenes. [video]

Darren Healy *Neal* • Viviana Verveen *Nuala* • Jeff O'Toole *Liam* • Mark Dunne *Sean* • Michael McElhatton *Detective Sergeant Hogan* ■ *Dir* Paul Tickell • *Scr* James Mathers, from a story by John Edwards, James Mathers

Crusoe ★★★ 15

Period adventure 1988 · US · Colour · 90mins

Daniel Defoe's classic allegory gets another makeover, this time with Aidan Quinn as the shipwrecked hero. His Robinson Crusoe is a slave trader whose moral failings are reversed first by his pet dog, then by an escaped slave whom he saves, and finally by a cannibal. Directed by Caleb Deschanel, better known as a cameraman, and superbly shot in the Seychelles, it's a generally impressive achievement that pushes its message home without undue force. AT [video]

Aidan Quinn *Crusoe* • Ade Sapara *The Warrior* • Elvis Payne *Runaway Slave* • Richard Sharp *Colcol* • Colin Bruce *Clerk* • Jimmy Nail *Tarik* • Timothy Spall *Reverend Milne* • Warren Clarke *Captain Lee* ■ *Dir* Caleb Deschanel • *Scr* Walon Green, Christopher Logue, from the novel *The Life and Adventures of Robinson Crusoe* by Daniel Defoe

Cry-Baby ★★★ 15

Musical parody 1989 · US · Colour · 81mins

John Waters's hilarious send-up of *Grease* and *Jailhouse Rock* revolves around juvenile delinquent Johnny Depp having the hots for square Amy Locane. A superb soundtrack mixes real throbbing golden oldies with wonderful rock 'n' roll parodies, and the usual hip cast (including Iggy Pop and porn queen Traci Lords) pushes the vivid cartoon caricatures as close to the edge as possible. The nostalgic delights in Waters's reform school drool are often more subtle than his other period offering, *Hairspray*, but it's still a polished debunking of pop culture from the "Pope of Trash". AJ. Contains swearing. [video]

Johnny Depp *Wade "Cry-Baby" Walker* • Amy Locane *Allison Vernon-Williams* • Susan Tyrrell *Ramona* • Polly Bergen *Mrs Vernon-Williams* • Iggy Pop *Belvedere* • Ricki Lake *Pepper* • Traci Lords *Wanda* • Kim McGuire *Hatchet-Face* • Troy Donahue *Hatchet's father* • Mink Stole *Hatchet's mother* • Joe Dallesandro *Milton's father* • Patricia Hearst *Wanda's mother* • Willem Dafoe *Hateful guard* • Mary Vivian Pearce *Picnic mother* ■ *Dir/Scr* John Waters (2)

The Cry Baby Killer ★★

Crime drama 1958 · US · BW · 61mins

Jack Nicholson's first big break – and his last for some time – was gaining the title role in this low-budget contribution to the juvenile delinquency cycle of the time. Nicholson mades his film debut as the frightened teenager who shoots two bullies and barricades himself in a storeroom with hostages. The siege that follows is well handled by director Jus Addiss, but Nicholson's part is too underwritten for him to make much of it. AE

Harry Lauter *Porter* • Jack Nicholson *Jimmy* • Carolyn Mitchell *Carole* • Brett Halsey *Manny* • Lynn Cartwright *Julie* • Ralph Reed *Joey* • John Shay *Gannon* • Barbara Knudson *Mrs Maxton* ■ *Dir* Jus Addiss • *Scr* Melvin Levy, Leo Gordon, from a story by Leo Gordon

Cry Danger ★★★

Crime drama 1951 · US · BW · 79mins

A former child actor and film editor, Robert Parrish made an impressive directorial debut with this tough thriller starring one-time crooner Dick Powell as an ex-convict on a quest to free a pal still in jail. The film is set in the ghetto area of Los Angeles, to allow Powell to hole up in a seedy trailer camp to stake out said friend's wife (played by Rhonda Fleming). Hot on atmosphere (provided by legendary cameraman and Robert Aldrich favourite Joseph Biroc) and tight on suspense, this was an auspicious debut from a still very interesting and under-rated director. TS

Dick Powell *Rocky Malloy* • Rhonda Fleming *Nancy* • Richard Erdman *Delong* • William Conrad *Castro* • Regis Toomey *Cobb* • Jean Porter *Darlene* • Jay Adler *Williams* ■ *Dir* Robert Parrish • *Scr* William Bowers, from a story by Jerome Cady

Cry for Happy ★

Romantic comedy
1961 · US · Colour · 110mins

A quartet of American navy photographers, on leave in Japan during the Korean War, become romantically entangled with four geisha girls who are attempting to found an orphanage. Starring Glenn Ford and Donald O'Connor, George Marshall's movie is a predictable, witless and desperately unfunny attempt at romantic comedy, while the portrayal of the girls is deeply patronising. RK

Glenn Ford *Andy Cyphers* • Donald O'Connor *Murray Prince* • Miiko Taka *Chiyoko* • James Shigeta *Suzuki* • Miyoshi Umeki *Harue* • Michi Kobi *Hanakichi* • Howard St John *Admiral Bennett* ■ *Dir* George Marshall • *Scr* Irving Brecher, from the novel by George Campbell

Cry for Me Billy ★★

Western 1972 · US · Colour · 87mins

Long in post-production and never properly released, this post-hippy western is not entirely without interest. Cliff Potts plays an alienated gunfighter who rescues an Indian girl after being appalled at the white man's treatment of the native American. When she's raped, he sets out on a violent quest for revenge. Director William A Graham can't really bring off this excursion into Anthony Mann territory. TS

Cliff Potts *Billy* • Oaxchitl *Indian girl* • Harry Dean Stanton *Luke Todd* • Don Wilbanks *Sergeant* • Woodrow Chambliss *Prospector* • Roy Jenson *Blacksmith* ■ *Dir* William A Graham • *Scr* David Markson

Cry Freedom ★★★★ PG

Biographical drama
1987 · UK · Colour · 151mins

This ambitious, worthy attempt by Richard Attenborough to re-create the success of *Gandhi* with another epic biographical portrait tells the story of the doomed South African civil rights leader Steve Biko. Attenborough is well served by the charismatic playing of Denzel Washington as the black activist and Kevin Kline as the liberal newspaper editor Donald Woods. The early scenes, in which the comfortably middle class Woods gradually has his eyes opened to the true horrors of the apartheid system, are sharply observed. The film loses its way a little when the attention switches to the plight of the Woods family, but their final attempts at flight are genuinely suspenseful. JF. Contains some violence and swearing. [video] DVD

Kevin Kline *Donald Woods* • Denzel Washington *Steve Biko* • Penelope Wilton *Wendy Woods* • John Hargreaves *Bruce* • Alec McCowen *Acting High Commissioner* • Kevin McNally *Ken* • Zakes Mokae *Father Kani* • Ian Richardson *State prosecutor* • Josette Simon *Dr Ramphele* • John Thaw *Kruger* • Timothy West *Captain de Wet* • Miles Anderson *Lemick* ■ *Dir* Richard Attenborough • *Scr* John Briley, from the non-fiction books *Biko* and *Asking for Trouble* by Donald Woods

A Cry from the Streets ★★★ U

Drama 1957 · UK · BW · 100mins

Dogmatic social worker Barbara Murray, who deals with underprivileged children, enlists the help of Max Bygraves as an assistant. He who saves the day when a child whose mother commits suicide goes on the run with the kids of a murderer – and a gun. Neither as melodramatic as it sounds, nor all doom and gloom, this is a decent attempt at realism, directed in quasi-documentary style by Lewis Gilbert. RK

Max Bygraves *Bill Lowther* • Barbara Murray *Ann Fairlie* • Colin Petersen *Georgie* • Dana Wilson *Barbie* • Kathleen Harrison *Mrs Farrer* • Mona Washbourne *Mrs Daniels* ■ *Dir* Lewis Gilbert • *Scr* Vernon Harris, from the novel *The Friend in Need* by Elizabeth Coxhead

Cry Havoc ★★★

Second World War melodrama
1943 · US · BW · 97mins

An interesting, accomplished cast does the *Tenko* routine as the likes of Joan Blondell and Ann Sothern pitch up on the island of Bataan during the height of Second World War hostilities. The material originated on the stage, and it shows in the movie's enclosed, claustrophobic look. However, despite the rather hackneyed dialogue and abundance of realistic make-up, this is a stirring, emotive tale. SH

Margaret Sullavan *Lieutenant Smith* • Ann Sothern *Pat* • Joan Blondell *Grace* • Fay Bainter *Captain Marsh* • Marsha Hunt *Flo Norris* • Ella Raines *Connie* • Frances Gifford *Helen* • Diana Lewis *Nydia* ■ *Dir* Richard Thorpe • *Scr* Paul Osborne, from the play *Proof Thro' the Night* by Allen R Kenward

A Cry in the Dark ★★★★ 15

Drama based on a true story
1988 · US/Aus · Colour · 116mins

This is an absolutely riveting and at times harrowing telling of the bizarre real-life story of Lindy Chamberlain, who claimed her baby was killed by a dingo at Ayers Rock in 1980. The movie covers a huge amount of ground: Aboriginal myths, the Chamberlains' Seventh Day Adventism, the media circus and the way the case challenged the legal system and obsessed Australians for years. Meryl Streep gives one of her best performances: a portrait of a tough, humourless woman who eventually earns our sympathy and pity. Sam Neill as her morose preacher husband is equally impressive. AT. Contains swearing and brief nudity. [video] DVD

Meryl Streep *Lindy Chamberlain* • Sam Neill *Michael Chamberlain* • Bruce Myles *Barker* • Charles Tingwell *Justice Muirhead* • Nick Tate *Charlwood* • Neil Fitzpatrick *Phillips* ■ *Dir* Fred Schepisi • *Scr* Robert Caswell, Fred Schepisi, from the non-fiction book *Evil Angels* by John Bryson

A Cry in the Night ★

Crime drama 1956 · US · BW · 75mins

Alan Ladd's Jaguar company made this rather sordid melodrama, with Ladd himself delivering the brief narration. It's all the fault of the parents: young Natalie Wood can't stand being at home with her domineering policeman father (Edmond O'Brien), and Raymond Burr's middle-aged Peeping Tom has been messed up by a possessive mother. The trouble starts when Burr, spying on Wood and boyfriend Richard Anderson in Lover's Lane, knocks him out and kidnaps her. There's never any doubt how it will end. AE

Edmond O'Brien *Taggart* • Brian Donlevy *Bates* • Natalie Wood *Liz* • Raymond Burr *Loftus* • Richard Anderson *Owen* • Irene Hervey *Helen* • Carol Veazie *Mrs Loftus* • Mary Lawrence *Madge* • Alan Ladd *Narrator* ■ *Dir* Frank Tuttle • *Scr* David Dortort, from the novel *All Through the Night* by Whit Masterson

Cry of the Banshee ★★ 15

Horror 1970 · UK · Colour · 83mins

The last period horror Vincent Price ever made finds the flamboyant villain back on *Witchfinder General* territory as an obsessed 16th-century witch-hunting magistrate hounded by demonic forces. Veteran actress Elisabeth Bergner (her name was misspelt on the original credits) plays the witch who unleashes werewolf-in-disguise Patrick Mower on the hedonistic patriarch. Director Gordon Hessler's lightweight chiller is a rather coy affair that's neither sexy nor spooky enough. AJ. Contains violence and nudity. [video]

Vincent Price *Lord Edward Whitman* • Elisabeth Bergner *Oona* • Essy Persson *Lady Patricia* • Hugh Griffith *Mickey* • Patrick Mower *Roderick* • Hilary Dwyer *Maureen* • Carl Rigg *Harry* ■ *Dir* Gordon Hessler • *Scr* Tim Kelly, Christopher Wicking, from a story by Tim Kelly

Cry of the City ★★★★

Film noir 1948 · US · BW · 95mins

One of the toughest and most uncompromising examples from that great period of 20th Century-Fox *film noir*, an emotive and exciting study of the relationship between one-time boyhood pals, gangster Richard Conte and cop Victor Mature. Richard Murphy's screenplay is adult and clever, and expressionist émigré director Robert Siodmak knows exactly how to paint this particular ultra-urban picture. For those who have been unable to take Mature seriously as an actor, this ranks with his best work. TS

Victor Mature *Lt Vittorio Candella* • Richard Conte *Martin Rome* • Fred Clark *Lt Jim Collins* • Shelley Winters *Brenda* • Betty Garde *Miss Florence Pruett* • Berry Kroeger *Niles* • Tommy Cook *Tony Rome* • Debra Paget *Teena Riconti* • Hope Emerson *Rose Given* • Roland Winters *Ledbetter* ■ *Dir* Robert Siodmak • *Scr* Richard Murphy, from the novel *The Chair for Martin Rome* by Henry Edward Helseth

Cry of the Hunted ★★★

Drama 1953 · US · BW · 78mins

Italian heart-throb Vittorio Gassman is an escaped convict being pursued through the boggy Louisiana bayous by officer Barry Sullivan. The few scenes with Polly Bergen – playing Sullivan's wife – were added later in an attempt to attract the female audience. But this is really a suspenseful chase movie, shot on authentically swampy locations by Joseph H Lewis. AT

Vittorio Gassman *Jory* • Barry Sullivan *Lt Tunner* • Polly Bergen *Janet Tunner* • William Conrad *Goodwin* • Mary Zavian *Ella* • Robert Burton *Warden Keeley* • Harry Shannon *Sheriff Brown* • Jonathan Cott *Deputy Davis* ■ *Dir* Joseph H Lewis • *Scr* Jack Leonard, from the story by Jack Leonard, Marion Wolfe

Cry of the Werewolf ★

Horror 1944 · US · BW · 62mins

Mild even by 1940s horror standards and utterly conventional in every respect, director Henry Levin's debut feature stars Nina Foch as queen of the Troiga gypsies. She murders a New Orleans museum curator to cover up the fact that she has inherited the curse of lycanthropy from her dead mother. Feeling far longer than it is, this banal potboiler lacks rudimentary suspense and even Foch's transformation takes place off-screen. AJ

Nina Foch *Celeste LaTour* • Stephen Crane *Bob Morris* • Osa Massen *Elsa Chauvet* • Blanche Yurka *Bianca* • Barton MacLane *Lt Barry Lane* ■ *Dir* Henry Levin • *Scr* Griffin Jay, Charles O'Neal, from a story by Griffin Jay

C

Cry Terror ★★★

Crime thriller 1958 · US · BW · 96mins

Low budget meets high suspense in this adroit thriller from writer/director Andrew L Stone, in which TV repairman James Mason, his wife Inger Stevens and his daughter Terry Ann Ross are held hostage by Rod Steiger, Angie Dickinson and Jack Klugman, who are plotting an extortion coup. Inventively contrived and executed, the action grips as it accelerates. TH

James Mason *Jim Molner* • Rod Steiger *Paul Hoplin* • Inger Stevens *Joan Molner* • Neville Brand *Steve* • Angie Dickinson *Kelly* • Kenneth Tobey *Frank Cole* • Jack Klugman *Vince* • Jack Kruschen *Charles Pope* • Terry Ann Ross *Pat Molner* ■ *Dir/Scr* Andrew L Stone

Cry, the Beloved Country ★★★★ PG

Drama 1951 · UK · BW · 99mins

Made in those grievous days of apartheid in South Africa, this adaptation of Alan Paton's stirring bestseller – with Canada Lee as the country minister looking for a lost son in Johannesburg – so obviously had its heart in the right place that it was hard to criticise. It still is, even in the post-apartheid era, because Zoltan Korda's direction, though naive, has a passionate directness that is timeless. One of the acting delights is Sidney Poitier as a young preacher who forgives all, but forgets nothing. TH [video]

Canada Lee *Stephen Kumalo* • Charles Carson *James Jarvis* • Sidney Poitier *Reverend Maimangu* • Joyce Carey *Margaret Jarvis* • Edric Connor *John Kumalo* • Geoffrey Keen *Father Vincent* ■ *Dir* Zoltan Korda • *Scr* Alan Paton, John Howard Lawson (uncredited), from the novel by Alan Paton

Cry, the Beloved Country ★★★★

Drama 1995 · S Afr/US · Colour · 111mins

This powerful adaptation of Alan Paton's 1940s-set racial drama centres on the converging lives of a black minister in rural South Africa and his white landowner neighbour. The first major feature to be shot in South Africa after the abolition of apartheid, Darrell James Roodt's film gains emotional resonance from the gentle, softly spoken sincerity of James Earl Jones as the pastor, devastated by the fate of his family in Johannesburg. Even if it occasionally feels a little manipulative (John Barry's score, for example), it is hard not to be affected. JC. Contains violence and swearing.

James Earl Jones *Reverend Stephen Kumalo* • Richard Harris *James Jarvis* • Charles S Dutton *John Kumalo* • Vusi Kunene *Father Msimangu* • Leleti Khumalo *Katie* • Dambisa Kente *Gertrude Kumalo* • Eric Miyeni *Absolom Kumalo* • Dolly Rathebe *Mrs Kumalo* ■ *Dir* Darrell James Roodt • *Scr* Ronald Harwood, from the novel by Alan Paton

Cry Vengeance ★★★

Crime drama 1954 · US · BW · 81mins

Mark Stevens, the handsome if rather bland leading man of Fox pictures of the 1940s, took on a tougher image in the 1950s. In this gripping crime drama, the first of five films he directed, Stevens plays a former detective who, after three years in prison, seeks revenge on the man he thinks framed him for a crime he didn't commit. A pulsating score and rapid editing helps give the film a lively pace, though the plot is somewhat convoluted and contrived. RB

Mark Stevens *Vic Barron* • Martha Hyer *Peggy Harding* • Skip Homeier *Roxey* • Joan Vohs *Lily Arnold* • Douglas Kennedy *Tino Morelli* • Don Haggerty *Lt Ryan* ■ *Dir* Mark Stevens • *Scr* Warren Douglas, George Bricker • *Editor* Elmo Veron • *Music* Paul Dunlap

Cry Wolf ★★ PG

Mystery 1947 · US · BW · 80mins

Screen icons Barbara Stanwyck and Errol Flynn were both past their box-office prime when they teamed up for this dour Warner Bros drama. When her husband kicks the bucket, Stanwyck returns to the old estate to find Flynn up to no good in the west wing. All very Charlotte Brontë, and very little fun thanks to Peter Godfrey's turgid direction. There's always pleasure to be gained from watching real movie stars go through their paces, but this *Old Dark House* tale is worthy of neither. TS [video]

Errol Flynn *Mark Caldwell* • Barbara Stanwyck *Sandra Marshall* • Geraldine Brooks *Julie Demarest* • Richard Basehart *James Demarest* • Jerome Cowan *Senator Charles Caldwell* • John Ridgely *Jackson Laidell* • Patricia White *Angela* ■ *Dir* Peter Godfrey • *Scr* Catherine Turney, from the novel by Marjorie Carleton

Crying Freeman ★★★ 18

Action drama
1995 · Fr/Jpn/Can/US · Colour · 97mins

Hong Kong-style action meets James Bond in a beautifully crafted adaptation of the cult Japanese comic strip. Enigmatic Mark Dacascos is the latest in a long line of human killing machines programmed by the Sons of the Dragon Society to respond to hypnotic signals. Because he sheds a tear after each contract killing, he earns the nickname "Crying Freeman". How he keeps his identity a secret fuels a cranked-up plot packed with inventive explosions, balletic gunplay, hyperkinetic stunts and forbidden love. AJ. Contains violence, swearing, sex scenes and nudity. [video] DVD

Mark Dacascos *Yo Hinomura/Freeman* • Julie Condra *Emu O'Hara* • Rae Dawn Chong *Detective Forge* • Byron Mann *Koh* • Mako *Shudo Shimizaki* • Tcheky Karyo *Detective Netah* ■ *Dir* Christophe Gans • *Scr* Christophe Gans, Thierry Cazals, from the comic book by Kazuo Koike, Ryoichi Ikegami

The Crying Game ★★★★ 18

Drama 1992 · UK · Colour · 107mins

Virtually ignored on its release, this offbeat tale went on to become a monster hit in America and even earned an Oscar for best original screenplay for writer/director Neil Jordan. It's a beguiling, eccentric blend of romantic drama and political thriller, and at its centre is a charismatic performance from Stephen Rea. He plays an IRA terrorist who flees to London after the botched kidnapping of a British soldier, played somewhat unconvincingly by Forest Whitaker. Ridden with guilt he locates the dead man's former lover (an extraordinary performance from Jaye Davidson that was deservedly rewarded with an Oscar nomination) and finds himself falling in love. JF. Contains violence, swearing and nudity. [video] DVD

Stephen Rea *Fergus* • Miranda Richardson *Jude* • Jaye Davidson *Dil* • Forest Whitaker *Jody* • Adrian Dunbar *Maguire* • Breffini McKenna [Breffni McKenna] *Tinker* • Jim Broadbent *Col* • Tony Slattery *Deveroux* • Shar Campbell *Bar performer* • David Crionelly *Security man* ■ *Dir/Scr* Neil Jordan

The Crystal Ball ★★★ U

Comedy 1943 · US · BW · 81mins

When gorgeous Texan Paulette Goddard fails to win a beauty contest, she takes up fake fortune-telling to earn a buck and gets involved with a bunch of swindlers. All ends happily when her shenanigans lead her to Ray Milland, the man of her dreams. An innocuous, slightly fantastical, but reasonably diverting comedy with a slapstick finale, this is nicely played and directed. RK

Ray Milland *Brad Cavanaugh* • Paulette Goddard *Toni Gerard* • Gladys George *Mme Zenobia* • Virginia Field *Jo Ainsley* • Cecil Kellaway *Pop Tibbets* • William Bendix *Biff Carter* • Mary Field *Foster* • Ernest Truex *Mr Martin* ■ *Dir* Elliott Nugent • *Scr* Virginia Van Upp, from a story by Steven Vas

Crystal Heart ★★ 15

Melodrama 1987 · US · Colour · 102mins

Mawkish and over-earnest, this drama misguidedly mixes music with a "disease of the week" scenario. Tawny Kitaen is the aspiring rock star who becomes infatuated with Lee Curreri, a young man suffering from an immune deficiency that keeps him literally sealed off from the rest of the world. Two leads are bland, and the lashings of sentiment are hard to digest. JF. Contains swearing, nudity. [video]

Lee Curreri *Christopher Newley* • Tawny Kitaen *Alley Daniels* • Lloyd Bochner *Frank Newley* • May Heatherly *Diana Newley* • Simon Andreu *Jean-Claude* • Marina Saura *Justine* ■ *Dir* Gil Bettman • *Scr* Linda Shayne, from a story by Alberto Vazquez-Figueroa

Crystal Voyager ★★ U

Documentary
1972 · US/Aus · Colour · 75mins

While not quite of the calibre of Bruce Brown's *The Endless Summer*, this documentary portrait of inventor extraordinaire George Greenough should keep armchair surf fans happy. Having already devised both the short board and the knee board, Greenough became a sports movie legend when he successfully pioneered a method of on-board filming to capture at first hand the intense experience of riding deep inside a breaker's "Green Room". DP [video] DVD

Dir David Elfick • *Scr* George Greenough

Crystalstone ★★★ PG

Adventure 1988 · Sp/UK · Colour · 94mins

An imaginative fantasy that captures the innocence and determination of a young brother and sister who, threatened with separation after their mother's death, run off. During their travels, they meet an odd old man who tells them a tale of an Aztec relic. This adventure, made for and about children in the Disney live-action tradition, is beautifully balanced and successfully conveys the emotional insecurity of childhood. JM [video]

Kamlesh Gupta *Pablo* • Laura Jane Goodwin *Maria* • Frank Grimes *Captain* • Edward Kelsey *Hook* • Sydney Bromley *Old man* • Terence Bayler *Policeman* • Patricia Conti *Filomena* ■ *Dir/Scr* Antonio Pelaez

Cuba ★★★★ 12

Period satirical drama
1979 · US · Colour · 117mins

In this hugely under-rated drama, Sean Connery stars as a British security adviser who washes up in Cuba during the last weeks of the Batista regime. He's been hired by the losing side and his growing doubts are set beside his love for a woman he first met in 1942, in Casablanca. This bracing satire features a great performance from Connery, while subplots spin off with a wealth of secondary characters as director Richard Lester weaves a fascinating tale about a country where romance, revolution and bombs co-exist. AT [video] DVD

Sean Connery *Robert Dapes* • Brooke Adams *Alexandra Pulido* • Jack Weston *Gutman* • Hector Elizondo *Ramirez* • Denholm Elliott *Skinner* • Martin Balsam *General Bello* • Chris Sarandon *Juan Pulido* ■ *Dir* Richard Lester • *Scr* Charles Wood

Cuba Crossing ★★

Spy drama 1980 · US · Colour · 90mins

In addition to *Cuba Crossing*, this little item has had at least four other titles at various times: *Key West Crossing*, which hinted at the main location; *The Mercenaries*, which pointed to the theme; *Assignment: Kill Castro*, which told of the story; and *Sweet Violent Tony*, which referred to the hero. Stuart Whitman plays a loner who runs a bar in the Florida Keys and thinks of bumping off the bearded, cigar-chomping one, while Robert Vaughn is his usual smooth and creepy self. AT

Stuart Whitman *Captain Tony Terracino* • Robert Vaughn *Hudd* • Woody Strode *Titi* • Sybil Danning *Veronica* • Raymond St Jacques *Bell* • Caren Kaye *Tracy* • Mary Lou Gassen *Maria* ■ *Dir/Scr* Chuck Workman

Cubbyhouse ★★ 15

Horror 2001 · Aus · Colour · 84mins

This tongue-in-cheek Aussie horror is a throwback to the 1980s slew of possessed building stories. The oddly un-menacing centre of demonic power is a shed in a quiet suburb, where single mother Belinda McClory hopes to start a new life with her three children. Its old fashioned innocence may amuse, but it barely delivers any shocks or suspense, which, coupled with the uninspired script and special effects, will make this far too anaemic for most horror fans. JC [video] DVD

Joshua Leonard *Danny* • Belinda McClory *Lynn Graham* • Jerome Ehlers *Harrison/Harrow* • Lauren Hewett *Bronwyn* • Craig McLachlan ■ *Dir* Murray Fahey • *Scr* Ian Coughlan, Murray Fahey

Cube ★★★★ 15

Science-fiction thriller
1997 · Can · Colour · 86mins

Six strangers wake up to find themselves in a 14ft by 14ft cube. When they try to get out, they find they are snared in a seemingly endless maze of interlocking cubicles armed with lethal booby traps. How did they get there? Why have they been incarcerated? Director Vincenzo Natali's extraordinary debut feature takes a unique idea and milks its potential to the maximum with panache and visual dexterity. Genuinely creepy and gory, this sci-fi horror puzzle is awash with bold ideas and unsettling tension. Two sequels (to date) followed. AJ. Contains swearing, violence. [video] DVD

Nicole de Boer *Leaven* • Nicky Guadagni *Holloway* • David Hewlett *Worth* • Andrew Miller *Kazan* • Julian Richings *Alderson* • Wayne Robson *Rennes* • Maurice Dean Wint *Quentin* ■ *Dir* Vincenzo Natali • *Scr* Vincenzo Natali, André Bijelic, Graeme Manson

The Cuckoo ★★★ 12

War comedy drama
2002 · Rus · Colour · 97mins

Writer/director Alexander Rogozhkin's sincere and often witty treatise on the futility of war and the barrier of language opens with an intense sequence in which Ville Haapasalo, a Finnish conscript in the Nazi army, breaks the shackle tethering him to a rock (he's been left as prey for Soviet snipers as punishment for his pacifism). But he's no safer once he reaches the hut of Lapp peasant Anni-Kristiina Juuso, as wounded Red Army trooper Viktor Bychkov mistakes him for a fascist that he's duty bound to kill. Beautifully photographed, this astute blend of satire, romance and mysticism cuts to the very heart of human nature. DP. In Russian, Finnish and Sami with English subtitles. Contains violence. DVD

Ville Haapasalo *Veiko* • Anni-Kristiina Juuso *Anni* • Viktor Bychkov *Ivan* ■ *Dir/Scr* Aleksandr Rogozhkin • *Cinematographer* Andrei Zhegalov

A Cuckoo in the Nest ★★★

Comedy 1933 · UK · BW · 87mins

Ben Travers's farces have dated badly on screen, though they still play perfectly well in their various current theatre versions. So the main pleasure in watching this stagey British talkie lies in its preservation of the original Aldwych company interpretation, as directed by chief *farceur* Tom Walls. Walls co-stars with Ralph Lynn in a slight but appealing saga. The most durable member of the cast is the still very funny Robertson Hare ("Oh, Calamity!") as a parson on a visit. TS

Tom Walls *Major Bone* • Ralph Lynn *Peter Wyckham* • Yvonne Arnaud *Marguerite Hickett* • Robertson Hare *Reverend Sioley-Jones* • Mary Brough *Mrs Spoker* • Veronica Rose *Barbara Wyckham* • Gordon James *Noony* ■ *Dir* Tom Walls • *Scr* Ben Travers, AR Rawlinson, from the play by Ben Travers

Cujo ★★ 18

Horror 1983 · US · Colour · 89mins

Add another title to the list of Stephen King movie adaptations that fail to ignite the screen. A rabid St Bernard traps spirited Dee Wallace and her son Danny Pintauro in a Ford Pinto and terrorises them for days in director Lewis Teague's predictable shocker, which sports a half-baked script and an altered, upbeat ending. The car siege should be a harrowing ordeal, but the suspense becomes laughably static, despite all the visual trickery thrown in to generate an interest that manifestly fails to materialise. AJ. Contains swearing and violence. [video] DVD

Dee Wallace [Dee Wallace Stone] *Donna Trenton* • Christopher Stone *Steve Kemp* • Danny Pintauro *Tad Trenton* • Daniel Hugh-Kelly *Vic Trenton* • Ed Lauter *Joe Camber* ■ *Dir* Lewis Teague • *Scr* Don Carlos Dunaway, Lauren Currier, from the novel by Stephen King

Cul-de-Sac ★★★ 15

Psychological comedy thriller
1966 · UK · BW · 100mins

In this surreal, macabre thriller, recluse Donald Pleasence strives to keep his young wife Françoise Dorléac cloistered for himself in a Holy Island castle, despite the attentions of gangsters-on-the-run Lionel Stander and Jack MacGowran. Fetishes abound in this, the most Buñuelian of all Roman Polanski's work, but weird slapstick comedy often undermines the deeply serious kinkiness. The result is an acquired taste. TH [video] DVD

Donald Pleasence *George* • Françoise Dorléac *Teresa* • Lionel Stander *Richard* • Jack MacGowran *Albert* • Iain Quarrier *Christopher* • Geoffrey Sumner *Christopher's father* • Renee Houston *Christopher's mother* • William Franklyn *Cecil* • Trevor Delaney *Nicholas* ■ *Dir* Roman Polanski • *Scr* Gérard Brach, Roman Polanski

The Culpepper Cattle Co ★★★★

Western 1972 · US · Colour · 92mins

This grim rite-of-passage western is superbly directed by Dick Richards, whose subsequent career failed to live up to such early promise. The extreme violence (tame by today's standards) earned it an X certificate in the UK. Gary Grimes plays the 16-year-old who sets out on a cattle drive alongside authentic western types such as Luke Askew and Bo Hopkins, both from Sam Peckinpah's repertory company. There are also superb performances from Billy "Green" Bush, as the hardy trail boss of the title, and Clint Eastwood regular Geoffrey Lewis. TS

Gary Grimes *Ben Mockridge* • Billy "Green" Bush [Billy Green Bush] *Frank Culpepper* • Luke Askew *Luke* • Bo Hopkins *Dixie Brick* • Geoffrey Lewis *Russ* • Wayne Sutherlin *Missoula* • Charles Martin Smith *Tim Slater* ■ *Dir* Dick Richards • *Scr* Eric Bercovici, Gregory Prentiss, from a story by Dick Richards

Cult of the Cobra ★★

Horror thriller 1955 · US · BW · 79mins

This is one of those inexplicable cases of a humdrum potboiler achieving cult recognition in later life. This is a war movie with a difference, in that American GIs face death, not from Nazi bullets, but an ancient curse. When a group of overly curious soldiers enter an Indian temple during a secret ceremony, they're followed home by an exotic serpent woman who starts bumping them off one by one. Francis D Lyon's direction is uninvolving, but his film is saved by solid performances and imaginative camerawork. RS

Faith Domergue *Lisa* • Richard Long *Paul Able* • Marshall Thompson *Tom Markel* • Kathleen Hughes *Julia* • Jack Kelly *Carl Turner* • Walter Coy *Inspector* • Myrna Hansen *Marian* • David Janssen *Rico Nardi* ■ *Dir* Francis D Lyon • *Scr* Jerry Davis, Cecil Maiden, Richard Collins, from a story by Jerry Davis

The Cup ★★★★ PG

Comedy 1999 · Bhu/Aus · Colour · 90mins

Directed by Khyentse Norbu, one of the most revered incarnate lamas in the Tibetan Buddhist hierarchy, this is Bhutan's first ever feature film. Played exclusively by non-professionals, it follows mischievous novice monk Jamyang Lodro in his bid to watch his hero Ronaldo play for Brazil in the 1998 World Cup final. Using shadow puppetry and satellite TV to highlight the need for tradition and progress to co-exist, this charmingly humorous tale also celebrates the exuberance of youth and the sagacity of the elderly, as Jamyang finds an unlikely ally in his venerable abbot. Beautifully shot in glowing colours, this is simply inspirational cinema. DP. In Hindi and Tibetan with English subtitles. [video]

Jamyang Lodro *Orgyen* • Orgyen Tobgyal *Geko* • Neten Chokling *Lodo* ■ *Dir/Scr* Khyentse Norbu • *Cinematographer* Paul Warren

Cup Final ★★★★ 15

Drama 1991 · Is · Colour · 104mins

It's good to see this thoughtful and accomplished piece of film-making finally reaching the wider audience it deserves. Set against the political complexities of the Middle East, this simple tale of war, humanity and football explores the relationship that develops between a Jewish soldier and his Arab jailer during the 1982 World Cup finals. The scenes depicting the Israeli invasion of Lebanon are rather tentatively handled, but director Eran Riklis is on much surer ground with the interaction between the two men, whose loathing turns to respect as the tournament progresses. DP. In Arabic and Hebrew with English subtitles. [video]

Moshe Ivgi *Cohen* • Muhamad Bacri [Muhamad Bakri] *Ziad* • Salim Dau *Mussa* • Basam Zuamut *Abu Eyash* • Yussef Abu Warda *George* ■ *Dir* Eran Riklis • *Scr* Eyal Halfon, from an idea by Eran Riklis

Curdled ★★ 18

Black comedy thriller
1995 · US · Colour · 85mins

This began life as a short film that inspired part of Quentin Tarantino's *Pulp Fiction*. He then turned executive producer to help director and co-writer Reb Braddock expand the original into a full-length movie. Itinerant cleaning maid Angela Jones discovers the identity of a serial killer from the debris left behind in his flat, but has difficulty proving it. The result has some neat touches, but it might have been better had it kept to its original duration. TH. Contains swearing, violence. [video] DVD

Angela Jones *Gabriela* • William Baldwin *Paul Guell* • Bruce Ramsay *Eduardo* • Lois Chiles *Katrina Brandt* • Barry Corbin *Lodger* • Mel Gorham *Elena* ■ *Dir* Reb Braddock • *Scr* John Maass, Reb Braddock

The Cure ★★★★ U

Silent comedy 1917 · US · BW · 23mins

Charles Chaplin's 1917 short is a ruthlessly comic and inventive frolic. When Charlie goes to stay at a spa for recovering alcoholics, gallons of liquor get dumped into the resort's water and change everyone into hyperactive lunatics. Our hero falls for Edna Purviance, as usual, and comes up against the massive Eric Campbell. This contains some remarkable comedy routines that Chaplin later said were derived from his days in music hall. TH [video]

Charles Chaplin *Alcoholic gentleman at spa* • Edna Purviance *Fellow guest at spa* • Eric Campbell *Man with gout* • John Rand *Male Nurse* • Albert Austin *Male Nurse* • Frank J Coleman *Proprietor* • James T Kelley *Ancient Bell Boy* ■ *Dir/Scr* Charles Chaplin

The Cure ★★★ 12

Drama 1995 · US · Colour · 94mins

A thoughtful drama dealing with the friendship between two boys, one of whom has contracted Aids from a blood transfusion. Directed by actor Peter Horton, this small, insightful movie deals with big issues and benefits enormously from a talented cast. Tough kid Brad Renfro and the poorly Joseph Mazzello are first-rate, skilfully supported by Annabella Sciorra as Mazzello's mother and Bruce Davison as his doctor. Believable and affecting. JC [video]

Joseph Mazzello *Dexter* • Brad Renfro *Erik* • Diana Scarwid *Gail* • Bruce Davison *Dr Stevens* • Annabella Sciorra *Linda* • Aeryk Egan *Tyler* • Delphine French *Tyler's girlfriend* • Andrew Broder *Tyler's buddy* ■ *Dir* Peter Horton • *Scr* Robert Kuhn

The Cure for Love ★★ U

Romantic comedy drama
1949 · UK · BW · 99mins

Adapted from a successful West End stage play, this English romantic comedy was a strange and awkward choice for revered actor Robert Donat, who produced, directed and starred. It concerns a soldier hero who, while on leave in his home town in Lancashire, falls in love with a London evacuee (real-life wife to be, Renée Asherson) and has difficulty finding the courage to tell his fiancée Dora Bryan. Stagey, dated, uncertain of its focus and only marginally amusing. RK

Robert Donat *Jack* • Renée Asherson *Milly* • Marjorie Rhodes *Mrs Hardacre* • Charles Victor *Henry* • Thora Hird *Mrs Dorbell* • Dora Bryan *Jenny* • Gladys Henson *Mrs Jenkins* • John Stratton *Sam* ■ *Dir* Robert Donat • *Scr* Robert Donat, Albert Fennell, Alexander Shaw, from the play by Walter Greenwood

Curious Dr Humpp ★★★

Cult erotic science fiction
1967 · Arg · BW · 85mins

This real oddity is one of the most bizarre mixes of sex, horror and sci-fi ever made. Forget the story about a voyeuristic mad scientist giving kidnapped girls aphrodisiacs; it's the fusion of paranoid fantasy, horrific morality play and soft-core banality that makes this Argentinian movie such a gob-smacker. Striking imagery, misshapen monsters, black-faced mutants, a talking brain from Italy and creatures playing weird musical instruments in foggy courtyards surrounded by zombies make this drama curiously unforgettable. AJ. Spanish dialogue dubbed into English.

Ricardo Bauleo • Gloria Prat • Aldo Barbero • Susana Beltran • Justin Martin • Michel Angel • Mary Albano • Al Bugatti ■ *Dir* Emilio Vieyra • *Scr* Emilio Vieyra, Raul Zorrilla

Curly Sue ★★ PG

Comedy 1991 · US · Colour · 97mins

Director John Hughes unexpectedly misses the target with this sentimental comedy about a young girl and her con artist travelling companion (James Belushi) who attempt to take Chicago lawyer Kelly Lynch for a ride. Belushi is always watchable, but even he can't make up for the cutesy performance of Alisan Porter in the title role. JB. Contains some swearing. [video]

James Belushi *Bill Dancer* • Kelly Lynch *Grey Ellison* • Alisan Porter *Curly Sue* • John Getz *Walker McCormick* • Fred Dalton Thompson *Bernard Oxbar* ■ *Dir/Scr* John Hughes

Curly Top ★★★ U

Musical 1935 · US · BW · 76mins

Shirley Temple at her exquisite best: a dimpled, ringleted moppet playing Cupid to her sister Rochelle Hudson and handsome John Boles, who adopts Temple and Hudson from an orphanage. This kind of movie made Temple a top movie star across the world and saved her studio, 20th Century-Fox, from bankruptcy. She's as good as she ever was here, revealing a talent and a surety of poise that's positively frightening in one so young. If the plot seems familiar, it's a reworking of that old stand-by *Daddy Long Legs*, given a new twist. TS

Shirley Temple *Elizabeth Blair* • John Boles *Edward Morgan* • Rochelle Hudson *Mary Blair* • Jane Darwell *Mrs Denham* • Rafaela Ottiano *Mrs Higgins* • Esther Dale *Aunt Genevieve Graham* • Etienne Girardo *Mr Wyckoff* • Maurice Murphy *Jimmie Rogers* ■ *Dir* Irving Cummings • *Scr* Patterson McNutt, Arthur Beckhard, from a story by Jean Webster

The Curse ★★★ 18

Horror 1987 · US · Colour · 82mins

Take method actor-turned-director David Keith, put him together with Italian rip-off producer Ovidio G Assonitis, and the result is very grisly food for thought. A glowing meteor crash lands near the Tennessee farm of redneck Claude Akins, mutating his produce and livestock before affecting the local community. There's a lot going on in this cynical chiller, though it's severely undercut once the film degenerates into formula zombie territory. However, Keith sustains a palpable sense of apocalyptic doom. AJ [video]

Wil Wheaton *Zachary Hayes* • Claude Akins *Nathan Hayes* • Malcolm Danare *Cyrus* • Cooper Huckabee *Dr Alan Forbes* • John Schneider *Carl Willis* • Amy Wheaton *Alice Hayes* • Steve Carlisle *Charley Davidson* ■ *Dir* David Keith • *Scr* David Chaskin, from the story *The Colour Out of Space* by HP Lovecraft

C

Curse II: The Bite ★★ 18

Horror thriller
1989 · US/It/Jpn · Colour · 93mins

Although it has absolutely nothing to do with *The Curse* (1987), opportunist Italian producer Ovidio G Assonitis tacked on the title to this insanely stupid snake spectacular. Jill Schoelen and boyfriend J Eddie Peck are driving through a nuclear testing ground in Arizona when a radioactive rattler bites Peck on the arm. The mutated venom mixes with his DNA and turns his arm into a snake. Daft glove-puppet special effects defuse the gore factor, but this is still entertaining trash. AJ

Jill Schoelen *Lisa* • J Eddie Peck *Clark* • Jamie Farr *Harry* • Savina Gersak *Iris* • Bo Svenson *Sheriff* • Marianne Muellerleile *Big Flo* ■ *Dir* Fred Goodwin [Federico Prosperi] • *Scr* Fred Goodwin, Susan Zelouf

Curse III: Blood Sacrifice ★ 18

Horror 1991 · US · Colour · 87mins

Completely unrelated to the previous two *Curse* movies, this catchpenny chiller (originally titled *Panga*) is set in early 1950s East Africa and concerns a plantation owner's pregnant wife (Jennilee Harrison) interrupting a witch doctor's black magic ceremony. For her sin, she is earmarked as sacrificial victim to a rubber monster. Christopher Lee lends gravity to the poorly shot production, which relies heavily on false scares, unconvincing gore and topless natives. AJ

Christopher Lee *Doctor Pearson* • Jenilee Harrison *Elizabeth Armstrong* • Henry Cele *Mletch* • Andre Jacobs *Geoff Armstrong* • Zoe Randall *Anthea Steed* ■ *Dir* Sean Barton • *Scr* John Hunt, Sean Barton, from a story by Richard Haddon Haines

The Curse of Frankenstein ★★★★ 15

Horror 1957 · UK · Colour · 79mins

This was the classic that single-handedly revived traditional British Gothic and firmly placed the "Hammer House of Horror" on the global gore map. Peter Cushing is the demented Baron who yearns to resurrect the dead, while Christopher Lee plays the hideous creature who proves his mad theories correct. With its gruesome atmosphere, unflinching direction and outstanding design, this phenomenally successful film was the first colour version of Mary Shelley's gallows fairy tale, setting a standard Hammer found it hard to live up to. The series continued the following year with *The Revenge of Frankenstein*. AJ DVD

Peter Cushing *Baron Victor Frankenstein* • Christopher Lee *The Creature* • Hazel Court *Elizabeth* • Robert Urquhart *Paul Krempe* • Valerie Gaunt *Justine* • Noel Hood *Aunt Sophia* ■ *Dir* Terence Fisher • *Scr* Jimmy Sangster, from the novel *Frankenstein* by Mary Shelley • *Art Director* Bernard Robinson

The Curse of the Cat People ★★★★ U

Horror fantasy 1944 · US · BW · 66mins

Producer Val Lewton originally wanted to call this picture *Aimée and Her Friend*, but RKO executives were so determined to cash in on Lewton's 1942 success, *Cat People*, that he was persuaded to change the title. Inspired by a Robert Louis Stevenson short story, it is more a study of child psychology than a horror film, but the brooding lighting, the all-pervading sense of menace and the occasional shock make for tense viewing. Simone Simon, the star of *Cat People*, is again superb as Irena, the cursed panther-woman who inspires pity rather than fear. One of the most charming chillers ever made. DP

Simone Simon *Irena* • Kent Smith *Oliver Reed* • Jane Randolph *Alice Reed* • Ann Carter *Amy* • Elizabeth Russell *Barbara* • Julia Dean *Julia Farren* • Eve March *Miss Callahan* • Erford Gage *Captain of the guard* ■ *Dir* Robert Wise, Gunther von Fritsch • *Scr* DeWitt Bodeen • *Cinematographer* Nicholas Musuraca

Curse of the Crimson Altar ★★

Horror 1968 · UK · Colour · 87mins

There are sacrifices galore, of course, as you'd expect from a title like this, but none was as great as that made by Boris Karloff, starring in a film with such a lacklustre script about devil worship in an old dark house. Not that Karloff cared much about quality, as he was enjoying the pleasure of being back in England, having taken a flat near Lord's in order to be close to his adored cricket. Christopher Lee co-stars. TH. Contains brief nudity.

Boris Karloff *Professor Marsh* • Christopher Lee *JD Morley* • Mark Eden *Robert Manning* • Virginia Wetherell *Eve* • Barbara Steele *Lavinia* • Rupert Davies *Vicar* • Michael Gough *Elder* • Rosemarie Reede *Esther* ■ *Dir* Vernon Sewell • *Scr* Mervyn Haisman, Henry Lincoln

The Curse of the Dragon ★★★ 15

Documentary
1993 · US · BW and Colour · 85mins

Narrated by *Star Trek*'s George Takei, this documentary tribute to Bruce Lee packs in plenty of information and insight. There are home movies of his early competition victories, interviews with fellow actors such as James Coburn and Chuck Norris and behind-the-scenes footage of stunt sequences from *Enter the Dragon*. Sadly, there are also shots of the funerals of both Bruce and his actor son Brandon, who was killed on the set of *The Crow*, which spark off a discussion about whether the family was cursed. Intriguing viewing. DP

George Takei *Narrator* ■ *Dir* Fred Weintraub, Tom Kuhn

Curse of the Fly ★★

Horror 1965 · UK · BW · 86mins

Brian Donlevy takes over from Vincent Price as the mad doctor experimenting with teleportation through the fourth dimension in this average second sequel to monster hit *The Fly*. Unfortunately, he still can't get the matter transmissions right, and the mutant results of his labours are locked in a closet. Journeyman director Don Sharp's talent for shock effects gets lost amid the stiff acting, slow pacing and cheap production values, but the odd moment of eerie atmosphere does surface. AJ

Brian Donlevy *Henri Delambre* • George Baker *Martin Delambre* • Carole Gray *Patricia Stanley* • Yvette Rees *Wan* • Bert Kwouk [Burt Kwouk] *Tai* • Michael Graham *Albert Delambre* • Jeremy Wilkin *Inspector Ronet* ■ *Dir* Don Sharp • *Scr* Harry Spalding, from characters created by George Langelaan

The Curse of the Jade Scorpion ★★ 12

Period comedy
2001 · US/Ger · Colour · 97mins

Woody Allen is in nostalgic mood for this handsome tribute to the 1940s crime B-movie. However, he misses the timbre of hard-boiled argot and allows his pastiche plot to meander. But what really prevents a potentially diverting project from taking off is the love-hate mismatch between Allen's hapless gumshoe and efficiency expert Helen Hunt, who have both been hypnotised into doing the bidding of nefarious showman David Ogden Stiers. Dan Aykroyd and Charlize Theron gamely boost underwritten supporting roles, but can't disguise the lethal lack of inspiration. DP DVD

Woody Allen *CW Briggs* • Helen Hunt *Betty Ann Fitzgerald* • Dan Aykroyd *Chris Magruder* • Charlize Theron *Laura Kensington* • Brian Markinson *Al* • Wallace Shawn *George Bond* • David Ogden Stiers *Eli Voytak "Voltan" Polgar* • Elizabeth Berkley *Jill* ■ *Dir/Scr* Woody Allen

The Curse of the Living Corpse ★

Horror 1964 · US · BW · 83mins

A millionaire vows to murder all his spiteful relatives if he is buried alive. When he is, a hooded maniac starts assassinating everyone in nasty ways. A drab attempt to emulate Roger Corman's Edgar Allan Poe adaptations, this laughably bad early gore movie from writer/producer/director Del Tenney has little to recommend it, besides the fact that it features Roy Scheider's film debut. AJ

Helen Warren *Abigail Sinclair* • Roy Scheider *Philip Sinclair* • Margot Hartman *Vivian Sinclair* • Robert Milli *Bruce Sinclair* • Hugh Franklin *James Benson* ■ *Dir/Scr* Del Tenney

The Curse of the Mummy's Tomb ★★ 15

Horror 1964 · UK · Colour · 76mins

After moderate success with *The Mummy* (1959), Hammer made several more films featuring the bandaged monster, though all lacked inspiration. In this, the second, there's the customary tomb opening, followed by the customary resurrection of its occupant. The mummy, played by forgotten bit player Dickie Owen, takes an unconscionably long time to go on his customary killing spree, though when it comes it does produce a few tense moments. DM

Terence Morgan *Adam Beauchamp* • Ronald Howard *John Bray* • Fred Clark *Alexander King* • Jeanne Roland *Annette Dubois* • John Paul *Inspector Mackenzie* • Jack Gwillim *Sir Giles* • George Pastell *Hashmi Bey* • Dickie Owen *Mummy* ■ *Dir* Michael Carreras • *Scr* Henry Younger [Michael Carreras]

The Curse of the Pink Panther ★★ PG

Comedy mystery
1983 · UK · Colour · 105mins

Without Peter Sellers, this seventh instalment in the comedy series produces negligible humour. The search for the amiable but idiotic Inspector Clouseau wavers when the inspector's vindictive boss (Herbert Lom) programmes the computer to select the world's worst detective for the job. A bumbling Ted Wass is chosen and sets about interviewing characters from previous movies. *Son of the Pink Panther* concluded the series in 1993. TH

David Niven *Sir Charles Litton* • Ted Wass *Clifton Sleigh* • Rich Little *Sir Charles Litton (voice)* • Robert Wagner *George Litton* • Herbert Lom *Dreyfus* • Joanna Lumley *Chandra* • Capucine *Lady Litton* • Robert Loggia *Bruno* • Harvey Korman *Professor Balls* • Burt Kwouk *Cato* • Leslie Ash *Juleta Shane* • Roger Moore *Jacques Clouseau* ■ *Dir* Blake Edwards • *Scr* Blake Edwards, Geoffrey Edwards

The Curse of the Werewolf ★★ 12

Horror 1961 · UK · Colour · 87mins

Hammer's stab at the werewolf legend may look tame compared to later computerised transformations, but this was shocking stuff in its day, and much horrid imagery was censored. Today the scenes with villagers muttering in the inn look like parody, and everything is so brightly lit there's not much atmosphere. There's also a long prologue that has little to do with the story of Oliver Reed, who goes on a killing spree every full moon. When Reed does appear, however, he gives a riveting performance. DM

Oliver Reed *Leon* • Clifford Evans *Alfredo* • Yvonne Romain *Servant girl* • Catherine Feller *Cristina* • Anthony Dawson *Marques Siniestro* • Josephine Llewellyn *Marquesa* • Richard Wordsworth *Beggar* ■ *Dir* Terence Fisher • *Scr* John Elder [Anthony Hinds], from the novel *The Werewolf of Paris* by Guy Endore

The Curse of the Wraydons ★★

Crime melodrama 1946 · UK · BW · 99mins

There was a time when Tod Slaughter was considered the scariest actor alive. It's hard to imagine that now, judging from his ultra-stagey performance in this dull adaptation of Maurice Sandoz's Victorian play *Springheeled Jack, the Terror of London*, which freely embroiders on the 19th-century legend of a leaping prowler. Larger-than-life Slaughter is always fun to watch, though, slicing the ham thick as a mad inventor who commits murder with a diabolical gizmo. A quaint diversion. AJ

Tod Slaughter *Philip Wraydon* • Bruce Seton *Captain Jack Clayton* • Gabriel Toyne *Lieutenant Payne* • Andrew Laurence *George Heeningham* • Lorraine Clews *Helen Sedgefield* • Pearl Cameron *Rose Wraydon* ■ *Dir* Victor M Gover • *Scr* Michael Barringer, from the play *Springheeled Jack, the Terror of London* by Maurice Sandoz

Cursed ★★ 15

Horror thriller
2005 · US/Ger · Colour · 96mins

Christina Ricci and Jesse Eisenberg star as siblings who are infected by a lycanthrope after a road accident. The events that follow, as the two slowly begin to transform, aren't so much scary as darkly amusing, with scriptwriter Kevin Williamson's adolescent witticisms and whines to the fore. However, Wes Craven's direction is surprisingly clumsy and the CGI effects are so appalling that they overshadow everything else, spoiling the creepy fun and turning a guilty pleasure into groan-worthy rubbish. SF

Christina Ricci *Ellie* • Joshua Jackson *Jake* • Jesse Eisenberg *Jimmy* • Judy Greer *Joannie* • Scott Baio • Milo Ventimiglia *Bo* • Kristina Anapau *Brooke* • Portia de Rossi *Zela* ■ *Dir* Wes Craven • *Scr* Kevin Williamson

Curtain Call ★★

Supernatural comedy
1998 · US · Colour · 95mins

James Spader moves into a New York apartment, unaware that his new home already has two tenants: the quarreling ghosts of two former Broadway stars, Caine and Maggie Smith. When they realise their new flatmate is having girlfriend troubles, the pair (whom only Stevenson can see and hear) decide to meddle, with supposedly hilarious results. Despite all-out efforts from the heavyweight cast, this is never more than mildly amusing. JB

James Spader *Stevenson Lowe* • Michael Caine *Max Gale* • Sam Shepard *Senator Will Dodge* • Buck Henry *Charles Van Allsburg* • Polly Walker *Julia Winston* • Maggie Smith *Lilly Marlowe* • Frank Whaley *Brett* • Valerie Perrine *Monica* ■ *Dir* Peter Yates • *Scr* Todd Alcott, from a story by Andrew S Karsch

Curtain Up ★★★ U

Comedy 1952 · UK · BW · 78mins

There's a nice irony in the fact that a film about a play in which the author refuses to sacrifice a single word of her text has been loosely adapted from the original stage show. Margaret Rutherford is in fine fettle as the persistent playwright, while Robert Morley gives a performance of polished petulance as the director of the down-at-heel stock company who insists on

U = SUITABLE FOR ALL Uc = SUITABLE FOR ALL, ESPECIALLY FOR YOUNG CHILDREN (VIDEO ONLY) PG = PARENTAL GUIDANCE

wholesale changes. This amusing dig at showbiz preciousness whiles away the time most agreeably. DP

Robert Morley *Harry* • Margaret Rutherford *Catherine* • Olive Sloane *Maud* • Joan Rice *Avis* • Charlotte Mitchell *Daphne* • Kay Kendall *Sandra* • Liam Gaffney *Norwood* • Margaret Avery (1) *Mary* ■ *Dir* Ralph Smart • *Scr* Michael Pertwee, Jack Davies, from the play *On Monday Next* by Philip King

Custer of the West ★★★ U

Western 1968 · US/Sp · Colour · 134mins

Intended as an epic spectacle, this became a miscasting mistake. British star Robert Shaw, as the native American-bashing general, is at odds with both accent and character, and the great *film noir* director Robert Siodmak has to make do with an inferior script that mixes fact with fiction. There are some fine battle sequences, though, and Custer's "Last Stand" makes a poignant finale, while Robert Ryan, as an army deserter, brands the screen with white-hot style. TH DVD

Robert Shaw *General George Custer* • Mary Ure *Elizabeth Custer* • Jeffrey Hunter *Lieutenant Benteen* • Ty Hardin *Major Marcus Reno* • Robert Ryan *Sergeant Mulligan* • Charles Stalnaker *Lieutenant Howells* • Robert Hall *Sergeant Buckley* • Lawrence Tierney *General Philip Sheridan* ■ *Dir* Robert Siodmak • *Scr* Bernard Gordon, Julian Halevy [Julian Zimet]

The Custodian ★★★ 15

Crime thriller 1993 · Aus · Colour · 105mins

Anthony LaPaglia adds an extra layer of class to an already impressive Australian corruption thriller, as a Machiavellian cop playing the internal affairs department and his ruthless, bent colleagues off against each other. Part of the film's appeal is that you're never quite sure which side LaPaglia is on, and some of the credit for that must go writer/director John Dingwall's intelligent script. The supporting performances are first rate, too. JF

Anthony LaPaglia *Quinlan* • Hugo Weaving *Church* • Barry Otto *Ferguson* • Kelly Dingwall *Reynolds* • Essie Davis *Jilly* • Bill Hunter *Managing director* • Skye Wansey *Claire* ■ *Dir/Scr* John Dingwall

Custody of the Heart ★★ PG

Drama 2000 · US · Colour · 87mins

An accomplished cast is wasted on this unexceptional TV movie, with Lorraine Bracco as the careerist whose spare time is divided between her family and disabled mother. Martin Donovan is miscast as the husband so emasculated by his wife's competence that he sues for divorce, while Bracco's decision to abandon her life and begin again in a renovated lighthouse detaches the plot from its semblance of reality and leaves it to drift into fanciful melodrama. DP DVD

Lorraine Bracco *Claire Raphael* • Martin Donovan (2) *Dennis Raphael* • Dennis Boutsikaris *Nick Brody* • Michael Cera *Johnny Raphael* • Charlotte Arnold *Kiki Raphael* ■ *Dir* David Hugh Jones [David Jones (3)] • *Scr* Marsha Norman, from the novel *A Woman's Place* by Barbara Delinsky

Cut ★★ 18

Horror spoof 2000 · Aus · Colour · 79mins

Those *Scream* sequels have so much to answer for, with their penchant for generic in-jokes and the paraphernalia of movie-making. Contributing a passable Parker Posey impression, Molly Ringwald plays the temperamental American star of a low-budget horror whose cast and crew keep falling victim to a masked, shears-wielding maniac. The odd gore gag pays off, but the filmic references are lame and the closing emphasis on the supernatural is as redundant as Kylie Minogue's cameo. DP

Molly Ringwald *Vanessa Turnbull* • Jessica Napier *Raffy Carruthers* • Sarah Kants *Hester Ryan* • Geoff Revell *Lossman* • Frank Roberts *Brad/Scar Man* • Kylie Minogue *Hilary Jacobs* • Stephen Curry *Rick Stephens* ■ *Dir* Kimble Rendall • *Scr* Dave Warner

A Cut Above ★★★ 15

Comedy drama 1989 · US · Colour · 105mins

Released in the States as *Gross Anatomy*, this lightweight *ER*-style frolic focuses on a group of young students getting to grips with grown-up medicine. Matthew Modine is the charismatic underachiever who refuses to play the competitive games set by harsh tutor Christine Lahti; Daphne Zuniga supplies the romantic interest and Zakes Mokae pops up as a wise old doctor. Director Thom Eberhardt does his best, but the script uneasily mixes slapstick with sentimentality. JF. Contains swearing. DVD

Matthew Modine *Joe Slovak* • Daphne Zuniga *Laurie Rorbach* • Christine Lahti *Dr Rachel Woodruff* • Todd Field *David Schreiner* • John Scott Clough *Miles Reed* • Alice Carter *Kim McCauley* • Robert Desiderio *Dr Banks* ■ *Dir* Thom Eberhardt • *Scr* Ron Nyswaner, Mark Spragg, Ron Nyswaner, Mark Spragg, from a story by Howard Rosenman, Alan Jay Glueckman, Stanley Isaacs, Mark Spragg

Cutaway ★★ 12

Action drama 2000 · US · Colour · 100mins

Director Guy Manos is a former skydiving world champion, so unsurprisingly the aerial sequences on show here are absolutely stunning. Unfortunately, as a writer (he co-scripted this with brother Greg) Manos is a brilliant parachutist. The lazy plot has Stephen Baldwin going undercover with a champion skydiving team which he believes are acting as drug-runners (or should that be drug-jumpers?). However, that is little more than appendage as Manos is more interested in the skydiving itself, so the result is an uncomfortable mixture of sporting movie clichés and psycho-babble. JF DVD

Tom Berenger *Redline* • Stephen Baldwin *Agent Vic Cooper* • Dennis Rodman *Turbo* • Ron Silver *Margate* • Maxine Bahns *Star* ■ *Dir* Guy Manos • *Scr* Greg Manos, Guy Manos

Cutter's Way ★★★★ 15

Crime drama 1981 · US · Colour · 104mins

This under-rated thriller, while occasionally overwrought, is also a study in moral responsibility. Disabled Vietnam veteran Cutter (John Heard) teams up with his gigolo friend Bone (Jeff Bridges) in a bid to expose tycoon Stephen Elliott as the murderer of a hitch-hiker. Cutter and Bone are seriously unlikeable characters, yet director Ivan Passer and writer Jeffrey Alan Fiskin make us see light in these hearts of darkness. Misunderstood at the time, it's now a worthy melodrama. Its original title, *Cutter and Bone*, was changed because the studio thought it sounded too much like surgery. TH. Contains swearing. DVD

Jeff Bridges *Richard Bone* • John Heard *Alex Cutter* • Lisa Eichhorn *Maureen "Mo" Cutter* • Ann Dusenberry *Valerie Duran* • Stephen Elliott *JJ Cord* • Arthur Rosenberg *George Swanson* • Nina Van Pallandt *Woman in hotel* ■ *Dir* Ivan Passer • *Scr* Jeffrey Alan Fiskin, from the novel *Cutter and Bone* by Newton Thornburg

CutThroat Island ★★ PG

Action adventure
1995 · US · Colour · 117mins

Renny Harlin's pirate picture has all the ingredients to shiver the timbers and it also boasts the best treasure map ever seen on screen, yet it has gone down in history as one of the biggest box-office disasters of recent times. Geena Davis and Matthew Modine swagger with suitable bravado, but their performances are sunk by the predictability of the action. Polished entertainment, but with a little more imagination it could have been exhilarating. DP. Contains violence and swearing. DVD

Geena Davis *Morgan Adams* • Matthew Modine *William Shaw* • Frank Langella *Captain Dawg Brown* • Maury Chaykin *John Reed* • Patrick Malahide *Ainslee* • Stan Shaw *Glasspoole* • Rex Linn *Mr Blair* • Paul Dillon *Snelgrave* ■ *Dir* Renny Harlin • *Scr* Robert King, Marc Norman, from a story by Michael Frost Beckner, James Gorman, Bruce A Evans, Raynold Gideon

Cutting Class ★★ 18

Comedy horror 1989 · US · Colour · 87mins

Notable only for featuring a very early performance from Brad Pitt, this is for shlock horror fans only. Jill Schoelen stars as an all-American cutie who has school jock Pitt for a boyfriend. When pupils start mysteriously dying, blame automatically falls on nutcase Donovan Leitch. But then Schoelen starts noticing Pitt isn't all he seems. Lines like "I am a murderer. Not as prestigious as a lawyer or a doctor, but the hours are good!" will have you reaching for the remote. LH DVD

Donovan Leitch *Brian Woods* • Jill Schoelen *Paula Carson* • Brad Pitt *Dwight Ingalls* • Roddy McDowall *Dr Dante* • Martin Mull *William Carson III* ■ *Dir* Rospo Pallenberg • *Scr* Steve Slavkin

The Cutting Edge ★★★ PG

Romantic sports drama
1992 · US · Colour · 97mins

An amiable romantic drama with DB Sweeney as the macho ice hockey player who is paired with snooty ice-skating hopeful Moira Kelly in a bid to win gold at the Olympics. Sweeney and Kelly spark off each other nicely and they are ably supported by the likes of Terry O'Quinn and Roy Dotrice. The skating scenes are splendidly staged, and director Paul Michael Glaser only loses his footing during the *Rocky*-style histrionics at the end. JF

DB Sweeney *Doug Dorsey* • Moira Kelly *Kate Moseley* • Roy Dotrice *Anton Pamchenko* • Terry O'Quinn *Jack Moseley* • Dwier Brown *Hale* • Chris Benson *Walter Dorsey* • Kevin Peeks *Brian* ■ *Dir* Paul M Glaser [Paul Michael Glaser] • *Scr* Tony Gilroy

Cutting It Short ★★★

Comedy 1980 · Cz · Colour · 98mins

Although a prize-winner at Venice, this chronicle of the early married life of screenwriter Bohumil Hrabal's parents ranks among Jirí Menzel's least trenchant satires on the Czech establishment. Effortlessly blending small-town period detail with whimsical character comedy, it charts brewery manager Jiri Schmitzer's attempts to curb the progressive inclinations of his beautiful, liberated wife (Magda Vasaryova) and the antics of his eccentric brother (Jaromir Hanzlik). Charmingly played and filmed, but rather lacking in bite. DP

Jiri Schmitzer *Francin* • Magda Vasaryova *Marja* • Jaromir Hanzlik *Pepin* • Rudolf Hrusinsky *Dr Gruntorad* • Oldrich Vlach *Ruzicka* • Frantisek Rehak *Vejvoda* • Petr Cepek • Oldrich Vizner *Barber* ■ *Dir* Jirí Menzel • *Scr* Jirí Menzel, Bohumil Hrabal

Cyborg ★★★ 18

Science-fiction adventure
1989 · US · Colour · 79mins

Director Albert Pyun's cheap sci-fi adventure features characters all named after electric guitars. Jean-Claude Van Damme is a futuristic mercenary hired to escort a cyborg carrying the antidote to a deadly plague that has almost wiped out mankind in the 21st century. Pyun piles on the trash, panache and gratuitous violence with cut-price style. AJ DVD

Jean-Claude Van Damme *Gibson Rickenbacker* • Deborah Richter *Nady Simmons* • Vincent Klyn *Fender Tremolo* • Alex Daniels *Marshall Strat* • Dayle Haddon *Pearl Prophet* • Blaise Loong *Furman Vox* • Rolf Muller *Brick Bardo* ■ *Dir* Albert Pyun • *Scr* Kitty Chalmers

Cyborg 2: Glass Shadow ★★★ 18

Science-fiction adventure
1993 · US · Colour · 95mins

A martial arts-fighting cyborg (Angelina Jolie) is created by a sinister US corporation to destroy a Japanese rival in an action-packed futuristic adventure with a fun cast. Hero Elias Koteas falls for the sexy humanoid, and together they fight drug-addicted bounty hunter Billy Drago and mercenary storm troopers. Michael Schroeder keeps everything bubbling along neatly in this violent fantasy, which has flashbacks to the Jean-Claude Van Damme original. AJ DVD

Elias Koteas *Colson "Colt" Ricks* • Angelina Jolie *Casella "Cash" Reese* • Billy Drago *Danny Bench* • Jack Palance *Mercy* • Allen Garfield *Martin Dunn* ■ *Dir* Michael Schroeder • *Scr* Ron Yanover, Mark Gelman, Michael Schroeder, from a story by Ron Yanover, Mark Gelman

Cyborg 3: The Recycler ★★★ 18

Science-fiction adventure
1994 · US · Colour · 87mins

This has a more thought-provoking script and better delineated characters than others in the series. Despicable "recycler" (bounty hunter) Richard Lynch preys on the comfort of benevolent humanoids. Scientist Zach Galligan and reproductive replicant Khrystyne Haje are caught up in the battle between bloodthirsty mankind and innocent robots for the right to procreate. Lynch takes magnetic evil to a new level of villainy. AJ DVD

Zach Galligan *Evans* • Malcolm McDowell *Lord Talon* • Michael Bailey Smith *Donovan* • Rebecca Ferratti *Elexia* • Khrystyne Haje *Cash* • Andrew Bryniarski *Jocko* • Richard Lynch *Lewellyn* ■ *Dir* Michael Schroeder • *Scr* Barry Victor, Troy Bolotnick

Cyborg Cop ★ 18

Science-fiction action
1993 · US · Colour · 92mins

David Bradley heads off to a Caribbean island in search of his missing brother. There he uncovers a secret organisation run by John Rhys-Davies that kidnaps innocent people and converts them into killer cyborgs. Seemingly filmed in abandoned buildings or vacant lots, this is a cheesy *Terminator* rip-off with unexceptional action scenes. The only reason there's a sequel is that both were filmed back to back. KB

David Bradley (4) *Jack Ryan* • John Rhys-Davies *Kessel* • Alonna Shaw *Cathy* • Todd Jensen *Phillip* • Rufus Swart *Cyborg* • Ron Smerczak *Callan* • Anthony Fridjohn *Hogan* ■ *Dir* Sam Firstenberg • *Scr* Greg Latter

Cyclo ★★★★★ 18

Crime drama
1995 · Fr/Viet · Colour · 123mins

In total contrast to the elegiac *Scent of Green Papaya*, this is a quite stunning achievement from Vietnamese director Tran Anh Hung. Tackling such complex themes as paternity, mother-child affinity and spiritual twinship, it is also an uncompromising portrait of life on the streets of Ho Chi Minh City. Le Van Loc is sensational as the teenage pedicab driver who falls in with gangster-pimp Tony Leung when his cycle is stolen. The camerawork is exceptional, with long, energetic takes arranged alongside slow, poetic images. Bold and brave, determined and disturbing, this is film-making of the highest order. DP. In Vietnamese with English subtitles.

Le Van Loc *The cyclo* • Tony Chiu-Wai Leung [Tony Leung (2)] *The poet* • Tran Nu Yen-Khe *The sister* • Nguyen Nhu Quynh *The madam* ■ *Dir* Tran Anh Hung • *Scr* Tran Anh Hung, Nguyen Trung Bing

The Cyclops ★

Science fiction 1957 · US · BW · 75mins

Director Bert I Gordon had an unhealthy fixation with giants: most of his output revolved around them, from colossal men to mutant ants. Even by Gordon's low standards, however, this is a seriously dumb film. Gloria Talbott plays a woman searching for her fiancé, who goes missing after his plane crashes in a radiation-polluted area. He subsequently turns up as a 50ft tall, one-eyed mutant. Guess the wedding's off, then. Bargain basement tosh that relies too heavily on a risible array of special effects, including giant spiders, lizards and rodents. RS

James Craig *Russ Bradford* • Gloria Talbott *Susan Winter* • Lon Chaney Jr *Martin Melville* • Tom Drake *Lee Brand* • Duncan "Dean" Parkin [Dean Parkin] *Bruce Barton/The Cyclops* • Vincente Padula [Vincent Padula] *The Governor* ■ *Dir/Scr* Bert I Gordon

Cynara ★★ PG

Melodrama 1932 · US · BW · 74mins

Directed by King Vidor, this story of marital infidelity has Ronald Colman's London barrister betraying his wife, Kay Francis, by falling for shopgirl Phyllis Barry. It's a tragedy, though the real drama was on the set, when Colman's dislike of the role led to press reports of his drunkenness. Colman sued Goldwyn for $1 million, dropped the case and brazenly announced his retirement. AT

Ronald Colman *Jim Warlock* • Kay Francis *Clemency Warlock* • Phyllis Barry *Doris Lea* • Henry Stephenson *John Tring* • Viva Tattersall *Milly Miles* • Florine McKinney *Garla* ■ *Dir* King Vidor • *Scr* Frances Marion, Lynn Starling, from the play by HM Harwood, Robert Gore-Brown, from the novel *An Imperfect Lover* by Robert Gore-Brown

Cynthia ★★ U

Comedy drama 1947 · US · BW · 98mins

Fifteen-year-old Elizabeth Taylor, already blossoming into sensuous young womanhood, is the eponymous heroine of this light domestic drama, directed by the expert Robert Z Leonard. It's the facile but reasonably involving tale of an adolescent girl fighting to loosen the controlling bonds of an over-protective mother (Mary Astor) and be allowed to go on her first date (with Jimmy Lydon). The young star is both appealing and convincing, and receives able support from Astor, George Murphy, SZ "Cuddles" Sakall and Gene Lockhart. RK

Elizabeth Taylor *Cynthia Bishop* • George Murphy *Larry Bishop* • SZ Sakall *Prof Rosenkrantz* • Mary Astor *Louise Bishop* • Gene Lockhart *Dr Fred I Jannings* • Spring Byington *Carrie Jannings* • Jimmy Lydon [James Lydon] *Ricky Latham* • Scotty Beckett *Will Parker* ■ *Dir* Robert Z Leonard • *Scr* Charles Kaufman, Harold Buchman, from the play *The Rich, Full Life* by Vina Delmar

Cypher ★★★ 15

Science-fiction action thriller
2002 · US · Colour and BW · 91mins

Director Vincenzo Natali's film features creative special effects and an amazingly sleek look, all elegantly presented with tricksy élan and stylish bravura. When accountant Jeremy Northam exchanges his dull grind for an excitement-filled existence as an industrial spy, he uncovers a sinister brainwashing operation. By playing with the boundaries between reason and madness, dreams and reality, and flashbacks and flash-forwards with some aplomb, Natali manages ultimately to boil down the extreme lengths an individual will go for true love. AJ DVD

Jeremy Northam *Morgan Sullivan* • Lucy Liu *Rita* • Nigel Bennett *Ed Finster* • Timothy Webber *Frank Calloway* • David Hewlett *Vergil Dunn* ■ *Dir* Vincenzo Natali • *Scr* Brian King

Cyrano de Bergerac ★★★ U

Period drama 1950 · US · BW · 112mins

Edmond Rostand's famous classic about the French army officer whose oversized nose prevents him declaring his love for the beautiful Roxane. Instead he woos her with poetic love letters on behalf of his young friend. This respectful screen translation stars José Ferrer as a dignified, moving Cyrano, a part he had played on Broadway and which here won him an Oscar for best actor. Michael Gordon directs in journeyman fashion, while William Prince and Mala Powers are adequate as the young lovers. RK

José Ferrer *Cyrano* • Mala Powers *Roxane* • William Prince *Christian* • Morris Carnovsky *Le Bret* • Ralph Clanton *de Guiche* • Lloyd Corrigan *Ragueneau* • Virginia Farmer *Duenna* ■ *Dir* Michael Gordon • *Scr* Carl Foreman, from the play by Edmond Rostand

Cyrano de Bergerac ★★★★★ U

Romantic drama 1990 · Fr · Colour · 137mins

An exceptional performance from Gérard Depardieu lights up this sumptuous adaptation of Edmond Rostand's classic play by director Jean-Paul Rappeneau. He thoroughly deserved his best actor prize at Cannes for the passion, wit and finesse he displays here as the noted swordsman and poet, whose search for happiness is hindered by his exceptionally large nose. Also worthy of mention are cinematographer Pierre Lhomme, art director Ezio Frigerio and Michèle Burke, who made the magnificent nose. Novelist Anthony Burgess supplied the English translation, brilliantly utilising the original's lyrical verse and treating audiences to subtitles of exquisite poetry. DP. In French with English subtitles. DVD

Gérard Depardieu *Cyrano de Bergerac* • Anne Brochet *Roxane* • Vincent Perez *Christian de Neuvillette* • Jacques Weber *Comte de Guiche* • Roland Bertin *Ragueneau* • Philippe Morier-Genoud *Le Bret* • Pierre Maguelon *Carbon de Castel-Jaloux* • Josiane Stoleru *Duenna* ■ *Dir* Jean-Paul Rappeneau • *Scr* Jean-Claude Carrière, Jean-Paul Rappeneau, from the play by Edmond Rostand

The Czech Dream ★★★ 12A

Documentary
2004 · Cz Rep/UK · Colour · 90mins

Film students Vit Klusak and Filip Remunda get their careers off to an impish start with this clever "provocumentary", in which they reveal just how rapidly the once-Communist citizens of the Czech Republic have acclimatised to capitalism. A state grant was secured to help advertise – through a splendid pastiche media campaign – the grand opening of a wholly fictitious hypermarket on the outskirts of Prague. The duo steer just the right side of a cynical candid-camera stunt, by emphasising the satirical ramifications of their hoax rather than the discomfort of those suckered by it. DP. In Czech with English subtitles. Contains swearing.

Dir Vit Klusak, Filip Remunda

D

D2: the Mighty Ducks ★★ U

Sports comedy 1994 · US · Colour · 102mins

The original *Mighty Ducks* was a bit of a surprise package, and it has gone on to spawn a couple of equally inoffensive if bland sequels. Emilio Estevez is once again the coach of the ragbag misfits, leading them to the Goodwill Games only to get seduced by the trappings of fame. Sam Weisman stages the ice hockey games with some flair. JF DVD

Emilio Estevez *Gordon Bombay* • Kathryn Erbe *Michele* • Michael Tucker *Tibbles* • Jan Rubes *Jan* • Carsten Norgaard *Wolf* ■ *Dir* Sam Weisman • *Scr* Steven Brill

D3: the Mighty Ducks ★★ PG

Sports comedy 1996 · US · Colour · 99mins

Original star Emilio Estevez makes a brief appearance in this third instalment in the successful but unremarkable franchise about the junior hockey team. In Robert Lieberman's contribution to the series, the Mighty Ducks – slightly more grown-up this time around – are bonafide champs, but they still find it difficult to adapt at their snooty new school. JF DVD

Emilio Estevez *Gordon Bombay* • Jeffrey Nordling *Coach Orion* • David Selby *Dean Buckley* • Heidi Kling *Casey* • Joshua Jackson *Charlie* • Joss Ackland *Hans* ■ *Dir* Robert Lieberman • *Scr* Steven Brill, from a story by Kenneth Johnson, Jim Burnstein, from characters created by Steven Brill

DC Cab ★★ 15

Comedy 1983 · US · Colour · 99mins

This uneasy mix of blue collar laughs and drama focuses on the battle between two rival groups of cabbies. There's an interesting cast, but it's unremarkable stuff and is only interesting as a career marker for fans of Joel Schumacher. JF

Max Gail *Harold* • Adam Baldwin *Albert* • Mr T *Samson* • Charlie Barnett *Tyrone* • Gary Busey *Dell* • DeWayne Jessie *Bongo* • Gloria Gifford *Miss Floyd* • Marsha Warfield *Ophelia* • Irene Cara ■ *Dir* Joel Schumacher • *Scr* Joel Schumacher, from a story by Topper Carew, Joel Schumacher

D-Day the Sixth of June ★★★ PG

Second World War romance
1956 · US · Colour · 101mins

This stirring and well-played romantic drama set at the time of the Normandy landings in 1944 shows the personal problems of officers encroaching on their work. Robert Taylor stars as the American serviceman who recalls his affair with Dana Wynter, while her fiancé Richard Todd was fighting in Africa. Aside from the familiar "stiff-upper-lip" heroics of the D-Day invasion, this offers some fine acting and action sequences. SH DVD

Robert Taylor (1) *Brad Parker* • Richard Todd *John Wynter* • Dana Wynter *Valerie* • Edmond O'Brien *Colonel Timmer* • John Williams *Brigadier Russell* • Jerry Paris *Raymond Boyce* • Robert Gist *Dan Stenick* • Richard Stapley *David Archer* • Alex Finlayson *Colonel Harkens* ■ *Dir* Henry Koster • *Scr* Ivan Moffat, Harry Brown, from the novel by Lionel Shapiro

DNA ★★★ 15

Science-fiction thriller
1996 · US · Colour · 93mins

Mark Dacascos is one of the more interesting and charismatic action heroes to have emerged in recent years, and his talent is well deployed in this otherwise formulaic thriller. He plays a doctor who is reluctantly coerced into tracking down mad scientist Jürgen Prochnow, who left him for dead years ago and has now regenerated an ancient, possibly alien, killing machine. Director William Mesa cheerfully splices together elements of *Jurassic Park* and *Predator* into an entertaining low-budget thriller. JF. Contains violence and swearing.

Mark Dacascos *Ash Mattley* • Jürgen Prochnow *Dr Carl Wessinger* • Robin McKee *Claire Sommers* • Roger Aaron Brown *Loren Azenfeld* • John H Brennan *Halton* ■ *Dir* William Mesa • *Scr* Nick Davis

DOA ★★★ PG

Film noir 1949 · US · BW · 83mins

This may not be the best *film noir* of the immediate postwar period, but it's one of the most unusual – how many people get to hunt for their own murderer? Edmond O'Brien responds to that unenviable challenge with grim determination in this slow-burning thriller that perhaps takes a mite too long to catch light. But once the scene is set, director Rudolph Maté takes us on a tortuous journey through the less salubrious parts of Los Angeles. Moodily shot by Ernest Laszlo and with a cracking score by Dimitri Tiomkin, it stands up well to the 1988 remake. DP DVD

Edmond O'Brien *Frank Bigelow* • Pamela Britton *Paula Gibson* • Luther Adler *Majak* • Beverly Campbell [Beverly Garland] *Miss Foster* • Lynn Baggett [Lynne Baggett] *Mrs Philips* • William Ching *Halliday* • Henry Hart *Stanley Philips* • Neville Brand *Chester* ■ *Dir* Rudolph Maté • *Scr* Russell Rouse, Clarence Green

DOA ★★★ 18

Music documentary
1980 · US · Colour · 89mins

A chaotic rockumentary detailing punk music's assault on comfortable America, set against the bleak backdrop of British daily life that spawned the movement. Extensive coverage of the Sex Pistols' US tour combines with rare footage of X-Ray Spex, Generation X, Sham 69 and the Rich Kids, plus a harrowing interview with a spaced-out Sid Vicious and Nancy Spungen, to give an overview of why punk scared the establishment so much. As a film, it's a complete shambles with some shining moments of frenzied energy and excitement. In other words, the perfect record of its subject matter. AJ

Dir Lech Kowalski

DOA ★★★★ 15

Crime thriller 1988 · US · Colour · 93mins

Dennis Quaid's gripping performance is just one reason why Rocky Morton and Annabel Jankel's smart and snappy retread of the memorable 1949 *film noir* is ripe for reappraisal. The *Max Headroom* creators begin their psycho thriller with the now famous exchange: "I wanna report a murder." "Whose?" "Mine!", and dress up the action with a smashing visual flash. Particularly impressive is the gimmick allying Quaid's deteriorating health to the colour draining out of the film, ending up in monochrome. A terrific touch in a thoroughly enjoyable remake. AJ. Contains violence swearing. DVD

Dennis Quaid *Dexter Cornell* • Meg Ryan *Sydney Fuller* • Charlotte Rampling *Mrs Fitzwaring* • Daniel Stern *Hal Petersham* •

Jane Kaczmarek *Gail Cornell* • Christopher Neame *Bernard* • Robin Johnson *Cookie Fitzwaring* • Rob Knepper [Robert Knepper] *Nicholas Lang* • Brion James *Detective Ulmer* ■ *Dir* Rocky Morton, Annabel Jankel • *Scr* Charles Edward Pogue, from a story by Charles Edward Pogue, Clarence Greene, Russell Rouse • *Cinematographer* Yuri Neyman

D-Tox ★ 18

Action thriller
2001 · US/Ger/Can · Colour · 91mins

After failing to catch the vicious serial killer responsible for the death of his girlfriend, detective Sylvester Stallone goes on an alcoholic bender and ends up in a detox programme for cops at a remote, snowbound facility in Wyoming. And, surprise, that's where the sadistic assassin is masquerading as one of the Betty Ford-style boozehounds. Derivative, nasty and just plain stupid. AJ ▭ DVD

Sylvester Stallone *Jake Malloy* • Tom Berenger *Hank* • Charles S Dutton *Hendricks* • Kris Kristofferson *Dr John "Doc" Mitchell* • Polly Walker *Jenny* • Sean Patrick Flanery *Connor* • Christopher Fulford *Frank Slater* ■ *Dir* Jim Gillespie • *Scr* Ron L Brinkerhoff, Patrick Kelly, from the novel *Jitter Joint* by Howard Swindle

Da ★★★ PG

Fantasy comedy drama
1988 · US · Colour · 97mins

Irish-American writer Martin Sheen returns to Ireland for the funeral of his father Barnard Hughes. However, no sooner is Sheen back on the old sod than the old sod materialises by his elbow, only too keen to reminisce about the old days. Adapted by Hugh Leonard from his own play, the film's theatrical roots are all too visible. Nevertheless, this is an unashamed heartstring-tugger that manages to be both funny and touching. SR ▭ DVD

Barnard Hughes *Da* • Martin Sheen *Charlie* • William Hickey *Drumm* • Doreen Hepburn *Mother* • Karl Hayden *Young Charlie* • Hugh O'Conor *Boy Charlie* • Ingrid Craigie *Polly* • Joan O'Hara *Mrs Prynne* ■ *Dir* Matt Clark • *Scr* Hugh Leonard, from his play and from his novel *Home before Night*

Dad ★★ PG

Drama 1989 · US · Colour · 112mins

This tries to provoke and uplift, but ends up being nothing more than an utterly false and manipulative melodrama. This is a shame because it starts well, yet from the moment Jack Lemmon falls ill, the film falls apart. Although his performance is not without its merits, it doesn't atone for the wild overplaying of Ted Danson as his son and the sloppy turn of Ethan Hawke as his grandson. DP ▭

Jack Lemmon *Jake Tremont* • Ted Danson *John Tremont* • Olympia Dukakis *Bette Tremont* • Kathy Baker *Annie* • Kevin Spacey *Mario* • Ethan Hawke *Billy Tremont* • Zakes Mokae *Dr Chad* • JT Walsh *Dr Santana* • Peter Michael Goetz *Dr Ethridge* ■ *Dir* Gary David Goldberg • *Scr* Gary David Goldberg, from the novel *Dad* by William Wharton

Dad and Dave: on Our Selection ★★★ PG

Period comedy drama
1995 · Aus · Colour and Sepia · 102mins

Since they were adapted by Raymond Longford in the silent era and Ken G Hall in the 1930s, the cod memoirs of Steele Rudd (written pseudonymously by Arthur Hoey) have fallen out of favour with Australian film-makers. Lampooning the caricature of the ocker Aussie, this revival not only reflects the nation's burgeoning self-image, but also reveals just how far cinema Down Under has come since the original series were produced. Leo McKern and Geoffrey Rush are ideally teamed as the Queenslanders striving to make the most of their unyielding farm, while Joan Sutherland provides the sense betwixt the bluster. DP DVD

Leo McKern *Dad Rudd* • Joan Sutherland *Mother Rudd* • Geoffrey Rush *Dave* • David Field *Dan* • Noah Taylor *Joe* • Essie Davis *Kate* • Celia Ireland *Sarah* ■ *Dir* George Whaley • *Scr* George Whaley, from stories by Steele Rudd [Arthur Hoey]

Dad Savage ★★ 18

Crime thriller 1997 · UK · Colour · 99mins

this is a downright strange British stab at a *Reservoir Dogs*-style crime thriller. Patrick Stewart is entirely unconvincing as the titular flower grower who has a hidden "pension fund" accrued from various illegal activities. His gang members' desire for the loot leads to murder, double-cross and all the other clichés of the genre. Alternately boring and confusing. JC. Contains violence and swearing. ▭

Patrick Stewart *Dad Savage* • Kevin McKidd *H* • Helen McCrory *Chris* • Joseph McFadden *Bob* • Marc Warren *Vic* • Jake Wood *Sav* ■ *Dir* Betsan Morris Evans • *Scr* Steven Williams

Daddy Day Care ★★ PG

Comedy 2003 · US · Colour · 88mins

What this lacks in originality it makes up for in cuteness and verve. Eddie Murphy and Jeff Garlin play sacked advertising executives who decide to set up a children's day-care centre; cue major mishaps as a house full of angel-faced youngsters turn into marauding monsters – much to the delight of rival childcare provider Anjelica Huston. Simplistic, and too sweet for mass appeal. SF ▭ DVD

Eddie Murphy *Charlie Hinton* • Jeff Garlin *Phil* • Steve Zahn *Marvin* • Regina King *Kim Hinton* • Kevin Nealon *Bruce* • Jonathan Katz *Mr Dan Kubitz* • Siobhan Fallon Hogan [Siobhan Fallon] *Peggy* • Anjelica Huston *Miss Harridan* ■ *Dir* Steve Carr • *Scr* Geoff Rodkey

Daddy Long Legs ★★★★

Silent comedy drama
1919 · US · BW · 85mins

In pigtails rather than her customary curls, 27-year-old Mary Pickford plays the rebellious youngster who leads a revolt against the prison-like conditions in her orphanage. There is much honest emotion along with the humour, while Marshall Neilan shows why he was her favourite director. (He also appears as a prospective suitor.) The girl's rich benefactor, the mysterious Daddy Long Legs, would register more importantly in later versions of the story, most notably the 1955 musical with Leslie Caron and Fred Astaire. AE

Mary Pickford *"Judy" Abbott* • Milla Davenport *Mrs Lippert* • Wesley Barry *Her pal* • Marshall Neilan *Jimmie McBride* ■ *Dir* Marshall Neilan • *Scr* Agnes Christine Johnston, from the novel and play by Jean Webster

Daddy Long Legs ★★★ U

Comedy drama 1931 · US · BW · 80mins

Mary Pickford's silent hit metamorphosed into one of 20th Century-Fox's hardy perennials, but this tale of a secret guardian falling for his young ward needed to be handled with extreme care on the grounds of taste. In this version, pretty Janet Gaynor, though a shade too old for the part, makes a charming foundling, Warner Baxter is a handsomely sturdy patron of at least a convincing age, and the whole story of their May-December relationship is deeply satisfying. TS

Janet Gaynor *Judy Abbott* • Warner Baxter *Jervis Pendleton* • Una Merkel *Sally McBride* • John Arledge *Jimmy McBride* • Claude Gillingwater Sr [Claude Gillingwater] *Riggs* • Kathlyn Williams *Mrs Pendleton* ■ *Dir* Alfred Santell • *Scr* Sonya Levien, SN Behrman, from the novel and play by Jean Webster

Daddy Long Legs ★★★★ U

Romantic musical comedy
1955 · US · Colour · 121mins

The third American screen version of Jean Webster's novel, this time with a perfectly cast Fred Astaire, who literally glides his way through the tissue-thin plot about an orphan falling for her playboy benefactor. This could be tasteless, bearing in mind the vast age gap, but it's a musical and the delightful Leslie Caron is the girl. Interestingly, this was released when rock 'n' roll was at its peak, and features the great Astaire doing the *Sluefoot*. (Watch Astaire's face: he's not joking.) A charming, old-fashioned musical. TS ▭

Fred Astaire *Jervis Pendleton* • Leslie Caron *Julie* • Terry Moore *Linda* • Thelma Ritter *Miss Pritchard* • Fred Clark *Griggs* ■ *Dir* Jean Negulesco • *Scr* Phoebe Ephron, Henry Ephron, from the novel and play by Jean Webster • *Music/lyrics* Johnny Mercer

Daddy-O ★ PG

Musical drama 1959 · US · Colour · 70mins

Here's an early embarrassment in the career of composer John Williams: a cheap and awful slice of teen schlock, its catchpenny title derived from then-contemporary slang. The negligible plot follows truck driver Dick Contino as he fights hoodlums and smashes a drugs ring, all the while singing forgettable tunes. This was already out of date by the time it was made. TS DVD

Dick Contino *Phil Sandifer* • Sandra Giles *Jana Ryan* • Bruno VeSota *Sidney Chillas* • Gloria Victor *Marcia* • Ron McNeil *Duke* ■ *Dir* Lou Place • *Scr* David Moessinger

Daddy's Dyin'... Who's Got the Will? ★★★ 15

Comedy drama 1990 · US · Colour · 92mins

Every now and then a director has to concede defeat and admit that a play with crackling dialogue and eccentric characters can get by without cinematic flourishes. Jack Fisk makes all the right choices in this adaptation of Del Shores's hit play and the result is an often hilarious comedy of dysfunctional family life. Beau Bridges has rarely been better as a white trash loudmouth, bullying his chalk-and-cheese sisters, who are played to perfection by Amy Wright, Tess Harper and Beverly D'Angelo. DP. Contains swearing and drug abuse. ▭

Beau Bridges *Orville Turnover* • Beverly D'Angelo *Evalita Turnover* • Tess Harper *Sara Lee* • Judge Reinhold *Harmony* • Amy Wright *Lurlene* • Patrika Darbo *Marlene Turnover* • Bert Remsen *Buford Turnover* • Molly McClure *Mama Wheelis* • Keith Carradine *Clarence* • Newell Alexander *Sid Cranford* ■ *Dir* Jack Fisk • *Scr* Del Shores, from his play

Daddy's Gone A-Hunting ★★

Thriller 1969 · US · Colour · 107mins

As both editor and director for ace horror producer Val Lewton, you would have expected Mark Robson to have made a better fist of this chiller. The thrills he concentrates on, however, are those of a sexual, rather than a suspenseful, nature and so the action is not as tense as it should be. Still, there are a couple of black comic touches, and Scott Hylands is convincingly deranged as he seeks revenge on Carol White for the abortion she kept secret from him. DP. Contains swearing.

Carol White *Cathy Palmer* • Scott Hylands *Kenneth Daly* • Paul Burke *Jack Byrnes* • Mala Powers *Meg Stone* • Rachel Ames *Dr Parkington's nurse* • Barry Cahill *FBI agent Crosley* • James Sikking [James B Sikking] *FBI Agent Menchell* ■ *Dir* Mark Robson • *Scr* Lorenzo Semple Jr, Larry Cohen

Dad's Army ★★★ U

Comedy 1971 · UK · Colour · 90mins

Dad's Army remains one of the best loved of all British comedy series. As with so many other TV spin-offs, the producers couldn't resist tinkering with the winning formula, and here we are treated to a Nazi invasion of Walmington-on-Sea that is somewhat at odds with the cosy incompetence that made the series so irresistible. But this is still great fun and it's always a pleasure to see such gifted character actors at work. DP ▭

Arthur Lowe *Captain Mainwaring* • John Le Mesurier *Sergeant Wilson* • Clive Dunn *Corporal Jones* • John Laurie *Private Frazer* • James Beck *Private Walker* • Arnold Ridley *Private Godfrey* • Ian Lavender *Private Pike* • Liz Fraser *Mrs Pike* • Bernard Archard *General Fuller* • Derek Newark *RSM* • Bill Pertwee *Hodges* • Frank Williams *Vicar* • Edward Sinclair *Verger* • Anthony Sager *Police sergeant* • Pat Coombs *Mrs Hall* ■ *Dir* Norman Cohen • *Scr* Jimmy Perry, David Croft, from their TV series

Daens ★★★★ 15

Period drama
1992 · Bel/Fr/Neth · Colour · 132mins

An Oscar-nominated journey through the life and hard times of a 19th-century Catholic priest in Flanders, who took on a political role in order to speak up for the downtrodden mill workers in the textile town of Aalst. The struggle between Father Adolf Daens and the establishment is spelled out in simple, didactic fashion. But the growling performance of Jan Decleir, as Daens, and a narrative anger that threatens immediate revolution both help to accelerate the drama into something to savour. TH. In Flemish with English subtitles. ▭

Jan Decleir *Adolf Daens* • Gérard Desarthe *Charles Woeste* • Antje De Boeck *Nette Scholliers* • Michael Pas *Jan De Meeter* ■ *Dir* Stijn Coninx • *Scr* François Chevallier, Stijn Coninx, from the novel *Pieter Daens* by Louis Paul Boon

Daffy Duck's Movie: Fantastic Island ★★★ U

Animation 1983 · US · Colour · 74mins

Directed by the legendary Friz Freleng and with voices by the great Mel Blanc, this is yet another collection of old Warner Bros cartoons combined and released under a new title. It's a veritable Who's Who of Looney Tunes/ Merrie Melodie favourites, with Sylvester and Tweety, Yosemite Sam (as a pirate), Foghorn Leghorn, Pepe LePew and Speedy Gonzales all putting in an appearance. However, there's the odd classic tucked away here, notably *Mutiny on the Bunny*, starring the irrepressible Bugs himself. DP ▭

Mel Blanc • June Foray • Les Tremayne ■ *Dir* Friz Freleng • *Scr* John Dunn, David Detiege, Friz Freleng

Daffy Duck's Quackbusters ★★★ U

Animated compilation
1988 · US · Colour · 75mins

Disney is the undoubted master of the animated feature, but when it comes to the five-minute cartoon, however, Warner Bros clearly has the edge. The best thing about compilation films like this one is that each component is a classic in its own right. In this neat spoof of *Ghostbusters*, Daffy, Bugs Bunny and Porky Pig join forces to rid the world of spooks. Younger viewers might not get all the subtle references to classic horror films, but *The Night of the Living Duck* and *The Duxorcist* are hilarious. DP ▭

Mel Blanc • Roy Firestone • BJ Ward ■ *Dir* Greg Ford, Terry Lennon

Dahmer ★★ 15

Biographical crime drama
2002 · US · Colour · 97mins

Exploring the adult life and motivations of notorious 1990s American serial killer Jeffrey Dahmer, David Jacobson avoids sensationalising the gruesome events that cost many young men their lives. He endeavours to rationalise Dahmer's deeds by balancing brief physical violence with the psychological turmoil that allegedly preceded it, but it's made less effective by Jeremy Renner's insipid central performance. SF. Contains swearing, violence, nudity. DVD

Jeremy Renner *Jeffrey Dahmer* • Bruce Davison *Lionel Dahmer* • Artel Kayaru *Rodney* • Matt Newton *Lance Bell* • Dion Basco *Khamtay* • Kate Williamson *Grandma* ■ *Dir/Scr* David Jacobson

Daisies ★★★★ 15

Comedy 1966 · Cz · Colour · 72mins

The two most significant female artists of the Czech New Wave collaborated on this anarchic assault on materialism. In addition to designing the stylised visuals, Ester Krumbachova co-wrote the screenplay with director Vera Chytilova, whose husband, Jaroslav Kucera, served as cinematographer. Employing collage, superimposition, symbolic *mise en scène* and prismatic distortion, they concoct a surrealist fantasy of the banality and conformity of Czech society as two girls, both named Marie, dupe several boorish males before indulging in an orgy of gleeful destruction. DP. In Czech with English subtitles.

Jitka Cerhova *Marie I* • Ivana Karbonova *Marie II* ■ *Dir* Vera Chytilova • *Scr* Vera Chytilova, Ester Krumbachova

Daisy Kenyon ★★★★

Romantic melodrama
1947 · US · BW · 98mins

Beginning with *Laura*, director Otto Preminger served up a dark and sinister series of movies throughout the 1940s, today labelled *film noir* but then just called thrillers. They're really melodramas at heart, served up with all the seaminess the censors and 20th Century-Fox would allow, and hold up well today as a consistently fine body of work. Here, Joan Crawford is Daisy, torn between Dana Andrews and Henry Fonda. There's also a surprisingly daring (for its day) subplot about child abuse. TS

Joan Crawford *Daisy Kenyon* • Dana Andrews *Dan O'Mara* • Henry Fonda *Peter* • Ruth Warrick *Lucile O'Mara* • Martha Stewart *Mary Angelus* • Peggy Ann Garner *Rosamund* • John Garfield *Man in restaurant* ■ *Dir* Otto Preminger • *Scr* David Hertz, from the novel by Elizabeth Janeway

Daisy Miller ★★★ U

Drama 1974 · US · Colour · 87mins

One of the key theme of Henry James's writings was the clash between American and European culture. So it's fascinating to watch a story in which surface actions are almost irrelevant being related by a director steeped in the storytelling traditions of John Ford and Howard Hawks. Peter Bogdanovich captures the styles, the manners and the atmosphere of late 19th-century Italy, but never comes close to conveying the inner life of the characters, which is precisely what interested James. The director was criticised for casting then-girlfriend Cybill Shepherd in the title role, and the film marked the beginning of his critical and commercial decline. DP DVD

Cybill Shepherd *Annie P "Daisy" Miller* • Barry Brown *Frederick Winterbourne* • Cloris Leachman *Mrs Ezra B Miller* • Mildred Natwick *Mrs Costello* • Eileen Brennan *Mrs Walker* • Duilio Del Prete *Mr Giovanelli* • James McMurtry *Randolph C Miller* • Nicholas Jones *Charles* ■ *Dir* Peter Bogdanovich • *Scr* Frederic Raphael, from the novel by Henry James

Dakota ★★ PG

Western 1945 · US · BW · 81mins

Big John Wayne found himself working out his Republic contract in this western directed by a studio hack, which despite a strong support cast, is fairly typical of that minor studio's output. Even the female lead is played by Vera Hruba Ralston, wife of the studio head. Wayne rides to the rescue of farmers whose valuable land is targeted by crooks, but his heart doesn't seem to be in it. TS

John Wayne *John Devlin* • Vera Hruba Ralston [Vera Ralston] *Sandy* • Walter Brennan *Captain Bounce* • Ward Bond *Jim Bender* • Ona Munson *"Jersey" Thomas* • Hugo Haas *Marko Poli* ■ *Dir* Joseph Kane • *Scr* Lawrence Hazard, Howard Estabrook, from a story by Carl Foreman

Dakota ★★ U

Drama 1987 · US · Colour · 91mins

After the success of *La Bamba*, Lou Diamond Phillips's next screen outing was a marked change of pace. He plays a teenager on the run, with all the usual adolescent hang-ups, who gets to grips with his life while working on a Texas ranch. Phillips smoulders away effectively enough and there are good supporting turns from a largely unknown cast, while Fred Holmes handles the directorial chores with some skill. JF

Lou Diamond Phillips *Dakota* • Eli Cummins *Walt* • DeeDee Norton *Molly* ■ *Dir* Fred Holmes • *Scr* Darryl Kuntz, Sara Lynn Kuntz

Dakota Incident ★ U

Western 1956 · US · Colour · 88mins

A dire western, this has an adequate cast – headed by Dale Robertson and Linda Darnell – hamstrung by pretentious dialogue and fuzzy characterisations. After interminable scenes in town setting up these boring characters, they set off on the stage to be attacked by Indians, but this only leads to more excessive gabbing after the group takes cover in a dry waterhole. It's a particular relief when Ward Bond's foolish windbag of a senator discovers that his sympathy for the Indians is not reciprocated. AE

Dale Robertson *John Banner* • Linda Darnell *Amy Clarke* • John Lund *Carter Hamilton* • Ward Bond *Senator Blakely* ■ *Dir* Lewis R Foster • *Scr* Frederic Louis Fox

Daleks – Invasion Earth 2150 AD ★★★ U

Science-fiction adventure
1966 · UK · Colour · 80mins

The second feature (after 1965's *Doctor Who and the Daleks*) starring Peter Cushing as the Doctor has the BBC's world famous Time Lord aiding human survivors in their future guerrilla war against the diabolical Daleks. *Independence Day* it's not, but director Gordon Flemyng keeps the colourful action moving swiftly along to cheap and cheerful effect. Yet, through all the mindless mayhem roll the impressive Daleks, one of science fiction's greatest alien creations. AJ DVD

Peter Cushing *Doctor Who* • Bernard Cribbins *Tom Campbell* • Ray Brooks *David* • Jill Curzon *Louise* • Roberta Tovey *Susan* • Andrew Keir *Wyler* • Godfrey Quigley *Dortmun* ■ *Dir* Gordon Flemyng • *Scr* Milton Subotsky

Dallas ★★ PG

Western 1950 · US · Colour · 90mins

Before his Oscar-winning role in *High Noon*, Gary Cooper's career was heading for the doldrums. Ageing and thought to be past his prime, he had become hard to cast, and in general his vehicles had become unworthy of their star. In this very average Warner Bros Technicolor western, Coop has little to do as a former Confederate officer seeking revenge by pretending to be a lawman, and looks uncomfortable doing it. TS

Gary Cooper *Blayde "Reb" Hollister* • Ruth Roman *Tonia Robles* • Steve Cochran *Bryant Marlow* • Raymond Massey *Will Marlow* • Barbara Payton *Flo* • Leif Erickson *Martin Weatherby* • Antonio Moreno *Felipe* • Jerome Cowan *Matt Coulter* • Reed Hadley *Wild Bill Hickok* ■ *Dir* Stuart Heisler • *Scr* John Twist, from his story

Dallas Doll ★★ 18

Comedy drama 1994 · US · Colour · 100mins

Australian director Ann Turner came seriously unstuck with this comedy drama, an unacknowledged reworking of Pier Paolo Pasolini's 1968 classic *Theorem*. Sandra Bernhard stars as a golf guru who disrupts the ordinary life of a middle-class Sydney family by raising their expectations of life and fulfilling their sexual fantasies. Bernhard has none of the mystery and charm Terence Stamp brought to *Theorem* and is never allowed to go into her customary overdrive. DP

Sandra Bernhard *Dallas Adair* • Victoria Longley *Rosalind* • Frank Gallacher *Stephen* • Jake Blundell *Charlie* • Rose Byrne *Rastus* • Jonathan Leahy *Eddy* • Douglas Hedge *Mayor Tonkin* • Melissa Thomas *Margaret* • Elaine Lee *Mrs Winthrop* • Alethea McGrath *Aunt Mary* • John Frawley *Mr Fellowes* • Roy Billing *Dave Harry* ■ *Dir/Scr* Ann Turner

The Daltons Ride Again ★★

Western 1945 · US · BW · 72mins

Five years after *When the Daltons Rode*, here they are again in a virtual remake. This time, though, it's a resolutely B-grade cast taking over from Randolph Scott and co, with the four outlaw brothers played here by Alan Curtis, Kent Taylor, Lon Chaney Jr and Noah Beery Jr. The quartet wreak havoc, just as they did in the earlier film, throughout Kansas before the all-action climactic bank raid. Efficient enough entertainment. TS

Alan Curtis *Emmett Dalton* • Kent Taylor *Bob Dalton* • Lon Chaney Jr *Grat Dalton* • Noah Beery Jr *Ben Dalton* • Martha O'Driscoll *Mary* • Jess Barker *Jeff* • Thomas Gomez *McKenna* ■ *Dir* Ray Taylor • *Scr* Roy Chanslor, Paul Gangelin, Henry Blankfort

The Dam Busters ★★★★★ U

Classic Second World War drama
1954 · UK · BW · 119mins

This thrilling drama about the bouncing bomb raid on the dams of the Ruhr valley is truly compelling viewing and stands among the best British movies about the Second World War. Indeed, thanks to its potent blend of scientific suspense and aerial action, accompanied by that stirring soundtrack, it has convinced generations of movie-watchers that the mission was a major turning point in the war rather than a risky venture that the brass hats considered something of a sideshow. Michael Redgrave puts a pinch too much bumbling boffin into his Barnes Wallis, but Richard Todd was never better as Wing Commander Guy Gibson, who led the raid. DP DVD

Richard Todd *Wing Commander Guy Gibson* • Michael Redgrave *Dr Barnes N Wallis* • Ursula Jeans *Mrs Wallis* • Basil Sydney *Sir Arthur Harris* • Patrick Barr *Captain Joseph Summers* • Ernest Clark *AVM Ralph Cochrane* • Derek Farr *Group Captain Whitworth* • Charles Carson *Doctor* • Stanley Van Beers *Sir David Pye* • Colin Tapley *Dr WH Glanville* • John Fraser *Flight Lieutenant Hopgood* • George Baker *Flight Lieutenant Maltby* • Robert Shaw *Flight Sergeant Pulford* ■ *Dir* Michael Anderson • *Scr* RC Sherriff, from the non-fiction book *The Dam Busters* by Paul Brickhill, from the story *Enemy Coast Ahead* by Wing Commander Guy Gibson

Damage ★★★ 18

Erotic drama 1992 · UK/Fr · Colour · 105mins

Louis Malle, directing his first English-language film since his return from America to France, employs an almost leisurely (but always exact) camera to highlight the emotional centre of this traumatic tale. Taken from Josephine Hart's bestseller by scriptwriter David Hare, the explosion of emotion is muted by moments of implausibility, caused by some widely varying acting styles. Whereas Miranda Richardson crumbles believably as the spurned wife, Juliette Binoche, as the object of an MP's lust, simply pouts seductively, while Jeremy Irons, as the politician, spends too much time behaving like a startled rabbit. JM. Contains swearing, sex scenes and nudity. DVD

Jeremy Irons *Stephen Fleming* • Juliette Binoche *Anna Barton* • Miranda Richardson *Ingrid Fleming* • Rupert Graves *Martyn Fleming* • Leslie Caron *Elizabeth Prideaux* • Ian Bannen *Edward Lloyd* • Gemma Clarke *Sally Fleming* • Peter Stormare *Peter* • Julian Fellowes *Donald Lindsay* ■ *Dir* Louis Malle • *Scr* David Hare, from the novel by Josephine Hart

Dames ★★★

Musical comedy 1934 · US · BW · 91mins

This is a super Depression-era musical, with wonderfully kaleidoscopic choreography from maestro Busby Berkeley. The dialogue is as witty as ever, but the blackmail-cum-putting on a show storyline is contrived, and the whole lacks the dazzle of stablemates *42nd Street* and the first two Berkeley *Gold Diggers*. No matter: the production numbers are sensational, and the cast, featuring witty Joan Blondell and wacky ZaSu Pitts, is compulsively watchable. TS

Joan Blondell *Mabel Anderson* • Dick Powell *Jimmy Higgens* • Ruby Keeler *Barbara Hemingway* • ZaSu Pitts *Mathilda Hemingway* • Hugh Herbert *Ezra Ounce* • Guy Kibbee *Horace* • Arthur Vinton *Bulger* • Phil Regan *Johnny Harris* • Busby Berkeley *Choreography* ■ *Dir* Ray Enright • *Scr* Delmer Daves, from a story by Robert Lord, Delmer Daves

Les Dames du Bois de Boulogne ★★★★★ PG

Drama 1946 · Fr · BW · 81mins

Robert Bresson's second feature, his last to use professional actors and be filmed in a studio, takes an anecdote from Diderot's *Jacques le Fataliste* and moves it to a 20th-century setting. When a man tells his girlfriend that he no longer loves her, she wreaks revenge by arranging a meeting between him and an ex-prostitute, only revealing her history after they marry. Jean Cocteau's screenplay brilliantly dissects the fable's ethical issues, while the director's austerity enhances the dramatic tension. RB. In French with English subtitles. DVD

Paul Bernard *Jean* • Maria Casarès *Hélène* • Elina Labourdette *Agnès* • Lucienne Bogaert *Agnès's mother* • Jean Marchat *Jacques* ■ *Dir* Robert Bresson • *Scr* Robert Bresson, Jean Cocteau, from the novel *Jacques le Fataliste et Son Maître* by Denis Diderot

Damien – Omen II ★★★ 18

Horror 1978 · US · Colour · 102mins

The Antichrist becomes an adolescent evil-doer in the second part of the satanic saga, which relies too openly on the same shock suspense tricks that made *The Omen* (1976) such a huge success. Here, Damien reads the Book of Revelations and discovers all about his true past. Don Taylor's direction is banal, but William Holden and Lee Grant handle their roles as Damien's marked foster parents with skill. The saga continued in 1980 with *The Final Conflict*. AJ. Contains violence and swearing. [VIDEO] DVD

William Holden (2) *Richard Thorn* • Lee Grant *Ann Thorn* • Jonathan Scott-Taylor *Damien Thorn* • Robert Foxworth *Paul Buher* • Nicholas Pryor *Charles Warren* • Lew Ayres *Bill Atherton* • Sylvia Sidney *Aunt Marion* • Lance Henriksen *Sergeant Neff* ■ *Dir* Don Taylor • *Scr* Stanley Mann, Michael Hodges, from characters created by David Seltzer

Damn Citizen ★★

Crime drama 1958 · US · BW · 88mins

Keith Andes plays the Second World War hero brought in to fight the corruption endemic in his native Louisiana. Filmed in and around New Orleans, Robert Gordon's picture has a documentary feel. Andes is not the most interesting of actors, however, and the screenplay follows a rather straightforward, predictable and episodic course. AE

Keith Andes *Colonel Francis C Grevemberg* • Maggie Hayes [Margaret Hayes] *Dorothy Grevemberg* • Gene Evans *Major Al Arthur* • Lynn Bari *Pat Noble* • Jeffrey Stone *Paul Musso* • Edward Platt *Joseph Kosta* • Ann Robinson *Cleo* • Sam Buffington *DeButts* ■ *Dir* Robert Gordon • *Scr* Stirling Silliphant

Damn Yankees ★★★ U

Musical 1958 · US · Colour · 105mins

After the success of *The Pajama Game*, Broadway's George Abbott and Hollywood's Stanley Donen teamed up again for this second show by the same writing team. Despite this talent, this time round the show didn't quite transfer, despite a supporting cast comprised entirely of the stage cast, and the retention of the original Bob Fosse choreography. The problem lies with Tab Hunter in the difficult leading role: to put it mildly, he lacks pizzazz. There's still a lot of fun to be gleaned, though: Gwen Verdon (Mrs Fosse) is a knockout, and Ray Walston is arguably the definitive movie Devil. TS [VIDEO]

Tab Hunter *Joe Hardy* • Gwen Verdon *Lola* • Ray Walston *Applegate* • Russ Brown *Van Buren* • Shannon Bolin *Meg Boyd* • Nathaniel Frey *Smokey* • Jimmie Komack *Rocky* • Rae Allen *Gloria* • Robert Shafer *Joe Boyd* • Jean Stapleton *Sister* • Albert Linville *Vernon* • Bob Fosse *Mambo dancer* ■ *Dir* George Abbott, Stanley Donen • *Scr* George Abbott, from the play *Damn Yankees!* by Douglas Wallop, George Abbott, from the novel *The Year The Yankees Lost the Pennant* by Douglas Wallop

Damnation ★★★ 15

Drama 1988 · Hun · BW · 114mins

Long after Gabor Medvigy's meandering monochrome images have faded, the unrelenting bleakness of Bela Tarr's study of an all-encompassing obsession will linger in the mind. Whether it's the sight of outcast Miklos B Szekely peering through the rain to watch his married lover (Vali Kerekes) singing at the Titanic Bar or the shocking finale, the film exercises a compulsion that is never diminished by its pessimism. This intense picture could almost be called an apocalyptic *noir*. DP. In Hungarian with English subtitles. DVD

Miklos B Szekely *Karrer* • Vali Kerekes *The singer* ■ *Dir* Bela Tarr • *Scr* Bela Tarr, Laszlo Krasznahorkai

Damnation Alley ★ PG

Science-fiction adventure 1977 · US · Colour · 87mins

An utterly pedestrian adaptation of Roger Zelazny's much-admired novel, this takes place after a nuclear holocaust and features psychedelic visual effects that are really quite awful. Five survivors cross America in a futuristic tank driven by George Peppard, looking for others after receiving mystery radio signals. Lacklustre acting, tedious exposition and laughable rubber monsters damn this regrettable misfire. AJ. Contains violence and swearing. [VIDEO]

Jan-Michael Vincent *Tanner* • George Peppard *Denton* • Dominique Sanda *Janice* • Paul Winfield *Keegan* • Jackie Earle Haley *Billy* ■ *Dir* Jack Smight • *Scr* Alan Sharp, Lukas Heller, from the novel by Roger Zelazny

The Damned ★★

Science fiction 1961 · UK · BW · 94mins

A downbeat financial disaster from Hammer, this clearly reflects the troubled shoot, the creative differences between director Joseph Losey and the cost-conscious House of Horror, and the delayed release in butchered form. While on holiday in Weymouth, and after being mugged by biker gang leader Oliver Reed, American boat owner Macdonald Carey stumbles on a secret government programme in which radioactive children are being schooled to repopulate the planet after a nuclear war. The plot never really fuses to create the powerful Orwellian fable the film was once acclaimed as. AJ

Macdonald Carey *Simon Wells* • Shirley Anne Field *Joan* • Viveca Lindfors *Freya Nelson, sculptress* • Alexander Knox *Bernard, scientist* • Oliver Reed *King* • Walter Gotell *Maj Holland* • Brian Oulton *Mr Dingle* • Kenneth Cope *Sid* ■ *Dir* Joseph Losey • *Scr* Evan Jones, from the novel *The Children of Light* by HL Lawrence

The Damned ★★★★ 18

Drama 1969 · It/W Ger · Colour · 146mins

Luchino Visconti's grand-operatic account views the rise of Fascism in the 1930s through an upper-class household (clearly based on the Krupps) as they murder and blackmail each other for the ownership of an armaments factory. Helmut Berger is the son who sleeps with his mother (Ingrid Thulin); Dirk Bogarde, as the mother's lover, looks bemused by all these unloosed deviations; and the whole is decked out in what amounts to Nazi chic. Ponderous, but still a remarkable work. TH. Italian dialogue dubbed into English. Contains violence, sex scenes. [VIDEO] DVD

Dirk Bogarde *Friedrich Bruckmann* • Ingrid Thulin *Baroness Sophie von Essenbeck* • Helmut Griem *Aschenbach* • Helmut Berger *Martin von Essenbeck* • Charlotte Rampling *Elisabeth Thallman* ■ *Dir* Luchino Visconti • *Scr* Luchino Visconti, Nicola Badalucco, Enrico Medioli • *Cinematographer* Pasqualino De Santis, Armando Nannuzzi

The Damned Don't Cry ★★★

Crime drama 1950 · US · BW · 100mins

A splendidly titled but resolutely low-rent Joan Crawford vehicle. It's a steamy crime drama, in which Vincent Sherman fails to rein in Crawford's excesses. She chews the scenery and her men as only she can, but is as splendid as ever. Pity the males are rather a let-down. TS

Joan Crawford *Ethel Whitehead* • David Brian *George Castleman* • Steve Cochran *Nick Prenta* • Kent Smith *Martin Blackford* • Hugh Sanders *Grady* • Selena Royle *Patricia Longworth* ■ *Dir* Vincent Sherman • *Scr* Harold Medford, Jerome Weidman, from a story by Gertrude Walker

Damned River ★ 18

Action adventure 1989 · US · Colour · 91mins

A crude exploitation effort directed by Michael Schroeder, who once worked for Paul Bartel and made his directing debut with the mordantly funny *Out of the Dark*. This second effort about a bunch of young Americans shooting the rapids in Zimbabwe isn't up to par, being a rip-off of *Deliverance*. AT [VIDEO]

Stephen Shellen *Ray* • Lisa Aliff *Anne* • John Terlesky *Carl* • Marc Poppel *Luke* • Bradford Bancroft *Jerry* • Louis Van Niekerk *Von Hoenigen* ■ *Dir* Michael Schroeder, John Crowther • *Scr* Bayard Johnson

A Damsel in Distress ★★★ U

Musical comedy 1937 · US · BW · 96mins

Adapted by PG Wodehouse from a play that was based on his own novel, this was Fred Astaire's second film without Ginger Rogers. But he's in sparkling form as a dance star attempting to trip the light fantastic with aristocratic Joan Fontaine. Hermes Pan's choreography won an Oscar, but every step is pure Astaire, and Fontaine (who was better known as a dramatic actress) never misses a beat. George Burns and Gracie Allen also show why they are so fondly remembered. DP [VIDEO]

Fred Astaire *Jerry Halliday* • George Burns • Gracie Allen • Joan Fontaine *Lady Alyce Marshmorton* • Reginald Gardiner *Keggs* • Ray Noble *Reggie* • Constance Collier *Lady Caroline Marshmorton* • Montagu Love *Lord John Marshmorton* ■ *Dir* George Stevens • *Scr* PG Wodehouse, SK Lauren, Ernest Pagano, from a play by PG Wodehouse, Ian Hay, from a novel by PG Wodehouse

Dan Candy's Law ★★★

Historical western 1973 · Can · Colour · 90mins

Donald Sutherland shines as Dan Candy, the rangy Mountie who always gets his man.This is based on the true story of Almighty Voice (Gordon Tootoosis), a Cree Indian fugitive who evaded the Canadian Mounties for more than a year. The plot may not be up to much, but it's most interesting as a chance to see how conflict between white police officers and native American Indians was dealt with back in the 1970s and for Claude Fournier's stunning photography, evoking the brutality of the rugged Canadian landscape. FL

Donald Sutherland *Sgt Dan Candy* • Kevin McCarthy *Sgt Malcolm Grant* • Chief Dan George *Sounding Sky* • Gordon Tootoosis *Almighty Voice* ■ *Dir* Claude Fournier • *Scr* George Malko

Dance Academy ★★ PG

Dance drama 1988 · US/It · Colour · 101mins

This borrows shamelessly from *Fame* and countless other musicals, in which a staid institution is shaken to its foundations by a new style that the kids love and the teachers simply don't understand. Here, it's a few funky jazz steps from Tony Dean Fields that divide a ballet school that is on its uppers and needs that magical something to revive its fortunes. The school principal is Julie Newmar, TV's Catwoman. DP [VIDEO]

Tony Dean Fields [Tony Fields] *Moon* • Galyn Gorg *Jana* • Scott Grossman *Tommy* • Eliska Krupka *Patrizia* • Steve La Chance *Vince* • Paula Nichols *Paula* • Julie Newmar *Miss McKenzie* ■ *Dir* Ted Mather • *Scr* Ted Mather, Guido DeAngelis

Dance, Fools, Dance ★★★

Crime drama 1931 · US · BW · 81mins

Joan Crawford – young, bright-eyed and light years away from the monster image for which she is more familiar – stars in this Depression-era drama as the spoilt daughter of a stockbroker who loses everything when the market crashes. Left with nothing, Joan becomes a cub reporter and goes undercover to investigate bootlegging gangster Clark Gable. Tightly directed by Harry Beaumont, this is a compact, suspenseful and entertaining film. RK

Joan Crawford *Bonnie Jordan* • Lester Vail *Bob Townsend* • Cliff Edwards *Bert Scranton* • William Bakewell *Rodney Jordan* • William Holden (1) *Stanley Jordan* • Clark Gable *Jake Luva* • Earle Foxe *Wally Baxter* ■ *Dir* Harry Beaumont • *Scr* Aurania Rouverol, Richard Schayer, from a story by Aurania Rouverol

D

Dance, Girl, Dance ★★

Musical 1940 · US · BW · 89mins

Lucille Ball and Maureen O'Hara are ambitious chorus girls in Maria Ouspenskaya's dance troupe. While O'Hara aspires to being a classical ballerina, Ball is happy to become a successful stripper. Both are in love with Louis Hayward. Pioneering female director Dorothy Arzner, who took over at short notice after filming commenced, does her best with an inadequate script and a miscast O'Hara; she manages to bring the film to life from time to time – usually when Ball is on screen. RK

Lucille Ball *Bubbles* • Maureen O'Hara *Judy* • Louis Hayward *Jimmy Harris* • Ralph Bellamy *Steve Adams* • Virginia Field *Elinor Harris* • Maria Ouspenskaya *Madame Basilova* • Mary Carlisle *Sally* • Katherine Alexander *Miss Olmstead* • Edward Brophy *Dwarfie* ■ *Dir* Dorothy Arzner • *Scr* Tess Slesinger, Frank Davis, from a story by Vicki Baum

The Dance Goes On ★★

Drama 1990 · Can · Colour · 110mins

A drama that's something of a family affair, with its young star, Matthew James Almond, being the son of writer/director Paul Almond and his ex-wife Geneviève Bujold, who has a supporting role here. Almond Jr plays a cynical city slicker who plans to flog the family farm to fund his flashy lifestyle. This mildewed situation is taken at a snail's pace by Almond Sr and played with such agonising sincerity that you've lost patience before a voice is raised in anger. At least rural Quebec looks beautiful. DP

James Keach *James Smith* • Matthew James Almond *Rick Smith* • Cary Lawrence *Molly Mackenzie* • Geneviève Bujold *Rick's mother* ■ *Dir/Scr* Paul Almond

Dance Hall ★★

Drama 1950 · UK · BW · 80mins

Several of Ealing's biggest talents collaborated on this downbeat drama, which fully captures the sense of austerity that pervaded postwar Britain. With Alexander Mackendrick among the screenwriters, Douglas Slocombe behind the camera, Seth Holt at the editing desk and Michael Balcon producing, one can't question the film's pedigree. However, director Charles Crichton settles for too many caricatures in this story of four women who assert the independence they gained doing war work. DP

Donald Houston *Phil* • Bonar Colleano *Alec* • Petula Clark *Georgie Wilson* • Natasha Parry *Eve* • Jane Hylton *Mary* • Diana Dors *Carol* • Gladys Henson *Mrs Wilson* • Sydney Tafler *Manager* • Douglas Barr *Peter* • Kay Kendall *Doreen* • Eunice Gayson *Mona* • Dandy Nichols *Mrs Crabtree* ■ *Dir* Charles Crichton • *Scr* EVH Emmett, Diana Morgan, Alexander Mackendrick

Dance Little Lady ★★ U

Drama 1954 · UK · Colour · 87mins

Terence Morgan made something of a habit of being horrid to little Mandy Miller on screen in the mid-1950s. He was her father in *Mandy*, the moving Ealing drama about deafness, and here he is the unscrupulous stage father who is determined to see her name in lights. The dance sequences are fine, but the poor production values ruin the look of the film. DP

Terence Morgan *Mack Gordon* • Mai Zetterling *Nina Gordon* • Guy Rolfe *Dr John Ransome* • Mandy Miller *Jill Gordon* • Eunice Gayson *Adele* • Reginald Beckwith *Poldi* • Ina De La Haye *Madame Bayanova* • Harold Lang *Mr Bridson* • Richard O'Sullivan *Peter* • Jane Aird *Mary* ■ *Dir* Val Guest • *Scr* Val Guest, Doreen Montgomery, from a story by R Howard Alexander, Alfred Dunning

D

Dance Me Outside ★★★

Drama 1994 · US/Can · Colour · 84mins

Thankfully avoiding the cinematic clichés of the past about native North Americans, this movie examines their lives in a contemporary context with seriousness and wit. Ryan Rajendra Black and Adam Beach are the young men on a Canadian reservation constantly diverted from fulfilling their ambitions by booze and drugs, while the racist killer of a dance-hall girl gets off with a light sentence, angering the community. The mix of quirky humour and sententious drama doesn't always blend, but this look at a nation within a nation still has considerable power. TH. Contains violence and swearing.

Ryan Rajendra Black *Silas Crow* • Adam Beach *Frank Fencepost* • Jennifer Podemski *Sadie Maracle* • Michael Greyeyes *Gooch* • Lisa Lacroix [Lisa LaCroix] *Illiana* • Kevin Hicks *Robert McVay* • Rose Marie Trudeau *Ma Crow* • Sandrine Holt *Poppy* ■ *Dir* Bruce McDonald • *Scr* Bruce McDonald, Don McKellar, John Frizzell, from the novel by WP Kinsella

The Dance of Death ★★

Drama 1969 · UK · Colour · 148mins

One of Sir Laurence Olivier's last stage performances is captured on film in this static version of the National Theatre production of August Strindberg's classic play. Cantankerous sea captain Olivier and wife Geraldine McEwan continuously bicker on their island home and turn what's left of their marriage into a war zone. As a record of Olivier's mesmerising stagecraft, it's a must. As a film, though, it's a torpid bore, with the camera placed in one position throughout the angst-ridden action. AJ

Laurence Olivier *Edgar* • Geraldine McEwan *Alice* • Robert Lang *Kurt* • Janina Faye *Judith* • Malcolm Reynolds *Allan* • Carolyn Jones *Jenny* • Maggie Riley *Kristin* ■ *Dir* David Giles • *Scr* CD Locock, from the play by August Strindberg

Dance of Dust ★★★

Documentary drama
1991 · Iran · Colour · 73mins

With its avowal of dialogue and its almost surreal desert images, this is a hypnotic study of an unspeakably harsh lifestyle. Mahmood Khosravi works in a brick kiln, where his back-breaking routine is relieved only by the sound of whispering voices telling him of realms beyond his imagination. However, with the arrival of Limua Ravi and her mother, in search of seasonal work, his life takes on a new purpose. It's sometimes difficult to understand the precise symbolism of the various daily rituals, but this is a striking example of how rarely the commercial sector exploits cinema's visual power. DP. In Turkmen, Arabic and English with English subtitles.

Mahmood Khosravi *Ilia* • Limua Rahi *Limua* ■ *Dir/Scr* Abolfazl Jalili • *Cinematographer* Ata Hayati

Dance of the Dwarfs ★★

Horror action adventure
1983 · US/Phil · Colour · 93mins

Anthropologist Deborah Raffin hires drunken loser helicopter pilot Peter Fonda to fly her in the jungle to find a missing scientist investigating reports of a lost tribe of pygmy reptile men in a weak mix of adventure horror conventions. Ignore the unremarkable special effects and there's some acting sparks to enjoy as the mismatched couple first grate on each other's nerves and then gradually find points of mutual interest. But it's generally cut-rate fare. AJ

Deborah Raffin *Dr Evelyn Howard* • Peter Fonda *Harry Bediker* • John Amos *Esteban* ■ *Dir* Gus Trikonis • *Scr* GW King, Larry H Johnson, Michael Viner, from the novel by Geoffrey Household

Dance of the Wind ★★★ U

Drama
1997 · UK/Ger/Ind/Fr/Neth · Colour · 82mins

Celebrating the oral tradition of Indian classical music and stressing the need for ancient art to survive the passage of time, Rajan Khosa's debut feature is a simple, but affecting, delight. In a film that rings with echoes and duets. Besides showing the teeming streets of Delhi, there's a much reduced socio-political element to the story of a singer (Kitu Gidwani) who rediscovers the voice (provided by Shweta Zaveri) she lost on the death of her mother and mentor through her relationship with divine urchin Roshan Bano. DP. In Hindi with English subtitles. [video]

Kitu Gidwani *Pallavi Sehgel* • Bhaveen Gossain *Ranmal* • BC Sanyal *Munir Baba* • Roshan Bano *Tara* ■ *Dir* Rajan Khosa • *Scr* Robin Mukherjee, Rajan Khosa

Dance with a Stranger ★★★★ 15

Biographical drama
1984 · UK · Colour · 97mins

Miranda Richardson is incandescent as Soho nightclub hostess Ruth Ellis, the last woman to be hanged in Britain, in this absorbing, brutal account of the infamous 1955 murder case. Sticking closely to the facts about why she shot her aristocratic lover, racing driver David Blakely (Rupert Everett), this film from director Mike Newell has a great sense of period and strikes the exact balance between fascination and luridness. AJ. Contains violence, sex scenes, swearing, nudity. [video] DVD

Miranda Richardson *Ruth Ellis* • Rupert Everett *David Blakely* • Ian Holm *Desmond Cussen* • Matthew Carroll *Andy* • Tom Chadbon *Anthony Findlater* • Jane Bertish *Carole Findlater* • David Troughton *Cliff Davis* • Paul Mooney *Clive Gunnel* • Stratford Johns *Morrie Conley* • Joanne Whalley *Christine* • Susan Kyd *Barbara* • Lesley Manville *Maryanne* ■ *Dir* Mike Newell • *Scr* Shelagh Delaney

Dance with Me ★★ PG

Romantic drama
1998 · US · Colour · 121mins

Think *Strictly Ballroom* with a mambo beat and you'll easily figure out the entire plot of this easy on the eye dance drama from director Randa Haines. Chayanne plays a Cuban youngster who gets a job as a handyman at a Houston dance studio working for Kris Kristofferson, whom he believes to be his father. There he meets Vanessa L Williams, and it's not long before the two of them are steaming up the dance floor with their stunningly choreographed Latin numbers. Forget the clichéd plot and performances and just enjoy those salsa dance moves. JB [video]

Vanessa L Williams *Ruby* • Chayanne *Rafael* • Kris Kristofferson *John* • Joan Plowright *Bea* • Jane Krakowski *Patricia* • Beth Grant *Lovejoy* ■ *Dir* Randa Haines • *Scr* Daryl Matthews • *Choreographer* Daryl Matthews, Liz Curtis

Dance with Me Henry ★★ U

Comedy 1956 · US · BW · 80mins

This was Bud Abbott and Lou Costello's last film together, and it's obvious that their comic partnership had reached the end of its tether. Here Lou plays the owner of an amusement park who becomes involved in Bud's gambling debts. When a district attorney is murdered, Lou finds he's being pursued by the police *and* the mob. The boys strive hard to make it work, and the strain shows. TH

Lou Costello *Lou Henry* • Bud Abbott *Bud Flick* • Gigi Perreau *Shelley* ■ *Dir* Charles Barton • *Scr* Devery Freeman, from a story by William Kozlenko, Leslie Kardos

Dancehall Queen ★★ 15

Musical dance drama
1996 · Jam · Colour · 96mins

Knowing patois is a useful skill when it comes to understanding this Jamacian street film. Audrey Reid stars as a single mother, struggling to survive by selling drinks outside popular dance halls, while predatory men are after her 15-year-old daughter. Adopting a mystery persona, Reid starts wowing in the dance halls. The soundtrack is as atmospheric as walking through the Notting Hill Carnival, but the sudden shift from Reid's extremely grim life into comedy doesn't quite hang together. LH [video] DVD

Audrey Reid *Marcia* • Carl Davis *Uncle Larry* • Paul Campbell *Priest* • Pauline Stone-Myrie *Mrs Gordon* ■ *Dir* Don Letts, Rick Elgood • *Scr* Suzanne Fenn, Don Letts, Ed Wallace, from an idea by Don Letts, Ed Wallace

Dancer in the Dark ★★★ 15

Musical drama
2000 · Den/Fr · Colour · 134mins

Lars von Trier is an excellent director of shocking and innovative material, and here he combines that ability with an old-fashioned musical subplot. Pop singer Björk wavers between raw and amateurish as a Czech immigrant in 1960s small-town America. Suffering from an inherited condition of encroaching blindness, she works relentlessly to earn the money for an operation that will save her ten-year-old son from the same fate. The elfin Björk is every inch the victim, but Trier's unremittingly fatalistic narrative does not make this easy viewing. AC. Contains violence. [video] DVD

Björk *Selma Jezková* • Catherine Deneuve *Kathy* • David Morse *Bill* • Peter Stormare *Jeff* • Udo Kier *Dr Pokorny* • Joel Grey *Oldrich Novy* ■ *Dir/Scr* Lars von Trier

Dancer, Texas Pop 81 ★★★ PG

Comedy drama 1998 · US · Colour · 97mins

Since they were 11, a group of small-town Texans have vowed to explore the wider world. But when it comes to leaving, everyone has an excuse to stay. Shot in just 25 days by debutant Tim McCanlies, this rites-of-passage picture deserves to reach a much wider audience. It's funny without being trite and moving without being corny. Moreover, it's spiritedly performed by the teenage cast. DP [video]

Breckin Meyer *Keller Coleman* • Ethan Embry *Squirrel* • Peter Facinelli *Terrell Lee Lusk* • Eddie Mills *John Hemphill* • Ashley Johnson *Josie* • Patricia Wettig *Mrs Lusk* • Alexandra Holden *Vivian* • Michael O'Neil *Mr Lusk* ■ *Dir/Scr* Tim McCanlies

The Dancer Upstairs ★★★ 15

Political thriller
2002 · US/Sp · Colour · 127mins

Vivified by José Luis Alcaine's predatory camerawork, John Malkovich's directorial debut owes a sizeable debt to the brand of political thriller perfected by Costa-Gavras. Javier Bardem excels as the Latin American lawyer-turned-cop who is constantly hindered by official corruption and public indifference as he agonisingly comes to realise that ballet teacher Laura Morante is associated with the perpetrators of a series of terrorist assaults. Despite a surfeit of contrivances and the unconvincing tension between leads who are romantic soulmates but idealogical adversaries, it's an arresting blend of policier and sociological treatise. DP [video] DVD

Javier Bardem *Agustin Rejas* • Laura Morante *Yolanda* • Juan Diego Botto *Sucre* • Elvira Minguez *Llosa* • Alexandra Lencastre *Sylvina* • Oliver Cotton *General Merino* ■ *Dir* John Malkovich • *Scr* Nicholas Shakespeare, from his novel

Dancers ★★ PG

Drama 1987 · US · Colour · 94mins

The flowing blond locks of Mikhail Baryshnikov tumble over both stage and boudoir in this infamous raunchy ballet movie. Director Herbert Ross's version of a dance soap works moderately well on a light, inconsequential level, with Julie Kent making a bright debut as the latest ingénue to get Baryshnikov's tights in a twist. Despite all that, the dancing throughout is a marvellous treat. SH. Contains some swearing. [video]

Mikhail Baryshnikov *Anton (Tony)* • Alessandra Ferri *Francesca* • Leslie Browne *Nadine* • Thomas Rall [Tommy Rall] *Patrick* • Lynn Seymour *Muriel* • Victor Barbee *Wade* ■ *Dir* Herbert Ross • *Scr* Sarah Kernochan

Dances with Wolves ★★★★★ 15

Epic western 1990 · US · Colour · 172mins

Kevin Costner's directorial debut, the first western to win the best picture Oscar for 60 years, is a heartfelt attempt to create a frontier epic and to atone for Hollywood's shameful depiction of native American life. Costner himself plays the depressed, battle weary Union officer, a Civil War hero who, given the choice, opts for a remote posting in South Dakota to see the frontier before it disappears. Costner directs with a clear passion for the subject, and proves that epic westerns can still work if their heart is in the right place, the characters are real and the cinematography is stunning. DP. Some Sioux dialogue with English subtitles. Contains violence, brief nudity. [video] DVD

Kevin Costner *Lieutenant John Dunbar/ Dances with Wolves* • Mary McDonnell *Stands with a Fist* • Graham Greene (2) *Kicking Bird* • Rodney A Grant *Wind in His Hair* • Floyd Red Crow Westerman *Chief Ten Bears* • Tantoo Cardinal *Black Shawl* • Robert Pastorelli *Timmons* • Charles Rocket *Lieutenant Elgin* • Maury Chaykin *Major Fambrough* ■ *Dir* Kevin Costner • *Scr* Michael Blake, from the novel by Michael Blake • *Cinematographer* Dean Semler

Dancin' thru the Dark ★★★ 15

Comedy drama 1989 · UK · Colour · 91mins

Director Mike Ockrent takes a minor Willy Russell play and turns it into a pleasant screen diversion. On the eve of Claire Hackett and Con O'Neill's wedding, both her hen party and his stag "do" end up at the same nightclub. Cue an avalanche of Scouse home truths and tart comedy, especially when it's revealed the bride's ex-boyfriend is in the house band. Although the script lacks Russell's trademark bite and wit, Ockrent gets good performances from the lead actors. AJ [video]

Claire Hackett *Linda* • Con O'Neill *Peter* • Colin Welland *Manager* • Willy Russell

Sourface • Julia Deakin *Bernadette* • Angela Clarke *Maureen* • Sandy Hendrickse *Carol* • Louise Duprey *Frances* • Simon O'Brien *Kav* • Conrad Nelson *Dave* • Mark Womack *Eddie* • Andrew Naylor *Billy* • Peter Watts *Robbie* ■ *Dir* Mike Ockrent • *Scr* Willy Russell, from his play *Stags and Hens*

Dancing at Lughnasa ★★★ PG

Period drama 1998 · UK/Ire · Colour · 90mins

Director Pat O'Connor stumbles a little with this rather meandering adaptation of Brian Friel's acclaimed play about five unmarried sisters living in rural Ireland in the 1930s, with Meryl Streep as Kate, the eldest. Into this secluded world comes their elder brother Michael Gambon, a missionary in Africa who has been seduced by "heathen" ways, and Rhys Ifans, sister Catherine McCormack's ex-lover and the father of her child. However, O'Connor spends too much time dwelling on the beautiful Irish countryside for the pace ever to move above a slow crawl. That said, the cast all perform superbly. JB. Contains some swearing. DVD

Meryl Streep *Kate Mundy* • Michael Gambon *Father Jack Mundy* • Catherine McCormack *Christina Mundy* • Kathy Burke *Maggie Mundy* • Sophie Thompson *Rose Mundy* • Brid Brennan *Agnes Mundy* • Rhys Ifans *Gerry Evans* • Darrell Johnston *Michael Mundy* • Lorcan Cranitch *Danny Bradley* ■ *Dir* Pat O'Connor • *Scr* Frank McGuinness, from the play by Brian Friel

Dancing at the Blue Iguana ★★ 18

Drama 2000 · US/UK · Colour · 118mins

The most credible scenes in Michael Radford's film about the lives of Los Angeles strippers are those that feature the disrobing of his committed female cast. This ensemble drama, created through an improvisational workshop, has some shining performances, notably Daryl Hannah as the dizzy Angel and Jennifer Tilly's brassy Jo. However, there's nowhere near enough material for a full-length movie, and this too often veers from depressing authenticity to unconvincing caricature. JC DVD

Daryl Hannah *Becky Willow, "Angel"* • Jennifer Tilly *Ellen Taylor, "Jo"* • Sandra Oh *Cathy, "Jasmine"* • Charlotte Ayanna *Jessie* ■ *Dir* Michael Radford • *Scr* Michael Radford, David Linter, from improvisational workshops

Dancing Co-Ed ★★

Musical comedy 1939 · US · BW · 82mins

The co-ed of the title is 19-year-old Lana Turner, at the gateway to major stardom at MGM, playing a college student with show biz ambitions who triumphs in both classroom and theatre. Flimsy nonsense, but one which serves its purpose as a star vehicle for the "sweater girl". RK

Lana Turner *Patty Marlow* • Richard Carlson *Pug Braddock* • Artie Shaw • Ann Rutherford *Eve* • Lee Bowman *Freddie Tobin* • Leon Errol *Sam "Pops" Marlow* • Roscoe Karns *Joe Drews* • Monty Woolley *Prof Lange* • Thurston Hall *HW Workman* ■ *Dir* S Sylvan Simon • *Scr* Albert Mannheimer, from a story by Albert Treynor

Dancing in the Dark ★★★ U

Musical comedy 1949 · US · Colour · 89mins

Former vaudeville star George Jessel forged a later career as producer of musicals at 20th Century-Fox, of which this is an interesting example, since it's set in the Fox studio itself (glamorous, and also cheap). Debonair William Powell is most welcome as a former star, now down on his luck and working as a talent scout, who discovers pert Betsy Drake in a plot twist that will have you hollering "enough!". But the real joke for insiders is Adolphe Menjou's uncanny impersonation of Fox boss Darryl F Zanuck. A pleasing time-waster. TS

William Powell *Emery Slide* • Mark Stevens *Bill Davis* • Betsy Drake *Julie* • Adolphe Menjou *Grossman* • Randy Stuart *Rosalie* • Lloyd Corrigan *Barker* • Hope Emerson *Mrs Schlaghammer* ■ *Dir* Irving Reis • *Scr* Mary C McCall Jr, Marion Turk, Jay Dratler, from the musical *Bandwagon* by George S Kaufman, Howard Dietz, Arthur Schwartz

Dancing in the Dark ★★★ 15

Drama 1986 · Can · Colour · 98mins

The mundane existence of a middle-class housewife begins to take its toll on her sanity in this dour Canadian drama. Recalled through confessions to a psychiatrist in flashback, Martha Henry's 20-year marriage to Neil Munro seems like a life sentence, as each meal and chore is greeted with the same self-centred boorishness. Lifting mannerisms from Jack Lemmon in full midlife crisis, Munro comes across as thoughtless, but he has none of the maliciousness that drives nosey neighbour Carole Galloway to destroy their far from happy home. DP

Martha Henry *Edna* • Neil Munro *Harry* • Rosemary Dunsmore *Nurse* • Richard Monette *Doctor* • Elena Kudaba *Edna's roommate* • Brenda Bazinet *Susan* ■ *Dir* Leon Marr • *Scr* Leon Marr, from the novel by Joan Barfoot

Dancing Lady ★★★

Musical 1933 · US · BW · 92mins

This vintage MGM musical melodrama teams two of the great sex symbols of their day, Joan Crawford and Clark Gable; they were real-life lovers off screen, and it shows. The *ménage à trois* is aptly completed by suave Franchot Tone, a future Mr Joan Crawford. Fred Astaire makes his movie debut, playing himself and bringing some dignity to the ridiculously tasteless production number, *Let's Go Bavarian*. There's also an appearance by the Three Stooges, though they are nothing short of embarrassing. TS

Joan Crawford *Janie Barlow* • Clark Gable *Patch Gallagher* • Franchot Tone *Tod Newton* • Fred Astaire • Nelson Eddy • May Robson *Dolly Todhunter* • Winnie Lightner *Rosette Henrietta La Rue* • Robert Benchley *Ward King* • Ted Healy *Steve* ■ *Dir* Robert Z Leonard • *Scr* Allen Rivkin, PJ Wolfson, from the novel by James Warner Bellah

The Dancing Masters ★★ PG

Comedy 1943 · US · BW · 63mins

One of the decidedly non-vintage films that Laurel and Hardy made for 20th Century-Fox in the 1940s. Considerably below their best, they play struggling dance school patrons, whose client Trudy Marshall is in love with would-be inventor Robert Bailey. The boys stage some madcap schemes in a bid to raise money for Bailey, but the drippy lovers are given far too much screen time. Not even the presence of Margaret Dumont and Robert Mitchum in a bit part can enliven the proceedings. DP

Stan Laurel *Stan* • Oliver Hardy *Ollie* • Trudy Marshall *Mary Harlan* • Robert Bailey *Grant Lawrence* • Matt Briggs *Wentworth Harlan* • Margaret Dumont *Mrs Harlan* • Bob Mitchum [Robert Mitchum] *Mickey* ■ *Dir* Mal St Clair [Malcolm St Clair] • *Scr* W Scott Darling, from a story by George Bricker

Dancing with Crime ★★

Crime drama 1946 · UK · BW · 82mins

Real-life newly-weds Richard Attenborough and Sheila Sim co-star in this stark crime quickie, which also marks the feature debut of Dirk Bogarde as a bobby on the beat. Attenborough is a cabbie who becomes the scourge of black marketeers when he investigates the suspicious death of an army pal (Bill Owen). With Sim going undercover at the local dance hall, the film will evoke memories of Saturday nights gone by. DP

Richard Attenborough *Ted* • Sheila Sim *Joy* • Barry K Barnes *Paul* • Garry Marsh *Sergeant Murray* • John Warwick *Inspector Carter* • Judy Kelly *Toni* • Barry Jones *Gregory* • Bill Owen *Dave* • Diana Dors *Hostess* • Dirk Bogarde *Policeman* ■ *Dir* John Paddy Carstairs • *Scr* Brock Williams, Peter Fraser

The Dancing Years ★★ U

Musical drama 1949 · UK · Colour · 98mins

A love affair between young composer Dennis Price and star of the musical stage Giselle Preville falters through a misunderstanding which leads her to leave him and marry prince Anthony Nicholls. Directed by Harold French, this screen transfer of a musical by Ivor Novello is outmoded, sickly sweet and devoid of what charm the original stage show offered. The debonair Price is hardly a natural for the genre, but the film does offer plenty of Novello's melodies. RK

Dennis Price *Rudi Kleiber* • Gisèle Préville *Maria Zeitler* • Patricia Dainton *Grete* • Anthony Nicholls *Prince Reinaldt* ■ *Dir* Harold French • *Scr* Warwick Ward, Jack Whittingham, from an operetta by Ivor Novello

Dandin ★★★★

Comedy 1988 · Fr · Colour · 116mins

Based on Molière's comedy *Georges Dandin*, this rumbustious tale of greed, suspicion and debasement is a lesser-known example of the playwright's genius for exposing the complexities and absurdities of human nature. Roger Planchon keeps this cruellest of comedies racing along, drawing an excellent performance from Claude Brasseur as the peasant who suffers an endless round of humiliations after he takes a wife to improve his social standing. He is ably supported by Zabou as his spouse, and Daniel Gélin as the father-in-law who is the chief architect of his misery. DP. In French with English subtitles.

Claude Brasseur *Georges Dandin* • Zabou *Angélique* • Daniel Gélin *M de Sotenville* • Nelly Borgeaud *Mme de Sotenville* ■ *Dir* Roger Planchon • *Scr* Roger Planchon, from the play *Georges Dandin* by Molière

A Dandy in Aspic ★★

Spy drama 1968 · UK · Colour · 100mins

The spy cycle of the 1960s produced a handful of serious espionage dramas, one of which is this unsuccessful, two-dimensional adaptation of Derek Marlowe's complex novel. Laurence Harvey is dull as the double agent assigned by British Intelligence to kill himself. Bodies pile up so fast, it becomes almost impossible to know who is doing what to whom. It cannot have helped that director Anthony Mann died during production; the film was completed by Harvey. DM

Laurence Harvey *Alexander Eberlin* • Tom Courtenay *Gatiss* • Mia Farrow *Caroline* • Lionel Stander *Sobakevich* • Harry Andrews *Intelligence Chief Fraser* • Peter Cook *Prentiss* • Per Oscarsson *Pavel* • Barbara Murray *Heather Vogler* • Richard O'Sullivan *Nevil* ■ *Dir* Anthony Mann, Laurence Harvey • *Scr* Derek Marlowe, from his novel

Danger beneath the Sea ★★ 12

Action adventure 2001 · US · Colour · 88mins

This macho submarine story wheels out tried-and-trusted elements – rookie captain, resentful second in command, communications breakdown, potential mutiny and in the end... Well, you'll have to watch this to see whether director Jon Cassar has the courage to break with tradition. But he does keep the tension surprisingly high considering the plot is a rust bucket (though the enemy is, somewhat unusually, North Korea) and the cast is decidedly third division. DP DVD

Casper Van Dien *Commander Sheffield* • Gerald McRaney *Admiral Justice* • Stewart Bick *Lt Commander Albert Kenner* • Tammy Isbell *Lt Clare Holliday* • Ron White *CPO Pete Le Croix* ■ *Dir* Jon Cassar

Danger by My Side ★

Crime thriller 1962 · UK · BW · 63mins

The road to justice leads to a Soho nightclub in this tawdry British B-movie. The hit-and-run murder, the sleazy club scenes, the heist and the motor-launch finale are all executed with the minimum of imagination as Maureen Connell puts her personal safety on the line while helping the police catch her detective-brother's killers. Charles Saunders's poor pacing leaves the cast high and dry. DP

Anthony Oliver *Inspector Willoughby* • Maureen Connell *Lynne* • Alan Tilvern *Venning* • Bill Nagy *Sam Warren* • Sonya Cordeau *Francine Dumont* ■ *Dir* Charles Saunders • *Scr* Ronald C Liles, Aubrey Cash

Danger: Diabolik ★★★

Crime comedy 1967 · It/Fr · Colour · 98mins

Based on a cult comic strip, this mix of fantasy and madcap criminality is directed with mischievous glee by horror specialist Mario Bava. Utilising stylised sets and encouraging his multi-national cast to camp it, Bava arrives at a *Barbarella*-style romp, a comparison that is reinforced by the presence of John Phillip Law as the master criminal who curries favour with the populace by destroying Italy's tax records. The press conference given by pompous minister Terry-Thomas, under the influence of laughing gas, is riotously funny. DP

John Phillip Law *Diabolik* • Marisa Mell *Eva Kant* • Michel Piccoli *Inspector Ginko* • Adolfo Celi *Ralph Valmont* • Terry-Thomas *Minister of Finance* ■ *Dir* Mario Bava • *Scr* Mario Bava, Dino Maiuri, Brian Degas, Tudor Gates, from a story by Angela Giussani, Luciana Giussani, Dino Maiuri, Adriano Baracco

Danger Lights ★★

Comedy drama 1930 · US · BW · 87mins

Beefy Louis Wolheim and dapper Robert Armstrong lock in conflict over Jean Arthur, against a background of problems in running a railway. A melange of romance, melodrama and macho tension, this mediocre movie is of interest in that it saw the short-lived launch (by RKO) of a new "wide stereoscopic" process. The technique, and Karl Struss's cinematography, does add a dimension of depth to the proceedings, but the huge costs involved made this the first and last time the experiment was attempted. RK

Louis Wolheim *Dan Thorn* • Robert Armstrong *Larry Doyle* • Jean Arthur *Mary Ryan* • Hugh Herbert *Professor* • Frank Sheridan *Ed Ryan* ■ *Dir* George B Seitz • *Scr* James Ashmore Creelman, Hugh Herbert

Danger – Love at Work ★★★

Comedy 1937 · US · BW · 81mins

The Viennese-born Otto Preminger had only directed one film in Germany when he was given a contract at 20th Century-Fox. This enjoyable screwball comedy was the second picture he made for the studio. The inconsequential plot involves Jack Haley as a lawyer sent to a small town to buy up a piece of property owned by an eccentric family. But it is the cast that makes the movie: Mary Boland at her most scatterbrained, pert Ann Sothern, fussy Edward Everett Horton and demented John Carradine. RB

Ann Sothern *Toni Pemberton* • Jack Haley *Henry MacMorrow* • Mary Boland *Mrs Alice Pemberton* • Edward Everett Horton *Howard Rogers* • John Carradine *Herbert Pemberton* • Walter Catlett *Uncle Alan* ■ *Dir* Otto Preminger • *Scr* James Edward Grant, Ben Markson, from a story by James Edward Grant

Danger Patrol ★★ U

Adventure 1937 · US · BW · 59mins

This RKO second feature looks at the foolhardy men who transport dangerous nitroglycerin to oil fields to quench fires. Because of the pedestrian direction by the prolific journeyman Lew Landers, the potentially explosive material fails to catch alight. However, it's good to see veteran character actor Harry Carey in a leading role. He is a driver who is opposed to his daughter (pretty Sally Eilers) marrying a man in the same dangerous profession. RB

Sally Eilers *Cathie Street* • John Beal *Dan Loring* • Harry Carey *Sam "Easy" Street* • Frank M Thomas *Rocky Sanders* • Edward Gargan *Gabby Donovan* ■ *Dir* Lew Landers • *Scr* Sy Bartlett, from a story by Helen Vreeland, Hilda Vincent

Danger Route ★

Spy thriller 1967 · UK · Colour · 92mins

This is a sloppily constructed spy thriller that aims for the gloss, levity and excitement of a Bond movie and misses by a mile. Director Seth Holt goes off on so many tangents that the central plot – about agent Richard Johnson's mission to kill a Soviet scientist before he can pass secrets to the Americans – is completely obscured. Dismal. DP

Richard Johnson *Jonas Wilde* • Carol Lynley *Jocelyn* • Barbara Bouchet *Mari* • Sylvia Syms *Barbara Canning* • Gordon Jackson *Stern* • Harry Andrews *Canning* • Diana Dors *Rhoda Gooderich* • Maurice Denham *Peter Ravenspur* • Sam Wanamaker *Lucinda* ■ *Dir* Seth Holt • *Scr* Meade Roberts, from the novel *The Eliminator* by Andrew York

Danger Within ★★★ U

Second World War drama
1958 · UK · BW · 96mins

Anyone who has seen Billy Wilder's PoW-camp classic *Stalag 17* will find this workmanlike British imitation somewhat predictable. The story has a whodunnit element that is cleverly and wittily plotted, but prisoners and guards alike are cardboard cutouts and it takes some competent character acting to make them even half credible. Richard Attenborough and Bernard Lee come off best, while Richard Todd trots out all his gruff officer mannerisms. Director Don Chaffey sustains the suspense with unfussy ease. DP

Richard Todd *Lt Col David Baird* • Bernard Lee *Lt Col Huxley* • Michael Wilding *Maj Charles Marquand* • Richard Attenborough *Capt Bunter Phillips* • Dennis Price *Capt Rupert Callender* • Donald Houston *Capt Roger Byford* • Michael Caine ■ *Dir* Don Chaffey • *Scr* Bryan Forbes, Frank Harvey, from the novel by Michael Gilbert

Danger Zone ★★ 18

Action adventure 1996 · US · Colour · 88mins

In this fairly routine straight-to-video adventure, Billy Zane plays a mine inspector in a small African state who is duped into carrying the can for a catastrophic spillage of lethal toxic waste supplied by CIA agent and former buddy Robert Downey Jr. Or is the plot thicker than it seems? The two leads are charismatic and the action rattles along nicely, but the ecological message begins to grate and the supporting cast struggles to make an impression. JF. Contains violence. DVD

Billy Zane *Rick Morgan* • Robert Downey Jr *Jim Scott* • Ron Silver *Dupont* • Cary-Hiroyuki Tagawa *Chang* • Lisa Collins *Dr Kim Woods* ■ *Dir* Allan Eastman • *Scr* Jeff Albert

Dangerous ★★★★ PG

Melodrama 1935 · US · BW · 75mins

Bette Davis won her first Oscar (the second was for *Jezebel*) for this fine melodrama about an alcoholic star, although at the time it was felt that the Academy Award was a compensatory one for Davis not winning the previous year as the spiteful Mildred in *Of Human Bondage*. Seen today, Davis's performance here is truly magnificent and splendidly overblown, with all those mannerisms well under control as Warner Bros veteran director Alfred E Green hands the movie to her on a platter. TS

Bette Davis *Joyce Heath* • Franchot Tone *Don Bellows* • Margaret Lindsay *Gail Armitage* • Alison Skipworth *Mrs Williams* • John Eldredge *Gordon Heath* • Dick Foran *Teddy* • Pierre Watkin *George Sheffield* ■ *Dir* Alfred E Green • *Scr* Laird Doyle

Dangerous Afternoon ★★ U

Crime drama 1961 · UK · BW · 61mins

Former editor Charles Saunders turned out a series of unexceptional movies after taking to directing, including this negligible crime drama. The story – about an escaped convict whose refuge for former women prisoners is threatened by a blackmailer – began life on stage, and Saunders does little to open out the long-forgotten play. Neither Howard Pays nor Ruth Dunning look comfortable before the camera and it's theatre stalwart Nora Nicholson who stands out. DP

Ruth Dunning *Miss Frost* • Nora Nicholson *Mrs Sprule* • Joanna Dunham *Freda* • Howard Pays *Jack Loring* • May Hallatt *Miss Burge* ■ *Dir* Charles Saunders • *Scr* Brandon Fleming, from a play by Gerald Anstruther

Dangerous Beauty ★★★ 15

Period romance 1997 · US · Colour · 111mins

Catherine McCormack co-stars with the glamorous city of Venice in this picturesque feminist fable, based on the biography of real-life 16th-century courtesan and poet Veronica Franco. McCormack lusts after impoverished aristocrat Rufus Sewell and an education, but is denied both by the prejudices of the time. Director Marshall Herskovitz splashes out on atmosphere and McCormack delivers her witty lines with aplomb, but the climax is too melodramatic to be credible. Also known as *The Honest Courtesan*. TH. Contains violence, swearing, sex scenes, nudity.

Catherine McCormack *Veronica Franco* • Rufus Sewell *Marco Venier* • Oliver Platt *Maffio Venier* • Moira Kelly *Beatrice Venier* • Fred Ward *Domenico Venier* • Jacqueline Bisset *Paola Franco* ■ *Dir* Marshall Herskovitz • *Scr* Jeannine Dominy, from the biography by Margaret Rosenthal

Dangerous Corner ★★

Mystery melodrama 1934 · US · BW · 66mins

The only reason for sticking with this – and it's a long wait – is the double ending retained from JB Priestley's play. Starring Virginia Bruce, Conrad Nagel and Melvyn Douglas, this abridged screen version makes heavy weather of an after-dinner discussion between a publisher and friends about the apparent suicide of one of their group and the disappearance of valuable bonds. Director Phil Rosen's handling of the drama is dreary. AE

Melvyn Douglas *Charles* • Conrad Nagel *Robert* • Virginia Bruce *Olwen* • Erin O'Brien-Moore *Freda* • Ian Keith *Martin* • Betty Furness *Betty* ■ *Dir* Phil Rosen • *Scr* Anne Morrison Chapin, Madeleine Ruthven, from the play by JB Priestley

Dangerous Exile ★★★ PG

Swashbuckling adventure
1957 · UK · Colour · 87mins

Stylishly shot by Geoffrey Unsworth and featuring a rousing score by Georges Auric, this historical adventure makes up for its cumbersome plot with some slick swashbuckling and an unrelenting pace. Louis Jourdan is the aristocrat who smuggles the son of Louis XVI across the channel to prevent the rabid revolutionaries from getting their egalitarian mitts on him. This kind of romp wasn't really Irish director Brian Desmond Hurst's strong suit, but he keeps the action rattling along. DP

Louis Jourdan *Duc de Beauvais* • Belinda Lee *Virginia Traill* • Keith Michell *Colonel St Gerard* • Richard O'Sullivan *Louis* • Martita Hunt *Aunt Fell* • Finlay Currie *Mr Patient* • Anne Heywood *Glynis* ■ *Dir* Brian Desmond Hurst • *Scr* Robin Estridge, Patrick Kirwan, from the novel *A King Reluctant* by Vaughan Wilkins

Dangerous Female ★★★★

Crime drama 1931 · US · BW · 80mins

This is the first film version of *The Maltese Falcon*, retitled for release in Britain and subsequent TV screenings to avoid confusion with John Huston's 1941 Humphrey Bogart classic. There's another version as well, called *Satan Met a Lady*, released in 1936, in which the legendary falcon became a ram's horn. This early Warner Bros melodrama is faithful to the great Dashiell Hammett novel, and Ricardo Cortez is a much more womanising Sam Spade than Bogie. TS

Bebe Daniels *Ruth Wonderly* • Ricardo Cortez *Sam Spade* • Dudley Digges *Kaspar Gutman* • Una Merkel *Effie Perine* • Robert Elliott *Detective Dundy* • J Farrell MacDonald *Polhouse* ■ *Dir* Roy Del Ruth • *Scr* Maude Fulton, Lucien Hubbard, Brown Holmes, Dashiell Hammett, from the novel *The Maltese Falcon* by Dashiell Hammett

Dangerous Game ★ 18

Drama 1993 · US · Colour · 104mins

Abel Ferrara aims to give us an unadorned insight into the film-making process and show how on-set tensions can often result in great art. Instead, he came up with a pretentious folly, in which an over-indulged cast bandy expletives and gorge themselves in an orgy of grandiloquence and gesturing. A best-forgotten aberration. DP. Contains violence, swearing, sex scenes, drug abuse and nudity.

Madonna *Sarah Jennings* • Harvey Keitel *Eddie Israel* • James Russo *Francis Burns* • Nancy Ferrara *Madlyn Israel* • Reilly Murphy *Tommy* • Victor Argo *Director of photography* • Leonard Thomas *Prop guy* • Christina Fulton *Blonde* ■ *Dir* Abel Ferrara • *Scr* Abel Ferrara, Nicholas St John

Dangerous Ground ★★ 18

Crime thriller
1996 · S Afr/US · Colour and BW · 91mins

This is a well-meaning but botched study of crime in post-apartheid Johannesburg. Sex, drugs and corruption in the new South Africa is an interesting concept, but the potentially fascinating political undercurrents aren't explored. Darrell James Roodt's film suffers from unconvincing characters, over-ripe dialogue and ineffectual stabs at social comment. JC. Contains violence, swearing, drug abuse and nudity.

Ice Cube *Vusi* • Elizabeth Hurley *Karin* • Sechaba Morojele *Ernest* • Ving Rhames *Muki* • Thokozani Nkosi *Young Vusi* • Ron Smerczac [Ron Smerczak] *Interrogation policeman* ■ *Dir* Darrell James Roodt • *Scr* Greg Latter, Darrell James Roodt

Dangerous Intentions ★★ 15

Drama based on a true story
1995 · US · Colour · 92mins

Queen of the true-life TV movie, Donna Mills plays the battered wife of nasty Corbin Bernsen, who eventually summons up the courage to leave him, only to discover that he has no intention of allowing her to break up the family. A routine, undistinguished outing. JF. Contains violence, swearing. DVD

Donna Mills *Beth Williamson* • Corbin Bernsen *Tim Williamson* • Robin Givens *Kaye* • Allison Hossack *Terri* • Sheila Larken *Nancy Boyle* • Ken Pogue *Andrew Madden* • Anna Ferguson *Alice Madden* ■ *Dir* Michael Toshiyuki Uno • *Scr* David J Hill

Dangerous Liaisons ★★★★ 15

Period drama 1988 · US · Colour · 114mins

Stephen Frears's richly textured production of the scandalous 18th-century "sex as power play" novel is a handsome homage to the idea that women lose out in a man's world even where they at first appear to be in control. The extraordinary performances of Glenn Close, as the vindictive Marquise de Merteuil, and Michelle Pfeiffer, as the pure wife despoiled by the slimy Valmont (John Malkovich) on a wager, help make this chilling depiction of an era's corruption totally believable. Malkovich, though, seems ill-cast, with none of the necessary seduction in his portrayal. That aside, this remains a treat for eye and mind. TH. Contains sex scenes, nudity. DVD

Glenn Close *Marquise de Merteuil* • John Malkovich *Vicomte de Valmont* • Michelle Pfeiffer *Madame de Tourvel* • Swoosie Kurtz *Madame de Volanges* • Keanu Reeves *Chevalier Dancény* • Mildred Natwick *Madame de Rosemonde* • Uma Thurman *Cécile de Volanges* • Peter Capaldi *Azolan* • Joe Sheridan *Georges* ■ *Dir* Stephen Frears • *Scr* Christopher Hampton, from his play *Les Liaisons Dangereuses*, from the novel by Choderlos de Laclos • *Production Designer* Stuart Craig • *Set Designer* Gerard James • *Costume Designer* James Acheson

The Dangerous Lives of Altar Boys ★★ 15

Part-animated drama
2001 · US · Colour · 100mins

Director Peter Care, making his feature debut, reveals his rock video roots at every turn in this sketchy rites-of-passage tale that mixes live action and comic book-style animation. It follows four 1970s Catholic schoolboys (including Kieran Culkin and Emile Hirsch) as they rebel against their lives and the strict educational regime of nun Sister Assumpta (co-producer Jodie Foster). The film tries hard to be edgy, but the story is too fragmented to support such jarring techniques and the characters are underdeveloped. SF. Contains swearing, sexual references, drug abuse. DVD

Kieran Culkin *Tim Sullivan* • Jena Malone *Margie Flynn* • Emile Hirsch *Francis Doyle* • Vincent D'Onofrio *Father Casey* • Jodie Foster *Sister Assumpta* • Jake Richardson *Wade* • Tyler Long *Joey* ■ *Dir* Peter Care

Dangerous Minds ★★★ 15

Drama based on a true story
1995 · US · Colour · 94mins

With an entire romantic subplot involving Andy Garcia ending up on the cutting-room floor, this schoolroom drama may have gained a singularity of purpose, but it definitely lost a much-needed release from the intensity of the classroom crusade. Although not a convincing ex-Marine, Michelle Pfeiffer turns in a solid performance as she tries to give her deprived students some sort of chance in life.

Screenwriter Ronald Bass pushes his luck linking Bob Dylan and Dylan Thomas, and the results-by-reward policy will have many teachers up in arms. DP. Contains swearing and some violence. DVD

Michelle Pfeiffer *LouAnne Johnson* • George Dzundza *Hal Griffith* • Courtney B Vance *Mr George Grandey* • Robin Bartlett *Ms Carla Nichols* • Bruklin Harris *Callie Roberts* • Renoly Santiago *Raul Sanchero* ■ *Dir* John N Smith • *Scr* Ronald Bass, Elaine May (uncredited), from the book *My Posse Don't Do Homework* by LouAnne Johnson

Dangerous Mission ★ U

Crime thriller 1954 · US · Colour · 74mins

Originally filmed in 3-D, this is widely acknowledged as one of the worst films made during the great stereoscopic experiment of the early 1950s. Victor Mature gives one of his most convincing impressions of a cardboard cut-out as a New York lawman who treks into Montana's Glacier National Park to prevent hoodlum Vincent Price from rubbing out Piper Laurie, the runaway witness to a gangland shooting. Directed by Louis King with little sense of adventure. DP

Victor Mature *Matt Hallett* • Piper Laurie *Louise Graham* • William Bendix *Joe Parker* • Vincent Price *Paul Adams* • Betta St John *Mary Tiller* ■ *Dir* Louis King • *Scr* Horace McCoy, WR Burnett, Charles Bennett, from a story by Horace McCoy, James Edmiston

Dangerous Money ★

Mystery 1946 · US · BW · 65mins

Sidney Toler rings up his 21st and penultimate appearance as Earl Derr Biggers's Oriental sleuth Charlie Chan. The slim plot has the duo trying to figure out who bumped off a government agent. Terry Morse was no great shakes as a director, but with its caricatured suspects and stock whodunnit situations, the script would have defeated even Hitchcock. DP

Sidney Toler *Charlie Chan* • Gloria Warren *Rona Simmonds* • Victor Sen Yung *Jimmy Chan* • Rick Vallin *Tao Erickson* • Joseph Crehan *Capt Black* • Willie Best *Chattanooga* ■ *Dir* Terry Morse • *Scr* Miriam Kissinger, from characters created by Earl Derr Biggers

Dangerous Moonlight ★★★ U

Second World War drama 1941 · UK/US · BW · 97mins

This is the wartime movie remembered for its Richard Addinsell score, which introduced to the world the massively popular (and ultra-corny) *Warsaw Concerto*, as irredeemably romantic pianist Anton Walbrook never stops playing it. The impossibly lovely Sally Gray is the American journalist Walbrook marries and who helps the musician recover his memory after a brush with a German bomber. However, it's awfully dull and not particularly well directed, but it's such potent tosh, why quibble? TS

Anton Walbrook *Stefan Radetzky* • Sally Gray *Carole Peters* • Derrick de Marney *Mike Carroll* • Percy Parsons *Bill Peters* • Keneth Kent *De Guise* ■ *Dir* Brian Desmond Hurst • *Scr* Shaun Terence Young, Brian Desmond Hurst, Rodney Ackland, from a story by Shaun Terence Young

Dangerous Moves ★★★ PG

Drama 1984 · Swi · Colour · 100mins

Richard Dembo's directorial debut may have landed the best foreign film Oscar, but it scarcely ranks among the worthiest winners of the award. Somewhat labouring the strategic comparisons, he uses the World Chess Championship in Geneva as a metaphor for the Cold War. Ailing Soviet Grand Master Michel Piccoli (in imperious form) enjoins battle with Alexandre Arbatt, a Russian who defected to the west. While there's a sly wit underlying the suspense, what stands out is the way ruthless cunning impinges on the cerebral jousting. DP. In French with English subtitles.

Michel Piccoli *Akiva Liebskind* • Alexandre Arbatt *Pavius Fromm* • Leslie Caron *Henia* • Liv Ullmann *Marina* • Daniel Olbrychski *Tac-Tac* • Michel Aumont *Kerossian* ■ *Dir/Scr* Richard Dembo

A Dangerous Pledge ★★★

Silent drama 1920 · Swe · BW · 78mins

A scarcity of prints has caused Victor Sjöström's reputation as a director to be dimmed. But, as anyone familiar with Ingmar Bergman's *Wild Strawberries* will know, he has a formidable screen presence. So the restoration of this droll melodrama presents an overdue opportunity to study him in action on both sides of the camera. As the miserly pawnbroker presented with a waif as a loan bond, Sjöström achieves a curmudgeonly compassion that is enlivened by the occasional twinkle in the eye. It's not the masterpiece some have claimed, if only because of the acting imbalance. But it's certainly impressive. DP

Victor Sjöström *Master Sammel Eneman* • Concordia Selander *Mother Boman* • Greta Almroth *Tora, her daughter* • Harald Schwenzen *Knut, sailor* ■ *Dir* Victor Sjöström • *Scr* Hjalmar Bergman

A Dangerous Profession ★★

Crime drama 1949 · US · BW · 79mins

A fast-moving, comfortably familiar and thoroughly forgettable crime programme-filler, in which ex-cop George Raft, now a partner in a bail bond company with Pat O'Brien, decides to investigate the mysterious death of a suspect (Bill Williams) he has bailed out. Could his interest in the dead man's pretty widow (Ella Raines) have anything to do with his determination to solve the crime? RK

George Raft *Kane* • Pat O'Brien *Farley* • Ella Raines *Lucy* • Bill Williams *Brackett* • Jim Backus *Ferrone* • Roland Winters *McKay* • Betty Underwood *Elaine* ■ *Dir* Ted Tetzlaff • *Scr* Martin Rackin, Warren Duff

A Dangerous Summer ★★★ 15

Thriller 1981 · Aus · Colour · 85mins

Tom Skerritt, James Mason and Wendy Hughes star in this little-seen Australian adventure, directed by Quentin Masters (*The Stud*). American businessman Skerritt discovers that his high hopes for a mountain resort could go up in smoke. Exciting bush fire sequences help to leaven the somewhat stolid plot. RT

Tom Skerritt *Howard Anderson* • Ian Gilmour *Steve Adams* • James Mason *George Engels* • Wendy Hughes *Sophie McCann* ■ *Dir* Quentin Masters • *Scr* Quentin Masters, David Ambrose

Dangerous When Wet ★★★ U

Musical comedy 1953 · US · Colour · 95mins

An utterly meaningless (but smart) title for one of Esther Williams's most amiable musical comedies, in which she and her whole health-nut family are persuaded to swim the English Channel. There's a super live/animated sequence featuring Tom and Jerry, and a marvellous moment when the film stops for a number by Barbara Whiting, playing Esther's peppy younger sister. Williams married her leading man in this movie in reality, and became Mrs Fernando Lamas. TS

Esther Williams *Katy* • Fernando Lamas *André Lanet* • Jack Carson *Windy Webbe* • Charlotte Greenwood *Ma Higgins* • Denise Darcel *Gigi Mignon* • William Demarest *Pa Higgins* • Donna Corcoran *Junior Higgins* • Barbara Whiting *Suzie Higgins* ■ *Dir* Charles Walters • *Scr* Dorothy Kingsley

A Dangerous Woman ★★★ 18

Thriller 1993 · US · Colour · 97mins

Directed with sensitivity by Stephen Gyllenhaal, and given greater depth than the Hollywood norm by his writer-wife, Naomi Foner, this is a slow-burning drama with a surprisingly subtle starring performance from Debra Winger as an emotionally disturbed woman trying to come to terms with life in small-town America. A chain of events involving her aunt Barbara Hershey, failed writer Gabriel Byrne and sleazy local petty criminal David Strathairn pushes the childlike Winger to the psychotic edge in a slightly mannered, yet affecting tale. AJ

Debra Winger *Martha Horgan* • Barbara Hershey *Frances Beecham* • Gabriel Byrne *Colin Mackey* • Chloe Webb *Birdie* • David Strathairn *Getso* • John Terry *Steve Bell* • Laurie Metcalf *Anita Bell* • Maggie Gyllenhaal *Patsy* • Jacob Gyllenhaal [Jake Gyllenhaal] *Edward* ■ *Dir* Stephen Gyllenhaal • *Scr* Naomi Foner, from a novel by Mary McGarry Morris

Dangerous Years ★★★

Crime 1947 · US · BW · 62mins

Marilyn Monroe has an early role in this interesting little movie that broached the subject of teenage delinquency, a growing problem in the postwar years. Former "Dead End Kid" William (Billy) Halop is a disoriented youth, raised in an orphanage, who turns to crime and is ultimately tried for murder. Ann E Todd, an accomplished and popular child actress of the time, added the "E" to her name to avoid confusion with British star Ann Todd. TV

Billy Halop *Danny Jones* • Ann E Todd *Doris Martin* • Jerome Cowan *Weston* • Anabel Shaw *Connie Burns* • Richard Gaines *Edgar Burns* • Marilyn Monroe *Evie* ■ *Dir* Arthur Pierson • *Scr* Arnold Belgard

Dangerously Close ★★ 18

Crime thriller 1986 · US · Colour · 90mins

What begins as an intriguing suspense movie, about student vigilantes who take their self-appointed enforcement policies too far, degenerates into a sloppy thriller once the bodies of low-income pupils start piling up. John Stockwell, who also co-wrote the poorly conceived script, stars as the leader of "The Sentinels", a bunch of neo-Nazi bully boys who patrol their affluent high school rooting out "undesirables". The young cast is improbably good-looking, while Albert Pyun directs with consummate anonymity. RS

John Stockwell *Randy McDevitt* • J Eddie Peck *Donny Lennox* • Carey Lowell *Julie* • Bradford Bancroft *Krooger Raines* • Don Michael Paul *Ripper* • Thom Mathews *Brian Rigletti* • Jerry Dinome *Lang Bridges* • Madison Mason *Corrigan* • Dedee Pfeiffer *Nikki* ■ *Dir* Albert Pyun • *Scr* Scott Fields, John Stockwell, Marty Ross, from a story by Marty Ross

Dangerously They Live ★★★

Second World War spy drama 1942 · US · BW · 76mins

A Warner Bros wartime melodrama mixing spies and medicine, starring the great John Garfield (*The Postman Always Rings Twice*), miscast as a doctor caught up with a kidnapped Allied secret agent, fetchingly played by Nancy Coleman. Tosh, of course, and Garfield is wasted in a routine role, but it helped wake up American audiences to the fact that there was a war on. Writer Marion Parsonnet is better known for *Gilda*, which also features similar Nazi stuff. TS

John Garfield *Dr Michael Lewis* • Nancy Coleman *Jane* • Raymond Massey *Dr Ingersoll* • Moroni Olsen *Mr Goodwin* • Esther Dale *Dawson* • Lee Patrick *Nurse Johnson* • John Ridgely *John* ■ *Dir* Robert Florey • *Scr* Marion Parsonnet, from his story

Daniel ★★ 15

Drama 1983 · US · Colour · 129mins

EL Doctorow's adaptation of his own novel about the famous Rosenberg spying case becomes a worthy, talkie drama that might just have caught fire had it had a stronger cast. Timothy Hutton plays a student who investigates the events that led to the execution of both his parents in the 1950s. Both were convicted of selling atomic secrets to the Russians and, as Hutton's work proceeds, flashbacks take us through a 20-year period of war, Cold War and general paranoia. Often vague and muddled, it's filled with psychobabble. AT

Timothy Hutton *Daniel Isaacson* • Mandy Patinkin *Paul Isaacson* • Lindsay Crouse *Rochelle* • Edward Asner *Jacob Ascher* • Ellen Barkin *Phyllis Isaacson* • Julie Bovasso *Frieda Stein* • Tovah Feldshuh *Linda Mindish* • Joseph Leon *Selig Mindish* • Amanda Plummer *Susan Isaacson* ■ *Dir* Sidney Lumet • *Scr* El Doctorow, from his novel *The Book of Daniel*

Daniel and the Devil ★★

Fantasy drama 1941 · US · BW · 107mins

Variously known as *All That Money Can Buy* and *The Devil and Daniel Webster*, this features a fine musical score that rightly won an Academy Award for composer Bernard Herrmann. Would that the rest of the movie were as good. New England farmer James Craig (wholly inadequate and utterly charmless) sells his soul to scene-stealing, wicked Walter Huston's Mr Scratch. Lawyer Daniel Webster, portrayed by Edward Arnold, is hijacked into the story to plead Craig's case. This is a rigidly humourless and prosaic telling of an old, old story. It has many admirers, but it hasn't really worn very well. TS

Edward Arnold *Daniel Webster* • Walter Huston *Mr Scratch* • James Craig *Jabez Stone* • Jane Darwell *Ma Stone* • Simone Simon *Belle* • Gene Lockhart *Squire Slossum* • John Qualen *Miser Stevens* ■ *Dir* William Dieterle • *Scr* Dan Totheroh, from the story *The Devil and Daniel Webster* by Stephen Vincent Benet

Daniel Boone, Trail Blazer ★★ PG

Adventure 1957 · US · Colour · 72mins

This lively film has its own little place in movie history as the final picture shot in Hollywood using two-colour stock (modern films are three-colour). Bruce Bennett, who made his name as Tarzan in the mid-1930s, stars as the legendary frontiersman guiding a wagon train from North Carolina to Kentucky. Lon Chaney Jr is on form as his sidekick, but the performances merit a better script. DP

Bruce Bennett *Daniel Boone* • Lon Chaney Jr *Blackfish* • Faron Young *Faron Callaway* • Kem Dibbs *Girty* • Damian O'Flynn *Andy Callaway* • Jacqueline Evans *Rebecca Boone* • Nancy Rodman *Susannah Boone* • Freddy Fernandez *Israel Boone* • Carol Kelly *Jemima Boone* ■ *Dir* Albert C Gannaway, Ismael Rodriguez • *Scr* Tom Hubbard, John Patrick

Daniel Defoe's Robinson Crusoe ★★ 12

Adventure drama 1996 · US · Colour · 86mins

Pierce Brosnan makes an unconvincing job of playing Daniel Defoe's famous castaway in this dismally dumbed-down screen bowdlerisation. Ian Hart cameos as the novelist to set up the tale of shipwreck and survival, but the events that unfold in this dramatisation often bear little resemblance to those in the novel. Much time is spent dwelling on Brosnan's relationships with Lysette Anthony and Polly Walker, while William Takalu's Friday is almost completely a figment of the screenwriters' imaginations. DP

Pierce Brosnan *Robinson Crusoe* • William Takaku *Patek* • Polly Walker *Mary* • Ian Hart *Daniel Defoe* • James Frain *Robert* • Damian Lewis *Patrick* ■ *Dir* Rod Hardy, George Miller (1) • *Scr* Christopher Lofren, Tracy Keenan Wynn, Christopher Canaan, David Stevens, from the novel *The Life and Strange Surprising Adventures of Robinson Crusoe* by Daniel Defoe

D

Danielle Steel's Changes ★★ PG

Romantic drama 1991 · US · Colour · 91mins

Michael Nouri stars in this fluffy TV movie as a widowed surgeon who starts a new life with Cheryl Ladd's TV news reporter. There are all the twists, turns and heartbreaks you'd expect from a Danielle Steel adaptation. JB DVD

Cheryl Ladd *Melanie Adams* • Michael Nouri *Peter Hallam* • Christie Clark *Valerie Adams* • Renee O'Connor *Jessica Adams* • Christopher Gartin *Mark Hallam* • Ami Foster *Pam Hallam* • Joseph Gordon-Levitt *Matthew Hallam* ■ *Dir* Charles Jarrott • *Scr* Susan Nanus, from the novel by Danielle Steel

Danielle Steel's Daddy ★★ PG

Romantic drama 1991 · US · Colour · 91mins

One of the more enjoyable (and less schmaltzy) adaptations of a Danielle Steel romantic novel, with *Dallas* star Patrick Duffy trying to cope after his wife, Kate Mulgrew (of *Star Trek: Voyager* fame), leaves him and their children. Look out for Ben Affleck in an early role. JB DVD

Patrick Duffy *Oliver Watson* • Lynda Carter *Charlotte Sampson* • Kate Mulgrew *Sarah Watson* • John Anderson *George Watson* • Ben Affleck *Benjamin Watson* • Jenny Lewis *Melissa Watson* • Matthew Lawrence *Sam Watson* ■ *Dir* Michael Miller (2) • *Scr* L Virginia Browne, from the novel by Danielle Steel

Danielle Steel's Fine Things ★ PG

Melodrama 1990 · US · Colour · 137mins

This overblown TV melodrama details the traumas of a recently widowed man who has to fight for custody of his stepdaughter. Oscar-winner Cloris Leachman shines like a beacon, while her fellow cast members give performances that make American daytime soaps look like *cinéma vérité*. JB. Contains swearing. DVD

DW Moffett *Bernie Fine* • Tracy Pollan *Liz O'Reilly* • Judith Hoag *Molly Jones* • Cloris Leachman *Ruth Fine* • Noley Thornton *Jane O'Reilly* ■ *Dir* Tom Moore • *Scr* Peter Lefcourt, from the novel by Danielle Steel

Danielle Steel's Full Circle ★★ 12

Melodrama 1996 · US · Colour · 87mins

Teri Polo plays a career woman who falls for the wealthy father (Corbin Bernsen) of her best friend, much to the dismay of her mother. Bernsen sensibly plays this with a light touch, but the melodramatic twists and turns of the story may be too much even for hardened lovers of kitsch. JF DVD

Teri Polo *Tana Roberts* • Corbin Bernsen *Harrison Winslow* • Eric Lutes *Drew Lands* • Reed Diamond *Harry Winslow* • Erika Slezak *Jean Roberts* • Allison Smith *Averill Merritt* • Nicolas Coster *Arthur Durning* ■ *Dir* Bethany Rooney • *Scr* Karol Ann Hoeffner, from the novel by Danielle Steel

Danielle Steel's Heartbeat ★★ PG

Romantic drama 1992 · US · Colour · 88mins

What do heavily moistened lips, tans as burnished as copper pans and several heaving cleavages signify? Yet another Danielle Steel blockbuster, busting its unsubtle way on to the screens. Two lovelorn TV producers get their edits in a twist, as they do, and both are already carrying enough emotional baggage to kit out the safari department at Harrods. SH DVD

John Ritter *Bill Grant* • Polly Draper *Adrian Townsend* • Nancy Morgan *Zelda* • Kevin Kilner *Steven Townsend* • Michael Lembeck *Ted* ■ *Dir* Michael Miller (2) • *Scr* Jan Worthington, from the novel by Danielle Steel

Danielle Steel's Kaleidoscope ★★★ 15

Melodrama 1990 · US · Colour · 89mins

Although film adaptations often disappoint, Danielle Steel fans need not worry, for this tense TV movie misses none of the author's melodramatic tricks as three sisters, parted on the horrific deaths of their parents, reunite to discover they not only have little in common, but also have dark secrets to hide. Jaclyn Smith suffers in style as the sibling scarred by hardship. DP DVD

Jaclyn Smith *Hilary Walker* • Perry King *John Chapman* • Patricia Kalember *Alexandra* • Claudia Christian *Meagan Kincaide* • Donald Moffat *Arthur Patterson* • Colleen Dewhurst *Margaret Gorham* ■ *Dir* Jud Taylor • *Scr* Karol Ann Hoeffner, from the novel by Danielle Steel

Danielle Steel's Mixed Blessings ★★ 12

Romantic drama 1995 · US · Colour · 86mins

Three couples deal with pregnancy, adoption and infertility in this weepie based on the Danielle Steel novel. The plot is predictable, but the TV-based cast gives its all. Director Bethany Rooney makes sure every moment is a three-hankie one. JB DVD

Gabrielle Carteris *Diana Douglas* • Bruce Greenwood *Andy Douglas* • Scott Baio *Charlie Winwood* • Julie Condra *Barbie Winwood* • Alexandra Paul *Beth* • Bess Armstrong *Pilar Coleman* • James Naughton *Brad Coleman* • Bruce Weitz *Dr Alex Johnson* ■ *Dir* Bethany Rooney • *Scr* L Virginia Browne, Rebecca Soladay, from the novel by Danielle Steel

Danielle Steel's No Greater Love ★★ PG

Period romantic drama 1996 · US · Colour · 86mins

This frothy melodramatic confection, takes in cataclysmic world news (the sinking of the *Titanic*) and reduces it to a facile excuse for showing us yet another of Steel's strong, brave and well turned-out women battling the odds. The cast has been wheeled out on castors and it runs through its hand-wringing paces as if the script is being relayed by hidden short-wave radio. SH DVD

Kelly Rutherford *Edwina Winfield* • Chris Sarandon *Sam Horowitz* • Nicholas Campbell *Stone* • Daniel Hugh-Kelly *Ben Jones* • Simon MacCorkindale *Patrick Kelly* • Michael Landes *George Winfield* ■ *Dir* Richard Heffron [Richard T Heffron] • *Scr* Carmen Culver from the novel by Danielle Steel

Danielle Steel's Once in a Lifetime ★★★ PG

Romantic drama 1994 · US · Colour · 87mins

Get out those hankies, this is one of the weepier movie adaptations of a Danielle Steel novel. Lindsay Wagner, ex-Bionic Woman and queen of the TV movie, plays an author reluctant to love again after her husband and daughter are killed in a fire. On top of all this, her young son is deaf. There's no prize for guessing who rescues our heroine from all this – TV-movie king Barry Bostwick. JB DVD

Lindsay Wagner *Daphne Fields* • Barry Bostwick *Dr Matthew Dane* • Duncan Regehr *Justin* • Amy Aquino *Barbara* • Rex Smith *Jeffrey Fields* • Jessica Sinegal *Aimee* ■ *Dir* Michael Miller (2) • *Scr* Syrie Astrahan James, from the novel by Danielle Steel

Danielle Steel's Palomino ★★ PG

Romantic drama 1991 · US · Colour · 91mins

There's enough corn to fill you up for a lifetime in this TV adaptation of Danielle Steel's novel. Lindsay Frost plays the photographer who retreats to a ranch after her marriage ends, and subsequently falls in love with rough and ready ranch hand Lee Horsley, from the wrong side of the tracks. Featuring Eva Marie Saint and Rod Taylor, both of whom should have known better. JB DVD

Lindsay Frost *Samantha Taylor* • Lee Horsley *Tate* • Eva Marie Saint *Caroline* • Rod Taylor *Bill* ■ *Dir* Michael Miller (2) • *Scr* Karol Ann Hoeffner, from the novel by Danielle Steel

Danielle Steel's A Perfect Stranger ★★ 12

Romantic drama 1994 · US · Colour · 87mins

From the moment you see the author's name in the title, you know what to expect of this glitzy TV melodrama. Luxury, deception and no little passion are all to the fore here as ambitious attorney Robert Urich finds himself falling for Stacy Haiduk, the trophy wife of terminally ill millionaire Darren McGavin. Strictly for soap fans and Steel readers only. DP DVD

Robert Urich *Alex Hale* • Stacy Haiduk *Raphaella Phillips* • Marion Ross *Charlotte Brandon* • Darren McGavin *John Henry Phillips* • Susan Sullivan *Kaye* • Holly Marie Combs *Amanda* ■ *Dir* Michael Miller (2) • *Scr* Jan Worthington, from the novel by Danielle Steel

Danielle Steel's Remembrance ★★ PG

Romantic drama 1996 · US · Colour · 87mins

Eva LaRue may not be in the same league as Joan Crawford and Barbara Stanwyck, but she suffers nobly as the Italian wife of an American army officer frozen out of the family by hellish mother-in-law Angie Dickinson. Directed with exemplary overstatement by Bethany Rooney, this is undemanding escapism. DP DVD

Angie Dickinson *Margaret Fullerton* • Eva LaRue *Serena Fullerton* • Jeffrey Nordling *Brad Fullerton* • James Calvert *Teddy Fullerton* ■ *Dir* Bethany Rooney • *Scr* David Ambrose, from the novel by Danielle Steel

Danielle Steel's Secrets ★★ 15

Romantic drama 1992 · US · Colour · 89mins

Scandals, love affairs and skeletons-in-the-closet are suffered by Tinseltown's rich and famous. Christopher Plummer is the TV producer who experiences a few steamy moments of his own, while the cast of his show spends more time jumping in and out of bed than it does filming the series. Silly, over-the-top, and, if you watch for too long, scarily addictive. JB DVD

Christopher Plummer *Mel Wexler* • Stephanie Beacham *Sabina Quarles* • Linda Purl *Jane Adams* • Gary Collins *Zack Taylor* • Ben Browder *Bill Warwick* • Josie Bissett *Gaby Smith* • John Bennett Perry *Dan Adams* ■ *Dir* Peter H Hunt • *Scr* William Bast, Paul Huson, from the novel by Danielle Steel

Danielle Steel's Star ★★ 15

Romantic melodrama
1993 · US · Colour · 92mins

Beverly Hills 90210's Jennie Garth plays a rising young star of the entertainment world who has put her personal tragedies behind her, but remains haunted by her first love Craig Bierko. Director Michael Miller revels in the melodramatic clichés, and the result is an undemanding slice of romantic tosh. JF DVD

Jennie Garth *Crystal Wyatt* • Craig Bierko *Spencer Hill* • Ted Wass *Ernie* • Terry Farrell *Elizabeth* ■ *Dir* Michael Miller (2) • *Scr* Claire Labine, Danielle Steel, from the novel by Danielle Steel

Danielle Steel's Vanished ★★ PG

Melodrama 1995 · US · Colour · 86mins

George Hamilton reveals that beneath the tan there beats the heart of a heel in this TV movie. Refusing to forgive ex-wife Lisa Rinna for the death of their son, Hamilton jets to the States to kidnap the child she's since had with new beau Robert Hays. Director George Kaczender works overtime to make us believe in this tosh and its cardboard characters, but this is still tiresome viewing. DP DVD

Lisa Rinna *Marielle Delauney* • George Hamilton *Malcolm Patterson* • Robert Hays *John Taylor* • Maurice Godin *Charles Delauney* • Daniela Akerblom *Brigitte* • Alex D Linz *Teddy* ■ *Dir* George Kaczender • *Scr* Kathleen Rowell, from the novel by Danielle Steel

Danny Boy ★ U

Drama 1941 · UK · BW · 79mins

What on earth was someone of Ann Todd's stature doing in a piece of sentimental nonsense like this? Admittedly, she was returning to films after a two-year absence, but she is woefully miscast as a singer hitting the road to find her estranged husband and son, who have become buskers. Slipshod. DP

Ann Todd *Jane Kay* • Wilfrid Lawson *Jack Newton* • John Warwick *Nick Carter* • Grant Tyler *Danny* • David Farrar *Harold Martin* ■ *Dir* Oswald Mitchell • *Scr* Vera Allinson

Dante's Inferno ★★★

Drama 1935 · US · BW · 89mins

As the title implies, there is an absolutely super vision of hell, replete with nudity. Most of the screen time, however, is taken up with a Spencer Tracy–Claire Trevor romance; the two Broadway actors acquit themselves well, assuring themselves of future Hollywood success. Tracy's bombast suits his role as a carnival barker owner who gets too big for his boots, and watch closely for a young dancer called Rita Cansino, before she altered her hairline and changed her surname to Hayworth. The film shows its age, though, so viewers should be tolerant. TS

Spencer Tracy *Jim Carter* • Claire Trevor *Betty McWade* • Henry B Walthall *Pop McWade* • Scotty Beckett *Sonny* • Alan Dinehart *Jonesy* • Rita Cansino [Rita Hayworth] *Speciality dancer* ■ *Dir* Harry Lachman • *Scr* Philip Klein, Robert Yost, from a story by Cyrus Wood, adapted by Edmund Goulding

Dante's Peak ★★★ 12

Disaster action adventure
1997 · US · Colour · 108mins

Pierce Brosnan's vulcanologist sees the warning signs for major lava problems in the small mountainside town but no one will believe him, in a typically FX-orientated 1990s disaster flick. Like the same year's larger-scale *Volcano*, this has some corking digital magma and a lot of cardboard in its path. Director Roger Donaldson papers over dialogue and character deficiencies with some exciting set pieces. Brosnan and Linda Hamilton offer serviceable performances, but they're battling against more than just the elements. JC [video] DVD

Pierce Brosnan *Harry Dalton* • Linda Hamilton *Rachel Wando* • Jamie Renee Smith *Lauren Wando* • Jeremy Foley *Graham Wando* • Elizabeth Hoffman *Ruth* • Charles Hallahan *Paul Dreyfus* • Grant Heslov *Greg* ■ *Dir* Roger Donaldson • *Scr* Leslie Bohem

Danton ★★★★ PG

Historical drama
1982 · Fr/Pol · Colour · 130mins

With Agnieszka Holland among the scriptwriting team and the great Polish director Andrzej Wajda behind the camera, it's easy to read this passionate account of the political ambushing of one of the key figures of the French Revolution as an allegorical study of the Solidarity movement. Gérard Depardieu gives arguably the finest performance of his career as the corrupt but committed man of the people, impressing both with his public oratory and his bitter ideological feuds with Wojciech Pszoniak's Robespierre. Although Wajda's free with the facts, he captures the fervour and fury of the period superbly. DP. In French with English subtitles. Contains violence and brief nudity. [video]

Gérard Depardieu *Georges Danton* • Wojciech Pszoniak *Maximilien Robespierre* • Patrice Chéreau *Camille Desmoulins* • Angela Winkler *Lucile Desmoulins* ■ *Dir* Andrzej Wajda • *Scr* Jean-Claude Carrière, Andrzej Wajda, Agnieszka Holland, Boleslaw Michalek, Jacek Gasiorowski, from the play *The Danton Affair* by Stanislawa Przybyszewska

Danzón ★★★ PG

Drama 1991 · Mex · Colour · 101mins

The danzón is a type of Latin American dance that recalls with wistful good humour the heartbreaks and missed opportunities of the performer. This sedate Mexican melodrama takes its cue from the gentle rhythms of such song-and-dance routines, as telephonist Maria Rojo is tempted by the attentions of a younger man in the course of her search for her missing dancing partner. Directed by Maria Novaro, the film lacks focus, and the routines, while hypnotic, no substitute for a more substantial plot. DP. In Spanish with English subtitles. [video]

Maria Rojo *Julia* • Carmen Salinas *Doña Ti* • Blanca Guerra *La Colorada* • Tito Vasconcelos *Susy* • Victor Carpinteiro *Rubén* • Margarita Isabel *Silvia* • Cheli Godinez *Tere* ■ *Dir* Maria Novaro • *Scr* Beatriz Novaro, Maria Novaro

Darby O'Gill and the Little People ★★★ U

Fantasy 1959 · US · Colour · 86mins

Tall-tale teller extraordinaire Albert Sharpe does a deal with the leprechauns (led by Jimmy O'Dea) to ensure daughter Janet Munro's happiness with the Sean Connery. Although Connery looks a little uneasy at having to sing, the performances are largely fine. But this is all about special effects, ranging from the mischievous imps on horseback to the terrifying arrival of the ghostly Costa Bower or Death Coach. DP [video]

Albert Sharpe *Darby O'Gill* • Jimmy O'Dea *King Brian* • Janet Munro *Katie* • Sean Connery *Michael McBride* • Kieron Moore *Pony Sugrue* • Estelle Winwood *Sheelah* • Walter Fitzgerald *Lord Fitzpatrick* ■ *Dir* Robert Stevenson • *Scr* Lawrence E Watkin, from the Darby O'Gill stories by HT Kavanagh

Darby's Rangers ★★

Second World War drama
1958 · US · BW · 105mins

This overlong, routine, dreary-looking drama follows American commandos in front-line action in north Africa and Italy during the Second World War. Charlton Heston signed up for the lead, but Jack L Warner apparently welched on the deal. Veteran director William A Wellman had to settle for young TV stars James Garner and Edd Byrnes and European newcomer Etchika Choureau, who struggle to make an impression. AE

James Garner *Major William Darby* • Etchika Choureau *Angelina De Lotta* • Jack Warden *Master Sergeant Saul Rosen* • Edward Byrnes [Edd Byrnes] *Lieutenant Arnold Dittman* • Venetia Stevenson *Peggy McTavish* • Torin Thatcher *Sergeant McTavish* • Peter Brown *Rollo Burns* • Joan Elan *Wendy Hollister* • Stuart Whitman *Hank Bishop* ■ *Dir* William A Wellman • *Scr* Guy Trosper, from a book by Major James Altieri

Daredevil ★★ 15

Action fantasy 2003 · US · Colour · 99mins

There are redeeming features to this Marvel comic adaptation – not least its strong visuals and attractive cast – but these do not add up to a satisfying whole. As a child, Matt Murdock is blinded by radioactive waste that simultaneously heightens his other senses. He grows up to be a New York lawyer (played by Ben Affleck) who doubles as a nocturnal crime-fighter. The flabby narrative introduces a soppy love story involving Jennifer Garner and a cursory game of cat-and-mouse against Colin Farrell's poorly sketched villain, but the action is sapped of clarity by rushed editing. AC. Contains violence, swearing. [video] DVD

Ben Affleck *Matthew "Matt" Murdock/ Daredevil* • Jennifer Garner *Elektra Natchios* • Michael Clarke Duncan *Wilson Fisk/Kingpin* • Colin Farrell (2) *Bullseye* • Joe Pantoliano *Ben Urich* • Jon Favreau *Franklin "Foggy" Nelson* • David Keith *Jack Murdock* • Kevin Smith (2) *Jack Kirby, lab assistant* • Stan Lee *Old man at crossing* ■ *Dir* Mark Steven Johnson • *Scr* Mark Steven Johnson, from stories and characters created by Stan Lee, Bill Everett, Frank Miller

Daria the Movie: Is It Fall Yet? ★★★

Animated comedy
2000 · US/S Kor · Colour · 75mins

If you've never before encountered MTV's withering anithesis to Beavis and Butt-head, this smart feature-length cartoon is going to turn you into a huge fan of Daria Morgendorffer. You don't need to know that she despairs of all the jocks and bubble-heads in her class or that her home life isn't exactly peachy-creamy, either. You'll soon come to appreciate her unerring accuracy with a stinging one-liner as she arrives up at summer camp, the OK to Cry Corral, where her prickly pragmatism causes more wounds than it heals. If only more American comedy was this subtle. DP

Tracy Grandstaff *Daria Morgendorffer* • Sarah Drew *Stacy Rowe* • Bart Fasbender *Andrew Landon* • Alvaro J Gonzalez *Trent Lane* • Amanda Fox *Katherine "Kay" Sloane* ■ *Dir* Karen Disher, Guy Moore • *Scr* Glenn Eichler, Peggy Nicoll

The Daring Dobermans ★★★

Crime caper 1973 · US · Colour · 90mins

The Doberman Gang had a group of thieves training some Doberman dogs to commit the perfect bank robbery. In this follow-up, the Dobermans are being trained by a new group of criminal masterminds, but their plans could be thwarted after a young boy, who loves the dogs, tries to set them free. Simple stuff for kids, this is most impressive for the clever use of the dogs. A second sequel, *The Amazing Dobermans*, completed the series. JB

Charles Knox Robinson • Tim Considine • David Moses • Claudio Martinez • Joan Caulfield ■ *Dir* Byron Ross Chudnow • *Scr* Alan Alch, Jack Kaplan

Daring Game ★★ U

Action adventure
1968 · US · Colour · 100mins

A *Mission Impossible*-style adventure with Lloyd Bridges liberating a professor and his daughter from the clutches of a Latin American dictator. This mission, shot in Florida, involves skydiving as well as scuba diving. The director, Laslo Benedek, had his brief moment in the early 1950s with *Death of a Salesman* and *The Wild One* but here he's just a journeyman controlled by producer Ivan Tors who had a wildlife park called Africa, USA. AT

Lloyd Bridges *Vic Powers* • Nico Minardos *Ricardo Balboa* • Michael Ansara *President Eduardo Delgado* • Joan Blackman *Kathryn Carlyle* • Shepperd Strudwick *Dr Carlyle* • Alex Montoya *General Tovrea* • Irene Dailey *Mrs Carlyle* ■ *Dir* Laslo Benedek • *Scr* Andy White, from a story by Andy White, Art Arthur

The Dark ★★ 15

Science-fiction horror
1979 · US · Colour · 86mins

This disjointed sci-fi horror movie was started by director Tobe Hooper as a fully fledged horror, then completed by John "Bud" Cardos when something more *Alien*-inspired was required. A confusing mix of supernatural slasher and intergalactic monster movie, this features a murderous alien stalking LA. Little happens between the attacks, all predicted by a mystic, and the murders themselves have minimal impact thanks to Cardos's unimaginative restraint. AJ. Contains violence, swearing and a sex scene. [video]

William Devane *Ray Warner* • Cathy Lee Crosby *Zoe Owens* • Richard Jaeckel *Detective Mooney* • Warren Kemmerling *Captain Speer* • Biff Elliot *Bresler* ■ *Dir* John "Bud" Cardos • *Scr* Stanford Whitmore

Dark Alibi ★

Mystery 1946 · US · BW · 61mins

The first eight entries in the Charlie Chan series after it transferred from Fox to Monogram were bashed out by journeyman writer George Callahan and the strain was readily evident by his swansong, in which as much emphasis is placed on humour as on the clues. Sidney Toler investigates who is responsible for leaving fake fingerprints at the scenes of crimes to implicate innocent people. Slapdash. DP

Sidney Toler *Charlie Chan* • Mantan Moreland *Birmingham* • Ben Carter *Carter* • Benson Fong *Tommy Chan* • Teala Loring *June* ■ *Dir* Phil Karlson • *Scr* George Callahan, from characters created by Earl Derr Biggers

The Dark Angel ★★★ U

Romantic drama 1935 · US · BW · 101mins

One of the great four-hankie melodramas, this is the talkie remake of a famous Guy Bolton play originally filmed in 1925 with Ronald Colman and Vilma Banky. Here Merle Oberon gives an Oscar-nominated performance as Kitty Vane, loved by upright Herbert Marshall and war-blinded Fredric March. This is an expertly crafted "woman's picture" in which Oberon, shorn of her trademark fashionable hairstyles and expensive wardrobes, is a revelation. The creaky theatrical origins seep through now and then, but acerbic co-scriptwriter Lillian Hellman keeps bathos at bay, and the result is a mighty fine wallow. TS [video]

Fredric March *Alan Trent* • Merle Oberon *Kitty Vane* • Herbert Marshall *Gerald Shannon* • Janet Beecher *Mrs Shannon* • John Halliday *Sir George Barton* • Henrietta Crosman *Granny Vane* ■ *Dir* Sidney Franklin • *Scr* Lillian Hellman, Mordaunt Shairp, from the play by Guy Bolton

Dark Angel ★★★ 18

Science-fiction thriller
1989 · US · Colour · 87mins

Dolph Lundgren gives one of his best performances as a Houston detective on the trail of an intergalactic drug dealer in this smartly scripted and crisply directed science-fiction spin on the buddy cop movie. The alien pusher has come to Earth to obtain a substance produced within the human body that is much sought after as a narcotic on his planet. The stock ingredients are all well proportioned in a cracking yarn that's exciting and full of extra twists. AJ [video] DVD

Dolph Lundgren *Jack Caine* • Brian Benben *Laurence Smith* • Betsy Brantley *Diane Pollon* • Matthias Hues *Talec* • David Ackroyd *Switzer* • Jim Haynie *Captain Malone* ■ *Dir* Craig R Baxley • *Scr* Jonathan Tydor, Leonard Maas Jr

The Dark at the Top of the Stairs ★★

Drama 1960 · US · Colour · 123mins

The William Inge play on which this memoir of life in 1920s Oklahoma is based won the Pulitzer Prize. Unfortunately, whatever merit the original might have had as a theatrical experience has been dissipated here by Delbert Mann's reverential approach to its themes of sexual awakening, family discord, class snobbery and anti-Semitism. Its attitudes have become so outdated that they are likely to breach even the most flexible code of political correctness. DP

Robert Preston *Rubin Flood* • Dorothy McGuire *Cora Flood* • Eve Arden *Lottie* • Angela Lansbury *Mavis Pruitt* • Shirley Knight *Reenie Flood* • Lee Kinsolving *Sammy Golden* ■ *Dir* Delbert Mann • *Scr* Irving Ravetch, Harriet Frank Jr, from the play by William Inge

The Dark Avenger ★★★ U

Swashbuckling drama
1955 · US/UK · Colour · 84mins

Before he stiffened up into arthritic gestures that passed for acting, Errol Flynn made this final parry-and-lunge costumed swashbuckler. Its story – about an English prince fighting off Peter Finch and his unmerry French conspirators and safeguarding Joanne Dru in the process – is no history lesson, but tuition on how to get away with Flynn's kind of daredevilry. It's a small-scale epic that does his roistering reputation no discredit, for he was, indeed, a class act. TH

Errol Flynn *Prince Edward* • Joanne Dru *Lady Joan Holland* • Peter Finch *Count de Ville* • Yvonne Furneaux *Marie* • Patrick Holt *Sir Ellys* • Michael Hordern *King Edward III* • Moultrie Kelsall *Sir Bruce* • Robert Urquhart *Sir Philip* ■ *Dir* Henry Levin • *Scr* Daniel B Ullman, Phil Park (uncredited) • *Cinematographer* Guy Green

The Dark Backward ★★ 15

Comedy fantasy 1991 · US · Colour · 99mins

Writer/director Adam Rifkin has scripted a number of idiosyncratic movies (*Small Soldiers*, *Mousehunt*), but this early entry in his oeuvre is really off the wall. Judd Nelson is a garbage collector who dreams of becoming a stand-up comic, but who only succeeds in getting noticed when a third arm starts to grow out of his back. An eclectic cast and the extraordinary premise failed to make this a cult hit, but it gets an "A" for effort. DF [video]

Judd Nelson *Marty Malt* • Bill Paxton *Gus* • Wayne Newton *Jackie Chrome* • Lara Flynn Boyle *Rosarita* • James Caan *Dr Scurvy* • Rob

Lowe *Dirk Delta* • King Moody *Twinkee Doodle* • Claudia Christian *Kitty* • Adam Rifkin *Rufus Bing* ■ *Dir/Scr* Adam Rifkin

Dark Blue ★★★ 15

Police thriller
2002 · US/Ger/UK · Colour · 113mins

This routine thriller is given some much needed impact by a muscular performance from Kurt Russell. Set in the run-up to the LA riots, it follows Russell's uncompromising cop as he keeps the peace with extreme prejudice, carrying on the corruption that has been handed down through generations in the face of a new breed of policeman (represented here by Ving Rhames). It's marred by obvious plotting, grating dialogue and a distinct lack of rounded characterisations, but this comes to life when Russell is on the screen. IF. Contains violence, swearing and sex scenes. DVD

Kurt Russell *Eldon Perry* • Scott Speedman *Bobby Keough* • Michael Michele *Beth Williamson* • Brendan Gleeson *Jack Van Meter* • Ving Rhames *Arthur Holland* • Lolita Davidovich *Sally Perry* • Dash Mihok *Gary Sidwell* ■ *Dir* Ron Shelton • *Scr* David Ayer, from a story by James Ellroy

Dark Blue World ★★★ 12

Second World War romantic drama
2001 · Cz Rep/UK/Ger · Colour · 108mins

Jan Sverak, director of the Oscar-winning *Kolya*, reunites with his screenwriter father Zdenek for this engaging memoir about the Czech pilots who flew alongside the RAF during the Second World War. Neatly dovetailing dogfights with domestic drama, the film avoids stereotype and sentiment, as Ondrej Vetchy and his rookie pal Krystof Hadek discover that their mutual attraction to sailor's wife Tara FitzGerald is infringing on their mission. DP. In Czech, English and German with subtitles. Contains violence. DVD

Ondrej Vetchy *Lt Frantisek "Franta" Slama* • Krystof Hadek *Karel Vojtisek* • Tara FitzGerald *Susan Whitmore* • Oldrich Kaiser *Machaty* • Hans-Jorg Assmann *Doctor Blaschke* • Charles Dance *Wing Commander Bentley* ■ *Dir* Jan Sverak • *Scr* Zdenek Sverak

Dark City ★★★

Mystery drama
1950 · US · BW · 97mins

Don DeFore loses all the company cash in a rigged poker game, then hangs himself. It's a fabulous *noir* opening, but director William Dieterle fails to maintain the tight suspense as Charlton Heston, here making his feature debut, is stalked by DeFore's psychotic brother. That said, it's a typically well-crafted Paramount production, and Lizabeth Scott smoulders seductively. TS

Charlton Heston *Danny Haley* • Lizabeth Scott *Fran* • Don DeFore *Arthur Winant* • Jack Webb *Augie* • Ed Begley *Barney* • Henry Morgan [Harry Morgan] *Soldier* • Mark Keuning *Billy Winant* • Mike Mazurki *Sidney Winant* ■ *Dir* William Dieterle • *Scr* Larry Marcus, John Meredyth Lucas, from a story by Larry Marcus

Dark City ★★★

Political thriller
1990 · UK/Zim · Colour · 98mins

This taut thriller manages to say more about life in South Africa under apartheid than numerous more overtly political tracts. The immediate presumption that black people must be guilty of a township crime, the brutality of the security forces and the bias of the legal system are all exposed in Chris Curling's hard-hitting film. Reinforcing these abuses is the struggle of seven suspects to prove they are innocent of the murder of a prominent councillor, which may or may not be bound up with a burglary at the mayor's house. DP

Sello Maake Ka-Ncube *Victor Mtetwa* • Vusi Dibakwane *Edison* • Thapelo Mafokeng *Mayor Seko* • Ernest Ndlovu *Reverend Bricks* • Moses Mphahlele *Oscar* • Pierre Knoesen *Major Fisher* • Charles Pillai *Reddy* ■ *Dir* Chris Curling • *Scr* David Lan

Dark City ★★★★ 15

Science-fiction fantasy thriller
1998 · US · Colour · 96mins

Director Alex Proyas lends a potent gothic atmosphere to this dreamlike *film noir* fantasy about a race of mysterious bald figures who continually reconfigure a surreal, gloomy city and its inhabitants as some sort of weird experiment. As with *The Crow*, Proyas employs every striking camera angle in his visual vocabulary, breathing dread into the overhanging *Batman*-style architecture. The effects are impressively realised, too, as buildings stretch and widen before our eyes. Although overshadowed by the film's visual flair, the eclectic cast adds a splash of colour to the shadowy surroundings. JC DVD

Rufus Sewell *John Murdoch* • Kiefer Sutherland *Dr Daniel Schreber* • Jennifer Connelly *Emma Murdoch* • Richard O'Brien *Mr Hand* • Ian Richardson *Mr Book* • Colin Friels *Walenski* • Mitchell Butel *Husselbeck* • Frank Gallacher *Stromboli* • Melissa George *May* • William Hurt *Inspector Frank Bumstead* ■ *Dir* Alex Proyas • *Scr* Alex Proyas, Lem Dobbs, David S Goyer, from a story by Alex Proyas • *Cinematographer* Dariusz Wolski

Dark Command ★★ U

Western
1940 · US · BW · 95mins

After John Wayne's success in *Stagecoach*, his home studio, Republic, promoted him from B-westerns to this big-budget effort. Wayne is the simple cowpoke who successfully runs for marshal to impress his girl and, as a result, the much better qualified other candidate, Walter Pidgeon, turns to a life of crime. Raoul Walsh directs and the film lurches between static dialogue scenes and bursts of action. AE

John Wayne *Bob Seton* • Claire Trevor *Mary McCloud* • Walter Pidgeon *William Cantrell* • Roy Rogers *Fletch McCloud* • George "Gabby" Hayes *Doc Grunch* • Porter Hall *Angus McCloud* ■ *Dir* Raoul Walsh • *Scr* Grover Jones, Lionel Hauser, F Hugh Herbert, from the novel by WR Burnett

The Dark Corner ★★★

Film noir
1946 · US · BW · 99mins

Although relatively unknown, this is a rattlingly good and cleverly plotted *film noir*, skilfully directed by Henry Hathaway. It's marred only by too-obvious studio sets and a bland leading man in Mark Stevens, who's not quite tough enough as the private eye framed by his former partner. Still, there's a nicely etched performance from, of all people, Lucille Ball as a hard-boiled secretary, and welcome character work from art dealer Clifton Webb and thug William Bendix. TS

Mark Stevens *Bradford Galt* • Lucille Ball *Kathleen* • Clifton Webb *Hardy Cathcart* • William Bendix *White Suit* • Kurt Kreuger *Tony Jardine* • Cathy Downs *Mari Cathcart* • Reed Hadley *Lt Frank Reeves* • Constance Collier *Mrs Kingsley* ■ *Dir* Henry Hathaway • *Scr* Jay Dratler, Bernard Schoenfeld, from a short story by Leo Rosten • *Cinematographer* Joseph MacDonald [Joe MacDonald]

The Dark Crystal ★★★★ PG

Fantasy adventure
1982 · UK · Colour · 87mins

Few film-makers feel at home in the realms of fantasy, but Jim Henson had an affinity with the magical. Although *The Dark Crystal* emerged from the darker side of his imagination, it's still a mesmerising picture that will enchant older children and adults alike. The story is a basic slice of sword and sorcery, following Jen and Kira as they attempt to restore a splinter of a crystal that will free the "Mystics" from the tyranny of the "Skeksis". However, there is a liberal sprinkling of Muppet-style humour to enliven the adventure, and, with the exception of the "Gelflings", the creatures are inspired. DP DVD

Stephen Garlick *Jen* • Billie Whitelaw *Aughra* • Lisa Maxwell *Kira* • Barry Dennen *Chamberlain* • Michael Kilgarriff *General* • Percy Edwards *Fizzgig* ■ *Dir* Jim Henson, Frank Oz • *Scr* David Odell, from a story by Jim Henson

Dark Days ★★★ 15

Documentary
2000 · US · BW · 78mins

British film-maker Marc Singer spent two years underground shooting his debut feature, a compassionate documentary about the inhabitants of the Amtrak tunnel network beneath New York's Pennsylvania Station. With his monochrome imagery evoking Depression-era photojournalism, Singer makes the distinction between homeless and hopeless, as he captures the ingenious ways his articulate subjects survive in their subterranean world. Yet there is also genuine pain in the frank discussion of the way in which drugs robbed some of life, if not hope. Less convincing, however, is the "happy ending", when the Amtrakers are resettled in above-ground accommodation. DP DVD

Dir Marc Singer • *Cinematographer* Marc Singer • *Editor* Melissa Neidich • *Music* DJ Shadow

Dark Eyes ★★ PG

Romantic comedy
1987 · It · Colour · 112mins

In addition to winning the best actor prize at Cannes, Marcello Mastroianni landed an Oscar nomination for his bravura performance in this self-conscious amalgamation of four Chekhov short stories. Directing with a fine eye for period detail, Nikita Mikhalkov robs the action of its social and pyschological subtlety by calling for grandiloquent gestures and stereotypical characterisations, which turn delicate situations into potboiler set pieces. As an ageing playboy, the ever astute Mastroianni is able to give a shaded performance. DP. In Italian with English subtitles.

Marcello Mastroianni *Romano* • Silvana Mangano *Elisa* • Marthe Keller *Tina* • Elena Sofonova *Anna* • Pina Cei *Elisa's mother* ■ *Dir* Nikita Mikhalkov • *Scr* Alexander Adabashian, Nikita Mikhalkov, Suso Cecchi D'Amico, from the short stories *Anna around the Neck, The Lady with the Little Dog, My Wife, The Name-Day Party* by Anton Chekhov

Dark Eyes of London ★★★ PG

Horror
1939 · UK · BW · 72mins

In one of the most effective examples of screen *Grand Guignol*, Bela Lugosi is at his evil best as the director of an insurance company who kills his clients so he can collect on their policies. Disguised as the kindly old proprietor of a home for the blind, he carries out his nefarious swindles with the assistance of a hideous giant. Based on an Edgar Wallace novel, this British-made shocker, directed by Walter Summers, is both bleak and remarkably scary for the time. AJ

Bela Lugosi *Dr Orloff* • Hugh Williams *Inspector Holt* • Greta Gynt *Diana Stuart* • Edmond Ryan [Edmon Ryan] *Lt O'Reilly* • Wilfrid Walter *Jake, the Monster* • Alexander Field *Grogan* ■ *Dir* Walter Summers • *Scr* Patrick Kirwan, Walter Summers, John Argyle, from a novel by Edgar Wallace

Dark Habits ★★★ 15

Comedy
1983 · Sp · Colour · 110mins

Pedro Almodóvar's third feature is a Buñuelian satire on religious hypocrisy bedecked in the most gloriously tacky Catholic kitsch. Seeking sanctuary after her lover's overdose, hard-nosed chanteuse Cristina Sánchez Pascual is shocked by what she finds inside the Convent of Humble Redeemers. But while it's tempting to mock the nuns in Julieta Serrano's charge – with Carmen Maura devoting herself to a menagerie, Marisa Paredes experiencing ecstatic visions and Chus Lampreave devouring pulp fiction – the film is as much about the irredeemable decadence of the secular world as it is about the sins committed beyond the cloisters. DP. In Spanish with English subtitles.

Cristina Sánchez Pascual *Yolanda Bell* • Willmore [Will More] *Jorge* • Julieta Serrano *Mother Julia* • Marisa Paredes *Sister Estiércol* • Mary Carrillo *Marquesa* • Carmen Maura *Sister Perdida* • Chus Lampreave *Sister Rata de Callejón* ■ *Dir/Scr* Pedro Almodóvar

The Dark Half ★★★ 18

Horror
1991 · US · Colour · 116mins

Timothy Hutton does his finest work in years in this Stephen King adaptation. He plays a bestselling writer whose emerging supernatural side manifests itself in the form of a brutal serial killer who starts stalking the New England family home. George A Romero makes this both possible and frightening by twisting the usual slasher genre conventions, but spoils the build-up with an overblown ending. AJ. Contains violence, swearing. DVD

Timothy Hutton *Thad Beaumont/George Stark* • Michael Rooker *Sheriff Alan Pangborn* • Amy Madigan *Liz Beaumont* • Julie Harris *Reggie Delesseps* • Robert Joy *Fred Clawson* • Rutanya Alda *Miriam Cowley* • Chelsea Field *Annie Pangborn* • Kent Broadhurst *Mike Donaldson* ■ *Dir* George A Romero • *Scr* George A Romero, from the novel by Stephen King

Dark Harbor ★★

Thriller
1998 · US · Colour · 88mins

Polly Walker and Alan Rickman star in this average thriller, directed by Adam Coleman Howard. They play a squabbling couple, struggling through a storm to reach the ferry that will take them to their island home. However, their problems *really* begin when they pick up a battered boy (Norman Reedus). Walker and Rickman are fine as the icy marrieds. For all that, this is one of those films that just doesn't hang together. LH

Alan Rickman *David Weinberg* • Polly Walker *Alexis Chandler Weinberg* • Norman Reedus *Young man* ■ *Dir* Adam Coleman Howard • *Scr* Adam Coleman Howard, Justin Lazard

Dark Horse ★★ 15

Drama
1992 · US · Colour · 70mins

After her mother dies, teenager Ari Meyers goes out of her way to get into trouble to get some attention from her workaholic dad played by Ed Begley Jr. Ordered to do community service at a local horse ranch, she learns to love horses with the help of ranch owner Mimi Rogers. The kid's a brat, Rogers is sleepwalking, and who told Ed Begley Jr he could act? There's a twist at the end, but only lovers of weepy drama will make it that far. ST

Mimi Rogers *Dr Susan Hadley* • Ed Begley Jr *Jack Mills* • Ari Meyers *Allison Mills* • Samantha Eggar *Mrs Curtis* • Tab Hunter *Perkins* • Chad Smith *Clint* ■ *Dir* David Hemmings • *Scr* JE MacLean, from a story by Tab Hunter

Dark Intruder ★★★

Horror 1965 · US · BW · 58mins

Murders occurring in turn-of-the-century San Francisco are traced back to Sumerian devil creatures by a psychic investigator in this pilot for a horror series. (The show, to be called *Black Cloak*, never materialised, so the pilot was given a theatrical release.) Superior make-up effects and a nifty HP Lovecraft-style atmosphere add power to the supernatural shocks, while future *Naked Gun* star Leslie Nielsen proves once again what a loss he was to straight melodrama. AJ

Leslie Nielsen *Brett Kingsford* • Gilbert Green *Harvey Misbach* • Charles Bolender *Nikola* • Mark Richman [Peter Mark Richman] *Robert Vandenburg* • Judi Meredith *Evelyn Lang* • Werner Klemperer *Prof Malaki* ■ *Dir* Harvey Hart • *Scr* Barre Lyndon

Dark Journey ★★★ U

First World War spy drama
1937 · UK · BW · 80mins

Vivien Leigh runs a Stockholm dress shop during the First World War. In reality, though, she's a double agent working for the Allies. Complications ensue when she becomes emotionally involved with a German baron (the silkily threatening Conrad Veidt) who cottons on to the truth. Producer Alexander Korda brought out all the big guns for this spy drama: Victor Saville directs, Georges Périnal and Harry Stradling provide some beautiful photography, while Richard Addinsell supplies the score. Meticulously wrought tosh. RK

Conrad Veidt *Baron Karl Von Marwitz* • Vivien Leigh *Madeleine Goddard* • Joan Gardner *Lupita* • Anthony Bushell *Bob Carter* • Ursula Jeans *Gertrude* • Margery Pickard *Colette* • Eliot Makeham *Anatole* • Austin Trevor *Dr Muller* ■ *Dir* Victor Saville • *Scr* Arthur Wimperis, from a story by Lajos Biró

The Dark Light ★

Crime thriller 1951 · UK · BW · 66mins

Imagine *Shallow Grave* shot in a lighthouse with a cast of no-hopers and the budget of a public information film, and you'll have some idea of what this dismal Hammer offering is like. "Quota quickie" veteran Vernon Sewell gets matters off to a promising start as a desperate gang of bank robbers are rescued from the stormy sea by a lighthouse crew, but tosses away the dramatic possibilities of the claustrophobic setting. DP

Albert Lieven *Mark* • David Greene *Johnny* • Norman Macowan *Rigby* • Martin Benson *Luigi* • Catherine Blake *Linda* • Jack Stewart *Matt* ■ *Dir/Scr* Vernon Sewell

The Dark Mirror ★★★★ PG

Psychological thriller
1946 · US · BW · 81mins

This near-classic thriller from director Robert Siodmak stars Lew Ayres as a psychologist trying to discover which twin sister is a killer. Nunnally Johnson's script springs few real surprises, raiding the textbooks of Freud, but Siodmak pulls out all the melodramatic stops with low-key lighting and weird camera angles. Dimitri Tiomkin's music, meanwhile, heaves like an ocean in a bad mood, and, as the two sisters, Olivia de Havilland seems to be saying, "Bette Davis, eat your heart out." AT [video]

Olivia de Havilland *Terry Collins/Ruth Collins* • Lew Ayres *Dr Scott Elliott* • Thomas Mitchell *Detective Stevenson* • Richard Long *Rusty* • Charles Evans *District Attorney Girard* ■ *Dir* Robert Siodmak • *Scr* Nunnally Johnson, from the novel by Vladimir Pozner • *Cinematographer* Milton Krasner

Dark of the Sun ★★ 15

Adventure 1967 · UK · Colour · 96mins

A tough colonial adventure, based on a Wilbur Smith novel that follows Rod Taylor and Jim Brown as they become entangled in the civil war in the Congo in 1960. Taylor is the man of no principle, until the script's sermonising gets to him, while Brown, as his buddy, plays the Congo native with a conscience. Directed on location by Jack Cardiff, a former ace cameraman, the film's schoolboy heroics sit awkwardly beside its political rhetoric. AT. Contains violence, swearing. [video]

Rod Taylor *Captain Bruce Curry* • Yvette Mimieux *Claire* • Jim Brown *Sergeant Ruffo* • Kenneth More *Dr Wreid* • Peter Carsten *Henlein* • Olivier Despax *Surrier* ■ *Dir* Jack Cardiff • *Scr* Quentin Werty, Adrian Spies, from the novel by Wilbur A Smith

Dark Passage ★★★ 15

Film noir thriller 1947 · US · BW · 101mins

Escaped convict Humphrey Bogart changes his appearance with plastic surgery and hides out with artist Lauren Bacall while he attempts to prove he is innocent of his wife's murder. The third Bogart–Bacall outing, written and directed by Delmer Daves, is slick and efficient, yet somewhat disappointing. The first 40 minutes or so are ingeniously photographed from Bogart's subjective point of view, tantalisingly keeping us waiting for the star's appearance. Otherwise, the movie is a low-key affair. RK [video] DVD

Humphrey Bogart *Vincent Parry* • Lauren Bacall *Irene Jansen* • Bruce Bennett *Bob* • Agnes Moorehead *Madge Rapf* • Tom D'Andrea *Sam* • Clifton Young *Baker* ■ *Dir* Delmer Daves • *Scr* Delmer Daves, from the novel *Dark Passage* by David Goodis

The Dark Past ★★★ PG

Crime drama 1948 · US · BW · 71mins

A moody remake of 1939's *Blind Alley*, the melodrama about a demented thug holding the local psychologist hostage while the latter tries to talk the convict into reasoning out why he turned bad. It always was a good plot, and here skilled director Rudolph Maté brings light and shade to bear on this once trail-blazing subject. A crew cut and highly strung William Holden makes a brave stab at the killer, but Lee J Cobb brings real Method intensity to the understanding psychiatrist. TS [video]

William Holden (2) *Al Walker* • Nina Foch *Betty* • Lee J Cobb *Dr Andrew Collins* • Adele Jergens *Laura Stevens* • Stephen Dunne [Steve Dunne] *Owen Talbot* • Lois Maxwell *Ruth Collins* • Berry Kroeger *Mike* • Steven Geray *Professor Fred Linder* • Wilton Graff *Frank Stevens* • Robert Osterloh *Pete* ■ *Dir* Rudolph Maté • *Scr* Philip MacDonald, Michael Blankfort, Albert Duffy, Malvin Wald, Oscar Saul, from the play *Blind Alley* by James Warwick

Dark Places ★★

Horror 1973 · UK · Colour · 90mins

Asylum administrator Robert Hardy inherits a supposedly haunted mansion where some grisly deaths occurred and a great deal of money is hidden. Psychiatrist Christopher Lee and his sister, Joan Collins, plot to cheat him out of his estate, despite the murderous spiritual presence of its previous owner. Leaden sub-Hammer horror, directed with little flair by veteran Don Sharp and containing inert performances across the board. AJ

Christopher Lee *Dr Mandeville* • Joan Collins *Sarah* • Robert Hardy *Edward/Andrew* • Herbert Lom *Prescott* • Jane Birkin *Alta* • Carleton Hobbs *Old Marr* ■ *Dir* Don Sharp • *Scr* Ed Brennan, Joseph Van Winkle

Dark Prince – the Legend of Dracula ★★★ 18

Horror 2000 · US · Colour · 87mins

A highly romanticised, yet basically accurate, telling of how 15th-century Romanian warlord Vlad Tepes became the brutal blood-drinking tyrant of Eastern European folklore and the basis for Bram Stoker's Dracula character. All the infamous atrocities are present and correct in this swashbuckling horror telemovie and B-movie maestro Joe Chappelle makes the most out of its low budget and Romanian locations. The final shift into fantasy is a little awkwardly done but overall it's impressive. AJ [video] DVD

Rudolf Martin *Vlad the Impaler* • Michael Sutton *Radu* • Christopher Brand *Bruno* • Peter Weller *Father Stefan* • Jane March *Lidia* • Roger Daltrey *King Janos* ■ *Dir* Joe Chappelle • *Scr* Tom Baum [Thomas Baum]

The Dark Road ★★

Drama 1948 · UK · BW · 74mins

This was Alfred Goulding's first feature after directing Laurel and Hardy in *A Chump at Oxford* in 1940. With his background in comedies, he struggles with this grim tale tracing the life and crimes of a surly borstal boy. To his credit, he achieves a certain cheap realism and catches the argot of postwar criminality. But neither Charles Stuart, as the delinquent who drifts from petty larceny to jewel robbery, nor Joyce Linden, as the girl he exploits, are up to the task. DP

Charles Stuart *Sidney Robertson* • Joyce Linden *Ann* • Antony Holles • Roddy Hughes • Patricia Hicks ■ *Dir* Alfred Goulding

The Dark Side of the Heart ★★★

Romance 1992 · Arg/Can · Colour · 127mins

Eliseo Subiela confirms his reputation as Argentina's most ambitious auteur with this literate study of lust, death, poetry and the true value of money. Weary of his art, Darío Grandinetti writes only when he needs cash, and then only accepts commissions from a lovesick chef. His unworldliness stands in stark contrast to the work ethic of prostitute Sandra Bellesteros, yet together they enjoy a passionate relationship. DP. In Spanish with English subtitles.

Darío Grandinetti *Oliverio* • Sandra Ballesteros *Ana* • Nacha Guevara *Muerte* • André Melançon *Erik* ■ *Dir/Scr* Eliseo Subiela

Dark Star ★★★★ PG

Science fiction 1973 · US · Colour · 79mins

In director John Carpenter's impressive feature debut, hippy spacemen fight boredom on a 20-year mission to seek out and destroy unstable planets. Produced as a film project at the University of Southern California for just $60,000, this sly parody begins as a satire on *2001: a Space Odyssey*. However, it quickly moves into original territory as the cabin-fevered crew cope with a vicious alien stowaway, a nagging computer and a thermo-nuclear device that's all set to explode. Witty, profound and cleverly scored by Carpenter with a selection of electronic country and western tunes. AJ. Contains some swearing. [video] DVD

Brian Narelle *Doolittle* • Andreijah Pahich *Talby* • Carl Kuniholm *Boiler* • Dan O'Bannon *Pinback* • Joe Sanders *Powell* ■ *Dir* John Carpenter • *Scr* John Carpenter, Dan O'Bannon

Dark Summer ★★ 12

Drama 1994 · UK · Colour · 70mins

As the familiar Scouse skyline recedes, to be replaced by sobering images of urban decay, there's a glimmer that Charles Teton's debut feature is going to deal with the real Liverpool, rather than the melodramatised *Brookside* version. But the social implications of the relationship between black labourer Steve Ako and Joeline Garnier-Joel, his white boss's daughter, are soon forgotten, as Ako embarks on a boxing career that will cost him everything. Director Teton's advertising background is proclaimed in almost every self-consciously grubby shot. DP

Steve Ako *Abraham Wilson* • Joeline Garnier-Joel *Jess Shepherd* • Bernie Deasy *Amateur coach* • Chris Darwin *Alan Shepherd* • Dermott Mulholland ■ *Dir* Charles Teton • *Scr* Charles Teton, with additional material from Bernie Deasy, Steve Cheers, Bernd Lubke

Dark Tower ★ 18

Supernatural horror thriller
1989 · US · Colour · 91mins

Michael Moriarty plays an investigator called in when a supernatural force starts bumping off people in a skyscraper. This appalling mix of *Omen*-style operatic deaths and *Poltergeist* scares ran into production problems, and Hammer veteran Freddie Francis was replaced as director. The cast weren't so lucky. RS [video]

Michael Moriarty *Dennis Randall* • Jenny Agutter *Carolyn Page* • Carol Lynley *Tilly Ambrose* • Theodore Bikel *Dr Max Gold* • Anne Lockhart *Elaine* • Kevin McCarthy *Sergie* ■ *Dir* Freddie Francis • *Scr* Robert J Avrech, Ken Wiederhorn, Ken Blackwell, from a story by Robert J Avrech

Dark Victory ★★★★ PG

Melodrama 1939 · US · BW · 100mins

Possibly the best terminal illness movie prior to *Love Story*, and easily surpassing that tear-jerker in style, this Bette Davis vehicle boasts one of her best performances as heiress Judith Traherne, tragically stricken with a brain tumour. The condition means that she will go blind before dying, and so paves the way for a death scene so memorably heart-rending (aided by a knockout Max Steiner score which the star loathed) that it took Davis to the number one female movie star slot in the US. All of those classy Warner Bros production values are well in evidence, hiding the fact that this is really a load of old codswallop. Humphrey Bogart performs as though he knows he's been miscast. Remade in Britain in 1963 as *Stolen Hours*, starring Susan Hayward. TS [video]

Bette Davis *Judith Traherne* • George Brent *Dr Frederick Steele* • Humphrey Bogart *Michael O'Leary* • Geraldine Fitzgerald *Ann King* • Ronald Reagan *Alec Hamin* • Henry Travers *Dr Parsons* • Cora Witherspoon *Carrie Spottswood* • Virginia Brissac *Martha* ■ *Dir* Edmund Goulding • *Scr* Casey Robinson, from the play by George Emerson Brewer Jr, Bertram Bloch

Dark Victory ★★

Romantic drama 1976 · US · Colour · 90mins

In this TV-movie remake of the classy 1939 Bette Davis/George Brent version, Elizabeth Montgomery stars as a cancer-stricken TV producer with no time for a personal life, who falls for the doctor who discovers the seriousness of her condition. While competent, she's not in Davis's class and director Robert Butler's funereal pacing doesn't help matters. Anthony Hopkins surpasses the efforts of Brent, playing the solicitous doctor, but it's hardly a stretch for him. DP

Elizabeth Montgomery *Katherine Merrill* • Anthony Hopkins *Dr Michael Grant* • Michele Lee *Dolores Marsh* • Janet MacLachlan *Eileen* • Michael Lerner *Manny* • John Elerick *Jeremy* • Herbert Berghof *Dr Kassiter* • Vic Tayback *Archie* ■ *Dir* Robert Butler • *Scr* M Charles Cohen, from the play by George Emerson Brewer Jr, Bertram Bloch

D

Dark Water ★★★★ 15

Supernatural horror
2002 · Jpn · Colour · 96mins

Much less contrived and infinitely more sinister than *Ring* and its sequels, Hideo Nakata's nerve-fraying film about a mother's desperate search for a missing child reclaims the horror movie from the slasher antics that prevail on either side of the Pacific. Hitomi Kuroki is outstanding as the divorcee whose paranoia on learning that a kidnapper once inhabited an upstairs room increases in proportion to the oozing stain on her ceiling. But the real star is the rundown Tokyo tenement whose scuffed colours and enveloping shadows are eerily evoked in Junichiro Hayashi's lowering photography. Stylish, atmospheric and very disturbing. DP. In Japanese with English subtitles. DVD

Hitomi Kuroki *Yoshimi Matsubara* • Rio Kanno *Ikuko Matsubara, aged six* • Mirei Oguchi *Mitsuko Kawai* • Asami Mizukawa *Ikuko Hamada, aged 16* ■ *Dir* Hideo Nakata • *Scr* Yoshihiro Nakamura, Ken-ichi Suzuki, from a novel by Koji Suzuki

Dark Waters ★★ U

Drama 1944 · US · BW · 85mins

Merle Oberon lends her exotic allure to this Andre De Toth-directed melodrama set in the Louisiana bayou. Oberon plays an heiress traumatised by the shipping accident in which her parents died, while Thomas Mitchell plays the malcontent who, sensing her incipient madness, hopes to push her over the edge and collect the money. Franchot Tone is the kindly medic who also takes a fancy to his patient. It's juicily acted when the script allows, with some good moments. AT

Merle Oberon *Leslie Calvin* • Franchot Tone *Dr George Grover* • Thomas Mitchell *Mr Sydney* • Fay Bainter *Aunt Emily* • John Qualen *Uncle Norbert* • Elisha Cook Jr *Cleeve* • Rex Ingram (2) *Pearson Jackson* ■ *Dir* Andre De Toth • *Scr* Joan Harrison, Marian Cockrell, Arthur Horman, from the novel by Frank Cockrell, Marian Cockrell

Dark Waters ★★ 18

Horror 1993 · Rus/Ukr · Colour · 93mins

A tepid chiller relating the quest of British girl Louise Salter to discover the secrets of a mysterious sect on a Russian island that's somehow linked to her late father. Zombie nuns and malevolent forces spring into action in this beautifully photographed but pretentious horror, strangely bereft of the jolts and gore that are the usual currency of the genre. A good attempt by director Mariano Baino to wed classic Italian fantasy imagery within a dreamy, atmospheric landscape, but the ultimate result is an awkwardly weird wash-out. AJ. Russian dialogue dubbed into English.

Louise Salter *Elizabeth* • Venera Simmons • Maria Kapnist ■ *Dir* Mariano Baino • *Scr* Mariano Baino, Andrew Bark

The Dark Wind ★★★ 15

Crime mystery 1991 · US · Colour · 106mins

Rookie native American cop Lou Diamond Phillips tracks down a group of murderous drug dealers operating on the Navajo reservations in this intermittently fascinating adaptation of Tony Hillerman's novel. Despite much artistic licence taken with the book's characters, director Errol Morris makes superb use of the magnificent Arizona and New Mexico locations and gives this unusual thriller an intensely brooding atmosphere. Although Indian leaders objected to the ancient rites depicted, they're an intriguing aspect which sets the film apart from other similarly-styled cop adventures. AJ

Lou Diamond Phillips *Officer Jim Chee* • Fred Ward *Lieutenant Joe Leaphorn* • Gary Farmer *Sheriff Albert "Cowboy" Dashee* • John Karlen *Jake West* • Lance Baker *Mr Archer* • Gary Basaraba *Larry* ■ *Dir* Errol Morris • *Scr* Eric Bergren, Neal Jimenez, Mark Horowitz, from the novel by Tony Hillerman

Darkbreed ★★★ 18

Science-fiction horror
1996 · US · Colour · 91mins

Jack Scalia wages a one-man war against an alien invasion force in a mindlessly enjoyable blend of *The X-Files*, *The Invaders* and *The A-Team*. The former astronaut learns Earth is about to be taken over by the dark breed, a deadly race of parasites, so he embarks on a mission to destroy a canister containing their eggs. Wall-to-wall violence, action and mayhem ensue in a cliché-ridden plot which contains the odd flash of impressive special effects. AJ. Contains violence, and some swearing.

Jack Scalia *Nicholas Saxon* • Donna W Scott *Deborah* • Jonathan Banks *Joseph Shay* • Robin Curtis *Marian* ■ *Dir* Richard Pepin • *Scr* Richard Preston Jr

Darker than Amber ★★

Crime thriller 1970 · US · Colour · 97mins

Thriller writer John D MacDonald's detective Travis McGee (in his only cinematic outing, though a series was mooted) is incarnated by likeable Rod Taylor, and glossily filmed on exotic Caribbean and Miami locations. Watch for Jane Russell's penultimate screen appearance. TS

Rod Taylor *Travis McGee* • Suzy Kendall *Vangie/Merrimay* • Theodore Bikel *Meyer* • Jane Russell *Alabama Tiger* • James Booth *Burk* ■ *Dir* Robert Clouse • *Scr* Ed Waters, from the novel by John D MacDonald

The Darkest Light ★★★ 12

Drama 1999 · UK · Colour · 90mins

This post-millennial downer outlines the never-ending misfortunes of Stephen Dillane and Kerry Fox's Yorkshire family. It's only when their daughter (Keri Arnold) and her Indian schoolmate think they've seen a vision of the Virgin Mary on the moors that Simon Beaufoy's contemplation on the true meaning of faith gathers momentum. The film is well acted, but the subject matter is so depressing that even those with patience to wallow in misery will find it a long haul. AJ. Contains swearing. DVD

Keri Arnold *Catherine* • Stephen Dillane *Tom* • Kerry Fox *Sue* • Kavita Sungha *Uma* • Jason Walton *Matthew* • Nisha K Nayar *Nisha* • Nicholas Hope *Father Mark* ■ *Dir* Simon Beaufoy, Bille Eltringham • *Scr* Simon Beaufoy

Darklands ★★★ 18

Horror thriller 1996 · UK · Colour · 86mins

Although it's a virtual rip-off of *The Wicker Man*, this shocker is an impressively dark and reasonably frightening tale of pagan ritual and human sacrifice. Journalist Craig Fairbrass investigates a series of killings in south Wales and learns, too late, that he has a terrifying part to play in blood-soaked rites aimed at regenerating an ancient religion. While Fairbrass lacks the range to milk his part for every shaded nuance, Julian Richards's feature debut proves the spirit of Hammer lives on. AJ. Contains swearing, nudity and violence.

Craig Fairbrass *Frazer Truick* • Rowena King *Rachel Morris* • Jon Finch *David Keller* • David Duffy *Carver* • Roger Nott *Dennis Cox* • Richard Lynch *Salvy* • Nicola Branson *Becky* ■ *Dir/Scr* Julian Richards

Darkman ★★★★ 18

Fantasy horror 1990 · US · Colour · 91mins

Independent director Sam Raimi's first studio movie is a splashy amalgam of *The Phantom of the Opera* and *Doctor X*, with a perfectly cast Liam Neeson donning synthetic flesh masks to take revenge on the mobsters who disfigured him. Pathos and tragedy are always lurking beneath the horrific surface of this take on classic 1930s *Grand Guignol*, given a nifty 1990s spin by exaggerated camera moves and psychedelic visuals. A tasty buffet of gothic moodiness, startling make-up effects and expressionistic artifice, this is Raimi on virtuoso form. AJ. Contains swearing and violence. DVD

Liam Neeson *Peyton Westlake/Darkman* • Frances McDormand *Julie Hastings* • Colin Friels *Louis Strack Jr* • Larry Drake *Robert G Durant* • Nelson Mashita *Yakitito* • Jessie Lawrence Ferguson *Eddie Black* • Rafael H Robledo *Rudy Guzman* • Danny Hicks *Skip* • Theodore Raimi [Ted Raimi] *Rick* ■ *Dir* Sam Raimi • *Scr* Chuck Pfarrer, Sam Raimi, Ivan Raimi, Daniel Goldin, Joshua Goldin, from a story by Sam Raimi • *Cinematographer* Bill Pope

Darkman II: the Return of Durant ★★★ 18

Fantasy horror
1995 · US/Can · Colour · 88mins

This direct-to-video sequel is as dynamic and fast-paced as its predecessor, thanks to director Bradford May taking more than a few leaves out of the Sam Raimi style book. Arnold Vosloo takes over from Liam Neeson as the synthetic mask-wearing Dr Peyton Westlake.The formula is 1940s pulp fiction with a twist of black comedy and some superior special effects, and it all works like a charm for an effective reprise. AJ. Contains violence and swearing. DVD

Arnold Vosloo *Dr Peyton Westlake/Darkman* • Larry Drake *Robert G Durant* • Renee O'Connor *Laurie Brinkman* • Kim Delaney *Jill Randall* • Lawrence Dane *Dr Alfred Hathaway* • Jesse Collins *Dr David Brinkman* • David Ferry *Eddie* ■ *Dir* Bradford May • *Scr* Steve McKay, Chuck Pfarrer, from a story by Robert Eisele, Lawrence Hertzog, from characters created by Sam Raimi

Darkman III: Die Darkman Die ★★★ 15

Fantasy horror 1996 · US · Colour · 83mins

In this second sequel, the "Urban Bigfoot" is pitted against evil drug baron Jeff Fahey, who is determined to learn the secret of deformed superhero Peyton Westlake's strength. With executive producer Sam Raimi and returning director/cameraman Bradford May maintaining the quality and integrity of both previous adventures, and with a well-realised script accenting character as much as explosive gimmicks, this comic-strip horror escapade is a worthwhile addition to the series. AJ. Contains violence and swearing. DVD

Jeff Fahey *Peter Rooker* • Arnold Vosloo *Dr Peyton Westlake/Darkman* • Roxann Biggs-Dawson [Roxann Biggs] *Angela Rooker* • Darlanne Fluegel *Dr Bridget Thorne* • Alicia Panetta *Jenny Rooker* ■ *Dir* Bradford May • *Scr* Mike Werb, Michael Colleary, from characters created by Sam Raimi

Darkness ★★ 15

Horror mystery
2002 · Sp/US · Colour · 84mins

This is a messy and muddled supernatural tale about an American family moving into a Spanish country house that seems to be haunted by the ghosts of six local children who disappeared 40 years earlier. The solid cast tries its best to invoke shuddery suspense as the relentlessly silly and repetitive plot unfolds, but the slow pace of this low-voltage formula horror defeats them at every bland turn. Although beautifully shot, the parade of familiar clichés adds up to an empty exercise in technique. AJ DVD

Anna Paquin *Regina* • Lena Olin *Maria* • Iain Glen *Mark* • Giancarlo Giannini *Albert Rua* • Fele Martínez *Carlos* • Stephan Enquist *Paul* • Fermí Reixach *Villalobos* ■ *Dir* Jaume Balagueró • *Scr* Jaume Balagueró, Fernando de Felipe

Darkness before Dawn ★★★ 15

Drama based on a true story
1992 · US · Colour · 92mins

Stephen Lang portrays a recovering drug addict, who finds inspiration in the strength of a woman (Meredith Baxter) working at the clinic that is treating him. Until, that is, he discovers that her troubles are worse than his. Not a load of laughs in this TV movie, but sufficient drama. PF. Contains drug abuse. DVD

Meredith Baxter *Mary Ann Thompson* • Stephen Lang *Guy Grand* ■ *Dir* John Patterson • *Scr* Karen Hall

Darkness Falls ★ 15

Psychological thriller
1998 · UK · Colour · 87mins

Ray Winstone and Sherilyn Fenn co-star in this poorly directed, badly acted drama. Winstone plays a man teetering on the edge of insanity following a car crash which has left his pregnant wife in a coma. Tricking his way into the Isle of Man home of obnoxious businessman Tim Dutton and his neglected wife (Fenn), Winstone holds them at gunpoint. Clunkingly awful. JB. Contains swearing. DVD

Sherilyn Fenn *Sally Driscoll* • Ray Winstone *John Barrett* • Tim Dutton *Mark Driscoll* • Anita Dobson *Mrs Hayter* • Bryan Pringle *Clive Hayter* • Robin McCaffrey *Jane Barrett* • Michael Praed *Hit man* • Oliver Tobias *Simpson* ■ *Dir* Gerry Lively • *Scr* John Howlett, from the play *Dangerous Obsession* by NJ Crisp

Darkness Falls ★ 15

Horror 2003 · US · Colour · 82mins

This risible slice of low-grade horror hokum has two attractive 20-somethings and a nine-year-old terrorised by the "Tooth Fairy", the legendary witch of the small New England town, Darkness Falls. The airborne harridan can only survive in the dark – cue much lurking in the shadows. The biggest shock of the film is that the limp effects are by the usually excellent Stan Winston. Laughably bad. AS DVD

Chaney Kley *Kyle Walsh* • Emma Caulfield *Caitlin* • Lee Cormie *Michael* • Grant Piro *Larry* • Sullivan Stapleton *Matt* • Steve Mouzakis *Dr Murphy* ■ *Dir* Jonathan Liebesman • *Scr* John Fasano, James Vanderbilt, Joe Harris, from a story by Joe Harris, from his short film *Tooth Fairy*

Darkness in Tallinn ★★★★ 15

Crime thriller
1993 · Fin/Est · BW and Colour · 95mins

If you can excuse the transition from monochrome to colour and Ilkka Jarvilaturi's determination to include every conceivable directorial flourish, then you're in for a treat with this Estonian heist movie. As the power-station worker persuaded by his pregnant wife to assist in the theft of the national treasury on its return from safe-keeping in Paris, Ivo Uukkivi gives a wonderfully bemused performance that gains a harder edge as the blood begins to flow. But this isn't just a quirky *film noir*. It's also a fascinating portrait of a long-oppressed country still not sure of its fate despite regaining independence. Produced with backing from the United States and Sweden. DP. In Estonian and Russian with English subtitles. [VIDEO]

Ivo Uukkivi *Toivo* • Milena Gulbe *Maria* • Monika Mager *Terje* • Enn Klooren *Mihhail "Misha"* • Vaino Laes *Andres* ■ *Dir* Ilkka Jarvilaturi • *Scr* Ilkka Jarvilaturi, Paul Kolsby

Darling ★★★★ 15

Drama 1965 · UK · BW · 121mins

At every turn of his Oscar-winning script, Frederic Raphael invites us to admire just how clever he's been in dissecting the shallowness of celebrity and the gullibility of the public. Yet no matter how much we want to resist falling under the spell of such a self-congratulatory piece of work, there's no denying that this is both an astute snapshot of a moment in time and a wicked insight into the national character that still has relevance today. Julie Christie thoroughly merited her Oscar as the immoral starlet hellbent on fame and Dirk Bogarde is equally splendid. DP [VIDEO] DVD

Laurence Harvey *Miles Brand* • Dirk Bogarde *Robert Gold* • Julie Christie *Diana Scott* • Roland Curram *Malcolm* • José-Luis De Villalonga *Cesare* • Alex Scott (1) *Sean Martin* ■ *Dir* John Schlesinger • *Scr* Frederic Raphael, from a story by Frederic Raphael, John Schlesinger, Joseph Janni

Darling, How Could You! ★★

Comedy 1951 · US · BW · 95mins

This adaptation was to be Gloria Swanson's follow-up to *Sunset Boulevard*. When she refused to test for the role, however, it was given to Joan Fontaine. Quickly shot using the Washington Square sets left over from *The Heiress*, this tale of an imaginative daughter who erroneously thinks her mother is having an affair is not one of director Mitchell Leisen's better efforts. Despite some very funny lines, the pace is too lethargic, while the playing is more cute than charming. TV

Joan Fontaine *Alice Grey* • John Lund *Dr Robert Grey* • Mona Freeman *Amy* • Peter Hanson *Dr Steve Clark* • David Stollery *Cosmo* • Virginia Farmer *Fanny* ■ *Dir* Mitchell Leisen • *Scr* Dodie Smith, Lesser Samuels, from the play *Alice-Sit-by-the-Fire* by JM Barrie

Darling Lili ★★★ U

Spy drama 1970 · US · Colour · 135mins

This lengthy First World War charade is an under-rated and utterly charming valentine from director Blake Edwards to his wife, Julie Andrews, who takes the lead role of a Mata Hari-type figure. The star is marvellously supported by dashing air ace Rock Hudson and British satirist Lance Percival in his best film role. The film was shot by *Red River* cinematographer Russell Harlan, and also boasts some marvellous aerial dogfight sequences. It does take itself rather too seriously at times, though, and non-Andrews fans should avoid it. TS

Julie Andrews *Lili Smith* • Rock Hudson *Major William Larrabee* • Jeremy Kemp *Kurt von Ruger* • Lance Percival *TC* • Michael Witney *Youngblood Carson* • Jacques Marin *Major Duvalle* • André Maranne *Lt Liggett* ■ *Dir* Blake Edwards • *Scr* Blake Edwards, William Peter Blatty

D'Artagnan's Daughter ★★★ 15

Period adventure 1994 · Fr · Colour · 124mins

Costume adventures might not be what we expect from Bertrand Tavernier, but his enthusiasm for this spirited romp is evident in the panache of his direction. Sophie Marceau leaves her convent to coax father Philippe Noiret out of retirement in order to save Louis XIV's throne. With Claude Rich and Charlotte Kady providing disdainful villainy, this is fun, but prone to longueurs and incongruous slapstick. DP. In French with English subtitles. Contains violence, nudity. [VIDEO]

Sophie Marceau *Eloise* • Philippe Noiret *D'Artagnan* • Claude Rich *Duke of Crassac* • Sami Frey *Aramis* • Jean-Luc Bideau *Athos* • Raoul Billerey *Porthos* • Charlotte Kady *Scarlet woman* • Nils Tavernier *Quentin* ■ *Dir* Bertrand Tavernier • *Scr* Michel Leviant, from the novel *Vingt Ans Après* by Alexandre Dumas

The Darwin Adventure ★★ U

Biographical drama
1972 · UK · Colour · 90mins

A biopic about Charles Darwin, whose voyages to South America and the Galapagos Islands aboard HMS *Beagle* fuelled his theory of natural selection, a theory that shocked the religious establishment of the Victorian world. In a subject far more suited to the television drama or mini-series, this is a sketchy effort that convinces us of Darwin's importance but turns his romantic life into soap opera. AT

Nicholas Clay *Charles Darwin* • Susan Macready *Emma Wedgewood* • Ian Richardson *Captain Fitzroy* • Robert Flemyng *Professor Henslow* ■ *Dir* Jack Couffer • *Scr* William Fairchild, from a story by Jack Couffer, Max Bella

DARYL ★★★ PG

Science-fiction drama
1985 · US · Colour · 95mins

Although highly derivative, this New Age fairy tale is a charming, lightweight diversion about a Florida couple whose lives are transformed after fostering a young boy suffering from what they believe to be amnesia. When they learn DARYL actually stands for Data Analysing Robot Youth Lifeform, the real drama unfolds as they fight to stop his termination by Pentagon intelligence agents. The plot's formulaic, but this is nicely written and well acted. AJ [VIDEO] DVD

Mary Beth Hurt *Joyce Richardson* • Michael McKean *Andy Richardson* • Barret Oliver *Daryl* • Colleen Camp *Elaine Fox* • Kathryn Walker *Ellen Lamb* • Josef Sommer *Dr Jeffrey Stewart* ■ *Dir* Simon Wincer • *Scr* David Ambrose, Allan Scott, Jeffrey Ellis

A Date with a Dream ★★ U

Comedy 1948 · UK · BW · 58mins

In only his second credited role, Terry-Thomas starred in this feeble comedy with brothers Len and Bill Lowe, playing the members of an ENSA trio who reunite after the war to revive their hopes of showbiz success. The nightclub routines are pretty awful and director Dicky Leeman hasn't a clue how to structure a narrative. But Jean Carson spares everyone's blushes as the girl they all fall for, and Norman Wisdom makes his feature debut. DP

Terry-Thomas *Terry* • Jean Carson *Jean* • Len Lowe *Len* • Bill Lowe *Bill* • Wally Patch *Uncle* • Norman Wisdom *Shadow boxer* ■ *Dir* Dicky Leeman • *Scr* Robert S Baker, Monty Berman, Dicky Leeman

Date with an Angel ★★ PG

Fantasy comedy romance
1987 · US · Colour · 100mins

Musician Michael E Knight saves a beautiful angel (Emmanuelle Béart) from drowning in a swimming pool. He then starts wondering if he should go ahead with his marriage to Phoebe Cates, the daughter of a cosmetics tycoon (David Dukes) who tries to make Béart his new cover girl. As wet as the nearly-drowned angel's wings, this otherworldly tosh marked an inauspicious American debut for French actress Béart after the success of *Manon des Sources*. TH [VIDEO]

Michael E Knight *Jim Sanders* • Phoebe Cates *Patty Winston* • Emmanuelle Béart *Angel* • David Dukes *Ed Winston* • Phil Brock *George* • Albert Macklin *Don* • Peter Kowanko [Pete Kowanko] *Rex* ■ *Dir/Scr* Tom McLoughlin

A Date with Judy ★★★ U

Musical comedy 1948 · US · Colour · 113mins

This utterly charming musical dates from MGM's greatest period, though it may be a little overlong and twee for today's tastes. Sweet Jane Powell plays the title role, but Richard Thorpe's film also gives the young and oh-so-beautiful Elizabeth Taylor a chance to shine. Wallace Beery is top-billed, but he was near the end of this life and Technicolor wasn't kind to him. Still, at least he gets to perform with Carmen Miranda. The song *It's a Most Unusual Day* was a huge hit. TS

Wallace Beery *Melvin R Foster* • Jane Powell *Judy Foster* • Elizabeth Taylor *Carol Pringle* • Carmen Miranda *Rosita Conchellas* • Xavier Cugat *Cugat* • Robert Stack *Stephen Andrews* ■ *Dir* Richard Thorpe • *Scr* Dorothy Cooper, Dorothy Kingsley, Aleen Leslie

A Date with the Falcon ★★

Detective mystery 1941 · US · BW · 63mins

Following *The Gay Falcon*, this was the second film in the 16-episode *Falcon* series, with which RKO followed their *Saint* movies. Here the suave investigator (George Sanders) and his nervy sidekick (Allen Jenkins) get involved in the case of a kidnapped scientist. Typical of the plethora of "gentleman sleuth" second features popular in the 1930s and 1940s, it's of little interest now, though Sanders is always a pleasure to watch. RK

George Sanders *Falcon* • Wendy Barrie *Helen Reed* • James Gleason *O'Hara* • Allen Jenkins *Goldy* • Mona Maris *Rita Mara* • Victor Kilian *Max* • Frank Moran *Dutch* ■ *Dir* Irving Reis • *Scr* Lynn Root, Frank Fenton, from the character created by Michael Arlen

Daughter of Darkness ★★

Crime drama 1948 · UK · BW · 91mins

This brooding, violent melodrama concerns an Irish servant girl (Siobhan McKenna) who is not only a nymphomaniac, but also a psychopathic killer given to murdering her admirers. Directed by Lance Comfort, this British offering is an opportunity to see McKenna, one of the most compelling of Irish stage actresses, portraying a maniac with full-blooded commitment. Little else to recommend it, though. RK

Anne Crawford *Bess Stanforth* • Maxwell Reed *Dan* • Siobhan McKenna *Emily Beaudine* • George Thorpe *Mr Tallent* • Barry Morse *Robert Stanforth* • Liam Redmond *Father Cocoran* • Honor Blackman *Julie Tallent* ■ *Dir* Lance Comfort • *Scr* Max Catto, from his play *They Walk Alone*

Daughter of Dr Jekyll ★

Horror 1957 · US · BW · 69mins

Dr Jekyll doesn't actually appear in this unusual take on the gothic classic. Instead, the film tells of his less well-known daughter, who, upon landing in England to claim her father's inheritance, is blamed for a series of grisly murders. The result is a hotch-potch of vampire, werewolf and Jekyll-and-Hyde elements, all searching in vain for a coherent storyline. A masterclass of abysmal acting. RS

John Agar *George Hastings* • Gloria Talbott *Janet Smith* • Arthur Shields *Dr Lomas* • John Dierkes *Jacob* • Martha Wentworth *Mrs Merchant* ■ *Dir* Edgar G Ulmer • *Scr* Jack Pollexfen

The Daughter of Rosie O'Grady ★★★ U

Musical comedy 1950 · US · Colour · 103mins

An unpretentious, charming Warner Bros period musical with an attractive cast, headed by June Haver, a former Fox blonde who married Fred MacMurray and whose talent and appeal tend to be forgotten nowadays. Debonair singer Gordon MacRae and talented dancer Gene Nelson provide solid support, but look out for that young teenager: it's Debbie Reynolds, making her movie musical debut. TS

June Haver *Patricia O'Grady* • Gordon MacRae *Tony Pastor* • James Barton *Dennis O'Grady* • Debbie Reynolds *Maureen O'Grady* • SZ "Cuddles" Sakall [SZ Sakall] *Miklos Teretzky* • Gene Nelson *Doug Martin* • Sean McClory *James Moore* • Marsha Jones *Katie O'Grady* • Jane Darwell *Mrs Murphy* ■ *Dir* David Butler • *Scr* Jack Rose, Melville Shavelson, Peter Milne, from a story by Jack Rose, Melville Shavelson • *Music Director* Ray Heindorf

Daughter of the Nile ★★★ PG

Drama 1987 · Tai · Colour · 83mins

The least typical entry in Hou Hsiao-Hsien's filmography, this Taipei tale of family in-fighting and social frustration dazzles with its urban iconography – the neon signs, the designer clothes, the blaring pop music and the Japanese time-travel comic books that keep schoolgirl Yang Lin sane, as she tries to tend house, hold down a fast-food job and prevent her cop father and gangster brother from tearing each other apart. Hou blends wit with warmth in exploring both the complex web of relationships and the ambitions that drive his superbly realised characters. DP. In Mandarin and Hokkien with English subtitles.

Yang Lin *Lin Hsiao-yang* • Kao Jai *Lin Hsiao-fang* • Yang Fan *Ah-sang* ■ *Dir* Hou Hsiao-Hsien • *Scr* Zhu Tianwen

Daughters Courageous ★★★

Drama 1939 · US · BW · 106mins

Wandering Claude Rains returns to his cosy home town just in time to stop wife Fay Bainter marrying Donald Crisp and to deal with daughter Priscilla Lane's engagement to John Garfield. Put over with fluent ease, this sentimental and lightweight movie is almost as charming as its blockbusting predecessor, *Four Daughters*, which had made an instant star of Warner Bros newcomer Garfield the previous year. Rushing to capitalise on that success, the studio recycled the formula, re-employing the same director (Michael Curtiz) and cast. *Four Wives* continued the story. RK

Claude Rains *Jim Masters* • John Garfield *Gabriel Lopez* • Jeffrey Lynn *Johnny Heming* • Fay Bainter *Nan Masters* • Donald Crisp *Sam Sloane* • May Robson *Penny* • Frank McHugh *George* • Dick Foran *Eddie Moore* • George Humbert *Manuel Lopez* • Berton Churchill *Judge Hornsby* • Priscilla Lane *Buff Masters* • Rosemary Lane *Tinka Masters* • Lola Lane *Linda Masters* ■ *Dir* Michael Curtiz • *Scr* Julius J Epstein, Philip C Epstein, from the play *Fly Away Home* by Irving White, Dorothy Bennett

Daughters of Darkness ★★★★ 18

Horror 1970 · Bel/Fr/W Ger · Colour · 95mins

The legend of Elizabeth Bathory (who Hammer lionised in *Countess Dracula*) provides the inspiration for this lyrically erotic, art house shocker, expertly directed by the Belgian Harry Kümel. Delphine Seyrig is the well-preserved *haute couture* vampire who insinuates her evil self on an unsuspecting honeymoon couple at a luxurious seaside hotel in Ostend. Explicitly sexual and violent, the haunting atmosphere, Seyrig's brilliant performance and the always striking imagery make this European chiller a stunning masterwork. AJ. A French language film.

Delphine Seyrig *Countess Bathory* • Daniele Ouimet *Valerie* • John Karlen *Stefan Chiltern* • Andrea Rau *Ilona Harczy* ■ *Dir* Harry Kümel • *Scr* Harry Kümel, Pierre Drouot, JJ Amiel • *Cinematographer* Van Der Enden

Daughters of Satan ★ 18

Horror 1972 · US · Colour · 86mins

A bottom-of-the-barrel horror, notable only for putting future *Magnum PI* star Tom Selleck on the road to fame. He's an art collector whose wife buys a painting of three witches being burned at the stake and gradually becomes possessed by the one she resembles. Featuring terrible dialogue and soap-opera dramatics. AJ DVD

Tom Selleck *James Robertson* • Barra Grant *Chris Robertson* • Tani Phelps Guthrie [Tani Guthrie] *Kitty Duarte* • Vic Silayan *Dr Dangal* ■ *Dir* Hollingsworth Morse • *Scr* John C Higgins, from a story by John Bushelman

Daughters of the Dust ★★★★ PG

Experimental period drama
1991 · US · Colour · 107mins

Completed over several years, Julie Dash's low-budget feature debut is a poetic tribute to African culture, the oral tradition and the spirit of the Gullah people, who owe their descent to the freed slaves who settled on the islands off the coasts of South Carolina and Georgia. Set in 1902, the film uses a gathering that precedes the mainland odyssey of five women to explore questions of race, sex and family as well as nationality and exile. The imagery impresses, with the naturally-lit colours given a sense of history remembered by Dash's stylised use of slow motion. DP

Adisa Anderson *Eli Peazant* • Cheryl Lynn Bruce *Viola* • Cora Lee Day *Nana Peazant* • Kaycee Moore *Haagar* • Alva Rogers *Eula Peazant* • Bahni Turpin *Iona Peazant* • Trula Hoosier *Trula* ■ *Dir/Scr* Julie Dash

Dave ★★★★ 15

Political comedy
1993 · US · Colour · 105mins

Part-time presidential impersonator Kevin Kline is called into the White House when the real president suffers a stroke. However, he soon begins to get a taste for the job, much to the horror of shifty White House aide Frank Langella. Kline is excellent as both the naive stand-in and the ruthless president, while Sigourney Weaver is fine as the bitter First Lady who begins to see her "husband" in a new light. Look out for Oliver Stone, playing himself, trying to convince a disbelieving chat-show host that there is another conspiracy afoot. A delightful, gentle satire on the Washington scene. JF DVD

Kevin Kline *Dave Kovic/President Bill Mitchell* • Sigourney Weaver *Ellen Mitchell* • Frank Langella *Bob Alexander* • Kevin Dunn *Alan Reed* • Ving Rhames *Duane Stevenson* • Ben Kingsley *Vice-President Nance* • Charles Grodin *Murray Blum* • Faith Prince *Alice* ■ *Dir* Ivan Reitman • *Scr* Gary Ross

David ★★★★ U

Drama 1979 · W Ger · Colour · 125mins

One of the most powerful films ever made about the Holocaust, this adaptation of Joel Konig's fact-based book isn't primarily about courage or heroic charity. Instead, it's a harrowing study of the gnawing terror that was part of everyday life for Jews living under the Nazi tyranny. Director Peter Lilienthal refuses to sentimentalise the humanity of the decent few, or reduce the endless round of concealment and escape to mere action set pieces. With Mario Fischel's determination born out of fear as the hunted teenager and Walter Taub outstanding as his Rabbi father, this thoroughly merited its Golden Bear at Berlin. DP. In German with English subtitles.

Walter Taub *Rabbi Singer* • Irena Vrkljan *Wife* • Eva Mattes *Toni* • Mario Fischel *David* ■ *Dir* Peter Lilienthal • *Scr* Jurek Becker, Ulla Ziemann, Peter Lilienthal, from the novel by Joel Konig

David and Bathsheba ★★

Biblical drama 1951 · US · Colour · 115mins

Gregory Peck is the King of Israel, who spots Susan Hayward's red-headed Bathsheba going about her ablutions and is instantly smitten, subsequently incurring the wrath of God and having to atone for his sins. More of a plodding, pompous moral debate than an epic, Henry King's movie eschews a lot of the DeMille-style orgies and battles one would expect. Peck manages to exude nobility and Hayward is ravishing, in a Kansas farmgirl sort of way. AT

Gregory Peck *David* • Susan Hayward *Bathsheba* • Raymond Massey *Nathan* • Kieron Moore *Uriah* • James Robertson-Justice *Abishai* • Jayne Meadows *Michal* ■ *Dir* Henry King • *Scr* Philip Dunne

David and Lisa ★★★

Drama based on a true story
1962 · US · BW · 93mins

David and Lisa are mental patients. He's autistic, obsessively tidy and hates being touched; she's a schizophrenic who talks only in gobbledegook rhymes, or else doesn't talk at all. On the one hand, this seems like a typical slice of American psychobabble about misunderstood kids. The acting, however, raises the story to an entirely different level – the performances of Keir Dullea and Janet Margolin are totally sincere and deeply touching. AT

Keir Dullea *David* • Janet Margolin *Lisa* • Howard Da Silva *Dr Swinford* • Neva Patterson *Mrs Clemens* • Clifton James *John* • Richard McMurray *Mr Clemens* • Nancy Nutter *Maureen* • Matthew Anden *Simon* ■ *Dir* Frank Perry • *Scr* Eleanor Perry, from a non-fiction book by Dr Theodore Isaac Rubin

David and Lisa ★★★ PG

Drama 1998 · US · Colour · 86mins

This is a well-meaning TV remake of the 1962 original, but what was innovative back then now feels very dated and similar to countless other dysfunctional teen movies. At a boarding school for emotionally disturbed adolescents, a hostile loner who detests being touched falls in love with a childlike girl who only speaks in rhyme. Sidney Poitier gives a sympathetic performance as the caring psychiatrist, and the film, while slow-paced, is moving. MC DVD

Sidney Poitier *Dr Jack Miller* • Lukas Haas *David* • Brittany Murphy *Lisa* • Debi Mazar *Maggie* • Allison Janney *Alix* • Kim Murphy *Natalie* ■ *Dir* Lloyd Kramer • *Scr* Lloyd Kramer, from the 1962 film

David Copperfield ★★★★★ U

Classic drama 1935 · US · BW · 124mins

This immaculately cast and designed David O Selznick production for MGM remains the definitive version of Charles Dickens's vaguely autobiographical classic novel. While Basil Rathbone is Mr Murdstone to a T, and there couldn't possibly be any other Aunt Betsey Trotwood than Edna May Oliver, the real casting coups are Lennox Pawle's perfect Mr Dick and Roland Young's Uriah Heep. If the great WC Fields makes Micawber a star turn, it's no bad thing, and both Freddie Bartholomew and Frank Lawton as the young and the grown-up David, respectively, could not be bettered. This film is a richly entertaining reminder of what Hollywood, and especially MGM, did best. TS

WC Fields *Mr Micawber* • Lionel Barrymore *Dan Peggotty* • Freddie Bartholomew *David as a child* • Maureen O'Sullivan *Dora* • Madge Evans *Agnes* • Edna May Oliver *Aunt Betsey* • Lewis Stone *Mr Wickfield* • Frank Lawton *David as a man* • Elizabeth Allan *Mrs Copperfield* • Roland Young *Uriah Heep* • Basil Rathbone *Mr Murdstone* • Elsa Lanchester *Clickett* • Jean Cadell *Mrs Micawber* • Jessie Ralph *Nurse Peggotty* • Lennox Pawle *Mr Dick* • Una O'Connor *Mrs Gummidge* ■ *Dir* George Cukor • *Scr* Howard Estabrook, Hugh Walpole, from the novel by Charles Dickens • *Cinematographer* Oliver T Marsh • *Editor* Robert J Kern

David Holzman's Diary ★★

Satire 1968 · US · BW · 74mins

Considered daring and experimental in its day, Jim McBride's directorial debut is a *cine-vérité* counterculture classic that now looks dull and pretentious. LM Kit Carson plays film-maker Holzman, who decides to record his own life for a couple of weeks and, in the self-obsessed process, loses his girlfriend. There are some interesting moments, plus the sort of avant-garde imagery that would soon enter the mainstream, but overall this 1960s curio is a self-indulgent exercise. AJ

LM Kit Carson *David Holzman* • Eileen Dietz *Penny Wohl* • Louise Levine *Sandra* • Lorenzo Mans *Pepe* ■ *Dir* Jim McBride • *Scr* LM Kit Carson, Jim McBride

David's Mother ★★★ PG

Drama 1994 · US · Colour · 92mins

Kirstie Alley proves herself a capable dramatic actress in this sensitive TV movie, as a mother who devotes her life to the care of her autistic son. Alley won an Emmy for her performance, as did Michael Goorjian, who plays David as a teenager. The script presents genuine situations and emotions without resorting to platitudes or easy sentiment, and gives the powerhouse cast plenty to get its teeth into. DP DVD

Kirstie Alley *Sally Goodson* • Sam Waterston *John* • Stockard Channing *Bea* • Michael Goorjian *David aged 17* • Chris Sarandon *Phillip* • Phylicia Rashad *Gladys* • Steve Ivany *David aged 59* ■ *Dir* Robert Allan Ackerman • *Scr* Bob Randall, from the play by Walt Lloyd

Davy Crockett and the River Pirates ★★★ U

Western adventure
1956 · US · Colour · 86mins

Davy Crockett was a phenomenon of the 1950s. Originally intended only for Disney's US TV shows, the noble buckskin-clad frontiersman swept the world after Uncle Walt strung some episodes together and released them in cinemas. This was the second theatrical outing, a feast of fun that falls clearly into two halves. The more enjoyable first part pits Crockett (Fess Parker) against self-styled "King of the River", splendidly hammed by Jeff York, while the second half deals with Indian confrontations. TS

Fess Parker *Davy Crockett* • Buddy Ebsen *George Russel* • Jeff York *Mike Fink* • Kenneth Tobey *Jocko* • Clem Evans *Cap'n Cobb* • Irving Ashkenazy *Moose* • Mort Mills *Sam Mason* ■ *Dir* Norman Foster • *Scr* Norman Foster, Tom Blackburn

Davy Crockett, King of the Wild Frontier ★★★ U

Western adventure
1955 · US · Colour · 88mins

The first of two cinema features, both adapted from a TV series produced by the Disney studio, about the legendary backwoodsman who became a congressman and died at the Alamo. Crockett is one of America's most bizarre, contradictory and elusive historical personages, but this movie simply prints the legend. Fess Parker, a jovial, athletic type, plays Crockett and successfully turned the coonskin hat into the fashion accessory most demanded by children in the mid-1950s, plus there's that hit theme song to hum along with as well. AT

Fess Parker *Davy Crockett* • Buddy Ebsen *George Russel* • Basil Ruysdael *Andrew Jackson* • Hans Conried *Thimblerig* • William Bakewell *Tobias Norton* • Kenneth Tobey *Colonel Jim Bowie* • Pat Hogan *Chief Red Stick* • Helene Stanley *Polly Crockett* ■ *Dir* Norman Foster • *Scr* Tom Blackburn

Dawg ★★ 15

Romantic comedy
2001 · US · Colour · 80mins

Denis Leary finds himself playing a disreputable likely lad in this over-calculating hybrid of *The Bachelor* and *Liar, Liar*. Reteaming with *Double Whammy* co-star Elizabeth Hurley, he mugs knowingly as a playboy who will inherit his grandmother's millions if he succeeds in apologising personally to each and every woman he's wronged. Unfortunately, Victoria Hochberg is clearly striving to make an impression on her feature debut and pushes too hard with both the character comedy and the innuendo. DP DVD

Denis Leary *Doug "Dawg" Munford* • Elizabeth Hurley *Anna Lockheart* • Steffani Brass *Lindsay Anne Wickman* • Eddie Adams (2) *Young Dawg* ■ *Dir* Victoria Hochberg • *Scr* Ken Hastings

Dawn! ★★★ U

Biographical drama
1979 · Aus · Colour · 111mins

Dawn Fraser is the only swimmer in Olympic history to win the same event at three consecutive games, taking the 100 metres freestyle gold at Melbourne, Rome and Tokyo. She also set 27 world records, making her one of the most remarkable swimmers of all time. Avoiding the usual sports biopic formula of running through the list of achievements by means of a few phoney action sequences, director Ken Hannam explores the strain such success exerts and the flatness of life away from the roar of the crowd. Bronwyn Mackay-Payne is magnificent in the title role. DP

Bronwyn Mackay-Payne *Dawn* • Tom Richards *Harry* • John Diedrich *Gary* • Bunney Brooke *Mum* • Ron Haddrick *Pop* ■ *Dir* Ken Hannam • *Scr* Joy Cavill

Dawn at Socorro ★★★

Western 1954 · US · Colour · 80mins

One of the last western co-features in rich Technicolor, before Eastman Colour took over, and jolly splendid it looks, too, with glistening saloon interiors and bright location exteriors. But veteran director George Sherman brings his usual lack of style to bear and fails to get the best out of the sexually-charged co-starring of rugged Rory Calhoun and fiery Piper Laurie, both of whom are excellent in what is basically a routine plot. TS

Rory Calhoun *Brett Wade* • Piper Laurie *Rannah Hayes* • David Brian *Dick Braden* • Kathleen Hughes *Clare* • Alex Nicol *Jimmy Rapp* • Edgar Buchanan *Sheriff Cauthen* • Lee Van Cleef *Earl Ferris* ■ *Dir* George Sherman • *Scr* George Zuckerman • *Cinematographer* Carl Guthrie

Dawn of the Dead ★★★★ 18

Horror 1978 · US · Colour · 139mins

With its shopping mall setting, some see this astoundingly violent sequel to the classic *Night of the Living Dead* as a satirical attack on American consumerism and shallow materialistic values. Others merely see it as the greatest zombie fantasy of all time as the reawakened dead resume their cannibalistic stalking of the living. Cynical, devastating and relentless, Romero's masterpiece about the American Dream turning into a terrifying nightmare is an ideal blend of black comedy and harrowing carnage. Romero completed his trilogy with 1985's *Day of the Dead*. AJ. Contains swearing and violence. [VIDEO] DVD

David Emge *Stephen* • Ken Foree *Peter* • Scott Reiniger *Roger* • Gaylen Ross *Francine* • David Crawford *Dr Foster* • David Early *Mr Berman* • George A Romero *TV director* ■ *Dir/Scr* George A Romero • *Music* Dario Argento and the Goblins

Dawn of the Dead ★★★ 18

Horror 2004 · US/Jpn/Fr · Colour · 95mins

Director Zack Snyder's remake of George A Romero's 1978 zombie horror is an efficient exercise in recycling. Romero's original screenplay acts as the flesh and bones for James Gunn's updated script, in which a group of survivors, including a nurse (Sarah Polley) and a police officer (Ving Rhames), find refuge from a plague of zombies in a shopping precinct. This is a gruesome but entertaining big-budget take on the horror classic, but Snyder's film lacks the satirical edge that gave Romero's original so much bite. TH. Contains violence. [VIDEO] DVD

Sarah Polley *Ana Clark* • Ving Rhames *Kenneth* • Jake Weber *Michael* • Mekhi Phifer *Andre* • Ty Burrell *Steve* • Michael Kelly (2) *CJ* • Kevin Zegers *Terry* • Lindy Booth *Nicole* ■ *Dir* Zack Snyder • *Scr* James Gunn (2), from the film by George A Romero

Dawn of the Mummy ★ 18

Horror 1981 · US · Colour · 86mins

The bright arc lights used for a photo shoot in an Egyptian tomb revive the ancient pharaoh and his slave army in this dispiriting mix of Hammer horror and extreme zombie violence. Completely vapid, with ham acting and shameless mugging galore, this can only be recommended to splatter addicts. AJ [VIDEO] DVD

Brenda King • Barry Sattels • George Peck • John Salvo • Joan Levy • Diane Beatty ■ *Dir* Frank Agrama [Farouk Agrama] • *Scr* Daria Price, Ronald Dobrin, Frank Agrama, from a story by Ronald Dobrin, Daria Price

The Dawn Patrol ★★

First World War drama
1930 · US · BW · 105mins

This famous flying picture was Howard Hawks's first talkie, but he ran into problems with Howard Hughes, producer/director of the rival *Hell's Angels*. Hughes tried to prevent the Hawks movie from going into production, even suing writer John Monk Saunders. The story concerns a squadron of British flyers stoically running near-suicidal bombing raids over Germany during the First World War. Hawks later made far better flying pictures; this one is hampered by the primitive talkie technology, the artificiality of the dialogue and the performances which are as wooden as the rickety planes. AT

Richard Barthelmess *Dick Courtney* • Douglas Fairbanks Jr *Douglas Scott* • Neil Hamilton *Major Brand* • William Janney *Gordon Scott* • James Finlayson *Field Sergeant* ■ *Dir* Howard Hawks • *Scr* Howard Hawks, Dan Totheroh, Seton I Miller, from the story *The Flight Commander* by John Monk Saunders • *Music* Leo F Forbstein

The Dawn Patrol ★★★★ U

First World War melodrama
1938 · US · BW · 98mins

A marvellously unsentimental First World War melodrama, this remake of the Howard Hawks classic movie is actually better cast (Errol Flynn, David Niven and Basil Rathbone all on top form) and better directed (by Edmund Goulding) than the original. It incorporates library material and action sequences from Hawks's movie, and there's a very real sense of the passion and futility of war in the gripping screenplay that realistically conveys horror among comrades and grace under pressure. This is a very fine film indeed. TS [VIDEO]

Errol Flynn *Captain Courtney* • David Niven *Lieutenant Scott* • Basil Rathbone *Major Brand* • Donald Crisp *Phipps* • Melville Cooper *Sergeant Watkins* • Barry Fitzgerald *Music* • Carl Esmond *Von Mueller* • Peter Willes *Hollister* • Morton Lowry *Donnie Scott* • Michael Brooke *Squires* • James Burke *Flaherty* ■ *Dir* Edmund Goulding • *Scr* Seton I Miller, Dan Totheroh, from the story *The Flight Commander* by John Monk Saunders

The Dawn Rider ★★ U

Western 1935 · US · BW · 53mins

An uninspiring John Wayne programme filler, from that period when he was trapped in Lone Star westerns before his resurrection in *Stagecoach* nine years later. The Duke is chasing his father's murderer, who turns out to be Denny Meadows, who later changed his name to Dennis Moore and propped up many a B-movie. Cinematographer Archie Stout ended his career with Wayne, working on some of the Duke's more famous Warner Bros movies, but his work here is purely functional. TS [VIDEO] DVD

John Wayne *John Mason* • Marion Burns *Alice* • Yakima Canutt *Barkeeper* • Reed Howes *Ben* • Denny Meadows [Dennis Moore] *Rudd* • Bert Dillard *Buck* • Jack Jones (1) *Black* ■ *Dir* RN Bradbury [Robert N Bradbury] • *Scr* RN Bradbury, from a story by Lloyd Nosler

The Dawning ★★★★ PG

Period drama 1988 · UK · Colour · 93mins

Rebecca Pidgeon made her debut in this striking film about pre-Partition Ireland. Pidgeon, stifled by living with aunt Jean Simmons and disabled grandfather Trevor Howard (in his last role), falls in love with bumbling city boy Hugh Grant. When she meets an enigmatic stranger (Anthony Hopkins), however, suddenly her world begins to turn on its head. Avoiding heavy-handedness or didacticism, director Robert Knights cleverly depicts the rise of the Irish Republican Army through Pidgeon's own progression from naive teenager to adult woman. LH [VIDEO]

Anthony Hopkins *Major Angus Barry/Cassius* • Rebecca Pidgeon *Nancy Gulliver* • Jean Simmons *Aunt Mary* • Trevor Howard *Grandfather* • Tara MacGowran *Maeve* • Hugh Grant *Harry* • Ronnie Masterson *Bridie* ■ *Dir* Robert Knights • *Scr* Moira Williams, from the novel *The Old Jest* by Jennifer Johnston

The Day after Tomorrow ★★★★ 12

Disaster movie 2004 · US · Colour · 118mins

This jaw-dropping disaster movie makes director Roland Emmerich's previous outings feel like expensive dress rehearsals. This cautionary tale piles on the Hollywood excess to deliver a US-centred thrill-ride in which global warming abruptly pushes the planet into a new ice age during one incredible, worldwide superstorm. Though there's a human element, focusing on climatologist Dennis Quaid's cross-country journey to Manhattan to rescue his trapped son, Jake Gyllenhaal, it's the weather effects that take centre stage. Never mind that the dialogue is often cheesy and the performances melodramatic, what counts here is the enormous entertainment factor. SF [VIDEO] DVD

Dennis Quaid *Professor Jack Hall* • Jake Gyllenhaal *Sam Hall* • Ian Holm *Professor Terry Rapson* • Emmy Rossum *Laura Chapman* • Sela Ward *Doctor Lucy Hall* • Dash Mihok *Jason Evans* • Jay O Sanders *Frank Harris* • Austin Nichols *JD* • Arjay Smith *Brian Parks* • Tamlyn Tomita *Janet Tokada* • Glenn Plummer *Luther* • Adrian Lester *Simon* • Kenneth Welsh *Vice President Becker* ■ *Dir* Roland Emmerich • *Scr* Jeffrey Nachmanoff, Roland Emmerich, from a story by Roland Emmerich

A Day at the Races ★★★ U

Comedy 1937 · US · BW · 104mins

The Marx Brothers' second film for MGM was hidebound by the decision to overload the mayhem with mediocre musical interludes that the studio bigwigs believed would give the picture more class. The inconsistent support playing similarly saps much of the energy, undoing the sterling work of the wonderful Margaret Dumont. The trio's own performances are splendid, with the "Tootsie frootsie ice cream" sketch standing as the best of the Chico-Groucho wordplay routines. DP [VIDEO] DVD

Groucho Marx *Dr Hugo Z Hackenbush* • Chico Marx *Tony* • Harpo Marx *Stuffy* • Allan Jones *Gil* • Maureen O'Sullivan *Judy* • Margaret Dumont *Mrs Upjohn* ■ *Dir* Sam Wood • *Scr* Robert Pirosh, George Seaton, George Oppenheimer, from a story by Robert Pirosh, George Seaton

Day Dreams ★★★★★ U

Silent comedy 1922 · US · BW · 21mins

Whether he's being pursued by an army of policemen on to a ferry, or walking round and round a ship's paddle-wheel like a hamster, Buster Keaton is just trying to prove his love for Renée Adorée. He wants to show her he can get – and keep – a job in the city. But since the jobs include working as a street-sweeper and as a nurse in a pet hospital, it takes a lot of persuasion. An early Keaton three-reeler, this manages to insert elements of surreality into even the humdrum. TH [VIDEO] DVD

Buster Keaton *The young man* • Renée Adorée *The girl* • Joe Keaton *Her father* • Edward F Cline [Edward Cline] *Stage manager* ■ *Dir* Buster Keaton, Eddie Cline [Edward Cline] • *Scr* Buster Keaton, Edward F Cline

Day for Night ★★★★★ PG

Drama 1973 · Fr · Colour · 110mins

The winner of the best foreign film Oscar, this is an exhilarating celebration of the movie-making process. Everything that could possibly go wrong on François Truffaut's film-within-the-film, *Meet Pamela*, does so in spades. Yet Truffaut's character battles on in the search for meaningful art. Regular collaborator Jean-Pierre Léaud is on cracking form as the actor who falls in love with leading lady Jacqueline Bisset, who spoofs her own image to perfection. There are also lovely supporting turns from Valentina Cortese and Nathalie Baye, while novelist Graham Greene (billed as Henry Graham) pops up in a cameo that was something of a practical joke at Truffaut's expense. DP. In French and English with subtitles. [VIDEO] DVD

François Truffaut *Ferrand* • Jacqueline Bisset *Julie* • Jean-Pierre Léaud *Alphonse* • Valentina Cortese *Severine* • Jean-Pierre Aumont *Alexandre* • Jean Champion *Bertrand* • Dani *Lilianne* • Alexandra Stewart *Stacey* • Bernard Menez *Bernard* • Nike Arrighi *Odile* • Nathalie Baye *Assistant* • Bernard Menez *Bernard* ■ *Dir* François Truffaut • *Scr* François Truffaut, Suzanne Schiffman, Jean-Louis Richard

The Day I Became a Woman ★★★★ PG

Drama 2000 · Iran · Colour · 74mins

A short story trilogy using the three stages of womanhood as its basis, Marziyeh Meshkini's first feature examines the restraints Iranian society places upon its women. Each has its own distinctive tone: the heartfelt simplicity of a young girl's last hour of play before taking the chador contrasts with the frantic satire of a husband's bid to prevent his wife from competing in a cycle race and, in the final surreal story, the disarming irony of an old lady atoning for a lifetime's drudgery by spending her savings on household gadgets. Infused with a graceful naturalism and lacking any sense of sermonising, this is a truly touching film that should bring its director as much acclaim as her renowned husband, Mohsen Makhmalbaf, who wrote and produced this. DP. In Farsi with English subtitles. [VIDEO] DVD

Fatemeh Cherag Akhar *Hava* • Shabnam Toloui *Ahoo* • Azizeh Sedighi *Hoora* ■ *Dir* Marziyeh Meshkini • *Scr* Mohsen Makhmalbaf, Marziyeh Meshkini, from short stories by Mohsen Makhmalbaf

D

A Day in October ★★★ 15

Second World War drama
1991 · US/Den · Colour · 96mins

Such was Denmark's antipathy to the invading Nazis and its sense of indivisible nationhood that only a relatively small percentage of its Jewish population was consigned to concentration camps. This melodrama concentrates on the heroism of a single family whose protection of a wounded partisan led to the mass exodus of Danish Jews to Sweden. Kenneth Madsen's uplifting film is given additional power by the understated performances of DB Sweeney and Daniel Benzali. DP [VIDEO]

DB Sweeney *Niels Jensen* • Kelly Wolf *Sara Kublitz* • Tovah Feldshuh *Emma Kublitz* • Daniel Benzali *Solomon Kublitz* • Ole Lemmeke *Larson* • Kim Romer *Arne* ■ *Dir* Kenneth Madsen • *Scr* Damian F Slattery

A Day in the Death of Joe Egg ★★★★

Black comedy drama
1971 · UK · Colour · 108mins

The fate of a child with cerebral palsy might not appear suitable material for a black comedy. Yet Peter Nichols's adaptation of his own hit play is less concerned with euthanasia than with the very human emotions being experienced by the girl's angst-ridden parents. Faced with constant shifts in tone, director Peter Medak prevents the action from becoming either tasteless or sentimental, thanks, largely, to the exceptional performances of Alan Bates and Janet Suzman. Free of the Brechtian devices that characterised the stage version, this is a provocative look at people under pressure and the transience of love. DP. Contains swearing and nudity.

Alan Bates *Brian* • Janet Suzman *Sheila* • Peter Bowles *Freddie* • Sheila Gish *Pam* • Joan Hickson *Grace* • Elizabeth Robillard *Jo* • Murray Melvin *Doctor* ■ *Dir* Peter Medak • *Scr* Peter Nichols, from his play

Day of Atonement ★★ 18

Thriller 1992 · Fr/It · Colour · 96mins

France's answer to *The Godfather*, this long-winded gangster movie is the sequel to director Alexandre Arcady's 1982 hit, *La Grand Pardon*, which also starred French heavy Roger Hanin. The first film dealt mainly with the internecine war conducted by Franco-Algerian Jewish gangsters; this sequel changes only in location: the film was shot mainly in Miami, allowing Christopher Walken to play a drug baron and the son of a former Nazi who fled to Chile. AT

Roger Hanin *Raymond Bettoun* • Richard Berry *Maurice Bettoun* • Jennifer Beals *Joyce Feranti* • Jill Clayburgh *Sally White* • Gérard Darmon *Roland Bettoun* • Christopher Walken *Pasco Meisner* ■ *Dir* Alexandre Arcady • *Scr* Alexandre Arcady, Daniel Saint-Hamont

A Day of Fury ★★

Western 1956 · US · Colour · 77mins

A moody little western, very much of its time, with rebel Dale Robertson finding himself outside civic convention in a conservative frontier town. It has its moments, but Robertson is both too bland and too old for the role, and the direction is very average. TS

Dale Robertson *Jagade* • Mara Corday *Sharman Fulton* • Jock Mahoney *Marshal Allan Burnett* • Carl Benton Reid *Judge John J McLean* ■ *Dir* Harmon Jones • *Scr* James Edmiston, Oscar Brodney, from a story by James Edmiston

Day of the Animals ★★★ 15

Horror 1977 · US · Colour · 92mins

One of the best movies made by horror hack William Girdler, who died in a tragic helicopter accident just as he was about to hit the big time with *The Manitou*. Ecological erosion of the ozone layer causes wild creatures to attack a group of Californian hikers in this creditable effort. Bears, wolves, vultures, snakes, dogs and rats (in a truly amazing forest ranger attack) all get in on the menacing act that's beautifully photographed and directed for lively shock value and welcome chuckles between the carnage. AJ

Christopher George *Steve Buckner* • Leslie Nielsen *Paul Jensen* • Lynda Day George *Terry Marsh* • Richard Jaeckel *Taylor MacGregor* • Michael Ansara *Daniel Santee* ■ *Dir* William Girdler • *Scr* William Norton, Eleanor Norton, from a story by Edward E Montoro

Day of the Bad Man ★★

Western 1958 · US · Colour · 82mins

A routine western, enhanced by the majestic photography of Irving Glassberg that gives the small tale a certain grandeur. Ageing Fred MacMurray stars as a judge who's trying to maintain law and order until the hour arrives when a condemned outlaw goes to the gallows. Director Harry Keller pays far too much attention to MacMurray's grim features, but there is the compensation of some irresistible western stalwarts in the cast. TS

Fred MacMurray *Judge Jim Scott* • Joan Weldon *Myra Owens* • John Ericson *Sheriff Barney Wiley* • Robert Middleton *Charlie Hayes* • Marie Windsor *Cora Johnson* • Edgar Buchanan *Sam Wyckoff* • Skip Homeier *Howard Hayes* • Lee Van Cleef *Jake Hayes* ■ *Dir* Harry Keller • *Scr* Lawrence Roman, from a story by John M Cunningham

The Day of the Beast ★★★★ 18

Black comedy horror
1995 · Sp/It · Colour · 99mins

Spanish director Alex de la Iglesia's highly engaging continental smash hit is a wicked parody of doom prophecy movies such as *The Omen*, with a dash of *Die Hard* thrown in. This scintillating and original spoof effortlessly mixes the sinister with the absurd, as three very unusual wise men search for the birth place of the Antichrist in Madrid on Christmas Eve. A screwball horror that's packed with demons, demises and diverting detail, it's as much a serious indictment of the way the media distorts reality as it is a clever genre satire. AJ. In Spanish with English subtitles. Contains violence, swearing and nudity.

Alex Angulo *Angel Berriartua* • Armando De Razza *Ennio Lombardi* • Santiago Segura *Jose Maria* • Terele Pávez *Rosario* • Nathalie Sesena *Mina* • Jaime Blanch *Toyota 1* • Maria Grazia Cucinotta *Susana* ■ *Dir* Alex de la Iglesia • *Scr* Alex de la Iglesia, Jorge Guerricaechevarría

Day of the Dead ★★★★ 18

Horror 1985 · US · Colour · 100mins

After *Night of the Living Dead* (1968) and *Dawn of the Dead* (1978), George A Romero ends his trilogy in a sophisticated, disturbing and horrifying way. Scientists in an underground missile base try to find ways of domesticating and controlling the cannibalistic zombie hordes so they can be re-integrated into society. Investing the living, rotting corpses with human touches (they shave and listen to personal stereos) is a stroke of genius on Romero's part, and one that makes his unnervingly bleak world vision both an intellectual and terrifying shock to the system. AJ. Contains violence and swearing. DVD

Lori Cardille *Sarah* • Terry Alexander *John* • Joseph Pilato *Captain Rhodes* • Jarlath Conroy *McDermott* • Antone DiLeo Jr [Anthony DiLeo Jr] *Miguel* • Richard Liberty *Dr Logan* • Howard Sherman *Bub* ■ *Dir/Scr* George A Romero

The Day of the Dolphin ★★ PG

Drama 1973 · US · Colour · 100mins

George C Scott takes on one of the biggest challenges of his career by conducting meaningful conversations with dolphins. He even teaches his pet dolphin endearments like "Fa" and "Pa". But this isn't a Flipperish, Disney-pic. Indeed, things get decidedly bleak when it's revealed that Scott's dolphins are destined to be used as sentient torpedoes in a plot to assassinate the President aboard his yacht. Georges Delerue's score is a high point. AT

George C Scott *Dr Jake Terrell* • Trish Van Devere *Maggie Terrell* • Paul Sorvino *Mahoney* • Fritz Weaver *Harold DeMilo* • Jon Korkes *David* • Edward Herrmann *Mike* • Leslie Charleson *Maryanne* ■ *Dir* Mike Nichols • *Scr* Buck Henry, from a novel by Robert Merle

Day of the Evil Gun ★★ PG

Western 1968 · US · Colour · 89mins

Originally planned as a TV movie, this western starts out as an unofficial and wholly competent remake of *The Searchers*. Glenn Ford and Arthur Kennedy bond surprisingly well as they survive all manner of perils in a bid to rescue Ford's family from the Apache, and there's solid support from the under-rated Dean Jagger as an untrustworthy Indian trader. But the action takes an unexpected and rather improbable turn, which rather spoils the film. DP

Glenn Ford *Lorn Warfield* • Arthur Kennedy *Owen Forbes* • Dean Jagger *Jimmy Noble* • John Anderson *Captain Jefferson Addis* • Paul Fix *Sheriff Kelso* • Nico Minardos *DeLeon* • Dean Stanton [Harry Dean Stanton] *Sergeant Parker* ■ *Dir* Jerry Thorpe • *Scr* Charles Marquis Warren, Eric Bercovici, from the novel by Charles Marquis Warren

The Day of the Jackal ★★★★★ 15

Thriller 1973 · UK/Fr · Colour · 136mins

A magnificent script from Kenneth Ross and a masterly central performance from Edward Fox form the backbone of this big-screen version of Frederick Forsyth's bestselling novel, but it's Fred Zinnemann's matchless direction that makes it such compelling viewing. The pacing of the picture is superb, a methodical accumulation of detail that is as fastidious as Fox's preparation for his mission to assassinate General de Gaulle. Although the action crisscrosses Europe, there's no postcard prettiness, just a sure grasp of the atmosphere of each place before getting down to the business of the scene. Remade in 1997 as *The Jackal*, starring Bruce Willis. DP. Contains violence, swearing and brief nudity. DVD

Edward Fox *The Jackal* • Michael Lonsdale [Michel Lonsdale] *Claude Lebel* • Alan Badel *Minister* • Tony Britton *Inspector Thomas* • Adrien Cayla-Legrand *President* • Cyril Cusack *Gunsmith* • Donald Sinden *Mallinson* • Derek Jacobi *Caron* • Eric Porter *Colonel Rodin* • Delphine Seyrig *Colette de Montpelier* • Timothy West *Berthier* ■ *Dir* Fred Zinnemann • *Scr* Kenneth Ross, from the novel by Frederick Forsyth

The Day of the Locust ★★★★ 18

Drama 1975 · US · Colour · 137mins

This chronicle of Hollywood losers, eaten up by ambition but possessing no talent, gets lavish coverage from British director John Schlesinger. Karen Black stars as a would-be starlet, the daughter of drunken vaudevillian Burgess Meredith, who takes Donald Sutherland for a ride and almost snares sketch artist William Atherton as well. Adapted from Nathanael West's famous novel about early Tinseltown, the film sprawls too indulgently but remains enormously watchable throughout. TH. Contains violence, nudity and sex scenes. DVD

Donald Sutherland *Homer Simpson* • Karen Black *Faye Greener* • Burgess Meredith *Harry Greener* • William Atherton *Tod Hackett* • Geraldine Page *Big Sister* ■ *Dir* John Schlesinger • *Scr* Waldo Salt, from the novel by Nathanael West

Day of the Outlaw ★★★

Western 1959 · US · BW · 92mins

A fine bleak winter western from veteran director Andre De Toth, who manages to emphasise every nuance of rage in anti-McCarthyite screenwriter Philip Yordan's bitter isolationist allegory. Rugged Robert Ryan is the rancher who finally makes a stand against Burl Ives's gang of renegade cut-throats. The snow-covered landscape (beautifully photographed in stark black and white by Russell Harlan) makes the tale seem even bleaker, with the climactic gunfight in a blizzard quite remarkable. TS

Robert Ryan *Blaise Starrett* • Burl Ives *Jack Bruhn* • Tina Louise *Helen Crane* • Alan Marshal *Hal Crane* • Nehemiah Persoff *Dan* • Venetia Stevenson *Ernine* • Donald Elson *Vic* ■ *Dir* Andre De Toth • *Scr* Philip Yordan

The Day of the Triffids ★★★ 15

Science-fiction horror
1962 · UK · Colour · 94mins

A meteor shower blinds all but a few Earthlings, leaving society at the mercy of carnivorous plants from outer space in this rather disappointing version of John Wyndham's classic sci-fi novel. While the Triffids themselves are efficiently bizarre and menacing, Steve Sekely's barely competent direction hardly provides the sinister spores with a shining showcase. Freddie Francis directed the lighthouse scenes, added later in a bravura effort to beef up the chills. AJ DVD

Howard Keel *Bill Masen* • Janette Scott *Karen Goodwin* • Nicole Maurey *Christine Durrant* • Kieron Moore *Tom Goodwin* • Mervyn Johns *Mr Coker* • Alison Leggatt *Miss Coker* • *Dir* Steve Sekely • *Scr* Philip Yordan, from the novel by John Wyndham

Day of the Wolves ★★

Crime drama 1973 · US · Colour · 95mins

A thoughtful B-picture thriller, this has former sheriff Richard Egan battling against a weird conspiracy by a mysterious gang who want to cut off his home town for three days to prepare for the "ultimate heist". Martha Hyer, in one of her final screen appearances, is Egan's reward for his courage. The director is Ferde Grofe Jr, and there's a touch of science-fiction to spice up the tension. TH

Richard Egan *Pete Anderson* • Rick Jason *Number Four* • Martha Hyer *Mrs Anderson* • Jan Murray *Uncle Murray* ■ *Dir/Scr* Ferde Grofe Jr

Day of Wrath ★★★★★ PG

Period drama 1943 · Den · BW · 92mins

Put to the stake for witchcraft, Anna Svierkier places a curse on the pastor (Thorkild Roose) who condemned her. Disaster and death are then visited upon Roose and his family, beginning with his discovery that his wife Lisbeth Movin is having an affair with a younger man (Preben Lerdoff Rye). Made by Denmark's great genius of the cinema, Carl Th Dreyer, this is an uncompromising vision of human frailty, stupidity, bigotry and cruelty, made all the more horrifying by the startling beauty of its images. Not easy, but rewarding. RK. In Danish with English subtitles.

Thorkild Roose *Absalon Pedersson* • Lisbeth Movin *Anne, his wife* • Sigrid Neiiendam *Merete, his mother* • Preben Lerdorff Rye *Martin, his son* ■ *Dir* Carl Th Dreyer • *Scr* Carl Th Dreyer, Mogens Skot-Hansen, Poul Knudsen, from the play and novel *Anne Pedersdotter* by Hans Wiers-Jenssens

A Day on the Grand Canal with the Emperor of China ★★★

Documentary 1988 · US · Colour · 46mins

Rejoicing under the alternative title *Surface Is Illusion but So Is Depth*, this is a predictably lucid yet surprisingly entertaining treatise on the rigidity of western artistic traditions. Illustrating his thesis by contrasting a 72-ft long scroll by the 17th-century Chinese painter Wang Hui with a Venetian cityscape by Canaletto, David Hockney demonstrates how much more imaginatively the Oriental artist has used perspective and iconography than his High Renaissance counterpart. With Philip Haas freeing the camera to rove around the sights witnessed by the Emperor on his progress, this can be classed alongside the artistic documentaries of Luciano Emmer. DP

Dir Philip Haas • *Scr* David Hockney

Day One ★★★★

Second World War drama
1989 · US · Colour · 141mins

The spectre of nuclear warfare is made real and immediate in this TV movie based on the true story of the Second World War Manhattan Project's race to build the first atomic bomb. David W Rintels's taut script, veteran Joseph Sargent's insightful direction and a splendid cast make this Emmy-winning production gleam with the feeling of living history. Moving, frightening and richly rewarding. MC

John McMartin *Dr Arthur Compton* • Brian Dennehy *General Leslie Groves* • Richard Dysart *President Harry S Truman* • Michael Tucker *Leo Szilard* • Hume Cronyn *James F Byrnes* • Hal Holbrook *General George Marshall* ■ *Dir* Joseph Sargent • *Scr* David W Rintels, from the book *Day One: Before Hiroshima and After* by Peter Wyden

The Day the Earth Caught Fire ★★★

Science-fiction drama
1961 · UK · BW · 98mins

Atomic explosions at the two poles put the planet on a collision course with the Sun in this bleak British doomsday vision. With the emphasis on the reactions of some London journalists to the impending catastrophe rather than elaborate special effects, this tautly intelligent sci-fi thriller hits all the right buttons, helped by a script full of fatalistic quips and apocalyptic cynicism. Engrossing, with a memorable fade-out on two possible newspaper headlines. AJ

Leo McKern *Bill Maguire* • Janet Munro *Jeannie* • Edward Judd *Peter Stenning* • Michael Goodliffe *Night editor* • Bernard Braden *News editor* • Reginald Beckwith *Harry* • Gene Anderson *May* • Austin Trevor *Sir John Kelly* • Renée Asherson *Angela* • Michael Caine *Policeman* ■ *Dir* Val Guest • *Scr* Val Guest, Wolf Mankowitz

The Day the Earth Stood Still ★★★★★ U

Classic science-fiction drama
1951 · US · BW · 88mins

Coming just four months after Christian Nyby and Howard Hawks had unleashed *The Thing from Another World* upon a petrified Cold War public, director Robert Wise's sci-fi classic was a welcome sign of hope that we might not be going up in flames after all. From Bernard Herrmann's otherworldly score to Lyle Wheeler and Addison Hehr's deceptively simple designs, this has had an incalculable influence on big screen science-fiction. For all its philosophical solemnity and heavy-handed religious symbolism, Edmund H North's script deftly pokes fun at the Red-baiters who had done so much to foster the nuclear scare, while his notion that children accept without question what grown-ups are too cynical to see has continued to resurface throughout the blockbuster era. DP [video] DVD

Michael Rennie *Klaatu* • Patricia Neal *Helen Benson* • Hugh Marlowe *Tom Stevens* • Sam Jaffe *Dr Barnhardt* • Billy Gray *Bobby Benson* • Frances Bavier *Mrs Barley* • Lock Martin *Gort* ■ *Dir* Robert Wise • *Scr* Edmund H North, from the short story *Farewell to the Master* by Harry Bates

The Day the Fish Came Out ★★

Satire 1967 · UK/Gr · Colour · 109mins

Michael Cacoyannis's follow-up to his highly acclaimed *Zorba the Greek* couldn't have been more different, or more of a disappointment: a ham-fisted satire that falls prisoner to the modish mood of its time. Tom Courtenay and Colin Blakely play Nato airmen whose plane, carrying a pair of H-bombs and a doomsday weapon, ditches in the sea near a Greek island. Cacoyannis struggles to integrate the clashing styles of farce and realism into any coherent whole. RS

Tom Courtenay *Navigator* • Sam Wanamaker *Elias* • Colin Blakely *Pilot* • Candice Bergen *Electra* • Ian Ogilvy *Peter* ■ *Dir/Scr* Michael Cacoyannis

The Day the Sun Turned Cold ★★★★ 12

Drama based on a true story
1994 · HK · Colour · 100mins

Taken as a political allegory or an Oedipal melodrama, Ho Yim's award-winning film is both troubling and compelling. It scarcely matters whether Si Ching Gao Wa (a powerful Mongolian actress who also starred in the director's 1984 breakthrough, *Homecoming*) actually killed her husband. What is so intriguing is why her son (Tao Chung Wa) would betray her to the authorities, and why he would wait a decade before doing so. Based on true events and told in a measured, unsettlingly realistic manner, this provocative picture will linger long in the mind. DP. In Mandarin with English subtitles.

Si Ching Gao Wa *Pu Fengying, the mother* • Tao Chung Wa *Guan Jian, the son* • Ma Jingwu *Guan Shichang, the father* ■ *Dir* Ho Yim • *Scr* Ho Yim, Wang Xing Dong

The Day the World Ended ★★ PG

Science fiction 1956 · US · BW · 79mins

The first science-fiction film from cult director Roger Corman has seven survivors of a nuclear war fighting off atomic radiation mutants from their mountain retreat. Not much else happens in this cheesy yet ludicrously entertaining fright flick, which transposes the Garden of Eden myth into an uncertain future. The ads at the time promised "a new high in naked shrieking terror", but the only shrieks to be heard now will be ones of laughter at the three-eyed, four-armed monster suits. AJ [video] DVD

Richard Denning *Rick* • Lori Nelson *Louise* • Adele Jergens *Ruby* • Touch Connors [Mike Connors] *Tony* • Paul Birch *Maddison* ■ *Dir* Roger Corman • *Scr* Lou Rusoff, from his story

The Day the World Ended ★★ 15

Science-fiction horror
2001 · US · Colour · 86mins

Despite taking its title from Roger Corman's 1956 B-movie about radiation-induced mutants, this TV remake is most indebted to *Invasion of the Body Snatchers*. No one believes youngster Bobby Edner's claims that recent murders are the work of his biological father, who he believes is an extraterrestrial. Predictable and one-dimensional. DP DVD

Randy Quaid *Dr Michael McCann* • Bobby Edner *Benjamin James McCann* • Nastassja Kinski *Dr Jennifer Stillman* • Harry Groener *Sheriff* • Lee DeBroux *Harlan* • Stephen Tobolowsky *Ed Turner* ■ *Dir* Terence Gross • *Scr* Max Enscoe, Annie de Young, from a story by Brian King

The Day They Gave Babies Away ★★ U

Period drama 1957 · US · Colour · 102mins

A rather curious account of the hardships and tragedies faced by a mid-19th-century Scottish immigrant family in the American backwoods, this stars the unlikely pairing of Britain's Glynis Johns and the hunky, pre-*High Chaparral* Cameron Mitchell. The result is little more than a plodding seasonal tear-jerker, but, despite the weak characterisation and mediocre direction, it's good to see the famously husky-voiced Johns as a doughty pioneer wife. RK

Glynis Johns *Mamie Eunson* • Cameron Mitchell *Robert Eunson* • Rex Thompson *Robbie Eunson* • Patty McCormack *Annabelle Eunson* ■ *Dir* Allen Reisner • *Scr* Dale Eunson, Katherine Eunson

The Day They Robbed the Bank of England ★★★ U

Crime caper 1960 · UK · BW · 84mins

In 1901, Irish nationalists plot to rob the Old Lady of Threadneedle Street of its gold bullion, taking it through the sewers and down the River Thames. Both a heist thriller and a sophisticated political drama, this was directed by John Guillermin, who makes the most of the planning and features some clever use of locations, but most eyes will be on Peter O'Toole as the young security guard Fitch. David Lean saw his performance and cast him in *Lawrence of Arabia*. AT

Aldo Ray *Norgate* • Elizabeth Sellars *Iris Muldoon* • Hugh Griffith *O'Shea* • Peter O'Toole *Fitch* • Kieron Moore *Walsh* • Albert Sharpe *Tosher* • John Le Mesurier *Green* • Joseph Tomelty *Cohoun* ■ *Dir* John Guillermin • *Scr* Howard Clewes, Richard Maibaum, from the novel by John Brophy

The Day Time Ended ★

Science fiction
1980 · US/Sp · Colour · 80mins

Jim Davis's family moves into a solar-powered desert home, only to find they're slap-bang in the middle of a time vortex that lures visiting aliens to warn them about Earth's imminent destruction. A nonsensical blend of cardboard special effects, this is a crudely assembled affair. AJ

Jim Davis *Grant* • Christopher Mitchum *Richard* • Dorothy Malone *Ana* • Marcy Lafferty *Beth* • Scott Kolden *Steve* • Natasha Ryan *Jenny* ■ *Dir* John "Bud" Cardos • *Scr* Wayne Schmidt, J Larry Carroll, David Schmoeller, from a story by Steve Neill

A Day to Remember ★★ U

Drama 1953 · UK · BW · 91mins

This mix of poignant drama and postcard comedy follows Cockney darts captain Stanley Holloway as he leads his team on a day trip to Boulogne. A host of familiar faces take caricature cameos. However, the stories that linger longest in the mind are those owing least to contrivance: notably widower James Hayter's return to his honeymoon hotel, and ex-soldier Donald Sinden's reunion with Odile Versois, the beauty he'd known as a child during the war. DP

Stanley Holloway *Charley Porter* • Donald Sinden *Jim Carver* • Joan Rice *Vera Mitchell* • Odile Versois *Martine Berthier* • James Hayter *Fred Collins* • Harry Fowler *Stan Harvey* • Edward Chapman *Mr Robinson* • Peter Jones *Percy Goodall* • Bill Owen *Shorty Sharpe* • Meredith Edwards *Bert Tripp* • George Coulouris *Captain* • Vernon Gray *Marvin* • Thora Hird *Mrs Trott* • Theodore Bikel *Henri Dubot* ■ *Dir* Ralph Thomas • *Scr* Robin Estridge, from the novel *The Hand and the Flower* by Jerrard Tickell

The Day Will Dawn ★★★ U

Second World War romance
1942 · UK · BW · 98mins

Markedly less restrained than many other British tales of wartime resistance, this well-meaning flag-waver is still far more effective than the majority of have-a-go Hollywood movies on the same theme. The story of a British journalist liaising with the Norwegian underground to help destroy a German U-boat base is merely par for the course. What sets this apart is a remarkable cast of British stalwarts, not one of whom puts a foot wrong. DP

Ralph Richardson *Lockwood* • Deborah Kerr *Kari Alstead* • Hugh Williams *Colin Metcalfe* • Griffith Manes *Inspector Gunter* • Francis L Sullivan *Wettau* • Roland Culver *Naval Attaché* • Niall MacGinnis *Olaf* • Finlay Currie *Alstead* ■ *Dir* Harold French • *Scr* Terence Rattigan, Anatole de Grunwald, Patrick Kirwan, from a story by Frank Owen

Daybreak ★★

Period romance 1931 · US · BW · 72mins

Ramon Novarro stars as a handsome Austrian guardsman who falls in love with the appealing Helen Chandler in this period romance. Although the film is elegantly and sensitively directed by Frenchman Jacques Feyder, with a supporting cast that includes the redoubtable C Aubrey Smith, it failed to appeal to the public then and is unlikely to do so now. RK

Ramon Novarro *Willi* • Helen Chandler *Laura* • Jean Hersholt *Herr Schnabel* • C Aubrey Smith *Gen von Hartz* ■ *Dir* Jacques Feyder • *Scr* Ruth Cummings, Cyril Hume, Zelda Sears, from the play by Arthur Schnitzler

Daybreak ★★ PG

Crime drama 1946 · UK · BW · 77mins

At the time, the producers Muriel and Sydney Box complained that their British melodrama had been held up by censorship and ruined by cuts. It is hard to see how it could have worked, even in its entirety, as Eric Portman portrays an unemployed hangman seeking revenge on the Swedish lover (Maxwell Reed) of his wife (Ann Todd). Despite Portman's usual magnetism, the result is quite laughable. TH [video]

Eric Portman *Eddie* • Ann Todd *Frankie* • Maxwell Reed *Olaf* • Edward Rigby *Bill Shackle* • Bill Owen *Ron* • Jane Hylton *Doris* • Eliot Makeham *Mr Bigley* • Margaret Withers *Mrs Bigley* • John Turnbull *Superintendent* • Maurice Denham *Inspector* ■ *Dir* Compton Bennett • *Scr* Muriel Box, Sydney Box, from a play by Monckton Hoffe

D

Daybreak ★

Drama 2000 · UK · Colour · 95mins

Director Bernard Rudden's debut feature is British independent cinema at its worst. It centres on an Edinburgh nightclub, where the DJ (played by Flash) is losing money almost as quickly as viewers will lose patience with the pretentious burblings of New Age oddball Shauna MacDonald or the sham patter that Jean-Philippe Ecoffey feeds Gaynor Purvis in trying to persuade her to become a French porn star. Almost unwatchable. DP

Shauna MacDonald *Emily* • Gaynor Purvis *Anna* • Jean-Philippe Ecoffey *Pierrot* • Flash *Jed* • Diane Bell *Eve* ■ *Dir/Scr* Bernard Rudden

Daybreak ★★★★ 15

Drama 2003 · Swe · Colour · 108mins

Two posh couples gather for a dinner party where adulterous secrets and other lies spill out. Meanwhile, a bitter middle-aged woman seeks revenge on the ex-husband who threw her over for a younger version. In another part of town, a builder is hired for a bizarre job, bricking in the windows and doors of a survivalist couple trying to reject society. This brooding drama, almost a black comedy in places, stands several cuts above the norm, because its three strands aren't forced to intersect too closely and feel like well-hewn short stories in themselves. Out of the impressive ensemble, Bergman favourite Pernilla August and Ann Petren, as two different spurned wives, particularly standout, the first all icy dignity, the second a hellcat bent on vengeance. LF. In Swedish with English subtitles. Contains swearing and sexual references.

Pernilla August *Agnes* • Jakob Eklund *Rickard* • Marie Richardson *Sofie* • Leif Andree *Mats* • Peter Andersson *Olof* • Ann Petren *Anita* • Sanna Krepper *Petra* • Ingvar Hirdwall *Knut* • Marika Lindstrom *Mona* • Magnus Krepper *Anders* ■ *Dir/Scr* Bjorn Runge

Daydream Believer ★★ 15

Romantic comedy drama
1991 · Aus · Colour · 81mins

Beginning with unpleasant scenes of child abuse, this film lurches forward in time to find the child in question has grown into the timid Miranda Otto, whose tactic in times of stress is to imagine she's a horse. There is some heavy-handed satire at the expense of wealthy businessman Martin Kemp and a last-minute rescue worthy of a silent melodrama. DP. Contains swearing, violence, nudity. [video]

Miranda Otto *Nell* • Martin Kemp *Digby* • Anne Looby *Margot* • Alister Smart *Ron* • Gia Carides *Wendy* • Bruce Venables *Stu* ■ *Dir* Kathy Mueller • *Scr* Saturday Rosenberg

Daylight ★★★ 12

Disaster movie 1996 · US · Colour · 109mins

This is an involving tale about a group of motorists who become trapped in a New York tunnel under the Hudson River following a horrific pile-up. Director Rob Cohen's classy contribution to the 1990s disaster movie resurgence is less reliant on slick visual effects than most, and Sylvester Stallone displays more vulnerability than expected as the leader of an escape party. Cohen's orchestration of the requisite action scenes is impressive. JC. Contains violence and swearing. DVD

Sylvester Stallone *Kit Latura* • Amy Brenneman *Madelyne Thompson* • Viggo Mortensen *Roy Nord* • Dan Hedaya *Frank Kraft* • Jay O Sanders *Steven Crighton* • Karen Young *Sarah Crighton* • Claire Bloom *Eleanor Trilling* • Sage Stallone *Vincent* ■ *Dir* Rob Cohen • *Scr* Leslie Bohem

Daylight Robbery ★★ U

Drama 1964 · UK · BW · 57mins

In the same year that he co-starred with The Beatles in *A Hard Day's Night*, Norman Rossington found himself up to his neck in trouble in this lively production from the Children's Film Foundation. The focus of the action falls on a kid quartet that gets locked overnight in a department store and thwarts the knockabout efforts of a gang of incompetent crooks. Michael Truman directs without much invention. DP

Trudy Moors *Trudy* • Janet Hannington *Janet* • Kirk Martin *Kirk* • Darryl Read *Darryl* • Douglas Robinson *Gangster* • John Trenaman *Gangster* • Gordon Jackson • Ronald Fraser ■ *Dir* Michael Truman • *Scr* Dermot Quinn, from a story by Frank Wells

The Days ★★★

Drama 1993 · Chi · BW · 75mins

Wang Xiaoshuai's subtle drama looks at a couple of Beijing art tutors whose common bonds can't save their ailing relationship, especially when professional success passes from one to the other. Dipping into images of modern China for added emphasis, *The Days* elegantly employs style, music and an unfussy narrative to comment on the duo, the choice of black and white over colour simply reinforcing the lyrical beauty. The writer/director found it impossible to secure state approval and distribution and was blacklisted as a result; his film has yet to be seen in China. JM. In Mandarin with English subtitles.

Yu Hong *Chun* • Liu Xiaodong *Dong* • Wang Xiaoshuai *Narrator* ■ *Dir/Scr* Wang Xiaoshuai

Days and Nights in the Forest ★★★★

Drama 1969 · Ind · BW · 115mins

Satyajit Ray was personally encouraged in his early film career by the great French director Jean Renoir, and his influence is clearly evident in this Bengali reworking of the classic featurette *Une Partie de Campagne*. Seeking to escape from the stress of Calcutta, four friends travel to the forest, where their encounters and misadventures cause them to take stock of their lives. Supremely capturing the glow of a summer's day and taking sly shots at the bourgeois mentality, Ray draws inspired performances from the leading quartet. DP. In Bengali with English subtitles.

Soumitra Chatterjee *Ashim* • Subhendu Chatterjee *Sanjoy* • Samit Bhanja *Harinath* • Robi Ghosh *Sekhar* ■ *Dir* Satyajit Ray • *Scr* Satyajit Ray, from the novel by Suil Ganguly

Days of Being Wild ★★★★ 12

Drama 1990 · HK · Colour · 90mins

This stylish, intricately structured drama not only harks back to the 1960s, but also explores the fears attending Hong Kong's handover to China. Leslie Cheung excels as a rebel with the cause of tracing his Filipino mother, callously leaving the broken hearts of waitress Maggie Cheung and showgirl Carina Lau in his wake. Two years in production and strikingly shot by Christopher Doyle, Wong Kar-Wai's second feature was such a flop at the domestic box office that a sequel was abandoned. However, internationally, it confirmed Wong's reputation as a rising art house star. DP. In Cantonese with English subtitles. DVD

Leslie Cheung *Yuddy* • Maggie Cheung *Su Lizhen* • Tony Chiu-Wai Leung [Tony Leung (2)] *Smirk* • Carina Lau *Fung-Ying* ■ *Dir/Scr* Wong Kar-Wai

Days of Glory ★★

Second World War romantic drama
1944 · US · BW · 85mins

Gregory Peck made his Hollywood debut in this, playing a Russian patriot fighting the Nazi invaders. Designed to show how friendly Uncle Sam was with Uncle Joe Stalin, it's never more than a B-picture, efficiently directed by Jacques Tourneur and co-starring Tamara Toumanova, a prima ballerina who grandly resisted Hollywood's efforts to turn her into a star. AT

Gregory Peck *Vladimir* • Tamara Toumanova *Nina* • Lowell Gilmore *Semyon* • Maria Palmer *Yelena* • Alan Reed *Sasha* • Hugo Haas *Fedor* ■ *Dir* Jacques Tourneur • *Scr* Casey Robinson, from a story by Melchior Lengyel

Days of Heaven ★★★★ PG

Drama 1978 · US · Colour · 88mins

This truly extraordinary visual treat from director Terrence Malick and Oscar-winning cinematographer Nestor Almendros was not a great commercial success, but has inspired film and particularly commercial directors for over a decade. Malick, who has only made two other films (*Badlands* and *The Thin Red Line*), takes a couple of disenfranchised labourers, Richard Gere and Brooke Adams, and Gere's little sister Linda Manz, and sets them down in the golden vastness of the Texas wheatfields. A tragedy-strewn love triangle develops between Gere, Adams and their employer, Sam Shepard, though Malick steps back from the narrative to give us a curiously disembodied elegy on poverty and freedom. SH. Contains violence, swearing and brief nudity. DVD

Richard Gere *Bill* • Brooke Adams *Abby* • Sam Shepard *Farmer* • Linda Manz *Linda* • Robert Wilke [Robert J Wilke] *Farm foreman* • Jackie Shultis *Linda's friend* • Stuart Margolin *Mill foreman* ■ *Dir/Scr* Terrence Malick

Days of Thrills and Laughter ★★★ U

Compilation 1961 · US · BW · 89mins

Film purists baulk at these Robert Youngson compilations but they did achieve a cinema release, and as a result became, for many, an introduction to the wonderful world of silent cinema. At the time, it was difficult, or more accurately, impossible to see pre-sound movies in anywhere near decent copies with proper projection. This is a fine selection (albeit with added commentary by Jay Jackson, music and a little juggling with projection speeds) and includes the work of such geniuses as Charlie Chaplin, Harry Langdon, Laurel and Hardy, Douglas Fairbanks (Sr, of course!) and queen of the serials, Pearl White. For those who have never seen them, this is a good introduction and will fuel the desire to view more from this fabulous period when the movies were young. TS

Jay Jackson *Narrator* ■ *Dir/Scr* Robert Youngson

Days of Thunder ★★★ 15

Sports drama 1990 · US · Colour · 107mins

This flashy action picture resulted in Tom Cruise's marital union with co-star Nicole Kidman. Motor sport movies have a lousy track record at the box office and this cliché-ridden stock car action movie was a costly flop. Reworking many of the themes in Howard Hawks's *The Crowd Roars*, Robert Towne's script must have looked a sure-fire winner, and there's little wrong with Tony Scott's zippy race sequences or Robert Duvall's performance as Cruise's manager. DP. Contains swearing. DVD

Tom Cruise *Cole Trickle* • Robert Duvall *Harry Hogge* • Nicole Kidman *Dr Claire Lewicki* • Randy Quaid *Tim Daland* • Cary Elwes *Russ Wheeler* • Michael Rooker *Rowdy Burns* • Fred Dalton Thompson *Big John* • John C Reilly *Buck Bretherton* • JC Quinn *Waddell* ■ *Dir* Tony Scott • *Scr* Robert Towne, from a story by Robert Towne, Tom Cruise

Days of Wine and Roses ★★★★ PG

Drama 1962 · US · BW · 112mins

For those who know Jack Lemmon only as one half of *The Odd Couple*, or as a Grumpy Old Man, this will be a revelation: he's in heart-rending dramatic mode as an advertising executive, driven to drink by his work and taking wife Lee Remick along for the alcoholic ride. Adapted by JP Miller from his own TV play, the film is directed by Blake Edwards with a poignancy you don't expect, and acted by Lemmon and Remick with a force that remains memorable long after viewing. TH DVD

Jack Lemmon *Joe Clay* • Lee Remick *Kirsten Arnesen* • Charles Bickford *Ellis Arnesen* • Jack Klugman *Jim Hungerford* • Alan Hewitt *Leland* • Tom Palmer *Ballefoy* • Debbie Megowan *Debbie* ■ *Dir* Blake Edwards • *Scr* JP Miller, from his television play

A Day's Pleasure ★★★ U

Silent comedy drama
1919 · US · BW · 18mins

In this Charlie Chaplin two-reeler, the comedy is condensed into a chaotic family outing on the river, where sea-sickness afflicts every passenger on a crowded cruiser. Edna Purviance is along for the ride, while Jackie Coogan makes his first appearance with Chaplin; he would later co-star with the great man in *The Kid* (1921). TH

Charles Chaplin *Father* • Edna Purviance *Mother* • Tom Wilson *Cop* • Sydney Chaplin [Syd Chaplin] *Father* • Jackie Coogan *Boy* ■ *Dir/Scr* Charles Chaplin

Dayton's Devils ★★ U

Adventure drama
1968 · US · Colour · 100mins

1950s action hunk Rory Calhoun, Leslie Nielsen (in his screen heavy days) and other unsocial types launch a daring raid on a military base and steal a $1.5 million payroll. Taking every cliché out of the heist movie manual, there's a lot of screen time devoted to the planning of the robbery. Then there's a chase, followed by those other key ingredients of the genre: the sudden twist and the ironic ending. AT

Leslie Nielsen *Frank Dayton* • Rory Calhoun *Mike Page* • Lainie Kazan *Leda Martell* • Hans Gudegast [Eric Braeden] *Max Eckhart* • Barry Sadler *Barney Barry* • Pat Renella *Claude Sadi* • Georg Stanford Brown *Theon Gibson* ■ *Dir* Jack Shea • *Scr* Fred De Gorter, from a story by Fred De Gorter

The Daytrippers ★★★★ 15

Comedy 1998 · US · Colour · 83mins

All of the mother-in-law-from-hell jibes that comedians used to make are on display in this sparky story about relationships among a family of oddballs. Led by dominating mother Anne Meara, the clan drives to the city to track down the husband (Stanley Tucci) whom Hope Davis thinks has been unfaithful. Davis is fairly sane about the whole issue, which is more than can be said about the rest of the family, with Meara being the wackiest of the lot. Writer/director Greg Mottola has contrived some great one-liners, but his one flaw is that the mother-in-law is almost too obnoxious. TH. Contains swearing. DVD

Hope Davis *Eliza* • Stanley Tucci *Louis D'Amico* • Parker Posey *Jo Malone* • Liev Schreiber *Carl* • Anne Meara *Rita Malone* • Pat McNamara *Jim Malone* • Campbell Scott *Eddie* ■ *Dir/Scr* Greg Mottola

Dazed and Confused ★★★★ 18

Comedy drama 1993 · US · Colour · 97mins

Some of Hollywood's hottest young talent cut their teeth on this ultra-hip movie, among them Matthew McConaughey and Milla Jovovich. But it's Jason London and Rory Cochrane who carry this freewheeling story, as a couple of high school wasters on the last day of the summer term. After giving voice to the disconnected youth of Austin, Texas, in his highly influential debut feature *Slacker*, director Richard Linklater here employs a pseudo-documentary style to expose teenage life in the raw, with all the attendant angst, arrogance, aggression and amorousness. This honest and incisive portrait is both funny and scary and ranks among the very best high school movies. AJ. Contains swearing and drug abuse. DVD

Jason London *Randy "Pink" Floyd* • Sasha Jenson *Don Dawson* • Rory Cochrane *Slater* • Wiley Wiggins *Mitch Kramer* • Michelle Burke *Jodi Kramer* • Shawn Andrews *Pickford* • Anthony Rapp *Tony* • Adam Goldberg *Mike* • Christin Hinojosa *Sabrina* • Milla Jovovich *Michelle* • Matthew McConaughey *Wooderson* • Ben Affleck *O'Bannion* ■ *Dir/Scr* Richard Linklater

De Sade ★★

Biographical drama
1969 · US/W Ger · Colour · 107mins

Begun by director Cy Endfield and completed by Roger Corman (uncredited), it's a beautiful-looking muddle of historical fact and hysterical fiction, with fuzzy fantasy and soft-core orgies punctuating the hopelessly contrived flow. Keir Dullea does his best as the marquis, but the Eurotrash supporting cast and John Huston's embarrassing turn as de Sade's cruel father places this squarely in the "interesting flop" category. AJ

Keir Dullea *Marquis de Sade* • Senta Berger *Anne de Montreuil* • Lilli Palmer *Mme de Montreuil* • John Huston *Abbé de Sade* • Anna Massey *Renée de Montreuil* • Ute Levka *Rose Keller* ■ *Dir* Cy Endfield • *Scr* Richard Matheson, Peter Berg

The Dead ★★★★ U

Period drama 1987 · US/UK · Colour · 79mins

This beautifully judged adaptation of James Joyce's story about a family Christmas party in turn-of-the-century Dublin is a fitting swan song to director John Huston's distinguished career. Huston captures the national character with a deft economy that few film-makers could hope to emulate. But it's the quality of the ensemble acting that makes this warm, nostalgic and intimate drama such a moving experience. Anjelica Huston is superb, with the speech in which she describes her lost love possibly the high spot of her career. Donal McCann also impresses as her regretful husband, while Donal Donnelly is outstanding as the tiddly Freddy Malins. DP

Anjelica Huston *Gretta Conroy* • Donal McCann *Gabriel Conroy* • Rachael Dowling *Lily* • Cathleen Delaney *Aunt Julia Morkan* • Helena Carroll *Aunt Kate Morkan* • Ingrid Craigie *Mary Jane* • Dan O'Herlihy *Mr Browne* • Frank Patterson *Bartell D'Arcy* • Donal Donnelly *Freddy Malins* ■ *Dir* John Huston • *Scr* Tony Huston, from the short story by James Joyce

Dead Again ★★★ 15

Thriller 1991 · US · Colour and BW · 103mins

The present is tense because the past is imperfect in Kenneth Branagh's determinedly old-fashioned thriller in the Hitchcock tradition. He's a cynical LA private detective hired to research the background of amnesiac mystery woman Emma Thompson, who's obsessed by scissors and tormented by nightmares from someone else's life. An enjoyably overdone, stylish mix of *film noir* trivia and eccentric plotting, director Branagh's darkly delicious reincarnation parody will keep you guessing right up until the OTT finale. AJ. Contains swearing. DVD

Kenneth Branagh *Mike Church/Roman Strauss* • Emma Thompson *Grace/Margaret Strauss* • Derek Jacobi *Franklyn Madson* • Andy Garcia *Gray Baker* • Wayne Knight *"Piccolo" Pete* • Hanna Schygulla *Inge* • Campbell Scott *Doug* • Gregor Hesse *Frankie* ■ *Dir* Kenneth Branagh • *Scr* Scott Frank

Dead & Buried ★★ 18

Horror thriller 1981 · US · Colour · 93mins

In his final film role Jack Albertson plays a mad mortician who revives the dead in a sleepy New England town, and then murders people to supply him with fresh corpses. James Farentino is the perplexed local sheriff. Uneven but pleasingly gory with standout make-up effects from Stan Winston. This film became one of many caught up in the UK's "video nasties" controversy of the 1980s and was denied a certificate for almost ten years. RS DVD

James Farentino *Sheriff Dan Gillis* • Melody Anderson *Janet Gillis* • Jack Albertson *G William Dobbs* • Dennis Redfield *Ron* • Nancy Locke *Linda* • Lisa Blount *Girl on the beach* • Robert Englund *Harry* ■ *Dir* Gary A Sherman [Gary Sherman] • *Scr* Ronald Shusett, Dan O'Bannon, from a story by Jeff Miller

The Dead and the Deadly ★★★★ 18

Supernatural comedy drama
1983 · HK · Colour · 97mins

Rightly considered one of the best supernatural comedies ever made in Hong Kong, this is a mix of kung fu, Chinese spiritualism and knockabout fun. Diminutive Wu Ma (who also directs) is killed while attempting an inheritance swindle, and his ghost takes over the body of hulking martial arts superstar Samo Kam-Bo Hung to get his revenge. It takes Cherry Cho-Hung Chung's battle with some supernatural powers, however, to put things right. Played for laughs rather than thrills, Wu's film has a seductively mystic feel. DP. In Cantonese and Mandarin with English subtitles.

Samo Kam-Bo Hung [Sammo Hung] • Cherry Cho-Hung Chung [Cherie Chung] ■ *Dir* Wu Ma • *Scr* Samo Kam-Bo Hung [Sammo Hung], Barry Ping-Yiu Wong

Dead Babies ★★★ 18

Black comedy 2000 · UK · Colour · 100mins

Adapted from the cult novel by Martin Amis and helmed by independent stage director William Marsh, this is a quirky heightened-reality effort about the extremes society will go to for new thrills and kicks. Updating the novel's action from the early 1970s, Marsh sets his movie in the near future where a group of upper-class misfits performs a controlled experiment with a new superdrug invented by a Charles Manson-style chemistry professor (played by Marsh). Loaded with disturbing imagery, gruesome special effects and startling sex scenes, this somewhat heavy-handed social critique raises provocative questions. AJ

Paul Bettany *Quentin* • Olivia Williams *Diana* • Charlie Condou *Giles* • Alexandra Gilbreath *Celia* • Cristian Solimeno *Andy* • Andy Nyman *Keith* • William Marsh *Marvel* ■ *Dir* William Marsh • *Scr* William Marsh, from the novel by Martin Amis

Dead Badge ★★★ 18

Crime thriller 1995 · US · Colour · 89mins

Clichés abound in this police drama about a cop (Brian Wimmer) investigating the death of a fellow officer and finding himself up to his eyes in corruption. Sounds completely missable, doesn't it? However, thanks to the gritty feel and some strong performances from a top-notch cast, this is a well paced and quite interesting tale. JB

Brian Wimmer *Dan Sampson* • M Emmet Walsh *Sgt Miller* • James B Sikking *Wheeler/Feld* • Yaphet Kotto *Capt Hunt* • Marta DuBois *Billie Torres* • Olympia Dukakis *Dr Doris Ric* ■ *Dir/Scr* Douglas Barr

Dead-Bang ★★★ 18

Detective action thriller
1989 · US · Colour · 101mins

Don Johnson stars in this thriller as a cop with the usual hang-ups – divorced, kids, workaholic, hot temper, tendency to kill people. On the trail of a cop killer, he winds up in Nowhere, Oklahoma, home of white supremacists who plan the overthrow of the US government. Director John Frankenheimer pumps this up nicely, orchestrating some clever twists, cleanly-shot action and some very quirky characterisation. AT

Don Johnson *Jerry Beck* • Bob Balaban *Elliot Webly* • William Forsythe *Arthur Kressler* • Penelope Ann Miller *Linda* • Frank Military *Bobby Burns* • Tate Donovan *John Burns* • Antoni Stutz *Ray* • Mickey Jones *Sleepy* ■ *Dir* John Frankenheimer • *Scr* Robert Foster

Dead Beat ★★★

Crime thriller 1994 · US · Colour · 92mins

A serial killer chiller, set in New Mexico in 1965, with Bruce Ramsay playing an Elvis-fixated psychopath whose band of disciples include little lost rich girl Natasha Gregson Wagner and snivelling acolyte Balthazar Getty. Adam Dubov's directorial debut was co-produced by the actor Christopher Lambert, while the casting of Natalie Wood's daughter and Jean-Paul Getty's great-grandson adds a certain *frisson* to the proceedings. AT

Bruce Ramsay *Kit* • Balthazar Getty *Rudy* • Natasha Gregson Wagner *Kirsten* • Meredith Salenger *Donna* • Deborah Harry *Mrs Kurtz* • Sara Gilbert *Martha* • Max Perlich *Jimmie* • Alex Cox *English teacher* ■ *Dir* Adam Dubov • *Scr* Adam Dubov, Janice Shapiro

Dead before Dawn ★★ 15

Thriller 1993 · US · Colour · 93mins

In a made-for-TV film that cries out for an actress with a greater range, Cheryl Ladd is merely adequate as the wife threatened by her murderous husband and forced to seek assistance from the FBI. However, director Charles Correll does come up with the odd suspenseful and atmospheric scene. JM. Contains swearing. DVD

Cheryl Ladd *Linda DeSilva Edelman* • Jameson Parker *Robert Edelman* • GW Bailey *Masterson* • Keone Young *James Young* • Kim Coates *Zack* • Matt Clark *John DeSilva* • Hope Lange *Virginia DeSilva* ■ *Dir* Charles Correll • *Scr* John Ireland, from a story by Ricky Blackwood

Dead Bolt Dead ★★ 15

Crime drama 1999 · UK · Colour · 89mins

This low-budget crime thriller, framed around two simultaneous sieges after a botched hit, is weighed down at first by self-consciously snappy dialogue, but later settles into a reasonably interesting battle of wills between captor and hostages. Neil Stuke is well cast as a laid-back assassin and there's some palpable friction as crime boss James Laurenson awaits his fate. JC DVD

Ariyon Bakare *Thug* • Monique de Villiers *Wife* • James Laurenson *Boss* • Neil Stuke *Assassin* • Ronnie McCann *Driver* ■ *Dir* James Rogan • *Scr* Paul de Villiers

Dead Calm ★★★★ 15

Thriller 1988 · Aus · Colour · 96mins

Nicole Kidman and director Phillip Noyce were catapulted into the Hollywood frontline by this scary revel. It's an ingenious psychological thriller in the grand Hitchcock tradition, with a very simple premise: a couple (Kidman and Sam Neill) take a yachting trip to try to recover from the death of their young son, but when they rescue the sole survivor (Billy Zane) from a sinking schooner, things take a very nasty turn. Noyce expertly cranks up the tension to fever pitch and you'll be screaming with delicious panic in one of the best ocean-going shockers since *Jaws*. AJ. Contains swearing, violence, nudity. DVD

Sam Neill *John Ingram* • Nicole Kidman *Rae Ingram* • Billy Zane *Hughie Warriner* • Rod Mullinar *Russell Bellows* • Joshua Tilden *Danny* ■ *Dir* Phillip Noyce • *Scr* Terry Hayes, from the novel by Charles Williams

The Dead Can't Lie ★★★ 15

Supernatural thriller
1988 · US · Colour · 93mins

Playboy Colin Bruce is being pursued by his dead wife, the immaculately groomed Virginia Madsen, and hires hard-boiled private eye Tommy Lee Jones to give her back the jewels that she was buried with, in order to be left alone. Needless to add, the detective falls for the ghost. There's a bewhiskered Frederic Forrest as a Russian Orthodox priest and some smart dialogue about Lillian Gish, but it's probably too pretentious for some tastes, and Lloyd Fonvielle has never managed anything so original again. TS. Contains swearing, nudity.

Tommy Lee Jones *Eddie Martel Mallard* • Virginia Madsen *Rachel Carlyle* • Colin Bruce *Charlie Rand* • Kevin Jarre *Tim* • Denise Stephenson *Debbie* • Frederic Forrest *Father George* ■ *Dir/Scr* Lloyd Fonvielle

Dead Cert ★★

Sports drama 1974 · UK · Colour · 99mins

Co-adapted from Dick Francis's runaway bestseller by former racing pundit Lord Oaksey, this tale of death and doping on the eve of the Grand National is a desperate stab for a box-office hit by director Tony Richardson. The authentic atmosphere of stableyards and racecourses that characterises Francis's thrillers has been missed by a lot more than a short head here. It's hardly an impenetrable mystery, but it passes the time. DP

Judi Dench *Laura Davidson* • Michael Williams *Sandy* • Scott Antony *Alan* • Ian Hogg *Bill Davidson* • Nina Thomas *Penny* • Mark Dignam *Clifford Tudor* • Julian Glover *Lodge* ■ *Dir* Tony Richardson • *Scr* Tony Richardson, John Oaksey, from the novel by Dick Francis

The Dead Don't Dream ★★

Western 1948 · US · BW · 62mins

The splendid title can't disguise the fact that this is a rather routine Hopalong Cassidy programme filler, actually the penultimate of that series's amazing 66 entries. Although the series was drawing to its end, a whole new, and largely children's, audience discovered Hoppy on television re-runs and advertising promotions, and silver-haired William Boyd became popular all over again. TS

William Boyd (1) *Hopalong Cassidy* • Andy Clyde *California Carlson* • Rand Brooks *Lucky Jenkins* • John Parrish *Jeff Potter* • Leonard Penn *Earl Wesson* • Mary Tucker *Mary Benton* ■ *Dir* George Archainbaud • *Scr* Francis Rosenwald, from characters created by Clarence E Mulford

Dead End ★★★★ PG

Crime drama 1937 · US · BW · 87mins

A marvellously evocative, albeit resolutely studio-bound, version of Sidney Kingsley's fine play, brilliantly directed by William Wyler from an adaptation by Lillian Hellman. The streets and gutters of production designer Richard Day's magnificent set are a little too clean, a little too well lit, but this is a fine work with brilliant performances, particularly from Sylvia Sidney and then new face Humphrey Bogart. Though Joel McCrea is a shade too bland as the worthy hero, the youngsters in the movie went on to their own series success, initially as the Dead End Kids, and, eventually, as the Bowery Boys. TS

Sylvia Sidney *Drina* • Joel McCrea *Dave* • Humphrey Bogart *Baby Face Martin* • Wendy Barrie *Kay* • Claire Trevor *Francie* • Allen Jenkins *Hunk* • Marjorie Main *Mrs Martin* • Billy Halop *Tommy* • Huntz Hall *Dippy* • Bobby Jordan *Angel* • Gabriel Dell *TB* • Bernard Punsley *Milty* • Charles Peck *Philip Griswold* • Leo Gorcey *Spit* ■ *Dir* William Wyler • *Scr* Lillian Hellman, from the play by Sidney Kingsley • *Cinematographer* Gregg Toland

Dead End ★★★ 15

Supernatural horror thriller
2003 · Fr · Colour · 79mins

This horror film twists a traditional Christmas drive to visit in-laws into a ghostly nightmare of death and terror, after dad Ray Wise decides to take his family on an unfamiliar short cut. Wise draws together the mishmash of schlock, chills and dark comedy with a delightfully over-the-top performance. His melodramatic outbursts, as his loved-ones fall prey to a mysterious woman in white, are as unnerving as they are humorous, adding genuine eccentricity to a feature that often tries too hard to be weird. SF. Contains swearing and violence. DVD

Ray Wise *Frank Harrington* • Alexandra Holden *Marion Harrington* • Lin Shaye *Laura Harrington* • Mick Cain *Richard Harrington* • Billy Asher *Brad Miller* • Amber Smith *Lady in white* ■ *Dir/Scr* Jean-Baptiste Andrea, Fabrice Canepa

Dead End Kids ★★★

Experimental documentary drama
1986 · US · Colour and BW · 87mins

This blend of eyewitness testimonies, scholarly articles and interviews attempts to put a satirical spin on the history of the nuclear industry. Lacking the cutting edge of that similarly cynical scrapbook, *The Atomic Café*, JoAnne Akalaitis's production is so in thrall of the text, it's as if the camera is bolted down. However, the performances of the self-effacing ensemble (most of whom take dual roles) are excellent, and there are cameo roles for David Byrne and Philip Glass, who composed the score. DP

Ellen McElduff *Television host/Army Stenographer/Schoolteacher* • Ruth Maleczech *Marie Curie* • George Bartenieff *Faust/Gen Groves* • David Brisbin *Nightclub comic/Gen Farrell* ■ *Dir* JoAnne Akalaitis • *Scr* JoAnne Akalaitis, from her play

D

Dead Funny ★★★

Comedy mystery
1995 · US/UK · Colour · 91mins

At the start of this comedy, Andrew McCarthy lies on the kitchen table, impaled by a samurai sword and completely dead. When his girlfriend (Elizabeth Peña) comes home and discovers him, she opens a bottle of champagne and calls a friend over. That's when the flashbacks begin, showing how McCarthy's practical joker reached such a pretty pass. The slightly nerdy McCarthy is well-cast here, and Peña makes her museum employee a very wacky character. The film's charms are perhaps too slight to make it memorable, however. AT

Elizabeth Peña *Vivian Saunders* • Andrew McCarthy *Reggie Barker* • Paige Turco *Louise* • Blanche Baker *Barbara* • Allison Janney *Jennifer* • Adelle Lutz *Mari* • Lisa Jane Persky *Sarah* ■ *Dir* John Feldman • *Scr* John Feldman, Cindy Oswin

Dead Heart ★★ 18

Detective thriller
1996 · Aus · Colour · 101mins

When it comes to depicting the Aborigines on screen, the infringement of tribal rights seems to be the only topic producers consider worth tackling. Consequently, what we have here is another thriller in which the clash of progress and tradition results in a murder, which is investigated by a well-intentioned white cop. Bryan Brown uncovers evidence of bootlegging, adultery and black magic with grim determination. DP. Contains swearing, violence and nudity.

Bryan Brown *Ray Lorkin* • Ernie Dingo *David* • Angie Milliken *Kate* • Aaron Pedersen *Tony* • Lewis Fitz-Gerald *Les* • John Jarratt *Charlie* ■ *Dir/Scr* Nicholas Parsons

Dead Heat ★★★ 18

Comedy horror 1988 · US · Colour · 80mins

Just when you thought nothing original could be made of the buddy-cop genre, along comes Mark Goldblatt's outlandish horror comedy. Treat Williams and Joe Piscopo star as cops who uncover a scheme by batty old Vincent Price to resuscitate the dead. In a movie that's imaginative and disgusting in equal measure, a butcher shop full of meat comes alive to do battle with the heroes, while Williams himself hilariously turns into a zombie and has 12 hours to solve the case before decomposition sets in. RS

Treat Williams *Roger Mortis* • Joe Piscopo *Doug Bigelow* • Darren McGavin *Dr Ernest McNab* • Lindsay Frost *Randi James* • Vincent Price *Arthur P Loudermilk* • Clare Kirkconnell *Rebecca Smythers* • Keye Luke *Mr Thule* ■ *Dir* Mark Goldblatt • *Scr* Terry Black

Dead Heat ★★ 15

Crime drama 2002 · Can · Colour · 93mins

The plot of this horse-racing thriller is more than a little convoluted, as Kiefer Sutherland's weak-hearted Boston cop comes up against mobster Daniel Benzali when he falls in with stepbrother Anthony LaPaglia's idea of buying a horse. The banter between Sutherland and LaPaglia is brisk, but it's essentially an old-fashioned B-movie. DP. Contains swearing. DVD

Kiefer Sutherland *Pally LaMarr* • Radha Mitchell *Charlotte LaMarr* • Anthony LaPaglia *Ray LaMarr* • Lothaire Bluteau *Tony LaRoche* • Daniel Benzali *Frank Finnegan* ■ *Dir/Scr* Mark Malone

Dead Heat on a Merry-Go-Round ★★ PG

Crime caper 1966 · US · Colour · 102mins

There's little to distinguish this crime caper from others of its ilk, though it does give Harrison Ford fans the opportunity to see their hero make his big-screen debut. Few could carry off the wisecracking tough guy act better than James Coburn, but even he seems to be going through the motions here as he robs the bank at Los Angeles airport during the arrival of the Russian premier. The action gets bogged down in its own cleverness, while writer/director Bernard Girard can't sustain either momentum or interest. DP DVD

James Coburn *Eli Kotch* • Camilla Sparv *Inger Knudson* • Aldo Ray *Eddie Hart* • Nina Wayne *Frieda Schmid* • Robert Webber *Milo Stewart* • Rose Marie *Margaret Kirby* • Todd Armstrong *Alfred Morgan* • Harrison Ford *Bellhop* ■ *Dir/Scr* Bernard Girard

Dead Letter Office ★★★

Drama 1998 · Aus · Colour · 95mins

John Ruane's surreal, often lyrical drama is both sad and uplifting. Set in an office for undeliverable mail that is under threat of mechanisation, this tale of damaged people and indefatigable hope turns on the unlikely relationship between new employee Mirando Otto (who still writes to her long-absent father) and her Chilean boss George DelHoyo, who was driven from his homeland because of his political views. Both powerful and poignant. DP. In English and Spanish with subtitles. Contains swearing and a sex scene.

George DelHoyo *Frank Lopez* • Miranda Otto *Alice* • Nicholas Bell *Kevin* • Georgina Naidu *Mary* • Syd Brisbane *Peter* • Barry Otto *Gerald Urquhart* • Vanessa Steele *Carmen* ■ *Dir* John Ruane • *Scr* Deborah Cox

Dead Man ★★★ 18

Western 1995 · US/Ger · BW · 116mins

Johnny Depp stars as a mundane clerk who arrives in the shoot-'em-up Wild West town of Machine to take a job as an accountant, only to find the position has been filled. Things go from bad to worse when he accidentally kills a man and is pursued as a gunslinger. Independent director Jim Jarmusch's black-and-white take on the cowboy movie is as bizarre and deadpan as his usual work, but it's enlivened by appearances from the likes of John Hurt and, briefly, Robert Mitchum. TH. Contains swearing and brief nudity.

Johnny Depp *William Blake* • Crispin Glover *Train fireman* • Gibby Haines *Man with gun in alley* • George Duckworth *Man at end of street* • Richard Boes *Man with wrench* • John Hurt *John Scholfield* • John North *Mr Olafsen* • Robert Mitchum *John Dickinson* • Mili Avital *Thel Russell* • Gabriel Byrne *Charlie Dickinson* • Lance Henriksen *Cole Wilson* • Gary Farmer *Nobody* • Iggy Pop *Salvatore "Sally" Jenko* ■ *Dir/Scr* Jim Jarmusch

Dead Man on Campus ★★ 15

Comedy 1998 · US · Colour · 90mins

Tom Everett Scott and Mark-Paul Gosselaar are on the verge of being kicked out of school because of low grades. When they discover a clause in the school constitution saying they will get automatic A's if a roommate commits suicide, they set about finding a suitably depressed person to share with. It's amiably played, but the direction lacks bite. JF. Contains swearing, sexual references.

Tom Everett Scott *Josh* • Mark-Paul Gosselaar *Cooper* • Poppy Montgomery *Rachel* • Lochlyn Munro *Cliff* • Randy Pearlstein *Buckley* • Corey Page *Matt* • Alyson Hannigan *Lucy* • Dave Ruby *Zeke* ■ *Dir* Alan Cohn • *Scr* Michael Traeger, Mike White, from a story by Adam Larson Broder, Anthony Abrams

Dead Man Walking ★★★★ 15

Prison drama based on a true story
1995 · US · Colour · 117mins

Sean Penn gives a chilling and mesmerising portrayal of sociopathy, as Matthew Poncelet, a white trash multiple killer on death row with no sense of remorse. His sparring partner is Susan Sarandon, in an Oscar-winning performance as Sister Helen Prejean, the nun who became Poncelet's spiritual adviser during his final countdown, and whose book about the experience was the inspiration for the film. Sarandon's nun is a sort of social worker with faith, whose sexually charged chats with Penn take us into the heart of the debate about capital punishment. But director Tim Robbins's refusal to make a clear judgement on the issue is frustrating. AT. Contains violence, swearing and brief nudity. DVD

Susan Sarandon *Sister Helen Prejean* • Sean Penn *Matthew Poncelet* • Robert Prosky *Hilton Barber* • Raymond J Barry *Earl Delacroix* • R Lee Ermey *Clyde Percy* • Celia Weston *Mary Beth Percy* • Lois Smith *Helen's mother* ■ *Dir* Tim Robbins • *Scr* Tim Robbins, from the book by Sister Helen Prejean

Dead Man's Curve ★★★★ 15

Black comedy 1997 · US · Colour · 86mins

This twisted comedy thriller becomes addictive viewing, thanks to the completely bonkers and mesmerising performance from young actor Matthew Lillard. Three roommates (Lillard, Michael Vartan and Randall Batinkoff) learn that their college has an unspoken rule that, should a student commit suicide, the students sharing their room are automatically awarded perfect grades for the rest of the academic year because they have had to suffer such a trauma. So, it's not long before Vartan and Lillard have offed their best pal and this is only the beginning of double-crossing, back-stabbing and murder on campus. Written and directed with a wicked gleam in his eye by Dan Rosen. JB. Contains swearing, sex scenes and violence. DVD

Matthew Lillard *Tim* • Michael Vartan *Chris* • Randall Batinkoff *Rand* • Keri Russell *Emma* • Tamara Craig Thomas *Natalie* • Anthony Griffith *Detective Schipper* • Bo Dietl *Detective Amato* ■ *Dir/Scr* Dan Rosen

Dead Man's Evidence ★★ U

Spy drama 1962 · UK · BW · 67mins

This provides a sobering insight into how the rest of the British film industry was handling espionage thrillers while Terence Young was making *Dr No*. With his heyday as TV's William Tell already behind him, Conrad Phillips stars as a spy sent to investigate when the body of a defector is washed up on an Irish beach. Francis Searle's direction is as perfunctory as Arthur La Bern and Gordon Wellesley's script. DP

Conrad Phillips *David Baxter* • Jane Griffiths *Linda Howard* • Veronica Hurst *Gay Clifford* • Ryck Rydon *Fallon* ■ *Dir* Francis Searle • *Scr* Arthur La Bern, Gordon Wellesley, from a story by Arthur La Bern

Dead Man's Eyes ★★

Mystery 1944 · US · BW · 64mins

Lon Chaney Jr returns for another in Universal's *Inner Sanctum* series, this time as a struggling artist whose sudden blindness threatens his engagement to Jean Parker and leads to a double murder. Dwight Babcock's screenplay introduces a sinister sci-fi element, as surgeon Jonathan Hale offers Chaney the hope of restored sight through a pioneering cornea transplant. But the emphasis is firmly on suspense, as first eye donor Edward Fielding and then scheming model Acquanetta bite the dust. Reginald Le Borg's direction is steady instead of taut, but Chaney is typically sympathetic as the gentle giant with a talent for misfortune. DP

Lon Chaney [Lon Chaney Jr] *Dave Stuart* • Jean Parker *Heather "Brat" Hayden* • Paul Kelly (1) *Dr Alan Bittaker* • Thomas Gomez *Captain Drury* • Jonathan Hale *Dr Sam Welles* • Edward Fielding *Dr Stanley "Dad" Hayden* • Acquanetta *Tanya Czoraki* ■ *Dir* Reginald Le Borg • *Scr* Dwight V Babcock

Dead Man's Float ★★

Crime adventure 1980 · Aus · Colour · 75mins

Bill Hunter may be the only familiar face in this children's adventure, but his young co-stars turn in spirited performances as they abandon their obsession with surfing to prevent drug smugglers from operating on their beach. Director Peter Sharp sets the scene with broad strokes, making the villains doltish in spite of their dark trade. However, it's in the depiction of the kids that the film scores. DP

Sally Boyden *Anne* • Greg Rowe *Johnny* • Jacqui Gordon *Sue* • Rick Ireland *Pete* • Bill Hunter *Eddie Bell* • Sue Jones *Shirley Bell* • John Heywood *Captain Collins* • Gus Mercurio *Mr Dobraski* ■ *Dir* Peter Sharp • *Scr* Roger Carr, from his novel

Dead Man's Folly ★★★ PG

Murder mystery 1986 · US · Colour · 89mins

While not perhaps among Agatha Christie's best mysteries, this slick TV movie will still keep you guessing whodunnit. As the fastidious Belgian detective Hercule Poirot, Peter Ustinov is invited to organise a murder hunt for a village fête only to find himself confronted with the real thing. In a case where nearly everybody is a thoroughly nasty piece of work, there is plenty of scope for the support cast to ham it up. DP

Peter Ustinov *Hercule Poirot* • Jean Stapleton *Mrs Oliver* • Constance Cummings *Mrs Folliat* • Tim Pigott-Smith *Sir George Stubbs* • Jonathan Cecil *Hastings* • Kenneth Cranham *Inspector Bland* • Susan Wooldridge *Miss Brewis* • Christopher Guard *Alec Legge* • Jeff Yagher *Eddie South* ■ *Dir* Clive Donner • *Scr* Rod Browning, from the novel by Agatha Christie

Dead Man's Shoes ★★★ 18

Crime thriller 2004 · UK · Colour · 86mins

This morally ambiguous shocker features an uncomfortably matter-of-fact performance from co-writer Paddy Considine. He plays a tortured ex-army man who returns to the rural Midlands village of his youth to take revenge on a drugs gang who used and abused his younger, mentally challenged brother (Toby Kebbell). With many of the cast being non-actors and much of the dialogue improvised, there's a strong sense of realism that makes the violence portrayed so much more horrific, and edgy laughs soon degenerate into grim brutality. SF. Contains swearing, violence and drug abuse. DVD

Paddy Considine *Richard* • Gary Stretch *Sonny* • Toby Kebbell *Anthony* • Stuart Wolfenden *Herbie* • Neil Bell *Soz* • Paul Sadot *Tuff* ■ *Dir* Shane Meadows • *Scr* Paddy Considine, Shane Meadows

Dead Men Can't Dance ★★ 15

War action adventure
1997 · US · Colour · 93mins

They can't act, either, and the same can be said for the cast of this war drama about the first women to be accepted into the ranks of the US Rangers. Borrowing heavily from *Full Metal Jacket*, director Stephen M Anderson charts the progress of a group of women through the Rangers training programme; we then see them in action in the demilitarised zone outside North Korea. Some good action scenes, but nothing to keep you on the edge of your seat. ST DVD

Michael Biehn *Hart* • Kathleen York *Victoria Elliot* • Adrian Paul *Shooter* • R Lee Ermey *Pullman T Fowler* • Shawnee Smith *Sgt Addie Cooper* • Joel McKinnon Miller *Bearclaw* • John Carroll Lynch *Sgt Plonder* • Grace Zabriskie *Brig Gen Burke* ■ *Dir* Stephen M Anderson [Steve Anderson] • *Scr* Bill Kerby, Mark Sevi, Paul Sinor

Dead Men Don't Die ★ PG

Black comedy 1991 · US · Colour · 94mins

Elliott Gould, whose career seemed to peak in the mid-1970s, here stars in a dire comedy about a newsreader who is shot dead and then brought back to life by his voodoo-chanting cleaning lady. It's all completely silly, with Gould lumbering from one pratfall to another, looking uncomfortable throughout. Well worth avoiding. JB. Contains violence and swearing.

Elliott Gould *Barry Barron* • Melissa Anderson [Melissa Sue Anderson] *Dulcie Niles* • Mark Moses *Jordan Penrose* ■ *Dir/Scr* Malcolm Marmorstein

Dead Men Don't Wear Plaid ★★★★ PG

Detective spoof 1982 · US · BW · 84mins

Steve Martin's early collaborations with director and co-writer Carl Reiner still rank among his best. This ingenious spoof finds Martin as a hard-boiled private eye with a dangerous phobia about cleaning women who gets involved in a supremely silly story involving a cheese professor and sinister Nazis. However, this provides the slenderest of excuses for Martin to be spliced into an array of classic movies and swap dumb dialogue with stars such as Bette Davis, Burt Lancaster, Barbara Stanwyck, Ray Milland in some of their most famous roles. There are some wonderful moments for film buffs, Martin is on inspired form and Rachel Ward is a revelation in a rare comic role. JF. Contains swearing. DVD

Steve Martin *Rigby Reardon* • Rachel Ward *Juliet Forrest* • Carl Reiner *Field Marshal Von Kluck* • Reni Santoni *Carlos Rodriguez* • George Gaynes *Dr Forrest* ■ *Dir* Carl Reiner • *Scr* George Gipe, Carl Reiner, Steve Martin

Dead of Night ★★★★★ PG

Portmanteau horror 1945 · UK · BW · 98mins

Ealing will for ever be associated with its celebrated comedies, but this chilling quintet deserves to be considered among the studio's finest achievements. Including stories penned by HG Wells and EF Benson, *Dead of Night* illustrates how ghost stories should be filmed. Alberto Cavalcanti's "The Ventriloquist's Dummy" episode has lost none of its shocking power, thanks largely to Michael Redgrave's astonishing performance, which ranks among the best of his career. There's also much to raise the hair on the back of the neck in Robert Hamer's "The Haunted Mirror", while the linking story involving architect Mervyn Johns brings it all to a nightmarish conclusion. DP DVD

Mervyn Johns *Walter Craig* • Roland Culver *Eliot Foley* • Mary Merrall *Mrs Foley* • Anthony Baird *Hugh Grainger* • Judy Kelly *Joyce Grainger* • Sally Ann Howes *Sally O'Hara* • Michael Allen (1) *Jimmy Watson* • Googie Withers *Joan Courtland* • Ralph Michael *Peter Courtland* • Michael Redgrave *Maxwell Frere* ■ *Dir* Alberto Cavalcanti, Basil Dearden, Robert Hamer, Charles Crichton • *Scr* John Baines, Angus MacPhail, TEB Clarke, from stories by HG Wells, EF Benson, John Baines, Angus MacPhail

Dead of Night ★★★ 15

Horror 1972 · Can/UK/US · Colour · 84mins

This cross between *The Monkey's Paw* and *Night of the Living Dead* is a tense low-budget horror gem. Distraught mother Lynn Carlin wishes her son Richard Backus would return from an unspecified war, clearly Vietnam. But when he does, it's as a walking corpse who syringes blood from his victims to sate his grisly appetite. With chilling make-up effects by writer Alan Ormsby and Tom Savini, it's a brilliantly sick and unpretentious allegory. AJ

John Marley *Charles Brooks* • Lynn Carlin *Christine Brooks* • Henderson Forsythe *Dr Philip Allman* • Richard Backus *Andy Brooks* • Anya Ormsby *Cathy Brooks* • Jane Daly *Joanne* ■ *Dir* Bob Clark • *Scr* Alan Ormsby

Dead of Night ★★

Horror 1997 · US · Colour · 95mins

This is the tale of a lovelorn vampire searching for his dead spouse and leaving a trail of victims in his wake. Kristoffer Tabori, the son of legendary film director Don Siegel and actress Viveca Lindfors, directs but falls a long way short of his father's achievements in a disappointing horror outing. Genre fans should look out for Kathleen Kinmont (*Bride of Re-Animator*) in the less-than-stellar cast. JF

John Enos III [John Enos] *Woods* • Kathleen Kinmont *Katherine* • Robert Knepper *Christian* • Alex Rocco *Bukowski* • Paul Winfield *Vernon* ■ *Dir* Kristoffer Tabori • *Scr* Karen Kelly

Dead of Winter ★★★ 15

Thriller 1987 · US · Colour · 96mins

It's slightly disconcerting to see Arthur Penn, the highly distinctive director of *Bonnie and Clyde* and *Alice's Restaurant*, switching to formula. That said, it's a pleasure to see a film where suspense is sustained by craft rather than through wham-bam action or gore. Penn allows Mary Steenburgen to relish no less than three roles, while Roddy McDowall is an unnerving study in controlled evil as the assistant to Jan Rubes's eccentric doctor. JM

Mary Steenburgen *Katie McGovern/Julie Rose/Evelyn* • Roddy McDowall *Thomas Franklin Murray* • Jan Rubes *Dr Joseph Lewis* • William Russ *Rod Sweeney* • Mark Malone *Roland McGovern* • Ken Pogue *Officer Mullavy* • Wayne Robson *Officer Huntley* ■ *Dir* Arthur Penn • *Scr* Marc Shmuger, Mark Malone

Dead on Sight ★★

Crime thriller 1994 · US · Colour · 90mins

A college professor who lectures on serial killers is obsessively tracking down the killer of his wife with the help of one of his students, herself haunted by a terrifying childhood episode. There are more psychological hang-ups here than in Dr Freud's casebook, and they manifest themselves in visions, dreams and flashbacks. Jennifer Beals plays the traumatised student, with Daniel Baldwin as the troubled professor, although neither is helped by Ruben Preuss's too-flashy direction. AT. Contains swearing and violence.

Jennifer Beals *Rebecca* • Daniel Baldwin *Caleb O'Dell* • William H Macy *Stephen Meeker* • Kurtwood Smith *Tommy* • Eleanor Comegys *Stephanie* ■ *Dir* Ruben Preuss • *Scr* Lewis Green

Dead Pigeon on Beethoven Street ★★ 15

Detective mystery
1972 · W Ger · Colour · 86mins

Near the end of a long working career veteran maverick director Samuel Fuller managed to put together this turgid hotch-potch of half-baked ideas, funded by German television and filmed entirely in Germany. Hard to tell if this is genuine tongue-in-cheek spy stuff or just inept movie storytelling, but Fuller's fans seem eager to accord Sam the benefit of the doubt. There's no excusing the wooden performances from Glenn Corbett or Christa Lang (Mrs S Fuller) in the leading roles, though. TS

Glenn Corbett *Sandy* • Christa Lang *Christa* • Sieghardt Rupp *Kessin* • Anton Diffring *Mensur* • Alex D'Arcy *Novka* • Anthony Chinn *Fong* ■ *Dir/Scr* Samuel Fuller

Dead Poets Society ★★★★ PG

Drama 1989 · US · Colour · 123mins

Peter Weir's warm, touching tale struck a chord with audiences around the world. Robin Williams is the unconventional teacher at a stuffy boys' school in late-1950s America, who awakens a love of poetry and writing among a disparate group of troubled adolescents headed by Robert Sean Leonard and Ethan Hawke. However, the individualism he fosters eventually leads to tragedy. The two young leads turn in subtle performances and, if Tom Schulman's Oscar-winning screenplay does lurch occasionally into mawkish melodrama, it's lusciously photographed and genuinely moving. JF DVD

Robin Williams *John Keating* • Robert Sean Leonard *Neil Perry* • Ethan Hawke *Todd Anderson* • Josh Charles *Knox Overstreet* • Gale Hansen *Charlie Dalton* • Dylan Kussman *Richard Cameron* • Allelon Ruggiero *Steven Meeks* • James Waterston *Gerard Pitts* • Norman Lloyd *Mr Nolan* • Kurtwood Smith *Mr Perry* ■ *Dir* Peter Weir • *Scr* Tom Schulman • *Cinematographer* John Seale

The Dead Pool ★★ 18

Crime thriller 1988 · US · Colour · 87mins

"Dirty" Harry Callahan's fifth outing finds the San Francisco detective looking decidedly ropey around the edges. Clint Eastwood goes through his iconic paces and directs the film in all but name; the actual credit, however, goes to Buddy Van Horn, Clint's stuntman. It's a flaccid, silly and extremely sadistic tale involving a demented movie fan who bumps off minor celebrities, with Liam Neeson co-starring as a British horror film director. TS. Contains violence and swearing. DVD

Clint Eastwood *Inspector Harry Callahan* • Patricia Clarkson *Samantha Walker* • Evan C Kim [Evan Kim] *Al Quan* • Liam Neeson *Peter Swan* • David Hunt *Harlan Rook* ■ *Dir* Buddy Van Horn • *Scr* Steve Sharon, from a story by Steve Sharon, Durk Pearson, Sandy Shaw, from the character created by Harry Julian Fink, RM Fink

Dead Presidents ★★★ 18

Crime drama 1995 · US · Colour · 114mins

In the Hughes Brothers' brutal 1970s drama, Bronx boy Larenz Tate returns from a tour of duty of Vietnam to find his urban life just as screwed-up as the war. Armed robbery seems the only solution. It's interesting to see the "coming home" story told from a black perspective, and there are some stunning sequences. However, the film's tone is so grim, and the characters so superficial, that it never quite sucks you in. Great period detail and a superb soundtrack of soul classics, though. JC. Contains sex scenes, swearing, violence. DVD

Larenz Tate *Anthony Curtis* • Keith David *Kirby* • Chris Tucker *Skip* • Freddy Rodriguez *Jose* • Rose Jackson *Juanita Benson* • N'Bushe Wright *Delilah Benson* • Alvaletah Guess *Mrs Benson* • James Pickens Jr *Mr Curtis* ■ *Dir* Albert Hughes, Allen Hughes • *Scr* Michael Henry Brown, from a story by Albert Hughes, Allen Hughes, Michael Henry Brown, from the story *Specialist No 4 Haywood T "The Kid" Kirkland* by Wallace Terry

D

Dead Reckoning ★★★★ U

Film noir 1947 · US · BW · 96mins

Humphrey Bogart stars in this hardboiled thriller, with sultry Lizabeth Scott as the duplicitous dame. The plot is very ordinary – war veteran Bogart trying to find out who killed his buddy – but the dialogue is as sharp as a razor: in one scene, Bogie confides of chanteuse Scott, "Maybe she was all right, and maybe Christmas comes in July." Watch out for Morris Carnovsky in one of his last roles before he was blacklisted during the McCarthy witch-hunt, here playing a villainous nightclub owner. With this talent at his disposal, director John Cromwell steps back and just lets his cast get on with it. TS DVD

Humphrey Bogart *Rip Murdock* • Lizabeth Scott *Coral Chandler* • Morris Carnovsky *Martinelli* • Charles Cane *Lt Kincaid* • William Prince *Johnny Drake* • Marvin Miller *Krause* • Wallace Ford *McGee* ■ *Dir* John Cromwell • *Scr* Oliver HP Garrett, Steve Fisher, Allen Rivkin (adaptation), from an unpublished story by Gerald Adams [Gerald Drayson Adams], Sidney Biddell

Dead Ringer ★★★ PG

Melodrama 1964 · US · BW · 111mins

This is a late Bette Davis vehicle in which she stars as twins. Under the gritty direction of her *Now, Voyager* co-star Paul Henreid she's in post-*Baby Jane* mode, as one sister kills the other and takes her place in the mansion on the hill. It's good to see 1960s stalwarts like Peter Lawford and Karl Malden with something to get their teeth into. TS

Bette Davis *Margaret/Edith* • Karl Malden *Sergeant Jim Hobbson* • Peter Lawford *Tony Collins* • Philip Carey *Sergeant Ben Hoag* • Jean Hagen *Dede* • George Macready *Paul Harrison* • Estelle Winwood *Matriarch* ■ *Dir* Paul Henreid • *Scr* Albert Beich, Oscar Millard, from the story *La Otra* by Rian James

Dead Ringers ★★★★ 18

Psychological thriller
1988 · Can · Colour · 110mins

This finely wrought urban horror tale was inspired by the true story of identical twin gynaecologists who were found dead on New York's Upper East Side in 1975. Here, with the setting transposed to Toronto, Jeremy Irons expertly plays both Beverly and Elliot Mantle, with Geneviève Bujold as the internationally famous, infertile actress who, quite literally, can't choose between them. Director David Cronenberg here demonstrates a uniquely distressing and subtle talent, and the result is enough to put you off visiting fertility clinics for ever. TS. Contains violence, swearing, a sex scene and nudity. DVD

Jeremy Irons *Beverly/Elliot Mantle* • Geneviève Bujold *Claire Niveau* • Heidi Von Palleske *Dr Cary Weiler* • Barbara Gordon *Danuta* • Shirley Douglas *Laura* • Stephen Lack *Anders Wolleck* • Nick Nichols *Leo* • Lynne Cormack *Arlene* ■ *Dir* David Cronenberg • *Scr* David Cronenberg, Norman Snider, from the book *Twins* by Bari Wood, Jack Geasland

D

Dead Run ★★ U

Spy comedy
1967 · Fr/W Ger/It · Colour · 96mins

A tongue-in-cheek spy thriller with CIA agent Peter Lawford and the Mafia both chasing a petty thief who has inadvertently run off with an attaché case containing top, top secret papers. In fact, the papers are just our old friend the MacGuffin, since the movie is really all about Lawford's smarmy womanising and gentle spoofing from French director Christian-Jaque. AT. French dialogue dubbed into English.

Georges Geret *Carlos* • Peter Lawford *Dain* • Ira von Fürstenberg *Suzanne* • Maria Grazia Buccella *Anna* • Horst Frank *Manganne* • Werner Peters *Bardieff* • Jean Tissier *Adelgate* ■ *Dir* Christian-Jaque • *Scr* Michel Levine, Christian-Jaque, Pascal Jardin, Dany Tyber, from the novel by Robert Scheckley

Dead Sexy ★★ 18

Murder mystery thriller
2001 · US · Colour · 85mins

This is a by-the-numbers retread of *Basic Instinct*, with Shannon Tweed as a cop tracking a serial killer who's targeting high-class prostitutes. The plot, which sees Tweed going undercover and falling for the enigmatic chief suspect, offers nothing new, although the handful of bedroom sequences are far more explicit than many of its kind. JC DVD

Shannon Tweed *Kate McBain* • John Enos *Blue* • Kenneth White *Capt Snyder* • Eric Keith *Billy Trainer* ■ *Dir* Robert Angelo • *Scr* Elroy Canton, Anthony Laurence Greene

Dead Silent ★★

Thriller 1999 · US · Colour · 105mins

Arlen Aguayo-Stewart is a youngster who has remained mute since witnessing her parents' murder at the hands of the Mob. There are no prizes for guessing what's hidden inside her favourite doll or for seeing through the façade of seemingly nice neighbour Rob Lowe, who offers to protect the girl and her aunt, student doctor Catherine Mary Stewart. Unconvincing. DP. Contains violence, swearing, sex scenes and brief nudity.

Catherine Mary Stewart *Julia Kerbridge* • Rob Lowe *Kevin Finney* • Larry Day *Sitton* • Sean Devine *Dakins* • Allen Altman *Harmon* ■ *Dir* Roger Cardinal • *Scr* Ed Fitzgerald, Paul Koval

Dead Women in Lingerie ★★

Mystery thriller 1990 · US · Colour · 89mins

Great title, shame about the film. In this feeble spoof on the gumshoe genre, John Romo plays a private eye who finds it more and more difficult to disentangle himself from a murder case. This kind of Chandleresque lampoon requires a cool nerve and steady hand, but Erica Fox's lame thriller is much too frenetic to make any kind of satirical impact. TH

John Romo *Nick* • Maura Tierney *Molly Field* • Jerry Orbach *Bartoli* • Maria Strova *Carmen* • Dennis Christopher *Lapin* • Jeanne Sal *Bing* • David S Cameron *Lt North* ■ *Dir* Erica Fox • *Scr* Erica Fox, John Romo

Dead Wrong ★★ 15

Romantic adventure
1983 · Can · Colour · 93mins

An air of leaden predictability hangs over this tale, in which romance and crime combine in true B-movie style. Perhaps the action might have been more credible had it not been Britt Ekland playing the feisty Mountie agent who helps impoverished fisherman Winston Rekert fight off the Columbian mafiosi who have commandeered his boat for a drug run. Her derring-do has a distinct *Charlie's Angels* feel to it, as she takes on all comers without a hair falling out of place. DP

Britt Ekland *Priscilla "Penny" Lancaster* • Winston Rekert *Sean Phelan* • Dale Wilson *Mike Brady* • Jackson Davies *Inspector Fred Foster* • Alex Daikun *Stranger* • Leon Bibb *Bahama Jones* • Annie Kidder *Didi* ■ *Dir* Len Kowalewich • *Scr* Ron Graham

The Dead Zone ★★★ 18

Horror 1983 · US · Colour · 103mins

In this engrossing yet strangely unembellished adaptation of Stephen King's bestseller by director David Cronenberg, Christopher Walken plays the teacher who wakes up from a coma to find he has acquired the ability to foresee the future. As his value to society increases, his life crumbles, especially when he envisions the horrifying truth of mankind's destiny under the possible control of evil politician Martin Sheen. While it has none of Cronenberg's usual bracing style, it is thoughtful and moving at times, with Walken, Sheen and Brooke Adams giving top-notch performances. AJ. Contains violence, swearing and brief nudity. DVD

Christopher Walken *Johnny Smith* • Brooke Adams *Sarah Bracknell* • Tom Skerritt *Sheriff George Bannerman* • Herbert Lom *Dr Sam Weizak* • Anthony Zerbe *Roger Stuart* • Colleen Dewhurst *Henrietta Dodd* • Martin Sheen *Greg Stillson* ■ *Dir* David Cronenberg • *Scr* Jeffrey Boam, from the novel by Stephen King

Deadfall ★

Crime thriller 1968 · UK · Colour · 126mins

This insufferably pretentious twaddle from Bryan Forbes masquerades as a heist movie, as Michael Caine teams up with husband-and-wife Eric Portman and Giovanna Ralli for an audacious robbery. The excessive Freudian psychodrama comes complete with a song from Shirley Bassey. Sadly, the film doesn't provide any workaday thrills, and also fatally lacks a sense of humour. AT

Michael Caine *Henry Clarke* • Giovanna Ralli *Fe Moreau* • Eric Portman *Richard Moreau* • Nanette Newman *Girl* • David Buck *Salinas* • Carlos Pierre *Antonio* • Leonard Rossiter *Fillmore* ■ *Dir* Bryan Forbes • *Scr* Bryan Forbes, from the novel by Desmond Cory • *Music* John Barry (1)

Deadfall ★★ 18

Crime thriller 1993 · US · Colour · 94mins

Half-homage, half send-up of *film noir*, this stars James Coburn and Michael Biehn as father-and-son conmen. When son accidentally kills father early on, it instigates an incredibly complicated plot. Generally regarded as a misfire, it's worth a look for its pedigree: director Christopher Coppola is Francis's nephew and he casts his brothers, Nicolas Cage and Marc Coppola, and his aunt Talia Shire. AT DVD

Michael Biehn *Joe Donan* • James Coburn *Mike Donan* • Nicolas Cage *Eddie* • Sarah Trigger *Diane* • Charlie Sheen *Steve* • Talia Shire *Sam* • Angus Scrimm *Dr Lyme* • Peter Fonda *Pete* • Marc Coppola *Bob* ■ *Dir* Christopher Coppola • *Scr* Christopher Coppola, Nick Vallelonga

Deadhead Miles ★★

Comedy road movie
1972 · US · Colour · 93mins

After making the sublime cult movie *The Unholy Rollers*, director Vernon Zimmerman tried to match it with this offbeat road movie about a long-distance trucker and the wacky people he meets en route. Despite an inspired and often hilarious script by Terrence Malick, and Alan Arkin acting his socks off, the end result is a meandering muddle that remained unreleased for over ten years. Eminently watchable and absolutely terrible by turns. AJ

Alan Arkin *Cooper* • Paul Benedict *Tramp* • Hector Elizondo *Bad character* • Oliver Clark *Durazno* • Charles Durning *Red ball rider* • Lawrence Wolf *Pineapple* • Barnard Hughes *Old man* • William Duell *Auto parts salesman* • Loretta Swit *Woman with glass eye* • John Milius *2nd state trooper* • Ida Lupino *She* • George Raft ■ *Dir* Vernon Zimmerman • *Scr* Terrence Malick

Deadlier than the Male ★ 12

Mystery adventure
1966 · UK · Colour · 96mins

James Bond, who made his first screen appearance four years earlier, might have got away with this unpleasant mix of sex and sadism, but fascist-minded "Bulldog" Drummond (Richard Johnson) just isn't nonchalant enough to make it palatable. He's in hot pursuit of Nigel Green's lady killers (Elke Sommer and Sylva Koscina), who wipe out opposition to his takeover bids. Johnson reprised the role in 1969's *Some Girls Do*. TH DVD

Richard Johnson *Hugh "Bulldog" Drummond* • Elke Sommer *Irma Eckman* • Sylva Koscina *Penelope* • Nigel Green *Carl Petersen* • Suzanna Leigh *Grace* • Steve Carlson (2) *Robert Drummond* ■ *Dir* Ralph Thomas • *Scr* Jimmy Sangster, David Osborn, Liz Charles-Williams, from a story by Jimmy Sangster, from the novels by Sapper [HC McNeile]

Deadline at Dawn ★★

Mystery 1946 · US · BW · 83mins

This was the only movie directed by the Group Theater of New York's influential left-winger Harold Clurman, and dismayingly pretentious it is, too, despite a sterling performance from Susan Hayward as a dancer trying to clear a sailor (the undercast Bill Williams) of murder. The picture has a screenplay by Clifford Odets, who knew the theatre milieu well. Clurman turned out to be an inept director in this medium, failing to make much of the opportunities to hand. TS

Susan Hayward *June Goff* • Paul Lukas *Gus* • Bill Williams *Alex Winkley* • Joseph Calleia *Bartelli* • Osa Massen *Helen Robinson* • Lola Lane *Edna Bartelli* • Jerome Cowan *Lester Brady* • Marvin Miller *Sleepy Parsons* ■ *Dir* Harold Clurman • *Scr* Clifford Odets, from a novel by William Irish [Cornell Woolrich]

Deadline – USA ★★★

Crime drama 1952 · US · BW · 86mins

A clever but improbable tale, with Humphrey Bogart lending his formidable presence to the role of a hard-boiled newspaper editor trying to persuade proprietor Ethel Barrymore not to sell her Pulitzer Prize-winning journal, while he simultaneously confronts the mob and argues before the bench over the obligations of the press to its readers. It's an interesting subject, shot in the offices of the New York *Daily News*, but dully filmed. TS

Humphrey Bogart *Ed Hutcheson* • Ethel Barrymore *Mrs Garrison* • Kim Hunter *Nora* • Ed Begley *Frank Allen* • Warren Stevens *Burrows* • Paul Stewart *Thompson* • Martin Gabel *Rienzi* • Joseph De Santis [Joe De Santis] *Schmidt* ■ *Dir/Scr* Richard Brooks

Deadlocked ★★ 12

Crime drama 2000 · US · Colour · 86mins

There's a hint of the storyline that informed the Denzel Washington vehicle *John Q* in this courtroom TV drama, in which anxious father Charles S Dutton takes both the jury and the victim's husband hostage to ensure his son gets a fair trial. The problem is that while Dutton gives a typically imposing performance, the remainder of the cast is unable to attain the same level of conviction. DP DVD

David Caruso *Ned Stark* • Charles S Dutton *Jacob Doyle* • Jo D Jonz *Demond Doyle* • John Finn *Jake Fisque* • Diego Wallraff *Sergeant DeLucca* • Malcolm Stewart *Richard Castlemore* ■ *Dir* Michael W Watkins [Michael Watkins] • *Scr* David Rosenfelt, Erik Jendresen, from a story by David Rosenfelt

Deadly ★★ 15

Thriller 1991 · Aus · Colour · 101mins

Presenting a stark view of life among Australia's Aboriginal population, this thriller from director Esben Storm misses many of the chances it had to both excite and enlighten. The script teasingly suggests that many of the country's ingrained attitudes derive from the macho image of the Aussie male, but Storm shies away from this point to concentrate on a clichéd examination of racism. Similarly, the story of a cop given one last chance after he accidentally kills a girl on a drugs bust falls flat because there's nothing mysterious about the case he takes on in the outback. DP

Jerome Ehlers *Tony Bourke* • Frank Gallacher *Mick Thornton* • Lydia Miller *Daphne* • John Moore (2) *Eddie* • Caz Lederman *Irene* • Bill Hunter *Bar owner* ■ *Dir* Esben Storm • *Scr* Esben Storm, Ranald Allan

Deadly Advice ★ 15

Black comedy 1993 · UK · Colour · 86mins

Sadly, this dreary farce starring Jane Horrocks is low on laughs as the spirits of infamous British murderers such as Dr Crippen dole out advice to henpecked Horrocks on how best to kill her domineering mother, Brenda Fricker. This semi-detached suburban shocker misses by miles. AJ

Jane Horrocks *Jodie Greenwood* • Brenda Fricker *Iris Greenwood* • Imelda Staunton *Beth Greenwood* • Jonathan Pryce *Dr Ted Philips* • Edward Woodward *Major Herbert Armstrong* • Billie Whitelaw *Kate Webster* • Hywel Bennett *Dr Crippen* • Jonathan Hyde *George Joseph Smith* • John Mills *Jack the Ripper* • Ian Abbey *Bunny* • Eleanor Bron *Judge* ■ *Dir* Mandie Fletcher • *Scr* Glenn Chandler

The Deadly Affair ★★★★ 15

Spy drama 1966 · UK · Colour · 106mins

James Mason worked regularly with Sidney Lumet on both stage and television, but this gripping adaptation of a John le Carré novel was their first film collaboration. Mason gives a studied performance as the intelligence officer investigating the suspicious suicide of a diplomat, with the ever-dependable Harry Andrews also on bristling form as a no-nonsense copper. Director Lumet expertly weaves Mason's deplorable domestic situation into the equation, coaxing an unsympathetic portrayal from Harriet Andersson as Mason's promiscuous wife. DP

James Mason *Charles Dobbs* • Simone Signoret *Elsa Fennan* • Maximilian Schell *Dieter Frey* • Harriet Andersson *Ann Dobbs* • Harry Andrews *Inspector Mendel* • Kenneth Haigh *Bill Appleby* • Lynn Redgrave *Virgin* • Roy Kinnear *Adam Scarr* ■ *Dir* Sidney Lumet • *Scr* Paul Dehn, from the novel *Call for the Dead* by John le Carré

The Deadly Bees ★

Horror 1967 · UK · Colour · 83mins

Suzanna Leigh plays the pop singer who visits a remote island to recover from exhaustion. There she meets an insane beekeeper who breeds a strain of mutant bee that attacks a certain scent. This is one of the worst films Oscar-winning cinematographer-turned-director Freddie Francis ever made for Hammer rivals Amicus – a lacklustre plod through obvious red herrings and banal dialogue. AJ

Suzanna Leigh *Vicki Robbins* • Frank Finlay *Manfred* • Guy Doleman *Hargrove* • Catherine Finn *Mrs Hargrove* • John Harvey *Thompson* • Michael Ripper *Hawkins* • Anthony Bailey

Compere • Tim Barrett *Harcourt* ■ *Dir* Freddie Francis • *Scr* Robert Bloch, Anthony Marriott, from the novel *A Taste of Honey* by HF Heard

Deadly Blessing ★★★ 18

Horror 1981 · US · Colour · 97mins

This early nerve-jangler from horrormeister Wes Craven turns an everyday woman-in-peril terror tale into an epic of vindictive evil. In the rural serenity of eastern Pennsylvania, young widow Maren Jensen is persecuted by a religious cult led by Ernest Borgnine backed up by demonic forces that not even Sharon Stone, in her second movie role, can withstand. Snake-haters should beware of one shock scene, but it engenders a chilling despair that makes the ending all the more scary. TH. Contains violence, swearing and nudity. [VIDEO]

Ernest Borgnine *Isaiah* • Maren Jensen *Martha* • Susan Buckner *Vicky* • Sharon Stone *Lana* • Jeff East *John Schmidt* • Lisa Hartman *Faith* • Lois Nettleton *Louisa* • Coleen Riley *Melissa* ■ *Dir* Wes Craven • *Scr* Wes Craven, Glenn M Benest, Matthew Barr

The Deadly Companions ★★★

Western 1961 · US · Colour · 93mins

Sam Peckinpah made his debut as a movie director with this often gripping psychological western, which concentrates on the interaction of its quartet of key characters before it bursts into violent life on the streets of a ghost town. As the rose among three thorns, Maureen O'Hara is excellent, but it's the posturing between gunmen Brian Keith, Chill Wills and Steve Cochran that holds the attention. The direction is tentative at times, but the script is rock solid. DP

Maureen O'Hara *Kit* • Brian Keith *Yellowleg* • Steve Cochran *Billy* • Chill Wills *Turk* • Strother Martin *Parson* • Will Wright *Doctor* • Jim O'Hara *Cal* ■ *Dir* Sam Peckinpah • *Scr* AS Fleischman, from his novel

Deadly Force ★ 18

Crime drama 1983 · US · Colour · 95mins

Wings Hauser plays a half-crazy ex-cop who's so obnoxious, we are actually pleased when his former colleagues harass him as he pounds the streets of LA looking for a serial killer. Despite violence, swearing and a sweaty Hauser taking his clothes off, this plays like a disappointing TV production. KB [VIDEO]

Wings Hauser *Stoney Cooper* • Joyce Ingalls *Eddie Cooper* • Paul Shenar *Joshua Adams* • Al Ruscio *Sam Goodwin* • Arlen Dean Snyder *Ashley Maynard* • Lincoln Kilpatrick *Otto Hoxley* ■ *Dir* Paul Aaron • *Scr* Ken Barnett, Barry Schneider, Robert Vincent O'Neil

Deadly Friend ★★ 18

Horror 1986 · US · Colour · 86mins

In this daft horror yarn from Wes Craven, Matthew Laborteaux is the teen genius whose robot is destroyed shortly before his girlfriend is killed. Naturally, he decides to plant the robot's brain into his girl's head – but things don't go as planned. The plot bears a remarkable resemblance to the cult shocker *Re-Animator*, made the year before, but this is still an enjoyable, if unscary piece of entertainment. JB [VIDEO]

Matthew Laborteaux *Paul* • Kristy Swanson *Samantha* • Anne Twomey *Jeannie Conway* • Michael Sharrett *Tom* • Richard Marcus *Harry* • Anne Ramsey *Elvira Williams* • Russ Marin *Dr Johanson* • Andrew Roperto *Carl Denton* ■ *Dir* Wes Craven • *Scr* Bruce Joel Rubin, from the novel *Friend* by Diana Henstell

Deadly Game ★★

Drama 1982 · W Ger · Colour · 87mins

Hungarian director Karoly Makk helms this routine thriller about a game warden caught up in a murderous *ménage à trois* with the mistress of the estate on which he works. Stunning mountain scenery is the wrong location for a *film noir* as it's virtually impossible to create the characteristic intensity and menace in such wide open spaces. Barbara Sukowa is fine as the *femme fatale*, but Helmut Berger fails to convey the warden's conflict between ambition, lust and conscience. DP. German dialogue dubbed into English.

Helmut Berger *Boris* • Mel Ferrer *Stephan* • Barbara Sukowa *Daniela* • Karin Baal *Anna* • Josef Kroner [Jozef Kroner] *Marek* ■ *Dir* Karoly Makk • *Scr* Karsten Peters

The Deadly Game ★★★ PG

Drama 1986 · US · Colour · 107mins

That superb character actor John Lithgow is here given the chance to get his teeth into a decent leading role in co-writer/director Marshall Brickman's wry drama, which is also known as *The Manhattan Project*. Lithgow is entirely persuasive as the nuclear physicist slowly emerging from the protective cocoon of his intellect and beginning to understand the ramifications of his work when his girlfriend's teenage son enters a homemade bomb for a science fair. The moral is rather hammered home in the later stages, but there is plenty of clever chat and an ingeniously comic heist. DP [VIDEO]

John Lithgow *John Mathewson* • Christopher Collet *Paul Stephens* • Cynthia Nixon *Jenny Anderman* • Jill Eikenberry *Elizabeth Stephens* • John Mahoney *Lt Col Conroy* ■ *Dir/Scr* Marshall Brickman

Deadly Hero ★★★ 18

Crime thriller 1976 · US · Colour · 97mins

A taut, complex thriller in which Diahn Williams is first assaulted by James Earl Jones and then tormented by the cop (Don Murray) who saves her. This is a real Hitchcockian conceit – one twist deserves another as Williams experiences the full frying pan and fire proverb. Jones is truly scary, Murray creepily effective and note the screen debut of Treat Williams, who was once tipped to be the new Pacino. AT [VIDEO]

Don Murray *Ed Lacy* • Diahn Williams *Sally Deveraux* • James Earl Jones *Rabbit* • Lilia Skala *Mrs Broderick* • George S Irving *Reilly* • Treat Williams *Billings* • Charles Siebert *Baker* ■ *Dir* Ivan Nagy • *Scr* George Wislocki

Deadly Illusion ★★ 15

Action crime thriller
1987 · US · Colour · 86mins

Also known as *Love You to Death*, this thriller was written and co-directed by Larry Cohen, acclaimed creator of exuberant and full-blooded horror films. This might explain why there are some exotic touches of humour in this generic story of private detective Billy Dee Williams who battles to clear his name after he is framed for murder. Morgan Fairchild co-stars. TH [VIDEO]

Billy Dee Williams *Hamberger* • Vanity *Rina* • Morgan Fairchild *Jane/Sharon* • John Beck *Alex Burton* • Joe Cortese *Detective Lefferts* • Michael Wilding [Michael Wilding Jr] *Costillion* • Dennis Hallahan *Fake Burton* • Allison Woodward *Nancy Costillion* ■ *Dir* William Tannen (2), Larry Cohen • *Scr* Larry Cohen

The Deadly Mantis ★★

Science-fiction thriller
1957 · US · BW · 78mins

The dawning of the atomic age gave rise to an invasion of big bug movies, but this perfunctorily-directed, would-be sci-fi epic from Nathan Juran isn't in the same league as *Them!* or *Tarantula*. Still, there's something cathartic about watching a giant praying mantis, awoken from its arctic slumber by nuclear testing, laying waste to tourist attractions in New York and Washington DC. Starring Craig Stevens, then famous as television's Peter Gunn. RS

Craig Stevens *Colonel Joe Parkman* • William Hopper *Dr Ned Jackson* • Alix Talton *Marge Blaine* • Donald Randolph *General Mark Ford* ■ *Dir* Nathan Juran • *Scr* Martin Berkeley, from a story by William Alland

Deadly Nightshade ★★ PG

Crime drama 1953 · UK · BW · 58mins

In spite of its penury, this typical 1950s British crime quickie – about an escaped convict who unwittingly assumes the identity of a spy – is curiously engaging. Director John Gilling throws in a few Cornish coastal views, but he's mostly confined to unconvincing sets. The cheapskate look only adds to the charm. DP [VIDEO]

Emrys Jones *Robert Matthews/John Barlow* • Zena Marshall *Ann Farrington* • John Horsley *Inspector Clements* • Joan Hickson *Mrs Fenton* • Hector Ross *Canning* ■ *Dir* John Gilling • *Scr* Lawrence Huntington

Deadly Pursuit ★★★ 15

Action thriller 1988 · US · Colour · 105mins

This solid thriller treads too much familiar ground to stand out from the pack. Sidney Poitier stars as a lawman saddled with a mismatched partner (Tom Berenger) who gives him as much trouble as the bad guy. The fact that Berenger's girlfriend Kirstie Alley is directly in danger from the crazed killer comes as no surprise, either. The performances are pretty good, while British director Roger Spottiswoode makes the most of the great outdoors and stages a couple of pulsating action sequences. DP. Contains swearing and violence. [VIDEO] DVD

Sidney Poitier *Warren Stantin* • Tom Berenger *Jonathan Knox* • Kirstie Alley *Sarah* • Clancy Brown *Steve* • Richard Masur *Norman* ■ *Dir* Roger Spottiswoode • *Scr* Harv Zimmel, Michael Burton, Daniel Petrie Jr, from a story by Harv Zimmel

The Deadly Trackers ★★★ 15

Western 1973 · US · Colour · 100mins

Richard Harris stars as a peace-loving sheriff who becomes a vengeance-seeking animal after his wife and son are killed by Rod Taylor and his vile gang. Rated PG in America but given an X certificate on its release in Britain, the picture has an intense physicality as Harris undergoes his usual sado-masochistic, Brando-esque voyage of self-denial, self-discovery and self-parody. Samuel Fuller began the film in Spain, but the footage was scrapped and the film was restarted in Mexico with Barry Shear as director. A fascinating rag-bag of a movie. AT [VIDEO]

Richard Harris *Kilpatrick* • Rod Taylor *Brand* • Al Lettieri *Gutierrez* • Neville Brand *Choo Choo* • William Smith *Schoolboy* • Paul Benjamin *Jacob* • Pedro Armendáriz Jr *Blacksmith* ■ *Dir* Barry Shear • *Scr* Lukas Heller, from the story *Riata* by Samuel Fuller

The Deadly Trap ★

Psychological spy thriller
1971 · Fr/It · Colour · 97mins

Neorealist French director René Clément was well past his prime when he tackled this lacklustre thriller, a hotch-potch of soap-opera dramatics, murder and espionage. Faye Dunaway and Frank Langella try to give the sub-Hitchcock plot an edge, but the leisurely pace and colour-supplement locations do little to inspire any tension or suspension of disbelief. AJ

Faye Dunaway *Jill Hallard* • Frank Langella *Philip Hallard* • Barbara Parkins *Cynthia* • Michèle Lourié *Kathy* • Patrick Vincent *Patrick* ■ *Dir* René Clément • *Scr* Sidney Buchman, Eleanor Perry, from the novel *The Children Are Gone* by Arthur Cavanaugh, adapted by Daniel Boulanger, René Clément

Deadly Vows ★★ 15

Drama based on a true story
1994 · US · Colour · 93mins

In this TV movie, Gerald McRaney is the trucker whose delusions of grandeur prompt him to enter into a bigamous marriage and then conspire with his new bride to murder his first wife. McRaney is suitably unhinged, but writer Philip Rosenberg fails to fully flesh out the other characters, so that Peggy Lipton and Josie Bissett are left with nothing to do but react to their husband's perverse and, ultimately, deadly fantasies. DP. Contains violence and swearing. [VIDEO] DVD

Gerald McRaney *Tom Weston* • Peggy Lipton *Nancy Weston* • Josie Bissett *Bobbi Gilbert* ■ *Dir* Alan Metzger • *Scr* Philip Rosenberg

Deadly Weapons ★ 18

Crime drama 1974 · US · Colour · 71mins

The talk of the town in 1974, this diabolically bad crime drama is little more than a freak show designed to exhibit the 73-inch bust of its star, credited as Zsa Zsa on the film and as Chesty Morgan in the advertising. Chesty tracks down the racketeers who killed her boyfriend and takes revenge by smothering them with her mammoth mammaries. Because director Doris Wishman appears to have learned nothing about film technique since she began making nude flicks in the early 1960s, and because Chesty cannot act, a little of this nonsense goes a long way. DM [VIDEO] DVD

Zsa Zsa [Chesty Morgan] *Crystal Davies* • Harry Reems *Tony* • Greg Reynolds *Larry* ■ *Dir* Doris Wishman • *Scr* JJ Kendall

Deadly Whispers ★★ 15

Thriller 1995 · US · Colour · 90mins

This TV movie deals with the familiar phenomenon of a loved one at a police press conference becoming the prime suspect in the murder investigation. Tony Danza stars as the father who vows to apprehend his daughter's killer, only for the evidence to begin stacking up against him, but Pamela Reed turns in the strongest performance as his wife. Directed with some skill, but unrelentingly melodramatic. DP [VIDEO] DVD

Tony Danza *Tom Acton* • Pamela Reed *Carol Acton* • Ving Rhames *Detective Jackson* • Heather Tom *Kathy Acton* • Sean Haberle *Jim* ■ *Dir* Bill Norton [Bill L Norton] • *Scr* Dennis Turner, from the novel by Ted Schwarz

Deal of the Century ★★ 15

Satirical black comedy
1983 · US · Colour · 94mins

Given the talent on show, this brackish political satire has to go down as a major disappointment. Chevy Chase, Sigourney Weaver and Gregory Hines are the trio who luck into the weapons deal of century, only to find things go horribly wrong. The performances are likeable enough, but the screenplay by Paul Brickman lacks focus and William Friedkin's direction never strikes the right tone. JF [VIDEO]

Chevy Chase *Eddie Muntz* • Sigourney Weaver *Mrs De Voto* • Gregory Hines *Ray Kasternak* • Vince Edwards *Frank Stryker* • William Marquez *General Cordosa* ■ *Dir* William Friedkin • *Scr* Paul Brickman

Dealers ★★★ 15

Drama 1989 · UK · Colour · 87mins

This somewhat impoverished imitation of *Wall Street* would have been a much better movie had it stuck to the clinical, cynical depiction of life in the City rather than veering off into the realms of predictable thrillerdom. Rebecca De Mornay and Paul McGann might be the headliners, but there's nothing new about the way their love-hate relationship shifts once they start pulling in the big bucks. Derrick O'Connor, on the other hand, gives a compelling performance as the former whizzkid hooked on the devil's dandruff. DP [video] DVD

Paul McGann *Daniel Pascoe* • Rebecca De Mornay *Anna Schuman* • Derrick O'Connor *Robby Barrell* • John Castle *Frank Mallory* • Paul Guilfoyle (2) *Lee Peters* • Rosalind Bennett *Bonnie* • Adrian Dunbar *Lennox Mayhew* • Nicholas Hewetson *Jamie Dunbar* • Sara Sugarman *Elana* • Dikran Tulaine *Wolfgang* • Douglas Hodge *Patrick Skill* ■ *Dir* Colin Bucksey • *Scr* Andrew MacLear

Dealing: or the Berkeley-to-Boston Forty-Brick Lost-Bag Blues ★★

Comedy 1971 · US · Colour · 88mins

In the ranking of stupid titles, this must come near the top. It's one of those "youth movies", made in the wake of *Easy Rider* by Paul Williams, whose previous effort was the 1970 political drama *The Revolutionary*. The aforementioned bricks are made of marijuana and ferried between the two college campuses on opposite coasts of America. One of the oddest relics of the counterculture, it co-stars Barbara Hershey and John Lithgow (making his screen debut) and is based on a novel by "Michael Douglas" – in fact, a pseudonym for Michael Crichton. AT

Barbara Hershey *Susan* • Robert F Lyons *Peter* • Charles Durning *Murphy* • Joy Bang *Sandra* • John Lithgow *John* • Ellen Barber *Annie* • Gene Borkan *Musty* ■ *Dir* Paul Williams • *Scr* Paul Williams, David Odell, from a novel by Michael Douglas [Michael Crichton]

Dear America: Letters Home from Vietnam ★★★★ PG

Documentary
1987 · US · Colour and BW · 82mins

Rarely has the horror of the Vietnam war been brought home with such immediacy and power. Director Bill Couturie ploughed through thousands of missives for this highly personal history, appositely and soberingly illustrated by footage gleaned from the archives of NBC and the Department of Defense, much of it previously unseen. Read with selfless sincerity and dramatic simplicity by the likes of Robert De Niro, Sean Penn, Michael J Fox and Kathleen Turner, the letters heartrendingly demonstrate how the naive optimism turned into grim disenchantment of senseless slaughter and humiliating defeat. DP [video]

Dir Bill Couturie • *Scr* from the non-fiction book *Dear America: Letters Home from Vietnam* by Bernard Edelman

Dear Brigitte ★★★ U

Comedy 1966 · US · Colour · 100mins

Directed by Henry Koster, veteran of light-hearted family entertainment, this incident-packed comedy stars James Stewart and Glynis Johns and features a charming cameo from Brigitte Bardot, playing herself. Pro-arts professor Stewart has an eight-year-old son (Billy Mumy) who, much to his father's annoyance, is revealed to be a mathematical genius. The boy also writes love letters to Bardot and dreams of going to France to meet her. Lots of twists and turns ensue, with Stewart and Johns giving typically [expert] performances. RK

[Ste]wart *Robert Leaf* • Fabian *Kenneth* [...]ns *Vina* • Cindy Carol *Pandora* • Billy Mumy [Bill Mumy] *Erasmus* • John Williams *Upjohn* • Ed Wynn *Captain* • Brigitte Bardot ■ *Dir* Henry Koster • *Scr* Hal Kanter, from the novel *Erasmus with Freckles* by John Haase

Dear Diary ★★★★★ 15

Biographical comedy drama
1994 · It/Fr · Colour · 100mins

Nanni Moretti is the maverick genius of modern Italian cinema. Here he abandons the formulas of traditional film-making and embarks upon a personal journey that takes him to a movie theatre, the site of Pier Paolo Pasolini's murder, the Aeolian Islands and his own doctor's surgery. The side swipes at Roman architecture, *Henry: Portrait of a Serial Killer*, teenagers, television and the Italian health service are as sharp as they are quirky. Each section of this three-part pseudo-documentary contains a memorable moment, whether it's Moretti's encounter with Jennifer Beals or the relaying of soap-opera plotlines across Stromboli. Unhurried, unusual and unmissable. DP. In Italian and French with English subtitles. [video]

Nanni Moretti • Giovanna Bozzolo *Actor in Italian film* • Sebastiano Nardone *Actor in Italian film* • Antonio Petrocelli *Actor in Italian film* • Giulio Base *Car driver* • Jennifer Beals ■ *Dir/Scr* Nanni Moretti

Dear Frankie ★★★★ 12A

Drama 2003 · UK · Colour · 104mins

Single mum Emily Mortimer tries to protect her young deaf son from the truth about his abusive father in this poignant Scottish drama from first-time feature director Shona Auerbach. Jack McElhone is wonderfully natural as nine-year-old Frankie, who corresponds religiously with his absentee dad, unaware that it's his devoted mother who's picking up the letters and faking the replies. Mortimer is particularly appealing, while Gerard Butler has magnetic allure as the stranger she pays to temporarily masquerade as Frankie's father. With its sincere and perceptive script, the beautifully shot film vividly captures its complex characters. SF. Contains swearing.

Emily Mortimer *Lizzie* • Gerard Butler *The Stranger* • Jake McElhone *Frankie* • Sharon Small *Marie* • Mary Riggans *Nell* • Jayd Johnson *Catriona* • Sean Brown *Ricky Monroe* ■ *Dir* Shona Auerbach • *Scr* Andrea Gibb

Dear God ★★ PG

Comedy 1996 · US · Colour · 107mins

Comedian Greg Kinnear – who was nominated for an Oscar for his work in *As Good As It Gets* – got his first leading role in this lightweight comedy about a petty criminal who takes it upon himself to read and reply to the many letters written to God when he's made to work for the post office. Cute, inoffensive stuff, perfect for a rainy afternoon and enlivened by Kinnear's enjoyable performance. JB [video] DVD

Greg Kinnear *Tom Turner* • Laurie Metcalf *Rebecca Frazen* • Maria Pitillo *Gloria McKinney* • Tim Conway *Herman Dooly* • Hector Elizondo *Vladek Vidov* • Jon Seda *Handsome* • Roscoe Lee Browne *Idris Abraham* • Anna Maria Horsford *Lucille* • Rue McClanahan *Mom Turner* ■ *Dir* Garry Marshall • *Scr* Warren Leight, Ed Kaplan

Dear Heart ★★★★

Romantic comedy 1964 · US · BW · 96mins

Forlorn small-town postmistress Geraldine Page – in New York for a post office convention – causes trouble when she falls for delegate Glenn Ford, who's betrothed to, but not enamoured of, widow Angela Lansbury. Written by Tad Mosel, a great name from early American TV, it's properly sentimental without being mawkish, while Page, clutching isolation to herself as steadfastly as a security blanket, is touchingly true as a middle-aged woman teetering on the edge of the eccentricity. TH

Glenn Ford *Harry Monk* • Geraldine Page *Evie Jackson* • Michael Anderson Jr *Patrick* • Barbara Nichols *June* • Patricia Barry *Mitchell* • Charles Drake *Frank Taylor* • Angela Lansbury *Phyllis* ■ *Dir* Delbert Mann • *Scr* Tad Mosel, from his story *The Out-of-Towners*

Dear John ★★★

Romantic drama 1964 · Swe · BW · 110mins

Nominated for a best foreign film Oscar, this was Lars Magnus Lindgren's fourth feature. Yet for all its success, he would make only three more films. It has sea captain Jarl Kulle's romance with waitress Christina Schollin skilfully interspersed with flashbacks detailing their pre-stories – he was abandoned by his wife and she was so hurt by the man who left her pregnant that she is now suspicious of Kulle's eager intentions. Watchfully played. DP. In Swedish with English subtitles.

Jarl Kulle *John* • Christina Schollin *Anita* • Helena Nilsson *Helena* • Morgan Andersson *Raymond* ■ *Dir* Lars Magnus Lindgren • *Scr* Lars Magnus Lindgren, from the novel by Olle Lansberg

Dear Mr Prohack ★★★ U

Romantic comedy 1949 · UK · BW · 91mins

Cecil Parker, one of Britain's best and most distinctive stiff-upper-lip character actors, takes a title role tailor-made for his screen persona. He plays an adept government Treasury official who comes into a fortune, but proves rather less competent at handling his own money. His unwise investments and the foolish extravagances of his family make for what is essentially a one-joke comedy that eventually runs out of steam, but there's fun to be had along the way. RK

Cecil Parker *Arthur Prohack* • Glynis Johns *Mimi Warburton* • Hermione Baddeley *Eve Prohack* • Dirk Bogarde *Charles Prohack* • Sheila Sim *Mary Prohack* • Heather Thatcher *Lady Maslam* • Denholm Elliott *Oswald Morfey* • Ian Carmichael *Hatter* ■ *Dir* Thornton Freeland • *Scr* Ian Dalrymple, Donald Bull, from the play *Mr Prohack* by Edward Knoblock, Arnold Bennett, from the novel by Arnold Bennett

Dear Murderer ★★ PG

Crime thriller 1947 · UK · BW · 90mins

When wealthy London businessman Eric Portman learns his wife Greta Gynt has had an affair during his absence, he murders the man. When he discovers she has a new lover (Maxwell Reed), he frames him for the crime. A nifty but thoroughly unpleasant British thriller, in which the protagonists are so vile we can only rejoice when they get their comeuppance. RK [video]

Eric Portman *Lee Warren* • Greta Gynt *Vivien Warren* • Dennis Price *Richard Fenton* • Jack Warner *Inspector Pembury* • Maxwell Reed *Jimmy Martin* ■ *Dir* Arthur Crabtree • *Scr* Muriel Box, Sydney Box, Peter Rogers, from the play *Dear Murderer* by St John L Clowes

Dear Ruth ★★★

Comedy 1947 · US · BW · 95mins

William Holden co-stars with Paramount's briefly popular Joan Caulfield in this adaptation of Norman Krasna's hit Broadway play about a pen-pal relationship with a difference. Mayhem ensues as a result of a recalcitrant, precocious and idealistic schoolgirl (bouncy Mona Freeman) corresponding with a soldier on active duty, using elder sister Caulfield's name. Director William D Russell deftly controls the polished cast in this endearing and delightful comedy. Two inferior sequels, *Dear Wife* and *Dear Brat*, followed. RK

Joan Caulfield *Ruth Wilkins* • William Holden (2) *Lt William Seacroft* • Edward Arnold *Judge Harry Wilkins* • Mary Philips *Edith Wilkins* • Mona Freeman *Miriam Wilkins* • Billy De Wolfe *Albert Kummer* • Virginia Welles *Martha Seacroft* ■ *Dir* William D Russell • *Scr* Arthur Sheekman, from the play by Norman Krasna

Dear Wendy ★★★★ 15

Drama
2005 · Den/Ger/UK/Fr · Colour · 105mins

America's love affair with guns is cleverly satirised in this thought-provoking drama from Thomas Vinterberg. In a mature and convincing performance, Jamie Bell plays a fervent pacifist in a poor American mining town who sets up a secret gun-worshiping club. The flamboyantly styled organisation becomes a means of mental empowerment for other local outcasts. It's quirky and imaginatively constructed, with every element from soundtrack to costumes serving a vital function. Yet most crucially the picture is also a stinging comment on individuality and intolerance, resulting in a shocking and tragic climax. SF. Contains swearing and violence.

Jamie Bell *Dick* • Bill Pullman *Krugsby* • Michael Angarano *Freddie* • Danso Gordon *Sebastian* • Chris Owen *Huey* • Alison Pill *Susan* • Mark Webber *Stevie* • Novella Nelson *Clarabelle* ■ *Dir* Thomas Vinterberg • *Scr* Lars von Trier

Dear Wife ★★ U

Comedy 1949 · US · BW · 88mins

This sequel to the successful comedy *Dear Ruth* (1947) was directed by Richard Haydn with the same leading players. The plot finds William Holden married to Joan Caulfield and running against his father-in-law Edward Arnold for the state senate, while younger sister Mona Freeman continues on her socially conscious way. Freeman almost steals the show from the more seasoned players. *Dear Brat* concluded the series in 1951. RK

William Holden (2) *Bill Seacroft* • Joan Caulfield *Ruth Seacroft* • Billy De Wolfe *Albert Kummer* • Mona Freeman *Miriam Wilkins* • Edward Arnold *Judge Wilkins* ■ *Dir* Richard Haydn • *Scr* Arthur Sheekman, N Richard Nash, from characters created by Norman Krasna

Death and the Maiden ★★★★ 18

Drama 1994 · UK/US/Fr · Colour · 99mins

Adapted for the screen by Rafael Yglesias and Ariel Dorfman from Dorfman's play, this is an anguished tour de force, in which a traumatised woman turns her living room into a court to try the neighbour she believes raped and tortured her during a previous fascist dictatorship. Outstandingly played by Sigourney Weaver and Ben Kingsley (as her possible tormentor), the effective three-hander succeeds because of a dreadful electricity sparking between the two leads, while Stuart Wilson, as her husband, tries not to get burned. Director Roman Polanski keeps this notable film as claustrophobic as a coffin. TH. Contains violence, swearing and nudity. [video]

Sigourney Weaver *Paulina Escobar* • Ben Kingsley *Dr Roberto Miranda* • Stuart Wilson (1) *Gerardo Escobar* • Krystia Mova *Dr Miranda's wife* • Rodolphe Vega *Dr Miranda's son* ■ *Dir* Roman Polanski • *Scr* Rafael Yglesias, Ariel Dorfman, from the play by Ariel Dorfman

Death at Clover Bend ★★

Crime thriller 2001 · US · Colour · 84mins

Director Michael Vickerman makes the most of the cramped locale after

Robert Urich's LAPD marksman and his holidaying family get caught up in David Keith's raid on a gas station. But the denouement is never in doubt, especially once Urich's wife, Erin Gray, catches a stray bullet. Urich and Keith strike sparks in several macho exchanges and also fight a battle with a script that fails to develop either their characters or any suspense. DP

Robert Urich *Bill Clayton* • David Keith *Mcgrary* • Erin Gray *Betty Clayton* • Barry Corbin *Cotton* • Dwayne Adway *Jones* ■ *Dir* Michael Vickerman

Death Becomes Her ★★★★ PG

Black comedy 1992 · US · Colour · 99mins

See Meryl Streep and Goldie Hawn as you've never seen them before, enlivening this special-effects laden, extremely dark comedy from Robert Zemeckis. Superbitch actress Streep and novelist Hawn are the present and former loves of plastic surgeon-turned-mortician Bruce Willis, whose talents can't compete with witch Isabella Rossellini's devilish gift of eternal youth. Zemeckis's under-rehearsed direction is at odds with a savagely delicious script and inspired casting: both leading ladies are superbly acerbic as they try to outbitch each other, while Willis is a pleasant surprise as the put-upon hubby in this quirky but most enjoyable oddity. SH. Contains swearing. [video] DVD

Meryl Streep *Madeline Ashton* • Bruce Willis *Ernest Menville* • Goldie Hawn *Helen Sharp* • Isabella Rossellini *Lisle Von Rhuman* • Ian Ogilvy *Chagall* • Adam Storke *Dakota* • Nancy Fish *Rose* ■ *Dir* Robert Zemeckis • *Scr* Martin Donovan, David Koepp

Death before Dishonor ★★ 18

Action adventure 1987 · US · Colour · 89mins

Rambo rides again in this rather second-rate thriller, with Fred Dryer as the Stallone-like hero, a marine with a short fuse hunting the Middle Eastern terrorists who've kidnapped his pal, colonel Brian Keith. There are some nasty moments, and there's little redeeming humour in this gung-ho, jingoistic gobbledegook. TH. Contains violence and swearing. [video]

Fred Dryer *Sergeant Jack Burns* • Joey Gian *Ramirez* • Sasha Mitchell *Ruggieri* • Peter Parros *James* • Brian Keith *Colonel Halloran* • Paul Winfield *Ambassador* • Joanna Pacula *Elli* ■ *Dir* Terry J Leonard • *Scr* John Gatliff, Lawrence Kubik, from their story

Death by Hanging ★★★★

Black comedy based on a true story
1968 · Jpn · BW · 117mins

If Akira Kurosawa was Japan's most American director, then Nagisa Oshima is its most European. The influence of Brecht, Buñuel, Godard and Dusan Makavejev can all be felt in this stylised account of a true story, which typifies Oshima's combative approach to both film-making and politics. Charged with the murder and rape of two girls, a first-generation Korean student (Yun-Do Yun) survives the noose but loses his memory. So his jailers subject him to a macabre and increasingly menacing reconstruction of his alleged crimes. A scathing denunciation of capital punishment and Japan's almost institutionalised hatred of the Korean community. DP. In Japanese with English subtitles.

Yun-Do Yun *R* • Kei Sato *Head Of Execution Ground* • Fumio Watanabe *Education officer* • Toshiro Ishido *Chaplain* • Masao Adachi *Security officer* • Mutsuhiro Toura *Doctor* • Nagisa Oshima *Narrator* ■ *Dir* Nagisa Oshima • *Scr* Tsutomu Tamura, Mamoru Sasaki, Michinori Fukao, Nagisa Oshima

Death Collector ★★★ 15

Crime drama 1976 · US · Colour · 88mins

Joe Cortese gets a job as a debt collector and gets caught up in the Mafia lifestyle, with suitably violent consequences. Although considered nothing more than a *Mean Streets* clone at the time, in retrospect director Ralph DeVito's gritty drama foreshadows many of the themes Martin Scorsese would later explore in *GoodFellas* and *Casino*. (Look out for Joe Pesci, the star of those two movies, in one of his earliest roles.) Great goon dialogue and quirky details set this apart. AJ [video]

Joe Cortese *Jerry Bolanti* • Lou Criscuolo *Anthony Iadavia* • Joe Pesci *Joey* • Bobby Alto *Serge* • Frank Vincent *Bernie Feldshuh* • Keith Davis *Marley* • Jack Ramage *Herb Greene* • Anne Johns *Paula* • Bob D'Andrea *Neil* ■ *Dir/Scr* Ralph DeVito

Death Drums along the River ★★ PG

Crime mystery 1963 · UK · Colour · 79mins

British veteran director Lawrence Huntington fetched up in South Africa in the days when it wasn't politically kosher to do so, to deliver this strangely appealing update of the hoary old Edgar Wallace imperialist saga *Sanders of the River*. The film features Richard Todd attempting to resuscitate his career by playing the police inspector. He reprised the role in 1965's *Coast of Skeletons*. TS [video]

Richard Todd *Inspector Harry Sanders* • Marianne Koch *Dr Inge Jung* • Vivi Bach *Marlene* • Walter Rilla *Dr Schneider* • Jeremy Lloyd *Hamilton* ■ *Dir* Lawrence Huntington • *Scr* Harry Alan Towers, Nicolas Roeg, Kevin Kavanagh, Lawrence Huntington, from the novel *Sanders of the River* by Edgar Wallace

Death Game ★★

Thriller 1976 · US · Colour · 86mins

San Francisco architect Seymour Cassel lets two hitch-hikers, Sondra Locke and Colleen Camp, into his house where they proceed to seduce, bind and torture him. This is an unnerving psychodrama, with sleazy sex and compelling depravity oozing from every exploitative frame. A prime example of 1970s post-Manson paranoia, the ridiculous twist ending lets this down. AJ

Sondra Locke *Jackson* • Colleen Camp *Donna* • Seymour Cassel *George Manning* • Beth Brickell *Karen Manning* • Michael Kalmansohn *Delivery boy* • Ruth Warshawsky *Mrs Grossman* ■ *Dir* Peter S Traynor • *Scr* Anthony Overman, Michael Ronald Ross

Death Hunt ★★★ 18

Thriller adventure based on a true story
1981 · US · Colour · 97mins

Charles Bronson is up to his macho tricks again in this violent adventure that trades on his *Death Wish* persona. He plays a trapper in the Canadian Rockies who is wrongly accused of murder and goes on the run, pursued by Mountie Lee Marvin. Director Peter Hunt does a decent job of shaping the borderline exploitation thrills into a highly watchable form, and the crisp photography helps enormously. Animal lovers, beware: there's a very graphic dog fight. AJ. Contains violence and swearing. [video]

Charles Bronson *Albert Johnson* • Lee Marvin *Sergeant Edgar Millen* • Angie Dickinson *Vanessa McBride* • Andrew Stevens *Alvin Adams* • Carl Weathers *Sundog* • William Sanderson *Ned Warren* • Jon Cedar *Hawkins* ■ *Dir* Peter Hunt • *Scr* Michael Grais, Mark Victor • *Cinematographer* James Devis

Death in a French Garden ★★★★ 18

Thriller 1985 · Fr · Colour · 97mins

Teasing and dripping with style, this is that rare blend of form and content that engages both the eye and the mind. Through elliptical editing and arch manipulation of his characters, director Michel Deville leaves us as baffled as his hero, a young guitar teacher played by Christophe Malavoy. Not only does he discover his affair with his pupil's mother (Nicole Garcia) is being filmed; he also learns he's being stalked by the gay assassin who's been hired to kill his employer (Michel Piccoli). The ambiguity and elegance may not be to all tastes, but the performances, especially Piccoli's, are excellent. DP. In French with English subtitles. [video] DVD

Michel Piccoli *Graham Tombsthay* • Nicole Garcia *Julia Tombsthay* • Anémone *Edwige Ledieu* • Christophe Malavoy *David Aurphet* • Richard Bohringer *Daniel Forest* ■ *Dir* Michel Deville • *Scr* Michel Deville, Rosalinde Damamme, from the novel *Sur la Terre comme au Ciel* by René Belletto

Death in Brunswick ★★★★ 15

Black comedy 1990 · Aus · Colour · 103mins

Now here is the Sam Neill you won't have seen before. He's on cracking form as a cook in a sleazy restaurant in the Brunswick area of Melbourne, who hopes that an affair with waitress Zoe Carides will help him escape his domineering mother. But the only bodily contact he gets is with the corpse of his Turkish colleague in this black comedy that works best during the restaurant scenes as the dialogue fizzes and the racial mix bubbles. DP. Contains violence, swearing, nudity. [video] DVD

Sam Neill *Carl Fitzgerald* • Zoe Carides *Sophie Papafagos* • John Clarke (2) *Dave* • Yvonne Lawley *Mrs Fitzgerald* • Nico Lathouris *Mustafa* • Nicholas Papademetriou *Yanni Voulgaris* ■ *Dir* John Ruane • *Scr* John Ruane, Boyd Oxlade, from the novel by Boyd Oxlade

Death in Small Doses ★★★ 15

Courtroom drama based on a true story
1995 · US · Colour · 91mins

Directed by Sondra Locke, this TV movie is based on a true story in which landscape gardener Richard Thomas is charged with poisoning his wife Glynnis O'Connor by lacing her vitamin pills with arsenic. However, all is not as it seems as the watertight case proves to have more holes than a Gruyère cheese. Locke knows when to press the suspense button and there are solid performances. DP [video] DVD

Richard Thomas *Richard Lyon* • Tess Harper *Assistant DA Jerri Sims* • Glynnis O'Connor *Nancy Lyon* • Gary Frank *Bill Dillard Jr* ■ *Dir* Sondra Locke • *Scr* Scott Swanton

Death in the Garden ★★★

Thriller 1956 · Fr/Mex · Colour · 95mins

Devised to exploit the success of *The Wages of Fear*, this jungle western was originally to be scripted by Jean Genet as a vehicle for Yves Montand. Luis Buñuel accepted the directorial reins with reluctance, yet he manages to explore his key themes of bourgeois avarice, religious hypocrisy and sexual repression while following a motley crew as it escapes across hostile terrain after a South American uprising. The perils encountered are drearily generic, but Buñuel still transforms this gloriously photographed Eden into a gruellingly perilous place. DP. In French with English subtitles.

Simone Signoret *Djin* • Georges Marchal *Shark* • Charles Vanel *Castin* • Tito Junco *Chenko* • Michel Piccoli *Father Lisardi* ■ *Dir* Luis Buñuel • *Scr* Luis Buñuel, Luis Alcoriza, Raymond Queneau, Gabriel Arout, from a novel by José André Lacour • *Cinematographer* Jorge Stahl

Death in the Shadows ★★★ 15

Drama based on a true story
1998 · US · Colour · 90mins

Believe it or not, *The Fugitive* – about an innocent doctor wrongly accused of murder – was actually based on a real story. In this TV movie, however, events have moved on and are now seen through the eyes of the physician's grown-up son. Peter Strauss plays the brilliant but arrogant surgeon Sam Sheppard, while Henry Czerny is his son, who starts digging into his father's case with the help of a local lawyer. An intriguing spin on a now-familiar tale. JF [video] DVD

Peter Strauss *Dr Sam Sheppard* • Henry Czerny *Sam "Chip" Reese Sheppard* • Lindsay Frost *Marilyn Sheppard* ■ *Dir* Peter Levin • *Scr* Adam Greenman, from the non-fiction book *Memory of Justice: the True Story of the Sam Sheppard Murder Case* by Cynthia L Cooper, Sam Reese Sheppard

Death in the Sun ★

Action adventure
1975 · W Ger/S Afr · Colour · 95mins

Trevor Howard and Christopher Lee put in fine cameo performances in an otherwise amateur exploitation thriller shot in Zimbabwe with a stupid script, inept direction and mediocre photography. In an East African British colony under threat from a Mau-Mau style uprising, farmer Howard's daughter is graphically raped by an albino native (Horst Frank in a totally unconvincing coat of whitewash). AJ

Christopher Lee *Bill* • James Faulkner *Terrick* • Trevor Howard *Johannes* • Horst Frank *Whispering Death* • Sybil Danning *Sally* • Sascha Hehn *Peter* • Sam Williams *Katchemu* ■ *Dir* Jürgen Goslar • *Scr* Scot Finch, from the novel *Whispering Death* by Daniel Carney

Death in Venice ★★★★★ 15

Period drama 1971 · It/Fr · Colour · 125mins

Former matinée idols Dirk Bogarde and Silvana Mangano increased their standing with art house audiences after this sumptuous reworking of Thomas Mann's novella. Bogarde's composer (an author in the original) arrives in Venice amid rumours of a cholera epidemic, troubled that he can no longer experience emotion, but the sight of Mangano's teenage son, Bjorn Andresen, stirs long dormant feelings. Luchino Visconti was a master of colour composition and here he has created a haunting work that is as operatic as it is cinematic. It is perhaps too sedate in places, but the shimmering photography more than compensates. DP [video] DVD

Dirk Bogarde *Gustav von Aschenbach* • Bjorn Andresen *Tadzio* • Silvana Mangano *Tadzio's mother* • Marisa Berenson *Frau von Aschenbach* • Mark Burns *Alfred* ■ *Dir* Luchino Visconti • *Scr* Luchino Visconti, Nicola Badalucco, from the novella by Thomas Mann • *Cinematographer* Pasquale De Santis [Pasqualino De Santis] • *Art Director* Ferdinando Scarfiotti • *Costume Designer* Piero Tosi

Death Japanese Style ★★★★ 18

Black comedy
1984 · Jpn · Colour and BW · 123mins

The high cost of dying in Japan is shrewdly, albeit sometimes crudely, satirised by director Juzo Itami, whose deconstruction of a three-day wake for a bad-tempered elder by his daughter and son-in-law is as wild as it is witty. Seemingly inspired by his own experiences, Itami establishes the samurai-slash style of film-making railing at a society that has lost touch with its traditions – a style he was to reinforce with his subsequent, better-known comedy *Tampopo*. TH. In Japanese with English subtitles.

Tsutomu Yamazaki *Wabisuke Inoue* • Nobuko Miyamoto *Chizuko Amamiya* • Kin Sugai *Kikue Amamiya* • Shuji Otaki *Shokichi Amamiya* • Ichiro Zaitsu *Satomi* ■ *Dir/Scr* Juzo Itami

The Death Kiss ★★★

Mystery 1933 · US · BW and Tinted · 74mins

Director Edwin L Marin's potboiler is an old-fashioned Hollywood thriller in every sense. Bela Lugosi plays the manager of Tinseltown's Tiffany Studios where a murder is committed on the set of a new production. While no great shakes in the mystery department, this is an intriguing behind-the-scenes look at the motion picture mechanics of the era. For Lugosi fans this is a fascinating artefact from the horror star's golden period. AJ

David Manners *Franklyn Drew* • Adrienne Ames *Marcia Lane* • Bela Lugosi *Joseph Steiner* • John Wray *Detective Lieut Sheehan* • Vince Barnett *Officer Gulliver* • Alexander Carr *Leon A Grossmith* • Edward Van Sloan *Tom Avery* ■ *Dir* Edwin L Marin • *Scr* Gordon Kahn, Barry Barringer, Joe Traub, from the novel by Madelon St Denis

Death Line ★★★★ 18

Horror 1972 · UK · Colour · 83mins

Reactionary cop Donald Pleasence investigates mysterious disappearances in the London Underground and makes the startling discovery that a colony of cannibals has existed in the creepy tunnels since a Victorian cave-in disaster. Strong stuff in its day, Gary Sherman never directed a better movie than this grisly chiller, which provides dark scares while presenting an effective commentary on violence. An under-rated slice of British horror, this manages to be eerie, touching, melancholic and imaginative to a degree rarely seen in the genre. Highly recommended. AJ

Donald Pleasence *Inspector Colquhoun* • Christopher Lee *Stratton-Villiers* • Norman Rossington *Detective Rogers* • David Ladd *Alex Campbell* • Sharon Gurney *Patricia Wilson* ■ *Dir* Gary Sherman • *Scr* Ceri Jones, from the story *Death Line* by Gary Sherman

Death Machine ★★★ 18

Science-fiction horror
1994 · UK · Colour · 111mins

Homegrown director Stephen Norrington fashions a distinctly un-British but hugely entertaining techno-thriller. Set in the near future, the story pits hi-tech weapons firm executive Ely Pouget and a gang of terrorists against barmy scientist Brad Dourif and his bone-crunching killing machine in a deserted office building. There's little in the way of character development, but former effects man Norrington never lets the pace slacken for a minute and designs some ingenious action sequences. JF

Brad Dourif *Jack Dante* • Ely Pouget *Hayden Cale* • William Hootkins *John Carpenter* • John Sharian *Sam Raimi* • Martin McDougall *Yutani* • Richard Brake *Scott Ridley* • Rachel Weisz *AN Other personnel manager* ■ *Dir/Scr* Stephen Norrington

Death of a Bureaucrat ★★★★

Black comedy 1966 · Cub · BW · 84mins

Tomás Gutiérrez Alea achieved international acclaim with this deliciously macabre comedy. Produced for the state-run ICAIC, it reveals an unexpected tolerance on the part of the Castro regime, as the satire at its expense is both funny and far from flattering. Frustrated at every turn by red tape, Salvador Wood has to resort to graverobbing to retrieve the union card his recently widowed aunt requires for her pension. Shot through with a Buñuelian strain of humour, Alea's approach also owes a good deal to silent slapstick and the anti-establishment ethos of contemporary Czech cinema. DP. In Spanish with English subtitles.

Salvador Wood *Nephew* • Silvia Planas *Aunt* • Manuel Estanillo *Bureaucrat* • Gaspar De Santelices *Nephew's boss* ■ *Dir* Tomás Gutiérrez Alea • *Scr* Alfredo Del Cueto, Ramón Suárez, Tomás Gutiérrez Alea

Death of a Cheerleader ★★★ 12

Mystery drama 1994 · US · Colour · 87mins

This isn't in the same league as the witty 1993 Holly Hunter film *The Positively True Adventures of the Alleged Texas Cheerleader-Murdering Mom*, but still provides a gripping portrait of high-school politics. Student Tori Spelling delights in tormenting the school's geeks, including bright-but-plain Kellie Martin, but then turns up dead. Director William A Graham sympathetically chronicles the complex pressures of adolescent life. JF. Contains swearing, violence and drug abuse. DVD

Kellie Martin *Angela Delvecchio* • Tori Spelling *Stacy Lockwood* • Valerie Harper *Mrs Delvecchio* • Terry O'Quinn *Ed Saxe* • James Avery *Agent Gilwood* • Andy Romano *Mr Delvecchio* • Margaret Langrick *Jill Anderson* ■ *Dir* William A Graham • *Scr* Dan Bronson, from a story by Dan Bronson, Randall Sullivan, from an article by Randall Sullivan

Death of a Cyclist ★★★★

Drama 1955 · Sp/It · BW · 85mins

One of the key films in the establishment of a neorealist tradition in 1950s Spanish cinema, this *noir*ish thriller boldly attempted social criticism at a time of severe censorship. It was unsurprising that the Franco regime should insist that university professor Alberto Closas and his mistress Lucia Bosé should pay the ultimate penalty for the hit-and-run death of a worker, but Juan Antonio Bardem still paints an unflattering portrait of the Madrid bourgeoisie. Hardly sophisticated, but historically significant. DP. In Spanish with English subtitles.

Lucia Bosé *Maria Jose* • Alberto Closas *Juan* • Otello Toso *Miguel* • Carlos Casaravilla *Rafa* ■ *Dir* Juan Antonio Bardem • *Scr* Juan Antonio Bardem, from a story by Luis F de Igoa

Death of a Gunfighter ★★★

Western 1969 · US · Colour · 94mins

A fine, grim western bearing all the hallmarks of its uncredited director, the great Don Siegel, who took over from Robert Totten after Totten fell out with star Richard Widmark. The credit was given to that alias agreed by the Directors Guild, one Allen Smithee (this was, in fact, the first feature to bear the name). Widmark is once again compulsively watchable as a former gunman-turned-marshal while Lena Horne is brilliantly cast as his woman. This may be too downbeat and slow for many tastes, but the casting of Widmark and Horne makes it an interesting collector's item. TS

Richard Widmark *Marshal Frank Patch* • Lena Horne *Claire Quintana* • Carroll O'Connor *Lester Locke* • David Opatoshu *Edward Rosenbloom* • Kent Smith *Andrew Oxley* ■ *Dir* Allen Smithee [Robert Totten], Allen Smithee [Don Siegel] • *Scr* Joseph Calvelli, from the novel by Lewis B Patten

Death of a Salesman ★★★★

Drama 1951 · US · BW · 111mins

This powerful and generally faithful film version of Arthur Miller's hit Broadway play – the tragedy of a mediocre individual trying to understand his life of failure – replaced the original stage star, Lee J Cobb, with screen veteran Fredric March. Sad for Cobb when some other members of the stage production – Mildred Dunnock as the wife, Cameron Mitchell as one of his two sons – were retained, but March is superb as the despairing salesman and gained an Oscar nomination. (He lost to Humphrey Bogart in *The African Queen*.) The theatrical transitions to flashbacks might have been avoided, but this is highly commendable work by director Laslo Benedek. AE

Fredric March *Willy Loman* • Mildred Dunnock *Linda Loman* • Kevin McCarthy *Biff* • Cameron Mitchell *Happy* • Howard Smith *Charley* • Royal Beal *Ben* ■ *Dir* Laslo Benedek • *Scr* Stanley Roberts, from the play by Arthur Miller

Death of a Salesman ★★★ PG

Drama 1985 · US · Colour · 130mins

Dustin Hoffman re-creates his Broadway role as Willy Loman, the ageing commercial traveller trapped in his vision of the go-getting American Dream, in director Volker Schlöndorff's fascinating version of Arthur Miller's play. Hoffman starts at the top of his voice and continues in the same vein, as if still playing to the back row, though Kate Reid, as Loman's long-suffering wife, and Stephen Lang and Emmy Award-winning John Malkovich as their sons, give more subtle performances. TH DVD

Dustin Hoffman *Willy Loman* • Kate Reid *Linda Loman* • John Malkovich *Biff Loman* • Stephen Lang *Happy Loman* • Charles Durning *Charley* • Louis Zorich *Ben* ■ *Dir* Volker Schlöndorff • *Scr* Arthur Miller, adapted from the original Broadway production staged by Michael Rudman

Death of a Schoolboy ★★★ PG

Biographical drama
1990 · Austria · Colour · 89mins

Austrian director Peter Patzak's film about the assassination of Archduke Franz Ferdinand in Sarajevo was full of possibilities. The spark that ignited the "tinderbox of Europe" was provided by Gavrilo Princip, a member of the Black Hand freedom fighters, but this biopic gives us too few insights into either the tense political situation in the summer of 1914 or the convictions that drove the boy to murder. It's handsomely mounted and the performances are earnest, but also ponderous. DP. Some German dialogue dubbed into English.

Reuben Pillsbury *Gavrilo* • Christopher Chaplin *Trifco* • Robert Munic *Cabri* • Sinolicka Trpkova *Sophia* • Hans Michael Rehberg *School director* • Philippe Léotard *Dr Levin* • Alexis Arquette *Milan* • Alan Cox *Anarchist* ■ *Dir* Peter Patzak • *Scr* David Anthony, Peter Patzak, from the book by Hans Konig

Death of a Scoundrel ★★

Crime drama 1956 · US · BW · 119mins

This *film à clef* on the life of Serge Rubenstein is something of a family affair, with George Sanders getting the chance to betray real-life brother Tom Conway and seduce then wife Zsa Zsa Gabor. Overlong and repetitive, the action follows Sanders as he treads the familiar path from stony-broke immigrant to spendthrift playboy. DP

George Sanders *Clementi Sabourin* • Yvonne De Carlo *Bridget Kelly* • Zsa Zsa Gabor *Mrs Ryan* • Victor Jory *Leonard Wilson* • Nancy Gates *Stephanie North* • John Hoyt *Mr O'Hara* • Coleen Gray *Mrs Van Renassalear* • Lisa Ferraday *Zina Monte* • Tom Conway *Gerry Monte* ■ *Dir/Scr* Charles Martin

Death of a Soldier ★★ 18

War drama based on a true story
1985 · Aus · Colour · 92mins

This is something of a departure for French-born, Australian-raised film-maker Philippe Mora. Although there are some expressionistic touches, the action is much less stylised than in his earlier documentaries. Rugged performances from James Coburn and Bill Hunter convey some of the tensions that arise between the US Army and the authorities Down Under during the hunt for a GI (Reb Brown) suspected of strangling several Melbourne women. DP. Contains violence, swearing and nudity.

James Coburn *Major Patrick Danneberg* • Reb Brown *Private Edward J Leonski* • Bill Hunter *Detective Sergeant "Bluey" Adams* • Maurie Fields *Detective Sergeant Ray Martin* • Belinda Davey *Margot Saunders* • Max Fairchild *Major William Fricks* ■ *Dir* Philippe Mora • *Scr* William Nagle

Death of an Angel ★

Crime drama 1951 · UK · BW · 64mins

When Jane Baxter, the wife of a country doctor is murdered, suspicion falls on her husband Patrick Barr, his new young assistant Raymond Young, his daughter Julie Somers and the local bank manager Russell Waters. Whodunnit? Suffice to say suspense is minimal in this British murder mystery, directed at a snail's pace by Charles Saunders. RK

Jane Baxter *Mary Welling* • Patrick Barr *Robert Welling* • Julie Somers *Judy Welling* • Jean Lodge *Ann Marlow* • Raymond Young *Chris Boswell* • Russell Waters *Walter Grannage* • Russell Napier *Superintendent Walshaw* • Katie Johnson *Sarah Oddy* ■ *Dir* Charles Saunders • *Scr* Reginald Long, from the play *This Is Mary's Chair* by Frank King

Death of an Angel ★★★ 12

Drama 1985 · US · Colour · 91mins

Cult indoctrination and its attendant psychological problems are snapped into sharp focus in this psychological thriller. Bonnie Bedelia goes to Mexico to wrest her impressionable daughter, Pamela Ludwig, from the evil clutches of a religious sect and its charismatic leader, Nick Mancuso. The superior cast and intelligent treatment of religious power-plays elevate this thriller above the norm. AJ DVD

Bonnie Bedelia *Grace* • Nick Mancuso *Father Angel* • Pamela Ludwig *Vera* • Alex Colon *Robles* ■ *Dir/Scr* Petru Popescu

The Death of Mario Ricci ★★★★ PG

Mystery romance
1983 · Fr/Swi · Colour · 100mins

A Swiss investigative journalist comes to a remote mountain village to interview an expert on famine. The man appears to be on the edge of a nervous breakdown, which is somehow connected with the mystery surrounding the death of Mario Ricci, an Italian immigrant worker. Brilliantly assembled by Swiss director Claude Goretta, with a central performance by Gian Maria Volonté that deservedly won him the best actor award at Cannes, the film is redolent with atmosphere, tension and visual flair. RK. In French with English subtitles.

Gian Maria Volonté *Bernard Fontana* • Magali Noël *Solange* • Heinz Bennent *Henri Kremer* • Mimsy Farmer *Cathy Burns* • Jean-Michel Dupuis *Didier Meylan* ■ *Dir* Claude Goretta • *Scr* Claude Goretta, Georges Haldas

The Death of the Incredible Hulk ★★ PG

Action adventure 1990 · US · Colour · 94mins

One of a number of TV movie spin-offs from the wearisome series, this has Bill Bixby still searching for a way of ridding himself of the alter ego who ruins all his clothes. Here he finds a sympathetic scientist (Philip Sterling) to help reverse the genetic process only to find himself the target of evil terrorists. Green-dyed Lou Ferrigno once again ripples his muscles, but the playing and the direction are as bland as usual. JF [video] DVD

Bill Bixby *Dr David Banner* • Lou Ferrigno *The Hulk* • Elizabeth Gracen *Jasmin* • Philip Sterling *Dr Ronald Pratt* • Andreas Katsulas *Kasha* • Carla Ferrigno *Bank clerk* ■ *Dir* Bill Bixby • *Scr* Gerald DiPego, from characters created by Stan Lee, Jack Kirby

Death on the Nile ★★ PG

Murder mystery 1978 · UK · Colour · 133mins

The biggest mystery here is how director John Guillermin managed to take a splendid Agatha Christie novel, some stunning scenery and a stellar cast and produce such a disappointing film. The only thing fatal about the first half of this picture is its pace. Peter Ustinov clearly enjoys his first outing as the fastidious Belgian super-sleuth Hercule Poirot and there's some delicious overplaying by Maggie Smith and Angela Lansbury. Yet David Niven and Bette Davis are wasted, and George Kennedy and Lois Chiles are simply dreadful. DP [video] DVD

Peter Ustinov *Hercule Poirot* • Jane Birkin *Louise Bourget* • Lois Chiles *Linnet Ridgeway* • Bette Davis *Mrs Van Schuyler* • Mia Farrow *Jacqueline de Bellefort* • Jon Finch *Mr Ferguson* • Olivia Hussey *Rosalie Otterbourne* • IS Johar *Manager of the Karnak* • George Kennedy *Andrew Pennington* • Angela Lansbury *Mrs Salome Otterbourne* • Simon MacCorkindale *Simon Doyle* • David Niven *Colonel Rice* • Maggie Smith *Miss Bowers* • Jack Warden *Dr Bessner* • Harry Andrews *Barnstaple* • Sam Wanamaker *Rockford* ■ *Dir* John Guillermin • *Scr* Anthony Shaffer, from the novel by Agatha Christie

Death on the Set ★

Crime mystery 1935 · UK · BW · 72mins

This barnstorming baloney stars Henry Kendall as both an American gangster and his movie-directing lookalike. Blackmail leads to murder, with Kendall-the-gangster trying to pin the dirty deed on leading lady Jeanne Stuart. Leslie S Hiscott's direction is blissfully free of suspense. DP

Henry Kendall *Cayley Morden/Charlie Marsh* • Jeanne Stuart *Lady Blanche* • Eve Gray *Laura Lane* • Lewis Shaw *Jimmy Frayle* • Garry Marsh *Inspector Burford* • Wally Patch *Sergeant Crowther* • Alfred Wellesley *Studio manager* • Rita Helsham *Constance Lyon* ■ *Dir* Leslie S Hiscott [Leslie Hiscott] • *Scr* Michael Barringer, from the novel by Victor MacClure

Death Race 2000 ★★★ 18

Futuristic action satire
1975 · US · Colour · 76mins

An ultra-violent, action-packed satire set in the future showing the fascist American government sponsoring a nationally televised road race where drivers score points for ramming pedestrians. The event is staged to pacify the ravenous public's lust for blood and stop them from getting involved with revolutionaries determined to overthrow the President. Although very graphic and bloody, light-hearted direction by Paul Bartel keeps the subversive demolition derby on an amusing track. AJ. Contains violence, swearing and brief nudity. [video] DVD

David Carradine *Frankenstein* • Simone Griffeth *Annie* • Sylvester Stallone *Machine Gun Joe Viterbo* • Mary Woronov *Calamity Jane* • Roberta Collins *Mathilda the Hun* • Martin Kove *Nero the Hero* • Louisa Moritz *Myra* • Don Steele *Junior Bruce* ■ *Dir* Paul Bartel • *Scr* Robert Thom, Charles B Griffith, from a story by Ib Melchior

Death Rides a Horse ★★ 15

Spaghetti western
1967 · It · Colour · 110mins

This overlong but spirited spaghetti western confidently uses the tried and tested clichés of the genre: the greenhorn gunfighter joining forces with a master marksman; the baddies turned upstanding leaders of the community; and the duellist with an empty gun. John Phillip Law is the youth searching for his parents' murderers, the same people Lee Van Cleef is hunting after they put him in jail. With stylish direction and a neat twist in the tale, this is an efficient horse opera. AJ. Italian dialogue dubbed into English. [video]

John Phillip Law *Bill* • Lee Van Cleef *Ryan* • Luigi Pistilli *Wolcott* • Anthony Dawson [Antonio Margheriti] *Manina* • José Torres (1) *Pedro* ■ *Dir* Giulio Petroni • *Scr* Luciano Vincenzoni

Death Takes a Holiday ★★★

Fantasy romance 1934 · US · BW · 79mins

A witty and sophisticated Paramount fable with a clever, though wordy, screenplay. It stars Fredric March as a very urbane grim reaper visiting Earth to learn how he is perceived and discover why humans are so scared of him. He takes the form of a handsome prince, only to fall in love during a palazzo house party. Director Mitchell Leisen keeps this bubbling along at a very healthy 79 minutes, which really makes you wonder how the 1998 remake *Meet Joe Black* clocked in at a grim three hours. TS

Fredric March *Prince Sirk* • Evelyn Venable *Grazia* • Sir Guy Standing [Guy Standing] *Duke Lambert* • Katherine Alexander *Alda* • Gail Patrick *Rhoda* • Helen Westley *Stephanie* • Kathleen Howard *Princess Maria* • Kent Taylor *Corrado* ■ *Dir* Mitchell Leisen • *Scr* Maxwell Anderson, Gladys Lehman, Walter Ferris, from the play by Alberto Casella

Death to Smoochy ★★ 15

Black comedy
2002 · US/UK · Colour · 105mins

This odd mix of comedy and drama stars Robin Williams as a sleazy psychotic children's entertainer on TV who finds himself sacked for taking backhanders. In his place, young, idealistic Edward Norton is hired, who dresses up as a Barney-like character named Smoochy. The darkly comic elements work brilliantly, but someone obviously got nervous about such a dark look at children's TV and decided to make it as cute and fluffy as Smoochy by the end. JB [video] DVD

Robin Williams *Rainbow Randolph* • Edward Norton *Sheldon Mopes/Smoochy the Rhino* • Catherine Keener *Nora Wells* • Danny DeVito *Burke Bennett* • Jon Stewart *Marion Frank Stokes* • Harvey Fierstein *Merv Green* • Pam Ferris *Tommy Cotter* ■ *Dir* Danny DeVito • *Scr* Adam Resnick

Death Train ★ 18

Horror 1989 · US · Colour · 90mins

The usual contingent of sex-obsessed American college kids go on a school trip to Yugoslavia and get trapped by Satan-worshippers on a possessed steam train because one of the girls is picked to be the Devil's bride. Forgettable in every respect, this sports a half-baked, thrown-together plot, incredibly inane dialogue and obvious train miniatures. AJ [video]

Mary Kohnert *Beverly* • Bo Svenson *Professor Andromolek* • Victoria Zinny *Beverly's mother* • Savina Gersak *Sara* ■ *Dir* Jeff Kwitny • *Scr* Sheila Goldberg

Death Train ★★ 15

Action thriller
1993 · UK/Cro/US · Colour · 94mins

In this minor TV movie, based on the Alistair MacLean novel, renegade Russian general Christopher Lee is exporting nuclear weapons to Iraq to start a revolution and Patrick Stewart is in charge of the UN army task force deciding to call in drunken ex-SAS officer Pierce Brosnan to head the mission. Cue the ripe dialogue, very tepid thrills and typical low-rent action in a would-be tough thriller. The stellar cast doesn't help much. AJ. Contains swearing and violence. [video] DVD

Pierce Brosnan *Mike Graham* • Patrick Stewart *Malcolm Philpott* • Alexandra Paul *Sabrina Carver* • Ted Levine *Alex Tierney* • Christopher Lee *General Benin* • John Abineri *Leitzig* • Nic D'Avirro *Rodenko* • Clarke Peters *Whitlock* ■ *Dir* David S Jackson [David Jackson] • *Scr* David S Jackson, from the novel by Alistair MacLean

Death Valley ★★ 18

Crime thriller 1982 · US · Colour · 84mins

Low-grade "stalk and slash" movie, focusing on a young boy visiting his mother in Arizona who unwittingly becomes the target of a psychopath. Director Dick Richards succeeds in creating a low quota of suspense, but he allows the predictable plot to be hampered by inferior acting. RS [video]

Paul Le Mat *Mike* • Catherine Hicks *Sally* • Stephen McHattie *Hal* • Wilford Brimley *Sheriff* • Peter Billingsley *Billy* • Edward Herrmann *Paul* • Jack O'Leary *Earl* ■ *Dir* Dick Richards • *Scr* Richard Rothstein

Death Vengeance ★★★ 18

Action crime drama
1982 · US · Colour · 91mins

As *Death Wish* rip-offs go, Lewis Teague's film is fairly close to the cream of the crop. Tom Skerritt is excellent as a Philadelphia shopkeeper who organises a vigilante group to crack down on local deviants, becoming a media celebrity by default. The pace is lively, but Teague tries to have his cake and eat it, denouncing violent retribution on the one hand while succumbing to crowd-pleasing mayhem on the other. RS [video]

Tom Skerritt *John D'Angelo* • Patti LuPone *Lisa D'Angelo* • Michael Sarrazin *Vince Morelli* • Yaphet Kotto *Ivanhoe Washington* • David Rasche *Michael Taylor* • Donna DeVarona *Sara Rogers* • Gina DeAngelis *Vera D'Angelo* • Jonathan Adam Sherman *Danny D'Angelo* ■ *Dir* Lewis Teague • *Scr* Tom Hedley, David Zelag Goodman

Death Warrant ★★★ 18

Action thriller
1990 · US/Can · Colour · 85mins

Even for a Jean-Claude Van Damme movie, this is an excessively violent, if clinically efficient, exercise in body pulverising. Van Damme stars as a maverick Royal Canadian Mountie, sent to a prison where there's been a series of grisly unsolved murders. There he comes face to face with an old foe: the psychopathic "Sandman", played with zealous enthusiasm by Patrick Kilpatrick. To some extent this marked a career breakthrough for Van Damme, who got to play not just a kickboxer, but – hey! – an *undercover* kickboxer. Deran Sarafian's direction is brutally efficient, but fans won't be disappointed. RS [video] DVD

Jean-Claude Van Damme *Louis Burke* • Cynthia Gibb *Amanda Beckett* • Robert Guillaume *Hawkins* • George Dickerson *Tom Vogler* • Art LaFleur *Sergeant DeGraf* • Patrick Kilpatrick *Naylor, "The Sandman"* ■ *Dir* Deran Sarafian • *Scr* David S Goyer

Death Wish ★★★ 18

Crime thriller 1974 · US · Colour · 89mins

This is the highly controversial sleaze epic that finally made Charles Bronson a star in America, and set a regrettable trend for ultra-violent vigilante thrillers. Bronson mechanically plays liberal architect Paul Kersey, who takes matters into his own hands after his wife is killed and his daughter is raped by a Manhattan gang (led by Jeff Goldblum in his film debut). Director Michael Winner's blood-lusting shocker is as intense and upsetting as it is morally reprehensible, and was very influential in its day, but spawned a series of dismal sequels. AJ. Contains violence, swearing and nudity. [video]

Charles Bronson *Paul Kersey* • Hope Lange *Joanna Kersey* • Vincent Gardenia *Frank Ochoa* • Steven Keats *Jack Toby* • William Redfield *Sam Kreutzer* • Stuart Margolin *Aimes Jainchill* • Jeff Goldblum *Mugger* ■ *Dir* Michael Winner • *Scr* Wendell Mayes, from the novel by Brian Garfield

D

Death Wish II ★ 18

Crime thriller 1981 · US · Colour · 85mins

Charles Bronson takes his lone vigilante act to Los Angeles in this crudely exploitative, belated first sequel to Michael Winner's trend-setting trash thriller. Beginning as it means to go on with the rape and murder of Bronson's Spanish maid, it would be offensive if it weren't so laughably over the top. AJ. Contains swearing, violence, nudity. [video] DVD

Charles Bronson *Paul Kersey* • Jill Ireland *Geri Nichols* • Vincent Gardenia *Frank Ochoa* • JD Cannon *New York DA* • Anthony Franciosa *LA Police Commissioner* • Ben Frank *Lieutenant Mankiewicz* • Robin Sherwood *Carol Kersey* ■ *Dir* Michael Winner • *Scr* David Engelbach, from characters created by Brian Garfield

Death Wish 3 ★ 18

Crime thriller 1985 · US · Colour · 86mins

With any remaining shred of political subtlety erased by the appallingly exploitative *Death Wish II*, director Michael Winner continues his freelance vigilante saga in ludicrously over-the-top mode. This time a pack of punks and gay Hell's Angels terrorises a Manhattan apartment block. Ridiculous and revolting. AJ [video]

Charles Bronson *Paul Kersey* • Deborah Raffin *Kathryn Davis* • Ed Lauter *Richard Striker* • Martin Balsam *Bennett* • Gavan O'Herlihy *Fraker* • Kirk Taylor *Giggler* • Alex Winter *Hermosa* ■ *Dir* Michael Winner • *Scr* Don Jakoby, Michael Edmonds, from characters created by Brian Garfield

Death Wish 4: the Crackdown ★ 18

Crime thriller 1987 · US · Colour · 94mins

Crusading vigilante architect Charles Bronson cleans up three crack-dealing LA syndicates after one causes the death of his girlfriend's (Kay Lenz) daughter in this shoddily staged sequel. J Lee Thompson takes over the directing ropes from Michael Winner and incredibly does an even lousier job marshalling the brain-damaged plot, inane dialogue and senseless violence. Awful. AJ [video]

Charles Bronson *Paul Kersey* • Kay Lenz *Karen Sheldon* • John P Ryan *Nathan White* • Perry Lopez *Ed Zacharias* • Soon-Teck Oh *Detective Nozaki* • George Dickerson *Detective Reiner* • Jesse Dabson *Randy Viscovich* • Dana Barron *Erica Sheldon* ■ *Dir* J Lee Thompson • *Scr* Gail Morgan Hickman, from characters created by Brian Garfield

Death Wish V: the Face of Death ★ 18

Crime thriller 1994 · US · Colour · 91mins

Charles Bronson's one-man crusade against low-lifes continues when his girlfriend, fashion designer Lesley-Anne Down, is slaughtered by her mobster ex-lover Michael Parks. Absolute dross, with transvestite henchmen and acid attacks barely livening up the formulaic violence. AJ. Contains swearing, violence and nudity.

Charles Bronson *Paul Kersey* • Lesley-Anne Down *Olivia Regent* • Erica Lancaster *Chelsea Regent* • Michael Parks *Tommy O'Shea* • Saul Rubinek *Brian Hoyle* ■ *Dir* Allan Goldstein [Allan A Goldstein] • *Scr* Stephen Peters, from characters created by Brian Garfield

D

Deathmask ★

Crime drama 1984 · US · Colour · 103mins

This is a tasteless, plotless thriller in which a medical examiner investigates the murder of a young boy in an attempt to ease the guilt of not being able to save his own daughter from her untimely death. Directed by Richard Friedman and starring Farley Granger, this is nasty stuff. JB

Farley Granger *Doug Andrews* • Lee Bryant *Jane Andrews* • John McCurry *Jim O'Brien* • Arch Johnson *Dr Riordan* • Barbara Bingham *Suzy Andrews* • Danny Aiello *Captain Mike Gress* ■ *Dir* Richard Friedman • *Scr* Jeffrey Goldenberg, Richard Friedman

Deathsport ★★

Science fiction 1978 · US · Colour · 82mins

Ranger guides David Carradine and Claudia Jennings battle the evil Statesmen, futuristic Hell's Angels who ride cycles called Death Machines, in a banal reworking of *Death Race 2000*. It's set in the post-apocalyptic year 3000, and mixes cheap *Star Wars* tricks and cannibal mutants into the vehicular violence. There's lots of fiery crashes and gory comedy, but little sense in a movie shot separately by directors Henry Suso and Allan Arkush and then literally stuck together. AJ

David Carradine *Kaz Oshay* • Claudia Jennings *Deneer* • Richard Lynch *Ankar Moor* • William Smithers *Doctor Karl* • David McLean *Lord Zirpola* • Jesse Vint *Polna* ■ *Dir* Henry Suso, Allan Arkush • *Scr* Henry Suso, Donald Steward, from a story by Frances Doel

Deathtrap ★★ PG

Thriller 1982 · US · Colour · 111mins

The play by Ira Levin was a particularly clever piece of stagecraft that, like *Sleuth*, was heavily dependent on the theatre itself to make its tricks work. No matter how well director Sidney Lumet manages to disguise the theatricality, and despite hard work by leads Michael Caine and Christopher Reeve, the basic plot devices sink the project cinematically. TS. Contains some swearing.

Michael Caine *Sidney Bruhl* • Christopher Reeve *Clifford Anderson* • Dyan Cannon *Myra Elizabeth Maxwell Bruhl* • Irene Worth *Helga Ten Dorp* • Henry Jones *Porter Milgrim* ■ *Dir* Sidney Lumet • *Scr* Jay Presson Allen, from the play by Ira Levin

Deathwatch ★★★

Drama 1966 · US · BW · 88mins

In the 1960s, an awkward translation of Jean Genet's difficult play, about the rivalries and tensions between three convicts (one awaiting execution) in a prison cell, had a surprisingly successful run in Los Angeles. This film is basically a record of that production with a new prologue and flashbacks added. It is still heavy going, but the Method-influenced performances are good. One of the inmates is played by Leonard Nimoy, just before he found fame in *Star Trek*, another by Paul Mazursky, who went on to write and direct films such as *Down and Out in Beverly Hills* and *Bob & Carol & Ted & Alice*. DM

Leonard Nimoy *Jules LeFranc* • Michael Forest *Greeneyes* • Paul Mazursky *Maurice* • Robert Ellenstein *Guard* • Gavin Macleod *Emil* ■ *Dir* Vic Morrow • *Scr* Barbara Turner, Vic Morrow, from the play *Haute Surveillance* by Jean Genêt and translated by Bernard Frechtman as *Deathwatch*

Deathwatch ★★★ 15

Science-fiction satire
1980 · Fr/W Ger · Colour · 124mins

This futuristic discourse on the intrusiveness of television is much bleaker and censorious than either Didier Grousset's *Kamikaze* or *The Truman Show*. With Glasgow providing the desolate backdrop, this shows how easy it is to commit acts of psychological trespass, as Harvey Keitel uses a miniature camera implanted in his skull to record the final days of the terminally ill Romy Schneider for unscrupulous Harry Dean Stanton's TV show. DP

Romy Schneider *Katherine Mortenhoe* • Harvey Keitel *Roddy* • Harry Dean Stanton *Vincent Ferriman* • Thérèse Liotard *Tracey* • Max von Sydow *Gerald Mortenhoe* ■ *Dir* Bertrand Tavernier • *Scr* Bertrand Tavernier, David Rayfiel, from the novel *The Continuous Katherine Mortenhoe (The Unsleeping Eye)* by David Compton

Deathwatch ★ 15

Horror 2002 · UK/Ger · Colour · 91mins

If war is hell, this combat-themed chiller from debutant writer/director Michael J Bassett isn't much better. *Billy Elliot's* Jamie Bell plays the youngest recruit of a First World War platoon that's lost deep in enemy territory, but takes refuge in an uncharted trench where the men are systematically picked off by a seemingly supernatural assassin. Bassett's lumbering direction blasts any horror or suspense clean out of the target area. AJ DVD

Jamie Bell *Charlie Shakespeare* • Hugo Speer *Sergeant Tate* • Matthew Rhys *"Doc" Fairweather* • Andy Serkis *Private Quinn* • Laurence Fox *Captain Jennings* • Dean Lennox Kelly *McNess* ■ *Dir/Scr* Michael J Bassett

The Debt Collector ★★★★ 18

Drama 1999 · UK · Colour · 105mins

As hard-hitting as a kick in the stomach, this gritty Scottish drama is outstanding on all fronts. First-time director Anthony Neilson has crafted a visceral and cathartic tale with virtuoso skill, combining tragedy on a Shakespearean scale with vibrant colour and superb camera control. Billy Connolly stars as a reformed ex-con and now successful sculptor whose violent past comes back to haunt him in the shape of his arresting officer, Ken Stott. Stott takes it upon himself to deal Connolly true retribution for his crimes, and in the process both they and their families suffer severe repercussions. LH. Contains violence, sexual threat and swearing. DVD

Billy Connolly *Nickie Dryden* • Ken Stott *Gary Keltie* • Francesca Annis *Val Dryden* • Iain Robertson *Flipper* • Annette Crosbie *Lana* • Alastair Galbraith *Colquhoun* ■ *Dir/Scr* Anthony Neilson • *Music* Adrian Johnston • *Cinematographer* Dick Pope

The Debut ★★ 15

Comedy drama 2000 · US · Colour · 84mins

Co-writer/director Gene Cajayon's independent labour of love was an unexpected success in its native America. Yet though Cajayon's obvious passion is admirable, this low-budget drama about teenage outsider Dante Basco, who's rejected his Filipino heritage, is largely clichéd, exploring its themes of alienation and misplaced identity with a clumsy lack of imagination. It's also badly acted overall, with wannabe artist Basco particularly wooden. SF. In English and Tagalog with subtitles. Contains swearing and violence. DVD

Dante Basco *Ben Mercado* • Eddie Garcia *Grandpa Mercado* • Tirso Cruz III *Roland Mercado* • Gina Alajar *Gina* • Darion Basco *Augusto* • Dion Basco *Rommel* • Derek Basco *Edwin Mercado* • Bernadette Balagtas *Rose Mercado* • Joy Bisco *Annabelle* ■ *Dir* Gene Cajayon • *Scr* Gene Cajayon, John Manal Castro

Los Debutantes ★★★ 18

Crime thriller 2003 · Chil · Colour · 114mins

Director Andrés Waissbluth demonstrates once again the camera's talent for deception in this simmering Chilean thriller. By revealing events from the viewpoint of each of his three main protagonists, Waissbluth is able to withhold the significance of seemingly minor events until we are as deeply embroiled in underworld danger as Néstor Cantillana and Juan Pablo Miranda, the shanty-town brothers who have fallen for Antonella Ríos, the slinky dancer lover of Santiago mobster Alejandro Trejo. Although Waissbluth's blend of Cagney, *film noir* and Tarantino doesn't always gel, this is still satisfyingly nasty. DP. In Spanish with English subtitles. Contains sex scenes, drug abuse.

Antonella Ríos *Gracia* • Néstor Cantillana *Silvio* • Juan Pablo Miranda *Victor* • Eduardo Barril *Don Marco* • Alejandro Trejo *Don Pascual* ■ *Dir* Andrés Waissbluth • *Scr* Andrés Waissbluth, Julio Rojas

A Decade under the Influence ★★★ 15

Documentary
2003 · US · Colour and BW · 109mins

The final film from Ted Demme (he died during post-production), this covers much the same ground as *Easy Riders, Raging Bulls*, but is an all together slicker affair. That's said, this is not without its flaws. On the plus side, the movie clips and archival footage are stitched together with wit and flair, while the extended interviews not only feature the usual suspects (Scorsese, Coppola, Altman), but lesser known figures such as John G Avildsen and Marshall Brickman. However, that's also one of the downsides: by casting the net so wide, there's no real thematic focus, while the interviewees themselves get a fairly easy ride from their inquisitors, who include film-makers Neil LaBute and Alexander Payne, as well as Demme and co-director Richard LaGravenese. JF DVD

Dir/Scr Richard LaGravenese, Ted Demme

Decadence ★ 18

Comedy 1993 · UK/Ger · Colour · 113mins

This pretentious film version of his own play is a virtual textbook on how not to make the transition from stage to screen. Stephen Berkoff, who both directs and stars alongside Joan Collins, can't bear to excise a single rhyming couplet, resulting in interminable monologues interspersed with bouts of lame slapstick, plus bizarre cameos. The leads play dual roles from different ends of the social spectrum, but plot comes a poor second to the author's laboured satire on the privileged classes. NS

Steven Berkoff *Steve/Les/Helen's "Couturier"* • Joan Collins *Helen/Sybil* • Christopher Biggins *Entourage* • Michael Winner *Entourage* • Marc Sinden *Entourage* ■ *Dir* Steven Berkoff • *Scr* Steven Berkoff, from his play

The Decameron ★★★★ 18

Period drama
1970 · It/Fr/W Ger · Colour · 106mins

This was the first film in Pier Paolo Pasolini's trilogy based on famous medieval story cycles – *The Canterbury Tales* and *Arabian Nights* being the others. The director himself plays Giotto, seen working on a fresco while around him revolve eight of Boccaccio's bawdy tales of sexual deception, which involve lascivious nuns, a false saint and three brothers who kill their sister's lover. Untrammelled by any Freudian or religious guilt, this episodic movie captures much of the spirit of the original. RB. In Italian with English subtitles.

Franco Citti *Ciappelletto* • Ninetto Davoli *Andreuccio of Perugia* • Angela Luce *Peronella* • Patrizia Capparelli *Alibech* • Jovan Jovanovic *Rustico* • Gianni Rizzo *Head friar* • Pier Paolo Pasolini *Giotto* ■ *Dir* Pier Paolo Pasolini • *Scr* Pier Paolo Pasolini, from the stories by Giovanni Boccaccio • *Cinematographer* Tonino Delli Colli • *Art Director* Dante Ferretti

Decameron Nights ★★★

Period adventure 1953 · UK · Colour · 93mins

Suave Louis Jourdan plays both yarnspinner Boccaccio and the leads in a trio of stories, framed by a device whereby he and Joan Fontaine flee 14th-century Florence to escape the plague, holing up in her villa. Unsurprisingly, Fontaine co-stars in the three tales as well. The result is diverting and mildly risqué tosh, beautifully photographed in rich Technicolor by talented cameraman Guy Green. Director Hugo Fregonese knows how to get the most out of this kind of flamboyant material. TS

Joan Fontaine *Fiametta/Ginerva/Isabella/Bartolomea* • Louis Jourdan *Boccaccio/Paganino/Giulio/Bertrando* • Binnie Barnes *Contessa/Old witch/Nerina* • Godfrey Tearle *Ricciardo/Bernabo* • Joan Collins *Pampinea/Maria* • Mara Lane *Girl in Villa* • George Bernard *Messenger* • Bert Bernard *Messenger* ■ *Dir* Hugo Fregonese • *Scr* George Oppenheimer, from the stories by Giovanni Boccaccio

Decasia ★★★ U

Experimental movie 2002 · US · BW · 67mins

Exploring the fragility of nitrate film stock and the transience of the human endeavours it records, Bill Morrison's experimental feature is both a fascinating study of decay and a visually arresting display of melancholic beauty. Originally commissioned for a multimedia stage show, this moving collage of old film footage occasionally suffers from the relentless drone of Michael Gordon's score. But the manner in which the mottled patches of corrupted celluloid obscure or reveal objects, change the nature and/or pace of the imagery or simply achieve their own abstract patterns, becomes as entrancing as it is entertaining. DP

Dir/Scr Bill Morrison

Deceived ★★★ 15

Psychological thriller
1991 · US · Colour · 103mins

Goldie Hawn takes a break from her usually frothy comedies for this flawed but mildly diverting thriller. Hawn is happily married to John Heard, only to discover after his accidental death that she knew very little about him. Despite her best efforts, Hawn lacks credibility in the pivotal role, so it's left to the ever-excellent Heard to make the most of what is, sadly, one of his rare leading roles. Damian Harris, son of actor Richard Harris, generates some suspense as director, but the climax is just plain silly. JF. Contains swearing, and some violence. DVD

Goldie Hawn *Adrienne Saunders* • John Heard *Jack Saunders* • Ashley Peldon *Mary Saunders* • Robin Bartlett *Charlotte* • Tom Irwin *Harvey Schwartz* • Amy Wright *Evelyn Wade* • Kate Reid *Rosalie* ■ *Dir* Damian Harris • *Scr* Mary Agnes Donoghue, Derek Saunders [Bruce Joel Rubin], from a story by Mary Agnes Donoghue

D

The Deceivers ★★ 15

Drama 1988 · UK · Colour · 98mins

In the absence of regular partner James Ivory, producer Ismail Merchant has managed to miss both the rousing adventure and the intriguing ideas contained in John Masters's novel of cultism and culture clash. Part of the problem lies with director Nicholas Meyer, who is unsure whether to opt for mini-series glossiness or schlock goriness as a secret cult is linked to a spate of murders that disturb the peace of 1820s India. DP [video] DVD

Pierce Brosnan *William Savage* • Saeed Jaffrey *Hussein* • Shashi Kapoor *Chandra Singh* • Helen Michell *Sarah Wilson* • Keith Michell *Colonel Wilson* • David Robb *George Angelsmith* • Tariq Yunus *Feringea* ■ *Dir* Nicholas Meyer • *Scr* Michael Hirst, from the novel by John Masters

December ★★ PG

Second World War drama
1991 · US · Colour · 87mins

The month in question is December 1941; the subject is the "day of infamy", as FDR famously described the Japanese attack on Pearl Harbor. That event has been used as the basis for several movies, but this one rings the changes by focusing on five high school seniors deciding whether to enlist, be drafted or register as conscientious objectors. The cast is led by Balthazar Getty as a gung-ho teenager too young to join up. AT [video]

Balthazar Getty *Allister Gibbs* • Jason London *Russell Littlejohn* • Brian Krause *Tim Mitchell* • Wil Wheaton *Kipp Gibbs* • Chris Young *Stuart Brayton* • Robert Miller *Headmaster Thurston* • Ann Hartfield *Mrs Langley* • Soren Bailey *Billy Wade* ■ *Dir/Scr* Gabe Torres

December Bride ★★★ PG

Period drama 1990 · UK · Colour · 84mins

On the surface yet another tale of undisclosed paternity from the Emerald Isle, this is, in fact, a careful and sincere study of the problems that have divided the Irish people throughout the 20th century. Saskia Reeves impresses as the maid whose simultaneous affairs with brothers Donal McCann and Ciaran Hinds scandalise the God-fearing members of an isolated farming community. But what elevates this film above the average melodrama is French cinematographer Bruno de Keyzer's brooding views of the austere Northern Ireland coastline and director Thaddeus O'Sullivan's avoidance of sensationalism. DP [video]

Saskia Reeves *Sarah* • Donal McCann *Hamilton Echlin* • Ciaran Hinds *Frank Echlin* • Patrick Malahide *Sorleyson* • Brenda Bruce *Martha* • Michael McKnight *Fergus* • Dervla Kirwan *Young Martha* • Peter Capaldi *Young Sorleyson* • Geoffrey Golden *Andrew Echlin* ■ *Dir* Thaddeus O'Sullivan • *Scr* David Rudkin, from the novel by Sam Hanna Bell

Deception ★★★★ PG

Melodrama 1946 · US · BW · 107mins

It's music, music, music as the great film composer Eric Wolfgang Korngold (*The Adventures of Robin Hood, The Sea Hawk*) receives as much of a showcase here as does star Bette Davis, who plays a pianist whose patron is suave composer/conductor Claude Rains. This is splendid stuff, brilliantly orchestrated in both senses as Bette lies to her husband, refugee cellist Paul Henreid, about her former relationship with Rains. Rains gets the best lines, and delivers them quite superbly, but Davis is at her best in what was to be one of her last great melodramas for Warner Bros. TS [video]

Bette Davis *Christine Radcliffe* • Paul Henreid *Karel Novak* • Claude Rains *Alexander Hollenius* • John Abbott *Bertram Gribble* • Benson Fong *Manservant* • Richard Walsh *Porter* ■ *Dir* Irving Rapper • *Scr* John Collier, Joseph Than, from the play *Jealousy (Monsieur Lamberthier)* by Louis Verneuil

Deception ★★★ 15

Thriller 2000 · US · Colour · 99mins

This entertaining thriller benefits greatly from a few fun plot twists and a colourful cast. Ben Affleck is an ex-con who assumes the identity of his dead cellmate in order to hook up with the guy's gorgeous pen-pal girlfriend (Charlize Theron). They share a few passionate moments before her nasty brother, sleazy Gary Sinise, coerces Affleck into robbing a casino. Sinise plays his role with just the right touch of menace and humour, but Affleck is out of his league as an action hero. John Frankenheimer's direction is only workmanlike. ST. Contains violence, swearing and sex scenes. [video] DVD

Ben Affleck *Rudy Duncan* • Charlize Theron *Ashley* • Gary Sinise *Gabriel* • Clarence Williams III *Merlin* • Dennis Farina *Jack Bangs* • James Frain *Nick* • Donal Logue *Pug* ■ *Dir* John Frankenheimer • *Scr* Ehren Kruger

Decision at Sundown ★★ U

Western 1957 · US · Colour · 77mins

Western star Randolph Scott hit a winning streak when he teamed up with director Budd Boetticher and writer Burt Kennedy on such gems as *The Tall T* and *Comanche Station*. This is visually less impressive, set in town rather than out in the wide open spaces, while the plot – about Randy's personal feud with local bigwig John Carroll – is rather verbose. AE

Randolph Scott *Bart Allison* • John Carroll *Tate Kimbrough* • Karen Steele *Lucy Summerton* • Valerie French *Ruby James* • Noah Beery Jr *Sam* • John Archer *Dr Storrow* • Andrew Duggan *Sheriff Swede Hansen* ■ *Dir* Budd Boetticher • *Scr* Charles Lang, from a story by Vernon L Fluharty

Decision before Dawn ★★★

Spy drama 1951 · US · BW · 119mins

This is a long and distinctly sombre spy drama, with Oskar Werner playing a German PoW who agrees to spy against his own people, apparently motivated by the belief that he can help shorten the war and save lives. The Americans send him back home loaded up with espionage tricks, giving rise to a moral conundrum: is he a traitor, a hero or simply a martyr-in-waiting? The most impressive aspect of the film is the location shooting in a bombed-out postwar Germany. It received a best picture Oscar nomination, the second in a row for director Anatole Litvak. AT

Richard Basehart *Lt Rennick* • Gary Merrill *Colonel Devlin* • Oskar Werner *Happy* • Hildegarde Neff *Hilde* • Dominique Blanchar *Monique* • OE Hasse *Oberst Von Ecker* • Wilfried Seyfert [Wilfried Seyferth] *SS Man Scholtz* • Hans Christian Blech *Tiger* ■ *Dir* Anatole Litvak • *Scr* Peter Viertel, from the novel *Call It Treason* by George Howe • *Cinematographer* Frank Planer [Franz Planer]

The Decks Ran Red ★★

Crime 1958 · US · BW · 84mins

James Mason plays the captain of a rusty old freighter whose crew unscrupulous deckhand Broderick Crawford is planning to murder so he can scuttle the ship and claim the salvage money. Mason, however, foils the plan with a little help from the cook's wife (beautiful Dorothy Dandridge), Director Andrew Stone maintains the tension here, but the film is sunk by his banal dialogue. RB

James Mason *Capt Edwin Rumill* • Dorothy Dandridge *Mahia* • Broderick Crawford *Henry Scott* • Stuart Whitman *Leroy Martin* • Katharine Bard *Joan Rumill* • Jack Kruschen *Alex Cole* • John Gallaudet *"Bull" Pringle* ■ *Dir/Scr* Andrew Stone [Andrew L Stone]

Decline and Fall... of a Birdwatcher ★

Satire 1968 · UK · Colour · 123mins

Ex-documentary director John Krish has a stab at Evelyn Waugh's partly autobiographical 1928 work, *Decline and Fall*. It was a vainglorious attempt, as the joys of this hilarious comedy of upper-class manners lie solely on the page; neither Krish nor his trio of scriptwriters have the satirical wit or irreverent verve to translate them to the screen. Their cause isn't helped by Robin Phillips's ghastly performance as Paul Pennyfeather. DP

Robin Phillips *Paul Pennyfeather* • Donald Wolfit *Dr Fagan* • Genevieve Page *Margot Beste-Chetwynde* • Robert Harris *Prendergast* • Leo McKern *Captain Grimes* • Colin Blakely *Philbrick* • Rodney Bewes *Arthur Potts* • Donald Sinden *Prison governor* ■ *Dir* John Krish • *Scr* Ivan Foxwell, Alan Hackney, Hugh Whitemore, from the novel *Decline and Fall* by Evelyn Waugh

The Decline of the American Empire ★★★★ 18

Comedy drama 1986 · Can · Colour · 97mins

Nominated for a best foreign film Oscar, this sophisticated satire on the sexual mores of a group of ageing intellectuals is superbly structured by Québecois director Denys Arcand. Having shown us the quartet of history tutors and their four female friends separately expressing their forthright views on physical pleasure, he then brings them together for a dinner party at which bourgeois discretion is soon forgotten amid the seepage of guilty secrets. As revealing as the bristling dialogue, flashbacks seamlessly punctuate the action to shade in the fascinating characters. DP. In French with English subtitles. [video] DVD

Pierre Curzi *Pierre* • Rémy Girard *Remy* • Yves Jacques *Claude* • Daniel Briere *Alain* • Dominique Michel *Dominique* • Louise Portal *Diane* • Dorothée Berryman *Louise* • Genevieve Rioux *Danielle* • Gabriel Arcand *Mario* ■ *Dir/Scr* Denys Arcand

The Decline of Western Civilization ★★★★

Music documentary
1980 · US · Colour · 100mins

Penelope Spheeris's cult documentary takes an unflinching and non-judgemental look at the Los Angeles punk scene at the fag end of the 1970s. She blends live performances from anonymous bands such as Circle Jerks, Black Flag and Fear (who were a particular favourite of John Belushi) with revealing contributions from managers, fans and the group members themselves. While most use the camera as a mirror for their preening, some are surprisingly articulate about their lifestyle – the downside of which is illustrated in the interview with Darby Crash, lead singer of the Germs, who ended up on a mortuary slab before the film was even released. This is the first in a trilogy of rock documentaries made by Spheeris that, viewed today, seem like valuable cultural documents. RS

Dir/Scr Penelope Spheeris

The Decline of Western Civilization Part II: the Metal Years ★★★ 18

Music documentary
1988 · US · Colour · 88mins

A great companion piece to *This Is Spinal Tap*, Penelope Spheeris's documentary follow-up to her revealing record of the Los Angeles punk scene at the end of the 1970s exposes the less than blemish-free world of Heavy Metal music. MTV-style concert footage is mixed with unplugged, warts-and-all interviews with the likes of Kiss, Ozzy Osbourne and Alice Cooper; Guns N' Roses declined to appear. Unsurprisingly, common themes broached are groupies, booze and drugs: Steve Tyler of Aerosmith freely admits "millions went up my nose". Utterly compelling, insightful and often hilarious. RS [video]

Dir Penelope Spheeris

The Decline of Western Civilization Part III ★★★

Music documentary
1997 · US · Colour · 89mins

Searing final chapter in Penelope Spheeris's trilogy of music documentaries, focusing this time not on the rock personalities themselves, but on the disenfranchised Hollywood waifs who make up the dwindling audience of Los Angeles's contemporary punk/metal scene. Grimmer in tone than its two predecessors, this wounded film maps out a generation of no-hopers with a bleak vision of the future. Despite Spheeris's exploitative interview techniques, this deservedly won the Freedom of Expression award at Robert Redford's Sundance film festival. RS

Dir Penelope Spheeris

Deconstructing Harry ★★★ 18

Comedy drama 1997 · US · Colour · 91mins

Woody Allen's tumultuous private life seems to spill sourly into this bad-taste story about a novelist, Harry Block (Allen), whose friends and relatives are used as thinly-disguised characters in his books, despite screams of protest from those he exploits. Block is suffering from a lack of inspiration for his latest book and is as out of focus with life as actor Robin Williams is – literally – out of focus in one of the film's funniest ideas. Rarely has Allen's use of a movie as a psychiatrist's couch been quite so evident. TH. Contains swearing and sex scenes. [video] DVD

Caroline Aaron *Doris* • Woody Allen *Harry Block* • Kirstie Alley *Joan* • Bob Balaban *Richard* • Richard Benjamin *Ken* • Eric Bogosian *Burt* • Billy Crystal *Larry* • Judy Davis *Lucy* • Hazelle Goodman *Cookie* • Mariel Hemingway *Beth Kramer* • Amy Irving *Jane* • Julie Kavner *Grace* • Julia Louis-Dreyfus *Leslie* • Demi Moore *Helen* • Elisabeth Shue *Fay* • Stanley Tucci *Paul Epstein* • Robin Williams *Mel* ■ *Dir/Scr* Woody Allen

Dee Snider's Strangeland ★

Horror thriller 1998 · US · Colour · 91mins

Yes, *that* Dee Snider – the bizarre former lead singer of Twisted Sister. If you remember the band, you'll have some idea of what's on offer here: sleaze and nastiness galore, with a bit of tasteless humour thrown in. The story, such as it is, involves a man who uses the internet to lure people into his clutches, whereupon he subjects them to 18-certificate tortures. JB

Dee Snider *Captain Howdy/Carleton Hendricks* • Elizabeth Peña *Toni Gage* • Brett Harrelson *Steve Christian* • Kevin Gage *Detective Mike Gage* • Amy Smart *Angela* • Robert Englund *Jackson Roth* • Linda Cardellini *Genevieve Gage* ■ *Dir* John Pieplow • *Scr* Dee Snider

The Deep ★★★ 15

Adventure 1977 · US · Colour · 119mins

Jacqueline Bisset in a wet T-shirt, Donna Summer's titular disco hit and *Jaws* author Peter Benchley co-scripting from his own novel were enough to make this soggy sea saga of rival divers after shipwrecked drugs a major box-office hit. With 40 per cent of his action taking place underwater in creepy depths, director Peter Yates doesn't have to do much to keep tension on an even keel, and the mean moray eel sequence is a real shocker when it arrives. But slick photography aside, the silly script and two-dimensional characterisations succeed in sinking plausibility every time reality threatens to surface. AJ. Contains violence, swearing and brief nudity. DVD

Robert Shaw *Romer Treece* • Jacqueline Bisset *Gail Berke* • Nick Nolte *David Sanders* • Louis Gossett [Louis Gossett Jr] *Henri Cloche* • Eli Wallach *Adam Coffin* • Robert Tessier *Kevin* ■ *Dir* Peter Yates • *Scr* Peter Benchley, Tracey Keenan Wynn, from the novel by Peter Benchley

D

Deep Blue ★★★ PG

Documentary
2003 · UK/Ger · Colour · 90mins

Filmed over three years off the Maldives, Azores, Caymans, Bermuda and Antarctica, this off-shoot of David Attenborough's BBC television series, *The Blue Planet*, provides a visually striking and occasionally harrowing insight into the staggering diversity of marine life. A sense of ever-present danger pervades the footage of dolphins, penguins, seals and baby whales. But it's the inhabitants of the seemingly more tranquil world 5000 metres below the surface that catch the eye and it's a shame that Michael Gambon's commentary couldn't have been more informative, especially as some of the more ethereal ocean-bed species had never been seen before, let alone photographed. DP DVD

Michael Gambon *Narrator* ■ *Dir/Scr* Alastair Fothergill, Andy Byatt

The Deep Blue Sea ★★★

Drama 1955 · UK · Colour · 98mins

Beautiful, middle-aged Vivien Leigh leaves her husband, a judge, and the comfort of her home to live in drab digs and continue an affair with Kenneth More, an attractive younger man. An ex-RAF pilot, Moore is unable to adjust to postwar life, and he is also losing interest in Leigh, which leads her to a suicidal crisis. Terence Rattigan's famous and oft-revived play is a sharply observed and emotionally searing period piece. All the more pity, then, that the film fails to capture the emotion of the original and is visually sub-standard. RK

Vivien Leigh *Hester* • Kenneth More *Freddie Page* • Eric Portman *Miller* • Emlyn Williams *Sir William Collyer* • Moira Lister *Dawn Maxwell* • Alec McCowen *Ken Thompson* • Dandy Nichols *Mrs Elton* • Arthur Hill *Jackie Jackson* • Miriam Karlin *Barmaid* • Sidney James *Man in street* ■ *Dir* Anatole Litvak • *Scr* Terence Rattigan, from his play

Deep Blue Sea ★★★ 15

Science-fiction action thriller
1999 · US · Colour · 100mins

In this popcorn thriller, three genetically mutated, super-intelligent sharks stalk the marooned members of an underwater research facility. A B-movie cast struggles gamely with the hopelessly mundane dialogue, but director Renny Harlin's film remains afloat through sheer nerve, technical prowess and some truly spectacular shock moments. The result is a gory, trashy blockbuster that succeeds despite its waterlogged script. AJ. Contains violence and swearing. DVD

Saffron Burrows *Dr Susan McAlester* • Thomas Jane *Carter Blake* • LL Cool J *Sherman "Preacher" Dudley* • Jacqueline McKenzie *Janice Higgins* • Michael Rapaport *Tom "Scog" Scoggins* • Stellan Skarsgård *Jim Whitlock* • Samuel L Jackson *Russell Franklin* ■ *Dir* Renny Harlin • *Scr* Duncan Kennedy, Donna Powers, Wayne Powers

Deep Cover ★★★★ 18

Crime thriller 1992 · US · Colour · 103mins

One of the most under-rated cop thrillers of the 1990s, this is an exhilarating and intelligent examination of blurred lines between those who break the law and those who enforce it. A suitably intense Laurence (still being billed as Larry) Fishburne is the undercover detective who sets out to unravel a major drugs ring by forming a curious alliance with shady, neurotic lawyer Jeff Goldblum. It's their relationship that forms the heart of the movie and both deliver superb performances. However, director Bill Duke doesn't stint on the action sequences and delivers some stunningly choreographed slices of screen mayhem. JF DVD

Larry Fishburne [Laurence Fishburne] *Russell Stevens Jr/John Q Hull* • Jeff Goldblum *David Jason* • Victoria Dillard *Betty McCutcheon* • Charles Martin Smith *Carver* • Sydney Lassick *Gopher* • Clarence Williams III *Taft* ■ *Dir* Bill Duke • *Scr* Henry Bean, Michael Tolkin

Deep Crimson ★★★ 18

Crime drama
1996 · Mex/Fr/Sp · Colour · 109mins

Dedicated to Leonard Kastle, who covered the same true-life case in *The Honeymoon Killers*, this Mexican melodrama is notable for both the genuine passion of its grotesque protagonists and the muted savagery of their crimes. Posing as brother and sister, corpulent nurse Regina Orozco and temperamental gigolo Daniel Gimenez Cacho prey on lonely-heart widows with an insouciance that is hideous in its pitilessness. DP. In Spanish with English subtitles. Contains violence, swearing, sex scenes.

Daniel Gimenez Cacho *Nicolas Estrella* • Regina Orozco *Coral Fabre* • Marisa Paredes *Irene Gallardo* • Veronica Merchant *Rebeca Sampedro* • Julieta Egurrola *Juanita Norton* • Rosa Furman *Mrs Silberman* ■ *Dir* Arturo Ripstein • *Scr* Paz Alicia Garciadiego

Deep End 

Drama 1970 · US/W Ger · Colour · 91mins

This is one of the strangest movies to come out of the Swinging Sixties. Directed by Polish émigré Jerzy Skolimowski, it's set in the grottily dank Chelsea public baths. John Moulder-Brown – a callow, haunted-looking 15-year-old – and Jane Asher are the employees, who swap changing rooms so he can please the ladies (including bosomy football fanatic Diana Dors) and she can pleasure the gents. The pool provides the film's central metaphor and some bizarre, shocking things happen in it. AT

Jane Asher *Susan* • John Moulder-Brown *Mike* • Karl Michael Vogler *Swimming instructor* • Christopher Sandford *Fiance* • Diana Dors *Lady client* ■ *Dir* Jerzy Skolimowski • *Scr* Jerzy Skolimowski, Jerzy Gruza, Boleslaw Sulik

The Deep End ★★★ 15

Drama 2001 · US · Colour · 96mins

In spite of her association with the British avant-garde (mainly thanks to her collaboration with the late Derek Jarman), Tilda Swinton is particularly convincing as a white-collar American housewife under duress. While her husband is away on naval duties, she finds it's actually her son who's in deep water as he dabbles in underage sex with an older man. Her attempts to intervene result in disaster; Swinton ends up with blood on her hands and Goran Visnjic's blackmailer at her door. Swinton's icy demeanour adds to this chilly thriller, which attacks the steely veneer of American middle-class life with a sledgehammer. LH DVD

Tilda Swinton *Margaret Hall* • Goran Visnjic *Alek Spera* • Jonathan Tucker *Beau Hall* • Peter Donat *Jack Hall* • Josh Lucas *Darby Reese* ■ *Dir* Scott McGehee, David Siegel • *Scr* Scott McGehee, David Siegel, from the novel *The Blank Wall* by Elizabeth Sanxay Holding

The Deep End of the Ocean ★★ 12

Drama 1999 · US · Colour · 103mins

Michelle Pfeiffer plays the mother whose life is turned upside down after her toddler son goes missing, never, it seems, to be seen again. How she and her family (including older son Jonathan Jackson and husband Treat Williams) cope or, more to the point, *don't* cope is really the stuff of TV movies, and there's little here to raise this above that status. Whoopi Goldberg, as the cop in charge of the case, adds little interest. JB. Contains swearing. DVD

Michelle Pfeiffer *Beth Cappadora* • Treat Williams *Pat Cappadora* • Jonathan Jackson *Vincent Cappadora, aged 16* • John Kapelos *George Karras* • Ryan Merriman *Sam* • Whoopi Goldberg *Candy Bliss* ■ *Dir* Ulu Grosbard • *Scr* Stephen Schiff, from the novel by Jacquelyn Mitchard

Deep Impact ★★★★ 12

Science-fiction drama
1998 · US · Colour · 116mins

A huge comet is on a collision course with Earth in director Mimi Leder's disaster movie, which gains a certain amount of credibility by highlighting the human side of the impending catastrophe. The frightening scenario focuses on TV reporter Téa Leoni, who uncovers the story after teenage stargazer Elijah Wood discovers the wayward mass, and on astronaut Robert Duvall as he and his colleagues try to destroy the threat in space. Using her trademark documentary-style realism and frenzied camerawork, Leder adds gripping immediacy to this loose remake of 1951's *When Worlds Collide*, capping it all with a spectacular trail of epic destruction. AJ. Contains swearing. DVD

Robert Duvall *Spurgeon Tanner* • Téa Leoni *Jenny Lerner* • Elijah Wood *Leo Biederman* • Vanessa Redgrave *Robin Lerner* • Maximilian Schell *Jason Lerner* • Morgan Freeman *President Tom Beck* • James Cromwell *Alan Rittenhouse* ■ *Dir* Mimi Leder • *Scr* Michael Tolkin, Bruce Joel Rubin

Deep in My Heart ★★★ U

Musical biography
1954 · US · Colour · 126mins

Under-rated in its day, this is the fictionalised biopic of composer Sigmund Romberg, of *The Student Prince* and *Desert Song* fame, featuring a cast of MGM contract stars performing magnificently. Most of it was directed by Stanley Donen, though ace choreographers Robert Alton and Jack Donohue helped out, and the whole is held together by the bravura performance of José Ferrer as Romberg. Good fun all round, and quite moving, too. TS DVD

José Ferrer *Sigmund Romberg* • Merle Oberon *Dorothy Donnelly* • Helen Traubel *Anna Mueller* • Doe Avedon *Lillian Romberg* • Walter Pidgeon *JJ Shubert* • Paul Henreid *Florenz Ziegfeld* • Tamara Toumanova *Gaby Deslys* • Paul Stewart *Bert Towsend* • Rosemary Clooney • Gene Kelly • Fred Kelly • Jane Powell • Vic Damone • Ann Miller • Cyd Charisse • Howard Keel • Tony Martin ■ *Dir* Stanley Donen • *Scr* Leonard Spigelgass, from the biography by Elliott Arnold

Deep Red ★★★ 18

Murder mystery 1975 · It · Colour · 121mins

Playing sinister games with doubles and mirrors, Dario Argento draws on a wealth of movie references to give this stylised chiller its unnerving atmosphere. What's most striking, however, is his incessant use of a fluid camera that fills each meticulously constructed sequence with unease. David Hemmings becomes obsessed with tracking down a killer, only for his classical musician to soon find himself being pursued as both suspect and target. Argento's delight in eccentric props and erratic angles, together with his reliance on pop psychology, help make this a fascinating odyssey into psychosis, despite its flaws. DP. In Italian with English subtitles. DVD

David Hemmings *Marcus Daly* • Daria Nicolodi *Gianna* • Gabriele Lavia *Carlo* • Clara Calamai *Marta* • Macha Méril *Helga* ■ *Dir* Dario Argento • *Scr* Dario Argento, Bernardino Zapponi

Deep Rising ★★ 15

Futuristic action horror
1998 · US · Colour · 101mins

Tremors meets *Titanic* in this dopey sea-monster movie from Stephen Sommers. It's a tepid horror tale in which a hi-tech pleasure cruiser on its maiden voyage is overrun by modern-day pirates, then attacked by a multi-tentacled, Hydra-like creature. The film navigates an ocean of hilarious monster-movie clichés and derivative special-effects sequences, while Treat Williams does a poor Kurt Russell impression. AJ. Contains violence and swearing. DVD

Treat Williams *John Finnegan* • Famke Janssen *Trillian* • Anthony Heald *Simon Canton* • Kevin J O'Connor *Joey Pantucci* • Wes Studi *Hanover* • Derrick O'Connor *Captain* • Jason Flemyng *Mulligan* • Cliff Curtis *Mamooli* ■ *Dir/Scr* Stephen Sommers

The Deep Six ★★ U

Second World War drama
1958 · US · Colour · 108mins

When Alan Ladd turned producer/star through his Jaguar company just after his career peaked with *Shane*, he stuck to formula film-making with old cronies. *The Deep Six* is a wartime drama set on a cruiser in the Pacific, the main complication being whether Ladd's Quaker beliefs will get in the way of his duties as the ship's gunnery officer. The issue is never properly resolved, but the film is slickly made and quite watchable. AE

Alan Ladd *Alec Austen* • Dianne Foster *Susan Cahill* • William Bendix *Frenchy Shapiro* • Keenan Wynn *Lt Cdr Edge* • James Whitmore *Cdr Meredith* • Efrem Zimbalist Jr *Lt Blanchard* • Jeanette Nolan *Mrs Austen* ■ *Dir* Rudolph Maté • *Scr* John Twist, Harry Brown, Martin Rackin, from the novel by Martin Dibner

Deep Throat ★★★ 18

Erotic comedy 1972 · US · Colour · 50mins

The most infamous, commercially successful and influential hard-core movie ever produced made Linda Lovelace an overnight sensation and director Gerard Damiano the leading light of fashionable "porno chic". Ground-breaking because it made watching porn acceptable, the film itself is badly made and full of stupid humour and dull stretches. It's important to note that Lovelace is not a sexual object being used by male abusers, but a take-charge, independent woman pursuing pleasure for her own needs. AJ DVD

Linda Lovelace • Harry Reems • Dolly Sharp • Carol Connors • William Love • Ted Street ■ *Dir/Scr* Gerard Damiano

Deep Valley ★★★

Drama 1947 · US · BW · 103mins

This is one of director Jean Negulesco's better movies, with Ida Lupino as a parent-dominated farm girl who shelters a convict (played by Dane

U = SUITABLE FOR ALL Uc = SUITABLE FOR ALL, ESPECIALLY FOR YOUNG CHILDREN (VIDEO ONLY) PG = PARENTAL GUIDANCE

Clark) after he escapes from a chain gang. Clark's scenes with Lupino are extremely touching, in a screenplay which boasts added dialogue by William Faulkner. There's a fine Max Steiner score, and a special bonus comes from some attractive location shooting, brought about by the lucky fact that a studio strike prevented the use of the Warners backlot. TS

Ida Lupino *Libby* • Dane Clark *Barry* • Wayne Morris *Barker* • Fay Bainter *Mrs Saul* • Henry Hull *Mr Saul* • Willard Robertson *Sheriff* • Rory Mallinson *Foreman* • Jack Mower *Supervisor* ■ *Dir* Jean Negulesco • *Scr* Salka Viertel, Stephen Morehouse Avery, from the novel by Dan Totheroh

DeepStar Six ★ 15

Science-fiction horror
1989 · US · Colour · 94mins

An experimental underwater colony disturbs a prehistoric sea creature in this shallow combination of *Alien* and *Jaws*. Directed by Sean S Cunningham, the originator of the *Friday the 13th* series, this soggy farrago sinks fast in an ocean of technical mumbo jumbo, murky model work and outrageously bad acting. The rubber monster looks like a giant, cross-eyed lobster, while Cunningham is completely out of his depth in his attempts to scare up tides of terror from an unfathomable and laughable script. AJ [VIDEO] DVD

Taurean Blacque *Laidlaw* • Nancy Everhard *Joyce Collins* • Greg Evigan *McBride* • Miguel Ferrer *Snyder* • Nia Peeples *Scarpelli* • Matt McCoy *Richardson* • Cindy Pickett *Diane Norris* • Marius Weyers *Van Gelder* ■ *Dir* Sean S Cunningham • *Scr* Lewis Abernathy, Geof Miller, from a story by Lewis Abernathy

The Deer Hunter ★★★★★ 18

War drama 1978 · US · Colour · 175mins

Michael Cimino's multi-Oscar winner was the first major movie about the Vietnam War and it remains one of the finest and most controversial, notably for the harrowing sequence in which American PoWs are forced by their Vietcong captors to play Russian roulette, a compelling if historically dubious metaphor for the war. Starring Robert De Niro, Christopher Walken, John Savage and John Cazale, this is a modern version of the Second World War drama *The Best Years of Our Lives*, showing how men and America itself cope with the horrors of war and its aftermath. With its mournful guitar theme, this intense drama lingers long in the memory and elevated Cimino to the front rank of American directors. But his next film was the notorious flop *Heaven's Gate*, and he has only worked occasionally since. AT. Contains violence, swearing. [VIDEO] DVD

Robert De Niro *Michael Vronsky* • John Cazale *Stan, "Stosh"* • John Savage *Steven* • Christopher Walken *Nick* • Meryl Streep *Linda* • George Dzundza *John* • Chuck Aspegren *Axel* • Shirley Stoler *Steven's mother* • Rutanya Alda *Angela* ■ *Dir* Michael Cimino • *Scr* Deric Washburn, from a story by Michael Cimino, Deric Washburn, Louis Garfinkle, Quinn K Redeker • *Cinematographer* Vilmos Zsigmond • *Editor* Peter Zinner • *Music* Stanley Myers

The Deerslayer ★★ U

Historical adventure
1957 · US · Colour · 76mins

An adaptation of James Fenimore Cooper's classic adventure, with Lex Barker as the hunter who teams up with his Mohican blood brother, Chingachgook (Carlos Rivas), to rescue a trapper and his two daughters from nasty Indians. A dead duck as far as suspense is concerned, back projection and indoor sets make this seem as artificial as the acting. TH

Lex Barker *The Deerslayer* • Rita Moreno *Hetty* • Forrest Tucker *Harry Marsh* • Cathy O'Donnell *Judith* • Jay C Flippen *Old Tom Hutter* • Carlos Rivas *Chingachgook* • John Halloran *Old warrior* ■ *Dir* Kurt Neumann • *Scr* Carroll Young, Kurt Neumann, from the novel by James Fenimore Cooper

Deewaar: Let's Bring Our Heroes Home ★★ 18

War drama 2004 · Ind · Colour · 160mins

Milan Luthria's politically contentious adventure stars Amitabh Bachchan as the leader of a unit of Indian soldiers who are captured behind the lines in Pakistani Kashmir. However, Akshaye Khanna carries as much of the plot, as the mild-mannered son forced to dig deep to rescue his father. Producer Gaurang Doshi insists that this isn't jingoistic propaganda, but while jailer Kay Kay and cynical prisoner Sanjay Dutt are presented in a positive light, they're nowhere near as noble as their subcontinental counterparts. DP. In Hindi with English subtitles. [VIDEO] DVD

Amitabh Bachchan *Ranvir Kaul* • Sanjay Dutt *Khan* • Akshaye Khanna *Gaurav Kaul* • Amrita Rao *Radhika* • KK Menon *Sohail* • Tanuja *Ranvir Kaul's wife* • Raghuvir Yadav *Jata* ■ *Dir* Milan Luthria • *Scr* Shridhar Raghavan, Kashyap

Def by Temptation ★★ 18

Horror 1990 · US · Colour · 94mins

A hip-hop, skip and a jump away from the generic blaxploitation of the 1970s, this initially stylish, erotic and funny mix of *Abby* and *House Party* loses momentum as it wends its way through over-familiar territory. Producer, director and writer James Bond III (really!) also stars as a redneck divinity student, in New York for a final fling before entering the ministry. However, he soon falls prey to Cynthia Bond, an ancient demon who cruises uptown singles bars. Daft special effects and formula blood-letting is jazzed up with perverse sexual twists and a great soundtrack. AJ [VIDEO] DVD

James Bond III *Joel* • Cynthia Bond *Temptress* • Kadeem Hardison *K* • Bill Nunn *Dougy* • Minnie Gentry *Grandma* • Samuel L Jackson *Minister Garth* • Melba Moore *Madam Sonya* ■ *Dir/Scr* James Bond III • *Cinematographer* Ernest R Dickerson

Def-Con 4 ★★★ 15

Action adventure 1984 · US · Colour · 83mins

This post-apocalyptic action film doesn't have the budget to provide too many futuristic thrills, yet what it lacks in hardware trappings it more than makes up for in imaginative staging. While radiation-ravaged America is overrun by as many ideas lifted from better science-fiction entries (*WarGames, The Terminator*) as it is with sadistic punks and militant cannibals, this low-rent *Mad Max* remains a watchable enough potboiler before it degenerates into a routine cat-and-mouse chase. AJ. Contains violence. [VIDEO] DVD

Lenore Zann *JJ* • Maury Chaykin *Vinny* • Kate Lynch *Jordan* • Kevin King *Gideon Hayes* • John Walsch *Walker* • Tim Choate *Howe* • Jeff Pustil *Lacey* ■ *Dir/Scr* Paul Donovan

The Defector ★★

Spy drama 1966 · W Ger/Fr · Colour · 68mins

This muddled European spy drama was the last film of the great Montgomery Clift, here looking tired and displaying little of the talent that illuminated *From Here to Eternity* and *A Place in the Sun*. A hackneyed Cold War drama, which was heavily truncated for its British release, it also stars Clift's loyal friend Roddy McDowall, who was on board to guide him through his barbiturate and alcohol-induced haze, and ends up giving the better performance. TS

Montgomery Clift *Professor James Bower* • Hardy Kruger *Peter Heinzman* • Roddy McDowall *CIA Agent Adams* • Macha Méril *Frieda Hoffman* • Christine Delaroche *Ingrid* • David Opatoshu *Orlovsky* • Hannes Messemer *Dr Saltzer* • Jean-Luc Godard *Orlovsky's friend* ■ *Dir* Raoul Lévy • *Scr* Robert Guenette, Lewis Gannet, Peter Francke, Raoul Lévy, from the novel *The Spy* by Paul Thomas

Defence of the Realm ★★★★ PG

Thriller 1985 · UK · Colour · 91mins

The role of the sozzled veteran reporter who for once finds himself involved in a meaningful story is brought wonderfully to life by Denholm Elliott, here trying to clear the name of an MP who's forced to resign after a sex scandal. Gabriel Byrne, as Elliott's ambitious young colleague, is less effective, but the film has plenty of tension and co-star Greta Scacchi proves a worthy accomplice. This unsettling movie proves the truth of the maxim that *all* governments are up to no good. TH [VIDEO] DVD

Gabriel Byrne *Nick Mullen* • Greta Scacchi *Nina Beckman* • Denholm Elliott *Vernon Bayliss* • Ian Bannen *Dennis Markham* • Fulton Mackay *Victor Kingsbrook* • Bill Paterson *Jack Macleod* • David Calder *Harry Champion* • Robbie Coltrane *Leo McAskey* ■ *Dir* David Drury • *Scr* Martin Stellman

The Defender ★★ 18

Martial arts action drama
1994 · HK · Colour · 88mins

Jet Li's Hong Kong movies tend to be all-action affairs showcasing his extraordinary martial arts skills. However, director Corey Yuen decides to throw some romantic melodrama and a couple of moments of ill-advised comic relief into this story. As a result, Li often looks uncomfortable as the impassive elite Red Army officer detailed to protect murder witness Christy Chung. The fight sequences are typically explosive, but this isn't one of Li's best. DP. Cantonese and Mandarin dialogue dubbed into English. Contains violence and swearing. [VIDEO] DVD

Jet Li *John Chang* • Christy Chung *Michelle Yeung* • Ngai Sing *Wong* • Kent Cheng *Charlie Leung* • Leung Wing-Chung *Ken* ■ *Dir* Corey Yuen • *Scr* Gordon Chan

Defending Your Life ★★ PG

Comedy drama 1991 · US · Colour · 106mins

Director/star Albert Brooks here takes a ham-fisted run at judgement after demise, one of the most abused movie concepts since the glorious *A Matter of Life and Death*, with heaven portrayed as a large shopping mall complete with shuttle trucks and revolving doors. This is an "ordinary Joe" version of the tale, and Brooks's ensuing "trial" for entry through the non-pearly gates is an example of movie-making at its most tedious, and not even Meryl Streep in her heyday can enliven events. SH. Contains swearing. [VIDEO]

Albert Brooks *Daniel Miller* • Meryl Streep *Julia* • Rip Torn *Bob Diamond* • Lee Grant *Lena Foster* • Buck Henry *Dick Stanley* ■ *Dir/Scr* Albert Brooks

Defenseless ★★★ 18

Thriller 1991 · US · Colour · 99mins

In this intriguing thriller, Barbara Hershey stars as a lawyer who is drawn into a murderous conspiracy when her former lover and client (JT Walsh) is found dead. With Sam Shepard, Mary Beth Hurt and Sheree North offering strong support, the playing of the classy cast can't be faulted, and director Martin Campbell skilfully sustains the suspense throughout. JF. Contains violence, swearing and brief nudity. [VIDEO]

Barbara Hershey *TK Katwuller* • Sam Shepard *George Beutel* • Mary Beth Hurt *Ellie Seldes* • JT Walsh *Steven Seldes* • Kellie Overbey *Janna Seldes* • Jay O Sanders *Bull Dozer* ■ *Dir* Martin Campbell • *Scr* James Hicks, from the story by Jeff Burkhart, James Hicks

Defiance ★★★ 15

Action drama 1979 · US · Colour · 102mins

Jan Michael Vincent is pitted against a vicious New York street gang in this weirdly engaging, if violent combination of vintage *Boys Town* melodrama, serial western and 1979's *The Warriors*. No prizes for guessing who tames who, though. The old-fashioned "man against the world" plot gains extra interest from the strong supporting cast, gritty dialogue and John Flynn's atmospheric direction. AJ. Contains violence and swearing. [VIDEO]

Jan-Michael Vincent *Tommy Gamble* • Theresa Saldana *Marsha Bernstein* • Fernando Lopez *"Kid"* • Danny Aiello *Carmine* • Art Carney *Abe* • Santos Morales *Paolo* • Rudy Ramos *Angel Cruz* ■ *Dir* John Flynn • *Scr* Thomas Michael Donnelly, from a story by Thomas Michael Donnelly, Mark Tulin

The Defiant ★★★

Drama 1972 · US · Colour · 88mins

Based on a story by Brazilian author Jorge Amado, this is the heartfelt story of a gang of orphans who steal food in order to survive. Also known as *The Wild Pack* and *The Sandpit Generals*, Hall Bartlett's drama won the Grand Prize at the Moscow Film Festival, presumably because of the optimistic comradeship the film engenders. Its attitudes come across as dated and quaint, but it's still worth a look. TH

Kent Lane *Bullet* • Tisha Sterling *Dora* • John Rubinstein *Professor* • Alejandro Rey *Father Jose Pedro* • Butch Patrick *No Legs* ■ *Dir* Hall Bartlett • *Scr* Hall Bartlett, from the story *Capitaes da Areira* by Jorge Amado

The Defiant Ones ★★★★ U

Crime drama 1958 · US · BW · 96mins

This still powerful drama was, in its day, a superb cinematic strike for racial equality. Two convicts, one black, one white, find themselves shackled together in their escape from a chain gang in the Deep South. Tony Curtis plays the bigoted "Joker" Jackson, and Sidney Poitier leapt to stardom as the angry, articulate Noah Cullen. This is one of under-rated Stanley Kramer's finest humanitarian movies, and the Oscar-winning story and screenplay were co-written by blacklisted actor Nedrick Young. TS [VIDEO] DVD

Tony Curtis *John "Joker" Jackson* • Sidney Poitier *Noah Cullen* • Theodore Bikel *Sheriff Max Muller* • Charles McGraw *Captain Frank Gibbons* • Lon Chaney Jr *Big Sam* • King Donovan *Solly* • Claude Akins *Mac* ■ *Dir* Stanley Kramer • *Scr* Nathan E Douglas [Nedrick Young], Harold Jacob Smith

Le Défroqué ★★★★

Religious drama 1953 · Fr · BW · 93mins

Having already won the Best Actor at Venice for his performance in *Monsieur Vincent* (1947), Pierre Fresnay plays a very different kind of priest in this cogent, if melodramatic treatise on faith and the nature of goodness, which earned Léo Joannon the Best Director prize at Berlin. Abandoning his vocation after his experiences in a Nazi prison camp, Fresnay is guided back towards Catholicism by Pierre Trabaud, who was inspired to his calling by his friend's essential humanity. It's an intense and often traumatic experience, heightened by Fresnay's courageously honest performance. DP. In French with English subtitles.

Pierre Fresnay *Maurice Morand* • Pierre Trabaud *Gérard Lacassagne* • Nicole Stéphane *Catherine Grandpré* • Marcelle Géniat *Mme Morand* • Léo Joannon *Canon*

Jousseaume • Jacques Fabbri *Soldier* ■ *Dir* Léo Joannon • *Scr* Léo Joannon, Denys de La Patellière

Déjà Vu ★ 15

Supernatural thriller
1984 · UK · Colour · 90mins

An apt title for a movie sporting the age-old soul transference plot, but with nothing tweaked to make it unique or remotely interesting. The ghost of a prima ballerina is upsetting writer Nigel Terry and his wife, Jaclyn Smith. When tarot card reader Shelley Winters regresses Terry back to the 1930s, it turns out that he was a choreographer in love with the dancer, and that Smith is her reincarnation. Hokey and unconvincing stuff, based on Trevor Meldal-Johnson's novel *Always*. AJ

Jaclyn Smith *Maggie Rogers/Brooke Ashley* • Nigel Terry *Gregory Thomas/Michael Richardson* • Claire Bloom *Eleanor Harvey* • Shelley Winters *Olga Nabokov* • Richard Kay *William Tanner in 1935* • Frank Gatliff *William Tanner in 1984* • Michael Ladkin *Willmer* ■ *Dir* Anthony Richmond [Tonino Ricci] • *Scr* Ezra D Rappaport, Anthony Richmond [Tonino Ricci], Arnold Schmidt, Joane A Gil, from the novel *Always* by Trevor Meldal-Johnson

Déjà Vu ★★ 15

Romance 1997 · US/UK · Colour · 117mins

Starting as a short story in 1974, Henry Jaglom's study of love perhaps owes more to his own sudden bliss than to his success in shaping some recalcitrant material into a screenplay. Since he met and married Victoria Foyt, Jaglom admits to toning down the autobiographical content of his films, sadly depriving them of the idiosyncracies that made them so fascinating. This is clearly a love letter to Foyt, with Stephen Dillane taking the Jaglom part of the man whose world is turned upside down by a chance encounter with a woman he feels he's known forever. DP. Contains swearing.

Stephen Dillane *Sean Elias* • Victoria Foyt *Dana Howard* • Vanessa Redgrave *Skelly* • Glynis Barber *Claire Stoner* • Michael Brandon *Alex* • Vernon Dobtcheff *Konstantine* ■ *Dir* Henry Jaglom • *Scr* Henry Jaglom, Victoria Foyt

Delayed Action ★★

Crime drama 1954 · UK · BW · 60mins

Melancholic author Robert Ayres has a change of heart after accepting a notorious gang's offer of a tidy nest egg if he takes responsibility for their crimes before topping himself. Quitting features after 21 years of unbroken mediocrity, John Harlow shows a sure sense of pace and atmosphere that would serve him well in television. DP

Robert Ayres *Ned Ellison* • Alan Wheatley *Mark Cruden* • June Thorburn *Ann Curlew* • Michael Kelly (1) *Lobb* • Bruce Seton *Sellers* ■ *Dir* John Harlow • *Scr* Geoffrey Orme

Delbaran ★★★★ PG

Drama 2001 · Iran/Jpn/Neth · Colour · 96mins

Once again combining compassionate realism with uncompromising visual poetry, director Abolfazl Jalili explores the plight of the exile in this exacting, authentic examination of lost innocence. Set on the Iran-Afghanistan border, it's an object lesson in the symbolic and psychological use of landscape, as young Afghan refugee Kaim Alizadeh runs errands across the scrub for the owner of an isolated Iranian café, who is suspected of smuggling by a laconic local cop. Jalili invests this episodic tale with world-weary wit and an unstinting respect for the forgotten victims of war. DP. In Farsi with English subtitles.

Kaim Alizadeh *Kaim* • Rahmatollah Ebrahimi *Khan* • Hossein Hashemian *Hossein* • Ahmad Mahdavi *Officer Mahdavi* • Ebrahim Ebrahimzadeh *Hunter* ■ *Dir* Abolfazl Jalili • *Scr* Abolfazl Jalili, from a story by Reza Saberi

A Delicate Balance ★★★ PG

Drama 1973 · US/UK · Colour · 128mins

Despite an extraordinary cast, this version of Edward Albee's Pulitzer Prize-winning play – directed by Tony Richardson for TV's American Film Theatre – is a stiff narrative about a neurotic Connecticut family that goes to war with itself. Katharine Hepburn, Paul Scofield, Lee Remick, Joseph Cotten and Betsy Blair pull out the dramatic stops, but the result remains defiantly stagebound. TH DVD

Katharine Hepburn *Agnes* • Paul Scofield *Tobias* • Lee Remick *Julia* • Kate Reid *Claire* • Joseph Cotten *Harry* • Betsy Blair *Edna* ■ *Dir* Tony Richardson • *Scr* Edward Albee, from his play

The Delicate Delinquent ★★★ U

Comedy 1957 · US · BW · 103mins

Although mooted as a Dean Martin and Jerry Lewis vehicle, the strain was beginning to show in *Pardners* (1956). So Lewis went solo for the first time, with Darren McGavin in the cop role earmarked for Martin. As the titular "teenager", Lewis's mix of schmaltz and slapstick ensured he maintained his public popularity. Today both subject and title have lost their resonance, but in the days of *The Blackboard Jungle* these antics passed for satire. TS

Jerry Lewis *Sidney Pythias* • Darren McGavin *Mike Damon* • Martha Hyer *Martha Henshaw* • Robert Ivers *Monk* • Horace McMahon *Captain Riley* • Richard Bakalyan *Artie* • Joseph Corey *Harry* • Mary Webster *Patricia* ■ *Dir/Scr* Don McGuire

Delicatessen ★★★★ 15

Black comedy fantasy
1990 · Fr · Colour · 95mins

Jean-Pierre Jeunet and Marc Caro made their feature debut with this gloriously surreal comedy. Rarely can a film have had so many disparate influences. In addition to the visual inspiration of French comic books and the eccentricity of Heath Robinson, there are references to the poetic realism of Marcel Carné and René Clair, as well as the darker visions of David Lynch and Terry Gilliam. The gallery of grotesques gathered at butcher Jean-Claude Dreyfus's tenement participate in some of the funniest set pieces of recent years, most notably the deliriously unerotic sex scene and Sylvie Laguna's preposterous suicide attempts. DP. In French with English subtitles. Contains violence and nudity. DVD

Dominique Pinon *Louison* • Marie-Laure Dougnac *Julie Clapet* • Jean-Claude Dreyfus *The Butcher* • Karin Viard *Mademoiselle Plusse* • Ticky Holgado *Monsieur Tapioca* • Anne-Marie Pisani *Madame Tapioca* • Jacques Mathou *Roger Cube* • Rufus *Robert Cube* • Jean-François Perrier *Monsieur Interligator* • Sylvie Laguna *Madame Interligator* ■ *Dir/Scr* Jean-Pierre Jeunet, Marc Caro

Delicious ★★★ U

Musical romantic comedy
1931 · US · BW · 102mins

Silent superstars Charles Farrell and Janet Gaynor teamed for the ninth time in this romantic comedy directed by David Butler, which marked the first occasion that George and Ira Gershwin composed directly for the screen. The musical highlight is undoubtedly the extract from George's *New York Rhapsody*, but the fantasy sequence in which Gaynor's Scottish immigrant is welcomed by the Statue of Liberty and Swedish valet El Brendel's parodic love song are good fun. However, the rocky road to romance throws up few novelties, while Virginia Cherrill (who would exel later in the year in Chaplin's *City Lights*) is disappointingly gauche as Farrell's spiteful fiancée. DP

Janet Gaynor *Heather Gordon* • Charles Farrell *Larry Beaumont* • El Brendel *Jansen* • Raul Roulien *Sascha* • Lawrence O'Sullivan *O'Flynn* • Manya Roberti *Olga* • Virginia Cherrill *Diana* • Olive Tell *Mrs Van Bergh* • Mischa Auer *Mischa* ■ *Dir* David Butler • *Scr* Guy Bolton, Sonya Levien, from a story by Guy Bolton

The Delinquents ★

Drama 1957 · US · BW · 71mins

Robert Altman's first feature, directed in his beloved home town of Kansas City, is a fascinating, if cheesy relic of its era. Tom Laughlin plays a good boy who gets mixed up in a street gang with his girlfriend (Rosemary Howard), whose parents think she is not old enough to go steady. Julia Lee sings *The Dirty Rock Boogie* – and sadly, that's as good as it gets. TH

Tom Laughlin *Scotty* • Peter Miller (1) *Cholly* • Richard Bakalyan *Eddy* • Rosemary Howard *Janice* • Helene Hawley *Mrs White* • Leonard Belove *Mr White* • Lotus Corelli *Mrs Wilson* • James Lantz *Mr Wilson* • Christine Altman *Sissy* ■ *Dir/Scr* Robert Altman

The Delinquents ★★ 15

Romantic drama
1989 · Aus · Colour · 100mins

At the height of her soap opera/pop singer fame, *Neighbours* star Kylie Minogue made her feature film debut in this passable tale of teenage torment set in 1950s Australia. Minogue and Charlie Schlatter co-star as the misunderstood young lovers ignoring adult condemnation in director Chris Thomson's tear-jerker, based on the novel by Criena Rohan, tennis player Pat Cash's aunt. AJ

Kylie Minogue *Lola Lovell* • Charlie Schlatter *Brownie Hansen* • Desirée Smith *Mavis* • Todd Boyce *Lyle* • Angela Punch McGregor *Mrs Lovell* • Lynette Curran *Mrs Hansen* ■ *Dir* Chris Thomson • *Scr* Mac Gudgeon, Clayton Frohman, Dorothy Hewitt, from a novel by Criena Rohan

Delirious ★★ PG

Comedy 1991 · US · Colour · 91mins

Soap opera scriptwriter John Candy is knocked unconscious, wakes up inside his own fictional TV serial *Beyond Our Dreams*, and watches in comic horror as his own romantic plotlines backfire. Written by former James Bond screenwriter Tom Mankiewicz, this tediously strained fiasco hinges on lovelorn Candy's magical ability to manipulate lathered events by typing them out seconds before they happen. A game cast is wasted in this painfully unfunny affair. AJ DVD

John Candy *Jack Gable* • Emma Samms *Rachel Hedison/Laura* • Mariel Hemingway *Janet Dubois/Louise* • Raymond Burr *Carter Hedison* • Dylan Baker *Blake Hedison* • Charles Rocket *Ty Hedison* • David Rasche *Dr Paul Kirkland/Dennis* • Jerry Orbach *Lou Sherwood* • Robert Wagner *Jack Gates* ■ *Dir* Tom Mankiewicz • *Scr* Fred Freeman, Lawrence J Cohen

Deliverance ★★★★★ 18

Thriller 1972 · US · Colour · 104mins

John Boorman's provocative adult thriller – best, if most uncomfortably, remembered for the sexual assault of Ned Beatty's townie by venal hillbillies in the Appalachian mountains – is about more than shock tactics. It charts the gradual erosion of "civilisation" by the elements, as four men on a back-to-nature canoe holiday, led by the macho Burt Reynolds, meet with disaster and destiny. It works as a piece of straightforward suspense cinema, with an uneasy atmosphere conjured from the off with the iconic "duelling banjos" scene, but it also resonates as a metaphor about masculinity under threat. AC. Contains swearing and violence. DVD

Jon Voight *Ed Gentry* • Burt Reynolds *Lewis Medlock* • Ned Beatty *Bobby Trippe* • Ronny Cox *Drew Ballinger* • Bill McKinney *Mountain man* • Herbert "Cowboy" Coward *Toothless man* • James Dickey *Sheriff Bullard* ■ *Dir* John Boorman • *Scr* James Dickey, from his novel • *Cinematographer* Vilmos Zsigmond • *Editor* Tom Priestley

The Delivery ★★★ 18

Crime thriller
1998 · Neth/Bel · Colour · 95mins

While Roel Reiné's flashy thriller has neither the gloss of *Nikita* nor the innovation of *Run Lola Run*, it still makes for energetic entertainment. The pulsing sex scenes and the explosive finale are disingenuously derivative of generic Hollywood fodder. But – thanks primarily to the untimely interventions of one-time terrorist Aurélie Meriel – it's the unpredictability of the plotting that gives small-time losers Freddy Douglas and Fedja van Huet's Ecstasy-smuggling trip from the Netherlands to Spain its edge. DP. In Dutch, French and Spanish with English subtitles. DVD

Fedja Van Huet *Alfred* • Freddy Douglas *Guy* • Aurélie Meriel *Loulou* • Esmée de la Bretonière *Anna* • Jonathan Harvey *Marc* ■ *Dir* Roel Reiné • *Scr* David Hilton, from a story by Roel Reiné

Della ★★

Drama 1965 · US · Colour · 70mins

Joan Crawford's once-glittering career was in terminal decline by the time this dreary TV movie was made. In an attempt to capture the *film noir* style that had made her name, Crawford plays a mother who keeps her beautiful daughter prisoner in a vast mansion. Sadly, despite the promising premise, the end result is a boring and predictable mess, only saved from total failure by Crawford's valiant attempt to rise above the material. JB

Joan Crawford *Della Chappel* • Paul Burke *Bernard "Barney" Stafford* • Diane Baker *Jenny Chappel* • Charles Bickford *Hugh Stafford* • Richard Carlson *David Stafford* ■ *Dir* Robert Gist • *Scr* Richard Alan Simmons

De-Lovely ★★ PG

Musical biographical drama
2004 · US/Lux · Colour and BW · 119mins

This biopic opens with ailing composer Cole Porter (an admirable Kevin Kline) being transported to a theatre where a stage musical based on his life is apparently in rehearsal. Flashbacks then move the action from the expat scene in Paris to Broadway and Hollywood, with the homosexual Porter's complicated marriage to wealthy socialite Linda Lee (an adequate Ashley Judd) given as the inspiration behind his most unforgettable songs. Director Irwin Winkler's pretentious folly may be clunky but at least this pretentious folly looks fabulous. Still, Porter's scintillating songs occur at regular enough intervals to keep interest afloat. AJ DVD

Kevin Kline *Cole Porter* • Ashley Judd *Linda Porter* • Kevin McNally *Gerald Murphy* • Allan Corduner *Monty Woolley* • Sandra Nelson *Sara Murphy* • Keith Allen *Irving Berlin* • James Wilby *Edward Thomas* • John Barrowman *Night and Day • performer* • Kevin McKidd *Bobby Reed* • Peter Polycarpou *Louis B Mayer* • Jonathan Pryce *Gabe* ■ *Dir* Irwin Winkler • *Scr* Jay Cocks

The Delta Factor ★

Adventure 1970 · US · Colour · 91mins

Mickey Spillane himself backed this adaptation of one of his lesser-known novels, but Christopher George is a poor man's James Bond as an adventurer recruited by the CIA to head an undercover mission. Stingy on the action, this would-be international drama is more confusing than intriguing, while a ridiculous subplot about an imprisoned scientist seems tacked-on by director Tay Garnett as an excuse to have a bloody jailbreak. This was the last professional assignment for veteran film-maker Raoul Walsh, who receives a co-writing credit. RS

Christopher George *Morgan* • Yvette Mimieux *Kim Stacy* • Diane McBain *Lisa Gordot* • Ralph Taeger *Art Keefer* • Yvonne De Carlo *Valerie* • Sherri Spillane *Rosa* ■ *Dir* Tay Garnett • *Scr* Tay Garnett, Raoul Walsh, from the novel by Mickey Spillane

Delta Fever ★ 15

Drama 1988 · US · Colour · 90mins

Watching this straight-to-video teen action movie, you get some idea of how low Martin Landau's career had sunk before he made the remarkable comeback that started with successive Oscar nominations for *Tucker: the Man and His Dream* and *Crimes and Misdemeanors*, and culminated in an Academy Award for his portrayal of Bela Lugosi in *Ed Wood*. This is not only a bad film, but it is also a shocking advertisement for water-skiing and American family values. DP. Contains violence. [VIDEO]

Tom Eplin *Nick Ramsey* • Leif Garrett *Lance Stanford* • Katherine Kelly Lang *Jillian Downey* • Martin Landau *William "Bud" Ramsey* • Denver Pyle *Walt Downey* • Wendie Jo Sperber *Claire* • Will Bledsoe *Bryce* ■ *Dir* William Webb • *Scr* Reed Steiner, from a story by Tom Eplin

The Delta Force ★★ 15

Action adventure
1986 · US · Colour · 123mins

Middle-eastern terrorists menace a planeload of Hollywood has-beens in an exploitative, revisionist version of the actual 1985 skyjacking of a TWA flight in Athens. The surprisingly accurate first half supplies some swift-paced tension before low-rent action hero Chuck Norris arrives on the scene, riding a rocket-armed motorcycle and destroying all credibility along with the baddies. Despite the abrupt change from jet-powered realism to cartoon wish-fulfilment, the constant catalogue of cheap thrills keeps boredom at bay. AJ [VIDEO] DVD

Chuck Norris *Major Scott McCoy* • Lee Marvin *Colonel Nick Alexander* • Martin Balsam *Ben Kaplan* • Joey Bishop *Harry Goldman* • Robert Forster *Abdul* • Lainie Kazan *Sylvia Goldman* • George Kennedy *Father O'Malley* • Hanna Schygulla *Ingrid* • Susan Strasberg *Debra Levine* • Bo Svenson *Captain Campbell* • Robert Vaughn *General Woolbridge* • Shelley Winters *Edie Kaplan* ■ *Dir* Menahem Golan • *Scr* Menahem Golan, James Bruner

Delta Force 2 ★ 18

Action adventure
1990 · US · Colour · 105mins

At least the original had Lee Marvin in the cast; for this clumsy sequel we're left with just stone-face Chuck Norris, whose neck muscles do most of the acting. Where the original explored the theme of political terrorism (albeit with zero subtlety), the follow-up has Norris leading his marines against the drug cartels of Colombia. A second sequel, without Norris, followed in 1991. RS [VIDEO] DVD

Chuck Norris *Colonel Scott McCoy* • Billy Drago *Ramon Cota* • John P Ryan *General Taylor* • Richard Jaeckel *John Page* • Begona Plaza *Quinquina* • Paul Perri *Major Bobby Chavez* • Hector Mercado *Miguel* • Mark Margolis *General Olmedo* ■ *Dir* Aaron Norris • *Scr* Lee Reynolds, from characters created by James Bruner, Menahem Golan

Delta of Venus ★★ 18

Erotic drama 1995 · Fr/US · Colour · 97mins

Soft-core king Zalman King is only interested in the salacious element in Anaïs Nin's oeuvre, so the result here is a beautifully packaged but stunningly dull tale set in 1940s Paris, punctuated by pop promo-style sex scenes. Audie England plays the writer who discovers a profitable sideline in writing rude stories. The performers look good but struggle to bring even a touch of credibility to their roles. JF. Contains swearing, sex scenes, drug abuse and nudity. [VIDEO] DVD

Audie England *Elena* • Costas Mandylor *Lawrence* • Eric Da Silva *Marcel* • Marek Vasut *Luc* • Emma Louise Moore *Ariel* ■ *Dir* Zalman King • *Scr* Elisa Rothstein, Patricia Louisiana Knop, from the novel by Anaïs Nin

Delta Pi ★ 18

Comedy 1985 · US · Colour · 84mins

Possibly the only feature-length film ever devoted to the noble sport of mud wrestling, this sploshed on to the UK market as *Mugsy's Girls*. The plot focuses on a group of female students who take to the mucky ring in a bid to save their sorority. Among those getting dirty are Laura Branigan, a one-hit American rock wonder in the late 1980s and – more mind-bogglingly – veteran Oscar-winning actress Ruth Gordon. Unspeakably bad. JF [VIDEO]

Ruth Gordon *Mugsy* • Eddie Deezen *Lane* • James Marcel *Shawn* • Steve Brodie *Jack Enoff* • Laura Branigan *Monica* ■ *Dir/Scr* Kevin Brodie

Deluge ★★★

Disaster movie 1933 · US · BW · 68mins

Long believed lost, director Felix E Feist's feature debut was rediscovered in 1987 and immediately hailed as one of Hollywood's earliest "disaster" movies. It combines special effects work with footage of an actual Californian earthquake to depict the tidal wave that engulfs the Eastern seaboard and leaves Sidney Blackmer to romance Peggy Shannon in the belief that his wife and family have perished. Elements of *Waterworld* can be detected in their battle against evil Fred Kohler and his band of outlaws, although the sentimental resolution to Lois Wilson's unexpected reappearance was pure melodrama. DP

Peggy Shannon *Claire Arlington* • Lois Wilson *Helen Webster* • Sidney Blackmer *Martin Webster* • Matt Moore *Tom* • Fred Kohler *Jephson* • Ralf Harolde *Norwood* • Edward Van Sloan *Prof Carlysle* • Samuel Hinds [Samuel S Hinds] *Chief prosecutor* ■ *Dir* Felix E Feist [Felix Feist] • *Scr* John Goodrich, Warren B Duff [Warren Duff], from the novel *Deluge; a Romance* by S Fowler Wright

Delusion ★★★

Thriller 1991 · US · Colour · 88mins

A little-seen but engaging thriller that provides a new twist in the "yuppie in peril" genre, with Jim Metzler getting caught up with a hitman and a showgirl on the road. The cast is largely unfamiliar, with the exception of the always reliable Jerry Orbach, but Carl Colpaert directs the proceedings with panache. JF. Contains swearing, violence and nudity.

Jim Metzler *George O'Brien* • Jennifer Rubin *Patti* • Kyle Secor *Chevy* • Jerry Orbach *Larry* • Robert Costanzo *Myron Sales* ■ *Dir* Carl Colpaert • *Scr* Kurt Voss, Carl Colpaert

Delusions of Grandeur ★★★

Period comedy 1971 · Fr · Colour · 108mins

Gérard Oury – never the subtlest of film-makers – casts restraint aside in this bawdy lampoon. Such excess won't suit all devotees of costume drama, but it's pitched perfectly for Louis De Funès. The actor gleefully overplays every scene as the jilted noble seeking revenge on the King of Spain by arranging for his wife to commit adultery with valet Yves Montand, who bears a striking resemblance to the monarch's cousin. Beautifully shot by Henri Decaë and lavishly designed by Georges Wakhevitch, this is still something of an acquired taste. DP. French dialogue dubbed into English.

Yves Montand *Blaze* • Louis De Funès *Salluste* • Alberto de Mendoza *King* • Karin Schubert *Queen* • Gabriele Tinti *Cesar* • Alice Sapritch *Dona Juna* • Don Jaime De Mora *Priego* ■ *Dir* Gérard Oury • *Scr* Gerard Oury, Marcel Jullian, Daniele Thompson, from the play *Ruy Blas* by Victor Hugo

Dementia 13 ★★★ 15

Horror 1963 · US · BW · 74mins

A series of axe murders marks the anniversary of a little girl's drowning at an eerie Irish castle. This is a passable horror whodunnit, directed by Francis Ford Coppola, aged 24, on a $22,000 budget. The future leading light of Hollywood convinced Ireland's prestigious Abbey Players to appear for minimum wages, begged William Campbell and Patrick Magee to star and used the same sets as the Roger Corman production he was assisting on. Those sets give an atmospheric patina to the proceedings, despite numerous continuity errors and poor production values. A seminal minor classic. AJ [VIDEO] DVD

William Campbell *Richard Haloran* • Luana Anders *Louise Haloran* • Bart Patton *Billy Haloran* • Mary Mitchel *Kane* • Patrick Magee *Justin Caleb* • Eithne Dunn *Lady Haloran* • Peter Read *John Haloran* • Karl Schanzer *Simon* ■ *Dir/Scr* Francis Ford Coppola

Demetrius and the Gladiators ★★★ PG

Epic 1954 · US · Colour · 96mins

In this sequel to *The Robe*, Victor Mature – the custodian of Christ's bloodstained garment – tries to keep it from falling into the clutches of Caligula. Forced to become a gladiator, Mature's antics in the arena arouse the passion of Messalina (Susan Hayward), the wife of stuttering Claudius (Barry Jones), and antagonise Caligula, played by the scene-stealing and deliriously camp Jay Robinson. The result is a juicy excursion into ancient Rome which lacks the oppressive religiosity of the first film. AT [VIDEO] DVD

Victor Mature *Demetrius* • Susan Hayward *Messalina* • Michael Rennie *Peter* • Debra Paget *Lucia* • Anne Bancroft *Paula* • Jay Robinson *Caligula* • Barry Jones *Claudius* • Ernest Borgnine *Strabo* ■ *Dir* Delmer Daves • *Scr* Philip Dunne, from characters created by Lloyd C Douglas

The Demi-Paradise ★★★ U

Second World War drama
1943 · UK · BW · 114mins

In this wartime propaganda piece from director Anthony Asquith, Laurence Olivier stars as a heavily accented Russian visitor who comes to England and finds a country stuffed to the brim with national stereotypes. In his wisdom, however, he manages to see beyond the peculiarities and, after falling in love with Penelope Dudley Ward, appreciates England for what it really is. This being wartime, and him being the inventor of a new type of ship's propeller, it's all jolly timely and actually quite charming. TS

Laurence Olivier *Ivan Dimitrevitch Kouzenetsoff* • Penelope Dudley Ward *Ann Tisdall* • Marjorie Fielding *Mrs Tisdall* • Margaret Rutherford *Rowena Ventnor* • Felix Aylmer *Mr Runalow* • Edie Martin *Aunt Winnie* • Joyce Grenfell *Mrs Pawson* • Wilfrid Hyde White *Waiter* ■ *Dir* Anthony Asquith • *Scr* Anatole de Grunwald

Demobbed ★ U

Comedy 1944 · UK · BW · 95mins

This civvy street comedy is fast, furious and totally unfunny. Despite their music hall experience, neither Nat Jackley nor famed female impersonator Norman Evans had appeared in features before. Their greenness causes them both to pitch to the back of the gallery, thus emphasising the lack of wit in the screenplay. Irredeemable tosh. DP

Nat Jackley *Nat* • Norman Evans *Norman* • Dan Young *Dan* • Betty Jumel *Betty* • Tony Dalton *Billy Brown* • Jimmy Plant *Graham* • Anne Firth *Norma Deane* ■ *Dir* John E Blakeley • *Scr* Roney Parsons, Anthony Toner, from a story by Julius Cantor, Max Zorlini

D

The Democratic Terrorist ★★★

Action thriller
1992 · Ger/Swe · Colour · 96mins

Swedish actor Stellan Skarsgård has become an international star thanks to his excellent performances in films such as *Good Will Hunting*. Earlier in his career he was known throughout northern Europe for complex characterisations such as the secret agent in this tense thriller. The story intriguingly sets the Baader-Meinhof terrorist group on a mission to destroy European unity, with Skarsgård a target for both sides. Briskly directed by Per Berglund, this is essentially low-budget Bond, but none the worse for that. DP. In Swedish, Norwegian and German with English subtitles. Contains violence, swearing and nudity.

Stellan Skarsgård *Captain Carl Hamilton* • Katja Flint *Monika* • Karl Heinz Maslo *Werner* • Heikko Deutschmann *Martin* • Burkhard Dreist *Horst* • Ulrich Tukur *Siegfried Maak* ■ *Dir* Per Berglund • *Scr* Hans Iverberg, from the novel by Jan Guillou

Demolition Man ★★★★ 15

Science-fiction thriller
1993 · US · Colour · 110mins

Sylvester Stallone wisely keeps his tongue stuck firmly in his cheek in this pretension-free, futuristic thriller. He plays a tough cop whose unconventional methods land him in a cryogenic prison. Decades later, he is defrosted to hunt down an old sparring partner, the spectacularly psychopathic Wesley Snipes, who has escaped from his deep frozen state and is creating havoc in the now crime-free Los Angeles (renamed San Angeles). The writers have a lot of fun sending up modern-day political correctness, while director Marco Brambilla delivers the goods when it comes to the action set pieces. JF. Contains swearing and violence. [VIDEO] DVD

Sylvester Stallone *John Spartan* • Wesley Snipes *Simon Phoenix* • Sandra Bullock *Lenina Huxley* • Nigel Hawthorne *Dr Raymond Cocteau* • Benjamin Bratt *Alfredo Garcia* • Bob Gunton *Chief George Earle* • Glenn Shadix *Associate Bob* • Denis Leary *Edgar Friendly* ■ *Dir* Marco Brambilla • *Scr* Daniel Waters, Robert Reneau, Peter M Lenkov, from a story by Peter M Lenkov, Robert Reneau

Demon House ★ 18

Horror 1997 · US · Colour · 81mins

The second sequel to *Night of the Demons* reverts back to the gory stupidity of the cheap original rather than the imaginatively delirious outrage of its immediate predecessor. The floating demon Angela (played once more by Amelia Kinkade) returns to annihilate another group of dumb teenagers who hide out in her ancestral home after shooting a cop on Halloween. Gratuitous nudity, derivative violence and amateurish acting condemn this cliché-ridden nonsense to the bottom of the barrel. AJ [VIDEO] DVD

Amelia Kinkade *Angela* • Kris Holdenreid *Vince* • Gregory Calpakis *Nick* • Stephanie Bauder *Holly* • Patricia Rodriguez *Abbie* • Larry Day *Larry* ■ *Dir* Jimmy Kaufman [Jim Kaufman] • *Scr* Kevin S Tenney

Demon Seed ★★★★ 15

Science-fiction horror
1977 · US · Colour · 90mins

This literate sci-fi take on *Rosemary's Baby* is as weird, provocative and compelling as you would expect from Donald Cammell, the co-director of *Performance*. Julie Christie is dazzling as the victim of a power-crazed computer that decides it's greater than its genius creator and malfunctions to conceive a child. This claustrophobic cautionary tale shrouds its incredible special effects in a powerful hallucinatory atmosphere, with Robert Vaughn providing the creepily compelling voice of the machine. AJ. Contains violence, swearing and nudity.

Julie Christie *Dr Susan Harris* • Fritz Weaver *Dr Alex Harris* • Gerrit Graham *Walter Gabler* • Berry Kroeger *Petrosian* • Lisa Lu *Dr Soon Yen* • Larry J Blake *Cameron* • John O'Leary *Royce* • Robert Vaughn *Proteus IV* ■ *Dir* Donald Cammell • *Scr* Robert Jaffe, Roger O Hirson, from the novel by Dean R Koontz

Demonlover ★★

Thriller
2002 · Fr/Jpn/Mex/US · Colour · 130mins

This combination of cyber-thriller and capitalist condemnation begins inticingly, as Paris-based executive Connie Nielsen displays a ruthless streak in negotiating a lucrative deal with a Japanese animation studio specialising in 3-D pornography. But the narrative spirals out of control following an eye-popping sampling of animé ingenuity. Nielsen's duels with assistant Chloë Sevigny and bitter rival Gina Gershon become increasingly implausible, while her liaison with colleague Charles Berling is left hanging. DP. In French, English and Japanese with subtitles. Contains violence, swearing and sex scenes.

Connie Nielsen *Diane de Monx* • Charles Berling *Hervé Le Millinec* • Chloë Sevigny *Elise Lipsky* • Gina Gershon *Elaine Si Gibril* • Jean-Baptiste Malartre *Henri-Pierre Volf* • Dominique Reymond *Karen* • Edwin Gerard *Edward Gomez* • Thomas M Pollard *Rodney LaCruz, American lawyer* ■ *Dir/Scr* Olivier Assayas

Demons of the Mind ★★★ 18

Psychological drama
1971 · UK · Colour · 84mins

As the 1970s dawned, Hammer tried different avenues of horror to survive the chilling competition. This was an experiment by director Peter Sykes to foster the artier side of the genre by delving deep into the psychological roots of the madness afflicting a troubled aristocratic family and the dark reasons why the baron keeps his children locked up in his Bavarian castle. Acted with a conviction way beyond the call of duty by a strong cast, it's ambitious, difficult, often intelligent stuff. AJ. Contains swearing.

Paul Jones *Carl Richter* • Gillian Hills *Elizabeth Zorn* • Robert Hardy *Baron Frederic Zorn* • Michael Hordern *Priest* • Patrick Magee *Dr Falkenberg* • Shane Briant *Emil Zorn* • Yvonne Mitchell *Aunt Hilda* ■ *Dir* Peter Sykes • *Scr* Christopher Wicking, from a story by Frank Godwin, Christopher Wicking

Demonstone ★★

Action horror 1989 · Aus · Colour · 92mins

Tough major R Lee Ermey teams up with ex-marine Jan-Michael Vincent to solve a series of grisly murders in Manila in a movie that's more action adventure than horror film. Political intrigue, machine gun battles and car crashes take precedence over the limited special effects, which involve such old-fashioned tricks as glowing eyes and images turning negative. AJ

R Lee Ermey *Major Joe Haines* • Jan-Michael Vincent *Andrew Buck* • Nancy Everhard *Sharon Gale* • Pat Skipper *Tony McKee* • Peter Brown *Admiral* • Joonee Gamboa *Senator Belfardo/Chief pirate* • Rolando Tinio *Professor Olmeda* ■ *Dir* Andrew Prowse • *Scr* John Trayne, David Phillips, Frederick Bailey

Denise Calls Up ★★★ 15

Romantic comedy
1995 · US · Colour · 79mins

People fall in love without holding hands; women have babies without a mate; and friends stay close for years without ever seeing each other. Writer/director Hal Salwen's sophisticated cautionary fable is bound to strike a communication chord with those who feel technology has a lot to answer for. This perceptive and consistently funny look at lifestyles today shows a small group of workaholic New Yorkers conducting their lives over the telephone to such an extent that they have forgotten how to interact on a human level. AJ

Tim Daly [Timothy Daly] *Frank Oliver* • Caroleen Feeney *Barbara* • Dan Gunther *Martin Wiener* • Dana Wheeler-Nicholson *Gale* • Liev Schreiber *Jerry* • Aida Turturro *Linda* • Alanna Ubach *Denise* ■ *Dir/Scr* Hal Salwen

Dennis ★★★ PG

Comedy 1993 · US · Colour · 91mins

Directed by Nick Castle, who played the murderous Shape in *Halloween*, this adaptation of Hank Ketcham's comic strip was released as *Dennis the Menace* in the USA, but shortened simply to *Dennis* in this country to avoid confusion with *The Beano*'s tousle-haired terror. Often very funny, but just as often painfully poor, the film was co-written and produced by John Hughes, who seems to have cobbled it together from ideas left over from *Home Alone*. Mason Gamble just gets by as the mischievous imp; Walter Matthau, however, is brilliant as his long-suffering victim, Mr Wilson. DP. Contains some violence.

Walter Matthau *Mr Wilson* • Mason Gamble *Dennis Mitchell* • Joan Plowright *Martha Wilson* • Christopher Lloyd *Switchblade Sam* • Lea Thompson *Alice Mitchell* • Robert Stanton *Henry Mitchell* • Amy Sakasitz *Margaret Wade* • Kellen Hathaway *Joey* • Paul Winfield *Chief of Police* • Natasha Lyonne *Polly* ■ *Dir* Nick Castle • *Scr* John Hughes, from characters created by Hank Ketcham

Dennis the Menace Strikes Again ★★ U

Comedy 1998 · US · Colour · 71mins

Don Rickles and Betty White appear as Dennis's (Justin Cooper) neighbours, Mr and Mrs Wilson. If the first five minutes – featuring a menagerie of escaped animals and Rickles's wagon ride down a flight of stairs half-naked – don't send you off screaming, then perhaps you'll enjoy the appearance of George Kennedy as Dennis's grandfather. The child actors play their cartoon counterparts with varying degrees of success, but for adults, watching Rickles provides most of the fun. ST

Justin Cooper *Dennis Mitchell* • Don Rickles *Mr Wilson* • George Kennedy *Grandpa* • Brian Doyle-Murray *Professor* • Carrot Top *Sylvester* • Betty White *Mrs Wilson* • Dwier Brown *George Mitchell* • Heidi Swedberg *Alice Mitchell* • George Wendt *Cop* ■ *Dir* Charles T Kanganis • *Scr* Tim McCanlies, from a story by Tim McCanlies, Jeff Schechter, from characters created by Hank Ketcham

The Dentist ★★★★ U

Comedy 1932 · US · BW · 20mins

Based on a sketch first performed in the Earl Carroll Vanities, this marked WC Fields's debut for slapstick supremo Mack Sennett. Having forbidden his daughter to marry the ice man and endured golfing hell, Fields is next tormented by a bearded patient and Elise Cavanna's stubborn tooth. (The shots in which she throws her legs around his waist to assist his merciless assault with the dental pliers were excised for TV screenings until the 1970s.) The film established the Fields persona that would serve him to the end of his career. DP DVD

WC Fields *Dentist* • "Babe" Kane [Marjorie Kane] *Daughter* • Arnold Gray *Arthur the iceman* • Dorothy Granger *Patient (Miss Peppitone)* • Elise Cavanna *Patient (Miss Mason)* ■ *Dir* Leslie Pearce • *Scr* WC Fields

The Dentist ★★★ 18

Horror 1996 · US · Colour · 88mins

A gory oral scare-fest from director Brian Yuzna, the producer of *Re-Animator*. Corbin Bernsen is the Beverly Hills dentist who goes murderously crazy when his professional and private lives stop conforming to his impossibly high standards. As paranoia sets in, he fights the moral decay contaminating his world with the sharp tools of his trade. The dental torture that follows is both grisly and hilariously funny, though *The Dentist II* is even better. AJ. Contains violence. DVD

Corbin Bernsen *Dr Feinstone* • Linda Hoffman *Brooke* • Molly Hagan *Jessica* • Ken Foree *Detective Gibbs* • Virginya Keehne *Sarah* • Patty Toy *Karen* • Jan Hoag *Candy* • Christa Sauls *April Reign* • Tony Noakes *Detective Sunshine* • Earl Boen *Marvin Goldblum* • Michael Stadvec *Matt* ■ *Dir* Brian Yuzna • *Scr* Stuart Gordon, Dennis Paoli, Charles Finch

The Dentist II ★★★ 18

Horror thriller 1998 · US · Colour · 93mins

The tagline "You know the drill" sums it all up rather nicely. But if you don't, here's a résumé. The original *Dentist* was a surprisingly funny and nasty horror that sent blackboard-scraping chills up the spine. The good news is that Brian Yuzna's sequel is just as black, just as gruesome and will convince another generation of fans to put the annual dental check-up on hold. Corbin Bernsen is back as the psychotic gum mutilator, resuming practice after escaping from an asylum. JF. Contains violence, nudity and some swearing. DVD

Corbin Bernsen *Dr Lawrence Caine* • Linda Hoffman *Brooke Sullivan* • Jillian McWhirter *Jamie Devers* • Susanne Wright *Bev Trotter* • Wendy Robie *Bernice* • Clint Howard *Mr Toothache* ■ *Dir* Brian Yuzna • *Scr* Richard Dana Smith, from characters created by Stuart Gordon, Dennis Paoli, Charles Finch

Dentist in the Chair ★★ U

Comedy 1960 · UK · BW · 75mins

Bob Monkhouse co-wrote and stars in this unremarkable little comedy, which will only have viewers in fits if they have been subjected to laughing gas. If the flimsy plot about stolen instruments at a dental training school isn't bad enough, the ghastly gags will set your teeth on edge. Numbing the pain, however, are the willing performances of Monkhouse and Kenneth Connor, and typically sound comic support from Eric Barker. DP

Bob Monkhouse *David Cookson* • Peggy Cummins *Peggy Travers* • Kenneth Connor *Sam Field* • Eric Barker *The Dean* • Ronnie Stevens *Brian Dexter* • Vincent Ball *Michaels* ■ *Dir* Don Chaffey • *Scr* Val Guest, Bob Monkhouse, George Wadmore, from the novel by Matthew Finch

Dentist on the Job ★ PG

Comedy 1961 · UK · BW · 84mins

A year after cutting his teeth on *Dentist in the Chair*, Bob Monkhouse returned in this disappointing sequel with a script that's so full of cavities you'll soon be wincing with pain and crying out for laughing gas. Newly qualified Monkhouse beams his way through a series of gags that could easily have been extracted from the *Doctor in the House* reject file. DP

Bob Monkhouse *David Cookson* • Kenneth Connor *Sam Field* • Ronnie Stevens *Brian Dexter* • Shirley Eaton *Jill Venner* • Eric Barker *Colonel JJ Proudfoot/Dean* • Richard Wattis *Macreedy* • Reginald Beckwith *Duff* • Charles Hawtrey *Pharmacist* • Graham Stark *Man* ■ *Dir* CM Pennington-Richards • *Scr* Hazel Adair, Hugh Woodhouse, Bob Monkhouse

Denver & Rio Grande ★★★ U

Western 1952 · US · Colour · 88mins

Renowned for the climactic head-on collision involving a pair of antique steam trains, this solid programmer succeeds in overcoming its clichés and stereotypes to produce a rattling good yarn. The feud between Edmond O'Brien of the titular railroad and Sterling Hayden of the Canyon City and San Juan runs along predictable lines, with the latter devoting more time to sabotaging his rival's efforts than concentrating on his own. But director Byron Haskin keeps the pace brisk and allows dependable supports to ply their stalwart trade. DP

Edmond O'Brien *Jim Vesser* • Sterling Hayden *McCabe* • Dean Jagger *General Palmer* • Laura Elliott *Linda Prescott* • Lyle Bettger *Johnny Buff* • J Carrol Naish *Harkness* • ZaSu Pitts *Jane* ■ *Dir* Byron Haskin • *Scr* Frank Gruber

Deranged ★★★ 18

Horror 1974 · US · Colour · 82mins

Based on the abhorrent real-life crimes of cannibal killer Ed Gein, who inspired *Psycho* and *The Texas Chain Saw Massacre*, this ghoulish shocker was disowned by its producer for being too repellently realistic. Roberts Blossom plays a sexually repressed mummy's boy who preserves the old dear's corpse and murders people to keep her company. Blossom gives a standout central performance, managing the near-impossible feat of making a sympathetic character out of a psychopathic killer. RS. Contains violence and some swearing.

Roberts Blossom *Ezra Cobb* • Cosette Lee *Ma Cobb* • Robert Warner *Harlan Kootz* • Marcia Diamond *Jenny Kootz* • Robert McHeady *Sheriff* • Marian Waldman *Maureen Selby* • Jack Mather *Drunk* ■ *Dir* Jeff Gillen, Alan Ormsby • *Scr* Alan Ormsby

Derby Day ★★★ U

Drama 1952 · UK · BW · 81mins

An engaging, absorbing look at the various flotsam and jetsam that pit themselves against the Fates at Epsom Downs on Derby Day. This is the early 1950s, when the British class system was firmly rooted and unassailable, and director Herbert Wilcox nicely milks its rituals and nuances at a great cultural event. The portmanteau cast effortlessly goes through its paces with aplomb and confidence. We have been here many times before, but it's still fun. SH

Anna Neagle *Lady Helen Forbes* • Michael Wilding *David Scott* • Googie Withers *Betty Molloy* • John McCallum *Tommy Dillon* • Peter Graves (1) *Gerald Berkeley* • Suzanne Cloutier *Michele Jolivet* • Gordon Harker *Joe Jenkins* • Gladys Henson *Gladys* ■ *Dir* Herbert Wilcox • *Scr* Monckton Hoffe, John Baines, Alan Melville, from a story by Arthur Austie

Derrida ★★★ PG

Documentary 2001 · US · Colour · 85mins

Apart from Jacques Derrida's recollections of encountering anti-Semitism as a Jewish youth in Vichy-ruled Algeria, this documentary portrait of the influential philosopher has few revelations to offer. At times, its sole purpose seems to be to display the intellectual acuity of director Kirby Dick and on-screen interviewer (and former student of Derrida's) Amy Ziering Kofman. However, there is a playfulness in the way that Derrida evades their attempts to lure him into philosophical pitfalls or expose the contradictions in the theories that laid the basis for Deconstructionism – that is, breaking down language to expose ideological bias. Making valid points about the nature of academic, biographical and cinematic truth, this is intriguing but somewhat specialised. DP. In English and French with subtitles. DVD

Dir Kirby Dick, Amy Ziering Kofman

Dersu Uzala ★★★ U

Period adventure
1975 · USSR/Jpn · Colour · 134mins

Anxious to appear open to cultural exchange, the Soviet Union gave Japanese maestro Akira Kurosawa untold roubles and all of Siberia's wilderness to play with for this eco-epic. It's a vast tone poem, set in the early 20th century when an expedition led by Yuri Solomin sets out to map the icy wastes. And that's it, really: a collection of episodes showing man's attempts to come to terms with nature at its toughest. There are some great moments, but there are also long periods when the camera just stares meaningfully at nothing. AT. In Russian with English subtitles. DVD

Maxim Munzuk *Dersu Uzala* • Yuri Solomin *Captain Arseniev* • A Pyatkov *Olentiev* • V Kremena *Turtygin* • S Chokmorov *Chang-Bao* • S Danilchenko *Anna* ■ *Dir* Akira Kurosawa • *Scr* Akira Kurosawa, Yuri Nagibin, from the novel by Vladimir Arseniev

The Descent ★★★★ 18

Horror 2005 · UK · Colour · 99mins

An all-female extreme caving expedition goes horribly wrong when six friends end up in an uncharted system and encounter a monstrous cannibal race in Neil Marshall's brilliantly constructed panic attack. Desperation, betrayals and imploding relationships prove as fatal to the girls as the subterranean threat. From the high impact opening shock to the poignantly bleak ending, this is super-scary and vicious – edgy British horror at its very best. AJ

Shauna Macdonald *Sarah* • Natalie Mendoza *Juno* • Alex Reid *Beth* • Saskia Mulder *Rebecca* • Nora-Jane Noone *Holly* • MyAnna Buring *Sam* ■ *Dir/Scr* Neil Marshall

Descent into Hell ★★★

Crime thriller 1986 · Fr · Colour · 90mins

This is a tidy enough thriller, but it lacks both the hard-boiled edge and star credibility that would raise it above the average. Claude Brasseur is sufficiently world-weary as the alcoholic author who accidentally kills a petty thief while vacationing in Haiti. But Sophie Marceau, as the trophy wife who helps conceal his crime, is short on *femme* fatality. DP. French dialogue dubbed into English.

Claude Brasseur *Alan Kolber* • Sophie Marceau *Lola Kolber* • Sidiki Bakaba [Sijiri Bakaba] *Theophile Bijou* • Hyppolyte Girardot *Philippe Devignat* • Gérard Rinaldi *Elvis* • Marie Dubois *Lucette Beulemans* • Betsy Blair *Mrs Burns* ■ *Dir* Francis Girod • *Scr* Francis Girod, Jean-Loup Dabadic, from the novel *The Wounded and the Slain* by David Goodis

Desert Bloom ★★★★ PG

Drama 1985 · US · Colour · 101mins

In this period piece director Eugene Corr splendidly captures the simmering, underlying tensions and almost childlike incredulity of a 1950s America heralding in the nuclear age. The bigger issues of the Bomb are used to add colour to an enclosed tale of dysfunctional family life, wonderfully played by Jon Voight as the drunken stepfather of young Annabeth Gish and Ellen Barkin as her sexy aunt. Corr takes an age to establish his characters and plot, but once up and running there isn't a more atmospheric film about pre-Kennedy America. SH. Contains some swearing.

Annabeth Gish *Rose* • Jon Voight *Jack* • JoBeth Williams *Lily* • Ellen Barkin *Starr* • Jay Underwood *Robin* • Desiree Joseph *Dee Ann* • Dusty Balcerzak *Barbara Jo* • Allen Garfield *Mr Mosol* • Tressi Loria *Shelly* ■ *Dir* Eugene Corr • *Scr* Eugene Corr, from a story by Linda Remy, Eugene Corr

Desert Blue ★★★ 15

Comedy drama 1998 · US · Colour · 86mins

Two travellers, father John Heard and daughter Kate Hudson, get trapped in a rural backwater after a chemical truck spillage. Their encounters with the town's restless youth expose personal prejudices and result in an unlikely romance between snobbish Hudson and bad boy Brendan Sexton III. Christina Ricci and Ben Affleck's brother Casey also appear. LH

Brendan Sexton III *Blue Baxter* • Kate Hudson *Skye* • John Heard *Father* • Christina Ricci *Ely* • Casey Affleck *Pete* • Sara Gilbert *Sandy* • Ethan Suplee *Cale* • Michael Ironside *Agent Bellows* ■ *Dir/Scr* Morgan J Freeman

The Desert Fox ★★★ PG

Second World War action drama
1951 · US · BW · 84mins

James Mason – an actor memorable for playing charming villains – stars as Field Marshal Erwin Rommel, who was known as a professional soldier rather than a Nazi sadist. Filmed not in North Africa but Borrego Springs, California, Henry Hathaway's film begins as a wartime adventure, then turns into a study of disenchantment as Rommel, beaten by Montgomery's 8th Army, returns to Germany and joins the plot against Hitler. There's a good supporting cast and Hathaway directs with solid assurance. Mason reprised his role in the sequel, *The Desert Rats*. AT DVD

James Mason *Erwin Rommel* • Cedric Hardwicke *Dr Karl Strolin* • Jessica Tandy *Frau Rommel* • Luther Adler *Hitler* • Everett Sloane *General Burgdorf* • Leo G Carroll *Field Marshal Von Rundstedt* • George Macready *General Fritz Bayerlein* ■ *Dir* Henry Hathaway • *Scr* Nunnally Johnson, from the biography by Desmond Young

Desert Fury ★★★

Drama 1947 · US · Colour · 96mins

Lizabeth Scott runs away from school and heads home to Nevada where her mom, Mary Astor, runs a gambling house and where the men get very steamed up indeed. There's widowed gambler John Hodiak, his henchman Wendell Corey and the most virile cop west of the Pecos, Burt Lancaster, in his third screen outing. It's really a western in modern dress, a display of macho posturing that's ridiculous and gripping at the same time. AT

John Hodiak *Eddie Bendix* • Lizabeth Scott *Paula Haller* • Burt Lancaster *Tom Hanson* • Wendell Corey *Johnny Ryan* • Mary Astor *Fritzie Haller* • Kristine Miller *Claire Lindquist* • William Harrigan *Judge Berle Lindquist* • James Flavin *Pat Johnson* ■ *Dir* Lewis Allen • *Scr* Robert Rossen, from the novel *Desert Town* by Ramona Stewart

Desert Hearts ★★★★ 18

Drama 1985 · US · Colour · 87mins

One of the very few truly risk-taking movies to come out of the mid-1980s, this tale of lesbian love in Reno was a deserved critical success at the time. Natalie Cooper's intriguing, intelligent screenplay gives great roles to Helen Shaver and Patricia Charbonneau, and the resulting juxtaposition – of a disillusioned older woman falling for a younger, freer spirit – works a treat. What scenes of carnal knowledge there are – for this is a film about relationships and prejudice – are deftly handled without sensationalism. This is one of those seminal pictures that show what Hollywood can do when it casts fear aside. SH

Helen Shaver *Vivian Bell* • Patricia Charbonneau *Cay Rivvers* • Audra Lindley *Frances Parker* • Andra Akers *Silver Dale* • Dean Butler *Darrell* • Gwen Welles *Gwen* ■ *Dir* Donna Deitch • *Scr* Natalie Cooper, from the novel *Desert of the Heart* by Jane Rule

Desert Heat ★★ 18

Action drama 1999 · US · Colour · 91mins

This violent variation on *High Plains Drifter* confirmed suspicions of Jean-Claude Van Damme's commercial decline. Pat Morita mugs shamelessly as the eccentric handyman who helps Van Damme's suicidal, motorbiking former hit man rid a desert town of a gang of vicious drug dealers. Laced with native American mysticism and crude comedy, the story follows predictable lines. DP DVD

Jean-Claude Van Damme *Eddie Lomax* • Nikki Bokal *Carol* • Larry Drake *Ramsey Hogan* • Bill Erwin *Eli Hamilton* • Neil Delama *Lester* ■ *Dir* Danny Mulroon [John G Avildsen] • *Scr* Tom O'Rourke

Desert Legion ★★ U

Swashbuckling adventure
1953 · US · Colour · 85mins

Alan Ladd stars in this B-grade swashbuckler as a soldier in the Foreign Legion who survives an ambush and is nursed back to health by the alluring Arlene Dahl. Dahl lives in a hidden city called Madara, and enlists Ladd to help keep it from the clutches of villain Richard Conte. Comic relief comes from Ladd's buddy, Akim Tamiroff. AT

Alan Ladd *Paul Lartel* • Richard Conte *Crito/Calif* • Arlene Dahl *Morjana* • Akim Tamiroff *Private Plevko* • Leon Askin *Major Vasil* • Oscar Beregi *Khalil* • Anthony Caruso *Lieutenant Messaoud* • Don Blackman *Kumbaba* ■ *Dir* Joseph Pevney • *Scr* Irving Wallace, Lewis Meltzer, from the novel *The Demon Caravan* by George Arthur Surdez

Desert Mice ★★ U

Second World War comedy
1959 · UK · BW · 83mins

The feeble title pun on "Desert Rats" (the nickname given to the British troops who fought against Rommel in North Africa) rather sets the tone for this overlookable comedy from director Michael Relph. Full of predictable characters, humdrum incidents and gags that would have lowered the morale of even the most battle-hardened tommy, it accompanies an Ensa concert party on its tour of army camps. Sid James, Dora Bryan and Irene Handl prove again to be reliable troupers, but Alfred Marks lacks the presence to carry the lead. DP

Alfred Marks *Major Poskett* • Sidney James *Bert Bennett* • Dora Bryan *Gay* • Dick Bentley *Gavin O'Toole* • Reginald Beckwith *Fred* • Irene Handl *Miss Patch* • Liz Fraser *Edie* ■ *Dir* Michael Relph • *Scr* David Climie

Desert Passage ★★

Western 1952 · US · BW · 62mins

After 12 years of grinding out nearly 50 B-westerns for RKO Radio with occasional (and sometimes memorable) appearances in bigger pictures, Tim Holt turned in his saddle and – save some fleeting later appearances – retired from the big screen. Far from ending the series on a high note, this one cuts back on action and atmosphere with most of the scenes located indoors at a hostelry. The story is lively enough, though, with Holt and sidekick Richard Martin driving a stagecoach carrying loot coveted by various parties. AE

Tim Holt *Tim* • Joan Dixon *Emily* • Walter Reed *Carver* • Richard Martin (1) *Chito Rafferty* • Dorothy Patrick *Rosa* • John Dehner *Bronson* ■ *Dir* Lesley Selander • *Scr* Norman Houston

The Desert Rats ★★★ U

Second World War action drama
1953 · US · BW · 84mins

A rather aloof desert-stormer, meant as a follow-up to *The Desert Fox*, and again boasting James Mason as Field Marshal Rommel, this time ordering the Battle of Tobruk against Allied forces that include Richard Burton commanding Aussie troops. Burton has his own problems with his cowardly old schoolteacher turned volunteer Robert Newton, but still manages to bring down Rommel's forces. TH DVD

Richard Burton *Captain MacRoberts* • Robert Newton *Bartlett* • Robert Douglas *General* • Torin Thatcher *Barney* • Chips Rafferty *Smith* • Charles Tingwell *Lieutenant Carstairs* • James Mason *Rommel* • Charles Davis *Pete* ■ *Dir* Robert Wise • *Scr* Richard Murphy

The Desert Song ★★

Musical 1929 · US · BW and Colour · 125mins

An early sound version of the Sigmund Romberg operetta about a seemingly wimpish Briton who, as the mysterious "Red Shadow", leads a revolt against villainous Arabs. Remade in 1944 and 1953, this rendition is worth seeing, not for its competence, but for its unintentional laughs. John Boles sings adequately, despite his stiff upper lip, while Carlotta King has a certain winsome banality as the girl who despises him at first. TH

John Boles *The Red Shadow* • Carlotta King *Margot* • Louise Fazenda *Susan* • Johnny Arthur *Benny Kidd* • Edward Martindel *Gen Bierbeau* • Jack Pratt *Pasha* • Myrna Loy *Azuri* ■ *Dir* Roy Del Ruth • *Scr* Harvey Gates, from the operetta by Sigmund Romberg, Otto Harbach, Lawrence Schwab, Frank Mandel, Oscar Hammerstein II

The Desert Song ★★★ U

Musical 1944 · US · Colour · 94mins

The second of three screen versions of the operetta about the romantic, heroic leader of a band of Riffs in North Africa who fight off their evil oppressors. This version was given contemporary relevance by having the villains as Nazis and the hero (Dennis Morgan) an American in disguise who, with his band of men, sabotages the building of a railway track. Directed by Robert Florey, this romantic nonsense can't miss for fans of Romberg's lush and rousing melodies, which include *One Alone* and *The Riff Song*. RK

Dennis Morgan *Paul Hudson* • Irene Manning *Margot* • Bruce Cabot *Col Fontaine* • Victor Francen *Caid Yousseff* • Lynne Overman *Johnny Walsh* • Gene Lockhart *Pere FanFan* • Faye Emerson *Hajy* • Marcel Dalio *Tarbouch* ■ *Dir* Robert Florey • *Scr* Robert Buckner, from the operetta by Sigmund Romberg, Otto Harbach, Lawrence Schwab, Frank Mandel, Oscar Hammerstein II

The Desert Song ★★★ U

Musical 1953 · US · Colour · 105mins

This handsomely mounted Warner Bros remake of Sigmund Romberg's popular operetta is easy enough on the eye, and easier still on the ear. But the good-looking Gordon MacRae is miscast as the young American anthropologist doubling by night as El Khobar, avenger of the desert Riffs. Still, Kathryn Grayson sings *One Alone* as if her life depended on it, and Raymond Massey is perfect as the cruel and villainous sheik. TS

Kathryn Grayson *Margot* • Gordon MacRae *Paul Bonnard/El Khobar* • Steve Cochran *Captain Fontaine* • Raymond Massey *Yousseff* • Dick Wesson *Benjy Kidd* • Allyn McLerie [Allyn Ann McLerie] *Azuri* • Ray Collins *General Birabeau* ■ *Dir* Bruce Humberstone [H Bruce Humberstone] • *Scr* Roland Kibbee, from the operetta by Sigmund Romberg, Otto Harbach, Lawrence Schwab, Frank Mandel, Oscar Hammerstein II

Desert Thunder ★★ 15

Action thriller 1998 · US · Colour · 82mins

Set in the aftermath of Operation Desert Storm, this gung-ho action thriller pits retired flyboy Daniel Baldwin and a *Dirty Dozen*-style squadron against a top secret chemical weapons plant with thuddingly predictable consequences. The macho posturing is hard to swallow, but the flying sequences are surprisingly effective, all the more so considering they were supervised by that master of B-movie schtick, Jim Wynorski. DP DVD

Daniel Baldwin • Richard Tyson *Streets* • Tim Abell • Marc Casabani *Hassim* • Stacy Haiduk ■ *Dir* Jim Wynorski • *Scr* Lenny Juliano

The Desert Trail ★★ U

Western 1935 · US · BW · 54mins

Trapped at Monogram Studios and contracted to a seemingly relentless series of B-westerns, John Wayne managed to hone his persona and learn screencraft in routine films such as this one. Director Cullin Lewis (Lewis Collins) does what he can with the desperately average "mistaken identity" plot, but there's not much to work with. The script is by Lindsley Parsons, who went on to become a prolific producer. TS DVD

John Wayne *John Scott* • Mary Kornman *Anne* • Paul Fix *Jim* • Eddy Chandler *Kansas Charlie* • Carmen Laroux *Juanita* • Lafe McKee *Sheriff Barker* • Al Ferguson *Pete* ■ *Dir* Cullen Lewis [Lewis D Collins] • *Scr* Lindsley Parsons

The Deserted Station ★★★★

Drama 2002 · Iran/Fr/Neth · Colour · 93mins

Ali Reza Raisian's third feature reverberates with the preoccupations of Iran's most pre-eminent film-maker, Abbas Kiarostami, upon whose story it is based. A car breakdown sets up a trademark Kiarostami investigation of town and country mores, in which the wife's minding of the nearby shanty school (while the teacher goes off to help her husband fix the car) permits a revealing insight into the impact of rural poverty on the virtually forgotten local women and children. Leila Hatami produces a touching display of compassion and shame, as she explores a near-dormant desert railway line, but Raisian also injects plenty of humour into his humanistic approach to the subject matter. DP. In Farsi with English subtitles.

Leila Hatami *The Wife* • Nezam Manouchehri *The Husband* • Mehran Rajabi *Feizollah* ■ *Dir* Ali Reza Raisian • *Scr* Kambozia Partovi, from a short story by Abbas Kiarostami

The Deserter ★★ 15

Western 1971 · It/Yug · Colour · 94mins

A lot of familiar western faces are in this cavalry versus Indians epic, but since this is a Euro-western, shot in Yugoslavia, there are also several Italians, plus Yugoslavian heart-throb Bekim Fehmiu in the title role. Hollywood director Burt Kennedy – noted for maintaining a sharp pace and no messing about – somehow talked John Huston into a cameo appearance. AT

Bekim Fehmiu *Captain Victor Kaleb* • John Huston *General Miles* • Richard Crenna *Major Wade Brown* • Chuck Connors *Reynolds* • Ricardo Montalban *Natachai* • Ian Bannen *Crawford* • Brandon de Wilde *Ferguson* • Slim Pickens *Tattinger* • Albert Salmi *Schmidt* • Woody Strode *Jackson* • Patrick Wayne *Bill Robinson* ■ *Dir* Burt Kennedy • *Scr* Clair Huffaker, from a story by Stuart J Byrne, William H James

Design for Living ★★★

Romantic comedy drama
1933 · US · BW · 86mins

A famous Noël Coward play becomes a minor work in the canon of the great Ernst Lubitsch. His usually witty visual style is seemingly cramped by having to rely too much on the master's witticisms, as translated into movietalk by ace scenarist Ben Hecht. Of course, in this famous *ménage à trois* tale, Gary Cooper and Fredric March are super fun. But why on earth are they both in such a dither over the self-regarding Miriam Hopkins? Edward Everett Horton saves this show single-handed as Max Plunkett, the stuffed shirt Hopkins eventually marries. TS

Fredric March *Tom Chambers* • Gary Cooper *George Curtis* • Miriam Hopkins *Gilda Farrell* • Edward Everett Horton *Max Plunkett* • Franklin Pangborn *Mr Douglas* • Isabel Jewell *Lisping Stenographer* • Harry Dunkminson *Mr Egelbauer* • Helena Phillips *Mrs Egelbauer* ■ *Dir* Ernst Lubitsch • *Scr* Ben Hecht, from the play by Nöel Coward

Design for Scandal ★★★ U

Romantic comedy 1941 · US · BW · 84mins

The last movie the fabulous Rosalind Russell made under her MGM contract is a deft romantic comedy based on a clever idea: ace newshound Walter Pidgeon is sent out to dish some dirt on squeaky-clean judge Russell, and falls for her. Screenwriter Lionel Houser provides some sparkling repartee, and director Norman Taurog keeps the froth moving along at a brisk pace. Mix in those glossy MGM production values and you have a very watchable time-filler. TS

Rosalind Russell *Judge Cornelia Porter* • Walter Pidgeon *Jeff Sherman* • Edward Arnold *Judson M Blair* • Lee Bowman *Walter Caldwell* • Jean Rogers *Dotty* • Donald Meek *Mr Wade* • Guy Kibbee *Judge Graham* ■ *Dir* Norman Taurog • *Scr* Lionel Houser

The Designated Mourner ★★

Drama 1997 · UK · Colour · 94mins

Anyone familiar with Wallace Shawn's earlier screenwriting effort *My Dinner with Andre* (which he co-scripted with theatre director Andre Gregory) will know what to expect from this chat-fest: a lament on the passing of high art in an age of middlebrow mediocrity. Set in an unnamed country on the edge of revolution, the action centres around the discussions between shiftless intellectual Mike Nichols, his wife Miranda Richardson, and her poet father, David De Keyser. Focusing on the dialogue rather than seeking ways to open out Shawn's stage play, director David Hare slams the door shut on all but the cognoscenti. DP. Contains swearing.

Mike Nichols *Jack* • Miranda Richardson *Judy* • David De Keyser *Howard* ■ *Dir* David Hare • *Scr* Wallace Shawn, from his play

Designing Woman ★★★★ U

Romantic comedy
1957 · US · Colour · 117mins

This has a nicely punning title, plus a witty Oscar-winning screenplay by George Wells that seems to have missed its decade, despite having sophisticated and assured comedy direction from MGM ace Vincente Minnelli. With its plot about a fashion designer and crusading sports columnist getting married, it's reminiscent of a Spencer Tracy/Katharine Hepburn comedy. Lauren Bacall gives good value, but Gregory Peck lacks the lightness of touch required. The original idea was suggested by MGM's great costume designer, Helen Rose. TS

Gregory Peck *Mike Hagen* • Lauren Bacall *Marilla Hagen* • Dolores Gray *Lori Shannon* • Sam Levene *Ned Hammerstein* • Tom Helmore *Zachary Wilde* • Mickey Shaughnessy *Maxie Stulz* • Jesse White *Charlie Arneg* ■ *Dir* Vincente Minnelli • *Scr* George Wells, from an idea by Helen Rose

Desire ★★★★

Romantic comedy 1936 · US · BW · 95mins

To evade detection at the Spanish border, a glamorous lady jewel thief hides the pearls she stole in Paris by dropping them into the pocket of an unsuspecting American motor car designer. In the course of her manoeuvrings to retrieve them, she falls in love with him. Marlene Dietrich and Gary Cooper star in this scintillating romantic comedy, produced by Ernst Lubitsch and full of the "Lubitsch touch." RK

Marlene Dietrich *Madeleine de Beaupré* • Gary Cooper *Tom Bradley* • John Halliday *Margoli, Carlos* • William Frawley *Mr Gibson* • Ernest Cossart *Aristide Duval* • Akim Tamiroff *Police Official* • Alan Mowbray *Dr Edouard Pauquet* ■ *Dir* Frank Borzage • *Scr* Edward Justus Mayer, Waldemar Young, Samuel Hoffenstein, from the play *Die Schönen Tage von Aranjuez* by Hans Szekely, RA Stemmle

Desire & Hell at Sunset Motel ★★★ 15

Comedy thriller 1991 · US · Colour · 95mins

1950s nostalgia meets oddball *film noir* when bombshell Sherilyn Fenn and her toy salesman husband (Whip Hubley) shack up in a dingy motel on the way to Disneyland. The deliberately convoluted plot involves Hubley hiring David Hewlett to spy on Fenn and her new lover, while the latter (David Johansen) plots to kill her spouse. Corkscrew twists abound, but for all its attempts to be wacky, erotic and offbeat, Alan Castle's crafty nightmare comedy remains little more than an interesting diversion. AJ

Sherilyn Fenn *Bridey DeSoto* • Whip Hubley *Chester DeSoto* • David Hewlett *Deadpan Winchester* • David Johansen *Auggie March* • Paul Bartel *Manager* • Kenneth Tobey *Captain Holiday* • Parker Whitman *Boss* • Shannon Sturges *Louella* ■ *Dir/Scr* Alan Castle

Desire in the Dust ★★

Drama 1960 · US · BW · 102mins

This tale of lust, death and madness in the Deep South generates much heat but little light. Shot in black-and-white CinemaScope by Lucien Ballard, this good-looking film involves ex-convict Ken Scott who, having taken a manslaughter rap for his lover Martha Hyer, returns home to put the cat among the pigeons. These include Hyer's father Raymond Burr, a political bigwig with ambitions, and her mother Joan Bennett, who has gone insane. Decently enough acted. RK

Raymond Burr *Colonel Ben Marquand* • Martha Hyer *Melinda Marquand* • Joan Bennett *Mrs Marquand* • Ken Scott *Lonnie Wilson* • Brett Halsey *Dr Ned Thomas* • Edward Binns *Luke Connett* ■ *Dir* William F Claxton • *Scr* Charles Lang, from the novel by Harry Whittington

Desire Me ★★

Drama 1947 · US · BW · 90mins

The first MGM film to be released with no director credit is pretty silly, but it's no worse and a good deal glossier than most Hollywood pap. Greer Garson is told by buddy Richard Hart that hubby Robert Mitchum was killed in the war; naturally, he wasn't. The director who took his name off the film was George Cukor, and both Mervyn LeRoy and Jack Conway allegedly directed bits. Not that bad. TS

Greer Garson *Marise Aubert* • Robert Mitchum *Paul Aubert* • Richard Hart *Jean Renaud* • Morris Ankrum *Martin* • George Zucco *Father Donnard* • Cecil Humphreys *Dr Andre Leclair* • David Hoffman *Postman* • Florence Bates *Mrs Lannie, "Joo-Lou"* ■ • *Scr* Marguerite Roberts, Zoe Akins

Desire under the Elms ★★ PG

Drama 1958 · US · BW · 106mins

Eugene O'Neill's gloomy drama is about New Englander Burl Ives's hot young wife (a virtually incomprehensible Sophia Loren) falling for his son (an overtly sensitive Anthony Perkins). This is overblown melodrama, pure and simple, but director Delbert Mann opts for realism, despite that fact that Daniel Fapp's crystal-clear (and Oscar-nominated) VistaVision photography reveals every phoney set and emotion for what it is. TS DVD

Sophia Loren *Anna Cabot* • Anthony Perkins *Eben Cabot* • Burl Ives *Ephraim Cabot* • Frank Overton *Simeon Cabot* • Pernell Roberts *Peter Cabot* • Rebecca Welles *Lucinda* • Jean Willes *Florence* ■ *Dir* Delbert Mann • *Scr* Irwin Shaw, from the play by Eugene O'Neill

Desiree ★★★ U

Historical romance
1954 · US · Colour · 105mins

Marlon Brando as Napoleon may seem like ideal casting – indeed, the "Great Mumbler" looks and sounds splendid – but it's clear from his sleepwalking performance that the star himself regarded this as a chore. Nevertheless, there is a splendid coronation sequence and some elegant costumes, plus a lovely Josephine played by Merle Oberon. The title role went to the lovely Jean Simmons; she and Brando would do much better work together the following year in *Guys and Dolls*. TS

Marlon Brando *Napoleon Bonaparte* • Jean Simmons *Desiree Clary* • Merle Oberon *Josephine* • Michael Rennie *Bernadotte* • Cameron Mitchell *Joseph Bonaparte* • Elizabeth Sellars *Julie* • Charlotte Austin *Paulette* • Cathleen Nesbitt *Madame Bonaparte* • Evelyn Varden *Marie* ■ *Dir* Henry Koster • *Scr* Daniel Taradash, from the novel by Annemarie Selinko • *Costume Designer* André Hubert, Charles Le Maire

Desk Set ★★★★ U

Romantic comedy
1957 · US · Colour · 103mins

The wit of the original title was lost in the UK when it was released as *His Other Woman*. But the sparkle in this penultimate pairing of the great Spencer Tracy and the wonderful Katharine Hepburn still endures, even if the slight plot – Tracy plays an efficiency expert hired to automate Hepburn's office – seems stretched. Watching their on-screen clash from the sidelines are splendid comic players Gig Young and Joan Blondell, and director Walter Lang sensibly lets the stars get on with it. TS

Spencer Tracy *Richard Sumner* • Katharine Hepburn *Bunny Watson* • Gig Young *Mike Cutler* • Joan Blondell *Peg Costello* • Dina Merrill *Sylvia* • Sue Randall *Ruthie* • Neva Patterson *Miss Warringer* ■ *Dir* Walter Lang • *Scr* Phoebe Ephron, Henry Ephron, from the play by William Marchant

Despair ★★★ 15

Drama 1978 · W Ger · Colour · 114mins

A whiff of *Satan's Brew* pervades Rainer Werner Fassbinder's dark drama of dual identity and the desire for death. However, there's none of the grubbiness of that showy experiment in this tale, set in pre-Nazi Germany, which – as you would expect of a screenplay adapted by Tom Stoppard from a novel by Vladimir Nabokov – has an ingenuity to match its erudition. Warning of the perils of confusing life with art, Fassbinder uses Dirk Bogarde's failed bid to pass himself off as a murdered tramp to explore the inevitability of fascism and the indolence of the individual. DP [video]

Dirk Bogarde *Hermann Herman* • Andréa Ferréol *Lydia Herman* • Volker Spengler *Ardalion* • Klaus Löwitsch *Felix Weber* • Alexander Allerson *Mayer* • Bernhard Wicki *Orlovius* • Peter Kern *Muller* ■ *Dir* Rainer Werner Fassbinder • *Scr* Tom Stoppard, from a novel by Vladimir Nabokov

Desperado ★★★★ 18

Action adventure
1995 · US · Colour · 100mins

The quirky no-budget charm of *El Mariachi* may have gone, but director Robert Rodriguez clearly revels in the chance to splash out with the backing of a studio to remake his modest debut feature. Antonio Banderas assumes the mantle of the mysterious guitar-playing stranger who arrives south of the border seeking vengeance against an evil drugs baron and keeps his tongue wedged firmly in cheek as he carries out his acrobatic slaughter of hordes of bad guys. The result is joyful mayhem. Banderas reprised his role in the 2003 sequel, *Once upon a Time in Mexico*. JF. Contains violence, swearing, drug abuse, sex scenes and nudity. [video] DVD

Antonio Banderas *El Mariachi* • Joaquim de Almeida *Bucho* • Salma Hayek *Carolina* • Steve Buscemi *Buscemi* • Cheech Marin [Richard "Cheech" Marin] *Short bartender* • Quentin Tarantino *Pick-up guy* ■ *Dir/Scr* Robert Rodriguez

The Desperado Trail ★★ U

Western 1965 · W Ger/Yug · Colour · 92mins

In this "sauerkraut" western, Harald Reinl dispenses with the frontier romanticism that characterises the source material and introduces a couple of novel twists into the proceedings. Winnetou and his pioneer pal, Old Shatterhand resolve a land war started by an unscrupulous rancher.Reinl lets a native American horde ride to the rescue instead of the cavalry and then he allows his noble hero to die. Pierre Brice would return to fight another day alongside (one-time Tarzan) Lex Barker. DP. A German language film.

Lex Barker *Old Shatterhand* • Pierre Brice *Winnetou* • Rik Battaglia *Rollins* • Ralf Wolter *Sam Hawkins* • Carl Lange *Governor* • Sophie Hardy *Ann* ■ *Dir* Harald Reinl • *Scr* Harald G Petersson, Joachim Bartsch, from the novel *Winnetou, der Röte Gentleman* by Karl Friedrich

The Desperadoes ★★ U

Western 1943 · US · Colour · 86mins

Historically important as Columbia's first feature in Technicolor, this large-scale western has the dubious benefits of some rather garish art direction and some strangely-lit night sequences. The star teaming of Randolph Scott and Glenn Ford makes this routinely plotted tale very watchable, though neither had fully developed their screen persona: Scott isn't quite taciturn enough, and Ford is still very much the juvenile in a role that calls for more maturity. TS

Randolph Scott *Sheriff Steve Upton* • Glenn Ford *Cheyenne Rogers* • Claire Trevor *The Countess* • Evelyn Keyes *Allison McLeod* • Edgar Buchanan *Uncle Willie McLeod* • Guinn "Big Boy" Williams *Nitro Rankin* • Raymond Walburn *Judge Cameron* • Porter Hall *Banker Stanton* ■ *Dir* Charles Vidor • *Scr* Robert Carson, from a story by Max Brand

The Desperados ★★ 15

Western 1969 · US/Spa · Colour · 86mins

Jack Palance – clearly off his rocker and loving every minute – plays a parson who takes his three boys off on an orgy of rape and pillage after the American Civil War. Oldest son Vince Edwards leaves Dad and settles in Texas; six years later, they meet again. Shot in Spain for financial reasons, Henry Levin's film is pretty shoddy in all departments. AT [video]

Vince Edwards *David Galt/David Whitaker* • Jack Palance *Parson Josiah Galt* • George Maharis *Jacob Galt* • Neville Brand *Sheriff Kilpatrick* • Sylvia Syms *Laura* • Christian Roberts *Adam Galt* • Kate O'Mara *Adah* ■ *Dir* Henry Levin • *Scr* Walter Brough, from a story by Clarke Reynolds

Desperate ★★★★

Film noir 1947 · US · BW · 71mins

Director Anthony Mann made a knockout series of B-thrillers in the 1940s that were notable for their cracking pace and economic use of sets and lighting. In this fine example, Steve Brodie plays an honest trucker who is forced to flee the Mob after he gets caught up in a warehouse caper and the killing of a cop. The movie is one virtually continuous flight and has a terrific twist at the end, while there's real directorial skill up there on the screen. TS

Steve Brodie *Steve Randall* • Audrey Long *Anne Randall* • Raymond Burr *Walt Radak* • Douglas Fowley *Pete* • William Challee *Reynolds* • Jason Robards [Jason Robards Sr] *Ferrari* • Freddie Steele *Shorty* ■ *Dir* Anthony Mann • *Scr* Harry Essex, Martin Rackin, from a story by Dorothy Atlas, Anthony Mann

Desperate Characters ★★★

Drama 1971 · US · Colour · 87mins

Shirley MacLaine heads a cast of little-known screen actors in a nightmare glimpse into the horrors of Manhattan life, as perceived, written and directed by Broadway playwright Frank D Gilroy. Covering 48 hours in the life of MacLaine and her husband (Kenneth Mars), there's no conventional narrative, just a series of incidents that reflect the breakdown of urban life and the struggle to live with it. Downbeat, Yet beautifully constructed and acutely observed. RK

Shirley MacLaine *Sophie* • Kenneth Mars *Otto* • Gerald S O'Loughlin *Charlie* • Sada Thompson *Claire* • Jack Somack *Leon* • Chris Gampel *Mike* • Mary Ellen Hokanson *Flo* • Robert Bauer *Young man* • Carol Kane *Young girl* ■ *Dir* Frank D Gilroy • *Scr* Frank D Gilroy, from the novel by Paula Fox

The Desperate Hours ★★★★ PG

Thriller 1955 · US · BW · 107mins

Superbly directed by William Wyler, this searing adaptation of author Joseph Hayes's Broadway hit features the last great villainous performance of Humphrey Bogart, playing an escaped convict holding Fredric March and his family hostage in their own house. The location becomes unbearably claustrophobic as March summons up hidden strengths to protect his loved ones from a criminal who has no redeeming features. This was the first movie to be filmed in black-and-white VistaVision ("motion picture high fidelity"), and the depth of field and overall quality of Lee Garmes's photography is superb. TS DVD

Humphrey Bogart *Glenn* • Fredric March *Dan Hilliard* • Arthur Kennedy *Jesse Bard* • Martha Scott *Eleanor Hilliard* • Dewey Martin *Hal* • Gig Young *Chuck* • Mary Murphy *Cindy* • Richard Eyer *Ralphie* ■ *Dir* William Wyler • *Scr* Joseph Hayes, from his novel and play

Desperate Hours ★★★ 15

Thriller 1990 · US · Colour · 100mins

Michael Cimino's combustible thriller stars Mickey Rourke as the psychotic gangster who invades the suburban home of Anthony Hopkins and Mimi Rogers. Cimino breaks free of the story's stage origins (there are some vivid scenes in the Colorado wilderness) and updates William Wyler's 1955 film version by having Hopkins's marriage on the verge of collapse. The result bristles with drama and visual spectacle. AT. Contains violence and swearing. [video]

Mickey Rourke *Michael Bosworth* • Anthony Hopkins *Tim Cornell* • Mimi Rogers *Nora Cornell* • Lindsay Crouse *Chandler* • Kelly Lynch *Nancy Breyers* • Elias Koteas *Wally Bosworth* • Mike Nussbaum *Mr Nelson* ■ *Dir* Michael Cimino • *Scr* Lawrence Konner, Mark Rosenthal, Joseph Hayes, from the film, novel and play by Joseph Hayes • *Cinematographer* Douglas Milsome

Desperate Journey ★★★ PG

Second World War adventure
1942 · US · BW · 103mins

Superstar Errol Flynn was medically unfit for military service, but fought the Second World War memorably on screen in a series of Warner Bros action adventures, invariably directed with great pace by Raoul Walsh. Here, Flynn and four other RAF recruits crash-land in Germany and attempt to make their way back to England. "Now for Australia and a crack at the Japs!" says our Errol, though another memorable line – "They know but one command – attack!" – was deleted after previews. (Flynn was embroiled in a rape scandal at the time.) TS [video]

Errol Flynn *Flight Lieutenant Terrence Forbes* • Ronald Reagan *Flying Officer Johnny Hammond* • Raymond Massey *Major Otto Baumeister* • Nancy Coleman *Kaethe Brahms* • Alan Hale *Flight Sergeant Kirk Edwards* • Arthur Kennedy *Flying Officer Jed Forrest* • Sig Rumann [Sig Ruman] *Preuss* ■ *Dir* Raoul Walsh • *Scr* Arthur T Horman, from his story *Forced Landing*

Desperate Justice ★★★ PG

Drama 1993 · US · Colour · 88mins

Aside from a charismatically blunt role in *Victor/Victoria* (which scooped her an Oscar nomination), Lesley Ann Warren has more often been at the centre of efficient yet mundane offerings. This is a surprisingly hard-edged TV outing, in which she plays a mother so distraught over her daughter's assault that she shoots the suspected attacker. Director Armand Mastroianni is admirably unsentimental in his approach. JM [video] DVD

Lesley Ann Warren *Carol Sanders* • Bruce Davison *Bill Sanders* • Missy Crider *Jill Sanders* • Allison Mack *Wendy Sanders* • Annette O'Toole *Ellen Wells* • David Byron *Frank Warden* • Shirley Knight *Bess Warden* ■ *Dir* Armand Mastroianni • *Scr* John Robert Bensink, from the novel by Richard Speight

Desperate Living ★★★★ 18

Satirical melodrama
1977 · US · Colour · 90mins

This lurid ensemble melodrama is John Waters's most "serious" work. Peggy Gravel is a highly strung, bourgeois housewife whose quest for self-actualisation and liberation leads her to a fascistic royal kingdom ruled by the very pink and vulgar Queen Carlotta (played respecitvely by Mink Stole and Edith Massey, two Waters regulars). The villagers are commanded to walk and dress backwards, while sex changes, rabies and auto-castration all work their magic into the plot. A woman's picture *par bizarre excellence*, the film may look cheap and cluttered, but it comes with a poignant ending that is endearingly apocalyptic. DM [video]

Mink Stole *Peggy Gravel* • Edith Massey *Queen Carlotta* • Liz Renay *Muffy St Jacques* • Susan Lowe *Mole McHenry* • Mary Vivian Pearce *Princess Coo-Coo* • Jean Hill *Grizelda Brown* • Brook Blake *Bosley Gravel Jr* • Cookie Mueller *Flipper* ■ *Dir/Scr* John Waters (2)

Desperate Measures ★★

Thriller 1995 · Ger/US · Colour · 90mins

This rather tasteless thriller chronicles the attempt of a childless American couple to kidnap the baby of the German nanny they had hired in the middle of what turned out to be a phantom pregnancy. For all the leering malevolence of Matt McCoy and Marita Geraghty, however, director Nikolai Müllerschön fails to generate a sense of menace. DP

Nicolette Krebitz *Anna Richter* • Matt McCoy *Derek Mitchelson* • Marita Geraghty *Carla Mitchelson* • Marco Leonardi *Eddie Sanchez* • Paul Winfield *William Stone* • Carroll Baker *Elaine Mitchelson* ■ *Dir* Nikolai Müllerschön • *Scr* Jennifer Grusskopf

Desperate Measures ★★ 15

Thriller 1998 · US · Colour · 96mins

A good premise, a great cast and an excellent director (Barbet Schroeder) amount to very little in a dumb thriller that rapidly goes downhill. Andy Garcia stars as a policeman who needs the rare bone marrow of the very unhinged Michael Keaton in order to save his ill son. Initially a intriguing, this disappointingly develops into an implausible action thriller as the overacting Keaton runs amok in a hospital and Garcia begins to regret his decision. JC [video] DVD

Michael Keaton *Peter McCabe* • Andy Garcia *Frank Connor* • Brian Cox *Captain Jeremiah Cassidy* • Marcia Gay Harden *Dr Samantha Hawkins* • Erik King *Nate Oliver* • Efrain Figueroa *Vargus* • Joseph Cross *Matthew Conner* • Janel Maloney *Sarah Davis* ■ *Dir* Barbet Schroeder • *Scr* David Klass

Desperate Moment ★★★ U

Mystery thriller 1953 · UK · BW · 88mins

This was one of several films in which handsome young Dirk Bogarde played a fugitive on the run, prior to consolidating his popularity and stardom with the following year's *Doctor in the House*. The meaningless title conceals a ludicrous plot in which Bogarde, believing girlfriend Mai Zetterling is dead, confesses to a murder he did not commit. When he discovers she is still alive, they go off to catch the real villain. Director Compton Bennett fails to get a grip on the narrative, but the stars make it entertaining enough that you don't really care what's going on. TS

Dirk Bogarde *Simon von Halder* • Mai Zetterling *Anna de Burgh* • Philip Friend *Robert Sawyer* • Albert Lieven *Paul* • Frederick Wendhousen *Grote* • Carl Jaffe *Becker* • Gerard Heinz *Bones* • André Mikhelson

Inspector ■ *Dir* Compton Bennett • *Scr* Patrick Kirwan, George H Brown, from the novel by Martha Albrand

The Desperate Ones ★★

Second World War drama
1967 · US/ Sp · Colour · 104mins

Alexander Ramati, a novelist turned film-maker, displayed a deep social conscience and interest the Second World War, especially the experiences of its Jewish and gypsy victims. Regrettably his sturdy movies, such as this and *The Assisi Underground*, lack filmic quality, despite having international star casts. This drama stars his friend Maximillian Schell and Raf Vallone, and tells of prisoners who escape a Siberian prison camp and make a perilous journey to join the Polish army. BB

Maximilian Schell *Marek* • Raf Vallone *Victor* • Irene Papas *Ajmi* • Theodore Bikel *Kisielev* • Maria Perschy *Marusia* • Fernando Rey *Ibram* ■ *Dir* Alexander Ramati • *Scr* Alexander Ramati, from his novel *Beyond the Mountains*

Desperate Remedies ★★★ 18

Period drama 1993 · NZ · Colour · 89mins

The liaisons are more dangerous, the ladies more wicked and the obsessions even more magnificent in this extraordinary historical (not to say hysterical) soap opera from New Zealand. Fabulously stylised sets, amazing design and deafening opera music accompany this gaudy Brontë-esque tale about the fall of high society draper Jennifer Ward-Lealand when she hires a penniless immigrant to marry her opium-addicted sister. John Waters camp meets Pedro Almodovar's kitsch imagery in this little gem, co-directed by Stewart Main and Peter Wells. AJ. Contains violence, swearing, drug abuse and nudity.

Jennifer Ward-Lealand *Dorothea Brook* • Kevin Smith (1) *Lawrence Hayes* • Lisa Chappell *Anne Cooper* • Cliff Curtis *Fraser* • Michael Hurst *William Poyser* • Kiri Mills *Rose* ■ *Dir/Scr* Stewart Main, Peter Wells • *Production Designer* Michael Kane • *Set Designer* Shane Radford

Desperate Search ★★★

Adventure drama 1952 · US · BW · 71mins

This is a tight little drama, beautifully directed by Joseph H Lewis, who became the cult director of such terrific films as *Gun Crazy* and *The Big Combo*. The always under-rated Howard Keel, a major star over this period, said that this unheralded little black-and-white movie was his personal favourite among his films, and he and Jane Greer are exceptionally fine as the parents of two children who are missing after a plane crash. TS

Howard Keel *Vince Heldon* • Jane Greer *Julie Heldon* • Patricia Medina *Nora Stead* • Keenan Wynn *"Brandy"* • Robert Burton *Wayne* • Lee Aaker *Don* ■ *Dir* Joseph Lewis [Joseph H Lewis] • *Scr* Walter Doniger, from the novel by Arthur Mayse

Desperately Seeking Susan ★★★★ 15

Screwball comedy thriller
1985 · US · Colour · 99mins

A delightful and funny movie, most notable for the fact that Madonna is actually very good in it. She's the free-living, wildly dressed Susan who trades messages with her lover in the *New York Times*, while Rosanna Arquette is Roberta, the bored housewife who follows the ads until a bump on the head leads her to believe she actually is Susan. The two lead women are tough and desirable at the same time, and they are ably supported by Mark Blum as Roberta's moronic husband and Aidan Quinn as the man even the strongest woman could not resist being rescued by. Utterly charming. JB. Contains swearing. DVD

Rosanna Arquette *Roberta Glass* • Madonna *Susan* • Aidan Quinn *Dez* • Mark Blum *Gary Glass* • Robert Joy *Jim* • Laurie Metcalf *Leslie Glass* • Will Patton *Wayne Nolan* • Steven Wright *Larry Stillman* • John Turturro *Ray* ■ *Dir* Susan Seidelman • *Scr* Leora Barish

Destination Gobi ★★ U

Second World War drama
1953 · US · Colour · 89mins

A US Navy contingent sent to observe weather conditions in the Gobi desert join forces with the Mongol hordes to fight the Japanese. Richard Widmark delivers his usual no-nonsense performance in this load of old nonsense, which claims to be a true story. Robert Wise keeps the desert scenery shifting while the story remains fairly static. AT

Richard Widmark *CPO Sam McHale* • Don Taylor *Jenkins* • Casey Adams [Max Showalter] *Walter Landers* • Murvyn Vye *Kengtu* • Darryl Hickman *Wilbur Cohen* • Martin Milner *Elwood Halsey* ■ *Dir* Robert Wise • *Scr* Everett Freeman, from a story by Edmund G Love

Destination Inner Space ★★★

Science fiction 1966 · US · Colour · 81mins

When a UFO is discovered at the bottom of the sea near a marine research facility, divers are sent to investigate, only to find a giant amphibian creature with a destructive agenda. Director Francis D Lyon keeps the pace lively, while the underwater scenes are especially well handled. There's also a nicely observed battle of wits between the scientists – keen to study the new species of alien – and the military, who are ever eager to drop a bomb on whatever they don't understand. RS

Scott Brady *Cmdr Wayne* • Sheree North *Sandra* • Gary Merrill *Dr Le Satier* • Mike Road *Hugh Maddox* • Wende Wagner *Rene* • John Howard (1) *Dr James* ■ *Dir* Francis D Lyon • *Scr* Arthur C Pierce

Destination Moon ★★★ U

Science-fiction adventure
1950 · US · Colour · 91mins

Intended to be the first realistic film about space exploration, producer George Pal's fun effort was beaten into cinemas by the exploitation quickie *Rocketship X-M*. But that didn't have an animated lecture on the principles of space travel hosted by Woody Woodpecker! Co-scripted by science-fiction great Robert A Heinlein, the pedestrian tale of man's first lunar landing has dated badly. Yet the enthralling look, taken straight from the pulp fiction illustrations of the day, is enchanting and colourful and the special effects (which won an Oscar) are impressive for the era. AJ

Warner Anderson *Dr Charles Cargraves* • John Archer *Jim Barnes* • Tom Powers *Gen Thayer* • Dick Wesson *Joe Sweeney* • Erin O'Brien-Moore *Emily Cargraves* • Ted Warde *Brown* ■ *Dir* Irving Pichel • *Scr* Rip van Ronkel, Robert A Heinlein, James O'Hanlon • *Special Effects* Lee Zavitz • *Cartoon Sequence* Walter Lantz • *Production Designer* Ernst Fegte

Destination Murder ★★

Thriller 1950 · US · BW · 72mins

Stanley Clements had played young thug roles in some decent movies (notably *Going My Way*). Married to Oscar-winning actress Gloria Grahame, he never managed to turn his teenage toughness into adult charm. This is an average Clements B-movie, of interest only to collectors, though Joyce MacKenzie makes a pert co-star. TS

Joyce MacKenzie *Laura Mansfield* • Stanley Clements *Jackie Wales* • Hurd Hatfield *Stretch Norton* • Albert Dekker *Armitage* • Myrna Dell *Alice Wentworth* • James Flavin *Lt Brewster* ■ *Dir* Edward L Cahn • *Scr* Don Martin

Destination Tokyo ★★★ U

Second World War drama
1943 · US · BW · 129mins

Flag-wavers rarely come as patriotic as this: more than two hours with Cary Grant and John Garfield as they steer their submarine towards Tokyo. Their mission is to land a meteorologist secretly in Japan to tell an aircraft carrier's bombers when the weather will be clear enough for an attack. Getting there is the real story as the sub runs the underwater gauntlet of depth charges and the usual on-board mishaps. Grant, as the captain, does his best in a cardboard role, though Garfield does better as the womaniser with no women around. AT

Cary Grant *Captain Cassidy* • John Garfield *Wolf* • Alan Hale *Cookie* • John Ridgely *Reserve* • Dane Clark *Tin Can* • Warner Anderson *Executive* • William Prince *Pills* • Robert Hutton *Tommy* • Tom Tully *Mike* ■ *Dir* Delmer Daves • *Scr* Albert Maltz, Delmer Daves, from a story by Steve Fisher

Les Destinées Sentimentales ★★★★ 12

Period drama
2000 · Fr/Swi · Colour · 172mins

Adapted with literary respect and cinematic assurance, Olivier Assayas's condensation of Jacques Chardonne's three-volume novel is a remarkable achievement. The visual style is wholly modern, yet never detracts from either the sense of period or the gravity of the themes. The story follows pastor Charles Berling from his desertion of both the church and his adulterous wife (Isabelle Huppert), through his marriage to the inexperienced Emmanuelle Béart and his ongoing obsession with reviving the family porcelain business. Epic, elegant and expertly acted. DP. In French with English subtitles. DVD

Emmanuelle Béart *Pauline* • Charles Berling *Jean Barnery* • Isabelle Huppert *Nathalie* • Olivier Perrier *Philippe Pommerel* • ' [Dominique Reymond] *Julie Desca* • André Marcon *Paul Desca* • Alexandra London *Louise Desca* • Julie Depardieu *Marcelle* ■ *Dir* Olivier Assayas • *Scr* Jacques Fieschi, Olivier Assayas, from a novel by Jacques Chardonne

Destiny ★★★★

Silent fantasy drama
1921 · Ger · BW · 79mins

Luis Buñuel once claimed that *Destiny* "opened my eyes to the poetic expressiveness of the cinema". This dark and mystical allegory was Fritz Lang's first notable critical success, and it remains impressive for its range of mood, the mastery of its visual composition, its extravagant settings and its special effects. Written by Lang with Thea von Harbou (whom he married in 1924), it's the story of a wife (Lil Dagover) who begs Death to spare her husband's life. RB

Lil Dagover *Fiancée/Zobeide/Fiametta/Tiao Tsien* • Walter Janssen *Fiancé/European/Liang* • Bernhard Goetzke *Death/El Mot/Archer* • Rudolf Klein-Rogge *Girolamo* • Lewis Brody *The Moor* ■ *Dir* Fritz Lang • *Scr* Fritz Lang, Thea von Harbou

Destiny of a Man ★★★★

Second World War drama
1959 · USSR · BW · 102mins

Having left his wife and children to fight on the Front during the Second World War, Sergei Bondarchuk is taken prisoner by the Nazis and sent to a concentration camp. He escapes and returns home to find that his family is dead. A powerfully realistic and much acclaimed Russian film, this marks the directing debut of the legendary actor Bondarchuk. He gives a searing portrayal of an ordinary man's despair and courage, and he captures all too graphically the horror of the war as experienced by the Russians. Winner of the best film award at the first Moscow Film Festival, this is heavyweight stuff. RK. Russian dialogue dubbed into English.

Sergei Bondarchuk *Andrei Sokolov* • Zinaida Kirienko *Irina* • Pavlik Boriskin *Vanyushka* • Pavel Volkov *Ivan Timofeyevich* • Yuri Averin *Myuller* ■ *Dir* Sergei Bondarchuk • *Scr* Yuri Lukin, Fyodor Shakhmagonov, from a novel by Mikhail Sholokhov

Destiny Turns on the Radio ★ 15

Comedy fantasy 1995 · US · Colour · 98mins

This self-consciously quirky comedy has a clumsy dollop of mysticism dumped on top. Dylan McDermott stars as an escaped convict returning to Las Vegas to reclaim his stolen cash; Nancy Travis plays his singer ex-girlfriend. Both give charmless performances, while Quentin Tarantino's turn as a supernatural stalker could be the worst acting work by a director ever. JC

Dylan McDermott *Julian* • James LeGros *Thoreau* • Quentin Tarantino *Johnny Destiny* • Nancy Travis *Lucille* • James Belushi *Tuerto* • Janet Carroll *Escabel* ■ *Dir* Jack Baran • *Scr* Robert Ramsey, Matthew Stone

Destroy All Monsters ★★★ PG

Science-fiction fantasy
1968 · Jpn · Colour · 85mins

Alien Kilaaks unleash Toho Studios' entire repertory company of rubber-suited, scaly behemoths to raze a selection of capital cities in this, the ultimate Japanese monster movie. Godzilla attacks New York, Mothra invades Peking and Rodan obliterates Moscow, while Wenda, Baragon and Spigas, the mega-spider from *Son of Godzilla*, all make appearances. This mighty marathon features a zany comic-strip plot, hilariously wooden acting, atrocious dubbing and special effects miniatures that make *Thunderbirds* look like *Terminator 2*. What are you waiting for? Set the video immediately! AJ. Japanese dialogue dubbed into English.

Akira Kubo *Capt Katsuo Yamabe* • Jun Tazaki *Dr Yoshido* • Yoshio Tsuchiya *Dr Otani* • Kyoko Ai *Queen of the Kilaaks* ■ *Dir* Ishiro Honda [Inoshiro Honda] • *Scr* Kaoru Mabuchi, Ishiro Honda

Destroyer ★★

Action thriller 1988 · US · Colour · 94mins

Former football player Lyle Alzado plays a vicious serial killer on his way to the electric chair who vanishes mysteriously during a sudden prison riot. Eighteen months later, a film crew headed by Anthony Perkins arrives at the abandoned prison to shoot a women-in-prison movie. Then the crew start disappearing... Perkins displays a flair for light comedy as the B-director who takes his craft very seriously, while Alzado has definite screen presence. However, most of the proceedings are predictable. KB

Anthony Perkins *Director Edwards* • Lyle Alzado *Ivan Moser* • Deborah Foreman *Susan Malone* • Clayton Rohner *David Harris* • Jim Turner *Rewire* • Lannie Garrett *Sharon Fox* • Tobias Andersen *Russell* • *Dir* Robert Kirk • *Scr* Peter Garrity, Rex Hauck

The Destructors ★

Science-fiction spy adventure
1968 · US · Colour · 96mins

There's little doubt that the low-budget nature of this feeble sci-fi thriller undermines its credibility, while the rabid Cold War xenophobia does nothing for its contemporary appeal. But it's equally obvious that special agent Richard Egan's heart isn't in the search for a consignment of laser rubies that have been stolen from a top secret lab. Michael Ansara valiantly attempts some sinister villainy, but how seriously can you take a swimsuit tycoon masquerading as a spy? DP

Richard Egan *Dan Street* • Patricia Owens *Charlie* • John Ericson *Dutch Holland* • Michael Ansara *Count Mario Romano* • Joan Blackman *Stassa* • David Brian *Hogan* ■ *Dir* Francis D Lyon • *Scr* Larry E Jackson, Arthur C Pierce

Destry ★★★

Western 1954 · US · Colour · 94mins

Good fun, especially for fans of baby-faced Audie Murphy and lovers of Universal westerns of the 1950s, until you realise this is a remake of the superb James Stewart/Marlene Dietrich film *Destry Rides Again*, itself a reworking of an early Tom Mix classic. It isn't up to those distinguished predecessors, and shouldn't really be judged against them as it was made for a whole new generation of film-goers. TS

Audie Murphy *Tom Destry* • Mari Blanchard *Brandy* • Lyle Bettger *Decker* • Lori Nelson *Martha Phillips* • Thomas Mitchell *Rags Barnaby* • Edgar Buchanan *Mayor Hirim Sellers* • Wallace Ford *Doc Curtis* • Alan Hale Jr *Jack Larson* ■ *Dir* George Marshall • *Scr* Edmund H North, DD Beauchamp, from a story by Felix Jackson, from the novel *Destry Rides Again* by Max Brand

Destry Rides Again ★★★★★ PG

Comedy western 1939 · US · BW · 90mins

Remembered today for its rollicking good humour and the fabulous Marlene Dietrich performing *See What the Boys in the Back Room Will Have*, this is one of those comedy westerns that has a universal appeal. Lanky and lovable James Stewart is Tom Destry, who manages to clean up the lawless town of Bottleneck by using a slow drawl rather than a quick draw. Chief villain is scowling, snide Brian Donlevy, and there's marvellous character support. Dietrich, cast against type, and Stewart, in his first western lead, strike sparks off one another (and in real life, too!), and the cat-fight between Dietrich and Una Merkel has never been bettered. Director George Marshall keeps well back, and some may find his style rather flat, but he created a comedy classic. TS [video]

Marlene Dietrich *Frenchy* • James Stewart *Tom Destry* • Mischa Auer *Boris Callahan* • Charles Winninger *"Wash" Dimsdale* • Brian Donlevy *Kent* • Allen Jenkins *Gyp Watson* • Warren Hymer *Bugs Watson* • Una Merkel *Lily Belle Callahan* ■ *Dir* George Marshall • *Scr* Felix Jackson, Henry Meyers, Gertrude Purcell, from the novel by Max Brand

The Detective ★★★ 15

Crime drama 1968 · US · Colour · 109mins

Cynical New York police detective Frank Sinatra is called upon to solve a case involving the brutal murder of a gay man. What follows is a hard-hitting, well-paced drama that takes swipes at slipshod policing and corruption in City Hall and features one of Sinatra's best performances. Sadly, the film's attitude towards homosexuality and sex in general – considered daring back in 1968 – is very dated. SR . Contains violence. [video]

Frank Sinatra *Joe Leland* • Lee Remick *Karen Leland* • Ralph Meeker *Curran* • Jack Klugman *Dave Schoenstein* • Jacqueline Bisset *Norma MacIver* • Horace McMahon *Farrell* • Lloyd Bochner *Dr Roberts* • William Windom *Colin MacIver* • Robert Duvall *Nestor* • Sugar Ray Robinson *Kelly* ■ *Dir* Gordon Douglas • *Scr* Abby Mann, from the novel by Roderick Thorp

Detective ★★★ 15

Detective thriller 1985 · Fr · Colour · 93mins

It's rare that one of French director Jean-Luc Godard's movies actually aims to entertain but this does, being a jokey movie about detective movies in which various characters try to solve a murder committed in a Paris hotel two years earlier. The plot sprouts myriad subplots and Godard dedicates the picture to Clint Eastwood, John Cassavetes and cult 1940s director Edgar G Ulmer. Newish things Nathalie Baye and Johnny Hallyday pleased the contemporary audience, while New Wave icons Claude Brasseur and Jean-Pierre Léaud bring nostalgia to the party. AT. In French with English subtitles. Contains swearing. [video] DVD

Claude Brasseur *Emile Chenal* • Nathalie Baye *Francoise Chenal* • Johnny Hallyday *Jim Fox-Warner* • Laurent Terzieff *Detective William Prospero* • Jean-Pierre Léaud *Nephew* • Alain Cuny *Old Mafioso* • Stephane Ferrara *Tiger Jones* • Emmanuelle Seigner *Grace Kelly, miancée* • Julie Delpy *Wise young girl* ■ *Dir* Jean-Luc Godard • *Scr* Alain Sarde, Philippe Setbon, Anne-Marie Mieville, Jean-Luc Godard

Detective Story ★★★★

Crime drama 1951 · US · BW · 117mins

Sidney Kingsley's smash-hit play about the ugliness of life as seen from the squad room of a drab police station loses none of its claustrophic intensity on screen under William Wyler's resourceful direction. Kirk Douglas is memorable as the cop who despises weakness and wrongdoing, only to find that his intolerance is his undoing. But many others are equally good, including William Bendix (fellow cop), Eleanor Parker (Douglas's wife) and George Macready (despicable abortionist). Only the wet young lovers (Cathy O'Donnell and Craig Hill) are a pain, but at least the Hollywood censors permitted abortion to be retained as an issue. AE

Kirk Douglas *Det James McLeod* • Eleanor Parker *Mary McLeod* • William Bendix *Det Lou Brody* • Lee Grant *Shoplifter* • Bert Freed *Det Dakis* • Frank Faylen *Det Gallagher* • Horace McMahon *Lt Monaghan* • Craig Hill *Arthur Kindred* • George Macready *Karl Schneider* • Joseph Wiseman *Charley Gennini* • Cathy O'Donnell *Susan Carmichael* ■ *Dir* William Wyler • *Scr* Philip Yordan, Robert Wyler, from the play by Sidney Kingsley

Determination of Death ★★

Crime drama 2001 · US · Colour · 100mins

Everywhere you look in Michael Miller's unoriginal crime drama, there's a familiar face. If only he'd found something more productive for them to do. There's an element of suspense in the storyline, which sees Marc Singer, the abusive husband of Michele Greene, seemingly meeting a sticky end on a hunting trip. Despite his family's concern over the ensuing insurance investigation, you'll have to be totally lost in the ironing not to twig what's really going on. DP

Michele Greene *Katie Williams* • Marc Singer *Reese Williams* • Veronica Hamel *Virginia "Ginny" Halloran* • John Ratzenberger *Charlie Halloran* • William Katt *John Logan* • George Dzundza *Mac* ■ *Dir* Michael Miller (2) • *Scr* Sharon Barry McTigue, James Hirsch, from a story by Sharon Barry McTigue

Deterrence ★★★ 15

Political thriller
1999 · US/Fr · Colour · 99mins

In this bomb-crisis thriller, Kevin Pollak stars as the harassed US president, stranded in a diner in the Colorado backwoods and attempting to avert a nuclear catastrophe. Writer/director Rod Lurie cleverly leads us into a gradual acceptance of the unlikely situation through excellent use of the claustrophobic setting. Sheryl Lee Ralph and Timothy Hutton give steady performances as the security advisers who seek to persuade Pollak to disengage his sensibilities in dealing with a rampant Iraq. DP [video]

Kevin Pollak *President Walter Emerson* • Timothy Hutton *Marshall Thompson* • Sean Astin *Ralph* • Sheryl Lee Ralph *Gayle Redford* • Clotilde Courau *Katie* • Badja Djola *Harvey* ■ *Dir/Scr* Rod Lurie

Detour ★★★★ U

Cult thriller 1945 · US · BW · 65mins

A remarkably pacey and stylish B-movie thriller that's now rightly recognised as a minor classic. It's a fitting tribute to skilled director Edgar G Ulmer, who made this hard-boiled little gem in just six days. Lead Tom Neal's lack of acting ability actually helps the stark tale of a hitch-hiker buffeted by fate, and the remarkable Ann Savage creates the kind of *femme fatale* you wouldn't want to meet in the dark. The clever use of night shooting and a score seemingly made up from Chopin's out-takes enhance the grimy tale which is a deeply satisfying example of what enthusiasts today refer to as *film noir*. TS [video]

Tom Neal *Al Roberts* • Ann Savage *Vera* • Claudia Drake *Sue* • Edmund MacDonald *Charles Haskell Jr* • Tim Ryan *Diner proprietor* • Esther Howard *Hedy* • Roger Clark *Dillon* ■ *Dir* Edgar G Ulmer • *Scr* Martin Goldsmith

Detour ★

Crime thriller 1992 · US · Colour · 89mins

This obscure, no-budget thriller has more than a touch of the Ed Woods about it. Seemingly a remake of a well-respected 1945 thriller that starred Tom Neal, this one stars Tom Neal Jr as the hitch-hiker who gets caught up with *femmes fatales*. Junior is no better an actor than his father. JF

Tom Neal Jr *Al Roberts* • Lea Lavish *Vera* • Erin McGrane *Sue Harvey* • Duke Howze *Charles Haskell* • Susanna Foster *Evvy* • Brad Bittiker *Cowboy* ■ *Dir* Wade Williams III • *Scr* Roger Hull, Wade Williams III, from the 1945 film

Detroit 9000 ★★ 18

Blaxploitation crime thriller
1973 · US · Colour · 102mins

A crudely photographed and relentlessly violent cops-and-robbers thriller, blaxploitation style. Jewel thieves make off with $400,000 of loot from attendees at a black congressman's fundraiser in Detroit, the murder capital of the world. Two cops – one black, the other white – are assigned to the case, which plonks the usual clichés (pimps, thugs, hookers and racial hatreds) into a mediocre police procedural. AJ [video]

Alex Rocco *Lieutenant Danny Bassett* • Hari Rhodes *Sergeant Jesse Williams* • Vonetta McGee *Roby Harris* • Ella Edwards *Helen* • Scatman Crothers *Reverend Markham* ■ *Dir* Arthur Marks • *Scr* Orville Hampton, from a story by Arthur Marks, Orville Hampton

Detroit Rock City ★★★ 15

Comedy 1999 · US · Colour · 90mins

High school and the 1970s have always been popular topics in Hollywood. In *Detroit Rock City* they meet head on, with a bit of road movie and country mouse comedy thrown in for good measure. With only the soundtrack to nail down the period, there's a universality about the adventures of four lads bunking off to Motown for a rock concert. The inevitabilities are given nostalgic bravura by the pace and idiosyncrasy of *Mousehunt* scribe Adam Rifkin's direction. DP. Contains swearing and sexual references. [video] DVD

Edward Furlong *Hawk* • Giuseppe Andrews *Lex* • James DeBello *Trip* • Sam Huntington *Jeremiah "Jam" Bruce* • Gene Simmons • Paul Stanley • Shannon Tweed *Amanda Finch* ■ *Dir* Adam Rifkin • *Scr* Carl V Dupré • *Producer* Gene Simmons, Barry Levine, Kathleen Haase

Deuce Bigalow: Male Gigolo ★★ 15

Comedy 1999 · US · Colour · 88mins

Pitched low and hitting even lower, Mike Mitchell's taste-free comedy is an addition to a mainstream "smut glut" spawned by the success of *There's Something about Mary* and *American Pie*. Rob Schneider plays an idiot aquarist who, while fish-sitting for a male escort, gets hooked into servicing a clientele of his own. His customers embrace every physical and mental imperfection, from Tourette syndrome to missing limbs. DA [video] DVD

Rob Schneider *Deuce Bigalow* • Arija Bareikis *Kate* • William Forsythe *Detective Chuck Fowler* • Eddie Griffin *TJ* • Oded Fehr *Antoine LeConte* • Gail O'Grady *Claire* • Richard Riehle *Bob Bigalow* ■ *Dir* Mike Mitchell • *Scr* Harris Goldberg, Rob Schneider

Le Deuxième Souffle ★★★

Crime thriller 1966 · Fr · BW · 149mins

From the opening homage to *A Man Escaped*, the influence of Robert Bresson can be felt throughout this intense investigation into that old cliché about honour among thieves. Yet this *noir*-ish mix of poetic realism and police procedural also bears the imprint of Jean-Pierre Melville, even though the thrilling mountain heist is less typical of his precise style than the cat-and-mouse confrontation between escaped gangster Lino Ventura and circumspect detective Paul Meurisse. DP. In French with English subtitles.

Lino Ventura *Gustave Minda* • Paul Meurisse *Inspector Blot* • Raymond Pellegrin *Paul Ricci* • Christine Fabrega *Manouche* • Pierre Zimmer *Orloff* • Marcel Bozzuffi *Ricci* ■ *Dir* Jean-Pierre Melville • *Scr* Jean-Pierre Melville, José Giovanni, from a novel by José Giovanni

Dev ★★★ 15

Drama 2004 · Ind · Colour · 164mins

Director Govind Nihalani virtually guarantees success to this project by bringing together Indian cinema legends Amitabh Bachchan and Om Puri. Unemployed law graduate Fardeen Khan singles out Bachchan's police commissioner as his target for revenge after his father falls victim to political violence. With Puri trying to prevent Bachchan from jeopardising his career by engaging in a personal feud and Kareena Kapoor seeking to channel her boyfriend's rage, this is a hard-hitting political drama. DP. In Hindi with English subtitles. [video] DVD

Amitabh Bachchan *Dev Pratap Singh* • Om Puri *Tejinder Khosla* • Amrish Puri *Chief Minister Bhandarker* • Fardeen Khan *Farhaan* • Kareena Kapoor *Aaliya* ■ *Dir* Govind Nihalani • *Scr* Meenakshi Sharma

Devdas ★★★ PG

Musical romantic drama
2002 · Ind · Colour · 184mins

There have been numerous adaptations of Sarat Chandra Chatterjee's novel, but this is flattered by the exhilarating presence of

D

Madhuri Dixit. She revels in the role of the Calcutta courtesan who attempts to console country boy Shah Rukh Khan, as he battles with the bottle and his remorse at leaving behind childhood sweetheart, Aishwarya Rai. Director Sanjay Leela Bhansali wisely allows Dixit full rein but it's the magnificent sets and costumes that made this version the most expensive Hindi film ever produced. DP. In Hindi with English subtitles. DVD

Shah Rukh Khan *Devdas Mukherjee* • Aishwarya Rai *"Paro" Parvati* • Madhuri Dixit *Chandramukhi* • Jackie Shroff *Chunnilal* ■ *Dir* Sanjay Leela Bhansali • *Scr* Prakash Kapadia, Sanjay Leela Bhansali, from the novel by Sarat Chandra Chatterjee • *Music/Lyrics* Ismail Darbar

D

Devi ★★★★ PG

Drama 1960 · Ind · BW · 100mins

Examining religious fanaticism, Satyajit Ray's first film after the completion of the Apu trilogy was briefly banned for being disrespectful towards the goddess Kali. But this is as much a study of rural superstition and the passing of a traditional way of life as a calculated assault on the Hindu faith. Exceptionally played, if occasionally melodramatic, it also explores the position of women in Indian society, as Chhabi Biswas destroys his 17-year-old daughter-in-law (Sharmila Tagore) after becoming convinced she is a divine reincarnation. Ray enhances his powerful story with some hauntingly stylised imagery. DP. In Bengali with English subtitles.

Soumitra Chatterjee *Umaprasad* • Sharmila Tagore *Doyamoyee* • Karuna Bannerjee *Harasundari* • Chhabi Biswas *Kalikinkar Roy* ■ *Dir/Scr* Satyajit Ray

The Devil and Max Devlin ★★ PG

Comedy 1981 · US · Colour · 91mins

Despite a wicked turn from Bill Cosby as Satan, this mawkish tale has little in the way of uplifting charm. The hell sequences are easily the most inspired thanks to their devilish design, and the dastardly dialogue between Cosby and sinner Elliott Gould also entertains. But the rest centres on the wishes Gould grants the gullible in return for their souls and is short on laughs and awash with sentiment. DP DVD

Elliott Gould *Max Devlin* • Bill Cosby *Barney Satin* • Susan Anspach *Penny Hart* • Adam Rich *Toby Hart* • Julie Budd *Stella Summers* • David Knell *Nerve Nordlinger* • Sonny Shroyer *Big Billy* • Charles Shamata [Chuck Shamata] *Jerry* ■ *Dir* Steven Hilliard Stern • *Scr* Mary Rodgers, from a story by Mary Rodgers, Jimmy Sangster

The Devil and Miss Jones ★★★ U

Comedy 1941 · US · BW · 92mins

Jean Arthur's smart, sassy brittleness can brighten up any comedy – including this one, which has a touch of Frank Capra in its bogus courting of socialist issues. Arthur plays a shopgirl who suddenly comes face to face with the big boss, zillionaire Charles Coburn, when he decides to get a taste of real life by posing as a shop assistant himself. It has its moments, but what it really needs is a proper leading man. Instead it has Robert Cummings, whose main interest is forming a union. AT

Jean Arthur *Mary Jones* • Robert Cummings *Joe* • Charles Coburn *John P Merrick* • Edmund Gwenn *Hooper* • Spring Byington *Elizabeth* • SZ Sakall *George* • William Demarest *First detective* • Walter Kingsford *Allison* • Montagu Love *Harrison* ■ *Dir* Sam Wood • *Scr* Norman Krasna

Devil and the Deep ★★

Drama 1932 · US · BW · 72mins

Submarine commander Charles Laughton (in his first American film) is consumed with jealousy every time anybody so much as glances in the direction of his glamorous wife Tallulah Bankhead. When he discovers she has formed a more-than-friendly alliance with Gary Cooper, Laughton takes extreme measures that backfire on him. Boasting an appearance by newcomer Cary Grant, this melodrama contrives to be both overheated and undernourished. RK

Tallulah Bankhead *Diana Sturm* • Gary Cooper *Lt Sempter* • Charles Laughton *Cmdr Charles Sturm* • Cary Grant *Lt Jaeckel* • Paul Porcasi *Hassan* • Juliette Compton *Mrs Planet* ■ *Dir* Marion Gering • *Scr* Benn W Levy, from a story by Harry Hervey, from the novel *Sirènes et Tritons, le Roman du Sous-marin* by Maurice Larrouy

The Devil and the Nun ★★★★

Supernatural drama based on a true story 1960 · Pol · BW · 105mins

The winner of the Special Jury prize at Cannes, this intensely disturbing drama is based on the same occurrences at the French convent of Loudun that inspired Ken Russell's *The Devils*. While certainly a stylised representation, director Jerzy Kawalerowicz's version exhibits considerably more restraint in depicting the demonic possession of Ursuline superior Lucyna Winnicka, whose lusts not only consume the other sisters, but also drive devout exorcist Mieczyslaw Voit to murder in a bid to win her favour. DP. In Polish with English subtitles.

Lucyna Winnicka *Mother Joan of the Angels* • Mieczyslaw Voit *Father Jozef Suryn/Rabbi* • Anna Ciepielewska *Sister Malgorzata* • Maria Chwalibog *Awdosia* • Kazimierz Fabisiak *Father Brym* ■ *Dir* Jerzy Kawalerowicz • *Scr* Tadeusz Konwicki, Jerzy Kawalerowicz, from a story by Jaroslaw Iwaszkiewicz

The Devil at Four o'Clock ★★★ PG

Disaster adventure 1961 · US · Colour · 121mins

Director Mervyn LeRoy always enjoyed an exotic location, and this overlong Pacific island-set hokum was probably more fun to make than it is to watch. Our advice is to park your brains and enjoy old-fashioned Hollywood as it lurches into the 1960s, exploding volcano and all. Cast as an agnostic convict, Frank Sinatra gets a chance to act with his idol Spencer Tracy, who never turned down an opportunity to play a priest, his original calling. Compulsively viewable because of the sheer star power on display. TS

Spencer Tracy *Father Matthew Doonan* • Frank Sinatra *Harry* • Kerwin Mathews *Father Joseph Perreau* • Jean-Pierre Aumont *Jacques* • Grégoire Aslan *Marcel* • Alexander Scourby *Governor* • Barbara Luna *Camille* • Cathy Lewis *Matron* ■ *Dir* Mervyn LeRoy • *Scr* Liam O'Brien, from the novel by Max Catto

Devil Bat ★★

Horror 1940 · US · BW · 68mins

One of the better-known films from Bela Lugosi's sad years on Poverty Row. In this tedious and predictable shocker, the *Dracula* star is in his other customary role, playing a mad scientist who takes revenge on his enemies by setting his giant killer bats on them. Although he is laughably hammy, fans rate his performance better than those he would later give for Monogram. DM

Bela Lugosi *Dr Paul Carruthers* • Suzanne Kaaren *Mary Heath* • Dave O'Brien *Johnny Layton* • Guy Usher *Henry Morton* • Yolande Mallott *Maxine* • Donald Kerr *One Shot Maguire* • Edward Mortimer *Martin Heath* ■ *Dir* Jean Yarbrough • *Scr* John Thomas Neville, from a story by George Bricker

The Devil Commands ★★★

Horror 1941 · US · BW · 61mins

Boris Karloff grabs the attention in one of the weirdest movies he made, playing an unhinged scientist trying to communicate with the dead (specifically, his late wife) via a brain-wave recording contraption and stolen corpses. Vastly under-rated, time has been kind to director Edward Dmytryk's macabre miniature. Today, the quaint surrealist touches of wired-up bodies in diving suits give it a strangely quirky atmosphere, while Anne Revere's evil spiritualist adds further chills in a must-see for Karloff collectors. AJ

Boris Karloff *Dr Julian Blair* • Richard Fiske (1) *Dr Richard Sayles* • Amanda Duff *Anne Blair* • Anne Revere *Mrs Walters* • Ralph Penney *Karl* • Dorothy Adams *Mrs Marcy* ■ *Dir* Edward Dmytryk • *Scr* Robert D Andrews, Milton Gunzberg, from the novel *The Edge of Running Water* by William Sloane

Devil Dogs of the Air ★★

Drama 1935 · US · BW · 86mins

This is a very average piece of Marine Flying Corps hokum, with James Cagney and Pat O'Brien striking sparks off each other and air sequences that are a combination of back projection and library shots. It moves fast and looks good, but relies too much on the personalities of its stars. TS

James Cagney *Thomas Jefferson "Tommy" O'Toole* • Pat O'Brien *Lt Bill Brannigan* • Margaret Lindsay *Betty Roberts* • Frank McHugh *Crash Kelly* • Helen Lowell *Ma Roberts* ■ *Dir* Lloyd Bacon • *Scr* Malcolm Stuart Boylan, Earl Baldwin

The Devil-Doll ★★★ PG

Horror 1936 · US · BW · 78mins

The sight of Lionel Barrymore in drag adds a note of merriment to this engagingly bizarre tale of terror, which was the penultimate movie from director Tod Browning, Hollywood's first master of the macabre. Barrymore plays a wrongly convicted criminal who escapes from prison and poses as a sweet old dollmaker, exacting his revenge by using a serum that shrinks people to Barbie size. The scares may be dated, but the miniaturised special effects, relying on oversized props, are still enthralling, and the offbeat fantasy atmosphere is highly unusual. AJ

Lionel Barrymore *Paul Lavond, "Madame Mandelip"* • Maureen O'Sullivan *Lorraine Lavond* • Frank Lawton *Toto* • Robert Greig *Emil Coulvet* • Lucy Beaumont *Madame Lavond* • Henry B Walthall *Marcel* ■ *Dir* Tod Browning • *Scr* Garret Fort, Guy Endore, Erich von Stroheim, from a story by Tod Browning, from the novel *Burn, Witch, Burn!* by Abraham Merritt

Devil Doll ★★ 15

Horror 1964 · UK · BW · 76mins

A cheap British shocker that owes more than a little to the classic ventriloquist episode in *Dead of Night*. Surprisingly highly regarded in some quarters, this low budget exploitation movie features Bryant Halliday as the Great Vorelli, who can transfer souls into his ventriloquist's dummy. TS

Bryant Halliday *The Great Vorelli* • William Sylvester *Mark English* • Yvonne Romain *Marianne* • Sandra Dorne *Vorelli's assistant* • Karel Stepanek *Dr Heller* • Francis De Wolff *Dr Keisling* • Nora Nicholson *Aunt Eva* • Philip Ray *Uncle Walter* ■ *Dir* Lindsay Shonteff • *Scr* George Barclay [Ronald Kinnoch], Lance Z Hargreaves, from a story by Frederick E Smith

Devil Girl from Mars ★★ U

Science fiction 1954 · UK · BW · 73mins

This rare UK contribution to the 1950s sci-fi boom enjoys a certain cult status in the States. Presumably this owes much to the sight of leather-clad Martian Patricia Laffan, as she patrols the Scottish Highlands in search of men to repopulate her ailing planet. It certainly can't be down to the dialogue or the hammed-up performances of journalist Hugh McDermott, model Hazel Court or escaped criminal Peter Reynolds. DP

Hugh McDermott *Michael Carter* • Hazel Court *Ellen Prestwick* • Patricia Laffan *Nyah* • Peter Reynolds *Albert Simpson* • Adrienne Corri *Doris* • Joseph Tomelty *Prof Hennessy* ■ *Dir* David MacDonald • *Scr* John C Maher, James Eastwood, from their play

Devil in a Blue Dress ★★★★ 15

Crime thriller 1995 · US · Colour · 97mins

After his brilliant thriller *One False Move*, director Carl Franklin makes all the right moves with this *film noir*. It's a supremely stylish thriller that has Denzel Washington as a man with time on his hands who's hired to find a politician's girlfriend (Jennifer Beals), and in the process is framed for murder. The film has a timberyard full of sawn-off dialogue and enough high-voltage tension to work an electric chair. TH. Contains violence, swearing, sex scenes and nudity. DVD

Denzel Washington *Ezekial "Easy" Rawlins* • Tom Sizemore *Dewitt Albright* • Jennifer Beals *Daphne Monet* • Don Cheadle *Mouse* • Maury Chaykin *Matthew Terell* • Terry Kinney *Todd Carter* • Mel Winkler *Joppy* • Albert Hall *Odell* • Lisa Nicole Carson *Coretta James* ■ *Dir* Carl Franklin • *Scr* Carl Franklin, from the novel by Walter Mosley

Devil in the Flesh ★★★

Romance 1947 · Fr · BW · 77mins

Set during the last months of the First World War, this once controversial love story stars Micheline Presle as a young wife who embarks on an affair with a 17-year-old schoolboy (Gérard Philipe) while her husband is fighting at the Front. Directed by the Claude Autant-Lara, the film sparked outrage in certain quarters for its uncritically sympathetic portrayal of lovers betraying a soldier away at war. Viewed now, it can be seen as a richly romantic and sensuous tale, supported by two touching lead performances. RB. A French language film.

Micheline Presle *Marthe Grangier* • Gérard Philipe *François Jaubert* • Jean Debucourt *M Jaubert* • Denise Grey *Mme Grangier* • Pierre Palau *M Marin* • Jean Varas *Jacques Lacombe* • Jeanne Pérez *Mme Marin* • Jacques Tati *Soldier in blue* ■ *Dir* Claude Autant-Lara • *Scr* Jean Aurenche, Pierre Bost, from the novel *Le Diable au Corps* by Raymond Radiguet

The Devil Is a Sissy ★★

Drama 1936 · US · BW · 91mins

Three New York schoolboys – rich kid Freddie Bartholomew, middle-class Jackie Cooper, and slum child Mickey Rooney – team up and get into trouble. Deftly directed by WS Van Dyke, this was designed to showcase three members of MGM's impressive roster of juvenile actors. Cooper was already an established star, Bartholomew was on the way up and Rooney was the least-known – though he would become the biggest name and most enduring talent of the three. RK

Freddie Bartholomew *Claude* • Jackie Cooper *"Buck" Murphy* • Mickey Rooney *"Gig" Stevens* • Ian Hunter *Jay Pierce* • Peggy Conklin *Rose* • Katherine Alexander *Hilda Pierce* • Gene Lockhart *Mr Murphy* ■ *Dir* WS Van Dyke • *Scr* John Lee Mahin, Richard Schayer, from a story by Rowland Brown

The Devil Is a Woman
★★★★★

Romantic drama 1935 · US · BW · 79mins

The film that archivist John Kobal described as "a shower of diamonds" and the one that Marlene Dietrich felt best captured her beauty was the final of seven vehicles engineered for her by director Josef von Sternberg, the "Leonardo of the lenses". In it she plays a seductress who, during carnival week in the south of Spain, finds her two most devoted infatuees in a duel for her attentions. A triumph of lighting, make-up and design, this is high camp stylisation of an unusually luxuriant kind, relentlessly amusing but not remotely silly. Even bemused viewers will delight at Dietrich's sublimely ridiculous costumes as well as some of Hollywood's most awe-inspiring imagery. The unobtainable object of desire has never been more sumptuously captured. DO

Marlene Dietrich *Concha Perez* • Lionel Atwill *Don Pasqual* • Cesar Romero *Antonio Galvan* • Edward Everett Horton *Don Paquito* • Alison Skipworth *Señora Perez* • Don Alvarado *Morenito* • Tempe Pigott *Tuerta* • Paco Moreno *Secretary* ■ *Dir* Josef von Sternberg • *Scr* John Dos Passos, SK Winston, from the novel and play *La Femme et le Pantin (The Woman and the Puppet)* by Pierre Louys • *Cinematographer* Josef von Sternberg, Lucien Ballard • *Costume Designer* Travis Banton • *Art Director* Josef von Sternberg, Hans Dreier

The Devil Makes Three
★★ U

Drama 1952 · US · BW · 90mins

This so-so thriller, filmed in Bavaria, enabled MGM to satisfy the "I must do non-musicals" clause in Gene Kelly's contract and use up their postwar frozen Deutschmarks. Andrew Marton directs with verve but little regard for pace; he also fails to stop a miscast Kelly mugging as a counterintelligence officer who returns to Munich to find the German family who saved his life during the war. Pier Angeli brightens up the grim proceedings. TS

Gene Kelly *Capt Jeff Eliot* • Pier Angeli *Wilhelmina Lehrt* • Richard Rober *Col James Terry* • Richard Egan *Lt Parker* • Claus Clausen *Heisemann* • Wilfried Seyferth *Hansig* ■ *Dir* Andrew Marton • *Scr* Jerry Davis, from the story by Lawrence Bachmann [Lawrence P Bachmann]

Devil on Horseback
★★ U

Drama 1954 · UK · BW · 93mins

Juvenile star Jeremy Spenser plays the young son of a miner who becomes a successful jockey, but his cruel tendency to flog the horses has disastrous consequences. Directed by Cyril Frankel, this is well acted, strong on atmosphere and story, but lacks pace and the racing sequences are disappointing. RK

Googie Withers *Mrs Jane Cadell* • John McCallum *Charles Roberts* • Jeremy Spenser *Moppy Parfitt* • Meredith Edwards *Ted Fellowes* • Liam Redmond *"Scarlett" O'Hara* • Sam Kydd *Darky* • Malcolm Knight *Squib* ■ *Dir* Cyril Frankel • *Scr* Neil Paterson, Montagu Slater, from a story by James Curtis

The Devil, Probably
★★ 18

Drama 1977 · Fr · Colour · 91mins

Although it won a prestigious award at Berlin, Robert Bresson's most earnest film is also his least engaging. In having 20-year-old student Antoine Monnier pay a junkie to stage his "suicide" in Père Lachaise (the Parisian cemetery containing many national luminaries), Bresson is clearly lamenting the death of individualism in an indifferent world. However, he is unable to find a suitable motive for the crime. Militant ecologist Henri de Maublanc blames society's ills on pollution and famine, but others seek political, spiritual, cultural and psychological causes. Each case is cogently argued, but the debate never fires the intellect. DP. In French with English subtitles. [VIDEO]

Antoine Monnier *Charles* • Tina Irissari *Alberte* • Henri de Maublanc *Michel* • Laelita Carcano *Edwige* • Regis Hanrion *Dr Mime* • Nicolas Deguy *Valentin* • Geoffroy Gaussen *Bookseller* ■ *Dir/Scr* Robert Bresson

The Devil Rides Out
★★★ 15

Horror 1968 · UK · Colour · 91mins

As a Satanic spectacular, this is the business, even if, for once in a Hammer horror, Christopher Lee is on the side of virtue. Director Terence Fisher searches for credibility in Dennis Wheatley's trashy tale of the Duc de Richleau (Lee) trying to save Patrick Mower's soul from the clutches of Charles Gray, a rotted limb of Satan. Whatever cynical giggles this might cause are soon flattened by the deadpan approach, some seriously orgiastic production numbers and a scary script from the ever-reliable Richard Matheson. TH [VIDEO] DVD

Christopher Lee *Duc de Richleau* • Charles Gray *Mocata* • Nike Arrighi *Tanith* • Leon Greene *Rex* • Patrick Mower *Simon* • Gwen Ffrangcon-Davies *Countess* • Sarah Lawson *Marie* • Paul Eddington *Richard* ■ *Dir* Terence Fisher • *Scr* Richard Matheson, from the novel by Dennis Wheatley

The Devil-Ship Pirates
★★★ PG

Period swashbuckling drama
1964 · UK · Colour · 82mins

Christopher Lee received top-billing for the first time in this agreeable Hammer excursion into swashbuckling costume drama. He's the Spanish captain looting the English coast during the Armada era, who hits on a daring plan to save his crew when his ship runs aground – seal off the area and convince the locals Spain has conquered England. Hammer delivers its usual top-notch production values and Lee indulges in some splendid swordfighting. AJ [VIDEO] DVD

Christopher Lee *Captain Robeles* • Andrew Keir *Tom* • John Cairney *Harry* • Duncan Lamont *Bosun* • Michael Ripper *Pepe* • Ernest Clark *Sir Basil* • Barry Warren *Manuel* ■ *Dir* Don Sharp • *Scr* Jimmy Sangster

The Devil Thumbs a Ride
★★★

Thriller 1947 · US · BW · 62mins

Short and sharp, writer/director Felix Feist's low-budget gem features a no-nonsense performance from Lawrence Tierney. Here he plays a hitch-hiker, picked up by innocent motorist Ted North, who soon reveals himself to be an amoral killer. Tierney's electrifying presence overcomes the talky script and lifts this rarely seen thriller to the status of minor classic. AJ

Lawrence Tierney *Steve* • Ted North *Jimmy* • Nan Leslie *Carol* • Betty Lawford *Agnes* • Andrew Tombes *Joe Brayden* • Harry Shannon *Owens* • Glenn Vernon *Jack* • Marian Carr *Diane* ■ *Dir* Felix Feist • *Scr* Felix Feist, from the novel by Robert C DuSoe

The Devil to Pay
★★★ U

Comedy 1930 · US · BW · 69mins

Ronald Colman's dashing good looks made him a star in the silent era, but what really catapulted him to the ranks of the all-time movie greats was the coming of sound. It revealed an elegant speaking voice that, when gently softened for the American market, became every male's ideal. Here Colman plays the son of a wealthy man who falls for a beautiful socialite (Loretta Lynn) when he returns to London from Africa. It creaks a bit now, but confirms Colman's magnetic screen presence. TS [VIDEO]

Ronald Colman *Willie Leeland* • Loretta Young *Dorothy Hope* • Florence Britton *Susan Leeland* • Frederick Kerr *Lord Leeland* • David Torrence *Mr Hope* • Mary Forbes *Mrs Hope* • Paul Cavanagh *Grand Duke Paul* • Myrna Loy *Mary Carlyle* ■ *Dir* George Fitzmaurice • *Scr* Benjamin Glazer, Frederick Lonsdale, from a play by Frederick Lonsdale

The Devils
★★★★ 18

Historical drama
1971 · UK · Colour · 106mins

Ken Russell's adaptation of Aldous Huxley's *The Devils of Loudun* is repulsive, hysterical, disturbing, overwhelming, stunning, compelling and fascinating. For once, Russell's surreal hallucinogenic style matches his frenzied material and, while condemned as being anti-religious, this is in fact a highly moral tale of absolute faith. In one of the most controversial and censored films of all time, Oliver Reed gives his best ever performance as the 17th-century French priest destroyed by political manipulators, and Vanessa Redgrave is almost as good as a humpbacked nun; Derek Jarman's sets are nearly a match for them both, however. AJ. Contains violence, swearing, sex scenes, drug abuse and nudity. [VIDEO]

Oliver Reed *Father Urbain Grandier* • Vanessa Redgrave *Sister Jeanne* • Dudley Sutton *Baron de Laubardemont* • Max Adrian *Ibert* • Gemma Jones *Madeleine* • Murray Melvin *Mignon* • Michael Gothard *Father Barre* • Georgina Hale *Philippe* ■ *Dir* Ken Russell • *Scr* Ken Russell, from the play by John Whiting, from the novel *The Devils of Loudun* by Aldous Huxley

The Devil's Advocate
★★ PG

Drama 1977 · W Ger · Colour · 104mins

Based on the novel by Morris West, who also wrote the script, this moral fable stars John Mills as a terminally ill Catholic priest who comes to Rome in 1958 to decide if a man executed 14 years earlier deserves canonisation. This is strangely uninvolving, due mainly to having English actors play Italian characters. Tackling the persecution of the Jews as well as homosexuality within the priesthood, Guy Green's movie is also overloaded with would-be significance. AT [VIDEO]

John Mills *Monsignor Blaise Meredith* • Stéphane Audran *Contessa* • Jason Miller *Dr Meyer* • Paola Pitagora *Nina* • Leigh Lawson *Nerone* • Timothy West *Anselmo* • Patrick Mower *Il Lupo* • Raf Vallone *Aurelio* • Daniel Massey *Black* ■ *Dir* Guy Green • *Scr* Morris West, from his novel

The Devil's Advocate
★★ 18

Supernatural thriller
1997 · US · Colour · 137mins

Keanu Reeves plays a hotshot lawyer from Florida who's lured to a New York law firm run by Al Pacino, whose character name, John Milton, is an unsubtle signpost to the diabolical turn of events. The heavy-handed dropping of clues, including supernatural visions from Reeves's ignored wife, Charlize Theron, makes the eventual revelation a very tardy one as far as the viewer is concerned. It's not remotely believable, and is directed with po-faced urgency. AT. Contains swearing, violence and sex scenes. [VIDEO] DVD

Keanu Reeves *Kevin Lomax* • Al Pacino *John Milton* • Charlize Theron *Mary Ann Lomax* • Jeffrey Jones *Eddie Barzoon* • Judith Ivey *Mrs Lomax* • Connie Nielsen *Christabella* • Craig T Nelson *Alexander Cullen* • Don King ■ *Dir* Taylor Hackford • *Scr* Jonathan Lemkin, Tony Gilroy, Andrew Neiderman

The Devil's Arithmetic
★★★ 12

Second World War fantasy drama
1999 · US · Colour · 91mins

A modern teenager, Kirsten Dunst, who only grudgingly accepts the Jewish faith, finds herself swept into the life of a Nazi death camp prisoner when she is asked to "open the front door" at a Seder feast. There, like a refugee Dorothy in *The Wizard of Oz*, she experiences all the Holocaust horrors first hand and learns to understand why traditions are so important to her people. Gritty and raw, if sometimes over-preachy, this historical semi-fantasy packs a punch. AJ [VIDEO] DVD

Kirsten Dunst *Hannah Stern* • Brittany Murphy *Rivkah* • Paul Freeman *Rabbi* • Mimi Rogers *Lenore Stern* • Louise Fletcher *Aunt Eva* • Nitzan Sharron *Ariel* • Shelly Skandrani *Leah* ■ *Dir* Donna Deitch • *Scr* Robert J Avrech, from the novel by Jane Yolen

The Devil's Backbone
★★★★ 15

Period supernatural horror
2001 · Sp/Mex · Colour · 107mins

This allegorical ghost story is set near the end of the Spanish Civil War when ten-year-old Fernando Tielve is sent to a remote orphanage, reputedly haunted by the ghost of a dead boy. There Tielve uncovers a secret involving sadistic young caretaker Eduardo Noriega, who surely represents fascism in the film's vivid metaphor for the war. Mexican director Guillermo del Toro relies on the power of suggestion and sound for the chilling, ever-present horror as the fates of the orphans and their guardians become tragically inter-linked. Though the whodunnit takes a fairly predictable course, the striking imagery is simply poetic. AC. In Spanish with English subtitles. Contains violence, swearing and sex scenes. [VIDEO] DVD

Marisa Paredes *Carmen* • Eduardo Noriega (2) *Jacinto* • Federico Luppi *Casares* • Fernando Tielve *Carlos* • Iñigo Garcés *Jaime* ■ *Dir* Guillermo del Toro • *Scr* Guillermo del Toro, Antonio Trashorras, David Munoz • *Cinematographer* Guillermo Navarro

Devil's Bait
★★ U

Drama 1959 · UK · BW · 58mins

A baker doesn't get on very well with his wife. When he discovers rats on his premises, he hires a rat-catcher who is totally blotto and mixes the cyanide in one of the baker's baking tins. Ah, we think in a Hitchcockian way, now the baker will serve his wife a suspect scone and she'll pass away. But no: all that happens is that a couple of picnickers are sold some poisoned bread and the police are called in to find them. This takes the sting out of the tale, but the cast makes this pass very quickly. AT

Geoffrey Keen *Joe Frisby* • Jane Hylton *Ellen Frisby* • Gordon Jackson *Det Sgt Malcolm* • Dermot Kelly *Mr Love* • Eileen Moore *Barbara* • Molly Urquhart *Mrs Tanner* • Rupert Davies *Landlord* ■ *Dir* Peter Graham Scott • *Scr* Peter Johnston, Diana K Watson

The Devil's Brigade
★★ PG

Second World War adventure
1968 · US · Colour · 130mins

A blatant rip-off of Robert Aldrich's *The Dirty Dozen*, albeit based on truth, with William Holden ordered to train a bunch of thugs to fight the Nazis in the Norwegian mountains. The usual tensions break out and the action scenes are routinely directed by Andrew V MacLaglen. The normally exuberant Holden seems becalmed by the surrounding cheerlessness, though the picture did reunite him with his real-life friend Cliff Robertson. AT DVD

William Holden (2) *Lt Col Robert T Frederick* • Cliff Robertson *Major Alan Crown* • Vince Edwards *Major Cliff Bricker* • Michael Rennie *Lt Gen Mark Clark* • Dana Andrews *Brig Gen Walter Naylor* • Andrew Prine *Theodore Ransom* • Claude Akins *Rocky Rockman* • Richard Jaeckel *Greco* ■ *Dir* Andrew V McLaglen • *Scr* William Roberts, from the book by Robert H Adleman, Col George Walton

Devil's Canyon ★★

Western 1953 · US · Colour · 89mins

Originally filmed in 3-D, this RKO western is actually more of a thriller, as psychotic killer Stephen McNally attempts to wreak revenge on fellow inmate Dale Robertson, a former US marshal serving ten years for his involvement in a fatal shoot-out. Virginia Mayo helps McNally escape from jail, but no prizes for guessing who she ends up with. The period realism of the Arizona Territorial Prison setting makes this an unusual time-passer, but it's all a bit grim, and a stronger cast would have helped. TS

Dale Robertson *Billy Reynolds* • Virginia Mayo *Abby Nixon* • Stephen McNally *Jesse Gorman* • Arthur Hunnicutt *Frank Taggert* • Robert Keith (1) *Steve Morgan* • Jay C Flippen *Captain Wells* ■ *Dir* Alfred Werker • *Scr* Frederick Hazlitt Brennan, Harry Essex, from a story by Bennett R Cohen, Norton S Parker • *Cinematographer* Nicholas Musuraca

Devil's Cargo ★★

Detective mystery 1948 · US · BW · 63mins

Two years after RKO dropped the Falcon franchise, it was snapped up by Poverty Row unit Film Classics, who changed the amateur sleuth's name to Michael Waring and installed professional magician John Calvert in the role. While this enabled Calvert to slip in a couple of conjuring tricks, it did little to bridge the charisma gap left by his predecessors. The formula remained unchanged, however, with Rochelle Hudson's husband facing jail for the murder of her putative lover. Roscoe Karns provides incompetent police support, while Theodore von Eltz and Lyle Talbot head the list of suspects. *Appointment with Murder* was the next instalment. DP

John Calvert *Michael Waring/The Falcon* • Rochelle Hudson *Margo Delgado* • Roscoe Karns *Lieutenant Hardy* • Lyle Talbot *Johnny Morello* • Theodore von Eltz *Thomas Mallon* ■ *Dir* John F Link • *Scr* Don Martin, from a story by Robert Tallman, Jason James, from the character created by Michael Arlen

Devil's Child ★★ 15

Supernatural thriller
1997 · US · Colour · 83mins

Kim Delaney plays a wealthy woman who meets the man of her dreams. In fact, she's so happy she initially fails to spot that he has "666" tattooed on his forehead. Delaney shrieks convincingly in all the right places, but Matthew Lillard steals this TV movie. Bobby Roth's direction is competent, though he doesn't generate enough frights. JF. Contains violence, swearing and sex scenes. DVD

Kim Delaney *Nikki DeMarco* • Thomas Gibson *Alexander Cole* • Colleen Flynn *Ruby* • Matthew Lillard *Tim* • Grace Zabriskie *Rose DeMarco* • Christopher John Fields *Father Darcy* • Larry Holden *Todd Gilman* • Paul Bartel *Dr Zimmerman* • Tracey Walter *Ezra Hersch* ■ *Dir* Bobby Roth • *Scr* Pablo F Fenjves, from a story by Laurence Minkoff, Pablo F Fenjves

The Devil's Disciple ★★ U

Period comedy drama
1959 · US/UK · BW · 83mins

Burt Lancaster took a shine to George Bernard Shaw's comedy of mistaken identity, set during the American War of Independence. So he lured his buddy Kirk Douglas and Laurence Olivier into co-starring with him and hired Alexander Mackendrick to direct. Mackendrick later quit and was replaced by Guy Hamilton. Like so many Shavian adaptations, it sits on the screen like a lump of stodge, the stilted dialogue slowing up the action. Lancaster plays a preacher; Douglas is the good-for-nothing who gets mistaken for him. Olivier, as a British general, plays to the gallery. AT

Burt Lancaster *Anthony Anderson* • Kirk Douglas *Richard Dudgeon* • Laurence Olivier *General Burgoyne* • Janette Scott *Judith Anderson* • Eva Le Gallienne *Mrs Dudgeon* • Harry Andrews *Major Swindon* ■ *Dir* Guy Hamilton • *Scr* John Dighton, Roland Kibbee, from the play by George Bernard Shaw

Devil's Doorway ★★★ U

Western 1950 · US · BW · 84mins

Robert Taylor gives one of his best performances as the Shoshone Indian who fights with distinction in the Civil War but is deprived of his valuable Wyoming spread by racists taking advantage of new homesteading laws. The contrived introduction of an inexperienced female lawyer to argue his case does little to lighten the mood of stark hopelessness. This is a visually powerful film thanks to the keen eye of director Anthony Mann and his cameraman John Alton. AE

Robert Taylor (1) *Lance Poole* • Louis Calhern *Verne Coolan* • Paula Raymond *Orrie Masters* • Marshall Thompson *Rod MacDougall* • James Mitchell *Red Rock* • Edgar Buchanan *Zeke Carmody* • Rhys Williams *Scotty MacDougall* • Spring Byington *Mrs Masters* ■ *Dir* Anthony Mann • *Scr* Guy Trosper

The Devil's Eye ★★ PG

Comedy 1960 · Swe · BW · 83mins

This laboured comedy is one of Ingmar Bergman's poorest pictures. From the moment Gunnar Bjornstrand appears to introduce the methodology, theatricality rests heavily on both the staging and the performances. Jarl Kulle injects a little verve as the playboy released from Hell to seduce parson's daughter Bibi Andersson, thus removing the sty her purity has caused in the devil's eye. DP. In Swedish with English subtitles.

Jarl Kulle *Don Juan* • Bibi Andersson *Britt-Marie* • Axel Duberg *Jonas, her fiancé* • Nils Poppe *Pastor, her father* • Gertrud Fridh *Pastor's wife* • Sture Lagerwall *Pablo* • Stig Järrel *Satan* • Gunnar Björnstrand *Actor* ■ *Dir* Ingmar Bergman • *Scr* Ingmar Bergman, from the radio play *Don Juan Returns* by Oluf Bang

Devil's Gate ★★★ 12A

Mystery drama 2002 · UK · Colour · 99mins

This old-fashioned melodrama is steeped in gothic bleakness, thanks to the Shetland locations. Laura Fraser reluctantly returns to the island of Devil's Gate after receiving a phone call from ex-boyfriend Callum Blue, who tells her that her estranged father (Tom Bell) is dying. Furious to discover the injuries have been exaggerated, she finds herself caught in a web of secrets and intrigue. Director Stuart St Paul's otherworldly tale may be a little overwrought at times, but its careful plotting and attention to character detail make for refreshing viewing. BP

Laura Fraser *Rachael* • Callum Blue *Rafe* • Luke Aikman *Matt* • Tom Bell *Jake* • Roger Ashton-Griffiths *Eagle* • Patrick Gordon *Clem* • Lynda Bellingham *Marlene* ■ *Dir* Stuart St Paul • *Scr* Stuart St Paul, Trevor Todd

The Devil's General ★★★

War drama 1955 · W Ger · BW · 96mins

Featuring an award-winning performance from Curt Jurgens and based on a play by Carl Zuckmayer, this West German-made drama was inspired by the life of Ernst Udets, the highest-ranking German air ace to have survived the Great War, who took his own life just prior to the Second World War because of his disgust with Hitler. Jurgens is General Harras, a loyal patriot and officer, driven to extremes by his abhorrence of the Nazi regime. Well made and engrossing. RB. In German with English subtitles.

Curt Jurgens *General Harras* • Victor de Kowa *Schmidt-Lausitz* • Karl John *Oderbruch* • Eva-Ingeborg Scholz *Fräulein Mohrungen* • Marianne Koch *Dorothea Geiss* • Albert Lieven *Oberst Eilers* ■ *Dir* Helmut Käutner • *Scr* Georg Hurdalek, Helmut Käutner, from a play by Carl Zuckmayer

The Devil's Hairpin ★★

Sports drama 1957 · US · Colour · 83mins

In his second film as director, Cornel Wilde plays a washed-up racing champ who runs a bar and has a drunken girlfriend (Jean Wallace, the star's real-life wife). Goaded into making a comeback, Wilde has to fight his inner demons, which stem from the time when he almost killed his brother. It's a corny story, but petrol-heads should enjoy the racing footage and the sight of some lovely 1950s cars. AT

Cornel Wilde *Nick Jargin* • Jean Wallace *Kelly* • Arthur Franz *Rhinegold* • Mary Astor *Mrs Jargin* • Paul Fix *Doc* • Larry Pennell *Johnny* ■ *Dir* Cornel Wilde • *Scr* James Edmiston, Cornel Wilde, from the novel *The Fastest Man on Earth* by James Edmiston

The Devil's Holiday ★★★

Drama 1930 · US · BW · 80mins

A young manicurist (Nancy Carroll) on the make is rescued from amorality and transformed by the strength of a young man's love. A morality play for its time that has little bearing on life now, this nonetheless remains a tender love story and is sensitively directed by Edmund Goulding, who also wrote it. The film boasts a genuinely affecting performance by Carroll, who narrowly lost the 1929/30 best actress Oscar to Norma Shearer. RK

Nancy Carroll *Hallie Hobart* • Phillips Holmes *David Stone* • James Kirkwood *Mark Stone* • Hobart Bosworth *Ezra Stone* • Ned Sparks *Charlie Thorne* • Morgan Farley *Monkey McConnell* • Jed Prouty *Kent Carr* • Paul Lukas *Dr Reynolds* ■ *Dir* Edmund Goulding • *Scr* Edmund Goulding, from his story

The Devil's in Love ★★

Medical drama 1933 · US · BW · 70mins

A morose-looking Victor Jory (a late replacement for Warner Baxter) stars as the French army doctor falsely accused of murder who runs off to help the poor in Africa. There he falls in love with missionary's niece Loretta Young, here at her most exquisitely beautiful. The contrived and predictable storyline remains watchable thanks to intelligent, lively direction from Wilhelm (later William) Dieterle and a surprise appearance from Bela Lugosi as a military prosecutor. AE

Victor Jory *Lt Andre Morand/Paul Vernay* • Loretta Young *Margot LeSesne* • Vivienne Osborne *Rena* • David Manners *Jean* • C Henry Gordon *Capt Radak* • Herbert Mundin *Bimpy* • Emil Chautard [Emile Chautard] *Father Carmion* • J Carrol Naish *Salazar* • Bela Lugosi *Military prosecutor* ■ *Dir* Wilhelm Dieterle [William Dieterle] • *Scr* Howard Estabrook, from a story by Harry Hervey

Devil's Island ★★

Drama 1940 · US · BW · 65mins

After treating a wounded political revolutionary, respected brain surgeon Boris Karloff is unjustly sentenced to ten years imprisonment on the notorious Devil's Island. There he must survive barbaric conditions and preserve his humanity in the shadow of the guillotine. Condemned by the French government on its first outing, the film was heavily censored and re-released a year later. Karloff's convincing performance holds director William Clemens's reasonable adventure/exposé together. AJ

Boris Karloff *Dr Charles Gaudet* • Nedda Harrigan *Mme Lucien* • James Stephenson *Colonel Armand* • Adia Kuznetzoff *Pierre* • Rolla Gourvitch *Colette* • Will Stanton *Bobo* • Edward Keane *Dr Duval* • Robert Warwick *Demontre* • Pedro De Cordoba *Marcal* ■ *Dir* William Clemens • *Scr* Kenneth Garnet, Don Ryan, from the story *The Return of Doctor X* by Anthony Coldeway, Raymond Schrock

Devil's Island ★★★ 15

Period drama
1996 · Ice/Ger/Nor/Den · Colour · 103mins

Set in the immediate postwar era, this cocked snook at American imperialism is not so self-satisfied as to ignore the very real problems caused by Iceland's cultural, as well as geographical, isolation. A product of the Reykjavik slums, Baltasar Kormákur can almost be excused for his arrogance on returning from visiting his runaway mother in the States. However, our sympathy remains with his put-upon brother Sveinn Geirsson, whose hopes are left as bereft as the abandoned barracks in which his family now lives. Eccentric but engaging. DP. In English and Icelandic with subtitles. Contains swearing, violence.

Baltasar Kormakur *Baddi Tomasson* • Gisli Halldorsson *Tommi Tomasson* • Sigurveig Jonsdottir *Karolina Tomasson* • Halldora Geirhardsdottir *Dolli* • Sveinn Geirsson *Danni Tomasson* • Gudmundur Olafsson *Grettir* ■ *Dir* Fridrik Thor Fridriksson • *Scr* Einar Kárason

Devils of Darkness ★ 15

Horror 1964 · UK · Colour · 84mins

The first British vampire movie to use a contemporary setting finds undead Hubert Noel posing as an artist in Brittany. There he heads a cult of devil worshippers who indulge in orgies with exotic snake dancers and sacrifice innocent tourists on their graveyard crypt altar. Little sense of terror, or even atmosphere, is raised in this undistinguished, stilted dud. AJ

William Sylvester *Paul Baxter* • Hubert Noel [Hubert Noël] *Count Sinistre/Armond du Moliere* • Tracy Reed *Karen* • Carole Gray *Tania* • Diana Decker *Madeline Braun* • Rona Anderson *Anne Forest* • Peter Illing *Inspector Malin* ■ *Dir* Lance Comfort • *Scr* Lyn Fairhurst

Devils on the Doorstep ★★★★

Second World War black comedy drama
2000 · Chi · Colour and BW · 162mins

Treading the fine line between collaboration and resistance, Jiang Wen's sprawling study of life in an isolated Chinese village in the last days of the Japanese occupation provides a fascinating insight into a forgotten aspect of the Second World War. The director also stars as the nobody who suddenly becomes the centre of attention after two prisoners – a Japanese soldier and a Chinese translator – are billeted in his house for interrogation. However, it soon becomes clear the hostages have been abandoned and Jiang is forced to make the unenviable choice between disposing of them or risking his own neck to save them. DP. In Mandarin and Japanese with English subtitles.

Jiang Wen *Ma Dasan* • Jiang Hongbo *Yu'er* • Teruyuki Kagawa *Kosaburo Hanaya* • Yuan Ding *Dong Hanchen* ■ *Dir* Jiang Wen • *Scr* You Fengwei, Shi Jianquan, Shu Ping, Jiang Wen, from a story by Jiang Wen, Shu Ping, from the novella *Shengcun* by You Fengwei

The Devil's Own ★★ 15

Thriller 1997 · US · Colour · 106mins

Bedevilled by production problems (constant script changes, disenchanted Brad Pitt wanting to quit, changes in the political situation while shooting), it's hardly surprising that director Alan J Pakula's IRA thriller is a fudged disappointment. Harrison Ford is the New York cop who takes Irish émigré Pitt into his home without realising he's a wanted terrorist on a missile-buying mission for the Republican cause. Both dramatically and politically incorrect. AJ. Contains swearing and violence. [VIDEO] DVD

Harrison Ford *Tom O'Meara* • Brad Pitt *Frankie McGuire, "Rory Devaney"* • Margaret Colin *Sheila O'Meara* • Rubén Blades *Edwin "Eddie" Diaz* • Treat Williams *Billy Burke* • George Hearn *Peter Fitzsimmons* • Mitchell Ryan *Chief Jim Kelly* • Natascha McElhone *Megan Doherty* • David O'Hara *Martin MacDuff* ■ *Dir* Alan J Pakula • *Scr* David Aaron Cohen, Vincent Patrick, Kevin Jarre

The Devil's Playground ★★ U

Western 1946 · US · BW · 65mins

This was the first of 12 Hopalong Cassidy features to be produced by their star, silver-haired William Boyd. Boyd ensured his character operated according to a rigid ethical code, unusual considering that Hopalong dressed entirely in black, the clothing usually worn by the western villain, and rode a lone range. Here, he's accompanied by sidekick Andy Clyde and his trusty steed Topper. An excellent example of a series western, and a fine introduction to Clarence E Mulford's gentleman cowboy. TS

William Boyd (1) *Hopalong Cassidy* • Andy Clyde *California Carlson* • Rand Brooks *Lucky Jenkins* • Elaine Riley *Mrs Evans* • Robert Elliott *Judge Morton* • Joseph J Greene *Sheriff* ■ *Dir* George Archainbaud • *Scr* Doris Schroeder, from a story by Ted Wilson, from characters created by Clarence E Mulford

The Devil's Playground ★★★ 15

Drama 1976 · Aus · Colour · 94mins

A nicely structured, if a tad po-faced look at the awkward sexual awakenings of boys at a Roman Catholic boarding school, made by Australian writer/director Fred Schepisi and based on his childhood experiences. Schepisi's intelligent screenplay gives the little-known Australian cast a chance to indulge in a great deal of entertaining breast-beating. But he doesn't take us any deeper into the issue than a legion of others before him. SH [VIDEO]

Arthur Dignam *Brother Francine* • Nick Tate *Brother Victor* • Simon Burke *Tom Allen* • Charles McCallum *Brother Sebastian* • John Frawley *Brother Celian* • Jonathan Hardy *Brother Arnold* • Gerry Duggan *Father Hanrahan* ■ *Dir/Scr* Fred Schepisi

The Devil's Rain ★★★

Horror 1975 · US/Mex · Colour · 85mins

A colourful, if confusing Satanic shocker with coven leader Ernest Borgnine searching for an ancient book that will enable him to deliver a fresh batch of souls to the prince of darkness. Worth persevering through the muddled set-up for the effects-laden climax where most of the cast members are reduced to screaming, oozing slime. Also notable for the sight of *Star Trek*'s William Shatner tied naked to a sacrificial altar, and a brief appearance from John Travolta. AJ

Ernest Borgnine *Jonathan Corbis* • Eddie Albert *Dr Richards* • Ida Lupino *Mrs Preston* • William Shatner *Mark Preston* • Keenan Wynn *Sheriff Owens* • Tom Skerritt *Tom Preston* • Joan Prather *Julie Preston* • John Travolta *Danny* ■ *Dir* Robert Fuest • *Scr* Gabe Essoe, James Ashton, Gerald Hopman

The Devil's Rejects ★★★ 18

Horror 2005 · US/Ger · Colour · 109mins

Rob Zombie follows up his 2001 debut *House of 1000 Corpses* with a pitch-black sequel that's bigger and nastier in every way. The film swaps the original's flashy visuals and surreal atmosphere for unflinching brutality and ultra-gritty realism. The crimes of the depraved Firefly family finally catch up with them, forcing the serial-killing Otis (Bill Moseley), Baby (Sheri Moon) and Captain Spaulding (Sid Haig) to run for their lives. This boasts grainy, 1970s-style cinematography and an evocative period soundtrack. If Zombie hasn't yet entirely found his own voice, he still demonstrates greater confidence and skill here. SF Contains violence and swearing.

Sid Haig *Captain Spaulding* • Bill Moseley *Otis* • Sheri Moon *Baby* • William Forsythe *Sheriff John Wydell* • Leslie Easterbrook *Mother Firefly* • Matthew McGrory *Tiny* ■ *Dir* Rob Zombie • *Scr* Rob Zombie, from his characters

The Devil's Wanton ★★★

Drama 1949 · Swe · BW · 72mins

Based on his own script, Ingmar Bergman's first important film contains many of his later philosophical preoccupations, particularly his view of a Godless, loveless universe. Over-ambitious, though interesting in the light of its creator's entire oeuvre, it tells of a director and writer who become embroiled in the wretched life of a suicidal prostitute. Made very cheaply and using sets from another movie, it made no profit but enhanced Bergman's reputation in Sweden. However, he had to wait six years for *Smiles of a Summer's Night* to make his name internationally. RB. In Swedish with English subtitles.

Doris Svedlund *Birgitta-Carolina Soderberg* • Birger Malmsten *Thomas* • Eva Henning *Sofi* • Hasse Ekman *Martin Grande* • Stig Olin *Peter* • Irma Christenson *Linnea* • Anders Henrikson *Paul* ■ *Dir/Scr* Ingmar Bergman

Devotion ★★★ U

Biographical drama 1946 · US · BW · 106mins

Writers are notoriously difficult to portray on film: since writing is an intellectual concept and cinema a visual medium, how does one convey what makes a writer write? Director Curtis Bernhardt doesn't bother with such ramifications, though. Olivia de Havilland and Ida Lupino play Charlotte and Emily Brontë, both of whom lust after Paul Henreid, while Arthur Kennedy is excellent as the alcoholic Bramwell. This romanticised saga could be about anybody, but it's still a splendid period melodrama. TS

Ida Lupino *Emily Brontë* • Olivia de Havilland *Charlotte Brontë* • Nancy Coleman *Anne Brontë* • Paul Henreid *Nicholls* • Sydney Greenstreet *Thackeray* • Arthur Kennedy *Branwell Brontë* • Dame May Whitty *Lady Thornton* ■ *Dir* Curtis Bernhardt • *Scr* Keith Winter, from a story by Theodore Reeves

Dharam Veer ★★★ PG

Fantasy adventure
1977 · Ind · Colour · 154mins

Take a deep breath before settling down with this swashbuckling fairy tale because the action is as spectacular as it is complicated. Wild tigers, wise hawks, wicked princes and heroic gypsies all have their part to play here, but the core plotline concerns Dharmendra and Jeetendra as twin boys separated at birth. One is raised in luxury, the other as a woodcutter's son, but romance and a court conspiracy bring them together. Director Manmohan Desai specialised in lost brother stories with the focus firmly on escapism. DP. In Hindi with English subtitles. [VIDEO]

Dharmendra *Dharam* • Jeetendra *Veer* • Pran *Hunter* • Zeenat Aman *Princess* ■ *Dir* Manmohan Desai • *Scr* Prayag Raj, KB Pathak

Dhoom ★★★ 12

Action thriller 2004 · Ind · Colour · 128mins

Director Sanjay Gadhvi places the emphasis in this rousing adventure firmly on adrenalin action, as detective Abhishek Bachchan enlists the help of motorcycle rebel Uday Chopra to nab suave crook John Abraham. Consequently, Esha Deol and Rimi Sen are confined to love-interest musical interludes, as Gadhvi glorifies the speeding machines and their photogenic riders. Style unashamedly triumphs over substance throughout, but the story rattles along and the set pieces are very slickly staged. DP. In Hindi with English subtitles. [VIDEO] DVD

Abhishek Bachchan *Jai Dixit* • John Abraham *Kabir* • Uday Chopra *Ali* • Esha Deol *Sheena* • Rimi Sen *Sweety Dixit* ■ *Dir* Sanjay Gadhvi • *Scr* Vijay Krishna Acharya

Les Diables ★★★★ 15

Drama 2002 · Fr/Sp · Colour · 105mins

By opening with the song from Charles Laughton's *The Night of the Hunter*, director Christophe Ruggia here alerts us to the fact that Adèle Haenel and Vincent Rottiers are children in peril. However, there's no single villain in the mould of Robert Mitchum's manic preacher, but an entire society that has failed the mentally traumatised girl and her tougher brother, who were abandoned by their mother and now seek to survive either inside institutions or on the run. Ruggia pulls off a dramatic coup midway through, but the strength of this affecting film lies in its authenticity, sensitivity and the intensity of the performances. DP. In French with English subtitles.

Adèle Haenel *Chloé* • Vincent Rottiers *Joseph* • Rochdy Labidi *Karim* • Jacques Bonnaffé *Doran* • Aurélia Petit *Joseph's mother* • Galamelah Lagraa *Djamel* ■ *Dir* Christophe Ruggia • *Scr* Christophe Ruggia, Olivier Lorelle

Diabolically Yours ★★★

Psychological thriller
1967 · Fr · Colour · 93mins

Diabolically dubbed, more like. This excellent Gallic thriller, the last film made by master director Julien Duvivier (*Pépé le Moko*), was distributed worldwide in a version that saddled handsome Alain Delon and sexy Senta Berger with bland American accents, a poor decision that seriously affects the credibility of their characters. Not that it really matters, for this is one of those glossy French thrillers where the goodies are good-looking, the baddies are slimy and all the plot twists unravel by the end. TS. French dialogue dubbed into English.

Alain Delon *Pierre* • Senta Berger *Christiane* • Sergio Fantoni *Freddie* • Peter Mosbacher *Kim* ■ *Dir* Julien Duvivier • *Scr* Julien Duvivier, Paul Gégauff, from the novel by Louis Thomas

Diabolique ★★ 18

Thriller 1996 · US · Colour · 102mins

If ever a film didn't need a Hollywood remake, it's Henri-Georges Clouzot's superb, twist-packed 1954 thriller *Les Diaboliques*, about a corpse that refuses to stay dead. Director Jeremiah Chechik hasn't got the foggiest idea how to create atmosphere, relying instead on melodramatic performances and the odd thunderstorm. Sharon Stone is suitably icy and Chazz Palminteri loathsome as the husband, but they deserve better than this. JC. Contains violence, swearing, nudity. [VIDEO] DVD

Sharon Stone *Nicole Horner* • Isabelle Adjani *Mia Baran* • Chazz Palminteri *Guy Baran* • Kathy Bates *Shirley Vogel* • Spalding Gray *Simon Veatch* • Shirley Knight *Edie Danziger* • Allen Garfield *Leo Kaztman* ■ *Dir* Jeremiah Chechik • *Scr* Don Roos, from the 1954 film *Les Diaboliques*

Les Diaboliques ★★★★★ 15

Thriller 1954 · Fr · BW · 116mins

When a sadistic headmaster's wife and mistress plot together to kill him – and then find his body is missing – the result is a brilliantly nasty thriller from Henri-Georges Clouzot. Paul Meurisse is the headmaster, Simone Signoret the mistress and Vera Clouzot the wife, while the climax is one of cinema's most diabolical scenes. The film has a graveyard gloom to match the school's oppressive atmosphere of neglect, while the final shot marvellously suggests unpleasantness to come. A masterpiece in its own terrifying way. TH. In French with English subtitles. [VIDEO] DVD

Simone Signoret *Nicole Horner* • Vera Clouzot *Christina Delassalle* • Paul Meurisse *Michel Delassalle* • Charles Vanel *Inspector Fichet* • Pierre Larquey *M Drain* • Noël Roquevert *M Herboux* • Jean Brochard *Plantiveau* • Thérèse Dorny *Mme Herboux* • Michel Serrault *Raymond* ■ *Dir* Henri-Georges Clouzot • *Scr* Henri-Georges Clouzot, Jérôme Géromini, Frédéric Grendel, René Masson, from the novel *Celle Qui N'Etait Plus* by Pierre Boileau, Thomas Narcejac • *Cinematographer* Armand Thirard

D

Diabolo Menthe ★★★★ 12

Romantic drama 1977 · Fr · Colour · 96mins

Director Diane Kurys also wrote the script for this highly-rated French film, an insightful portrayal of early adolescence that was extensively based on her own experiences. The film follows a rebellious schoolgirl through her spell at a stuffy French lycée. It's a rollercoaster ride whose ups and downs encompass sadistic teachers and first periods, parental divorce and first love. Kurys would later draw on other life experiences for such films as *Cocktail Molotov* and *C'est la Vie*, but this is widely regarded as the best of her bunch. DA. In French with English subtitles. Contains some sexual references. [VIDEO]

Eléonore Klarwein *Anne Weber* • Odile Michel *Frederique Weber* • Anouk Ferjac *Madame Weber* • Coralie Clément *Perrine Jacquet* • Marie Véronique Maurin *Muriel Cazau* • Valérie Stand *Martine Dubreuil* ■ *Dir/Scr* Diane Kurys

Diagnosis: Murder ★★

Crime thriller 1974 · UK · Colour · 90mins

Psychiatrist Christopher Lee is suspected of murdering his wife after she disappears. The twist is that he was planning to murder her anyway so he could be with his mistress. This tepid made-for-television thriller received a brief theatrical release thanks to its star cast, which includes Jon Finch, Judy Geeson and Tony Beckley. A stoic performance from Lee and a few whodunnit wrinkles along the way make it of passing interest. AJ

Jon Finch *Inspector Lomax* • Judy Geeson *Helen* • Christopher Lee *Dr Stephen Hayward* • Tony Beckley *Sergeant Green* • Dilys Hamlett *Julia Hayward* • Jane Merrow *Mary Dawson* • Colin Jeavons *Bob Dawson* ■ *Dir* Sidney Hayers • *Scr* Philip Levene

Dial M for Murder ★★★★ PG

Thriller 1954 · US · Colour · 100mins

Alfred Hitchcock only took on this version of Frederick Knott's play to fulfil his Warners contract, and such was his lack of interest in the project that he claimed he could have phoned in his direction and that the action wouldn't have been any less interesting if he had staged it in a phone box. But as Ray Milland plots to bump off wife Grace Kelly there are plenty of deft touches that loudly proclaim "genius at work". Milland's sinister sophistication catches the eye, but Kelly's subtly shaded suffering is superb. Remade with Michael Douglas and Gwyneth Paltrow in 1998 as *A Perfect Murder*. DP DVD

Ray Milland *Tony Wendice* • Grace Kelly *Margot Wendice* • Robert Cummings *Mark Halliday* • John Williams *Chief Inspector Hubbard* • Anthony Dawson *Captain Lesgate* • Patrick Allen *Pearson* • George Leigh *William* • George Alderson *Detective* • Robin Hughes *Police sergeant* ■ *Dir* Alfred Hitchcock • *Scr* Frederick Knott, from his play

The Diamond ★★

Crime drama 1954 · UK · BW · 83mins

A rare UK venture into 3-D, this crime programme-filler was shot in a process called Spacemaster. The action follows American detective Dennis O'Keefe as he teams with British bobby Philip Friend to uncover how a batch of synthetic diamonds links two seemingly unconnected incidents – a bullion robbery and the disappearance of an atomic scientist. Mostly shown in its flat format, the film was jointly directed by its star and Montgomery Tully, who was something of a dab hand at atmosphere-free mysteries. DP

Dennis O'Keefe *Treasury Agent Joe Dennison* • Margaret Sheridan *Marlene Miller* • Philip Friend *Chief Inspector McClaren* • Alan Wheatley *Thompson Blake* • Francis De Wolff *Yeo* ■ *Dir* Dennis O'Keefe, Montgomery Tully • *Scr* John C Higgins, from the novel *Rich Is the Treasure* by Maurice Procter

Diamond City ★★ U

Drama 1949 · UK · BW · 90mins

A mediocre attempt by the British film industry to transplant the wide-open spaces, excitement and gunslinging of the American western to the veldts of South Africa. Stolid David Farrar tries to bring law and order to the titular diamond-mining town, which takes some doing as the movie was shot at Denham Studios in London. Rank starlets Honor Blackman and Diana Dors play saloon girls and have a catfight, but there's little else to recommend in this lacklustre oddity. AJ

David Farrar *Stafford Parker* • Honor Blackman *Mary Hart* • Diana Dors *Dora* • Niall MacGinnis *Hans Muller* • Andrew Crawford *David Raymond* • Mervyn Johns *Hart* ■ *Dir* David MacDonald • *Scr* Roland Pertwee, from a story by Roger Bray

Diamond Head ★★★

Melodrama 1962 · US · Colour · 106mins

Charlton Heston plays a powerful landowner with ambitions to be Hawaii's senator. When his sister Yvette Mimieux plans to marry Polynesian James Darren (in heavy make-up), Heston does everything he can to prevent it – despite having a Hawaiian mistress who's pregnant with his child. This isn't the Hawaii of grass skirts, ukeleles, hula-hula and aloha. Instead it's the exotic setting for a no-holds-barred melodrama, with Heston simmering impressively like the Diamond Head volcano of the title. AT

Charlton Heston *Richard Howland* • Yvette Mimieux *Sloan Howland* • George Chakiris *Dr Dean Kahana* • France Nuyen *Mei Chen* • James Darren *Paul Kahana* • Aline MacMahon *Kapiolani Kahana* ■ *Dir* Guy Green • *Scr* Marguerite Roberts

The Diamond Queen ★★ U

Period adventure 1953 · US · Colour · 76mins

A swashbuckler about a French adventurer (Fernando Lamas) who goes to India in search of a jewel fit for the crown of Louis XIV. There he finds a big, fat, sparkly diamond attached to Maya, queen of Nepal (Arlene Dahl), who is herself attached to the Great Mogul, a jealous cove played by Sheldon Leonard. As usual with these essays in exotica, there's a lot of silly dialogue, lavish costumes and lascivious dance routines. Lamas and Dahl married shortly after the film was completed. AT

Fernando Lamas *Jean Tavernier* • Arlene Dahl *Maya* • Gilbert Roland *Baron Paul de Cabannes* • Sheldon Leonard *Great Mogul* • Jay Novello *Gujar* • Michael Ansara *Jumla* • Richard Hale *Gabriel Tavernier* ■ *Dir* John Brahm • *Scr* Otto Englander, from his story

Diamond Skulls ★★★ 18

Drama 1989 · UK · Colour · 83mins

In its own quiet way, Gabriel Byrne's CV is one of the most impressive in modern cinema. Here he opts for a picture that might not have rung too many box-office bells, but which has a couple of interesting ideas and offers him a chance to extend his already considerable range of characters. In a rare venture into fictional films, documentary specialist Nick Broomfield only scratches the surface of his themes of class responsibility and dangerous obsession. Yet he maintains the dramatic tension more than adequately. DP. Contains violence, swearing, sex scenes.

Gabriel Byrne *Lord Hugo Buckton* • Amanda Donohoe *Ginny Buckton* • Douglas Hodge *Jamie* • Sadie Frost *Rebecca* • Matthew Marsh *Raul* • Michael Hordern *Lord Crewne* • Judy Parfitt *Lady Crewne* • Ralph Brown *Jack* • Ian Carmichael *Exeter* ■ *Dir* Nick Broomfield • *Scr* Tim Rose Price, from an idea by Nick Broomfield, Tim Rose Price

Diamonds ★ PG

Crime drama 1975 · US/Is · Colour · 103mins

A heist picture with Robert Shaw in a dual role as two brothers: one a jewel thief, the other a security expert. This sort of set-up is both technically cumbersome and rather tiresome, and the film does not disappoint on either count, being very tedious and shoddily made. Shelley Winters contributes an excruciating cameo. AT

Robert Shaw *Charles/Earl Hodgson* • Richard Roundtree *Archie* • Barbara Seagull [Barbara Hershey] *Sally* • Shelley Winters *Zelda Shapiro* • Shai K Ophir *Moshe* • Gadi Yageel *Gaby* ■ *Dir* Menahem Golan • *Scr* Menaham Golan, David Paulsen, from a story by Menaham Golan

Diamonds ★★

Comedy drama
1999 · US/Ger · Colour · 91mins

To see Kirk Douglas slowed by both his own physical disability and a banal script is sad indeed. The 83-year-old actor plays a man who, like himself, is suffering from the aftereffects of a stroke. His son (Dan Aykroyd) wants him to go into a home, but Dad, who used to be a boxer, wants to stay independent. Deciding to pick up the gems he was once paid to throw a fight, Douglas, his son and grandson (Corbin Allred) drive to Reno. The dialogue is tedious and the ideas are older than Douglas himself; he deserves better than this. TH

Kirk Douglas *Harry* • Lauren Bacall *Sin-Dee* • Dan Aykroyd *Lance* • Corbin Allred *Michael* • Jenny McCarthy *Sugar* • Kurt Fuller *Moses* • Mariah O'Brien *Tiffany* • John Landis *Gambler* ■ *Dir* John Asher [John Mallory Asher] • *Scr* Allan Aaron Katz

Diamonds Are Forever ★★ PG

Spy adventure 1971 · UK · Colour · 114mins

After *You Only Live Twice*, Sean Connery said "Never again", but after George Lazenby's sole effort in *On Her Majesty's Secret Service*, Connery was lured back for a fee of more than $1 million, which he donated to the Scottish International Educational Trust. One of the weakest Bonds, its plot about diamond smuggling develops rather tiresomely, while Connery simply goes through the motions. The Las Vegas sequences have some dash, and Bruce Glover and Putter Smith make an intriguing double-act as gay hitmen. AT DVD

Sean Connery *James Bond* • Jill St John *Tiffany Case* • Charles Gray *Blofeld* • Lana Wood *Plenty O'Toole* • Jimmy Dean *Willard Whyte* • Bruce Cabot *Saxby* • Putter Smith *Mr Kidd* • Bruce Glover *Mr Wint* • Norman Burton *Felix Leiter* • Joseph Furst *Dr Metz* • Bernard Lee *"M"* • Desmond Llewelyn *"Q"* • Leonard Barr *Shady Tree* • Lois Maxwell *Miss Moneypenny* ■ *Dir* Guy Hamilton • *Scr* Richard Maibaum, Tom Mankiewicz, from the novel by Ian Fleming

Diamonds for Breakfast ★★ U

Crime caper 1968 · UK · Colour · 102mins

Coming off Visconti's *The Stranger*, Marcello Mastroianni clearly felt the need for an easier assignment, and he sleepwalks through this dotty crime caper that, like so many 1960s co-productions, sought to reproduce the suave heroism of the Bond movies. He plays a shop-owner who is fourth in line to the Russian throne. Debutant director Christopher Morahan failed to invest much fun or excitement into this tale of an impoverished nobleman's bid to swipe the Romanov gems with the help of seven sexy assistants. DP

Marcello Mastroianni *"Nicky", Grand Duke Nicholas* • Rita Tushingham *Bridget* • Elaine Taylor *Victoria* • Maggie Blye *Honey* • Francesca Tu [Francisca Tu] *Jeanne* • Warren Mitchell *Popov* • Leonard Rossiter *Inspector* ■ *Dir* Christopher Morahan • *Scr* Pierre Rouve, NF Simpson, Ronald Harwood

Diamonds in the Rough ★★

Crime comedy 1996 · US · Colour · 100mins

There's so much plot packed into this breakneck crime comedy that it's hard to keep track of just who is duping whom. Jim Gray and David Richard star as a couple of delivery drivers who find themselves up to their necks in gangsters, crooked cops and jealous hairdressers after they're tricked into a diamond robbery by receptionist Michelle Verhunce. The ensuing mayhem is taken at a ferocious clip by writer/director Serge Rodnunsky. DP

Jim Gray *Erick* • David Richard *Ralph* • Michelle Verhunce *Gina* • Gina La Piana *Maria* • Jonathan Lutz *Detective Michaels* ■ *Dir/Scr* Serge Rodnunsky

Diamonds on Wheels ★★ U

Action adventure
1973 · UK/US · Colour · 81mins

This generally robust children's thriller, one of Disney's British productions, centres on a 24-hour car rally. Three teenagers (one of whom is Peter Firth) enter the race, unaware of stolen diamonds hidden in their car. The villains (Barry Jackson and Dudley Sutton) give chase. Unfortunately the film runs out of steam when it leaves the racetrack. Director Jerome Courtland was a juvenile lead in Hollywood in the 1940s. DM

Peter Firth *Robert Stewart* • Dudley Sutton *Finch* • Andrew McCulloch *Billy* • Cynthia Lund *Susan Stewart* • Derek Newark *Mercer* • George Sewell *Henry* • Spencer Banks *Charlie Todd* • Barry Jackson *Wheeler* ■ *Dir* Jerome Courtland • *Scr* William Robert Yates, from the novel *Nightmare Rally* by Pierre Castex

Diana & Me ★★

Romantic comedy
1997 · Aus · Colour · 97mins

Toni Collette plays a frumpy Australian innocent whose name, Diana Spencer, wins her a trip to London. There her efforts to meet her namesake lead to much crossing of paths, misadventures with paparazzi Dominic West and her transformation from geek to chic. Written and produced before the Princess of Wales's death, this reeks of bad taste, despite the addition of an opening scene that turns the rest of the movie into a flashback. AME

Toni Collette *Diana Spencer* • Dominic West *Rob Naylor* • Malcolm Kennard *Mark Fraser* • Victoria Eagger *Carol* • John Simm *Neil* • Serena Gordon *Lady Sarah Myers-Booth* • Roger Barclay *Richard* • Tom Hillier *Neville* • Jerry Hall • Bob Geldof • Kylie Minogue ■ *Dir* David Parker • *Scr* Matt Ford, from a screenplay (unproduced) by Elizabeth Coleman

Diane ★★ U

Historical romance
1955 · US · Colour · 110mins

"Sweater girl" Lana Turner is in period costume as Diane de Poitier, the love consultant to French king Pedro Armendáriz who nevertheless falls for the king's son, Roger Moore. Stuffed to the frills with Hollywood detail, this lavish production does benefit from its majestic score by the great Miklos Rozsa. The dialogue, however, betrays none of the usual wit and grace of its writer, Christopher Isherwood. TH

Lana Turner *Diane* • Roger Moore *Prince Henri* • Pedro Armendáriz *Francis I* • Marisa Pavan *Catherine de Medici* • Cedric Hardwicke *Ruggieri* • Torin Thatcher *Count de Breze* • Taina Elg *Alys* ■ *Dir* David Miller • *Scr* Christopher Isherwood, from the novel *Diane de Poitier* by John Erskine

Diary for My Children ★★★★ PG

Political biographical drama
1982 · Hun · BW · 106mins

Winner of the special jury prize at Cannes, this is the first part of Marta Mészáros's superb *Diary* trilogy. Based on her own experiences in Budapest after her family returned from exile in the Soviet Union, the film gives such a precise portrait of a nation coming to terms with the strictures of communism that it was not shown in the west until 1984. Although time and place are established with great skill, the direction is curiously dispassionate for an autobiography. DP. In Hungarian with English subtitles.

Zsuzsa Czinkoczi *Juli* • Anna Polony *Magda* • Jan Nowicki *Janos* • Tamas Toth *Janos's son* • Mari Szemes *Grandmother* • Pal Zolnay *Grandfather* ■ *Dir/Scr* Marta Mészáros

Diary for My Father and Mother ★★★

Political biographical drama
1990 · Hun · Colour and BW · 110mins

The concluding part of director Marta Mészáros's autobiographical trilogy, which began with *Diary for My Children* and continued with *Diary for My Loves*. Tracing the course and consequences of the 1956 uprising in Hungary, the film is more focused on historical events than its predecessors. So, while those familiar with the central characters will have an advantage, the action should still be comprehensible to new viewers. Mészáros spins her complex web of shifting loyalties, dubious motives and personal crises with great skill. DP. In Hungarian with English subtitles.

Zsuzsa Czinkoczi *Juli* • Jan Nowicki *Janos* • Mari Torocsik *Vera* • Ildiko Bansagi *Ildi* • Anna Polony *Magda* • Lajos Balazsovits • Jolan Jaszai • Irina Kouberskaya ■ *Dir* Marta Mészáros • *Scr* Marta Mészáros, Eva Pataki

Diary for My Loves ★★★★ PG

Political biographical drama
1987 · Hun · Colour and BW · 130mins

The second sequel to *Diary for My Children* takes events from the death of Stalin to the 1956 Hungarian uprising. Again, Marta Mészáros humanises this momentous period by focusing on Zsuzsa Czinkoczi, the 18-year-old girl whose determination to use her Moscow film scholarship to trace her imprisoned father results in a relationship with activist Jan Nowicki. Acted with integrity and consistently probing the psychological depths of its characters, this is a highly personal yet acutely political film. DP. In Hungarian with English subtitles.

Zsuzsa Czinkoczi *Juli* • Anna Polony *Magda* • Jan Nowicki *Janos* • Pal Zolnay *Grandfather* • Mari Szemes *Grandmother* • Irina Kouberskaya *Anna Pavlova* • Adel Kovats *Natacha* ■ *Dir* Marta Mészáros • *Scr* Marta Mészáros, Eva Pataki

Diary of a Chambermaid ★★★

Drama 1946 · US · BW · 86mins

Although ostensibly a vehicle for Paulette Goddard, penned and co-produced by her then-husband, Burgess Meredith, this is also a bold attempt by Jean Renoir to make a comedy of domestic manners in the style of his own *La Règle du Jeu*, within the strictures of the Hollywood system. While his intentions are undermined by the inconsistent playing of a seemingly well-chosen cast, Meredith's adaptation and Renoir's direction are not without merit. DP

Paulette Goddard *Celestine* • Burgess Meredith *Capt Mauger* • Hurd Hatfield *Georges* • Francis Lederer *Joseph* • Judith Anderson *Mme Lanlaire* • Florence Bates *Rose* • Irene Ryan *Louise* ■ *Dir* Jean Renoir • *Scr* Burgess Meredith, from the novel by Octave Mirbeau

The Diary of a Chambermaid ★★★★ 12

Drama 1964 · Fr/It · BW · 93mins

Shifting the action from the turn of the century to 1928, Luis Buñuel's reworking of Octave Mirbeau's novel is far more savage than Jean Renoir's 1946 version. Buñuel scathingly reveals the fascist tendencies of the French bourgeoisie, while simultaneously presenting a hilarious gallery of grotesques for us to laugh at. Jeanne Moreau plays Célestine as a cooly calculating customer, while Michel Piccoli's rakish husband and Georges Géret's bigoted gamekeeper are both suitably loathsome. A mercilessly bitter film, undeservedly overshadowed by the director's other masterpieces. DP. In French with English subtitles. [video] DVD

Jeanne Moreau *Célestine* • Georges Géret [Georges Geret] *Joseph* • Michel Piccoli *M Monteil* • Françoise Lugagne *Mme Monteil* • Daniel Ivernel *Capitaine Mauger* • Jean Ozenne *M Rabour* • Gilberte Géniat *Rose* • Jean-Claude Carrière *Curé* ■ *Dir* Luis Buñuel • *Scr* Luis Buñuel, Jean-Claude Carrière, from the novel by Octave Mirbeau

Diary of a City Priest ★★

Drama 2001 · US · Colour · 78mins

Based on the autobiography of Catholic priest Father John McNamee, this worthy drama owes an obvious debt to Georges Bernanos's, *Diary of a Country Priest*, which was memorably filmed in 1950 by Robert Bresson. David Morse's inner-city cleric feels the agony of loneliness and the demands on his faith as he ministers to his Philadelphia parishioners. Director Eugene Martin tries to emulate Bresson's pared down approach, but the decision to animate some of the saints in the stained-glass windows of St Malachy's church to turn Morse's deliberations into dialogue was a miscalculation. DP

David Morse *Father John McNamee* • John Ryan *Father Dave Hagan* • Phillip Goodwin *St Francis of Assisi* • Ana Reeder *St Therese* • Robert Sella *St Malachy* • Judy Bauerlein *Sister Mary* ■ *Dir* Eugene Martin • *Scr* Eugene Martin, from the autobiography by Father John McNamee

Diary of a Country Priest ★★★★★ U

Drama 1950 · Fr · BW · 114mins

One of the most influential films ever made, this sublime masterpiece shows how an adaptation can remain faithful to its source while still being wholly cinematic. Building atmosphere, character and content through the gradual accumulation of detail, director Robert Bresson minutely captures the agony, humility and despair suffered by a dying priest who feels he has failed in his mission to increase the holiness of his flock. Claude Laydu, whose first film this was, is utterly convincing in the lead role, and the result is an almost spiritual experience. Although Bresson was forced by his distributors to cut 40 minutes, this is nonetheless a glorious example of the power that cinema can attain. DP. In French with English subtitles.

Claude Laydu *Priest of Ambricourt* • Nicole Ladmiral *Chantal* • Nicole Maurey *Mademoiselle Louise* • Marie-Monique Arkell *Countess* • Armand Guibert *Priest of Torcy* • Jean Riveyre *Count* • Jean Danet *Olivier* ■ *Dir* Robert Bresson • *Scr* Robert Bresson, from the novel by Georges Bernanos • *Cinematographer* Léonce-Henri Burel

Diary of a Hitman ★★ 18

Crime thriller 1992 · US · Colour · 86mins

This ambitious but gloomy existential thriller never really shakes off its stage origins despite an impressive cast. Forest Whitaker plays a world-weary assassin who has an attack of conscience when he is hired to kill Sherilyn Fenn and her Aids-afflicted child. The performances are impressively low-key, but it's just a little too talky and static. JF [video]

Forest Whitaker *Dekker* • Sherilyn Fenn *Jain* • Sharon Stone *Kiki* • Seymour Cassel *Koenig* • James Belushi *Shandy* • Lewis Smith *Zidzyk* ■ *Dir* Roy London • *Scr* Kenneth Pressman, from his play *Insider's Price*

Diary of a Lost Girl ★★★★★ PG

Silent drama 1929 · Ger · BW · 74mins

It took German director GW Pabst to recognise the unique qualities of Louise Brooks, ill-used by Hollywood. Having made the exquisite bob-haired actress into an enduring icon with *Pandora's Box*, charting the decline and fall of the amoral Lulu, this followed immediately. This time Brooks's heroine descends into degradation as an innocent victim of circumstance, suffering harsh and painful cruelties at the hands of a social order dominated by sex, money and hypocrisy. Massacred by the censors – apparently almost half the film was excised before its release – but what remains is an absorbing masterpiece of silent cinema. RK [video]

Louise Brooks *Thymiane Henning* • Josef Rovensky *Robert Henning* • Fritz Rasp *Meinert* • Edith Meinhard *Erika* • Vera Pawlowa *Aunt Frieda* • André Roanne *Count Osdorff* • Arnold Korff *Elder Count Osdorff* • Andrews Engelmann *Director of reform school* ■ *Dir* GW Pabst • *Scr* Rudolf Leonhardt, from the novel *Das Tagebuch einer Verlorenen* by Margarethe Boehme

Diary of a Mad Housewife ★★★★

Drama 1970 · US · Colour · 94mins

An acerbic, witty and perceptive peek at the world of American housewife Carrie Snodgress, married to ineffable snob Richard Benjamin and locked into an affair with suave author Frank Langella. Snodgress was never this good again (she was nominated for an Oscar for her performance). Benjamin virtually repeated his smarmy performance in *Marriage of a Young Stockbroker* the following year. TS

Richard Benjamin *Jonathan Balser* • Frank Langella *George Prager* • Carrie Snodgress *Tina Balser* • Lorraine Cullen *Sylvie Balser* • Frannie Michel *Liz Balser* • Lee Addoms *Mrs Prinz* ■ *Dir* Frank Perry • *Scr* Eleanor Perry, from the novel by Sue Kaufman

Diary of a Madman ★★

Horror 1963 · US · Colour · 96mins

Nineteenth-century French magistrate Vincent Price inherits an invisible evil spirit when he accidentally kills a condemned murderer in prison. This entity, the "Horla", then forces him to slash to death Nancy Kovack, the opportunistic model who has been posing for his amateur sculptures. Then he discovers the Horla responds unfavourably to fire. Standard horror fare, with a neat period atmosphere and Price having another shuddery field day in a tailor-made histrionic role. AJ

Vincent Price *Simon Cordier* • Nancy Kovack *Odette* • Chris Warfield *Paul* • Elaine Devry *Jeanne* • Stephen Roberts *Rennedon* • Lewis Martin *Priest* • Ian Wolfe *Pierre* • Edward Colmans *Andre* • Mary Adams *Louise* ■ *Dir* Reginald Le Borg • *Scr* Robert E Kent, from the story *La Horla* by Guy de Maupassant

Diary of a Serial Killer ★ 18

Thriller 1997 · US · Colour · 88mins

While investigating transvestite nightlife, a struggling freelance writer stumbles across a serial killer in action. But rather than report the crime to the driven detective in charge of the case, he strikes up a bizarre deal to document the killer's motives and handiwork. A promising concept is ruined by the soap opera approach and the miscast lead actors. AJ. Contains swearing and violence. [video] DVD

Gary Busey *Nelson Keece* • Michael Madsen *Haynes* • Arnold Vosloo *Stefan* • Julia Campbell *Juliette* • Reno Wilson *Larou* ■ *Dir* Alan Jacobs, Joshua Wallace • *Scr* Jennifer Badham-Stewart, Christopher Koefoed

Diary of a Sex Addict ★★★ 18

Erotic thriller 2001 · US · Colour · 93mins

Less trashy than the title suggests, this is actually a frank and troubling attempt to seriously tackle a genuine addiction. Michael Des Barres offers just the right combination of charm and sleaze as the English married restaurant owner who leads a voracious double life, while Rosanna Arquette and Nastassja Kinski add further credibility as wife and psychiatrist, respectively. Shot on digital video with jump cuts that emphasise Des Barres mounting mental anxiety, this is a fairly convincing portrait of a rarely tackled psychological problem. JC [video] DVD

Rosanna Arquette *Grace Horn* • Nastassja Kinski *Jane Bordeaux* • Michael Des Barres *Sammy Horn* • Ed Begley Jr *Dr Aaron Spencer* • Alexandra Paul *Katherine* ■ *Dir* Joseph Brutsman • *Scr* Tony Peck, Joseph Brutsman

The Diary of Anne Frank ★★★★★ U

Drama based on a true story
1959 · US · BW · 176mins

This is a marvellous screen version of the most moving stories to emerge from the tragedy of the Second World War, about a Jewish girl forced to hide from the Nazis in occupied Amsterdam. It's beautifully directed by George Stevens in claustrophobic black-and-white CinemaScope, and superbly cast, with doe-eyed Millie Perkins near-perfect as Anne, the role that made Susan Strasberg a star on stage. Shelley Winters garnered a best supporting Oscar, and Academy Awards also rightly went to the camerawork and art direction. Under-rated on its release, this is not as well-known as it deserves. TS [video] DVD

Millie Perkins *Anne Frank* • Joseph Schildkraut *Otto Frank* • Shelley Winters *Mrs Van Daan* • Ed Wynn *Mr Dussell* • Richard Beymer *Peter Van Daan* • Gusti Huber *Mrs Frank* • Lou Jacobi *Mr Van Daan* • Diane Baker *Margot Frank* ■ *Dir* George Stevens • *Scr* Frances Goodrich, Albert Hackett, from their play, from the diary by Anne Frank • *Cinematographer* William C Mellor • *Art Director* Lyle Wheeler, George W Davis • *Music* Alfred Newman

D

The Diary of Lady M ★★ 18

Drama
1992 · Swi/Bel/Sp/Fr · Colour · 112mins

Resuming low-budget film-making after a couple of high-profile ventures, Alain Tanner directs what is clearly a vanity project. As the tempestuous leader of an all-girl cabaret act, Mézières is not afraid to flaunt herself as she seduces both Catalan artist Juanjo Puigcorbé and his black wife, Félicité Wouassi. With so much soft-focus sex and so many scenes of Mézières writhing with her pen as she commits her *pensées* to paper, this feels more like a porn flick than the work of a major art house talent. Wincingly trite. DP. French dialogue with English subtitles.

Myriam Mézières *M* • Juanjo Puigcorbé *Diego* • Félicité Wouassi *Nuria* • Nanou • Marie Peyrucq-Yamou • Gladys Gambie ■ *Dir* Alain Tanner • *Scr* Myriam Mézières

The Diary of Major Thompson ★★★ U

Comedy 1955 · Fr · BW · 87mins

The last outing for Hollywood writer/director Preston Sturges, who by the time he made this in France seemed more interested in running restaurants than making films. Britain's debonair Jack Buchanan, at the end of his career, still sparkles and is remarkably well-cast. There's much to enjoy in this semi-sophisticated farce with a genuinely Gallic air, faithfully based on author Pierre Daninos's very popular book. But be warned: the crude dubbing mars the American version. TS. A French language film.

Jack Buchanan *Major Thompson* • Martine Carol *Martine* • Noël-Noël *Taupin* ■ *Dir* Preston Sturges • *Scr* Preston Sturges, from the novel *Les Carnets du Major Thompson* by Pierre Daninos

Dick ★★★ 12

Comedy 1999 · US · Colour · 90mins

Clueless meets *All the President's Men* in this comedy, which stars Kirsten Dunst and Michelle Williams as two dim teens who stumble into the Watergate break-in and soon find themselves working as presidential dogwalkers for "Tricky Dick". It playfully tweaks at the Watergate myths, with the girls becoming fixtures in the Nixon White House and eventually serving as "Deep Throat". Williams's taped confession of her crush on the president is a high point, as is Dan Hedaya as a foul-mouthed Nixon. ST [video] DVD

Kirsten Dunst *Betsy Jobs* • Michelle Williams *Arlene Lorenzo* • Dan Hedaya *President Richard M Nixon* • Dave Foley *Bob Haldeman* • Harry Shearer *G Gordon Liddy* • Ana Gasteyer *Rosemary Woods* • Will Ferrell *Bob Woodward* • Bruce McCulloch *Carl Bernstein* • Teri Garr *Helen Lorenzo* ■ *Dir* Andrew Fleming • *Scr* Andrew Fleming, Sheryl Longin

Dick Tracy ★★ PG

Detective adventure 1945 · US · BW · 58mins

Cartoonist Chester Gould's square-jawed detective had a remarkable career that culminated when Warren

Beatty played him in the 1990 all-star extravaganza. This was the first Dick Tracy feature, though the sleuth had previously appeared in four superb serials, incarnated by rugged Ralph Byrd. This flick isn't terribly good; the detective is played by Morgan Conway, who completed two features before public demand had him replaced with Byrd. More cheap than cheerful. TS

Morgan Conway *Dick Tracy* • Anne Jeffreys *Tess Trueheart* • Mike Mazurki *Splitface* • Jane Greer *Judith Owens* • Lyle Latell *Pat Patton* • Joseph Crehan *Chief Brandon* • Mickey Kuhn *Tracy Jr* • Trevor Bardette *Prof Starling* • Morgan Wallace *Steven Owens* ■ *Dir* William Berke • *Scr* Eric Taylor, from the comic strip by Chester Gould

Dick Tracy ★★★★ PG

Detective adventure 1990 · US · Colour · 100mins

A strange yet successful departure for Warren Beatty, who nurtured this marvellous-looking rendition of the 1940s comic strip for several years and through many rewrites. Beatty takes the title role as the laconic and almost monosyllabic detective surrounded by villains of a more colourful hue, such as Al Pacino as Big Boy. The film was received with faint but reverential praise at the time, though Beatty fails to inject the enterprise with any great depth or warmth. A near-perfect example, however, of how to bring florid characters off the page and on to the screen. SH. DVD

Warren Beatty *Dick Tracy* • Madonna *Breathless Mahoney* • Al Pacino *Big Boy Caprice* • Glenne Headly *Tess Trueheart* • Charlie Korsmo *Kid* • Mandy Patinkin *88 Keys* • Charles Durning *Chief Brandon* • Paul Sorvino *Lips Manlis* • William Forsythe *Flattop* • Dustin Hoffman *Mumbles* • James Caan *Spaldoni* • Kathy Bates *Mrs Green* • Dick Van Dyke *Da Fletcher* • Estelle Parsons *Mrs Trueheart* • Jim Wilkey *Stooge* ■ *Dir* Warren Beatty • *Scr* Jim Cash, Jack Epps Jr, from the comic strip by Chester Gould • *Cinematographer* Vittorio Storaro • *Art Director* Richard Sylbert, Rick Simpson

Dick Tracy Meets Gruesome ★★ PG

Detective adventure 1947 · US · BW · 62mins

A rare instance of one of those weirdly named cartoon creations sharing title billing with our hero, and rightly so, since Gruesome is played by the great Boris Karloff, top-billed over cinema-goers' favourite Dick Tracy, Ralph Byrd. This was the last Tracy movie until Warren Beatty donned the fedora four decades later, and the plot's a hoot: Karloff uses deep-freeze gas to hold people in place while he robs banks. TS DVD

Boris Karloff *Gruesome* • Ralph Byrd *Dick Tracy* • Anne Gwynne *Tess Trueheart* • Edward Ashley *LE Thal* • June Clayworth *Dr IM Learned* • Lyle Latell *Pat Patton* • Tony Barrett *Melody* • Skelton Knaggs *X-Ray* • Jim Nolan *Dan Sterne* • Joseph Crehan *Chief Brandon* ■ *Dir* John Rawlins • *Scr* Robertson White, Eric Taylor, from a story by William H Graffis, Robert E Kent, from the comic strip by Chester Gould

Dick Tracy vs Cueball ★★ PG

Detective adventure 1946 · US · BW · 59mins

The second of RKO's Dick Tracy B-movies, with the detective portrayed by the vapid Morgan Conway; Ralph Byrd, who had played the role more convincingly for Republic, would return to the part in the last two RKO films. This is an apprentice work for director Gordon M Douglas and he keeps the pace up well. Sadly, the production values are shoddy. TS DVD

Morgan Conway *Dick Tracy* • Anne Jeffreys *Tess Trueheart* • Lyle Latell *Pat Patton* • Rita Corday *Mona Clyde* • Ian Keith *Vitamin Flintheart* • Dick Wessel *Cueball* • Douglas Walton *Priceless* • Esther Howard *Filthy Flora* • Joseph Crehan *Chief Brandon* ■ *Dir* Gordon M Douglas [Gordon Douglas] • *Scr* Dane Lussier, Robert E Kent, from a story by Luci Ward, from the comic strip by Chester Gould

Dick Tracy's Dilemma ★★ PG

Detective adventure 1947 · US · BW · 57mins

In the penultimate feature in the RKO series, the studio at last realised the wisdom of casting Ralph Byrd as Chester Gould's comic-strip detective. Byrd, who had previously played Tracy in four Republic serials, seemed born to play the role, and audiences warmed to him. Though unadventurous, it's a perfectly respectable addition to the series. TS DVD

Ralph Byrd *Dick Tracy* • Kay Christopher *Tess Trueheart* • Lyle Latell *Pat Patton* • Jack Lambert *The Claw* • Ian Keith *Vitamin Flintheart* • Bernadene Hayes *Longshot Lillie* ■ *Dir* John Rawlins • *Scr* Robert Stephen Brode, from the comic strip by Chester Gould

Dick Turpin – Highwayman ★★ U

Period drama 1956 · UK · Colour · 26mins

There may not be a lot to detain the casual viewer in this brisk tale of highway robbery, which sees Philip Friend stealing the golden dowry of Diane Hart, only for a mutual attraction to develop between them. However, David Paltenghi's slickly directed short is significant in that it launched Hammer Films' very own widescreen process, Hammerscope, which would be used on such prestige projects as *The Abominable Snowman* (1957). DP

Philip Friend *Dick Turpin* • Diane Hart *Liz* • Allan Cuthbertson *Redgrove* • Gabrielle May *Genevieve* • Hal Osmond *Mac* • Raymond Rollett *Hawkins* • Norman Mitchell *Rooks* ■ *Dir* David Paltenghi • *Scr* Joel Murcott

Dickie Roberts: Former Child Star ★★★ 12

Comedy 2003 · US · Colour · 94mins

There are more laughs than you might expect in this light-hearted vehicle from David Spade. He plays a washed-up former child star who, having missed his real-life childhood, is unable to generate the emotion necessary to clinch a possible movie comeback. To solve the problem, he moves in with an all-American family. The screenplay degenerates into schmaltz occasionally but Spade creates an unusual character who, despite being self-obsessed, is oddly vulnerable and likeable. AS DVD

David Spade *Dickie Roberts* • Mary McCormack *Grace Finney* • Jon Lovitz *Sidney Wernick* • Craig Bierko *George Finney* • Alyssa Milano *Cyndi* • Rob Reiner • Scott Terra *Sam Finney* • Jenna Boyd *Sally Finney* • Edie McClurg *Mrs Gertrude* ■ *Dir* Sam Weisman • *Scr* Fred Wolf, David Spade

The Dictator ★★

Period romance 1935 · UK/Ger · BW · 87mins

Among the most expensive pictures then produced in Britain, this costume drama had prestige written all over it. It boasted lavish sets by the Russian designer André Andreyev and sumptuous cinematography by Franz Planer. It even had a fascinating story to tell, as Denmark's 18th-century ruler Charles VII is deposed by his wife, Caroline Mathilde, and a German doctor who falls in love with her on a medical visit. But under the direction of Victor Saville, the action is suffocated by too much pomp. DP

Clive Brook *Struensee* • Madeleine Carroll *Queen Caroline* • Emlyn Williams *King Charles VII* • Alfred Drayton *Brandt* • Nicholas Hannen *Goldberg* • Helen Haye *Queen Mother Juliana* ■ *Dir* Victor Saville • *Scr* Benn Levy, Hans Wilhelm, HG Lustig, Michael Logan, from a story by HG Lustig, Michael Logan

Did You Hear the One about the Traveling Saleslady? ★ U

Comedy 1968 · US · Colour · 96mins

A showcase for the larger-than-life comedy monster Phyllis Diller, here playing a travelling saleslady who roams the west peddling player pianos. Her career is derailed when she arrives in a small town and her Pianola throws a fit. Local inventor Bob Denver claims he can fix her instrument, but instead embroils her in a number of farcical situations. A charmless offering. DF

Phyllis Diller *Agatha Knabenshu* • Bob Denver *Bertram Webb* • Joe Flynn *Shelton* • Eileen Wesson *Jeanine* • Jeanette Nolan *Ma Webb* • Paul Reed *Pa Webb* • Bob Hastings *Lyle* • David Hartman *Constable* ■ *Dir* Don Weis • *Scr* John Fenton Murray, from a story by Jim Fritzell, Everett Greenbaum

Didier ★★★

Fantasy sports comedy 1997 · Fr · Colour · 105mins

A bizarre but funny and offbeat French comedy from actor/director Alain Chabat. Jean-Pierre Bacri discovers his friend's pet pooch has miraculously turned into a man (Chabat). Capitalising on the canine's capability with balls, Bacri hires the man/dog out as a top footballer. Managing to weave into this farcical tale the odd poignant comment on racial tolerance, this is a darn sight better than your average "straight" sports movie, while Chabat is quite remarkable in the title role. LH. A French language film.

Alain Chabat *Didier* • Jean-Pierre Bacri *Costa* • Isabelle Gelinas *Maria* • Caroline Cellier *Annabelle* • Lionel Abelanski • Jean-Marie Frin • Michel Bompoil ■ *Dir/Scr* Alain Chabat

Didn't Do It for Love ★★★ 18

Documentary 1997 · Ger · Colour · 78mins

This is a compelling portrait of Norwegian-born sexual pioneer Eva Norvind, a heaven-sent subject for German documentary film-maker and feminist, Monika Treut. Norvind started out as the pin-up girl of 1960s Mexican cinema who thought nothing of sleeping with powerful men to espouse the causes of free love, birth control and female emancipation. She then resurfaced in the 1970s as a hostess to the New York intelligentsia, before reinventing herself as Ava Taurel, the city's leading dominatrix. Today, she's a respected authority on sexuality and criminal psychology. Treut unflinchingly allows the 54-year-old to exhibit her fascinating ideas about female gender. DP

Dir/Scr Monika Treut • *Cinematographer* Ekkehart Pollack, Christopher Landerer

Die Another Day ★★★★ 12

Spy adventure 2002 · UK/US · Colour · 126mins

There are only two "cons" to the 20th James Bond adventure, and both involve Madonna – firstly, the singer's grating theme song and secondly her dire cameo as a fencing instructor. These trivialities aside, the much loved franchise has rarely looked better, even if the plotline is more preposterous than ever. Such continued vigour is largely down to director Lee Tamahori's fluid style and the relentless pace which effortlessly propels the film's intense action around the globe. Pierce Brosnan, as a betrayed and vengeful 007, is on particularly fine form, while the introduction of Halle Berry as an equal, if underdeveloped, female sidekick is a definite coup. SF DVD

Pierce Brosnan *James Bond* • Halle Berry *Jinx* • Toby Stephens *Gustav Graves* • Rosamund Pike *Miranda Frost* • Rick Yune *Zao* • Judi Dench *M* • John Cleese *Q* • Michael Madsen *Damian Falco* • Will Yun Lee *Colonel Moon* • Kenneth Tsang *General Moon* • Samantha Bond *Miss Moneypenny* • Madonna *Verity, fencing instructor* ■ *Dir* Lee Tamahori • *Scr* Neal Purvis, Robert Wade, from characters created by Ian Fleming

Die! Die! My Darling ★★★

Horror thriller 1964 · UK · Colour · 96mins

For its first suspense thriller in colour, Hammer turned to specialist genre screenwriter Richard (*The Incredible Shrinking Man*) Matheson and asked Tallulah Bankhead to star as a *Baby Jane*-inspired mad matron. Despite being intoxicated throughout the entire shoot, the legendary Broadway diva (in her last screen performance) produced a venomous characterisation of terrifying intensity as the religious fanatic keeping her dead son's fiancée (Stefanie Powers) a prisoner in her rambling mansion. Donald Sutherland plays Bankhead's imbecile handyman in one of Hammer's best stabs at the *Psycho*-style chiller. AJ

Tallulah Bankhead *Mrs Trefoile* • Stefanie Powers *Pat Carroll* • Peter Vaughan *Harry* • Maurice Kaufman *Alan Glentower* • Yootha Joyce *Anna* • Donald Sutherland *Joseph* • Robert Dorning *Ormsby* ■ *Dir* Silvio Narizzano • *Scr* Richard Matheson, from the novel *Nightmare* by Anne Blaisdell

Die Hard ★★★★★ 18

Action thriller 1988 · US · Colour · 126mins

This is the action thriller that minted Bruce Willis's career, launched a franchise and still stands as a giant of the genre. It places a group of people in peril (office workers at a Christmas party in an otherwise empty Los Angeles skyscraper) when suave Alan Rickman's Euro-terrorists take them hostage. One man (Willis, naturally) is charged with saving them. Director John McTiernan handles the bravura, vertigo-inducing set pieces with aplomb and the script oozes dry wit, but the star of the show is Willis, as a resourceful but world-weary off-duty cop, who just wants to get home for Christmas dinner. AC. Contains violence, swearing, drug abuse and nudity. DVD

Bruce Willis *John McClane* • Alan Rickman *Hans Gruber* • Bonnie Bedelia *Holly Gennaro McClane* • Reginald VelJohnson *Sergeant Al Powell* • Paul Gleason *Dwayne T Robinson* • De'Voreaux White *Argyle* • William Atherton *Thornburg* • Hart Bochner *Harry Ellis* • James Shigeta *Takagi* • Alexander Godunov *Karl* ■ *Dir* John McTiernan • *Scr* Jeb Stuart, Steven E de Souza, from the novel *Nothing Lasts Forever* by Roderick Thorp

Die Hard 2: Die Harder ★★★★ 18

Action thriller 1990 · US · Colour · 118mins

Bruce Willis wonders aloud how it could happen to him again, but dons the white singlet anyway for another hugely entertaining slice of action hokum. Director Renny Harlin makes no attempt to re-create the intriguing battle of wits in the original between Alan Rickman and Willis, and instead cheerfully piles on increasingly grander set pieces. This time around Willis uncovers a terrorist plot on the ground and in the air as he waits for his wife to fly in to a snowbound Washington airport. Bonnie Bedelia is once again Willis's jinxed spouse, while Reginald VelJohnson and William Atherton reprise their roles from the original. JF. Contains swearing, violence, brief nudity. DVD

Bruce Willis *John McClane* • Bonnie Bedelia *Holly McClane* • William Atherton *Dick*

Thornberg • Reginald VelJohnson *Al Powell* • Franco Nero *General Ramon Esperanza* • William Sadler *Colonel Stuart* • John Amos *Captain Grant* • Dennis Franz *Carmine Lorenzo* • Art Evans *Barnes* ■ *Dir* Renny Harlin • *Scr* Steven E de Souza, Doug Richardson, from the novel *58 Minutes* by Walter Wager

Die Hard with a Vengeance ★★★★ 15

Action thriller 1995 · US · Colour · 122mins

Mad bomber Jeremy Irons keeps Bruce Willis and Samuel L Jackson on their toes in this third instalment of the *Die Hard* series, with a set of Simple Simon tasks that give a high-speed 20th-century labours-of-Hercules twist to the plot. Jackson and Willis make a testy duo, trading quips and insults at a pace that matches the breathless action. Returning to the fray after missing the first sequel, John McTiernan directs with a gleeful disregard for narrative logic, especially in the closing stages. Cracking entertainment, though. DP DVD

Bruce Willis *John McClane* • Jeremy Irons *Simon/Peter Gruber* • Samuel L Jackson *Zeus Carver* • Graham Greene (2) *Joe Lambert* • Colleen Camp *Connie Kowalski* • Larry Bryggman *Arthur Cobb* • Anthony Peck *Ricky Walsh* • Nick Wyman *Targo* ■ *Dir* John McTiernan • *Scr* Jonathan Hensleigh, from characters created by Roderick Thorp

Die Laughing ★ PG

Black comedy 1980 · US · Colour · 101mins

Former teen star Robby Benson was perhaps overstretched in this crass chase caper, in which he stars, co-wrote the screenplay and composed the simply atrocious songs. The inane plot has a San Francisco cabbie hiding a dead scientist's pet monkey from Russian spies to prevent them learning the formula for a plutonium bomb. The quality cast can't drag this up from the mire. DP

Robby Benson *Pinsky* • Linda Grovenor *Amy* • Charles Durning *Arnold* • Elsa Lanchester *Sophie* • Bud Cort *Mueller* • Rita Taggart *Thelma* ■ *Dir* Jeff Werner • *Scr* Jerry Segal, Robby Benson, Scott Parker, from a story by Scott Parker

Die, Monster, Die! ★★ 12

Horror 1965 · US/UK · Colour · 75mins

Former Roger Corman art director Daniel Haller's feature debut is a creditable genre effort in spite of itself. Scientist Nick Adams turns up at a remote village to visit his fiancée Suzan Farmer and her crippled father Boris Karloff only to find that a recently crash-landed meteorite is causing strange mutations. Haller gets the most chills from the visual components of his terror tale, rather than from the muddled script and weak acting. AJ DVD

Boris Karloff *Nahum Witley* • Nick Adams *Stephen Reinhart* • Freda Jackson *Letitia Witley* • Suzan Farmer *Susan Witley* ■ *Dir* Daniel Haller • *Scr* Jerry Sohl, from the novel *The Colour out of Space* by HP Lovecraft

Die Screaming Marianne ★★ 15

Horror thriller 1970 · UK · Colour · 96mins

This cheaply-made, sensational suspense thriller was filmed during a transitional period that took British director Pete Walker from skin flicks to cult horror films. The plot involves a variety of shady characters trying to force dancer Susan George to reveal the number of a Swiss bank account. Although crudely done by today's standards, some sequences have a certain noteworthy flair. The film was shot in and around Walker's holiday retreat in the Algarve, which adds to the appeal. DM DVD

Susan George *Marianne* • Barry Evans *Eli Frome* • Christopher Sandford *Sebastian Smith* • Judy Huxtable *Hildegarde* • Leo Genn *Judge* • Kenneth Hendel *Rodriguez* • Anthony Sharp *Registrar* • Martin Wyldeck *Policeman* ■ *Dir* Pete Walker • *Scr* Murray Smith

Die Watching ★★★ 18

Thriller 1993 · US · Colour · 81mins

B-movie king Tim Thomerson is underused here as the detective in charge of a serial murder investigation; somehow we're supposed to believe that Christopher Atkins can carry the film as the antisocial serial murderer. Atkins' character makes erotic videos and occasionally strangles the women who star in them. The police start to suspect him about the same time he falls in love with a local artist. Trashy but titillating, with some hilariously absurd fright effects. ST

Christopher Atkins *Michael Terrence* • Vali Ashton *Nola Carlisle* • Tim Thomerson *Detective Lewis* • Carlos Palomino *Detective Barry* • Mike Jacobs Jr *Adam Parker* ■ *Dir* Charles Davis • *Scr* Kenneth J Hall

Dieu A Besoin des Hommes ★★★★

Period religious drama
1950 · Fr · BW · 100mins

Pierre Fresnay delivers another inspirational display in Jean Delannoy's steady adaptation of Henri Queffelec's fact-based novel. Set on the Breton island of Sein in the 1850s, it chronicles the clash between the Catholic hierarchy and a solicitous sacristan who assumes clerical responsibility for a community of scavenging scoundrels after their curé absconds. Admired within church circles for its compassion and humility, and by critics for its literacy, scenic realism and impeccable playing. DP. In French with English subtitles.

Pierre Fresnay *Thomas Gourvennec* • Madeleine Robinson *Jeanne Gourvennec* • Andrée Clément *Kerneis* • Jean Brochard *Kerhervé, the priest* • Daniel Gélin *Joseph Le Berre* ■ *Dir* Jean Delannoy • *Scr* Jean Aurenche, Pierre Bost, from the novel *Un Recteur de l'Ile de Sein* by Henri Queffelec

Different for Girls ★★★ 15

Comedy drama 1996 · UK · Colour · 92mins

What's Rupert Graves to do? His best mate (Steven Mackintosh) has had a sex change since they last met, and now he's finding himself attracted to her. That's the dilemma in director Richard Spence's decidedly offbeat romantic comedy. What follows is sometimes awkward, sometimes emotionally remote but, because of Graves and Mackintosh's fine acting, always watchable. Thanks to the perceptive dialogue and barbed humour, this is a heart-warming tale of sexual confusion and love against the odds. AJ. Contains violence, swearing and nudity.

Steven Mackintosh *Kim Foyle* • Rupert Graves *Paul Prentice* • Miriam Margolyes *Pamela* • Saskia Reeves *Jean Payne* • Charlotte Coleman *Alison* • Neil Dudgeon *Neil Payne* ■ *Dir* Richard Spence • *Scr* Tony Marchant

A Different Story ★★ 15

Drama 1978 · US · Colour · 103mins

A ridiculously dated melodrama about homosexual Perry King marrying lesbian Meg Foster to avoid deportation and how they unexpectedly fall in love with each other. Director Paul Aaron's homophobic soap opera-style treatment reinforces every old-fashioned cliché about the ability of gay closet cases to "go straight" and advocates what a fine goal that is. Hopelessly naive when it isn't being insulting, but well acted. AJ

Perry King *Albert* • Meg Foster *Stella* • Valerie Curtin *Phyllis* • Peter Donat *Sills* • Richard Bull *Mr Cooke* • Barbara Collentine *Mrs Cooke* • Guerin Barry *Ned* • Doug Higgins *Roger* ■ *Dir* Paul Aaron • *Scr* Henry Olek

Dig! ★★★ 15

Music documentary
2004 · US · Colour · 107mins

In 1996, Ondi Timoner planned a low-budget film about ten unknown bands. She wound up focusing on two, The Brian Jonestown Massacre and The Dandy Warhols. The resulting film, assembled from 1,500 hours of footage shot over seven years, makes a compelling, instructive and rough-edged documentary about the vagaries of underground rock crossing over to the mainstream. This becomes apparent as the Warhols find chart success, while the BJM, led by deranged, self-appointed visionary Anton Newcombe, descend into violence, recrimination and drug abuse. By turns hilarious and shocking, and narrated by affable Warhols frontman Courtney Taylor. AC. Contains swearing and drug abuse.

Courtney Taylor (2) *Narrator* ■ *Dir* Ondi Timoner

Digby, the Biggest Dog in the World ★★ U

Comedy fantasy 1973 · UK · Colour · 84mins

While Peter Sellers was a natural before a movie camera, his fellow Goons never really found a screen niche. Spike Milligan, for example, looks singularly lost in this children's comedy about a nosey pooch who guzzles down a sample of miracle plant food and just keeps growing. Even the versatile Jim Dale struggles to make a go of Michael Pertwee's script, which is essentially a one-gag shaggy dog story. DP

Jim Dale *Jeff Eldon* • Spike Milligan *Dr Harz* • Angela Douglas *Janine* • John Bluthal *Jerry* • Norman Rossington *Tom* • Milo O'Shea *Dr Jameson* • Richard Beaumont *Billy White* • Dinsdale Landen *Colonel Masters* • Garfield Morgan *Rogerson* • Victor Spinetti *Professor Ribart* ■ *Dir* Joseph McGrath • *Scr* Michael Pertwee, from a story by Charles Isaacs, from the book *Hazel* by Ted Key

Digging to China ★★ PG

Drama 1998 · US · Colour · 94mins

Evan Rachel Wood plays Harriet, a ten-year-old girl who dreams of escaping her suffocating life with her alcoholic mother (Cathy Moriarty) and promiscuous sister (Mary Stuart Masterson) in this drama, the directorial debut of actor Timothy Hutton. Things perk up when Wood forms an unlikely friendship with the mentally disabled Kevin Bacon, though some scenes between the two are so sentimental they lean towards the unbearable. LH

Kevin Bacon *Ricky Schroth* • Mary Stuart Masterson *Gwen Frankovitz* • Cathy Moriarty *Mrs Frankovitz* • Evan Rachel Wood *Harriet Frankovitz* • Marian Seldes *Leah Schroth* ■ *Dir* Timothy Hutton • *Scr* Karen Janszen

Digimon the Movie ★★ PG

Animated adventure
1999 · Jpn/US · Colour · 88mins

For those of you in blissful ignorance, Digimon are digital monsters – Pokémon-type cartoon characters who inhabit the computer world and can evolve into powerful warriors. The Digimon are linked to the real world via a bunch of "digidestined" youngsters who join forces with them to defeat the forces of evil. Originally a TV series, this is *Digimon's* first cinema outing, and it loosely links together three tales of perils facing the virtual world, the real world, or both. The animation is rather better than Pokémon – although that isn't saying much. DA DVD

Lara Jill Miller *Kari/Young Kari* • Joshua Seth *Young Tai/Tai* • Bob Papenbrook *Red Greymon* ■ *Dir* Mamoru Hosoda, Shigeyasu Yamauchi • *Scr* Reiko Yoshida, Jeff Nimoy, Bob Buchholz

Dil Se... ★★★ 12

Musical romantic drama
1998 · Ind · Colour · 157mins

Proving that mainstream Indian cinema doesn't necessarily have to be dressed up in Bollywood razzmatazz, this stylish melodrama uses a doomed romance to analyse the subcontinent's political heritage. Director Mani Rathnam may utilise songs to explore his characters' emotions, but he refuses to allow the escapist elements to dominate the story of radio journalist Shahrukh Khan's obsession with provincial girl Manisha Koirala who, unbeknown to him, is a key figure in a terrorist plot. DP. In Hindi with English subtitles. Contains violence. DVD

Shahrukh Khan [Shah Rukh Khan] *Amar* • Manisha Koirala *Meghna* ■ *Dir* Mani Rathnam • *Scr* Mani Ratnam, from a story by Mani Ratnam

Dilemma ★

Drama 1962 · UK · BW · 67mins

What would you do if you came home and found your wife missing and a dead body in the bath? Bury the corpse beneath the floorboards? Surely not. Then again, if you were the returning wife, would you condone your husband's actions and spend the rest of your life confined to the house for fear of discovery? Well, this is the situation in which Peter Halliday and Ingrid Hafner find themselves in this risible slice of everyday life. No wonder British B-movies of the 1960s have such an awful reputation. DP

Peter Halliday *Harry Barnes* • Ingrid Hafner *Jean Barnes* • Patricia Burke *Mrs Jones* • Patrick Jordan *Inspector Murray* • Joan Heath *Mrs Barnes* • Robert Dean *Doctor* ■ *Dir* Peter Maxwell • *Scr* Pip Baker, Jane Baker

Dillinger ★★★★ PG

Crime biography 1945 · US · BW · 66mins

This is an extraordinarily effective Monogram B-movie, very successful in its day and still playing theatrically over 20 years later in a double-bill with the 1959 film, *Al Capone*. Budget limitations are obvious, but a tough, tight, Oscar-nominated screenplay by Phil Yordan more than compensates. The persuasive direction is by the eclectic Max Nosseck, while Lawrence Tierney wields a tight lip as public enemy number one John Dillinger. Tierney displayed the same uncompromising leathery quality as the ringleader in *Reservoir Dogs*. TS

Lawrence Tierney *Dillinger* • Anne Jeffreys *Helen* • Edmund Lowe *Specs* • Eduardo Ciannelli *Marco Minnelli* • Marc Lawrence (1) *Doc* • Elisha Cook Jr *Kirk* • Ralph Lewis *Tony* • Ludwig Stossel *Otto* ■ *Dir* Max Nosseck • *Scr* Leon Charles, Phil Yordan

Dillinger ★★★★ 18

Crime biography 1973 · US · Colour · 106mins

Warren Oates gives a wonderfully slimy performance as gangster John Dillinger in this bullet-laced biography from director John Milius. Dillinger blazed his way to notoriety during the 1930s and was the first man to be tagged public enemy number one, and here he's pursued across America by FBI man Ben Johnson. The movie was a coup for debut director John Milius, a hoodlum history that is small-scale but devastating all the same. TH. Contains violence and swearing.

Warren Oates *John Dillinger* • Ben Johnson *Melvin Purvis* • Michelle Phillips *Billie*

Frechette • Cloris Leachman *Anna Sage* • Harry Dean Stanton *Homer Van Meter* • Geoffrey Lewis *Harry Pierpont* • John Ryan [John P Ryan] *Charles Mackley* • Richard Dreyfuss *George "Baby Face" Nelson* • Steve Kanaly *Lester "Pretty Boy" Floyd* ■ *Dir/Scr* John Milius

Dillinger and Capone ★★★ 15

Period crime drama
1995 · US · Colour · 90mins

What could have been a run-of-the-mill gangster picture is given a boost by an interesting and intriguing plot. In 1934, criminal John Dillinger was gunned down by the Feds outside the Biograph Theater in Chicago. In this film, though, it's not Dillinger who gets killed but his brother, and the FBI are unaware of their error. A few years later, Al Capone, who knows the former bank robber's secret, holds John Dillinger's family hostage to get him to recover money Capone has stashed in a Chicago hotel. The film moves briskly along, in part thanks to Jon Purdy's strong direction, but mainly due to the talents of his cast. JB DVD

Martin Sheen *John Dillinger* • F Murray Abraham *Al Capone* • Catherine Hicks *Abigail Dalton* • Michael Oliver *Sam Dalton* • Don Stroud *George* • Anthony Crivello *Lou Gazzo* • Stephen Davies *Cecil* • Clint Howard *Bobo* ■ *Dir* Jon Purdy • *Scr* Michael B Druxman

Dilwale Dulhania Le Jayenge ★★★ PG

Romantic drama
1995 · Ind · Colour · 181mins

Some of the locations may be European, but this is as traditional a Bollywood masala as you could wish for. Shahrukh Khan and Kajol star as Londoners who fall in love during a month's vacation on the continent, but standing in the way of their happiness is an arranged marriage. With his father (acclaimed director Yash Chopra) acting as producer, Aditya Chopra could hardly go wrong with this debut outing. It's lively and packed with mischievous contrivance. DP. In Hindi with English subtitles. VIDEO DVD

Shahrukh Khan [Shah Rukh Khan] *Raj Malhotra* • Kajol *Simran* • Amrish Puri *Chaudhry Baldev Singh* • Farida Jalal *Lajwanti* ■ *Dir/Scr* Aditya Chopra

Dim Sum: a Little Bit of Heart ★★★★ U

Comedy
1985 · US · Colour · 83mins

Delicate but deceptively spicy, this delicious film shows just how easy it is to appear selfless while acting purely out of self-interest. Taking his stylistic cue from Yasujiro Ozu, director Wayne Wang allows the story to develop in its own time and space while drawing us into the world of San Francisco's Chinese community. This enables us to appreciate more fully the emotional games being played out by the elderly Kim Chew, her westernised daughter Laureen Chew and her roguish uncle Victor Wong, all of whom dissemble in their relationships to avoid making difficult decisions. DP VIDEO

Laureen Chew *Geraldine Tam* • Kim Chew *Mrs Tam* • Victor Wong (2) *Uncle Tam* • Ida FO Chung *Auntie Mary* • Cora Miao *Julia* • John Nishio *Richard* • Amy Hill *Amy Tam* • Keith Choy *Kevin Tam* ■ *Dir* Wayne Wang • *Scr* Terrel Seltzer, from an idea by Terrel Seltzer, Laureen Chew, Wayne Wang

Dimples ★★★ U

Period musical drama
1936 · US · BW · 78mins

This was one of Shirley Temple's biggest hits and a good of example of why she became the world's biggest box-office draw. Young Shirley had a tremendous instinctive talent, something that her detractors are impervious to. Here she sings (and swings) *Oh Mister Man up in the Moon* and *Hey, What Did the Bluebird Say?* with great aplomb, and swaps dialogue with screen grandad Frank Morgan like the seasoned trouper she is. As a well-meaning kiddie in mid-19th century New York, she's irresistible. TS

Shirley Temple *Sylvia Dolores Appleby, "Dimples"* • Frank Morgan *Professor Eustace Appleby* • Helen Westley *Mrs Caroline Drew* • Robert Kent *Allen Drew* • Delma Byron *Betty Loring* • Astrid Allwyn *Cleo Marsh* • Stepin Fetchit *Cicero* ■ *Dir* William A Seiter • *Scr* Arthur Sheekman, Nat Perrin, from an idea by Nunnally Johnson

Diner ★★★★ 15

Comedy drama 1982 · US · Colour · 105mins

This gentle, warm-hearted film about a group of young men in 1950s Baltimore was director Barry Levinson's debut feature and it remains among his finest work. It's a sympathetic portrait of youth on the threshold of adulthood that's episodic in structure; it also happens to be rather funny. In addition, Levinson shows a remarkable eye for talent. At the time, most of the performers were far from being household names; Steve Guttenberg, Mickey Rourke, Ellen Barkin, Kevin Bacon, Daniel Stern and Paul Reiser all boosted their careers after appearing in this movie. JF. Contains swearing. VIDEO

Steve Guttenberg *Eddie* • Mickey Rourke *Boogie* • Ellen Barkin *Beth* • Kevin Bacon *Fenwick* • Daniel Stern *Shrevie* • Timothy Daly *Billy* • Paul Reiser *Modell* • Kathryn Dowling *Barbara* ■ *Dir/Scr* Barry Levinson

Le Dîner de Cons ★★★★ 15

Comedy 1998 · Fr · Colour · 76mins

Despite frequently betraying its stage origins, Francis Veber's splutteringly funny farce is a model of snowball comedy. From the moment publisher Thierry Lhermitte agrees to exhibit matchstick model-maker Jacques Villeret at one of his clique's "idiot dinners", his idyllic existence begins to fall apart as this balding bundle of good intentions dismantles his deceptions with devastating artlessness. Lhermitte is selfless as the despicable straight man, but Villeret has fashioned a masterly creation: a buffoonish descendant of Stan Laurel and Inspector Clouseau, whose every word and gesture has catastrophic consequences. DP. In French with English subtitles. VIDEO DVD

Jacques Villeret *François Pignon* • Thierry Lhermitte *Pierre Brochant* • Francis Huster *Leblanc* • Alexandra Vandernoot *Christine* • Daniel Prévost *Cheval* • Catherine Frot *Marlène* • Edgar Givry *Cordier* • Christian Pereira *Sorbier* ■ *Dir* Francis Veber • *Scr* Francis Veber, from his play

Dingo ★★

Drama 1991 · Aus/Fr · Colour · 108mins

Miles Davis and Michel Legrand are the true stars here for producing a jazz score that, for all its geniality, this Australian drama scarcely deserves. Rolf De Heer attempts to impart a fantastical element to this middling meditation on dreams and destiny, in which a chance meeting with a legendary trumpeter transforms the life of a Poona Flats wannabe. Colin Friels impresses as he strives to fulfil his ambition, but co-star Davis gives a one-note performance. DP

Colin Friels *John "Dingo" Anderson* • Miles Davis *Billy Cross* • Helen Buday *Jane Anderson* • Joe Petruzzi *Peter* • Bernadette Lafont *Angie Cross* • Steve Shaw *Archie* • Helen Doig *Ruth* • Daniel Scott *Young John* ■ *Dir* Rolf De Heer • *Scr* Marc Rosenberg

Dinner at Eight ★★★★ PG

Comedy drama 1933 · US · BW · 106mins

A sumptuously produced (by David O Selznick) all-star MGM extravaganza, based on the witty George S Kaufman/ Edna Ferber Broadway success, but with an even smarter screenplay by Frances Marion, Herman J Mankiewicz and the mordant Donald Ogden Stewart. In the distinguished company of Marie Dressler, Wallace Beery and a couple of Barrymores, blonde bombshell Jean Harlow really shines, and affords Dressler the opportunity for one of cinema's greatest ever last lines. Director George Cukor proved himself highly skilled at handling this kind of super-production; in its day, this was a popular and critical hit. Well worth watching. TS VIDEO

Marie Dressler *Carlotta Vance* • John Barrymore *Larry Renault* • Wallace Beery *Dan Packard* • Jean Harlow *Kitty Packard* • Lionel Barrymore *Oliver Jordan* • Lee Tracy *Max Kane* • Edmund Lowe *Dr Wayne Talbot* • Billie Burke *Mrs Oliver Jordan* • Madge Evans *Paula Jordan* • Jean Hersholt *Joe Stengel* ■ *Dir* George Cukor • *Scr* Frances Marion, Herman J Mankiewicz, Donald Ogden Stewart, from the play by George S Kaufman, Edna Ferber

Dinner at the Ritz ★★★ U

Romantic thriller 1937 · UK · BW · 77mins

Despite the enchanting presence of French actress Annabella (the future Mrs Tyrone Power), this thriller suffers from slack pacing and a hackneyed plot. Annabella plays the daughter of a murdered banker who comes to London to find the men responsible, with a little help from David Niven's government agent. A period artefact now, this was once considered the epitome of chic. TS DVD

David Niven *Paul de Brack* • Annabella *Ranie Racine* • Paul Lukas *Philip de Beaufort* • Romney Brent *Jimmy Raine* • Francis L Sullivan *Brogard* • Stewart Rome *Racine* ■ *Dir* Harold D Schuster [Harold Schuster] • *Scr* Roland Pertwee, from a story by Roland Pertwee, Romney Brent

Dinner Rush ★★★★ 15

Comedy drama 2000 · US · Colour · 94mins

Director Bob Giraldi displays a mastery of texture and character in this delightful comedy drama set in a fashionable Manhattan restaurant. Danny Aiello exudes understated charm as the prosperous owner, who's dismayed that his family trattoria is forgoing traditional food for the flashy nouvelle cuisine that is the trademark of his talented chef son (star-in-the-making Edoardo Ballerini). During one fraught night, he and his staff must deal with mobsters wanting a piece of the action, a demanding food critic (played by an irresistible Sandra Bernhard), a lengthy power cut and various other diversions. Filmed in Giraldi's own restaurant, this is a finely polished gem. JC. Contains violence, swearing and sex scenes. VIDEO DVD

Danny Aiello *Louis* • Edoardo Ballerini *Udo* • Vivian Wu *Nicole* • Mike McGlone *Carmen* • Kirk Acevedo *Duncan* • Sandra Bernhard *Jennifer Freeley* • Summer Phoenix *Marti* ■ *Dir* Bob Giraldi • *Scr* Rick Shaughnessy, Brian Kalata

Dinner with Friends ★ 15

Drama 2001 · US · Colour · 90mins

Director Norman Jewison trades subtle observations for ham-fisted showiness in this made-for-cable adaptation of a Pulitzer Prize-winning play. Applying over simplistic rationale to the idiosyncrasies of human relationships, he ploughs into the intimate nitty-gritty of romance and betrayal like an intrusive voyeur. This emotionally hollow melodrama throws up cliché after cliché, as idyllic couple Dennis Quaid and Andie MacDowell find their friends' divorce threatening their own perfect marriage. SF VIDEO DVD

Dennis Quaid *Gabe* • Andie MacDowell *Karen* • Greg Kinnear *Tom* • Toni Collette *Beth* ■ *Dir* Norman Jewison • *Scr* Donald Margulies, from his play

Dino ★★

Drama 1957 · US · BW · 94mins

From the era when juvenile delinquency was all the rage comes this predictably moral story of teenager Sal Mineo who has a hard time in reform school and an even harder time trying to stay straight outside. Adapted by Reginald Rose from his TV play, it has the many of the same concerns he revealed in *12 Angry Men.* Nowadays, though, it looks rather subdued. TH

Sal Mineo *Dino* • Brian Keith *Sheridan* • Susan Kohner *Shirley* • Frank Faylen *Mandel* • Joe De Santis *Mr Minetta* • Penny Santon *Mrs Minetta* • Pat DeSimone *Tony* • Richard Bakalyan *Chuck* ■ *Dir* Thomas Carr • *Scr* Reginald Rose, from his TV play

Dinosaur ★★★ PG

Animated adventure
2000 · US · Colour · 82mins

While the story isn't exactly Kafka – abandoned baby dinosaur is raised by lemurs until they have to flee during a fiery meteor storm and join other dinosaurs on a treacherous trek to a new land – the animation is excellent. DB Sweeney and Julianna Margulies give life to their characters and there is solid vocal support from the rest of the cast in this ambitious Disney movie. JB VIDEO DVD

DB Sweeney *Aladar* • Alfre Woodard *Plio* • Ossie Davis *Yar* • Samuel E Wright *Kron* • Julianna Margulies *Neera* • Joan Plowright *Baylene* • Della Reese *Eema* ■ *Dir* Eric Leighton, Ralph Zondag • *Scr* John Harrison, Robert Nelson Jacobs, from a screenplay (unproduced) by Walon Green, from a story by Thom Enriquez, John Harrison, Robert Nelson Jacobs, Ralph Zondag

Dinosaurus! ★★

Fantasy 1960 · US · Colour · 82mins

Jurassic Park this ain't! A caveman, a friendly brontosaurus and a nasty T-Rex are disturbed from their slumber on a tropical island by construction workers in one of the funniest monster movies ever made. Best described as a prehistoric take on the Three Stooges' brand of comedy, viewers will shake their heads in dismay at the cheap mindlessness. Still, lousy special effects and worse acting make it hilariously compulsive viewing. AJ

Ward Ramsey *Bart Thompson* • Paul Lukather *Chuck* • Kristina Hanson *Betty Piper* • Alan Roberts *Julio* • Gregg Martell *Prehistoric man* • Fred Engelberg *Mike Hacker* ■ *Dir* Irvin S Yeaworth Jr • *Scr* Jean Yeaworth, Dan E Weisburd, from an idea by Jack H Harris

Dionysus in '69 ★★★

Documentary 1970 · US · BW · 90mins

At the outset of his career, Brian De Palma operated on the fringes of the New York avant-garde. Consequently, a self-conscious straining for effect informs this documentary as it seeks to match in visual terms the experimental nature of the Performance Group's adaptation of Euripides's *Bacchae.* Devised by Richard Schechner, the production encouraged audiences at the Performing Garage to participate in the play to achieve "total theatre". By using hand-held cameras and gimmicky devices like split screens, De Palma and fellow film-makers Robert Fiore and Bruce Joel Rubin attempt to capture the energy of the experience, but only partially succeed. DP

William Finley *Dionysus* • William Shephard *Pentheus* • Joan MacIntosh *Agave* ■ *Dir* Brian

De Palma, Bruce Fiore, Bruce Rubin [Bruce Joel Rubin] • *Scr* from the play *Dionysus in '69* by Richard Schechner, from the play *Bacchae* by Euripedes

Diplomatic Courier ★★★ U

Spy drama 1952 · US · BW · 97mins

A rattlingly good Cold War thriller, shot on European locations, with Tyrone Power's blandness offset by his female co-stars: Soviet agent Hildegarde Neff and American tourist Patricia Neal. Look out too for Karl Malden, Lee Marvin and Charles Bronson on their respective paths to stardom. With hindsight, the "secret agenda" plot seems chillingly appropriate. Underrated and well worth a look. TS

Tyrone Power *Mike Kells* • Patricia Neal *Joan Ross* • Stephen McNally *Colonel Cagle* • Hildegarde Neff *Janine* • Karl Malden *Ernie* • James Millican *Sam Carew* • Stefan Schnabel *Platov* ■ *Dir* Henry Hathaway • *Scr* Casey Robinson, Liam O'Brien, from the novel *Sinister Errand* by Peter Cheyney

Diplomatic Immunity ★ 18

Action thriller 1991 · US · Colour · 90mins

TV star Bruce Boxleitner gets to kick some bad guy's butt in this plodding revenge thriller. His daughter is murdered, but her killer is set free because he has diplomatic immunity. Dad is an ex-marine, so he thinks nothing of hopping on a plane and pursuing said baddie to Paraguay. Cue grunting and punching. JB [video]

Bruce Boxleitner *Cole Hickel* • Billy Drago *Cowboy* • Tom Breznahan *Klaus Hermann* • Christopher Neame *Stefan Noll* • Fabiana Udenio *Teresa Escobal* • Matthias Hues *Gephardt* • Meg Foster *Gerta Hermann* • Robert Forster *Stonebridge* ■ *Dir* Peter Maris • *Scr* Randall Frakes, Richard Donn, Jim Trombetta, from the novel *The Stalker* by Theodore Taylor

Diplomatic Siege ★★ 15

Action thriller 1999 · US · Colour · 90mins

This boasts a better than average cast although that's probably more about the stars' current standing in Hollywood than the class of this bog-standard straight-to-video actioner. The reality-defying plot has Peter Weller and Daryl Hannah trapped in a US embassy taken over by terrorists. Tom Berenger, playing a US general, turns up to do little more than pick up his wages, leaving Weller and Hannah to wrestle with an illogical plot and lame dialogue. JF DVD

Peter Weller *Steve Mitchell* • Daryl Hannah *Erica Long* • Tom Berenger *Buck Swain* • Adrian Pintea *Goran* ■ *Dir* Gustavo Graef-Marino • *Scr* Mark Amin, Sam Bernard, Kevin Bernhardt, Robert Boris

Dirigible ★★★

Adventure 1931 · US · BW · 104mins

Made some years before his sentimental association with small-town America transformed him into a Hollywood great, this reminds us that Frank Capra also worked in other genres. Two navy pilots experiment with airships, one of which crashes in the Antarctic, resulting in a three-way tug of war between the fame-seeking pilot, his wife and a colleague who covets her. Capra knows how to build and sustain action, but he is less sure with the mush of romance that, at times, sets the film in cement. JM

Jack Holt *Jack Bradon* • Ralph Graves *Frisky Pierce* • Fay Wray *Helen* • Hobart Bosworth *Rondelle* • Roscoe Karns *Sock McGuire* • Harold Goodwin (1) *Hansen* • Clarence Muse *Clarence* ■ *Dir* Frank Capra • *Scr* Jo Swerling, Dorothy Howell, from a story by Lieutenant Commander Frank W Weed

El Dirigible ★★

Drama 1994 · Urug · BW and Colour · 80mins

Inspired by the suicide of Baltasar Brum, the nation's youngest president, this broad comedy was only the second feature to be completed in Uruguay since the 1950s. Unfortunately, director Pablo Dotta fritters away the interesting subject by indulging a penchant for elliptical construction that muddles proceedings rather than imbuing them with a sense of mystery. As the journalist trying to recover a stolen video interview with a reclusive author who witnessed Brum's demise, Laura Schneider gives a spirited performance. DP. In Spanish with English subtitles.

Laura Schneider *The Frenchwoman* • Marcello Buquet *Translator* • Ricardo Espalter *Police detective* • Eduardo Miglionico • Gonzalo Cardozo *Snotty* ■ *Dir/Scr* Pablo Dotta

The Dirt Bike Kid ★★★ PG

Fantasy comedy 1986 · US · Colour · 86mins

Fans of the *Herbie* movies should enjoy this similar tale of a boy with a bike that has a mind of its own. Peter Billingsley is the young teen in question, and he seems to have fun playing a character who is continually getting into the sorts of trouble only his wonder bike can get him out of. Not exactly memorable, but amusing nonetheless. JB [video]

Peter Billingsley *Jack Simmons* • Stuart Pankin *Mr Hodgkins* • Anne Bloom *Janet Simmons* • Patrick Collins *Mike* • Sage Parker *Miss Clavell* • Chad Sheets *Bo* • Gavin Allen *Max* • Danny Breen *Flaherty* ■ *Dir* Hoite C Caston • *Scr* David Brandes, Lewis Colick, from a story by J Halloran [Julie Corman]

Dirty Dancing ★★★★ 15

Romantic drama 1987 · US · Colour · 95mins

This sentimental but never cloying tale of sexual awakening at a Jewish holiday camp in 1963 became a much-loved blockbuster and kick-started major industry careers for its production team. The casting is perfect, with ex-dancer Patrick Swayze as the sexy dancing coach and Jennifer Grey as the middle-class teenager, and their relationship never strikes a false note. But what really makes the film unmissable is the fabulous dancing which, despite being highly erotic, is never tacky. SH. Contains swearing. [video] DVD

Jennifer Grey *Frances "Baby" Houseman* • Patrick Swayze *Johnny Castle* • Jerry Orbach *Dr Jake Houseman* • Cynthia Rhodes *Penny Johnson* • Jack Weston *Max Kellerman* • Jane Brucker *Lisa Houseman* • Kelly Bishop *Marjorie Houseman* • Lonny Price *Neil Kellerman* ■ *Dir* Emile Ardolino • *Scr* Eleanor Bergstein • *Choreographer* Kenny Ortega, Miranda John Pritchett

Dirty Dancing 2 ★★ PG

Romantic drama 2003 · US · Colour · 82mins

This tale of polar opposites brought together by dance is a thematic reworking, rather than a sequel, to the 1987 hit. Set in Havana in 1958, it sees Romola Garai's American teen shocking her rich father's country club set by falling for fancy-footed local waiter Diego Luna. Though the two are attractive together, their dancing lacks fire and there's no sense of the sexual tension that ignited the original. Having Patrick Swayze pop up in a dance teacher cameo doesn't help either – he makes poor Luna look clumsy in comparison. SF [video] DVD

Diego Luna *Javier Suarez* • Romola Garai *Katey Miller* • Sela Ward *Jeannie Miller* • John Slattery *Bert Miller* • Jonathan Jackson *James Phelps* • January Jones *Eve* • Mika Boorem *Susie Miller* • Patrick Swayze *Dance instructor* ■ *Dir* Guy Ferland • *Scr* Boaz Yakin, Victoria Arch, from a story by Kate Gunzinger, Peter Sagal

Dirty Deeds ★★ 18

Crime comedy
2002 · Aus/UK · Colour · 93mins

This Australian import tries hard to achieve the cool, off-beam sensibility of recent British gangster films but, despite creditable performances, winds up a jarring melange of mismatched styles and iffy plotting. This follows the travails of a local crime boss (Bryan Brown) as he attempts to ward off the Chicago Mafia (in the corpulent shape of John Goodman) who are in town to muscle in on his slot-machine racket. Director David Caesar's uncertain direction and hectic editing obscure the film's strengths, particularly the always entertaining Brown and Goodman. AS [video] DVD

Bryan Brown *Barry Ryan* • Toni Collette *Sharon Ryan* • John Goodman *Tony Testano* • Sam Neill *Det-Sgt Ray Murphy* • Sam Worthington *Darcy* • Kestie Morassi *Margaret* • Felix Williamson *Sal Cassela* • William McInnes *Hollywood* ■ *Dir/Scr* David Caesar

Dirty Dingus Magee ★★ PG

Comedy western 1970 · US · Colour · 86mins

Frank Sinatra plays a literally lousy outlaw in this vulgar, gross and bawdy comedy western, but he only succeeds in looking anachronistically stupid. There's a nice cast of old western reliables on hand to keep director Burt Kennedy's film watchable, plus a gem of a performance from the under-rated Lois Nettleton. TS [video]

Frank Sinatra *Dingus Magee* • George Kennedy *Hoke Birdsill* • Anne Jackson *Belle Kops* • Lois Nettleton *Prudence* • Jack Elam *John Wesley Hardin* • Michele Carey *Anna Hotwater* • John Dehner *General* • Harry Carey Jr *Stuart* ■ *Dir* Burt Kennedy • *Scr* Frank Waldman, Tom Waldman, Joseph Heller, from the novel *The Ballad of Dingus Magee* by David Markson

The Dirty Dozen ★★★★ 15

Second World War action adventure
1967 · US/UK · Colour · 143mins

One of the smash hits of its year, this action-packed war movie is violent and amoral, and fans would say all the better for it. Whatever your tastes, there's no denying director Robert Aldrich's consummate skill with such material or the powerhouse impact of the starry all-male cast headed by Lee Marvin, factors that have helped maintain the film's popularity. The violence is in fact mild by today's standards, but it nevertheless leaves a nasty taste in the mouth as a group of sociopaths are released from jail on a suicide mission to murder Nazis, and the movie rightly earned its original "X" certificate. John Poyner won the best sound effects Oscar for his superb soundtrack. TS [video] DVD

Lee Marvin *Major Reisman* • Ernest Borgnine *General Worden* • Charles Bronson *Joseph Wladislaw* • Jim Brown *Robert Jefferson* • John Cassavetes *Victor Franko* • Richard Jaeckel *Sgt Bowren* • George Kennedy *Maj Max Armbruster* • Trini Lopez *Pedro Jiminez* • Ralph Meeker *Capt Stuart Kinder* • Robert Ryan *Col Everett Dasher Breed* • Telly Savalas *Archer Maggott* • Donald Sutherland *Vernon Pinkley* • Clint Walker *Samson Posey* • Robert Webber *Colonel Denton* ■ *Dir* Robert Aldrich • *Scr* Lukas Heller, Nunnally Johnson, from the novel by EM Nathanson

The Dirty Game ★★

Portmanteau spy drama
1965 · Fr/It/W Ger · BW · 91mins

This deglamorising spy compendium is patchy in the extreme. The first section has Vittorio Gassman going undercover in Rome to kidnap a jet fuel specialist; the second involves rival detachments of frogmen doing battle beneath the Gulf of Aden. The Le Carré-esque conclusion affords Henry Fonda the opportunity to demonstrate what a superb actor he is – even though he utters no more than a couple of lines of dialogue. DP

Henry Fonda *Kourlov* • Robert Ryan *General Bruce* • Vittorio Gassman *Perego* • Annie Girardot *Nanette* • Bourvil *Laland* • Robert Hossein *Dupont* • Peter Van Eyck *Berlin CIA head Petchatkin* • Maria Grazia Buccella *Natalia* ■ *Dir* Terence Young, Christian-Jaque, Carlo Lizzani, Werner Klinger • *Scr* Jo Eisinger, Jacques Laborie, Jacques Remy, Ennio De Concini, Christian-Jaque, from a screenplay (unproduced) by Philippe Bouvard

Dirty Harry ★★★★★ 18

Crime thriller 1971 · US · Colour · 102mins

Movie history might have run differently had Frank Sinatra not injured his hand, causing him to relinquish the role of renegade cop "Dirty" Harry Callahan to Clint Eastwood. This is the first, and best, outing for Eastwood's San Francisco police inspector, in which he tramples on the American Constitution to bring gibbering psychopath Andrew Robinson to justice. A masterpiece of action movie-making, directed by Don Siegel with his usual toughness and crisp efficiency, and acted by Clint with the characteristic hard-boiled traits that are now part of his screen persona and cinema folklore. Armed with a darkly cynical and smart script, this original generates an excitement that none of the four sequels (*Magnum Force*, *The Enforcer*, *Sudden Impact* and *The Dead Pool*) could match. AJ. Contains violence, swearing and brief nudity. [video] DVD

Clint Eastwood *Harry Callahan* • Harry Guardino *Lieutenant Bressler* • Reni Santoni *Chico* • John Vernon *Mayor* • Andy Robinson [Andrew Robinson] *Killer* • John Larch *Chief* • John Mitchum *DeGeorgio* • Mae Mercer *Mrs Russell* ■ *Dir* Don Siegel • *Scr* Harry Julian Fink, Rita M Fink, Dean Riesner, from a story by Harry Julian Fink, Rita M Fink • *Cinematographer* Bruce Surtees

Dirty Little Billy ★★★

Western 1972 · US · Colour · 92mins

Rarely has a myth been so muddied as that of Billy the Kid in this early revisionist western, in which the lad is seen before notoriety gave him outlaw celebrity. Director Stan Dragoti's often surreal visuals mesmerise, with Coffeyville, Kansas, seen as a slop-bucket community from which Billy is only too happy to escape. The fictionalised antihero of the Wild West is played here by Michael J Pollard as a mentally challenged eccentric, which tends to subtract some sympathy from his situation. TH. Contains swearing.

Michael J Pollard *Billy Bonney* • Lee Purcell *Berle* • Richard Evans *Goldie Evans* • Charles Aidman *Ben Antrim* • Dran Hamilton *Catherine McCarty* • Willard Sage *Henry McCarty* • Josip Elic *Jawbone* • Mills Watson *Ed* ■ *Dir* Stan Dragoti • *Scr* Stan Dragoti, Charles Moss • *Cinematographer* Ralph Woolsey

Dirty Mary Crazy Larry ★★ 15

Action adventure 1974 · US · Colour · 88mins

Peter Fonda steals $150,000 from a supermarket, buys a souped-up car and hits the road with Susan George and Adam Roarke, pursued by cop Vic Morrow. Still trading on his *Easy Rider* image, Fonda drifts through what rapidly becomes a demolition derby with pit stops for disputes over George's sexual favours. As one would expect, the cars crash and career spectacularly and the California scenery is often eye-catching. AT [video]

Peter Fonda *Larry* • Susan George *Mary* • Adam Roarke *Deke* • Vic Morrow *Franklin* • Kenneth Tobey *Donohue* • Roddy McDowall *Stanton* ■ *Dir* John Hough • *Scr* Leigh Chapman, Antonio Santean, from the novel *The Chase* by Richard Unekis

D

Dirty Pictures ★★ 18

Drama documentary
2000 · US · Colour · 99mins

Despite winning a Golden Globe, this made-for-TV film is a messy account of the trial of Cincinnati gallery director Dennis Barrie, who was arrested for staging a supposedly obscene exhibition of images by the controversial photographer, Robert Mapplethorpe. James Woods seizes upon the role and is well supported by Diana Scarwid as the wife forced to endure his pillorying by the forces of moralising conservatism. But Frank Pierson's decision to stud the action with archival and talking-head interjections proves a fatal miscalculation. DP

James Woods *Dennis Barrie* • Diana Scarwid *Dianne Barrie* • Craig T Nelson *Sheriff Simon Leis* • Leon Pownall *Prouty* • David Huband *Sirkin* ■ *Dir* Frank Pierson • *Scr* Ilene Chaiken

Dirty Pretty Things ★★★ 15

Drama 2002 · UK/US · Colour · 93mins

Stephen Frears here provides a distinctive insight into illegal immigrants living a hidden, knife-edge existence in London. Chiwetel Ejiofor is all soulful integrity as a Nigerian taxi driver who moonlights as a night porter in a hotel, while *Amélie's* Audrey Tautou elicits sympathy as a downtrodden Turkish asylum seeker. Aided by accomplished cinematographer Chris Menges, Frears's depiction of a seedy London is impressive, though the script's intrusive thriller elements dent the film's overall credibility. JC. Contains violence, swearing and sex scenes. DVD

Chiwetel Ejiofor *Okwe* • Audrey Tautou *Senay* • Sergi Lopez *Sneaky* • Sophie Okonedo *Juliette* • Benedict Wong *Guo Yi* • Sotigui Kouyate *Shinti* • Abi Gouhad *Shinti's son* ■ *Dir* Stephen Frears • *Scr* Steven Knight

Dirty Rotten Scoundrels ★★★ PG

Comedy 1988 · US · Colour · 105mins

A proficient remake of the old David Niven/Marlon Brando caper movie *Bedtime Story* that cruises by on star power alone. Michael Caine is the veteran conman making a comfortable living on the Riviera, who takes brash American Steve Martin under his wing. However, the pair fall out when they compete to take rich heiress Glenne Headly to the cleaners. Caine more than holds his own against the manic Martin and, if the script holds few surprises, the south of France looks great and director Frank Oz ensures the action slips along smoothly. Frothy fun. JF. Contains swearing. DVD

Michael Caine *Lawrence Jamieson* • Steve Martin *Freddy Benson* • Glenne Headly *Janet Colgate* • Anton Rodgers *Inspector André* • Barbara Harris *Fanny Eubanks* • Ian McDiarmid *Arthur* • Dana Ivey *Mrs Reed* ■ *Dir* Frank Oz • *Scr* Dale Launer, Stanley Shapiro, Paul Henning

A Dirty Shame ★★★ 18

Satirical comedy 2004 · US · Colour · 88mins

It's filthy! It's disgusting! It's another film by John Waters. After the Hollywood satire *Cecil B Demented*, Waters is back to subvert suburbia with another bad-taste comedy. Tracey Ullman stars as a repressed woman who resists the advances of her husband (Chris Isaak) and locks her daughter (Selma Blair, with comically distended breasts) in her room to prevent her working in a strip club. Then she's involved in an accident, wakes with uncontrollable lust and falls in with sex guru Johnny Knoxville. John Waters's desire to outrage is as strong as ever, but can't compensate for a patchy script. TH. Contains sexual references.

Tracey Ullman *Sylvia Stickles* • Johnny Knoxville *Ray-Ray Perkins* • Selma Blair *Caprice Stickles* • Chris Isaak *Vaughn Stickles* • Suzanne Shepherd *Big Ethel* • Mink Stole *Marge the Neuter* • Patricia Hearst *Paige* ■ *Dir/Scr* John Waters (2)

Dirty Weekend ★★ 18

Thriller 1992 · UK · Colour · 96mins

Directed by Michael Winner, this was released to a crescendo of controversy concerning its gross violence, regarded as a sort of *Death Wish* in a skirt. Lia Williams plays a much-abused young woman who is egged on by a Brighton clairvoyant to take her revenge on all men. She takes the advice very much to heart, using the knife he gives her to gruesome effect. JF. Contains sex scenes, violence, swearing.

Lia Williams *Bella* • Ian Richardson *Nimrod* • David McCallum *Reggie* • Rufus Sewell *Tim* • Miriam Kelly *Marion* • Sylvia Syms *Mrs Crosby* • Shaughan Seymour *Charles* • Christopher Adamson *Serial Killer* • Sean Pertwee ■ *Dir* Michael Winner • *Scr* Michael Winner, from the novel by Helen Zahavi

Dirty Work ★★★ 12

Comedy 1998 · US · Colour · 78mins

Saturday Night Live alumnus Norm MacDonald and Artie Lange play a couple of losers who discover their vocation in life: being paid to play humiliating pranks on behalf of wronged victims. Chevy Chase pops up as a cheerfully amoral surgeon, and there's a nicely grumpy turn from Jack Warden as MacDonald's dad. Despite losing its nerve by the end, it is for the most part a crudely nasty treat. JF. Contains swearing and sexual references.

Norm MacDonald *Mitch* • Artie Lange *Sam* • Christopher McDonald *Travis Cole* • Traylor Howard *Kathy* • Chevy Chase *Dr Farthing* • Don Rickles *Hamilton* • Jack Warden *Pops* • Chris Farley • Gary Coleman • Adam Sandler ■ *Dir* Bob Saget • *Scr* Fred Wolf, Norm Macdonald, Frank Sebastiano

The Disappearance ★★★ 15

Crime drama
1977 · Can/UK · Colour · 87mins

Few titles have proved as prophetic, for this elegantly-mounted mystery promptly vanished from screens as quickly as it arrived. A shame, for there is much to admire in this tale of a hitman, played by a suitably haunting Donald Sutherland, pondering the disappearance of his wife while planning his next job. Beautifully shot on location in icy Canada, a symbol of the assassin's frozen emotions, the British supporting cast shine. Only Stuart Cooper's somewhat arty approach to Paul Mayersberg's admittedly confusing script lets the side down. RS DVD

Donald Sutherland *Jay* • Francine Racette *Celandine* • David Hemmings *Edward* • Virginia McKenna *Catherine* • Christopher Plummer *Deverell* • John Hurt *Atkinson* • David Warner *Burbank* ■ *Dir* Stuart Cooper • *Scr* Paul Mayersberg, from the novel *Echoes of Celandine* by Derek Marlowe • *Cinematographer* John Alcott

The Disappearance of Aimee ★★★★

Mystery drama 1976 · US · Colour · 110mins

Based on a true story, this fascinating TV movie involves the disappearance of evangelist Aimee Semple McPherson (played by Faye Dunaway) in 1926. When she returned, Aimee claimed she had been abducted. Her mother, however, believed she had run off to have an affair, and the events became a national scandal. The story is handled in a gripping manner by director Anthony Harvey (*The Lion in Winter*), but it's the performances which keep you pinned to your seat. JB

Faye Dunaway *Sister Aimee McPherson* • Bette Davis *Minnie Kennedy* • James Sloyan *District Attorney Asa Keyes* • James Woods *Assistant DA Joseph Ryan* • John Lehne *Captain Cline* • Lelia Goldoni *Emma Shaffer* ■ *Dir* Anthony Harvey • *Scr* John McGreevey

The Disappearance of Finbar ★★★ 15

Drama
1996 · Ire/UK/Swe/Fr · Colour · 100mins

The title refers to the vanishing act of a failed young Irish footballer from his home on a Dublin housing estate. Initially a mournful study of the repercussions of Finbar's (Jonathan Rhys) departure, the film takes on an altogether more humorous tone when his best friend (Luke Griffin) embarks on a Scandinavian odyssey to seek some answers. There are a few oddly appealing moments, although the film possesses the strange look of two different movies spliced together. Not without charm. JC. Contains swearing and a sex scene. DVD

Luke Griffin *Danny Quinn* • Jonathan Rhys Meyers *Finbar Flynn* • Sean McGinley *Detective Roche* • Fanny Risberg *Abbi* • Marie Mullen *Ellen Quinn* • Lorraine Pilkington *Katie Dunnigan* • Sean Lawlor *Michael Flynn* ■ *Dir* Sue Clayton • *Scr* Sue Clayton, Dermot Bolger, from the novel *The Disappearance of Rory Brophy* by Carl Lombard

The Disappearance of Garcia Lorca ★★★

Mystery thriller
1997 · US/Fr · Colour · 114mins

After a teenage encounter with Spanish writer Federico Garcia Lorca (Andy Garcia), Esai Morales grows up determined to return to Spain and uncover the truth behind the great man's disappearance and untimely death. His amateur murder investigation suggests that, while a dead poet can be a national hero, a live one can be a national threat. Based on the speculations of author Ian Gibson, this is an interesting study of Lorca and the Spanish civil war, but not an altogether successful one. LH

Andy Garcia *Federico Garcia Lorca* • Esai Morales *Ricardo* • Edward James Olmos *Roberto Lozano* • Jeroen Krabbé *Colonel Aguirre* • Giancarlo Giannini *Taxi* • Miguel Ferrer *Centeno* • Marcela Walerstein *Maria Eugenia* • Eusebio Lázaro *Vicente Fernandez* ■ *Dir* Marcos Zurinaga • *Scr* Marcos Zurinaga, Juan Antonio Ramos, Neil Cohen, from the non-fiction books *The Assassination of Federico Garcia Lorca* , *Federico Garcia Lorca: A Life* by Ian Gibson

The Disappearance of Kevin Johnson ★★★ 15

Mystery thriller
1995 · US/UK · Colour · 101mins

A whodunnit thriller set in the movie world featuring Pierce Brosnan, Dudley Moore and James Coburn playing themselves. Filmed in mock-documentary style and unfolding like a real-life piece of investigative journalism, the twists and turns come thick and fast, with the suspense increasing as the surprise ending veers into view. Fascinating, original and hugely entertaining. AJ. Contains swearing and sexual references.

Pierce Brosnan • James Coburn • Dudley Moore • Alexander Folk *Police Detective* • Carl Sundstrom *Security Guard* • Bridget Baiss *Gayle Hamilton* • Ian Ogilvy *Gary* • Charlotte Brosnan *Amy* ■ *Dir/Scr* Francis Megahy

Disappearing Acts ★★★ 15

Romantic drama
2000 · US · Colour · 110mins

Another classy HBO production, this emotionally complex drama follows the glorious ups and moving downs in the relationship between builder Wesley Snipes and aspiring singer Sanaa Lathan. The two leads are superb, and neither they nor director Gina Prince-Bythewood flinch from the raw truths of love and relationships in the modern age. JF DVD

Wesley Snipes *Franklin Swift* • Sanaa Lathan *Zora Banks* • John Amos *Mr Swift* • CCH Pounder *Mrs Swift* • Regina Hall *Portia* ■ *Dir* Gina Prince-Bythewood • *Scr* Lisa Jones, from the novel by Terry McMillan

Disclosure ★★ 18

Thriller 1994 · US · Colour · 122mins

Demi Moore plays Michael Douglas's former lover, who is promoted above him in a computer corporation. When Moore seeks to rekindle their passion, the now-married Douglas has second thoughts at a vital moment, and the much-miffed Moore accuses him of sexual harassment. This is a self-important and unintentionally funny thriller about corporate power and sexual equality, though there is too much emphasis on computer gizmos and cyber-babble. AT. Contains swearing and sex scenes. DVD

Michael Douglas *Tom Sanders* • Demi Moore *Meredith Johnson* • Donald Sutherland *Bob Garvin* • Roma Maffia *Catherine Alvarez* • Caroline Goodall *Susan Hendler* • Dennis Miller *Mark Lewyn* • Rosemary Forsyth *Stephanie Kaplan* • Dylan Baker *Philip Blackburn* • Nicholas Sadler *Don Cherry* ■ *Dir* Barry Levinson • *Scr* Paul Attanasio, from the novel by Michael Crichton

Disco Pigs ★★ 15

Drama 2001 · UK/Ire · Colour · 89mins

This twisted rites-of-passage tale is an overwrought drama that doesn't quite come up with the goods. Inseparable since birth, next-door neighbours Cillian Murphy and Elaine Cassidy have grown up together as though they were twins – even having their own special language. But when they are prised apart on their 17th birthday, all hell breaks loose. Kirsten Sheridan's already precarious feature debut then collapses into a mêlée of sickening violence. DP DVD

Elaine Cassidy *Sinead, "Runt"* • Cillian Murphy *Darren, "Pig"* • Brian F O'Byrne *Runt's dad* • Eleanor Methven *Pig's mam* • Geraldine O'Rawe *Runt's mam* • Darren Healy *Marky* ■ *Dir* Kirsten Sheridan • *Scr* Enda Walsh, from her play

The Discreet Charm of the Bourgeoisie ★★★★★ 15

Comedy drama 1972 · Fr · Colour · 97mins

Brilliantly interweaving a sequence of disrupted dinners, three diversionary tales and a quartet of awakenings that alert us to the fact we have been sharing a dream, this sharply satirical and teasingly structured picture is one of Luis Buñuel's finest achievements as both film-maker and social commentator. At once a delightful comedy and a clinical assault on the bastions and behaviour of the bourgeoisie, it touches on all the director's favourite themes: sexual repression, religious hypocrisy and patriarchal paranoia. The playing is exceptional, though Fernando Rey, Delphine Seyrig and Michel Piccoli merit special mention. DP. In French with English subtitles.

Fernando Rey *Ambassador* • Delphine Seyrig *Mme Simone Thévenot* • Stéphane Audran *Mme Alice Sénéchal* • Bulle Ogier *Florence* • Jean-Pierre Cassel *M Sénéchal* • Paul Frankeur *M Thévenot* • Julien Bertheau *Bishop*

Dufour • Claude Piéplu *Colonel* • Michel Piccoli *Home Secretary* ■ *Dir* Luis Buñuel • *Scr* Luis Buñuel, Jean-Claude Carrière

The Dish ★★★★ 12

Comedy drama 2000 · Aus · Colour · 96mins

When Neil Armstrong became the first man to walk on the Moon on 20 July 1969, he was watched by a global TV audience of 600 million people. But how many of them had even heard of the Australian town of Parkes in New South Wales, whose radio telescope of transmitted the pictures? Not many, and that's the arresting premise of this gentle, human comedy. A heart-warming tale of small-town folk getting on with the business of making history, it's full of self-deprecating, irreverent Aussie humour, typified by Roy Billing's local mayor and Tayler Kane's security guard, who takes his job very seriously indeed. Sam Neill supplies a dignified authority – and a star name, of course. AC. Contains swearing. [VIDEO] DVD

Sam Neill *Cliff Buxton* • Kevin Harrington *Ross "Mitch" Mitchell* • Tom Long *Glenn Latham* • Patrick Warburton *Al Burnett* • Genevieve Mooy *May McIntyre* • Tayler Kane *Rudi Kellerman* • Bille Brown *Prime minister* • Roy Billing *Mayor Bob McIntyre* ■ *Dir* Rob Sitch • *Scr* Santo Cilauro, Tom Gleisner, Jane Kennedy, Rob Sitch

Disha ★★★

Drama 1990 · Ind · Colour · 130mins

For this naturalistic town-and-country tale, Sai Paranjpye firmly roots the characters in their environment and makes evocative use of Bombay's teeming textile quarter. Nana Patekar and Raghuvir Yadav arrive in the city, seeking work after their farms are parched by drought. But the most compelling drama takes place back home, where Patekar's wife (Shabana Azmi) falls for the boss of a thriving factory, and Yadav's brother (Om Puri) goes divining to save his homestead. DP. In Hindi with English subtitles.

Shabana Azmi • Nana Patekar *Vasant* • Raghuvir Yadav *Soma* • Om Puri • Nilu Phule • Rajshree Sawant ■ *Dir/Scr* Sai Paranjpye

Dishonored ★★★★★

First World War spy drama
1931 · US · BW · 91mins

An erotic dream doubling as a First World War espionage drama, this extraordinary work was the third of director Josef von Sternberg's celebrated collaborations with Marlene Dietrich, and casts the latter as "Agent X-27" and Victor McLaglen as her rival and sexual plaything, "Agent H-14". Rivalling Garbo's *Mata Hari*, which was released the same year, it was a huge box-office hit, luring audiences with its promise of sex and spying. As the sultry spy doomed by her predatory nature, Dietrich is radiant and poised in a performance that is at once controlled and all over the place, the result of von Sterrnberg's customary exactitude. AT

Marlene Dietrich *Magda/X-27* • Victor McLaglen *Colonel Kranau* • Gustav von Seyffertitz *Secret Service head* • Warner Oland *Colonel von Hindau* • Lew Cody *Colonel Kovrin* • Barry Norton *Young lieutenant* • Davison Clark *Court-martial officer* • Wilfred Lucas *General Dymov* ■ *Dir* Josef von Sternberg • *Scr* Daniel N Rubin, from the story *X-27* by Josef von Sternberg • *Cinematographer* Lee Garmes

Dishonored Lady ★★

Crime 1947 · US · BW · 85mins

Produced by Hedy Lamarr herself, this screen version of a Broadway hit finds her playing a neurotic magazine editor who goes off the rails and attempts to kill herself by driving her car into a garden wall. Luckily for her, said wall belongs to a psychiatrist! Alas, her shady past catches up with her and she's accused of murder. The wordy script and Robert Stevenson's pedestrian direction are drawbacks, but Lamarr does reasonably well. AT

Hedy Lamarr *Madeleine Damien* • Dennis O'Keefe *Dr David Cousins* • John Loder *Felix Courtland* • William Lundigan *Jack Garet* • Morris Carnovsky *Dr Caleb* • Paul Cavanagh *Victor Kranish* • Douglass Dumbrille *District attorney* ■ *Dir* Robert Stevenson • *Scr* Edmund H North, from the play by Edward Sheldon, Margaret Ayer Barnes

Disney's The Kid ★★★ PG

Comedy fantasy 2000 · US · Colour · 99mins

Bruce Willis here returns to *The Sixth Sense* territory, starring alongside youngster Spencer Breslin in a film that has a tinge of the supernatural about it. Willis plays a heartless image consultant in need of redemption. Initially puzzled by the child who seems to be following him, Willis comes to realise that Breslin is in fact his younger self. Confronted by the past, the gruff adult has a chance to change his present-day existence for the better. The story is unalloyed by sentimentality and rings as true as a school bell. TH [VIDEO] DVD

Bruce Willis *Russ Duritz* • Spencer Breslin *Rusty Duritz* • Emily Mortimer *Amy* • Lily Tomlin *Janet* • Chi McBride *Kenny* • Jean Smart *Deirdre Lafever* • Dana Ivey *Dr Alexander* ■ *Dir* Jon Turteltaub • *Scr* Audrey Wells

Disorderlies ★ PG

Comedy 1987 · US · Colour · 82mins

Rappers the Fat Boys' attempt to break into the movies is unlikely to stand the test of time. This Three Stooges-influenced screwball comedy sees the boys coming to the aid of millionaire Ralph Bellamy, who's about to be murdered by an evil nephew. Bellamy's career survived this turkey unscathed but the Fat Boys' bumbling soon wears thin. RS [VIDEO]

Damon Wimbley *Kool Rock* • Darren Robinson *Buffy* • Mark Morales *Markie* • Ralph Bellamy *Albert Dennison* • Tony Plana *Miguel* • Anthony Geary *Winslow Lowry* • Marco Rodriguez *Luis Montana* • Troy Beyer *Carla* ■ *Dir* Michael Schultz • *Scr* Mark Feldberg, Mitchell Klebanoff

The Disorderly Orderly ★★★ U

Comedy 1964 · US · Colour · 89mins

Jerry Lewis's comic genius is very much a matter of taste. In France he's virtually canonised; elsewhere, though, he has admirers and detractors in equal parts. This is exactly the type of movie that tends to infuriate both parties. It's very, very funny, with a wonderful climactic chase and a particularly hysterical moment where Lewis has sympathy pains with the choleric Alice Pearce. However, the film also contains some of the most melancholy and cloying sentiment in the whole of Lewis's oeuvre. TS

Jerry Lewis *Jerome Littlefield* • Glenda Farrell *Dr Jean Howard* • Everett Sloane *Mr Tuffington* • Karen Sharpe *Julie Blair* • Kathleen Freeman *Maggie Higgins* • Del Moore *Dr Davenport* • Susan Oliver *Susan Andrews* • Alice Pearce *Talkative patient* • Jack E Leonard *Fat Jack* ■ *Dir* Frank Tashlin • *Scr* Frank Tashlin, from a story by Norm Liebmann, Ed Haas

Disorganized Crime ★★ 15

Crime comedy 1989 · US · Colour · 97mins

In what could have been a jolly roller-coaster ride, a group of criminals mooch about expectantly as they wait for the mastermind behind their latest heist to show up, but the movie deteriorates all too swiftly. Still, the assembled actors, including Corbin Bernsen and Lou Diamond Phillips, fight gamely with the lousy script, managing to create the occasional flicker of interest. SH. Contains violence, swearing. [VIDEO]

Hoyt Axton *Sheriff Henault* • Corbin Bernsen *Frank Salazar* • Rubén Blades *Carlos Barrios* • Fred Gwynne *Max Green* • Ed O'Neill *George Denver* • Lou Diamond Phillips *Ray Forgy* ■ *Dir/Scr* Jim Kouf

A Dispatch from Reuters ★★★ U

Biographical drama 1940 · US · BW · 98mins

In the last of its series of high-minded historical biographies, Warner Bros squeezes a surprising amount of tense drama out of the story of Julius Reuter, whose passion for spreading the news goes from pigeon post to establishing his famous impartial wire service. Relishing a peaceful character part for once, Edward G Robinson is eminently watchable as Reuter, while director William Dieterle, teamed with ace cameraman James Wong Howe, gives the film pace and visual distinction. AE

Edward G Robinson *Julius Reuter* • Edna Best *Ida Magnus* • Albert Basserman *Franz Geller* • Gene Lockhart *Bauer* • Otto Kruger *Dr Magnus* • Nigel Bruce *Sir Randolph Persham* ■ *Dir* William Dieterle • *Scr* Milton Krims

Disraeli ★★

Biographical drama 1929 · US · BW · 90mins

This stolid biopic of the prime minister and Victorian novelist stars a monocled George Arliss. The real Mrs Arliss, Florence, gets to play Mrs Disraeli as well. On the political front, it's the race to purchase the Suez Canal in front of the Russians that commands the PM's attention, but on the domestic front it's romantic matchmaking. AT

George Arliss *Disraeli* • Joan Bennett *Lady Clarissa Pevensey* • Florence Arliss *Lady Mary Beaconfield* • Anthony Bushell *Charles, Lord Deeford* • David Torrence *Sir Michael, Lord Probert* ■ *Dir* Alfred E Green • *Scr* Julien Josephson, from the play by Louis Napoleon Parker

Distance ★★★

Drama 2001 · Jpn · Colour · 132mins

Inspired by events surrounding the sarin gas attack on the Tokyo subway, this tale tracks the reunion of four very different people whose cult member relatives sacrificed themselves in a bid to poison Tokyo's water supply. The shooting style alternates between hand-held cameras for the scenes in the woodland cabin where the quartet are forced to spend the night, and more carefully composed flashbacks to illustrate their relationships with their loved ones. Koreeda Hirokazu's largely improvised mood piece ultimately lacks the focus and resonance to match its sincere objectives. DP. In Japanese with English subtitles.

Tadanobu Asano *Koichi* • Arata *Atsushi Mizuhara* • Yusuke Iseya *Masaru Enoki* • Yui Natsukawa *Kiyoka Yamamoto* ■ *Dir/Scr* Hirokazu Koreeda

Distant Drums ★★ U

Period adventure 1951 · US · Colour · 99mins

This Warner Bros adventure can't technically be termed a western – it's set in Florida – but deals with a familiar theme, as Seminole Indians go on the warpath against an expeditionary force in 1840. The supporting cast is way below par, and the whole thing is held together by the sheer star power of Cooper. If it all seems a little familiar, that's because director Raoul Walsh has reworked his own controversial Second World War drama *Objective, Burma!*. TS

Gary Cooper *Captain Quincy Wyatt* • Mari Aldon *Judy Beckett* • Richard Webb *Richard Tufts* • Ray Teal *Private Mohair* • Arthur Hunnicutt *Monk* • Robert Barrat *General Zachary Taylor* • Clancy Cooper *Sergeant Shane* ■ *Dir* Raoul Walsh • *Scr* Niven Busch, Martin Rackin, from a story by Niven Busch

Distant Harmony ★★★

Music documentary
1987 · US · Colour · 85mins

Seeing that *From Mao to Mozart: Isaac Stern in China* won the Oscar for best documentary, it's easy to see why DeWitt Sage was tempted to record Luciano Pavarotti's 1986 visit to the Forbidden City. Where Stern placed himself at the service of budding Chinese musicians, however, Pavarotti is content to be treated like a celebrity. Sage follows the legendary tenor at a respectable distance, capturing the inevitable culture clashes with a wry detachment. Once he reaches the Great Hall and the focus shifts firmly to music, though, you can almost forgive him for everything. DP

Dir DeWitt Sage

Distant Justice ★★ 18

Thriller 1992 · Jpn/US · Colour · 87mins

A routine title for a routine thriller about a committed police chief who throws away the rulebook to help a friend track down the man who killed his wife and kidnapped his child. The result is less than arresting, though Hollywood veteran George Kennedy turns in a better performance than the material merits. DA [VIDEO]

Bunta Sugawara *Rio Yuki* • David Carradine *Joe Foley* • George Kennedy *Tom Bradfield* • Yoko Nogiwa *Hiroko* • Eric Lutes *Charlie Givens* • Sakura Sugawara *Sakura* ■ *Dir* Toru Murakawa • *Scr* Toshiyuki Tabe

Distant Thunder ★★★★

Drama 1973 · Ind · Colour · 101mins

This harrowing drama, set during the famine that ravaged Bengal in the early 1940s, is one of Satyajit Ray's most politically committed films. Yet it retains the humanism and concern for character that makes his work so compelling. While the railings at the caste system and government corruption make for powerful viewing, it's the slow realisation of a Brahmin and his wife that people matter more than rigid rules that makes this an unmissable experience. DP. In Bengali with English subtitles.

Soumitra Chatterjee *Gangacharan* • Babita *Ananga* • Sandhya Roy *Chutki* • Ramesh Mukherjee *Biswas* • Chitra Bannerjee • Govinda Chakravarty • Noni Ganguly • Seli Pal • Suchita Roy ■ *Dir/Scr* Satyajit Ray

Distant Thunder ★★★ 18

Drama 1988 · Can/US · Colour · 109mins

This co-production casts the admirable John Lithgow as a traumatised Vietnam vet who has abandoned society for life in the wilds. Karate Kid Ralph Macchio plays the teenage son he deserted as a toddler. Thanks mainly to Lithgow, who doesn't know how to give a bad performance, this occasionally violent film holds the attention, despite struggling at times to keep its maudlin elements in check. PF. Contains swearing. [VIDEO]

John Lithgow *Mark Lambert* • Ralph Macchio *Jack Lambert* • Kerrie Keane *Char* • Reb Brown *Harvey Nitz* • Janet Margolin *Barbara Lambert* • Denis Arndt *Larry* • Jamey Sheridan *Moss* • Tom Bower *Louis* ■ *Dir* Rick Rosenthal • *Scr* Robert Stitzel, from a story by Robert Stitzel, Deedee Wehle

A Distant Trumpet ★★★★

Western 1964 · US · Colour · 117mins

The last film from veteran director Raoul Walsh is impressive: a handsome, intelligent cavalry western, superbly scored by Max Steiner and ravishingly shot by William Clothier. Walsh makes partial reparation to the hordes of Indians slaughtered in previous westerns by using subtitles in an attempt to preserve their dignity, and the complex military themes are well handled. What lets this fine movie down, though, is the casting. Newlyweds Troy Donahue and Suzanne Pleshette are just too 1960s in hairstyle and attitude to convince us they belong in Walsh's Old West. TS. Some native American dialogue with English subtitles.

Troy Donahue *Second Lt Matthew Hazard* • Suzanne Pleshette *Kitty Mainwaring* • Diane McBain *Laura Greenleaf* • James Gregory *General Alexander Quait* • William Reynolds *Lt Mainwaring* • Claude Akins *Seely Jones* ■ *Dir* Raoul Walsh • *Scr* John Twist, Richard Fielder, Albert Beich, from the novel by Paul Horgan

Distant Voices, Still Lives ★★★★★ 15

Drama 1988 · UK · Colour · 80mins

Never has song been used so poignantly as in Terence Davies's painful, yet curiously fond recollection of postwar Liverpool. The popular tunes that punctuate the ritualistic round of family gatherings and boozer sing-songs jarringly counterpoint the irrational violence perpetrated by Pete Postlethwaite's short-fused father. Unflinchingly depicting both the beatings and their consequences, Davies brings a bruising realism to the stylised series of vignettes, which adeptly avoid the patronising tone that jaundices so many portraits of working-class life. DP. Contains violence and swearing.

Freda Dowie *Mother* • Pete Postlethwaite *Father* • Angela Walsh *Eileen* • Dean Williams *Tony* • Lorraine Ashbourne *Maisie* • Marie Jelliman *Jingles* • Sally Davies *Eileen as a child* • Nathan Walsh *Tony as a child* • Susan Flanagan *Maisie as a child* • Michael Starke *Dave* ■ *Dir/Scr* Terence Davies

The Distinguished Gentleman ★★★ 15

Comedy 1992 · US · Colour · 107mins

Eddie Murphy plays a smooth talking grifter who sets his sights on the ultimate con – politics. However, on his election as a senator, he quickly learns that the biggest villains are in Washington. Director Jonathan Lynn, of *Yes, Minister* fame, is a lot gentler on the American political scene than he was with our own, but there are some neat satirical jibes and he gives free rein to Murphy, who delivers a relaxed performance. JF. Contains swearing and nudity. DVD

Eddie Murphy *Thomas Jefferson Johnson* • Lane Smith *Dick Dodge* • Sheryl Lee Ralph *Miss Loretta* • Joe Don Baker *Olaf Andersen* • Kevin McCarthy *Terry Corrigan* • Charles S Dutton *Elijah Hawkins* • Noble Willingham *Zeke Bridges* • James Garner *Jeff Johnson* ■ *Dir* Jonathan Lynn • *Scr* Marty Kaplan, from a story by Marty Kaplan, Jonathan Reynolds

Distortions ★★★ 18

Thriller 1987 · US · Colour · 94mins

Ever wonder what happened to Piper Laurie in between *The Hustler* and *Twin Peaks*? Apparently she was in training for her role in David Lynch's weird but wonderful TV series, appearing in Armand Mastroianni's almost equally bizarre thriller. Olivia Hussey's husband meets a violent end following an encounter with a gigolo. Presented with his charred remains, his widow starts to experience disturbing hallucinations under the malign influence of Laurie, who is holding her captive. Not well-known, but worth seeking out for lovers of suspense. RT

Olivia Hussey *Amy* • Piper Laurie *Margot* • Steve Railsback *Scott* • Rita Gam *Mildred* • June Chadwick • Terence Knox ■ *Dir* Armand Mastroianni • *Scr* John F Goff

Disturbed ★★ 18

Psychological horror thriller
1990 · US · Colour · 93mins

This low-budget thriller from director Charles Winkler, son of *Rocky* producer Irvin stars a blond Malcolm McDowell as a psychiatrist who probably needs more treatment than the whole ward of stereotypical nuts he treats, especially when a patient he murdered returns to haunt him. McDowell's broad brush strokes are in tune with Winkler's demented camerawork. RS

Malcolm McDowell *Dr Derek Russell* • Geoffrey Lewis *Michael* • Priscilla Pointer *Nurse Francine* • Pamela Gidley *Sandy Ramirez* • Irwin Keyes *Pat Tuel* • Clint Howard *Brian* ■ *Dir* Charles Winkler • *Scr* Charles Winkler, Emerson Bixby

Disturbing Behaviour ★★ 15

Thriller 1998 · US · Colour · 83mins

Bad kids in a small town are turning good after undergoing experimental psychological treatment in this tepid teen variation on *The Stepford Wives*. Trouble is, they turn homicidal when sexually aroused, and it seems high school student James Marsden is the only one to notice. Director David Nutter brings some of his trademark *X Files* moodiness to the material, but he can't seem to decide what sort of film he's making. A statement about individuality versus conformity? Or just another run-of-the-mill slash-fest? AJ. Contains swearing. DVD

Bruce Greenwood *Dr Caldicott* • Katie Holmes *Rachel Wagner* • William Sadler *Dorian Newberry* • Nick Stahl *Gavin Strick* • Steve Railsback *Officer Cox* • James Marsden *Steve Clark* • Tobias Mehler *Andy Effkin* ■ *Dir* David Nutter • *Scr* Scott Rosenberg

Diva ★★★★ 15

Cult crime drama 1981 · Fr · Colour · 112mins

Considered one of the masterpieces of *cinéma du look* (the name given to French films of the 1980s in which style took precedence over content), *Diva* marked the directorial debut of Jean-Jacques Beineix. It's a dazzling job, brimful with bravura camera movements and ultra-chic images. The tale of two tapes (one a bootlegged recording of an opera star, the other incriminating evidence against a police inspector) rather gets lost as Beineix experiments with styles ranging from the Feuillade serials of the early years of the last century to the New Wave of the 1950s and 1960s. Yet this remains compelling viewing, if only for the amazing performance of Dominique Pinon (*Delicatessen*). DP. In French with English subtitles. Contains violence, swearing, nudity. DVD

Frédéric Andrei *Jules* • Wilhelmenia Wiggins Fernandez *Cynthia Hawkins* • Richard Bohringer *Gorodish* • Thuy An Luu *Alba* • Jacques Fabbri *Inspector Jean Saporta* • Chantal Deruaz *Nadia Kalonsky* • Roland Bertin *Simon Weinstadt* ■ *Dir* Jean-Jacques Beineix • *Scr* Jean-Jacques Beineix, Jean Van Hamme, from the novel by Delacorta • *Cinematographer* Philippe Rousselot

The Dive ★ 15

Thriller 1989 · Nor/UK · Colour · 92mins

It may be one of Norway's biggest box-office successes, but this pedestrian deep sea action thriller really only merits "nul point". A dangerous rescue operation is launched when a group of divers is trapped underwater, but the formulaic plot poses a far bigger threat to the proceedings than the treacherous ocean currents. Nicely shot in shimmering dark hues, but hopeless in the suspense and empathy departments. AJ

Michael Kitchen *Bricks* • Frank Grimes *Dobs* • Bjorn Sundquist *Gunnar* • Marika Lagercrantz *Ann* • Sverre Anker Ousdal *Captain* • Nils Ole Oftebro *Akselsen* ■ *Dir* Tristan De Vere Cole • *Scr* Leidulv Risan, Carlos Wigan

Dive Bomber ★★★ PG

Wartime drama 1941 · US · Colour · 126mins

This wonderful flying drama features Errol Flynn and Fred MacMurray in fine fettle for a *Boys' Own* treat directed by Michael Curtiz. Ostensibly a piece of serious research into pilot blackout, it gives all concerned a roaring excuse to slap each other about in friendly fashion in a flurry of patched leather elbows. If your idea of a good film is the wind in your hair and aerial thrills, this is for you. SH DVD

Errol Flynn *Lieutenant Doug Lee* • Fred MacMurray *Commander Joe Blake* • Ralph Bellamy *Dr Lance Rogers* • Alexis Smith *Linda Fisher* • Regis Toomey *Tim Griffin* • Robert Armstrong *Art Lyons* • Allen Jenkins *Lucky Dice* ■ *Dir* Michael Curtiz • *Scr* Frank Wead, Robert Buckner, from the story *Beyond the Blue Sky* by Frank Wead

The Divided Heart ★★ U

Drama 1954 · UK · BW · 89mins

This British melodrama would be dismissed as sentimental tosh if it wasn't based on a true story that hit the headlines following the end of the Second World War. Drawing on the actual records of the case, director Charles Crichton uses a series of artful flashbacks to pad out the courtroom battle at the centre of the action, as biological mother Yvonne Mitchell fights Cornell Borchers for custody of the child Borchers adopted. Crichton lays on the pathos so thickly that the emotional drama never really tugs at our heartstrings. DP

Cornell Borchers *Inga* • Yvonne Mitchell *Sonja* • Armin Dahlen *Franz* • Alexander Knox *Chief Justice* • Geoffrey Keen *Marks* • Michel Ray *Toni* • Martin Keller *Toni* • Liam Redmond *First Justice* • Eddie Byrne *Second Justice* ■ *Dir* Charles Crichton • *Scr* Jack Whittingham, Richard Hughes

Divided We Fall ★★★★ PG

Second World War drama
2000 · Cz Rep · Colour · 117mins

Inspired by a true story, Jan Hrebejk's film takes a darkly comic approach to the hideous events of the Holocaust. Any hope married couple Boleslav Polivka and Anna Siskova may have of keeping a low profile during the German occupation of their small Czech town is shattered by the sudden reappearance of a Jewish friend who had been sent to a concentration camp earlier in the war. They decide to hide the refugee in their larder, despite the fact their nosey neighbour is a Nazi lackey. The performances are first rate in a film in which only fact could be this fantastic while managing to be comic, appalling and poignant. DP. In Czech with English subtitles. Contains violence. DVD

Boleslav Polivka *Josef Cizek* • Anna Siskova *Marie Cizkova* • Jaroslav Dusek *Horst Prohaska* • Csongor Kassai *David Wiener* • Jiri Kodet *Dr Fiser-Rybar* ■ *Dir* Jan Hrebejk • *Scr* Petr Jarchovsky, from his novel *Musime si Pomahat*

Divine ★★★

Comedy drama 1935 · Fr · BW · 82mins

Colette provided the original story for this engaging work, plus some dialogue for the adaptation by Jean-Georges Auriol and director Max Ophüls. It tells of a young girl who leaves the countryside hoping to become a successful singer in Paris. She suffers problems and heartaches along the way, especially in the handsome form of Georges Rigaud as a milkman. The central theme – so beloved by Colette – shows the transformation of Simone Berriau into a woman of the world. BB. In French with English subtitles.

Simone Berriau *Ludivine, "Divine" Jarisse* • Catherine Fonteney *Mme Jarisse* • Yvette Lebon *Roberte* • Jorge Rigaud [Georges Rigaud] *Antonin* • Philippe Hériat *Lutuf Allah, the fakir* ■ *Dir* Max Ophüls • *Scr* Colette, Jean-Georges Auriol, Max Ophüls, from the novel *L'Envers du Music-Hall* by Colette

The Divine Comedy ★★

Psychological drama
1992 · Por · Colour · 140mins

This densely symbolic tract has little in common with Dante's medieval masterpiece, even though it shares such themes as faith and truth, sin and delusion. Veteran Portuguese director Manoel de Oliveira also scripted this portrait of an asylum where every patient believes themselves to be a character from the Bible or from *Crime and Punishment*. This is a wordy picture that is rarely enlightening or engrossing. DP. In Portuguese with English subtitles.

Maria de Medeiros *Sonya* • Miguel Guilherme *Raskolnikov* • Luis Miguel Cintra *The prophet* • Mario Viegas *The philosopher* • Leonor Silveira *Eve* • Diogo Doria *Ivan* • Paulo Matos *Jesus* • Carlos Gomes *Adam* • Ruy Furtado *The director* ■ *Dir/Scr* Manoel de Oliveira

Divine Intervention ★★★ 15

Political comedy drama
2002 · Fr/Ger/Mor/Neth · Colour · 89mins

Subtitled "A Chronicle of Love and Pain", writer/director Elia Suleiman's quirky take on life in the occupied territories is strewn with poignant insights into coping in a divided society. The Nazareth-set opening vividly illustrates a number of neighbourhood tensions that serve as a backdrop to the romantic trysts between Suleiman and his Palestinian girlfriend, Manal Khader. However, for every astute incident, there are gross misfires. DP. In Arabic and Hebrew with English subtitles. Contains swearing and violence. DVD

Elia Suleiman *ES* • Manal Khader *Woman* • Nayef Fahoum Daher *Father* • George Ibrahim *Santa Claus* • Jamal Daher *Jamal* • Amer Daher *Auni* ■ *Dir/Scr* Elia Suleiman

The Divine Lady ★★★

Silent historical drama
1928 · US · BW · 100mins

Director Frank Lloyd won an early Oscar for this story of Emma, Lady Hamilton, Nelson's mistress and one of the most notorious women in English history. Corinne Griffith has a generous sweep of personality as Emma, though her performance pales in comparison with Vivien Leigh's in *That Hamilton Woman* (1941). The historical detail is taken very much for granted, and the film's appeal at the time was mainly due to its novelty. TH

Corinne Griffith *Emma, Lady Hamilton* • Victor Varconi *Lord Nelson* • HB Warner *Sir William Hamilton* • Ian Keith *Greville* • William Conklin *Romney* • Marie Dressler *Mrs Hart* ■ *Dir* Frank Lloyd • *Scr* Harry Carr (titles), Edwin Justus Mayer (titles), Forrest Halsey, from the novel *The Divine Lady: a Romance of Nelson and Emma Hamilton* by E Barrington

Divine Madness ★★★ 15

Concert movie 1980 · US · Colour · 82mins

Shot over four days using up to 20 cameras, Michael Ritchie's record of Bette Midler's shows at the Pasadena Civic Auditorium broke the mould for concert films in terms of look and technique. Backed by the Harlettes, Bette blazes through songs and comic routines with the kind of unfettered energy that is sometimes the undoing of her feature work. Midler has an amazing range as a singer, but there's nothing particularly new in her interpretations, unlike her mix of stand-up and sketches that are as varied as her outlandish costumes. There's little sense of "being there", however, and ultimately the exercise seems rather clinical. DP. Contains swearing. [VIDEO]

Dir Michael Ritchie • *Scr* Jerry Blatt, Bette Midler, Bruce Vilanch

Divine Secrets of the Ya-Ya Sisterhood ★★ 12

Comedy drama 2002 · US · Colour · 111mins

Sandra Bullock plays the writer who has issues with her mother, so her mother's friends (Shirley Knight, Fionnula Flanagan and Maggie Smith) kidnap her so they can explain all the things her mother went through that turned her into the hard-drinking, bitchy woman she is now. Ashley Judd and Ellen Burstyn are terrific as the past and present version of Bullock's mum, but the story doesn't flow properly and is let down by a final revelation that isn't much of a surprise. JB. Contains swearing and violence. [VIDEO] DVD

Sandra Bullock *Sidda Lee Walker* • Ellen Burstyn *Vivi* • Fionnula Flanagan *Teensy* • James Garner *Shep Walker* • Ashley Judd *Younger Vivi* • Shirley Knight *Necie* • Angus MacFadyen *Connor McGill* • Maggie Smith *Caro* • Gina McKee *Genevieve* ■ *Dir* Callie Khouri • *Scr* Mark Andrus, from the novels *Divine Secrets of the Ya-Ya Sisterhood*/*Little Altars Everywhere* by Rebecca Wells

The Divine Woman

Silent romantic drama 1928 · US · BW

A long-lost treat for Greta Garbo fans, this film is now one of the American Film Institute's "most wanted" movies. The divine Greta starts out as a Breton peasant girl and ends up taking Paris – and lover Lars Hanson – by storm. Directed by by Garbo's fellow Swede, Victor Seastrom. TS

Greta Garbo *Marianne* • Lars Hanson *Lucien* • Lowell Sherman *Legrand* • Polly Moran *Mme Pigonier* • Dorothy Cumming *Mme Zizi Rouck* • John Mack Brown [Johnny Mack Brown] *Jean Lery* • Cesare Gravina *Gigi* • Paulette Duval *Paulette* ■ *Dir* Victor Seastrom [Victor Sjöström] • *Scr* Dorothy Farnum, John Colton (titles), from the play *Starlight* by Gladys Unger

Le Divorce ★★★ 12

Romantic comedy drama
2003 · US/UK · Colour · 112mins

This romantic comedy drama from director James Ivory and producer Ismail Merchant is a convoluted look at French and American sexual attitudes. Kate Hudson arrives in Paris just as her pregnant stepsister Naomi Watts is deserted by husband Melvil Poupaud. Hudson then starts an affair with his uncle Thierry Lhermitte, Glenn Close contributes to the proceedings as an expatriate American writer and Leslie Caron has a callously disapproving eye for everyone. More shallow than profound, but there are some satisfying moments. TH. Contains some swearing. [VIDEO] DVD

Kate Hudson *Isabel Walker* • Naomi Watts *Roxeanne "Roxy" de Persand* • Glenn Close *Olivia Pace* • Stockard Channing *Margreeve Walker* • Sam Waterston *Chester Walker* • Thierry Lhermitte *Edgar Cosset* • Leslie Caron *Suzanne de Persand* • Bebe Neuwirth *Julia Manchevering* • Matthew Modine *Tellman* • Stephen Fry *Piers Janely* • Melvil Poupaud *Charles-Henri de Persand* ■ *Dir* James Ivory • *Scr* Ruth Prawer Jhabvala, James Ivory, from the novel by Diane Johnson

Divorce American Style ★★★

Satirical comedy
1967 · US · Colour · 109mins

This sophisticated, brilliantly cast comedy is compulsive viewing. The title, taken from the 1961 Italian original, masks a witty tale of contemporary mores in which separating spouses Dick Van Dyke and Debbie Reynolds take a baleful look at the effects of divorce on their friends. Jason Robards is brilliant as a man so crippled by alimony payments he's desperate to pair off ex-wife Jean Simmons, while Van Johnson makes even a used car salesman seem boyishly beguiling. Some may find it an acquired taste. TS

Dick Van Dyke *Richard Harmon* • Debbie Reynolds *Barbara Harmon* • Jason Robards *Nelson Downes* • Jean Simmons *Nancy Downes* • Van Johnson *Al Yearling* • Joe Flynn *Lionel Blandsforth* • Shelley Berman *David Grieff* • Martin Gabel *Dr Zenwinn* ■ *Dir* Bud Yorkin • *Scr* Norman Lear, from a story by Robert Kaufman

Divorce – Italian Style ★★★★

Black comedy 1961 · It · BW · 103mins

It's not often that a foreign language film takes a mainstream Oscar, so the success of Pietro Germi and his fellow screenwriters suggests this wicked black comedy is doubly special. For all the ingenuity of the script, though, it's Marcello Mastroianni (who added an Oscar nomination to his Golden Globe and Bafta victories) that makes these sinister Sicilian shenanigans so memorable. He plays the lovesick husband who opts to kill his shrewish wife (Daniella Rocca) rather than divorce her; in Italy, that's the easier option! Mastroianni expertly combines deadpan suavity with impeccable comic timing, while Germi directs with flair. DP. An Italian language film.

Marcello Mastroianni *Ferdinando Cefalu* • Daniela Rocca *Rosalie Cefalu* • Stefania Sandrelli *Angela* • Leopoldo Trieste *Carmelo Patane* • Odoardo Spadaro *Don Gaetano* ■ *Dir* Pietro Germi • *Scr* Pietro Germi, Ennio DeConcini, Alfredo Giannetti

The Divorce of Lady X ★★★ U

Comedy 1938 · UK · Colour · 87mins

Producer Alexander Korda used marvellous early three-strip Technicolor to give this piece of screwball whimsy a special lustre. The film starred his wife-to-be Merle Oberon, who plays a party-goer trapped in a London hotel by one of those fogs so beloved of Americans. The Technicolor works, but Oberon doesn't: comedy wasn't her forte. Laurence Olivier does little more than pout, so the acting honours are stolen by Ralph Richardson and Binnie Barnes. The film's quite amusing, though, in its daffy way. TS [VIDEO]

Merle Oberon *Leslie Steele* • Laurence Olivier *Logan* • Binnie Barnes *Lady Mere* • Ralph Richardson *Lord Mere* • Morton Selten *Lord Steele* • JH Roberts *Slade* • Gertrude Musgrove *Saunders* • Gus McNaughton *Waiter* • Eileen Peele *Mrs Johnson* ■ *Dir* Tim Whelan • *Scr* Ian Dalrymple, Arthur Wimperis, Lajos Biró, Robert Sherwood [Robert E Sherwood], from the play *Counsel's Opinion* by Gilbert Wakefield

Divorce Wars ★★★★

Drama 1982 · US · Colour · 100mins

This cleverly scripted and insightful domestic drama about a divorce lawyer who can't solve the problems within his own marriage is co-written and directed by the talented Donald Wrye, whose work includes the Jack Lemmon version of *The Entertainer*. As the high-powered attorney, Tom Selleck proves yet again what a personable actor he is, and he's well teamed here with Jane Curtin. This made-for-TV drama is also worth catching for the last screen appearance of Joan Bennett, whose film career began in 1916 and includes such highlights as *Little Women* and *Father of the Bride*. TS

Tom Selleck *Jack Kaiser* • Jane Curtin *Vickey Kaiser* • Candy Azzara *Sylvia Bemous* • Joan Bennett *Adele Burgess* • Maggie Cooper *Leslie Fields* • Charles Haid *Fred Bemous* ■ *Dir* Donald Wrye • *Scr* Donald Wrye, Linda Elstad, from a story by Linda Elstad

The Divorcee ★★★

Romantic drama 1930 · US · BW · 83mins

Norma Shearer won her best actress Academy Award for the spunky, sexy performance on display here. This may surprise viewers who only recall her as the grand queen of the lot in her later roles at a prestige-conscious MGM run by her husband, Irving Thalberg. In fact, this movie was based on a novel so racy that the author published it anonymously, and much of that substance (though not the actual plot) is on screen in those halcyon pre-Code days. Shearer plays a woman having an affair with a man loved by another woman. All a bit creaky now. TS

Norma Shearer *Jerry* • Chester Morris *Ted* • Conrad Nagel *Paul* • Robert Montgomery *Don* • Florence Eldridge *Helen* • Helene Millard *Mary* • Robert Elliott *Bill* • Mary Doran *Janice* ■ *Dir* Robert Z Leonard • *Scr* Nick Grinde, Zelda Sears, John Meehan, from the novel *Ex-Wife* by Ursula Parrott

Divorcing Jack ★★★ 15

Comedy thriller
1998 · UK/Fr · Colour · 105mins

Virtuoso character actor David Thewlis utterly dominates this chase thriller set in Northern Ireland, in which he plays a drunken, foul-mouthed reporter whose life is in ruins. Robert Lindsay co-stars as an ambitious politician and Rachel Griffiths is great as a nun with a gun. The picture barely stops for breath, while Thewlis, with his grotty wardrobe, filthy hair and unshaven face, is a very different action hero. AT. Contains swearing, violence, sex scenes. [VIDEO] DVD

David Thewlis *Dan Starkey* • Rachel Griffiths *Lee Cooper* • Robert Lindsay *Michael Brinn* • Jason Isaacs *"Cow Pat" Keegan* • Laura Fraser *Margaret* • Richard Gant *Charles Parker* • Laine Megaw *Patricia Starkey* • Kitty Aldridge *Agnes Brinn* ■ *Dir* David Caffrey • *Scr* Colin Bateman, from his novel

Dixie ★★★ U

Musical biographical drama
1943 · US · Colour · 89mins

A big hit in its day, this Bing Crosby vehicle purports to be the biography of Daniel Decatur Emmett, the man who wrote the South's most famous marching song. With its corny sentiment and minstrel shows, it's rather difficult, especially if you don't warm to Bing. But there's a notable screen debut from comedian Billy de Wolfe, and the 1940s Technicolor is simply sumptuous. TS

Bing Crosby *Dan Emmett* • Dorothy Lamour *Millie Cook* • Billy De Wolfe *Mr Bones* • Marjorie Reynolds *Jean Mason* • Lynne Overman *Mr Whitlock* • Eddie Foy Jr *Mr Felham* • Raymond Walburn *Mr Cook* • Grant Mitchell *Mr Mason* ■ *Dir* A Edward Sutherland • *Scr* Darrell Ware, Claude Binyon, from the story by William Rankin

Dixie Dynamite ★

Action crime drama
1976 · US · Colour · 88mins

This "good ol' boy" nonsense from director Lee Frost is punishment for the eyes, while the soundtrack, which includes songs by Duane Eddy, gives the ears a bashing too. Warren Oates stars as a motorcycle racer enlisted by two sisters to exact revenge upon the trigger-happy sheriff who killed their moonshiner father. Exuberant action, risible dialogue. RS

Warren Oates *Mack* • Christopher George *Sheriff Phil Marsh* • Jane Anne Johnstone *Dixie* • Kathy McHaley *Patsy* ■ *Dir* Lee Frost • *Scr* Lee Frost, Wes Bishop

Django ★★★★ 18

Spaghetti western
1966 · It/Sp · Colour · 86mins

Switching effortlessly from the gritty realism of the mud-splattered streets to the stylised violence of the machine-gun shoot-outs, this superior spaghetti western from Sergio Corbucci owes as much to the Japanese samurai film as it does to the Hollywood horse opera. Franco Nero stars as the avenging angel who uses the armoury he keeps in a coffin to settle the feud between Mexican general Angel Alvarez and Civil War veteran Jose Bodalo and his red-hooded horsemen. Packed with floggings, ambushes and robberies, with a little ear-eating for good measure, this is not one for the faint-hearted. The 30-plus *Django* movies truly represent the foundation of the genre. DP. Italian dialogue dubbed into English. [VIDEO] DVD

Franco Nero *Django* • Loredana Nusciak *Maria* • Jose Bodalo *Major Jackson* • Angel Alvarez *General Hugo Rodrigues* ■ *Dir* Sergio Corbucci • *Scr* Sergio Corbucci, Bruno Corbucci, Franco Rossetti, Jose G Maesso

Django Kill ★★★ 15

Spaghetti western
1967 · It/Sp · Colour · 111mins

Giulio Questi began his career as an assistant to Federico Fellini, which might explain why this surreal film feels like a spaghetti *Satyricon*. Tomas Milian takes on the role of the avenging gunslinger made famous by Franco Nero, finding a unique solution to a feud over a stolen gold shipment. But the plot is almost irrelevant in what is considered by many to be the most violent western ever made. Providing a bizarre balance to the brutality, there's a melodramatic band of outlaws and a parrot who's a gunfight aficionado. DP. Italian dialogue dubbed into English. DVD

Tomas Milian *Django* • Piero Lulli *Oaks* • Milo Quesada *Tembler* • Paco Sanz *Hagerman* • Roberto Camardiel *Sorro* • Marilu Tolo *Flory* • Raymond Lovelock *Evan* • Patrizia Valturri *Lizabeth* ■ *Dir* Giulio Questi • *Scr* Giulio Questi, Franco Arcalli

Django the Bastard ★★★ 12

Western 1970 · It · Colour · 94mins

This is among the best films in this seminal spaghetti series. Antonio de Teffe(who also co-wrote) stars as the Civil War veteran who takes revenge on the Confederate officers who slaughtered his comrades. Stately, stylish and prone to sudden eruptions of violence (most notably the massacre of a band of Mexican desperados), this Wild West ghost story was clearly an influence on Clint Eastwood's *High Plains Drifter*. DP. Italian dialogue dubbed into English. [VIDEO]

Antonio de Teffe *Django* • Rada Rassimov *Alethea* • Paolo Gozlino *Rod Murdoch* • Lu Kanante *Luke Murdoch* ■ *Dir* Sergio Garrone • *Scr* Anthony de Teffe, Sergio Garrone

Djomeh ★★★★

Romantic drama 2000 · Iran · Colour · 94mins

Hassan Yektapanah was a former assistant director to acclaimed Iranian film-maker Abbas Kiarostami and invests his debut feature with the affecting humanism that makes his mentor's work so sincere. The film follows the day-to-day life of Djomeh

(Jalil Nazari), an Afghan immigrant who has moved to Iran for reasons of the heart rather than war or poverty. Although primarily a treatise on exile and local schisms within Islam, this is also a charming tale of doomed devotion, as Djomeh quaintly pays court to an Iranian shopgirl. DP. In Farsi with English subtitles.

Jalil Nazari *Djomeh* • Mahmoud Behraznia *Mr Mahmoud* • Mahbobeh Khalili *Setareh* • Rashid Akbari *Habib* ■ *Dir/Scr* Hassan Yektapanah

D

Do Bigha Zameen ★★★ U

Drama 1953 · Ind · BW · 88mins

This is a fascinating hybrid of Bollywood musical and postwar European film-making. It's a shamelessly emotive melodrama, and Balraj Sahni gives the performance of his career as the peasant drawn to the city to save his home from unscrupulous speculators. The key inspiration is that of the Italian neorealist Vittorio De Sica, not only in the authentic use of location and the resort to sentimental humanism, but also in the plot borrowings from *Bicycle Thieves* and *Shoeshine*. DP. In Hindi with English subtitles.

Balraj Sahni *Shambhu* • Ratan Kumar *Kanhaiya* • Murad *Sapru* • Nirupa Roy *Paro* ■ *Dir* Bimal Roy • *Scr* Hrishikesh Mukherjee, from a story by Salil Choudhury

Do I Love You? ★★ 18

Romantic comedy drama
2003 · UK · Colour · 72mins

Focusing on an interlocking group of young London lesbians, writer/director Lisa Gornick's debut is a mischievous and occasionally perceptive take on modern-day love, life and sexuality. Marina (Gornick herself) is pushed into an emotional crisis when her girlfriend (Raquel Cassidy) starts to get uncomfortably serious about their romance. Gornick paints a picture of queer culture that humorously reassesses popular misconceptions, while the wooden actors at least deliver her cheeky dialogue with enthusiasm. SF. Contains swearing and sexual references.

Lisa Gornick *Marina, woman on bike* • Raquel Cassidy *Romy, Marina's girlfriend* • Ruth Posner *Paula, Marina's mother* • Brendan Gregory *Stefan, Marina's father* • Sarah Patterson *Louise, a columnist* • Kemal Sylvester *Greg, Louise's boyfriend* • Kate McGoldrick *Alice, a photographer* • Harri Alexander *Lois, Alice's girlfriend* • Caitlin Morrow *Susie, Marina's ex-girlfriend* ■ *Dir/Scr* Lisa Gornick

Do Not Disturb ★★★

Comedy 1965 · US · Colour · 101mins

By the time this movie was made, the 1960s were swinging and sunny Doris Day had developed a chic and slightly risqué image, promoted by her producer/husband Martin Melcher. Here, Day and screen husband Rod Taylor suspect each other of varying infidelities abroad, but the pair deserve much better. Taylor was capable in his prime of enlivening mediocre material, and here he proves a worthy successor to Rock Hudson as a foil for Day. TS

Doris Day *Janet Harper* • Rod Taylor *Mike Harper* • Hermione Baddeley *Vanessa Courtwright* • Sergio Fantoni *Paul Bellari* • Reginald Gardiner *Simmons* • Maura McGiveny *Claire Hackett* • Aram Katcher *Culkos* • Leon Askin *Langsdorf* • Pierre Salinger *American consul* ■ *Dir* Ralph Levy • *Scr* Milt Rosen, Richard Breen [Richard L Breen], from the play *Some Other Love* by William Fairchild

Do the Right Thing ★★★★ 18

Drama 1989 · US · Colour · 114mins

Spike Lee's fierce racial drama concentrates on one sweltering day in New York where simmering racial tensions are about to explode. The focal point becomes a pizza parlour run by Danny Aiello, who refuses to replace his old Italian photographs with pictures of black heroes. Lee himself is excellent as Aiello's delivery boy, but the playing of the ensemble cast is exemplary and, although there are a dozen different storylines, Lee effortlessly meshes them together without losing sight of his central theme. Add to that Ernest Dickerson's bright, vibrant cinematography and the superb soundtrack, and the result is an exhilarating, passionate and often very funny modern classic. JF. Contains swearing. DVD

Danny Aiello *Sal* • Spike Lee *Mookie* • John Turturro *Pino* • Richard Edson *Vito* • Ossie Davis *Da Mayor* • Ruby Dee *Mother Sister* • Giancarlo Esposito *Buggin' Out* • Bill Nunn *Radio Raheem* • Rosie Perez *Tina* • John Savage *Clifton* • Sam Jackson [Samuel L Jackson] *Mister Señor Love Daddy* ■ *Dir/Scr* Spike Lee

Do You Love Me? ★★★ U

Musical 1946 · US · Colour · 90mins

The 1940s Technicolor of this charming 20th Century-Fox musical shows off Maureen O'Hara's flowing red tresses a treat. She's a college dean and she's loved by band vocalist Dick Haymes, who proves yet again that he was one of the greatest ever singers of slow-tempo ballads. Harry James, one of the biggest band stars of the period, also appears, while Reginald Gardiner provides the laughs. TS

Maureen O'Hara *Katherine Hilliard* • Dick Haymes *Jimmy Hale* • Harry James *Barry Clayton* • Reginald Gardiner *Herbert Benham* • Richard Gaines *Ralph Wainwright* • Stanley Prager *Dilly* • BS Pully *Taxi driver* • Chick Chandler *Earl Williams* • Alma Kruger *Mrs Crackleton* ■ *Dir* Gregory Ratoff • *Scr* Robert Ellis, Helen Logan, Dorothy Bennett, from a story by Bert Granet

Do You Remember Love ★★★★ PG

Drama 1985 · US · Colour · 92mins

Joanne Woodward won an Emmy for her role in this made-for-TV movie about how the family of a middle-aged college professor copes when she contracts Alzheimer's. Scriptwriter Vickie Patik also walked away with an award for her moving script, which pulls no punches and steers clear of melodrama, However, most plaudits should go to director Jeff Bleckner and the cast, which also includes *LA Law*'s Susan Ruttan and Ron Rifkin (*The Negotiator, LA Confidential*). JB

Joanne Woodward *Barbara Wyatt-Hollis* • Richard Kiley *George Hollis* • Geraldine Fitzgerald *Lorraine Wyatt* • Jim Metzler *Tom Hollis* • Jordan Charney *Marvin Langdon* • Ron Rifkin *Gerry Kaplan* • Susan Ruttan *Julie Myers* ■ *Dir* Jeff Bleckner • *Scr* Vickie Patik

The Doberman Gang ★★

Crime caper 1972 · US · Colour · 86mins

A low-budget comedy about a gang of bungling bank robbers who come up with the idea of training a pack of dogs to do the job for them. They even name the pooches after legendary gangsters: Dillinger, Bonnie and Clyde and so on. The canines pull off the caper to plan, but are less keen on handing over the dough. It's not Shakespeare, but once you've bought the premise it has its moments. Two sequels (*The Daring Dobermans* and *The Amazing Dobernans*) followed. PF

Byron Mabe *Eddie Newton* • Hal Reed *Barney Greer* • Julie Parrish *June* • Simmy Bow *Sammy* • Jojo D'Amore *Jojo* • John Tull *Pet shop owner* • Jay Paxton *Bank manager* • Diane Prior *Sandy* ■ *Dir* Byron Ross Chudnow • *Scr* Louis Garfinkle, Frank Ray Perilli

Dobermann ★★★★ 18

Crime thriller 1997 · Fr · Colour · 98mins

Wildly stylish, this tongue-in-cheek cops and robbers tale bursts with dazzling technical trickery, explosive action scenes and deranged performances, particularly from Tcheky Karyo as the scariest cop who ever lived. Jan Kounen's comic-strip concoction has a fairly simplistic plot, but slick, sexy camerawork and editing, plus super-cool criminal posturing from Vincent Cassel and Monica Bellucci give the film a dynamic edge over the majority of recent foreign language thrillers. If you can stomach the extreme violence, this is a heart-pumping, high-speed chase through the more commercial district of French cinema. JC. In French with English subtitles. Contains violence, sex scenes and drug abuse. DVD

Vincent Cassel *Yann LePentrec, "Le Dob"* • Monica Bellucci *Nathalie, "Nat la gitane"* • Tcheky Karyo *Chief Inspector Sauveur Christini* • Antoine Basler *Jean-Claude Ayache, "Mosquito"* • Dominique Bettenfeld *Elie Frossard, "Padre"* ■ *Dir* Jan Kounen • *Scr* Jan Kounen, Joël Houssin, from the novels by Joël Houssin

Doc ★★★★ 15

Western 1971 · US · Colour · 91mins

A flawed but fascinating account of the famous gunfight at the OK Corral with Stacy Keach as Doc Holliday, Faye Dunaway as his girlfriend Katie Elder, and Harris Yulin especially impressive as the political opportunist Wyatt Earp. The shoot-out, when it comes, is impressively handled by director Frank Perry, who successfully avoids mimicking previous versions, notably Ford's *My Darling Clementine* and John Sturges's two films on the same subject. Shorn of many of the familiar trappings, this account may disappoint traditional western fans, but its focus on Holliday's disenchantment seems to be a little parable about the moral bankruptcy of Nixon's America. AT

Stacy Keach *Doc Holliday* • Faye Dunaway *Kate Elder* • Harris Yulin *Wyatt Earp* • Mike Witney [Michael Witney] *Ike Clanton* • Denver John Collins *Kid* ■ *Dir* Frank Perry • *Scr* Pete Hamill

Doc Hollywood ★★★ 15

Romantic comedy
1991 · US · Colour · 98mins

A diverting, folksy comedy, in which Michael J Fox plays an ambitious California-bound intern who finds himself press-ganged into becoming a doctor in a small South Carolina community. Revelling in local idiosyncrasies, director Michael Caton-Jones gives the film a lovely golden glow and produces a Capra-like hymn to the small town. There are fine performances from Fox and a talented supporting cast; look out for a neat cameo from George Hamilton. JF. Contains swearing and nudity.

Michael J Fox *Dr Benjamin Stone* • Julie Warner *Lou* • Barnard Hughes *Dr Hogue* • Woody Harrelson *Henry "Hank" Gordon* • David Ogden Stiers *Nick Nicholson* • Frances Sternhagen *Lillian* • George Hamilton *Dr Halberstrom* • Bridget Fonda *Nancy Lee* • Mel Winkler *Melvin* ■ *Dir* Michael Caton-Jones • *Scr* Jeffrey Price, Peter S Seaman, Daniel Pyne, from the novel *What?...Dead Again* by Neil B Shulman

Doc Savage: the Man of Bronze ★★ PG

Fantasy adventure
1975 · US · Colour · 96mins

George Pal was a legendary figure in the worlds of sci-fi and fantasy, but this, his swan-song film as a producer, is not the best way to remember him. The story is taken from the ever-popular Doc Savage books of the 1930s, with television's Tarzan, Ron Ely, in the title role. Despite director Michael Anderson's admirable attempts to insert some knowing humour, this remains a rather tame and routine adventure. JF. Contains some violence and swearing.

Ron Ely *Doc Savage* • Paul Gleason *Long Tom* • Bill Lucking [William Lucking] *Renny* • Michael Miller (1) *Monk* • Eldon Quick *Johnny* • Darrell Zwerling *Ham* • Paul Wexler *Captain Seas* • Janice Heiden *Andriana* ■ *Dir* Michael Anderson • *Scr* George Pal, Joe Morhaim, from the novel by Kenneth Robeson

The Docks of New York ★★★★

Silent drama 1928 · US · BW · 60mins

Josef von Sternberg's movie flopped in America, mainly because it was previewed the same week as the first talkie, *The Jazz Singer*. (A singular case of bad timing.) Over the years, though, the picture has been rediscovered as a highly effective melodrama about a ship's stoker who saves a streetwalker from suicide, marries her and then takes the blame when she's accused of murder. The film's romantic fatalism is compelling, and von Sternberg creates some stunning imagery out of his low-life settings. AT

George Bancroft *Bill Roberts* • Betty Compson *Sadie* • Olga Baclanova *Lou* • Clyde Cook *"Sugar" Steve* • Mitchell Lewis *Third Engineer* • Gustav von Seyffertitz *"Hymn Book" Harry* • Guy Oliver *The Crimp* • May Foster *Mrs Crimp* ■ *Dir* Josef von Sternberg • *Scr* Jules Furthman • *Cinematographer* Harold Rosson

Docks of New York ★★

Crime comedy drama
1945 · US · BW · 61mins

One of the last gasps of the *East Side Kids*, made shortly before star Leo Gorcey picked up the franchise and continued the series as *The Bowery Boys*. It's the same mixture as usual, involving some mayhem around stolen jewellery, while Huntz Hall's mugging over-compensates for the absence of series regulars Gabriel Dell and Bobby Jordan, both off working for Uncle Sam. Movie buffs should note that the Carlyle Blackwell Jr who appears here is *not* the infamous fashion critic "Mr Blackwell", as has been claimed. TS

Leo Gorcey *Muggs McGinnis* • Huntz Hall *Glimpy* • Billy Benedict *Skinny* • Bud Gorman *Danny* • Mende Koenig *Sam* • Gloria Pope *Saundra* • Carlyle Blackwell Jr *Marty* • George Meeker *Naclet* • Betty Blythe *Mrs Darcy* ■ *Dir* Wallace Fox • *Scr* Harvey Gates

Docteur Petiot ★★★★ 15

Biographical drama
1990 · Fr · Colour and BW · 97mins

While most people are now familiar with the Holocaust heroics of Raoul Wallenberg and Oskar Schindler, the hideous crimes of Marcel Petiot have largely gone unrecorded. This chilling film recounts the career of one of France's most notorious serial killers, who conned Jews into believing he could smuggle them to Argentina before murdering them and incinerating their bodies. Michel Serrault is quite superb, whether reassuring loved ones or hurtling round the darkened streets, with his cape billowing like a vampire. Christian de Chalonge's flamboyant direction exploits every cinematic trick in the book to create an authentic and genuinely horrific atmosphere. DP. In French with English subtitles.

Michel Serrault *Docteur Petiot* • Pierre Romans *Ivan Drezner* • Zbigniew Horoks *Nathan Guzik* • Bérangère Bonvoisin *Georgette Petiot* • Aurore Prieto *Madame Guzik* ■ *Dir* Christian de Chalonge • *Scr* Dominique Garnier, Christian de Chalonge

The Doctor ★★★★ 15

Drama 1991 · US · Colour · 117mins

William Hurt stars as a glib, egotistical doctor who's forced to re-appraise his life when he's diagnosed as suffering from cancer. When the tables are turned and he becomes a patient, he begins to realise the shortcomings of his profession. As moral issues come under the microscope (a rare enough event in Hollywood), Hurt makes a credible transition from blunt medical hard-nut to "born again" doctor with a conscience, and the probing script and first-class performances (from Hurt and Elizabeth Perkins as a fellow patient) prevent this harrowing drama from becoming an empty exercise in Hollywood schmaltz. JM [video] DVD

William Hurt *Dr Jack McKee* • Christine Lahti *Anne McKee* • Elizabeth Perkins *June* • Mandy Patinkin *Murray* • Adam Arkin *Eli* • Charlie Korsmo *Nicky* • Wendy Crewson *Dr Leslie Abbott* ■ *Dir* Randa Haines • *Scr* Robert Caswell, from the memoirs *A Taste of My Own Medicine* by Ed Rosenbaum

The Doctor and the Devils ★★★ 15

Historical crime drama
1985 · UK · Colour · 88mins

A rather earnest resurrection of the Burke and Hare bodysnatchers tale, pitched more as a dark moral fable than a horror film. Based on a script written by Dylan Thomas in the 1940s (unproduced because of censor problems), producer Mel Brooks got veteran Hammer horror director/ cinematographer Freddie Francis to rework it. The result is high on period detail, but low on *Grand Guignol* chills. AJ. Contains violence, swearing, nudity and sex scenes. [video]

Timothy Dalton *Dr Thomas Rock* • Jonathan Pryce *Robert Fallon* • Twiggy *Jenny Bailey* • Julian Sands *Dr Murray* • Stephen Rea *Timothy Broom* • Phyllis Logan *Elizabeth Rock* ■ *Dir* Freddie Francis • *Scr* Ronald Harwood, from a screenplay (unproduced) by Dylan Thomas

The Doctor and the Girl ★★

Medical drama 1949 · US · BW · 97mins

In his first picture for MGM, under the competent direction of Curtis Bernhardt, Glenn Ford plays an idealistic medic who eschews the rewards of becoming a specialist in order to help the underprivileged. RK

Glenn Ford *Dr Michael Corday* • Charles Coburn *Dr John Corday* • Gloria De Haven [Gloria DeHaven] *Fabienne Corday* • Janet Leigh *Evelyn Heldon* • Bruce Bennett *Dr Alfred Norton* • Nancy Davis *Mariette* ■ *Dir* Curtis Bernhardt • *Scr* Theodore Reeves, from the novel *Bodies and Souls* by Maxence van der Meersch

Doctor at Large ★★★ U

Comedy 1957 · UK · Colour · 94mins

In this third entry in the series inspired by the novels of Richard Gordon, Dirk Bogarde, as accident-prone houseman Simon Sparrow, once again escapes the confines of St Swithin's in order to explore pastures new, in this case a country practice where virtually nothing goes right. But it's only once he's back under the beady gaze of James Robertson-Justice that the film comes to life. Amiable enough, but everyone is just a touch off colour, and the film shows signs of the terminal decline that would set in after Bogarde quit the series. DP [video] DVD

Dirk Bogarde *Simon Sparrow* • Muriel Pavlow *Joy* • Donald Sinden *Benskin* • James Robertson-Justice *Sir Lancelot Spratt* • Shirley Eaton *Nan* • Derek Farr *Dr Potter-Shine* • Michael Medwin *Bingham* • Lionel Jeffries *Dr Hackett* ■ *Dir* Ralph Thomas • *Scr* Nicholas Phipps, Richard Gordon, from the novel by Richard Gordon

Doctor at Sea ★★ PG

Comedy 1955 · UK · Colour · 89mins

Appearing in her first British film and still a year away from taking world cinema by storm in *And God Created Woman*, Brigitte Bardot here provides Dirk Bogarde with a welcome distraction from the miserable seasickness he experiences away from the terra firma of St Swithin's. Despite the lively rapport between the stars, however, the second of Rank's popular series is short on truly comic incident, and the shipboard location is limiting. DP [video] DVD

Dirk Bogarde *Simon Sparrow* • Brigitte Bardot *Helene Colbert* • Brenda de Banzie *Muriel Mallet* • James Robertson-Justice *Captain Hogg* • Maurice Denham *Easter* • Michael Medwin *Trail* • Hubert Gregg *Archer* ■ *Dir* Ralph Thomas • *Scr* Nicholas Phipps, Richard Gordon, Jack Davies, from the novel by Richard Gordon

Doctor Blood's Coffin ★★

Horror 1960 · UK · Colour · 92mins

Director Sidney J Furie cut his teeth on such British programme fillers as this cheap and cheerful *Frankenstein*-flavoured tale. Doctor Kieron Moore experiments in bringing the dead back to life while his fetching nurse (Hazel Court) screams a lot amid the lurid, Hammer Horror-style glossiness. Enhanced by its Cornish tin-mine setting, Furie's cardboard suspense shocker is hardly a classic, but still great fun. AJ

Kieron Moore *Dr Peter Blood* • Hazel Court *Linda Parker* • Ian Hunter *Dr Robert Blood* • Fred Johnson *Tregaye (Morton)* • Kenneth J Warren *Sergeant Cook* • Andy Alston *Beale* • Paul Stockman *Steve Parker* • John Ronane *Hanson* • Gerald C Lawson *Morton (Sweeting)* ■ *Dir* Sidney J Furie • *Scr* Jerry Juran, James Kelly, Peter Miller, from a story by Jerry Juran

Dr Broadway ★★

Crime comedy drama
1942 · US · BW · 68mins

Anthony Mann's first feature film is a tight little thriller revolving around a Times Square medic who finds himself becoming a detective in a murder mystery. The second-league cast is headed by the competent Macdonald Carey and Jean Phillips, usually Ginger Rogers's stand-in. Various Broadway characters people the plot, there is some good location work and Mann keeps the action moving smartly. RB

Macdonald Carey *Dr Timothy "Doc" Kane* • Jean Phillips *Connie Madigan* • J Carrol Naish *Jack Venner* • Richard Lane *Patrick Doyle* • Edward Ciannelli [Eduardo Ciannelli] *Vic Telli* • Joan Woodbury *Margie Dove* • Arthur Loft *Captain Mahoney* • Warren Hymer *Maxie the goat* ■ *Dir* Anthony Mann • *Scr* Art Arthur, from the short story by Borden Chase

Dr Bull ★★★ U

Drama 1933 · US · BW · 79mins

The folksy wisdom and whimsical humour of Will Rogers seem hopelessly old-fashioned today, but in the first third of this century he was one of the biggest stars in the States. The first of his three collaborations with John Ford sees Rogers playing a small-town GP making light of his limited resources and the suspicions of would-be patients. Ford, who was a sucker for this brand of homespun philosophising, loved the film, although modern audiences will probably find it somewhat twee. DP

Will Rogers *Dr Bull* • Vera Allen *Janet Cardmaker* • Marian Nixon *May Tripping* • Howard Lally *Joe Tripping* • Berton Churchill *Herbert Banning* • Louise Dresser *Mrs Banning* • Andy Devine *Larry Ward* • Rochelle Hudson *Virginia Banning* ■ *Dir* John Ford • *Scr* Paul Green, Jane Storm, from the novel *The Last Adam* by James Gould Cozzens

Dr Caligari ★★★

Horror comedy 1989 · US · Colour · 80mins

Under the pseudonym "Rinse Dream", Stephen Sayadian directed *Cafe Flesh* (1982), an influential slice of expressionist porn. This, his only mainstream film to date, is Sayadian's similarly styled version of *The Cabinet of Dr Caligari* (1919), with Caligari played by a woman (model Madeleine Reynal) who presides over bizarre experiments at her sanatorium. Sick humour, stupid dialogue and emetic effects will repel most viewers, but lovers of the truly outré should seek out this amazing product of a warped imagination. DM

Madeleine Reynal *Dr Caligari* • Fox Harris *Dr Avol* • Laura Albert *Mrs Van Houten* • Jennifer Balgobin *Ramona Lodger* • John Durbin *Gus Pratt* • Gene Zerna *Les Van Houten* • David Parry *Dr Lodger* ■ *Dir* Stephen Sayadian • *Scr* Jerry Stahl, Stephen Sayadian

Dr Crippen ★★ PG

Biographical crime drama
1962 · UK · BW · 94mins

Considering the notoriously sordid subject matter, director Robert Lynn's true crime case history should have been a far more riveting affair than this so-so account. But you can't blame Donald Pleasence, at his sinister best playing the monstrous doctor who murders his persecuting wife in order to elope with his typist lover. Told in flashback as Crippen stands trial, this remains remote and uninvolving because of the deliberately austere quasi-documentary stance. AJ [video]

Donald Pleasence *Dr Hawley Harvey Crippen* • Coral Browne *Belle Crippen* • Samantha Eggar *Ethel Le Neve* • Donald Wolfit *RD Muir* • James Robertson-Justice *Captain Kendall* • Geoffrey Toone *Mr Tobin* • Oliver Johnston *Lord Chief Justice* ■ *Dir* Robert Lynn • *Scr* Leigh Vance • *Photography* Nicolas Roeg

Dr Cyclops ★★★

Science-fiction thriller
1940 · US · Colour · 78mins

Ernest B Schoedsack, co-director of the original *King Kong*, returns to the fantasy genre with this wonderfully weird tale of a mad scientist (Albert Dekker) who miniaturises explorers in his Amazon jungle laboratory. Borrowing ideas from *Kong* special effects man Willis O'Brien, Schoedsack crafts a well-mounted science-fiction thriller, the first of its kind in vivid Technicolor. The standard plot now looks hackneyed, but the impressive props make this a lot of fun. AJ

Albert Dekker *Dr Thorkel* • Janice Logan *Dr Mary Mitchell* • Thomas Coley *Bill Stockton* • Charles Halton *Dr Bulfinch* • Victor Kilian *Steve Baker* • Frank Yaconelli *Pedro* • Bill Wilkerson *Silent Indian* • Allen Fox *Cab driver* • Paul Fix *Dr Mendoza* • Frank Reicher *Prof Kendall* ■ *Dir* Ernest B Schoedsack • *Scr* Tom Kilpatrick • *Special Effects* Farciot Edouard

Doctor Detroit ★★ 15

Comedy 1983 · US · Colour · 86mins

Featuring Dan Aykroyd in his first leading role after the death of his partner John Belushi, this comedy is only a partial success. The plot, which finds Aykroyd's mild-mannered college teacher getting mixed up with some hookers, gives him full rein to showcase all of his comic talents, and he is particularly good as a ludicrously OTT pimp. However, he is let down by a loose script and crude direction by Michael Pressman. JF [video]

Dan Aykroyd *Clifford Skridlow* • Howard Hesseman *Smooth Walker* • TK Carter *Diavolo Washington* • Donna Dixon *Monica McNeil* • Lynn Whitfield *Thelma Cleland* • Lydia Lei *Jasmine Wu* • Fran Drescher *Karen Blittstein* ■ *Dir* Michael Pressman • *Scr* Carl Gottlieb, Robert Boris, Bruce Jay Friedman, from the novel *Detroit Abe* by Bruce Jay Friedman

Doctor Dolittle ★★★ U

Musical fantasy adventure
1967 · US · Colour · 138mins

Children will revel in this infamous musical comedy based on Hugh Lofting's stories, but this was a costly disaster in its day which almost killed off 20th Century-Fox. Its longevity belies a thumpingly leaden affair, in which Rex Harrison is squeakily embarrassing as the dotty doc. There are some good tunes, including the Oscar-winning *Talk to the Animals*, and the special effects also won an Academy Award, but overall it is rather a bore. To adults, that is; children find it entertaining enough. SH [video]

Rex Harrison *Doctor John Dolittle* • Anthony Newley *Matthew Mugg* • Peter Bull *General Bellowes* • William Dix *Tommy Stubbins* • Portia Nelson *Sarah Dolittle* • Samantha Eggar *Emma Fairfax* • Richard Attenborough *Albert Blossom* • Norma Varden *Lady Petherington* ■ *Dir* Richard Fleischer • *Scr* Leslie Bricusse, from the stories by Hugh Lofting • *Music/ Lyrics* Leslie Bricusse

Doctor Dolittle ★★★ PG

Fantasy comedy 1998 · US · Colour · 81mins

After the success of *The Nutty Professor*, Eddie Murphy completed the transformation from foul-mouthed, fast-talking comic to all-round family entertainer with this high-grossing film. Murphy plays a doctor whose life is turned upside down when his old childhood gift – the ability to "talk to the animals" – returns. Cue lots of juvenile gags from a host of guest voices. JF. Contains swearing. [video] DVD

Eddie Murphy *Dr John Dolittle* • Ossie Davis *Archer Dolittle* • Oliver Platt *Dr Mark Weller* • Peter Boyle *Calloway* • Richard Schiff *Dr Gene Reiss* • Kristen Wilson *Lisa* • Jeffrey Tambor *Dr Fish* • Kyla Pratt *Maya* ■ *Dir* Betty Thomas • *Scr* Nat Mauldin, Larry Levin, from stories by Hugh Lofting

Dr Dolittle 2 ★★ PG

Fantasy comedy 2001 · US · Colour · 83mins

The tedious central plot of this sequel sees Eddie Murphy coaching a slovenly circus bear (voiced by Steve Zahn) to be an alpha male, attract a mate and save an endangered forest from destruction. The parade of supporting species with human characteristics is much the same as its far funnier predecessor, but the main story is flat and charmless, and the pace is leaden. JC [video] DVD

Eddie Murphy *Dr John Dolittle* • Kristen Wilson *Lisa Dolittle* • Jeffrey Jones *Joseph Potter* • Kevin Pollak *Jack Riley/Crocodile* • Raven-Symone *Charisse Dolittle* • Kyla Pratt *Maya Dolittle* • Steve Zahn *Archie* • Lisa Kudrow *Ava* • Isaac Hayes *Possum* • Richard C Sarafian *God Beaver* ■ *Dir* Steve Carr • *Scr* Larry Levin, from the stories by Hugh Lofting

Dr Ehrlich's Magic Bullet ★★★

Biographical drama 1940 · US · BW · 102mins

Edward G Robinson plays the German doctor who discovered a cure for syphilis – not celibacy but the drug Salvarsan – and won a Nobel Prize in 1908. A tricky subject for a Warner Bros biopic in 1940, but everything is done in the most tasteful manner. The original story by Norman Burnside was thoroughly rewritten with the help of John Huston and Heinz Herald, cutting out all the romantic twaddle to concentrate on Ehrlich peering through a microscope. It's absorbing viewing, and Robinson later regarded it as his finest performance. AT

Edward G Robinson *Dr Paul Ehrlich* • Ruth Gordon *Mrs Ehrlich* • Otto Kruger *Dr Emil von Behring* • Donald Crisp *Minister Althoff* • Maria Ouspenskaya *Franziska Speyer* • Montagu Love *Professor Hartmann* • Sig Rumann [Sig Ruman] *Dr Hans Wolfert* ■ *Dir*

William Dieterle • *Scr* John Huston, Heinz Herald, Norman Burnside, from a story by Norman Burnside

Doctor Faustus ★★★ PG

Drama 1967 · UK/It · Colour · 88mins

Christopher Marlowe's play – about the man who sold his soul to the devil – was a favourite of Richard Burton's, who may have looked at Faust and seen himself, the great stage actor who willingly sold out to Hollywood and celebrity. Casting himself as Faust and his wife Elizabeth Taylor as Helen of Troy, Burton put the play on at Oxford and then used all his box-office clout to produce and co-direct this screen version. To his credit, Burton took with him his co-director and the Oxford cast, though the result is more a fascinating record of the stage production – Burton's reading of Marlowe's verse is magnificent – than a fully realised film. AT

Richard Burton *Doctor Faustus* • Elizabeth Taylor *Helen of Troy* • Andreas Teuber *Mephistopheles* • Ian Marter *Emperor* • Elizabeth O'Donovan *Empress* • David McIntosh *Lucifer* • Jeremy Eccles *Beelzebub* • Ram Chopra *Valdes* • Richard Carwardine *Cornelius* ■ *Dir* Richard Burton, Nevill Coghill • *Scr* Nevill Coghill, from the play by Christopher Marlowe

Doctor Françoise Gailland ★★★

Drama 1975 · Fr · Colour · 100mins

Annie Girardot won a César (the French equivalent of an Oscar) for her performance in this three-hankie weepie. Also known as *No Time for Breakfast*, the film sticks pretty closely to the classic "women's picture" formula of the careerist whose professional ambitions are compromised by events in her personal life. Girardot skilfully captures first the anger, then the courage of the eponymous cancer victim, while Jean-Pierre Cassel and Isabelle Huppert offer selfless support. DP. French dialogue dubbed into English.

Annie Girardot *Françoise Gailland* • Jean-Pierre Cassel *Daniel Letessier* • François Périer *Gérard Gailland* • Isabelle Huppert *Elisabeth Gailland* • William Coryn *Julien Gailland* ■ *Dir* Jean-Louis Bertucelli • *Scr* André G Brunelin, Jean-Louis Bertucelli, from the novel *Un Cri* by Noelle Loriot

Dr Giggles ★ 18

Horror 1992 · US · Colour · 91mins

Heard the one about the kid sent mad by his father's surgical obsessions, who escapes from an asylum years later and turns up in his home town to wreak vengeance? Of course you have. An ultra-derivative medical *Halloween*, there isn't one iota of originality in this comatose collection of "Dr Kill-Dare" clichés. AJ. Contains swearing, violence.

Larry Drake *Evan Rendell* • Holly Marie Combs *Jennifer Campbell* • Glenn Quinn *Max Anderson* • Cliff De Young *Tom Campbell* • Richard Bradford *Officer Hank Magruder* • Keith Diamond *Officer Joe Reitz* • Michelle Johnson *Tamara* ■ *Dir* Manny Coto • *Scr* Manny Coto, Graeme Whifler

Dr Gillespie's Criminal Case ★★★

Medical drama 1943 · US · BW · 88mins

With James Craven stepping into the shoes vacated by Phil Brown, this entry in MGM's popular medical series continues the plotline started in *Calling Dr Gillespie*. Upset by former fiancée Donna Reed's romance with sergeant Michael Duane, Craven's homicidal maniac reduces Blair General to chaos, and the venerable senior surgeon is forced to call on junior doctors Van Johnson and Keye Luke for assistance. DP

Lionel Barrymore *Dr Leonard Gillespie* • Van Johnson *Dr Randall Adams* • Donna Reed *Marcia Bradburn* • Keye Luke *Dr Lee Wong How* • James Craven *Roy Todwell* • Nat Pendleton *Joe Wayman* • Alma Kruger *Molly Byrd* • Margaret O'Brien *Margaret* • Walter Kingsford *Dr Walter Carew* • Nell Craig *Nurse Parker* • Michael Duane *Sergeant Orisin* ■ *Dir* Willis Goldbeck • *Scr* Martin Berkeley, Harry Ruskin, Lawrence P Bachmann, from characters created by Max Brand

Dr Gillespie's New Assistant ★★★

Medical drama 1942 · US · BW · 87mins

Bereft of Dr Kildare, MGM entrusted new director Willis Goldbeck with the task of resuscitating its long-running medical series by contriving a contest to find a personable assistant to crotchety surgeon Lionel Barrymore. In setting three interns each a tricky case to diagnose, the studio sought to showcase star-in-waiting Van Johnson, while Goldbeck aimed to add a touch of topicality by having Keye Luke decamp partway through to join the Chinese nationalist army. DP

Lionel Barrymore *Dr Leonard Gillespie* • Van Johnson *Dr Randall Adams* • Susan Peters *Mrs Howard Young* • Richard Quine *Dr Dennis Lindsey* • Keye Luke *Dr Lee Wong How* • Nat Pendleton *Joe Wayman* • Alma Kruger *Molly Byrd* • Horace McNally [Stephen McNally] *Howard Young* • Nell Craig *Nurse Parker* ■ *Dir* Willis Goldbeck • *Scr* Martin Berkeley, Harry Ruskin, Lawrence P Bachmann, from characters created by Max Brand

Doctor Glas ★★★

Drama 1968 · Den · BW · 83mins

This is the bleakest of Mai Zetterling's directorial ventures. Collaborating on both screenplay and staging with husband David Hughes, she has created an unflinching study of isolation, despair and the contrast between physical and spiritual love. The triangle that forms between doctor Per Oscarsson, pastor Ulf Palme and his loyally chaste wife Lone Hertz will ultimately end in murder. DP

Per Oscarsson *Dr Glas* • Ulf Palme *Pastor Gregorius* • Lone Hertz *Helga Gregorius* • Nils Eklund *Markel* • Bente Dessau *Eva Martens* • Lars Lunoe *Klas Recke* ■ *Dir* Mai Zetterling • *Scr* Mai Zetterling, David Hughes, from the novel *Doktor Glas* by Hjalmar Soderberg

Dr Goldfoot and the Bikini Machine ★★ PG

Comedy 1965 · US · Colour · 84mins

Very much a product of the Swinging Sixties, this slice of tosh combines several of the elements that made AIP films so popular at the drive-ins. Vincent Price plays the eponymous doctor, who creates female robots so they can marry rich men and line his coffers. Susan Hart plays the female lead, and Frankie Avalon and Dwayne Hickman are also along for the ride. Even Annette Funicello drops in! It's all a little too daft, though, and the humour is positively leaden. TS

Vincent Price *Dr Goldfoot* • Frankie Avalon *Craig Gamble* • Dwayne Hickman *Todd Armstrong* • Susan Hart *Diane* • Jack Mullaney *Igor* • Fred Clark *DJ Pevney* • Annette Funicello *Girl in the Stock* ■ *Dir* Norman Taurog • *Scr* Elwood Ullman, Robert Kaufman, from a story by James Hartford

Dr Goldfoot and the Girl Bombs ★★

Comedy 1966 · US/It · Colour · 85mins

Only in the mid-1960s could you have got away with a film like this! Thanks to cult Italian horror director Mario Bava, this sequel to *Dr Goldfoot and the Bikini Machine* piles on the style, but rather loses out in the fun stakes. Still, Vincent Price is his usual hammy self as Dr Goldfoot, who gets backing from China to start a war between the Americans and the Soviets using sexy robot girls with bombs implanted in their navels. RS

Vincent Price *Dr Goldfoot* • Fabian *Bill Dexter* • Franco Franchi *Franco* • Ciccio Ingrassia *Ciccio* • Laura Antonelli *Rosanna* ■ *Dir* Mario Bava • *Scr* Louis M Heyward, Castellano Pipolo, Robert Kaufman, from a story by James Hartford

Dr Heckyl & Mr Hype ★★

Comedy 1980 · US · Colour · 97mins

Oliver Reed tackles the title role in a clumsy comedy that mixes the Jekyll and Hyde idea with elements of *The Nutty Professor*. Reed is engagingly grotesque – bulbous nose, mangy skin, the works – as a scientist who overdoses on an experimental diet formula and transforms into a dashing playboy with a predilection for killing. Reed enters into the rollicking spirit of the piece, but director Charles B Griffith ruins it with laboured dialogue and stilted slapstick. RS

Oliver Reed *Dr Heckyl/Mr Hype* • Sunny Johnson *Coral Careen* • Maia Danziger *Miss Finebum* • Virgil Frye *Lieutenant Mack Druck "Il Topo"* • Mel Welles *Dr Hinkle* • Kedrick Wolfe *Dr Lew Hoo* • Jackie Coogan *Sergeant Fleacollar* ■ *Dir/Scr* Charles B Griffith

Doctor in Clover ★★ PG

Comedy 1966 · UK · Colour · 96mins

The penultimate entry in the seven-film series based on the comic novels of Richard Gordon is possibly the least strong in terms of incident, but there are some pleasing performances. Demonstrating his flair for the debonair, Leslie Phillips just about makes the whole thing worthwhile, but even he struggles with the anaemic story in which a romance and a new wonder drug complicate his hectic love life. DP DVD

Leslie Phillips *Dr Gaston Grimsdyke* • James Robertson-Justice *Sir Lancelot Spratt* • Shirley Anne Field *Nurse Bancroft* • John Fraser *Dr Miles Grimsdyke* • Joan Sims *Matron Sweet* • Fenella Fielding *Tatiana Rubikov* ■ *Dir* Ralph Thomas • *Scr* Jack Davies, from characters created by Richard Gordon

Doctor in Distress ★★ PG

Comedy 1963 · UK · Colour · 98mins

What a cast! What a letdown! After a one-film absence, Dirk Bogarde reluctantly returned to the role of Simon Sparrow in this muddled comedy and immediately announced he'd never step inside St Swithin's again. Faced with a script that reads like a medical school rag mag, the cast plods through the picture as though under anaesthetic. James Robertson-Justice has the most fun as the lovesick Lancelot Spratt and Leo McKern as a film producer flirting with starlet Jill Adams takes a pot shot at movie moguls. DP DVD

Dirk Bogarde *Dr Simon Sparrow* • Samantha Eggar *Delia* • James Robertson-Justice *Sir Lancelot Spratt* • Mylène Demongeot *Sonja* • Donald Houston *Major French* • Barbara Murray *Iris* • Dennis Price *Blacker* • Peter Butterworth *Ambulance driver* • Leo McKern *Heilbronn* ■ *Dir* Ralph Thomas • *Scr* Nicholas Phipps, Ronald Scott Thorn, from characters created by Richard Gordon

Doctor in Love ★★ PG

Comedy 1960 · UK · Colour · 92mins

Though a box-office hit in its day, this comedy is even more episodic than others in the long-running series and comes over now as a thin excuse for a series of risqué encounters and double entendres. Leslie Phillips is impeccable as a philandering doctor finding the country air conducive to consultancies of the canoodling kind, and the supporting cast is as solid as ever. The film fails, however, because of Michael Craig, who is not only no Dirk Bogarde, but also no comedian. DP DVD

Michael Craig *Dr Richard Hare* • Virginia Maskell *Dr Nicola Barrington* • Leslie Phillips *Dr Tony Burke* • James Robertson-Justice *Sir Lancelot Spratt* • Carole Lesley *Kitten Strudwick* • Liz Fraser *Leonora* • Joan Sims *Dawn* • Nicholas Parsons *Dr Hinxman* • Irene Handl *Professor MacRitchie* ■ *Dir* Ralph Thomas • *Scr* Nicholas Phipps, from characters created by Richard Gordon

Doctor in the House ★★★★ U

Comedy 1954 · UK · Colour · 87mins

This film launched the popular St Swithin's series and made a matinée idol out of Dirk Bogarde. Following a class of students through their training, it delights in the dark side of hospital humour, with the medical misadventures providing much better entertainment than the romantic interludes. Kenneth More, Donald Sinden and Donald Houston are on top form as the duffers doing retakes, while Bogarde oozes charm and quiet comic flair. But stealing all their thunder is James Robertson-Justice as Sir Lancelot Spratt. DP DVD

Dirk Bogarde *Simon Sparrow* • Muriel Pavlow *Joy* • Kenneth More *Grimsdyke* • Donald Sinden *Benskin* • Kay Kendall *Isobel* • James Robertson-Justice *Sir Lancelot Spratt* • Donald Houston *Taffy* • Suzanne Cloutier *Stella* ■ *Dir* Ralph Thomas • *Scr* Nicholas Phipps, from the novel by Richard Gordon

Doctor in Trouble ★★ PG

Comedy 1970 · UK · Colour · 86mins

The seventh and last movie to be culled from Richard Gordon's bestselling series was based on a book called *Doctor on Toast*, which would have been a pretty apt title for this innocently smutty film, as it feels as if it has been warmed up from the left-overs of *Doctor at Sea*. Any enjoyment there is comes from the bullish performance of Leslie Phillips as the medic-turned-steward on board a luxury liner. DP DVD

Leslie Phillips *Dr Burke* • Harry Secombe *Llewellyn Wendover* • James Robertson-Justice *Sir Lancelot Spratt* • Angela Scoular *Ophelia O'Brien* • Irene Handl *Mrs Dailey* • Robert Morley *Captain George Spratt* • Freddie Jones *Master-at-Arms* • Joan Sims *Russian captain* • John Le Mesurier *Purser* • Simon Dee *Basil Beauchamp* • Graham Chapman *Roddy* ■ *Dir* Ralph Thomas • *Scr* Jack Davies, from the novel *Doctor on Toast* by Richard Gordon

Dr Jekyll and Mr Hyde ★★★ PG

Silent horror 1920 · US · Tinted · 62mins

Based on Thomas Russell Sullivan's Victorian stage adaptation and steeped in the attitudes of that era, this is generally considered to be the best silent version of Robert Louis Stevenson's classic story. It's hopelessly dated by modern standards, though, while John Barrymore slices the ham far too thickly. His Jekyll isn't the villain of the piece so much as his girlfriend's father, played by Brandon Hurst. It's Hurst who suggests idealist Jekyll experiments with the good and evil sides of human nature, and he's also the one who deliberately leads him into temptation with silent goddess Nita Naldi. AJ DVD

John Barrymore *Dr Henry Jekyll/Mr Edward Hyde* • Martha Mansfield *Millicent Carew* • Nita Naldi *Gina* • Brandon Hurst *Sir George Carew* • Charles Lane (1) *Dr Richard Lanyon* • Louis Wolheim *Music hall proprietor* ■ *Dir* John S Robertson • *Scr* Clara S Beranger, from the novel *The Strange Case of Dr Jekyll and Mr Hyde* by Robert Louis Stevenson

Dr Jekyll and Mr Hyde
★★★★ 12

Horror 1931 · US · BW · 91mins

Robert Louis Stevenson's oft-told split personality tale receives its most stylish, erotic and exciting treatment under Rouben Mamoulian's sure direction. Fredric March deservedly won the best actor Oscar – shared with Wallace Beery in *The Champ* – for his tormented performance; the single-take transformation scenes are particularly impressive. Also memorable is the smouldering sensuality of Miriam Hopkins as the prostitute who's the object of his evil attentions. This enduring adaptation is totally satisfying. AJ VIDEO DVD

Fredric March *Dr Henry Jekyll/Mr Hyde* • Miriam Hopkins *Ivy Pearson* • Rose Hobart *Muriel Carew* • Holmes Herbert *Dr Lanyon* • Halliwell Hobbes *Brig Gen Carew* • Edgar Norton *Poole* • Arnold Lucy *Utterson* • Colonel McDonnell *Hobson* • Tempe Pigott *Mrs Hawkins* ■ *Dir* Rouben Mamoulian • *Scr* Samuel Hoffenstein, Percy Heath, from the novel *The Strange Case of Dr Jekyll and Mr Hyde* by Robert Louis Stevenson • *Cinematographer* Karl Struss • *Art Director* Hans Dreier • *Make-up* Wally Westmore

Dr Jekyll and Mr Hyde
★★★ 12

Horror 1941 · US · BW · 108mins

Director Victor Fleming's first film after *Gone with the Wind* was this lavish MGM treatment of Robert Louis Stevenson's classic cautionary tale. With the accent on the bad doctor's emotional turmoil rendered in complex Freudian terms to little dramatic effect rather than the horror of the situation, it's a poor, if at times scary relation to the superior 1931 version, which starred Fredric March. Spencer Tracy adds scant shading to either side of his split personality, despite an impressive and sinister transformation montage. Worth seeing for the luminescent Ingrid Bergman. AJ DVD

Spencer Tracy *Dr Harry Jekyll/Mr Hyde* • Ingrid Bergman *Ivy Peterson* • Lana Turner *Beatrix Emery* • Donald Crisp *Sir Charles Emery* • Ian Hunter *Dr John Lanyon* • Barton MacLane *Sam Higgins* • C Aubrey Smith *The bishop* • Peter Godfrey *Poole* ■ *Dir* Victor Fleming • *Scr* John Lee Mahin, from the novel *The Strange Case Of Dr Jekyll and Mr Hyde* by Robert Louis Stevenson

Dr Jekyll and Ms Hyde
★ 12

Comedy 1995 · US · Colour · 86mins

This dire, unfunny and completely unnecessary comic twist on Robert Louis Stevenson's classic tale stars Tim Daly as Jekyll's descendant, a gormless fellow who has the unhappy knack of turning into trampy vamp Helen Hyde (Sean Young). Neither funny nor frightening, the only really scary thing in the movie is Young's bad acting. As you would expect, this lamentable affair ended up in bargain video bins everywhere. JB. Contains swearing and nudity. VIDEO

Sean Young *Helen Hyde* • Tim Daly [Timothy Daly] *Dr Richard Jacks* • Lysette Anthony *Sarah Carver* • Stephen Tobolowsky *Oliver Mintz* • Harvey Fierstein *Yves DuBois* • Thea Vidale *Valerie* • Jeremy Piven *Pete Walston* • Polly Bergen *Mrs Unterveldt* ■ *Dir* David F Price • *Scr* Tim John, Oliver Butcher, William Davies, William Osborne, from a story by David F Price, from the novel *The Strange Case of Dr Jekyll and Mr Hyde* by Robert Louis Stevenson

Dr Jekyll and Sister Hyde
★★★ 18

Horror 1971 · UK · Colour · 93mins

Written by Brian Clemens (longtime writer and producer of *The Avengers* TV series), this bizarre bisexual take on the split personality classic even includes the grave robbers Burke and Hare and a Jack the Ripper subplot. While not quite living up to its initial hype – "the transformation of a man into a woman will take place before your very eyes", warned the ads – it's still mid-range Hammer horror with extra heat supplied by solid Ralph Bates and Martine Beswick as the good and evil flip sides. AJ. Contains violence, brief nudity. VIDEO DVD

Ralph Bates *Dr Jekyll* • Martine Beswick *Sister Hyde* • Gerald Sim *Professor Robertson* • Lewis Fiander *Howard* • Dorothy Alison *Mrs Spencer* • Neil Wilson *Older policeman* • Ivor Dean *Burke* • Paul Whitsun-Jones *Sergeant Danvers* • Philip Madoc *Byker* • Tony Calvin *Hare* • Susan Brodrick *Susan* ■ *Dir* Roy Ward Baker • *Scr* Brian Clemens, from the novel *The Strange Case of Dr Jekyll and Mr Hyde* by Robert Louis Stevenson

Dr Kildare Goes Home
★★★ U

Medical drama 1940 · US · BW · 78mins

The fifth entry in MGM's popular hospital series is one of the few to move the action away from Blair General. Lew Ayres is impeccable as the idealistic young medic, who this time around sacrifices his chances of promotion by going off to help his country doctor father set up a clinic. Lionel Barrymore's wheelchair-bound Dr Gillespie is less visible than usual, replaced by veteran character actor Samuel S Hinds, playing Kildare's father. RK

Lew Ayres *Dr James Kildare* • Lionel Barrymore *Dr Leonard Gillespie* • Laraine Day *Mary Lamont* • Samuel S Hinds *Dr Stephen Kildare* • Gene Lockhart *George Winslow* • John Shelton *Dr Davidson* • Nat Pendleton *Wayman* ■ *Dir* Harold S Bucquet • *Scr* Harry Ruskin, Goldbeck Willis, from a story by Max Brand, Goldbeck Willis

Dr Kildare's Crisis
★★★

Medical drama 1940 · US · BW · 74mins

The "crisis" in the sixth movie in the long-running medic series is one that personally affects young Dr James Kildare (Lew Ayres): his future brother-in-law may be suffering from epilepsy, a disease which could run in the family. Unusually for this B-movie series, the unfortunate patient is played by Robert Young, a star from MGM's A-company. Otherwise the regulars are in place. RK

Lew Ayres *Dr James Kildare* • Robert Young (1) *Douglas Lamont* • Lionel Barrymore *Dr Leonard Gillespie* • Laraine Day *Mary Lamont* • Emma Dunn *Mrs Martha Kildaire* • Nat Pendleton *Joe Wayman* • Bobs Watson *Tommy* ■ *Dir* Harold S Bucquet • *Scr* Harry Ruskin, Willis Goldbeck, from a story by Max Brand, Willis Goldbeck

Dr Kildare's Strange Case
★★★

Medical drama 1940 · US · BW · 76mins

An even bigger hit than the previous three pictures in the Dr Kildare series, this one concerns the use of electric shock therapy to cure a mental patient. The medical techniques might be somewhat dated, but the ethical questions remain valid in this snappy entry. Lew Ayres is again the perfect foil for Lionel Barrymore's irascible Dr Gillespie, who is bossed about in turn by Alma Kruger's Nurse Molly Byrd. RK

Lew Ayres *Dr James Kildare* • Lionel Barrymore *Dr Leonard Gillespie* • Laraine Day *Mary Lamont* • Shepperd Strudwick *Dr Gregory Lane* • Samuel S Hinds *Dr Stephen Kildare* • Emma Dunn *Martha Kildare* • Alma Kruger *Molly Byrd* • Nat Pendleton *Wayman* ■ *Dir* Harold S Bucquet • *Scr* Harry Ruskin, Willis Goldbeck, from a story by Max Brand, Willis Goldbeck

Dr Kildare's Victory
★★★

Medical drama 1941 · US · BW · 92mins

His fiancée having been killed off in the previous movie, *Dr Kildare's Wedding Day*, the eponymous medic seeks solace by falling for socialite patient Ann Ayars. This was the only picture in the 15-film series directed by WS Van Dyke, although the style differs not a jot from the others. It was released just before the news broke of Lew Ayres's conscientious objection to the war, which led him to be dropped by MGM after nine appearances as Dr Kildare. Blair General functioned without him for a further six titles. RK

Lew Ayres *Dr James Kildare* • Lionel Barrymore *Dr Leonard Gillespie* • Robert Sterling *Dr Roger Winthrop* • Ann Ayars *Edith "Cookie" Charles* • Jean Rogers *Annabelle Kirke* • Alma Kruger *Molly Byrd* • Walter Kingsford *Dr Walter Carew* • Nell Craig *Nurse Parker* ■ *Dir* Major WS Van Dyke II [WS Van Dyke] • *Scr* Harry Ruskin, Willis Goldbeck, from a story by Joseph Harrington, from characters created by Max Brand

Dr Kildare's Wedding Day
★★★

Medical drama 1941 · US · BW · 82mins

Laraine Day was gaining a large following as Mary Lamont, the dedicated nurse and fiancée of Dr Kildare (Lew Ayres), when MGM, who had been grooming her for bigger pictures, decided to have her killed by a truck. The elegant brunette, who had featured in eight Kildare episodes, was never again able to find a distinctive screen image. Up-and-coming comic Red Skelton provides some comic relief in this ironically titled and somewhat gloomy episode,. RK

Lew Ayres *Dr James Kildare* • Lionel Barrymore *Dr Leonard Gillespie* • Laraine Day *Mary Lamont* • Red Skelton *Vernon Briggs* • Fay Holden *Mrs Bartlett* • Walter Kingsford *Dr Walter Carew* • Samuel S Hinds *Dr Stephen Kildare* • Nils Asther *Constanzo Labardi* ■ *Dir* Harold S Bucquet • *Scr* Willis Goldbeck, Harry Ruskin, from a story by Ormond Ruthven, Lawrence P Bachmann, from characters created by Max Brand

Dr M
★★ 18

Horror thriller
1989 · W Ger/It/Fr · Colour · 111mins

Even Claude Chabrol's failures make for more interesting viewing than the latest bland Hollywood offering. This is a case in point. Set in a futuristic Berlin, the action centres on the evil schemes of Alan Bates, a media mogul who has obviously been modelled on Fritz Lang's hypnotising hoodlum Dr Mabuse. The story is jumbled and the acting unrestrained, but it's worth a look. DP. Contains violence and swearing. VIDEO

Alan Bates *Dr Marsfeldt* • Jennifer Beals *Sonja Vogler* • Jan Niklas *Klaus Hartmann* • Hanns Zischler *Moser* • Benoît Régent *Stieglitz* • William Berger *Penck* • Alexander Radszun *Engler* ■ *Dir* Claude Chabrol • *Scr* Sollace Mitchell, from a story by Thomas Bauermeister, from the novel *Dr Mabuse, der Spieler* by Norbert Jacques

Dr Mabuse, the Gambler
★★★★ PG

Silent crime thriller
1922 · Ger · BW · 270mins

Director Fritz Lang's famous anti-totalitarianism silent allegory about a mad professor (Rudolf Klein-Rogge) trying to take over the world could be hard work for today's audiences. Despite being superbly designed, the plots-within-plots, characters in disguises and weird coincidental plot twists might prove childish and tiresome to some. Many, though, will attest to Lang's wit and cleverness at putting one over on the future Nazis by satirising the ideas of fascism. This was originally shown in two halves; the first is the more entertaining. TS DVD

Rudolf Klein-Rogge *Dr Mabuse* • Alfred Abel *Graf Told* • Aud Egede Nissen *Cara Carozza* • Gertrude Welcker *Graefin Told* • Paul Richter *Edgar Hull* • Bernhard Goetzke *von Wenk* • Hans Adalbert von Schlettow *Georg* • Georg John *Pesch* ■ *Dir* Fritz Lang • *Scr* Fritz Lang, Thea von Harbou, from the novel *Dr Mabuse, der Spieler* by Norbert Jacques

Dr Morelle – the Case of the Missing Heiress
★

Detective drama 1949 · UK · BW · 73mins

The first (and last) of an intended series based on a popular radio detective, this undistinguished B-feature murder mystery is typical of the early postwar output of Hammer before it discovered horror. Directed by Godfrey Grayson, it stars Valentine Dyall as Doctor Morelle, the sleuth who solves the murder of an heiress. AE

Valentine Dyall *Dr Morelle* • Julia Lang *Miss Frayle* • Philip Leaver *Samuel Kimber* • Jean Lodge *Cynthia Mason* • Peter Drury *Peter* ■ *Dir* Godfrey Grayson • *Scr* Ambrose Grayson, Roy Plomley, from a radio series by Ernest Dudley and a play by Wilfred Burr

Dr No
★★★★★ PG

Spy adventure 1962 · UK · Colour · 105mins

The James Bond series started in great style with this cleverly conceived dose of sheer escapism that, unlike later episodes, remained true to the essence of Ian Fleming's super-spy novels. Director Terence Young set the 007 standard with terrific action sequences, highly exotic atmosphere and witty humour. There was also the sex, of course, and bikini-clad Ursula Andress couldn't have asked for a better star-making entrance. Looking back, it's understandable why this caused so much excitement as it was entirely different from anything else. Sean Connery is perfect as the debonair and ruthless secret agent with a licence to kill. AJ VIDEO DVD

Sean Connery *James Bond* • Ursula Andress *Honey* • Joseph Wiseman *Dr No* • Jack Lord *Felix Leiter* • Bernard Lee *"M"* • Anthony Dawson *Professor Dent* • John Kitzmiller *Quarrel* • Zena Marshall *Miss Taro* • Eunice Gayson *Sylvia* • Lois Maxwell *Miss Moneypenny* • Lester Prendergast *Puss Feller* • Reggie Carter *Jones* • Peter Burton *Major Boothroyd* ■ *Dir* Terence Young • *Scr* Richard Maibaum, Johanna Harwood, Berkely Mather, from the novel by Ian Fleming

Dr Phibes Rises Again
★★★ 15

Horror 1972 · UK · Colour · 84mins

Vincent Price returns as the ingenious doctor, now in Egypt searching for the elixir of life, but continuing to outwit enemies with macabre murders, each grislier and funnier than the last. While it's not as splendid as *The Abominable Dr Phibes*, this sequel is mounted with lavish care by Robert Fuest, director of several classic episodes of *The Avengers*, and still scores high in the squirm and chuckle departments, thanks to Price's perfect timing and grandiose camp relish. AJ VIDEO DVD

Vincent Price *Dr Anton Phibes* • Robert Quarry *Biederbeck* • Valli Kemp *Vulnavia* • Hugh Griffith *Ambrose* • John Thaw *Shavers* • Keith Buckley *Stuart* • Lewis Fiander *Baker* ■ *Dir* Robert Fuest • *Scr* Robert Fuest, Robert Blees, from characters created by James Whiton, William Goldstein

Doctor Rhythm
★★ U

Musical comedy 1938 · US · BW · 81mins

On the surface, this is a vapid, well below-average Bing Crosby flick. Connoisseurs should note, however, that the wondrous Beatrice Lillie co-stars as one Lorelei Dodge-Blodgett and performs her famous stage and record sketch, *Two Dozen Double Damask Dinner Napkins*. The silly plot, based on a story by O Henry, has Crosby as a doctor pretending to be a cop to stop Lillie's niece marrying a fortune-hunter. TS

Bing Crosby *Bill Remsen* • Mary Carlisle *Judy* • Beatrice Lillie *Lorelei Dodge-Blodgett* • Andy Devine *O'Roon* • Laura Hope Crews *Mrs Twombling* ■ *Dir* Frank Tuttle • *Scr* Jo Swerling, Richard Connell, from the story *The Badge of Policeman O'Roon* by O Henry

D

Dr Seuss' The Cat in the Hat ★★ PG

Fantasy comedy adventure
2003 · US · Colour · 78mins

The much loved children's book gets turned into big-screen mush in this colourful but lifeless adaptation, which makes scant use of Dr Seuss's wonderful rhymes and pacing, instead delivering a horribly self-aware vehicle for Mike Myers's ego. There's little magic or charm here as youngsters Dakota Fanning and Spencer Breslin find a rainy day at home lifted by the mysterious appearance of a giant talking feline. Though the kids are great and the CGI fish hugely entertaining, Myers's Cat is just plain annoying. SF DVD

Mike Myers *The Cat* • Alec Baldwin *Quinn* • Kelly Preston *Mom* • Dakota Fanning *Sally* • Spencer Breslin *Conrad* • Amy Hill *Mrs Kwan* • Sean Hayes *Mr Humberfloob/The Fish* • Dan Castellaneta *Thing 1/Thing 2* • Victor Brandt *Narrator* ■ *Dir* Bo Welch • *Scr* Alec Berg, David Mandel, Jeff Schaffer, from the story by Dr Seuss

Doctor Sleep ★★★

Psychological thriller
2002 · UK · Colour · 108mins

In Nick Willing's dark, gruesome thriller, Goran Visnjic plays a London-based hypnotherapist with the creepy ability to read people's minds. Brittle detective Shirley Henderson thinks Visnjic can get through to the girl (Sophie Stuckey) who hasn't spoken since she escaped from the clutches of a serial killer. The plot stretches credibility, but the leads are solid and there are some spooky moments. RT. Contains violence, swearing.

Goran Visnjic *Dr Michael Strother* • Shirley Henderson *Detective Janet Losey* • Miranda Otto *Clara Strother* • Paddy Considine *Elliot* • Claire Rushbrook *Grace* • Fiona Shaw *Catherine Lebourg* • Corin Redgrave *Clements* ■ *Dir* Nick Willing • *Scr* Nick Willing, William Brookfield, from the novel by Madison Smartt Bell

Dr Socrates ★★★

Crime drama 1935 · US · BW · 71mins

Paul Muni was the Marlon Brando of the 1930s, in technique if not in looks. His method of character establishment from the inside out earned him starring roles in many worthy biographies, so this was a welcome change of pace: a gangster thriller in which he plays the small-town doctor who is forced to treat wounded mobsters. There's wonderfully brisk direction by William Dieterle and a blustering performance by Barton MacLane as the gang leader nearly, but not quite, upstaging Muni. Remade in 1939 as *King of the Underworld*, starring Humphrey Bogart. TH

Paul Muni *Dr Caldwell* • Ann Dvorak *Josephine Gray* • Barton MacLane *Red Bastian* • Raymond Brown *Ben Suggs* • Ralph Remley *Bill Payne* • Hal K Dawson *Mel Towne* ■ *Dir* William Dieterle • *Scr* Robert Lord, Mary C McCall Jr, from a story by WR Burnett

Dr Strangelove, or How I Learned to Stop Worrying and Love the Bomb ★★★★★ PG

Satirical comedy 1963 · UK · BW · 90mins

Is this the way the world ends, not with a bang but a simper? Stanley Kubrick's ferocious Cold War satire makes us smile through gritted teeth as unhinged general Sterling Hayden sends a squadron of nuclear bombers to attack Russia and trigger an apocalypse-laden doomsday machine. Peter Sellers's trio of performances (bemused airman, confused president and defused US Nazi adviser, re-armed by the prospect of world annihilation) spirals from gentle humour to surreal horror. The scenes in which Hayden raves about "bodily fluids" and Pentagon general George C Scott rants about statistical deaths were obviously inspired by Sellers's genius. Kubrick's unsparing disgust with our warlike instincts has never been so obvious nor so grimly comic. TH. Contains swearing. DVD

Peter Sellers *Group Captain Lionel Mandrake/President Merkin Muffley/Dr Strangelove* • George C Scott *General "Buck" Turgidson* • Sterling Hayden *General Jack D Ripper* • Keenan Wynn *Colonel "Bat" Guano* • Slim Pickens *Major TJ "King" Kong* • Peter Bull *Ambassador de Sadesky* • Tracy Reed *Miss Scott* • James Earl Jones *Lieutenant Lothar Zogg* ■ *Dir* Stanley Kubrick • *Scr* Stanley Kubrick, Terry Southern, Peter George, from the novel *Red Alert* by Peter George • *Cinematographer* Gilbert Taylor • *Art Director* Ken Adam • *Editor* Anthony Harvey

Dr Syn ★★★

Adventure 1937 · UK · BW · 81mins

George Arliss retired from movies after starring in this sprightly 19th-century smuggling adventure. By day the respected vicar of Dymchurch, Arliss uses the cover of darkness to masquerade as the ruthless Dr Syn, daredevil brigand and scourge of the Kent coast. Defying his 69 years and reputation for stuffiness, Arliss gives a rousing performance, while Roy William Neill directs with atmospheric efficiency. DP

George Arliss *Dr Syn* • John Loder *Denis Cobtree* • Margaret Lockwood *Imogene* • Roy Emerton *Captain Howard Collyer* • Graham Moffatt *Jerry Jerk* • Frederick Burtwell *Rash* • George Merritt *Mipps* ■ *Dir* Roy William Neill • *Scr* Roger Burford, Michael Hogan, from the novel by Russell Thorndike

Dr Syn, Alias the Scarecrow ★★★ U

Adventure 1963 · US · Colour · 97mins

Patrick McGoohan sails through this Disney frolic as the kindly vicar of Dymchurch by day who becomes the notorious smuggler Dr Syn by night. George Cole, Michael Hordern, Kay Walsh and a host of other stalwarts add to the quaint Georgian atmosphere, augmented by some nice photography (by Paul Beeson) of authentic Kentish locations. Made for American TV, the film was originally shown in three episodes as *The Scarecrow of Romney Marsh* but was released theatrically overseas. AT

Patrick McGoohan *Dr Syn* • George Cole *Mr Mipps* • Michael Hordern *Squire Banks* • Tony Britton *Bates* • Geoffrey Keen *General Pugh* • Eric Flynn *Philip Brackenbury* • Kay Walsh *Mrs Waggett* ■ *Dir* James Neilson • *Scr* Robert Westerby, from the novel *Christopher Syn* by Russell Thorndike, William Buchanan

Dr T & the Women ★★ 12

Satirical romance
2000 · US · Colour · 116mins

The usually excellent Robert Altman stumbles with this disappointing tale of a gynaecologist who adores women, despite the fact that all the females he knows make his life worse rather than better. While Richard Gere gives a nice, understated performance, the accomplished actresses are stuck with trying to make the best out of some badly written caricatures. JB. Contains nudity, sexual references. DVD

Richard Gere *Dr Sullivan "Dr T" Travis* • Helen Hunt *Bree Davis* • Farrah Fawcett *Kate Travis* • Laura Dern *Peggy* • Shelley Long *Carolyn* • Tara Reid *Connie Travis* • Kate Hudson *Dee Dee Travis* • Liv Tyler *Marilyn* ■ *Dir* Robert Altman • *Scr* Anne Rapp

The Doctor Takes a Wife ★★★

Screwball comedy 1940 · US · BW · 88mins

A delectable Loretta Young and an amiable Ray Milland co-star in this romantic comedy that's in the always entertaining screwball tradition. She is a writer and an ardent feminist who's opposed to marriage; he teaches at medical school but is angling for promotion to professor. When a publicity stunt leads to their being mistaken for a newly married couple, she smells a new bestseller in the situation, while he discovers that the supposed change in his marital status will bring him his desired professional status. The pair take an apartment together and masquerade as man and wife with inevitable results. RK

Loretta Young *June Cameron* • Ray Milland *Dr Timothy Sterling* • Reginald Gardiner *John Pierce* • Gail Patrick *Marilyn Thomas* • Edmund Gwenn *Dr Lionel Sterling* • Frank Sully *Slapcovitch* ■ *Dir* Alexander Hall • *Scr* George Seaton, Ken Englund, from a story by Aleen Leslie

Dr Terror's House of Horrors ★★★ PG

Horror 1964 · UK · Colour · 93mins

Vampires, werewolves, crawling hands, voodoo curses and creeping vines – they're all present and enjoyably correct in the first, and best, fun fright anthology from the Amicus horror factory, Hammer's only real 1960s rival. Peter Cushing is the tarot card reader telling five men on a train their grim fortunes. Director Freddie Francis delivers a fair quota of entertaining shocks with his trademark visual flair, and it's a joy to see DJ-turned-actor Alan Freeman at the mercy of that peculiar writhing plant. AJ DVD

Peter Cushing *Dr Schreck* • Christopher Lee *Franklyn Marsh* • Roy Castle *Biff Bailey* • Donald Sutherland *Bob Carroll* • Neil McCallum *Jim Dawson* • Alan Freeman *Bill Rogers* • Max Adrian *Dr Blake* • Edward Underdown *Tod* ■ *Dir* Freddie Francis • *Scr* Milton Subotsky

Doctor Who and the Daleks ★★★ U

Science-fiction adventure
1965 · UK · Colour · 79mins

The first big-screen outing for the BBC's ever-popular sci-fi TV series has Peter Cushing playing the time-travelling Doctor with amiable seriousness as he pits his wits against those mobile knobbly tin cans forever shrieking "Exterminate". Lacking the bite and inventiveness that set the landmark series apart, this spin-off unwisely injects humour into its sparse scenario. Despite the many faults, it's still a slick slice of enjoyable mayhem. *Daleks – Invasion Earth 2150AD* followed in 1966. AJ DVD

Peter Cushing *Dr Who* • Roy Castle *Ian* • Jennie Linden *Barbara* • Roberta Tovey *Susan* • Barrie Ingham *Alydon* • Geoffrey Toone *Temmosus* • Mark Peterson *Elydon* • John Brown *Antodus* • Michael Coles *Ganatus* ■ *Dir* Gordon Flemyng • *Scr* Milton Subotsky, from the BBC TV series by Sydney Newman, from characters created by Terry Nation

Doctor X ★★★

Horror 1932 · US · Colour · 76mins

This is a weird mix of effective horror, creaky haunted house clichés and dated comic relief, the latter single-handedly disrupting the sombre mood created by director Michael Curtiz as police hunt for the "Full Moon Killer" among a group of eccentric medics. Considered a classic mainly for the scary "synthetic flesh" sequence, the film's more tiresome moments are masked by energetic lead performances. This was the first horror film to be shot in colour. AJ

Lionel Atwill *Dr Xavier* • Fay Wray *Joan Xavier* • Lee Tracy *Lee Taylor* • Preston Foster *Dr Wells* • John Wray *Dr Haines* • Harry Beresford *Dr Duke* • Arthur Edmund Carewe *Dr Rowitz* ■ *Dir* Michael Curtiz • *Scr* Robert Tasker, Earl Baldwin, from a play by Howard W Comstock, Allen C Miller

Doctor Zhivago ★★★★★ PG

Romantic epic 1965 · US · Colour · 191mins

This adaptation of Boris Pasternak's classic novel has all the sweep and stateliness that characterised David Lean's mastery of the epic. At its centre is the star-crossed romance between married physician and poet Omar Sharif and dressmaker's daughter Julie Christie, whose passionate encounters are played out against the backdrop of the Great War and the Russian Revolution. The scene is set superbly, thanks largely to John Box's brilliant designs for both the plush and the poverty-ridden quarters of Moscow, and to Freddie Young's atmospheric cinematography. Moreover, the ever-meticulous Lean retains the intimacy of the love story within the sweep of momentous historical events. DP DVD

Omar Sharif *Yuri Zhivago* • Julie Christie *Lara* • Geraldine Chaplin *Tonya Gromeko* • Rod Steiger *Komarovsky* • Alec Guinness *Yevgraf Zhivago* • Tom Courtenay *Pasha Antipov/Strelnikov* • Ralph Richardson *Alexander* • Siobhan McKenna *Anna Gromeko* • Rita Tushingham *Girl* • Bernard Kay *Bolshevik* • Klaus Kinski *Kostoyed* ■ *Dir* David Lean • *Scr* Robert Bolt, from the novel by Boris Pasternak

The Doctor's Dilemma ★★ U

Comedy 1958 · UK · Colour · 99mins

Anthony Asquith fails to breathe life into this fast-fading satire on the foibles of Harley Street. Self-obsessed artist Dirk Bogarde improves the worse his tuberculosis becomes, but Leslie Caron never captures the stubborn devotion that inspires her fight to save him. George Bernard Shaw's comedy might have been scalpel-sharp back in 1903, but the foundation of the National Health Service rather blunted its edge. DP

Leslie Caron *Mrs Jennifer Dubedat* • Dirk Bogarde *Louis Dubedat* • Alastair Sim *Cutler Walpole* • Robert Morley *Sir Ralph Bloomfield-Bonington* • John Robinson (1) *Sir Colenso Ridgeon* • Felix Aylmer *Sir Patrick Cullen* • Peter Sallis *Picture gallery secretary* ■ *Dir* Anthony Asquith • *Scr* Anatole de Grunwald, from the play by George Bernard Shaw

Doctor's Orders ★★ U

Comedy 1934 · UK · BW · 69mins

John Mills stars as a medical student whose romantic plans are complicated when his father (Leslie Fuller), a travelling medicine man, is revealed to be a carnival confidence trickster. The result is a flimsy, music hall-style comedy which gives the then-popular Leslie Fuller plenty of opportunities to deliver his trademark bombast as the quack whose heart turns out to be in the right place. AT

Leslie Fuller *Bill Blake* • John Mills *Ronnie Blake* • Marguerite Allan *Gwen Summerfield* • Mary Jerrold *Mary Blake* • Ronald Shiner *Miggs* • Georgie Harris *Duffin* • Felix Aylmer

Sir Daniel Summerfield • William Kendall *Jackson* ■ *Dir* Norman Lee • *Scr* Clifford Grey, RP Weston, Bert Lee, from a story by Clifford Grey, Syd Courtenay, Lola Harvey

Doctors' Wives ★★★ 18

Medical drama 1970 · US · Colour · 97mins

Based on the principle that "if you can't beat 'em, join 'em", this attempts to be a super-sudsy soap opera like the ones TV was using to gnaw away at cinema attendances. Like *Peyton Place*, it's built around a community going through the usual rituals (neurosis, adultery, murder), though the acting is considerably classier: a young Gene Hackman, Dyan Cannon, Rachel Roberts and Carroll O'Connor. Distinguished screenwriter Daniel Taradash (*Rancho Notorious*) does not distinguish himself. TH [video]

Dyan Cannon *Lorrie Dellman* • Richard Crenna *Pete Brennan* • Gene Hackman *Dave Randolph* • Carroll O'Connor *Joe Gray* • Rachel Roberts (1) *Della Randolph* • Janice Rule *Amy Brennan* • Diana Sands *Helen Straughn* • Ralph Bellamy *Jake Porter* ■ *Dir* George Schaefer • *Scr* Daniel Taradash, from the novel by Frank G Slaughter

Dodes'ka-Den ★★★★

Fantasy drama 1970 · Jpn · Colour · 139mins

After a five-year break (during which time he bailed on *Tora! Tora! Tora!*), Akira Kurosawa returned to make his first film in colour. Adapted from a collection of short stories, this affecting study of the hopes, fears and bitter realities of a group of slum dwellers originally ran for 244 minutes. Sensitively played and demonstrating an instinctive genius for colour, the gently paced mix of fantasy and melodrama typifies Kurosawa's essential humanity. Despite receiving an Oscar nomination for best foreign film, it was dismissed by the critics. Soon afterwards, the director attempted suicide. DP. In Japanese with English subtitles.

Yoshitaka Zushi *Rokkuchan* • Kin Sugai *Rokkuchan's mother* • Junzaburo Ban *Yukichi Shima* • Kiyoko Tange *Mrs Shima* • Hisashi Igawa *Masuo Masuda* • Hideko Okiyama *Masuda's wife* ■ *Dir* Akira Kurosawa • *Scr* Akira Kurosawa, Hideo Oguni, Shinobu Hashimoto, from a short story collection by Shugoro Yamamoto

Dodge City ★★★★ PG

Western 1939 · US · Colour · 99mins

Errol Flynn rides into Dodge, sees that "knavery is rampant" (as *Variety* described it in 1939) and sets about cleaning up the town with military precision. Why Warner Bros couldn't come clean and call him Wyatt Earp is a mystery. It's knockabout stuff, exuberantly directed in lush early Technicolor by Michael Curtiz, and is in sharp contrast to John Ford's later *My Darling Clementine* as well as more recent, revisionist trawls through the Earp legend. Flynn is in swashbuckling mode and Olivia de Havilland, as usual, is the woman in his life. AT [video]

Errol Flynn *Wade Hatton* • Olivia de Havilland *Abbie Irving* • Ann Sheridan *Ruby Gilman* • Bruce Cabot *Jeff Surrett* • Frank McHugh *Joe Clemens* • Alan Hale *Rusty Hart* • John Litel *Matt Cole* • Henry Travers *Dr Irving* ■ *Dir* Michael Curtiz • *Scr* Robert Buckner

Dodgeball: a True Underdog Story ★★★ 12

Sports comedy
2004 · US/Ger · Colour · 88mins

This slight and silly comedy features a hyper-energetic Ben Stiller and an almost catatonic Vince Vaughn. Vaughn owns a run-down gym and Stiller wants to take it over. Only by forming a dodgeball team and going to Las Vegas to win $50,000 in the national championships can Vaughn and his rag-tag band of under-achievers save the day. Along the way the underdogs are whipped into shape by Rip Torn's insane coach and challenged by a variety of bizarre opponents. It's daft, but is delivered with such good-natured spirit that it's easy to succumb to its simple-minded charms. GM. Contains swearing, sexual references. [video] DVD

Vince Vaughn *Peter La Fleur* • Ben Stiller *White Goodman* • Christine Taylor *Kate Veatch* • Rip Torn *Patches O'Houlihan* • Justin Long *Justin* • Stephen Root *Gordon* • Chris Williams *Dwight* • Hank Azaria *Young Patches O'Houlihan* ■ *Dir/Scr* Rawson Marshall Thurber

Dodsworth ★★★★ PG

Romantic drama 1936 · US · BW · 96mins

William Wyler's masterly film of Sinclair Lewis's novel has Walter Huston, Ruth Chatterton, Mary Astor and David Niven giving wonderful performances. It's a full-blown romance with a darker edge, gleamingly shot and nominated for seven Oscars, winning one for art direction. Producer Sam Goldwyn was offered the book for $20,000 and turned it down, thinking it would make a lousy movie. Sidney Howard subsequently adapted it into a Broadway hit starring Huston and Fay Bainter, and Goldwyn ended up buying the screen rights for $165,000. AT [video]

Walter Huston *Sam Dodsworth* • Ruth Chatterton *Fran Dodsworth* • Paul Lukas *Arnold Iselin* • Mary Astor *Edith Cortright* • David Niven *Lockert* • Gregory Gaye *Kurt von Obersdorf* • Maria Ouspenskaya *Baroness von Obersdorf* • Odette Myrtil *Madame de Penable* ■ *Dir* William Wyler • *Scr* Sidney Howard, from his play, from the novel by Sinclair Lewis • *Art Director* Richard Day

Dog Day Afternoon ★★★★ 15

Crime drama 1975 · US · Colour · 119mins

This is a film about a bank robbery, the proceeds of which are needed to pay for a sex-change operation. Weird but apparently true. From this material, Sidney Lumet creates a marvellous patchwork of a movie, cutting between the inept but passionate bank robbers (Al Pacino and John Cazale) whose bungled heist turns into a hostage situation, the corpulent cop leading the police siege (Charles Durning) and the mob that gathers outside the bank. Pacino's performance (which earned him a fourth Oscar nomination) is a multilayered display. AT. Contains violence, swearing. [video] DVD

Al Pacino *Sonny Wortzik* • John Cazale *Sal* • Charles Durning *Moretti* • Chris Sarandon *Leon Shermer* • Sully Boyar *Mulvaney* • Penelope Allen *Sylvia* • James Broderick *Sheldon* • Carol Kane *Jenny* • Beulah Garrick *Margaret* ■ *Dir* Sidney Lumet • *Scr* Frank Pierson, from an article by BF Kluge, Thomas Moore • *Cinematographer* Victor J Kemper

Dog Days ★★★ 18

Drama 2001 · Austria/Ger · Colour · 121mins

Filmed over three hot Viennese summers, director Ulrich Seidl's award-winning debut feature draws heavily on his documentary experience to give fictional events an unnervingly authentic feel. Bleak humour underlies some of the improvised situations, most notably those involving compulsive hitch-hiker Maria Hofstatter and ageing widower Erich Finsches and his housekeeper, Gerti Lehner. As each vignette is played out before the remorseless camera, a scathing picture of contemporary Austria emerges. DP. In German with English subtitles. [video] DVD

Maria Hofstätter *Anna, the hitch-hiker* • Alfred Mrva *Hruby, the alarm systems man* • Erich Finsches *Walter, the old man* • Gerti Lehner *Walter's housekeeper* • Franziska Weiss *Klaudia, the young girl* • Rene Wanko *Mario, Klaudia's boyfriend* ■ *Dir* Ulrich Seidl • *Scr* Ulrich Seidl, Veronika Franz

Dog Eat Dog ★★ 15

Comedy drama
2000 · UK/Ger · Colour · 89mins

Director Moody Shoaibi's low-budget film focuses on four cash-strapped Londoners who concoct a scheme to kidnap a celebrity writer's pet dog. But their get-rich-quick scheme goes literally to the dogs when they inadvertently petnap the pooch of a local crime boss (overplayed by Gary Kemp). The young black leads do their best, but this is not as quirky and original as it thinks it is. DA [video] DVD

Mark Tonderai *Rooster* • Nathan Constance *Jess* • David Oyelowo *CJ* • Crunski *Chang* • Gary Kemp *Jesus* • Alan Davies *Phil* • Melanie Blatt *Kelly* • Steve Toussaint *Darcy* • Ricky Gervais *Bouncer* ■ *Dir* Moody Shoaibi • *Scr* Moody Shoaibi, Mark Tonderai

A Dog of Flanders ★★ U

Drama 1959 · US · Colour · 96mins

Based on Ouida's novel which was twice filmed as a silent, this lachrymose picture epitomises Hollywood's vision of family entertainment in the late 1950s. However, while youngsters will delight in the restoration of the abandoned pup, they may find the gentle adventures of his young master rather hard going. Alan Ladd's son David Ladd stars as the orphan hero. DP

David Ladd *Nello* • Donald Crisp *Daas* • Theodore Bikel *Piet* • Max Croiset *Mr Cogez* • Monique Ahrens *Corrie* • Siobhan Taylor *Alois* ■ *Dir* James B Clark • *Scr* Ted Sherdeman, from the novel by Ouida

A Dog of Flanders ★★ U

Period drama 1999 · US · Colour · 96mins

This is the fourth film version of Ouida's famous story, but never before has it been adapted with such disregard for its humbling simplicity. Director Kevin Brodie's bid to make the trials of an orphan artist accessible for today's youngsters is laudable enough and he makes splendid use of the Flemish locations. However, the cast (with the honorable exception of Jack Warden's grandfather) singularly fails to invest the action with human warmth. DP [video]

Jon Voight *Michel La Grande* • Jack Warden *Jehan Daas* • Steven Hartley *Carl Cogez* • Bruce McGill *William the blacksmith* • Jeremy James Kissner *Older Nello* • Jesse James *Young Nello* • Cheryl Ladd *Anna Cogez* ■ *Dir* Kevin Brodie • *Scr* Kevin Brodie, Robert Singer, from the story by Ouida

Dog Park ★★

Romantic comedy
1998 · Can · Colour · 91mins

It's a well-known fact that the best way to meet people is by walking the dog, and Bruce McCulloch's film is built around just such a premise. Luke Wilson stars as a recently dumped bloke who gets the hots for Natasha Henstridge in the park; sadly, she only has eyes for her dog. Meanwhile, Wilson's angst at being chucked by Kathleen Robertson is affecting their dog. Fluffy fare. LH

Natasha Henstridge *Lorna* • Luke Wilson *Andy* • Kathleen Robertson *Cheryl* • Janeane Garofalo *Jeri* • Bruce McCulloch *Jeff* • Kristin Lehman *Keiran* • Amie Carey *Rachel* • Gordon Currie *Trevor* ■ *Dir/Scr* Bruce McCulloch

Dog Soldiers ★★★★ 15

Horror 2001 · UK/Lux · Colour · 100mins

Don't be disheartened by the British film industry's dismal record with horror movies – this is as scary, funny and exhilarating as any Hollywood fright-fest. A bunch of jaded British soldiers on weekend manoeuvres (and hence with limited live ammunition) stumble across the scene of a savage werewolf attack and hightail it to a secluded farmhouse, battling to make it through till dawn against wave after wave of hirsute assaults. This is a sensational debut from writer/director Neil Marshall, which explodes into life in the first 20 minutes and rarely pauses for breath. JC. Contains violence. [video] DVD

Sean Pertwee *Sgt Harry Wells* • Kevin McKidd *Lawrence Cooper* • Liam Cunningham *Capt Richard Ryan* • Emma Cleasby *Megan* • Darren Morfitt *Spoon* • Chris Robson *Joe Kirkley* ■ *Dir/Scr* Neil Marshall

Dog Star Man ★★★★

Experimental silent drama
1964 · US · Colour and BW · 78mins

The most famous work produced by avant-gardist Stan Brakhage is a masterpiece of superimpositional editing that recalls the pioneering work of Dziga Vertov. Following a prelude, the four parts of the piece (approximating the seasons) trace the stages of human life from cradle to grave, while also frequently alluding to the evolution of artistic endeavour. Utterly devoid of narrative, this dazzling silent collage of frantic camera movements, boldly coloured fragments and poetic diversions is impossible to appreciate in a single viewing. Brakhage later unravelled the multiple imagery for a 270-minute exposition entitled *The Art of Vision*. DP

Stan Brakhage *Dog Star Man* • Jane Brakhage *Woman* ■ *Dir/Scr* Stan Brakhage

The Dog Who Stopped the War ★★★ U

Drama 1984 · Can · Colour · 86mins

This is the story a snowball fight that escalates into a neighbourhood war. Director André Melançon coaxes spirited performances from his young cast, with Cédric Jourde doing well as the cunning peace envoy, but, as you might expect, the hound steals every scene. Glorious photography adds to the enjoyment of this lovely little film from Quebec. DP. French dialogue dubbed into English. [video]

Cédric Jourde *Luke* • Julien Elie *Mark* • Maripierre Arseneau-d'Anou *Sophie* • Duc Minh Vu *Warren* • Luc Boucher *Johnny* • Gilbert Monette *George* ■ *Dir* André Melançon • *Scr* Danyèle Patenaude • *Cinematographer* François Protat

Dogfight ★★★★ 15

Romantic drama 1991 · US · Colour · 89mins

Barely seen on its original release, this poignant drama only emphasises what cinema lost with the death of River Phoenix. Most young actors could have carried off the role of the rookie marine who squires sensitive peacenik Lili Taylor to a pre-Vietnam "ugly date" party. But few would have brought such truth to a story so dependent on genuine emotion. Taylor is equally impressive, swallowing her hurt to discover what lies beneath an exterior necessarily toughened by boot camp. Directed by Nancy Savoca with an impeccable grasp of the mood of Kennedy's America, this is a must for more than just Phoenix fans. DP [video]

River Phoenix *Birdlace* • Lili Taylor *Rose* • Richard Panebianco *Berzin* • Anthony Clark *Oakie* • Mitchell Whitfield *Benjamin* • Holly Near *Rose Snr* ■ *Dir* Nancy Savoca • *Scr* Bob Comfort

Dogma ★★★★ 15

Religious satire 1999 · US · Colour · 122mins

Kevin Smith tackles the subject of religion with a wickedly humorous touch that unsurprisingly offended some Catholic groups when the film was released. Matt Damon and Ben Affleck star as two fallen angels who discover there is a loophole which will allow them back into heaven, obliterating the Earth in the process. Non-believer Linda Fiorentino is called upon to stop them, with the help of two guardians (recurring characters Jay and Silent Bob, played by Jason Mewes and Smith himself). While the film does not work on every level, Smith again delivers a unique script and some terrifically funny performances. JB DVD

Ben Affleck *Bartleby* • George Carlin *Cardinal Glick* • Matt Damon *Loki* • Linda Fiorentino *Bethany* • Salma Hayek *Serendipity* • Jason Lee *Azrael* • Jason Mewes *Jay* • Alan Rickman *Metatron* • Chris Rock *Rufus* • Bud Cort *John Doe Jersey* • Alanis Morissette *God* • Kevin Smith (2) *Silent Bob* • Janeane Garofalo *Clinic girl* ■ *Dir/Scr* Kevin Smith (2)

Dogmatic ★★

Fantasy comedy 1996 · Can · Colour · 91mins

How many dogs have their own websites? Well, the one devoted to Barkley, the Jack Russell star of this comedy, is full of choice morsels – such as the fact he was named after a character in *Out of Africa* and that his tail-wagging scenes were performed by a stunt double. He plays a pooch called Rocky, who is struck by lightning while out walking with his master, Michael Riley, causing their personalities to be exchanged. DP

Michael Riley *Dennis Winslow* • Leila Kenzle *Amy* • David Leisure *Pal Acres* • Rick Ducommun *George* • Eugene Levy *Larry Palmer* ■ *Dir* Neill Fearnley • *Scr* George Zaloom, "ZA K"

Dogpound Shuffle ★★★

Comedy drama 1974 · Can · Colour · 100mins

So often a scene-stealing character actor, Ron Moody gets a rare crack at a lead in this amiable piece of family entertainment. As the one-time vaudevillian desperate to raise $30 to get his beloved pet out of the dog pound, he demonstrates some of the soft-shoe style that made him such a hit as Fagin in *Oliver!* There's also some unselfish support from David Soul, who calls on his experiences as a pop singer for his tuneful turn as the washed-up prizefighter who becomes Moody's song-and-dance partner. DP

Ron Moody *Steps* • David Soul *Pritt* • Pamela McMyler *Pound lady* • Ray Strickland *Mr Lester Jr* • Raymond Sutton *Pound Attendant* ■ *Dir/Scr* Jeffrey Bloom

Dogs ★

Horror 1976 · US · Colour · 89mins

This low-budget howler fails to convince with its tale of a pack of killer hounds on the loose in an isolated college campus. David McCallum struggles gamely as a biology professor whose students end up as Winalot chunks. If movies were dogs, this would be a shih-tzu. RS

David McCallum *Harlan Thompson* • George Wyner *Michael Fitzgerald* • Eric Server *Jimmy Goodmann* • Sandra McCabe *Caroline Donoghue* • Sterling Swanson *Dr Martin Koppelman* • Holly Harris *Mrs Koppelman* ■ *Dir* Burt Brinckerhoff • *Scr* O'Brian Tomalin

A Dog's Best Friend ★★

Adventure drama 1960 · US · BW · 70mins

There are shades of Rin Tin Tin in this tale of a wounded German Shepherd who befriends an emotionally scarred orphan. Roger Mobley turns in a creditable display of simmering resentment, which quickly deflects into terror once he realises his new pal has witnessed a murder and that the killer is now on their trail. Edward L Cahn demonstrates both a B-movie sensibility honed over 30 years and a keen grasp of what keeps kids on the edge of their seats. DP

Bill Williams *Wes Thurman* • Marcia Henderson *Millie Thurman* • Roger Mobley *Pip Wheeler* • Charles Cooper *Bill Beamer* • Dean Stanton [Harry Dean Stanton] *Roy Janney* • Roy Engel *Sheriff Dan Murdock* ■ *Dir* Edward L Cahn • *Scr* Orville H Hampton

Dogs in Space ★★★★ 18

Drama 1986 · Aus · Colour · 104mins

This appealingly quirky snapshot of punk life Down Under in the late 1970s marked the film debut of the INXS singer Michael Hutchence, who plays a heroin-taking wannabe rock star. The film focuses on struggling band Dogs in Space, led by Hutchence, plus their friends and hangers-on as they drift from party to gig to another party. The soundtrack, which mixes Aussie punk with Iggy Pop and Brian Eno, is superb, while the direction – from pop promo man Richard Lowenstein – is surprisingly unflashy. JF DVD

Michael Hutchence *Sam* • Saskia Post *Anna* • Nique Needles *Tim* • Deanna Bond *Girl* • Tony Helou *Luchio* • Chris Haywood *Chainsaw man* • Peter Walsh *Anthony* • Laura Swanson *Clare* ■ *Dir/Scr* Richard Lowenstein

The Dogs of War ★★ 15

Action drama 1980 · UK · Colour · 102mins

Unleashed upon the big screen from Frederick Forsyth's thriller, these hounds unfortunately have been muzzled and boast too few snarls. Christopher Walken plays the disillusioned mercenary caught up in a dastardly plot to take over a West African state, but any possible thrills are overpowered by too much explanation. John Irvin's direction of the macho passions on display is both predictable and unfocused. TH. Contains violence, swearing. DVD

Christopher Walken *Jamie Shannon* • Tom Berenger *Drew* • Colin Blakely *North* • Hugh Millais *Endean* • Paul Freeman *Derek* • JoBeth Williams *Jessie* ■ *Dir* John Irvin • *Scr* Gary DeVore, George Malko, from the novel by Frederick Forsyth

Dogtanian – the Movie ★★ U

Animated adventure
1989 · Sp · Colour · 93mins

This full-length version of the popular Spanish cartoon series sticks closely to the familiar Dumas story. Like most other animated spin-offs, however, characters who are comfortable companions for 20 minutes become insufferable after an hour. A brash, yappy pup, Dogtanian is the least likeable of the Muskehounds, and we don't get nearly enough of the foxy Cardinal Richelieu as he plots an alliance with England. DP

Dir Luis Ballester • *Scr* from characters created by Claudio Biem Boyd, from the novel *The Three Musketeers* by Alexandre Dumas

Dogtown and Z-Boys ★★★ 15

Documentary 2001 · US · Colour · 90mins

Narrated by Sean Penn and recalling the reverential style that characterised Bruce Brown's 1960s surf movies, this is a fond, but fatally self-mythologising memoir of the Zephyr skateboarding team. Known as the Z-Boys, these kids from the rundown LA neighbourhood of Dogtown rode their boards to national celebrity in the mid-1970s and revolutionised this distinctive urban sport. The unfussy contemporary footage of the team performing gravity-defying stunts in both local competitions and drained swimming pools is priceless. Less valuable, however, are the nostalgic insights provided by Jay Adams, Tony Alva and director Stacy Peralta, with the latter in particular suffering from an overblown sense of his own significance. DP. Contains swearing. DVD

Sean Penn *Narrator* ■ *Dir* Stacy Peralta • *Scr* Stacy Peralta, Craig Stecyk • *Cinematographer* Peter Pilafian

Dogville ★★★★ 15

Drama
2003 · Den/Swe/UK/Fr/Neth · Col · 170m

Director Lars von Trier abandons the restrictions that he devised for Dogme 95 and sets himself a new batch of creative dilemmas in this defiantly stylised picture that's played out on a single sound stage, with buildings and landmarks being suggested by outlines and props rather than existing as authentic sets. The ensemble cast is excellent, but it's Nicole Kidman who fixes the attention, playing the Depression-era runaway who places herself at the disposal of the residents of a Rocky Mountain backwater in return for their protection from the Mob. A sobering study in human frailty. (Made with additional funding from Norway, Germany and Finland.) DP. Contains violence. DVD

Nicole Kidman *Grace* • Harriet Andersson *Gloria* • Lauren Bacall *Ma Ginger* • Jean-Marc Barr *The man with the big hat* • Paul Bettany *Tom Edison* • Blair Brown *Mrs Henson* • James Caan *The big man* • Patricia Clarkson *Vera* • Jeremy Davies *Bill Henson* • Ben Gazzara *Jack McKay* • Philip Baker Hall *Tom Edison Sr* • Udo Kier *The man in the coat* • Chloë Sevigny *Liz Henson* • Stellan Skarsgård *Chuck* ■ *Dir/Scr* Lars von Trier

Dogwatch ★★ 18

Crime thriller 1997 · US · Colour · 95mins

Sam Elliott and Paul Sorvino star in a hard-hitting crime thriller about a tough San Francisco cop who discovers his late partner wasn't exactly on the right side of the law. Having killed the man he thinks is responsible for his friend's death, detective Elliott and his new partner Esai Morales become entangled in two murder investigations. Seedy and humourless. RT. Contains swearing and violence. DVD

Sam Elliott *Charlie Falon* • Esai Morales *Murrow* • Paul Sorvino *Delgoti* • Dan Lauria *Halloway* • Richard Gilliland *Orlanski* • Mimi Graven *Sally* ■ *Dir* John Langley • *Scr* Martin Zurla, from a story by Dan Lauria, Martin Zurla

Doin' Time on Planet Earth ★★ 15

Comedy 1988 · US · Colour · 79mins

Nicholas Strouse is a teenager who, in the course of his search for a date for his brother's wedding, comes to believe he is an alien from outer space. Candice Azzara and Adam West are two other potential aliens who believe Strouse holds the information that will lead them all home. It all has something to do with the wedding being on a blue moon and in Strouse's father's revolving restaurant. A supposed comedy that's too complicated to be funny. ST

Nicholas Strouse *Ryan Richmond* • Matt Adler *Dan Forrester* • Andrea Thompson *Lisa Winston* • Martha Scott *Virginia Camalier* • Adam West *Charles Pinsky* • Hugh Gillin *Fred Richmond* • Timothy Patrick Murphy *Jeff Richmond* • Candice Azzara [Candy Azzara] *Edna Pinsky* ■ *Dir* Charles Matthau • *Scr* Darren Star, from a story by Andrew Licht, Jeffrey A Mueller, Darren Star

Doing Time for Patsy Cline ★★★

Comedy road movie
1997 · Aus · Colour · 93mins

Miranda Otto teams up with real-life paramour Richard Roxburgh in a genial Aussie road movie with a country and western twang. Matt Day is a young innocent off to seek fame and fortune in Nashville. En route he hooks up with drug-dealing rogue Roxburgh and his redheaded girlfriend Otto, who harbours her own dreams of stardom. Things go pear-shaped when the trio get busted by the police. Attractively played by the three leads, the end result has a rich vein of self-mocking humour that leavens the rather heavy-handed stab at third-act pathos. NS

Matt Day *Ralph* • Richard Roxburgh *Boyd* • Miranda Otto *Patsy* • Gus Mercurio *Tyrone* • Tony Barry *Dwayne* • Kiri Paramore *Ken* ■ *Dir/Scr* Chris Kennedy

La Dolce Vita ★★★★★ 15

Classic drama 1960 · It/Fr · BW · 167mins

Winner of the Palme d'Or at Cannes, this sprawling, scathing satire on the decadence of contemporary Italy and the hypocrisy of the Catholic Church confirmed Federico Fellini's reputation for flamboyant, controversial imagery. Marcello Mastroianni is outstanding as the journalist who, by day, jostles with the paparazzi in the hunt for movie stars, miraculous visitations and flying statues of Christ. By night, he indulges his passion for intellectual pretension and the indolent delights of the jet set. A dire warning that Italy was still politically and socially prone to the false promises of fascism, this almost Dantesque odyssey so drained its Oscar-nominated director, he did not make another feature for three years. DP. In Italian with English subtitles. Contains violence, swearing. DVD

Marcello Mastroianni *Marcello Rubini* • Anita Ekberg *Sylvia* • Anouk Aimée *Maddalena* • Yvonne Furneaux *Emma* • Magali Noël *Fanny* • Alain Cuny *Steiner* • Nadia Gray *Nadia* • Lex Barker *Robert* • Annibale Ninchi *Marcello's father* ■ *Dir* Federico Fellini • *Scr* Federico Fellini, Ennio Flaiano, Tullio Pinelli, Brunello Rondi, from a story by Federico Fellini, Ennio Flaiano, Tullio Pinelli

Dolina Mira ★★★

Second World War drama
1956 · Yug · BW · 82mins

John Kitzmiller was still a GI when he was first cast in such neorealist classics as Roberto Rossellini's *Paisà* (1946), but it was the African-American's performance in this Yugoslav drama that earned him the Best Actor prize at Cannes. Again playing a Second World War soldier, Kitzmiller strikes up a charming relationship with Evelyne Wohlfeiler and the other waifs he encounters on their search for a valley that has escaped the Nazi blight. DP. A Slovenian language film.

John Kitzmiller • Evelyne Wohlfeiler *Lotti* • Tugo Stiglic *Marko* • Boris Kralj *Strumfuhrer* • Maks Furijan *Scharfuhrer* • Cuk Janez *Vodnik* ■ *Dir* France Stiglic • *Scr* Ivan Ribic

Dollar ★★★

Comedy 1938 · Swe · BW · 88mins

Having found stardom in romantic melodramas, Ingrid Bergman took a bit of a risk making this frantic comedy. As usual, she carried it off with the ease and grace that made her one of the finest actresses in cinema history. What with illicit romances, false suspicions, gambling debts, stock market crashes, secret pacts and mysterious illnesses, the plot concocted by Gustaf Molander takes credibility to its elastic limit. DP. In Swedish with English subtitles.

Georg Rydeberg *Kurt Balzar* • Ingrid Bergman *Julia Balzar* • Kotti Chave *Louis Brenner* • Tutta Rolf *Sussi Brenner* • Håkan Westergren *Ludvig von Bathwyhl* • Birgit Tengroth *Katja* • Elsa Burnett *Mary Jonstone* • Edvin Adolphson *Dr Jonsson* ■ *Dir* Gustaf Molander • *Scr* Stina Bergman, Gustaf Molander, from the play by Hjalmar Bergman

Dollar for the Dead ★★ PG

Western 1998 · US · Colour · 94mins

This is a commendable but flawed attempt to re-create the spaghetti western style of Sergio Leone, right down to shooting on the same Spanish sets Leone used. Director Gene Quintano also recalls John Woo in the two-fisted action and non-stop gunplay that feature throughout. Emilio Estevez comes to the aid of a crippled Civil War veteran, and the pair hitch up to re-assemble a treasure map embossed on four leather holsters. Out to stop them are "The Regulators" and a renegade troop of US cavalry. JF DVD

Emilio Estevez *The Cowboy* • William Forsythe *Dooley* • Howie Long *Reager* • Joaquim de Almeida *Friar Ramon* • Jonathan Banks *Skinner* • Ed Lauter *Colby* • Lance Kinsey *Tracker* • Jordi Mollà *Federal Captain* ■ *Dir/Scr* Gene Quintano

Dollar Mambo ★★★

Musical drama 1993 · Pan · Colour · 80mins

Re-enacting actual events, this mix of dance and mime proves that the musical is a suitable vehicle for political comment. Once more, Mexican director Paul Leduc employs a diversity of dance styles as the American invasion of Panama brings a halt to the lively entertainment at a downtown cabaret, where comics, magicians and showgirls provide the exploited workers with an escape from their toils. The shift in tone, once the gas-masked soldiers violate the bar and drive a dancer to suicide, is deeply disturbing. DP. In Spanish with English subtitles.

Roberto Sosa • Dolores Pedro • Javier Molina • Kandido Uranga ■ *Dir* Paul Leduc • *Scr* Paul Leduc, Jaime Aviles, Jose Jaquin Blanco, Hector Ortego, Juan Tovar

Dollars ★★★ 15

Crime comedy 1971 · US · Colour · 120mins

Never anything less than hugely enjoyable, this often frantic caper stars Warren Beatty as a bank security expert dedicated to crime and Goldie Hawn as his happy hooker accomplice. Although there is little chemistry between the leads and the direction is occasionally over-elaborate, the thefts from the deposit boxes of three criminal heavies are conducted with training-manual precision, while the finale has all the intricacy of a Buster Keaton chase. DP

Warren Beatty *Joe Collins* • Goldie Hawn *Dawn Divine* • Gert Fröbe *Mr Kessel* • Robert Webber *Attorney* • Scott Brady *Sarge* • Arthur Brauss *Candy Man* • Robert Stiles *Major* ■ *Dir/Scr* Richard Brooks

The Dollmaker ★★★★ PG

Drama 1984 · US · Colour · 137mins

This was Jane Fonda's first venture into small-screen movies, and she won an Emmy for her performance. After her husband lands a key wartime job in Detroit, Fonda's only escape from the trials of raising five children away from their Kentucky home comes from carving wooden dolls. The star reveals an intensity which has often been missing in the latter part of her career, although it helps that she's working with superior material. DP

Jane Fonda *Gertie Nevels* • Levon Helm *Clovis Nevels* • Geraldine Page *Mrs Kendrick* • Amanda Plummer *Marnie Childers* • Susan Kingsley *Sophronie* • Ann Hearn *Max* • Bob Swan *Victor* • Nikki Creswell *Cassie Nevels* • David Dawson *Amos Nevels* ■ *Dir* Daniel Petrie • *Scr* Susan Cooper, Hume Cronyn, from the novel by Harriette Arnow

Dolls ★★ 18

Comedy horror 1987 · US · Colour · 74mins

A novel variation on the 1980s "stalk and slash" movie, replacing the usual lone killer with knife-wielding mannequins. Director Stuart Gordon carved out something of a niche for himself as a gore fiend with such films as *Re-Animator*, but this film – about a disparate group of travellers holed up in a spooky mansion inhabited by an ageing couple who make homicidal puppets – is fairly restrained and has a perverse sense of humour. RS

Ian Patrick Williams *David Bower* • Carolyn Purdy-Gordon *Rosemary Bower* • Carrie Lorraine *Judy Bower* • Guy Rolfe *Gabriel Hartwicke* • Hilary Mason *Hilary Hartwicke* • Bunty Bailey *Isabel Prange* • Cassie Stuart *Enid Tilley* • Stephen Lee *Ralph Morris* ■ *Dir* Stuart Gordon • *Scr* Ed Naha

Dolls ★★★★ 12

Drama 2002 · Jpn · Colour · 108mins

Opening with a traditional *bunraku* puppet production of 18th-century playwright Monzaemon Chikamatsu's *The Courier for Hell*, this highly stylised and mournfully elegiac study of doomed romance recalls director Takeshi Kitano's previous production, *Hana-Bi*. Cinematographer Katsumi Yanagijima gloriously captures the colours of the changing seasons, as Kitano links three tales that demonstrate the exquisite agony of love: a young careerist seeks to atone for his jilted fiancée's maddening grief; an elderly yakuza hopes to re-ignite a forgotten passion; and a fan endures blindness to prove his fidelity to a disfigured pop star. The stately pacing may dissuade some, but the subtle symbolism and exquisite staging will have most viewers falling under its hypnotic spell. DP. In Japanese with English subtitles. DVD

Miho Kanno *Sawako* • Hidetoshi Nishijima *Matsumoto* • Tatsuya Mihashi *Hiro, the boss* • Chieko Matsubara *Ryoko, the woman in the park* • Kyoko Fukada *Haruna Yamaguchi, the pop star* • Tsutomu Takeshige *Nukui, the fan* ■ *Dir/Scr* Takeshi Kitano

A Doll's House ★★★

Drama 1973 · US · Colour · 85mins

Derived from the 1971 Broadway production directed by Patrick Garland, this version of Ibsen's classic play about the way marriage straitjackets women stars Claire Bloom as Nora, the flirtatious child-wife who gradually takes on an independence of spirit which resounds like the final slam of the symbolic door. She has some fine support by Anthony Hopkins and Ralph Richardson, though the result is a bit too earnest. TH

Claire Bloom *Nora Helmer* • Anthony Hopkins *Torvald Helmer* • Ralph Richardson *Dr Rank* • Denholm Elliott *Krogstad* • Anna Massey *Kristine Linde* • Edith Evans *Anne-Marie* ■ *Dir* Patrick Garland • *Scr* Christopher Hampton, from the play by Henrik Ibsen

A Doll's House ★★★★ PG

Drama 1973 · UK · Colour · 102mins

This adaptation (by playwright David Mercer) of Ibsen's play appeared the same time as the other 1973 version. Directed by Joseph Losey, however, it's the more cinematic, with its use of location (Norway) and camerawork (a mobile witness of events). Jane Fonda as Nora speaks up a little too blatantly for early women's liberation, but David Warner and Trevor Howard sustain Ibsen's then-revolutionary arguments with a subtlety that carries the play's message across time. TH

Jane Fonda *Nora* • David Warner *Torvald* • Trevor Howard *Dr Rank* • Delphine Seyrig *Kristine Linde* • Edward Fox *Krogstad* • Anna Wing *Anne-Marie* ■ *Dir* Joseph Losey • *Scr* David Mercer, from the play by Henrik Ibsen

The Dolly Sisters ★★★

Musical biography 1945 · US · Colour · 113mins

Produced by vaudeville legend George Jessel, this zesty biopic of Hungarian singing sensations Jenny and Rosie Dolly was tailor-made for the talents of Betty Grable and June Haver. The story follows a predictable route as the girls bid farewell to cuddly uncle SZ Sakall to make it big the world over and romance John Payne and Frank Latimore respectively. Blending period and newly penned tunes (including the Oscar-nominated *I Can't Begin to Tell You*), this colourful turn-of-the-century romp became one of 20th Century-Fox's most profitable musicals. DP

Betty Grable *Jenny* • June Haver *Rosie* • John Payne *Harry Fox* • SZ Sakall *Uncle Latsie* • Reginald Gardiner *Duke* • Frank Latimore *Irving Netcher* ■ *Dir* Irving Cummings • *Scr* John Larkin, Marian Spitzer

Dolores Claiborne ★★★★ 18

Mystery drama 1995 · US · Colour · 126mins

Kathy Bates, who won an Oscar for her performance in the film version of Stephen King's novel *Misery*, here stars in another King adaptation, this time as a housekeeper accused of killing her elderly employer. Jennifer Jason Leigh co-stars as Bates's daughter, who suspects her mother is guilty of more than one killing. There are magnificent portrayals all round, especially from Christopher Plummer as a retired and vengeful cop, but Bates steals every scene. TH. Contains violence and swearing. DVD

Kathy Bates *Dolores Claiborne* • Jennifer Jason Leigh *Selena St George* • Judy Parfitt *Vera Donovan* • Christopher Plummer *Detective John Mackey* • David Strathairn *Joe St George* • Eric Bogosian *Peter* • John C Reilly *Constable Frank Stamshaw* • Ellen Muth *Young Selena* ■ *Dir* Taylor Hackford • *Scr* Tony Gilroy, from the novel by Stephen King

Domestic Disturbance ★★★ 12

Thriller 2001 · US · Colour · 85mins

Vince Vaughn plays a monstrous stepfather with such finger-licking menace that even good-guy John Travolta has a job keeping up with his sinister machinations. Travolta plays the divorced father who is drawn into ex-wife Teri Polo's life with wealthy new husband Vaughn when son Matt O'Leary witnesses his stepdad's particular brand of murder and mayhem. This keeps up the suspense quotient, but can't overcome its stereotypical treatment of characters and events, in spite of a sleazy performance from Steve Buscemi as a seedy blackmailer. TH DVD

John Travolta *Frank Morrison* • Vince Vaughn *Rick Barnes* • Teri Polo *Susan Morrison Barnes* • Matt O'Leary *Danny Morrison* • Ruben Santiago-Hudson *Sgt Edgar Stevens* • Susan Floyd *Diane* • Angelica Torn *Patty* • Steve Buscemi *Ray Coleman* ■ *Dir* Harold Becker • *Scr* Lewis Colick, from a story by Lewis Colick, William S Comanor, Gary Drucker

Dominick and Eugene ★★★ 15

Drama 1988 · US · Colour · 104mins

Have the Kleenex handy when you watch this heart-rending tale of brotherly love, originally known here as *Nicky and Gino*. In a welcome change from his more usual villainous roles, Ray Liotta is a bright medical student devoted to his mentally disabled twin, Tom Hulce. But, if Liotta pursues his career, who will look after his brother? Overly sentimental perhaps, but compassionate and superbly played by the two leads. AJ. Contains violence and swearing.

Tom Hulce *Dominick "Nicky" Luciano* • Ray Liotta *Eugene "Gino" Luciano* • Jamie Lee Curtis *Jennifer Reston* • Todd Graff *Larry "Snake" Higgins* • Bill Cobbs *Jesse Johnson* • David Strathairn *Martin Chernak* ■ *Dir* Robert M Young • *Scr* Alvin Sargent, Corey Blechman, from a story by Danny Porfirio

Dominique ★★

Thriller 1978 · UK · Colour · 99mins

This daft thriller – about a husband who drives his crippled wife mad and then has to cope with her ghostly presence after she dies – is a variation on the old haunted house routine that offers few surprises and a lot of padding. The cast, however, is good, with perpetually perplexed Cliff Robertson and the lovely Jean Simmons. An expert at action movies, director Michael Anderson comes over all arty here and denies us the jolts the story promises. AT

Cliff Robertson *David Ballard* • Jean Simmons *Dominique Ballard* • Jenny Agutter *Ann Ballard* • Simon Ward *Tony Calvert* • Ron Moody *Doctor Rogers* • Judy Geeson *Marjorie Craven* • Michael Jayston *Arnold Craven* • Flora Robson *Mrs Davis* • David Tomlinson *Solicitor* • Jack Warner *George* ■ *Dir* Michael Anderson • *Scr* Edward Abraham, Valerie Abraham

The Domino Principle ★★ 15

Political thriller 1977 · US · Colour · 97mins

This feeble thriller – also known as *The Domino Killings* – has Gene Hackman as an expert marksman sprung from prison by an unnamed government agency and assigned to shoot an international bigwig. Adam Kennedy adapts his own novel, while director Stanley Kramer assembles a first-rate cast. The result, however, is a third-rate intrigue that is neither deep nor complex – just obscure. TH 

Gene Hackman *Roy Tucker* • Candice Bergen *Ellie* • Richard Widmark *Tagge* • Mickey Rooney *Spiventa* • Edward Albert *Ross Pine* • Eli Wallach *General Tom Reser* • Ken Swofford *Warden Ditcher* ■ *Dir* Stanley Kramer • *Scr* Adam Kennedy, from his novel

Don ★★★★

Drama 1998 · Iran · Colour · 90mins

Continuing the Iranian tradition of outstanding performances by non-professional juveniles, Farhad Bahremand proves persistent, resourceful, impudent and tragically vulnerable in this lacerating realist satire from the ever-contentious Abolfazl Jalili. As his junkie father forgot to register his birth, the nine-year-old is ineligible for the ID card that would enable him to attend school and earn the meagre wage needed by his destitute family. But the camera can only watch helplessly as Farhad pleads with both jobsworth civil servants to secure his papers and exploitative employers. Affecting, amusing and deeply depressing. DP. In Farsi with English subtitles.

Farhad Bahremand *Farhad* • Bakhtiyar Bahremand • Farzad Helili ■ *Dir/Scr* Abolfazl Jalili

Don Giovanni ★★★

Opera 1979 · Fr/It/W Ger · Colour · 184mins

Joseph Losey spent much time in France towards the end of his career, and it was there that he made this labour of love. Mozart's opera tells of a libertine who is offered redemption by the father of one of his conquests; it has been filmed many times, though never as sumptuously as this. Beautiful scenery and voices make this ideal for those who love opera but can't afford Covent Garden prices. FL. In Italian with English subtitles.

Ruggero Raimondi *Don Giovanni* • John Macurdy *The Commander* • Edda Moser *Donna Anna* • Kiri Te Kanawa *Donna Elvira* • Kenneth Riegel *Don Ottavio* • José Van Dam

Leporello • Teresa Berganza *Zerlina* • Malcolm King *Masetto* ■ *Dir* Joseph Losey • *Scr* Patricia Losey, Joseph Losey, Frantz Salieri, from the opera *Don Giovanni* by Wolfgang Amadeus Mozart, Lorenzo Da Ponte

The Don Is Dead ★★ 18

Crime drama 1973 · US · Colour · 108mins

In this hastily produced rip-off of *The Godfather*, Anthony Quinn is the Mafia boss while Robert Forster is the hothead who precipitates a gang war. It might have passed muster as a mobster pic had it been released before Francis Ford Coppola's Oscar-winning epic, but coming after it only emphasises the film's failings. Director Richard Fleischer is no slouch when it comes to action sequences, however, and the climactic raid on the enemy HQ is particularly impressive. AT

Anthony Quinn *Don Angelo* • Frederic Forrest *Tony* • Robert Forster *Frank* • Al Lettieri *Vince* • Angel Tomkins *Ruby* • Charles Cioffi *Orlando* ■ *Dir* Richard Fleischer • *Scr* Marvin H Albert, from his novel, adapted by Michael Philip Butler, Christopher Trumbo

Don Juan ★★★★

Silent romantic drama
1926 · US · BW · 93mins

Historically important, this was Warner Bros's (and indeed Hollywood's) first synchronised sound movie. No dialogue or songs – they would come the following year with *The Jazz Singer* – the film has a synchronised score and some pointed (though shamefully non-synchronised) sound effects. Yet this would have been a spectacular success with or without sound, the title role being tailor-made for the great John Barrymore, who clearly revels in the part. The beautiful young Mary Astor reforms the Don, while Estelle Taylor makes a super Lucretia Borgia. The expensive production is exceptionally well directed by Alan Crosland, who would also direct that Jolson milestone. TS

John Barrymore *Don Juan* • Mary Astor *Adriana Della Varnese* • Willard Louis *Perdillo* • Estelle Taylor *Lucretia Borgia* • Helene Costello *Rena, Adriana's maid* • Myrna Loy *Maria, Lucretia's maid* • Jane Winton *Beatrice* • John Roche *Leandro* • Warner Oland *Caesar Borgia* ■ *Dir* Alan Crosland • *Scr* Bess Meredyth, from the poem by Lord Byron

Don Juan DeMarco ★★★★ 15

Romantic drama 1995 · US · Colour · 93mins

Lunatics take over the asylum again in an enchanting feel-good fable showcasing a masked Johnny Depp as the world's greatest lover on the verge of suicide. As a burnt-out shrink, Marlon Brando must prick the cod Casanova's fantasy bubble in therapy sessions, where his exaggerated Mexican past and hopelessly romantic conquests are revealed in mythic flashback, or have him committed. Instead, through Depp's grandiose, poetic delusions, Brando re-examines the importance of passion in his own marriage to Faye Dunaway. A scintillating lyrical tone makes director Jeremy Leven's film a wonderfully funny, touching odyssey. AJ. Contains swearing and nudity. DVD

Marlon Brando *Jack Mickler* • Johnny Depp *Don Juan DeMarco* • Faye Dunaway *Marilyn Mickler* • Géraldine Pailhas *Dona Ana* • Bob Dishy *Dr Paul Showalter* • Rachel Ticotin *Dona Inez* • Talisa Soto *Dona Julia* ■ *Dir* Jeremy Leven • *Scr* Jeremy Leven, from a character created by Lord Byron

Don Juan 73, or If Don Juan Were a Woman ★★ 18

Drama 1973 · Fr/It · Colour · 89mins

Brigitte Bardot still looks stunning at 39, but her films were not getting much better; this was one of the last she made before vanishing from showbusiness altogether. Roger Vadim's film centres on three traumatic affairs involving the same libertine woman. Notorious for a lesbian bed scene between Bardot and British actress Jane Birkin, this marked the first time the French superstar had ever appeared full-frontal before cameras. RS. French dialogue dubbed into English.

Brigitte Bardot *Jeanne* • Jane Birkin *Clara* • Maurice Ronet *Pierre* • Mathieu Carrière *Paul* • Robert Hossein *Prevost* • Michèle Sand *Leporella* • Robert Walker Jr *Young Spaniard* ■ *Dir* Roger Vadim • *Scr* Jean Cau, Roger Vadim, Jean-Pierre Petrolacci

Don Q, Son of Zorro ★★★

Silent swashbuckling adventure
1925 · US · BW · 111mins

Here's an early version of the Zorro tale, with the original swashbuckling hero, Douglas Fairbanks, playing both father and son. In fact, Fairbanks had already played the swish swordsmith in *The Mark of Zorro* in 1920, but this time round he had more money and Mary Astor as his co-star. While due allowance should be made for the histrionic acting, this remains a key Fairbanks adventure, with spectacular sets and rousing action. AT

Douglas Fairbanks *Don Cesar de Vega/Zorro* • Mary Astor *Dolores de Muro* • Donald Crisp *Don Sebastian* • Stella de Lanti *The Queen* • Warner Oland *Archduke Paul of Austria* • Jean Hersholt *Don Fabrique* • Albert MacQuarrie *Col Matsado* • Lottie Pickford Forrest *Lola* ■ *Dir* Donald Crisp • *Scr* Jack Cunningham • *Art Director* Edward M Langley

Don Quixote ★★★ U

Musical adventure drama
1932 · UK/Fr · BW · 78mins

Cervantes's epic novel had already been adapted nine times before the exiled GW Pabst shot this rather stilted version with the great Russian vocalist Feodor Chaliapin. The supporting cast depended on the language you spoke: George Robey played the English Sancho Panza, while Dorville was his French counterpart. Chaliapin, who occasionally exceeds his thespian limitations, still produces moments of real pathos. Pabst is ill-served by song composer Jacques Ibert, but the cinematography is sublime. DP

Feodor Chaliapin *Don Quixote* • George Robey *Sancho Panza* • Sidney Fox *The Niece* • Miles Mander *The Duke* • Oscar Asche *Police Captain* • Dannio *Carrasco* • Emily Fitzroy *Sancho's wife* • Frank Stanmore *Priest* ■ *Dir* GW Pabst • *Scr* Paul Morand, Alexandre Arnoux, from the novel *El Ingenioso Hidalgo Don Quijote de la Mancha* by Miguel de Cervantes Saavedra • *Cinematographer* Nicolas Farkas, Paul Portier

Don Quixote ★★★★★ U

Adventure drama
1957 · USSR · Colour · 106mins

Having already played Alexander Nevsky and Ivan the Terrible for Eisenstein, Nikolai Cherkassov confirmed his status as one of Soviet cinema's finest actors by playing Cervantes's eccentric knight. With the Crimea standing in for the Spanish plains, the film achieves a picaresque sweep through Grigori Kozintsev's majestic use of widescreen colour. Assuredly staging such classic episodes as the encounter with the windmills, he wisely prevents the finale from becoming too maudlin. Yet it's the delightful performances that sustain the novel's wit and warmth, with Cherkassov expertly conveying Quixote's delusional pride and naive idealism, and Yuri Tolubeyev bringing a earthy loyalty to Sancho Panza.. DP. Russian dialogue dubbed into English.

Nikolai Cherkassov *Don Quixote* • Yuri Tolubeyev *Sancho Panza* • T Agamirova *Altisidora* • V Freindlich *Duke* • L Vertinskaya *Duchess* • G Vitsin *Carrasco* • L Kasyanova *Aldonsa* ■ *Dir* Grigori Kozintsev • *Scr* Yevgeni Shvarts, from the novel *El Ingenioso Hidalgo Don Quijote de la Mancha* by Miguel de Cervantes Saavedra

Don Quixote ★★★ U

Dance 1973 · Aus · Colour · 111mins

Co-directed by Robert Helpmann and Rudolf Nureyev, this film of Marius Petipa's light-hearted romantic ballet doesn't have much to do with tilting windmills. Instead it deals with a barber (Nureyev) who woos and wins his sweetheart with the aid of Helpmann's misguided knight and Sancho Panza (Ray Powell). Cinematographer Geoffrey Unsworth uses overhead shots to capture the full scale of the action; as a result, you feel as if you're in the frame instead of just watching it. FL

Robert Helpmann *Don Quixote* • Ray Powell *Sancho Panza* • Rudolf Nureyev *Basilio* • Francis Croese *Lorenzo* • Lucette Aldous *Kitri* • Colin Peasley *Gamache* • Marilyn Rowe *Street dancer* • Kelvin Coe *Espada* ■ *Dir* Rudolf Nureyev, Robert Helpmann

Don Quixote ★★★ PG

Adventure drama
2000 · US · Colour · 139mins

John Lithgow and Bob Hoskins headline Peter Yates's marathon TV feature. Lithgow is quite magnificent in a role he'd long hoped to play. He invites genuine pathos as the delusional knight whose undimmed sense of chivalry is responsible for sending devoted squire Sancho Panza in search of challenges to please the fair Dulcinea. The Spanish locations are exploited to the full, but Yates finds no solution to the fragmentary nature of the novel. DP DVD

John Lithgow *Don Quixote/Don Alonso* • Bob Hoskins *Sancho Panza* • James Purefoy *Sampson Carrasco* • Lambert Wilson *Duke* • Isabella Rossellini *Duchess* • Vanessa L Williams *Dulcinea/Aldonza* • Amelia Warner *Antonia* ■ *Dir* Peter Yates • *Scr* John Mortimer, from the novel *El Ingenioso Hidalgo Don Quijote de la Mancha* by Miguel de Cervantes Saavedra

Dona Flor and Her Two Husbands ★★ 18

Romantic comedy
1977 · Bra · Colour · 104mins

This wants to be a smart, sexy satire. But it's little more than an upmarket *pornochanchada*, the soft-core comedy that dominates Brazilian film-making. There are some flashes of intelligence in the way Sonia Braga exploits the security offered by living husband Mauro Mendonca, while also accepting vigorous advances from her ex-husband's ghost (Jose Wilker). Sally Field starred in the witless American remake, *Kiss Me Goodbye*. DP. A Portuguese language film.

Sonia Braga *Dona Flor* • José Wilker *Vadinho* • Mauro Mendonca *Teodoro* • Dinorah Brillanti *Rozilda* • Nelson Xavier *Mirandao* • Arthur Costa Filho *Carlinhos* ■ *Dir* Bruno Barreto • *Scr* Bruno Barreto, from the novel *Doña Flor e Seus Dois Maridos* by Jorge Amado

Dona Herlinda and Her Son ★★★★ 15

Comedy 1986 · Mex · Colour · 89mins

This gay comedy from Mexican director Jaime Humberto Hermosillo is a low-budget satire of sexual manners, as doctor Marco Antonio Trevino marries to placate his matchmaking mother, Guadalupe Del Toro, while still cohabiting with his music student lover, Arturo Meza. Mocking machismo, romance, sexual duplicity and social snobbery, the picture benefits from some adroit playing and a sharp script based on Hermosillo's own experiences as a homosexual in an unsympathetic society. DP. In Spanish with English subtitles.

Guadalupe Del Toro *Dona Herlinda* • Arturo Meza *Ramon* • Marco Antonio Trevino *Rodolfo* • Leticia Lupersio *Olga* • Angelica Guerrero *Ramon's mother* • Donato Castaneda *Ramon's father* • Guillermina Alba *Billy* ■ *Dir/Scr* Jaime Humberto Hermosillo

Donnie Brasco ★★★★ 18

Crime drama 1997 · US · Colour · 121mins

In this 1970s-set crime drama, Al Pacino stars as a sleazeball who inducts young Brasco, played by Johnny Depp, into the codes and "family" values of organised crime. In fact, Depp is an FBI undercover agent whose job threatens his marriage to Anne Heche as well as his life. Directed by Mike Newell, the film develops nicely as Depp finds himself becoming rather fond of his monstrous mentor. The period setting – a world of tacky shirts, fur collars and plastic lawns – is also beautifully evoked. AT. Contains swearing, violence and a sex scene. DVD

Al Pacino *Lefty Ruggiero* • Johnny Depp *Joe Pistone/"Donnie Brasco"* • Michael Madsen *Sonny Black* • Bruno Kirby *Nicky* • James Russo *Paulie* • Anne Heche *Maggie Pistone* • Zeljko Ivanek *Tim Curley* • Gerry Becker *Dean Blandford* ■ *Dir* Mike Newell • *Scr* Paul Attanasio, from a non-fiction book by Joseph D Pistone, Richard Woodley

Donnie Darko ★★★★ 15

Psychological fantasy drama
2001 · US · Colour · 108mins

Jake Gyllenhaal is an introverted student in therapy who keeps having visions of a 6ft tall rabbit that tells him the end of the world is imminent and forces him to commit acts of vandalism while sleepwalking. Director Richard Kelly's powerfully affecting meditation on parallel universes, time travel and paranoid schizophrenia is a stunningly crafted and hypnotic masterwork that opens up intriguing new genre avenues. The additional material included in the director's cut has divided critics. Some feel that adding to the coherence of the narrative has compromised the teasing mystery of the film, while others have welcomed the chance to see the film as Kelly intended. AJ. Contains drug abuse, violence, swearing. DVD

Jake Gyllenhaal *Donnie Darko* • Jena Malone *Gretchen Ross* • Drew Barrymore *Karen Pomeroy* • Mary McDonnell *Rose Darko* • Holmes Osborne *Eddie Darko* • Katharine Ross *Dr Lilian Thurman* • Patrick Swayze *Jim Cunningham* • Noah Wyle *Dr Monnitoff* • Maggie Gyllenhaal *Elizabeth Darko* ■ *Dir/Scr* Richard Kelly

The Donor ★★

Medical thriller 1994 · US · Colour · 94mins

Jeff Wincott is one of many who have attempted to follow in the Hollywood footsteps of Jean-Claude Van Damme and failed. His English is better and so is his acting, but he isn't exactly pin-up material. In this flawed but intriguing thriller, he gets the opportunity to flex something other than his muscles playing a stuntman who, discovering that he has been the victim of some smash-and-grab organ surgery, sets out to uncover the conspiracy. The story stretches credibility, but the action powers along. JF. Contains swearing, violence, sex scenes.

Jeff Wincott *Billy Castle* • Michelle Johnson *Dr Lucy Flynn* • Gordon Thomson *Dr Jonathan Cross* ■ *Dir* Damian Lee • *Scr* Neal Dobrofsky, Tippi Dobrofsky

D

Donovan's Brain ★★★

Science fiction 1953 · US · BW · 83mins

Directed with unnerving seriousness by MGM journeyman Felix Feist, this is the most faithful and easily the best adaptation of Curt Siodmak's fiendish novel. The tale of doctor Lew Ayres's struggle with the maniacal powers of a dead industrialist's transplanted brain is given chilling credibility by the extraordinary range of expressions Ayres assumes whenever he's gripped by the millionaire's insane desire to destroy his family and former associates. Gene Evans and Nancy Davis (Ronald Reagan's future first lady) are on hand to provide effectively uncomprehending support. DP

Lew Ayres *Dr Patrick J Corey* • Gene Evans *Dr Frank Schratt* • Nancy Davis *Janice Cory* • Steve Brodie *Herbie Yocum* • Lisa K Howard *Chloe Donovan* ■ *Dir* Felix Feist • *Scr* Felix Feist, from the novel by Curt Siodmak

Donovan's Reef ★★★ U

Comedy drama 1963 · US · Colour · 104mins

This ramshackle but enjoyable South Sea island romp was the last teaming of the great director John Ford and his friend John Wayne. Elizabeth Allen co-stars as the prim Bostonian whose presence on a Pacific island disturbs the drinking and brawling lifestyle of the Duke and his crony Lee Marvin. There's a seasonal touch involving Dorothy Lamour and a children's Christmas, though the best thing here is the Technicolor photography by William Clothier. TS [video] DVD

John Wayne *"Guns" Donovan* • Lee Marvin *"Boats" Gilhooley* • Jack Warden *"Doc" Dedham* • Elizabeth Allen *Amelia Dedham* • Cesar Romero *Andre de Lage* • Dorothy Lamour *Fleur* • Jacqueline Malouf *Lelani* • Mike Mazurki *Sergeant Menkowicz* ■ *Dir* John Ford • *Scr* Frank Nugent, James Edward Grant, from a story by Edmund Beloin, from material by James Michener (uncredited)

Don's Party ★★★★ 18

Black comedy 1976 · Aus · Colour · 86mins

Set on election night, 1969, this savage black comedy lifts the lid off suburban Australia and exposes all the prejudice and resentment simmering underneath. The dialogue crackles with offensive opinions and lacerating insults as the 11 guests throw off their ill-fitting gentility and let rip at one another as the beer flows and the results come in. Bruce Beresford paces the descent into uncivil war to perfection, while the cast are uniformly excellent in turning grotesque caricatures into credible specimens of boorish humanity. DP [video]

Ray Barrett *Mal* • Claire Binney *Susan* • Pat Bishop *Jenny* • Graeme Blundell *Simon* • John Hargreaves *Don Henderson* • Harold Hopkins *Cooley* • John Gorton ■ *Dir* Bruce Beresford • *Scr* David Williamson, from his play

Don't Be a Menace to South Central while Drinking Your Juice in the Hood ★ 15

Comedy 1996 · US · Colour · 85mins

It's a great title, and there's no denying that the ghetto drama genre is ripe for send-up, but this is dire. It squanders its comic potential through lazy spoofing, ramshackle plotting and tasteless jokes. Not even the presence of what appears to be the entire Wayans family can save this sorry mess. JF DVD

Shawn Wayans *Ashtray* • Marlon Wayans *Loc Dog* • Tracey Cherelle Jones *Dashiki* • Chris Spencer *Preach* • Suli McCullough *Crazy Legs* • Helen Martin *Grandma* • Isaiah Barnes *Doo Rag* • Lahmard Tate *Ashtray's father* • Keenen Ivory Wayans *Mailman* • Craig Wayans *First thug* ■ *Dir* Paris Barclay • *Scr* Shawn Wayans, Marlon Wayans, Phil Beauman

Don't Bother to Knock ★★★ PG

Thriller 1952 · US · BW · 76mins

Marilyn Monroe was just a year away from stardom when she made this hysterical melodrama, which finds her trading twitches with that master of mannered mania, Richard Widmark. As the suicidal babysitter confronted by Widmark's leering hotel guest, Monroe occasionally looks close to the edge. Alas, this lacks both the psychological depth and the necessary suspense to distract us from the stilted acting and laboured direction. Anne Bancroft impresses in her feature debut, but it's the cast-against-type Monroe who catches the eye. DP [video] DVD

Richard Widmark *Jed Towers* • Marilyn Monroe *Nell* • Anne Bancroft *Lyn Leslie* • Donna Corcoran *Bunny* • Jeanne Cagney *Rochelle* • Lurene Tuttle *Ruth Jones* • Elisha Cook Jr *Eddie* • Jim Backus *Peter Jones* • Verna Felton *Mrs Ballew* ■ *Dir* Roy Baker [Roy Ward Baker] • *Scr* Daniel Taradash, from the novel by Charlotte Armstrong

Don't Bother to Knock ★★ PG

Comedy 1961 · UK · Colour · 84mins

This is a leaden romp that starts out smug and ends up tasteless. Considering he also produced the project, Richard Todd looks distinctly uncomfortable as the philandering travel agent who discovers, to girlfriend June Thorburn's horror, that all his European flirtations have arrived at his Edinburgh home at once. Thanks to Geoffrey Unsworth and Anne V Coates respectively, it has better photography and editing than it deserves. DP [video]

Richard Todd *Bill Ferguson* • Nicole Maurey *Lucille* • Elke Sommer *Ingrid* • June Thorburn *Stella* • Rik Battaglia *Giulio* • Judith Anderson *Maggie* • Dawn Beret *Harry* • Scott Finch *Perry* • Eleanor Summerfield *Mother* • John Le Mesurier *Father* • Warren Mitchell *Waiter* ■ *Dir* Cyril Frankel • *Scr* Denis Cannan, Frederick Gotfurt, Frederic Raphael, from the novel *Love from Everybody* by Clifford Hanley

Don't Cry, It's Only Thunder ★★★

War drama 1982 · US · Colour · 108mins

This Vietnam drama looks at a topic that few war movies examine. Dennis Christopher is outstanding as an initially selfish army medic who is saddled with the responsibility of helping nuns take care of war orphans. The movie shows us the human cost of armed conflict, not just by examining its helpless victims, but also by making Christopher and his fellow soldiers evolve and grow over time. However, the subplot involving Christopher's relationship with doctor Susan Saint James feels unfinished. KB

Dennis Christopher *Brian* • Susan Saint James *Katherine* • Lisa Lu *Sister Marie* • Thu Thuy *Sister Hoa* • Mai Thi Lien *Anh* • Truong Minh Hai *Duc* • Robert Englund *Tripper* • James Whitmore Jr *Major Flaherty* ■ *Dir* Peter Werner • *Scr* Paul Hensler

Don't Drink the Water ★★

Comedy 1969 · US · Colour · 98mins

Woody Allen's sharp and angry stage play is bloated to portly buffoonry to suit comic actor Jackie Gleason, with Allen's words rewritten for the screen by RS Allen and Harvey Bullock. Gleason stars as a Jewish caterer who is forced to take refuge in the American embassy in Vulgaria. He's suspected of spying by East European officials when he takes some snaps at the airport, and then tries to flee the fictional Iron Curtain country. TH

Jackie Gleason *Walter Hollander* • Estelle Parsons *Marion Hollander* • Ted Bessell *Axel Magee* • Joan Delaney *Susan Hollander* • Michael Constantine *Krojack* • Howard St John *Ambassador Magee* • Danny Meehan *Kilroy* • Richard Libertini *Father Drobney* ■ *Dir* Howard Morris • *Scr* RS Allen, Harvey Bullock, from the play by Woody Allen

Don't Ever Leave Me ★★ U

Comedy 1949 · UK · BW · 80mins

Petula Clark is on typically ebullient form, playing the spoiled daughter of a star actress who is kidnapped by a wily old crook, only to fall for his grandson and refuse to go home. Jimmy Hanley simply has to look fetching in the latter role, but as the older man veteran character actor Edward Rigby relishes the chance to display a little Dickensian devilment. Arthur Crabtree's direction fails to hit a consistent tone. DP [video]

Petula Clark *Sheila Farlaine* • Jimmy Hanley *Jack Denton* • Hugh Sinclair *Michael Farlaine* • Linden Travers *Mary Lamont* • Anthony Newley *Jimmy Knowles* ■ *Dir* Arthur Crabtree • *Scr* Robert Westerby, from the novel *The Wide Guy* by Anthony Armstrong

Don't Forget You're Going to Die ★★★

Drama 1995 · Fr · Colour · 118mins

This uncompromising study of a life cut short by Aids-related illness earned a certain notoriety for its terrifyingly realistic depiction of drug use and sexual oblivion. Xavier Beauvois's art historian accidentally becomes HIV-positive at the hands of a careless doctor, and his friendship with Roschdy Zem's trafficker casts a chilling pall of despair and self-destruction over affairs. The gloom doesn't dissipate even as Beauvois experiences happiness during his brief affair with student Chiara Mastroianni. DP. In French with English subtitles.

Xavier Beauvois *Benoit* • Chiara Mastroianni *Claudia* • Roschdy Zem *Omar* • Bulle Ogier *Benoit's mother* • Emmanuel Salinger *Military doctor* • Jean-Louis Richard *Benoit's father* • Jean Douchet *Jean-Paul* ■ *Dir* Xavier Beauvois • *Scr* Xavier Beauvois, Anne-Marie Sauzeau, Emmanuel Salinger, Zoubir Tligui

Don't Get Me Started ★

Comedy drama
1994 · UK/Ger · Colour · 76mins

Re-edited after its disastrous Cannes showing under its original title *Psychotherapy*, Arthur Ellis's feature debut comes as a major disappointment following such acclaimed shorts as *A Turnip Head's Guide to Alan Parker*. Caught between sinister satire and symbolic *film noir*, Ellis gives too little direction to a cast which is consequently unable to strike a consistent tone. Trevor Eve is particularly exposed as the happily married man whose pent-up frustration, brought on by quitting smoking, is indicative of a murderous past. DP

Trevor Eve *Jack Lane* • Steven Waddington *Jerry Hoff* • Marion Bailey *Gill Lane* • Ralph Brown *Larry Swift* • Marcia Warren *Pauline Lewis* ■ *Dir/Scr* Arthur Ellis

Don't Give Up the Ship ★★★ U

Comedy 1959 · US · BW · 88mins

This very, very funny Jerry Lewis vehicle comes from the period when Lewis had just split with Dean Martin and was still trying to establish his solo style. The wonderful wacky plot involves Jerry and sidekick Mickey Shaughnessy looking for a naval battleship that Lewis commanded during the Second World War and is now lost. (Don't ask!) Classy rich girl Dina Merrill turns in a mighty cute performance that makes you regret that she semi-retired from the screen in 1989 in order to run RKO Pictures with her husband, Ted Hartley. TS

Jerry Lewis *John Paul Steckler* • Dina Merrill *Ensign Benson* • Diana Spencer *Prudence Trabert* • Mickey Shaughnessy *Stan Wychinski* • Robert Middleton *Admiral Bludde* • Gale Gordon *Congressman Mandeville* • Mabel Albertson *Mrs Trabert* ■ *Dir* Norman Taurog • *Scr* Herbert Baker, Edmund Beloin, Henry Garson, from a story by Ellis Kadison

Don't Go Breaking My Heart ★★★ PG

Romantic comedy
1999 · UK · Colour · 89mins

Jenny Seagrove stars with *ER* heart-throb Anthony Edwards in this feel-good romantic comedy. She plays a widowed gardening expert who, through accident and misadventure, becomes involved with visiting American sports therapist Edwards. The only fly in the ointment is Charles Dance in a ridiculously over-the-top role as Edwards's love rival. Viewed as a superficial piece of fluffy nonsense, the film is enormously enjoyable, thanks largely to the charm and warmth of the two stars, and some genuinely moving moments. JF. Contains swearing. [video]

Anthony Edwards *Tony Dorfman* • Jenny Seagrove *Suzanne Brody* • Charles Dance *Frank* • Jane Leeves *Juliet* • Tom Conti *Doctor Fiedler* • Linford Christie • Ben Reynolds *Ben* ■ *Dir* Willi Patterson • *Scr* Geoff Morrow

Don't Go in the House ★ 18

Horror 1979 · US · Colour · 75mins

Offensive and simple-minded, this movie's only point of interest is the anti-feminist slant it shares with many late 1970s and early 1980s horror movies. Dan Grimaldi turns psycho when his mother suddenly dies. Extremely poor photography and bad lighting make it even more of an ordeal. KB [video]

Dan Grimaldi *Donny Kohler* • Charlie Bonet *Ben* • Bill Ricci *Vito* • Robert Osth *Bobby Tuttle* • Dennis Hunt *Locker room worker* • John Hedberg *Locker room worker* • Ruth Dardick *Mrs Kohler* • Johanna Brushay *Kathy Jordan* ■ *Dir* Joseph Ellison • *Scr* Joseph Ellison, Ellen Hammill, Joseph Masefield

Don't Go Near the Water ★★★ U

Comedy 1957 · US · Colour · 106mins

Patchy but always amiable and sometimes hilarious, this slapstick comedy deals with the problems faced by a naval public relations unit on a South Pacific island in attempting to promote a wholesome image of the service with little or no experience of ever having been at sea. Glenn Ford and Gia Scala are top-billed, but the standouts are Fred Clark, on top form as the irascible commanding officer, and burly Mickey Shaughnessy as a most unfortunate choice of sailor to thrust into the spotlight. AE

Glenn Ford *Lieutenant Max Siegel* • Gia Scala *Melora* • Earl Holliman *Adam Garrett* • Anne Francis *Lieutenant Alice Tomlen* • Keenan Wynn *Gordon Ripwell* • Fred Clark *Lieutenant Commander Clinton Nash* • Russ Tamblyn *Ensign Tyson* ■ *Dir* Charles Walters • *Scr* Dorothy Kingsley, George Wells, from the novel by William Brinkley

Don't Just Lie There, Say Something! ★ PG

Comedy 1973 · UK · Colour · 87mins

The Whitehall farces may have delighted London theatre-goers from the 1950s to the 1970s, but they have never worked on the screen. This film reduces the precise timing of the double entendres, the bedroom entrances and exits and the dropped-trouser misunderstandings to the level of clumsy contrivance, which not even the slickest of players can redeem. Few *farceurs* are as practised as Leslie

Phillips and Brian Rix, but they are powerless to save this. DP DVD

Leslie Phillips *Sir William* • Brian Rix *Barry Ovis* • Joanna Lumley *Miss Parkyn* • Joan Sims *Birdie* • Derek Royle *Wilfred Potts* • Peter Bland *Inspector Ruff* • Katy Manning *Damina* ■ *Dir* Bob Kellett • *Scr* Michael Pertwee, from his play

Don't Just Stand There ★★★

Comedy drama 1968 · US · Colour · 99mins

This clever comedy is given added appeal by the pairing of the extremely likeable Robert Wagner and Mary Tyler Moore. The two join forces to search for novelist Glynis Johns, who has only managed to pen the first half of her new book. Harvey Korman pops up en route to great effect, and director Ron Winston papers over the holes in the script by keeping the pace at fever pitch. Glossy production values, period Technicolor and Techniscope lensing lend this artefact a quaint charm. TS

Robert Wagner *Lawrence Colby* • Mary Tyler Moore *Martine Randall* • Glynis Johns *Sabine Manning* • Barbara Rhoades *Kendall Flanagan* • Harvey Korman *Merriman Dudley* • Vincent Beck *Painter* • Joseph Perry *Jean-Jacques* ■ *Dir* Ron Winston • *Scr* Charles Williams, from his novel *The Wrong Venus*

Don't Knock the Rock ★★ U

Musical 1956 · US · BW · 84mins

Quickie producer Sam Katzman's follow-up to the enormously successful *Rock around the Clock* also features the airwave-shattering Bill Haley and the Comets. There's great period value in this movie: kiss-curled Haley and his great line-up playing numbers like *Hook, Line and Sinker*, and the fabulous Little Richard at his peak performing *Long Tall Sally* and *Tutti Frutti*. But it lacks the innocence of its predecessor and looks as if it was thrown together in a hurry. TS

Bill Haley • Little Richard • Alan Dale *Arnie Haines* • Alan Freed • The Treniers • Patricia Hardy *Francine MacLaine* • Fay Baker *Arlene MacLaine* ■ *Dir* Fred F Sears • *Scr* Robert E Kent, James B Gordon

Don't Look Back ★★★★

Music documentary 1967 · US · BW · 95mins

Fans of Bob Dylan will need no encouragement to watch this brilliantly filmed record of his British tour in 1965, the year of *Subterranean Homesick Blues*. But film enthusiasts should also note that this is also a fine example of the craft of director/cameraman DA Pennebaker, one of the masters of *cinéma vérité*. Pennebaker just followed Dylan around, picking up truthful insights along the way, including revelatory moments with Joan Baez, Alan Price and, particularly, Dylan's manager Albert Grossman. The end result, edited down from over 20 hours of material, is a telling portrait of a unique performer at the height of his powers. TS

Dir DA Pennebaker

Don't Look Now ★★★★★ 15

Supernatural thriller
1973 · UK/It · Colour · 105mins

A fiercely erotic scene of love-making between Donald Sutherland and Julie Christie forms the sensual core of this supernatural chiller, which offers a time-distorted vision of terror set in wintertime Venice, portrayed here as a hostile city of brooding silences and fog-shrouded canals. After the death of their small daughter, church restorer Sutherland and wife Christie take their grief with them to Italy, where the spectral presence of their child draws them into a labyrinth of cryptic signs and doom-laden portents. Adapted from a Daphne du Maurier short story, this is director Nicolas Roeg's masterpiece; the fear-drenched mood of alienation is sustained right up until the unforgettable final shot. TH. Contains violence, swearing, a sex scene and nudity. DVD

Donald Sutherland *John Baxter* • Julie Christie *Laura Baxter* • Hilary Mason *Heather* • Clelia Matania *Wendy* • Massimo Serato *Bishop Barbarrigo* • Renato Scarpa *Inspector Longhi* • David Tree *Anthony Babbage* ■ *Dir* Nicolas Roeg • *Scr* Allan Scott, Chris Bryant, from a short story by Daphne du Maurier • *Cinematographer* Anthony Richmond [Anthony B Richmond] • *Editor* Graeme Clifford • *Music* Pino Donaggio

Don't Look Now... We're Being Shot At ★★

Second World War comedy
1966 · Fr · Colour · 130mins

Shot by Jean Renoir's nephew, Claude, and with a score by France's finest film composer, Georges Auric, it is directed with gleeful assurance by Gérard Oury. The stars are our own Terry-Thomas, the gently comedic Bourvil and practised farceur Louis De Funès. Why, then, does this story of an RAF pilot sheltered from the incompetent Nazis by the Resistance manage to be less funny than *'Allo, 'Allo*? DP. French dialogue dubbed into English.

Terry-Thomas *Reginald* • Bourvil *Augustin Bouvet* • Louis De Funès *Stanislas Lefort* • Claudio Brook *Peter Cunningham* • Marie Dubois *Juliette* • Benno Sterzenbach *Col Achbach* • Colette Brosset *Madame Germaine* ■ *Dir* Gérard Oury • *Scr* Gérard Oury, Georges Tabet, André Tabet

Don't Make Waves ★★★

Comedy 1967 · US · Colour · 97mins

Ealing expatriate Alexander Mackendrick, better known for *Whisky Galore!* and *Sweet Smell of Success*, directs this good-natured satire on Californian lifestyles. Tony Curtis gives a clever performance as a tourist who gets a job selling swimming pools. However, the real revelation is the witty comic playing of Sharon Tate, tragically murdered by the Manson "family" two years later. The Byrds provide the title song for this wacky film, which is nostalgically rooted in the early days of psychedelia. TS

Tony Curtis *Carlo Cofield* • Claudia Cardinale *Laura Califatti* • Sharon Tate *Malibu* • Robert Webber *Rod Prescott* • Joanna Barnes *Diane Prescott* • David Draper *Harry Hollard* • Mort Sahl *Sam Lingonberry* • Edgar Bergen *Madame Lavinia* • Ann Elder *Millie Gunder* ■ *Dir* Alexander Mackendrick • *Scr* Ira Wallach, George Kirgo, Maurice Richlin, from the novel *Muscle Beach* by Ira Wallach

Don't Move ★★★ 15

Drama 2004 · It/Sp/UK · Colour · 122mins

Penélope Cruz puts in an unglamorous but moving performance in this powerful and challenging drama. Co-writer/director Sergio Castellitto himself takes the lead role as a wealthy surgeon who's forced to remember a secret and tragic past when his daughter is involved in a road accident. As the girl lies comatose, he reflects on an extramarital affair that he enjoyed with downtrodden, working-class cleaner (Cruz). The passion that he recalls is obsessive and often ugly, born from rape and punctuated by sexual and emotional sadism. The film is difficult to watch but brilliantly acted, though the tacky soundtrack lowers the tone. SF. In Italian with English subtitles. Contains swearing and sex scenes.

Sergio Castellitto *Timoteo* • Penélope Cruz *Italia* • Claudia Gerini *Elsa* • Angela Finocchiaro *Ada* • Marco Giallini *Manlio* • Pietro De Silva *Alfredo* • Elena Perino *Angela* ■ *Dir* Sergio Castellitto • *Scr* Margaret Mazzantini, Sergio Castellitto, from the novel *Non ti muovere* by Margaret Mazzantini

Don't Move, Die and Rise Again ★★★★ 12

Period drama 1989 · USSR · BW · 102mins

Winner of the Camera d'Or at Cannes for the best debut feature, this is a bleak study of the way Japanese PoWs were treated by their Soviet captors in the Stalinist era of the mid-1940s. Faithfully re-creating the ghastly conditions in which everyone lived and worked in a remote mining town, director Vitaly Kanevsky is keen to point out that the Russian miners were as much in captivity as the prisoners, and they wouldn't be able to go home once hostilities ended. The presence of two children, playing happily amid the degradation, only reinforces Kanevsky's depressing but well-made point. Sobering and provocative. DP. In Russian with English subtitles.

Dinara Drukarova *Galiia* • Pavel Nazarov *Valerka* • Elena Popova *Nina* • Valery Ivchenko • Vyacheslav Bambushek • Vadim Ermolaev ■ *Dir/Scr* Vitaly Kanevsky

Don't Raise the Bridge, Lower the River ★★ U

Comedy 1968 · UK · Colour · 95mins

Jerry Lewis is quite hopelessly adrift and desperately unfunny in an awkward UK adaptation of humorist Max Wilk's novel. It's ham-fistedly directed by former actor Jerry Paris, and concerns Lewis's plans to steal a high-speed oil drill and peddle the plans to oil-rich Arabs. The Brits acquit themselves well, particularly co-star Terry-Thomas, while Patricia Routledge registers strongly as a lascivious Girl Guide leader. Yet both pace and tone are uncertain, and Lewis's performance is embarrassingly undirected. TS

Jerry Lewis *George Lester* • Terry-Thomas *H William Homer* • Jacqueline Pearce *Pamela Lester* • Bernard Cribbins *Fred Davies* • Patricia Routledge *Lucille Beatty* • Nicholas Parsons *Dudley Heath* • Michael Bates *Dr Spink* • Colin Gordon *Mr Hartford* ■ *Dir* Jerry Paris • *Scr* Max Wilk, from his novel

Don't Say a Word ★★★ 15

Thriller 2001 · US/Aus · Colour · 108mins

Michael Douglas plays a psychiatrist, whose comfortable existence is shattered when his young daughter is kidnapped. The ransom for her return is a six-digit number, locked in the memory of near-catatonic mental patient Brittany Murphy. Douglas must therefore delve into the girl's damaged psyche, retrieve the number and deliver it to kidnapper Sean Bean – and he has one day to do it. While the premise is ludicrous and some of the plot developments heavily signposted, thanks to compelling performances and pacey direction, this adds up to an enjoyable ride. JB. Contains violence and swearing. DVD

Michael Douglas *Dr Nathan Conrad* • Sean Bean *Patrick B Koster* • Brittany Murphy *Elisabeth Burrows* • Skye McCole Bartusiak *Jessie Conrad* • Guy Torry *Martin J Dolen* • Jennifer Esposito *Det Sandra Cassidy* • Shawn Doyle *Russel Maddox* • Famke Janssen *Aggie Conrad* • Oliver Platt *Dr Louis Sachs* ■ *Dir* Gary Fleder • *Scr* Anthony Peckham, Patrick Smith Kelly, from the novel by Andrew Klavan

Don't Take It to Heart ★★★ U

Comedy 1944 · UK · BW · 86mins

Written and directed by Jeffrey Dell, this haunted house comedy is a triumph of eccentricity over substance. It was made during wartime, but only the British could find propaganda value in a film in which the aristocracy triumphs over the beastly nouveaux riches thanks to an alliance between a ghost and a lawyer. Although Richard Greene and Patricia Medina are the leads, it's the supporting cast that takes the acting honours, with Alfred Drayton hissable as the tycoon trying to land Brefni O'Rorke's stately pile at a knockdown price. DP

Richard Greene *Peter Hayward* • David Horne *Sir Henry Wade* • Patricia Medina *Lady Mary* • Alfred Drayton *Mr Pike* • Joan Hickson *Mrs Pike* • Richard Bird *Ghost Arthur* • Wylie Watson *Harry Bucket* • Brefni O'Rorke *Lord Chaunduyt* ■ *Dir/Scr* Jeffrey Dell

Don't Talk to Strange Men ★★

Thriller 1962 · UK · BW · 65mins

A worthy little feature with a social message that's more interesting now for its depiction of early 1960s Britain. But director Pat Jackson's thriller still has relevance today. Christina Gregg is the young girl in trouble after disobeying the instruction of the title, while Gillian Lind and Cyril Raymond are her very middle-class parents. TS

Christina Gregg *Jean Painter* • Janina Faye *Ann Painter* • Conrad Phillips *Ron* • Dandy Nichols *Molly* • Cyril Raymond *Mr Painter* • Gillian Lind *Mrs Painter* • Gwen Nelson *Mrs Mason* ■ *Dir* Pat Jackson • *Scr* Gwen Cherrell

Don't Tell Mom the Babysitter's Dead ★★ 15

Comedy 1991 · US · Colour · 100mins

The children of the Crandell family are forced to fend for themselves when their elderly and decidedly crotchety babysitter drops dead while their mother is on holiday in Australia. This reasonably engaging comedy fantasy from Stephen Herek veers uneasily from slightly adult comedy to farcical teenage wish-fulfilment. Nevertheless, it remains remarkably good-humoured throughout such awkward shifts in tone. AJ. Contains swearing. DVD

Christina Applegate *Sue Ellen "Swell" Crandell* • Joanna Cassidy *Rose Lindsey* • John Getz *Gus Brandon* • Josh Charles *Bryan* • Keith Coogan *Kenny Crandell* • Concetta Tomei *Mom Crandell* • David Duchovny *Bruce* • Kimmy Robertson *Cathy* ■ *Dir* Stephen Herek • *Scr* Neil Landau, Tara Ison

The Doolins of Oklahoma ★★ U

Western 1949 · US · BW · 89mins

Meet the Doolin gang: not in the same league as the James boys or the Daltons, but a lively bunch of bank robbers nonetheless. Their leader is played by Randolph Scott, who decides to turn over a new leaf, marry a deacon's daughter (Virginia Huston) and take up farming, only to find his past won't leave him alone. This is no great shakes as a western, yet it's briskly directed by Gordon Douglas. AE

Randolph Scott *Bill Doolin* • George Macready *Sam Hughes* • Louise Allbritton *Rose of Cimarron* • John Ireland *Bitter Creek* • Virginia Huston *Elaine Burton* • Charles Kemper *Arkansas* • Noah Beery Jr *Little Bill* • Dona Drake *Cattle Annie* ■ *Dir* Gordon Douglas • *Scr* Kenneth Gamet

Doom Asylum ★

Horror 1987 · US · Colour · 78mins

It's six movies for the price of one as a lovesick zombie terrorises and murders a female rock band in an abandoned mental asylum. This is a feeble fright farce, tricked out with endless slow-motion sex fantasies and puzzling pans to a TV screen, which shows five extended clips of the best scenes from British horror icon Tod Slaughter's 1930s and 1940s movies. A ludicrous hotch-potch. AJ

Patty Mullen *Judy/Kiki* • Ruth Collins *Tina* • Kristin Davis *Jane* • William Hay *Mike* • Kenny L Price *Dennis* ■ *Dir* Richard Friedman • *Scr* Rick Marx, from the story by Richard Friedman, Steve Menkin, Rick Marx

Doom Generation ★★★ 18

Road movie 1995 · US/Fr · Colour · 80mins

Gregg Araki succeeds triumphantly in both shocking the prudish and exhibiting his technical mastery in what he describes as his first heterosexual outing. This is a self-satisfied affair that too often thinks a cinematic in-joke or a cheap shot at middle American mores is more important than expanding the characters of teenage lovers Rose McGowan and James Duval and their maniacal mentor, Johnathon Schaech. Araki glamorises the sex as much as the violence, but the sight of a shopkeeper's severed head continuing to scream will be most people's abiding memory. DP [VIDEO]

James Duval *Jordan White* • Rose McGowan *Amy Blue* • Johnathon Schaech *Xavier Red, "X"* • Cress Williams *Peanut* • Skinny Puppy *Gang of goons* • Dustin Nguyen *Quickiemart clerk* • Margaret Cho *Clerk's wife* • Lauren Tewes *TV anchorwoman* • Christopher Knight (2) *TV anchorman* ■ *Dir/Scr* Gregg Araki

The Doomsday Flight ★★★

Thriller 1966 · US · Colour · 96mins

Only the fifth TV movie to be released in the United States, although released theatrically in the UK, this hijack thriller had to be withdrawn by Universal after it inspired a copycat extortion bid. Scripted by *Twlight Zone* creator Rod Serling, it features Edmond O'Brien, who has planted a bomb aboard an internal flight that's primed to go off if the plane dips beneath 5,000 feet. With *Hawaii Five-O* star Jack Lord as the agent sent to deal with the crisis and a nerve-jangling soundtrack from composer Lalo Schifrin, this is an entertaining roller-coaster ride. DP

Jack Lord *Special Agent Frank Thompson* • Edmond O'Brien *The Man* • Van Johnson *Captain Anderson* • Katherine Crawford *Jean* • John Saxon *George Ducette* • Michael Sarrazin *Army corporal* • Ed Asner [Edward Asner] *Feldman* ■ *Dir* William A Graham • *Scr* Rod Serling

Doomsday Man ★★

Futuristic thriller 1998 · US · Colour · 89mins

This futuristic thriller hits all the right buttons but still fails to excite. Yancy Butler plays the spirited soldier assigned to track down mad researcher James Marshall, who has made off with a lethal biological weapon from a top-secret base. The cast is better than average with the actors enthusiastically giving it their best shot. Director William Greenblatt scores in the action sequences, but this is predictable fare. JF

Yancy Butler *Kate* • Esai Morales *Mike Banks* • James Marshall *Tom Banks* • Renee Griffin *Jill* ■ *Dir* William R Greenblatt • *Scr* Andrew Stein

Doomwatch ★★ 12

Mystery thriller 1972 · UK · Colour · 88mins

As a spin-off from an ecological BBC TV series, this crash-landed in the swamp of horror instead of on the firmer ground of science fact or fiction. John Paul, Ian Bannen and Judy Geeson look suitably intense as an investigation is mounted into the effects of a sunken oil tanker on the inhabitants of an island off the Cornish coast only to discover something nastily mutated in the biological woodshed. Risibly alarmist, but the environmental dangers it pinpoints are only too topical. TH [VIDEO] DVD

Ian Bannen *Dr Del Shaw* • Judy Geeson *Victoria Brown* • John Paul *Dr Quist* • Simon Oates *Dr Ridge* • George Sanders *Admiral* • Percy Herbert *Hartwell* • Geoffrey Keen *Sir Henry Layton* • Joseph O'Conor *Vicar* ■ *Dir* Peter Sasdy • *Scr* Clive Exton, from the TV series by Kit Pedler, Gerry Davis

The Door in the Floor ★★★★ 15

Drama 2004 · US · Colour · 110mins

Tod Williams's discreet drama is based on the first third of John Irving's novel *A Widow for One Year*. Jeff Bridges and Kim Basinger star as a couple whose teenage sons died in an accident some years ago. The tragedy has crushed the marriage and not even the couple's four-year-old daughter (Elle Fanning, sister of Dakota) can ease their sorrow. Bridges has descended into drinking and womanising, while Basinger begins a relationship with her husband's 16-year-old assistant (Jon Foster). This is a mature, subtle and surprising drama. KK. Contains swearing, sex scenes.

Jeff Bridges *Ted Cole* • Kim Basinger *Marion Cole* • Jon Foster *Eddie O'Hare* • Mimi Rogers *Evelyn Vaughn* • Elle Fanning *Ruth Cole* • Bijou Phillips *Alice* • Louis Arcella *Eduardo Gomez* ■ *Dir* Tod Williams • *Scr* Tod Williams, from the novel *A Widow for One Year* by John Irving

Door-to-Door Maniac ★

Crime thriller 1961 · US · BW · 75mins

Country-and-western singer Johnny Cash does himself few favours by appearing in this turgid and trashy thriller as a guitar-toting thug who extorts money from a bank president while holding his wife for ransom. Cash sings two songs: the extraordinary *I've Come to Kill* and *Five Minutes to Live*. The latter doubled as the movie's original title; the film was re-released as *Door-to-Door Maniac* with an additional rape scene. AJ

Johnny Cash *Johnny Cabot* • Donald Woods *Ken Wilson* • Cay Forrester *Nancy Wilson* • Pamela Mason [Pamela Kellino] *Ellen* • Midge Ware *Doris* • Vic Tayback *Fred* • Ronnie Howard [Ron Howard] *Bobby* • Merle Travis *Max* ■ *Dir* Bill Karn • *Scr* MK Forrester, Robert L Joseph, from a story by Palmer Thompson

The Door with Seven Locks ★★★

Horror mystery
1962 · W Ger/Fr · BW · 89mins

This brisk horror mystery is one of many Edgar Wallace adaptations made in Germany from the late 1950s to the early 1970s. Harking back to silent expressionism, director Alfred Vohrer reworks the "old dark house" format to eerie effect, as Scotland Yard detective Heinz Drache and sidekick Eddi Arent investigate the serial killing of victims linked by the keys that are found on their bodies and an eccentric millionaire. Equally intriguing for the viewer is the sight of Klaus Kinski letting slip vital clues in one of his earliest roles. DP. In German with English subtitles.

Heinz Drache *Inspector Richard "Dick" Martin* • Sabine Sesselmann *Sybil Lansdown* • Hans Nielsen *Mr Haveloc* • Gisela Uhlen *Emely Cody* • Pinkas Braun *Dr Antonio Staletti* • Werner Peters *Bertram Cody* • Klaus Kinski *Pheeny* ■ *Dir* Alfred Vohrer • *Scr* Harald Petersson Giertz [Harald G Petersson], from a novel by Edgar Wallace

The Doors ★★★ 18

Musical biography
1991 · US · Colour · 134mins

Although the title would have you believe that this is a biopic of the entire band, we learn next to nothing about Ray Manzarek, John Densmore or Robby Krieger, as the emphasis is so firmly on the Doors's charismatic, enigmatic frontman, Jim Morrison. Unfortunately, co-writer/director Oliver Stone is so preoccupied with exploring the native American influences on Morrison's music and re-creating the sights and sounds of the 1960s that we discover precious little about Morrison either. Val Kilmer does, however, pull off a remarkable impression of the vocalist. DP. Contains violence, swearing, sex scenes, drug abuse, nudity. [VIDEO] DVD

Val Kilmer *Jim Morrison* • Meg Ryan *Pamela Courson* • Kyle MacLachlan *Ray Manzarek* • Kevin Dillon *John Densmore* • Frank Whaley *Robby Krieger* • Billy Idol *Cat* • Dennis Burkley *Dog* • Josh Evans *Bill Siddons* • Michael Madsen *Tom Baker* • Kathleen Quinlan *Patricia Kennealy* ■ *Dir* Oliver Stone • *Scr* Oliver Stone, J Randall Johnson, Randy Johnson, Ralph Thomas, from the non-fiction book *Riders on the Storm* by John Densmore

Doorway to Hell ★★★

Crime melodrama 1931 · US · BW · 78mins

The chief of a bootlegging outfit decides to retire and hands over his racketeering interests to another. But he finds himself embroiled in the underworld again after his wife leaves him and his young brother is killed by his former rivals. Oscar-nominated for its story and directed with tough brio by Archie Mayo for Warner Bros, the studio that put the gangster movie on the map, the film stars clean-cut, good-looking Lew Ayres as the troubled gangster and James Cagney as the man who takes over his empire. RK

Lewis Ayres [Lew Ayres] *Louis Ricarno* • Dorothy Mathews *Doris* • Leon Janney *Jackie Lamarr* • Robert Elliott *Capt O'Grady* • James Cagney *Steve Mileway* • Jerry Mandy *Joe* • Noel Madison *Rocco* ■ *Dir* Archie Mayo • *Scr* George Rosener, from the story *A Handful of Clouds* by Rowland Brown

Doppelganger ★★ 18

Horror 1993 · US · Colour · 100mins

Three years before becoming one of the first victims of the *Scream* franchise, Drew Barrymore was the star of her own hokey slasher flick, playing a young woman terrorised by an evil alter ego who's killing off her family in New York. Moving out to Los Angeles, Drew begins an affair with her new roommate. But is it her or her doppelgänger that he's fallen in love with? This intriguing premise is stifled by Avi Nesher's predictable and at times crass direction. RS [VIDEO] DVD

Drew Barrymore *Holly Gooding* • George Newbern *Patrick Highsmith* • Dennis Christopher *Dr Heller* • Sally Kellerman *Sister Jan* • Leslie Hope *Elizabeth* • George Maharis *Wallace* ■ *Dir/Scr* Avi Nesher

Doss House ★★

Detective drama 1933 · UK · BW · 52mins

John Baxter, an unsung hero of British cinema, made quota quickies and immensely popular regional comedies. His "serious" films began in tandem with the great 1930s documentary movement and introduced realist fiction. This feature debut tells of a journalist and a detective who infiltrate a doss house to trap a criminal taking refuge among the down and outs. Heavily atmospheric, it was described as a "descent into hell" story, and Baxter remade it, indifferently, as *Judgment Deferred* (1951). BB

Frank Cellier *Editor* • Arnold Bell *Reporter* • Herbert Franklyn *Detective* • Mark Daly *Shoeblack* • Edgar Driver *Catsmeat Man* ■ *Dir* John Baxter • *Scr* Herbert Ayres

Dot and the Kangaroo ★★ Uc

Part-animated adventure
1976 · Aus · Colour · 71mins

Based on the children's character created by Ethel Pedley, this is the first of Yoram Gross's series of live-action/animation films about the little red-headed girl who can talk to animals. There isn't much to get excited about in the story, in which Dot gets lost in the Australian bush and is helped out by a kindly kangaroo, and the songs will hardly set toes a-tapping, but the blend of cartoon characters and real wildlife footage is neatly done. Seven further films followed. DP [VIDEO]

Robyn Moore *Dot* ■ *Dir* Yoram Gross • *Scr* Yoram Gross, John Palmer, from a character created by Ethel Pedley

The Dot and the Line ★★★★★ U

Animated romantic comedy
1965 · US · Colour · 10mins

It's perhaps ironic that Chuck Jones, the king of personality animation (the art of conveying the interior life of a character through their facial and physical movements) should win one of his three Oscars for a film about three faceless, limbless geometric shapes. Yet such is his genius there's no doubting the emotional depth of the three protagonists in this charming short: an immature pink dot, the straight black line who loves her and the coarse, hairy squiggle she prefers. This masterpiece – created in the midst of his under-rated Tom and Jerry series – remains unique in his output. Layout artist Maurice Noble's colourful designs contribute enormously in suggesting character mood, and there's another superb soundtrack, this time with elegant music by Eugene Poddany and subtle narration by the great Robert Morley. CLP

Robert Morley *Narrator* ■ *Dir* Chuck Jones • *Scr* Juster Norton, from his story

Dot the i ★★ 15

Romantic thriller
2003 · UK/Sp · Colour · 87mins

This curious mix of romance and psychological chills stars Gael García Bernal as a wannabe actor-cum-waiter in London who falls for Natalia Verbeke on the eve of her marriage to the staid but wealthy James D'Arcy. As she agonises over the choice between love and security, she also has the unsettling feeling that she is being watched by a mysterious stranger. You will probably think that you have it all figured out half way through, but then director Matthew Parkhill pulls out a far-fetched twist that derails all the good work that went before. JF DVD

Gael García Bernal *Kit* • Natalia Verbeke *Carmen* • James D'Arcy *Barnaby* • Tom Hardy *Tom* • Charlie Cox *Theo* ■ *Dir/Scr* Matthew Parkhill

Double Bunk ★★

Comedy 1961 · UK · BW · 94mins

There's more pleasure to be had from spotting the support cast than from following the stars in some vintage British movies, and this under-directed comedy about honeymooners racing their houseboat is no exception. The nominal lead is Ian Carmichael, displaying his usual Hugh Grant-like dottiness. But he had lost his ability to carry a picture by this point, and lovely though Thora Hird's daughter Janette Scott may be, she's no great shakes as an actress. TS

Ian Carmichael *Jack Goddard* • Janette Scott *Peggy Deeley* • Liz Fraser *Sandra* • Sidney James *Sid Randall* • Dennis Price *Leonard Watson* • Reginald Beckwith *Alfred Harper* • Irene Handl *Mrs Harper* • Noel Purcell *O'Malley* • Miles Malleson *Reverend Thomas* ■ *Dir/Scr* CM Pennington-Richards

Double Cross ★★ U

Spy drama 1955 · UK · BW · 71mins

This benefits from its Cornish locations and director Anthony Squire's tight use of the cramped conditions on board a cross-channel fishing boat. Otherwise, it's B-business as usual, as salmon poacher Donald Houston realises mysterious passengers Anton Diffring and Delphi Lawrence have tricked him into ferrying Cold War secrets. DP

Donald Houston *Albert Pascoe* • Fay Compton *Alice Pascoe* • Anton Diffring *Dmitri Krassin* • Delphi Lawrence *Anna Krassin* • Allan Cuthbertson *Clifford* • William Hartnell *Whiteway* • Frank Lawton *Chief Constable* • Raymond Francis *Inspector Harris* ■ *Dir* Anthony Squire • *Scr* Anthony Squire, Kern Bennett, from the novel *The Queer Fish* by Kern Bennett

Double Crossbones ★★★ U

Satire 1951 · US · Colour · 75mins

This smashing Donald O'Connor vehicle uses all of Universal's pirate-ship sets and costumes in a jolly tale of an apprentice shopkeeper who is mistaken for a famous buccaneer. Alan Napier makes a splendid Captain Kidd, and Hope Emerson is a fearsome Ann Bonney. However, the real pleasure is the sumptuous Technicolor, which makes the whole shebang seem rather better than it is. Fans of *Against All Flags* will have fun recognising props, while the narration is by Jeff Chandler, star of *Yankee Pasha*. TS

Donald O'Connor *Davy Crandell* • Helena Carter *Lady Sylvia Copeland* • Will Geer *Tom Botts* • John Emery *Governor Elden* • Hope Emerson *Mistress Ann Bonney* • Charles McGraw *Capt Ben Wickett* • Alan Napier *Capt Kidd* • Jeff Chandler *Narrator* ■ *Dir* Charles T Barton [Charles Barton] • *Scr* Oscar Brodney

Double Dare ★★★

Comedy thriller 1981 · Fr · Colour · 100mins

Miou-Miou and Gérard Lanvin, who first worked together in *café-théâtre*, are here reunited by veteran director Georges Lautner for this sprightly comedy thriller. It's a frothy story that has Lanvin steal a judge's robes to escape his trial, only for Miou-Miou to insist he accompanies her to Nice and solve a murder mystery. There's plenty of spark between the leads and screen legend Renée Saint-Cyr (the director's mother) contributes a neat cameo. DP. French dialogue dubbed into English.

Miou-Miou *Julie Boucher* • Gérard Lanvin *Gerard Louvier* • Renée Saint-Cyr *Madame Bertillon* • Julien Guiomar *Raymond* • Michel Galabru *Bailiff* ■ *Dir* Georges Lautner • *Scr* Jean-Marie Poiré

Double Deal ★★ 15

Romantic crime drama
1981 · Aus · Colour · 86mins

This self-consciously smart-aleck thriller sat on the shelf for three years, and it's easy to see why. Brian Kavanagh tries desperately to deceive us as bored fashion model Angela Punch McGregor and criminal biker Warwick Comber play an increasingly far-fetched game of cat and mouse with her tycoon husband (Louis Jourdan) and his secretary (Diana Craig). Banal. DP [video]

Louis Jourdan *Peter Sterling* • Angela Punch McGregor *Christina Sterling* • Diane Craig *June Stevens* • Warwick Comber *Young man* • Peter Cummins *Detective Mills* • Bruce Spence *Doug Mitchell* • June Jago *Mrs Coolidge* ■ *Dir/Scr* Brian Kavanagh

Double Dragon ★★★ 12

Martial arts adventure
1994 · US · Colour · 91mins

In the ravaged, flooded Los Angeles of 2007, Mark Dacascos and Scott Wolf are streetwise youths who come upon one half of an ancient Chinese talisman, which gives awesome power to whoever possesses both halves. Unfortunately, the other portion is owned by unscrupulous gang boss Robert Patrick and his phalanx of gigantic henchmen. Decent effects and a wisecracking screenplay lift James Yukich's movie above the usual futuristic fare. JF [video] DVD

Robert Patrick *Koga Shuko* • Mark Dacascos *Jimmy Lee* • Scott Wolf *Billy Lee* • Kristina Malandro Wagner *Linda Lash* • Julia Nickson [Julia Nickson-Soul] *Sartori Imada* • Alyssa Milano *Marian Delario* ■ *Dir* James Yukich • *Scr* Michael Davis, Peter Gould, from a story by Neal Shusterman, Paul Dini

Double Dynamite ★★ U

Comedy 1951 · US · BW · 77mins

Thanks to a favour from a bookie (Nestor Paiva), a decent young bank clerk (Frank Sinatra) wins a fortune on a race. When $75,000 goes missing from the bank, however, the clerk's fiancée (Jane Russell) and unconventional waiter friend (Groucho Marx) are convinced he stole his new-found wealth. Apart from an occasional laugh supplied by Groucho, this is a thin and dismally unfunny comedy that does nothing for anybody, especially the audience. RK [video]

Jane Russell *Mildred "Mibs" Goodhug* • Groucho Marx *Emil J Keck* • Frank Sinatra *Johnny Dalton* • Don McGuire *Bob Pulsifer Jr* • Howard Freeman *RB Pulsifer Sr* • Harry Hayden *JL McKissack* • Nestor Paiva *"Hot Horse" Harris* • Lou Nova *Max* ■ *Dir* Irving Cummings • *Scr* Melville Shavelson, Harry Crane, from a story by Leo Rosten, from a character created by Mannie Manheim

Double Edge ★★

Political drama 1992 · Is · Colour · 86mins

Assigned to Israel for three weeks, intrepid reporter Faye Dunaway finds herself drawn to both sides in the Arab/Israeli conflict. But when she writes about a family of Palestinian resistance fighters, the story gets her into trouble both politically and emotionally. Dunaway isn't at her most charismatic here, but the film is interesting enough and the ending has a nice punch. ST

Faye Dunaway *Faye Milano* • Amos Kollek *David* • Muhamad Bacri [Muhamad Bakri] *Mustafa Shafik* • Makram Khouri *Ahmed Shafik* • Michael Schneider *Max* • Shmuel Shiloh *Moshe* • Anat Atzmon *Censor* ■ *Dir/Scr* Amos Kollek

Double Exposure ★ U

Detective thriller 1954 · UK · BW · 63mins

John Bentley stars in this missable British B-movie. Director John Gilling, who went on to make several Hammer horrors, tries to bring some mystery and tension to the story of a private eye investigating the apparent suicide of an advertising executive's wife. However, the cardboard sets, static performances and his own perfunctory script end up defeating him. AT

John Bentley *Pete Fleming* • Rona Anderson *Barbara Leyland* • Garry Marsh *Daniel Beaumont* • Alexander Gauge *Denis Clayton* • Maxine Goldner *Ingeborg Wells* • John Horsley *Lamport* • Rick Rydon *Trixon* • Frank Forsyth *Inspector Grayle* ■ *Dir* John Gilling • *Scr* John Gilling, from a story by John Roddick

Double Impact ★★★ 18

Action thriller 1991 · US · Colour · 105mins

Yet to convincingly handle one role, Jean-Claude Van Damme was a tad ambitious to take on two in this otherwise straightforward action thriller. In a performance that adds a new meaning to the term identical twins, Van Damme is equally wooden as the two brothers – one good, one a bit of a rogue – who are reunited to avenge the death of their parents. However, there's plenty of biffing, kicking and explosions for those who like that sort of thing. JF. Contains swearing, violence, drug abuse and nudity. [video] DVD

Jean-Claude Van Damme *Chad Wagner/Alex Wagner* • Geoffrey Lewis *Frank Avery* • Alan Scarfe *Nigel Griffith* • Alonna Shaw *Danielle Wilde* • Cory Everson *Kara* • Philip Yan Kin Chan [Philip Chan] *Raymond Zhang* • Bolo Yeung *Moon* ■ *Dir* Sheldon Lettich • *Scr* Sheldon Lettich, Jean-Claude Van Damme, from a story by Sheldon Lettich, Jean-Claude Van Damme, Steve Meerson, Peter Krikes

Double Indemnity ★★★★★ PG

Classic film noir 1944 · US · BW · 103mins

Billy Wilder's classic thriller, with its crackling screenplay co-written by Raymond Chandler, is one of the best-loved examples of *film noir* ever made. Based on a short story by James M Cain (author of *The Postman Always Rings Twice*), it follows definitive *femme fatale* Barbara Stanwyck as she seduces insurance salesman Fred MacMurray into murdering – then feigning the accidental death of – her husband Tom Powers, before claiming the premium on the latter's life. However, dogged insurance investigator Edward G Robinson smells a rat and suspects Stanwyck of murder. Wilder was nominated for an Oscar, as was John F Seitz's cinematography and Miklos Rozsa's atmospheric score, while in the best actress category Stanwyck lost out to Ingrid Bergman for *Gaslight*. TS DVD

Fred MacMurray *Walter Neff* • Barbara Stanwyck *Phyllis Dietrichson* • Edward G Robinson *Barton Keyes* • Porter Hall *Mr Jackson* • Jean Heather *Lola Dietrichson* • Tom Powers *Mr Dietrichson* • Byron Barr *Nino Zachette* ■ *Dir* Billy Wilder • *Scr* Billy Wilder, Raymond Chandler, from the novella by James M Cain, as serialised in *Liberty* magazine

Double Jeopardy ★★★ 18

Drama 1992 · US · Colour · 99mins

Rachel Ward is perfectly cast as the sexy *femme fatale* who tempts married Bruce Boxleitner away from his family and gets him involved in a murder in this made-for-cable thriller. It benefits from the top-notch performances of its cast and the taut direction of Lawrence Schiller. JB [video] DVD

Bruce Boxleitner *Jack Hart* • Rachel Ward *Lisa Burns* • Sela Ward *Karen Hart* • Sally Kirkland *Detective Camden* • Whitney Porter [Whitney Danielle Porter] *Sascha* ■ *Dir* Lawrence Schiller • *Scr* Craig Tepper, Monte Stettin, from a story by Craig Tepper

Double Jeopardy ★★★ 15

Action thriller
1999 · US/Ger · Colour · 100mins

This revenge thriller was a big hit in the US, where women lined up to see wronged wife Ashley Judd get her own back on her evil, cheating partner. What starts off as a romantic sailing trip turns into a nightmare when she wakes up one morning surrounded by coastguards with her spouse (Bruce Greenwood) missing and pools of blood all over the boat. Sent to prison for his murder, she discovers he faked his own death and has run off with their child and her best friend. Judd gives a believable performance, but Tommy Lee Jones gives a sub-*Fugitive* turn as the federal officer on her trail. Completely preposterous. JB [video] DVD

Tommy Lee Jones *Travis Lehman* • Ashley Judd *Libby Parsons* • Bruce Greenwood *Nick Parsons* • Annabeth Gish *Angie* • Benjamin Weir *Matty aged 4* ■ *Dir* Bruce Beresford • *Scr* David Weisberg, Douglas S Cook

A Double Life ★★★ PG

Crime drama 1947 · US · BW · 99mins

Debonair Ronald Colman won his only Oscar for his performance in this overtly theatrical melodrama about an actor who becomes dangerously absorbed with his stage roles in real life. As Colman is about to play Othello, Signe Hasso is the Desdemona who's under threat. Colman is an unlikely Moor, but he cleverly manages to convince, aided by George Cukor's adroit direction and the brilliant Oscar-winning score. The story, however, remains resolutely silly as Colman becomes increasingly unhinged during his stint in the Shakespearean tragedy. TS [video]

Ronald Colman *Anthony John* • Signe Hasso *Brita* • Edmond O'Brien *Bill Friend* • Shelley Winters *Pat Kroll* • Ray Collins *Victor Donlan* • Philip Loeb *Max Lasker* • Millard Mitchell *Al Cooley* ■ *Dir* George Cukor • *Scr* Ruth Gordon, Garson Kanin • *Music* Miklos Rozsa

The Double Life of Véronique ★★★★ 15

Drama 1991 · Fr/Pol · Colour · 93mins

A slight but mesmerising tale from Polish director Krzysztof Kieslowski, this disappointed some critics on its release after the scope of his monumental *Ten Commandments*. However, this is also a work of great intelligence, with its discussion of the fragility of humanity, the perils of ambition and the possibility that we may all have a spiritual twin somewhere in the world, as troubling and provocative as anything broached in his earlier work. Irène Jacob won the best actress prize at Cannes for her subtle dual performance. DP. In Polish and French with English subtitles. Contains nudity. [video]

Irène Jacob *Weronika/Véronique* • Philippe Volter *Alexandre Fabbri* • Halina Gryglaszewska *Aunt* • Kalina Jedrusik *Gaudy woman* • Aleksander Bardini *Orchestra conductor* • Wladyslaw Kowalski *Weronika's father* ■ *Dir* Krzysztof Kieslowski • *Scr* Krzysztof Kieslowski, Krzysztof Piesiewicz

The Double McGuffin ★★ PG

Mystery 1979 · US · Colour · 93mins

Despite the presence of screen heavies Ernest Borgnine and George Kennedy, this is a children's film about a plot to kill a middle-eastern head of state, played with mind-boggling implausibility by Elke Sommer. Also involved are a bunch of wholesome American kids who try and avert the assassination. The setting is a real bonus – Charleston in South Carolina, America's most beautiful city. There is an introduction from an uncredited Orson Welles, who explains what a MacGuffin is. AT [video]

Ernest Borgnine *Firat* • George Kennedy *Chief Talasek* • Elke Sommer *Prime Minister Kura* • Ed "Too Tall" Jones *First assassin* • Lyle Alzado *Second assassin* • Rod Browning *Moras* • Orson Welles *Narrator* ■ *Dir* Joe Camp • *Scr* Joe Camp, from a story by Richard Baker, Joe Camp

The Double Man ★★ PG

Spy thriller 1967 · UK · Colour · 100mins

A miscast Yul Brynner plays two characters, one American and one German, and makes both of these tight-lipped agents equally dull. The real surprise is that this Swiss-located Elstree-based murk is directed by the redoubtable Franklin J Schaffner, best remembered for *Patton* and *Planet of the Apes*. Goes to show that, no matter how talented a director is, if it's not in the script it'll never be on the screen. Cameraman Denys Coop at least ensures the movie looks fetching. TS [video]

Yul Brynner *Dan Slater/Kalmar* • Britt Ekland *Gina* • Clive Revill *Frank Wheatley* • Anton Diffring *Col Berthold* • Moira Lister *Mrs Carrington* • Lloyd Nolan *Edwards* • David Bauer *Miller* ■ *Dir* Franklin J Schaffner • *Scr* Henry S Maxfield

Double Nickels ★

Action drama 1977 · US · Colour · 89mins

Shots of fast cars stand in for a credible plot in this story of a highway patrolman (played by director and co-writer Jack Vacek) who repossesses cars on the side. The problems start when his boss George Cole has him stealing vehicles instead of reclaiming them. A clumsy, amateurish series of car chases ensues in a film that quickly grinds to a halt. TH

Jack Vacek *Smokey* • Ed Abrams *Ed* • Patrice Schubert *Jordan* • George Cole *George* • Heidi Schubert *Tami* ■ *Dir* Jack Vacek • *Scr* Jack Vacek, Patrice Schubert, Jack Vacek

Double Platinum ★★ PG

Musical drama 1999 · US · Colour · 86mins

Diana Ross, the most successful female recording artist of all time, here stars with teen sensation Brandy, a pretender to her crown. Ross is a struggling lounge singer who abandons her daughter Brandy to pursue her showbiz dream. Flash forward 18 years, and Ross is now a massive star to whom Kayla – ignorant of her origins and just embarking on her own warbling career – goes to for advice. Fans will enjoy the tunes, but not the creaking melodrama. JF [video] DVD

Diana Ross *Olivia King* • Brandy Norwood [Brandy] *Kayla Harris* • Christine Ebersole *Peggy* • Allen Payne *Ric Ortega* • Brian Stokes Mitchell *Adam Harris* • Roger Rees *Marc Reckler* • Samantha Brown *Royana* ■ *Dir* Robert Allan Ackerman • *Scr* Nina Shengold

Double Take ★ 18

Crime thriller 1997 · US · Colour · 82mins

Craig Sheffer plays a successful author who witnesses a murder. His testimony puts the gunman away, but a few days later he spots the imprisoned man's twin on the street. With the help of the accused man's wife (Brigitte Bako), Sheffer discovers there is much more going on here than a case of mistaken identity. Slow and not very exciting, with lots of plot twists, none of which make any sense whatsoever. ST [video]

Craig Sheffer • Costas Mandylor • Brigitte Bako ■ *Dir* Mark L Lester • *Scr* Ed Rugoff, Ralph Rugoff

Double Take ★★ 12

Action comedy thriller
2001 · US · Colour · 84mins

This remake of the 1957 Rod Steiger thriller *Across the Bridge* leaves little taste of the original. Comedy matters as much as suspense, as banker Orlando Jones heads to Mexico to clear his name, only to find himself in even deeper trouble after he swaps identities with jive-talking hustler Eddie Griffin who knows more than he should. The byplay between Jones and Griffin fitfully amuses, but this is a disappointing venture. DP. Contains violence and swearing. [video] DVD

Orlando Jones *Daryl Chase* • Eddie Griffin *Freddy Tiffany* • Gary Grubbs *Timothy Jarret McReady* • Daniel Roebuck *Agent Norville* • Benny Nieves *Agent Martinez* • Garcelle Beauvais *Chloe* ■ *Dir* George Gallo • *Scr* George Gallo, from the film *Across the Bridge* by Guy Elmes, Denis Freeman, from the story by Graham Greene (1)

Double Tap ★★★ 18

Action crime thriller
1997 · US · Colour · 86mins

Heather Locklear plays an undercover agent assigned to track down a lethal assassin whose trademark is the "double tap" – two bullets to the head. Locklear is surprisingly convincing, Stephen Rea is his usual lugubrious self and there's a solid cast of supporting players. Director Greg Yaitanes displays a quirky eye for detail. JF. Contains swearing, violence and sex scenes. DVD

Stephen Rea *Cypher* • Heather Locklear *Katherine* • Peter Greene *Nash* • Mykelti Williamson *Hamilton* • Kevin Gage *Burke* • Robert LaSardo *Rodriguez* • Richard Edson *Fischer* ■ *Dir* Greg Yaitanes • *Scr* Erik Saltzgaber, Alfred Gough, Miles Millar

Double Team ★★ 18

Action adventure 1997 · US · Colour · 89mins

Here Tsui Hark supplies a hyper-realistic surface sheen and loads of slow-motion violence, but gets no closer to drawing out a convincing performance from the Belgian star Jean-Claude Van Damme. Tsui also has to cope with another non-actor, in the shape of basketball legend Dennis Rodman. His ludicrous hair and clothes do at least deflect attention from his unfunny performance as a mysterious gun-runner, who helps Van Damme track down master criminal Mickey Rourke. JF. Contains violence and swearing. [video] DVD

Jean-Claude Van Damme *Jack Quinn* • Dennis Rodman *Yaz* • Mickey Rourke *Stavros* • Paul Freeman *Goldsmythe* • Natacha Lindinger *Kath* • Valeria Cavalli *Dr Maria Trifioli* ■ *Dir* Tsui Hark • *Scr* Don Jakoby, Paul Mones, from a story by Don Jakoby

Double Threat ★

Erotic thriller 1992 · US · Colour · 96mins

Sally Kirkland plays an ageing actress who reluctantly agrees to have a body double come in for her sex scenes. Unfortunately, her boyfriend and co-star (Andrew Stevens) takes a shine to the stand-in, and a twisted tale of lust, jealousy and revenge ensues. This has all the melodrama of a daytime soap and is just as predictable. ST

Sally Kirkland *Monica Martel* • Andrew Stevens *Eric Cline* • Anthony Franciosa *Crocker Scott* • Sherrie Rose *Lisa Shane* • Richard Lynch *Fenich* • Chick Vennera *Stephen Ross* ■ *Dir/Scr* David A Prior

Double Trouble ★ U

Musical drama 1967 · US · Colour · 87mins

Arguably the worst of the stream of pap movies the great Elvis Presley found himself trapped in by dint of manager Colonel Tom Parker's wheeling and dealing, this substandard frolic is actually set in a nonexistent England (filmed on a badly designed MGM set in Culver City) in a pathetic nod to the shift in musical culture at the time. Elvis sings one decent rock number, *Long-Legged Girl (with the Short Dress on)*, but this is truly lame-brained nonsense. TS [video] DVD

Elvis Presley *Guy Lambert* • Annette Day *Jill Conway* • John Williams *Gerald Waverly* • Yvonne Romain *Claire Dunham* • Harry Wiere • Herbert Wiere • Sylvester Wiere • Chips Rafferty *Archie Brown* • Norman Rossington *Arthur Babcock* ■ *Dir* Norman Taurog • *Scr* Jo Heims, from a story by Marc Brandel

Double Trouble ★ 18

Action comedy 1992 · US · Colour · 83mins

The Barbarian Brothers (David and Peter Paul) usually have a lot of fun in their movies, but here they seem sullen and subdued, even during their requisite comic banter. A sloppy cop is forced to team up with his twin, a high-class thief, to bust a diamond operation helmed by Roddy McDowall. Though it's designed as a comedy with some action elements, there is always a feeling of hostility in the background and the savage killings sour what laughter the film provokes. KB [video]

Peter Paul *Peter Jade* • David Paul *David Jade* • Roddy McDowall *Chamberlain* • Adrienne-Joi Johnson *Danitra* • Collin Bernsen *Whitney Regan* • David Carradine *Mr C* • Bill Mumy *Bob* • James Doohan *Chief O'Brien* • Troy Donahue *Leonard Stewart* ■ *Dir* John Paragon • *Scr* Jeffrey Kerns, Kurt Wimmer, from a story by Chuck Osborne, Kurt Wimmer

Double Vision ★★ 18

Thriller 2002 · Tai/HK · Colour · 108mins

One-time critic Chen Kuo-fu attempts to cross the divide between art house and the mainstream with this serial killer thriller only to come up way short. The opening segment, in which world-weary Taipei cop Tony Leung Ka-fai investigates a series of inventively grisly murders, is darkly intriguing. But once he's teamed with FBI agent David Morse, the story spirals into culture-clashing caricature and flights of fantasy. DP. In Mandarin, Hokkien and English with subtitles. DVD

Tony Leung Ka-fai [Tony Leung (1)] *Huang Huo-tu* • David Morse *Kevin Richter* • Rene Lui *Ching-fang* • Leon Dai *Li Feng-bo* • Yang Kuei-Mei *Coroner* ■ *Dir* Chen Kuo-fu • *Scr* Chen Kuo-fu, Su Chao-Bin • *Cinematographer* Arthur Wong

Double Wedding ★★★ U

Screwball comedy 1937 · US · BW · 86mins

This wonderfully wacky farce stars William Powell as an eccentric artist and Myrna Loy as a bossy designer, bent on forcing her feisty, movie-mad sister (Florence Rice) to marry conservative John Beal. At the time, several reviewers thought this frolic too European in tone – hardly surprising, since it's loosely based on Ferenc Molnar's play, *Great Love*. A silly cavil really, since the whole purpose of these beautifully produced MGM comedies was simply to entertain, which this one most certainly does. TS

William Powell *Charlie Lodge* • Myrna Loy *Margit Agnew* • Florence Rice *Irene Agnew* • John Beal *Waldo Beaver* • Jessie Ralph *Mrs Kensington Bly* • Edgar Kennedy *Spike* • Sidney Toler *Keough* ■ *Dir* Richard Thorpe • *Scr* Jo Swerling, Waldo Salt, from the play *Great Love* by Ferenc Molnar

Double Whammy ★ 15

Black comedy drama
2001 · US/Ger · Colour · 96mins

The quirky charm of writer/director Tom DiCillo has deserted him in this grating comedy. Denis Leary gives a typically one-note performance as a cop whose debilitating back problem in the middle of attempted heroism has made him a New York laughing stock, while a decorative Elizabeth Hurley as his chiropractor (and love interest) suggests that her *Austin Powers* comic assurance was a fluke. A total misfire from start to finish. JC [video] DVD

Denis Leary *Det Ray Pluto* • Elizabeth Hurley *Dr Ann Beamer* • Steve Buscemi *Jerry Cubbins* • Luis Guzman *Juan Benitez* • Chris Noth [Christopher Noth] *Chick Dmitri* • Keith Knobbs *Duke* ■ *Dir/Scr* Tom DiCillo

Double X: the Name of the Game ★ 15

Crime drama 1991 · UK · Colour · 93mins

Some people never learn. Even in the darkest days of the low-budget crime drama, few films plumbed the depths reached by this atrocity. Norman Wisdom does his best to convince as a petty crook trying to keep his daughter out of the clutches of a criminal gang, but such is the awfulness of director Shani S Grewal's dialogue that Wisdom raises more laughs than he used to get in his sentimental comedies. DP. Contains violence and swearing. [video]

Simon Ward *Edward Ross* • William Katt *Michael Cooper* • Norman Wisdom *Arthur Clutton* • Bernard Hill *Iggy Smith* • Gemma Craven *Jenny Eskridge* • Leon Herbert *Ollie* • Derren Nesbitt *Minister* ■ *Dir* Shani S Grewal • *Scr* Shani S Grewal, from the short story *Vengeance* by David Fleming

Dougal and the Blue Cat ★★★ U

Animated adventure
1970 · Fr · Colour · 78mins

Did you know that Dougal was called Pollux in the original French version of *The Magic Roundabout*? In this awesomely weird feature spin-off, the cynical shaggy dog is the only creature who can prevent the devious double act of Buxton the Cat and Madame Blue from stealing Zebedee's moustache and taking control of the Magic Garden. Directed with typically surreal inventiveness by Serge Danot, this zany adventure is made all the more hilarious by the crackling dialogue penned and delivered by Eric Thompson, father of Emma. DP [video]

Eric Thompson *Narrator/Dougal/Zebedee/Florence/Dylan/Buxton* • Fenella Fielding *Madame Blue* ■ *Dir* Serge Danot, Eric Thompson • *Scr* Serge Danot, Jacques Josselin, Eric Thompson

D

Doughboys ★★

First World War comedy
1930 · US · BW · 80mins

Buster Keaton, the comic genius who made his reputation in the silent era, took quite a risk with this, his first talkie. It's the tale of a rich man joining the army by mistake, and was based on Keaton's own experiences during the First World War. Directed by Edward Sedgwick, the film works reasonably well, though sound was never Buster's natural medium. TH

Buster Keaton *Elmer* • Sally Eilers *Mary* • Cliff Edwards *Nescopeck* • Edward Brophy *Sgt Brophy* • Victor Potel *Svendenburg* • Arnold Korff *Gustave* • Frank Mayo *Capt Scott* ■ *Dir* Edward Sedgwick • *Scr* Al Boasberg, Sidney Lazarus, Richard Schayer, from a story by Al Boasberg, Sidney Lazarus

The Doughgirls ★★★

Wartime comedy 1944 · US · BW · 101mins

This bowdlerised screen version of Joseph A Fields's Broadway hit about the wartime housing shortage in Washington DC is still very funny, but it's a long way behind other movies on the same subject (*The More the Merrier*, for example). Warner Bros contract players get a chance to shine in this ensemble comedy, particularly Ann Sheridan, Alexis Smith and Jane Wyman (then married to Ronald Reagan). Once again, however, the priceless Eve Arden – here playing a Russian – effortlessly walks away with every scene she's in. TS

Jack Carson *Arthur Halstead* • Jane Wyman *Vivian Halstead* • John Ridgely *Julian Cadman* • Ann Sheridan *Edna Stokes* • Charles Ruggles *Slade* • Alexis Smith *Nan* • Craig Stevens *Tom* • Eve Arden *Natalia* ■ *Dir* James V Kern • *Scr* James V Kern, Sam Hellman, from a play by Joseph A Fields

Doug's 1st Movie ★★★ U

Animated adventure
1999 · US · Colour · 77mins

As an introduction to a much-loved American children's TV character for wider audiences, this full-length Disney animation does a fairly successful job, with a tale hingeing on a now-familiar eco-message. A squidgy, pollution-induced monster (named after *Moby Dick* writer Herman Melville) is found by oddball high-school student Doug Funnie and his friend Skeeter in a lake owned by wicked tycoon Bill Bluff. The cautionary conclusion will be easily understood by the three-to-eight-year-olds at which it's aimed. TH [video]

Thomas McHugh *Doug Funnie/Lincoln* • Fred Newman *Skeeter/Mr Dink/Porkchop/Ned* • Chris Phillips *Roger Klotz/Boomer/Larry/Mr Chiminy* • Constance Shulman *Patti Mayonnaise* • Frank Welker *Herman Melville* ■ *Dir* Maurice Joyce • *Scr* Ken Scarborough

Le Doulos ★★★ 12

Crime drama 1962 · Fr · BW · 106mins

Jean-Pierre Melville's flawed but fascinating crime thriller – a tribute to the classic American gangster movies of the 1930s and 1940s – casts Jean-Paul Belmondo as an underworld figure and police informer for whom treachery is a religion. First he helps an ex-con plan a heist; then he betrays him. Then he plans the man's escape from prison. Oh, and he kills his girlfriend, too. Look out for the famous nine-minute take in the policeman's office: Melville insisted the camera crew wore black and donned face masks to eliminate the risk of reflection in the windows and mirrors. AT. In French with English subtitles. Contains violence. DVD

Jean-Paul Belmondo *Silien* • Serge Reggiani *Maurice* • Monique Hennessy *Therese* • René Lefèvre *Gilbert* • Jean Desailly *Inspector* • Michel Piccoli *Leader* • Carl Studer *Kern* ■ *Dir* Jean-Pierre Melville • *Scr* Jean-Pierre Melville, from the novel by Pierre Lesou

The Dove ★★★ PG

Biographical adventure
1974 · US/UK · Colour · 99mins

Gregory Peck produced this beautifully shot family film, based on a true story, in which a 16-year-old boy comes of age during a five-year solo circumnavigation of the globe in a small boat. Part travelogue, part round-the-world adventure, the film makes you yearn for the days when not every city, beach and seaside town was over-developed, and features accomplished performances from a young Joseph Bottoms as the intrepid sailor, Deborah Raffin and Dabney Coleman. Charles Jarrott lovingly directs. JB

Joseph Bottoms *Robin Lee Graham* • Deborah Raffin *Patti Ratteree* • John McLiam *Lyle Graham* • Dabney Coleman *Charles Huntley* • John Anderson *Mike Turk* • Colby Chester *Tom Barkley* • Ivor Barry *Kenniston* ■ *Dir* Charles Jarrott • *Scr* Peter Beagle, Adam Kennedy, from the non-fiction book by Robin Lee Graham, Derek Gill

Down among the Z-Men ★ U

Comedy 1952 · UK · BW · 67mins

Although Peter Sellers, Harry Secombe and Spike Milligan co-starred in *Penny Points to Paradise* (1951), this was the only time all four founders of *The Goon Show* appeared together on celluloid. However, Michael Bentine's turn as a mad professor is just one of many space-fillers in this dismal army romp. Gone is the zany humour that made the radio show essential listening and, in its place, comes crude slapstick and obvious observation. Director Maclean Rogers fails to disguise the cheapness of the production or the bankruptcy of the plot, which is held together with interminable numbers from the camp radio programme. DP DVD

Peter Sellers *Major Bloodnock* • Harry Secombe *Harry Jones* • Spike Milligan *Private Eccles* • Michael Bentine *Professor Osrick Purehart* • Carole Carr *Carole Gayley* ■ *Dir* Maclean Rogers • *Scr* Jimmy Grafton, France Charles

Down and Dirty ★★★ 15

Comedy 1976 · It · Colour · 111mins

Ettore Scola directs this raucous comedy, which exploits the conventions of neorealism to mock its sentimental attitude to poverty. Set in a crumbling shanty town on the outskirts of Rome, the film introduces us to a gallery of grotesques, none more revolting than Nino Manfredi's one-eyed patriarch, whose vulgarity and greed bring out the darker side of his desperate relations. Although graphic in his depiction of their squalor, Scola refuses to portray the poor as innocent victims of an invidious system, but also refrains from cruelty in satirising their low expectations and boorish behaviour. DP. In Italian with English subtitles.

Nino Manfredi *Giacinto* • Francesco Anniballi *Domizio* • Maria Bosco *Gaetana* • Giselda Castrini *Lisetta* ■ *Dir* Ettore Scola • *Scr* Ruggero Maccari, Ettore Scola

Down and Out in Beverly Hills ★★★ 15

Comedy 1986 · US · Colour · 103mins

This box-office smash hit provided Nick Nolte with a choice comic role, and he makes the most of it. But there's something a shade too frantic and nervy about the film's pace and the performances of Bette Midler and Richard Dreyfuss as the *nouveau riche* Beverly Hills couple who find themselves giving house room to Nolte's hobo. Some very funny set pieces, usually involving the family dog, and the occasional unerring spotlight on snobbery make it a movie worth watching, but it's not a patch on the classic French original *Boudu Saved from Drowning*. SH. Contains some swearing and nudity.

Nick Nolte *Jerry Baskin* • Bette Midler *Barbara Whiteman* • Richard Dreyfuss *Dave Whiteman* • Little Richard *Orvis Goodnight* • Tracy Nelson *Jenny Whiteman* • Elizabeth Peña *Carmen* • Evan Richards *Max Whiteman* • Donald F Muhich *Dr Von Zimmer* ■ *Dir* Paul Mazursky • *Scr* Paul Mazursky, Leon Capetanos, from the film *Boudu, Saved from Drowning* by Jean Renoir, from the play by René Fauchois

Down Argentine Way ★★★ U

Musical 1940 · US · Colour · 88mins

When this movie was first shown in cinemas, Argentina was as alien to American movie audiences as Mars, and the kind of Latin music presented here by Carmen Miranda was tremendously exciting. It's important to bear that in mind as you watch this witless farrago set in an Argentina that never gets off the 20th Century-Fox backlot (though Miranda's numbers were filmed in New York where she was starring on Broadway). Betty Grable became a star after replacing an indisposed Alice Faye, and Miranda became a sensation. The 1940s Technicolor is nice, but the supporting cast leaves a lot to be desired. TS

Don Ameche *Ricardo Quintana* • Betty Grable *Glenda Crawford* • Carmen Miranda • Charlotte Greenwood *Binnie Crawford* • J Carrol Naish *Casiano* • Henry Stephenson *Don Diego Quintana* • Katharine Aldridge *Helen Carson* ■ *Dir* Irving Cummings • *Scr* Darrell Ware, Karl Tunberg, from a story by Rian James, Ralph Spence

Down by Law ★★★★ 15

Black comedy 1986 · US · BW · 102mins

Jim Jarmusch's uneven but stylish *comédie noire* is an astute mixture of prison picture, road movie and downbeat screwball. Posturing hard men Tom Waits and John Lurie find themselves sharing a cell after they are framed for transporting a corpse and corrupting a minor respectively. Their petty feuding is interrupted by chatty new cellmate Roberto Benigni, who soon devises an escape plan. As the excellent soundtrack testifies, Waits and Lurie are more effectively paired as songwriters than performers, but they offer solid support to the brilliant Benigni, whose prattling is a joy. DP. Contains swearing. DVD

Tom Waits *Zack* • John Lurie *Jack Romano* • Roberto Benigni *Roberto* • Nicoletta Braschi *Nicoletta* • Ellen Barkin *Laurette* • Billie Neal *Bobbie* ■ *Dir/Scr* Jim Jarmusch

Down from the Mountain ★★ PG

Music documentary
2000 · US · Colour · 94mins

Such has been the success of the soundtrack album to *O Brother, Where Art Thou* that the Coen brothers facilitated a reunion of some of the greatest names in bluegrass music at the Ryman Theatre in Nashville. They even had the foresight to hire DA Pennebaker – the godfather of the rockumentary – to film the event. Unfortunately, Pennebaker and co-directors Chris Hegedus and Nick Doob fail to capture the magic of the concert. Compounding the predictable shooting style is a lack of backstage bustle, which is disappointing considering the bonhomie of the rehearsal scenes. DP DVD

Dir Nick Doob, Chris Hegedus, DA Pennebaker

Down in the Delta ★★★

Drama 1997 · US · Colour · 111mins

Any film with the wonderful Alfre Woodard is worth catching, so don't miss this moving drama directed by the poet Maya Angelou. Woodard is the Chicago mother packed off with her children to a Mississippi backwater to escape the perils of the inner city streets. While Angelou loads on the family values theme a little thickly in places, this is nonetheless an enjoyable and heartrending picture, given extra weight by some classy performances from Loretta Devine, Esther Rolle and Wesley Snipes. JB

Alfre Woodard *Loretta* • Al Freeman Jr *Earl* • Mary Alice *Rosa Lynn* • Esther Rolle *Annie* • Loretta Devine *Zenia* • Wesley Snipes *Will* • Mpho Koaha *Thomas* • Kulani Hassen *Tracy* ■ *Dir* Maya Angelou • *Scr* Myron Goble

Down Mexico Way ★★ U

Western 1941 · US · BW · 79mins

A popular Gene Autry feature, this western has a little more action than most, plus a fair amount of well-known songs. Maybe that's why Joseph Santley, better known for musicals than westerns, was hired to direct. The plot's a nothing about Autry chasing some conmen who are posing as movie-makers. TS

Gene Autry *Gene* • Smiley Burnette *Frog* • Fay McKenzie *Maria Elena* • Harold Huber *Pancho Grande* • Sidney Blackmer *Gibson* • Joe Sawyer *Allen* • Andrew Tombes *Mayor Tubbs* • Murray Alper *Flood* • Paul Fix *Davis* • Duncan Renaldo *Juan* ■ *Dir* Joseph Santley • *Scr* Olive Cooper, Albert Duffy, from the story by Stuart McGowan, Dorrell McGowan

Down Periscope ★★ 12

Comedy 1996 · US · Colour · 88mins

Frasier's Kelsey Grammer is a useless submarine commander who will be kicked out of the navy unless he can train a hapless crew in an old boiler of a sub how to outmanoeuvre the entire fleet. Director David S Ward has done this type of slapstick so many times before that he's run out of ideas. Grammer is funny, however. JB. Contains swearing. DVD

Kelsey Grammer *Lt Commander Thomas Dodge* • Lauren Holly *Lt Emily Lake* • Rob Schneider *Executive Officer Martin Pascal* • Harry Dean Stanton *Howard* • Bruce Dern *Admiral Yancy Graham* • William H Macy *Captain Knox* • Ken Hudson Campbell *Buckman* • Toby Huss *Nitro* • Rip Torn *Admiral Winslow* ■ *Dir* David S Ward • *Scr* Hugh Wilson, Eliot Wald, Andrew Kurtzman, from a story by Hugh Wilson

Down Three Dark Streets ★★★ U

Detective crime drama
1954 · US · BW · 85mins

When an FBI agent dies, a colleague takes on his caseload and finds himself caught up in three different crimes involving car theft, a gangster on the run and an extortion racket. Broderick Crawford stars as the investigator, while Martha Hyer makes an excellent gangster's moll. Ruth Roman and Marisa Pavan also appear, as a widow under threat and a blind girl respectively. In the best tradition of gritty, low-key crime thrillers, Arnold Laven's movie keeps the suspense going all the way to the final fade. RK

Broderick Crawford *Ripley* • Ruth Roman *Kate Martel* • Martha Hyer *Connie Anderson* • Marisa Pavan *Julie Angelino* • Casey Adams [Max Showalter] *Dave Millson* • Kenneth Tobey *Zack Stewart* • Gene Reynolds *Vince Angelino* • William Johnstone *Frank Pace* ■ *Dir* Arnold Laven • *Scr* Bernard C Schoenfeld, The Gordons [Gordon Gordon, Margaret Gordon], from their novel *Case File FBI*

Down to Earth ★★★ U

Musical fantasy 1947 · US · Colour · 96mins

Along the same lines as the following year's *One Touch of Venus*, and incorporating a couple of characters directly from 1941's *Here Comes Mr Jordan*, this Columbia musical boasts two significant assets: Rita Hayworth and Technicolor. Some may find this whimsy about the goddess of dance (Hayworth) landing on Earth to help Larry Parks jazz up a musical show tiresome, but still much pleasure to be had. TS

Rita Hayworth *Terpsichore/Kitty Pendleton* • Larry Parks *Danny Miller* • Marc Platt *Eddie Marin* • Roland Culver *Mr Jordan* • James Gleason *Max Corkle* • Edward Everett Horton *Messenger 7013* • Adele Jergens *Georgia Evans* • George Macready *Joe Mannion* ■ *Dir* Alexander Hall • *Scr* Edwin Blum, Don Hartman, from the characters created by Harry Segall in his play *Heaven Can Wait*

Down to Earth ★★ 12

Fantasy comedy 2001 · US · Colour · 83mins

Chris Rock plays an unfunny stand-up comedian who is taken before his time and has to be returned to Earth by Mr King (Chazz Palminteri, playing God's right-hand man like a Mafia consiglieri). Trouble is, the comedian's original body has been cremated, and the only alternative has just been vacated by a fat-cat white businessman who's been bumped off by his wife and her lover. Rock tries hard – too hard at times. DA DVD

Chris Rock *Lance Barton* • Regina King *Sontee* • Chazz Palminteri *King* • Eugene Levy *Keyes* • Whitney Daniels *Frankie Faison* • Mark Addy *Cisco* • Greg Germann *Sklar* • Jennifer Coolidge *Mrs Wellington* ■ *Dir* Chris Weitz, Paul Weitz • *Scr* Chris Rock, Lance Crouther, Ali Le Roi, Louis CK, from the film *Heaven Can Wait* by Elaine May, Warren Beatty, from the play *Heaven Can Wait* by Harry Segall

Down to the Sea in Ships ★★★ U

Adventure 1949 · US · BW · 120mins

Henry Hathaway keeps this rousing whaling adventure firmly on course. Lionel Barrymore is his cantankerous self as a 19th-century seafarer whose grandson (Dean Stockwell) is torn between the old methods of the family firm and the modern techniques of first mate Richard Widmark. Hathaway makes the most of the set pieces, but the real highlight is the playing of such stalwarts as Cecil Kellaway, Gene Lockhart and Harry Davenport. DP

Richard Widmark *Dan Lunceford* • Lionel Barrymore *Captain Bering Joy* • Dean Stockwell *Jed Joy* • Cecil Kellaway *Slush Tubbs* • Gene Lockhart *Andrew Bush* • Berry Kroeger *Manchester* • John McIntire *Thatch* • Henry Morgan [Harry Morgan] *Britton* • Harry Davenport *Mr Harris* ■ *Dir* Henry Hathaway • *Scr* John Lee Mahin, Sy Bartlett, from a story by Sy Bartlett, from the film by John LE Pell

Down to You ★★ 12

Romantic comedy
2000 · US · Colour · 87mins

This teenage romance details the relationship between two New York college kids. Freddie Prinze Jr and Julia Stiles make attractive leads, but Kris Isacsson's film is marred by irritating voiceovers, asides to camera and loads of cracker-barrel philosophising about life and love. There's a fine supporting performance from Henry Winkler, but the picture would have benefited from a less smart-aleck approach. DA. Contains sexual references, swearing. [VIDEO] DVD

Freddie Prinze Jr *Al Connelly* • Julia Stiles *Imogen* • Shawn Hatosy *Eddie Hicks* • Selma Blair *Cyrus* • Zak Orth *Monk Jablonski* • Ashton Kutcher *Jim Morrison* • Rosario Dawson *Lana* • Henry Winkler *Chef Ray* ■ *Dir/Scr* Kris Isacsson

Down Twisted ★ 15

Crime caper 1987 · US · Colour · 84mins

Hack director Albert Pyun strikes again with this international robbery caper, in which a wealthy art collector hires some thieves to steal the ancient symbol of a small country. Naturally, the thieves pull a double cross. The cinematography is unusually competent for Pyun, but the ham-fisted editing and terrible acting let the side down. Look out for *Friends* star Courteney Cox as a waitress. ST [VIDEO]

Carey Lowell *Maxine* • Charles Rocket *Reno* • Trudi Dochtermann *Michelle* • Thom Mathews *Damalas* • Norbert Weisser *Deltoid* • Linda Kerridge *Soames* • Courteney Cox *Tarah* ■ *Dir* Albert Pyun • *Scr* Gene O'Neill, Noreen Tobin, from a story by Albert Pyun

Down with Love ★★★ 12

Period romantic comedy
2003 · US/Ger · Colour · 97mins

This frothy confection satirises and celebrates the sex comedies of the late 1950s and 60s. Renée Zellweger and Ewan McGregor aren't the most obvious stand-ins for Doris Day and Rock Hudson, but both hit the mark amusingly. Zellweger plays the new writing sensation who has produced a bestseller claiming that women can consign romance to the garbage heap, while McGregor's cocky journalist plots to disprove her theories publicly. This is shot in faux Technicolor with sublimely kitsch decor and a soundtrack choreographed to every accentuated footstep. JC [VIDEO] DVD

Renée Zellweger [Renee Zellweger] *Barbara Novak* • Ewan McGregor *Catcher Block* • Sarah Paulson *Vikki Hiller* • David Hyde Pierce *Peter "Mac" MacMannus* • Rachel Dratch *Gladys* • Jack Plotnick *Maurice* • Tony Randall *Theodore Banner* • Jeri Ryan *Gwendolyn* ■ *Dir* Peyton Reed • *Scr* Eve Ahlert, Dennis Drake

Downfall ★★★★ 15

Second World War historical drama
2004 · Ger/Austria/It · Colour · 155m

The final days of the Third Reich are claustrophobically re-created in this acutely observed, Oscar-nominated drama. Made by German director Oliver Hirschbiegel, it's a ground-breaking attempt to confront the ghosts of his country's Nazi past. It's grotesquely surreal, as key personnel – among them Hitler's mistress Eva Braun (Juliane Köhler) – plot and party underground, while outside ordinary Berliners face the Allied advance. Such chilling matter-of-factness makes for a gripping experience, with Bruno Ganz's uncomfortably humanised Hitler particularly riveting. Rich period detail complements the superb acting, adding extra depth to a feature that's so eerily realistic, it's like watching history being replayed. SF. In German with English subtitles.

Bruno Ganz *Adolf Hitler* • Alexandra Maria Lara *Traudl Junge* • Corinna Harfouch *Magda Goebbels* • Ulrich Matthes *Joseph Goebbels* • Juliane Köhler *Eva Braun* • Heino Ferch *Albert Speer* • Christian Berkel *Professor Schenck* • Matthias Habich *Professor Werner Haase* • Thomas Kretschmann *Hermann Fegelein* ■ *Dir* Oliver Hirschbiegel • *Scr* Bernd Eichinger, from the non-fiction book *Inside Hitler's Bunker: the Last Days of the Third Reich* by Joachim Fest and from the memoirs *Until the Final Hour: Hitler's Last Secretary* by Traudl Junge, Melissa Müller

The Downfall of Osen ★★★

Drama 1935 · Jpn · BW · 78mins

Kenji Mizoguchi made 55 films between 1922 and 1935, of which only six have survived. However, while the director dismissed many of the pictures completed in this period, this moving drama is not only predicative of his recurrent themes, but also demonstrates considerable technical innovation. The story of servant girl Isuzu Yamada's bid to help Daijiro Natsukawa enter medical school by becoming a prostitute echoes the sacrifice of Mizoguchi's own geisha sister. The stylised realism and the inventive use of flashbacks give the film its historical value. DP. A Japanese language film.

Isuzu Yamada *Osen* • Daijiro Natsukawa *Sokichi Hata* • Mitsusaburo Ramon *Ukiki* • Shin Shibata *Kumazawa* • Genichi Fujii *Matsuda* • Mitsuru Tojo *Kanya* • Junichi Kitamura *Sakazuki no Keishiro* ■ *Dir* Kenji Mizoguchi • *Scr* Tatsunosuke Takashima, from the short story *Baishoku Kamonanban* by Kyoka Izumi • *Cinematographer* Shigeto Miki [Minoru Miki]

Downhill ★★★

Silent drama 1927 · UK · BW · 80mins

Many were disappointed by Alfred Hitchcock's reunion with Ivor Novello following their triumph with *The Lodger*. Yet this adaptation of a play Novello co-penned perfectly exploits his matinée status as it depicts his decline from public school hero to Marseilles bum – all in the name of honour. Exploring social hypocrisy and the chasm that separates the classes, Hitchcock proves himself again the master of psychological insight, while his use of location is impeccable. It's unabashed melodrama, but wholly cinematic. DP

Ivor Novello *Roddy Berwick* • Lilian Braithwaite *Lady Berwick* • Ian Hunter *Archie* • Robin Irvine *Tim Wakely* • Isabel Jeans *Julia* • Sybil Rhoda *Sybil Wakely* • Ben Webster *Dr Dawson* ■ *Dir* Alfred Hitchcock • *Scr* Eliot Stannard, from the play by David L'Estrange [Ivor Novello], Constance Collier

Downhill Racer ★★ PG

Action drama 1969 · US · Colour · 101mins

The first project from Robert Redford's own production company Wildwood, this skiing potboiler – low on plot, high on downhill racing – has the whiff of vanity about it. Redford stars as a handsome if egocentric skier being groomed as Olympic champion by hard-headed coach Gene Hackman, who later complained of feeling like "a high-priced extra". Inevitably, there is a girl, but the sport takes precedence and the appeal of the film, directed by Michael Ritchie (making his feature debut) lies in the well handled action sequences. AC [VIDEO]

Robert Redford *David Chappellet* • Gene Hackman *Eugene Claire* • Camilla Sparv *Carole Stahl* • Joe Jay Jalbert *Tommy Erb* • Timothy Kirk *DK Bryan* • Dabney Coleman *Mayo* • Jim McMullan *Johnny Creech* ■ *Dir* Michael Ritchie • *Scr* James Salter, from the novel *The Downhill Racers* by Oakley Hall

Downtime ★ 15

Romantic thriller
1997 · UK/Fr · Colour · 86mins

Two people from totally different backgrounds fall in love while trapped in a dangerously derelict lift in a Newcastle high rise. Even dafter than it sounds, this ludicrous fiasco switches between low-rent suspense and glib, socially-aware drama. No one acts sensibly in Bharat Nalluri's dumb mix of *Die Hard* and Barbara Cartland, while the hostage crisis finale defies belief. AJ. Contains swearing and some violence. [VIDEO] DVD

Paul McGann *Rob* • Susan Lynch *Chrissy* • Tom Georgeson *Jimmy* • David Roper *Mike* • Denise Bryson *Jan* • Adam Johnston *Jake* • David Horsefield *Kevin* • Stephen Graham *Jacko* ■ *Dir* Bharat Nalluri • *Scr* Caspar Berry

Downtown ★★★ 18

Action comedy 1990 · US · Colour · 91mins

Great things were predicted for Anthony Edwards after he scored as "Goose" in *Top Gun*. That he has achieved them on TV in *ER* and not on the big screen could be owing to a string of mediocre films, though this buddy cop movie is far from his worst. Comedy specialist Richard Benjamin is perhaps not the best director for a tough crime picture and there's nothing new or profound about his slant on white liberalism versus black realism. At least Edwards and co-star Forest Whitaker give their characters some depth. DP. Contains swearing, violence. [VIDEO] DVD

Anthony Edwards *Alex Kearney* • Forest Whitaker *Dennis Curren* • Penelope Ann Miller *Lori Mitchell* • Joe Pantoliano *White* • David Clennon *Jerome Sweet* • Art Evans *Henry Coleman* • Kimberly Scott *Christine Curren* ■ *Dir* Richard Benjamin • *Scr* Nat Mauldin

Downtown 81 ★★ 15

Documentary drama
1981 · US · Colour · 71mins

Started by fashion photographer Edo Bertoglio back in 1980, only to be abandoned through lack of funds, this snapshot of Manhattan subculture was rediscovered by producer Maripol in the late 1990s, who attempted to tidy up the disjointed narrative by adding a voiceover from Slam star Saul Williams. Some may question whether this often aimless and frequently pretentious picture was worth the effort. But it does afford the opportunity to see Jean Michel Basquiat in a quasi-autobiographical tale about a struggling artist whose wish is granted by bag lady Debbie Harry. Moreover, it also provides performance records of several then-critical bands, including Tuxedomoon, Kid Creole and the Coconuts and James White and the Blacks. DP [VIDEO]

Jean Michel Basquiat *Jean* • Deborah Harry *Fairy godmother/Bag lady* • Anna Schroeder *Beatrice, the Love Interest* • Saul Williams *Narrator* ■ *Dir* Edo Bertoglio • *Scr* Glenn O'Brien

Dracula ★★★★ PG

Classic horror 1931 · US · BW · 71mins

One of the most famous horror movies ever made, director Tod Browning's seminal classic is, by today's standards, rather talky, stagebound and bloodless. Most of its important chills occur off-screen, too. But it remains the most subtly romantic and highly atmospheric rendition of Bram Stoker's tale of the Transylvanian count's parasitic trip to London, with Browning orchestrating the opening scenes to macabre perfection. Bela Lugosi's star turn (he'd been in the stage version since 1927) is an impressive film debut. A neglected sequel, *Dracula's Daughter*, followed five years later. AJ [VIDEO] DVD

Bela Lugosi *Count Dracula* • Helen Chandler *Mina Seward* • David Manners *Jonathan Harker* • Dwight Frye *Renfield* • Edward Van Sloan *Dr Van Helsing* • Herbert Bunston *Dr Seward* • Frances Dade *Lucy Weston* ■ *Dir* Tod Browning • *Scr* Garrett Fort, from the novel by Bram Stoker and the play by Hamilton Deane, John Balderston • *Cinematographer* Karl Freund • *Art Director* Charles D Hall • *Make-up* Jack Pierce

Dracula ★★★ 15

Horror 1974 · US · Colour · 93mins

Originally made for American television, this adaptation of the Bram Stoker classic was given a theatrical release overseas, albeit in a pared-down version. Jack Palance gives one of his better performances as a sympathetic, Byronic Dracula, a Transylvanian count motivated by love as much as bloodlust. Veteran screenwriter Richard Matheson scripts this under-rated and well-appointed adaptation, which offers refreshing new slants on the usual undead clichés. AJ [VIDEO]

Jack Palance *Count Dracula* • Simon Ward *Arthur Holmwood* • Nigel Davenport *Dr Van Helsing* • Pamela Brown *Mrs Westerna* • Fiona Lewis *Lucy Westerna* • Penelope Horner *Mina Murray* • Murray Brown *Jonathan Harker* ■ *Dir* Dan Curtis • *Scr* Richard Matheson, from the novel by Bram Stoker

Dracula ★★★★ 15

Horror 1979 · US · Colour · 104mins

Like the 1931 version of Bram Stoker's tale, this streamlined remake is based on the hoary 1920s stage play, with the emphasis less on the supernatural horror and more on the Transylvanian count's seduction techniques. Frank Langella, fresh from the hit Broadway version, turns on the sensuality to great effect in director John Badham's stylishly atmospheric retread, with Laurence Olivier passionately histrionic as his nemesis, Van Helsing. While it's crafted as mainstream melodrama, there are enough chills to satisfy a more hardened horror crowd. AJ [VIDEO]

Frank Langella *Dracula* • Laurence Olivier *Van Helsing* • Donald Pleasence *Seward* • Kate Nelligan *Lucy* • Trevor Eve *Harker* • Jan Francis *Mina* • Janine Duvitski *Annie* • Tony Haygarth *Renfield* • Teddy Turner *Swales* ■ *Dir* John Badham • *Scr* WD Richter, from the play by Hamilton Deane, John Balderston, from the novel by Bram Stoker

Dracula AD 1972 ★★ 18

Horror 1972 · UK · Colour · 91mins

For this entry in their enduring *Dracula* series, Hammer relocated the count to swinging Chelsea, where he's holed up in a deconsecrated King's Road church and putting the bite on hippy layabouts. Derided at the time as a monumental misjudgement on the House of Horror's part, this slice of bell-bottomed phoniness can now be enjoyed as a camp period piece. Despite the mod trappings, Christopher Lee and Peter Cushing are as convincing as ever in their familiar roles, and director Alan Gibson keeps things moving at a fine pace. AJ [VIDEO]

Christopher Lee *Count Dracula* • Peter Cushing *Professor Van Helsing* • Stephanie Beacham *Jessica* • Christopher Neame *Johnny* • Michael Coles *Inspector* • Marsha A Hunt *Gaynor* • Caroline Munro *Laura* ■ *Dir* Alan Gibson • *Scr* Don Houghton, from the characters created by Bram Stoker

Dracula: Dead and Loving It ★ PG

Comedy horror 1995 · US · Colour · 90mins

Mel Brooks's run of cinematic disappointments continues with this woeful spoof on vampire movies. Leslie Nielsen is dreadfully miscast as the count, although most of the blame must be levelled at director Brooks and his co-writers, who not only show no understanding of the genre they're sending up but who also seem to have forgotten how to actually write a remotely funny gag. JF [VIDEO]

Leslie Nielsen *Dracula* • Peter MacNicol *Renfield* • Steven Weber *Jonathan Harker* • Amy Yasbeck *Mina* • Lysette Anthony *Lucy* • Harvey Korman *Dr Seward* • Mel Brooks *Professor Van Helsing* • Mark Blankfield *Martin* ■ *Dir* Mel Brooks • *Scr* Mel Brooks,

D

Rudy DeLuca, Steve Haberman, from a story by Rudy DeLuca, Steve Haberman, from the characters created by Bram Stoker

Dracula Has Risen from the Grave ★★★ 15

Horror 1968 · UK · Colour · 88mins

A weak priest provides the blood that revives the evil Count Dracula and becomes his servant in a typical dose of vampire flesh-creeping from the Hammer House of Horror. A minor triumph of style over content, the third sequel to Hammer's 1958 classic succeeds by virtue of Freddie Francis's adventurous direction and his ability to extract religious irony from the formulaic script. Moody red filters are used to enhance the sanguinary motifs, while the ever-reliable Christopher Lee evokes supernatural menace. AJ DVD

Christopher Lee *Count Dracula* • Rupert Davies *Monsignor* • Veronica Carlson *Maria* • Barbara Ewing *Zena* • Barry Andrews *Paul* • Ewan Hooper *Priest* • Michael Ripper *Max* • Marion Mathie *Anna* ■ *Dir* Freddie Francis • *Scr* John Elder [Anthony Hinds], from the characters created by Bram Stoker

Dracula: Pages from a Virgin's Diary ★★★ 12

Silent dance horror
2002 · Can · BW and Colour · 74mins

Bram Stoker's *Dracula* is re-interpreted as a gothic ballet in cult Canadian director Guy Maddin's sumptuous take on the classic vampire novel. Beautifully performed by the Royal Winnipeg Ballet, it's stylishly shot as a silent movie in black and white with occasional tints of colour. By sticking closely to the original text, Maddin's storyline is more full-bodied than many other Stoker adaptations, while the cinematography and art direction complement company choreographer Mark Godden's elegant dance movements. SF DVD

Zhang Wei-Qiang *Dracula* • Tara Birtwhistle *Lucy Westenra* • David Moroni *Dr Van Helsing* • CindyMarie Small *Mina Murray* • Johnny Wright *Jonathan Harker* ■ *Dir* Guy Maddin • *Scr* from the ballet by Mark Godden, from the novel by Bram Stoker • *Cinematographer* Paul Suderman

Dracula – Prince of Darkness ★★★★ 15

Horror 1965 · UK · Colour · 86mins

Two English couples dare to go travelling through the Carpathian mountains in one of the best in the Hammer Dracula series. Veteran horror director Terence Fisher brings out the innate sexuality in the tightly plotted story and Christopher Lee is awesome as the dreaded count, despite having no dialogue. The gruesome sequence where the infamous bloodsucker is resurrected in a perverse religious ritual still retains its shock value, with scream queen Barbara Shelley's demise just as memorable. Andrew Keir is no real substitute for Peter Cushing (glimpsed in the prologue lifted from the studio's 1958 *Horror of Dracula* blockbuster), but in every other respect this is a text-book example of top-grade ghoulish horror. AJ DVD

Christopher Lee *Count Dracula* • Barbara Shelley *Helen Kent* • Andrew Keir *Father Sandor* • Francis Matthews *Charles Kent* • Suzan Farmer *Diana Kent* • Charles Tingwell *Alan Kent* • Thorley Walters *Ludwig* • Walter Brown *Brother Mark* ■ *Dir* Terence Fisher • *Scr* John Sansom, from the characters created by Bram Stoker

Dracula, Prisoner of Frankenstein ★

Horror 1972 · Sp · Colour · 86mins

Spanish hack director Jesus Franco intended to make a parody of horror myths, but had neither the talent nor the budget to pull off the conceit. This sorry spectacle has Dr Frankenstein (a slumming Dennis Price) reviving Dracula (Franco regular Howard Vernon) with a nightclub singer's blood, so that he can use his vampire acolytes to conquer the world. Featuring lousy make-up and shoddy special effects. AJ. Spanish dialogue dubbed into English.

Dennis Price *Dr Frankenstein* • Howard Vernon *Dracula* • Alberto Dalbes • Genevieve Deloir ■ *Dir/Scr* Jesus Franco

Dracula 2001 ★★ 15

Horror 2000 · US · Colour · 94mins

Count Dracula (Gerard Butler) crosses the Atlantic to New Orleans, seeking Van Helsing's Basin Street-based daughter, Justine Waddell. It's up to antique dealer Jonny Lee Miller (in hilarious "diamond geezer" mode) and Virgin store sales assistant Waddell to thwart the Count's family reunion plans. Patrick Lussier's attempt to inject hip life into vampire mythology by giving it a *Scream* spin is pretty much an all-round disaster because the plot is plodding and schematic, tarted up with rock video imagery and camera trickery. Released in the US as *Dracula 2000*. AJ DVD

Jonny Lee Miller *Simon* • Christopher Plummer *Abraham Van Helsing/Matthew Van Helsing* • Justine Waddell *Mary* • Gerard Butler *Dracula* • Jennifer Esposito *Solina* • Omar Epps *Marcus* • Colleen Ann Fitzpatrick [Colleen Fitzpatrick] *Lucy* • Sean Patrick Thomas *Trick* ■ *Dir* Patrick Lussier • *Scr* Joel Soisson, from a story by Joel Soisson, Patrick Lussier

Dracula vs Frankenstein ★ 15

Horror 1970 · US · Colour · 90mins

Director Al Adamson surely ranks alongside Ed Wood as one of the genre's true incompetents. This is arguably his crowning glory – a hilarious mix of bad music, teenage dopeheads, beach parties and unconvincing monsters. Horror veterans J Carrol Naish and Lon Chaney Jr (who both never made another film) look thoroughly embarrassed, while the plot is a complete shambles. A must for all bad movie lovers. RS DVD

J Carrol Naish *Dr Frankenstein* • Lon Chaney Jr *Groton, the Mad Zombie* • Regina Carrol *Judith* • John Bloom (1) *The Monster* • Anthony Eisley *Mike Howard* • Russ Tamblyn *Rico* • Jim Davis *Sgt Martin* • Zandor Vorkov *Count Dracula* ■ *Dir* Al Adamson • *Scr* William Pugsley, Samuel M Sherman

Dracula's Daughter ★★★ PG

Horror 1936 · US · BW · 68mins

Edward Van Sloan's Von Helsing returns to face the undead once more in the neglected sequel to the 1931 *Dracula*. Gloria Holden became the first female vampire star, stalking the streets looking for a cure for her nocturnal agitations. In another first for the genre, she looks for young model Marguerite Churchill with more than blood-sucking in mind. Moody and beautifully shot, this is saturated with bleak hopelessness. AJ

Otto Kruger *Dr Jeffrey Garth* • Gloria Holden *Countess Marya Zaleska* • Marguerite Churchill *Janet Blake* • Irving Pichel *Sandor* • Edward Van Sloan *Dr Von Helsing* • Nan Grey *Lili* • Hedda Hopper *Lady Esme Hammond* ■ *Dir* Lambert Hillyer • *Scr* Garrett Fort, from a story by John Balderston, Oliver Jeffries [David O Selznick], from the short story *Dracula's Guest* by Bram Stoker • *Cinematographer* George Robinson

Dracula's Widow ★ 18

Horror 1988 · US · Colour · 81mins

Emmanuelle star Sylvia Kristel makes a poor and remarkably unsexy vampire in an anaemic addition to the undead genre from director Christopher Coppola, Francis Ford's nephew. As "the true wife of Dracula", Kristel arrives in Hollywood and takes up residence in a wax museum, whose owner (Lenny Von Dohlen) she enslaves. Transforming into an ugly monster and a laughably mechanical bat, Kristel slaughters a devil cult and seeks out a descendant of her husband's nemesis, Von Helsing. A pathetic wash-out. AJ

Sylvia Kristel *Vanessa* • Josef Sommer *Lieutenant Lannon* • Lenny Von Dohlen *Raymond Everett* • Marc Coppola *Brad* • Stefan Schnabel *Von Helsing* • Rachel Jones *Jenny* ■ *Dir* Christopher Coppola • *Scr* Kathryn Ann Thomas, Christopher Coppola

Drag ★★

Comedy 1929 · US · BW · 118mins

Richard Barthelmess, the publisher of a local Vermont newspaper, marries Alice Day, despite his attraction to socialite Lila Lee. His wife is inseparable from her parents, however, which causes friction in their relationship. Directed by Frank Lloyd, this unexceptional romantic comedy is a good example of its type, with a plot typical of the period and genre. DF

Richard Barthelmess *David Carroll* • Lucien Littlefield *Pa Parker* • Alice Day *Allie Parker* • Katherine Ward *Ma Parker* • Tom Dugan *Charlie Parker* • Lila Lee *Dot* ■ *Dir* Frank Lloyd • *Scr* Bradley King, Gene Towne, from the novel by William Dudley Pelley

The Dragnet ★★★★

Silent crime drama 1928 · US · BW

This lost film by Josef von Sternberg features George Bancroft as a duped chief of detectives and lovely Evelyn Brent, who leaves gang boss William Powell for the dogged Bancroft. The screenplay was partly the work of two men who would help shape the style of Hollywood storytelling over the next few decades – Jules Furthman (*Shanghai Express*, *The Big Sleep*) and Herman J Mankiewicz (*Citizen Kane*). The camerawork is by the great Harold Rosson (*Singin' in the Rain*). TS

George Bancroft *Two-Gun Nolan* • Evelyn Brent *The Magpie* • William Powell *Dapper Frank Trent* • Fred Kohler *"Gabby" Steve* • Francis McDonald *Sniper Dawson* • Leslie Fenton *Shakespeare* ■ *Dir* Josef von Sternberg • *Scr* Jules Furthman, Charles Furthman, Herman J Mankiewicz (titles), from the story *Nightstick* by Oliver HP Garrett • *Editor* Helen Lewis

Dragnet ★★★ PG

Police drama 1954 · US · Colour · 88mins

This spin-off from the famous American radio and TV series finds Jack Webb directing himself as Sergeant Joe Friday of the LAPD. The main problem with TV spin-offs is what works at 30 minutes doesn't always work at three times the length. This is certainly true of *Dragnet*, with its emphasis on police procedure making it look like a "How to Be a Detective" recruitment film. Nevertheless, it offers a nostalgic look at the days before *Dirty Harry* and *The French Connection* came along. AT

Jack Webb *Sergeant Joe Friday* • Ben Alexander *Officer Frank Smith* • Richard Boone *Captain Hamilton* • Ann Robinson *Grace Downey* • Stacy Harris *Max Troy* • Virginia Gregg *Ethel Marie Starkie* • Victor Perrin *Adolph Alexander* • Georgia Ellis *Belle Davitt* ■ *Dir* Jack Webb • *Scr* Richard L Breen

Dragnet ★★ PG

Spoof police drama
1987 · US · Colour · 101mins

It's a trawl through the comic depths for this parody of Jack Webb's 1950s TV series. Dan Aykroyd is the deadpan nephew of Webb's Sergeant Joe Friday, lumbered with an amoral, dishevelled partner in Tom Hanks and battling with porn king Dabney Coleman and satanist Christopher Plummer. A virgin sacrifice is the least of it and, as far as laughs are concerned, the most of it, despite the talents of Aykroyd and Hanks. TH. DVD

Dan Aykroyd *Det Sgt Joe Friday* • Tom Hanks *Pep Streebek* • Christopher Plummer *Rev Jonathan Whirley* • Harry Morgan *Captain Bill Gannon* • Alexandra Paul *Connie Swail* • Jack O'Halloran *Emil Muzz* • Dabney Coleman *Jerry Caesar* • Bruce Gray *Mayor Parvin* ■ *Dir* Tom Mankiewicz • *Scr* Dan Aykroyd, Alan Zweibel, Tom Mankiewicz

Dragon Seed ★★

War drama 1944 · US · BW · 147mins

This MGM version of life in China during the 1937 Japanese invasion couldn't have been more wierdly cast if they'd put all the studio contract players' names in a hat and just shaken them out. But if you can believe a Chinese, Bryn Mawr-accented Katharine Hepburn, you'll probably accept her extended family of Walter Huston, Akim Tamiroff and Aline MacMahon. The last credit of MGM's great contract director Jack Conway, this is one of Hollywood's most misconceived movies. TS

Katharine Hepburn *Jade* • Walter Huston *Ling Tan* • Aline MacMahon *Mrs Ling Tan* • Akim Tamiroff *Wu Lien* • Turhan Bey *Lao Er* • Hurd Hatfield *Lao San* • Frances Rafferty *Orchid* • Agnes Moorehead *3rd cousin's wife* • Lionel Barrymore *Narrator* ■ *Dir* Jack Conway, Harold S Bucquet • *Scr* Marguerite Roberts, Jane Murfin, from the novel by Peal S Buck • *Producer* Pandro S Berman

Dragon: the Bruce Lee Story ★★★★ 15

Biographical drama
1993 · US · Colour · 119mins

Adapted from the book by Lee's wife, Linda Lee Cadwell (played in the film by Lauren Holly), this is a curious mix of traditional Hollywood biography and Hong Kong ghost story. Jason Scott Lee (no relation) captures Bruce's exuberance and finesse with considerable skill. Directed with panache by Rob Cohen, the rags-to-riches tale, which sees Lee rise from street kid to martial arts master, is pretty standard stuff. Yet what's so fascinating is the insight into the private torment that the film suggests led to Lee's death. DP. Contains violence. DVD

Jason Scott Lee *Bruce Lee* • Lauren Holly *Linda Lee* • Robert Wagner *Bill Krieger* • Michael Learned *Vivian Emery* • Nancy Kwan *Gussie Yang* • Lim Kay Tong *Philip Tan* • Ric Young *Bruce's father* • Wang Luoyong *Yip man* • Sterling Macer Jr *Jerome Sprout* ■ *Dir* Rob Cohen • *Scr* Edward Khmara, John Raffo, Rob Cohen, from the non-fiction book *Bruce Lee: The Man Only I Knew* by Linda Lee Cadwell

Dragonard ★ 18

Period drama 1987 · US · Colour · 85mins

Part bodice ripper, part slave drama, this 18th-century tale is a tough movie to figure out. On a British island in the Caribbean, the governor is killed the same night his daughter seduces a slave. The slave is accused of murder; when he can't be found, new governor Oliver Reed (even more over-the-top than usual) begins torturing the island's black population. Every now and then a rape scene is thrown in, just to make this disgusting display more intolerable. ST

Oliver Reed *Captain Shanks* • Eartha Kitt *Naomi* • Annabel Schofield *Honore* • Claudia Udy *Arabella* • Patrick Warburton *Richard Abdee* • Drummond Marais *Pierre* • Dennis Folbigge *Governor* ■ *Dir* Gérard Kikoine • *Scr* Peter Welbeck [Harry Alan Towers], Rick Marx, from a novel by Rupert Gilchrist

Dragonflies ★★★ 15

Psychological drama
2001 · Nor/Swe · Colour · 104mins

This shoestring Norwegian drama offers a refreshing, rural variation on a well-worn theme. Kim Bodnia is an ex-con whose simply idyll with pregnant lover Maria Bonnevie is disrupted by the unexpected arrival of a ghost from his past, an old "friend" (played by Mikael Persbrandt) recently released from jail. But director Marius Holst seems uncertain whether to stage the intruder's quest for revenge and lust for Bonnevie as a psychological drama or a thriller; a dilemma that's exacerbated by his decision to allow the cast to improvise much of the dialogue. Ambitious, moody, but lacking in intensity. DP. In Norwegian with English subtitles. DVD

Maria Bonnevie *Maria* • Kim Bodnia *Eddie* • Mikael Persbrandt *Kullman* • Tord Peterson *Sven* • Skarpjordet. Thomas *Thomas* ■ *Dir* Marius Holst • *Scr* Nicolaj Frobenius, Marius Holst, from the short story *Natt til Mork Morgen* by Ingvar Ambjornsen

Dragonfly ★★ 12

Supernatural romantic drama
2002 · US · Colour · 99mins

Kevin Costner stars as an ER doctor who is devastated by the death of his pregnant wife (Susanna Thompson) while on a Red Cross mission in Venezuela. Costner becomes convinced that she is trying to contact him from "beyond", and an encounter with Linda Hunt's eccentric nun sends him off on a jungle adventure. Sadly, the understated performance of Costner can't rescue this schmaltzy misfire. LH DVD

Kevin Costner *Joe Darrow* • Joe Morton *Hugh Campbell* • Ron Rifkin *Charlie Dickinson* • Linda Hunt *Sister Madeline* • Susanna Thompson *Emily Darrow* • Kathy Bates *Miriam Belmont* ■ *Dir* Tom Shadyac • *Scr* David Seltzer, Brandon Camp, Mike Thompson, from a story by Brandon Camp, Mike Thompson

DragonHeart ★★★ PG

Fantasy adventure
1996 · US · Colour · 98mins

Sean Connery lends his distinctive burr to Draco, a 10th-century dragon who joins forces with an itinerant knight (Dennis Quaid). The result is a likeable, if a tad over-eager mix of derring-do and special effects, which has everything from wicked kings and poetic monks to romantic encounters and revolting peasants. Quaid gives a rousing performance, while Pete Postlethwaite is charmingly awkward as the religious wayfarer with a penchant for rhyming couplets. As the dastardly despot, however, David Thewlis belongs in a pantomime. DP DVD

Dennis Quaid *Bowen* • Sean Connery *Draco* • David Thewlis *Einon* • Pete Postlethwaite *Gilbert* • Dina Meyer *Kara* • Jason Isaacs *Felton* • Brian Thompson *Brok* • Lee Oakes *Young Einon* • Julie Christie *Aislinn* • John Gielgud *King Arthur* ■ *Dir* Rob Cohen • *Scr* Charles Edward Pogue, from a story by Patrick Read Johnson, Charles Edward Pogue

Dragonheart: a New Beginning ★★ PG

Fantasy adventure
1999 · US · Colour · 80mins

Chris Masterson headlines this efficient sequel to Rob Cohen's medieval adventure. However, the stable lad with ambitions of knighthood is largely overshadowed by the presence of Drake, the junior dragon who was hatched and nurtured in the crypt of a monastery. As in the original, the CGI work is impressive, although Robby Benson is no substitute for Sean Connery in the voiceover department. Lots of action, but it's the byplay between boy and beast that kids will most enjoy. DP DVD

Chris Masterson *Geoff* • Harry Van Gorkum *Osric/Old Bowen* • Rona Figueroa *Princess Lian* • Matt Hickey *Mansel* • Henry O *Kwan* • Robby Benson *Drake the dragon* ■ *Dir* Doug Lefler • *Scr* Shari Goodhartz, from characters created by Charles Edward Pogue, Patrick Read Johnson

Dragonslayer ★★★ PG

Fantasy adventure
1981 · US · Colour · 104mins

The early 1980s brought a rash of fantasy adventures, ranging from the camp fun of *Conan the Barbarian* to such dire examples as *The Sword and the Sorcerer*. This film, which follows a magician's assistant on his quest to kill a dragon, is aimed more at a family audience, though it's not without its violent moments, and it benefits from a good cast that includes Ralph Richardson. The effects aren't bad either. JF DVD

Peter MacNicol *Galen* • Caitlin Clarke *Valerian* • Ralph Richardson *Ulrich* • John Hallam *Tyrian* • Peter Eyre *Casiodorus* • Albert Salmi *Greil* • Chloe Salaman *Princess Elspeth* • Roger Kemp *Horsrik* • Ian McDiarmid *Brother Jacopus* ■ *Dir* Matthew Robbins • *Scr* Hal Barwood, Matthew Robbins

Dragonworld ★★ U

Fantasy 1994 · US · Colour · 82mins

Although the setting looks suspiciously like the eastern European castle cult horror producer Charles Band used for his more adult films, this is a charming if slight tale of a boy's friendship with a baby dragon. The effects aren't up too much, but it is a curiously innocent affair, and John Woodvine and Andrew Keir add a bit of class. A made-for-TV sequel followed in 1997. JF

Sam Mackenzie *John McGowan* • Brittney Powell *Beth Armstrong* • John Calvin *Bob Armstrong* • Courtland Mead *Young Johnny McGowan* • Lila Kaye *Mrs Cosgrove* • John Woodvine *Lester MacIntyre* • Andrew Keir *Angus McGowan* ■ *Dir* Ted Nicolaou • *Scr* Suzanne Glazener Naha, Ted Nicolaou, from a story by Charles Band

Dragonwyck ★★★ PG

Gothic melodrama 1946 · US · BW · 98mins

This preposterous old tosh, a sort of Manderley-on-the-Hudson, marked distinguished film-maker Joseph L Mankiewicz's directorial debut. He does well by the material, but the casting leaves a lot to be desired. Top-billed Gene Tierney is a lovely governess, but Vincent Price hams quite extraordinarily as the sadistic master of the estate, while Glenn Langan is truly hopeless as the local doctor. There's pleasure to be had from watching these ludicrous performances on phoney sets, but you can't escape the feeling that it was meant to be taken seriously. TS DVD

Gene Tierney *Miranda Wells* • Walter Huston *Ephraim Wells* • Vincent Price *Nicholas Van Ryn* • Glenn Langan *Dr Jeff Turner* • Anne Revere *Abigail Wells* • Spring Byington *Magda* ■ *Dir* Joseph L Mankiewicz • *Scr* Joseph L Mankiewicz, from the novel by Anya Seton

Dragoon Wells Massacre ★★ PG

Western 1957 · US · Colour · 82mins

This brisk, good-looking western that benefits greatly from CinemaScope and the camerawork of William Clothier, who also shot *The Alamo* and *Cheyenne Autumn*. The plot is routine, but Barry Sullivan and *High Noon's* Katy Jurado make the most of their roles. He's a killer, she's a hooker; they are forced to join together to protect themselves from marauding Apaches. TS

Barry Sullivan *Link Ferris* • Dennis O'Keefe *Captain Matt Riordan* • Mona Freeman *Ann Bradley* • Katy Jurado *Mara Fay* • Jack Elam *Tioga* • Sebastian Cabot *Jonah* • Casey Adams [Max Showalter] *Phillip Scott* • Trevor Bardette *Marshal Bill Haney* ■ *Dir* Harold Schuster • *Scr* Warren Douglas, from a story by Oliver Drake

Dragstrip Girl ★★

Drama 1957 · US · BW · 69mins

Only the smouldering presence of 1950s cult sexpot Fay Spain in the title role makes this AIP cheapie at all watchable. Spain showed better form in higher-budgeted movies such as *Al Capone* (opposite Rod Steiger) and *God's Little Acre* (supporting Robert Ryan and Aldo Ray), but she did not achieve lasting fame. Here she transcends the material in this banal teen flick about hot-rod racing. TS

Fay Spain *Louise Blake* • Steven Terrell *Jim Donaldson* • John Ashley *Fred Armstrong* • Tommy Ivo *Rick Camden* • Frank Gorshin *Tommy* • Judy Bamber *Rhoda, the blonde* ■ *Dir* Edward L Cahn • *Scr* Lou Rusoff

Dramatic School ★★★ U

Drama 1938 · US · BW · 80mins

Luise Rainer, a fragile and hard-to-cast talent, made precious few movies after her back-to-back best actress Oscars for *The Great Ziegfeld* (1936) and *The Good Earth* (1937). In all of them, however, she was superb. In this MGM drama reminiscent of the popular *Stage Door*, her co-stars are the up-and-coming Lana Turner and the lovely Paulette Goddard – but it's Rainer's movie through and through. TS

Luise Rainer *Louise* • Paulette Goddard *Nana* • Lana Turner *Mado* • Alan Marshal *Andre D'Abbencourt* • Anthony Allan [John Hubbard] *Fleury* • Henry Stephenson *Pasquel Sr* • Genevieve Tobin *Gina Bertier* • Gale Sondergaard *Madame Charlot* • Ann Rutherford *Yvonne* • Margaret Dumont *Teacher* • Dick Haymes *Student* ■ *Dir* Robert B Sinclair • *Scr* Ernst Vadja, Mary C McCall Jr, from the play *School of Drama* by Hans Szekely, Zoltan Egyed

Drango ★★ U

Western drama 1957 · US · Colour · 92mins

Jeff Chandler is Drango, a Union officer who faces considerable hostility when he takes charge of a small town in Georgia in the aftermath of the Civil War. The issues are poorly developed, and writer/producer Hall Bartlett rather awkwardly shares the direction with Jules Bricken. But Joanne Dru and Julie London make forceful leading ladies, and there's a surprising but effective appearance from British actor Ronald Howard. AE

Jeff Chandler *Drango* • John Lupton *Marc* • Joanne Dru *Kate* • Morris Ankrum *Calder* • Julie London *Shelby* • Donald Crisp *Allen* • Ronald Howard *Clay* ■ *Dir* Hall Bartlett, Jules Bricken • *Scr* Hall Bartlett

The Draughtsman's Contract ★★★★★ 15

Period drama 1982 · UK · Colour · 103mins

Peter Greenaway's first commercially released feature film is a calling card of dazzling virtuosity. A 17th-century draughtsman (Anthony Higgins) is hired to make 12 drawings of a country estate, and is paid in sexual favours by the landowner's wife and daughter (Janet Suzman and Anne Louise Lambert). The possibility of his drawings being an artistic witness to murder is deftly, tantalisingly displayed and his ultimate downfall from arrogant posturing is a lesson in class-distinction, only to be expected from the aristocratic world he's tried to enter. Michael Nyman's minimalist music reinforces the remarkable visuals in this clever and witty ground-breaking debut. TH DVD

Anthony Higgins *Mr Neville* • Janet Suzman *Mrs Herbert* • Anne Louise Lambert *Mrs Talmann* • Neil Cunningham *Mr Noyes* • Hugh Fraser *Mr Talmann* • Dave Hill *Mr Herbert* ■ *Dir/Scr* Peter Greenaway

Drawn to the Flame ★★

Erotic drama 1997 · US · Colour · 92mins

The storyline is usually an irrelevance where erotica is concerned. Yet there's always that lingering hope that a female director can bring something to the party other than a misty lens. However, Valerie Landsburg cranks out more formulaic soft-focus fumblings in this drama, as Lisa Welti's Hollywood agent returns to her sleepy home town to settle her father's estate and take the odd trip down lovers' lane. DP

Lisa Welti *Mary* • Jodi Verdu *Sarah* • Spencer Garrett ■ *Dir* Valerie Landsburg

Dream a Little Dream ★ 15

Comedy drama 1989 · US · Colour · 110mins

Yet another body-swap movie with nothing new to offer. Here Jason Robards ends up in the body of spotty 16-year-old Corey Feldman after the latter crashes into his meditation session on a bicycle. The problem is that Feldman is utterly incapable of acting like an elderly man in a youngster's body, thus defeating the entire premise of the film. For some unknown reason, a sequel followed six years later. LH

Corey Feldman *Bobby Keller* • Corey Haim *Dinger* • Jason Robards *Coleman Ettinger* • Piper Laurie *Gena Ettinger* • Harry Dean Stanton *Ike Baker* • Meredith Salenger *Lainie Diamond* ■ *Dir* Marc Rocco • *Scr* Daniel Jay Franklin, Marc Rocco, DE Eisenberg, from a story by Daniel Jay Franklin

Dream Demon ★ 18

Fantasy thriller 1988 · UK · Colour · 85mins

This tragic British answer to Freddy Krueger – "A Nightmare on Sloane Street" – is about as scary as a trip to Harvey Nichols. Jemma Redgrave is the upper-class socialite hunted by the press and suffering dream premonitions about her friends dying. A pointless terror exercise with awful performances that kill the lame premise of Hooray Henry horror stone dead. AJ

Jemma Redgrave *Diana Markham* • Kathleen Wilhoite *Jenny Hoffman* • Timothy Spall *Peck* • Jimmy Nail *Paul* • Mark Greenstreet *Oliver* • Susan Fleetwood *Deborah* • Annabelle Lanyon *Little Jenny* • Nickolas Grace *Jenny's father* ■ *Dir* Harley Cokliss • *Scr* Harley Cokliss, Christopher Wicking

Dream Flights ★★★

Drama 1983 · USSR · Colour · 90mins

Although he regularly collaborated with Andrei Tarkovsky, Oleg Yankovsky gives his most electrifying performance in this finely judged tragicomedy from Roman Balayan. As a 40-year-old charmer with an underdeveloped sense of responsibility, he is forced to re-evaluate his priorities when his adulterous private life and directionless career begin to collapse around him. The result is a fascinating study of Soviet socio-sexual mores. DP. In Russian with English subtitles.

Oleg Yankovsky *Sergei Makarov* • Lyudmila Gurchenko *Larisa* • Oleg Tabakov *Nikolai "Kolya" Pavlovich* • Liudmila Ivanova *Nina Sergeyevna* • Liudmila Zorina *Natasha*

D

Makarov • Elena Kostina *Alisa* • Oleg Menshikov *Alisa's friend* ■ *Dir* Roman Balayan • *Scr* Viktor Merezhko

Dream for an Insomniac

★★★ 15

Romantic comedy
1996 · US · BW and Colour · 83mins

This charming, feel-good romantic comedy is admittedly about as solid as a grass hut in a hurricane. Ione Skye is the sleep-disordered romantic who, with best friend Jennifer Aniston, is determined to make it big in Hollywood. But her life gets complicated by the arrival of hunky kindred spirit MacKenzie Astin, who has a girlfriend. Filmed in a mixture of black and white and colour, this has enough good lines to keep you smiling and the young cast members deliver attractive performances. JF. Contains swearing, sexual references. DVD

Ione Skye *Frankie* • Jennifer Aniston *Allison* • MacKenzie Astin *David Schrader* • Michael Landes *Rob* • Robert Kelker-Kelly *Trent* • Seymour Cassel *Uncle Leo* • Sean San Jose Blackman *Juice* • Michael Sterk *B J* • Leslie Stevens (3) *Molly* ■ *Dir/Scr* Tiffanie DeBartolo

Dream Girl

★★

Comedy 1948 · US · BW · 85mins

Elmer Rice's Broadway satire, a vehicle for his wife Betty Field, is turned into a fun-fest for Paramount's reigning laff queen Betty Hutton. She hams every line and milks every gag as a daydreamer who imagines she's an understudy to an opera star or a broken-hearted whore. Hutton was immensely popular in the 1940s, but as a distaff version of *The Secret Life of Walter Mitty* this just doesn't cut it. A lowbrow romp. TS

Betty Hutton *Georgina Allerton* • Macdonald Carey *Clark Redfield* • Patric Knowles *Jim Lucas* • Virginia Field *Miriam Allerton Lucas* • Walter Abel *George Allerton* • Peggy Wood *Lucy Allerton* • Carolyn Butler *Claire* • Lowell Gilmore *George Hand* ■ *Dir* Mitchell Leisen • *Scr* Arthur Sheekman, from the play by Elmer Rice • *Music* Victor Young

The Dream Life of Angels

★★★★ 18

Drama 1998 · Fr · Colour · 108mins

Elodie Bouchez and Natacha Régnier shared the best actress prize at Cannes for their work in Erick Zonca's painfully realistic debut. Bouchez particularly impresses as the optimistic drifter whose creativity and resourcefulness see her through the daily crises that consistently floor her cynical new friend, who has become morbidly dependent on a doomed love affair with a rich man. Although prone to disconcerting moments of melodrama, this is still a provocative study of dislocation and isolation. DP. In French with English subtitles. Contains sex scenes.

Elodie Bouchez *Isa* • Natacha Régnier *Marie* • Grégoire Colin *Chriss* • Patrick Mercado *Charly* • Jo Prestia *Fredo* • Francine Massenhave *Attendant* • Zivko Niklevski *Yugoslav patron* ■ *Dir* Erick Zonca • *Scr* Erick Zonca, Roger Bohbot, Virginie Wagon, Pierre Schoeller, Frederic Carpentier, Pierre Chosson, Jean-Daniel Magnin

Dream Lover

★ 15

Psychological thriller
1986 · US · Colour · 99mins

This dreadful mess of a movie purports to explore the repercussions of extensive "dream therapy" on a young girl desperate to rid herself of a recurring nightmare. The cast does its best to pick its way through a minefield of psychobabble and histrionics, but Alan J Pakula directs with a leaden hand and somnambulistic air. One movie without any redeeming features whatsoever. SH. Contains violence, swearing and nudity.

Kristy McNichol *Kathy Gardner* • Ben Masters *Michael Hansen* • Paul Shenar *Ben Gardner* • Justin Deas *Kevin McCann* • John McMartin *Martin* • Gayle Hunnicutt *Claire* ■ *Dir* Alan J Pakula • *Scr* Jon Boorstin

Dream Lover

★★ 18

Thriller 1993 · US · Colour · 99mins

Successful architect James Spader meets the woman of his dreams (*Twin Peaks* star Mädchen Amick) and, after a whirlwind romance, they get married. But slowly (very slowly!) he begins to wonder about her real motives in director Nicholas Kazan's low-key suspense thriller. While Kazan has fun setting up the stock situations and spinning plot threads off in surprising directions, this lethargically paced drama comes off as part *Suspicion*, part *Body Heat* – without the stylish flair of either. AJ. Contains violence, swearing, sex scenes and nudity.

James Spader *Ray Reardon* • Mädchen Amick *Lena Reardon* • Bess Armstrong *Elaine* • Fredrick Lehne [Fredric Lehne] *Larry* • Larry Miller *Norman* • Kathleen York *Martha* • Kate Williamson *Mrs Sneeder* ■ *Dir/Scr* Nicholas Kazan

The Dream Machine

★★ PG

Action comedy 1990 · US · Colour · 82mins

Corey Haim reprises his cheeky charmer persona to outwit bumbling grown-ups. Here he plays a student who rather implausibly is presented with the car of his dreams, only to discover that the previous owner is dead in the boot and that the killer wants the body back. With a cast of unknowns, this rests on the leading man's charisma. If you're not a fan now, this won't win you over. JF. Contains violence and swearing.

Corey Haim *Barry Davis* • Evan Richards *Meese* • Jeremy Slate *Mr Chamberlain* • Susan Seaforth Hayes [Susan Seaforth] *Margo Chamberlain* • Randall England *Lance* • Susan Kent *Jean Davis* • James MacKrell *Claude Davis* ■ *Dir* Lyman Dayton • *Scr* Eric Hendershot

A Dream of Kings

★★★★

Drama 1969 · US · Colour · 110mins

Anthony Quinn transfers his "Zorba the Greek" persona to urban Chicago in this powerful portrayal of a Graeco-American paterfamilias. It's a neglected, marvellous, warm-hearted movie that works brilliantly – unless, of course, you're one of the many who has developed an aversion to Quinn's salt-of-the-earth, all-purpose ethnic mensch. Here he's exceptionally fine as the gambler-philosopher trying to raise the money to send his dying son to Greece. Irene Papas is well cast as Quinn's wife, but tragic beauty Inger Stevens steals the film as the young widow Quinn has an affair with. It's a beautifully observed movie, excellently directed by Daniel Mann. TS

Anthony Quinn *Matsoukas* • Irene Papas *Caliope* • Inger Stevens *Anna* • Sam Levene *Cicero* • Val Avery *Fatsas* • Tamara Daykarhanova *Mother-in-law* • Peter Mamakos *Falconis* ■ *Dir* Daniel Mann • *Scr* Harry Mark Petrakis, Ian Hunter, from the novel by Harry Mark Petrakis

A Dream of Passion

★ 18

Drama 1978 · Gr · Colour · 101mins

A thick pall of pretension hangs over this rancid cocktail of Greek myth and art house angst. Melina Mercouri gnaws her way through the scenery with a voracious appetite as the Greek actress who sees Ellen Burstyn's murderous American mother as the perfect publicity ruse for her new production of *Medea*. So far so ghastly. But once the women begin to merge emotionally *à la* Ingmar Bergman's *Persona*, the entire edifice comes tumbling down. DP. An English/Greek language film.

Melina Mercouri *Maya* • Ellen Burstyn *Brenda* • Andreas Voutsinas *Kostas* • Despo Diamantidou *Maria* • Dimitris Papamichael *Dimitris/Jason* • Yannis Voglis *Edward* ■ *Dir* Jules Dassin • *Scr* Jules Dassin, from the play *Medea* by Euripides

Dream Street

★★

Silent drama 1921 · US · BW · 102mins

A heavily melodramatic outing from the great silent movie maestro DW Griffith, who actually wrote his own pseudonymous screenplay for this sub-*Broken Blossoms* tale. It's inspired by two *Limehouse Nights* short stories by *Blossoms* author Thomas Burke. The result is uncomfortably racist and shows few signs of Griffith's undoubted picture-making genius, as dancer Carol Dempster inadequately serves as an obsessive sex object, whose very existence causes death, mayhem and destruction. Overlong and stilted it may be, but it's not without a certain watchability. TS

Carol Dempster *Gypsy Fair* • Ralph Graves *James "Spike" McFadden* • Charles Emmett Mack *Billy McFadden* • Edward Peil [Edward Peil Sr] *Swan Way* • WJ Ferguson *Gypsy's father* • Porter Strong *Samuel Jones* ■ *Dir* DW Griffith • *Scr* Roy Sinclair [DW Griffith], from the short stories *Gina of the Chinatown* and *The Sign of the Lamp* by Thomas Burke

The Dream Team

★★★★ 15

Comedy 1989 · US · Colour · 107mins

This light-hearted spin on *One Flew over the Cuckoo's Nest* has a group of inmates from a psychiatric hospital slipping the leash while on a day trip to New York. For Michael Keaton, in the year he became a superstar in *Batman*, the role offered the chance to return to what he does best – the silver-tongued, lovable rogue. He also benefits from a gallery of accomplished supporting players, most notably an anally retentive Christopher Lloyd. Director Howard Zieff makes an occasional attempt at seriousness, but keeps the laughs flowing smoothly. JF. Contains violence, swearing, drug abuse and brief nudity. DVD

Michael Keaton *Billy Caulfield* • Christopher Lloyd *Henry Sikorsky* • Peter Boyle *Jack McDermott* • Stephen Furst *Albert Ianuzzi* • Dennis Boutsikaris *Dr Weitzman* • Lorraine Bracco *Riley* • Milo O'Shea *Dr Newald* • Philip Bosco *O'Malley* ■ *Dir* Howard Zieff • *Scr* Jon Connolly, David Loucka

Dream Wife

★★ U

Comedy 1953 · US · BW · 98mins

Cary Grant and Deborah Kerr dull? Well, they certainly are in this feeble slapstick concoction, a rare excursion into directing from screenwriter Sidney Sheldon. Grant's engaged to Kerr but falls for Betta St John, who has been trained to please men. Grant and Kerr teamed up again to far better effect in *An Affair to Remember*, but Sidney Sheldon made an even more wretched film (*The Buster Keaton Story*) before becoming a novelist. TS

Cary Grant *Clemson Reade* • Deborah Kerr *Effie* • Walter Pidgeon *Walter McBride* • Betta St John *Tarji* • Eduard Franz *Khan* • Buddy Baer *Vizier* • Les Tremayne *Ken Landwell* • Gloria Holden *Mrs Landwell* • Steve Forrest *Louis* ■ *Dir* Sidney Sheldon • *Scr* Sidney Sheldon, Herbert Baker, Alfred Lewis Levitt, from a story by Alfred Lewis Levitt

Dream with the Fishes

★★★ 18

Black comedy drama
1996 · US · Colour · 92mins

Darkly melancholic, but also charmingly offbeat, Finn Taylor's directorial debut offers a moving study of loss and obsession. *Scream* star David Arquette, who also co-produced, plays a grieving, voyeuristic loner who gradually comes out of his shell when he gets mixed up with the dying Brad Hunt. Hunt is determined to live his final days to the full – which, in his case, means nude bowling, nude bank robbery and giving LSD to traffic policemen. All the performances are first-rate, and Taylor's vision is both quirky and lyrical. JF. Contains swearing, nudity, violence.

David Arquette *Terry* • Brad Hunt *Nick* • Cathy Moriarty *Aunt Elise* • Kathryn Erbe *Liz* • Patrick McGaw *Don* • JE Freeman *Joe, Nick's father* • Timi Prulhiere *Michelle* • Anita Barone *Mary* ■ *Dir* Finn Taylor • *Scr* Finn Taylor, from a story by Jeffrey Brown, Finn Taylor

Dreamboat

★★★ U

Satirical comedy 1952 · US · BW · 83mins

This very funny satire on the early days of television was made when TV was a novelty newcomer and not yet a threat to cinemas. Ginger Rogers is delightful as a silent-movie queen who revives her popularity by presenting her old movies on TV, annoying her former co-star Clifton Webb, now ensconced in "the groves of Academe". The best bits are the re-creations of the silent movies. Rogers and Webb are particularly fetching as their younger selves, while Elsa Lanchester is a joy as Webb's lustful superior. TS

Clifton Webb *Thornton Sayre* • Ginger Rogers *Gloria* • Anne Francis *Carol Sayre* • Jeffrey Hunter *Bill Ainslee* • Elsa Lanchester *Dr Coffey* • Fred Clark *Sam Levitt* • Paul Harvey *Harrington* ■ *Dir* Claude Binyon • *Scr* Claude Binyon, from a story by John D Weaver

Dreamcatcher

★★ 15

Science-fiction horror
2003 · US/Aus · Colour · 128mins

Four childhood friends on a hunting trip rescue a deranged oddball who, it soon emerges, is host to some sort of alien parasite. While they attempt to evade the monster, the military – in the shape of Morgan Freeman – arrives, determined to eradicate all trace of the shape-shifting beastie. Despite a screenplay co-written by William Goldman, initially effective atmospherics and creditable performances, this is soon hobbled by poor quality CGI and an abysmally incoherent final act. AS DVD

Morgan Freeman *Colonel Abraham Curtis* • Thomas Jane *Dr Henry "H" Devlin* • Jason Lee *Jim "Beaver" Clarendon* • Damian Lewis *Professor Gary "Jonesy" Jones* • Timothy Olyphant *Pete Moore* • Tom Sizemore *Captain Owen Underhill* • Donnie Wahlberg *Douglas "Duddits" Cavell* ■ *Dir* Lawrence Kasdan • *Scr* Lawrence Kasdan, William Goldman, from the novel by Stephen King

Dreamchild

★★★ PG

Fantasy drama 1985 · UK · Colour · 94mins

This is a fascinating and imaginative, if seriously flawed exploration of the real-life person on whom the Reverend Charles Dodgson (aka Lewis Carroll) allegedly based his fictional character Alice. Coral Browne gives a deeply layered performance as the 80-year-old Alice Hargreaves, traumatised by her recollections of the famous relationship, while Dennis Potter's screenplay is typically taut and riveting. There are more red herrings here than in the North Sea, and Browne has a love interest that is rather unnecessary. SH

Coral Browne *Mrs Alice Hargreaves* • Ian Holm *Reverend Charles Dodgson* • Peter Gallagher *Jack Dolan* • Caris Corfman *Sally Mackeson* • Nicola Cowper *Lucy* • Jane Asher *Mrs Liddell* ■ *Dir* Gavin Millar • *Scr* Dennis Potter

Dreamer ★ PG

Drama 1979 · US · Colour · 86mins

One-dimensional actor Tim Matheson gets to show off his lack of acting skills once again in a sporting drama set around the heady world of bowling. The title of this yawnsome movie could also be used to describe director Noel Nosseck, who must have been in a comatose state when he decided this would make good entertainment. JB. Contains swearing.

Tim Matheson *Dreamer* • Susan Blakely *Karen* • Jack Warden *Harry* • Richard B Shull *Taylor* • Barbara Stuart *Angie* • Owen Bush *Fan* • Marya Small *Elaine* ■ *Dir* Noel Nosseck • *Scr* James Proctor, Larry Bishoff

The Dreamers ★★★★ 18

Period drama
2003 · Fr/It/UK/US · Colour · 110mins

During the revolutionary spring of 1968 in France, twins Louis Garrel and Eva Green invite American fellow student Michael Pitt to stay at their parents' Paris apartment. There they test each other's cinematic, emotional, sexual and political ideals to see how far they will go. The fact the trio are film fanatics enables director Bernardo Bertolucci to explore a cineaste edge to their passions, and the vintage film clips give the drama further stylish resonance. Pitt is wonderful as the sexually awakened naif who slowly comes to terms with Euro sophistication and the *Blowin' in the Wind* tenor of the times. Erotically explicit, this is a stunning return to form from the taboo-challenging director. AJ. In English and French with subtitles. DVD

Michael Pitt *Matthew* • Eva Green *Isabelle* • Louis Garrel *Théo* • Robin Renucci *Father* • Anna Chancellor *Mother* • Florian Cadiou *Patrick* ■ *Dir* Bernardo Bertolucci • *Scr* Gilbert Adair, from his novel *The Holy Innocents*

Dreaming ★★ U

Comedy 1944 · UK · BW · 78mins

Comedians Bud Flanagan and Chesney Allen from the Crazy Gang star in this gently naive comedy produced by Britain's Ealing Studios. It's about a soldier who gets a knock on his head and drifts into a dream world. The dreams feature appearances from music hall turns such as xylophonist Teddy Brown and violinist Alfredo Campoli, plus cameos from famous jockeys Gordon Richards and Dick Francis in an attempt to comfort wartime audiences. TH

Bud Flanagan *Bud* • Chesney Allen *Ches* • Hazel Court *Wren/Avalah/Miss Grey* • Dick Francis *Sir Charles Paddock* • Philip Wade *Dr Goebbels* • Gerry Wilmott *United States General* • Peter Bernard *American soldier* • Ian MacLean *General* • Gordon Richards ■ *Dir* John Baxter • *Scr* Bud Flanagan [Dennis O'Keefe], Reginald Purdell

Dreaming of Joseph Lees ★★ 12

Drama 1998 · US/UK · Colour · 88mins

Filmed on the Isle of Man, standing in for 1950s Somerset, this rural melodrama is heavy going, despite some glowingly worthy performances. Samantha Morton falls in love with geologist Rupert Graves, her cousin; when he takes off, she marries pig farmer Lee Ross. Then Graves returns, re-igniting passions. Eric Styles's direction is overwrought, while Catherine Linstrum's script is declamatory and stagey. TH. Contains violence, sexual references.

Samantha Morton *Eva Babbins* • Rupert Graves *Joseph Lees* • Lee Ross *Harry Flite* • Miriam Margolyes *Signora Caldoni* • Frank Finlay *Eva's father* • Holly Aird *Maria Flite, Harry's sister* • Nicholas Woodeson *Mr Dian* ■ *Dir* Eric Styles • *Scr* Catherine Linstrum

Dreams ★★★

Drama 1955 · Swe · BW · 86mins

Sophisticated fashion photographer Eva Dahlbeck and jaunty model Harriet Andersson go to Gothenberg where the former attempts to revive an affair with married man Ulf Palme, and the latter has a flirtation with rich, retired diplomat Gunnar Bjornstrand. The gap between illusion and reality in Ingmar Bergman's film is reflected in the literal translation of the original Swedish title, *Women's Dreams*, while the casting of the lead actresses mirrors the shifting moods of the piece, alternately light-hearted and sombre. RB. A Swedish language film.

Harriet Andersson *Doris* • Eva Dahlbeck *Susanne* • Gunnar Björnstrand *The consul* • Ulf Palme *Henrik Lobelius* • Inga Landgré *Marta Lobelius* • Sven Lindberg *Palle* • Naima Wifstrand *Mrs Aren* • Benkt-Ake Benktsson *Magnus* ■ *Dir/Scr* Ingmar Bergman

Dreams That Money Can Buy ★★★★ 12

Experimental portmanteau drama
1946 · US · Colour and BW · 79mins

This intriguing experiment in psychoanalytical surrealism (which took three years to complete) represents the most astonishing avant-garde collaboration in film history. Corralled by German Dadaist Hans Richter, the creative team comprises Max Ernst, Marcel Duchamp, Man Ray, Alexander Calder and Fernand Léger, while Louis Applebuam, Paul Bowles, John Cage, David Diamond, John Latouche and Darius Milhaud contributed to the score. A mysterious young man discovers he has a gift for dreaming and begins selling his bizarre visions to needy clients. Strikingly photographed by Arnold Eagle, the various vignettes range from the eccentric and satirical to the dazzling and disturbing, and their visual and psychological impact is mesmerising. DP. Contains nudity, violence.

Jack Bittner *Joe/"Narcissus"* • Dorothy Griffith *Girl* ■ *Dir* Hans Richter • *Scr* Hans Richter, Max Ernst, Fernand Léger, Man Ray, Marcel Duchamp, Alexander Calder

Dreamscape ★★ 15

Science-fiction thriller
1984 · US · Colour · 94mins

Psychic Dennis Quaid enters the American president's guilt-plagued nuclear nightmares to save him from a paranormal assassin in this workmanlike fantasy thriller. The perfectly cast actors fly as high as they can with the intriguing concept, but the script is mediocre and lacks any real excitement. The main pleasure of this efficient piece of film-making comes from the dream sequences that punctuate the political thriller framework. AJ DVD

Dennis Quaid *Alex Gardner* • Max von Sydow *Dr Paul Novotny* • Christopher Plummer *Bob Blair* • Eddie Albert *President* • Kate Capshaw *Dr Jane Devries* • David Patrick Kelly *Tommy Ray Glatman* • George Wendt *Charlie Prince* ■ *Dir* Joseph Ruben • *Scr* Joseph Ruben, David Loughery, Chuck Russell, from a story by David Loughery

Dressed to Kill ★★★★ 18

Thriller 1980 · US · Colour · 100mins

Brian De Palma does his witty Hitchcock imitation again, and adds his own trademark layers of macabre black comedy and visual ingenuity to the *Psycho*-influenced proceedings. After sex-starved housewife Angie Dickinson is murdered with a razor in a lift, her son Keith Gordon and prostitute Nancy Allen (then the director's wife) join forces to track down the killer. An eyebrow-raising performance from Michael Caine keeps this clever shocker moving along nicely, as De Palma's brilliant sleight-of-hand direction pulls out all the suspense stops, providing some unforgettable jolts. AJ. Contains swearing, violence, sex scenes and nudity. DVD

Michael Caine *Dr Robert Elliott* • Angie Dickinson *Kate Miller* • Nancy Allen *Liz Blake* • Keith Gordon *Peter Miller* • Dennis Franz *Detective Marino* • David Margulies *Dr Levy* ■ *Dir/Scr* Brian De Palma • *Editor* Jerry Greenberg • *Music* Pino Donaggio

The Dresser ★★★★ PG

Drama 1983 · UK · Colour · 113mins

The inspiration for Ronald Harwood's play came from his own experiences as Sir Donald Wolfit's dresser in the 1950s. Wolfit was an actor/manager of enormous girth and even greater eccentricity. To play the Wolfit character, Albert Finney also borrowed from Laurence Olivier and Charles Laughton, creating a vivid composite of a man who had "flashes of greatness". Getting Finney into his costumes is Tom Courtenay, giving another splendid performance: small-scale, seedy and obsequious. Both Finney and Courtenay were rightly nominated for Oscars. AT. Contains some swearing. DVD

Albert Finney *Sir* • Tom Courtenay *Norman* • Edward Fox *Oxenby* • Zena Walker *Her Ladyship* • Eileen Atkins *Madge* • Michael Gough *Frank Carrington* • Cathryn Harrison *Irene* • Betty Marsden *Violet Manning* • Sheila Reid *Lydia Gibson* ■ *Dir* Peter Yates • *Scr* Ronald Harwood, from his play

The Dressmaker ★★★★ 15

Second World War drama
1988 · UK · Colour · 91mins

It is 1944, and Joan Plowright defends Merseyside against the Germans. This is an excellent example of what the British do best: honourable thespians acting their utility socks off; an adaptation of a novel by Beryl Bainbridge, written with great skill and flair by the always interesting John McGrath; and lots of moody shots of Liverpool under fire. Courage, fear, repression and sex with GIs are all mixed into this glorious, tautly acted vehicle. It can all seem a trifle claustrophobic at times, but this is a minor quibble in a masterly movie. SH

Joan Plowright *Nellie* • Billie Whitelaw *Margo* • Jane Horrocks *Rita* • Peter Postlethwaite [Pete Postlethwaite] *Jack* • Tim Ransom *Wesley* • Rosemary Martin *Mrs Manders* • Pippa Hinchley *Valerie* • Tony Haygarth *Mr Manders* • Michael James-Reed *Chuck* ■ *Dir* Jim O'Brien • *Scr* John McGrath, from the novel by Beryl Bainbridge

Dreyfus ★★★ U

Historical drama 1931 · UK · BW · 96mins

An extremely worthy British reworking of a notable German success, this makes a deliberate shifting of emphasis, since the Dreyfus case was not only a staggering miscalculation of justice but also a national manifestation of anti-Jewish feeling. The famous case tells of a Jew in the French general staff who is framed for treason and sent to Devil's Island. Later movie versions of the tale – most notably *The Life of Emile Zola* and the under-rated *I Accuse!* – may be more accessible, but there's no doubting this film's sincerity. TS

Cedric Hardwicke *Alfred Dreyfus* • Charles Carson *Col Picquart* • George Merritt *Emile Zola* • Sam Livesey *Labori* • Beatrix Thompson *Lucie Dreyfus* • Garry Marsh *Major Esterhazy* ■ *Dir* FW Kraemer, Milton Rosmer • *Scr* Reginald Berkeley, Walter C Mycroft, from the play *The Dreyfus Case* by Wilhelm Herzog, Hans Rehfisch

The Drifter ★★ 18

Thriller 1988 · US · Colour · 81mins

What at first appears like another spin on the *Play Misty for Me* formula turns into quite a satisfying, low-budget thriller. Kim Delaney stars as a fashion designer whose one-night stand with a mysterious hitch-hiker (Miles O'Keeffe) turns into a nightmare when he won't leave her alone. Director Larry Brand, who also makes an appearance as a cop, does a reasonably effective job within the narrow parameters and Delaney makes a totally believable heroine. RS

Kim Delaney *Julia* • Timothy Bottoms *Arthur* • Al Shannon *Kriger* • Miles O'Keeffe *Trey* • Anna Gray Garduno *Matty* • Loren Haines *Willie Monroe* ■ *Dir/Scr* Larry Brand • *Executive Producer* Roger Corman

Drifting Clouds ★★★★ PG

Romance 1996 · Fin/Ger/Fr · Colour · 92mins

Aki Kaurismäki considers this urban morality tale to be a mix of *Bicycle Thieves* and *It's a Wonderful Life*. Yet the bright colours and ironic soundtrack make it a Helsinki version of *The Umbrellas of Cherbourg*, as waitress Kati Outinen and and her ex-tram driver husband Kari Vaananen unite to overcome the humiliations of poverty and menial employment. Minutely observed, perfectly paced and beautifully underplayed by the director's stock company, this is an affectionate portrait of real people surviving slings and arrows with a decency and determination. DP. In Finnish with English subtitles.

Kati Outinen *Ilona Koponen* • Kari Vaananen *Lauri Koponen* • Elina Salo *Mrs Sjoholm* • Sakari Kuosmanen *Melartin* • Markku Peltola *Lajunen* ■ *Dir/Scr* Aki Kaurismäki

Driftwood ★★★ U

Drama 1946 · US · BW · 84mins

A charmingly bucolic tale about likeable doctor Walter Brennan, who looks after an orphan waif who's never before strayed from the backwoods, winsomely played by nine-year-old Natalie Wood. Though some may feel Wood's performance a tad calculated, she shows all the early glimmerings of that bright shining talent that rightly made her a major star of the 1950s and 1960s. Veteran director Allan Dwan wisely keeps the sentimentality reined in. TS

Ruth Warrick *Susan* • Walter Brennan *Murph* • Dean Jagger *Dr Steve Webster* • Charlotte Greenwood *Mathilda* • Natalie Wood *Jenny* • Margaret Hamilton *Essie Keenan* ■ *Dir* Allan Dwan • *Scr* Mary Loos, Richard Sale

Driftwood ★ 18

Drama 1996 · Ire/UK · Colour · 100mins

Alone on a windswept island, Anne Brochet gets to roll her eyes as the seemingly normal sculptress who helps amnesiac castaway James Spader. Her kindness is gradually replaced by violent hysteria as her new lover threatens to return to civilisation. Spader offers only distracted hesitancy, so the burden of dramatic impetus falls on Brochet, who responds with a display of desperate theatricality. DP DVD

James Spader *The Man* • Anne Brochet *Sarah* • Barry McGovern *McTavish* • Anna Massey *Mother* • Aiden Grenell *Father* • Kevin McHugh *Motorcycle driver* ■ *Dir* Ronan O'Leary • *Scr* Richard MN Waring, Ronan O'Leary

The Driller Killer ★★ 18

Horror 1979 · US · Colour · 94mins

Abel Ferrara's notorious contribution to Do-It-Yourself serial slaying is actually an amateurish, art house affair that hardly deserves the "video nasty" label it received in the early 1980s. A disturbed artist is continually thwarted in his career. Noisy neighbours are his first targets as he enforces his own brand of peace and quiet with his Black and Decker. When it was finally released on video in the UK in 1999, 54 seconds were cut, and some of the more gratuitous scenes of violence were toned down via optical editing. JF. Contains swearing, violence and sex scenes. [subtitles] DVD

Jimmy Laine [Abel Ferrara] *Reno* • Carolyn Marz *Carol* • Baybi Day *Pamela* • Harry Schultz *Dalton Briggs* • Alan Wynroth *Landlord* • Maria Helhoski *Nun* • James O'Hara *Man in church* ■ *Dir* Abel Ferrara • *Scr* Nicholas St John

D

Drive ★★★ 18

Martial arts thriller
1997 · US · Colour · 99mins

Mark Dacascos stars in this outrageously violent martial arts adventure with vaguely sci-fi overtones. Taking unemployed songwriter Kadeem Hardison hostage, superhuman fighter Dacascos goes on the run and fights endless acrobatic villains for no reason whatsoever. Forget the story – it's the endless parade of Jackie Chan-style stunts, hardcore gore and bizarre humour that matter in this turbo-charged *Lethal Weapon* clone. AJ. Contains swearing, violence. [subtitles] DVD

Mark Dacascos *Toby Wong* • Kadeem Hardison *Malik Brody* • John Pyper-Ferguson *Vic Madison* • Brittany Murphy *Deliverance Bodine* • Tracey Walter *Hedgehog* • James Shigeta *Mr Lau* • Masaya Kato *Advanced model* • Dom Magwili *Mr Chow* ■ *Dir* Steve Wang • *Scr* Scott Phillips

Drive a Crooked Road ★★★

Crime drama 1954 · US · BW · 82mins

A prime example of a Hollywood B-melodrama, this was originally shown in the UK as the support to Alec Guinness's *Father Brown*. Director Richard Quine's first thriller, this tautly paced Columbia action tale reminds us of what a talented film-maker he was and how under-rated he is today. The style may be a little drawn-out for contemporary tastes, and star Mickey Rooney's tendency to chew the scenery has not worn well, but Dianne Foster is an attractive foil. TS

Mickey Rooney *Eddie Shannon* • Dianne Foster *Barbara Mathews* • Kevin McCarthy *Steve Norris* • Jack Kelly *Harold Baker* • Harry Landers *Ralph* • Jerry Paris *Phil* • Paul Picerni *Carl* • Dick Crockett *Don* ■ *Dir* Richard Quine • *Scr* Blake Edwards, Richard Quine (adaptation), from a story by James Benson Nablo

Drive, He Said ★★★

Drama 1971 · US · Colour · 90mins

In the mid-1960s Jack Nicholson took a shine to Jeremy Larner's novel, which fused basketball (one of Nicholson's obsessions) with the activities of campus radicals during the escalation of the Vietnam War. Five years later, Nicholson had become a star but realised he couldn't play a basketball star. So he turned director and delivered this funky piece, which has lofty ambitions but never quite comes together. There's a fascinating cast, including Nicholson's friends Robert Towne, Karen Black and Bruce Dern. AT

William Tepper *Hector* • Karen Black *Olive* • Michael Margotta *Gabriel* • Bruce Dern *Bullion* • Robert Towne *Richard* • Henry Jaglom *Conrad* ■ *Dir* Jack Nicholson • *Scr* Jack Nicholson, Jeremy Larner, from the novel by Jeremy Larner

Drive Me Crazy ★★★ 12

Romantic comedy
1999 · US · Colour · 87mins

Made specifically for teenage girls (it stars *Sabrina the Teenage Witch's* Melissa Joan Hart and has a title song by Britney Spears), this is a slight but sweet romantic comedy that doesn't break any new ground yet features some nice performances. Hart plays a high school senior who is looking for a date to take her to the prom. When the school jock directs his attentions elsewhere, she sets her sights on the brooding boy next door (Adrian Grenier), though he needs a major makeover before she'll consider going out with him. JB [subtitles] DVD

Melissa Joan Hart *Nicole Maris* • Adrian Grenier *Chase Hammond* • Stephen Collins *Mr Maris* • Mark Metcalf *Mr Rope* • William Converse-Roberts *Mr Hammond* • Faye Grant *Mrs Maris* • Susan May Pratt *Alicia* • Kris Park *Ray Neeley* ■ *Dir* John Schultz • *Scr* Rob Thomas, from the novel *How I Created My Perfect Dream Date* by Todd Strasser

Driven ★★★ PG

Sports action drama
2001 · US/Can · Colour · 111mins

In an attempt to regain pole position as an action man, Sylvester Stallone not only stars in this monument to racing cars and breakneck effects, but also wears his screenwriter/co-producer cap, too. He plays a veteran race driver who's brought out of retirement by wheelchair-bound buddy Burt Reynolds to help his hotshot protégé Kip Pardue beat German ace Til Schweiger to the world championship. The formulaic tale is directed with minimal imagination by Renny Harlin, but, if high speed chases, races and crashes are your thing, then the director delivers the goods with aplomb. TH [subtitles] DVD

Sylvester Stallone *Joe Tanto* • Burt Reynolds *Carl Henry* • Kip Pardue *Jimmy Bly* • Stacy Edwards *Lucretia "Luc" Jones* • Til Schweiger *Beau Brandenburg* • Gina Gershon *Cathy* ■ *Dir* Renny Harlin • *Scr* Sylvester Stallone, from a story by Sylvester Stallone, Jan Skrentny, Neal Tabachnick

The Driver ★★★★ 15

Crime thriller 1978 · US · Colour · 86mins

The story of a getaway driver who has no life outside his work is pared down to its absolute existential essentials in Walter Hill's terrific thriller. Critics thought that the writer/director was paying tribute to Jean-Pierre Melville's 1967 classic *Le Samouraï*, though he denied he'd ever seen it. But Ryan O'Neal wears the same trenchcoat as Alain Delon; he also has the same cool demeanour and ruthless tunnel vision. The car chases are amazing, but it's O'Neal's calm you remember, together with its unravelling, as Isabelle Adjani and cop Bruce Dern get under his skin. AT [subtitles] DVD

Ryan O'Neal *The Driver* • Bruce Dern *The Detective* • Isabelle Adjani *The Player* • Ronee Blakley *The Connection* • Matt Clark *Red plain-clothes man* • Felice Orlandi *Gold plain-clothes man* • Joseph Walsh *Glasses* • Rudy Ramos *Teeth* ■ *Dir/Scr* Walter Hill

The Driver's Seat ★★ 15

Drama 1975 · It · Colour · 93mins

"It's not sex I want," says Elizabeth Taylor at the outset of this obscure melodrama, "but death." She also says she has used up all her supply of happiness, a line that one of her biographers pounced upon, claiming the movie was deeply personal. It's a doom-laden affair, acted with such seriousness it rates as a camp send-up of Antonioni's meditations on urban alienation. Taylor is simply playing herself as a cultural icon; Andy Warhol makes an appropriately fleeting appearance. AT [subtitles]

Elizabeth Taylor *Lise* • Ian Bannen *Richard* • Guido Mannari *Carlo* • Mona Washbourne *Mrs Fiedke* • Maxence Mailfort *Bill* • Andy Warhol ■ *Dir* Giuseppe Patroni-Griffi • *Scr* Raffaele La Capria, Giuseppe Patroni-Griffi, from the novel by Muriel Spark

Driving Force ★★ 15

Science-fiction adventure
1988 · Aus · Colour · 90mins

Wouldn't it be nice, just once, if, after an apocalyptic nuclear disaster, the Earth was ruled by ruthless, neatly dressed accountants and clerks rather than the leather-clad bikers who inevitably run riot? This is another substandard excursion into *Mad Max* territory, with Sam Jones as the moody hero fighting off the bad guys led by fellow straight-to-video star Don Swayze (Patrick's brother). The requisite explosions are loud but staged with little originality or flair. JF. Contains violence, swearing and nudity. [subtitles]

Sam Jones • Catherine Bach • Angel Cook • Don Swayze ■ *Dir* Andrew Prowse • *Scr* Patrick Edgeworth

Driving Me Crazy ★★ PG

Comedy 1991 · US · Colour · 103mins

Released in the States as *Dutch*, this was the first sign that teenpic wunderkind John Hughes was beginning to run out of ideas. This story of a sulky kid travelling through America for Thanksgiving in the company of his mother's beau may well strike you as familiar – think *Planes, Trains and Automobiles*, also penned by Hughes. Long on contrivance and short on comedy, this film will soon drive you crazy, too. DP. Contains swearing. [subtitles]

Ed O'Neill *Dutch Dooley* • Ethan Randall [Ethan Embry] *Doyle Standish* • JoBeth Williams *Natalie Standish* • Ari Meyers *Brock* • Christopher McDonald *Reed Standish* • EG Daily [Elizabeth Daily] *Halley* ■ *Dir* Peter Faiman • *Scr* John Hughes

Driving Miss Daisy ★★★★ U

Drama 1989 · US · Colour · 94mins

This small, unassuming movie went up against the big guns of Hollywood and emerged with a best picture Oscar. It charts the deepening relationship between an elderly widow and her black chauffeur in Atlanta. Miss Daisy (Oscar-winner Jessica Tandy) is an independent former schoolteacher with a will of iron, until she crashes her new car and cannot get insurance on another. So her son (Dan Aykroyd) arranges a chauffeur (Morgan Freeman). The story covers the years from 1948 until 1973 – a period of racial strife and the civil rights movement – attaining the status of allegory in the process. AT [subtitles] DVD

Jessica Tandy *Miss Daisy Werthan* • Morgan Freeman *Hoke Colburn* • Dan Aykroyd *Boolie Werthan* • Patti LuPone *Florine Werthan* • Esther Rolle *Idella* • Joann Havrilla *Miss McClatchey* • William Hall Jr *Oscar* • Alvin M Sugarman *Dr Weil* ■ *Dir* Bruce Beresford • *Scr* Alfred Uhry, from his play

Drôle de Drame ★★★★

Period black comedy
1937 · Fr · BW · 109mins

Set in Edwardian London, this witty and anarchic farce was the second of director Marcel Carné's seven collaborations with screenwriter Jacques Prévert; they went on to make the classic *Les Enfants du Paradis* in 1945. Played to perfection by a superb cast, the film involves a mystery writer (Michel Simon) accused by a visiting bishop (Louis Jouvet) of murdering his wife (Françoise Rosay). Jean-Louis Barrault appears as an animal-lover who kills butchers. RB. In French with English subtitles.

Louis Jouvet *Archibald Soper, Bishop of Bedford* • Françoise Rosay *Margaret Molyneux* • Michel Simon *Irwin Molyneux/Félix Chapel* • Jean-Louis Barrault *William Kramps* • Jean-Pierre Aumont *Billy* • Nadine Vogel *Eva* • Pierre Alcover *Inspector Bray* • Henri Guisol *Buffington* • Jean Marais *Fatigued reveller* ■ *Dir* Marcel Carné • *Scr* Jacques Prévert, from the novel *His First Offence* by J Storer-Clouston

Drôle de Félix ★★★ 15

Road movie 2000 · Fr · Colour · 91mins

Writer/directors Olivier Ducastel and Jacques Martineau explore the nature of kinship and modern French attitudes to race and sexuality in this ambling road movie. Travelling from Dieppe to Marseille to meet the father he never knew, Sami Bouajila encounters anti-Arab prejudice and homophobic ignorance at every turn. But he also finds acceptance among diverse members of his wider "family", including a randy railway worker, a world-weary fisherman, a vibrantly rebellious "grandmother" (a scene-stealing turn from Patachou) and an independent-minded "sister" (the ever-feisty Ariane Ascaride). Wry and touching. DP. In French with English subtitles. [subtitles] DVD

Sami Bouajila *Félix* • Patachou *Mathilde* • Ariane Ascaride *Isabelle* • Pierre-Loup Rajot *Daniel* • Charly Sergue *Jules* • Maurice Bénichou *Fisherman* ■ *Dir/Scr* Olivier Ducastel, Jacques Martineau

Drop Dead Darling ★★★

Comedy 1966 · UK · Colour · 100mins

British director Ken Hughes is an unsung British talent, responsible for, among other films, *The Trials of Oscar Wilde* and *Chitty Chitty Bang Bang*. This handsome Shepperton-shot farce, released in the USA as *Arrivederci, Baby!*, offers a bravura role to the terrific Tony Curtis, as a charming Bluebeard, and some plum lines and opportunities for grimacing to the irascible Lionel Jeffries. Tastelessness abounds, but for once it's deliberate, and the Panavision and Technicolor photography is extremely glossy. TS

Tony Curtis *Nick Johnson* • Zsa Zsa Gabor *Gigi* • Rosanna Schiaffino *Francesca* • Lionel Jeffries *Parker* • Nancy Kwan *Baby* • Fenella Fielding *Fenella* • Anna Quayle *Aunt Miriam* • Warren Mitchell *Count de Rienzi/Maximilian* • Mischa Auer *Romeo* ■ *Dir* Ken Hughes • *Scr* Ken Hughes, from a story by Ken Hughes, Ronald Harwood, suggested by the novel *The Careful Man* by Richard Deming • *Cinematographer* Denys Coup

Drop Dead Fred ★★ 15

Fantasy comedy 1991 · US · Colour · 94mins

A high-energy performance by Rik Mayall in the title role is the chief interest in this largely uninteresting and unfunny comedy. It's the story of a grown woman (Phoebe Cates) who is revisited by the imaginary friend of her childhood (Mayall), on a mission to cheer her up at a bad time. A nice idea falls between all available stools and ends up as a mess on the floor. PF. Contains swearing. [subtitles] DVD

Phoebe Cates *Elizabeth Cronin* • Rik Mayall *Drop Dead Fred* • Marsha Mason *Polly* • Tim Matheson *Charles Cronin* • Bridget Fonda *Annabella* • Carrie Fisher *Janie* • Keith Charles *Murray* • Ashley Peldon *Young Elizabeth* • Daniel Gerroll *Nigel* ■ *Dir* Ate De Jong • *Scr* Carlos Davis, Anthony Fingleton, from a story by Elizabeth Livingston

Drop Dead Gorgeous ★★★ 15

Black comedy 1999 · US · Colour · 93mins

A sophisticated black comedy in mockumentary style, this traces a small-town beauty pageant from the auditions to the glitz and glamour of the finals. Kirsten Dunst, a sweet girl from a trailer-trash background, is pitted against spoilt little rich bitch Denise Richards. Meanwhile, someone in town is knocking off their competition. Ellen Barkin and Kirstie Alley are both entertaining as the girls' cat-fighting moms, and overall this is a refreshing and ironic take on suburban American life. Better than your average Hollywood fare. LH. Contains swearing and sexual references. [VIDEO] DVD

Kirstie Alley *Gladys Leeman* • Ellen Barkin *Annette Atkins* • Kirsten Dunst *Amber Atkins* • Denise Richards *Becky Leeman* • Allison Janney *Loretta* • Will Sasso *Hank Vilmes* • Mindy Sterling *Iris Clark* • Sam McMurray *Lester Leeman* • Adam West ■ *Dir* Michael Patrick Jann • *Scr* Lona Williams

DROP Squad ★★ 15

Satirical drama 1994 · US · Colour · 83mins

"DROP" stands for "Deprogramming and Restoration of Pride", and is the name of a group that attempts to persuade African-Americans that they have "sold out" their culture. The tone of this drama from Spike Lee's production company is a tad strident, as advertising executive Eriq La Salle proves a tough nut for the group to crack. Not as balanced as it should be, given the controversial subject matter, but well performed. JF [VIDEO]

Eriq La Salle *Bruford Jamison Jr* • Vondie Curtis-Hall *Rocky* • Ving Rhames *Garvey* • Leonard Thomas *XB* • Michael Ralph *Trevor* • Billy Williams *Huey* • Eric A Payne [Eric Payne] *Stokeley* • Vanessa Williams *Mali* ■ *Dir* David Johnson • *Scr* David Johnson, Butch Robinson, David Taylor from the short film *The Session* by David Taylor

Drop Zone ★★★ 15

Thriller 1994 · US · Colour · 101mins

You go for years without seeing a movie about skydiving and then suddenly, like buses, two of them come along at the same time – this and the Charlie Sheen vehicle *Terminal Velocity*. This is the pick of the pair: an exhilarating ride, directed by action specialist John Badham with his usual flair and eye for spectacular set pieces. Wesley Snipes exudes charisma as the US marshal who sets out to hunt down the parachuting crooks. Gary Busey delivers another entertainingly villainous performance, while Yancy Butler is equally good as Snipes's reluctant partner. JF. Contains swearing, violence. [VIDEO] DVD

Wesley Snipes *Pete Nessip* • Gary Busey *Ty Moncrief* • Yancy Butler *Jessie Crossman* • Michael Jeter *Earl Leedy* • Corin Nemec *Selkirk* • Kyle Secor *Swoop* • Luca Bercovici *Jagger* • Malcolm-Jamal Warner *Terry Nessip* ■ *Dir* John Badham • *Scr* Peter Barsocchini, John Bishop, from a story by Tony Griffin

Drowning by Numbers ★★★★ 18

Black comedy drama
1988 · UK · Colour · 113mins

In one of writer/director Peter Greenaway's darkest comedies, three generations of womenfolk, all named Cissie Colpitts, drown their menfolk with the acquiescence of local coroner Bernard Hill. Joan Plowright, Juliet Stevenson and Joely Richardson are delightfully lethal as the scheming trio, while Greenaway indulges his obsessions with word games, lists and the ache of mortality. Michael Nyman's score builds momentum, even though there isn't any, and it's luminous and lurid in equal measure. TH [VIDEO]

Bernard Hill *Madgett* • Joan Plowright *Cissie Colpitts 1* • Juliet Stevenson *Cissie Colpitts 2* • Joely Richardson *Cissie Colpitts 3* • Jason Edwards *Smut* • Bryan Pringle *Jake* • Trevor Cooper *Hardy* • David Morrissey *Bellamy* ■ *Dir/Scr* Peter Greenaway

Drowning Mona ★★ 12

Black comedy 2000 · US · Colour · 92mins

This lame comedy starts out in a promising fashion by having Bette Midler killed during the opening credits. Alas, it quickly goes downhill. Police chief Danny DeVito is dealing with a much bigger mystery than discovering who offed Midler, the most hated resident of Verplanck, NY: he has to find someone who *didn't* want her dead. Nick Gomez's movie desperately wants to be a quirky black farce, but ends up more like an episode of *White Trash Family Feud*. You want to be amused by these characters, but they're just too stupid to be funny. ST [VIDEO] DVD

Danny DeVito *Chief Wyatt Rash* • Bette Midler *Mona Dearly* • Neve Campbell *Ellen Rash* • Jamie Lee Curtis *Rona Mace* • Casey Affleck *Bobby Calzone* • William Fichtner *Phil Dearly* • Will Ferrell *Cubby* ■ *Dir* Nick Gomez • *Scr* Peter Steinfeld

The Drowning Pool ★★★ 12

Mystery thriller 1975 · US · Colour · 103mins

Paul Newman's second outing (after 1966's *Harper*) as novelist Ross MacDonald's private detective Lew Harper sees him plunging into a swamp of Deep South greed and murder when he's called to oil baroness Joanne Woodward's bayou home to investigate a blackmail plot. The title refers to a hydrotherapy bath in an abandoned mental home, which is typical of the oddball eccentricity of the film and its characters. It's a pity that Stuart Rosenberg's direction is so straightforward because the impenetrable plot needs a more bizarre approach to keep us interested. TH [VIDEO]

Paul Newman *Lew Harper* • Joanne Woodward *Iris Devereaux* • Anthony Franciosa *Chief Broussard* • Murray Hamilton *JJ Kilbourne* • Gail Strickland *Mavis Kilbourne* • Melanie Griffith *Schuyler Devereaux* • Linda Haynes *Gretchen* • Richard Jaeckel *Lieutenant Franks* ■ *Dir* Stuart Rosenberg • *Scr* Tracy Keenan Wynn, Lorenzo Semple Jr, Walter Hill, from the novel by Ross MacDonald

Drugstore Cowboy ★★★★ 18

Drama 1989 · US · Colour · 97mins

This provocative drama set in early 1970s Oregon looks at the sordid life of four junkies who rob pharmacies to support their habits. Director Gus Van Sant brings an extraordinary visual style to this credible, non-judgemental portrayal of addiction, which is based on an unpublished semi-autobiographical novel by prisoner James Fogle. Matt Dillon gives a compelling performance and *The Naked Lunch* author William S Burroughs appears in a cameo as a priest turned dope fiend. There's a good oldies soundtrack, too. AJ. Contains violence, swearing, drug abuse. [VIDEO] DVD

Matt Dillon *Bob Hughes* • Kelly Lynch *Dianne Hughes* • James Remar *Gentry* • James LeGros *Rick* • Heather Graham *Nadine* • Beah Richards *Drug counsellor* • Grace Zabriskie *Bob's mother* • Max Perlich *David* • William S Burroughs *Tom the Priest* • Eric Hull *Druggist* ■ *Dir* Gus Van Sant • *Scr* Gus Van Sant, Daniel Yost, from a novel by James Fogle

Druids ★ 12

Period epic
2001 · Fr/Can/Bel · Colour · 109mins

It is 60 BC, ancient France, a time of alarming fright wigs and even dodgier accents. Well, at least that's the case in this hilariously bad historical epic, which finds proud Gallic tribal leader Christopher Lambert trying to unite his squabbling countrymen against the devious Julius Caesar (a spectacularly miscast Klaus Maria Brandauer). Director Jacques Dorfmann stages the battle scenes with an astounding lack of inspiration. JF [VIDEO]

Christophe Lambert [Christopher Lambert] *Vercingétorix* • Klaus Maria Brandauer *Caesar* • Max von Sydow *Guttuart* • Inés Sastre *Epona* • Bernard-Pierre Donnadieu *Dumnorix* ■ *Dir* Jacques Dorfmann • *Scr* Rospo Pallenberg, Norman Spinrad, Jacques Dorfmann, from a story by Anne de Leuselec, Jacques Dorfmann

The Drum ★★★★ U

Adventure 1938 · UK · Colour · 89mins

AEW Mason, author of *The Four Feathers*, wrote this story especially for producer Alexander Korda as a vehicle for the talented 14-year-old star of *Elephant Boy*, Sabu. The youngster delivers a truly beguiling performance as Prince Azim, forced from his inheritance by his uncle, the swinish villain Raymond Massey. It's ravishingly photographed in three-strip Technicolor. This is a stirring reminder of what British cinema was once about: telling a tale of the courageous struggle between right and wrong with an unerring sense of patriotism. TS [VIDEO]

Sabu *Prince Azim* • Raymond Massey *Prince Ghul* • Valerie Hobson *Mrs Carruthers* • Roger Livesey *Captain Carruthers* • Desmond Tester *Bill Holder* • Martin Walker *Herrick* • David Tree *Lieutenant Escott* • Francis L Sullivan *Governor* ■ *Dir* Zoltan Korda • *Scr* Arthur Wimperis, Patric Kirwan, Hugh Gray, Lajos Biró (adaptation), from the novel by AEW Mason

Drum ★ 18

Drama 1976 · US · Colour · 99mins

While *Mandingo* walked the tightrope between exploitation and gothic melodrama, this wretched sequel has no pretensions at all. It's a real cheapo, with Warren Oates as a slave breeder and Yaphet Kotto as one of his purchases. Things get seriously bogged down in a plot about interbreeding, before Kotto turns into Spartacus and instigates a very bloody slave revolt. AT [VIDEO]

Warren Oates *Hammond Maxwell* • Ken Norton *Drum* • Isela Vega *Marianna* • Pam Grier *Regine* • Yaphet Kotto *Blaise* • John Colicos *DeMarigny* • Fiona Lewis *Augusta Chauvet* ■ *Dir* Steve Carver • *Scr* Norman Wexler, from the novel by Kyle Onstott

Drum Beat ★★★ U

Western 1954 · US · Colour · 107mins

Alan Ladd brings an end to the Indian Wars in this fact-based western, which gave Charles Bronson his first starring role. Writer/director Delmer Daves toiled away in the public record office in order to be as impartial as possible in his account of the 1869 Modoc uprising. The script has an intelligence that matches his earlier *Broken Arrow*, one of the first Hollywood features to see the Wild West from the native American perspective. J Peverell Marley's views of the Oregon/California landscape are stunning. DP

Alan Ladd *Johnny MacKay* • Charles Bronson *Captain Jack* • Audrey Dalton *Nancy Meek* • Marisa Pavan *Toby* • Robert Keith (1) *Bill Satterwhite* • Rodolfo Acosta *Scarface Charlie* • Warner Anderson *General Canby* • Elisha Cook Jr *Crackel* ■ *Dir/Scr* Delmer Daves

Drumline ★★ PG

Musical drama 2002 · US · Colour · 113mins

The clichés are reeled out with depressingly rhythmic precision in this lame remix of *Fame* and *Bring It On*. Nick Cannon is the rebellious but intuitively brilliant drummer who shakes up a starchy college marching band that is battling to unseat the flashy reigning champions. The best bits are the admittedly brilliantly choreographed musical set pieces, but the non-musical antics will leave most just brassed off. JF [VIDEO] DVD

Nick Cannon *Devon Miles* • Zoë Saldana *Laila* • Orlando Jones *Dr Lee* • Leonard Roberts *Sean Taylor* • G Q *Jayson* • Jason Weaver *Ernest* • Earl C Poitier *Charles* • Candace Carey *Diedre* ■ *Dir* Charles Stone III • *Scr* Tina Gordon Chism, Shawn Schepps, from a story by Shawn Schepps

Drums across the River ★★ PG

Western 1954 · US · Colour · 74mins

This very average Audie Murphy western is somewhat redeemed by nice 1950s Technicolor and a very short running time. The plot – about how deceitful whites stole gold from the native Americans – deserves a better treatment, but the baby-faced Murphy, a former war hero, makes a sympathetic leading man. Among the support, Hugh O'Brian shows signs of star quality. TS [VIDEO]

Audie Murphy *Gary Brannon* • Lisa Gaye *Jennie Marlowe* • Lyle Bettger *Frank Walker* • Walter Brennan *Sam Brannon* • Mara Corday *Sue* • Hugh O'Brian *Morgan* • Jay Silverheels *Taos* • Regis Toomey *Sheriff Beal* ■ *Dir* Nathan Juran • *Scr* John K Butler, Lawrence Roman, from a story by John K Butler

Drums along the Mohawk ★★★★ PG

Western 1939 · US · Colour · 99mins

One of the most beautiful and distinguished achievements of early colour, this fine movie tends to be overlooked among the other highlights of 1939, Hollywood's *annus mirabilis*. This is effectively a pre-western, dealing with Indian raids against the early settlers during the American War of Independence. It contains a rather disturbing anti-British bias, not for the first time from ace director John Ford. Taken as a romantic action adventure, though, it rattles along. Claudette Colbert is a little too well groomed for the frontier, but Henry Fonda seems perfectly at home. TS DVD

Claudette Colbert *Lana "Magdelana" Martin* • Henry Fonda *Gilbert Martin* • Edna May Oliver *Mrs Sarah McKlennar* • Eddie Collins *Christian Reall* • John Carradine *Caldwell* • Dorris Bowdon *Mary Reall* • Jessie Ralph *Mrs Weaver* ■ *Dir* John Ford • *Scr* Lamar Trotti, Sonya Levien, from a novel by Walter D Edmonds • *Cinematographer* Bert Glennon, Ray Rennahan • *Art Director* Richard Day, Mark-Lee Kirk

Drunken Angel ★★★★ PG

Drama 1948 · Jpn · BW · 93mins

This is notable as the first major screen appearance of Toshiro Mifune, whom director Akira Kurosawa would cast in virtually every one of his subsequent films. Later films such as *Rashomon* and *The Seven Samurai* made Mifune a star, but in this early work he plays a volatile gangster who has a bullet removed by a drunken doctor. When the doctor, played by another Kurosawa favourite, Takashi Shimura, also discovers that Mifune is suffering from tuberculosis, he is inexorably drawn into his patient's underworld of crime and violence. Part realist drama, part gangster movie, this is a gripping story that also casts an observant eye over the evolving postwar Japanese society. AT. In Japanese with English subtitles. [VIDEO]

Toshiro Mifune *Matsunaga* • Takashi Shimura *Dr Sanada* • Reisaburo Yamamoto *Okada* • Michiyo Kogure *Nanse* • Chiefko Nakakita *Miyo* • Noriko Sengoku *Gin* • Choko Lida *Old Maid Servant* ■ *Dir* Akira Kurosawa • *Scr* Keinosuke Uegusa, Akira Kurosawa

Drunken Master ★★★★ 15

Martial arts action comedy
1978 · HK · Colour · 106mins

This was the film that saw Jackie Chan crowned as the clown prince of kung fu. As the legendary folk hero, Wong Fei-Hung, who is forced to suffer the humiliations of uncle Yuen Hsiao Tian's pitiless training programme, Chan frequently reveals why he's so often acclaimed as Hong Kong's answer to Buster Keaton. But not everything is as gloriously knockabout as the final fight with the eight

D

immortals, with the roadside encounter with assassin Huang Cheng Li being particularly brutal. Two sequels were released in 1994. DP. A Cantonese language film. DVD

Jackie Chan *Wong Fei-Hung* • Yuen Hsiao Tian [Simon Yuen] *Sam Seed* • Huang Cheng Li [Hwang Jang Lee] *Thunderfoot* • Michelle Yeoh ■ *Dir* Yuen Woo-Ping • *Scr* Hsiao Lung, Ng See Yuen

Dry Cleaning ★★

Black comedy 1997 · Fr/Sp · Colour · 97mins

Unsure whether to be a comedy of sexual manners or a bawdy farce, this study of the repressed desires that simmer beneath even the most respectable bourgeois exteriors ends up more amusing than outrageous. Miou-Miou and Charles Berling give sporting performances as the staid marrieds whose fascination with bisexual drag artist Stanislas Merhar prompts them to offer him a job in their dry-cleaning shop. Contrived. DP. A French language film.

Miou-Miou *Nicole Kunstler* • Charles Berling *Jean-Marie Kunstler* • Stanislas Merhar *Loic* • Mathilde Seigner *Marylin* • Nanou Meister *Yvette* • Noe Pflieger *Pierre* • Michel Bompoil *Robert* • Christopher King *Steve* ■ *Dir* Anne Fontaine • *Scr* Gilles Taurand, Anne Fontaine

Dry Rot ★★ U

Comedy 1956 · UK · BW · 85mins

Maurice Elvey was one of the longest-serving of all British directors, claiming to have shot over 300 films. This was his penultimate picture and, in keeping with many of the comedies that occupied his twilight years, it's not very good. This tale of crooked bookies plods along more slowly than a doped horse. Thankfully, those expert *farceurs* Ronald Shiner, Brian Rix and Sid James give polished performances. DP

Ronald Shiner *Alf Tubbs* • Brian Rix *Fred Phipps* • Peggy Mount *Sgt Fire* • Lee Patterson *Danby* • Sidney James *Flash Harry* • Christian Duvaleix *Polignac* • Joan Sims *Beth* • Heather Sears *Susan* ■ *Dir* Maurice Elvey • *Scr* John Chapman, from his play

A Dry White Season ★★★ 15

Drama 1989 · US · Colour · 102mins

This worthy drama sees Marlon Brando deliver one of his most passionate performances in a long time, even if it is in a supporting role. Donald Sutherland stars as the ordinary white South African who is awakened to the injustices of the repressive apartheid regime; Brando is the liberal lawyer who helps him challenge the establishment. Aided by a star-studded support cast, director Euzhan Palcy succeeds in producing a compelling and disturbing portrait of the brutality in pre-Mandela South Africa. JF. Contains violence and swearing.

Donald Sutherland *Ben du Toit* • Janet Suzman *Susan du Toit* • Zakes Mokae *Stanley Makhaya* • Jürgen Prochnow *Captain Stolz* • Susan Sarandon *Melanie Bruwer* • Marlon Brando *Ian McKenzie* • Winston Ntshona *Gordon Ngubene* • Thoko Ntshinga *Emily* ■ *Dir* Euzhan Palcy • *Scr* Euzhan Palcy, Colin Welland, from the novel by André Brink

DuBarry Was a Lady ★★★

Musical comedy 1943 · US · Colour · 96mins

Cole Porter's risqué musical play was a hit on Broadway in 1939, but arrived on the screen four years later as a bowdlerised Red Skelton/Lucille Ball vehicle. Lucy, MGM's resident chirpy redhead, never looked lovelier than here, and newcomer Gene Kelly learned from this film never to look down at his feet again while dancing. It's an amiable romp, officially credited to director Roy Del Ruth, though the choreography is by Charles Walters, who began a distinguished career with this movie. TS

Lucille Ball *May Daly/Madame DuBarry* • Red Skelton *Louis Blore/King Louis* • Gene Kelly *Alec Howe/Black Arrow* • Douglass Dumbrille *Willie/Duc De Rigor* • Rags Ragland *Charlie/Dauphin* • Donald Meek *Mr Jones/Duc De Choiseul* • George Givot *Cheezy/De Roqueford* • Zero Mostel *Rami the Swami/Cagliostro* ■ *Dir* Roy Del Ruth • *Scr* Irving Brecher, Nancy Hamilton, Wilkie Mahoney, Albert Mannheimer, Jack McGowan, Charles Sherman, Mary C McCall, from a play by BG De Sylva, Herbert Fields • *Music* Cole Porter

Dublin Nightmare ★★ U

Murder mystery 1958 · UK · BW · 63mins

A Canadian photographer in Dublin discovers that his "dead" wartime friend is really an IRA leader. Sounds familiar? It should: this is a totally shameless B-movie rip-off of *The Third Man*, with Dublin substituted for Vienna and the IRA taking the place of penicillin. William Sylvester and Marla Landi are perfectly adequate stand-ins for Joseph Cotten and Alida Valli. TS

William Sylvester *John Kevin* • Marla Landi *Anna* • Richard Leech *Steven Lawlor* • William Sherwood *Edward Dillon* • Harry Hutchinson *"Vulture"* • Helen Lindsay *Mary O'Callaghan* • Jack Cunningham *Inspector O'Connor* ■ *Dir* John Pomeroy • *Scr* John Tully

The Duchess and the Dirtwater Fox ★★ PG

Comedy western 1976 · US · Colour · 99mins

George Segal and Goldie Hawn co-star as a gambler and a dance hall girl thrown together in adversity who pull off a few judicious scams. They fight, they make up, they swindle each other, he tells an awful lot of old Jewish jokes and we laugh – but not for long. Segal often seems to think that all he has to do is stand around and wink at the camera a few times and that will suffice. Hawn, meanwhile, remains an over-rated actress for some, and this movie will do nothing to change their opinion. SH

George Segal *Charlie Malloy* • Goldie Hawn *Amanda Quaid* • Conrad Janis *Gladstone* • Thayer David *Widdicombe* • Jennifer Lee (1) *Trollop* • Roy Jenson *Bloodworth* • Pat Ast *Dance hall girl* • Sid Gould *Rabbi* ■ *Dir* Melvin Frank • *Scr* Barry Sandler, Jack Rose, Melvin Frank, from a story by Barry Sandler

Duck Dodgers in the 24½ Century ★★★★★

Animated science-fiction comedy
1953 · US · Colour · 7mins

One of Chuck Jones's best-remembered cartoons, this sci-fi spoof has Daffy Duck, in the guise of space explorer Duck Dodgers, sent to Planet X in search of Illudium Phosdex, the shaving cream atom. With "eager young space cadet" Porky Pig, Dodgers does battle with an effeminate alien (christened Marvin Martian in 1979's *The Bugs Bunny/Road Runner Movie*) that results in the destruction of the planet for which they are fighting (a serious point made lightly, as usual, by Jones). This was one of a brilliant series of shorts in which Jones placed Daffy's inflated ego in various postmodernist, generic surroundings, yet it has become the most famous, probably thanks to the timelessness of its targets, the purity of its humour and the witty designs of layout artist Maurice Noble. CLP

Mel Blanc *Daffy Duck/Porky Pig/Marvin Martian* ■ *Dir* Chuck Jones • *Scr* Michael Maltese

Duck Season ★★★ 15

Comedy 2004 · Mex · BW · 83mins

Rarely has boredom been so engagingly presented on screen as in this Mexican comedy. Adolescent friends Diego Cataño and Daniel Miranda are home alone and set for a perfect Sunday until impoverished pizza delivery man Enrique Arreola arrives – 11 seconds late so they refuse to pay him – and won't leave the high-rise apartment without his money. Director Fernando Eimbcke never forces the issues and subtly laces the standoff with moments of wry wit and touching humanity. DP. In Spanish with English subtitles. Contains swearing and some drug abuse. DVD

Enrique Arreola *Ulises* • Diego Cataño *Moko* • Daniel Miranda *Flama* • Danny Perea *Rita* ■ *Dir* Fernando Eimbcke • *Scr* Fernando Eimbcke, Paula Markovitch, Felipe Cazals

Duck Soup ★★★★★ U

Comedy 1933 · US · BW · 65mins

The Marx Brothers reached peaks of anarchic brilliance in this comedy masterpiece, which burst upon audiences four years after their primitive feature debut in *The Cocoanuts*. Groucho, Chico, Harpo and the uncharismatic Zeppo are all entangled in a runaway satire that finds Groucho as a Ruritanian leader going to war because he's paid a month's advance rent on the battlefield. What helps make this the funniest Marx Brothers' film – besides the absence of the romantic interludes which dogged later outings – are the exchanges between Groucho and Margaret Dumont, plus a stunningly surreal mirror sequence. Classic quips, classy delivery. TH DVD

Groucho Marx *Rufus T Firefly* • Harpo Marx *Pinky* • Chico Marx *Chicolini* • Zeppo Marx *Bob Roland* • Margaret Dumont *Mrs Gloria Teasdale* • Raquel Torres *Vera Marcal* • Louis Calhern *Ambassador Trentino of Sylvania* • Edmund Breese *Zander* • Leonid Kinskey *Agitator* • Charles B Middleton [Charles Middleton] *Prosecutor* ■ *Dir* Leo McCarey • *Scr* Burt Kalmar, Harry Ruby, Arthur Sheekman, Nat Perrin

Duck Tales: the Movie – Treasure of the Lost Lamp ★★★ U

Animated adventure
1990 · US · Colour · 70mins

Scrooge McDuck and the ever-troublesome Huey, Dewey and Louie go in search of a genie's lamp before it falls into the evil clutches of Merlock in this Disney animated adventure with an *Indiana Jones* twist. Alan Young (who once chatted to Mr Ed, the talking horse) voices Uncle Scrooge, while Christopher Lloyd brings some menace to the villain. It all feels a touch rough-and-ready, but younger children will lap it up. DP DVD

Alan Young *Scrooge McDuck* • Terence McGovern [Terry McGovern] *Launchpad McQuack* • Russi Taylor *Huey/Dewey/Louie/Webby* • Richard Libertini *Dijon* • Christopher Lloyd *Merlock* • June Foray *Mrs Featherby* • Chuck McCann *Duckworth* ■ *Dir* Bob Hathcock • *Scr* Alan Burnett

Dude, Where's My Car? ★ 15

Comedy 2000 · US · Colour · 79mins

The daft title is the most amusing thing about this embarrassing, laugh-free exercise in teen idiocy. Seann William Scott and Ashton Kutcher are the pot-smoking dumb chums, who awaken from a night of hedonism to discover Kutcher's car is missing and re-trace their movements. A witless, pointless shambles. JC. Contains swearing. DVD

Ashton Kutcher *Jesse* • Seann William Scott *Chester* • Kristy Swanson *Christie Boner* • Jennifer Garner *Wanda* • Marla Sokoloff *Wilma* • David Herman *Nelson* ■ *Dir* Danny Leiner • *Scr* Philip Stark

Dudes ★★★ 15

Comedy 1987 · US · Colour · 86mins

Penelope Spheeris made her name chronicling the punk scene, but is now better known for mainstream comedies such as *Wayne's World*. Here, Jon Cryer and Daniel Roebuck play New York punks hunting the renegade biker gang, led by Lee Ving, who murdered their buddy Flea (later to find fame as a member of the Red Hot Chili Peppers). The western elements are clumsily crafted on to the tale, but it's still an enjoyably offbeat ride. JF

Jon Cryer *Grant* • Daniel Roebuck *Biscuit* • Flea *Milo* • Lee Ving *Missoula* • Billy Ray Sharkey *Blix* • Glenn Withrow *Wes* • Michael Melvin *Logan* • Axxel G Reese *Red* ■ *Dir* Penelope Spheeris • *Scr* Randall Jahnson

Dudley Do-Right ★★ PG

Comedy 1999 · US · Colour · 73mins

Brendan Fraser, who scored a surprise hit in 1997 with *George of the Jungle*, brings another of Jay Ward's cartoon favourites to life, though with considerably less success. Director Hugh Wilson seems to be aiming for an affectionate live-action tribute to the likeably dumb Mountie of the title (Fraser) as he does battle with his nemesis, Snidely Whiplash (Alfred Molina). The actors enthusiastically enter into the spirit of tomfoolery, but there's far too much reliance on slapdash slapstick. JF DVD

Brendan Fraser *Dudley Do-Right* • Sarah Jessica Parker *Nell Fenwick* • Alfred Molina *Snidely Whiplash* • Alex Rocco *The Chief* • Eric Idle *The Prospector* • Robert Prosky *Inspector Fenwick* ■ *Dir* Hugh Wilson • *Scr* Hugh Wilson, from characters created by Jay Ward

Duel ★★★★★ PG

Thriller 1971 · US · Colour · 85mins

Made for TV by a 20-something Steven Spielberg, this thriller proved such a hit that it enjoyed a theatrical release in Europe and launched the young director's career in movies. The pitch is simplicity itself: businessman Dennis Weaver in his red Plymouth Valiant is terrorised by an anonymously-driven truck on a stretch of Californian desert highway. There's barely any dialogue – it's all palm-moistening, tyre-squealing action – but once you've seen it, you'll never forget it. It works as a parable about urban paranoia or as a rollercoaster thriller that never lets up. The truck itself prefigures Spielberg's shark in *Jaws* as a marauding screen monster with a personality of its own. AC DVD

Dennis Weaver *David Mann* • Jacqueline Scott *Mrs Mann* • Eddie Firestone *Cafe owner* • Lou Frizzell *Bus driver* • Gene Dynarski *Man in cafe* • Lucille Benson *Lady at Snakarama* ■ *Dir* Steven Spielberg • *Scr* Richard Matheson, from his story

The Duel ★★★ 12A

War drama 2004 · Iran · Colour · 133mins

This fast-moving Iranian combat tale will surprise those who may be expecting the usual social realist output associated with the region. Among the most expensive movies ever made in the country, writer/director Ahmadreza Darvish's film is set during the days of the Iran-Iraq War and ably conveys the chaos of the conflict. He also keeps us guessing as to the contents of a safe that Pejman Bazeghi is detailed to recover – a mission that culminates in the soldier serving 20 years for treason. DP. In Farsi with English subtitles.

Saeed Rad *Eskandar* • Pejman Bazeghi *Zeynal* • Kambiz Dirbaz *Yahya* • Anooshirvan Arjmand *Latif* • Parvis Parastoee *Yusef* • Abolfazl Shah Karam *Mansur* • Parivash Nazarieh *Salimeh* ■ *Dir/Scr* Ahmadreza Darvish

Duel at Diablo ★★★ 15

Western 1966 · US · Colour · 100mins

Co-producer/director Ralph Nelson's well-intentioned attempt to liberalise the western explores racist themes using an international cast. Unfortunately, it doesn't quite succeed, partly because the eclectic casting gets in the way of the authenticity. There is plenty of action, however, and a considerable amount of violence, as a cavalry troop escorting a wagon train of explosives out west is beset by Indians and riven by internal racial conflict. Sidney Poitier looks ill at ease, but a grim and quietly snarling James Garner provides the strength of the movie. TS [video]

James Garner *Jess Remsberg* • Sidney Poitier *Toller* • Bill Travers *Lieutenant McAllister, "Scotty"* • Bibi Andersson *Ellen Grange* • Dennis Weaver *Willard Grange* • William Redfield *Sergeant Ferguson* • John Hoyt *Chata* ■ *Dir* Ralph Nelson • *Scr* Marvin H Albert, Michael M Grilikhes, from the novel *Apache Rising* by Marvin H Albert

The Duel at Silver Creek ★★ U

Western 1952 · US · Colour · 73mins

This minor and utterly unremarkable Audie Murphy western somewhat surprisingly bears the name of ace *Dirty Harry* director Don Siegel. Unfortunately, it's absolutely devoid of the personal style Siegel brought to such low-budget films as *Invasion of the Body Snatchers* and *Riot in Cell Block 11*. But Murphy and Siegel fans won't want to miss it, and the supporting cast, including a pre-stardom Lee Marvin, also makes it watchable. TS [video] DVD

Audie Murphy *Silver Kid* • Faith Domergue *Opal Lacey* • Stephen McNally *Lightning Tyrone* • Susan Cabot *Dusty Fargo* • Gerald Mohr *Rod Lacey* • Eugene Iglesias *Johnny Sombrero* • Lee Marvin *Tinhorn Burgess* • Walter Sande *Pete Fargo* ■ *Dir* Don Siegel • *Scr* Gerald Adams [Gerald Drayson Adams], Joseph Hoffman, from a story by Gerald Adams [Gerald Drayson Adams]

Duel in the Jungle ★★★ PG

Adventure 1954 · UK · Colour · 97mins

This entertaining, if a little simplistic, action adventure is a real tribute to its producer, Marcel Hellman. The Technicolor photography, shot on location in Rhodesia by Erwin Hillier, is thrilling, and the film reunites the co-stars of *State Fair* (1945), Dana Andrews and Jeanne Crain. David Farrar steals the acting thunder as the villain, while Hollywood veteran director George Marshall keeps the tension taut. TS [video]

Dana Andrews *Scott Walters* • Jeanne Crain *Marian Taylor* • David Farrar *Perry Henderson/Arthur Henderson* • Patrick Barr *Superintendent Roberts* • George Coulouris *Captain Malburn* • Charles Goldner *Martell* • Wilfrid Hyde White *Pitt* ■ *Dir* George Marshall • *Scr* Sam Marx, TJ Morrison, from a story by SK Kennedy

Duel in the Sun ★★★★ PG

Western melodrama
1946 · US · Colour · 129mins

Producer David O Selznick intended this costly production to be the equal of his *Gone with the Wind*. It certainly managed to offend church leaders and censorship boards alike with its sex content. Starring Jennifer Jones and Gregory Peck, it became (unsurprisingly) a mammoth hit – second only to *The Best Years of Our Lives* in the box-office tally for the entire decade – and is much admired today. The infamous finale is both ludicrous and stunning, as Jones and Peck, both dying, orgasmically crawl towards each other as the desert sun blazes down. It was this that led audiences to refer to the movie as *Lust in the Dust*. TS [video] DVD

Jennifer Jones *Pearl Chavez* • Joseph Cotten *Jesse McCanles* • Gregory Peck *Lewt McCanles* • Lionel Barrymore *Senator McCanles* • Herbert Marshall *Scott Chavez* • Lillian Gish *Laura Belle McCanles* • Walter Huston *Jubal Crabbe, the sinkiller* • Charles Bickford *Sam Pierce* • Butterfly McQueen *Vashti* • Otto Kruger *Mr Langford* • Orson Welles *Narrator* ■ *Dir* King Vidor • *Scr* David O Selznick, Oliver HP Garrett, from the novel by Niven Busch

Duel of Champions ★★ PG

Period drama 1961 · It/Sp · Colour · 85mins

Already looking ill, Alan Ladd clearly feels uncomfortable in his period costume and delivers his lines with the conviction of a man who'd rather be somewhere else. However, this sword-and-sandal romp, in which Rome and Alba decide to let two teams of three brothers fight the final battle of their war, did give him the chance to co-star with daughter Alana. DP. Italian dialogue dubbed into English. [video]

Alan Ladd *Horatio* • Franca Bettoja *Marcia* • Franco Fabrizi *Curiazio* • Robert Keith (1) *King of Rome* • Jacques Sernas *Marcus* • Andrea Aureli *King of Alba* • Mino Doro *Caio* • Alana Ladd *Scilla* ■ *Dir* Ferdinando Baldi, Terence Young • *Scr* Carlo Lizzani, Ennio De Concini, Giuliano Montaldo, from a story by Luciano Vincenzoni

Duel of the Titans ★★★ U

Period adventure 1961 · It · Colour · 105mins

Two of the finest exponents of the spaghetti western join forces on this superior sword-and-sandal offering. Sergio Corbucci called the shots, while Sergio Leone was among the septet of screenwriters. There's also an impressive double act in front of the camera, with ex-Mr Universe Steve Reeves teaming with one-time Tarzan Gordon Scott as the founders of Rome, Romulus and Remus. Even the supporting cast is better than average, with Virna Lisi providing the glamour and Massimo Girotti the gravitas. DP. Italian dialogue dubbed into English.

Steve Reeves *Romulus* • Gordon Scott *Remus* • Virna Lisi *Julia* • Massimo Girotti *Tazio* • Jacques Sernas *Curzio* ■ *Dir* Sergio Corbucci • *Scr* Sergio Corbucci, Sergio Leone, Luciano Martino, Sergio Prosperi, Franco Rossetti, Ennio De Concini, Duccio Tessari

The Duellists ★★★★ PG

Period drama 1977 · UK · Colour · 95mins

Set against the heavyweight hostilities of the Napoleonic Wars, the small-time conflict of hussars Harvey Keitel and Keith Carradine – challenging each other over the years to a series of duels – might seem ludicrously beside the point. But Keitel's manic man of honour is a character whose chilling fixation says something about the wider conflict and humankind's need to struggle. This was director Ridley Scott's first feature after graduating from commercials, and it comes across as a coldly brilliant portrait of obsession. TH [video] DVD

Keith Carradine *Armand d'Hubert* • Harvey Keitel *Gabriel Feraud* • Albert Finney *Fouché* • Edward Fox *Colonel* • Cristina Raines *Adèle* • Robert Stephens *General Treillard* • Tom Conti *Dr Jacquin* • Diana Quick *Laura* ■ *Dir* Ridley Scott • *Scr* Gerald Vaughan-Hughes, from the novella *The Duel* by Joseph Conrad

Duet for One ★★★★ 15

Drama 1986 · UK · Colour · 102mins

Julie Andrews gives a moving, unsentimental performance as a concert violinist whose life is shattered, in slow motion, by the onset of multiple sclerosis. Saccharine music aside, director Andrei Konchalovsky ensures the story – which echoes the real-life experience of cellist Jacqueline du Pré – has real conviction, with Alan Bates movingly surly as Julie's composer husband and Max von Sydow disagreeably callous as the death-fearing psychotherapist. TH [video]

Julie Andrews *Stephanie Anderson* • Alan Bates *David Cornwallis* • Max von Sydow *Dr Louis Feldman* • Rupert Everett *Constantine Kassanis* • Margaret Courtenay *Sonia Randvich* • Cathryn Harrison *Penny Smallwood* ■ *Dir* Andrei Konchalovsky • *Scr* Tom Kempinski, Jeremy Lipp, Andrei Konchalovsky, from the play by Tom Kempinski

Duets ★★★ 15

Comedy drama 2000 · US · Colour · 107mins

Directed by Bruce Paltrow and starring his daughter Gwyneth, this follows six would-be singers as they travel across America to take part in a big-money karaoke competition. The movie takes its time fleshing out its characters, who range from a starstruck waitress to an escaped con, and there are some terrific performances, notably from Paul Giamatti as a burned-out rep and singer Huey Lewis as a veteran karaoke hustler. Ironically, the most insipid performance comes from Miss Paltrow, though she does display a decent, non-dubbed singing voice. Otherwise, mature and entertaining character-driven drama. DA [video] DVD

Gwyneth Paltrow *Liv* • Maria Bello *Suzi Loomis* • Scott Speedman *Billy Hannon* • André Braugher *Reggie Kane* • Paul Giamatti *Todd Woods* • Huey Lewis *Ricky Dean* • Angie Dickinson *Blair* ■ *Dir* Bruce Paltrow • *Scr* John Byrum

Duffy ★★

Crime caper 1968 · UK · Colour · 101mins

Portraitist Donald Cammell broke into films as the co-author of this slipshod heist caper that would have you believe its anarchic chaos is really ultra-chic comedy. Compounding the script's lack of focus is director Robert Parrish's preoccupation with flashy visuals and the Mediterranean locations, which leaves his cast floundering. James Coburn is particularly bemused as the hippy drifter hired by half-brothers James Fox and John Alderton to rob their mean-spirited millionaire father, James Mason. Fox turns in a wildly mannered performance that's almost as eccentric as his fashion sense. DP

James Coburn *Duffy* • James Mason *Calvert* • James Fox *Stefane* • Susannah York *Segolene* • John Alderton *Anthony* • Barry Shawzin *Bakirgian* • Carl Duering *Bonivet* ■ *Dir* Robert Parrish • *Scr* Donald Cammell, Harry Joe Brown Jr, from a story by Donald Cammell, Harry Joe Brown Jr, Pierre De La Salle

Duffy's Tavern ★ U

Musical comedy 1945 · US · BW · 97mins

This revue-style aberration from a distinguished studio (Paramount) hangs dozens of embarrassed-looking contract stars performing second-rate songs and sketches on to a paper-thin excuse for a plot. They are supposedly putting on a benefit show for innkeeper Ed Gardner (whose popular radio show of the same title gave rise to the idea). RK

Bing Crosby • Betty Hutton • Paulette Goddard • Alan Ladd • Dorothy Lamour • Eddie Bracken • Brian Donlevy • Sonny Tufts • Veronica Lake • Arturo de Cordova • Barry Fitzgerald *Bing Crosby's father* • Ed Gardner *Archie/Ed Gardner* ■ *Dir* Hal Walker • *Scr* Melvin Frank, Norman Panama, Abram S Burrows [Abe S Burrows], Barney Dean, George White, Eddie Davis, Matt Brooks, from the radio series by Ed Gardner

The Duke of West Point ★★ U

Drama 1938 · US · BW · 109mins

Minor South African star Louis Hayward was as bland a leading man as they came. He made this feature between playing the Saint and the Man in the Iron Mask, in what could be considered the peak of his career. Co-star Joan Fontaine makes a charming ingénue, three years before tremulously winning an Oscar for Alfred Hitchcock's *Suspicion*. However, the real star of the movie is America's military academy West Point, whose governors recognised the recruitment value of such films. TS

Louis Hayward *Steven Early* • Joan Fontaine *Ann Porter* • Tom Brown *Sonny Drew* • Richard Carlson *Jack West* • Alan Curtis *Cadet Strong* • Donald Barry *Cadet Grady* • Gaylord Pendleton [Steve Pendleton] *Cadet Rains* • Charles D Brown *Doc Porter* • Jed Prouty *Mr Drew* ■ *Dir* Alfred E Green • *Scr* George Bruce

D

The Duke Wore Jeans ★★ U

Musical 1958 · UK · BW · 89mins

Where movies are concerned, a single Tommy Steele is usually one too many, but two are more than flesh and blood can bear. Here he plays a likely lad who helps a charmless lookalike noble to escape being married off to feisty princess June Laverick. The "trading places" plot is an old chestnut of drama and the jerry-built sets and fifth-rate pop songs that adorn this tosh considerably scuff the sheen. DP

Tommy Steele *Tony Whitecliffe/Tommy Hudson* • June Laverick *Princess Maria* • Michael Medwin *Cooper* • Eric Pohlmann *Bastini* • Alan Wheatley *King of Ritallia* • Mary Kerridge *Queen* • Ambrosine Philpotts *Duchess* • Clive Morton *Lord Whitecliffe* ■ *Dir* Gerald Thomas • *Scr* Norman Hudis, from a story by Lionel Bart, Michael Pratt

Dulcima ★★

Drama 1971 · UK · Colour · 97mins

John Mills gives a rambunctious performance as the Gloucestershire farmer who risks losing his carefully stashed wealth when he falls in lust with gold-digging Carol White. Writer/director Frank Nesbitt indulges in a little crude comedy, and Mills can't quite manage to avoid caricature. By the time White seduces gamekeeper Stuart Wilson, however, the tone has descended to the level of penny-dreadful melodrama. DP

Carol White *Dulcima Gaskain* • John Mills *Mr Parker* • Stuart Wilson (1) *Gamekeeper* • Bernard Lee *Mr Gaskain* • Sheila Raynor *Mrs Gaskain* • Dudley Foster *Symes* • Cyril Cross *Harris* • Neil Wilson *Auctioneer* ■ *Dir* Frank Nesbitt • *Scr* Frank Nesbitt, from a story by HE Bates

Dum ★★ 12

Musical action drama
2002 · Ind · Colour · 170mins

Corruption has been a popular theme of Bollywood "socials" for decades. There are usually few grey areas in these morality melodramas and director E Niwas is not about to break the mould with this "good cop, bad cop" story. Having dreamed of serving his country, Vivek Oberoi is horrified by the methods employed by superior Atul Kulkarni, but how is a rookie policeman going to expose the crimes of such a respected colleague? Playing heavily on the notion of performing one's civic duty in difficult times, this is hardly a subtle movie, stopping just short of being outright propaganda. DP. A Hindi language film. [video] DVD

Vivek Oberoi *Uday Shinde* • Atul Kulkarni *Shankar* • Diya Mirza *Kaveri* • Sushant *Mohan* • Govind Namdeo *Deshmukh* • Yashpal Sharma *Babu Kasai* ■ *Dir* E Niwas • *Scr* E Niwas, Mehran, from a story by Bunty Soorma

Duma ★★★ U

Adventure drama
2005 · US · Colour · 100mins

This handsome adventure drama from *Black Stallion* director Carroll Ballard tells the story of a white South African boy (Alexander Micheletos), and Duma, the young cheetah he has grown up with. When they have to leave the family farm and move to the big city, the boy is determined to release the cheetah back into the wild and embarks on a hazardous trek across the desert, joined by the mysterious Eamonn Walker. The film benefits from some spectacular wildlife photography and solid acting, plus an unsentimental storyline. DA

Alexander Michaletos *Xan* • Eamonn Walker *Rip* • Campbell Scott *Peter* • Hope Davis *Kristin* ■ *Dir* Carroll Ballard • *Scr* Karen Janszen, Mark St Germain, from a story by Carol Flint, Karen Janszen, from the non-fiction book *How It Was with Dooms: a True Story from Africa* by Carol Cawthra Hopcraft, Xan Hopcraft

D

Dumb and Dumber ★★★★ 12

Comedy 1994 · US · Colour · 106mins

With Jim Carrey, there are no half measures. So you'll either love this as one of his finest moments or loathe it as a perfect example of mind-numbing Hollywood cinema. But even the harshest critic will find it hard to suppress a couple of chuckles during this cheerfully moronic mix of slapstick, sight gags and toilet humour. Carrey and Jeff Daniels play two of the world's stupidest people who set off on a chaotic road trip when they attempt to return Lauren Holly's missing briefcase. Disengage the brain and enjoy. JF. Contains violence and nudity. DVD

Jim Carrey *Lloyd Christmas* • Jeff Daniels *Harry Dunne* • Lauren Holly *Mary Swanson* • Mike Starr *Joe Mentalino* • Karen Duffy *JP Shay* • Charles Rocket *Nicholas Andre* • Victoria Rowell *Athletic beauty* • Teri Garr *Helen Swanson* ■ *Dir* Peter Farrelly • *Scr* Peter Farrelly, Bennett Yellin, Bobby Farrelly

Dumb and Dumberer: When Harry Met Lloyd ★★ 12

Comedy 2003 · US/Ger · Colour · 81mins

This belated prequel boasts neither of the original stars; Eric Christian Olsen and Derek Richardson step into Lloyd and Harry's shoes and do a pretty decent job. The plot has the doltish duo meeting for the first time and going on to foil a plot by corrupt principal Eugene Levy to embezzle school funds. This sometimes stoops lower than a limbo dancer in its search for easy laughs but for the young audience it's aimed at, this is diverting enough tosh. DA DVD

Eric Christian Olsen *Lloyd Christmas* • Derek Richardson *Harry Dunne* • Rachel Nichols *Jessica* • Cheri Oteri *Ms Heller* • Luis Guzman *Ray* • Elden Henson *Turk* • Mimi Rogers *Mrs Dunne* • Eugene Levy *Principal Collins* ■ *Dir* Troy Miller • *Scr* Troy Miller, Robert Brenner, from a story by Robert Brenner, from characters created by Peter Farrelly, Bennett Yellin, Bobby Farrelly

Dumbo ★★★★★ U

Classic animation
1941 · US · Colour · 60mins

Although directed by Ben Sharpsteen, every frame of this story from the Disney studio of the outcast elephant with huge ears was personally approved by Uncle Walt himself. The film won an Oscar for its score, but it's songs such as *When I See an Elephant Fly* and *Baby of Mine* (from the heartbreaking mother-child reunion) that linger in the memory. On the animation side, the highlight is the parade of pink elephants after Dumbo and Timothy Mouse get tipsy. Made for a fraction of the cost of previous Disney animations, this may be one of the studio's shortest features, but it's also among the best. DP DVD

Edward Brophy *Timothy Mouse* • Herman Bing *Ringmaster* • Verna Felton *Elephant* • Sterling Holloway *Stork* • Cliff Edwards *Jim Crow* ■ *Dir* Ben Sharpsteen • *Scr* Joe Grant, Dick Huemer, from a book by Helen Aberson, Harold Pearl • *Music/lyrics* Frank Churchill, Oliver Wallace, Ned Washington

Dummy ★★★ 15

Comedy drama 2002 · US · Colour · 101mins

This potentially poor taste comedy confirmed Adrien Brody as an edgy actor who is willing to tackle unconventional projects. But good though he is as a slow-witted New Jerseyite who takes up ventriloquism to try to conquer his painful reticence, his efforts are restricted by director Greg Pritikin's screenplay, which lurches between quirky Jewish humour and cloying sentimentality. DP DVD

Adrien Brody *Steven* • Milla Jovovich *Fangora* • Illeana Douglas *Heidi* • Vera Farmiga *Lorena* • Jessica Walter *Fern* • Ron Leibman *Lou* • Jared Harris *Michael* ■ *Dir/Scr* Greg Pritikin

Dune ★★★ 15

Science-fiction drama
1984 · US · Colour · 130mins

Frank Herbert's mammoth cult novel, about the competition between two warring families for control of a barren planet renowned for its mind-expanding "spice", is converted by director David Lynch into a dense, swirling mass of religious symbolism and mysticism. Lynch was, reportedly, unhappy with the final cut, but his film is visually stunning and many of the scenes are among the most memorable and original of the genre. Kyle MacLachlan stars as the "messiah" alongside an amazing cast. While it is unwieldy and confusing, it's not as bad as it seemed on release. AJ. Contains violence, swearing. DVD

Kyle MacLachlan *Paul Atreides* • Francesca Annis *Lady Jessica* • Brad Dourif *Piter De Vries* • José Ferrer *Padishah Emperor Shaddam IV* • Linda Hunt *Shadout Mapes* • Freddie Jones *Thufir Hawat* • Richard Jordan *Duncan Idaho* • Virginia Madsen *Princess Irulan* • Silvana Mangano *Reverend Mother Ramallo* • Kenneth McMillan *Baron Vladimir Harkonnen* • Patrick Stewart *Gurney Halleck* • Sting *Feyd Rautha* • Dean Stockwell *Dr Wellington Yueh* • Max von Sydow *Dr Kynes* • Sean Young *Chani* ■ *Dir* David Lynch • *Scr* David Lynch, from the novel by Frank Herbert

Dungeons & Dragons ★ 12

Fantasy adventure
2000 · US/Cz Rep · Colour · 103mins

Courtney Solomon's belated and instantly redundant screen version of the popular role-playing game has Empress Savina (Thora Birch) wanting equality for all citizens in the mythical kingdom of Izmer. But villainous Jeremy Irons plots to establish his own tyrannical rule. The perilous task of stopping him falls to thieves Justin Whalin and Marlon Wayans, apprentice magic user Zoe McLellan, dwarf Lee Arenberg and elf Kristen Wilson. Shifting uneasily from banal adventure and arch brutality to unintentional hilarity and pantomime camp, this is scuppered by some dire performances. AJ DVD

Jeremy Irons *Profion* • Justin Whalin *Ridley Freeborn* • Marlon Wayans *Snails* • Zoe McLellan *Marina Pretensa* • Thora Birch *Empress Savina* • Kristen Wilson *Norda* • Richard O'Brien *Xilus* • Tom Baker *Halvarth* • Lee Arenberg *Elwood Gutworthy* ■ *Dir* Courtney Solomon • *Scr* Topper Lilien, Carroll Cartwright

Dunkirk ★★★ PG

Second World War drama
1958 · UK · BW · 129mins

This Ealing reconstruction of the evacuation of Dunkirk is impressive in its scale and authenticity, but slightly disappointing in its writing and execution. John Mills, Richard Attenborough and Bernard Lee scarcely have to act as their respective parts – a corporal lost on the beaches, a snivelling stay-at-home and a cynical reporter – are so cleverly tailor-made. Director Leslie Norman handles the manoeuvres with skill and does well to maintain the docudramatic feel, in spite of some shoddy dialogue, but his approach is too reverential. DP

John Mills *Binns* • Bernard Lee *Charles Foreman* • Richard Attenborough *Holden* • Robert Urquhart *Mike* • Ray Jackson *Barlow* • Meredith Edwards *Dave Bellman* • Anthony Nicholls *Military spokesman* • Michael Shillo *Jouvet* ■ *Dir* Leslie Norman • *Scr* David Divine, WP Lipscomb, from the novel *The Big Pick-Up* by Elleston Trevor and the play *Dunkirk* by Lt Col Ewen Butler, Maj JS Bradford • *Producer* Michael Balcon

Dunston Checks In ★★★ PG

Comedy 1996 · Can · Colour · 84mins

Early Tarzan films led the way, with the ape-man's own furry jungle swinger, Cheetah. Now there's Dunston, an orang-utan acting as the unwilling sidekick to a snooty English peer (Rupert Everett) who wants to use him to burgle New York's Majestic Hotel. It's amiable tosh, but Dunston's antics are as delightfully appealing as Faye Dunaway's rudely ruthless proprietor is unattractive. TH DVD

Jason Alexander *Robert Grant* • Faye Dunaway *Mrs Dubrow* • Eric Lloyd *Kyle Grant* • Rupert Everett *Lord Rutledge* • Graham Sack *Brian* • Paul Reubens *La Farge* • Glenn Shadix *Lionel Spalding* • Nathan Davis *Victor* ■ *Dir* Ken Kwapis • *Scr* John Hopkins, Bruce Graham, from a story by John Hopkins

The Dunwich Horror ★★ 18

Horror 1970 · US · Colour · 84mins

Lovers of HP Lovecraft's stories had to wait until *Re-Animator* to see full justice done to his full-blooded *Necronomicon* tales. Back in the 1960s, fans made do with fun fiascos from the Roger Corman scrap heap. In this comic caper, a hopelessly miscast Sandra Dee plays a student who is the drugged victim of a fertility rite, set up by the hammy Dean Stockwell in his bid to restore ancient powers of evil. AJ. Contains violence.

Sandra Dee *Nancy Walker* • Dean Stockwell *Wilbur Whateley* • Ed Begley *Dr Henry Armitage* • Sam Jaffe *Old Whateley* • Donna Baccala *Elizabeth Hamilton* • Joanne Moore Jordan *Lavinia* • Talia Coppola [Talia Shire] *Cora* ■ *Dir* Daniel Haller • *Scr* Curtis Lee Hanson, Henry Rosenbaum, Ronald Silkosky, from the story by HP Lovecraft

Durango Kids ★★

Fantasy adventure
2000 · US · Colour · 87mins

There's an old-fashioned feel about this time-travelling adventure from debutant director Ashton Root. But despite the wealth of incident, it's hard to see it capturing the imagination of youngsters reared on high-concept action and special effects. Set in the town of Ouray, Colorado, the action shifts between 1891 and the present day, as a quartet of school pals encounters bandits and frontiersmen while searching for lost gold and the solution to an age-old mystery. DP

Brendon Ryan Barrett *Taylor* • Taylor Root *Spencer* • Curtis Williams *Cameron* • Caitlin Barrett *Katie* ■ *Dir/Scr* Ashton Root

During One Night ★★

Second World War drama
1961 · UK · BW · 85mins

Sidney J Furie's Second World War drama has a whiff of controversy about it, as it explores the then taboo topics of virginity and impotence. Don Borisenko headlines as the USAF pilot who goes AWOL after a buddy is castrated during a mission, but his brushes with the military police and a sympathetic padre are nowhere near as involving as his encounters with a young Susan Hampshire. DP

Susan Hampshire *Jean* • Don Borisenko *David* • Sean Sullivan *Major* • Joy Webster *Prostitute* • Jackie Collins *Girl* • Tom Busby *Sam* ■ *Dir/Scr* Sidney J Furie

Dust ★★★ 18

Drama 1985 · Fr/Bel · Colour · 85mins

Adapted from JM Coetzee's novel *In the Heart of the Country*, this brooding South African drama gives Trevor Howard the opportunity to explore a fully rounded character after years of formulaic cameos. As the boorish farmer who seduces the wife of his black foreman, he chillingly conveys the arrogance of supremacy and the lust of isolation. Yet it's Jane Birkin, as the daughter who becomes increasingly jealous of her father's new flame, who provides both the film's emotional core and its shocking resolution. Directed with extreme care, this is stern stuff. DP

Jane Birkin *Magda* • Trevor Howard *Father* • John Matshikiza *Hendrik* • Nadine Uwampa *Klein Anna* • Lourdes Christina Sayo Momoboko *Old Anna* • René Diaz *Jacob* • Tom Vrebos *Piet* ■ *Dir* Marion Hänsel • *Scr* Marion Hänsel, from the novel *In the Heart of the Country* by JM Coetzee

Dust ★★ 18

Drama
2001 · UK/Ger/It/Mac/US · Colour · 119mins

This brutal, depressing film alternates between a contemporary New York drama and an early-20th-century "Wild East" blood bath. This is an awkward combination, and is not aided by an unappealing quartet of protagonists. Its starting point is the attempted robbery of an apartment by petty thief Adrian Lester, who is wounded by owner Rosemary Murphy. For some reason, she decides to recall the origins of her ancestors, namely two brothers (a pair of shaky performances from David Wenham and Joseph Fiennes) who end up as fierce adversaries in the wilds of Macedonia. JC DVD

Joseph Fiennes *Elijah* • David Wenham *Luke* • Adrian Lester *Edge* • Anne Brochet *Lilith* • Nikolina Kujaca *Neda* • Rosemary Murphy *Angela* ■ *Dir/Scr* Milcho Manchevski

Dust Be My Destiny ★★

Crime drama 1939 · US · BW · 88mins

A routine melodrama redeemed by the ever-excellent John Garfield. He's ideally cast as an innocent on the run, fleeing a murder rap. In jail, he falls for Priscilla Lane, the work-farm boss's stepdaughter, while newspaper editor Alan Hale takes an interest in his case. The story's more than a mite overfamiliar, and little more originality wouldn't have gone amiss. TS

John Garfield *Joe Bell* • Priscilla Lane *Mabel* • Alan Hale *Mike Leonard* • Frank McHugh *Caruthers* • Billy Halop *Hank* • Bobby Jordan *Jimmy* • Charley Grapewin *Pop* • Henry Armetta *Nick* ■ *Dir* Lewis Seiler • *Scr* Robert Rossen, from a novel by Jerome Odlum

Dust Devil ★★★★ 18

Horror thriller 1992 · UK · Colour · 103mins

Richard Stanley's surreal serial killer horror thriller is a landmark British film of the 1990s. Combining African tribal myths with spaghetti western folklore, the *Hardware* director's highly personal magical mystery tour through sweeping Namibian vistas is an embarrassment of cinematic riches. It's a hallucinogenic eye-popper, a political allegory – accent on the gory – that bursts with atmospheric moodiness. Robert Burke is a forbidding presence

 U = SUITABLE FOR ALL Uc = SUITABLE FOR ALL, ESPECIALLY FOR YOUNG CHILDREN (VIDEO ONLY) PG = PARENTAL GUIDANCE

as "The Hitcher from Hell", spinning an illusory web of dream-like terror around his suicidal victims. AJ. Contains violence, swearing, sex scenes and nudity.

Robert Burke *Dust Devil/"Hitch"* • Chelsea Field *Wendy Robinson* • Zakes Mokae *Ben Mukurob* • John Matshikiza *Joe Niemand* • Rufus Swart *Mark Robinson* • William Hootkins *Captain Cornelius Beyman* • Marianne Sägebrecht *Dr Leidzinger* ■ *Dir/Scr* Richard Stanley

Dust in the Wind ★★★ 15

Romantic drama
1987 · Tai · Colour · 109mins

While not Hou Hsiao-Hsien's most ambitious picture, this bittersweet tale of country mice finding love in the big city, only to drift apart when patriotic duty calls, is full of human foibles and shrewd observations. As the teenagers leaving their mining village to complete their studies in Taipei, Wang Ching-Won and Xin Shufen have an honesty that reinforces the film's social realism, while the director's command of their environment is impeccable. For all the implied criticisms of Taiwan and China, however, it's a fairly noncommital picture. DP. In Hokkien and Mandarin with English subtitles.

Wang Ching-Won *Wan* • Xin Shufen *Huen* • Che'en Shu-Fang *Huen's mother* • Li Tianlu *Grandpa* ■ *Dir* Hou Hsiao-Hsien • *Scr* Wu Nien-Jen, Chu Tien-Wen

Dust of Life ★★★

Drama 1994 · Fr/Alg/HK · Colour · 87mins

This grinding study of institutionalised brutality and indomitable hope provides telling insights into a neglected aspect of the Vietnam War. Despised for being the son of an African-American, Daniel Guyant is sent to a labour camp. Although he eventually makes an almost suicidal bid for freedom, director Rachid Bouhareb is more concerned with depicting the harsh conditions inside the compound and the way Guyant responds to them. Uncompromisingly photographed and played with courage and conviction. DP. In French with English subtitles.

Daniel Guyant *Son* • Gilles Chitlaphone *Bob* • Leon Outtrabady *Shrimp* • Jehan Pages *Little Hai* • Lam Siu Lin *Greaser* • Yann Roussel *Steel Muscles* • William Low *Commander* ■ *Dir* Rachid Bouchareb • *Scr* Rachid Bouchareb, Bernard Gesbert, from the novel *La Colline de Fanta* by Duyen Ahn

Dusting Cliff 7 ★★ 18

Action thriller 1996 · US · Colour · 88mins

The budget for this action thriller precludes any eye-popping pyrotechnics, while the ham-fisted direction prevents either pace or palpable tension. However, the real problem is the script, which is not only strewn with dismal dialogue, but also fails to present the villainous Lance Henriksen with a credible motive for pinching the nuclear and chemical weapons buried somewhere in the desert beneath Cliff 7. DP. Contains violence and swearing.

Lance Henriksen *Roger McBride* • Nancy Allen *Anna Bishop* • Scott Lincoln *Brock Daniels* • Dean Scofield *Mitch Stevens* • Ashley Buccille *Carrie Bishop* ■ *Dir* William H Molina • *Scr* Jim Menza, Charles Philip Moore, Justin J Stanley, William H Molina

Dusty ★★★

Drama 1982 · Aus · Colour · 90mins

Bill Kerr made his name on radio as one of Tony Hancock's sidekicks. But, in later years, his grizzled features suited him for roles in a number of Australian outdoor dramas. Here he plays a bushman turned shepherd who trains an abandoned wild hound (Dusty) into a champion sheepdog. Kerr is superb as the outsider whose loyalties lie with the wilds. DP

Bill Kerr *Tom* • Noel Trevarthen *Harry* • Carol Burns *Clara* • John Stanton *Railey Jordan* ■ *Dir* John Richardson • *Scr* Sonia Borg, from a novel by Frank Dalby Davison

Dusty Ermine ★★

Crime drama 1936 · UK · BW · 85mins

This is far from the best film made by the recently rediscovered director Bernard Vorhaus. However, detective Anthony Bushell's pursuit of criminal peer Ronald Squire is not without its moments of tension and droll humour. Jane Baxter provides the glamour, but the real interest lies in the supporting performances of Felix Aylmer and Margaret Rutherford. DP

Jane Baxter *Linda Kent* • Anthony Bushell *Inspector Forsyth* • Ronald Squire *Jim Kent* • Margaret Rutherford *Miss Butterby* • Davina Craig *Goldie* • Athole Stewart *Mr Kent* • Felix Aylmer *Assistant commissoner* ■ *Dir* Bernard Vorhaus • *Scr* L du Garde Peach, Michael Hankinson, Arthur Macrae, Paul Hervey Fox, H Fowler Mear, from the play by Neil Grant

Dutchman ★★

Drama 1966 · UK · BW · 54mins

Ostensibly, this shows how sadistic white woman Shirley Knight persecutes and eventually assaults black man Al Freeman Jr on the New York subway. But while there are multiple layers of socio-political symbolism beneath the surface, the action is so slow and portentous you soon tire of searching for them. Editor Anthony Harvey made his directorial debut with this 54-minute film. He earned an Oscar nomination for his first feature, *The Lion in Winter*. DP

Shirley Knight *Lula* • Al Freeman Jr *Clay* • Frank Lieberman *Subway Rider* • Robert Calvert *Subway Rider* • Howard Bennett *Subway Rider* • Sandy McDonald *Subway Rider* • Denis Peters *Subway Rider* ■ *Dir* Anthony Harvey • *Scr* Anthony Harvey, from the play by LeRoi Jones

Duty Free Marriage ★★★

Romantic drama
1980 · Hun/Fin · Colour · 100mins

While gently mocking the national characteristics of its principals, this Finnish-Hungarian co-production also had the more serious purpose of attacking the 1981 immigration laws that forbade Hungarians who married outside the country from returning home within five years. Pausing for some acerbic asides on generational and town-and-country politics, János Zsombolyai seamlessly segues from comedy into drama as Mari Kiss's marriage of convenience to Tom Wentzel's Finnish bachelor takes a turn for the worse once they realise its impact on his family and her friends. Direct, disarming and delightful. DP. In Hungarian with English subtitles.

Mari Kiss *Mari* • Tom Wentzel *Pekka* • Cecilia Esztergályos *Ili* • Agi Margittay *Agi* ■ *Dir* János Zsombolyai • *Scr* János Zsombolyai, Akos Kertesz, from a story by János Zsombolyai

D'Ye Ken John Peel? ★★

Drama 1934 · UK · BW · 84mins

This is a crusty old melodrama in which Leslie Perrins chews the scenery with a delicious lack of restraint, playing the dastardly rogue whose idea of payment for an outstanding debt is to marry the debtor's daughter. But fear not for Winifred Shotter: riding to the rescue is Waterloo veteran John Garrick, who knows a thing or two about delivering damsels from distress. Hardly a lost classic. DP

John Garrick *Major John Peel* • Winifred Shotter *Lucy Merrall* • Stanley Holloway *Sam Small* • John Stuart *Captain Moonlight* • Leslie Perrins *Mr Craven* • Mary Lawson *Toinette* ■ *Dir* Henry Edwards • *Scr* H Fowler Mear, from a story by Charles Cullum

Dying of Laughter ★★★

Black comedy 1999 · Sp · Colour · 105mins

Maverick director Alex de la Iglesia returns to the realms of pitch-black comedy with this macabre tale of a comedy double act whose success disguises a pathological rivalry. Superb performances from the dashingly witty El Gran Wyoming and his put-upon stooge, Santiago Segura, are the key to this scathing memoir of Spanish light entertainment during two decades of almost ceaseless socio-political upheaval. Yet the romantic feuds, drug-induced separations and explosive reunions would be nothing without the knowing kitsch of the decor and the irreverence of the direction. DP. In Spanish with English subtitles.

Santiago Segura *Nino* • El Gran Wyoming *Bruno* • Alex Angulo *Julian* • Carla Hidalgo *Laura* • Eduardo Gomez *El Pobre Tino* ■ *Dir* Alex de la Iglesia • *Scr* Alex de la Iglesia, Jorge Guerricaechevarría

Dying Young ★★ 15

Romantic drama
1991 · US · Colour · 106mins

Joel Schumacher's tear-jerker leaves one wishing that the terminally sick rich lad at the centre of this interminable nonsense had died even younger (or at least before the cameras arrived). Campbell Scott tries hard in a thankless role, made all the more difficult by the fact that Schumacher only has eyes for Julia Roberts as the blowsy girl from the wrong side of the tracks who answers Scott's advert for a carer. DP. Contains swearing, nudity. DVD

Julia Roberts *Hilary O'Neil* • Campbell Scott *Victor Geddes* • Vincent D'Onofrio *Gordon* • Colleen Dewhurst *Estelle Whittier* • David Selby *Richard Geddes* • Ellen Burstyn *Mrs O'Neil* • Dion Anderson *Cappy* • Daniel Beer *Danny* ■ *Dir* Joel Schumacher • *Scr* Richard Friedenberg, from the novel by Marti Leimbach

Dynamite ★★★ U

Drama 1929 · US · BW · 69mins

The first talkie from producer/director Cecil B DeMille, one of the few directors (along with Hitchcock and Spielberg) whose name is always instantly recognised by the public. This is very typical of DeMille, with a love triangle involving a condemned murderer (Charles Bickford), a giddy socialite (Kay Johnson) and a noble hero (Conrad Nagel), all thrown together in a mammoth mine disaster. The cave-in is spectacular, the costumes are splendid and the bathrooms are lavish. TS

Conrad Nagel *Roger Towne* • Kay Johnson *Cynthia Crothers* • Charles Bickford *Hagon Derk* • Julia Faye *Marcia Towne* • Muriel McCormac *Katie Derk* • Tyler Brooke *Life of the Party* • Joel McCrea *Marco the Sheik* ■ *Dir* Cecil B DeMille • *Scr* Jeanie Macpherson, John Howard Lawson, Gladys Unger, from a story by Jeanie Macpherson

Dynamite Chicken ★★ 18

Satirical documentary
1971 · US · Colour · 75mins

Only the 1960s could have given birth to a concept like this: a "multi-media mosaic" of American pop culture that incorporates rock footage, animation, newsreels and nudity. By turns offensive and enlightening, there are all too brief glimpses of such 20th-century icons as Jimi Hendrix, John and Yoko, the Velvet Underground and Lenny Bruce, and far too many shots of hippies doing what hippies did back then. A pre-fame Richard Pryor provides ironic comedy links. Even for curiosity seekers it's a real mixed bag. RS

Joan Baez • Richard Pryor • Ron Carey • Marshall Efron • Lisa Ryan • Paul Krasner • Leonard Cohen • John Lennon • Ondine • Andy Warhol ■ *Dir/Scr* Ernest Pintoff

Dynamite Man from Glory Jail ★★★

Melodrama 1971 · US · Colour · 97mins

James Stewart plays a habitual criminal who is released after 40 years in jail and wants to claim $25,000 of prison pay that he has banked legitimately. But the bank manager has run off with it, forcing Stewart back to his old ways. The star chews up the scenery, while George Kennedy, Strother Martin and a young Kurt Russell offer expert support. AT

James Stewart *Mattie Appleyard* • George Kennedy *Doc Council* • Anne Baxter *Cleo* • Strother Martin *Lee Cottrill* • Kurt Russell *Johnny Jesus* • William Windom *Roy K Sizemore* ■ *Dir* Andrew V McLaglen • *Scr* James Lee Barrett, from the novel by Davis Grubb

D

E' Lollipop ★★ U

Drama 1975 · S Afr · Colour · 92mins

Young Muntu Ndebele finds himself cast adrift in Harlem after an airport mix-up sees him separated from José Ferrer, the priest escorting him from South Africa. He's only here in America to cheer up his buddy, fellow orphan Norman Knox, who is recovering from emergency surgery. Asserting that racial tolerance could become a reality if only we adopted the innocence of children, this well-meaning melodrama might have preached more forcibly had it not resorted so readily to sentimentality. DP

José Ferrer *Father Alberto* • Karen Valentine *Carol Anne* • Bess Finney *Sister Marguerita* • Muntu Ndebele *Tsepo* • Norman Knox *Jannie* • Bingo Mbonjeni *Cash general* • Simon Sabela *Rakwaba* ■ *Dir* Ashley Lazarus • *Scr* Ashley Lazarus, from a story by Andre Pieterse

ET the Extra-Terrestrial ★★★★★ U

Classic science-fiction adventure 1982 · US · Colour · 109mins

Steven Spielberg's ode to aliens could also be seen as a tribute to all the loners of the world, as little ET, abandoned by his extraterrestrial pals, has to cope on Earth until they can come back and rescue him. Luckily, he's befriended by an equally lonely little boy, played by Henry Thomas, who proceeds to teach his alien chum how to talk, dress up in women's clothes and guzzle beer. Much has been made of the changes and additions to the anniversary edition, but this is no extended director's cut; the alterations are minimal. Some of ET's facial expressions have been enhanced with computer animation, there are five additional minutes of footage that were left out of the original and – significantly in the current political climate – the guns carried by the government agents have been digitally replaced by walkie-talkies. However, 20 years after its first release, this is still a special, delightful adventure. JB DVD

Henry Thomas *Elliott* • Dee Wallace [Dee Wallace Stone] *Mary* • Peter Coyote *Keys* • Robert MacNaughton *Michael* • Drew Barrymore *Gertie* • KC Martel *Greg* • Sean Frye *Steve* • Tom Howell [C Thomas Howell] *Tyler* • Erika Eleniak *Pretty girl* ■ *Dir* Steven Spielberg • *Scr* Melissa Mathison • *Cinematographer* Allen Daviau • *Music* John Williams • *Special Effects* Carlo Rambaldi

Each Dawn I Die ★★★ PG

Prison drama 1939 · US · BW · 87mins

What's lacking in credibility is made up for in ferocious energy here, as James Cagney portrays a framed campaigning reporter who is sent to prison and brutalised into throwing in his lot with a crime boss. Sombre undercurrents run below the routine melodrama, with the reporter believing he's been betrayed by both life and by fellow convict George Raft. Cagney gives it all he's got. TH

James Cagney *Frank Ross* • George Raft *"Hood" Stacey* • Jane Bryan *Joyce Conover* • George Bancroft *Warden John Armstrong* • Stanley Ridges *Meuller* • Alan Baxter *Polecat Carlisle* ■ *Dir* William Keighley • *Scr* Norman Reilly Raine, Warren Duff, Charles Perry, from the novel by Jerome Odlum

The Eagle ★★★★ U

Silent adventure 1925 · US · BW · 70mins

A film of enormous curiosity value because Rudolph Valentino's penultimate surge before he died shows – in his smouldering-eyed, he-man presence – just what his attraction was to those women who formed a cult after his death. As a modern-day Robin Hood, the "Black Eagle", Valentino makes a sinewy play for Vilma Banky, while being ironically observed by Tsarina Louise Dresser, who puts herself about as much as the hero. Much parodied since its release, it still has charisma – and that's because of Valentino: his star quality was so great he only needed one to tango. TH DVD

Rudolph Valentino *Vladimir Dubrovsky* • Vilma Banky *Mascha Troekouroff* • Louise Dresser *Czarina* • Albert Conti *Kuschka* • James A Marcus *Kyrilla Troekouroff* • George Nichols *Judge* • Carrie Clark Ward *Aunt Aurelia* ■ *Dir* Clarence Brown • *Scr* Hans Kräly

The Eagle and the Hawk ★★★★

War drama 1933 · US · BW · 63mins

A mordant and very bitter "lost generation" First World War tale, with a quite superb cast to do it justice. You couldn't wish for better than Fredric March as the disaffected leader of a British flying squadron, Cary Grant as his truculent air gunner, Jack Oakie as his best mate and Carole Lombard as March's London society doll. Reissue prints give Mitchell Leisen his due as assistant director, but first time out the full credit went to Stuart Walker alone. TS

Fredric March *Jeremiah Young* • Cary Grant *Henry Crocker* • Jack Oakie *Mike Richards* • Carole Lombard *Beautiful lady* • Sir Guy Standing [Guy Standing] *Major Dunham* • Forrester Harvey *Hogan* • Kenneth Howell *John Stevens* ■ *Dir* Stuart Walker • *Scr* Bogart Rogers, Seton I Miller, from the story by John Monk Saunders

The Eagle Has Landed ★★★ 15

Second World War adventure 1976 · UK · Colour · 117mins

This far-fetched but entertaining thriller stars Michael Caine as an unlikely German colonel who leads a task force that infiltrates an English village in 1943 with the aim of kidnapping prime minister Winston Churchill. Even more unlikely is English-hating Donald Sutherland's Irish accent allied with the cut-glass tones of Jenny Agutter, who plays the local girl he falls for. As a lurking party, the Germans aren't very convincing, but director John Sturges puts some hefty action into the untidy package, while Donald Pleasence's impersonation of Heinrich Himmler is totally credible. TH. Contains swearing, violence. DVD

Michael Caine *Colonel Kurt Steiner* • Donald Sutherland *Liam Devlin* • Robert Duvall *Colonel Max Radl* • Jenny Agutter *Molly Prior* • Donald Pleasence *Heinrich Himmler* • Anthony Quayle *Admiral Wilhelm Canaris* • Jean Marsh *Joanna Grey* • John Standing *Father Philip Verecker* • Judy Geeson *Pamela Verecker* ■ *Dir* John Sturges • *Scr* Tom Mankiewicz, from the novel by Jack Higgins

The Eagle Has Two Heads ★★★

Drama 1948 · Fr · BW · 94mins

Jean Cocteau's film of his play, *L'Aigle à Deux Têtes*, with Jean Marais – the hero of Cocteau's *Orphée* and star of the stage version – as a 19th-century anarchist who falls in love with the king's widow when he plans to assassinate her. The fact that he's also a dead ringer for the deceased king complicates matters, as do the plans of the queen's enemies. Less of an achievement than Cocteau's better-known movies – such as *Blood of a Poet* (1930) – this has an exuberant romanticism that's hard to resist. AT. In French with English subtitles.

Edwige Feuillère *The Queen* • Jean Marais *Stanislas* • Sylvia Monfort *Edith de Berg* • Jean Debucourt *Felix de Willenstein* • Jacques Varennes *Count de Foehn* • Abdallah *Tony* ■ *Dir* Jean Cocteau • *Scr* Jean Cocteau, from his play *L'Aigle à Deux Têtes*

Eagle in a Cage ★★★★

Historical drama 1971 · UK · Colour · 102mins

Napoleon's frustrating last years in exile on the tiny, remote island of St Helena make for a compelling drama. Seizing one of the best roles of his career, Kenneth Haigh is superb as the unbowed Bonaparte, and he's beautifully supported by John Gielgud, Ralph Richardson and Billie Whitelaw. Producer/screenwriter Millard Lampell had already nursed this project into an Emmy award-winning TV production starring Trevor Howard in 1965, and his bitter experience of exile, as a blacklisted writer during the McCarthy era, resonates resonates in his understanding of the deposed conqueror. AME

John Gielgud *Lord Sissal* • Ralph Richardson *Sir Hudson Lowe* • Billie Whitelaw *Madame Bertrand* • Kenneth Haigh *Napoleon Bonaparte* • Moses Gunn *General Gourgaud* • Ferdy Mayne *Count Bertrand* • Lee Montague *Cipriani* • Georgina Hale *Betty Balcombe* ■ *Dir* Fielder Cook • *Scr* Millard Lampell

Eagle's Wing ★★★ PG

Western 1978 · UK · Colour · 99mins

Anthony Harvey's strange, myth-laden movie pits two deeply troubled men against each other in a spiritual and material battle for the prize of a white stallion named Eagle's Wing. As, respectively, cowboy and native American Indian, Martin Sheen and Sam Waterston are both superb in their playing of traditional enemies who recognise in each other the same desire to acquit themselves bravely in the critical eyes of their communities. The movie loses a certain momentum as Harvey piles subplot upon subplot, but otherwise this intelligent western is a treat. SH

Martin Sheen *Pike* • Sam Waterston *White Bull* • Harvey Keitel *Henry* • Stéphane Audran *Widow* • Caroline Langrishe *Judith* • John Castle *Priest* • Jorge Luke *Red Sky* • Jose Carlos Ruis *Lame Wolf* • Manuel Ojeda *Miguel* ■ *Dir* Anthony Harvey • *Scr* John Briley, from a story by Michael Syson

The Ear ★★★★

Political thriller 1969 · Cz · BW · 93mins

This is one of the films "banned forever" by the Czech government in 1969, which finally emerged to great acclaim following the Velvet Revolution 20 years later. Directed with awesome control by Karel Kachyna, *The Ear* is a blistering combination of political allegory and domestic drama. Radoslav Brzobohaty is the epitome of paranoia as the minor official who arrives home from a blood-letting party function convinced that he is next in line for dismissal and arrest. His feuds with wife Jirina Bohdalova as they strip the house of incriminating evidence are excruciating in their bitterness. DP. In Czech with English subtitles.

Jirina Bohdalova *Anna* • Radoslav Brzobohaty *Ludvik* • Gustav Opocensky *Conrade* • Miloslav Holub [Miroslav Holub] *General* • Lubor Tokos *Minister* ■ *Dir* Karel Kachyna • *Scr* Karel Kachyna, Jan Prochazka, from a story by Jan Prochazka

Earl Carroll Vanities ★★ U

Musical 1945 · US · BW · 91mins

Princess Drina (Constance Moore) comes to New York to try to raise some money for her impoverished country. Desperate situations call for desperate measures, and she finds herself starring on Broadway in one of Earl Carroll's musical extravaganzas and receiving the romantic attentions of Dennis O'Keefe. Directed by Joseph Santley and offering some lively production numbers, this is still a candidate for the "Most Idiotic Musical of All Time" award. RK

Dennis O'Keefe *Danny Baldwin* • Constance Moore *Drina* • Eve Arden *Tex Donnelly* • Otto Kruger *Earl Carroll* • Alan Mowbray *Grand Duke Paul* • Stephanie Bachelor *Claire Elliott* ■ *Dir* Joseph Santley • *Scr* Frank Gill Jr, from a story by Cortland Fitzsimmons

The Earl of Chicago ★★

Comedy drama 1940 · US · BW · 87mins

Robert Montgomery stars as a Chicago gangster who inherits a title – and a castle! Accompanied by crooked lawyer Edward Arnold, he visits a very backlot England where he encounters butler Edmund Gwenn and solicitor Reginald Owen. Directed by MGM hack Richard Thorpe, who does what he can, this wasn't amusing then and sorely tries the patience now. TS

Robert Montgomery *"Silky" Kilmount* • Edward Arnold *"Doc" Ramsey* • Reginald Owen *Gervase Gonwell* • Edmund Gwenn *Munsey* • EE Clive *Redwood* • Norma Varden *Maureen Kilmount* • Halliwell Hobbes *Lord Chancellor* ■ *Dir* Richard Thorpe • *Scr* Lesser Samuels, from a story by Charles de Grandcourt, Gene Fowler, Brock Williams

The Early Bird ★★ U

Comedy 1965 · UK · Colour · 93mins

Well past his movie sell-by date, Norman Wisdom is powerless to prevent this dreary dairy comedy from turning sour. The satirical jibes at large-scale automation are nowhere near sharp enough, while the tribute to Britain's fast-fading family firms is too twee. As co-scriptwriter, Wisdom must shoulder much of the blame himself, as regular straight men Jerry Desmonde and Edward Chapman are as solid as rocks and longtime director Robert Asher gives his star plenty of leeway. DP DVD

Norman Wisdom *Norman Pitkin* • Edward Chapman *Mr Grimsdale* • Jerry Desmonde *Hunter* • Paddie O'Neil *Mrs Hoskins* • Bryan Pringle *Austin* • Richard Vernon *Sir Roger* • John Le Mesurier *Colonel Foster* ■ *Dir* Robert Asher • *Scr* Jack Davies, Norman Wisdom, Eddie Leslie, Henry Blyth

Early Frost ★ 18

Crime thriller 1981 · Aus · Colour · 86mins

This is a weak Australian thriller about a private detective who finds a corpse while working on a divorce case and suspects murder, even though a verdict of accidental death is recorded. The paranoia inherent in the situation is underplayed, while the ham-fisted actors give no indication that they know what they are doing. JB

Guy Doleman *Mike Hayes* • Diana McLean *Val Meadows* • Jon Blake *Peter Meadows* • Janet Kingsbury *Peg Prentice* • Kit Taylor *Paul Sloane* ■ *Dir/Scr* Terry O'Connor

An Early Frost ★★★★ 15

Drama 1985 · US · Colour · 96mins

One of the first dramas on TV to tackle the subject of Aids, this is a poignant and powerful movie about a son who has to tell his parents he is both homosexual and has an Aids-related disease. Aidan Quinn gives a moving performance as the son, while Gena Rowlands and Ben Gazzara are superb as his mum and dad. Subsequent movies on the subject, such as the Tom Hanks Oscar-winner *Philadelphia*, have lapsed into sentimentality, but director John Erman successfully manages to keep the schmaltz in check and produce a touching and effective film. JB

Aidan Quinn *Michael Pierson* • Gena Rowlands *Katherine Pierson* • Ben Gazzara *Nick Pierson* • Sylvia Sidney *Beatrice McKenna* • DW Moffett *Peter Hilton* • John Glover *Victor Dimato* • Sydney Walsh *Susan Maracek* ■ *Dir* John Erman • *Scr* Ron Cowen, Daniel Lipman, from a story by Sherman Yellen

Early Spring ★★★★

Drama 1956 · Jpn · BW · 144mins

Stylistically and thematically, the postwar films of Yasujiro Ozu are very much alike – even their titles (*Late Spring, Early Summer, Late Autumn*) are confusingly similar – yet each one is a gem. In this mature work, young clerk Ryo Ikebe finds temporary respite from the boredom of his job and his marriage in a brief affair with the firm's flirt. The characteristically slight plot, involving a modern Japanese couple, unravels slowly with great formal beauty, economy, lucidity and humour. The outdoor scenes are limited to brief glimpses or to pauses in the action. RB. In Japanese with English subtitles.

Chikage Awashima *Masako* • Ryo Ikebe *Sugiyama* • Keiko Kishi *"Goldfish"* • Chishu Ryu *Onodera* • So Yamamura *Kawai* • Haruko Sugimura *Masako's mother* • Kuniko Miyake *Sakae* • Eijiro Tono *Hattori* ■ *Dir* Yasujiro Ozu • *Scr* Yasujiro Ozu, Kogo Noda

Early Summer ★★★★

Drama 1951 · Jpn · BW · 150mins

Few could manipulate screen space and time better than director Yasujiro Ozu. Precious little appears to happen in these two-and-a-half hours, yet they seem to fly by as the director's deceptively inobtrusive style draws you ever more deeply into the lives of Setsuko Hara and her family. As the devoted daughter who suddenly refuses to accept her ageing parents' choice of husband, Hara gives a wonderfully nuanced performance of quiet determination and dignity. But it's the way in which Ozu slowly accumulates detail and gently forces the characters to reveal themselves that makes this simple human drama so compelling. DP. In Japanese with English subtitles.

Setsuko Hara *Noriko* • Chishu Ryu *Koichi* • Kuniko Miyake *Fumiko* • Chikage Awashima *Aya Tamura* • Chieko Higashiyama *Shige* • Zen Murase *Minoru* • Ichiro Sugai *Shukichi* • Haruko Sugimura *Tami Yabe* ■ *Dir* Yasujiro Ozu • *Scr* Yasujiro Ozu, Kogo Noda

Earth ★★★★★ U

Silent drama 1930 · USSR · BW · 83mins

Among the most moving films ever made, director Alexander Dovzhenko's hymn of praise to his native Ukraine comes as close as any silent picture to achieving cinematic poetry. Paced to match the gentle rhythms of nature, the story of the feud between a family of wealthy kulaks and some idealistic collective farmers has a pronounced political purpose. But it's primarily a celebration of the unending cycle of birth, love and death, hence the funeral of the murdered village chairman ending with a life-giving shower of summer rain. Combining lyrical beauty with simple truth, this is a masterpiece with a soul. DP. A Russian language film.

Stepan Shkurat *Opanas Trubenko* • Semyon Savshenko *Vasil Trubenko* • Pyotr Masokha *Khoma Belokon* • Mikola Nademski *Grandfather Semion Trubenko* • Nikolai Mikhailov *Father Gerasim* • Yelena Maksimova *Natalka* ■ *Dir/Scr* Alexander Dovzhenko

Earth ★★★ 15

Political romantic drama
1998 · Ind/Can · Colour · 101mins

This is a disturbing depiction of Muslims, Hindus and Sikhs literally tearing each other apart. Considering the complexity of the political situation in late-1940s India, Deepa Mehta admirably delineates the rivalries, though it's only when independence is declared and Lahore erupts into sickening violence that the extent of these enmities becomes apparent. The plot is provocative, the acting committed, but dramatically it's something of a disappointment. DP. In English and Hindi with subtitles. Contains swearing.

Maaia [Maia Sethna] *Lenny Sethna* • Nandita Das *Shanta (Lenny's ayah)* • Aamir Khan *Dil Nawaz (Ice Candy man)* • Rahul Khanna *Hasan (Masseur)* • Kulbhushan Kharbanda *Imam Din* • Kitu Gidwani *Bunty Sethna* ■ *Dir* Deepa Mehta • *Scr* Deepa Mehta, from the autobiography *Cracking India* by Bapsi Sidhwa

The Earth Dies Screaming ★

Science fiction 1964 · UK · BW · 66mins

Great title, boring movie, even though it's only an hour long! Veteran horror director Terence Fisher hit the bottom of the alien-invasion barrel with the first in his off-Hammer sci-fi trilogy that continued with the better *Island of Terror* and *Night of the Big Heat*. Test pilot Willard Parker returns to England and finds the entire population wiped out by robots that kill by touch and then re-animate their victims as eyeless zombies. A dud. AJ

Willard Parker *Jeff Nolan* • Virginia Field *Peggy Taggett* • Dennis Price *Quinn Taggett* • Vanda Godsell *Violet Courtland* ■ *Dir* Terence Fisher • *Scr* Henry Cross [Harry Spalding]

Earth Girls Are Easy ★★★★ PG

Musical satire 1988 · US · Colour · 100mins

Three randy aliens (Jeff Goldblum, Jim Carrey and Damon Wayans) crash-land in LA and are given a guided tour through Planet Hollywood's craziness by two beautician Valley Girls in this enormously entertaining musical comedy. Geena Davis and Julie Brown are terrific in a popcorn movie that's full of bitchy one-liners and frothy fantasy. There's no attempt at a reality check in this hairsprayed *Lost in Space*, just breezy glitz, garish glamour and *Grease*-type songs in a trash setting. AJ DVD

Geena Davis *Valerie Dale* • Jeff Goldblum *Mac* • Jim Carrey *Wiploc* • Damon Wayans *Zebo* • Julie Brown *Candy Pink* • Charles Rocket *Ted* • Michael McKean *Woody* ■ *Dir* Julien Temple • *Scr* Julie Brown, Charlie Coffey, Terrence E McNally

Earth vs the Flying Saucers ★★ U

Science-fiction fantasy
1956 · US · BW · 79mins

Commendable only for special effects genius Ray Harryhausen's flying saucers trashing Washington DC's landmarks, this routine potboiler lifts most of its plot from HG Wells's *The War of the Worlds*. Hero scientist Hugh Marlowe, back in the nation's capital after surviving *The Day the Earth Stood Still*, slows down the plodding story even further by embarking on a sluggish romantic interlude with Joan Taylor. For serial Harryhausen freaks only. AJ DVD

Hugh Marlowe *Dr Russell A Marvin* • Joan Taylor *Carol Marvin* • Donald Curtis *Major Huglin* • Morris Ankrum *General Hanley* • John Zaremba *Professor Kanter* • Tom Browne Henry [Thomas Browne Henry] *Admiral Enright* • Grandon Rhodes *General Edmunds* • Larry Blake [Larry J Blake] *Motorcycle officer* ■ *Dir* Fred F Sears • *Scr* George Worthing Yates, Raymond T Marcus [Bernard Gordon], from a story by Curt Siodmak, from the article *Flying Saucers from Outer Space* by Major Donald E Keyhoe

Earth vs the Spider ★ 15

Science-fiction horror
1958 · US · BW · 72mins

A high-school biology teacher finds a "dead" giant spider and puts it in the gym. But when the local rock 'n' roll band starts practising for the prom, the mutation wakes up and rampages around town sucking the vital fluids from terrified teenagers. It sounds like trashy fun, and it is for about five minutes, but then the dreadful special effects and awful performances lose their camp lustre. AJ DVD

Edward Kemmer *Mr Kingman* • June Kenny *Carol Flynn* • Gene Persson *Mike Simpson* • Gene Roth *Sheriff Cagle* • Hal Torey *Mr Simpson* • June Jocelyn *Mrs Flynn* ■ *Dir* Bert I Gordon • *Scr* Laszlo Gorog

Earthbound ★

Science-fiction drama
1981 · US · Colour · 94mins

Pandemonium breaks out in the town of Gold Rush when a disabled spaceship lands in its midst and the humanoid cargo seeks out grandfather Burl Ives for help. Evil government agent Joseph Campanella is convinced the aliens are anything but benevolent in this tiresome retread of sci-fi clichés without an iota of style. AJ

Burl Ives *Ned Anderson* • Christopher Connelly *Zef* • Meredith MacRae *Lara* • Joseph Campanella *Conrad* • Todd Porter *Tommy* • Marc Gilpin *Dalem* • Elissa Leeds *Teva* ■ *Dir* James L Conway • *Scr* Michael Fisher

The Earthling ★★ PG

Adventure drama
1980 · Aus · Colour · 96mins

Terminally ill William Holden gives recently orphaned Ricky Schroder a crash course in life and survival techniques in the Australian outback. Overly sentimental, there is also an inordinate number of shots featuring cuddly koalas and loping kangaroos. Holden has an undeniable craggy charm, though Schroder isn't as cute as he could have been. AT

William Holden (2) *Patrick Foley* • Ricky Schroder [Rick Schroder] *Shawn Daley* • Jack Thompson *Ross Daley* • Olivia Hamnett *Bettina Daley* • Alwyn Kurts *Christian Neilson* • Redmond Phillips *Bobby Burns* ■ *Dir* Peter Collinson • *Scr* Lanny Cotler

Earthly Possessions ★★ 15

Drama 1999 · US · Colour · 98mins

A trip to the local bank goes horribly wrong for preacher's wife Susan Sarandon when she's taken hostage by robber Stephen Dorff. Far from playing the victim, Sarandon manages to help Dorff escape and get his pregnant girlfriend Elisabeth Moss out of a home for unwed mothers. Sarandon does a great line in bored housewives, but her talents are smothered in James Lapine's mediocre TV movie. LH DVD

Susan Sarandon *Charlotte Emery* • Stephen Dorff *Jake Simms Jr* • Jay O Sanders *Zack Emery* • Elisabeth Moss *Mindy* • Phoebe Lapine *Cheerleader No 1* • Anna Menken *Cheerleader No 2* ■ *Dir* James Lapine • *Scr* Steven Rogers, from the novel by Anne Tyler

Earthquake ★★★★ PG

Disaster movie 1974 · US · Colour · 117mins

As usual in disaster movies, "the big one" hits Los Angeles at the worst possible moment for the cast in this highly enjoyable hokum. The first hour builds up the tension with tremor suspense before the entire city is razed spectacularly to the ground; the dam-busting sequence has since inspired a Universal theme park favourite. Mark Robson's star-packed extravaganza deservedly won a special achievement Oscar for best visual effects. An "8" on the entertainment Richter scale. AJ DVD

Charlton Heston *Stuart Graff* • Ava Gardner *Remy Graff* • George Kennedy *Lew Slade* • Lorne Greene *Sam Royce* • Geneviêve Bujold *Denise Marshall* • Richard Roundtree *Miles Quade* • Marjoe Gortner *Jody* • Barry Sullivan *Dr Stockle* • Lloyd Nolan *Dr Vance* • Victoria Principal *Rosa* • Walter Matuschanskavasky [Walter Matthau] *Drunk* ■ *Dir* Mark Robson • *Scr* George Fox, Mario Puzo

E

East Is East ★★★★ 15

Comedy drama 1999 · UK · Colour · 92mins

This 1970s-set culture-clash comedy drama is thoroughly accessible and doesn't take itself too seriously as it follows the travails of a Pakistani dad, now married to an English woman, who is desperate that his sons buckle under and accept arranged marriages. The boys, heady with teenage freedom and feeling "British" as opposed to "Asian", are resistant, and family wrangling ensues. Funny, charming and refreshing, this is a great little film. LH. Contains swearing, violence. DVD

Om Puri *George Khan* • Linda Bassett *Ella Khan* • Jordan Routledge *Sajid Khan* • Archie Panjabi *Meenah Khan* • Emil Marwa *Maneer Khan* • Chris Bisson *Saleem Khan* • Jimi Mistry *Tariq Khan* • Raji James *Abdul Khan* ■ *Dir* Damien O'Donnell • *Scr* Ayub Khan-Din, from his play

East LA Warriors ★★ 15

Crime drama 1989 · US · Colour · 121mins

Cliché-ridden, low-budget thriller with a largely Mexican cast and some spurious nods to mythicism. Lawrence Hilton-Jacobs is the best-known face in the largely unknown cast, while writer Raymond Martino would go on to the heights of making vehicles for *Playboy* star Anna Nicole Smith. JF DVD

Tony Bravo *Aurelo* • Kamar Reyes *Paulo Santees* • William Smith *Mr Martel* • Lawrence Hilton-Jacobs *Chesare* ■ *Dir* Addison Randall • *Scr* Addison Randall, Raymond Martino

East Lynne ★★★★

Melodrama 1931 · US · BW · 102mins

One of the greatest Victorian melodramas becomes a surprisingly credible movie in the skilled hands of director Frank Lloyd, who has assembled an immaculate cast to bring conviction to a story that is, quite frankly, twaddle. Ann Harding is both beautiful and touching as the fallen woman struggling to regain her child, while Clive Brook and Conrad Nagel are both sturdy and excellent. Art director Joseph Urban's European re-creations on the backlot would be used again and again. TS

Ann Harding *Lady Isabella* • Clive Brook *Captain Levinson* • Conrad Nagel *Robert Carlyle* • Cecilia Loftus *Cornelia Carlyle* • Beryl Mercer *Joyce* • OP Heggie *Earl of Mount Severn* ■ *Dir* Frank Lloyd • *Scr* Bradley King, Tom Barry, from the novel by Mrs Henry Wood

East of Eden ★★★★ PG

Drama 1955 · US · Colour · 112mins

John Steinbeck's sprawling novel becomes a sprawling movie about two brothers vying for their father's love. It's Cain and Abel territory and the Biblical parallels are exploited well by Elia Kazan and writer Paul Osborn. The film has dated, but it's still worth seeing, for one main reason: James Dean's first starring role. Kazan was set on casting Marlon Brando, but when he met Dean – "a heap of twisted legs and denim rags, looking resentful for no particular reason" – he recognised the potential. AT DVD

James Dean *Cal Trask* • Julie Harris *Abra* • Raymond Massey *Adam Trask* • Jo Van Fleet *Kate Trask* • Burl Ives *Sheriff* • Richard Davalos *Aron Trask* • Albert Dekker *Will* • Lois Smith *Ann* • Harold Gordon *Albrecht* ■ *Dir* Elia Kazan • *Scr* Paul Osborn, from the novel by John Steinbeck

East of Elephant Rock ★★

Drama 1976 · UK · Colour · 92mins

Judi Bowker guns down her lover in a jealous rage and pleads self-defence. Don Boyd's film is carried along by the momentum of a cracking story and an urge to see just how much lower it can descend. The Sri Lankan countryside, however, looks amazing. DP. Contains some nudity.

John Hurt *Nash* • Jeremy Kemp *Harry Rawlins* • Judi Bowker *Eve Proudfoot* • Christopher Cazenove *Robert Proudfoot* • Anton Rodgers *Mackintosh* ■ *Dir* Don Boyd • *Scr* Don Boyd, from a story by Richard Boyle, James Atherton

East of Piccadilly ★★

Crime drama 1940 · UK · BW · 78mins

This sordid murder mystery was an unusual offering to place before a country at war. Director Harold Huth paints a fascinating portrait of Soho in the late 1930s, but his handling of the whodunnit is much less assured. Red herrings abound as reporter Judy Campbell and crime writer Sebastian Shaw debate whether a waiter, an actor or a Soviet spy is responsible for a series of murders with a silk stocking. DP

Judy Campbell *Penny Sutton* • Sebastian Shaw *Tamsie Green* • Niall MacGinnis *Joe* • Henry Edwards *Inspector* • George Pughe *Oscar Juloff* • Martita Hunt *Ma* ■ *Dir* Harold Huth • *Scr* J Lee Thompson, Lesley Storym, from the novel by Gordon Beckles

East of Sudan ★★ U

Period adventure 1964 · UK · Colour · 84mins

A lacklustre adventure about a small group who escape an outpost in the Sudan. The central characters are army regular Anthony Quayle and governess Sylvia Syms, and their relationship forms the subplot in this piece of hokum. Director Nathan Juran had the good sense to use British cameraman Wilkie Cooper on five films including this one and his contribution, in colour and Techniscope, enhances a rather dull movie. BB

Anthony Quayle *Richard Baker* • Sylvia Syms *Margaret Woodville* • Derek Fowlds *Murchison* • Jenny Agutter *Asua* • Johnny Sekka *Kimrasi* • Harold Coyne *Major Harris* ■ *Dir* Nathan Juran • *Scr* Jud Kinberg

East of Sumatra ★★ U

Action adventure 1953 · US · Colour · 81mins

A thinly disguised western, set in the Pacific, with Jeff Chandler as a macho American mining engineer. Thanks to his boss John Sutton he soon falls foul of the island's ruler Anthony Quinn, whose alluring native fiancée, is played by actress Suzan Ball. Quinn and Ball also worked together on *City beneath the Sea* but the latter died tragically in 1955 of bone cancer. AT

Jeff Chandler *Duke Mullane* • Marilyn Maxwell *Lory Hale* • Anthony Quinn *Kiang* • Suzan Ball *Minyora* • John Sutton *Daniel Catlin* • Jay C Flippen *Mac* • Scatman Crothers *Baltimore* • Peter Graves (2) *Cowboy* ■ *Dir* Budd Boetticher • *Scr* Frank Gill Jr, Jack Natteford (adaptation), from a story by Louis L'Amour

East of the River ★★

Crime drama 1940 · US · BW · 73mins

This is a lazy piece of backlot movie-making that did little for the burgeoning reputation of John Garfield. As the Italian-American wastrel, envious of adopted brother William Lundigan's looks and education, Garfield strikes a series of pseudo-Cagney poses as he struts around New York with his Mob buddies after a stretch in San Quentin. Things only begin to warm up when Lundigan pinches Garfield's girl, Brenda Marshall. DP

John Garfield *Joe Lorenzo* • Brenda Marshall *Laurie Romayne* • Marjorie Rambeau *Mama Teresa Lorenzo* • George Tobias *Tony* • William Lundigan *Nick Lorenzo* • Moroni Olsen *Judge Davis* ■ *Dir* Alfred E Green • *Scr* Fred Niblo Jr, from a story by John Fante, Ross B Willis

East Side of Heaven ★★★ U

Musical comedy 1939 · US · BW · 87mins

Dripping in sentimentality, but nonetheless sweet-natured, this comedy marks the debut of 10-month-old Baby Sandy, a girl here cast as a boy (who would know!) who went on to become the star of her own series of movies. In this one, though, she is the excuse for star Bing Crosby to croon a handful of songs as a singing cab driver, saddled with the care of an abandoned baby. RK

Bing Crosby *Denny Martin* • Joan Blondell *Mary Wilson* • Mischa Auer *Nicky* • Irene Hervey *Mona* • Jerome Cowan *Claudius De Wolfe* • Robert Kent *Cyrus Barrett Jr* • C Aubrey Smith *Cyrus Barrett Sr* ■ *Dir* David Butler • *Scr* William Conselman, from a story by David Butler, Herbert Polesie

East Side, West Side ★★

Drama 1949 · US · BW · 107mins

James Mason is married to Barbara Stanwyck, but unable to resist playing away with Ava Gardner. Stanwyck, meanwhile, does her best to be all saintly and forgive him, while war veteran Van Heflin offers her all the comfort he can muster. Smoothly performed by the appealing cast and smothered in Miklos Rozsa's syrupy music, this overcooked melodrama is an old-time soap opera. AT

Barbara Stanwyck *Jessie Bourne* • James Mason *Brandon Bourne* • Van Heflin *Mark Dwyer* • Ava Gardner *Isabel Lorrison* • Cyd Charisse *Rosa Senta* • Nancy Davis *Helen Lee* • Gale Sondergaard *Nora Kernan* • William Conrad *Lieutenant Jacobi* ■ *Dir* Mervyn LeRoy • *Scr* Isobel Lennart, from the novel by Marcia Davenport

East-West ★★★ 12

Period romantic drama
1999 · Fr/Rus/Sp/Bul · Colour · 119mins

Régis Wargnier's Oscar-nominated period piece not only sheds light on a little-known episode in Soviet history, but also provides plenty of satisfyingly dramatic incident. The teaming of Oleg Menshikov and Sandrine Bonnaire is crucial, as they provide the emotional core of this stark exposé of the conditions that greet a White Russian exile and his French wife on accepting Stalin's duplicitous postwar amnesty. However, the secondary characters are also well delineated, particularly Catherine Deneuve's touring stage diva. DP. In French and Russian with English subtitles. DVD

Sandrine Bonnaire *Marie* • Catherine Deneuve *Gabrielle Develay* • Oleg Menshikov *Alexei Golovin* • Sergei Bodrov Jr *Sasha* • Ruben Tapiero *Seryozha aged 7* • Erwan Baynaud *Seryozha aged 14* • Grigori Manukov *Pirogov* • Tatyana Dogilova *Olga* ■ *Dir* Régis Wargnier • *Scr* Régis Wargnier, Sergei Bodrov, Rustam Ibragimbekov, Louis Gardel

Easter Parade ★★★★★ U

Classic musical 1948 · US · Colour · 98mins

Originally intended as a re-teaming of Judy Garland and Gene Kelly under Vincente Minnelli's direction after *The Pirate*, this turned out to be one of MGM's great seasonal delights. Producer Arthur Freed coaxed Fred Astaire out of retirement when Kelly broke his ankle, and entrusted the direction to the brilliant craftsman Charles Walters, and the result was simply wonderful. Aided by terrific Irving Berlin songs and radiant Technicolor design – all browns and greens – Astaire, Garland and Walters made an all-time classic, with Fred and Judy particularly outstanding in the perennial favourite *A Couple of Swells*. The screenplay is witty, co-star Ann Miller dances up a storm, and this is the one opportunity to enjoy the talents of Astaire and Garland on screen together. TS DVD

Judy Garland *Hannah Brown* • Fred Astaire *Don Hewes* • Peter Lawford *Jonathan Harrow III* • Ann Miller *Nadine Hale* • Jules Munshin *François* • Clinton Sundberg *Mike, the bartender* • Jeni LeGon *Essie* ■ *Dir* Charles Walters • *Scr* Frances Goodrich, Albert Hackett, Sidney Sheldon, Guy Bolton, from a story by Frances Goodrich, Albert Hackett • *Cinematographer* Harry Stradling • *Art Director* Cedric Gibbons, Jack Martin Smith • *Music/lyrics* Irving Berlin

Easy Come, Easy Go ★★ U

Musical adventure
1967 · US · Colour · 90mins

One of the weakest of Elvis Presley's later Paramount vehicles, this is almost as embarrassing for audiences as it clearly is for Elvis himself, dealing both with stupid and intractable material about finding lost treasure, and demeaning songs like "Yoga Is as Yoga Does". The humour is feeble and invariably tasteless (anti-beatnik jokes in the 1960s?) and it's tough to watch Elsa Lanchester used as a figure of fun. The garish Technicolor just about makes this watchable. TS DVD

Elvis Presley *Ted Jackson* • Dodie Marshall *Jo Symington* • Elsa Lanchester *Madame Neherina* • Pat Priest *Dina Bishop* • Pat Harrington *Judd Whitman* • Skip Ward *Gil Carey* • Sandy Kenyon *Lt Schwartz* • Frank McHugh *Captain Jack* ■ *Dir* John Rich • *Scr* Allan Weiss, Anthony Lawrence

The Easy Life ★★★★

Drama 1962 · It · BW · 105mins

Writer/director Dino Risi established himself as one of the most scathing critics of Italian complacency during the economic boom of the late 1950s. He was at his sharpest with this tragicomedy, in which cynical waster Vittorio Gassman sets about corrupting idealistic student Jean-Louis Trintignant. Risi gets the most out of his exceptional cast during Trintignant's meeting with Gassman's daughter, Catherine Spaak. DP. In Italian with English subtitles.

Vittorio Gassman *Bruno Cortona* • Jean-Louis Trintignant *Roberto Mariani* • Catherine Spaak *Lilly, Bruno's daughter* • Luciana Angiolillo *Bruno's wife* • Linda Sini *Aunt Lidia* • Corrado Olmi *Alfredo* ■ *Dir* Dino Risi • *Scr* Dino Risi, Ettore Scola, Ruggero Maccari

Easy Living ★★★★

Screwball comedy 1937 · US · BW · 87mins

A smashing slapstick comedy, due mainly to the cracking script by Preston Sturges. The story is simple: a fur coat thrown out of a window gets simple stenographer Jean Arthur mistaken for a millionaire's mistress, leading to all sorts of misunderstandings. Arthur shows what a gifted comedian she was, coping beautifully with the wisecracks and pratfalls Sturges provides. Edward Arnold and Ray Milland also give spot-on performances, and there's a spectacular update on the old custard pie fight set in a New York automat. AT

Jean Arthur *Mary Smith* • Edward Arnold *JB Ball* • Ray Milland *John Ball Jr* • Luis Alberni *Mr Louis Louis* • Mary Nash *Mrs Ball* • Franklin Pangborn *Van Buren* • William Demarest *Wallace Whistling* ■ *Dir* Mitchell Leisen • *Scr* Preston Sturges

Easy Living ★★★ PG

Romantic drama 1949 · US · BW · 76mins

Based on an Irwin Shaw story, this tale of a retiring football player worried about his pension is smart, sassy and very satisfying. Victor Mature is cleverly cast as the New York Chiefs' ex-star halfback, and he gets terrific support from Lizabeth Scott as his overspending spouse and Lucille Ball as the team secretary who has the hots for him. Talented director Jacques Tourneur makes this work far better than anyone could expect. TS

Victor Mature *Pete Wilson* • Lucille Ball *Anne* • Lizabeth Scott *Liza Wilson* • Sonny Tufts *Tim McCarr* • Lloyd Nolan *Lenahan* • Paul Stewart *Argus* • Jack Paar *"Scoop" Spooner* • Jeff Donnell *Penny McCarr* ■ *Dir* Jacques Tourneur • *Scr* Charles Schnee, from the story *Education of the Heart* by Irwin Shaw

Easy Money ★★ U

Portmanteau comedy drama
1947 · UK · BW · 89mins

This portmanteau picture is based partly on a play by Arnold Ridley about four characters who dream of winning the pools in the era of postwar austerity, when thousands lived in hope of a windfall. Frankly, none of the tales is particularly original and the ones involving crooked Dennis Price and meek Mervyn Johns are decidedly ropey. But Edward Rigby's generosity towards his beloved band and the arguments that divide Jack Warner's family are rather neatly played. DP

Greta Gynt *Pat Parsons* • Jack Warner *Phillip Stafford* • Marjorie Fielding *Ruth Stafford* • Yvonne Owen *Carol Stafford* • Jack Watling *Dennis Stafford* • Petula Clark *Jackie Stafford* • Mabel Constanduros *Grandma* • Mervyn Johns *Herbert Atkins* • Joan Young *Agnes Atkins* • Dennis Price *Joe Henty* • Bill Owen *Mr Lee* ■ *Dir* Bernard Knowles • *Scr* Muriel Box, Sydney Box, from the play by Arnold Ridley (first story)

Easy Money ★★ 15

Comedy 1983 · US · Colour · 95mins

The quick-fire vulgarity of Rodney Dangerfield isn't to everyone's taste, but even doubters will find to difficult to stifle the odd chuckle at this cheerfully crude comedy. The plot bears more than a passing resemblance to *Brewster's Millions*: slob-about-town Dangerfield has a year to clean up his act or face forfeiting millions from an inheritance. Joe Pesci scores in an early comic outing, and look out for Jennifer Jason Leigh in a small supporting role. JF

Rodney Dangerfield *Monty* • Joe Pesci *Nicky* • Geraldine Fitzgerald *Mrs Monahan* • Candy Azzara *Rose* • Taylor Negron *Julio* • Val Avery *Louie* • Jeffrey Jones *Clive* • Tom Ewell *Scrappleton* • Jennifer Jason Leigh *Allison* ■ *Dir* James Signorelli • *Scr* Rodney Dangerfield, Michael Endler, PJ O'Rourke, Dennis Blair

Easy Rider ★★★★★ 18

Cult road movie 1969 · US · Colour · 91mins

As laid-back as the machines straddled by Dennis Hopper and Peter Fonda in their search for "the real America", and as hip as a whole drop-out generation, this magical mystery tour of the US has a casual conviction that outstrips Hopper's own on-the-run direction to touch a mythic nerve. Jack Nicholson's boozy lawyer successfully articulates the yearning of the alienated young. That the film ends in sullen and sudden death raises it to the power of allegory, and its success proved there was an audience and a need that the box-office pundits didn't even know existed. The studios tried desperately to repeat its low-budget magic, but couldn't. It just didn't equate with the usual Hollywood formula; it had created its own. TH.

Contains sex scenes, drug abuse and brief nudity. [video] DVD

Peter Fonda *Wyatt/"Captain America"* • Dennis Hopper *Billy* • Jack Nicholson *George Hanson* • Phil Spector *Connection* • Antonio Mendoza *Jesus* • Warren Finnerty *Rancher* • Tita Colorado *Rancher's wife* • Robert Walker Jr *Jack* • Keith Green *Sheriff* • Toni Basil *Mary* • Karen Black *Karen* ■ *Dir* Dennis Hopper • *Scr* Dennis Hopper, Peter Fonda, Terry Southern • *Cinematographer* Laszlo Kovacs

Easy Riders, Raging Bulls ★★★ 15

Documentary
2003 · US/UK/Can · Colour · 113mins

Based on Peter Biskind's eponymous bestseller and narrated by William H Macy, this is a solid survey of that brief golden age between the studio and blockbuster eras, when Hollywood permitted its auteurs to make films for adults that reflected the social, moral and political crises affecting America. Stripping away Biskind's penchant for gossip, Kenneth Bowser concentrates on the movies and the people who made them. He largely has to settle for archival contributions from such big guns as Francis Ford Coppola and Martin Scorsese, although the likes of Dennis Hopper and Peter Bogdanovich offer plenty of original insights. DP [video] DVD

Dir Kenneth Bowser • *Scr* Kenneth Bowser, from the non-fiction book by Peter Biskind

Easy to Love ★★

Romantic comedy 1934 · US · BW · 62mins

The stylishness of the playing keeps this mildly sophisticated, if rather old-fashioned marital comedy alive now as it did on its release. Adolphe Menjou and pert blonde Genevieve Tobin star as a married couple whose relationship founders when she finds him romancing a glamorous brunette and retaliates by claiming to be having an affair herself. A brief running time is advantageous to the one-idea plot; so is the polished cast. RK

Genevieve Tobin *Carol Townsend* • Adolphe Menjou *John Townsend* • Mary Astor *Charlotte Hopkins* • Edward Everett Horton *Eric Schulte* • Patricia Ellis *Janet Townsend* • Guy Kibbee *Justice of the Peace* • Hugh Herbert *Detective John McTavish* ■ *Dir* William Keighley • *Scr* Carl Erickson, Manuel Seff, David Boehm (adaptation, from the play *As Good as News* by Thompson Buchanan

Easy to Love ★★★ U

Musical 1953 · US · Colour · 95mins

There's not too much plot and few memorable songs (except for the Cole Porter title classic), but stunning Esther Williams needs no such help. This MGM musical is a perfectly constructed vehicle for the swimming star whose bossy, no-nonsense screen personality is well suited to this Florida-set satire on advertising. Lovers of high camp will cherish ace choreographer Busby Berkeley's contribution to the water ballets, stacking bodies upon water-skis with perfect symmetry. TS

Esther Williams *Julie Hallerton* • Van Johnson *Ray Lloyd* • Tony Martin *Barry Gordon* • John Bromfield *Hank* • Edna Skinner *Nancy Parmel* • King Donovan *Ben* • Paul Bryar *Mr Barnes* • Carroll Baker *Clarice* ■ *Dir* Charles Walters • *Scr* Laslo Vadnay, William Roberts, from a story by Laslo Vadnay

Easy to Wed ★★★

Musical 1946 · US · Colour · 110mins

Although it lacked the star power of the original, MGM could have no complaints about the performances in this remake of its 1936 screwball classic, *Libeled Lady*. Keenan Wynn is no substitute for Spencer Tracy, but he barks admirably as the editor who sends reporter Van Johnson to charm heiress Esther Williams out of a suit against their paper. The leads can't match the chemistry of William Powell and Myrna Loy, but they still look good together, while Lucille Ball, in one of her breakthrough roles, is every bit as sparky as Jean Harlow. DP

Van Johnson *Bill Stevens Chandler* • Esther Williams *Connie Allenbury* • Lucille Ball *Gladys Benton* • Keenan Wynn *Warren Haggerty* • Cecil Kellaway *JB Allenbury* • June Lockhart *Babs Norvell* ■ *Dir* Edward Buzzell • *Scr* Dorothy Kingsley, from the film *Libeled Lady* by Maurine Watkins, Howard Emmett Rodgers, George Oppenheimer

Easy Virtue ★★★

Silent drama 1927 · UK · BW · 79mins

This early Alfred Hitchcock film sees him still developing his distinctive style. This is an adaptation of Nöel Coward's play about a charming divorcee (Isabel Jeans) with a scandal in her past, who marries into a staid provincial family with predictable results. It's well scripted by Eliot Stannard, and captures the essence of the play even without Coward's witty dialogue. In one of the best scenes, when the hero is proposing to the heroine over the telephone, Hitch cuts away from them and cleverly shows only the reactions on the face of the telephone operator. RB

Isabel Jeans *Larita Filton* • Robin Irvine *John Whittaker* • Franklin Dyall *Mr Filton* • Enid Stamp-Taylor *Sarah* • Violet Farebrother *Mrs Whittaker* • Darcia Deane *Marion Whittaker* ■ *Dir* Alfred Hitchcock • *Scr* Eliot Stannard, from the play by Nöel Coward

Easy Wheels ★ 15

Action adventure comedy
1989 · US · Colour · 90mins

The battle of the sexes meets the biker movie in this action comedy from director David O'Malley. She-Wolf (Eileen Davidson) and Bruce (Paul Le Mat) are the rival gang leaders whose clashes lead the girls to take increasingly desperate measures: kidnapping girl babies and turning them over to wolves to toughen them up. If you're looking for sophisticated comedy and trenchant social comment, this is the wrong film. RT [video]

Paul Le Mat *Bruce* • Eileen Davidson *She-Wolf* • Marjorie Bransfield *Wendy* • Jon Menick *Professor* • Barry Livingston *Reporter* • George Plimpton • Ted Raimi ■ *Dir* David O'Malley • *Scr* David O'Malley, Ivan Raimi

Eat a Bowl of Tea ★★★ 15

Comedy drama 1989 · US · Colour · 98mins

In his early films, Wayne Wang was more interested in the behaviour of his characters in specific cultural and social situations than he was in exploring their motives and emotions. While this made his work intriguing, it often lacked depth. Here the period atmosphere enhances a story about Chinese immigrants in postwar America, but again, beneath the layers of detail and quirky characterisation, there is scant substance. As a result, this is engaging, but ultimately unsatisfying. DP. In English and Mandarin with subtitles. [video]

Victor Wong (2) *Wah Gay* • Russell Wong *Ben Loy* • Cora Miao *Mei Oi* • Eric Chi Wai Tsang [Eric Tsang] *Ah Song* • Lau Siu-Ming *Lee Gong* • Wu Ming Yu *Mei Oi's mother* • Hui Funi *Ben Loy's mother* ■ *Dir* Wayne Wang • *Scr* Judith Rascoe, from the novel by Louis Chu

Eat and Run ★★★ 15

Science-fiction comedy
1986 · US · Colour · 80mins

This spoof on the "creature features" of the 1950s revolves around a king-sized alien whose favourite discovery on Earth turns out to be Italian food. Devouring an Italian sausage maker helps his appetite on its way, though it soon brings Irish cop Ron Silver on his trail. Certain humorous interludes are just too slack to hit home, but Silver, a much underused actor, acquits himself well at the centre of this amiable nonsense. JM [video]

Ron Silver *Mickey McSorely* • Sharon Schlarth *Judge Cheryl Cohen* • RL Ryan *Murray Creature* • John F Fleming *Police captain* • Derek Murcott *Sorely McSorely* • Robert Silver *Pusher* • Mimi Cecchini *Grandmother* • Tony Moundroukas *Zepoli kid* ■ *Dir* Christopher Hart • *Scr* Stan Hart, Christopher Hart

Eat Drink Man Woman ★★★★ PG

Comedy drama 1994 · Tai · Colour · 119mins

Although the prime influence on Taiwanese director Ang Lee's stately style and several of the film's themes is the Japanese genius Yasujiro Ozu, there is more than a hint of Woody Allen in this complex ensemble comedy. The action flits between the problems facing each member of master chef Lung Sihung's family, and the performances are light and believable, the dialogue full of wit and wisdom. DP. In Mandarin with English subtitles. [video]

Lung Sihung *Mr Chu* • Wang Yu-wen *Jia-ning* • Wu Chien-lien *Jia-chien* • Yang Kuei-Mei *Jia-jen* • Sylvia Chang *Jin-rong* • Winston Chao *Li Kai* • Chen Chao-jung *Guo Lun* ■ *Dir* Ang Lee • *Scr* Ang Lee, Wang Hui-ling, James Schamus

Eat My Dust! ★

Comedy action adventure
1976 · US · Colour · 88mins

Charles B Griffith, the prolific writer of Roger Corman's best movies, turned director with this inept car crash comedy starring the famous Howard family of Ron, father Rance and brother Clint. Nothing more than a patchy excuse to destroy automobiles, trucks, boats and buildings on the cheap in a frantic demolition derby, while dumb cops and grease monkey Ron Howard's romantic interest look on in bemusement. A crashing bore. AJ

Ron Howard *Hoover Niebold* • Chrissie Norris *Darlene* • Warren Kemmerling *Sheriff Harry Niebold* • Dave Madden *Big Bubba Jones* • Rance Howard *Deputy Clark* • Clint Howard *Georgie* ■ *Dir/Scr* Charles B Griffith

Eat the Peach ★★★ PG

Comedy drama 1986 · Ire · Colour · 91mins

Armed with a true story, a tight budget and a video of the Elvis Presley vehicle *Roustabout*, director Peter Ormrod comes up with an engaging film whose main fault is its determination to be offbeat. As the jobless duo who set out to build a "Wall of Death", Stephen Brennan and Eamon Morrissey have a likeable loopiness, though the rascally side to their characters is perhaps overdone. Memorable moments include the sight of Brennan's small daughter tricycling around the lower wall, though there's a lot of dull stuff in between. DP [video]

Eamon Morrissey *Arthur* • Stephen Brennan *Vinnie Galvin* • Catherine Byrne *Nora Galvin* • Niall Toibin *Boots* • Joe Lynch *Boss Murtagh* • Tony Doyle *Sean Murtagh* • Takashi Kawahara *Bunzo* • Victoria Armstrong *Vicky Galvin* ■ *Dir* Peter Ormrod • *Scr* Peter Ormrod, John Kelleher, from an idea by Peter Ormrod

Eat the Rich ★★ 15

Comedy 1987 · UK · Colour · 84mins

When a waiter loses his job at trendy London restaurant Bastards, he plots with a band of revolutionaries to put its customers on the menu. Peter Richardson's film is more of a student prank than a subversive satire. Of the main performers, Nosher Powell is memorable as a Home Secretary who behaves like a Kray brother. However, the movie's main fascination lies in its array of cameos, from Paul McCartney and Bill Wyman to Koo Stark and French and Saunders. AT [video]

Lanah Pellay *Alex* • Nosher Powell *Nosher* • Fiona Richmond *Fiona* • Ronald Allen *Commander Fortune* • Lemmy *Spider* • Robbie Coltrane *Jeremy* • Kathy Burke *Kathy* • Miles Copeland *Derek* • Adrian Edmondson *Charles* • Dawn French *Debbie Draws* • Jools Holland *"Sun" Reporter* • Rik Mayall *Micky* • Shane McGowan *Terrorist* • Nigel Planer *DHSS manager* • Miranda Richardson *DHSS blonde* • Jennifer Saunders *Lady Caroline* • Sandie Shaw *Edgeley's girlfriend* • Koo Stark *Hazel* • Ruby Wax *Bibi de Coutts* • Bill Wyman *Toilet victim* • Paul McCartney ■ *Dir* Peter Richardson • *Scr* Peter Richens, Peter Richardson

E

Eaten Alive ★★ 18

Horror thriller 1976 · US · Colour · 81mins

Tobe Hooper's little-seen follow-up to his seminal *Texas Chain Saw Massacre* is a heavily stylised tale that incorporates the shock value of the EC horror comics of the 1950s. Neville Brand stars as the psychopathic proprietor of a rundown hotel who feeds guests to his pet crocodile. While the film is perhaps guilty of perpetuating the myth that all backwoods yokels are a couple of strings short of a banjo, the goofy plot and impressive production design win the day. RS [video] DVD

Neville Brand *Judd* • Mel Ferrer *Harvey Wood* • Carolyn Jones *Miss Hattie* • Marilyn Burns *Faye* • William Finley *Roy* • Stuart Whitman *Sheriff Martin* • Robert Englund *Buck* ■ *Dir* Tobe Hooper • *Scr* Alvin L Fast, Mardi Rustam, Kim Henkel

Eating ★★★

Comedy drama 1990 · US · Colour · 110mins

A group of women talk about food and life at a birthday party, yet, fascinating though the interchanges and revelations are, they don't merit 110 minutes. The performances, however, are sparkling, with birthday girls Mary Crosby (30), Lisa Richards (40) and Marlena Giovi (50) revelling in a script exploring the ways in which women view food as both a comfort and a scourge. This is very much an ensemble piece, but mouthy Frances Bergen, mousy Daphna Kastner and bitchy Gwen Welles do stand out. DP

Lisa Richards *Helene* • Mary Crosby *Kate* • Marlena Giovi *Sadie* • Gwen Welles *Sophie* • Nelly Alard *Martine* • Frances Bergen *Mrs Williams* • Daphna Kastner *Jennifer* • Elizabeth Kemp *Nancy* • Rachelle Carson *Cathy* • Toni Basil *Jackie* • Marina Gregory *Lydia* ■ *Dir/Scr* Henry Jaglom

Eating Raoul ★★★★ 18

Black comedy 1982 · US · Colour · 79mins

Paul and Mary Bland (brilliantly portrayed by director Paul Bartel and actress Mary Woronov) finance their dream restaurant by advertising for wealthy swingers and then killing them off during sex for their cash. Handyman Robert Beltran muscles in on the action by selling the bodies to a dog food factory. A cute black comedy, hilariously sending up California culture and executed with sadistic glee by all concerned. Bartel turned his cult sleeper into an off-Broadway musical in 1992. AJ [video] DVD

Paul Bartel *Paul Bland* • Mary Woronov *Mary Bland* • Robert Beltran *Raoul* • Susana Saiger *Doris the Dominatrix* • Ed Begley Jr *Hippy* • Dan Barrows *Bobbie R* • Richard Blackburn *James* • Ralph Brannen *Paco* • Buck Henry *Mr Leech* ■ *Dir* Paul Bartel • *Scr* Paul Bartel, Richard Blackburn

L'Eau Froide ★★★★

Drama 1994 · Fr · Colour · 92mins

This is a frank yet tender insight into troubled adolescence from director

Olivier Assayas. Virginie Ledoyen gives a heartrending performance as the mentally fragile product of a broken home who goes on the run with short-fused Parisian schoolboy Cyprien Fouquet after her father puts her in an institution. Shot with energy and authenticity, yet without condescension, the film not only captures the anxiety of youth, but also the feel of the early 1970s. DP. In French with English subtitles.

Virginie Ledoyen *Christine* • Cyprien Fouquet *Gilles* • Laszlo Szabo *Gilles's father* • Jean-Pierre Darroussin *Inspector* • Dominique Faysse *Christine's mother* • Smail Mekki *Mourad* • Jackie Berroyer *Christine's father* ■ *Dir/Scr* Olivier Assayas

E

Eaux d'Artifice ★★★★ U

Experimental fantasy
1953 · US · Tinted · 12mins

Having been frustrated in his attempts to direct again following the acclaim for *Fireworks* (1947), Kenneth Anger finally completed this elegiac companion piece in 1953. Part of the Magick Lantern Cycle and inspired by the ending to Ronald Firbank's novel, *Valmouth*, this baroque fantasy features the diminutive and fabulously dressed Carmillo Salvatorelli wandering through an ornate Italian garden to the strains of Vivaldi. The use of gargoyles, grottoes, staircases and fountains makes this a formally fascinating film, whose atmosphere is further enhanced by an inky blue tint that makes the play of light on water all the more mesmerising. DP

Carmillo Salvatorelli *Water Witch* ■ *Dir/Scr* Kenneth Anger • *Cinematographer* Kenneth Anger

Ebirah, Horror of the Deep ★★ U

Horror 1966 · Jpn · Colour · 83mins

Or *Godzilla versus the Sea Monster*, as it was known everywhere else. In his sixth screen outing, the king of the monsters and his one-time arch enemy, Mothra, hiss and make up to battle the evil giant lobster Ebirah, being used as a p(r)awn by the nasty Red Bamboo gang seeking world domination. Typical Japanese monster fare featuring cardboard mayhem, laughable special effects and failed comedy sees Godzilla play football. Total trash? Naturally. Absolutely unmissable? Of course. AJ. Japanese dialogue dubbed into English. [subtitles]

Akira Takarada • Toru Watanabe • Hideo Sunazuka • Kumi Mizuno • Jun Tazaki ■ *Dir* Jun Fukuda • *Scr* Shinichi Sekizawa

Echo of Diana ★★ U

Spy drama 1963 · UK · BW · 61mins

In this low-budget spy drama, the newshound leads are two Australian actors, Vincent Ball and Betty McDowall, which makes a refreshing change from the usual fading Hollywood stars. Their noses for a story begin to twitch when a mysterious death puts them on the track of one of the most alfresco covert operations you are ever likely to clap eyes on. Director Ernest Morris does well to sustain it for an hour. DP

Vincent Ball *Bill Vernon* • Betty McDowall *Joan Scott* • Geoffrey Toone *Colonel Justin* • Clare Owen *Pam Jennings* • Peter Illing *Kovali* ■ *Dir* Ernest Morris • *Scr* Reginald Hearne

Echo Park ★★★ 15

Comedy drama
1985 · Aus/US · Colour · 84mins

This story of a trio of losers – Susan Dey as the aspiring actress reduced to working in a sleazy bar, Tom Hulce as a song-writing pizza boy and Michael Bowen body-building himself up to disappointment – has moments of real truth and affection from its director Robert Dornhelm. As a study in human relationships it doesn't exactly resound with insight, but it almost – but not quite – reminds us of *Jules et Jim*. TH. Contains swearing and sexual references. [subtitles] DVD

Tom Hulce *Jonathan* • Susan Dey *May* • Michael Bowen *August* • Christopher Walker *Henry Greer* • Shirley Jo Finney *Gloria* • Heinrich Schweiger *August's father* • Richard "Cheech" Marin *Syd* • John Paragon *Hugo* ■ *Dir* Robert Dornhelm • *Scr* Michael Ventura

Echoes ★★ 15

Fantasy thriller 1983 · US · Colour · 85mins

Despite the efforts of director Arthur Allan Seidelman and an intriguing Freudian premise, this psychological thriller fails to live up to its promise. Art student Richard Alfieri keeps dreaming that his twin brother – who died before birth – is determined to kill him and take over his body. Girlfriend Nathalie Nell mops his fevered brow, while oldsters Gale Sondergaard, Mercedes McCambridge and Ruth Roman offer fine support. Alas, it becomes rather melodramatic. TH [subtitles]

Richard Alfieri *Michael Durant/Dream Michael* • Nathalie Nell *Christine* • Mercedes McCambridge *Lillian Gerben* • Ruth Roman *Michael's mother* • Gale Sondergaard *Mrs Edmunds* ■ *Dir* Arthur Allan Seidelman • *Scr* Richard J Anthony

Echoes of a Summer ★

Drama 1976 · US/Can · Colour · 99mins

Jodie Foster assaults the tear ducts by playing a 12-year-old with a terminal heart condition. Facing certain death with startling courage, she makes life a little easier for her parents, played by Lois Nettleton and Richard Harris. Foster, who looks more like a boy than a girl in some scenes, is an odd blend of natural talent and applied emotion, although her love affair with Brad Savage is unspeakably yucky. AT

Richard Harris *Eugene Striden* • Lois Nettleton *Ruth Striden* • Geraldine Fitzgerald *Sara* • William Windom *Doctor Hallett* • Brad Savage *Phillip Anding* • Jodie Foster *Deirdre Striden* ■ *Dir* Don Taylor • *Scr* Robert L Joseph

The Eclipse ★★★★ PG

Romantic drama 1962 · Fr/It · BW · 123mins

This troubling, stylised film completed director Michelangelo Antonioni's "alienation trilogy". As in *L'Avventura* and *La Notte*, Monica Vitti is at the centre of events, here ending a passionless affair with the bookish Francisco Rabal to indulge in a fling with her mother's stockbroker, Alain Delon. Returning to his recurrent themes of the desensitising impact of urban life and the hopelessness of love, Antonioni presents his bleakest portrait of the modern age, with the famous seven-minute, 58-shot montage of cold, impersonal buildings symbolising the city's final victory over its inhabitants. DP. In Italian with English subtitles. [subtitles] DVD

Monica Vitti *Vittoria* • Alain Delon *Piero* • Lilla Brignone *Vittoria's mother* • Francisco Rabal *Riccardo* • Louis Seignier *Ercoli* • Rossana Rory *Anita* • Mirella Ricciardi *Marta* ■ *Dir* Michelangelo Antonioni • *Scr* Michelangelo Antonioni, Tonino Guerra, Elio Bartolini, Ottiero Ottieri

Ecoute Voir... ★★★

Crime drama 1978 · Fr · Colour · 125mins

Argentinian director Hugo Santiago is renowned for his rather strange political commentaries, and this film is no exception. The gracious Catherine Deneuve stars as a private detective hired to investigate and expose a sinister cult. Her trail leads to a mansion house in the middle of nowhere, where the group is attempting to interrupt radio waves with subliminal propaganda. Atmospheric and stylishly shot, the film's moodiness is compounded by a great soundtrack. LH. In French with English subtitles.

Catherine Deneuve *Claude Alphand* • Sami Frey *Arnaud* • Anne Parillaud *Chole* • Florence Delay *Flora* • Antoine Vitez *Sect man* • Didier Haudepin *Secretary* ■ *Dir* Hugo Santiago • *Scr* Hugo Santiago, Claude Ollier

Ecstasy ★★★★

Drama 1933 · Cz · BW · 68mins

It's difficult to separate this Czech film from the furore it created at the time; it was banned outright in Germany and cut to ribbons by the rest of the world. However, it was imported into the USA and shown privately all over Hollywood, where its star – the young Heidi Kiesler – would be imported and renamed Hedy Lamarr, becoming one of Tinseltown's loveliest love goddesses. The reason is a famous sequence where Hedy is swimming in the nude; her horse runs off with her clothes, so she runs starkers through the woods. In another famous sequence, she discovers and demonstrates sexual pleasure in extreme close-up. Director Gustav Machaty creates a wondrous mood, and the overall (uncut) movie is one of cinema's great sensual masterpieces. TS. In Czech with English subtitles.

Hedy Kiesler [Hedy Lamarr] *Eva* • Jaromir Rogoz *Emile* • Aribert Mog *Adam* • Leopold Kramer *Eva's father* ■ *Dir* Gustav Machaty • *Scr* Gustav Machaty, Franz Horky, Vitezslav Nezval, Jacques A Koerpel

Ed ★ PG

Sports comedy 1996 · US · Colour · 90mins

Even the struggling actor Matt LeBlanc portrays in hit series *Friends* would have passed on this dim-witted family comedy, in which the star plays second fiddle to an ape. The Ed of the title is the chimpanzee mascot of a struggling baseball team who becomes the star player and helps LeBlanc out of his pitching slump. The primate gets the best lines – and all he does is grunt and shriek. JF [subtitles]

Matt LeBlanc *Jack Cooper* • Jayne Brook *Lydia* • Jack Warden *Chubb* • Bill Cobbs *Tippet* ■ *Dir* Bill Couturie • *Scr* David Mickey Evans, from a story by Janus Cercone, Ken Richards

Ed Gein ★★ 15

Biographical horror
2000 · US · Colour · 85mins

In what is claimed to be the definitive true-life story of the Wisconsin farmer-turned-cannibal killer, whose 1957 case inspired a host of horror movies, director Chuck Parello has gone for simple storytelling rather than grit and gore. He delivers so many "spooky neighbour" clichés and shows so little of Gein's crimes that he never even scratches the surface of explaining what made the man actually tick. Steve Railsback, in the title role, has no depth or range, while the sporadic special effects are so poor that they give the whole production a made-for-television ambience. SF [subtitles] DVD

Steve Railsback *Ed Gein* • Carrie Snodgress *Augusta Gein* • Sally Champlin *Mary Hogan* • Carol Mansell *Colette* • Nancy Linehan Charles *Eleanor* • Pat Skipper *Sheriff Jim Stillwell* ■ *Dir* Chuck Parello [Charles Parello] • *Scr* Stephen Johnston

Ed McBain's 87th Precinct ★★★ 12

Crime drama 1995 · US · Colour · 85mins

Ed McBain has long been a staple of American crime fiction and, despite its TV roots, this film does full justice to his streetwise sense of realism. Randy Quaid is perfectly cast as the cynical veteran detective who teams up with the younger Alex McArthur to track down the killer of a star athlete. The two leads are backed up with scene-stealing turns from Ving Rhames and Ron Perkins. Director Bruce Paltrow admirably keeps the tension on the boil. JF DVD

Randy Quaid *Steve Carella* • Alex McArthur *Bert Kling* • Deanne Bray *Teddy* • Ving Rhames *Brown* • Eddie Jones *Lieutenant Byrnes* • Alan Blumenfeld *Ollie Weeks* • Ron Perkins *Meyer* ■ *Dir* Bruce Paltrow • *Scr* Dan Levine, Mike Krohn, from the novel *Lightning* by Ed McBain [Evan Hunter]

Ed Wood ★★★★★ 15

Biographical drama 1994 · US · BW · 121mins

Only one of cinema's finest directors could have so lovingly crafted this homage to one of its worst. Tim Burton's wonderful celebration of awful art, and the fascination it continues to exert, traces the weird career of Edward D Wood Jr, from his autobiographical exploitation quickie *Glen or Glenda* to his "masterpiece", the truly terrible *Plan 9 from Outer Space*. Johnny Depp is amazing as director Wood in Burton's black-and-white evocation of 1950s life in Grade Z-land, and Martin Landau deservedly won an Oscar for his uncanny impersonation of Wood's low-rent inspiration, Bela Lugosi. AJ. Contains swearing and drug abuse. [subtitles] DVD

Johnny Depp *Ed Wood* • Martin Landau *Bela Lugosi* • Sarah Jessica Parker *Dolores Fuller* • Patricia Arquette *Kathy O'Hara* • Jeffrey Jones *Criswell* • GD Spradlin *Reverend Lemon* • Vincent D'Onofrio *Orson Welles* • Bill Murray *John "Bunny" Breckinridge* • Mike Starr *Georgie Weiss* ■ *Dir* Tim Burton • *Scr* Scott Alexander, Larry Karaszewski, from the book *Nightmare of Ecstasy* by Rudolph Grey

Eddie ★★★ 12

Sports comedy drama
1996 · US · Colour · 96mins

The newly appointed basketball coach for the legendary New York Knicks is both an obsessive fan and a woman (motormouth Whoopi Goldberg). The Knicks' actual team doesn't appear, by the way, but the screen side does comprise various real-life hoop heroes. Not bad of its kind, with Goldberg taking no nonsense from the NBA stars, and there are also some stimulating slam-dunk sequences. JC. Contains swearing. [subtitles]

Whoopi Goldberg *Edwina "Eddie" Franklin* • Frank Langella *Wild Bill Burgess* • Dennis Farina *Coach Bailey* • Richard Jenkins *Assistant Coach Zimmer* • Lisa Ann Walter *Claudine* • John Benjamin Hickey *Joe Nader* • Troy Beyer *Beth Hastings* ■ *Dir* Steve Rash • *Scr* John Connolly, David Loucka, Eric Champnella, Keith Mitchell, Steve Zacharias, Jeff Buhai, from a story by John Connolly, David Loucka, Steve Zacharias, Jeff Buhai

Eddie and the Cruisers ★★ PG

Drama 1983 · US · Colour · 91mins

Intriguing, if not completely successful spin on the rock movie, which also provided an early platform for two actors on the verge of stardom. Tom Berenger plays a musician who, along with journalist Ellen Barkin, sets out to uncover the mystery behind the demise of his band Eddie and the Cruisers, the archetypal one-hit wonders who fell apart when the lead singer abruptly vanished. Director Martin Davidson manages to sidestep some of the more obvious rock clichés, but it falls apart near the end and, sadly, the music isn't very memorable. JF [subtitles]

Tom Berenger *Frank Ridgeway* • Michael Paré *Eddie Wilson* • Joe Pantoliano *"Doc" Robbins* • Matthew Laurance *Sal Amato* • Helen Schneider *Joann Carlino* • David Wilson *Kenny Hopkins* • Michael "Tunes" Antunes *Wendell*

Newton • Ellen Barkin *Maggie Foley* ■ *Dir* Martin Davidson • *Scr* Martin Davidson, Arlene Davidson, from a novel by PF Kluge

Eddie and the Cruisers II: Eddie Lives! ★★ PG

Drama 1989 · US/Can · Colour · 99mins

The 1983 original was a big video hit, so this belated, cliché-ridden sequel brings Eddie (Michael Paré) back from the dead – or at least back from the blue-collar identity he's been hiding behind since his supposed fatal accident. Once again, Eddie's music has become popular and his cynical record company smells a money-making cash-in. Unless they're fans of 1980s soft rock, most people would advise Eddie not to give up his day job. JF

Michael Paré *Eddie Wilson/Joe West* • Marina Orsini *Diane* • Bernie Coulson *Rick* • Matthew Laurance *Sal* • Michael Rhoades *Dave Pagent* • Larry King • Bo Diddley • Martha Quinn *Music video hostess* ■ *Dir* Jean-Claude Lord • *Scr* Charles Zev Cohen, Rick Doehring, from characters created by PF Kluge

The Eddie Cantor Story ★★ U

Biographical musical
1953 · US · Colour · 116mins

The tale of how Israel Iskowitz, a poor Jewish boy from the Lower East Side of New York, became the rich and famous Hollywood star Eddie Cantor, has all the usual rags-to-riches ingredients and successfully invokes the atmosphere of vaudeville where Eddie started out as an entertainer. A number of his best songs (*If You Knew Susie*, *Making Whoopee*) are included, too, but the lack of a star personality, allied to a weak script, makes for an unengaging showbiz biopic. RK

Keefe Brasselle *Eddie Cantor* • Marilyn Erskine *Ida* • Aline MacMahon *Grandma Esther* • Arthur Franz *Harry Harris* • Alex Gerry *David Tobias* • Greta Granstedt *Rachel Tobias* • Gerald Mohr *Rocky* • William Forrest *Ziegfeld* ■ *Dir* Alfred E Green • *Scr* Sidney Skolsky, Ted Sherdeman, Jerome Weidman, from a story by Sidney Skolsky

Eddie Macon's Run ★★ 15

Action crime drama
1983 · US · Colour · 90mins

This uncomfortable late Kirk Douglas flick gives second billing to John Schneider, one of the stars of *The Dukes of Hazzard*. Like that TV show, this is little more than a prolonged celluloid chase, with a fair amount of crashes and smashes. Douglas shouldn't of been doing this kind of stuff at this stage of his career, but John Goodman does makes his movie debut here. TS

Kirk Douglas *Marzack* • John Schneider *Eddie Macon* • Lee Purcell *Jilly Buck* • Leah Ayres *Chris* • Lisa Dunsheath *Kay Potts* • Tom Noonan *Daryl Potts* • John Goodman *Hebert* ■ *Dir* Jeff Kanew • *Scr* Jeff Kanew, from the novel by James McLendon

Eddie Murphy Raw ★★ 18

Comedy 1987 · US · Colour · 86mins

This overlong and poorly shot concert film of Eddie Murphy's one-man show is for die-hard fans only. Murphy may be a phenomenon as a movie star, but his stand-up routine leaves much to be desired – a foul-mouthed concoction trading on racial and sexual stereotypes that effortlessly offends majority tastes. His frenetic energy and delivery are impressive, though, and his comic imitation of Bill Cosby is inspired. Watch for the uproarious fictional prologue set in a 1960s Murphy household. RS DVD

Eddie Murphy • Tatyana Ali *Singing child* • Billie Allen *Eddie's aunt* • Clebert Ford *Uncle Lester* • Geri Gibson *Second card player* • Samuel L Jackson *Eddie's uncle* ■ *Dir* Robert Townsend • *Scr* Eddie Murphy, Keenen Ivory Wayans

The Eddy Duchin Story ★★★★ U

Biographical drama
1956 · US · Colour · 117mins

This is a deeply satisfying weepie, filmed in CinemaScope, about the New York society pianist struck down by leukaemia in his prime. Though the actual illness isn't named, the scenes in which Duchin, sympathetically portrayed by a mature Tyrone Power, takes leave of his son (Rex Thompson) are unbearably moving. This is a film strong on romance, and Power's relationship with the lovely Kim Novak is superbly orchestrated by director George Sidney against exquisite New York locations in autumnal colours. TS

Tyrone Power *Eddy Duchin* • Kim Novak *Marjorie Oelrichs* • Victoria Shaw *Chiquita* • James Whitmore *Lou Sherwood* • Rex Thompson *Peter Duchin as a boy* • Shepperd Strudwick *Mr Wadsworth* • Frieda Inescort *Mrs Wadsworth* • Gloria Holden *Mrs Duchin* • Gregory Gaye *Philip* ■ *Dir* George Sidney (2) • *Scr* Samuel Taylor, from a story by Leo Katcher

Eden Valley ★★★ 15

Drama 1994 · UK · Colour · 40mins

A slow, lyrical, almost impressionistic effort by the Amber Films collective, featuring famous harness racing family the Laidlers. You either find these working-class denizens of the North East fascinating, or you don't. Most of us uneasily straddle the two camps, one of which says that the work of Amber and its ilk is vital in keeping alive the drama and tension of dying ways of life, while the other says it is like watching paint dry, complete with impenetrable accents. SH

Brian Hogg *Hoggy* • Darren Bell *Billy* • Mike Elliot *Danker* • Jimmy Killeen *Probation officer* • Wayne Buck *Young lad* • Kevin Buck *Young lad* ■ *Dir/Scr* Richard Grassick, Ellen Hare, Sirkka Liisa Konttinen, Murray Martin, Pat McCartny, Lorna Powell, Pete Roberts

The Edge ★★★ 15

Action adventure
1997 · US · Colour · 112mins

A mediocre survival story is turned into an eminently watchable action adventure by the performances of Anthony Hopkins and Alec Baldwin. Hopkins plays a billionaire who suspects fashion photographer Baldwin covets his beautiful young wife (Elle Macpherson). When their plane crashes in the Alaskan wilderness, the rivals must learn to depend on each other to survive. Lee Tamahori's direction is enhanced by David Mamet's hard-boiled dialogue and Donald M McAlpine's awesome camerawork. TH DVD

Anthony Hopkins *Charles Morse* • Alec Baldwin *Robert Green* • Elle Macpherson *Mickey Morse* • Harold Perrineau *Stephen* • LQ Jones *Styles* • Kathleen Wilhoite *Ginny* ■ *Dir* Lee Tamahori • *Scr* David Mamet

Edge of Darkness ★★★ PG

Second World War drama
1943 · US · BW · 114mins

This impressively grim Warner Bros war movie about the Norwegian Resistance features a stellar cast headed up by unlikely Scandinavians Errol Flynn, Ann Sheridan and Walter Huston. Flynn acquits himself well, and the film is expertly directed by veteran Lewis Milestone and superbly photographed by Sid Hickox. There's also fine support work, and this is stirring stuff, overtly propagandist when it was made but still pretty potent today. TS

Errol Flynn *Gunnar Brogge* • Ann Sheridan *Karen Stensgard* • Walter Huston *Dr Martin Stensgard* • Nancy Coleman *Katja* • Helmut Dantine *Captain Koenig* • Judith Anderson *Gerd Bjarnesen* • Ruth Gordon *Anna Stensgard* • John Beal *Johann Stensgard* • Morris Carnovsky *Sixtus Andresen* ■ *Dir* Lewis Milestone • *Scr* Robert Rossen, from the novel by William Woods

Edge of Doom ★★ PG

Drama 1950 · US · BW · 93mins

This is one of those "street punk" dramas that John Garfield used to swallow whole. Unfortunately, all Farley Granger can manage in the way of torment are a few scowls and sulks as he tries to prevent kindly priest Dana Andrews from discovering that he's guilty of murdering the cleric who denied his mother a decent funeral. Mark Robson's inconsistent direction is disappointing. DP

Dana Andrews *Father Roth* • Farley Granger *Martin Lynn* • Joan Evans *Rita Conroy* • Robert Keith (1) *Det Mandel* • Paul Stewart *Craig* • Mala Powers *Julie* ■ *Dir* Mark Robson • *Scr* Philip Yordan, from a novel by Leo Brady

Edge of Eternity ★★★ U

Western 1959 · US · Colour · 79mins

A moderately exciting modern-day western, with lawman Cornel Wilde pursuing murderer Mickey Shaughnessy towards the Grand Canyon and a cable-car climax. The overall effect is marred only by some cheap back projection that jars against the footage of the real thing. *Dirty Harry* director Don Siegel does wonders with the low budget and his short schedule, but even he can't get a performance out of Victoria Shaw. TS

Cornel Wilde *Les Martin* • Victoria Shaw *Janice Kendon* • Mickey Shaughnessy *Scotty O'Brien* • Edgar Buchanan *Sheriff Edwards* • Rian Garrick *Bob Kendon* • Jack Elam *Bill Ward* ■ *Dir* Donald Siegel [Don Siegel] • *Scr* Knut Swenson [Marion Hargrove], Richard Collins, from a story by Ben Markson, Knut Swenson [Marion Hargrove]

Edge of Sanity ★ 18

Psychological horror
1989 · UK · Colour · 87mins

Anthony Perkins turns into a cocaine-snorting killer after experiments with a new drug backfire. Perkins, giving the most outrageous performance of his career, dwells more on the psychological change in his character than the physical one. No ghoulish make-up here, then; just a look that makes him come across like a hungover Iggy Pop. Director Gérard Kikoine learnt his trade making French porno movies. RS DVD

Anthony Perkins *Dr Henry Jekyll/Mr Jack Hyde* • Glynis Barber *Elisabeth Jekyll* • David Lodge *Gabriel Underwood* • Sarah Maur-Thorp *Susannah* • Ben Cole *Johnny* • Ray Jewers *Newcomen* ■ *Dir* Gérard Kikoine • *Scr* JP Felix, Ron Raley, from the novel *Dr Jekyll and Mr Hyde* by Robert Louis Stevenson

Edge of the City ★★★

Drama 1957 · US · BW · 85mins

A dated and hectoring liberal drama about the destructive friendship between troubled loner John Cassavetes and hard-working labourer Sidney Poitier. Owing much to *On the Waterfront*, released three years earlier, the picture also followed teen dramas such as *Rebel without a Cause* and *The Blackboard Jungle* by taking delinquency out of the classroom and into the world of work. Despite its sledgehammer script and direction, it can still be enjoyed for the acting and the realistic location photography. AT

John Cassavetes *Axel North* • Sidney Poitier *Tommy Tyler* • Jack Warden *Charles Malik* • Kathleen Maguire *Ellen Wilson* • Ruby Dee *Lucy Tyler* • Robert F Simon *Mr Nordmann* • Ruth White *Mrs Nordmann* ■ *Dir* Martin Ritt • *Scr* Robert Alan Aurthur, from his TV play *A Man Is Ten Feet Tall*

The Edge of the Horizon ★★★

Drama 1993 · Fr/Por · Colour · 91mins

Portugal is the poor relation of European cinema; until recently, even its greatest film-maker, Manoel de Oliveira, struggled to find financial backing. Director Fernando Lopes accepted French funding for this atmospheric *film noir*, which stars Claude Brasseur as a pathologist whose life is transformed when he begins to delve into the criminal past of a corpse that appears to be his younger self. This is as much an exercise in style as it is a thriller, with Lopes bathing Lisbon's backstreets in shadow to keep us as much in the dark as Brasseur himself. DP. In Portuguese with English subtitles.

Claude Brasseur *Spino* • Andréa Ferréol *Francesca* • Ana Padrão *Prostitute* • Antonio Valero *Alvaro* ■ *Dir* Fernando Lopes • *Scr* Christopher Frank, Jean Nachbaur, from the novel *Il Filo dell'Orizzonte* by Antonio Tabucchi

The Edge of the World ★★★★ U

Drama 1937 · UK · BW · 71mins

Made by Michael Powell, arguably the British cinema's most profoundly creative director, this is a fictional account of the harsh lives led by a dwindling community off the Scottish mainland. Filmed on the island of Foula, whose real-life inhabitants play the village people, it stars Niall MacGinnis, John Laurie, Finlay Currie and Belle Chrystall, all superb. But it is the landscape, and the spirit of a way of life being slowly but inevitably eroded, that dominate this poignant, elegiac tale of life, love and death. In 1978, Powell returned to the isle and shot a prologue and epilogue to the film, retitling the new version *Return to the Edge of the World*. RK DVD

John Laurie *Peter Manson* • Belle Chrystall *Ruth Manson* • Niall MacGinnis *Andrew Gray* • Finlay Currie *James Gray* • Eric Berry *Robbie Manson* • Michael Powell *Yachtsman* ■ *Dir/Scr* Michael Powell

Edison, the Man ★★★ U

Biographical drama 1940 · US · BW · 106mins

In a movie that contains almost as much sentimental invention as the practical kind, Thomas Alva Edison emerges as the sort of against-all-odds, American pioneer that Hollywood loves. Despite the sanitisation, Spencer Tracy offers a convincing study of the inventor, stubbornly fighting trials and tribulations and constructing the light bulb in a radiant sequence as exciting as any thriller. A sequel to Mickey Rooney's *Young Tom Edison*, Clarence Brown's film takes itself much more seriously. TH

Spencer Tracy *Thomas Alva Edison* • Rita Johnson *Mary Stilwell* • Lynne Overman *Bunt Cavatt* • Charles Coburn *General Powell* • Gene Lockhart *Mr Taggart* • Henry Travers *Ben Els* ■ *Dir* Clarence Brown • *Scr* Talbot Jennings, Bradbury Foote, from a story by Dore Schary, Bradbury Foote

Edith and Marcel ★ PG

Biographical romantic drama
1983 · Fr · Colour · 140mins

When Patrick Dewaere killed himself early in the production, Marcel Cerdan Jr stepped up from technical adviser to play his famous boxing father in this account of his love affair with "the little sparrow", Edith Piaf. If Claude Lelouch had captured just a modicum of the passion the couple generated, this might have been a compelling picture. But he spends too much time

E

on an irrelevant subplot involving a bibliophile and a prisoner of war. Lethargic, pretentious and wasteful. DP. In French with English subtitles.

Evelyne Bouix *Edith Piaf/Margot de Villedieu* • Jacques Villeret *Jacques Barbier* • Francis Huster *Francis Roman* • Jean-Claude Brialy *Loulou Barrier* • Jean Bouise *Lucien Roupp* • Marcel Cerdan Jr *Marcel Cerdan* • Charles Aznavour ■ *Dir/Scr* Claude Lelouch

Ed's Next Move ★★★ 15

Romantic comedy 1996 · US · Colour · 83mins

This is an engaging comedy about a Wisconsin nerd, Matt Ross (the Ed in question), going to the Big Apple and falling for musician Callie Thorne. Fortunately, Ross's worldly wise roommate Kevin Carroll is on hand to take him to diners and pump him with advice about women. Writer/director John Walsh makes an impressive debut with this low-budget feature. Romantic comedy is one of the toughest genres to crack; this one just about makes the grade. LH

Matt Ross *Eddie Brodsky* • Callie Thorne *Lee Nicol* • Kevin Carroll *Ray Obregon* • Ramsey Faragallah *Dr Banarjee* ■ *Dir/Scr* John Walsh

Edtv ★★★★ 12

Comedy 1999 · US · Colour · 117mins

Director Ron Howard's delightfully soft-centred rumination on the excesses of television has suffered in the wake of *The Truman Show*, but comparisons with the Jim Carrey blockbuster are misplaced. Howard's comedy drama is more concerned with "feel-good" laughs and formulaic romantic complications than hard-edged satire, and it doesn't disappoint in delivering sheer enjoyment. Matthew McConaughey gives a winning performance as the small-town video store assistant who agrees to be filmed 24 hours a day by a camera crew for a ratings-hungry cable network. Hardly subtle yet highly entertaining, despite its deliberately unchallenging fuzziness. AJ DVD

Matthew McConaughey *Ed Pekurny* • Ellen DeGeneres *Cynthia Topping* • Jenna Elfman *Shari* • Woody Harrelson *Ray Pekurny* • Sally Kirkland *Jeanette* • Martin Landau *Al* • Rob Reiner *Whitaker* • Dennis Hopper *Hank* • Elizabeth Hurley *Jill* • Michael Moore (2) *Panel member* • Clint Howard *Ken* ■ *Dir* Ron Howard • *Scr* Lowell Ganz, Babaloo Mandel, from the film *Louis XIX: Roi des Ondes* by Emile Gaudreault, Sylvie Bouchard

Educating Rita ★★★★ 15

Comedy drama 1983 · UK · Colour · 106mins

A joy from start to finish, largely thanks to Willy Russell's crisp adaptation of his successful stage play and the lead players' divine suitability for the roles. Julie Walters is great as the sassy and streetwise heroine, eager for higher learning but smart enough to spot Michael Caine's foibles at a hundred paces, and Caine has one of his best ever roles as the drink-sodden, cynical lecturer. Some felt that Walters's portrayal patronised bright, working-class girls, but she brings genuine warmth to the part. SH. Contains swearing. DVD

Michael Caine *Dr Frank Bryant* • Julie Walters *Rita "Susan" White* • Michael Williams *Brian* • Maureen Lipman *Trish* • Jeananne Crowley *Julia* • Malcolm Douglas *Denny* • Godfrey Quigley *Rita's father* ■ *Dir* Lewis Gilbert • *Scr* Willy Russell, from his play

The Education of Little Tree ★★ PG

Drama 1997 · US/Can · Colour · 110mins

Quiet, thoroughly tasteful account of a part-Cherokee boy (Joseph Ashton) struggling to come to terms with the white man's world when he goes to live with his grandparents in 1930s America. James Cromwell adds suitable moral authority to a moving tale which is occasionally a touch too reverential. Based on the novel by Forrest Carter, which was originally regarded as autobiographical before the author was revealed as a former white supremacist. JF DVD

Joseph Ashton *Little Tree* • James Cromwell *Granpa* • Tantoo Cardinal *Granma* • Leni Parker *Martha* • Rebecca Dewey *Dolly* • William Rowat *Henry* • Robert Daviau *Ralph* • Graham Greene (2) *Willow John* ■ *Dir* Richard Friedenberg • *Scr* Richard Friedenberg, from the novel by Forrest Carter

The Edukators ★★★ 15

Crime comedy drama 2004 · Ger/Austria · Colour · 129mins

Director Hans Weingartner here highlights some telling contrasts between the revolutionary fervour of 1960s youth and the more emotive radicalism of the modern antiglobalisation movement. Daniel Brühl and Stipe Erceg star as flatmates and mischievous activists, who break into luxury homes to daub sinister slogans and rearrange the occupants' possessions. The romantic triangle between the two friends and Erceg's girlfriend (Julia Jentsch) intrudes upon the action that ensues when they kidnap businessman Burghart Klaussner. Brühl and Klaussner impress, but the plotting and dialogue lack precision. DP. In German with English subtitles. Contains swearing.

Daniel Brühl *Jan* • Julia Jentsch *Jule* • Stipe Erceg *Peter* • Burghart Klaussner *Hardenberg* • Peer Martiny *Villa owner* • Petra Zieser *Villa owner's wife* • Laura Schmidt *Villa owner's daughter* • Sebastian Butz *Villa owner's son* ■ *Dir* Hans Weingartner • *Scr* Katharina Held, Hans Weingartner

Edward, My Son ★★

Drama 1949 · US/UK · BW · 112mins

This reeks of theatricality, and the fault lies with the gimmick-ridden play on which it was based; co-written by actor Robert Morley as a vehicle for himself, it traced an ailing marriage and deliberately refrained from showing the eponymous Edward on stage. The film, which awkwardly preserves the same convention, features Hollywood import Spencer Tracy, uncomfortable as the despotic dad, and Deborah Kerr, unconvincing as his alcoholic missus. It's a bleak piece, and director George Cukor seems at a loss depicting the English class system. TS

Spencer Tracy *Arnold Boult* • Deborah Kerr *Evelyn Boult* • Ian Hunter *Dr Larry Woodhope* • Leueen MacGrath *Eileen Perrin* • James Donald *Bronton* • Mervyn Johns *Harry Simpkin* • Harriette Johns *Phyllis Mayden* • Felix Aylmer *Mr Hanray* • Walter Fitzgerald *Mr Kedner* ■ *Dir* George Cukor • *Scr* Donald Ogden Stewart, from the play by Robert Morley, Noel Langley

Edward Scissorhands ★★★★★ PG

Fantasy 1990 · US · Colour · 100mins

Tim Burton's bewitchingly oddball "Beauty and the Beast" fairy tale is a masterpiece and one of the best fantasy films ever made. Its haunting power, exquisite charm and dark romance are a match for the spellbinding work of Hans Christian Andersen, while Johnny Depp's sensitive performance as scientist Vincent Price's "Punkenstein" creation is a revelation. Humanoid Edward's inability to touch the things he loves because of his razor and scissor appendages makes for potent symbolism of the highest mythic order. The finale packs an unforgettable emotional wallop, assisted by Danny Elfman's gloriously magical score. AJ. Contains swearing, violence. DVD

Johnny Depp *Edward Scissorhands* • Winona Ryder *Kim Boggs* • Dianne Wiest *Peg Boggs* • Anthony Michael Hall *Jim* • Kathy Baker *Joyce Monroe* • Vincent Price *Inventor* • Alan Arkin *Bill Boggs* ■ *Dir* Tim Burton • *Scr* Caroline Thompson, from a story by Caroline Thompson, Tim Burton • *Cinematographer* Stefan Czapsky • *Art Director* Bo Welch

Edward II ★★ 18

Historical drama 1991 · UK · Colour · 86mins

Director Derek Jarman's adaptation of Christopher Marlowe's play of court favouritism and lethal power games behind the throne is both a challenging and off-putting experience. Telling the admittedly compelling story of Britain's only acknowledged homosexual monarch, whose preference for his male lover rather than Queen Isabella led to a civil war, Jarman turns the grim 16th-century drama into a typically radical and confrontational polemic about the evils of homophobia, stylishly staged in modern dress. Steven Waddington is a handsome, if tiresome Edward, while Tilda Swinton makes the best impression as his cruelly-rejected queen. AJ

Steven Waddington *Edward II* • Tilda Swinton *Isabella* • Andrew Tiernan *Gaveston* • Nigel Terry *Mortimer* • Dudley Sutton *Bishop of Winchester* • Kevin Collins *Lightborn* • John Lynch *Spencer* • Jerome Flynn *Kent* ■ *Dir* Derek Jarman • *Scr* Derek Jarman, Stephen McBride, Ken Butler, from the play by Christopher Marlowe

The Eel ★★★ 18

Drama 1997 · Jpn · Colour · 111mins

The joint winner of the 1997 Palme d'Or, this is a curious, sometimes powerful tale of one man's isolated existence, interlaced with fantasy, farce and a fish. Some will be touched by director Shohei Imamura's story of a reformed wife-killer whose only real friend is his pet eel. Others will be mystified by the near-silent central character, the dreamlike moments and a bizarre comedy subplot involving unidentified flying objects. At times gentle and poignant, at others shockingly brutal, *The Eel* is striking, but difficult to get to grips with. JC. In Japanese with English subtitles. Contains violence and nudity.

Koji Yakusho *Takuro Yamashita* • Misa Shimizu *Keiko Hattori* • Fujio Tsuneta *Jiro Nakajima* • Mitsuko Baisho *Misako Nakajima* ■ *Dir* Shohei Imamura • *Scr* Motofumi Tomikawa, Shohei Imamura, Daisuke Tengan, from the novel *Sparkles in the Darkness* by Akira Yoshimura

The Effect of Gamma Rays on Man-in-the-Moon Marigolds ★★

Drama 1972 · US · Colour · 100mins

Although it won him a Pulitzer Prize, Paul Zindel's play feels like a clumsy pastiche of Tennessee Williams. So while it's possible to see why Paul Newman might be drawn to a film of the project, it's hard to see what he felt he could bring to the story of an unkempt widow struggling to raise her chalk-and-cheese daughters, given his refusal to explore its deeper emotional resonances. Clearly the chance of working with his wife Joanne Woodward and daughter Nell Potts was an incentive, but his stagey direction leaves them straining for the effects he is reluctant to broach. DP

Joanne Woodward *Beatrice* • Nell Potts *Matilda* • Roberta Wallach *Ruth* • Judith Lowry *Nanny* • Richard Venture *Floyd* • Estelle Omens *Floyd's wife* • Carolyn Coates *Granny's daughter* • Will Hare *Junk man* • Jess Osuna *Sonny* ■ *Dir* Paul Newman • *Scr* Alvin Sargent, from the play by Paul Zindel

Effi Briest ★★★★ U

Period drama 1974 · W Ger · BW · 134mins

Teenager Effi (Hanna Schygulla) is forced into an unsuitable marriage in Fassbinder's adaptation of Theodor Fontane's classic 19th-century novel. A lonely existence drives Effi to infidelity, and her husband's later discovery of the affair has tragic consequences. Despite an increasingly tempestuous professional relationship with Schygulla, Fassbinder has created a stylised but truly literary film. Using elegant monochrome photography and with mirrors reflecting the artifice of Effi's world, the director treats the original text with awed reverence. DP. In German with English subtitles.

Hanna Schygulla *Effi Briest* • Wolfgang Schenck *Baron Geert von Instetten* • Ulli Lommel *Major Crampas* • Lilo Pempeit *Frau Briest* • Herbert Steinmetz *Herr Briest* • Hark Bohm *Gieshuebler* ■ *Dir* Rainer Werner Fassbinder • *Scr* Rainer Werner Fassbinder, from the novel by Theodor Fontane

The Egg and I ★★★ U

Comedy 1947 · US · BW · 107mins

This massively popular film version of Betty MacDonald's autobiographical bestseller follows a couple of city slickers who buy a clapped-out old farmhouse and renovate it. Claudette Colbert is delightful as the newlywed who discovers on her wedding night that her husband, attractively played by a wry Fred MacMurray, wants to be a chicken farmer. Producer/director/screenwriter Chester Erskine perhaps keeps events on too even a keel, but it still makes for a very pleasant, if undramatic, whole. The picture also marks the first appearance of Ma and Pa Kettle (Marjorie Main and Percy Kilbride), who were later given their own series by Universal. TS

Claudette Colbert *Betty* • Fred MacMurray *Bob* • Marjorie Main *Ma Kettle* • Percy Kilbride *Pa Kettle* • Louise Allbritton *Harriet Putnam* • Richard Long *Tom Kettle* • Billy House *Billy* ■ *Dir* Chester Erskine • *Scr* Chester Erskine, Fred F Finklehoffe, from the autobiography by Betty MacDonald

The Egyptian ★★

Historical epic 1954 · US · Colour · 138mins

Even Michael Curtiz has difficulty in jollying up this solemn, overlong historical epic about the search for God in ancient Egypt. The dishy but wooden Edmund Purdom in the leading role doesn't help matters, and neither does hunky Victor Mature. The excellent music is a singular collaboration between Alfred Newman and Bernard Herrmann, while Leon Shamroy's colour CinemaScope photography was nominated for an Oscar. The less said about the script, the better. AT

Edmund Purdom *Sinuhe* • Jean Simmons *Merit* • Victor Mature *Horemheb* • Peter Ustinov *Kaptah* • Gene Tierney *Baketamon* • Michael Wilding *Akhnaton* ■ *Dir* Michael Curtiz • *Scr* Philip Dunne, Casey Robinson, from the novel by Mika Waltari

The Eiger Sanction ★★ 15

Spy thriller 1975 · US · Colour · 113mins

Conceived as a Bond-style adventure and having been rejected by Paul Newman, this story was picked up by Clint Eastwood, who turned it into a critical and box-office failure. In the weakest of his self-directed movies, Eastwood plays a mountaineering art collector and former spy who agrees to climb the Eiger and eliminate an agent in return for preferential tax status. It often looks spectacular, but the lacklustre dialogue and performances let the film down. AT DVD

Clint Eastwood *Jonathan Hemlock* • George Kennedy *Ben Bowman* • Vonetta McGee *Jemima Brown* • Jack Cassidy *Miles Mellough*

• Heidi Brühl *Mrs Montaigne* • Thayer David *Dragon* • Reiner Schoene *Freytag* • Michael Grimm *Meyer* ■ *Dir* Clint Eastwood • *Scr* Hal Dresner, Warren B Murphy, Rod Whitaker, from the novel by Trevanian

8½ ★★★★★ 15

Drama 1963 · It · BW · 132mins

Having made six features and three short films, director Federico Fellini reckoned that this mesmerising insight into the creative process took his tally of movies to eight-and-a-half. The winner of the best foreign language film Oscar, this is a complex, painfully honest study of a man in a personal and professional crisis. After *La Dolce Vita*, Fellini was faced with the problem of repeating his success and this soul-searching film, with its mix of daydreams, memories, nightmares and frustrating confrontations, is a fantasy chronicle of his attempts to sustain his reputation as a cinematic genius. As the tormented film-maker, the exceptional Marcello Mastroianni is superbly supported by Anouk Aimée and Claudia Cardinale. DP. In Italian with English subtitles.

Marcello Mastroianni *Guido Anselmi* • Claudia Cardinale *Claudia* • Anouk Aimée *Luisa Anselmi* • Sandra Milo *Carla* • Rossella Falk *Rossella* • Barbara Steele *Gloria Morin* • Mario Pisu *Mezzabotta* • Guido Alberti *Producer* ■ *Dir* Federico Fellini • *Scr* Federico Fellini, Tullio Pinelli, Ennio Flajano, Brunello Rondi, from a story by Federico Fellini, Ennio Flajano • *Music* Nino Rota • *Costume Designer* Piero Gherardi

8½ Women ★★ 15

Comedy drama
1999 · Neth/UK/Lux/Ger · Colour · 115mins

Intended as a tribute to Federico Fellini, Peter Greenaway's misfiring comedy seeks to explore man's tendency to idealise women. However, such is Greenaway's preoccupation with referencing cultural history that he fails to capitalise on the themes and relationships that arise when widowed businessman John Standing and son Matthew Delamere open their doors to various disaffected women. This is less misogynist than angrier critics would have you believe, yet it's still unworthy of its auteur. DP DVD

John Standing *Philip Emmenthal* • Matthew Delamere *Storey Emmenthal* • Vivian Wu *Kito* • Shizuka Inoh *Simato* • Barbara Sarafian *Clothilde* • Kirina Mano *Mio* • Toni Collette *Griselda* • Amanda Plummer *Beryl* • Polly Walker *Palmira* ■ *Dir/Scr* Peter Greenaway

Eight Days a Week ★★★ 15

Comedy 1996 · US · Colour · 89mins

Writer/director Michael Davis made his feature debut with this coming-of-age comedy. The story focuses on Joshua Schaefer's passion for his neighbour Keri Russell and the romantic vigil with which he hopes to win her heart. More a crash course in suburban living than a guide to successful courting, this often wincingly accurate insight into confused male adolescence may not be the ultimate teen pic, but it's far from being the worst. DP DVD

Joshua Schaefer *Peter* • Keri Russell *Erica* • RD Robb *Matt* • Mark Taylor *Peter's father* • Marcia Shapiro *Peter's mother* • Johnny Green (3) *Nick* • Buck Kartalian *Nonno* • Catherine Hicks *Ms Lewis* ■ *Dir/Scr* Michael Davis (3)

8 Heads in a Duffel Bag ★ 15

Black comedy 1997 · US · Colour · 94mins

Tom Schulman makes his directorial debut with a lame comedy that doesn't have enough laughs. Joe Pesci plays a Mob hitman whose bag of heads gets mixed up with one belonging to a medical student. Pesci and most of the supporting cast simply mug their way through the "hilarious" proceedings. JB DVD

Joe Pesci *Tommy Spinelli* • Andy Comeau *Charlie* • Kristy Swanson *Laurie Bennett* • Todd Louiso *Steve* • George Hamilton *Dick Bennett* • Dyan Cannon *Annette Bennett* • David Spade *Ernie* • Anthony Mangano *Rico* ■ *Dir/Scr* Tom Schulman

800 Leagues down the Amazon ★★

Period adventure
1993 · US/Mex · Colour · 88mins

This unprepossessing costume adventure was directed by Luis Llosa, who returned to the Amazon in 1997 for the laugh-a-minute monster movie *Anaconda*. Barry Bostwick stars as a wealthy plantation owner escorting his daughter, Daphne Zuniga, to her wedding. However, they reckoned without the perils of the river and the schemes of bounty hunter Adam Baldwin. A bigger budget would have done nothing to improve the long-winded script. DP. Contains violence.

Daphne Zuniga *Minha* • Barry Bostwick *Garral* • Adam Baldwin *Koja* • Tom Verica *Monoel* • EE Ross *Frolgoso* ■ *Dir* Luis Llosa • *Scr* Laura Schiff, Jackson Barr, from the novel by Jules Verne

Eight Iron Men ★★

Second World War drama
1952 · US · BW · 80mins

Burt Lancaster starred in the original Broadway stage flop but wisely skipped producer Stanley Kramer's film version several years later. It was left to a cast of virtual unknowns to play the front-line infantrymen who refuse to abandon a comrade pinned down in a shell-hole in this stagebound drama. There's little action and much talk before the ironic conclusion, but Lee Marvin makes a strong impression in his first big break. AE

Bonar Colleano *Colucci* • Arthur Franz *Carter* • Lee Marvin *Mooney* • Richard Kiley *Coke* • Nick Dennis *Sapiros* • James Griffith *Ferguson* ■ *Dir* Edward Dmytryk • *Scr* Harry Brown, from the play *A Sound of Hunting* by Harry Brown

Eight Legged Freaks ★★ 12

Science-fiction horror comedy
2001 · US/Aus · Colour · 95mins

David Arquette and Kari Wuhrer fight chemically mutated spiders in a rural mining town in this tongue-in-cheek take on the creature features of the 1950s and early 60s. With its blend of absurd set pieces, hammy acting and deliberately exaggerated dialogue, the movie works hard to capture the kitsch spirit of its predecessors. Though it's too self-conscious and heavy handed to succeed entirely, there's much to enjoy, not least watching Scarlett Johansson battling for survival in a scatty supporting role. SF DVD

David Arquette *Chris McCormack* • Kari Wuhrer *Sheriff Sam Parker* • Scott Terra *Mike Parker* • Scarlett Johansson *Ashley Parker* • Doug E Doug *Harlan* • Rick Overton *Deputy Pete Willis* • Leon Rippy *Mayor Wade* ■ *Dir* Ellory Elkayem • *Scr* Jesse Alexander, Ellory Elkayem, from a story by Elkayem, Randy Kornfield

Eight Men Out ★★★ 15

Drama based on a true story
1988 · US · Colour · 114mins

John Cusack and Charlie Sheen star in a low-key and serious exposé of corruption in the American baseball game when, in 1919, the Chicago White Sox threw the World Series. When the truth became known, it was quickly dubbed the Black Sox Scandal. Written and directed by John Sayles, the picture details the social and economic stresses of the time that led the players into the clutches of hustlers and organised crime. It's a sad and compelling piece that is totally convincing and doesn't require a knowledge of baseball. AT DVD

John Cusack *Buck Weaver* • Charlie Sheen *Hap Felsch* • John Mahoney *Kid Gleason* • DB Sweeney *"Shoeless" Joe Jackson* • Clifton James *Charles Comiskey* • Eliot Asinof *Heydler* • David Strathairn *Eddie Cicotte* • John Sayles *Ring Lardner* ■ *Dir* John Sayles • *Scr* John Sayles, from the novel by Eliot Asinof

8 Mile ★★★★ 15

Drama 2002 · US/Ger · Colour · 105mins

Director Curtis Hanson puts a new spin on the familiar "triumph against the odds" genre with this slick showcase for the talents of superstar rapper Eminem. Aspiring rap artist "Rabbit" hopes to escape his bleak life in Detroit's 8 Mile district. But, after losing his job and his (pregnant) girlfriend, he's forced to work in a soul-destroying factory and to live with his alcoholic mother (Kim Basinger) and her lover. While it doesn't break any new ground, Hanson's film delivers a compellingly gritty account of growing up in poverty, but the real revelation here is Eminem, who delivers a likeable, honest performance. AS. Contains violence, swearing, drug abuse, sex scene, nudity. DVD

Eminem [Marshall Mathers] *Jimmy "Rabbit" Smith* • Kim Basinger *Stephanie* • Brittany Murphy *Alex* • Mekhi Phifer *Future* • Evan Jones *Cheddar Bob* • Omar Benson Miller *Sol George* • Eugene Byrd *Wink* • De'Angelo Wilson *DJ Iz* ■ *Dir* Curtis Hanson • *Scr* Scott Silver

8mm ★★ 18

Mystery thriller
1999 · US/Ger · Colour · 118mins

Joel Schumacher directs this disappointing and depressing thriller. Honourable private detective Nicolas Cage is hired by a wealthy widow to uncover the identity of a teenage girl, whom the widow believes has been murdered in a reel of pornographic film found among her late husband's belongings. The trail leads a surprisingly bland Cage through LA's hardcore underworld, but the movie does have one saving grace in Joaquin Phoenix's jaded sex-shop assistant. JF. Contains violence, swearing, sex scenes and nudity. DVD

Nicolas Cage *Tom Welles* • Joaquin Phoenix *Max California* • James Gandolfini *Eddie Poole* • Peter Stormare *Dino Velvet* • Anthony Heald *Longdale* • Chris Bauer *Machine* • Catherine Keener *Amy Welles* ■ *Dir* Joel Schumacher • *Scr* Andrew Kevin Walker

8 Million Ways to Die ★★★ 18

Crime thriller 1986 · US · Colour · 110mins

Oliver Stone wrote the original script of this urban thriller, intending to direct it himself. But financial problems led to a delay and, when Hal Ashby was brought in to direct, Robert Towne rewrote the script uncredited. Stone disowns it, Ashby was reportedly fired near the end of production and few people ever saw it. On the credit side, there are some vivid locations and a decent cast: Jeff Bridges as the cop with a drink problem, Rosanna Arquette as the mobster's moll and Andy Garcia as a drug dealer. AT

Jeff Bridges *Matthew Scudder* • Rosanna Arquette *Sarah* • Alexandra Paul *Sunny* • Randy Brooks *Chance* • Andy Garcia *Angel Maldonado* • Lisa Sloan *Linda Scudder* ■ *Dir* Hal Ashby • *Scr* Oliver Stone, David Lee Henry, Robert Towne (uncredited), from the novel by Lawrence Block

Eight O'Clock Walk ★★ PG

Drama 1953 · UK · BW · 83mins

Richard Attenborough finds himself on trial for his life in this lukewarm legal drama. Typically with courtroom pictures, there's too much chat and not enough action, although father-and-son barristers Ian Hunter and Derek Farr enjoy a few jousts before the verdict is returned. The problem is that, no matter how damning the evidence, you never believe for a second that cabbie Attenborough is guilty of murder. DP

Richard Attenborough *Tom Manning* • Derek Farr *Peter Tanner* • Cathy O'Donnell *Jill Manning* • Ian Hunter *Geoffrey Tanner* • Maurice Denham *Horace Clifford* • Bruce Seton *DCI* • Harry Welchman *Justice Harrington* • Kynaston Reeves *Mr Munro* ■ *Dir* Lance Comfort • *Scr* Katherine Strueby, Guy Morgan, from a story by Jack Roffey, Gordon Harbord

Eight on the Lam ★★ U

Comedy 1967 · US · Colour · 107mins

There was safety in numbers for Bob Hope at this stage of a career that wasn't just flagging but seemed at half-mast. A few years after *The Seven Little Foys* this came along, with Bob as a nervous bank clerk accused of embezzlement who goes on the run with his seven children. Not even the acerbic wit of Phyllis Diller can cut through the bland sentimentality. TH

Bob Hope *Henry Dimsdale* • Phyllis Diller *Golda* • Jonathan Winters *Jasper Lynch* • Shirley Eaton *Ellie Barton* • Jill St John *Monica* • Stacey Maxwell *Linda* • Kevin Brody *Steve* ■ *Dir* George Marshall • *Scr* Albert E Lewin, Burt Styler, Bob Fisher, Arthur Marx, from a story by Bob Fisher, Arthur Marx

8 Seconds ★★ PG

Drama based on a true story
1994 · US · Colour · 100mins

Bareback riding has never looked so easy as in this biopic of Lane Frost, whose brief career saw him become one of America's youngest ever rodeo champions. Such is the predictability of the bucking sequences that it's almost a relief to be plunged into Lane's marital misery and his search for the popularity. Luke Perry and Cynthia Geary are well matched as the ill-fated Frosts, but the action is just too tame to thrill. DP DVD

Luke Perry *Lane Frost* • Stephen Baldwin *Tuff Hedeman* • Cynthia Geary *Kellie Frost* • James Rebhorn *Clyde Frost* • Red Mitchell *Cody Lambert* • Carrie Snodgress *Elsie Frost* ■ *Dir* John G Avildsen • *Scr* Monte Merrick

8 Women ★★★★ 15

Musical murder mystery comedy
2001 · Fr/It · Colour · 106mins

This crackles with catty quips and also serves up an intriguing murder mystery in which eight women are trapped in an isolated country house with a murderer either on the loose or among their number. The costumes and sets both reference and satirise the styles of the 1950s, are photographed in loving colour by Jeanne Lapoirie. The stellar cast is sublime, but Isabelle Huppert takes the honours as the dowdy sister of glamorous matriarch Catherine Deneuve. Holding it all together is the slick direction of François Ozon, whose blend of Agatha Christie and Douglas Sirk is as precise as it is mischievous. DP. In French with English subtitles. Contains swearing. DVD

Danielle Darrieux *Mamy* • Catherine Deneuve *Gaby* • Isabelle Huppert *Augustine* • Emmanuelle Béart *Louise* • Fanny Ardant *Pierrette* • Virginie Ledoyen *Suzon* • Ludivine Sagnier *Catherine* • Firmine Richard *Mme Chanel* ■ *Dir* François Ozon • *Scr* François Ozon, from the play *8 Femmes* by Robert Thomas

18 Again! ★★ PG

Comedy 1988 · US · Colour · 95mins

George Burns did the majority of his best work on stage, radio and TV with his wife Gracie Allen. However, most viewers will remember him as a mischievous old man in films like *The Sunshine Boys* and *Oh, God!* Either of these would better have shown off the talents of the veteran trouper, who died shortly after his 100th birthday, as he's given little screen time in this non-starting "body swap" comedy that crept in at the end of the cycle that began with *Big* and *Vice Versa*. DP

George Burns *Jack Watson* • Charlie Schlatter *David Watson* • Tony Roberts *Arnold* • Anita Morris *Madelyn* • Miriam Flynn *Betty* • Jennifer Runyon *Robin* • Red Buttons *Charlie* • George DiCenzo *Coach* ■ *Dir* Paul Flaherty • *Scr* Josh Goldstein, Jonathan Prince

E

1871 ★★ 15

Period romantic drama
1989 · UK · Colour · 100mins

Ken McMullen's drama, set during the time of the Paris Commune, focuses on actors from Ramborde's Theatre. Ana Padrao is the actress with the complicated love life, caught between John Lynch and Roshan Seth during this turbulent period of French history. Directed with awkward solemnity by McMullen, the actors give of their all, but that turns out to be not much. TH

Ana Padrão *Severine* • John Lynch *O'Brien* • Roshan Seth *Lord Grafton* • Jack Klaff *Cluseret* • Timothy Spall *Ramborde* • Maria de Medeiros *Maria* • Jacqueline Dankworth *Street singer* • Ian McNeice *Prince of Wales* • Dominique Pinon *Napoleon III* • Med Hondo *Karl Marx* ■ *Dir* Ken McMullen • *Scr* Terry James, James Leahy, Ken McMullen

1860 ★★★

Historical political drama
1933 · It · BW · 75mins

Alessandro Blasetti was one of the major directors of the Italian cinema of the 1930s, and was a direct influence on Luchino Visconti. Describing the events surrounding the battle of Calatafimi in May 1860 when the Sicilians rose up and defeated the troops of the King of Naples, the film avoids many of the rhetorical postures of the other historical epics made in Fascist Italy at the time. The use of non-professional actors, actual landscapes and regional dialects makes it a precursor of neorealism. RB. An Italian language film.

Aida Bellia *Gesuzza* • Giuseppe Gullino *Carmeliddu* ■ *Dir/Scr* Alessandro Blasetti

Eighteen Springs ★★★★

Romantic melodrama
1997 · HK · Colour · 125mins

This film is a consummate piece of storytelling, in which director Ann Hui combines glorious visuals and simple human truths with typical sensitivity and insight. Set in 1930s Shanghai, it focuses on the thwarted passion of Wu Chien-lien and Leon Lai, who are first kept apart by his parents' determination that he marries the wealthy Annie Wu, and then by the intervention of her prostitute sister Anita Mui, whose businessman husband has designs of his own on the demure Wu. Linked by the lovers' melancholic narration, this is intricate, delicate and compelling. DP. In Cantonese with English subtitles.

Lai Ming [Leon Lai] *Shen Shijun* • Wu Chien-lien *Gu Manzhen* • Mui Yim-Fong [Anita Mui] *Gu Manlu* • Ge You *Zhu Hongcai* • Wang Lei *Xu Shuhui* • Wu Chenjun [Annie Wu] *Shi Cuizhi* ■ *Dir* Hui On-Wah [Ann Hui] • *Scr* John Chan [Chan Kin Chung], from the novel *Half a LIfetime's Romance* by Eileen Chang

The Eighteenth Angel ★★ 15

Horror
1997 · US · Colour · 84mins

Soon after the unexplained death of his wife, Christopher McDonald accompanies his daughter, Rachael Leigh Cook, on a modelling assignment to Italy. There she becomes the target of a mysterious sect of priests preparing for the return of Satan. More Bible-based horror from David Seltzer, writer of *The Omen*, who clearly should get out a bit more if these sloppy seconds are anything to go by. Some reasonable chills register along the way, despite the film's obvious contrivances. AJ

Christopher McDonald *Hugh Stanton* • Rachael Leigh Cook *Lucy Stanton* • Stanley Tucci *Todd Stanton* • Wendy Crewson *Norah Stanton* • Maximilian Schell *Father Simeon* ■ *Dir* William Bindley • *Scr* David Seltzer

The Eighth Day ★★★ PG

Drama
1996 · Bel · Colour · 112mins

A sentimental, life-affirming movie from Belgium that highlights the friendship between a corporate businessman who loathes his existence and a man with Down's syndrome who embraces life. Daniel Auteuil and Pascal Duquenne (who shared the best actor prize at Cannes) are both excellent, and their *Rain Man*-style relationship has some profoundly touching moments. However, director Jaco Van Dormael (*Toto the Hero*) strives a little too hard for profundity, decorating the film with poetic images of nature. JC. In French with English subtitles.

Daniel Auteuil *Harry* • Pascal Duquenne *Georges* • Miou-Miou *Julie* • Isabelle Sadoyan *Georges's mother* • Henri Garcin *Company director* • Michele Maes *Nathalie* • Laszlo Harmati *Luis Mariano* • Helene Roussel *Julie's mother* ■ *Dir/Scr* Jaco Van Dormael

84 Charing Cross Road ★★★★ U

Biographical drama
1986 · UK · Colour · 95mins

Adapted from Helene Hanff's bestselling account of her dealings with the staff of a London bookshop, this is an absolute delight. Building his film around the letters exchanged between Hanff and manager Frank Doel, director David Jones manages to create utterly credible characters, convey something of the beauty of books and make some telling comparisons between the gloomy reserve of postwar Britain and the effervescence of Cold War America. However, what makes this gentle drama so compelling are the performances of Anne Bancroft and Anthony Hopkins, who ingeniously fashion a romance between two people who never meet. DP DVD

Anne Bancroft *Helene Hanff* • Anthony Hopkins *Frank Doel* • Judi Dench *Nora Doel* • Jean De Baer *Maxine Bellamy* • Maurice Denham *George Martin* • Eleanor David *Cecily Farr* • Mercedes Ruehl *Kay* • Daniel Gerroll *Brian* • Wendy Morgan *Megan Wells* ■ *Dir* David Jones (3) • *Scr* Hugh Whitemore, from the book by Helene Hanff

84 Charlie Mopic ★★★ 18

War drama
1989 · US · Colour · 90mins

This eye-opening film about the Vietnam War has a viewpoint that neither waves flags nor wastes blame, as it follows a two-man documentary film crew accompanying a platoon "to record procedures peculiar to the combat situation". Such is the skill of writer/director Patrick Duncan that it all comes across as reality. The constant slang, though, is a barrier to our understanding, while the continual hand-held camera becomes too unsettling. TH. Contains swearing.

Jonathan Emerson *LT* • Nicholas Cascone *Easy* • Jason Tomlins *Pretty Boy* • Christopher Burgard *Hammer* • Glenn Morshower *Cracker* • Richard Brooks *OD* • Byron Thomas *Mopic* ■ *Dir/Scr* Patrick Duncan

Eighty Steps to Jonah ★★

Drama
1969 · US · Colour · 107mins

Vegas vocalist Wayne Newton turns up in this sentimental tale of an innocent man on the run who poses as a handyman in a children's summer camp for the blind. The treatment of the story stays just a shade this side of saccharine. Several familiar faces, such as Mickey Rooney, turn up in small roles. British jazz pianist George Shearing, himself born blind, provides the score. JG

Wayne Newton *Mark Jonah Winters* • Jo Van Fleet *Nonna* • Keenan Wynn *Barney Glover* • Diana Ewing *Tracy* • Slim Pickens *Scott* • RG Armstrong *Mackray* • Brandon Cruz *Little Joe* • Erin Moran *Kim* • Mickey Rooney *Wilfred Bashford* • Sal Mineo *Jerry Taggart* ■ *Dir* Gerd Oswald • *Scr* Frederic Louis Fox, from a story by Gerd Oswald, Frederic Louis Fox

80,000 Suspects ★★

Thriller
1963 · UK · BW · 116mins

This epidemic movie seems to have everything going for it – a bit of cod science, millions being threatened by malevolent micro-organisms and a race against time involving the daredevil doctor and the unsuspecting carrier, but it doesn't come off. More emphasis is placed on repairing the hero's marriage than on preventing disaster, which should add a human dimension to the tale, but here deprives the picture of suspense. DP

Claire Bloom *Julie Monks* • Richard Johnson *Steven Monks* • Yolande Donlan *Ruth Preston* • Cyril Cusack *Father Maguire* • Michael Goodliffe *Clifford Preston* • Mervyn Johns *Buckridge* • Kay Walsh *Matron* • Norman Bird *Mr Davis* • Basil Dignam *Medical officer* ■ *Dir* Val Guest • *Scr* Val Guest, from the novel *The Pillars of Midnight* by Elleston Trevor

Ek Aur Ek Gyarah ★★ PG

Musical action comedy
2003 · Ind · Colour · 156mins

While there's plenty of plot in this frantic crime comedy, the laughs are in short supply. Govinda teams up with Sanjay Dutt as a couple of wasters who are forced to flee to Nepal, having fallen foul of gangster Ashish Vidyarthi. However, their only hope of escape is cop Jackie Shroff, who is more interested in recovering a secret weapon stolen by Vidyarthi and his brother, Gulshan Grover. With Amrita Arora and Nandini Singh providing romantic distractions, this is brash fun that's unfortunately hamstrung by endless contrivance. DP. A Hindi language film. DVD

Govinda *Sitara* • Sanjay Dutt *Taraji* • Jackie Shroff • Amrita Arora • Nandini Singh • Gulshan Grover ■ *Dir* David Dhawan • *Scr* Yunus Sajawal

Ek Hi Rasta ★★★ U

Drama
1956 · Ind · BW · 153mins

Baldev Raj Chopra was already one of India's most influential film critics when he turned director in 1951. This was one of the first features made for his own production company BR Films, which was renowned for tackling key social issues within the context of commercial pictures. With a title meaning "The Only Way", this is ostensibly an old-fashioned melodrama about revenge, murder and thwarted passion, with a villain straight out of a penny-dreadful. Yet it is also a heartfelt protest about the Hindu custom preventing the remarriage of widows. DP. In Hindi and Urdu with English subtitles.

Ashok Kumar • Sunil Dutt • Meena Kumari • Daisy Irani • Jeevan ■ *Dir* BR Chopra

El ★★★★

Black comedy drama
1953 · Mex · BW · 100mins

Exploring Luis Buñuel's perennial themes of sexual terror, religious hypocrisy and bourgeois indolence, this seething melodrama was based on Mercedes Pinto's autobiographical novel. Buñuel also drew inspiration from his insanely jealous brother-in-law and his own emotional conflicts. Amazingly, the film was poorly received on its Mexican release, but the tale of 40-year-old Catholic virgin Arturo De Cordova's descent into paranoia after marrying the much younger Delia Garces is a probing study of moral and psychological collapse, stuffed with moments of inspired surrealism. DP. A Spanish language film.

Arturo de Cordova *Francisco Galvan de Montemayor* • Delia Garces *Gloria* • Luis Beristain *Raul Conde* • Aurora Walker *Senora Esperanza Peralta* • Carlos Martinez Baena *Padre Velasco* • Manuel Donde *Pablo* ■ *Dir* Luis Buñuel • *Scr* Luis Buñuel, Luis Alcoriza, from the novel *Pensamientos* by Mercedes Pinto

El Dorado ★★★★★ PG

Western
1967 · US · Colour · 121mins

"Ride, boldly ride…" sings George Alexander over the Remington-styled western paintings that accompany the titles to this elegiac masterwork, a fabulously entertaining tale from ace director Howard Hawks. Gunfighter John Wayne is a flawed hero, whose actions lead to a boy's suicide in a superbly staged preface to the plot, and whose resulting wounds dictate the pace and outcome of the movie. More than a match for the Duke is the great Robert Mitchum, in one of his best screen roles as an alcoholic sheriff. This film suffered on its release by comparison to Hawks's earlier western masterpiece *Rio Bravo*, but with the passing of time this screen meditation on ageing proves to be one of the most pleasurable of all Hollywood movies. TS DVD

John Wayne *Cole Thornton* • Robert Mitchum *JP Harrah* • James Caan *Mississippi* • Charlene Holt *Maudie* • Michele Carey *Joey MacDonald* • Arthur Hunnicutt *Bull Harris* • RG Armstrong *Kevin MacDonald* • Edward Asner *Bart Jason* • Johnny Crawford *Luke MacDonald* ■ *Dir* Howard Hawks • *Scr* Leigh Brackett, from the novel *The Stars in Their Courses* by Harry Brown

El Dorado ★★★ 15

Adventure
1988 · Sp/Fr · Colour · 122mins

Director Carlos Saura's re-creation of the doomed 1560 expedition to find the fabled New World land of El Dorado is historically accurate, earnestly played and magnificently photographed by Teo Escamilla. Saura succeeds in conveying the mix of greed and reckless folly that inspired the conquistadors to risk all in the pursuit of wealth and power, but it never comes close to topping the achievement of *Aguirre, Wrath of God*, Werner Herzog's remarkable account of the same story made 16 years earlier. DP. In Spanish with English subtitles. Contains violence.

Omero Antonutti *Lope de Aguirre* • Eusebio Poncela *Fernando de Guzman* • Lambert Wilson *Pedro de Ursua* • Gabriela Roel *Dona Ines* • José Sancho *Juan de la Bandera* • Feodor Atkine *Montoya* • Patxi Bisquert *Pedrarias* ■ *Dir/Scr* Carlos Saura

Election ★★★★ 15

Satirical comedy
1999 · US · Colour · 98mins

Topping the league table of recent high-school movies, this is the rightful heir to the John Hughes youth-antics tradition. The casting of Matthew Broderick as a devoted teacher trying to prevent manipulative overachiever

Reese Witherspoon from becoming student president is inspired. Director/ co-writer Alexander Payne is repaid by his star with a performance of sincere, if muddled idealism. Pitted against jock Chris Klein and his lesbian sister (Jessica Campbell making a revelatory debut), Witherspoon's blend of corruption and compassion slyly satirises contemporary American politics, while George Washington Carver High serves as a microcosm of *fin-de-siècle* society. Astute, offbeat and uproarious. DP [video] DVD

Matthew Broderick *Jim McAllister* • Reese Witherspoon *Tracy Flick* • Chris Klein *Paul Metzler* • Phil Reeves *Walt Hendricks* • Mark Harelik *Dave Novotny* • Delaney Driscoll *Linda Novotny* • Molly Hagan *Diane McAllister* • Jessica Campbell *Tammy Metzler* ■ *Dir* Alexander Payne • *Scr* Alexander Payne, Jim Taylor, from the novel by Tom Perrotta

Electra Glide in Blue ★★★ 18

Crime drama 1973 · US · Colour · 108mins

A cult movie of its day, this abrasive mix of black comedy and satire made a one-hit wonder of its director, record producer James William Guercio. Robert Blake gives one of his best performances as a diminutive motorcycle cop who justifies his tough-guy act by claiming to be the exact same height as Alan Ladd. After some of the most graphic violence then seen on screen, the ending is something of a cop-out, but Conrad Hall's photography is outstanding. DP [video]

Robert Blake *John Wintergreen* • Billy Green Bush *Zipper Davis* • Mitchell Ryan *Harve Poole* • Jeannine Riley *Jolene* • Elisha Cook [Elisha Cook Jr] *Willie* • Royal Dano *Coroner* ■ *Dir* James William Guercio • *Scr* Robert Boris, Michael Butler, from a story by Robert Boris, Rupert Hitzig

Electric Dreams ★ PG

Romantic comedy
1984 · US/UK · Colour · 92mins

"Computers are alive" is the theme of this daft romantic comedy. Lenny Von Dohlen plays a geeky architect whose new computer comes to life when champagne is spilt over it. Both owner and computer then fall for girl-next-door Virginia Madsen. Shot by director Steve Barron in the style of a pop promo, this starts brightly enough but soon disintegrates. LH [video]

Lenny Von Dohlen *Miles* • Virginia Madsen *Madeline* • Maxwell Caulfield *Bill* • Bud Cort *Edgar* • Don Fellows *Ryley* • Alan Polonsky *Frank* • Wendy Miller *Computer clerk* • Harry Rabinowitz *Conductor* • Miriam Margolyes *Ticket girl* • Koo Stark *Soap opera girl* ■ *Dir* Steve Barron • *Scr* Rusty Lemorande

The Electric Horseman ★★★ PG

Comedy western
1979 · US · Colour · 120mins

Despite its title and the sparks-flying relationship between Robert Redford and Jane Fonda, this early eco-warning tale about mindless consumerism carries too little charge. When Redford, a down-on-his-luck rodeo rider, saves a thoroughbred horse from corporate greed, it all becomes excessively preachy under Sydney Pollack's heavy direction: he doesn't seem able to film a sunset without silhouetting people against it. It means well, but moral fables need more subtlety. TH [video]

Robert Redford *Sonny Steele* • Jane Fonda *Hallie Martin* • Valerie Perrine *Charlotta* • Willie Nelson *Wendell* • John Saxon *Hunt Sears* • Nicholas Coster [Nicolas Coster] *Fitzgerald* • Allan Arbus *Danny* • Wilford Brimley *Farmer* • Will Hare *Gus* ■ *Dir* Sydney Pollack • *Scr* Robert Garland, from a screenplay (unproduced) by Robert Garland, Paul Gaer, from a story by Shelly Burton

Electric Moon ★★ 15

Satirical drama 1992 · UK · Colour · 102mins

There's a distinct Ealing feel to this wry satire on themed holidays, which are seemingly designed to reinforce patronising perceptions of an idealised past. But there are also acerbic asides on India's colonial legacy and its predilection for bureacratic pettifogging. Director Pradip Krishen reduces the western tourists to hideous stereotypes, yet he takes such a time doing so that the film fails to gain any momentum until rulebook martinet Naseeruddin Shah and duplicitous lodge manager Roshan Seth begin to feud over the latter's bogus safari operation. DP

Roshan Seth *Ranveer* • Naseeruddin Shah *Rambuhj Goswami* • Leela Naidu *Socks/ Sukanya* • Gerson Da Cunha *Bubbles/Raja Ran Bikram Singh* • Raghubir Yadav [Raghuvir Yadav] *Boltoo* ■ *Dir* Pradip Krishen • *Scr* Arundhati Roy

Elektra ★★

Drama 1962 · Gr · BW · 113mins

This is the first entry in Michael Cacoyannis's Euripides trilogy, which he completed with *The Trojan Women* (1971) and *Iphigenia* (1976). It may have garnered international critical acclaim (including a gong at Cannes) but, for all the spartan beauty of the Mycenae locations, Cacoyannis's fussy use of tight close-ups and jarring flashbacks too often hold the action to ransom. Irene Papas's histrionics in the title role are also detrimental. DP. In Greek with English subtitles.

Irene Papas *Elektra* • Aleka Katselli *Clytemnestra* • Yannis Fertis *Orestes* • Theano Ioannidou *Chorus leader* • Notis Peryalis *Electra's husband* • Takis Emmanuel *Pylades* • Phoebus Rhazis *Aegisthus* ■ *Dir* Michael Cacoyannis • *Scr* Michael Cacoyannis, from the play by Euripides

Elektra ★★ 12

Martial arts action fantasy
2005 · US · Colour · 92mins

Daredevil's lady friend Elektra gets a solo outing in this insipid adventure based on the spin-off Marvel comic book. Resuming events where the Ben Affleck vehicle ended, Jennifer Garner's warrior is literally back from the dead and working as a hired assassin. But when she's asked to kill a father and daughter on the run from a supernatural martial arts syndicate, Elektra's past and conscience catch up with her. The film is glossy and stylish, but Garner lacks charisma and the fight action is unimpressive. SF. Contains violence. [video] DVD

Jennifer Garner *Elektra Natchios* • Terence Stamp *Stick* • Goran Visnjic *Mark Miller* • Kirsten Prout *Abby Miller* • Cary-Hiroyuki Tagawa *Roshi* • Will Yun Lee *Kirigi* • Chris Ackerman *Tattoo* • Edson T Ribeiro *Kinkou* • Colin Cunningham *McCabe* ■ *Dir* Rob Bowman • *Scr* Raven Metzner, Zak Penn, Stuart Zicherman, from the Marvel character created by Frank Miller

The Element of Crime ★★★★ 15

Fantasy crime mystery
1984 · Den · Colour · 99mins

Lars von Trier's debut feature is a ragbag of visual allusions to everything from German expressionism and Hollywood *noir* to the self-reflexivity of the *Nouvelle Vague* and the grim poetry of Andrei Tarkovsky. Yet shamus Michael Elphick's quest to unmask the mathematically minded serial perpetrator of the "Lotto murders" makes for compelling viewing. With Esmond Knight leading a first-rate multinational ensemble cast, this was rightly hailed as the work of a master-in-waiting. DP [video] DVD

Michael Elphick *Fisher* • Esmond Knight *Osborne* • Me Me Lai *Kim* • Jerold Wells *Police Chief Kramer* • Ahmed El Shenawi *Therapist* • Astrid Henning-Jensen *Osborne's housekeeper* • Janos Hersko *Coroner* • Stig Larsson *Coroner's assistant* • Lars von Trier *Schmuck of Ages* ■ *Dir* Lars von Trier • *Scr* Lars von Trier, Niels Vorsel

Elementary School ★★★

Comedy 1991 · Cz · Colour · 100mins

Jan Sverak made his feature debut with this powerful drama. Written by and starring Sverak's father, Zdenek, this largely autobiographical story focuses on life in Prague during the interlude between liberation from the Nazis and subjugation by the Communists. In addition to Zdenek and leading Czech actor Rudolf Hrusinsky, the cast also includes legendary film-makers Jirí Menzel and Karel Kachyna in cameo roles. The film was nominated for an Oscar, but the Sveraks were to go one better with the enchanting *Kolya*, which won the 1996 Academy Award for best foreign language film. DP. In Czech with English subtitles.

Jan Triska *Igor Hnizdo* • Zdenek Sverak *Soucek* • Libuse Safrankova *Mrs Soucek* • Rudolf Hrusinsky *Schoolmaster* • Daniela Kolarova *Miss Maxova* • Vaclav Jakoubek *Eda* • Jirí Menzel *Doctor* • Karel Kachyna *School inspector* ■ *Dir* Jan Sverak • *Scr* Zdenek Sverak

Elena et les Hommes ★★★ U

Period romantic drama
1956 · Fr/Ital · Colour · 62mins

This deceptively lightweight period piece from writer/director Jean Renoir provides a glistening showcase for Ingrid Bergman. She plays a beautiful woman in Paris at the end of the 19th century looking for a wealthy meal ticket who gradually learns about the true meaning of love. Renoir's main concern is evoking the colour and gaiety of the time, and the result is an enchanting romantic fable. JF. In French with English subtitles.

Ingrid Bergman *Elena* • Mel Ferrer *Henri de Chevincourt* • Jean Marais *Rollan* • Jean Richard *Hector* • Magali Noël *Lolotte* • Juliette Greco *Miarka* • Pierre Bertin *Martin-Michaud* • Jean Castanier *Isnard* ■ *Dir/Scr* Jean Renoir

Eleni ★★★ PG

Biographical drama
1985 · US · Colour · 110mins

What was uplifting on the page comes out flatly on film, in this re-creation of Nicholas Gage's book about his real-life search for the executioners of his peasant mother, who sacrificed herself to save her children from the communist faction that took over her Greek village. Although Kate Nelligan as Eleni gives a poignant performance in flashback, it's the search for truth by John Malkovich (as Gage) that holds what tension there is. TH [video] DVD

Kate Nelligan *Eleni Gatzoyiannis* • John Malkovich *Nicholas Gage* • Linda Hunt *Katina* • Oliver Cotton *Katis* • Ronald Pickup *Spiro Skevis* • Glenne Headly *Joan* • Alfred Molina *Young Christos* ■ *Dir* Peter Yates • *Scr* Steve Tesich, from the book by Nicholas Gage

Elenya ★★★ PG

Second World War drama
1992 · UK · Colour · 78mins

This Second World War tale, about a young woman of Italian descent living with her aunt in the Welsh countryside, feels dispiritingly familiar. Pascale Delafouge Jones superbly plays the ostracised girl, while Klaus Behrendt is utterly believable as the German pilot she befriends after he crashes in the woods. It's all skilfully portrayed and consummately photographed, yet one cannot shake off the lingering feeling that Hayley Mills might bound in at any moment. So much talent on display – a pity it's not put to better use. SH [video]

Margaret John *Old Elenya* • Pascale Delafouge Jones *Young Elenya* • Seiriol Tomos *Glyn* • Sue Jones-Davies *Maggie* • Iago Wynn Jones *Sidney* • Llio Millward *Schoolteacher* • Klaus Behrendt *Franz* ■ *Dir/Scr* Steve Gough

Elephant ★★★ 15

Drama 2003 · US · Colour · 78mins

Director Gus Van Sant's Palme d'Or-winning film documents a normal day at an ordinary American high school. Except this day ends in a senseless massacre, much like the Columbine killings to which it alludes. The main characters are real students, and their casual encounters and improvised snatched conversations are detailed in long travelling shots before Alex Frost and Eric Deulen enter school carrying assault weapons. It's either a disturbingly poetic disaster movie or an arty view of a contemporary malaise, but by not apportioning blame, Van Sant's drama raises more questions than it answers. AJ [video] DVD

Alex Frost *Alex* • Eric Duelen *Eric* • John Robinson (3) *John McFarland* • Elias McConnell *Elias* • Jordan Taylor *Jordan* • Carrie Finklea *Carrie* • Nicole George *Nicole* • Brittany Mountain *Brittany* • Timothy Bottoms *Mr McFarland* ■ *Dir/Scr* Gus Van Sant

The Elephant and the Bicycle ★★★

Drama 1995 · Cub · Colour · 81mins

Cuban director Juan Carlos Tabio is best known for the Oscar-nominated gay classic *Strawberry and Chocolate*, which he directed with Tomas Gutierrez Alea. In keeping with the worldwide celebrations to mark the centenary of cinema, this film recalls the glorious silent days when movies were presented by travelling showmen and Douglas Fairbanks was the king of the swashbucklers. Cleverly contrasting the action of Fairbanks's stirring version of *Robin Hood* with events in Cuba on the eve of the Machado coup, the film has its share of quirky characters, but it rather lacks pace. DP. In Spanish with English subtitles.

Luis Alberto Garcia *Isleño* • Lilian Vega *Marina* • Daisy Granados • Raul Pomares • Adolfo Llaurado • Marta Farre ■ *Dir* Juan Carlos Tabio • *Scr* Eliseo Alberto Diego

Elephant Boy ★★ U

Adventure 1937 · UK · BW · 78mins

In 1936, the British-based movie mogul Alexander Korda dispatched the famed documentarist Robert Flaherty to India to make a version of Rudyard Kipling's *Toomai of the Elephants*. Flaherty discovered Sabu, who was a 12-year-old stable boy to a maharajah, and cast him in the leading role; he then shot some 50 hours of footage and returned to England with fine images but no story. Korda then put his brother Zoltan to work to patch things together. The result, predictably, is a bit of a mess, but it retains its exoticism. Sabu became an overnight sensation. AT [video]

Sabu *Toomai* • Walter Hudd *Petersen* • Allan Jeayes *Machua Appa* • WE Holloway *Father* • Bruce Gordon (1) *Rham Lahl* • DJ Williams *Hunter* • Wilfrid Hyde White *Commissioner* • Iravatha *Kala Nag* ■ *Dir* Robert Flaherty, Zoltan Korda • *Scr* John Collier, Akos Tolnay, Marcia de Silva, from the novel *Toomai of the Elephants* by Rudyard Kipling

An Elephant Called Slowly ★★ U

Adventure 1969 · UK · Colour · 87mins

Director James Hill tries to do for elephants what he did for lions in *Born Free* (1966), though with rather less success. The wildlife story again involves Virginia McKenna and Bill Travers, this time trying to protect three orphaned baby elephants. In the process they rub shoulders with the real-life Adamsons, the couple they played in the earlier film. Alas, the film failed to please audiences. FL

Virginia McKenna *Ginny* • Bill Travers *Bill* • Vinay Inambar *Mr Mophagee* • Joab Collins *Henry* • Ali Twaha *Mutiso* ■ *Dir* James Hill • *Scr* Bill Travers, James Hill

Elephant Juice ★★ 18

Comedy drama
1999 · US/UK · Colour · 83mins

Pitched as a penetrating look at the relationship merry-go-round in modern-day London, this arch comedy drama is a banal bust. In her British film debut, French star Emmanuelle Béart plays a city whizzkid whose engagement to handsome artist Daniel Lapaine causes her close circle of friends to re-evaluate their own lives. Secret affairs, crises of conscience and a suicide attempt lead to a ho-hum happy ending in a mundane soap opera. AJ. Contains swearing, nudity. DVD

Emmanuelle Béart *Jules* • Sean Gallagher *Billy* • Daniel Lapaine *Will* • Mark Strong *Frank* • Daniela Nardini *Daphne* • Kimberly Williams *Dodie* • Lennie James *Graham* • Lee Williams *George* ■ *Dir* Sam Miller • *Scr* Amy Jenkins, from an idea by Amy Jenkins, Sam Miller

The Elephant Man ★★★★ PG

Biographical drama 1980 · US · BW · 118mins

Probably the closest director David Lynch has got to the mainstream – outside of the disastrous *Dune* – this stylish, poignant drama is based on the true story of the horrifically disfigured John Merrick (a superb, unrecognisable John Hurt) who battled the prejudices of Victorian society. Full marks, too, for Freddie Francis's striking black-and-white photography and the excellent playing from a top-drawer cast (Anthony Hopkins, Anne Bancroft, John Gielgud). Made, surprisingly, by comic Mel Brooks's production company. JF DVD

John Hurt *John Merrick* • Anthony Hopkins *Frederick Treves* • Anne Bancroft *Mrs Madge Kendal* • John Gielgud *Carr Gomm* • Wendy Hiller *Mothershead* • Freddie Jones *Bytes* • Michael Elphick *Night porter* • Hannah Gordon *Mrs Treves* ■ *Dir* David Lynch • *Scr* Christopher de Vore, Eric Bergren, David Lynch, from the non-fiction books *The Elephant Man: A Study In Human Dignity* by Ashley Montagu and *The Elephant Man and Other Reminiscences* by Sir Frederick Treves • *Make-up* Christopher Tucker

Elephant Walk ★★★ U

Drama
1954 · US · Colour · 102mins

Peter Finch marries Elizabeth Taylor and takes her back to Ceylon where his tea plantation has been established right in the path of commuting pachyderms. But domestic squabbles, an outbreak of typhoid and the promised elephant stampede do not prevent our heroes from producing a good, strong, freshly-brewed cuppa in this sold Imperial melodrama. In shots of the early car journey from the airport the eagle-eyed may spot Vivien Leigh, who was originally cast as Finch's wife. But Leigh's illness in Ceylon led to complications, and she then suffered a nervous breakdown. AT

Elizabeth Taylor *Ruth Wiley* • Dana Andrews *Dick Carver* • Peter Finch *John Wiley* • Abraham Sofaer *Appuhamy* • Abner Biberman *Dr Pereira* • Noel Drayton *Planter Atkinson* • Rosalind Ivan *Mrs Lakin* ■ *Dir* William Dieterle • *Scr* John Lee Mahin, from the novel by Robert Standish

11 Harrowhouse ★★

Crime comedy
1974 · UK · Colour · 108mins

This overeager comedy foolhardily attempts to send up the heist caper. Only the bullish playing saves the day, as Aram Avakian's direction is so slipshod that the enterprise has descended into low farce long before the extended chase finale. Hard though Charles Grodin and Candice Bergen try as the ingenious vacuuming jewel thieves, they're totally outclassed by a venerable supporting cast that includes a deliciously embittered James Mason, a gloriously sniffy John Gielgud and an unashamedly barnstorming Trevor Howard. Fun but forgettable. DP

Charles Grodin *Chesser* • Candice Bergen *Maren* • John Gielgud *Meecham* • Trevor Howard *Clyde Massey* • James Mason *Watts* • Peter Vaughan *Coglin* • Helen Cherry *Lady Bolding* • Jack Watson *Miller* • Jack Watling *Fitzmaurice* ■ *Dir* Aram Avakian • *Scr* Jeffrey Bloom, Charles Grodin, from the novel *11 Harrowhouse Street* by Gerald A Browne

11'09''01 – September 11 ★★★ 12

Portmanteau documentary
2002 · Fr · Colour and BW · 128mins

Cinema seizes its responsibility to reflect reality, rather than simply provide an escape from it, in this laudably even-handed omnibus. While all involved express sympathy with those personally affected by the Twin Towers tragedy, more militant film-makers such as Ken Loach and Youssef Chahine are prepared to challenge the ethics of postwar US foreign policy, while others including Amos Gitai and Danis Tanovic prefer to highlight the many local tragedies that were eclipsed by the overwhelming media response to the attack and its geo-political ramifications. The project's sincerity is indisputable, but the quality of the contributions is decidedly mixed. Alejandro González Iñárritu's courageous blend of darkness, evocative sound and horrifying flashes of the towers being the artistic highlight and Shohei Imamura's obscure allegory the nadir. The contributions came from Iran, France, Egypt, Bosnia-Herzegovina, Borkina Faso, the UK, Mexico, Israel, India, the US and Japan. DP DVD

Dir Samira Makhmalbaf, Claude Lelouch, Youssef Chahine, Danis Tanovic, Idrissa Ouedraogo, Ken Loach, Alejandro González Iñárritu, Amos Gitai, Mira Nair, Sean Penn, Shohei Imamura • *Scr* Samira Makhmalbaf, Claude Lelouch, Pierre Uytterhoeven, Youssef Chahine, Danis Tanovic, Idrissa Ouedraogo, Paul Laverty, Ken Loach, Vladimir Vega, Alejandro González Iñárritu, Amos Gitaï, Marie Josée Sanselme, Sabrina Dhawan, Sean Penn, Daisuke Tengan

Elf ★★★ PG

Christmas comedy fantasy
2003 · US · Colour · 92mins

Director Jon Favreau's sweet seasonal comedy relies entirely on the talents of Will Ferrell, who plays an adult raised from a baby by Santa's little helpers. Ferrell discovers the existence of his real father (James Caan in full-bore Scrooge mode) and heads for New York. Despite modern special effects trickery, this strives for the feel of vintage Disney through twee settings and storybook narration from Bob Newhart. Dispensing decorations and sugary snacks with a beaming grin, Ferrell is the life and soul of an otherwise unexceptional Christmas celebration. JC DVD

Will Ferrell *Buddy* • James Caan *Walter* • Bob Newhart *Papa Elf* • Edward Asner *Santa* • Mary Steenburgen *Emily* • Zooey Deschanel *Jovie* • Daniel Tay *Michael* • Michael Lerner *Fulton* ■ *Dir* Jon Favreau • *Scr* David Berenbaum

Elisa ★★ 15

Drama
1994 · Fr · Colour · 110mins

Jean Becker is a master at combining the commercial with the psychological. He is also clearly fascinated by the way in which disturbed teenage girls resolve their problems. Vanessa Paradis uses her wiles to right a past wrong, though her pin-up looks prevent her from carrying off the part of a tough little hussy – a sizeable drawback considering she's on screen for much of the film. Unfortunately, the same cannot be said of the underused Gérard Depardieu. DP. In French with English subtitles.

Vanessa Paradis *Marie* • Gérard Depardieu *Jacques Lébovitch* • Clothilde Courau [Clotilde Courau] *Solange* • Sekkou Sall *Ahmed* • Florence Thomassin *Elisa* • Michel Bouquet *Samuel* • Philippe Léotard *Smoker* ■ *Dir* Jean Becker • *Scr* Jean Becker, Fabrice Carazo

Elizabeth ★★★★ 15

Historical drama
1998 · UK · Colour · 118mins

This Elizabethan political thriller charting the turbulent life and times of the self-proclaimed "Virgin Queen" is given a vivid contemporary focus by Indian director Shekhar Kapur's keen visual eye. A far cry from the usual "frock opera", this sumptuous biography is a thoughtful and dramatic triumph, with Australian actress Cate Blanchett revelatory as the strong-willed monarch who nimbly transforms from naive girlhood to true majesty, assisted by Sir Francis Walsingham (*Shine's* Geoffrey Rush). Richard Attenborough, Joseph Fiennes and ex-footballer Eric Cantona flesh out an interesting cast. School history lessons were never this good! AJ. Contains violence and sex scenes. DVD

Cate Blanchett *Elizabeth I* • Geoffrey Rush *Sir Francis Walsingham* • Richard Attenborough *Sir William Cecil* • John Gielgud *The Pope* • Fanny Ardant *Mary of Guise* • Terence Rigby *Bishop Gardiner* • Christopher Eccleston *Duke of Norfolk* • Amanda Ryan *Lettice Howard* • Kathy Burke *Queen Mary Tudor* • Joseph Fiennes *Robert Dudley, Earl of Leicester* • Wayne Sleep *Dance tutor* • Angus Deayton *Woad, Chancellor of the Exchequer* • Eric Cantona *Monsieur de Foix* ■ *Dir* Shekhar Kapur • *Scr* Michael Hirst

Elizabeth of Ladymead ★★

Period drama
1948 · UK · Colour · 107mins

This is a disappointing pageant, in which a concussed Anna Neagle imagines herself in various incarnations during a turbulent century of change. In 1854, she's a devotee of women's rights awaiting news of the conflict in the Crimea. By the post-Boer War era, she's become sufficiently independent to run the family estate. However, things take a sordid turn around the Treaty of Versailles, when her reckless behaviour drives her husband to suicide. DP

Anna Neagle *Elizabeth* • Hugh Williams *John, 1946* • Nicholas Phipps *John, 1854* • Michael Laurence *John, 1919* • Bernard Lee *John, 1903* ■ *Dir* Herbert Wilcox • *Scr* Frank Harvey, Nicholas Phipps, from a play by Frank Harvey

Ella Enchanted ★★★ PG

Comedy fantasy adventure
2004 · US/UK/Ire · Colour · 92mins

Fairy tales are engagingly deconstructed in director Tommy O'Haver's overly spiced-up adaptation. Spirited Anne Hathaway plays Ella of Frell, cursed at birth to obey every command, who navigates her way through a revisionist onslaught of villainous stepsisters, enslaved ogres and show-tune singing elves to conquer her fears and uncover a plot to kill the handsome Prince Charmont (Hugh Dancy). Blending contemporary morals, pop culture references, exemplary fantasy vistas and classic hit songs, this is a camp mess but an appealing one. AJ DVD

Anne Hathaway *Ella of Frell* • Hugh Dancy *Prince Charmont* • Cary Elwes *Sir Edgar* • Aidan McArdle *Slannen of Pim* • Joanna Lumley *Dame Olga* • Minnie Driver *Mandy* • Jimi Mistry *Benny* • Eric Idle *Narrator* • Vivica A Fox *Lucinda Perriweather* • Patrick Bergin *Sir Peter* • Steve Coogan *Heston* ■ *Dir* Tommy O'Haver • *Scr* Laurie Craig, Karen McCullah Lutz, Kirsten Smith, Jennifer Heath, Michelle J Wolff, from the novel by Gail Carson Levine

Ellery Queen Master Detective ★★

Detective mystery 1940 · US · BW · 67mins

Ellery Queen, one of the most successful fictional detectives of all time, didn't have much luck with his movie incarnations, eventually finding his natural home on TV. Here, Queen is portrayed by an embarrassed Ralph Bellamy as a comic bumbling dolt. Bellamy only played Queen on four occasions, leaving the role to William Gargan in 1942 for three futher films, but the damage was done. TS

Ralph Bellamy *Ellery Queen* • Margaret Lindsay *Nikki Porter* • Charley Grapewin *Inspector Queen* • James Burke *Sergeant Velie* • Michael Whalen *Dr James Rogers* • Marsha Hunt *Barbara Braun* • Fred Niblo *John Braun* ■ *Dir* Kurt Neumann • *Scr* Eric Taylor, from a story by Ellery Queen [Frederic Dannay, Manfred Bennington Lee]

Ellie ★ 15

Comedy
1984 · US · Colour · 85mins

A soft-core sex comedy, somewhat dignified by the presence of Shelley Winters, but mainly a pretext for *Penthouse* pet Sheila Kennedy to pose in any number of designer underwear outfits – and sometimes less. The latter has more curves than a mountain road as a virginal country girl, besieged by Winters's three sons after her wheelchair-bound father is murdered. Kennedy swears vengeance, a campaign that almost always involves taking off her clothes, and starts bumping off the sons. AT

Sheila Kennedy *Ellie* • Shelley Winters *Cora* • Edward Albert *Tom* • Pat Paulsen *Sheriff* • George Gobel *Preacher* ■ *Dir* Peter Wittman • *Scr* Glenn Allen Smith

Elling ★★★★ 15

Comedy drama
2001 · Nor · Colour · 88mins

Nominated for the 2002 best foreign film Oscar, director Petter Naess's adaptation effectively combines offbeat comedy with poignant insight. Discovered hiding in a cupboard after the death of his mother, 40-something Elling (Per Christian Ellefsen) is taken in to an institution where he meets the dull-witted Sven Nordin. Two years later, they are installed in an Oslo flat where Nordin's interest is diverted by pregnant neighbour Marit Pia Jacobsen, and Elling copes by writing poetry. Without a single patronising moment, this is a perceptive portrait of life on the margins. DP. In Norwegian with English subtitles.

Per Christian Ellefsen *Elling* • Sven Nordin *Kjell Bjarne* • Per Christensen *Alfons Jorgensen* • Jørgen Langhelle *Frank Asli* • Marit Pia Jacobsen *Reidun Nordsletten* • Hilde Olausson *Gunn* • Ola Otnes *Hauger* • Eli-Anne Linnestad [Eli Anne Linnestad] *Johanne* ■ *Dir* Petter Naess • *Scr* Axel Hellstenius, from the novel *Brothers in Blood* by Ingvar Ambjornsen

Elmer Gantry ★★★★★ PG

Drama
1960 · US · Colour · 140mins

Seldom does the cinema see such a perfect match of star and role as here, with Burt Lancaster as the conman who finds evangelism as easy to sell as vacuum cleaners. Lancaster rightly won the best actor Oscar for the finest performance of his career; the film also picked up Oscars for director Richard Brooks's screenplay and Shirley Jones's supporting turn as a vengeful prostitute. Also brilliantly cast is Jean Simmons as Sister Sharon Falconer, whose sincerity, like Gantry's, is never questioned. John Alton's colour photography is superb, but it's Brooks's handling of the key scenes that makes this film a Hollywood classic. TS [video] DVD

Burt Lancaster *Elmer Gantry* • Jean Simmons *Sister Sharon Falconer* • Arthur Kennedy *Jim Lefferts* • Shirley Jones *Lulu Bains* • Dean Jagger *William L Morgan* • Patti Page *Sister Rachel* • Edward Andrews *George Babbitt* • John McIntyre [John McIntire] *Rev Pengilly* • Joe Maross *Pete* ■ *Dir* Richard Brooks • *Scr* Richard Brooks, from the novel by Sinclair Lewis

Eloge de l'Amour ★★★★★ PG

Experimental drama
2001 · Fr/Swi · BW and Colour · 94mins

Already renowned for a career studded with memorable and revolutionary work, Jean-Luc Godard here produces an experimental meditation on the nature of love which ranks as one of his finest achievements. It's essentially a Teach Yourself Guide to the stylistic gimmicks – non-linear narrative, unusual editing techniques, varying visual textures – and ideological concerns – the "Hollywoodisation" of culture, the elusiveness of history and memory – that have pre-occupied the maverick maestro throughout his life. The consciously convoluted story concerns film-maker Bruno Putzulu's attempt to study the four stages of love – meeting, passion, separation and reconciliation – through the eyes of three couples. The contrast between the melancholic monochrome of the opening section and the lustrous high-resolution digital colour of the conclusion would have been enough to set it apart. But Godard's precise dissection of American cultural arrogance and the sly asides on the nature of heroism and the value of history lend a razor-sharp edge to this masterpiece. DP. In French with English subtitles. [video] DVD

Bruno Putzulu *Edgar* • Cécile Camp *The woman* • Jean Davy *Grandfather* • François Verny *Grandmother* • Philippe Lyrette *Philippe, Edgar's assistant* • Audrey Klebaner *Eglantine* ■ *Dir/Scr* Jean-Luc Godard • *Cinematographer* Christophe Pollock, Julien Hirsch

Elstree Calling ★★

Comedy musical 1930 · UK · BW · 86mins

Hollywood had already produced several lavish musical revues to exploit sound and showcase contract artists when Britain's Elstree studio cobbled together this pathetically tatty-looking variety show, done against cardboard-looking sets. The production numbers are laughably bad, far funnier than the dire comedy sketches. There is historical interest in the performances of music-hall stars Will Fyffe and Lily Morris and the fact that the really dreadful spoof of *The Taming of the Shrew* and other linking material were directed by Alfred Hitchcock. DM

Tommy Handley *Compère* ■ *Dir* Alfred Hitchcock, André Charlot, Jack Hubert, Paul Murray • *Scr* Adrian Brunel, Val Valentine, Walter Mycroft

The Elusive Pimpernel ★★ U

Period adventure
1950 · UK · Colour · 104mins

This version of Baroness Orczy's *The Scarlet Pimpernel* is one of Michael Powell and Emeric Pressburger's lesser efforts; Powell had at one stage wanted the project to be a musical and called what he ended up with "a terrible mess". This is a little harsh, though, since the film is not without its moments of colour and excitement. David Niven is as suave as ever in the title role of the jaunty Englishman who, beneath his carefree exterior, dedicates himself to the task of saving French aristocrats from the revolutionary guillotine. PF [video]

David Niven *Sir Percy Blakeney* • Margaret Leighton *Marguerite Blakeney* • Jack Hawkins *Prince of Wales* • Cyril Cusack *Chauvelin* • Robert Coote *Sir Andrew Ffoulkes* • Edmond Audran *Armand St Juste* • Danielle Godet *Suzanne de Tournai* ■ *Dir* Michael Powell, Emeric Pressburger • *Scr* Michael Powell, Emeric Pressburger, from the novel *The Scarlet Pimpernel* by Baroness Orczy

Elves ★ 18

Horror 1989 · US · Colour · 89mins

The budget for this seems to have been almost entirely spent on star Dan Haggerty (playing a department store Santa), possibly explaining why there is only one stiff animatronic elf, despite the plural title. Haggerty investigates his predecessor's castration, with plenty of Nazis, incest, rape, drugs, and other questionable elements thrown in. KB [video]

Dan Haggerty • Deanna Lund • Julie Austin • Borah Silver ■ *Dir* Jeffrey Mandel • *Scr* Mike Griffin, Bruce Taylor, Jeff Mandel

Elvira Madigan ★★★ PG

Romantic drama
1967 · Swe · Colour · 85mins

This true tale of doomed love and flouted convention will either have you sobbing uncontrollably or wincing at its overt sentimentality. Director Bo Widerberg shot the illicit romance between a tightrope artist and a married soldier in hazy pastels, thus enhancing both the picturesque delights of the Swedish countryside and the beauty of Pia Degermark, who won the best actress prize at Cannes. DP. In Swedish with English subtitles. [video] DVD

Pia Degermark *Elvira* • Thommy Berggren *Sixten* • Lennart Malmer *Friend* • Nina Widerberg *Girl* • Cleo Jensen *Cook* ■ *Dir* Bo Widerberg • *Scr* Bo Widerberg, from the song *Visan om den Sköna Konstberiderskan Elvira Madigans Kälek och Grymma Död* by Johan Lindström Saxon

Elvira, Mistress of the Dark ★ 15

Comedy 1988 · US · Colour · 91mins

A distinctly American phenomenon, Elvira (real name Cassandra Peterson) is a camp vampette, an amalgam of Morticia Addams and Dolly Parton, who hosts horror movie nights on television. Graduating to her own feature movie, Peterson is cast as, well, a television horror movie host who inherits a haunted house. Horror buffs may get a kick out of the numerous references to the genre, but the rest of us will be bored by the predictable plot and unimpressed with the shoddy effects. RS [video] DVD

Cassandra Peterson *Elvira* • W Morgan Sheppard [Morgan Sheppard] *Vincent Talbot* • Daniel Greene *Bob Redding* • Susan Kellermann *Patty* • Jeff Conaway *Travis* • Edie McClurg *Chastity Pariah* • Kurt Fuller *Mr Glotter* • Pat Crawford Brown *Mrs Meeker* • Lee McLaughlin *Earl Hooter* ■ *Dir* James Signorelli • *Scr* Sam Egan, John Paragon, Cassandra Peterson

Elvis! Elvis! ★★★

Drama 1977 · Swe · Colour · 101mins

Although the King made 33 films himself, most of them unworthy of his immense talent, he has since been posthumously immortalised in such diverse works as Tony Scott's *True Romance* and Jim Jarmusch's *Mystery Train*. This charming Swedish picture therefore forms part of an eclectic sub-genre: the non-Elvis Elvis movie. It's a domestic drama, based on a real boy whose mother was so obsessed with Elvis she saddled her son with his moniker. Leisurely directed by Kay Pollak, this is a sweet film, with cinematography from Mikael Salomon. TS. In Swedish with English subtitles.

Lele Dorazio *Elvis* • Lena-Pia Bernhardsson *Elvis's mother* • Fred Gunnarsson *Elvis's father* • Elisaveta *Elvis's grandmother* • Allan Edwall *Elvis's grandfather* ■ *Dir* Kay Pollak • *Scr* Kay Pollak, Maria Gripe, from the book *Elvis Karlsson* by Maria Gripe

Elvis on Tour ★★★ PG

Music documentary
1972 · US · Colour · 89mins

Essential viewing for Elvis fans as the King goes on stage, but the raw energy of his 1950s performances and songs are long gone. The then-fashionable multiscreen technique here becomes tiresome: the King only needs one screen to himself. Still, the material is mesmerising for fans, and there's also a skilful trawl through Elvis's earlier life for non-devotees. Interesting to note that a youngster in the cutting rooms graduated from a similiar role on the multiscreen *Woodstock*: an assistant film editor named Martin Scorsese. TS [video]

Dir Pierre Adidge, Robert Abel

Elvis: That's the Way It Is ★★★★ U

Music documentary
1970 · US · Colour · 94mins

A magnificent record of the King's return to live performances, stunningly filmed in Las Vegas. More than just a documentary, this is a carefully-crafted Metro special, filmed in Panavision by the great cameraman Lucien Ballard (*The Wild Bunch*) under the canny direction of Denis Sanders. The film is shot through with Presley's delicious sense of self-mockery, but the real pleasure comes from watching one of the greatest performers of the 20th century doing what he does best. Preserved here are great performances of such standards as *Suspicious Minds*, *You've Lost That Lovin' Feeling* and the electric *I Just Can't Help Believing*. Forget the 30-odd Hollywood movies that preceded this – here's the real thing. TS [video] DVD

Dir Denis Sanders

Elvis – the Movie ★★★★ U

Biographical drama
1979 · US · Colour · 163mins

John Carpenter's made-for-TV version of the Elvis Presley saga, which was sadly truncated on its cinema release in the UK, is a detailed and truthful account of one of the most potent myths of modern popular culture. Kurt Russell, though no lookalike, makes a fine job of playing Presley – as a child actor, he played alongside the King in a scene in *It Happened at the World's Fair* – while Shelley Winters is particularly moving as Elvis's tragic mother, Gladys. For those who don't know the story, this is a worthwhile introduction – a biopic made with respect and affection. TS [video]

Kurt Russell *Elvis Presley* • Shelley Winters *Gladys Presley* • Bing Russell *Vernon Presley* • Robert Gray *Red West* • Season Hubley *Priscilla Presley* • Pat Hingle *Colonel Tom Parker* • Abi Young *Natalie Wood* ■ *Dir* John Carpenter • *Scr* Anthony Lawrence

Elvjs & Merilijn ★★★

Drama 1998 · It · Colour · 93mins

Although Armando Manni's directorial debut isn't without humour, the tragedy of the Balkans always impinges on the story of Goran Navojec and Edyta Olszowka, the winners of a *Stars in Their Eyes*-type contest, who see their prize trip to Italy as the start of something big. But the Bulgarian Elvis and the Romanian Marilyn Monroe are soon confronted with the realities of the region, with the suicide of Yugoslav colonel Toni Bertorelli taking the sheen off Olszowka's dayglow dreams. The descent into porn is badly mismanaged, but the leads retain our sympathy. DP. In Italian, Romanian, Bulgarian, Serbo-Croat and French with English subtitles.

Edyta Olszowka *Ileana/Merilijn* • Goran Navojec *Nicolaj/Elvjs* • Giorgio Faletti *Gino* • Toni Bertorelli *Colonel* • Julietta Koleva *Eva Petrova* • Sasa Vulicevic *Goran* • Margaretha Von Kraus *Ileana's mother* • Mariana Jichich *Nicolaj's wife* ■ *Dir* Armando Manni • *Scr* Armando Manni, Massimo Torre, from their story

E

Embassy ★★

Spy drama 1972 · UK · Colour · 89mins

Few actors can look more quietly harassed than Max von Sydow and, as the Soviet defector coming in from the cold to the protective warmth of the US embassy in Beirut, he looks even more disturbed than usual. He has good reason for alarm, as KGB agent Chuck Connors is out to get him and there's an awful lot of over-emphatic dialogue to get through, a task that overwhelms most of the cast. Mediocre. TH

Richard Roundtree *Shannon* • Chuck Connors *Kesten* • Marie-José Nat *Laure* • Ray Milland *Ambassador* • Broderick Crawford *Dunninger* • Max von Sydow *Gorenko* • David Bauer *Kadish* ■ *Dir* Gordon Hessler • *Scr* William Fairchild, from a novel by Stephen Coulter

Embrace of the Vampire ★ 18

Erotic horror 1994 · US · Colour · 88mins

Virginal Alyssa Milano falls under vampire Martin Kemp's spell in the days leading up to her 18th birthday, after which she must choose between a mortal existence or immortality with her undead lover. Poorly scripted with inane dialogue and virtually no plot, the whole reason for this contrived fantasy's existence is to show Milano's nude body at every available opportunity. That aside, there's nothing else worth watching in an aimless and sleep-inducing production. AJ [video] DVD

Alyssa Milano *Charlotte* • Jennifer Tilly *Marika* • Martin Kemp *Vampire* • Harrison Pruett *Chris* • Charlotte Lewis *Sarah* • Jordan Ladd *Eliza* ■ *Dir* Anne Goursaud • *Scr* Nicole Coady, Halle Eaton, Rick Bitzelberger

Embryo ★ 15

Science-fiction drama
1976 · US · Colour · 103mins

Frankenstein rides again in director Ralph Nelson's update. Rock Hudson gives one of his worst performances as the scientist who invents a hormone enabling foetuses to grow rapidly to maturity outside the womb. When he develops gorgeous Barbara Carrera, she turns into a homicidal maniac looking for the formula to stop her accelerated ageing. Embarrassing dialogue and nauseating special effects test the patience. AJ [video] DVD

Rock Hudson *Dr Paul Holliston* • Diane Ladd *Martha* • Barbara Carrera *Victoria* • Roddy McDowall *Riley* • Anne Schedeen *Helen* • John Elerick *Gordon* ■ *Dir* Ralph Nelson • *Scr* Anita Doohan, Jack W Thomas

The Emerald Forest ★★★ 15

Drama 1985 · UK · Colour · 108mins

Director John Boorman teaches us a conservation lesson, with his son Charley as the boy kidnapped in the jungles of the Amazon. Found by his engineer father Powers Boothe, the wild child ponders whether a return to civilisation is worth it, while dad wonders if his dam-building is of any value. Such weighty matters are unbalanced by Charley's awkward acting and an over-earnest approach, though the film's appeal is strengthened by Philippe Rousselot's breathtakingly beautiful photography. TH. Contains violence, drug abuse and nudity. DVD

Powers Boothe *Bill Markham* • Charley Boorman *Tommy* • Meg Foster *Jean Markham* • Estee Chandler *Heather* • Dira Paes *Kachiri* • William Rodriquez *Young Tommy* • Eduardo Conde *Uwe Werner* • Rui Polonah *Wanadi* ■ *Dir* John Boorman • *Scr* Rospo Pallenberg

Emergency ★★ U

Drama 1962 · UK · BW · 64mins

Francis Searle's anaemic little movie re-creates the agony of an estranged couple and their young daughter who is in desperate need of a blood donor. Glyn Houston is the earnest Scotland Yard flatfoot looking for likely candidates while the parents Zena Walker and Dermot Walsh look suitably in need of tranquillisers. Things get quite dramatic before the hour and the budget is up, in this remake of Lewis Gilbert's *Emergency Call* (1952). DP

Glyn Houston *Inspector Harris* • Zena Walker *Joan Bell* • Dermot Walsh *John Bell* • Colin Tapley *Dr Lloyd* • Garard Green *Professor Graham* • Anthony Dawes *Sergeant Phillips* ■ *Dir* Francis Searle • *Scr* Don Nicholl, James O'Connolly, from a story by Lewis Gilbert, Vernon Harris

Emergency Call ★★ U

Medical drama 1952 · UK · BW · 90mins

A small child with a rare blood type needs a transfusion to pull through a critical operation, and the only donors available are a boxer at a career crossroads, a black sailor with attitude and a killer on the run. Director Lewis Gilbert manages to take this cliché-ridden mishmash and mould it into a mildly diverting and well-edited drama. Remade ten years later as *Emergency*. DP

Jack Warner *Inspector Lane* • Anthony Steel *Dr Carter* • Joy Shelton *Laura Bishop* • Sidney James *Danny Marks* • Freddie Mills *Tim Mahoney* • Earl Cameron *George Robinson* • John Robinson (1) *Dr Braithwaite* • Thora Hird *Mrs Cornelius* • Eric Pohlmann *Flash Harry* • Sydney Tafler *Brett* ■ *Dir* Lewis Gilbert • *Scr* Lewis Gilbert, Vernon Harris

The Emigrants ★★★

Period epic 1971 · Swe · Colour · 150mins

Oscar-nominated for best picture in 1972, this adaptation of Vilhelm Moberg's novels was followed by *The New Land* – which was also nominated, this time for best foreign film. Not content with co-scripting and directing this cross-continental epic, Jan Troell also shot and edited the imposing imagery that so powerfully conveys the pain of leaving Sweden for ever and the enormity of the challenge awaiting farmer Max von Sydow and his wife Liv Ullmann on the plains of Minnesota. It's often grindingly slow, but it's impossible not to be moved by the dangers and hardships they face en route to their new home. DP. Swedish dialogue dubbed into English.

Max von Sydow *Karl Oskar* • Liv Ullmann *Kristina* • Eddie Axberg *Robert* • Pierre Lindstedt *Arvid* • Allan Edwall *Danjel* • Monica Zeterlund *Ulrika* • Hans Alfredson *Jonas Petter* ■ *Dir* Jan Troell • *Scr* Bengt Forslund, Jan Troell, from the novels by Vilhelm Moberg

Emil and the Detectives ★★ U

Crime comedy adventure
1964 · US · Colour · 92mins

There's a Children's Film Foundation feel to this Disney version of Erich Kästner's ever-popular novel about a boy who stumbles across a master criminal's plan to rob Berlin's richest bank. Walter Slezak plays the Baron with an unnecessarily pantomimic brio, but most under-tens will be too busy identifying with the heroic Bryan Russell to notice. DP

Walter Slezak *Baron* • Bryan Russell *Emil* • Roger Mobley *Gustav* • Heinz Schubert *Grundeis* • Peter Ehrlich *Muller* • Cindy Cassell *Pony* • Elsa Wagner *Nana* ■ *Dir* Peter Tewksbury • *Scr* AJ Carothers, from the novel *Emil und die Detektiven* by Erich Kästner

Emile ★★★ 15

Drama 2003 · Can/UK/Nor · Colour · 92mins

Centred on a subtle performance by Ian McKellen, this is a gentle and endearing tale about guilt, betrayal and resentment. McKellen's ageing professor is poignantly frail and flawed as he struggles with the ghosts of his past, stirred up during a trip from England to Canada to receive an honorary degree. Though his journey to redemption relies more on reflection than action, the emotional repercussions of his stay with his only living relatives (Deborah Kara Unger and newcomer Theo Crane) are thoroughly absorbing. SF

Ian McKellen *Emile* • Deborah Kara Unger *Nadia/Nadia's mother* • Chris William Martin [Chris Martin (2)] *Carl* • Tygh Runyan *Freddy* • Ian Tracey *Tom* • Janet Wright *Alice* • Nancy Sivak *Superintendent* • Theo Crane *Maria/ Nadia, aged 10* ■ *Dir/Scr* Carl Bessai

Eminent Domain ★★ 15

Political thriller
1991 · Can/Fr/Is · Colour · 106mins

Donald Sutherland is the Politburo official who finds himself out in the cold in this Kafkaesque thriller, set in pre-Solidarity Poland. More sinisterly, Sutherland can't find anyone to explain his sudden loss of power and status. Anne Archer and Bernard Hepton co-star in a film that has its intriguing aspects, but whose confusions and complexities may be a bit of a "trial" for some viewers. DA

Donald Sutherland *Josef Borski* • Anne Archer *Mira* • Bernard Hepton *Slovak* • Jodhi May *Ewa* • Paul Freeman *Ben* • Anthony Bate *Kowal* • Pip Torrens *Anton* • Françoise Michaud *Nicole* • Yves Beneyton *Roger* • Denys Fouqueray *Dr Marwicz* ■ *Dir* John Irvin • *Scr* Andrzej Krakowski, Richard Greggson, from a story by Andrzej Krakowski

Emma ★★★

Melodrama 1932 · US · BW · 71mins

A marvellous showcase for MGM superstar Marie Dressler, here cast as a long-suffering servant condemned to watch the family she has tended turn against her in her unuseful old age. In other hands this could be a recipe for gibbering bathos, but the great Dressler convinces with every single movement and gesture. (She was rightly nominated for an Academy Award.) Jean Hersholt is also excellent as the man of the house, and there's fine support from youngsters Richard Cromwell and Myrna Loy. TS

Marie Dressler *Emma Thatcher* • Richard Cromwell *Ronnie Smith* • Jean Hersholt *Mr Smith* • Myrna Loy *Isabelle* • John Miljan *District attorney* ■ *Dir* Clarence Brown • *Scr* Leonard Praskins, Zelda Sears

Emma ★★★★ U

Period romantic drama
1996 · UK/US · Colour · 116mins

Gwyneth Paltrow made her mark as the quintessential Jane Austen heroine in this convincing period romance from writer/director Douglas McGrath. Paltrow stars as the strong-willed matchmaker who entangles her friend (Toni Collette) in hopeless passion while trying to uncover the identity of her own true soulmate. Laced with wit, sophistication and a host of fine supporting performances (Jeremy Northam, Alan Cumming, Juliet Stevenson), this bright drama weaves a magical spell, with Paltrow at its charming centre. AJ DVD

Gwyneth Paltrow *Emma* • Toni Collette *Harriet* • Alan Cumming *Mr Elton* • Jeremy Northam *Mr Knightley* • Ewan McGregor *Frank Churchill* • Greta Scacchi *Mrs Weston* • Juliet Stevenson *Mrs Elton* • Polly Walker *Jane Fairfax* • Sophie Thompson *Miss Bates* • Phyllida Law *Mrs Bates* • James Cosmo *Mr Weston* • Denys Hawthorne *Mr Woodhouse* ■ *Dir* Douglas McGrath • *Scr* Douglas McGrath, from the novel by Jane Austen

Emmanuelle ★★ 18

Erotic drama 1974 · Fr · Colour · 89mins

Possibly the best-known porn film in the world, this made Sylvia Kristel an international star and spawned countless imitations. So is it any good? It's artfully shot by director Just Jaeckin, the Thailand locations are occasionally stunning and Kristel disrobes with some elegance. However, acting is far from her strong suit, and the dialogue and story, about the sexual awakening of a young woman, is banal. JF. In French with English subtitles. DVD

Sylvia Kristel *Emmanuelle* • Alain Cuny *Mario* • Daniel Sarky *Jean* • Jeanne Colletin *Ariane* • Marika Green *Bee* • Christine Boisson *Marie-Ange* ■ *Dir* Just Jaeckin • *Scr* Jean-Louis Richard, from the novel by Emmanuelle Arsan

Emmanuelle 2 ★★ 18

Erotic drama 1975 · Fr · Colour · 87mins

In this first sequel (one of eight starring Sylvia Kristel), the scene shifts from Bangkok to Hong Kong and then Bali – not that you'd notice, however, as most of the action takes place in soft-focus close-up. The Dutch actress invests the round of sexual encounters with a modicum of eroticism, but it's clear that director Francis Giacobetti was not interested in the psychological aspects of Kristel's wanderlust. *Goodbye Emmanuelle* followed. DP. French dialogue dubbed into English. DVD

Sylvia Kristel *Emmanuelle* • Umberto Orsini *Jean* • Catherine Rivet *Anna-Maria* • Frédéric Lagache *Christopher* • Caroline Laurence *Ingrid* • Florence Lafuma *Laura* ■ *Dir* Francis Giacobetti • *Scr* Bob Elia, Francis Giacobetti, from the novel by Emmanuelle Arsan

Emmanuelle IV ★★ 18

Erotic drama 1983 · US · Colour · 85mins

By this stage in her career, Sylvia Kristel must have been tired of disrobing in exotic locations, but she hung around for a token role in the opening scenes of this leaden sequel, six years after *Goodbye Emmanuelle*. To get around her absence for the majority of the movie, the writers came up with a simple solution: Kristel this time travels to Brazil for plastic surgery and, hey presto, a younger Emmanuelle is born in the shape of Mia Nygren. For completists only, who'd probably be interested in the five subsequent unremarkable sequels in which Kristel makes an appearance. JF. French dialogue dubbed into English - checked bfi. DVD

Sylvia Kristel *Emmanuelle* • Mia Nygren *Emmanuelle IV* • Patrick Bauchau *Marc* • Deborah Power *Dona* • Sophie Berger *Maria* ■ *Dir* Francis Giacobetti • *Scr* Francis Leroi, Iris Letans, from the novel by Emmanuelle Arsan

Emma's War ★★ PG

Drama 1985 · Aus · Colour · 92mins

This is notable only for the fact that it was one of Lee Remick's last features before her tragic death from cancer at just 55. Struggling to find depth in a film in which image takes precedence over content, she plays a lonely, drunken mother who drags her daughters away from their blissful boarding school existence and deposits them in a rundown outback town where very little ever happens. Tom Cowan's photography neatly suggests the contrasting atmosphere of the two places, but the patchwork screenplay flits between episodes with no dramatic focus. DP DVD

Lee Remick *Anne Grange* • Miranda Otto *Emma Grange* • Bridey Lee *Laurel Grange* • Terence Donovan *Frank Grange* • Mark Lee *John Davidson* • Pat Evison *Miss Arnott* • Donal Gibson *Hank* • Grigor Taylor *Dr Friedlander* • Noeline Brown *Mrs Mortimer* • Rebel Russell *Miss Gunz* ■ *Dir* Clytie Jessop • *Scr* Peter Smalley, Clytie Jessop

Emotional Backgammon ★ 15

Romantic drama 2003 · UK · Colour · 93mins

Leon Herbert helms the first feature by a black British director for over a decade. He also plays the tough character who uses backgammon strategy to guide tailor Wil Johnson through his romantic entanglements with Brazilian girlfriend Daniela Lavender, who is being advised by her embittered best friend, Jacqueline de Peza. Misogyny informs the trite dialogue and the tone of the unpersuasive performances. DP

Wil Johnson *John* • Daniela Lavender *Mary* • Leon Herbert *Steve* • Jacqueline de Peza *Jane* • Bob Mercer *Paul* ■ *Dir* Leon Herbert • *Scr* Leon Herbert, Matthew Hope

The Emperor and the Assassin ★★★ 12

Historical drama
1999 · Chi/Jpn/Fr · Colour · 154mins

Despite four attempts at reworking this five-chaptered historical epic, Chen Kaige has again succumbed to the pictorialism that blighted *Temptress Moon* (1996). Embroidering the fragmentary facts known about Ying Zheng's unification of China in the late third century BC, Chen concocts a story of such complexity and specialised significance that it's difficult not only to keep track of events, but also to invest much emotional energy in the central characters. DP. In Mandarin with English subtitles. DVD

Gong Li *Lady Zhao* • Zhang Fengyi *Jing Ke* • Li Xuejian *Ying Zheng, King of Qin* • Wang Zhiwen *Marquis Changxin* ■ *Dir* Chen Kaige • *Scr* Wang Peigong, Chen Kaige

The Emperor Jones ★★

Drama 1933 · US · BW · 81mins

The commanding presence and glorious voice of Paul Robeson dominate this screen version of Eugene O'Neill's play; indeed, it's an indication of his stature that he was given the lead at a time when few black actors starred in Hollywood movies. Scriptwriter DuBose Heyward opens out the play to include Jones's earlier life as a railroad porter before following him to the West Indies, where he becomes the tyrannical ruler of a remote isle. Despite a wealth of incident, the pacing is stilted and the film fails to capture the fatalism of the original. TV

Paul Robeson *Brutus Jones* • Dudley Digges *Smithers* • Frank Wilson *Jeff* • Fredi Washington *Undine* • Ruby Elzy *Dolly* • George Haymid Stamper *Lem* • Jackie Mayble *Marcella* • Blueboy O'Connor *Treasurer* ■ *Dir* Dudley Murphy • *Scr* DuBose Heyward, from the play by Eugene O'Neill

Emperor of the North ★★★★ 15

Action adventure
1973 · US · Colour · 120mins

This addictively tough action adventure follows a railway guard (Ernest Borgnine) who is proud of the fact that no tramp, especially not Lee Marvin, rides his train for free. Robert Aldrich's direction comes at the viewer like an express train and, typically fusing darkness with wit, creates a symbolic tale of the Depression, even if the drifter in this film is rather absurdly elevated to hero status. The Aldrich express does screech to a halt now and again with rather more chat than action, but there is enough pulsating drama and compelling background detail to keep you glued. JM

Lee Marvin *A-No 1* • Ernest Borgnine *Shack* • Keith Carradine *Cigaret* • Charles Tyner *Cracker* • Malcolm Atterbury *Hogger* • Simon Oakland *Policeman* • Harry Caesar *Coaly* ■ *Dir* Robert Aldrich • *Scr* Christopher Knopf

The Emperor Waltz ★★★

Musical comedy 1948 · US · Colour · 107mins

Legend has it that this is Billy Wilder's worst movie, though it does have its delectably barmy moments. Set in the Austrian Tyrol, it stars Bing Crosby and his pet pooch, Buttons, peddling gramophones to the European nobility. Crosby falls for a countess, Joan Fontaine, while Buttons falls for a poodle. It's a fable about American enterprise and a lament for a Europe buried beneath the ruins of war. For collectors of kitsch, this all-yodelling comedy is essential viewing. AT

Bing Crosby *Virgil H Smith* • Joan Fontaine *Countess Johanna Augusta Franziska Von Stolzenberg-Stolzenberg* • Roland Culver *Baron Holenia* • Lucile Watson *Princess Bitotska* • Richard Haydn *Emperor Franz Josef* • Harold Vermilyea *Chamberlain* • John Goldsworthy *Obersthofmeister* • Sig Ruman *Dr Zwieback* ■ *Dir* Billy Wilder • *Scr* Charles Brackett, Billy Wilder

The Emperor's Candlesticks ★★★ U

Period spy drama 1937 · US · BW · 88mins

In the early 20th century, rival spies William Powell and Luise Rainer make the mistake of hiding their vital documents in a pair of candlesticks. This leads the stylish pair on a chase round Europe during which – of course – they fall in love. Lavishly mounted, acted as if the hokum were serious, and well directed by George Fitzmaurice, this is a charming, elegant tale of impeccably dressed and well-connected spies, adapted from a novel by Baroness Orczy, creator of *The Scarlet Pimpernel*. RK

William Powell *Baron Stephan Wolensky* • Luise Rainer *Countess Olga Mironova* • Robert Young (1) *Grand Duke Peter* • Maureen O'Sullivan *Maria Orlech* • Frank Morgan *Col Baron Suroff* • Henry Stephenson *Prince Johann* • Bernadene Hayes *Mitzi Reisenbach* • Donald Kirke *Anton* • Douglass Dumbrille *Korum* ■ *Dir* George Fitzmaurice • *Scr* Monckton Hoffe, Harold Goldman, Herman Mankiewicz (uncredited), Hugh Mills (uncredited), John Meehan (uncredited), Erich von Stroheim (uncredited), from a story by Baroness Orczy, from her novel

The Emperor's Club ★★★ PG

Drama 2002 · US · Colour · 104mins

This sentimenal film about a committed, but flawed, teacher says nothing new, but at least the acting makes it worthwhile. Posh prep school Classics professor Kevin Kline is so obsessed with teaching that he cuts himself off from Embeth Davidtz, his one true love. Now his hopes are centred on unruly student Emile Hirsch, who slowly conforms to the ideals of scholarship but then turns on his teacher. The idea buckles under the weight of the clichés. TH DVD

Kevin Kline *William Hundert* • Emile Hirsch *Sedgewick Bell* • Steven Culp *Older Martin Blythe* • Embeth Davidtz *Elizabeth* • Patrick Dempsey *Older Louis Masoudi* • Joel Gretsch *Older Sedgewick Bell* • Edward Herrmann *Headmaster Woodbridge* • Rob Morrow *James Ellerby* ■ *Dir* Michael Hoffman • *Scr* Neil Tolkin, from the short story *The Palace Thief* by Ethan Canin

The Emperor's New Clothes ★★ U

Musical fantasy 1987 · US · Colour · 80mins

Simple but pleasant enough fare for children, this musical reworking of the old folk tale features veteran comedian Sid Caesar as the pompous monarch being conned by tailor Robert Morse, whose beneath clothes are so "fine and delicate" they're invisible. Director David Irving plays it all with an obvious turn, but it's bound to reach its young audience. TH

Sid Caesar *The Emperor* • Robert Morse *Henry* • Jason Carter *Nicholas* • Lysette Anthony *Gilda* • Clive Revill *Prime Minister* • Julian Joy-Chagrin [Julian Chagrin] *Duke* • Eli Gorenstein *Sergeant* ■ *Dir* David Irving • *Scr* Anna Mathias, Len Talan, David Irving, from the fairy tale by Hans Christian Andersen

The Emperor's New Clothes ★★★ PG

Period comedy 2001 · UK/It/Ger · Colour · 106mins

Alan Taylor's period comedy recalls the offbeat charm of his debut *Palookaville*. But while it's undoubtedly literate and nimbly executed, it lacks the brio to match its conceit. Ian Holm revels in the dual role of the deposed emperor striving to regain his throne and the lookalike he's left in St Helena to disguise his flight. There are plenty of smiles as he treks across Europe, but once he reaches Paris and becomes enamoured of feisty melon-seller Iben Hjejle, the slick revisionism descends into historical cornball. DP

Ian Holm *Napoleon Bonaparte/Eugene Lenormand* • Iben Hjejle *Pumpkin* • Tim McInnerny *Dr Lambert* • Nigel Terry *Montholon* • Hugh Bonneville *Bertrand* • Murray Melvin *Antommarchi* • Eddie Marsan *Marchand* • Clive Russell *Sgt Justin Bommel* ■ *Dir* Alan Taylor • *Scr* Kevin Molony, Alan Taylor, Herbie Wave, from the novel *The Death of Napoleon* by Simon Leys

The Emperor's New Groove ★★★★ U

Animated comedy 2000 · US · Colour · 78mins

In this refreshingly hip take on the mismatched buddy genre, Emperor Kuzco (David Spade) is the arrogant young ruler of a mythical South American kingdom, who is transformed into a llama by his power-hungry adviser, Yzma (Eartha Kitt), and cast into the jungle. Kuzco's only chance to reclaim his throne rests with affable peasant Pacha (John Goodman), whose picturesque village was due to be razed to accommodate the Emperor's new summer palace. Spade brings his rapier-like sarcasm, vocal dexterity and brilliant timing to the proceedings. This colourful, stylish and more adult endeavour has the character-driven pace missing from recent Disney animations. AJ DVD

David Spade *Kuzco/Kuzco Llama* • John Goodman *Pacha* • Eartha Kitt *Yzma* • Patrick Warburton *Kronk* • Wendie Malick *Chicha* ■ *Dir* Mark Dindal • *Scr* David Reynolds, from a story by Chris Williams, Mark Dindal • *Music* John Debney • *Music/Lyrics* Sting, David Hartley

The Emperor's Shadow ★★★★

Historical epic 1996 · HK · Colour · 123mins

A tragedy of epic proportions, this is, nevertheless, a very human story in which love is destroyed by the misuse of power. Wen Jiang gives a towering performance as Ying Zheng, the emperor who united China in the second century BC and whose dictatorial treatment of his childhood friend Gao Jianli results in the death of his own daughter. Ge You is also impressive as Gao, the enslaved musician whose acts of defiance topple the imperial edifice. But it's the way in which Zhou Xiaowen combines sweeping scale with intimate detail that gives the film both its power and its subtle contemporary subtext. DP. In Cantonese with English subtitles.

Jiang Wen *Ying Zheng* • Ge You *Gao Jianli* • Xu Qing *Ying Yueyang* ■ *Dir* Zhou Xiaowen • *Scr* Lu Wei

Empire ★★ 15

Crime drama 2002 · US · Colour · 95mins

Urban dramas don't get any more derivative than this hackneyed debut from Franc Reyes. Starring John Leguizamo, it tells the story of a South Bronx drugs dealer who teams up with a Wall Street hotshot (a slimy Peter Sarsgaard) to try to escape the ghetto. While Leguizamo runs rings around his co-stars in the central role, the mediocrity of the plot does him no favours. SF. Contains swearing, violence, sex scenes, drug abuse. DVD

John Leguizamo *Victor Rosa* • Peter Sarsgaard *Jack* • Denise Richards *Trish* • Vincent Laresca *Jimmy* • Isabella Rossellini *La Colombiana* • Sonia Braga *Iris* • Delilah Cotto *Carmen* • Nestor Serrano *Rafael Menendez* ■ *Dir/Scr* Franc Reyes • *Cinematographer* Kramer Morgenthau

Empire City ★★ 15

Thriller 1991 · US · Colour · 78mins

Underachieving American action man Michael Paré sleepwalks through a wannabe *film noir* that is nothing more than a patchwork of police thriller clichés loosely strung together. How many times have we seen macho cops saddled with partners they neither want nor need? In this instance, Paré is paired with Mary Mara, who proves to be more than a match for him as they bicker their way through an investigation of murder in high places. DP. Contains violence, swearing.

Michael Paré *Joe Andre* • Mary Mara *Nancy Krause* • Beau Starr *Lieutenant Bob Conway* • Peter Frechette *Graham MacGowan* • Ron Vawter *Lieutenant Spinell* • Kelly Carnahan *Robin Christopher* ■ *Dir/Scr* Mark Rosner

Empire of the Ants ★ 15

Science-fiction drama 1977 · US · Colour · 85mins

This tacky tale of tepid terror is just another poverty-row, giant-insect tale from schlock director Bert I Gordon, featuring Joan Collins up to her designer khakis in mud fighting off laughably phoney mutant ants. She's the head swindler of a housing development consortium on a resort island where radiation waste has been dumped. In between the slipshod special effects, the actors bicker a lot while trying to escape the boring menace. AJ DVD

Joan Collins *Marilyn Fryser* • Robert Lansing *Dan Stokely* • John David Carson *Joe Morrison* • Albert Salmi *Sheriff Art Kincade* • Jacqueline Scott *Margaret Ellis* • Pamela Shoop *Coreen Bradford* • Robert Pine *Larry Graham* • Edward Power *Charlie Pearson* ■ *Dir* Bert I Gordon • *Scr* Jack Turley, from a story by Bert I Gordon, from a story by HG Wells

Empire of the Sun ★★★ PG

Second World War drama 1987 · US · Colour · 146mins

Steven Spielberg's drama set in China during the Second World War is a glossy and rather tame affair, based on JG Ballard's semi-autobiographical novel. Bland Christian Bale plays 11-year-old Jim, who is separated from his family in Shanghai and ends up in a Japanese internment camp. The film has its heroic moments and scenes that depict the horror of war through the eyes of a child. However, despite the presence of such talents as John Malkovich, Miranda Richardson and Nigel Havers, this never depicts the true effects of armed conflict. JB. Contains swearing. DVD

Christian Bale *Jim Graham* • John Malkovich *Basie* • Miranda Richardson *Mrs Victor* • Nigel Havers *Dr Rawlins* • Joe Pantoliano *Frank Demerest* • Leslie Phillips *Maxton* • Robert Stephens *Mr Lockwood* • Burt Kwouk *Mr Chen* • Paul McGann *Lt Price* ■ *Dir* Steven Spielberg • *Scr* Tom Stoppard, from the novel by JG Ballard

E

Empire Records ★★★ 12

Comedy drama 1995 · US · Colour · 86mins

This likeable if faintly preposterous teen flick is set around one day in the life of a small independent music store, run by Anthony LaPaglia, which is about to be taken over by a record giant. Liv Tyler looks suitably winsome but is overshadowed by co-stars Renee Zellweger and Rory Cochrane, while Maxwell Caulfield enjoys himself as a spoilt teen idol. Director Allan Moyle demonstrates a keen understanding of adolescent angst, though the film as a whole has a distinctly old-fashioned feel. JF. Contains swearing and drug abuse. DVD

Anthony LaPaglia *Joe* • Rory Cochrane *Lucas* • Johnny Whitworth *A J* • Liv Tyler *Corey* • Renee Zellweger *Gina* • Robin Tunney *Debra* • Ethan Randall [Ethan Embry] *Mark* • Maxwell Caulfield *Rex* • Debi Mazar *Jane* ■ *Dir* Allan Moyle • *Scr* Carol Heikkinen

Employees' Entrance ★★★

Drama 1933 · US · BW · 74mins

This rather daring film was one of many in the early 1930s that led to the introduction of the censorious Hay's Code. Warren William stars as the tyrannical owner of a huge New York department store, whose only concerns are power, money and women. He gives a job to Loretta Young, after she has slept with her future boss. When she falls in love and marries an ambitious salesman, matters are brought to a climax. Briskly directed by Roy Del Ruth, this is eventful, well-acted entertainment. BB

Warren William *Kurt Anderson* • Loretta Young *Madeline Walters* • Wallace Ford *Martin West* • Alice White *Polly Dale* • Hale Hamilton *Monroe* • Albert Gran *Denton Ross* ■ *Dir* Roy Del Ruth • *Scr* Robert Presnell, from a play by David Boehm

The Empty Beach ★★★ 18

Crime drama 1985 · Aus · Colour · 86mins

Bryan Brown takes a walk on the seamy side of Sydney in this violent Australian *film noir* about a hard-boiled gumshoe, who is hired by a wealthy widow to solve the mystery of her hubby's disappearance. This may not be the most original film, but it rates as a perfectly acceptable Australian take on a familiar genre. PF. Contains swearing.

Bryan Brown *Cliff Hardy* • Anna Maria Monticelli [Anna Jemison] *Anne Winter* • Ray Barrett *MacLeary* • John Wood *Parker* • Nick Tate *Brian Henneberry* • Belinda Giblin *Marion Singer* ■ *Dir* Chris Thomson • *Scr* Keith Dewhurst, from the novel by Peter Corris

The Empty Canvas ★

Drama 1963 · Fr/It · BW · 104mins

When Bette Davis met Damiano Damiani, the Italian cult director clearly lost. In one of her strangest roles, the bitch goddess does her utmost to save her artist son, Horst Buchholz, from his obsessive love for model Catherine Spaak. Davis is all at sea in an avant-garde melodrama, in which her determination to stay in front of 1960s cameras is her only steely motivation. A sad experience. AJ. Some dialogue dubbed into English.

Bette Davis *Dino's mother* • Horst Buchholz *Dino* • Catherine Spaak *Cecilia* • Isa Miranda *Cecilia's mother* • Lea Padovani *Balestrieri's widow* • Daniela Rocca *Rita* • Georges Wilson *Cecilia's father* • Leonida Repaci *Balestrieri* ■ *Dir* Damiano Damiani • *Scr* Damiano Damiani, Tonino Guerra, Ugo Liberatore, from the novel *La Noia* by Alberto Moravia

The Empty Table ★★★★ PG

Drama 1985 · Jpn · Colour · 141mins

A modest, tradition-minded Japanese family suddenly realise that their son is a terrorist and that they will be stigmatised because of his actions. Set in the 1970s, when the much-feared Japanese Red Army were committing outrages across the world, this Masaki Kobayashi picture (his last) is slow to unfold yet presents the world of the terrorist and his family with unusual insight, taking a real event – a televised police raid on the terrorists' mountain training centre in 1970 – as its starting point. AT. In Japanese with English subtitles.

Tatsuya Nakadai *Nobuyuki Kidoji* • Mayumi Ogawa *Yukimo Kidoji* • Kie Nakai *Tamae Kidoji* • Kiichi Nakai *Otohiko Kidoji* • Takayuki Takemoto *Osamu Kidoji* • Shima Iwashita *Kiwa Nakahara* • Mikijiro Hira *Kawabe's lawyer* ■ *Dir* Masaki Kobayashi • *Scr* Masaki Kobayashi, from a story by Fumiko Enchi

En Face ★★★

Thriller 1999 · Fr · Colour · 90mins

Director Mathias Ledoux reworks the old dark house theme to good advantage in this stealthy thriller. Jean-Hugues Anglade and Clotilde Courau play the impoverished couple who are delighted to accept the bequest of a Montmartre townhouse from a mysterious neighbour. However, no sooner have they settled in than they realise their benefactor was a voyeur and that the maid (Christine Boisson) he stipulated should remain in their employ is almost as sinister as the suspicions Anglade begins to harbour against his wife. Eerily unnerving. DP. In French with English subtitles.

Jean-Hugues Anglade *Jean* • Clotilde Courau *Michelle* • Christine Boisson *Clemence* • José Garcia *Hugo* ■ *Dir* Mathias Ledoux • *Scr* Valerie Guignabodet

En Plein Coeur ★★ 15

Drama 1998 · Fr · Colour · 97mins

It's hard to believe this adaptation of Georges Simenon's novel was made by the same Pierre Jolivet who directed that intense morality tale, *Force Majeure*. Gone is the depth of characterisation and the probing intellect; in their place comes a designer *noir* style. In the absence of psychological truth, actorly earnestness scarcely atones. Yet Carole Bouquet is credibly crushed as her lawyer husband Gérard Lanvin defends wild child Virginie Ledoyen on a robbery charge, only to fall for her charms in the process. DA. In French with English subtitles. [VIDEO]

Gérard Lanvin *Michel* • Virginie Ledoyen *Cécile* • Carole Bouquet *Viviane* • Guillaume Canet *Vincent* • Aurelie Verillon *Samira* • Denis Podalydès *Martorel* ■ *Dir* Pierre Jolivet • *Scr* Roselyne Bosch, from the novel *En Cas de Malheur* by Georges Simenon

En Toute Innocence ★★★

Psychological thriller
1987 · Fr · Colour · 95mins

Alain Jessua's adaptation relies heavily on the animosity generated by Michel Serrault and Nathalie Baye, as they finagle in a deadly game of wits. Architect Serrault catches daughter-in-law Baye in her lover's embrace. But before he can inform his son, François Dunoyer is involved in an auto smash that leaves him paralysed and mute. Played out in an atmosphere of guilt, mistrust and fearful ambition, this is a deeply disconcerting thriller. DP. In French with English subtitles.

Michel Serrault *Paul Duchene* • Nathalie Baye *Catherine* • François Dunoyer *Thomas* • Suzanne Flon *Clemence* • Philippe Caroit *Didier* • Sylvie Fennec *Geneviève* ■ *Dir* Alain Jessua • *Scr* Alain Jessua, Luc Béraud, Dominique Roulet, from the novel *Suicide à l'Amiable* by André Lay

Enchanted April ★★ U

Romantic drama 1991 · UK · Colour · 89mins

Genteel to the point of tedium, this British period piece relies on its four female stars – Oscar-nominated Joan Plowright, Miranda Richardson, Josie Lawrence and Polly Walker – who play four women bonding on an Italian holiday while waiting for their male partners. The women are worth the wait, but otherwise this has all the careful, itemised hallmarks of a made-for-TV movie. Director Mike Newell went on to make the box-office hit *Four Weddings and a Funeral*. TH [VIDEO]

Miranda Richardson *Rose Arbuthnot* • Josie Lawrence *Lotty Wilkins* • Polly Walker *Lady Caroline Dester* • Joan Plowright *Mrs Fisher* • Alfred Molina *Mellersh Wilkins* • Michael Kitchen *George Briggs* • Jim Broadbent *Frederick Arbuthnot* • Davide Manuli *Beppo* ■ *Dir* Mike Newell • *Scr* Peter Barnes, from the novel by Elizabeth von Arnim

The Enchanted Cottage ★★★★ U

Romantic drama 1945 · US · BW · 92mins

One of the great romances of the cinema, this tale of two society misfits depends very heavily on a serious suspension of disbelief from its audience. Writer Arthur Pinero referred to the original as a fable, and was very aware of its low credibility factor. But the First World War update works superbly, and director John Cromwell achieves a perfect tone. As it's a Hollywood movie, leads Dorothy McGuire and Robert Young aren't disfigured or plain enough. Give your heart to it, rather than your mind, and you'll love it. TS

Dorothy McGuire *Laura Pennington* • Robert Young (1) *Oliver Bradford* • Herbert Marshall *John Hillgrove* • Mildred Natwick *Mrs Abigail Minnett* • Spring Byington *Violet Price* • Hillary Brooke *Beatrice Alexander* • Richard Gaines *Frederick Price* • Alec Englander *Danny* • Mary Worth *Mrs Stanton* ■ *Dir* John Cromwell • *Scr* DeWitt Bodeen, Herman J Mankiewicz, from the play by Sir Arthur Wing Pinero [Arthur Wing Pinero]

Enchantment ★★★ U

Romantic drama 1948 · US · BW · 96mins

Films following events in an English stately home have long held an attraction for American audiences. This one has the unusual distinction of being told by the ancestral pile itself. Based on a novel by Rumer Godden, it was advertised by RKO as "just about the most wonderful love story ever filmed". Of course it's nothing of the sort. However, David Niven gives a good account of himself as the hot-blooded lover in the first half and the wise old head in the second. DP [VIDEO]

David Niven *General Sir Roland Dane* • Teresa Wright *Lark Ingoldsby* • Evelyn Keyes *Grizel Dane* • Farley Granger *Pilot Pax Masterson* • Jayne Meadows *Selina Dane* • Leo G Carroll *Proutie* • Philip Friend *Pelham Dane* ■ *Dir* Irving Reis • *Scr* John Patrick, from the novel *Take Three Tenses* by Rumer Godden

Encore ★★★

Portmanteau drama 1951 · UK · BW · 88mins

Without ever really exerting a grip, this portmanteau picture, based on the stories of W Somerset Maugham, is a diverting collection of passable vignettes. The direction is pedestrian, but the performances of a fine cast of British stalwarts save the day. Nigel Patrick and Roland Culver give a polished demonstration of comic timing in *The Ant and the Grasshopper*, while Glynis Johns and Terence Morgan struggle to find the pathos in *Gigolo and Gigolette*. Best of all, however, is Kay Walsh, chattering in *Winter Cruise*. DP

Nigel Patrick *Tom Ramsey* • Roland Culver *George Ramsey* • Alison Leggatt *Freda Ramsey* • Kay Walsh *Miss Reid* • Noel Purcell *Captain* • Ronald Squire *Doctor* • Glynis Johns *Stella Cotman* • Terence Morgan *Syd Cotman* ■ *Dir* Harold French, Pat Jackson, Anthony Pelissier • *Scr* TEB Clarke, Arthur Macrae, Eric Ambler, from the short stories *The Ant and the Grasshopper*, *Gigolo and Gigolette* and *Winter Cruise* by W Somerset Maugham

Encounter at Raven's Gate ★★★★ 15

Science-fiction thriller
1988 · Aus · Colour · 85mins

This standout Australian science-fiction thriller involves a paroled ex-convict, his brother, the brother's bored wife and the strange phenomena that occur at Raven's Gate farm – perhaps the work of visiting evil aliens. Director Rolf De Heer allows the viewer's imagination to go into overdrive thanks to creepy photography and evocative use of sound – both of which create more edge-of-seat menace than using cheap UFO effects or rubber monsters. Tense, engrossing and packed with unusual incident (the sky raining dead birds), this atmospheric gem is a fine example of low-budget success. AJ [VIDEO]

Steven Vidler *Eddie Cleary* • Celine Griffin *Rachel Cleary* • Ritchie Singer *Richard* • Vincent Gil *Felix Skinner* • Saturday Rosenberg *Annie* • Terry Camilleri *Dr Hemmings* ■ *Dir* Rolf De Heer • *Scr* Marc Rosenberg, Rolf De Heer, James Michael Vernon

The End ★ 15

Comedy 1978 · US · Colour · 96mins

Burt Reynolds directed himself in this tasteless mishmash so, presumably, Jerry Belson's script must have meant something to him. It means nothing to us, however, as a bearded Reynolds discovers he's medically doomed and starts to square his conscience with a life that has been totally selfish. Hamming is the order of the dying day – with Dom DeLuise coming a close second to the star. TH [VIDEO]

Burt Reynolds *Wendell Sonny Lawson* • Dom DeLuise *Marlon Borunki* • Sally Field *Mary Ellen* • Strother Martin *Dr Waldo Kling* • David Steinberg *Marty Lieberman* • Joanne Woodward *Jessica* • Norman Fell *Dr Samuel Krugman* • Myrna Loy *Maureen Lawson* ■ *Dir* Burt Reynolds • *Scr* Jerry Belson

End of a Priest ★★★★

Comedy drama 1969 · Cz · BW · 82mins

Evald Schorm's tragicomic parable was withdrawn in 1973 for supposedly championing Christian morality over socialist truth. Twinkling with dark satirical gems, it traces the misadventures of Vlastimil Brodsky, a bellringer who poses as a pastor to cash in on the benevolence of parishioners desperate to re-embrace the old religion. However, the local teacher, Jan Libicek, is unconvinced by his piety and sets him up with a prostitute in order to expose his duplicity. Artfully juxtaposing bibilical *bon mots* with Communist slogans, it's a sly inversion of the cosy world of Giovanni Guareschi's Don Camillo. DP. In Czech with English subtitles.

Vlastimil Brodsky *Sexton* • Jana Brejchova *Majka* • Jan Libicek *Village teacher* • Zdena Skvorecka *Anna* • Jaroslav Satoransky *Tonik* ■ *Dir* Evald Schorm • *Scr* Evald Schorm, Josef Skvorecky, from the story *Fararuv Konec* by Josef Skvorecky

End of Days ★★★ 18

Supernatural action thriller
1999 · US · Colour · 127mins

While Arnold Schwarzenegger's amateurish emoting never rings true in the role of a run-down, suicidal, alcoholic ex-cop, the "Devil searching for his bride" story provides some decent popcorn entertainment. Gabriel Byrne, meanwhile, rises above the clumsily structured and wholly derivative script to give an attention-grabbing performance as a very laid-back Prince of Darkness. JC. Contains swearing, violence, nudity. [VIDEO] DVD

Arnold Schwarzenegger *Jericho Cane* • Gabriel Byrne *The Man* • Kevin Pollak *Chicago* • Robin Tunney *Christine York* • CCH Pounder *Detective Marge Francis* • Rod Steiger *Father Kovak* • Miriam Margolyes *Mabel* ■ *Dir* Peter Hyams • *Scr* Andrew W Marlowe

The End of Innocence ★★

Drama 1990 · US · Colour · 102mins

Actress Dyan Cannon writes, directs and stars in this drama about one woman's disappointments and setbacks. Evidently Cannon – who gets to scream, rant and wave her legs around – saw this as an opportunity to flex her creative muscle. For the viewer, though, it's a rather depressing and relentless tale, made even more so by the final appearance of Rebecca Schaeffer, who was tragically murdered at the age of 21. JB

Dyan Cannon *Stephanie Lewis* • John Heard *Dean* • George Coe *Dad* • Lola Mason *Mom* • Rebecca Schaeffer *Stephanie at 18* • Stephen Meadows *Michael* • Michael Madsen *Earl* ■ *Dir/Scr* Dyan Cannon

The End of St Petersburg ★★★★ PG

Silent political drama
1927 · USSR · BW · 68mins

Commissioned as part of the tenth anniversary celebrations of the Russian Revolution, the film was shot by the great Russian director Vsevolod Pudovkin at the same time and place (Leningrad) as Sergei Eisenstein's more famous *October* (1928). Both films dealt with the storming of the Winter Palace and the triumph of the Bolsheviks, but Pudovkin's film was shown two months before *October* and was the more popular version. The events were witnessed through the eyes of a central character (an uneducated peasant boy), someone with whom audiences could identify. Not as dazzling technically as *October*, it has some marvellous montage sequences and much emotional appeal. RB [VIDEO] DVD

A Chistyakov *Worker* • Vera Baranovskaya *His wife* • Ivan Chuvelov *Ivan, a peasant* • V Chuvelov *Friend from the village* • A Gromov *Revolutionary* ■ *Dir* Vsevolod I Pudovkin • *Scr* Nathan Zarkhi, from the poem *The Bronze Horseman* by Vsevolod I Pudovkin, from the novel *St Petersburg* by Andrey Biely

The End of Summer ★★★★★ U

Drama 1961 · Jpn · Colour · 98mins

Yasujiro Ozu's penultimate film shows a deep concern for the everyday life of his middle-class characters. An elderly widower, much to the dismay of his three daughters, decides to resume a relationship with his former mistress. Although the film is presented from the viewpoint of a Japanese family, it addresses universal themes governing relationships. Ozu uses delicate colour and shoots long scenes with his camera at a constant height to reveal both the inner truth and outer manifestation of life, which he depicts with rigorous perception. BB. In Japanese with English subtitles. [video] DVD

Ganjiro Nakamura *Manbei Kohayagawa* • Setsuko Hara *Akiko Kohayagawa* • Yoko Tsukasa *Noriko Kohayagawa* • Michiyo Aratama *Fumiko Kohayagawa* • Yumi Shirakawa *Takako* ■ *Dir* Yasujiro Ozu • *Scr* Kogo Noda, Yasujiro Ozu • *Cinematographer* Asakazu Nakai

The End of the Affair ★★★★ PG

Wartime romantic drama
1954 · UK · BW · 101mins

Graham Greene's mystical, semi-autobiographical novel of doomed romance is convincingly brought to life by director Edward Dmytryk and contains a trio of powerful star performances from Deborah Kerr, John Mills and the outstanding Peter Cushing. Only miscast lead Van Johnson fails to achieve the requisite Catholic angst, which is certainly suggested but not really explored by Stephen Murray as the all-important priest. TS [video]

Deborah Kerr *Sarah Miles* • Van Johnson *Maurice Bendrix* • John Mills *Albert Parkis* • Peter Cushing *Henry Miles* • Michael Goodliffe *Smythe* • Stephen Murray *Father Crompton* ■ *Dir* Edward Dmytryk • *Scr* Lenore Coffee, from the novel by Graham Greene

The End of the Affair ★★★★ 18

Wartime romantic drama
1999 · US/UK · Colour · 97mins

Graham Greene's literary style was always consciously cinematic, but he has been singularly ill-served by those translating his novels to the screen. However, Neil Jordan has made a laudable attempt at conveying the characters' inner lives in this second filming of Greene's most autobiographical fiction. The story of doomed adultery between writer Ralph Fiennes and married Julianne Moore has a delicious sense of stolen joy. With Ian Hart outstanding as the detective hired by the jealous Fiennes, and Stephen Rea no less impressive as Moore's stuffy husband, this is an admirable study of adult emotion. DP. Contains sex scenes. [video] DVD

Ralph Fiennes *Maurice Bendrix* • Julianne Moore *Sarah Miles* • Stephen Rea *Henry Miles* • Ian Hart *Mr Parkis* • Jason Isaacs *Father Smythe* • James Bolam *Mr Savage* ■ *Dir* Neil Jordan • *Scr* Neil Jordan, from the novel by Graham Greene

End of the Century: the Story of the Ramones ★★★ 15

Music documentary
2003 · US · Colour · 107mins

Although hailed as the godfathers of punk, the Ramones never quite achieved the commercial success of the many British bands that followed in their wake. Consequently, Joey, Dee Dee, Johnny and Tommy were more familiar with the seedy underside of the rock dream, as they succumbed to the excesses of touring and growing creative differences. Michael Gramaglia and Jim Field's documentary uses archive material and exclusive interviews to explore the band's personal demons and assess their musical legacy. Almost a decade in the making, this is a comprehensive look at the band, albeit a touch short on previously unseen material. DP DVD

Dir Michael Gramaglia, Jim Fields

The End of the Day ★★★★

Drama 1939 · Fr · BW · 93mins

The least penetrating of the poetic realist allegories on the ruinous decadence of prewar France, this is still a superbly realised and desperately sad film. Director Julien Duvivier creates a tangible atmosphere of melancholic pride in which his exceptional cast essay the various retired actors who have lost their very identities after years of playing roles on and off the stage. Each performance is a gem, from failed classicist Victor Francen's attempts to insinuate himself into Madeleine Ozeray's affections, to the fury of ladies' man Louis Jouvet. But, as ever, it's Michel Simon, as a lifelong understudy, who steals the show. DP. In French with English subtitles.

Arquillieres [Alexandre C Arquillière] *Monsieur Lucien* • Michel Simon *Cabrissade* • Victor Francen *Gilles Marny* • Louis Jouvet *Raphaël Saint-Clair* • Madeleine Ozeray *Jeannette* • Gabrielle Dorziat *Madame Chabert* • Sylvie *Madame Tusini* ■ *Dir* Julien Duvivier • *Scr* Charles Spaak, Julien Duvivier

End of the Game ★★★

Mystery drama
1976 · W Ger/It · Colour · 106mins

It's role reversal time, with actor Maximilian Schell taking the director's chair, and director Martin Ritt making a rare foray in front of the cameras. Ritt neatly plays a dying police commissioner who makes one last attempt to catch the master criminal he's been hunting for the last 30 years. Jon Voight, Robert Shaw and Donald Sutherland are the better-known acting names in a complicated but rewarding Euro-thriller. DA

Jon Voight *Walter Tschantz* • Jacqueline Bisset *Anna Crawley* • Martin Ritt *Hans Barlach* • Robert Shaw *Richard Gastman* • Helmut Qualtinger *Von Schwendi* • Gabriele Ferzetti *Dr Lutz* • Rita Calderoni *Nadine* • Friedrich Dürrenmatt *Friedrich* • Donald Sutherland *Corpse* ■ *Dir* Maximilian Schell • *Scr* Friedrich Dürrenmatt, Bo Goldmann, Maximilian Schell, from the novel *The Judge and His Hangman* by Friedrich Dürrenmatt

The End of the Golden Weather ★★★ PG

Drama 1992 · NZ · Colour · 98mins

This cult oddity may be too eccentric for some. Director Ian Mune and playwright Bruce Mason adapted Mason's one-man show about the imaginary world of a 12-year-old boy (Stephen Fulford). The gaggle of grotesques on parade lacks a single redeeming feature; meanwhile, the age gap between the adolescent boy and his father widens to a predictable chasm. Unlike the curate's egg, this family drama really is good in parts. TH. Contains some swearing. [video]

Stephen Fulford *Geoff* • Stephen Papps *Firpo* • Paul Gittins *Dad* • Gabrielle Hammond *Mum* • David Taylor *Ted* • Alexandra Marshall *Molly* ■ *Dir* Ian Mune • *Scr* Ian Mune, Bruce Mason, from the play by Bruce Mason

End of the Line ★★★ PG

Drama 1987 · US · Colour · 103mins

It's man versus the system time again in a warm and touching drama about tradition and doing the right thing. Shocked when they hear the news that their freight depot is about to be closed down, railway workers Wilford Brimley and Levon Helm steal a locomotive and head to corporate headquarters in Chicago to make their feelings known to the chairman, Henderson Forsyth. Beautifully played by the down-home lead duo, they don't come more graceful than this. AJ [video]

Wilford Brimley *Will Haney* • Levon Helm *Leo Pickett* • Mary Steenburgen *Rose Pickett* • Barbara Barrie *Jean Haney* • Henderson Forsythe *Thomas Clinton* • Bob Balaban *Warren Gerber* • Kevin Bacon *Everett* • Holly Hunter *Charlotte* ■ *Dir* Jay Russell • *Scr* Jay Russell, John Wohlbruck

The End of the River ★★ U

Drama 1947 · UK · BW · 79mins

A curio, produced by Michael Powell and Emeric Pressburger and directed by Derek Twist, who had edited Powell's 1937 semi-documentary about Shetland islanders, *The Edge of the World*. The all-purpose exotic Sabu here plays Manoel, forced to leave his jungle home for the corrupt and dirty city and finding himself on trial for murder. Despite a good cast and the Brazilian locations, the results are both confusing and disappointing. AT [video]

Sabu *Manoel* • Bibi Ferreira *Teresa* • Esmond Knight *Dantos* • Robert Douglas *Mr Jones* • Antoinette Cellier *Conceicao* • Torin Thatcher *Lisboa* • Orlando Martins *Harrigan* • Raymond Lovell *Colonel Porpino* • James Hayter *Chico* ■ *Dir* Derek Twist • *Scr* Wolfgang Wilhelm, from the novel *Death of a Common Man* by Desmond Holdridge

End of the Road ★

Comedy drama 1970 · US · Colour · 110mins

One day, a visiting alien may alight upon a can of film containing this movie. After ten minutes, he'll switch it off and say to his alien comrade, "Fancy a beer, mate?" For few movies are as boringly awful as this one. It's a counterculture affair with psychedelic trips, mental illness and a graphic message about abortion. AT

Stacy Keach *Jake Horner* • Harris Yulin *Joe Morgan* • Dorothy Tristan *Rennie Morgan* • James Earl Jones *Doctor D* • Grayson Hall *Peggie Rankin* • Ray Brock *Sniper Man/Mrs Dockey* • James Coco *School Man* • Oliver Clark *Dog Man* ■ *Dir* Aram Avakian • *Scr* Dennis McGuire, Terry Southern, Aram Avakian, from the novel *The End of the Road* by John Barth

End of the World ★

Science fiction 1977 · US · Colour · 86mins

Space invaders use a Californian convent as a base of operations in their plot to blow up the Earth because mankind is polluting the universe. Christopher Lee lends a modicum of dignity to the incredibly tacky proceedings as a Catholic priest and his extraterrestrial double who is controlling the murderous alien nuns. Tedious junk with a has-been cast. AJ

Christopher Lee *Father Pergado/Zindar* • Sue Lyon *Sylvia Boran* • Kirk Scott *Professor Andrew Boran* • Dean Jagger *Ray Collins* • Lew Ayres *Beckerman* • Macdonald Carey *John Davis* • Liz Ross *Sister Patrizia* ■ *Dir* John Hayes • *Scr* Frank Ray Perilli

The End of the World (in Our Usual Bed in a Night Full of Rain) ★★

Drama 1978 · It/US · Colour · 104mins

The first in a four-picture deal with Warners, this turned out to be the only film controversial Italian director Lina Wertmuller made in the States. Despite working once more with her favourite star, Giancarlo Giannini, Wertmuller lets herself be weighed down by polemic in this talkative confrontation between old-world machismo and self-assertive feminism. The observations are worth making, but the flashback structure does little to make things more accessible. DP. Contains swearing.

Giancarlo Giannini *Paolo* • Candice Bergen *Lizzy* • Anne Byrne *Friend* • Flora Carabella *Friend* • Mario Scarpetta *Friend* ■ *Dir/Scr* Lina Wertmuller

The End of Violence ★★★ 15

Thriller 1997 · US/Ger/Fr · Colour · 116mins

As a mysterious figure (Gabriel Byrne) uses surveillance cameras to keep watch over the city, a Hollywood producer (Bill Pullman), who's become rich thanks to the public's thirst for blood, is kidnapped by inept gangsters. Escaping, he goes undercover and finds kindness on the streets; his wife (Andie MacDowell), meanwhile, tries to find him. The result is an uneasy mix of Fritz Lang determinism and Frank Capra optimism, but, in the hands of director Wim Wenders, it makes for a very watchable and oddly poignant film. TH. Contains swearing. [video]

Bill Pullman *Mike* • Andie MacDowell *Paige* • Gabriel Byrne *Ray* • Loren Dean *Doc* • Traci Lind *Cat* • Rosalind Chao *Claire* • K Todd Freeman *Six* • Chris Douridas *Technician* ■ *Dir* Wim Wenders • *Scr* Nicholas Klein, from a story by Wim Wenders, Nicholas Klein

Endangered Species ★★★ 15

Drama based on a true story
1982 · US · Colour · 92mins

A burnt-out New York cop moves west to investigate a series of cattle mutilations in director Alan Rudolph's offbeat thriller, based on a true-life incident. Is it the work of aliens performing surgical experiments as UFO fanatics speculate? Or does the answer lie with a covert germ warfare research programme? Local sheriff JoBeth Williams teams up with hard-nosed Robert Urich to expose the conspiracy in a suspense mystery with an edgy difference. AJ [video]

Robert Urich *Ruben Castle* • JoBeth Williams *Harriet Purdue* • Paul Dooley *Joe Hiatt* • Hoyt Axton *Ben Morgan* • Peter Coyote *Steele* • Marin Kanter *MacKenzie Castle* • Gailard Sartain *Mayor* • Dan Hedaya *Peck* • Harry Carey Jr *Dr Emmer* ■ *Dir* Alan Rudolph • *Scr* Alan Rudolph, John Binder, from a story by Judson Klinger, Richard Woods

Endless Love ★★ 15

Romantic drama
1981 · US · Colour · 110mins

Vaguely interesting for causing controversy at the time, this tacky tale of illicit teenage romance hasn't aged particularly well. Martin Hewitt and Brooke Shields are the mismatched youngsters who fall in love, much to the disapproval of the latter's father (Don Murray). Director Franco Zeffirelli brings a modicum of class and style to the affair, but not enough to overcome the cloying sentimentality on show. Watch for Tom Cruise, making his feature debut. JF [video]

Brooke Shields *Jade Butterfield* • Martin Hewitt *David Axelrod* • Shirley Knight *Anne Butterfield* • Don Murray *Hugh Butterfield* • Richard Kiley *Arthur Axelrod* • Beatrice Straight *Rose Axelrod* • James Spader *Keith* • Tom Cruise *Billy* ■ *Dir* Franco Zeffirelli • *Scr* Judith Rascoe, from the novel by Scott Spencer

Endless Night ★★★ 15

Psychological thriller
1971 · UK · Colour · 95mins

A torrid sex scene shatters the carefully established suspense in this dark thriller – hardly the kind of thing you'd expect in an Agatha Christie mystery. But then, this is not a typical offering from the queen of crime. Comedy specialist Sidney Gilliat keeps you guessing here as American heiress Hayley Mills becomes convinced that not even husband Hywel Bennett and best friend Britt Ekland can protect her. DP [video]

Hayley Mills *Ellie* • Hywel Bennett *Michael* • Britt Ekland *Greta* • George Sanders *Lippincott* • Per Oscarsson *Santonix* • Peter Bowles *Reuben* • Lois Maxwell *Cora* ■ *Dir* Sidney Gilliat • *Scr* Sidney Gilliat, from the novel by Agatha Christie

E

The Endless Summer ★★★

Documentary 1964 · US · Colour · 91mins

Two surfers, Mike Hynson and Robert August, travel the world in search of the "perfect wave" in this classic surfing documentary put together by film-maker Bruce Brown. Capturing the subculture at the precise time it was having the most profound influence on popular music and Californian lifestyles, the duo visit the virgin beaches of Africa, Australia, New Zealand, Tahiti and Hawaii for time-elapsed sunsets and fabulous shots of them riding wild surf. Groovy music by the Sandals, a five-piece surfing outfit, accompany the beautiful images and Brown's hip surfer-speak is a history lesson in itself. AJ DVD

Bruce Brown *Narrator* ■ *Dir/Scr* Bruce Brown • *Cinematographer* Bruce Brown

The Endless Summer II ★★ U

Documentary 1994 · US · Colour · 105mins

Twenty-eight years on, the search for the "perfect wave" continues with tanned and toned beach boys Pat O'Connell and Robert "Wingnut" Weaver being followed around the world by all-round film-maker Bruce Brown. This time it's Alaska, Bali, Fiji, France and Java getting the photographic picture postcard treatment. Fans of the original will be equally impressed by this stunningly-shot document, despite Brown's narration being slightly more pretentious and irritating. AJ DVD

Dir Bruce Brown • *Scr* Bruce Brown, Dana Brown

Endurance ★★★ U

Sports documentary drama
1998 · US/UK/Ger · Colour · 94mins

Bud Greenspan may have supervised the Atlanta Olympic sequences, but this portrait of the veteran Ethiopian distance runner, Haile Gebrselassie, is very much the work of ethnographer Leslie Woodhead. The athlete's young nephew, Yonas Zergaw, plays him in a series of dramatic reconstructions showing how he ran 12 miles every day to the school nearest his home village of Asela and then relocated to Addis Ababa in the hope of emulating his 10,000-metre hero, Miruts Yifter ("The Shifter"). With Haile's sister, Shawanness, playing their mother, and his wife Alem Tellahun as herself, this is a stirring study of raw ambition and awesome dedication. DP. An English/Amharic language film.

Haile Gebrselassie • Bekele Gebrselassie • Alem Tellahun • Yonas Zergaw *Young Haile Gebrselassie* • Shawanness Gebrselassie *Haile's mother* • Tedesse Haile *Haile's father* ■ *Dir* Leslie Woodhead, Bud Greenspan • *Scr* Leslie Woodhead

The Endurance: Shackelton's Legendary Antarctic Expedition ★★★

Documentary
2000 · US/UK · Colour and BW · 97mins

The intrepid durability of Ernest Shackleton's 1914 Antarctic expedition throughout its ill-fated bid to cross the polar continent on foot was captured first hand by Australian cameraman Frank Hurley. Much of his tinted footage appears in this blindly admiring account. But George Butler's documentary also draws heavily on Caroline Alexander's meticulous book to piece together an exact chronology. Narrator Liam Neeson links the various archival clips, interviews, graphic sequences and dramatic reconstructions to paint a portrait of an inspired leader, while also considering the validity of the exploration business. However, its main fascination is Hurley's extraordinary imagery. DP

Liam Neeson *Narrator* ■ *Dir* George Butler • *Scr* Caroline Alexander, Joseph Dorman, from a non-fiction book by Caroline Alexander

Enduring Love ★★ 15

Psychological thriller
2004 · UK/US · Colour · 96mins

A bizarre accident links two strangers in director Roger Michell's illogical and annoying metaphysical thriller. After attempting to halt a runaway hot-air balloon, which results in a man falling to his death, Daniel Craig is mercilessly stalked by fellow would-be rescuer Rhys Ifans, who believes himself in love with Craig. Wilfully obscure, this corrosive and bitter tale is bolstered by expert performances from Craig and Ifans, but it just isn't enough. AJ. Contains swearing and violence. DVD

Daniel Craig *Joe Rose* • Rhys Ifans *Jed* • Samantha Morton *Claire* • Bill Nighy *Robin* • Susan Lynch *Rachel* • Helen McCrory *Mrs Logan* • Andrew Lincoln *TV producer* • Corin Redgrave *Professor* ■ *Dir* Roger Michell • *Scr* Joe Penhall, from the novel by Ian McEwan

Enemies, a Love Story ★★★★ 15

Comedy drama 1989 · US · Colour · 114mins

A wonderfully lyrical and multi-layered ensemble piece, about the painful, tangled relationships of a group of Jewish immigrants in postwar New York. The acting is simply sublime, particularly from Lena Olin as a disturbed but passionate Holocaust survivor and Ron Silver as her emotionally repressed, egocentric lover. Director Paul Mazursky has fashioned a deeply moving, thought-provoking movie which, despite suffering marginally from insufficient light and shade, challenges the mind while stirring the heart. SH. Contains swearing, sex scenes, nudity.

Anjelica Huston *Tamara* • Ron Silver *Herman Broder* • Lena Olin *Masha* • Margaret Sophie Stein *Yadwiga* • Judith Malina *Masha's mother* • Alan King *Rabbi Lembeck* • Rita Karin *Mrs Schreier* ■ *Dir* Paul Mazursky • *Scr* Roger L Simon, Paul Mazursky, from the novel by Isaac Bashevis Singer

The Enemy ★★

Action thriller
2000 · US/Lux · Colour · 101mins

There's something uncomfortably old-fashioned about this thriller. It lacks the zip of today's modern action thrillers, and the casting doesn't help either, with neither Luke Perry nor Olivia D'Abo being memorable as the scientist and secret agent, out to rescue Perry's father (Horst Bucholtz) from terrorists who want him to hand over a lethal chemical weapon. JF

Luke Perry *Mike Ashton* • Olivia D'Abo *Penny Johnson* • Roger Moore *Robert Ogilvy* • Tom Conti *John Creger* • Horst Buchholz *George Ashton* ■ *Dir* Tom Kinninmont • *Scr* John Penney, from the novel *The Enemy* by Desmond Bagley

Enemy at the Gates ★★ 15

Second World War drama
2001 · US/Ger/UK/Ire · Colour · 125mins

Featuring three miscast stars, director Jean-Jacques Annaud's uninspiring drama focuses on the battle for Stalingrad. According to Annaud's version of events, the lengthy conflict (summer 1942 to February 1943) boiled down to a sniper duel between legendary Russian shepherd Jude Law and German nobleman Ed Harris. Soviet propaganda genius Joseph Fiennes elevates Law to folk hero status, but they both fall in love with Rachel Weisz. This is saddled with a spectacularly awful script. AJ. Contains violence. DVD

Jude Law *Vassily Zaitsev* • Joseph Fiennes *Danilov* • Rachel Weisz *Tania* • Bob Hoskins *Nikita Khrushchev* • Ed Harris *Major König* • Ron Perlman *Koulikov* • Eva Mattes *Mother Filipov* ■ *Dir* Jean-Jacques Annaud • *Scr* Alain Godard, Jean-Jacques Annaud, from the novel by William Craig, and from the novel *Vendetta* by Derek Lambert

The Enemy Below ★★★★ PG

Second World War drama
1957 · US · Colour · 93mins

This is one of the best submarine movies, a stunning drama about a Second World War German U-boat and the US destroyer that's stalking it, whose captains only meet in the final reel. As the respective skippers, Curt Jurgens and Robert Mitchum turn in fine performances. The special effects won an Oscar, but it is the direction by Dick Powell that is really remarkable – his taut handling of the action makes this one of his finest movie achievements. The film was actually based on a real story, written into novel form by wartime submarine captain DA Rayner. TS DVD

Robert Mitchum *Captain Murrell* • Curt Jurgens *Von Stolberg* • Al Hedison [David Hedison] *Lieutenant Ware* • Theodore Bikel *Schwaffer* • Russell Collins *Doctor* • Kurt Kreuger *Von Holem* • Frank Albertson *Chief Petty Officer Crain* ■ *Dir* Dick Powell • *Scr* Wendell Mayes, from the novel by DA Rayner • *Special Effects (Audible)* Walter Rossi

Enemy Mine ★★★★ 15

Science-fiction fantasy
1985 · US · Colour · 89mins

Earthman Dennis Quaid and lizard-like alien Louis Gossett Jr (virtually unrecognisable under very impressive scaly make-up) crash-land on an unknown planet and learn that co-operation equals survival. Director Wolfgang Petersen makes this racial tolerance plea in outer space disguise a satisfying blend of action spills and emotional thrills. It touches both the brain and heart, remaining true to its pulp science-fiction roots while never being anything less than engrossing entertainment. AJ. Contains some violence and swearing. DVD

Dennis Quaid *Willis Davidge* • Louis Gossett Jr *Jeriba Shigan* • Brion James *Stubbs* • Richard Marcus *Arnold* • Carolyn McCormick *Morse* • Bumper Robinson *Zammis* • Jim Mapp *Old Drac* • Lance Kerwin *Wooster* ■ *Dir* Wolfgang Petersen • *Scr* Edward Khmara, from a story by Barry Longyear

An Enemy of the People ★★★ U

Period drama 1977 · US · Colour · 106mins

Action hero Steve McQueen peers through a thicket of beard to take on a much-coveted role as the doctor whose warning that the local spa is polluted leads to antagonism from the small town's inhabitants. George Schaefer's direction is as worthy as McQueen's performance, but Charles Durning's counterbalance to the doctor's righteous indignation shows us what real acting is, and how dull McQueen seems in comparison. TH

Steve McQueen *Dr Thomas Stockmann* • Charles Durning *Peter Stockmann* • Bibi Andersson *Catherine Stockmann* • Eric Christmas *Morten Kiil* • Michael Cristofer *Hovstad* • Richard A Dysart [Richard Dysart] *Aslaksen* • Michael Higgins *Billing* ■ *Dir* George Schaefer • *Scr* Alexander Jacobs, from the play by Henrik Ibsen, adapted by Arthur Miller

An Enemy of the People ★★ U

Drama 1989 · Ind · Colour · 95mins

In many ways this adaptation of Ibsen's play (also released as *Ganashatru*) was a courageous enterprise, as director Satyajit Ray was returning to work after a four-year hiatus following a heart attack and was forbidden to shoot on location by his doctors. However, while we can forgive the studio-bound feel, it's hard to ignore the fact that this is a dull film made almost interminable by the impossibly earnest performance of Soumitra Chatterjee as the doctor trying to close a temple following the contamination of its water supply. DP. In Bengali with English subtitles.

Soumitra Chatterjee *Dr Ashok Gupta* • Ruma Guha-Thakurta *Maya Gupta* • Dhritiman Chatterjee *Nichit Gupta* • Mamata Shankar *Ranu Gupta* • Dipankar Dey *Haridas Bagchi* ■ *Dir* Satyajit Ray • *Scr* Satyajit Ray, from the play by Henrik Ibsen

Enemy of the State ★★★★ 15

Thriller 1998 · US · Colour · 131mins

Expert direction by Tony Scott and a winning central performance by Will Smith give this cracking hi-tech thriller extra edge and appeal. When an incriminating tape revealing the murder of congressman Jason Robards accidentally ends up in Smith's possession, he finds himself relentlessly pursued by corrupt Jon Voight and his posse of electronic trackers, who use spy satellites, transmitters and all manner of undercover gizmos to trace him. An exciting action adventure that's both intriguing and thought-provoking. AJ. Contains swearing, violence. DVD

Will Smith *Robert Clayton Dean* • Gene Hackman *Brill* • Jon Voight *Reynolds* • Lisa Bonet *Rachel Banks* • Regina King *Carla Dean* • Ian Hart *Bingham* • Jason Lee *Zavitz* • Gabriel Byrne *"Brill"* • Jason Robards *Hammersly* • Tom Sizemore *Pintero* ■ *Dir* Tony Scott • *Scr* David Marconi

Enemy Territory ★★ 18

Action 1987 · US · Colour · 85mins

Gary Frank plays an insurance agent whose job takes him into a dangerous part of the city. He and telephone man Ray Parker Jr are quickly targeted by a vicious street gang, and spend the rest of the movie hiding and trying to get out of the building. The better parts of the film are those that don't take themselves completely seriously, including Jan-Michael Vincent as a paranoid ex-soldier who has converted his apartment into a bunker. KB

Gary Frank *Barry* • Ray Parker Jr *Jackson* • Jan-Michael Vincent *Parker* • Frances Foster *Elva Briggs* • Tony Todd *The count* • Stacey Dash *Toni Briggs* • Deon Richmond *Chet* • Tiger Haynes *Barton* ■ *Dir* Peter Manoogian • *Scr* Stuart M Kaminsky, Bobby Liddell, from a story by Stuart M Kaminsky

The Enemy Within ★★★ 12

Thriller 1994 · US · Colour · 86mins

Would anyone dare to challenge the authority of Uncle Sam and overthrow an elected US government? That's the intriguing premise behind this efficient remake of the 1964 film *Seven Days in May*. By TV movie standards, a strong cast has been assembled here, and the performances are professional, but it lacks the raw power of the original. RT. Contains swearing and violence. DVD

Forest Whitaker *Colonel Mac Casey* • Sam Waterston *President William Foster* • Dana Delany *Chief of Staff Betsy Corcoran* • Jason Robards *General Lloyd* • Josef Sommer *Secretary of Defense Potter* • George Dzundza *Jake* ■ *Dir* Jonathan Darby • *Scr* Ron Bass [Ronald Bass], Darryl Ponicsan, from the film *Seven Days in May* by Rod Serling, from the novel *Seven Days in May* by Fletcher Knebel, Charles Waldo Bailey

L'Enfance Nue ★★★

Drama 1968 · Fr · Colour · 83mins

Co-produced by François Truffaut this is a remarkable first feature from director Maurice Pialat, especially since the participants are not professional actors. This sensitive yet unsentimental tale focuses on a ten-year-old boy who is abandoned by his mother. Handed over to the social services, he is treated with dispassion and becomes a teenage nightmare when placed with foster parents. This extremely well-observed docudrama takes all perspectives into account, while the relationship the child develops with his aged grandmother, Marie Marc, is particularly touching. LH. In French with English subtitles.

Michel Terrazon *François* • Linda Gutemberg *Simone* • Raoul Billerey *Roby* • Pierette Deplanque *Josette* • Marie-Louise Thierry *Mme Minguet* • Rene Thierry *M Minguet* • Henri Puff *Raoul* • Marie Marc *Meme* • Maurice Coussoneau *Letillon* ■ *Dir/Scr* Maurice Pialat

L'Enfant Sauvage ★★★★ U

Period drama based on a true story
1970 · Fr · BW · 82mins

This is a historical drama that eschews costume finery in favour of philosophical debate. The film tackles such complex notions as natural law, the supremacy of society, the right to resist injustice and the conflict between scientific research and emotional subjectivity, but it is also a very human tale. Set in 1798, it relates the true story of Victor (Jean-Pierre Cargol), the forest foundling who is introduced to the basics of civilisation by Dr Jean Itard (François Truffaut). Making pleasing use of antiquated cinematic devices and actual journal extracts, this has a documentary feel that makes it more authentic and fascinating. DP. In French with English subtitles. DVD

Jean-Pierre Cargol *Victor, the boy* • Paul Villé *Rémy* • François Truffaut *Dr Jean Itard* • Françoise Seigner *Madame Guérin* • Claude Miller *Monsieur Lemeri* • Annie Miller *Madame Lemeri* ■ *Dir* François Truffaut • *Scr* François Truffaut, Jean Gruault, from the non-fiction book *Mémoire et Rapport sur Victor de L'Aveyron* by Jean-Marc Gaspard Itard

Les Enfants de Lumière ★★★★★

Compilation
1995 · Fr · BW and Colour · 102mins

Several fictional features and personal memoirs were commissioned to commemorate the centenary of cinema, but few celebrate film's unique ability to entertain, move, provoke or reminisce with such charm and intelligence as this superb French compilation. Divided thematically, this priceless collection of greatest clips features a *Who's Who* of French film, with Gérard Philipe and Jean Marais rubbing shoulders with the great Jean Gabin and Jean-Louis Barrault, and Arletty, Michèle Morgan and Simone Signoret competing for the soft-focus spotlight. The brainchild of top producer Jacques Perrin, it also has the benefit of a spine-tingling score from Michel Legrand. DP. In English and French with subtitles.

Anthony Valentine *Narrator* ■ *Dir* André Asseo, Pierre Billard, Alain Corneau, Claude Miller, Claude Sautet

Les Enfants du Paradis ★★★★★ PG

Classic drama 1945 · Fr · BW · 181mins

The most courageous and elegant act of defiance in cinema history, this beautiful tale of Parisian popular theatre in the early 19th century was shot under the noses of the Gestapo towards the end of the Second World War. Determined to premiere the picture in a liberated France, director Marcel Carné tolerated all manner of delays, including the absence of cast members sent on missions for the Resistance. On the surface, the film is a tale of unrequited love, but it is in fact a tribute to the indomitable spirit of Free France, as personified by Garance (Arletty), the legendary actress who resists all attempts to possess her. DP. In French with English subtitles. VIDEO DVD

Arletty *Garance* • Jean-Louis Barrault *Baptiste Debureau* • Pierre Brasseur *Frédérick Lemaître* • Marcel Herrand *Lacenaire* • Pierre Renoir *Jéricho, the old clothes man* • Maria Casarès *Natalie* • Etienne Decroux *Anselme Debureau* ■ *Dir* Marcel Carné • *Scr* Jacques Prévert, Marcel Carné, from an idea by Jacques Prévert, Marcel Carné • *Art Director* Alexandre Trauner, Léon Barsacq, Raymond Gabutti

Les Enfants du Siècle ★★★ 15

Biographical period drama
1999 · Fr/UK · Colour · 108mins

Diane Kurys examines the pre-Chopin love life of the 19th-century French writer George Sand. Juliette Binoche gives a steady performance as Sand (the pen name of Baroness Dudevant), a fiercely independent mother of two, who leaves her husband to pursue a career in literature. Much of the focus, however, falls on her passionate relationship with poet Alfred de Musset (Benoît Magimel), who is driven by self-doubt and family disapproval into a life of debauchery and regret, while Sand finds solace with Italian physician Stefano Dionisi. This was cut by almost half an hour for its belated UK release. DP. In French with English subtitles.

Juliette Binoche *George Sand* • Benoît Magimel *Alfred de Musset* • Stefano Dionisi *Pietro Pagello* • Robin Renucci *François Buloz* • Karin Viard *Marie Dorval* • Isabelle Carré *Aimée d'Alton* • Patrick Chesnais *Gustave Planche* ■ *Dir* Diane Kurys • *Scr* Diane Kurys, Murray Head, François-Olivier Rousseau

Les Enfants Terribles ★★★★ 12

Drama 1949 · Fr · BW · 100mins

Budgetary restraint goes a long way to explaining the effectiveness of this adaptation of Jean Cocteau's 1929 novel. By shooting much of the action in his own apartment and on the stage of the Théâtre Pigalle, director Jean-Pierre Melville was able to reproduce the simmering claustrophobia that makes the obsessive relationship between brother and sister Edouard Dermit and Nicole Stéphane so intense. Although Cocteau narrates and directed the seaside scene, the film's erotic tension and visual poetry are down to Melville's finesse, which ensures that the tale becomes troubling tragicomedy instead of melodramatic high camp. DP. In French with English subtitles. VIDEO DVD

Nicole Stéphane *Elisabeth* • Edouard Dermithe *Paul* • Jacques Bernard *Gerad* • Renée Cosima *Dargelos/Agathe* • Roger Gaillard *Gerard's Uncle* • Melvyn Martin *Michael* • Jean Cocteau *Narrator* ■ *Dir* Jean-Pierre Melville • *Scr* Jean Cocteau, Jean-Pierre Melville, from the novel by Jean Cocteau

L'Enfer ★★★ 15

Thriller 1994 · Fr · Colour · 98mins

L'Enfer, or *Hell*, began in 1964 as a movie starring Romy Schneider and Serge Reggiani and directed by Henri-Georges Clouzot. Shortly after shooting started, Reggiani quit through illness; then Clouzot himself was felled by a heart attack. After Clouzot's death in 1977 the project pass to Claude Chabrol. It's a story about pathological jealousy, acted to the hilt by the sensuous Emmanuelle Béart, whose character is married to seething hotel owner François Cluzet. Things get seriously out of control, tipping the picture quickly into the realm of black comedy. AT. A French language film. VIDEO DVD

Emmanuelle Béart *Nelly* • François Cluzet *Paul* • Nathalie Cardone *Marylin* • André Wilms *Doctor Arnoux* • Marc Lavoine *Martineau* • Christiane Minazzoli *Madame Vernon* • Dora Doll *Madame Chabert* • Mario David *Duhamel* ■ *Dir* Claude Chabrol • *Scr* Henri-Georges Clouzot, José-André Lacour

The Enforcer ★★★★ PG

Crime drama 1951 · US · BW · 84mins

This terrific Warner Bros crime drama features Humphrey Bogart on the right side of the law for once, closing in on a gang of professional killers with the help of key witnesses, including Zero Mostel in one of his last movie roles before he was blacklisted during the communist witch-hunt. Bretaigne Windust takes the credit as director, though most of the film was actually directed by the uncredited Raoul Walsh. Unusually, there's no romance to slow down the action as it moves to a riveting finale. TS VIDEO

Humphrey Bogart *Martin Ferguson* • Zero Mostel *"Big Babe" Lazich* • Ted De Corsia *Joseph Rico* • Everett Sloane *Albert Mendoza* • Roy Roberts *Captain Frank Nelson* • Lawrence Tolan *"Duke" Tiano* • King Donovan *Sergeant Whitlow* • Robert Steele [Bob Steele] *Herman* ■ *Dir* Bretaigne Windust • *Scr* Martin Rackin

The Enforcer ★★ 18

Crime thriller 1976 · US · Colour · 92mins

The identikit collection of corrupt cops and crazed killers confronting Clint Eastwood's Harry Callahan in this third film in the *Dirty Harry* series is hardly a match for the no-nonsense lawman's unique talents. Only Harry's new partner (played with spirit by Tyne Daly) has any depth, but this intriguing relationship is wasted in a welter of sexist one-liners. Fans would have to wait seven years for Harry's fourth outing, *Sudden Impact*. DP. Contains violence, swearing, nudity. VIDEO DVD

Clint Eastwood *Harry Callahan* • Tyne Daly *Kate Moore* • Bradford Dillman *Captain McKay* • Harry Guardino *Lieutenant Bressler* • DeVeren Bookwalter *Bobby Maxwell* • John Mitchum *DiGeorgio* • John Crawford *Mayor* ■ *Dir* James Fargo • *Scr* Stirling Silliphant, Dean Reisner, from characters created by Harry Julian Fink, RM Fink

The Enforcer ★★ 18

Martial arts action thriller
1995 · HK · Colour · 100mins

An early attempt by Jet Li to move on from the historical martial arts epics which made his name into more western-friendly action roles, this is a proficient but unconvincing thriller. Playing a Beijing cop who goes undercover to infiltrate a Hong Kong crime syndicate, Li's dazzling fight skills are well to the fore. However, the dubbing is atrocious and the screen time given over to the precocious Tse Miu, who plays his adoring son, introduces an unwelcome dose of sentimentality. JF. Cantonese dialogue dubbed into English. VIDEO DVD

Jet Li *Kung Wei* • Anita Mui *Anna* • Tse Mui *Johnny* • Yu Rong Guang *Po Kwong* ■ *Dir* Corey Yuen • *Scr* Sandy Shaw, Wong Jing

England Made Me ★★★★

Drama 1973 · UK · Colour · 100mins

Graham Greene's least-known novel was the inspiration behind this under-rated film which, like *Cabaret* the year before, offers a fascinating glimpse of pre-Second World War Germany. Michael York plays a sponging Englishman whose dealings with Peter Finch's sinister financier almost lead him to become incestuously involved with his own sister (Hildegard Neil). The potential for atmosphere is vividly explored by director Peter Duffell. TH

Peter Finch *Erich Krogh* • Michael York *Anthony Farrant* • Hildegard Neil *Kate Farrant* • Michael Hordern *F Minty* • Joss Ackland *Hiller* • Tessa Wyatt *Liz Davidge* • Michael Sheard *Fromm* • William Baskiville [Bill Baskiville] *Stein* ■ *Dir* Peter Duffell • *Scr* Peter Duffell, Desmond Cory, from the novel by Graham Greene

English, August ★★★

Drama 1994 · Ind · Colour · 118mins

Based on the cult novel by Upamanyu Chatterjee, this was among the first Indian independent productions to score at the box-office and helped usher in a new generation of non-Bollywood, English-language movie-makers. What makes this all the more remarkable was that the film marked director Dev Benegal's feature debut. It's an iconoclastic comedy drama in which a civil servant struggles to find his niche in Madna (reputedly the subcontinent's hottest little town) against a backdrop of drugs, infidelity, pornography and corruption. DP. In Hindi and English with subtitles.

Tanvi Azmi *Malti Srivastava* • Rahul Bose *Agastya Sen* • Shivaji Satham *Govinde Sathe* • Salim Shah *Ravi Srivastava* • Yogendra Tikku *Kumar* ■ *Dir* Dev Benegal • *Scr* Dev Benegal, Upamanyu Chatterjee, from a novel by Upamanyu Chatterjee

The English Patient ★★★★★ 15

Second World War romantic drama
1996 · US · Colour · 155mins

Inevitably recalling *Lawrence of Arabia* with its desert setting and epic sweep, this skilful adaptation of Michael Ondaatje's difficult novel is at heart two love stories, one in the present, the other told in flashback. Ralph Fiennes is the hideously burned "English patient" tended to by Juliette Binoche's nurse in an Italian monastery at the end of the Second World War. His story, torrid and dangerous, is pieced together gradually, while Binoche falls in love with a bomb disposal officer (Naveen Andrews). Fiennes is in fact a Hungarian, a mapmaker charting the Sahara who got caught up in the war and in an affair with the unhappily married Kristin Scott Thomas. It's an ambitious film, and director Anthony Minghella's skill lies equally in his screenplay, which delivers explanation only in fragments but keeps us involved for what is an epic running time. LH. Contains violence, swearing and sex scenes. VIDEO DVD

Ralph Fiennes *Count Laszlo Almasy* • Juliette Binoche *Hana* • Willem Dafoe *Caravaggio* • Kristin Scott Thomas *Katharine Clifton* • Naveen Andrews *Kip* • Colin Firth *Geoffrey Clifton* • Julian Wadham *Madox* • Jürgen Prochnow *Major Müller* • Kevin Whately *Hardy* ■ *Dir* Anthony Minghella • *Scr* Anthony Minghella, from the novel by Michael Ondaatje

English without Tears ★★

Romantic comedy 1944 · UK · BW · 88mins

Five years after screenwriters Terence Rattigan and Anatole de Grunwald and cinematographer Bernard Knowles collaborated on the witty comedy of manners *French without Tears*, they reunited for this less perceptive, but still amusing, satire on the leisured classes at war. While the romance between wealthy ATS girl Penelope Ward and butler Michael Wilding had its social significance, the attack on the League of Nations would have struck the loudest chord with contemporary audiences. DP

Michael Wilding *Tom Gilbey* • Lilli Palmer *Brigid Knudsen* • Penelope Ward *Joan Heseltine* • Claude Dauphin *Jean de Freyeinet* • Roland Culver *Sir Cosmo Brandon* • Peggy Cummins *Bobby Heseltine* • Margaret Rutherford *Lady Christabel Beauclerk* ■ *Dir* Harold French • *Scr* Terence Rattigan, Anatole de Grunwald

The Englishman Who Went up a Hill, but Came down a Mountain ★★★ PG

Romantic comedy
1995 · UK · Colour · 95mins

Hugh Grant does what he does best – mildly bumbling, nice Englishness – in this engaging slice of whimsy, which harks back to the Ealing comedies of old. Grant plays a cartographer who is called upon to rule on whether a Welsh village's beloved landmark is a hill or a mountain. The canny locals are determined it's the latter and proceed to run rings around the hapless Grant. The plot is about as a slight as the slope in question, but the talented playing of the cast makes it a modest treat. JF DVD

Hugh Grant *Reginald Anson* • Tara FitzGerald *Betty of Cardiff* • Colm Meaney *Morgan the Goat* • Ian Hart *Johnny Shellshocked* • Kenneth Griffith *Reverend Jones* • Ian McNeice *George Garrad* • Robert Blythe *Ivor the Grocer* • Robert Pugh *Williams the Petroleum* ■ *Dir* Christopher Monger • *Scr* Christopher Monger, from a story by Ifor David Monger, Ivor Monger

Enigma ★★ 15

Thriller 1982 · UK/Fr · Colour · 122mins

This Cold War thriller is neither one thing nor another, and seems to have suffered some post-production rethinking plot-wise. The classy cast pretends they know what's going on as the KGB try to kill five dissidents in the west, only to find their way barred by unlikely CIA agent Martin Sheen. The title of this Anglo-French co-production is rather apt. TS

Martin Sheen *Alex Holbeck* • Brigitte Fossey *Karen* • Sam Neill *Dimitri Vasilkov* • Derek Jacobi *Kurt Limmer* • Michel Lonsdale *Bodley* • Frank Finlay *Canarsky* • David Baxt *Melton* • Kevin McNally *Bruno* ■ *Dir* Jeannot Szwarc • *Scr* John Briley, from the novel *Enigma Sacrifice* by Michael Barak

Enigma ★★★ 15

Second World War romantic thriller
2001 · UK/US/Neth/Ger · Colour · 116mins

Acting as an antidote to the Hollywood heroism of *U-571*, in which a German code machine is recovered by the US Navy during the Second World War, this concentrates on the quiet, bookish pluck of our own code-breakers at Bletchley Park. Dougray Scott plays the fragile but brilliant Tom Jericho, back at his desk after a nervous breakdown and drawn into a race against time to crack the latest German cipher. He also suspects that Saffron Burrows, with whom he is infatuated, is a spy. This well-acted wartime intrigue is commendable for the intelligence it assumes on the part of the audience, but the effect is spoiled somewhat by a superfluous, *Boys' Own* adventure ending. AC. Contains violence, swearing and a sex scene. DVD

Dougray Scott *Tom Jericho* • Kate Winslet *Hester* • Saffron Burrows *Claire* • Jeremy Northam *Wigram* • Nikolaj Coster Waldau [Nikolaj Coster-Waldau] *"Puck" Pukowski* • Tom Hollander *Logie* • Corin Redgrave *Admiral Trowbridge* ■ *Dir* Michael Apted • *Scr* Tom Stoppard, from the novel by Robert Harris

The Enigma of Kaspar Hauser ★★★★ PG

Period drama based on a true story
1974 · W Ger · Colour · 105mins

The Nuremberg of the 1820s is here seen through the eyes of Kaspar Hauser, the real-life child genius who was dumped in the town square after a lifetime of beatings and sensory deprivation. Werner Herzog's fact-based drama, though ostensibly the tale of one man's response to civilisation, is really a study of landscape, and more a film about awakening than socio-political values. Yet it's easy to sneer at the smug bourgeois attitudes of the townsfolk and be captivated by Bruno S's eager expression as he drinks in sights and sounds like a greedy, excited child. DP. In German with English subtitles.

Bruno S *Kaspar* • Brigitte Mira *Kathe, the servant* • Willy Semmelrogge *Circus director* • Hans Musaus *Unknown man* • Michael Kroecher *Lord Stanhope* • Henry van Lyck *Captain* ■ *Dir/Scr* Werner Herzog

L'Ennui ★★★ 18

Erotic comedy drama
1998 · Fr · Colour · 116mins

Director Cédric Kahn explores the struggle for power that underpins many relationships in this erotic comedy drama. However, with its repeated acts of perfunctory sex and the slow descent into manic envy by an intellectually moribund academic, this adaptation of Alberto Moravia's novel might have made for heavy going, were it not for the outstanding performances of Charles Berling and Sophie Guillemin. As the physically unremarkable, socially inept teenager fuelling her lover's neurosis, the debuting Guillemin is a revelation, while Berling's midlife misery is agonisingly persuasive. DP. In French with English subtitles. DVD

Charles Berling *Martin* • Sophie Guillemin *Cécilia* • Arielle Dombasle *Sophie* • Robert Kramer *Leopold Meyers* • Alice Grey *Cécilia's mother* • Maurice Antoni *Cécilia's father* ■ *Dir* Cédric Kahn • *Scr* Cédric Kahn, Laurence Ferreira Barbosa, Gilles Taurand, from the novel *La Noia* by Alberto Moravia

Enormous Changes at the Last Minute ★★★

Drama 1983 · US · Colour · 98mins

Also known as *Trumps*, this is a collection of three dramas (two filmed in 1982 and one back in 1978) based on the stories of Grace Paley. While the trio don't completely work together, this is nonetheless an interesting group of stories about women living in New York and their relationships with their families and the men in their lives. The impressive cast includes David Strathairn, Ellen Barkin and Kevin Bacon, while writer John Sayles went on to direct *Eight Men Out*. JB

Maria Tucci *Alexandra* • Ellen Barkin *Virginia* • Lynn Milgrim *Faith* • Sudie Bond *Mrs Raftery* • Kevin Bacon *Dennis* • Didi Velez *Blanca* • David Strathairn *Jerry* • Jeffrey DeMunn *Ricardo* ■ *Dir* Mirra Bank, Ellen Hovde, Muffie Meyer • *Scr* John Sayles, Susan Rice, from stories by Grace Paley

Enough ★ 15

Thriller 2002 · US · Colour · 110mins

The issue of domestic violence is exploited for cheap thrills in this tawdry cat-and-mouse thriller. Jennifer Lopez, lip-glossed to perfection, works through a catalogue of female stereotypes, from blushing bride to spousal punching bag to mother who fights back. For all its gut-churning brutality, the film remains a grotesque mockery of reality. SF DVD

Jennifer Lopez *Slim* • Billy Campbell [Bill Campbell] *Mitch* • Juliette Lewis *Ginny* • Dan Futterman *Joe* • Fred Ward *Jupiter* • Jim Toller *Bill Cobbs* • Tessa Allen *Gracie* • Noah Wyle *Robbie* ■ *Dir* Michael Apted • *Scr* Nicholas Kazan

Enron: the Smartest Guys in the Room ★★★ 15

Documentary 2005 · US · Colour · 109mins

A solidly but not over-imaginatively assembled documentary, this tells how Enron, one of the mightiest and most well-regarded corporations on Wall Street was revealed to be a house of trick cards, built on greed, deceit and political opportunity. Based on a bestseller co-written by Bethany McLean, the first reporter to break the scandal of Enron's misdeeds, the film traces how top executives Kenneth Lay and Jeff Skilling manipulated the energy market, embezzled employee pension funds, and engineered the Californian "energy crisis" to push up the price of electricity. Director Alex Gibney painstakingly unpacks the facts through charts and interviews, so one need not possess a business degree to understand what went wrong. LF. Contains swearing.

Peter Coyote *Narrator* ■ *Dir* Alex Gibney • *Scr* Alex Gibney, from the non-fiction book *The Smartest Guys in the Room: the Amazing Rise and Scandalous Fall of Enron* by Bethany McLean, Peter Elkind

Ensign Pulver ★★

Comedy drama 1964 · US · Colour · 104mins

A prime example of how a bad idea can result in a worse movie. *Mister Roberts* had been an overwhelming triumph on stage and screen. So, spurred on by the fact that Jack Lemmon had won an Oscar as Ensign Pulver, Warner Bros decided to push out the boat once more. Robert Walker Jr tries valiantly to recapture the impishness of the wheeler-dealer Pulver, but never emerges from the shadow of his predecessor. DP

Robert Walker Jr *Ensign Pulver* • Burl Ives *Captain* • Walter Matthau *Doc* • Tommy Sands *Bruno* • Millie Perkins *Scotty* • Kay Medford *Head nurse* • Larry Hagman *Billings* • Gerald S O'Loughlin *LaSueur* • Sal Papa *Gabrowski* • James Coco *Skouras* • Jack Nicholson *Dolan* ■ *Dir* Joshua Logan • *Scr* Joshua Logan, Peter S Feibleman, from characters created by Joshua Logan, Thomas Heggen

Enter Arsene Lupin ★★

Crime 1944 · US · BW · 71mins

Hungarian exile and one-time cinematographer Charles Korvin made his acting debut here as writer Maurice Leblanc's notorious gentleman thief. But for once, purloining gems and avoiding the clutches of inspector J Carrol Naish are nowhere near as important as stealing the heart of Ella Raines. Sloppily scripted by Bertram Millhauser and directed with little suspense by Ford Beebe. DP

Charles Korvin *Arsene Lupin* • Ella Raines *Stacie* • J Carrol Naish *Ganimard* • George Dolenz *Dubose* • Gale Sondergaard *Bessie Seagrave* • Miles Mander *Charles Seagrave* • Leyland Hodgson *Constable Ryder* ■ *Dir* Ford Beebe • *Scr* Bertram Millhauser, from characters created by Maurice Leblanc

Enter Laughing ★★★ U

Comedy 1967 · US · Colour · 110mins

...and exit giggling at director Carl Reiner's adaptation of the play based on his early career experiences. Reni Santoni is the young man who defies mother Shelley Winters and decides to become a professional actor. He goes through the usual rituals of acceptance before realising his dream. Very astute and witty stuff, with José Ferrer's turn as a pompous producer worth the price of admission alone. TH

Reni Santoni *David Kolowitz* • José Ferrer *Mr Marlowe* • Shelley Winters *Mrs Kolowitz* • Elaine May *Angela* • Jack Gilford *Mr Foreman* • Janet Margolin *Wanda* • David Opatoshu *Mr Kolowitz* • Michael J Pollard *Marvin* ■ *Dir* Carl Reiner • *Scr* Joseph Stein, Carl Reiner, from the play by Joseph Stein, from the novel by Carl Reiner

Enter Madame! ★★

Musical comedy drama
1933 · US · BW · 81mins

Cary Grant, the wealthy husband of tantrum-throwing opera star Elissa Landi, has to cope with playing second fiddle to both her career and her entourage of peculiar characters. This film version of a 1920 Broadway hit comedy fails to survive the transfer to another medium or the passage of time. The coolly lovely Landi was hardly the ideal choice for this extrovert role, but Grant exudes his usual easy charm. RK

Elissa Landi *Lisa Della Robbia* • Cary Grant *Gerald Fitzgerald* • Lynne Overman *Mr Farnum* • Sharon Lynne *Flora Preston* • Michelette Burani *Bice* • Paul Porcasi *Archimede* • Adrian Rosley *Doctor* • Cecilia Parker *Aline Chalmers* ■ *Dir* Elliott Nugent • *Scr* Charles Brackett, Gladys Lehman, from the play by Gilda Varesi Archibald, Dorothea Donn-Byrne

Enter the Dragon ★★★★ 18

Martial arts adventure
1973 · US · Colour · 99mins

Bruce Lee, the "Fred Astaire of martial arts", is at his balletic, brilliant best in this kung fu classic that, tragically, proved to be his last completed film. When his sister commits suicide rather than succumb to the henchmen of a ruthless master criminal, Lee leaves the Shaolin temple where he teaches kung fu and spiritual discipline to become a James Bond-style secret agent. When he arrives at an island fortress to take part in a notoriously brutal martial arts tournament, he finds himself having to smash an opium ring and a white slavery racket. Director Robert Clouse produces a series of intricate and athletic fight scenes that, in the opinion of many aficionados, have yet to be bettered. DP. Contains violence, swearing, drug abuse and nudity. DVD

Bruce Lee *Lee* • John Saxon *Roper* • Jim Kelly *Williams* • Kien Shih *Han* • Bob Wall [Robert Wall] *Oharra* • Ahna Capri *Tania* • Angela Mao Ying *Su-Lin* • Betty Chung *Mei Ling* ■ *Dir* Robert Clouse • *Scr* Michael Allin

Enter the Ninja ★★★ 18

Martial arts action
1981 · US · Colour · 91mins

After the kung fu mania of the early 1970s came a spate of movies relishing the silent but lethal killing machine that is the Japanese ninja. Evil Filipino crime baron Christopher George is intimidating a farmer into giving him his precious land, but he reckons without visiting friend and ninja Franco Nero who makes short shrift of various henchmen until he is forced into a real ninja-style showdown with far-eastern superstar Sho Kosugi. Two sequels followed in 1983. JF DVD

Franco Nero *Cole* • Susan George *Mary-Ann Landers* • Sho Kosugi *Hasegawa* • Alex Courtney *Frank Landers* • Will Hare *Dollars* • Zachi Noy *The "Hook"* • Dale Ishimoto *Komori* • Christopher George *Charles Venarius* ■ *Dir* Menahem Golan • *Scr* Dick Desmond

The Entertainer ★★★ PG

Drama 1960 · UK · BW · 99mins

John Osborne's follow-up to his ground-breaking *Look Back in Anger* brought Laurence Olivier to the world of kitchen-sink drama. Olivier gives a stunning performance as music-hall has-been Archie Rice, a seedy vaudeville artist who brings misery to all who know him. It was a personal triumph for Olivier on stage but, in enshrining the legendary actor's performance on celluloid, director Tony

Escapade in Japan ★★★U

Adventure 1957 · US · Colour · 92mins

Teresa Wright and Cameron Mitchell play the worried parents whose child goes missing in Japan when his flight crash lands. It's really a *Boys' Own* adventure, geared for the whole family and cleverly directed for maximum sentiment by veteran Arthur Lubin. Mitchell makes the most of a rare leading role, and youngsters Jon Provost and Roger Nakagawa give sound performances. Take a closer look at that rangy serviceman called Dumbo – it's Clint Eastwood. TS

Teresa Wright *Mary Saunders* • Cameron Mitchell *Dick Saunders* • Jon Provost *Tony Saunders* • Roger Nakagawa *Hiko* • Kuniko Miyake *Michiko* • Susumu Fujita *Kei Tanaka* • Clint Eastwood *Dumbo* ■ *Dir* Arthur Lubin • *Scr* Winston Miller

Escape ★★

Drama 1930 · UK · BW · 70mins

Impresario Basil Dean, who had taken only tentative steps into silent cinema, broke into talkies with this tale of a fugitive on Dartmoor. Unfortunately, his inexperience with both the camera and the primitive sound technology further compound the staginess of his own adaptation of John Galsworthy's tedious play. Sir Gerald du Maurier also struggles, often failing to rein in an effusiveness designed to hit the back of the stalls. The supporting cast boasts some of the biggest names in British theatre, but the episodic structure and the cluttered staging leave them all looking amateurish. DP

Gerald du Maurier *Captain Matt Denant* • Edna Best *Shingled lady* • Gordon Harker *Convict* • Horace Hodges *Gentleman* • Madeleine Carroll *Dora* • Mabel Poulton *Girl of the town* • Lewis Casson *Farmer* ■ *Dir* Basil Dean • *Scr* Basil Dean, John Galsworthy, from the play by John Galsworthy

Escape ★★U

Second World War drama
1940 · US · BW · 103mins

Robert Taylor stars as an American travelling to Germany in a desperate bid to rescue his mother (Russian actress Alla Nazimova) from a Nazi concentration camp. He's helped by countess Norma Shearer, a German-American whose lover is the dastardly Conrad Veidt, a Nazi general. All very starry and, alas, all very phoney. AT

Norma Shearer *Countess Von Treck* • Robert Taylor (1) *Mark Preysing* • Conrad Veidt *Gen Kurt Von Kolb* • Alla Nazimova *Emmy Ritter* • Felix Bressart *Fritz Keller* • Albert Bassermann [Albert Basserman] *Dr Arthur Henning* • Philip Dorn *Dr Ditten* ■ *Dir* Mervyn LeRoy • *Scr* Arch Oboler, Marguerite Roberts, from a novel by Ethel Vance

The Escape Artist ★★PG

Drama 1982 · US · Colour · 89mins

Ryan O'Neal's son Griffin holds his own in this mishmash of vaudeville and small town corruption. Bragging that he will escape a prison sentence within an hour cues a flashback for O'Neal about his childhood in theatre. Exploited by his aunt and uncle, who perform "the best escape act since Houdini" he hones his skills and escapes, lifting the wallet of the vindictive son of the local major, Raul Julia. Julia then sends his goons to threaten the boy. This is a mess of a film and far too formulaic. LH [VIDEO]

Griffin O'Neal *Danny Masters* • Raul Julia *Stu Quinones* • Teri Garr *Arlene* • Gabriel Dell *Uncle Burke* • Desi Arnaz *Mayor Quinones* • John P Ryan *Vernon* • Elizabeth Daily *Sandra* • M Emmet Walsh *Fritz* • Jackie Coogan *Magic shop owner* ■ *Dir* Caleb Deschanel • *Scr* Melissa Mathison, Stephen Zito, from the novel by David Wagoner

Escape by Night ★★

Crime drama 1953 · UK · BW · 78mins

Something of an improvement on the usual hokum churned out by low-budget expert John Gilling, this drama lacks any of the menace or desperation with which it would have been saturated by even the most pedestrian Hollywood B-movie director. Yet Sid James gives a solid performance as the vice boss on the run who holds a journalist hostage, and he is well supported by Bonar Colleano as the crusading reporter after an exclusive. DP

Bonar Colleano *Tom Buchan* • Andrew Ray *Joey Weston* • Sidney James *Gino Rossini* • Ted Ray *Mr Weston* • Simone Silva *Rosetta Mantania* • Patrick Barr *Inspector Frampton* ■ *Dir/Scr* John Gilling

Escape from Alcatraz ★★★★15

Prison drama based on a true story
1979 · US · Colour · 107mins

Don Siegel did much to establish his reputation with *Riot in Cell Block 11* in 1954. He went back behind bars for this tough and compelling reconstruction of the only successful escape from San Francisco's notorious island prison in its 29-year history. Driven stir crazy by the strictures of warden Patrick McGoohan's regime and the brutality of his fellow inmates, Clint Eastwood plans an ingenious bid for freedom with Fred Ward and Jack Thibeau. Blessed with expert performances, Siegel shoots the preparations with an attention to detail that exerts as strong a grip as the escape itself. DP [VIDEO] DVD

Clint Eastwood *Frank Morris* • Patrick McGoohan *Warden* • Roberts Blossom *Chester "Doc" Dalton* • Jack Thibeau *Clarence Anglin* • Fred Ward *John Anglin* • Paul Benjamin *English* • Larry Hankin *Charley Butts* ■ *Dir* Don Siegel • *Scr* Richard Tuggle, from the book by J Campbell Bruce

Escape from Fort Bravo ★★★PG

Western 1953 · US · Colour · 94mins

Intended for 3-D but ultimately shown flat, this otherwise impressive early John Sturges western suffers from the use of obvious studio exteriors in many key sequences. On location, though, in the dust of the desert as Mescalero Indians menace the escapees, the use of landscape is mighty fine. Union captain William Holden is suitably rugged, lovely Eleanor Parker is deceptively charming, and honourable Confederate leader John Forsythe reminds you of what a boring movie actor he was before his hair turned blue in TV's *Dynasty*. TS [VIDEO]

William Holden (2) *Captain Roper* • Eleanor Parker *Carla Forester* • John Forsythe *Captain John Marsh* • William Demarest *Campbell* • William Campbell *Cabot Young* • Polly Bergen *Alice Owens* • Richard Anderson *Lieutenant Beecher* • Carl Benton Reid *Colonel Owens* ■ *Dir* John Sturges • *Scr* Frank Fenton, from a story by Michael Pate, Phillip Rock

Escape from LA ★★15

Futuristic action thriller
1996 · US · Colour · 96mins

In John Carpenter's shambolic, big-budget sequel to his superior *Escape from New York*, Kurt Russell returns as macho hero Snake Plissken, who is blackmailed into scouring the City of Angels for a doomsday device stolen by the president's daughter. Apart from the witty, face-lifted zombie section, this unexciting rehash lacks the sharp black comedy of the original. AJ [VIDEO] DVD

Kurt Russell *Snake Plissken* • AJ Langer *Utopia* • Steve Buscemi *"Map to the Stars" Eddie* • George Corraface [Georges Corraface] *Cuervo Jones* • Stacy Keach *Malloy* • Michelle Forbes *Brazen* • Pam Grier *Hershe* • Jeff Imada *Saigon Shadow* • Cliff Robertson *President* • Peter Fonda *Pipeline* • Paul Bartel *Congressman* ■ *Dir* John Carpenter • *Scr* John Carpenter, Debra Hill, Kurt Russell, from characters created by John Carpenter, Nick Castle

Escape from New York ★★★15

Futuristic action thriller
1981 · US · Colour · 94mins

Sullen Kurt Russell impersonates Clint Eastwood in director John Carpenter's tough futuristic western that never fulfils the ingenuity of its premise. Manhattan island is a maximum security prison where the president's plane has crashed. This is certainly one of Carpenter's slickest looking films, with the presence of Lee Van Cleef reinforcing its Sergio Leone associations. But, despite a marvellous night-time opening sequence, this slice of escapism often disappoints, though it still rates higher than the poor sequel *Escape from LA*. AJ. Contains swearing, violence. [VIDEO] DVD

Kurt Russell *Snake Plissken* • Lee Van Cleef *Bob Hauk* • Donald Pleasence *President* • Isaac Hayes *Duke of New York* • Adrienne Barbeau *Maggie* • Harry Dean Stanton *"Brain"* • Ernest Borgnine *Cabby* ■ *Dir* John Carpenter • *Scr* John Carpenter, Nick Castle

Escape from Sobibor ★★★★15

War drama based on a true story
1987 · UK/US · Colour · 142mins

This is a compelling account of the escape from a Nazi death camp deep in the Polish countryside, concocted by a cabal of Jewish workers and Soviet soldiers. Over 250,000 million people died in the Sobibor gas chambers. In comparative terms, the fact that more than 300 prisoners fled from this hellhole may seem slight. But their achievement remains one of the most audacious acts of courage in the entire Second World War. Alan Arkin is excellent as the ringleader, while Rutger Hauer and Joanna Pacula head a superb ensemble cast. But the key component is Jack Gold's directorial restraint and this TV film deservedly won two Golden Globes. DP [VIDEO]

Alan Arkin *Leon Feldhendler* • Rutger Hauer *Sasha* • Joanna Pacula *Luka* • Emil Wolk *Samuel* • Hartmut Becker *Sgt Wagner* • Jack Shepherd *Itzhak* • Kurt Raab *Sgt Frenzel* ■ *Dir* Jack Gold • *Scr* Reginald Rose, from the non-fiction book by Richard Rashke

Escape from the Planet of the Apes ★★★★PG

Science-fiction adventure drama
1971 · US · Colour · 93mins

The third in the popular movie series sees Roddy McDowall and Kim Hunter land in present-day California after surviving the catastrophe that ended *Beneath the Planet of the Apes*. It's very much a film of two halves, the first being an amusing collection of observations on modern life, as seen through the eyes of the more advanced apes. The second half, is much darker, with the arrogant and fearful humans being driven to unspeakable cruelty to protect their future. An intelligent script, capable direction and solid performances add up to a fine film. *Conquest of the Planet of the Apes* (1972) followed. DP [VIDEO] DVD

Roddy McDowall *Cornelius* • Kim Hunter *Zira* • Bradford Dillman *Dr Lewis Dixon* • Natalie Trundy *Dr Stephanie Branton* • Eric Braeden *Dr Otto Hasslein* • William Windom *The President* • Sal Mineo *Milo* • Albert Salmi *E-1* • Jason Evers *E-2* • John Randolph *Chairman* ■ *Dir* Don Taylor • *Scr* Paul Dehn, from characters created by Pierre Boulle

Escape from Zahrain ★★U

Action thriller 1962 · US · Colour · 93mins

Well-upholstered but ultimately mundane would-be thriller set in the Middle East. Yul Brynner leads a motley crew across the Panavisioned desert to find guest star James Mason. Such worthies as Sal Mineo and Jack Warden are along for the (underscripted) ride, but veteran director Ronald Neame shows little sense of dramatic pacing despite the handsome location photography. TS

Yul Brynner *Sharif* • Sal Mineo *Ahmed* • Madlyn Rhue *Laila* • Jack Warden *Huston* • James Mason *Johnson* ■ *Dir* Ronald Neame • *Scr* Robin Estridge, from a novel by Michael Barrett • *Cinematographer* Ellsworth Fredericks

E

Escape Me Never ★★★

Melodrama 1935 · UK · BW · 101mins

The smash-hit play was especially written by Margaret Kennedy to exploit the considerable abilities of star Elisabeth Bergner. This unsurprising film version, directed by Bergman's husband Paul Czinner, is virtually a transcript of the show, even down to the same male smoothie leads (Hugh Sinclair and Griffith Jones). The tale is pure tosh, involving unwed mother Bergner going nuts over no-good cad composer Sinclair. But it does reveal Bergner's range, and you'll be surprised at how charming, delightful, sexy and talented the lady is. TS

Elisabeth Bergner *Gemma Jones* • Hugh Sinclair *Sebastian Sanger* • Griffith Jones *Caryl Sanger* • Penelope Dudley Ward *Fenella McClean* • Irene Vanbrugh *Mrs McClean* • Leon Quartermaine *Mr McClean* ■ *Dir* Paul Czinner • *Scr* Carl Zuckmayer, Robert J Cullen, from the novel *The Fool of the Family* and the play *Escape Me Never* by Margaret Kennedy

Escape Me Never ★★

Melodrama 1947 · US · BW · 103mins

This idiotically cast remake of the old Elisabeth Bergner vehicle has Ida Lupino as the Bergnerian waif (you're no waif, Ida) and Errol Flynn as the caddish composer she falls for. Only skilled Eleanor Parker really convinces as Flynn's fling after he marries Lupino. British expatriate director Peter Godfrey does what he can with this stale tosh, though the Erich Wolfgang Korngold score does go some way to mitigate the silliness. TS

Errol Flynn *Sebastian Dubrok* • Ida Lupino *Gemma Smith* • Eleanor Parker *Fenella MacLean* • Gig Young *Caryl Dubrok* • Reginald Denny *Ivor MacLean* • Isobel Elsom *Mrs MacLean* • Albert Basserman *Professor Heinrich* • Ludwig Stossel *Mr Steinach* ■ *Dir* Peter Godfrey • *Scr* Thomas Williamson, from the novel *The Fool of the Family* and the play *Escape Me Never* by Margaret Kennedy

Escape Route ★★U

Spy thriller 1952 · UK · BW · 79mins

George Raft gives a fair impression of a man who has had his arms welded to his sides in this dismissable quickie thriller. One of the handful of films Raft made in Europe after his Hollywood fortunes dipped, it's a lightweight affair in which he plays a FBI agent called in to discover who is smuggling scientists to the east. The villain's identity is painfully obvious, as is the distaste with which undercover operative Sally Gray smooches her ageing co-star. DP

George Raft *Steve Rossi* • Sally Gray *Joan Miller* • Clifford Evans *Michael Grand* • Reginald Tate *Colonel Wilkes* • Patricia Laffan *Miss Brooks* • Frederick Piper *Inspector Reid* • Roddy Hughes *Porter* • John Warwick *Brice* ■ *Dir* Seymour Friedman, Peter Graham Scott • *Scr* John V Baines, Nicholas Phipps

Escape to Athena ★★ PG

Second World War adventure
1979 · UK · Colour · 114mins

Despite the best efforts and intentions of mogul Lew Grade, most of his film-producing legacy is, regrettably, a pile of old tosh. This is a prime example: a slight plot combines an ancient treasure caper with a Second World War escape adventure, and wastes the talents of such diverse names as David Niven, Elliott Gould, Claudia Cardinale and Sonny Bono. And they aren't even the leads! TS [video] DVD

Roger Moore *Major Otto Hecht* • Telly Savalas *Zeno* • David Niven *Professor Blake* • Claudia Cardinale *Eleana* • Stefanie Powers *Dottie Del Mar* • Richard Roundtree *Nat Judson* • Sonny Bono *Bruno Rotelli* • Elliott Gould *Charlie Dane* • William Holden (2) *Prisoner* ■ *Dir* George Pan Cosmatos • *Scr* Richard S Lochte, Edward Anhalt, from a story by Richard S Lochte, George Pan Cosmatos

Escape to Burma ★★ PG

Adventure 1955 · US · Colour · 83mins

One of the last films to be directed by veteran Allan Dwan, this trite melodrama contributed to the decline of RKO. Barbara Stanwyck and Robert Ryan, who were so good together in the same studio's *Clash by Night*, are wasted here as lovers in the jungle whose tryst is disturbed by David Farrar when he tries to arrest Ryan for murder. There's a final twist, but by then you'll be numb with boredom, despite the dutiful performances. TS [video]

Barbara Stanwyck *Gwen Moore* • Robert Ryan *Jim Brecan* • David Farrar *Cardigan* • Murvyn Vye *Makesh* • Lisa Montell *Andora* • Robert Warwick *Sawbwa* ■ *Dir* Allan Dwan • *Scr* Talbot Jennings, Hobart Donavan, from the story *Bow Tamely to Me* by Kenneth Perkins

Escape to Victory ★★★ PG

Second World War drama
1981 · US · Colour · 111mins

Can you imagine what this corny prisoner-of-war picture would have been like if producer Freddie Fields had not secured the services of Michael Caine, Sylvester Stallone, Max von Sydow and a squad of international footballing legends? It's pretty obvious that director John Huston didn't quite know what to make of it all, but his sure touch and Pelé's football choreography turn this into a rousing romp, made all the more enjoyable by the shocking performances of the players. Escapist entertainment in every sense. DP [video]

Sylvester Stallone *Robert Hatch* • Michael Caine *John Colby* • Pelé *Luis Fernandez* • Bobby Moore *Terry Brady* • Osvaldo Ardiles *Carlos Rey* • Paul Van Himst *Michel Fileu* • Kazimierz Deyna *Paul Wolchek* • Hallvar Thorensen *Gunnar Hilsson* • Mike Summerbee *Sid Harmor* • Co Prins *Pieter Van Beck* • Russell Osman *Doug Clure* • John Wark *Arthur Hayes* • Soren Linsted *Erik Borge* • Kevin O'Callaghan *Tony Lewis* • Max von Sydow *Major Karl Von Steiner* • Daniel Massey *Colonel Waldron* • Tim Pigott-Smith *Rose* ■ *Dir* John Huston • *Scr* Evan Jones, Yabo Yablonsky, from a story by Yabo Yablonsky, Djordje Milicevic, Jeff Maguire

Escape to Witch Mountain ★★★ U

Science-fiction drama
1975 · US · Colour · 90mins

With actors such as Ray Milland, Eddie Albert and Donald Pleasence treating this Disney children's movie as seriously as any other adult-themed film they might tackle, the result is pacey, scary and sentimental. Milland is oozingly malevolent as the villain who wants to use the clairvoyant powers of two youngsters for his own nefarious ends. Plenty of thrills, even if it is a bit dated. Bette Davis appears in the follow-up movie, *Return from Witch Mountain*. TH [video] DVD

Kim Richards *Tia Malone* • Ike Eisenmann *Tony Malone* • Ray Milland *Aristotle Bolt* • Eddie Albert *Jason O'Day* • Donald Pleasence *Lucas Deranian* • Walter Barnes *Sheriff Purdy* ■ *Dir* John Hough • *Scr* Robert Malcolm Young, from the novel by Alexander Key

Escape under Pressure ★★ 12

Action drama 2000 · US · Colour · 87mins

Jean Pellerin takes an eternity to get Rob Lowe's army engineer, his classics professor wife Larissa Miller, diverse baddies and a statue of Artemis on to a boat travelling between Athens and Lesbos. Connoisseurs of crassness will enjoy the flashback to ancient Greece and the cheap imitations of *Titanic*. Released on video and DVD in the UK as *The Cruel Deep*. DP. Contains swearing and violence. [video] DVD

Rob Lowe *John Spencer* • Craig Wasson *Elgin Bates* • Larissa Miller *Chloe Spencer* • Harry Van Gorkum *Crowley* • Scott Anthony Viscomi *Nikos Gravas* ■ *Dir* Jean Pellerin • *Scr* Martin Lazarus

Escapement ★★

Mystery thriller 1958 · UK · BW · 77mins

Also known under the more lurid title of *The Electronic Monster* this underwhelming British thriller has Rod Cameron investigating an actor's death at a clinic specialising in electronic hypnosis. Barely mesmerising, it was one of those zero-budget British movies that gave refuge to B-picture stars from Hollywood, in this case Mary Murphy and Cameron, former Fred MacMurray stand-in. TH

Rod Cameron *Keenan* • Mary Murphy *Ruth* • Meredith Edwards *Dr Maxwell* • Peter Illing *Zekon* • Kay Callard *Laura Maxwell* • Carl Jaffe *Dr Erich Hoff* ■ *Dir* Montgomery Tully • *Scr* Charles Eric Maine, J MacLaren-Ross, from the novel by Charles Eric Maine

The Escapist ★★

Action adventure 1983 · US · Colour · 87mins

One of those belting movies that contains such an overdose of wacky plotlines you can only sit and gawp. Bill Shirk wants to be the greatest escapologist in the world, so director Eddie Beverly Jr has him buried alive, stuck underwater and making the acquaintance of several deadly animals. All phobics are thus well catered for in this substandard action adventure, in which great flurries of melodramatic activity paper over absolutely nothing of substance. SH

Bill Shirk *Shirk* • Milbourne Christopher *Weiss* • Peter Lupus *Sharky* • Dick the Bruiser *Bruiser* • Gary Todd *Doug Meyers* • Terri Mann *Polly* • Cynthia Johns *Stormy* ■ *Dir* Eddie Beverly Jr • *Scr* Stephen Meyers

The Escapist ★★ 15

Thriller 2002 · UK · Colour · 86mins

The perfect life of pilot Jonny Lee Miller is torn apart when psychotic criminal Andy Serkis breaks into his home and murders his pregnant wife. After faking his death, Miller packs a life of crime into a few months, getting sent to higher and higher security prisons until he and Serkis meet again. Despite a highly charged plot and great use of locations, this unconvincing thriller is full of stereotypical prison characters and revenge-movie clichés. JF. Contains violence and swearing. [video] DVD

Jonny Lee Miller *Denis* • Andy Serkis *Ricky Barnes* • Gary Lewis *Ron* • Jodhi May *Christine* • Paloma Baeza *Valerie* • Vas Blackwood *Vin* • Philip Barantini *Joey* ■ *Dir* Gillies MacKinnon • *Scr* Nick Perry

The Escort ★★★ 18

Drama 1999 · Fr/UK · Colour · 101mins

Daniel Auteuil here plays a Frenchman in London who discovers he can make big bucks as a male escort. The action has a bitter tang of authenticity, as the opportunistic Auteuil preys on bored socialites, timid housewives and lonely hearts. But his relationships with fellow gigolo Stuart Townsend and single-mother hooker Liza Walker are less persuasive, diverting us into the realms of melodrama. DP. In English and French with subtitles. Contains swearing, sex scenes and violence. [video] DVD

Daniel Auteuil *Pierre* • Stuart Townsend *Tom* • Liza Walker *Kim* • Noah Taylor *Gem* • Frances Barber *Jessica* • Claire Skinner *Patricia* ■ *Dir* Michel Blanc • *Scr* Michel Blanc, from an idea by Hanif Kureishi

Escort West ★★★ U

Western 1959 · US · BW · 76mins

Produced by John Wayne's brother, Robert E Morrison, this was too modest a venture to interest the big man himself. So Victor Mature takes the lead as the ex-Confederate soldier heading west with his young daughter. Along the way he picks up two sisters (Elaine Stewart and Faith Domergue) and their wounded servant (Rex Ingram), all survivors of an Indian attack. This is a cut above the average thanks to an eventful narrative and well-developed characters. AE

Victor Mature *Ben Lassiter* • Elaine Stewart *Beth Drury* • Faith Domergue *Martha Drury* • Reba Waters *Abbey Lassiter* • Noah Beery Jr *Jamison* • Leo Gordon *Vogel* • Rex Ingram (2) *Nelson* • John Hubbard *Lieutenant Weeks* • Harry Carey Jr *Travis* • Slim Pickens *Wheeler* ■ *Dir* Francis D Lyon • *Scr* Leo Gordon, Fred Hartsook, from a story by Steven Hayes

Eskiya ★★★★ 15

Drama 1996 · Tur · Colour · 127mins

Turkey's biggest ever box-office hit, this astute drama exploits Hollywood convention to produce a film few in America would have the wit to make. Yavuz Turgul turns Istanbul into a hostile wilderness as Kurdish bandit Sener Sen returns from 35 years in jail to take his revenge on the friend who not only betrayed him, but also stole his girl. Rambling and brimming over with life, this is an engrossing mix of social comment, unassuming heroism, wry humour and shameless sentiment, with the relationship between the bandit and a brash street rogue symbolising what young and old can learn from each other. DP. In Turkish with English subtitles.

Sener Sen *Baran* • Ugur Yucel *Cumali* • Sermin Sen *Keje* • Yasim Salkim *Emel* ■ *Dir/Scr* Yavuz Turgul

Espionage ★★★ U

Adventure drama 1937 · US · BW · 66mins

Suave Edmund Lowe and romantic Madge Evans (a former child star) make a sophisticated pair as rival reporters tracking down arms tycoon Paul Lukas on the Orient Express. It manages to be as slick and fast-paced as the train on which most of the action takes place. RB

Edmund Lowe *Kenneth* • Madge Evans *Patricia* • Paul Lukas *Kronsky* • Ketti Gallian *Sonia* • Richard "Skeets" Gallagher *Brown* • Frank Reicher *Von Cram* • Billy Gilbert *Turk* • Robert Graves *Duval* ■ *Dir* Kurt Neumann • *Scr* Manuel Seff, Leonard Lee, Ainsworth Morgan, from a play by Walter Hackett

Les Espions ★★★ PG

Spy thriller 1957 · Fr/It · BW · 121mins

While maybe not of the same calibre as *Les Diaboliques*, Henri-Georges Clouzot's adaptation is still clearly the work of a master of suspense. Everything about this tale of espionage and deception is open to question, whether it's the existence of a top secret nuclear device, the intentions of the Soviet and American agents who come clamouring after it or the motives of a sanitorium director who allows the intriguing charade to be played out under his roof. Curt Jurgens and Peter Ustinov stand out in a splendid international cast, but the real star is the director. DP. In French with English subtitles. DVD

Gérard Séty *Malic* • Curd Jürgens [Curt Jurgens] *Visitor* • Vera Clouzot *Patient* • Peter Ustinov *Russian agent* • Sam Jaffe *American agent* • Martita Hunt *Nurse* • OE Hasse *Vogel* ■ *Dir* Henri-Georges Clouzot • *Scr* Henri-Georges Clouzot, Jérôme Géromini, from the novel *Midnight Patient* by Egon Hostowsky

Essex Boys ★★★ 18

Crime drama based on a true story
1999 · UK · Colour · 97mins

This slick British crime thriller breaks no new ground and tries too hard to be tough. Yet interest is sustained by taut pacing, a nicely murky plot and spirited performances from Alex Kingston, Tom Wilkinson, Charlie Creed-Miles and a scenery-chewing Sean Bean. The story centres on a young minicab driver (Creed-Miles) who is hired by a hard man fresh out of prison. He then finds himself in the firing line when a major drug deal prompts a power struggle among rival elements of the Essex criminal fraternity. DA. Contains violence, swearing, drug abuse and sex scenes. [video] DVD

Sean Bean *Jason Locke* • Alex Kingston *Lisa Locke* • Charlie Creed-Miles *Billy Reynolds* • Tom Wilkinson *John Dyke* • Larry Lamb *Peter Chase* • Terence Rigby *Henry Hobbs* • Billy Murray *Perry Elley* • Amelia Lowdell *Nicole* ■ *Dir* Terry Winsor • *Scr* Jeff Pope, Terry Winsor

Esther and the King ★

Biblical drama
1960 · US/It · Colour · 109mins

Biblical stuff and nonsense, with Joan Collins marrying the Persian king to stop the oppression of the Jews and save the throne from various plots and assassins. Shot in Italy like so many Hollywood epics, it veers between the laughable and the plodding, and you'd never guess that Hollywood action maestro Raoul Walsh directed it. AT

Joan Collins *Esther* • Richard Egan *King Ahasuerus* • Denis O'Dea *Mordecai* • Sergio Fantoni *Haman* • Rick Battaglia [Rik Battaglia] *Simon* • Renato Baldini *Klydrathes* ■ *Dir* Raoul Walsh • *Scr* Raoul Walsh, Michael Elkins • *Cinematographer* Mario Bava

Esther Kahn ★★ 15

Period drama 2000 · Fr/UK · Colour · 148mins

Set in London at the turn of the 19th century, this drawn-out period tale charts the progress of a Jewish seamstress from East End backstreet to West End acclaim playing Hedda Gabler. In his first film in English, French director Arnaud Desplechin neither captures the imagination nor exploits such compelling themes as poverty, sexual betrayal and personal ambition. Even more fatally, he fails to coax any emotion out of his lead actress, Summer Phoenix. DP

Summer Phoenix *Esther Kahn* • Ian Holm *Nathan Quellen* • Frances Barber *Rivka Kahn* • Fabrice Desplechin *Philippe Haygard* • Ian Bartholomew *Norton, Shylock's director* • Emmanuelle Devos *Sylvia l'Italienne* • Anton Lesser *Sean* ■ *Dir* Arnaud Desplechin • *Scr* Arnaud Desplechin, Emmanuel Bourdieu, from a story by Arthur Symons

Esther Waters ★★ U

Period melodrama 1948 · UK · BW · 105mins

This tawdry adaptation plunges between the two stools of heritage production and sensationalist melodrama. Dirk Bogarde is suitably scurrilous as a rascally footman, but the action slows fatally when he is off screen, with Kathleen Ryan facing all her trials (single motherhood, the workhouse and Bogarde's drinking) with sulkiness rather than dignity. DP

Kathleen Ryan *Esther Waters* • Dirk Bogarde *William Latch* • Cyril Cusack *Fred Parsons* • Ivor Barnard *Randal* • Fay Compton *Mrs Barfield* • Margaret Diamond *Sarah Tucker* • Morland Graham *Ketley* ■ *Dir* Ian Dalrymple, Peter Proud • *Scr* Michael Gordon, William Rose, from a novel by George Moore

The Eternal ★ 15

Horror 1998 · US · Colour · 91mins

A ludicrous mixture of Irish whimsy, Druid folklore and zombie witches, this is a mind-boggling mistake. Allison Elliott plays an alcoholic New Yorker who returns to the Emerald Isle to visit her uncle (Christopher Walken) and becomes possessed by the spirit of a 2,000-year-old witch whose remains have been discovered in the local peat bog. This simple-minded shocker is one of the daftest horror movies ever made. AJ DVD

Alison Elliott (2) *Nora/Niamh* • Jared Harris *Jim* • Christopher Walken *Bill Ferriter* • Rachel O'Rourke *Alice* • Lois Smith *Mrs Ferriter* • Karl Geary *Sean* ■ *Dir/Scr* Michael Almereyda

Eternal Love ★★★

Silent romantic drama
1929 · US · BW · 71mins

Set in 1812, this features John Barrymore and Camilla Horn as the Swiss couple who take to the Alps after being wrongfully accused of murdering her husband. Released in the midst of the talkie furore, Ernst Lubitsch's silent swansong comes complete with occasional sound effects, most notably during the climactic avalanche. It was ignored by contemporary audiences and hasn't been of much interest to critics since – perhaps because it stands in such stark contrast to the frothy farces that came to be seen as Lubitsch's trademark in Hollywood. DP

John Barrymore *Marcus Paltram* • Camilla Horn *Ciglia* • Victor Varconi *Lorenz Gruber* • Hobart Bosworth *Reverend Tass* • Bodil Rosing *Housekeeper* • Mona Rico *Pia* ■ *Dir* Ernst Lubitsch • *Scr* Hans Kraly, Katherine Hilliker (titles), HH Caldwell (titles), from the novel *Der König der Bernina, Roman aus dem Schweizerischen* by Jakob Christoph Heer

Eternal Love ★★★ PG

Romantic drama 1943 · Fr · BW · 107mins

The subject of endless debates about whether this updating of the legend of Tristan and Isolde had pro-Nazi sympathies, this is also a film that leaves one wondering how much better it might have been had screenwriter Jean Cocteau also directed instead of the more literal Jean Delannoy. Permanently on set, Cocteau clearly influenced the fairy-tale setting, the dreamy atmosphere and the rather bloodless acting of doomed lovers Jean Marais and Madeleine Sologne. The result is pompous, perhaps, but undeniably arresting and affecting. DP. In French with English subtitles.

Madeleine Sologne *Nathalie* • Jean Marais *Patrice* • Yvonne de Bray *Gertrude* • Jane Marken *Anne* • Jean Murat *Marc* • Pierre Piéral *Achille* • Roland Toutain *Lionel* ■ *Dir* Jean Delannoy • *Scr* Jean Cocteau

Eternal Revenge ★★

Thriller 1999 · US/Can · Colour · 94mins

This serial killer TV thriller proves too much of a stretch for former *Baywatch* star Alexandra Paul. With the men dropping like nine pins at her college reunion, Philadelphia cop Paul begins to suspect that the victims may all be linked by a heinous act from their reckless youth. A plodding plot and dismal dialogue. DP

Alexandra Paul *Laura Underwood* • Michelle Johnson *Vicky Mayerson* • Eric Davis *Scotty Flannigan* • Anthony Michael Hall *Brian Cutler* ■ *Dir* Marc S Grenier • *Scr* Neil Goldberg

Eternal Sunshine of the Spotless Mind ★★★★ 15

Romantic comedy drama
2003 · US · Colour · 103mins

In this inventive collaboration with music video director Michel Gondry, Jim Carrey and Kate Winslet meet by chance, and lose their minds over each other. Literally. After their affair ends, Winslet decides she can't live with the memories and goes to Lacuna Inc, a quirky, modest business that erases unwanted recollections. Carrey then discovers what she's done and decides to follow suit. This outing from Kaufman's oddball imagination is wonderfully intriguing, often touching and typically convoluted. The only minor quibbles are Carrey's understated performance and a slightly lacklustre ending. BP. Contains swearing. DVD

Jim Carrey *Joel Barish* • Kate Winslet *Clementine Kruczynski* • Kirsten Dunst *Mary* • Mark Ruffalo *Stan* • Elijah Wood *Patrick* • Tom Wilkinson *Dr Howard Mierzwiak* • Jane Adams (2) *Carrie* • David Cross (2) *Rob* ■ *Dir* Michel Gondry • *Scr* Charlie Kaufman, from a story by Charlie Kaufman, Michel Gondry, Pierre Bismuth

Eternally Yours ★★★

Romantic drama 1939 · US · BW · 99mins

Lightweight but endearing romance from an era when Hollywood really knew how to cook this recipe properly, featuring the lovely Loretta Young involved with magician David Niven in a vicissitude-strewn marriage. Director Tay Garnett brings his aerial knowledge to bear on some scenes, but seems generally content to let the movie coast along on the charms of the leading players. TS

David Niven *Tony Halstead* • Loretta Young *Anita Halstead* • Broderick Crawford *Don Barnes* • Hugh Herbert *Benton* • Billie Burke *Aunt Abby* • C Aubrey Smith *Bishop Hubert Peabody* • ZaSu Pitts *Carrie Bingham* • Eve Arden *Gloria* ■ *Dir* Tay Garnett • *Scr* Gene Towne, Graham Baker, John Meehan

Eternity ★★ 18

Fantasy drama 1990 · US · Colour · 121mins

Jon Voight battles it out with Armand Assante in medieval times, losing his beloved Eileen Davidson in the process. Then the temporal rug is pulled out from under events and moved to the present-day where Voight is a do-gooder at odds with Assante, a right-wing tycoon. This laboured what-goes-around-comes-around reincarnation tale is a mixture of half-baked metaphysics and fantasy. TH

Jon Voight *James/Edward* • Armand Assante *Sean/Roni* • Eileen Davidson *Valerie/Dahlia* • Wilford Brimley *Eric/King* • Kaye Ballard *Selma/Sabrina* • Steven Keats *Harold/Tax collector* • Lainie Kazan *Bernice/Mother* ■ *Dir* Steven Paul • *Scr* Jon Voight, Steven Paul, Dorothy Koster Paul

Eternity and a Day ★★★ PG

Drama 1998 · Gr/Fr/It/Ger · Colour · 127mins

Winner of the Palme d'Or at Cannes, this meditation on memory and mortality follows dying writer Bruno Ganz around Salonika as he seeks to atone for a life of self-obsession by helping a young Albanian refugee. Switching lyrically between a sunlit past filled with missed opportunities and the murky moodiness of the poet's present, director Theo Angelopoulos is overdeliberate in both his pacing and symbolism. For all its epic scope and its sublime camera movements, this is never as provocative as Angelopoulos's impressive 1995 film, *Ulysses' Gaze*. DP. In Greek with English subtitles.

Bruno Ganz *Alexandre* • Isabelle Renaud *Anna* • Fabrizio Bentivoglio *The Poet* • Despina Bebedeli *Mother* • Achileas Skevis *The Child* • Vassilis Seimenis *Son-in-law* ■ *Dir* Theo Angelopoulos • *Scr* Theo Angelopoulos, Petros Markaris, Tonino Guerra, Giorgio Silvagni

Ethan Frome ★★★

Period drama
1993 · US/UK · Colour · 107mins

This adaptation of the Edith Wharton novel is a bleak, dark affair, but rewarding. Liam Neeson is the proud farmer trapped in a cold marriage with Joan Allen who finds love in the shape of her cousin, Patricia Arquette. The three leads bring resonance to the doom-laden story and, although it can be heavy going at times, it remains a moving experience. JF

Liam Neeson *Ethan Frome* • Patricia Arquette *Mattie Silver* • Joan Allen *Zeena Frome* • Tate Donovan *Reverend Smith* • Katharine Houghton *Ruth Hale* • Stephen Mendillo *Ned Hale* • Deborah Ayer *Young Ruth* • Jay Goede *Denis Eady* ■ *Dir* John Madden • *Scr* Richard Nelson, from the novel by Edith Wharton

L'Etoile du Nord ★★ PG

Period crime drama
1982 · Fr · Colour · 123mins

This is not one of the more successful adaptations of a Georges Simenon novel. Philippe Noiret is suitably mysterious as the seemingly urbane traveller regaling landlady Simone Signoret with his tales of North African adventure. But, considering the psychological sophistication of the César-winning screenplay, the flashbacks to Noiret's shipboard encounter with Signoret's gold-digging daughter Fanny Cottençon (who also won a César) and wealthy Egyptian Gamil Ratib are handled with insufficient finesse. DP. A French language film. In French with English subtitles

Simone Signoret *Madame Baron* • Philippe Noiret *Edouard* • Fanny Cottençon *Sylvie* • Julie Jezequel *Antoinette* • Jean-Yves Chatelais *Valesco* • Gamil Ratib *Nemrod* ■ *Dir* Pierre Granier-Deferre • *Scr* Pierre Granier-Deferre, Michel Grisolia, Jean Aurenche, from the novel *La Locataire* by Georges Simenon

Etre et Avoir ★★★★ U

Documentary 2002 · Fr · Colour · 99mins

In this delightful documentary, 55-year-old teacher Georges Lopez reflects on his two decades at a tiny school in the rural Auvergne as he prepares his penultimate year group for their uncertain future. Lopez handles the various personality clashes, domestic crises and learning difficulties of the children in his care with patience, professionalism and pride. Capturing the sense of community and conveying the pivotal role Lopez has played in so many lives, director Nicolas Philibert's film is a fond and fascinating portrait of an unassuming local hero. DP. In French with English subtitles. DVD

Dir/Scr Nicolas Philibert

Eu Sei Que Vou Te Amar ★★★

Drama 1986 · Bra · Colour · 110mins

Fernanda Torres shared the Best Actress prize at Cannes for her work in this intense study of a marriage in crisis, which also reflects the political uncertainty of its time. Yet, without the counterbalancing performance of Thales Pan Chacon, this would have been as askew an enterprise as Vittorio De Sica's *Indiscretion of an American Wife*, in which Montgomery Clift's Method style completely overwhelms Jennifer Jones. In some ways, this is an inversion of that film, as an estranged Brazilian couple meet to discuss their problems and the chances of a reconciliation. DP. In Portuguese with English subtitles.

Fernanda Torres • Thales Pan Chacon ■ *Dir/Scr* Arnaldo Jabor

Eugenio ★★★ 15

Romantic drama 2002 · It · Colour · 93mins

Veteran actor Giancarlo Giannini excels in this earnest, if occasionally calculating study of a resilient 50-something with Down's Syndrome who inspires confidence in a recovering accident victim. His inspiring performance relies wholly on an understanding of the character rather than special make-up. But the screenplay lapses too often into heart-tugging melodrama, particularly once Giannini is reunited with Giuliana de Sio, the object of a childhood crush who just happens to be wheelchair-bound Chiara de Bonis's estranged mother. DP. In Italian with English subtitles. Contains swearing.

Giancarlo Giannini *Eugenio* • Giuliana de Sio *Elena* • Jacques Perrin *Federico* • Chiara de Bonis *Laura/Young Elena* ■ *Dir* Francisco José Fernandez

Eureka ★★ 18

Drama 1982 · UK · Colour · 123mins

Gene Hackman would be given an extract from the Bible every night to get him in the mood for the following day's shooting, but it made director Nicolas Roeg's weird self-indulgence no clearer. Hackman plays a gold prospector who strikes it rich but not lucky; instead he becomes paranoid, especially when his daughter (Theresa Russell) marries a fortune-hunter. Villainous Joe Pesci settles it all in a welter of slaughter which solves most problems, but not Roeg's oblique story-telling. TH DVD

Gene Hackman *Jack McCann* • Theresa Russell *Tracy* • Rutger Hauer *Claude Maillot Van Horn* • Jane Lapotaire *Helen McCann* • Mickey Rourke *Aurelio D'Amato* • Ed Lauter *Charles Perkins* • Joe Pesci *Mayakofsky* • Helena Kallianiotes *Frieda* • Corin Redgrave *Worsley* ■ *Dir* Nicolas Roeg • *Scr* Paul Mayersberg, from the novel *Who Killed Sir Harry Oakes?* by Marshall Houts

Eureka ★★★★ 15

Psychological road movie
2000 · Jpn · Sepia · 2108mins

Director Shinji Aoyama has called this extraordinary film "a prayer for modern man, who is searching for the courage to go on living". The story follows coach driver Koji Yakusho and siblings Aoi and Masaru Miyazaki, who are the only survivors of a tragic bus hijacking. Two years after the incident, Yakusho seeks out the traumatised teenagers and suggests a cross-country journey to salve their damaged souls. Aoyama's meditation on redemption allows for a measured discussion of memory, regret and the gradual erosion of cultural identity, while the decision to print Masaki Tamura's CinemaScope imagery in monochrome enhances the action's ethereal aura. DP. In Japanese with English subtitles. DVD

Koji Yakusho *Makoto Sawai* • Aoi Miyazaki *Kozue Tamura* • Masaru Miyazaki *Naoki Tamura* • Yohichiroh Saitoh *Akihiko* • Sayuri Kokusho *Yumiko* • Ken Mitsuishi *Shigeo* ■ *Dir/Scr* Shinji Aoyama

Eureka Stockade ★★ U

Adventure 1949 · UK · BW · 101mins

This is the story of the clashes between police and miners during the Australian gold rush of the 1850s after the government tried to restrict the miners' freedom of movement. Chips Rafferty plays the sharpest thorn in the authorities' side, but despite the obvious research and the efforts at authenticity, it's a stodgy film that hasn't worn the years well. AT

Chips Rafferty *Peter Lalor* • Jane Barrett *Alicia Dunne* • Jack Lambert *Commissioner Rede* • Peter Illing *Raffaello* • Gordon Jackson *Tom Kennedy* • Ralph Truman *Gov Hotham* • Sydney Loder *Vern* • John Fernside *Sly grog seller* ■ *Dir* Harry Watt • *Scr* Harry Watt, Walter Greenwood, from a story by Harry Watt

Europa ★★★★ 15

Political thriller
1991 · Den · Colour and BW · 107mins

Lars von Trier's mesmerising study of a defeated nation is a bold and imaginative attempt to fuse Kafkaesque paranoia with a mix of visual styles. Max von Sydow's opening narration, when combined with hypnotic shots of a maze of railway tracks, creates an atmosphere of uncertainty that pervades the rest of the picture. Jean-Marc Barr gives a suitably wide-eyed performance as the American sleeping-car conductor caught between the occupying Allies, Nazi partisans and the railway company in postwar Germany. DP. In English and German with subtitles. Contains violence. VIDEO DVD

Jean-Marc Barr *Leopold Kessler* • Barbara Sukowa *Katharina Hartmann* • Udo Kier *Lawrence Hartmann* • Ernst-Hugo Jaregard *Uncle Kessler* • Erik Merk *Pater* • Jørgen Reenberg *Max Hartmann* • Henning Jensen *Siggy* • Eddie Constantine *Colonel Harris* • Max von Sydow *Narrator* ■ *Dir* Lars von Trier • *Scr* Lars von Trier, Niels Vorsel

Europa, Europa ★★★★ 15

Second World War biography
1991 · Fr/Ger · Colour · 107mins

This extraordinary story proves once again that truth is stranger than fiction. Marco Hofschneider is hugely impressive as Salomon Perel, the Jewish teenager who fled to Soviet-occupied Poland to escape the Nazi tyranny, only to become accepted as a loyal Aryan after he was captured by the advancing Germans. Agonisingly hiding the physical clues to his extraction, he becomes a hero of the Hitler Youth and even manages to romance rabid anti-Semite Julie Delpy. Holland's wonderfully understated direction allows the cruel ironies to bite harder and she makes chilling use of the paraphernalia of totalitarianism. DP. In German with English subtitles. Contains nudity. VIDEO DVD

Marco Hofschneider *Young Salomon Perel* • Julie Delpy *Leni* • André Wilms *Robert* • Salomon Perel *Old Salomon Perel* • Ashley Wanninger *Gerd* • René Hofschneider *Isaak Perel* • Piotr Kozlowski *David Perel* ■ *Dir* Agnieszka Holland • *Scr* Agnieszka Holland, from the memoirs by Salomon Perel

Europa '51 ★★★

Drama 1952 · It · BW · 118mins

This is probably the best of the four spiritual melodramas Ingrid Bergman made with her husband Roberto Rossellini. Bergman plays a superficial American society woman living in Rome who believes she is the cause of her young son's suicide. She seeks salvation by tending the poor and the sick, much to the incomprehension of her bourgeois husband (Alexander Knox). Giulietta Masina plays a factory girl whom Bergman rescues. Rossellini's unfussy direction creates a genuine feeling of spirituality. RB. In Italian with English subtitles.

Ingrid Bergman *Irene Girard* • Alexander Knox *George Girard* • Ettore Giannini *Andrea* • Giulietta Masina *Passerotto* • Sandro Franchina *Michele* • Teresa Pellati *Ines* ■ *Dir* Roberto Rossellini • *Scr* Roberto Rossellini, Sandro De Leo, Mario Pannunzio, Ivo Perilli, Brunello Rondi, Diego Fabbri, Donald Ogden Stewart (English dialogue)

The Europeans ★★★★ U

Period drama 1979 · UK · Colour · 87mins

James Ivory came closer than anyone to translating the near-unfilmable Henry James to the screen with this beautifully-judged drama. Aided, as ever, by the impeccable production values of Ismail Merchant and the intelligent writing of Ruth Prawer Jhabvala, Ivory's take on cross-continental snobbery is deliciously played by an immaculate, if unfamiliar cast. Returning to 1850s Boston, Lee Remick expertly keeps the lid on a performance that begged extravagance, thus ensuring that her gold-digging countess remains sympathetic for all her schemes and jibes. Elegant, witty and highly literate. DP VIDEO DVD

Lee Remick *Eugenia* • Robin Ellis *Robert Acton* • Wesley Addy *Mr Wentworth* • Tim Choate *Clifford Wentworth* • Lisa Eichhorn *Gertrude Wentworth* • Nancy New *Charlotte Wentworth* • Kristin Griffith *Lizzie Acton* ■ *Dir* James Ivory • *Scr* Ruth Prawer Jhabvala, from the novel by Henry James

EuroTrip ★★★ 15

Comedy 2004 · US · Colour · 88mins

There's something to offend almost everybody in this raucous and rude teen sex comedy in which an American student (Scott Mechlowitz) embarks on a trip across Europe in search of an internet friend he has accidentally dumped, believing her to be a he. In the process every European stereotype is wheeled out, but despite the gleefully crude xenophobia there are enough laughs in this good-natured follow-up to 2000's *Road Trip* to keep the less easily shocked amused. AS. Contains swearing, sex scenes and nudity. VIDEO DVD

Scott Mechlowicz *Scotty Thomas* • Michelle Trachtenberg *Jenny* • Jacob Pitts *Cooper Harris* • Travis Wester *Jamie* • Jessica Boehrs *Mieke* • Lucy Lawless *Madame Vandersexxx* • Vinnie Jones *Mad Maynard* • Matt Damon *Donny* • Kristin Kreuk *Fiona* ■ *Dir* Jeff Schaffer • *Scr* Alec Berg, David Mandel, Jeff Schaffer

Eva ★★★★ 15

Drama 1962 · Fr/It · BW · 104mins

This simmering study of obsession provides Jeanne Moreau with one of the meatiest roles of her career. As the ruthless opportunist exploiting the weakness of successful novelist Stanley Baker, she presents in many ways the darker side of Catherine, the character she played the previous year in François Truffaut's *Jules et Jim* – a perfect woman whose middle name is trouble. It's as if Michelangelo Antonioni had decided to make a *film noir*, as director Joseph Losey turns Venice into a city of lost souls, over which hangs the sour odour of lust and greed. DP VIDEO

Jeanne Moreau *Eva Olivier* • Stanley Baker *Tyvian* • Virna Lisi *Francesca Ferrara* • Giorgio Albertazzi *Braneo Maloni* • James Villiers *Arthur McCormick* • Riccardo Garrone *Michele* • Lisa Gastoni *The redhead* • Checco Rissone *Pieri* ■ *Dir* Joseph Losey • *Scr* Hugo Butler, Evan Jones, from the novel *Eve* by James Hadley Chase

Eve and the Handyman ★ PG

Sex comedy 1961 · US · Colour · 64mins

Sex film pioneer Russ Meyer's follow-up to his classic nudie-cutie *Immoral Mr Teas* is another leering peep show featuring his then wife Eve in all the pin-up roles. She's a ribald detective shadowing comic handyman Anthony-James Ryan as he plies his trade among beatnik artists, saucy hitch-hikers and naked sunbathers. Barely watchable in these more enlightened times, this may be of quaint historical interest to those into glamour magazine nostalgia. AJ VIDEO

Anthony-James Ryan *Handyman* • Eve Meyer *Eve* ■ *Dir/Scr* Russ Meyer

Eve of Destruction ★ 18

Science-fiction thriller
1991 · US · Colour · 95mins

This female version of *The Terminator* features an eye-catching performance from Dutch star Renée Soutendijk as a scientist who creates a cyborg in her own image, which then runs amok with a thermonuclear bomb in its womb. Gregory Hines plays the cop tracking her down, while Duncan Gibbins directs with some verve. However, the interesting premise isn't explored amid the explosions and fifth-rate effects. RS VIDEO

Gregory Hines *Jim McQuade* • Renée Soutendijk *Dr Eve Simmons/Eve VIII* • Michael Greene *General Curtis* • Kurt Fuller *Schneider* • John M Jackson *Peter Arnold* • Loren Haynes *Steve the robot* ■ *Dir* Duncan Gibbins • *Scr* Duncan Gibbins, Yale Udoff

The Eve of St Mark ★★★

Second World War drama
1944 · US · BW · 96mins

Maxwell Anderson's flag-waving Broadway play was a key wartime work, written in a form of blank verse and extremely emotive for an audience with sons and relatives at war immediately after Pearl Harbor. To its credit, the movie doesn't greatly expand the piece, although it does expurgate some of the original dialogue. The barrack room scenes in particular convey the heartfelt feelings of the time, despite serious undercasting owing to the fact that 20th Century-Fox's top leading men were themselves in the forces. TS

Anne Baxter *Janet Feller* • William Eythe *Private Quizz West* • Michael O'Shea *Private Thomas Mulveray* • Vincent Price *Private Francis Marion* • Ruth Nelson *Nell West* • Ray Collins *Deckman West* • Stanley Prager *Private Glinka* • Henry Morgan [Harry Morgan] *Private Shevlin* ■ *Dir* John M Stahl • *Scr* George Seaton, from the play by Maxwell Anderson

Evel Knievel ★★

Biographical drama
1971 · US · Colour · 88mins

George Hamilton stars as the famed daredevil motorcyclist, reflecting on major events that have shaped his life in this mildly diverting film biography of one of the great cultural figures of the 1970s. The script is guilty of too much cod philosophising, but Marvin J Chomsky's film is redeemed by some truly wonderful stock footage of Knievel in action. This is not to be confused with *Viva Knievel!*, which appeared six years later and featured the man playing himself. RS

George Hamilton *Evel Knievel* • Sue Lyon *Linda* • Bert Freed *Doc Kincaid* • Rod Cameron *Charlie Kresson* • Dub Taylor *Turquoise Smith* ■ *Dir* Marvin J Chomsky • *Scr* Alan Caillou, John Milius

Evelyn ★★★ PG

Drama based on a true story
2002 · Ire/UK/US/Ger · Colour · 90mins

Triumph-over-adversity stories don't come much more manipulative than this syrupy, true-life drama set in 1950s Ireland. A warm, if contrived, account of paternal love, this stars Pierce Brosnan as a charismatic single father struggling to bring up a trio of cutesy kids after his wife abandons them. Doyle is devastated when the authorities force his brood into care and what follows is a poignant, albeit predictable, courtroom battle to get them back. Endearing performances add colour and weight to an essentially simplistic tale. SF VIDEO DVD

Pierce Brosnan *Desmond Doyle* • Aidan Quinn *Nick Barron* • Julianna Margulies *Bernadette Beattie* • Sophie Vavasseur *Evelyn Doyle* • Alan Bates *Tom Connolly* • Hugh McDonagh *Maurice Doyle* • Frank Kelly *Henry Doyle* ■ *Dir* Bruce Beresford • *Scr* Paul Pender

Evelyn Prentice ★★★

Mystery melodrama 1934 · US · BW · 78mins

Star power makes this overheated soap opera of infidelity, murder and courtroom revelations seem better than it is. William Powell and Myrna Loy were teamed for the third time in this tale of a lawyer, suspected of philandering by his wife, who promptly gets involved with a blackmailing gigolo. The plot convolutions stretch credibility to breaking point, but the film is saved by its cast. Rosalind Russell makes her screen debut as a client of Powell's. TV

William Powell *John Prentice* • Myrna Loy *Evelyn Prentice* • Una Merkel *Amy Drexel* • Rosalind Russell *Nancy Harrison* • Isabel Jewell *Judith Wilson* • Harvey Stephens *Lawrence Kennard* • Edward Brophy *Eddie Delaney* ■ *Dir* William K Howard • *Scr* Lenore Coffee, from the novel by WE Woodward

Even Cowgirls Get the Blues ★★ 15

Comedy adventure
1993 · US · Colour · 92mins

In this misfiring comedy, Uma Thurman is lumbered with the role of a fashion model with abnormally long thumbs, who takes to hitch-hiking and ends up at the Rubber Rose Ranch, which is inhabited by lesbian cowgirls. Adapted from a bizarre novel by Tom Robbins, it's a belated flower-power idea that's decidedly below par. A miscalculation for director Gus Van Sant. TH VIDEO

Uma Thurman *Sissy Hankshaw* • Lorraine Bracco *Delores Del Ruby* • Noriyuki "Pat" Morita [Pat Morita] *The Chink* • Angie Dickinson *Miss Adrian* • Keanu Reeves *Julian Gitchie* • John Hurt *The Countess* • Rain Phoenix *Bonanza Jellybean* • Ed Begley Jr *Rupert* • Carol Kane *Carla* • Sean Young *Marie Barth* • Crispin Glover *Howard Barth* • Roseanne Arnold [Roseanne Barr] *Madame Zoe* • Buck Henry *Dr Dreyfus* • Grace Zabriskie *Mrs Hankshaw* • Heather Graham *Cowgirl Heather* ■ *Dir* Gus Van Sant • *Scr* Gus Van Sant, from the novel by Tom Robbins

Even Dwarfs Started Small ★★★ PG

Drama 1970 · W Ger · BW · 89mins

With this, his second feature film, Werner Herzog joined the elite of the new German cinema. Like his debut, *Signs of Life* (1968), the movie is set on an island, here used as a penal colony, and the allegorical story illuminates Herzog's unflattering view of humankind. The volcanic terrain houses only dwarfs, who indulge in increasingly rebellious acts against authority. Herzog made better films and documentaries than this darkly comic attack on institutionalism, but this disturbing work foreshadows his later extremism. BB. In German with English subtitles. VIDEO

Helmut Döring *Hombre* • Gerd Gickel *Pepe* • Paul Glauer *Deputy* • Erna Gschwendtner *Azucar* ■ *Dir/Scr* Werner Herzog

The Evening Star ★★★ 15

Drama 1996 · US · Colour · 123mins

This disappointing but still interesting sequel to *Terms of Endearment* picks up the story more than a decade later. Shirley MacLaine returns as eccentric matriarch Aurora, now of pensionable age but just as feisty as she struggles to bring up her late daughter's children. Despite a brief cameo from MacLaine's fellow *Endearment* Oscar-winner Jack Nicholson, and strong performances by Juliette Lewis and Miranda Richardson, this never truly sparkles, largely due to a lacklustre script, but it does touch the heart. JB. Contains swearing, nudity. [video]

Shirley MacLaine *Aurora Greenway* • Bill Paxton *Jerry Bruckner* • Juliette Lewis *Melanie Horton* • Miranda Richardson *Patsy Carpenter* • Ben Johnson *Arthur Cotton* • Jack Nicholson *Garrett Breedlove* • Scott Wolf *Bruce* • George Newbern *Tommy Horton* • Marion Ross *Rosie Dunlop* ■ *Dir* Robert Harling • *Scr* Robert Harling, from the novel by Larry McMurtry

Evensong ★★★ U

Musical drama 1934 · UK · BW · 81mins

Evelyn Laye plays an Irish opera singer pursued by the likes of handsome Archduke Carl Esmond. Some may find this saga poignant; others will think it unbearably silly and slow. However, Fritz Kortner makes a powerful contribution as the impresario, and if you peer hard enough you'll spot Alec Guinness in a small role. It's impossible not to enjoy a film that contains dialogue such as "My cousin has been assassinated at Sarajevo – God only knows what this is going to lead to!" TS [video]

Evelyn Laye *Irela/Maggie O'Neil* • Fritz Kortner *Kober* • Alice Delysia *Mme Valmond* • Carl Esmond *Archduke Theodore* • Emlyn Williams *George Murray* • Muriel Aked *Tremlowe* • Patrick O'Moore *Bob McNeil* • Alec Guinness *Soldier* ■ *Dir* Victor Saville • *Scr* Edward Knoblock, Dorothy Farnum, from the play by Edward Knoblock, Beverley Nichols, from the novel by Beverley Nichols

Event Horizon ★★★ 18

Science-fiction horror
1997 · US/UK · Colour · 91mins

This is an enjoyable slice of space splatter from British director Paul Anderson. The *Event Horizon* of the title is an experimental spacecraft that has been missing for years but has just been located. A rescue team, led by Laurence Fishburne, is sent to retrieve it, but it soon becomes apparent that it's in the grip of a malevolent force. Fishburne, Sam Neill, Joely Richardson and Sean Pertwee bring some class to the determinedly B-movie dialogue, and Anderson delivers some nasty sequences that will please horror fans. JF. Contains violence, swearing, nudity. [video] DVD

Laurence Fishburne *Miller* • Sam Neill *Weir* • Kathleen Quinlan *Peters* • Joely Richardson *Starck* • Richard T Jones *Cooper* • Jason Isaacs *DJ* • Sean Pertwee *Smith* ■ *Dir* Paul Anderson • *Scr* Philip Eisner

Ever After: a Cinderella Story ★★★★ PG

Romantic fantasy
1998 · US · Colour · 116mins

As Baz Luhrmann did with *William Shakespeare's Romeo + Juliet*, director Andy Tennant brings new freshness and vitality to the Cinderella story in a delightful reworking that treats the legend as if it were hard historical fact. All the pantomime sorcery and comical sidekicks have been jettisoned, and the result allows the romance between feisty servant girl Drew Barrymore and Dougray Scott's handsome prince to shine even brighter. Anjelica Huston re-interprets the evil stepmother role with deft assurance, and Leonardo da Vinci makes a surprising fairy godmother figure. A handsomely mounted epic. AJ. Contains swearing. [video] DVD

Drew Barrymore *Danielle* • Anjelica Huston *Baroness Rodmilla* • Dougray Scott *Prince Henry* • Patrick Godfrey *Leonardo da Vinci* • Megan Dodds *Marguerite* • Melanie Lynskey *Jacqueline* • Timothy West *King Francis* • Judy Parfitt *Queen Marie* ■ *Dir* Andy Tennant • *Scr* Andy Tennant, Susannah Grant, Rick Parks, from the story *Cinderella* by Charles Perrault

Ever in My Heart ★★

Drama 1933 · US · BW · 70mins

This far-fetched weepie presents Barbara Stanwyck as an upper-crust New Englander defiantly marrying a good German who's forced by anti-Hun fervour to return home during the First World War. They meet again: she as a frontline canteen worker, he as a German spy. Ever-reliable Stanwyck gives it all she's got and almost manages to draw some warmth from Otto Kruger as the love of her life, but the cursory direction of Archie Mayo deprives it of any real impact. AE

Barbara Stanwyck *Mary Archer* • Otto Kruger *Hugo Wilbrandt* • Ralph Bellamy *Jeff* • Ruth Donnelly *Lizzie* • Laura Hope Crews *Grandma Archer* • Frank Albertson *Sam* • Ronnie Crosby *Teddy* • Clara Blandick *Anna* ■ *Dir* Archie Mayo • *Scr* Bertram Milhauser, from a story by Beulah Marie Dix, Bertram Milhauser

Evergreen ★★★ U

Musical comedy 1934 · UK · BW · 89mins

Unquestionably British musical star Jessie Matthews's most popular movie, a Michael Balcon-produced trifle directed by Victor Saville about a girl posing as her own music-hall star mum, a situation which naturally evokes complications when romance arrives. Jessie is quite lovely, sumptuously photographed by Glen MacWilliams, and given to wearing endearing see-through gowns. TS [video]

Jessie Matthews *Harriet Green/Harriet's daughter* • Sonnie Hale *Leslie Benn* • Betty Balfour *Maudie* • Barry Mackay *Tommy Thompson* • Ivor MacLaren *Marquis of Staines* • Hartley Power *Treadwell* • Patrick Ludlow *Lord Shropshire* • Betty Shale *Mrs Hawkes* ■ *Dir* Victor Saville • *Scr* Emlyn Williams, Marjorie Gaffney, from the play by Benn W Levy

An Everlasting Piece ★★★★ 15

Comedy 2000 · US · Colour · 99mins

Belfast in the 1980s is the somewhat unlikely setting for director Barry Levinson's eccentric comedy. Barry McEvoy (who also wrote the hilarious script) and Brian F O'Byrne work as hairdressers in a prison asylum, relieving their boredom with lame attempts at poetry. When deranged hairpiece kingpin Billy Connolly (an all-too-brief cameo) is incarcerated, the pair decide to go into business as the "Piece People". With much-needed help from McEvoy's mouthy girlfriend (an ebullient performance from Anna Friel), they soon find themselves in competition with some ludicrously named rivals. Mining a broad vein of comedy, the action moves swiftly without descending into total farce. SS. Contains swearing. [video] DVD

Barry McEvoy *Colm O'Neill* • Brian F O'Byrne *George* • Anna Friel *Bronagh* • Pauline McLynn *Gerty* • Billy Connolly *Scalper* ■ *Dir* Barry Levinson • *Scr* Barry McEvoy

Eversmile, New Jersey ★★ PG

Road movie 1989 · Arg/UK · Colour · 87mins

This production must rank as one of the most unusual entries on the CV of star Daniel Day-Lewis. He plays a bike-riding dentist preaching the gospel of good dental hygiene with missionary zeal in the most far-flung parts of Argentina. The film's quirkiness is initially rather appealing, but it rapidly palls. DA [video] DVD

Daniel Day-Lewis *Fergus O'Connell* • Mirjana Jokovic *Estela* • Gabriela Acher *Celeste* • Ignacio Quiros *The "Boss"* • Boy Olmi *Radio announcer* • Alberto Benegas *Sheriff* • Ruben Patagonia *Butler* • Matias Puelles *Child* • Eduardo Santoro *Party guest* ■ *Dir* Carlos Sorin • *Scr* Jorge Goldenberg, Roberto Sheuer, Carlos Sorin

Every Breath ★★★ 18

Erotic thriller 1993 · US · Colour · 84mins

Above average, straight-to-video thriller which places more emphasis on suspense than steamy thrills. Judd Nelson plays an out-of-work actor who gets caught up in a bizarre love triangle with the beautiful Joanna Pacula and her rich husband, Patrick Bauchau. You can see the plot twists coming a mile off, but it's put together with some style, and Bauchau steals every scene he's in. JF [video]

Judd Nelson *Jimmy* • Joanna Pacula *Lauren* • Patrick Bauchau *Richard* • Willie Garson *Bob* • Rebeca Arthur *Mimi* • John Pyper Ferguson *Hal* • Cynthia Brimhall *Kris* • Kathleen Beaton *Kim* ■ *Dir* Steve Bing • *Scr* Andrew Fleming, Steve Bing, Judd Nelson

Every Day's a Holiday ★★★

Comedy 1937 · US · BW · 78mins

Deprived of her salty dialogue by the censors, there's little Mae West can do but sing and flounce, but she still does it better than anybody else. In this average vehicle, she's a delight, disguised as a French singer to escape New York detective Edmund Lowe because she sold Herman Bing the Brooklyn Bridge. Lloyd Nolan plays Lowe's crooked boss and there's a rare glimpse of Louis Armstrong for good measure. TS

Mae West *Peaches O'Day* • Edmund Lowe *Captain Jim McCarey* • Charles Butterworth *Larmadou Graves* • Charles Winninger *Von Reighle Van Pelter Van Doon* • Walter Catlett *Nifty Bailey* • Lloyd Nolan *Honest John Quade* • Louis Armstrong • Herman Bing *Fritz Krausmeyer* ■ *Dir* A Edward Sutherland • *Scr* Mae West

Every Day's a Holiday ★★ U

Musical comedy 1964 · UK · Colour · 89mins

Director James Hill's attempt to take the Swinging Sixties to the seaside is often laughably bad. John Leyton is the nominal star of this talent-show farrago, although the musical headliners are Freddie and the Dreamers, who were trying to match the movie achievements of the Beatles in *A Hard Day's Night*. However, no film with cinematography by Nicolas Roeg can be dismissed out of hand, and Ron Moody and Liz Fraser provide accomplished comic support. DP [video]

Freddie and the Dreamers *The Chefs* • John Leyton *Gerry Pullman* • Mike Sarne [Michael Sarne] *Timothy Gilbin* • Ron Moody *Professor Bastinado* • Liz Fraser *Miss Slightly* • Grazina Frame *Christina Barrington de Witt* • Susan Baker *Susan* ■ *Dir* James Hill • *Scr* Anthony Marriott, Jeri Matos, James Hill, from the story by Anthony Marriott

Every Girl Should Be Married ★★ U

Romantic comedy 1948 · US · BW · 81mins

This lightweight movie was the 55th of Cary Grant's 74 films, and the star used his considerable sway to cast his future wife Betsy Drake in the female lead. This film is an unworthy vehicle: it's not only the title that renders it desperately old-fashioned in today's post-feminist world, but there's also a rather unpalatable plotline about a paediatrician (Grant) and a department store clerk (Drake) who wants to get married at all costs. TS [video]

Cary Grant *Dr Madison Brown* • Betsy Drake *Anabel Sims* • Franchot Tone *Roger Sanford* • Diana Lynn *Julie Hudson* • Alan Mowbray *Mr Spitzer* • Elisabeth Risdon *Mary Nolan* ■ *Dir* Don Hartman • *Scr* Stephen Morehouse Avery, Don Hartman, from a story by Eleanor Harris

Every Home Should Have One ★ 15

Comedy 1970 · UK · Colour · 93mins

This dismal comedy was co-scripted by Marty Feldman, Barry Took and Denis Norden, and it boasts a top-notch comic cast. But their efforts are totally overshadowed by a shambolic, leering performance from Feldman, making only his second screen appearance, as a mad advertising executive who devises a series of steamy commercials for a brand of frozen porridge. DP. Contains swearing, sex scenes and brief nudity. [video]

Marty Feldman *Teddy* • Shelley Berman *Nat Kaplan* • Judy Cornwell *Liz* • Julie Ege *Inga Giltenberg* • Patrick Cargill *Wallace Trufitt MP* • Jack Watson *McLaughlin* • Patience Collier *Mrs Levin* • Penelope Keith *Lotte von Gelbstein* • Dinsdale Landen *Reverend Mellish* ■ *Dir* Jim Clark • *Scr* Marty Feldman, Barry Took, Denis Norden, from a story by Milton Shulman, Herman Kretzmer

Every Little Crook and Nanny ★★★

Comedy 1972 · US · Colour · 92mins

A glorious piece of self-guying from Victor Mature illuminates this hit-and-miss mob comedy, though we don't spend nearly enough time in his company. Instead we get Lynn Redgrave, mugging for all she's worth, as a nanny who abducts the son of a Mafia godfather (guess who?). If only Cy Howard had written himself a better script; he might not have had to direct with such frenetic energy. But it's worth waiting for the odd sightings of Mature, whose knowing performance compares favourably with the fading film star he played in *After the Fox*. DP

Lynn Redgrave *Miss Poole, Nanny* • Victor Mature *Carmine Ganucci* • Paul Sand *Benny Napkins* • Maggie Blye *Stella* • Austin Pendleton *Luther* • John Astin *Garbugli* • Dom DeLuise *Azzecca* • Louise Sorel *Marie* • Phillip Graves *Lewis Ganucci* ■ *Dir* Cy Howard • *Scr* Cy Howard, Jonathan Axelrod, Robert Klane, from a novel by Ed McBain [Evan Hunter]

Every Picture Tells a Story ★★ PG

Biographical drama
1984 · UK · Colour · 82mins

Director James Scott recalls the troubled adolescence that helped shape his father William's sensibilities in this portrait of the artist as a young man. It begins as an unsentimental study of working-class life in Scotland and Northern Ireland in the early 1920s. Phyllis Logan is typically assured as William's mother, and the trio playing the growing boy do well. Once Alex Norton (who plays Scott senior) departs the scene, however, the action starts to falter in this visually impressive but dramatically flawed film. DP

Phyllis Logan *Agnes Scott* • Alex Norton *William Scott Sr* • Leonard O'Malley *William aged 15-18* • John Docherty *William aged 11-14* • Mark Airlie *William aged 5-8* • Natasha Richardson *Miss Bridle* ■ *Dir* James Scott • *Scr* Shane Connaughton

Every Sunday ★★★ U

Musical 1936 · US · BW · 10mins

This enchanting featurette was designed by MGM as a screen test for young contractees Judy Garland and Deanna Durbin. They play a pair of teenage friends who save a Sunday afternoon park orchestra from closure by taking to the bandstand to modernise the repertoire, singing a song each and a duet. MGM ended up retaining Garland, while Durbin went off to Universal, where her string of hits saved the studio from bankruptcy. Historic, and a must for fans. RK

Judy Garland *Judy* • Deanna Durbin *Edna* ■ *Dir* Felix E Feist [Felix Feist] • *Scr* Mauri Grashin

Every Time We Say Goodbye ★★ 15

Romantic drama
1986 · US/Is · Colour · 93mins

After a string of comedy successes Tom Hanks took his first crack at something weightier in this modest romantic drama. He plays a Second World War pilot stationed near Jerusalem who falls for a local Jewish girl (Cristina Marsillach), much to the anger of her family. Hanks looks a little uncomfortable in the lead role and there are hardly any familiar faces in the supporting cast. However, director Moshe Mizrahi does pull the right emotional strings. JF

Tom Hanks *David* • Cristina Marsillach *Sarah* • Benedict Taylor *Peter* • Anat Atzmon *Victoria* • Gila Almagor *Lea* • Moni Moshanov *Nessin* ■ *Dir* Moshe Mizrahi • *Scr* Moshe Mizrahi, Rachel Fabien, Leah Appet, from a story by Moshe Mizrahi

Every Which Way but Loose ★★★ 15

Comedy drama 1978 · US · Colour · 109mins

Clint Eastwood cruises through this coarse comedy as a travelling prizefighter whose best buddy is a beer-swilling, lowlife orang-utan named Clyde. There are plenty of lively scenes to keep fans satisfied, and Eastwood just about manages to avoid being made a monkey of by his scene-stealing co-star. His romantic hankerings after country singer Sondra Locke don't add much to the brew, though. It did such good box-office that Eastwood was tempted back into a feeble sequel, *Any Which Way You Can*. DP. Contains violence, swearing and brief nudity.

Clint Eastwood *Philo Beddoe* • Sondra Locke *Lynn Halsey-Taylor* • Geoffrey Lewis *Orville* • Ruth Gordon *Ma* • Beverly D'Angelo *Echo* • Walter Barnes *Tank Murdock* • Sam Gilman *Fat man's friend* ■ *Dir* James Fargo • *Scr* Jeremy Joe Kronsberg

Everybody Does It ★★★ U

Comedy 1949 · US · BW · 97mins

This very funny remake of *Wife, Husband and Friend* sensibly retains Nunnally Johnson's clever script almost word for word, but is far better cast than that 1939 Loretta Young vehicle. Celeste Holm is simply terrific as a woman who wants to sing opera but can't, while Paul Douglas is no less fine as her husband, who *can* sing opera but doesn't! Elsewhere Linda Darnell is lovely as the local neighbourhood diva. This trifle is lightly directed by Edmund Goulding, and is consistantly amusing throughout. TS

Paul Douglas *Leonard Borland* • Linda Darnell *Cecil Carver* • Celeste Holm *Doris Borland* • Charles Coburn *Major Blair* • Millard Mitchell *Mike Craig* • Lucile Watson *Mrs Blair* • John Hoyt *Wilkins* • Leon Belasco *Hugo* ■ *Dir* Edmund Goulding • *Scr* Nunnally Johnson, from a story by James M Cain

Everybody Sing ★★★ U

Musical 1938 · US · BW · 91mins

Best-known today as a sparkling young Judy Garland flick, this was actually one of those "crazy family" movies so popular in the 1930s. Judy is the second daughter, to lovely Lynne Carver, of Reginald Owen and actress Billie Burke, who puts on a show with cook Fanny Brice and Allen Jones. Judy sings five numbers, all especially arranged for her by her mentor, the great Roger Edens, and reveals that magnificent talent that only a year later would make her an international star in *The Wizard of Oz*. TS

Allan Jones *Ricky Saboni* • Fanny Brice *Olga Chekaloff* • Judy Garland *Judy Bellaire* • Reginald Owen *Hillary Bellaire* • Billie Burke *Diana Bellaire* • Reginald Gardner *Jerrold Hope* • Lynne Carver *Sylvia Bellaire* • Monty Woolley *John Fleming* ■ *Dir* Edwin L Marin • *Scr* Florence Ryerson, Edgar Allan Woolf, James Gruen, from their story • *Music Director* Roger Edens

Everybody Wins ★ 15

Mystery drama 1990 · UK · Colour · 92mins

This is a sort of thriller, with Nick Nolte as a widowed private eye hired and then seduced by mysterious Debra Winger, who wants him to open up an old murder case. Winger is given reams of dialogue to declaim and some utterly unplayable scenes to wade through. Arthur Miller is a great playwright, but he can't write a decent screenplay. AT

Debra Winger *Angela Crispini* • Nick Nolte *Tom O'Toole* • Will Patton *Jerry* • Jack Warden *Judge Harry Murdoch* • Judith Ivey *Connie* • Frank Converse *Charlie Haggerty* • Kathleen Wilhoite *Amy* • Frank Military *Felix* ■ *Dir* Karel Reisz • *Scr* Arthur Miller

Everybody's All-American ★★★ 15

Drama 1988 · US · Colour · 121mins

Dennis Quaid plays a legendary American football star in this saga of sporting success and failure that begins in the Eisenhower era of flash cars, material plenty and patriotism. Quaid marries a local beauty queen (Jessica Lange), and the film charts 25 turbulent years in their lives. It's over-plotted, though Lange's performance, as always, lifts the essentially lightweight material. AT

Dennis Quaid *Gavin Grey* • Jessica Lange *Babs Rogers Grey* • Timothy Hutton *Donnie "Cake"* • John Goodman *Ed Lawrence* • Carl Lumbly *Narvel Blue* • Raymond Baker [Ray Baker] *Bolling Kiely* • Savannah Smith Boucher *Darlene Kiely* • Patricia Clarkson *Leslie Stone* ■ *Dir* Taylor Hackford • *Scr* Tom Rickman, from the novel by Frank Deford

Everybody's Baby: the Rescue of Jessica McClure ★★★ PG

Drama based on a true story
1989 · US · Colour · 90mins

A strong, highly experienced TV-movie cast here re-enacts the true story of a Texas toddler who plunged into a disused well. Though the ensuing nail-biting rescue attempt created world headlines, it has to be said that this is not a complicated tale and the ending is never in doubt. But, given those limitations, writer David Eyre Jr does a fine job of holding our interest until the thankfully robust finale. SH DVD

Beau Bridges *Richard Czeh* • Roxana Zal *Cissy McClure* • Pat Hingle *Fire Chief James Roberts* • Patty Duke *Carolyn Henry* • Will Oldham *Chip McClure* ■ *Dir* Mel Damski • *Scr* David Eyre Jr

Everybody's Fine ★★★ PG

Drama 1990 · It/Fr · Colour · 120mins

Marcello Mastroianni has a ball as an elderly father of five who travels all over Italy to visit his now grown-up clan and gets some shocks when he discovers his children haven't quite turned out as he expected. There's a welcome appearance by Michèle Morgan as a Rimini widow, but this is predominantly a showcase for the delightful Mastroianni, who makes the most of the opportunity. Director/co-writer Giuseppe Tornatore finds room for sentimentality in an otherwise cynical tale. AT. In Italian with English subtitles.

Marcello Mastroianni *Matteo Scuro* • Michèle Morgan *Woman on train* • Marino Cenna *Canio* • Roberto Nobile *Guglielmo* • Valeria Cavalli *Tosca* • Norma Martelli *Norma* ■ *Dir* Giuseppe Tornatore • *Scr* Giuseppe Tornatore, Tonino Guerra, Massimo De Rita, from a story by Giuseppe Tornatore

Everyone Says I Love You ★★★★ 12

Musical comedy 1996 · US · Colour · 96mins

This musical from Woody Allen dares to be different – none of the cast can sing. This is a comedy of frustrated emotions, in which Allen tries to woo Julia Roberts, his ex-wife (played by Goldie Hawn) takes charge of an ex-convict and her daughter (Drew Barrymore) is absorbed by teenage angst. Despite revisiting the usual Allen themes, this is a bold departure from the norm. Characters suddenly launch into songs and there's a wonderful dance sequence on the banks of the Seine, but the lack of musical skills can be a little distracting. The result, though, is strangely endearing. TH. Contains swearing. DVD

Woody Allen *Joe* • Alan Alda *Bob* • Goldie Hawn *Steffi* • Julia Roberts *Von* • Drew Barrymore *Skylar* • Edward Norton *Holden* • Natasha Lyonne *DJ* • Gaby Hoffmann *Lane* • Natalie Portman *Laura* • Lukas Haas *Scott* • Tim Roth *Charles Ferry* ■ *Dir/Scr* Woody Allen

Everything I Have Is Yours ★★ U

Musical 1952 · US · Colour · 91mins

Sumptuously Technicolored starring vehicle for the marvellous MGM dance team of Marge and Gower Champion, who shot to fame together in the smash hit *Show Boat* the previous year. Unfortunately, all the MGM gloss in the world can't help this frankly tasteless tale of a pregnant Marge wondering if partner Gower is faithful. There are, though, some knockout dance numbers along the way. TS

Marge Champion *Pamela Hubbard* • Gower Champion *Chuck Hubbard* • Dennis O'Keefe *Alec Tackabury* • Monica Lewis *Sybil Meriden* • Dean Miller *Monty Dunston* • Eduard Franz *Phil Meisner* • Elaine Stewart *Showgirl* ■ *Dir* Robert Z Leonard • *Scr* George Wells

Everything Is Thunder ★★★

First World War drama
1936 · UK/US · BW · 77mins

This oddly titled film struck a chord with the great writer (and film critic) Graham Greene, who identified with the original novel's complicated plot involving disguises, human frailty and men in hiding, fearful of discovery by the police and betrayal. Constance Bennett is cast as a prostitute (only hinted at because of censorship rules) who helps Canadian officer and PoW Douglass Montgomery escape. There's a twist, involving her lover's sacrifice, that contributes to the pace of this intelligent entertainment. BB

Constance Bennett *Anna* • Douglass Montgomery *Hugh McGrath* • Oscar Homolka *Detective Goertz* • Roy Emerton *Kostner* • Frederick Lloyd *Muller* ■ *Dir* Milton Rosmer • *Scr* Marion Dix, John Orton, from a novel by Jocelyn L Hardy

Everything Put Together ★★

Drama 2000 · US · Colour · 87mins

This harrowing movie from director Marc Forster begins with the exploration of the agony of losing a newborn baby to Sudden Infant Death Syndrome. But while Radha Mitchell's display of emotion is excruciating to watch, the narrative and style of the piece – it's shot on digital video – are less impressive. Forster is too dependent on cheap visual tricks to suggest Mitchell's teetering sanity, and he seems more interested in achieving a pseudo-horror atmosphere than considering emotional implications. DP. Contains swearing.

Radha Mitchell *Angie* • Justin Louis *Russ* • Megan Mullally *Barbie* • Catherine Lloyd Burns *Judith* • Matt Malloy *Dr Reiner* • Michele Hicks *April* • Mark Boone Junior *Bill* • Judy Geeson *Angie's mother* • Alan Ruck *Kessel* ■ *Dir* Marc Forster • *Scr* Catherine Lloyd Burns, Marc Forster, Adam Forgash

Everything That Rises ★★★★ PG

Western drama 1998 · US · Colour · 90mins

A heart-warming and uplifting look at the harsh struggles faced by contemporary American farmers. Dennis Quaid and Mare Winningham are the credible heroes of this gritty TV movie, who face the challenges and seemingly insurmountable obstacles placed before them, including their son's disability and bank loan problems, with vim, vigour and personal sacrifice. Beautifully acted, this realistic drama makes for refreshing, thought-provoking and compelling viewing. AJ

Dennis Quaid *Jim Clay* • Mare Winningham *Kyle Clay* • Harve Presnell *Garth* • Meat Loaf *Red* • Ryan Merriman *Nathan Clay* • Bruce McGill *Alan Jamison* • Denise Durham *Red's wife* ■ *Dir* Dennis Quaid • *Scr* Mark Spragg

Everything You Always Wanted to Know about Sex ... but Were Afraid to Ask ★★★ 18

Comedy 1972 · US · Colour · 84mins

Woody Allen's third outing as actor/writer/director, made in the days when his films were largely an excuse to string together a relentless series of gags, is one of his least satisfying pictures. But this seven-story sex-manual parody does have its redeeming features. The razor-sharp Michelangelo Antonioni spoof and Lou Jacobi's ill-timed experiment in cross-dressing are neatly done, but Gene Wilder's affair with a sheep is rather woolly and the "What's My Perversion?" panel game quickly runs out of steam. The best is left to last, as Woody and his fellow sperms prepare to parachute to unknown glory. DP. Contains sex scenes. DVD

Woody Allen *Victor/Fabrizio/Fool/Sperm* • John Carradine *Doctor Bernardo* • Lou Jacobi *Sam* • Louise Lasser *Gina* • Anthony Quayle *King* • Tony Randall *Operator* • Lynn Redgrave *Queen* • Burt Reynolds *Switchboard* • Gene Wilder *Doctor Ross* • Jack Barry ■ *Dir* Woody Allen • *Scr* Woody Allen, from a non-fiction book by Dr David Reuben

Eve's Bayou ★★★★ 15

Drama 1997 · US · Colour and BW · 104mins

"The summer I killed my father, I was ten years old," begins this remarkable Louisiana-set drama, the promising debut of Kasi Lemmons. The hero/antihero is Dr Batiste (Samuel L Jackson), a loving father and womanising local physician who, one summer night in 1962, is not discreet enough in his philandering. Jackson is a charismatic presence, but the focus is on the women of the family, and Lemmons's impressive screenplay and direction allow her female cast to shine. Recollections play false in this Tennessee Williams-style story in which atmosphere is as important as drama. TH. Contains swearing.

Samuel L Jackson *Louis Batiste* • Lynn Whitfield *Roz Batiste* • Debbi Morgan *Mozelle Batiste Delacroix* • Vondie Curtis-Hall *Julian Grayraven* • Branford Marsalis *Harry Delacroix* • Lisa Nicole Carson *Matty Mereaux* • Meagan Good *Cisely Batiste* • Jurnee Smollett *Eve Batiste* ■ *Dir/Scr* Kasi Lemmons

The Evictors ★★ 18

Horror 1979 · US · Colour · 88mins

When city newly-weds rent a lonely farm in an isolated village in Arizona, the locals view them with distrust, while it appears the previous owners are refusing to stay buried. Director Charles B Pierce generates a convincing sense of place and community amid the requisite splatter, and the final twist is just good enough to catch you off guard. RS

Vic Morrow *Jake Rudd* • Michael Parks *Ben Watkins* • Jessica Harper *Ruth Watkins* • Sue Ane Langdon *Olie Gibson* • Dennis Fimple *Bumford* • Bill Thurman *Preacher Higgins* • Jimmy Clem *Buckner* • Harry Thomasson *Wheeler* ■ *Dir* Charles B Pierce • *Scr* Charles B Pierce, Paul Fisk, Garry Rusoff

Evidence of Love ★★★★ 18

Crime drama based on a true story
1990 · US · Colour · 90mins

This TV movie tells the true tale about a supposedly kindly, decent, devout Texas housewife who beat her best friend to death with an axe. The build-up and backdrop to this grim event are filtered through the trial with tremendous insight and a hefty dramatic punch by director Stephen Gyllenhaal. However, it is Barbara Hershey's soulful performance you'll remember. JM DVD

Barbara Hershey *Candy Morrison* • Brian Dennehy *Ed Reivers* • John Terry *Stan Blankenship* • Richard Gilliland *Dale Morrison* • Lee Garlington *Peggy Blankenship* • Hal Holbrook *Dr Beardsley* • Matthew Posey *Norman Billings* ■ *Dir* Stephen Gyllenhaal • *Scr* Cynthia Cidre, from the non-fiction book by John Bloom, Jim Atkinson

The Evil ★★

Horror 1978 · US · Colour · 89mins

Joanna Pettet and Richard Crenna want to convert an old mansion into a drug rehabilitation centre. Problem is it's packed with poltergeists, and when Crenna unleashes a hostile force in the cellar, their existence turns into a shutter-banging, corpse-finding nightmare. Victor Buono turns up at the entertaining climax in a white suit and horns as the Devil in this low-rent version of *The Haunting*. Shoddy special effects undercut most of the horror in this rather routine outing. AJ

Richard Crenna *CJ* • Joanna Pettet *Caroline* • Andrew Prine *Raymond* • Cassie Yates *Mary* • Lynne Moody *Felicia* • Victor Buono *The Devil* ■ *Dir* Gus Trikonis • *Scr* Donald G Thompson

Evil ★★★ 15

Period drama
2003 · Swe/Den · Colour · 113mins

In 1950s Sweden, Andreas Wilson plays an unruly teenager who is sent by his mother to a strict boarding school. There he finds an institution run by a cadre of sadistic prefects whose violent bullying is all but ignored by the staff. Wilson is more than serviceable as the plucky teen who must stand up both for himself and his friend Henrik Lundstrom. But, while competently acted and directed, this doesn't reveal anything new. AS. In Swedish with English subtitles. Contains violence and swearing.

Andreas Wilson *Erik Ponti* • Henrik Lundstrom *Pierre Tanguy* • Gustaf Skarsgard *Otto Silverhielm* • Linda Zilliacus *Marja* • Jesper Salen *Dahlen* • Filip Berg *Johan* • Johan Rabaeus *Erik's stepfather* • Marie Richardson *Erik's mother* ■ *Dir* Mikael Hafstrom • *Scr* Mikael Hafstrom, Hans Gunnarsson, from the novel *Ondskan* by Jan Guillou

The Evil beneath Loch Ness ★ 15

Action fantasy 2001 · US · Colour · 82mins

The Loch Ness Monster legend gets a farcically absurd overhaul in a rock-bottom monstrosity. Scientist Patrick Bergin is called in to investigate new sightings of Nessie and deals with the usual dire warnings from the locals and his ex-wife (Lysette Anthony, playing a character named Elizabeth "Lizzie" Borden!). Tedious juvenile tosh with the one pathetic special effect of the swimming monster repeated ad nauseam. AJ DVD

Patrick Bergin *Richard Blay* • Lysette Anthony *Elizabeth Borden* • Brian Wimmer *Case* • Lysa Apostle *Julie* ■ *Dir* Chuck Comisky • *Scr* Shane Bitterling, Justin Stanley

The Evil Dead ★★★★ 18

Horror 1983 · US · Colour · 79mins

Director Sam Raimi burst onto the horror scene with this crude cult favourite that's short on story but long on excessive gore and innovative camera work (future director Joel Coen was the assistant editor). An evil force tries to destroy five friends on vacation in a backwoods cabin when they discover an ancient Sumerian Book of the Dead. Cue all manner of vicious zombies, giggling ghouls and hideous demons going overboard in a relentless blood-splattering, pus-spurting attack. The only way to kill them is to hack them to pieces, so sit back and watch the body parts and viscera fly in this essential 1980s horror. AJ. Contains swearing and violence. DVD

Bruce Campbell *Ash* • Ellen Sandweiss *Cheryl* • Betsy Baker *Linda* • Hal Delrich *Scott* • Sarah York *Shelly* ■ *Dir/Scr* Sam Raimi

Evil Dead II ★★★ 18

Horror comedy 1987 · US · Colour · 80mins

Director Sam Raimi's thrill-packed heaven for gore-hounds starts with an embellished recap of the original film before spinning off into another possession tale, with hopeless hero Ash (Bruce Campbell) again trying to repel a nasty demonic onslaught. Flashy special effects, hysterical scare tactics and Three Stooges-style farce combine with Raimi's trademark dizzying camera angles and manic wit for a breathless roller-coaster ride through twisted genre conventions. A disappointing second sequel, *Army of Darkness*, followed. AJ DVD

Bruce Campbell *Ash* • Sarah Berry *Annie* • Dan Hicks [Danny Hicks] *Jake* • Kassie Wesley *Bobby Joe* • Theodore Raimi [Ted Raimi] *Possessed Henrietta* • Denise Bixler *Linda* • Richard Domeier *Ed* • John Peaks *Professor Raymond Knowby* • Lou Hancock *Henrietta* ■ *Dir* Sam Raimi • *Scr* Sam Raimi, Scott Spiegel

Evil Ed ★ 18

Horror comedy 1995 · Swe · Colour · 89mins

A young film editor is hired to censor the gruesome bits out of a horror series. He begins to lose his mind and turns into a murderer in this low-budget genre comedy from Sweden. Packed with fake gore, unfunny gags and dreadful acting, this film pays insulting lip-service the argument that screen violence leads to violent behaviour, which looks decidedly hollow in context. An unmemorable bust. AJ. Contains violence.

Johan Rudeback *Edward Svensson* • Olof Rhodin *Sam Campbell* • Gert Fylking *Nurse* • Per Loftberg *Nick* • Cecelia Ljung *Barbara* ■ *Dir* Anders Jacobsson • *Scr* Anders Jacobsson, Goran Lundstrom

Evil of Frankenstein ★★

Horror 1964 · UK · Colour · 86mins

The third of Hammer's *Frankenstein* films (after *The Curse of Frankenstein* and *The Revenge of Frankenstein*) and the least interesting of all. Peter Cushing lends his usual conviction to the mad doctor part, this time bringing his brain-damaged creation back to life with the help of a mesmerist. Lumbering direction by Freddie Francis matches the gait of New Zealand wrestler Kiwi Kingston as the bolted one. *Frankenstein Created Woman* (1966) continued the series. AJ

Peter Cushing *Baron Frankenstein* • Peter Woodthorpe *Zoltan* • Sandor Eles *Hans* • Kiwi Kingston *Creature* • Duncan Lamont *Chief of Police* • Katy Wild *Beggar girl* ■ *Dir* Freddie Francis • *Scr* John Elder

Evil Roy Slade ★★★★

Comedy western 1971 · US · Colour · 97mins

Penned by Garry Marshall and Jerry Belson, this under-rated, made-for-TV western spoof is a splendid showcase for John Astin who, apart from his stint as Gomez in *The Addams Family* TV series, never quite fulfilled his comic potential. Timing every set piece and throwaway gag with equal precision, he revels in the role of the west's most loathsome bandit, who is determined to go straight and win the heart of schoolteacher Pamela Austin. Milton Berle and Mickey Rooney are standouts, while Dick Shawn nearly steals the show as a hilariously incompetent lawman. DP

Mickey Rooney *Nelson Stool* • Dick Shawn *Marshal Bing Bell* • Henry Gibson *Clifford Stool* • Dom DeLuise *Logan Delp* • Edie Adams *Flossie* • Pamela Austin *Betsy Potter* • Milton Berle *Harry Fern* • John Astin *Evil Roy Slade* • Pat Morita *Turhan* • Penny Marshall *Bank teller* • John Ritter *Minister* ■ *Dir* Jerry Paris • *Scr* Jerry Belson, Garry Marshall

Evil Spirits ★★

Mystery horror 1991 · US · Colour · 95mins

Psycho undergoes a sex change, as batty landlady Karen Black is apparently bumping off her low-life boarders and banking their social security cheques, while psychically conversing with her husband's wheelchair-bound, mummified corpse. Supposedly a gory black comedy, the only laughs to be had are unintentional ones, although the above-average celebrity horror cast, including Hammer starlet Martine Beswick, plus the odd atmospheric gothic image, will hold the interest of genre enthusiasts. AJ

Karen Black *Mrs Purdy* • Michael Berryman *Mr Balzac* • Arte Johnson *Lester Potts* • Virginia Mayo *Mrs Wilson* • Martine Beswick *Vanya* • Bert Remsen *Mr Wilson* • Mikel Angel *Willie* ■ *Dir* Gary Graver • *Scr* Mikel Angel

The Evil That Men Do ★ 18

Action thriller 1984 · US · Colour · 85mins

With its numerous beatings and rapes, this repellent film surely ranks as Charles Bronson's most depraved picture – quite a feat! Ol' stone eyes stars as a professional hitman coaxed out of retirement to deal with a torturer working in an oppressed South American country. Action veteran J Lee Thompson suffers from muddled ethics – by taking the moral high ground, the film is guilty of revelling in the scenes of torture it supposedly decries. RS. Contains violence, swearing, drug abuse and nudity. DVD

Charles Bronson *Holland* • Theresa Saldana *Rhiana Hidalgo* • Joseph Maher *Dr Clement Molloch* • José Ferrer *Dr Hector Lomelin* • Rene Enriquez *Max Ortiz* • John Glover *Briggs* • Raymond St Jacques *Randolph* • Antoinette Bower *Claire* ■ *Dir* J Lee Thompson • *Scr* David Lee Henry, John Crowther, from the novel by Lance R Hill

The Evil Trap ★★★

Thriller 1975 · Fr · Colour · 93mins

Yves Boisset had several run-ins with the censor for the decidedly left-wing content of his grittily realistic *policiers*. However, suspense is more to the fore here, as governess Marlène Jobert searches for her young charge before she's framed for his murder by kidnapper Tomas Milian. Jobert exhibits the emotional fragility of a woman fresh out of a clinic, and Milian is a study in malevolence. But Thomas Waintrop is outstanding as the brattish tycoon's nephew who barely deserves rescuing. DP. French dialogue dubbed into English.

Marlène Jobert *Julie* • Tomas Milian *Thompson* • Thomas Waintrop *Thomas* • Michael Lonsdale [Michel Lonsdale] *Mostri* ■ *Dir* Yves Boisset • *Scr* Yves Boisset, from the novel *O Dingos, O Châteaux* by Jean-Patrick Manchette

Evil under the Sun ★★★ PG

Murder mystery 1982 · UK · Colour · 111mins

This is a typically polished whodunnit, which sees Peter Ustinov make his second appearance as the fussy Belgian detective Hercule Poirot. You won't use up too many little grey cells figuring out who is responsible for the murder of actress Diana Rigg, but there's enormous pleasure to be had from sitting through the picture while waiting to be proved right. Majorca looks hot, but it would have been nice if the producers had retained the original Cornish setting. DP DVD

Peter Ustinov *Hercule Poirot* • Colin Blakely *Sir Horace Blatt* • Jane Birkin *Christine Redfern* • Nicholas Clay *Patrick Redfern* • Maggie Smith *Daphne Castle* • Roddy McDowall *Rex Brewster* • Sylvia Miles *Myra Gardener* • James Mason *Odell Gardener* • Denis Quilley *Kenneth Marshall* • Diana Rigg *Arlena Marshall* ■ *Dir* Guy Hamilton • *Scr* Anthony Shaffer, from the novel by Agatha Christie

Evil Woman ★ 15

Comedy
2001 · US/Aus/Can · Colour · 92mins

Released under the title *Saving Silverman* in the US, this crass comedy has a splendidly surreal premise: Neil Diamond is enlisted by flatmates Jack Black and Steve Zahn to save buddy Jason Biggs from the matrimonial clutches of bunny-boiling girlfriend Amanda Peet. All promise and precious little delivery, this is mean-spirited, unfunny and overplayed. DA DVD

Jason Biggs *Darren Silverman* • Steve Zahn *Wayne* • Jack Black *J D* • Amanda Peet *Judith* • R Lee Ermey *Coach* • Amanda Detmer *Sandy* • Neil Diamond ■ *Dir* Dennis Dugan • *Scr* Hank Nelken, Greg DePaul

Evita ★★★ PG

Musical biography
1996 · US · Colour · 134mins

Madonna's most successful foray into movies, taken from one of the most successful musicals of recent years, casts her as the woman who became mother-figure to Argentina through marriage to President Juan Perón (Jonathan Pryce). Director Alan Parker eschews explanatory dialogue to link the music, resulting in a curiously airless and enigmatic piece which never involves us in the traumas of Evita or Argentina. Antonio Banderas, meanwhile, co-stars as the Everyman revolutionary whose appearance and reappearance in Evita's life is never fully explained. TH DVD

Madonna *Eva Perón* • Antonio Banderas *Ché* • Jonathan Pryce *Juan Perón* • Jimmy Nail *Agustín Magaldi* • Victoria Sus *Doña Juana* • Julian Littman *Brother Juan* • Olga Merediz *Blanca* • Laura Pallas *Elisa* • Andrea Corr *Perón's mistress* ■ *Dir* Alan Parker • *Scr* Alan Parker, Oliver Stone, from the musical by Andrew Lloyd Webber, Tim Rice

Evolution ★★★ PG

Science-fiction action comedy
2001 · US · Colour · 97mins

Ivan Reitman's lightweight but amiably daft science-fiction comedy features laid-back performances and a tongue-in-cheek approach, but it lacks wit and sparkle. Fortunately, it does boast the considerable comic charm of David Duchovny and Orlando Jones (as college professors), Seann William Scott (as an aspiring fireman) and Julianne Moore (as a government scientist), while the loose Darwinian concept allows for an entertainingly mad menagerie of regenerated digital creatures. JC DVD

David Duchovny *Dr Ira Kane* • Orlando Jones *Dr Harry Block* • Seann William Scott *Wayne* • Julianne Moore *Allison* • Ted Levine *General Woodman* • Ethan Suplee *Deke* • Katharine Towne *Nadine* • Dan Aykroyd *Governor Lewis* ■ *Dir* Ivan Reitman • *Scr* David Diamond, David Weissman, Don Jakoby, from a story by Don Jakoby

E

Ex-Lady ★

Drama 1933 · US · BW · 67mins

Warners Bros gave Bette Davis her first "official" starring role, that of a woman with startlingly progressive attitudes to sex and marriage that moderate when love enters her life. Davis described the result as a shaming "piece of junk", critics and audiences agreed, and her official leading lady status was delayed for a year or two. RK

Bette Davis *Helen Bauer* • Gene Raymond *Don Peterson* • Frank McHugh *Hugo Van Hugh* • Monroe Owsley *Nick Malvyn* • Claire Dodd *Iris Van Hugh* • Kay Strozzi *Peggy Smith* ■ *Dir* Robert Florey • *Scr* David Boehm, from the story by Edith Fitzgerald, Robert Riskin

The Ex-Mrs Bradford ★★★

Comedy mystery 1936 · US · BW · 81mins

A fast-moving screwball farce, delightfully teaming a post-*Thin Man* William Powell with the lovely Jean Arthur. The sophisticated Powell is a surgeon this time, investigating a murder in which a black widow spider was the weapon. It's all good, clean fun, with a marvellous supporting cast of RKO regulars, notably cop James Gleason and Eric Blore, typecast as a butler. It's not directed too well, but it's always a pleasure to view such endearing stars. TS

William Powell *Dr Bradford* • Jean Arthur *Paula Bradford* • James Gleason *Inspector Corrigan* • Eric Blore *Stokes* • Robert Armstrong *Nick Martel* • Lila Lee *Miss Prentiss* • Grant Mitchell *Mr Summers* ■ *Dir* Stephen Roberts • *Scr* Anthony Veiller, from a story by James Edward Grant

Excalibur ★★★★ 15

Action fantasy
1981 · UK/US · Colour · 134mins

Director John Boorman's vivid and passionate telling of the Arthurian legend is a thoroughly convincing visualisation of the Knights of the Round Table myth within Dark Ages history. Masterfully intermingling fable and magic with a gritty reality, Boorman explores the cosmic duality of good versus evil, paganism versus Christianity, mighty Merlin versus malevolent Morgana, with eccentric élan. The search for the Holy Grail and the final battle are simply stunning sequences, and, while the dizzying pace leaves scant time for proper characterisation, Nicol Williamson, Nigel Terry and Helen Mirren make their mark. AJ. Contains some violence and brief nudity. DVD

Nigel Terry *King Arthur* • Helen Mirren *Morgana* • Nicol Williamson *Merlin* • Nicholas Clay *Lancelot* • Cherie Lunghi *Guenevere* • Paul Geoffrey *Perceval* • Robert Addie *Mordred* • Gabriel Byrne *Uther Pendragon* • Liam Neeson *Gawain* • Corin Redgrave *Duke of Cornwall* • Patrick Stewart *Leondegrance* ■ *Dir* John Boorman • *Scr* Rospo Pallenberg, John Boorman, from the prose romance *Le Morte d'Arthur* by Thomas Malory

Excess Baggage ★ 12

Romantic comedy adventure
1997 · US · Colour · 96mins

In the first film from her production company First Kiss, Alicia Silverstone stars as an annoying, spoiled brat who fakes her own kidnapping by locking herself in the trunk of her car. She then gets snatched for real when thief Benicio Del Toro steals it in this dire comedy adventure. Lacking in laughs, romance and action, the film plods along painfully, with only the reliable Christopher Walken injecting any entertaining moments. JB DVD

Alicia Silverstone *Emily* • Benicio Del Toro *Vincent* • Christopher Walken *Ray* • Jack Thompson *Alexander* • Harry Connick Jr *Greg* • Nicholas Turturro *Stick* • Michael Bowen *Gus* • Robert Wisden *Detective Sims* ■ *Dir* Marco Brambilla • *Scr* Max D Adams, Dick Clement, Ian La Frenais, from a story by Max D Adams

Excessive Force ★★★ 18

Thriller 1993 · US · Colour · 82mins

Thomas Ian Griffith has always stood out from the ranks of action heroes as someone who can act a bit. He's never really crossed over into the mainstream but his thrillers usually deliver the goods, and this is no exception. He's helped by an outstanding supporting cast that includes Burt Young, as a gangster who murders Griffith's police colleagues in revenge for a drugs bust, prompting our moody hero to take the law into his own hands. JF

Thomas Ian Griffith *Terry McCain* • Lance Henriksen *Devlin* • Burt Young *Sal DiMarco* • James Earl Jones *Jake* • Charlotte Lewis *Anita Gilmour* • Tom Hodges *Dylan* • Tony Todd *Frankie Hawkins* • Randy Popplewell *Tony* ■ *Dir* Jon Hess • *Scr* Eric Rhodes

The Executioner ★★ PG

Spy drama 1970 · UK · Colour · 105mins

This convoluted spy drama finds George Peppard playing a British secret agent uncovering treachery within his department and collusion within the CIA. Peppard looks rather lost amid a cast of English stalwarts, while director Sam Wanamaker seems far more interested in scoring points about the British class system than concentrating on plot logic and suspense. AT

George Peppard *John Shay* • Joan Collins *Sarah Booth* • Judy Geeson *Polly Bendel* • Oscar Homolka *Racovsky* • Charles Gray *Vaughan Jones* • Nigel Patrick *Colonel Scott* • George Baker *Philip Crawford* ■ *Dir* Sam Wanamaker • *Scr* Jack Pulman, from a story by Gordon McDonell

The Executioner of Venice ★★★

Period swashbuckling adventure
1963 · It · Colour · 90mins

Director Luigi Capuano is often referred to as the Italian Michael Curtiz because he specialised in highly colourful, continental costume epics, always managing to give even the most predictable plots a high energy lift. Here's one of his best: a smooth spectacle about pirate bands operating in the Adriatic, in which hero Lex Barker is torn between duty and romance with Venetian vixen Sandra Panaro. An effervescent swashbuckler laced with modest suspense. AJ. Italian dialogue dubbed into English.

Lex Barker *Sandrigo* • Sandra Panaro [Alessandra Panaro] *Leonora* • Mario Petri *Guarnieri* • Guy Madison *Rodrigo Zeno* ■ *Dir* Luigi Capuano • *Scr* Luigi Capuano, Arpad De Riso

Executive Action ★★★★ PG

Political thriller 1973 · US · Colour · 86mins

Unshown on TV for many years, this drama about the Kennedy assassination in Dallas makes for absolutely riveting viewing. It shows how a shadowy group of businessmen and military leaders (including Robert Ryan and Burt Lancaster) plots to kill JFK, who has "gone soft on communism and the blacks". Brilliantly organised, the film describes how the shooters plan their kill as well as the search for a fall guy, Lee Harvey Oswald. It's as tense as *The Day of the Jackal*, only this time the question is not how does he fail, but how do they get away with it? AT

Burt Lancaster *Farrington* • Robert Ryan *Foster* • Will Geer *Ferguson* • Gilbert Green *Paulitz* • John Anderson *Halliday* • Paul Carr *Gunman Chris* • Colby Chester *Tim* • Ed Lauter *Operation chief, team A* ■ *Dir* David Miller • *Scr* Dalton Trumbo, from a story by Donald Freed, Mark Lane

Executive Decision ★★★ 15

Action thriller 1996 · US · Colour · 127mins

In this competent thriller, director Stuart Baird makes good use of the set pieces, diverting attention from the once far-fetched but now rather chilling plot in which David Suchet's gang of Arab terrorists is headed towards the US in a hijacked jumbo jet with enough stolen Russian nerve gas to kill millions of Americans. Steven Seagal and Kurt Russell share top billing as part of an elite team that sets out in a stealth bomber to defuse the situation. Mindless fun. JF. Contains violence, swearing. DVD

Kurt Russell *David Grant* • Steven Seagal *Lt Col Austin Travis* • Halle Berry *Jean* • John Leguizamo *Rat* • Oliver Platt *Cahill* • Joe Morton *Cappy* • David Suchet *Nagi Hassan* • BD Wong *Louie* ■ *Dir* Stuart Baird • *Scr* Jim Thomas, John Thomas

Executive Power ★★

Political thriller 1998 · US · Colour · 115mins

The real-life scandals of the Clinton era are probably more compelling than events in this slow-moving potboiler. In a plot obviously inspired by the suicide of one of Bill Clinton's friends, Vince Foster, disillusioned ex-Secret Service agent Nick finds himself investigating the mysterious death of a presidential adviser. What makes this movie so frustrating is that a character's motivation at any given time is apparently dictated solely by what is needed to keep the action going. ST

Craig Sheffer *Nick* • John Heard *Walker* • William Atherton *President Fields* • Joanna Cassidy *First Lady* • Denise Crosby *Christine Rolands* ■ *Dir/Scr* David Corley

Executive Suite ★★★★ U

Drama 1954 · US · BW · 104mins

Cameron Hawley's novel about a boardroom battle for power seemed an unlikely subject for a glossy MGM movie. However, in the hands of editor turned director Robert Wise, this gritty drama is riveting, helped by an all-star cast. William Holden heads the corporate suits, and there's particularly strong support from Fredric March, Nina Foch and Walter Pidgeon. But what dignifies the whole proceedings is, uniquely for Hollywood, the absence of a music score. TS

William Holden (2) *McDonald Walling* • June Allyson *Mary Blemond Walling* • Barbara Stanwyck *Julia O Tredway* • Fredric March *Loren Phineas Shaw* • Walter Pidgeon *Frederick Y Alderson* • Shelley Winters *Eva Bardeman* • Paul Douglas *Josiah Walter Dudley* • Louis Calhern *George Nyle Caswell* • Nina Foch *Erica Martin* ■ *Dir* Robert Wise • *Scr* Ernest Lehman, from the novel by Cameron Hawley

Executive Target ★★★ 18

Action thriller 1996 · US · Colour · 91mins

Essentially a series of increasingly spectacular car chases, this cheap and cheerful action thriller makes for entertainingly stupid viewing. Michael Madsen stars as the stunt driver who's sprung from prison by a shady organisation to help kidnap the president (Roy Scheider) when he's visiting Los Angeles. Keith David is splendidly over-the-top as the chief villain, while director Joseph Merhi just can't wait to smash up more vehicles. Great fun. JF. Contains violence, swearing and nudity. DVD

Michael Madsen *Nick James* • Roy Scheider *President Carlson* • Keith David *Lamar Quentin* • Angie Everhart *Lacey* • Dayton Callie *Bela* ■ *Dir* Joseph Merhi • *Scr* Jacobsen Hart, Dayton Callie

The Exile ★★ U

Historical drama 1947 · US · BW · 91mins

Douglas Fairbanks Jr not only stars as the exiled Charles II; he also wrote the script and produced the picture. So what we see is evidence of a star's clout rather than his talent, since it's a poorly written piece of historical flummery that gives Fairbanks a number of women to romance while hiding from Cromwell's agents in Europe. As one would expect of director Max Ophüls, it contains some sensuous camerawork. Original prints were in sepia tones. AT

Douglas Fairbanks Jr *Charles Stuart* • Maria Montez *The Countess* • Paula Croset [Rita Corday] *Katie* • Henry Daniell *Colonel Ingram* • Nigel Bruce *Sir Edward Hyde* • Robert Coote *Pinner* • Otto Waldis *Jan* • Eldon Gorst *Seymour* ■ *Dir* Max Ophüls • *Scr* Douglas Fairbanks Jr, from the novel *His Majesty, the King* by Cosmo Hamilton

Exiles ★★★

Road movie drama
2004 · Fr/Jap · Colour · 104mins

This amiable, exotic road movie won Tony Gatlif the best director prize at the 2004 Cannes film festival, but the film's spicy charms might not be to everyone's tastes. Romain Duris and Lubna Azabal are sitting round naked in their Paris flat one day and decide to make a pilgrimage to Algeria, where both their families hail from. En route, the two meet gypsies, seductive flamenco dancers and, once in Algeria, hostile locals. There's not really a lot of plot here, but Gatlif's camera lingers lovingly on his sexy stars and serves up big dollops of funky, world music on the soundtrack. LF. In French, Arabic, Romany and Spanish with English subtitles. Contains nudity and sex scenes.

Romain Duris *Zano* • Lubna Azabal *Naima* • Leila Makhlouf *Leila* • Habib Cheik *Habib* • Zouhir Gacem *Said* ■ *Dir/Scr* Tony Gatlif

eXistenZ ★★★★ 15

Futuristic thriller
1999 · Can/UK · Colour · 96mins

It seems that David Cronenberg cannot shake off his obsession with "body horror". Though this futuristic virtual-reality thriller sidesteps the more explicit visceral gore of *The Fly* and *Videodrome*, it nonetheless involves pulsating computer-game consoles and handsets that plug directly into the flesh. Despite the usual high degree of visual invention and good lead performances from Jude Law (as a security guard) and Jennifer Jason Leigh (as creator of the eponymous game), the movie is not quite up there with Cronenberg's best; it's hard to escape the nagging feeling that virtual reality is slightly old hat. AC. Contains violence and swearing. DVD

Jennifer Jason Leigh *Allegra Geller* • Jude Law *Ted Pikul* • Ian Holm *Kiri Vinokur* • Don McKellar *Yevgeny Nourish* • Callum Keith Rennie *Hugo Carlaw* • Sarah Polley *Merle* • Christopher Eccleston *Levi* • Willem Dafoe *Gas* ■ *Dir/Scr* David Cronenberg • *Cinematographer* Peter Suschitzky

Exit in Red ★ 18

Erotic mystery drama
1996 · US · Colour · 94mins

The *Wild Orchid* pair of Mickey Rourke and Carré Otis are reunited for this would-be erotic thriller. This time around, though, there's barely enough steam to fog up a pocket mirror. Rourke is the psychiatrist with a past trying to set up a new life with lawyer Otis who gets involved in a complex murder plot when he meets sexy Annabel Schofield. Sloppily acted and directed. JF [video] DVD

Mickey Rourke *Ed Altman* • Anthony Michael Hall *Nick* • Carré Otis *Kate* • Annabel Schofield *Ally* • Johnny Venocur *Cop* • Robert F Lyons *Detective Vollers* ■ *Dir* Yurek Bogayevicz • *Scr* David Womark

Exit to Eden ★ 18

Sex comedy 1994 · US · Colour · 109mins

This unfunny sex comedy is only worth catching if you can stomach the sight of Dan Aykroyd in bondage gear. Aykroyd and Rosie O'Donnell play a pair of investigators going "undercover" at an S&M resort run by Dana Delany, while *Strictly Ballroom* star Paul Mercurio wanders around in something resembling a nappy. A career low for all. JB [video] DVD

Dana Delany *Lisa Emerson* • Paul Mercurio *Elliot Slater* • Rosie O'Donnell *Sheila* • Dan Aykroyd *Fred* • Hector Elizondo *Martin Halifax* • Stuart Wilson (1) *Omar* • Iman *Nina* ■ *Dir* Garry Marshall • *Scr* Deborah Amelon, Bob Brunner, from the novel by Anne Rice

Exit Wounds ★★ 18

Action drama
2001 · US/Aus · Colour · 97mins

Action star Steven Seagal, looking far from the svelte fast-moving hero he should be, plays a disgraced cop who is transferred to a tough inner city precinct, where he discovers his new colleagues are selling heroin to drug dealers. Seagal's performance in this comeback film is typically wooden, and the Toronto locations are hardly convincing as Detroit. However, rapper DMX provides some relief from the usual shenanigans. JF. Contains swearing, violence, nudity. [video] DVD

Steven Seagal *Orin Boyd* • DM X *Latrell Walker* • Isaiah Washington *George Clark* • Anthony Anderson *TK* • Michael Jai White *Strutt* • Bill Duke *Hinges* • Jill Hennessy *Annette Mulcahy* • Tom Arnold *Henry Wayne* ■ *Dir* Andrzej Bartkowiak • *Scr* Ed Horowitz, Richard D'Ovidio, from the novel by John Westermann

Exodus ★★★★ PG

Epic drama 1960 · US · Colour · 199mins

Leon Uris's bestseller gets the Otto Preminger treatment in this accomplished, epic retelling of events leading to the birth of Israel in 1948. With a script by former blacklistee Dalton Trumbo, this is a gritty, forthright and marvellously cinematic experience, if a long one. Some critics weren't happy about the all-star cast, though it's hard to imagine better than Paul Newman as Haganah leader Ari Ben Canaan or Eva Marie Saint as nurse Kitty Fremont. Sal Mineo was nominated for best supporting actor as freedom fighter Dov Landau, but the Oscar went to Ernest Gold's marvellously grandiose music, which has achieved classic status. TS [video] DVD

Paul Newman *Ari Ben Canaan* • Eva Marie Saint *Kitty Fremont* • Ralph Richardson *Gen Sutherland* • Peter Lawford *Maj Caldwell* • Lee J Cobb *Barak Ben Canaan* • Sal Mineo *Dov Landau* • John Derek *Taha* • Hugh Griffith *Mandria* • Gregory Ratoff *Lakavitch* ■ *Dir* Otto Preminger • *Scr* Dalton Trumbo, from the novel by Leon Uris

The Exorcist ★★★★★ 18

Horror 1973 · US · Colour · 132mins

One of the most talked-about and reviled horror movies of all time. Unbelievably scary when it first came out, its overall impact has been lessened by time and repeated genre duplication. But the macabre, obscene demonstrations of manifest evil still retain their power to startle and nauseate, particularly Linda Blair's "head-turning" antics as the obsessed child. Aside from the graphic and revolutionary special effects, director William Friedkin dwells on the allegorical religious subtleties, making this a richly satisfying experience for horror aficionados. Special mention should go to Robert Knudson and Chris Newman, for their marvellous, Oscar-winning use of sound. AJ. Contains violence, swearing and sexual references. [video] DVD

Ellen Burstyn *Mrs MacNeil* • Max von Sydow *Father Merrin* • Lee J Cobb *Lieutenant Kinderman* • Kitty Winn *Sharon* • Jack MacGowran *Burke Dennings* • Jason Miller *Father Karras* • Linda Blair *Regan MacNeil* • Reverend William O'Malley *Father Dyer* • Wallace Rooney *Bishop* • Mercedes McCambridge *Voice of the Demon* ■ *Dir* William Friedkin • *Scr* William Peter Blatty, from his novel • *Cinematographer* Owen Roizman • *Art Director* Bill Malley • *Make-up* Dick Smith • *Sound* Robert Knudsen, Chris Newman

Exorcist II: The Heretic ★★★ 18

Horror 1977 · US · Colour · 112mins

The jury is still out on this critical and financial disaster, tampered with by the studio after audiences cracked up at the devilish finale. The focus here is on the quest of Father Richard Burton to quell the demon still present within Linda Blair, now in therapy to combat recurring nightmares. Yes, Burton overplays the doom-laden script. And, yes, all the African mumbo jumbo is bewildering. But director John Boorman deliberately accents the weighty mythological angles to create a film as complex and intellectual as it is visceral, and his daring approach is overdue for reappraisal. AJ [video] DVD

Linda Blair *Regan MacNeil* • Richard Burton *Father Lamont* • Louise Fletcher *Dr Gene Tuskin* • Max von Sydow *Father Merrin* • Kitty Winn *Sharon* • Paul Henreid *The Cardinal* • James Earl Jones *Older Kokumo* • Ned Beatty *Edwards* ■ *Dir* John Boorman • *Scr* William Goodhart, from characters created by William Peter Blatty

The Exorcist III ★★★ 18

Horror 1990 · US · Colour · 105mins

Director William Peter Blatty's official sequel to his original story is an intellectual suspense chiller. Lieutenant Kinderman (George C Scott replacing Lee J Cobb from the original terror classic) investigates a series of sacrilegious murders by the Gemini Killer, who may be a servant of the Devil. Relying heavily on static shots, elongated close-ups and academic dialogue to convey the real horror of life, sin and unbelief, Blatty's film is full of unexpected surprises, quirkiness and one absolutely frightening moment of pure shock. AJ [video] DVD

George C Scott *Lieutenant William Kinderman* • Ed Flanders *Father Dyer* • Brad Dourif *The Gemini Killer* • Jason Miller *Patient X* • Nicol Williamson *Father Morning* • Nancy Fish *Nurse Allerton* • Samuel L Jackson *Dream blind man* ■ *Dir* William Peter Blatty • *Scr* William Peter Blatty, from his novel *Legion*

Exorcist: the Beginning ★ 15

Horror 2004 · US · Colour · 108mins

This sloppy prequel is the crudest of shockers. Paul Schrader was removed as director after his cut was deemed too cerebral, but could it have been worse than Renny Harlin's bad B-movie? Future Georgetown exorcist Father Merrin (Stellan Skarsgård) loses his faith during the Nazi occupation of Holland and rediscovers it in a remote area of Kenya in 1949. There he examines a 5th-century church, mistakenly built on the spot where Lucifer fell, where evil and CGI hyenas lurk. The cast fails to rise above the clichéd gruesomeness. AJ. Contains violence. DVD

Stellan Skarsgård *Father Lankester Merrin* • James D'Arcy *Father Francis* • Izabella Scorupco *Dr Sarah Novack* • Remy Sweeney *Joseph* • Julian Wadham *Major Granville* • Andrew French *Chuma* • Ralph Brown *Sergeant Major* • Ben Cross *Semelier* • Alan Ford *Jeffries* ■ *Dir* Renny Harlin • *Scr* Alexi Hawley, from a story by William Wisher, Caleb Carr, from characters created by William Peter Blatty

Exotica ★★★★ 18

Drama 1994 · Can · Colour · 103mins

Prying behind the façade of the respectable is director Atom Egoyan's stock-in-trade. In this pulsating study of need, isolation and fantasy, he effortlessly slips between past and present to create myriad plot strands that he finally ties together with a mastery few can match. The scenes within the strip club of the title drip with erotic tension, reinforced by the sinister DJ-ing of Elias Koteas, the seductive dancing of Mia Kirshner and the disturbing willingness of auditor Bruce Greenwood to succumb to her charms. Add in a smuggling operation centred on a pet shop and you have a truly provocative movie. DP. Contains swearing and nudity. [video]

Bruce Greenwood *Francis* • Mia Kirshner *Christina* • Elias Koteas *Eric* • Don McKellar *Thomas* • Arsinée Khanjian *Zoe* • David Hemblen *Inspector* • Sarah Polley *Tracey* • Victor Garber *Harold* ■ *Dir/Scr* Atom Egoyan

Expect No Mercy ★ 18

Science-fiction action
1995 · Can · Colour · 90mins

Wolf Larson plays the kind of megalomaniac who sports long blond hair and runs one of those hi-tech labs/fight schools. Of course, no one running such places is ever up to any good, so it falls to Federal agents Billy Blanks and Jalal Merhi to go undercover and save the day. The attempt to portray virtual reality and hi-tech on a small budget make the movie come across as one big eyesore. KB [video] DVD

Billy Blanks *Justin Vanier* • Wolf Larson *Warbeck* • Laurie Holden *Vicki* • Jalal Merhi *Eric* • Brett Halsey *Bromfield* ■ *Dir* Zale Dalen • *Scr* J Stephen Maunder

The Experiment ★★★ 18

Psychological prison thriller
2000 · Ger · Colour · 113mins

This taut German thriller was inspired by the notorious 1971 Stanford Prison Experiment, in which college students were asked to take part in a two-week simulation of prison life. Director Oliver Hirschbiegel builds the tension brilliantly, only to dilute its intensity with unnecessary diversions and an unimaginative all-action finale. The feud between former journalist Moritz Bleibtreu and latent fascist Justus von Dohnányi soon descends into generic macho posturing. DP. In German with English subtitles. [video] DVD

Moritz Bleibtreu *Tarek Fahd, No 77* • Edgar Selge *Professor Dr Klaus Thon* • Christian Berkel *Robert Steinhoff, No 38* • Justus von Dohnányi *Berus* • Maren Eggert *Dora* • Andrea Sawatzki *Dr Jutta Grimm* ■ *Dir* Oliver Hirschbiegel • *Scr* Mario Giordano, Christoph Darnstädt, Don Bohlinger, from the novel *Black Box* by Mario Giordano

Experiment in Terror ★★

Thriller 1962 · US · BW · 123mins

This is an unlikely offering from director Blake Edwards. Teaming up here with Lee Remick, Edwards goes berserk with his camera, which goes everywhere, searching for a bug's-eye view and then a bird's, making the audience rather dizzy if not very scared. Problem is, this isn't a horror movie but an overlong glossy B-movie thriller, about a bank cashier (Remick) forced to embezzle by a killer. AT

Glenn Ford *John Ripley* • Lee Remick *Kelly Sherwood* • Stefanie Powers *Toby* • Roy Poole *Brad* • Ned Glass *Popcorn* • Anita Loos *Lisa* • Patricia Huston *Nancy* • Ross Martin *Red Lynch* • Clifton James *Captain Moreno* ■ *Dir* Blake Edwards • *Scr* Gordon Gordon, Mildred Gordon, from their novel *Operation Terror*

Experiment Perilous ★★★

Period melodrama 1944 · US · BW · 91mins

This clever but wordy suspense drama is expertly directed by the talented Jacques Tourneur. Insane husband Paul Lukas and glamorous wife Hedy Lamarr are embroiled in a psychological battle of wits, with George Brent as the psychiatrist trying to rescue Lamarr. Written and produced by Warren Duff, the movie is helped by the 1903 period art direction, which was Oscar nominated. TS

Hedy Lamarr *Allida Bedereaux* • George Brent *Dr Huntington Bailey* • Paul Lukas *Nick Bedereaux* • Albert Dekker *Claghorne* • Carl Esmond *Maitland* • Olive Blakeney *Cissie* • *Dir* Jacques Tourneur • *Scr* Warren Duff, from the novel by Margaret Carpenter

The Expert ★★ 18

Action adventure 1994 · US · Colour · 94mins

Cult favourite Larry Cohen had a hand in the script, so this is a notch above the usual straight-to-video fodder. Jeff Speakman plays a police instructor seeking to avenge himself on the serial killer (Michael Shaner) who murdered his sister and is now on death row. To get to him, Speakman must break into prison. Speakman's unflashy fighting style is impressive, the set pieces are nicely choreographed and Shaner makes for a creepy villain. JF [video] DVD

Jeff Speakman *John Lomax* • Michael Shaner *Martin Kagan* • Wolfgang Bodison *Dan Mason* • Alex Datcher *Dr Alice Barnes* • James Brolin *Warden Munsey* • Jim Varney ■ *Dir* Rick Avery • *Scr* Larry Cohen, Max Allan Collins, from a story by Jill Gatsby

The Experts ★ 15

Spy comedy 1989 · US · Colour · 89mins

John Travolta spent a long time in the wilderness before Quentin Tarantino rejuvenated his career in *Pulp Fiction*, and this is an excellent example of the drivel he was making. This part screwball comedy, part Cold War satire stars Travolta, Arye Gross and Travolta's now-wife Kelly Preston in a tale of slick city types inveigled into aiding the dreaded "Ruskies" in their secret project to replicate American suburbia. Quite why the KGB should waste its valuable time on such futility is never sufficiently explained. SH [video]

John Travolta *Travis* • Kelly Preston *Bonnie* • Arye Gross *Wendell* • Deborah Foreman *Jill* • James Keach *Yuri* • Charles Martin Smith *Cameron Smith* ■ *Dir* Dave Thomas • *Scr* Nick Thile, Steven Greene, Eric Alter, from a story by Steven Greene, Eric Alter

Explorers ★★★ U

Science-fiction adventure
1985 · US · Colour · 104mins

This is a minor entry in the Joe Dante canon, but an amusing family yarn all the same. A pre-fame Ethan Hawke and River Phoenix team up with Jason

Presson as a trio of kids who build their own spacecraft and set off on the adventure of a lifetime. The youngsters are uniformly excellent, Mary Kay Place and Dante regular Dick Miller stand out among the grown-ups, and the tone is refreshingly unpatronising and unsentimental. JF [video] DVD

Ethan Hawke *Ben Crandall* • River Phoenix *Wolfgang Müller* • Jason Presson *Darren Woods* • Amanda Peterson *Lori Swenson* • Dick Miller *Charlie Drake* • James Cromwell *Mr Müller* • Dana Ivey *Mrs Müller* • Leslie Rickert *Neek* • Mary Kay Place *Mrs Crandall* ■ *Dir* Joe Dante • *Scr* Eric Luke

E

The Explosive Generation ★★

Drama 1961 · US · BW · 89mins

Teen-angst movie about high school students who support their teacher (William Shatner) when he gets fired for teaching them about the birds and the bees. It seems that the students' parents can't talk to their kids about anything, and are shocked by the frankness of the discussion in the classroom. One of literally scores of movies Hollywood made at the time about teenage delinquency, shot on a slender budget by debutant director Buzz Kulik, a graduate of live TV. AT

William Shatner *Peter Gifford* • Patty McCormack *Janet Sommers* • Lee Kinsolving *Dan Carlyle* • Billy Gray *Bobby Herman Jr* • Steve Dunne *Bobby Herman Sr* • Arch Johnson *Mr Sommers* • Virginia Field *Mrs Sommers* • Beau Bridges *Mark* ■ *Dir* Buzz Kulik • *Scr* Joseph Landon

Exposé ★★★ 18

Erotic thriller 1975 · UK · Colour · 79mins

Director James Kenelm Clarke's erotic thriller stars Udo Kier as the novelist whose attempts to meet his deadline are hampered by a sexy typist with a hidden agenda (Linda Hayden) and his former girlfriend (played by 1970s sex starlet Fiona Richmond). Without much competition, the film stood out as a well photographed and reasonably well written (although completely illogical) example of the genre. It is markedly superior to Clarke's subsequent films with Richmond, and, after being saddled with being a British "video nasty", it developed a cult following. DM. Contains violence, swearing, sex scenes and nudity. [video]

Udo Kier *Paul Martin* • Linda Hayden *Linda Hindstatt* • Fiona Richmond *Suzanne* • Patsy Smart *Mrs Aston* ■ *Dir/Scr* James Kenelm Clarke

Exposed ★★ 15

Drama 1983 · US · Colour · 95mins

Before *Reservoir Dogs* star Harvey Keitel became cool he appeared in this tepid thriller as a terrorist who crosses paths with jet-set model Nastassja Kinski when she's not romancing violinist Rudolf Nureyev. Kinski has travelled to the big city to become a concert pianist. Supposedly sexy and arty, this is neither. JB [video]

Nastassia Kinski [Nastassja Kinski] *Elizabeth Carlson* • Rudolf Nureyev *Daniel Jelline* • Harvey Keitel *Rivas* • Ian McShane *Greg Miller* • Bibi Andersson *Margaret* • Ron Randell *Curt* • Pierre Clémenti *Vic* • Dov Gottesfeld *Marcel* • James Russo *Nick* ■ *Dir/Scr* James Toback

Exposure ★★

Thriller 2000 · US · Colour · 92mins

Ron Silver may not always land the choicest roles, but he usually gives a decent performance. He easily handles his lead role in this uninspired thriller, playing a photographer who becomes suspected of the murder of a model. But, other than using Elizabeth Hawthorne to play the detective on the case, director David Blyth can't lift the material above the average. DP Contains violence, swearing, sex scenes and nudity.

Ron Silver *Gary Whitford* • Alexandra Paul *Jackie Steerman* • Susan Pari *Elaine Drury/Anne* • Paul Gittins *Paul Steerman* • Elizabeth Hawthorne *Detective Shoorwell* ■ *Dir* David Blyth • *Scr* Ian Coughlan

Expresso Bongo ★★★★ PG

Musical 1959 · UK · BW · 101mins

This isn't only a fascinating snapshot of Soho in the skiffle and coffee bar era, but it's also one of the best musicals ever produced in this country. Oozing the easy charm and shiftless opportunism that had just served him so well in *Room at the Top*, Laurence Harvey is perfectly cast as the talent agent hoping to get rich quick through rookie rocker Cliff Richard, who, for all his raw appeal, is also very religious. Val Guest captures the fads and fashions of the late 1950s, but it's Wolf Mankowitz's crackling script that gives the film its authenticity. DP [video]

Laurence Harvey *Johnny Jackson* • Sylvia Syms *Maisie King* • Yolande Donlan *Dixie Collins* • Cliff Richard *Bongo Herbert* • Meier Tzelniker *Mayer* • Ambrosine Philpotts *Lady Rosemary* • Eric Pohlmann *Leon* ■ *Dir* Val Guest • *Scr* Wolf Mankowitz, from a play by Julian More, Wolf Mankowitz

The Exquisite Sinner ★★

Silent romantic melodrama 1926 · US · BW

Renée Adorée is a gypsy girl and Myrna Loy a "living statue" in this starring vehicle for Conrad Nagel. He plays a young Frenchman who eschews conventional society to seek liberation with a band of wandering gypsies. This is a silent collector's piece for admirers of Josef von Sternberg, here directing his third Hollywood film and his first for MGM. The studio disliked the film (and von Sternberg, who soon left for Paramount) and extensive retakes were filmed by Phil Rosen, but the film still bears the hallmarks of Hollywood's master visual stylist. RK

Conrad Nagel *Dominique Prad* • Renée Adorée *Silda, the gypsy maid* • Paulette Duval *Yvonne* • Frank Currier *Colonel* • George K Arthur *His orderly* • Myrna Loy *The living statute* ■ *Dir* Josef von Sternberg, Phil Rosen • *Scr* Josef von Sternberg, Alice DG Miller, Joe Farnham [Joseph Farnham] (titles), from the novel *Escape* by Alden Brooks

Exquisite Tenderness ★★★ 18

Horror 1995 · US/Ger/Can · Colour · 95mins

Side effects from pituitary gland experiments turn former doctor Sean Haberle into a slobbering maniac in this crackpot chiller from director Carl Schenkel. A ghoulish and garish exercise in retro-slasher nostalgia, Schenkel's Hitch-cocktail of nightmare imagery, tasteless violence and lip-smacking gore is both terribly enjoyable and enjoyably terrible. Luckily, Haberle sews up hospital administrator Charles Dance's mouth so no one has to endure his terrible American accent for too long! An entertaining, if overwrought spectacular. AJ [video] DVD

Isabel Glasser *Dr Theresa McCann* • James Remar *Dr Benjamin Hendricks* • Sean Haberle *Dr Julian Matar* • Charles Dance *Dr Ed Mittlesbay* • Peter Boyle *Lieutenant Daryl McEllwaine* • Malcolm McDowell *Dr Roger Stein* • Charles Bailey-Gates *Sgt Ross* • Gregory West *Tommy Beaton* ■ *Dir* Carl Schenkel • *Scr* Patrick Cirillo, from a screenplay (unproduced) by Bernard Sloane

Extension du Domaine de la Lutte ★★★★ 18

Drama 1999 · Fr · Colour · 115mins

Dismissed in France for lacking the literary precision of Michel Houellebecq's cult novel, this is, nevertheless, a deliciously melancholic insight into the psyche of the bourgeois male, caught between the last flickerings of professional and romantic ambition and the resigned acceptance of middle-aged mediocrity. The byplay between the world-weary Philippe Harel and José Garcia's overeager IT virgin is keenly observed and superbly controlled. Harel's misanthropic musings on everything from buying a bed to the artistic failings of modern cinema give the film its sardonic charm DP. In French with English subtitles. [video]

Philippe Harel *Our Hero* • José Garcia *Raphaël Tisserand* • Catherine Mouchet *Psychologist* • Cécile Reigher *Catherine Lechardey* ■ *Dir* Philippe Harel • *Scr* Philippe Harel, Michel Houellebecq, from the novel *Extension du Domaine de la Lutte* by Michel Houellebecq

The Exterminating Angel ★★★★ 12

Satirical drama 1962 · Mex · BW · 89mins

Luis Buñuel turns his attention to another of his favourite targets, the middle classes, in this searing condemnation of convention and outmoded morality. Clearly revealing his surrealist roots, this blackly comic film ingeniously uses a nightmare dinner party to make the terrifying assertion that the bourgeois lifestyle is every bit as hideous and limiting as any concentration camp regime. Brilliantly played, this is one of Buñuel's most pessimistic films, and its chilling ending will leave you dumbstruck. DP. In Spanish with English subtitles. [video]

Silvia Pinal *Letitia* • Jacqueline Andere *Alicia Roc* • José Baviera *Leandro* • Augusto Benedico *Doctor* • Luis Beristain *Cristian Ugalde* • Antonio Bravo *Russell* • Claudio Brook *Julio, majordomo* • Cesar Del Campo *Colonel* • Rosa Elena Durgel *Silvia* ■ *Dir* Luis Buñuel • *Scr* Luis Buñuel, Luis Alcoriza, from the play *Los Naufragos de la Calle de la Providencia* by José Bergamin

The Exterminator ★★ 18

Crime drama 1980 · US · Colour · 94mins

For a straightforward tale of violent revenge, this is a surprisingly influential film in straight-to-video circles. Avenging Vietnam vet Robert Ginty was henceforth known as Robert "Exterminator" Ginty, and became quite a draw in his own right. Here Ginty is on the trail of the murderous gang that beat up his comrade. He finds himself using his brutal combat skills to tackle the CIA, the cops and the crime families who are all after his blood. JF [video] DVD

Christopher George *Detective James Dalton* • Samantha Eggar *Dr Megan Stewart* • Robert Ginty *John Eastland* • Steve James (1) *Michael Jefferson* • Tony DiBenedetto *Chicken Pimp* • Dick Boccelli *Gino Pontivini* • Patrick Farrelly *CIA Agent Shaw* • Michele Harrell *Maria Jefferson* ■ *Dir/Scr* James Glickenhaus

Exterminator 2 ★★ 18

Crime thriller 1980 · US · Colour · 83mins

In this unimaginatively titled sequel set in sleazy New York street crime circles. Robert Ginty, star of the original, is once again on the violent revenge trail, this time because some very bad people, led by a mysterious master criminal, have been picking on his girlfriend. Blaxploitation star Mario Van Peebles and a young John Turturro turn up in supporting roles. JF [video]

Robert Ginty *Johnny Eastland* • Mario Van Peebles *X* • Deborah Geffner *Caroline* • Frankie Faison *Be Gee* • Scott Randolph *Eyes* • Reggie Rock Bythewood *Spider* • Bruce Smolanoff *Red Rat* • John Turturro *1st guy* ■ *Dir/Scr* Mark Buntzman, William Sachs

The Extra Day ★★ U

Portmanteau drama
1956 · UK · Colour · 83mins

Had this portmanteau picture been shot in Italy or France in the same period, the five short stories about the mundane lives of some movie extras would have been made with *bona fide* bit players rather than with a cast comprising a second division Hollywood star, a faded French siren and umpteen ubiquitous British character actors. Sid James comes closest to convincing us he's a real human being, but the trite tales and the bogus behind-the-scenes atmosphere render this merely a disappointing curio. DP

Richard Basehart *Joe Blake* • Simone Simon *Michele Blanchard* • George Baker *Steven Marlow* • Josephine Griffin *Toni Howard* • Colin Gordon *Sir George Howard* • Laurence Naismith *Kurt Vorn* • Charles Victor *Bert* • Sidney James *Barney West* • Joan Hickson *Mrs West* ■ *Dir/Scr* William Fairchild

Extralarge: Moving Target ★★

Detective drama
1990 · It/US · Colour · 88mins

Best known for his partnership with Terence Hill in spaghetti westerns and comedy action films, Bud Spencer (real name Carlo Pedersoli) here finds himself pounding a Florida beat with former *Miami Vice* star Philip Michael Thomas. As private eyes in possession of a nuclear secret wanted by both desperate assassins and crooked CIA agents, it doesn't take a genius to work out that much tyre tread will be lost before it's all quiet on the waterfront. It's lively, but it doesn't have that *Vice*-like grip. This was the first in a series of seven *Extralarge* made-for-TV movies. DP

Bud Spencer *Jack "Extralarge" Costello* • Philip Michael Thomas *Dumas* • Juan Fernandez *Rashid* • Vivian Ruiz *Mrs Martinez* • Lou Bedford *Sam* • Jackie Davis *Harry* ■ *Dir/Scr* Enzo G Castellari

The Extraordinary Seaman ★★

Second World War comedy
1969 · US · Colour · 80mins

David Niven was going through a rough patch at this point in his career and with this movie he hit a positive thicket. Alan Alda, Mickey Rooney and Jack Carter, on the run from the Japanese, find a natty Niven living on a beached ship in the Philippines. Faye Dunaway joins the crew, which is consolation for nobody but her agent, as action director John Frankenheimer just can't get to grips with this. TH

David Niven *Lieutenant Commander Finchhaven* • Faye Dunaway *Jennifer Winslow* • Alan Alda *Lieutenant JG Morton Krim* • Mickey Rooney *Cook 3rd Class W WJ Oglethorpe* • Jack Carter *Gunner's Mate Orville Toole* • Juano Hernandez *Ali Shar* • Manu Tupou *Seaman 1st Class Lightfoot Star* • Barry Kelley *Admiral Barnwell* ■ *Dir* John Frankenheimer • *Scr* Phillip Rock, Hal Dresner, from a story by Phillip Rock

Extreme Close-Up ★★

Drama 1973 · US · Colour · 80mins

Television reporter James McMullan, working on a series about invasion of privacy, gets sucked into the kind of sexual voyeurism he's seeking to expose when he spies on a woman in the block opposite him. Although the script by *Jurassic Park's* Michael Crichton cleverly plays with *Rear Window* and *Peeping Tom* motifs, Jeannot Szwarc's direction can't elevate the material from superficial, seedy exploitation. AJ

James McMullan [Jim McMullan] *John Norman* • Kate Woodville *Sally Norman* • James A Watson Jr *Cameraman* ■ *Dir* Jeannot Szwarc • *Scr* Michael Crichton

Extreme Measures ★★★ 15

Mystery thriller
1996 · US/UK · Colour · 113mins

In this silly but enjoyable *Coma*-style medical thriller, Hugh Grant stars as a doctor who uncovers dastardly deeds involving homeless patients at a big city hospital. Grant is out-acted and outclassed at every turn by co-star Gene Hackman, who chews up the scenery and spits it out as the revered surgeon who is Grant's number one suspect. Director Michael Apted's film contains no surprises, but it does have a few laughs thanks to Grant and Hackman (unintentionally and intentionally, respectively). JB. Contains violence, swearing. [VIDEO] DVD

Hugh Grant *Dr Guy Luthan* • Gene Hackman *Dr Lawrence Myrick* • Sarah Jessica Parker *Jodie Trammel* • David Morse *Frank Hare* • Bill Nunn *Detective Burke* • John Toles-Bey *Bobby* • Paul Guilfoyle (2) *Dr Jeffery Manko* • David Cronenberg *Hospital lawyer* ■ *Dir* Michael Apted • *Scr* Tony Gilroy, from the novel by Michael Palmer

Extreme Ops ★★ 12

Action thriller
2003 · UK/Ger/US/Lux/Can · Col · 89m

This flick aims to be the ultimate action movie – celebrating extreme snowboarding – but our attention gets swept away by an avalanche of clichés. A film-making crew led by Rufus Sewell is in the Austrian Alps to record the ski stylings of gold-medallist Bridgette Wilson-Sampras, but then they spot a Serbian war criminal. Director Christian Duguay's narrative loses out to the obvious – including some rather fake-looking CGI effects. TH [VIDEO] DVD

Devon Sawa *Will* • Bridgette Wilson-Sampras [Bridgette Wilson] *Chloe* • Rupert Graves *Jeffrey* • Rufus Sewell *Ian* • Heino Ferch *Mark* • Joe Absolom *Silo* • Klaus Lowitsch [Klaus Löwitsch] *Pavle* ■ *Dir* Christian Duguay • *Scr* Michael Zaidan, from a story by Timothy Scott Bogart, Mark Mullin

Extreme Prejudice ★★★ 18

Action thriller 1987 · US · Colour · 100mins

Director Walter Hill, initially revered for his unravelling of the male psyche and his lyrical expression of violence (à la Sam Peckinpah), has in recent years simply settled for violent action. He pokes wry fun here at the central clichéd conflict between two old pals who each end up on opposite sides of the law. Hill is also aided by two actors who exude tough-guy behaviour with ease: Nick Nolte as the Texas Ranger and Powers Boothe as the chum-turned-drug lord. JM. Contains violence, swearing, sex scenes, drug abuse and nudity. [VIDEO] DVD

Nick Nolte *Jack Benteen* • Powers Boothe *Cash Bailey* • Michael Ironside *Major Paul Hackett* • Maria Conchita Alonso *Sarita Cisneros* • Rip Torn *Sheriff Hank Pearson* • Clancy Brown *Sergeant McRose* • Matt Mulhern *Sergeant Coker* • William Forsythe *Sergeant Atwater* ■ *Dir* Walter Hill • *Scr* Deric Washburn, Harry Kleiner, from a story by John Milius, Fred Rexer

Extremities ★★ 18

Drama 1986 · US · Colour · 84mins

Is *Extremities* controversial or exploitative? There's a large helping of both as Farrah Fawcett escapes a would-be rapist (James Russo) only for him to return and terrorise her. The surprise comes when she turns the tables on him, but this leads to a relentless catalogue of brutality that never truly tackles the sensitive subject at hand. JB [VIDEO] DVD

Farrah Fawcett *Marjorie* • James Russo *Joe* • Diana Scarwid *Terry* • Alfre Woodard *Patricia* • Sandy Martin *Officer Sudow* • Eddie Velez *1st officer* ■ *Dir* Robert M Young • *Scr* William Mastrosimone, from his play

The Eye ★★★★ 15

Psychological horror thriller
2002 · HK/Sing · Colour · 95mins

Directors Danny and Oxide Pang focus on a blind violinist in this superbly controlled chiller. Tapping into the terror of anticipation, the brothers unnerve us from the off with Lee Sin-Je's first blurred images of the world following a corneal transplant. However, it's the succeeding nightmares, shifting scenes and ghostly apparitions that prove to be the most disturbing and send Lee and counsellor Lawrence Chou to the Thai village where her psychic donor met her grisly end. With eye-catching effects and a tingling score, this is a stylish blend of the psychological and the visceral. DP. In Cantonese, Mandarin and Thai with English subtitles. Contains violence. [VIDEO] DVD

Lee Sin-Je *Man* • Lawrence Chou *Dr Wah* • Chutcha Rujinanon *Ling* • Candy Lo *Man's sister* • Pierre Ping *Dr Eak* ■ *Dir* Oxide Pang, Danny Pang • *Scr* Jojo Yuet-Chun Hui, Oxide Pang, Danny Pang

The Eye 2 ★★★

Psychological horror thriller
2004 · HK/Sing · Colour · 90mins

Bearing minimal relation to their *Eye* concept, the Pang brothers' follow-up delves into the very interesting creepy-crawl space between western urban legend and eastern Buddhist undercurrents. Qi Shu is the pregnant woman cursed with the ability to see ghosts. Featuring the now standard girl-with-long-dark-hair-over-eyes Asian cliché image, the Pangs take a far more novel approach in introducing the unexpected apparitions accompanied by surprise sound effects. In a remarkably elegant sequence, a slow-motion floating spirit terrorises charismatic Taiwanese star Qi in a lift. It's a tad too long, but this crisply shot, jolting philosophy lesson is a slick shock package. AJ. In Mandarin and Thai with English subtitles.

Qi Shu *Joey Cheng* • Jesdaporn Pholdee *Sam* • Eugenia Yuan *Yuen Chi-Kei* ■ *Dir/Scr* Pang Brothers [Oxide Pang], Pang Brothers [Danny Pang]

An Eye for an Eye ★★

Western 1966 · US · Colour · 91mins

Robert Lansing sets out to find the gang who murdered his wife and child. Teaming up with younger bounty hunter Pat Wayne (son of the Duke), they get badly shot up when they find nasty Slim Pickens and his cronies. Lansing is shot through his gun hand and Wayne is blinded, so they combine talents. This plot twist gives this western a certain novelty value and makes the biblical title doubly allusive, but otherwise it's poorly acted and sluggishly directed. AT

Robert Lansing *Talion* • Pat Wayne [Patrick Wayne] *Benny* • Slim Pickens *Ike Slant* • Gloria Talbott *Bri Quince* • Paul Fix *Quince* • Strother Martin *Trumbull* • Henry Wills *Charles* • Jerry Gatlin *Jonas* • Clint Howard *Jo-Hi* ■ *Dir* Michael Moore (1) • *Scr* Bing Russell, Sumner Williams

An Eye for an Eye ★★ 18

Martial arts action thriller
1981 · US · Colour · 99mins

When this was made, Chuck Norris just about ruled supreme in the martial arts stakes, and, though he was no Bruce Lee, this is a serviceable enough vehicle for his talents. He is his usual monosyllabic self as the former cop who launches a destructive private war against the Triads after the death of his partner. Quite what Christopher Lee is doing here is anybody's guess, but there are enough fights and set pieces to keep genre fans contented. JF [VIDEO]

Chuck Norris *Sean Kane* • Christopher Lee *Morgan Canfield* • Richard Roundtree *Capt Stevens* • Matt Clark *Tom McCoy* • Mako *James Chan* • Maggie Cooper *Heather Sullivan* • Rosalind Chao *Linda Chan* ■ *Dir* Steve Carver • *Scr* William Gray, James Bruner, from a story by James Bruner

Eye for an Eye ★★★ 18

Thriller 1995 · US · Colour · 97mins

The casting of Sally Field as a gun-toting vigilante and Kiefer Sutherland as an out-and-out baddie gives novelty value to this revenge thriller from director John Schlesinger. Field plays a woman who is catapulted into a world of terror when her daughter is raped and murdered. Forensic evidence points to Sutherland, but when he escapes jail on a legal technicality Field sets out to exact her own form of justice. Field is perhaps a touch too mumsy to convince totally in her role, though Sutherland clearly relishes playing a lowlife killer. JF. Contains violence and swearing. [VIDEO] DVD

Sally Field *Karen McCann* • Ed Harris *Mack McCann* • Olivia Burnette *Julie McCann* • Alexandra Kyle *Megan McCann* • Kiefer Sutherland *Robert Doob* • Joe Mantegna *Detective Sergeant Denillo* • Beverly D'Angelo *Dolly Green* • Darrell Larson *Peter Green* ■ *Dir* John Schlesinger • *Scr* Amanda Silver, Rick Jaffa, from the novel by Erika Holzer

Eye of God ★★★ 15

Drama 1997 · US · Colour · 79mins

This labyrinthine tale of passion, violence and religious fanaticism in small-town America is held together by a simmering performance from Kevin Anderson, who leaves jail to marry Martha Plimpton, the burger waitress who's been writing to him during his sentence for assault. But cutting across this uneasy romance is sheriff Hal Holbrook's attempt to coax the truth from terrified teenager Nick Stahl, found dazed and bloodied. Director Tim Blake Nelson plays fast and loose with the narrative structure, but it's worth staying the course. DP [VIDEO] DVD

Martha Plimpton *Ainsley Dupree* • Kevin Anderson *Jack Stillings* • Hal Holbrook *Sheriff Sam Rogers* • Nick Stahl *Tom Spencer* • Margo Martindale *Dorothy* • Mary Kay Place *Claire Spencer* • Richard Jenkins *Willard Sprague* ■ *Dir* Tim Blake Nelson • *Scr* Tim Blake Nelson, from his play

Eye of the Beholder ★ 18

Thriller
1999 · Can/UK/US/Aus · Colour · 100mins

In this stodgy combination of ersatz James Bond and sub-Hitchcock thriller, secret service agent Ewan McGregor is assigned to follow serial killer Ashley Judd. However, because the seductive assassin reminds him of his long-lost daughter, he darts all over the world obsessively spying on her. Stephan Elliott's farcical potboiler paints itself into far too many ludicrous corners, while McGregor does little with a thankless role. AJ [VIDEO] DVD

Ewan McGregor *The Eye* • Ashley Judd *Joanna Eris* • kd lang *Hilary* • Jason Priestley *Gary* ■ *Dir* Stephan Elliott • *Scr* Stephan Elliott, from the novel by Marc Behm

Eye of the Cat ★★★

Thriller 1969 · US · Colour · 100mins

Riddled with laughable lines and so many plot potholes that the story forever teeters on the brink of collapse, it's hard to believe that this rickety chiller was penned by Joseph Stefano, the man who wrote the screenplay for *Psycho*. What keeps you watching are the performances of the three leads, who play it with earnest conviction. Eleanor Parker particularly enjoys herself as the disabled *grande dame*, whose house full of cats thwarts the gold-digging ambitions of nephew Michael Sarrazin and his accomplice, Gayle Hunnicutt. DP

Michael Sarrazin *Wylie* • Gayle Hunnicutt *Kassia* • Eleanor Parker *Aunt Danny* • Tim Henry *Luke* • Laurence Naismith *Dr Mills* • Jennifer Leak *Poor Dear* • Linden Chiles *Bendetto* • Mark Herron *Bellemondo* ■ *Dir* David Lowell Rich • *Scr* Joseph Stefano

Eye of the Devil ★★

Horror 1966 · UK · BW · 95mins

Controversial in its day, and extensively cut for American release, director J Lee Thompson's daft occult thriller concerns a French nobleman sacrificing himself to the grape gods to improve the vintage of his faltering vineyard. David Niven and Deborah Kerr add considerable authority to the silly premise. Warlock David Hemmings and witch Sharon Tate have their moments turning a toad into a dove and hypnotising the locals. AJ

Deborah Kerr *Catherine de Montfaucon* • David Niven *Philippe de Montfaucon* • Donald Pleasence *Pere Dominic* • Edward Mulhare *Jean-Claude Ibert* • Flora Robson *Countess Estell* • Emlyn Williams *Alain de Montfaucon* • David Hemmings *Christian de Caray* • Sharon Tate *Odile* • John Le Mesurier *Dr Monnet* ■ *Dir* J Lee Thompson • *Scr* Robin Estridge, Dennis Murphy, from the novel *Day of the Arrow* by Philip Loraine

Eye of the Killer ★★★ 15

Crime thriller 1999 · US · Colour · 96mins

Kiefer Sutherland doesn't disappoint in this straight-to-video thriller as a detective who develops psychic skills that come in handy when he has to track down a serial killer. Not the brainiest of scripts, and some of the cast just turned up to pick up their pay slips, but fans of the genre will enjoy guessing the outcome. Also known as *After Alice*. JB. Contains swearing and violence. [VIDEO] DVD

Kiefer Sutherland *Detective Mickey Hayden* • Henry Czerny *Harvey* • Polly Walker *Dr Vera Swann* • Gary Hudson *John Hatter* • Ronn Sarosiak *Ray Coombs* ■ *Dir* Paul Marcus • *Scr* Jeff Miller

Eye of the Needle ★★★ 15

Second World War spy thriller
1981 · UK · Colour · 108mins

This is a film version of Ken Follett's novel about a lethal Nazi agent who has somehow managed to infiltrate the lower reaches of, er, British Rail during the war. This might seem an unglamorous base of operations from which to subvert the Allied war effort, but Donald Sutherland as the Nazi keeps the suspenseful story of murder, romance and intrigue on the right track. PF [VIDEO]

Donald Sutherland *Henry Faber* • Kate Nelligan *Lucy Rose* • Ian Bannen *Percy Godliman* • Christopher Cazenove *David Rose* • Faith Brook *Lucy's mother* • Barbara Ewing *Mrs Garden* • David Hayman *Canter* ■ *Dir* Richard Marquand • *Scr* Stanley Mann, from the novel by Ken Follett

Eye of the Storm ★★

Psychological crime thriller
1991 · Ger/US · Colour · 98mins

More a character study than a straight horror film, this teenage *Psycho* fails to capitalise on its flashy build-up and only really comes alive at the end. After their parents' murder, two brothers take over the family's remote desert motel. However, things go pear-shaped when drunken Dennis Hopper and his trashy young wife Lara Flynn Boyle arrive. Director Yuri Zeltser keeps us pondering as to which of the boys will emerge as the Norman Bates-style nutter. RS. Contains violence, drug abuse and swearing.

Craig Sheffer *Ray* • Bradley Gregg *Steven* • Lara Flynn Boyle *Sandra Gladstone* • Leon Rippy *Sheriff* • Dennis Hopper *Marvin Gladstone* ■ *Dir* Yuri Zeltser • *Scr* Yuri Zeltser, Michael Stewart

Eye of the Stranger ★ 15

Action mystery 1993 · US · Colour · 96mins

Writer/director/actor David Heavener casts himself in the Clint Eastwood role as the nameless stranger who wanders into a small town. Corrupt mayor Martin Landau seems to be calling all the shots, but the stranger sets about bringing him and his cronies to justice for an unsolved murder. Many fights and meaningful shots of the stranger's boots follow. Inept and cliché-ridden. ST

David Heavener *Stranger* • Martin Landau *Mayor Howard Baines* • Sally Kirkland *Lori* • Don Swayze *Rudy* • Stella Stevens *Doc* • Sy Richardson *Jeb* • Joe Estevez *Sheriff* • John Pleshette *Joe* • Thomas F Duffy *Ballack* ■ *Dir/Scr* David Heavener

Eye of the Tiger ★★ 18

Thriller 1986 · US · Colour · 87mins

Framed for a crime he didn't commit, Vietnam veteran Gary Busey goes home after his release from jail to take vengeance on the real culprits, biker drug-dealers led by William Smith. Wire decapitations, dynamite stuck in people's orifices and Busey's RV customised with cannons are the various methods of dispatch in this violent and unpleasant thriller. AJ. Contains violence and swearing.

Gary Busey *Buck Matthews* • Yaphet Kotto *JB Deveraux* • Seymour Cassel *Sheriff* • Bert Remsen *Father Healey* • Jorge Gil *Jamie* • William Smith *Blade* • Kimberlin Ann Brown *Dawn* • Denise Galik *Christie* ■ *Dir* Richard C Sarafian • *Scr* Michael Montgomery

Eye Witness ★★★

Courtroom drama 1949 · UK · BW · 105mins

Also known as *Your Witness*, Robert Montgomery's fourth credited directorial outing is a compact courtroom drama, laced with a little amateur sleuthing. Just about every scene contains a venerable British character actor, from wrongly accused war hero Michael Ripper to judge Felix Aylmer. But it's Montgomery's hotshot American attorney who dominates the proceedings, as he searches for the mysterious poetry-loving woman who can corroborate Ripper's plea of self-defence. Slow in places, but steadily directed, well acted and satisfying. DP

Robert Montgomery *Adam Heyward* • Leslie Banks *Colonel Summerfield* • Patricia Wayne [Patricia Cutts] *Alex Summerfield* • Felix Aylmer *Judge* • Harcourt Williams *Beamish* • Andrew Cruickshank *Sir Adrian Horth, KC* • Wylie Watson *Widgery* • Michael Ripper *Sam Baxter* ■ *Dir* Robert Montgomery • *Scr* Hugo Butler, Ian McLellan Hunter, William Douglas Home, from a story by Hugo Butler

Eyes in the Night ★★★

Crime drama 1942 · US · BW · 79mins

This superior MGM thriller is a bit too polished to be a *film noir*. Starring avuncular character actor Edward Arnold as a blind detective, it's one of those formula movies offered to gifted new directorial talent, in this case the young Fred Zinnemann. The nominal star is Ann Harding, but Donna Reed shows she has real star quality. TS

Edward Arnold *Captain Duncan Maclain* • Ann Harding *Norma Lawry* • Donna Reed *Barbara Lawry* • Allen Jenkins *Marty* • John Emery *Paul Gerente* • Horace McNally [Stephen McNally] *Gabriel Hoffman* • Katherine Emery *Cheli Scott* ■ *Dir* Fred Zinnemann • *Scr* Guy Trosper, Howard Emmett Rogers, from the novel *Odor of Violets* by Baynard Kendrick

Eyes of a Stranger ★ 18

Horror 1980 · US · Colour · 79mins

Jennifer Jason Leigh stars in this voyeuristic and distasteful horror as the blind and deaf sister of TV anchorwoman Lauren Tewes. During the Miami summer, serial killer John DiSanti has been raping and murdering local women. Tewes discovers the killer is her next-door neighbour, and attempts to prove his guilt before he comes after her and the defenceless Leigh. Extremely exploitative. LH

Lauren Tewes *Jane* • Jennifer Jason Leigh *Tracy* • John DiSanti *Stanley Herbert* • Peter DuPre *David* • Gwen Lewis *Debbie* • Kitty Lunn *Annette* ■ *Dir* Ken Wiederhorn • *Scr* Mark Jackson, Eric L Bloom

Eyes of an Angel ★★

Adventure crime drama
1991 · US · Colour · 91mins

John Travolta stars as a single parent, struggling to bring up his daughter Ellie Raab. Only released on the coat-tails of its star's post-*Pulp Fiction* comeback, this violent story follows Raab as she nurses a mobster's injured Doberman back to health, not realising that her involvement with the pooch will have her and Travolta fleeing Chicago. It really is no surprise to learn Robert Harmon's movie failed to find a distributor for four years. LH

John Travolta *Bobby* • Ellie Raab *The Girl* • Tito Larriva *Cissy* • Richard Edson *Goon* • Vincent Guastaferro *Goon* • Jeffrey DeMunn *Georgie* • Jacqueline Pulliam *Gloria* ■ *Dir* Robert Harmon • *Scr* Robert Stitzel

Eyes of Laura Mars ★★★ 15

Psychological thriller
1978 · US · Colour · 99mins

Designed as a vehicle for Barbra Streisand (who sings the theme song), this movie ended up starring Faye Dunaway as the glamorous photographer who develops a psychic link with a killer and witnesses his gruesome murders while they are being committed. Co-written by John Carpenter, it's a standard slasher melodrama given a glitzy face-lift and, because Dunaway blends sex with sadism in her chic layouts (her gallery photos were actually taken by Helmut Newton), there's a great deal of pop analysis on exploitative images. Decently done, though surface gloss always wins out over deeper psychological substance. AJ DVD

Faye Dunaway *Laura Mars* • Tommy Lee Jones *Detective John Neville* • Brad Dourif *Tommy Ludlow* • René Auberjonois *Donald Phelps* • Raul Julia *Michael Reisler* • Frank Adonis *Sal Volpe* • Michael Tucker *Bert* • Lisa Taylor *Michele* ■ *Dir* Irvin Kershner • *Scr* John Carpenter, David Zelag Goodman

The Eyes of Tammy Faye ★★★ 12

Documentary 2000 · US/UK · Colour · 78mins

Fenton Bailey and Randy Barbato's portrait of American TV evangelist Tammy Faye Bakker Messner is like the lady herself – kitsch, melodramatic and endearingly camp. Narrated by celebrity drag artist RuPaul, it's an absorbing exposé of how she and her ex-husband Jim Bakker became the biggest names in the "electric church", only for scandal in the 1980s to destroy their multi-million dollar empire. With heavily made-up eyes often brimming with tears, Tammy Faye emotes her way through her turbulent life story, turning it into pure soap opera. Though her viewpoint is central, she doesn't hijack proceedings entirely, and there's plenty of talking head interviews and archive footage for balance. The result is a visually stimulating and comprehensive feature that really gets to the heart of its subject matter. SF DVD

RuPaul *Narrator* ■ *Dir* Fenton Bailey, Randy Barbato

Eyes of the Spider ★★★

Crime thriller 1999 · Jpn · Colour · 83mins

Shot along with *Serpent's Path* in a phenomenal four-week burst of creativity, this is a somewhat disappointing conclusion to the adventures of callously cool opportunist Sho Aikawa. Ordered by crime boss Ren Osugi to eliminate an old friend (Dankan), Aikawa presents a knowing variation on the Takeshi Kitano type of hoodlum – part eccentric, part homicidal time bomb – while director Kiyoshi Kurosawa typically laces the story with offbeat characters and disconcerting details. However, the shift from Seijun Suzuki-style yakuza comedy to psychological thriller lacks conviction. DP. A Japanese language film.

Sho Aikawa *Niijima* • Ren Osugi • Shun Sugata • Susumu Terajima • Dankan ■ *Dir* Kiyoshi Kurosawa • *Scr* Yoichi Nishiyama, Kiyoshi Kurosawa

Eyes Wide Shut ★★★ 18

Psychological drama
1999 · US/UK · Colour · 152mins

Full of trademark themes and characteristic compositions, Stanley Kubrick's final film is also his most fascinatingly flawed. With its style often resembling 1970s European art house movies, it lacks the morbidity to pass as a Buñuelian satire, while it is far too stately and serious to succeed as a commercial enterprise. Tom Cruise – as the doctor recklessly seeking a means of avenging his wife's fantasised infidelity – is too controlled for his character's fraught nocturnal adventures to be plausible. Nicole Kidman as his wife is less visible, though she simmers with the potential for erotic danger. Despite expectations, this is a disappointingly conservative conclusion to a career spent pushing back cinematic boundaries. DP DVD

Tom Cruise *Dr William Harford* • Nicole Kidman *Alice Harford* • Sydney Pollack *Victor Ziegler* • Marie Richardson *Marion Nathanson* • Rade Serbedzija *Milich* • Todd Field *Nick Nightingale* • Vinessa Shaw *Domino* • Alan Cumming *Desk clerk* ■ *Dir* Stanley Kubrick • *Scr* Stanley Kubrick, Frederic Raphael, from the novella *Traumnovelle* by Arthur Schnitzler

Eyes without a Face ★★★★★ 18

Horror 1959 · Fr/It · BW · 86mins

This is one of the most haunting horror films ever made. Director Georges Franju made his name with a series of inspired documentary shorts, and it's the realism of his approach that makes his "poetic fantasy" so unnerving. There's nothing of the hammy Hollywood mad scientist in Pierre Brasseur, as he and assistant Alida Valli resort to murder in order to rebuild the face of his daughter, Edith Scob. Franju's control of atmosphere is masterly, Eugen Schüfftan's photography is outstanding, and Auguste Capelier deserves a mention for designing Scob's unforgettable mask. DP. In French with English subtitles. Contains violence.

Pierre Brasseur *Professor Génessier* • Alida Valli *Louise* • Edith Scob *Christiane* • François Guérin *Jacques* • Juliette Mayniel *Edna Gruber* ■ *Dir* Georges Franju • *Scr* Jean Redon, Georges Franju, Jean Redon, Claude Sautet, Pierre Boileau, Thomas Narcejac, from the novel *Les Yeux sans Visage* by Jean Redon • *Music* Maurice Jarre

Eyewitness ★★★

Crime drama 1956 · UK · BW · 82mins

Donald Sinden, a rather bland leading man on both stage and screen before this was made, successfully attempts a rather different role, conveying all the ruthlessness of the heartless killer as he tries to rub out the witness to a crime. He is effectively supported by Muriel Pavlow (as his would-be victim), while director Muriel Box unfurls the suspense with a good sense of timing. JM

Donald Sinden *Wade* • Muriel Pavlow *Lucy Church* • Belinda Lee *Penny* • Michael Craig *Jay Church* • Nigel Stock *Barney* • Susan Beaumont *Probationer nurse* • David Knight *Mike* ■ *Dir* Muriel Box • *Scr* Janet Green

Eyewitness ★★ 15

Thriller 1970 · UK · Colour · 87mins

Why did a playwright of the calibre of Ronald Harwood bother himself with this adaptation of Mark Hebden's minor "cry wolf" thriller? It's hardly original stuff, and the threadbare plot leaves players a lot more experienced than Mark Lester looking forlorn. Lester is wincingly wide-eyed as the fanciful child whose account of a murder is disbelieved by all and sundry. Second-time director John Hough is still too obsessed with "meaningful" angles and camera trickery to concern himself with the pivotal performance. DP

Mark Lester (2) *Timothy, "Ziggy"* • Lionel Jeffries *Colonel* • Susan George *Pippa* • Tony Bonner *Tom* • Jeremy Kemp *Galleria* • Peter Vaughan *Paul* • Peter Bowles *Victor* • Betty Marsden *Madame Robiac* ■ *Dir* John Hough • *Scr* Ronald Harwood, from the novel by Mark Hebden

Eyewitness ★★★ 15

Thriller 1981 · US · Colour · 97mins

Shy night janitor William Hurt foolishly pretends to know something about a murder at his building in order to get close to TV newswoman Sigourney Weaver in this sub-"Hitch" cocktail of New York paranoia and fairy-tale romance from director Peter Yates. This is a slick and enjoyable thriller, with Yates deftly moving his classy cast through one mind-bending plot contortion after another and the suspense becomes truly nail-biting. The film may be more familiar by its British title, *The Janitor*. AJ

William Hurt *Daryll Deever* • Sigourney Weaver *Tony Sokolow* • Christopher Plummer *Joseph* • James Woods *Aldo* • Irene Worth *Mrs Sokolow* • Kenneth McMillan *Mr Deever* • Pamela Reed *Linda* • Morgan Freeman *Lieutenant Black* ■ *Dir* Peter Yates • *Scr* Steve Tesich

The FBI Story ★★★★ PG

Crime drama 1959 · US · Colour · 142mins

Virtually a potted history of America's Federal Bureau of Investigation under its now notorious head, J Edgar Hoover, directed by *Little Caesar's* Mervyn LeRoy and given tremendous credibility and heart by James Stewart. The device of telling the story through the eyes and exploits of one agent, who takes on everyone from the Klan to the mob to the Nazi secret service, verges on the unlikely, but is colourfully told against the backdrop of Stewart's domestic life. Vera Miles is impressive as his wife, and there's a marvellous supporting cast. TS

James Stewart *Chip Hardesty* • Vera Miles *Lucy Hardesty* • Murray Hamilton *Sam Crandall* • Larry Pennell *George Crandall* • Nick Adams *John Graham* • Diane Jergens *Jennie, as an adult* • Jean Willes *Anna Sage* • Joyce Taylor *Anne, as an adult* ■ *Dir* Mervyn LeRoy • *Scr* Richard L Breen, John Twist, from the book by Don Whitehead

F for Fake ★★★ PG

Documentary
1973 · Fr/Iran/W Ger · Colour · 84mins

Much of this sly treatise on deception was shot by François Reichenbach for a TV documentary on art forger supreme, Elmyr de Hory. When news broke that his biographer, Clifford Irving, had also faked his life of Howard Hughes, Orson Welles jumped at the chance to use Reichenbach's footage and added to it sequences of prestidigitation, confessional pieces on his own chicanery and a marvellously convoluted story about Oja Kodar and some Picasso paintings. Welles opens the film by promising to tell the absolute truth for one hour. DP

Oja Kodar *The Girl* • Orson Welles • Joseph Cotten *The Guest* ■ *Dir* Orson Welles • *Scr* from a original by Clifford Irving

FM ★★

Music drama 1977 · US · Colour · 104mins

It tells you something when a soundtrack album ends up being more popular than the film it's taken from. Such was the case for John A Alonzo's debut feature, a sketch-driven take on life at a progressive rock station in 1970s Los Angeles. Michael Brandon stars as a DJ determined to keep commercialism at bay, who leads a revolt when the playlist becomes too square for his liking. Amiable enough, but a deeply flawed product. RS

Michael Brandon *Jeff Dugan* • Eileen Brennan *Mother* • Alex Karras *Doc Holiday* • Cleavon Little *Prince* • Martin Mull *Eric Swan* • Cassie Yates *Laura Coe* • Norman Lloyd *Carl Billings* • James Keach *Lieutenant Reach* • Linda Ronstadt • Jimmy Buffett • Tom Petty ■ *Dir* John A Alonzo • *Scr* Ezra Sacks

FP1 ★★

Science-fiction drama
1932 · UK/Ger · BW · 74mins

An early instance of trilingual film-making, this sci-fi melodrama was a German venture with different casts for the German, French and English versions under one director, Karl Hartl. The best scenes show planes using the huge floating aerodrome in the middle of the Atlantic Ocean that serves as a stopping point for flights between Europe and America. The shorter British version stars Conrad Veidt as the aviator and inventor who saves the base from a sabotage attempt. Like modern "Europuddings", it met with mixed success. AE

Conrad Veidt *Maj Ellisen* • Leslie Fenton *Capt Droste* • Jill Esmond *Claire* • George Merritt *Lubin* • Donald Calthrop *Photographer* • Warwick Ward *1st Officer* • Philip Manning *Doctor* • Nicholas Hannen *Matthias* ■ *Dir* Karl Hartl • *Scr* Walter Reisch, Kurt Siodmak [Curt Siodmak], Robert Stevenson, Peter Macfarlane, from a story by Walter Reisch, Kurt Siodmak [Curt Siodmak]

FTA ★★

Political documentary
1972 · US · Colour · 96mins

The makers of this documentary claimed the title stood for "Free the Army" or even, bearing in mind the project's collaborative nature, "Free Theatre Associates". But few doubted what the "F" signified, in light of Jane Fonda's well-publicised stance against the Vietnam War. She insisted that the shows were staged as a feminist response to the girlie entertainment being offered to the troops by the likes of Bob Hope, but the army saw only antiwar propaganda and kept the troupe off its bases. DP

Jane Fonda • Donald Sutherland • Pamela Donegan • Len Chandler • Rita Martinson • Holly Near ■ *Dir* Francine Parker • *Scr* Michael Alaimo, Pamela Donegan, Jane Fonda, Robin Menken, Holly Near, Donald Sutherland, Dalton Trumbo

FTW ★★★ 18

Crime thriller 1994 · US · Colour · 97mins

The initials stand for Frank T Wells, the rodeo rider played by Mickey Rourke. After serving ten years for manslaughter, Wells is determined to revive his rodeo career and gets drawn into an affair with Lori Singer, who pays for his career on the proceeds of bank robberies. It's a peculiar mix, populated by assorted low-lifes and shot amid the spectacular scenery of Montana. AT. Contains swearing and sex scenes. DVD

Mickey Rourke *Frank T Wells* • Lori Singer *Scarlett Stuart* • Brion James *Sheriff Rudy Morgan* • Peter Berg *Clem* ■ *Dir* Michael Karbelnikoff • *Scr* Mari Kornhauser, from a story by Sir Eddie Cook

FX: Murder by Illusion ★★★★ 15

Crime thriller 1985 · US · Colour · 108mins

In this compulsively watchable thriller set in the intriguing world of special effects, Bryan Brown stars as an ace film technician who's hired by the US government to stage the fake assassination of a mobster-turned-informant. When the assignment takes a number of violent twists, Brown ends up on the run, armed only with his bag of tricks to expose corruption in high places. For both action fans and gore hounds, this is fast-paced fun. AJ. Contains violence, swearing. DVD

Bryan Brown *Rollie Tyler* • Brian Dennehy *Leo McCarthy* • Diane Venora *Ellen* • Cliff De Young *Lipton* • Mason Adams *Colonel Mason* • Jerry Orbach *Nicholas DeFranco* • Joe Grifasi *Mickey* ■ *Dir* Robert Mandel • *Scr* Robert T Megginson, Gregory Fleeman

FX 2 ★★★ 15

Crime thriller
1991 · UK/US · Colour · 107mins

Bryan Brown returns as the special effects whizz in this sequel, which, while lacking the fresh ingenuity of the original, remains a sly, entertaining thriller. This time Brown gets mixed up with crooked law enforcement officers, among others, but again runs rings around the crooks with the use of his incredible skills. Brian Dennehy once more provides solid support, while the under-rated Richard Franklin directs with some style and an appropriate light touch. JF. Contains violence, swearing and nudity.

Bryan Brown *Rollie Tyler* • Brian Dennehy *Leo McCarthy* • Rachel Ticotin *Kim Brandon* • Joanna Gleason *Liz Kennedy* • Philip Bosco *Ray Silak* • Kevin J O'Connor *Matt Neely* ■ *Dir* Richard Franklin • *Scr* Bill Condon, from characters created by Robert T Megginson, Gregory Freeman

The Fabulous Baker Boys ★★★★ 15

Romantic drama
1989 · US · Colour · 108mins

This sophisticated salute to family, romance, friends and disillusionment is pure bliss from start to finish. Real-life brothers Jeff and Beau Bridges play the cocktail lounge piano players of the title whose volatile relationship explodes when they employ sultry torch singer Michelle Pfeiffer to revitalise their tired act. Sweetly directed by Steve Kloves, the film zeroes in on many universal truths along its delightful way, with the fabulous Bridges boys' faultless timing and underplaying allowing Pfeiffer to shine. AJ. Contains swearing. DVD

Jeff Bridges *Jack Baker* • Michelle Pfeiffer *Susie Diamond* • Beau Bridges *Frank Baker* • Ellie Raab *Nina* • Jennifer Tilly *Monica Moran* • Xander Berkeley *Lloyd* • Dakin Matthews *Charlie* • Gregory Itzin *Vince Nancy* • Wendy Girard *Donna Baker* ■ *Dir/Scr* Steve Kloves

The Fabulous Dorseys ★★ U

Biographical musical
1947 · US · BW · 83mins

Warring bandleaders Tommy and Jimmy Dorsey were stolid and ageing when they played themselves in this rather lacklustre biopic, which is best enjoyed simply as a visual record of their music. The storytelling is perfunctory and the Dorsey Brothers themselves are no actors. Perhaps the most telling fact about them is that they were prepared to portray themselves on screen constantly battling with each other, and that it took the death of their father to bring them together. TS DVD

Tommy Dorsey • Jimmy Dorsey • Janet Blair *Jane Howard* • Paul Whiteman • William Lundigan *Bob Burton* • Sara Allgood *Mrs Dorsey* • Arthur Shields *Mr Dorsey* • James Flavin *Gorman* ■ *Dir* Alfred E Green • *Scr* Richard English, Art Arthur, Curtis Kenyon

The Face ★★ 15

Drama 1996 · US · Colour · 89mins

Yasmine Bleeth stars in this hokey but fun TV drama. She plays a shy, disfigured woman who ends up in prison after being set up by smooth womaniser James Wilder. While serving her sentence she is given a new look by a plastic surgeon that changes her life for ever. The performances are lacklustre but director Jack Bender paces the action so you can overlook the daft plot. JF DVD

Yasmine Bleeth *Emily Gilmore* • James Wilder *Alec Dalton* • Robin Givens *Claudia* • Richard Beymer *Dr Matthew Sheridan* ■ *Dir* Jack Bender • *Scr* Duane Poole, from a book by Marvin Werlin, Mark Werlin

Face ★★★ 18

Crime thriller 1997 · UK · Colour · 101mins

Robert Carlyle, who became a star after two movies and a TV series (*Trainspotting, The Full Monty, Hamish Macbeth*), here plays a thief seeking a traitor in his gang following a bungled robbery. The film is simple-mindedly clichéd and as predictable as a calendar. Still, there are terrific performances from Carlyle, Ray Winstone, Peter Vaughan and Sue Johnston, while director Antonia Bird shows that screen violence is not just a game that boys can play. TH. Contains violence, swearing. DVD

Robert Carlyle *Ray* • Ray Winstone *Dave* • Steven Waddington *Stevie* • Philip Davis *Julian* • Damon Albarn *Jason* • Lena Headey *Connie* • Peter Vaughan *Sonny* • Sue Johnston *Alice* ■ *Dir* Antonia Bird • *Scr* Ronan Bennett

The Face at the Window ★★

Crime melodrama 1939 · UK · BW · 66mins

Arguably barnstormer Tod Slaughter's best performance (surely no one ever called it acting?) was in this third version of a Parisian *Petit Guignol* about a revived presumed-dead body, revealing our hero and his mad brother to be serious bank robbers. Slaughter chews a good deal of scenery, while director George King sometimes lets the pace drag. TS

Tod Slaughter *Chevalier Del Gardo* • Marjorie Taylor *Cecile De Brisson* • John Warwick *Lucien Cortier* • Leonard Henry *Gaston* • Aubrey Mallalieu *De Brisson* ■ *Dir* George King • *Scr* AR Rawlinson, Randall Faye, from the play by F Brooke Warren

The Face behind the Mask ★★★★

Horror 1941 · US · BW · 68mins

Peter Lorre is ideally cast in this low-budget gem, as the watchmaker disfigured in a fire who turns to crime and romances a blind girl with tragic results. A truly haunting expressionist B-movie garnished with gruesome poetry, Robert Florey's subtle direction turns a stock horror situation on its head and gives threatening tension to the simmering, sinister undercurrent. A magical mood piece. AJ

Peter Lorre *Janos Szabo* • Evelyn Keyes *Helen Williams* • Don Beddoe *Jim O'Hara* • George E Stone *Dinky* • John Tyrell *Watts* • Stanley Brown *Harry* • Al Seymour *Benson* • James Seay *Jeff* • Warren Ashe *Johnson* ■ *Dir* Robert Florey • *Scr* Allen Vincent, Paul Jarrico, from a story by Arthur Levinson, from a radio play by Thomas Edward O'Connell

A Face in the Crowd ★★★★

Satirical drama 1957 · US · BW · 125mins

Andy Griffith gives the performance of his career as "Lonesome" Rhodes, the small-town philosopher who is discovered by a TV producer (Patricia Neal) and rocketed to fame, fortune and corruption. Director Elia Kazan and writer Budd Schulberg had previously collaborated on *On the Waterfront*, both winning Oscars. Although less celebrated, this film remains topical in the media-obsessed 1990s. Watch out for Lee Remick in her first film. RT

Andy Griffith *"Lonesome" Rhodes* • Patricia Neal *Marcia Jeffries* • Anthony Franciosa *Joey Kiely* • Walter Matthau *Mel Miller* • Lee Remick *Betty Lou Fleckum* • Percy Waram *Colonel Hollister* • Rod Brasfield *Beanie* • Charles Irving *Mr Luffler* ■ *Dir* Elia Kazan • *Scr* Budd Schulberg, from his short story *The Arkansas Traveler* • *Art Director* Richard Sylbert, Paul Sylbert

A Face in the Rain ★★

Second World War drama
1963 · US · BW · 80mins

Third-rung war movie with Rory Calhoun as an American agent dropped behind enemy lines in Italy where the wife of the local resistance leader is having an affair with a Gestapo officer. That's terribly inconvenient for Calhoun who's trapped in their apartment. Apart from its notably ironic climax, the movie offers an assortment of thrills, some tension and a nicely orchestrated chase across the rooftops. AT

Rory Calhoun *Rand* • Marina Berti *Anna* • Niall MacGinnis *Klaus* • Massimo Giuliani *Paolo* •

Danny Ryais • Peter Zander ■ *Dir* Irvin Kershner • *Scr* Hugo Butler, Jean Rouverol, from a story by Guy Elmes

Face of a Fugitive ★★★ U

Western 1959 · US · Colour · 80mins

This intriguing minor western is particularly well directed by Paul Wendkos and stars Fred MacMurray as a bank robber trying to shake off his past and settle down in a new town. MacMurray is a shade too old and staid for his role (and, besides, his toupee never really convinces), but watch out for then-newcomer James Coburn, who takes over the screen every time he appears. Wendkos made a number of highly regarded low-budget films around this period before basing his career in television. TS

Fred MacMurray *Jim Larson/Ray Kincaid* • Lin McCarthy *Mark Riley* • Dorothy Green *Ellen Bailey* • Alan Baxter *Reed Williams* • Myrna Fahey *Janet* • James Coburn *Purdy* • Francis De Sales *Allison* ■ *Dir* Paul Wendkos • *Scr* David T Chantler, Daniel B Ullman, from the story *Long Gone* by Peter Dawson

Face of a Stranger ★★

Romantic drama 1978 · US · Colour · 97mins

Also known as *The Promise*, this is an archetypal weepie about a woman (Kathleen Quinlan) who is disfigured in a car accident and accepts money for her reconstructive surgery from her fiancé's mother. The condition for this generosity is that she must move away and never see him again. It's predictable stuff, but Stephen Collins gives a nice turn as the lover Quinlan will, of course, cross paths with again (if true love has anything to do with it) and Beatrice Straight has fun as the mother from hell. JB

Kathleen Quinlan *Nancy/Marie* • Stephen Collins *Michael Hillyard* • Beatrice Straight *Marion Hillyard* • Laurence Luckinbill *Dr Gregson* • William Prince *George Calloway* • Michael O'Hare *Ben Avery* ■ *Dir* Gilbert Cates • *Scr* Garry Michael White, from a story by Fred Weintraub, Paul Heller

The Face of Another ★★★★ 12

Drama 1966 · Jpn · BW · 121mins

A compelling treatise on identity and the correlation between physique and personality, this was Hiroshi Teshigahara's first feature since *Woman of the Dunes*. Shades of Franju's *Eyes without a Face* fall upon the action, as Tatsuya Nakadai dons a mask to disguise the hideous disfigurement incurred in an industrial accident. But, is it the mask that prompts him to discard his wife on a spurious charge of adultery, or the same desperate feelings of alienation that drive scarred Miki Irie to commit incest with her devoted brother? Disturbing, but absorbing. DP. In Japanese with English subtitles. DVD

Machiko Kyo *Mrs Okuyama* • Tatsuya Nakadai *Mr Okuyama* • Mikijiro Hira • Miki Irie ■ *Dir* Hiroshi Teshigahara • *Scr* Kobo Abe, from the novel *Tanin No Kao* by Kobo Abe

The Face of Fear ★★★★

Drama 1971 · US · Colour · 75mins

You'll have some idea of the quality of this TV movie when you learn it was executive produced by Quinn Martin, the man responsible for such gems as *The Untouchables*, *The Fugitive* and *The Streets of San Francisco*. It stars Elizabeth Ashley as the leukemia-stricken Iowa teacher who hires a hitman to spare her the agonies of a slow death – only to discover she isn't fatally ill! Ashley seems genuinely terrified, but the acting honours go to Ricardo Montalban and Jack Warden as the cops racing against time to find her unknown assassin. DP

Ricardo Montalban *Sgt Frank Ortega* • Jack Warden *Lt George Coye* • Elizabeth Ashley *Sally Dillman* • Dane Clark *Tamworth* • Roy Poole *Glenn Kennedy* • Charles Dierkop *Patsy Fain* • Burr DeBenning *Fennington* • Regis J Cordic *Dr Landsteiner* ■ *Dir* George McCowan • *Scr* Edward Hume, from the novel *Sally* by EV Cummingham

Face of Fire ★★

Drama 1959 · US/UK · BW · 80mins

This obscure film of some ambition founders in trying to expand a short story by the eminent Stephen Crane into a feature-length drama. In turn-of-the-century New England, James Whitmore plays a much-loved handyman who becomes hideously disfigured after saving a small boy from a fire and finds people can no longer stand him. Curiously, this was made in Sweden under the direction of Albert Band, with a largely Hollywood cast that includes Cameron Mitchell and Royal Dano. AE

Cameron Mitchell *Ned Trescott* • James Whitmore *Monk Johnson* • Bettye Ackerman *Grace Trescott* • Miko Oscard *Jimmie Trescott* • Royal Dano *Jake Winter* • Robert F Simon *The Judge* • Richard Erdman *Al Williams* ■ *Dir* Albert Band • *Scr* Louis Garfinkle, from the story *The Monster* by Stephen Crane

The Face of Fu Manchu ★★★ PG

Horror 1965 · UK · Colour · 92mins

The first and best of Christopher Lee's portrayals of mystery writer Sax Rohmer's insidious East-Asian arch villain. Here he plans to conquer the world with a poison gas invented by a German professor held prisoner in his secret HQ under the Thames – very handy for those Chinese water tortures. Propelled by an eerie opening, this atmospheric comic strip fantasy is skilfully assembled, and Nigel Green is superb as Fu Manchu's Scotland Yard nemesis, Nayland Smith. The series continued the following year with *The Brides of Fu Manchu*. AJ DVD

Christopher Lee *Fu Manchu* • Nigel Green *Nayland Smith* • James Robertson-Justice *Sir Charles Fortesque* • Howard Marion-Crawford *Dr Walter Petrie* • Tsai Chin *Lin Tang* • Joachim Fuchsberger *Carl Jansen* • Karin Dor *Maria* • Walter Rilla *Professor Muller* ■ *Dir* Don Sharp • *Scr* Harry Alan Towers, from characters created by Sax Rohmer

Face/Off ★★★★ 18

Action thriller 1997 · US · Colour · 133mins

Nicolas Cage has lost his face and now he wants it back. Problem is, it's attached to John Travolta whose own face has been stitched on to Cage. Cage is a terrorist who, having planted a bomb somewhere in LA, is put into a coma by his FBI agent nemesis (Travolta). This is when the plastic surgery comes in – it is the only way to dupe Cage's associates into revealing the bomb's location. The mix of bizarre plotting, high-octane thrills and sentimental drama doesn't always jell, but director John Woo more than delivers in the overblown action stakes. AT. Contains swearing and violence. DVD

John Travolta *Sean Archer* • Nicolas Cage *Castor Troy* • Joan Allen *Eve Archer* • Alessandro Nivola *Pollux Troy* • Gina Gershon *Sasha Hassler* • Dominique Swain *Jamie Archer* • Nick Cassavetes *Dietrich Hassler* • Harve Presnell *Lazarro* ■ *Dir* John Woo • *Scr* Mike Werb, Michael Colleary

Face the Music ★★

Crime drama 1954 · UK · BW · 84mins

This adequate mystery offers a rare nice guy outing to soulless screen villain Alex Nicol, slumming in Britain after his Hollywood career went into a decline. Looking nothing like a trumpeter, he goes underground to prove his innocence when he is accused of murdering a singer. In one of his last assignments before becoming Hammer's horror maestro, director Terence Fisher never manages to intrigue. DP

Alex Nicol *James Bradley* • Eleanor Summerfield *Barbara Quigley* • John Salew *Max Marguiles* • Paul Carpenter *Johnny Sutherland* • Geoffrey Keen *Maurice Green* ■ *Dir* Terence Fisher • *Scr* Ernest Borneman, from his novel

Face to Face ★★ U

Portmanteau drama 1952 · US · BW · 89mins

Inspired by portmanteau movies, such as *Dead of Night* and *Forever and a Day*, which glued several short stories together, a young millionaire named Huntington Hartford somehow persuaded RKO to revive the format. John Brahm's section is a version of Joseph Conrad's *The Secret Sharer*, with James Mason hiding a murder suspect on his ship. Bretaigne Windust's film is *The Bride Comes to Yellow Sky*, based on a Stephen Crane story, with Robert Preston as a Texan sheriff whose fiancée is threatened by a long-time adversary. The fiancée is played by Marjorie Steele, who was married to Hartford. Both stories are effectively told on dime budgets, and audiences stayed away in droves. AT

James Mason *Captain* • Gene Lockhart *Capt Archbold* • Michael Pate *Swimmer* • Albert Sharpe *1st Mate* • Robert Preston *Sheriff* • Marjorie Steele *Bride* • Minor Watson *Bad man* • Dan Seymour *Drummer* • James Agee *Prisoner* ■ *Dir* John Brahm, Bretaigne Windust • *Scr* Aeneas MacKenzie, James Agee, from the short story *The Secret Sharer* by Joseph Conrad, from the short story *The Bride Comes to Yellow Sky* by Stephen Crane

Face to Face ★★★ 15

Western 1967 · It/Sp · Colour · 90mins

This is less a spaghetti western than a political parable. Gian Maria Volonté gives a highly persuasive performance as a college professor who discovers a talent for banditry when sent to recover his health at a small western town. But the subtext is too often thrust to the fore, with the result that the exploits of the prof and his gang become an irrelevance as writer/director Sergio Sollima sermonises on the misuse of power and the rule of fear. Ennio Morricone contributes a typically poignant score. DP. Italian dialogue dubbed into English.

Gian Maria Volonté *Brad Fletcher* • Tomas Milian *Solomon "Beauregard" Bennett* • William Berger *Charles Siringo* • Jolanda Modio *Marie* • Carole Andre *Cattle Annie* • Gianni Rizzo *Williams* ■ *Dir/Scr* Sergio Sollima • *Music* Ennio Morricone

Face to Face ★★

Drama 1976 · Swe · Colour · 135mins

Originally presented as a four-part TV series, this intense, personal drama suffers from its drastic truncation. After a string of successes, Ingmar Bergman allows introspection to get the better of him with this tiresome study of suppressed trauma, which is so riddled with familiar images and themes it often feels like a bad homage by a slavish acolyte. Fortunately, while Bergman loses himself in unresolved homosexual subplots and stylised dream sequences, Liv Ullmann turns in a compelling performance as a psychiatist. DP. In Swedish with English subtitles.

Liv Ullmann *Dr Jenny Isaksson* • Erland Josephson *Dr Tomas Jacobi* • Gunnar Björnstrand *Grandfather* • Aino Taube-Henrikson *[Aino Taube] Grandmother* • Kari Sylwan *Maria* • Sif Raud *Elizabeth Wankel* • Sven Lindberg *Dr Erik Isaksson* • Tore Segelcke *The lady* ■ *Dir/Scr* Ingmar Bergman

Face Value ★★

Mystery thriller 2001 · US · Colour · 90mins

Scott Baio is ill at ease in this routine thriller as a disgraced police cadet who comes to LA and gets rather too involved in the affairs of a glamorous pal. Things might have worked better had director Michael Miller stuck to credible situations. But Baio gets caught up with drug dealers and turns out to be a hunk in nerd's clothing. DP

Scott Baio *Barry Rengler* • Krista Allen *Syd* • James Wilder *Tim Gates* • Sandra Hess *Cat* • Tracey Walter *Leon Gates* ■ *Dir* Michael Miller (2) • *Scr* James G Hirsch

Faces ★★★★ 15

Drama 1968 · US · BW · 124mins

A challenging, gritty example of 1960s New American cinema from John Cassavetes, that combines Method acting with the cinematic techniques of the French New Wave. The marriage of Californian liberals John Marley and Lynn Carlin is on the rocks and after yet another row he storms out to spend the night with prostitute Gena Rowlands, while she finds solace in the arms of disco-dancing hippy Seymour Cassel. The picture originally lasted six hours and there are still places where some judicious cutting would not go amiss. But the improvised performances are exceptional, with Marley and Rowlands every bit as impressive as the Oscar-nominated Carlin and Cassel. DP

John Marley *Richard Forst* • Gena Rowlands *Jeannie Rapp* • Lynn Carlin *Maria Forst* • Fred Draper *Freddie* • Seymour Cassel *Chet* • Val Avery *McCarthy* • Dorothy Gulliver *Florence* • Joanne Moore Jordan *Louise* • Darlene Conley *Billy Mae* ■ *Dir/Scr* John Cassavetes

Faces in the Dark ★★

Thriller 1960 · UK · BW · 84mins

This tale of blindness and rage should have been a real nail-biter, but ex-documentary director David Eady doesn't have the thriller instinct and throws away countless opportunities to make the tension unbearable. Mild-mannered John Gregson is the blind person under threat. DP

John Gregson *Richard Hammond* • Mai Zetterling *Christiane Hammond* • Michael Denison *David Merton* • John Ireland *Max Hammond* • Tony Wright *Clem* • Nanette Newman *Janet* • Valerie Taylor *Miss Hopkins* ■ *Dir* David Eady • *Scr* Ephraim Kogan, John Tully, from the novel by Pierre Boileau, Thomas Narcejac

Faces of Children ★★★

Silent drama 1925 · Swi/Fr · BW · 114mins

Having experimented with expressionism in his early career, Belgian-born Jacques Feyder refined his poetic realist style in this sentimental tale of motherly love. But not even a director with his visual gifts could completely eradicate the melodramatic miming endemic in silent acting. Consequently, the performances work against the stylised authenticity of the sets, although the story itself is more than a little contrived. Child star Jean Forest is the pick of the cast, as the boy who expresses his resentment at his father's remarriage by tormenting his new stepsister, Arlette Peyran. DP

Jean Forest *Jean Amsler* • Rachel Devirys *Jeanne Dutois* • Victor Vina *Piérre Amsler* • Arlette Peyran *Arlette Dutois* • Pierrette Houyez *Pierrette Amsler* • Henri Duval *Canon Taillier* • Suzy Vernon *Jean's mother* ■ *Dir* Jacques Feyder • *Scr* Jacques Feyder, Françoise Rosay

Facing the Enemy ★★

Thriller 2001 · US · Colour · 98mins

The screen career of Maxwell Caulfield (*Grease 2*) continues to disappoint in this wildly contrived thriller from director Robert Malenfant. Caulfield plays a maniac who's convinced that cop Lynden Ashby was responsible for the death of his wife. Given that Ashby's missus, played by Alexandra Paul, has still to forgive him for the fact that their son shot himself with his service gun. DP

Maxwell Caulfield *Harlan Moss* • Linden Ashby *Griff McCleary* • Alexandra Paul *Olivia McCleary* • Melanie Wilson *Cassie Ives* • Bruce Weitz *Lt Carl Runyon* ■ *Dir* Robert Malenfant • *Scr* Martin Kitrosser

Facing Window ★★★ 15

Romantic drama
2003 · It/UK/Tur/Por · Colour · 106mins

Director Ferzan Ozpetek has always exhibited an atmospheric sense of place and he makes the most of the backstreets of Rome in this sincere study of suppressed secrets and second chances. Evoking the fears and prejudices of Italy's fascist past, this focuses on discontented housewife Giovanna Mezzogiorno, who enlists the help of handsome neighbour Raoul Bova to solve the mystery of amnesiac camp survivor Massimo Girotti. Veteran actor Girotti, who first came to prominence in the neorealist era, manages a moving display of wounded bemusement, but the culinary symbolism occasionally feels strained. DP. In Italian with English subtitles. Contains swearing.

Giovanna Mezzogiorno *Giovanna* • Massimo Girotti *Davide* • Raoul Bova *Lorenzo* • Filippo Nigro *Filippo* • Serra Yilmaz *Emine* • Massimo Poggio *Younger Davide* • Ivan Bachhi *Simone* ■ *Dir* Ferzan Ozpetek • *Scr* Gianni Romoli, Ferzan Ozpetek

The Facts of Life ★★★

Comedy 1960 · US · BW · 103mins

This pairs two of the screen's greatest clowns (though both Bob Hope and Lucille Ball play virtually straight parts here) as married – but not to each other– lovers desperately trying to consummate their affair, and being thwarted at every turn. Naughty rather than raunchy, it was deemed suitable as a saucy dish to present to the Queen at that year's Royal Film Performance. Their engaging teamwork makes this little flick memorable. TS

Bob Hope *Larry Gilbert* • Lucille Ball *Kitty Weaver* • Ruth Hussey *Mary Gilbert* • Don DeFore *Jack Weaver* • Louis Nye *Charles Busbee* • Philip Ober *Doc Mason* • Marianne Stewart *Connie Mason* • Peter Leeds *Thompson* • Hollis Irving *Myrtle Busbee* ■ *Dir* Melvin Frank • *Scr* Norman Panama, Melvin Frank • *Costume Designer* Edith Head

The Faculty ★★★ 15

Science-fiction horror thriller
1998 · US · Colour · 99mins

Scream writer Kevin Williamson teams up with *From Dusk till Dawn* director Robert Rodriguez for this enjoyable reworking of alien invasion movies, bolstered by Williamson's patented in-jokes and genre subversions. This succeeds through assured performances from the teenage cast, zippy direction and the writer's refusal to take even the most tense moments seriously. Despite a disappointing reliance on digital effects in the final third, this is classy entertainment. JC. Contains violence, swearing, drug abuse, nudity. [video] DVD

Josh Hartnett *Zeke* • Elijah Wood *Casey* • Salma Hayek *Nurse Harper* • Robert Patrick *Coach Willis* • Piper Laurie *Mrs Olson* • Clea DuVall *Stokely* • Jordana Brewster *Delilah* • Laura Harris *Marybeth* • Shawn Hatosy *Stan* • Famke Janssen *Miss Burke* ■ *Dir* Robert Rodriguez • *Scr* Kevin Williamson, from a story by David Wechter, Bruce Kimmel

Fade to Black ★★★ 18

Horror 1980 · US · Colour · 97mins

When a movie fanatic's loser lifestyle tips him over the edge into insanity, he embarks on a killing spree disguised as his favourite film characters. Vernon Zimmerman turns in an intelligent and imaginative movie, with plenty of cinematic references and in-jokes to enjoy, but an excess of violence leaves a bitter aftertaste. Dennis Christopher's carefully judged central performance is made ridiculous by turning him into just another slasher killer. RS [video]

Dennis Christopher *Eric* • Linda Kerridge *Marilyn* • Tim Thomerson *Dr Moriarty* • Morgan Paull *Gary* • Hennen Chambers *Bart* • Marya Small *Doreen* • Mickey Rourke *Richie* ■ *Dir/Scr* Vernon Zimmerman

Fahrenheit 451 ★★★ 12

Science-fiction drama
1966 · UK · Colour · 107mins

The only film François Truffaut directed in English, this adaptation of Ray Bradbury's deeply troubling novel promises much but is sadly flawed. Syd Cain's futuristic sets cleverly convey the menace and desperation of a society in which books are banned and burned, Cyril Cusack's fire chief is hugely resistible as he unquestioningly performs his duty and Julie Christie superbly judges the contrasts in her dual role. But Oskar Werner seems to have lost the plot, and, as he's its driving force, this is a major stumbling block. DP [video] DVD

Oskar Werner *Montag* • Julie Christie *Linda/Clarisse* • Cyril Cusack *Captain* • Anton Diffring *Fabian* • Jeremy Spenser *Man with apple* • Alex Scott (1) *Henry Brulard* ■ *Dir* François Truffaut • *Scr* François Truffaut, Jean-Louis Richard, David Rudkin, Helen Scott, from the novel by Ray Bradbury • *Cinematographer* Nicolas Roeg

Fahrenheit 9/11 ★★★★ 15

Political documentary
2004 · US · Colour · 122mins

Michael Moore's controversial Palme d'Or winning documentary is a blistering attack on George W Bush's administration. The film investigates the legitimacy of Bush's presidency, his links to the Bin Laden family, the role oil played in the response to the World Trade Center attacks and how the pursuit of the Taliban led to the Iraq War. He even takes us up to the abuse of Iraqi prisoners by US soldiers that dominated the news in the first half of 2004. The assembled news footage and street interviews are always riveting, contentious and one-sided. This agitprop reflection on the dubious agenda of American foreign policy inevitably preaches to the converted, but it also uncovers or highlights many thought-provoking facts. AJ [video] DVD

Dir/Scr Michael Moore (2)

Fail-Safe ★★★★ PG

Drama 1964 · US · BW · 107mins

This follows the same flight path as *Dr Strangelove* as a squadron of US planes, loaded with nuclear bombs, accidentally sets off to devastate Moscow and cannot be halted from its doomsday mission. Director Sidney Lumet builds the tension from neurotic jitters (Larry Hagman as presidential interpreter) through to psychotic jeopardy (Walter Matthau's anti-Soviet professor urging the Armageddon sanction) when fail-safe devices fail and American president Henry Fonda has to warn his Soviet counterpart that the world is heading into nightmare. By telling it straight, the idea loses a certain satirical edge, but gains a hint of reality. TH [video]

Henry Fonda *The President* • Walter Matthau *Groeteschele* • Frank Overton *General Bogan* • Dan O'Herlihy *General Black* • Fritz Weaver *Colonel Cascio* • Larry Hagman *Buck* • Edward Binns *Colonel Grady* • William Hansen *Secretary Swenson* ■ *Dir* Sidney Lumet • *Scr* Walter Bernstein, from the novel by Eugene Burdick, Harvey Wheeler

Fail Safe ★★★ PG

Political thriller 2000 · US · BW · 84mins

Remaking the 1964 Sidney Lumet Cold War classic about a president who nukes New York in atonement for a rogue missile's decimation of Moscow was a challenge in itself. But to do it in one take and in letterboxed black and white was asking a lot of even this talented cast. Yet, director Stephen Frears achieves a judicious blend of suspense and philosophising, as the various hawks and doves seek to sway Richard Dreyfuss while George Clooney's plane gets ever closer to its target. DP [video] DVD

George Clooney *Col Grady* • Noah Wyle *Buck* • Richard Dreyfuss *President* • Hank Azaria *Professor Groeteschele* • Brian Dennehy *Gen Bogan* • Harvey Keitel *Warren Black* • Don Cheadle *Pierce* • James Cromwell *Gordon Knapp* • Sam Elliott *Congressman Tom Raskob* ■ *Dir* Stephen Frears • *Scr* Walter Bernstein, from the novel by Harvey Wheeler, Eugene Burdick

Fair Game ★★ 15

Action drama 1995 · US · Colour · 86mins

T-shirt clad Cindy Crawford gets chased by baddies and falls into the water a lot, and that's about it. If you can believe supermodel Crawford (in her big Hollywood debut) is a high-powered lawyer then you will probably just about swallow the nonsensical story about Russian villains who are convinced she has some valuable information about their American operation. Some enjoyably destructive set pieces aside, the only fun to be had is savouring Steven Berkoff's over-the-top performance. JF. Contains swearing, violence and nudity. [video] DVD

William Baldwin *Detective Max Kirkpatrick* • Cindy Crawford *Kate McQuean* • Steven Berkoff *Kazak* • Christopher McDonald *Lieutenant Mayerson* • Miguel Sandoval *Juantorena* • Salma Hayek *Rita* ■ *Dir* Andrew Sipes • *Scr* Charlie Fletcher, from the novel by Paula Gosling

Fair Warning ★★

Mystery 1937 · US · BW · 68mins

One of those 20th Century-Fox programme fillers made swiftly and cheaply, invariably on existing sets, intended as little more than support for the main feature, and undeniably fascinating to view today. This western features John Howard Payne, playing a swimming instructor involved in murder. Top-billed, however, is the excellent J Edward Bromberg, whose career would be tragically cut short by the communist witch-hunt (he was blacklisted and died in London in 1951 at the age of 48). TS

J Edward Bromberg *Matthew Jericho* • Betty Furness *Kay Farnham* • John Howard Payne [John Payne] *Jim Preston* • Victor Kilian *Sam* • Billy Burrud *Malcolm Berkhardt* • Gavin Muir *Herbert Willett* • Gloria Roy *Grace Hamilton* ■ *Dir* Norman Foster • *Scr* Norman Foster, Saul Elkins (uncredited), from the short story *Paradise Canyon Mystery* by Philip Wylie

Fair Wind to Java ★★★ PG

Adventure 1953 · US · Colour · 87mins

Fred MacMurray stars as a seafaring skipper in this rip-roaring adventure, racing against time and pirate Robert Douglas to recover a hoard of diamonds before Krakatoa erupts, and romancing Vera Ralston along the way. Unfortunately, the film is spoiled by its cheap studio backdrops and hopeless effects – you'll fall about laughing when the volcano blows. Still, there's much to enjoy, including Victor McLaglen as a drunken sailor. TS [video]

Fred MacMurray *Captain Boll* • Vera Ralston *Kim Kim* • Robert Douglas *Pulo Besar/St Ebenezer* • Victor McLaglen *O'Brien* • John Russell *Flint* • Buddy Baer *Kung* • Claude Jarman Jr *Chess* • Grant Withers *Jason Blue* ■ *Dir* Joseph Kane • *Scr* Richard Tregaskis, from the novel by Garland Roark

Fairy Tale for Seventeen Year Olds ★★★

Drama 1986 · Viet · BW · 77mins

Vietnamese films were shot in black and white until the mid-1980s, but few directors turned this budgetary constraint to such striking advantage as Nguyen Xuan Son in this touching home-front drama. Making particularly effective use of moonlight and reflective surfaces, the director brings a dreamlike quality to the tale of the teenager whose impression of the bitterly fought civil war is romanticised by her love for a handsome soldier at the front. However, he also depicts, all too realistically, the quiet heroism of those left behind as they endure the unbearable pain of waiting and hoping. DP. A Vietnamese language film.

Vy Le • Tranh Hahn • Tu Thanh ■ *Dir* Nguyen Xuan Son • *Scr* Trinh Thanh Nha

F

FairyTale: a True Story ★★★★ U

Period drama based on a true story
1997 · US · Colour · 93mins

Charles Sturridge lyrically directs this family tale, based on the true story of two young girls who, in 1917, produced photographs of a group of winged, fairy-like creatures they had taken at the bottom of their garden. The story follows the controversy that surrounded the photographs – were they real or were they faked? Luminaries such as Sir Arthur Conan Doyle (Peter O'Toole) and Harry Houdini (Harvey Keitel) debated the authenticity of the pictures. It's beautifully filmed, with nice special effects by Tim Webber, and Sturridge infuses the it with a sense of wonder and romanticism that contrasts with the more sombre backdrop of the First World War. JB [video]

Florence Hoath *Elsie Wright* • Elizabeth Earl (2) *Frances Griffiths* • Paul McGann *Arthur Wright* • Phoebe Nicholls *Polly Wright* • Bill Nighy *Edward Gardner* • Bob Peck *Harry Briggs* • Harvey Keitel *Harry Houdini* • Peter O'Toole *Sir Arthur Conan Doyle* • Mel Gibson *Frances' father* ■ *Dir* Charles Sturridge • *Scr* Ernie Contreras, from a story by Ernie Contreras, Albert Ash, Tom McLoughlin

Faithful ★ 15

Comedy 1996 · US · Colour · 87mins

Actor/scriptwriter Chazz Palminteri isn't so lucky with this adaptation of his stage play as he was with *A Bronx Tale*. In director Paul Mazursky's hands, Palminteri's three-hander turns into bland fare, showing little insight and featuring Cher in one of her worst performances. She plays the wife of Ryan O'Neal, who has hired hitman Palminteri to kill her on their 20th wedding anniversary. A depressingly flat, entertainment-free zone. AJ [video]

Cher *Margaret O'Donnell* • Chazz Palminteri *Tony* • Ryan O'Neal *Jack O'Donnell* • Paul Mazursky *Dr Susskind* • Amber Smith *Debbie* • Elisa Leonetti *Maria* ■ *Dir* Paul Mazursky • *Scr* Chazz Palminteri

Faithless ★★★

Melodrama 1932 · US · BW · 76mins

Made at the height of the Depression, this movie canters through a melodramatic story about a spoiled socialite who plumbs the depths before love saves the day. Tallulah Bankhead plays the daughter of a banker whose business has failed. She rejects Robert Montgomery despite the fact that she loves him, and sponges off acquaintances, eventually becoming mistress to one of them. This pre-Hays Code film ran into censorship problems in Britain because of its outspokenness, but audiences were unenthusiastic. BB

Tallulah Bankhead *Carol Morgan* • Robert Montgomery *Bill Wade* • Hugh Herbert *Mr Peter M Blainey* • Maurice Murphy *Anthony Wade* • Sterling Holloway *Reporter* • Charles Williams *Reporter* ■ *Dir* Harry Beaumont • *Scr* Carey Wilson, from a story by Mildred Cram

Faithless ★★★★ 15

Drama 2000 · Swe/Nor/Fin · Colour · 147mins

Given the history between director Liv Ullmann and screenwriter Ingmar Bergman, it's tempting to speculate on the autobiographical content of this intense study of infidelity and inspiration. It explores the impact of Lena Endre's affair with director Krister Henriksson on both her conductor husband, Thomas Hanzon, and their young daughter. Further blurring the line between fiction and reality, Bergman has Endre relate her story to Erland Josephson, a blocked scenarist whose relationship to the flashback events is never clarified. This is complex, mature and engrossing cinema from a master artist and his remarkable protégée. DP. In Swedish with English subtitles. DVD

Lena Endre *Marianne Vogler* • Erland Josephson *Bergman* • Krister Henriksson *David* • Thomas Hanzon *Markus* • Michelle Gylemo *Isabelle* • Juni Dahr *Margareta* ■ *Dir* Liv Ullmann • *Scr* Ingmar Bergman

Fakers ★★ 15

Comedy crime caper
2004 · UK · Colour · 81mins

There's something endearingly reminiscent of the 1960s about this watchable crime caper. Matthew Rhys plays a small-time conman who's in debt to London crime lord Art Malik. When Rhys stumbles across a lost sketch by an Italian master, he sees a way of wiping his slate clean – he commissions several copies and seeks to flog them to some of London's less scrupulous art dealers over the course of a single morning. This is well cast and decently made, but it lacks big-screen appeal. DA. Contains swearing. DVD

Matthew Rhys *Nick Edwards* • Kate Ashfield *Eve Evans* • Tom Chambers *Tony Evans* • Art Malik *Foster Wright* • Tony Haygarth *Phil Norris* • Edward Hibbert *Edward Fisher* • Paul Clayton *Gordon Price* • Larry Lamb *Harvey Steed* • Rula Lenska *Sylvia Creat* ■ *Dir* Richard Janes • *Scr* Paul Gerstenberger

The Falcon and the Co-Eds ★★

Detective mystery 1943 · US · BW · 68mins

Logic was never the byword of this RKO series, but utter confusion reigns in this seventh entry. Tom Conway investigates the death of a professor at a girls' school and, while the screenwriters pretty adept at bumping off suspects, the motives are so obscure that repeated viewing of Conway's accusatory summation only reveals additional loose ends and inconsistencies. No wonder William Clemens directed at such a lick. Still, this is entertaining. DP

Tom Conway *Tom Lawrence/The Falcon* • Jean Brooks *Vicky Gaines* • Rita Corday *Marguerita Serena* • Amelita Ward *Jane Harris* • Isabel Jewell *Mary Phoebus* • George Givot *Dr Anatole Graelich* • Cliff Clark *Timothy Donovan* • Ed Gargan [Edward Gargan] *Bates* ■ *Dir* William Clemens • *Scr* Ardel Wray, Gerald Geraghty, from the story by Ardel Wray, from the character created by Michael Arlen

The Falcon and the Snowman ★★★ 15

Spy drama based on a true story
1985 · US · Colour · 125mins

A convoluted spy thriller, with Timothy Hutton as a college dropout who obtains US secrets and, with his drug-addicted buddy Sean Penn, passes them on to the Soviet embassy in Mexico. The movie is about the motives for treason and the loss of moral purpose in America, underlined by some heavy-handed flashbacks to Vietnam, the Kennedys, Martin Luther King and even John Lennon. Directed with customary visual flair by John Schlesinger, it's undeniably gripping, if a little long and unfocused. AT. Contains violence and swearing.

Timothy Hutton *Christopher Boyce* • Sean Penn *Daulton Lee* • Pat Hingle *Mr Boyce* • Richard Dysart *Dr Lee* • Lori Singer *Lana* • David Suchet *Alex* • Dorian Harewood *Gene* • Priscilla Pointer *Mrs Lee* ■ *Dir* John Schlesinger • *Scr* Steven Zaillian, from the book by Robert Lindsey

The Falcon in Danger ★★

Detective mystery 1943 · US · BW · 70mins

When $100,000 in securities goes missing and two corpses show up, who better to solve the mystery than debonair detective the Falcon (Tom Conway)? The sixth entry in RKO's B-movie series is far from the most suspenseful. Indeed, apart from the opening sequence, in which an empty plane crashes at an airport and a couple of assassination attempts take place, the mystery is often forced to take a backseat to the Falcon's romance with Amelita Ward. DP

Tom Conway *The Falcon* • Jean Brooks *Iris* • Elaine Shepard *Nancy* • Amelita Ward *Bonnie* • Cliff Clark *Donovan* • Ed Gargan [Edward Gargan] *Bates* • Clarence Kolb *Palmer* • Felix Basch *Morley* • Richard Davies *Ken* ■ *Dir* William Clemens • *Scr* Fred Niblo Jr, Craig Rice, from the character created by Michael Arlen

The Falcon in Hollywood ★★

Detective mystery 1944 · US · BW · 67mins

Hooray for Hollywood, because without the trip around RKO's back lot and visits to such landmarks as the Hollywood Bowl, this whodunnit would have been over in two reels. The vacationing Tom Conway clearly revels in being surrounded by beautiful starlets as he tries to discover who killed the acting ex of a costume designer on the eve of her wedding to a hotshot director. This tenth outing for the RKO hero is a ploddingly predictable thriller. DP

Tom Conway *Tom Lawrence/The Falcon* • Barbara Hale *Peggy Callahan* • Veda Ann Borg *Billie* • Jean Brooks *Roxanna* • Rita Corday *Lilli D'Allio* • John Abbott *Martin Dwyer* • Sheldon Leonard *Louie* ■ *Dir* Gordon Douglas • *Scr* Gerald Geraghty, from the character created by Michael Arlen

The Falcon in Mexico ★★

Detective mystery 1944 · US · BW · 70mins

According to Hollywood legend, the location footage used in this puzzling ninth series entry was borrowed from Orson Welles's infamously scuppered documentary, *It's All True*. Certainly, the Mexican vistas add to the appeal of this typical mystery, in which Tom Conway allies with artist's daughter Martha MacVicar to discover how her long-dead father could have painted a portrait of Cecilia Callejo. With a trio of murders, a couple of unnecessary musical interludes and one near miss, this is certainly a busy picture. DP

Tom Conway *Tom Lawrence/The Falcon* • Mona Maris *Raquel* • Martha MacVicar *Barbara Wade* • Nestor Paiva *Manuel Romero* • Mary Currier *Paula Dudley* • Cecilia Callejo *Dolores Ybarra* ■ *Dir* William Berke • *Scr* Gerald Geraghty, George Worthing Yates, from the character created by Michael Arlen

The Falcon in San Francisco ★★★

Detective mystery 1945 · US · BW · 65mins

Joseph H Lewis's sole entry in RKO's long-running crime series (the eleventh) is undoubtedly the most stylish. It's also the funniest, with Tom Conway's doltish sidekick Edward Brophy spending as much time searching for a wife as he does looking for clues to solve the case. A murder on a train sparks this lively adventure, in which the Falcon plays nursemaid to orphaned Sharyn Moffett while trying to clear Rita Corday of involvement with a gang of silk smugglers. DP

Tom Conway *Tom Lawrence/The Falcon* • Rita Corday *Joan Marshall* • Edward S Brophy [Edward Brophy] *Goldie Locke* • Sharyn Moffett *Annie Marshall* • Fay Helm *Doreen Temple* ■ *Dir* Joseph H Lewis • *Scr* Robert Kent, Ben Markson, from a story by Robert Kent, from the character created by Michael Arlen

The Falcon Out West ★★

Detective mystery 1944 · US · BW · 64mins

Tom Conway finds himself in sagebrush country after millionaire Lyle Talbot collapses inexplicably on a New York dance floor. A trip to his ranch in Texas, in the unwelcome company of inspector Cliff Clark and his doltish sidekick Don Douglas, reveals the culprit, but not before Conway has survived two attempts on his life. Not one of the best in the series, with the script idly coasting along on western clichés. DP

Tom Conway *The Falcon* • Barbara Hale *Marion* • Don Douglas *Hayden* • Carole Gallagher *Vanessa* • Joan Barclay *Mrs Irwin* • Cliff Clark *Inspector Donovan* • Ed Gargan [Edward Gargan] *Bates* • Minor Watson *Caldwell* ■ *Dir* William Clemens • *Scr* Billy Jones, Morton Grant, from the character created by Michael Arlen

The Falcon Strikes Back ★★★

Detective mystery 1943 · US · BW · 65mins

One of the finest slapstick stooges since the silent era, Edgar Kennedy steals the show here as a malevolent puppeteer caught up in the same war bond scam for which the police want to question our dapper hero, The Falcon (Tom Conway), after he is found unconscious alongside a very dead bank manager. Dashing off the playful dialogue with aplomb, Conway relishes his first solo outing as the crime fighter in this fifth instalment of the long-running series. Clearly, the superior direction of Edward Dmytryk suited him in this slickly staged mystery. DP

Tom Conway *The Falcon* • Harriet Hilliard [Harriet Nelson] *Gwynne Gregory* • Jane Randolph *Marcia Brooks* • Edgar Kennedy *Smiley Dugan* • Cliff Edwards *Goldie* • Rita Corday *Mia Bruger* • Erford Gage *Rickey Davis* ■ *Dir* Edward Dmytryk • *Scr* Edward Dein, Gerald Geraghty, from a story by Stuart Palmer, from the character created by Michael Arlen

The Falcon Takes Over ★★★

Detective mystery 1942 · US · BW · 63mins

Raymond Chandler's *Farewell, My Lovely* was the inspiration for George Sanders's penultimate outing as Michael Arlen's suave sleuth. (Sanders handed over the role to his real-life brother Tom Conway in *The Falcon's Brother*). An escaped convict, a priceless necklace and a clever impostor are the plot strands that Irving Reis weaves together at breakneck speed. The third, and easily the best, entry in RKO's ever-enjoyable series. DP

George Sanders *The Falcon* • Lynn Bari *Ann Riordan* • Allen Jenkins *Goldie Locke* • James Gleason *Inspector Mike O'Hara* • Helen Gilbert *Diana Kenyon* • Ward Bond *Moose Malloy* • Ed Gargan [Edward Gargan] *Bates* ■ *Dir* Irving Reis • *Scr* Lynn Root, Frank Fenton, from the character created by Michael Arlen and the novel *Farewell, My Lovely* by Raymond Chandler

Falcons ★★ 15

Drama
2002 · Ice/UK/Nor/Ger/Fr · Colour · 91mins

Beautifully photographed by Harald Paalgard, but utterly lacking in logic and precision, this bizarre road movie never seems sure where it's heading. Initially, it appears as though American jailbird Keith Carradine has arrived in Iceland intent on either self-discovery or suicide. But he is then distracted by eccentric artist Margret Vilhjalmsdottir, who is taking care of a rescued falcon and so begins a meandering journey across the northlands. Director Fridrik Thor Fridriksson seems as lost as everyone on screen. DP. In Icelandic and English with subtitles. DVD

Keith Carradine *Simon* • Margret Vilhjalmsdottir *Dua* • Ingvar E Sigurdsson *Cop* ■ *Dir* Fridrik Thor Fridriksson • *Scr* Fridrik Thor Fridriksson, Einar Karason

The Falcon's Adventure ★★

Detective mystery 1946 · US · BW · 61mins

Considering the uninspiring job he did on *The Falcon in Mexico*, it's rather surprising that RKO executives let William Berke direct the 13th entry in this ever-lively series. It turned out to be the troubleshooter's final assignment for the studio, however, as Tom Conway cancels his vacation to keep both Madge Meredith and a formula for synthetic industrial diamonds out of the hands of the villains who have framed him for her father's murder. John Calvert took over the role of the Falcon for a further three adventures, beginning with *Devil's Cargo* (1948). DP

Tom Conway *The Falcon* • Madge Meredith *Louisa Braganza* • Edward S Brophy [Edward Brophy] *Goldie* • Robert Warwick *Sutton* • Myrna Dell *Doris* • Steve Brodie *Benny* • Ian Wolfe *Denison* • Carol Forman *Helen* ■ *Dir* William Berke • *Scr* Aubrey Wisberg, Robert Kent, from the character created by Michael Arlen

The Falcon's Alibi ★★

Detective mystery 1946 · US · BW · 62mins

This twelfth entry is one of the weakest in the series, a tale of jewel theft and murders that leaves you doubting Tom Conway's powers of detection. A waiter, a hotel guest and sassy band singer Jane Greer all bite the dust before Conway finally twigs who's responsible for the theft of Esther Howard's pearls, which he was supposed to protect. DP

Tom Conway *The Falcon* • Rita Corday *Joan* • Vince Barnett *Goldie* • Jane Greer *Lola* • Elisha Cook Jr *Nick* • Emory Parnell *Metcalf* • Al Bridge *Inspector Blake* • Esther Howard *Mrs Peabody* ■ *Dir* Ray McCarey • *Scr* Paul Yawitz, from a story by Dane Lussier, Manny Seff, from the character created by Michael Arlen

The Falcon's Brother ★★

Detective mystery 1942 · US · BW · 62mins

George Sanders handed over the reins of RKO's popular B-franchise to his brother Tom Conway during this disappointing thriller, the fourth in the 16-film series. The war rears its ugly head for the only time in the series, as Conway arrives in South America in time to help Sanders track down some Fifth Columnists. Directed with brisk efficiency, but little imagination. Conway went on to star as the Falcon a further nine times, beginning with 1943's *The Falcon Strikes Back*. DP

George Sanders *Gay Lawrence* • Tom Conway *Tom Lawrence* • Jane Randolph *Marcie Brooks* • Don Barclay *Lefty* • Cliff Clark *Inspector Timothy Donovan* ■ *Dir* Stanley Logan • *Scr* Stuart Palmer, Craig Rice, from the character created by Michael Arlen

Fall ★★ 18

Romantic drama 1997 · US · Colour · 86mins

Directed by, written by and starring Eric Schaeffer this is a romantic drama with a refreshingly realistic edge. Despite the totally obvious premise – Schaeffer meets model Amanda De Cadenet, they have steamy sex and then part, as she's married – it moves from semi-soft-porn style rot to become an interesting drama about how the two of them can genuinely remain friends. De Cadenet is watchable and Schaeffer handles his role and a sharp script with skill. LH. Contains swearing and sex scenes.

Eric Schaeffer *Michael Shiver* • Amanda De Cadenet *Sarah Easton* • Rudolf Martin *Philippe* • Francie Swift *Robin* • Lisa Vidal *Sally* ■ *Dir/Scr* Eric Schaeffer

Fall into Darkness ★★ 15

Mystery thriller 1996 · US · Colour · 87mins

The execution is pretty routine, but there is more intrigue than usual in this made-for-TV thriller. Tatyana Ali plays a brilliant music student who falls victim to a young socialite's plan to avenge her brother's death. The playing of Ali and her co-star Jonathan Brandis is bland, but there are enough twists and turns in the plot to keep the viewer guessing. JF. Contains swearing and violence. DVD

Tatyana M Ali [Tatyana Ali] *Sharon McKay* • Jonathan Brandis *Chad Lear* • Charlotte Ross *Ann Price* • Sean Murray (2) *Jerry Price* • Paul Scherrer *Paul Lear* ■ *Dir* Mark Sobel • *Scr* JB White, from the novel by Christopher Pike

The Fall of Babylon ★★★

Silent historical epic 1919 · US · BW · 82mins

DW Griffith's 1916 epic *Intolerance* contained four separate stories, virtually bankrupted Griffith, and audiences found it far too much to swallow in one gulp. So Griffith took out the juiciest story, about a mountain girl who loves Belshazzar and protects him against the evil high priest of Bel, added some new scenes and released the "new" film in 1919. There's lashings of sex and violence, and that staggering set filled with elephant statues and thousands of semi-naked extras. The penalty is Griffith's overlay of moral indignation." AT

Tully Marshall *The High Priest of Bel* • Constance Talmadge *The Mountain girl* • Elmer Clifton *The Rhapsode* • Alfred Paget *Prince Belshazzar* • Carl Stockdale *Nabonidus, King of Babylonia* • Seena Owen *Attarea, favorite of Belshazzar* ■ *Dir/Scr* DW Griffith • *Cinematographer* GW Bitzer [Billy Bitzer]

The Fall of the House of Usher ★★★★ 12

Horror 1960 · US · Colour · 78mins

The huge success of this elegant tale of foreboding horror, based on an Edgar Allan Poe story of substance (unlike some later knock-offs), cemented director Roger Corman's artistic style and developed Vincent Price's "Master of the Macabre" persona. Price is superb as the white-haired, hypersensitive recluse Roderick Usher who has a demented obsession with his ancestors. Lavishly produced, visually gorgeous and still scary after all these years. AJ DVD

Vincent Price *Roderick Usher* • Mark Damon *Philip Winthrop* • Myrna Fahey *Madeline Usher* • Harry Ellerbe *Bristol* ■ *Dir* Roger Corman • *Scr* Richard Matheson, from the story by Edgar Allan Poe • *Cinematographer* Floyd Crosby

The Fall of the Roman Empire ★★★★ U

Historical epic 1964 · US · Colour · 172mins

Producer Samuel Bronston's legacy of six European-shot epics looks more cherishable as the years pass, and leaves one aching to see them once more in their full cinematic glory. This fine example has excellent chariot action and a wonderful, if brief, performance by Alec Guinness. Sophia Loren has seldom looked lovelier, and the screenplay with its nods to historian Edward Gibbon is resolutely intelligent. The distinguished support cast ensures that the long movie never palls, and Anthony Mann directs with his usual finesse. TS DVD

Sophia Loren *Lucilla* • Stephen Boyd *Livius* • Alec Guinness *Marcus Aurelius* • Christopher Plummer *Commodus* • James Mason *Timonides* • Omar Sharif *Sohamus* • Anthony Quayle *Verulus* • John Ireland *Ballomar* • Mel Ferrer *Cleander* • Eric Porter *Julianus* ■ *Dir* Anthony Mann • *Scr* Ben Barzman, Basilio Franchina, Philip Yordan • *Cinematographer* Robert Krasker • *Music* Dmitri Tiomkin

Fall Time ★★ 18

Crime thriller 1994 · US · Colour · 84mins

Mickey Rourke's career decline continued with this daft, muddled crime thriller. He and Stephen Baldwin (wildly over the top) play two vicious bank robbers who kidnap a trio of prank-loving teenagers whom they mistakenly believe are planning to rob a bank they have already targeted. In director Paul Warner's hands the film lurches clumsily from one unlikely situation to the next. JF. Contains violence and swearing.

Mickey Rourke *Florence* • Stephen Baldwin *Leon* • Sheryl Lee *Patty* • Sammy Kershaw *Officer Donny* • Jason London *Tim* • David Arquette *David* ■ *Dir* Paul Warner • *Scr* Steven Alden, Paul Skemp

Fallen ★★★ 15

Supernatural thriller
1998 · US · Colour · 119mins

In this convoluted, *Omen*-esque chiller, Denzel Washington gives a strong central performance as a Manhattan homicide detective pursuing a supernatural serial killer. The initial development of the tale is intriguing, with seemingly disparate strands of information gradually combining into the discovery of a vengeful ancient god. But the atmosphere is only fitfully scary because of writer/producer Nicholas Kazan's loose-ended, pretentiously unresolved script. AJ. Contains swearing, violence. DVD

Denzel Washington *John Hobbes* • John Goodman *Jonesy* • Donald Sutherland *Lieutenant Stanton* • Embeth Davidtz *Gretta Milano* • James Gandolfini *Lou* • Elias Koteas *Edgar Reese* • Gabriel Casseus *Art* ■ *Dir* Gregory Hoblit • *Scr* Nicholas Kazan

Fallen Angel ★★★★ PG

Film noir 1945 · US · BW · 95mins

This terrific Fox *film noir* was directed by Otto Preminger in the wake of his classic *Laura*. Slightly softened by the casting of Alice Faye, who was ill at ease in a leading role, it is greatly enhanced by the presence of Dana Andrews and Linda Darnell. They're a nervy opportunist and sexy paramour respectively in a knockout plot involving Andrews's wish to quit respectable Faye for bad girl Darnell. Watch Andrews – his quizzical, deadpan features always seemed more alert for Preminger than under any other director. TS DVD

Alice Faye *June Mills* • Dana Andrews *Eric Stanton* • Linda Darnell *Stella* • Charles Bickford *Mark Judd* • Anne Revere *Clara Mills* • Bruce Cabot *Dave Atkins* • John Carradine *Professor Madley* • Percy Kilbride *Pop* ■ *Dir* Otto Preminger • *Scr* Harry Kleiner, from the novel by Marty Holland

Fallen Angels ★★★★ 15

Comedy drama 1995 · HK · Colour · 96mins

Asian film-maker Wong Kar-Wai always offers skewed and original views of a seemingly familiar world, accompanied by weirdly inappropriate pop music. Here the director takes his peripatetic camera on a vivid trip through the neon-soaked nightlife of Hong Kong as hitman Leon Lai comes into contact with three other frustrated lost souls. The multilayered story blends riveting philosophical musings on missed opportunities, the impermanence of memory and the inevitability of loneliness, brilliantly serving it all up in a *Pulp Fiction*-style wrapper. AJ. In Cantonese with English subtitles.

Leon Lai *Wong Chi-Ming* • Takeshi Kaneshiro *He Zhiwu* • Charlie Yeung *Cherry* • Michelle Reis *Agent* • Karen Mok *Blondie* ■ *Dir/Scr* Wong Kar-Wai

The Fallen Idol ★★★★ PG

Thriller 1948 · UK · BW · 91mins

While working as a film critic in the 1930s, Graham Greene noticed Carol Reed's developing directorial talent. This was the first of their three collaborations as writer and director, and what a minor masterpiece it is. Bobby Henrey gives an exceptional performance as the ambassador's son whose attempts to help the butler he idolises only land the latter in hot water with the police after the suspicious death of the butler's wife. Credit is also due to Ralph Richardson and Michèle Morgan for allowing the boy to steal every scene in the interest of suspense. DP DVD

Ralph Richardson *Baines* • Michèle Morgan *Julie* • Bobby Henrey *Felipe* • Sonia Dresdel *Mrs Baines* • Denis O'Dea *Inspector Crowe* • Walter Fitzgerald *Dr Fenton* • Dandy Nichols *Mrs Patterson* • Bernard Lee *Detective Hart* • Jack Hawkins *Detective Lake* ■ *Dir* Carol Reed • *Scr* Graham Greene, Lesley Storm, William Templeton, from the short story *The Basement Room* by Graham Greene

The Fallen Sparrow ★★★ PG

Spy drama 1943 · US · BW · 93mins

In this entertaining though sometimes unintelligible spy drama, there's a strong feeling of a left-leaning plot that's been knobbled by the studio. Tough guy John Garfield gives a great performance as the battle weary veteran who returns from the hell of an internment camp in the Spanish Civil War only to find he's being chased by Nazi agents in the US. Maureen O'Hara is on hand to help, but this *film noir*-like material needed a tighter hand on the tiller than studio hack Richard Wallace. TS

John Garfield *Kit* • Maureen O'Hara *Toni Donne* • Walter Slezak *Dr Skaas* • Patricia Morison *Barby Taviton* • Martha O'Driscoll *Whitney Hamilton* • Bruce Edwards *Ab Parker* ■ *Dir* Richard Wallace • *Scr* Warren Duff, from the novel by Dorothy B Hughes

Falling Down ★★★★ 18

Satirical thriller
1992 · US/Fr · Colour · 107mins

Made from a script rejected by every major Hollywood studio, this is a storming portrait of inner-city life in America. That stateside critics were virtually unanimous in condemning it as a dangerous and irresponsible fantasy says more about the insecurities of the world's sole remaining superpower than it does about the merits of Joel Schumacher's bold, believable and darkly funny film. As the headlines never cease to remind us, the idea that an ordinary Joe can snap and go on a violent spree is depressingly feasible. Michael Douglas gives a superb performance and he's matched by the excellent Robert Duvall. Courageous, mature film-making. DP. Contains swearing and violence. DVD

Michael Douglas *D-Fens, William Foster* • Robert Duvall *Prendergast* • Barbara Hershey *Beth* • Rachel Ticotin *Sandra* • Tuesday Weld *Mrs Prendergast* • Frederic Forrest *Surplus Store owner* • Lois Smith *D-Fens's mother* • Joey Hope Singer *Adele* ■ *Dir* Joel Schumacher • *Scr* Ebbe Roe Smith

Falling from Grace ★★ 15

Drama 1992 · US · Colour · 96mins

Rock star John Mellencamp made his directorial debut with this tale of a country singer who discovers he has few fans in his home town. Larry McMurtry wrote the screenplay, but this is closer to *Texasville* than it is to *The Last Picture Show*, with such clichéd characters as a brutal father, an envious brother and an embittered old flame moping around this dead-end part of Indiana. The storyline is unlikely in the extreme, but this is still an astute portrait of the delusions that attend celebrity. DP

John Mellencamp *Bud Parks* • Mariel Hemingway *Alice Parks* • Claude Akins *Speck Parks* • Dub Taylor *Grandpa Parks* • Kay Lenz *PJ Parks* • Larry Crane *Ramey Parks* • Kate Noonan *Linda* ■ *Dir* John Mellencamp • *Scr* Larry McMurtry

Falling in Love ★★★ PG

Romantic drama
1984 · US · Colour · 101mins

Robert De Niro and Meryl Streep are such dramatic heavyweights it's difficult to see them as ordinary people involved in a typical affair. Yet this succeeds thanks to their subtle performances, as the separately married Manhattan commuters whose daily contact becomes mutual obsession. Ulu Grosbard's stilted direction is a hindrance, but De Niro and Streep more than compensate. TH. Contains swearing. DVD

Meryl Streep *Molly Gilmore* • Robert De Niro *Frank Raftis* • Harvey Keitel *Ed Lasky* • Jane Kaczmarek *Ann Raftis* • George Martin (1) *John Trainer* • David Clennon *Brian Gilmore* • Dianne Wiest *Isabelle* ■ *Dir* Ulu Grosbard • *Scr* Michael Christofer

Falling in Love Again ★★★ 15

Romantic comedy drama
1980 · US · Colour · 98mins

Elliott Gould is perfectly cast as the New Yorker in midlife crisis, remembering the girl he loved and won when they were both much younger. Unfortunately, his wife Susannah York couldn't make a success of their married life. For all its spot-on observations, this comedy drama about an American hero who can't come to terms with the way things are is introspective and narcissistic. York's younger self is played by Michelle Pfeiffer with an inner glow that suggested stardom was ahead. TH DVD

Elliott Gould *Harry Lewis* • Susannah York *Sue Lewis* • Michelle Pfeiffer *Sue Wellington* • Kaye Ballard *Mrs Lewis* • Stuart Paul *Pompadour/Young Harry* • Robert Hackman *Mr Lewis* • Steven Paul *Stan the Con* • Todd Helper *Alan Childs* ■ *Dir* Steven Paul • *Scr* Steven Paul, Ted Allan, Susannah York, from a story by Hank Paul, Steven Paul

The Falls ★★★★ PG

Science-fiction drama
1980 · UK · Colour · 186mins

Peter Greenaway is at his most mischievously accessible and intellectually sophisticated in this pastiche documentary chronicling the impact of an unexplained phenomenon dubbed the "Violent Unknown Event" (VUE) on 92 people whose surnames are all contain the word "Fall". The accompanying commentary, delineating the biographies of these eccentric unfortunates, is stuffed with literate wordplay, surreal concepts, numerical sequences and satirical asides, as Greenaway links the VUE with various bizarre ornithological and linguistic manifestations. The use of found footage and photography is equally inspired, as it enables Greenaway to demonstrate his visual acuity while reinforcing this unique enterprise's Pythonesque absurdity. DP DVD

Colin Cantlie *Narrator* • Hilary Thompson *Narrator* • Sheila Canfield *Narrator* • Adam Leys *Narrator* • Serena MacBeth *Narrator* • Martin Burrows *Narrator* ■ *Dir/Scr* Peter Greenaway • *Cinematographer* Mike Coles, John Rosenberg • *Music* Michael Nyman, Brian Eno, John Hyde, Keith Pendlebury

False Identity ★★ 15

Thriller 1990 · US · Colour · 94mins

James Keach directs his brother Stacy in this suspense thriller about a man who returns home after nearly 20 years in prison, unable to remember much of his past. Keach is terrific as the disturbed ex-con and is given impressive support from Geneviève Bujold (*Coma*) and Veronica Cartwright (*Alien*), but this is eventually spoiled by a badly fitting finale. Shame, because otherwise this is a well-played and interesting drama. JB

Stacy Keach *Harlan Errickson/Ben Driscoll* • Geneviève Bujold *Rachel Roux* • Tobin Bell *Marshall Errickson* • Veronica Cartwright *Vera Errickson* • Mimi Maynard *Audrey* • Mike Champion [Michael Champion] *Luther* ■ *Dir* James Keach • *Scr* Sandra K Bailey

False Paradise ★★ U

Western 1948 · US · BW · 59mins

One of the last of the Hopalong Cassidy series, this standard western potboiler has William Boyd (who by this time was his own producer and about to transfer to TV) outshooting the usual villains and coming out with the heroine on his arm. Andy Clyde is in attendance in his usual sidekick role as California Carlson; so is regular director George Archainbaud. AT

William Boyd (1) *Hopalong Cassidy* • Andy Clyde *California Carlson* • Rand Brooks *Lucky Jenkins* ■ *Dir* George Archainbaud • *Scr* Doris Schroeder, Harrison Jacobs

Fame ★★★ 15

Musical drama 1980 · US · Colour · 128mins

This musical drama from director Alan Parker might not be as much fun as *Bugsy Malone* and the songs aren't a patch on those in *The Commitments*, but it is, nevertheless, a thoroughly entertaining look at life in New York's High School for the Performing Arts (and, more to the point, it's miles better than the TV series that followed). Interestingly enough, none of the cast playing in a film all about making it big has gone on to become a movie star. DP. Contains swearing, drug abuse, a sex scene and brief nudity. DVD

Eddie Barth *Angelo* • Irene Cara *Coco Hernandez* • Lee Curreri *Bruno Martelli* • Laura Dean *Lisa Monroe* • Antonia Franceschi *Hilary Van Doren* • Boyd Gaines *Michael* • Albert Hague *Shorofsky* • Tresa Hughes *Naomi Finsecker* • Gene Anthony Ray *Leroy Johnson* • Debbie Allen *Lydia* ■ *Dir* Alan Parker • *Scr* Christopher Gore

Fame Is the Spur ★★★

Drama 1947 · UK · BW · 115mins

Labour's first prime minister, Ramsay MacDonald, was supposedly the inspiration for Howard Spring's bestseller, which is the source for director Roy Boulting's political drama. Yet Nigel Balchin's screenplay owes more to melodramatic contrivance than to historical fact, as Michael Redgrave rises from the north country slums to high office by waving his grandfather's trusty sword during his rabble-rousing speeches, and exploiting friends and foes alike. It's a powerhouse performance, but such is Redgrave's dominance that there's little room for other characters to develop. DP

Michael Redgrave *Hamer Radshaw* • Rosamund John *Ann Radshaw* • Bernard Miles *Tom Hanaway* • Hugh Burden *Arnold Ryerson* • Jean Shepherd *Mrs Radshaw* • Guy Verney *Grandpa* ■ *Dir* Roy Boulting • *Scr* Nigel Balchin, from a book by Howard Spring

Familia Rodante ★★ 15

Road movie drama
2004 · Arg/Sp/Ger/Bra · Colour · 103mins

Pablo Trapero's stalling trans-Argentinian road movie begins promisingly, as 80-something Graciana Chironi and her family cram into a rickety camper van to attend a wedding on the Brazilian border. However, their archetypically dysfunctional crises soon begin to grate. The desire to show how today's unbearable trials become tomorrow's cherished memories is laudable, but Trapero's execution is flat. DP. In Spanish with English subtitles. Contains swearing.

Graciana Chironi *Emilia* • Liliana Capurro *Marta* • Ruth Dobel *Claudia* • Bernardo Forteza *Oscar* • Federico Esquerro *Claudio* • Laura Glave *Paola* • Leila Gómez *Nadia* • Nicolás López *Matias* ■ *Dir/Scr* Pablo Trapero

The Family ★★★★

Drama 1987 · It/Fr · Colour · 130mins

Without once leaving the symbolically decorated apartment of an upper-middle-class Roman family, this increasingly static conversation piece explores 80 years of Italian national and domestic trauma through the eyes of one man and his quarrelsome kinsmen. Leading an ensemble cast of uniform excellence, Vittorio Gassman laments his decision to marry Stefania Sandrelli instead of her sister, Fanny Ardant, while director Ettore Scola shifts effortlessly between melodrama and comedy, while passing insightful comments on the national character. DP. In Italian with English subtitles.

Vittorio Gassman *Carlo/Carlo's grandfather* • Fanny Ardant *Adriana* • Stefania Sandrelli *Beatrice* • Andrea Occhipinti *Carlo, as a young man* • Jo Champa *Adriana, as a young woman* ■ *Dir* Ettore Scola • *Scr* Ruggero Maccari, Furio Scarpelli, Ettore Scola

A Family Affair ★★

Comedy 1937 · US · BW · 68mins

Worthy of a modest footnote in cinema history as being the first in the long-running Andy Hardy series – 15 films in all. Mickey Rooney plays the small-town American teen whose father is the local judge – the role played here by Lionel Barrymore, later inherited by Lewis Stone. Rooney falls for a girl, while his dad has work-related problems. As per the series which followed, it's a hymn to all things American, land of the free and, it seems, of the cute and precocious. AT

Lionel Barrymore *Judge Hardy* • Mickey Rooney *Andy Hardy* • Cecilia Parker *Marian Hardy* • Eric Linden *Wayne Trenton* • Charley Grapewin *Frank Redmond* • Spring Byington *Mrs Hardy* • Julie Haydon *Joan Hardy* ■ *Dir* George B Seitz • *Scr* Kay Van Riper, from the play *Skidding* by Aurania Rouverol

Family Album ★★

Romantic comedy
1994 · Sp · Colour · 92mins

Marta Balletbò-Coll made her feature debut with this lesbian love story, which took a mere 14 days to shoot. She also stars as the Barcelona tour guide who uses all her powers of persuasion to prevent bisexual seismologist, Desi del Valle, from terminating their hesitant romance and taking a job abroad. As with so many low-budget projects, it's a highly talkative affair, with Balletbò-Coll declaiming at length about past lovers. Eager and amiable, but short on substance and style. DP

Desi del Valle *Montserrat Ehrzman-Rosas* • Marta Balletbò-Coll *Anna Giralt-Romaguera* • Montserrat Gausachs *Marta L Puig* • Emili Remolins Casas *Man at the computer* • Josep Maria Brugues *Jordi* ■ *Dir* Marta Balletbò-Coll • *Scr* Marta Balletbò-Coll, Ana Simon Cerezo

Family Business ★★★ 15

Comedy drama 1989 · US · Colour · 109mins

The line-up is mouthwatering (Sean Connery, Dustin Hoffman and Matthew Broderick, plus director Sidney Lumet), but the result is something of a disappointment. Connery plays an irascible, old-school thief and Hoffman is his bitter son who is now desperately trying to go straight. However, he is reluctantly drawn back into a life of crime when he learns that his own son (Broderick) is about to go to work with grandpa in the family business. The scenes between the leads are superb, but all three are poorly served by an ill-focused script and surprisingly sluggish direction. JF. Contains swearing, violence. DVD

Sean Connery *Jessie McMullen* • Dustin Hoffman *Vito McMullen* • Matthew Broderick *Adam McMullen* • Rosana De Soto *Elaine McMullen* • Janet Carroll *Margie* • Victoria Jackson *Christine* • Bill McCutcheon *Doheny* • Deborah Rush *Michele Dempsey* ■ *Dir* Sidney Lumet • *Scr* Vincent Patrick, from his book

The Family Jewels ★ U

Comedy 1965 · US · Colour · 99mins

After the split with comedy partner Dean Martin, the unique talents of Jerry Lewis made him one of those performers you just couldn't ignore. But the man who influenced Jim Carrey and Adam Sandler began at one point to overreach himself and this movie is a sorry reminder of that period. Here, Lewis plays seven roles as potential guardians of precocious little Donna Butterworth, heiress to a fortune. He also directed this clumsy, mawkish and unfunny load of old tripe. RS

Jerry Lewis *Willard Woodward/Everett Peyton/James Peyton/Eddie Peyton/Julius Peyton/"Bugs" Peyton/Skylock Peyton* • Sebastian Cabot *Dr Matson* • Donna Butterworth *Donna Peyton* • Jay Adler *Attorney* ■ *Dir* Jerry Lewis • *Scr* Jerry Lewis, Bill Richmond

Family Life ★★★

Drama 1971 · UK · Colour · 107mins

This is a harrowing study of mental illness and the methods of treating it. Making only his third feature, director Ken Loach was already employing the uncompromisingly realistic style that has since become his trademark and some of the scenes in which teenager Sandy Ratcliff is subjected to electroconvulsive therapy are among the most traumatic of his career. Rarely has family life been presented in such a gloomy light, and Bill Dean and Grace Cave deserve much credit for depicting such thoroughly detestable parents. Over-manipulative, maybe, but still deeply disturbing. DP. Contains violence and swearing.

Sandy Ratcliff *Janice Baildon* • Bill Dean *Mr Baildon* • Grace Cave *Mrs Baildon* • Malcolm Tierney *Tim* • Hilary Martyn *Barbara Baildon* • Michael Riddall *Dr Donaldson* • Alan MacNaughtan *Mr Carswell* • Johnny Gee *Man in garden* ■ *Dir* Ken Loach • *Scr* David Mercer, from his TV play *In Two Minds*

The Family Man ★★★ 12

Seasonal romantic fantasy
2000 · US · Colour · 129mins

Nicolas Cage is the high-powered businessman who goes to bed in his designer Manhattan apartment on Christmas Eve, but wakes up in a suburban home on Christmas Day, complete with wife, dog and kids. It seems he's getting the chance to see what his life would have been like had he stayed with his college sweetheart Téa Leoni instead of pursuing a highly successful life in the fast lane. Cage is fun as the fish out of water trying to adapt to school runs and working at a local tyre company, and Leoni is spot-on as his harassed wife. JB DVD

Nicolas Cage *Jack Campbell* • Téa Leoni *Kate* • Don Cheadle *Cash* • Jeremy Piven *Arnie* • Saul Rubinek *Alan Mintz* • Josef Sommer *Lassiter* ■ *Dir* Brett Ratner • *Scr* David Diamond, David Weissman

Family Plan ★ PG

Comedy 1997 · US · Colour · 92mins

Leslie Nielson has persisted with the spoofery that relaunched his career, with patchy results. With this turkey, however, he hits a new low. After the death of an old friend, the bungling Nielson finds himself in charge of a crumbling summer camp for orphans; Judge Reinhold is the slimy businessman out to convert the property into a holiday resort. JF. Contains some swearing. DVD

Leslie Nielsen *Harry Haber* • Judge Reinhold *Jeffrey Shayes* • Eddie Bowz *Matt Nolan* • Emily Procter *Julie Rubins* ■ *Dir* Fred Gerber • *Scr* Paul Bernbaum

Family Plot ★★★★ PG

Comedy thriller 1976 · US · Colour · 115mins

Fifty years after he made what he regarded as his directorial debut, Alfred Hitchcock signed off with this gently twisting thriller. Hitchcock coaxes along a deliciously contrived plot that sets kidnappers William Devane and Karen Black on a collision course with fake medium Barbara Harris and her partner Bruce Dern as they search for a missing heir. The performances are perfect, and it is to Hollywood's shame that it has not made better use of such gifted players since. DP DVD

Karen Black *Fran* • Bruce Dern *Lumley* • Barbara Harris *Blanche* • William Devane *Adamson* • Ed Lauter *Maloney* • Cathleen Nesbitt *Julia Rainbird* • Katherine Helmond *Mrs Maloney* • Warren J Kemmerling [Warren Kemmerling] *Grandison* ■ *Dir* Alfred Hitchcock • *Scr* Ernest Lehman, from the book *The Rainbird Pattern* by Victor Canning

Family Prayers ★★ PG

Drama 1991 · US · Colour · 104mins

Producer Scott Rosenfelt's directorial debut brims over with credible detail about growing up Jewish in the late 1960s. Tzvi Ratner-Stauber makes a good impression as the sheltered teenager confronted with both the bickering of his gambling father (Joe Mantegna) and his end-of-tether mother (Anne Archer), and the harsh facts of life that he learns from Paul Reiser, the tutor preparing him for his bar mitzvah. Let down by the sentimental script. DP

Joe Mantegna *Martin Jacobs* • Anne Archer *Rita Jacobs* • Paul Reiser *Dan Linder* • Patti LuPone *Aunt Nan* • Tzvi Ratner-Stauber *Andrew Jacobs* • Allen Garfield *Cantor* ■ *Dir* Scott Rosenfelt • *Scr* Steve Ginsberg

A Family Thing ★★ 15

Comedy drama 1996 · US · Colour · 104mins

Robert Duvall and James Earl Jones take centre stage in this charming if somewhat flimsy comedy drama. Duvall plays a good ole boy from Arkansas who is astonished to discover on his mother's death that his real mum was a black servant. He then reluctantly sets out to meet his half-brother, city cop Jones. The sparring of the two grumpy old men overcomes the deficiencies in plot and the sentimentality in a script co-written by Billy Bob Thornton. JF. Contains swearing and brief violence. [video]

Robert Duvall *Earl Pilcher, Jr* • James Earl Jones *Ray Murdoch* • Michael Beach *Virgil* • Irma P Hall *Aunt T* • Grace Zabriskie *Ruby* • Regina Taylor *Ann* • Mary Jackson *Carrie* ■ *Dir* Richard Pearce • *Scr* Tom Epperson, Billy Bob Thornton

Family Viewing ★★★★ 18

Satirical drama 1987 · Can · Colour · 86mins

Atom Egoyan makes inspired use of camcorder footage in this remarkable satire on dysfunctional nuclear family life. Delving into the darkest corners of society, Egoyan emerges with a story about a quiet teenager Aidan Tierney who finds refuge with his institutionalised grandmother away from the sexual obsessions of his seemingly respectable father and stepmother. Exploring themes that recur in all his films, this is a sly, sharp and often touching picture. DP

David Hemblen *Stan* • Aidan Tierney *Van* • Gabrielle Rose *Sandra* • Arsinée Khanjian *Aline* • Selma Keklikian *Armen* • Jeanne Sabourin *Aline's Mother* • Rose Sarkisyan *Van's Mother* ■ *Dir/Scr* Atom Egoyan

The Family Way ★★★★ 15

Comedy drama 1966 · UK · Colour · 110mins

Considered somewhat risqué in its day, this gentle comedy can now be seen as a fond portrait of an era when sex was still taboo. Complete with a score by Paul McCartney, it recounts the experience of so many 1960s' newlyweds who had to share a house with their in-laws for much of the early part of their married lives. Hywel Bennett is bang on form as the husband so wound up by cohabitation that he is unable to consummate his marriage to the equally impressive Hayley Mills. But it's her real-life dad, John Mills, who steals the show with a splendid study in working-class cantankerousness, along with award-winner Marjorie Rhodes. DP [video] DVD

Hayley Mills *Jenny Piper* • Hywel Bennett *Arthur Fitton* • John Mills *Ezra Fitton* • Marjorie Rhodes *Lucy Fitton* • Avril Angers *Liz Piper* • John Comer *Leslie Piper* • Wilfred Pickles *Uncle Fred* • Barry Foster *Joe Thompson* ■ *Dir* Roy Boulting • *Scr* Bill Naughton, Roy Boulting, Jeffrey Dell, from the play *All in Good Time* by Bill Naughton • *Music* Paul McCartney

The Famous Sword ★★★

Period drama 1945 · Jpn · BW · 66mins

Keen to keep working, but reluctant to shoot the kind of propaganda demanded by the government, Kenji Mizoguchi spent the Second World War making historical dramas. This was his last solo wartime project and scrupulously avoids any overtly political message. Instead, it serves up a tale of daughterly determination and loyal devotion, in which apprentice swordmaker Shotaro Hanayagi seeks the assistance of master craftsman Eijiro Yanagi in making the weapon that will enable Isuzu Yamada to avenge her murdered father. While nowhere near as impressive as his work either side of the war, this is anything but anodyne entertainment. DP. In Japanese with English subtitles.

Shotaro Hanayagi *Kiyone Sakurai* • Isuzu Yamada *Sasae Onoda* • Ichijiro Oya *Kozaemon Onoda* • Eijiro Yanagi *Kiyohide Yamatomori* • Kan Ishii *Kiyotsugu* ■ *Dir* Kenji Mizoguchi • *Scr* Matsutaro Kawaguchi

The Fan ★★

Drama 1949 · US · BW · 79mins

This is director Otto Preminger's rather dull, abridged version of Oscar Wilde's witty play, *Lady Windermere's Fan*. Although the screenplay was co-authored by famed wit Dorothy Parker, this is an updated and desecrated version of the plot, suffering from the heavy-handed directorial style. Jeanne Crain and Richard Greene are colourless Windermeres, George Sanders is a dull Lord Darlington, and, in her last movie, the lovely Madeleine Carroll a wan Mrs Erlynne. TS

Jeanne Crain *Lady Windermere* • Madeleine Carroll *Mrs Erlynne* • George Sanders *Lord Darlington* • Richard Greene *Lord Windermere* • Martita Hunt *Duchess of Berwick* ■ *Dir* Otto Preminger • *Scr* Walter Reisch, Dorothy Parker, Ross Evans, from the play *Lady Windermere's Fan* by Oscar Wilde

The Fan ★★★ 18

Thriller 1981 · US · Colour · 90mins

Fans of charismatic old-timers will enjoy this thriller about glamorous stage star Lauren Bacall being pursued by psychotic stalker Michael Biehn. The excellent James Garner appears as Bacall's ex-husband, and Maureen Stapleton plays her secretary. But it's Bacall's picture, and she has no problems convincing us she's a star. AT [video]

Lauren Bacall *Sally Ross* • James Garner *Jake Berman* • Maureen Stapleton *Belle Goldman* • Hector Elizondo *Ralph Andrews* • Michael Biehn *Douglas Breen* • Anna Maria Horsford *Emily Stolz* • Kurt R Johnson *David Branum* ■ *Dir* Edward Bianchi • *Scr* Priscilla Chapman, John Hartwell, from the novel by Bob Randall

The Fan ★★ 15

Thriller 1996 · US · Colour · 111mins

Robert De Niro is the psycho fan from hell and the object of his obsession is baseball star Wesley Snipes. It's when the San Francisco Giant team member hits a losing streak that the pitiful loser moves into action with fatal consequences. Despite being directed by Tony Scott with flash and dash, his over-vigorous use of mannered camera angles does nothing for this implausible plot that's short of both suspense and surprise. AJ [video] DVD

Robert De Niro *Gil Renard* • Wesley Snipes *Bobby Rayburn* • Ellen Barkin *Jewel Stern* • John Leguizamo *Manny* • Benicio Del Toro *Juan Primo* • Patti D'Arbanville-Quinn [Patti D'Arbanville] *Ellen Renard* ■ *Dir* Tony Scott • *Scr* Phoef Sutton, from the story by Peter Abrahams

Fanci's Persuasion ★★★

Surreal comedy fantasy
1994 · US · Colour · 80mins

Something of a hit on the gay and lesbian festival circuit, Charles Herman-Wurmfeld's directorial debut is a modern fairy tale that sets out to prove that "love is a many-gendered thing". As Jessica Patton prepares for her marriage to her girlfriend, the whole of San Francisco falls under a magical spell that forces people to reveal their true sexual identity and forsake their stubborn prejudices. The tone is decidedly romantic. DP

Jessica Patton *Fanci* • Justin Bond *Irene Wiesenthal* • Robert Coffman *Irving Wiesenthal* • Boa *Loretta* • Alyssa Wendt ■ *Dir* Charles Herman-Wurmfeld • *Scr* Charles Herman-Wurmfeld, Caroline Juliet Libresco

Fancy Pants ★★★ U

Musical comedy 1950 · US · Colour · 92mins

A riotous teaming of Bob Hope and Lucille Ball in yet another reworking of *Ruggles of Red Gap*. This finds Hope out West again, after his success as *The Paleface*. Hope makes not the slightest attempt to "buttle" in the English manner, but Ball is excellent as a rootin' tootin' tomboy heiress. Director George Marshall simply indulges them. TS

Bob Hope *Humphrey* • Lucille Ball *Agatha Floud* • Bruce Cabot *Cart Belknap* • Jack Kirkwood *Mike Floud* • Lea Penman *Effie Floud* • Hugh French *George Van-Basingwell* ■ *Dir* George Marshall • *Scr* Edmund Hartmann [Edmund L Hartmann], Robert O'Brien, from the story *Ruggles of Red Gap* by Harry Leon Wilson

Fandango ★★★ 15

Comedy drama 1985 · US · Colour · 86mins

Not only the first film to give an indication of Kevin Costner's star power, but also a crucial point in his career, as the director here, Kevin Reynolds, became a firm friend and went on to make *Robin Hood: Prince of Thieves* and *Waterworld* with him. This gently quirky rites-of-passage comedy drama began life as a student project for Reynolds, and follows five college friends in the early 1970s who set off on one last adolescent adventure before entering adulthood. Costner shines as the anarchic unofficial leader of the group, but he is more than matched by Judd Nelson, who turns in a powerful, mature performance. JF. Contains swearing and brief nudity. [video]

Kevin Costner *Gardner Barnes* • Judd Nelson *Phil Hicks* • Sam Robards *Kenneth Waggener* • Chuck Bush *Dorman* • Brian Cesak *Lester* • Elizabeth Daily *Judy* ■ *Dir* Kevin Reynolds • *Scr* Kevin Reynolds, from his short film

Fanfan la Tulipe ★★★★ 12

Satirical historical romance
1951 · Fr · BW · 95mins

A glorious spoof on the Hollywood swashbuckler. Beautifully designed, and filmed with a real feel for both the period trappings and the energetic action by cinematographer Christian Matras, the plot is fabulously preposterous, as Gérard Philipe confounds bandits and the Austrian army to win the heart of princess Sylvie Pelayo. With a sparkling script, a dashing lead and solid support from the likes of Gina Lollobrigida as Fanfan's mentor, it's no wonder Christian-Jaque won the best director prize at Cannes. DP. In French with English subtitles. DVD

Gérard Philipe *Fanfan la Tulipe* • Gina Lollobrigida *Adeline* • Noël Roquevert *Fier-à-Bras* • Olivier Hussenot *Tranche Montagne* • Marcel Herrand *Louis XV* • Jean-Marc Tennberg *Lebel* • Jean Parédès *Captain de la Houlette* ■ *Dir* Christian-Jaque • *Scr* Christian-Jaque, René Wheeler, Henri Jeanson, from a story by René Wheeler, René Fallet

Fanny ★★★★

Drama 1932 · Fr · BW · 126mins

Coming between *Marius* and *César*, the central segment of writer Marcel Pagnol's Marseille trilogy is easily the best directed. However, not even Marc Allégret could get much of a performance out of Orane Demazis, Pagnol's wife at the time. The rest of the cast are impeccable, though, with Raimu outstanding as the wily bar owner who persuades seafaring son Pierre Fresnay to abandon all claim to the child who has now found a father in widowed sailmaker, Fernand Charpin. The perfectly observed ambience and subtly shaded characters make this a joy to behold. DP. In French with English subtitles.

Orane Demazis *Fanny* • Raimu *César* • Fernand Charpin *Panisse* • Pierre Fresnay *Marius* • Alida Rouffe *Honorine* • Robert Vattier *Mr Brun* ■ *Dir* Marc Allégret • *Scr* Marcel Pagnol, from his play, from his books *Marseilles Trilogy*

Fanny ★★

Drama 1961 · US · Colour · 133mins

Stripped of its songs, Joshua Logan's reworking of his own 1954 Broadway production might have the striking Technicolor photography of Jack Cardiff in its corner, but it is utterly devoid of the local colour that made the 1932 adaptation of Marcel Pagnol's Marseille trilogy so enchanting. Charles Boyer is slyly charming as the waterfront bar owner who competes with sailmaker Maurice Chevalier for the affections of waif Leslie Caron, after lover Horst Buchholz leaves her pregnant. Cardiff and Boyer were well worth their Oscar nominations, but it's harder to see why this merited a best picture nod. DP

Leslie Caron *Fanny* • Maurice Chevalier *Panisse* • Charles Boyer *César* • Horst Buchholz *Marius* • Baccaloni [Salvatore Baccaloni] *Escartifique* • Lionel Jeffries *M Brun* • Raymond Bussires *Admiral* • Victor Francen *Louis Panisse* ■ *Dir* Joshua Logan • *Scr* Julius J Epstein, from a play by SN Behrman, Joshua Logan, from the play by Marcel Pagnol, from the books *Marseilles Trilogy* by Marcel Pagnol

Fanny and Alexander ★★★★★ 15

Period drama
1982 · Swe/Fr/W Ger · Colour · 188mins

The warmth, humour and compassion of this wonderful turn-of-the-century family saga make it one of the most accessible movies ever made by Sweden's greatest director Ingmar Bergman. The story, which covers two years in the life of a well-to-do household as seen through the eyes of a small boy, is rendered all the more fascinating by the autobiographical elements that Bergman has included and by Sven Nykvist's Oscar-winning photography. The film takes us on a magical tour of the child's encounters with his oppressive, puritanical stepfather, his loving mother and his extended family in an atmosphere that is both cosy and scary. The result is an unmissable experience from a master film-maker. TH. In Swedish with English subtitles. [video] DVD

Gunn Wallgren *Grandmother Helena Ekdahl* • Börje Ahlstedt *Professor Carl Ekdahl* • Christina Schollin *Lydia Ekdahl* • Allan Edwall *Oscar Ekdahl* • Ewa Fröling *Emilie Ekdahl* • Pernilla Allwin *Fanny Ekdahl* • Bertil Guve *Alexander Ekdahl* • Jarl Kulle *Gustav Adolf Ekdahl* • Mona Malm *Alma Ekdahl* • Pernilla Wallgren [Pernilla August] *Maj* • Gunnar Björnstrand *Filip Landahl* • Jan Malmsjö *Bishop Edvard Vergerus* • Erland Josephson *Isak Jacobi* ■ *Dir/Scr* Ingmar Bergman • *Cinematographer* Sven Nykvist

Fanny & Elvis ★★ 15

Romantic comedy
1999 · UK/Fr · Colour · 106mins

This soppy second-chance romance marks the directorial debut of writer Kay Mellor (best know for TV's *Band of Gold*), in which a budding Barbara Cartland finds millennial love with a much-married car dealer. Were it not for the knowing performances of Kerry Fox and Ray Winstone, the stodginess of Mellor's staging and the laziness of her script would be all the more apparent. DP. Contains swearing and sex scenes. [video] DVD

Kerry Fox *Kate* • Ray Winstone *Dave* • Ben Daniels *Andrew* • David Morrissey *Rob* • Jennifer Saunders *Roanna* • Colin Salmon *Alan* • Gaynor Faye *Samantha* • William Ash *Rick* ■ *Dir/Scr* Kay Mellor

Fanny by Gaslight ★★★ PG

Period drama 1944 · UK · BW · 102mins

This Gainsborough picture is more luridly Hogarthian than usual. Despite being visually sanitised, director Anthony Asquith's film doesn't hesitate in drawing attention to the sleazier corners of Victorian society. Phyllis Calvert is the politician's illegitimate daughter about to become bawdyhouse baggage, while James Mason and Stewart Granger swagger in appropriate fashion. It seems innocent now, but it caused quite a fuss in its day. How low can décolletage get? TH

Phyllis Calvert *Fanny* • James Mason *Lord Manderstoke* • Stewart Granger *Harry Somerford* • Wilfrid Lawson *Chunks* • Jean Kent *Lucy* • Margaretta Scott *Alicia* • Nora Swinburne *Mrs Hopwood* • Cathleen Nesbitt *Kate Somerford* ■ *Dir* Anthony Asquith • *Scr* Doreen Montgomery, Aimee Stuart, from a novel by Michael Sadleir

F

Fanny Hill ★★ 18

Period erotic romp
1983 · UK · Colour · 86mins

Although considerably classier than Russ Meyer's 1964 version, this is still a disappointingly bawdy dramatisation of John Cleland's 1749 erotic classic. Director Gerry O'Hara sets out to titillate rather than explore the sordid events behind the transformation of Lisa Raines from a comely country girl into a practised woman of pleasure. Moreover, this rambunctious approach leaves the admirably willing Oliver Reed and Shelley Winters little option but to go for pantomimic caricature, while Raines's shortcomings are as apparent as her charms. DP

Lisa Raines *Fanny Hill* • Oliver Reed *Lawyer* • Wilfrid Hyde White *Mr Barville* • Shelley Winters *Mrs Cole* • Alfred Marks *Lecher* ■ *Dir* Gerry O'Hara • *Scr* Stephen Chesley, from the novel *Fanny Hill – Memoirs of a Woman of Pleasure* by John Cleland

Fanny Hill: Memoirs of a Woman of Pleasure ★

Period erotic romp
1964 · US/W Ger · BW · 104mins

Hilariously hyped at the time as a "female *Tom Jones*", this is notorious flesh merchant Russ Meyer's brush with the classics. In this case Meyer characteristically exploits the bawdy 18th-century novel about a young woman who finds herself working in a brothel, but his direction lacks any style or discernible talent. This is amateurish drivel that fails as comedy, titillation or historical fiction. RS

Miriam Hopkins *Mrs Maude Brown* • Leticia Roman *Fanny Hill* • Walter Giller *Hemingway* • Alex D'Arcy *The Admiral* • Helmut Weiss *Mr Dinklespieler* • Chris Howland *Mr Norbert* • Ulli Lommel *Charles* • Cara Garnett *Phoebe* ■ *Dir* Russ Meyer • *Scr* Robert Hill, from the novel *Fanny Hill; or, Memoirs of a Woman of Pleasure* by John Cleland

Fantasia ★★★★★ U

Classic animation
1940 · US · Colour · 114mins

A tremendous leap into the light, which won a special Oscar for Walt Disney and conductor Leopold Stokowski, and a mighty innovation in feature-length cartoons as a concert of classical music is made visually articulate – from Bach to Stravinsky to Tchaikovsky. Beethoven's *Pastoral* gets the kitsch treatment with cute mythology, and Mussorgsky's *Night on Bald Mountain* is a *danse macabre* of opened graves and broom-riding witches. Mickey Mouse even appears as Dukas's *Sorcerer's Apprentice*. Most successful are Bach abstractions, while the dying dinosaurs of Stravinsky's *Rite of Spring* is a massive decimation of reptiles – and affirmation for life. A high-voltage masterpiece which showed what could be achieved with a marriage of the technical (multiplane cameras, stereo sound) and the creative. TH DVD

Deems Taylor • Leopold Stokowski conducting the Philadelphia Symphony Orchestra ■ *Dir* Samuel Armstrong, James Algar, Bill Roberts, Paul Satterfield, Hamilton Luske, Jim Handley, Ford Beebe, Norman Ferguson, Wilfred Jackson

Fantasia 2000 ★★★ U

Animation 1999 · US · Colour · 71mins

The first release of the 21st century, and the only animated feature to be made in the giant IMAX format, Disney's long-awaited follow-up to the 1940 classic *Fantasia* is something of a disappointment. For while the spectacle is impressive, the artistic content is regrettably lacklustre. An ecological theme informs the visuals for Beethoven's *Fifth Symphony*, Respighi's *Pines of Rome* and Stravinsky's *Firebird Suite*; and Mickey Mouse returns for a underwhelming digital remastering of *The Sorcerer's Apprentice*. More of a one-off than the future of animation, but worth catching for the experience. DP DVD

James Levine conducting the Chicago Symphony Orchestra • Steve Martin • Itzhak Perlman • Quincy Jones • Bette Midler • James Earl Jones • Penn [Penn Jillette] *Penn Jillette* • Teller • Angela Lansbury ■ *Dir* Pixote Hunt, Hendel Butoy, Eric Goldberg, James Algar, Francis Glebas, Paul Brizzi, Gaetan Brizzi, Don Hahn

The Fantasist ★★ 18

Thriller 1986 · Ire · Colour · 94mins

Quite why director Robin Hardy never managed to live up to the huge potential of cult classic *The Wicker Man* remains a perplexing mystery. His only other feature film is an intriguing but confused chiller about a young woman (Moira Harris) heading to the bright lights of Dublin, only to fall into the radar of a disturbed psychopath who is terrorising the city. The slasher elements of the tale just don't gel with the setting and the psychological musings don't ring true either. JF

Moira Harris *Patricia Teeling* • Christopher Cazenove *Inspector McMyler* • Timothy Bottoms *Danny Sullivan* • John Kavanagh *Robert Foxley* • Mick Lally *Uncle Lar* ■ *Dir* Robin Hardy • *Scr* Robin Hardy, from the novel *Goosefoot* by Patrick McGinley

Fantastic Planet ★★★★ PG

Animated science-fiction fantasy
1973 · Fr/Cz · Colour · 69mins

A remarkable animated French/Czech science-fiction fantasy conceived by Roland Topor and René Laloux, depicting the odd happenings on planet Yagam. There, humans, called Oms, are pets of the giant Draags, and numerous allegorical references are imaginatively drawn as a war breaks out between the two factions. A fascinating fable utilising impressive organic design, surreal composition and stunning visuals, this Cannes award-winner is highly intriguing and compulsive viewing. AJ. French dialogue dubbed into English.

Barry Bostwick • Marvin Miller • Olan Soule • Cynthia Alder • Nora Heflin • Hal Smith • Mark Gruner • Monika Ramirez • Janet Waldo ■ *Dir* René Laloux • *Scr* René Laloux, from the book *Oms en Serie* by Stefan Wul

Fantastic Voyage ★★★★ U

Science-fiction adventure
1966 · US · Colour · 96mins

Shrunken doctors in a mini-sub journeying through the body of a dying Czech scientist to perform interior brain surgery provide the plot for this wonderfully ludicrous 1960s classic. An interesting cast includes secret agent Stephen Boyd, Raquel Welch in a tight diving suit and Donald Pleasence in danger from rampaging white corpuscles. Director Richard Fleischer's deft execution and tremendous special effects for the time make for an imaginative guided tour through the bloodstream to witness the wonders of the heart, lungs and other assorted organs, along with the requisite doses of sex, suspense and sabotage. AJ DVD

Stephen Boyd *Grant* • Raquel Welch *Cora Peterson* • Donald Pleasence *Dr Michaels* • Edmond O'Brien *General Carter* • Arthur O'Connell *Colonel Donald Reid* • William Redfield *Captain Bill Owens* • Arthur Kennedy *Dr Duval* ■ *Dir* Richard Fleischer • *Scr* Harry Kleiner, David Duncan, from the novel by Otto Klement, Jay Lewis Bixby • *Art Director* Jack Martin Smith, Dale Hennesey • *Cinematographer* Ernest Laszlo

The Fantasticks ★★

Musical romance 1995 · US · Colour · 86mins

Based on the long-running New York musical, this was made in 1995 but not released until 2000. Why MGM held it in limbo for five years is a sign of the film's dated feel and its failings. Joel Grey and Brad Sullivan play farmers who invent a fictitious feud to encourage their offspring Jean Louisa Kelly and Joe McIntyre to fall in love. Theatrical scenes set against the sweeping Arizona landscape date back to the 1950s but the songs themselves have a sweet and redeeming ring to them. LH

Joel Grey *Bellamy* • Bernard Hughes *Henry* • Jean Louisa Kelly *Luisa* • Joe McIntyre *Matt* • Jonathon Morris *El Gallo* • Brad Sullivan *Hucklebee* ■ *Dir* Michael Ritchie • *Scr* Tom Jones, Harvey Schmidt, from their play

Le Fantôme de la Liberté ★★★★ 15

Surreal drama 1974 · Fr · Colour · 99mins

Luis Buñuel's penultimate film shows him as mordantly comic and subversive as ever, but this series of loosely linked surreal sketches betrays a certain fatigue and laziness. The title refers to Karl Marx's phrase, and Buñuel's theme seems to be that most people are really afraid of freedom. The best-remembered sequence has elegant guests seated on individual lavatories around a table from which they excuse themselves to go and have a meal in a little room behind a locked door. Audacious, certainly, but it lacks the discreet charm of the other episodic French movies of his late period. RB. In French with English subtitles.

Michel Lonsdale *Hatter* • Jean-Claude Brialy *M Foucauld* • Michel Piccoli *Second Prefect of Police* • Adriana Asti *Prefect's sister* • Julien Bertheau *First Prefect of Police* • Adolfo Celi *Docteur Legendre* • Monica Vitti *Mme Foucauld* ■ *Dir* Luis Buñuel • *Scr* Luis Buñuel, Jean-Claude Carrière

Far and Away ★★ 15

Romantic period adventure
1992 · US · Colour · 134mins

In this curious, frothy 19th-century period piece, Tom Cruise somewhat unbelievably earns his living as a bare knuckle fighter, while his co-star and then real-life wife Nicole Kidman flounces around, tossing pre-Raphaelite curls. Directed with predictable gloss and visual panache by Ron Howard, and with a soundtrack featuring the stirring strains of Irish singer Enya, this is a movie that bounces along on a sea of ripped petticoats, horse whips and rotten teeth. SH. Contains violence, swearing and brief nudity. DVD

Tom Cruise *Joseph Donelly* • Nicole Kidman *Shannon Christie* • Thomas Gibson *Stephen* • Robert Prosky *Daniel Christie* • Barbara Babcock *Nora Christie* • Cyril Cusack *Danty Duff* • Colm Meaney *Kelly* • Eileen Pollock *Molly Kay* • Michelle Johnson *Grace* ■ *Dir* Ron Howard • *Scr* Bob Dolman, from a story by Ron Howard, Bob Dolman

Far Away ★★★

Drama 2001 · Fr/Sp · Colour · 120mins

André Téchiné explores the plight of the would-be immigrant in this credible, but unfocused drama. Employing a digi-video style for added immediacy, he concentrates on the human drama rather than dwelling on its socio-political considerations, while bringing unbearable tension to the drug smuggling and money laundering sequences. Yet, a surfeit of sub-plots distracts from the central premise, which sees trucker Stéphane Rideau promise to smuggle Mohamed Hamaidi from Tangiers to Spain if he can effect a reconciliation with Rideau's estranged girlfriend, Lubna Azabal. DP. In French, English, Arabic and Spanish with subtitles.

Stéphane Rideau *Serge* • Lubna Azabal *Sarah* • Mohamed Hamaidi *Said* • Yasmina Reza *Emily* ■ *Dir* André Téchiné • *Scr* André Téchiné, Faouzi Bensaïdi, Faouzi, Mehdi Ben Attia

The Far Country ★★★ U

Western 1954 · US · Colour · 93mins

This is a beautifully made western, set in snowy gold rush territory. James Stewart's character is unusual for a movie hero of this period: he's basically self-absorbed, a ruthless loner, a contrast to the remarkably affable villain, played with relish by John McIntire. This concept of character reversal doesn't quite come off, but director Anthony Mann's striking use of landscape and the intense and satisfying fury of the action sequences more than compensate. TS

James Stewart *Jeff Webster* • Ruth Roman *Ronda Castle* • Corinne Calvet *Renee Vallon* • Walter Brennan *Ben Tatem* • John McIntire *Mr Gannon* • Jay C Flippen *Rube* • Henry Morgan [Harry Morgan] *Ketchum* • Jack Elam *Newberry* ■ *Dir* Anthony Mann • *Scr* Borden Chase

Far East ★

Action drama 1982 · Aus · Colour · 107mins

Director John Duigan bit off more than he could chew with this excursion into the thriller genre. Clearly he aimed to explore the nature of post-colonial rule and the iniquities of expatriate opulence within a *Casablanca*-like framework. Unfortunately the romance between Koala Klub boss Bryan Brown and married good-time-gal Helen Morse is so devoid of passion that you never begin to care what happens to them. Derivative, disappointing and dull. DP

Bryan Brown *Morgan Keefe* • Helen Morse *Jo Reeves* • John Bell *Peter Reeves* • Raina McKeon *Rosita Constanza* • Henry Duval *Rudolf DeCruz* ■ *Dir/Scr* John Duigan

Far from Heaven ★★★★★ 12

Romantic drama
2002 · US/Fr · Colour · 102mins

An exquisite evocation of the 1950s tear-jerkers of director Douglas Sirk, Todd Haynes's gorgeously designed, stunningly photographed, ravishingly scored and beautifully acted melodrama is an immaculate masterpiece. Julianne Moore plays a housewife in 1957 Connecticut who, reeling from the discovery of husband Dennis Quaid's homosexuality, develops an attraction to her black gardener (Dennis Haysbert). This is a perfectly pitched synthesis of Sirkian themes: middle-class conformity, hypocrisy and self-delusion. Without a trace of intrusive irony, lush images illustrate a taboo-breaking story without suffering from the restrictions of that time. AJ. Contains swearing. [video] DVD

Julianne Moore *Cathy Whitaker* • Dennis Quaid *Frank Whitaker* • Dennis Haysbert *Raymond Deagan* • Patricia Clarkson *Eleanor Fine* • Viola Davis *Sybil* • James Rebhorn *Dr Bowman* • Celia Weston *Mona Lauder* ■ *Dir/Scr* Todd Haynes • *Cinematographer* Edward Lachman [Ed Lachman] • *Music* Elmer Bernstein

Far from Home ★★ 18

Horror thriller 1989 · US · Colour · 85mins

Drew Barrymore kicked off her Lolita phase (*Poison Ivy* was the highpoint) with this rather undistinguished straight-to-video thriller. While on a cross-country trip, Matt Frewer and daughter Barrymore are forced to take refuge in a run-down trailer park when their vehicle breaks down. Barrymore shows that she possessed the talent to make the transition from child to grown-up star, although the way director Meiert Avis lingers over her is a little distasteful. JF [video]

Matt Frewer *Charlie Cross* • Drew Barrymore *Joleen Cross* • Richard Masur *Duckett* • Karen Austin *Louise* • Susan Tyrrell *Agnes Reed* • Anthony Rapp *Pinky Sears* • Jennifer Tilly *Amy* ■ *Dir* Meiert Avis • *Scr* Tommy Lee Wallace, from a story by Theodore Gershuny

Far from Home: the Adventures of Yellow Dog ★★★ U

Adventure 1994 · US · Colour · 77mins

This adventure, in which a golden labrador sticks by his teenage master, Jesse Bradford, after their boat capsizes in the wilds of British Columbia, thankfully lacks the sentiment of the Lassie era. Some of the survival methods might prove too strong for youngsters (although many will revel in the insect eating), but there is enough exciting action to keep them amused. DP [video] DVD

Mimi Rogers *Katherine McCormick* • Bruce Davison *John McCormick* • Jesse Bradford *Angus McCormick* • Tom Bower *John Gale* • Joel Palmer *Silas McCormick* • Josh Wannamaker *David Finlay* • Margot Finley *Sara* ■ *Dir/Scr* Phillip Borsos

Far from the Madding Crowd ★★★ U

Period romantic drama
1967 · UK · Colour · 155mins

Helped by the shimmering photography of Nicolas Roeg and hindered by a straitjacket of a script by Frederic Raphael, this laudable, lengthy adaptation of Thomas Hardy's classic novel might have benefited from a less respectful treatment. Director John Schlesinger fails to impose his own personality on the proceedings and, consequently, he never challenges his cast to explore the emotional depths of their characters. Julie Christie narrowly misses the spirit of Bathsheba, and Terence Stamp just doesn't convince as one of her three besotted suitors. DP [video] DVD

Julie Christie *Bathsheba Everdene* • Terence Stamp *Sergeant Troy* • Peter Finch *William Boldwood* • Alan Bates *Gabriel Oak* • Fiona Walker *Liddy* • Prunella Ransome *Fanny Robin* • Alison Leggatt *Mrs Hurst* ■ *Dir* John Schlesinger • *Scr* Frederic Raphael, from the novel by Thomas Hardy

Far from Vietnam ★★★

Experimental political documentary
1967 · Fr · BW and Colour · 120mins

For all the rhetoric spouted in this passionate protest against American involvement in Vietnam, it's the dreadful simplicity of the combat footage that has the most powerful effect. The opening sequence, for example, which juxtaposes US preparations for an air raid and the terrified response it evokes in Hanoi, makes for chilling viewing over 30 years on. There's undoubted socio-artistic integrity in Jean-Luc Godard's emotive confession and Alain Resnais's assessment of the war's morality, while the film is edited with supreme propagandist skill by Chris Marker. Far more revealing, however, are the American TV clips exposing the extent to which the nation was divided by the conflict. DP. In French and English with subtitles.

Dir Alain Resnais, William Klein, Joris Ivens, Agnès Varda, Claude Lelouch, Jean-Luc Godard • *Editor* Chris Marker

The Far Frontier ★★ U

Western 1949 · US · Colour · 68mins

Routine Roy Rogers fodder, given a little more glitz than usual for being filmed in the cheap colour process Trucolor, and notable for being the last time sidekick Andy Devine rode with the (self-styled) King of the Cowboys. The plot's not without interest either, dealing as it does with illegal wetbacks, outlaws smuggled back into the US from Mexico. TS

Roy Rogers • Gail Davis *Susan Hathaway* • Andy Devine *Judge Cookie Bullfincher* • Francis Ford *Alf Sharper* • Roy Barcroft *Bart Carroll* • Clayton Moore *Tom Sharper* • Robert Strange *Willis Newcomb* • Holly Bane *Rocco* ■ *Dir* William Witney • *Scr* Sloan Nibley

The Far Horizons ★★ U

Historical adventure
1955 · US · Colour · 107mins

Canoes replace horses in this American frontier saga that takes dramatic liberties with the real-life expedition of Lewis and Clark up the Missouri river into the Northwest. The journey goes on far too long but is often spectacularly beautiful to behold. Fred MacMurray is the stern-jawed Lewis while Charlton Heston plays the virile Clark who forgets the girl back home (Barbara Hale) when he runs into Donna Reed's Indian maiden. AE

Fred MacMurray *Meriwether Lewis* • Charlton Heston *William Clark* • Donna Reed *Sacajawea* • Barbara Hale *Julia Hancock* • William Demarest *Sergeant Gass* • Alan Reed *Charboneau* • Eduardo Noriega (1) *Cameahwait* ■ *Dir* Rudolph Maté • *Scr* Winston Miller, Edmund H North, from the novel *Sacajawea of the Shoshones* by Della Gould Emmons

Far North ★★ 15

Drama 1988 · US · Colour · 84mins

Playwright Sam Shepard's feature film debut as director stars his real-life partner Jessica Lange. Despite Lange's abilities, this still manages to be a major head-banging exercise in dragging Freudian clichés through the farm dust of Minnesota. The cast is impeccable, but Shepard's tediously tangled script and lumpen direction badly let it down. SH. Contains swearing. [video]

Jessica Lange *Kate* • Charles Durning *Bertrum* • Tess Harper *Rita* • Donald Moffat *Uncle Dane* • Ann Wedgeworth *Amy* • Patricia Arquette *Jilly* • Nina Draxten *Gramma* • Pearl Fuller *Older Nurse* ■ *Dir/Scr* Sam Shepard

A Far Off Place ★★ PG

Adventure 1993 · US · Colour · 102mins

This is a disappointingly Disneyfied adaptation of two Laurens van der Post novels. As a highly acclaimed cinematographer, debuting director Mikael Salomon clearly knows where to place his camera. Yet, in dumbing down the ecological themes for his adolescent audience, he inadvertently patronises Sarel Bok, the Kalahari bush guide who leads imperilled teens Reese Witherspoon and Ethan Randall across the desert and out of the clutches of evil ivory hunter Jack Thompson. DP. Contains violence. [video]

Reese Witherspoon *Nonnie Parker* • Ethan Randall [Ethan Embry] *Harry Winslow* • Jack Thompson *John Ricketts* • Maximilian Schell *Colonel Mopani Theron* • Sarel Bok *Xhabbo* • Robert Burke *Paul Parker* • Patricia Kalember *Elizabeth Parker* • Daniel Gerroll *John Winslow* ■ *Dir* Mikael Salomon • *Scr* Robert Caswell, Jonathan Hensleigh, Sally Robinson, from the books *A Story Like the Wind* and *A Far Off Place* by Laurens van der Post • *Cinematographer* Juan Ruiz-Anchia

Faraway, So Close ★★★ 15

Fantasy drama
1993 · Ger · BW and Colour · 138mins

Wim Wenders's sequel to *Wings of Desire* is as visually beautiful and sweet-natured as the original. Fallen angel Bruno Ganz now runs a pizza restaurant, which makes his ghostly pal Otto Sander want a slice of mortality for himself. Unfortunately, he ends up working for illegal arms dealer Horst Buchholz. Wenders's mix of recent German history with weighty metaphysical concerns again uses stark black and white to depict the angels' viewpoint. AJ. In English and German with subtitles. Contains violence, swearing. [video]

Otto Sander *Cassiel* • Peter Falk • Horst Buchholz *Tony Baker* • Nastassja Kinski *Raphaela* • Heinz Ruhmann *Konrad* • Bruno Ganz *Damiel* • Solveig Dommartin *Marion* • Rüdiger Vogler *Phillip Winter* • Lou Reed • Willem Dafoe *Emit Flesti* • Mikhail Gorbachev ■ *Dir* Wim Wenders • *Scr* Wim Wenders, Ulrich Zieger, Richard Reitinger, from a story by Wim Wenders

The Farewell – Brecht's Last Summer ★★ 12

Period biographical drama
2000 · Ger/Pol · Colour · 88mins

An air of melancholy hangs heavily over this slow-moving memoir of Bertolt Brecht's final visit to his summer retreat. The intensity of director Jan Schütte's film – set in 1956, a time of political turmoil behind the Iron Curtain – compensates for the a certain lack of humanity. Disappointingly, Brecht (Josef Bierbichler) is something of a marginal figure, with the focus instead on his devoted wife, Helene Weigel (Monica Bleibtreu). Sincere but inaccessible. DP. In German with English subtitles. [video] DVD

Josef Bierbichler *Bertolt Brecht* • Monica Bleibtreu [Monika Bleibtreu] *Helene Weigel* • Jeanette Hain *Käthe Reichel* • Elfriede Irrall *Elisabeth Hauptmann* • Margit Rogall *Ruth Berlau* • Samuel Fintzi *Wolfgang Harich* ■ *Dir* Jan Schütte • *Scr* Klaus Pohl

Farewell, Home Sweet Home ★★★

Comedy drama
1999 · Fr/Swi/It · Colour · 118mins

Comprised of an eliding series of fluent long takes, this Parisian satire is a determinedly eccentric study of exclusion, exile, privilege and poverty, as well as social and sexual hypocrisy. With the rich envying the dispossessed's lack of responsibility and the poor coveting the good life, everyone, in their own peculiar way, is seeking an escape from their fate. Yet it's only the wealthy family's downtrodden head (played by director Otar Iosseliani), who makes the break by sailing away with his hobo soulmate, just as his once rebellious son, Nico Tarielashvili, leaves jail for château indolence. Scarcely penetrating, but superbly controlled. DP. In French with English subtitles.

Nico Tarielashvili *Son* • Lily Lavina *Mother* • Philippe Bas *Moto driver* • Stephanie Hainque *Girl at bar* • Otar Iosseliani *Father* ■ *Dir/Scr* Otar Iosseliani

Farewell My Concubine ★★★★★ 15

Epic drama 1993 · HK/Chi · Colour · 150mins

Banned for a time in China, Oscar nominated and joint winner of the Palme d'Or at Cannes in 1993 with Jane Campion's *The Piano*, Chen Kaige's fifth feature sweeps impressively across 50 years of Chinese history to trace the shifting relationship between Peking opera singers Zhang Fengyi and Leslie Cheung. A reluctance to explore, with any depth, Cheung's gay love for his friend Zhang and a rather prosaic presentation of the political events that rocked China after 1925 are the only quibbles one can have with this majestic and often riveting piece of film-making. Both men give remarkable performances, as does the beguiling Gong Li as Zhang's put-upon wife. DP. In Mandarin with English subtitles. [video]

Leslie Cheung *Douzi/Cheng Dieyi (young man)* • Zhang Fengyi *Shitou/Duan Xiaolou (young man)* • Gong Li *Juxian* • Lu Qi *Guan Jifa* • Ying Da *Na Kun* • Ge You *Master Yuan* • Li Chun *Xiao Si (teenager)* • Lei Han *Xiao Si (adult)* • Ma Mingwei *Douzi (child)* • Yin Zhi *Douzi (teenager)* • Fei Yang *Shitou (child)* • Zhao Hailong *Shitou (teenager)* ■ *Dir* Chen Kaige • *Scr* Lillian Lee, Lu Wei

Farewell, My Love ★★

Action thriller 1999 · US · Colour · 90mins

Gabrielle Fitzpatrick is the sole survivor of an attack on her family by Ed Lauter's Russian gang, whose entire life has been geared towards exacting revenge. Robert Culp's rival Mob, meanwhile, is convinced her vigilante spree will spark a turf war and decides to kidnap her. The cast rallies doggedly, but the lumpen direction confounds its efforts. DP

Gabrielle Fitzpatrick *Brigit Faure* • Phillip Rhys *Luc* • Brion James *Renault* • Adam Baldwin *Jimmy, the bartender* • Robert Culp *Reilly* • Ed Lauter *Sergei Karpov* ■ *Dir/Scr* Randall Fontana

Farewell My Lovely ★★★★★ PG

Classic film noir 1944 · US · BW · 91mins

Also known by its American title *Murder, My Sweet*, this terrific adaptation of the Raymond Chandler novel was the movie that established former crooner Dick Powell's new hard-boiled image. He out-Bogies Bogart playing the impoverished private eye Philip Marlowe, caught up in two tough and nasty cases that eventually dovetail into one. Quintessential *film noir*, this is superbly directed by Edward Dmytryk, with an economic use of voiceover that now stands as a skilful example of the device. Mike Mazurki is a perfect Moose Malloy, but it's Claire Trevor as Velma that you'll remember. Parts of the plot were used previously in *The Falcon Takes Over*, and the film was later remade with Robert Mitchum as Marlowe, but this tight black-and-white masterpiece is as good as it gets. TS [video] DVD

Dick Powell *Philip Marlowe* • Claire Trevor *Mrs Grayle/Velma Valento* • Anne Shirley *Ann Grayle* • Otto Kruger *Jules Amthor* • Mike Mazurki *Moose Malone* • Miles Mander *Mr Grayle* • Douglas Walton *Lindsay Marriott* ■ *Dir* Edward Dmytryk • *Scr* John Paxton, from the novel by Raymond Chandler

Farewell, My Lovely ★★★★ 15

Detective drama 1975 · US · Colour · 91mins

This is a richly atmospheric and affectionate tribute to Raymond Chandler and 1940s *film noir*, with Robert Mitchum as Philip Marlowe. It's amazing that Mitchum came so late to the role that he seems born to play. The corrupt mess of Los Angeles hangs on those rumpled eyelids as he gives a mesmeric performance of world-weariness. Also impressive is Charlotte Rampling as the alluring Velma, who gives Mitchum a smile that, he says, he can feel in his hip pocket. The director is Dick Richards, who chose to make this rather than *Jaws*. Look out for Sylvester Stallone, just a year before *Rocky* shot him to world stardom. AT DVD

Robert Mitchum *Philip Marlowe* • Charlotte Rampling *Mrs Velma Grayle* • John Ireland *Lieutenant Nulty* • Sylvia Miles *Mrs Jessie Florian* • Jack O'Halloran *Moose Malloy* • Harry Dean Stanton *Billy Rolfe* • Sylvester Stallone *Kelly/Jonnie* ■ *Dir* Dick Richards • *Scr* David Zelag Goodman, from the novel by Raymond Chandler

A Farewell to Arms ★★★ PG

First World War romantic drama
1932 · US · BW · 75mins

Time has not been terribly kind to this adaptation of Ernest Hemingway's First World War love story about an English nurse and an American ambulance driver. But, in 1932, Helen Hayes and Gary Cooper (accompanied by Wagner on the soundtrack) created tidal waves of tears in movie theatres. Still worth seeing for those classically romantic performances and for the Oscar-winning photography by Charles Lang. AT DVD

Gary Cooper *Lieutenant Frederic Henry* • Helen Hayes *Catherine Barkley* • Adolphe Menjou *Major Rinaldi* • Mary Philips *Helen Ferguson* • Jack LaRue *Priest* • Blanche Frederici *Head nurse* • Henry Armetta *Bonello* ■ *Dir* Frank Borzage • *Scr* Benjamin Glazer, Oliver HP Garret, from the novel by Ernest Hemingway

A Farewell to Arms ★★★ 15

First World War romantic drama
1957 · US · Colour · 146mins

Ambulance driver Rock Hudson is wounded in Italy during the First World War and, while recovering from his injuries, falls in love with nurse Jennifer Jones. Jones was married to the film's producer, David O Selznick, who not only wanted to pay adoring tribute to his wife's beauty, but also sought to repeat the huge success of his earlier blockbuster *Gone with the Wind*. As a result, this is overblown and compulsively enjoyable (even with its disturbing depiction of war). AT DVD

Rock Hudson *Lt Frederic Henry* • Jennifer Jones *Catherine Barkley* • Vittorio De Sica *Major Alessandro Rinaldi* • Mercedes McCambridge *Miss Van Campen* • Kurt Kasznar *Bonello* • Oscar Homolka *Dr Emerich* • Elaine Stritch *Helen Ferguson* • Alberto Sordi *Father Galli* ■ *Dir* Charles Vidor • *Scr* Ben Hecht, from the novel by Ernest Hemingway

Farewell to the King ★ PG

Second World War adventure
1988 · US · Colour · 112mins

Captain Nigel Havers (poorly cast) treks into Borneo's heart of darkness and discovers jungle "King" Nick Nolte, who's gone native to the strains of Basil Poledouris's score. Unsurprisingly, this militaristic nonsense is written and directed by John Milius, co-screenwriter of *Apocalypse Now*, who completely fails to uncover any significant resonance in his own material. TS. Contains some violence and swearing. DVD

Nick Nolte *Learoyd* • Nigel Havers *Captain Fairbourne* • Frank McRae *Sergeant Tenga* • James Fox *Colonel Ferguson* • Marilyn Tokuda *Yoo* • Marius Weyers *Conklin* ■ *Dir* John Milius • *Scr* John Milius, from the book *L'Adieu au Roi* by Pierre Shoendoerffer

Fargo ★★★★★ 18

Black comedy thriller
1995 · US · Colour · 93mins

The Coen brothers (director/writer Joel, producer/writer Ethan) are on top form with this quirky, unconventional, comedy-tinged crime thriller set in snowy Minnesota. Amateur kidnappers Steve Buscemi and Peter Stormare leave a trail of dead bodies that is investigated, with rare instinct and understanding, by heavily pregnant police chief Frances McDormand (who won an Oscar for her performance). Supposedly inspired by a true story, the Coens neatly subvert thriller clichés for their own surreal and philosophical ends, while retaining the genre's old-fashioned virtues and screw-tightening tension. While sweet-natured mirth is combined with deliciously twisted malice, and gory horror merges with offbeat humour, the whole is set against an extraordinary winter wonderland backdrop. A modern masterpiece. AJ DVD

Frances McDormand *Marge Gunderson* • Steve Buscemi *Carl Showalter* • Peter Stormare *Gaear Grimsrud* • William H Macy *Jerry Lundegaard* • Harve Presnell *Wade Gustafson* • Kristin Rudrud *Jean Lundegaard* • Tony Denman *Scotty Lundegaard* • Kurt Schweickhardt *Car salesman* ■ *Dir* Joel Coen • *Scr* Ethan Coen, Joel Coen • *Producer* Ethan Coen • *Cinematographer* Roger Deakins

Farinelli il Castrato ★★★★ 15

Biographical drama
1994 · Bel/Fr/It · Colour · 106mins

Not since *Amadeus* has a film made classical music so popular as this bizarre take on the musical past. Stéfano Dionisi stars as castrated singer Farinelli, one of a select band of 18th-century tonal high-fliers, whose emasculated voice can drive an audience of women wild with lust, and who is forever feuding with his more virile brother and arguing with the composer Handel. In the film, Farinelli's reedy resonance is the digital result of combining counter-tenor with soprano. Passionless vocals, maybe, but this is an emotion-charged story. TH. In French and Italian with English subtitles. Contains sex scenes. DVD

Stefano Dionisi *Farinelli/Carlo Broschi* • Enrico Lo Verso *Riccardo Broschi* • Elsa Zylberstein *Alexandra* • Caroline Cellier *Margaret Hunter* • Marianne Basler *Countess Mauer* • Jacques Boudet *Philip V* • Graham Valentine *The Prince of Wales* • Jeroen Krabbé *Handel* ■ *Dir* Gérard Corbiau • *Scr* Andrée Corbiau, from a screenplay (unproduced) by Andrée Corbiau, Gérard Corbiau

The Farm: Angola, USA ★★★

Documentary 1996 · US · Colour · 90mins

The Shawshank Redemption superbly captured the bleakness of prison life – but this is the real McCoy. This acclaimed documentary focuses on Angola Prison, a facility that is home for 5,000 convicts facing life sentences, the majority of whom will never seen the outside world again. It's essentially a day in the life of a number of the prisoners, with co-director Wilbert Rideau sympathetically listening to the sobering, thoughtful insights of the felons as they desperately cling to the remote hope of one day leaving the facility. JF

Bernard Addison *Narrator* ■ *Dir* Jonathan Stack, Liz Garbus, Wilbert Rideau

The Farmer Takes a Wife ★★★ U

Period romantic drama
1935 · US · Colour · 93mins

Henry Fonda made his movie debut in this charming romance set along the Erie Canal in the 1850s, and created a screen persona that would endure for five decades. Determined, caring and trustworthy, he was virtually the American ideal. Janet Gaynor and Fonda are well matched under the direction of Victor Fleming who, refreshingly, elects to shoot mainly in the open, away from studio backdrops. Never a studio to waste a good property, 20th Century-Fox dusted this off as a Betty Grable vehicle in 1953, but Dale Robertson was no substitute for Fonda. TS

Janet Gaynor *Molly Larkins* • Henry Fonda *Dan Harrow* • Charles Bickford *Jotham Klore* • Slim Summerville *Fortune Friendly* • Andy Devine *Elmer Otway* • Roger Imhof *Sam Weaver* • Jane Withers *Della* • Siegfried Rumann [Sig Ruman] *Blacksmith* ■ *Dir* Victor Fleming • *Scr* Edwin Burke, from the play by Frank B Elser, Marc Connelly, from the novel *Rome Haul* by Walter D Edmonds

The Farmer Takes a Wife ★★ U

Period musical 1953 · US · Colour · 80mins

This is an ill-advised musical remake of the 1935 period romance. Dale Robertson steps into Henry Fonda's shoes as the 19th-century land-lover who signs on to a barge on the Erie Canal to raise the money to buy a farm. But he lacks the naiveté of the young Fonda, while brassy Betty Grable has none of the wide-eyed idealism that made Janet Gaynor so persuasive as the barge cook who comes to share his dream. Harold Arlen and Dorothy Fields's blaring songs, Arthur E Arling's garish photography and director Henry Levin's idea of cosy nostalgia don't help much either. DP

Betty Grable *Molly* • Dale Robertson *Daniel Harrow* • Thelma Ritter *Lucy Cashdollar* • John Carroll *Jotham Klore* • Eddie Foy Jr *Fortune Friendly* • Charlotte Austin *Pearl* ■ *Dir* Henry Levin • *Scr* Walter Bullock, Sally Benson, Joseph Fields, from the play by Frank B Elser, Marc Connelly, from the novel *Rome Haul* by Walter D Edmonds • *Music* Cyril Mockridge • *Music/lyrics* Harold Arlen, Dorothy Fields

The Farmer's Daughter ★★★ U

Comedy drama 1946 · US · BW · 96mins

Loretta Young picked up her best actress Oscar for this strangely accented, but utterly charming, performance as Katrin Holstrom, a fictionalised Swede who comes to Washington as a lady's maid and ends up running for Congress opposing the man she loves. Holstrom's really an RKO mouthpiece for producer Dore Schary's Hollywood-liberal political views, but the original play *Hulda, Daughter of Parliament* was, amazingly, a hit in Finland. Eventually Schary took over MGM from the ousted reactionary Louis B Mayer, and Young became one of the brightest names in the early days of television. TS

Loretta Young *Katrin Holstrom* • Joseph Cotten *Glenn Morley* • Ethel Barrymore *Mrs Morley* • Charles Bickford *Clancy* • Rose Hobart *Virginia* • Rhys Williams *Adolph* ■ *Dir* HC Potter • *Scr* Allen Rivkin, Laura Kerr, from the play *Hulda, Daughter of Parliament* by Juhni Tervataa

The Farmer's Wife ★★★ U

Silent comedy 1928 · UK · BW · 97mins

Eden Phillpott's play had been a long-running hit in the West End before Alfred Hitchcock translated it to the screen. It's a comedy of rural manners, as widower Jameson Thomas alights on the village's eligible spinsters before coming to appreciate the charms of his loyal housekeeper, Lilian Hall-Davis. But Hitchcock adds a veneer of social suspense that renders the farmer's search as much a study in gender and class as a melodramatic romance. There's also plenty of coarse clowning from Gordon Harker, as Thomas's handyman. DP DVD

Jameson Thomas *Samuel Sweetland* • Lillian Hall-Davis *Araminta Dench* • Gordon Harker *Churdles Ash* • Gibb McLaughlin *Henry Coaker* • Maud Gill *Thirza Tapper* • Louie Pounds *Widow Windeatt* ■ *Dir* Alfred Hitchcock • *Scr* Eliot Stannard, from the play by Eden Phillpotts, from the novel *Widecombe Fair* by Eden Phillpotts

Fascination ★★ 18

Erotic horror 1979 · Fr · Colour · 78mins

More nonsensical soft-core horror trash from French hack director Jean Rollin. This turn-of-the-century fairy tale combines ritual slaughter, cannibal orgies and exploitation gore. A hunky thief comes between two lesbian vampires. It's better than some of Rollin's yawn-inducing efforts, thanks to halfway-decent acting. However, it's still a slow-moving bore thanks to Rollin's camera dwelling on the visual properties of naked bodies, fabrics and furnishings above the thin plot. AJ. In French with English subtitles.

Franca Mai *Elisabeth* • Brigitte Lahaie *Eva* ■ *Dir/Scr* Jean Rollin

Fashions of 1934 ★★★

Musical comedy 1934 · US · BW · 78mins

A *Prêt-à-Porter* for the 1930s? Not really, but it's actually a lot more fun than Robert Altman's 1990s take on *haute couture*. Smooth charmer William Powell and glamorous assistant Bette Davis play the visiting Americans who succeed in running rings around the snooty, fashion-conscious inhabitants of Paris. Director William Dieterle spares no expense in invoking a dizzying world of elegant artifice, and there's sharp playing from the two leads. JF

William Powell *Sherwood Nash* • Bette Davis *Lynn Mason* • Frank McHugh *Snap* • Verree Teasdale *Grand Duchess Alix* • Reginald Owen *Oscar Baroque* • Henry O'Neill *Duryea* • Philip Reed *Jimmy* • Hugh Herbert *Joe Ward* ■ *Dir* William Dieterle • *Scr* F Hugh Herbert, Gene Markey, Kathryn Scola, Carl Erickson, from a story by Harry Collins, Warren Duff

Fast and Furious ★★

Comedy mystery 1939 · US · BW · 73mins

This was the last of three features (after *Fast Company* and 1939's *Fast and Loose*) written for MGM by the clever and witty Harry Kurnitz, here starring suave Franchot Tone and sexy Ann Sothern as the rare book dealers. This particular episode proved a training ground for Busby Berkeley, best known for his ground-breaking flamboyant choreography, who had left his home studio Warner Bros to establish himself as a "serious" director over at MGM. Despite the sparseness of the budget, it was a competent enough effort. TS

Franchot Tone *Joel Sloane* • Ann Sothern *Garda Sloane* • Ruth Hussey *Lily Cole* • Lee Bowman *Mike Stevens* • Allyn Joslyn *Ted Bentley* • John Miljan *Erie Bartell* ■ *Dir* Busby Berkeley • *Scr* Harry Kurnitz

Fast and Loose ★★

Comedy 1930 · US · BW · 70mins

Miriam Hopkins was to become one of the brightest stars of the 1930s, but few would have guessed from her screen debut in this comedic misfire. Despite a script co-written by Preston Sturges, the story is a conventional rich-girl-falls-for-poor-boy affair. Carole

Lombard, in the smaller role of a chorus girl who reforms Hopkins's playboy brother, comes off better, though Fred C Newmeyer's stilted direction favours no one. TV

Miriam Hopkins *Marion Lenox* • Carole Lombard *Alice O'Neil* • Frank Morgan *Bronson Lenox* • Charles Starrett *Henry Morgan* • Henry Wadsworth *Bertie Lenox* • Winifred Harris *Carrie Lenox* • Herbert Yost *George Grafton* ■ *Dir* Fred C Newmeyer • *Scr* Doris Anderson, Jack Kirkland, Preston Sturges, from the play *The Best People* by David Gray, Avery Hopwood

Fast and Loose ★★

Comedy mystery 1939 · US · BW · 79mins

The sequel to *Fast Company*, which starred Melvyn Douglas and Florence Rice as married sleuths, this one stars Robert Montgomery trying to discover what's happened to a collection of manuscripts which vanish from a library, and Rosalind Russell as his wife who complicates the situation. An undemanding piece of fluff, with the stars on good form. MGM made a further film, *Fast and Furious*, before abandoning the format which was a rip-off of *The Thin Man* series. AT

Robert Montgomery *Joel Sloane* • Rosalind Russell *Garda Sloane* • Reginald Owen *Vincent Charlton* • Ralph Morgan *Nicholas Torrent* • Etienne Girardot *Christopher Oates* • Alan Dinehart *David Hilliard* ■ *Dir* Edwin L Marin • *Scr* Harry Kurnitz

The Fast and the Furious ★★★★ 15

Action thriller
2001 · US/Ger · Colour · 102mins

Director Rob Cohen's pedal-to-the-metal thriller has fabulous customised cars, scantily clad babes, moody hunks, bare-knuckle brawls and a boot full of turbo-charged stunts to spare. Vin Diesel is the champion of LA's illegal street racing subculture, where gangs organise cash-prize races between souped-up cars. But is his crew of tuned-up misfits, including girlfriend Michelle Rodriguez, behind a spate of recent truck hijackings? That's what cop Paul Walker goes undercover to find out, falling in love with Diesel's sister Jordana Brewster in the process. Electrifying. Followed by *2 Fast 2 Furious* in 2003. AJ [video] DVD

Paul Walker *Brian Earl Spilner/Officer Brian O'Conner* • Vin Diesel *Dominic Toretto* • Michelle Rodriguez *Letty* • Jordana Brewster *Mia Toretto* • Rick Yune *Johnny Tran* • Chad Lindberg *Jesse* ■ *Dir* Rob Cohen • *Scr* Gary Scott Thompson, Erik Bergquist, David Ayer, from a story by Gary Scott Thompson, from an article by Ken Li

Fast Break ★★★

Comedy 1979 · US · Colour · 107mins

One of the first attempts to duplicate the "worst – insert activity – team in the world whipped into shape by dedicated coach" formula that originated from *The Bad News Bears*, is one of the best. Basketball is the sport this time, with Gabe Kaplan playing the New York coach hired by a small college to produce a winning team, doing so by recruiting a number of eccentric players. Instead of concentrating on the usual story clichés, the movie is content to focus on the players, who are not just funny, but surprisingly well-rounded characters. There's also some great basketball action. KB

Gabe Kaplan *David Greene* • Harold Sylvester *DC* • Mike Warren [Michael Warren] *Preacher* • Bernard King *Hustler* • Reb Brown *Bull* • Mavis Washington *Swish* ■ *Dir* Jack Smight • *Scr* Sandy Stern [Sandor Stern], from a story by Marc Kaplan

Fast Charlie: the Moonbeam Rider ★★ PG

Action adventure 1978 · US · Colour · 94mins

This is an adequate action drama laced with barbed comedy about a disenchanted First World War soldier (David Carradine) who deserts his unit to enter the first transcontinental motorcycle race. Authentic production design, and credible support from Brenda Vaccaro as his faithful groupie, add class to another B-movie from the Roger Corman production conveyor belt. AJ [video]

David Carradine *Charlie Swattle* • Brenda Vaccaro *Grace Wolf* • LQ Jones *Floyd Bevins* • RG Armstrong *Al Barber* • Terry Kiser *Lester Neal* • Jesse Vint *Calvin Hawk* ■ *Dir* Steve Carver • *Scr* Michael Gleason, from the story by Ed Spielman, Howard Friedlander

Fast Company ★★

Comedy mystery 1938 · US · BW · 73mins

Melvyn Douglas and Florence Rice star as amateur detectives who specialise in finding stolen and bogus books but find themselves also caught up in a murder. The background of book auctions has some interest and Douglas is always an exceptionally smooth performer, though Rice never had the star appeal MGM initially thought she had. It was the first in a three-part series about married detectives – *Fast and Loose* and *Fast and Furious* followed. AT

Melvyn Douglas *Joel Sloane* • Florence Rice *Garda Sloane* • Claire Dodd *Julia Thorne* • Shepperd Strudwick *Ned Morgan* • Louis Calhern *Elias Z Bannerman* • Nat Pendleton *Paul Torison* • Douglass Dumbrille *Arnold Stamper* ■ *Dir* Edward Buzzell • *Scr* Marco Page, Harold Tarshis, from a story by Marco Page, Harry Kurnitz

Fast Food ★★★ PG

Comedy 1989 · US · Colour · 88mins

Anything goes in the burger wars – including spiking the sauce with an aphrodisiac. Students and scam artists Clark Brandon and Randal Patrick take on ruthless burger king Jim Varney whose expansion plans threaten their friend Tracy Griffith's gas station. This good-natured comedy boasts some decent jokes and an eccentric cast that includes Melanie Griffith's half-sister, Tracy, Michael J Pollard from *Bonnie and Clyde* and ex-porn star Traci Lords. AT [video]

Clark Brandon *Auggie* • Randal Patrick *Drew* • Tracy Griffith *Samantha* • Michael J Pollard *Bud* • Lanny Horn *Calvin* • Jim Varney *Wrangler Bob Bundy* • Blake Clark *EG McCormick* • Traci Lords *Dixie Love* ■ *Dir* Michael A Simpson • *Scr* Randal Patrick, Clark Brandon, Lanny Horn, from a story by Scott B Sowers, Jim Bastille

Fast Food ★ 18

Comedy drama 1998 · UK · Colour · 95mins

Stewart Sugg, in his directorial debut, dishes up an overcooked, indigestible mess that borrows indiscriminately from *A Clockwork Orange*, *Blue Velvet* and diverse Scorsese and Tarantino pictures. Of the five friends reunited after decades of disappointment, only Douglas Henshall comes remotely close to giving a performance as he tries to save blind hooker Emily Woof from his safe-blowing mates and her savage pimp. A new low for the homegrown crime movie. DP [video]

Douglas Henshall *Benny* • Emily Woof *Letitia/Claudia* • Miles Anderson *Dwayne* • Gerard Butler *Jacko* • Danny Midwinter *Bisto* • Sean Hughes ■ *Dir/Scr* Stewart Sugg

The Fast Lady ★★★ PG

Comedy 1963 · UK · Colour · 94mins

Despite driving up too many B roads, this story of a civil servant (Stanley Baxter), his car (a Bentley) and the girl on whom he dotes (Julie Christie) has such a degree of fresh-faced innocence that you appreciate the film's charm rather than notice the rambling plot. This Rank movie is tackled with relish by the cast: Christie is simpering and decent, Baxter is spot-on with his "gormless comic" style and James Robertson-Justice booms throughout. JM [video] DVD

James Robertson-Justice *Charles Chingford* • Leslie Phillips *Freddy Fox* • Stanley Baxter *Murdoch Troon* • Kathleen Harrison *Mrs Staggers* • Julie Christie *Claire Chingford* • Dick Emery *Shingler* ■ *Dir* Ken Annakin • *Scr* Jack Davies, Helen Blyth, from a story by Howard Keble

Fast Money ★★ 18

Action crime romance
1995 · US · Colour · 88mins

This rehash of the old thief-and-innocent-bystander-together-on-the-run formula is no great shakes, but it passes the time well enough. The twist comes with the sexes being reversed: Yancy Butler plays Francesca, a car thief with a liking for luxury vehicles, who is on the run after causing a major accident. Along for the ride is Matt McCoy, an unassuming reporter minding his business on a mundane assignment. The action sequences are fine but the main attraction here is the chemistry between the actors. KB. Contains swearing and violence. [video]

Yancy Butler *Francesca* • Matt McCoy *Jack* • John Ashton *Lt Diego* • Trevor Goddard *Regy* • Jacob Witkin *Stewart* • Patrika Darbo *Teebou* ■ *Dir/Scr* Alexander Wright [Alex Wright]

Fast Times at Ridgemont High ★★★★ 18

Comedy 1982 · US · Colour · 85mins

Amy Heckerling's insightful, sympathetic and still very funny foray into high school life is a stunning exception to the spate of dreadful post-*Animal House* teen sex comedies. Thoughtfully adapted by Cameron Crowe from his own novel, on the surface it's just another episodic story of high school students trying to lose their virginity – except this also chronicles serious issues such as teenage pregnancy along with the usual hi-jinks. It also boasts a quite astonishing cast of then unknowns: Jennifer Jason Leigh, Phoebe Cates, Judge Reinhold, Forest Whitaker, Eric Stoltz, Anthony Edwards and, best of all, Sean Penn as a permanently stoned surfer, the template for everybody from Bill and Ted to Beavis and Butthead. JF [video] DVD

Sean Penn *Jeff Spicoli* • Jennifer Jason Leigh *Stacy Hamilton* • Judge Reinhold *Brad Hamilton* • Robert Romanus *Mike Damone* • Brian Backer *Mark Ratner* • Phoebe Cates *Linda Barrett* • Forest Whitaker *Charles Jefferson* • Eric Stoltz *Stoner Bud* • Anthony Edwards *Stoner Bud* ■ *Dir* Amy Heckerling • *Scr* Cameron Crowe, from his novel

Fast-Walking ★★ 18

Comedy drama 1982 · US · Colour · 111mins

This prison drama has James Woods in a typically amoral role as a guard who becomes involved in a plot to assassinate black activist Robert Hooks. There are some good performances from Tim McIntire, M Emmet Walsh and the ever-reliable Woods, but these accomplished actors can't hide the fact that this is a rather nasty and unpleasant film. JB. Contains swearing and violence. [video]

James Woods *Miniver* • Kay Lenz *Moke* • Tim McIntire *Wasco* • Robert Hooks *Galliot* • M Emmet Walsh *Sergeant Sanger* • Susan Tyrrell *Evie* • Charles Weldon *Jackson* ■ *Dir* James B Harris • *Scr* James B Harris, from the novel *The Rap* by Ernest Brawley

Faster, Pussycat! Kill! Kill! ★★★★ 18

Cult satirical melodrama
1965 · US · BW · 83mins

Three go-go dancers, led by *femme fatale* Tura Satana, go on a wild crime spree in California in Russ Meyer's cult favourite. After indulging in kidnapping, theft, murder and wanton exposure of their seemingly limitless cleavages, the crazy-for-kicks chicks take the Battle of the Sexes to the extreme, drawing some hapless males into a violently perverse cat-and-mouse game. This double-entendre parade through the seamier side of the Swinging Sixties is the definitive Meyer movie. AJ. Contains violence and sex scenes. [video] DVD

Tura Satana *Varla* • Haji *Rosie* • Lori Williams *Billie* • Susan Bernard [Sue Bernard] *Linda* • Stuart Lancaster *Old man* • Paul Trinka *Kirk* • Dennis Busch *Vegetable* ■ *Dir* Russ Meyer • *Scr* Jack Moran, from a story by Russ Meyer

F

The Fastest Guitar Alive ★★ U

Musical comedy western
1966 · US · Colour · 87mins

Roy Orbison is barely recognisable without his trademark shades in this shameless exploitation offering, but there's no mistaking that magical voice. A curious hybrid of matinée horse opera and teen drive-in picture, it casts him as a Confederate spy who becomes a fugitive after being trapped behind enemy lines at the end of the American Civil War. It's more a knockabout adventure than a genuine western, with the Big O (who hides a rifle behind his guitar) coming over as an uncomfortable throwback to such singing cowboys as Hopalong Cassidy and Roy Rogers. DP

Roy Orbison *Johnny Banner* • Sammy Jackson *Steve Menlo* • Maggie Pierce *Flo Chestnut* • Joan Freeman *Sue Chestnut* • Lyle Bettger *Charlie Mansfield* • John Doucette *Sheriff Max Cooper* • Patricia Donahue *Stella* ■ *Dir* Michael Moore (1) • *Scr* Robert E Kent

The Fastest Gun Alive ★★★ U

Western 1956 · US · BW · 85mins

Glenn Ford is trying to live down his father's gunslinging past by working as a town storekeeper, when Broderick Crawford blasts in, exposing Ford and taunting him with his father's name. Russ Tamblyn has some knockabout moments at a barn dance, and Jeanne Crain is earnest and pretty as the pleading wife, but Ford shines, giving an outstanding performance in a taut, under-rated western. TS [video]

Glenn Ford *George Temple* • Jeanne Crain *Dora Temple* • Broderick Crawford *Vinnie Harold* • Russ Tamblyn *Eric Doolittle* • Allyn Joslyn *Harvey Maxwell* • Leif Erickson *Lou Glover* • Noah Beery Jr *Dink Wells* ■ *Dir* Russell Rouse • *Scr* Frank D Gilroy, Russell Rouse, Frank D Gilroy

Fat Albert ★★

Fantasy comedy adventure
2004 · US · Colour · 100mins

This live action update of the 1970s cartoon series is probably too sugary for today's savvy youngsters. The original series, created by Bill Cosby (he serves as producer here and also pops up in a cameo), was centred around the feel-good antics of a gang of young black youths. Here the cartoon characters literally climb out of the TV set to help a lonely young teen (Kyla Pratt). Keenan Thompson makes a good fist of the fleshed out Fat Albert, but this is as much out of step with modern tastes as the cartoon characters are in the real world. JF

Kenan Thompson *Fat Albert* • Kyla Pratt *Doris* • Shedrack Anderson III *Rudy* • Jermaine

Williams *Mushmouth* • Keith Robinson *Bill* • Alphonso McAuley *Bucky* • Aaron A Frazier *Old Weird Harold* • Marques B Houston [Marques Houston] *Dumb Donald* • Bill Cosby ■ *Dir* Joel Zwick • *Scr* William H Cosby Jr [Bill Cosby], Charles Kipps

Fat City ★★★★

Sports drama 1972 · US · Colour · 96mins

Strip away the sleaziness of the setting and you have that old Hollywood standby, *A Star Is Born*, recycled as a boxing picture. Stacy Keach (in a role offered first to Marlon Brando) is the boxer on the slide and Jeff Bridges is the one on the rise. John Huston, who directed wearing an oxygen mask owing to acute emphysema, shot the picture on skid row in Stockton, California, and aimed for a grimly realistic, but not seedy, look. The result is a minor classic, necessarily brutal but with humanity and an underlying optimism. AT. Contains violence and swearing.

Stacy Keach *Billy Tully* • Jeff Bridges *Ernie Munger* • Susan Tyrrell *Oma* • Candy Clark *Faye* • Nicholas Colasanto *Ruben* • Art Aragon *Babe* • Curtis Cokes *Earl* • Sixto Rodriguez *Lucero* • Billy Walker *Wes* ■ *Dir* John Huston • *Scr* Leonard Gardner, from his novel • *Cinematographer* Conrad Hall

Fat Slags ★ 15

Comedy 2004 · UK · Colour · 72mins

This crude, one-note live-action adaptation of *Viz* comic's regular strip aims low and still manages to misfire. Fiona Allen and Sophie Thompson don fat suits to bring Sandra and Tracy, *Viz*'s booze-swilling, kebab-scoffing nymphos, to life. The girls' "star quality" is spotted by media baron Sean Cooley (Jerry O'Connell), after he receives a reality-altering bump on the head. Around this crass premise, the scattershot approach encompasses poorly handled gross-out slapstick and misjudged celebrity cameos. IF. Contains swearing and sexual references. VIDEO DVD

Sophie Thompson *Tracey* • Fiona Allen *Sandra* • Jerry O'Connell *Sean Cooley* • James Dreyfus *Fidor* • Anthony Head *Victor* • Michael Greco *Niarchos* • Geri Halliwell *Paige* • Tom Goodman-Hill *Baz* • Henry Miller *Dave* • Naomi Campbell *Sales assistant* • Angus Deayton *Maurice* • Dolph Lundgren *Randy* ■ *Dir* Ed Bye • *Scr* William Osborne, from characters created by Chris Donald, Simon Donald [uncredited]

Fatal Attraction ★★★★ 18

Thriller 1987 · US · Colour · 114mins

This is the movie that helped create a new genre: the psychotic female from hell. Glenn Close is the obsessed woman driven to extreme lengths when she discovers that Michael Douglas is not going to leave his wife (Anne Archer) for her. Close is excellent in a thankless role, while Douglas established himself as the troubled icon of middle-class America. The movie's message (it's all right to have an affair as long as it's not with a nutcase) is more than a little dubious, but there is no denying its slick power and director Adrian Lyne milks the tension for all it's worth. However, he had to reshoot the movie's climax after test audiences gave the thumbs down to his first ending. Lyne later got the chance to reinstate the original ending with his director's cut. JF. Contains violence, swearing, sex scenes and nudity. VIDEO DVD

Michael Douglas *Dan Gallagher* • Glenn Close *Alex Forrest* • Anne Archer *Beth Gallagher* • Ellen Hamilton Latzen *Ellen Gallagher* • Stuart Pankin *Jimmy* • Ellen Foley *Hildy* • Fred Gwynne *Arthur* • Meg Mundy *Joan Rogerson* ■ *Dir* Adrian Lyne • *Scr* James Dearden

Fatal Beauty ★★ 18

Comedy thriller 1987 · US · Colour · 99mins

Director Tom Holland loses his humorous touch with this lukewarm vehicle for Whoopi Goldberg. Goldberg stars as a tough narcotics cop on the trail of some drug-dealing bad guys. This gives her an excuse to totter around in ill-advised prostitute disguise, while Cheech Marin, Rubén Blades and Sam Elliott (as Goldberg's love interest) try their best to pretend they're in a movie worth sitting through. JB. Contains swearing. VIDEO

Whoopi Goldberg *Rita Rizzoli* • Sam Elliott *Mike Marshak* • Rubén Blades *Carl Jimenez* • Harris Yulin *Conrad Kroll* • Brad Dourif *Leo Nova* • Cheech Marin [Richard "Cheech" Marin] *Bartender* ■ *Dir* Tom Holland • *Scr* Hilary Henkin, Dean Riesner

Fatal Bond ★★

Thriller 1991 · Aus · Colour · 89mins

The *Exorcist* spoof *Repossessed* aside, Linda Blair rarely breaks out of straight-to-video mode these days, and even a change of continents here fails to provide a remedy. In this seedy, supposedly erotic thriller, Blair is the bored suburbanite who falls for smouldering drifter Jerome Ehlers, who may or may not be a psychopathic killer. The Australian locations are a pleasant change, but the storyline is far-fetched. JF. Contains swearing, violence and nudity.

Linda Blair *Leonie Stevens* • Jerome Ehlers *Joe Martinez* • Stephen Leeder *Anthony Boon* • Donal Gibson *Rocky Bargetta* • Caz Lederman *Detective Chenko* • Joe Bugner *Miller* • Roger Ward *Greaves* ■ *Dir* Vincent Monton • *Scr* Phillip Avalon

Fatal Instinct ★★★ 15

Spoof thriller 1993 · US · Colour · 86mins

Panned on its original release, this boasts some slick gags and several knowing performances. The problem is, it's often far too clever for its own good. Veteran director Carl Reiner has got the look and feel of latter-day *films noirs* off to a T, and he is well served by Armand Assante as a cop who doubles as a lawyer for the people he arrests, Kate Nelligan as his blatantly adulterous wife and Sherilyn Fenn and Sean Young as his *femmes fatales*. DP. Contains swearing and sex scenes. VIDEO DVD

Armand Assante *Ned Ravine* • Sherilyn Fenn *Laura* • Kate Nelligan *Lana Ravine* • Sean Young *Lola Cain* • Christopher McDonald *Frank Kelbo* • James Remar *Max Shady* ■ *Dir* Carl Reiner • *Scr* David O'Malley

Fatal Lady ★★

Murder mystery 1936 · US · BW · 75mins

Walter Pidgeon returned to Hollywood from the Broadway stage to play opposite Mary Ellis in this ill-conceived attempt to turn the leading lady of stage musicals into a movie name. She plays an opera star suspected of murder, but the title of this hackneyed backstage drama proved sadly prophetic for Ellis, whose casting as a prima donna seemed both appropriate and unsympathetic. TS

Mary Ellis *Marion Stuart/Marla Delasano/Malevo* • Walter Pidgeon *David Roberts* • Ruth Donnelly *Melba York* • Norman Foster *Phillip Roberts* • Guy Bates Post *Feodor Glinka* • John Halliday *Romero Fontes* ■ *Dir* Edward Ludwig • *Scr* Samuel Ornitz, Horace McCoy, from a story by Harry Segall

Fatal Mission ★★

War drama 1990 · US · Colour · 84mins

"Nothin's guaranteed in the 'Nam'", or so declares American "black" operations agent Peter Fonda at the beginning of this movie. What is guaranteed is that you will have flashbacks to *Hell in the Pacific* about halfway through. Fonda assassinates a Communist leader, and while trying to escape, is taken prisoner by a Chinese agent, played by Tia Carrere. Together they find out that everyone's against them, and they have to rely on each other to survive. ST

Peter Fonda *Ken Andrews* • Tia Carrere *Mai Chong* • Mako *Trang* • Ted Markland *CIA Man* • Jim Mitchum [James Mitchum] *Captain Bauer* • Felind Obach *NVA Sergeant Tuong* • Joonee Gamboa *NVA Captain Hao* • Joe Mari *Vietnam general* ■ *Dir* George Rowe • *Scr* Anthony Gentile, John Gentile, George Rowe, Chosei Funahara, Peter Fonda, from a story by Erlinda Quiaoit Rowe

Le Fate Ignoranti ★★★ 15

Drama 2001 · Fr/It · Colour · 105mins

The theme of clashing cultures recurs throughout director Ferzan Ozpetek's work, but here the Turkish-born film-maker shifts the emphasis from ethnic to sexual matters with a tale of grief, shock and acceptance. When medical worker Margherita Buy is widowed, she sets out to find the woman she suspects of having been her husband's mistress, but is confronted with Stefano Accorsi, a younger man with whom her husband had a long-term affair. Their relationship is soon strewn with contrived twists and facile resolutions, while the tension that existed in their early meetings dissipates into cosiness as Buy becomes part of Accorsi's eccentric coterie. DP. In Italian and Turkish with English subtitles. VIDEO DVD

Margherita Buy *Antonia* • Stefano Accorsi *Michele* • Serra Yilmaz *Serra* • Andrea Renzi *Massimo* • Gabriel Garko *Ernesto* • Erica Blanc *Veronica* • Rosaria De Cicco *Luisella* ■ *Dir* Ferzan Ozpetek • *Scr* Gianni Romoli, Ferzan Ozpetek

Fate Is the Hunter ★★★

Mystery drama 1964 · US · BW · 106mins

Glenn Ford leads the investigation into an air crash for which his friend, pilot Rod Taylor, is thought to be responsible. Flashbacks show us what might have happened, until Ford and sole survivor Suzanne Pleshette restage the flight to solve the mystery. A lot of interesting detail and a surprising cast make this quite watchable, though Ford is fairly glum throughout. AT

Glenn Ford *Sam McBane* • Nancy Kwan *Sally Fraser* • Rod Taylor *Capt Jack Savage* • Suzanne Pleshette *Martha Webster* • Jane Russell *Jane Russell, guest star* • Wally Cox *Ralph Bundy* • Mary Wickes *Mrs Llewelyn* • Dorothy Malone *Lisa Bond* ■ *Dir* Ralph Nelson • *Scr* Harold Medford, from the novel by Ernest K Gann

Father ★★★

Drama 1990 · Aus · Colour · 106mins

The father is Max von Sydow, a German living in Melbourne with his daughter (Carol Drinkwater), son-in-law and two grandchildren. A nice, happy family, until grandad is suddenly charged with committing wartime atrocities and is put on trial. While not in the same league as Costa-Gavras's *Music Box*, this is nevertheless a gripping drama, superbly played by von Sydow. The film explores the themes of guilt and the nature of truth with skill, even drawing parallels with the son-in-law's experiences in Vietnam. AT. Contains swearing and nudity.

Max von Sydow *Joe Mueller* • Carol Drinkwater *Anne Winton* • Julia Blake *Iya Zetnick* • Steve Jacobs *Bobby Winton* • Simone Robertson *Rebecca Winton* • Kahli Sneddon *Amy Winton* • Nicholas Bell *Paul Jamieson* ■ *Dir* John Power • *Scr* Tony Cavanaugh, Graham Hartley

Father and Son ★★★ PG

Drama 2003 · Rus/Ger/It/Fr/Neth/Swi · Col · 82m

After the period exuberance of *Russian Ark*, Aleksandr Sokurov retreats into the more personal mood that characterised *Mother and Son* in this awkward companion piece. Aleksandr Burov's glowing golden imagery is the film's undoubted glory. But despite the psychological estrangement that contrasts with their easy physicality, the relationship between war veteran Andrei Shetinin and his motherless soldier son Alexei Neimyshev is so intense that there's no room for onlookers. Moving, stylish, but frustratingly inaccessible. DP. In Russian with English subtitles. DVD

Andrei Shetinin *Father* • Alexei Neimyshev *Son* • Aleksandr Razbash *Neighbour* • Marina Zasukhina *Girlfriend* ■ *Dir* Aleksandr Sokurov • *Scr* Sergei Potepalov

Father Brown ★★★★ U

Comedy thriller 1954 · UK · BW · 93mins

Although occasionally overdoing the unworldliness, Alec Guinness brings GK Chesterton's sermonising sleuth to rich and vigorous life in this hugely enjoyable comedy thriller from director Robert Hamer, who also made Guinness's classic comedy *Kind Hearts and Coronets*. Fans of the original stories might be a tad aggrieved by the slight shift of period and the marked reduction in religious undertone, but the case of St Augustine's Cross is nevertheless packed with incident and intrigue. Peter Finch is languidly villainous as Flambeau and Joan Greenwood huskily seductive as the devout Lady Warren, but it's Cecil Parker's bishop and Ernest Thesiger's doddering librarian who stay longest in the memory. DP

Alec Guinness *Father Brown* • Joan Greenwood *Lady Warren* • Peter Finch *Flambeau* • Cecil Parker *Bishop* • Bernard Lee *Inspector Valentine* • Sidney James *Parkinson* • Gérard Oury *Inspector Dubois* • Ernest Thesiger *Vicomte* ■ *Dir* Robert Hamer • *Scr* Thelma Schnee, Maurice Rapf, Robert Hamer, from the characters created by GK Chesterton

Father Came Too ★★

Comedy 1963 · UK · Colour · 92mins

This is a disappointing outing, considering that it had all the makings of being an amusing inversion of the old mother-in-law joke. James Robertson-Justice stars as the father-in-law from hell who shatters the bliss of newlyweds Stanley Baxter and Sally Smith with his tactless intrusions and incessant hectoring. Such is his dominance of the action that there simply aren't enough gags to go around, leaving Leslie Phillips and Ronnie Barker twiddling their thumbs on the periphery. DP

James Robertson-Justice *Sir Beverley Grant* • Leslie Phillips *Roddy Chipfield* • Stanley Baxter *Dexter Munro* • Sally Smith *Juliet Munro* • Ronnie Barker *Josh* • James Villiers *Benzil Bulstrode* ■ *Dir* Peter Graham Scott • *Scr* Jack Davies, Henry Blyth

Father Dear Father ★★ U

Comedy 1972 · UK · Colour · 94mins

Based on the enduring sitcom first shown in 1968, this, as with most film versions of popular TV shows, lacks the cosy comic consistency of the original, even though it retains most of the cast. Guest stars Beryl Reid, Donald Sinden and Richard O'Sullivan are given too little to do as novelist Patrick Cargill's marriage to his agent is jeopardised by his trouble-prone daughters. DP VIDEO

Patrick Cargill *Patrick Glover* • Natasha Pyne *Anna* • Ann Holloway *Karen* • Noel Dyson *Nanny* • Beryl Reid *Mrs Stoppard* • Donald Sinden *Philip* • Richard O'Sullivan *Richard* •

Jack Watling *Bill Mossman* ■ *Dir* William G Stewart • *Scr* Johnnie Mortimer, from the TV series by Johnnie Mortimer, Brian Cooke

Father Goose ★★★ U

Second World War comedy drama
1964 · US · Colour · 116mins

Cary Grant stars as a boozy beach bum caught up in Second World War heroics involving a gaggle of schoolgirls and their teacher, Leslie Caron. Grant is terrific, as ever, and his air of discomfort certainly helps the plot, but you have to wonder if a comedy about the Japanese invasion of the Pacific is actually a good idea. The Hollywood Academy thought so, and writers Peter Stone and Frank Tarloff won an Oscar for their screenplay. TS

Cary Grant *Walter Eckland* • Leslie Caron *Catherine Freneau* • Trevor Howard *Frank Houghton* • Stephanie Berrington *Elizabeth* • Jennifer Berrington *Harriet* • Jack Good *Stebbings* ■ *Dir* Ralph Nelson • *Scr* Frank Tarloff, Peter Stone, from the story *A Place of Dragons* by SH Barnett

Father Hood ★ PG

Crime comedy 1993 · US · Colour · 91mins

This dislikeable family comedy is really only for diehard Patrick Swayze fans. He plays the supposedly lovable rogue who sets off on the adventure of a lifetime with his two young kids who have been languishing in horrid foster care. The tone veers between naturalistic drama and simple-minded slapstick, and not even a talented supporting cast can rescue this sinking ship. JF. Contains some violence and swearing.

Patrick Swayze *Jack Charles* • Halle Berry *Kathleen Mercer* • Sabrina Lloyd *Kelly Charles* • Brian Bonsall *Eddie Charles* • Michael Ironside *Jerry* • Diane Ladd *Rita* ■ *Dir* Darrell James Roodt • *Scr* Scott Spencer

Father of the Bride ★★★★ U

Comedy 1950 · US · BW · 88mins

Spencer Tracy has seldom been better than here in the title role. His gnarled face is peerless when confronted with so much frustration, and his retelling of the events leading up to the debris that was once his home is a joy. Joan Bennett co-stars as his wife and Elizabeth Taylor plays the bride who's impending nuptials lead to chaos. Director Vincente Minnelli keeps up a sprightly pace and gets the most out of the witty screenplay. This film was so successful that it inspired a sequel – *Father's Little Dividend* – and, four decades on, the inferior remake with its own follow-up (both starring Martin and Keaton). TS

Spencer Tracy *Stanley T Banks* • Joan Bennett *Ellie Banks* • Elizabeth Taylor *Kay Banks* • Don Taylor *Buckley Dunstan* • Billie Burke *Doris Dunstan* • Leo G Carroll *Mr Massoula* • Moroni Olsen *Herbert Dunstan* • Melville Cooper *Mr Tringle* ■ *Dir* Vincente Minnelli • *Scr* Albert Hackett, Francis Goodrich, from the novel by Edward Streeter

Father of the Bride ★★★★ PG

Comedy 1991 · US · Colour · 100mins

The original 1950 marriage-go-round starring Spencer Tracy is given an amiable 1990s work-out by the *Baby Boom* and *Private Benjamin* husband-and-wife team of Charles Shyer and Nancy Meyers. Steve Martin shines as the anxious parent who can't find a single thing to like about his daughter's perfect fiancé, while continually counting the ceremony costs. Diane Keaton gives him sparkling back-up as the uncomplaining wife, but it's Martin Short who steals the entire movie as the camp wedding organiser. AJ DVD

Steve Martin *George Banks* • Diane Keaton *Nina Banks* • Kimberly Williams *Annie Banks* • Kieran Culkin *Matty Banks* • George Newbern *Bryan MacKenzie* • Martin Short *Franck Eggelhoffer* • BD Wong *Howard Weinstein* ■ *Dir* Charles Shyer • *Scr* Nancy Meyers, Charles Shyer, from the film by Frances Goodrich, Albert Hackett, from the novel by Edward Streeter

Father of the Bride Part 2 ★★ PG

Comedy 1995 · US · Colour · 101mins

This loose version of 1951's *Father's Little Dividend* is full of false emotion, lame humour and pointless details. Steve Martin's peaceful life is upset this time by the simultaneous pregnancies of both his wife (Diane Keaton) and his newly-married daughter (Kimberly Williams). Although flashes of Martin's comic genius occasionally shine through the syrupy script, the verbal comedy on offer is dim-witted. AJ DVD

Steve Martin *George Banks* • Diane Keaton *Nina Banks* • Martin Short *Franck Eggelhoffer* • Kimberly Williams *Annie Banks-MacKenzie* • George Newbern *Bryan MacKenzie* • Kieran Culkin *Matty Banks* ■ *Dir* Charles Shyer • *Scr* Nancy Meyers, Charles Shyer, from the film *Father's Little Dividend* by Albert Hackett, Frances Goodrich, from the characters created by Edward Streeter

Father to Be ★★★

Comedy drama 1979 · Swe · Colour · 107mins

This Swedish film takes a different slant on the expectant father scenario, as directed by Lasse Hallström. In the film's defence, it can be said that, through the use of live-action and animated daydreams, it does manage to be occasionally amusing before it goes off at a post-natal tangent. The big plus is Magnus Harenstam as the diligent father-to-be. DP. In Swedish with English subtitles.

Magnus Härenstam *Bosse* • Anki Liden *Lena* • Micha Gabay *Bosse's pal* • Ulf Brunnberg *Bjorn* ■ *Dir/Scr* Lasse Hallström

Father Was a Fullback ★★★

Comedy 1949 · US · BW · 78mins

This is one of those post-*Life with Father* movies, where the mother actually runs the household and the father manages to preserve the illusion of being boss in his own home. Here, Maureen O'Hara rules the roost while Fred MacMurray buckles down on the gridiron as the football coach to a losing college team. Their extended family includes a very young Natalie Wood, a charming Betty Lynn, an irascible Thelma Ritter and crooner Rudy Vallee. Pleasant lightweight fare. TS

Fred MacMurray *George Cooper* • Maureen O'Hara *Elizabeth Cooper* • Betty Lynn *Connie Cooper* • Rudy Vallee *Mr Jessop* • Thelma Ritter *Geraldine* • Natalie Wood *Ellen Cooper* ■ *Dir* John M Stahl • *Scr* Aleen Leslie, Casey Robinson, Mary Loos, Richard Sale, from a play by Clifford Goldsmith

Fatherland ★★★ 15

Political drama
1986 · UK/Ger · Colour · 104mins

To borrow a footballing cliché, this is a film of two halves. The opening section is classic Ken Loach, even though the setting might be unfamiliar. Making his screen debut, Gerulf Pannach is suitably despondent as the liberated East German folk singer whose creativity dries up after he exchanges the political restrictions of the Communist bloc for the capitalist demands of his new American record label. But the fascinating case study of clashing cultures is disappointingly sacrificed for a thriller subplot, as Pannach goes in search of his missing father in England. DP. In German and English with subtitles.

Gerulf Pannach *Drittemann* • Fabienne Babe *Emma* • Cristine Rose *Lucy* • Sigfrit Steiner *James Dryden* • Robert Dietl *Lawyer* • Heike Schrotter *Marita* • Stephan Samuel *Max* ■ *Dir* Ken Loach • *Scr* Trevor Griffiths

A Father's Betrayal ★★★ 15

Drama 1997 · US · Colour · 87mins

Brian Dennehy both directs and stars in this high-quality, made-for-TV drama. He plays a ruthless attorney slowly rebuilding his relationship with his estranged son Reed Diamond. All that changes, however, when a friend of his son's (Alice Krige) accuses his father of raping her. Dennehy is in commanding form and his direction is equally dependable. He also draws good performances from a talented cast. DP. Contains violence. DVD

Brian Dennehy *Ed Brannigan Sr* • Lynn Redgrave *Monica Brannigan* • Reed Diamond *Ed Brannigan Jr* • Alice Krige *Rebecca Daly* ■ *Dir* Brian Dennehy • *Scr* Joe Cacaci

A Father's Choice ★★

Drama 2000 · US · Colour · 97mins

Mini-series and TV-movie stalwart Peter Strauss plays a rodeo rider in this hugely unpersuasive tale about a self-serving macho man getting in touch with his feelings. The cause of his transformation is the arrival of his estranged daughters, who fetch up on the plains after their mother is murdered. DP

Peter Strauss *Charlie "Mac" McClain* • Mary McDonnell *Susan Shaw* • Michelle Trachtenberg *Kelly McClain* • Yvonne Zima *Chris McClain* • Susan Hogan *Gayle Miller* • Roger R Cross *Detective Ross* • Eddie Velez *Detective Cortez* ■ *Dir* Christopher Cain • *Scr* Richard Leder

Fathers' Day ★★ 12

Comedy 1997 · US · Colour · 95mins

This surprisingly unfunny comedy stars Billy Crystal and Robin Williams as two men who are both told by Nastassja Kinski that they are the father of her wayward missing teenage son, in an attempt to get them to help her find him. This had the potential to be hilarious, but instead falls flat thanks to a weak script, which even the combined comedic talents of Williams and Crystal can't perk up. JB DVD

Robin Williams *Dale Putley* • Billy Crystal *Jack Lawrence* • Julia Louis-Dreyfus *Carrie Lawrence* • Nastassja Kinski *Collette Andrews* • Charlie Hofheimer *Scott Andrews* ■ *Dir* Ivan Reitman • *Scr* Lowell Ganz, Babaloo Mandel, from the film *Les Compères* by Francis Veber

Father's Doing Fine ★★★ U

Comedy 1952 · UK · Colour · 83mins

A certain bourgeois self-satisfaction permeates this superficial situation comedy. However, such is the precision of Henry Cass's direction and the exuberance of the performances that it's difficult not to be sucked into this frantic world of scatterbrained daughters, disastrous share deals and crooked butlers. Seemingly a door can't open without a fresh crisis breezing in, but Heather Thatcher's ennobled widow takes it all in her stride, unlike Richard Attenborough's nerve-jangled father-to-be. The pace disguises the fact that the humour has dated somewhat. DP

Richard Attenborough *Dougall* • Heather Thatcher *Lady Buckering* • Noel Purcell *Shaughnessy* • George Thorpe *Dr Drew* • Diane Hart *Doreen* • Susan Stephen *Bicky* • Mary Germaine *Gerda* • Virginia McKenna *Catherine* • Sidney James *Taxi driver* ■ *Dir* Henry Cass • *Scr* Anne Burnaby, from the play *Little Lambs Eat Ivy* by Noel Langley

Father's Little Dividend ★★★ U

Comedy 1951 · US · BW · 81mins

Director Vincente Minnelli was reunited with Spencer Tracy, Joan Bennett, Elizabeth Taylor and Don Taylor for this sequel to their 1950 smash hit *Father of the Bride*. The dividend, of course, is a grandchild, which leads Tracy into dialogue of the "coochy, coochy, coo" variety. Minnelli shot the film in only 22 days while the sets for the final ballet in *An American in Paris* were being constructed. AT DVD

Spencer Tracy *Stanley Banks* • Joan Bennett *Ellie Banks* • Elizabeth Taylor *Kay Dunstan* • Don Taylor *Buckley Dunstan* • Billie Burke *Doris Dunstan* • Moroni Olsen *Herbert Dunstan* ■ *Dir* Vincente Minnelli • *Scr* Frances Goodrich, Albert Hackett, from the characters created by Edward Streeter

Fathom ★★★ U

Spoof spy adventure
1967 · UK · Colour · 100mins

Fresh from the success of their 1966 big-screen version of *Batman*, writer Lorenzo Semple Jr and director Leslie H Martinson came up with this sprightly spoof, which combines the frenetic pace of a crime caper with the flashiness of a Bond movie. Shifting from the search for a lost H-bomb trigger to a race for a priceless statuette, the plot is almost an irrelevance as agents Raquel Welch and Tony Franciosa hurtle around the Mediterranean. Revelling in the sunny locations and the shenanigans, Welch gives one of her best performances in an often disappointing career. DP

Raquel Welch *Fathom Harvill* • Tony Franciosa [Anthony Franciosa] *Peter Merriweather* • Ronald Fraser *Douglas Campbell* • Greta Chi *Jo-May Soon* • Richard Briers *Timothy* ■ *Dir* Leslie H Martinson • *Scr* Lorenzo Semple Jr, from the novel by Larry Forrester

Fatma ★★★

Drama 2001 · Tun/ Fr · Colour · 124mins

Despite focusing on controversial topics such as rape, family tradition and professional prejudice, this authentic-looking, if formulaic, drama from director Khaled Ghorbal presents a surprisingly positive perspective on the status of Tunisian women. The restrained realism helps to illustrate the frank exploration of the attitudes that educated women take towards sex. But what lends the film an intimacy to match its honesty, is the performance of Awatef Jendoubi as a young woman who refuses to bow to societal pressure whether in pursuit of her career or the man she loves. DP. In Arabic with English subtitles.

Awatef Jendoubi *Fatma* • Nabila Guider *Samira* • Bagdadi Aoum *Aziz* • Amel Safta *Radhia* ■ *Dir/Scr* Khaled Ghorbal

Fatso ★★

Comedy 1979 · US · Colour · 93mins

Anne Bancroft is such an attractively classy actress you'd expect her debut as feature director to be the same. Sadly, not. Following the death of an obese cousin, Dom DeLuise is trying to lose weight, hoping both to stay alive and impress Bancroft. The results are mawkish and crude, with enough jokes about excrement to fill a bucket. Bancroft should have known better, though she contributes a performance, to contrast with that of DeLuise, that is as elegant as the rest of the movie should have been. TH

Dom DeLuise *Dominick DiNapoli* • Anne Bancroft *Antoinette* • Ron Carey *Frankie* • Candice Azzara [Candy Azzara] *Lydia* • Michael Lombard *Charlie* ■ *Dir/Scr* Anne Bancroft

Faust ★★★★★ PG

Classic silent fantasy
1926 · Ger · BW · 115mins

This is as much a masterpiece of design as a triumph for the director and his international cast. Inspired by the paintings of Caspar David Friedrich, Robert Herlth and Walter Röhrig brought all their Expressionist expertise to sculpting light, smoke and steam into the malevolent atmosphere that FW Murnau required for Faust's epic duel with Mephistopheles. Emil Jannings makes an imposing demon, Swedish star Gösta Ekman unassumingly transforms from decrepitude to youth and the untried Camilla Horn is suitably pure as the misused Marguerite (a role that was rejected by Lillian Gish). DP DVD

Gösta Ekman (1) *Faust* • Emil Jannings *Mephistopheles* • Camilla Horn *Marguerite* • Frida Richard *Marguerite's mother* • William Dieterle *Valentin, Marguerite's brother* • Yvette Guilbert *Marthe Schwerdtlein, Marguerite's aunt* • Eric Barclay *Duke of Parma* • Hanna Ralph *Duchess of Parma* ■ *Dir* Friedrich W Murnau [FW Murnau] • *Scr* Hans Kyser, from the play *The Tragical History of Doctor Faustus* by Christopher Marlowe, from the writings *Faust: eine Tragödie* by Johann Wolfgang von Goethe • *Cinematographer* Carl Hoffman

Faust ★★★★★ 12

Part-animated fantasy
1994 · UK/Cz Rep/Fr · Colour · 92mins

Jan Svankmajer is the undisputed king of the puppet film, equally at ease with marionettes, claymation and stop-motion animation. His version of *Alice's Adventures in Wonderland* put a dark, disturbing slant on a much-loved fantasy, and here he succeeds in adding a chilling new dimension to the legend of *Faust*. Largely set inside a timelessly magical theatre in modern-day Prague, the mind-bending action is littered with surreal images, satirical asides and serious messages. Petr Cepek gives a remarkable performance, never once betraying the fact that his co-stars are inanimates. This is beautiful, troubling and unmissable. DP

Petr Cepek *Faust* • Andrew Sachs ■ *Dir/Scr* Jan Svankmajer

Faust: Love of the Damned ★ 18

Erotic horror 2001 · US/Sp · Colour · 96mins

Brian Yuzna's shocker is an appallingly bad devil-in-disguise version of *The Crow*. Shattered after the murder of his girlfriend by a criminally demonic sect called The Hand, Mark Frost signs away his soul to the Devil in return for vengeance on her killers. But the satanic pact also means he's transformed into a sick superhero, armed with long metal claws, who must play a vital part in a black magic ritual. A crude dud. AJ DVD

Mark Frost *John Jaspers/Faust* • Isabel Brook *Dr Jade de Camp* • Andrew Divoff *M* • Jeffrey Combs *Lt Margolies* • Monica Van Campen *Claire* ■ *Dir* Brian Yuzna • *Scr* David Quinn, from the comic book *Faust* by Tim Vigil, David Quinn

Fausto ★★★ 15

Comedy drama 1992 · Fr · Colour · 78mins

In spite of an ebullient performance from Jean Yanne as a kindly, hunchbacked tailor, this fashion fantasy is as flimsy and improbable as the grass suits that make orphan Ken Higelin the toast of the catwalks. This wry tale captures the eccentricity of the 1960s quite well, but Higelin's rags-to-riches odyssey is devoid of conflict, and relies on the talents of Higelin's corpulent pal, François Hauteserre, and his lusty relationship with garage owner's daughter, Florence Darel. Optimistic, if naive, this will still make you smile. DP. In French with English subtitles.

Jean Yanne *Mietek* • Ken Higelin *Fausto* • Florence Darel *Tonie* • François Hauteserre *Raymond* • Maurice Bénichou *Lucien* • Bruce Myers *Roger* • Marianne Groves *Myriam* ■ *Dir* Rémy Duchemin • *Scr* Richard Morgiève, Rémy Duchemin, from the novel by Richard Morgiève

Fausto 5.0 ★★★ 18

Science-fiction drama
2001 · Sp · Colour · 94mins

Faust is something of an obsession with the Catalan La Fura dels Baus company – this film follows on from a multimedia play and an opera, both inspired by Goethe's version of the legend. It's unlikely their predecessors could boast such effective performances as those given here by Miguel Angel Sola, as a cancer specialist on the verge of suicide, and Eduard Fernández, as the one-time patient out for revenge following botched surgery. Pedro del Rey's ethereal imagery swathes the action in malevolence, but the female characters are marginalised. DP. In Spanish with English subtitles.

Miguel Angel Sola *Fausto* • Eduard Fernández *Santos* • Najwa Nimri *Julia* • Juan Fernandez *Quiroga* • Raquel Gonzáles *Margarita* ■ *Dir* Isidro Ortiz, Alex Ollé, Carlos Padrissa • *Scr* Fernando León de Aranoa

The Favor ★★ 15

Romantic comedy
1994 · US · Colour · 93mins

The main point of interest in this misguided romantic comedy is the appearance of Brad Pitt, before he established himself as one of Hollywood's leading pin-ups. The starring role goes to Harley Jane Kozak, who gets involved in all sorts of entanglements when she sets up best friend Elizabeth McGovern with old flame Ken Wahl. The supporting cast can't be faulted, but the script is short on decent gags and the direction clumsy. JF. Contains swearing.

Harley Jane Kozak *Kathy* • Elizabeth McGovern *Emily* • Bill Pullman *Peter* • Brad Pitt *Elliott* • Larry Miller *Joe Dubin* • Ken Wahl *Tom Andrews* • Ginger Orsi *Gina* • Leigh Ann Orsi *Hannah* ■ *Dir* Donald Petrie • *Scr* Sara Parriot, Josann McGibbon

Les Favoris de la Lune ★★★ 15

Comedy drama 1984 · Fr/It · Colour · 101mins

Hurtling round Paris in pursuit of such artefacts as a priceless set of chinaware and a period nude, the various characters in Otar Iosseliani's frantic comedy don't have time to develop in the traditional sense. Nor does Iosseliani have the chance to dwell on his highly potent themes – the acquisitiveness of modern society and the consequent reduction of art to a lifestyle commodity. Yet the madcap interaction of the scheming gunsmith, the cuckolded locksmith and the burglar training his son remains hugely diverting in its own right. DP. In French with English subtitles.

Alix de Montaigu *Delphine LaPlace* • Pascal Aubier *Monsieur LaPlace* • Gaspard Flori *Christian LaPlace* • Emilie Aubry *Lucie LaPlace* • Hans Peter Cloos *Monsieur Duphour-Paquet* • Maïté Nahyr *Madeleine Duphour-Paquet* • Julie Aubier *Sabine Duphour-Paquet* • Baptiste Blanchet *Marc Duphour-Paquet* • Katja Rupé *Clair* ■ *Dir* Otar Iosseliani • *Scr* Gérard Brach

The Favour, the Watch and the Very Big Fish ★★ 15

Comedy 1991 · Fr/UK · Colour · 84mins

In this would-be surreal comedy, Bob Hoskins plays a photographer of religious tableaux involved with Natasha Richardson, who does orgiastic voiceovers for porn movies. When her ex-boyfriend Jeff Goldblum is released from jail, he agrees to pose for Hoskins as Christ, but the problems start when he tries to work miracles. Director Ben Lewin has a leaden approach to this Loony Toon-style farce, whose title whets the appetite. The execution, however, leaves a lot to be desired. TH

Bob Hoskins *Louis Aubinard* • Jeff Goldblum *Pianist* • Natasha Richardson *Sybil* • Michel Blanc *Norbert* • Jacques Villeret *Charles* • Angela Pleasence *Elizabeth* • Jean-Pierre Cassel *Zalman* ■ *Dir* Ben Lewin • *Scr* Ben Lewin, from the short story *Rue Saint-Sulpice* by Marcel Aymé

Fazil ★★

Silent romantic drama
1928 · US · BW · 88mins

Rudolph Valentino in *Son of the Sheik* inspired a flurry of exotic imitations, including this dated melodrama from the Fox studio, directed by Howard Hawks – his sixth silent movie. It features Charles Farrell as a petulant Arab prince who meets a pretty Parisienne, played by Norwegian actress Greta Nissen, and whisks her off to marriage and Mecca. However her liberated European ways clash with Arab tradition and his visits to his harem. Apparently this was quite sexy for its time, but is now only of interest as an early piece from a great American director. AT

Charles Farrell *Prince Fazil* • Greta Nissen *Fabienne* • Mae Busch *Helene Debreuze* • Vadim Uraneff *Ahmed* • Tyler Brooke *Jacques Debreuze* • Eddie Sturgis *Rice* • Josephine Borio *Aicha* • John Boles *John Clavering* • John T Murray *Gondolier* ■ *Dir* Howard Hawks • *Scr* Seton I Miller, Philip Klein (adaptation), from the play *L'Insoumise* by Pierre Frondaie

Fear ★★★

Drama 1954 · It/W Ger · BW · 91mins

A German industrialist's wife, who had an affair while her husband was in a PoW camp during the Second World War, finds herself blackmailed by her former lover's mistress. Ingrid Bergman stars in this German-Italian co-production, which marks the last of the six films she made with her writer/director husband, Roberto Rossellini, during her exile from Hollywood. A combination of psychological thriller and marital drama, the film is a rather lumbering affair but, thanks to the presence of the star, and the style of the director, it holds one's interest. RK. In German with English subtitles.

Ingrid Bergman *Irene Wagner* • Mathias Wieman *Professor Albert Wagner* • Renate Mannhardt *Joanna Schultze* • Kurt Kreuger *Heinz Baumann* • Elise Aulinger *Martha* ■ *Dir* Roberto Rossellini • *Scr* Roberto Rossellini, Sergio Amidei, Franz Graf Treuberg, from the novel *Der Angst* by Stefan Zweig

Fear ★★ 18

Action adventure 1988 · US · Colour · 91mins

Yet another therapy session for America on the Vietnam couch, it's just a shame the rest of us have to suffer. This one follows a tiresomely predictable course as a family are held hostage in their isolated cabin by a gang of escaped cons, one of whom is played by Frank Stallone, brother of the more famous Sly. Fellow con Robert Factor turns out to be a pscho, but luckily dad (Cliff De Young) shares his Vietnam background and fights back thanks to various ingenious booby traps. Debut director Robert A Ferretti does his best with a restrictive budget but this is a lost cause. RS

Cliff De Young *Don Haden* • Kay Lenz *Sharon Haden* • Robert Factor *Jack Gracie* • Scott Schwartz *Brian Haden* • Geri Betzler *Jennifer Haden* • Frank Stallone *Robert Armitage* ■ *Dir* Robert A Ferretti • *Scr* Rick Scarry, Kathryn Connell, from a story by Robert A Ferretti

The Fear ★ 18

Horror 1995 · US · Colour · 101mins

A group of students are taken on an experimental "Coming to Terms with Fear" weekend only to find themselves being bumped off by Morty, the killer wooden mannequin, and confessor figure of sad student psychologist Eddie Bowz. A perfunctory attempt at *Elm Street*-style slasher horror with a paucity of imagination that, like the vengeful Morty himself, is in dire need of a further polish. AJ DVD

Eddie Bowz *Richard* • Leland Hayward *Vance* • Erick Weiss *Morty* • Vince Edwards *Uncle Pete* • Ann Turkel *Leslie* • Heather Medway *Ashley* • Darin Heames *Troy* • Wes Craven *Dr Arnold* ■ *Dir* Vincent Robert • *Scr* Ron Ford, from a story by Ron Ford, Greg H Sims

Fear ★★★ 18

Psychological thriller
1996 · US · Colour · 92mins

Would you trust Mark Wahlberg with your 16-year-old daughter? Of course you wouldn't! But when the Walker family first meet her latest date, they think he's a saint with a great body. Alas, he soon turns into the "Boyfriend from Hell" in director James Foley's tautly constructed, albeit predictable thriller. The plot may be contrived, yet Foley adds a few more complexities than usual, while an excellent cast brings credibility to the relationships in crisis. AJ DVD

Mark Wahlberg *David McCall* • Reese Witherspoon *Nicole Walker* • William L Petersen *Steve Walker* • Amy Brenneman *Laura Walker* • Alyssa Milano *Margo Masse* ■ *Dir* James Foley • *Scr* Christopher Crowe

Fear and Desire ★

War drama 1953 · US · BW · 68mins

Stanley Kubrick believed his first feature – about a platoon of soldiers in an unspecified war fighting behind enemy lines – was "a serious effort, ineptly done", so he tried to suppress it. He was right to do so; for, despite some striking imagery, what wrecks the movie – made with money borrowed from relatives – are the uniformly terrible performances and the atrocious dialogue. AT

Frank Silvera *Mac* • Kenneth Harp *Lt Corby* • Virginia Leith *The Girl* • Paul Mazursky *Sidney* • Steve Coit *Fletcher* ■ *Dir* Stanley Kubrick • *Scr* Howard O Sackler, Stanley Kubrick

Fear and Loathing in Las Vegas ★★★ 18

Road movie 1998 · US · Colour · 113mins

This was always going to be a challenging experiment, even for maverick director Terry Gilliam (who replaced Alex Cox in pre-production). Hunter S Thompson's distinctive prose survives nearly intact and, although Johnny Depp brings an amusingly twitchy energy to the role of gonzo journalist Raoul Duke, this brave film falls short of capturing the book's vibrancy. The pace is a bit too fast to allow the audience to clamber on board, however, so one can only watch in bemused admiration as it zooms past. DP. Contains drug abuse and swearing. DVD

Johnny Depp *Raoul Duke* • Benicio Del Toro *Dr Gonzo* • Tobey Maguire *Hitchhiker* • Ellen Barkin *North Star waitress* • Gary Busey *Highway patrolman* • Christina Ricci *Lucy* • Mark Harmon *Magazine reporter* • Cameron Diaz *Blonde TV reporter* • Lyle Lovett *Road* person ■ *Dir* Terry Gilliam • *Scr* Terry Gilliam, Tony Grisoni, Tod Davies, Alex Cox, from the novel by Hunter S Thompson

Fear and Trembling

★★★★ 12A

Comedy 2003 · Fr · Colour · 106mins

This is a stingingly satirical insight into Japanese corporate culture. Despite being born in Tokyo and still fluent in the language, Sylvie Testud's eager Belgian intern falls foul of her employers because of her inability to appreciate the rigidity of their hierarchical structure. Working predominantly in Japanese, Alain Corneau directs with a sly surety that reinforces the comic potential of the various cultural chasms without indulging in racial stereotyping. DP. In Japanese and French with English subtitles. Contains violence and sexual references.

Sylvie Testud *Amélie* • Kaori Tsuji *Miss Fubuki Mori* • Taro Suwa *Monsieur Saito* • Bison Katayama *Monsieur Omochi* • Yasunari Kondo *Monsieur Tenshi* • Sokyu Fujita *Monsieur Haneda* • Gen Shimaoka *Monsieur Unagi* ■ *Dir* Alain Corneau • *Scr* Alain Corneau, from the novel *Stupeur et Tremblements* by Amélie Nothomb

Fear, Anxiety, and Depression

★★

Comedy 1989 · US · Colour · 85mins

Those familiar with Todd Solondz's *Welcome to the Dollhouse* and *Happiness* won't be entirely surprised by the title of this earlier effort. The themes explored with so successfully in the later films are all bubbling away under the surface of this loser romance. Solondz plays the Woody Allen-esque hero on the unblinking lookout for love but finding only ugliness and disappointment in his choice of partner. This film suffers from an overdose of wackiness and is too forced to be entirely believable. AJ

Todd Solondz *Ira Ellis* • Max Cantor *Jack* • Alexandra Gersten *Janice* • Jane Hamper *Junk* • Stanley Tucci *Donny* ■ *Dir/Scr* Todd Solondz

Fear City

★★★ 18

Crime drama 1984 · US · Colour · 91mins

Melanie Griffith makes an early appearance in this vivid, exploitatitive shocker from director Abel Ferrara. The future star of *Working Girl* plays a stripper in mid-town Manhattan, helping out talent agent Tom Berenger just as a homicidal maniac is going about slaughtering professional striptease artists. Scenes of both straight and gay sex, not to mention the multiple murders, have a raw and visceral impact, and Ferrara turns up the heat with such expertise you rather wish he wouldn't. TH [video]

Tom Berenger *Matt Rossi* • Billy Dee Williams *Al Wheeler* • Jack Scalia *Nicky Piacenza* • Melanie Griffith *Loretta* • Rossano Brazzi *Carmine* • Rae Dawn Chong *Leila* • Joe Santos *Frank* • Michael V Gazzo *Mike* ■ *Dir* Abel Ferrara • *Scr* Nicholas St John

Fear Eats the Soul

★★★★ 15

Romantic drama
1973 · W Ger · Colour · 89mins

Rainer Werner Fassbinder's affecting film uses an unconventional love story to attack the prejudices inherent in German society in the early 1970s. As the widowed cleaner and the Moroccan mechanic whose cross-cultural age-gap romance is frowned upon by their family and friends, Brigitte Mira and El Hedi Ben Salem are so convincing it's easy to forget they are merely playing roles. Fassbinder also impresses as Mira's loathsome son-in-law, but it's the deceptive simplicity of his direction that elevates this incisive drama above the more popular period pieces of his later career. DP. In German with English subtitles. [video]

Brigitte Mira *Emmi* • El Hedi Ben Salem *Ali* • Barbara Valentin *Barbara* • Irm Hermann *Krista* • Peter Gauhe *Bruno* • Karl Scheydt *Albert* • Rainer Werner Fassbinder *Eugen* ■ *Dir/Scr* Rainer Werner Fassbinder

Fear in the Night

★★★★

Film noir 1947 · US · BW · 72mins

This is the sort of B-movie that used to be called a "sleeper". A highly original thriller with a literally nightmarish quality, it is based on a book by *noir* specialist Cornell Woolrich (*Rear Window*), and the requisite *noir* elements of paranoia and uncertainty are evident in this tale of a man whose horrific dream seems to have truly taken place. The film's grip is maintained from the haunting opening, set in a room composed entirely of mirrored doors, and Jack Greenhalgh's stylised photography enhances the moody narrative. The hero is a suitably anguished DeForest Kelley, who would achieve fame many years later as Dr "Bones" McCoy in *Star Trek*. Director Maxwell Shane made the same story again, as *Nightmare*, in 1956. TV

Paul Kelly (1) *Cliff Herlihy* • DeForest Kelley *Vince Grayson* • Ann Doran *Lil Herlihy* • Kay Scott *Betty Winters* • Robert Emmett Keane *Lewis* • Jeff York *Torrence* • Charles Victor *Capt Warner* ■ *Dir* Maxwell Shane • *Scr* Maxwell Shane, from the short story *Nightmare* by William Irish [Cornell Woolrich]

Fear in the Night

★★★ 15

Drama 1972 · UK · Colour · 91mins

This school chiller gets off to a cracking start with an eerie title sequence that concludes with a genuine shock. Peter Cushing, complete with an artificial arm and a genius for appearing when least expected, is on creepy form as a demented headmaster who plays sound effects records to re-create the atmosphere of his fire-damaged school. Judy Geeson is admirably ill at ease, while Ralph Bates and Joan Collins whip up some truly malevolent passion. More fun than frightening. DP. Contains violence and swearing. [video]

Peter Cushing *Michael Carmichael* • Joan Collins *Molly Carmichael* • Ralph Bates *Robert Heller* • Judy Geeson *Peggy Heller* • James Cossins *Doctor* ■ *Dir* Jimmy Sangster • *Scr* Jimmy Sangster, Michael Syson

Fear Is the Key

★★★ 15

Action thriller 1972 · UK · Colour · 100mins

This satisfying action thriller, based on an Alistair MacLean novel, has Barry Newman pursuing stolen jewels as well as vengeance for his wife and child who died aboard a hijacked plane. An excitingly staged car chase gets things off to a cracking start and Newman makes a convincingly hyped-up hero. It also marks the screen debut of Ben Kingsley. AT [video]

Barry Newman *John Talbot* • Suzy Kendall *Sarah Ruthven* • John Vernon *Vyland* • Dolph Sweet *Jablonski* • Ben Kingsley *Royale* • Ray McAnally *Ruthven* • Peter Marinker *Larry* ■ *Dir* Michael Tuchner • *Scr* Robert Carrington, from the novel by Alistair MacLean

Fear No Evil

★★ 18

Supernatural horror
1980 · US · Colour · 94mins

In director Frank LaLoggia's ambitious feature debut, Lucifer is reincarnated as an American high school student who does battle with two archangels in disguise. The acting is on the amateurish side, and the story loses its way in some aimless subplots. Yet this is still a strangely affecting vision of low-budget armageddon whose punk rock soundtrack is augmented by an elaborate symphonic score. AJ [video]

Stefan Arngrim *Andrew* • Elizabeth Hoffman *Mikhail/Margaret Buchanan* • Frank Birney *Father Daly* • Kathleen Rowe McAllen *Gabrielle/Hulie* • Daniel Eden *Tony* • Jack Holland *Rafael/Father Damon* • Barry Cooper *Mr Williams* ■ *Dir/Scr* Frank LaLoggia

Fear of a Black Hat

★★★ 15

Spoof documentary
1992 · US · Colour · 81mins

Sampling freely from Rob Reiner's cult heavy metal comedy, this music-biz spoof could have been retitled "This Is Spinal Rap". Although it treads warily in places, the script scores countless direct hits as it follows the career of the rapping trio NWH (Niggaz with Hats). The blurred line between commercial success and social protest, the ludicrous press conference generalisations and the intrigues among the entourage are all keenly observed. Even the band members' names are spot on – Tone-Def, Tasty Taste and Ice Cold. But the music can't hold a candle to the cod anthems of the mighty *Tap*. DP. Contains sex scenes, swearing and nudity. [video]

Mark Christopher Lawrence *Tone Def* • Larry B Scott *Tasty Taste* • Rusty Cundieff *Ice Cold* • Kasi Lemmons *Nina Blackburn* • Howie Gold *Guy Friesh* • G Smokey Campbell *First backstage manager* ■ *Dir/Scr* Rusty Cundieff

Fear of Fear

★★★★

Psychological drama
1976 · W Ger · Colour · 88mins

Comfortable conformity is cited as the first sign of madness in this little-known film from Rainer Werner Fassbinder, originally made for television. Shot with a measured intensity, Margit Carstensen's slow decline into misery is charted with the apprehensive potency of a thriller. Will she commit suicide like her dishevelled neighbour? Or will she reconcile herself to her bourgeois ordinariness and resume her life without recourse to adulterous affairs or chemical solace? Challenging and irresistible. DP

Margit Carstensen *Margot* • Ulrich Faulhaber *Kurt* • Brigitte Mira *Mother* • Irm Hermann *Lore* • Armin Meier *Karli* • Adrian Hoven *Dr Merck* • Kurt Raab *Herr Bauer* • Ingrid Caven *Edda* • Lilo Pempeit *Mrs Schall* ■ *Dir* Rainer Werner Fassbinder • *Scr* Rainer Werner Fassbinder, from an idea by Asta Scheib • *Cinematographer* Jürgen Jüges, Ulrich Prinz

Fear on Trial

★★★★

Drama based on a true story
1975 · US · Colour · 100mins

This outstanding TV movie tells the tragic true story of television personality John Henry Faulk, who fell victim to the McCarthyite blacklist in the 1950s and, with his career ruined, decided to sue for libel. William Devane gives a moving performance as Faulk and George C Scott is magnificent as his lawyer. This riveting saga is expertly told by director Lamont Johnson. TV producers David Susskind and Mark Goodson play themselves, and Bruce Geller, the creator of TV series *Mission: Impossible*, plays his real-life father, the presiding judge in the case. TS

George C Scott *Louis Nizer* • William Devane *John Henry Faulk* • Dorothy Tristan *Laura Faulk* • William Redfield *Stan Hopp* • Bruce Geller *Judge Abraham N Geller* • David Susskind • Mark Goodson ■ *Dir* Lamont Johnson • *Scr* David W Rintels, from an autobiography by John Henry Faulk

Fear Strikes Out

★★★★

Biographical sports drama
1957 · US · BW · 102mins

Director Robert Mulligan's feature film debut is a harrowing and intense biopic of Boston Red Sox baseball star Jim Piersall, superbly portrayed by Anthony Perkins, whose later mannerisms are held well in check as he movingly conveys Piersall's breakdown. Karl Malden has a tendency to over-emote but under Mulligan's direction, he gives a fine performance as the over-ambitious father, whose behaviour had such a devastating impact on his son. This is a touching and tragic tale, beautifully photographed in stunning black-and-white VistaVision by Haskell Boggs, and featuring a fine early score from Elmer Bernstein. TS

Anthony Perkins *Jimmy Piersall* • Karl Malden *John Piersall* • Norma Moore *Mary Teevan* • Adam Williams *Dr Brown* • Perry Wilson *Mrs John Piersall* • Peter Votrian *Jimmy Piersall as a boy* • Dennis McMullen *Phil* ■ *Dir* Robert Mulligan • *Scr* Ted Berkman, Raphael Blau, from the autobiography by James A Piersall, Albert S Hirshberg

Fear X

★★★ 12

Psychological thriller
2002 · Den/UK/Can/Nor · Colour · 87mins

The American author of *Last Exit to Brooklyn* and *Requiem for a Dream* teams up with the Danish director of *Pusher* and *Bleeder* on this elusive search for truth. Intense yet measured, what makes this fascinating is the steely performance of John Turturro. He plays a Wisconsin security guard who's obsessed with discovering the reason for his wife's murder in the car park of the mall where he works. Guilty cop James Remar's torment is conveyed with equally brooding introspection, but this tense psychological thriller falls apart in the final act. DP. Contains violence. DVD

John Turturro *Harry Cain* • Deborah Kara Unger *Kate* • Stephen McIntyre *Phil* • William Allen Young *Agent Lawrence* • Eugene M Davis [Gene Davis] *Ed* • Mark Houghton *Diner cop* • Jacqueline Ramel *Claire* • James Remar *Peter* ■ *Dir* Nicolas Winding Refn • *Scr* Nicolas Winding Refn, Hubert Selby Jr

FearDotCom

★ 18

Horror thriller
2002 · US/UK/Ger/Lux · Colour · 97mins

Detective Stephen Dorff and public health inspector Natascha McElhone investigate a snuff torture website causing phobic death to all who log on in this nonsensical chiller. Director William Malone's *Ring* rip-off with a monochromatic murkiness stolen from *Se7en*. The real torture comes from having to sit through such ugly trash, loaded with empty scares, dreadful acting and joyless style. AJ [video] DVD

Stephen Dorff *Det Mike Reilly* • Natascha McElhone *Terry Huston* • Stephen Rea *Alistair Pratt, "The Doctor"* • Udo Kier *Polidori* • Amelia Curtis *Denise Stone* • Jeffrey Combs *Styles* • Nigel Terry *Turnbull* ■ *Dir* William Malone • *Scr* Josephine Coyle, from a story by Moshe Diamant

Fearless

★★★ 15

Drama 1993 · US · Colour · 116mins

Containing sequences of astonishing power, this is an intense drama about the pain of loss and the stress of surviving a near-death experience. Director Peter Weir has spent his career studying people trapped in unfamiliar environments, but here plane-crash survivor Jeff Bridges is a stranger to his own self. Unfortunately, the film struggles to live up to its breathtaking opening, and neither the heartrending scenes between Bridges and Oscar-nominated fellow survivor Rosie Perez nor his exchanges with

F

incomprehending wife Isabella Rossellini are quite as compelling. DP. Contains violence and swearing.

Jeff Bridges *Max Klein* • Isabella Rossellini *Laura Klein* • Rosie Perez *Carla Rodrigo* • Tom Hulce *Brillstein* • John Turturro *Dr Bill Perlman* • Benicio Del Toro *Manny Rodrigo* • Deirdre O'Connell *Nan Gordon* • John de Lancie *Jeff Gordon* ■ *Dir* Peter Weir • *Scr* Rafael Yglesias, from his novel

The Fearless Vampire Killers ★★★★ 12

Horror comedy 1967 · US · Colour · 103mins

Want to know where *Interview with the Vampire* found most of its best ideas? Look no further than this lyrical exploration of undead myths that's poised on the knife edge of Hammer nightmare and *Carry On* farce. Eerie, funny, scary and brilliantly baroque, Roman Polanski's astoundingly beautiful tour de force features two genre firsts – a Jewish vampire unaffected by the crucifix and a gay vampire – plus his ill-fated wife-to-be Sharon Tate in her best role. It's worth seeing for the breathtaking ballroom mirror sequence alone. AJ. Contains some violence. DVD

Jack MacGowran *Professor Abronsius* • Roman Polanski *Alfred* • Alfie Bass *Shagal* • Jessie Robins *Mrs Shagal* • Sharon Tate *Sarah Shagal* • Ferdy Mayne *Count Von Krolock* • Iain Quarrier *Herbert Von Krolock* • Terry Downes *Koukol* ■ *Dir* Roman Polanski • *Scr* Gerald Brach, Roman Polanski

The Fearmakers ★

Political drama 1958 · US · BW · 84mins

This preposterous right-wing melodrama has Dana Andrews returning to his Washington-based public relations firm only to find that his partner has mysteriously disappeared. The agency has been taken over by communists, whose agenda includes rigging opinion polls and promoting an end to the Cold War. A demeaning assignment for talented director Jacques Tourneur. AE

Dana Andrews *Alan Eaton* • Dick Foran *Jim McGinnis* • Mel Tormé *Barney Bond* • Marilee Earle *Lorraine Dennis* • Veda Ann Borg *Vivian Loder* • Kelly Thordsen *Harold Loder* ■ *Dir* Jacques Tourneur • *Scr* Elliot West, Chris Appley, from a novel by Darwin L Teilhet

A Feast at Midnight ★★ PG

Comedy 1994 · UK · Colour · 106mins

Stereotypes abound in this nostalgic fantasy on the cruelty and cameraderie of public school life. Freddie Findlay attempts to win over the bullies by starting the secret "Scoffers Society"; its aim is to sample culinary delights denied them by the strict health food regime imposed by headmaster Robert Hardy. Completing this familiar rites-of-passage recipe is a little romance; Findlay dotes on Lisa Faulkner, daughter of stern Latin master Christopher Lee. DP

Christopher Lee *Longfellow (Raptor)* • Robert Hardy *Headmaster* • Freddie Findlay *Magnus* • Aled Roberts *Goof* • Andrew Lusher *Tava* • Sam West [Samuel West] *Chef* • Lisa Faulkner *Miss Charlotte* • Edward Fox *Magnus's father* ■ *Dir* Justin Hardy • *Scr* Justin Hardy, Yoshi Nishio

Feast of July ★★ 15

Romantic period drama
1995 · UK · Colour · 111mins

The title promises a feast, but this melancholy story set in late 19th-century England offers slim pickings. Embeth Davidtz plays a young woman deserted by her lover (Greg Wise) who is taken in by a rural family, headed by Tom Bell. She befriends his three sons and, when two of them go to war, falls for the youngest, simple-minded Ben Chaplin. Christopher Menaul directs this with an emphasis on melodramatic flourishes. TH DVD

Embeth Davidtz *Bella Ford* • Tom Bell *Ben Wainwright* • Gemma Jones *Mrs Wainwright* • James Purefoy *Jedd Wainwright* • Ben Chaplin *Con* • Kenneth Anderson *Matty Wainwright* • Greg Wise *Arch Wilson* ■ *Dir* Christopher Menaul • *Scr* Christopher Neame, from the novel by HE Bates • *Executive Producer* Ismail Merchant

Federal Hill ★★★

Drama 1994 · US · BW · 100mins

Boyz 'n the Hood Italian-style, as a gang of Rhode Island punks struggle to make sense of their lives as they hurtle down a drug-fuelled, self-destructive path. Nicholas Turturro (John's younger brother) stars as a jewel thief who specialises in random violence with his gang. Independent film-maker Michael Corrente's cutting edge black-and-white effort infuses the *Mean Streets* genre with a new raw, raucous and insightful energy helped enormously by a powerhouse performance from Turturro as a screwed-up psycho thief. AJ

Nicholas Turturro *Ralph* • Anthony DeSando *Nicky* • Libby Langdon *Wendy* • Michael Raynor *Frank* • Jason Andrews *Bobby* • Robert Turano *Joey* ■ *Dir/Scr* Michael Corrente

Federal Protection ★★ 18

Action thriller 2002 · US · Colour · 89mins

This darkly comedic crime thriller demonstrates that Anthony Hickox has a knack for set pieces that he's not quite capable of carrying over into his general storytelling. Car thief Armand Assante's experiences under the witness protection programme are formulaic, as his relationship with new neighbour Angela Featherstone prompts her cheating husband and disloyal sister (David Lipper and Dina Meyer) to sell him out to the Mob for the bounty. DP DVD

Armand Assante *Frank Carbone/Howard Akers* • Angela Featherstone *Leigh Kirkindall* • Dina Meyer *Bootsie Cavander* • David Lipper *Denny Kirkindall* ■ *Dir* Anthony Hickox • *Scr* Craig Smith

Fedora ★★★★ PG

Drama 1978 · W Ger/Fr · Colour · 108mins

This is director Billy Wilder's bittersweet tale about a fabled, Garbo-esque star of the 1930s who appears to have the secret of youth and lives in seclusion in Corfu. William Holden, the hero of Wilder's *Sunset Boulevard*, is the independent producer who worms his way into Fedora's secret and tries to coax her out of retirement. Yes, there are flaws and some unintentional laughs – Michael York as a living screen legend? – but this is also a richly comic, deeply melancholy movie, enriched by Wilder's long perspective on the picture business. AT

William Holden (2) *Barry Detweiler* • Marthe Keller *Fedora* • José Ferrer *Dr Vando* • Hildegarde Neff *Countess Sobryanski* • Frances Sternhagen *Miss Balfour* • Michael York • Henry Fonda ■ *Dir* Billy Wilder • *Scr* Billy Wilder, IAL Diamond, from the novel *Crowned Heads* by Thomas Tryon

Feds ★★ 15

Comedy 1988 · US · Colour · 79mins

Before her searching, scorching performance in *The Hand That Rocks the Cradle*, Rebecca De Mornay made an unimpressive living playing anaemic, pretty blondes. As one of two female students who are aspiring FBI agents, she encounters male prejudice on a grand scale. All comic efforts in this direction seem to delight in the obvious, yet De Mornay herself has the right, light touch. JM. Contains violence and swearing.

Rebecca De Mornay *Ellie DeWitt* • Mary Gross *Janis Zuckerman* • Ken Marshall *Brent Sheppard* • Fred Dalton Thompson *Bill Belecki* • Larry Cedar *Howard Butz* • James Luisi *Sperry* • Raymond Singer *Hupperman* ■ *Dir* Dan Goldberg • *Scr* Len Blum, Dan Goldberg

Feeling Minnesota ★★ 18

Romantic comedy drama
1996 · US · Colour · 94mins

In this quirky, low-budget film, Cameron Diaz plays the bride who ditches her husband-to-be (Vincent D'Onofrio) on her wedding day to run off with his estranged, wayward brother (Keanu Reeves), only to have her fiancé and an assortment of heavies come after them. Amusingly odd rather than hilariously funny – and with a liberal splattering of violence and bad language – this has its moments, but is perhaps of most appeal to fans of the two leads. JB. Contains swearing, violence and sex scenes. DVD

Keanu Reeves *Jjaks* • Vincent D'Onofrio *Sam* • Cameron Diaz *Freddie* • Delroy Lindo *Red* • Courtney Love *Rhonda, the waitress* • Tuesday Weld *Nora* • Dan Aykroyd *Ben* • Levon Helm *Bible salesman* ■ *Dir/Scr* Steven Baigelman

Feeling Sexy ★★★

Comedy 1999 · Aus · Colour · 121mins

This shrewdly observed comedy centres on doctor's wife Susie Porter, as she bids to break free from the petty constraints of middle-class mediocrity and find sexual and artistic fulfilment. Playfully contrasting runny noses and dirty dishes with the temptations of adultery and tattoos, Davida Allen clearly has innate sympathy for this Brisbane Bovary, whose desire to rekindle the flame of courtship finds new expression when she develops a crush on one of her life-class students. Feisty, fantasy-prone and fiercely honest, the voluptuous Porter excels. DP

Susie Porter *Vicki* • Tamblyn Lord *Greg* • Amanda Muggleton *Vicki's mum* ■ *Dir/Scr* Davida Allen

Feet First ★★ U

Comedy 1930 · US · BW · 69mins

Harold Lloyd raids his own gag store to refloat this feeble comedy after it runs aground during an over-long sea voyage. Stowing away on a Honolulu liner to press his romantic suit with Barbara Kent, Lloyd's timid go-getter gets himself trapped in a mail sack, which just happens to land on a builder's hoist outside a skyscraper. Although much of the high-rise slapstick that follows is borrowed from *Safety Last*, the business with the gyrating fire hose is both inspired and hilarious. However, it comes too late to save a picture hamstrung by Lloyd's discomfort with dialogue. DP

Harold Lloyd *Harold Horne* • Robert McWade *John Tanner* • Lillianne Leighton *Mrs Tanner* • Barbara Kent *Mary* • Alec Francis [Alec B Francis] *Old timer* • Noah Young *Ship's officer* • Henry Hall (1) *Endicott* ■ *Dir* Clyde Bruckman • *Scr* Felix Adler, Lex Neal, Paul Gerard Smith, from a story by John Grey, Alfred A Cohn, Clyde Bruckman

Felicia's Journey ★★★★ 12

Psychological thriller
1999 · UK/Can · Colour · 111mins

Pregnant Irish innocent Felicia (Elaine Cassidy) travels to Birmingham to find her lover, who has joined the British Army. There she is befriended by Hilditch (Bob Hoskins), a factory catering manager with a sinister interest in young girls. All the tabloid elements of a lurid thriller are here, but Canadian director Atom Egoyan avoids the obvious in his adaptation of William Trevor's novel. The result is a small masterpiece of atmosphere and insight that reveals the extraordinary in the everyday, with performances that transform the story into a scary fairy tale. TH DVD

Bob Hoskins *Hilditch* • Elaine Cassidy *Felicia* • Claire Benedict *Miss Calligary* • Brid Brennan *Mrs Lysaght* • Peter McDonald *Johnny* • Gerard McSorley *Felicia's father* • Arsinée Khanjian *Gala* ■ *Dir* Atom Egoyan • *Scr* Atom Egoyan, from the novel by William Trevor

Felix the Cat: the Movie ★ U

Animated fantasy 1989 · US · Colour · 78mins

Felix the Cat made his debut as an animated short as far back as 1919, but this attempt to update the feline hero for a new generation is a monumental clanger and an insult to kids with even the merest of imaginations. Surrealism abounds as Felix goes on a quest to rescue a princess, encountering Mizards (mice with bodies of lizards) and a rhinoceros on a tightrope. Bland and uninspired. RS

Chris Phillips • Maureen O'Connell • Peter Neuman • Alice Playten • Susan Montanaro • Don Oriolo ■ *Dir* Tibor Hernadi • *Scr* Don Oriolo, Pete Brown, from a story and cartoon character created by Don Oriolo

Fellini's Roma ★★★ 15

Experimental comedy documentary
1972 · It/Fr · Colour · 117mins

Posing as a documentary, this mix of memories, fantasies and idle musings confirms Federico Fellini's visual genius, while also exposing his reckless lack of intellectual rigour. Beginning with youthful impressions of the Eternal City gained from his home town of Rimini, Fellini recalls people and place as the fancy takes him (hence the film's much-criticised shapelessness). Whether reminiscing or chatting to the likes of Marcello Mastroianni, Anna Magnani and Gore Vidal, he makes a companionable, if occasionally overbearing guide. But it's the 1940s music-hall show, the unearthing of an ancient villa and the clerical fashion parade that reveal the maverick maestro close to his best. DP. An Italian language film. DVD

Federico Fellini • Peter Gonzales *Fellini, age 18* • Stefano Mayore *Fellini as a child* • Pia De Doses *Princess* • Renato Giovannelli *Cardinal Ottaviani* • Fiona Florence *Young prostitute* • Anna Magnani • Gore Vidal • Marcello Mastroianni ■ *Dir* Federico Fellini • *Scr* Federico Fellini, Bernardino Zapponi

Fellow Traveller ★★★★ 15

Political drama
1989 · UK/US · Colour · 97mins

The title refers to someone with Communist sympathies, and this TV movie deals with that terrible time in Hollywood when the blacklist was in force, a serious subject only rarely tackled by Hollywood itself. A genuinely political film, directed (by the under-rated Philip Saville) in anger, and played to perfection by the cast. The look and feel of the 1950s, and in particular the early birth pangs of commercial television in England are beautifully conjured up, and you'll never view Richard Greene's *The Adventures of Robin Hood* TV series in quite the same way again. TS

Ron Silver *Asa Kaufman* • Imogen Stubbs *Sarah Aitchison* • Daniel J Travanti *Jerry Leavy* • Hart Bochner *Clifford Byrne* • Katherine Borowitz *Joan Kaufman* • Julian Fellowes *D'Arcy* • Richard Wilson *Sir Hugo Armstrong* ■ *Dir* Philip Saville • *Scr* Michael Eaton

Female ★★★

Romantic comedy drama
1933 · US · BW · 65mins

A splendid starring vehicle for the largely forgotten Ruth Chatterton, this comedy/drama presents her as an intelligent and liberated female who runs a car manufacturing company and seduces the better-looking male employees for amorous relief. Her astonishing mansion marks an early screen appearance for Frank Lloyd Wright's Ennis House in the Hollywood Hills. Skilfully directed by Michael Curtiz (with uncredited assistance from William A Wellman), the film rapidly loses conviction when dreary George Brent (Chatterton's real-life husband at the time) comes along and is supposed to bowl her over. AE

Ruth Chatterton *Alison Drake* • George Brent *Jim Thorne* • Lois Wilson *Harriet* • Johnny Mack Brown *George C Cooper* • Ruth Donnelly *Miss Frothingham* • Ferdinand Gottschalk *Pettigrew* ■ *Dir* Michael Curtiz • *Scr* Gene Markey, Kathryn Scola, from the novel by Donald Henderson Clarke

The Female Animal ★

Romantic drama 1958 · US · BW · 82mins

Saved from a serious injury by handsome George Nader, movie star Hedy Lamarr moves him into her beach house as both caretaker and lover. It's only a matter of time before her adopted daughter Jane Powell falls for him, too, as does former actress Jan Sterling. This inept and dreary movie is pulp melodrama of the worst kind. RK

Hedy Lamarr *Vanessa Windsor* • Jane Powell *Penny Windsor* • Jan Sterling *Lily Frayne* • George Nader *Chris Farley* • Jerry Paris *Hank Lopez* ■ *Dir* Harry Keller • *Scr* Robert Hill, from a story by Albert Zugsmith

The Female Bunch ★ 18

Drama 1969 · US · Colour · 80mins

Women's Lib meets Russ Meyer-style sexploitation in this insane movie shot at the Spahn ranch, a disused film set occupied by the Manson "family" around the time of the notorious murders. About a group of man-hating women living on a secluded farm who run drugs across the Mexican border, you'd think a movie filled with bouts of lesbianism, drug-taking, nudity, sadism and *tom thumb* actor Russ Tamblyn having his face branded would be fun – wrong! And spare a thought for poor old Lon Chaney Jr in his last ever role as a hired hand. RS

Russ Tamblyn *Bill* • Jennifer Bishop (1) *Grace* • Lon Chaney Jr *Monty* • Nesa Renet *Sandy* • Geoffrey Land *Jim* • Regina Carrol *Waitress* ■ *Dir* Al Adamson, John "Bud" Cardos • *Scr* Jale Lockwood, Brent Nimrod, from a story by Raphael Nussbaum

The Female Jungle ★ PG

Crime drama 1955 · US · BW · 70mins

Lawrence Tierney stars as a police sergeant found drunk at the scene of an actress's murder in this below average whodunnit that's mainly of interest because it features the first significant film role of 1950s sex bomb Jayne Mansfield. She was only paid $150 for her performance, but it typecast her as the dumb blonde/nymphomaniac for the rest of her tragically short life. AJ DVD

Lawrence Tierney *Sergeant Stevens* • John Carradine *Claude Almstead* • Jayne Mansfield *Candy Price* • Burt Kaiser *Alec Voe* • Kathleen Crowley *Peggy Voe* • James Kodl *Joe* ■ *Dir* Bruno VeSota • *Scr* Bruno VeSota, Burt Kaiser

Female on the Beach ★★

Crime drama 1955 · US · BW · 96mins

Joan Crawford plays a widow who moves in to a beach house and quickly falls in love with Jeff Chandler, who may have murdered the previous occupant. This successful melodrama kept Crawford's career moving, gave her some great opportunities to model some beachwear and to deliver some hilarious dialogue. Things get pretty steamy towards the end, but the final product is silly rather than sexy. AT

Joan Crawford *Lynn Markham* • Jeff Chandler *Drummond Hall* • Jan Sterling *Amy Rawlinson* • Cecil Kellaway *Osbert Sorenson* • Judith Evelyn *Eloise Crandall* • Natalie Schafer *Queenie Sorenson* ■ *Dir* Joseph Pevney • *Scr* Robert Hill, Richard Alan Simmons, from the play *The Besieged Heart* by Robert Hill

Female Perversions ★★ 18

Drama 1996 · US/Ger · Colour · 108mins

Tilda Swinton is a high-powered lawyer with judicial aspirations, who is outwardly a model of femininity but is plagued by neuroses. She has a stormy relationship with her sister Amy Madigan, a compulsive shoplifter. Secrets are unravelled and kit is taken off, but despite the promise of something interesting to come, it never actually arrives as Susan Streitfeld (making her directorial debut) gets bogged down in her own pretentiousness. JB. Contains swearing, sex scenes, violence. DVD

Tilda Swinton *Evelyn "Eve" Stephens* • Amy Madigan *Madelyn Stephens* • Karen Sillas *Renee* • Frances Fisher *Annunciata* • Laila Robins *Emma* • Paulina Porizkova *Langley Flynn* ■ *Dir* Susan Streitfeld • *Scr* Susan Streitfeld, Julie Hebert, from the non-fiction book *Female Perversions: the Temptations of Emma Bovary* by Louise J Kaplan

Female Trouble ★★★★ 18

Satirical melodrama
1974 · US · Colour · 93mins

Along with *Pink Flamingos*, this is the film that gained cult director John Waters his trophy for spectacularly redefining melodrama. A twisted parallel of *Mildred Pierce*, it features the transvestite Divine on a perverse quest for self-realisation, following a disastrous Christmas morning in which her parents fail to deliver the requested cha-cha heels. The squeamish solo delivery of her baby is the first scene in what turns out to be a true mother-and-daughter-from-hell scenario, with Mink Stole as the insufferable brat. An unhinged celebration of bad taste. DO

Divine *Dawn Davenport/Earl Peterson* • David Lochary *Donald Dasher* • Mary Vivian Pearce *Donna Dasher* • Mink Stole *Taffy Davenport* • Edith Massey *Aunt Ida Nelson* • Cookie Mueller *Concetta* • Susan Walsh *Chiclet* • Michael Potter *Gater* ■ *Dir/Scr* John Waters (2)

The Female Vampire ★ 18

Erotic horror
1973 · Fr/Bel/Por · Colour · 91mins

In this ludicrous vampire tale, Lina Romay stars as a countess who seduces all and sundry. Jesus Franco dwells on badly executed bloodsucking, crass nudity and pointless zooms in what turned out to be one of his most popular poverty-row quickies. Ponderous and artlessly shot. AJ. Contains violence, sex scenes and nudity.

Lina Romay *Countess Irina Karlstein* • Jack Taylor *Baron Von Rathony* • Jess Franck [Jesus Franco] *Dr Roberts* • Jean-Pierre Bouyxou *Dr Orloff* ■ *Dir/Scr* Jesus Franco

The Feminine Touch ★★★

Comedy 1941 · US · BW · 97mins

This entertaining Rosalind Russell comedy vehicle has a knockout central idea: Russell is the wife of writer Don Ameche, who's just penned a book on jealousy, and she thinks he's fooling around with the lovely Kay Francis. Well, who wouldn't? There's lots of MGM gloss, and star-to-be Van Heflin in sterling support as the publisher who has his eye on Russell. Director Woody Van Dyke II piles on the pace, and the cast simply couldn't be more glamorous – watch how both Francis and Russell are exquisitely back-lit, and not just in their close-ups. TS

Rosalind Russell *Julie Hathaway* • Don Ameche *John Hathaway* • Kay Francis *Nellie Woods* • Van Heflin *Elliott Morgan* • Donald Meek *Captain Makepeace Liveright* • Gordon Jones *Rubber-legs Ryan* ■ *Dir* WS Van Dyke II [WS Van Dyke] • *Scr* George Oppenheimer, Edmund L Hartmann, Ogden Nash

The Feminine Touch ★★ U

Romantic drama 1956 · UK · Colour · 91mins

This mediocre drama was among the last batch of films made at the famous Ealing Studios. Director Pat Jackson had made his name with realistic docudramas during the Second World War, but this tale of trainee nurses was a far cry from his earlier hospital picture *White Corridors*. Diana Wynyard stands out as Matron, but the five girls we follow are a pretty tepid bunch. DP

George Baker *Dr Jim Alcott* • Belinda Lee *Susan Richards* • Delphi Lawrence *Pat Martin* • Adrienne Corri *Maureen O'Brien* • Henryetta Edwards *Ann Bowland* • Barbara Archer *Liz Jenkins* • Diana Wynyard *Matron* ■ *Dir* Pat Jackson • *Scr* Ian McCormick, from the book *A Lamp Is Heavy* by Sheila Mackay Russell

Une Femme Est une Femme ★★★ PG

Comedy drama 1961 · Fr · Colour · 79mins

French New Wave director Jean-Luc Godard's third feature is often described as a homage to the Hollywood musical. Shot in colour and CinemaScope, it is also a love letter to its radiant star Anna Karina, whom Godard married shortly after the film was completed. She plays a stripper who badly wants a child, and when her boyfriend Jean-Claude Brialy won't give her one, so to speak, she turns to his best friend, Jean-Paul Belmondo. Back in 1961, its New Wave freshness took the breath away. AT. In French with English subtitles. DVD

Anna Karina *Angéla* • Jean-Claude Brialy *Emile Recamier* • Jean-Paul Belmondo *Alfred Lubitsch* • Nicole Paquin *Suzanne* • Marie Dubois *First prostitute* • Marion Sarraut *Second prostitute* • Jeanne Moreau *Woman in bar* ■ *Dir* Jean-Luc Godard • *Scr* Jean-Luc Godard, from an idea by Geneviève Cluny

Femme Fatale ★★ 15

Thriller 1991 · US · Colour · 92mins

Colin Firth plays an unbelievably naive Englishman abroad in Los Angeles who falls for the beautiful Lisa Zane, only for her to disappear suddenly. He then discovers she has a sinister past. Firth does his best with his material, but Ms Zane (Billy's sister in real life) lacks the lure of a true *femme fatale*. There are some interesting ideas explored here, but the end result is a muddled mess. JF. Contains swearing, violence and sex scenes.

Colin Firth *Joe Prince* • Lisa Zane *Elizabeth/Cynthia/Maura* • Billy Zane *Elijah* • Scott Wilson *Dr Beaumont* • Lisa Blount *Jenny* • Suzanne Snyder *Andrea* • Pat Skipper *Ted* ■ *Dir* Andre Guttfreund • *Scr* Michael Ferris, John D Brancato

Femme Fatale ★★★ 15

Crime thriller 2002 · Fr · Colour · 109mins

Can reclusive French Ambassador's wife Rebecca Romijn-Stamos hide her former identity as a jewel thief when secret snaps taken by paparazzi photographer Antonio Banderas alert her former partners in crime into reclaiming stolen diamonds? Complete with a mind-bending last-act shift in reality many will find a complete cheat, Brian De Palma's audaciously seductive deception is a bold and imaginative exercise in film-making craft, with Romijn-Stamos a duplicitous blonde heroine in the best Hitchcock tradition. AJ. In English and French with subtitles. DVD

Rebecca Romijn-Stamos *Laure Ash* • Antonio Banderas *Nicolas Bardo* • Peter Coyote *Watts* • Gregg Henry *Shiff* • Rie Rasmussen *Veronica* • Eriq Ebouaney *Black Tie* • Edouard Montoute *Racine* • Thierry Frémont *Serra* ■ *Dir/Scr* Brian De Palma

Une Femme Française ★★ 18

Drama 1994 · Fr/UK/Ger · Colour · 94mins

Daniel Auteuil and Emmanuelle Béart's off-screen relationship terminated during the production of this uninvolving story, set either side of the Second World War. The merest hint of their private tensions might have sparked this ponderous melodrama into life. He plays a prisoner-of-war betrayed by his wife both during his incarceration and after their reconciliation. She plays the wife, who spends much of the time pouting seductively with her young German lover (Gabriel Barylli). DP. Contains violence.

Emmanuelle Béart *Jeanne* • Daniel Auteuil *Louis* • Gabriel Barylli *Mathias Behrens* • Jean-Claude Brialy *Arnoult* • Geneviève Casile *Solange* • Heinz Bennent *Andreas* • Michel Etcheverry *Charles* ■ *Dir* Régis Wargnier • *Scr* Régis Wagnier, Alain Le Henry

La Femme Infidèle ★★★★ 15

Thriller 1968 · Fr/It · Colour · 94mins

Director Claude Chabrol's masterly thriller stars the stunning Stéphane Audran as the unfaithful wife of the title, whose husband kills her lover, then dumps him in a lake. Owing much to Hitchcock, this is an elegant, tense and wickedly funny satire on the middle classes, performed to perfection by Audran, Michel Bouquet as the decidedly creepy husband, and Maurice Ronet as the doomed lover. This was the first in a magnificent run of thrillers from Chabrol in which the main characters were always called Charles and Hélène. AT. In French with English subtitles. DVD

Stéphane Audran *Hélène Desvallees* • Michel Bouquet *Charles Desvallees* • Maurice Ronet *Victor Pegala* • Serge Bento *Bignon* • Michel Duchaussoy *Police Officer Duval* • Guy Marly *Police Officer Gobet* ■ *Dir/Scr* Claude Chabrol

La Femme Publique ★★★★

Crime drama 1984 · Fr · Colour · 105mins

Made shortly after he left his native Poland for France, Andrzej Zulawski's dazzling picture occasionally lacks focus, but there's no denying the ingenuity of its story, its Dostoevskian preoccupations and its delirious style. There's a *Pygmalion* feel to tyrannical director Francis Huster's relationship with ambitious actress Valérie Kaprisky. But the more bizarre incidents occur, as Huster pursues the wife of Czech exile Lambert Wilson, who finds himself charged with the murder of a Lithuanian archbishop. DP. In French with English subtitles.

Francis Huster *Lucas Kesling* • Valérie Kaprisky *Ethel* • Lambert Wilson *Milan Mliska* • Diane Delor *Elena* • Roger Dumas *Photographer* ■ *Dir* Andrzej Zulawski • *Scr* Andrzej Zulawski, Dominique Garnier

FernGully: the Last Rainforest ★★ U

Animated fantasy
1992 · Aus · Colour · 72mins

Many critics felt this eco-worthy cartoon force-fed its tale of planet-saving too strenuously. The criticism was a bit unfair, as the story of a fairy, a fruit bat and a tiny lumberjack battling a malevolent spirit bent on destruction is well-meaning and thoroughly entertaining for youngsters. Its target audience won't mind the preachiness and adults can be sure of the film's good intentions. A sequel, *Ferngully 2: the Magical Rescue* followed in 1997. TH DVD

Samantha Mathis *Crysta* • Jonathan Ward *Zak* • Robin Williams *Batty Koda* • Christian Slater *Pips* • Tim Curry *Hexxus* • Grace Zabriskie *Magi Lune* • Geoffrey Blake *Ralph* • Robert Pastorelli *Tony* ■ *Dir* Bill Kroyer • *Scr* Jim Cox, from stories by Diana Young

Ferris Bueller's Day Off ★★★★ 15

Comedy 1986 · US · Colour · 98mins

Matthew Broderick – worshipped by students, scourge of teachers – decides to play truant and whisks chum Alan Ruck and girlfriend Mia Sara off to the big city for an adventure; uptight Dean of Students Jeffrey Jones is determined to catch him in the act. It's a simple story, but this remains the most fully rounded of writer/director John Hughes's teen comedies, although once again it's marred slightly by Hughes's familiar undercurrent of sentimentality. Broderick is likeable as the arrogant, spoilt brat, while Ruck is excellent as his melancholy friend. JF DVD

Matthew Broderick *Ferris Bueller* • Alan Ruck *Cameron Frye* • Mia Sara *Sloane Peterson* • Jeffrey Jones *Ed Rooney* • Jennifer Grey *Jeanie Bueller* • Cindy Pickett *Katie Bueller* • Lyman Ward *Tom Bueller* • Edie McClurg *School secretary* • Charlie Sheen *Garth Volbeck* ■ *Dir/Scr* John Hughes

Ferry to Hong Kong ★★ U

Drama 1958 · UK · Colour · 98mins

Directed on location by Lewis Gilbert, the script was extensively rewritten and then ad-libbed by Orson Welles, who clashed loudly with co-star Curt Jurgens. For Welles, this "holiday" – he boycotted the premiere and never saw the finished film – was his first visit to Macao where he hatched the idea of filming Isak Dinesen's *The Immortal Story*. Welles hit the markets for Chinese bric-a-brac and even hijacked Gilbert's camera equipment to shoot some background footage, which eventually found its way into his 1968 film. AT

Curt Jurgens *Mark Conrad* • Orson Welles *Captain Hart* • Sylvia Syms *Liz Ferrers* • Jeremy Spenser *Miguel Henriques* • Noel Purcell *Joe Skinner* • Margaret Withers *Miss Carter* ■ *Dir* Lewis Gilbert • *Scr* Vernon Harris, Lewis Gilbert

Festen ★★★ 15

Drama 1998 · Den · Colour · 100mins

This is the first feature made under film-making collective Dogme 95's "vow of chastity". A Danish patriarch celebrates his 60th birthday, but his son decides to reveal a few family secrets. But while the severity of the themes and the immediacy of the video imagery give the disastrous family reunion the same sort of visceral thrill induced by the first films of the *nouvelle vague*, this is more a shakycam soap opera than a mould-breaking masterpiece. However, any film that can tumble complacent audiences out of their seats has to be applauded. DP. In Danish with English subtitles. DVD

Ulrich Thomsen *Christian* • Henning Mortizen *Helge* • Thomas Bo Larsen *Michael* • Paprika Steen *Helene* • Birthe Neuman *Elsa* • Trine Dyrholm *Pia* ■ *Dir* Thomas Vinterberg • *Scr* Thomas Vinterberg, Mogens Rukov

Festival ★★★ 18

Black comedy drama
2005 · UK · Colour · 107mins

Annie Griffin makes her feature debut with this comedy that follows a motley band of stars and misfits in their attempts to survive the annual Edinburgh Festival. Griffin mixes drama and black comedy, rough Scottish characters and seemingly sophisticated foreigners, producing something that confounds expectations, challenges stereotypes and leaves viewers unsure whether to laugh or cry. For the most part the shifts in tone work, though the sex scenes are uncomfortably frank. BP. Contains sex scenes and swearing.

Daniela Nardini *Joan Gerard* • Clive Russell *Brother Mike* • Lyndsey Marshal *Faith Myers* • Stephen Mangan *Sean Sullivan* • Amelia Bulmore ■ *Dir/Scr* Annie Griffin

Festival Express ★★★★ 15

Music documentary
2003 · UK/Neth · Colour · 85mins

This fascinating rock documentary belatedly puts together footage of the 1970 trans-Canada train tour undertaken by some of the world's top musicians, including The Band, Grateful Dead and Janis Joplin. The ramshackle tour, in which the musicians jammed en route and alighted to play a series of gigs, was a financial disaster. This had little effect on the morale of the performers, however, who treated the trip as a five-day party – an attitude that comes across in on- and off-stage footage that's surprisingly revealing, especially considering the on-the-hoof way in which it was filmed. Contemporary interviews with some of the surviving players give added insight, making this a must-see for fans of the people involved and connoisseurs of rock lore. DA. Contains swearing. DVD

Dir Bob Smeaton • *Cinematographer* Peter Biziou, Bob Fiore

Festival in Cannes ★★★

Romantic comedy drama
2001 · US/Fr · Colour · 99mins

Filmed at Cannes during the 1999 festival and strewn with guest stars, this is an agile examination of the way in which an event designed to celebrate cinematic excellence has become a tawdry circus characterised by commercial frenzy. Director Henry Jaglom is well served here by a cast attuned to his method of unrehearsed improvisation. Greta Scacchi is particularly impressive as the star peddling a low-budget personal project, as is Anouk Aimée as a fading art house star undecided whether to headline Scacchi's indie or cameo in a blockbuster. DP

Anouk Aimée *Millie Marquand* • Greta Scacchi *Alice Palmer* • Maximilian Schell *Viktor Kovner* • Ron Silver *Rick Yorkin* • Zach Norman *Kaz Naiman* • Peter Bogdanovich *Milo* • Jenny Gabrielle *Blue* ■ *Dir* Henry Jaglom • *Scr* Henry Jaglom, Victoria Foyt

Fetishes ★★★ 18

Documentary 1996 · UK · Colour · 77mins

Nick Broomfield's documentary about sadomasochism made its TV debut in defiance of the triumphant publicity tag "the film that Channel 4 dared not show". Having already made the controversial *Chicken Ranch*, which detailed the comings and goings at a real-life brothel, this wasn't the first time Broomfield had explored the sex sector. But the man who has also tackled Margaret Thatcher, Eugene Terreblanche and Courtney Love without batting an eyelid is clearly less than comfortable with Mistress Raven and the other occupants of New York's Pandora's Box club. Disturbingly compelling, this is a judgement-free, if graphic, insight into a highly singular world. DP. Contains swearing and sex scenes. DVD

Dir Nick Broomfield

Le Feu Follet ★★★★ 15

Drama 1963 · Fr/It · BW · 103mins

Released as *The Fire Within* in the States and sometimes called *Will o' the Wisp* in this country, Louis Malle's drama is widely regarded as one of his best. The story of an alcoholic who visits his friends in the hope of finding a reason to live could, in the wrong hands, have been an unbearably maudlin and melodramatic affair. But Malle shuns sentiment and turns this into a painfully truthful study of self-realisation. Maurice Ronet (the forgotten actor of the French New Wave) is outstanding as Alain Leroy, subtly earning our sympathy without ever really deserving it. DP. In French with English subtitles.

Maurice Ronet *Alain Leroy* • Léna Skerla *Lydia* • Yvonne Clech *Madamoiselle Farnoux* • Hubert Deschamps *D'Averseau* • Jean-Paul Moulinot *Dr La Barbinais* • Mona Dol *Madame La Barbinais* • Jeanne Moreau *Jeanne* ■ *Dir* Louis Malle • *Scr* Louis Malle, from the novel by Pierre Drieu la Rochelle

The Feud ★★★ 15

Comedy 1989 · US · Colour · 93mins

In small-town America, the Beeler and the Bullard families start a feud when Dolf Beeler brandishes a cigar in the Bud Bullard's non-smoking hardware store. The row escalates and the hardware store becomes a smoking one – it's burned down in an arson attack. Then a car is bombed, people get killed and, of course, in the tradition of *Romeo and Juliet*, there's a love affair across the divide. Set in a sunny Eisenhower era of happy families, optimism and cars that look like spaceships, this is a deftly-made black comedy. AT

René Auberjonois *Reverton* • Joe Grifasi *Bud Bullard* • Ron McLarty *Dolf Beeler* • David Strathairn *The Stranger* • Gale Mayron *Bernice Beeler* • Scott Allegrucci *Tony Beeler* • Lynne Killmeyer *Eva Bullard* ■ *Dir* Bill D'Elia • *Scr* Bill D'Elia, Robert Uricola, from the novel by Thomas Berger

Fever ★★★

Crime drama 1988 · Aus · Colour · 86mins

Popular Australian actor Bill Hunter here plays a good detective who turns bad when he discovers a suitcase full of drug money. Gleefully returning home to share a new life with his wife, he unfortunately interrupts her in a bit of extramarital lovemaking... There are excellent performances all around, with a twist some may see coming. Still, it's a fun caper. ST

Bill Hunter *Jack Welles* • Gary Sweet *Jeff* • Mary Regan *Leanne Welles* • Jim Holt *Morris* ■ *Dir* Craig Lahiff • *Scr* John Emery

A Fever in the Blood ★★

Political comedy drama
1961 · US · BW · 118mins

A judge, a district attorney and a senator are all campaigning for State Governor. Unfortunately their involvement in a murder case may thwart their ambitions. Exactly how are the three gubernatorial candidates involved and is one of them the killer? Directed by veteran Vincent Sherman, it's a workmanlike job with a decent cast headed by Efrem Zimbalist Jr. AT

Efrem Zimbalist Jr *Judge Leland Hoffman* • Angie Dickinson *Cathy Simon* • Jack Kelly *Dan Callahan* • Don Ameche *Senator AS Simon* • Ray Danton *Marker* • Herbert Marshall *Governor Thornwall* ■ *Dir* Vincent Sherman • *Scr* Roy Huggins, Harry Kleiner, from the novel by William Pearson

Fever Pitch ★★ 15

Drama 1985 · US · Colour · 91mins

Poor old Ryan O'Neal. In the 1970s he was the envy of Hollywood, but within a decade his career was seriously off the boil and only badly scripted roles, such as this as a sports writer who becomes addicted to gambling, seem to have popped through his letterbox. This film also marks a decline in fortunes for writer/director Richard Brooks. JB. Contains swearing.

Ryan O'Neal *Taggart* • Catherine Hicks *Flo* • Giancarlo Giannini *Charley* • Bridgette Andersen *Amy* • Chad Everett *Dutchman* • John Saxon *Sports editor* • Hank Greenspun *Sun Publisher* • Keith Hefner *Casino boss* ■ *Dir/Scr* Richard Brooks

Fever Pitch ★★★★ 15

Romantic comedy
1996 · UK · Colour · 98mins

This is a hugely entertaining reworking of Nick Hornby's runaway bestseller. But although the film is based on a football fanatic's memoir, don't despair – there's much more to this romantic comedy than football. Colin Firth and best buddy Mark Strong buzz off to Highbury or are glued to the box, while girlfriend Ruth Gemmell and flatmate Holly Aird pass acerbic asides about how incapable the lads are of growing up. Football, fads, fashion aberrations and long-gone TV shows will ensure this story is instantly recognisable, not only to nearly every 30-something male in the country, but also to their long-suffering female kin. DP. Contains swearing and sexual references. DVD

Colin Firth *Paul Ashworth* • Ruth Gemmell *Sarah Hughes* • Neil Pearson *Paul's dad* • Lorraine Ashbourne *Paul's mum* • Mark Strong *Steve* • Holly Aird *Jo* • Ken Stott *Ted, the headmaster* • Stephen Rea *Ray, the governor* • Luke Aikman *Young Paul* ■ *Dir* David Evans • *Scr* Nick Hornby, from his book

A Few Good Men ★★★★ 15

Courtroom drama
1992 · US · Colour · 132mins

The ultimate rebel Jack Nicholson has a ball playing the ultimate establishment figure in this star-laden, rather old-fashioned courtroom drama. In fact, Nicholson's role of the obsessive, hard-nosed marine officer is little more than a scene-stealing cameo. The two leads are Tom Cruise and Demi Moore, who play naval lawyers trying to discover the truth behind the death of a marine. It's crisply directed by Rob Reiner, who once again shows that he is comfortable with numerous styles of film-making and, if it becomes a little talky at times, the climactic fireworks between Nicholson and Cruise make for compulsive viewing. JF. Contains swearing and violence. DVD

Tom Cruise *Lt Daniel Kaffee* • Jack Nicholson *Col Nathan R Jessep* • Demi Moore *Lt Cmdr JoAnne Galloway* • Kevin Bacon *Capt Jack Ross* • Kiefer Sutherland *Lt Jonathan Kendrick* • Kevin Pollak *Lt Sam Weinberg* • James Marshall *Private First Class Louden Downey* • JT Walsh *Lt Col Matthew Markinson* ■ *Dir* Rob Reiner • *Scr* Aaron Sorkin, from his play

Fiddler on the Roof ★★★★ U

Musical comedy drama
1971 · US · Colour · 171mins

This film version of one of the greatest, most heartbreaking of all Broadway shows really should have been no less than magnificent, given its source and the opportunities it presents to create movie magic. Through the tale of Tevye and his search for husbands for his five daughters, director Norman Jewison describes the tragic background to the expulsion of the Jews from the Ukraine and the dissolution of their traditions. As Tevye the garrulous milkman, Topol is memorable, and to have his performance (he played the part on the London stage) preserved on film is a major plus. The generally unfamiliar supporting cast is exceptionally well chosen, but the real gem is the Oscar-winning soundtrack. TS [video] DVD

Topol *Tevye* • Norma Crane *Golde* • Leonard Frey *Motel* • Molly Picon *Yente* • Paul Mann *Lazar Wolf* • Rosalind Harris *Tzeitel* • Michele Marsh *Hodel* • Neva Small *Chava* • Michael Glaser [Paul Michael Glaser] *Perchik* • Raymond Lovelock *Fyedka* ■ *Dir* Norman Jewison • *Scr* Joseph Stein, from his book of the stage musical, from stories by Sholom Aleichem • *Cinematographer* Oswald Morris • *Music* Jerry Bock • *Lyrics* Sheldon Harnick

Fiddlers Three ★★

Comedy 1944 · UK · BW · 88mins

The follow-up to *Sailors Three* is a cheap and cheerful reworking of Eddie Cantor's *Roman Scandals*. A bolt of lightning transports stars Tommy Trinder, Sonny Hale and Wren Diana Decker back to ancient Rome, where she takes the eye of the emperor Nero, and Tommy has to resort to a Carmen Miranda disguise to save her. The gags are poor and the songs are even worse, but any escape from the war was welcome and, with Francis L Sullivan camping it up as Nero, there were a few cheerful digs at Mussolini and his allies along the way. DP

Tommy Trinder *Tommy* • Frances Day *Poppaea* • Sonnie Hale *Professor* • Francis L Sullivan *Nero* • Diana Decker *Lydia* • Elisabeth Welch *Thora* ■ *Dir* Harry Watt • *Scr* Harry Watt, Diana Morgan, Angus MacPhail

La Fidélité ★★ 15

Drama 2000 · Fr · Colour · 166mins

Andrzej Zulawski here directs his real-life partner, Sophie Marceau, in a reckless updating of Madame de la Fayette's novel *La Princesse de Clèves*. What starts promisingly as a scathing dissection of modern cultural vacuity soon takes a turn for the worse as Marceau's Canadian photographer tumbles into bed with children's book publisher Pascal Greggory, forming a bond that compels her to reject the passionate advances of sexy colleague Guillaume Canet. Pretentious. DP. In French with English subtitles.

Sophie Marceau *Clélia* • Pascal Greggory *Clève* • Guillaume Canet *Nemo* • Magali Noël *Clélia's mother* ■ *Dir* Andrzej Zulawski • *Scr* Andrzej Zulawski, from the novel *La Princesse de Clèves* by Madame de La Fayette

The Field ★★★ 15

Drama 1990 · UK · Colour · 105mins

Critics and audiences alike were rather underwhelmed by Jim Sheridan's follow-up to the phenomenally successful *My Left Foot*. His attempt to create a rural drama akin to those premiered in the heyday of Dublin's Abbey Theatre results in an overbrewed poteen that intoxicates only to leave you with dulled senses. Richard Harris received an Oscar nomination for his imposing performance as the grouchy farmer fighting to save "his" land, but it is the understated playing of John Hurt and Brenda Fricker that provides the real backbone of this handsome, arresting production. DP. Contains violence and swearing. [video] DVD

Richard Harris *"Bull" McCabe* • Sean Bean *Tadgh McCabe* • Tom Berenger *Peter, the American* • Frances Tomelty *The widow* • Brenda Fricker *Maggie McCabe* • John Hurt *"Bird" O'Donnell* • Ruth McCabe *First tinker woman* ■ *Dir* Jim Sheridan • *Scr* Jim Sheridan, from a play by John B Keane

Field of Dreams ★★★★ PG

Fantasy drama 1989 · US · Colour · 101mins

This fantasy drama from director Phil Alden Robinson is a delightful blend of the blind-fate story and the more fanciful feel-good corn of Frank Capra. Kevin Costner, as an Iowan farmer, is the epitome of dignified determination as he accedes to a ghostly voice and turns the field on which the family depends for its livelihood into a baseball pitch. The underestimated Amy Madigan gives a good account of herself as his trusting wife, while Ray Liotta, Burt Lancaster and Frank Whaley represent the spirit world with distinction. DP [video] DVD

Kevin Costner *Ray Kinsella* • Amy Madigan *Annie Kinsella* • Gaby Hoffman [Gaby Hoffmann] *Karin Kinsella* • Ray Liotta *"Shoeless" Joe Jackson* • Timothy Busfield *Mark* • James Earl Jones *Terence Mann* • Burt Lancaster *Dr "Moonlight" Graham* • Frank Whaley *Archie Graham* • Dwier Brown *John Kinsella* ■ *Dir* Phil Alden Robinson • *Scr* Phil Alden Robinson, from the novel *Shoeless Joe* by WP Kinsella

The Fiend ★★★

Horror 1971 · UK · Colour · 91mins

This unnerving stalk 'n' slash horror offering marries religious mania to *Peeping Tom*-style voyeuristic repression. With an opening in which a christening is cross-cut with a murder, it's clear that emotionally stunted Tony Beckley is not going to be fit to wear the policeman's uniform that he hides behind while pursuing his savage quest. When his diabetic mother (Ann Todd) suffers under manic Bible-thumping Patrick Magee, Beckley demonstrates the full horror of his insanity. Director Robert Hartford-Davis can't be accused of subtlety, but this is still a disturbing film. DP

Ann Todd *Birdie Wemys* • Patrick Magee *Minister* • Tony Beckley *Kenny Wemys* • Madeline Hinde *Brigitte Lynch* • Suzanna Leigh *Paddy Lynch* • Percy Herbert *Commissionaire* • David Lodge *CID Inspector* ■ *Dir* Robert Hartford-Davis • *Scr* Brian Comport

The Fiend Who Walked the West ★★★

Western 1958 · US · Colour · 100mins

Take two top Hollywood writers, a highly experienced director and a great cameraman and set them loose on a revamp of the scary urban-based thriller, *Kiss of Death* (which made a star out of Richard Widmark in 1947). The result? A blend of gothic horror, western and *film noir*. Robert Evans (later a producer of fine films such as *Chinatown*) gives a memorably over-the-top performance as a baby-faced psychotic who gets out of prison and embarks on a mission to kill the friends and family of former cellmate, Hugh O'Brian. A must-see curiosity. BB

Hugh O'Brian *Dan Hardy* • Robert Evans *Felix Griffin* • Dolores Michaels *May* • Linda Cristal *Ellen Hardy* • Stephen McNally *Emmett* ■ *Dir* Gordon Douglas • *Scr* Harry Brown, Philip Yordan, from the film *Kiss of Death* by Ben Hecht, Charles Lederer, Eleazar Lipsky • *Cinematographer* Joseph MacDonald [Joe MacDonald]

Fiend without a Face ★★★ PG

Science-fiction horror 1957 · UK · BW · 70mins

Canadian atomic experiments cause human thoughts to transform into brain-sucking creatures in a grisly little 1950s number featuring unusually graphic special effects for the period. Arthur Crabtree's *Quatermass*-style shocker starts off pretty ordinarily but, once the flying spinal cords whip into throat-choking action, the screams you hear may well be your own! British to the core, despite the pseudo-American trappings and the presence of fading Hollywood actor Marshall Thompson taking centre stage. AJ DVD

Marshall Thompson *Major Jeff Cummings* • Terence Kilburn [Terry Kilburn] *Captain Chester* • Kynaston Reeves *Professor Walgate* • Stanley Maxted *Colonel Butler* • Michael Balfour *Sergeant Kasper* • Kim Parker *Barbara* ■ *Dir* Arthur Crabtree • *Scr* Herbert J Leder, from a story by Amelia Reynolds Long

The Fiendish Plot of Dr Fu Manchu ★ PG

Comedy 1980 · US · Colour · 100mins

There's no escaping the fact that the last film Peter Sellers made was also his worst (mercifully he didn't live to see two later *Pink Panther* out-take abominations). It was a bad idea in the first place to have Sellers play both the Oriental master villain and his dogged pursuer, Nayland Smith, but he spends so much time in disguise that it's sometimes hard to remember who he's supposed to be. DP [video]

Peter Sellers *Dr Fu Manchu/Nayland Smith* • Helen Mirren *Alice Rage* • David Tomlinson *Sir Roger Avery* • Sid Caesar *Joe Capone* • Stratford Johns *Ismail* • John Le Mesurier *Perkins* ■ *Dir* Piers Haggard • *Scr* Jim Moloney, Rudy Dochtermann, from characters created by Sax Rohmer

Fierce Creatures ★★ 12

Comedy 1997 · US/UK · Colour · 89mins

John Cleese reassembled the team from *A Fish Called Wanda* for this soft-hearted caper. Cleese plays the new manager appointed by an Australian media mogul to jazz up a local zoo by adopting a "fierce creatures only" policy. Sadly, this follow-up lacks the magic of the original, and, despite the valiant efforts of a host of familiar faces, that vital spark is largely missing. JF [video] DVD

John Cleese *Rollo Lee* • Jamie Lee Curtis *Willa Weston* • Kevin Kline *Vince McCain/Rod McCain* • Michael Palin *Bugsy Malone* • Ronnie Corbett *Reggie Sealions* • Carey Lowell *Cub Felines* • Robert Lindsay *Sydney Small Mammals* ■ *Dir* Fred Schepisi, Robert Young (2) • *Scr* John Cleese, Iain Johnstone, from an idea by Terry Jones, Michael Palin

The Fiercest Heart ★★ U

Adventure 1961 · UK · Colour · 89mins

This decidedly anti-colonial tale is really nothing more than a western transferred to the South African veld. Set in 1837, director George Sherman replaces wagon train adventure with a great Boer trek, while the usual fugitive outlaw figure becomes a political prisoner who escapes from a British internment camp and finds redemption in the arms of a pioneering woman. Stuart Whitman combines ruggedness and rigidity in about equal measure, and Juliet Prowse is just as inanimate. Thank heavens for Raymond Massey's performance as a community elder. DP

Stuart Whitman *Bates* • Juliet Prowse *Francina* • Ken Scott *Harry Carter* • Raymond Massey *Willem* • Geraldine Fitzgerald *Tante Maria* • Rafer Johnson *Nzobo* • Michael David *Barent* ■ *Dir* George Sherman • *Scr* Edmund H North, from the novel by Stuart Cloete

Fiesta ★★★

Musical 1947 · US · Colour · 102mins

This sumptuous MGM production filmed on location down Mexico way and in glorious Technicolor, is little more than a starring vehicle for ultra-glamorous Esther Williams. She looks ravishing in a torero's outfit in a sort of Shakespearean plot in which she has to disguise herself as her twin brother – dashing screen newcomer Ricardo Montalban. Montalban falls for the equally ravishing Cyd Charisse, and the two of them get to indulge in a brace of fiery dance duets. Meanwhile, sister Esther finds romance with John Carroll. Tosh, of course, but done with style, and it's simply fabulous to look at. TS

Esther Williams *Maria Morales* • Akim Tamiroff *Chato Vasquez* • Ricardo Montalban *Mario Morales* • John Carroll *Jose "Pepe" Ortega* • Mary Astor *Senora Morales* • Cyd Charisse *Conchita* ■ *Dir* Richard Thorpe • *Scr* George Bruce, Lester Cole

La Fièvre Monte à el Pao ★★★

Drama 1959 · Fr/Mex · BW · 100mins

Part potboiler, part acute political analysis, this cynical drama unfolds on an island off the coast of a Latin American republic with a large population of jailbirds and political prisoners from the mainland. When the governor is assassinated, Gérard Philipe, his former secretary and a man of ideals, takes care of matters until a new governor (Jean Servais) is appointed. The director's cynical message – that individuals are forced to bow to systems – comes through loud and clear, but Philipe, making his last film before his early death, is unable to inject life into his ill-defined role. RB. A French language film.

Gérard Philipe *Ramón Vásquez* • Maria Felix *Inés Rojas* • Jean Servais *Alejandro Gual* • Victor Junco *Indarte* • Roberto Cañedo *Coronel Olivares* • Andres Soler *Carlos Barreiro* • Domingo Soler *Juan Cárdenas* ■ *Dir* Luis Buñuel • *Scr* Luis Buñuel, Luis Alcoriza, Charles Dorat, Louis Sapin, Henry Castillou, from the novel by Henry Castillou

15 ★★★ 18

Drama 2003 · Sing · Colour · 96mins

Royston Tan's uncompromising take on teenage ennui caused outrage in its native Singapore. The story of five young people living on the fringes of society is played out by actual street kids, who re-enact their own experiences of drug abuse, promiscuity and violence. Sequences containing an animated guide to suicide and a rap tribute to the Lion City's most feared street gangs reveal the director's outspoken support for these nonconformists. However, Tan's background in music videos lends the film a self-consciously modish look, which somewhat swamps the fragile feelings of these young rebels. DP. In Mandarin, Hokkien, Malay and Hindi with English subtitles.

Shaun Tan *Shaun* • Melvin Chen *Melvin* • Erick Chun *Erick* • Melvin Lee *Armani* • Vynn Soh *Vynn* ■ *Dir/Scr* Royston Tan

15 Minutes ★★ 18

Thriller 2001 · US · Colour · 115mins

This New York cop thriller with a social conscience teams old dog Robert De Niro with hip young gunslinger Edward Burns, throwing in *Frasier* star Kelsey Grammer for light relief. But while this purports to be a savage indictment of tabloid TV – De Niro's cop feeds crime exclusives to Grammer's news hack in return for exposure – it's merely a glossy sham. As our disparate heroes pursue two implausible Eastern Europeans who are recording their murderous crime spree on videotape, any subtlety of message is swamped by the welter of join-the-dots action. AC. Contains violence and swearing. [video] DVD

Robert De Niro *Eddie Fleming* • Edward Burns *Jordy Warsaw* • Kelsey Grammer *Robert Hawkins* • Avery Brooks *Leon Jackson* • Melina Kanakaredes *Nicolette Karas* • Karel Roden *Emil Slovak* • Oleg Taktarov *Oleg Razgul* • Kim Cattrall *Cassandra* • Charlize Theron *Rose Hearn* ■ *Dir/Scr* John Herzfeld

Fifth Avenue Girl ★★

Comedy 1939 · US · BW · 82mins

The girl is poor-but-honest Ginger Rogers (a tad too old for the role) who's "adopted" by millionaire Walter Connolly for a night to be his companion, in order to compensate himself for familial neglect. Some nice left-wing barbs in here, but overall there's a rather unsavoury and unfamiliar taste to director Gregory La Cava's misanthropic view of human behaviour. TS

Ginger Rogers *Mary Grey* • Walter Connolly *Mr Borden* • Verree Teasdale *Mrs Borden* • James Ellison *Michael* • Tim Holt *Tim Borden* • Kathryn Adams *Katherine Borden* ■ *Dir* Gregory La Cava • *Scr* Allan Scott

The Fifth Element ★★★★ PG

Science-fiction action adventure
1997 · Fr · Colour · 121mins

Ancient evil returns to destroy the galaxy in director Luc Besson's ultra-hip, socially conscious and clever film. Laconic former government agent Bruce Willis is forced to save the universe when the secret key to stopping this happening literally falls into his cab in 23rd-century New York. This superb flight of imagination soars into original terrain for an inventive roller-coaster ride; the satire is slick, the visuals unusual and the thrills futuristic. Gary Oldman is great as *haute-couture* corruption personified. AJ. Contains violence, swearing and nudity. DVD

Bruce Willis *Korben Dallas* • Gary Oldman *Zorg* • Ian Holm *Cornelius* • Milla Jovovich *Leeloo* • Chris Tucker *Ruby Rhod* • Luke Perry *Billy* • Brion James *General Munro* • Lee Evans *Fog* ■ *Dir* Luc Besson • *Scr* Luc Besson, Robert Mark Kamen

The Fifth Floor ★

Psychological thriller
1980 · US · Colour · 87mins

This is bargain-basement stuff about a woman mistakenly admitted to a mental hospital, after being poisoned at a disco. Populated by the usual crazies and a depraved orderly (Bo Hopkins), it's definitely not the place for a nice girl, particularly when she's sane. Howard Avedis's direction reaches no heights and is as predictable as a calendar. TH

Bo Hopkins *Carl* • Dianne Hull *Kelly McIntire* • Patti D'Arbanville *Cathy Burke* • Sharon Farrell *Melanie* • Mel Ferrer *Dr Coleman* • Robert Englund *Benny* ■ *Dir* Howard Avedis • *Scr* Meyer Dolinsky, from a story by Howard Avedis, Marlene Schmidt

The 5th Monkey ★★

Adventure 1990 · US · Colour · 95mins

Ben Kingsley's film career has taken some peculiar turns since his Oscar-winning portrayal of Gandhi in 1982. Here he finds himself deep in the Amazon rainforest attempting to sell some rare monkeys in order to make enough money to marry his true love. This meandering tale makes the most of the Brazilian landscape, but fails to sustain interest in Kingsley's ultimate goal, and its sermon on the need for conservation is overzealously preached. DP. Contains violence.

Ben Kingsley *Cunda* • Mika Lins *Octavia* • Vera Fischer *Mrs Watts* • Silvia De Carvalho *Maria* • Carlos Kroeber *Mr Garcia* ■ *Dir* Eric Rochat • *Scr* Eric Rochat, from the novel *Le Cinquième Singe* by Jacques Zibi

The Fifth Musketeer ★★ 15

Period adventure
1979 · Austria · Colour · 115mins

Yet another rehash of *The Man in the Iron Mask*, with Beau Bridges rather poorly cast in the dual role as Louis XIV and his incarcerated twin brother. Sylvia Kristel – famous as the heroine of the soft-porn *Emmanuelle* films – plus Ursula Andress join an impressive roster of slumming veterans, including Rex Harrison, Olivia de Havilland and Jose Ferrer. Ken Annakin directs without fuss but the whole thing has the heaviness one expects from a Euro-pudding movie. AT

Beau Bridges *King Louis/Philippe* • Sylvia Kristel *Marie-Thérèse* • Ursula Andress *Madame De La Vallière* • Cornel Wilde *D'Artagnan* • Ian McShane *Fourquet* • Lloyd Bridges *Aramis* • Alan Hale Jr *Porthos* • Olivia de Havilland *Queen Anne* • José Ferrer *Athos* • Rex Harrison *Colbert* ■ *Dir* Ken Annakin • *Scr* David Ambrose, from a screenplay (unproduced) by George Bruce, from the novel *The Man in the Iron Mask* by Alexandre Dumas

Fifty/Fifty ★★★ 15

Action adventure 1991 · US · Colour · 96mins

Directed by actor Charles Martin Smith (*American Graffiti*), this decent little action adventure concerns two wisecracking mercenaries taking a job from the CIA to overthrow a South East Asian dictator. Along the way they have to train a guerrilla army and spar romantically for the favour of a pretty rebel soldier. The two tough guys are played by Peter Weller and Robert Hays, and they have a lot of chemistry together. The dialogue is surprisingly good, but in the end the setup is more fun than the pay-off. ST

Peter Weller *Jake Wyer* • Robert Hays *Sam French* • Charles Martin Smith *Martin Sprue* • Ramona Rahman *Suleta* • Lim Kay Tong *Akhantar* ■ *Dir* Charles Martin Smith • *Scr* Michael Butler, Dennis Shryack, Jeff Levine, LeeAnn Lanctos, Chris Wood

50 First Dates ★★★ 12

Romantic comedy
2004 · US · Colour · 94mins

Only the grumpiest viewer could fail to be charmed by this sweet comedy. Featuring one of Adam Sandler's least goofy performances, it's a simple and undemanding story, with genuine warmth beneath the slapstick. Drew Barrymore plays a car-crash survivor whose short term memory loss means she wakes up every morning with no knowledge of the day before. For laid-back, would-be suitor Sandler this means repeating their first date over and over again, an amusing concept laced with poignancy. SF. Contains drug abuse. DVD

Adam Sandler *Henry Roth* • Drew Barrymore *Lucy Whitmore* • Rob Schneider *Ula* • Sean Astin *Doug Whitmore* • Lusia Strus *Alexa* • Dan Aykroyd *Dr Keats* • Amy Hill *Sue* • Allen Covert *Ten Second Tom* • Blake Clark *Marlin Whitmore* ■ *Dir* Peter Segal • *Scr* George Wing

The 51st State ★★ 18

Action comedy drama
2001 · UK/Can · Colour · 88mins

This glossy, visceral crime thriller from director Ronny Yu is a mere exercise in noisy excess, yet a few elements mark it out as something slightly unusual. The script about a master chemist trying to sell the ultimate in designer drugs was sent to Samuel L Jackson by a first-time writer and off-licence worker, and then given the go-ahead. It's also set in less than glamorous Liverpool; streetwise Jackson's pharmacist hero wears a kilt and his sidekick Robert Carlyle is a rabid football fan. JC. Contains violence, swearing and drug abuse. DVD

Samuel L Jackson *Elmo McElroy* • Robert Carlyle *Felix De Souza* • Emily Mortimer *"Dakota"* • Rhys Ifans *Iki* • Ricky Tomlinson *Durant* • Sean Pertwee *Virgil Kane* • Meat Loaf *The Lizard* ■ *Dir* Ronny Yu • *Scr* Stel Pavlou

55 Days at Peking ★★★★ U

Historical drama
1963 · US · Colour · 147mins

This is an intelligent historical epic about the Boxer rebellion of 1900 when extremists besieged the compound of international diplomats. Charlton Heston stars in this Philip Yordan-scripted Chinese drama, filmed in a custom-built Peking, one of the most spectacular sets ever created. Switching smoothly between the wider political sphere and the personal dilemmas of the key players – Heston, David Niven, Ava Gardner – the movie is a carefully balanced study of principle and courage in action, partly directed by Nicholas Ray who suffered a heart attack during production and whose work was completed by second unit director Andrew Marton and an uncredited Guy Green. AT

Charlton Heston *Major Matt Lewis* • Ava Gardner *Baroness Natalie Ivanoff* • David Niven *Sir Arthur Robertson* • Flora Robson *Dowager Empress Tzu Hsi* • John Ireland *Sergeant Harry* • Harry Andrews *Father de Bearn* ■ *Dir* Nicholas Ray • *Scr* Philip Yordan, Bernard Gordon, Robert Hamer

54 ★★★ 15

Drama 1998 · US · Colour · 89mins

Vividly capturing the atmosphere of Studio 54 and the energy of the disco era, this ambitious chronicle of the notorious 1970s nightclub from writer/director Mark Christopher is only let down by a formulaic plot. Ryan Phillippe plays the hunky bartender from New Jersey who gains a surrogate family when he is sucked into the decadent, glitzy lifestyle of the spaced-out "in-crowd". Mike Myers is terrific as Steve Rubell, the club's permanently stoned, homosexual emcee, but it's the hedonistic circus atmosphere evoked by Christopher that makes this superficial yet captivating. AJ. Contains swearing, sex scenes and drug abuse. DVD

Ryan Phillippe *Shane O'Shea* • Salma Hayek *Anita* • Neve Campbell *Julie Black* • Mike Myers *Steve Rubell* • Sela Ward *Billie Auster* • Breckin Meyer *Greg Randazzo* • Sherry Stringfield *Viv* ■ *Dir/Scr* Mark Christopher

52 Pick-Up ★★★ 18

Crime thriller 1986 · US · Colour · 103mins

The 1980s saw two versions of Elmore Leonard 's *52 Pick-Up*, both made by the same company. The first was *The Ambassador*, made in 1984; for the second, made two years later, they kept Leonard's original title and storyline and sensibly asked the novelist to write the script himself. Director John Frankenheimer is way below his best form but still keeps the plot simmering, while Roy Scheider is excellent as the man whose mistress has been murdered because he won't pay the blackmailers. Fans will not be disappointed. AT DVD

Roy Scheider *Harry Mitchell* • Ann-Margret *Barbara Mitchell* • Vanity *Doreen* • John Glover *Alan Raimy* • Robert Trebor *Leo Franks* • Lonny Chapman *Jim O'Boyle* • Kelly Preston *Cini* • Doug McClure *Mark Averson* ■ *Dir* John Frankenheimer • *Scr* John Steppling, Elmore Leonard, from the novel by Elmore Leonard

Fight Club ★★★★★ 18

Satirical drama 1999 · US · Colour · 133mins

Chuck Palahniuk's bestseller is boldly brought to the screen by director David Fincher. The result is a shocking, provocative and highly amusing macho fantasy, as insomniac loser Edward Norton teams up with seditionary soap salesman Brad Pitt to form a no-holds-barred fight club as an outlet for their directionless aggression. The growing cult's Project Mayhem takes subversive vandalism into the outside world with a series of ludicrous acts of sabotage. Fincher's satirical fable brilliantly plays with cinematic conventions and climaxes with a shock twist. This charged slice of nihilistic angst is a mesmerising ride through the 1990s male psyche, aided by elaborate production design, unconventional editing, startling images and superlative acting from the leads. AJ. Contains violence, swearing and sex scenes. DVD

Brad Pitt *Tyler Durden* • Edward Norton *Narrator* • Helena Bonham Carter *Marla Singer* • Meat Loaf Aday [Meat Loaf] *Robert Paulsen* • Jared Leto *Angel Face* • Rachel Singer *Chloe* ■ *Dir* David Fincher • *Scr* Jim Uhls, from the novel by Chuck Palahniuk • *Cinematographer* Jeff Cronenweth • *Music* The Dust Brothers

The Fighter ★★

Drama 1952 · US · BW · 78mins

Jack London's short story *The Mexican* is turned into a nothing B-movie. Richard Conte becomes a prizefighter to raise money for the revolution against a local bigwig who is responsible for the slaughter of his village. He decides to take on a big name fighter. Conte is not leading man material, Vanessa Brown is the vague love interest and Lee J Cobb is busking between better assignments. Only James Wong Howe's camerawork has any class. AT

Richard Conte *Filipe Rivera* • Lee J Cobb *Durango* • Vanessa Brown *Kathy* • Frank Silvera *Paulino* • Roberta Haynes *Nevis* • Hugh Sanders *Roberts* ■ *Dir* Herbert Kline • *Scr* Herbert Kline, Aben Kandel, from the short story *The Mexican* by Jack London

Fighter Squadron ★★ U

Second World War drama
1948 · US · Colour · 94mins

This routine Warner Bros war flick is of moderate interest in that it stars the ever-watchable Edmond O'Brien and Robert Stack as the flyboys struggling against both clichés and Technicolor make-up. It's of more interest today as it features the extremely gauche premiere appearance of superstar-to-be Rock Hudson, cast on looks alone by legendary director Raoul Walsh, and whose single-line performance (requiring a phenomenal amount of takes to get right) is barely acceptable. The rest of the movie just about passes muster. TS

Edmond O'Brien *Maj Ed Hardin* • Robert Stack *Capt Stu Hamilton* • John Rodney *Col Bill Brickley* • Tom D'Andrea *Sgt Dolan* • Henry Hull *Brig Gen Mike McCready* • Rock Hudson *Lieutenant* ■ *Dir* Raoul Walsh • *Scr* Seton I Miller, Martin Rackin

Fighting Caravans ★★★ U

Western 1931 · US · BW · 88mins

This excellent, if dated, early Gary Cooper western features him as a young wagon train guide. Fresh from *Morocco* opposite Marlene Dietrich, he is here well paired with striking French actress Lili Damita. Ernest Torrence and Tully Marshall reprise the old-timers they played in *The Covered Wagon*, while Fred Kohler contributes some lively villainy that leads to a spectacular climactic attack by Indians as the travellers cross a river. AE

Gary Cooper *Clint Belmet* • Lili Damita *Felice* • Ernest Torrence *Bill Jackson* • Fred Kohler *Lee Murdock* • Tully Marshall *Jim Bridger* ■ *Dir* Otto Brower, David Burton • *Scr* Edward E Paramore Jr, Keene Thompson, Agnes Brand Leahy, from a novel by Zane Grey

Fighting Father Dunne ★

Drama 1948 · US · BW · 92mins

This simply awful drama has Pat O'Brien in his customary role as a Catholic priest with a heart as big as Ireland. This time he fights on behalf of orphaned newsboys in St Louis and tries to find them a home. Based on a true story, it was made to prove that movie studios were not merely money machines but were at the service of humanity. However, this woeful effort is only for those in need of a cringe. AT

Pat O'Brien *Father Peter Dunne* • Darryl Hickman *Matt Davis* • Charles Kemper *Emmett Mulvey* • Una O'Connor *Miss O'Rourke* ■ *Dir* Ted Tetzlaff • *Scr* Martin Rackin, Frank Davis, from a story by William Rankin

The Fighting Kentuckian ★★★ U

Historical adventure 1949 · US · BW · 99mins

This is a genuine curio. Produced by the Duke himself, it details an interesting historical anomaly – the settling in America of Napoleon's exiled officers and their relatives immediately after the defeat at Waterloo. The political aspect isn't really explored, though, merely serving as a background for a rollicking romance with lots of fighting. Wayne's sidekick is Oliver Hardy, who acquits himself well without his usual partner, Stan Laurel; indeed, he's the best reason for viewing. TS

John Wayne *John Breen* • Vera Ralston *Fleurette DeMarchand* • Philip Dorn *Colonel Georges Geraud* • Oliver Hardy *Willie Paine* • Marie Windsor *Ann Logan* • John Howard (1) *Blake Randolph* • Hugo Haas *General Paul DeMarchand* ■ *Dir/Scr* George Waggner

Fighting Mad ★★

Action drama 1976 · US · Colour · 87mins

A sleazy, low-budget effort from the Roger Corman factory, with Peter Fonda as an Arkansas rancher's son who declares war on big-business interests and does a Rambo when intimidation turns into murder. Paying a certain amount of lip service to environmental issues, this is really just an excuse to justify some vigilante violence and to allow novice writer/director Jonathan Demme a few opportunities to show off. AT. Contains violence, swearing and nudity

Peter Fonda *Tom Hunter* • Lynn Lowry *Lorene Maddox* • John Doucette *Jeff Hunter* • Philip Carey *Pierce Crabtree* • Scott Glenn *Charlie Hunter* • Kathleen Miller *Carolee Hunter* ■ *Dir/Scr* Jonathan Demme

Fighting Man of the Plains ★★ U

Western 1949 · US · Colour · 93mins

Randolph Scott stars as a former Quantrill's Raider, cleaning up a town with the help of outlaw Jesse James, in this sturdy Fox western from skilled producer Nat Holt. As James, Holt cast newcomer Dale Robertson, who later achieved fame in such TV series as *Tales of Wells Fargo* and *The Iron Horse*. Look out for *Gone with the Wind*'s carpetbagger Victor Jory. TS

Randolph Scott *Jim Dancer* • Bill Williams *Johnny Tancred* • Victor Jory *Dave Oldham* • Jane Nigh *Florence Peel* • Douglas Kennedy *Ken Vedder* • Joan Taylor *Evelyn Slocum* • Dale Robertson *Jesse James* ■ *Dir* Edwin L Marin • *Scr* Frank Gruber, from his novel *Fighting Man*

The Fighting O'Flynn ★★★ U

Period swashbuckling adventure 1948 · US · BW · 94mins

This rousing Napoleonic swashbuckler gives Douglas Fairbanks Jr copious opportunities to prove himself a chip off the old block. He certainly cuts a dash as the Irishman dividing his energies between thwarting the French and foiling obnoxious viceregal aide Richard Greene's plans to marry Helena Carter. But his co-written screenplay also contains elements of knowing humour at the expense of both the genre and the Fairbanks legend, as he ceaslessly jousts and duels, trysts and jests. DP

Douglas Fairbanks Jr *The O'Flynn* • Helena Carter *Lady Benedetta* • Richard Greene *Lord Sedgemouth* • Patricia Medina *Fancy Free* • Arthur Shields *Dooley* • JM Kerrigan *Timothy* • Lumsden Hare *Viceroy* ■ *Dir* Arthur Pierson • *Scr* Douglas Fairbanks Jr, Robert Thoeren, from the novel *The O'Flynn* by Justin Huntly McCarthy

The Fighting Prince of Donegal ★★ U

Swashbuckling adventure 1966 · UK · Colour · 105mins

The title tells all – buckles swashed and derring-do done. Peter McEnery is the rebel in Ireland during Elizabethan times, wooing Susan Hampshire and battling a villainous Gordon Jackson, leader of the British troops who kidnaps McEnery's true love and mother. Aimed directly at youngsters – who may well overlook the cut-out castle and the cast-offs dialogue – director Michael O'Herlihy's noisy movie is enjoyable enough. TH

Peter McEnery *Red Hugh* • Susan Hampshire *Kathleen* • Tom Adams *Henry O'Neill* • Gordon Jackson *Capt Leeds* • Andrew Keir *MacSweeney* • Norman Wooland *Sir John Perrott* ■ *Dir* Michael O'Herlihy • *Scr* Robert Westerby, from the novel *Red Hugh, Prince of Donegal* by Robert T Reilly

The Fighting Seabees ★★★ U

Second World War drama 1944 · US · BW · 99mins

Although denied military service during the Second World War, John Wayne did his fair share of fighting on screen in propaganda movies such as this one, which is based on a true story. He stars as the boss of a construction company who orders his workers to take up arms against the invading Japanese. Wayne's hot-headedness causes his buddy's death, leading him to demolish all the enemy in sight, blasting his way to glory. Borden Chase's screenplay worked then, and it almost works now, and if you're a fan of the Duke, give it a try. TS

John Wayne *Wedge Donovan* • Susan Hayward *Constance Chesley* • Dennis O'Keefe *Lt Cmdr Bob Yarrow* • William Frawley *Eddie Powers* • Leonid Kinskey *Johnny Novasky* • Jim Kerrigan [JM Kerrigan] *Sawyer Collins* ■ *Dir* Edward Ludwig • *Scr* Borden Chase, Aeneas MacKenzie, from a story by Borden Chase

The Fighting 69th ★★ PG

First World War drama 1940 · US · BW · 86mins

James Cagney joins up for the First World War, but breaks down under fire in the trenches. His cowardice results in him sending up a star shell, giving away his regiment's position, causing many deaths. Fortunately there's a kindly, sympathetic priest at hand – good heavens, it's Pat O'Brien, what a surprise – who cures Cagney and gets him firing on all cylinders. A cynical piece of studio propaganda, efficiently directed by William Keighley. AT

James Cagney *Jerry Plunkett* • Pat O'Brien *Father Duffy* • George Brent *Wild Bill Donovan* • Jeffrey Lynn *Joyce Kilmer* • Alan Hale *Sgt Big Mike Wynn* • Frank McHugh *"Crepe Hanger" Burke* ■ *Dir* William Keighley • *Scr* Norman Reilly Raine, Fred Niblo Jr, Dean Franklin

Fighting Stock ★★

Comedy 1935 · UK · BW · 72mins

While at film company Gainsborough, producer Michael Balcon demonstrated a highly catholic taste in comedy, including a yen for the Aldwych farces of Ben Travers, whom Balcon hired to write this comedy. This is not one of the strongest Balcon/Travers collaborations, but brigadier Tom Walls and bumbling nephew Ralph Lynn are on top of their game as they tackle a crotchety neighbour and deliver niece Marie Lohr from blackmailers during a stay in a country cottage. DP

Tom Walls *Sir Donald Rowley* • Ralph Lynn *Sidney* • J Robertson Hare [Robertson Hare] *Duck* • Marie Lohr *Barbara Rivers* • Lesley Wareing *Eileen Rivers* • Veronica Rose *Diana Rivers* ■ *Dir* Tom Walls • *Scr* Ben Travers

The Fighting Sullivans ★★★★ U

Biographical drama 1944 · US · BW · 107mins

Unbearably moving (because you know the outcome) true story of the five brothers of a single family who enlisted, fought, and died together in the Second World War (the American Navy consequently banned all family members from serving on the same ship). A superb cast does full justice to the tragedy of the brothers from Iowa, whose ship was sunk at Guadalcanal. Although the Sullivans are played by virtual unknowns, exceptionally fine acting is provided by top-billed Anne Baxter as the wife of Al Sullivan, the last to enlist, and in particular by Thomas Mitchell and Selena Royle as the boys' parents. TS DVD

Anne Baxter *Katherine Mary* • Thomas Mitchell *Thomas F Sullivan* • Selena Royle *Alleta Sullivan* • Edward Ryan *Albert Leo Sullivan* • Trudy Marshall *Genevieve "Gen" Sullivan* • John Campbell *Francis Henry Sullivan* • James Cardwell *George Thomas Sullivan* • John Alvin *Madison "Matt" Abel Sullivan* • George Offerman Jr *Joseph Eugene Sullivan* • Ward Bond *Commander Robinson* • Bobby Driscoll *Al as a child* ■ *Dir* Lloyd Bacon • *Scr* Mary C McCall Jr, from a story by Edward Doherty, Jules Schermer

The Fighting Temptations ★★ PG

Musical comedy 2003 · US · Colour · 117mins

Director Jonathan Lynn (the co-creator of *Yes, Minister*) is rarely in control of the tone or pacing of this messy amalgam of African-American social attitudes and musical tastes. Cuba Gooding Jr clowns to excess as the cynical ad executive determined to galvanise the choristers at his aunt's church in order to inherit her fortune. But the diverse singing styles of Melba Moore, T-Bone and Beyoncé Knowles, and a feisty turn from LaTanya Richardson, provide some compensation. DP DVD

Cuba Gooding Jr *Darrin Hill* • Beyoncé Knowles *Lilly* • Mike Epps *Lucius* • Steve Harvey *Miles the DJ* • LaTanya Richardson *Paulina Pritchett* • Faith Evans *Maryann Hill* • Angie Stone *Alma* • Melba Moore *Bessie Cooley* ■ *Dir* Jonathan Lynn • *Scr* Elizabeth Hunter, Saladin K Patterson, from a story by Elizabeth Hunter

Figures in a Landscape ★★★

Thriller 1970 · UK · Colour · 108mins

A nightmare vision of a repressive future? A treatise on the survival of the fittest and the corruption of the innocent? Take your pick in Robert Shaw's reworking of Barry England's novel about two escaped prisoners (Shaw and Malcolm McDowell) who resort to violence to evade the dogged pursuit of a helicopter pilot. Director Joseph Losey cleverly uses the rugged landscape to show the hopelessness of their situation. By keeping the characters at a distance, however, he stops us sharing their plight. DP

Robert Shaw *MacConnachie* • Malcolm McDowell *Ansell* • Henry Woolf *Helicopter pilot* • Christopher Malcolm *Helicopter observer* • Pamela Brown *Widow* • Andrew Bradford *Soldier* ■ *Dir* Joseph Losey • *Scr* Robert Shaw, from the novel by Barry England • *Cinematographer* Henri Alekan

The File of the Golden Goose ★

Crime thriller 1969 · UK · Colour · 109mins

Sam Wanamaker was talented in many fields, but he was not a good film director as this (the first of his five feature outings behind the camera) testifies. Admittedly the ponderous tale of American agent Yul Brynner's pursuit of international counterfeiters is hardly riveting material, but it would be markedly less irksome to watch if it had not been so baldly padded out with uninspired tableaux of the London landscape. This goose is a turkey. TS

Yul Brynner *Peter Novak* • Charles Gray *Nick "the Owl" Harrison* • Edward Woodward *Peter Thompson* • John Barrie *Sloane* ■ *Dir* Sam Wanamaker • *Scr* John C Higgins, James B Gordon, from a story by John C Higgins

The File on Thelma Jordon ★★★

Film noir 1949 · US · BW · 100mins

Barbara Stanwyck is a murder suspect who works her spell on a hapless assistant DA, played to meek perfection by Wendell Corey. He has her acquitted, but discovers her true motives. It's as if Stanwyck had somehow survived *Double Indemnity* and this is what happened after she killed Fred MacMurray. In these thrillers Stanwyck has a terrific, deadly allure and the moody lighting and the music conspire with her, keeping the men fluttering around her like moths to a flame. A second-string *film noir* maybe, but director Robert Siodmak orchestrates it with flair. AT

Barbara Stanwyck *Thelma Jordon* • Wendell Corey *Cleve Marshall* • Paul Kelly (1) *Miles Scott* • Joan Tetzel *Pamela Marshall* • Stanley Ridges *Kingsley Willis* • Richard Rober *Tony Laredo* ■ *Dir* Robert Siodmak • *Scr* Ketti Grings, from a story by Marty Holland

F

La Fille de l'Air ★★ 15

Action drama 1992 · Fr · Colour · 102mins

Béatrice Dalle is devastated when her ex-convict lover (Thierry Fortineau) is arrested and imprisoned for armed robbery. Having served time herself for complicity, she plots to free Fortineau with the help of his brother, a small-time crook. Maroun Bagdadi's film climaxes with a reconstruction of an actual jailbreak that took place in 1980s France, and the action scenes are thrilling. Characterisation is thin on the ground, however. LH. In French with English subtitles.

Béatrice Dalle *Brigitte* • Hippolyte Girardot *Philippe* • Thierry Fortineau *Daniel* • Jean-Claude Dreyfus *Marcel* • Roland Bertin *Mr Lefort* ■ *Dir* Maroun Bagdadi • *Scr* Dan Franck, Florence Quentin, Maroun Bagdadi, from a book by Nadine Vaujour

Film ★★★

Experimental comedy drama 1965 · US · BW · 21mins

Written by playwright Samuel Beckett of *Waiting for Godot* fame, *Film* is notable not only for its ambiguity, but also for bringing Buster Keaton back from semi-retirement. Paring cinema down to its visual essentials, it's a parable of an old man fending off the futility of existence and his own obscurity. It hardly goes out of its way to explain itself but it's good to see Buster back again and wielding unusual silent power. TH

Buster Keaton *O* ■ *Dir* Alan Schneider • *Scr* Samuel Beckett • *Cinematographer* Boris Kaufman

Un Filme Falado ★★★

Drama 2003 · Por/Fr/It · Colour · 96mins

Language may be exclusive, but culture is universal according to Manoel de Oliveira in this engaging guided tour around the Mediterranean. With cinematographer Emmanuel Machuel providing picturesque views of the landmarks between Lisbon and Cairo, Leonor Silveira regales eight-year-old daughter Filipa de Almeida with the myths and mistakes of past civilisations, while casting aspersions on our own age of disposable art and crass celebrity. De Oliveira is less surefooted in the scenes centring on singer Irene Papas, businesswoman Catherine Deneuve and ex-model Stefania Sandrelli, who join captain John Malkovich at his table. DP. In Portuguese, French, Italian, English and Greek with subtitles.

Leonor Silveira *Rosa Maria* • John Malkovich *Captain John Walesa* • Catherine Deneuve *Delfina* • Stefania Sandrelli *Francesca* • Irene Papas *Helena* • Filipa de Almeida *Maria Joana* • Luis Miguel Cintra *Portuguese actor* ■ *Dir/Scr* Manoel de Oliveira

The Filth and the Fury ★★★ 15

Music documentary
2000 · UK/US · Colour · 103mins

Director Julien Temple revisits *The Great Rock 'n' Roll Swindle* for a second look at the band with the gift of the gob: the Sex Pistols. Sidelining self-serving manager Malcolm McLaren, this punk retrospective combines comments from surviving band members with unseen archive footage and TV appearances, including the notorious encounter with Bill Grundy. The result is a more accurate and less sensationalised account of the era of safety-pinned, one-chord wonders. This really is essential viewing for anyone who was there, anyone who wasn't there but wishes they were, and even for anyone who wasn't there and is glad they weren't. DA. Contains swearing, drug abuse and sex scenes. DVD

Dir Julien Temple

Final Analysis ★★ 15

Psychological thriller
1992 · US · Colour · 119mins

With an alluring surface gloss that suggests more than is there, and a plot so clumsy that it regularly trips over itself, it is astonishing that the quality cast is able to salvage anything from the wreckage of this film. Uma Thurman is psychiatrist Richard Gere's patient and Kim Basinger is Thurman's married sister with whom he soon becomes involved. As the twists and turns in the story stretch credibility to breaking point, it's Basinger who brings character and determination to the heart of the film. JM. Contains violence, swearing, nudity. DVD

Richard Gere *Isaac Barr* • Kim Basinger *Heather Evans* • Uma Thurman *Diana Baylor* • Eric Roberts *Jimmy Evans* • Paul Guilfoyle (2) *Mike O'Brien* • Keith David *Detective Huggins* ■ *Dir* Phil Joanou • *Scr* Wesley Strick, from a story by Robert Berger, Wesley Strick

Final Appointment ★★ U

Crime drama 1954 · UK · BW · 65mins

Despite cutting a dash in low-budget fare such as this, John Bentley never quite made it as a movie star. Here he plays a reporter who links a series of killings to a wartime court martial. With help from assistant Eleanor Summerfield, he tracks down the sole surviving officer involved in the trial, but there's a sting in the tail. There was an equally undistinguished sequel. DP

John Bentley *Mike Billings* • Eleanor Summerfield *Jenny Drew* • Hubert Gregg *Hartnell* • Liam Redmond *Inspector Corcoran* • Meredith Edwards *Tom Martin* • Jean Lodge *Laura Robens* • Sam Kydd *Vickery* • Charles Farrell *Percy* • Arthur Lowe *Barratt* ■ *Dir* Terence Fisher • *Scr* Kenneth Hayles, from a story by Sidney Nelson, Maurice Harrison

Final Approach ★ 15

Thriller 1991 · US · Colour · 96mins

This *Twilight Zone*-style science-fiction thriller tries for zest, but lacks any originality. Debut director Eric Steven Stahl emphasises technology over content in this tale of a test pilot, played by the traditionally dour James B Sikking, who is interrogated after an accident involving a top secret plane. The always reliable Hector Elizondo plays the psychiatrist probing his past. Gimmicky and uninvolving, this is notable only for its pioneering use of digital sound. RS

James B Sikking *Colonel Jason J Halsey* • Hector Elizondo *Dr Dio Gottlieb* • Madolyn Smith Osborne [Madolyn Smith] *Casey Halsey* • Kevin McCarthy *General Geller* • Cameo Kneuer *Brooke Halsey* ■ *Dir* Eric Steven Stahl • *Scr* Eric Steven Stahl, Gerald Laurence

Final Chapter – Walking Tall ★ 18

Action crime drama
1977 · US · Colour · 108mins

This is the concluding episode of an unpleasant trilogy of films, based on the real-life exploits of Tennessee sheriff Buford Pusser, energetically wielding his baseball bat in the one-man fight against bad-doers. This was the second outing in the lead for Bo Svenson, who had taken over from Joe Don Baker, and he brings all of his non-star appeal to the role. The clumsy script lurches between cornball schmaltz and hyper-violence. RS

Bo Svenson *Buford Pusser* • Margaret Blye [Maggie Blye] *Luan* • Forrest Tucker *Grandpa Pusser* • Lurene Tuttle *Grandma Pusser* • Morgan Woodward *The Boss* • Leif Garrett *Mike Pusser* ■ *Dir* Jack Starrett • *Scr* Howard B Kreitsek, Samuel A Peeples

Final Combination ★★ 18

Crime thriller 1993 · US · Colour · 89mins

A (failed) bid to turn former British light middleweight boxing champ Gary Stretch into a Hollywood action star, this sometimes unsavoury serial-killer outing also features hard working *Reservoir Dogs* cult actor Michael Madsen as the dogged cop on his trail. Stretch is actually quite menacing as a wandering parcel of psychotic knuckles who has left a trail of pulped faces across the USA. JF. Contains swearing, violence and sex scenes.

Michael Madsen *Det Matt Dickson* • Lisa Bonet *Catherine Briggs* • Gary Stretch *Richard Welton* • Tim Russ *Det Chuck Rowland* • Damian Chapa *Donato* • Carmen Argenziano *Lt Stein* • Eric DaRe *Bouncer* ■ *Dir* Nigel Dick • *Scr* Larry Golin, Jonathan Tydor

The Final Comedown ★★

Blaxploitation thriller
1972 · US · Colour · 83mins

A fairly average slice of blaxploitation, although with a stronger political slant than usual. This stars Billy Dee Williams as a young black man who gets mixed up with a Black Panther style organisation who set out to make their mark in the cosy white middle-class suburbs. The political message is a little muddled and, as is often the case with these Blaxploitation thrillers, the 1970s fashions provide the most entertainment. JF

Billy Dee Williams *Johnny Johnson* • D'Urville Martin *Billy Joe Ashley* • Celia Kaye *Rene Freeman* • Raymond St Jacques *Imir* ■ *Dir/Scr* Oscar Williams

The Final Countdown ★★★ PG

Science-fiction thriller
1980 · US · Colour · 98mins

What would have happened if the Americans possessed modern aircraft carriers and nuclear weapons during the time of the attack on Pearl Harbor? That's the ingenious premise of this absorbing thriller as Kirk Douglas and Martin Sheen sail into a time warp, and have the power to alter history at the touch of a button. Reminiscent of the *Twilight Zone* but on a big budget, the film was given unprecedented access to film aboard the USS *Nimitz*. AT DVD

Kirk Douglas *Captain Matthew Yelland* • Martin Sheen *Warren Lasky* • Katharine Ross *Laurel Scott* • James Farentino *Commander Richard Owens* • Ron O'Neal *Commander Dan Thurman* • Charles Durning *Senator Samuel Chapman* • Victor Mohica *Black Cloud* ■ *Dir* Don Taylor • *Scr* David Ambrose, Gerry Davis, Thomas Hunter, Peter Powell

The Final Curtain ★★★ 15

Black comedy drama
2002 · UK · Colour · 79mins

Director Patrick Harkins, in his debut, occasionally attempts to make too much of an impression in this satire on TV quiz shows, transient celebrity and the ruthlessness of showbusiness. However, Peter O'Toole is in bravura mood as the veteran UK TV presenter whose decision to allow novelist Adrian Lester to pen his biography coincides with a battle to sell the concept of his family-friendly format to an American network in the face of fierce competition from his grotesque rival, Aidan Gillen. Barnstorming, if unsubtle, fun. DP DVD

Peter O'Toole *JJ Curtis* • Adrian Lester *Jonathan Stitch* • Aidan Gillen *Dave Turner* • Julia Sawalha *Karen* • Ralph Brown *Timothy* • Henry Goodman • Patrick Malahide • Ian McNeice ■ *Dir* Patrick Harkins • *Scr* John Hodge

The Final Cut ★★ 18

Action thriller 1995 · US · Colour · 95mins

The Keanu Reeves hit *Speed* sparked a brief craze for mad bomber movies, including this watchable straight-to-video thriller. Sam Elliott plays a former bomb disposal expert called in to find out who is blowing up members of his old squad, only to find himself becoming the prime suspect. The explosive set pieces are spectacular enough, though the plotting won't exactly tax the brain. JF DVD

Sam Elliott *John Pierce* • Amanda Plummer *Rothstein* • John Hannah *Gilmore* • Matt Craven *Lloyd* • Charles Martin Smith *Captain Weldon Mamet* • Anne Ramsay *Sergeant Kathleen Hardy* ■ *Dir* Roger Christian • *Scr* Raul Inglis, from a story by Crash Leyland

Final Cut ★ 18

Drama 1998 · UK · Colour · 90mins

This mock-docudrama was released, tellingly, at the height of "Cool Britannia", when a homegrown product, from pop to art, was greeted with exaggerated fanfare. Jude Law, then-spouse Sadie Frost and a bunch of stage schoolmates play themselves in a sleazy, North London-set chamber piece about backstabbing, drug-taking and deceit among a group of stage schoolmates. The material is thin (Law is dead, leaving a videotape that exposes the gang's double-dealing at a wake) and the net result is like watching someone else's home movie. AC. Contains swearing. DVD

Ray Winstone *Ray* • Jude Law *Jude* • Sadie Frost *Sadie* • Holly Davidson *Holly* • John Beckett *John* • Mark Burdis *Mark* • Perry Benson *Tony* • Lisa Marsh *Lisa* ■ *Dir/Scr* Ray Burdis, Dominic Anciano

The Final Cut ★★ 15

Futuristic science-fiction thriller
2004 · Can/US/Ger · Colour · 90mins

Robin Williams delivers here another performance of subtle understatement. He plays a "cutter", whose job is to splice together the memories of the recently deceased into a visual tribute of the dead person's life. However, an assignment to work on the life of one of the key executives involved in the controversial memory technology not only attracts the attention of opponents of the process – led by former cutter Jim Caviezel – but reawakens some buried secrets of his own. Omar Naim never really exploits the premise's full potential and this runs out of steam. JF. Contains violence, swearing and sexual references.

Robin Williams *Alan Hackman* • Mira Sorvino *Delila* • Mimi Kuzyk *Thelma* • Thom Bishops *Hasan* • Jim Caviezel *Fletcher* • Brendan Fletcher *Michael* • Vincent Gale *Simon* ■ *Dir/Scr* Omar Naim

The Final Days ★★★★ U

Historical drama
1989 · US · Colour · 144mins

Fans of Oliver Stone's *Nixon* can enjoy another portrayal of the flawed president in this drama originally shown on US television. This time it's veteran character actor Lane Smith playing Richard Nixon, from Watergate through to resignation disgrace, with Richard Kiley as Special White House Counsel and Theodore Bikel as Henry Kissinger. Directed by Richard Pearce with a real feel for gathering tension, this was based on Bob Woodward and Carl Bernstein's book, *All the President's Men*. TH DVD

Lane Smith *Richard Nixon* • Richard Kiley *J Fred Buzhardt* • David Ogden Stiers *General Alexander Haig* • Ed Flanders *Leonard Garment* • Theodore Bikel *Henry Kissinger* ■ *Dir* Richard Pearce • *Scr* Hugh Whitemore, from a book by Bob Woodward, Carl Bernstein

Final Destination ★★★ 15

Horror thriller 2000 · US · Colour · 93mins

The X-Files veteran James Wong makes his feature debut with this entertaining thriller, in which the principals are named after movie horror legends. It's as if the teen slasher and the disaster flick had met in the *Twilight Zone*, as Devon Sawa's premonition of a midair disaster comes explosively true and Death begins to stalk those who escaped thanks to Sawa's timely intervention. The premise is flawed and the exposition clumsy, but the methods of demise are as hilarious as they're ingenious. DP. Contains violence, swearing. DVD

Devon Sawa *Alex Browning* • Ali Larter *Clear Rivers* • Kerr Smith *Carter Horton* • Kristen Cloke *Valerie Lewton* • Seann William Scott *Billy Hitchcock* • Chad E Donella *Tod Waggner* • Amanda Detmer *Terry Chaney* ■ *Dir* James Wong • *Scr* Glen Morgan, James Wong, Jeffrey Reddick, Lara Fox, from a story by Jeffrey Reddick

Final Destination 2 ★★★ 15

Horror thriller 2002 · US · Colour · 86mins

David R Ellis directs this effective sequel to the sleeper hit. This time around it's perturbed teenager AJ Cook who prompts Death to resume his stalking, after her premonitions save her and a group of motorists from a freeway pile-up. While the film is no more sophisticated than the original, Ellis's skilful manipulation of horror conventions demonstrates a thorough understanding of the genre. A tense mix of innovative gore sequences and irony-laden dialogue, this is an over-the-top thrill-ride with no pretensions. SF DVD

Ali Larter *Clear Rivers* • AJ Cook *Kimberly Corman* • Michael Landes *Officer Thomas Burke* • Terrence "T C" Carson *Eugene Dix* • Jonathan Cherry *Rory* • Keegan Connor Tracy *Kat* • Sarah Carter *Shaina* • Lynda Boyd *Nora Carpenter* ■ *Dir* David R Ellis • *Scr* J Mackye Gruber, Eric Bress, from a story by J Mackye Gruber, Eric Bress, Jeffrey Reddick, from characters created by Jeffrey Reddick

Final Fantasy: the Spirits Within ★★★ PG

Animated science-fiction adventure
2001 · Jpn/US · Colour · 101mins

Japan's long-running computer-game franchise provides the bare, thematic bones for this 100-per-cent computer-animated movie. The film follows the quest of brilliant young scientist Dr Aki Ross (voiced by *ER's* Ming-Na) to find a peaceful end to the ongoing war between mankind and invading "phantoms" in 2065. The story is simple sci-fi stuff, but it's strong and intelligent enough to prevent this being merely an expensive ($140 million) exhibition match for the US-Japanese animators. That said, it's a truly state-of-the-art display although there is a rubbery quality to the human characters. AC [VIDEO] DVD

Ming-Na *Dr Aki Ross* • Alec Baldwin *Capt Gray Edwards* • Ving Rhames *Ryan* • Steve Buscemi *Neil* • Peri Gilpin *Jane* • Donald Sutherland *Dr Sid* • James Woods *General Hein* • Keith David *Council member* • Jean Simmons *Council member* ■ *Dir* Hironobu Sakaguchi, Motonori Sakakibara • *Scr* Al Reinert, Jeff Vintar, from a story by Hironobu Sakaguchi

Final Mission ★★ 15

Action thriller 1993 · US · Colour · 87mins

This straight-to-video thriller comes up with some nice spins on the *Top Gun* formula. The setting is a secret defence project where a group of crack flyers is undergoing a secret virtual reality programme. When some of his fellow pilots start to crack up, Billy Wirth suspects a conspiracy. There are good turns from Corbin Bernsen and Steve Railsback, but budgetary constraints mean that a lot of the ideas aren't fully realised. JF [VIDEO] DVD

Billy Wirth *Tom Waters* • Corbin Bernsen *General Breslaw* • Elizabeth Gracen *Caitlin Cole* • Steve Railsback *Colonel Anderson* ■ *Dir* Lee Redmond • *Scr* Sam Montgomery, Lee Richmond, Ernst Sheldon Jr

The Final Programme ★★

Science-fiction fantasy
1973 · UK · Colour · 83mins

The sight of the misshapen messiah will certainly send shudders down the spine of those who have stuck with the stylised imagery and apocalyptic incidents that comprise this baffling adaptation of one of Michael Moorcock's "Jerry Cornelius" stories. Patrick Magee, Graham Crowden and George Coulouris make fearsome adversaries, but Jon Finch's bid to save both his sister and the planet are confounded by director Robert Fuest's preoccupation with look over logic. DP

Jon Finch *Jerry Cornelius* • Jenny Runacre *Miss Brunner* • Hugh Griffith *Professor Hira* • Patrick Magee *Dr Baxter* • Sterling Hayden *Major Wrongway Lindbergh* • Graham Crowden *Dr Smiles* • George Coulouris *Dr Powys* ■ *Dir* Robert Fuest • *Scr* Robert Fuest, from the novel by Michael Moorcock

The Final Test ★★★ U

Comedy 1953 · UK · BW · 87mins

Inspired by Don Bradman's famous second-ball dismissal in his final Test match, this charming film was adapted by Terence Rattigan from his own TV play. Jack Warner gives a no-nonsense performance as the old pro, only to be totally outplayed by Robert Morley as the poet who'd give anything to be a cricketer (much to the bewilderment of Warner's pretentious son, Ray Jackson). Anthony Asquith directs with a straight bat, producing a picture that is as quintessentially English as *Test Match Special*. Cricketing legends including Len Hutton, Denis Compton and Alec Bedser have cameos. DP [VIDEO]

Jack Warner *Sam Palmer* • Robert Morley *Alexander Whitehead* • Brenda Bruce *Cora* • Ray Jackson *Reggie Palmer* • George Relph *Syd Thompson* • Adrianne Allen *Aunt Ethel* • Len Hutton *Frank Jarvis* • Denis Compton • Alec Bedser ■ *Dir* Anthony Asquith • *Scr* Terence Rattigan, from his TV play

Find the Lady ★ U

Crime thriller 1956 · UK · BW · 56mins

Former editor Charles Saunders never really established himself behind the camera and was saddled with too many bargain-basement B-movies such as this one. Released a year after *The Ladykillers*, this is a straight variation on the theme of a gang of crooks holing up in an elderly woman's home. Lacking in suspense and played without a hint of naturalism, this thriller does at least have the advantage of being mercifully brief. DP

Donald Houston *Bill* • Beverley Brooks *June* • Mervyn Johns *Mr Hurst* • Kay Callard *Rita* • Maurice Kaufmann *Nicky* ■ *Dir* Charles Saunders • *Scr* Kenneth R Hayles, from a story by Paul Erickson, Dermot Palmer

Find the Lady ★ PG

Comedy 1976 · Can/UK · Colour · 85mins

Hardly a film to boost the reputation of British or Canadian movie-making, this politically incorrect comedy is packed with the kind of raucous humour that rocks pubs towards last orders. John Candy and Lawrence Dane star as incompetent cops stomping their way through the upper classes in search of a missing socialite. DP [VIDEO]

Lawrence Dane *Detective Sergeant Roscoe Broom* • John Candy *Officer Kopek* • Mickey Rooney *Trigger* • Dick Emery *Leo-Hugo* • Peter Cook *JK Lewenhak* • Alexandra Bastedo *Victoria* ■ *Dir* John Trent • *Scr* Kenneth R Hughes

Finders Keepers ★ U

Musical comedy 1966 · UK · Colour · 85mins

Five years after they made *The Young Ones*, Cliff Richard and Robert Morley were reunited for this dismal romp that, more significantly, marked the end of Cliff's screen collaboration with The Shadows. Written by Michael Pertwee, the story of a clean-cut combo who find an American atom bomb off the Spanish coast is too ridiculous to contemplate and, for once, Cliff doesn't have any decent songs to distract us from its shortcomings. DP [VIDEO]

Cliff Richard *Cliff* • Robert Morley *Colonel Roberts* • Bruce Welch • Hank Marvin *Hank Marvin* • Brian Bennett • John Rostill • John Le Mesurier *Mr X* ■ *Dir* Sidney Hayers • *Scr* Michael Pertwee, from a story by George H Brown • *Music/lyrics* The Shadows

Finders Keepers ★ 15

Comedy 1984 · US · Colour · 91mins

A deeply depressing blip on Richard Lester's directorial career, this is a misguided, laugh-free comedy caper. Lightweights Michael O'Keefe and Beverly D'Angelo find themselves caught in an increasingly hysterical chase for a fortune hidden in a coffin. Pamela Stephenson is among those who bravely hide their embarrassment. Notable mainly for an early film appearance by Jim Carrey. JF [VIDEO]

Michael O'Keefe *Michael Rangeloff* • Beverly D'Angelo *Standish Logan* • Pamela Stephenson *Georgiana Latimer* • Louis Gossett Jr *Century* • Ed Lauter *Josef Sirola* • Jim Carrey *Lane Biddlecoff* ■ *Dir* Richard Lester • *Scr* Ronny Graham, Terence Marsh, Charles Dennis, from the novel *The Next to Last Train Ride* by Charles Dennis

Finders Keepers, Lovers Weepers ★★ 18

Crime drama 1968 · US · Colour · 71mins

This uncharacteristic crime drama from soft-core sex director Russ Meyer has too much moralising and a crueller edge than normal. Sleazy topless nightclub owner Paul Lockwood, his unfaithful wife and her bartender lover are held captive by two burglars employed by the tough brothel madam he's seeing on the sly. Sadly, Meyer's psychodrama has little of his trademark titillation, sexual satire or broad humour. AJ. Contains nudity. [VIDEO]

Anne Chapman *Kelly* • Paul Lockwood *Paul Lockwood, actor* • Gordon Wescourt *Ray* • Duncan McLeod *Cal* • Robert Rudelson *Feeny* • Lavelle Roby *Claire* • Jan Sinclair *Christiana* • Joey Duprez *Joy* • Nick Wolcuff *Nick* ■ *Dir* Russ Meyer • *Scr* Richard Zachary, from a story by Russ Meyer

Finding Forrester ★★★ 12

Drama 2000 · US/Can · Colour · 130mins

Sean Connery stars in this Gus Van Sant-directed drama about literary aspirations. Connery (who also co-produced) plays an elderly, reclusive writer, a JD Salinger-like figure seemingly crippled by the success of his first novel. Living in the Bronx he befriends black teenager Robert Brown, a basketball ace with a brilliant literary streak, forced to downplay his intelligence. An unlikely friendship grows, as Forrester recognises and nurtures this talent – despite opposition from F Murray Abraham's malicious professor. This film has a mood and tempo that transcend manipulated cosiness. TH [VIDEO] DVD

Sean Connery *William Forrester* • Rob Brown *Jamal Wallace* • F Murray Abraham *Professor Crawford* • Anna Paquin *Claire Spence* • Busta Rhymes *Terrell* • April Grace *Ms Joyce* • Michael Pitt *Coleridge* • Michael Nouri *Dr Spence* ■ *Dir* Gus Van Sant • *Scr* Mike Rich

Finding Graceland ★★ PG

Road movie 1999 · US · Colour · 92mins

Depressed following the death of his wife, Johnathon Schaech takes to the road in his beaten-up car and picks up Harvey Keitel who insists he's the real Elvis. So do most of the awe-struck people they encounter on the road to Graceland in a whimsical saga about finding oneself and being true to your own feelings. Religious metaphor and *Blue Suede Shoes* nostalgia make for an uneasy mix and it does teeter on the edge of open-mouthed stupidity. But Elvis fans will love it, and Bridget Fonda is wonderful as a Marilyn Monroe impersonator. AJ DVD

Harvey Keitel *Elvis* • Bridget Fonda *Ashley* • Johnathon Schaech *Byron Gruman* • Gretchen Mol *Beatrice Gruman* • David Stewart *Purvis* ■ *Dir* David Winkler • *Scr* Jason Horwitch, from a story by David Winkler, Jason Horwitch

Finding Nemo ★★★★ U

Animated comedy adventure
2003 · US · Colour · 96mins

This computer-generated animated feature is a rainbow-hued delight, overflowing with innovation and vitality. Australia's Great Barrier Reef provides a stunning starting point for this aquatic fable, as single-parent clown fish Marlin (voiced by Albert Brooks) sees his beloved only son, Nemo, netted by a scuba diver. From then on, it's a non-stop journey of visual excitement, as the distraught father sets off to rescue his offspring, encountering a host of colourful characters along the way. The voice casting is inspired, with Willem Dafoe, Geoffrey Rush and Eric Bana among those contributing supplementary texture to this marvellous sensory experience. SF [VIDEO] DVD

Albert Brooks *Marlin* • Ellen DeGeneres *Dory* • Alexander Gould *Nemo* • Willem Dafoe *Gill* • Geoffrey Rush *Nigel* • Barry Humphries *Bruce* • Austin Pendleton *Gurgle* • John Ratzenberger *Fish school voice* • Allison Janney *Peach* • Eric Bana *Anchor* ■ *Dir* Andrew Stanton, Lee Unkrich • *Scr* Andrew Stanton, Bob Peterson, David Reynolds, from a story by Andrew Stanton

Finding Neverland ★★★★ PG

Period drama based on a true story
2004 · US · Colour · 96mins

Fantasy and reality combine to magical effect in this deeply affecting and beautifully crafted account of the creation and evolution of the children's classic *Peter Pan*. A perfectly cast Johnny Depp portrays the young-at-heart Scottish playwright J M Barrie, whose career is reinvigorated when he befriends the four fatherless Llewelyn Davies boys and their recently widowed mother Sylvia (Kate Winslet). Depp is magnificent, alternating between playful and sensitive as the joys and tragedies of this inspirational relationship unfold. It's a performance of genuine emotion, superbly complemented by Winslet's tender turn. SF [VIDEO] DVD

Johnny Depp *Sir James Matthew Barrie* • Kate Winslet *Sylvia Llewelyn Davies* • Julie Christie *Mrs Emma du Maurier* • Radha Mitchell *Mary Ansell Barrie* • Dustin Hoffman *Charles Frohman* • Kelly Macdonald *"Peter Pan"* • Ian Hart *Sir Arthur Conan Doyle* • Eileen Essell *Mrs Snow* • Paul Whitehouse *Stage manager* • Freddie Highmore *Peter Llewelyn Davies* ■ *Dir* Marc Forster • *Scr* David Magee, from the play *The Man Who Was Peter Pan* by Allan Knee

Finding North ★★★ 15

Road movie 1997 · US · Colour · 90mins

Tanya Wexler's feature debut takes an off-the-beaten-track approach to the road movie. Mixing gentle character comedy with life-affirming revelation, it features John Benjamin Hickey as a man with a mission – a Texan quest set by his dead lover – who is joined by Wendy Makkena as a just-sacked, 30-something Brooklynite desperate to escape the clutches of her shrewish Jewish mother. Played to the pleasingly melancholic strains of a country soundtrack, the film tackles the Aids issue with sensitivity and avoids unnecessary sentimentality. But the central relationship feels forced, with the sparky Makkena getting too little response from Hickey's self-pitying stuffed shirt. DP. Contains swearing. [VIDEO] DVD

Wendy Makkena *Rhonda Portelli* • John Benjamin Hickey *Travis Furlong* • Anne Bobby *Debi* • Rebecca Creskoff *Gina* • Angela Pietropinto *Mama Portelli* ■ *Dir* Tanya Wexler • *Scr* Kim Powers

A Fine Madness ★★★

Black comedy 1966 · US · Colour · 105mins

This is probably the darkest screwball comedy ever made and it undoubtedly would have been bleaker still if studio boss Jack Warner hadn't demanded last-minute changes. Sean Connery gives a most vigorous performance as a poet devoid of inspiration and driven to distraction by the women in his life. Often painfully funny, but it's pretty misogynistic, with Joanne Woodward and Jean Seberg doing well with a script that has no time for them. DP

Sean Connery *Samson Shillitoe* • Joanne Woodward *Rhoda Shillitoe* • Jean Seberg *Lydia West* • Patrick O'Neal *Dr Oliver West* • Colleen Dewhurst *Dr Vera Kropotkin* • Clive Revill *Dr Menken* ■ *Dir* Irvin Kershner • *Scr* Elliot Baker, from his novel

A Fine Mess ★ PG

Comedy 1986 · US · Colour · 86mins

Had Blake Edwards swapped the word "hideous" for "fine", he would have been nearer the mark. Ted Danson hits an all-time career low as an actor who stumbles upon a plot to dope a horse before the big race, only to find himself hurtling around Los Angeles in some of the most shambolic chase sequences you've ever seen. Worse still are villains Richard Mulligan and Stuart

F

Margolin, whose unrestrained mugging is embarrassing to watch. DP

Ted Danson *Spence Holden* • Howie Mandel *Dennis Powell* • Richard Mulligan *Wayne "Turnip" Farragalla* • Stuart Margolin *Maurice "Binky" Dzundza* • Maria Conchita Alonso *Claudia Pazzo* • Jennifer Edwards *Ellen Frankenthaler* • Paul Sorvino *Tony Pazzo* • Dennis Franz *Phil* ■ *Dir/Scr* Blake Edwards

A Fine Pair ★

Crime comedy drama
1968 · It · Colour · 89mins

Director Francesco Maselli never comes to terms with the tone or the pacing of this crass crime caper. The basic premise is sound enough, with Claudia Cardinale suckering New York cop Rock Hudson into "returning" the priceless jewels that a thief of her acquaintance has stolen from an Austrian villa. Hudson looks bored and the romantic by-play between the leads is tiresome. DP. Italian dialogue dubbed into English.

Rock Hudson *Captain Mike Harmon* • Claudia Cardinale *Esmeralda Marini* • Tomas Milian *Roger* • Leon Askin *Chief Wellman* ■ *Dir* Francesco Maselli • *Scr* Francesco Maselli, Luisa Montagnana, Larry Gelbart, Virgil C Leone, from a story by Luisa Montagnana

The Finest Hour ★★ 15

War action thriller
1991 · US · Colour · 100mins

Before Rob Lowe discovered there was more fun to be had in sending up his smoothie image than in playing it straight, he found himself relegated to straight-to-video fare such as this tired thriller. He plays a cocky young SEAL recruit who falls out with his best buddy Gale Hansen over a girl, in between fighting the Iraqis. Melanie Griffith's less famous half-sister Tracy pops up in support, but pretty locations fail to compensate for the hackneyed script. JF. Contains swearing, violence and brief nudity.

Rob Lowe *Hammer* • Gale Hansen *Dean* • Tracy Griffith *Barbara* • Eb Lottimer *Bosco* • Baruch Dror *Greenspan* • Daniel Dieker *Albie* • Michael Fountain *Carter* ■ *Dir* Shimon Dotan • *Scr* Shimon Dotan, Stuart Schoffman

The Finger Points ★★

Crime drama 1931 · US · BW · 87mins

Richard Barthelmess stars as a low-paid newspaper reporter who compromises his integrity by allowing gang leaders to buy his silence. Like the curate's egg, this low-key crime drama is good in parts. Fay Wray is the girl who attempts to get Barthelmess to mend his ways, Clark Gable appears as a gangster, and John Francis Dillon directs competently enough. RK

Richard Barthelmess *Breckenridge Lee* • Fay Wray *Marcia Collins* • Regis Toomey *Charlie "Breezy" Russell* • Clark Gable *Louis Blanco* • Robert Elliott *City editor* ■ *Dir* John Francis Dillon • *Scr* Robert Lord, from a story by John Monk Saunders, WR Burnett

Fingers ★★★★ 18

Psychological drama
1978 · US · Colour · 89mins

James Toback's directorial debut is a strangely erotic and ominously threatening drama about a concert pianist who also collects debts for the Mob. The edgy direction and Harvey Keitel's compelling performance caught the attention of several major critics, including David Thomson and Pauline Kael, but the film did not find an audience. Toback is undeniably talented, but wayward, and his career has never really got going, but as studio-financed oddities go, this one is unmissable. AT

Harvey Keitel *Jimmy Angelelli* • Tisa Farrow *Carol* • Jim Brown *Deems* • Michael V Gazzo *Ben Angelelli* • Marian Seldes *Mother* • Carole Francis *Christa* • Georgette Muir *Anita* • Danny Aiello *Butch* ■ *Dir/Scr* James Toback

Fingers at the Window ★

Horror mystery 1942 · US · BW · 80mins

Mad, bad Basil Rathbone impersonates the head of an asylum and hypnotises the inmates to carry out a string of axe murders. Actor Lew Ayres and his girlfriend Laraine Day (stars of the popular *Dr Kildare* series at the time) follow the trail of the "Robot Murders" (as the posters hyped it) and bring Rathbone to justice. A very dated chiller, weakly directed, with a cast acting as if they were all indeed under hypnosis! AJ

Lew Ayres *Oliver Duffy* • Laraine Day *Edwina Brown* • Basil Rathbone *Dr H Santelle* • Walter Kingsford *Dr Cromwell* • Miles Mander *Dr Kurt Immelman* ■ *Dir* Charles Lederer • *Scr* Rose Caylor, Lawrence P Bachmann, from a story by Rose Caylor

Finian's Rainbow ★★★ U

Musical 1968 · US · Colour · 180mins

Although it ran for 725 performances on Broadway, it's tempting to suggest that the reason this satirical musical took 21 years to make it to the screen was because studio executives recognised that its magic worked best on the stage. Even old hands would have struggled to balance the whimsical story of a leprechaun searching for his stolen gold with sharp insights into racism and greed. Directing his first film for a major studio, Francis Ford Coppola fumbles both fantasy and sermon. However, Fred Astaire is as watchable as ever. DP DVD

Fred Astaire *Finian McLonergan* • Petula Clark *Sharon McLonergan* • Tommy Steele *Og* • Don Francks *Woody* • Barbara Hancock *Susan the Silent* • Keenan Wynn *Judge Billboard Rawkins* ■ *Dir* Francis Ford Coppola • *Scr* EY Harburg, Fred Saidy, from their play

Finishing School ★★

Drama 1934 · US · BW · 70mins

Frances Dee has the leading role of the pupil at an exclusive girls' school who becomes pregnant, but most interest in this drama now resides in a perky performance by Ginger Rogers. She plays Dee's madcap roommate dispensing the wisecracks, and Billie Burke also has fun as Dee's selfish mother. RKO made the film a test of new directorial talent by teaming one of the film's writers, Wanda Tuchock, with an editor, George Nichols Jr. Only Nichols continued directing. AE

Frances Dee *Virginia Radcliff* • Billie Burke *Mrs Radcliff* • Ginger Rogers *Pony* • Bruce Cabot *MacFarland* • John Halliday *Mr Radcliff* • Beulah Bondi *Miss Van Alstyn* ■ *Dir* Wanda Tuchock, George Nichols Jr • *Scr* Wanda Tuchock, Laird Doyle, from a story by David Hempstead, from the play *These Days* by Katherine Clugston

Fiorile ★★★★ 12

Drama 1993 · It/Fr/Ger · Colour · 113mins

Tracing an ancestral curse over 200 years, the three stories in this elegant outing possess all the passion and wonderment we've come to expect from the Taviani brothers. Related by a father to his children as they visit their grandfather, the accounts are neatly woven into the journey and punctuated by the kids' increasingly anxious questions. With the cast playing multiple roles, the action has a neorealist feel in spite of the period opulence, most evident in the Napoleonic episode. Magisterial film-making from one of cinema's most accomplished storytelling duos. DP. In Italian with English subtitles.

Claudio Bigagli *Corrado/Alessandro* • Galatea Ranzi *Elisabetta/Elisa* • Michael Vartan *Jean/Massimo* • Lino Capolicchio *Luigi* • Constanze Engelbrecht *Juliette* • Athina Cenci *Gina* ■ *Dir* Paolo Taviani, Vittorio Taviani • *Scr* Paolo Taviani, Vittorio Taviani, Sandro Petraglia, from a story by Paolo Taviani, Vittorio Taviani

Fire ★★★★ 15

Drama 1996 · Can/Ind · Colour · 107mins

Parodying the traditions of the traditional masala melodrama and opening Deepa Mehta's controversial "elements" trilogy, this was one of the first Indian films to depict adultery, pornography, masturbation and lesbianism. Deprived of love in a patriarchal society, Shabana Azmi succumbs to the advances of her equally neglected sister-in-law, Nandita Das. With the exception of Ranjit Chowdhry's embittered servant, the males are rather crudely caricatured, but the female leads exhibit a courage that matches Mehta's bold discussion of such themes as arranged marriage, sexual emancipation, spiritual enslavement and disappointed ambition. DP. Contains swearing and some sex scenes.

Shabana Azmi *Radha* • Nandita Das *Sita* • Kulbhushan Kharbanda *Ashok* • Jaaved Jaaferi *Jatin* • Ranjit Chowdhry *Mundu* • Kushal Rekhi *Biji* ■ *Dir/Scr* Deepa Mehta

Fire and Ice ★★ PG

Political thriller 1962 · Fr · BW · 100mins

This unremarkable story of jealousy and political zealotry offers passing insights into the concerns of the day, but now seems almost ridiculously earnest. Full of the kind of brooding, meaningful conversations seized upon by the detractors of art house cinema, it makes too little of the doomed romantic triangle that is formed when activist Jean-Louis Trintignant leaves his actress wife Romy Schneider in the care of liberal Henri Serre while he plots the assassination of a politician. DP. French dialogue dubbed into English. DVD

Romy Schneider *Anne* • Jean-Louis Trintignant *Clément* • Henri Serre *Paul* • Diana Lepvrier *Cécile* • Pierre Asso *Serge* • Jacques Berlioz *Le Père* • Armand Meffre *André* • Clara Tambour *Marthe* ■ *Dir/Scr* Alain Cavalier

Fire and Ice ★★ PG

Animated fantasy 1983 · US · Colour · 78mins

Ralph Bakshi teams with legendary fantasy artist Frank Frazetta and comic-book masters Roy Thomas and Gerry Conway for this showdown between good and evil set in mystical prehistoric times. With the figures being Rotoscoped (traced on to celluloid from live-action footage), the animation has a realistic feel. DP DVD

Susan Tyrrell *Juliana* • Maggie Roswell *Teegra* • William Ostrander *Taro/Larn* • Stephen Mendel *Nekron* • Clare Nono *Tutor* • Alan Koss *Envoy* • Hans Howes *Defender Captain* ■ *Dir* Ralph Bakshi • *Scr* Roy Thomas, Gerry Conway, from a story and characters created by Ralph Bakshi, Frank Frazetta

Fire Down Below ★★

Romantic adventure
1957 · UK · Colour · 115mins

Corny, only vaguely watchable melodrama, with Jack Lemmon and Robert Mitchum as smuggling partners who fall out over Rita Hayworth. Hayworth is on board Mitchum's ship, trying to get to the West Indies so she can get a passport, when the boat catches fire, creating much back-projected action. The film wastes its top-rank cast and was shot in Britain on a tiny budget by producers "Cubby" Broccoli and Irving Allen. AT

Rita Hayworth *Irena* • Jack Lemmon *Tony* • Robert Mitchum *Felix* • Herbert Lom *Harbour master* • Bonar Colleano *Lt Sellers* • Anthony Newley *Miguel* ■ *Dir* Robert Parrish • *Scr* Irwin Shaw, from a novel by Max Catto

Fire Down Below ★★ 18

Action adventure
1997 · US · Colour · 100mins

Steven Seagal proves he is no tree-hugging peacenik in this eco-thriller. Joined by Harry Dean Stanton and a grizzled Kris Kristofferson in a tale of environmental mayhem in rural Tennessee, he plays a federal agent on a twin mission to track down the killer of a colleague and destroy the industrialist who has been poisoning the local water supply. As usual Seagal's fists and boots do most of the talking, but fans will enjoy an unexpected treat as he warbles a folk song over the credits. JF. Contains swearing and violence. DVD

Steven Seagal *Jack Taggart* • Marg Helgenberger *Sarah Kellogg* • Stephen Lang *Earl* • Brad Hunt *Orin Jr* • Kris Kristofferson *Orin Sr* • Harry Dean Stanton *Cotton* ■ *Dir* Felix Enriquez Alcala • *Scr* Jeb Stuart, Philip Morton, from a story by Jeb Stuart

A Fire Has Been Arranged ★★ U

Comedy 1935 · UK · BW · 66mins

Bud Flanagan and Chesney Allen are on leave from most of the Crazy Gang, playing former convicts who go back to retrieve their plunder only to find that it's now covered by a building. The film's title suggests their possible solution to this problem. As comedy it relies too much on Flanagan and Allen's very fragile star-quality, though it does contain a "turn" by the magnificent Robb Wilton. TH DVD

Bud Flanagan *Bud* • Chesney Allen *Ches* • Mary Lawson *Betty* • Robb Wilton *Oswald* • Harold French *Toby* • Alastair Sim *Cutte* ■ *Dir* Leslie Hiscott • *Scr* H Fowler Mear, Michael Barringer, from a story by H Fowler Mear, James Carter

Fire, Ice and Dynamite ★★ PG

Action drama
1990 · W Ger · Colour · 101mins

Having turned in his Walther PPK after 1985's *A View to a Kill*, Roger Moore found himself back in Bond territory – but only in terms of the daft plot and emphasis on stunts. Moore plays a wealthy man who fakes his own death and sets up an elaborate series of Olympic-type sports contests pitting his stepchildren against his creditors. The winners will get their hands on his fortune. This harmless time-waster is worth catching only for the stunning ski set pieces and for Moore's famous charm. RS DVD

Roger Moore *Sir George/McVay* • Connie de Groot *Lucy* • Geoffrey Moore *Dudley* • Simon Shepherd *Alexander* • Shari Belafonte-Harper [Shari Belafonte] *Serena* • Uwe Ochsenknecht *Victor* • Isaac Hayed ■ *Dir* Willy Bogner • *Scr* Tony Williamson, Willy Bogner

Fire in the Sky ★★★ 15

Science-fiction drama
1993 · US · Colour · 104mins

A small-town lumberjack vanishes in the woods and his colleagues claim he was kidnapped by aliens. Problem is, the investigating officer here is sceptical James Garner and he suspects foul play. Director Robert Lieberman wisely concentrates on the emotional impact of the event on a close-knit circle of friends and family, although the eventual revelation of the abduction is genuinely scary. DB Sweeney shines in the lead role, although old pro Garner effortlessly steals every scene. JF. Contains some swearing. DVD

DB Sweeney *Travis Walton* • Robert Patrick *Mike Rogers* • Craig Sheffer *Allan Dallis* • Peter Berg *David Whitlock* • Henry Thomas *Greg Hayes* • Bradley Gregg *Bobby Cogdill* • James Garner *Lieutenant Frank Watters* ■ *Dir* Robert Lieberman • *Scr* Tracy Tormé, from the book *The Walton Experience* by Travis Walton

Fire Maidens from Outer Space ★ U

Science fiction 1956 · UK · BW · 79mins

Life is such a trial for the female lost civilisation of Atlantis, stranded on the 13th moon of Jupiter. They wear bathing suits with little skirts, lie around in flames all day for extra energy, perform dances to Borodin's music and fight a lumpy-faced creature in ill-fitting tights. Bottom-of-the-barrel lunatic nonsense. AJ

Anthony Dexter *Luther Blair* • Susan Shaw *Hestia* • Paul Carpenter *Larson* • Harry Fowler *Sydney Stanhope* • Jacqueline Curtiss *Duessa* • Sidney Tafler [Sydney Tafler] *Dr Higgins* ■ *Dir/Scr* Cy Roth

Fire over England ★★★★ U

Historical adventure 1937 · UK · BW · 91mins

This spectacular adventure, set in the Elizabethan past, is memorable not just for early sword- and word-play by Laurence Olivier, but for its political context – it's a call to arms against the growing forces of Nazism in Europe. Olivier is the young nobleman seeking revenge for the death of his father at the hands of the Spanish Inquisition, and warning Queen Elizabeth (Flora Robson) about the imminent Armada invasion. Raymond Massey sneers a lot as Philip II of Spain, while director William K Howard's lavish production design works hard to divert attention from uneven dialogue matched to fervent jingoism. Great fun, though. TH

Flora Robson *Queen Elizabeth* • Raymond Massey *Philip of Spain* • Leslie Banks *Leicester* • Laurence Olivier *Michael Ingolby* • Vivien Leigh *Cynthia* • Morton Selten *Burleigh* • Tamara Desni *Elena* • Lyn Harding *Sir Richard Ingolby* • James Mason *Hillary Vane* ■ *Dir* William K Howard • *Scr* Clemence Dane, Sergei Nolbandov, from a novel by AEW Mason • *Photography* James Wong Howe • *Costume Design* Rene Hubert

Fire Sale ★★

Comedy 1977 · US · Colour · 88mins

Alan Arkin's second outing as a feature director is a wild farce that most contemporary critics denounced as distasteful. It's certainly on the dark side, with basketball coach Arkin adopting a troublesome black kid solely to secure him for his under-achieving team; meanwhile his brother Rob Reiner persuades crazed uncle Sid Caesar to torch the family department store by convincing him it's a Nazi stronghold. Arkin labours over too many misfiring gags and this clumsy comedy refuses to catch light. DP

Alan Arkin *Ezra Fikus* • Rob Reiner *Russel Fikus* • Vincent Gardenia *Benny Fikus* • Anjanette Comer *Marion Fikus* • Barbara Dana *Virginia* • Sid Caesar *Sherman* ■ *Dir* Alan Arkin • *Scr* Robert Klane, from his novel

Fire with Fire ★★ 15

Romantic drama 1986 · US · Colour · 99mins

This dull tale of teenage angst is not as salacious as it first sounds. Prim Virginia Madsen's hormones go into overdrive when she catches sight of mean and moody junior convict Craig Sheffer, much to the disapproval of all those around her. Madsen and Sheffer do their best with the clichéd material and there's good support from Jon Polito, but the story has been better told elsewhere. JF

Virginia Madsen *Lisa Taylor* • Craig Sheffer *Joe Fisk* • Jon Polito *Boss* • Jeffrey Jay Cohen [JJ Cohen] *Mapmaker* • Kate Reid *Sister Victoria* • Jean Smart *Sister Marie* ■ *Dir* Duncan Gibbins • *Scr* Bill Phillips, Warren Skaaren, Paul Boorstin, Sharon Boorstin

The Fireball ★★ U

Sports drama 1950 · US · BW · 83mins

Multi-talented diminutive dynamo Mickey Rooney is the star of this unappealing drama about an orphan with a complex about his height who sets out to become a roller-skating champion, exhibiting ruthless ambition along the way. Rooney fans will be familiar with his brash, cocky brilliance but, although his presence enlivens this lacklustre movie, the character he plays is an unattractive one. Tay Garnett directs for 20th Century-Fox, whose relatively unknown contract player Marilyn Monroe appears. RK

Mickey Rooney *Johnny Casar* • Pat O'Brien *Father O'Hara* • Beverly Tyler *Mary Reeves* • James Brown (1) *Allen* • Marilyn Monroe *Polly* • Ralph Dumke *Bruno Crystal* ■ *Dir* Tay Garnett • *Scr* Tay Garnett, Horace McCoy

Fireball 500 ★★★ U

Action drama 1966 · US · Colour · 90mins

A beach party movie with those icons of sand, sea and swimwear – Frankie Avalon, Fabian and the adorable Annette Funicello. The two boys are rivals for the girl as they race souped-up cars for her pleasure and get into hot water with illicit booze. The whole thing exudes an innocence and charm, as well as some very twangy, singalong tunes. Perhaps not quite up to the standards of previous William Asher beach epics, this is still unmissable for 1960s culture-vultures. AT

Frankie Avalon *Dave* • Annette Funicello *Jane* • Fabian *Leander* • Chill Wills *Big Jaw* • Harvey Lembeck *Charlie Bigg* • Julie Parrish *Martha* ■ *Dir* William Asher • *Scr* William Asher, Leo Townsend

Firebird 2015 AD ★

Science fiction 1980 · US · Colour · 97mins

Petrol is in such short supply in the 21st century that the government orders all cars to be destroyed. When their owners start getting wiped out, too, it's up to illegal bands of motorcyclists to take the law into their own hands. Poorly written and directed, this *Mad Max* rip-off has minor futuristic fantasy touches but plenty of stunt action for those who like that sort of thing. AJ

Darren McGavin *Red* • Doug McClure *McVain* • George Touliatos *Indy* • Mary Beth Rubens *Jill* ■ *Dir* David M Robertson • *Scr* Barry Pearson, Biff McGuire, Maurice Hurley

The Firechasers ★★ U

Crime thriller 1970 · UK · Colour · 101mins

Chad Everett, a teen heart-throb in the US 1970s TV series *Medical Center*, stars in this, a TV movie in America, and a supporting theatrical film over here. Director Sidney Hayers keeps up the pace as insurance investigator Everett hunts an arsonist throughout a London peopled with well-known British character actors. He's aided by lovely Anjanette Comer, and they make a glamorous, if improbable, twosome. TS

Chad Everett *Quentin Barnaby* • Anjanette Comer *Toby Collins* • Keith Barron *Jim Maxwell* • Joanne Dainton *Valerie Chrane* • Rupert Davies *Prentice* • Roy Kinnear *Roscoe* ■ *Dir* Sidney Hayers • *Scr* Philip Levene

Firecreek ★★★ 12

Western 1968 · US · Colour · 99mins

James Stewart here succumbs to the notorious "yup-nope" syndrome, playing a monosyllabic part-time sheriff defending his fellow townsfolk from outlaw Henry Fonda and his gang of layabout thugs. Cast against type, Fonda obviously liked his role so much he became even more villainous for Sergio Leone's *Once upon a Time in the West*, released in Italy the same year. While this doesn't bear serious comparison with Leone's classic spaghetti western, it's entertaining enough. TH. Contains violence.

James Stewart *Johnny Cobb* • Henry Fonda *Larkin* • Inger Stevens *Evelyn* • Gary Lockwood *Earl* • Dean Jagger *Whittier* • Ed Begley *Preacher Broyles* ■ *Dir* Vincent McEveety • *Scr* Calvin Clements

The Firefly ★★★ U

Period musical 1937 · US · BW · 138mins

"There's a song in the air, but the gay senorita doesn't seem to care... " Yes, it's the *Donkey Serenade* movie, with Allan Jones singing his heart out to vivacious Jeanette MacDonald, winning her from stern Warren William during the Spanish Peninsular War, as she takes a break from her regular singing swain Nelson Eddy. MGM's production is so glossy and the film's length so nearly unendurable that its flimsy origins are all but forgotten under Robert Z "Pops" Leonard's classy direction. TS

Jeanette MacDonald *Nina Maria Azara* • Allan Jones *Don Diego Manrique De Lara* • Warren William *Colonel De Rougemont* • Douglass Dumbrille *Marquis De Melito* ■ *Dir* Robert Z Leonard • *Scr* Frances Goodrich, Albert Hackett, Ogden Nash, from the operetta by Otto A Harbach [Otto Harbach] • *Music* Rudolf Friml • *Music Director* Herbert Stothart

Firefox ★★ 15

Spy thriller 1982 · US · Colour · 119mins

Clint Eastwood (as director) every now and then delivers up a boring, emotionless film and this violent Cold War affair is hard going for even the most dedicated of fans. Eastwood plays a disillusioned flier who is sent across the Iron Curtain to steal a new Russian jet and bring it home. The supporting Britpack hams it up for all it's worth, but, while there are some decent flying sequences, Eastwood's heart doesn't appear to be in it. JF. Contains swearing. DVD

Clint Eastwood *Mitchell Gant* • Freddie Jones *Kenneth Aubrey* • David Huffman *Buckholz* • Warren Clarke *Pavel Upenskoy* • Ronald Lacey *Semelovsky* ■ *Dir* Clint Eastwood • *Scr* Alex Lasker, Wendell Wellman, from the novel by Craig Thomas

Firehead ★★ 15

Science-fiction action adventure
1991 · US · Colour · 83mins

Scientist Chris Lemmon (sounding and acting like his father Jack) and CIA agent Gretchen Becker team up to track down Soviet defector Brett Porter who can shoot laser beams from his eyes, move molecules and start fires. Christopher Plummer needs Porter to kill the president and start a Third World War, while Martin Landau is a retired admiral. A fuzzy muddle. AJ. Contains violence and swearing

Christopher Plummer *Colonel Garland Vaughn* • Chris Lemmon *Warren Hart* • Martin Landau *Admiral Pendleton* • Gretchen Becker *Melia Buchanan* • Brett Porter *Ivan Tibor* ■ *Dir* Peter Yuval • *Scr* Peter Yuval, Jeff Mandel

Firelight ★★★ 15

Period romantic drama
1997 · US/UK · Colour · 99mins

Tissues at the ready for this sugary 19th-century tale of a mother's love. Swiss governess Sophie Marceau agrees to conceive a child for English aristocrat Stephen Dillane, who takes the child back to his wife. A few years later the pair cross paths again when he takes her on as nanny to their daughter. The two leads seem uncomfortable with their roles, but the story is interesting enough and is enlivened by a strong performance by Dominique Belcourt as their daughter, and a supporting cast that includes Joss Ackland. JB. Contains some swearing and a sex scene.

Sophie Marceau *Elisabeth Laurier* • Stephen Dillane *Charles Godwin* • Kevin Anderson *John Taylor* • Lia Williams *Constance* • Dominique Belcourt *Louisa Godwin* • Joss Ackland *Lord Clare* ■ *Dir/Scr* William Nicholson

Fireman Save My Child ★★★

Sports comedy 1932 · US · BW · 67mins

Joe E Brown, who was to the mouth what Jimmy Durante was to the nose, is fairly amusing as a dopey, peanut-munching hick fireman who's also a crack baseball player. He manages to get to the big league, and is torn between the girl back home in Kansas and the sophisticated city girl. Naturally, simple values triumph at the end of this serio-comic movie. RB

Joe E Brown *Smokey Joe Grant* • Evalyn Knapp *Sally Toby* • Lilian Bond [Lillian Bond] *June Farnum* • Guy Kibbee *Pop Devlin* • Richard Carle *Dan Toby* ■ *Dir* Lloyd Bacon • *Scr* Ray Enright, Robert Lord, Arthur Caesar, from a story by Ray Enright, Robert Lord, Arthur Caesar, Lloyd Bacon

Fireman Save My Child ★★ U

Comedy 1954 · US · BW · 80mins

Abbott and Costello were the original stars of this slapdash comedy but their withdrawal made room for the less than stellar talents of Hugh O'Brian and Buddy Hackett. However, this silly tale set in an early 20th-century San Francisco fire department, is enlivened by the eccentric presence of Spike Jones and his City Slickers. The film bears no resemblance to the superior 1932 Joe E Brown comedy of the same name. RB

Spike Jones *Lieutenant McGinty* • Buddy Hackett *Smokey* • Hugh O'Brian *Smitty* • Adele Jergens *Harry's wife* • Tom Brown *Captain Bill Peters* ■ *Dir* Leslie Goodwins • *Scr* Lee Loeb, John Grant

The Fireman's Ball ★★★★ U

Political satire 1967 · Cz/It · Colour · 69mins

Director Milos Forman's last film in Czechoslovakia before his American exile begins as a gently mocking comedy of small-town manners, but ends as a blazing allegorical satire on the incompetence, insularity and ideological idiocy of the state. Amid the wealth of comic detail that surrounds the ball held to celebrate a veteran fire chief's retirement, it's easy to forget that the real theme of this socialist realist parody is the Stalinist purges of the 1950s. But the chaotic beauty contest, the theft of the lottery prizes and the discomfort of the guest of honour can all be enjoyed without a deep knowledge of Czech politics. DP. In Czech with English subtitles.

Vaclav Stockel *Fire brigade commander* • Josef Svet *Old man* • Jan Vostrcil *Chairman of committee* • Josef Kolb *Josef* • Frantisek Debelka *First committee member* • Josef Sebanek *Second committee member* ■ *Dir* Milos Forman • *Scr* Milos Forman, Ivan Passer, Jaroslav Papousek

Firepower ★★★ 15

Action thriller 1979 · UK · Colour · 99mins

One of the easiest jobs in film criticism is to knock the work of Michael Winner. But he's not always deserved the pannings he's received and this fast-moving (if admittedly empty-headed) thriller is no worse than many other luxury location jaunts that have escaped without censure. From the opening scene in which Sophia Loren's husband is killed, to the highly predictable denouement, there are

F

explosions and car chases aplenty. On the plus side, Loren and James Coburn do make an attractive couple. Winner also edited the film under the pseudonym Arnold Crust. DP

Sophia Loren *Adele Tasca* • James Coburn *Jerry Fanon/Eddie* • OJ Simpson *Catlett* • Eli Wallach *Sal Hyman* • Anthony Franciosa *Dr Felix* • Vincent Gardenia *Frank Hull* • Victor Mature *Harold Everett* ■ *Dir* Michael Winner • *Scr* Gerald Wilson, from a story by Bill Kerby, Michael Winner

Fires on the Plain ★★★★★

Second World War drama
1959 · Jpn · BW · 107mins

This is cinema's most terrifying study of the Second World War. Adapted by director Kon Ichikawa's wife, Natto Wada, from the novel by Shohei Ooka, Ichikawa's masterpiece has an other-worldly feel. Desperate, cannibalistic Japanese soldiers are left to fend for themselves on the Philippine island of Leyte, its desolate landscape littered with ominous fires. As the tubercular trooper who wanders the landscape in search of food and shelter, and whose infirmity delivers him from the hellish nightmare of survival, the almost wordless Eiji Funakoshi reacts to the atrocities he witnesses with such genuine horror that their impact becomes all the more immediate. DP. In Japanese with English subtitles.

Eiji Funakoshi *Tamura* • Osamu Takizawa *Yasuda* • Mickey Curtis *Nagamatsu* • Mantaro Ushio *Sergeant* • Kyu Sazanka *Army surgeon* • Yoshihiro Hamaguchi *Officer* • Asao Sano *Soldier* • Masaya Tsukida *Soldier* • Hikaru Hoshi *Soldier* ■ *Dir* Kon Ichikawa • *Scr* Natto Wada, from the novel by Shohei Ooka

Fires Were Started ★★★★ U

Second World War documentary drama
1943 · UK · BW · 63mins

Humphrey Jennings was the poet of the British Documentary Movement. Yet, he reined in his imaginative impulses to record the grim reality of the Blitz in what ranks among the finest Home Front films of the Second World War. As in all good propaganda, it's simplicity that makes the most impact. In depicting the Auxiliary Fire Service as a dedicated team, whose cameraderie is evident both at work and play, Jennings is able to inspire audience confidence in their quiet heroism, while also extolling their essential humanity. DP

Dir/Scr Humphrey Jennings

Fires Within ★★ 15

Romantic drama 1991 · US · Colour · 83mins

What makes this film, made by the talented Australian director Gillian Armstrong, disappointing is that its story of Cuban refugees in America throws up some fascinating political points, which are evaded by the pedestrian script. Greta Scacchi as a Cuban housewife is a rotten bit of casting, but she, Jimmy Smits and Vincent D'Onofrio (as her new lover) try to wring every ounce of significance out of the potentially interesting plot. DP. Contains swearing. DVD

Jimmy Smits *Nestor* • Greta Scacchi *Isabel* • Vincent D'Onofrio *Sam* • Luis Avalos *Victor Hernandez* • Bertila Damas *Estella Sanchez* • Bri Hathaway *Maribi* ■ *Dir* Gillian Armstrong • *Scr* Cynthia Cidre, Peter Barsocchini

Firestarter ★★ 15

Supernatural drama
1984 · US · Colour · 109mins

Stephen King's work has suffered mixed fortune at the hands of film-makers and this early folly is not one of the better adaptations. Drew Barrymore is the girl with very fiery thoughts that are connected to the sinister experiments dad and mum (David Keith and Heather Locklear) underwent. Despite a starry cast, there's little here in the way of frights or suspense. JF DVD

David Keith *Andrew McGee* • Drew Barrymore *Charlie McGee* • Freddie Jones *Dr Joseph Wanless* • Heather Locklear *Vicky McGee* • Martin Sheen *Captain Hollister* • George C Scott *John Rainbird* • Art Carney *Irv Manders* • Louise Fletcher *Norma Manders* ■ *Dir* Mark L Lester • *Scr* Stanley Mann, from the novel by Stephen King • *Music* Tangerine Dream

Firestorm ★★ 15

Action adventure 1998 · US · Colour · 85mins

Former American football star Howie Long stars as a daredevil bush fire fighter who finds himself caught up in a lethal forest blaze started by a group of escaped convicts hunting for their buried loot. Long is short on talent, William Forsythe effortlessly steals the show as a psychotic robber, and director Dean Semler struggles away from the action sequences. JF. Contains swearing, violence. DVD

Howie Long *Jesse* • Scott Glenn *Wynt* • William Forsythe *Shaye* • Suzy Amis *Jennifer* • Christianne Hirt *Monica* ■ *Dir* Dean Semler • *Scr* Chris Soth, Graham Yost

Firetrap ★★ 15

Disaster movie 2001 · US · Colour · 94mins

Dean Cain headlines this competently made disaster movie. Director Harris Done efficiently reworks the *Towering Inferno* formula, thanks to some impressive effects. The opening segment, in which Cain's super-crook poses as a fireman in order to facilitate the purloining of a cutting-edge microchip, lacks suspense. But the action really begins to hot up once he's called upon to rescue his target's trapped employees. DP DVD

Dean Cain *Max Hooper* • Richard Tyson *Paul Brody* • Mel Harris *Cordelia* • Lori Petty *Lucy* ■ *Dir* Harris Done • *Scr* Diane Fine, Richard Preston Jr

Firewalker ★ 15

Western adventure
1986 · US · Colour · 100mins

Chuck Norris here attempts to do something that he has absolutely no knack for – comedy. Neither does his co-star Louis Gossett Jr, though he at least keeps some dignity, even when he's forced to speak Pig Latin. The two stars play mercenary adventurers who are hired by Melody Anderson to find an ancient treasure south of the border, with danger, cardboard sets, and stereotypes at every turn. KB

Chuck Norris *Max Donigan* • Louis Gossett Jr *Leo Porter* • Melody Anderson *Patricia Goodwyn* • Will Sampson *Tall Eagle* • Sonny Landham *El Coyote* • John Rhys-Davies *Corky Taylor* ■ *Dir* J Lee Thompson • *Scr* Robert Gosnell, from a story by Jeffrey M Rosenbaum, Norman Aladjem, Robert Gosnell

Fireworks ★★★★ 15

Psychological fantasy
1947 · US · Colour and BW Tinted · 13mins

Although best known for his notorious *Hollywood Babylon* exposés, Kenneth Anger has been a fixture of American avant-garde cinema since 1947, when at 17 he filmed this remarkable short – a "psycho-dramatic trance film" which remains perhaps the peak of his oeuvre. Set against the music of Respighi, this surreal visual poem combines phallic imagery and references to Christmas, the US navy and innocent youth for an orgasmically violent gay fantasy in which Anger is punished for lusting after a hunky sailor. The film's pièta sequence – featuring a bruised Anger collapsed in the sailor's arms – and blatant sexual imagery would qualify it as an audacious and accomplished work for anyone, let alone a teenager. DP

Kenneth Anger *Dreamer* • Bill Seltzer *Bare-chested sailor* • Gordon Gray *Body-bearing sailor* ■ *Dir* Kenneth Anger • *Cinematographer* Kenneth Anger • *Music* Ottorino Respighi

The Firm ★★★★ 15

Thriller 1993 · US · Colour · 148mins

After running rings around the US Navy in *A Few Good Men*, Tom Cruise returned to the courtroom for this big-screen adaptation of John Grisham's bestseller. The result is a lavish, star-studded legal thriller that is never less than engrossing. Cruise is a rising young lawyer who gets a dream job with a prestigious law firm only to discover that it offers more than just legal advice to one particularly sinister client. The ever excellent Gene Hackman is his jaded superior, but, as good as they are, the two stars are outshone by the seemingly never-ending parade of star supporting turns. JF. Contains swearing, violence and a sex scene. DVD

Tom Cruise *Mitch McDeere* • Jeanne Tripplehorn *Abby McDeere* • Gene Hackman *Avery Tolar* • Hal Holbrook *Oliver Lambert* • Terry Kinney *Lamar Quinn* • Wilford Brimley *William Devasher* • Ed Harris *Wayne Tarrance* • Holly Hunter *Tammy Hemphill* • David Strathairn *Ray McDeere* ■ *Dir* Sydney Pollack • *Scr* David Rabe, Robert Towne, David Rayfiel, from the novel by John Grisham

First a Girl ★★★ U

Musical comedy 1935 · UK · BW · 88mins

A popular hit for British screen sweetheart Jessie Matthews, this tuneful comedy plunders a German film called *Viktor und Viktoria* and was itself later reworked by director Blake Edwards as a vehicle for his wife Julie Andrews as *Victor/Victoria*. Whichever way you look at it, this is a highly unconvincing tale of cross-dressing about a girl who impersonates a female impersonator. Matthews brings it all off charmingly, singing and dancing her merry way in a relatively lavish Michael Balcon production, directed by Victor Saville without a hint of subtext. TS

Jessie Matthews *Elizabeth* • Sonnie Hale *Victor* • Griffith Jones *Robert* • Anna Lee *Princess* • Alfred Drayton *McIntosh* • Constance Godridge *Darryl* • Martita Hunt *Seraphina* ■ *Dir* Victor Saville • *Scr* Marjorie Gaffney, from the play *Viktor und Viktoria* by Reinhold Schünzel

First Blood ★★★ 15

Action drama 1982 · US · Colour · 89mins

Although two jingoistic sequels reduced Vietnam veteran John Rambo (Sylvester Stallone) to an indestructible cartoon figure, the film that introduced him is an involving tale of an ostracised loner pushed too far. Brian Dennehy is on fine snarling form as a bigoted small-town sheriff, the catalyst for a woodland cat-and-mouse chase in which his experienced quarry quickly assumes the feline role. The warfare is tautly assembled by director Ted Kotcheff and Stallone portrays Rambo with enough wounded conviction to forgive some of his increasingly far-fetched escapes. JC. Contains violence, swearing, nudity. DVD

Sylvester Stallone *John Rambo* • Richard Crenna *Colonel Trautman* • Brian Dennehy *Sheriff Will Teasle* • David Caruso *Mitch* • Jack Starrett *Galt* ■ *Dir* Ted Kotcheff • *Scr* Michael Kozoll, William Sackheim, Q Moonblood [Sylvester Stallone], from a book by David Morrell • *Music* Jerry Goldsmith

First Daughter ★★

Thriller 1999 · US/Aus · Colour · 94mins

Mariel Hemingway is the unlikely secret service agent who has been demoted to baby-sitting the president's daughter (Monica Keena). However, when American militia types kidnap Keena while on an adventure holiday, it's up to Hemingway and white-water rafter Doug Savant to get her back. Pretty unexceptional, but this TV movie was popular enough to spawn a sequel. JF

Mariel Hemingway *Alex McGregor* • Doug Savant *Grant Carlson* • Monica Keena *Jess Hayes* • Diamond Dallas Page *Dirk Lindman* • Gregory Harrison *President Jonathan Hayes* ■ *Dir* Armand Mastroianni • *Scr* Chad Hayes, Carey Hayes

First Daughter ★★ PG

Romantic comedy
2004 · US · Colour · 101mins

Katie Holmes plays the dutiful daughter of the US president (Michael Keaton), who is looking forward to asserting her independence when she heads off to college. The secret service and tabloid reporters make life difficult, but things start to look up when she falls for fellow student Marc Blucas. The direction here by Forest Whitaker (who also narrates) is proficient enough, but what starts off as a fairy-tale romp gets drearily serious midway through. JF DVD

Katie Holmes *Samantha Mackenzie* • Marc Blucas *James Lamson* • Amerie [Amerie Rogers] *Mia* • Michael Keaton *President John Mackenzie* • Margaret Colin *Melanie Mackenzie* • Lela Rochon Fuqua [Lela Rochon] *Liz Pappas* • Michael Milhoan *Agent Bock* • Dwayne Adway *Agent Dylan* • Forest Whitaker *Narrator* ■ *Dir* Forest Whitaker • *Scr* Jessica Bendinger, Kate Kondell, from a story by Jessica Bendinger, Jerry O'Connell

The First Deadly Sin ★★ 15

Mystery 1980 · US · Colour · 107mins

After a hiatus of ten years, Frank Sinatra returned to the screen as a cop on the verge of retirement whose last case is a series of grisly murders. Faye Dunaway plays his wife, who's in hospital connected to a dialysis machine. No prizes for guessing whodunnit, and apart from some fairly gory details this is no different than a routine episode of *Kojak*. The very quick of eye might just be able to spot Bruce Willis wearing a big cap in a restaurant doorway. AT

Frank Sinatra *Edward Delaney* • Faye Dunaway *Barbara Delaney* • David Dukes *Daniel Blank* • George Coe *Dr Bernardi* • Brenda Vaccaro *Monica Gilbert* • Martin Gabel *Christopher Langley* ■ *Dir* Brian G Hutton • *Scr* Mann Rubin, Lawrence Sanders

First Do No Harm ★★★ PG

Drama based on a true story
1997 · US · Colour · 90mins

Only Meryl Streep could turn a standard disease-of-the-week TV movie into something special. Her mannered performance as a mother trying to get the best treatment for her epileptic son, while also struggling with marital and financial problems, is yet another of her class acts. Seth Adkins also shines as her son in this gruelling drama, which informs about epilepsy while making pertinent statements about society's attitude towards the condition. AJ DVD

Meryl Streep *Lori Reimuller* • Fred Ward *Dave Reimuller* • Seth Adkins *Robbie Reimuller* • Margo Martindale *Marjean* • Allison Janney *Dr Abbasac* • Oni Faida Lampley *Marisha Warren* ■ *Dir* Jim Abrahams • *Scr* Ann Beckett

First Family ★★ 15

Comedy 1980 · US · Colour · 95mins

A disappointing debut for director Buck Henry, whose screenplays for *The Graduate* and *What's Up, Doc?* showed he was adept at both satire and screwball. Here he tackles political satire but without political sting. The absurd plot concerns the kidnapping of

American president Bob Newhart's daughter, Gilda Radner, by an African tribe. Despite the comedy credentials of the strong cast, this witless witness to the wonders of the White House fails as entertainment. TH

Gilda Radner *Gloria Link* • Bob Newhart *President Manfred Link* • Madeline Kahn *Constance Link* • Richard Benjamin *Press Secretary Bunthorne* • Bob Dishy *Vice President Shockley* • Buck Henry *Father Sandstone* ■ *Dir/Scr* Buck Henry

The First Great Train Robbery ★★★ 12

Period crime thriller
1978 · UK · Colour · 107mins

Sumptuously shot on location in Ireland by Geoffrey Unsworth, this allegedly true heist movie is a kind of "Butch Connery and the Sutherland Kid". Written and directed by Michael Crichton from his own novel, it features a pair of Victorian villains, played by Sean Connery and Donald Sutherland, who set out to steal gold destined for the army in the Crimea from a moving train. Crichton fails to sustain the tension of the robbery and too often lets the comedy run unchecked, but it's still a smashing piece of escapism. DP DVD

Sean Connery *Edward Pierce* • Donald Sutherland *Agar* • Lesley-Anne Down *Miriam* • Alan Webb *Edgar Trent* • Malcolm Terris *Henry Fowler* • Wayne Sleep *Clean Willy* • Michael Elphick *Burgess* ■ *Dir* Michael Crichton • *Scr* Michael Crichton, from his novel

First Kid ★★ PG

Comedy 1996 · US · Colour · 95mins

This sugary family comedy was presumably designed as a vehicle for American comedy favourite Sinbad. He plays a secret service agent who gets the task of babysitting the US president's spoilt son (Brock Pierce). However, it's not long before the big guy warms to his charge and starts teaching him some valuable life lessons. It's predictable stuff, though the slapstick humour will delight youngsters. JF

Sinbad *Sam Simms* • Brock Pierce *Luke Davenport* • Blake Boyd *Dash* • Timothy Busfield *Woods* • Art LaFleur *Morton* • Lisa Eichhorn *Linda Davenport* • James Naughton *President Davenport* • Sonny Bono *Congressman Sonny Bono* ■ *Dir* David Mickey Evans • *Scr* Tim Kelleher

First Knight ★★★ PG

Adventure 1995 · US · Colour · 128mins

If Kevin Costner can play Robin Hood with an American accent, then what's to stop Richard Gere giving Lancelot a Philadelphia twang? Gere is suitably dashing as the most independent knight of the Round Table, while Julia Ormond is ravishing as the constantly imperilled Guinevere. Stealing every scene, however, is Sean Connery, who, as a legend in his own lifetime, has no difficulty conveying the regal bearing of the once and future king. Very 1990s, yet curiously and unashamedly old-fashioned. DP. Contains some violence. DVD

Sean Connery *King Arthur* • Richard Gere *Lancelot* • Julia Ormond *Lady Guinevere* • Ben Cross *Malagant* • Liam Cunningham *Sir Agravaine* • Christopher Villiers *Sir Kay* ■ *Dir* Jerry Zucker • *Scr* William Nicholson

First Lady ★★★

Comedy 1937 · US · BW · 83mins

This classy, clever and sophisticated screen adaptation of the George S Kaufman/Katharine Dayton Broadway play offers a strong role to the elegant Kay Francis as an ambitious politician's wife, schemingly shoving her husband Preston Foster into a campaign against crooked judge Walter Connolly. There's little doubt that the message here is that Washington women are the real power behind the throne. A little wordy, and not overly cinematic, but well worth dipping into. TS

Kay Francis *Lucy Chase Wayne* • Anita Louise *Emmy Page* • Verree Teasdale *Irene Hibbard* • Preston Foster *Stephen Wayne* • Walter Connolly *Carter Hibbard* • Victor Jory *Senator Keane* ■ *Dir* Stanley Logan • *Scr* Rowland Leigh, from the play by George S Kaufman, Katharine Dayton

The First Legion ★★★ U

Drama 1951 · US · BW · 86mins

Charles Boyer gives a fine performance as the former criminal attorney turned priest who investigates an apparent miracle at a Jesuit seminary. Made entirely on location at a Spanish-style inn, this is one of director Douglas Sirk's lesser-known films from the 1950s but it's skilfully directed, smoothly acted (though it takes time to accept comedian William Demarest as a Monsignor) and lighter in tone than might be expected. The ending is a mushy attempt to keep believers as well as sceptics happy. AE

Charles Boyer *Father Marc Arnoux* • William Demarest *Monsignor Michael Carey* • Lyle Bettger *Dr Peter Morrell* • Barbara Rush *Terry Gilmartin* • Leo G Carroll *Fr Paul Duquesne* ■ *Dir* Douglas Sirk • *Scr* Emmett Lavery

First Love ★★ U

Romance 1939 · US · BW · 80mins

Only significant now for Deanna Durbin receiving her first proper screen kiss, from Robert Stack in his movie debut, and that's about it. Hard to imagine the impact nowadays, but when singing superstar Durbin puckered up to receive her sensational smackeroo from handsome Stack, audiences were enthralled. As for the plot, it's a version of Cinderella with orphan Deanna hived off to an aunt and uncle. All rather charming, and Durbin sings a few choice songs. TS DVD

Deanna Durbin *Constance Harding* • Robert Stack *Ted Drake* • Eugene Pallette *James Clinton* • Helen Parrish *Barbara Clinton* • Lewis Howard *Walter Clinton* • Leatrice Joy *Grace Clinton* ■ *Dir* Henry Koster • *Scr* Bruce Manning, Lionel Houser

First Love ★★★★

Romance 1970 · W Ger/Swi · Colour · 92mins

A classy adaptation of the Turgenev story about an adolescent boy who becomes infatuated with the flirtatious girl next door. She plays with him, then rejects him. John Moulder-Brown is suitably callow-looking as the boy, while Dominique Sanda is radiantly beautiful and alluring. Impeccably shot by Ingmar Bergman's cameraman, Sven Nykvist, it marked the directing debut of Maximilian Schell; his style is a little academic at times, yet he assembles a fine supporting cast that includes playwright John Osborne. AT

John Moulder-Brown *Alexander* • Dominique Sanda *Sinaida* • Maximilian Schell *Father* • Valentina Cortese *Mother* • Marius Goring *Dr Lushin* • John Osborne *Maidanov* ■ *Dir* Maximilian Schell • *Scr* Maximilian Schell, John Gould, from a story by Ivan Turgenev

First Love ★★ 15

Romantic drama 1977 · US · Colour · 87mins

This is a sentimental tale about a romance between college students William Katt and Susan Dey that turns sour when Katt discovers Dey is involved with a much older man. Because this was made in the 1970s, there are lots of intense discussions about sex, but Dey looks uncomfortable leaving her *Partridge Family* goody two-shoes image behind to play a woman with at least two men on the go. JB. Contains swearing.

William Katt *Elgin Smith* • Susan Dey *Caroline* • John Heard *David* • Beverly D'Angelo *Shelley* • Robert Loggia *John March* • Tom Lacy *Professor Oxtan* • Swoosie Kurtz *Marsha* ■ *Dir* Joan Darling • *Scr* Jane Stanton Hitchcock, David Freeman, from the short story *Sentimental Education* by Harold Brodkey

First Man into Space ★★ PG

Science-fiction adventure
1958 · UK · BW · 73mins

Cosmic rays mutate Earth's first astronaut into a marauding monster with a taste for blood in this briskly efficient B-movie from the golden era of British science fiction. Director Robert Day goes for both pity and scares by engendering sympathy for the one-eyed malformation while delivering uneasy shocks. Lacklustre acting from Marshall Thompson doesn't help his cause, but Marla Landi screaming every time the slime-encrusted alien appears does add an unintentional streak of light entertainment. AJ

Marshall Thompson *Commander CE Prescott* • Marla Landi *Tia Francesca* • Bill Edwards *Lt Dan Prescott* • Robert Ayres *Captain Ben Richards* • Bill Nagy *Wilson* • Carl Jaffe *Dr Paul von Essen* ■ *Dir* Robert Day • *Scr* John C Cooper, Lance Z Hargreaves, from a story by Wyott Ordung

First Men in the Moon ★★★ U

Science-fiction adventure
1964 · UK · Colour · 98mins

Outstanding special effects from stop-motion magician Ray Harryhausen add further lustre to director Nathan Juran's colourfully engaging tale, adapted from the HG Wells novel, about a Victorian lunar expedition. Lionel Jeffries is splendid as the eccentric professor who uses his antigravity paint invention to achieve liftoff in this light-hearted adventure. Jeffries, Edward Judd and Martha Hyer are then captured by insectoid creatures and menaced by a Moon caterpillar in this highly enjoyable flight of sheer fantasy. AJ DVD

Edward Judd *Arnold Bedford* • Lionel Jeffries *Cavor* • Martha Hyer *Kate Callender* • Erik Chitty *Gibbs* • Betty McDowall *Maggie* ■ *Dir* Nathan Juran • *Scr* Nigel Kneale, Jan Read, from the novel by HG Wells

First Monday in October ★★★ 15

Comedy drama 1981 · US · Colour · 93mins

There is far too much chat, even for a courtroom movie, but, if you plan your tea breaks for the segments in which the American political and legal systems are discussed, this is quite a likeable romantic comedy of sorts. Jill Clayburgh does a sterling job as the first female Supreme Court judge, whose strict principles alienate and then attract shabby liberal colleague Walter Matthau. The leads make better adversaries than possible partners and their jousting alone sustains the interest. DP. Contains swearing.

Walter Matthau *Dan Snow* • Jill Clayburgh *Ruth Loomis* • Barnard Hughes *Chief Justice Crawford* • Jan Sterling *Christine Snow* • James Stephens *Mason Woods* ■ *Dir* Ronald Neame • *Scr* Jerome Lawrence, Robert E Lee, from their play

First Name: Carmen ★★ 18

Drama 1983 · Fr/Swi · Colour · 80mins

Ostensibly a film about a terrorist called Carmen X, this is actually a movie about the problems of making movies, interspersed with recitals of Beethoven string quartets and long sessions with director Jean-Luc Godard, sitting in a lunatic asylum and burbling on about himself, life and art. Maybe Godard thought this could be his $8\frac{1}{2}$, and that a few explicit sex scenes would somehow attract an audience. Some of it is actually rather charming, but for most viewers this will be maddening. AT. In French with English subtitles. DVD

Maruschka Detmers *Carmen X* • Jacques Bonnaffé *Joseph Bonnaffe* • Myriem Roussel *Claire* • Christophe Odent *Gang leader* • Jean-Luc Godard *Uncle Jean* • Hippolyte Girardot *Fred* ■ *Dir* Jean-Luc Godard • *Scr* Anne-Marie Miéville

The First of May ★★

Drama 2000 · US · Colour · 111mins

Debutant director Paul Sirmons's account of an orphan runaway's adventures with a discontented pensioner has its heart in the right place, but this family movie suffers from the fact that it's too darn sweet for its own good. There are nice cameos from Mickey Rooney and baseball legend Joe DiMaggio, but the kitsch quotient rises unchecked and Sirmons allows young Dan Byrd to overplay almost all of his big scenes. DP

Julie Harris *Carlotta* • Mickey Rooney *Boss Ed* • Robin O'Dell *Michelle* • Joe DiMaggio ■ *Dir* Paul Sirmons • *Scr* Gary Rogers

The First of the Few ★★★ U

Second World War biographical drama
1942 · UK · BW · 113mins

Offered contracts and any number of enticing star roles after *Gone with the Wind*, Leslie Howard chose to leave Hollywood and return to England to make films designed to boost wartime morale. Here, he directs and stars as visionary aircraft designer RJ Mitchell, the father of the Spitfire. The fine cast includes Rosamund John as his wife and David Niven as the test pilot, while William Walton's fine score sums up an entire era of flying pictures. It was Howard's final screen performance: his plane was shot down in 1943 on a mission that immediately became shrouded in mystery – one that has never been explained. AT DVD

Leslie Howard *RJ Mitchell* • David Niven *Geoffrey Crisp* • Rosamund John *Diana Mitchell* • Roland Culver *Commander Bride* • Annie Firth [Anne Firth] *Miss Harper* • David Horne *Higgins* ■ *Dir* Leslie Howard • *Scr* Antone de Grunwald, Miles Malleson, from a story by Henry C James, Katherine Strueby

The First Power ★★ 18

Horror thriller 1990 · US · Colour · 94mins

Detective Lou Diamond Phillips catches the Pentagram Killer – so called because he carves that sign on his victims' chests – and sends him to the gas chamber. From there his demonic spirit transfers into a succession of weak bodies and continues the murderous spree. Phillips and clairvoyant Tracy Griffith (half-sister of Melanie) try to stop the carnage. A few eerie moments and a couple of excellent stunts are lost in the poor continuity, sloppy framing and senseless plot. AJ

Lou Diamond Phillips *Russell Logan* • Tracy Griffith *Tess Seaton* • Jeff Kober *Patrick Channing* • Mykel T Williamson [Mykelti Williamson] *Detective Oliver Franklin* • Elizabeth Arlen *Sister Marguerite* ■ *Dir/Scr* Robert Resnikoff

The First Rebel ★★★ U

Western 1939 · US · BW · 70mins

Originally titled *Allegheny Uprising* and retitled for the UK, this super little pre-American War of Independence western benefited from its casting, reteaming the leads from *Stagecoach*, John Wayne and Claire Trevor. Wayne smashes evil Brian Donlevy's illicit liquor trade as well as dealing with snarling British officer George Sanders and finding the time to romance Trevor. The film is helped immensely by the somewhat expressionistic lighting from master cinematographer Nicholas Musuraca. TS/AE

John Wayne *Jim Smith* • Claire Trevor *Janie* • Brian Donlevy *Callendar* • George Sanders *Capt Swanson* • Wilfrid Lawson *MacDouglas* • Robert Barrat *Duncan* ■ *Dir* William A Seiter • *Scr* PJ Wolfson

The First Teacher ★★★★

Period drama 1965 · USSR · BW · 98mins

Andrei Konchalovsky made his directorial debut with this scrupulous adaptation of Chingiz Aitmatov's novel of post-Revolutionary progress. Employing mostly non-professional performers and utilitising a lyrical realism, he captures the dignity of the conquered Kirghiz kulaks while contrasting their Muslim fundamentalism with the intractable steppe terrain. Bolot Beishenaliev is hugely sympathetic as the ex-Red Army recruit sent to open the region's first school, but it was Natalya Arinbasarova, as the teenager whose father refuses to let her marry an outsider, who took the acting honours at the Venice Film Festival. DP. In Russian with English subtitles.

Bolot Beishenaliev *Dyuishen* • Natalya Arinbasarova *Altinai* ■ *Dir* Andrei Mikhalkov-Konchalovsky [Andrei Konchalovsky] • *Scr* Andrei Konchalovsky, Chingiz Aitmatov, Boris Dobrodeyev, from a novel by Chingiz Aytmatov

The First Texan ★★ U

Biographical western
1956 · US · Colour · 82mins

Joel McCrea stars as Sam Houston, the man who avenges the fall of the Alamo and becomes the first president of the new Republic of Texas. It's a sluggish picture, more talk than action until the well-staged climactic battle of San Jacinto, but McCrea gives a sincere performance as the man who bides his time and Felicia Farr displays spirit in a humdrum romantic role. AE

Joel McCrea *Sam Houston* • Felicia Farr *Katherine* • Jeff Morrow *Jim Bowie* • Wallace Ford *Delaney* • Abraham Sofaer *Don Carlos* • Jody McCrea *Baker* ■ *Dir* Byron Haskin • *Scr* Dan Ullman [Daniel B Ullman]

The First Time ★★

Comedy 1969 · US · Colour · 89mins

A limp coming-of-age comedy about a teenager who cons his two friends into believing that Buffalo is a buzzing, switched-on place and that losing one's virginity there is as easy as falling off a log. It isn't, of course, and various comic complications ensue. It's really just a pale imitation of *The Graduate* with the gorgeous Jacqueline Bisset as the rather intimidating seductress who isn't actually a prostitute, as the boys think. AT

Jacqueline Bisset *Anna* • Wes Stern *Kenny* • Rick Kelman *Mike* • Wink Roberts *Tommy* • Gerard Parkes *Charles* • Sharon Acker *Pamela* • Cosette Lee *Grandmother* • Vincent Marino *Frankie* ■ *Dir* James Neilson • *Scr* Jo Heims, Roger Smith, from a story by Bernard Bassey

First Time Felon ★★★ 15

Drama based on a true story
1997 · US · Colour · 105mins

The American concept of boot camps for young criminals has been championed by a number of British politicians. Perhaps they saw this TV movie. Omar Epps plays a young gang member who opts for the new justice programme after being convicted of drug-dealing. Initially rebellious, he and his fellow teens get the chance to prove themselves when they are called in to help a flood-threatened town. Actor-turned-director Charles S Dutton maintains a realistic, even tone throughout and elicits fine performances from his cast. JF. Contains swearing, violence.

Omar Epps *Greg Yance* • Delroy Lindo *Calhoun* • Rachel Ticotin *McBride* • Justin Pierce *Eddie* • Lucinda Jenney *Sharon* • Jo D Jonz *Pookie* ■ *Dir* Charles S Dutton • *Scr* Daniel Therriault

First to Fight ★★ U

Second World War drama
1967 · US · Colour · 97mins

Chad Everett – a minor TV star and even less of a movie star – plays a marine who returns from Guadalcanal as a war hero, marries, becomes a drill instructor but craves to be back on the front line. Sent back to Pacific, Everett cracks up and turns into a dribbling wreck. A young Gene Hackman is on hand to encourage Everett to further heroics. Never more than a B-movie, though a fairly costly one, this war drama pushes all the right patriotic buttons. AT

Chad Everett *Jack Connell* • Marilyn Devin *Peggy Sanford* • Dean Jagger *Lt Col Baseman* • Bobby Troup *Lt Overman* • Claude Akins *Capt Mason* • Gene Hackman *Sgt Tweed* ■ *Dir* Christian Nyby • *Scr* Gene L Coon

The First Travelling Saleslady ★ U

Comedy 1956 · US · Colour · 92mins

You could charitably view this as an early feminist tract, but actually it's a deadly dull, badly-paced "comedy" about a corset saleswoman out West reduced to hawking barbed wire. Played by the totally miscast Ginger Rogers, interest now would come from a very young and bronzed Clint Eastwood playing Carol Channing's Cavalry boyfriend. Director Arthur Lubin, who also produced this farrago allegedly once intended for Mae West, supervises matters as though he wishes he were somewhere else. TS

Ginger Rogers *Rose Gillray* • Barry Nelson *Charles Masters* • Carol Channing *Molly Wade* • David Brian *James Carter* • James Arness *Joel Kingdom* • Clint Eastwood *Jack Rice* ■ *Dir* Arthur Lubin • *Scr* Stephen Longstreet, Devery Freeman

The First Wives Club ★★★★ PG

Comedy 1996 · US · Colour · 98mins

Olivia Goldsmith's bestselling novel is turned into a hilarious film by *Police Academy* director Hugh Wilson. Hollywood divas Goldie Hawn, Bette Midler and Diane Keaton give sparkling performances as the three wealthy New Yorkers who have been deserted by their husbands in favour of much younger women (including *Sex and the City's* Sarah Jessica Parker and *Showgirls* star Elizabeth Berkley). Instead of sitting back and taking it, the trio unites to exact revenge and gain financial control, with Midler stealing the show from her two co-stars as the most deliciously vicious of them all. Terrific stuff. JB DVD

Goldie Hawn *Elise Elliot Atchison* • Bette Midler *Brenda Morelli Cushman* • Diane Keaton *Annie MacDuggan Paradise* • Maggie Smith *Gunilla Garson Goldberg* • Sarah Jessica Parker *Shelly Stewart* • Dan Hedaya *Morty Cushman* • Stockard Channing *Cynthia Swann Griffin* • Elizabeth Berkley *Phoebe LaVelle* ■ *Dir* Hugh Wilson • *Scr* Robert Harling, from the novel by Olivia Goldsmith

First Yank into Tokyo ★

Second World War action drama
1945 · US · BW · 82mins

Less than a month after the fall-out settled on the ruins of Hiroshima and Nagasaki, RKO rushed out this programme-filler about the atomic bomb. In fact, it was originally a drama about a new super-gun but a few twiddles to the dialogue and a few new scenes gave the film an unexpected immediacy. It's rubbish, of course, with Tom Neal playing a soldier who undergoes plastic surgery and sneaks into Japan to obtain weaponry information from a captive scientist. AT

Tom Neal *Major Ross* • Barbara Hale *Abby Drake* • Marc Cramer *Jardine* • Richard Loo *Colonel Okanura* • Keye Luke *Haan-Soo* • Leonard Strong *Major Nogira* ■ *Dir* Gordon Douglas • *Scr* J Robert Bren, from a story by J Robert Bren, Gladys Atwater

The First Year ★★★ U

Drama 1932 · US · BW · 81mins

Janet Gaynor and Charles Farrell were indisputably Hollywood's sweethearts in the immediate pre-sound era, and carried on as a strictly professional perfect screen couple for a while through the early talkie years. This is a well-scripted tale of a newlywed couple's attempt to settle down and, though both Gaynor and Farrell are a shade long in the tooth for the roles, they play together superbly, with great charm and élan. TS

Janet Gaynor *Grace Livingston* • Charles Farrell *Tommy Tucker* • Minna Gombell *Mrs Barstow* • Leila Bennett *Hattie* • Dudley Digges *Dr Anderson* • Robert McWade *Fred Livingston* • George Meeker *Dick Loring* ■ *Dir* William K Howard • *Scr* Lynn Starling, from a play by Frank Craven

Firstborn ★★ 15

Drama 1984 · US · Colour · 96mins

In a prime example of a film that engages interest only to dramatically lose it with the denouement, Teri Garr is a divorcee with two sons who picks up a lover that her boys realise is totally unsavoury. However by playing on her self-doubt he manages to drive a wedge between the mother and her sons. Peter Weller is excellent as the sinister suitor and Garr is convincing as the neurotic mother, but the plausible set-up is thrown away by actions more akin to *Death Wish* than domestic melodrama. FL

Teri Garr *Wendy* • Peter Weller *Sam* • Christopher Collet *Jake* • Corey Haim *Brian* • Sarah Jessica Parker *Lisa* • Richard Brandon *Dad* ■ *Dir* Michael Apted • *Scr* Ron Koslow

Fish and Elephant ★★★

Romantic comedy drama
2001 · Chi · Colour · 96mins

Former TV host Li Yu made Chinese cinema history with this 16mm outing, which was the first lesbian movie to be completed on mainland China. Shot without official sanction, it's a partially improvised blend of sex comedy and generational satire that follows Beijing zoo keeper Pan Yi's bid to thwart her mother's matchmaking activities, while maintaining a discreet silence about her relationship with dressmaker, Shi Tou. Pan's blind dates provide the comic highlights. But a subplot about the murder of an abusive father proves as distracting as the director's occasionally wayward visuals. DP. In Mandarin with English subtitles.

Pan Yi *Xiao Qun* • Shi Tou *Xiao Ling* • Zhang Jilian *Mother* • Zhang Qianqian *Junjun* ■ *Dir/Scr* Li Yu

A Fish Called Wanda ★★★★★ 15

Comedy 1988 · UK/US · Colour · 108mins

This hilarious tale of criminal incompetence and transatlantic eccentricity is easily John Cleese's finest achievement since *Fawlty Towers*. He excels as the uptight London barrister who becomes the dupe of scheming American thief Jamie Lee Curtis and her doltishly macho lover, Kevin Kline. But Cleese must share the credit for the film's international success with director Charles Crichton, who was the perfect choice for this sparkling blend of Ealing and Monty Python. Every piece of verbal or physical humour is a model of timing and restraint, and this sparkling comedy also has an underlying darkness that recalls the work of Preston Sturges and Billy Wilder. Praise doesn't come much higher than that. DP. Contains swearing, violence, sex scenes and nudity. DVD

John Cleese *Archie Leach* • Jamie Lee Curtis *Wanda* • Kevin Kline *Otto* • Michael Palin *Ken* • Maria Aitken *Wendy* • Tom Georgeson *George* • Patricia Hayes *Mrs Coady* • Geoffrey Palmer *Judge* • Cynthia Caylor [Cynthia Cleese] *Portia* ■ *Dir* Charles Crichton • *Scr* John Cleese, from a story by Charles Crichton, John Cleese

The Fish That Saved Pittsburgh ★★

Comedy 1979 · US · Colour · 104mins

A hopelessly muddled basketball comedy that attempts to cash in on the disco craze. The loosely plotted story focuses on a dire team that in desperation turns to the stars (the astrological ones, that is) in an attempt to get back on the winning track. Real-life basketball greats Kareem Abdul-Jabbar and Julius Erving are teamed with some talented comedy performers but no one really gets the chance to shine. JF

Julius "Dr J" Erving *Moses Guthrie* • Jonathan Winters *HS/Harvey Tilson* • Meadowlark Lemon *Reverend Grady Jackson* • M Emmet Walsh *Wally Cantrell* • Stockard Channing *Mona Mondieu* • Kareem Abdul-Jabbar ■ *Dir* Gilbert Moses • *Scr* Jaison Starkes, Edmond Stevens, from a story by Gary Stromberg, David Dashev

The Fisher King ★★★★★ 15

Fantasy drama 1991 · US · Colour · 131mins

The Arthurian legend of a maimed warrior healed by the innocence of "a perfect fool" is given a magical update by director Terry Gilliam, tripping the light fantastic in his highly individual manner in this fantasy drama. Gilliam has an eerie knack of wringing visionary heart-tugging power from unsentimental if bizarre material, and Jeff Bridges's mythical search for redemption in the enchanted kingdom of New York fits the bill exactly. A magnificent perusal into what fires and feeds the soul, with super-tramp Robin Williams keeping his trademark zaniness in check until it really counts. But it's Oscar-winner Mercedes Ruehl's electrifying portrayal of moral betrayal that you'll remember long after the fade-out. AJ. Contains swearing, some violence and brief nudity. DVD

Robin Williams *Parry* • Jeff Bridges *Jack Lucas* • Amanda Plummer *Lydia* • Mercedes Ruehl *Anne Napolitano* • Michael Jeter *Homeless cabaret singer* • Adam Bryant *Radio engineer* • David Hyde Pierce *Lou Rosen* ■ *Dir* Terry Gilliam • *Scr* Richard LaGravenese

FIST ★★★ PG

Drama 1978 · US · Colour · 130mins

Sylvester Stallone made a brave attempt to get away from his *Rocky* image in this unflattering portrayal of the American trade union movement. He plays Johnny Kovak, who rises to the leadership of the Federation of Interstate Truckers but finds that power corrupts. The result is not wholly one-dimensional and there are moments of real dramatic conviction. Director Norman Jewison supplies the visual punch to this drama, but Stallone is outclassed by Rod Steiger and Peter Boyle. TH. Contains swearing. DVD

Sylvester Stallone *Johnny Kovak* • Rod Steiger *Senator Andrew Madison* • Peter Boyle *Max Graham* • Melinda Dillon *Anna Zerinkas* • David Huffman *Abe Belkin* • Kevin Conway *Vince Doyle* • Tony LoBianco *Babe Milano* ■ *Dir* Norman Jewison • *Scr* Sylvester Stallone, Joe Eszterhas, from articles by Joe Eszterhas

Fist of Fury ★★★ 18

Martial arts drama
1972 · HK · Colour · 98mins

Despite a troubled shoot, this remains an essential Bruce Lee vehicle. Dating from his Hong Kong days, he plays a martial arts student who sets out to avenge the death of his beloved mentor. He uncovers a gang of smugglers who killed his boxing master when he discovered their plots. The uninitiated will cringe at the dumb script and amateurish direction, but the fight scenes, choreographed by Lee, are breathtaking and his athletic charisma will win over doubters. JF. Cantonese dialogue dubbed into English. [video] DVD

Bruce Lee *Chen Chen* • Nora Miao *Yuan Le-Erh* • James Tien *Fan Chun-Hsia* • Robert Baker (1) *Russian boxer* ■ *Dir/Scr* Lo Wei

Fist of Legend ★★★ 18

Period martial arts
1994 · HK · Colour · 99mins

This thriller is a virtual remake of Bruce Lee's *Fist of Fury* and more than holds its own in comparison. Set in the 1930s, Jet Li is the martial arts expert who returns to his old academy – now under the control of the Japanese – to avenge the death of his beloved tutor. The striking period settings provide a sumptuous backdrop to some superbly choreographed fight sequences devised by Yuen Woo-Ping, now better known to western audiences for his work on *Crouching Tiger, Hidden Dragon* and *The Matrix*. JF. Cantonese and Japanese dialogue dubbed into English. [video] DVD

Jet Li *Chen Zhen* • Shinobu Nakayama *Mitsuko Yamada* • Chin Siu-hou *Huo Ting-en* • Ada Choi *Xian-Hong/So Lan* • Yasuaki Kurata *Fumio Funakoshi, Mitsuko's uncle* ■ *Dir* Gordon Chan • *Scr* Yip Kwong-Kim, Lan Kai-To

Fist of the North Star ★★ 18

Animated science-fiction adventure
1986 · Jpn · Colour · 111mins

Based on a Japanese *manga* of the same name, this animated movie gained instant cult status because of the extremely violent and gory deaths many of the grotesque characters suffer. One "hero" aims get his girlfriend back from the brute who beat him up and left him for dead, but there is not much else going on in this story about various martial arts factions and *Mad Max*-like gangs constantly at each other's throats in a post-apocalypse world. KB. Japanese dialogue dubbed into English. [video] DVD

John Vickery *Ken* • Melodee Spivack *Julia* • Wally Burr *Raoh* • Michael McConnohie *Shin* • Gregory Snegoff *Rei* • Tony Oliver *Bat* • Holly Sidell *Lynn* ■ *Dir* Toyoo Ashida • *Scr* Susumu Takahisa, from the graphic novels by Buronson Hara, Tetsuo Hara

Fist of the North Star ★★ 18

Science-fiction martial arts adventure
1995 · US · Colour · 88mins

Martial arts star Gary Daniels is Kenshiro, the warrior on a mission to restore peace between the warring factions in his post-apocalyptic kingdom. Evil chief Lord Shin (Costas Mandylor) has other ideas. This resembles a bad spaghetti western unceremoniously placed in a science-fiction setting, and Tony Randel's direction fails to match the hyper-kinetic quality of the original popular *manga* series, despite plenty of goofy action spiced up with gore. AJ. Contains violence, swearing. [video] DVD

Gary Daniels *Kenshiro* • Malcolm McDowell *Ryuken* • Costas Mandylor *Lord Shin* • Dante Basco *Bat* • Nalona Herron *Lynn* • Melvin Van Peebles *Asher* • Chris Penn *Jackal* ■ *Dir* Tony Randel • *Scr* Peter Atkins, Tony Randel, from the graphic novels by Buronson Hara, Tetsuo Hara

A Fistful of Dollars ★★★★★ 15

Classic spaghetti western
1964 · It/W Ger/Sp · Colour · 95mins

Based on Akira Kurosawa's 1961 samurai classic *Yojimbo*, this was the first "spaghetti" western to find a worldwide audience. Director Sergio Leone's daringly brilliant use of extreme close-up and compensational depth, and his unflinching depiction of violence, gave the western a new lease of life. Clint Eastwood became an international superstar for his portrayal of the Man with No Name, insisting that much of his dialogue was cut to increase the drifter's air of mystery. Gian Maria Volonté lends excellent support as the snarling Ramon, and Ennio Morricone's minimalist score is a gem. What became known as Leone's *Dollars* trilogy continued with *For a Few Dollars More*. DP [video] DVD

Clint Eastwood *The Man with No Name* • Marianne Koch *Marisol* • John Wels [Gian Maria Volonté] *Ramon Rojo* • Pepe Calvo *Silvanito* • Wolfgang Lukschy *John Baxter* • Sieghardt Rupp *Esteban Rojo* • Antonio Prieto *Benito Rojo* • Margarita Lozano *Consuela Baxter* • Daniel Martin *Julian* • Carol Brown [Bruno Carotenuto] *Antonio Baxter* • Benito Stefanelli *Rubio* • Richard Stuyvesant [Mario Brega] *Chico* • Josef Egger *Piripero* ■ *Dir* Sergio Leone • *Scr* Sergio Leone, Duccio Tessari, Victor A Catena, G Schock, from the film *Yojimbo* by Akira Kurosawa, Ryuzo Kikushima, Hideo Oguni, from the novel *Red Harvest* by Dashiell Hammett

A Fistful of Dynamite ★★★ 15

Spaghetti western
1971 · It · Colour · 150mins

This spaghetti western from master chef Sergio Leone was originally called *Duck, You Sucker!*, a title that is perhaps more in tune with the film's jokey intentions. Rod Steiger stars as a peasant who becomes involved with fugitive IRA explosives expert James Coburn and the Mexican Revolution. There's nothing really funny about Coburn as a walking arsenal, but Leone manages more laughs than you'd expect, thanks to his actors' gift for deadpan comedy. TH. Some dialogue dubbed into English. Contains violence, swearing. [video] DVD

Rod Steiger *Juan Miranda* • James Coburn *Sean Mallory* • Romolo Valli *Dr Villega* • Maria Monti *Adolita* • Rik Battaglia *Santerna* • Franco Graziosi *Governor* ■ *Dir* Sergio Leone • *Scr* Sergio Leone, Luciano Vicenzoni, Sergio Donati, from a story by Sergio Leone

A Fistful of Fingers ★★ 15

Western spoof 1995 · UK · Colour · 77mins

Shot in Somerset on a minuscule budget, this spoof western from self-confessed Sam Raimi fan, director Edgar Wright features *Monty Python* slapstick, *Airplane!*-style gags and Sergio Leone references. The Man With No Name, his face smeared in fake five o'clock shadow, pursues the outlaw Squint, wearing a false moustache, across the Mendips in Wright's game homage. Although most of the humour falls flat, it's hard not to enjoy the sheer gung ho ingenuity of this movie. AJ [video]

Graham Low *No Name/Walter Marshall* • Martin Curtis *Running Sore* • Oliver Evans *The Squint* • Quentin Green *Jimmy James* • Jeremy Beadle • Nicola Stapleton *Pint-sized hussy* ■ *Dir/Scr* Edgar Wright

Fists in the Pocket ★★★★ 12

Drama 1965 · It · BW · 104mins

Shot on a shoestring, Marco Bellocchio's debut feature is an aggressive, semi-autobiographical assault on family life and bourgeois parochialism. Raging at the restrictions of small-town, middle-class life, the film uses epilepsy and blindness as symbols of social malaise to which teenager Lou Castel can only respond with increasingly frenzied acts of violence when he tries to escape the family by getting married. Typified by Castel's astonishing portrayal of pent-up fury, the bruising backstreet authenticity is amazing for its time. Thanks to Bellocchio's controlled direction and Alberto Marrama's no-nonsense imagery, this study of mental instability and murder is totally convincing. DP. An Italian language film. Contains violence. [video]

Paola Pitagora *Giulia* • Lou Castel *Sandro* • Marino Mase *Augusto* • Liliana Gerace *The Mother* • Pier Luigi Troglio *Leone* • Jean MacNeil *Lucia* ■ *Dir/Scr* Marco Bellocchio

Fitzcarraldo ★★★★★ PG

Drama 1982 · W Ger · Colour · 150mins

This is German director Werner Herzog's true masterpiece, a labour of love that almost engulfed him. It is the story of a quest by the titular man in a white suit to build an opera house in the South American jungle, funded by profits from a rubber plantation that requires him to drag a 320-ton steamship over a mountain. This, the film's central motif, Herzog actually did. Klaus Kinski, so vivid in many of Herzog's films, again brings an imperious presence. There is far more to this lengthy film than a boat going up a hill, but it crowns an unforgettable piece of cinema. The making of this epic (captured in the 1982 documentary *Burden of Dreams*) sometimes threatens to eclipse the work itself, but that would be a tragedy. AC. In German with English subtitles. [video] DVD

Klaus Kinski *Fitzcarraldo* • Claudia Cardinale *Molly* • José Lewgoy *Don Aquilino* • Paul Hittscher *Paul* • Miguel Angel Fuentes *Cholo* ■ *Dir/Scr* Werner Herzog

Fitzwilly ★★ U

Comedy 1967 · US · Colour · 102mins

What with Edith Evans compiling a dictionary for people who can't spell and butler Dick Van Dyke heading a crime syndicate to prevent her discovering that the family fortune has given out, this keeps threatening to turn into a gleeful screwball romp. That it fails to do so is mostly down to the killjoy direction of Delbert Mann, who doesn't seem to appreciate the comic potential of the situations and Isobel Lennart's gag-packed script. DP

Dick Van Dyke *Fitzwilliam* • Barbara Feldon *Juliet Nowell* • Edith Evans *Victoria Woodworth* • John McGiver *Albert* • Harry Townes *Mr Nowell* • Sam Waterston *Oliver* ■ *Dir* Delbert Mann • *Scr* Isobel Lennart, from the novel *A Garden of Cucumbers* by Poyntz Tyler

Five ★★★

Drama 1951 · US · BW · 90mins

Former radio producer turned exploitation merchant Arch Oboler has some interesting gimmick-laden films to his credit, most notably the first movie in 3-D, the notorious *Bwana Devil*. The gimmick here is both the title and the plot, which deals with the last five survivors after the Earth has been devastated by a (then topical) A-bomb blast. The trouble is, it's all rather static and cheap-looking, and it's awfully hard to care about these particular survivors, a group of unknowns who have remained as such. However, the dialogue is clever and the situations, though contrived, are nonetheless intriguing. TS

William Phipps *Michael* • Susan Douglas *Roseanne* • James Anderson (2) *Eric* • Charles Lampkin *Charles* ■ *Dir/Scr* Arch Oboler

Five ★★★ U

Experimental documentary drama
2003 · Iran/Fr/Jap · Colour · 74mins

Subtitled "5 Long Takes Dedicated to Yasujiro Ozu", this is an homage to those Zen-inspired "pillow shots" that the Japanese maestro used to insert between scenes. Emulating Ozu's fixed-camera perspective, Abbas Kiarostami considers, in turn, a piece of driftwood on the low tide, daytrippers strolling along a seaside promenade, some dogs romping on a beach, a paddling of indecisive ducks and an impenetrable nocturnal pond scene accompanied by a deafening chorus of frogs. Fittingly, each vignette is divided by enchanting musical interludes. This rigorous experimental exercise – filmed entirely without dialogue – won't appeal to everyone, but those who appreciate sly visual humour and cinematic poetry will find much to enjoy. DP

Dir/Scr Abbas Kiarostami

Five against the House ★★

Crime drama 1955 · US · BW · 83mins

This heist thriller, in which five students plan to rob an allegedly secure casino in Reno, cashes in on two winning movie formulas of the time: the "perfect robbery" and the "teenage-angst drama". Guy Madison makes a lacklustre hero, quite upstaged by Brian Keith as the psychotic member of the gang. Kim Novak's allure, plus Phil Karlson's zippy direction, make for a decent B-movie with a ludicrously cod-Freudian ending. AT

Guy Madison *Al Mercer* • Kim Novak *Kay Greylek* • Brian Keith *Brick* • Alvy Moore *Roy* • William Conrad *Eric Berg* • Kerwin Mathews *Ronnie* ■ *Dir* Phil Karlson • *Scr* Stirling Silliphant, William Bowers, John Barnwell, from a story by Jack Finney

Five Branded Women ★★

Second World War drama
1960 · US/It/Yug · BW · 103mins

A stellar cast has far too little asked of it in this uncompromising exploration of Yugoslav resistance during the Second World War. The scene in which the women have their heads shaved for dallying with Nazi officer Steve Forrest is easily the most disturbing of the picture, as the later guerrilla encounters differ little from the combat sequences seen in a dozen other war movies. Martin Ritt's direction doesn't shy away from the cruel realities of Partisan activity, but its brutal intensity makes it rather heavy going. DP

Van Heflin *Velko* • Silvana Mangano *Jovanka* • Vera Miles *Daniza* • Barbara Bel Geddes *Marja* • Jeanne Moreau *Ljuba* • Richard Basehart *Captain Reinhardt* • Harry Guardino *Branco* • Carla Gravina *Mira* ■ *Dir* Martin Ritt • *Scr* Ivo Perilli, from the novel by Ugo Pirro

Five Came Back ★★★

Adventure drama 1939 · US · BW · 75mins

Pilot Chester Morris crashes his plane in the Andes and can only take off again with the titular five. Of the 12 on board, who will escape the dreaded headhunters of the Amazon? Lucille Ball? John Carradine? C Aubrey Smith? Wendy Barrie? This is still gripping, though showing its age now. Director John Farrow liked the plot so much he remade it in 1956 as *Back from Eternity*. TS

Chester Morris *Bill* • Lucille Ball *Peggy* • Wendy Barrie *Alice Melhorne* • John Carradine *Crimp* • Allen Jenkins *Peter* • C Aubrey Smith *Prof Henry Spengler* ■ *Dir* John Farrow • *Scr* Jerry Cady [Jerome Cady], Dalton Trumbo, Nathanael West, from a story by Richard Carroll

5 Card Stud ★★★ 12

Western 1968 · US · Colour · 98mins

When a cardsharp is lynched by the five men he cheated, the men themselves start dying mysteriously. This neat little mystery is really Agatha Christie's *Ten Little Indians* transposed to the Wild West, with Dean Martin as a cardplayer turned detective and Robert Mitchum as a preacher. Made during a brief fad for poker pictures (*The Cincinnati Kid*, *Kaleidoscope*, and *Big Deal at Dodge City* were others), it exists solely on the laconic charm of its two stars. AT DVD

Dean Martin *Van Morgan* • Robert Mitchum *Reverend Rudd* • Roddy McDowall *Nick Evers* • Inger Stevens *Lily Langford* • Katherine Justice *Nora Evers* • John Anderson *Marshal Dana* • Yaphet Kotto *Little George* ■ *Dir* Henry Hathaway • *Scr* Marguerite Roberts, from a novel by Roy Gaulden

Five Children and It ★★ U

Period fantasy adventure
2004 · UK/Fr/US · Colour · 85mins

If it wasn't for the splendid voice talent of comedian Eddie Izzard as the titular sand fairy "It", this family adventure would be a lacklustre affair. During the First World War, five London siblings are evacuated to their unconventional uncle Kenneth Branagh's seaside mansion. There the youngsters discover an irritable, ancient Psammead (Izzard), who possesses amazing wish-granting powers. This offers a flat script, school play-style over-acting and poor special effects. SF DVD

Kenneth Branagh *Uncle Albert* • Zoë Wanamaker *Martha* • Eddie Izzard *It* • Freddie Highmore *Robert* • Jonathan Bailey *Cyril* • Jessica Claridge *Anthea* • Poppy Rogers *Jane* • Tara FitzGerald *Mother* • John Sessions *Peasemarsh* • Norman Wisdom *Nesbit* ■ *Dir* John Stephenson • *Scr* David Solomons, from the novel by E Nesbit

Five Corners ★★★ 15

Thriller 1987 · US · Colour · 89mins

It's the cast of this virtually unreleased movie that catches the eye: Jodie Foster, Tim Robbins and John Turturro. It's set in the Bronx in 1964 where Foster has been nearly raped, Turturro emerges from jail for said crime, and Robbins is about to go south to join the civil rights movement. After much scene-setting, Turturro goes completely crazy. As a coming-of-age drama, it offers nothing new, and the film's shifts of mood from comedy to drama to horror are over-calculated, but the three young stars are always worth watching. AT. Contains violence, swearing.

Jodie Foster *Linda* • Tim Robbins *Harry Fitzgerald* • Todd Graff *James* • John Turturro *Heinz Sabantino* • Elizabeth Berridge *Melanie* • Rose Gregorio *Mrs Sabantino* ■ *Dir* Tony Bill • *Scr* John Patrick Shanley

Five Days from Home ★

Action drama 1978 · US · Colour · 108mins

With less than a week of his sentence to go, convicted killer George Peppard escapes from jail in order to be with his critically ill son. Peppard turned director for the first and last time with this drama in which he also takes the lead role as the ex-cop whose victim was his wife's lover. The sentimentality of the story will probably leave you feeling a bit nauseous. AT

George Peppard *TM Pryor* • Neville Brand *Inspector Markley* • Sherry Boucher *Wanda Dulac* • Victor Campos *Jose Stover* • Robert Donner *Baldwin* ■ *Dir* George Peppard • *Scr* William Moore

Five Days One Summer ★★ PG

Drama 1982 · US · Colour · 103mins

Fred Zinnemann's last film is a very personal tale, but not, alas, obvious screen material. Sean Connery goes climbing in the Swiss Alps with young Betsy Brantly, whom he introduces as his wife. Zinnemann knows how to tell a tale, and the use of Alpine scenery is striking, but the film never really builds up steam and isn't helped by the fragmentary story-telling and flashback structure. Despite the stellar presence of Connery, the chemistry simply isn't there. TS

Sean Connery *Douglas* • Betsy Brantley *Kate* • Lambert Wilson *Johann* • Jennifer Hilary *Sarah* • Isabel Dean *Kate's mother* • Gérard Buhr *Brendel* • Anna Massey *Jennifer Pierce* ■ *Dir* Fred Zinnemann • *Scr* Michael Austin, from the short story *Maiden Maiden* by Kay Boyle

Five Easy Pieces ★★★★★ 15

Drama 1970 · US · Colour · 94mins

Jack Nicholson's in his prime in this accomplished drama. Here he's lean and hungry, fresh from *Easy Rider* and in cahoots with several of the best indie film-makers of the time: director Bob Rafelson, producer Bert Schneider and writers Carole Eastman and Robert Towne. Nicholson is simply magnetic as Bobby Dupea, emotionally repressed and unable to adjust to the two worlds he inhabits among blue-collar oil-riggers and the family home, a sort of Ibsen commune devoted to maths and Mozart. The film, superbly directed by Rafelson, shifts the late 1960s hippy drop-out genre into the Ingmar Bergman class: it's cerebral, moving and witty. AT DVD

Jack Nicholson *Robert Eroica Dupea* • Karen Black *Rayette Dipesto* • Susan Anspach *Catherine Van Oost* • Lois Smith *Partita Dupea* • Billy "Green" Bush [Billy Green Bush] *Elton* • Fannie Flagg *Stoney* • Ralph Waite *Carl Fidelio Dupea* ■ *Dir* Bob Rafelson • *Scr* Adrien Joyce [Carole Eastman], from a story by Bob Rafelson, Joyce Rafelson

Five Finger Exercise ★

Melodrama 1962 · US · BW · 111mins

Peter Shaffer's successful stage play here becomes an embarrassing showcase for the rasping charm of Rosalind Russell, a culture vulture who's married to thick Jack Hawkins and fancies egghead German tutor Maximilian Schell, who tries to commit suicide because he feels alienated. The original was set in London but this is set on the Columbia backlot in Hollywood, and is hopelessly stagebound. AT

Rosalind Russell *Louise Harrington* • Jack Hawkins *Stanley Harrington* • Maximilian Schell *Walter* • Richard Beymer *Philip Harrington* • Annette Gorman *Pamela Harrington* ■ *Dir* Daniel Mann • *Scr* Frances Goodrich, Albert Hackett, from the play by Peter Shaffer

5 Fingers ★★★ U

Spy drama 1952 · US · BW · 103mins

Loosely based on fact, this stars James Mason as the Albanian valet who, while serving the British Ambassador to Turkey, peddles secrets to the Germans. Michael Rennie is the detective trying to plug the leak, while Danielle Darrieux is a mysterious countess. It's a sophisticated and often witty affair dominated by Mason's suave duplicity. AT DVD

James Mason *Cicero* • Danielle Darrieux *Anna* • Michael Rennie *George Travers* • Walter Hampden *Sir Frederic* • Oscar Karlweis *Moyzisch* • Herbert Berghof *Col von Richter* • John Wengraf *Von Papen* ■ *Dir* Joseph L Mankiewicz • *Scr* Michael Wilson, from the book *Operation Cicero* by LC Moyzisch

Five Gates to Hell ★

War drama 1959 · US · BW · 88mins

Before he became known as the author of *Tai-Pan*, James Clavell persuaded Fox to let him write, produce and direct this frenzied war melodrama. Seven Red Cross nurses are captured and abused by Indo-Chinese guerrillas, but live to wreak a violent revenge on their captors. The result is in such bad taste, it's surprising it didn't develop a cult following. AE

Neville Brand *Chen Pamok* • Dolores Michaels *Athena* • Patricia Owens *Joy* • Ken Scott *Dr John Richter* • Nobu McCarthy *Chioko* ■ *Dir/Scr* James Clavell

Five Golden Dragons ★★ PG

Action crime drama
1967 · UK · Colour · 100mins

The most appealing thing about this unashamed slice of hokum are the villains – Christopher Lee, George Raft, Brian Donlevy and Dan Duryea as members of a secret sect in Hong Kong. The hero, Hollywood has-been Robert Cummings, washes up there and finds himself caught between the Dragons and local Mafioso. An outrageously hammy Klaus Kinski also pops up in this lively affair that fleeces everything from *The World of Suzie Wong* to the *Fu Manchu* films. AT

Robert Cummings *Bob Mitchell* • Rupert Davies *Comm Sanders* • Margaret Lee *Magda* • Klaus Kinski *Gert* • Brian Donlevy *Dragon* • Dan Duryea *Dragon* • Christopher Lee *Dragon* • George Raft *Dragon* ■ *Dir* Jeremy Summers • *Scr* Peter Welbeck [Harry Alan Towers] • *Cinematographer* John von Kotze

Five Graves to Cairo ★★★★

Second World War drama
1943 · US · BW · 96mins

This minor but hugely enjoyable Billy Wilder picture stars Erich von Stroheim as Field Marshal Rommel, holed up in a fly-blown hotel during the North Africa campaign. Franchot Tone is a British spy posing as a club-footed waiter, Anne Baxter is a French maid, Peter Van Eyck a Nazi sadist and Fortunio Bonanova an Italian buffoon who bursts into opera. Despite a few token shots of tanks in the desert, this is the Second World War played indoors as a game of charades, role-playing and racial stereotyping. Tense and hilarious, it's a smashing entertainment, and von Stroheim is utterly magnificent. AT

Franchot Tone *Cpl John Bramble* • Anne Baxter *Mouche* • Akim Tamiroff *Farid* • Erich von Stroheim *Field Marshal Rommel* • Peter Van Eyck *Lt Schwegler* • Fortunio Bonanova *General Sabastiano* • Miles Mander *British Colonel* ■ *Dir* Billy Wilder • *Scr* Charles Brackett, Billy Wilder, from the play *Hotel Imperial* by Lajos Biró

Five Guns West ★★ U

Western 1955 · US · Colour · 81mins

A piece of movie history was forged here with the directing debut of Roger Corman, who became the acknowledged master and exploiter of the B-movie and the sponsor of such talents as Bogdanovich, Coppola, Scorsese and Demme. It's a sort of Civil War spy story about a deserter, stolen gold, a list of Confederate agents and five convicted murderers who are let out of jail to catch the deserter. Starring wooden John Lund and Dorothy Malone, it's unmissable for students of modern Hollywood. AT

John Lund *Govern Sturges* • Dorothy Malone *Shalee* • Mike Connors *Hale Clinton* • Bob Campbell *John Candy* • Jonathan Haze *Billy Candy* • Paul Birch *JC Haggard* • James Stone *Uncle Mime* • Jack Ingram *Jethro* • Larry Thor *Confederate captain* ■ *Dir* Roger Corman • *Scr* R Wright Campbell

The Five Heartbeats ★★★ 15

Musical drama 1991 · US · Colour · 116mins

Having made a sensational debut with the blistering satire *Hollywood Shuffle*, Robert Townsend slightly missed his step with this overlong, but still essentially enjoyable, tribute to African-American singing groups like the Dells (on whom this film is loosely based), who struggled in the shadow of Motown in the 1960s. The familiar round of minor gigs, auditions and disappointments is trotted out in textbook fashion, but it's lovingly done and slickly played. DP. Contains violence and swearing.

Robert Townsend *Donald "Duck" Matthews* • Michael Wright *Eddie King Jr* • Leon Robinson [Leon] *James Thomas "JT" Matthews* • Harry Lennix *Terence "Dresser" Williams* • Tico Wells *Anthony "Choirboy" Stone* • Diahann Carroll *Eleanor Porter* ■ *Dir* Robert Townsend • *Scr* Robert Townsend, Keenen Ivory Wayans

Five Miles to Midnight ★★

Drama 1963 · US/Fr/It · BW · 108mins

Sophia Loren slowly goes stark, staring mad. Well, she is married to Anthony Perkins who unfortunately (for her) survives a plane crash and continues to torment her and everyone else who thinks he's dead. Meanwhile, he plans to take advantage of his timely demise by defrauding the insurance company – with the help of his unwilling spouse. Fans of melodrama will enjoy this juicy item that sometimes seems Hitchcockian in tone but most of the time exists in a world of its own. AT

Sophia Loren *Lisa Macklin* • Anthony Perkins *Robert Macklin* • Gig Young *David Barnes* • Jean-Pierre Aumont *Alan Stewart* • Yolande Turner *Barbara Ford* ■ *Dir* Anatole Litvak • *Scr* Peter Viertel, Hugh Wheeler

The Five Obstructions ★★★★ 15

Part-animated documentary drama
2003 · Den/Bel/Swi/Fr · Col/BW · 87m

In 1967, the Danish director Jorgen Leth made a short film called *The Perfect Human*, in which the behaviour patterns of Claus Nissen and Maiken Algren were analysed as though they were lab specimens. Over 30 years later, Lars von Trier – clearly still amused by the restrictive approach imposed by his Dogme 95 experiment – challenged his mentor to remake his film only to constantly find ways of hindering its progress. This is not only a fascinating insight into the cinematic process, but also a tribute to Leth's directorial ingenuity, as he endeavours to complete three live-action and one animated variation on his intriguing theme. DP. In Danish, English, French and Spanish with subtitles. Contains some swearing and sex scenes. DVD

Jorgen Leth *The man* • Daniel Hernández Rodríguez *The man (Cuba)* • Jacqueline Arenal *Woman 1 (Cuba)* • Patrick Bauchau *M Rukov, the man (Brussels)* • Alexandra Vandernoot *The woman (Brussels)* • Claus Nissen *The man (1967)* • Maiken Algren *The woman (1967)* ■ *Dir* Jorgen Leth, Lars von Trier • *Scr* Lars von Trier, Jorgen Leth, Asger Leth, from the film *The Perfect Human* (1967) by Jorgen Leth, Ole John

The Five Pennies ★★★★ U

Musical biographical drama
1959 · US · Colour · 117mins

After the success of James Stewart in *The Glenn Miller Story*, glossy bandleader biopics enjoyed a brief vogue, and this dramatic but schmaltzy Paramount music-fest was one of the best. Danny Kaye is perfectly cast as cornettist "Red" Nichols, whose life seemed like a scriptwriter's invention. When his daughter Dorothy (played as a teenager by a wonderful Tuesday Weld) contracted polio, he threw away his instrument, only to enjoy a revival as her health improved. There's a super jam session with Louis Armstrong, plus some fine new songs, including a lovely *Lullaby in Ragtime* from the film's associate producer Sylvia Fine (Mrs Danny Kaye). A 1950s studio crowd-pleaser. TS

Danny Kaye *Loring "Red" Nichols* • Barbara Bel Geddes *Bobbie Meredith* • Louis Armstrong • Bob Crosby *Wil Paradise* • Harry Guardino *Tony Valani* • Susan Gordon *Dorothy Nichols, aged six* • Tuesday Weld *Dorothy aged 12–14* • Bob Hope ■ *Dir* Melville Shavelson • *Scr* Melville Shavelson, Jack Rose, from a story by Robert Smith

The Five Senses ★★★★ 15

Drama 1999 · Can · Colour · 104mins

The danger of making a film about genetic stereotyping is that contrivance will undermine inspiration, yet Canadian director Jeremy Podeswa avoids any such pitfalls in this accomplished ensemble drama. Although it takes time to introduce us to the cake-maker with no taste, the cleaner with a nose for romance, the optician who's going deaf and the masseuse with an irresponsible teenage daughter, their stories soon interweave into a satisfying whole. With a splendid cast led by Mary-Louise Parker, this is a genuinely sensual experience which suggests people should trust their senses more and their emotions less. DP. Contains swearing and sex scenes.

Mary-Louise Parker *Rona* • Pascale Bussières *Gail* • Richard Clarkin *Raymond* • Brendan Fletcher *Rupert* • Marco Leonardi *Roberto* • Nadia Litz *Rachel* • Molly Parker *Anna Miller* ■ *Dir/Scr* Jeremy Podeswa

Five Star Final ★★★

Crime drama 1931 · US · BW · 90mins

This stars Edward G Robinson as a decent editor who is ordered by his proprietor to sink the tone of the stories he prints into the gutter to raise his newspaper's circulation. Two suicides ensue when a scandal breaks on the front page. Wearing its social conscience on its rolled-up sleeve, the picture, directed by Mervyn LeRoy, remains gripping, and the excellent Robinson is well supported by HB Warner, Frances Starr and Boris Karloff as a shifty reporter. AT

Edward G Robinson *Randall* • Marian Marsh *Jenny Townsend* • HB Warner *Michael Townsend* • Anthony Bushell *Philip Weeks* • George E Stone *Ziggie Feinstein* • Frances Starr *Nancy Voorhees Townsend* • Ona Munson *Kitty Carmody* • Boris Karloff *"Reverend" Vernon Isopod* ■ *Dir* Mervyn LeRoy • *Scr* Byron Morgan, Robert Lord, from the play *Late Night Final* by Louis Weitzenkorn

Five Steps to Danger ★★ U

Spy melodrama 1957 · US · BW · 80mins

This lame-brained B-thriller stars Ruth Roman as a "mystery woman" in possession of a secret code, who finds herself the target of communist agents. Werner Klemperer, the son of the famous conductor Otto, plays a shifty psychiatrist. The main reason for watching is Sterling Hayden, a major actor who never became a star; his career was handicapped by his "friendly" testimony before the anti-communist McCarthy hearings and by an obsession with the sea which took him on long and arduous voyages. AT

Ruth Roman *Ann Nicholson* • Sterling Hayden *John Emmett* • Werner Klemperer *Dr Simmons* • Richard Gaines *Dean Brant* • Charles Davis *Kirk* • Jeanne Cooper *Helen Bethke* ■ *Dir* Henry S Kesler • *Scr* Henry S Kesler, from a story by Donald Hamilton

The 5,000 Fingers of Dr T ★★★★★ U

Fantasy adventure
1953 · US · Colour · 88mins

Criminally neglected for far too long, producer Stanley Kramer's offbeat children's nightmare, co-written by Ted Geisel (better known as Dr Seuss), is one of the best surrealistic fantasies Hollywood has ever made. Tommy Rettig hates his piano lessons so much he dreams of being forced to play the world's largest keyboard by mad musician Dr Terwilliker (the nastily marvellous Hans Conried) along with 500 other captive boys. Look for the anti-communist propaganda (symbolised by the red smoke) as the children are slave-driven to ignite an atomic bomb by their manic playing. Hugely imaginative, fun, scary and visually dazzling – the sets and backdrops are simply stunning. AJ

Peter Lind Hayes *Mr Zabladowski* • Tommy Rettig *Bart Collins* • Mary Healy *Mrs Collins* • Hans Conried *Dr Terwilliker* • John Heasley *Uncle Whitney* • Robert Heasley *Uncle Judson* • Noel Cravat *Sergeant Lunk* • Henry Kulky *Stroogo* ■ *Dir* Roy Rowland • *Scr* Ted "Dr Seuss" Geisel, Allan Scott, from a story by Ted "Dr Seuss" Geisel • *Cinematographer* Franz Planer • *Art Director* Rudolph Sternad

5x2 ★★★★ 15

Romantic drama 2004 · Fr · Colour · 90mins

One of France's most prolific film-makers, director François Ozon shows no sign of a lapse in quality with this meticulously composed, astutely acted study of a marriage in crisis. Adopting a reverse chronology, Ozon tells the story of the deteriorating relationship between Valéria Bruni-Tedeschi and the womanising Stéphane Freiss, from their divorce to first meeting. As Ozon expertly allows pertinent details to seep into the scenario, Bruni-Tedeschi proves anything other than a helpless victim in a performance of exquisite emotional intensity. DP. In French with English subtitles. Contains swearing and sex scenes.

Valéria Bruni-Tedeschi *Marion Ferron* • Stéphane Freiss *Gilles Ferron* • Géraldine Pailhas *Valérie* • Françoise Fabian *Monique Chabart* • Michael Lonsdale [Michel Lonsdale] *Bernard Chabart* • Antoine Chappey *Christophe Ferron* • Marc Ruchmann *Mathieu* ■ *Dir/Scr* François Ozon

Five Weeks in a Balloon ★ U

Period comedy 1962 · US · Colour · 101mins

Pop go entertainment values in this Jules Verne adventure that is inflated beyond all probability by disaster movie maestro Irwin Allen, who here made the wrong sort of disaster. Cedric Hardwicke, singer Fabian and Red Buttons are members of a 19th-century British expedition floating over Africa, while Peter Lorre joins them for the dramatic ride. The inclusion of Fabian just shows how desperate the movie is to attract attention. TH

Red Buttons *Donald O'Shay* • Fabian *Jacques* • Barbara Eden *Susan Gale* • Cedric Hardwicke *Fergusson* • Peter Lorre *Ahmed* • Richard Haydn *Sir Henry Vining* ■ *Dir* Irwin Allen • *Scr* Charles Bennet, Irwin Allen, Albert Gail, from the novel by Jules Verne

Five Women around Utamaro ★★★★

Period melodrama 1946 · Jpn · BW · 106mins

Returning to the theme of female emancipation that had preoccupied him in the mid-1930s, Kenji Mizoguchi was prevented from using this film to celebrate Japan's new-found democracy and the concept of liberation through eroticism by the production guidelines issued by the US occupying force. Consequently, he found himself the subtextual subject of this exploration of the complex relationships and social injustices that inspired the 18th-century Edo printmaker, Utamaro. In depicting the twilight world of the geishas and the artist's struggle for creative freedom, screenwriter Yoshikata Yoda provides a dramatic core that enables Mizoguchi to conduct formal experiments reflecting Utamaro's style. DP. In Japanese with English subtitles.

Minosuke Bando *Utamaro* • Kotaro Bando *Seinosuke Koide* • Kinuyo Tanaka *Okita* • Kowasaki Hiroko *Oran* • Izuka Toshiko *Takasode* ■ *Dir* Kenji Mizoguchi • *Scr* Yoshikata Yoda, from the novel *Utamaro O Meguru Gonin no Onna* by Kanji Kunideda

Fixed Bayonets ★★★

War drama 1951 · US · BW · 91mins

War may be hell, but for writer/director Samuel Fuller it's also a character workout that can temper personalities for the worse or the better. In this familiar story of a lost platoon fighting a rearguard action in Korea, it is Richard Basehart who is fused by events into purposeful command. Although the film never reaches the poetic heights of Lewis Milestone's similar *A Walk in the Sun*, there's the same understanding that men in battle are really at war within themselves. TH

Richard Basehart *Corporal Denno* • Gene Evans *Sergeant Rock* • Michael O'Shea *Sergeant Lonergan* • Richard Hylton *Wheeler* • Craig Hill *Lieutenant Gibbs* • Skip Homeier *Whitey* ■ *Dir* Samuel Fuller • *Scr* Samuel Fuller, from the novel by John Brophy

The Fixer ★★

Drama 1968 · US · Colour · 132mins

This lumbering epic stars Alan Bates as a Jewish opportunist in tsarist Russia who claims to be a Gentile and insinuates his way into the management of a brick factory. There's a rape charge, imprisonment, humiliation and constant fear of exposure and a new wave of pogroms. Based on Bernard Malamud's novel, screenwriter Dalton Trumbo and director John Frankenheimer take on some mighty themes and turn them into a scaled-down *Doctor Zhivago*, complete with a tacky Maurice Jarre score. Tedious and turgid. AT

Alan Bates *Yakov Bok* • Dirk Bogarde *Bibikov* • Georgia Brown *Marfa Golov* • Hugh Griffith *Lebedev* • Elizabeth Hartman *Zinaida* • Ian Holm *Grubeshov* • David Warner *Count Odoevsky* • Carol White *Raisl* ■ *Dir* John Frankenheimer • *Scr* Dalton Trumbo, from the novel by Bernard Malamud • *Music* Maurice Jarre

Fixing the Shadow ★★★ 18

Crime drama 1994 · US · Colour · 96mins

This engrossing look at the machinations of undercover police work is uncomfortably shoe-horned into an imperfect update of the old American Indian legend of the title, about a young brave running from his shadow and then descending into the land of shadows to retrieve it. Charlie Sheen is the cop recruited by the FBI to infiltrate a biker gang who finds his life strangely mirroring the fable. This never quite achieves the depth, grit or emotional power it strives for. AJ [VIDEO]

Charlie Sheen *Dan* • Linda Fiorentino *Renee* • Michael Madsen *Blood* • Courtney B Vance *Conroy* • Rip Torn *Prescott* • Larry Ferguson *Kelly* ■ *Dir/Scr* Larry Ferguson

Fiza ★★★ 12

Drama 2000 · Ind · Colour · 166mins

Stylishly photographed by Santosh Sivan, this is both a domestic melodrama and an insight into political extremism in modern-day India. However, debut director Khalid Mohamed is deflected from his purpose by the dance routines and comic subplots that are *de rigueur* in Bollywood blockbusters. Karisma Kapoor is earnest in the title role as she challenges the system in a bid to find her long-lost brother, Hrithik Roshan, but she's sidelined in the second half of the story, as the traumatised Roshan struggles to settle back into everyday life. DP. In Hindi and Urdu with English subtitles. [VIDEO] DVD

Karisma Kapoor [Karishma Kapoor] *Fiza* • Hrithik Roshan *Amaan* • Jaya Bhaduri [Jaya Bachchan] *Nishatbi* ■ *Dir/Scr* Khalid Mohamed

The Flame and the Arrow ★★★ U

Romantic swashbuckling adventure
1950 · US · Colour · 87mins

This exuberant swashbuckler stars Burt Lancaster, playing a Robin Hood-style character from northern Italy who woos Virginia Mayo while taking on Robert Douglas's land-owning monster. Lancaster's soul mate on the swinging chandeliers is Nick Cravat (his former circus partner), who was brought into the picture to ensure that the acrobatics went smoothly. AT

Burt Lancaster *Dardo* • Virginia Mayo *Anne* • Robert Douglas *Alessandro* • Aline MacMahon *Nonna Bartoli* • Nick Cravat *Piccolo* ■ *Dir* Jacques Tourneur • *Scr* Waldo Salt, from his story *The Hawk and the Arrow*

The Flame Barrier ★★ U

Science fiction 1958 · US · BW · 71mins

This post-Sputnik scare story was designed to cash in on public disquiet at venturing beyond the final frontier. The star of the show (or villain of the piece depending on your viewpoint) is art director James D Vance, who designed the heat-emitting cannibal protoplasm attached to the satellite that has crash-landed in the Yucatan jungle. There's a Val Lewton feel to the sequences in which explorer Arthur Franz locates the craft, but director Paul Landres is at the mercy of his cut-price special effects and the limited talents of his cast. DP

Arthur Franz *Dave Hollister* • Kathleen Crowley *Carol Dahlmann* • Robert Brown *Matt Hollister* • Vincent Padula *Julio* ■ *Dir* Paul Landres • *Scr* Pat Fielder, George Worthing Yates, from a story by George Worthing Yates

Flame in the Streets ★★ PG

Drama 1961 · UK · Colour · 89mins

Released at a time when "kitchen sink" realism was all the rage, this adaptation by Ted Willis of his own play suffers from the uncomfortable worthiness that blighted the efforts of so many British film-makers trying to tackle thorny social issues. John Mills rises above the old-fashioned liberalism to capture the confused bluster of the trade unionist who defends a black shop steward, but cannot tolerate the prospect of his daughter Sylvia Syms marrying Jamaican teacher Johnny Sekka. Brenda de Banzie's performance as his scornful, snobbish wife is badly misjudged. DP [VIDEO]

John Mills *Jacko Palmer* • Sylvia Syms *Kathie Palmer* • Brenda de Banzie *Nell Palmer* • Johnny Sekka *Peter Lincoln* • Earl Cameron *Gabriel Gomez* ■ *Dir* Roy Baker [Roy Ward Baker] • *Scr* Ted Willis, from his play *Hot Summer Night*

The Flame of New Orleans ★★

Comedy 1941 · US · BW · 79mins

A frothy comedy from French director René Clair, his first effort on his wartime sojourn in Hollywood. Phoney countess Marlene Dietrich leaves her rich but dull new husband Roland Young at the altar and sails away with rough-trade sea captain Bruce Cabot, disguising herself in the process. However, a shadowy figure from her European past appears and threatens her plans. This twist on the old gold-digger formula offers only middling entertainment, and shows just how ordinary Dietrich could be. AT

Marlene Dietrich *Claire Ledeux* • Bruce Cabot *Robert Latour* • Roland Young *Charles Giraud* • Mischa Auer *Zolotov* • Andy Devine *First sailor* • Frank Jenks *Second sailor* ■ *Dir* René Clair • *Scr* Norman Krasna

Flame of the Barbary Coast ★★★ U

Western 1945 · US · BW · 91mins

This earthquake adventure was a big picture for Republic, was trumpeted as the studio's "tenth anniversary production". John Wayne excels as a cattleman, competing with slimy Joseph Schildkraut for the attentions of Ann Dvorak. The low budget is evident in the ropey old stock shots and inadequate sets, though the production received Oscar nominations for its sound and score. TS

John Wayne *Duke Fergus* • Ann Dvorak *Flaxen Tarry* • Joseph Schildkraut *Tito Morell* • William Frawley *Smooth Wylie* • Virginia Grey *Rita Dane* • Russell Hicks *Cyrus Danver* ■ *Dir* Joseph Kane • *Scr* Borden Chase

Flame Top ★★★

Biographical drama
1980 · Fin · Colour · 150mins

One of the most expensive films ever made in Finland, this historical epic chronicles the life of the prolific and reclusive novelist, Maiju Lassila. Forced to flee St Petersburg after the murder of a Tsarist official, Lassila worked for the most part in abject poverty, enduring a tempestuous relationship with ex-actress Olga Esempio (passionately played by Rea Mauranen), before participating in the Bolshevik revolt in Helsinki. Faced with portraying such a complex character, Asko Sarkola is a touch too self-effacing. But the stately pacing lends suitable weight to unfamiliar events. DP. In Finnish with English subtitles.

Asko Sarkola *Maiju Lassila* • Rea Mauranen *Olga Esempio* • Kari Franck *Publisher* • Esko Salminen *Stationmaster* • Ari Suonsuu *Errand boy* • Tuomo Railo *Olga's young son* ■ *Dir/Scr* Pirjo Honkasalo, Pekka Lehto

Flamenco ★★ U

Documentary 1995 · Sp · Colour · 98mins

Celebrating the rich diversity and vibrant durability of the flamenco, Carlos Saura has created a handsome tribute to the various song, dance and instrumental styles that have evolved since the mid-19th century. However, in electing not to subtitle the lyrics, he deprives the uninitiated of the opportunity to enter fully into the passion and spirit of the music. The music is sublime, but Vittorio Storaro's lighting changes feel overly familiar, while Saura's approach is that of the antiquarian, not the artist. DP. A Spanish language film. DVD

Dir/Scr Carlos Saura • *Cinematographer* Vittorio Storaro • *Art Director* Rafael Palmero

Flaming Creatures ★★★

Experimental movie 1963 · US · BW · 45mins

A landmark experimental movie that paved the way for the acceptance of underground culture (specifically Andy Warhol's work) and a higher profile depiction of on-screen homosexuality. An elliptical mesh of tableaux featuring drag queens in various states of orgiastic behaviour, director Jack Smith's sexual apocalypse pilfers a kitsch range of Hollywood imagery from Marilyn Monroe and Josef von Sternberg to Maria Montez and Busby Berkeley movies and shakes them up with taboo-ridden acts of wanton lust. Ground-breaking in its day for its pivotol fusion of outrageous performance art, sumptuous surfaces, twisted text and camp, it remains a fascinating shock to the system. AJ

Francis Francine • Delores Flores • Joel Markman • Shirley ■ *Dir/Scr* Jack Smith (2)

Flaming Star ★★★★ PG

Western 1960 · US · Colour · 88mins

Originally intended as a vehicle for Marlon Brando, this immensely dignified and astoundingly violent (for its time) western became the second movie after *King Creole* to prove Elvis Presley could act. Here he plays an unhappy misfit, who must take sides when his mother's people (he is half native American) decide to go on the warpath. The tension, under the brilliant direction of Don Siegel, is beautifully sustained, and the outdoor colour and CinemaScope photography is outstanding. This was to be the last shot Presley would get at a decent acting role with a major director – after this his film career took a major turn for the worse. TS DVD

Elvis Presley *Pacer Burton* • Steve Forrest *Clint Burton* • Barbara Eden *Roslyn Pierce* • Dolores Del Rio *Neddy Burton* • John McIntire *Sam Burton* • Rudolph Acosta [Rodolfo Acosta] *Buffalo Horn* ■ *Dir* Don Siegel • *Scr* Clair Huffaker, Nunnally Johnson, from the novel by Clair Huffaker • *Cinematographer* Charles Clarke

The Flamingo Kid ★★★ 15

Comedy drama 1984 · US · Colour · 95mins

Garry Marshall didn't stray far from his *Happy Days* sitcom roots with this slight but affectionate teenage comedy drama set in the early 1960s. Matt Dillon plays the working class kid, attempting to better himself by working at an exclusive private club, who finds himself in a paternal tug of war between rich smoothie Richard Crenna and his own blue-collar dad, played by Hector Elizondo. The period trappings are lovingly re-created, as are the sounds of the era, and the script is a cut above the norm. JF DVD

Matt Dillon *Jeffrey Willis* • Richard Crenna *Phil Brody* • Hector Elizondo *Arthur Willis* • Jessica Walter *Phyllis Brody* • Fisher Stevens *Hawk Ganz* • Brian McNamara *Steve Dawkins* ■ *Dir* Garry Marshall • *Scr* Garry Marshall, Neal Marshall, from a story by Neal Marshall

Flamingo Road ★★★

Melodrama 1949 · US · BW · 94mins

After leaving MGM under a cloud and winning her Oscar in 1945 for *Mildred Pierce* at Warner Bros, Joan Crawford played a string of *femme fatale/grande dame* roles, making mincemeat of weak leading men. Here Crawford is reunited with the brilliant director Michael Curtiz, portraying a carnival dancer stranded in deepest Florida, trapped between two men and swapping cheap philosophy with sinister sheriff Sydney Greenstreet. A torrid treat. TS

Joan Crawford *Lane Bellamy* • Zachary Scott *Fielding Carlisle* • Sydney Greenstreet *Titus Semple* • David Brian *Dan Reynolds* • Gladys George *Lute-Mae Sanders* • Virginia Huston *Annabelle Weldon* • Fred Clark *Doc Waterson* ■ *Dir* Michael Curtiz • *Scr* Robert Wilder, Edmund H North, from the play by Robert Wilder, Sally Wilder

Flap ★

Comedy drama 1970 · US · Colour · 105mins

You would need the world's most powerful microscope to spot any trace of the director of *The Third Man* in this utterly dismal effort. It stars Anthony Quinn as an Indian chief who starts an uprising in order to draw attention to the economic plight of all native Americans. Carol Reed's movie is pitched as a slapstick comedy and Quinn's role as a drunken lecher is far more insulting than sympathetic. AT

Anthony Quinn *Flapping Eagle* • Claude Akins *Lobo Jackson* • Tony Bill *Eleven Snowflake* • Victor Jory *Wounded Bear Mr Smith* • Don Collier *Mike Lyons* • Shelley Winters *Dorothy Bluebell* ■ *Dir* Carol Reed • *Scr* Clair Huffaker

Flareup ★★ 15

Thriller 1969 · US · Colour · 93mins

A little-seen Raquel Welch vehicle which makes for diverting enough viewing. The star plays a Las Vegas dancer who attracts the unwelcome attentions of a psychopath, who rather unreasonably blames her for all his own personal problems. It's actually an early example of the *Fatal Attraction* genre that became so popular in the 1980s and 1990s, so it makes for an interesting curiosity. JF

Raquel Welch *Michele* • James Stacy *Joe Brodnek* • Luke Askew *Alan Morris* • Don Chastain *Lieutentant Manion* • Ron Rifkin *"Sailor"* • Jean Byron *Jerri Benton* ■ *Dir* James Neilson • *Scr* Mark Rogers

Flash Gordon ★★★ U

Science-fiction adventure
1936 · US · BW · 205mins

This is the feature-length condensation of the original 13-part *Flash Gordon* serial which inspired director George Lucas to create *Star Wars*. Breathless cliffhangers and vintage action meets cheesy special effects and hilarious overacting as charismatic hero Flash (former Olympic athlete Larry "Buster" Crabbe), along with Dale Arden (Jean Rogers) and Dr Zarkov (Frank Shannon), prevent Ming the Merciless (Charles Middleton) of the Planet Mongo conquering Earth. It's non-stop thrill-a-minute stuff (thanks to the ruthless editing) as Flash battles one adversary after another. The best of the Crabbe trilogy of *Flash Gordon* films, which in included *Flash Gordon's Trip to Mars* and *Flash Gordon Conquers the Universe*. AJ

Larry "Buster" Crabbe *Flash Gordon* • Jean Rogers *Dale Arden* • Charles Middleton *Ming the Merciless* • Priscilla Lawson *Princess Aura* • John Lipson *King Vultan* • Richard Alexander *Prince Barin* • Frank Shannon *Dr Zarkov* ■ *Dir* Frederick Stephani • *Scr* Frederick Stephani, George Plympton, Basil Dickey, Ella O'Neill, from the comic strip by Alex Raymond

Flash Gordon ★★★ PG

Science-fiction fantasy
1980 · US · Colour · 106mins

Aiming for the tongue-in-cheek frivolity of the fabulous Buster Crabbe adventures of the 1930s, Mike Hodges's big-budget fantasy is great fun, providing you ignore the plot altogether and concentrate on the corny performances and cheesy special effects. Although Ornella Muti makes a wonderfully witty Princess Aura, it's Max von Sydow who runs away with the picture as the dastardly Emperor Ming. However, the sheer badness of Sam J Jones as Flash (whose dialogue had to be dubbed by another actor) and Melody Anderson as Dale Arden also adds to the charm of this sci-fi pantomine. DP DVD

Sam J Jones [Sam Jones] *Flash Gordon* • Melody Anderson *Dale Arden* • Topol *Dr Hans Zarkov* • Max von Sydow *Emperor Ming* • Ornella Muti *Princess Aura* • Timothy Dalton *Prince Barin* • John Osborne *Arborian priest* • Richard O'Brien *Fico* ■ *Dir* Mike Hodges • *Scr* Lorenzo Semple Jr, Michael Allin, from the characters created by Alex Raymond • *Music* Queen, Howard Blake

A Flash of Green ★★★★

Drama 1984 · US · Colour · 131mins

Ed Harris once again proves what a superb actor he is, in this drama with an ecological theme, based on the John D MacDonald novel. He plays a Florida reporter who betrays more than just his profession when he agrees to help a corrupt official win backing for a controversial housing development. Victor Nunez's (*Ulee's Gold*) film boasts both classy direction and a strong cast. Gripping stuff. JB

Ed Harris *Jimmy Wing* • Blair Brown *Kate Hubble* • Richard Jordan *Elmo Bliss* • George Coe *Brian Hass* • Joan Goodfellow *Mitchie* • Jean De Baer *Jackie Halley* • John Glover *Ross Halley* ■ *Dir* Victor Nunez • *Scr* Victor Nunez, from the novel by John D MacDonald

Flashback ★★★ 15

Comedy action road movie
1990 · US · Colour · 103mins

This entertaining trip through flower power nostalgia stars Dennis Hopper, having a ball sending up his old screen persona. He is a 1960s activist, on the run for two decades, who is finally nabbed by the FBI but then proceeds to run rings around his fresh-faced captor, Kiefer Sutherland. The stars spark off each other nicely and there are also some neat supporting turns from Richard Masur, Carol Kane and Michael McKean as frustrated middle-aged hippies. The script lacks any real satirical bite, but it is nice to see Hopper in one of his rare non-psycho roles and director Franco Amurri keeps the action zipping along. JF DVD

Kiefer Sutherland *John Buckner* • Dennis Hopper *Huey Walker* • Carol Kane *Maggie* • Cliff De Young *Sheriff Hightower* • Michael McKean *Hal* • Richard Masur *Barry* • Paul Dooley *Donald R Stark, FBI Director* ■ *Dir* Franco Amurri • *Scr* David Loughery

Flashdance ★★★ 15

Musical drama 1983 · US · Colour · 90mins

Jennifer Beals stars as a welder by day and exotic dancer by night. But what she really, really wants is to join the Pittsburgh Ballet. Her dream ambition and fluffy romance with Michael Nouri look welded together from other Hollywood fairy tales of fame and fortune, yet director Adrian Lyne caught the post-disco visual mood of the time to win over even the most cynical viewer. The title song (sung by Irene Cara) won an Oscar. AJ. Contains swearing and nudity. DVD

Jennifer Beals *Alex Owens* • Michael Nouri *Nick Hurley* • Lilia Skala *Hanna Long* • Sunny Johnson *Jeanie Szabo* • Kyle T Heffner *Richie* ■ *Dir* Adrian Lyne • *Scr* Joe Eszterhas, Tom Hedley, from a story by Tom Hedley

Flashfire ★★ 18

Thriller 1993 · US · Colour · 84mins

This thriller starts well enough, with a ferocious blaze and the murder of cop Billy Zane's partner. But invention is at a premium once Zane joins up with feisty hooker Kristin Minter, who witnessed the murder, and they have to rely on their wits to stay one step ahead of Zane's crooked colleagues and a gang of arsonists. Carelessly directed by Elliot Silverstein, this muddled tale of corruption and conspiracy comes to an abrupt and highly unsatisfactory conclusion. DP. Contains swearing, violence. DVD

Billy Zane *Jack Flinder* • Louis Gossett Jr *Ben Durand* • Kristin Minter *Lisa Cates* • Louis Giambalvo *Al Sherwin* • Tom Mason *Art Cantrell* • Caroline Williams *Ann* ■ *Dir* Elliot Silverstein • *Scr* John Warren, Dan York

Flashpoint ★★★ 15

Thriller 1984 · US · Colour · 89mins

Despite its title and the combustible chemistry of its two leads (Kris Kristofferson and Treat Williams as US border patrolmen), this is rather a damp squib with a final revelation route-mapped all too obviously. The guards, who fear replacement by computer techology, find a jeep buried in the desert complete with a skeleton and a lot of loot. They start making enquiries about where the cash came from, before keeping the money; soon both the baddies and the FBI (or are they one and the same?) are on their trail. There's a fascinatingly eerie sense of location, but the characters are as chaotic as the narrative. TH [video]

Kris Kristofferson *Bob Logan* • Treat Williams *Ernie Wiatt* • Kevin Conway *Brook* • Joaquin Martinez *Pedroza* • Rip Torn *Sheriff Wells* • Guy Boyd *Lambasino* ■ *Dir* William Tannen (2) • *Scr* Michael Butler, Dennis Shryack, from the novel by George La Fountaine

Flatliners ★★★ 15

Supernatural thriller
1990 · US · Colour · 114mins

Is there life after death? Kiefer Sutherland, Julia Roberts and Kevin Bacon are among the medical students who are trying to find the answer by inducing their own temporary deaths in this gothic mix of old dark house and hi-tech laboratory. Schumacher puts more flash than flesh on the story, but still delivers the expected chills with cool efficiency. Trouble is, the afterlife stuff is rather too crudely clichéd. TH. Contains violence, swearing and a sex scene. [video] DVD

Kiefer Sutherland *Nelson Wright* • Julia Roberts *Rachel Mannus* • Kevin Bacon *David Labraccio* • William Baldwin *Joe Hurley* • Oliver Platt *Randy Steckle* • Kimberly Scott *Winnie Hicks* • Joshua Rudoy *Billy Mahoney* ■ *Dir* Joel Schumacher • *Scr* Peter Filardi • *Cinematographer* Jan De Bont

The Flavour of Green Tea over Rice ★★★★ U

Drama 1952 · Jpn · BW · 115mins

Yasujiro Ozu explores the nature of deceit and companionship in this wry yet ultimately touching study of arranged marriage. In showing how a discontented executive (Shin Saburi) and his free-spirited wife (Michiyo Kogure) work through the crisis in their relationship, he highlights the shifting social priorities of the bourgeoisie while also evoking a fond nostalgia for the recent past. It remains a recognisably intimate Ozu offering, in spite of the diversity of locations, frequency of camera movements and rhythmic cutting. DP. In Japanese with English subtitles. DVD

Shin Saburi • Michiyo Kogure • Koji Tsuruta • Keiko Tsushima • Kuniko Miyake • Chikage Awashima • Chishu Ryu ■ *Dir* Yasujiro Ozu • *Scr* Yasujiro Ozu, Kogo Noda

The Flaw ★

Crime drama 1954 · UK · BW · 60mins

Director Terence Fisher, best known for his work at Hammer films, does all that can be expected with this ominously titled thriller starring John Bentley. Well-cast as a sinisterly suave racing driver, Bentley easily upstages Donald Houston, who is the lawyer trying to thwart Bentley's plans to bump off his wealthy wife, Rona Anderson. The feeble script betrays the fact this is pure B-fodder, remade from a 1933 film, but adding nothing. DP

John Bentley *Paul Oliveri* • Donald Houston *John Millway* • Rona Anderson *Monica Oliveri* • Doris Yorke *Mrs Bower* • Tonia Bern *Vera* ■ *Dir* Terence Fisher • *Scr* Brandon Fleming

Flawless ★★ 15

Comedy drama 1999 · US · Colour · 110mins

Utterly schematic, hopelessly old-fashioned and totally bogus, director Joel Schumacher's highly personal comedy drama nevertheless delivers some camp laughs along its uneven, manipulative route. After suffering a stroke, homophobic security guard Robert De Niro is rehabilitated by drag queen Philip Seymour Hoffman. Deflating the simplistic morality fable is a vicious subplot involving stolen Mob money that Hoffman may have hidden to pay for a sex-change operation. AJ [video] DVD

Robert De Niro *Walt Koontz* • Philip Seymour Hoffman *Rusty Zimmerman* • Barry Miller *Leonard Wilcox* • Wilson Jermaine Heredia *Cha-Cha* • Daphne Rubin-Vega *Tia* ■ *Dir/Scr* Joel Schumacher

A Flea in Her Ear ★★★

Farce 1968 · US/Fr · Colour · 94mins

Doppelgängers, mistaken identity, mad chases and misunderstandings abound in this movie adaptation (by *Rumpole* creator John Mortimer) of a Feydeau farce which had scored a considerable success in London at the National Theatre. Rex Harrison stars in the double role of barrister Victor Chandebisse and hotel porter Poche, and Rosemary Harris is Gabrielle, Victor's suspicious and jealous wife. The Anglo-French cast are all on form in this classic Gallic sex comedy which was considered quite risqué in its time and was given an X certificate on release in the UK. DF

Rex Harrison *Victor Chandebisse/Poche* • Rosemary Harris *Gabrielle Chandebisse* • Louis Jourdan *Henri* • Rachel Roberts (1) *Suzanne* • John Williams *Dr. Finache* • Grégoire Aslan *Max* • Edward Hardwick *Pierre* ■ *Dir* Jacques Charon • *Scr* John Mortimer, from the play by John Mortimer, from the play *La Puce à l'Oreille* by Georges Feydeau

Fled ★★ 18

Action thriller 1996 · US · Colour · 93mins

This far-fetched action thriller has one black and one white convict (Laurence Fishburne and Stephen Baldwin) handcuffed together as they escape from a chain gang. The exit has been organised with the knowledge of the law enforcement agencies, who have their sights set on a South American narcotics boss. Director Kevin Hooks fills in the spaces between the audience's gasps of incredulity with fist-fights. TH. Contains swearing, violence and brief nudity. [video]

Laurence Fishburne *Charles Piper* • Stephen Baldwin *Mark Dodge* • Will Patton *Matthew Gibson* • Robert John Burke [Robert Burke] *Pat Schiller* • Robert Hooks *Lieutenant Clark* • Salma Hayek *Cora* ■ *Dir* Kevin Hooks • *Scr* Preston A Whitmore II

The Fleet's In ★★★ U

Musical comedy 1942 · US · BW · 93mins

This daft Paramount wartime crowd-pleaser has shy sailor William Holden taking on a bet to kiss sultry nightclub chanteuse Dorothy Lamour. Funny newcomer Betty Hutton in support became a star virtually overnight, and Jimmy Dorsey and his Orchestra feature prominently. It's all very 1940s, but alas director Victor Schertzinger died before the movie opened. Nevertheless the plot would continue to be used in Paramount pictures right up to Elvis Presley's comeback film *GI Blues* in 1960. TS

Dorothy Lamour *The Countess* • William Holden (2) *Casey Kirby* • Eddie Bracken *Barney Waters* • Betty Hutton *Bessie* • Cass Daley *Cissie* • Gil Lamb *Spike* ■ *Dir* Victor Schertzinger • *Scr* Walter DeLeon, Ralph Spence, Sid Silvers, from the play *Sailor Beware!* by Kenyon Nicholson, Charles Robinson, from a story by Monte Brice, J Walter Ruben

Flesh ★★★★

Drama 1932 · US · BW · 95mins

A wonderfully melancholic study of tragic wrestler Wallace Beery and his obsessional passion for moll Karen Morley, who's emotionally involved with nasty Ricardo Cortez. This is full-blown melodrama, superbly directed by the great John Ford, someone never afraid to tackle meaty material. The insights into the world of professional wrestling are fascinating and revelatory, especially the differences in the "sport" between Germany (where the tale begins) and the USA, while the brilliant Beery produces another fine performance. TS

Wallace Beery *Polikai* • Karen Morley *Laura Nash* • Ricardo Cortez *Nicky* • Jean Hersholt *Mr Herman* • John Miljan *Joe Willard* • Vince Barnett *Waiter* ■ *Dir* John Ford • *Scr* Moss Hart, Leonard Praskins, Edgar Allan Woolf, from a story by Edmund Goulding

Flesh ★★★ 18

Cult erotic drama 1968 · US · Colour · 85mins

Set in the demimonde of male prostitutes and extroverted transvestites typical of producer Andy Warhol, director Paul Morrissey's gutter graphic sex farce was an early attempt by the pop art icon to cross over from underground cinema into the mainstream arena. With no story structure as such, Morrissey is content to focus on the fringe elements of society in a series of Manhattan vignettes, revolving around the nearly always naked Joe Dallesandro, who is either hustling gays to get money for his bad-tempered wife or having sex with assorted weirdos. A frank walk on the wild side. AJ [video] DVD

Joe Dallesandro *Joe* • Geraldine Smith *Gerry* • John Christian *Young man* • Maurice Braddell *Artist* • Barry Brown *Boy on street* • Candy Darling *Blonde on sofa* • Jackie Curtis *Redhead on sofa* • Patti D'Arbanville *Gerry's girl friend* ■ *Dir/Scr* Paul Morrissey

Flesh + Blood ★★★ 18

Period epic
1985 · US/Neth · Colour · 126mins

Dutch director Paul Verhoeven's first Hollywood movie is a medieval epic which delivers the titular ingredients in proverbial buckets. It also boasts sumptuous music and splendid camerawork by Verhoeven regulars Basil Poledouris and Jan De Bont. Tough and witty, the film stars Rutger Hauer as a guerrilla warrior and Jennifer Jason Leigh as the virgin he kidnaps and rapes. It's a spectacle that anticipates Verhoeven's later films by pushing back the boundaries of sex and violence. AT [video] DVD

Rutger Hauer *Martin* • Jennifer Jason Leigh *Agnes* • Tom Burlinson *Steven* • Jack Thompson *Hawkwood* • Fernando Hillbeck *Arnolfini* • Susan Tyrrell *Celine* ■ *Dir* Paul Verhoeven • *Scr* Paul Verhoeven, Gerald Soeteman, from a story by Gerald Soeteman

Flesh and Bone ★★★★ 15

Mystery drama 1993 · US · Colour · 121mins

Dennis Quaid and Meg Ryan (then husband and wife) turn in two of their best performances in director Steve Kloves's unsettling modern *film noir*. James Caan is the psychotic cowhand who discovers his son Quaid is in love with the sole survivor of a family he murdered when she was a child. But will Ryan remember his face? Combining a fascinating fatalism with uncompromising black humour, this expert thriller evokes a haunting moodiness that never loses its grip as it turns up the subtle suspense to full throttle. AJ. Contains swearing and sex scenes. [video] DVD

Dennis Quaid *Arlis Sweeney* • Meg Ryan *Kay Davies* • James Caan *Roy Sweeney* • Christopher Rydell *Reese Davies* • Gwyneth Paltrow *Ginnie* • Scott Wilson *Elliot* ■ *Dir/Scr* Steve Kloves

Flesh and Fantasy ★★★

Supernatural portmanteau
1943 · US · BW · 92mins

New York wits Robert Benchley and David Hoffman link these three tales of the supernatural as they discuss dreams and elements of the supernatural. This leads into the three stories: the first is *Cinderella* with a twist, starring Betty Field and Robert Cummings; the second and best is an adaptation of Oscar Wilde's *Lord Arthur Saville's Crime* with Edward G Robinson shocked to learn from a spiritualist that he's about to become a murderer; and finally, Barbara Stanwyck's ghostly presence makes circus tightrope walker Charles Boyer lose his balance. Like all portmanteau films, a mixed blessing, but Julien Duvivier directs them all stylishly. AT

Edward G Robinson *Marshall Tyler* • Charles Boyer *Paul Gaspar* • Barbara Stanwyck *Joan Stanley* • Betty Field *Henrietta* • Robert Cummings *Michael* • Robert Benchley *Doakes* • David Hoffman *Davis* ■ *Dir* Julien Duvivier • *Scr* Ernest Pascal, Samuel Hoffenstein, Ellis St Joseph, from stories by Ellis St Joseph, Oscar Wilde (*Lord Arthur Saville's Crime,),* *Laslo Vadnay*

Flesh and Fury ★★

Sports drama 1952 · US · BW · 82mins

This was the 27-year-old Tony Curtis's 12th film and the first in which he relied on his acting ability rather than just his "pretty-boy" image. He plays a deaf-mute boxer besotted by good-time girl Jan Sterling. He's saved by honest reporter Mona Freeman, but on the way to that salvation there's time for boxing, an operation to restore his hearing and other complications. Curtis's performance gives some indication of the heights he would occasionally scale in future years. BB

Tony Curtis *Paul Callan* • Jan Sterling *Sonya Bartow* • Mona Freeman *Ann Hollis* • Wallace Ford *Jack Richardson* • Connie Gilchrist *Mrs Richardson* • Katherine Locke *Mrs Hollis* ■ *Dir* Joseph Pevney • *Scr* Bernard Gordon, from a story by William Alland

Flesh and the Devil ★★★★ U

Silent drama 1926 · US · BW · 112mins

Greta Garbo glows like a luminous icon of yearning with John Gilbert as one of her lovers in a film whose tremendous success was as much to do with the stars' off-screen affair as the story. Garbo – helped by William Daniels's lustrous camerawork – is a Countess-temptress who inspires a duel between her husband and a soldier, which – subtracted from its notorious sex scenes – was touched with the absurdity of the over-melodramatic. It was Garbo's third film for MGM, and director Clarence Brown poured her more than competently into the mould of a *femme fatale*. TH [video]

John Gilbert (1) *Leo von Harden* • Greta Garbo *Felicitas von Eltz* • Lars Hanson *Ulrich von Kletzingk* • Barbara Kent *Hertha Prochvitz* • William Orlamond *Uncle Kutowski* • George Fawcett *Pastor Voss* ■ *Dir* Clarence Brown • *Scr* Benjamin F Glazer [Benjamin Glazer], from the novel *Es War; Roman in Zwei Banden* by Herman Sudermann

The Flesh and the Fiends ★★★

Horror 1959 · UK · BW · 93mins

This explicitly scary and darkly atmospheric retelling the Burke and

Hare story stars Peter Cushing, exceptional as the coldly ambitious Dr Knox who scandalises the medical profession when he strikes a fatal bargain with two grave robbers to supply him with fresh corpses for experiments. The grimy poverty of 19th-century Edinburgh provides a vivid background to this unflinching shocker, which uses stark black-and-white imagery to startling effect. AJ

Peter Cushing *Dr Robert Knox* • Donald Pleasence *William Hare* • June Laverick *Martha* • George Rose *William Burke* • Dermot Walsh *Dr Geoffrey Mitchell* • Renee Houston *Helen Burke* • Billie Whitelaw *Mary Patterson* ■ *Dir* John Gilling • *Scr* John Gilling, Leon Griffiths, from a story by John Gilling

The Flesh Eaters ★★★★

Horror 1964 · US · BW · 89mins

Stylishly directed, well acted and featuring some spectacular gore effects for the period, director Jack Curtis' s splendidly convincing comic fantasy is long overdue for discovery as one of the most accomplished and influential shockers spearheading the nasty strain of American gothic. Filmed in 1960-61 in suburban New York but not released until 1964, it features pilot Byron Sanders and two passengers, alcoholic movie star Rita Morley and her secretary Barbara Wilkin, who crash on a small island where mad Nazi scientist Martin Kosleck is creating tiny carnivorous sea creatures. A must for connoisseurs of the bizarre. AJ

Martin Kosleck *Peter Bartell* • Rita Morley *Laura Winters* • Byron Sanders *Grant Murdock* • Ray Tudor *Omar* • Barbara Wilkin *Jan Letterman* ■ *Dir* Jack Curtis (2) • *Scr* Arnold Drake

Flesh Feast ★

Horror 1970 · US · Colour · 72mins

What do Hollywood glamour queens do when they retire? Play homicidal maniacs, of course. The trend started memorably with *What Ever Happened to Baby Jane?* but hit rock bottom with this tasteless and cheap mess of a movie. Lured back to the screen long after her glory days of the 1940s, Veronica Lake (in her last film) plays a scientist conducting anti-ageing experiments using live maggots that devour old skin tissue. RS

Veronica Lake *Dr Elaine Frederick* • Phil Philbin *Ed Casey* • Heather Hughes *Kristine* • Martha Mischon • Yanka Mann • Dian Wilhite • Chris Martell ■ *Dir* Brad F Grinter • *Scr* Brad F Grinter, Thomas Casey

Flesh for Frankenstein ★★★ 18

Horror 1974 · It/Fr/US · Colour · 90mins

Explicit blood-letting and violence overwhelm director Paul Morrissey's shockingly funny exposé of the venal grime behind Victorian aristocracy. Udo Kier is wonderfully arrogant as the Nietzschean Baron dismembering the local townspeople to build the perfect Aryan male and his female mate. Originally shown in excellent Space-Vision 3-D (the reason why sharp instruments are constantly being thrust into the camera) a strong stomach is still needed to witness the flattened down lurid gore and sickening splatter. Full of camp quotable dialogue, this was produced by, among others, Andy Warhol and Carlo Ponti. AJ [video]

Joe Dallesandro *Nicholas* • Udo Kier *Frankenstein* • Monique Van Vooren *Katrin* • Arno Juerging *Otto* • Srdjan Zelenovic *Male monster* ■ *Dir* Paul Morrissey, Antonio Margheriti • *Scr* Paul Morrissey, Tonino Guerra

Flesh Gordon ★★ 18

Science-fiction sex comedy
1974 · US · Colour · 84mins

This limp sex spoof of the Flash Gordon Saturday morning pictures adventure series became a theatrical, and then later, video hit. Jason Williams in the title role, Suzanne Fields, John Hoyt and a cameo from real-life porn star Candy Samples supply the talent. The Earth is being bombarded with a sex ray from the Planet Porno, and Flesh Gordon is the man to save us from our naughty selves. Not hilarious, but harmless all the same. JF [video] DVD

Jason Williams *Flesh Gordon* • Suzanne Fields *Dale Ardor* • Joseph Hudgins *Dr Flexi Jerkoff* • John Hoyt *Professor Gordon* • William Hunt [William Dennis Hunt] *Emperor Wang* • Craig T Brandy *(uncredited) Voice of the monster* • Candy Samples ■ *Dir* Howard Ziehm, Michael Benveniste • *Scr* Michael Benveniste

Flesh Gordon Meets the Cosmic Cheerleaders ★ 18

Science-fiction sex comedy
1989 · Can · Colour · 98mins

Director Howard Ziehm's sequel to his equally amateurish, but far superior, 1972 fantasy romp, resembles a bad home movie. This time all the charm, endearingly rock-bottom special effects and film buff cleverness is non-existent. Well-endowed Flesh (kick-boxer Vince Murdocco) goes to rescue his kidnapped girlfriend Robyn Kelly, but the mission is derailed by sex-starved Cosmic Cheerleaders from a planet inhabited by impotent men. A dreadfully unfunny fiasco. AJ [video] DVD

Vince Murdocco *Flesh Gordon* • Tony Travis *Dr Flexi Jerkoff* • Robyn Kelly *Dale Ardor* • William Hunt [William Dennis Hunt] *Emperor Wang* ■ *Dir* Howard Ziehm • *Scr* Doug Frisby, Howard Ziehm

The Flesh Is Weak ★

Crime drama 1957 · UK · BW · 88mins

John Derek – the future husband of Ursula Andress, Linda Evans and Bo Derek – takes on the sordid role of a Soho racketeer. He has an affair with innocent country girl Milly Vitale, frames her and watches her go to jail. However, a journalist manages to get Vitale to talk about her corruptor. Pretending to be a socially responsible look at the world of prostitution and campaigning for its legalisation, this is actually a cheapo melodrama. AT

John Derek *Tony Giani* • Milly Vitale *Marissa Cooper* • William Franklyn *Lloyd Buxton* • Martin Benson *Angelo Giani* • Freda Jackson *Trixie* • Norman Wooland *Insp Kingcombe* ■ *Dir* Don Chaffey • *Scr* Leigh Vance

The Flesh of the Orchid ★★★

Drama 1974 · Fr/It/W Ger · Colour · 105mins

This is less an exercise in hard-boiled fiction than in *Grand Guignol*. Exploiting expressionist visuals and allowing his cast to play at fever pitch, Patrice Chéreau clearly hopes to bring a sense of theatrical menace to his slow-burning tale of greed and revenge. Edwige Feuillère hits the right note of hysteria as the wicked aunt who has her niece consigned to an asylum in a bid to seize her inheritance, while Bruno Cremer is charismatically sinister as the stranger who helps confound her schemes. But Charlotte Rampling is less successful as the put-upon heiress who gets help from an unexpected source. DP. French dialogue dubbed into English.

Charlotte Rampling *Claire* • Bruno Cremer *Louis* • Edwige Feuillère *Aunt* • Simone Signoret *Lady Vamos* • Hugues Quester *Son* • Alida Valli *Woman* ■ *Dir* Patrice Chéreau • *Scr* Jean-Claude Carrière, Patrice Chéreau, from the novel by James Hadley Chase

Fleshtone ★★ 18

Erotic thriller 1994 · US · Colour · 86mins

Before relaunching his acting career on *EastEnders*, Martin Kemp wiled away the years in straight-to-video land. In this thriller, one of his less distinguished efforts, he is somewhat unconvincingly cast as a painter who becomes a murder suspect when he gets hooked on a sex chat-line. It's the usual mix of soft lighting, mild eroticism and a plot twist you will see coming a mile off. JF [video] DVD

Martin Kemp *Matthew Greco* • Lise Cutter • Tim Thomerson ■ *Dir/Scr* Harry Hurwitz

Fletch ★★★ PG

Comedy adventure
1985 · US · Colour · 94mins

Chevy Chase, one of the original *Saturday Night Live* team, stars in the first of two outings as the investigative reporter with a sideline in disguises and witty repartee. Seized from Malibu beach (where he is disguised as a beach bum) by a millionaire who orders his own murder, Chase stumbles and bumbles through a corkscrew plot that fits his comic frame like a bespoke suit. Sleek, glossy and often very funny indeed, the inventive script is by Andrew Bergman, who went on to direct *The Freshman* and *Honeymoon in Vegas*. AT [video] DVD

Chevy Chase *IM Fletcher, "Fletch"* • Joe Don Baker *Chief Karlin* • Dana Wheeler-Nicholson *Gail Stanwyk* • Tim Matheson *Alan Stanwyk* • M Emmet Walsh *Dr Dolan* • George Wendt *Fat Sam* • Geena Davis *Larry* ■ *Dir* Michael Ritchie • *Scr* Andrew Bergman, from the novel by Gregory McDonald

Fletch Lives ★★ PG

Comedy adventure
1989 · US · Colour · 90mins

Chevy Chase reprises his role as the daffy investigative reporter in this adult comedy, but this time he's not blessed with a sharp enough script. Fletch is one of those characters that you either find irresistibly funny and folksy, or merely the celluloid celebration of the nightmare passenger you find yourself sitting beside in a plane. The plot, such as it is, doesn't so much revolve around Chase in a variety of ill-fitting disguises, as spin mercilessly out of control. SH. Contains swearing. [video]

Chevy Chase *Fletch* • Julianne Phillips *Becky Ann Culpepper* • Hal Holbrook *"Ham" Johnson* • R Lee Ermey *Jimmy Lee Farnsworth* • Richard Libertini *Frank Walker* • Randall "Tex" Cobb *Ben Dover* ■ *Dir* Michael Ritchie • *Scr* Leon Capetanos, from characters created by Gregory McDonald

Un Flic ★★★ 12

Crime thriller 1972 · Fr · Colour · 98mins

Jean-Pierre Melville wound down his incalculably influential career with this return to his favourite stomping ground, the *film noir*. This may not be his most innovative work, but the duel between cop Alain Delon and drug-smuggling bank robber Richard Crenna does contain some of his most audacious set pieces. The narrative gets a little messy in places as Melville experiments with elliptical editing and shifting time frames. Delon is typically laconic, however, while Catherine Deneuve delivers a virtually silent performance as his mistress. DP. French dialogue dubbed into English. [video] DVD

Alain Delon *Coleman* • Catherine Deneuve *Cathy* • Richard Crenna *Simon* • Riccardo Cucciolla *Paul* • Michael Conrad *Costa* • André Pousse *Albouis* • Paul Crauchet *Morand* ■ *Dir/Scr* Jean-Pierre Melville

Flight ★★

Action drama 1929 · US · BW · 116mins

Jack Holt and Ralph Graves star in this Frank Capra talkie. It's a military adventure, dealing with America's invasion of Nicaragua. Because the US Navy cooperated fully with the production, loaning the unit its base and equipment in San Diego, the movie has some spectacular aerial sequences. Unfortunately the same cannot be said for the familiar love triangle storyline. AT

Jack Holt *Panama Williams* • Ralph Graves *Lefty Phelps* • Lila Lee *Elinor* • Alan Roscoe *Major* • Harold Goodwin (1) *Steve Roberts* ■ *Dir* Frank Capra • *Scr* Howard J Green, Frank Capra, from a story by Ralph Graves

Flight Command ★★

Second World War drama
1940 · US · BW · 115mins

MGM prepared Americans for war by sending Robert Taylor aloft as a recently qualified Naval pilot who helps design a fog landing system, saving the squadron commander in the process and making widowed Ruth Hussey go all dewy-eyed. There's enough plot for a dozen movies, so emotions tend to suffer from serious air turbulence and even Red Skelton, in his second film, hasn't much time for his comedy schtick. AT

Robert Taylor (1) *Ensign Alan "Pensacola" Drake* • Ruth Hussey *Lorna Gary* • Walter Pidgeon *Squadron Cdr Bill Gary* • Paul Kelly (1) *Lt Cmdr "Dusty" Rhodes* • Shepperd Strudwick *Lt Jerry Banning* • Red Skelton *Lt "Mugger" Martin* ■ *Dir* Frank Borzage • *Scr* Wells Root, Cdr Harvey Haislip, from the story by Cdr Harvey Haislip, John Sutherland

Flight for Freedom ★★ U

Romantic drama 1943 · US · BW · 101mins

This thinly disguised biopic is clearly based on noted aviatrix Amelia Earhart, and her last mysterious journey. Though the movie was sanctioned by Earhart's widower, publisher Charles Palmer Putnam, he wouldn't let RKO use her name, and you can't blame him after seeing this melodramatic nonsense. Rosalind Russell made her debut for the studio as the plucky flier, cast opposite a happy-go-lucky Fred MacMurray. Preposterous stuff, leadenly directed. TS

Rosalind Russell *Tonie Carter* • Fred MacMurray *Randy Britton* • Herbert Marshall *Paul Turner* • Edward Ciannelli [Eduardo Ciannelli] *Johnny Salvini* • Walter Kingsford *Admiral Graves* ■ *Dir* Lothar Mendes • *Scr* Oliver HP Garrett, SK Lauren, Jane Murfin, from a story by Horace McCoy

Flight from Ashiya ★★

Action drama
1964 · US/Jpn · Colour · 102mins

A mega-macho trio – Yul Brynner, Richard Widmark, George Chakiris – are engulfed by sentimentality and self-doubt as members of a US rescue mission at sea. They're trying to save the survivors of a storm-battered cargo ship off the Japanese coast but all three have psychological problems to overcome before they can get to grips with the elements. Far from being a robust action adventure, the extensive flashback sequences turn this into a glorified high-seas soap. TH

Yul Brynner *Sgt Mike Takashima* • Richard Widmark *Col Glenn Stevenson* • George Chakiris *Lt John Gregg* • Suzy Parker *Lucille* • Shirley Knight *Caroline* • Danièle Gaubert *Leila* ■ *Dir* Michael Anderson • *Scr* Elliott Arnold, Waldo Salt, from the novel by Elliott Arnold

Flight from Glory ★★

Action drama 1937 · US · BW · 66mins

An RKO B-movie, inspired by the success of MGM's classier *Night Flight*, which boasted two Barrymores and Clark Gable flying air freight across the Andes. Here it's still the Andes, but the cast only gets as high up the stellar scale as Chester Morris and Van Heflin, who have both lost their licences in America and now fly supplies to a remote mountain mining camp. When they're not in the air, romance blossoms between head honcho Morris and Whitney Bourne, Heflin's new bride. AT

Chester Morris *Smith* • Whitney Bourne *Lee Wilson* • Onslow Stevens *Ellis* • Van Heflin *George Wilson* • Richard Lane *Hanson* • Paul Guilfoyle (1) *Jones* ■ *Dir* Louis Friedlander [Lew Landers] • *Scr* David Silverstein, John Twist, from a story by Robert D Andrews

Flight of Fancy ★★

Drama 2000 · US · Colour · 98mins

A lonely lad learns a bit about life and a lot about himself through his encounter with an intriguing stranger. Bored with his mundane island existence and unhappy with mother Talisa Soto's relationship with dull Miguel Sandoval, young Kristian de la Osa has his hopes raised when Dean Cain arrives in his bi-plane. Cain makes a suitably dashing penny-dreadful hero, but director Noel Quinones douses his dealings with the kid in queasy sentiment. DP

Dean Cain *Clay* • Talisa Soto *Mercedes* • Miguel Sandoval *Frank* • Kristian de la Osa *Gabriel* ■ *Dir* Noel Quinones • *Scr* Mark Kemble, Noel Quinones, Tom Musca

Flight of the Albatross ★★★

Drama 1995 · Ger/NZ · Colour · 93mins

Unlike most children's dramas, this cinematic collaboration between New Zealand and Germany treats its audience with respect by tackling such serious subjects as conservation and the notion that cultural difference represents a challenge and not a threat. As the New Yorker who comes to the Great Kauri island in the South Pacific to visit her scientist mother, Julia Brendler is refreshingly unprecocious. The way her friendship develops with Maori Emile Taungaroa, as they tend an injured albatross, makes the issues seem alive rather than contrived. DP

Jack Thompson *Mike* • Taungaroa Emile *Mako* • Julia Brendler *Sarah* • Suzanne von Borsody *Claudia* • Pete Smith *Huka* • Diana Ngaromotu-Heka *Mari* ■ *Dir* Werner Meyer • *Scr* Riwia Brown, from the novel by Deborah Savage, Philippe Campbell

Flight of the Doves ★★★ U

Adventure drama 1971 · UK · Colour · 97mins

Director Ralph Nelson followed the success of the controversial *Soldier Blue* with this charming piece of Irish whimsy that may be too self-consciously cute for adult tastes. Beautifully shot on location by ace cinematographer Harry Waxman, this blithe tale charts the trials and tribulations of a pair of Liverpudlian children who, quite unaccountably, keep running into English character actors such as Ron Moody, Stanley Holloway and Willie Rushton. There's a lovely performance from the marvellous Dorothy McGuire, and Roy Budd's score is great. TS [VIDEO] DVD

Ron Moody *Hawk Dove* • Jack Wild *Finn Dove* • Dorothy McGuire *Granny O'Flaherty* • Stanley Holloway *Judge Liffy* • Helen Raye *Derval Dove* • William Rushton *Tobias Cromwell* ■ *Dir* Ralph Nelson • *Scr* Frank Gabrielson, Ralph Nelson, from a novel by Walter Macken

Flight of the Innocent ★★ 18

Thriller 1993 · It/Fr · Colour · 100mins

After an arresting opening, in which a young boy witnesses the slaughter of both his family and a kidnapped child, Carlo Carlei's film lapses into a shameless sentimentality that fatally undermines the initial naturalism. Manuel Colao gives a remarkable performance as the hill urchin who seeks refuge in the city, but he has one too many narrow escapes, and is accepted too readily by grieving parents Francesca Neri and Jacques Perrin, for this melodramatic tale to truly convince. DP. In Italian with English subtitles. [VIDEO]

Manuel Colao *Vito* • Francesca Neri *Marta Rienzi* • Jacques Perrin *Davide Rienzi* • Federico Pacifici *Scarface* • Sal Borgese *Vito's father* ■ *Dir* Carlo Carlei • *Scr* Carlo Carlei, Gualtiero Rosella, from a story by Carlo Carlei

Flight of the Intruder ★★ 15

War drama 1991 · US · Colour · 109mins

Gung-ho bombast is definitely macho director John Milius's forte. Unfortunately, it can't save this claustrophobic and endlessly talky drama, set during the winding-down stages of the Vietnam War. Milius co-wrote *Apocalypse Now*, but this moralistic study of the vainglorious US military effort isn't in the same class. The high-profile cast does what it can considering the ideological script, but it's fighting as much of a losing battle as the one depicted. AJ [VIDEO] DVD

Danny Glover *Commander Frank Camparelli* • Willem Dafoe *Lieutenant Commander Virgil Cole* • Brad Johnson *Lieutenant Jake* • Rosanna Arquette *Callie* ■ *Dir* John Milius • *Scr* Robert Dillon, David Shaber, from a novel by Stephen Coonts

Flight of the Navigator ★★★ U

Science-fiction adventure 1986 · US · Colour · 85mins

This appealing children's adventure has just enough quirky touches to keep adults involved as well. Joey Cramer is the youngster who goes missing at the age of 12, only to turn up eight years later completely unchanged. It soon becomes apparent that his disappearance is linked to alien space travel. The scenes where Cramer attempts to get to grips with the fact that he has missed out on eight years of his life are neatly handled by director Randal Kleiser, who proves equally adept at the action sequences. JF [VIDEO] DVD

Joey Cramer *David Freeman* • Veronica Cartwright *Helen Freeman* • Cliff De Young *Bill Freeman* • Sarah Jessica Parker *Carolyn McAdams* • Howard Hesseman *Dr Faraday* • Paul Mall [Paul Reubens] *Max* ■ *Dir* Randal Kleiser • *Scr* Michael Burton, Matt MacManus, from a story by Mark H Baker

The Flight of the Phoenix ★★★★ PG

Adventure drama 1965 · US · Colour · 136mins

James Stewart's plane crashes in the desert and when, after days in the sweltering heat, you think he might take a juicy bite out of Richard Attenborough, Peter Finch or Hardy Kruger to get some protein, a plan is hatched to build a smaller plane out of the wreckage. This survivalist epic has all the expected ingredients and more – Attenborough's nerves are shattered, Kruger is the embodiment of Germanic efficiency, Finch is stiff-upper-lipped, Stewart is Charles Lindbergh with a wing down, and all of them sweat and grow beards with customary skill. Director Robert Aldrich keeps things boiling for perhaps longer than is necessary but delivers a genuinely exciting climax. AT DVD

James Stewart *Frank Towns* • Richard Attenborough *Lew Moran* • Peter Finch *Captain Harris* • Hardy Kruger *Heinrich Dorfmann* • Ernest Borgnine *Trucker Cobb* • Ian Bannen *Crow* • Ronald Fraser *Sergeant Watson* ■ *Dir* Robert Aldrich • *Scr* Lukas Heller, from the novel by Elleston Trevor

Flight of the Phoenix ★★★ 12

Action adventure 2004 · US · Colour · 108mins

This remake adds little to the 1965 original, save some superior special effects, but it's a decent enough adventure yarn. The plot remains much the same: the survivors of a plane crash in the desert and seek to escape by building a second craft from the wreckage of the first. Dennis Quaid assumes the role of the pilot originally played by James Stewart, while Giovanni Ribisi steps into Hardy Kruger's shoes to play the aircraft designer who conceives the idea of a new plane to rise phoenix-like from the ashes of the old. DA. Contains swearing. [VIDEO] DVD

Dennis Quaid *Frank Towns* • Giovanni Ribisi *Elliott* • Tyrese Gibson *AJ* • Miranda Otto *Kelly* • Hugh Laurie *Ian* • Tony Curran *Rodney* • Kirk Jones *Jeremy* • Jacob Vargas *Sammi* • Scott Michael Campbell *Liddle* • Kevork Malikyan *Rady* ■ *Dir* John Moore (3) • *Scr* Frank Scott, Edward Burns, from the film by Lukas Heller, from the novel by Elleston Trevor

The Flight of the White Heron ★★★ U

Documentary 1954 · UK · Colour · 95mins

This little seen documentary is not just significant because it chronicles the first extensive Commonwealth tour undertaken by the Queen after her coronation, but because it was also the first time the new widescreen colour process, CinemaScope, was used in a British non-fiction film. As close-ups were still regarded as intrusive in those pre-paparazzi days, the producers scrupulously stuck to atmospheric overviews, which not only enhance the spectacle of such events as the Dunedin Highland Games, the Aboriginal corroboree and the Bondi Beach surf carnival, but also showed off Scope's unique visual potential. DP

Leslie Mitchell *Narrator* ■ • *Producer* Jack Ramsden • *Supervising Producer* Gordon Craig • *Cinematographer* Paul Wyand, Norman Fisher, Mark McDonald

The Flight That Disappeared ★ U

Science fiction 1961 · US · BW · 72mins

Three nuclear scientists are on board a plane headed for Washington, armed with plans for a powerful super-bomb. Their flight reaches an altitude that suddenly shifts them into another dimension, where a jury representing future generations subjects them to a trial for their warrior invention. A slight plea-for-pacifism ethical drama further let down by a confusing script and shoddy production values. AJ

Craig Hill *Tom Endicott* • Paula Raymond *Marcia Paxton* • Dayton Lummis *Dr Morris* • Gregory Morton *Examiner* ■ *Dir* Reginald Le Borg • *Scr* Ralph Hart, Judith Hart, Owen Harris

Flight to Fury ★★

Crime adventure drama 1966 · US/Phil · BW · 80mins

Amazingly, Jack Nicholson wrote the script for this jungle potboiler on the ship that was taking him and the crew to the Philippines where the film was to be shot. By the time they landed in Manila, Nicholson had finished his first solo screenplay. Not surprisingly he wrote the best part for himself, that of a psychopathic gem smuggler, member of a gang whose plane crashes in the jungle where they fight bandits and each other over a cache of stolen diamonds. Directed on a shoestring budget with credible gusto by Monte Hellman. RS

Dewey Martin *Joe Gaines* • Fay Spain *Destiny Cooper* • Jack Nicholson *Jay Wickam* • Jacqueline Hellman [Jaclyn Hellman] *Gloria Walsh* ■ *Dir* Monte Hellman • *Scr* Jack Nicholson, from a story by Monte Hellman, Fred Roos

Flight to Mars ★ U

Science fiction 1951 · US · Colour · 71mins

A ramshackle space opera in comic-strip style about mankind's first landing on Mars and the discovery of an advanced, dying underground civilisation plotting an Earth invasion because they are running low on resources. Shot in 11 days by quickie merchants Monogram Studios, this uninspired pulp nonsense. AJ [VIDEO]

Marguerite Chapman *Alita* • Cameron Mitchell *Steve* • Arthur Franz *Jim* • Virginia Huston *Carol* • John Litel *Dr Lane* • Richard Gaines *Prof Jackson* ■ *Dir* Lesley Selander • *Scr* Arthur Strawn

Flight to Tangier ★ U

Action drama 1953 · US · Colour · 89mins

Joan Fontaine's career was on the slide when she agreed to star in this overly complicated chase melodrama, although Jack Palance must have welcomed the chance to play a romantic lead, abdicating the villainy to Robert Douglas. Set in contemporary Tangier, writer/director Charles Marquis Warren's picture is peopled by mysterious characters behaving strangely. It was originally made for screening in 3-D, which would have provided a welcome distraction. AE

Joan Fontaine *Susan* • Jack Palance *Gil Walker* • Corinne Calvet *Nicole* • Robert Douglas *Danzar* • Marcel Dalio *Gogo* ■ *Dir/Scr* Charles Marquis Warren

The Flintstones ★★ U

Comedy 1994 · US · Colour · 86mins

The casting is almost perfect, the re-creation of Bedrock is masterly and the special effects are clever without being overly intrusive. And yet this live-action version of the classic 1960s TV cartoon series is lacklustre. The boisterous fun that made the Hanna-Barbera original so endearing has been lost and not even John Goodman's exuberant Fred or Elizabeth Taylor's sly mother-in-law can atone. The comic slapstick will appeal to youngsters, but the film isn't that funny. DP [VIDEO] DVD

John Goodman *Fred Flintstone* • Elizabeth Perkins *Wilma Flintstone* • Rick Moranis *Barney Rubble* • Rosie O'Donnell *Betty Rubble* • Kyle MacLachlan *Cliff Vandercave* • Halle Berry *Miss Stone* • Elizabeth Taylor *Pearl Slaghoople* ■ *Dir* Brian Levant • *Scr* Tom S Parker, Jim Jennewein, Steven E de Sousa, from the animated TV series by William Hanna, Joseph Barbera

The Flintstones in Viva Rock Vegas ★★★ PG

Comedy 2000 · US · Colour · 87mins

It's yabba-dabba-two time as Fred and Barney first meet Wilma and Betty in a belated prequel to 1994's live-action original. The first half is cuter, with the trademark retro gizmos, while the more plot-driven second half could tax pre-adolescent patience as Fred seeks to win Wilma's hand by striking it rich in Vegas. The casting is variable: Mark Addy looks the part as Fred, but underplays it; Stephen Baldwin's Barney is too gormless and two feet too tall. The girls, though, are great, with Jane Krakowski a nicely traditional Betty, and Kristen Johnston a voluptuous Wilma. DA [VIDEO] DVD

Mark Addy *Fred Flintstone* • Stephen Baldwin *Barney Rubble* • Kristen Johnston *Wilma Slaghoople* • Jane Krakowski *Betty O'Shale* • Joan Collins *Pearl Slaghoople* • Alan Cumming

F

The Great Gazoo/Mick Jagged • Harvey Korman *Col Slaghoople* ■ *Dir* Brian Levant • *Scr* Harry Elfont, Deborah Kaplan, Jim Cash, Jack Epps Jr, from the animated TV series by William Hanna, Joseph Barbera

Flipper ★★★ U

Adventure 1963 · US · Colour · 86mins

There can hardly be a baby boomer in Britain who didn't follow the adventures of Flipper the dolphin on TV at one time or another during the 1960s. Well, this is the film that inspired the series. Produced by Ivan Tors, who specialised in animal adventures, this is a delight from start to finish, with Luke Halpin excelling as the small boy who befriends and tames the mischievous, scene-stealing dolphin. A sequel, *Flipper's New Adventure*, followed and it was remade in 1996. DP DVD

Chuck Connors *Porter Ricks* • Luke Halpin *Sandy Ricks* • Kathleen Maguire *Martha Ricks* • Connie Scott *Kim Parker* • Jane Rose *Hettie White* • Joe Higgins *LC Porett* ■ *Dir* James B Clark • *Scr* Arthur Weiss, from a story by Ricou Browning, Jack Cowden

Flipper ★★ PG

Adventure 1996 · US · Colour · 91mins

Elijah Wood goes to spend the summer on an island near Florida with his fisherman uncle Paul Hogan. The island's fisherfolk turn nasty when Wood befriends a dolphin they suspect of eating all the local catch, but the tables are turned when the duo discovers a gang of hunters polluting the in-shore waters with toxic waste. A formula family film, but with idyllic locations and an upbeat soundtrack. JF DVD

Paul Hogan *Porter* • Elijah Wood *Sandy* • Jonathan Banks *Dirk Moran* • Bill Kelley *Tommy* • Chelsea Field *Cathy* • Isaac Hayes *Sheriff Buck Cowan* • Luke Halpin *Bounty fisherman* ■ *Dir* Alan Shapiro • *Scr* Alan Shapiro, from the film by Arthur Weiss, from a story by Ricou Browning, Jack Cowden

Flipper's New Adventure ★★★ PG

Adventure 1964 · US · Colour · 97mins

Following the success of the previous year's *Flipper*, cinema's most adorable dolphin returned for another adventure in the company of Luke Halpin as Sandy. Fearing they are to be separated, the duo flee to a remote island, where they encounter a British family, whose yachting holiday has been hijacked by pirates. With Pamela Franklin and Francesca Annis making early screen appearances, this exciting story makes splendid use of both its exotic locations and its aquatic superstar. TS

Luke Halpin *Sandy Ricks* • Pamela Franklin *Penny* • Tom Helmore *Sir Halsey Hopewell* • Helen Cherry *Julia* • Francesca Annis *Gwen* ■ *Dir* Leon Benson • *Scr* Art Arthur, from a story by Ivan Tors, from characters created by Ricou Browning, Jack Cowden

Flipping ★★★ 18

Crime drama 1996 · US · Colour · 98mins

Despite the off-putting title, this is an atmospheric crime thriller, set on the seedy streets of Hollywood. David Amos is one of group of tough-guy collectors working for for local crime boss Keith David. The trouble starts when the boys decide they would be better off with David out of the way. An interesting twist is Amos's unexpected relationship with cop David Proval. Sharply written and directed, this is smarter than your average crime yarn. DA. Contains swearing, violence.

Keith David *Leo Richards* • David Proval *Billy White* • David Amos *Michael Moore* • Barry Primus *Joey* • Mike Starr *CJ* • Gene Mitchell *Shot* ■ *Dir/Scr* Gene Mitchell

Flirt ★★ 15

Comedy drama
1995 · US/Ger/Jpn · Colour · 83mins

Independent director Hal Hartley has a vision as quirky as it is emotionally contained, and this is a whimsy in which the same idea is put through three transformations. New Yorker Bill Sage wonders if he should reject his lover, only to find a suicide attempt getting in the way; in Berlin, Dwight Ewell wonders about his own future; in Tokyo Miho Nikaido (Hartley's wife) engages with a visiting film director (Hartley himself). Some emotional home truths are learned, but the structure is too self-conscious to appeal to those who aren't in on the joke. TH. In English, German and Japanese with subtitles.

Bill Sage *Bill (New York)* • Martin Donovan (2) *Walter (New York)* • Parker Posey *Emily (New York)* • Dwight Ewell *Dwight (Berlin)* • Geno Lechner *Greta (Berlin)* • Miho Nikaido *Miho (Tokyo)* • Chikako Hara *Yuki (Tokyo)* • Hal Hartley *Hal (Tokyo)* ■ *Dir/Scr* Hal Hartley

Flirtation Walk ★★★ U

Musical comedy 1934 · US · BW · 98mins

Dedicated to the West Point Military Academy, this lively musical goes a fair way to both glamourising and glorifying that legendary institution. It also provides an ideal arena for that likeable twosome of Dick Powell and Ruby Keeler (he's a cadet, she's the general's daughter) who get to croon and stroll along a very studio-bound vision of the eponymous "walk". Director Frank Borzage makes heavy weather of the simplistic plotting, but the film was popular enough to earn a best picture Oscar nomination. TS

Dick Powell *Dick "Canary" Richard Palmer* • Ruby Keeler *Kit Fitts* • Pat O'Brien *Scrapper Thornhill* • Ross Alexander (1) *Oskie* • John Arledge *Spike* • John Eldredge *Lt Robert Biddle* • Henry O'Neill *Gen Jack Fitts* ■ *Dir* Frank Borzage • *Scr* Delmer Daves, from a story by Lou Edelman, Delmer Daves

Flirting ★★★★★ 15

Comedy drama 1989 · Aus · Colour · 94mins

Director John Duigan began the coming-of-age story of Danny Embling in the wonderful *The Year My Voice Broke*, and continues it in this even more enjoyable and moving comedy drama. Noah Taylor reprises his role as the young boy who moves from his small Australian outback town to an all-boys boarding school. Across the lake is an all-girls school, and it is during one of the occasions where the two schools get together that he meets and falls in love with a beautiful young Ugandan pupil (Thandie Newton, making her film debut). A true gem, Duigan's film is also notable for a brief appearance by Nicole Kidman, back on her native soil. JB

Noah Taylor *Danny Embling* • Thandie Newton *Thandiwe Adjewa* • Nicole Kidman *Nicola Radcliffe* • Bartholomew Rose *"Gilby" Fryer* • Felix Nobis *Jock Blair* • Josh Picker *"Baka" Bourke* • Marc Gray *Christopher Laidlaw* ■ *Dir/Scr* John Duigan

Flirting with Disaster ★★★ 15

Comedy road movie
1996 · US · Colour · 88mins

This madcap, country-crossing comedy makes up in eccentric characterisation what it occasionally loses in control. As the orphan hoping to trace his roots before naming his new baby, Ben Stiller is suitably neurotic as ditzy psychologist Téa Leoni leads him up endless blind alleys. Cameos by adoptive parents Mary Tyler Moore and George Segal, and ageing hippies Alan Alda and Lily Tomlin steal Stiller's thunder and further marginalise the under-used Patricia Arquette. Great screwball, shame about the slapstick. DP DVD

Ben Stiller *Mel Coplin* • Patricia Arquette *Nancy Coplin* • Téa Leoni *Tina Kalb* • Mary Tyler Moore *Mrs Coplin* • George Segal *Mr Coplin* • Alan Alda *Richard Schlicting* • Lily Tomlin *Mary Schlicting* • Richard Jenkins *Paul* • Josh Brolin *Tony* ■ *Dir/Scr* David O Russell

Floating Life ★★

Drama 1996 · Aus · Colour · 98mins

Despite earlier misgivings, China's takeover of Hong Kong disturbed comparatively few indigenous families. This modest Australian film tells the story of one elderly couple who decide to uproot and join their daughter (Annie Yip) in Sydney. A nicely observed and occasionally poignant piece of work, it entertainingly depicts a small-scale human dilemma, but ultimately is well meaning rather than distinguished. BB. In English, German and Cantonese with English subtitles.

Annette Shun Wah *Yen* • Annie Yip *Bing* • Anthony Wong (2) *Gar Ming* • Edwin Pang *Pa Chan* • Cecilia Fong Sing Lee *Ma Chan* ■ *Dir* Clara Law • *Scr* Eddie LC Fong [Eddie Ling-Ching Fong], Clara Law

Floating Weeds ★★ PG

Drama 1959 · Jpn · Colour · 113mins

Based on the same story that inspired his silent 1934 drama, *A Story of Floating Weeds*, this was among Yasujiro Ozu's weakest postwar pictures. For once his nostalgic yearnings seem to have got the better of him, as there are few contemporary resonances in this story of a travelling Kabuki player who hurts his mistress by interfering in the love life of his estranged son. Kenji Mizoguchi's regular cinematographer Kazuo Miyagawa gives the seascapes a lustre that only occasionally illuminates the rest of the production. DP. In Japanese with English subtitles. DVD

Ganjiro Nakamura *Komajuro Arashi* • Haruko Sugimura *Oyoshi* • Hiroshi Kawaguchi *Kiyoshi* • Machiko Kyo *Sumiko* • Ayako Wakao *Kayo* • Chishu Ryu *Theatre owner* ■ *Dir* Yasujiro Ozu • *Scr* Yasujiro Ozu, Kogo Noda, from a story by Yasujiro Ozu, from the 1934 film *Ukigusa Monogatari [A Story of Floating Weeds]* by Tadao Ikeda

The Flood ★★★

Drama 1993 · Rus/Fr · Colour · 97mins

This adaptation of Yevgyeni Zamyatin's novel concentrates on the emotions experienced by a childless woman when her respectable husband falls for their adopted teenage daughter. Renowned for her ability to convey psychological depth, Isabelle Huppert gives an expert reading of the transformation of humiliation and acceptance into jealousy and recrimination, as she rebels against both her situation and a discriminatory society. Director Igor Minayev's visual sense is acute, although some may find his pacing too precise. DP. A French language film.

Isabelle Huppert *Sofia* • Boris Nevzorov *Trofim* • Masha Lipkina *Ganka* • Svetlana Kryuchkova *Pelagia* ■ *Dir* Igor Minayev • *Scr* Jacques Baynac, Igor Minayev, from a novel by Yevgyeni Zamyatin

Floods of Fear ★★ 12

Drama 1958 · UK · BW · 80mins

Ealing Studios veteran Charles Crichton didn't do his reputation any favours with this sentimental melodrama. Basically an ensemble chamber piece revolving around four people trapped by floods in a gloomy house, the predictable plot barely keeps credibility afloat as an escaped convict eventually redeems himself through decisive action when tragedy looms. Well performed by an able cast, this is typical, and unremarkable, 1950s British B-movie fare. AJ. Contains swearing and violence.

Howard Keel *Donovan* • Anne Heywood *Elizabeth Matthews* • Cyril Cusack *Peebles* • Harry H Corbett *Sharkey* • John Crawford *Jack Murphy* • Eddie Byrne *Sheriff* • John Phillips (1) *Dr Matthews* ■ *Dir* Charles Crichton • *Scr* Vivienne Knight, Charles Crichton, from the novel by John Hawkins, Ward Hawkins

Floodtide ★★

Romantic drama 1949 · UK · BW · 89mins

The grim grandeur of the Clyde shipyards provides the setting for this lacklustre melodrama which trades on the British docudramatic tradition while dealing in potboiling clichés. Having alienated his farming family by decamping to Glasgow, Gordon Jackson rises from engineer to designer at Jack Lambert's yard. But it still takes an act of reckless heroism on the eve of a prestigious launch to convince him Jackson is the right man for daughter, Rona Anderson. DP

Gordon Jackson *David Shields* • Rona Anderson *Mary Anstruther* • John Laurie *Joe Drummond* • Jack Lambert *Anstruther* • Janet Brown *Rosie* • Elizabeth Sellars *Judy* • Jimmy Logan *Tim Brogan* ■ *Dir* Frederick Wilson • *Scr* George Blake, Donald B Wilson, Frederick Wilson

The Floorwalker ★★★★ U

Silent comedy 1916 · US · BW · 24mins

Chaplin makes the most of a look-alike scenario, as he discovers he's a ringer for the floorwalker in a large department store. He indulges in some of his greatest pratfalls and seriously falls for Edna Purviance. Basically a series of revue turns, with him skidding and dancing around, it is more reliant on plot than many of his early films at this time. It's a frivolity, with escapades on the escalator, but nevertheless offers some acute insights into the almost Dickensian society of the day. TH

Charles Chaplin *Tramp* • Edna Purviance *Secretary* ■ *Dir* Charles Chaplin • *Scr* Charles Chaplin, Vincent Bryan

The Florentine Dagger ★

Murder mystery 1935 · US · BW · 69mins

This routine whodunnit concerns a murder and the subsequent attempts to unravel the mysterious circumstances surrounding the crime. A serviceable company of second-division Warner Bros players plod through a screenplay that manages to dilute an intriguing novel by Ben Hecht into an uninvolving B-pic. If only Hecht had written the screenplay, the result might have been more worthy. RK

Donald Woods *Juan Cesare* • Margaret Lindsay *Florence Ballau* • C Aubrey Smith *Dr Gerard Lytton* • Henry O'Neill *Victor Ballau* • Robert Barrat *Captain* • Florence Fair *Teresa* ■ *Dir* Robert Florey • *Scr* Tom Reed, Brown Holmes, from a novel by Ben Hecht

Florian ★★ U

Period adventure drama
1940 · US · BW · 92mins

The title role is taken by a Lippizaner stallion, a member of Franz Josef's court and waited on hand and hoof by stable boy Robert Young. Like *Black Beauty*, all sorts of misadventures befall the horse. He goes from the circus, through the war and finally to America where he pulls a junk cart. But fear not, this is an MGM picture and Florian can't end up in the glue factory, can he? AT

Robert Young (1) *Anton Ervan* • Helen Gilbert *Duchess Diana* • Charles Coburn *Hofer* • Lee Bowman *Archduke Oliver* • Reginald Owen *Emperor Franz Josef* • Lucile Watson *Countess* • Irina Baronova *Trina* ■ *Dir* Edwin L

Marin • *Scr* Noel Langley, James Kevin McGuinness, Geza Herczeg, from the novel *Florian, das Pferd des Kaisers* by Felix Salten

Floundering ★★

Drama 1994 · US · Colour · 97mins

The psychological aftermath of the LA riots is examined in an offbeat but muddled look at the unravelling life of one resident. This doesn't pull any punches in its portrayal of crumbling social and political values, but its air of self-importance doesn't encourage identification with James LeGros, nor do his pretentious ramblings about spirituality. JC

James LeGros *John Boyz* • John Cusack *JC* • Ethan Hawke *Jimmy* • Maritza Rivera *Elle* • Steve Buscemi *Ned* • Billy Bob Thornton *Gun clerk* ■ *Dir/Scr* Peter McCarthy

Flower Drum Song ★★ U

Musical comedy 1961 · US · Colour · 132mins

Interminable and grotesquely over-produced (by the king of "camp" glamour Ross Hunter) this screen version of Rodgers and Hammerstein's Broadway success about life in San Francisco's Chinatown was woefully patronising and under-directed by Henry Koster. On Broadway, the tale had charm and style but this overblown and overlong movie just lies there and dies there. However, there's some bracing choreography from clever Hermes Pan and mercifully the endearing score has survived almost intact. TS

Nancy Kwan *Linda Low* • James Shigeta *Wang Ta* • Miyoshi Umeki *Mei Li* • Juanita Hall *Auntie* • Jack Soo *Sammy Fong* • Benson Fong *Wang Chi-Wang* • Reiko Sato *Helen Chao* ■ *Dir* Henry Koster • *Scr* Joseph Fields, from the novel by CY Lee and the book of the musical by Joseph Fields • *Cinematographer* Russell Metty

The Flower of Evil ★★★★ 15

Mystery drama 2002 · Fr · Colour · 104mins

Both Nathalie Baye and Suzanne Flon impress in this acute dissection of bourgeois mores. But while Baye's mayoral campaign in a mixed-class neighbourhood of Bordeaux makes for easy satire, the exposure of Flon's past re-opens the scars inflicted by the Nazi Occupation. The sexual antics of Bernard Le Coq's philandering pharmacist and the pseudo-incestuous affair between his son, Benoît Magimel, and Baye's daughter, Mélanie Doutey, add to the sense of family strife, making Claude Chabrol's tale of domestic intrigue a morbidly fascinating experience. DP. In French with English subtitles.

Benoît Magimel *François Vasseur* • Nathalie Baye *Anne Charpin-Vasseur* • Mélanie Doutey *Michèle Charpin-Vasseur* • Suzanne Flon *Aunt Line* • Bernard Le Coq *Gérard Vasseur* • Thomas Chabrol *Matthieu Lartigue* ■ *Dir* Claude Chabrol • *Scr* Louise L Lambrichs, Caroline Eliacheff, Claude Chabrol

The Flower of My Secret ★★★★ 15

Drama 1995 · Sp/Fr · Colour · 101mins

This constitutes a marked change of pace for the cult Spanish director Pedro Almodóvar. Here he tones down his usual camp satirical sensibilities to tell the engaging story of a romance novelist (Marisa Paredes) whose work is suffering because her marriage is falling apart. And that's not all: her best friend is betraying her, her half-blind mother and her sister are driving her crazy, and her maid's son has plagiarised one of her manuscripts. Paredes gives an extraordinary performance as the writer in crisis, in a lush tragicomedy that boasts a scorching script, sharp visual contrasts and moments of truly biting humour. AJ. In Spanish with English subtitles. Contains swearing. [VIDEO]

Marisa Paredes *Leo* • Juan Echanove *Angel* • Imanol Arias *Paco* • Carmen Elias *Betty* • Rossy de Palma *Rosa* • Chus Lampreave *Mother* • Joaquin Cortes *Antonio* • Manuela Vargas *Blanca* ■ *Dir/Scr* Pedro Almodóvar

Flowers and Trees ★★★★

Animated musical comedy 1932 · US · Colour · 8mins

This classic short cartoon was not only Disney's first full colour film, it was the first film anyone had shot in Technicolor's then-new three-strip process, to which Disney had bought exclusive rights in animation for three years. The basic story, in which a romance between two anthropomorphic trees is threatened by a covetous stump, has been so often imitated it may now seem twee, yet the personality animation and use of colour are so sophisticated that its beauty outweighs any contemporary qualms, turning datedness into period charm. It created a sensation among 1930s audiences and won an Academy Award (the first animated film to do so). CLP

Dir Burt Gillett

Flowers in the Attic ★★ 15

Horror 1987 · US · Colour · 87mins

VC Andrews's twisted Gothic bestseller gets a rather sanitised makeover in this big screen adaptation. Victoria Tennant is unconvincing in the villainous role of a loopy widow who keeps her own children prisoners in a creepy old mansion while she plots to rid her parents (Louise Fletcher and Nathan Davis) of their fortune. Director Jeffrey Bloom raises the odd fright, but the finale is plain silly. JF [VIDEO] DVD

Clare C Peck *Narrator* • Victoria Tennant *Corinne* • Kristy Swanson *Cathy* • Jeb Stuart Adams *Chris* • Louise Fletcher *Grandmother* • Ben Ganger *Cory* • Nathan Davis *Grandfather* ■ *Dir* Jeffrey Bloom • *Scr* Jeffrey Bloom, from the novel by VC Andrews

Flowers of Shanghai ★★★★

Period drama 1998 · Tai/Jpn · Colour · 125mins

This is a masterclass in studio stylisation from Taiwanese director Hou Hsiao-Hsien. His meticulous compositions and unobtrusive camera movements capture both the traditional atmosphere and the impending sense of change hanging over a Shanghai "flower house", which is more a place of education and intrigue than a brothel. This is a ruthless world of exploitation, enslavement and emotional blackmail, in which the women use everything at their disposal to retain the favour of their wealthy callers. DP. A Mandarin language film.

Tony Chiu-Wai Leung [Tony Leung (2)] *Wang Lingsheng* • Michiko Hada *Crimson* • Michelle Reis *Emerald* • Carina Lau *Pearl* • Jack Kao *Luo* • Vicky Wei [Wei Hsiao-Hui] *Jasmin* ■ *Dir* Hou Hsiao-Hsien • *Scr* Chu Tian-Wen, from the novel *Haishang hua liezhuang (Biographies of Flowers of Shanghai)* by Han Ziyun

Flubber ★★★ U

Comedy 1997 · US · Colour · 90mins

This continues Hollywood's obsession with souping-up the hit comedies of the past – in this case *The Absent-Minded Professor* (1961) – with today's sophisticated special effects. Robin Williams plays a scientist who becomes so immersed in creating a new energy source that he once again misses his own wedding. But this time he has an excuse, because he has invented Flubber – a substance like rubber that generates its own energy, wreaking havoc everywhere it goes. Kids will love it. JF [VIDEO] DVD

Robin Williams *Professor Philip Brainard* • Marcia Gay Harden *Sara Jean Reynolds* • Christopher McDonald *Wilson Croft* • Raymond J Barry *Chester Hoenicker* • Clancy Brown *Smith* • Ted Levine *Wesson* • Wil Wheaton *Bennett Hoenicker* • Edie McClurg *Martha George* ■ *Dir* Les Mayfield • *Scr* John Hughes, Bill Walsh, from the story *A Situation of Gravity* by Samuel W Taylor

The Fluffer ★★★ 18

Erotic drama 2001 · US · Colour · 90mins

The adult entertainment industry is the focus for a contemporary reworking of the traditional love triangle theme in this dark and occasionally humorous drama. This interweaves the turbulent lives of an adult movie star, his stripper girlfriend and a cameraman so enamoured with the star that he'll perform the most intimate of on-set functions for him. Though the story unfolds against a gay porn setting which may marginalise the film's appeal, the directors present a story that is of relevance to audiences of all sexual persuasions. SF [VIDEO] DVD

Scott Gurney *Michael "Mike" Rossini/Johnny Rebel* • Michael Cunio *Sean McGinnis* • Roxanne Day *Babylon* • Taylor Negron *Tony Brooks* • Deborah Harry *Marcella* ■ *Dir* Richard Glatzer, Wash West [Wash Westmoreland] • *Scr* Wash West [Wash Westmoreland]

Fluffy ★★ U

Comedy 1965 · US · Colour · 91mins

The eponymous animal is a lion who has the misfortune to be engaged in research with Professor Tony Randall who – by way of that research – falls in love with Shirley Jones. We keep watching, hoping that Randall will rise above the script, and that Jones will burst into song; a waste of the two stars – and the lion. TH

Tony Randall *Daniel Potter* • Shirley Jones *Janice Claridge* • Edward Andrews *Griswald* • Ernest Truex *Claridge* • Jim Backus *Sergeant* • Frank Faylen *Catfish* • Howard Morris *Sweeney* ■ *Dir* Earl Bellamy • *Scr* Samuel Roeca

Fluke ★★★ PG

Fantasy drama 1995 · US · Colour · 91mins

A well-meaning adaptation of James Herbert's fantasy adventure about a man protecting his family from villainous intent when reincarnated as a dog after a fatal car crash. Directed by co-writer Carlo Carlei with razzle-dazzle visuals, what is basically a children's story becomes accessible to adults thanks to the serious issues. Good voiceover work from Matthew Modine and Samuel L Jackson, plus fine performances from human stars Nancy Travis and Eric Stoltz add to a charming tale that some will find slightly sappy. AJ [VIDEO] DVD

Matthew Modine *Thomas Johnson/Fluke* • Nancy Travis *Carol Johnson* • Eric Stoltz *Jeff Newman* • Max Pomeranc *Brian Johnson* • Samuel L Jackson *Rumbo* ■ *Dir* Carlo Carlei • *Scr* Carlo Carlei, James Carrington, from the novel by James Herbert

The Fly ★★★ 15

Horror 1958 · US · Colour · 89mins

No match for the superior David Cronenberg remake, but still a slick slice of absurdist 1950s' sci-fi in its own right. Based on a *Playboy* short story, with a script by *Shogun* writer James Clavell, the plot has matter-transmitter experiments giving Al Hedison (later David Hedison) the head and arm of a common house fly, while Vincent Price, as Hedison's brother, has histrionics about family curses. Enjoyably unsettling once past the inconsistencies of the premise, this plush flesh-crawler includes many marvellous moments. Two sequels, *Return of the Fly* (1959) and *Curse of the Fly* (1965), followed. AJ [VIDEO] DVD

Al Hedison [David Hedison] *Andre* • Patricia Owens *Helene* • Vincent Price *François* • Herbert Marshall *Inspector Charas* • Kathleen Freeman *Emma* • Betty Lou Gerson *Nurse Andersone* • Charles Herbert *Philippe* ■ *Dir* Kurt Neumann • *Scr* James Clavell, from a short story by George Langelaan

The Fly ★★★★ 18

Horror 1986 · US · Colour · 91mins

It's easy to see why visceral visionary David Cronenberg wanted to remake the landmark 1958 chiller about scientific experiments in molecular teleportation. It plunges into the same primal territory he explored in *Shivers*, *Rabid* and *Videodrome* by regurgitating his deep-seated fears of ageing, disease, deformity and the beast within. Only Cronenberg can get away with working out his raw phobias on screen while being poignantly witty and repulsively entertaining at the same time. Jeff Goldblum's sensitive performance takes the edge off the grisly special effects, but many will find it hard to get past the gooey gore. AJ. Contains violence, swearing and a sex scene. [VIDEO] DVD

Jeff Goldblum *Seth Brundle* • Geena Davis *Veronica Quaife* • John Getz *Stathis Borans* • Joy Boushel *Tawny* • Les Carlson *Dr Cheevers* • George Chuvalo *Marky* • David Cronenberg *Gynaecologist* ■ *Dir* David Cronenberg • *Scr* Charles Edward Pogue, David Cronenberg, from a short story by George Langelaan

The Fly II ★★ 18

Horror 1989 · US · Colour · 100mins

Special effects and make-up artist-turned-director Chris Walas puts too much emphasis on gore galore and pays scant attention to plot. Eric Stoltz does what he can encased in rubber as the misunderstood larva, but it goes without saying that this obvious sequel has none of the sly subtlety, horrific elegance or poignant humour David Cronenberg brought to his superior 1986 film. AJ. Contains swearing and violence. [VIDEO] DVD

Eric Stoltz *Martin Brundle* • Daphne Zuniga *Beth Logan* • Lee Richardson *Anton Bartok* • John Getz *Stathis Borans* • Frank Turner *Dr Shepard* ■ *Dir* Chris Walas • *Scr* Mick Garris, Jim Wheat, Frank Darabont, Ken Wheat, from a story by Mick Garris

Fly Away Home ★★★★ U

Drama based on a true story 1996 · US · Colour · 102mins

No one captures the inspirational beauty of nature better than director Carroll Ballard, who also made *Never Cry Wolf* and the excellent *Black Stallion*. This exhilarating picture gets off to a painful start with a fatal road accident. But the mood changes from despair to determination as Anna Paquin channels her grief into the rearing of some orphan goslings, and learning to fly a microlight plane to guide her feathered family to its winter breeding ground. With selfless support from Jeff Daniels as Paquin's inventor father and from the geese themselves (stealing every scene, whether waddling comically or flying majestically), this impeccably photographed film is an unbounded delight. DP [VIDEO] DVD

Jeff Daniels *Thomas Alden* • Anna Paquin *Amy Alden* • Dana Delany *Susan Barnes* • Terry Kinney *David Alden* • Holter Graham *Barry Strickland* ■ *Dir* Carroll Ballard • *Scr* Robert Rodat, Vince McKewin, from the autobiography by Bill Lishman

Fly by Night ★★

Crime thriller 1942 · US · BW · 74mins

This unassuming little thriller stars B-movie regular Richard Carlson and former child star Nancy Kelly as two innocents ensnared in the world of espionage and a mysterious weapon known only as G-32. Carlson is accused of killing an inventor, and escapes to try to prove his innocence. Making only his second US movie, director Robert Siodmak makes the most of his slender resources. AT

Nancy Kelly *Pat Lindsey* • Richard Carlson *Jeff Burton* • Albert Basserman *Dr Storm* • Martin Kosleck *George Taylor* • Nestor Paiva *Grube* • Walter Kingsford *Heydt* ■ *Dir* Robert Siodmak • *Scr* Jay Dratler, F Hugh Herbert, from a story by Ben Roberts, Sidney Sheldon

The Flying Deuces ★★ U

Comedy 1939 · US · BW · 64mins

Notwithstanding a script co-written by silent star Harry Langdon and direction by comedy specialist A Edward Sutherland, this is one of the weaker Laurel and Hardy pictures. Mostly pilfered from the four-reeler *Beau Hunks* and the feature *Bonnie Scotland*, the comic material is simply spread too thinly, and time hangs heavily between the Paris opening, the pair's jaunty dance on arrival at the Foreign Legion fort and the careering plane finale. DP DVD

Stan Laurel *Stan* • Oliver Hardy *Ollie* • Jean Parker *Georgette* • Reginald Gardiner *François* • Charles Middleton *Commandant* ■ *Dir* A Edward Sutherland • *Scr* Ralph Spence, Alfred Schiller, Charles Rogers, Harry Langdon

Flying down to Rio ★★★ U

Musical 1933 · US · BW · 85mins

When it was first shown, the stars of this film were glamorous Dolores Del Rio and dashing Gene Raymond, backed by perfect Depression-era deco sets and design and imaginative choreography. But the real significance and most of the pleasure of this film today lies in the casting of two featured players who, although they knew each other in their pre-Hollywood days in New York, had never danced together until this movie. And when they did, screen history was made. Their names were Fred Astaire and Ginger Rogers. TS

Dolores Del Rio *Belinha* • Gene Raymond *Roger Bond* • Raul Roulien *Julio Rubeiro* • Ginger Rogers *Honey Hale* • Fred Astaire *Fred Ayres* • Blanche Friderici *Dona Helena de Rezende* ■ *Dir* Thornton Freeland • *Scr* Cyril Hume, HW Hanemann, Erwin Gelsey, from a play by Anne Caldwell, from a story by Lou Brock

The Flying Eye ★★★ U

Adventure 1955 · UK · BW · 53mins

The special effects may look like something cobbled together on *Blue Peter*, but who could resist a film in which a character called Colonel Audacious and his trusty sidekick Bunstuffer use a model plane with an all-seeing TV eye to confound some enemy spies? Adapted from a novel by John Newton Chance, this ripping yarn was one of the Children's Film Foundation's most enjoyable offerings, with Geoffrey Sumner revelling in the role of the eccentric inventor and David Hannaford contributing some oafish derring-do. It's dated, of course, but will evoke pleasant memories for ex-Saturday matinée aficionados. DP

David Hannaford *Bunstuffer* • Julia Lockwood *Angela* • Harcourt Williams *Professor* • Ivan Craig *Mayer* • Geoffrey Sumner *Col Audacious* ■ *Dir* William C Hammond • *Scr* William C Hammond, Ken Hughes, Darrell Catling, from a novel by John Newton Chance

Flying 55 ★★ U

Crime drama 1939 · UK · BW · 71mins

As with so many horse-racing melodramas, this Edgar Wallace story is pretty heavy going until we reach the course, when all the clichés and caricatures are forgotten in that frantic dash for the line. Wallace could never be accused of stinting on incident as family feuds, race fixing, blackmail and romance are all brought under starters' orders by no-nonsense director, Reginald Denham. Derrick de Marney and Nancy Burne are the stars, but it's Marius Goring who contributes the only worthwhile performance. DP

Derrick de Marney *Bill Urquhart* • Nancy Burne *Stella Barrington* • Marius Goring *Charles Barrington* • John Warwick *Jebson* • Peter Gawthorne *Jonas Urquhart* • DA Clarke-Smith *Jacques Gregory* ■ *Dir* Reginald Denham • *Scr* Victor M Greene, Vernon Clancey, Kenneth Horne, from the novel by Edgar Wallace

Flying Leathernecks ★★ PG

Second World War action drama
1951 · US · Colour · 97mins

Another disappointing early work from Nicholas Ray, this is a trite reworking of many familiar themes and characters. John Wayne and Robert Ryan seem ill-at-ease in their leading roles, flying studio mock-ups of planes against Technicolor back projection and dutifully conveying a gung-ho spirit without any real enthusiasm. Acting honours are stolen by veteran Jay C Flippen, well cast as a wily sergeant; however, this is just corny, obvious and not really good enough. TS

John Wayne *Major Dan Kirby* • Robert Ryan *Captain Carl Griffin* • Don Taylor *Lieutenant "Cowboy" Blithe* • William Harrigan *Curan* • Jay C Flippen *Master Sergeant Clancy* ■ *Dir* Nicholas Ray • *Scr* James Edward Grant, from a story by Kenneth Gamet

The Flying Saucer ★★ PG

Science-fiction spy drama
1949 · US · BW · 75mins

Although many 1950s sci-fi movies were allegories for the Red Threat, Mikel Conrad's UFO drama comes right out and accuses the Soviets of using space to compromise American security. However, he takes his time getting there both as writer/director and as the government agent who wanders round Alaska seeking witnesses to the mysterious phenomenon that has been illuminating the night sky. It's xenophobic propaganda from start to finish. But, if nothing else, the film led to the word "disc" being dropped in favour of "saucer" to describe extraterrestrial craft. DP

Mikel Conrad *Mike Trent* • Pat Garrison *Vee Langley* • Hantz Von Teuffen *Hans* • Lester Sharpe *Col Marikoff* • Russell Hicks *Hank Thorn* • Denver Pyle *Turner* ■ *Dir* Mikel Conrad • *Scr* Howard Irving Young, Mikel Conrad, from a story by Mikel Conrad

The Flying Scot ★ U

Crime thriller 1957 · UK · BW · 70mins

The most noteworthy thing about this crime programme-filler is that it was scripted by Norman Hudis, who wrote six *Carry On* films. As with most British B-movies of the period, a clutch of transatlantic stars were imported to raise the profile, but they couldn't do much to distract from the mediocrity of this train robbery thriller. DP

Lee Patterson *Ronnie* • Kay Callard *Jackie* • Alan Gifford *Phil* • Margaret Withers *Lady* • Mark Baker *Gibbs* • Jeremy Bodkin *Charlie* ■ *Dir* Compton Bennett • *Scr* Norman Hudis, from a story by Ralph Smart, Jan Read

Flying Tigers ★★ PG

Second World War drama
1942 · US · BW · 97mins

A very average wartime John Wayne feature, singing the praises of the American Volunteer Group, the mercenaries who fought for China's freedom against superior Japanese odds in the days before Pearl Harbor. Director David Miller provides some well-staged action sequences, but Wayne and his co-star John Carroll struggle with the contrived plot. TS

John Wayne *Jim Gordon* • John Carroll *Woody Jason* • Anna Lee *Brooke Elliott* • Paul Kelly (1) *Hap Davis* • Gordon Jones *Alabama Smith* • Mae Clarke *Verna Bales* ■ *Dir* David Miller • *Scr* Kenneth Gamet, Barry Trivers, from a story by Kenneth Gamet

Flynn ★★★ 18

Biographical drama
1995 · Aus · Colour · 95mins

Even if only half of the stories are true, dashing screen legend Errol Flynn packed enough incident into his lifetime to provide material for at least three movies. This Australian biography concentrates on his pre-Hollywood, hell-raising days, with Guy Pearce (*LA Confidential*) enjoying himself as the young Flynn, a rampant womaniser, gold prospector and possible killer. Steven Berkoff and John Savage also get into the spirit of things, while director Frank Howson whips it along at an entertaining pace. JF

Guy Pearce *Errol Flynn* • Steven Berkoff *Klaus Reicher* • John Savage *Joe Stromberg* • Claudia Karvan *Penelope Watts* • Will Gluth *Professor Flynn* ■ *Dir* Frank Howson • *Scr* Frank Howson, Alister Webb

Focus ★★ 12

Period drama 2001 · US · Colour · 102mins

This study of anti-Semitism in postwar America is based on the little-known novel by playwright Arthur Miller. Having each been mistaken for Jews in the past, William H Macy and wife Laura Dern are appalled to find themselves being invited to participate in Meat Loaf Aday's lynch-mob persecution of newsvendor David Paymer, after he's falsely implicated in the murder of a Puerto Rican woman in their Brooklyn neighbourhood. While his message is valid, debutant director Neal Slavin's overbearing approach debilitates the drama. DP DVD

William H Macy *Larry Newman* • Laura Dern *Gertrude Hart* • David Paymer *Finkelstein* • Meat Loaf Aday [Meat Loaf] *Fred* ■ *Dir* Neal Slavin • *Scr* Kendrew Lascelles, from the novel by Arthur Miller

The Fog ★★★ 15

Horror 1980 · US · Colour · 85mins

Director John Carpenter isn't at the peak of his form here, but this is still a reasonable enough shocker about spectral pirates who terrorise a coastal town. Losing dramatic focus by switching between two heroines who never meet – disc jockey Adrienne Barbeau (then married to Carpenter) and Jamie Lee Curtis (starring with real-life mum Janet Leigh for the first time) – Carpenter leans hard on cheap scare tactics more than subtle suspense. However, some sequences do turn the tension dial up quite high. AJ. Contains violence. DVD

Adrienne Barbeau *Stevie Wayne* • Hal Holbrook *Father Malone* • Jamie Lee Curtis *Elizabeth Solley* • Janet Leigh *Kathy Williams* • Tom Atkins *Nick Castle* • John Houseman *Machen* ■ *Dir* John Carpenter • *Scr* John Carpenter, Debra Hill • *Cinematographer* Dean Cundey • *Music* John Carpenter

Fog Island ★

Mystery 1945 · US · BW · 69mins

Uninviting tale about the search for treasure on an isolated isle, with character actors George Zucco and Lionel Atwill wading through fog-shrouded dullness, not alleviated by the cumbersome direction. Zucco plays a once-rich man who invites those he thinks are responsible for his downfall to his island. AJ

George Zucco *Leo Grainger* • Lionel Atwill *Alec Ritchfield* • Jerome Cowan *Kavanaugh* • Sharon Douglas *Gail* • Veda Ann Borg *Sylvia* ■ *Dir* Terry Morse • *Scr* Pierre Gendron, from the story by Bernadine Angus

The Fog of War: Eleven Lessons from the Life of Robert S McNamara ★★★★ PG

Documentary 2003 · US · Colour · 102mins

Robert McNamara, who served Presidents Kennedy and Johnson as defence secretary, remains a vivid figure in the US, where a generation quivered in the shadow of nuclear war during the Cuban Missile Crisis and later protested when thousands were sent to die in Vietnam. Here, the 85-year-old reflects on a career of conflict, from his involvement in the firebombing of Japan during the Second World War to the Vietnam debacle. The film's title suggests that war is rarely a matter of black and white, and this is reinforced with some remarkable revelations and insights from McNamara. The overall impression – perhaps carefully constructed – is of a principled man who still believes that on the big issues he was right. Errol Morris won the best documentary Oscar for this feature. BP DVD

Dir Errol Morris • *Music* Philip Glass

Fog over Frisco ★

Crime drama 1934 · US · BW · 69mins

As a San Francisco heiress and archetypal bad girl, Bette Davis flounces and emotes with breathtaking conviction, lighting a fiery path through the inane plot and cardboard characters that surround her. It's often unintentionally funny: watch it and relish Margaret Lindsay as Bette's loyal sister, bravely maintaining dignity as she utters dialogue that beggars belief. RK

Bette Davis *Arlene Bradford* • Margaret Lindsay *Val Bradford* • Lyle Talbot *Spencer Carleton* • Arthur Byron *Everett Bradford* • Hugh Herbert *Izzy Wright* • Douglass Dumbrille *Joshua Maynard* ■ *Dir* William Dieterle, Daniel Reed • *Scr* Robert N Lee, Eugene Solow, from the story by George Dyer

Fogbound ★★★ 18

Drama 2002 · Neth/UK · Colour · 98mins

Roman Polanski's *Knife in the Water* is clearly the inspiration for director and co-writer Ate De Jong's simmering thriller in which a 30-something trio's dark secrets slowly emerge after they become marooned on a mountain road. Ben Daniels's flashbacks to revolutionary France are an attempt to explain his reluctance to have children with Orla Brady, who, tiring of their decade-long marriage, has embarked on an affair with old friend Luke Perry. Such devices do strain credibility, but De Jong exploits the psycho-sexual intrigue to escalate the dramatic tension, while the performances are admirably restrained. DP

Luke Perry *Bob* • Ben Daniels *Leo* • Orla Brady *Ann* • Jeroen Krabbé *Dr Duff* • Stephanie Leonidas *Annette, aged 16* • Elliott Jordan *Boy, aged 16* • Daniella Isaacs *Annette, aged ten* • Mike Walther *Boy, aged ten* ■ *Dir* Ate De Jong • *Scr* Ate De Jong, Michael Lally

Folies Bergère ★★★

Musical 1935 · US · BW · 104mins

This super 20th Century-Fox musical revolves around one of the studio's many stock plots. Here it's the one about mistaken identity. Maurice Chevalier is in his prime here as both Folies star and pompous aristocrat, getting involved with Folies co-star Ann Sothern and beautiful baroness Merle Oberon, whose scenes slow down the pace somewhat. Nevertheless, the musical numbers are elaborate, and there's a knockout (though tasteless) dance finale which won choreographer Dave Gould an Oscar. TS

Maurice Chevalier *Eugene Charlier/Baron Cassini* • Merle Oberon *Baroness Genevieve Cassini* • Ann Sothern *Mimi* • Walter Byron *Rene* • Lumsden Hare *Gustave* • Eric Blore *François* ■ *Dir* Roy Del Ruth • *Scr* Bess Meredyth, Hal Long, from the play *The Red Cat* by Hans Adler, Rudolph Lothar

Folks! ★ 15

Comedy 1992 · US · Colour · 108mins

This terrible "comedy" drove a stake into the heart of Tom Selleck's career. He plays a broker whose world falls apart when he is investigated for insider trading. Senility and attempted suicide are among supposed comic effects, as Selleck wanders around wondering how he ended up in this dreadful film. JB [video] DVD

Tom Selleck *Jon Aldrich* • Don Ameche *Harry Aldrich* • Anne Jackson *Mildred Aldrich* • Christine Ebersole *Arlene Aldrich* • Wendy Crewson *Audrey Aldrich* • Robert Pastorelli *Fred* ■ *Dir* Ted Kotcheff • *Scr* Robert Klane

Follow a Star ★★ U

Comedy 1959 · UK · BW · 99mins

If you can follow the plot of this Norman Wisdom comedy, you'll find faint echoes of *Singin' in the Rain*. Norman is the tailor's assistant whose voice celebrity Jerry Desmonde mimes to, without rewarding the little man's services. Norman's humour knows no restraint or timing, which makes him schmaltzily tedious, especially as he can only sing in the presence of his wheelchair-bound girlfriend June Laverick. TH [video] DVD

Norman Wisdom *Norman Truscott* • June Laverick *Judy* • Jerry Desmonde *Vernon Carew* • Hattie Jacques *Dymphna Dobson* • Richard Wattis *Dr Chatterway* • John Le Mesurier *Birkett* • Fenella Fielding *Lady Finchington* ■ *Dir* Robert Asher • *Scr* Jack Davies, Henry Blyth, Norman Wisdom

Follow Me ★★

Detective comedy
1971 · UK · Colour · 95mins

Adapted from Peter Shaffer's play *The Public Eye*, this one-hour comedy is inexcusably strung out to 95 minutes by the playwright and the director, Carol Reed. While some of this time is justifiably taken up with photographer Christopher G Challis's loving images of London, too much is occupied with Topol's ham-fisted buffoonery. He plays a detective hired by priggish accountant Michael Jayston to spy on his free-spirited wife Mia Farrow. DP

Mia Farrow *Belinda* • Topol *Julian Cristoforou* • Michael Jayston *Charles* • Margaret Rawlings *Mrs Sidley* • Annette Crosbie *Miss Framer* ■ *Dir* Carol Reed • *Scr* Peter Shaffer, from his play *The Public Eye*

Follow Me, Boys! ★★ U

Romantic comedy
1966 · US · Colour · 115mins

In a far cry from his *film noir* tough-guy stance in the 1940s, the hit TV series *My Three Sons* gave actor Fred MacMurray a completely new avuncular image, and he spent much of his later career portraying a good guy at Disney. Here he plays a scout leader in a small-town saga of rather limited charm. The supporting cast is full of seasoned veterans, none more impressive than silent movie great Lillian Gish. The Technicolor is nice but, to be honest, it's a long slog through the corn. TS [video]

Fred MacMurray *Lemuel Siddons* • Vera Miles *Vida Downey* • Lillian Gish *Hetty Seibert* • Charlie Ruggles [Charles Ruggles] *John Everett Hughes* • Elliott Reid *Ralph Hastings* • Kurt Russell *Whitey* ■ *Dir* Norman Tokar • *Scr* Louis Pelletier, based on the novel God and My Country by MacKinley Kantor

Follow That Dream ★★★ U

Musical drama 1962 · US · Colour · 105mins

This easy-going rustic drama stars Elvis Presley as a wide-eyed country boy. This was not intended as a vehicle for Elvis (the real stars are Arthur O'Connell and a troublesome homestead) but it benefits from Presley's laid-back performance as an unsophisticated hillbilly. Director Gordon Douglas seems at a loss over what to do during Elvis's (too) few songs, and directs him lying down and looking rather uncomfortable most of the time, especially during the obvious miming of the title number. TS [video]

Elvis Presley *Toby Kwimper* • Arthur O'Connell *Pop Kwimper* • Anne Helm *Holly Jones* • Joanna Moore *Alicia Claypoole* • Jack Kruschen *Carmine* ■ *Dir* Gordon Douglas • *Scr* Charles Lederer, from the novel *Pioneer, Go Home* by Richard Powell

Follow the Boys ★★★★ U

Musical comedy 1944 · US · BW · 119mins

A wonderful nostalgic treat that has now become a quintessential wartime artefact. This all-star review produced by ace packager Charles K Feldman was released by Universal as a tribute to the US forces (the "boys" of the title). It actually has a plot of sorts, with George Raft and Vera Zorina splitting up – somewhat improbably – so that Raft can organise USO shows, but, oh what shows! Here's Orson Welles famously sawing Marlene Dietrich in half, WC Fields demonstrating his great *Ziegfeld Follies* pool hall routine and Jeanette MacDonald reviving *Beyond the Blue Hoizon*. Of course it's a little long, but what would you cut? TS

George Raft *Tony West* • Vera Zorina *Gloria Vance* • Grace McDonald *Kitty West* • Charles Grapewin [Charley Grapewin] *Nick West* • George Macready *Walter Bruce* • Jeanette MacDonald • Orson Welles • Marlene Dietrich • Donald O'Connor • WC Fields • Lon Chaney Jr • Randolph Scott • Dinah Shore • Artur Rubinstein • Maria Montez • Sophie Tucker ■ *Dir* Edward Sutherland [A Edward Sutherland] • *Scr* Lou Breslow, Gertrude Purcell

Follow the Boys ★★ U

Romantic comedy
1963 · US · Colour · 95mins

Sequel of sorts to MGM's popular 1960 teenage romp *Where the Boys Are* (itself ludicrously remade in 1984) substituting the French Riviera for Florida's Fort Lauderdale and reuniting two of the female stars that made the first one so sassy – swingin' Connie Francis and kooky Paula Prentiss. It's a pleasure to look at in but frankly it smacks of desperation, with the cast too old for this would-be romp. TS

Connie Francis *Bonnie Pulaski* • Paula Prentiss *Toni Denham* • Ron Randell *Cmdr Ben Bradville* • Janis Paige *Liz Bradville* • Russ Tamblyn *Lt "Smitty" Smith* • Dany Robin *Michele* ■ *Dir* Richard Thorpe • *Scr* David T Chantler, David Osborn, from a story by Lawrence P Bachmann

Follow the Fleet ★★★★ U

Musical comedy 1936 · US · BW · 110mins

Shore-leave sailors Fred Astaire and Randolph Scott breeze into town and fall for sisters Ginger Rogers and Harriet Nelson (billed here as Harriet Hilliard). The Scott/Hilliard romance plays second fiddle to that of the swaggering Astaire and the equally sassy Rogers. The settings might not be the Art Deco delights of the couple's other pictures and not all of Irving Berlin's songs would make his greatest hits compilation, but the song-and-dance duo are as captivating as ever and *Let's Face the Music and Dance* ranks as one of their finest routines. DP [video] DVD

Fred Astaire *"Bake" Baker* • Ginger Rogers *Sherry Martin* • Randolph Scott *Bilge Smith* • Harriet Hilliard [Harriet Nelson] *Connie Martin* • Astrid Allwyn *Iris Manning* • Betty Grable *Showgirl* • Harry Beresford *Captain Ezra Hickey* • Russell Hicks *Jim Nolan* • Lucille Ball *Kitty Collins* ■ *Dir* Mark Sandrich • *Scr* Dwight Taylor, Allan Scott, from the play *Shore Leave* by Hubert Osborne, from the musical *Hit the Deck* by Herbert Fields

Follow the Leader ★★

Comedy adventure 1944 · US · BW · 64mins

The East Side Kids were headed for a wartime rut by the time they delivered this instalment, a reiteration of their usual shtick as Muggs and Glimpy (that's Leo Gorcey and Huntz Hall, not yet the Bowery Boys) try to flush out a bad 'un from among the kids. In Second World War Hollywood, that's a subtext that means watch out for informers or fifth columnists in your neighbourhood. TS

Leo Gorcey *Muggs McGinnis* • Huntz Hall *Glimpy Freedhoff* • Dave Durand *Danny* • Bud Gorman *James Aloysius "Skinny" Bogerty* • Bobby Stone *Speed* • Jimmy Strand *Dave* • Gabriel Dell *WW "Fingers" Belmont* • Jack LaRue *Larry* • Joan Marsh *Millie McGinnis* ■ *Dir* William Beaudine • *Scr* William X Crowley, Beryl Sachs, from a story by Ande Lamb

Follow the Sun: the Ben Hogan Story ★★ U

Sports biography 1951 · US · BW · 93mins

Frederick Hazlitt Brennan adapted his own *Reader's Digest* article for this stodgy biopic that cashes in on Ben Hogan's recovery from a serious injuries received in a car crash to win the US Open in 1950. Glenn Ford's own golfing proficiency makes him a credible lead, but director Sidney Lanfield lashes on the melodrama, both during Hogan's impoverished Texan childhood and his battle for fitness alongside his devoted wife, played by Anne Baxter. DP [video]

Glenn Ford *Ben Hogan* • Anne Baxter *Valerie Hogan* • Dennis O'Keefe *Chuck Williams* • June Havoc *Norma* • Larry Keating *Jay Dexter* • Roland Winters *Dr Graham* • Nana Bryant *Sister Beatrice* ■ *Dir* Sidney Lanfield • *Scr* Frederick Hazlitt Brennan, from his article in *Reader's Digest*

Following ★★★ 15

Thriller 1998 · UK · BW · 70mins

Shot around Soho at weekends on 16mm monochrome, Christopher Nolan's feature debut is a tortuous flashback thriller that attempts one twist too many. The opening segment is filled with sinister promise, as people-watching wannabe novelist Jeremy Theobald is played at his own game by Alex Haw, a burglar who claims to be able to define his victims' personalities by their possessions. Alarm bells sound once Lucy Russell joins the fray, however, as intriguing character study is abandoned for structural and narrative contrivance. This is a misfire, but a fascinating and unusual one. DP [video] DVD

Jeremy Theobald *The young man* • Alex Haw *Cobb* • Lucy Russell *Blonde* • John Nolan *Policeman* • Dick Bradsell *Bald guy* • Gillian El-Kadi *Home owner* • Jennifer Angel *Waitress* • Nicolas Carlotti *Barman* ■ *Dir/Scr* Christopher Nolan

Folly to Be Wise ★★★

Comedy 1952 · UK · BW · 91mins

Based on the James Bridie play that gently mocked the popular BBC radio debate programme *The Brains Trust*, this Frank Launder and Sidney Gilliat comedy seems so satisfied with its central idea that it neglects to flesh it out with wit. The various members of the splendid cast seem all too aware that they are marking time between those marvellous moments when army chaplain Alastair Sim loses control of his squabbling panellists, but they are powerless to raise the tempo. DP

Alastair Sim *Captain Paris* • Roland Culver *George Prout* • Elizabeth Allan *Angela Prout* • Martita Hunt *Lady Dodds* • Miles Malleson *Dr Hector McAdam* • Colin Gordon *Professor James Mutch* • Edward Chapman *Joseph Byres* ■ *Dir* Frank Launder • *Scr* Frank Launder, John Dighton, from the play *It Depends What You Mean* by James Bridie

Food of Love ★★ 15

Romantic comedy
1997 · UK/Fr · Colour · 108mins

This romantic comedy set in the world of amateur dramatics subjects a willing cast to situations and dialogue worthier of a weekend playwright than someone of Stephen Poliakoff's reputation. Wearily touching on such themes as the town and country divide, middle-age regret and the continuing relevance of theatre, the action follows banker Richard E Grant's attempt to relive an idyllic summer by taking his long-disbanded thesping troupe back to a sleepy rural village for a production of *Twelfth Night*. What follows is cringingly predictable. DP

Richard E Grant *Alex Salmon* • Nathalie Baye *Michèle* • Joe McGann *Sam* • Juliet Aubrey *Madeline* • Lorcan Cranitch *Luke* • Penny Downie *Mary* • Holly Davidson *Jessica* • Tameka Empson *Alice* • Sylvia Syms *Mrs Harvey-Brown* ■ *Dir/Scr* Stephen Poliakoff

Food of Love ★★★ 15

Drama 2002 · Sp/Ger · Colour · 104mins

Despite the occasional lapses into taste, David Leavitt's novel has been adapted with a mischievously seductive air by Catalan veteran Ventura Pons. The action centres on talented music student Kevin Bishop's tortuous liaisons with classical pianist Paul Rhys and his manager-lover, Allan Corduner. But contrasted with Bishop's discovery that he isn't concert calibre is stage mother Juliet Stevenson's realisation of her son's sexuality and the need for them to re-adjust their relationship. Pitched perfectly between vulgarity and vulnerability, Stevenson's turn is the standout in this ribald chamber play. DP [video] DVD

Juliet Stevenson *Pamela Porterfield* • Paul Rhys *Richard Kennington* • Allan Corduner *Joseph* • Kevin Bishop *Paul Porterfield* • Geraldine McEwan *Novotna* ■ *Dir* Ventura Pons • *Scr* Ventura Pons, from the novel *The Page Turner* by David Leavitt

The Food of the Gods ★★ 18

Science-fiction horror
1975 · US · Colour · 84mins

This "revenge of nature" thriller owes much to big bug movies of the 1950s like but lacks the charm that made those schlock classics so memorable. Still, it's tough to dislike a movie that incorporates giant chickens and rats in its tale of a remote island where a mystery substance has caused the creatures to grow to an abnormal size. The special effects that are so crucial in making a picture like this work are variable at best, but director Bert I Gordon conjures up some gruesome set-piece deaths. RS [video]

Marjoe Gortner *Morgan* • Pamela Franklin *Lorna Scott* • Ralph Meeker *Jack Bensington* • Ida Lupino *Mrs Skinner* • Jon Cypher *Brian* • Belinda Balaski *Rita* • Tom Stovall *Tom* • John McLiam *Mr Skinner* ■ *Dir* Bert I Gordon • *Scr* Bert I Gordon, from the novel by HG Wells

Food of the Gods II ★ 18

Science-fiction horror
1989 · Can · Colour · 82mins

A completely unnecessary sequel to a dire original. Research scientist Paul

Coufos uses a growth hormone to increase the size of lab rats and animal activists release the king-sized rodents into the streets. The rat puppets and over-sized model rodent heads are ludicrous and laughable more than scary and suspense-inducing. AJ

Paul Coufos *Prof Neil Hamilton* • Lisa Schrage *Alex Reed* • Colin Fox *Edmund Delhurst* • Frank Moore *Jacques* • Real Andrews *Mark* ■ *Dir* Damian Lee • *Scr* Richard Bennett, E Kim Brewster, from a story by Richard Bennett

The Fool ★★★ U

Drama 1990 · UK · Colour · 140mins

This is a beautifully detailed account of Victorian life in London, with Derek Jacobi as the humble clerk who leads a double life by also posing as a businessman who's accepted in high social circles – a gem of paste in a chandelier of diamonds. Director Christine Edzard needs a stronger narrative, and her superb cast can't prevent the characters from resembling the Cruikshank-illustrated cartoons of Victorian social historian Henry Mayhew. TH

Derek Jacobi *Sir John/Mr Frederick* • Cyril Cusack *The Ballad Seller* • Ruth Mitchell *The Girl* • Maria Aitken *Lady Amelia* • Irina Brook *Georgiana Shillibeer* • Paul Brooke *Lord Paramount* • Richard Caldicot *Duke* • Rosalie Crutchley *Mrs Harris* • Patricia Hayes *The Dowager* ■ *Dir* Christine Edzard • *Scr* Christine Edzard, Olivier Stockman

Fool for Love ★★★ 15

Drama 1985 · US · Colour · 102mins

Kim Basinger acts her sexual socks off in Robert Altman's adaptation of a theatrical production that works well as a piece of cinema, while still retaining its stifling atmosphere. Sam Shepard takes the starring role in his own play, about a past, semi-incestuous love that overshadows the present, and lends a special power to his role as a hick, driven by furies that would not disgrace a Greek tragedy. TH. Contains violence, swearing. DVD

Sam Shepard *Eddie* • Kim Basinger *May* • Harry Dean Stanton *Old man* • Randy Quaid *Martin* • Martha Crawford *May's mother* • Louise Egolf *Eddie's mother* • Sura Cox *Teenage May* • Jonathan Skinner *Teenage Eddie* ■ *Dir* Robert Altman • *Scr* Sam Shepard, from his play

The Fool Killer ★★★

Period thriller 1965 · US · BW · 101mins

The story of an orphan boy's adventures just after the end of the Civil War proves to be an unusual experience. Initially the boy – played by actor Eddie Albert's son, Edward – runs into a reclusive eccentric named Dirty Jim Jelliman (Henry Hull, relishing the role) who tells him yarn after yarn about the Fool Killer, a legendary slayer of idiots. The boy then encounters Anthony Perkins, a traumatised former soldier who may or may not be the eponymous axe-wielder. Surely not? AT

Anthony Perkins *Milo Bogardus* • Edward Albert *George Mellish* • Dana Elcar *Mr Dodd* • Henry Hull *Dirty Jim Jelliman* • Salome Jens *Mrs Dodd* • Charlotte Jones (1) *Mrs Ova Fanshawe* • Arnold Moss *Rev Spotts* ■ *Dir* Servando Gonzalez • *Scr* David Friedkin, Morton Fine, from a novel by Helen Eustis

Foolin' Around ★★ PG

Romantic comedy
1980 · US · Colour · 95mins

Another would-be zany comedy, with not-too-bad performances from the stars, but a silly script. Gary Busey plays an innocent farm boy turned student who woos gorgeous Annette O'Toole. Of course, she turns out to be very rich and already engaged to another man. Busey was in his mid-30s when he played this role, but he tries his best despite this miscasting, and the uneven direction. SG

Gary Busey *Wes McDaniels* • Annette O'Toole *Susan Carlson* • John Calvin *Whitley* • Eddie Albert *Daggett* • Cloris Leachman *Samantha Carlson* • Tony Randall *Peddicord* • Michael Talbott *Clay* ■ *Dir* Richard T Heffron • *Scr* Mike Kane, David Swift

Foolish Heart ★★

Romantic drama
1998 · Arg/Bra/Fr · Colour · 132mins

Clearly autobiographical but clumsily constructed, this is a two-act melodrama that neither involves nor convinces. The film begins with Argentine teenager Juan (Walter Quiroz) tasting first love with the mentally unstable Maria Luiza Mendonca during a project to photograph the human soul. Settling for fame as a movie director, the adult Juan (Miguel Angel Sola) returns home to visit his ailing father and embarks on another affair, this time with the impoverished Xuxa Lopes. DP. In Spanish with English subtitles.

Miguel Angel Sola *Juan as an adult* • Walter Quiroz *Juan as an adolescent* • Maria Luiza Mendonca *Ana* • Xuxa Lopes *Lilith* ■ *Dir* Hector Babenco • *Scr* Hector Babenco, Ricardo Piglia, from an idea by Hector Babenco

Foolish Wives ★★★

Silent drama 1920 · US · BW · 107mins

A legendary silent movie which cost more and took longer to make than DW Griffith's epic *Intolerance*. Originally running for five hours, it's an incredibly lavish study of corruption and sexual obsession, set largely in the casinos, hotels, cafés and boudoirs of Monte Carlo and ends, appropriately enough for a satire, in the city's sewers. A fake count seduces rich ladies, but when he tries it with an ambassador's wife he runs out of luck. Today's viewers will have problems with the pacing, the wayward plotting and the acting styles, but director Erich von Stroheim's vision of decadence still seems impressive. AT

Rudolph Christians *Andrew J Hughes* • Miss Du Pont *Helen, his wife* • Maude George *Princess Olga Petschnikoff* • Mae Busch *Princess Vera Petschnikoff* • Erich von Stroheim *Count Sergius Karamzin, Captain of Third Hussars, Imperial Russian Army* ■ *Dir* Erich von Stroheim • *Scr* Erich von Stroheim, Marian Ainslee (titles)

Fools ★

Romantic drama 1970 · US · Colour · 93mins

This dumb (and aptly titled) drama, set in San Francisco, is about the romance between an ageing star of horror movies and the neglected wife of a lawyer. Indifferently written, directed and acted, it's a shoddy vehicle for its two "name" stars – Jason Robards and Katharine Ross. DA

Jason Robards *Matthew South* • Katharine Ross *Anais* • Scott Hylands *David Appleton* • Marc Hannibal *Dog owner* ■ *Dir* Tom Gries • *Scr* Robert Rudelson

Fools for Scandal ★★

Comedy 1938 · US · BW · 80mins

Mervyn LeRoy directs Carole Lombard (sublime) and Fernand Gravet (engaging) in this mind-bendingly silly romantic comedy which starts out very well indeed in a cardboard, studio-built Paris. The action then moves to London, where penniless French aristocrat and master chef Gravet pursues famous movie star Lombard in an attempt to woo her away from her stuffy insurance man (Ralph Bellamy). The piece progressively disintegrates but there are some laughs along the way, and the stars, particularly Lombard, almost survive the chaos into which they are thrown. RK

Carole Lombard *Kay Winters* • Fernand Gravet *René* • Ralph Bellamy *Phillip Chester* • Allen Jenkins *Dewey Gibson* • Isabel Jeans *Lady Paula Malverton* • Marie Wilson *Myrtle* • Marcia Ralston *Jill* ■ *Dir* Mervyn LeRoy • *Scr* Herbert Fields, Joseph Fields, Irving Brecher, from the play *Return Engagement* by Nancy Hamilton, James Shute, Rosemary Casey

Fool's Gold ★★ U

Western 1946 · US · BW · 63mins

Silent screen matinée idol William Boyd achieved a memorable second career in the sound era as the black-clad, silver-haired gentleman cowboy with the improbable name of Hopalong Cassidy. The movies were little more than cheap programme fillers, but the character whose popularity was fuelled by comic books and personal appearances was immensely dignified and endearing, and movies like this one, in which "Hoppy" is memorably teamed with sidekick Andy Clyde, were fast-paced, fun, and mercifully short in duration. The series would find a whole new audience on television, making William Boyd a very rich actor. TS

William Boyd (1) *Hopalong Cassidy* • Andy Clyde *California Carlson* • Rand Brooks *Lucky Jenkins* • Robert Emmett Keane *Professor Dixon* • Jane Randolph *Jessie Dixon* • Steve Barclay [Stephen Barclay] *Bruce Landy* ■ *Dir* George Archainbaud • *Scr* Doris Schroeder, from characters created by Clarence E Mulford

Fools of Fortune ★★★ 15

Drama 1990 · UK · Colour · 104mins

It's the 1920s in Ireland, and the wealthy Quinton family are shocked when their rural splendour is shattered by the British army of the time, the Black and Tans, who burn the house and massacre some of the family. Survivors include Julie Christie and her son, Iain Glen, whose childhood sweetheart grows into Mary Elizabeth Mastrantonio. But politics continue to play a major role in this absorbing but curiously reticent family saga. AT

Iain Glen *Willie Quinton* • Mary Elizabeth Mastrantonio *Marianne* • Julie Christie *Mrs Quinton* • Michael Kitchen *Mr Quinton* • Niamh Cusack *Josephine* • Tom Hickey *Father Kilgarriff* • John Kavanagh *Johnny Lacy* • Mick Lally *Mr Derenzy* • Niall Toibin *Lanigan* ■ *Dir* Pat O'Connor • *Scr* Michael Hirst, from the novel by William Trevor

Fools Rush In ★★

Romantic comedy 1949 · UK · BW · 81mins

Kenneth Horne was one of the brightest British radio stars of the 1950s and 1960s, but the stage play that inspired this timid sitcom is a far cry from the irreverent comedy that enlivened *Beyond Our Ken* and *Round the Horne*. Sally Ann Howes postpones her wedding to reunite her supposedly caddish father, Guy Rolfe, with mother Nora Swinburne. The cast frantically over-compensates for the flimsy script. DP

Sally Ann Howes *Pamela Dickson* • Guy Rolfe *Paul Dickson* • Nora Swinburne *Angela Dickson* • Nigel Buchanan *Joe Trent* • Raymond Lovell *Sir Charles Leigh* • Thora Hird *Mrs Coot* ■ *Dir* John Paddy Carstairs • *Scr* Geoffrey Kerr, from the play by Kenneth Horne

Fools Rush In ★★★ 12

Romantic comedy
1997 · US · Colour · 104mins

Ignored on its cinema release, this romantic comedy is well worth seeking out. *Friends* star Matthew Perry plays a New Yorker on business in Las Vegas who has a one night stand with beautiful Mexican Salma Hayek, only for her to reappear three months later to tell him she's pregnant with his baby. The road to true happiness is littered with problems, with her traditional parents (and his snobby Wasp-ish ones) being the butt of many a joke along the way. Matthew's real-life dad, John Bennett Perry plays, of course, Matthew's dad. JB. Contains sexual references. DVD

Matthew Perry *Alex* • Salma Hayek *Isabel* • Jon Tenney *Jeff* • Carlos Gomez *Chuy* • Tomas Milian *Tomas* • Siobhan Fallon *Lanie* • John Bennett Perry *Richard* ■ *Dir* Andy Tennant • *Scr* Katherine Reback, from a story by Joan Taylor, Katherine Reback

Football Days ★★

Sports comedy
2003 · Sp/Azerbaijan · Colour · 118mins

David Serrano made his directorial debut with this brisk, but formulaic battle-of-the-sexes romp. Ernesto Alterio emerges from jail, convinced he's acquired an insight into the male psyche and forms a football team to help his friend Alberto San Juan cope with his romantic problems with Alterio's sister, Natalia Verbeke. It's soon obvious that every player is blighted by relationship strife, but too few of them are sufficiently well drawn for us to care. There's the odd funny moment, but little inspiration or consistency. DP. In Spanish with English subtitles.

Alberto San Juan *Jorge* • Ernesto Alterio *Antonio* • Natalia Verbeke *Violeta* • María Esteve *Carla* • Fernando Tejero *Serafín* • Roberto Alamo *Ramon* • Secun de la Rosa *Gonzalo* • Ponce Pere *Carlos* ■ *Dir/Scr* David Serrano

The Football Factory ★★★ 18

Drama 2004 · UK · Colour · 87mins

Director/writer Nick Love takes an unflinching look at soccer hooliganism and the thugs who get their kicks from it. Portraying several weeks in the lives of a "firm" of Chelsea supporters, it is a decently acted and well-made film, but what is less evident is its moral stance. While not openly condoning the brutality it depicts, the movie doesn't actively condemn it either. Love's film is at its best when things are kept gritty, with Frank Harper in menacing form as an ageing hooligan who's old enough to know better. However, the crisis of conscience faced by Danny Dyer's character is less well handled. DA. Contains swearing, violence and drug abuse. DVD

Danny Dyer *Tommy Johnson* • Frank Harper *Billy Bright* • Tamer Hassan *Jack* • Roland Manookian *Zeberdee* • Neil Maskell *Rod* • Dudley Sutton *Bill Farrell* • Jamie Foreman *Cabbie* ■ *Dir* Nick Love • *Scr* Nick Love, from the novel by John King

Footlight Parade ★★★★ U

Musical 1933 · US · BW · 99mins

James Cagney, hoofer extraordinaire, is better remembered for being the 1930s' top gangster than as a rival to Fred Astaire. This typically fast-paced Warner Bros extravaganza is a showcase for Cagney at full pelt, playing an extrovert producer staging those now-forgotten prologues to the main feature. In this movie, Cagney has the benefit of the genius choreography of Busby Berkeley at his peak. Witty, well cast and as brash as they come, this is a real treat. TS

James Cagney *Chester Kent* • Joan Blondell *Nan Prescott* • Dick Powell *Scotty Blair* • Ruby Keeler *Bea Thorn* • Guy Kibbee *Silas Gould* ■ *Dir* Lloyd Bacon, Busby Berkeley • *Scr* Manuel Seff, James Seymour, from a story by Robert Lord, Peter Milne

Footlight Serenade ★★ U

Musical 1942 · US · BW · 80mins

Not to be confused with Warner Bros's wonderful *Footlight Parade*, this is an average wartime 20th Century-Fox Betty Grable vehicle, though with a little more humour than most of its ilk. The film contains some very pleasing performances, including a lightly self-mocking one from hulk Victor Mature as a Broadway-bound boxer. Phil Silvers and Jane Wyman are also impressive, but Grable is not at her best, and her leading man is the terminally bland John Payne. TS

John Payne *Bill Smith* • Betty Grable *Pat Lambert* • Victor Mature *Tommy Lundy* • Jane Wyman *Flo Laverne* • James Gleason *Bruce McKay* • Phil Silvers *Flap* • Cobina Wright Jr *Estelle Evans* • June Lang *June* • Frank Orth *Doorman* • Mantan Moreland *Dresser* ■ *Dir* Gregory Ratoff • *Scr* Robert Ellis, Helen Logan, Lynn Starling, from the story *Dynamite* by Fidel LaBarba, Kenneth Earl

Footloose ★★★ 15

Musical drama 1984 · US · Colour · 99mins

Kevin Bacon stars as a free-spirited teenager fighting small-minded minister John Lithgow in a small town where rock 'n' roll and dancing are illegal. The cast performs wonders with a story that hits the drivel button and becomes overly sentimental far too frequently. Kenny Loggins's tunes aren't half bad (the title track got to number six in the UK charts), and the energy raised during the finger-snapping dance numbers is infectious. AJ. Contains violence, swearing and brief nudity. DVD

Kevin Bacon *Ren MacCormack* • Lori Singer *Ariel Moore* • John Lithgow *Reverend Moore* • Dianne Wiest *Vi Moore* • Christopher Penn [Chris Penn] *Willard* • Sarah Jessica Parker *Rusty* • John Laughlin *Woody* • Elizabeth Gorcey *Wendy Jo* ■ *Dir* Herbert Ross • *Scr* Dean Pitchford • *Music* Kenny Loggins

Footrot Flats: the Dog's Tale ★★★

Animation 1986 · NZ · Colour · 71mins

Down Under, Murray Ball's newspaper cartoon strip *Footrot Flats* is as big as *The Gambols*, and this feature film became one of New Zealand's biggest releases. Here, the nice-but-dim sheep farmer with a passion for rugby crosses swords with the fearsome Crocopigs and Murphy's hellhounds, aided and abetted by his loyal canine companion. An acquired taste, perhaps, but well worth a watch. JF

John Clarke (2) *Wal* • Peter Rowley *Dog* • Rawiri Paratene *Rangi* • Fiona Samuel *Cheeky Hobson/Pongo* • Peter Hayden *Cooch/Irish Murphy* • Dorothy McKegg *Aunt Dolly* ■ *Dir* Murray Ball • *Scr* Murray Ball, Tom Scott

Footsteps in the Dark ★★

Comedy mystery 1941 · US · BW · 96mins

This flat-footed comedy thriller features Errol Flynn looking distinctly uncomfortable in a suit and bow-tie as the investment banker who moonlights as a mystery writer called FX Pettijohn. Flynn's Holmesian character cruises the streets, discovers a murder and sets out to solve it. Warner Bros, buckling under Flynn's demands to be relieved of his swashbuckles, had in mind a *Thin Man*-style adventure and missed by yards, if not miles. AT

Errol Flynn *Francis Warren* • Brenda Marshall *Rita Warren* • Ralph Bellamy *Dr Davis* • Alan Hale *Inspector Mason* • Lee Patrick *Blondie White* • Allen Jenkins *Wilfred* • Lucile Watson *Mrs Archer* • William Frawley *Hopkins* ■ *Dir* Lloyd Bacon • *Scr* Lester Cole, John Wexley, from the play *Blondie White* by Ladislaus Fodor [Ladislas Fodor], Bernard Merivale, Jeffrey Dell

Footsteps in the Fog ★★★

Thriller 1955 · UK/US · Colour · 89mins

Handsome Stewart Granger and his then wife, the lovely Jean Simmons, returned to Britain at the peak of their international stardom for this suspenseful and atmospheric Victorian melodrama. In a Columbia Studios tale of lust and blackmail, the under-rated Granger is particularly effective as the murderer, his unique combination of matinée idol looks and ability to appear at ease in period clothing being used to good effect. The Technicolor photography and the clever Shepperton studio interiors also complement him perfectly. Well worth catching. TS

Stewart Granger *Stephen Lowry* • Jean Simmons *Lily Watkins* • Bill Travers *David MacDonald* • Ronald Squire *Alfred Travers* • Finlay Currie *Inspector Peters* • Belinda Lee *Elizabeth Travers* • William Hartnell *Herbert Moresby* • Frederick Leister *Doctor Simpson* ■ *Dir* Arthur Lubin • *Scr* Dorothy Reid, Leonore Coffee, Arthur Pierson, from the novel *The Interruption* by WW Jacobs

For a Few Dollars More ★★★★★ 15

Classic spaghetti western
1965 · It/W Ger/Sp · Colour · 125mins

The second instalment of Sergio Leone's *Dollars* trilogy (after *A Fistful of Dollars*) is the best and most influential of the three. Honing the stylised visuals and dark humour of the original, Leone takes this opportunity to develop such future genre staples as the uneasy alliance against a common foe and the three-way shoot-out. But, while the pursuit of bandit Gian Maria Volonté by bounty hunters Clint Eastwood (motivated by greed) and Lee Van Cleef (driven by revenge) forms the core of the action, it's the attention to everyday detail and the symbols of a passing era (religion and the railroad) that give this operatic classic its distinctive aura. *The Good, the Bad and the Ugly* concluded the trilogy. DP. Some dialogue dubbed into English. DVD

Clint Eastwood *Man with No Name* • Lee Van Cleef *Colonel Douglas Mortimer* • Gian Maria Volonté *Indio* • Josef Egger *Old man over railway* • Rosemary Dexter *Colonel's sister* • Mara Krup *Hotel manager's wife* • Klaus Kinski *Hunchback* ■ *Dir* Sergio Leone • *Scr* Sergio Leone, Luciano Vincenzoni, from a story by Sergio Leone, from a story by Fulvio Morsella • *Music* Ennio Morricone

For Better and for Worse ★★

Romantic comedy
1993 · Fr/US · Colour · 89mins

There's nothing worse than a low-concept comedy in which the central contrivance is matched only by the decrepitude of the dialogue. This, for example, was progressing along quite nicely as a wedding nerves romp, with some broad class divide satire thrown in for good measure. But then the groom's practical joking buddy send an invitation to the Pope, which is accepted. This is as lightweight as a handful of confetti. DP

Patrick Dempsey *Robert Faldo* • Kelly Lynch *Catherine Vernet* • Gérard Rinaldi *Touchet* • Marion Peterson *Françoise* • Catherine Alcover *Carmina Faldo* • Nicolas Vogel *Joseph Faldo* • Marianne Borgo *Nathalie Vernet* ■ *Dir* Paolo Barzman • *Scr* Tony Gilroy

For Better, for Worse ★★★ U

Romantic comedy
1954 · UK · Colour · 84mins

Almost comforting in its snug predictability, this adaptation of Arthur Watkyn's stage play is now more noteworthy for its unworldly, sit-comic depiction of young bourgeois marriage than its actual entertainment value. There's a definite rapport between impoverished Dirk Bogarde and his bride, Susan Stephen, but the reliance on disapproving in-laws, nosey neighbours and dodgy tradesmen for laughs could easily have worn thin were it not for the accomplished supporting cast. DP

Dirk Bogarde *Tony Howard* • Susan Stephen *Anne Purves* • Cecil Parker *Anne's father* • Eileen Herlie *Anne's mother* • Dennis Price *Debenham* • Sidney James *Foreman* ■ *Dir* J Lee Thompson • *Scr* J Lee Thompson, from the play by Arthur Watkyn

For Better or for Worse ★★ 15

Spy spoof 1990 · US · Colour · 89mins

This spy spoof starring *Sex and the City*'s Kim Cattrall is like a distaff version of *True Lies*, with Cattrall as the undercover agent who has kept her business a secret from her fiancé (he thinks she's a travel agent). When the pair marry, Cattrall gives up her job and intends to settle down into a normal life, but her boss has one last dangerous assignment for her to carry out. It's a rather obvious comedy, but the two leads are good value. DF

Kim Cattrall *Chris Nelson* • Robert Hays *Sean McDonald* • Leigh Taylor-Young *Doris Kent* • Jonathan Banks *Pitt* • Christopher Lee *Lazos* ■ *Dir* Gene Quintano • *Scr* Gene Quintano, Jerry Lazarus, from a story by Gene Quintano

For Better or Worse ★★★ 12

Romantic comedy
1995 · US · Colour · 85mins

Also known as *Stranger Things*, this comedy marked the directorial debut of *Seinfeld* co-star Jason Alexander. While there's no shortage of kooky characters and slick wisecracks, the storyline takes some swallowing as love-scarred loser Alexander finds himself on the lam with his new sister-in-law (Lolita Davidovich) after his crooked brother (James Woods) bungles a robbery. It's overly reliant on Alexander's manic melancholia, and the farce is too often encumbered by pathos. But Davidovich is pleasingly feisty, and there's a wonderful double act from Joe Mantegna and Jay Mohr as the world's dumbest gangsters. DP. Contains violence and swearing.

Jason Alexander *Michael Makeshift* • James Woods *Reggie* • Lolita Davidovich *Valerie* • Joe Mantegna *Stone* • Jay Mohr *Dwayne* • Beatrice Arthur *Beverly* • Robert Constanzo *Landlord* • Rip Torn • Rob Reiner ■ *Dir* Jason Alexander • *Scr* Jeff Nathanson

For Ever Mozart ★★

Experimental drama
1996 · Fr/Swi · Colour · 85mins

This wayward effort from Jean-Luc Godard consists of four short films glued together – "which do not necessarily form a whole" – but could also be called "30 people in search of a story". Most viewers might well be in search of the exit after 20 minutes or so which is, loosely, about the conflict in Bosnia and about the film-making process. Thus businessmen, philospophers, film producers and Serbian fighters spout on about the war and the importance of culture. It's the movie an idealistic 19-year-old student might have made, but Godard was 65 at the time. The Mozart music is gloriously uplifting, though; the world premiere was held in Sarajevo. AT. In French with English subtitles.

Madeleine Assas *Camille, the director's daughter* • Frédéric Pierrot *Jerome, Camille's lover* • Ghalia Lacroix *Dzamila, Camille and Vicky's Arab maid* • Vicky Messica *Vicky Vitalis, the director* ■ *Dir/Scr* Jean-Luc Godard

For Heaven's Sake ★★★★

Silent comedy 1926 · US · BW · 58mins

After several years at Pathé, Harold Lloyd made his debut for Paramount with this sprightly slapstick classic, in which he took the "comedy of thrills" to new heights in a dazzling finale featuring a double-decker bus careering through the tightest city streets. Although playing a millionaire's son, Lloyd is still in characteristic go-getting mood as he sets out to woo Jobyna Ralston by supporting her father's mission. Although the scenes in the Bowery slums were intended to have some social impact, the emphasis is firmly on the comic, but none of the gags come close to the brilliance of the closing chase. DP

Harold Lloyd *J Harold Manners, the Uptown Boy* • Jobyna Ralston *Hope, the Downtown Girl* • Noah Young *Bull Brindle, the Roughneck* • James Mason [Jim Mason] *The Gangster* • Paul Weigel *Brother Paul, the Optimist* ■ *Dir* Sam Taylor • *Scr* John Grey, Ted Wilde, Clyde Bruckman

For Heaven's Sake ★★★

Fantasy comedy 1950 · US · BW · 86mins

A bizarre but eminently watchable fantasy, saved from ignominy by the splendidly tongue-in-cheek acting of Clifton Webb and Edmund Gwenn as a pair of unlikely angels sent to watch over the unborn baby of Joan Bennett and Robert Cummings. What distinguishes this tale from other less successful "visitors from above" sagas is the spicy, gloriously witty script and the deft, easy direction of George Seaton. SH

Clifton Webb *Charles* • Joan Bennett *Lydia Bolton* • Robert Cummings *Jeff Bolton* • Edmund Gwenn *Arthur* • Joan Blondell *Daphne* • Gigi Perreau *Item* • Jack LaRue *Tony* • Harry Von Zell *Tex* • Tommy Rettig *Joe* ■ *Dir* George Seaton • *Scr* George Seaton, from the play *May We Come In?* by Harry Segall

For Hire ★★★ 15

Crime thriller 1997 · Can · Colour · 94mins

A nifty TV crime thriller with a superior plotline. Rob Lowe plays an aspiring actor who forms a friendship with shady author Joe Mantegna, only to find himself the prime suspect in a murder. Lowe is bland, but the reliable Mantegna more than compensates and director Jean Pellerin keeps you guessing right up to the end. JF. Contains swearing, violence. DVD

Rob Lowe *Mitch Lawrence* • Joe Mantegna *Lou Webber* • Charles Powell *Joe Watson* • Bronwen Booth *Faye Lawrence* • Steve Adams *Tom Kellman* ■ *Dir* Jean Pellerin • *Scr* Karen Erbach, Leah M Kerr, from their story

For Keeps ★★ 15

Comedy drama 1987 · US · Colour · 94mins

Molly Ringwald finds life tough as a teenage wife and mother when she gets pregnant by boyfriend Randall Batinkoff. Career and college ambitions have to be sacrificed and their relationship comes under enormous strain. Written by the team who collaborated on *About Last Night...* , this is lacking in depth or realism, with Ringwald portrayed as a special case rather than the archetypal girl-next-door. The intimate scenes between the two leads do have genuine heart though. LH

Molly Ringwald *Darcy Elliot* • Randall Batinkoff *Stan Bobrucz* • Kenneth Mars *Mr Bobrucz* • Miriam Flynn *Mrs Elliot* • Conchata Ferrell *Mrs Bobrucz* • John Zarchen *Chris* • Sharon Brown *Lila* ■ *Dir* John G Avildsen • *Scr* Tim Kazurinsky, Denise DeClue

For Love of Ivy ★★ PG

Romantic comedy
1968 · US · Colour · 100mins

Having taken Hollywood by storm with *In the Heat of the Night* and *Guess Who's Coming to Dinner*, Sidney Poitier clearly wanted to take a break from hard-hitting civil rights dramas. Daniel Mann's film is a much lighter affair, though there is still an underlying message. Poitier co-stars with Abbey Lincoln as a couple who are brought together by a liberal white family desperate to keep their treasured home-help. This worthy attempt at depicting everyday black life veers uncomfortably between the preachy and the patronising. DP DVD

Sidney Poitier *Jack Parks* • Abbey Lincoln *Ivy Moore* • Beau Bridges *Tim Austin* • Nan Martin *Doris Austin* • Lauri Peters *Gena Austin* • Carroll O'Connor *Frank Austin* • Leon Bibb *Billy Talbot* ■ *Dir* Daniel Mann • *Scr* Robert Alan Aurthur, from a story by Sidney Poitier

For Love of the Game ★★ 12

Sports drama 1999 · US · Colour · 132mins

Kevin Costner is the legendary but ageing baseball pitcher desperate to prove there's life in the old dog yet in this glossy but overblown sports drama. A distracted Costner strives to focus long enough to pitch the perfect game, but is hampered by injuries and thoughts of partner Kelly Preston, who's made a sudden decision to dump him. Long-winded and oversentimental. DA DVD

Kevin Costner *Billy Chapel* • Kelly Preston *Jane Aubrey* • John C Reilly *Gus Sinski* • Jena Malone *Heather* • Brian Cox *Gary Wheeler* • JK Simmons *Frank Perry* • Vin Scully • Steve Lyons ■ *Dir* Sam Raimi • *Scr* Dana Stevens, from a novel by Michael Shaara

For Love or Country: the Arturo Sandoval Story ★★★ 12

Biographical drama
2000 · US · Colour · 115mins

With standout performances from Andy Garcia as trumpeter Arturo Sandoval and Charles S Dutton as jazz legend Dizzy Gillespie, this compelling biopic also provides keen insights into the clash between political security and personal expression that dominated life in Castro's post-coup Cuba. This TV movie concentrates on the dilemma that made Sandoval's plight even more unbearable – his passion for his wife Mia Maestro, a committed Communist. Director Joseph Sargent laudably strives to avoid propagandising melodramatics. DP DVD

Andy Garcia *Arturo Sandoval* • Mia Maestro *Marienela* • Gloria Estefan *Emilia* • David Paymer *Embassy interviewer* • Charles S Dutton *Dizzy Gillespie* ■ *Dir* Joseph Sargent • *Scr* Timothy J Sexton

For Love or Money ★★

Comedy 1963 · US · Colour · 107mins

Oh dear, one of those would-be Swinging Sixties comedies from Universal, all gloss and glitz, but with little charm or humour. Despite the presence of a glowing Mitzi Gaynor, clever Gig Young and watchable Thelma Ritter, this attempt at levity is sunk by a desperately unfunny performance from a totally miscast Kirk Douglas, as the attorney hired by Ritter to find husbands for her three daughters. Director Michael Gordon might have been hoping for another *Pillow Talk*, but Douglas's grimacing would sink a battleship. TS

Kirk Douglas *Deke Gentry* • Mitzi Gaynor *Kate Brasher* • Gig Young *"Sonny" John Dayton Smith* • Thelma Ritter *Chloe Brasher* • Julie Newmar *Bonnie Brasher* • William Bendix *Joe Fogel* ■ *Dir* Michael Gordon • *Scr* Michael Morris, Larry Markes

For Love or Money ★★ PG

Comedy 1993 · US · Colour · 91mins

Michael J Fox plays a smooth concierge who is desperate to open his own hotel, but to do that he needs the help of slimy millionaire Anthony Higgins, and Higgins's mistress (Gabrielle Anwar) happens to be the girl Fox loves. Director Barry Sonnenfeld seems strangely ill-at-ease with the material, and he is not helped by a script that swings from wild farce to slushy romance. Released on video in the UK as *The Concierge*. JF

Michael J Fox *Doug Ireland* • Gabrielle Anwar *Andy Hart* • Anthony Higgins *Christian Hanover* • Michael Tucker *Mr Wegman* • Bob Balaban *Mr Drinkwater* • Isaac Mizrahi *Julian Russell* • Patrick Breen *Gary Taubin* • Udo Kier *Mr Himmelman* ■ *Dir* Barry Sonnenfeld • *Scr* Mark Rosenthal, Lawrence Konner

For Me and My Gal ★★★★ U

Musical 1942 · US · BW · 103mins

This is a fabulous star vehicle for Judy Garland, who glows with talent and basks in the best songs and production values that MGM could bestow on her. The studio also gave her a new leading man, a dancer with a neon smile who had impressed Broadway critics as John O'Hara's heel in *Pal Joey*. His name? Gene Kelly, here making a stunning movie debut. Director Busby Berkeley uses his leads brilliantly and, while Kelly's character is not the most endearing ever, the plot's engrossing. TS

Judy Garland *Jo Hayden* • George Murphy *Jimmy K Metcalf* • Gene Kelly *Harry Palmer* • Marta Eggerth *Eve Minard* • Ben Blue *Sid Simms* • Horace McNally [Stephen McNally] *Bert Waring* • Keenan Wynn *Eddie Milton* • Richard Quine *Danny Hayden* ■ *Dir* Busby Berkeley • *Scr* Richard Sherman, Fred F Finklehoffe, Sid Silvers, Jack McGowan, Irving Brecher, from the story *The Big Time* by Howard Emmett Rogers • *Cinematographer* William Daniels [William H Daniels]

For Pete's Sake ★★ PG

Comedy 1974 · US · Colour · 86mins

This is one of those specially constructed star vehicles, but this time the wheels fell off with Barbra Streisand on board. It arrived with much ballyhoo and crept away shamefacedly after a major critical mauling. Streisand looks bewildered and lost as a debt-ridden wife forced to mix in unsavoury company. This smacks of shoving a famous name into a hastily put together dollar earner. Except it wasn't. SH. Contains swearing. DVD

Barbra Streisand *Henry* • Michael Sarrazin *Pete* • Estelle Parsons *Helen* • Molly Picon *Mrs Cherry* • William Redfield *Fred* • Louis Zorich *Nick* • Vivian Bonnell *Loretta* • Heywood Hall Broun *Judge Hiller* ■ *Dir* Peter Yates • *Scr* Stanley Shapiro, Maurice Richlin

For Queen and Country ★★★ 15

Thriller 1988 · UK/US · Colour · 100mins

Scriptwriter Martin Stellman made his directorial debut with this odd drama set against the gloomy backdrop of the Thatcher years of mid-1980s Britain. In an unusual bit of casting, Denzel Washington stars as the Caribbean-born Falklands war veteran who returns home to his grim South London council estate, only to be told he is no longer a British citizen. It's all rather depressing stuff, but Stellman's own script captures the mood of the time intelligently and it is backed up by a nice (if unevenly accented) performance by Washington. JB DVD

Denzel Washington *Reuben* • Dorian Healy *Fish* • Amanda Redman *Stacey* • George Baker *Kilcoyne* • Bruce Payne *Colin* • Sean Chapman *Bob* • Geff Francis *Lynford* • Craig Fairbrass *Challoner* ■ *Dir* Martin Stellman • *Scr* Martin Stellman, Trix Worrell

For Richer or Poorer ★★ 12

Comedy 1997 · US · Colour · 110mins

TV stars Kirstie Alley and Tim Allen star in this sitcom-style comedy about a bickering married couple who hide out in an Amish community because the Inland Revenue Service is after them for unpaid taxes. Allen and Alley don the costumes, leave their materialistic life behind and, of course, rekindle the love they lost while he was making money and she was getting manicures. JB. Contains some swearing.

Tim Allen *Brad Sexton* • Kirstie Alley *Caroline Sexton* • Jay O Sanders *Samuel Yoder* • Michael Lerner *Phil Kleinman* • Wayne Knight *Bob Lachman* ■ *Dir* Bryan Spicer • *Scr* Jana Howington, Steve LuKanic

For the Boys ★★★ 15

Drama 1991 · US · Colour · 138mins

Bette Midler scooped an Oscar nomination and gave one of the best performances of her career in this otherwise overblown showbiz drama that traces the love-hate relationship of a comedy duo who only ever seem to speak to each other when America is at war. You'd expect better material from *River's Edge* screenwriter Neal Jimenez and Woody Allen's longtime collaborator Marshall Brickman, and the action sags badly when Midler is off screen. Given little to do but sulk, smarm and shout, James Caan looks distinctly uncomfortable throughout. DP. Contains swearing. DVD

Bette Midler *Dixie Leonard* • James Caan *Eddie Sparks* • George Segal *Art Silver* • Patrick O'Neal *Shephard* • Christopher Rydell *Danny* • Arye Gross *Jeff Brooks* • Norman Fell *Sam Schiff* • Rosemary Murphy *Luanna Trott* ■ *Dir* Mark Rydell • *Scr* Marshall Brickman, Neal Jimenez, Lindy Laub, from the story by Neal Jimenez, Lindy Laub

For the First Time ★★ U

Musical romance
1959 · US/It/W Ger · Colour · 97mins

Actually, for the last time, since this was tenor Mario Lanza's final movie. He had decided not to fulfil a concert commitment for mobster Lucky Luciano, and tragically was discovered dead in a hospital bed soon afterwards. The incidents, apparently, were not connected. This is the one where he falls for a deaf girl and belts out *Ave Maria* to her, to test whether she can actually hear. TS

Mario Lanza *Tonio "Tony" Costa* • Johanna Von Koczian *Christa Bruckner* • Zsa Zsa Gabor *Gloria de Vadnuz* • Kurt Kasznar *Ladislas Tabory* • Hans Sohnker [Hans Söhnker] *Professor Albert Bruckner* • Peter Capell *Leopold Huebner* • Renzo Cesana *Angelo* ■ *Dir* Rudolph Maté • *Scr* Andrew Solt

For the Love of Ada ★★ PG

Comedy 1972 · UK · Colour · 84mins

The 70-something romance of Ada Cresswell and Walter Bingley never made for scintillating sitcom viewing, even though the 1970 TV series was popular in its day. This movie spin-off, set on the couple's first wedding anniversary, is leisurely in the extreme, as the writers struggle to fill the extra hour. While the by-play between widow Irene Handl and Wilfred Pickles (as the gravedigger who'd buried her husband) is engaging enough, this may be too gentle for modern tastes. DP DVD

Irene Handl *Ada Bingley* • Wilfred Pickles *Walter Bingley* • Barbara Mitchell *Ruth Pollit* • Jack Smethurst *Leslie Pollit* • Arthur English *Arthur* • Andria Lawrence *Sandra* • Larry Martyn *Brian* ■ *Dir* Ronnie Baxter • *Scr* Harry Driver, Vince Powell

For the Love of Benji ★★ U

Adventure 1977 · US · Colour · 83mins

Three years after his surprise hit *Benji*, director Joe Camp finally got round to making a second film about the smart little stray. Patsy Garrett and Cynthia Smith return for this perfectly acceptable adventure, set amid the splendours of Athens, in which our canine hero escapes from the clutches of a spy ring with a secret code written on his paw. The plot could have used a touch more imagination, but this sequel is better than the later addition, *Benji the Hunted* (1987). DP

Patsy Garrett *Mary* • Cynthia Smith *Cindy* • Allen Fiuzat *Paul* • Ed Nelson *Chandler Dietrich* • Art Vasil *Stelios* • Peter Bowles *Ronald* • Bridget Armstrong *Elizabeth* ■ *Dir* Joe Camp • *Scr* Joe Camp, from a story by Ben Vaughn, Joe Camp

For the Love of Mary ★★

Musical comedy 1948 · US · BW · 90mins

Deanna Durbin stars as a telephonist at the White House, striking up a relationship with the president (never seen) after she suffers an attack of hiccups. He helps her to sort out her romantic problems. Directed by Frederick De Cordova, this is characteristic Durbin flimflam, allowing the star to break into song from time to time and providing fairly painless entertainment. This unremembered movie was one of her two last. RK

Deanna Durbin *Mary Peppertree* • Edmond O'Brien *Lt Tom Farrington* • Don Taylor *David Paxton* • Jeffrey Lynn *Phillip Manning* • Ray Collins *Harvey Elwood* • Hugo Haas *Gustav Heindel* • Harry Davenport *Justice Peabody* ■ *Dir* Frederick De Cordova • *Scr* Oscar Brodney

For the Love of Mike ★★★

Silent romantic drama
1927 · US · BW · 75mins

Having parted acrimoniously from baby-faced clown Harry Langdon, Frank Capra sought to to rebuild his career with this adaptation. It was a commercial failure, but it contains traces of the comic sentimentality that would underpin the classic "Capra-corn" formula. Set in the New York slums, the story opens with German grocer Ford Sterling, Jewish tailor George Sidney and Irish street-cleaner Hugh Cameron raising an abandoned baby. However, Ben Lyon falls from grace at Yale and endures a few trials and tribulations before returning to the straight and narrow and the arms of the debuting Claudette Colbert. DP

Claudette Colbert *Mary* • Ben Lyon *Mike* • George Sidney (1) *Abraham Katz* • Ford Sterling *Herman Schultz* • Hugh Cameron *Patrick O'Malley* ■ *Dir* Frank Capra • *Scr* J Clarkson Miller, from the story *Hell's Kitchen* by John Moroso

For the Love of Mike ★★ U

Western 1960 · US · Colour · 88mins

Danny Bravo is a young native American boy who enters his horse in a race so he can win the prize money to build a new church. It's enough to bring tears to the eyes of local priest Richard Basehart, local doctor Stuart Erwin and, indeed, to Bravo's horse, but no one has told the local mountain lion (who does everything but wear a black hat) that little Danny is off limits as prey. But let us not be cynical: this is a story that celebrates the human spirit, directed with Bressonian intensity by George Sherman. AT

Richard Basehart *Father Phelan* • Stuart Erwin *Dr Mills* • Arthur Shields *Father Walsh* • Armando Silvestre *Tony Eagle* • Elsa Cardenas *Mrs Eagle* • Michael Steckler *Ty Corbin* • Rex Allen • Danny Bravo *Michael* ■ *Dir* George Sherman • *Scr* DD Beauchamp

For the Moment ★★

Second World War romantic drama
1994 · Can · Colour · 120mins

This provided the first major overseas starring role for Russell Crowe and is an unassuming but nicely played drama, filmed and set in Canada. Crowe is the Australian pilot who is sent to Canada for bomber training in 1942, where he falls for local lass Christianne Hirt – the only problem being that she is already married. There are a number of other romantic subplots but, unsurprisingly, it is

Crowe who catches the eye. While the material is overly familiar, this is a watchable enough affair. JF

Russell Crowe *Lachlan* • Christianne Hirt *Lill* • Wanda Cannon *Betsy* • Scott Kraft *Zeek* • Peter Outerbridge *Johnny* ■ *Dir/Scr* Aaron Kim Johnston

For Their Own Good ★★★ PG

Drama based on a true story
1993 · US · Colour · 91mins

The thorny issue of a woman's right to have a family versus the employer's interests, is given a new twist in this TV movie. Produced by Jon Avnet (director of *Fried Green Tomatoes at the Whistle Stop Cafe*) this stars Elizabeth Perkins as a young woman who challenges her employer's ultimatum that she agree to a sterilisation or lose her job. Thought-provoking stuff. JB VIDEO DVD

Elizabeth Perkins *Sally Thompson* • Charles Haid *Frank Souter* • Gary Basaraba *Roy Wheeler* • Laura San Giacomo *Jo Mandell* • CCH Pounder *Naomi Brinker* • Kelli Williams *Erma* • David Purdham *Jim Davis* ■ *Dir* Ed Kaplan • *Scr* Ed Kaplan, from a story by Clifford Campion, William Wages

For Those in Peril ★★★ U

Second World War drama
1943 · UK · BW · 66mins

Documentarist Harry Watt and future Ealing comedy scribe TEB Clarke united for this flagwaver directed by Charles Crichton, making his directorial debut. About the rivalry between David Farrar's air-sea rescue unit and a bigger patrol boat, the action sags a little as ace pilot Ralph Michael has to learn the importance of teamwork. However, the scenes in which he races against time to fish survivors out of the drink before a Nazi craft reaches them have an exciting, pseudo-newsreel feel, thanks to Douglas Slocombe's fine photography. DP

David Farrar *Murray* • Ralph Michael *Rawlings* • Robert Wyndham *Leverett* • John Slater *Wilkie* • John Batten *Wireless operator* • Robert Griffith *Griffiths* • Peter Arne *Junior officer* • James Robertson-Justice *Operations room officer* ■ *Dir* Charles Crichton • *Scr* Harry Watt, JOC Orton, TEB Clarke, from a story by Richard Hillary

For Those Who Think Young ★★ U

Romantic comedy
1964 · US · Colour · 96mins

Named after a Pepsi slogan (indeed, this beach movie was among the earliest Hollywood pictures to feature product placement), it's the tired old story of a group of high-school kids whose hi-jinks are jeopardised by a square grown-up. The cast gives it a certain cachet, but United Artists would do considerably better with their other 1964 teen-market offering, *A Hard Day's Night*. DP

James Darren *Gardner "Ding" Pruitt III* • Pamela Tiffin *Sandy Palmer* • Woody Woodbury • Paul Lynde *Sid Hoyt* • Tina Louise *Topaz McQueen* • Nancy Sinatra *Karen Cross* • Bob Denver *Kelp* • Ellen McRae [Ellen Burstyn] *Dr Pauline Taylor* ■ *Dir* Leslie H Martinson • *Scr* James O'Hanlon, George O'Hanlon, Dan Beaumont, from a story by Dan Beaumont

For Valour ★★★

Comedy 1937 · UK · BW · 94mins

Adapted for the screen from his own hit play, this Ben Travers comedy keeps promising to burst into life, but is eventually snuffed out by the endless round of deceptions and misunderstandings that were the trademark of his celebrated Aldwych productions. Expert farceurs Tom Walls and Ralph Lynn are as happy as sandboys in their dual roles but, while Walls plays father and son with the customary glint in his eye, Lynn fails to bring the same vim to the part of a Boer War veteran as he does to his shady, silly-ass grandson. DP

Tom Walls *Doubleday/Charlie Chisholm* • Ralph Lynn *Major Pyke/Willie Pyke* • Veronica Rose *Phyllis Chisholm* • Joan Marion *Clare Chester* • Hubert Harben *Mr Gallop* • Henry Longhurst *Inspector Harding* ■ *Dir* Tom Walls • *Scr* Ben Travers, from his play

For Whom the Bell Tolls ★★★ U

War drama 1943 · US · Colour · 124mins

Gary Cooper and Ingrid Bergman turn Ernest Hemingway's classic of the Spanish Civil War into a star vehicle made for two, while director Sam Wood scrubs this tale – about an American who joins a loyalist partisan group – clean of political taint (there's no mention of Franco, for example). The focus on Cooper's love for Bergman works well enough because of the quality of the two actors. However, it was Katina Paxinou as a peasant woman who won the Oscar, perhaps for the sense of reality she brought to the sanitisation. TH VIDEO DVD

Ingrid Bergman *Maria* • Gary Cooper *Robert Jordan* • Akim Tamiroff *Pablo* • Katina Paxinou *Pilar* • Vladimir Sokoloff *Anselmo* • Arturo de Cordova *Agustin* • Mikhail Rasumny *Rafael* ■ *Dir* Sam Wood • *Scr* Dudley Nichols, from the novel by Ernest Hemingway

For Your Eyes Only ★★★ PG

Spy adventure 1981 · UK · Colour · 122mins

Number 12 in the 007 series provides no real surprises, with the exception perhaps of Roger Moore, who gets the chance to show a little bit more grit than usual. The plot revolves around the hunt for a device from a sunken spy ship, with French star Carole Bouquet providing a little class as the girl who may hold the key to the puzzle. If Julian Glover is rather subdued as the number one villain, there is a colourful turn from *Fiddler on the Roof* star Topol as a rogue with shifting loyalties. Bond veteran John Glen ensures that the set pieces are spectacular enough and thankfully plays down the gadgetry. JF. Contains violence and swearing. VIDEO DVD

Roger Moore *James Bond* • Carole Bouquet *Melina* • Topol *Columbo* • Lynn-Holly Johnson *Bibi* • Julian Glover *Kristatos* • Cassandra Harris *Lisl* • Jill Bennett *Brink* • Michael Gothard *Locque* • Lois Maxwell *Moneypenny* • Desmond Llewelyn *"Q"* • Charles Dance *Claus* • John Wells *Denis* • Janet Brown *Prime Minister* ■ *Dir* John Glen • *Scr* Richard Maibaum, Michael G Wilson, from the short stories *For Your Eyes Only* and *Risico* by Ian Fleming

Forbidden ★★

Melodrama 1932 · US · BW · 87mins

An undistinguished entry in the Frank Capra canon. Barbara Stanwyck is a spinster who goes on a cruise and falls for married district attorney Adolphe Menjou. Regardless of the script, Capra could usually be relied upon to bring lightness and brisk wit to any storyline. In this case he fails – the only redeeming features being the performance of Stanwyck and fine photography from Joseph Walker. SH

Barbara Stanwyck *Lulu Smith* • Adolphe Menjou *Bob Grover* • Ralph Bellamy *Al Holland* • Dorothy Peterson *Helen* • Thomas Jefferson *Winkinson* ■ *Dir* Frank Capra • *Scr* Jo Swerling, from a story by Frank Capra

Forbidden ★★

Crime drama 1953 · US · BW · 84mins

Tough-guy Tony Curtis is dispatched to Macao by a gang of criminals to bring back, by force if necessary, Joanne Dru, the widow of a racketeer who possesses incriminating evidence against them. Much cross and double-cross later, involving among other things Macao's chief criminal (Lyle Bettger), the plot complications are resolved and love triumphs. This sub-*noir* gangster film-cum-romance is good-looking and technically proficient, but otherwise downbeat and dreary. RK

Tony Curtis *Eddie Darrow* • Joanne Dru *Christine Lawrence* • Lyle Bettger *Justin Keit* • Marvin Miller *Cliff Chalmer* • Victor Sen Yung *Allan* • Alan Dexter *Barney* ■ *Dir* Rudolph Maté • *Scr* William Sackheim, Gil Doud, from a story by William Sackheim

Forbidden ★★ 18

Erotic drama 2002 · US · Colour · 80mins

Renee Rea stars in this soft-core thriller, which is a minor improvement on the usual erotic trash. The plot is resolutely banal, as Rea's secret encounter with Dillon Silver at his bachelor party rears its head at the most inopportune moment. But director Robert Kubilos and screenwriter Eric Mittleman succeed in creating suspenseful, as well as sexual, tension. DP. Contains swearing, violence, sex scenes and nudity. DVD

Renee Rea *Nikki/Monique* • Dillon Silver *Jason* • Tracy Ryan *Lisa* • Jason Schnuit *Andy* ■ *Dir* Robert Kubilos • *Scr* Eric Mittleman

Forbidden Cargo ★★ PG

Crime drama 1954 · UK · BW · 82mins

Customs agent Nigel Patrick tries to stop drug smugglers from polluting our shores in this cosy but rather unexciting thriller. Patrick is supported by a cast of British stalwarts that includes Joyce Grenfell (as a bird-watcher named Lady Flavia Queensway), Elizabeth Sellars, Jack Warner and Terence Morgan. AT VIDEO

Nigel Patrick *Michael Kenyon* • Elizabeth Sellars *Rita Compton* • Terence Morgan *Roger Compton* • Jack Warner *Alec White* • Greta Gynt *Madame Simonetta* • Theodore Bikel *Max* • Joyce Grenfell *Lady Flavia Queensway* ■ *Dir* Harold French • *Scr* Sydney Box

Forbidden Island ★★

Adventure 1959 · US · Colour · 65mins

An adventure star of the 1930s and 1940s, Jon Hall is a little bit long in the tooth for this slice of hokum about skin-divers and a sunken treasure ship. The divers fall out in their search for a priceless emerald but the problem, as ever, with these underwater malarkies is that it's hard to fathom who's who behind the masks. Critics at the time were hard pressed to decide whether the colour process was deliberately stylised or just messed up in the lab. AT

Jon Hall *Dave Courtney* • Nan Adams *Joanne* • John Farrow *Stuart Godfrey* • Jonathan Haze *Jack Mautner* • Greigh Phillips *Dean Pike* ■ *Dir/Scr* Charles B Griffith

Forbidden Planet ★★★★★ U

Classic science-fiction adventure
1956 · US · Colour · 94mins

What unknown terror roams the planet Altair-4 killing everyone apart from tormented scientist Morbius (Walter Pidgeon) and his daughter Altaira (Anne Francis)? Starship commander Leslie Nielsen finds out in one of the finest science-fiction films ever made. Loosely based on Shakespeare's *The Tempest*, which explains its overall intelligence, this is an enthralling eye-popper. The super monster effects (created by Disney animators) and outstanding technology include the unforgettable Robby the Robot, the subterranean Krell city, Morbius's futuristic home and an impressive array of space vehicles. AJ VIDEO

Walter Pidgeon *Dr Morbius* • Anne Francis *Altaira* • Leslie Nielsen *Commander Adams* • Warren Stevens *Lieutenant "Doc" Ostrow* • Jack Kelly *Lieutenant Farman* • Richard Anderson *Chief Quinn* • Earl Holliman *Cook* • Marvin Miller *Robby the Robot* ■ *Dir* Fred McLeod Wilcox [Fred M Wilcox] • *Scr* Cyril Hume, from a story by Irving Block, Allen Adler • *Cinematographer* George Folsey • *Special Effects* A Arnold Gillespie, Warren Newcombe, Irving G Ries, Joshua Meador

Forbidden Sins ★★ 18

Erotic thriller 1998 · US · Colour · 93mins

Shannon Tweed is a lawyer who gets drawn into shady goings-on a strip club run by Corbin Timbrook. He has been charged with murdering one of his strippers, but things start getting complicated when Tweed falls for her client. But director Robert Angelo is more interested in getting his cast to disrobe, with Tweed and enthusiastic newcomer Amy Lindsay leading the way. JF VIDEO DVD

Shannon Tweed *Maureen Doherty* • Corby Timbrook *David Mulholland* • Myles O'Brien *John Doherty* • Kirstine Calstrand *Virginia Hill* • Amy Lindsay *Molly Malone* ■ *Dir* Robert Angelo • *Scr* Daryl Haney, Hel Styverson

Forbidden Valley ★★ U

Western 1938 · US · BW · 67mins

One of those perfectly competent but utterly routine westerns made by Universal, starring the amiable Noah Beery Jr. Here he plays a boy living in a remote mountain hideaway because his father, Samuel S Hinds, has been wrongly accused of murder. Beery's isolated existence begins to change when he encounters wealth in the pert shape of Frances Robinson. This was remade in colour as *Sierra* in 1950 with Audie Murphy. TS

Noah Beery Jr *Ring* • Frances Robinson *Wilda* • Fred Kohler Sr [Fred Kohler] *Regan* • Alonzo Price *Indian Joe* • Samuel S Hinds *Hazzard* • Stanley Andrews *Lanning* • Spencer Charters *Dr Scudd* ■ *Dir* Wyndham Gittens • *Scr* Wyndham Gittens, from the novel *Mountains Are My Kingdom* by Stuart Hardy

Force Majeure ★★★

Drama 1989 · Fr · Colour · 86mins

This is a dark deliberation on the contention that the modern age is not a time of heroes. Patrick Bruel and François Cluzet are the holidaying friends who face a moral dilemma when a fellow backpacker is sentenced to death for drug-trafficking. In a film in which dialogue is at a premium, much depends on the physical performances of the cast, and Bruel and Cluzet manage to convey a range of contradictory emotions without ever resorting to histrionics. Difficult and often self-conscious, but give it a go. DP. In French with English subtitles.

Patrick Bruel *Philippe* • François Cluzet *Daniel* • Kristin Scott Thomas *Katia* • Alan Bates *Malcolm* • Sabine Haudepin *Jeanne* • Thom Hoffman *Hans* • Lucienne Hamon *Philippe's mother* • Marc Jolivet *Journalist* ■ *Dir* Pierre Jolivet • *Scr* Pierre Jolivet, Oliver Schatzky

Force of Arms ★★

Second World War drama
1951 · US · BW · 98mins

William Holden and Nancy Olson star in this war movie, directed by the man who made *Casablanca*. In fact, it's a remake of Hemingway's *A Farewell to Arms*, first filmed in 1932 and updated to the Second World War. Holden's GI falls for Olson's nurse during the Italian campaign; he is then reported missing after a terrible battle. It's nothing special, despite Holden's romantic appeal. A further remake followed in 1957, reverting to Hemingway's original title. AT

William Holden (2) *Peterson* • Nancy Olson *Eleanor* • Frank Lovejoy *Maj Blackford* • Gene Evans *McFee* • Dick Wesson *Klein* • Paul Picerni *Sheridan* • Katherine Warren *Maj*

Waldron, WAC • Ross Ford *Hooker* ■ *Dir* Michael Curtiz • *Scr* Orin Jannings, from the story *Italian Story* by Richard Tregaskis

Force of Evil ★★★★ PG

Film noir 1948 · US · BW · 74mins

This is a truly remarkable one-off, a quintessential *film noir* filmed on authentic New York locations by the great cinematographer George Barnes with dialogue in blank verse, co-written and directed by Abraham Polonsky. The plot revolves around corruption in the numbers racket, and holding it all together is a remarkably intense performance by John Garfield, doing some of his career best screen work here. But, be warned, this bleak and sordid philosophical allegory may not be to everyone's taste. Polonsky was blacklisted following the McCarthy witch-hunt and did not direct again until 1969. TS

John Garfield *Joe Morse* • Beatrice Pearson *Doris Lowry* • Thomas Gomez *Leo Morse* • Howland Chamberlin *Freddy Bauer* • Roy Roberts *Ben Tucker* • Marie Windsor *Edna Tucker* • Paul McVey *Hobe Wheelock* • Tim Ryan *Johnson* ■ *Dir* Abraham Polonsky • *Scr* Abraham Polonsky, Ira Wolfert, from the novel *Tucker's People* by Ira Wolfert

A Force of One ★★ 15

Martial arts 1979 · US · Colour · 85mins

Between the death of Bruce Lee and the emergence of Jackie Chan, martial arts fans had to make do with the plank of wood that was Chuck Norris, the six-times world karate champion. Displaying all his customary charm, the hairy one is characteristically cast as a Vietnam vet fighting cop-killing drug dealers in a small Californian town. This has about as much life as an opponent who's just been felled by Norris. RS DVD

Jennifer O'Neill *Detective Mandy Rust* • Chuck Norris *Matt Logan* • Clu Gulager *Dunne* • Ron O'Neal *Rollins* • Bill Wallace *Jerry Sparks* • Eric Laneuville *Charlie Logan* • James Whitmore Jr *Moskowitz* • Clint Ritchie *Melrose* ■ *Dir* Paul Aaron • *Scr* Ernest Tidyman, from a story by Pat Johnson

Force 10 from Navarone ★★ 15

Second World War drama
1978 · UK · Colour · 113mins

A totally unnecessary and belated follow-up to the massive 1961 smash hit, *The Guns of Navarone*. The cast here is no match for the original's; this time round, a tired Robert Shaw (in his penultimate picture), a pre-superstardom Harrison Ford and a mannered Edward Fox are faced not only with the enemy, but also with a cliché-ridden script. Director Guy Hamilton's uninspired movie begins with the climax of the earlier film, then spends an inordinate amount of time before reaching its own explosive finale. TS. Contains swearing.

Robert Shaw *Mallory* • Harrison Ford *Barnsby* • Edward Fox *Miller* • Barbara Bach *Maritza* • Franco Nero *Lescovar* • Carl Weathers *Weaver* • Richard Kiel *Drazac* • Angus MacInnes *Reynolds* ■ *Dir* Guy Hamilton • *Scr* Robin Chapman, from a story by Carl Foreman, from the novel by Alistair MacLean

Forced March ★★★ 15

Drama 1989 · US/Hun · Colour · 99mins

An ambitious film within a film about a fading US actor who travels to Hungary to star in a biography of a Hungarian-Jewish poet who died during the Holocaust. Rick King's film mixes scenes of the actor making the film with scenes from the film he's making; it also explores the cast members' varying commitment to the project. Style sometimes gets in the way of content, but this remains a powerful drama, with Chris Sarandon impressive at the head of a predominantly European cast. DA

Chris Sarandon *Kline/Miklos Radnoti* • Renée Soutendijk *Myra* • Josef Sommer *Father* • John Seitz *Hardy* ■ *Dir* Rick King • *Scr* Dick Atkins, Charles K Bardosh

Forced Vengeance ★★ 18

Martial arts thriller
1982 · US · Colour · 85mins

Chuck Norris may yet learn that slick karate chops and macho grunting are no substitute for acting. Looking for the most part here as if he's reading his lines off another actor's forehead, Norris only begins to add any character to the film when he stops talking and gets on with the action. At that point, the tightly choreographed martial arts sequences, the movie's sole blessing, come into their own. JM. Contains swearing and nudity.

Chuck Norris *Josh Randall* • Mary Louise Weller *Claire Bonner* • Camila Griggs *Joy Paschal* • Michael Cavanaugh *Stan Raimondi* • David Opatoshu *Sam Paschal* ■ *Dir* James Fargo • *Scr* Franklin Thompson

Forces of Nature ★★ 12

Romantic comedy
1998 · US · Colour · 101mins

Unfortunately, the forces at work in this romantic comedy starring Sandra Bullock and Ben Affleck fail to muster much chemistry between the two leads. He is fine as the strait-laced groom-to-be who has a *Planes, Trains and Automobiles*-style trip to his wedding, but Bullock is miscast as the quirky gal who may tempt him away from his waiting bride (Maura Tierney). Director Bronwen Hughes never brings enough farcical humour or a sense of impending catastrophe to the adventure. JB. Contains swearing and sexual references. DVD

Sandra Bullock *Sarah Lewis* • Ben Affleck *Ben Holmes* • Maura Tierney *Bridget* • Steve Zahn *Alan* • Blythe Danner *Virginia* • Ronny Cox *Hadley* • Michael Fairman *Richard* ■ *Dir* Bronwen Hughes • *Scr* Marc Lawrence

Forces' Sweetheart ★ U

Comedy 1953 · UK · BW · 73mins

Having starred with Peter Sellers and Spike Milligan in *Down among the Dead Men* the previous year, Harry Secombe and Michael Bentine re-team for this dismally unfunny uniform debacle. Hy Hazell is the object of everyone's attention, while veteran comic Freddie Frinton has the few good lines there are. DP

Hy Hazell *Judy James* • Harry Secombe *Private Llewellyn* • Michael Bentine *Flight Lt Robinson* • Freddie Frinton *Aloysius Dimwitty* • John Ainsworth *Lt Robinson* • Kenneth Henry *Tommy Tupp* ■ *Dir/Scr* Maclean Rogers

A Foreign Affair ★★★★

Romantic comedy drama
1948 · US · BW · 116mins

Iowa congresswoman Jean Arthur is sent to postwar Berlin to check on things, and runs into a thriving black market, corrupt GIs and a seductive Marlene Dietrich who's having affairs with an American army captain and a former Nazi. Not for nothing is Arthur's character called Frost and the question is, will she melt? Brimming with great lines, the film's weakness is John Lund as the US soldier. but its strength is Arthur's brave performance and director Billy Wilder's take on the ruins of the city he once lived in. Only he could have toured the bomb sites and stuck *Isn't It Romantic?* on the soundtrack. Comedies come no blacker or harsher than this. AT

Jean Arthur *Phoebe Frost* • Marlene Dietrich *Erika von Schluetow* • John Lund *Capt John Pringle* • Millard Mitchell *Col Rufus J Plummer* • Peter Von Zerneck *Hans Otto Birgel* • Stanley Prager *Mike* • Bill Murphy *Joe* ■ *Dir* Billy Wilder • *Scr* Charles Brackett, Billy Wilder, Richard Breen [Richard L Breen], Robert Harari, from a story by David Shaw, Irwin Shaw (uncredited) • *Cinematographer* Charles B Lang Jr [Charles Lang] • *Costume Designer* Edith Head

Foreign Affaires ★★ U

Comedy 1935 · UK · BW · 69mins

Written by Ben Travers in the style of his Aldwych farces, this hit-and-miss affair features the accomplished team of Tom Walls and Ralph Lynn who trot out their familiar mannerisms as the artful gambler and silly-ass car dealer who find themselves being duped in a crooked Nice casino. However, it's the estimable Robertson Hare who steals the show, with his shockable pomposity and his immaculate comic timing. Walls also directs, but his theatrical expertise renders the action stiff and stagey. DP

Tom Walls *Capt Archibald Gore* • Ralph Lynn *Jefferson Darby* • Robertson Hare *Mr Hardy Hornett* • Norma Varden *Mrs Hardy Hornett* • Marie Lohr *Mrs Cope* • Diana Churchill *Sophie* ■ *Dir* Tom Walls • *Scr* Ben Travers

Foreign Body ★ 15

Comedy 1986 · UK · Colour · 106mins

This is one of those comedies that manages to be both unfunny and offensive. Victor Banerjee stars as Indian immigrant Ram Das, who gets a job as a bus conductor in England until he is convinced by his cousin (Warren Mitchell, complete with blacked-up face) to pose as a private doctor. Despite an impressive cast, this is fumbled at every turn. JB

Victor Banerjee *Ram Das* • Warren Mitchell *IQ Patel* • Amanda Donohoe *Susan Partridge* • Eve Ferret *Norah Plumb* • Geraldine McEwan *Lady Ammanford* • Trevor Howard *Dr Stirrup* • Denis Quilley *Prime Minister* • Anna Massey *Miss Furze* ■ *Dir* Ronald Neame • *Scr* Celine La Freniere, from a novel by Roderick Mann

Foreign Correspondent ★★★★ PG

Spy thriller 1940 · US · BW · 115mins

This immensely pleasurable spy story is set on the eve of the Second World War and ends with American reporter Joel McCrea warning of the danger to come. Director Alfred Hitchcock makes the most of some great set pieces, many of which are now acknowledged as key moments in the Hitchcock canon: an Amsterdam assassination (on a huge interior set) as umbrellas close ranks in the rain; tense moments inside a vast Dutch windmill; a plane crash where the air supply on board is slowly draining away; a remarkable sequence in Westminster Cathedral. The plot's twists and turns are cleverly and wittily maintained, and the supporting cast is impeccably chosen. The propagandist aspects have dated the film, and it is also impaired by the lightweight casting of McCrea and Laraine Day in the leading roles. No matter, this is still marvellous. TS DVD

Joel McCrea *Johnny Jones/Huntley Haverstock* • Laraine Day *Carol Fisher* • Herbert Marshall *Stephen Fisher* • George Sanders *Scott Ffolliott* • Albert Basserman *Van Meer* • Robert Benchley *Stebbins* • Edmund Gwenn *Rowley* • Eduardo Ciannelli *Krug* ■ *Dir* Alfred Hitchcock • *Scr* Charles Bennett, Joan Harrison, James Hilton, Robert Benchley • *Cinematographer* Rudolph Maté

Foreign Intrigue ★★

Spy drama 1956 · US · Colour · 99mins

Shot on location in Europe, this stars a trenchcoat-clad Robert Mitchum at his most laconic in a movie whose murky plot and even murkier colour photography leave much to be desired. This was allegedly based on the Cold War experiences of its writer/producer/director Sheldon Reynolds, whose adventures formed the basis for a TV series from which this plodding film is a spin-off. TS

Robert Mitchum *Dave Bishop* • Genevieve Page *Dominique* • Ingrid Tulean [Ingrid Thulin] *Brita* • Frederick O'Brady [Frédéric O'Brady] *Spring* • Eugene Deckers *Sandoz* • Inga Tidblad *Mrs Lindquist* ■ *Dir* Sheldon Reynolds • *Scr* Sheldon Reynolds, Harry Jack Bloom, Gene Levitt

Foreign Student ★★ 15

Period drama 1994 · US/Fr · Colour · 91mins

This American co-produced melodrama was adapted from the bestselling memoirs of French film-maker Philippe Labro. Debuting director Eva Sereny capably captures the atmosphere of mid-1950s Virginia, but Robin Givens is too modern to convince as the black teacher being romanced by visiting student Marco Hofschneider. The book's fond nostalgia has been turned into mildly sensationalist sentiment, and any sense of passion or social insight is lost in the trite script. DP. Contains swearing, nudity.

Robin Givens *April* • Marco Hofschneider *Philippe Le Clerc* • Rick Johnson (2) *Cal Cate* • Charlotte Ross *Sue Ann* • Edward Herrmann *Zach Gilmore* ■ *Dir* Eva Sereny • *Scr* Menno Meyjes, from the novel by Philippe Labro

The Foreman Went to France ★★★ U

Second World War comedy drama
1941 · UK · BW · 81mins

Charles Frend edited some of the most impressive British pictures of the 1930s, including *Goodbye, Mr Chips*. He later graduated to direction during the Second World War and shot three of the most interesting docudramas of the conflict. This engaging flag-waver was based on the true-life exploits of Melbourne Johns, who crossed the Channel to smuggle vital machine tools back to Blighty. Clifford Evans and Constance Cummings tackle the mission with suitable gravitas, while troopers Gordon Jackson and Tommy Trinder provide some light relief. AJ

Tommy Trinder *Tommy* • Constance Cummings *Anne* • Clifford Evans *Fred Carrick* • Robert Morley *French mayor* • Gordon Jackson *Jock* • Ernest Milton *Stationmaster* ■ *Dir* Charles Frend • *Scr* John Dighton, Angus MacPhail, Leslie Arliss, from a story by JB Priestley • *Music* William Walton

The Forest Rangers ★★★

Romantic action drama
1942 · US · Colour · 86mins

The claws are out as two of Hollywood's most glamorous and popular leading ladies of the period, Paulette Goddard and Susan Hayward, compete for the affections of he-man forest ranger Fred MacMurray. A romantic action drama, with one of the ladies getting her man to the altar but nobly rescuing her rejected rival from a spectacular forest fire, this is formulaic but fun hokum in Technicolor. The scenery helps. RK

Fred MacMurray *Don Stuart* • Paulette Goddard *Celia Huston* • Susan Hayward *Tana Mason* • Lynne Overman *Jammer Jones* • Albert Dekker *Twig Dawson* • Eugene Pallette *Mr Howard Huston* • Regis Toomey *Frank Hatfield* ■ *Dir* George Marshall • *Scr* Harold Shumate, from the short story by Thelma Strabel

Forever ★

Fantasy mystery 1993 · US · Colour · 93mins

Movie fact meets movie fiction in this low-grade supernatural thriller which seeks to exploit the real-life unsolved murder of Irish-born director William Desmond Taylor in 1920s Hollywood. When a rock video director moves into the former home of a murdered film-maker he cranks up an old moviola and the celluloid personalities inside come to life, including Mary Pickford and "Fatty" Arbuckle. It sounds great, but a messy script and cack-handed direction consign it to the bin. RS

Sally Kirkland *Angelica* • Sean Young *Mary Miles Minter* • Keith Coogan *Ted Dickson* • Diane Ladd *Mabel Normand* • Terence Knox *Wallace Reid* • Nicholas Guest *Billy Baldwin* • Ashley Hester *Mary Pickford* ■ *Dir* Thomas Palmer Jr • *Scr* Jackelyn Giroux, Thomas Palmer Jr

Forever Amber ★★★ U

Historical melodrama
1947 · US · Colour · 132mins

Otto Preminger's lavish costume drama was based on Kathleen Winsor's notorious novel about a sultry wench romping from bed to bed on her way up the social ladder in the time of Charles II. Amber is portrayed with competent efficiency by Linda Darnell, who was one of Hollywood's biggest stars of the 1940s, but, after Fox ended her studio contract, a virtual unknown by the late 1950s. The film may be short on finesse but it is long on period colour and Hollywood production values. PF

Linda Darnell *Amber St Clair* • Cornel Wilde *Bruce Carlton* • Richard Greene *Lord Harry Almsbury* • George Sanders *King Charles II* • Glen Langan [Glenn Langan] *Rex Morgan* • Richard Haydn *Earl of Radcliffe* • Jessica Tandy *Nan Britton* • Anne Revere *Mother Red Cap* ■ *Dir* Otto Preminger • *Scr* Philip Dunne, Ring Lardner Jr, Jerome Cady, from the novel by Kathleen Winsor

Forever and a Day ★★★★

Period drama 1943 · US · BW · 104mins

No less than 21 writers – ranging from Christopher Isherwood to RC Sheriff – are credited with writing this all-star curio, plus seven directors and a mere four cameramen. It charts the history of a London mansion from 1804 to the Blitz, when it was converted into a residential hotel; as many stars as possible enter its impressive portals. An uneven film, obviously, and a bit rushed, but some episodes are outstanding and the whole enterprise is to be commended: everyone worked for free and profits were given to Anglo-American war charities. AT

Anna Neagle *Miriam (Susan)* • Ray Milland *Bill Trimble* • Claude Rains *Pomfret* • C Aubrey Smith *Adm Trimble* • Dame May Whitty *Mrs Trimble* • Gene Lockhart *Cobblewick* • Ray Bolger *Sentry* • Edmund Gwenn *Stubbs* • Lumsden Hare *Fitts* • Stuart Robertson *Lawyer* • Charles Coburn *Sir William* • Jessie Matthews *Mildred* • Charles Laughton *Bellamy* • Montagu Love *Sir John Bunn* • Reginald Owen *Mr Simpson* • Cedric Hardwicke *Dabb* • Buster Keaton *Dabb's assistant* • Ida Lupino *Jenny* • Merle Oberon *Marjorie* ■ *Dir* René Clair, Edmund Goulding, Cedric Hardwicke, Frank Lloyd, Victor Saville, Robert Stevenson, Herbert Wilcox • *Scr* Charles Bennett, CS Forester, Lawrence Hazard, Michael Hogan, WP Lipscomb, Alice Duer Miller, John Van Druten, Alan Campbell, Peter Godfrey, SM Herzig, Christopher Isherwood, Gene Lockhart, RC Sherriff, Claudine West, Norman Corwin, Jack Hartfield, James Hilton, Emmett Lavery, Frederick Lonsdale, Donald Ogden Stewart, Keith Winters

Forever, Darling ★★ U

Comedy 1956 · US · Colour · 90mins

Lucille Ball and Desi Arnaz's second attempt to become stars of the big screen together after the popular and stylish Vincente Minnelli-directed *The Long, Long Trailer* was this unfunny lark, in which guardian angel James Mason attempts to sort out the tribulations in their screen marriage. It doesn't sound particularly funny, and it wasn't, despite having Alexander Hall as director, who'd already had notable success with angels in *Here Comes Mr Jordan* and *Down to Earth*. Mason is a joy to watch, (even if he does look embarrassed about the material), but it's an unworthy vehicle for American TV's greatest stars. TS

Lucille Ball *Susan Vega* • Desi Arnaz *Lorenzo Xavier Vega* • James Mason *Guardian angel* • Louis Calhern *Charles Y Bewell* • John Emery *Dr Edward R Winter* • John Hoyt *Bill Finlay* • Natalie Schafer *Millie Opdyke* ■ *Dir* Alexander Hall • *Scr* Helen Deutsch

Forever England ★★ PG

First World War drama
1935 · UK · BW · 67mins

This was the first fictional film made with the full co-operation of the Royal Navy, including ships and technical advisers, and, not surprisingly, the Senior Service emerges with all colours flying. After a slow start, director Walter Forde cranks up the pace as able seaman John Mills is rescued from the wreck of HMS *Rutland* by the German battleship *Zeithen*. Crude but exciting, this was remade in 1953 as *Sailor of the King*. DP

John Mills *Albert Brown* • Betty Balfour *Elizabeth Brown* • Barry Mackay *Lt Somerville* • Jimmy Hanley *Ginger* • Howard Marion-Crawford *Max* ■ *Dir* Walter Forde • *Scr* Michael Hogan, Gerard Fairlie, JOC Horton, from a novel by CS Forester

Forever Female ★★★

Comedy 1953 · US · BW · 93mins

Adapted and updated out of all recognition from an old JM Barrie play, this comedy about the Broadway theatre is haunted by the ghost of *All about Eve* (1950), but is nonetheless bitchy, witty and romantic in its own right. A chic Ginger Rogers plays an ageing Broadway actress, married to producer Paul Douglas. Desperate to regain her former star status, Rogers competes with ambitious youngster Patricia Crowley for the lead in a new play, and falls for its author, William Holden. Polished entertainment, directed by old hand Irving Rapper of *Now Voyager* fame. RK

Ginger Rogers *Beatrice Page* • William Holden (2) *Stanley Krown* • Paul Douglas *E Harry Phillips* • Patricia Crowley [Pat Crowley] *Clara Mootz* • James Gleason *Eddie Woods* • Jesse White *Willie Wolfe* • Marjorie Rambeau ■ *Dir* Irving Rapper • *Scr* Julius J Epstein, Philip G Epstein, from the play *Rosalind* by JM Barrie

Forever Lulu ★ 18

Comedy adventure
1987 · US · Colour · 86mins

Yikes, is this bad! Fresh-faced debutant Alec Baldwin must have wondered what sort of business he was getting into as he watched Israeli director Amos Kollek cobble together this unmitigated disaster of a movie. It was much worse for German star Hanna Schygulla because she had placed an international reputation on the line (although heaven only knows why). Debbie Harry got it right, however – cameo, get paid and run. DP. Contains swearing and nudity

Hanna Schygulla *Elaine Hines* • Deborah Harry *Lulu* • Alec Baldwin *Buck* • Annie Golden *Diana* • Paul Gleason *Robert* • Dr Ruth Westheimer • Raymond Serra *Alphonse* • George Kyle *Pepe* ■ *Dir/Scr* Amos Kollek

Forever Mine ★★ 15

Romantic crime drama
1999 · UK/US · Colour · 112mins

It's hard to believe that this weak, over-played picture was scripted and directed by the writer of such greats as *Taxi Driver* and *Raging Bull*. Sporting ineffective scar make-up, Joseph Fiennes stars as a financier, whose affair with married Gretchen Moll when he was a young cabana boy sparks a 16-year vendetta against her husband Ray Liotta. With his dodgy accent and clumsy dialogue, Fiennes is as unconvincing as the film, while Moll is merely window dressing. SF. Contains swearing, sex scenes. DVD

Joseph Fiennes *Manuel Esquema/Alan Riply* • Ray Liotta *Mark Brice* • Gretchen Mol *Ella Brice* • Vincent Laresca *Javier* • Kevi Katsuras • Shannon Lawson • Lindsey Connell ■ *Dir/Scr* Paul Schrader • *Music* Angelo Badalamenti

Forever Young ★★ 15

Drama 1984 · UK · Colour and BW · 80mins

This tangled tale of faded fame and unresolved differences is told via a series of bitterly nostalgic flashbacks. Although Nicholas Gecks is now a priest and James Aubrey a teacher, they were once part of a 1950s rock band. Their rivalry resurfaces, as reunion bonhomie is replaced by competition for the attention of single mother Karen Archer, which has a traumatic effect on her altar boy son. The monochrome memoirs make more impact than the modern-day melodrama. DP

James Aubrey *James* • Nicholas Gecks *Father Michael* • Alec McCowen *Father Vincent* • Karen Archer *Mary* • Joseph Wright *John* • Liam Holt *Paul* • Jane Forster *Cathy* ■ *Dir* David Drury • *Scr* Ray Connolly

Forever Young ★★★ PG

Romantic fantasy 1992 · US · Colour · 97mins

Mel Gibson obviously had to dig deep to find the enthusiasm to carry off this tired role of a cryogenic Rip Van Winkle who wakes 53 years after he has been frozen and forgotten. Hollywood used to churn out this kind of fluff with practised ease and it's a pity director Steve Miner couldn't have found the same winning formula in here. That said, the reunions are touching, Jamie Lee Curtis provides charming support, and we're spared the usual smug time-lapse jokes. DP DVD

Mel Gibson *Daniel McCormick* • Jamie Lee Curtis *Claire* • Elijah Wood *Nat* • Isabel Glasser *Helen* • George Wendt *Harry* • Joe Morton *Cameron* ■ *Dir* Steve Miner • *Scr* Jeffrey Abrams

Forget Me Never ★★★ PG

Drama based on a true story
1999 · US/Can · Colour · 85mins

Mia Farrow gives a sensitive portrayal in this TV movie of an intelligent woman succumbing to the creeping cruelty of Alzheimer's disease. As a lawyer who hides her suspicions to protect husband Martin Sheen from the stress of her condition, she conveys an inner strength that he's unable to match when she grows increasingly dependent on a fellow sufferer for support. Sadly, director Robert Ackerman can't always distinguish between poignancy and melodrama. DP

Mia Farrow *Diane McGowin* • Martin Sheen *Jack* • Colm Feore *Albert* ■ *Dir* Robert Allan Ackerman • *Scr* Renee Longstreet, from a story by H Haden Yelin

Forget-Me-Not ★★ U

Romantic drama 1936 · UK · BW · 68mins

In spite of the plea in the title, this badly dated melodrama is all too forgettable. Co-directed by Zoltan Korda and Stanley Irving, it begins on board a ship and spends the rest of its time inside hotel rooms and opera houses as Joan Gardner tries to choose between sailor Ivan Brandt and widowed singer Beniamino Gigli, whose appeal lies wholly in his magical voice. The direction is manipulative, the script sentimental and the performances painful. DP

Beniamino Gigli *Enzo Curti* • Joan Gardner *Helen* • Ivan Brandt *Hugh Anderson* • Hugh Wakefield *Curti's manager* • Jeanne Stuart *Irene* ■ *Dir* Zoltan Korda, Stanley Irving • *Scr* Hugh Gray, Arthur Wimperis

Forget Mozart ★★★

Historical detective thriller
1985 · Cz/W Ger · Colour · 93mins

As anyone who has seen *Amadeus* will know, slighted court composer Antonio Salieri considered himself responsible for Mozart's death. But masons, music-hall managers, monarchs – among others – all come under investigation in this complex costume thriller, as secret policeman Armin Mueller-Stahl seeks a darker explanation that will satisfy his conspiracy theories. While it lacks the scale of Milos Forman's Oscar-winner, this is still a stylish picture. DP. In German with English subtitles.

Max Tidof *Mozart* • Armin Mueller-Stahl *Count Pergen* • Catarina Raacke *Konstanze* • Wolfgang Preiss *Swieten* • Uwe Ochsenknecht *Schikaneder* • Winfried Glatzeder *Salieri* ■ *Dir* Slavo Luther [Miloslav Luther] • *Scr* Zdenek Mahler

Forget Paris ★★★ 12

Romantic comedy
1995 · US · Colour · 97mins

This romantic comedy has a cosily familiar feel to it – perhaps that's because it has borrowed its anecdotal flashback structure from *Broadway Danny Rose*, its initial premise from *Avanti!* and much of what happens thereafter from *When Harry Met Sally...* The film is well played – though Winger isn't really cut out for comedy – and has both wit and insight. Its plus points are diminished, however, by the nagging sense of *déjà vu*. DP

Billy Crystal *Mickey Gordon* • Debra Winger *Ellen Andrews* • Joe Mantegna *Andy* • Cynthia Stevenson *Liz* • Richard Masur *Craig* • Julie Kavner *Lucy* ■ *Dir* Billy Crystal • *Scr* Billy Crystal, Lowell Ganz, Babaloo Mandel

The Forgotten ★★ 12

Psychological mystery thriller
2004 · US · Colour · 87mins

Joseph Ruben's psychological thriller has no real tension, relying instead on a handful of ruthlessly effective jolts to convey its air of unseen menace. In another of her tormented mother roles, Julianne Moore plays a woman grieving over the death of her eight-year-old son. Told by her psychiatrist (Gary Sinise) that the boy never existed, she's stunned to find all evidence of the child has disappeared and sets out to prove that she's not delusional. While Moore works hard, her performance is undermined by a weak script and ridiculous storyline. SF. Contains swearing, violence. DVD

Julianne Moore *Telly Paretta* • Dominic West *Ash Correll* • Gary Sinise *Dr Jack Munce* • Alfre Woodard *Detective Ann Pope* • Linus Roache *Friendly Man* • Anthony Edwards *Jim Paretta* • Robert Wisdom *Carl Dayton* • Jessica Hecht *Eliot* ■ *Dir* Joseph Ruben • *Scr* Gerald DiPego

Forgotten Sins ★★ 15

Drama based on a true story
1996 · US · Colour · 87mins

John Shea is the father who finds his life turning into a nightmare after his grown-up daughters accuse him of abuse, following therapy to release repressed memories. Despite the well-rounded performances of Shea and Willam Devane, this controversial subject is treated in a trivial fashion in this TV movie. JB DVD

William Devane *Dr Richard Ofshe* • John Shea *Matthew Bradshaw* • Bess Armstrong *Roberta Bradshaw* • Dean Norris *Carl Messenger* • Brian Markinson *Lowell Hart* ■ *Dir* Dick Lowry • *Scr* TS Cook, from articles in *The New Yorker* by Lawrence Wright

The Formula ★★ 15

Thriller 1980 · US · Colour · 112mins

This thriller about a Nazi process for synthetic fuel prompted such an acrimonious bust-up between writer Steve Shagan and director John Avildsen that the latter campaigned to remove his name from the credits. At stake was the relative emphasis to be placed on the narrative and on the theory that the oil business was exploiting the world by suppressing this ingenious formula. Marlon Brando is a mumbling tycoon, while George C Scott is as baffled as we are. DP

George C Scott *Lieutenuant Barney Caine* • Marlon Brando *Adam Steiffel* • Marthe Keller *Lisa* • John Gielgud *Dr Abraham Esau* • GD Spradlin *Clements* ■ *Dir* John G Avildsen • *Scr* Steve Shagan, from his novel

Formula for Death ★★★ 15

Thriller 1995 · US · Colour · 89mins

If we tell you that this TV movie is also known as *Virus* and was taken from a Robin Cook novel entitled *Outbreak*, you'll have a pretty shrewd idea what it's all about. And, although not on a par with the film of Cook's best-known book, *Coma*, this is still quite a decent little thriller, even though the audience will probably have twigged who was responsible for the spread of a supposedly extinct plague, long before ace medical researcher Nicollette Sheridan. DP. Contains some violence and sexual references. DVD

Nicollette Sheridan *Dr Marissa Blumenthal* • William Devane *Dr Ralph Harbuck* • William Atherton *Dr Reginald Holloway* • Stephen Caffrey *Tad Shockley* • Dakin Matthews *Cyrill Dubcheck* • Barry Corbin *Dr Jack Clayman* ■ *Dir* Armand Mastroianni • *Scr* Roger Young, from the novel *Outbreak* by Robin Cook

Forrest Gump ★★★★ 12

Comedy drama 1994 · US · Colour · 136mins

Winner of six Oscars, including best picture, actor and director, this was a box-office hit in America, though its simple-minded patriotism was greeted with a certain cynicism in Europe. Gump, played by Tom Hanks, is a chump: a semi-literate everyman who drifts through recent American history and emerges triumphant. He's an athlete, war hero and hokey southern savant, a one-man palliative for a nation's political and moral bankruptcy. Hanks's performance is truly remarkable and, this being a Robert Zemeckis film, the effects are stunning: Gump meeting people such as JFK and Nixon is amazingly believable. AT. Contains violence, swearing and drug abuse. DVD

Tom Hanks *Forrest Gump* • Gary Sinise *Lieutenant Dan Taylor* • Robin Wright [Robin Wright Penn] *Jenny Curran* • Sally Field *Mrs Gump* • Mykelti Williamson *Benjamin Buford "Bubba" Blue* • Rebecca Williams *Nurse at park bench* • Michael Conner Humphreys *Young Forrest* ■ *Dir* Robert Zemeckis • *Scr* Eric Roth, from the novel by Winston Groom

The Forsaken ★★ 18

Horror 2001 · US · Colour · 86mins

A vampire yarn for the slacker generation sees hapless film editor Kerr Smith on a long-distance drive to Florida. Having picked up hitch-hiker Brendan Fehr – who just happens to be a vampire slayer – Smith then falls into the clutches of a vanload of young bloodsuckers who roam the highways and byways of America's southwest. Johnathon Schaech as the black-clad boss vamp with killer cheekbones provides some much needed charisma, but his efforts are largely wasted on material that has "straight-to-video" stamped all over it. DA DVD

Kerr Smith *Sean* • Brendan Fehr *Nick* • Izabella Miko *Megan* • Phina Oruche *Cym* • Simon Rex *Pen* • Carrie Snodgress *Ina* • Johnathon Schaech *Kit* ■ *Dir/Scr* JS Cardone

Forsaking All Others ★★★

Comedy 1934 · US · BW · 82mins

Clark Gable and Joan Crawford team up yet again for this smart MGM comedy. Gable wants to propose to childhood friend Crawford, but she's engaged to Robert Montgomery. Need you ask about the outcome? The under-rated WS "Woody" Van Dyke directs adroitly, while Crawford seems to undergo more costume changes than in her entire career (and that's saying something). The ineffable Charles Butterworth offers a beautifully timed supporting performance, while the feline Frances Drake plays Montgomery's other woman. TS

Joan Crawford *Mary Clay* • Clark Gable *Jeff Williams* • Robert Montgomery *Dill Todd* • Charles Butterworth *Shep* • Billie Burke *Paula* • Frances Drake *Connie* • Rosalind Russell *Eleanor* ■ *Dir* WS Van Dyke • *Scr* Joseph L Mankiewicz, from a play by Edward Barry Roberts, Frank Morgan Cavett

The Forsyte Saga ★★ U

Melodrama 1949 · US · Colour · 112mins

While Greer Garson looks splendid as "That Forsythe Woman" (the US title of the film), the courageously cast Errol Flynn is by far the best thing in this stilted picture, giving a performance of considerable restraint and depth. The leaden pace shown here proves that imported British director Compton Bennett's *The Seventh Veil* was just a lucky fluke, as the *Saga* is barely touched upon and, despite the high production values, this spiritually undernourished, empty feature is no match for the later BBC serial. TS

Errol Flynn *Soames Forsyte* • Greer Garson *Irene Forsyte* • Walter Pidgeon *Young Jolyon Forsyte* • Robert Young (1) *Philip Bosinney* • Janet Leigh *June Forsyte* • Harry Davenport *Old Jolyon Forsyte* ■ *Dir* Compton Bennett • *Scr* Ivan Tors, James B Williams, Arthur Wimperis, from the novel *The Man of Property*, the first book in the trilogy *The Forsyte Saga* by John Galsworthy

Fort Algiers ★★ U

Adventure 1953 · US · BW · 79mins

A Foreign Legion adventure showcasing exotic Yvonne De Carlo (born Peggy Middleton in Vancouver) and dashing Argentinian Carlos Thompson. The stars quickly became a couple in real life, but here they pale beside big Raymond Burr, swarthy Anthony Caruso and angst-ridden Leif Erickson as the heavies. Of course, the Arabs are bad, the French are dashing, and Yvonne's a secret agent posing as a cabaret singer. Time-wasting nonsense. TS

Yvonne De Carlo *Yvette* • Carlos Thompson *Jeff* • Raymond Burr *Amir* • Leif Erickson *Kalmani* • Anthony Caruso *Chavez* • John Dehner *Major Colle* ■ *Dir* Lesley Selander • *Scr* Theodore St John, Frederick Stephani

Fort Apache ★★★★★ U

Western 1948 · US · BW · 128mins

This magnificent western – one of the highlights of American cinema – is a satisfying, finely crafted work, not least because of Ford's ability to create a tangible sense of time and place in a displaced community against the majestic surroundings of his beloved Monument Valley. Ford regular Henry Fonda is particularly outstanding, cast against type as an embittered martinet officer. Fonda breaks a peace deal with Apache leader Cochise, an agreement that was originally engineered by John Wayne, in one of his finest, most delicate portrayals. The life of the cavalry – its music, its women, its mythology – is all superbly realised. TS DVD

John Wayne *Captain York* • Henry Fonda *Lt Col Owen Thursday* • Shirley Temple *Philadelphia Thursday* • Pedro Armendáriz *Sergeant Beaufort* • Ward Bond *Sgt Maj Michael O'Rourke* • George O'Brien *Captain Collingwood* • John Agar *Lieutenant Michael O'Rourke* • Victor McLaglen *Sergeant Festus Mulcahy* • Miguel Inclan *Chief Cochise* ■ *Dir* John Ford • *Scr* Frank S Nugent, from the story *Massacre* by James Warner Bellah • *Cinematographer* Archie Stout • *Music* Richard Hageman

Fort Apache, the Bronx ★★★★

Crime drama 1981 · US · Colour · 123mins

Hard-boiled and hard-pressed, cop Paul Newman tries to control crime on New York's mean streets in a tremendously exciting urban western that's laced with taut suspense and grisly shocks. Pam Grier gives an electric performance as a psychotic hooker – just watch for that razor blade between her teeth. It was highly controversial (the Bronx community complained about misrepresentation), but is still highly recommended. AJ. Contains swearing, violence, sex scenes, brief nudity and drug abuse.

Paul Newman *John Murphy* • Edward Asner *Captain Dennis Connolly* • Ken Wahl *Corelli* • Danny Aiello *Morgan* • Rachel Ticotin *Isabella* • Pam Grier *Charlotte* • Kathleen Beller *Theresa* • Tito Goya *Jumper/Detective* • Miguel Pinero *Hernando* ■ *Dir* Daniel Petrie • *Scr* Heywood Gould

Fort Massacre ★★ U

Western 1958 · US · Colour · 80mins

Shot in colour and CinemaScope and featuring the ever-dependable Joel McCrea (he of the laughing eyes) this is a strictly by-the-book western. McCrea is leading a troop on a mission into Indian territory, inevitably landing in constant skirmishes with those who previously owned the land. Entertaining, but unsurprising. BB

Joel McCrea *Vinson* • Forrest Tucker *McGurney* • Susan Cabot *Piute girl* • John Russell *Travis* • Anthony Caruso *Pawnee* • Denver Pyle *Collins* ■ *Dir* Joseph M Newman • *Scr* Martin Goldsmith

Fort Saganne ★★★★ 15

Historical adventure
1984 · Fr · Colour · 173mins

This long and lavish desert adventure pulls out all the stops for location shooting, almost rivalling *Lawrence of Arabia*, and casts four of France's biggest stars: Gérard Depardieu, Philippe Noiret, Catherine Deneuve and Sophie Marceau. The result is an exhausting but impressive drama in which Depardieu's legionnaire expands the French Empire from the back of a camel just prior to the First World War. Acting honours go to Noiret's ambitious and choleric officer, but the star of the show is cameraman Bruno Nuytten, whose images of Mauritania will take your breath away. AT. In French with English subtitles.

Gérard Depardieu *Charles Saganne* • Philippe Noiret *Dubreuilh* • Catherine Deneuve *Louise Tissot* • Sophie Marceau *Madeleine De Saint Ilette* • Michel Duchaussoy *Baculard* ■ *Dir* Alain Corneau • *Scr* Alain Corneau, Henri DeTurenne, Louis Gardel, from the novel by Louis Gardel

Fort Worth ★★ U

Western 1951 · US · Colour · 80mins

The last film of veteran director Edwin L Marin is little more than a routine western, with a fairly innocuous plot that deals with the coming of newsprint to the west. Rugged Randolph Scott makes a most unlikely newspaper editor, and his predictable reversion to gunplay denudes the movie of any real suspense, but it's never less than watchable. TS

Randolph Scott *Ned Britt* • David Brian *Blair Lunsford* • Phyllis Thaxter *Flora Talbot* • Helena Carter *Amy Brooks* • Dick Jones [Dickie Jones] *Luther Wick* ■ *Dir* Edwin L Marin • *Scr* John Twist, from his story *Across the Panhandle*

Fortress ★★★ 18

Science-fiction action thriller
1992 · Aus/US · Colour · 91mins

An entertaining science-fiction thriller, with Christopher Lambert sent to a maximum security prison for conceiving a second child – a crime in director Stuart Gordon's imaginatively rendered totalitarian future. There he suffers hi-tech torture and intense corruption while planning a daring break out. Violent, inventive and lots of intriguing fun, Gordon makes this fantasy a suspenseful roller-coaster ride, despite its pulp limitations. AJ. Contains violence, swearing, nudity. DVD

Christopher Lambert *John Brennick* • Kurtwood Smith *Prison Director Poe* • Loryn Locklin *Karen Brennick* • Lincoln Kilpatrick *Abraham* • Clifton Gonzalez Gonzalez [Clifton Collins Jr] *Nino* ■ *Dir* Stuart Gordon • *Scr* Steve Feinberg, Troy Neighbors

Fortress 2: Re-entry ★★ 15

Futuristic action thriller
1999 · US/Lux · Colour · 88mins

Eight years after the moderately successful *Fortress*, Christopher Lambert is called back to reprise his role as a rebel imprisoned by an evil global corporation. Here, he's incarcerated aboard an orbiting space slammer. Escaping involves lots of running down corridors and much noisy mayhem. Less glossy and violent than the original. DA DVD

Christopher Lambert *John Brennick* • Patrick Malahide *Peter Teller* • Liz May Brice *Elena Rivera* • Anthony C Hall *Marcus Jackson* • Willie Garson *Stanley Nussbaum* ■ *Dir* Geoff Murphy • *Scr* John Flock, Peter Doyle, from a story and characters created by Steven Feinberg, Troy Neighbors

The Fortune ★★

Comedy 1975 · US · Colour · 87mins

Stockard Channing easily outshines Warren Beatty and Jack Nicholson, while David Shire's jazz arrangements are a major delight, in this occasionally tacky story set in the 1920s. Beatty and Nicholson are two incompetent con-men trying to extract money from an heiress. Director Mike Nichols has an impressive track-record, but here his style seems tastelessly gauche. TH

Jack Nicholson *Oscar* • Warren Beatty *Nicky* • Stockard Channing *Freddie* • Florence Stanley *Mrs Gould* • Richard B Shull *Chief Detective* • Tom Newman *John the barber* ■ *Dir* Mike Nichols • *Scr* Adrien Joyce

Fortune and Men's Eyes ★★

Prison drama
1971 · US/Can · Colour · 102mins

Homosexual activity and brutality in men's prisons were the themes of John Herbert's powerful Broadway play. However, although Herbert himself wrote the screenplay, the film version is far more exploitative, and seems to have lost the plea for prison reform on the way. Nevertheless, it still packs a certain punch, given its story of a young man having to submit to being sodomised regularly by his "protector". The original director Jules Schwerin was replaced by Harvey Hart, and many scenes had to be reshot. RB

Wendell Burton *Smitty* • Michael Greer *Queenie* • Zooey Hall *Rocky* • Danny Freedman *Mona* • Larry Perkins *Screwdriver* • James Barron *Holyface Peters* • Lazaro Perez *Catso* • Jon Granik *Sgt Gritt* ■ *Dir* Harvey Hart • *Scr* John Herbert, from his play

The Fortune Cookie

★★★★ U

Comedy 1966 · US · BW · 120mins

Billy Wilder's first teaming of Walter Matthau and Jack Lemmon crackles throughout. Matthau is amoral lawyer "Whiplash Willie" who sees an opportunity to cash in when his brother-in-law, hapless cameraman Harry (Lemmon) is injured at a football game. Typically mining his drama from the collision between affectionate comedy and spiky cynicism, Wilder squeezes telling performances from his two stars. Matthau's lugubrious eccentricity won him an Oscar for best supporting actor, while Lemmon conveys the decency familiar from his role in *The Apartment*. AJ [video] DVD

Jack Lemmon *Harry Hinkle* • Walter Matthau *Willie Gingrich* • Ron Rich *Luther "Boom-Boom" Jackson* • Cliff Osmond *Mr Purkey* • Judi West *Sandy Hinkle* • Lurene Tuttle *Mother Hinkle* • Harry Holcombe *O'Brien* ■ *Dir* Billy Wilder • *Scr* Billy Wilder, IAL Diamond

Fortune Hunters

★★ U

Comedy adventure
1999 · US · Colour · 87mins

The producers clearly think they're being cute in teaming Richard (*The Waltons*) Thomas and Maureen (*The Brady Bunch*) McCormick as the discontented parents of dysfunctional kids, Alison Lohman and Andrew Sandler. But the scheme backfires, as they deliver woefully stagey performances as the family is forced to pull together in order to find a misplaced lottery ticket. Cornball misadventures abound as they hurtle round town without raising a single laugh. DP DVD

Richard Thomas *Ted Hunter* • Maureen McCormick *Betsy Hunter* • C Thomas Howell *Valentino* • Corey Feldman *Charles* • Estelle Getty *Sister Rosanne* • Randy Travis *Man in jail cell* • Kaye Ballard *Mrs Crabby* • Alison Lohman *Courtney Hunter* • Adam Sandler *Shane Hunter* ■ *Dir* Neil Mandt • *Scr* Gregory Poppen, from the story *The $30,000 Bequest* by Mark Twain

Fortune Is a Woman

★★

Mystery 1956 · UK · BW · 94mins

This fair-to-middling thriller by Frank Launder and Sidney Gilliat is all plot and no point. Borrowing from a thousand and one *films noirs*, it follows the misfortunes of Jack Hawkins, an insurance assessor whose investigation of a series of fires draws him into murder, marriage and blackmail with a fatalistic inevitability. Hawkins lacks the vulnerability that Edward G Robinson brought to similar films, while Arlene Dahl's *femme fatale* lacks allure. DP

Jack Hawkins *Oliver Branwell* • Arlene Dahl *Sarah Moreton* • Dennis Price *Tracey Moreton* • Violet Farebrother *Mrs Moreton* • Ian Hunter *Clive Fisher* • Christopher Lee *Charles Highbury* ■ *Dir* Sidney Gilliat • *Scr* Sidney Gilliat, Frank Launder, Val Valentine, from the novel by Winston Graham

40 Carats

★★ PG

Comedy 1973 · US · Colour · 108mins

This would-be sprightly comedy suffers from severe central miscasting. Swedish import Liv Ullmann doesn't fit into the sophisticated New York whirl presented here, and no matter how hard she tries, her affair with younger Edward Albert remains unconvincing. But debonair Gene Kelly, as her ex-husband, is a joy to discover in this wisp of fluff, despite his awkward toupee. TS [video]

Liv Ullmann *Ann Stanley* • Edward Albert *Peter Latham* • Gene Kelly *Billy Boylan* • Binnie Barnes *Maud Ericson* • Deborah Raffin *Trina Stanley* ■ *Dir* Milton Katselas • *Scr* Leonard Gershe, from the play by Jay Presson Allen, Pierre Barillet, Jean-Pierre Gredy

40 Days and 40 Nights

★★★ 15

Romantic comedy
2002 · US/Fr/UK/Can · Colour · 91mins

Josh Hartnett casts himself into the sexual wilderness in this comedy about celibacy that is less crude than most teen-orientated offerings, and is even rather cute. Hartnett plays the recently dumped Matt, whose large number of one-night stands have left him depressed and doubting the existence of his soul. To rectify his shallowness, he swears off sex for Lent, but the very next day meets the woman of his dreams. His only remaining option is to woo her the old-fashioned way. Handled with humour and charm, while Hartnett proves to be an appealing comic lead. LH [video] DVD

Josh Hartnett *Matt Sullivan* • Shannyn Sossamon *Erica Sutton* • Vinessa Shaw *Nicole* • Paulo Costanzo *Ryan* • Maggie Gyllenhaal *Sam* • Griffin Dunne *Jerry* ■ *Dir* Michael Lehmann • *Scr* Robert Perez

48 HRS

★★★★ 15

Action thriller 1982 · US · Colour · 96mins

Trading Places apart, Eddie Murphy has never been better than in this, his exhilarating debut, still one of the best "buddy" cop thrillers to be made. Murphy is the con who is sprung from prison by racist cop Nick Nolte in an attempt to track down psychopathic duo James Remar and Sonny Landham, who have escaped from a chain gang and are now back in town. Nolte and Murphy are perfectly paired: the latter all smooth charm and wisecracks, the former the rough, gruff straight man. Murphy's taming of a redneck bar deserves its place in the cinematic history books, while director Walter Hill also delivers the goods in the action stakes with some beautifully orchestrated shoot-ups and chases. Followed by the uninspired *Another 48 HRS* in 1990. JF. Contains swearing, violence and nudity. [video] DVD

Nick Nolte *Detective Jack Cates* • Eddie Murphy *Reggie Hammond* • Annette O'Toole *Elaine* • Frank McRae *Captain Haden* • James Remar *Albert Ganz* ■ *Dir* Walter Hill • *Scr* Roger Spottiswoode, Walter Hill, Larry Gross, Steven E de Souza

Forty Guns

★★★ PG

Western 1957 · US · BW · 76mins

Samuel Fuller was one of American cinema's true mavericks who eventually found a comfortable base at 20th Century-Fox, turning out a series of lurid melodramas that later achieved cult status, including this stylishly photographed CinemaScope western. Barbara Stanwyck (slightly too old) plays a ruthless Arizona rancher who is a law unto herself, until marshal Barry Sullivan turns up. Good fun. TS DVD

Barbara Stanwyck *Jessica Drummond* • Barry Sullivan *Griff Bonnell* • Dean Jagger *Ned Logan* • John Ericson *Brockie Drummond* ■ *Dir/Scr* Samuel Fuller

40 Guns to Apache Pass

★★ PG

Western 1966 · US · Colour · 91mins

Audie Murphy made his penultimate screen appearance in this low-budget western from B-movie specialist William Witney. Although it's briskly and efficiently made, it's never anything more than routine, with Murphy leading his bluecoats into brutal action against the Apache, only to discover that the tribe isn't his most pressing problem. DP [video]

Audie Murphy *Captain Coburn* • Michael Burns *Doug* • Kenneth Tobey *Corporal Bodine* • Laraine Stephens *Ellen* • Robert Brubaker *Sergeant Walker* ■ *Dir* William Witney • *Scr* Willard Willingham, Mary Willingham

The 49th Man

★★★ U

Spy drama 1953 · US · BW · 72mins

Worried about a foreign power smuggling an atomic bomb into the US, the Navy plans an elaborate hoax to test the readiness of the security services. That's one twist in the plot; the next is such a humdinger that one becomes genuinely concerned for the survival of Nevada and for the devious mind of the screenwriter Harry Essex. Designed to reassure Middle America about communist invasion and atomic terrorism, this B-movie has a sense of urgency and suitably awed acting. AT

John Ireland *John Williams* • Richard Denning *Paul Regan* • Suzanne Dalbert *Margo Wayne* • Robert Foulk *Commander Jackson* • Touch Connors [Mike Connors] *Lt Magrew* • Richard Avonde *Buzz Olin* ■ *Dir* Fred F Sears • *Scr* Harry Essex, from a story by Ivan Tors

49th Parallel

★★★★ U

Second World War drama
1941 · UK · BW · 116mins

Sponsored by the Ministry of Information and 18 months in the making, this is one of the best propaganda films produced in Britain during the Second World War. With a stellar cast and a rousing score by Ralph Vaughan Williams, Michael Powell and Emeric Pressburger's gripping action drama thoroughly merited its Oscar for best original story and its nominations for best picture and screenplay. Eric Portman gives the finest performance of his career as the officer of a bombed U-boat who has to lead his surviving crew across the Canadian wilderness to neutral America. Laurence Olivier's French-Canadian accent has to be heard to be believed. DP [video] DVD

Eric Portman *Lt Ernst Hirth* • Laurence Olivier *Johnnie Barras* • Leslie Howard *Philip Armstrong Scott* • Anton Walbrook *Peter* • Raymond Massey *Andy Brock* • Glynis Johns *Anna* • Niall MacGinnis *Vogel* ■ *Dir* Michael Powell • *Scr* Rodney Ackland, Emeric Pressburger, from a story by Emeric Pressburger • *Cinematographer* Freddie Young • *Editor* David Lean

Forty Pounds of Trouble

★★★ U

Comedy 1962 · US · Colour · 105mins

An immensely likeable reworking of the Damon Runyon tale, filmed in 1934 and 1980 as *Little Miss Marker* and in 1949 as *Sorrowful Jones*. This time it's amiable Tony Curtis as the gambling house manager who's left holding the baby, a situation that prompts nightclub chanteuse Suzanne Pleshette to lure him away from his ex-wife. What's surprising, given its lightness of content, is that it marked the feature debut of Canadian director Norman Jewison, later responsible for such worthy classics as *In the Heat of the Night* and *Fiddler on the Roof*. TS

Tony Curtis *Steve McLuskey* • Phil Silvers *Bernie Friedman* • Suzanne Pleshette *Chris Lockwood* • Claire Wilcox *Penny Piper* • Larry Storch *Floyd* • Howard Morris *Julius* • Edward Andrews *Herman* • Stubby Kaye *Cranston* • Warren Stevens *Swing* ■ *Dir* Norman Jewison • *Scr* Marion Hargrove, from the short story *Little Miss Marker* by Damon Runyon

42nd Street

★★★★★ U

Musical 1933 · US · BW · 85mins

One of the most important and enjoyable musicals of all time, this sizzling Warner Bros movie is also one of the best loved of the early talking pictures. The film is recognised as a masterpiece, not merely for its racy dialogue and lavish costumes, or for its now-classic "newcomer goes on instead of indisposed star" plot, but also for affording kaleidoscope choreographer Busby Berkeley a chance to show off. The production cost a then-mammoth $400,000 and it shows. This is as entertaining as it gets, with a knockout cast headed by Warner Baxter as the stressed Broadway director and Bebe Daniels as his star. Dick Powell and Ruby Keeler feature in roles that would turn them into household favourites, and a newcomer called Ginger Rogers plays Anytime Annie. TS [video]

Warner Baxter *Julian Marsh* • Bebe Daniels *Dorothy Brock* • Ruby Keeler *Peggy Sawyer* • Dick Powell *Billy Lawler* • George Brent *Pat Denning* • Una Merkel *Lolly* • Ginger Rogers *Anytime Annie* • Guy Kibbee *Abner Dillon* ■ *Dir* Lloyd Bacon • *Scr* James Seymour, Rian James, from a novel by Bradford Ropes • *Producer* Darryl F Zanuck • *Cinematographer* Sol Polito • *Music/lyrics* Harry Warren, Al Dubin

Forty Thousand Horsemen

★★

First World War drama
1941 · Aus · BW · 80mins

For 30 years, Charles Chauvel was Australia's first and possibly only major director. It was Chauvel who, in 1933, gave Errol Flynn his screen debut as Fletcher Christian in the docudrama *In the Wake of the Bounty*. This is Chauvel's big movie about the Australian Light Horse regiment's role in Palestine during the First World War. The action easily outclasses the quieter moments, involving a romance between an Aussie soldier and a beautiful French girl, which are rather awkward and poorly acted. AT

Grant Taylor *Red Gallagher* • Betty Bryant *Juliet Rouget* • Chips Rafferty *Jim* • Pat Twohill *Larry* • Harvey Adams *Von Hausen* • Eric Reiman *Von Schiller* • Joe Valli *Scotty* ■ *Dir* Charles Chauvel • *Scr* Elsa Chauvel

La Forza del Destino

★★ U

Opera 1949 · It · BW · 102mins

The least assured of the operas filmed by veteran director Carmine Gallone in the immediate postwar period, this tale of forbidden love, unsuspecting camaraderie and bitter revenge is also considered one of Verdi's lesser works. However, legendary baritone Tito Gobbi stars as the rebel who is forced to flee to Europe after killing his lover's disapproving father. The plot marginalises Nelly Corradi (voiced by Caterina Mancini) by having her become a penitent hermit. But the relationship between Gobbi and her soldier brother, Gino Sinimberghi (sung by Galliano Masini) is well developed. DP. In Italian with English subtitles.

Caterina Mancini • Galliano Masini • Tito Gobbi • Nelly Corradi • Gino Sinimberghi ■ *Dir* Carmine Gallone

Foul Play

★★★ PG

Comedy thriller 1978 · US · Colour · 110mins

This incredibly silly but enjoyable comedy stars Goldie Hawn as a librarian who discovers a plot to kill the visiting Pope. Chevy Chase has one of his best roles as the detective who doesn't believe Hawn's life is in danger, and the cast also features Burgess Meredith and Dudley Moore having a whale of a time in between car chases and assassination attempts. Undemanding fun. JB. Contains some swearing. [video]

Goldie Hawn *Gloria Mundy* • Chevy Chase *Tony Carlson* • Dudley Moore *Stanley Tibbets* • Burgess Meredith *Mr Hennesey* • Rachel Roberts (1) *Gerda Casswell* • Brian Dennehy *Fergie* ■ *Dir/Scr* Colin Higgins

The Fountain

★★

First World War drama
1934 · US · BW · 80mins

This creaky and dated melodrama, faithfully (but slowly) directed by John Cromwell, is about a married Dutch

F

woman who falls for a handsome British officer billeted on her family during the First World War. This tedious tale is redeemed somewhat by the casting – particularly the superbly serene but under-rated Ann Harding – and the conflict engendered when her German husband, Paul Lukas, returns. TS

Ann Harding *Julie Von Narwitz* • Brian Aherne *Lewis Allison* • Paul Lukas *Rupert Von Narwitz* • Jean Hersholt *Baron Van Leyden* • Ralph Forbes *Ballater* ■ *Dir* John Cromwell • *Scr* Jane Murfin, Samuel Hoffenstein, from the novel by Charles Morgan

The Fountain ★★★

Comedy 1988 · USSR · Colour · 100mins

With its mock realist portrait of everyday life, Yuri Mamin's satire cheekily compares the Soviet state to a dilapidated apartment block, which begins to crumble further when Kazakh farmer Asankul Kuttubaev comes to stay with his daughter and her bureaucrat husband. The symbolism of this *perestroika* comedy is blatant, but there is a charm about the havoc wreaked by this innocent abroad, as he approaches modern appliances with a mixture of awe and disgust at what he sees as reckless waste. DP. In Russian with English subtitles.

Zhanna Kerimtaeva *Maya* • Viktor Mikhailov *Mitrofanov* • Asankul Kuttubaev *Kerbabaev* • Sergei Dontsov *Lagutin* ■ *Dir* Yuri Mamin • *Scr* Vladimir Vardunas

The Fountainhead ★★★ PG

Drama 1949 · US · BW · 107mins

A genuine oddity in 1940s Hollywood studio film-making, this is a deliriously entertaining adaptation by Ayn Rand of her novel inspired by the life of architect Frank Lloyd Wright. At its core is a smouldering, over-the-top love struggle between Gary Cooper and Patricia Neal as the uncompromising maverick and the cultured beauty who uneasily surrenders to him. The script is a crazed cocktail of stilted dialogue, libertarian platitudes and unhinged innuendo. Not quite qualifying as bizarre, the film certainly operates on its own near-ridiculous level, heightened by striking close-ups, *noirish* passages and some superbly expressionistic interiors. DO. Contains some violence.

Gary Cooper *Howard Roark* • Patricia Neal *Dominique Francon* • Raymond Massey *Gail Wynand* • Kent Smith *Peter Keating* • Robert Douglas *Ellsworth M Toohey* • Henry Hull *Henry Cameron* • Ray Collins *Enright* ■ *Dir* King Vidor • *Scr* Ayn Rand, from her novel • *Cinematographer* Robert Burks • *Art Director* John Holden, Edward Carrere • *Set Decorator* William Kuehl

Four Adventures of Reinette and Mirabelle ★★★★ U

Drama 1986 · Fr · Colour · 94mins

Concentrating on the contrasting attitudes of two talkative teens, this rare non-series picture from French auteur Eric Rohmer makes light of its minuscule budget and inexperienced cast to provide another richly layered and hugely satisfying drama. A sophisticated spin on the town and country mouse fable, this is a film of incidents rather than adventures, with the eccentric Joëlle Miquel landing herself in scrapes that alternately amuse and irritate her more sophisticated Parisian pal, Jessica Forde. The endless stream of chat is never less than absorbing. DP. In French with English subtitles.

Joëlle Miquel *Reinette* • Jessica Forde *Mirabelle* • Philippe Laudenbach *Waiter* • Yasmine Haury *Kleptomaniac* • Marie Rivière *Hustler* • Béatrice Romand *Inspector* • Géraud Courant *Inspector* ■ *Dir/Scr* Eric Rohmer

4 Clowns ★★★★★ U

Comedy compilation 1970 · US · BW · 95mins

From innocence to insolence – they don't make them like this any more. Robert Youngson's compilation of comic cuts from the early days of film comedy reveals Laurel and Hardy, Buster Keaton and the undervalued Charley Chase (in his magnificent *Limousine Love*, among others) as creatures of infinite grace and wit. You can even forgive the film's sometimes patronising ho-ho commentary for showing us the dizzying standards from which so many of today's comedians have fallen. Here's a golden age which has lost none of its lustre. TH

Buster Keaton • Charley Chase • Stan Laurel • Oliver Hardy ■ *Dir* Robert Youngson

Four Daughters ★★★★ U

Romantic drama 1938 · US · BW · 89mins

A big-box office winner in its day, and deservedly so. Claude Rains is simply wonderful as the musical father watching over the lives and loves of his four disparate daughters. This is a prime example of what can be achieved with an ostensibly soapy outline: small-town life with all its foibles, but with a top-notch cast that includes John Garfield in his first role. What could have been an exercise in hoary old clichés and character stereotyping emerges as a fascinating, subtle look at the complexities of parenthood and community life. So popular was the film that it spawned that the cast were brought together for a follow-up (*Daughters Courageous*), two proper sequels (*Four Wives* and *Four Mothers*) and in 1955 Frank Sinatra took over Garfield's role for a remake, *Young at Heart*. SH

Claude Rains *Adam Lemp* • May Robson *Aunt Etta* • Priscilla Lane *Ann Lemp* • Lola Lane *Thea Lemp* • Rosemary Lane *Kay Lemp* • Gale Page *Emma Lemp* • Dick Foran *Ernest* ■ *Dir* Michael Curtiz • *Scr* Julius J Epstein, Lenore Coffee, from the novel *Sister Act* by Fannie Hurst

Four Days ★★ 15

Crime thriller 1999 · Can · Colour · 85mins

Teenager Kevin Zegers, seeing his father William Forsythe shot during a bank robbery, grabs the money and heads north hoping his dad will follow, not knowing that another gangster, Colm Meaney, is following him on his journey. Unfortunately, despite nice performances from Zegers and Forsythe, this suffers from some rather questionable plot twists and an over the top turn from Lolita Davidovich as the local floozy. JB

Kevin Zegers *Simon* • Lolita Davidovich *Chrystal* • Colm Meaney *Fury* • William Forsythe *Milt* • Anne-Marie Cadieux *Feather* ■ *Dir* Curtis Wehrfritz • *Scr* Pinckney Benedict, from the novel by John Buell

Four Days in September ★★★★

Drama based on a true story 1997 · Bra · Colour · 105mins

Returning home after a decade in the States, Bruno Barreto landed an Oscar nomination for this political drama, based on the autobiography of revolutionary-turned-journalist Fernando Gabeira. Set in 1969, with Brazil under a military dictatorship, the film recalls the abduction of American ambassador Charles Burke Elbrick by the MR-8 movement in a bid to secure the release of 15 political prisoners and publicise its cause. Playing fair with all the participants, this is a gripping reconstruction, with the friendship between ambassador Alan Arkin and journalist Pedro Cardoso humanising a tense situation. DP. In Portuguese with English subtitles.

Alan Arkin *Charles Burke Elbrick* • Pedro Cardoso *Fernando Gabeira/Paulo* • Fernanda Torres *Maria* • Luiz Fernando Guimaraes *Marcao* • Claudia Abreu *Renee* • Nelson Dantas *Toledo* • Matheus Nachtergaele *Jonas* • Marco Ricca *Henrique* ■ *Dir* Bruno Barreto • *Scr* Leopoldo Serran, from the novel *O Que E Isso, Companheiro?* by Fernando Gabeira

The Four Days of Naples ★★★★

Second World War drama 1962 · It · BW · 119mins

The raw courage of a proud people rising against the Nazi yoke is brought home with eloquence and power in this Oscar-nominated drama from director Nanni Loy. Comparisons with Roberto Rossellini's *Rome, Open City* are somewhat flattering, but what this account of the events of September 1943 shares with that neorealist masterpiece is a sense of immediacy, as the Neopolitan population rebelled against a dictate that all males between the ages of five and 50 should be dispatched to labour camps. The ensemble playing is exceptional, with the standout being Domenico Formato as the barricade boy-hero, Gennaro Capuozzo. DP. In Italian with English subtitles.

Lea Massari *Maria* • Jean Sorel *Livornese* • Franco Sportelli *Professor Rosati* • Charles Belmont *Sailor* • Gian Maria Volonté *Stimolo* • Frank Wolff *Salvatore* • Domenico Formato *Gennaro Capuozzo* ■ *Dir* Nanni Loy • *Scr* Pasquale Festa Campanile, Massimo Franciosa, Nanni Loy, Carlo Benari, from a story by Vasco Pratolini, Pasquale Festa Campanile, Massimo Franciosa

The Four Deuces ★★ 12

Crime drama 1976 · US · Colour · 84mins

Jack Palance here takes on an almost benevolent aspect as a gangland boss during the Prohibition era – both his gang and and his gambling establishment bear the name of the film's title. What redeems him this time is the love he bears for Carol Lynley and it's this romance that gives the film's violent action and romance its raison d'être. An oddball spin on the genre. TH DVD

Jack Palance *Vic* • Carol Lynley *Wendy* • Warren Berlinger *Chico* • Adam Roarke *Ross* • EJ Peaker *Lory* ■ *Dir* William H Bushnell Jr • *Scr* C Lester Franklin, from a story by Don Martin

Four Dogs Playing Poker ★★★ 15

Crime mystery thriller 1999 · US · Colour · 92mins

Four art thieves lose their stolen $1 million object before they can deliver it to bad guy Forest Whitaker, so they decide to insure each of themselves for a million, then secretly assign one of their number to kill one of the others in order to collect the insurance and pay their debt – except no one will know who is to be the killer and who the victim. Like the British *Shallow Grave*, this gets interesting when they turn against and suspect each other. The script is quite weak, but there are some fun performances. JB DVD

Olivia Williams *Audrey* • Balthazar Getty *Julian* • Stacy Edwards *Holly* • Daniel London *Kevin* • Tim Curry *Felix* • Forest Whitaker *Ellington* • George Lazenby *Carlo* ■ *Dir* Paul Rachman • *Scr* Thomas Durham, William Quist

The Four Feathers ★★★

Silent war adventure 1929 · US · BW · 81mins

This spectacular version of AEW Mason's famous novel was the last major Hollywood film to be made without any spoken dialogue, carrying only music and sound effects. Richard Arlen is the young officer given white feathers for displaying cowardice by three fellow soldiers – William Powell, Clive Brook and Theodore von Eltz – and his fiancée, played by Fay Wray in an early association with the *King Kong* team of Ernest B Schoedsack and Merian C Cooper. They began their film careers making wild-life documentaries and spent a year in Africa filming dramatic sequences with hippos and baboons – scenes that are well integrated into the story of Arlen redeeming himself in action. AE

Richard Arlen *Harry Faversham* • Fay Wray *Ethne Eustace* • Clive Brook *Lt Durrance* • William Powell *Capt Trench* • Theodore von Eltz *Lt Castleton* • Noah Beery Sr [Noah Beery] *Slave trader* • Zack Williams *Idris* • Noble Johnson *Ahmed* ■ *Dir* Merian C Cooper, Ernest B Schoedsack, Lothar Mendes • *Scr* Howard Estabrook, Hope Loring, from the novel by AEW Mason • *Producer* David Selznick [David O Selznick]

The Four Feathers ★★★★★ U

Classic war adventure 1939 · UK · Colour · 109mins

This screen version of AEW Mason's rousing adventure is one of the finest films made by the Korda brothers – producer Alexander, director Zoltan and art director Vincent. Everything about it is spot on: the tightly constructed script by RC Sherriff, Lajos Biró and Arthur Wimperis; the rich colours and evocative location work of cinematographers Georges Perinal, Osmond Borradaile and Jack Cardiff; the perfectly paced editing of William Hornbeck and Henry Cornelius; and the pounding score by Miklos Rozsa. And we've not even begun to extol the virtues of the performances. It's a gem! (Korda made a thinly disguised remake of his classic in 1955 as *Storm over the Nile*.) DP DVD

John Clements *Harry Faversham* • Ralph Richardson *Captain John Durrance* • C Aubrey Smith *General Burroughs* • June Duprez *Ethne Burroughs* • Allan Jeayes *General Faversham* • Jack Allen *Lieutenant Willoughby* • Donald Gray *Peter Burroughs* • Frederick Culley *Dr Sutton* ■ *Dir* Zoltan Korda • *Scr* RC Sherriff, Lajos Biró, Arthur Wimperis, from the novel by AEW Mason

The Four Feathers ★★★ 15

Period war adventure 2002 · US/UK · Colour · 125mins

In visual terms, Shekhar Kapur's filming of AEW Mason's novel has the grandiose qualities to justify a new interpretation. The film's major action sequence – a desert battle between a meagre British contingent and a vast Sudanese army – certainly reaches the thrill levels of *Zulu*. Its pacing and casting, however, have significant flaws, with too many drawn-out, talky sequences. Heath Ledger has heroic appeal as the disgraced officer who adopts a secret Arabic identity to assist his battalion, but Wes Bentley and Kate Hudson are stiff and unconvincing. JC DVD

Heath Ledger *Harry Feversham* • Wes Bentley *Jack Durrance* • Kate Hudson *Ethne Eustace* • Djimon Hounsou *Abou Fatma* • Michael Sheen *Trench* • Alex Jennings *Colonel Hamilton* • Tim Pigott-Smith *General Feversham* • Kris Marshall *Castelton* • Rupert Penry-Jones *Willoughby* ■ *Dir* Shekhar Kapur • *Scr* Michael Schiffer, Hossein Amini, from the novel by AEW Mason

4 for Texas ★★ PG

Comedy western 1963 · US · Colour · 110mins

This overlong, over-indulgent comedy western is sometimes quite amusing, despite the rather tiresome antics of Frank Sinatra and Dean Martin (whose production company made the film). They play the rivals who unite to defeat baddies Victor Buono and Charles Bronson. At least Sinatra had the good sense to hire a decent director in Robert Aldrich and no film that succeeds in roping in the excesses of

Martin and Bronson can be totally unwatchable. TS

Frank Sinatra *Zack Thomas* • Dean Martin *Joe Jarrett* • Anita Ekberg *Elya Carlson* • Ursula Andress *Maxine Richter* • Charles Bronson *Matson* • Victor Buono *Harvey Burden* • Edric Connor *Prince George* ■ *Dir* Robert Aldrich • *Scr* Teddi Sherman, Robert Aldrich

Four Frightened People ★★★

Adventure 1934 · US · BW · 77mins

Silly but entertaining survivalist melodrama, shot partly in Hawaii, with Claudette Colbert, Herbert Marshall and others hacking through the Malayan jungle because an on-board epidemic forces them to jump from a Dutch coastal steamer. Even away from ancient Rome, Cecil B DeMille still asks Colbert to strip off and take a bath – DeMille, you will recall, got Colbert bathing in ass's milk in *The Sign of the Cross*, and she was semi-naked throughout *Cleopatra*. AT

Claudette Colbert *Judy Cavendish* • Herbert Marshall *Arnold Ainger* • Mary Boland *Mrs Mardick* • William Gargan *Stewart Corder* • Leo Carrillo *Montague* ■ *Dir* Cecil B DeMille • *Scr* Bartlett Cormack, Lenore Coffee, from the novel by E Arnot Robertson

Four Girls in White ★★

Drama 1939 · US · BW · 73mins

MGM clearly released this hospital melodrama hoping to repeat the success of its new *Doctor Kildare* series. However, the nursing quartet of the title spend as much time flirting with the doctors and orderlies as they do ministering to their patients. Sara Haden is suitably starchy as the martinet matron and Una Merkel and Buddy Ebsen provide some cornball comic relief. But the main focus falls on the rivalry between Florence Rice and single mother Mary Howard for the attention of Doctor Alan Marshal, which ends with a tragedy that will have you reaching for the tissues. DP

Florence Rice *Norma Page* • Una Merkel *Gertie Robbins* • Ann Rutherford *Patricia Page* • Mary Howard *Mary Forbes* • Alan Marshal *Dr Stephen Melford* ■ *Dir* S Sylvan Simon • *Scr* Dorothy Yost, from a story by Nathalie Bucknall, Endre Boehm

Four Guns to the Border ★★ U

Western 1954 · US · Colour · 82mins

Youthful Rory Calhoun and Colleen Miller convey some unusually uninhibited (for the time) moments of passion in this otherwise routine western, handsomely photographed by Russell Metty. The title refers to Calhoun and his three pals, who rob a bank and hightail it for Mexico, only to be sidetracked into rescuing Miller and her old rancher father from an Apache ambush. Actor Richard Carlson does a capable job as director. AE

Rory Calhoun *Ray Cully* • Colleen Miller *Lolly Bhumer* • George Nader *Bronco* • Walter Brennan *Simon Bhumer* • Nina Foch *Maggie Flannery* • John McIntire *Dutch* ■ *Dir* Richard Carlson • *Scr* George Van Marter, Franklin Coen, from a story by Louis L'Amour

The Four Horsemen of the Apocalypse ★★★

Silent First World War drama
1921 · US · BW · 114mins

So much of this film is rubbish, and the stuff about two brothers fighting on opposing sides in the First World War is extremely tedious. However, in those scenes where Latin heart-throb Rudolph Valentino dances the tango or simply glowers dangerously, one is suddenly confronted with one of the most powerful of screen legends. Director Rex Ingram handles the apocalyptic climax very well. AT

Rudolph Valentino *Julio Desnoyers* • Alice Terry *Marguerite Laurier* • Pomeroy Cannon *Madariaga, the Centaur* • Josef Swickard *Marcelo Desnoyers* • Brinsley Shaw *Celendonio* • Alan Hale *Karl von Hartrott* • Bridgetta Clark *Dona Luisa* • Mabel Van Buren *Elena* ■ *Dir* Rex Ingram (1) • *Scr* June Mathis, from the novel *Los Cuatro Jinetes del Apocalipsis* by Vicente Blasco Ibáñez

The Four Horsemen of the Apocalypse ★★★

Second World War drama
1962 · US · Colour · 153mins

This study of an Argentinian family torn apart by war became indelibly famous as the silent movie in which Rudolph Valentino danced the tango and catapulted to stardom. However, despite the array of talent on display and some stunning CinemaScope photography, this would-be extravaganza stubbornly remains earthbound. It's not helped by the grievous miscasting of the usually dependable Glenn Ford in the Valentino role, while updating the story to the Second World War doesn't wash. But the vision of the Four Horsemen from the Book of Revelations, riding to the strains of André Previn's potent score, is genuinely impressive. TS

Glenn Ford *Julio Desnoyers* • Ingrid Thulin *Marguerite Laurier* • Charles Boyer *Marcelo Desnoyers* • Lee J Cobb *Julio Madariaga* • Paul Henreid *Etienne Laurier* ■ *Dir* Vincente Minnelli • *Scr* Robert Ardrey, John Gay, from the novel *Los Cuatro Jinetes del Apocalipsis* by Vicente Blasco Ibáñez • *Cinematographer* Milton Krasner

The 400 Blows ★★★★★ PG

Drama 1959 · Fr · BW · 95mins

Former critic François Truffaut made his feature debut with this largely autobiographical drama. Made for a mere $75,000, it has echoes of Jean Vigo's *Zéro de Conduite*, although the influence of Jean Renoir and Italian neorealism is also evident. Introducing the character of Antoine Doinel, the story paints a grimly authentic portrait of troubled adolescence, with 13-year-old actor Jean-Pierre Léaud effortlessly conveying both mischief and vulnerability in the lead role. The film won Truffaut the best director's prize at Cannes and sent ripples around world cinema with its audacious freeze-frame finale. The character of Antoine Doinel (and, indeed, Léaud himself) was to grow and mature through four further Truffaut films: *Love at Twenty* (1962), *Stolen Kisses* (1968), *Bed and Board* (1970) and *Love on the Run* (1979). DP. In French with English subtitles. [video] DVD

Jean-Pierre Léaud *Antoine Doinel* • Claire Maurier *Mme Doinel* • Albert Rémy *M Doinel* • Guy Decomble *Teacher* • Patrick Auffay *René Bigey* • Georges Flamant *M Bigey* ■ *Dir* François Truffaut • *Scr* François Truffaut, Marcel Moussy, from a story by François Truffaut • *Cinematographer* Henri Decaë

Four in the Morning ★★★★

Drama 1965 · UK · BW · 93mins

The title's a clever pun, since the film deals with the time of a young girl's drowning, and with the (unrelated) trials and tribulations of two unnamed couples. Acclaimed in its day as a sharp slice of British neorealism, talented director/writer Anthony Simmons has done nothing quite as good. Judi Dench won a Bafta award for her role, while Ann Lynn, Norman Rodway and Brian Phelan have seldom been better. The bleak score by John Barry is superb. TS

Ann Lynn *Girl* • Brian Phelan *Boy* • Judi Dench *Wife* • Norman Rodway *Husband* • Joe Melia *Friend* ■ *Dir/Scr* Anthony Simmons

The Four Just Men ★★★

Drama 1939 · UK · BW · 87mins

Gathering war clouds cast their shadows over this adaptation of novelist Edgar Wallace's ingenious imperial thriller. Produced by Michael Balcon at Ealing, it defiantly suggests that Britain could never fall under the sway of a dictator. But in all other respects it's a rollicking *Boys' Own* adventure, with some of the most fiendishly comic-book murders you will ever see. Hugh Sinclair, Frank Lawton, Griffith Jones and Francis L Sullivan unite gallantly to prevent treacherous Basil Sydney from helping enemy agents sabotage the Suez Canal. DP

Hugh Sinclair *Humphrey Mansfield* • Griffith Jones *James Brodie* • Francis L Sullivan *Leon Poiccard* • Frank Lawton *Terry* • Anna Lee *Ann Lodge* • Alan Napier *Sir Hamar Ryman MP* ■ *Dir* Walter Forde • *Scr* Angus MacPhail, Sergei Nolbandov, Roland Pertwee, from a novel by Edgar Wallace

4 Little Girls ★★★★ 15

Documentary
1997 · US · BW and Colour · 102mins

Spike Lee's Oscar-nominated account of the murder of four young African-Americans by white supremacist bombers is as chilling as it is compelling. Using interviews, cuttings and archive footage to establish the segregational fervour that existed in Birmingham, Alabama in 1963, Lee not only describes how Carol Denise McNair, Cynthia Wesley, Addie Mae Collins and Carole Rosamund Robertson met their fate, but also suggests how much poorer the world has been for their loss. The arrogance of Klan killer Robert Chambliss is hard to bear, but nothing prepares you for the morgue photographs of the dead girls. Not to be ignored. DP [video] DVD

Dir Spike Lee

Four Men and a Prayer ★★★

Mystery drama 1938 · US · BW · 85mins

In spite of a slow start and a humdrum romantic diversion, this is a serviceable adventure mystery from master director John Ford. The gung-ho quartet of the title are the sons of old soldier C Aubrey Smith, who come face to face with a gang of gun-runners while investigating their father's death. Although George Sanders and William Henry have some fun back in Blighty, Richard Greene and David Niven get rather bogged down feuding over Loretta Young in Buenos Aires. The Brits are solid, but it's the acting of supports Alan Hale and John Carradine that catches the eye. DP

George Sanders *Wyatt Leigh* • David Niven *Christopher Leigh* • Richard Greene *Geoff Leigh* • William Henry *Rodney Leigh* • Loretta Young *Lynn Cherrington* • C Aubrey Smith *Colonel Loring Leigh* • J Edward Bromberg *General Torres* • Alan Hale *Furnoy* • John Carradine *General Adolfo Arturo Sebastian* ■ *Dir* John Ford • *Scr* Richard Sherman, Sonya Levien, Walter Ferris, from the novel by David Garth

Four Mothers ★★★ U

Drama 1941 · US · BW · 84mins

This is the last in a trilogy about small-town family life, sparked off by the huge success of *Four Daughters* in 1938, which was followed by the less compelling *Four Wives* in 1939. The Lemp sisters, played in all three films by the Lane sisters and Gale Page, are now happily married but they are plunged into financial disaster when one of the brothers-in-law loses all their money in a failed land scheme. Cosy, comforting nostalgia. RK

Priscilla Lane *Ann Lemp Dietz* • Rosemary Lane *Kay Lemp Forrest* • Lola Lane *Thea Lemp Crowley* • Gale Page *Emma Lemp Talbot* • Claude Rains *Adam Lemp* • Jeffrey Lynn *Felix Dietz* • Eddie Albert *Clint Forrest* • May Robson *Aunt Etta* ■ *Dir* William Keighley • *Scr* Stephen Morehouse Avery, from the short story *Sister Act* by Fannie Hurst

The Four Musketeers ★★★ PG

Swashbuckling comedy adventure
1974 · Pan/Sp · Colour · 102mins

This sequel was shot at the same time as its more illustrious predecessor *The Three Musketeers*, but without the knowledge of its cast, who sued producer Alexander Salkind for back-pay. The action brings Faye Dunaway to the fore, as she seeks to trap the dashing blades by imprisoning Michael York's beloved, Raquel Welch. There is a nice demonstration of screen villainy from Christopher Lee, but director Richard Lester can't resist tilting the swashbuckling into slapstick, with uneven results. Lester revisited the saga 15 years later with *The Return of the Musketeers*. DP [video] DVD

Oliver Reed *Athos* • Faye Dunaway *Milady de Winter* • Michael York *D'Artagnan* • Raquel Welch *Constance Bonancieux* • Richard Chamberlain *Aramis* • Frank Finlay *Porthos* • Simon Ward *Duke of Buckingham* • Christopher Lee *Rochefort* • Charlton Heston *Cardinal Richelieu* • Geraldine Chaplin *Anne of Austria* ■ *Dir* Richard Lester • *Scr* George MacDonald Fraser, from the novel *The Three Musketeers* by Alexandre Dumas

Four Nights of a Dreamer ★★★

Drama 1971 · Fr/It · Colour · 82mins

Having made his colour debut with *A Gentle Creature*, Robert Bresson returned to Dostoyevsky for this exploration of obsessive passion and the romantic treachery of nocturnal Paris. In relating the tale of an artist's love for the girl he dissuades from suicide, Bresson achieves an erotic realism that makes the promise of lasting love all the more tantalising and impossible. Sensitively played by Guillaume Des Forêts and Isabelle Weingarten, but with its occasionally precious visuals and stilted dialogue, this is one of Bresson's few disappointments. DP. In French with English subtitles.

Isabelle Weingarten *Marthe* • Guillaume Des Forêts *Jacques* • Jean-Maurice Monnoyer *The lodger* • Giorgio Maulini • Lydia Biondi [Lidia Biondi] *Marthe's mother* ■ *Dir* Robert Bresson • *Scr* Robert Bresson, from the story *White Nights* by Fyodor Dostoyevsky

The Four Poster ★★

Comedy drama 1953 · US · BW · 102mins

Although they were married in real life, Rex Harrison and Lilli Palmer were not perhaps the ideal couple to star in this adaptation. Spanning 45 years of marriage, this boudoir drama requires more raw emotion than the sophisticated spouses were prepared to invest, especially in the scene of the death of their soldier son. Informative, as well as amusing, the seven animated intrascenes were created by the UPA studio duo of John Hubley and Paul Julian. DP

Rex Harrison *John* • Lilli Palmer *Abby* ■ *Dir* Irving Reis • *Scr* Allan Scott, from the play by Jan de Hartog • *Music* Dmitri Tiomkin

Four Rooms ★ 18

Portmanteau comedy drama
1995 · US · Colour · 93mins

Proof that wonderkid Quentin Tarantino is fallible. He's the driving force behind this horribly botched portmanteau movie and he also directs and stars in one segment. Set in the same hotel, the four stories are loosely linked by inept bellboy Tim Roth. Allison Anders's story of a witches coven is slight and silly; Alexandre Rockwell fares little better in a farcical yarn of a lover's tiff; while Tarantino's effort barely passes muster as an anecdote. The best of the bunch is Robert Rodriguez's, a cartoon-like tale of Roth playing baby-sitter to a gangster's psychopathic children. JF

Tim Roth *Ted the Bellhop* • Lawrence Bender *Long Hair Yuppy Scum* • Marisa Tomei *Margaret* • Madonna *Elspeth* • Amanda De Cadenet *Diana* • Antonio Banderas *Man* • Salma Hayek *TV dancing girl* • Quentin Tarantino *Chester* • Bruce Willis *Leo* ■ *Dir/Scr* Allison Anders, Alexandre Rockwell, Robert Rodriguez, Quentin Tarantino

The Four Seasons ★★★ 15

Comedy drama 1981 · US · Colour · 103mins

Alan Alda's directorial debut is as waspishly decent-hearted as you'd expect, with its exploration of American middle-class habits. Three married couples regularly take their holidays together, but find this complacent routine faltering when one husband falls for a younger woman. A rather stodgy narrative is transcended by fine performances from Carol Burnett, Len Cariou, Sandy Dennis, Jack Weston and Alda himself. TH. Contains swearing and brief nudity.

Alan Alda *Jack Burroughs* • Carol Burnett *Kate Burroughs* • Len Cariou *Nick Callan* • Sandy Dennis *Anne Callan* • Rita Moreno *Claudia Zimmer* • Jack Weston *Danny Zimmer* • Bess Armstrong *Ginny Newley* • Elizabeth Alda *Beth* • Beatrice Alda *Lisa* ■ *Dir/Scr* Alan Alda

Four Sided Triangle ★★ PG

Science fiction 1953 · UK · BW · 77mins

When scientists Stephen Murray and John Van Eyssen fall in love with the same girl (Barbara Payton) they solve their rivalry by making a duplicate of her. One of the earliest Hammer movies made prior to their international breakthrough with *The Quatermass Experiment* and *The Curse of Frankenstein*, this slow moving cautionary tale is methodically directed by Terence Fisher with little of the flair he would soon be famous for. AJ DVD

Barbara Payton *Lena/Helen* • Percy Marmont *Sir Walter* • James Hayter *Dr Harvey* • Stephen Murray *Bill* • John Van Eyssen *Robin* • Glynn Dearman *Bill as a child* • Sean Barrett (1) *Robin as a child* ■ *Dir* Terence Fisher • *Scr* Terence Fisher, Paul Tabori, from the novel by William F Temple

Four Sons ★★★★

Silent First World War drama
1928 · US · BW · 100mins

This heartbreaking opus from the great director John Ford, about a widow whose sons fight on opposite sides during the First World War, is a formidable piece of cinema. There are few more moving moments than those in which the postman (superbly delineated by Albert Gran) arrives bearing news of the sons, while the long-suffering Bavarian mother is brilliantly portrayed by Margaret Mann. The climactic sequence of her finally arriving at New York's Ellis Island will leave no handkerchief dry, and was amazingly influential on film-makers as diverse as Elia Kazan and Francis Ford Coppola. Fox remade the story in 1940, but the addition of sound and the efforts of director Archie Mayo could not improve on Ford's film. TS

James Hall *Joseph Bernle* • Margaret Mann *Mother Bernle* • Earle Foxe *Von Stomm* • Charles Morton *Johann Bernle* • Francis X Bushman Jr [Ralph Bushman] *Franz Bernle* • George Meeker *Andres Bernle* • Albert Gran *Letter Carrier* ■ *Dir* John Ford • *Scr* Philip Klein, HH Caldwell (titles), Katherine Hilliker (titles), from the story *Grandmother Bernle Learns Her Letters* by Ida Alexa Ross Wylie

Four Sons ★★

Second World War drama
1940 · US · BW · 88mins

A remake of the 1928 silent picture, updated to cover Hitler's inexorable march into Czechoslovakia, an event which has a cataclysmic impact on a mother and her four sons. One flees to America, one becomes a Nazi, another joins the resistance and the youngest fights for the Third Reich in Poland. Guess which one survives? It probably served its propagandist purpose well enough in 1940, but it seems schematic nowadays. AT

Don Ameche *Chris* • Eugenie Leontovich *Frau Bernie* • Mary Beth Hughes *Anna* • Alan Curtis *Karl* • George Ernest *Fritz* • Robert Lowery *Joseph* • Lionel Royce *Max Sturm* ■ *Dir* Archie Mayo • *Scr* John Howard Lawson, Milton Sperling, from a story by IAR Wylie

Four Steps in the Clouds ★★★★

Comedy drama 1942 · It · BW · 96mins

After almost two decades of pompous propagandising, this charming comedy signalled a stylistic shift in Italian film-making. Its enshrinement as the herald of neorealism (courtesy of the fact its co-scenarist was Cesare Zavattini) is perhaps a little excessive, especially as its emphasis is more firmly on serenading the national spirit and satirising the contrasting temperaments of town and country than exposing the impoverishing legacy of fascism. But the nostalgic authenticity with which Alessandro Blasetti invests his delicate tale of deception, in which henpecked Gino Cervi poses as pregnant waif Adriana Benetti's husband, gives it an irresistible slice-of-life feel. Remade in 1995 as *A Walk in the Clouds*. DP. An Italian language film.

Gino Cervi *Paolo Bianchi* • Giuditta Rissone *Clara Bianchi* • Adriana Benetti *Maria* • Guido Celano *Pasquale, Maria's brother* • Aldo Silvani *Luca, Maria's father* ■ *Dir* Alessandro Blasetti • *Scr* Aldo De Benedetti, Giuseppe Amato, Alessandro Blasetti, Cesare Zavattini, from the story *Quattro Passi fra le Nuvole* by Cesare Zavattini, Piero Tellini

Four Times That Night ★★

Erotic comedy
1972 · It/W Ger · Colour · 90mins

This sex comedy was a distinct change of pace for Italian horror maestro Mario Bava. It clearly owes its genesis to Akira Kurosawa's landmark treatise on the nature of real and cinematic truth, *Rashomon*, as various witnesses try to account for the scratches that appear on Brett Halsey's forehead following a date with Daniela Giordano. This might have been a sordid little story had not Bava taken such a playful approach, but even then, it's definitely only a minor work. DP. Italian dialogue dubbed into English.

Daniela Giordano *Tina* • Brett Halsey *Gianni* • Michael Hinz *Sergio* • Dick Randall *Duccio* • Valeria Sabel ■ *Dir* Mario Bava • *Scr* Mario Moroni, Charles Ross

Four Weddings and a Funeral ★★★★★ 15

Comedy 1994 · UK · Colour · 112mins

No one could have foreseen that this glorified sitcom would change the nature of British screen comedy. The tale of a foppish bachelor, his eccentric friends and their romantic escapades is extremely funny, charming, poignant and never anything less than hugely enjoyable. Neatly structured and full of genuine warmth for its characters, Richard Curtis's Oscar-nominated screenplay is superbly observed and is well served by Mike Newell's deft direction. But more important to the film's enduring appeal is the individuality of the performances. Simon Callow and Kristin Scott Thomas are outstanding alongside star Hugh Grant, who became an overnight sensation. DP. Contains swearing DVD

Hugh Grant *Charles* • Andie MacDowell *Carrie* • Kristin Scott Thomas *Fiona* • James Fleet *Tom* • Simon Callow *Gareth* • John Hannah *Matthew* • David Bower *David* • Charlotte Coleman *Scarlett* • Corin Redgrave *Hamish* • Rowan Atkinson *Father Gerald* • Anna Chancellor *Henrietta* • Timothy Walker *Angus* • Rosalie Crutchley *Mrs Beaumont* ■ *Dir* Mike Newell • *Scr* Richard Curtis

Four Wives ★★

Drama 1939 · US · BW · 110mins

John Garfield caused a sensation in *Four Daughters* playing a brash misfit and musical genius who kills himself. This sequel keeps his memory alive as his young widow (Priscilla Lane) discovers she will be having his baby. Garfield also returns as a ghostly vision. The result is trite and overlong, but director Michael Curtiz still generates warmth between the characters and his fluid camera style keeps up the momentum. A further sequel, *Four Mothers*, followed. AE

Priscilla Lane *Ann Lemp Borden* • Rosemary Lane *Kay Lemp* • Lola Lane *Thea Lemp Crowley* • Gale Page *Emma Lemp* • Claude Rains *Adam Lemp* • John Garfield *Mickey Borden* ■ *Dir* Michael Curtiz • *Scr* Julius J Epstein, Philip G Epstein, Maurice Hanline, from the story *Sister Act* by Fannie Hurst

Four's a Crowd ★★ U

Romantic comedy 1938 · US · BW · 91mins

Errol Flynn as a PR man, Rosalind Russell as an ace reporter, Patric Knowles as a playboy newspaper proprietor and Olivia de Havilland as an heiress. Blend thoroughly and hand to Michael Curtiz for careful cooking. Sadly, though, the result lacks the sparkle promised by the cast and director, and the script is merely a rehash of other, better pictures, which gives it a rather jaded air. AT

Errol Flynn *Robert "Bob" Kensington Lansford* • Olivia de Havilland *Lorri Dillingwell* • Rosalind Russell *Jean Christy* • Patric Knowles *Patterson Buckley* • Walter Connolly *John P Dillingwell* • Hugh Herbert *Silas Jenkins* ■ *Dir* Michael Curtiz • *Scr* Casey Robinson, Sid Herzig, from the novel *All Rights Reserved* by Wallace Sullivan

Fourteen Hours ★★★★

Drama based on a true story
1951 · US · BW · 91mins

An exciting suspense drama about Richard Basehart threatening to end it all from a New York skyscraper, gutwrenchingly directed by Henry Hathaway and based on a real-life incident. The crowd of onlookers that gathers becomes a character in itself, with stars-to-be on view including Debra Paget and Jeffrey Hunter, plus the debut of young Grace Kelly, playing an estranged wife who is prompted by Basehart's plight to take another crack at marriage. Agnes Moorehead and Robert Keith are particularly effective as the would-be suicide's parents, but the movie's actual top-liner is tough cop Paul Douglas. TS

Paul Douglas *Dunnigan* • Richard Basehart *Robert Cosick* • Barbara Bel Geddes *Virginia* • Debra Paget *Ruth* • Agnes Moorehead *Mrs Cosick* • Robert Keith (1) *Mr Cosick* ■ *Dir* Henry Hathaway • *Scr* John Paxton, from the story *The Man on the Ledge* by Joel Sayre

1492: Conquest of Paradise ★★★★ 15

Historical drama
1992 · US/Sp/Fr/UK · Colour · 149mins

Three big films were made to mark the 500th anniversary of the discovery of the New World – a catastrophic *Carry On*, the dire *Christopher Columbus: the Discovery* and Ridley Scott's *1492: Conquest of Paradise*. Despite a rather wobbly first hour, when it's hard to understand Gérard Depardieu's accent or make out Sigourney Weaver's scheming Spanish queen in the gloomy light, the picture gathers momentum with the voyage, captures in dazzling imagery the actual discovery, and then produces a horrific and masterly final segment as Columbus returns on a second voyage to preside over slaughter and the raising of a giant church bell. This dark, bloody and brooding piece about colonial exploitation was woefully under-rated by many critics, and boasts an eerily atmospheric score by Vangelis. AT. Contains violence. DVD

Gérard Depardieu *Christopher Columbus* • Armand Assante *Sanchez* • Sigourney Weaver *Queen Isabel* • Loren Dean *Older Fernando* • Angela Molina *Beatrix* • Fernando Rey *Marchena* • Michael Wincott *Moxica* • Tcheky Karyo *Pinzon* • Kevin Dunn *Captain Mendez* ■ *Dir* Ridley Scott • *Scr* Roselyne Bosch

The Fourth Angel ★★ 15

Thriller 2001 · Can/UK · Colour · 91mins

Originally due for an earlier US release, director John Irvin's thoughtful revenge thriller had to give way to post-11 September sensitivity. On a holiday flight to India, the family of magazine editor Jeremy Irons are involved in a hijack and killed. When the hijackers are released on a technicality, Irons turns into a gun-wielding Charles Bronson clone and starts to hunt them down, bringing him to the attention of US agent, Forest Whitaker. Despite moderate tension and an interesting cast, Irvin stretches credibility to breaking point. AJ DVD

Jeremy Irons *Jack Elgin* • Forest Whitaker *Agent Jules Bernard* • Charlotte Rampling *Kate Stockton* • Jason Priestley *Davidson* • Ian McNeice *MI5 officer* ■ *Dir* John Irvin • *Scr* Allan Scott, from the novel by Robin Hunter

The Fourth Man ★★★★ 18

Black comedy thriller
1983 · Neth · Colour · 98mins

An early nightmarish, and typically allegorical, fantasy from Dutch director Paul Verhoeven and cinematographer-turned-director Jan De Bont. Homosexual writer Jeroen Krabbé suffers horrific premonitions after he meets attractive blonde Renée Soutendijk, whose last three husbands have all died in mysterious circumstances. Is he to be her fourth victim, lured into her black widow's web by her attractive bisexual lover Thom Hoffman? Obliquely eerie, explicitly erotic and perversely hilarious, this is an intricate, symbolic shocker. AJ. In Dutch with English subtitles. DVD

Jeroen Krabbé *Gerard Reve* • Renée Soutendijk *Christine Halsslag* • Thom Hoffman *Herman* • Dolf de Vries *Dr De Vries* • Geert De Jong *Ria* ■ *Dir* Paul Verhoeven • *Scr* Gerard Soeteman, from a novel by Gerard Reve • *Cinematographer* Jan De Bont

The Fourth Protocol ★★ 15

Spy thriller 1987 · UK · Colour · 113mins

Before getting his big break as 007, Pierce Brosnan tried his hand at life on the other side of the wall, playing a dastardly Russian spy out to blow up an American airbase in England. Michael Caine is the less-than-super agent out to stop him, and a familiar cavalcade of British actors (plus the odd visiting American) is on hand to help or hinder him. Tired and not particularly relevant. JF. Contains swearing, violence, nudity. DVD

Michael Caine *John Preston* • Pierce Brosnan *Major Valeri Petrofsky* • Joanna Cassidy *Irina Vassilieva* • Ned Beatty *General Borisov* • Ray

McAnally *General Karpov* ■ *Dir* John Mackenzie • *Scr* Frederick Forsyth, Richard Burridge, from the novel by Frederick Forsyth

The Fourth War ★★ 15

Thriller 1990 · US · Colour · 86mins

It's November 1988 and Roy Scheider is a gung-ho Vietnam veteran who embarks on a private war with Soviet hothead Jürgen Prochnow (himself an embittered casualty of Afghanistan) after he witnesses the death of a defector during one of his reckless sorties beyond the checkpoint. Recently the films of John Frankenheimer have been disappointing and this dreary piece of macho posturing is no exception. DP. Contains violence, swearing. [video]

Roy Scheider *Colonel Jack Knowles* • Jürgen Prochnow *Colonel NA Valachev* • Tim Reid *Lt Col Timothy Clark* • Lara Harris *Elena Novotna* • Harry Dean Stanton *General Roger Hackworth* ■ *Dir* John Frankenheimer • *Scr* Stephen Peters, Kenneth Ross, from the novel by Stephen Peters

The Fox ★★★

Drama 1967 · US · Colour · 110mins

From glamour girl to drama diva, Anne Heywood made the transition in fine style, marrying producer Raymond Stross and starring in this risqué adaptation of the DH Lawrence novella. It details the long-term relationship of lesbians Heywood and Sandy Dennis that's disrupted by the arrival of handyman Keir Dullea. Dennis's twitchiness is almost laughable at times, but Heywood's portrayal of dominance threatened by aching insecurity is memorably poignant. TH

Sandy Dennis *Jill* • Keir Dullea *Paul* • Anne Heywood *Ellen March* • Glyn Morris *Realtor* ■ *Dir* Mark Rydell • *Scr* Lewis John Carlino, Howard Koch, from the novella by DH Lawrence

Fox and His Friends ★★★★ 15

Drama 1975 · W Ger · Colour · 118mins

Director Rainer Werner Fassbinder also plays the title role of an unemployed carnival worker in this penetrating melodrama. Picked up by an antique dealer after winning the lottery and introduced into an effete bourgeois homosexual milieu, he is exploited, abused and driven to despair. The working class victim was based on Armin Meier, one of Fassbinder's former lovers, a young butcher to whom the film is dedicated. Although an honest portrayal of homosexual relationships, Fassbinder's absorbing film is ultimately more concerned with class exploitation. RB. In German with English subtitles. [video]

Rainer Werner Fassbinder *Fox* • Peter Chatel *Eugen* • Karl-Heinz Bohm [Karlheinz Böhm] *Max* • Harry Baer *Philip* • Adrian Hoven *Father* • Ulla Jacobsson *Mother* • Christiane Maybach *Hedwig* ■ *Dir* Rainer Werner Fassbinder • *Scr* Christian Hohoff, Rainer Werner Fassbinder

The Fox and the Hound ★★★ U

Animated adventure
1981 · US · Colour · 80mins

Disney animation was still reckoned to be in the doldrums when this charming tale of animal friendship was produced, and it probably has a lower profile than it deserves. A young hound pup is befriended by a fox cub and they become firm chums. Once grown, the hound warns his foxy friend to keep away from the hunt and his cruel master, but the fox proves his courage when he saves the hound from a marauding bear. Hound returns the favour when his wild friend is pursued by the pack in a family parable about the power of friendship. JF [video] DVD

Mickey Rooney *Tod* • Kurt Russell *Copper* • Pearl Bailey *Big Mama* • Jack Albertson *Amos Slade* • Sandy Duncan *Vixey* • Jeanette Nolan *Widow Tweed* ■ *Dir* Art Stevens, Ted Berman, Richard Rich • *Scr* Larry Clemmons, Ted Berman, Peter Young, Steve Hulett, David Michener, Burny Mattinson, Earl Kress, Vance Gerry, from the novel by Daniel P Mannix

Fox Movietone Follies of 1929 ★★

Musical 1929 · US · BW and Colour · 80mins

This was Fox's riposte to MGM's *The Broadway Melody* and *Hollywood Revue of 1929* and to Warner Bros' *Show of Shows*, all of which were star-packed extravaganzas designed to show off the new wonder of the age. Fox really went to town with this one: not only did it use early Technicolor, but the film was also shot in the 70mm process called Grandeur, with a separate soundtrack offering fantastic sound quality. Pity they didn't take as much care over the laboured plot, substandard songs and corny dance routines. For collectors of historic movie curios only. TS

John Breeden *George Shelby* • Lola Lane *Lila Beaumont* • DeWitt Jennings *Jay Darrell* • Sharon Lynne *Ann Foster* • Arthur Stone *Al Leaton* • Stepin Fetchit *Swifty* • Warren Hymer *Martin* ■ *Dir* David Butler, Marcel Silver • *Scr* David Butler, William K Wells

Foxes ★★★ 15

Drama 1980 · US · Colour · 101mins

Ex-TV commercial director Adrian Lyne made his feature film debut with this slick movie about four teenage girls and their problems with life and men. A young Jodie Foster is the straight arrow sorting out her friends, which include podgy, unloved Marilyn Kagan, compulsive liar Kandice Stroh, and abused hooker Cherie Currie. Foster's *Bugsy Malone* co-star Scott Baio provides the male interest, but it's really one to watch for the girls, who overcome the clichés. JB [video] DVD

Jodie Foster *Jeanie* • Scott Baio *Brad* • Sally Kellerman *Mary* • Randy Quaid *Jay* • Marilyn Kagan *Madge* • Kandice Stroh *Deirdre* • Lois Smith *Mrs Axman* • Adam Faith *Bryan* • Cherie Currie *Annie* ■ *Dir* Adrian Lyne • *Scr* Gerald Ayres • *Producer* David Puttnam, Gerald Ayres

The Foxes of Harrow ★★

Period drama 1947 · US · BW · 117mins

This overlong adaptation of Frank Yerby's popular Southern novel would have benefited from more sensible casting, Technicolor photography and a more involved director than John M Stahl at the helm. Rex Harrison is miscast as the Irish rogue who gambles his way to the top, while Maureen O'Hara plays her role with a grimness which suggests how unhappy she must have been to be subjected to her co-star's infamous on-set arrogance. The production values are undoubtably attractive, however, and the art direction was unsurprisingly nominated for an Oscar. TS

Rex Harrison *Stephen Fox* • Maureen O'Hara *Odalie D'Arceneaux* • Richard Haydn *Andre LeBlanc* • Victor McLaglen *Capt Mike Farrell* • Vanessa Brown *Aurore D'Arceneaux* • Patricia Medina *Desiree* • Gene Lockhart *The Vicomte* ■ *Dir* John M Stahl • *Scr* Wanda Tuchock, from the novel by Frank Yerby • *Art Director* Lyle Wheeler, Maurice Ransford

Foxfire ★★

Romantic drama 1955 · US · Colour · 91mins

A soppy concoction with Jeff Chandler as a half-breed Apache, a mining engineer digging for gold in Arizona and settling down to married bliss with Jane Russell. Yes, it's love across the cultural divide, but despite the improbability of the match, it carries on without batting an eyelid. The trade magazine *Variety* apparently described Chandler as "churlish", "surly" and generally a bit of a heel. AT

Jane Russell *Amanda* • Jeff Chandler *Jonathan Dartland* • Dan Duryea *Hugh Slater* • Mara Corday *Maria* • Robert Simon [Robert F Simon] *Ernest Tyson* • Frieda Inescort *Mrs Lawrence* • Barton MacLane *Jim Mablett* ■ *Dir* Joseph Pevney • *Scr* Ketti Frings, from a novel by Anya Seton

Foxfire ★★★ 18

Drama 1996 · US · Colour · 97mins

Four teenage girls discover their common strengths when they tire of an abusive teacher and the negligent school system that ignores him. Hedy Burress is the film's focus, with the ever-smirking Angelina Jolie as "Legs", the independent wanderer who floats into the lives of the other girls just as they need that extra push into rebellion. The male characters are painted rather flatly as either abusive or obtuse, mostly to give the girls more incentive to revolt. This probably would have had more impact if, like the book that inspired it, the film had been set in its original 1950s milieu. ST. Contains swearing, violence. [video]

Hedy Burress *Maddy Wirtz* • Angelina Jolie *Legs Sadovsky* • Jenny Lewis *Rita Faldes* • Jenny Shimizu *Goldie Goldman* • Sarah Rosenberg *Violet Kahn* ■ *Dir* Annette Haywood-Carter • *Scr* Elizabeth White, from the novel by Joyce Carol Oates

Foxhole in Cairo ★★

Spy drama 1960 · UK · BW · 83mins

Unremarkable wartime espionage drama, with James Robertson-Justice and Adrian Hoven as British and German spies playing hide and seek with the plans for El Alamein. Fenella Fielding makes a sexy Jewish resistance fighter saved by Robertson-Justice, who prevents the Desert Fox from winning the Battle of Algiers. Albert Lieven is a convincing Rommel and if you blink you'll miss Michael Caine as a German soldier. AT

James Robertson-Justice *Captain Robertson DSO* • Adrian Hoven *John Eppler* • Niall MacGinnis *Radek* • Peter Van Eyck *Count Almaszy* • Fenella Fielding *Yvette* • Albert Lieven *Rommel* • Michael Caine *Weber* ■ *Dir* John Moxey [John Llewellyn Moxey] • *Scr* Leonard Mosley, Donald Taylor, from the novel *The Cat and the Mice* by Leonard Mosley

Foxy Brown ★★ 18

Blaxploitation thriller
1974 · US · Colour · 87mins

"Don't mess aroun' with Foxy Brown" read the shoutline for Pam Grier's fourth collaboration with director Jack Hill. However, far more revealing is the poster copy that sums up the slam-bam nature of one of blaxploitation's low points: "She's got drive and that ain't jive. She don't bother to bring 'em back alive!" Posing as a hooker to snare the drug dealers who killed her cop boyfriend, Grier is so preoccupied with kinky sex and violence she has to leave what little acting there is to Antonio Fargas. DP [video] DVD

Pam Grier *Foxy Brown* • Antonio Fargas *Link Brown* • Peter Brown *Steve Elias* • Terry Carter *Michael Anderson* • Kathryn Loder *Katherine Wall* • Harry Holcombe *Judge Fenton* • Juanita Brown *Claudia* ■ *Dir/Scr* Jack Hill

Fragment of Fear ★★ 15

Thriller 1970 · UK · Colour · 91mins

The poster promised "A Phantasmagoria of Fright", but director Richard C Sarafian's disappointing adaptation of John Bingham's novel delivers very little of anything. The initial premise is promising. Writer David Hemmings is investigating the murder of his aunt (Flora Robson) in Pompeii. The problem is, he's a reformed drug addict, and clues to the mystery keep being complicated by weird hallucinations. Is he going insane? A Euro-pudding cast provides some answers before the whole flimsy farrago falls apart. AJ [video]

David Hemmings *Tim Brett* • Gayle Hunnicutt *Juliet Bristow* • Flora Robson *Lucy Dawson* • Wilfrid Hyde White *Mr Copsey* • Daniel Massey *Major Ricketts* • Adolfo Celi *Bardoni* ■ *Dir* Richard C Sarafian • *Scr* Paul Dehn, from the novel by John Bingham

Frailty ★★★ 15

Horror thriller
2001 · US/Ger · Colour · 95mins

The directorial debut of actor Bill Paxton is a haunting tale of a family torn apart by religious fanaticism and madness, steeped in a chilling "Southern Gothic" atmosphere. Texan Matthew McConaughey tells FBI agent Powers Boothe that the serial killer he is looking for is his brother and relates, in flashback, their horrifying family history. Using the "less is more" maxim – no gore, just powerful imagery – Paxton's assured, if morbidly bleak, creepshow is directed with artful precision. AJ [video] DVD

Bill Paxton *Dad* • Matthew McConaughey *Fenton Meiks/Adam Meiks* • Powers Boothe *Agent Wesley J Doyle* • Matt O'Leary *Young Fenton* • Luke Askew *Sheriff Smalls* • Jeremy Sumpter *Young Adam Meiks* • Derk Cheetwood *Agent Griffin Hull* • Melissa Crider [Missy Crider] *Becky* ■ *Dir* Bill Paxton • *Scr* Brent Hanley

Framed ★★

Crime drama 1947 · US · BW · 82mins

Even after *Gilda*, Glenn Ford was still serving time on the treadmill of Columbia's programme-fillers, this one a crime thriller in which he's an unemployed mining engineer who becomes the fall-guy for a bank robbery. He is set up by robber Janis Carter, who uses him because he looks like her accomplice Barry Sullivan, but she ends up falling for Ford instead. AT

Glenn Ford *Mike Lambert* • Janis Carter *Paula Craig* • Barry Sullivan *Stephen Price* • Edgar Buchanan *Jeff Cunningham* • Karen Morley *Mrs Price* • Jim Bannon *Jack Woodworth* ■ *Dir* Richard Wallace • *Scr* Ben Maddow, from the story by Jack Patrick

Framed ★ 18

Crime action 1975 · US · Colour · 100mins

You've seen this one a billion times before but never one more gratuitously violent. Nashville gambler Joe Don Baker is put in jail for accidentally killing a sheriff and, after being paroled, goes after the corrupt cops who set him up. This is a typical 1970s revenge saga characterised by reprehensible *Death Wish* viciousness. Unsurprising, really, as director, writer and star had previously collaborated on *Walking Tall*. AJ [video]

Joe Don Baker *Ron Lewis* • Conny Van Dyke *Susan Barrett* • Gabriel Dell *Vince Greeson* • John Marley *Sal Viccarrone* ■ *Dir* Phil Karlson • *Scr* Mort Briskin, from a novel by Art Powers, Mike Misenheimer

Framed ★★ 12

Crime thriller 2002 · US · Colour · 87mins

This twisting and occasionally explosive TV-movie crime thriller transposes Lynda La Plante's original story to a New York setting and provides a fascinating insight into the differences between British and American entertainment. Demoted for his association with a corrupt detective, NYPD cop Rob Lowe sees a chance for redemption when he arrests fugitive criminal Sam Neill in the Bahamas and grills him for information on a money-laundering case. However, Neill's smooth operator soon has Lowe tempted by the promise of the high life

F

that a bribe would guarantee. DP. Contains violence, swearing. DVD

Rob Lowe *Mike Santini* • Sam Neill *Eddie Meyers* • Alicia Coppola *Lucy Santini* • Howard Rosenstein *Eddie's Lawyer* • Philip Akin *Bahamian Superintendent* ■ *Dir* Daniel Petrie Jr • *Scr* Daniel Petrie Jr, from the TV serial by Lynda La Plante

Frameup ★★★

Crime comedy drama
1993 · US · Colour and BW · 91mins

Doomed young killers have long fascinated American directors (*Badlands, Natural Born Killers*) but this little-seen gem is one of the bleakest examinations of the subject. Howard Swain is the small-time crook who hooks up with bored waitress Nancy Carlin to make a new life in California. Their aimless road trip takes in sex, sightseeing and – finally – murder. Unlike other movies with similar themes, writer/director Jon Jost shows absolutely no sympathy for his pathetic leads, and although that provokes some uncomfortable laughs, his jarring vision chills to the bone. JF

Howard Swain *Ricky Lee Gruber* • Nancy Carlin *Beth-Ann Bolet* ■ *Dir/Scr* Jon Jost

Frances ★★★★ 15

Biographical drama
1982 · US · Colour · 133mins

Jessica Lange is mesmerising in this uneven biopic of the spirited, politically outspoken 1930s actress Frances Farmer, who fell from grace in Hollywood and ended up institutionalised in an asylum where she later underwent a lobotomy. Although the film only touches on the problems in Hollywood which Frances faced, instead focusing on her hospitalisations, this is an often riveting drama which benefits from a superb central performance from Lange (who at times looks eerily like Farmer), and solid support from Sam Shepard (as Farmer's love) and Kim Stanley as her fame-hungry mother. JB DVD

Jessica Lange *Frances Farmer* • Sam Shepard *Harry York* • Kim Stanley *Lillian Farmer* • Bart Burns *Ernest Farmer* • Christopher Pennock *Dick Steele* • James Karen *Judge* • Gerald S O'Loughlin *Lobotomy doctor* ■ *Dir* Graeme Clifford • *Scr* Eric Bergren, Christopher DeVore, Nicholas Kazan

Francesca and Nunziata ★★★

Period drama 2001 · It · Colour · 125mins

Lina Wertmuller renews her pivotal association with Giancarlo Giannini in this TV adaptation of a period novel. However, his indolent prince is somewhat marginalised as the focus centres on the feud between his rags-to-riches wife, Sophia Loren, and Claudia Genini, the daughter she adopted in an act of atonement for the recovery of ailing son, Raoul Bova. Typically, Wertmuller packs her melodrama with plenty of caustic comment, but, despite Loren's bravura, it's not one of her most compelling outings. DP. In Italian with English subtitles.

Sophia Loren *Francesca* • Giancarlo Giannini *Giordano* • Claudia Gerini *Nunziata* • Raoul Bova *Federico* • Carmen Femiano *Mariuccia* ■ *Dir* Lina Wertmuller • *Scr* Lina Wertmuller, Elvio Porta, from the novel *Francesca e Nunziata* by Maria Orsini Natale

Francesco ★ 12

Biographical religious drama
1989 · It/W Ger · Colour · 128mins

In 1966, Liliana Cavani made a TV biopic about St Francis of Assissi. Years later she persuaded backers to let her try again, using Herman Hesse's book, a bigger budget and imported star Mickey Rourke. Told in flashback, it recalls his life as a group of disciples remember his conversion in prison, after which he renounced worldly possessions. Rourke makes a muscular visionary, allowing Cavani to make use of Francesco shedding his clothes, but the script is risible, Rourke miscast and the docudrama unconvincing. BB. In English and Italian with subtitles. DVD

Mickey Rourke *Francesco* • Helena Bonham Carter *Chiara* • Paolo Bonacelli *Pietro Bernardone, Francesco's father* • Andréa Ferréol *Pica, Francesco's mother* • Hanns Zischler *Pope Innocence III* • Peter Berling *Guido, Bishop of Assisi* ■ *Dir* Liliana Cavani • *Scr* Liliana Cavani, Roberta Mazzoni, from the novel *Francis of Assisi* by Herman Hesse

The Franchise Affair ★★

Mystery 1950 · UK · BW · 88mins

Adapted from the novel by Josephine Tey (which was itself based on actual events), this tale of superstition and recrimination should keep us guessing right up to the moment the mystery is sensationally cleared up. But the presence of postwar British cinema's golden couple, Michael Denison and Dulcie Gray, deprives the story of much of its suspense. As one of the women accused of kidnap and torture by the hysterical Ann Stephens, Gray fails to generate sufficient ambiguity, while lawyer Denison's decency lacks the indignation that might have injected some much-needed impetus. DP

Michael Denison *Robert Blair* • Dulcie Gray *Marion Sharpe* • Anthony Nicholls *Kevin McDermott* • Marjorie Fielding *Mrs Sharpe* • Athene Seyler *Aunt Lin* • Ann Stephens *Betty Kane* ■ *Dir* Lawrence Huntington • *Scr* Robert Hall, Lawrence Huntington, from the novel by Josephine Tey

Francis ★★ U

Comedy 1949 · US · BW · 90mins

The adventures of Francis the talking mule (voiced by Chill Wills) proved so successful that they led to an unofficial comedy series, critically unloved but massively popular with the picture-going public. In this first entry, the pesky mule helps Donald O'Connor become a war hero. O'Connor felt that being Francis's stooge cost him true stardom, and he may not have been far wrong. The seven-strong series was used to try out new studio contractees – look out for Anthony (later Tony) Curtis in this one – while director Arthur Lubin later worked with another talking horse on TV's *Mr Ed*. TS

Donald O'Connor *Lt Peter Stirling* • Patricia Medina *Maureen Gelder* • ZaSu Pitts *Valerie Humpert* • Ray Collins *Colonel Hooker* • John McIntire *General Stevens* • Anthony Curtis [Tony Curtis] *Captain Jones* • Chill Wills *Francis the Talking Mule* ■ *Dir* Arthur Lubin • *Scr* David Stern, from his novel

Francis Covers the Big Town ★★ U

Comedy 1953 · US · BW · 86mins

Director Arthur Lubin broke a golden rule in the fourth entry in Universal's comedy series by allowing the talking mule to speak to someone other than Donald O'Connor. Francis is called upon to give evidence in court after O'Connor – now employed as a crime reporter on a newspaper because his buddy receives tip-offs from garrulous police horses – becomes embroiled in a murder case. DP

Donald O'Connor *Peter Stirling* • Yvette Duguay [Yvette Dugay] *Maria Scola* • Gene Lockhart *Tom Henderson* • Nancy Guild *Alberta Ames* • Larry Gates *Dan Austin* • Gale Gordon *Evans* • Chill Wills *Francis the Talking Mule* ■ *Dir* Arthur Lubin • *Scr* Oscar Brodney, from characters created by David Stern

Francis, God's Jester ★★★★ U

Biographical drama 1950 · It · BW · 96mins

Based on the writings of St Francis of Assisi and shot with such a firm grasp of period and place that it feels like a newsreel of 13th-century Italy, this truly inspiring picture is not a saintly homage, but a neorealist study in faith and human decency. Director Roberto Rossellini draws extraordinary performances from his mainly non-professional cast, notably from Nazario Gerardi, who was himself a Franciscan friar. Ironically, the only weak link is established star Aldo Fabrizi's eye-rolling villainy as a local warlord. Co-authored by Italian director Federico Fellini, the script focuses on the simple joys of life rather than theology and is guaranteed to raise the spirits. DP. In Italian with English subtitles.

Aldo Fabrizi *Nicolaio, the Tyrant* • Arabella Lemaitre *Saint Clair* • Brother Nazario Gerardi *Saint Francis* ■ *Dir* Roberto Rossellini • *Scr* Roberto Rossellini, Federico Fellini

Francis Goes to the Races ★★ U

Comedy 1951 · US · BW · 87mins

Following the success of *Francis*, Universal invited Donald O'Connor to reprise the role of Peter Stirling (the real name of David Stern, on whose novel the series was based), the trouble-prone everyman whose best buddy is a talking mule. Chill Wills also returned to voice the equine sage, with a brain as sharp as Bilko's, and he's soon feeding O'Connor with insider information after he lands a job at the rundown racing stable owned by Cecil Kellaway and niece Piper Laurie. DP

Donald O'Connor *Peter Stirling* • Piper Laurie *Frances Travers* • Cecil Kellaway *Colonel Travers* • Jesse White *Frank Damer* • Barry Kelley *Mallory* • Chill Wills *Francis the Talking Mule* ■ *Dir* Arthur Lubin • *Scr* Oscar Brodney, from a story by Robert Arthur, from characters created by David Stern

Francis Goes to West Point ★★ U

Comedy 1952 · US · BW · 81mins

Donald O'Connor here makes his third appearance in Universal's talking mule comedy series. Rewarded with a scholarship for preventing a calamity at an atomic plant, O'Connor finds life at the US Army academy tough going – all the more so having invented himself a pregnant wife. However, with the help of the scheming Francis (voiced as ever by Chill Wills), he comes to the fore during a big football game versus the Navy. Good-natured fun. DP

Donald O'Connor *Peter Stirling* • Lori Nelson *Barbara Atwood* • Alice Kelley *Cynthia Daniels* • Palmer Lee [Gregg Palmer] *William Norton* • William Reynolds *Wilbur Van Allen* • Les Tremayne *Col Daniels* • Chill Wills *Francis the Talking Mule* ■ *Dir* Arthur Lubin • *Scr* Oscar Brodney, from characters created by David Stern

Francis in the Haunted House ★★ U

Comedy 1956 · US · BW · 79mins

It was all change for the final entry in Universal's long-running B franchise. But despite Mickey Rooney's eager antics, Charles Lamont's bullish direction and Paul Frees's brave attempt to keep up Francis's equine quipping, what little magic this always amiable, but never remarkable series might have generated passed with the departure of their predecessors. Feeling eerily like "Abbott and Costello Meets Scooby Doo", this bland blend of knockabout and thrills is only likely to slow pulse rates. DP

Mickey Rooney *David Prescott* • Virginia Welles *Lorna MacLeod* • James Flavin *Chief Martin* • Paul Cavanagh *Neil Frazer* • Mary Ellen Kay *Lorna Ann* • David Janssen *Lt Hopkins* • Paul Frees *Francis the Talking Mule* ■ *Dir* Charles Lamont • *Scr* Herbert Margolis, William Raynor, from characters created by David Stern

Francis in the Navy ★★ U

War comedy 1955 · US · BW · 80mins

Tired of being upstaged by a musing mule, Donald O'Connor bade bon voyage to Universal's B series after this amiable comedy of errors, in which he plays a bosun, as well as the hapless Peter Stirling, who finds himself all at sea when he tries to prevent Francis from being sold off as army surplus. This sixth entry also ended Chill Wills's and Arthur Lubin's association with the franchise. However, it marked the second screen appearance of a young contract player named Clint Eastwood. DP

Donald O'Connor *Lt Peter Stirling/Slicker Donovan* • Martha Hyer *Betsy Donovan* • Richard Erdman *Murph* • Jim Backus *Cmdr Hutch* • Clint Eastwood *Jonesy* • David Janssen *Lt Anders* • Martin Milner *Rick* • Chill Wills *Francis the Talking Mule* ■ *Dir* Arthur Lubin • *Scr* Devery Freeman, from characters created by David Stern

Francis Joins the WACS ★★ U

Comedy 1954 · US · BW · 94mins

Having been content to steal the *Francis* franchise by voicing the talking mule, Chill Wills opted to take a key supporting role in the fifth entry. He plays a general who is convinced that women should have only a token role in the US Army. However, Lynn Bari is determined to prove otherwise and receives unexpected assistance from one-time second lieutenant Donald O'Connor, who has been assigned to her unit following a bureaucratic bungle. ZaSu Pitts reprises the role she took in the series opener. DP

Donald O'Connor *Peter Stirling* • Mamie Van Doren *Col Bunky Hilstrom* • Lynn Bari *Maj Louise Simpson* • ZaSu Pitts *Lt Valerie Humpert* • Joan Shawlee *Sgt Kipp* • Chill Wills *General Kaye* • Chill Wills *Francis the Talking Mule* ■ *Dir* Arthur Lubin • *Scr* Devery Freeman, from a story by Herbert Baker, from a character created by David Stern

Francis of Assisi ★ U

Biographical drama
1961 · US · Colour · 105mins

This stilted biopic of the patron saint of animals has a woefully miscast Bradford Dillman as Francis – only Pat Boone or Frankie Avalon could have been worse. Even more surprising is that Michael Curtiz should have agreed to direct it. Those expecting cuddly creatures will be disappointed, as this focuses on the life of Francis the warrior who, like El Cid before him, sorts out rival Christians and Arabs while fighting for Sicily's liberation before going into retreat. AT

Bradford Dillman *Francis Bernardone* • Dolores Hart *Clare Scefi* • Stuart Whitman *Paolo* • Pedro Armendáriz *Sultan* ■ *Dir* Michael Curtiz • *Scr* Eugene Vale, James Forsyth, Jack Thomas, from the novel *The Joyful Beggar* by Louis De Wohl

Frank and Jesse ★★ 15

Western 1995 · US · Colour · 101mins

Writer/director Robert Boris assembled a willing young cast for what he intended to be a revisionist western. But, the life and crimes of Frank and Jesse James have been re-examined so many times that there is little left to say. Boris predictably gives Rob Lowe's Jesse a conscience and suggests the James, Younger and Ford brothers were victims of a society that betrayed them after the South's defeat in the Civil War. But, more interestingly, he also explores the corruption and brutality of the forces of law and order, respresented by William Atherton's egotistical detective. DP. Contains violence. DVD

Rob Lowe *Jesse James* • Bill Paxton *Frank James* • Randy Travis *Cole Younger* • William Atherton *Allan Pinkerton* • Todd Field *Bob Younger* • Alexis Arquette *Charlie Ford* • Dana Wheeler-Nicholson *Annie* • Maria Pitillo *Zee James* ■ *Dir/Scr* Robert Boris

Frank Lloyd Wright ★★★★

Documentary
1997 · US · Colour and BW · 146mins

With exhaustive chronicles of the Civil War, the Wild West and the history of baseball already to his credit, documentarist Ken Burns here turns his attention to one of the 20th century's most influential and controversial artists. Inspired by nature in his crusade against Victorian fussiness, architect Frank Lloyd Wright may have had his personal problems and his share of criticism (particularly in his later career). But he emerges from this meticulously assembled portrait (combining archive material and expert analysis) as a visionary (albeit a swaggering one) whose monument, the Guggenheim Museum in New York, speaks eloquently of his genius. DP

Edward Herrmann *Narrator* ■ *Dir* Ken Burns, Lynn Novick • *Scr* Godfrey C Ward

Frankenhooker ★★★ 18

Comedy horror 1990 · US · Colour · 80mins

Cult director Frank Henenlotter sews together one of his best lampoons with this madcap gore parody revealing his usual bad taste and warped sense of humour. Mad inventor James Lorinz accidentally chops up his girlfriend in a power lawnmower, saves her head and finds body parts to remake her from prostitutes addicted to the drug he's developed. Pushing cartoon violence to the limit, Henenlotter's trump card is Lorinz, who turns in a charismatic performance laden with wit and pathos. AJ DVD

James Lorinz *Jeffrey Franken* • Patty Mullen *Elizabeth* • Louise Lasser *Jeffrey's Mom* • Charlotte Helmkamp *Honey* • Joseph Gonzalez *Zorro* • Shirley Stoler *Spike* • Lia Chang *Crystal* ■ *Dir* Frank Henenlotter • *Scr* Frank Henenlotter, Robert Martin

Frankenstein ★★★★★ PG

Classic horror 1931 · US · BW · 68mins

Shocking in its day, and still a genuinely creepy experience, director James Whale's primitive yet enthralling interpretation of Mary Shelley's classic tale of man playing God is the most influential genre movie ever made. Its success kick-started the golden age of horror for Universal Studios and provided inspiration for scores of imitators and successors. Boris Karloff breathes miraculous life into his definitive monster portrayal: the most touching moment is the creature reaching up to grasp a ray of sunlight. A superb cast, imaginative set design and Whale's innovative direction using bizarre camera angles create a remarkably tense and melancholy atmosphere. Karloff returned as the Monster in *Bride of Frankenstein* (1935). AJ DVD

Colin Clive *Dr Frankenstein* • ? [Boris Karloff] *The Monster* • Mae Clarke *Elizabeth* • John Boles *Victor* • Edward Van Sloan *Dr Waldman* • Dwight Frye *Fritz, the dwarf* • Frederick Kerr *Baron* • Lionel Belmore *Burgomaster* • Michael Mark *Ludwig, peasant father* ■ *Dir* James Whale • *Scr* Garrett Fort, Francis Edwards Faragoh, John L Balderston, Robert Florey, from the novel by Mary Shelley, from the play by Peggy Webling • *Cinematographer* Arthur Edeson • *Art Director* Charles D Hall • *Make-up* Jack Pierce

Frankenstein and the Monster from Hell ★★★ 15

Horror 1973 · UK · Colour · 90mins

The sixth Hammer *Frankenstein* (not counting 1970's aberration *The Horror of Frankenstein*) is a stylish return to their 1950s' gothic roots, and is a fitting end to the series. Peter Cushing returned as the obsessed Baron Frankenstein, this time creating a new monster (Dave Prowse) from the lunatic inmates of Carlsbad's asylum for the criminally insane. Hammer protégé Shane Briant engagingly plays his willing disciple, while Madeline Smith stars as a mute girl in this efficiently horrifying exercise, packed with gruesome close-ups and laboratory black humour. AJ DVD

Peter Cushing *Baron Frankenstein* • Shane Briant *Dr Simon Helder* • Dave Prowse *Creature* • Madeline Smith *Sarah, the Angel* • Bernard Lee *Tarmut* • Norman Mitchell *Policeman* • Patrick Troughton *Body snatcher* ■ *Dir* Terence Fisher • *Scr* John Elder [Anthony Hinds]

Frankenstein Conquers the World ★★

Monster horror
1964 · Jpn/US · Colour · 87mins

One of the more inventive re-workings of the *Frankenstein* myth collapses into a typical Toho monster battle in *Godzilla* director Inoshiro Honda's daffy spectacular. A young kid eats the Hiroshima-infected heart of the Frankenstein monster and grows into a 30-foot tall mutated caveman, who eventually saves Japan's rebuilding programme from the rampaging dinosaur Baragon. Nick Adams is the friendly American scientist in a ridiculous but still fun addition to the Japanese monster hall of fame. AJ

Nick Adams *Dr James Bowen* • Tadao Takashima *Dr Yuzo Kawaji* • Kumi Mizuno *Dr Sueko Togami* ■ *Dir* Inoshiro Honda • *Scr* Kaoru Mabuchi, from a synopsis by Jerry Sohl, from a story by Reuben Bercovitch

Frankenstein Created Woman ★★★ 15

Horror 1966 · UK · Colour · 87mins

This sequel to 1964's *Evil of Frankenstein* is considered by Hammer aficionados to be the best Frankenstein made by the House of Horror. The good doctor experiments with soul transference in this offbeat entry, re-animating the corpse of young Susan Denberg. The ever-dependable Peter Cushing gives it the soul of her boyfriend, who was wrongly guillotined for murder. The chilling result is a vengeful creature luring his/her enemies to their death. Terence Fisher's neat balance of psychological horror and murky sexuality makes this a fine addition to the genre. The series continued with *Frankenstein Must Be Destroyed* (1969). AJ DVD

Peter Cushing *Baron Frankenstein* • Susan Denberg *Christina* • Thorley Walters *Dr Hertz* • Robert Morris *Hans* • Peter Blythe *Anton* • Barry Warren *Karl* • Derek Fowlds *Johann* • Alan MacNaughtan *Kleve* ■ *Dir* Terence Fisher • *Scr* John Elder [Anthony Hinds]

Frankenstein Meets the Wolf Man ★★★ PG

Horror 1943 · US · BW · 73mins

The fifth feature in Universal's series was the first time two celebrity monsters shared the screen. Picking up where both *The Wolf Man* (1941) and *The Ghost of Frankenstein* (1942) left off, this entertaining sequel has werewolf Lon Chaney Jr seeking out the dead Frankenstein's diary, containing the cure for his lycanthropy, and stumbling across the monster (Bela Lugosi in his only appearance as the creature) encased in ice. Not particularly horrific, director Roy William Neill's monster mish-mash is still charming fun because of the skilled acting, cheap thrills and trademark Universal back-lot atmosphere. AJ

Lon Chaney Jr *The Wolf Man/Lawrence Talbot* • Ilona Massey *Baroness Elsa Frankenstein* • Patric Knowles *Dr Mannering* • Lionel Atwill *Mayor* • Bela Lugosi *Monster* • Maria Ouspenskaya *Maleva* ■ *Dir* Roy William Neill • *Scr* Curt Siodmak

Frankenstein Must Be Destroyed ★★★ 18

Horror 1969 · UK · Colour · 96mins

The fifth of Hammer's Frankenstein series (that began with 1957's *The Curse of Frankenstein*) is graced by an incisive performance from Peter Cushing, up to his old tricks as the Baron performing brain transplants. Freddie Jones is astonishing as the anguished victim of the transplant, whose wife fails to recognise him and rejects him, prompting a revenge plan. The gothic gore is once more directed with spirited skill and economy by Terence Fisher (his fourth in the series). Ralph Bates took over from Cushing for 1970's disappointing *The Horror of Frankenstein*. AJ DVD

Peter Cushing *Baron Frankenstein* • Simon Ward *Dr Karl Holst* • Veronica Carlson *Anna Spengler* • Freddie Jones *Prof Richter* • Thorley Walters *Insp Frisch* ■ *Dir* Terence Fisher • *Scr* Bert Batt, from a story by Anthony Nelson Keys, Bert Batt

Frankenstein – 1970 ★

Horror 1958 · US · BW · 82mins

This hugely inept plummet into gothic fakery is significant only in the fact that for the first time in his career Boris Karloff played the Baron and not the creature. Karloff is the grandson of the deceased and disfigured (courtesy of Nazi torturers) Baron Frankenstein, who finds himself so strapped for cash to buy an atomic reactor with which to resuscitate his latest creation that he allows a television crew into the family castle for a touch of *Through the Keyhole* Transylvanian-style. A total waste of time. Howard W Koch directs as if in a coma. RS

Boris Karloff *Baron Victor von Frankenstein* • Tom Duggan *Mike Shaw* • Jana Lund *Carolyn Hayes* • Don "Red" Barry [Donald Barry] *Douglas Row* ■ *Dir* Howard W Koch • *Scr* Richard Landau, George Worthing Yates, from a story by Aubrey Schenck, Charles A Moses

Frankenstein 90 ★★

Horror satire 1984 · Fr · Colour · 100mins

Director Alain Jessua makes a right hash of this madcap updating of Mary Shelley's much-abused fable. The idea of casting Jean Rochefort's eccentric scientist as a cybernetics specialist is valid enough, but the heavy-handed mix of pastiche and innuendo never comes close to amusing. With the body of a robot and a human face, Eddy Mitchell's "monster" is supposed to be mischievously amoral. But neither his fixation with Frankenstein's fiancée, Fiona Gélin, nor Rochefort's passion for nubile construct Herma Vos even hints at salaciousness. DP. In French with English subtitles.

Jean Rochefort *Victor Frankenstein* • Eddy Mitchell *Frank* • Fiona Gélin *Elizabeth* • Herma Vos *Adelaide* • Ged Marlon *Inspector* • Serge Marquand *Commissioner* ■ *Dir* Alain Jessua • *Scr* Alain Jessua, Paul Gégauff, from the novel by Mary Shelley

Frankenstein: the True Story ★★★★

Horror 1973 · US · Colour · 122mins

Kenneth Branagh's 1994 version of the classic horror tale (*Mary Shelley's Frankenstein*) made much of its fidelity to the source novel, but this earlier version remains among the most faithful of the *Frankenstein* adaptations. The production is notable for the sympathy with which the monster is portrayed by Michael Sarrazin, minus the once obligatory nuts and bolts, and his relationship with his creator (Leonard Whiting) has a tragic resonance. The film is intelligently scripted by Christopher Isherwood and boasts a distinguished cast of supporting players. AJ

James Mason *Dr Polidori* • Leonard Whiting *Dr Victor Frankenstein* • David McCallum *Henry Clerval* • Jane Seymour (2) *Agatha/Prima* • Michael Sarrazin *The creature* • Nicola Pagett *Elizabeth Fanschawe* • Ralph Richardson *Mr Lacey* • John Gielgud *Chief Constable* • Tom Baker *Sea captain* ■ *Dir* Jack Smight • *Scr* Christopher Isherwood, Don Bachardy, from the novel by Mary Shelley

Frankenstein Unbound ★★★ 18

Science-fiction horror
1990 · US · Colour · 82mins

After nearly 20 years in retirement as a director Roger Corman returned to the job with this engagingly loopy rewriting of the Frankenstein myth. Based on the novel by Brian W Aldiss, this camp confection jumbles time travel, Mary Shelley's circle of friends, her monstrous fictional creation, dream sequences and an apocalyptic future for a mind-boggling baroque soap opera. More fun and far scarier than any other recent *Frankenstein* you might care to mention. AJ. Contains violence and swearing.

John Hurt *Dr Joseph Buchanan* • Raul Julia *Dr Victor Frankenstein* • Bridget Fonda *Mary Godwin Shelley* • Jason Patric *Lord Byron* • Michael Hutchence *Percy Shelley* • Nick Brimble *The Monster* ■ *Dir* Roger Corman • *Scr* Roger Corman, FX Feeney, from the novel by Brian W Aldiss

Frankie & Johnny ★★ U

Musical comedy drama
1966 · US · Colour · 86mins

This is Elvis Presley's film version of the old jazz/folk song standard. It's gaudy and bright, but, like most of Presley's films from this period, it has an air of having just been thrown together. The Mississippi riverboat setting is undeniably attractive, but it's simply inexcusable to use repeat footage of the title number in the finale reprise. Presley and Donna Douglas pair sweetly together, and the songs pass muster, but this is merely a pleasant time-filler. TS DVD

Elvis Presley *Johnny* • Donna Douglas *Frankie* • Nancy Kovack *Nelly Bly* • Sue Ane Langdon *Mitzi* • Harry Morgan *Cully* • Audrey Christie *Peg* ■ *Dir* Frederick De Cordova • *Scr* Alex Gottlieb, from a story by Nat Perrin

Frankie & Johnny ★★★★ 15

Romantic drama
1991 · US · Colour · 112mins

A moving and often very funny romantic drama, with Al Pacino and Michelle Pfeiffer as the short-order cook and the waitress who fall hesitantly in love. It does take a major suspension of the imagination to see this gorgeous duo as lonely hearts rejects, but they act their way out of the hole. Pfeiffer in particular shows what a fine actress she can be with a good script. What lifts this particular romantic tale above the dross is the realistic air of vulnerability and fear that characterises the halting affair. SH. Contains swearing. DVD

Michelle Pfeiffer *Frankie* • Al Pacino *Johnny* • Hector Elizondo *Nick* • Nathan Lane *Tim* • Jane Morris *Nedda* • Greg Lewis *Tino* • Al Fann *Luther* • Kate Nelligan *Cora* ■ *Dir* Garry Marshall • *Scr* Terrence McNally, from his play *Frankie and Johnny in the Clair de Lune*

Frankie Starlight ★★★ 15

Romantic comedy
1995 · US/Ire · Colour · 96mins

Is this offbeat drama, based on the reminiscences of a dwarf novelist, a charmer that slipped through the net or a trifling whimsy? Co-scripted by Chet Raymo from his novel, the film has its moments, as wartime refugee Anne Parillaud falls for Irish customs officer Gabriel Byrne and then Texan drifter Matt Dillon. There are also two splendid performances from Alan Pentony and Corban Walker as the young and adult Frankie, the son whose love of stars and fascination with his mother's amours result in a bestseller. It's all amiable enough, but promises more than it delivers. DP. Contains swearing and nudity

Anne Parillaud *Bernadette De Bois* • Matt Dillon *Terry Klout* • Gabriel Byrne *Jack Kelly* • Rudi Davies *Emma Kelly* • Georgina Cates *Young Emma* • Corban Walker *Frank Bois* ■ *Dir* Michael Lindsay-Hogg • *Scr* Chet Raymo, Ronan O'Leary, from the novel *The Dork of Cork* by Chet Raymo

Frank's Greatest Adventure ★★

Satire 1967 · US · Colour · 78mins

Shot in 1965, shown at Cannes in 1967 and shelved until 1969, this satire is the first solo feature by the director of *The Right Stuff* and *The Unbearable Lightness of Being*, Philip Kaufman. It was also the first screen appearance by Jon Voight, who plays a Mafia victim who dreams of coming back from the dead to wipe everyone out in comic-strip fashion. It's very much a product of its time, influenced by the French New Wave, and feels rather dated now. AT

Jon Voight *Frank/False Frank* • Monique Van Vooren *Plethora* • Joan Darling *Lois* • Severn Darden *Doctor/Claude* • Anthony Holland *Alfred* • Lou Gilbert *Boss* • Ben Carruthers *The Cat* ■ *Dir/Scr* Philip Kaufman

Frantic ★★★★ 15

Thriller 1988 · US · Colour · 114mins

Roman Polanski makes this account of doctor Harrison Ford looking for his missing wife in an antagonistic Paris deeply disturbing. When Ford's wife Betty Buckley disappears from their hotel suite, reality becomes nightmare and solid citizen Ford resorts to increasingly desperate measures to find her. Emmanuelle Seigner, as a punkish free spirit, is a major flaw, but as a whole the movie is a bad dream of surreal, often funny, conviction. It's a Hitchcockian idea, but Polanski embellishes it with his own baleful theme of the uneasy nature of human existence. TH. Contains swearing, brief nudity and drug use. DVD

Harrison Ford *Dr Richard Walker* • Emmanuelle Seigner *Michelle* • Betty Buckley *Sondra Walker* • John Mahoney *Williams* • Jimmy Ray Weeks [Jimmie Ray Weeks] *Shaap* • Yorgo Voyagis *Kidnapper* • David Huddleston *Peter* • Gérard Klein *Gaillard* • Jacques Ciron *Hotel manager* ■ *Dir* Roman Polanski • *Scr* Gérard Brach, Roman Polanski

Frantz Fanon: Black Skin White Mask ★★★ 12

Drama documentary
1996 · UK/Fr · Colour · 68mins

Isaac Julien's portrait of the author of the freedom's fighter's "bible", *The Wretched of the Earth*, is a skilful combination of archive footage, contemporary interviews and dramatic reconstructions. Compelling, if erring slightly towards the hagiographic, Julien's film traces Fanon's life from his youth on Martinique, through his experience of fighting for France in the Second World War, to his gradual politicisation as a psychiatrist in Algeria during its struggle for independence. The staged elements aren't very persuasive, however, and Colin Salmon's static performance isn't helped along by the pious dialogue. DP

Colin Salmon *Frantz Fanon* • Al Nedjari *Algerian patient* • John Wilson *French policeman* • Ana Ramalho *French woman* • Noirín Ní Dubhgaill *Fanon's companion* ■ *Dir* Isaac Julien • *Scr* Isaac Julien, Mark Nash

Frasier, the Sensuous Lion ★

Comedy 1973 · US · Colour · 97mins

Once upon a time there was a lion in a California safari park that became famous because he sired 37 cubs from a harem of seven lionesses. The real Frasier died in 1972 but such was his fame that the park's proprietors conceived this crackpot movie in which Frasier starts talking in the manner of Francis, the Talking Mule. Michael Callan plays the animal behaviourist who becomes Frasier's buddy and confidante, learning what makes him such a great sexual athlete. AT

Michael Callan *Marvin Feldman* • Katherine Justice *Allison Stewart* • Victor Jory *Frasier (voice only)* • Frank De Kova *The man* ■ *Dir* Pat Shields • *Scr* Jerry Kobrin, from a story by Sandy Dore

Fratelli e Sorelle ★★★

Comedy drama 1992 · It/US · Colour · 92mins

The work of director Pupi Avati is virtually unknown outside his native Italy yet he's one of their best talents. This wry and penetrating social drama is the tale of two Italian boys who are transplanted to the States when their mother leaves her cheating husband to stay with her sister in St Louis. Observing the different ways in which these strangers in a strange land cope with their new situation, Avati has produced a complex, well observed and richly detailed study of the family in all its extended forms. AJ. In Italian with English subtitles.

Franco Nero *Franco* • Paola Quattrini *Lea* • Anna Bonaiuto *Gloria* • Lino Capolicchio *Aldo* • Stefano Accorsi *Matteo* • Christopher Marsh *Steve* ■ *Dir/Scr* Pupi Avati

Fraternity Row ★★★ 15

Drama 1977 · US · Colour · 94mins

A fascinating insight into upper-echelon America in the mid-1950s, this low-budget drama is a laudable blend of raw talent and professional nous. Director Thomas J Tobin and writer/producer Charles Gray Allison were able to draw on Hollywood guidance to complete this troubling picture about fraternity rituals, performed and shot by undergraduates at the University of Southern California. Although veteran Cliff Robertson provided the narration, only Robert Emhardt had much acting experience. Scott Newman, Paul's son, died in a drink/drugs accident the following year. DP

Peter Fox *Rodger Carter* • Gregory Harrison *Zac Sterling* • Scott Newman *Chunk Cherry* • Nancy Morgan *Jennifer Harris* • Wendy Phillips *Betty Ann Martin* • Robert Emhardt *Brother Bob Abernathy* • Cliff Robertson *Narrator* ■ *Dir* Thomas J Tobin • *Scr* Charles Gary Allison

Fraternity Vacation ★ 15

Comedy 1985 · US · Colour · 89mins

Yet another cheap teen comedy attempting to hijack the success of *Animal House* and *Porky's*. This one features a young Tim Robbins, who today possibly wishes he was holding the negative in one hand and a flaming torch in the other. Beer, sex, beer, wet T-shirts and beer all feature fairly prominently in this slender tale of college delinquents pursuing girls. The best reason to avoid this movie are the songs by Bananarama. RS

Stephen Geoffreys *Wendell Tvedt* • Sheree J Wilson *Ashley Taylor* • Cameron Dye *Joe Gillespie* • Leigh McCloskey *Charles "Chas" Lawlor III* • Tim Robbins *Larry "Mother" Tucker* • Britt Ekland *Evette* ■ *Dir* James Frawley • *Scr* Lindsay Harrison

Frauds ★★ 15

Black comedy thriller
1992 · Aus · Colour · 89mins

This cartoonish farce gives Phil Collins a wacky, black film role, but in the end it has to go down as a missed opportunity. The pop star plays a mysterious insurance broker who begins to terrorise Hugo Weaving and Josephine Byrnes when they resort to a financial scam to get themselves out of a business mess. Collins is occasionally very creepy, but director Stephan Elliott backs off when he could have gone for the jugular. JF. Contains violence, swearing.

Phil Collins *Roland* • Hugo Weaving *Jonathan* • Josephine Byrnes *Beth* • Peter Mochrie *Michael Allen* • Helen O'Connor *Margaret* • Andrew McMahon *Young Matthew* • Rebel Russell *Mother* • Colleen Clifford *Mrs Waterson* ■ *Dir/Scr* Stephan Elliott

Fraulein Doktor ★★

Wartime spy drama
1968 · It/Yug · Colour · 100mins

This is a hopelessly melodramatic account of the exploits of a real-life double agent (previously filmed as *Mademoiselle Docteur* in 1936). Eschewing his trademark realism, Italian director Alberto Lattuada here depicts espionage as a sexily glamorous game rather than a perilous round of treachery and deceit. Suzy Kendall shines as she plots the death of Lord Kitchener and seeks the formula for a hideous poisonous gas, but the excitement is only sporadic. DP

Suzy Kendall *Fraulein Doktor* • Kenneth More *Colonel Foreman* • James Booth *Meyer* • Capucine *Dr Saforet* • Alexander Knox *General Peronne* ■ *Dir* Alberto Lattuada • *Scr* Duilio Coletti, Stanley Mann, H AL Craig, Vittoriano Petrilli, Alberto Lattuada, from a story by Vittoriano Petrilli

Freaked ★★★ 15

Comedy horror 1993 · US · Colour · 81mins

Alex Winter co-directs this idiotic "tour de farce" on warp-drive with Tom Stern, his partner on the MTV series *The Idiot Box*. Winter also plays the arrogant Hollywood celebrity and spokesperson for a toxic chemical being pawned off to the Third World as a fertiliser. On a South American promotional tour, his entourage meet crazy Freak Show owner Randy Quaid, who uses the product to turn Winter into a headlining half man/half scaly beast. Forget the insane story, just laugh out loud at the amiable absurdity, and unsubtle send-ups of everything from *The Twilight Zone* to *Hollywood Squares*. AJ DVD

Alex Winter *Ricky Coogin* • Megan Ward *Julie* • Michael Stoyanov *Ernie* • Keanu Reeves *The Dog Boy (uncredited)* • Randy Quaid *Elijah C Skuggs* • William Sadler *Dick Brian* • Mr T *Bearded Lady* • Brooke Shields *Skye Daley* ■ *Dir/Scr* Alex Winter, Tom Stern

Freaks ★★★★ 15

Horror 1932 · US · BW · 62mins

Still banned in some countries, and suppressed in others for decades, this unique classic from Tod Browning remains one of the most nightmarish yet compassionate horror movies ever made. Browning cleverly draws the viewer into an enclosed carnival society (featuring real circus anatomical oddities essentially playing themselves) with its attendant bonds, codes and rituals, and then chillingly shows what happens when a "normal" human – conniving trapeze artist Olga Baclanova – breaks them with a swindling scam. A deserved cult masterpiece, this tale of the macabre with its blood-freezing shock ending is incredible, disturbing and, once seen, never forgotten. AJ DVD

Wallace Ford *Phroso* • Leila Hyams *Venus* • Olga Baclanova *Cleopatra* • Rosco Ates [Roscoe Ates] *Roscoe* • Henry Victor *Hercules* • Harry Earles *Hans* • Daisy Earles *Frieda* • Rose Dione *Madame Tetrallini* • Daisy Hilton *Siamese Twin* • Violet Hilton *Siamese Twin* ■ *Dir* Tod Browning • *Scr* Willis Goldbeck, Leon Gordon, Edgar Allan Woolf, Al Boasberg, from the book *Spurs* by Clarence Aaron "Tod" Robbins • *Cinematographer* Merritt B Gerstad • *Art Director* Cedric Gibbons

Freaky Friday ★★★ U

Comedy 1976 · US · Colour · 94mins

One of the very early body-swap movies, this was a precursor to *Vice Versa* and the blockbuster *Big*. This one undeservedly sank without trace, although it contains an effervescent performance from Jodie Foster, who switches places with her mother for a day. It's one of those movies that starts at a brisk trot, lapses into walking pace and winds up misfiring through sheer lack of gags. However, it's well worth catching for the performances of Foster and Barbara Harris as the mum. SH DVD

Barbara Harris *Ellen Andrews* • Jodie Foster *Annabel Andrews* • John Astin *Bill Andrews* • Patsy Kelly *Mrs Schmauss* • Dick Van Patten *Harold Jennings* • Vicki Schreck *Virginia* • Sorrell Booke *Mr Dilk* ■ *Dir* Gary Nelson • *Scr* Mary Rodgers, from her novel

Freaky Friday ★★★ PG

Comedy 2003 · US · Colour · 92mins

In this update of Disney's 1976 comedy, Jamie Lee Curtis and Lindsay Lohan star as a widowed psychiatrist and her teenage daughter. Curtis is about to get married again, but Lohan objects.Then a fairy-godmother figure at a Chinese restaurant puts a spell on their fortune cookies, and the transformation is made. Although the plot takes a familiar course from then on, director Mark Waters keeps up the comic momentum with skill and the two leads are excellent. TH DVD

Jamie Lee Curtis *Tess Coleman* • Lindsay Lohan *Anna Coleman* • Mark Harmon *Ryan* • Harold Gould *Grandpa* • Chad Michael Murray *Jake* • Stephen Tobolowsky *Mr Bates* • Christina Vidal *Maddie* • Ryan Malgarini *Harry Coleman* • Rosalind Chao *Pei-Pei* ■ *Dir* Mark Waters • *Scr* Heather Hach, Leslie Dixon, from the novel by Mary Rodgers

Freddie as FRO7 ★★ U

Animated spoof adventure
1992 · UK · Colour · 90mins

Technically, this ill-advised foray into full-length feature animation can't be faulted: the visuals are sumptuous and a distinguished cast of British actors provide the voices. The story, however, which revolves around a James Bond-style superagent who also happens to be a frog, is just plain daft, and there is little of the knowing humour which makes the new features from Walt Disney popular with adults as well as kids. JF

Ben Kingsley *Freddie the Frog* • Jenny Agutter *Daffers* • John Sessions *Scotty* • Brian Blessed *El Supremo* • Nigel Hawthorne *Brigadier G* • Michael Hordern *King* • Phyllis Logan *Nessie* • Jonathan Pryce *Trilby* • Billie Whitelaw *Messina* ■ *Dir* Jon Acevski • *Scr* Jon Acevski, David Ashton

Freddy Got Fingered ★ 18

Comedy 2001 · US · Colour · 83mins

If your idea of good viewing is seeing an actor of Rip Torn's quality being deluged by elephant semen, then MTV maverick Tom Green's hideous directorial debut is what you've been waiting for. Plunging vulgarity to new depths, the humour is more bestial than lavatorial, and makes the Farrelly brothers seem like choirboys. What attempts to pass for a plot centres on Green's inability to move out from the family home after his bid to become a Hollywood animator fails. DP DVD

Tom Green *Gord Brody* • Rip Torn *Jim Brody* • Marisa Coughlan *Betty* • Eddie Kaye Thomas *Freddy Brody* • Julie Hagerty *Julie Brody* • Anthony Michael Hall *Mr Davidson* • Stephen Tobolowsky *Uncle Neil* • Drew Barrymore *Mr Davidson's secretary* ■ *Dir* Tom Green • *Scr* Tom Green, Derek Harvie

Freddy vs Jason ★★ 18

Horror 2003 · US · Colour · 93mins

Ronny Yu's half-hearted direction comes as the only real shock worth mentioning in this pointlessly gory and daft affair that plays ludicrous havoc with the myths of both the *Elm Street* and *Friday the 13th* horror icons. Because the Springwood folk have drugged potential Freddy (Robert Englund) victims with a dream suppressant, the razor-gloved bogeyman has been rendered impotent. Freddy then coaxes Jason Voorhees (Ken Kirzinger) into causing machete mayhem. Cheap, chill-free claptrap. AJ DVD

Robert Englund *Freddy Krueger* • Ken Kirzinger *Jason Voorhees* • Monica Keena *Lori Campbell* • Jason Ritter *Will* • Kelly Rowland *Kia* • Katharine Isabelle *Gibb* • Christopher George Marquette *Linderman* • Brendan Fletcher *Mark* ■ *Dir* Ronny Yu • *Scr* Damian Shannon, Mark Swift, from characters created by Wes Craven, Victor Miller

Freddy's Dead: the Final Nightmare ★★ 18

Horror 1991 · US · Colour · 88mins

This gimmick-laden sixth instalment about the child-molesting dream-stalker's exploits in nightmare land is a virtual rehash of *A Nightmare on Elm Street 3: Dream Warriors*, with an astonishingly lame 3-D climax tacked on. Roseanne (Barr), Johnny Depp (who starred in the original) and Alice Cooper make cameo appearances to little effect. The series concluded with *Wes Craven's New Nightmare* (1994), in which the director took his saga into another realm altogether. AJ DVD

Robert Englund *Freddy Krueger* • Lisa Zane *Maggie Burroughs* • Shon Greenblatt *John* • Lezlie Deane *Tracy* • Ricky Dean Logan *Carlos* • Breckin Meyer *Spencer* • Yaphet Kotto *Doc* ■ *Dir* Rachel Talalay • *Scr* Michael DeLuca, from a story by Rachel Talalay, from characters created by Wes Craven

Free and Easy ★★

Comedy 1930 · US · BW · 73mins

Buster Keaton's career wobbled with his first sound film and never recovered. His great days as a silent comedian in creative charge of his work were over. His grave voice suited his demeanour, but MGM put him in a musical comedy as the hick who escorts Anita Page's beauty contest winner to Hollywood. They see celebrities at a premiere and he runs through the studio, bursting in on films in production and giving glimpses of stars and directors at work. It has none of the clever construction of Keaton's earlier comedies and it's a young Robert Montgomery who ends up getting the girl. AE

Buster Keaton *Elmer Butts* • Anita Page *Elvira* • Trixie Friganza *Ma* • Robert Montgomery *Larry* • Fred Niblo *Director* • Edgar Dearing *Officer* • Gwen Lee • John Miljan • Lionel Barrymore • Cecil B DeMille ■ *Dir* Edward Sedgwick • *Scr* Richard Schayer, Al Boasberg, Paul Dickey

Free Enterprise ★★★ 15

Comedy 1998 · US · Colour · 109mins

You can't keep a good geek down according to this slickly written indie comedy about a couple of *Star Trek* obsessives. Wannabe film-makers Eric McCormack and Rafer Weigel are inseparable. That is until McCormack meets comic-book goddess Audie England and Weigel discovers his hero, William Shatner, has feet of clay. Weigel and McCormack are impressive as the slacker incarnations of Kirk and Spock, but the star is the sportingly self-mocking Shatner. DP DVD

Rafer Weigel *Robert* • Eric McCormack *Mark* • Audie England *Claire* • William Shatner *Bill* • Patrick Van Horn *Sean* ■ *Dir* Robert Meyer Burnett • *Scr* Mark A Altman, Robert Meyer Burnett

Free Money ★ 15

Comedy 1998 · Can · Colour · 89mins

This moronic comedy has Marlon Brando reaching a career-low as a religious-nut prison warden, joining a completely wasted cast. This unfunny shambles starts with the double wedding of Brando's identical twin daughters, and it's downhill from there. Attempts at quirkiness fall flat, and the nonsensical plot developments include the dumbest prison break you've ever seen. JC DVD

Marlon Brando *Sven the Swede* • Mira Sorvino *Agent Karen Polarski* • Charlie Sheen *Bud* • Donald Sutherland *Judge Rolf Rausenberg* • Thomas Haden Church *Larry* • David Arquette ■ *Dir* Yves Simoneau • *Scr* Anthony Peck, Joseph Brutsman

A Free Soul ★★★★

Drama 1931 · US · BW · 93mins

When San Francisco society girl Norma Shearer, brought up to defy convention by her adored and adoring lawyer father Lionel Barrymore, rejects perfect suitor Leslie Howard for a liaison with gangster Clark Gable, the lives of father and daughter are almost destroyed. MGM wheeled out the big guns and high style for this melodrama which, seen today, is both gripping and fascinating. Shearer picked up one of her several Oscar nominations, as did director Clarence Brown. The best actor award went to Barrymore, who makes a climactic 14-minute courtroom speech. Remade in 1953 as *The Girl Who Had Everything*, starring Elizabeth Taylor. RK

Norma Shearer *Jan Ashe* • Leslie Howard *Dwight Winthrop* • Lionel Barrymore *Stephen Ashe* • Clark Gable *Ace Wilfong* • James Gleason *Eddie* • Lucy Beaumont *Grandma Ashe* • Claire Whitney *Aunt Helen* ■ *Dir* Clarence Brown • *Scr* John Meehan, from the novel by Adela Rogers St John, from the play by Willard Mack

Free Willy ★★★ U

Wildlife adventure
1993 · US · Colour · 107mins

This strong children's picture about a boy and his whale knows exactly which strings to pull and when. Australian director Simon Wincer combines animatronic models with shots of Keiko, the real-life killer whale that plays Willy, with great skill. The action away from the aqua park is suffocated by political correctness, family-bonding scenes and hammed-up villainy, but it's pretty hard to resist once Keiko and Jason James Richter are on screen together. DP DVD

Jason James Richter *Jesse* • Lori Petty *Rae Lindley* • Jayne Atkinson *Annie Greenwood* • August Schellenberg *Randolph Johnson* • Michael Madsen *Glen Greenwood* ■ *Dir* Simon Wincer • *Scr* Keith A Walker, Corey Blechman

Free Willy 2: the Adventure Home ★★ U

Wildlife adventure
1995 · US · Colour · 93mins

After all the fuss that followed the revelation that the real Willy was being kept in less than adequate conditions, the producers of this sequel decided to take no chances and used mostly model whales. Unfortunately, they opted for a plastic replica plot, too, with Jason James Richter once more standing between the friendly orca and some unscrupulous adults, this time with sassy half-brother Francis Capra in tow. Full of sentiment. DP DVD

Jason James Richter *Jesse* • Francis Capra *Elvis* • Mary Kate Schellhardt *Nadine* • August Schellenberg *Randolph* • Michael Madsen *Glen* • M Emmet Walsh *Wilcox* ■ *Dir* Dwight Little [Dwight H Little] • *Scr* Karen Janszen, Corey Blechman, John Mattson, from characters created by Keith A Walker, Corey Blechman

Free Willy 3: the Rescue ★★★ U

Wildlife adventure
1997 · US · Colour · 81mins

Jason James Richter returns for this third instalment of the eco-friendly killer-whale saga. However the drama here centres on ten-year-old Vincent Berry, who's horrified to discover that his fisherman father (Patrick Kilpatrick) is an illegal whale-hunter. Director Sam Pillsbury taps into America's male hunter myth, making Kilpatrick's re-evaluation a real wrench from tradition rather than just a sentimental change of heart. The whales are the big attraction, but this is also a subtly argued message movie. DP DVD

Jason James Richter *Jesse* • August Schellenberg *Randolph* • Annie Corley *Drew* • Vincent Berry *Max* • Patrick Kilpatrick *Wesley* • Tasha Simms *Mary* ■ *Dir* Sam Pillsbury • *Scr* John Mattson, from characters created by Keith A Walker, Corey Blechman

Freebie and the Bean ★★★ 18

Action comedy 1974 · US · Colour · 107mins

James Caan and Alan Arkin star in an early variation on the buddy cops routine that is dominated by a clutter of car crashes as our heroes pursue big-time mobster Jack Kruschen. Hugely tasteless (there are a flurry of racist jokes from Caan about Arkin's chicano origins), this is a film where most of the characters are treated with contempt, but director Richard Rush puts so much energetic inventiveness into the turbulence you're almost convinced he doesn't mean it. TH. Contains violence and swearing.

Alan Arkin *Bean* • James Caan *Freebie* • Loretta Swit *Meyers's wife* • Jack Kruschen *Red Meyers* • Mike Kellin *Lt Rosen* • Linda Marsh *Freebie's girl* • Valerie Harper *Bean's wife* ■ *Dir* Richard Rush • *Scr* Robert Kaufman, from a story by Floyd Mutrux

Freedom Radio ★★ PG

Second World War drama
1940 · UK · BW · 89mins

Raymond Huntley, later a fine comic stooge, is the sole reason for watching this outdated and often unintentionally funny flag-waver. Here he plays a truly sinister Nazi, but the rest of the cast are simply dreadful as they spout platitudes in clipped accents that are totally unsuited to their middle-European characters. Clive Brook and Derek Farr are embarrassingly earnest as the heads of a pirate radio station, but topping them is Diana Wynyard's ludicrously naive collaborator. DP

Clive Brook *Dr Karl Roder* • Diana Wynyard *Irena Roder* • Raymond Huntley *Rabenau* • Derek Farr *Hans Glaser* • Joyce Howard *Elly* • H Marion-Crawford [Howard Marion-Crawford] *Kummer* • John Penrose *Otto* ■ *Dir* Anthony Asquith • *Scr* Anatole de Grunwald, Basil Woon, Jeffrey Dell, Louis Golding, Gordon Wellesley, Bridget Boland, Roland Pertwee, from the story by Wolfgang Wilhelm, George Campbell

Freedom Road ★★ PG

Historical drama
1979 · US · Colour · 186mins

Two years after starring in *The Greatest*, Muhammad Ali appeared in this sprawling saga, originally a mini-series, edited down for release outside the United States. Ali, who rejected his original name of Cassius Clay because it was a slave name, plays an ex-slave who becomes a delegate to a state convention charged with rewriting the constitution of South Carolina. It was directed by the Hungarian-born director Jan Kadar, who died shortly after the film was completed. AT

Muhammad Ali *Gideon Jackson* • Kris Kristofferson *Abner Lait* • Ron O'Neal *Francis Cardozo* • Edward Herrmann *Stephen Holms* • Barbara-O Jones [Barbara O Jones] *Rachel Jackson* • Alfre Woodard *Katie* ■ *Dir* Jan Kadar • *Scr* David Zelag Goodman, from a novel by Howard Fast

Freedom Song ★★★ 12

Political drama 2000 · US · Colour · 111mins

Set in a small town in Mississippi in 1961, Phil Alden Robinson's fictional TV drama demonstrates that not every African-American approved of the battle against desegregation. Again belying his *Lethal Weapon* image, Danny Glover gives another powerhouse performance as the father fearful that son Vicellous Reon Shannon's involvement with Vondie Curtis-Hall's suffrage campaign will cause more harm than good. Sincere. DP

Danny Glover *Will Walker* • Vondie Curtis-Hall *Daniel Wall* • Vicellous Reon Shannon *Owen Walker* • Loretta Devine *Evelyn Walker* • Michael Jai White *Coleman Vaughnes* ■ *Dir* Phil Alden Robinson • *Scr* Phil Alden Robinson, Stanley Weiser

Freefall ★★★ 18

Action adventure 1994 · US · Colour · 96mins

Eric Roberts and Jeff Fahey were two of the most reliable draws on video throughout the 1990s and this thriller catches them in good form. Set in Africa, Roberts gets the good guy role, coming to the assistance of snapper Pamela Gidley who is caught up in a complex international conspiracy. Fahey exudes villainy with his usual style, while John Irvin's gritty direction makes good use of the stunning locations. JF DVD

Eric Roberts *Grant Orion* • Jeff Fahey *Dex Dellum* • Pamela Gidley *Katy Mazur* • Ron Smerczak *John Horner* ■ *Dir* John Irvin • *Scr* David Zito, Les Weldon

Freefall: Flight 174 ★★ PG

Drama based on a true story
1995 · US · Colour · 93mins

This in-flight entertainment is one of TV moviedom's better efforts, helped by the fact that it's based on an incident that occurred in 1983. William Devane, Shelley Hack and Mariette Hartley are put through their panic-station paces as Flight 174 mysteriously runs out of fuel in midair and the tense search begins for a landing site. There's enough low-rent suspense and ham acting on offer to make this enjoyable. AJ DVD

William Devane *Captain Bob Pearson* • Shelley Hack *Lynn Brown* • Scott Hylands *Maurice Quintal* • Mariette Hartley *Beth Pearson* •

Nicholas Turturro *Al Williams* ■ *Dir* Jorge Montesi • *Scr* Lionel Chetwynd, from the book *Freefall* by William Hoffer, Marilyn Hoffer

Freejack ★★ 15

Science-fiction adventure
1992 · US · Colour · 105mins

Based on an imaginative and surprising novel, this opts instead for sci-fi cliché and obvious thrills as Emilio Estevez is plucked from near-death in a racing accident to house the brain of a future-age Anthony Hopkins. Mick Jagger – in his first big screen dramatic role since 1970's *Performance* and *Ned Kelly* – suitably interprets his devious mercenary as a cynical yobbo, but it's a sin not to give talent like Hopkins and Rene Russo meatier roles. JM. Contains swearing and violence. DVD

Emilio Estevez *Alex Furlong* • Rene Russo *Julie Redlund* • Mick Jagger *Vacendak* • Anthony Hopkins *McCandless* • Jonathan Banks *Michelette* • David Johansen *Brad* • Amanda Plummer *Nun* • Grand L Bush *Boone* ■ *Dir* Geoff Murphy • *Scr* Steven Pressfield, Ronald Shusett, Dan Gilroy, from a story by Steven Pressfield, Ronald Shusett, from the novel *Immortality Inc* by Robert Sheckley

Freeway ★★★★ 18

Satirical thriller 1996 · US · Colour · 97mins

This deeply twisted version of *Little Red Riding Hood* brought the exceptionally talented Reese Witherspoon to the attention of a wider audience. She plays a feisty young teenager from a dysfunctional family who sets off to find her grandmother, falling foul of psycho Bob Wolverton (Kiefer Sutherland) en route. Witherspoon is a revelation as the foul-mouthed teenage rebel, Sutherland is great as her nemesis, and there are enjoyable cameos from Amanda Plummer, Dan Hedaya and Brooke Shields. JF DVD

Kiefer Sutherland *Bob Wolverton* • Reese Witherspoon *Vanessa* • Brooke Shields *Mimi Wolverton* • Wolfgang Bodison *Detective Breer* • Dan Hedaya *Detective Wallace* • Amanda Plummer *Ramona* ■ *Dir/Scr* Matthew Bright

Freeze Frame ★★★ 15

Crime thriller 2003 · UK/Ire · Colour · 95mins

Funnyman Lee Evans sheds his comic skin in this satisfying slice of low-budget paranoia. He delivers a supremely creepy performance as a misfit who's so traumatised by a near murder conviction that he constantly videotapes himself in case he needs a future alibi. First-time writer/director John Simpson makes imaginative use of modern visual technology, interweaving many different formats into an absorbing and atmospheric whole. The result is a genuinely disturbing and disorientating experience, only let down by a second-rate supporting cast. SF. Contains violence and swearing. DVD

Lee Evans *Sean Veil* • Sean McGinley *Detective Inspector Emeric* • Ian McNeice *Saul Seger* • Colin Salmon *Mountjoy* • Rachael Stirling *Katie Carter* • Rachel O'Riordan *Mary Shaw* • Andrew Wilson *Covert cameraman* • Andrea Grimason *Susan Jasper* • Martin McSharry *Sam Jasper* ■ *Dir/Scr* John Simpson

Freezer ★★★★ 18

Horror 2000 · Jpn · Colour · 102mins

Although its cult reputation rests on the fact that a respectable woman keeps the victims of her vengeful killings in huge chest freezers in her apartment, Takashi Ishii's chiller proves much more intriguing on a psychological than a visceral level. Having attempted to rebuild her life following a rape, Harumi Inoue's pitiless dispatching of the three perpetrators is presented as an agonised struggle between her repugnance at her actions and the need to end her nightmare. Consequently, the deaths are shown in all their cruelty to reflect her pain and desperation, which makes them all the more disturbing. DP. In Japanese with English subtitles. DVD

Harumi Inoue *Chihiro* • Shingo Tsurumi *Kojima* • Kazuki Kitamura *Hirokawa* • Shunsuke Matsuoka *Nogami* • Naoto Takenaka *Baba* ■ *Dir/Scr* Takashi Ishii

French Cancan ★★★ PG

Musical drama 1955 · Fr · Colour · 99mins

Director Jean Renoir's return to France after 15 years and his reunion with fellow legend Jean Gabin was not the cinema event buffs would hope, but there is still much to treasure in this exuberant tribute to the Moulin Rouge. The story – Gabin sets out to turn laundress Françoise Arnoul into a star – would not have been out of place in a glitzy Hollywood musical, but Renoir lovingly brings the glamorous world of the celebrated cancan to glorious life. JF. In French with English subtitles.

Jean Gabin *Danglard* • Maria Felix *La Belle Abesse* • Françoise Arnoul *Nini* • Jean-Roger Caussimon *Baron Walter* • Gianni Esposito *Prince Alexandre* • Philippe Clay *Casimir* ■ *Dir* Jean Renoir • *Scr* Jean Renoir, from an idea by André-Paul Antoine

The French Connection ★★★★★ 18

Crime drama 1971 · US · Colour · 99mins

Based on a real-life drugs bust by New York narcotics cops, director William Friedkin brings a fluid, documentary realism to Ernest Tidyman's adaptation that makes it one of the most influential movies of a very fertile decade for American film. Gene Hackman made his name (and won an Oscar) as wild-card detective "Popeye" Doyle, chasing down Fernando Rey's suave French drugs overlord. This is the underside of New York and a distinctly non-glamorous portrait of police life, where Hackman and sidekick Roy Scheider sit for hours in cars watching doorways and eating fast food, and action, like the film's iconic car chase beneath an elevated train track, is clumsy, real and dangerous. AC. Contains violence, swearing, drug abuse and brief nudity. DVD

Gene Hackman *Jimmy "Popeye" Doyle* • Fernando Rey *Alain Charnier* • Roy Scheider *Buddy Russo* • Tony LoBianco *Sal Boca* • Marcel Bozzuffi *Pierre Nicoli* • Frederic de Pasquale *Devereaux* • Bill Hickman *Mulderig* ■ *Dir* William Friedkin • *Scr* Ernest Tidyman, from the novel by Robin Moore • *Cinematographer* Owen Roizman

French Connection II ★★★★ 18

Thriller 1975 · US · Colour · 114mins

John Frankenheimer's sequel to *The French Connection* may be less believable than its predecessor, but it's still a cracking thriller. Here, New York cop "Popeye" Doyle (Gene Hackman brilliantly reprising his Oscar-winning role from the original) blunders into the French operation to uncover heroin-tsar Fernando Rey's drugs ring. There's a disturbing sequence that details Hackman's withdrawal after being forcibly addicted, but after that it's revenge and violence all the way. TH. Contains violence, swearing and drug abuse. DVD

Gene Hackman *"Popeye" Doyle* • Fernando Rey *Alain Charnier* • Bernard Fresson *Barthélemy* • Jean-Pierre Castaldi *Raoul Diron* • Charles Millot *Miletto* • Cathleen Nesbitt *Old lady* • Pierre Collet *Old pro* ■ *Dir* John Frankenheimer • *Scr* Robert Dillon, Laurie Dillon, Alexander Jacobs, from a story by Laurie Dillon, Robert Dillon

French Dressing ★★★

Comedy 1964 · UK · BW · 100mins

Ken Russell passed up the chance to direct the Cliff Richard musical *Summer Holiday*, choosing to break into feature films with this charming story partly inspired by Jacques Tati's *Monsieur Hulot's Holiday*. A deck-chair attendant (James Booth) at the seaside resort of Gormleigh-on-Sea (Herne Bay in disguise) aims to brighten things up by organising a film festival with a Bardot-like film star (Marisa Mell). Despite a nice cast, it was panned by critics at the time, but now seems rather cherishable. AT

James Booth *Jim* • Roy Kinnear *Henry* • Marisa Mell *Francoise Fayol* • Alita Naughton *Judy* • Bryan Pringle *Mayor* • Robert Robinson • Norman Pitt *Westebourne Mayor* • Henry McCarthy *Bridgemouth Mayor* ■ *Dir* Ken Russell • *Scr* Peter Myers, Ronald Cass, Peter Brett, Johnny Speight (additional dialogue), from a story by Peter Myers, Ronald Cass

French Kiss ★★★ 15

Romantic comedy
1995 · US · Colour · 106mins

This is one of director Lawrence Kasdan's most insubstantial movies, but this amiably fluffy confection is still enjoyable. Meg Ryan, in her trademark ditzy mode, sets off for France to reclaim wandering fiancé Timothy Hutton only to find herself stuck with slobby French thief Kevin Kline. The latter's role was reported to have been created for Gérard Depardieu, but Kline acquits himself well as the Gallic rogue and the chemistry between him and Ryan is spot on. JF. Contains swearing DVD

Meg Ryan *Kate* • Kevin Kline *Luc* • Timothy Hutton *Charlie* • Jean Reno *Jean-Paul* • François Cluzet *Bob* • Susan Anbeh *Juliette* • Renee Humphrey *Lilly* ■ *Dir* Lawrence Kasdan • *Scr* Adam Brooks

The French Lieutenant's Woman ★★★★ 12

Romantic drama
1981 · UK · Colour · 123mins

Director Karel Reisz and screenwriter Harold Pinter here take on the near-impossible filming of John Fowles's complex novel. Two stories are told in parallel, one of an affair between a disgraced Victorian governess and an English gentleman, and the other the relationship between the two film actors portraying the Victorian couple. Jeremy Irons and Meryl Streep feature in the dual roles. Victorian morality seeps hauntingly into every frame of the main story, which is decked out in convincing period detail and hangs on two scorching performances from Irons and Streep. JM. Contains swearing, sex scenes and brief nudity. DVD

Meryl Streep *Sarah Woodruff/Anna* • Jeremy Irons *Charles Smithson/Mike* • Hilton McRae *Sam* • Leo McKern *Dr Grogan* • Emily Morgan *Mary* • Charlotte Mitchell *Mrs Tranter* • Lynsey Baxter *Ernestina Freeman* • Jean Faulds *Cook* ■ *Dir* Karel Reisz • *Scr* Harold Pinter, from the novel by John Fowles • *Cinematographer* Freddie Francis • *Music* Carl Davis

The French Line ★★ U

Musical comedy 1954 · US · Colour · 98mins

Notorious in its day for Jane Russell's censor-provoking costume – the one with the crafty gaps in it – this was originally shot in 3-D to best show off Russell's assets. It was eventually released flat, which is how this would-be comedy well and truly falls. The songs are lacklustre, the supporting cast is second rate and Russell, sadly, is past her prime. Seen today, the film does contain a quaint period charm, and watch closely for Marilyn (soon to become Kim) Novak's siren debut as a fashion model. TS

Jane Russell *Mary Carson* • Gilbert Roland *Pierre DuQueene* • Arthur Hunnicutt *"Waco" Mosby* • Mary McCarty *Annie Farrell* • Joyce MacKenzie *Myrtle Brown* ■ *Dir* Lloyd Bacon • *Scr* Mary Loos, Richard Sale, from a story by Matty Kemp, Isabel Dawn

A French Mistress ★★ PG

Comedy 1960 · UK · BW · 93mins

Roy Boulting was past his comic prime by the time he made this underwhelming boys' school comedy, produced, as ever, by twin brother John, and co-scripted by longtime partner Jeffrey Dell. All those familiar faces should at least have given the action a certain cosy appeal, but veterans such as Cecil Parker, James Robertson-Justice and Raymond Huntley are left high and dry by a script that is little more than a bumper collection of sniggering bike-shed jokes about sex and French women. DP

Cecil Parker *Headmaster* • James Robertson-Justice *Robert Martin* • Ian Bannen *Colin Crane* • Agnes Laurent *Madeleine Lafarge* • Raymond Huntley *Reverend Edwin Peake* • Irene Handl *Staff Sergeant Hodges* • Edith Sharpe *Matron* • Kenneth Griffith *Mr Meade* • Michael Crawford *Kent* ■ *Dir* Roy Boulting • *Scr* Roy Boulting, Jeffrey Dell, from the play by Robert Monro

French Postcards ★★ 15

Romantic comedy drama
1979 · W Ger/Fr/US · Colour · 90mins

This tasteful older woman romance fails to capture the excitement of teenage initiation, despite a knowing display of exotic eccentricity from Marie-France Pisier as the tutor at the Institute of French Studies in Paris, whose unconventional methods cast a spell over impressionable all-American Miles Chapin. Fellow exchange students Debra Winger and David Marshall Grant also complete their rites of passage. But while the City of Light exerts its usual magic, it also exposes the banality of the American Dream. DP

Miles Chapin *Joel* • Blanche Baker *Laura* • David Marshall Grant *Alex* • Valérie Quennessen *Toni* • Debra Winger *Melanie* • Mandy Patinkin *Sayyid* • Marie-France Pisier *Mme Tessier* • Jean Rochefort *M Tessier* ■ *Dir* Willard Huyck • *Scr* Willard Huyck, Gloria Katz

French without Tears ★★★

Romantic comedy
1939 · UK/US · BW · 88mins

Although director Anthony Asquith refused to "open up" plays for the screen, his understanding of the intimate relationship between camera, actors and dialogue made his films surprisingly fluent. The cast adds lustre to the simple story of young men at a French language school in the south of France, who fall for the charms of visiting flirt, Ellen Drew. This comedy is a perfect example of how a frothy, very British battle-of-the-sexes romp can work as a witty screen diversion. Interesting, too, that the editor of this entertaining bit of fluff was a young man called David Lean, who would go on to greater things. BB

Ray Milland *Alan Howard* • Ellen Drew *Diana Lake* • Janine Darcey *Jacqueline Maingot* • David Tree *Chris Neilan* • Roland Culver *Commander Bill Rogers* • Guy Middleton *Brian Curtis* • Kenneth Morgan *Kenneth Lake* ■ *Dir* Anthony Asquith • *Scr* Anatole de Grunwald, Ian Dalrymple, from the play by Terence Rattigan

Frenchie ★★

Western 1950 · US · Colour · 80mins

Joel McCrea and Shelley Winters, the leads in this tame reworking of *Destry Rides Again*, simply can't match the star wattage generated by their counterparts in the classic 1939 western. Winters, in the Marlene Dietrich role, is typically brassy as the boss of a New Orleans gambling den who heads west to find her father's killers. But while he embodies decency, McCrea has none of the vulnerability that made James Stewart's everyman so appealing. DP

Joel McCrea *Tom Banning* • Shelley Winters *Frenchie Fontaine* • Paul Kelly (1) *Pete Lambert* • Elsa Lanchester *Countess* • Marie Windsor *Diane* • John Russell *Lance Cole* • John Emery *Clyde Gorman* • Regis Toomey *Carter* ■ *Dir* Louis King • *Scr* Oscar Brodney

Frenchman's Creek ★★★

Period romantic adventure
1944 · US · Colour · 113mins

Following the Oscar-winning success of *Rebecca*, Hollywood snapped up Daphne du Maurier's tale of an aristocratic woman who leaves her husband, goes to Cornwall and falls for a French pirate. Mitchell Leisen's direction typically concentrates on the colour scheme, the sets and costumes – he was once an art director – while the story rolls along by itself. Joan Fontaine is ideally cast as the imperious woman in the throes of passion but she's handicapped by the dullest of leading men – Ralph Forbes as the spineless husband and Arturo De Cordova as the pirate. AT

Joan Fontaine *Lady Dona St Columb* • Arturo de Cordova *French Pirate* • Basil Rathbone *Lord Rockingham* • Nigel Bruce *Lord Godolphin* • Cecil Kellaway *William* • Ralph Forbes *Harry St Columb* ■ *Dir* Mitchell Leisen • *Scr* Talbot Jennings, from the novel by Daphne du Maurier • *Costume Designer* Raoul Pène du Bois

Frenzy ★★★★ 18

Thriller 1972 · UK · Colour · 111mins

Alfred Hitchcock's penultimate film saw him return to his British roots with this thriller about a necktie murderer causing havoc in London. Jon Finch plays the chief suspect but, typically, Hitchcock is more interested in black humour than a simple whodunnit. Lots of typical Hitchcockian touches are on show – a roving, restless camera; dark shots of fleeing footsteps; a shocking corpse when least expected. *Sleuth* author Anthony Shaffer wrote the screenplay and there's plenty of other local talent on display, including Alec McCowen and the excellent Billie Whitelaw. While some regard this as inferior fare, it remains an unsettling piece. SH. Contains violence, swearing and sexual references. DVD

Jon Finch *Richard Blaney* • Alec McCowen *Chief Inspector Oxford* • Barry Foster *Robert Rusk* • Barbara Leigh-Hunt *Brenda Blaney* • Anna Massey *Babs Milligan* • Vivien Merchant *Mrs Oxford* • Bernard Cribbins *Felix Forsythe* • Billie Whitelaw *Hetty Porter* • Rita Webb *Mrs Rusk* • Jean Marsh *Monica Barley* ■ *Dir* Alfred Hitchcock • *Scr* Anthony Shaffer, from the novel *Goodbye Piccadilly, Farewell Leicester Square* by Arthur LaBern • *Cinematographer* Gilbert Taylor

Frequency ★★★★ 15

Fantasy thriller 2000 · US · Colour · 113mins

Via an ancient ham radio set, Jim Caviezel is able to speak to his beloved fireman dad (Dennis Quaid) across 30 years of time, on the day before the latter is due to die in a warehouse blaze. Forewarned by Caviezel, Quaid escapes his fate, but his survival changes history: suddenly, Caviezel's mum (Elizabeth Mitchell) no longer exists! Combining a relationship yarn with a race-against-time bid to hunt down a killer, *Frequency* plays like a big-budget episode of *The Twilight Zone*. Paradoxes appear as the film gets increasingly complex, but Quaid and Caviezel give fine performances and director Gregory Hoblit's only serious misjudgement is a slushy finale. DA. Contains violence and swearing. DVD

Dennis Quaid *Frank Sullivan* • Jim Caviezel *John Sullivan* • André Braugher *Satch DeLeon* • Elizabeth Mitchell *Julia Sullivan* • Noah Emmerich *Gordo Hersch* • Shawn Doyle *Jack Shepard* ■ *Dir* Gregory Hoblit • *Scr* Toby Emmerich

Fresh ★★★★ 18

Drama 1994 · US · Colour · 108mins

The frequently explored subject of ghetto life and drugs is wonderfully enlivened here by Boaz Yakin's direction and Sean Nelson's quietly contained performance as the 12-year-old trying to extricate himself from his squalid upbringing. He is well backed up by Samuel L Jackson as the father who has failed his son in every respect but has taught him to play chess. The absence of moralising and macho posturing gives authenticity and poignancy to the film, which stands as a great example of what African-American cinema can achieve. TH

Sean Nelson *Fresh* • Giancarlo Esposito *Esteban* • Samuel L Jackson *Sam* • N'Bushe Wright *Nicole* • Ron Brice *Corky* • Jean LaMarre *Jake* • José Zuniga *Lt Perez* • Luis Lantigua *Chuckie* ■ *Dir/Scr* Boaz Yakin

Fresh Horses ★★ 15

Romantic drama 1988 · US · Colour · 98mins

Andrew McCarthy co-stars with Molly Ringwald in this doom-laden story of ill-matched lovers. McCarthy is a university student who has a good marriage in prospect until he meets Ringwald, at which point common sense deserts him. She turns out to be an underage bride from the wrong side of the tracks, whose husband Viggo Mortensen may be a murderer. Far too superficial to work, McCarthy is very bland and Ringwald too one-dimensional to pull this off. LH

Molly Ringwald *Jewel* • Andrew McCarthy *Matt Larkin* • Patti D'Arbanville *Jean McBaine* • Ben Stiller *Tipton* • Doug Hutchinson *Sproles* ■ *Dir* David Anspaugh • *Scr* Larry Ketron, from his play

The Freshman ★★★★★ U

Silent comedy 1925 · US · BW · 69mins

The bespectacled comic innocence of Harold Lloyd here takes a tumble that does him no harm at all, as the nerdish new college student who, via a series of accidents, beomes an all-star football player and so wins the hand of Jobyna Ralson. A classic of Lloyd's "Cinderfella" kind of humour – the poor boy who makes good – and there are some sly digs at the way an American educational institute values brawn instead of brain to raise funds. The final game is a knockout in more ways than one. TH

Harold Lloyd *Harold "Speedy" Lamb* • Jobyna Ralston *Peggy* • Brooks Benedict *College cad* • James Anderson (1) *Chester A "Chet" Trask* • Hazel Keener *College belle* • Joseph Harrington *College tailor* • Pat Harmon *The coach* • Charles Stevenson *Assistant coach* ■ *Dir* Fred C Newmeyer, Sam Taylor • *Scr* John Grey, Ted Wilde, Tim Whelan, Sam Taylor, Clyde Bruckman, Lex Neal, Jean Havez

The Freshman ★★★★ PG

Comedy drama 1990 · US · Colour · 98mins

Here's a chance to see a mellow Marlon Brando in his greatest comedy performance. It's a case of self-parody as he plays a godfather figure making film student Matthew Broderick an offer he can't refuse: a job as a delivery boy, carting around exotic animals including a giant lizard. Andrew Bergman's glorious spoof of Mafia ways spends too long satirising film-study pretension, but spins its screwball antics along at such a pace you can forgive it almost anything. TH. Contains swearing. DVD

Marlon Brando *Carmine Sabatini* • Matthew Broderick *Clark Kellogg* • Bruno Kirby *Victor Ray* • Penelope Ann Miller *Tina Sabatini* • Frank Whaley *Steve Bushak* • Jon Polito *Chuck Greenwald* • Paul Benedict *Arthur Fleeber* ■ *Dir/Scr* Andrew Bergman

Freshman Fall ★★ 12

Drama 1996 · US · Colour · 90mins

This date-rape TV drama adds nothing new to a powerful subject. Director Bethany Rooney sets up her freshman tale with every campus cliché she can find to ensure we're behind demure Candace Cameron Bure, even before she's assaulted at a seniors' party. The devious, sensationalist resolution turns what purports to be a serious study of the aftershock of a terrifying ordeal into a below-average revenge movie. DP DVD

Candace Cameron Bure [Candace Cameron] *Melissa Connell* • Mark-Paul Gosselaar *Scott Baker* • Jenna Von Oy *Jordan* • Nikki Cox *Kellie* • Bess Armstrong *Denise Connell* • Lawrence Pressman *Edward Connell* ■ *Dir* Bethany Rooney • *Scr* Kathleen Rowell

Freud ★★

Biographical drama 1962 · US · BW · 140mins

Montgomery Clift seems the wrong choice to play Sigmund Freud, the father of psychoanalysis, while John Huston's style as director is far too direct to depict Freud's intricate early years. The nervous collapse of a young woman (Susannah York) helped the young doctor formulate his theory that the sexual instinct was the basis of human personality, leading to the revelation that came to be known as the Oedipus Complex. Everyone works hard to convince, but the use of dream sequences seems a curious cop-out. TH

Montgomery Clift *Sigmund Freud* • Susannah York *Cecily Koertner* • Larry Parks *Dr Joseph Breuer* • Susan Kohner *Martha Freud* • Eric Portman *Dr Theodore Meynert* ■ *Dir* John Huston • *Scr* Charles Kaufman, Wolfgang Reinhardt, from a story by Charles Kaufman

Frida ★★★★ 15

Biographical drama
2002 · US · Colour · 117mins

The extraordinary life of Mexican painter Frida Kahlo is told in fierce style by director Julie Taymor, who cleverly fuses the vivid events of Kahlo's turbulent existence with the stark images of her uncompromising self-portraits. Salma Hayek gives a career-best performance as the bisexual bohemian Marxist, whose physical suffering infused her challenging work. Charting her many affairs but mainly her stormy marriage to womanising artist Diego Rivera (Alfred Molina), Taymor's visually inventive narrative is both a riveting history lesson and a celebration of the artistic revolution in which Frida participated. AJ. Contains swearing and nudity. DVD

Salma Hayek *Frida Kahlo* • Alfred Molina *Diego Rivera* • Geoffrey Rush *Leon Trotsky* • Ashley Judd *Tina Modotti* • Antonio Banderas *David Alfaro Siqueiros* • Edward Norton *Nelson Rockefeller* • Valeria Golino *Lupe Marin* • Saffron Burrows *Gracie* • Mia Maestro *Cristina Kahlo* • Roger Rees *Guillermo Kahlo* ■ *Dir* Julie Taymor • *Scr* Clancy Sigal, Diane Lake, Gregory Nava, Anna Thomas, from the biography *Frida: a Biography of Frida Kahlo* by Hayden Herrera

Friday ★★★ 15

Comedy 1995 · US · Colour · 87mins

Rapper Ice Cube and Chris Tucker (in one of his first major roles) navigate an ordinary day in the ghetto through a haze of dope in this less preachy and more laid-back view of the "boyz" from the 'hood. Their love of the latter sees them fall foul of gun-toting gangsters, while the unemployed pair also have to endure lectures from their relatives, jealous partners and the neighbourhood bully. Director F Gary Gray (*The Negotiator*), sidesteps some of the usual clichés of the genre to deliver an affectionate, fresh portrait of inner city life. *Next Friday* followed in 1999. JF DVD

Ice Cube *Craig* • Chris Tucker *Smokey* • Nia Long *Debbie* • Tiny "Zeus" Lister Jr [Tom "Tiny" Lister Jr] *Deebo* • John Witherspoon *Mr Jones* • Anna Maria Horsford *Mrs Jones* • Regina King *Dana* • Paula Jai Parker *Joi* ■ *Dir* F Gary Gray • *Scr* Ice Cube, DJ Pooh

Friday Foster ★★★ 18

Blaxploitation crime drama
1975 · US · Colour · 86mins

Pam Grier – star of *Jackie Brown* – is here seen in an early role as a black "superwoman". She plays a fearless magazine photographer (a character taken from a comic strip) who blunders into a St Valentine's Day-style massacre involving a black millionaire. Grier is joined by a terrific black cast: Yaphet Kotto (cop), Godfrey Cambridge (crook), Eartha Kitt (fashion designer), Scatman Crothers (minister). The villainous mastermind (Jim Backus) is white, though. TH

Pam Grier *Friday Foster* • Yaphet Kotto *Colt Hawkins* • Godfrey Cambridge *Ford Malotte* • Thalmus Rasulala *Blake Tarr* • Eartha Kitt *Madame Rena* • Jim Backus *Enos Griffith* • Scatman Crothers *Reverend Noble Franklin* ■ *Dir* Arthur Marks • *Scr* Orville H Hampton, Arthur Marks, from a story by Arthur Marks

F

Friday Night Lights ★★★★ 12A

Sports drama based on a true story
2004 · US · Colour · 117mins

Billy Bob Thornton delivers yet another robust but nuanced performance in this atypical American football movie that focuses not on the highs and lows of winning and losing, but on the intolerable pressure that is put on players barely old enough to shave. Based on a true story, it centres on the Permian Panthers, a high-school football team from the small Texas town of Odessa, a place warped by its obsession with the game and oblivious to the human cost of this fixation. On one level, this is an intense and exciting sports drama, shot in grainy documentary style but with quick-fire editing. But it's also intelligent and undercut with a powerful sadness. AS

Billy Bob Thornton *Coach Gary Gaines* • Derek Luke *Boobie Miles* • Jay Hernandez *Brian Chavez* • Lucas Black *Mike Winchell* • Garrett Hedlund *Don Billingsley* • Tim McGraw *Charles Billingsley* • Connie Britton *Sharon Gaines* • Lee Thompson Young *Chris Comer* • Lee Jackson *Ivory Christian* ■ *Dir* Peter Berg • *Scr* Peter Berg, David Aaron Cohen, from the non-fiction book *Friday Night Lights: a Town, a Team and a Dream* by HG Bissinger [Buzz Bissinger]

Friday the Thirteenth ★★★★ U

Drama 1933 · UK · BW · 86mins

After a bus crashes, the preceding day in the lives of six passengers unfolds, before revealing which ones survive. The formula goes at least as far back as Thornton Wilder's 1927 novel *The Bridge of San Luis Rey*, but it's an intriguing one that is given an entertaining workout here. The episodes are neatly tied together with an adroit mixture of comedy and drama, while the top-notch cast includes Jessie Matthews and co-writer Emlyn Williams as a cunningly insinuating villain. TV

Sonnie Hale *Alf, the conductor* • Cyril Smith *Fred, the driver* • Max Miller *Joe* • Alfred

Drayton *Detective* • Eliot Makeham *Henry Jackson* • Ursula Jeans *Eileen Jackson* • DA Clarke-Smith *Max* • Edmund Gwenn *Wakefield* • Mary Jerrold *Flora Wakefield* • Gordon Harker *Hamilton Briggs* • Emlyn Williams *Blake* • Frank Lawton *Frank Parsons* • Belle Chrystall *Mary Summers* • Robertson Hare *Mr Lightfoot* • Martita Hunt *Agnes Lightfoot* • Jessie Matthews *Millie Adams* • Ralph Richardson *Horace, the schoolmaster* ■ *Dir* Victor Saville • *Scr* GH Moresby-White, Emlyn Williams, from a story by Sidney Gilliat, GH Moresby-White

Friday the 13th ★★★ 18

Horror 1980 · US · Colour · 90mins

Essentially a cheap rural rip-off of John Carpenter's hugely influential *Halloween*, this mix of bloody horror and teenage terror from low-budget sleaze merchant Sean Cunningham blazed the trail for the stalk-and-slash vogue of the 1980s. A catalogue of gruesome slaughter follows the re-opening of Camp Crystal Lake, long closed after a brutal unsolved murder. There are plenty of gory scares, while the audience sympathises with the counsellors under attack from a mystery assailant. AJ DVD

Betsy Palmer *Mrs Voorhees* • Adrienne King *Alice* • Harry Crosby *Bill* • Laurie Bartram *Brenda* • Mark Nelson *Ned* • Jeannine Taylor *Marcie* • Robbi Morgan *Annie* • Kevin Bacon *Jack* • Ari Lehman *Jason Voorhees* ■ *Dir* Sean S Cunningham • *Scr* Victor Miller

F

Friday the 13th Part 2 ★★ 18

Horror 1981 · US · Colour · 83mins

The first sequel to the surprise horror hit is a virtual retread of the original, except that it introduces maniac icon Jason Voorhees (here played by Warrington Gillette) into the mayhem mix, eager to butcher another camp full of sex-starved counsellors. No real surprises, just plenty of murders, with graphic impaling being the favourite. Steve Miner directs by the numbers because, in this mean-spirited slasher, it's the splatter that matters, not the dead-end cast. AJ DVD

Amy Steel *Ginny* • John Furey *Paul Holt* • Adrienne King *Alice* • Kirsten Baker *Terry* • Stuart Charno *Ted* • Warrington Gillette *Jason Voorhees* • Walt Gorney *"Crazy Ralph"* ■ *Dir* Steve Miner • *Scr* Ron Kurz, from characters created by Victor Miller

Friday the 13th Part III ★★ 18

Horror 1982 · US · Colour · 91mins

Jason donned his famous hockey mask for the first time in director Steve Miner's formula rehash of slasher gold. This time Jason carves his gory way through a crew of dim-witted teenagers renting a house on the shores of his beloved Camp Crystal Lake. Originally shot in 3-D to disguise the creative bankruptcy, Miner's body count machine still fails to tap into the insecurities that made the original so potent. AJ DVD

Dana Kimmell *Chris* • Paul Kratka *Rick* • Tracie Savage *Debbie* • Jeffrey Rogers *Andy* • Catherine Parks *Vera* • Richard Brooker *Jason Voorhees* ■ *Dir* Steve Miner • *Scr* Martin Kitrosser, Carol Watson, from characters created by Victor Miller, Ron Kurz

Friday the 13th: the Final Chapter ★★ 18

Horror 1984 · US · Colour · 91mins

The plot is as negligible as ever, the sex-obsessed teenagers interchangeable and the grisly murders all twists on the old favourites in director Joseph Zito's take on the Camp Crystal Lake blueprint. Special make-up genius Tom Savini gives the body count an extra dimension of charnel house nausea as machete-wielding Jason goes on the rampage again. Incredibly, Zito manages to create tension prior to each shock demise, and he also provides a truly nightmarish denouement. AJ DVD

Crispin Glover *Jimmy* • Erich Anderson *Rob* • Judie Aronson *Samantha* • Peter Barton *Doug* • Kimberly Beck *Trish* • Corey Feldman *Tommy* ■ *Dir* Joseph Zito • *Scr* Barney Cohen, from a story by Bruce Hidemi Sakow, from characters created by Victor Miller, Ron Kurz, Martin Kitrosser, Carol Watson

Friday the 13th: a New Beginning ★★★ 18

Horror 1985 · US · Colour · 87mins

Has Jason returned from the dead? Or is there a copycat killer doing a good impersonation of the Camp Crystal Lake nemesis? The setting for the fifth instalment is a rural rehab centre where Tommy Jarvis (John Shepherd) is still haunted by the memory of the hockey-masked murderer. Director Danny Steinmann tries hard to breathe fresh life into the hackneyed proceedings with a tongue-in-cheek script and more characterisation than the series is usually noted for. Beginning and ending with stylish nightmares, this features less blood than usual. AJ DVD

Melanie Kinnaman *Pam* • John Shepherd *Tommy Jarvis* • Shavar Ross *Reggie* • Marco St John *Sheriff Cal Tucker* • Richard Young *Matt Peters* • Juliette Cummins *Robin* ■ *Dir* Danny Steinmann • *Scr* Martin Kitrosser, David Cohen, Danny Steinmann, from a story by Martin Kitrosser, David Cohen

Friday the 13th Part VI: Jason Lives ★★★ 15

Horror 1986 · US · Colour · 83mins

A witty parody of a James Bond credits sequence immediately sets the tone for director Tom McLoughlin's slick and exuberant Jason sequel. Cleverly mining the undercurrent of humour inherent in the gory series, McLoughlin makes sure Jason's roller-coaster tracks are well-oiled and run smoothly in this vivid and creepy instalment. When Tommy Jarvis (Thom Mathews) digs up his grave to prove Jason's really dead, a bolt of lightning hits the corpse and turns it into a zombie. Cue inventive deaths galore and textbook scares. AJ DVD

Thom Mathews *Tommy Jarvis* • Jennifer Cooke *Megan Garris* • David Kagen *Sheriff Garris* • Kerry Noonan *Paula* • Renee Jones *Sissy* • Tom Fridley *Cort* • CJ Graham *Jason Voorhees* ■ *Dir* Tom McLoughlin • *Scr* Tom McLoughlin, from characters created by Victor Miller

Friday the 13th Part VII: the New Blood ★ 18

Horror 1988 · US · Colour · 84mins

Victim hears noise. Stops. Turns. Turns back. Jason appears from nowhere holding a machete/axe/spike... The Jason formula hits rock bottom with this static, boring and threadbare episode, directed by B-movie make-up man John Carl Buechler. *New Blood* contains virtually no blood; the only new addition to the nihilism is a telekinetic girl who may be able to destroy Jason with her psychic powers. AJ DVD

Lar Park-Lincoln *Tina* • Kevin Blair [Kevin Spirtas] *Nick* • Terry Kiser *Dr Crews* • Susan Jennifer Sullivan *Melissa* • Heidi Kozak *Sandra* • Kane Hodder *Jason* • William Butler *Michael* • Staci Greason *Jane* ■ *Dir* John Carl Buechler • *Scr* Daryl Haney, Manuel Fidello

Friday the 13th Part VIII: Jason Takes Manhattan ★★★ 18

Horror 1989 · US · Colour · 96mins

Director Rob Hedden's stylish attack on the Jason franchise lifts the fear formula a cut and a slash above the average. The title is a misnomer: it takes ages for Jason to carve up the Big Apple. Having been revived by an underwater electrical cable, he stows aboard a pleasure cruiser taking Crystal Lake graduates to New York. It's fun seeing the hockey-masked murderer stalking rat-infested mean streets instead of leafy glades, but this crisply photographed scare-fest surprisingly doesn't milk the new location for extra chills. The series continued with *Jason Goes to Hell: the Final Friday* in 1993. AJ DVD

Jensen Daggett *Rennie Wickham* • Scott Reeves *Sean Robertson* • Peter Mark Richman *Charles McCulloch* • Barbara Bingham *Colleen Van Deusen* • Kane Hodder *Jason* ■ *Dir* Rob Hedden • *Scr* Rob Hedden, from characters created by Victor Miller

Fried Green Tomatoes at the Whistle Stop Cafe ★★★★ PG

Drama 1991 · US · Colour · 124mins

Jessica Tandy received an Oscar nomination for her portrayal of a feisty old-timer in the American south, telling tales about the bigotry she encountered during her youth in the 1930s. Kathy Bates is almost as good as Tandy, playing a modern-day housewife and frump in the dumps, who visits Tandy in a nursing home and finds inspiration in her memories of the past. Essentially a story about friendship between two pairs of women, then and now, this could be classified as an intelligent woman's picture, but this truly uplifting and gratifying movie can and should be enjoyed by all. PF. Contains some violence and swearing. DVD

Mary Stuart Masterson *Idgie Threadgoode* • Mary-Louise Parker *Ruth* • Kathy Bates *Evelyn Couch* • Jessica Tandy *Ninny Threadgoode* • Gailard Sartain *Ed Couch* • Stan Shaw *Big George* • Cicely Tyson *Sipsey* • Gary Basaraba *Grady* ■ *Dir* Jon Avnet • *Scr* Fannie Flagg, Carol Sobieski, from the novel by Fannie Flagg

Frieda ★★★ PG

Drama 1947 · UK · BW · 94mins

Although there were plenty of tales of brave wartime resistance, few film-makers ventured into the darker territory of commitment to Nazism. Basil Dearden's bold bid to understand collaboration and the need to forgive, lapses into stereotype and melodrama rather too quickly. Yet the story of RAF officer David Farrar who returns to Blighty with Mai Zetterling – the German girl who helped him when he was a prisoner of war– still touches a few raw nerves. DP

David Farrar *Robert Dawson* • Glynis Johns *Judy Dawson* • Mai Zetterling *Frieda Dawson* • Flora Robson *Nell Dawson* • Albert Lieven *Richard Mannsfeld* ■ *Dir* Basil Dearden • *Scr* Ronald Millar, Angus MacPhail, from the play by Ronald Millar

Friendly Enemies ★★ U

Second World War drama
1942 · US · BW · 95mins

The title refers to two Germans who have been living in the USA for 40 years when the country enters the Second World War. Charles Winninger plays the one sympathetic to his fatherland's cause and Charles Ruggles his friend who supports the USA. The two old pros get a few laughs, but their tiresome verbal battles take up too much screen time until Winninger sees the light and joins his friend to trap a spy. Director Allan Dwan can do little to compensate for the static nature of the piece. TV

Charles Winninger *Karl Pfeiffer* • Charlie Ruggles [Charles Ruggles] *Heinrich Block* • James Craig *William Pfeiffer* • Nancy Kelly *June Block* • Otto Kruger *Anton Miller* • Ilka Gruning [Ilka Grüning] *Mrs Pfeiffer* ■ *Dir* Allan Dwan • *Scr* Adelaide Heilbron, from the play by Samuel Shipman, Aaron Hoffman

Friendly Fire ★★★★

Drama based on a true story
1979 · US · Colour · 147mins

The American media is obsessed with conspiracy theories. So it should come as no surprise to learn that this TV movie, chronicling the real-life efforts of Peg Mullen to compel Washington to reveal the circumstances of her son's death in Vietnam, won four Emmys, including best drama. Although both leads took acting awards, Carol Burnett's unswerving commitment is less subtly shaded than Ned Beatty's performance as her husband, torn between patriotism and the truth. With fine support from Sam Waterston and Timothy Hutton, this is a disturbing insight into both war and the state's ability to distort facts. DP

Carol Burnett *Peg Mullen* • Ned Beatty *Gene Mullen* • Sam Waterston *CDB Bryan* • Dennis Erdman *Sgt Michael Mullen* • Sherry Hursey *Mary Mullen* • Timothy Hutton *John Mullen* • Fanny Spiess *Pat Mullen* ■ *Dir* David Greene • *Scr* Fay Kanin, from the novel by CDB Bryan

Friendly Persuasion ★★★★ U

Period drama 1956 · US · Colour · 137mins

Gary Cooper is in fine form in this marvellously humane study of an Indiana Quaker family during the American Civil War. Director William Wyler's pacing is a little slow, with the story taking time to unravel, but the film has great charm and there are impressive performances from Dorothy McGuire as Cooper's wife and a young Anthony Perkins as the son with whom he clashes. The movie also boasts a superb score from Dmitri Tiomkin, plus ravishing location colour photography from Ellsworth Fredericks. It rightly received six Oscar nominations, including one for its blacklisted screenwriter, Michael Wilson. TS

Gary Cooper *Jess Birdwell* • Dorothy McGuire *Eliza Birdwell* • Marjorie Main *Widow Hudspeth* • Anthony Perkins *Josh Birdwell* • Richard Eyer *Little Jess* • Robert Middleton *Sam Jordan* • Phyllis Love *Mattie Birdwell* ■ *Dir* William Wyler • *Scr* Michael Wilson (uncredited), from the novel by Jessamyn West • *Cinematographer* Ellsworth Fredericks • *Music* Dmitri Tiomkin

Friends ★ 15

Drama 1971 · UK · Colour · 96mins

This is one of those innocent teenage movies where sweet fumbling results in pregnancy puzzlement. Set around a deserted beach in France, there's a lot of soft focus, numerous log-fires, connubial bliss by the cartload and an Elton John soundtrack. Both sets of parents pitch up to administer smacks all round, but not before the audience has been left feeling rather ill. An equally dire sequel, *Paul and Michelle*, followed. SH

Sean Bury *Paul Harrison* • Anicée Alvina *Michelle LaTour* • Ronald Lewis *Harrison* • Tony Robins *Mrs Gardner* ■ *Dir* Lewis Gilbert • *Scr* Jack Russell, Vernon Harris, from a story by Lewis Gilbert

Friends ★★★ 15

Drama 1993 · UK/Fr · Colour · 104mins

The versatile Kerry Fox stars as one of three friends who meet at university in South Africa. Fox is from a rich area of Johannesburg, while Michele Burgers is a poor Afrikaner and Dambisa Kente is a Zulu. This is one of those dramas in which important political and social issues are used as a background to the central theme of friendship. Here that friendship is severely tested when Fox's character plants a bomb as part of her anti-apartheid activities. Director

Elaine Proctor's debut feature is strong on setting and politics but the characters unfortunately lack the depth of their surroundings. JB

Kerry Fox *Sophie* • Dambisa Kente *Thoko* • Michele Burgers *Aninka* • Marius Weyers *Johan* • Tertius Meintjes *Jeremy* • Dolly Rathebe *Innocentia* • Wilma Stockenstrom *Iris* ■ *Dir/Scr* Elaine Proctor

Friends and Lovers ★★

Romantic drama 1931 · US · BW · 66mins

Adolphe Menjou and Laurence Olivier are British officers in India, rivals for the affections of *femme fatale* Lili Damita, whose scheming husband, Erich von Stroheim, isn't averse to a spot of blackmail. This risible melodrama has only its intriguing cast going for it. Interesting to see the 24-year-old Olivier, in one of his first Hollywood films and the always-hypnotic von Stroheim. Director Victor Schertzinger was co-credited with Max Steiner for the score. RB

Adolphe Menjou *Captain Roberts* • Lili Damita *Alva Sangrito* • Laurence Olivier *Lieutenant Nichols* • Erich von Stroheim *Victor Sangrito* • Hugh Herbert *McNellis* • Frederick Kerr *General Armstrong* ■ *Dir* Victor Schertzinger • *Scr* Wallace Smith, Jane Murfin, from the novel *Le Sphinx A Parlé* by Maurice De Kobra

Friends for Life ★★★ U

Drama 1955 · It · Colour · 90mins

Italian cinema has been blessed with several inspired performances by child actors, and Geronimo Meynier and Andrea Scire excel in this sensitive study of childhood friendship, although your response will very much depend on which version you see (unusually, the US ending is the more downbeat). However, Franco Rossi's deft direction ensures that Meynier's betrayal of Scire's motherless diplomat's son lingers in the mind, no matter what the denouement at Rome airport. Charmingly scored by Nino Rota, this is touching and authentic. DP. In Italian with English subtitles.

Geronimo Meynier *Mario* • Andrea Scire *Franco* • Luigi Tosi *Mario's father* • Vera Carmi *Mario's mother* • Carlo Tamberlani *Franco's father* • Paolo Ferrara *Professor Martenelli* • Marcella Rovena *English professor* ■ *Dir* Franco Rossi • *Scr* Ottavio Alessi, Leo Benvenuti, Piero De Bernardi, Gian-Domenico Giagni, Franco Rossi, Ugo Guerra

The Friends of Eddie Coyle ★★★★

Crime drama 1973 · US · Colour · 102mins

Robert Mitchum plays an ageing small-time gangster and cynical police informer who is relentlessly pursued by the mobsters he's betrayed. In a quality cast, Peter Boyle stands out as the hitman who's given the job of eliminating Mitchum. Peter Yates, the British director who forged his Hollywood reputation with the incredible car chase in *Bullitt*, gives this crime drama a more subtle power, turning the story into a fable about urban violence. TH. Contains violence and swearing.

Robert Mitchum *Eddie Coyle* • Peter Boyle *Dillon* • Richard Jordan *Dave Foley* • Steven Keats *Jackie* • Alex Rocco *Scalise* • Joe Santos *Artie Van* • Mitchell Ryan *Waters* ■ *Dir* Peter Yates • *Scr* Paul Monash, from the novel by George V Higgins

Fright ★★ 18

Thriller 1971 · UK · Colour · 83mins

Employing mental illness as fodder for horror movies, however unsettling, can produce masterpieces like *Psycho* and *Repulsion*. But exploitation is all too evident in this unpleasant tale of a young baby-sitter terrorised by an escaped lunatic. Ian Bannen jumps through hoops in an effort to make his role convincing but the formulaic direction reduces him to just another anonymous nutter. As the terrified heroine, Susan George alternates between pouting and screaming. RS

Susan George *Amanda* • Honor Blackman *Helen* • Ian Bannen *Brian* • John Gregson *Dr Cordell* • George Cole *Jim* • Dennis Waterman *Chris* • Tara Collinson *Tara* ■ *Dir* Peter Collinson • *Scr* Tudor Gates

Fright Night ★★★★ 18

Comedy horror 1985 · US · Colour · 102mins

Hugely entertaining horror spoof in which teenage B-movie buff William Ragsdale becomes convinced that new neighbour Chris Sarandon is a vampire responsible for a spate of brutal killings. Only when best pal Stephen Geoffreys has become Sarandon's slave and girlfriend Amanda Bearse has also fallen under his spell, does Ragsdale succeed in enlisting the help of "fearless" TV vampire hunter Roddy McDowall to end his reign of terror. Neatly parodying Hitchcock and John Hughes movies, writer/director Tom Holland litters his rattling story with as many laughs as jolts. DP. Contains violence and swearing. DVD

Chris Sarandon *Jerry Dandridge* • William Ragsdale *Charley Brewster* • Amanda Bearse *Amy Peterson* • Roddy McDowall *Peter Vincent* • Stephen Geoffreys *Evil Ed* • Jonathan Stark *Billy Cole* • Dorothy Fielding *Judy Brewster* ■ *Dir/Scr* Tom Holland

Fright Night Part 2 ★★ 18

Comedy horror 1988 · US · Colour · 99mins

The original *Fright Night* breathed a bit of knowing humour into the vampire genre, but this is an uninspired retread from horror sequel specialist Tommy Lee Wallace, also responsible for the dire *Halloween 3*. William Ragsdale returns as student Charley Brewster, who uncovers another coven of vampires when he falls for sexy Julie Carmen. Roddy McDowall also reprises his role as fearful vampire slayer Peter Vincent, but he can't breathe life into the worn-out script or Wallace's shapeless direction. JF

Roddy McDowall *Peter Vincent* • William Ragsdale *Charley Brewster* • Julie Carmen *Regine* • Traci Lin [Traci Lind] *Alex* • Jonathan Gries *Louie* ■ *Dir* Tommy Lee Wallace • *Scr* Tommy Lee Wallace, Tim Metcalfe, Miguel Tejada-Flores, from the characters created by Tom Holland

The Frightened City ★★ PG

Crime drama 1961 · UK · BW · 93mins

Limping along years after Hollywood's postwar exterior-location thrillers such as *The Naked City*, this British attempt at the genre just about manages to hold the interest. The story is about London gangsters falling out over a protection racket, and features a young Sean Connery (when he had hair) and a pre-*Pink Panther* Herbert Lom at his most seedily sinister. TH

Herbert Lom *Waldo Zhernikov* • John Gregson *Detective Inspector Sayers* • Sean Connery *Paddy Damion* • Alfred Marks *Harry Foulcher* ■ *Dir* John Lemont • *Scr* Leigh Vance, from a story by Leigh Vance, John Lemont

The Frightened Man ★★

Crime drama 1952 · UK · BW · 70mins

This is a dreary little quota quickie which draws on all the stock situations one associates with British B-thrillers. Director John Gilling makes solid use of the down-at-heel locations, but he fails to inject any suspense into the story (which he wrote) of a botched jewel robbery. Given little support by the rest of the cast, Dermot Walsh tries hard as the junk dealer's son who's thrown out of university and drawn into a life of crime. DP

Dermot Walsh *Julius Roselli* • Barbara Murray *Amanda* • Charles Victor *Mr Roselli* • John Blythe *Maxie* • Michael Ward *Cornelius* • Thora Hird *Vera* ■ *Dir/Scr* John Gilling

The Frighteners ★★★★ 15

Supernatural comedy thriller
1996 · NZ/US · Colour · 105mins

Peter Jackson explores the shockingly unhealthy paranormal bond between two lovers with record-breaking murder in mind. Hitting exactly the right balance between black comedy and jet-black chills, this cross between *Casper* and *The Silence of the Lambs* is another ghoulish masterpiece from the Kiwi eccentric, showcasing a dazzling array of computer-generated ghosts and blood-freezing poltergeist activity. Michael J Fox is ingeniously cast against type as a pseudo psychic dealing with all the nasty hereafter horror in a merrily menacing spectre spectacular. AJ DVD

Michael J Fox *Frank Bannister* • Trini Alvarado *Lucy Lynskey* • Peter Dobson *Ray Lynskey* • John Astin *The Judge* • Jeffrey Combs *Milton Dammers* • Dee Wallace Stone *Patricia Bradley* ■ *Dir* Peter Jackson • *Scr* Fran Walsh, Peter Jackson

Frightmare ★★★ 18

Horror 1974 · UK · Colour · 82mins

Reviled by critics, loved by gore-hounds, British exploitation director Pete Walker's Home Counties version of *The Texas Chain Saw Massacre* is a brutally effective shocker for all its cheap nastiness and graphic bloodletting. Walker regular Sheila Keith craves human flesh and her husband, Rupert Davies, looks on impotently as she pitchforks, axes and power drills the brains out of the local farming community lured to her cannibal domain by Tarot card readings. Morally twisted in Walker's signature way, this bleak vision of the triumph of evil over good is grisly, chilling and intense. AJ DVD

Rupert Davies *Edmund* • Sheila Keith *Dorothy* • Deborah Fairfax *Jackie* • Paul Greenwood *Graham* • Kim Butcher *Debbie* ■ *Dir* Pete Walker • *Scr* David McGillivray, from a story by Peter Walker (1)

Frightmare ★★ 18

Horror 1981 · US · Colour · 82mins

Horror movie stalwart Ferdy Mayne never quite hit the Hammer heights of Christopher Lee, but he's well cast here as an old horror movie icon, whose body is kidnapped by members of a horror film society. When his widow holds a séance the actor's reanimated corpse picks off the kids one by one in *Friday the 13th* style. An uneasy blend of homage, laughs and standard teens-in-jeopardy bloodletting. RS DVD

Ferdinand Mayne [Ferdy Mayne] *Conrad* • Luca Bercovici *Saint* • Nita Talbot *Mrs Rohmer* • Leon Askin *Wolfgang* • Jennifer Starrett *Meg* • Barbara Pilavin *Etta* • Carlene Olson *Eve* ■ *Dir/Scr* Norman Thaddeus Vane

The Fringe Dwellers ★★★ PG

Drama 1985 · Aus · Colour · 97mins

Good intentions abound in this story of a teenage girl who is determined to rouse her idle father into action so that they can move into a new housing development. But the characterisations are too broad, with nearly all the whites being loathsome and the Aborigines being cheerful in their poverty. However, Kristina Nehm gives a striking performance as the ambitious Trilby, with Ernie Dingo impressive as her shiftless lover, in this story of middle-class snobbery and Aboriginal exclusion. DP

Kristina Nehm *Trilby Comeaway* • Justine Saunders *Mollie Comeaway* • Bob Maza *Joe Comeaway* • Kylie Belling *Noonah Comewaway* • Denis Walker *Bartie Comeaway* ■ *Dir* Bruce Beresford • *Scr* Bruce Beresford, Rhoisin Beresford, from the novel by Nene Gare

Frisco Kid ★★

Adventure 1935 · US · BW · 77mins

James Cagney sports curly hair and wing collars in this late 19th century tale of the notorious Barbary Coast in San Francisco. The story of a young sailor's rise to prominence in a corrupt world is routine, with the heroine a crusading newspaper owner fighting to clean up the city. Even with the fast cutting we expect from Warner Bros, and a brief running time, the tale still flags and it's the dynamic Cagney who keeps it afloat. TV

James Cagney *Bat Morgan* • Margaret Lindsay *Jean Barrat* • Ricardo Cortez *Paul Morra* • Lili Damita *Bella Morra* • Donald Woods *Charles Ford* • Barton MacLane *Spider Burke* • George E Stone *Solly* ■ *Dir* Lloyd Bacon • *Scr* Warren Duff, Seton I Miller

The Frisco Kid ★★ PG

Comedy western
1979 · US · Colour · 113mins

A comedy drama that isn't as comic as it thinks it is, nor as dramatic as it should be. Gene Wilder stars as a novice rabbi sent to San Francisco and befriended by cowboy Harrison Ford on the way. There are some laughs to be had in the gaffes, but director Robert Aldrich inserts some violent action sequences into the episodic plot that jar with what should have been a much gentler affair. TH

Gene Wilder *Avram* • Harrison Ford *Tommy* • Ramon Bieri *Mr Jones* • Val Bisoglio *Chief Gray Cloud* • George DiCenzo *Darryl Diggs* • Leo Fuchs *Chief Rabbi* • Penny Peyser *Rosalie* • William Smith *Matt Diggs* ■ *Dir* Robert Aldrich • *Scr* Michael Elias, Frank Shaw

Frisk ★★

Erotic thriller 1995 · US · Colour · 88mins

Director Todd Verow's explicit shocker explores a gay man's increasingly baroque fantasies of sex and murder after he picks up a willing masochist. Intended as a serious look at the differing attitudes society has towards pain and pleasure, Verow's matter-of-fact approach renders the startling issues he tackles dull instead of riveting, while using such extreme imagery quickly becomes exploitation rather than argument. AJ. Contains swearing, sex and violence.

Michael Gunther *Dennis* • Raoul O'Connell *Kevin* • Jaie Laplante *Julian* • Mark Ewert *Young Dennis* • James Lyons *Gypsy Pete* • Dustin Schell *Snuff photographer* ■ *Dir* Todd Verow • *Scr* Todd Verow, George LaVoo, Jim Dwyer, from the novel by Dennis Cooper

Fritz the Cat ★★★ 18

Animated erotic comedy
1972 · US · Colour · 75mins

Radical and largely successful attempt on the part of director Ralph Bakshi to translate the underground comic character invented by Robert Crumb to the big screen. Fritz is an innocent at large at the fag end of the hippy wave. He rapidly discovers the joys of sex and student politics, before bumping painfully into various downsides of the counterculture like hard drugs and biker gangs. Quite shocking at the time, this remains a fun period artefact. Followed in 1974 by *Nine Lives of Fritz the Cat*. JF DVD

Skip Hinnant *Fritz the Cat* • Rosetta LeNoire • John McCurry • Judy Engles ■ *Dir* Ralph Bakshi • *Scr* Ralph Bakshi, from the character created by Robert Crumb

F

Frog Dreaming ★★★

Fantasy adventure
1985 · Aus · Colour · 93mins

In spite of a troubled shoot, this is an intriguing blend of childhood imagination and local mythology. Henry Thomas plays the gadget-obsessed American orphan who becomes fascinated with the legend of a fire-breathing spirit who supposedly inhabits an unmapped lake near his Australian guardian's bush home. Without any of the cloying sentimentality that blights so many Hollywood rites-of-passage pictures, this is far-fetched but enjoyable. DP

Henry Thomas *Cody Walpole* • Tony Barry *Gaza* • Rachel Friend *Wendy* • Tamsin West *Jane* • John Ewart *Sergeant Ricketts* • Dennis Miller *Mr Cannon* ■ *Dir* Brian Trenchard-Smith • *Scr* Everett DeRoche

F

The Frog Prince ★★★ 15

Romantic comedy
1984 · UK · Colour · 86mins

This charming tale of cross-cultural courtship is set in the pre-Swinging Sixties. Cartoonist Posy Simmonds's semi-autobiographical screenplay may indulge in a little cheap caricature where both the plainspeaking and bohemian French folk are concerned, but it, nevertheless, captures the hesitancy and naive emotionalism of first love with insight and affection. Director Brian Gilbert turns Paris into a key character, rather than just the beautiful backdrop to mousey exchange student Jane Snowden's relationship with the dashing Alexandre Sterling. DP

Jane Snowden *Jenny* • Alexandre Sterling *Jean-Philippe* • Jacqueline Doyen *Mme Peroche* • Raoul Delfosse *Monsieur Peroche* • Jeanne Herviale *Mme Duclos* ■ *Dir* Brian Gilbert • *Scr* Posy Simmonds, Brian Gilbert, from the story by Posy Simmonds

The Frogmen ★★★ U

Second World War action drama
1951 · US · BW · 96mins

Warners' veteran director Lloyd Bacon fetched up after the war at 20th Century-Fox as a sort of hack-of-all-trades. He has the benefit here of the studio's starry roster of male actors in a realistic and tense suspense drama about Pacific underwater demolition teams during the Second World War. Richard Widmark is the tough commander whose men resent him – naturally though, led by Dana Andrews, they eventually come to understand his uncompromising methods. TS

Richard Widmark *Lieutenant Commander John Lawrence* • Dana Andrews *Flannigan* • Gary Merrill *Lieutenant Commander Pete Vincent* • Jeffrey Hunter *Creighton* • Warren Stevens *Hodges* • Robert Wagner *Lieutenant Franklin* ■ *Dir* Lloyd Bacon • *Scr* John Tucker Battle, from a story by Oscar Millard

Frogs ★★

Horror 1972 · US · Colour · 90mins

One of the many ecologically-correct horror films of the 1970s and one of the silliest. Ray Milland is the wheelchair-bound Southern patriarch whose birthday celebrations are disrupted by a revolt of the swamp creatures he has tried to eliminate with DDT and insecticides. The intelligent frogs also enrol snakes, bugs and snapping turtles to leap around attacking the obvious upper-class types on their private island. AJ

Ray Milland *Jason Crockett* • Sam Elliott *Pickett Smith* • Joan Van Ark *Karen Crockett* • Adam Roarke *Clint Crockett* • Judy Pace *Bella Berenson* ■ *Dir* George McCowan • *Scr* Robert Hutchison, Robert Blees, from a story by Robert Hutchison

From Beyond ★★ 18

Science-fiction horror
1986 · US · Colour · 81mins

Following his gross-out hit *Re-Animator*, Stuart Gordon reunited leads Jeffrey Combs and Barbara Crampton in another HP Lovecraft-based splatter-fest. This sometimes crude clash of horror and sci-fi elements stars Combs as a typically unhinged scientist, whose experiments with the Resonator spark off the usual orgy of murder and mutilation, turning him into a mutated creature with increasingly rubbery effect. Sloppily directed, but you can't fault its energy and audacity. RS [video]

Jeffrey Combs *Crawford Tillinghast* • Barbara Crampton *Dr Katherine McMichaels* • Ken Foree *Bubba Brownlee* • Ted Sorel *Dr Edward Pretorius* ■ *Dir* Stuart Gordon • *Scr* Dennis Paoli, Stuart Gordon, Brian Yuzna, from the story by HP Lovecraft

From beyond the Grave ★★★ 15

Horror 1973 · UK · Colour · 94mins

Devilish antiques dealer Peter Cushing sells evil artefacts to unsuspecting shoppers in an above average anthology from British studio Amicus, linking four R Chetwynd-Hayes horror stories. Haunted mirrors, demonic oak doors, invisible elementals and black magic provide the shudder basics for director Kevin Connor, who complements each distinctive tale with atmospheric flourishes and eerie production values. Dotty psychic Margaret Leighton is a standout in the enthusiastic cast. AJ [video] DVD

Peter Cushing *Proprietor* • David Warner *Edward Charlton* • Wendy Allnutt *Pamela* • Donald Pleasence *Underwood* • Ian Bannen *Christopher Lowe* • Diana Dors *Mabel Lowe* • Angela Pleasence *Emily* • Margaret Leighton *Madame Orloff* • Ian Carmichael *Reggie Warren* • Ian Ogilvy *William Seaton* • Lesley-Anne Down *Rosemary Seaton* ■ *Dir* Kevin Connor • *Scr* Raymond Christodoulou, Robin Clarke, from the short story collection *The Unbidden* by R Chetwynd-Hayes

From Dusk till Dawn ★★★★ 18

Black comedy action horror
1995 · US · Colour · 103mins

Delivering everything you'd expect from a splatter-action horror bearing scriptwriter Quentin Tarantino's name, director Robert Rodriguez's in-your-face shocker juggles sharp dialogue, excessive violence, great special effects and bad taste with stylish verve. Tarantino and George Clooney are two crooks heading south of the border, who take preacher Harvey Keitel's family hostage and end up under attack from bloodthirsty vampires when they hide out at a sleazy Mexican bar. Energetic film-making and engaging performances keep this hilarious gore-fest firing on all its raucously tongue-in-cheek cylinders. AJ. Contains violence, swearing and nudity. [video] DVD

Harvey Keitel *Jacob Fuller* • George Clooney *Seth Gecko* • Quentin Tarantino *Richard Gecko* • Juliette Lewis *Kate Fuller* • Cheech Marin [Richard "Cheech" Marin] *Border guard/Chet Pussy/Carlos* • Salma Hayek *Santanico Pandemonium* • Fred Williamson *Frost* • Danny Trejo *Razor Charlie* • Marc Lawrence (1) *Old timer* ■ *Dir* Robert Rodriguez • *Scr* Quentin Tarantino, from a story by Robert Kurtzman

From Dusk till Dawn II: Texas Blood Money ★★ 18

Action horror 1999 · US · Colour · 84mins

The first of two made-for-video sequels to creator Quentin Tarantino's 1995 original is another road movie-cum-vampire shocker. Basically a reworking of the same plot, Robert Patrick and his lowlife gang plan a heist but get sidetracked by the bloodsucking undead inmates of the Titty Twister bar, the origin of the carnage in the first film. Patrick is hardly in the same charisma/machismo league as George Clooney but director Scott Spiegel keeps the re-heated action moving along at a lively pace. AJ [video] DVD

Robert Patrick *Buck* • Bo Hopkins *Sheriff Otis Lawson* • Duane Whitaker *Luther* • Muse Watson *CW* • Brett Harrelson *Ray Bob* • Raymond Cruz *Jesus* • Danny Trejo *Razor Eddie* • Bruce Campbell *Barry* • Tiffani-Amber Thiessen *Pam* ■ *Dir* Scott Spiegel • *Scr* Scott Spiegel, Duane Whitaker, from a story by Scott Spiegel, Boaz Yakin

From Dusk till Dawn 3: the Hangman's Daughter ★★ 18

Horror western 2000 · US · Colour · 89mins

The third in the series of vampire thrillers shifts virtually the same plot as the previous two back 100 years into the Old West to ring a few, but not enough, neat changes. A gang on the run from a gun-toting posse goes to ground in an out-of-the-way Mexican bar, which turns out to be a vampire lair. It's only the horrifically inventive ways of removing vast numbers of assorted body parts that counts in this average chiller. AJ [video] DVD

Marco Leonardi *Johnny Madrid* • Michael Parks *Ambrose Bierce* • Ara Celi *Esmeralda* • Danny Trejo *Razor Charlie* • Temuera Morrison *The Hangman* • Sonia Braga *Quixtla* • Rebecca Gayheart *Mary Newlie* ■ *Dir* PJ Pesce • *Scr* Alvaro Rodriguez, from a story by Alvaro Rodriguez, Robert Rodriguez

From Hell ★★★★ 18

Period horror 2001 · US · Colour · 117mins

Despite the gruesome nature of the Jack the Ripper's crimes, directors Allen and Albert Hughes resist the temptation to produce merely a blood-drenched whodunnit; this is a meticulous, gripping chiller that captivates on many levels. On the one hand, it's painstakingly crafted social history that captures the grime, grit and prejudices of a thoroughly hypocritical era. On the other, it's a grisly and horribly believable tale of greed, revenge and lunacy in which gore is only part of the film's pervading horror. Combined with the hypnotic camerawork and inspired performances, this ensures that the movie is both visually and intellectually engaging. SF [video] DVD

Johnny Depp *Inspector Frederick "Fred" Abberline* • Heather Graham *Mary Kelly* • Ian Holm *Sir William Gull* • Robbie Coltrane *Sgt Peter Godley* • Ian Richardson *Sir Charles Warren* • Jason Flemyng *John Netley* • Katrin Cartlidge *"Dark Annie" Chapman* ■ *Dir* Albert Hughes, Allen Hughes • *Scr* Terry Hayes, Rafael Yglesias, from the graphic novel by Alan Moore, Eddie Campbell

From Hell It Came ★★

Horror 1957 · US · BW · 70mins

Not a problem which pops up too often in *Gardeners' Question Time* – what do you do with a man-eating, walking tree? This is the dilemma facing Tod Andrews and Tina Carver when an island paradise becomes haunted by a sapling seeking revenge. The unknowns in the cast do their best to keep a straight face, but this really is one for trash fans. JF

Tod Andrews *Dr William Arnold* • Tina Carver *Dr Terry Mason* • Linda Watkins *Mrs Kilgore* • John McNamara *Dr Howard Clark* • Gregg Palmer *Kimo* • Robert Swan *Witch doctor Tano* ■ *Dir* Dan Milner • *Scr* Richard Bernstein, from a story by Richard Bernstein, Jack Milner

From Hell to Texas ★★★ U

Western 1958 · US · Colour · 99mins

Cowboy Don Murray accidentally kills a man and is relentlessly pursued by RG Armstrong as the victim's vengeful father. Murray's open, innocent face is perfect for this allegorical western, vividly directed by Henry Hathaway. The main interest today lies in the casting of Dennis Hopper, whose final confrontation with Murray is as taut as it is unpredictable, and Hathaway brilliantly frames the antagonists against the landscape. TS

Don Murray *Tod Lohman* • Diane Varsi *Juanita Bradley* • Chill Wills *Amos Bradley* • Dennis Hopper *Tom Boyd* • RG Armstrong *Hunter Boyd* • Jay C Flippen *Jake Leffertfinger* ■ *Dir* Henry Hathaway • *Scr* Robert Buckner, Wendell Mayes, from the book *The Hell Bent Kid* by Charles O Locke

From Hell to Victory ★★

Second World War drama
1979 · Fr/It/Sp · Colour · 102mins

In Umberto Lenzi's film, a group of friends of various nationalities face separation on the eve of the Second World War. They plan an annual reunion, of course, but how many of them will survive? The battle sequences are well mounted, but the highlight is George Hamilton's laughable French accent. DP

George Peppard *Brett Rosson* • George Hamilton *Maurice* • Horst Buchholz *Jurgen Dietrich* • Jean-Pierre Cassel *Dick Sanders* • Capucine *Nicole Levine* • Sam Wanamaker *Ray MacDonald* ■ *Dir* Hank Milestone [Umberto Lenzi] • *Scr* Umberto Lenzi, Jose Luis Martinez Molls, Gianfranco Clerici

From Here to Eternity ★★★★★ PG

Second World War drama
1953 · US · BW · 113mins

James Jones's bestseller was thought to be unfilmable – too sexy and too anti-militaristic for a start – but, as written by Daniel Taradash and directed by Fred Zinnemann, it became a classic and a box-office smash, nominated for 13 Oscars and winning eight of them. Set in the run-up to and during the Japanese attack on Pearl Harbor, it deals with life in the US forces overseas – the sexually predatory sergeant (Burt Lancaster), the frustrated wife (Deborah Kerr), the peace-loving bugler (Montgomery Clift), the persecuted Italian GI (Frank Sinatra) and the sadistic stockade sergeant (Ernest Borgnine). Lancaster and Kerr's embrace in the pounding surf gained instant fame. AT [video] DVD

Burt Lancaster *Sergeant Milton Warden* • Deborah Kerr *Karen Holmes* • Montgomery Clift *Robert E Lee Prewitt* • Frank Sinatra *Angelo Maggio* • Donna Reed *Alma/Lorene* • Ernest Borgnine *Sergeant "Fatso" Judson* • Philip Ober *Captain Dana Holmes* • Jack Warden *Corporal Buckley* ■ *Dir* Fred Zinnemann • *Scr* Daniel Taradash, from the novel by James Jones • *Cinematographer* Burnett Guffey • *Editor* William Lyon

From Hollywood to Deadwood ★★

Detective spoof 1989 · US · Colour · 90mins

Two gumshoes are hired to find an actress who's gone missing in mid-production in this spoof on the private eye genre from writer/director Rex Pickett. Evidently there was no time for retakes or a more considered script, as Pickett struggles to make the most of the interplay between Scott Paulin and Jim Haynie. Consequently, the few genuinely wry jabs at Hollywood's expense become lost amid the road movie clichés. JM. Contains swearing, violence and sex scenes.

Scott Paulin *Raymond Savage* • Jim Haynie *Jack Haines* • Barbara Schock *Lana Dark* • Jurgen Doeres *Steve Reese* • Chris Mulkey *Nick Detroit* • Mike Genovese *Ernie November* • Campbell Scott *Bobby* ■ *Dir/Scr* Rex Pickett

From Mao to Mozart: Isaac Stern in China ★★★★ U

Music documentary
1980 · US · Colour · 83mins

Winner of the Oscar for best documentary feature, Murray Lerner's reverential, yet revealing record of Isaac Stern's 1979 goodwill tour to China is remarkable on a number of levels. Apart from the violin virtuoso's eloquent playing, it is interesting to see the enthusiasm with which he was received and the passion for Western music that has been fostered under the communist system. There are sombre moments too, such as the old academic's memoir of the Cultural Revolution. But the scenes at the Peking Opera and those featuring the phenomenal child prodigies, give the film a sociological fascination to complement its sublime music. DP

Dir Murray Lerner • *Cinematographer* Nic Knowland, Nick Doob, David Bridges • *Editor* Tom Haneke

From Noon till Three ★★ 15

Comedy western 1976 · US · Colour · 95mins

An eccentric western, with Charles Bronson as an amateur gunfighter who returns from the dead after his former mistress (Jill Ireland) has embellished his clumsy exploits and turned him into a money-making legend. Writer/director Frank D Gilroy turns in a movie with few laughs and even fewer action highlights. Bronson, cast against type, lacks the necessary lightness for the role. AT [video]

Charles Bronson *Graham Dorsey* • Jill Ireland *Amanda Starbuck* • Douglas V Fowley [Douglas Fowley] *Buck Bowers* • Stan Haze *Ape* • Damon Douglas *Boy* • Hector Morales *Mexican* • Bert Williams *Sheriff* • Elmer Bernstein *Songwriter* ■ *Dir* Frank D Gilroy • *Scr* Frank D Gilroy, from his novel

From Russia with Love ★★★★ PG

Spy adventure 1963 · UK · Colour · 110mins

Ian Fleming received a useful boost to his sales when President Kennedy listed *From Russia with Love* as one of his ten favourite books. It is also one of the most popular Bond movies and a terrific thriller in its own right, owing much to Hitchcock and Carol Reed's *The Third Man* in its marvellous atmosphere of foreign intrigue. Superbly shot on location in Istanbul, and closely following Fleming's original story, the film has Sean Connery duped into smuggling a top secret communist decoding machine, plus blonde Russian diplomat Daniela Bianchi, from Turkey to the west via the Orient Express. AT [video] DVD

Sean Connery *James Bond* • Daniela Bianchi *Tatiana Romanova* • Pedro Armendáriz *Kerim Bey* • Lotte Lenya *Rosa Klebb* • Robert Shaw *Red Grant* • Bernard Lee *"M"* • Eunice Gayson *Sylvia Trench* • Walter Gotell *Morzeny* • Lois Maxwell *Miss Moneypenny* • Francis De Wolff *Vavra* • Desmond Llewelyn *Major Boothroyd* ■ *Dir* Terence Young • *Scr* Richard Maibaum, Johanna Harwood, from the novel by Ian Fleming • *Music* John Barry (1)

From the Earth to the Moon ★★ U

Science-fiction adventure
1958 · US · Colour · 99mins

This clunky sci-fi drama can't overcome the size of its budget, despite the cast of veterans who lurch through the material. This Jules Verne dramatisation stars Joseph Cotten and George Sanders as the rival scientists with differing views on space travel. It's nice to see Debra Paget as the leading lady, but ageing stars such as Henry Daniell and Melville Cooper only add to the morbid enjoyment. TS [video]

Joseph Cotten *Victor Barbicane* • George Sanders *Stuyvesant Nicholl* • Debra Paget *Virginia Nicholl* • Don Dubbins *Ben Sharpe* • Henry Daniell *Morgana* • Melville Cooper *Bancroft* ■ *Dir* Byron Haskin • *Scr* Robert Blees, James Leicester, from the novel by Jules Verne

From the Edge of the City ★★★ 18

Drama 1998 · Gr · Colour · 93mins

If this stark study of disenfranchised Russian émigrés operating on the outskirts of Athens proves anything, it's that, as far as cinema is concerned, the counterculture of the streets is the same no matter where you are. In following the misfortunes of a gang of pill-popping, petty thieving rent boys, director Constantinos Giannaris employs a technique that combines neorealistic episodes with talking head interviews and frantic time-lapse codas. While this adds immediacy, it distracts from the dramatic implications of Stathis Papadopoulos's dangerous liaison with prostitute Theodora Tzimou and her pimp Dimitris Papoulidis. DP. In Greek with English subtitles.

Stathis Papadopoulos *Sasha* • Costas Cotsianidis *Cotsian* • Panagiotis Chartomatsidis *Panagiotis* • Dimitris Papoulidis *Giorgos* • Theodora Tzimou *Natasha* • Anestis Polychronidis *Anestis* ■ *Dir/Scr* Constantinos Giannaris

From the Hip ★ 15

Courtroom comedy drama
1987 · US · Colour · 106mins

Oh dear, what has happened to Judd Nelson's career? From Brat Pack success in films such as *The Breakfast Club*, he has been reduced to making rubbish like this third-rate comedy. He's not the only one who would probably like to forget this tale of a lawyer who will do anything to clear his client of murder. JB [video]

Judd Nelson *Robin Weathers* • Elizabeth Perkins *Jo Ann* • John Hurt *Douglas Benoit* • Darren McGavin *Craig Duncan* ■ *Dir* Bob Clark • *Scr* David E Kelley, Bob Clark, from a story by David E Kelley

From the Life of the Marionettes ★★★★ 18

Drama
1980 · W Ger · BW and Colour · 99mins

Ingmar Bergman's second film made during his tax exile in Germany is superior to *The Serpent's Egg* (1977). Opening with the murder of a prostitute in a blood-red room, most of the film is shot in stark monochrome with an intense whiteness in the dream sequences. Balanced between the distancing device of Brechtian titles and the use of large closeups, Bergman creates a controlled case history in the German idiom. Many of the thoughts of the characters are delivered via speeches, most notably a monologue by an ageing gay man, a rarity in Bergman's female-dominated *oeuvre*. RB. In German with English subtitles. [video] DVD

Robert Atzorn *Peter Egermann* • Christine Buchegger *Katarina Egermann* • Martin Benrath *Mogens Jensen* • Rita Russek *Ka* • Lola Müthel *Cordelia Egermann* ■ *Dir/Scr* Ingmar Bergman • *Cinematographer* Sven Nykvist • *Art Director* Rolf Zehetbauer

From the Pole to the Equator ★★★ PG

Experimental documentary compilation
1987 · It/W Ger · Tinted · 97mins

Born in 1874, Luca Comerio was the official photographer to the Italian Royal Family, before turning to film-making in 1905. Over the next 23 years, he covered the globe capturing news events such as the 1911 invasion of Libya as well as making travelogues in areas as varied as the South Pole, India, Africa and Central Asia. This stylised compilation of his most representative imagery took over three years to assemble. Yervant Gianikian and Angela Ricci Lucchi sifted through miles of footage, which they then stretch-printed and tinted to produce a mesmerising – and often disconcerting – memoir of a bygone age of sporting savagery and imperial exploitation. DP. With subtitles. [video]

Dir Yervant Gianikian, Angela Ricci Lucchi

From the Terrace ★★ PG

Drama 1960 · US · Colour · 143mins

The combination of pedestrian direction and predictable plotting undermines Mark Robson's adaptation of John O'Hara's sprawling novel. Paul Newman goes through the motions as a Wall Street whizzkid who defies his well-heeled family to marry Joanne Woodward, only to risk losing her when he has a fling with Ina Balin. Newman is upstaged by his female co-stars, with Myrna Loy particularly effective playing against type as a boozing matriarch. A glitzy soap opera. DP [video]

Paul Newman *Alfred Eaton* • Joanne Woodward *Mary St John* • Myrna Loy *Martha Eaton* • Ina Balin *Natalie* • Leon Ames *Samuel Eaton* • Elizabeth Allen *Sage Rimmington* ■ *Dir* Mark Robson • *Scr* Ernest Lehman, from the novel by John O'Hara

From This Day Forward ★★★

Romantic drama 1946 · US · BW · 95mins

Mark Stevens stars as an unemployed ex-serviceman looking back to the days during the Depression when he met and married Joan Fontaine in this classy piece of escapism from RKO. Stevens struggles with his role, but his rather feeble performance is offset by the charm of Fontaine, even if you have to suspend disbelief to accept her as a working-class New Yorker. Once over that hurdle, relax and enjoy what was a box-office hit. TS

Joan Fontaine *Susan* • Mark Stevens *Bill Cummings* • Rosemary DeCamp *Martha* • Henry Morgan [Harry Morgan] *Hank* • Wally Brown *Jake* • Bobby Driscoll *Timmy* ■ *Dir* John Berry • *Scr* Hugo Butler, Garson Kanin, Edith R Sommer, Charles Schee, from the novel *All Brides Are Beautiful* by Thomas Bell

The Front ★★★ 15

Comedy drama 1976 · US · Colour · 90mins

Woody Allen too bland? Surprisingly, that's how he comes across in this Martin Ritt-directed exposé of Hollywood during the witch-hunt days of the 1950s, playing a cashier who agrees to lend his name as a cover for blacklisted scriptwriters. Allen simply puts his usual neurotic personality on hold until his character starts believing he's as good as the authors he's helping. Allen is dwarfed physically and dramatically by Zero Mostel. TH [video]

Woody Allen *Howard Prince* • Zero Mostel *Hecky Brown* • Herschel Bernardi *Phil Sussman* • Michael Murphy *Alfred Miller* • Andrea Marcovicci *Florence Barrett* ■ *Dir* Martin Ritt • *Scr* Walter Bernstein

The Front Page ★★★

Comedy drama 1931 · US · BW · 102mins

Ben Hecht and Charles MacArthur's stage success of 1928 was a natural for a movie adaptation: set mainly in the pressroom of a Chicago court-house, it's a gift for actors. Adolphe Menjou plays the powerful editor, Walter Burns, and Pat O'Brien is his ace reporter, Hildy Johnson. Spraying smart dialogue at the speed of Chicago's machine-guns, it carries its age with dignity. Remade – with a sex-change operation (Hildy becomes a woman) – as *His Girl Friday* in 1940, by Billy Wilder in 1974, and again in *Switching Channels* in 1988, by this time set in a TV newsroom. AT

Adolphe Menjou *Walter Burns* • Pat O'Brien *Hildy Johnson* • Mary Brian *Peggy* • Edward Everett Horton *Bensinger* • Walter Catlett *Murphy* ■ *Dir* Lewis Milestone • *Scr* Bartlett Cormack, Ben Hecht (uncredited), Charles Lederer (uncredited), from the play by Ben Hecht, Charles MacArthur

The Front Page ★★★★

Comedy drama 1974 · US · Colour · 104mins

Director Billy Wilder had already made one classic newspaper movie, *Ace in the Hole*, before he tackled Ben Hecht and Charles MacArthur's play, previously filmed in 1931. Preserving the Prohibition-era setting but rewriting nearly half the play's dialogue, Wilder and his co-writer, IAL Diamond, create a breathless, Faustian farce. Jack Lemmon stars as the hotshot reporter who's intent on getting married despite the fact that he has clearly sold his soul to the Devil incarnate, satanic editor Walter Burns, played by Walter Matthau. Lemmon and Matthau are on top form, although the endless shouting, no matter how clever the dialogue, gets a bit wearing. AT

Jack Lemmon *Hildy Johnson* • Walter Matthau *Walter Burns* • Carol Burnett *Mollie Malloy* • Susan Sarandon *Peggy Grant* • Vincent Gardenia *Sheriff* • David Wayne *Bensinger* • Allen Garfield *Kruger* ■ *Dir* Billy Wilder • *Scr* Billy Wilder, IAL Diamond, from the play by Ben Hecht, Charles MacArthur

Front Page Story ★★★ PG

Drama 1953 · UK · BW · 94mins

Back in the days when Rupert was only a bear in Fleet Street and British newspapers engaged in rivalries that were almost gentlemanly compared with today, editor Jack Hawkins has to choose between his job and his marriage to Elizabeth Allan, who sits at home and wonders where it all went wrong. Cosily dated, but an interesting sign of its times. TH [video]

Jack Hawkins *John Grant* • Elizabeth Allan *Susan Grant* • Eva Bartok *Mrs Thorpe* • Derek Farr *Teale* • Michael Goodliffe *Kennedy* ■ *Dir* Gordon Parry • *Scr* Jay Lewis, Jack Howells, William Fairchild, Guy Morgan, from the novel *Final Night* by Robert Gaines

Front Page Woman ★★★

Comedy drama 1935 · US · BW · 83mins

Bette Davis and George Brent co-star in this tale about two newspaper hounds, constantly trying to out-scoop and out-quip each other, before deciding to settle their professional differences in the traditional way of romantic comedies. It wins no prizes for realism in its depiction of newspaper life, but at least it scores some points for correctness ahead of its time on the working woman issue, and there's a good deal of enjoyment to be had en route to the rather predictable finale. PF

Bette Davis *Ellen Garfield* • George Brent *Curt Devlin* • Roscoe Karns *Toots* • Winifred Shaw *Inez Cordova* • Joseph Crehan *Spike Kiley* ■ *Dir* Michael Curtiz • *Scr* Roy Chanslor, Lillie Hayward, Laird Doyle, from the novel *Women Are Bum Newspapermen* by Richard Macauley

La Frontera ★★★ 15

Political drama
1991 · Chil/Sp · Colour · 115mins

Deftly revealing character through locale, Ricardo Larrain's debut feature (which won a Silver Bear at the Berlin Film Festival) is a precisely paced study of the loneliness of principle. As the Chilean maths teacher exiled to a coastal town that was once swept away by a tidal wave, Patricio Contreras combines commitment and resignation. There's amusement to be

F

had in the way he taunts his doltish police guards, but the core of the film lies in his tentative relationship with Gloria Laso, the daughter of a fugitive from Franco's Spain, and his uneasy friendship with a priest. DP. In Spanish with English subtitles.

Patricio Contreras *Ramiro Orellana* • Gloria Laso *Maite* • Hector Noguera *Father Patricio* • Alonso Venegas *Delegate* • Aldo Bernales *Diver* ■ *Dir* Ricardo Larrain • *Scr* Ricardo Larrain, Jorge Goldenberg

Frontier Badmen ★★ U

Western 1943 · US · BW · 77mins

The bland Robert Paige is surrounded by a highly watchable cast, notably the tormented Diana Barrymore, alcoholic daughter of John, as the romantic lead. Lon Chaney Jr features as a mean hired gun with a streak of sheer sadism unusual in a family-themed movie of this type, and Paige's sidekick is a young Noah Beery Jr. TS

Robert Paige *Steve* • Anne Gwynne *Chris* • Noah Beery Jr *Jim* • Diana Barrymore *Claire* • Leo Carrillo *Chinito* • Andy Devine *Slim* • Lon Chaney Jr *Chango* ■ *Dir* Ford Beebe • *Scr* Gerald Geraghty, Morgan B Cox

Frontier Gal ★★★

Comedy western 1945 · US · Colour · 84mins

This romantic western was one of the movies that made a star out of Yvonne De Carlo. Tight-lipped leading man Rod Cameron is her co-star, and the splendidly batty plot involves bandit Cameron marrying De Carlo and going on the run for six years, then returning to discover that he's now a father before ultimately throwing the villain over a cliff. Don't ask. De Carlo would gain icon status in *The Munsters* TV series, but Cameron was relegated to B-westerns. TS

Yvonne De Carlo *Lorena Dumont* • Rod Cameron *Johnny Hart* • Andy Devine *Big Ben* • Fuzzy Knight *Fuzzy* • Sheldon Leonard *Blackie* • Andrew Tombes *Judge Prescott* • Clara Blandick *Abigail* ■ *Dir* Charles Lamont • *Scr* Michael Fessier, Ernest Pagano

Frontier Horizon ★★ U

Western 1939 · US · BW · 54mins

This was John Wayne's last appearance in the *Three Mesquiteers* series before Republic finally promoted him to A-features. The dreary-as-usual plot has Wayne, Ray Corrigan and Raymond Hatton saving settlers from taking worthless land. Watch for young Phyllis Isley, who would transform herself into a major star under the name of Jennifer Jones. AE DVD

John Wayne *Stony Brooke* • Ray "Crash" Corrigan *Tucson Smith* • Raymond Hatton *Rusty Joslin* • Phyllis Isley [Jennifer Jones] *Celia* ■ *Dir* George Sherman • *Scr* Betty Burbridge, Luci Ward, from characters created by William Colt MacDonald

Frontier Marshal ★★★

Western 1939 · US · BW · 71mins

A marvellously authentic-looking version of the Wyatt Earp legend, the first sound western for director Allan Dwan. This stars the stone-faced Randolph Scott as the man who cleaned up the West, with debonair Cesar Romero as the doom-laden Doc Holliday, renamed for some reason as Doc Halliday. It may not be historically correct, but it's entertaining, with a cracking pace and some exciting moments. TS

Randolph Scott *Wyatt Earp* • Nancy Kelly *Sarah Allen* • Cesar Romero *Doc Halliday* • Binnie Barnes *Jerry* • John Carradine *Ben Carter* • Edward Norris *Dan Blackmore* • Lon Chaney Jr *Pringle* ■ *Dir* Allan Dwan • *Scr* Sam Hellman, from the novel *Wyatt Earp, Frontier Marshal* by Stuart N Lake

Frontier Outlaws ★★★ U

Western 1944 · US · BW · 58mins

Former Olympic gold medallist Buster Crabbe made 36 B-westerns for poverty row studio PRC from 1941 to 1946. This brisk 58-minute affair is one of the best, with enough action and humour to please all enthusiasts of old-fashioned, uncomplicated shoot-'em-ups. Crabbe's comic sidekick in all these films was played by Al "Fuzzy" St John, former Sennett comedian and nephew of "Fatty" Arbuckle, but there are more laughs than usual between the action episodes in this, due to a great courtroom turn by Emmett Lynn as an unconventional judge. TV

Buster Crabbe [Larry "Buster" Crabbe] *Billy Carson* • Al St John *Fuzzy Jones* • Frances Gladwin *Pat* • Marin Sais *Ma Clark* • Charles King (2) *Barlow* • Jack Ingram *Taylor* ■ *Dir* Sam Newfield • *Scr* Joe O'Donnell

Frozen Assets ★★ 15

Comedy 1992 · US · Colour · 97mins

If you were going to make a comedy about a sperm bank, you would think the only way to go is over the top. But director George Miller was unable or unwilling to enter the realms of cheerful tastelessness, and the result is a tepid comedy. Corbin Bernsen is the city high-flier who finds himself in charge of a small-town bank that doesn't deal in the usual commodities. Shelley Long spars with Bernsen, but an embarrassingly eccentric turn from Larry Miller hardly helps matters. JF. Contains swearing.

Shelley Long *Dr Grace Murdock* • Corbin Bernsen *Zach Shepard* • Larry Miller *Newton Patterson* • Dody Goodman *Mrs Patterson* • Matt Clark *JF Hughes* ■ *Dir* George Miller (1) • *Scr* Don Klein, Thomas Kartozian

The Frozen Dead ★★

Horror 1966 · UK · Colour and BW · 92mins

In this clinically ghoulish low-budget British shocker, imported American star Dana Andrews is set on reviving 1,500 top Nazi officials who've been in a deep freeze since the war. Though directed with a fatal lack of gusto by Herbert J Leder, the sheer delirium of the premise takes some beating. We have a row of severed arms, all neatly mounted and awaiting use, and a woman's severed head that lives in a box and, through mental telepathy, warns others of Andrews's nefarious scheme for jackbooted world domination. RS

Dana Andrews *Dr Norberg* • Anna Palk *Jean Norberg* • Philip Gilbert *Dr Ted Roberts* • Kathleen Breck *Elsa Tenney* • Karel Stepanek *Gen Lubeck* • Basil Henson *Tirpitz* • Edward Fox *Prisoner No 3* ■ *Dir* Herbert J Leder • *Scr* Herbert J Leder, from his story

The Frozen Ghost ★★

Psychological mystery
1944 · US · BW · 61mins

Lon Chaney Jr was never the most flexible of actors, but few could play innocents lured into iniquity with such lumbering geniality. In this *Inner Sanctum* instalment, he hits another streak of bad luck as a stage hypnotist whose career is ruined when a member of his audience dies during a show. However, things go from bad to worse after he lands a job at Tala Birell's wax museum and falls prey to a series of bizarre incidents designed to send him crazy. Abetted by a practised supporting cast, director Harold Young admirably exploits his atmospheric locations. DP

Lon Chaney [Lon Chaney Jr] *Alex Gregor/Gregor the Great* • Evelyn Ankers *Maura Daniel* • Milburn Stone *George Keene* • Douglass Dumbrille *Inspector Brant* • Martin Kosleck *Rudi Poldan* • Elena Verdugo *Nina Coudreau* ■ *Dir* Harold Young • *Scr* Bernard Schubert, Luci Ward, Henry Sucher, from a story by Harrison Carter, Henry Sucher

Fubar ★★ 15

Comedy 2002 · Can · Colour · 79mins

Michael Dowse's low-budget mockumentary is a curious affair. An offbeat look at life and friendship seen through the eyes of mullet-haired Canadian rock fans Terry and Dean (co-writers David Lawrence and Paul J Spence), it's one of those films that sounds so much more entertaining on paper than it actually is on screen. The "*Spinal Tap* meets Alan Partridge"-style stupidity soon wears thin. There are some hilarious scenes as the beer-swilling head-bangers engage with the bemused Calgary locals, but for the most part, the movie is crude and unfunny. SF. Contains swearing and sexual references.

Paul J Spence *Dean Murdoch* • David Lawrence *Terry Cahill* • Gordon Skilling *Farrel Mitchner* • Tracey Lawrence *Trixie Anderson* • Sage Lawrence *Chastity Anderson* • Rose Martin *Rose Murdoch* • Dr SC Lim *Dr SC Lim* • Jim Lawrence *Ron Miller* • Andrew Sparacino *Tron/Troy McRae* ■ *Dir* Michael Dowse • *Scr* Michael Dowse, David Lawrence, Paul J Spence, from an idea by David Lawrence, from a character created by North Darling

The Fugitive ★★★★ PG

Drama 1947 · US · BW · 99mins

Director John Ford's mesmerising version of *The Power and the Glory* – Graham Greene's novel about a "whisky priest"– was seriously compromised by the censorship of the time. But, despite the fact that the central relationship is no longer a sexual one and Henry Fonda's priest is not an alcoholic, it remains resolutely convincing. Pedro Armendáriz is particularly fine as the police lieutenant, and Dolores Del Rio smoulders as the woman, but the real star of this brooding opus is the magnificent outdoor photography from Gabriel Figueroa. TS

Henry Fonda *Fugitive/Priest* • Dolores Del Rio *Native woman/Maria Dolores* • Pedro Armendáriz *Police lieutenant* • J Carrol Naish *Police informer* • Leo Carrillo *Chief of police* • Ward Bond *El Gringo/James Calvert* ■ *Dir* John Ford • *Scr* Dudley Nichols, from the novel *The Power and the Glory* by Graham Greene

The Fugitive ★★★★ 15

Thriller 1993 · US · Colour and BW · 124mins

The original TV series of *The Fugitive* starring David Janssen ran for 120 episodes in the 1960s and attracted a cult following. Director Andrew Davis takes the bare bones of the source material and comes up with an unstoppable juggernaut, in which the suspense never lets up and the set pieces are truly epic. Harrison Ford is fine as the innocent surgeon who is wrongfully convicted of the murder of his wife and sets off to find the real killer. But the movie is stolen from under his nose by Tommy Lee Jones, who gives an Oscar-winning performance as the marshal doggedly pursuing the wanted man. Jones reprised his role in the disappointing *US Marshals*. JF. Contains violence and swearing. DVD

Harrison Ford *Dr Richard Kimble* • Tommy Lee Jones *Deputy Marshal Samuel Gerard* • Sela Ward *Helen Kimble* • Julianne Moore *Dr Anne Eastman* • Joe Pantoliano *Cosmo Renfro* ■ *Dir* Andrew Davis • *Scr* Jeb Stuart, David Twohy, from a story by David Twohy, from characters created by Roy Huggins

Fugitive from Justice ★★ 15

Drama based on a true story
1996 · US · Colour · 90mins

Another TV movie about parents kidnapping their own children to save them from an abusive spouse. From the opening shots you know where this awkwardly directed drama is going. Chris Noth does his best as a concerned father who fears that his boozy ex-wife (Loryn Locklin) and her low-life boyfriend are abusing his infant daughter. Singer Natalie Cole plays the head of the underground group that helps him. MC DVD

Chris Noth [Christopher Noth] *Larry Coster* • Loryn Locklin *Andrea Coster* • Megan Gallagher *Veronica* • Peter MacNicol *Roy Dowd* • Natalie Cole *Latisha Corbett* ■ *Dir* Chuck Bowman • *Scr* Joel Oliansky, Kurt Inderbitzen, Victoria Karess

The Fugitive Kind ★★ 15

Drama 1960 · US · BW · 116mins

Another emotional tale from Tennessee Williams, directed by Sidney Lumet, with Marlon Brando as a guitar-playing drifter who falls into the lap of Anna Magnani, a lonely woman trapped in a marriage to a dying man. There are subplots aplenty, and Joanne Woodward as well, but you get the feeling it's Williams throwing out his dirty washing and seeing how it falls. But, despite such prestige casting, audiences sensed a downer and stayed away in droves. AT

Marlon Brando *Val Xavier* • Anna Magnani *Lady Torrance* • Joanne Woodward *Carol Cutrere* • Maureen Stapleton *Vee Talbot* • Victor Jory *Jabe Torrance* ■ *Dir* Sidney Lumet • *Scr* Tennessee Williams, Meade Roberts, from the play *Orpheus Descending* by Tennessee Williams

Full Alert ★★★ 15

Crime action thriller
1997 · HK · Colour · 94mins

Ringo Lam (whose *City on Fire* was a big influence on *Reservoir Dogs*) directs this gripping crime thriller. The story focuses on the cat-and-mouse games between tough cop Lau Ching Wan and Francis Ng, who is planning the ultimate robbery at a race track. As usual, the action sequences are stunningly choreographed, but Lam is equally interested in the pyschological interplay between good and evil and Ng makes for an intriguingly sympathetic villain. JF. In Cantonese with English subtitles. DVD

Lau Ching Wan *Inspector Pao* • Francis Ng *Mak Kwan* • Blacky Ko [Ko Sau Leung] • Amanda Lee • Monica Chan ■ *Dir* Ringo Lam • *Scr* WK Lua, Ringo Lam, from a story by Ringo Lam

Full Circle ★★

Horror 1977 · UK/Can · Colour · 97mins

Director Richard Loncraine's competent adaptation is a slow-moving, supernatural tale more concerned with atmosphere than action. Mia Farrow is an unstable mother who, feeling responsible for the choking death of their daughter, leaves her husband Keir Dullea. Moving into an eerie house haunted by the spirit of a moody child, she becomes even more guilt-stricken and obsessed. Loncraine's lyrical chiller has its admirers, but most viewers will be three steps ahead of the catatonic Farrow. AJ

Mia Farrow *Julia Lofting* • Keir Dullea *Magnus Lofting* • Tom Conti *Mark* • Jill Bennett *Lily* • Robin Gammell *David Swift* • Cathleen Nesbitt *Mrs Rudge* • Anna Wing *Mrs Flood* ■ *Dir* Richard Loncraine • *Scr* Dave Humphries, Harry Bromley Davenport (adaptation), from the novel *Julia* by Peter Straub

Full Confession ★★

Crime drama 1939 · US · BW · 72mins

Victor McLaglen plays a ruthless killer who tells a priest of his crime. Since an innocent man (Barry Fitzgerald) is under sentence of death, can the priest convince McLaglen to confess? The interesting theme is marred by the script's heavy-handed piety and sanctimonious soul-searching, which John Farrow's slow-paced direction fails to counteract. TV

Victor McLaglen *McGinnis* • Sally Eilers *Molly* • Joseph Calleia *Father Loma* • Barry Fitzgerald *Michael O'Keefe* • Elisabeth Risdon *Norah O'Keefe* ■ *Dir* John Farrow • *Scr* Jerry Cady [Jerome Cady], from a story by Leo Birinski

Full Contact ★★★★ 18

Action thriller 1992 · HK · Colour · 92mins

Chow Yun-Fat is a Bangkok bouncer who takes violent revenge after an arms raid leads to a double-cross in this frantic "heroic bloodshed" thriller. Simon Yam, as a gay arms dealer dominates proceedings and Anthony Wong plays Chow's duplicitous friend. This is a film of flying metal, whether in the form of speeding cars, bikes or bullets. Ringo Lam's direction is electrifying, topping the armoured car robberies with a sensational nightclub shoot-out, in which the camera takes on the perspective of the bullets. DP. In Cantonese with English subtitles. Contains violence, swearing. VIDEO DVD

Chow Yun-Fat *Jeff* • Simon Yam *Judge* • Ann Bridgewater *Mona* • Anthony Wong (1) *Sam* • Bonnie Fu *Virgin* • Frankie Chin *Deano* ■ *Dir* Ringo Lam • *Scr* Nam Yin

A Full Day's Work ★★

Black comedy 1973 · Fr · Colour · 95mins

Actor Jean-Louis Trintignant makes his directorial debut with this undistinguished black comedy, following the murderous exploits of baker Jacques Dufilho, as he exacts his revenge on the jurors who sent his son to his death. As far as "chopping list" films go we're not exactly in Vincent Price territory. DP. French dialogue dubbed into English.

Jacques Dufilho *Gaston Rousseau, baker* • André Falcon *Director* • Luce Marquand *Mother* • Vittorio Caprioli *Mangiacavalo* ■ *Dir/Scr* Jean-Louis Trintignant

Full Eclipse ★★★ 18

Action horror thriller
1993 · US · Colour · 93mins

This imaginative werewolf romp is given lashings of style by horror director Anthony Hickox, which compensates for the general lack of blood-spilling enforced by its TV movie status. Hard-bitten urban cop Mario Van Peebles is tricked by Patsy Kensit into joining Bruce Payne's elite corps of crime-busting lycanthropes. A simple injection turns him into a furry vigilante with an appetite for criminal-ripping frenzies, performed with Hong Kong-inspired élan. AJ VIDEO DVD

Mario Van Peebles *Max Dire* • Patsy Kensit *Casey Spencer* • Bruce Payne *Adam Garou* • Anthony John Denison *Jim Sheldon* • Victoria Rowell *Anna Dire* • John Verea *Ramon Perez* ■ *Dir* Anthony Hickox • *Scr* Richard Christian Matheson, Michael Reaves

Full Fathom Five ★★

Action thriller 1990 · US · Colour · 82mins

Roger Corman once again demonstrates his unerring ability when it comes to spotting directorial talent. Carl Franklin is now acclaimed for his thrillers *One False Move* and *Devil in a Blue Dress*, but back in 1990 he was a jobbing TV actor. This blatant cash-in on *The Hunt for Red October* features Michael Moriarty as a submarine skipper on the trail of stolen nuclear craft. It's pretty undistinguished fare, although it obviously taught Franklin something. JF

Michael Moriarty *McKenzie* • Maria Rangel *Justine* • Diego Bertie *Miguel* • German Gonzales *Sebastian* ■ *Dir* Carl Franklin • *Scr* Bart Davis, from his novel

Full Frontal ★ 18

Romantic comedy drama
2002 · US · Colour · 96mins

Built on Dogme 95-style foundations – with actors doing their own hair and make-up and relinquishing their traditional on-set privileges – director Steven Soderbergh's apparent attempt to get back to his grittier roots isn't nearly as clever as he thinks it is. The basic scenario is a day in the life of LA's beautiful people; those featured are potential guests at the 40th birthday bash of movie producer Gus (David Duchovny). The glittering cast rambles its way through a plethora of human emotions, captured on grainy digital video for that extra touch of pretension. SF VIDEO DVD

David Duchovny *Gus* • Nicky Katt *Hitler* • Catherine Keener *Lee* • Mary McCormack *Linda* • David Hyde Pierce *Carl* • Julia Roberts *Francesca/Catherine* • Blair Underwood *Calvin/Nicholas* • David Fincher *Film director* ■ *Dir* Steven Soderbergh • *Scr* Coleman Hough

Full Metal Jacket ★★★★★ 18

War drama 1987 · UK · Colour · 111mins

Stanley Kubrick's penultimate film is a harrowing, foul-mouthed and violent Vietnam war drama. But, unlike the rainforest horrors of *Apocalypse Now* or *Platoon*, Kubrick's film begins with a long training camp sequence in America before moving to a bombed-out Vietnamese city. While its message is simple – innocent young Americans are taught to be machine-like killers – its technique is extraordinary. Because Kubrick refuses to travel any distance, it was shot entirely in Britain, with palm trees uprooted from Spain and Matthew Modine and a cast of relative unknowns uprooted from Hollywood. The performances are superb, especially Lee Ermey as the drill sergeant with a colourful vocabulary, Vincent D'Onofrio as the pathetic Private Pyle and Modine as the cynical recruit named Joker. AT VIDEO DVD

Matthew Modine *Private Joker* • Adam Baldwin *Animal Mother* • Vincent D'Onofrio *Leonard Lawrence, Private Gomer Pyle* • Lee Ermey [R Lee Ermey] *Gunnery Sergeant Hartman* • Dorian Harewood *Eightball* • Arliss Howard *Private Cowboy* ■ *Dir* Stanley Kubrick • *Scr* Stanley Kubrick, Michael Herr, Gustav Hasford, from the novel *The Short-Timers* by Gustav Hasford • *Art Director* Anton Furst

The Full Monty ★★★★★ 15

Comedy drama
1997 · UK/US · Colour · 87mins

When the going gets tough, the tough get go-going, as Robert Carlyle – a divorced father trying to maintain joint custody of his son – forms a strip act along with a group of other unemployed Sheffield steelworkers in director Peter Cattaneo's highly engaging, genuinely poignant and hilarious full-frontal comedy drama. Well endowed with side-splitting laughter, mined by a superb ensemble cast, it's about men's emotional shortcomings as much as their *Dirty Dancing* techniques. The many wonderful moments include the Chippendales of the North inadvertently gyrating to the radio in a dole queue – simply inspired. AJ. Contains swearing, nudity. VIDEO DVD

Robert Carlyle *Gaz* • Tom Wilkinson *Gerald* • Mark Addy *Dave* • Lesley Sharp *Jean* • Emily Woof *Mandy* • Steve Huison *Lomper* • Paul Barber *Horse* • Hugo Speer *Guy* • Deirdre Costello *Linda* • Bruce Jones *Reg* ■ *Dir* Peter Cattaneo • *Scr* Simon Beaufoy

Full Moon High ★★★ 15

Comedy horror 1982 · US · Colour · 90mins

Horror specialist Larry Cohen ventures into comedy with this parody of such 1950s' B-movies as *I Was a Teenage Werewolf*. But it's also a sort of *Back to the Future* with fangs, as Adam Arkin returns from Transylvania after years in a lycanthropic wilderness to discover that his old high school buddies have changed almost as drastically as he has. Playing down the special effects in order to concentrate on the social spoofing, this is a sharp and funny film. DP VIDEO

Adam Arkin *Tony Walker* • Elizabeth Hartman *Miss Montgomery* • Ed McMahon *Mr Walker* • Kenneth Mars • Roz Kelly • Joanne Nail • Pat Morita • Louis Nye ■ *Dir/Scr* Larry Cohen

Full Moon in Blue Water ★★ 15

Comedy drama 1988 · US · Colour · 90mins

Only Gene Hackman saves this from totally sinking. He plays the owner of a run-down Texas bar, who is obsessed by his long-lost wife despite the efforts of Teri Garr to grab him for herself. Full of the kind of eccentrics usually found in a Tennessee Williams play, the production veers too clumsily between engaging realism and overblown melodrama. TH. Contains swearing. VIDEO

Gene Hackman *Floyd* • Teri Garr *Louise* • Burgess Meredith *The General* • Elias Koteas *Jimmy* • Kevin Cooney *Charlie* • David Doty *Virgil* • Gil Glasgow *Baytch* ■ *Dir* Peter Masterson • *Scr* Bill Bozzone

Full Moon in Paris ★★★★ 15

Romantic comedy 1984 · Fr · Colour · 97mins

The fourth film in Eric Rohmer's *Comedies and Proverbs* series is a sublime example of the trouble we land ourselves in every time we open our mouths. In this delightful tale – surely no other film-maker has depicted with such consistency and accuracy exactly what it means to be human – Pascale Ogier's desire to spread her wings away from boyfriend Tcheky Karyo backfires when she's sucked into a new social world full of temptations and regrets. The daughter of popular star Bulle Ogier, Pascale won the best actress award at Venice, only to die shortly afterwards at the young age of 24. DP. In French with English subtitles. VIDEO DVD

Pascale Ogier *Louise* • Fabrice Luchini *Octave* • Tcheky Karyo *Rémi* • Christian Vadim *Bastien* • Virginie Thévenet *Camille* • Thérèse Liotard *Marianne* • Noël Coffman *Stanislas* ■ *Dir/Scr* Eric Rohmer

Full of Life ★★★

Comedy drama 1956 · US · BW · 90mins

The delightful Judy Holliday was rarely upstaged, but this warm family comedy is stolen by pudgy Salvatore Baccaloni, the Metropolitan Opera bass making his screen debut with a superb performance as her father-in-law. The film covers the final few days in Holliday's pregnancy with her first child, and the problems that arise when her husband's well-meaning but interfering Italian Catholic father comes to fix a hole in their floor. Holliday's anxieties are human and believable and the film has a beguiling charm. TV

Judy Holliday *Emily Rocco* • Richard Conte *Nick Rocco* • Salvatore Baccaloni *Papa Rocco* • Esther Minciotti *Mama Rocco* • Joe De Santis *Father Gondolfo* ■ *Dir* Richard Quine • *Scr* John Fante, from his novel

Fulltime Killer ★★★ 18

Action thriller 2002 · HK · Colour · 100mins

Consciously designed to appeal to Pan-Asian audiences, this country-hopping tale of two hitmen occasionally loses its way in dotting round the continent. However, co-directors Johnny To and Wai Ka-Fai make the most of the character contrasts and allow Andy Lau's film-mad ex-Olympian to exhibit plenty of crowd-pleasing bravura, while Takashi Sorimachi's Japanese veteran looks on with inscrutable disdain. Caught in the middle of their rivalry are Taiwanese video store assistant Kelly Lin and Singaporean Interpol agent Simon Yam. The action sequences are expertly contrived, but elsewhere the editing and effects are self-indulgently flamboyant. DP. In Cantonese, Mandarin, Japanese and English with subtitles. VIDEO DVD

Andy Lau *Tok* • Takashi Sorimachi *O* • Simon Yam *Lee* • Kelly Lin *Chin* ■ *Dir* Johnny To, Wai Ka-Fai • *Scr* Joey O'Bryan, Wai Ka-Fai, from a novel by Edmond Pang

The Full Treatment ★★

Mystery drama 1961 · UK · BW · 120mins

This sees racing driver Ronald Lewis follow his marriage to Diane Cilento with a serious head injury. French psychiatrist Claude Dauphin is supposed to be helping Lewis with some serious psychological problems but he's actually more interested in pursuing Cilento. The adult theme and a few sexy scenes earned this film an X certificate on release but it looks mild enough now and far too long. AT

Claude Dauphin *Dr David Prade* • Diane Cilento *Denise Colby* • Ronald Lewis *Alan Colby* • Françoise Rosay *Madame Prade* ■ *Dir* Val Guest • *Scr* Val Guest, Ronald Scott Thorn, from the novel by Ronald Scott Thorn

The Fuller Brush Girl ★★★ U

Crime comedy 1950 · US · BW · 85mins

Retaining a screenplay by Frank Tashlin, this is a remake of *The Fuller Brush Man*, filmed two years earlier as a slapstick vehicle for Red Skelton (who makes a fleeting, unbilled appearance here). However, the fresh twist is gender reversal, with Lucille Ball starring as the door-to-door saleswoman who finds herself involved in a murder investigation and forced into a series of crazy situations while fleeing the cops. Co-starring Eddie Albert as her clueless boyfriend, the movie fizzes along nicely in a cocktail of comic confusion. RK

Lucille Ball *Sally Elliott* • Eddie Albert *Humphrey Briggs* • Carl Benton Reid *Christy* • Gale Robbins *Ruby Rawlings* • Jeff Donnell *Jane Bixby* • Jerome Cowan *Harvey Simpson* • Red Skelton *Red Jones* ■ *Dir* Lloyd Bacon • *Scr* Frank Tashlin

The Fuller Brush Man ★★

Comedy mystery 1948 · US · BW · 91mins

Red Skelton's style of slapstick comedy isn't to all tastes but this is a better example than most. As a novice brush salesman, he has some fine moments going door-to-door but the picture is overburdened with a plot which makes him a murder suspect and involves a war surplus racket before the engaging climax in which the comic and his girlfriend Janet Blair are on the run from the heavies. AE

Red Skelton *Red Jones* • Janet Blair *Ann Elliot* • Don McGuire *Keenan Wallick* • Hillary Brooke *Mrs Trist* • Trudy Marshall *Sara Franzen* ■ *Dir* S Sylvan Simon • *Scr* Frank Tashlin, Devery Freeman, from the short story *Now You See It* by Roy Huggins

Fun ★★★ 18

Drama
1994 · Can/US · Colour and BW · 99mins

Director Rafal Zielinski's tale of two precocious teenagers committing murder to cement their friendship makes no effort to endear the gruesome girls to the viewer. That flaw, coupled with questionable psychology and a cop-out climax, severely undermines the *vérité* style that the director was aiming for, despite a tightly constructed plot in black and white for the present, glorious colour for the flashbacks and horribly compelling performances from Alicia Witt and Renee Humphrey. AJ

Renee Humphrey *Hilary* • Alicia Witt *Bonnie* • William R Moses *John* • Leslie Hope *Jane* • Ania Suli *Mrs Farmer* ■ *Dir* Rafal Zielinski • *Scr* James Bosley, from his play

Fun and Fancy Free ★★★ U

Part-animated musical fairy tale
1947 · US · Colour · 69mins

Disney's support for the war effort and the consequent diversion of the studio's resources, resulted in a series of packaged shorter cartoons during the late 1940s. This pairing of just two stories is one of the better pictures from that period. Jiminy Cricket's tale about Bongo the wandering bear is based on a Sinclair Lewis story, while Edgar Bergen's retelling of *Jack and the Beanstalk* is notable for being the last time Disney supplied the voice of Mickey. DP

Edgar Bergen • Dinah Shore *Narrator of Bongo* • Luana Patten • Anita Gordon *The Singing Harp* • Cliff Edwards *Jiminy Cricket* • Billy Gilbert *Willie the Giant* • Clarence Nash *Donald Duck* • Walt Disney *Mickey Mouse* • Pinto Covig *Goofy* ■ *Dir* Jack Kinney, Bill Roberts, Hamilton Luske, William Morgan • *Scr* Homer Brightman, Eldon Dedini, Lance Nolley, Tom Oreb, Harry Reeves, Ted Sears, from the short story *Bongo* by Sinclair Lewis in *Hearst's International-Cosmopolitan* and from the fairy tale *Jack and the Beanstalk*

Fun in Acapulco ★★★ U

Musical 1963 · US · Colour · 92mins

Elvis Presley performs a decidedly sub-standard score in a back-projected Mexico – though *Bossa Nova Baby* was a minor hit. The women, though, are pretty sensational: Ursula Andress, fresh from *Dr No*, plus beautiful Elsa Cardenas as a sexy lady bullfighter. Director Dick Thorpe once guided the King through the untamed *Jailhouse Rock*, but the results are much tamer here. Paul Lukas steals the show as a batty chef. TS DVD

Elvis Presley *Mike Windgren* • Ursula Andress *Margarita Dauphine* • Elsa Cardenas *Dolores Gómez* • Paul Lukas *Maximillian* • Larry Domasin *Raoul Almeido* ■ *Dir* Richard Thorpe • *Scr* Allan Weiss

Fun with Dick and Jane ★★★

Comedy 1977 · US · Colour · 99mins

The humour inherent in the title is somewhat lost on British audiences, since it's the name of a basic primary school book in the States. Dick (George Segal in top comic form) becomes unemployed, and with the help of his wife (Jane Fonda), decides to turn to crime. It's funny at first, but being out of work isn't much of a laugh really, and the gags become hard to sustain despite director Ted Kotcheff's pleasant handling of the situation. TS. Contains swearing.

George Segal *Dick Harper* • Jane Fonda *Jane Harper* • Ed McMahon *Charlie Blanchard* • Dick Gautier *Dr Will* • Allan Miller *Loan company manager* ■ *Dir* Ted Kotcheff • *Scr* David Giler, Jerry Belson, Mordecai Richler, from the story by Gerald Gaiser

The Funeral ★★★ 18

Crime drama 1996 · US · Colour · 95mins

Probably the most conventional, formal film in Abel Ferrara's 1990s canon, this crime drama, scripted by his longtime collaborator Nicholas St John, nevertheless touches upon familiar themes of guilt and redemption. Christopher Walken, for once relatively low-key, is the head of a gangster family trying to come to grips with the death of younger brother Vincent Gallo. Walken's subtle turn is matched by fine performances from Chris Penn, Isabella Rossellini and Annabella Sciorra. A little talky at times, this remains a thoughtful slow-burner. JF. Contains swearing, sex scenes and violence. DVD

Christopher Walken *Ray Tempio* • Chris Penn *Chez Tempio* • Vincent Gallo *Johnny* • Benicio Del Toro *Gaspare* • Annabella Sciorra *Jeanette* • Isabella Rossellini *Clara* • Gretchen Mol *Helen* • John Ventimiglia *Sali* ■ *Dir* Abel Ferrara • *Scr* Nicholas St John

Funeral Ceremony ★★★

Drama 1969 · Cz · BW · 79mins

Following the Soviet invasion of Czechoslovakia in 1968, four films were "banned forever" and several more were withdrawn without ever being screened. Twenty years after it was made, Zdenek Sirovy's powerful drama finally emerged as a result of the Velvet Revolution. Jaroslava Ticha gives a performance of determination and dignity as the widow demanding that her husband should be buried in the village from which he was driven during the Communist takeover of 1948. Josef Somr shows why he was one of the most significant figures of Czech cinema at the time. DP. In Czech with English subtitles.

Jaroslava Ticha • Josef Somr ■ *Dir* Zdenek Sirovy • *Scr* Zdenek Sirovy, from the novel by Eva Kanturkova

Funeral in Berlin ★★★ PG

Spy action drama 1966 · UK · Colour · 97mins

Following the success of *The Ipcress File*, Michael Caine returned as Harry Palmer in this dense thriller that is so full of ingenious plotlines that you need to have your wits about you. Caine travels behind the Iron Curtain to persuade communist spy boss Oscar Homolka to defect, only to run into Israeli agent Eva Renzi who is tracking down Nazi war criminals. The film blends action with sardonic humour, and it's all held together by Guy Hamilton's skilful, albeit rather dour, direction. Caine returned as Palmer in the less successful *Billion Dollar Brain* in 1967. DP

Michael Caine *Harry Palmer* • Eva Renzi *Samantha Steel* • Paul Hubschmid *Johnny Vulkan* • Oscar Homolka *Colonel Stok* • Guy Doleman *Ross* • Rachel Gurney *Mrs Ross* ■ *Dir* Guy Hamilton • *Scr* Evan Jones, from the novel by Len Deighton

The Funhouse ★★★ 18

Horror 1981 · US · Colour · 88mins

Director Tobe Hooper has lots of fun pulling the rug out from under the viewer's feet in this under-rated "frightmare". Four bored teenagers are challenged to spend the night in a spooky ghost train at the local carnival. Trouble is, a mutant albino wearing a Frankenstein mask knows they saw him kill a gypsy fortune teller and wants to eradicate all witnesses to his crime. It's full of clever twists, and Hooper elicits great tension from the simple cat-and-mouse concept. AJ

Elizabeth Berridge *Amy Harper* • Cooper Huckabee *Buzz* • Miles Chapin *Richie* • Largo Woodruff *Liz* • Shawn Carson *Joey Harper* ■ *Dir* Tobe Hooper • *Scr* Larry Block

Funny about Love ★★ 15

Comedy drama 1990 · US · Colour · 97mins

Despite the title, there is very little that is amusing in this lukewarm comedy. And that's quite surprising, considering the combined talents of a cast that includes Gene Wilder, Christine Lahti, Mary Stuart Masterson and Robert Prosky. This project was based on a magazine article – probably not a good omen for director Leonard Nimoy or his stars. JB. Contains swearing. DVD

Gene Wilder *Duffy Bergman* • Christine Lahti *Meg Lloyd* • Mary Stuart Masterson *Daphne Delillo* • Robert Prosky *Emil T Bergman* • Stephen Tobolowsky *Dr Hugo Blatt* ■ *Dir* Leonard Nimoy • *Scr* Norman Steinberg, David Frankel, from the article *Convention of the Love Goddesses* by Bob Greene

Funny Bones ★★★★ 15

Comedy drama
1994 · US/UK · Colour · 127mins

This wry and caustic examination of the nature of comedy gave British stand-up comedian Lee Evans the chance to shine in his movie debut, alongside American character actor Oliver Platt. Platt plays the son of a legendary comedian (played by legendary comedian Jerry Lewis), who arrives in Blackpool to buy comedy material that he intends to pass off as his own back home in America. He discovers he has a long-lost brother in in Evans, who has "funny bones" – he's effortlessly funny – whereas Platt isn't. How everything is resolved makes for eccentric viewing, with amusing highlights and quirky set pieces. AJ. Contains swearing. DVD

Oliver Platt *Tommy Fawkes* • Jerry Lewis *George Fawkes* • Lee Evans *Jack Parker* • Leslie Caron *Katie Parker* • Richard Griffiths *Jim Minty* • Oliver Reed *Dolly Hopkins* • George Carl *Thomas Parker* • Freddie Davies *Bruno Parker* ■ *Dir* Peter Chelsom • *Scr* Peter Chelsom, Peter Flannery

Funny Dirty Little War ★★★★ 15

War black comedy
1983 · Arg · Colour · 79mins

This mordantly comic film was Hector Olivera's international breakthrough, thanks to prizes at the Berlin Film Festival and critical acclaim. Such praise was deserved, since the Argentinian director combines robust humour with a fast-paced portrait of an imaginary war following Peron's return to power in 1974. A small town, Colonia Vela, near the capital is occupied by a group opposed to the army and fighting breaks out, with trapped civilians suffering torture and murder. A passionate view of turbulent South American politics. BB

Federico Luppi *Ignacio Fuentes* • Hector Bidonde *Suprino* • Victor Laplace *Reinaldo* • Rodolfo Ranni *Llanos* • Miguel Angel Sola *Juan* • Julio DeGrazia *Corporal Garcia* ■ *Dir* Hector Olivera • *Scr* Roberto Cossa, from a novel by Osvaldo Soriano

Funny Face ★★★★ U

Musical comedy 1957 · US · Colour · 103mins

With glowing Technicolor (photography by Ray June) and great Gershwin tunes, director Stanley Donen has created a film that looks as elegant today as it did when it first appeared. A satire on fashion magazines, the fabulous Fred Astaire stars as photographer Dick Avery (Richard Avedon was the film's consultant), who finds the face of his dreams (Audrey Hepburn) in a Greenwich Village bookstore, while Kay Thompson stands out as an imperious magazine editor. Scintillating, magical and above all romantic. TS DVD

Audrey Hepburn *Jo Stockton* • Fred Astaire *Dick Avery* • Kay Thompson *Maggie Prescott* • Michel Auclair *Prof Emile Flostre* • Robert Flemyng *Paul Duval* • Dovima *Marion* ■ *Dir* Stanley Donen • *Scr* Leonard Gershe, from his musical libretto *Wedding Day*

Funny Farm ★★ PG

Comedy 1988 · US · Colour · 97mins

Chevy Chase plays a sports hack who finds himself wrestling with life in the country. Quite why esteemed director George Roy Hill would want to build a film around the cheesy charm of Chase is beyond understanding. However, his smart mouth, wrap-around smirk and Tinseltown teeth do join forces to provide a degree of relaxed enjoyment, even when the gags stop being funny, which they too often do. By contrast, the final sequence is blessed with a comic vitality missing from much of the film. JM. Contains some swearing.

Chevy Chase *Andy Farmer* • Madolyn Smith *Elizabeth Farmer* • Joseph Maher *Michael Sinclair* • Jack Gilpin *Bud Culbertson* • Brad Sullivan *Brock* • MacIntyre Dixon *Mayor Barclay* ■ *Dir* George Roy Hill • *Scr* Jeffrey Boam, from the book by Jay Cronley

Funny Games ★★★ 18

Thriller 1997 · Austria · Colour · 104mins

Austrian director Michael Haneke's controversial cautionary tale is lauded in some circles for being an uncompromising study of on-screen violence and, in others, as the worst type of exploitation that panders to the same base instincts it purports to lay bare. Two young men inveigle their way into the holiday home of a middle-class family and subject them to degrading torture and sickening humiliation in a deconstruction of terror that's radical and thought-provoking, but also too clever by half. This is a powerful "shockumentary" that's hard to watch – deliberately. AJ. In German with English subtitles. Contains violence and swearing. DVD

Susanne Lothar *Anna* • Ulrich Mühe *Georg* • Frank Giering *Peter* • Arno Frisch *Paul* • Stefan Clapczynski *"Schorschi"* • Doris Kunstmann *Gerda* • Christoph Bantzer *Fred* • Wolfgang Glück *Robert* ■ *Dir/Scr* Michael Haneke

Funny Girl ★★★★ U

Biographical musical
1968 · US · Colour · 141mins

This was a spectacular switch from stage to screen for Barbra Streisand, replicating her Broadway triumph as legendary entertainer Fanny Brice. Streisand's bravura performance earned her a joint Oscar for best actress (she shared the honour with Katharine Hepburn) and the film was nominated for a further seven, including best score and best song. It traces Brice's rise from vaudeville to the Ziegfeld Follies by way of a troubled marriage to gambler Nick Arnstein, and Streisand is given fine support by the ultra-smooth Omar Sharif. The success of this marvellous film led to a sequel, *Funny Lady*, seven years later. AT DVD

Barbra Streisand *Fanny Brice* • Omar Sharif *Nick Arnstein* • Kay Medford *Rose Brice* • Anne Francis *Georgia James* • Walter Pidgeon *Florenz Ziegfeld* • Lee Allen *Eddie Ryan* • Mae Questel *Mrs Strakosh* ■ *Dir* William Wyler • *Scr* Isobel Lennart, from the musical by Jule Styne, Bob Merrill, Isobel Lennart

Funny Lady ★★★ PG

Biographical musical
1975 · US · Colour · 132mins

Barbra Streisand returns to the role of Ziegfeld Follies star Fanny Brice for producer Ray Stark (the man behind *Funny Girl*). This sequel suffers a little in the hands of choreographer-turned-director Herbert Ross, who can't quite control the clichés of the plot or the rowdy performance of James Caan. Still, the musical numbers are fine, and there's some fancy footwork from Ben Vereen, plus a welcome guest appearance from *Funny Girl* co-star Omar Sharif. TS DVD

Barbra Streisand *Fanny Brice* • James Caan *Billy Rose* • Omar Sharif *Nick Arnstein* • Roddy McDowall *Bobby* • Ben Vereen *Bert Robbins* • Carole Wells *Norma Butler* ■ *Dir* Herbert Ross • *Scr* Arnold Schulman, Jay Presson Allen, from a story by Arnold Schulman

The Funny Man ★★ 18

Horror comedy 1994 · UK · Colour · 88mins

Monty Python meets Freddy Krueger in a predictable drip-feed of gore, gags and groans in this horror tale spoof. Benny Young wins a haunted house in a poker game with Christopher Lee, and then falls prey to its fourth dimensional evil spirit incarnated as a demented jester. The harlequin from hell (Tim James) then indulges in wickedly droll murders as Young's friends are systematically disembowelled and dismembered. Debut director Simon Sprackling's slapdash comic strip shows some brutal invention, but for the most part it's a childish, witless endeavour. AJ. Contains swearing and violence.

Tim James *The Funny Man* • Christopher Lee *Callum Chance* • Ingrid Lacey *Tina Taylor* • Matthew Devitt *Johnny Taylor* • Chris Walker *Morgan "Hard Man"* • George Morton *Alan "Crap Puppeteer"* • Rhona Cameron *Thelma Fudd* ■ *Dir/Scr* Simon Sprackling

A Funny Thing Happened on the Way to the Forum ★★★ PG

Musical comedy
1966 · US/UK · Colour · 93mins

This toga-clad musical farce about ancient Roman scandals was the inspiration for Frankie Howerd's popular TV series, *Up Pompeii*. Richard Lester's undisciplined direction takes its cue from the great comic line-up: Zero Mostel as the slave seeking freedom; Phil Silvers as a Bilko-like brothel keeper; Jack Gilford as Hysterium; and the great Buster Keaton, in one of his last feature films, as a man who's lost his children. Ramshackle it may be but it retains the verve and humour of its Broadway origins. TH DVD

Zero Mostel *Pseudolus* • Phil Silvers *Lycus* • Jack Gilford *Hysterium* • Buster Keaton *Erronius* • Michael Crawford *Hero* • Annette Andre *Philia* • Patricia Jessel *Domina* • Michael Hordern *Senex* ■ *Dir* Richard Lester • *Scr* Melvin Frank, Michael Pertwee, from the musical by Burt Shevelove, Larry Gelbart • *Cinematographer* Nicolas Roeg • *Music/lyrics* Stephen Sondheim

The Furies ★★★★

Western 1950 · US · BW · 108mins

This intense, highly-charged account of power, passion, rivalry and revenge has much in common with Greek tragedy and is full of far-from-subtle Freudian elements. (Watch how Walter Huston and Barbara Stanwyck, as a father and daughter perpetually at odds, ease their faces closer until it seems they are about to kiss.) Expertly written by Charles Schnee and brilliantly directed by Anthony Mann, the film is powerfully performed. Franz Waxman's rousing score and Victor Milner's Oscar-nominated photography add to the pleasures of an overwrought but totally compelling piece. TV

Barbara Stanwyck *Vance Jeffords* • Walter Huston *TC Jeffords* • Wendell Corey *Rip Darrow* • Judith Anderson *Florence Burnett* • Gilbert Roland *Juan Herrera* • Thomas Gomez *El Tigre* • Beulah Bondi *Mrs Annaheim* ■ *Dir* Anthony Mann • *Scr* Charles Schnee, from the novel by Niven Busch

A Further Gesture ★★ 15

Political thriller
1996 · UK/Ger/Jpn/Ire · Colour · 96mins

Director Robert Dornhelm contributes little except melancholy to this barely coherent political thriller. Stephen Rea plays an escaped IRA prisoner who flees to the US and is asked by a group of Guatemalan immigrants to assist in an assassination attempt. There's precious little insight and even less drama to be found in Ronan Bennett's screenplay. TH. Contains swearing and violence.

Stephen Rea *Dowd* • Alfred Molina *Tulio* • Rosana Pastor *Monica* • Brendan Gleeson *Richard* • Jorge Sanz *Paco* • Pruitt Taylor Vince *Scott* • Frankie McCafferty *Danny* ■ *Dir* Robert Dornhelm • *Scr* Ronan Bennett, from an idea by Stephen Rea

Further up the Creek ★★ U

Comedy 1958 · UK · BW · 86mins

Made in something of a hurry by director Val Guest, as he sought to cash in on the success of *Up the Creek*, this sequel suffers from both indifferent plotting and the absence of Peter Sellers from the role of the scheming bosun. Exploiting the sale of his ship to the ruler of Algerocco by flogging tickets for a Mediterranean cruise, Frankie Howerd (not a natural before the movie camera) works every gag, as the floating con trick is called to action stations. DP DVD

David Tomlinson *Lt Fairweather* • Frankie Howerd *Bos'n* • Shirley Eaton *Jane* • Thora Hird *Mrs Galloway* • Lionel Jeffries *Steady Barker* ■ *Dir* Val Guest • *Scr* Val Guest, John Warren, Len Heath

Fury ★★★

Silent adventure 1923 · US · BW

This is an all-stops-out melodrama set aboard a sailing ship and at the docks of London and Glasgow. Richard Barthelmess plays the son of Tyrone Power (senior) whose wife, Dorothy Gish, has run off with another man – which proves to be upsetting for everyone. It was a big hit with 1920s audiences, who loved its heaving emotions and its vividly filmed depiction of life at sea. AT

Richard Barthelmess *Boy Leyton* • Tyrone Power *Captain Leyton* • Pat Hartigan *Morgan* • Barry Macollum *Looney Luke* • Dorothy Gish *Minnie* • Jessie Arnold *Boy's mother* ■ *Dir* Henry King • *Scr* Edmund Goulding

Fury ★★★★

Crime drama 1936 · US · BW · 92mins

Austrian-born director Fritz Lang's first American movie is a searing indictment of lynch law based on a true case. The film is given tremendous intensity by the naturalistic performances of leads Spencer Tracy, as the man unjustly accused, and Sylvia Sidney as his fiancée. This is an uncomfortable film to watch, with Joseph Ruttenberg's lighting deliberately expressionistic, but the second half fails to carry the conviction of the opening scenes, and a bizarre manic thrust takes over, perhaps intended to symbolise the unchannelled fury of the mob. TS

Spencer Tracy *Joe Wilson* • Sylvia Sidney *Katherine Grant* • Walter Abel *District Attorney* • Bruce Cabot *Kirby Dawson* • Edward Ellis *Sheriff* • Walter Brennan *"Bugs" Meyers* • George Walcott *Tom* ■ *Dir* Fritz Lang • *Scr* Bartlett Cormack, Fritz Lang, from the story *Mob Rule* by Norman Krasna

The Fury ★★★★ 18

Psychological horror
1978 · US · Colour · 113mins

Brian De Palma found himself in familiar territory with this follow-up to *Carrie* – an adaptation of John Farris's telekinetic conspiracy thriller. Adopting a broader suspense canvas than he'd utilised before (the action and slow motion sequences remain the best he's ever crafted), De Palma's gorgeous horror adventure concerns two teens with psychic powers who become pawns between spy factions. Ingeniously plotted, extravagantly staged and beautifully balanced between apocalyptic goriness and full-blooded pyrotechnic imagery, this nail-biting shocker is De Palma's most under-rated movie. AJ DVD

Kirk Douglas *Peter Sandza* • John Cassavetes *Childress* • Carrie Snodgress *Hester* • Charles Durning *Dr Jim McKeever* • Amy Irving *Gillian Bellaver* • Fiona Lewis *Dr Susan Charles* • Andrew Stevens *Robin Sandza* • Carol Rossen *Dr Ellen Lindstrom* ■ *Dir* Brian De Palma • *Scr* John Farris, from his novel

Fury at Furnace Creek ★★ U

Western 1948 · US · BW · 87mins

When General Blackwell (Robert Warwick) is accused of instigating an Indian massacre, his sons Victor Mature and Glenn Langan are determined to clear his name. The solution lies in the boom town of Furnace Creek where the head of a mining syndicate, well played by Albert Dekker, is revealed as the villain. AE

Victor Mature *Cash* • Coleen Gray *Molly Baxter* • Glenn Langan *Rufe* • Reginald Gardiner *Capt Walsh* • Albert Dekker *Leverett* ■ *Dir* H Bruce Humberstone • *Scr* Charles G Booth, Winston Miller, from the novel by David Garth

Fury at Showdown ★★★

Western 1957 · US · BW · 75mins

His pretty-boy days behind him, John Derek gives an intense performance as a complex cowboy in this atmospheric western. Derek tries to live down his reputation as a gunfighter by running a cattle ranch, while villains pressure him into selling his property. Directed with punch by Gerd Oswald and photographed beautifully by Joseph LaShelle, the film is quite an achievement considering it was shot in only five days. RB

John Derek *Brock Mitchell* • John Smith *Miley Sutton* • Carolyn Craig *Ginny Clay* • Nick Adams *Tracy Mitchell* • Gage Clarke *Chad Deasey* ■ *Dir* Gerd Oswald • *Scr* Jason James, from the novel by Lucas Todd

Fury at Smugglers Bay ★★★ PG

Period adventure 1961 · UK · BW · 82mins

Writer/director John Gilling's rumbustious tale of Cornish piracy has squire Peter Cushing and his gung-ho son John Fraser take on Bernard Lee and his band of smuggling cut-throats. This 1790s adventure is tantamount to an English western, with a saloon brawl, sword-wielding showdowns and a last-minute rescue. DP DVD

John Fraser *Chris Trevenyan* • Peter Cushing *Squire Trevenyan* • Bernard Lee *Black John* • June Thorburn *Jenny Trevenyan* • Michèle Mercier *Louise Lejeune* • George Coulouris *François Lejeune* • Miles Malleson *Duke of Avon* ■ *Dir/Scr* John Gilling

Futuresport ★★ 15

Science-fiction action drama
1998 · US · Colour · 86mins

This glossily unimaginative TV movie borrows so liberally from the far superior *Rollerball* as to appear totally redundant. Set in the future, a violent game is created in a bid to ease gang tensions, a sort of amalgam of basketball and rugby played on levitating skateboards with an electrified ball. The trio of stars – Dean Cain, Vanessa L Williams and Wesley Snipes – add much needed lustre to Ernest Dickerson's join-the-dots direction. RS. Contains swearing, violence and nudity. DVD

Wesley Snipes *Obike Fixx* • Dean Cain *Tremaine "Tre" Ramzey* • Vanessa L Williams *Alex Torres* • Bill Smitrovich *Coach Douglas Freeman* • Adrian Hughes ■ *Dir* Ernest R Dickerson • *Scr* Robert Hewitt Wolfe, from a story by Steve Dejarnatt, Robert Hewitt Wolfe

Futureworld ★★★ PG

Science-fiction thriller
1976 · US · Colour · 103mins

This inventive sci-fi thriller – the follow-up to the excellent *Westworld* – gives more than a nod in the direction of Don Siegel's classic *Invasion of the Body Snatchers*, with a story about the replacement of the world's ruling elite by lookalike robots. Less explosive than its predecessor, this is nevertheless an unnerving watch, and makes good use of early 3-D computer animation. DP DVD

Peter Fonda *Chuck Browning* • Blythe Danner *Tracy Ballard* • Arthur Hill *Duffy* • Yul Brynner *Gunslinger* • John Ryan [John P Ryan] *Dr Schneider* • Stuart Margolin *Harry* • Jim Antonio *Ron* • Allen Ludden *Game show host* ■ *Dir* Richard T Heffron • *Scr* Mayo Simon, George Schenck

Fuzz ★★ 18

Detective comedy
1972 · US · Colour · 89mins

Evan Hunter adapted this cynical cop comedy from one of the *87th Precinct* stories he wrote under his pseudonym Ed McBain. A series of vignettes involving a quartet of Boston cops is linked by ingenious bombings carried out by Yul Brynner. The standout scenes involve Burt Reynolds and Jack Weston posing as nuns, and Tom Skerritt and Raquel Welch trying to concentrate on a stakeout while sharing a sleeping bag. The characterisation is rounded and the station-house atmosphere well established, but the Keystone-style mayhem is slightly ham-fisted. DP

Burt Reynolds *Detective Carella* • Jack Weston *Detective Meyer* • Tom Skerritt *Detective Kling* • Yul Brynner *The Deaf Man* • Raquel Welch *Detective McHenry* • James McEachin *Detective Brown* ■ *Dir* Richard A Colla • *Scr* Evan Hunter, from the novel by Ed McBain [Evan Hunter]

The Fuzzy Pink Nightgown ★★ U

Comedy 1957 · US · BW · 87mins

Inspired by a true-life incident when actress Marie McDonald was purportedly kidnapped, then discovered wandering in the desert, this mild comedy tells a similar tale of a movie star (Jane Russell) kidnapped just before the release of her new film, *The Kidnapped Heiress*. Predictably, no one will believe the incident is not a publicity stunt and, just as predictably, Russell falls for handsome kidnapper Ralph Meeker. Russell took the blame for the film's commercial failure, stating that she insisted on black and white rather than colour and told director Norman Taurog to play up the romance at the expense of comedy. TV

Jane Russell *Laurel Stevens* • Ralph Meeker *Mike Valla* • Keenan Wynn *Dandy* • Adolphe Menjou *Arthur Martin* ■ *Dir* Norman Taurog • *Scr* Richard Alan Simmons, from the novel by Sylvia Tate

F

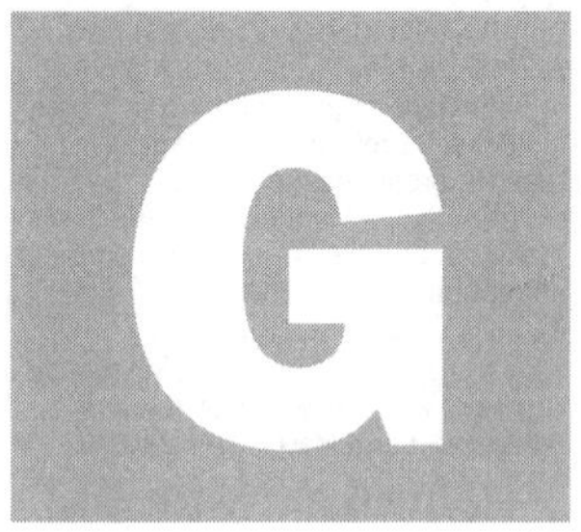

GI Blues ★★★ U

Musical 1960 · US · Colour · 99mins

Elvis Presley had been away for two years, heroically doing his military service, including a spell in Germany, and this comeback film was intended to capitalise on that. This movie substantially shifted Elvis's image – from the teenage rebel of *King Creole* to the all-American soldier boy. Sultry Juliet Prowse is the dancer he loses his heart to after he woos her for a $300 bet, and the songs are classy. TS DVD

Elvis Presley *Tulsa McCauley* • James Douglas *Rick* • Robert Ivers *Cookey* • Juliet Prowse *Lili* • Leticia Roman *Tina* • Sigrid Maier *Marla* • Arch Johnson *Sergeant McGraw* • The Jordanaires ■ *Dir* Norman Taurog • *Scr* Edmund Beloin, Henry Garson

GI Jane ★★ 15

Action drama
1997 · US/UK · Colour · 119mins

Demi Moore built up her body but forgot to spend equal time on her acting skills for this high-on-testosterone, low-on-brains action film from Ridley Scott. Moore stars as the first woman to train with the macho Navy SEALS as part of a government experiment. Expect lots of lingering shots of a very buff Demi flexing muscles, shaving her head and kicking male butt, but don't expect much in the way of great moments in acting. JB. Contains swearing, violence and brief nudity. DVD

Demi Moore *Lt Jordan O'Neil* • Viggo Mortensen *Master Chief John Urgayle* • Anne Bancroft *Lillian DeHaven* • Jason Beghe *Royce* • Scott Wilson *CO Salem* • Lucinda Jenney *Blondell* • Morris Chestnut *McCool* • Jim Caviezel *Slovnik* • Daniel Von Bargen *Theodore Hayes* ■ *Dir* Ridley Scott • *Scr* David N Twohy [David Twohy], Danielle Alexandra, from a story by Danielle Alexandra

GMT Greenwich Mean Time ★ 18

Drama 1998 · UK · Colour · 117mins

This is unconvincing, painfully clichéd garbage about a bunch of London-based friends who are torn apart by everything from jealousy to paralysis. For two unbearable hours, the film leaps clumsily between half a dozen plot strands, as poorly defined characters spew out corny dialogue and experience a couple of traumas each. The decent drum 'n' bass soundtrack helps a little, but this is still nothing short of an ordeal. JC

Alec Newman *Charlie* • Melanie Gutteridge *Lucy* • Georgia MacKenzie *Rachel* • Chiwetel Ejiofor *Rix* • Steve John Shepherd *Sam* • Alicya Eyo *Bobby* • Benjamin Waters *Bean* • Anjela Lauren Smith *Sherry* ■ *Dir* John Strickland • *Scr* Simon Mirren

"G" Men ★★★

Crime drama 1935 · US · BW · 84mins

This is a typically gritty Warner Bros gangster melodrama from the studio's greatest period, with James Cagney on the side of justice for once. Director William Keighley keeps the action cracking along, and there's terrific support from all those regular Warners character players, plus Ann Dvorak as Cagney's former girlfriend. But no one else really gets a look in, as this is Cagney's movie, a vehicle to show off the abilities of one of cinema's most talented stars in one of his best roles, fast talking, tough and terrific. TS

James Cagney *James "Brick" Davis* • Ann Dvorak *Jean Morgan* • Margaret Lindsay *Kay McCord* • Robert Armstrong *Jeff McCord* • Barton MacLane *Brad Collins* • Lloyd Nolan *Hugh Farrell* • William Harrigan *McKay* • Edward Pawley *Danny Leggett* ■ *Dir* William Keighley • *Scr* Seton I Miller, from the novel *Public Enemy No 1* by Gregory Rogers

G-Men from Hell ★★ 12

Action comedy fantasy
2000 · US · Colour · 94mins

Inspired by Michael Allred's comic-book, *Grafik Muzik*, this is a brilliant premise that loses its way as Christopher Coppola strives to reproduce the twisting complexities of hardboiled pulp. Escaping from Hell after a lifetime's iniquity, cops Tate Donovan and William Forsythe vow to go straight to avoid a reunion with the satanic Robert Goulet. However, decency becomes increasingly difficult as they investigate the murder of millionaire Barry Newman, who had hired them to keep tabs on his scheming wife, Vanessa Angel. DP

William Forsythe *Dean Crept* • Tate Donovan *Mike Mattress* • Bob Goldthwait [Bobcat Goldthwait] *Buster* • Barry Newman *Greydon Lake* • Vanessa Angel *Gloria Lake* • David Huddleston *Dr Boifford* • Kari Wuhrer *Marete* • Charles Fleischer *Martin/Pete* • Gregory Sporleder *Cheetah man* • Gary Busey *Lt Langdon* • Robert Goulet *Lucifer* ■ *Dir* Christopher Coppola • *Scr* Robert Cooper, Richard L Albert, Nicholas Johnson, from the comic book *Grafik Muzik* by Michael Allred

Gabbeh ★★★★ U

Fantasy documentary drama
1995 · Iran/Fr · Colour · 69mins

Woven by the nomadic Ghashgai tribe of south-eastern Iran, gabbehs are intricately designed carpets, laden with symbolic figures, like the one that comes to life in Mohsen Makhmalbaf's beautifully modulated, dazzlingly composed folk tale. Relating the story of Shaghayegh Djodat's love for an unnamed horseman and the conditions set on her by her father, it shows how Djodat wins the heart of the old man washing the carpet. As past and present intermingle, their shared emotions and experiences are reflected in the brightly coloured strands. Originally intended as a documentary about the weavers, this sublime cinematic poem fulfils its director's claim to be a "song of life". DP. In Farsi with English subtitles.

Shaghayegh Djodat *Gabbeh* • Abbas Sayahi *Poet/teacher* • Hossein Moharami *Old man* • Roghieh Moharami *Old woman* ■ *Dir/Scr* Mohsen Makhmalbaf

Gable and Lombard ★

Biographical romance
1976 · US · Colour · 131mins

A tragic romance is presented more like a screwball comedy in this disastrous biopic that shamefully insults its subjects. James Brolin is rigidly unconvincing as Clark Gable, while Jill Clayburgh brims over with anachronistic energy as Carole Lombard, the sparky actress who stole the King of Hollywood's heart and then broke it when she was killed in a plane crash on a wartime bond rally. Director Sidney J Furie fails to capture either the atmosphere of the period or the uniqueness of the relationship. DP

James Brolin *Clark Gable* • Jill Clayburgh *Carole Lombard* • Allen Goorwitz [Allen Garfield] *Louis B Mayer* • Red Buttons *Ivan Cooper* • Joanne Linville *Ria Gable* • Melanie Mayron *Dixie* • Carol McGinnis *Noreen* • Noah Keen *A Broderick* ■ *Dir* Sidney J Furie • *Scr* Barry Sandler

Gabriel & Me ★★ 15

Drama 2001 · UK · Colour · 83mins

Young Jimmy Spud (Sean Landless) wants to become a guardian angel and so he enlists the archangel Gabriel (Billy Connolly). After performing one feat of life-saving, Landless is convinced his powers are increasing. But will he be able to help when his father (Iain Glen in a standout performance) is diagnosed with terminal lung cancer? Udayan Prasad's direction is spirited enough to make the soul-searching gloom almost palatable, but Lee Hall's adaptation is too faithful to his original BBC radio play and the result is a depressing kitchen-sink saga. AJ. Contains swearing. DVD

Iain Glen *Dad* • David Bradley (3) *Grandad* • Sean Landless *Jimmy Spud* • Rosie Rowell *Mam* • Billy Connolly *Gabriel* ■ *Dir* Udayan Prasad • *Scr* Lee Hall, from his radio play *I Luv You Jimmy Spud*

Gabriel over the White House ★★★

Political fantasy 1933 · US · BW · 94mins

A witty and highly distinctive political satire starring Walter Huston as a rather corrupt president, who survives an accident, is visited by the Archangel Gabriel and goes on to save America from the Depression and gangsters. The picture's simple-minded patriotism has to be seen to be believed, though the film went through some political cartwheels of its own during production in order to assuage MGM boss Louis B Mayer's political sympathies. AT

Walter Huston *Judson Hammond* • Arthur Byron *Jasper Brooks* • Karen Morley *Pendota Molloy* • Franchot Tone *Hartley Beekman* • Dickie Moore *Jimmy Vetter* • C Henry Gordon *Nick Diamond* • David Landau *John Bronson* • Samuel Hinds [Samuel S Hinds] *Dr Eastman* • William Pawley *Borell* • Jean Parker *Alice Bronson* • Claire DuBrey *Nurse* ■ *Dir* Gregory La Cava • *Scr* Carey Wilson, Bertram Bloch, from the novel *Rinehard* by TF Tweed

Gabriela ★★ 18

Romantic drama 1983 · Bra · Colour · 99mins

Already the inspiration for a steamy TV soap, Jorge Amado's novel was adapted for the big screen by Bruno Barreto. Set in the 1920s, the action takes place in the scrubland village of Parati, where, despite a drought, bartender Marcello Mastroianni struggles to make a living – until he hires the shamelessly sensual Sonja Braga (reprising her role from the TV series) as his cook. Such is Barreto's fixation with Braga's body that the tone is risibly soft-core. DP. In Portuguese with English subtitles.

Sonia Braga *Gabriela* • Marcello Mastroianni *Nacib* • Antonio Cantafora *Tonico Bastos* • Paulo Goulart *Colonel Joao Fulgencio* ■ *Dir* Bruno Barreto • *Scr* Bruno Barreto, Leopoldo Serran, from the novel *Gabriela, Clove and Cinnamon* by Jorge Amado

Gaby ★★

Wartime romantic drama
1956 · US · Colour · 97mins

The third screen version of the play *Waterloo Bridge*, though still hidebound by censorship, was updated to the Second World War. It stars a beguiling Leslie Caron s the ballerina forced to become a prostitute through circumstance. John Kerr is gauche as her beau, but then who could ever erase memories of Robert Taylor and Vivien Leigh in the classic 1940 version? The film does have a quaint 1950s sheen, but director Curtis Bernhardt's pacing is slow, and the overall effect is dull. TS

Leslie Caron *Gaby* • John Kerr *Gregory Y Wendell* • Cedric Hardwicke *Mr Carrington* • Taina Elg *Elsa* • Margalo Gillmore *Mrs Carrington* • Scott Marlowe *Jan* • Ian Wolfe *Registrar* • Joe Di Reda *Allen* • Ruta Lee *Denise* ■ *Dir* Curtis Bernhardt • *Scr* Albert Hackett, Frances Goodrich, Charles Lederer, from the film *Waterloo Bridge* by SN Behrman, Paul H Rameau, George Froeschel, from the play by Robert E Sherwood

Gaby: a True Story ★★★ 15

Biographical drama
1987 · US · Colour · 109mins

Rachel Levin plays Gabriela Brimmer, the Mexico-born daughter of emigrant Austrian Jews, who used her left leg to communicate with a world that had condemned her to vegetative isolation. Argentinian actress Norma Aleandro was nominated for her supporting turn as the nanny who recognises the repressed intelligence of her charge and persuades despairing parents Liv Ullmann and Robert Loggia to further her education. Luis Mandoki melodramatises Levin's romance with fellow cerebral palsy victim Lawrence Monoson, but otherwise avoids overt sentimentality. DP

Liv Ullmann *Sari Brimmer* • Norma Aleandro *Florencia Morales, Gaby's Nurse* • Robert Loggia *Michel Brimmer* • Rachel Levin *Gabriela "Gaby" Brimmer* • Lawrence Monoson *Fernando* • Robert Beltran *Luis* ■ *Dir* Luis Mandoki • *Scr* Martin Salinas, Michael James Love, from a story by Luis Mandoki, from events narrated by Gabriela Brimmer

Gadjo Dilo ★★★ 15

Drama 1997 · Fr · Colour · 101mins

Director Tony Gatlif completes the "Gypsy Triptych" he began with *Les Princes* (1982) and *Latcho Drom* (1993) with this striking, if sentimentalised drama. As the young Parisian seduced by culture shock, Romain Duris seems too eager to conform. But Izidor Serban is mischievously grizzled as his surrogate father, and Rona Hartner brings a fierce sense of self-worth to the role of the enticing Romanian firebrand. While it seeks to score social points, this is more a celebration of the Romany lifestyle than a plea for greater tolerance. DP. In French with English subtitles. Contains swearing, sex scenes and sexual references.

Romain Duris *Stéphane* • Rona Hartner *Sabina* • Izidor Serban *Izidor* • Ovidiu Balan *Sami* • Angela Serban *Angela* • Aurica Ursan *Aurica* • Vasile Serban *Vasile* • Ioan Serban *Ioan* ■ *Dir/Scr* Tony Gatlif

Le Gai Savoir ★

Documentary drama
1968 · Fr · Colour · 95mins

This film marked Godard's irrevocable break with narrative cinema. It's supposed to be an adaptation of Swiss philosopher Jean Jacques Rousseau's novel about education, *Emile* – at least, that's what French TV commissioned. However, it consists mainly of Jean-Pierre Léaud and Juliet Berto sitting in a black void of a TV studio beneath a transparent umbrella to protect them from atomic radiation. Their chat consists of naive slogans, Maoist ideas and general ranting about the media and capitalism. Pretentious, incredibly boring and infuriating. AT. In French with English subtitles.

Juliet Berto *Patricia Lumumba* • Jean-Pierre Léaud *Emile Rousseau* ■ *Dir* Jean-Luc Godard • *Scr* Jean-Luc Godard, from the book *Emile* by Jean Jacques Rousseau

Gaiety George ★★★

Period musical biography
1946 · UK · BW · 98mins

Richard Greene, best known to a generation as TV's Robin Hood, here portrays the father figure of Edwardian musical comedy, George Edwardes, famous for his Gaiety Girls. He's called George Howard here, renamed perhaps because Greene totally fails to evoke Edwardes's trademark flamboyance and Irish vitality. A pallid Ann Todd doesn't add much as the love interest, and the film cries out for colour. However, the period atmosphere is well re-created, ingénue Hazel Court is particularly mesmerising, and the whole is not unwatchable. TS

Richard Greene *George Howard* • Ann Todd *Kathryn Davis* • Peter Graves (1) *Carter* • Hazel Court *Elizabeth Brown* • Leni Lynn *Florence Stephens* • Ursula Jeans *Isobel Forbes* • Morland Graham *Morris* • Frank Pettingell *Grindley* ■ *Dir* George King, Freddie Carpenter, Leontine Sagan • *Scr* Katherine Strueby, Basil Woon, from a story by Richard Fisher, Peter Cresswell

Gaily, Gaily ★★

Period comedy 1969 · US · Colour · 106mins

Released as *Chicago, Chicago* in the UK, this account of screenwriter Ben Hecht's early career should have been a stingingly satirical portrait of the Windy City at its breeziest. Instead, it's a crass comedy with the laughs writ large and the playing wildly over the top. Beau Bridges grows in confidence as the cub reporter who discovers that Melina Mercouri's "hotel" is a brothel. Director Norman Jewison spends more time showing off his gaudy period sets than on the story. DP

Beau Bridges *Ben Harvey* • Melina Mercouri *Queen Lil* • Brian Keith *Francis X Sullivan* • George Kennedy *Axel P Johanson* • Hume Cronyn *"Honest" Tim Grogan* • Margot Kidder *Adeline* • Wilfrid Hyde White *Governor* ■ *Dir* Norman Jewison • *Scr* Abram S Ginnes, from the memoirs by Ben Hecht

The Gal Who Took the West ★★ U

Comedy western 1949 · US · Colour · 84mins

This B-western was photographed by William H Daniels, Garbo's favourite cameraman, and his Arizona vistas are the sole reason for enduring this unfunny attempt to parody the conventions of the genre. Director Frederick De Cordova fails to invest the proceedings with any brio, hindered by a below-par screenplay that recounts the battle between cousins John Russell and Scott Brady for the affections of Yvonne De Carlo. DP

Yvonne De Carlo *Lillian Marlowe* • Charles Coburn *General Michael O'Hara* • Scott Brady *Lee O'Hara* • John Russell *Grant O'Hara* • Myrna Dell *Nancy* ■ *Dir* Frederick De Cordova • *Scr* William Bowers, Oscar Brodney, from their story

Gal Young Un ★★

Drama 1979 · US · Colour · 105mins

An early indie production from Victor Nunez, the future director of *Ruby in Paradise* and *Ulee's Gold*. Set in the 1930s in the backwoods of Florida, the story concerns a woman who has chosen to live a simple and solitary existence. A young bootlegger and conman, who comes out of nowhere, becomes romantically involved with her and fleeces her of her modest savings. Slow to unfold, earnest in tone and uneven in performance. AT

Dana Preu *Mattie Siles* • David Peck *Trax* • J Smith *Elly* • Gene Densmore *Storekeeper* • Jennie Stringfellow *Edna* • Tim McCormack *Blaine* • Casey Donovan *Jeb Lantry* • Mike Garlington *Eddy Lantry* • Marshall New *Edgar* • Bruce Cornwell *Phil* ■ *Dir* Victor Nunez • *Scr* Victor Nunez, from a story by Marjorie Kinnan Rawlings • *Cinematographer* Victor Nunez

Galaxina ★

Science-fiction spoof
1980 · US · Colour · 95mins

This spoof features lowbrow comedy, duff special effects and a central performance by Dorothy Stratten, murdered by her estranged husband on the very day it received its American premiere. The doomed starlet is the robot navigator on board a police spaceship. Few laughs and even fewer thrills are raised thanks to an unfocused script and haphazard direction. A sad epitaph. AJ

Dorothy Stratten *Galaxina* • Stephen Macht *Thor* • Ronald Knight *Ordric* • Lionel Smith *Maurice* • Tad Horino *Sam Wo* • Nancy McCauley *Elexia* • Avery Schreiber *Captain Butt* ■ *Dir/Scr* William Sachs

Galaxy Quest ★★★★ PG

Science-fiction spoof
1999 · US · Colour · 97mins

In this enormously entertaining send-up of the *Star Trek* universe, a bunch of actors from a cult sci-fi TV show are mistaken for the real thing and recruited to defend a dying alien race. It's an inspired premise, fired into orbit by a fantastic script, sublime visual effects and an absolutely perfect cast, including Tim Allen, Sigourney Weaver and Alan Rickman, hysterical as a grumpy British actor who hates his half-reptilian character. The story is so cleverly executed and the characters so nicely fleshed-out that it not only succeeds as a *Trek* spoof, a satire on the acting profession and a parody of sci-fi fans, but also as an original space saga. JC [VIDEO] DVD

Tim Allen *Jason Nesmith/Commander Peter Quincy Taggart* • Sigourney Weaver *Gwen DeMarco/Lt Tawny Madison* • Alan Rickman *Alexander Dane/Dr Lazarus* • Tony Shalhoub *Fred Kwan/Tech Sgt Chen* • Sam Rockwell *Guy Fleegman* • Daryl Mitchell *Tommy Webber/Laredo* • Enrico Colantoni *Mathesar* • Robin Sachs *Sarris* • Patrick Breen *Quellek* ■ *Dir* Dean Parisot • *Scr* Robert Gordon, David Howard, from a story by David Howard

Galileo ★★★ PG

Historical biography
1974 · UK/Can · Colour · 138mins

After fiddling on the roof for so long, Topol steps down to take on the role of the 17th-century Italian mathematician and astronomer whose heretical theories of the universe brought him into dangerous confrontation with the Roman Catholic church and the Inquisition. Adapted from the play by Bertolt Brecht and directed by Joseph Losey, this is a rather static production from the America Film Theatre. However the actors enliven the debate. TH DVD

Chaim Topol [Topol] *Galileo Galilei* • Edward Fox *Cardinal Inquisitor* • Colin Blakely *Priuli* • Georgia Brown *Ballad singer's wife* • Clive Revill *Ballad singer* • Margaret Leighton *Court lady* • John Gielgud *Old cardinal* • Michael Gough *Sagredo* • Michel Lonsdale *Cardinal Barberini (later Pope)* • Tom Conti *Andrea Sarti as a man* ■ *Dir* Joseph Losey • *Scr* Barbara Bray, Joseph Losey, Charles Laughton, from the play by Bertolt Brecht

The Gallant Blade ★★ U

Swashbuckling adventure
1948 · US · Colour · 80mins

Although it's set at the time of the Three Musketeers, this 17th-century swashbuckler lacks the wit that spices up the best screen adaptations of Alexandre Dumas's classic tale. Consequently, Larry Parks's thrusting young lieutenant is something of an earnest bore as he strives to prevent Victor Jory from kidnapping pacifist general George Macready and precipitating a war with Spain. He's even more of a dull dog when in pursuit of glamorous spy Marguerite Chapman, who herself lacks the venom of a Milady de Winter. DP

Larry Parks *Lt David Picard* • Marguerite Chapman *Nanon de Lartigues* • Victor Jory *Marshall Mordore* • George Macready *General Cadeau* • Edith King *Madame Chauvignac* ■ *Dir* Henry Levin • *Scr* Walter Ferris, Morton Grant, Wilfred H Pettitt, from a story by Ted Thomas, Edward Dein

The Gallant Hours ★★ U

Second World War biography
1960 · US · BW · 111mins

James Cagney gives a sober, po-faced performance as legendary American war hero Admiral William F Halsey, paying homage on bended knee to the man's formidable reputation. A strong cast, including Robert Montgomery Jr, Dennis Weaver and Ward Costello, admirably fleshes out the tale, but this all-American farrago centres firmly on Cagney, whose portrayal displays great grit but little light or shade. SH [VIDEO]

James Cagney *Admiral William F Halsey Jr* • Dennis Weaver *Lt Com Andy Lowe* • Ward Costello *Captain Harry Black* • Richard Jaeckel *Lt Com Roy Webb* • Les Tremayne *Captain Frank Enright* • Robert Burton *Maj Gen Roy Geiger* • Raymond Bailey *Maj Gen Archie Vandegrift* ■ *Dir* Robert Montgomery • *Scr* Frank D Gilroy, Beirne Lay Jr

Gallant Lady ★★★

Melodrama 1934 · US · BW · 81mins

Unmarried mother Ann Harding is forced to give up her baby son for adoption. Travelling abroad five years later, she meets widower Otto Kruger who is about to marry a woman whom his five-year-old son (Dickie Moore) intensely dislikes. No prizes for guessing who the boy really is, or who Kruger marries in the end. Melodramas about self-sacrificing mother love were popular in the 1930s. Though this is not the best example of the genre, it's stylishly directed by Gregory La Cava and engages the heart thanks to Harding, one of Hollywood's most sympathetic and gifted actresses. Remade in 1938 as *Always Goodbye* with Barbara Stanwyck. RK

Ann Harding *Sally Wyndham* • Clive Brook *Dan Pritchard* • Otto Kruger *Philip Lawrence* • Tullio Carminati *Count Carnini* • Dickie Moore *Deedy* ■ *Dir* Gregory La Cava • *Scr* Sam Mintz, from a story by Gilbert Emery, Douglas Doty, Franc Rhodes

Gallipoli ★★★★ PG

First World War drama
1981 · Aus · Colour · 106mins

Although its ultimate location is the Dardanelles front during the First World War, this landmark in the emergence of Australian cinema steers between overt pacifism and ANZAC pride to focus on the spirit of competition and camaraderie that underpins the national character. Peter Weir refuses to shirk the issue of imperial troops fighting European battles and admirably conveys the chaos and waste of warfare by pointedly contrasting the warren-like trenches with the sunlit acres of the opening scenes. But his interest clearly lies in the specific response to the situation of zealous sprinter Mark Lee and his cynical buddy, Mel Gibson. DP. Contains some swearing. [VIDEO] DVD

Mel Gibson *Frank Dunne* • Mark Lee *Archy Hamilton* • Bill Hunter *Major Barton* • Bill Kerr *Uncle Jack* • Robert Grubb *Billy Lewis* • Tim McKenzie *Barney Wilson* • David Argue *"Snowy"* • Ron Graham *Wallace Hamilton* • Harold Hopkins *Les McCann* ■ *Dir* Peter Weir • *Scr* David Williamson, from a story by Peter Weir, from the book *The Broken Years* by Bill Gammage and war histories by CEW Bean

Gallivant ★★★★ 15

Documentary 1996 · UK · Colour · 99mins

Cruelly overlooked on its original release, this offbeat documentary has more incident and intelligence than a barrow-load of blockbusters. Compiled from over 50 hours of interviews and travelogue footage, Andrew Kötting's odyssey around the British coastline is made all the more enchanting by the frank opinions of his grandmother, Gladys, and the courage of his daughter, Eden, who makes light of Joubert's Syndrome to communicate in sign language. With its experimental use of different camera angles and speeds, the style is occasionally fussy, but the eccentric encounters are priceless and highly revealing of our diverse national characteristics. DP. Contains swearing. [VIDEO]

Dir/Scr Andrew Kötting

Gambit ★★★ U

Crime comedy 1966 · US · Colour · 103mins

Falling into the trap of lighting up each surprise in neon well in advance, director Ronald Neame ensures that the unexpected here quickly becomes the expected and so contributes to the shallowness of the plot. However, events are regularly chirped up by Michael Caine and Shirley MacLaine, who feed their natural frivolity and nimble comic timing into the roles of a cockney crook and his Eurasian showgirl-turned-accomplice. Herbert Lom is also good fun as the hapless target of their wheeze. JM [VIDEO]

Shirley MacLaine *Nicole* • Michael Caine *Harry Deane* • Herbert Lom *Shahbandar* • Roger C Carmel *Ram* • Arnold Moss *Abdul* • John Abbott *Emile* • Richard Angarola *Colonel Salim* • Maurice Marsac *Hotel clerk* ■ *Dir* Ronald Neame • *Scr* Alvin Sargent, Jack Davies, from the novel by Sidney Carroll

The Gamble ★★★ 15

Period drama 1988 · It · Colour · 100mins

An entertaining costume romp, with Matthew Modine as an impoverished nobleman who wagers his life in a bid to to win back the family fortune from sinister countess Faye Dunaway. Though no great shakes, this is made with a certain panache and acted with tongues firmly in cheeks by the cast, which also includes Jennifer Beals. DA. An English/Italian language film. [VIDEO]

Matthew Modine *Francesco* • Jennifer Beals *Olivia* • Faye Dunaway *Countess* • Corinne Cléry ■ *Dir* Carlo Vanzina • *Scr* Enrico Vanzina, Carlo Vanzina, Livia Giampalmo, from a novel by Alberto Ongaro

The Gambler ★★★★ 18

Drama 1974 · US · Colour · 106mins

Quoting Dostoyevsky's gambling compulsion as an excuse for his own obsession, James Caan gives a remarkable performance as the university lecturer in hock to loan sharks for his debts. This was director Karel Reisz's most effective movie of those made during his brief stay in Hollywood. It's a film that takes its time, but the strong supporting actors give necessary substance to the movie's style. TH. Contains swearing. [VIDEO]

James Caan *Axel Freed* • Lauren Hutton *Billie* • Paul Sorvino *Hips* • Morris Carnovsky *AR Lowenthal* • Jacqueline Brookes *Naomi Freed* • Burt Young *Carmine* • Carmine Caridi *Jimmy* • Vic Tayback *One* • Steven Keats *Howie* ■ *Dir* Karel Reisz • *Scr* James Toback

The Gambler ★★★ 15

Drama 1997 · UK/Neth/Hun · Colour · 93mins

A starry cast and some beautiful locations enhance this adaptation of Fyodor Dostoyevsky's autobiographical novel. Hungarian director Karoly Makk employs the unusual device of the "novel within the film" to show how the writer came to pen his intense study of gambling fever. Stylistically, however, Makk has overloaded his dice and goes for broke on far too many occasions. Rising above the wordy script and the stiff staging, Michael Gambon and Jodhi May fascinate as the author and his young muse. However, the most remarkable performance comes from dual Oscar winner Luise Rainer, appearing in her first film in 54 years. DP. Contains some swearing and a sex scene.

Michael Gambon *Fyodor Dostoyevsky* • Jodhi May *Anna Snitkina* • Polly Walker *Polina* • Dominic West *Alexei* • John Wood *The General* • Johan Leysen *De Grieux* • Angeline Ball *Mlle Blanche* • Tom Jansen *Stellovsky* • Luise Rainer *Grandmother* • Gijs Scholten von Asschat *Maikov* ■ *Dir* Karoly Makk • *Scr* Katharine Ogden, Charles Cohen, Nick Dear, from the novel by Fyodor Dostoyevsky

The Gambler and the Lady ★★

Crime drama 1952 · UK · BW · 72mins

What went on behind the scenes of this Hammer production is far more interesting than the on-screen action. Although Pat Jenkins has his name on the picture, a variety of sources claim that Hollywood hack Sam Newfield co-directed; others assert that horror maestro Terence Fisher also had a hand in its making. The film itself is an unremarkable crime tale about a hard-bitten American gambler (Dane Clark) who discovers the English aristocracy is a much tougher nut to crack than the underworld. DP

Dane Clark *Jim Forster* • Kathleen Byron *Pat* • Naomi Chance *Lady Susan Willens* • Meredith Edwards *Dave* • Anthony Forwood *Peter Willens* • Eric Pohlmann *Arturo Colonna* • Julian Somers *Licasi* • Anthony Ireland *Farning* • Enzo Cottichia *Angelo Colonna* ■ *Dir* Pat Jenkins, Sam Newfield • *Scr* Sam Newfield

The Gamblers ★ U

Comedy drama 1969 · US · Colour · 91mins

A lacklustre caper movie starring Suzy Kendall, supposedly based on a Gogol play, and filmed in the spectacular Croatian seaboard city of Dubrovnik where gamblers, conmen and other dubious characters gather. As well as the usual Europudding cast, creating a gaggle of accents, it features a bulging swag-bag of movie plunder. Kendall doesn't have a lot to do except model some fancy frocks. AT

Suzy Kendall *Candace* • Don Gordon *Rooney* • Pierre Olaf *Cozzier* • Kenneth Griffith *Broadfoot* • Stuart Margolin *Goldy* • Richard Woo *Koboyashi* • Massimo Serato *Del Isolla* • Faith Domergue *Signora Del Isolla* • Relja Basic *Yakov* ■ *Dir* Ron Winston • *Scr* Ron Winston, from a play by Nikolai Gogol

Gambling, Gods and LSD ★★★

Documentary
2002 · Can/Swi · Colour · 180mins

Ten years in the making, this epic essay travels the world to meet mystics and junkies, sportsmen and card sharps, scientists and sex toy salesmen to discover the diversity of spiritual, natural and artificial means of satisfying humanity's basic need for pleasure and transcendence. Director Peter Mettler is as fascinated with the mundane as he is with the moving or the marvellous and, consequently, images of everyday bustle become as poignant as the more exotic happenings or landscapes. Occasionally, the observations of the interviewees are self-consciously eccentric and the presentation unduly flamboyant, but this still provides plenty to think about. DP

Dir/Scr Peter Mettler

Gambling Lady ★★★

Drama 1934 · US · BW · 66mins

Here's tough and sexy Barbara Stanwyck, on her way to becoming one of Hollywood's great ladies, cast as a professional gambler born on the wrong side of the tracks who enters high society through marriage to posh Joel McCrea. This is one of those swiftly-paced, tightly-knit melodramas that leave you gasping at the end of a comparatively short running time. Pat O'Brien is actually the nominal co-star, but McCrea has the more important role, and looks good with Stanwyck. TS

Barbara Stanwyck *Lady Lee* • Joel McCrea *Garry Madison* • Pat O'Brien *Charlie Lang* • C Aubrey Smith *Peter Madison* • Claire Dodd *Sheila Aiken* • Philip Reed *Steve* • Philip Faversham *Don* • Robert Barrat *Mike Lee* ■ *Dir* Archie Mayo • *Scr* Ralph Block, Doris Malloy, from a story by Doris Malloy

The Game ★★★ 15

Psychological thriller
1997 · US · Colour · 122mins

Michael Douglas is perfectly cast as the increasingly desperate pawn in this visually stylish thriller from *Se7en* director David Fincher, which successfully cranks up the suspense and continually questions what's real and what isn't. When hard-nosed businessman Douglas is given the ultimate birthday present by his brother Sean Penn – the chance to play an all-encompassing "reality game" that promises life-changing consequences – he gets swept into what he perceives as a paranoid conspiracy. Sadly, what starts off as a fascinating tale soon becomes glossy and trivial. AJ. Contains violence, swearing. DVD

Michael Douglas *Nicholas Van Orton* • Sean Penn *Conrad Van Orton* • Deborah Kara Unger *Christine* • James Rebhorn *Jim Feingold* • Peter Donat *Samuel Sutherland* • Carroll Baker *Ilsa* • Anna Katarina *Elizabeth* • Armin Mueller-Stahl *Anson Baer* ■ *Dir* David Fincher • *Scr* John Brancato, Michael Ferris

A Game for Vultures ★ 18

Political drama 1979 · UK · Colour · 108mins

Political strife in Rhodesia in the late 1970s is the backdrop for this dull and dusty home-grown epic. Richard Roundtree (*Shaft*) plays a black freedom fighter, increasingly angry at the British sanctions. Richard Harris finds it impossible to resist the charms of Joan Collins, while Ray Milland and Denholm Elliott round off a cast that's a lot better than the movie merits. A pretentious, shoddy mess. DA. Contains violence and swearing.

Richard Harris *David Swansey* • Richard Roundtree *Gideon Marunga* • Joan Collins *Nicolle* • Ray Milland *Colonel Brettle* • Sven-Bertil Taube *Larry Prescott* • Denholm Elliott *Raglan Thistle* • Jana Cilliers *Ruth Swansey* ■ *Dir* James Fargo • *Scr* Phillip Baird, from the novel by Michael Hartmann

The Game is Over ★

Drama romance 1966 · Fr/It · Colour · 98mins

Jane Fonda's second film with director/husband Roger Vadim was this mildly scandalous, updated version of Zola's novel *La Curée*, in which Fonda falls passionately in love with her stepson, played by Peter McEnery. She asks her husband for a divorce, but while she is away he pressures the stepson into a marriage with the daughter of a banker. Panned at the time, it nevertheless allowed Vadim plenty of opportunities to photograph her semi-naked. AT

Jane Fonda *Renée Saccard* • Peter McEnery *Maxime Saccard* • Michel Piccoli *Alexandre Saccard* • Tina Marquand [Tina Aumont] *Anne Sernet* • Jacques Monod *M Sernet* • Simone Valère *Mme Sernet* • Luong Ham Chau *Mr Chou* ■ *Dir* Roger Vadim • *Scr* Roger Vadim, Jean Cau, Bernard Frechtman, from the novel *La Curée* by Emile Zola

A Game of Death ★★

Thriller 1945 · US · BW · 72mins

Although modestly effective in its own low-budget way, director Robert Wise's version of writer Richard Connell's horror adventure yarn *The Most Dangerous Game* suffers in comparison to the classic 1932 interpretation. Edgar Barrier takes on the role of Kreiger, the Nazi lunatic hunting shipwreck survivors for sadistic sport on his isolated island. John Loder is the novelist washed up on his shores who turns the hunter into the hunted, with a certain degree of suspense. AJ

John Loder *Rainsford* • Audrey Long *Ellen* • Edgar Barrier *Kreiger* • Russell Wade *Robert* • Russell Hicks *Whitney* • Jason Robards [Jason Robards Sr] *Captain* • Gene Stutenroth [Gene Roth] *Pleshke* • Noble Johnson *Carib* • Robert Clarke *Helmsman* ■ *Dir* Robert Wise • *Scr* Norman Houston, from the story *The Most Dangerous Game* by Richard Connell

Game of Death ★ 18

Martial arts drama
1978 · HK · Colour · 96mins

When Bruce Lee died suddenly in 1973, the industry he helped bring to a wider audience lost no time in churning out a string of shabby exploitation pieces. This is one of the best known of his posthumous releases and one of the worst. The Lee character – predominantly stand-in Kim Tai Jong – finds himself up against gangster Dean Jagger, who kidnaps his girlfriend (Colleen Camp). Apart from a beautifully edited end sequence featuring Lee at his best, this is an embarrassing mess. JF. Contains swearing. DVD

Bruce Lee *Billy Lo* • Gig Young *Jim Marshall* • Dean Jagger *Dr Land* • Hugh O'Brian *Steiner* • Robert Wall *Carl Miller* • Colleen Camp *Ann Morris* • Kareem Abdul-Jabbar *Hakim* • Chuck Norris *Fighter* • Kim Tai Jong *Billy Lo* ■ *Dir* Robert Clouse • *Scr* Jan Spears

Game Over: Kasparov and the Machine ★★★ PG

Documentary
2003 · Can/UK · Colour · 84mins

No one was surprised when grandmaster Garry Kasparov defeated IBM's chess-playing computer, Deep Blue, in 1996. But when the result was reversed in a rematch a year later, the gasps of disbelief were almost immediately drowned out by cries of "foul", as the Russian accused the American corporation of behind-the-scenes shenanigans. The fact that Vikram Jayanti's compelling documentary so clearly shows disdain for the arrogance of the IBM programming team and includes excerpts from Raymond Bernard's silent classic *The Chess Player* raises doubts as to its impartiality. But, regardless of this misgiving, it's hard not to sympathise with Kasparov and his conspiracy theories. DP DVD

Dir Vikram Jayanti • *Cinematographer* Maryse Alberti

Gamera the Invincible ★★

Monster adventure 1965 · Jpn · BW · 86mins

Created by the Daiei Studio to rival Toho's *Godzilla*, Gamera is a giant prehistoric fire-breathing turtle, which is awakened by an atomic blast and spins its way to Tokyo, destroying all in its path. As with the original *Godzilla*, American stars Albert Dekker and Brian Donlevy make their appearance, in footage specially shot for the international market. Although competent in every standard Japanese monster-movie department, *Gamera* never really caught on outside its home turf despite numerous wacky sequels and a spectacular hi-tech refit in the 1990s. AJ. Japanese dialogue dubbed into English.

Albert Dekker *Secretary of Defense* • Brian Donlevy *General Terry Arnold* • Diane Findlay *WAF A/IC Susan Embers* • John Baragrey *Miles Standish* • Dick O'Neill *General O'Neill* • Ejii Funakoshi *Dr Hidaka* • Harumi Kiritachi *Kyoke* • Yoshiro Uchida *Toshio* ■ *Dir* Noriyaki Yuasa • *Scr* Fumi Takahashi, Richard Kraft, from an idea by Yonejiro Saito

Games ★★

Psychological drama
1967 · US · Colour · 100mins

Despite a multiplication of psychological double-crosses, Curtis Harrington's mystery drama never really involves us in the Manhattan machinations of fortune-hunting husband James Caan and his gullible wife Katharine Ross. Simone Signoret is the amateur medium who becomes embroiled in their games, peering into a crystal ball as murky as the plot. Had Harrington been concerned more with pace and less with style, the film might have worked. TH

Simone Signoret *Lisa* • James Caan *Paul* • Katharine Ross *Jennifer* • Don Stroud *Norman* • Kent Smith *Harry* • Estelle Winwood *Miss Beattie* • Marjorie Bennett *Nora* • Ian Wolfe *Dr Edwards* ■ *Dir* Curtis Harrington • *Scr* Gene Kearney, from a story by Curtis Harrington, George Edwards

The Games ★ PG

Sports drama 1970 · UK · Colour · 92mins

What real-life athletes such as technical adviser Gordon Pirie made of this sports drama about the build-up to the marathon at the Rome Olympics is anybody's guess. It's hard to know where to look, really. At the so-obvious cardboard cut-out crowds? At the mind-boggling casting of Michael Crawford as an ace marathon runner? Or at Ryan O'Neal as an all-round American good guy, competing despite a heart condition? A sprawling mess. TS

Michael Crawford *Harry Hayes* • Stanley Baker *Bill Oliver* • Ryan O'Neal *Scott Reynolds* • Charles Aznavour *Pavel Vendek* • Jeremy Kemp *Jim Harcourt* • Elaine Taylor *Christine* • Athol Compton *Sunny Pintubi* • Fritz Wepper *Kovanda* ■ *Dir* Michael Winner • *Scr* Erich Segal, from a novel by Hugh Atkinson

Gandhi ★★★★★ PG

Epic biographical drama
1982 · UK · Colour · 180mins

Richard Attenborough's stately biopic has historical scope, a sure command of thousands of extras and, most of all, the ability to focus on individual endeavour amid the spectacle. For this is one of the 20th century's most remarkable stories, that of the righteous Indian lawyer (a quietly inspirational performance by Ben Kingsley) who returned from racially segregated South Africa to drive the British out of his home country through successive acts of non-violent protest. The film begins with his assassination and flashes back to the key moments in a 30-year struggle. While Kingsley (who took one of eight Oscars) is the glue that holds this epic piece together, you must also relish the outstanding cast. AC DVD

Ben Kingsley *Mahatma Gandhi* • Candice Bergen *Margaret Bourke-White* • Edward Fox *General Dyer* • John Gielgud *Lord Irwin* • Trevor Howard *Judge Broomfield* • John Mills *The Viceroy* • Martin Sheen *Walker* • Rohini Hattangady *Kasturba Gandhi* • Roshan Seth *Pandit Nehru* ■ *Dir* Richard Attenborough • *Scr* John Briley • *Cinematographer* Billy Williams, Ronnie Taylor • *Editor* John Bloom • *Costume Designer* John Mollo, Bhanu Athaiya • *Production Designer* Stuart Craig

Gang Busters ★★

Crime drama 1955 · US · BW · 71mins

Cinematographer William H Clothier makes the most of the Oregon locations in this minor crime drama, giving the action a documentary feel, but director Bill Karn lacks the visual imagination to inject much life into a slow-moving story. Given a rare leading role after dozens of western supports, Myron Healey acquits himself well as Public Enemy No 4, who seems to spend as much time breaking out of jails as he does committing crimes. DP

Myron Healey *John Omar Pinson* • Don C Harvey *Detective Walsh* • Sam Edwards *Long* • Frank Gerstle *Detective Fuller* • Frank Richards *Slug Bennett* • Kate MacKenna *Aunt Jenny* • Rusty Wescoatt *Mike* • William Justine *Louie* ■ *Dir* Bill Karn • *Scr* Phillips H Lord

Gang Law ★★ 18

Crime drama 1999 · US · Colour · 92mins

This is slicker than Master P's earlier work, although its dubious moral message and ultra-violence occasionally makes for uncomfortable viewing. Master P's young brother Silkk the Shocker stars as an aspiring rapper who embraces a life of crime when his girlfriend is falsely imprisoned. There's a host of cameos from other rappers, while video stars Gary Busey, C Thomas Howell and Jeff Speakman add a smidgin of marquee value. JF [video] DVD

Gary Busey *Tully* • Silkk the Shocker *Kool* • Jeff Speakman *Master Keaton* • Snoop Dogg *C-Dawg* • Master P *Moe* • Shireen Crutchfield *LaShawna* • C Thomas Howell *Officer Roberts* ■ *Dir/Scr* Master P

Gang Related ★★★★ 15

Crime drama 1997 · US · Colour · 106mins

Tupac Shakur's final film offers a glimpse of what a fine, subtle actor he was becoming before his tragic early death. The acclaimed rap star plays a detective who, with partner James Belushi, has established a lucrative scam ripping off and killing drug dealers and pronouncing the deaths as "gang related". However, it all goes pear-shaped when their latest victim turns out to be an undercover drugs agent and the derelict they attempt to frame (Dennis Quaid) is discovered to have a surprising past. Writer/director Jim Kouf delivers the goods thriller-wise, while mining an unexpected seam of gallows humour. JF. Contains swearing, violence, nudity. [video] DVD

James Belushi *Detective Frank K Divinci* • Tupac Shakur *Detective Rodriguez* • Lela Rochon *Cynthia Webb* • Dennis Quaid *William Dane McCall/"Joe Doe"* • James Earl Jones *Arthur Baylor* • David Paymer *Elliot Goff* • Wendy Crewson *Helen Eden* • Gary Cole *Richard Simms* ■ *Dir/Scr* Jim Kouf

The Gang That Couldn't Shoot Straight ★★★ 15

Crime comedy 1971 · US · Colour · 92mins

This slapstick comedy about New York mobsters stars Jerry Orbach as the incompetent hood who makes a disastrous series of attempts to bump off a local Mafioso, played by gravel-voiced Lionel Stander. Directed at breakneck pace by James Goldstone and written by Waldo Salt, with an ear for the local South Brooklyn wisecrack, it's a bit hit and miss, but it's hard to dislike a mobster movie that features a cycle race and a lion on the loose. Most eyes will be on Robert De Niro as one of the Italian cyclists who becomes an illegal immigrant and a bogus priest. AT [video]

Jerry Orbach *Kid Sally* • Leigh Taylor-Young *Angela* • Jo Van Fleet *Big Momma* • Lionel Stander *Baccala* • Robert De Niro *Mario* • Irving Selbst *Big Jelly* • Herve Villechaize *Beppo* ■ *Dir* James Goldstone • *Scr* Waldo Salt, from the novel by Jimmy Breslin

Gang War ★★★

Crime drama 1958 · US · BW · 71mins

Long before the controversial *Death Wish*, Charles Bronson turned vigilante in this little-known crime thriller. Having witnessed a gangland murder, Bronson testifies in court and later finds his pregnant wife has been murdered in a revenge attack. When the police fail to arrest the killers, Bronson goes up against the Mob himself. Despite some naff scenes and a few dodgy performances, this B-movie is well worth seeking out. AT

Charles Bronson *Alan Avery* • Kent Taylor *Bryce Barker* • Jennifer Holden *Marie* • John Doucette *Maxie Matthews* • Gloria Henry *Edie Avery* • Gloria Grey *Marsha Brown* • Barney Phillips *Sam Johnson* • Ralph Manza *Axe Duncan* ■ *Dir* Gene Fowler Jr • *Scr* Louis Vittes, from the novel *The Hoods Take Over* by Ovid Demaris

The Gang's All Here ★★★

Crime comedy 1939 · UK · BW · 78mins

This Jack Buchanan vehicle is a sequel to his earlier *Smash and Grab*, which attempted to turn Buchanan and Elsie Randolph into a British Nick and Nora Charles (*The Thin Man*). He plays John Forrest, an insurance investigator who routs an American gang in a London nightclub with Googie Withers. Jack and Googie make a very smart coupling, and this was a big hit. TS

Edward Everett Horton *Treadwell* • Otto Kruger *Mike Chadwick* • Jack Buchanan *John Forrest* • Jack LaRue *Alberni* • Googie Withers *Alice Forrest* • Syd Walker *Younce* • David Burns *Beretti* • Walter Rilla *Prince Homouska* ■ *Dir* Thornton Freeland • *Scr* Ralph Spence

The Gang's All Here ★★ U

Musical 1943 · US · Colour · 103mins

Better known in the UK by the title *The Girls He Left Behind*, this is a mesmerisingly awful chunk of camp kitsch, designed and filmed in Technicolor so garish you'd be forgiven for thinking you'd fallen into a box of chocolates. The undoubted highlight is Carmen Miranda performing *The Lady in the Tutti Frutti Hat* while chorus girls do the most extraordinary things with giant bananas. This farrago proves that director Busby Berkeley left his taste behind him when he decamped to 20th Century-Fox. Painfully dated now, the film nominally stars Alice Faye. TS

Alice Faye *Eadie Allen* • Carmen Miranda *Dorita* • Phil Baker • Eugene Pallette *Mr Mason Sr* • Charlotte Greenwood *Mrs Peyton Potter* • Edward Everett Horton *Peyton Potter* ■ *Dir* Busby Berkeley • *Scr* Walter Bullock, from a story by Nancy Winter, George Root Jr, Tom Bridges

Gangs of New York ★★★★ 18

Period crime drama
2002 · US · Colour · 159mins

Director Martin Scorsese's brutal, occasionally muddled, but always riveting film about Manhattan gang warfare in the 1860s begins with a gruesome street battle between the Nativists and the Dead Rabbits. The latter's leader, Liam Neeson (a brief but striking appearance), is slaughtered in front of his young son. Sixteen years later, his son (played by Leonardo DiCaprio in a disappointingly one-note performance), insinuates himself into the gang in order to avenge his father. However, his evolving relationship with Nativist boss Daniel Day-Lewis provides the young man with a dilemma. If the film never marries its complex political intrigue with the more simplistic personal stories, the epic sweep is breathtaking, the attention to detail intoxicating and Day-Lewis's riveting turn is unmissable. IF. Contains violence, swearing, sex scenes and nudity. [video] DVD

Leonardo DiCaprio *Amsterdam Vallon* • Daniel Day-Lewis *William Cutting, "Bill the Butcher"* • Cameron Diaz *Jenny Everdeane* • Liam Neeson *Priest Vallon* • Jim Broadbent *William "Boss" Tweed* • John C Reilly *Happy Jack* • Henry Thomas *Johnny Sirocco* • Brendan Gleeson *Walter "Monk" McGinn* • Gary Lewis *Charles McGloin* • Stephen Graham *Shang* • Roger Ashton-Griffiths *PT Barnum* • David Hemmings *Mr Schermerhorn* • Barbara Bouchet *Mrs Schermerhorn* • Alec McCowen *Reverend Raleigh* • Michael Byrne *Horace Greeley* • Martin Scorsese *Wealthy homeowner* ■ *Dir* Martin Scorsese • *Scr* Jay Cocks, Steve Zaillian, Kenneth Lonergan, from the novel by Herbert Asbury

The Gangster ★

Film noir 1947 · US · BW · 83mins

A gloomy and largely unrevealing attempt to psychoanalyse a criminal mind. Barry Sullivan is the gangland leader who tries to be a nicer human being, but finds people still crossing the street to avoid him. Sullivan, never a front-rank actor, comes across as merely tedious, leaving Akim Tamiroff and Belita (a former ice-skater and down-market Sonja Henie) to try to lighten things up. This dime-budget production is dudsville all the way. DP

Barry Sullivan *Shubunka* • Belita *Nancy Starr* • Joan Lorring *Dorothy* • Akim Tamiroff *Nick Jammey* • Henry Morgan [Harry Morgan] *Shorty* • John Ireland *Karty* ■ *Dir* Gordon Wiles • *Scr* Daniel Fuchs, from his novel *Low Company*

Gangster No 1 ★★★ 18

Crime thriller 2000 · UK · Colour · 98mins

Following in the wake of *Lock, Stock and Two Smoking Barrels*, Paul McGuigan's thriller is another tale of London gangsters, though this time without the humour. As studies of pure evil go, however, it's very convincing. Malcolm McDowell plays a crime lord who looks back on the 1960s antics of his gang. Flashbacks show him played by the impressive Paul Bettany, whose psychotic behaviour leads to much blood-letting. This central section is stylistically superb, but the gratuitous violence and profanity also leave a nasty taste in the mouth. LH [video] DVD

Malcolm McDowell *Gangster 55* • David Thewlis *Freddie Mays* • Paul Bettany *Young Gangster* • Saffron Burrows *Karen* • Kenneth Cranham *Tommy* • Jamie Foreman *Lennie Taylor* • Andrew Lincoln *Maxie King* ■ *Dir* Paul McGuigan • *Scr* Johnny Ferguson, from the play by Louis Mellis, David Scinto

Gangster Story ★★★ PG

Crime drama 1959 · US · BW · 67mins

Inside every great Hollywood actor there's a would-be director trying to get out. Clint Eastwood, Mel Gibson and Kevin Costner are but three recent examples. Fans of Walter Matthau may be surprised to find that the untidy half of *The Odd Couple* made his directing debut as far back as 1959. He also stars in this crime drama as gangster Jack Martin, who finds himself in conflict with local hood Bruce McFarlan when he tries to muscle in on his territory. Not Oscar-winning stuff, but competent and absorbing. TH DVD

Walter Matthau *Jack Martin* • Carol Grace *Carol* • Bruce McFarlan *Earl Dawson* • Garrett Wallberg *Adolph* • Raiken Ben Ari *Hood* ■ *Dir* Walter Matthau • *Scr* Paul Purcell, from a story by Richard Grey, VJ Rhems

Gangway ★★★ U

Crime musical 1937 · UK · BW · 86mins

Try as they might, British producers of the 1930s always managed to be just out of time in their attempts to emulate the Hollywood musical. Jessie Matthews, therefore, didn't have much to beat to be hailed as the queen of the British equivalent, but her energy and charm enabled her to elevate the most mundane material and win fans on both sides of the Atlantic. The second of three films directed by her then husband Sonnie Hale, this is a lively crime comedy of errors. DP [video]

Jessie Matthews *Pat Wayne* • Barry Mackay *Inspector Bob Deering* • Olive Blakeney *Nedda Beaumont* • Nat Pendleton *"Smiles" Hogan* • Noel Madison *Mike Otterman* • Liane Ordeyne *Greta Brand* • Patrick Ludlow *Carl Freemason* • Alastair Sim *Taggett* ■ *Dir* Sonnie Hale • *Scr* Lesser Samuels, Sonnie Hale, from a story by Dwight Taylor

Ganja and Hess ★★★

Blaxploitation horror
1973 · US · Colour · 86mins

Lauded in some circles as one of the best movies to explore black culture seriously within a genre context and seen by others as just a dull vampire tale, director Bill Gunn's spiritual contemplation on African myth versus Christianity was severely cut and tampered with on its initial release and retitled *Blood Couple*. Duane Jones is an anthropologist studying the ancient religion of Myrthia. When he's stabbed by a sacrificial dagger, he becomes addicted to blood and resistant to death, and starts having visions of his native Africa. Thought-provoking, Gunn's offbeat tale is a haunting experience, with slow patches. AJ

Duane Jones *Dr Hess Green* • Marlene Clark *Ganja Meda* • Bill Gunn *George* • Sam Waymon *Reverend Luther Williams* • Leonard Jackson *Archie* • Candece Tarpley *Girl in bar* • Richard Harrow *Dinner guest* • John Hoffmeister *Jack Sargent* ■ *Dir/Scr* Bill Gunn

G

Gaolbreak ★ U

Crime drama 1962 · UK · BW · 62mins

This typically down-at-heel crime story from low-budget specialists Butcher's is spiced up by a subplot about an unwanted pregnancy. It features an early performance by Carol White, who found fame in Ken Loach's television play *Cathy Come Home* and his feature *Poor Cow*. Sadly, this tale has barely enough plot to make a TV episode, let alone keep a cinema audience happy, and seems stretched even at its one-hour running time. DP

Peter Reynolds *Eddie Wallis* • Avice Landone *Mrs Wallis* • David Kernan *Len Rogerson* • Carol White *Carol Marshall* • David Gregory *Ron Wallis* • John Blythe *Slim* • Robert Desmond *Page* • Geoffrey Hibbert *Dr Cambus* ■ *Dir* Francis Searle • *Scr* AR Rawlinson

Garage Olimpo ★★★★

Political drama
1999 · It/Fr/Arg · Colour · 98mins

Set inside a Buenos Aires torture chamber during the 1978 World Cup and directed by Marco Bechis with an unflinching sense of realism, this wrenching study of sadism and survival takes on the aspect of a psychological thriller, as slum teacher and anti-junta activist Antonella Costa seeks to exploit the susceptibility of her jailer (and family lodger), Carlos Echeverria. Highlighting the brutality of the military regime, this is also a scathing exposé of the ignorance and indifference of those Argentinians who were solely intent on keeping their heads down, while thousands around them disappeared. DP. In Spanish and Italian with English subtitles.

Antonella Costa *Maria Fabiani* • Carlos Echeverria *Felix* • Dominique Sanda *Diane* • Chiara Caselli *Ana* • Enrique Pineyro *Tigre* • Pablo Razuk *Texas* ■ *Dir* Marco Bechis • *Scr* Marco Bechis, Lara Fremder, from a story by Marco Bechis

Garam Hawa ★★★★

Drama 1973 · Ind · Colour · 146mins

Also known as *Scorching Winds*, this is the highly impressive debut feature from the socially committed Indian film-maker MS Sathyu. Set in northern India shortly after partition in 1947, it explores the problems faced by those Muslims who chose to stay rather than emigrate to the new state of Pakistan. Balraj Sahni (who died shortly after filming) gives a towering performance as the shoemaker whose family suffers in the face of prejudicial new laws and his refusal to leave his heritage behind. DP. An Urdu language film.

Balraj Sahni *Salim Mirza* • Shaukat Azmi *Jamila Mirza* • Gita *Amina* • Farouque Shaikh *Sikander* • Dinanath Zutshi *Halim Mirza* ■ *Dir* MS Sathyu • *Scr* Kaifi Azmi, Shama Zaidi, from a story by Ismat Chugtai

The Garbage Pail Kids Movie ★ PG

Comedy 1987 · US · Colour · 91mins

The movie spin-off from the Topps Company's bubble gum trading cards series is purposely offensive rubbish. The alien kids land on Earth in a dustbin and end up in Anthony Newley's shop. Unfortunately Newley's assistant takes the lid off the dustbin, subjecting us to a bad-taste mix of mean-spirited pranks, grotesque humour and knockabout violence. Director Rod Amateau's lousy movie is mindless trash. AJ

Anthony Newley *Captain Manzini* • MacKenzie Astin *Dodger* • Katie Barberi *Tangerine* • Ron MacLachlan *Juice* • Kevin Thompson *Ali Gator* • Phil Fondacaro *Greaser Greg* • Robert Bell [Robert N Bell] *Foul Phil* • Larry Green *Nat Nerd* • Arturo Gil *Windy Winston* ■ *Dir* Rod Amateau • *Scr* Rod Amateau, Melinda Palmer

Garbo Talks ★★★ 15

Comedy drama 1984 · US · Colour · 100mins

Director Sidney Lumet's fondness for social outsiders goes back to his first film, *12 Angry Men*, and the pattern continues with *Garbo Talks*, in which Anne Bancroft plays an affable but certifiable eccentric. The New York housewife is obsessed with the titular film star and addicted to supporting lost causes, as a result of which she is continually getting arrested. Ron Silver is suitably long-suffering as her exasperated but devoted son and Bancroft makes her character wholly credible. The result is a charming, if uneven film. TH DVD

Anne Bancroft *Estelle Rolfe* • Ron Silver *Gilbert Rolfe* • Carrie Fisher *Lisa Rolfe* • Catherine Hicks *Jane Mortimer* • Steven Hill *Walter Rolfe* • Howard Da Silva *Angelo Dokakis* • Dorothy Loudon *Sonya Apollinar* ■ *Dir* Sidney Lumet • *Scr* Larry Grusin

La Garce ★★

Drama 1984 · Fr · Colour · 90mins

This provocative drama dabbles in extreme situations, coldly enacted by a main trio of resistible characters. Isabelle Huppert's attempt to adopt a new personality after she is raped by cop Richard Berry is confounded by her decision to abandon her gangster lover Vittorio Mezzogiorno on her assailant's release from jail. For once, Huppert fails to get to grips with the complexities of her character. DP. French dialogue dubbed into English.

Isabelle Huppert *Aline/Edith* • Richard Berry *Lucien Sabatier* • Vittorio Mezzogiorno *Max* • Jean Benguigui *Rony* • Jean-Claude Leguay *Brunet* • Daniel Jegou *Dujarric* • Jenny Cleve *Mme Beffroit* • Jean-Pierre Bagot *Beffroit* ■ *Dir* Christine Pascal • *Scr* Andre Marc Delocque-Fourcaud, Laurent Heynemann, Pierre Fabre, Christine Pascal

Garde à Vue ★★★★

Crime drama 1981 · Fr · Colour · 88mins

By confining the bulk of the action in this tense murder investigation to a provincial police station, Claude Miller is able to control not only the steady flow of secrets and lies, but also the suspense levels, as detectives Lino Ventura and Guy Marchand seek to uncover prominent lawyer Michel Serrault's role in the rape and murder of a young girl. There are improbabilities in the plot, but such is the conviction of the exchanges that they serve only to deepen the mystery. Remade in Hollywood almost 20 years later as *Under Suspicion*, starring Morgan Freeman and Gene Hackman. DP. In French with English subtitles.

Lino Ventura *Inspector Antoine Gallien* • Michel Serrault *Jérôme Martinaud* • Guy Marchand *Inspector Marcel Belmont* • Romy Schneider *Chantal Martinaud* • Didier Agostini *Young policeman* • Patrick Depeyrat *1st policeman* • Pierre Maguelon *Adami* • Serge Malik *Mechanic* ■ *Dir* Claude Miller • *Scr* Claude Miller, Jean Herman, from the novel *Brainwash* by John Wainwright

The Garden ★★ 15

Experimental drama
1990 · UK · BW and Colour · 88mins

Derek Jarman's uncompromising experimental work is alternately moving, annoying and boring. Christianity, the media, police brutality, advertising, Aids, old age and repression are just some of the topics that make up this angry, non-narrative view of homosexual discrimination. Using camp, weird and shocking imagery, Jarman's political treatise is a graphically dense look at gay counterculture. Michael Gough (Alfred in the *Batman* films) supplies the narration. AJ DVD

Tilda Swinton *Madonna* • Johnny Mills *Lover* • Kevin Collins *Lover* • Pete Lee-Wilson *Devil* • Spencer Leigh *Mary Magdalene/Adam* • Jody Graber *Young boy* • Roger Cook *Christ* • Jessica Martin *Singer* • Michael Gough *Narrator* ■ *Dir/Scr* Derek Jarman

The Garden of Allah ★★★

Silent romance 1927 · US · BW · 82mins

Directing wife Alice Terry, Rex Ingram allows the camera to caress her face without capturing the barest flicker of emotion. As the monk who abandons his vocation to run away and marry her, Ivan Petrovich at least manages to express some of the torment experienced by the Trappist lured from the right path by worldly temptation. However, it's Marcel Vibert's sinister Arab who steals this stylish but ultimately limp melodrama. DP

Alice Terry *Domini Enfilden* • Ivan Petrovich *Father Adrien/Boris Androvsky* • Marcel Vibert *Count Anteoni* • HH Wright *Lord Rens* ■ *Dir* Rex Ingram (1) • *Scr* Willis Goldbeck, from the novel by Robert Hichens

The Garden of Allah ★ U

Romantic melodrama
1936 · US · Colour · 75mins

Directed with little sense of style or pace, and phoney beyond endurance in narrative and execution, this film is total rubbish and doesn't even appeal on the "so bad it's good" front. Marlene Dietrich and Charles Boyer look uncomfortable as they attempt to mouth unspeakable platitudes, but the early Technicolor photography is sumptuous. TS DVD

Marlene Dietrich *Domini Enfilden* • Charles Boyer *Boris Androvsky* • Basil Rathbone *Count Anteoni* • C Aubrey Smith *Father Roubier* • Tilly Losch *Irena* • Joseph Schildkraut *Batouch* • John Carradine *Sand diviner* ■ *Dir* Richard Boleslawski • *Scr* WP Lipscomb, Lynn Riggs, from the novel by Robert Hichens • *Cinematographer* Harold Rosson

Garden of Evil ★★ PG

Western 1954 · US · Colour · 96mins

This loose rehash of *The Treasure of the Sierra Madre* squanders its cast and devotes its energies to capturing the scenery with the new CinemaScope lens. Susan Hayward convinces adventurers Gary Cooper and Richard Widmark that "there's gold in them thar hills" – as well as a husband buried in the mine they're seeking. Indian attacks impede their progress, while Hayward makes the chaps break out in sweaty rivalry. AT DVD

Gary Cooper *Hooker* • Susan Hayward *Leah Fuller* • Richard Widmark *Fiske* • Cameron Mitchell *Luke Daly* • Hugh Marlowe *John Fuller* • Rita Moreno *Singer* • Victor Manuel Mendoza *Vicente Madariaga* • Fernando Wagner *Captain* ■ *Dir* Henry Hathaway • *Scr* Frank Fenton, from a story by Fred Freiberger, William Tunberg

The Garden of the Finzi-Continis ★★★★★

Second World War drama
1971 · It/W Ger · Colour · 95mins

Based on Giorgio Bassani's semi-autobiographical novel and the winner of the 1971 best foreign film Oscar, this sobering drama is something of a companion piece to Roberto Benigni's *Life Is Beautiful*. Eschewing both the neorealist flourishes that forged his reputation and the melodramatic excesses that marred it, Vittorio De Sica brilliantly employs flashbacks to explain the confidence of a Jewish family in their belief that Fascism will never breach the walls of their Ferrara home. Rarely has inevitability been so suspensefully presented – or faith in a doomed way of life so well portrayed – as in this exquisitely played and genuinely moving masterpiece. DP. In Italian with English subtitles.

Dominique Sanda *Micol* • Lino Capolicchio *Giorgio* • Helmut Berger *Alberto* • Fabio Testi *Malnate* • Romolo Valli *Giorgio's father* • Raffaele Curi *Ernesto* • Camillo Angelini-Rota *Micol's father* • Katina Viglietti *Micol's mother* • Inna Alexeieff *Micol's grandmother* ■ *Dir* Vittorio De Sica • *Scr* Cesare Zavattini, Vittorio Bonicelli, Ugo Pirro, Giorgio Bassani, from the novel by Giorgio Bassani

Garden of the Moon ★★ U

Musical 1938 · US · BW · 93mins

Busby Berkeley's dull direction of his last musical for Warner Bros is a far cry from the glorious inventiveness he brought to the musical numbers of *42nd Street* or *Gold Diggers of 1933*. Set in a nightclub called the Garden of the Moon run by a pushy and obnoxious Pat O'Brien, this spotlights John Payne as a bandleader and singer with Margaret Lindsay's publicity agent as his love interest. AE

Pat O'Brien *John Quinn* • Margaret Lindsay *Toni Blake* • John Payne *Don Vincente* • Johnnie Davis *Slappy Harris* • Melville Cooper *Maurice* • Isabel Jeans *Mrs Lornay* • Mabel Todd *Mary Stanton* • Penny Singleton *Miss Calder* ■ *Dir* Busby Berkeley • *Scr* Jerry Wald, Richard Macaulay, from the story by H Bedford-Jones, John Barton Browne

Garden State ★★★★ 15

Comedy drama 2003 · US · Colour · 98mins

Zach Braff's engaging charm and sharp comic timing played a big part in the success of the TV comedy series *Scrubs*. Those qualities are very much to the fore here, but it's his talents behind the camera as writer and director that really impress. The story is familiar enough: an actor is forced to re-examine his rather empty, aimless life when he returns to his home town in New Jersey for the funeral of his mother. But Braff's thoughtful, mature script neatly sidesteps most of the obvious clichés, while as a director he shows a fine eye for offbeat composition. The performances are uniformly excellent, too. DA. Contains swearing, sex scenes, drug abuse. DVD

Zach Braff *Andrew Largeman* • Ian Holm *Gideon Largeman* • Ron Leibman *Dr Cohen* • Method Man [Method Man] *Diego* • Natalie Portman *Sam* • Peter Sarsgaard *Mark* • Jean Smart *Carol* • Ann Dowd *Olivia* ■ *Dir/Scr* Zach Braff

The Gardener ★

Horror 1972 · US · Colour · 97mins

This mind-boggling trash was filmed in Puerto Rico and didn't see the light of day until the early 1980s. One-time Andy Warhol superstar Joe Dallesandro is a gardener with a wonderful gift for rearing exotic plants, but his female employers aren't enjoying such good health. It's hard to stay awake, but the ending, in which Dallesandro turns into a tree, just has to be seen. AJ

Katharine Houghton *Ellen Bennett* • Rita Gam *Helena Boardman* • Joe Dallesandro *Carl the gardener* • James Congdon *John Bennett* ■ *Dir/Scr* James H Kay III

Gardens of Stone ★★★ 15

War drama 1987 · US · Colour · 106mins

Francis Coppola returns to the subject of the Vietnam War in this quieter, more sombre film, set on the home front. James Caan gives a powerful performance as the combat veteran whose ambivalence towards the war and the military is combined with a romantic interest in antiwar journalist Anjelica Huston. The film was marred by the tragic death of Coppola's son, Giancarlo, in a boating accident during production. PF DVD

James Caan *Sgt Clell Hazard* • James Earl Jones *Sgt Major "Goody" Nelson* • DB Sweeney *Private Jackie Willow* • Anjelica Huston *Samantha Davis* • Dean Stockwell *Capt Homer Thomas* • Mary Stuart Masterson *Rachel Field* • Dick Anthony Williams *Sgt Slasher Williams* ■ *Dir* Francis Coppola [Francis Ford Coppola] • *Scr* Ronald Bass, from the novel by Nicholas Proffitt

Garfield ★★ U

Comedy 2004 · US · Colour · 76mins

Jim Davis's fat-cat comic strip gets the big-screen treatment here. In an inspired piece of casting, Bill Murray voices the sardonic, lasagne-loving feline, who here finds his lazy lifestyle threatened when owner Jon (Breckin Meyer) decides to adopt a dog to impress beautiful vet Liz (Jennifer Love Hewitt). Aimed squarely at a younger audience, it's miniscule plot barely does justice to Garfield's infamous dry wit. SF DVD

Breckin Meyer *Jon Arbuckle* • Jennifer Love Hewitt *Dr Liz Wilson* • Stephen Tobolowsky *Happy Chapman* • Bill Murray *Garfield* • Eve Brent *Mrs Baker* • Debra Messing *Arlene* • David Eigenberg *Nermal* ■ *Dir* Pete Hewitt [Peter Hewitt] • *Scr* Joel Cohen, Alec Sokolow, from the comic strip by Jim Davis

The Garment Jungle ★★★

Crime drama 1957 · US · BW · 87mins

A good hard-hitting example of 1950s Hollywood realism, this tackles the subject of labour unions in the clothing business. It is almost a pro-union retort by Columbia to the studio's own anti-union *On the Waterfront*, three years earlier. Lee J Cobb is the heavy, a union-bashing boss involved with gangster Richard Boone. The original (uncredited) director Robert Aldrich was taken off the film towards the end of shooting and replaced by Vincent Sherman. RB

Lee J Cobb *Walter Mitchell* • Kerwin Mathews *Alan Mitchell* • Gia Scala *Theresa Renata* • Richard Boone *Artie Ravidge* • Valerie French *Lee Hackett* • Robert Loggia *Tulio Renata* • Joseph Wiseman *Kovan* • Harold J Stone *Tony* ■ *Dir* Vincent Sherman • *Scr* Harry Kleiner, from the article *Gangsters in the Dress Business* by Lester Velie

Garv: Pride & Honour ★★★ 12A

Crime drama 2004 · Ind · Colour · 162mins

Actor Puneet Issar makes his feature directorial debut with this vigilante thriller exploring the link between organised crime and India's political establishment. Salman Khan headlines as the Mumbai cop who turns in his badge to exact revenge on Anupam Kher and the mobsters responsible for killing his partner and threatening his mother and sister during a gangland crackdown. Love interest Shilpa Shetty only comes into her own during the musical numbers, but these seem more of an intrusion than an asset to an otherwise tough tale. DP. In Hindi with English subtitles.

Amrish Puri *Samar Singh* • Salman Khan *Arjun Ranawat* • Arbaaz Khan *Hyder Ali* • Shilpa Shetty *Jannat* • Farida Jalal *Arjun's mother* • Anupam Kher ■ *Dir* Puneet Issar • *Scr* Puneet Issar, Deepali, from a story by Puneet Issar

Gas Attack ★★★

Drama 2001 · UK · Colour · 75mins

Shot on digital video and set in a rundown Glasgow housing estate, its subject matter may seem a touch sensational. But the idea that extremist thugs could consider infecting asylum seekers with an anthrax virus is truly terrifying. Director Kenneth Glenaan wisely adopts a rigidly realist tone to keep a lid on the melodrama, although he's ably abetted by a restrained performance from Sherko Zen-Aloush, as the Kurdish exile whose daughter, Benae Hassan, is stricken by a mystery ailment. DP

Sherko Zen-Aloush *Sherko* • Benae Hassan *Resa* • Robina Qureshi *Robina Dhoudy* • Morag Caulder *Annie* ■ *Dir* Kenneth Glenaan • *Scr* Rowan Joffe

Gas, Food, Lodging ★★★★ 15

Drama 1992 · US · Colour · 101mins

In this intelligent family drama, Brooke Adams stars as a single mother trying to hold down a job at a diner while coping with teenage daughters who are growing up too fast. Writer/director Allison Anders works wonders with a low budget and sketches a gritty, sympathetic portrait of lost dreams and the daily struggle of small-town American life. The cast, with Ione Skye and Fairuza Balk as the daughters, is exemplary, and there's even a decent turn from the usually wooden James Brolin. JF. Contains swearing and sex scenes. [video]

Brooke Adams *Nora Roberts* • Ione Skye *Trudi* • Fairuza Balk *Shade* • James Brolin *John Evans* • Robert Knepper *Dank* • David Landsbury *Hamlet Humphrey* • Chris Mulkey *Raymond* • Adam Biesk *Brett* ■ *Dir* Allison Anders • *Scr* Allison Anders, from the novel *Don't Look and It Won't Hurt* by Richard Peck

Gasbags ★★★ U

Second World War comedy
1940 · UK · BW · 77mins

Intended to boost wartime morale, this is the best film ever made by the Crazy Gang, the British comedy team led by Bud Flanagan and Chesney Allen. The plot includes a flying fish-and-chip shop, while the geriatric-looking Moore Marriott – a veteran of innumerable Will Hay films – plays a prisoner of war with plans for a secret weapon tattooed on his back. No wonder the Gang have designs on him. Director Marcel Varnel has just the right surreal touch to make it work and leave audiences laughing. TH

Bud Flanagan *Bud* • Chesney Allen *Ches* • Jimmy Nervo *Cecil* • Teddy Knox *Knoxy* • Charlie Naughton *Charlie* • Jimmy Gold *Goldy* • Moore Marriott *Jerry Jenkins* • Wally Patch *Sergeant Major* ■ *Dir* Marcel Varnel • *Scr* Val Guest, Marrott Edgar, from the story by Val Valentine, Ralph Smart

Gaslight ★★★ PG

Psychological drama 1940 · UK · BW · 88mins

Nowadays, most viewers will probably be more familiar with George Cukor's 1944 adaptation of Patrick Hamilton's stage success than with this British original. The Hollywood version is easily the better picture, with MGM's vision of Victorian London more atmospheric than the rough-and-ready one cobbled together here by British National. Diana Wynyard is streets behind Ingrid Bergman (who won an Oscar) as the terrorised wife, but Anton Walbrook is splendidly sinister and it is a great story. MGM bought up the prints of this to ensure that its remake had the field to itself. DP [video]

Anton Walbrook *Paul Mallen* • Diana Wynyard *Bella Mallen* • Cathleen Cordell *Nancy* • Robert Newton *Ullswater* • Frank Pettingell *Rough* • Jimmy Hanley *Cobb* • Minnie Rayner *Elizabeth* • Mary Hinton *Lady Winterbourne* ■ *Dir* Thorold Dickinson • *Scr* Ar Rawlinson, Bridget Boland, from the play *Angel Street* by Patrick Hamilton

Gaslight ★★★★ PG

Melodrama 1944 · US · BW · 108mins

Ingrid Bergman won her first best actress Oscar as the socialite slowly being driven mad (or is she really mad?) by suave husband Charles Boyer. This was released in Britain as *The Murder in Thornton Square*, to avoid confusion with the equally famous 1940 British version with Anton Walbrook and Diana Wynyard. MGM actually tried to suppress the first film when they remade it as this super glossy Bergman vehicle. It's a bit dated now, but still has much to offer, notably George Cukor's intelligent direction, which, combined with production designer Cedric Gibbons's terrific Victorian setting (the interior decoration won an Oscar), offers the radiant Bergman an opportunity that she seizes with all the acting tricks at her disposal. TS [video] DVD

Charles Boyer *Gregory Anton* • Ingrid Bergman *Paula Alquist* • Joseph Cotten *Brian Cameron* • Dame May Whitty *Miss Thwaites* • Angela Lansbury *Nancy Oliver* • Barbara Everest *Elizabeth Tompkins* • Eustace Wyatt *Budge* ■ *Dir* George Cukor • *Scr* John Van Druten, Walter Reisch, John L Balderston, from the play *Angel Street* by Patrick Hamilton

Gas-s-s-s, or It Became Necessary to Destroy the World in Order to Save It ★★

Comedy 1970 · US · Colour · 79mins

A nerve gas leak in Alaska kills everyone over 25 in this hopelessly surreal comedy from cult director Roger Corman. However, the expected Utopia doesn't materialise in a freewheeling romp that features Hell's Angels, Che Guevara, Edgar Allan Poe and Martin Luther King. Corman takes aim at too many hip targets and doesn't hit any of them successfully. After the film was heavily cut by his usual distributors, he set up his own production company, New World. A time-capsule oddity. AJ

Robert Corff *Coel* • Elaine Giftos *Cilla* • Bud Cort *Hooper* • Talia Coppola [Talia Shire] *Coralie* • Ben Vereen *Carlos* • Cindy Williams *Marissa* • Alex Wilson *Jason* • Lou Procopio *Marshall McLuhan* • Country Joe McDonald *FM Radio* ■ *Dir* Roger Corman • *Scr* George Armitage

The Gate ★★★ 15

Horror 1987 · US/Can · Colour · 82mins

Three kids (Stephen Dorff, Christa Denton and Louis Tripp) inadvertently open the gateway to hell in their back yard and unleash a horde of demonic midgets who are making way for the arrival of the Devil himself. Although full of plot holes bigger than the one in the garden, director Tibor Takacs's low-budget trip though *Gremlins* and *Poltergeist* territory has enough verve and gall to drag it above the usual level of popcorn horror fodder despite every twist being telegraphed well in advance. AJ [video] DVD

Stephen Dorff *Glen* • Christa Denton *Al* • Louis Tripp *Terry* • Kelly Rowan *Lori Lee* • Jennifer Irwin *Linda Lee* • Deborah Grover *Mom* • Scot Denton *Dad* • Ingrid Veninger *Paula* • Sean Fagan *Eric* ■ *Dir* Tibor Takacs • *Scr* Michael Nankin

Gate II ★ 15

Horror 1992 · Can · Colour · 88mins

Director Tibor Takacs returns, along with co-star Louis Tripp, to summon up more demonic minions in a senseless sequel to their goofily ghoulish original. This time Tripp uses his computer knowledge to escape the horror fantasy adventures incurred by the ceremony that makes his wishes come true in warped ways. Dull and unimaginative. AJ [video]

Louis Tripp *Terry* • Simon Reynolds *Moe* • James Villemaire *John* • Pamela Segall *Liz* • Neil Munro *Art* • James Kidnie *Mr Coleson* ■ *Dir* Tibor Takacs • *Scr* Michael Nankin

Gate of Flesh ★★★★ 18

Period drama 1964 · Jpn · Colour · 90mins

Two years before his cult action thriller *Tokyo Drifter*, Japanese director Seijun Suzuki courted controversy with this near-the-knuckle drama, set at the end of the Second World War. Entirely business minded, a group of Tokyo prostitutes govern themselves by strict rules (for instance, anyone who offers their services for free gets sadistically punished). These regulations have stark consequences for Yumiko Nogawa when she falls in love with a thief who hides out in the women's home. The naked beatings subsequently delivered add a sheen of edgy exploitation, but it's the dark reality of postwar life, not the titillation, that is Suzuki's masterstroke. SF. In Japanese with English subtitles. Contains violence, swearing and sex scenes. [video] DVD

Yumiko Nogawa *Maya* • Jo Shishido *Shintaro Ibuki* • Kayo Matsuo *Omino* • Misako Tominaga *Machiko* ■ *Dir* Seijun Suzuki • *Scr* Goro Tanada, from a novel by Taijiro Tamura

Gate of Hell ★★★★★

Period drama 1953 · Jpn · Colour · 91mins

Winner of an Oscar for best costume and an honorary statuette, as well as the Grand Prix (now Palme d'Or) at Cannes, this is one of the most sumptuously coloured films ever made. Shooting in Eastmancolor and employing the theories of "synaesthesia" learned from Sergei Eisenstein, director Teinosuke Kinugasa lovingly sculpts each image, whether it's from a battle or the doomed courtship of Machiko Kyo by the heroic samurai, Kazuo Hasegawa. Amid such physical beauty, it's too easy to forget the majesty of the performances, particularly Kyo's proud wife, who refuses to submit to either the lust of her suitor or the conventions of her time. DP. In Japanese with English subtitles.

Machiko Kyo *Lady Kesa* • Kazuo Hasegawa *Moritoh* • Isao Yamagata *Wataru* • Koreya Senda *Kiyomori* • Yataro Kurokawa *Shigemori* • Kikue Mohri *Sawa* • Kotaro Bando *Rokuroh* • Jun Tazaki *Kogenta* ■ *Dir* Teinosuke Kinugasa • *Scr* Teinosuke Kinugasa, from the play *Jigokumon* by Kan Kikuchi

Gates of Paris ★★★ U

Drama 1957 · Fr/It · BW · 100mins

René Clair's last film before his New Wave denunciation is an unexpectedly serious and grossly under-rated near neighbour of Marcel Carné's *Le Jour Se Lève*. Yet his return to poetic realism is only partially successful. Léon Barsacq's claustrophobic interiors are derivative to the point of cliché, while the *ménage à trois* of dipsomanic drifter Pierre Brasseur, his girlfriend Dany Carrel and fugitive killer Henri Vidal can only end in tragedy. However, there are flashes of the old inspiration, with troubadour Georges Brassens (in his only film) acting as a roving commentator on the action. DP. In French with English subtitles.

Pierre Brasseur *Juju* • Georges Brassens *L'Artiste* • Henri Vidal *Pierre Barbier* • Dany Carrel *Maria* • Raymond Bussières *Alphonse* • Amédée *Paolo* ■ *Dir* René Clair • *Scr* René Clair, Jean Aurel, from the novel *La Grande Ceinture* by René Fallet

A Gathering of Eagles ★★ U

Drama 1963 · US · Colour · 115mins

Colonel Rock Hudson arrives at a Strategic Air Command base, where he has control over nuclear warheads but not, it seems, over his indolent men or wife. This soggy drama strives to be a Cold War version of *From Here to Eternity*, but it's let down by Hudson's boring performance and a generally weak supporting cast. The film needs Elizabeth Taylor or Ava Gardner as the wife; instead it has Mary Peach. AT

Rock Hudson *Col Jim Caldwell* • Rod Taylor *Hollis Farr* • Mary Peach *Victoria Caldwell* • Barry Sullivan *Col Fowler* • Kevin McCarthy *Gen Kirby* • Henry Silva *Col Garcia* • Leora Dana *Mrs Fowler* • Robert Lansing *Sgt Banning* ■ *Dir* Delbert Mann • *Scr* Robert Pirosh, from a story by Sy Bartlett

Gator ★★★ 15

Action thriller 1976 · US · Colour · 111mins

Burt Reynolds resurrected Gator McKlusky, the demon driver character he created in *White Lightning*, for his directorial debut, a so-so action thriller. The moonshining ex-con is forced by federal agents to nail an old school friend who's now a corrupt politician. Surprisingly good-humoured, this features unconventional performances from Jack Weston and Jerry Reed. Reynolds employs more subtlety, both in front of and behind the camera, than one would expect from such a formula endeavour. AJ [video] DVD

Burt Reynolds *Gator McKlusky* • Jack Weston *Irving Greenfield* • Lauren Hutton *Aggie Maybank* • Jerry Reed *Bama McCall* • Alice Ghostley *Emmeline Cavanaugh* • Dub Taylor *Mayor Caffrey* • Mike Douglas *Governor* ■ *Dir* Burt Reynolds • *Scr* William Norton

Gattaca ★★★★ 15

Science-fiction thriller
1997 · US · Colour · 106mins

Before screenplay writer Andrew Niccol stood the science-fiction genre on its end with *The Truman Show*, he had already shaken it up with this superlative futuristic thriller (which he also directed), built around the controversial subject of genetic engineering. Ethan Hawke is the imperfect human with ambitions of joining a space mission, who illegally exchanges identities with Jude Law, a paraplegic with perfect DNA. Niccol mints a new genre vocabulary with his utterly absorbing, intelligent and suspenseful story. Stunningly designed, this cautionary tale has Hawke, Law and Uma Thurman giving accomplished performances. AJ. Contains violence, swearing, sex scenes and nudity. [video] DVD

Ethan Hawke *Jerome/Vincent* • Uma Thurman *Irene* • Jude Law *Eugene/Jerome* • Gore Vidal *Director Josef* • Xander Berkeley *Lamar* • Elias Koteas *Antonio* • Ernest Borgnine *Caesar* • Alan Arkin *Detective Hugo* • Loren Dean *Anton* ■ *Dir/Scr* Andrew Niccol

The Gaucho ★★★

Silent swashbuckling drama
1927 · US · BW and Colour · 96mins

The last but one of Douglas Fairbanks's silent swashbucklers is a virtual rehash of his two *Zorro* films and was based on a story by Fairbanks, using his customary pseudonym of Elton Thomas. Set in South America, it gives Fairbanks the chance to demonstrate his athletic skills while saving the peasants from exploitation. Fairbanks's wife, Mary Pickford, makes a brief appearance as Our Lady of the Shrine. Mexican actress Lupe Velez, who plays the heroine, was originally spotted in a Laurel and Hardy one-reeler. AT

Douglas Fairbanks *The Gaucho* • Lupe Velez *The Mountain Girl* • Geraine Greear *Girl of the Shrine* • Eve Southern *Girl of the Shrine, as a child* • Gustav von Seyffertitz *Ruiz, the Usurper* • Mary Pickford *Our Lady of the Shrine* ■ *Dir* F Richard Jones • *Scr* Lotta Woods, from a story by Douglas Fairbanks [Elton Thomas]

The Gauntlet ★★★ 18

Action crime drama
1977 · US · Colour · 104mins

Clint Eastwood stars in this effective action adventure as a discredited and dim cop escorting prostitute Sondra Locke to a trial in Phoenix, Arizona, with mobsters and corrupt officials trying to stop them. The shoot-outs prove less engaging than the mismatched couple's smart-talking infighting and, as director, Eastwood selflessly highlights his then-girlfriend Locke's acting range with understanding and precision. Well paced and compelling. AJ. Contains violence and swearing. DVD

Clint Eastwood *Ben Shockley* • Sondra Locke *Gus Mally* • Pat Hingle *Josephson* • William Prince *Blakelock* • Bill McKinney *Constable* • Michael Cavanaugh *Feyderspiel* • Carole Cook *Waitress* ■ *Dir* Clint Eastwood • *Scr* Michael Butler, Dennis Shryack

Gawain and the Green Knight ★★ U

Fantasy 1973 · UK · Colour · 107mins

With his first feature, *I, Monster*, Stephen Weeks reworked the Jekyll and Hyde story and this second effort takes on Arthurian legend. Murray Head is an appealing hero as Gawain, while the Green Knight – headless from the start – is played by the imposing Nigel Green, who died shortly after the film was completed. Weeks complained long and loud that the film was re-edited by the distributor and, in 1983, he had a second crack at the story as *Sword of the Valiant*. AT

Murray Head *Gawain* • Nigel Green *Green Knight* • Ciaran Madden *Linet* • Robert Hardy *Sir Bertilak* • David Leland *Humphrey* • Anthony Sharp *King* • Ronald Lacey *Oswald* • Murray Melvin *Seneschal* ■ *Dir* Stephen Weeks • *Scr* Stephen Weeks, Philip Breen

The Gay Adventure ★★

Portmanteau drama 1949 · UK · BW · 74mins

This rather insipid portmanteau picture, made in 1949 but held up for four years, follows three men travelling from France to London. They are an "ooh-la-la" Frenchman (Jean-Pierre Aumont), an "oh I say" Englishman (Richard Murdoch) and a "gee whizz" American (Burgess Meredith). They each fantasise differently about the same blonde they see on the train. The object of their lust is played by the wooden Paula Valenska. RB

Burgess Meredith *Dick* • Jean-Pierre Aumont *Andre Marchand* • Paula Valenska *Suzy/ Sonia/Hedy* • Kathleen Harrison *Isobel* • Richard Murdoch *David Felton* • Julian D'Albie *Waterhouse* • Jose de Almeyda *Jones* ■ *Dir* Gordon Parry • *Scr* Paul Darcy, Sid Colin, Anatole de Grunwald

The Gay Bride ★★

Comedy crime drama
1934 · US · BW · 80mins

The sublime Carole Lombard is wasted in this mishmash of crime melodrama and comedy. She marries gangster Nat Pendleton solely for his money and in anticipation of his early death. He duly gets himself killed and she moves on to another sucker. The supporting cast includes ZaSu Pitts, and the script promises much, but it runs out of steam far too soon. RK

Carole Lombard *Mary* • Chester Morris *Office boy* • ZaSu Pitts *Mirabelle* • Leo Carrillo *Mickey* • Nat Pendleton *Shoots Magiz* • Sam Hardy *Dingle* • Walter Walker *MacPherson* • Joe Twerp *Lafcadio* ■ *Dir* Jack Conway • *Scr* Bella Spewack, Sam Spewack, from the story *Repeal* by Charles Francis Coe

The Gay Caballero ★★ U

Western 1940 · US · BW · 57mins

This is Cesar Romero's third outing (after *The Cisco Kid and the Lady* and *The Return of the Cisco Kid*) as the ever so slightly camp cowboy, a role that suited the gay Romero perfectly. Running at less than an hour, it tells of Romero and his sidekick Chris-Pin Martin arriving in town and discovering that the Kid is presumed dead. While the plot about land rights seems hard-pressed to fill the time, this does offer B-movie thrills and a good villainess in Janet Beecher. AT

Cesar Romero *Cisco Kid* • Sheila Ryan *Susan Wetherby* • Robert Sterling *Billy Brewster* • Chris-Pin Martin *Gordito* • Janet Beecher *Kate Brewster* • Edmund MacDonald *Joe Turner* • Jacqueline Dalya *Carmelita* • Montague Shaw [C Montague Shaw] *George Wetherby* ■ *Dir* Otto Brower • *Scr* Albert Duffy, John Larkin, from a story by Walter Bullock, Albert Duffy, from characters created by O Henry

The Gay Deception ★★★ U

Romantic comedy 1935 · US · BW · 77mins

This gained an Academy Award nomination for best original story but it now seems routine. Francis Lederer is the prince working incognito as a bellboy in a New York hotel, and Frances Dee is the lottery winner who checks in to inject some luxury into her life. William Wyler's smooth direction, some clever comic details and spirited supporting work overcome the weak casting of the leads. AE

Francis Lederer *Sandro* • Frances Dee *Mirabel* • Benita Hume *Miss Channing* • Alan Mowbray *Lord Clewe* • Akim Tamiroff *Spellek* • Lennox Pawle *Consul General* • Adele St Maur *Lucille* • Luis Alberni *Ernest* ■ *Dir* William Wyler • *Scr* Stephen Morehouse Avery, Don Hartman

The Gay Desperado ★★

Musical comedy 1936 · US · BW · 88mins

Leo Carrillo is the small-time Mexican bandit who loves Hollywood gangster pictures and decides to remodel his gang on American lines. He also loves music and finds a way to get tenor Nino Martini to join his merry band. Ida Lupino is the heiress kidnapped along with her fiancé, James Blakeley. It's moderately engaging to see what a brilliant director (Rouben Mamoulian) makes of this broad comedy material and the images are often stunning, but the songs are second-rate and the humour becomes tiresome. AE

Ida Lupino *Jane* • Nino Martini *Chivo* • Leo Carrillo *Braganza* • Harold Huber *Campo* • James Blakeley *Bill* • Stanley Fields *Butch* ■ *Dir* Rouben Mamoulian • *Scr* Wallace Smith, from a story by Leo Birinski

The Gay Divorce ★★★★ U

Musical comedy 1934 · US · BW · 103mins

Hollywood censorship refused to acknowledge that a divorce could possibly be gay, in the old-fashioned sense of the word, and retitled the film *The Gay Divorcee*. Here in Britain, the title reverted back to that of the original stage show. This knock-out movie pairs Fred Astaire with perky Ginger Rogers in the leading roles for the first time – and how they shine. The plot's froth, but the sets (including a very deco Brighton) are ingenious, the score superb and the supporting cast witty and well chosen. TS

Fred Astaire *Guy Holden* • Ginger Rogers *Mimi* • Alice Brady *Aunt Hortense* • Edward Everett Horton *Egbert* • Erik Rhodes *Rodolfo Tonetti* • Eric Blore *Waiter* • Betty Grable *Hotel guest* ■ *Dir* Mark Sandrich • *Scr* George Marion Jr, Dorothy Yost, Edward Kaufman, from the musical by Dwight Taylor, Cole Porter

The Gay Falcon ★★★

Detective mystery 1941 · US · BW · 66mins

George Sanders takes on the role of writer Michael Arlen's debonair detective and ladies' man, Gay Lawrence (aka the Falcon) in this fast-moving detective mystery that delighted audiences and spawned 15 sequels over the next eight years, beginning with *A Date with the Falcon*. Cruising through a case involving jewel thieves and an insurance scam, Sanders not only proves his chauffeur (Allen Jenkins) innocent of murder and diamond robbery, but also revels in having Wendy Barrie and Anne Hunter squabble over him. DP

George Sanders *Gay Lawrence/The Falcon* • Wendy Barrie *Helen Reed* • Allen Jenkins *Goldy* • Anne Hunter *Elinor* • Gladys Cooper *Maxine* • Edward Brophy *Bates* • Arthur Shields *Waldeck* • Damian O'Flynn *Weber* ■ *Dir* Irving Reis • *Scr* Lynn Root, Frank Fenton, from the character created by Michael Arlen

Gay Purr-ee ★★★ U

Animated musical adventure
1962 · US · Colour · 84mins

This sophisticated and witty cartoon reunited Judy Garland with the composers from *The Wizard of Oz*, Harold Arlen and EY "Yip" Harburg. Mewsette the cat (voiced by Garland) leaves her country home seeking excitement in the big city (Paris) and soon runs into trouble. Adults will enjoy spotting the Impressionist landscapes used in some scenes.The kids may prefer that later feline adventure, Disney's *The Aristocats*, which was probably influenced by this film's character and style. TS

Judy Garland *Mewsette* • Hermione Gingold *Mme Rubens-Chatte* • Robert Goulet *Jaune-Tom* • Red Buttons *Robespierre* • Paul Frees *Meowrice* ■ *Dir* Abe Levitow • *Scr* Chuck Jones, Dorothy Jones, Ralph Wright

The Gay Sisters ★★★

Drama 1942 · US · BW · 109mins

A melodrama from the days when gay meant, well, gay. The title is ironic as Barbara Stanwyck, Geraldine Fitzgerald and Nancy Coleman are the conniving titular trio, bent on deviously securing an inheritance through Stanwyck secretly marrying sturdy George Brent. A supporting actor called Byron Barr played a character named Gig Young in this, and subsequently changed his professional name to that of his character. TS

Barbara Stanwyck *Fiona Gaylord* • George Brent *Charles Barclay* • Geraldine Fitzgerald *Evelyn Gaylord* • Donald Crisp *Ralph Pedloch* • Byron Barr [Gig Young] *Gig Young* • Nancy Coleman *Susanna Gaylord* • Gene Lockhart *Herschell Gibbon* • Larry Simms *Austin* ■ *Dir* Irving Rapper • *Scr* Lenore Coffee, from the novel by Stephen Longstreet

Gayab ★★ 12

Fantasy comedy
2004 · Ind · Colour · 132mins

Tusshar Kapoor's wish for invisibility is granted by a mysterious statue, and he becomes increasingly unhinged as his new powers transform his personality. He begins tinkering with the lives of his bickering parents, his trendy neighbour Antara Mali and her boyfriend, Ramman Trikha. This is patchily entertaining, if short on genuine comic invention, but the invisibility effects are tame and predictable. DP. In Hindi with English subtitles. Contains violence. DVD

Tusshar Kapoor *Vishnu Prasad* • Antara Mali *Mohini* • Raghuveer Yadav [Raghuvir Yadav] *Balwant Rai* • Ramman Trikha *Sameer* • Rashika Joshi *Shanti* ■ *Dir* Prawal Raman

The Gazebo ★★★

Black comedy 1959 · US · BW · 101mins

There's a small summerhouse in the grounds of a country estate under which there may – or may not be – a dead body. Likeable stars Glenn Ford and Debbie Reynolds are super together, and here they're close to their box-office prime and both are enchanting. They're nearly acted off the screen, though, by character stars John McGiver and Doro Merande. TS

Glenn Ford *Elliott Nash* • Debbie Reynolds *Nell Nash* • Carl Reiner *Harlow Edison* • John McGiver *Sam Thorpe* • Mabel Albertson *Mrs Chandler* • Martin Landau *The Duke* • Doro Merande *Matilda* • Bert Freed *Lieut Joe Jenkins* • ZaSu Pitts *Mrs MacGruder* ■ *Dir* George Marshall • *Scr* George Wells, from a play by Alec Coppel, from a story by Myra Coppel, Alec Coppel

Gazon Maudit ★★★ 18

Comedy 1995 · Fr · Colour · 102mins

Josiane Balasko wrote, directed and stars in this well-meaning but uneven French sex comedy. She plays a woman whose car breaks down near the home of Victoria Abril and her philandering husband Alain Chabat. Abril invites Balasko in, and it's not long before the two women are expressing their mutual appreciation of each other, much to the anger of Chabat. All three leads play their roles with farcical verve, but they are let down by Balasko's script. Sexy and amusing this is, but hilarious and original it is not. JB. In French with English subtitles. Contains swearing and nudity.

Victoria Abril *Loli* • Josiane Balasko *Marijo* • Alain Chabat *Laurent* • Ticky Holgado *Antoine* • Miguel Bose *Diego* • Catherine Hiegel *Dany* • Catherine Samie *Prostitute* • Catherine Lachens *Sopha* • Michèle Bernier *Solange* ■ *Dir/Scr* Josiane Balasko

The Geisha Boy ★★★ U

Comedy 1958 · US · Colour · 101mins

Jerry Lewis's frantic, jerk-around comedy style here got its most suitable director, who saw him simply as a cartoon with no connection to real life. That's because Frank Tashlin used to be a cartoonist himself, so the sight gags are often hilarious. The comedy works less well when third-rate magician Lewis joins an army tour of Japan and gets lumbered with a kid. Yet even when the twee flies thick and fast, there's some fun to be had. TH

Jerry Lewis *Gilbert Wooley* • Marie McDonald *Lola Livingston* • Robert Kazuyoshi Hirano *Mitsuo Watanabe* • Nobu Atsumi McCarthy [Nobu McCarthy] *Kimi Sikita* • Sessue Hayakawa *Mr Sikita* • Barton MacLane *Major Ridgley* • Suzanne Pleshette *Betty Pearson* • Ryuzo Demura *Ichiyama* ■ *Dir* Frank Tashlin • *Scr* Frank Tashlin, from a story by Rudy Makoul

Gen-X Cops ★★ 18

Martial arts comedy thriller
1999 · HK · Colour · 108mins

Not even a cameo from producer Jackie Chan can enliven this predictable Benny Chan actioner, in which twitchy inspector Eric Tsang trains a trio of slacker rookies to infiltrate arms dealer Toru Nakamora's gang. Moreover, there's nothing earth-shattering about the stunt pieces, but what really drags this into mediocrity are the performances of newcomers Nicholas Tse, Stephen Fung and Sam Lee. They waste one-liners and fight with the choreographed conviction of a boy band. A sequel followed in 2000. DP. Cantonese dialogue dubbed into English. [video] DVD

Nicholas Tse *Jack* • Stephen Fung *Match* • Sam Lee *Alien* • Toru Nakamura *Akatura* • Eric Tsang *Inspector Chan* • Daniel Wu *Danny* • Grace Yip *Y2K* • Jackie Chan *Fisherman* ■ *Dir* Benny Chan • *Scr* Benny Chan, Hui Koan, Peter Tsi, Lee Yee Wah

The Gendarme in New York ★ U

Comedy 1965 · Fr/It · Colour · 101mins

The second in Jean Girault's series of coarse, chaotic comedies makes the mistake of taking Sergeant Cruchot and his brigade of buffoons away from home. The plot has the St Tropez squad representing France at an international police conference in New York. The resulting farce is less funny than its predecessor, and also proved a misfire at the French box office. DP. French dialogue dubbed into English.

Louis De Funès *Sergeant Ludovic Cruchot* • Geneviève Grad *Nicole* • Michel Galabru *Gerber* • Jean Lefebvre *Fougasse* ■ *Dir* Jean Girault • *Scr* Jacques Vilfrid, Richard Balducci, Jean Girault, from a story by Richard Balducci

The Gendarme of St Tropez ★★ U

Comedy 1964 · Fr/It · Colour · 94mins

This was the first of six frantic farces starring Louis De Funès as the blusteringly incompetent Sergeant Ludovic Cruchot. French critics detested the series, though they initially proved hugely popular with the public. There's the vaguest hint of Clouseau in this first misadventure, as De Funès arrives to take up his new post and launches a crusade against the local nudists. However, much of the action is taken up with the apprehension of a gang of art thieves, thanks more to Cruchot's daughter (Geneviève Grad) than the efforts of his own Keystone-style cops. DP. French dialogue dubbed into English.

Louis De Funès *Sergeant Ludovic Cruchot* • Geneviève Grad *Nicole Cruchot* • Michel Galabru *Gerber* • Jean Lefebvre *Fougasse* • Christian Marin *Merlot* • Daniel Cauchy *Richard* • Jean-Paul Bertrand *Eddie* • Frank Vilcour *Jean-Luc* ■ *Dir* Jean Girault • *Scr* Richard Balducci, Jacques Vilfrid, Jean Girault, from the story by Richard Balducci

The Gendarme Wore Skirts ★

Comedy 1982 · Fr/It · Colour · 99mins

The *Gendarme of St Tropez* series never quite plumbed the depths of the *Police Academy* movies, but they came close with this final, undistinguished farce. Made four years after *The Spacemen of St Tropez* flopped, the film – in which Sergeant Cruchot's incompetent squad are sent into total disarray by the arrival of some female recruits – also proved to be Louis De Funès's last picture. DP. French dialogue dubbed into English.

Louis De Funès *Sergeant Ludovic Cruchot* • Michel Galabru *Inspector Gerber* • Maurice Risch *Beaupied* • Jacques François *Colonel* ■ *Dir* Jean Girault, Tony Aboyantz • *Scr* Jacques Vilfrid

Gendernauts ★★ 18

Documentary 1999 · Ger · Colour · 87mins

Long one of gay cinema's most provocative voices, cross-dressing German Monika Treut explores the world of transgender in this disappointingly traditional and uncharacteristically defensive documentary. Each TS she interviews has interesting things to say about gender as "performance" and the motives and impact of their sexual reassignment. But the refusal to stray outside their San Franciscan ghetto prevents any exploration of their social status, while the medical implications of their treatment are stubbornly ignored. It's eminently sympathetic, but a missed opportunity. DP

Dir/Scr Monika Treut • *Cinematographer* Elfi Mikesch

The Gene Krupa Story ★★★

Musical biography 1959 · US · BW · 101mins

This biopic, alternatively called *Drum Crazy*, tells the story of Krupa (Sal Mineo), the greatest jazz percussionist of his time, who was convicted on a drugs charge and then found that success drained away in the aftermath of the scandal. It's a whitewash job as far as it can be, but the jazz soundtrack is more than adequate. TH

Sal Mineo *Gene Krupa* • Susan Kohner *Ethel Maguire* • James Darren *Eddie Sirota* • Susan Oliver *Dorissa Dinell* • Yvonne Craig *Gloria Corregio* • Lawrence Dobkin *Speaker Willis* • Celia Lovsky *Mother* • Red Nichols ■ *Dir* Don Weis • *Scr* Orin Jannings

Généalogies d'un Crime ★★★

Mystery thriller
1997 · Fr/Por · Colour · 113mins

Exploring the essence of evil and positing predestination against conditioning, this is the ultimate cinematic riddle wrapped in a mystery inside an enigma. An intelligent film-maker with a healthy disregard for highbrow posturing, Raúl Ruiz approaches Hitchcock via Buñuel in this gnawingly complex thriller, in which flashbacks jostle with theoretical debates, as lawyer Catherine Deneuve seeks to establish whether Melvil Poupaud is a natural-born killer or was programmed by his eccentric psychologist aunt (also Deneuve) and her sinister mentor, Michel Piccoli. DP. In French with English subtitles.

Catherine Deneuve *Jeanne/Solange* • Michel Piccoli *Georges Didier* • Melvil Poupaud *René* • Andrzej Seweryn *Christian* • Bernadette Lafont *Esther* ■ *Dir* Raoul Ruiz [Raúl Ruiz] • *Scr* Pascal Bonitzer, Raoul Ruiz [Raúl Ruiz]

The General ★★★★★ U

Silent comedy 1927 · US · BW · 73mins

Buster Keaton's greatest movie is, some would argue, the finest silent screen comedy ever made. Stone-faced engineer Buster loves his vast steam locomotive, "The General", almost as much as his girlfriend (Marion Mack). When he is rejected by the Confederate Army, Mack brands him a coward and breaks off the engagement. Later, he risks all to pursue the train with her on board when it's stolen by Yankee spies. The humour ranges from the gentle to the exhilarating, while the drama of the railtrack-chase has a visual beauty that puts this comedy into the category of true classic. Buster Keaton's genius was not just in the nuts and bolts of invention, but in the creation of an endearing character. TH [video] DVD

Buster Keaton *Johnnie Gray* • Marion Mack *Annabelle Lee* • Charles Smith *Her father* • Frank Barnes (1) *Her brother* • Glen Cavender *Capt Anderson, chief spy* • Jim Farley [James Farley] *Gen Thatcher* • Frank Hagney *Recruiting officer* • Frederick Vroom *Confederate general* ■ *Dir* Buster Keaton, Clyde Bruckman • *Scr* Buster Keaton, Clyde Bruckman, Al Boasberg, Charles Smith, from the novel *The Great Locomotive Chase* by William Pittinger • *Cinematographer* J Devereaux Jennings

The General ★★★★★ 15

Biographical drama
1998 · Ire/UK · BW · 118mins

Brendan Gleeson gives a towering performance here as Martin Cahill, the man dubbed "Dublin's favourite gangster". This biopic looks back at Cahill's childhood and the events that led up to his murder in 1994, and shows him to be a ruthless criminal who, nevertheless, courted popular acclaim. Living on a grim Dublin estate with his beloved wife (Maria Doyle Kennedy) and her equally beloved sister (Angeline Ball) – with whom he had an affair – Cahill managed to keep one step ahead of police inspector Ned Kenny (Jon Voight). John Boorman's film is a brilliant example of storytelling and his excellent cast rises to the occasion, with Gleeson on career-best form as the fascinating yet flawed folk hero. TH. Contains swearing, violence and sexual references. [video]

Brendan Gleeson *Martin Cahill* • Adrian Dunbar *Noel Curley* • Sean McGinley *Gary* • Maria Doyle Kennedy *Frances* • Angeline Ball *Tina* • Jon Voight *Inspector Ned Kenny* • Eanna MacLiam *Jimmy* • Tom Murphy *Willie Byrne* ■ *Dir* John Boorman • *Scr* John Boorman, from the non-fiction book *The General: Godfather of Crime* by Paul Williams

General Della Rovere ★★★★

Second World War drama
1959 · It/Fr · BW · 131mins

The winner of the Golden Lion at Venice in 1959, this film relies totally on the astonishing performance of Vittorio De Sica. In attempting to recapture the neorealist glories of *Rome, Open City*, director Roberto Rossellini overstages the authenticity and misses the naturalism that characterised the performances in his epoch-making film. So it falls to one-time matinée idol De Sica to bring some life and truth to this sentimental tale. He's a swindler who is forced by the Nazis to impersonate a murdered resistance leader. Moving, darkly comic and inspirational. DP. In Italian with English subtitles.

Vittorio De Sica *Bardone/Grimaldi* • Hannes Messemer *Colonel Mueller* • Sandra Milo *Olga* • Giovanna Ralli *Valeria* • Anne Vernon *Chiara Fassio* • Vittorio Caprioli *Banchelli* • Ivo Garrani *Fabrizio* ■ *Dir* Roberto Rossellini • *Scr* Roberto Rossellini, Sergio Amidei, Diego Fabbri, Indro Montanelli, from a story by Indro Montanelli

The General Died at Dawn ★★

Adventure 1936 · US · BW · 97mins

The general is a Chinese warlord (a very cheesy Akim Tamiroff) and Gary Cooper is a mercenary whose plans to assist the oppressed peasants are thwarted by Madeleine Carroll robbing him on a train. There's a lot of plot here but, rather than treat it as a thick slice of hokum, with performances to match, playwright Clifford Odets, working on his first film, and director Lewis Milestone try to say great things about the human condition. The dialogue is mock-poetic mudcake that sticks to everything. AT

Gary Cooper *O'Hara* • Madeleine Carroll *Judy Perrie* • Akim Tamiroff *General Yang* • Dudley Digges *Mr Wu* • Porter Hall *Peter Perrie* • William Frawley *Brighton* • JM Kerrigan *Leach* • Philip Ahn *Oxford* ■ *Dir* Lewis Milestone • *Scr* Clifford Odets, from a novel by Charles G Booth • *Cinematographer* Victor Milner • *Music* Werner Janssen

The General Line ★★★★ PG

Silent political drama
1929 · USSR · BW · 100mins

Shot either side of his ill-received revolutionary masterpiece, *October*, this was an effort on the part of Sergei Eisenstein to return to official favour by enthusiastically promoting the Kremlin's policy of collectivisation. However, the experiments in tonal montage, which characterise Eisenstein's last silent feature, met with disapproval and he elected to go on a prolonged sabbatical. The film recalls the rural poetry of Dovzhenko's *Earth*, while Marfa Lapkina's weatherworn face triumphantly proclaims the effectiveness of the casting principle of typage. DP [video]

Marfa Lapkina *Marfa* • M Ivanin *Marfa's son* • Vasia Buzenkov *A komsomol, manager of dairy co* • Nejnikov *Mitrochkin, teacher* • Chukamariev *Kulak, peasant proprietor* • Kostia Vasiliev *Tractor driver* ■ *Dir/Scr* Sergei Eisenstein, Grigori V Aleksandrov

General Spanky ★★ U

Period comedy 1936 · US · BW · 71mins

Having charmed Depression audiences with their backstreet antics in dozens of Hal Roach shorts (including the 1936 Oscar-winner *Bored of Education*), the Our Gang kids were sorely out of their depth in this American Civil War adventure. Spanky McFarland and Billie Thomas are entrusted with protecting Philip Holmes's beloved, Rosina Lawrence, while he's away at the front. They form a tykes defence unit against Mississippi gambler Irving Pichel. DP

Spanky McFarland *Spanky* • Phillips Holmes *Marshall Vallent* • Ralph Morgan *Yankee general* • Irving Pichel *Captain Simmons* • Rosina Lawrence *Louella Blanchard* • Billie "Buckwheat" Thomas *Buckwheat* • Carl "Alfalfa" Switzer *Alfalfa* • Hobart Bosworth *Colonel Blanchard* ■ *Dir* Fred Newmeyer [Fred C Newmeyer], Gordon Douglas • *Scr* Richard Flournoy, Hal Yates, John Guedel, from a story by Richard Flournoy, Hal Yates, John Guedel

The General's Daughter ★★★ 18

Mystery thriller
1999 · US/Ger · Colour · 111mins

This moderately absorbing military whodunnit is let down by the lazy hamming of star John Travolta. He plays an armed forces cop called in to investigate the horrific rape and murder of a woman officer (Leslie Stefanson), who also happens to be the daughter of heavyweight military man James Cromwell. James Woods effortlessly steals the show as one of the prime murder suspects, but the wayward script's derivative twists and turns weaken what should have been a hard-hitting drama. JF. Contains violence and swearing. [video] DVD

John Travolta *Paul Brenner* • Madeleine Stowe *Sarah Sunhill* • James Cromwell *General Campbell* • Timothy Hutton *Colonel Kent* • Leslie Stefanson *Elisabeth Campbell* • Daniel Von Bargen *Chief Yardley* • Clarence Williams III *Colonel Fowler* • James Woods *Colonel Moore* ■ *Dir* Simon West • *Scr* Christopher Bertolini, William Goldman, from the novel by Nelson DeMille

A Generation ★★★★ 12

Second World War drama
1954 · Pol · BW · 83mins

Director Andrzej Wajda made his debut with this solemn tale of love, patriotism and party unity that opened the war trilogy completed by *Kanal* and *Ashes and Diamonds*. As much influenced by personal zeal as the socialist realism that the Polish state expected of its film-makers, this is a naive picture. But such is Wajda's commitment and his pictorial sense that we are carried along with the story of Tadeusz Lomnicki, the young woodworker whose passion for Urszula Modrzynska leads to his involvement with the resistance, the Warsaw ghetto and the communist agenda. Bursting with potential, the film also launched the acting careers of Roman Polanski and Zbigniew Cybulski. DP. In Polish with English subtitles. [video]

Tadeusz Lomnicki *Stach* • Urszula Modrzynska *Dorota* • Janusz Paluszkiewicz *Sekula* •

Ryszard Kotas *Jacek* • Roman Polanski *Mundek* • Zbigniew Cybulski *Kostek* ■ *Dir* Andrzej Wajda • *Scr* Bohdan Czeszko

Generation ★★

Comedy 1969 · US · Colour · 90mins

This generation-gap comedy, which betrays its Broadway origins, is not one of the high points of David Janssen's career. He plays an advertising executive, about to become a grandfather, who is horrified when his determined daughter decides to opt for a home birth. JG

David Janssen *Jim Bolton* • Kim Darby *Doris Bolton Owen* • Carl Reiner *Stan Herman* • Pete Duel *Walter Owen* • Andrew Prine *Winn Garand* • James Coco *Mr Blatto* • Sam Waterston *Desmond* • David Lewis (1) *Arlington* ■ *Dir* George Schaefer • *Scr* William Goodhart, from his play

Genevieve ★★★★ U

Comedy 1953 · UK · Colour · 82mins

Mocking many of the character traits that supposedly made this nation great, this is one of the most British of British films. The good-natured round of confrontations and calamities that befall John Gregson, Dinah Sheridan, Kenneth More and Kay Kendall are familiar to generations of movie-goers and, even though each disaster is more predictable than the last, there is pleasure to be had in observing the reactions of the childish, overzealous chauvinists and their teasing, long-suffering partners. DP DVD

Kenneth More *Ambrose Claverhouse* • John Gregson *Alan McKim* • Dinah Sheridan *Wendy McKim* • Kay Kendall *Rosalind Peters* • Geoffrey Keen *First traffic policeman* • Harold Siddons *Second traffic policeman* • Reginald Beckwith *JC Callahan* • Joyce Grenfell *Hotel proprietress* ■ *Dir* Henry Cornelius • *Scr* William Rose • *Music* Larry Adler

Genghis Khan ★ PG

Biographical adventure
1964 · US/UK/W Ger/Yug · Colour · 119mins

This shoddy-looking movie is one of those "sub-epics" that aim for the prestige and grandeur of *Ben-Hur* or *El Cid* yet fall dismally short. Omar Sharif is woefully miscast as the Mongol invader, riding across Yugoslavian locations and hacking extras to bloody bits in Henry Levin's slow-moving film. The supporting cast, however, offers a few diversions – James Mason and Robert Morley are especially silly as Chinamen. AT

Omar Sharif *Temujin-Genghis Khan* • Stephen Boyd *Jamuga* • James Mason *Kam Ling* • Eli Wallach *Shah of Khwarezm* • Françoise Dorléac *Bortei* • Telly Savalas *Shan* • Robert Morley *Emperor of China* • Yvonne Mitchell *Katke* • Woody Strode *Sengal* • Michael Hordern *Geen* ■ *Dir* Henry Levin • *Scr* Clarke Reynolds, Beverly Cross, from a story by Berkely Mather

Genocide ★★★★ 15

Documentary
1981 · US · Colour and BW · 83mins

Everything about this Oscar-winning documentary was calculated to ensure its academic expertise was delivered with maximum emotional impact. Winston Churchill's biographer, Martin Gilbert, joined Rabbi Marvin Hier among the screenwriters, while Elmer Bernstein's evocative score played behind the authoritative, but always compassionate tones of Orson Welles and Elizabeth Taylor. Yet, considering his exemplary use of interviews, public and private papers, and archive footage, one wonders why director Arnold Schwartzman felt he needed the Hollywood backing. The wealth of documentary evidence he presents in this survey of anti-Semitism and the barbaric atrocities committed by the Nazis is already so overwhelmingly powerful. DP

Elizabeth Taylor *Narrator* • Orson Welles *Narrator* ■ *Dir* Arnold Schwartzman • *Scr* Arnold Schwartzman, Martin Gilbert, Marvin Hier

A Gentle Creature ★★★★

Psychological drama
1969 · Fr · Colour · 88mins

Based on a story by his constant inspiration, Fyodor Dostoyevsky, this is Robert Bresson's first film in colour. The purity of his vision remains intact, however, as he once more employs the blend of naturalistic acting and precise, symbolic composition that established him as one of cinema's most rigorous auteurs. Dominique Sanda makes a remarkable debut as the wife whose suicide prompts a sequence of flashbacks, as her pawnbroker husband Guy Frangin seeks clues to her despair. This is more pessimistic than Bresson's earlier works, but the essential humanism is still evident. DP. In French with English subtitles.

Dominique Sanda *The wife* • Guy Frangin *The husband* • Jane Lobre *Anna* ■ *Dir* Robert Bresson • *Scr* Robert Bresson, from the short story *A Gentle Soul* by Fyodor Dostoyevsky

Gentle Giant ★★ U

Adventure 1967 · US · Colour · 92mins

When seven-year-old Clint Howard befriends a cuddly black bear cub, his daddy (Dennis Weaver) and mummy (Vera Miles) are surprisingly unperturbed. Set in Florida, this is a Disney-style animal adventure aimed primarily at uncritical youngsters and features Clint Howard (the younger brother of child actor-turned-director Ron Howard). The movie was deemed successful enough to spawn a TV series called *Gentle Ben*. AT

Dennis Weaver *Tom Wedloe* • Vera Miles *Ellen Wedloe* • Ralph Meeker *Fog Hanson* • Clint Howard *Mark Wedloe* • Huntz Hall *Dink* • Rance Howard *Tater* • Frank Schuller *Charlie* • Ric O'Feldman *Mate* ■ *Dir* James Neilson • *Scr* Edward J Lakso, Andy White, from the novel *Gentle Ben* by Walt Morey

The Gentle Gunman ★★★ U

Drama 1952 · UK · BW · 82mins

Dirk Bogarde wrote that this "wasn't a film I particularly wanted to make". Nontheless, playing an IRA activist who wants to step up the war against the British in 1941, he still does a good job as a man tormented by doubts. There are no doubts, though, for his brother (John Mills) who sees the war against the Nazis as more important and is put on IRA trial for his pains. This too-balanced approach to the Irish dilemma makes this otherwise thoughtful film too glib for its own good. TH

John Mills *Terence Sullivan* • Dirk Bogarde *Matt Sullivan* • Robert Beatty *Shinto* • Elizabeth Sellars *Maureen Fagan* • Barbara Mullen *Molly Fagan* • Eddie Byrne *Flynn* • Joseph Tomelty *Dr Brannigan* • Gilbert Harding *Henry Truethorne* • James Kenney *Johnny Fagan* ■ *Dir* Basil Dearden, Michael Relph • *Scr* Roger MacDougall, from his play

The Gentle Rain ★★

Romantic drama
1966 · US/Bra · Colour · 110mins

In Rio de Janeiro, a neurotic American girl falls for a man who has lost his power of speech following a traumatic accident. What should have been a tender tale about the problems of speaking and non-speaking people relating to each other becomes a routine and ultimately discreditable melodrama. Christopher George and Lynda Day do their best with less than credible material and the somewhat contrived ending. JG

Christopher George *Bill Patterson* • Lynda Day [Lynda Day George] *Judy Reynolds* • Fay Spain *Nancy Masters* • Maria Helena Dias *Gloria* • Lon Clark *Harry Masters* • Barbara Williams (1) *Girl friend* • Robert Assumpaco *Hotel manager* ■ *Dir* Burt Balaban • *Scr* Robert Cream

The Gentle Sex ★★★ U

Second World War drama
1943 · UK · BW · 88mins

Viewed today, this drama seems patronising in its depiction of the contribution made to the war effort by seven socially diverse women, who volunteer for service on the same day. Yet it served its purpose both as a morale booster and as a recruitment advertisement, thanks to some astute appeals to the patriotic spirit and some spunky acting by a top-notch cast. A week after the film was released, its co-director Leslie Howard was killed when his plane was shot down while he was on a secret mission to Portugal. DP

Joan Gates *Gwen* • Jean Gillie *Good Time Dot* • Joan Greenwood *Betty* • Joyce Howard *Ann Lawrence* • Rosamund John *Maggie Fraser* • Lilli Palmer *Erna* • Barbara Waring *Joan* • John Justin *David Sheridan* ■ *Dir* Leslie Howard, Maurice Elvey • *Scr* Moie Charles, Aimee Stuart, Roland Pertwee, Phyllis Rose, from a story by Moie Charles

The Gentle Trap ★

Thriller 1960 · UK · BW · 61mins

An utterly threadbare British B-movie about an apprentice locksmith who goes on the run from the police and local gangsters. It was made by the low-budget production company Butcher's, and everyone involved accordingly made a hash of it. Only devoted fans of its leading actor Spencer Teakle and actress Felicity Young, who plays a rather feeble *femme fatale*, will bother to watch. AT

Spencer Teakle *Johnny Ryan* • Felicity Young *Jean* • Dorinda Stevens *Mary* • Martin Benson *Ricky Barnes* • Dawn Brooks *Sylvia* • Arthur Hewlett *Sam* • Alan Edwards *Al Jenkins* • Hugh Latimer *Vic Carter* ■ *Dir* Charles Saunders • *Scr* Brock Williams, Alan Osborne, from the story by Guido Coen

A Gentleman after Dark ★★

Crime drama 1942 · US · BW · 76mins

Miriam Hopkins's career was on the wane when she teamed up with Brian Donlevy in this low-budget melodrama. Playing with her usual relish, she stars as a woman who isn't averse to a spot of blackmail. Husband Donlevy is prepared to break out of jail and sacrifice everything in order to deal with her and protect the honour of their daughter. Despite their efforts, this is past its sell-by date. AE

Brian Donlevy *Harry Melton* • Miriam Hopkins *Flo Melton* • Preston Foster *Tom Gaynor* • Harold Huber *Stubby* • Philip Reed *Eddie* • Gloria Holden *Miss Clark* ■ *Dir* Edwin L Marin • *Scr* Patterson McNutt, George Bruce, from a story by Richard Washburn Child

A Gentleman at Heart ★★ U

Comedy 1942 · US · BW · 66mins

Cesar Romero is given a rare chance to play the lead – rather than a loser in love to one of Fox's musical stars. He clearly enjoys himself in this slight comedy about shady dealings in the art world. As the bookie who discovers sculptors aren't the only chisellers where fine art is concerned, Romero more than holds his own against such notorious scene-stealers as Milton Berle. J Carrol Naish is also in fine fettle as a forger dashing off old masters to order, but Carole Landis is slightly miscast as the gallery manager who Romero romances. DP

Cesar Romero *Tony Miller* • Carole Landis *Helen Mason* • Milton Berle *Lucky Cullen* • J Carrol Naish *Gigi* • Richard Derr *Stewart Haines* • Rose Hobart *Claire Barrington* • Jerome Cowan *Finchley* • Elisha Cook Jr *Genius* ■ *Dir* Ray McCarey • *Scr* Lee Loeb, Harold Buchman, from the story *Masterpiece* by Paul Hervey

Gentleman Jim ★★★ U

Biographical drama 1942 · US · BW · 100mins

Errol Flynn stars as James J Corbett, the bank clerk who went on to become the first official heavyweight champion of the world. While Flynn regarded this performance as one of his best, there is disagreement as to whether the film's portrayal of a brash extrovert is a true reflection of Corbett's personality. Despite claiming to be based on his autobiography, the movie is somewhat fictionalised, although the actual fights are re-created with some care and it's pacily directed by action maestro Raoul Walsh. AT

Errol Flynn *James J Corbett* • Alexis Smith *Victoria Ware* • Jack Carson *Walter Lowrie* • Alan Hale *Pat Corbett* • John Loder *Clinton DeWitt* • William Frawley *Billy Delaney* • Minor Watson *Buck Ware* • Ward Bond *John L Sullivan* ■ *Dir* Raoul Walsh • *Scr* Vincent Lawrence, Horace McCoy, from the autobiography *The Roar of the Crowd* by James J Corbett

Gentleman's Agreement ★★★★ U

Drama 1947 · US · BW · 112mins

An eye-opener in its day, this exposure of racial prejudice in high society still has the power to compel. The story of magazine writer Gregory Peck, in one of his finest performances, passing himself off as a Jew to reveal anti-Semitism is not violently confrontational, but it is successful in showing that the subtle malaise is not recognised as such by the people who sustain it. Writer Moss Hart pressed all the politically correct postwar buttons, adapting Laura Z Hobson's controversial bestseller for rising young director Elia Kazan. Twentieth Century-Fox gave this blast at bigotry all the hype it needed and the result was Academy awards and nominations all round. TH DVD

Gregory Peck *Phil Green* • Dorothy McGuire *Kathy* • John Garfield *Dave* • Celeste Holm *Anne* • Anne Revere *Mrs Green* • June Havoc *Miss Wales* • Albert Dekker *John Minify* • Jane Wyatt *Jane* ■ *Dir* Elia Kazan • *Scr* Moss Hart, from the novel by Laura Z Hobson

Gentlemen Marry Brunettes ★★

Musical comedy 1955 · US · Colour · 106mins

Jeanne Crain and Jane Russell, showing a lot of leg and cleavage, play dual roles as brunette showgirl sisters in Paris and their blonde mother and aunt, who were the toast of Paris in the 1920s. Despite the gorgeous costumes by Travilla and Christian Dior, the Technicolor and CinemaScope, the chic Parisian settings and some good songs, this is an uninspired feeble farrago. RB

Jane Russell *Bonnie Jones/Mimi Jones* • Jeanne Crain *Connie Jones/Mitzi Jones* • Alan Young *Charlie Biddle/Mrs Biddle/Mr Biddle Sr* • Scott Brady *David Action* • Rudy Vallee • Guy Middleton *Earl of Wickenware* • Eric Pohlmann *Monsieur Ballard* • Ferdy Mayne *Monsieur Dufond* ■ *Dir* Richard Sale • *Scr* Mary Loos, Richard Sale, from the story *But Gentlemen Marry Brunettes* by Anita Loos

Gentlemen Prefer Blondes ★★★★ U

Musical comedy 1953 · US · Colour · 87mins

Marilyn Monroe's star was well into the ascendant when she portrayed writer Anita Loos's gold-digging Lorelei Lee in this scintillating 20th Century-Fox musical, cannily directed by Howard Hawks who had a clever understanding of how to exploit Monroe's star power. Monroe particularly shines in the superbly photographed (Harry J Wild) and brilliantly choreographed (Jack Cole) production numbers. The movie opens with a scene that uses the sparkling Technicolor to best effect, as Monroe and Jane Russell announce that they're just *Two Little Girls from Little Rock*, and it simply takes off from there. The men are underused and the third act is a flat and contrived letdown, but make no mistake – this is the movie that consolidated Monroe's stardom. TS [video] DVD

Marilyn Monroe *Lorelei Lee* • Jane Russell *Dorothy Shaw* • Charles Coburn *Sir Francis Beekman* • Elliott Reid *Malone* • Tommy Noonan *Gus Esmond* • George Winslow *Henry Spofford III* • Taylor Holmes *Gus Esmond Sr* ■ *Dir* Howard Hawks • *Scr* Charles Lederer, from the play by Anita Loos, Joseph Fields, from the novel by Anita Loos

Genuine Risk ★★ 18

Crime thriller 1990 · US · Colour · 85mins

Peter Berg plays an ex-con, gambler and all-round slacker who reluctantly takes a job with gangster Terence Stamp's outfit. Unfortunately, Berg's current lover Michelle Johnson is also bestowing her sexual favours on the villainous Stamp. The plot details are predictable, and Johnson remains little more than a cipher. RT [video]

Terence Stamp *Paul Hellwart* • Peter Berg *Henry* • Michelle Johnson *Girl* • MK Harris [Michael Harris (2)] *Cowboy Jack* • Teddy Wilson *Billy* • Sid Haig *Curly* ■ *Dir* Kurt Voss • *Scr* Kurt Voss, from a story by Larry J Rattner

Geordie ★★★ U

Drama 1955 · UK · Colour · 95mins

Scripted by those bastions of postwar British cinema, Frank Launder and Sidney Gilliat, this is a pleasing picture, yet unlike its central character it never really develops into anything substantial. The story of a Scottish gamekeeper's son who body-builds his way to the Olympics was given relevance by the 1956 Melbourne games, but, shorn of its topicality, the film is too dependent on that old British standby, whimsy, to rank among the best British comedies. Bill Travers could do with a little more charm to add to his brawn, but Alastair Sim is on hand to pep up the humour. DP [video]

Alastair Sim *Laird* • Bill Travers *Geordie MacTaggart* • Norah Gorsen *Jean Donaldson* • Molly Urquhart *Geordie's mother* • Francis De Wolff *Henry Samson* • Jack Radcliffe *Rev McNab* ■ *Dir* Frank Launder • *Scr* Frank Launder, Sidney Gilliat, from the novel by David Walker

George and Mildred ★ 15

Comedy 1980 · UK · Colour · 89mins

Brian Murphy and Yootha Joyce were consistently funny on TV as the Ropers, first in *Man about the House* and then in their own series *George and Mildred*. But this desperate, smutty comedy of errors is no laughing matter. Made a year after the series ended, it was a sad finale for Yootha Joyce, who died before the film was released. DP [video] DVD

Yootha Joyce *Mildred Roper* • Brian Murphy *George Roper* • Stratford Johns *Harry Pinto* • Norman Eshley *Jeffrey Fourmile* • Sheila Fearn *Ann Fourmile* • Kenneth Cope *Harvey* • David Barry *Elvis* ■ *Dir* Peter Frazer Jones • *Scr* Dick Sharples, from the characters created by Brian Cooke, Johnnie Mortimer

George Balanchine's The Nutcracker ★★ U

Ballet 1993 · US · Colour · 92mins

Director Emile Ardolino's version of Tchaikovsky's popular children's ballet remains stubbornly stagebound. Shooting from the stalls, Ardolino fails to capture the energy of the dancers, while the clumsily incorporated close-ups interfere with the action. Macaulay Culkin trained at the School of American Ballet, but he doesn't do much here as the prince who guides Jessica Lynn Cohen through his toyland kingdom. Kevin Kline's narration was a late addition, intended to make the story more accessible. DP

Kevin Kline *Narrator* • Macaulay Culkin *Nutcracker Prince* • Bart Robinson Cook *Herr Drosselmeier* • Jessica Lynn Cohen *Marie* • Darci Kistler *Sugarplum Fairy* • Damian Woetzel *Cavalier* • Kyra Nichols *Dewdrop* • Wendy Whelan *Coffee* • Margaret Tracey *Marzipan* ■ *Dir* Emile Ardolino • *Scr* Susan Cooper, from the story by ETA Hoffman

George in Civvy Street ★

Comedy 1946 · UK · BW · 88mins

From 1937-43 George Formby was Britain's biggest box-office draw and most of his hits had been directed by Marcel Varnel. This sad final collaboration, in which George returns from the army to run a dilapidated pub, is dispiritingly uninspired and the songs are a poor echo of Formby's earlier hits. Formby made no more films after this, and Varnel was killed the following year in a car crash. TV

George Formby *George Harper* • Rosalyn Boulter *Mary Colton* • Ronald Shiner *Fingers* • Ian Fleming *Uncle Shad* • Wally Patch *Sprout* • Philippa Hiatt *Lavender* • Enid Cruickshank *Miss Gummidge* • Mike Johnson *Toby* ■ *Dir* Marcel Varnel • *Scr* Peter Fraser, Ted Kavanagh, Max Kester, Gale Pedrick, from the story by Howard Irving Young

George of the Jungle ★★★ U

Comedy adventure 1997 · US · Colour · 87mins

This engagingly stupid spin on *Tarzan* packs in enough dim-witted slapstick to raise a chuckle from even the most sophisticated grown-ups. Brendan Fraser is George, who has been brought up by a group of brainy gorillas led by Ape (voiced by John Cleese). Unfortunately none of their intelligence has rubbed off on George, who has an unfortunate habit of swinging into trees. The fun slows down a little when he gets whisked back to the States by heiress Leslie Mann. Fraser didn't return for the 2003 straight-to-video sequel. JF [video] DVD

Brendan Fraser *George* • Leslie Mann *Ursula Stanhope* • Thomas Haden Church *Lyle Van de Groot* • Richard Roundtree *Kwame* • Greg Cruttwell *Max* • Holland Taylor *Beatrice Stanhope* • Kelly Miller *Besty* • John Cleese *Ape* ■ *Dir* Sam Weisman • *Scr* Dana Olsen, Audrey Wells, from a story by Dana Olsen, from the characters created by Jay Ward

The George Raft Story ★★

Biographical drama 1961 · US · BW · 105mins

Ray Danton stars as the Broadway dancer who became a racketeer and then a Hollywood actor, making his name as the coin-spinning hood in *Scarface*. Raft could never really duck charges of illegal activities and his movie career faded in the 1950s, as did his business career. Since this biopic was made when Raft was alive and kicking, it is necessarily uncontroversial and, therefore, somewhat dull. AT

Ray Danton *George Raft* • Jayne Mansfield *Lisa Lang* • Julie London *Sheila Patton* • Barrie Chase *June* • Barbara Nichols *Texas Guinan* • Frank Gorshin *Moxie Cusack* • Margo Moore *Ruth Harris* • Brad Dexter *Benny Siegel* • Neville Brand *Al Capone* ■ *Dir* Joseph M Newman • *Scr* Crane Wilbur

George Washington ★★★★ 12

Drama 2000 · US · Colour · 86mins

Rarely has the eccentric seemed so everyday or the desolate felt so welcoming as in this remarkable tale of social deprivation and juvenile innocence. Basking in its widescreen lyricism, the story – about a small-town black boy who refuses to allow the fragility of his skull to interfere with his superheroic ambitions – unfolds at its own gentle pace. This allows debutant director David Gordon Green to concentrate on the performances of his non-professional cast, who deliver their part-improvised lines with a delightfully unforced sense of poetry. Eschewing politics in favour of an extraordinary dream-like style, this takes the rites-of-passage picture to a whole new level. DP [video] DVD

Candace Evanofski *Nasia* • Donald Holden *George Richardson* • Damian Jewan Lee *Vernon* • Curtis Cotton III *Buddy* • Rachael Handy *Sonya* ■ *Dir/Scr* David Gordon Green

George Washington Slept Here ★★ U

Comedy 1942 · US · BW · 91mins

Although this is one of Jack Benny's better comedies, he's still somewhat miscast as the Manhattanite whose wife purchases a surprise new home – a house in the country in which Washington reputedly stayed. Far from idyllic, their new home lacks everything from running water to walls, and Benny naturally hates it. Directed by William Keighley, this is too calculated and predictable to be more than superficially amusing but it was just what wartime audiences wanted. AE

Jack Benny *Bill Fuller* • Ann Sheridan *Connie Fuller* • Charles Coburn *Uncle Stanley* • Percy Kilbride *Mr Kimber* • Hattie McDaniel *Hester* • William Tracy *Steve Eldridge* • Joyce Reynolds *Madge* • Lee Patrick *Rena Leslie* ■ *Dir* William Keighley • *Scr* Everett Freeman, from the play by George S Kaufman, Moss Hart

George White's 1935 Scandals ★★★ U

Musical 1935 · US · BW · 84mins

Ziegfeld's biggest rival, Broadway impresario George White, directs himself in this sequel to the previous year's *George White's Scandals*. Not surprisingly, he plays a Broadway impresario discovering small-town talent Alice Faye and making her into a star. The stage acts are enjoyable enough – comedian Ned Sparks, singer Cliff Edwards and tap-dancing Eleanor Powell making her debut. The inevitable love triangle here involves Faye, Powell and James Dunn. TH

Alice Faye *Honey Walters* • James Dunn *Eddie Taylor* • Ned Sparks *Elmer White* • Lyda Roberti *Manya* • Cliff Edwards *Dude Holloway* • Arline Judge *Midgie Malone* • Eleanor Powell *Marilyn Collins* • Emma Dunn *Aunt Jane* ■ *Dir* George White • *Scr* Jack Yellin, Patterson McNutt, from an idea by George White

George White's Scandals ★★★

Musical 1934 · US · BW · 83mins

George White's annual music revues had become a Broadway fixture by the early 1930s, so it seemed a good idea to put on a film version, with the impresario taking on the roles of producer, co-director and even actor. The result is merely a hackneyed backstage musical, but it gave Alice Faye a starring role in her first picture and her alluring performance won her a contract with Fox. Rudy Vallee and Jimmy Durante are the other topliners. This was popular enough to be followed by two more screen *Scandals*, in 1935 and 1945. AE

Rudy Vallee *Jimmy Martin* • Jimmy Durante *Happy McGillicuddy* • Alice Faye *Kitty Donnelly* • Adrienne Ames *Barbara Loraine* • Gregory Ratoff *Nicholas Mitwoch* • Cliff Edwards *Stew Hart* • George White ■ *Dir* George White, Thornton Freeland, Harry Lachman • *Scr* Jack Yellen, from a story by George White

George White's Scandals ★★ U

Musical 1945 · US · BW · 94mins

After two screen versions of Broadway impresario George White's musical revues in the mid-1930s, this belated follow-up was directed by Felix E Feist, with White producing. It's a patchy affair that provides a fine showcase for the nutty comedy of Joan Davis, including her take-off of *grande dames* of the theatre. Among the many guest performers are Gene Krupa and his band. George White doesn't appear this time round, but he's impersonated by Glenn Tryon. AE

Joan Davis *Joan Mason* • Jack Haley *Jack Williams* • Phillip Terry *Tom McGrath* • Glenn Tryon *George White* • Martha Holliday *Jill Martin* • Margaret Hamilton *Clarabell* • Ethel Smith ■ *Dir* Felix E Feist [Felix Feist] • *Scr* Hugh Wedlock, Howard Snyder, Parke Levy, Howard J Green, from a story by Hugh Wedlock, Howard Snyder

George's Island ★★

Adventure 1991 · Can · Colour · 89mins

This Canadian family film about a modern-day search for buried treasure is a muddled mix of pirate quest and foster-home drama. Ian Bannen is a class above everyone else, as the eccentric ex-sailor whose tales of Captain Kidd unlock his grandson's imagination. But the humour is flat and often nasty, and the story – which has more than a hint of the dark fantasies of Roald Dahl – is as entertaining as a long walk off a short plank. JC

Ian Bannen *Captain Waters* • Sheila McCarthy *Cloata Birdwood* • Maury Chaykin *Mr Droonfield* • Nathaniel Moreau *George Waters* • Vicki Ridler *Bonnie* • Brian Downey *Mr Beane* • Irene Hogan *Mrs Beane* • Gary Reineke *Captain Kidd* ■ *Dir* Paul Donovan • *Scr* Paul Donovan, Maura O'Connell

Georgette Meunier ★★

Satire 1988 · W Ger · Colour · 82mins

One to file under "bizarre". Directors Tania Stöcklin and Cyrille Rey-Coquais were seemingly under the illusion that they were creating a profound feminist statement on celluloid. In fact, apart from the odd striking image, this is a *pfennig*-dreadful in which Georgette (Tiziana Jelmini) is transformed from an ordinary girl engaged in an incestuous relationship with her brother into a merciless murderess who kills with kisses. Utterly resistible. DP. In German with English subtitles.

Tiziana Jelmini *Georgette* • Thomas Schunke *Emile* • Dina Leipzig *Esmeralda* • Miklos Königer *Leopold Zsoldos* • Frank Kunkel *Insect specialist* • Kio Cornel *Singer* • Joe Rey-Coquais *Adonis* ■ *Dir* Tania Stöcklin, Cyrille Rey-Coquais • *Scr* Tania Stöcklin, Cyrille Rey-Coquais, Felix Schneider-Henninger

Georgia ★★★ 15

Mystery thriller 1988 · Aus · Colour · 89mins

Australian director Ben Lewin attempts to merge Michelangelo Antonioni's *Blow Up* with Akira Kurosawa's *Rashomon* in this overambitious thriller. The opening is neat and intriguing, as a series of photographs puts tax fraud investigator Judy Davis on the track of a murderer. But, as the different witnesses give their versions of events through fragmentary

G

flashbacks, it becomes clear that Lewin is cheating on us: his mystery isn't that mysterious. Davis's typically solid performance just about holds things together. DP. Contains some violence, swearing and nudity.

Judy Davis *Nina Bailey/Georgia White* • John Bach *William Karlin* • Julia Blake *Elizabeth* • Marshall Napier *Frank LeMat* • Alex Menglet *Laszlo* • Lewis Fiander *Scarlatti* • Roy Baldwin *Librarian* • Keryn Boyer *First policewoman* ■ *Dir* Ben Lewin • *Scr* Ben Lewin, Joanna Murray-Smith, Bob Weis

Georgia ★★★

Musical drama
1995 · US/Fr · Colour · 113mins

Jennifer Jason Leigh and Mare Winningham compete in acting their socks off in this interesting, performance-led film from director Ulu Grosbard. Winningham is a successful folk singer with a husband and children, while Leigh is her more destructive, erratic and unpredictable sister, who sings in clubs but remains undiscovered. Written by Leigh's mother, Barbara Turner, the film has some uncomfortable moments, but it's worth persevering with for the impressive lead performances. JB

Jennifer Jason Leigh *Sadie* • Mare Winningham *Georgia* • Ted Levine *Jake* • Max Perlich *Axel* • John Doe *Bobby* • John C Reilly *Herman* • Jimmy Witherspoon *Trucker* • Jason Carter *Chasman* ■ *Dir* Ulu Grosbard • *Scr* Barbara Turner

Georgia, Georgia ★★

Drama 1972 · US/Swe · Colour · 84mins

A tale of pride and prejudice, written for the screen by author Maya Angelou, about a controversial mixed-race relationship between a black singer and a white photographer. The subject matter now looks somewhat dated, but the passion of the writing and performances still shines through. DA

Diana Sands *Georgia Martin* • Dirk Benedict *Michael Winters* • Minnie Gentry *Alberta Anderson* • Roger Furman *Herbert Thompson* • Terry Whitmore *Bobo* • Diana Kjaer *Brigit* ■ *Dir* Stig Bjorkman • *Scr* Maya Angelou

Georgy Girl ★★★★ 15

Comedy drama 1966 · UK · BW · 94mins

At the time a sexual show-stopper, this can now be seen as an unconscious parody of Swinging Sixties chic. It is saved from mere shock novelty by Lynn Redgrave's performance as the dowdy girl pursued by older employer James Mason, who finds her own identity looking after the illegitimate baby of flatmate Charlotte Rampling. Former TV director Silvio Narizzano piles on the tricks of cinematic trendiness, but it's the acting that stabilises the story into something memorable from a boringly self-conscious era. TH

Lynn Redgrave *Georgy* • James Mason *James Leamington* • Alan Bates *Jos* • Charlotte Rampling *Meredith* • Bill Owen *Ted* • Clare Kelly *Doris* • Denise Coffey *Peg* • Rachel Kempson *Ellen* ■ *Dir* Silvio Narizzano • *Scr* Margaret Forster, Peter Nichols, from the novel by Margaret Forster

Geppetto ★★ U

Musical fantasy 2000 · US · Colour · 84mins

This Disney TV movie adopts a pantomimic tone, combining cornball sentiment, knockabout comedy and slipshod ditties in an attempt to entertain family audiences. However, Drew Carey's performance as the woodcarver whose marionette son comes to life is eminently resistible, while his picaresque pursuit of Brent Spiner's puppet show is too episodic to involve. DP DVD

Drew Carey *Geppetto* • Seth Adkins *Pinocchio* • Julia Louis-Dreyfus *Blue Fairy* • Brent Spiner *Stromboli* • René Auberjonois *Professor Buonragazzo* • Wayne Brady *Lazardo* ■ *Dir* Tom Moore • *Scr* David Stern, from the story by Carlo Collodi

The German Sisters ★★★

Political drama
1981 · W Ger · Colour · 106mins

Margarethe von Trotta based this provocative drama on the true-life experiences of Christiane and Gudrun Ensslin. While this is a highly politicised film, there is also a pronounced personal emphasis, with magazine editor Jutta Lampe being shaken from her bourgeois lethargy by the state's insistence that the Stammheim prison death of her hunger-striking terrorist sister (Barbara Sukowa) was suicide. Von Trotta examines what causes individuals from identical backgrounds to depart in such radically different directions. DP. A German language film.

Jutta Lampe *Juliane* • Barbara Sukowa *Marianne* • Rüdiger Vogler *Wolfgang* • Doris Schade *Mother* • Vérénice Rudolph *Sabine* • Luc Bondy *Werner* • Franz Rudnick *Father* • Julia Biedermann *Marianne aged 16* • Ina Robinski *Juliane aged 17* ■ *Dir/Scr* Margarethe von Trotta

Germany in Autumn ★★★

Portmanteau documentary drama
1978 · W Ger · Colour and BW · 123mins

With its title bitterly evoking the idealism of *Heimat*, this portmanteau piece is an instant reaction to the events that rocked West Germany in the autumn of 1977: the storming of the hijacked plane at Mogadishu; the mysterious deaths of the Baader-Meinhof trio at Stammheim jail; and the murder of kidnapped industrialist Hans Martin Schleyer. Supervised by the father of New German cinema, Alexander Kluge, it's a mix of fictional and documentary vignettes from nine leading film-makers, with Rainer Werner Fassbinder's chilling conversation with his pro-authoritarian mother and Volker Schlöndorff's media spoof being the highlights. DP. In German with English subtitles.

Hannelore Hoger • Katja Rupé • Hans Peter Cloos • Angela Winkler • Franziska Walser • Vadim Glowna • Helmut Griem • Dieter Laser ■ *Dir* Alf Brustellin, Bernhard Sinkel, Hans Peter Cloos, Katja Rupé, Rainer Werner Fassbinder, Alexander Kluge, Beate Mainka-Jellinghaus, Maximiliane Mainka, Peter Schubert, Edgar Reitz, Volker Schlöndorff • *Scr* Heinrich Böll, Peter Steinbach, Alf Brustellin, Bernhard Sinkel, Hans Peter Cloos, Katja Rupé, Rainer Werner Fassbinder, Alexander Kluge, Beate Mainka-Jellinghaus, Maximiliane Mainka, Peter Schubert, Edgar Reitz, Volker Schlöndorff

Germany, Year Zero ★★★★ PG

Drama 1947 · It/W Ger/Fr · BW · 69mins

The number of studio-shot scenes in the concluding part of director Roberto Rossellini's war trilogy, which also includes *Rome, Open City* and *Paisà*, shows that he was already moving away from the neorealist style. Yet the documentary footage of a decimated Berlin is still enormously powerful. The shadow of Nazism hovers over this depiction of desperation, as 12-year-old Edmund Moeschke scavanges among the ruins to feed his family. His murder of his ailing father is harrowing, but the tiny human details with which Rossellini invests the crime make it somehow forgivable. DP. In German with English subtitles.

Edmund Moeschke *Edmund* • Franz Kruger *Edmund's father* • Barbara Hintz *Eva* • Werner Pittschau *Karlheinz* ■ *Dir* Roberto Rossellini • *Scr* Roberto Rossellini, Carlo Lizzani, Max Kolpet, from a story by Roberto Rossellini

Germinal ★★★ 15

Period drama
1993 · Fr/Bel/It · Colour · 151mins

Emile Zola's grimly realistic novel did much to highlight the miseries of French miners in the 1860s. In his pursuit of authenticity for this screen version of the tale, director Claude Berri broke the budget record for a French film. There's no doubt that the mining village is a masterpiece of period design and Yves Angelo's photography is often breathtaking, but the scale and sheen of the production in many ways count against this dour study of exploitative capitalism and stoic (rather than heroic) labour. Gérard Depardieu turns in another towering performance, but it's Miou-Miou and Judith Henry, as his wife and daughter, who impress most. DP. In French with English subtitles. Contains violence, sex scenes and nudity.

Renaud *Etienne Lantier* • Gérard Depardieu *Maheu* • Miou-Miou *Maheude* • Jean Carmet *Bonnemort* • Judith Henry *Catherine Maheu* • Jean-Roger Milo *Chaval* • Laurent Terzieff *Souvarine* • Jean-Pierre Bisson *Rasseneur* ■ *Dir* Claude Berri • *Scr* Claude Berri, Arlette Langmann, from the novel by Emile Zola

Geronimo ★★ U

Western 1939 · US · BW · 87mins

This lavish-looking Paramount western, with a B-feature cast headed by Preston Foster, is a real cheat. Its writer/director, the obscure Paul H Sloane, took his storyline from *The Lives of a Bengal Lancer*, integrated spectacular highlights from big-budget pictures such as *The Plainsman* and *Wells Fargo*, and gave the title character little screen time. At least he's portrayed by a real native American, Chief Thundercloud. AE

Preston Foster *Captain Starrett* • Ellen Drew *Alice Hamilton* • Andy Devine *Sneezer* • William Henry *Lt Steele* • Ralph Morgan *Gen Steele* • Gene Lockhart *Gillespie* • Marjorie Gateson *Mrs Steele* • Chief Thundercloud *Geronimo* ■ *Dir/Scr* Paul H Sloane

Geronimo ★★★ PG

Western 1962 · US · Colour · 98mins

Today, Chuck Connors might not seem a politically correct choice to play the famous Apache leader, but back in the 1960s this was the kind of role that consolidated the star power of the former professional baseball player. Connors looks good and acquits himself well and the landscapes – shot by Mexican cinematographer Alex Phillips – are stunning. Unfortunately, the script strays from the facts of the shameful story and fails to improve upon history. The eclectic casting is interesting, however. TS

Chuck Connors *Geronimo* • Kamala Devi *Teela* • Ross Martin *Mangus* • Pat Conway *Maynard* • Adam West *Delahay* • Lawrence Dobkin *General Crook* • Denver Pyle *Senator Conrad* ■ *Dir* Arnold Laven • *Scr* Pat Fielder, from a story by Arnold Laven, Pat Fielder

Geronimo: an American Legend ★★★★ 12

Western 1993 · US · Colour · 110mins

Many critics questioned whether Walter Hill's version of the story of the Chiricahua Apache was actually about him at all. The narration presents us with the wider picture from which to draw our conclusions. The film also caused a fuss over its depiction of the native Americans. Screenwriter John Milius and Hill present the massacres perpetrated by both sides as part and parcel of the struggle for nationhood, to be seen in the context of the times. While many will find this uncomfortable to watch, there's no denying the quality of Joe Alves's painstakingly authentic design or the lovingly re-created period feel of Lloyd Ahern's cinematography. The acting is also first rate. DP. Contains violence and swearing. DVD

Jason Patric *Lieutenant Charles Gatewood* • Gene Hackman *Brigadier General George Crook* • Robert Duvall *Al Sieber* • Wes Studi *Geronimo* • Matt Damon *Lieutenant Britton Davis* • Rodney A Grant *Mangas* • Kevin Tighe *Brigadier General Nelson Miles* • Steve Reevis *Chato* ■ *Dir* Walter Hill • *Scr* John Milius, Larry Gross, from a story by John Milius

Gerry ★★★ 15

Drama 2001 · US · Colour · 98mins

Co-written by director Gus Van Sant and joint leads Matt Damon and Casey Affleck, this follows two friends – both called Gerry – who embark on a wilderness trail only to get lost without any provisions. Unwinding at a snail's pace, with a simplistic storyline and barely any dialogue, this audacious allegory is either pretentious twaddle or a poetic masterpiece, depending on personal taste. Their predicament becomes riveting, made additionally entrancing by dreamy cinematography, breathtaking landscapes and hallucinatory cloud formations. SF. Contains swearing. DVD

Casey Affleck *Gerry* • Matt Damon *Gerry* ■ *Dir* Gus Van Sant • *Scr* Casey Affleck, Matt Damon, Gus Van Sant • *Cinematographer* Harris Savides

Gert and Daisy's Weekend ★★ U

Second World War comedy
1941 · UK · BW · 79mins

Elsie and Doris Waters had been radio stars for some 15 years before they made this rare sortie in front of the movie camera. Starring as the cockney tittle-tattles Gert and Daisy, they escort some East End evacuees to a country house, where the kids end up as chief suspects in a jewel robbery. The sisters usually wrote their own material and took great pains to be original. Consequently, they look distinctly unhappy with the rehashed gags on offer here. DP

Elsie Waters *Gert* • Doris Waters *Daisy* • Iris Vandeleur *Ma Butler* • John Slater *Jack Densham* • Elizabeth Hunt *Maisie Butler* • Wally Patch *Charlie Peters* • Annie Esmond *Lady Plumtree* • Aubrey Mallalieu *Barnes* • Gerald Rex *George the Terror* ■ *Dir* Maclean Rogers • *Scr* Maclean Rogers, Kathleen Butler

Gertie the Dinosaur ★★★★★

Classic silent animation 1914 · US · BW

This landmark in animation was originally designed as one half of a vaudeville routine in which its creator, celebrated newspaper cartoonist Winsor McCay, appeared in person to issue instructions to a drawn dinosaur on a screen. When the act ran its course, McCay added a live-action prologue in which he accepts a bet that he can bring a dinosaur to life, then reveals the painstaking process by which he succeeded. Often cited as the first animated film due to its tremendous impact, this wasn't even McCay's first, being preceded by two others, yet such is the credibility of its "leading lady" it can be seen as the first important work of the genre. McCay's true brilliance lies in his concept of the possibilities of animation: he never tries to reproduce live-action, but instead uses the medium to show that which couldn't be filmed, such as dancing bugs, flying houses, centaurs and dinosaurs. CLP

Dir/Scr Winsor McCay

Gertrud ★★★★★ PG

Drama 1964 · Den · BW · 112mins

Carl Th Dreyer was a filmic genius who never shied away from controversial themes or unconventional techniques.

This film is a troubling study of a married woman (played with great passion by Nina Pens Rode) who is prepared to sacrifice all in the impossible pursuit of love. In spite of the intimacy and intensity of the action, Dreyer opted to shoot in long takes with little camera movement, in order to emphasise the power of the words and performances. Much maligned on its release, this mesmerising picture was subsequently hailed as one of the most remarkable achievements of a brilliant career. DP. In Danish with English subtitles.

Nina Pens Rode *Gertrud Kanning* • Bendt Rothe *Gustav Kanning* • Ebbe Rode *Gabriel Lidman* • Baard Owe *Erland Jansson* • Axel Strøbye *Axel Nygren* • Karl Gustav Ahlefeldt • Vera Gebuhr *Kanning's maid* ■ *Dir* Carl Th Dreyer • *Scr* Carl Th Dreyer, from a play by Hjalmar Soderberg

Gervaise ★★★

Drama 1956 · Fr · BW · 115mins

René Clément's film is a solid version of Zola's *L'Assommoir*, which dealt with the ravages of alcoholism among the working classes of 19th-century Paris. Maria Schell is an 18-year-old washerwoman who is abandoned by the father of her two children. She then marries a roofing contractor, who turns to drink after an accident leaves him incapacitated. When Schell's first lover Armand Mestral returns, further catastrophes and humiliations ensue. Schell gives a performance that won her a prize at the Venice Festival but was widely criticised as an exercise in technique, lacking in conviction. AT. In French with English subtitles.

Maria Schell *Gervaise* • François Périer *Henri Coupeau* • Suzy Delair *Virginie* • Mathilde Casadesus *Madame Boche* • Armand Mestral *Lantier* • Jacques Harden *Goujet* ■ *Dir* René Clément • *Scr* Jean Aurenche, Pierre Bost, from the novel *L'Assommoir* by Emile Zola

Get Back ★★★ PG

Music documentary
1991 · UK · Colour and BW · 85mins

Having compiled the moving scrapbook that was shown on giant screens before each concert, Richard Lester was the natural choice for this rockumentary account of Paul McCartney's 1990 world tour. Valiantly attempting to update the busy visual style he pioneered on *A Hard Day's Night*, he slightly overdoes the trickery and spends a tad too long behind the scenes. However, his coverage of the gigs is exemplary, with Macca and his superb band rattling through Beatles anthems and solo favourites with genuine pleasure. DP

Dir Richard Lester

Get Carter ★★★★ 18

Crime thriller 1971 · UK · Colour · 106mins

This terrific, tough British thriller hides its story of raw revenge behind some fascinating Newcastle upon Tyne locations, courtesy of cinematographer Wolfgang Suschitzky, and its impact remains undiminished. Michael Caine is at his most impassively impressive as the London gangster who goes north after his brother is murdered and finds his teenage niece involved in a blue-film racket. Playwright John Osborne, appearing here as a North East crime boss, has a razor-slash presence, while director Mike Hodges keeps a firm hand on the surly proceedings. This is sex and death with a British accent. TH DVD

Michael Caine *Jack Carter* • John Osborne *Cyril Kinnear* • Ian Hendry *Eric Paice* • Britt Ekland *Anna Fletcher* • Bryan Mosley *Cliff Brumby* • Geraldine Moffat *Glenda* • Dorothy White *Margaret* • Alun Armstrong *Keith* ■ *Dir* Mike Hodges • *Scr* Mike Hodges, from the novel *Jack's Return Home* by Ted Lewis

Get Carter ★★ 15

Crime thriller 2000 · US · Colour · 98mins

An ill-advised remake of the Newcastle classic, with a moody Sylvester Stallone taking over the vengeful Carter role and the action relocated to America. Yet, this has few similarities to the outstanding original, replacing gritty direction with flashy surface gloss, Michael Caine's unremitting viciousness with Stallone's soft-centred bruiser, and Roy Budd's haunting score with a noisy rock remix. Caine himself has an ineffectual cameo and is on the receiving end of Jack Carter's most celebrated line, delivered by Stallone as if he's reading a shopping list. JC DVD

Sylvester Stallone *Jack Carter* • Miranda Richardson *Gloria Carter* • Rachael Leigh Cook *Doreen Carter* • Mickey Rourke *Cyrus Paice* • Michael Caine *Cliff Brumby* • Alan Cumming *Jeremy Kinnear* • Rhona Mitra *Geraldine* • Gretchen Mol *Audrey* ■ *Dir* Stephen Kay • *Scr* David McKenna, from the novel *Jack's Return Home* by Ted Lewis

Get Cracking ★★ U

Second World War comedy
1943 · UK · BW · 97mins

In the late 1930s and early 1940s, George Formby had been virtually the only home-grown talent who could match the popularity of the major Hollywood stars at the British box office. But by 1942 his star was showing signs of waning. This is pleasant enough, but it's hardly vintage Formby, offering a somewhat substandard story of rival village Home Guard units trying to outdo each other on manoeuvres. DF

George Formby *George Singleton* • Edward Rigby *Sam Elliott* • Frank Pettingell *Alf Pemberton* • Ronald Shiner *Everett Manley* • Dinah Sheridan *Mary Pemberton* • Wally Patch *Sgt Joe Preston* • Mike Johnson *Josh* ■ *Dir* Marcel Varnel • *Scr* L du Garde Peach

Get Crazy ★★★ 18

Musical comedy spoof
1983 · US · Colour · 88mins

A long-time employee of the legendary music venue Fillmore East in New York, director Allan Arkush was the right man for this rock-flavoured satire. A spoof comedy, in which a New Year's Eve concert is threatened by a trio of villains (Ed Begley Jr, Bobby Sherman and Fabian), it has actors playing musicians and vice versa. Malcolm McDowell plays a Mick Jagger-like character, while Lou Reed appears as a Dylan clone. The result is cartoonish fun. FL

Malcolm McDowell *Reggie Wanker* • [Allen Garfield] *Max Wolfe* • Daniel Stern *Neil* • Gail Edwards *Willy Loman* • Miles Chapin *Sammy Fox* • Ed Begley Jr *Colin Beverly* • Lou Reed *Auden* • Bobby Sherman *Mark* • Fabian Forte [Fabian] *Marv* • Mary Woronov *Violetta* • Dick Miller *Susie's dad* ■ *Dir* Allan Arkush • *Scr* Danny Opatoshu, Henry Rosenbaum, David Taylor

Get off My Back ★★

Drama 1965 · US · BW · 106mins

Richard Quine directs this curio about a drug rehab centre called Synanon, founded by Charles Dederich in California in the late 1950s. Using real Synanon residents as well as actors, its message is driven by subplots and incidents that could come from any Hollywood melodrama. Dederich, played by Edmond O'Brien, was the film's chief adviser. Slinky Eartha Kitt puts in an interesting performance as a former heroin addict. AT

Chuck Connors *Ben* • Stella Stevens *Joaney* • Alex Cord *Zankie Albo* • Richard Conte *Reid* • Eartha Kitt *Betty Coleman* • Edmond O'Brien *Chuck Dederich* • Barbara Luna *Mary* • Alejandro Rey *Chris* ■ *Dir* Richard Quine • *Scr* Ian Bernard, S Lee Pogostin, from a story by Barry Oringer, S Lee Pogostin

Get on the Bus ★★★ 15

Road movie 1996 · US · Colour · 116mins

On 16 October 1995, African-American men from all over the United States converged on Washington DC to unite in a historic moment of goodwill, known as the "Million Man March". This event serves as the inspiration for another controversial look at racial politics from Spike Lee. The focus is on 12 angry men from different backgrounds (cop, prisoner, student, gay couple, Denzel Washington wannabe) who travel from Los Angeles to the rally, embarking on personal voyages of discovery. Less confrontational than Spike Lee's usual output, the message is still hammered home. AJ

Richard Belzer *Rick* • De'Aundre Bonds *Junior* • André Braugher *Flip* • Thomas Jefferson Byrd *Evan Thomas Sr* • Gabriel Casseus *Jamal* • Albert Hall *Craig* • Hill Harper *Xavier* • Harry Lennix *Randall* • Bernie Mac *Jay* ■ *Dir* Spike Lee • *Scr* Reggie Rock Bythewood

Get out Your Handkerchiefs ★★★

Comedy 1977 · Fr/Bel · Colour · 108mins

The winner of the Oscar for best foreign film, this outrageous comedy stars Gérard Depardieu and Patrick Dewaere in a savage satire on the conventionality of middle-class life and the cosiness of commercial cinema. Depardieu reins in his natural ebullience as the husband who devotes himself to finding lovers for his discontented wife, Carol Laure, thus allowing 13-year-old Riton to steal the picture as the missing piece in their bizarre *ménage à trois*. Occasionally wildly wide of the mark, this provocative picture has something to offend everyone. DP. In French with English subtitles.

Gérard Depardieu *Raoul* • Patrick Dewaere *Stephane* • Carole Laure *Solange* • Riton *Christian Beloeil* • Michel Serrault *Neighbor* • Eléonore Hirt *Mrs Beloeil* • Jean Rougerie *Mr Beloeil* • Sylvie Joly *Passerby* ■ *Dir/Scr* Bertrand Blier

Get over It ★★★ 12

Romantic comedy
2001 · US · Colour · 82mins

Ben Foster plays a teenager who's dumped by his longtime girlfriend. He signs up to join her in the school's musical version of *A Midsummer Night's Dream* just so he can win her back. He's aided and abetted by his best friend's younger sister. As she's played by the drop-dead gorgeous Kirsten Dunst, there are no prizes for guessing that maybe young Foster is making moon-eyes in the wrong direction. Smartly written and sassily acted. DA DVD

Kirsten Dunst *Kelly* • Ben Foster *Berke Landers* • Melissa Sagemiller *Allison McAllister* • Sisqo *Dennis* • Shane West *Striker* • Colin Hanks *Felix* • Swoosie Kurtz *Beverly Landers* • Ed Begley Jr *Frank Landers* • Martin Short *Dr Desmond Forrest-Oates* ■ *Dir* Tommy O'Haver • *Scr* R Lee Fleming Jr

Get Real ★★ 15

Drama 1998 · UK/S Afr · Colour · 106mins

What's a 16-year-old school boy to do when he lives in Basingstoke, knows he's "dodgy" (in other words, gay) and fancies the head boy? Those are the problems facing Ben Silverstone. Director Simon Shore merely joins up the gay soap-opera dots and, despite encouraging an engaging central performance from Silverstone, does little more than indulge in a certain clichéd angst. AJ. Contains swearing and sex scenes.

Ben Silverstone *Steven Carter* • Brad Gorton *John Dixon* • Charlotte Brittain *Linda* • Stacy A Hart *Jessica* • Kate McEnery *Wendy* • Patrick Nielsen *Mark* • Tim Harris *Kevin* • James D White *Dave* ■ *Dir* Simon Shore • *Scr* Patrick Wilde, from his play *What's Wrong with Angry?*

Get Shorty ★★★★ 15

Crime comedy 1995 · US · Colour · 100mins

This adaptation of Elmore Leonard's novel explores the murky world of Hollywood's links to organised crime. John Travolta plays a Florida gangster who arrives in Tinseltown to collect a bad debt from Gene Hackman and decides to stay, importing his strong-arm methods into movie production. Made in the wake of *Pulp Fiction*, *Get Shorty* was the first attempt by a major studio to cash in on Quentin Tarantino's style. The performances by the impressive cast are exquisite: the jowly Travolta has tremendous charm but also considerable menace; Danny DeVito plays a movie star to perfection; and Hackman is a sheer delight as the purveyor of schlocky monster movies. A snazzy treat. AT. Contains violence, swearing. DVD

John Travolta *Chili Palmer* • Gene Hackman *Harry Zimm* • Rene Russo *Karen Flores* • Danny DeVito *Martin Weir* • Dennis Farina *Ray "Bones" Barboni* • Delroy Lindo *Bo Catlett* • James Gandolfini *Bear* • Jon Gries [Jonathan Gries] *Ronnie Wingate* • Rene Props *Nicki* ■ *Dir* Barry Sonnenfeld • *Scr* Scott Frank, from the novel by Elmore Leonard

Get to Know Your Rabbit ★★

Satirical comedy 1972 · US · Colour · 91mins

Bored with corporate politics, Tom Smothers abandons his conformist job to become an itinerant tap-dancing magician, with a little help from Orson Welles. He soon finds that his change of lifestyle hasn't freed him from the exploitative, money-obsessed world he is trying to escape. Director Brian De Palma's first big-budget feature is an overlong, uninspired parable for the time, with stagey performances. This was edited against De Palma's wishes and only a few flashes of his visual talent remain. AJ

Tom Smothers *Donald Beeman* • John Astin *Mr Turnbull* • Suzanne Zenor *Paula* • Samantha Jones *Susan* • Allen Goorwitz [Allen Garfield] *Vic* • Katharine Ross *Girl* • Orson Welles *Mr Delasandro* ■ *Dir* Brian De Palma • *Scr* Jordan Crittenden

Get Well Soon ★★ 15

Romantic black comedy
2001 · US · Colour · 90mins

A very offbeat satire about the cult of media personality, featuring Vincent Gallo as a revered talk show host suffering a nervous breakdown and Courteney Cox as his ex-wife, who still harbours feelings for him. The stars work well together and the script overflows with quirky, bittersweet twists and turns. It overdoses on its weirdness motif, however, weakened by a mental home subplot that verges on fantasy. This confused black comedy plays like a rough cut in need of pruning. JC DVD

Vincent Gallo *Bobby Bishop* • Courteney Cox *Lily* • Jeffrey Tambor • Tate Donovan • Anne Meara *Lily's mother* ■ *Dir/Scr* Justin McCarthy

Get Yourself a College Girl ★★

Musical comedy 1964 · US · Colour · 86mins

Student Mary Ann Mobley gets into trouble when she's exposed as the songwriter of some disreputable – but supposedly groovy – tunes. Fortunately, an ambitious senator (Willard

Waterman) is around to help out – in exchange for some youth "cred" with the voters. This would-be fun teen picture is saved by the appearance of a strange melange of musicians, including early Britpoppers the Dave Clark Five and the Animals. JG

Mary Ann Mobley *Terry* • Joan O'Brien *Marge* • Chris Noel *Sue* • Nancy Sinatra *Lynne* • Chad Everett *Gary* • Fabrizio Mioni *Armand* • Willard Waterman *Senator Hubert Morrison* ■ *Dir* Sidney Miller • *Scr* Robert E Kent

The Getaway ★★★★ 18

Crime thriller 1972 · US · Colour · 117mins

In this gripping, landmark thriller, ex-convict Steve McQueen and his wife Ali MacGraw head off to Mexico after a bank robbery backfires, pursued by psychotic partner-in-crime Al Lettieri and the heavily armed henchmen of crime boss Ben Johnson. Directed by the master of screen violence, Sam Peckinpah, it's a modern western, a tough, disconcerting fable exploring the human soul, set in the barren landscapes of the Texan desert. The charismatic McQueen has to face the unpalatable truth about how MacGraw secured his release from jail, as their relationship – literally – comes under fire in a hail of bullets. In real life, though, the stars fell in love and subsequently married. AT. Contains violence, swearing. DVD

Steve McQueen *"Doc" McCoy* • Ali MacGraw *Carol McCoy* • Ben Johnson *Jack Benyon* • Sally Struthers *Fran Clinton* • Al Lettieri *Rudy Butler* • Slim Pickens *Cowboy* • Richard Bright *Thief* • Jack Dodson *Harold Clinton* ■ *Dir* Sam Peckinpah • *Scr* Walter Hill, from the novel by Jim Thompson

The Getaway ★★★ 18

Crime thriller 1994 · US · Colour · 110mins

This remake of Sam Peckinpah's 1972 thriller re-uses much of Walter Hill's original script and stars Alec Baldwin and Kim Basinger in roles played originally by Steve McQueen and Ali MacGraw. Baldwin isn't in the same league as McQueen, but Roger Donaldson's picture has flair, and the female leads stand up to comparison. The story has a fair amount of tension, and the southwestern locations have an arid, end-of-the-line symbolism. AT. Contains swearing, violence, sex scenes and nudity.

Alec Baldwin *Carter "Doc" McCoy* • Kim Basinger *Carol McCoy* • Michael Madsen *Rudy Travis* • James Woods *Jack Benyon* • David Morse *Jim Deer Jackson* • Jennifer Tilly *Fran Carvey* • James Stephens *Harold Carvey* • Richard Farnsworth *Slim* ■ *Dir* Roger Donaldson • *Scr* Walter Hill, Amy Jones [Amy Jones Holden], from the novel by Jim Thompson

Getting Away with Murder ★ 15

Black comedy
1996 · US/Can · Colour · 87mins

It's a special sort of director who takes a talented comic cast – including Dan Aykroyd, Jack Lemmon and Lily Tomlin – and still manages to turn in a completely unfunny comedy. The problem here is that the material is weird rather than wacky, as professor Aykroyd discovers that his neighbour (Lemmon) is a Nazi war criminal and decides to murder him. Nasty and tasteless. JB

Dan Aykroyd *Jack Lambert* • Lily Tomlin *Inga Mueller* • Jack Lemmon *Max Mueller/Karl Luger* • Bonnie Hunt *Gail Holland* • Brian Kerwin *Marty Lambert* • Jerry Adler *Judge* • Andy Romano *Psychiatrist* ■ *Dir/Scr* Harvey Miller

Getting Even ★★ 18

Action thriller 1986 · US · Colour · 86mins

This uninspired hostage drama has a plot that ultimately stretches audience credibility too far. Joe Don Baker is an insane industrialist threatening to unleash a deadly flesh-eating gas upon the population of Dallas unless he's paid $50 million. Edward Albert is the rival businessman hot on his heels. Director Dwight H Little allows the pace to lag. RS

Edward Albert *Taggar* • Audrey Landers *Paige Starsen* • Joe Don Baker *King Kenderson* • Rod Pilloud *Doc* • Billy Streater *Ryder* • Blue Deckert *Kurt* • Caroline Williams *Molly* ■ *Dir* Dwight H Little • *Scr* M Phil Senini, Eddie Desmond, J Michael Liddle

Getting Even with Dad ★★ PG

Comedy 1994 · US · Colour · 104mins

Home Alone's Macaulay Culkin again proves more than a match for a whole bunch of adults with criminal tendencies in this inoffensive if grindingly obvious comedy. This time the victim of his machinations is his dad, crooked Ted Danson, who Culkin is trying to steer on to the straight and narrow. However, most of the humiliation is saved for Danson's inept sidekicks, Saul Rubinek and Gailard Sartain. Howard Deutch is a proficient enough second-division director, but he lets sentimentality to run riot. JF. Contains swearing. DVD

Macaulay Culkin *Timmy* • Ted Danson *Ray* • Glenne Headly *Theresa* • Saul Rubinek *Bobby* • Gailard Sartain *Carl* • Sam McMurray *Alex* • Hector Elizondo *Lt Romayko* • Sydney Walker *Mr Wankmueller* ■ *Dir* Howard Deutch • *Scr* Tom S Parker, Jim Jennewein

Getting Gertie's Garter ★★

Comedy 1945 · US · BW · 73mins

In this version of a bedroom-and-hayloft farce Dennis O'Keefe plays a newly-married scientist desperately trying to retrieve an engraved diamond-studded garter he gave his old flame Gertie, played by Marie "The Body" McDonald. His wife, played by Sheila Ryan, and Gertie's fiancé, Barry Sullivan, naturally misunderstand. AE

Dennis O'Keefe *Ken* • Marie McDonald *Gertie* • Barry Sullivan *Ted* • Binnie Barnes *Barbara* • Sheila Ryan *Patty* • J Carrol Naish *Charles, the butler* • Jerome Cowan *Billy* • Vera Marshe *Anna, the maid* ■ *Dir* Allan Dwan • *Scr* Allan Dwan, Karen De Wolf, from the play by Wilson Collison, Avery Hopwood

Getting Gotti ★★ 15

Crime drama based on a true story
1994 · US · Colour · 89mins

It was inevitable that Mafia boss John Gotti, a gangster obsessed with celebrity, would end up being the subject of a film. Anthony John Denison plays the infamous "Teflon Don", but events are seen from the perspective of the obsessed district attorney (Lorraine Bracco) who fought for years to nail the media-friendly mobster. Reasonably well played, although the treatment is a little too low-key. JF

Lorraine Bracco *Diane Giacalone* • Anthony John Denison *John Gotti* • Ellen Burstyn *Jo Giacalone* • Kathleen Laskey *Cassie* • August Schellenberg *Willie Boy Johnson* • Kenneth Welsh *Bennett* • Jeremy Ratchford *Harvey Sanders* • Ron Gabriel *Gravano* ■ *Dir* Roger Young • *Scr* James S Henerson

Getting In ★★★

Black comedy thriller
1994 · US · Colour · 94mins

Stephen Mailer is bound by family tradition to go to Johns Hopkins College to study medicine. A lacklustre exam performance sees him resorting to blackmail to eliminate the five people ahead of him on the reserve list. Unfortunately they're dropping down dead instead and, before he knows it, Gabriel's a murder suspect. Matthew Perry and Calista Flockhart are among the strong supporting cast in Doug Liman's directorial debut. Great gags make this enjoyable. LH

Stephen Mailer *Gabriel Higgs* • Kristy Swanson *Kirby Watts* • Andrew McCarthy *Rupert Grimm* • Dave Chappelle *Rom* • Matthew Perry *Randall Burns* • Calista Flockhart *Amanda Morel* ■ *Dir* Doug Liman • *Scr* PJ Posner, Joel Posner, Jonathan Lewin

Getting It Right ★★ 15

Romantic comedy
1989 · US · Colour · 97mins

A decade before her mould-breaking role in *Fight Club*, Helena Bonham Carter unsuccessfully tried to shake her period drama image in this uneven comedy. Jesse Birdsall is an inexperienced young man who finds himself pursued by three women, including Bonham Carter and Jane Horrocks. Based on Elizabeth Jane Howard's novel, this probably worked better on the page than it does on screen, but a classy cast makes it worth a look. JB

Jesse Birdsall *Gavin Lamb* • Helena Bonham Carter *Lady Minerva Munday* • Peter Cook *Mr Adrian* • John Gielgud *Sir Gordon Munday* • Jane Horrocks *Jenny* • Lynn Redgrave *Joan* • Shirley Anne Field *Anne* • Pauline Quirke *Muriel Sutton* ■ *Dir* Randal Kleiser • *Scr* Elizabeth Jane Howard, from her novel

The Getting of Wisdom ★★★ PG

Period drama 1977 · Aus · Colour · 97mins

Film-makers during the Australian New Wave of the 1970s had a flair for giving costume movies a resounding contemporary relevance. Here Bruce Beresford provides a few choice insights into the miseries of school life and the pain of lonely adolescence. He re-creates the atmosphere of a repressive turn-of-the-century boarding school with some care, but misses the sense of danger found in the original autobiographical novel by Henry Handel Richardson that caused a scandal on its publication. DP

Susannah Fowle *Laura Tweedle Rambotham* • Barry Humphries *Reverend Strachey* • John Waters (3) *Reverend Robert Shepherd* • Sheila Helpmann *Mrs Gurley* • Patricia Kennedy *Miss Chapman* • Kerry Armstrong *Kate Horner* • Celia De Burgh *MP* • Kim Deacon *Lilith Gordon* ■ *Dir* Bruce Beresford • *Scr* Eleanor Witcombe, from the novel by Henry Handel Richardson [Ethel Florence Richardson]

Getting Straight ★★★ 15

Comedy drama 1970 · US · Colour · 119mins

Made on the back of *Easy Rider* and the anti-Vietnam War campaign, this was one of several "campus movies" that enabled studio executives to look cool and save money on ties. Elliott Gould plays a Vietnam veteran who, resuming his university education, becomes embroiled in campus politics and involved with fashion victim Candice Bergen. Harrison Ford makes an early appearance in a film that is very much of its time. AT

Elliott Gould *Harry Bailey* • Candice Bergen *Jan* • Robert F Lyons *Nick* • Jeff Corey *Dr Willhunt* • Max Julien *Ellis* • Cecil Kellaway *Dr Kasper* • Jon Lormer *Vandenburg* • Leonard Stone *Lysander* • Harrison Ford *Jake* ■ *Dir* Richard Rush • *Scr* Robert Kaufman, from the novel by Ken Kolb

Gettysburg ★★★ PG

Historical war drama
1993 · US · Colour · 259mins

Ted Turner's company produced this ambitious account of the bloody battle of July 1863, which cost some 7,000 lives and secured final victory for the Union. With a running time considerably longer than *Gone with the Wind* – Turner's favourite movie – *Gettysburg* has time to consider both points of view, but it has only been going for 45 minutes before the cannons start firing. Spectacular in parts and dull in others, it makes the strategy of the battle clear but takes some liberties with the actual events. Turner makes an uncredited cameo appearance as a Confederate who gets shot when answering the call to advance. AT DVD

Tom Berenger *Lt Gen James Longstreet (Confederate)* • Martin Sheen *General Robert E Lee (Confederate)* • Stephen Lang *Maj Gen George E Pickett (Confederate)* • Richard Jordan *Brig Gen Lewis A Armistead (Confederate)* • George Lazenby *Brig Gen J Johnston Pettigrew (Confederate)* • Jeff Daniels *Colonel Joshua Lawrence Chamberlain (Federal)* • Sam Elliott *Brigadier General John Buford (Federal)* • C Thomas Howell *Lieutenant Thomas D Chamberlain (Federal)* • Maxwell Caulfield *Colonel Strong Vincent (Federal)* ■ *Dir* Ronald F Maxwell • *Scr* Ronald F Maxwell, from the novel *The Killer Angels* by Michael Shaara

Ghidrah, the Three-Headed Monster ★★★

Science-fiction horror
1965 · Jpn · Colour · 73mins

Ghidrah (or Ghidorah as Japanese movie-goers correctly know him) is a three-headed, fire-breathing dragon which lands on Earth and causes the usual global destruction. Godzilla (in his first adventure as a good monster) defends the planet, with help from Mothra and Rodan (Toho Studio's other big earners), defeating Ghidrah in a spectacular battle on Mount Fuji. With higher production values and better visual effects than normal, this engaging behemoth bash established the use of various monsters in combat combinations, which would increase in goofiness over the years. AJ. Japanese dialogue dubbed into English.

Yosuke Natsuki *Shindo* • Yuriko Hoshi *Naoko* • Hiroshi Koizumi *Professor Murai* • Takashi Shimura *Dr Tsukamoto* ■ *Dir* Ishiro Honda [Inoshiro Honda] • *Scr* Shinichi Sekizawa

Ghost ★★★★ 15

Romantic drama
1990 · US · Colour · 121mins

This romantic and glossy mix of the sentimental and the supernatural reaps higher rewards than Patrick Swayze's acting ability deserves. He's the murdered banker trying to warn girlfriend Demi Moore she's in mortal danger via psychic Whoopi Goldberg, who provides the comic moments so necessary to lighten the potentially maudlin atmosphere. In fact, she did it so well, she won a best supporting actress Oscar. The special effects are a real treat, the love-beyond-the-grave theme is touching and Swayze's ascent into heaven is a wonderful piece of schmaltz. TH. Contains swearing and violence. DVD

Patrick Swayze *Sam Wheat* • Demi Moore *Molly Jensen* • Whoopi Goldberg *Oda Mae Brown* • Tony Goldwyn *Carl Bruner* • Rick Aviles *Willie Lopez* • Gail Boggs *Louise* ■ *Dir* Jerry Zucker • *Scr* Bruce Joel Rubin

The Ghost ★★ 18

Action thriller 2000 · US · Colour · 82mins

Chung Lai throws herself into the role of a dispassionate Tong assassin forced to seek sanctuary in the States in Douglas Jackson's impoverished action thriller. Certainly, she has the looks and some good moves, but she is no Cheng Pei Pei or Michelle Yeoh, and is further hobbled by the plodding storyline. The lack of budget is palpable, and Michael Madsen's very average performance as a bounty hunter further testifies to his post-*Reservoir Dogs* decline. DP [video] DVD

Michael Madsen *Dan Olinghouse* • Cary-Hiroyuki Tagawa *Chang* • Chung Lai *Jing* • Brad Dourif *Lieutenant Garland* • Richard Hatch *Edward* ■ *Dir* Douglas Jackson • *Scr* Dave Tedder

The Ghost and Mr Chicken

★★ U

Comedy mystery 1966 · US · Colour · 89mins

Don Knotts made one of his more successful ventures on to the silver screen with this comedy chiller. He plays a typesetter for a local newspaper who yearns to be a proper journalist. He finally gets his big break with a piece about a supposedly haunted house, where two mysterious deaths took place 20 years earlier. The bad news for Luther is that he has to spend a night in the house. DF

Don Knotts *Luther Heggs* • Joan Staley *Alma* • Liam Redmond *Kelsey* • Dick Sargent *Beckett* • Skip Homeier *Ollie* • Reta Shaw *Mrs Maxwell* • Lurene Tuttle *Mrs Miller* • Philip Ober *Simmons* ■ *Dir* Alan Rafkin • *Scr* James Fritzell, Everett Greenbaum

The Ghost and Mrs Muir

★★★★ U

Romantic fantasy 1947 · US · BW · 99mins

This wonderfully romantic ghost story has ethereally beautiful Gene Tierney beguiled by bewhiskered sea captain Rex Harrison, himself long dead. A marvellously lyrical Bernard Herrmann score helps underline the poignancy of this enchanting tale, and Philip Dunne's literate screenplay avoids all the pitfalls normally associated with such delicate material. Today, the settings and pace may look studio-bound, but they suit the theatricality of the subject, and this superb original is far better than its spin-off TV series. TS [video] DVD

Gene Tierney *Lucy Muir* • Rex Harrison *Captain Daniel Gregg* • George Sanders *Miles Fairley* • Edna Best *Martha* • Vanessa Brown *Anna* • Anna Lee *Mrs Fairley* • Robert Coote *Coombe* • Natalie Wood *Young Anna* ■ *Dir* Joseph L Mankiewicz • *Scr* Philip Dunne, from the novel by RA Dick

The Ghost and the Darkness

★ 15

Period action adventure
1996 · US · Colour · 109mins

Screenwriter William Goldman wanted to tell the tale of the man-eating Tsavo lions terrorising the building of a railway in East Africa in the late 19th century, but producer Michael Douglas pulled rank and decided he would also star as the enigmatic big game hunter who assists Val Kilmer's engineer. Douglas and Kilmer did not hit it off on a stressful location shoot, and this fails to convince on any level. AC. Contains violence,swearing. [video] DVD

Michael Douglas *Remington* • Val Kilmer *John Patterson* • Bernard Hill *Dr Hawthorne* • John Kani *Samuel* • Tom Wilkinson *Beaumont* • Om Puri *Abdullah* • Emily Mortimer *Helena Patterson* ■ *Dir* Stephen Hopkins • *Scr* William Goldman, from the book *The Man-Eaters of Tsavo* by John Patterson

The Ghost Breakers ★★★★

Horror comedy mystery
1940 · US · BW · 83mins

Made to capitalise on the success the previous year of Bob Hope's comedy *The Cat and the Canary*, this lightning paced follow-up is even better than its money-spinning predecessor. Once again Hope and Paulette Goddard find themselves shacked up in a supposedly haunted house – this time it's her inherited mansion in an exotic Cuban locale. The same pleasing recipe of thrills, laughs and romance keep the potboiler simmering nicely with the added bonus of some truly spooky moments amid the fun. DF

Bob Hope *Larry Lawrence* • Paulette Goddard *Mary Carter* • Richard Carlson *Geoff Montgomery* • Paul Lukas *Parada* • Willie Best *Alex* • Pedro De Cordoba *Havez* • Virginia Brissac *Mother zombie* • Noble Johnson *Zombie* • Anthony Quinn *Ramon Mederos/ Francisco Mederos* • Lloyd Corrigan *Martin* ■ *Dir* George Marshall • *Scr* Walter DeLeon, from the play by Paul Dickey, Charles W Goddard

The Ghost Camera ★★ U

Crime mystery 1933 · UK · BW · 64mins

The much-maligned "quota quickie" proved an invaluable training ground for some of Britain's most talented individuals. Director Bernard Vorhaus clearly doesn't fit into that category, but his stars Ida Lupino, then a mere 19 years old, and a scarcely more experienced John Mills certainly do. Unfortunately, much of the action is dominated by Henry Kendall as the chemist-turned-sleuth seeking to use photographic evidence to prove Mills innocent of murder. DP [video]

Henry Kendall *John Grey* • Ida Lupino *Mary Elton* • John Mills *Ernest Elton* • S Victor Stanley *Albert Sims* • George Merritt *Inspector* • Felix Aylmer *Coroner* • Davina Craig *Amelia Wilkinson* • Fred Groves *Barnaby Rudd* ■ *Dir* Bernard Vorhaus • *Scr* H Fowler Mear, from a story by J Jefferson Farjeon

Ghost Catchers ★★★

Musical comedy 1944 · US · BW · 68mins

While it never quite recaptures the manic mayhem of the hilarious *Hellzapoppin'*, this is another riot of mirth and melody from stars Ole Olsen and Chic Johnson. The plot is as transparent as a spectre and the action pauses rather too readily for a song. But Chic and Ole are on rattlingly good form as they help the family in the mansion adjoining their nightclub solve their spook problem. DP

Ole Olsen *Ole* • Chic Johnson *Chic* • Gloria Jean *Melinda* • Martha O'Driscoll *Susanna* • Leo Carrillo *Jerry* • Andy Devine *Bear* • Lon Chaney Jr *Horsehead* • Kirby Grant *Clay* ■ *Dir* Edward F Cline [Edward Cline] • *Scr* Edmund L Hartmann, from the story *High Spirits* by Milt Gross, Edward F Cline [Edward Cline]

The Ghost Comes Home

★★ U

Comedy drama 1940 · US · BW · 78mins

Billie Burke and Frank Morgan star in this adaptation of a negligible stage play. Morgan is declared dead through a bureaucratic bungle and has to hide away in his own attic, because his family are happily living off his life insurance. The sequence in which Morgan has to don drag to foil snoopers is probably the highlight, while the nadir is daughter Ann Rutherford's romance with sappy John Shelton. DP

Frank Morgan *Vern Adams* • Billie Burke *Cora Adams* • Ann Rutherford *Billie Adams* • John Shelton *Lanny Shea* • Reginald Owen *Hemingway* • Donald Meek *Mortimer Hopkins Sr* ■ *Dir* William Thiele • *Scr* Richard Maibaum, Harry Ruskin, from the play *Der Mutige Seefahrer (The Courageous Seaman)* by George Kaiser [Georg Kaiser]

Ghost Dad ★ PG

Fantasy comedy 1990 · US · Colour · 80mins

Bill Cosby has had a disastrous time trying to transfer his TV popularity to the big screen. After the ill-conceived spy spoof *Leonard, Part 6* came this equally daft supernatural comedy directed by Sidney Poitier. Cosby plays a harassed businessman who is killed in a car accident and discovers he's been missing out on the joys of family life. Cosby mugs away for all he's worth, but good gags are few and far between. JF. Contains swearing. [video]

Bill Cosby *Elliot Hopper* • Kimberly Russell *Diane Hopper* • Denise Nicholas *Joan* • Ian Bannen *Sir Edith Moser* • Christine Ebersole *Carol* • Barry Corbin *Mr Collins* • Salim Grant *Danny Hopper* • Brooke Fontaine *Amanda Hopper* ■ *Dir* Sidney Poitier • *Scr* Chris Reese, Brent Maddock, SS Wilson, from a story by SS Wilson, Brent Maddock

Ghost Dog: the Way of the Samurai ★★★ 15

Crime drama 1999 · US/Fr · Colour · 110mins

Inspired by Jean-Pierre Melville's *Le Samouraï*, Jim Jarmusch's quirky crime drama creates a world of such deadpan solemnity that humour exists solely in the eye of the beholder. Forest Whitaker is perfectly at home here, as a bushido-obsessed hitman who communicates with his boss by pigeon and doesn't speak a word of his ice cream-selling best friend's language. The word laconic doesn't do justice to the film's tempo – though the outbursts of explosive violence tend to spoil the ambience. DP. Contains violence. [video] DVD

Forest Whitaker *Ghost Dog* • John Tormey *Louie* • Cliff Gorman *Sonny Valerio* • Henry Silva *Vargo* • Isaach de Bankole *Raymond* • Tricia Vessey *Louise Vargo* • Gene Ruffini *Old consigliere* ■ *Dir/Scr* Jim Jarmusch

The Ghost Goes West

★★★ U

Comedy 1935 · UK · BW · 78mins

One of the prestige pictures with which producer Alexander Korda hoped to capture a corner of the US market. This is a lightweight fantasy that gets by thanks to some expert playing and the assured touch of director René Clair, who was making his English language debut after a decade of making comedies in his native France. Although Clair's frothy style is somewhat stifled by Korda's delusions of grandeur, he coaxes an impish performance out of Robert Donat as the ghost haunting a Scottish castle transported to Florida by vulgar millionaire Eugene Pallette. DP [video]

Robert Donat *Murdoch/Donald Glourie* • Jean Parker *Peggy Martin* • Eugene Pallette *Joe Martin* • Elsa Lanchester *Lady Shepperton* • Ralph Bunker *Ed Bigelow* • Patricia Hilliard *Shepherdess* • Everley Gregg *Gladys Martin* ■ *Dir* René Clair • *Scr* Robert Sherwood [Robert E Sherwood], Geoffrey Kerr, René Clair, Lajos Biró, from the story *Sir Tristram Goes West* by Eric Keown

A Ghost in Monte Carlo

★★ PG

Period romantic drama
1990 · UK/US · Colour · 89mins

Fans of Barbara Cartland's rich settings, English poise and tales of improbable innocents ensnared by lascivious men may well enjoy this sugary made-for-TV contrivance, which is adapted from one of her novels. Others may find it unintentionally funny, as a decent cast is forced to recite slabs of dialogue to camera in what is, sadly, an unmoving romantic drama. JM [video] DVD

Lysette Anthony *Mistral* • Sarah Miles *Aunt Emilie* • Oliver Reed *Rajah* • Marcus Gilbert *Lord Robert Stanford* • Christopher Plummer *Grand Duke Ivan* • Samantha Eggar *Jeanne* • Fiona Fullerton *Lady Violet* • Jolyon Baker *Prince Nicholas* • Joanna Lumley *Lady Drayton* • Lewis Collins *Lord Drayton* • Gareth Hunt *Dulton* • Ron Moody *Alphonse* ■ *Dir* John Hough • *Scr* Terence Feely, from the novel by Barbara Cartland

The Ghost in the Invisible Bikini ★★ PG

Comedy horror 1966 · US · Colour · 79mins

Exploitation movies don't come much brighter and bolder than this. Forget the plot, some aimless drivel about newly deceased Boris Karloff trying to gain entry into heaven by doing a good deed. The real fun comes from watching an eclectic cast go through its paces, including Karloff, Nancy Sinatra and Basil Rathbone who, despite his advanced years, allegedly handled his own stunts in a swordfight with teen idol Tommy Kirk. RS [video]

Tommy Kirk *Chuck Phillips* • Deborah Walley *Lili Morton* • Aron Kincaid *Bobby* • Quinn O'Hara *Sinistra* • Jesse White *J Sinister Hulk* • Harvey Lembeck *Eric Von Zipper* • Nancy Sinatra *Vicki* • Basil Rathbone *Reginald Ripper* • Boris Karloff *Hiram Stokely, the corpse* ■ *Dir* Don Weis • *Scr* Louis M Heyward, Elwood Ullman, from a story by Louis M Heyward

Ghost in the Machine

★★★ 18

Science-fiction horror
1993 · US · Colour · 91mins

A byte-sized horror thriller from Rachel Talalay about a serial killer whose death during a freak electrical storm transforms him into a computer virus. His evil spirit then murderously stalks through Cleveland's communication networks using Karen Allen's lost address book. Engaging and fast-paced, it's a very contemporary tale, laced with inventive mayhem and cool wit, sparsely augmented by well-executed special effects. AJ. Contains swearing and violence. [video]

Karen Allen *Terry Munroe* • Chris Mulkey *Bram* • Ted Marcoux *Karl* • Wil Horneff *Josh Munroe* • Jessica Walter *Elaine* • Brandon Quintin Adams [Brandon Adams] *Frazer* • Rick Ducommun *Phil* • Nancy Fish *Karl's landlord* ■ *Dir* Rachel Talalay • *Scr* William Davis, William Osborne

Ghost in the Noonday Sun

★ PG

Comedy adventure
1973 · UK · Colour · 88mins

The history behind the making of this film is far more interesting than the tired shambles that eventually ended up on screen. Peter Sellers's career was at a low ebb at the time and the star hoped this desperately unfunny pirate romp about hidden treasure would revive it. He was wrong – the whole sorry mess never found its way inside cinemas. Modest laughs are to be had, especially during Spike Milligan's brief appearance, but this poor man's *Treasure Island* is for Sellers completists only. RS [video]

Peter Sellers *Dick Scratcher* • Anthony Franciosa *Pierre* • Spike Milligan *Bombay* • Clive Revill *Bay of Algier* • Peter Boyle *Ras Mohammed* • Richard Willis *Jeremiah* • James Villiers *Parsley-Freck* ■ *Dir* Peter Medak • *Scr* Evan Jones, Spike Milligan

Ghost in the Shell ★★★★ 15

Animated science-fiction
1995 · Jpn/UK · Colour · 82mins

This is a hypnotic, animated fusion of thrilling, highly cinematic action sequences and philosophical soul-searching. Dynamic use of traditional cel techniques and computer-aided artwork, a vivid *Blade Runner*-esque landscape and a curvy cyborg heroine make this even more of a visual feast than the previous *manga* benchmark *Akira*. The fluid elegance of the animation is matched by Kenji Kawai's haunting music and, although the script gets bogged down in its own artfulness, there's moody atmosphere here to match that in any Ridley Scott movie. JC. Japanese dialogue dubbed into English. [video] DVD

Richard George *Bateau* • Mimi Woods *Kusanagi* • William Frederick *Aramaki* • Abe Lasser *Puppet master* • Christopher Joyce *Togusa* • Mike Sorich *Ishikawa* ■ *Dir* Mamoru Oshii • *Scr* Kazunori Ito, from the graphic novel *Kokaku Kidotai* by Shirow Masamune

The Ghost of Frankenstein ★★ PG

Horror 1942 · US · BW · 67mins

Technically and artistically second-rate, the fourth episode in Universal's *Frankenstein* series sees Bela Lugosi back for a second stint as the vengeful Ygor. His brain gets transplanted by mistake into Lon Chaney Jr's creature by Dr Frankensein's second son, Cedric Hardwicke. Sloppy sequel continuity means characters who died in the previous *Son of Frankenstein* suddenly appear without explanation. The scant running time is bolstered by scenes from the original 1931 classic. Creaky more than creepy. AJ

Lon Chaney Jr *Monster* • Sir Cedric Hardwicke [Cedric Hardwicke] *Frankenstein* • Ralph Bellamy *Erik* • Lionel Atwill *Dr Bohmer* • Bela Lugosi *Ygor* • Evelyn Ankers *Elsa* • Janet Ann Gallow *Cloestine* • Barton Yarborough *Dr Kettering* ■ *Dir* Erle C Kenton • *Scr* Scott Darling, from the story by Eric Taylor

G

The Ghost of Greville Lodge ★★

Supernatural mystery
2000 · UK · Colour · 88mins

There's a hint of *The Children of Green Knowe* about orphan Jon Newman's arrival at his uncle's rambling country manor. But the action quickly turns into a more traditional supernatural mystery, as the teenager ventures through the doors of the forbidden west wing and stumbles upon clues to the secrets of the old dark old house. Newman isn't the best child actor this country has ever produced, but George Cole and Prunella Scales are always worth watching. DP

George Cole *Uncle James* • Prunella Scales *Sarah* • Jon Newman *James Greville* • Billy Smith *Ben* • Rebecca Weeks *Midge* ■ *Dir* Niall Johnson • *Scr* Niall Johnson, from the novel *Down Came a Blackbird* by Nicholas Wilde

The Ghost of St Michael's ★★★★ U

Comedy thriller 1941 · UK · BW · 78mins

Will Hay is back before the blackboard and on the trail of Nazi spies in this spooky comedy. Hay and his class of likely lads are evacuated to a castle on the Isle of Skye, which is haunted by a ghost whose skirling bagpipes are a portent of death. While the mystery is moderately baffling, the highlights are the classroom showdowns in which Hay's academic shortcomings are gleefully exposed by brainbox Charles Hawtrey. Hay is on fine form, and the ensemble cast is splendid. DP

Will Hay *William Lamb* • Claude Hulbert *Hilary Teasdale* • Charles Hawtrey *Percy Thorne* • Raymond Huntley *Mr Humphries* • Felix Aylmer *Dr Winter* • Elliot Mason *Mrs Wigmore* • John Laurie *Jamie* • Hay Petrie *Procurator Fiscal* • Roddy Hughes *Amberley* ■ *Dir* Marcel Varnel • *Scr* Angus MacPhail, John Dighton

The Ghost Ship ★★★

Psychological horror 1943 · US · BW · 69mins

A successful plagiarism suit kept this film from acclaimed low-budget producer Val Lewton out of circulation for a long time. It proves to be a highly effective psychological thriller rather than just another horror picture. Under Mark Robson's direction, the normally heroic Richard Dix gives a powerful performance as the mentally deranged ship's captain whose crew members die in mysterious circumstances. Young third officer, Russell Wade, rumbles his secret but can't convince any of his crew mates. AE

Richard Dix *Captain Stone* • Russell Wade *Tom Merriman* • Edith Barrett *Ellen Roberts* • Ben Bard *Bowns* • Edmund Glover *Jacob Winslow, "Sparks"* • Skelton Knaggs *Finn* • Tom Burton *Benson* • Steve Winston *Ausman* ■ *Dir* Mark Robson • *Scr* Donald Henderson Clarke, from a story by Leo Mittler

Ghost Ship ★ U

Horror 1952 · UK · BW · 71mins

Buying a vessel that's haunted, even at a bargain price, is asking for trouble, as the young couple played by Dermot Walsh and Hazel Court find out in this waterlogged British B-feature. After they discover that the previous owner killed his spouse and her lover on board, they're on their way to laying the ship's ghost. Vernon Sewell, who was able to combine film-making with a love of the sea, probably had more fun than the audience. AE

Dermot Walsh *Guy* • Hazel Court *Margaret* • Hugh Burden *Dr Fawcett* • John Robinson (1) *Dr Martineau* • Joss Ambler *Yard manager* • Joan Carol *Mrs Martineau* • Hugh Latimer *Peter* • Mignon O'Doherty *Mrs Manley* ■ *Dir* Vernon Sewell • *Scr* Vernon Sewell, Philip Thornton

Ghost Ship ★ 18

Science-fiction horror thriller
2002 · US/Aus · Colour · 86mins

A hackneyed and unsophisticated morality tale, this revolves around skipper Gabriel Byrne and his salvage team who think they've struck gold when they discover a mysterious, loot-filled cruise liner that's been lost at sea since the 1960s. The ineffectual performances and threadbare plot effectively eliminate tension. Turgid nonsense. SF DVD

Julianna Margulies *Maureen Epps* • Ron Eldard *Dodge* • Desmond Harrington *Jack Ferriman* • Isaiah Washington *Greer* • Gabriel Byrne *Sean Murphy* • Alex Dimitriades *Santos* ■ *Dir* Steve Beck • *Scr* Mark Hanlon, John Pogue, from a story by Mark Hanlon

Ghost Story ★★ 18

Horror 1974 · UK · Colour · 87mins

This is more an arty mood piece than a fully fledged horror outing by Stephen Weeks, one-time British genre hopeful and director of the equally idiosyncratic *I, Monster* and *Gawain and the Green Knight*. In England in the 1930s, a trio of friends are invited to test whether an ancestral mansion is haunted or not. One of them comes under the influence of an enigmatic doll, which relays psychic images of past events. Unexceptional special effects make this an interesting failure. AJ

Larry Dann *Talbot* • Murray Melvin *McFayden* • Vivian Mackerall *Duller* • Marianne Faithfull *Sophy* • Anthony Bate *Dr Borden* • Penelope Keith *Rennie* • Leigh Lawson *Robert* • Sally Grace *Girl* ■ *Dir* Stephen Weeks • *Scr* Rosemary Sutcliff, Stephen Weeks

Ghost Story ★★ 18

Horror 1981 · US · Colour · 105mins

Peter Straub's bestselling novel about four old-timers haunted by supernatural reminders of a past dark secret makes for pretty slow going here. Badly adapted by *Carrie* scriptwriter Lawrence D Cohen from the convoluted book, it's more a gothic soap opera than a horror film; in fact, most of the special effects were edited out prior to release. Yet it's worth watching for the skilled performances of veterans Fred Astaire, Melvyn Douglas, John Houseman and Douglas Fairbanks Jr (even if they're all miscast) and for the gifted Alice Krige as the central spectre. AJ. Contains nudity.

Fred Astaire *Ricky Hawthorne* • Melvyn Douglas *John Jaffrey* • Douglas Fairbanks Jr *Edward Wanderley* • John Houseman *Sears James* • Craig Wasson *Don/David* • Patricia Neal *Stella* • Alice Krige *Alma/Eva* ■ *Dir* John Irvin • *Scr* Lawrence D Cohen, from the novel by Peter Straub

Ghost Town ★★★ 18

Horror western 1988 · US · Colour · 81mins

"The good, the bad and the Satanic" ran the more than apt tagline for this inventive mix of western, ghost story and conventional splatter movie. Franc Luz stars as a sheriff who tracks down a missing girl to a zombie-populated town and finds himself drawn into a *High Noon*-style showdown with an evil gunslinger. Debut director Richard Governor achieves an eerie ghost town atmosphere and displays a deft talent for surreal touches. RS

Franc Luz *Langley* • Catherine Hickland *Kate* • Jimmie F Skaggs *Devilin* • Penelope Windust *Grace* • Bruce Glover *Dealer* • Zitto Kazann *Blacksmith* • Blake Conway *Harper* ■ *Dir* Richard Governor • *Scr* Duke Sandefur, from a story by David Schmoeller

The Ghost Train ★★★ U

Comedy mystery 1931 · UK · BW · 71mins

Walter Forde was clearly a big fan of this comedy chiller as, almost a decade after completing this version, he remade it as a wartime flag-waver with Arthur Askey. This story of a haunted country station may now seem short on suspense, but there are still laughs a-plenty as the husband-and-wife team of Jack Hulbert and Cicely Courtneidge take on a gang of smugglers bringing commie propaganda into England. The supporting cast is also first class. DP

Jack Hulbert *Teddy Deakin* • Cicely Courtneidge *Miss Bourne* • Ann Todd *Peggy Murdock* • Cyril Raymond *Richard Winthrop* • Allan Jeayes *Dr Sterling* • Donald Calthrop *Saul Hodgkin* • Angela Baddeley *Julia Price* • Henry Caine *Herbert Price* ■ *Dir* Walter Forde • *Scr* Angus MacPhail, Lajos Biró, Sidney Gilliat, from the play by Arnold Ridley

The Ghost Train ★★★ U

Comedy mystery 1941 · UK · BW · 81mins

Arthur Askey and Richard Murdoch, the stars of the hit radio show *Band Waggon*, were reunited for this flag-waving remake of the classic play by Arnold Ridley (Private Godfrey in *Dad's Army*) about a haunted country station. Try as director Walter Forde might to inject some atmosphere, there's a predictability about both the proceedings and the comedy. Askey was never at his best on screen and his energetic overacting has dated badly. DP

Arthur Askey *Tommy Gander* • Richard Murdoch *Teddy Deakin* • Kathleen Harrison *Miss Bourne* • Morland Graham *Dr Sterling* • Linden Travers *Julia Price* • Peter Murray Hill *Richard Winthrop* • Carole Lynn *Jackie Winthrop* • Raymond Huntley *John Price* ■ *Dir* Walter Forde • *Scr* Marriott Edgar, Val Guest, JOC Orton, Sidney Gilliat, from the play by Arnold Ridley

Ghost World ★★★ 15

Comedy drama
2001 · US/UK/Ger · Colour · 107mins

A scathing yet affectionate send-up of modern American culture, this traces the attempts of teenage misfit Thora Birch and her more level-headed friend Scarlett Johansson to survive life after high school. Terry Zwigoff delivers a poignant but darkly comic overview of human behaviour as he homes in on a cast of oddballs and eccentrics pigeonholed by society's prejudices. Though hampered by occasional self-conscious kookiness, the sharp dialogue and endearing performances keep this entertaining. SF. Contains sex scenes, swearing. DVD

Thora Birch *Enid* • Scarlett Johansson *Rebecca* • Steve Buscemi *Seymour* • Brad Renfro *Josh* • Illeana Douglas *Roberta* • Bob Balaban *Enid's dad* • Teri Garr *Maxine* ■ *Dir* Terry Zwigoff • *Scr* Daniel Clowes, Terry Zwigoff, from the graphic novel by Daniel Clowes

Ghostbusters ★★★★ PG

Supernatural comedy
1984 · US · Colour · 100mins

The often dazzling, special effects-driven slapstick tends to overshadow the fact that there are some slyer, more sophisticated laughs on offer in this blockbusting family comedy. Bill Murray is terrifically deadpan and sleazy as the dubious leader of a troupe of ghostbusters (writers Dan Aykroyd and Harold Ramis, plus Ernie Hudson) who are called into action when ancient spirits are let loose in New York. Sigourney Weaver shows an admirably light touch as a possessed cellist, and Rick Moranis also scores in his breakthrough movie. Director Ivan Reitman stages some spectacular set pieces, including an enjoyably daft finale. The concept was so successful that the film spawned a sequel and a cartoon series. JF. Contains swearing. DVD

Bill Murray *Dr Peter Venkman* • Dan Aykroyd *Dr Raymond Stantz* • Sigourney Weaver *Dana Barrett* • Harold Ramis *Dr Egon Spengler* • Rick Moranis *Louis Tully* • Annie Potts *Janine Melnitz* • Ernie Hudson *Winston Zeddemore* • William Atherton *Walter Peck* ■ *Dir* Ivan Reitman • *Scr* Dan Aykroyd, Harold Ramis

Ghostbusters II ★★★ PG

Supernatural comedy
1989 · US · Colour · 103mins

Having reassembled almost the entire team behind the first blockbuster, director Ivan Reitman was not prepared to mess with a successful formula. This time the self-styled ghostbusters – Bill Murray, Dan Aykroyd, Harold Ramis and Ernie Hudson – are called back into service when evil emanating from a painting Sigourney Weaver's boss Peter MacNicol has been restoring awakens spirits around New York. The effects are bigger and more spectacular than in the original, but Ramis and Aykroyd's script fails to sparkle and there is very little new here. JF. Contains swearing. DVD

Bill Murray *Dr Peter Venkman* • Dan Aykroyd *Dr Raymond Stantz* • Sigourney Weaver *Dana Barrett* • Harold Ramis *Dr Egon Spengler* • Rick Moranis *Louis Tully* • Ernie Hudson *Winston Zeddemore* • Annie Potts *Janine Melnitz* • Peter MacNicol *Janosz Poha* • Harris Yulin *Judge* ■ *Dir* Ivan Reitman • *Scr* Dan Aykroyd, Harold Ramis

Ghosts Can't Do It ★ 18

Erotic supernatural fantasy
1990 · US · Colour · 83mins

Execrable soft-core nonsense from director John Derek and his wife Bo. Billionaire Anthony Quinn commits suicide after a heart attack ruins his sex life with wife Bo Derek. The ludicrous plot then sees him return in ghostly form with a plan to kill handsome Leo Damien and take over his body so they can resume their erotic odyssey. An indescribably bad fantasy fiasco. AJ

Bo Derek *Kate* • Anthony Quinn *Scott* • Leo Damian *Fausto* • Don Murray *Winston* • Julie Newmar *Angel* ■ *Dir/Scr* John Derek

Ghosts in the Night ★★ U

Comedy drama 1943 · US · BW · 64mins

Bela Lugosi's second outing with the East Side Kids was something of a comedown from his first – the more than mediocre *Spooks Run Wild*. Ignore the title, as there isn't a single ghoul occupying that old deserted house. But there are plenty of fifth columnists, operating under the fanatical eye of spymaster Lugosi. Mugging in their usual unsubtle way, Huntz Hall and Leo Gorcey are torn between nabbing the Nazis and getting Hall's sister (played by Ava Gardner) to the church on time. DP

Leo Gorcey *Mugs McGinnis* • Huntz Hall *Glimpy Williams* • Bobby Jordan *Danny* • Bela Lugosi *Emil* • Ava Gardner *Betty Williams Gibson* • Rick Vallin *John "Jack" Gibson* • Sammy Morrison ["Sunshine Sammy" Morrison] *Scruno* • Billy Benedict *Benny* • Bobby Stone *Rocky/Dave* • Bill Bates *"Sleepy" Dave* ■ *Dir* William Beaudine • *Scr* Kenneth Higgins

Ghosts – Italian Style ★★★

Comedy 1967 · Fr/It · Colour · 92mins

Every genre went "Italian style" in the 1960s and this supernatural comedy is one of the better offshoots of that craze. Sophia Loren and Vittorio Gassman are an impoverished married couple offered free accommodation in an old palace. Of course, it's haunted. Meanwhile, Loren's would-be lover, Mario Adorf, has also moved into the palace and much amusement ensues when Gassman mistakes him for a ghost. Renato Castellani's romp scores much laughter from the hereafter. AJ. An Italian language film.

Sophia Loren *Maria* • Vittorio Gassman *Pasquale* • Mario Adorf *Alfredo* • Aldo Giuffre *Raffaele* • Margaret Lee *Sayonara* • Francesco Tensi *Professor Santanna* • Marcello Mastroianni *Headless ghost* ■ *Dir* Renato Castellani • *Scr* Renato Castellani, Adriano Baracco, Leo Benvenuti, Piero De Bernardi, Ernest Pintoff, from the play *Questi Fantasmi!* by Eduardo De Filippo

The Ghosts of Berkeley Square ★★★

Comedy 1947 · UK · BW · 100mins

Robert Morley and Felix Aylmer are wonderfully mischievous as the bungling 18th-century assassins who are cursed to haunt a luxurious town house until it is visited by a reigning monarch. Amusing interludes along the way include Ernest Thesiger's attempt to prove they're a hoax and the ghosts being mistaken for First World War spies. A great opportunity to watch an accomplished cast of British character actors go through its paces, and a spirited flight of fancy that takes several sly swipes at the British cinema of the period. DP

Robert Morley *General Burlap* • Felix Aylmer *Colonel Kelsoe* • Yvonne Arnaud *Millie* • Robert Beaumont *King's equerry* • Madge Brindley *Matron* • Strelsa Brown *Rajah's Amazon attendant* • Harry Fine *1914 Colonel* • Ronald Frankau *Tex* • Ernest Thesiger *Investigator* ■ *Dir* Vernon Sewell • *Scr* James Seymour, from the novel *No Nightingales* by Caryl Brahms, SJ Simon

Ghosts of Mississippi ★★★ 15

Drama based on a true story
1996 · US · Colour · 125mins

Also known as *Ghosts from the Past*, this fact-based drama stars Alec Baldwin as the lawyer who re-opened the case of Medgar Evers, a black civil rights leader murdered nearly 30 years before. A white man named Byron De La Beckwith (an over-the-top James Woods) had been charged with the crime, but was released when two white juries could not unanimously find him guilty. It's a moving true story and the cast is excellent. However, Rob Reiner's uninvolving direction fails to make the story as compelling or passionate as it should be, and what we end up with is something with the feel of a superior TV movie. JB. Contains violence and swearing. [video]

Alec Baldwin *Bobby DeLaughter* • Whoopi Goldberg *Myrlie Evers* • James Woods *Byron De La Beckwith* • Craig T Nelson *Ed Peters* • Susanna Thompson *Peggy Lloyd* • William H Macy *Charlie Crisco* ■ *Dir* Rob Reiner • *Scr* Lewis Colick

Ghosts... of the Civil Dead ★★★★ 18

Prison drama 1988 · Aus · Colour · 92mins

Prison pictures don't come much tougher than this. Directed with reckless visual energy by one-time pop promo producer John Hillcoat, this drama casts an unflinching eye over the brutalities perpetrated by the staff of a state-of-the-art, maximum security prison, packed to the rafters with violent offenders. Everything from drugs and starvation to rape and self-mutilation is charted as the film, through a series of flashbacks, reveals the motives for an explosive riot that rips through the hi-tech defences. Shot with a ruthless power, made all the more chilling by the relentlessly raw realism, this is a remarkable debut that is not for the faint-hearted. DP. Contains violence and swearing. [video]

Dave Field [David Field] *Wenzil* • Mike Bishop *David Yale* • Chris De Rose *Jack Grezner* • Nick Cave *Maynard* • Freddo Dierck *Robbins* • Vincent Gil *Ruben* • Bogdan Koca *Waychek* • Kevin Mackey *Glover* • Dave Mason *Lilly* ■ *Dir* John Hillcoat • *Scr* Nick Cave, Gene Conkie, Evan English, John Hillcoat, Hugo Race, John Flaus

The Ghoul ★★★★ PG

Horror 1933 · UK · BW · 69mins

Following his enormous success in the US, Boris Karloff returned home to England for this highly successful clone of *The Mummy*. Under eerily effective make-up, he's a cataleptic Egyptologist rising from the dead to recover a stolen talisman. Hugely atmospheric, if slow by today's standards, the macabre mood eventually gives way to sinister slapstick; yet Karloff's commanding presence elevates it to the level of seminal British *Grand Guignol*. It also marks Ralph Richardson's first screen appearance, here playing a fake priest. AT [video] DVD

Boris Karloff *Professor Morlant* • Cedric Hardwicke *Broughton* • Ernest Thesiger *Laing* • Dorothy Hyson *Betty Harlow* • Anthony Bushell *Ralph Morlant* • Kathleen Harrison *Kaney* • Harold Huth *Aga Ben Dragore* • DA Clarke-Smith *Mahmoud* • Ralph Richardson *Nigel Hartley* ■ *Dir* T Hayes Hunter • *Scr* Roland Pertwee, John Hastings Turner, Rupert Downing, L du Garde Peach, from the novel and play by Dr Frank King, Leonard J Hines

The Ghoul ★★ 18

Horror 1975 · UK · Colour · 89mins

Shot on leftover sets from *The Great Gatsby*, Freddie Francis's flapper fright-fest (produced by his son Kevin) eschews gore in favour of more traditional terror. It's an unsavoury tale about defrocked minister Peter Cushing trying to keep his cannibal son locked in the attic. Then Hammer scream queen Veronica Carlson's car breaks down on the foggy moors and... A nice feeling for the 1920s period atmosphere and a crazed performance from John Hurt give this fractured slow-mover a few extra kicks. AJ [video]

Peter Cushing *Dr Lawrence* • John Hurt *Tom Rawlings* • Alexandra Bastedo *Angela* • Gwen Watford *Ayah* • Veronica Carlson *Daphne* • Stewart Bevan *Billy* • Ian McCulloch *Geoffrey* • Don Henderson *The Ghoul* ■ *Dir* Freddie Francis • *Scr* John Elder [Anthony Hinds]

Ghoulies ★★ 15

Comedy horror 1985 · US · Colour · 77mins

Executive producer Charles Band, the self-styled B-movie king of 1980s schlock and cheap straight-to-video horror was responsible for this tacky imitation of *Gremlins*. Under the spell of his satanist father, Peter Liapis invokes a black magic ritual in the family mansion and conjures up midget demons from another dimension which go on a teen-killing spree. The result is low-grade trash with a cult cast and a self-mocking tone. The little devils returned for three sequels. AJ [video] DVD

Peter Liapis *Jonathan Graves* • Lisa Pelikan *Rebecca* • Michael Des Barres *Malcolm Graves* • Jack Nance *Wolfgang* • Peter Risch *Grizzel* • Tamara De Treaux *Greedigut* • Scott Thomson *Mike* ■ *Dir* Luca Bercovici • *Scr* Luca Bercovici, Jefery Levy

Gia ★★★ 18

Biographical drama
1998 · US · Colour · 119mins

Oscar-winner Angelina Jolie gives an early knockout performance in this dark and provocative TV movie. She stars as Gia Carangi, whose rise to fame as a supermodel in the 1970s brought tragedy as she became addicted to pills, cocaine and heroin. With its almost soft-core porn style, this is more an art house film then standard TV-movie fare. Strong performances by Mercedes Ruehl and Faye Dunaway give it a powerful punch. MC. Contains sex scenes and drug abuse. [video] DVD

Angelina Jolie *Gia Carangi* • Elizabeth Mitchell *Linda* • Mercedes Ruehl *Kathleen Carangi* • Faye Dunaway *Wilhemina Cooper* • Kylie Travis *Stephanie* ■ *Dir* Michael Cristofer • *Scr* Michael Cristofer, Jay McInerney

Giant ★★★★ PG

Epic drama 1956 · US · Colour · 192mins

James Dean's last film before his fatal car crash reveals him more as an icon for the time than an actor. He just doesn't convince as the middle-aged Jett Rink in the final half of this drama based on Edna Ferber's homage to Texas. But director George Stevens, who won an Oscar for the film, manages to compress some of the swashbuckling magic of oil barons and land exploitation into the three hours-plus running time. A lustrous Elizabeth Taylor plays the object of Dean's unrequited passion – unfortunately for him, she's married to manly Rock Hudson. Those elements and a tremendous scene in which Dean strikes oil make it an adventure of epic proportions. TH [video] DVD

Elizabeth Taylor *Leslie Benedict* • Rock Hudson *Bick Benedict* • James Dean *Jett Rink* • Mercedes McCambridge *Luz Benedict* • Carroll Baker *Luz Benedict II* • Dennis Hopper *Jordan Benedict III* • Sal Mineo *Angel Obregon III* • Jane Withers *Vashti Snythe* • Chill Wills *Uncle Rawley* ■ *Dir* George Stevens • *Scr* Fred Guiol, Ivan Moffat, from the novel by Edna Ferber

The Giant Behemoth ★★★

Science fiction 1959 · UK · BW · 71mins

Director Eugène Lourié cannibalised his own *The Beast from 20,000 Fathoms* and added sterling special effects by *King Kong* creator Willis O'Brien for another classic 1950s giant-monster-on-the-loose fantasy. This time a prehistoric dinosaur is revived by an atomic explosion and travels to London to wreak radioactive havoc. Lourié builds suspense and mood through evocative lighting and excellent use of O'Brien's stop-motion puppet. The director recycled the same story again for *Gorgo*. AJ

Gene Evans *Steve Karnes* • André Morell *Professor James Bickford* • John Turner *Ian Duncan* • Leigh Madison *Jeanie MacDougall* • Jack MacGowran *Dr Sampson* • Maurice Kaufmann *Submarine officer* • Henry Vidon *Tom* • Leonard Sachs *Scientist* ■ *Dir* Eugène Lourié, Douglas Hickox • *Scr* Eugène Lourié, Daniel James (uncredited), from a story by Robert Abel, Allen Adler

The Giant Gila Monster ★

Science-fiction horror
1959 · US · BW · 74mins

A badly rear-projected giant lizard stomps through model Texan towns and terrorises the local teens, who always seem to be having hot-rod races or rock 'n' roll dance hall parties. The creature is eventually beaten by one brave lad who drives a hot rod packed with explosives into the beast's belly. Unintentionally amusing rather than scary. AJ

Don Sullivan *Chace Winstead* • Lisa Simone *Lisa* • Shug Fisher *Mr Harris* • Jerry Cortwright *Bob* • Beverly Thurman *Gay* • Don Flournoy *Gordy* • Clarke Browne *Chuck* • Pat Simmons *Sherry* ■ *Dir* Ray Kellogg • *Scr* Jay Sims, Ray Kellogg, from a story by Ray Kellogg

The Giant of Marathon ★★ U

Historical adventure
1960 · It · Colour · 90mins

Steve Reeves abandons the role of Hercules (for which he was most famous) to squeeze his bronzed torso into the role of the Athenian warrior Philippides, who warns his fellow Greeks of a Persian invasion. It's not the worst of its kind by a long chalk, but it's sad to see B-movie maestro Jacques Tourneur reduced to muscle-bound mediocrity like this. DP

Steve Reeves *Philippides* • Mylène Demongeot *Andromeda* • Daniela Rocca *Karis* • Ivo Garrani *Creuso* • Philippe Hersent *Callimaco* • Sergio Fantoni *Teocrito* • Alberto Lupo *Milziade* • Daniele Varga *Dario, King of the Persians* ■ *Dir* Jacques Tourneur • *Scr* Ennio De Concini, Augusto Frassinetti, Bruno Vailati, from an idea by Raffaello Pacini, Alberto Barsanti

The Giant Spider Invasion ★

Science-fiction horror
1975 · US · Colour · 75mins

A rash of outsize spider sightings are traced to Wisconsin, but greedy farmer Robert Easton, thinking the radioactive spiders' eggs from another dimension are jewels, won't let the authorities investigate until it's too late. This irredeemable dreck has bottom-of-the-barrel special effects, including a Volkswagen in hairy drag masquerading as the largest spider of all. AJ

Barbara Hale *Dr Jenny Langer* • Steve Brodie *Dr Vance* • Leslie Parrish *Ev Kester* • Alan Hale Jr *Sheriff* • Robert Easton *Kester* • Kevin Brodie *Dave Perkins* • Christiane Schmidtmer *Helga* ■ *Dir* Bill Rebane, Richard L Huff • *Scr* Richard L Huff, Robert Easton

Gideon ★★

Comedy drama 1999 · US · Colour · 100mins

Christopher Lambert is surprisingly effective playing a child-man who is placed in a retirement home in rural South Carolina and slowly begins to transform the lives of its dissatisfied residents. The veteran stars in the supporting cast perform their stereotyped roles with aplomb, although Carroll O'Connor's bolshy cook, Mike Connors's ring-rusty boxer and Shirley Jones's frustrated artist are less showy than Charlton Heston's crusty philosophy professor. DP

Christopher Lambert *Gideon Dobbs* • Charlton Heston *Addison Sinclair* • Shelley Winters *Mrs Willows* • Carroll O'Connor *Leo Barnes* • Shirley Jones *Elly Morton* • Mike Connors *Harland Greer* • Barbara Bain *Sarah* • Crystal Bernard *Jean MacLemore* ■ *Dir* Claudia Hoover • *Scr* Brad Mirman

Gideon's Day ★★★★

Crime drama 1958 · UK · Colour · 90mins

Shown in America as *Gideon of Scotland Yard*, this cynical romp is extremely entertaining and contains a marvellous performance from Jack Hawkins as the Gideon of the title, who is followed by the camera on what must be the busiest day of his life. Hawkins was the only British actor to star for the three greatest American directors of their day: William Wyler in *Ben-Hur*, Howard Hawks in *Land of the Pharaohs* and John Ford here. TS

Jack Hawkins *Inspector George Gideon* • Dianne Foster *Joanna Delafield* • Anna Lee *Kate Gideon* • Anna Massey *Sally Gideon* • Andrew Ray *PC Simon Farnaby-Green* • Cyril Cusack *Herbert "Birdy" Sparrow* • James Hayter *Mason* • Ronald Howard *Paul Delafield* ■ *Dir* John Ford • *Scr* TEB Clarke, from the novel by JJ Marric [John Creasey]

Gideon's Trumpet ★★★★ U

Courtroom drama based on a true story
1980 · US · Colour · 103mins

Henry Fonda is marvellous in this TV movie based on a true-life court case that enshrined the principle of free representation in American legal history. Although not the obvious choice to play a semi-literate convict, Fonda manages to bring off the characterisation with a bravado that is both winning and warm. Also remarkably effective is José Ferrer as Fonda's lawyer, while John Houseman (who also executive produced) heads up a distinguished supporting cast. In a much-maligned genre, this is an example of the TV movie at its best, tackling a subject that cinema might regard as uncommercial. TS

Henry Fonda *Clarence Earl Gideon* • José Ferrer *Abe Fortas* • John Houseman *Chief Justice* • Fay Wray *Edna Curtis* • Sam Jaffe *1st Justice* • Dean Jagger *6th Justice* • Nicholas Pryor *Jacob* • William Prince *5th Justice* ■ *Dir* Robert Collins • *Scr* David W Rintels, from a story by Anthony Lewis

G

Gidget ★★★★ U

Romantic comedy
1959 · US · Colour · 95mins

A perfect period artefact, this quintessential California surf movie is actually much, much better than it should be – or was ever given credit for – largely thanks to the stylish direction by Paul Wendkos. Sandra Dee is the titular heroine and she became identified with the role, even though she didn't reprise it in the two sequels or in the two completely different TV series. Her beaus are James Darren and Cliff Robertson, and there is a very real sense of enjoyment when all three are together. The beach looks fabulous in CinemaScope and Eastmancolor and, if you let your hair down, you'll enjoy the period slang and good-time atmosphere. TS

Sandra Dee *Francie* • James Darren *Moondoggie* • Cliff Robertson *Kahoona* • Arthur O'Connell *Russell Lawrence* • Mary LaRoche *Dorothy Lawrence* • Joby Baker *Stinky* • Tom Laughlin *Lover Boy* ■ *Dir* Paul Wendkos • *Scr* Gabrielle Upton, from the novel by Frederick Kohner

Gidget Goes Hawaiian ★★

Romantic comedy
1961 · US · Colour · 101mins

There's a different Gidget (Deborah Walley had taken over from Sandra Dee), but otherwise things are much the same in this sequel to the surprise hit surf movie. Gidget and Jeff (nicknamed Moondoggie) split up after a misunderstanding and Gidget flies off with her parents to Hawaii, where she finds herself pursued by a number of boys and becomes a victim of gossip. Moondoggie turns up, and the rest is a tangle of rivalry, teenage jealousy and endless shots of surfing. DF

James Darren *Jeff* • Michael Callan *Eddie Horner* • Deborah Walley *Gidget* • Carl Reiner *Russ Lawrence* • Peggy Cass *Mitzie Stewart* • Eddie Foy Jr *Monty Stewart* • Vicki Trickett *Abby Stewart* ■ *Dir* Paul Wendkos • *Scr* Ruth Brooks Flippen, from the characters created by Frederick Kohner

Gidget Goes to Rome ★★ U

Romantic comedy
1963 · US · Colour · 103mins

Third film, third Gidget. This time Cindy Carol stars, although continuity is assured by the reappearance of James Darren as boyfriend Jeff. Here the couple travel to Rome where their relationship is tested by the attentions of two locals – Cesare Danova and Danielle de Metz. The *Gidget* series spawned a mini-industry, with TV movies and two series keeping the diminutive heroine on the small screen until the end of the 1980s. DF

Cindy Carol *Gidget* • James Darren *Jeff* • Jessie Royce Landis *Aunt Albertina* • Cesare Danova *Paolo Cellini* • Danielle De Metz *Daniela Serrini* • Joby Baker *Judge* • Trudi Ames *Libby* ■ *Dir* Paul Wendkos • *Scr* Ruth Brooks Flippen, Katherine Eunson, Dale Eunson, from the characters created by Frederick Kohner

The Gift ★★★ 15

Supernatural thriller
2000 · US · Colour · 107mins

Co-scripted by Billy Bob Thornton, this eerie tale sees widow Cate Blanchett blessed with ESP and roped into assisting the police find a missing woman. Her insights lead to the arrest of adulterous wife-batterer Keanu Reeves, but is he really the culprit? The strong cast rises above the rather predictable plotting and hackneyed final reel, and there are some genuinely scary moments along the way. The lack of emphasis on digital effects here is refreshing, and Reeves's ferocious turn is a real eye-opener. JC. Contains violence, swearing, sex scenes and nudity. DVD

Cate Blanchett *Annie Wilson* • Giovanni Ribisi *Buddy Cole* • Keanu Reeves *Donnie Barksdale* • Katie Holmes *Jessica King* • Greg Kinnear *Wayne Collins* • Hilary Swank *Valerie Barksdale* ■ *Dir* Sam Raimi • *Scr* Billy Bob Thornton, Tom Epperson

A Gift for Heidi ★★

Adventure
1958 · US · Colour · 71mins

It may be impossible to film Johanna Spyri's much-loved novel without lashings of sentimentality, but never has the little Alpine orphan found herself so immersed in sticky sweetness as in this glutinous fable. The gift in question is a set of carved wooden figures depicting Faith, Hope and Charity, the true meaning of which she comes to learn in the course of three tacky tales. Sandy Descher is just about bearable in the lead. DP

Sandy Descher *Heidi* • Douglas Fowley *Alm Uncle* • Van Dyke Parks *Peter* • Peter Capell *Doc* • Erik Jelde *Ernst* • Susan Sainio *Clara* • Oswald Ursteins *Carlo* • Clancy Cooper *Dr Roth* ■ *Dir* George Templeton • *Scr* Eugene Vale, David Dortort, from the characters created by Johanna Spyri

The Gift Horse ★★ U

Second World War drama
1951 · UK · BW · 101mins

Packed with stock situations, this unremarkable naval drama starts in 1940 on the broken-down tub presented to gung-ho captain Trevor Howard as part of a 50-destroyer loan made to Britain by neutral America. Director Compton Bennett stages the action with efficiency but no urgency, and Howard looks bored by the proceedings. DP

Trevor Howard *Lieutenant Commander Hugh Fraser* • Richard Attenborough *Dripper Daniels* • Sonny Tufts *Yank Flanagan* • James Donald *Lieutenant Richard Jennings* • Joan Rice *June Mallory* • Bernard Lee *Stripey Wood* • Dora Bryan *Glad* • Hugh Williams *Captain* ■ *Dir* Compton Bennett • *Scr* William Fairchild, William Rose, Hugh Hastings, from a story by Ivan Goff, Ben Roberts

The Gift of Love ★ U

Drama 1958 · US · Colour · 105mins

In 1946, Fox had a big hit with the very mushy *Sentimental Journey*, which worked because of the sincerity of Maureen O'Hara and the adroit direction of Walter Lang. This time round it's Lauren Bacall playing the dying wife who adopts a little girl to provide consolation for her husband after she's gone. Garish colour, the miscasting of Bacall and the crude direction of Jean Negulesco result in insufferable schmaltz. AE

Lauren Bacall *Julie Beck* • Robert Stack *Bill Beck* • Evelyn Rudie *Hitty* • Lorne Greene *Grant Allan* • Anne Seymour *McMasters* • Edward Platt *Dr Miller* • Joseph Kearns *Mr Rynicker* ■ *Dir* Jean Negulesco • *Scr* Luther Davis, from a story by Nelia Gardner White

The Gig ★★★ 15

Comedy drama 1985 · US · Colour · 87mins

This wistfully funny jazz movie stars Wayne Rogers, as a New York car dealer. He's been playing jazz trombone with a bunch of friends for years and books them into a swanky resort in the Catskill Mountains, the sort of place that usually hosts Jewish stand-ups and tea dances. Personally financed by its director, Frank D Gilroy, the film has a pleasingly sardonic edge, a tremendous sense of place and winning performances. AT

Wayne Rogers *Marty Flynn* • Cleavon Little *Marshall Wilson* • Andrew Duncan *Jack Larmon* • Daniel Nalbach *Arthur Winslow* • Jerry Matz *Aaron Wohl* • Warren Vache *Gil Macrae* • Joe Silver *Abe Mitgang* • Jay Thomas *Rick Valentine* • Stan Lachow *George* ■ *Dir/Scr* Frank D Gilroy

Gigi ★★★★★ PG

Musical 1958 · US · Colour · 110mins

Rightful winner of nine Academy Awards (including best picture), this is the last great musical from producer Arthur Freed. He coerced composers Lerner and Loewe into creating a screen original from Colette's tale following their sensational stage success with *My Fair Lady*. Superbly cast (Leslie Caron in the title role, Maurice Chevalier winning a special Oscar, Louis Jourdan), immaculately designed (for CinemaScope in Art Nouveau by Cecil Beaton) and impeccably directed by Vincente Minnelli, this is a sophisticated and entertaining musical treat. The story about the training of a young girl to become a courtesan is hardly the usual basis for a screen song-fest, but it's brilliantly and intelligently handled, with arguably the best sequences (the duet *I Remember It Well* and Gaston's soliloquy) directed by the uncredited Charles Walters, who had previously guided Caron in *Lili*. TS DVD

Leslie Caron *Gigi* • Maurice Chevalier *Honore Lachaille* • Louis Jourdan *Gaston Lachaille* • Hermione Gingold *Mme Alvarez* • Eva Gabor *Liane D'Exelmans* • Jacques Bergerac *Sandomir* • Isabel Jeans *Aunt Alicia* • John Abbott *Manuel* ■ *Dir* Vincente Minnelli • *Scr* Alan Jay Lerner, from the play by Anita Loos, from the novel by Colette • *Cinematographer* Joseph Ruttenberg • *Editor* Adrienne Fazan • *Art Director* William A Horning, Preston Ames • *Costume Designer* Cecil Beaton • *Music/lyrics* Frederick Loewe • *Lyrics* Alan Jay Lerner • *Music Director* Andre Previn

Gigli ★ 15

Romantic crime comedy
2003 · US · Colour · 116mins

There's no chemistry between Ben Affleck and Jennifer Lopez, starring as Mob operatives who kidnap the mentally challenged younger brother of a powerful federal prosecutor. Lopez is a new-age lesbian, and Affleck's Neanderthal hitman tries to prove that he's the solution to her sexual "affliction". Martin Brest's excruciating gangster comedy has absolutely no redeeming qualities at all. SF DVD

Ben Affleck *Larry Gigli* • Jennifer Lopez *Ricki* • Justin Bartha *Brian* • Lainie Kazan *Larry's mother* • Missy Crider *Robin* • Lenny Venito *Louis* • Christopher Walken *Det Stanley Jacobellis* • Al Pacino *Starkman* ■ *Dir/Scr* Martin Brest

Gigot ★★★ U

Comedy drama 1962 · US · Colour · 104mins

Director Gene Kelly embraces the inherent sentimentality in the touching tale of a Parisian mute and, aided by a magnificent performance in the title role by Jackie Gleason, achieves an almost Chaplinesque work of great poignancy. Understandably, and unfortunately, the film was re-edited by 20th Century-Fox when they realised what Kelly had delivered, and Kelly and Gleason always claimed that the original cut (no longer in existence) was far better than the one that survives. Not for all tastes, certainly, but interesting nonetheless. TS

Jackie Gleason *Gigot* • Katherine Kath *Colette* • Gabrielle Dorziat *Madame Brigitte* • Jean Lefebvre *Gaston* • Jacques Marin *Jean* • Albert Rémy *Alphonse* • Yvonne Constant *Lucille Duval* • Germaine Delbat *Madame Greuze* ■ *Dir* Gene Kelly • *Scr* John Patrick, from a story by Jackie Gleason

Gilda ★★★★★ PG

Classic film noir 1946 · US · BW · 104mins

"There never was a woman like Gilda!" shrieked the original poster (designed by James Bond title wizard Maurice Binder). And there never was anyone to capture the imagination like Rita Hayworth, whose first appearance in this movie is a classic star introduction. Highlights include her striptease (well, she takes off a glove!) and her voluptuous vamping of callow Glenn Ford, whose perverse relationship with his former boss and Gilda's husband George Macready seems to circumvent the censors by a mile. Columbia's low-lit studio-bound Buenos Aires setting is quintessential 1940s *film noir*, and the whole is a remarkable example of the Hollywood system turning dross into pure gold. TS DVD

Rita Hayworth *Gilda Mundson* • Glenn Ford *Johnny Farrell* • George Macready *Ballin Mundson* • Joseph Calleia *Obregon* • Steven Geray *Uncle Pio* • Joe Sawyer *Casey* • Gerald Mohr *Captain Delgado* ■ *Dir* Charles Vidor • *Scr* Marion Parsonnet, Jo Eisinger, from a story by EA Ellington

The Gilded Cage ★★

Thriller 1954 · UK · BW · 78mins

After a string of supporting roles for Universal in the early 1950s, Alex Nicol earned a dubious promotion to leading man in this British thriller, co-starring Clifford Evans. Director John Gilling tries to push this tale of art theft and murder along at a decent pace, but spotting who framed Nichol's brother is hardly taxing. DP

Alex Nicol *Steve Anderson* • Veronica Hurst *Marcia Farrell* • Clifford Evans *Ken Aimes* • Ursula Howells *Brenda Lucas* • Elwyn Brook-Jones *Bruno* • John Stuart *Harding* • Michael Alexander *Harry Anderson* • Trevor Reid *Inspector Brace* ■ *Dir* John Gilling • *Scr* Brock Williams, from a story by Paul Erickson

The Gilded Lily ★★★

Screwball comedy 1935 · US · BW · 82mins

This frothy Paramount comedy rode in on the back of the phenomenal success of Columbia's *It Happened One Night*. Critics and public alike were quick to make the connection with this new vehicle for Claudette Colbert. She's delightful as a New York secretary having to make up her mind between two suitors: a charming, wealthy but caddish English aristocrat (Ray Milland) and a standard-issue American newspaper reporter (Fred MacMurray). Deftly directed by Wesley Ruggles, the movie launched MacMurray to stardom, while raising Milland's Hollywood profile. RK

Claudette Colbert *Lillian David* • Fred MacMurray *Peter Dawes* • Ray Milland *Charles Gray/Granville* • C Aubrey Smith *Lloyd Granville* • Eddie Craven *Eddie* • Luis Alberni *Nate* • Donald Meek *Hankerson* ■ *Dir* Wesley Ruggles • *Scr* Claude Binyon, from a story by Melville Baker, Jack Kirkland

Gimme Shelter ★★★★ 15

Music documentary
1970 · US · Colour · 91mins

Rightly considered to be more of a 1960s watershed than Woodstock, the free concert given by the Rolling Stones at the Altamount Speedway in northern California will always be remembered for revealing the flip side of the decade of love and peace. The murder of a black spectator by a Hell's Angels bouncer during *Under My Thumb* and the violence that followed pervades this documentary, most memorably in the scene in which Mick Jagger and Charlie Watts view the incident on an editing machine. But there is also some mesmerising footage of the Stones, Jefferson Airplane and the Flying Burrito Brothers, and a slyly mocking portrait of showbiz lawyer Melvin Belli. DP [video]

Dir David Maysles, Albert Maysles, Charlotte Zwerin

Ginger & Fred ★★★★★ PG

Satirical comedy
1986 · It/Fr/W Ger · Colour · 127mins

Ginger Rogers tried to sue the production company behind this masterpiece from the great Italian director Federico Fellini – a move that now seems astonishingly myopic. The film itself pays tribute to Ginger; it also meditates on urban decay (exemplified by television's down-market values) while affirming the warmth of past love. Marcello Mastroianni and Guilietta Massina (Fellini's wife) play two elderly dancers who, having discreetly modelled themselves on Astaire and Rogers, are brought out of retirement for a TV show. Fellini's attack on tacky telly is as comic as it is wounding, but Mastroianni and Massina show that human emotion can win the day. TH. In Italian with English subtitles. [video]

Giulietta Masina *Amelia Bonetti, "Ginger"* • Marcello Mastroianni *Pippo Botticella, "Fred"* • Franco Fabrizi *Show host* • Frederick von Ledenburg *Admiral* • Augusto Poderosi *Transvestite* • Martin Maria Blau *Assistant producer* • Jacques Henri Lartigue *Flying priest* ■ *Dir* Federico Fellini • *Scr* Federico Fellini, Tonino Guerra, Tullio Pinelli

Ginger in the Morning ★★ PG

Road movie romance
1973 · US · Colour · 90mins

A young Sissy Spacek plays the titular Ginger – a gangly, free-spirited teenage hitch-hiker who gets a ride from lonely travelling salesman Monte Markham. This road movie slides effortlessly into a romance, as the unlikely mutual attraction between the conservative Joe and the wild child Ginger grows apace. However, although the landscape is lovely, the action is minimal. FL [video]

Monte Markham *Joe* • Sissy Spacek *Ginger* • Slim Pickens *Sheriff* • Mark Miller *Charlie* • Susan Oliver *Sugar* ■ *Dir* Gordon Wiles • *Scr* Mark Miller

Ginger Snaps ★★★★ 18

Horror 2000 · Can · Colour · 103mins

Director John Fawcett's highly sophisticated and disturbing horror gem avoids the popular tendency to parody. Teenager Katharine Isabelle is attacked by the legendary "Beast of Bailey Downs" and goes from being a death-obsessed Goth freak to a sexually charged dominatrix. Too terrified to confide in their home-loving mother (Mimi Rogers on fine form), and not wanting to go to the police when Isabelle's lust turns murderously savage, her younger sister Emily Perkins turns to enigmatic drug dealer Kris Lemche for help. Fawcett expertly puts the werewolf myth into the tortured adolescence melting pot and keeps the suspense high and the humour engaging in this wonderfully crafted chiller. Two less successful sequels followed. AJ. Contains sex scenes, violence, swearing. [video] DVD

Emily Perkins *Brigitte* • Katharine Isabelle *Ginger* • Kris Lemche *Sam* • Mimi Rogers *Pamela* • Jesse Moss *Jason* • Danielle Hampton *Trina* ■ *Dir* John Fawcett • *Scr* Karen Walton, from a story by Karen Walton, John Fawcett

The Gingerbread Man ★★★ 15

Thriller 1997 · US · Colour · 109mins

Robert Altman directs this conventional adaptation of a John Grisham story set in Savannah, Georgia. Kenneth Branagh brings a touch of bravado to the role of successful lawyer Rick Magruder, who becomes involved with a waitress (Embeth Davidtz) when she accuses her religious fanatic father (Robert Duvall) of pursuing her. Soon Branagh feels compelled to kidnap his own children to save them from danger, while the menacing atmosphere grows along with the threat of impending floods. TH. Contains swearing. [video] DVD

Kenneth Branagh *Rick Magruder* • Embeth Davidtz *Mallory Doss* • Robert Downey Jr *Clyde Pell* • Daryl Hannah *Lois Harlan* • Robert Duvall *Dixon Doss* • Tom Berenger *Pete Randle* • Famke Janssen *Leeanne* • Clyde Hayes *Carl Alden* ■ *Dir* Robert Altman • *Scr* Al Hayes, from a story by John Grisham

The Girl ★★★ 18

Erotic thriller
1986 · Swe/UK · Colour · 103mins

The seduction of a leading lawyer by a 14-year-old schoolgirl is the focus of this soft-core slice of Euro erotica. Seduction leads to lust, passion and murder, though not necessarily in that order. Starring Franco Nero and Bernice Stegers, with Christopher Lee in a small supporting role, the film starts strongly in a *Lolita* vein, but then the pace slackens. Oodles of sex and nudity, though, for those who like that sort of thing. DA [video]

Clare Powney *Pat, the girl* • Franco Nero *John Berg* • Bernice Stegers *Eva Berg* • Frank Brennan *Lindberg, reporter* • Mark Robinson *Hans, cab driver* • Clifford Rose *General Carlsson* • Rosie Jauckens *Mrs Carlsson* • Christopher Lee *Peter Storm* ■ *Dir* Arne Mattsson • *Scr* Ernest Hotch

Girl ★★★ 15

Comedy drama 1998 · US · Colour · 95mins

After a very promising comic start, in which the camera tracks down a suburban American street showing every garage full of aspiring but terrible teen rock bands, this quickly disintegrates and enters predictable territory. Dominique Swain stars as a high school girl on the verge of adulthood, who sleeps with ultra-cool, egocentric rock god Sean Patrick Flanery and must then work through her disillusionment when she realises he's a selfish pig. Very much a debut feature, this offers nothing original. LH. Contains swearing. [video] DVD

Dominique Swain *Andrea Marr* • Sean Patrick Flanery *Todd Sparrow* • Summer Phoenix *Rebecca Farnhurst* • Tara Reid *Cybil* • Selma Blair *Darcy* • Channon Roe *Kevin* • Portia Di Rossi [Portia de Rossi] *Carla* • Rosemary Forsyth *Mother* ■ *Dir* Jonathan Kahn • *Scr* David E Tolchinsky, from the novel by Blake Nelson

The Girl ★★ 15

Thriller 1999 · Fr/US · Colour · 83mins

With its mournful voiceover, lazy jazz score and casual shots of Paris, Sande Zeig's lesbian *noir* has all the attributes of a stylish tale of danger and deceit. But the pacing of its contrived storyline exposes the artifice of the dialogue and the limitations of the cast. Agatha de la Boulaye particularly struggles to bring to life the suit-clad American art student who risks her relationship with musician Sandra N'Kake to pursue a passion with chanteuse Claire Keim. DP. In English and French with subtitles. [video] DVD

Claire Keim *The girl* • Agatha de la Boulaye *The narrator* • Cyril Lecomte *The man* • Sandra N'Kake *Bu Save* • Ronald Guttman *Bartender* • Cyrille Hertel *Bodyguard* ■ *Dir* Sande Zeig • *Scr* Monique Wittig, Sande Zeig, from a story by Monique Wittig

The Girl and the General ★★

First World War drama
1967 · It/Fr · Colour · 103mins

Rod Steiger gives a lazy performance in this mediocre period drama. Clearly there's Method in his madness, but he often seems to be in a totally different movie from his co-stars, Virna Lisi and Umberto Orsini, as a peasant girl and a scheming soldier who kidnap a First World War general for a thousand lira reward. Nothing impresses about this Carlo Ponti production, not even the score by Ennio Morricone. DP. Italian dialogue dubbed into English.

Rod Steiger *General* • Virna Lisi *Ada* • Umberto Orsini *Private Tarasconi* • Toni Gaggia *Lieutenant* • Marco Mariani *Corporal* ■ *Dir* Pasquale Festa Campanile • *Scr* Luigi Malerba, Pasquale Festa Campanile, from a story by Massimo Franciosa, Pasquale Festa Campanile

A Girl Called Rosemarie ★★

Drama based on a true story
1996 · Ger · Colour · 133mins

Nina Hoss stars as a teenage delinquent whose habit of sleeping her way out of trouble resulted in her (still unsolved) murder. There's a wealth of plot to pack in, yet director Bernd Eichinger manages to locate the drama in an authentically seedy Frankfurt underworld, where Hoss encounters both blackmailing pimp Til Schweiger and mysterious Frenchman Mathieu Carrière. Accomplished, but detached. DP. In German with English subtitles.

Nina Hoss *Rosemarie Nitribitt* • Heiner Lauterbach *Hartog* • Mathieu Carrière *Fribert* • Horst Krause *Bruster* • Hannelore Elsner *Marga* • Katja Flint *Christine* • Til Schweiger *Nadler* ■ *Dir* Bernd Eichinger • *Scr* Bernd Eichinger, Uwe Wilhelm

The Girl Can't Help It ★★★★ U

Satirical musical comedy
1956 · US · Colour · 97mins

Witty, stylish, clever and (by today's standards) extraordinarily sexist, this hilarious satire on the juke-box industry is the rock 'n' roll movie *par excellence*. Pneumatic Jayne Mansfield is supported (if that's the word) by more than a dozen major music acts, including Little Richard, Eddie Cochran, Fats Domino and Gene Vincent. But director Frank Tashlin's viewpoint is pure acid, and only balladeer Julie London is filmed without cynicism. The use of CinemaScope is exemplary, and the movie is a perfect 1950s piece. TS [video] DVD

Tom Ewell *Tom Miller* • Jayne Mansfield *Jerri Jordan* • Edmond O'Brien *Murdock* • Henry Jones *Mousey* • John Emery *Wheeler* • Juanita Moore *Hilda* ■ *Dir* Frank Tashlin • *Scr* Frank Tashlin, Herbert Baker

Girl Crazy ★★★ U

Musical comedy 1943 · US · BW · 98mins

A magnificent George and Ira Gershwin score and the teaming of the fabulous Judy Garland with the irrepressible Mickey Rooney make this worth seeing. Admittedly, its attitudes have dated badly and, despite Garland looking lovelier than ever, the Rooney/Garland romance really doesn't gel. This was the second version of the Gershwin musical, first filmed in 1932. It was remade in 1965 as *When the Boys Meet the Girls*. TS

Mickey Rooney *Danny Churchill Jr* • Judy Garland *Ginger Gray* • Gil Stratton *Bud Livermore* • Robert E Strickland *Henry Lathrop* • Rags Ragland *"Rags"* • June Allyson *Speciality* • Nancy Walker *Polly Williams* • Guy Kibbee *Dean Phineas Armour* ■ *Dir* Norman Taurog • *Scr* Fred F Finklehoffe, Sid Silvers, Dorothy Kingsley, William Ludwig, from the play by George Gershwin, Ira Gershwin, Guy Bolton, Jack McGowan

G

The Girl from Manhattan ★★ U

Comedy drama 1948 · US · BW · 81mins

A scene-stealing turn from Charles Laughton as a saintly bishop is the highlight of this amiable, but mawkish comedy. Returning to her home town to find that uncle Ernest Truex's boarding house faces demolition, New York model Dorothy Lamour locks horns with the Reverend George Montgomery, who wants to build a new church on the land. However, they soon come to join forces against crooked property developer, Howard Freeman. There's little chemistry between Lamour and Montgomery. DP

Dorothy Lamour *Carol Maynard* • George Montgomery *Rev Tom Walker* • Charles Laughton *The Bishop* • Ernest Truex *Homer Purdy* • Hugh Herbert *Aaron Goss* • Constance Collier *Mrs Brooke* • William Frawley *Mr Bernouti* ■ *Dir* Alfred E Green • *Scr* Howard Estabrook

The Girl from Mexico ★

Comedy 1939 · US · BW · 71mins

Lupe Velez revived her Hollywood screen career with this limp slapstick comedy that exploited her tempestuous Latin image. She's hired by Donald Woods's advertising executive to sing on the radio in New York and sneaks out on the town with Leon Errol's Uncle Matt, shouting herself hoarse at a wrestling match and ruining her audition the next day. The film went down so well with American small-town audiences that it started the *Mexican Spitfire* series, which starred Lupe and Leon Errol. AE

Lupe Velez *Carmelita Fuentes* • Donald Woods *Dennis Lindsey* • Leon Errol *Uncle Matt* • Linda Hayes *Elizabeth Price* • Donald MacBride *Renner* • Edward Raquello *Tony Romano* • Elisabeth Risdon *Aunt Della* • Ward Bond *Mexican Pete* ■ *Dir* Leslie Goodwins • *Scr* Lionel Houser, Joseph A Fields, from a story by Lionel Houser

The Girl from Missouri ★★★

Romantic comedy 1934 · US · BW · 71mins

Anita Loos (*Gentlemen Prefer Blondes*) co-scripted this sharp, witty comedy, which stars blonde bombshell Jean Harlow, Franchot Tone and comedian Patsy Kelly. The women play a couple of chorus-line girls on the lookout for husbands, with Harlow determined to snare a millionaire while preserving her virginity until the right man comes along. Spirited entertainment, this has an excellent supporting cast. RK

Jean Harlow *Eadie Chapman* • Lionel Barrymore *TR Paige* • Franchot Tone *T "Tom" R Paige Jr* • Lewis Stone *Frank Cousins* • Patsy Kelly *Kitty Lennihan* • Alan Mowbray *Lord Douglas* • Clara Blandick *Miss Newberry* ■ *Dir* Jack Conway • *Scr* Anita Loos, John Emerson

The Girl from Paris ★★★ 15

Comedy drama
2001 · Fr/Bel · Colour · 98mins

Christian Carion's debut feature not only benefits from the striking Rhône-Alp scenery, but also the slow-burning chemistry between testy widower Michel Serrault and Mathilde Seigner, the disillusioned Parisienne who buys his rundown farm and transforms it into a thriving business. The insights into the agricultural year have undeniable charm, but there's also much to provoke in Carion's astute consideration of the need to temper tradition with change. Pitched between gritty realism and pastoral idyll, this is most satisfying. DP. In French with English subtitles. DVD

Michel Serrault *Adrien Rochas* • Mathilde Seigner *Sandrine Dumez* • Jean-Paul Roussillon *Jean Farjon* • Frédéric Pierrot *Gérard Chauvin* • Marc Berman *Stéphane* ■ *Dir* Christian Carion • *Scr* Christian Carion, Eric Assous

The Girl from Petrovka ★

Romantic comedy
1974 · US · Colour · 104mins

Goldie Hawn and Anthony Hopkins adopt thick Russian accents for this pathetic Cold War comedy. La Hawnska grows disenchanted with life in Russia and is romanced by American foreign correspondent Hal Holbrook. Hopkins is a black marketeer, a sort of Harry Lime figure. Subplots proliferate, but the story goes nowhere quickly. AT

Goldie Hawn *Oktyabrina* • Hal Holbrook *Joe* • Anthony Hopkins *Kostya* • Grégoire Aslan *Minister* • Anton Dolin *Ignatievitch, ballet master* • Bruno Wintzell *Alexander* • Zoran Andric *Leonid* • Hanna Hertelendy *Judge* ■ *Dir* Robert Ellis Miller • *Scr* Allan Scott, Chris Bryant, from the novel by George Feifer

Girl from Rio ★★ 15

Comedy 2001 · UK/Sp · Colour · 103mins

Writer/director Christopher Monger attempts to re-create that unique Ealing atmosphere with this tale of two cities, with the help of José Luis Alcaine's astute cinematography. But the film lapses into low farce as the location shifts from London to Rio. Hugh Laurie begins in admirably hangdog style as a cuckolded banker who finds his sole release in dance. Once he makes for Brazil, however, his character becomes a mere victim of circumstance – he's hurtled around Rio by taxi driver Santiago Segura in pursuit of the loot purloined from him by samba sensation Vanessa Nunes. Genial, but uninspired. DP

Hugh Laurie *Raymond* • Vanessa Nunes *Orlinda* • Santiago Segura *Paulo* • Lia Williams *Cathy* • Patrick Barlow *Strothers* • Nelson Xavier *Bichero* ■ *Dir* Christopher Monger • *Scr* Christopher Monger, from a screenplay (unproduced) by Francisco Lara, Julián Ibáñez

The Girl from 10th Avenue ★★★

Drama 1935 · US · BW · 68mins

A smashing first starring vehicle for wide-eyed Bette Davis, who grabs this daft melodrama between her teeth and never lets go. She's an honest working girl straightening out an alcoholic society type, while coping with the nuisance of a female nemesis who wants her man back. Bette remains unfazed, of course, and this leads to a verbal baiting, which precipitates a newspaper story causing the marriage to topple. It's great tosh, terrifically directed at a smart pace by Alfred E Green, who would later steer La Davis to her first Oscar with *Dangerous*. TS

Bette Davis *Miriam Brady* • Ian Hunter *Geoffrey Sherwood* • Colin Clive *John Marland* • Alison Skipworth *Mrs Martin* • John Eldredge *Hugh Brown* • Philip Reed *Tony Hewlett* ■ *Dir* Alfred E Green • *Scr* Charles Kenyon, from the play *Outcast* by Hubert Henry Davies

Girl Happy ★★ PG

Musical 1965 · US · Colour · 90mins

This is one of Elvis Presley's weaker vehicles and a sign that worse was to come. The King plays a rock 'n' roll musician doubling up as a chaperone for mobster's daughter Shelley Fabares. Presley displays his customary charm and gives those remarkable tonsils a real work-out on generally unworthy material. TS

Elvis Presley *Rusty Wells* • Shelley Fabares *Valerie Frank* • Harold J Stone *Big Frank* • Gary Crosby *Andy* • Joby Baker *Wilbur* • Nita Talbot *Sunny Daze* • Mary Ann Mobley *Deena* • Fabrizio Mioni *Romano* ■ *Dir* Boris Sagal • *Scr* Harvey Bullock, RS Allen

The Girl He Left Behind ★★★ U

Comedy 1956 · US · BW · 103mins

Studio chief Jack L Warner must have had high hopes of Tab Hunter and Natalie Wood as new stars, teaming them in both the western *The Burning Hills* and this army comedy. Under the direction of veteran David Butler, Hunter is well cast as a spoiled, insufferable and unwilling draftee in the peace-time army, who itches to get back to the girl he left behind (Wood). The comedy is familiar stuff, the film is overlong, but Wood is vivacious. AE

Tab Hunter *Andy Shaeffer* • Natalie Wood *Susan Daniels* • Jessie Royce Landis *Madeline Shaeffer* • Jim Backus *Sergeant Hanna* • Henry Jones *Hanson* • Murray Hamilton *Sergeant Clyde* • Alan King *Maguire* • James Garner *Preston* • David Janssen *Captain Genaro* ■ *Dir* David Butler • *Scr* Guy Trosper, from the novel by Marion Hargrove

The Girl Hunters ★★

Mystery thriller 1963 · UK · BW · 97mins

Author Mickey Spillane plays his own creation, hard-boiled private eye Mike Hammer, in this all-American B-movie that, for tax reasons, was based and financed in Britain. Little is made of a promising plot about murder and corruption in American politics, while Spillane is shown to have more ego than acting talent. British starlet Shirley Eaton plays a blonde *femme fatale* who, fatally, doesn't know one end of a shotgun from the other. AT

Mickey Spillane *Mike Hammer* • Shirley Eaton *Laura Knapp* • Scott Peters *Pat Chambers* • Hy Gardner • Lloyd Nolan *Art Rickerby* • Guy Kingsley Poynter *Dr Larry Snyder* • James Dyrenforth *Bayliss Henry* ■ *Dir* Roy Rowland • *Scr* Roy Rowland, Robert Fellows, from the novel by Mickey Spillane

A Girl in a Million ★★

Comedy 1946 · UK · BW · 91mins

An object lesson in how tastes change, this chauvinistic comedy made a star of Joan Greenwood in a role that basically dismisses women as blethering nuisances who should be seen and not heard. Having just escaped a shrewish wife, scientist Hugh Williams considers Greenwood the perfect mate, as she's been shell-shocked into silence. However, she recovers her speech once married and that's the start of the troubles. DP

Hugh Williams *Tony* • Joan Greenwood *Gay* • Basil Radford *Prendergast* • Naunton Wayne *Fotheringham* • Wylie Watson *Peabody* ■ *Dir* Francis Searle • *Scr* Sydney Box, Muriel Box

The Girl in a Swing ★

Thriller 1988 · UK/US · Colour · 117mins

An interminable and incomprehensible suspense thriller, long on atmosphere but short on sense, about an antiques dealer who, while on business abroad, becomes besotted with a German girl and quickly weds her. He ignores the fact that she's prone to delusions and other bizarre behaviour. A wilfully and irritatingly odd film. DA

Meg Tilly *Karin Foster* • Rupert Frazer *Alan* • Nicholas Le Prevost *The Vicar* • Elspet Gray *Mrs Dresland* • Lorna Heilbron *Flick* • Claire Shepherd *Angela* • Jean Boht *Mrs Taswell* • Sophie Thursfield *Deirdre* ■ *Dir* Gordon Hessler • *Scr* Gordon Hessler, from the novel by Richard Adams

The Girl in Black Stockings ★★

Murder mystery 1957 · US · BW · 75mins

Murder in a ritzy Utah resort hotel – with voluptuous blonde Mamie Van Doren as one of the female victims – places crippled hotel owner Ron Randell, his loving sister Marie Windsor, lawyer Lex Barker and a young Anne Bancroft under suspicion. Sheriff John Dehner investigates. Howard W Koch directs this efficient whodunnit, which has its roots in the Agatha Christie-style formula of having contrasting characters walled up in a confined location who all appear to have a motive to kill. RK

Lex Barker *David Hewson* • Anne Bancroft *Beth Dixon* • Mamie Van Doren *Harriet Ames* • Ron Randell *Edmund Parry* • Marie Windsor *Julia Parry* • John Dehner *Sheriff Holmes* • John Holland *Norman Grant* • Diana Vandervlis [Diana Van Der Vlis] *Louise Miles* ■ *Dir* Howard W Koch • *Scr* Richard Landau, from the story *Wanton Murder* by Peter Godfrey

A Girl in Every Port ★★

Silent comedy 1928 · US · BW

Director Howard Hawks would go on to better things, such as *Bringing Up Baby* and *To Have and Have Not*. This late silent-era vehicle for beefy Victor McLaglen is nobody's finest hour. The title tells the story: sailors McLaglen and Robert Armstrong chase women, date women and brawl over women during their travels around the four corners of the globe. Coarse-grained and only mildly amusing, the film's best episode features the always extraordinary Louise Brooks. RK

Victor McLaglen *Spike Madden* • Maria Casajuana *Chiquita* • Natalie Joyce *Girl in Panama* • Dorothy Mathews *Girl in Panama* • Elena Jurado *Girl in Panama* • Louise Brooks *Marie, girl in France* • Francis McDonald *Gang leader* • Phalba Morgan *Lena, girl in Holland* • Robert Armstrong *Salami* ■ *Dir* Howard Hawks • *Scr* Howard Hawks, Seton I Miller, from the story by James Kevin McGuinness

A Girl in Every Port ★ U

Comedy 1952 · US · BW · 82mins

A dire experience for Groucho Marx enthusiasts, as he appears with a real moustache and without his brothers, scouring the horizon for non-existent laughlines. The low-budget farce casts him as a fast-talking sailor, with William Bendix as his dim-witted pal. The pair try to put over a horse-race scam involving two identical nags, one fast and the other slow. AE

Groucho Marx *Benny Linn* • Marie Wilson *Jane Sweet* • William Bendix *Tim Dunnevan* • Don DeFore *Bert Sedgwick* • Gene Lockhart *Garvey* • Dee Hartford *Millicent* • Hanley Stafford *Navy Lieutenant* • Teddy Hart *"High Life"* ■ *Dir* Chester Erskine • *Scr* Chester Erskine, from the story *They Sell Sailors Elephants* by Frederick Hazlitt Brennan

Girl in the Headlines ★★★

Crime drama 1963 · UK · BW · 93mins

This sleazy whodunnit could have been compiled from a random leaf through the Sunday scandal sheets. At times it seems as if every known vice has been woven into the labyrinthine plot, which centres on the efforts of cop Ian Hendry to prise clues to the identity of a model's killer out of her friends and family. Hendry's commitment and the Watsonesque support of his sergeant (Ronald Fraser) keep you curious. DP

Ian Hendry *Inspector Birkett* • Ronald Fraser *Sergeant Saunders* • Margaret Johnston *Mrs Gray* • Natasha Parry *Perlita Barker* • Jeremy Brett *Jordan Barker* • Kieron Moore *Herter* • Peter Arne *Hammond Barker* • Jane Asher *Lindy Birkett* • Rosalie Crutchley *Maude Klein* ■ *Dir* Michael Truman • *Scr* Vivienne Knight, Patrick Campbell, Laurence Payne

The Girl in the News ★★★

Murder mystery 1940 · UK · BW · 78mins

Carol Reed churns out this workmanlike if rather transparent murder mystery. Margaret Lockwood heads a starry British cast as a nurse, whose patients have the unfortunate habit of dying after being poisoned. It's a pretty thankless role and she adequately performs the task of looking bewildered and persecuted. DP

Margaret Lockwood *Anne Graham* • Barry K Barnes *Stephen Farringdon* • Emlyn Williams *Tracy* • Roger Livesey *Bill Mather* • Margaretta Scott *Judith Bentley* • Wyndham Goldie *Edward Bentley* • Irene Handl *Miss Blaker* ■ *Dir* Carol Reed • *Scr* Sidney Gilliat, from the novel by Roy Vickers

The Girl in the Picture ★★ U

Crime drama 1956 · UK · BW · 63mins

Probably best known for his work at Disney in the 1960s, director Don Chaffey was still cutting his teeth on British B-movies when he completed this lacklustre thriller. The girl of the title is Junia Crawford, whom crime reporter Donald Houston is convinced holds the key to the murder story he's covering. As mysteries go, this is on the elementary side. DP

Donald Houston *John Deering* • Patrick Holt *Inspector Bliss* • Maurice Kaufmann *Rod Molloy* • Junia Crawford *Pat Dryden* • Paddy Joyce *Jack Bates* • John Miller *Duncan* ■ *Dir* Don Chaffey • *Scr* Paul Rogers

The Girl in the Picture ★★★ 15

Romantic comedy
1985 · UK · Colour · 84mins

John Gordon-Sinclair is the awkward wedding photographer who falls in and out of love with the beautiful Irina Brook. It never quite captures the quirky charm of Gordon-Sinclair's hit *Gregory's Girl*, but the playing in this gentle comedy is superb and it remains thoroughly enjoyable in an unassuming way. JF

John Gordon-Sinclair *Alan* • Irina Brook *Mary* • David McKay *Ken* • Gregor Fisher *Bill* • Caroline Guthrie *Annie* • Paul Young *Smiley* • Rikki Fulton *Minister* ■ *Dir/Scr* Cary Parker

The Girl in the Red Velvet Swing ★★ PG

Historical crime drama
1955 · US · Colour · 108mins

Remembered as the Hollywood debut, amid a fanfare of publicity, of Joan Collins, whose "come hither" charms are its chief focus, this is a suspect retelling of the notorious murder of the brilliant American architect Stanford White in 1906. He was shot in full view of the Manhattan crowds by Harry K Thaw, the unstable husband of White's mistress, showgirl Evelyn Nesbit. This is a superficial soap opera exercise. The young Collins makes a flashy and inadequate Nesbit, but Ray Milland is convincing. Visually excellent, though. RK

Ray Milland *Stanford White* • Joan Collins *Evelyn Nesbit Thaw* • Farley Granger *Harry K Thaw* • Luther Adler *Delphin Delmas* • Cornelia Otis Skinner *Mrs Thaw* • Glenda Farrell *Mrs Nesbit* • Frances Fuller *Mrs White* ■ *Dir* Richard Fleischer • *Scr* Walter Reisch, Charles Brackett

The Girl in White ★★ U

Biographical drama 1952 · US · BW · 93mins

From MGM – a studio with an ongoing devotion to hospital drama – comes this biopic adapted from Dr Emily Dunning's autobiography. Recounting her experiences as the first woman to storm the male bastions of medical practice in the slums of New York at the turn of the last century, the movie's only real narrative surprise – and its major mistake – is the miscasting of sunny girl-next-door June Allyson as the tough-minded medical pioneer. RK

June Allyson *Dr Emily Dunning* • Arthur Kennedy *Dr Ben Barringer* • Gary Merrill *Dr Seth Pawling* • Mildred Dunnock *Dr Marie Yeomans* • Jesse White *Alec* • Marilyn Erskine *Nurse Jane Doe* ■ *Dir* John Sturges • *Scr* Philip Stevenson, Allen Vincent, Irmgard von Cube, from the non-fiction book *Bowery to Bellevue: the Story of New York's First Woman Ambulance Surgeon* by Emily Dunning Barringer

Girl, Interrupted ★★★ 15

Drama based on a true story
1999 · US · Colour · 122mins

Set in a New England psychiatric institution in 1967, director/co-writer James Mangold's commendable drama has a similar agenda to Milos Forman's Oscar-winning classic *One Flew over the Cuckoo's Nest*, but never quite reaches the same peaks of poignancy. Mangold makes clever use of jarring narrative cuts to convey Winona Ryder's confused state of mind, Oscar winner Angelina Jolie is mesmerising as a pushy, pouting troublemaker, and Whoopi Goldberg does her best work in ages as a no-nonsense nurse. Well-intentioned but lightweight. JC. Contains swearing and sex scenes. DVD

Winona Ryder *Susanna Kaysen* • Angelina Jolie *Lisa* • Brittany Murphy *Daisy* • Clea DuVall *Georgina* • Whoopi Goldberg *Valerie* • Jeffrey Tambor *Dr Potts* • Jared Leto *Tobias Jacobs* • Vanessa Redgrave *Dr Wick* ■ *Dir* James Mangold • *Scr* Anna Hamilton Phelan, James Mangold, Susan Shilliday, Lisa Loomer, from the memoirs of Susanna Kaysen

Girl Loves Boy ★

Drama 1937 · US · BW · 77mins

Not a very original title – but the action is even less inspired. This halting melodrama stars Eric Linden, who gets his just desserts after he spurns the love of perky Cecilia Parker and chooses a gold-digging girl instead. This takes an eternity to reach its obvious conclusion. DP

Eric Linden *Robert Conrad* • Cecilia Parker *Dorothy McCarthy* • Roger Imhof *Charles Conrad* • Dorothy Peterson *Mrs McCarthy* • Pedro De Cordoba *Signor Montefiori* • Bernadene Hayes *Sally* • Rollo Lloyd *Dr Williams* ■ *Dir* Duncan Mansfield • *Scr* Duncan Mansfield, Carroll Graham

The Girl Most Likely ★★★ U

Musical comedy 1957 · US · Colour · 94mins

A winsome musical remake of the 1941 RKO Ginger Rogers hit *Tom, Dick and Harry*, this is a stylish, fun musical, albeit in a minor key. It's the last feature of veteran Mitchell Leisen, directed with wit and verve, and well served by some super choreography from the great Gower Champion. Jane Powell is perfect as the girl who can't choose a mate, and comedian Kaye Ballard is terrific in her first movie as Powell's best friend. The guys are lightweight but charming. TS

Jane Powell *Dodie* • Cliff Robertson *Pete* • Keith Andes *Neil* • Kaye Ballard *Marge* • Tommy Noonan *Buzz* • Una Merkel *Mom* • Kelly Brown *Sam* ■ *Dir* Mitchell Leisen • *Scr* Paul Jarrico (uncredited), Devery Freeman, from a story by Paul Jarrico (uncredited)

A Girl Named Tamiko ★★

Romantic drama
1962 · US · Colour · 110mins

Tough-guy director John Sturges was never really comfortable with melodrama. However, who could blame him for wanting to work in exotic Tokyo locations with lovely France Nuyen under the auspices of veteran producer Hal B Wallis? The film stars Laurence Harvey as a Russo-Chinese photographer who stops at nothing to get a US visa. It's all well made; unfortunately, it's also turgid, intractable and empty. That said, the solid cast helps make it watchable. TS

Laurence Harvey *Ivan Kalin* • France Nuyen *Tamiko* • Martha Hyer *Fay Wilson* • Gary Merrill *Max Wilson* • Michael Wilding *Nigel Costairs* • Miyoshi Umeki *Eiko* • Steve Brodie *James Hatten* • Lee Patrick *Mary Hatten* ■ *Dir* John Sturges • *Scr* Edward Anhalt, from a novel by Ronald Kirkbride

The Girl Next Door ★★★ U

Musical comedy 1953 · US · Colour · 91mins

Dan Dailey is always a pleasure to watch, his easy-going screen persona reflecting a versatile talent and likeable personality that was too often wasted in lightweight vehicles such as this. He stars as a cartoonist whose quiet life is disrupted when chanteuse June Haver moves in next door. There's nice support from crooner Dennis Day, best remembered from Jack Benny's TV and radio shows, and from the under-rated Cara Williams. TS

Dan Dailey *Bill Carter* • June Haver *Jeannie* • Dennis Day *Reed Appleton* • Billy Gray *Joe Carter* • Cara Williams *Rosie* • Natalie Schafer *Evelyn* • Clinton Sundberg *Samuels* • Hayden Rorke *Fields* ■ *Dir* Richard Sale • *Scr* Isobel Lennart, from a story by L Bush-Fekete [Ladislaus Bus-Fekete], Mary Helen Fay

The Girl Next Door ★★★ 15

Comedy 2004 · US · Colour · 104mins

The first half of this boisterous comedy plays like a hackneyed "boy meets girl" yarn, as nerdy high school over-achiever Emile Hirsch falls for his gorgeous new neighbour (Elisha Cuthbert), only to discover she's a former porn star. It's cliché-ridden nonsense, but then in a welcome shift, teen fodder suddenly turns into *Risky Business*-style hilarity. With likeable performances adding to the youthful vitality, the end result is an endearingly daft romp. SF. Contains swearing and sexual references. DVD

Emile Hirsch *Matthew Kidman* • Elisha Cuthbert *Danielle* • Timothy Olyphant *Kelly* • James Remar *Hugo Posh* • Chris Marquette [Christopher George Marquette] *Eli* • Paul Dano *Klitz* • Timothy Bottoms *Mr Kidman* • Donna Bullock *Mrs Kidman* ■ *Dir* Luke Greenfield • *Scr* Stuart Blumberg, David T Wagner, Brent Goldberg, from a story by David T Wagner, Brent Goldberg

The Girl of the Golden West ★★★ U

Musical 1938 · US · Sepia · 120mins

For its hit team of Jeanette MacDonald and Nelson Eddy, MGM bought the rights to a hoary old David Belasco stage melodrama. More than satisfactory for the duo's followers but hardly innovative in any way, this features MacDonald as the saloon proprietor in love with Eddy's dashing bandit and the object of sheriff Walter Pidgeon's affections. Sigmund Romberg and Gus Kahn wrote the score for the film. AE

Jeanette MacDonald *Mary Robbins* • Nelson Eddy *Ramerez/Lt Johnson* • Walter Pidgeon *Sheriff Jack Rance* • Leo Carrillo *Mosquito* • Buddy Ebsen *Alabama* • Leonard Penn *Pedro* • Priscilla Lawson *Nina Martinez* • Bob Murphy *Sonora Slim* ■ *Dir* Robert Z Leonard • *Scr* Isabel Dawn, Boyce DeGaw, from the play by David Belasco

Girl of the Night ★★

Drama 1960 · US · BW · 90mins

Anne Francis makes the most of her role as a reluctant prostitute relating her seamy adventures to oh-so-earnest psychiatrist Lloyd Nolan. She hopes these sessions will help her change her life. Presented as a "medical case history", this was quite outspoken for its time, athough it seems fairly tame today. The girl's tale, told in flashback, makes for dull viewing. RB

Anne Francis *Bobbie* • Lloyd Nolan *Dr Mitchell* • Kay Medford *Rowena* • John Kerr *Larry* • Arthur Storch *Jason Franklin Jr* • James Broderick *Dan Bolton* • Lauren Gilbert *Mr Shelton* • Eileen Fulton *Lisa* ■ *Dir* Joseph Cates • *Scr* Ted Berkman, Raphael Blau, from the book *The Call Girl* by Dr Harold Greenwald

The Girl of Your Dreams ★★★ 15

Period comedy 1998 · Sp · Colour · 110mins

Set in the aftermath of the Civil War, this perceptive comedy follows the misadventures of a Spanish film unit as it embarks upon a prestigious co-production at the legendary German UFA studios. Much of the attention is focused on the attempts of Spanish star Penélope Cruz to avoid the attentions of the lecherous Goebbels (Johannes Silberschneider). But director Fernando Trueba is also keen to explore the nature of propaganda and the ostensible differences between Franco and Hitler's brands of fascism. The final descent into farce is laboured and trite, but the political observations are astutely presented. DP. In Spanish and German with English subtitles. DVD

Penélope Cruz *Macarena Granada* • Antonio Resines *Blas Fontiveras* • Neus Asensi *Lucia Gandia* • Jesús Bonilla *Bonilla* • Loles Leon *Trini Moreno* • Jorge Sanz *Julian Torralba* • Hanna Schygulla *Magda Goebbels* • Johannes Silberschneider *Goebbels* ■ *Dir* Fernando Trueba • *Scr* Rafael Azcona, David Trueba, Carlos Lopez, Manuel Angel Egea

The Girl on a Motorcycle ★★★ 15

Romantic drama
1968 · UK/Fr · Colour · 86mins

This quintessential 1960s movie catches Marianne Faithfull on the cusp between beauty and seedy decline. She is required to do little more than sneer, pout and wrap her leather-encased limbs around said bike, but this image alone reduced a generation of males to pop-eyed slavering wrecks. The plot is as wafer thin but, with its gallery of cinematic icons of the day, the movie is still a delicious-looking curiosity. SH. Contains swearing, sex scenes and nudity. DVD

Marianne Faithfull *Rebecca* • Alain Delon *Daniel* • Roger Mutton *Raymond* • Marius Goring *Rebecca's father* • Catherine Jourdan *Catherine* • Jean Leduc *Jean* ■ *Dir* Jack Cardiff • *Scr* Ronald Duncan, Gillian Freeman, from the novel *La Motocyclette* by Andre Pieyre de Mandiargues

Girl on Approval ★★★

Drama 1962 · UK · BW · 79mins

This pithy little feature was made by Eyeline Films for the then-new British film company Bryanston. About the angst of foster parenting, this film provides excellent roles for the hitherto under-used Rachel Roberts and suave James Maxwell as the parents, and Annette Whitley as the lass up for fostering. Perhaps a little too self-consciously worthy, it is most interesting today for its view of the mores and fashions of what feels like a bygone age. TS

Rachel Roberts (1) *Anne Howland* • James Maxwell *John Howland* • Annette Whitley *Sheila* • John Dare *Stephen Howland* • Ellen McIntosh *Mary Gardner* • Michael Clarke *William Howland* ■ *Dir* Charles Frend • *Scr* Kathleen White, Kenneth Cavander, from a story by Kathleen White

The Girl on the Boat ★★ U

Comedy 1962 · UK · BW · 89mins

Norman Wisdom tried something different from his usual slapstick with this seagoing comedy romance taken from a story by PG Wodehouse. It doesn't work for Wisdom, though it does for the less mannered professionals in support such as Richard Briers, Millicent Martin and Athene Seyler. It bombed at the box office and Wisdom must have thought he could do nothing right. TH

Norman Wisdom *Sam* • Millicent Martin *Billie Bennett* • Richard Briers *Eustace Hignett* • Sheila Hancock *Jane* • Bernard Cribbins *Peters* • Athene Seyler *Mrs Hignett* • Philip Locke *Bream Mortimer* • Noel Willman *Webster* ■ *Dir* Henry Kaplan • *Scr* Reuben Ship, from the novel by PG Wodehouse

The Girl on the Bridge ★★★ 15

Romantic drama 1999 · Fr · BW · 87mins

Middle-aged knife thrower Daniel Auteuil talks the elfin Vanessa Paradis out of jumping off a bridge into the Seine, turning her desperation to his advantage by hiring her as his assistant. Their relationship deepens, and darkens, as they tour the south of France, although romance is hampered by the flings she has at every port of call – not to mention the daggers he flings at her every night. With Marianne Faithfull warbling on the soundtrack and sumptuous visuals from Jean-Marie Dreujou, this is an elegant, nostalgic treat that's short enough to leave you wanting more. NS. In French with English subtitles.

Vanessa Paradis *Adèle* • Daniel Auteuil *Gabor* • Demetre Georgalas *Takis* • Isabelle Petit-Jacques *The bride* • Frederic Pfluger *The contortionist* ■ *Dir* Patrice Leconte • *Scr* Serge Frydman

Girl on the Run ★★ U

Crime thriller 1958 · US · BW · 77mins

A programme filler that utilises the roster of contract actors Warner Bros built up for its many TV series in the 1950s and early 1960s. Made for US television but released in cinemas outside the USA as a supporting feature, this serves as a showcase for suave charmer Efrem Zimbalist Jr (from the studio's phenomenally successful television show *77 Sunset Strip*). His co-star here is Erin O'Brien, whose career never really took off. A pleasant enough crime thriller that's inoffensive, short and nothing special. TS

Efrem Zimbalist Jr *Stuart Bailey* • Erin O'Brien *Kathy Allen/Karen Shay* • Shepperd Strudwick *McCullough* • Edward Byrnes [Edd Byrnes] *Smiley* • Barton MacLane *Brannigan* • Ray Teal *Lieutenant Harper* • Vince Barnett *Janitor* ■ *Dir* Richard L Bare • *Scr* Marion Hargrove, from a story by Roy Huggins

Girl Rush ★★

Musical comedy 1944 · US · BW · 64mins

This B-movie is a real curio, so it's a shame it isn't very good. Alan Carney and Wally Brown are the two vaudevillians stranded during the gold rush days in San Francisco. A look down the cast list reveals a young Robert Mitchum in a minor role, showing little promise of the great screen career to come. The leading lady is sexy singer Frances Langford, and ditzy Vera Vague has some moments, but overall it's just daft. TS

Wally Brown *Jerry Miles* • Alan Carney *Mike Strager* • Frances Langford *Flo Daniels* • Robert Mitchum *Jimmy Smith* • Vera Vague [Barbara Jo Allen] *Suzie Banks* • Paul Hurst *Muley* • Patti Brill *Claire* • Sarah Padden *Emma* ■ *Dir* Gordon Douglas • *Scr* Robert E Kent, from a story by Laszlo Vadnay, Aladar Laszlo

The Girl Rush ★★★ U

Musical comedy 1955 · US · Colour · 84mins

Rosalind Russell goes to Las Vegas to claim her inheritance in a hotel but things aren't quite what they seem. Her hotel is on the skids thanks to the efforts of James Gleason and Russell is labouring under the impression that she owns half of another establishment – actually owned by Fernando Lamas. This needs a brassier personality than Russell. TH

Rosalind Russell *Kim Halliday* • Fernando Lamas *Victor Monte* • Eddie Albert *Elliot Atterbury* • Gloria DeHaven *Taffy Tremaine* • Marion Lorne *Aunt Clara* • James Gleason *Ether Ferguson* ■ *Dir* Robert Pirosh • *Scr* Robert Pirosh, Jerome Davis, from a story by Henry Ephron, Phoebe Ephron

Girl Shy ★★★★★ U

Silent comedy 1924 · US · BW · 88mins

The two sides of Harold Lloyd's screen persona are evident in this classic silent comedy. In the first half, Lloyd's inimitable Everyman pins his hopes of advancement on his book entitled "The Secrets of Making Love". Lloyd's timid tailor's assistant wins the heart of Jobyna Ralston, but he loses her to sleazy bigamist Carlton Griffin when his manuscript is rejected. However, when the publisher changes his mind, Lloyd shifts into fearless mode and hurtles across town using every means of transport he can commandeer to prevent Ralston's wedding. Lloyd's genius illuminates this breathtaking chase, which is both frantic and hilarious, thanks in no small part to the precision of the editing. DP

Harold Lloyd *Harold Meadows, the Poor Boy* • Jobyna Ralston *Mary Buckingham, the Rich Girl* • Richard Daniels *Jerry Meadows, the Poor Man* • Carlton Griffith *Ronald Devore, the Rich Man* ■ *Dir* Fred C Newmeyer, Sam Taylor • *Scr* from a story by Ted Wilde, Tim Whelan, Tommy Gray, Sam Taylor

Girl 6 ★★★★ 18

Comedy drama 1996 · US · Colour · 103mins

This light-hearted tale is free from the preachy philosophising often associated with film-maker Spike Lee. Theresa Randle gives the performance of her life as a struggling actress who decides to join a phone-sex agency after being asked to strip for casting director Quentin Tarantino. She becomes addicted to the buzz she gets from her conversations, as she takes on a variety of characters in order to feed the fantasies of her callers. This film lays itself wide open to every politically incorrect charge you could level at it, yet Lee comments on society's dual standards with regard to sexploitation without detracting from the humour of the piece. DP. Contains swearing, nudity.

Theresa Randle *Girl 6* • Isaiah Washington *Shoplifter* • Spike Lee *Jimmy* • Jenifer Lewis *Boss 1, Lil* • Debi Mazar *Girl 39* • Peter Berg *Caller 1, Bob* • Michael Imperioli *Scary caller 30* • Dina Pearlman *Girl 19* • Naomi Campbell *Girl 75* • Gretchen Mol *Girl 12* • Madonna *Boss 3* • John Turturro *Murray the agent* ■ *Dir* Spike Lee • *Scr* Suzan-Lori Parks

The Girl Who Had Everything ★

Crime drama 1953 · US · BW · 69mins

Elizabeth Taylor was hot from *Ivanhoe* and *A Place in the Sun* when MGM squandered her talents in this tepid remake of its torrid 1931 hit *A Free Soul*. Liz lacks the abandon required for the role of the spoiled daughter of a prosperous criminal lawyer who falls for his gangster client, Fernando Lamas. As the lawyer William Powell remains as suave as ever in his last role for the studio, while Lamas struggles with the part of the shady Romeo. Under Richard Thorpe's static direction the film didn't work and was pared down to B-feature length. AE

Elizabeth Taylor *Jean Latimer* • Fernando Lamas *Victor Y Ramondi* • William Powell *Steve Latimer* • Gig Young *Vance Court* • James Whitmore *Charles "Chico" Menlow* • Robert Burton *John Ashmond* • William Walker *Julian* • Harry Bartell *Joe* ■ *Dir* Richard Thorpe • *Scr* Art Cohn, from the novel *A Free Soul* by Adela Rogers St John

The Girl Who Knew Too Much ★★ U

Spy drama 1969 · US · Colour · 96mins

There's no sign of a Joker or a Riddler as the former Caped Crusader takes on the Red Menace. *Batman*'s Adam West stars in this spy film as an ex-CIA man who comes out of retirement to investigate communist infiltration of the mob. Nancy Kwan and Buddy Greco co-star. The Cold War theme seems very dated now and this is one of many non-classics on West's CV. TH

Adam West *Johnny Cain* • Nancy Kwan *Revel Drue* • Nehemiah Persoff *Lieutenant Crawford* • Buddy Greco *Lucky Jones* • Robert Alda *Kenneth Allardice* • Patricia Smith *Tricia Grinaldi* • David Brian *Had Dixon* ■ *Dir* Francis D Lyon • *Scr* Charles Wallace

Girl with a Pearl Earring ★★★★ 12

Period drama
2003 · UK/Lux/US · Colour · 95mins

British director Peter Webber makes an astonishing feature debut with this ravishing period drama. Based on the bestselling novel by Tracy Chevalier, it's an imaginary reconstruction of the story behind 17th-century Dutch master Johannes Vermeer's celebrated painting *Girl with a Pearl Earring*. Scarlett Johansson gives a heartbreakingly brilliant portrayal of Vermeer's housemaid and eventual muse. Drawn to the secretive artist (a brooding Colin Firth), she finds head and heart colliding to costly effect. The cinematography is intoxicating, transforming every detailed frame into a richly coloured *tableau vivant*, while Alexandre Desplat's beautiful score adds extra intensity. SF DVD

Colin Firth *Johannes Vermeer* • Scarlett Johansson *Griet* • Tom Wilkinson *Van Ruijven* • Judy Parfitt *Maria Thins* • Cillian Murphy *Pieter* • Essie Davis *Catharina Vermeer* • Joanna Scanlan *Tanneke* • Alakina Mann *Cornelia Vermeer* ■ *Dir* Peter Webber • *Scr* Olivia Hetreed, from the novel by Tracy Chevalier • *Cinematographer* Eduardo Serra

The Girl with Brains in Her Feet ★★★ 15

Comedy drama 1997 · UK · Colour · 98mins

This endearing coming-of-age tale, set in Leicester, centres on a fleet-footed 13-year-old schoolgirl whose career in athletics seems set to run and run. But only weeks before a major sports meet, she veers off track as a result of the twin distractions of adolescent angst and a dysfunctional home life. The film's feel of the real, plus sterling performances from its cast of relative unknowns, more than compensate for the enigmatic and off-putting title. DA

Amanda Mealing *Vivienne Jones* • Joanna Ward *Jacqueline "Jack" Jones* • Jamie McIntosh *"Poor Bastard"* • Jodie Smith *Maxine* • Richard Claxton *Steve Green* • John Thomson *Mr Loughborough* • Gareth Tudor-Price *Mr Roundhead* ■ *Dir* Roberto Bangura • *Scr* Jo Hodges

Girl with Green Eyes ★★★★ PG

Romantic drama 1963 · UK · BW · 92mins

This sensitive tale of opposites is blessed with a highly literate script and affecting performances. Rita Tushingham and Lynn Redgrave play the shopgirls who share a room but little else, until they meet shy writer Peter Finch. The decline in their relationship, as it transpires he prefers the mousey Tushingham to the blowsy Redgrave, is conveyed with great skill. Debutant director Desmond Davis wisely allows the cast to go about their business and captures the atmosphere of Dublin with the eye of an experienced cinematographer. DP

Peter Finch *Eugene Gaillard* • Rita Tushingham *Kate Brady* • Lynn Redgrave *Baba Brenan* • Marie Kean *Josie Hannigan* • Arthur O'Sullivan *Mr Brady* • Julian Glover *Malachi Sullivan* • TP McKenna *Priest* • Lislott Goettinger *Joanna* ■ *Dir* Desmond Davis • *Scr* Edna O'Brien, from her novel *The Lonely Girl*

The Girl with Red Hair ★★★ PG

Second World War drama
1981 · Neth · Colour · 113mins

The redhead in question is Hannie Schaft, a vigilante member of the Dutch resistance whose unconventional methods often brought her into conflict with her own superiors, as well as the Nazis. Renée Soutendijk plays her as an ordinary woman whose fierce patriotism drives her to abandon her ambitions and conquer a distaste for violence in order to become a ruthless killing machine. Debutant Ben Verbong directs with dignity and justified anger, but occasionally allows his generally intelligent depiction to lapse into cliché. DP. In Dutch with English subtitles.

Renée Soutendijk *Hannie Schaft* • Peter Tuinman *Hugo* • Ada Bouwman *Tinka* • Robert Delhez *Floor* • Johan Leysen *Frans* • Loes Luca *An* • Adrian Brine *German Officer* • Lineke Rijxman *Judith* ■ *Dir* Ben Verbong • *Scr* Ben Verbong, Pieter De Vos, from the novel by Theun De Vries

Girlfight ★★★★ 15

Sports drama 2000 · US · Colour · 106mins

Effortlessly linking an intense look at the lot of inner-city misfits, a fierce family drama and a sweetly engaging romance, debut director Karyn Kusama's boxing story is a lot more than a female *Rocky* set in an ultra-macho Latino landscape. Michelle Rodriguez, giving an inspiring if scary performance, enrols for fight lessons at the local male-dominated gym, and starts a tentative relationship with fellow boxer Santiago Douglas. But their burgeoning affair is put to the test when they're forced to fight in a gender-blind competition. This tense situation stays remarkably free of cliché and builds to a powerfully moving epiphany. AJ DVD

Michelle Rodriguez *Diana Guzman* • Jaime Tirelli *Hector* • Paul Calderon *Sandro Guzman* • Santiago Douglas *Adrian* • Ray Santiago *Tiny Guzman* ■ *Dir/Scr* Karyn Kusama

Girlfriends ★★★★

Comedy drama 1978 · US · Colour · 87mins

Claudia Weill directs what is a significant landmark in both women's film-making and American independent cinema. Smashing cosy studio stereotypes, she creates the kind of single women who might really dwell in rented apartments rather than exist solely in the hazy imagination of a Hollywood screenwriter. As wannabe photographer Susan, Melanie Mayron is fresh, honest and vulnerable, whether she's trying to break into the New York art scene or discussing men with her soon-to-be-married flatmate, Anita Skinner. Lightly played, keenly observed and superbly understated. DP

Melanie Mayron *Susan Weinblatt* • Eli Wallach *Rabbi Gold* • Anita Skinner *Anne Munroe* • Bob Balaban *Martin* • Christopher Guest *Eric* • Gina Rogak *Julie* • Amy Wright *Ceil* ■ *Dir* Claudia Weill • *Scr* Vicki Polon, from a story by Claudia Weill, Vicki Polon

Les Girls ★★★ U

Musical 1957 · US · Colour · 109mins

This late MGM musical was selected for its year's Royal Film Performance, and there was much discussion about how the Queen would relate to a sexy musical about the British upper classes in Paris. Others wondered how British audiences would get the point of a send-up of Marlon Brando's *The Wild One* when the original was still banned in Britain. Today it's fun to watch, risqué and disarming, but not really sophisticated enough. The girls are delightful, and Gene Kelly is as watchable as ever. Director George Cukor seems uncomfortable with the material, though, and the Cole Porter score is disappointing. TS

Gene Kelly *Barry Nichols* • Mitzi Gaynor *Joy Henderson* • Kay Kendall *Lady Wren* • Taina Elg *Angele Ducros* • Jacques Bergerac *Pierre Ducros* • Leslie Phillips *Sir Gerald Wren* • Henry Daniell *Judge* • Patrick Macnee *Sir Percy* ■ *Dir* George Cukor • *Scr* John Patrick, from a story by Vera Caspary

Girls about Town ★★

Comedy drama 1931 · US · BW · 80mins

This curiosity from George Cukor's early career hardly stacks up against the director's later work, but it shows clear signs of his legendary skill with actresses in the vivacious performances of Kay Francis and Lilyan Tashman. The duo play gold-diggers who enjoy a lavish lifestyle courtesy of the businessmen they "entertain". Joel McCrea is well cast as the rich sucker from out of town who wants to marry Francis. The film pre-dates the Hays Office clampdown on morality in Hollywood, which explains the relative latitude in plot and dialogue. AE

Kay Francis *Wanda Howard* • Joel McCrea *Jim Baker* • Lilyan Tashman *Marie Bailey* • Eugene Pallette *Benjamin Thomas* • Alan Dinehart *Jerry Chase* • Lucille Webster Gleason *Mrs Benjamin Thomas* • Anderson Lawler *Alex Howard* • George Barbier *Webster* ■ *Dir* George Cukor • *Scr* Raymond Griffith, Brian Marlow, from a story by Zoe Akins

Girls at Sea ★ U

Comedy 1958 · UK · Colour · 80mins

The cast in this tepid comedy does its level best to pep up the tired material, but there's only so much you can do with a story in which a captain has to keep his admiral from discovering three girls stranded on board after a dockside party. Ronald Shiner is cheeky and Michael Hordern is absent-mindedly authoritarian, but Guy Rolfe is as wooden as a figurehead. DP

Guy Rolfe *Captain* • Ronald Shiner *Marine Ogg* • Michael Hordern *Admiral Hewitt* • Alan White *Commander* • Anne Kimbell *Mary* • Nadine Tallier *Antoinette* • Fabia Drake *Lady Hewitt* • Mary Steele *Jill* • Teddy Johnson *Singer* ■ *Dir* Gilbert Gunn • *Scr* Gilbert Gunn, TJ Morrison, Walter C Mycroft, from the play *The Middle Watch* by Stephen King-Hall, Ian Hay

Girls Can Play ★

Crime drama 1937 · US · BW · 59mins

Rita Hayworth was several years away from her defining role in *Gilda* when she appeared in this forgettable B-movie. The plot bizarrely revolves around booze racketeer John Gallaudet and the female baseball team that represents one of his more legitimate business interests. When one of the girls is murdered, dull-witted cop Guinn Williams is assigned to the case. AE

Jacqueline Wells [Julie Bishop] *Ann Casey* • Charles Quigley *Jimmy Jones* • Rita Hayworth *Sue Collins* • John Gallaudet *Foy Harris* • George McKay *Sluggy* • Patricia Farr *Peanuts* • Guinn "Big Boy" Williams *Lt Flannigan* • Joseph Crehan *Brophy* ■ *Dir* Lambert Hillyer • *Scr* Lambert Hillyer, from a story by Albert DeMond

Girls Can't Swim ★★★ 15

Drama 1999 · Fr · Colour · 97mins

Subtle shifts in tone and contrasts in character are key to the success of writer/director Anne-Sophie Birot's assured feature debut. By delaying teenager Karen Alyx's arrival on the Breton coast, Birot builds up a one-sided picture of her friendship with the extrovert Isild Le Besco, who's been carried away by the temptations of post-school adolescence, while her intense, but manipulative friend mourns the death of her estranged father in Paris. Both leads impress, but there's also discreet support from Pascale Bussières and Marie Rivière as their mothers. DP. In French with English subtitles. [video] DVD

Isild Le Besco *Gwen* • Karen Alyx *Lise* • Pascale Bussières *Céline* • Pascal Elso *Alain* • Marie Rivière *Anne-Marie* • Yelda Reynaud *Solange* ■ *Dir/Scr* Anne-Sophie Birot

Girls! Girls! Girls! ★★★ U

Musical 1962 · US · Colour · 94mins

One of Presley's more enjoyable romps, this has colourful locations, a serviceable (though silly) plot and the usual attractive co-stars, including cult sex bomb Stella Stevens, who also gets to sing. Elvis plays a tuna boat fisherman in Hawaii who shows his underlying toughness in a brief but particularly revealing scene in which he tries to seduce rich girl Laurel Goodwin. The hit song was the superb *Return to Sender* and the rest of the score is quite bearable. TS [video] DVD

Elvis Presley *Ross Carpenter* • Stella Stevens *Robin Gantner* • Jeremy Slate *Wesley Johnson* • Laurel Goodwin *Laurel Dodge* • Benson Fong *Kin Yung* • Robert Strauss *Sam* • Guy Lee *Chen Yung* • Frank Puglia *Alexander Stavros* ■ *Dir* Norman Taurog • *Scr* Edward Anhalt, Allan Weiss, from a story by Allan Weiss

Girls in Uniform ★★★★

Drama 1931 · Ger · BW · 110mins

This landmark in gay cinema may no longer scandalise, but it remains a touching love story, as neurotic Hertha Thiele falls under the spell of teacher Dorothea Wieck, her only source of solace in a cold Prussian boarding school. Demonstrating a sympathetic understanding of the misery of teenage isolation, director Leontine Sagan also emphasises the importance of the individual in a society still ruled by the code of militarist uniformity. This subtly subversive picture was banned by the Nazis and many of its key personnel were forced into exile. DP. In German with English subtitles.

Emilia Unda *The Principal* • Dorothea Wieck *Fraulein von Bernburg* • Hedwig Schlichter *Fraulein von Kesten* • Hertha Thiele *Manuela von Meinhardie* • Ellen Schwannecke *Ilse von Westhagen* ■ *Dir* Leontine Sagan • *Scr* Christa Winsloe, FD Andam, from the play *Gestern und Heute* by Christa Winsloe

Girls Just Want to Have Fun ★★★ PG

Musical comedy 1985 · US · Colour · 88mins

American teen flicks are never short of clichés, and this musical comedy is no exception, packing in most of the genre conventions on the way to its wildly over-the-top, all-dancing finale. However, a confident performance by Sarah Jessica Parker rescues this outing from obscurity. She convincingly plays a high-school student who incurs her father's wrath by entering a dance competition. JM [video] DVD

Sarah Jessica Parker *Janey Glenn* • Helen Hunt *Lynne Stone* • Lee Montgomery *Jeff Malene* • Shannen Doherty *Maggie Malene* • Biff Yeager *Mr Malene* • Morgan Woodward *JP Sands* • Jonathan Silverman *Drew* ■ *Dir* Alan Metter • *Scr* Amy Spies

Girls' Night ★★★★ 15

Comedy drama
1997 · UK/US · Colour · 98mins

This comedy drama enables Brenda Blethyn to give another demonstration of everywoman bravura. She stars alongside Julie Walters, who matches Blethyn in every scene. The pair play two northern girls who work in an electrics factory and have been friends since school. When Walters discovers Blethyn has cancer, she decides to take her pal to Las Vegas. There they meet cowboy Kris Kristofferson and embark on an adventure to remember. Impressive and moving. JB. Contains sex scenes, swearing. [video] DVD

Brenda Blethyn *Dawn Wilkinson* • Julie Walters *Jackie Simpson* • Sue Cleaver *Rita* • Kris Kristofferson *Cody* • Meera Syal *Carmen* • Margo Stanley *Irene* • Maggie Tagney *Anne Marie* • George Costigan *Steve Wilkinson* ■ *Dir* Nick Hurran • *Scr* Kay Mellor

Girls' Town ★

Drama 1959 · US · BW · 92mins

After her questionable lifestyle involves her in the death of a young guy, bad girl Mamie Van Doren is sent to a correctional institution run by nuns. Trading off Van Doren's brassy, suggestive voluptuousness, the movie brings to mind a whole lexicon of adjectives, such as sleazy, tawdry and trashy. Its only point of interest is the inclusion of such musical luminaries as Mel Tormé, Paul Anka and The Platters in the cast. RK

Mamie Van Doren *Silver Morgan* • Mel Tormé *Fred Alger* • Paul Anka *Jimmy Parlow* • Ray Anthony *Dick Culdane* • Maggie Hayes [Margaret Hayes] *Mother Veronica* • Cathy Crosby *Singer* • Gigi Perreau *Serafina Garcia* • Elinor Donahue *Mary Lee Morgan* • Harold Lloyd Jr *Chip Gardner* ■ *Dir* Charles Haas • *Scr* Robert Smith, from a story by Robert Hardy Andrews

Girls Town ★★★ 15

Drama 1996 · US · Colour · 89mins

Made on a shoestring and largely improvised by the impressive ensemble, Jim McKay's small-town drama begins with a chillingly subtle opening sequence, in which evidence of a rape is planted in the soundtrack. From then on, however, it is inexorably drawn into melodrama, as three high school seniors decide to avenge the suicide of their best friend. Single mum Lili Taylor holds things together, with her relationship with abusive boyfriend John Ventimiglia providing greater dramatic interest than her antics with Bruklin Harris and Anna Grace. The plotting is shaky, but the dialogue rings true. DP [video]

Aunjanue Ellis *Nikki* • Bruklin Harris *Angela* • Anna Grace *Emma* • Lili Taylor *Patti Lucci* • Ramya Pratt *Tomy Lucci* • Asia Minor *Marlys Giovanni* • John Ventimiglia *Eddie* ■ *Dir* Jim McKay • *Scr* Jim McKay, Anna Grace, Bruklin Harris, Lili Taylor, Denise Casano

Giro City ★★★

Thriller 1982 · UK · Colour · 102mins

Glenda Jackson lends her talents to this social thriller, but not to much effect. Writer/director Karl Francis's film follows two members of a British investigative documentary team as they consider the plight of a Welsh farmer facing eviction, before going on to look into the activities of the IRA. But they end up having to compromise, in a film that has its heart is in the right place but lacks the substance or artistry to do its subjects justice. TH

Glenda Jackson *Sophie* • Jon Finch *O'Mally* • Kenneth Colley *Martin* • James Donnelly *James* • Emrys James *Tommy Williams* • Karen Archer *Brigitte* • Simon Jones *Henderson* • Huw Ceredig *Elwyn Davies* ■ *Dir/Scr* Karl Francis

Give a Girl a Break ★★★ U

Musical 1953 · US · Colour · 82mins

Directed by Stanley Donen and co-choreographed by Gower Champion, this is an enjoyable diversion from MGM's stable of musical talent and offers several dazzling dance routines to compensate for the totally unmemorable score. Champion plays the director of a forthcoming Broadway show from which the temperamental leading lady departs in a huff. The search for a replacement results in three possible contenders: mature Marge Champion (Gower's old flame and first choice); balletic Helen Woods (supported by the show's composer, Kurt Kasznar); and ingénue Debbie Reynolds, whose cause is championed by Gower's assistant, Bob Fosse. RK

Marge Champion *Madelyn Corlane* • Gower Champion *Ted Sturgis* • Debbie Reynolds *Suzy Doolittle* • Helen Wood *Joanna Moss* • Bob Fosse *Bob Dowdy* • Kurt Kasznar *Leo Belney* • Richard Anderson *Burton Bradshaw* • William Ching *Anson Pritchett* ■ *Dir* Stanley Donen • *Scr* Albert Hackett, Frances Goodrich, from a story by Vera Caspary • *Choreographer* Gower Champion, Stanley Donen

Give 'em Hell, Harry! ★★★

Comedy drama 1975 · US · Colour · 102mins

Actor James Whitmore's successful one-man show as US President Harry S Truman toured extensively in the USA and was brought to the screen by director Steve Binder. The timing seemed to be propitious. Richard Nixon was in disgrace after Watergate and Whitman's portrayal of Truman harked back to an era of cleaner, nobler politics. The 33rd US President, Truman was in office from 1945-53, ordering the bombing of Hiroshima and steering America through postwar prosperity and the first years of the Cold War. As for Whitmore, his virtuoso performance earned him an Oscar nomination. The film was recorded and edited together from two live performances in Seattle. AT

James Whitmore *Harry S Truman* ■ *Dir* Steve Binder • *Scr* Samuel Gallu

Give My Regards to Broad Street ★★ PG

Musical 1984 · UK · Colour · 108mins

Widely condemned as a worthless ego trip, Paul McCartney's musical fantasy is a great idea for a concept video that had the misfortune to be made into a feature film. The plot – about an ex-con and some missing tapes – is negligible, the references to Fellini's *8½* are laughable, and some of the musical sequences lack inspiration. However, fans will enjoy the Beatles classics and newer songs, such as *Ballroom Dancing*. DP [video]

Paul McCartney *Paul* • Bryan Brown *Steve* • Ringo Starr *Ringo* • Barbara Bach *Journalist* • Linda McCartney *Linda* • Tracey Ullman *Sandra* • Ralph Richardson *Jim* • George Martin (2) *Record producer* ■ *Dir* Peter Webb • *Scr* Paul McCartney • *Music* Paul McCartney

Give My Regards to Broadway ★★★ U

Musical 1948 · US · Colour · 88mins

Broadway movies with backstage emotions boiling over and the show going on regardless are a sub-genre all of their own, and this is one of the most amiable, even if it lacks the usual abundance of big production numbers. Charles Winninger is the old-timer who refuses to accept that the vaudeville tradition has had its day, and devotes his energy towards putting his children on the stage. Dan Dailey, as Winninger's son, proves yet again what a versatile actor he was. TH

Dan Dailey *Bert* • Charles Winninger *Albert* • Nancy Guild *Helen* • Charlie Ruggles [Charles Ruggles] *Toby* • Fay Bainter *Fay* • Barbara Lawrence *June* • Jane Nigh *May* • Charles Russell *Arthur Waldron Jr* • Sig Rumann [Sig Ruman] *Dinkel* ■ *Dir* Lloyd Bacon • *Scr* Samuel Hoffenstein, Elizabeth Reinhardt, from a story by John Klempner

Give Us the Moon ★★★ U

Comedy 1944 · UK · BW · 95mins

Made during the Second World War but set in the postwar future, this unusual British comedy is based on a Caryl Brahms and SJ Simon novel about a Soho club founded by a group of idlers who refuse to work. The satire is slight, but co-screenwriter and director Val Guest keeps it moving along nicely, and there's terrific work from stars Margaret Lockwood, Vic Oliver and Peter Graves. There's also a wonderfully brash performance from 14-year-old Jean Simmons as Lockwood's sister, demonstrating her future star quality. TS

Margaret Lockwood *Nina* • Vic Oliver *Sascha* • Peter Graves (1) *Peter Pyke* • Roland Culver *Ferdinand* • Max Bacon *Jacobus* • Frank Cellier *Pyke* • Jean Simmons *Heidi* • Irene Handl *Miss Haddock* ■ *Dir* Val Guest • *Scr* Val Guest, Howard Irving Young, Caryl Brahms, SJ Simon, from the novel *The Elephant Is White* by Caryl Brahms, by SJ Simon

Give Us This Day ★★

Drama 1949 · UK · BW · 119mins

Sam Wanamaker plays an Italian bricklayer in Brooklyn, whose dreams of owning his own house are brought crashing down by his naivety and the Depression. This movie pleads for our sympathy and every point is driven home with sledgehammer obviousness – it freely advertises its left-wing credentials because it was shot and financed in Britain. The director and writer had both been blacklisted as a result of the McCarthy witch-hunts – Dmytryk having already served a year in prison – and were living in exile along with Wanamaker who, though never blacklisted himself, thought it prudent to leave America. AT

Sam Wanamaker *Geremio* • Lea Padovani *Annunziata* • Kathleen Ryan *Kathleen* • Charles Goldner *Luigi* • Bonar Colleano *Julio* • William Sylvester *Giovanni* • Nino Pastellides *The Lucy* ■ *Dir* Edward Dmytryk • *Scr* Ben Barzman, from the novel *Christ in Concrete* by Pietro Di Donato

Give Us Tomorrow ★

Thriller 1978 · UK · Colour · 94mins

In trying to re-create the tension of a hostage situation following a bungled bank job, writer/director Donovan Winter shies away from portraying intimidation and human drama and instead plunges us into a risible debate on the iniquities of the class system. Derren Nesbitt's villain is far less scary than Sylvia Syms's affronted suburbanite. Hopeless. DP

Sylvia Syms *Wendy Hammond* • Derren Nesbitt *Ron* • James Kerry *Martin Hammond* • Donna Evans *Nicola Hammond* • Matthew Haslett *Jamie Hammond* • Alan Guy *Boy* • Victor Brooks *Superintendent* • Derek Anders *Inspector* ■ *Dir/Scr* Donovan Winter

The Given Word ★★★★

Drama 1962 · Bra · BW · 98mins

This scathing attack on the Brazilian Catholic Church is often claimed as a key entry in the *cinema nôvo* movement. But, with its theatrical structuring and traditional visuals, it owes more to the *chanchada* tradition of comic melodrama. However, the story of the farmer who vows to carry a cross to the local chapel in thanks for the recovery of his donkey still has the power to move and provoke. Director Anselmo Duarte exposes the unholy alliance of social corruption, political indolence and media manipulation that conspires to repress the impoverished people of Bahia. DP. In Portuguese with English subtitles.

Leonardo Vilar *Ze* • Gloria Menezes *Rosa* • Dionisio Azevedo *Father Olavo* • Norma Bengell *Marli* • Geraldo Del Rey *Bonitao/ "Handsome"* • Roberto Ferreira *Dede* • Othon Bastos *Reporter* • Gilberto Marques *Galego* ■ *Dir* Anselmo Duarte • *Scr* Anselmo Duarte, from the play *O Pagador de Promessas* by Alfredo Dias Gomes

The Gladiator ★★★ U

Comedy 1938 · US · BW · 72mins

The character Joe E Brown plays in this mischievous adaptation of Philip Wylie's novel was, allegedly, the inspiration for Superman. However, instead of being a repressed alien, Brown plays Hugo Kipp, a college weakling who allows himself to be injected with Lucien Littlefield's strength serum in order to become a football hero and subsequently impress both co-ed June Travis and his scathingly macho pa. Edward Sedgwick handles the slapstick with apolomb. DP

Joe E Brown *Hugo Kipp* • AJ "Man Mountain" Dean *Man Mountain Dean* • June Travis *Iris Bennett* • Dickie Moore *Bobby* • Lucien Littlefield *Prof Abner Danner* • Robert Kent *Tom Dixon* • Ethel Wales *Mrs Matilda Danner* ■ *Dir* Edward Sedgwick • *Scr* George Marion, Charlie Melson, James Mulhauser, Arthur Sheekman, Earle Snell, from a novel by Philip Wylie

Gladiator ★★★ 15

Action drama 1992 · US · Colour · 97mins

Cuba Gooding Jr plays a streetwise teenager who, along with alumnus James Marshall, is lured into the world of illegal boxing by a memorably sleazy Brian Dennehy. The plot is riddled with clichés, but this is much grittier territory than the airbrushed world of the *Rocky* films. The two leads are aided by a talented line-up of fine character actors, including John Heard, Robert Loggia and Ossie Davis. JF. Contains violence, swearing, nudity. DVD

James Marshall *Tommy Riley* • Cuba Gooding Jr *Lincoln* • Brian Dennehy *Jimmy Horn* • Robert Loggia *Pappy Jack* • Ossie Davis *Noah* • John Heard *John Riley* • Jon Seda *Romano* ■ *Dir* Rowdy Herrington • *Scr* Lyle Kessler, Robert Mark Kamen

Gladiator ★★★★★ 15

Period epic 2000 · US · Colour · 148mins

Ridley Scott and the boys from DreamWorks produced the first genuine Roman epic since 1964's *The Fall of the Roman Empire* with this virtual remake that deals with the transition of power from the sage-like Marcus Aurelius to his monstrous son, Commodus. The fictional hero, General Maximus, is Caesar's adopted heir, whom Commodus turns into an exile after killing his family. Becoming a gladiator, Maximus fights to avenge his loved ones and save the soul of Rome. The film's strengths are a fine script and excellent performances from Richard Harris and Oliver Reed, in his final film. Also superb is Joaquin Phoenix as the paranoid Commodus, while Russell Crowe is utterly convincing as the Conan/Spartacus-like hero. As always with Scott, the visuals are fabulous. AT. Contains violence. DVD

Russell Crowe *Maximus Decimus Meridius* • Joaquin Phoenix *Commodus* • Connie Nielsen *Lucilla* • Oliver Reed *Proximo* • Derek Jacobi *Gracchus* • Djimon Hounsou *Juba* • Richard Harris *Marcus Aurelius* • David Schofield *Falco* • John Shrapnel *Gaius* ■ *Dir* Ridley Scott • *Scr* David Franzoni, John Logan, William Nicholson, from a story by David Franzoni • *Cinematographer* John Mathieson

Glamour ★★

Melodrama 1934 · US · BW · 74mins

Ambitious chorus girl Constance Cummings becomes a successful Broadway star and leaves her husband Paul Lukas for her younger stage partner Phillip Reed. Everything is hunky-dory until Reed, in turns, dumps her. It's a trite tale, the only redeeming feature of which is the presence of the stylish, skilful and persuasive Constance Cummings, who is always worth watching. Otherwise this minor melodrama shows little sign of being directed by William Wyler. RK

Paul Lukas *Victor Banki* • Constance Cummings *Linda Fayne* • Phillip Reed [Philip Reed] *Lorenzo Valenti* • Doris Lloyd *Nana* • Joseph Cawthorn *Carl Ibsen* ■ *Dir* William Wyler • *Scr* Doris Anderson, Gladys Unger, LG Blochman, from the short story by Edna Ferber

The Glass Bottom Boat ★★★ U

Romantic comedy 1966 · US · Colour · 110mins

Doris Day shows a surprising affinity for satire in this Cold War spoof, starring as a publicist in a space laboratory who's falling in love with engineer boss Rod Taylor while writing a biography of him. Various governments are interested in Taylor's work and, as Day has a dog called Vladimir, she quickly becomes a Soviet suspect. Director Frank Tashlin was a former cartoonist and packs the film with sight gags, but Day rises above the slapstick. TH

Doris Day *Jennifer Nelson* • Rod Taylor *Bruce Templeton* • Arthur Godfrey *Axel Nordstrom* • John McGiver *Ralph Goodwin* • Paul Lynde *Homer Cripps* • Edward Andrews *General Wallace Bleecker* • Eric Fleming *Edgar Hill* • Dom DeLuise *Julius Pritter* • Robert Vaughn *Napoleon Solo* ■ *Dir* Frank Tashlin • *Scr* Everett Freeman

The Glass Cage ★

Crime drama 1955 · UK · BW · 75mins

John Ireland, best known for playing heavies in Hollywood B-movies, was lured to Britain for this low-budget crime drama. It's a promising but ultimately bungled yarn about a circus performer called the "Starving Man" (Eric Pohlmann) who fasts for a living. When he is found dead in his glass cage, investigations reveal that he had witnessed the murder of a blackmailer. Honor Blackman co-stars. AT

John Ireland *Pel* • Honor Blackman *Jenny* • Geoffrey Keen *Stanton* • Eric Pohlmann *Sapolio* • Sidney James *Tony Lewis* • Liam Redmond *Lindley* • Sydney Tafler *Rorke* • Valerie Vernon *Bella* ■ *Dir* Montgomery Tully • *Scr* Richard Landau, from the novel *The Outsiders* by AE Martin

The Glass Cage ★ 18

Erotic thriller 1996 · US · Colour · 91mins

This sordid tale of diamond smuggling and dirty dancing lurches from shoot-out to soft-core porn, while paying only passing attention to such trifles as character, originality and logic. As the gangster's moll condemned to gyrate at a New Orleans strip joint, Charlotte Lewis just manages to keep her dignity. The same cannot be said of Eric Roberts as a corrupt cop. DP. Contains violence, swearing, sex scenes, drug abuse and nudity.

Charlotte Lewis *Jaqueline* • Richard Tyson *Paul Yaeger* • Eric Roberts *Detective Montrachet* • Stephen Nichols *Renzi* • Joseph Campanella *LeBeque* • Richard Moll *Ian Dexter* ■ *Dir* Michael Schroeder • *Scr* Peter Yurksaitis, David Keith Miller

The Glass House ★★★★ 15

Prison drama 1972 · US · Colour · 90mins

Tom Gries had a chequered career: a one-time reporter, he produced B-pics such as *Donovan's Brain* (1953) before moving into television. He won his second Emmy for this no-nonsense, gritty prison drama. Based on a story co-written by Truman Capote, it stars Alan Alda as a college professor who falls foul of hardened lifer Vic Morrow after being jailed for manslaughter. Clu Gulager also impresses as a rookie guard. DP DVD

Vic Morrow *Hugo Slocum* • Alan Alda *Jonathan Paige* • Clu Gulager *Brain Courtland* • Billy Dee Williams *Lennox* • Kristoffer Tabori *Allan Campbell* • Dean Jagger *Warden Auerbach* ■ *Dir* Tom Gries • *Scr* Tracy Keenan Wynn, from a story by Truman Capote, Wyatt Cooper

The Glass House ★★★ 15

Psychological thriller 2001 · US · Colour · 101mins

Director Daniel Sackheim's big-screen debut is essentially an immaculately realised, join-the-dot chiller that utilises every spine-tingling trick at his disposal to elicit a powerful audience response. While there's no real innovation in this slickly enthralling tale of two orphans whose wealthy guardians are not at all what they seem, Sackheim still manages to infuse the film with a pleasing sophistication and freshness. Leelee Sobieski is a standout as the eldest child, sending hearts into mouths as she frantically battles to escape a terror no one will believe, while Stellan Skarsgård's reptilian sleaziness as her guardian is a joy to hate. SF DVD

Leelee Sobieski *Ruby Baker* • Diane Lane *Dr Erin Glass* • Stellan Skarsgård *Terry Glass* • Bruce Dern *Alvin Begleiter* • Kathy Baker *Nancy Ryan* • Trevor Morgan *Rhett Baker* • Chris Noth [Christopher Noth] *Uncle Jack* ■ *Dir* Daniel Sackheim • *Scr* Wesley Strick • *Cinematographer* Alar Kivilo

Glass Houses ★

Erotic drama 1972 · US · Colour · 90mins

We're in *Bob and Carol and Ted and Alice* territory – minus the big stars – with this story about the sexual revolution, set in California. The plot throws in adultery, environmental concerns and a *soupçon* of incest but hovers close to soft-core porn and the characters seem to spend a lot of time in the hot-tub. AT

Bernard Barrow *Victor* • Deirdre Lenihan *Kim* • Jennifer O'Neill *Jean* • Ann Summers *Wife* • Phillip Pine *Ted* • Clarke Gordon *Novelist* ■ *Dir* Alexander Singer • *Scr* Alexander Singer, Judith Singer

The Glass Key ★★

Crime drama 1935 · US · BW · 77mins

A dated but still absorbing adaptation of Dashiell Hammett's novel, with George Raft as the henchman of an allegedly corrupt politician (Edward Arnold) accused of murdering a senator's son. The dialogue is pure "movie talk", sometimes hovering close to screwball comedy. There is a decent sense of intrigue, but the visual atmospherics associated with *film noir* are conspicuously absent . AT

George Raft *Ed Beaumont* • Claire Dodd *Janet Henry* • Edward Arnold *Paul Madvig* • Rosalind Keith *Opal Madvig* • Ray Milland *Taylor Henry* • Robert Gleckler *Shad O'Rory* • [Guinn "Big Boy" Williams] *Jeff* • Tammany Young *Clarkie* ■ *Dir* Frank Tuttle • *Scr* Kathryn Scola, Kubec Glasmon, Harry Ruskin, from the novel by Dashiell Hammett

The Glass Key ★★★★

Film noir 1942 · US · BW · 85mins

The second, and far superior, version of Dashiell Hammett's novel, with Alan Ladd and Veronica Lake following up their first hit together, *This Gun for Hire*. Ladd plays the bodyguard to Brian Donlevy's politician, uncovering a murder plot, while Lake seesaws provocatively between them, finally settling on Ladd in one of those legendary screen clinches. The story's focus on the bodyguard gave Akira Kurosawa the idea for his masterly 1961 samurai drama *Yojimbo* and that, in turn, was acknowledged by Sergio Leone as the inspiration for *A Fistful of Dollars*. AT

Brian Donlevy *Paul Madvig* • Veronica Lake *Janet Henry* • Alan Ladd *Ed Beaumont* • Bonita Granville *Opal Madvig* • Richard Denning *Taylor Henry* • Joseph Calleia *Nick Varna* • William Bendix *Jeff* ■ *Dir* Stuart Heisler • *Scr* Jonathan Latimer, from the novel by Dashiell Hammett

The Glass Menagerie ★★★ U

Drama 1950 · US · BW · 107mins

This early film version of Tennessee Williams's play relies as much on star power as the mesmeric dialogue and the involving quality of the story. Gertrude Lawrence stars as the faded Southern belle mother, living in a run-down St Louis apartment with crippled, introverted daughter Jane Wyman and rebellious son Arthur Kennedy. Kirk Douglas is the gentleman caller, whose visit changes the family completely – Lawrence believes Douglas will sweep Wyman off her feet and into a wedding. Director Irving Rapper is demonstrably restrained. TH

Jane Wyman *Laura Wingfield* • Kirk Douglas *Jim O'Connor* • Gertrude Lawrence *Amanda Wingfield* • Arthur Kennedy *Tom Wingfield* • Ralph Sanford *Mendoza* • Ann Tyrrell *Clerk* • John Compton *Young man* • Gertrude Graner *Woman instructor* ■ *Dir* Irving Rapper • *Scr* Tennessee Williams, Peter Berneis, from the play by Tennessee Williams

The Glass Menagerie ★★★★ PG

Drama 1987 · US · Colour · 138mins

Paul Newman's reverent film version of one of Tennessee Williams's slighter fables stars his wife Joanne Woodward as a faded Southern belle and dominating mother who lives with her son John Malkovich and her crippled daughter Karen Allen in a delapidated St Louis apartment. Malkovich works in a warehouse to keep the family, while Allen spends her days polishing her collection of glass animals and wistfully waiting for a "gentleman caller" to whisk her away. Woodward's iron woman is a triumph, and Malkovich is easily her match. TH

Joanne Woodward *Amanda Wingfield* • John Malkovich *Tom Wingfield* • Karen Allen *Laura Wingfield* • James Naughton *The Gentleman Caller/Jim O'Connor* ■ *Dir* Paul Newman • *Scr* from a play by Tennessee Williams

The Glass Mountain ★★

Romantic drama 1949 · UK · BW · 107mins

In the second of their five screen twinnings, husband-and-wife team Michael Denison and Dulcie Gray experience a few marital difficulties after he returns from RAF duty obsessed with both an idea for an opera and Valentina Cortese, the partisan who rescued him from the mountain snow. The subject of couples forced apart because of differing wartime experiences is worthy of attention, but director Henry Cass struggles to prevent it being buried in an avalanche of sentimentality. DP

Michael Denison *Richard Wilder* • Dulcie Gray *Ann Wilder* • Valentina Cortese *Alida* • Tito Gobbi *Tito* • Sebastian Shaw *Bruce McLeod* • Antonio Centa *Gino* • Sidney King *Charles* • Elena Rizzieri *Singer* ■ *Dir* Henry Cass • *Scr* Joseph Janni, John Hunter, Emery Bonnet, John Cousins, Henry Cass

The Glass Shield ★★ 15

Police drama based on a true story 1995 · US/Fr · Colour · 105mins

A worthy if overelaborate thriller, this is based on a true story about the first black cop to be assigned to a Californian sheriff's department. Michael Boatman is the eager young recruit who finds himself contending with not only the racist attitudes of his all-white colleagues, but also a web of corruption that leads to the highest level. There's solid support from Lori Petty, rapper Ice Cube and old hand Michael Ironside, but director Charles Burnett occasionally gets too bogged down in the intricate plot to allow a real sense of excitement. JF [video]

Michael Boatman *JJ Johnson* • Lori Petty *Deputy Deborah Fields* • Ice Cube *Teddy Woods* • Elliott Gould *Greenspan* • Richard Anderson *Massey* • Don Harvey *Deputy Bono* • Michael Ironside *Baker* • Michael Gregory *Roy Bush* • Bernie Casey *Locket* ■ *Dir* Charles Burnett • *Scr* Charles Burnett, from the (unproduced) screenplay *One of Us* by Ned Walsh

The Glass Slipper ★★ U

Romantic fantasy 1955 · US · Colour · 93mins

This musical version of the Cinderella story, directed by Charles Walters, is solemnly narrated by Walter Pidgeon. It stars Leslie Caron and an awkwardly-cast Michael Wilding, who finds himself unsuitably involved in the ballet production numbers, choreographed by Roland Petit. These are, however, the highlights of a dull movie, in which Caron's heroine is perversely irritating, the ugly sisters even more perversely glamorous and Estelle Winwood's fairy godmother a winsome old bag. RK

Leslie Caron *Ella* • Michael Wilding *Prince Charles* • Keenan Wynn *Kovin* • Estelle Winwood *Mrs Toquet* • Elsa Lanchester *Widow Sonder* • Barry Jones *Duke* • Amanda Blake *Birdena* • Lisa Daniels *Serafina* ■ *Dir* Charles Walters • *Scr* Helen Deutsch

The Glass Wall ★★★

Drama 1953 · US · BW · 79mins

One of a handful of films made by Vittorio Gassman for MGM during his marriage to Shelley Winters. The Italian heart-throb plays an illegal immigrant in the USA, who is given refuge by social outcast Gloria Grahame and jazzman Jerry Paris. The atmospherically lit, documentary-style movie has a lively jazz score, and there are brief appearances by the likes of Jack Teagarden. It was the best of Gassman's Hollywood films; his marriage to Winters proved short-lived and he returned to Italy to resume his stage and screen career. RB

Vittorio Gassman *Peter* • Gloria Grahame *Maggie* • Ann Robinson *Nancy* • Douglas Spencer *Inspector Bailey* • Robin Raymond *Tanya* • Jerry Paris *Tom* • Elizabeth Slifer *Mrs Hinckley* ■ *Dir* Maxwell Shane • *Scr* Maxwell Shane, Ivan Tors

The Glass Web ★★

Crime drama 1953 · US · BW · 81mins

A TV producer is blackmailed by his former mistress: when she is murdered, the case is featured on the producer's show, *Crime of the Week*. Made when television was beginning to eat into cinema attendances, Jack Arnold's drama was originally filmed in 3-D, a gimmick intended to lure audiences away from their TV sets. However, the plot is tortuous and unfolds slowly, while Edward G Robinson, playing another of the film's blackmail victims, is given little opportunity to show his talents. AT

Edward G Robinson *Henry Hayes* • John Forsythe *Don Newell* • Kathleen Hughes *Paula Ranier* • Marcia Henderson *Louise Newell* • Richard Denning *Dave Markson* • Hugh Sanders *Lieutenant Stevens* • Clark Howat *Bob Warren* • Dick Stewart *Everett* ■ *Dir* Jack Arnold • *Scr* Robert Blees, Leonard Lee, from the novel by Max Simon Ehrlich

Glastonbury Fayre ★★★ 15

Music documentary 1973 · UK · Colour · 87mins

During the summer of 1971, an estimated 12,000 people packed into Worthy Farm in the Somerset countryside for the second Glastonbury Festival. Organised by Andrew Kerr and Arabella Churchill to coincide with the summer solstice, the fayre was a determined bid hold a music festival on a non-commercial basis. It leaned heavily towards medieval mysticism, and director Peter Neal's movie of the event successfully captures much of the unique atmosphere around the stage, as well as documenting the performances (from the likes of David Bowie, Fairport Convention, Gong and Traffic) on it. DP [video]

Dir Peter Neal • *Cinematographer* Nicolas Roeg

Glastonbury the Movie ★★★ 15

Music documentary 1995 · UK · Colour · 96mins

What a contradiction this is – a documentary celebrating Britain's thriving counterculture that proudly proclaims itself to be the first feature completed with National Lottery funding. Employing widely differing styles and film techniques, and shot over a number of years, this tribute is more concerned with the antics of the audience than with the acts on stage. The sideshows around this site of Arthurian legend are revealing and occasionally entertaining, but the refusal to present the sights and sounds in a cohesive way deprives the footage of any anthropological value. However, fans of the bands featured won't complain. DP [video]

Dir Robin Mahoney, William Beaton, Matthew Salkeld, Lisa Lake, Mike Sarne [Michael Sarne]

Gleaming the Cube ★★★ PG

Action adventure 1988 · US · Colour · 99mins

Despite the sometimes uneasy mix of children's caper and more adult action, this is, for the most part, an exhilarating ride. Christian Slater is the ace skateboarder who teams up with his chums and detective Steven Bauer to discover who murdered his adopted Vietnamese brother. Slater oozes charisma, and the stunning skateboarding sequences are expertly choreographed by director Graeme Clifford. JF. Contains swearing. [video] DVD

Christian Slater *Brian Kelly* • Steven Bauer *Detective Al Lucero* • Ed Lauter *Mr Kelly* • Micole Mercurio *Mrs Kelly* • Art Chudabala *Vinh Kelly* • Richard Herd *Ed Lawndale* • Tuan Le *Colonel Trac* • Min Luong *Tina Trac* ■ *Dir* Graeme Clifford • *Scr* Michael Tolkin

The Gleaners and I ★★★★

Documentary 2000 · Fr · Colour · 82mins

A profound portrait of necessity and eccentricity, Agnès Varda's documentary pays tribute to those who subsist on the margins of society. Tracing the venerable history of gleaning from medieval times, Varda travels across France to meet those who gather discarded items for survival, art and pleasure. Consciously engaging in some cinematic gleaning, she occasionally indulges herself with a charming diversion or striking image. Indeed, this is as poetic as a polemic can get. But beneath the gentle, humanist tone, there's a despair at the fact that so many people embrace a hand to mouth existence in a supposedly civilised state. DP. In French with English subtitles.

Dir/Scr Agnès Varda

Glen or Glenda ★ 15

Drama 1953 · US · BW · 70mins

The poster for Tim Burton's 1994 biopic *Ed Wood* featured a pink angora sweater – a homage to this 1950s gem. Edward D Wood Jr directs himself (billed as Daniel Davis) as Glen, the troubled transvestite who longs to share a wardrobe with his fiancée Dolores Fuller. The cross-dressing Wood aimed for a documentary realism in this plea for understanding. However, his juxtaposition of painfully earnest psychiatrist Timothy Farrell and a sneering Bela Lugosi rattling on about big green dragons quickly reduces the entire exercise to excruciating farce. So bad, it's unmissable. DP. Contains sexual references. [video]

Bela Lugosi *The Spirit* • Lyle Talbot *Police Inspector Warren* • Timothy Farrell *Dr Alton* • Daniel Davis [Edward D Wood Jr] *Glen/Glenda* • Dolores Fuller *Barbara* • "Tommy" Haines *Alan/Ann* ■ *Dir/Scr* Edward D Wood Jr

Glengarry Glen Ross ★★★★★ 15

Drama 1992 · US · Colour · 96mins

Director James Foley, working with a highly resonant screenplay by David Mamet, brings a palpable cinematic tension to what could have been a dry, theatrical piece. Rarely moving outside the real-estate office where four salesmen are under pressure to sell more or lose their jobs, the film speaks forcefully about decency being snuffed out by desire, good men taking wrong turnings despite their best efforts and the stench of the American Dream gone mad. Al Pacino, Jack Lemmon, Alan Arkin and Ed Harris all give note-perfect ensemble performances, Alec Baldwin appears in a telling cameo and there's a major early role for Kevin Spacey. JM. Contains swearing. [video] DVD

Al Pacino *Ricky Roma* • Jack Lemmon *Shelley "The Machine" Levene* • Alec Baldwin *Blake* • Ed Harris *Dave Moss* • Alan Arkin *George Aaronow* • Kevin Spacey *John Williamson* • Jonathan Pryce *James Lingk* ■ *Dir* James Foley • *Scr* David Mamet, from his play

The Glenn Miller Story ★★★★ U

Musical biographical drama 1953 · US · Colour · 107mins

This biopic of the legendary trombonist and band leader will always be the most fondly remembered collaboration between director Anthony Mann and star James Stewart. Whether struggling to find the style of swing that would set him apart from his contemporaries, enjoying the brief benefits of fame or romancing June Allyson, Stewart is perfect for the role. The supporting cast is impeccable and the music, adapted by Henry Mancini, is as bewitching as ever. DP [video]

James Stewart *Glenn Miller* • June Allyson *Helen Burger Miller* • Charles Drake *Don Haynes* • George Tobias *Si Schribman* • Henry Morgan [Harry Morgan] *Chummy MacGregor* • Marion Ross *Polly Haynes* • Irving Bacon *Mr Miller* ■ *Dir* Anthony Mann • *Scr* Valentine Davies, Oscar Brodney

The Glimmer Man ★★ 18

Action thriller 1996 · US · Colour · 87mins

Sandwiched between his eco-warrior outings *On Deadly Ground* and *Fire Down Below*, this has Steven Seagal going back to the no-brainer fare that made his name. It's a partial success, but ultimately it lacks the streamlined thrills of his early films. Here, New Age cop Seagal is set on the trail of a serial killer, only to discover his murky government past coming back to haunt him. JF. Contains swearing. [video] DVD

Steven Seagal *Jack Cole* • Keenen Ivory Wayans *Jim Campbell* • Bob Gunton *Frank Deverell* • Brian Cox *Mr Smith* • John M Jackson *Donald* • Michelle Johnson *Jessica* • Stephen Tobolowsky *Christopher Maynard* ■ *Dir* John Gray • *Scr* Kevin Brodbin

G

Glitter ★ PG

Musical romantic drama 2001 · US/Can · Colour · 100mins

This rags-to-riches vehicle for superstar diva Mariah Carey invites ridicule on almost every level. In her starring debut as a struggling backing singer hoisted into the big time, Carey possesses all the star quality of a pub karaoke singer but none of the memorable tunes. The gaudy 1980s setting provides a certain nostalgic amusement, though the rest of the limited entertainment on show is of the unplanned variety. JC [video] DVD

Mariah Carey *Billie Frank* • Max Beesley *Julian Dice* • Da Brat *Louise* • Tia Texada *Roxanne* • Valarie Pettiford *Lillian Frank* • Ann Magnuson *Kelly* ■ *Dir* Vondie Curtis-Hall • *Scr* Kate Lanier, from a story by Cheryl L West

A Global Affair ★★ U

Comedy 1964 · US · BW · 83mins

Bob Hope is a United Nations official who discovers that an abandoned baby is a good way to make yourself very popular with a bevy of international beauties. But is it Hope or the baby they're after? Not a highlight of Bob's post-*Road* career. TH

Bob Hope *Frank Larrimore* • Lilo Pulver [Liselotte Pulver] *Sonya* • Michèle Mercier *Lisette* • Elga Andersen *Yvette* • Yvonne De Carlo *Dolores* • Miiko Taka *Fumiko* • Robert Sterling *Randy* • Nehemiah Persoff *Sigura* ■ *Dir* Jack Arnold • *Scr* Arthur Marx, Bob Fisher, Charles Lederer, from a story by Eugene Vale

La Gloire de Mon Père ★★★ U

Biographical drama 1990 · Fr · Colour · 106mins

Drawn from film-maker Marcel Pagnol's autobiography, this is a handsome and beautifully acted piece of French heritage cinema. The kitsch quotient may be high, but the cast is fine, with Philippe Caubère neatly capturing the arrogance of the *petit bourgeois* and Nathalie Roussel dishing out fond reproaches with true maternal gentility. Even more impressive is Julien Ciamaca as the young Marcel, struggling to deal with his father's victory at *boules* and his celebrity after he bags a brace of partridge. Try not to let Vladimir Cosma's intrusive score spoil your enjoyment. DP. In French with English subtitles. DVD

Philippe Caubère *Joseph Pagnol* • Nathalie Roussel *Augustine Pagnol* • Thérèse Liotard *Aunt Rose* • Didier Pain *Uncle Jules* • Julien Ciamaca *Marcel aged 11* • Victorien Delamere *Paul aged 5* • Joris Molinas *Lili Des Bellons* • Paul Crauchet *Mond Des Parpaillouns* ■ *Dir* Yves Robert • *Scr* Lucette Andrei, Jérôme Tonnerre, Louis Nucera, Yves Robert, from the autobiography by Marcel Pagnol

Gloria ★★★★ 15

Thriller 1980 · US · Colour · 116mins

Gena Rowlands was Oscar-nominated for her formidably engaging performance in this terrific thriller. She plays a not-so-dumb broad living in the Bronx who takes charge of a half-Puerto Rican boy (John Adames) whose parents have been killed by the Mafia. Holding an account book of gangster dealings, she and the boy go on the run from the Mob, until she turns and stands her ground. Director John Cassavetes deftly matches his trademark freewheeling camerawork to his wife Rowlands's brassy, endearing portrayal. TH DVD

Gena Rowlands *Gloria Swenson* • Tony Knesich *First gangster* • Gregory Cleghorne *Kid in elevator* • Buck Henry *Jack Dawn* • John Adames *Phil Dawn* • Julie Carmen *Jeri Dawn* • Jessica Castillo *Joan Dawn* • Tom Noonan *Second gangster* • Ronald Maccone *Third gangster* ■ *Dir/Scr* John Cassavetes

Gloria ★★ 15

Crime drama 1998 · US · Colour · 102mins

Sharon Stone, together with a small, orphaned Hispanic boy (Jean-Luke Figueroa) and a computer disc of Mafia info, is pursued by the Mob. Stone's attempt to emulate Gena Rowlands's hard-as-nails moll in John Cassavetes's 1980 social thriller is undercut by Sidney Lumet's lacklustre direction. It's a pity for Stone's sake – she's an enterprising actress who should be admired for taking dramatic chances. Cardboard characters and cut-out situations are all that are left here, without any acknowledgement of Cassavetes's original. TH DVD

Sharon Stone *Gloria* • Jean-Luke Figueroa *Nicky* • Jeremy Northam *Kevin* • Cathy Moriarty *Diane* • George C Scott *Ruby* • Mike Starr *Sean* • Barry McEvoy *Terry* • Don Billett *Raymond* • Bonnie Bedelia *Brenda* ■ *Dir* Sidney Lumet • *Scr* Steven Antin, from the film by John Cassavetes

Glory ★★★★ 15

Historical war drama
1989 · US · Colour · 117mins

This Civil War tale is a long overdue tribute to America's first black regiment to go into combat, the 54th Massachusetts Voluntary Infantry. The details are culled partly from the letters of the 54th's commander, Colonel Robert Gould Shaw (played by Matthew Broderick), a sensitive 25-year-old (but already a veteran) from an abolitionist family who's determined to lead his men into full battle. His racist superiors won't even allow the soldiers boots, and the troops resent the young white man's leadership, especially runaway slave Denzel Washington. While there is some stereotyping, the lasting impression is of Washington's performance and the plight of the men. Fabulously photographed by Freddie Francis, it features brilliantly staged (and shockingly violent) battle scenes. AT. Contains swearing. DVD

Matthew Broderick *Colonel Robert Gould Shaw* • Denzel Washington *Trip* • Morgan Freeman *John Rawlins* • Cary Elwes *Cabot Forbes* • Jihmi Kennedy *Sharts* • André Braugher *Thomas Searles* • John Finn *Sergeant Mulcahy* • Donovan Leitch *Charles Morse* ■ *Dir* Edward Zwick • *Scr* Kevin Jarre, from the books *Lay This Laurel* by Lincoln Kirstein and *One Gallant Rush* by Peter Burchard, and the letters of Robert Gould Shaw

Glory Alley ★

Drama 1952 · US · BW · 79mins

MGM was trying to find roles for Leslie Caron after *An American in Paris* and wanted to see if Ralph Meeker had the makings of a star. This stilted, dreary drama was no help to either of them; nor did it enhance the reputation of its director, Raoul Walsh. Meeker is the boxer accused of cowardice who goes off to become a hero in Korea. AE

Ralph Meeker *Socks Barbarrosa* • Leslie Caron *Angela* • Kurt Kasznar *Judge* • Gilbert Roland *Peppi Donnato* • John McIntire *Gabe Jordan* • Louis Armstrong *Shadow Johnson* • Jack Teagarden • Larry Gates *Dr Robert Ardley* ■ *Dir* Raoul Walsh • *Scr* Art Cohn

Glory & Honor ★★★ PG

Biographical adventure drama
1998 · US · Colour · 90mins

Not many people know that, when Captain Robert Peary claimed the honour of being the first man to reach the North Pole, he was accompanied by his African-American assistant. That's the premise of this high-quality TV movie about nonstop adventure in the icy wastes. The master/servant relationship was gradually eroded as the stalwart Henson (played by Delroy Lindo) turned out to be invaluable, and his willingness to learn Inuit ways was an important factor in the success of the team. JF. Contains some swearing and brief nudity.

Delroy Lindo *Matthew Henson* • Henry Czerny *Robert Peary* • Bronwen Booth *Josephine Peary* • Kim Staunton *Lucy Ross* ■ *Dir* Kevin Hooks • *Scr* Jeffrey Lewis, Susan Rhinehart, from a story by Robert Caputo

Glory Boy ★

Drama 1971 · US · Colour · 102mins

Disillusioned soldier Michael Moriarty brings two fellow Vietnam servicemen home to his father's dilapidated farm. Mitchell Ryan is the psychopathic sergeant who taunts Moriarty's patriotic father, played by veteran character actor Arthur Kennedy, and then forces himself on a young hitch-hiker, Topo Swope. Director Edwin Sherin allows a seemingly bold attempt to convey the dehumanising effect of the Vietnam War to degenerate into a sordid tale of rape and murder. AE

Michael Moriarty *Trubee Pell* • Arthur Kennedy *Walter Pell* • William Devane *Jimmy Pilgrim* • Mitchell Ryan *Sergeant Martin Flood* • Topo Swope *Helen* • Lloyd Gough *Dr Paul* • Ford Rainey *Sheriff Coleman* • Peter Donat *Car salesman* ■ *Dir* Edwin Sherin • *Scr* Stanford Whitmore, from the novel *The Old Man's Place* by John Sanford

The Glory Brigade ★★★ U

War drama 1953 · US · BW · 81mins

Victor Mature stars in this tale of conflict between American and Greek soldiers, fighting alongside one another during the Korean War. The film's portrayal of smart Americans and peasant Greeks seems dubious by today's standards, but director Robert D Webb specialised in action scenes and acquits himself well enough, while Lee Marvin makes a strong impression in an early starring role. The real Korean War ended only a month after this film was released. AT

Victor Mature *Lieutenant Sam Prior* • Alexander Scourby *Lieutenant Niklas* • Lee Marvin *Corporal Bowman* • Richard Egan *Sergeant Johnson* • Nick Dennis *Corporal Marakis* • Roy Roberts *Sergeant Chuck Anderson* • Alvy Moore *Private Stone* • Russell Evans *Private Taylor* ■ *Dir* Robert D Webb • *Scr* Franklin Coen

Glory Daze ★★

Comedy drama 1995 · US · Colour · 104mins

This pointless movie about pointless people will be of interest mainly to admirers of Ben Affleck and Matt Damon. Affleck takes the lead role as one of a gang of rich college seniors, all living in the same boarding house and fearing graduation day and the cruel realities of life beyond. There are a few laughs, but on the whole nothing much happens and a stream of bad language and scenes of boozing are supposed to make up for it. RS

Ben Affleck *Jack* • Sam Rockwell *Rob* • French Stewart *Dennis* • Alyssa Milano *Chelsea* • Megan Ward *Joannie* • Vinnie DeRamus *Mickey* • Matthew McConaughey *Rental truck guy* • Matt Damon *Edgar Pudwhacker* • Hong Vien *Slosh* ■ *Dir/Scr* Rich Wilkes

The Glory Guys ★★★

Western 1965 · US · Colour · 119mins

A large-budget and largely competent western, written by Sam Peckinpah, this focuses on a US cavalry action against the Indians and conflict within the ranks. Tom Tryon is pretty nondescript in the leading role, playing a cavalry officer loath to send his recruits into combat. Andrew Duggan does better as the general who's less fussed at the prospect of losing a few men, while a young James Caan catches the eye as a bull-headed soldier. The brutal plot takes to unfold, but builds to a rousing finale. PF

Tom Tryon *Demas Harrod* • Harve Presnell *Sol Rogers* • Senta Berger *Lou Woodard* • Andrew Duggan *General McCabe* • James Caan *Dugan* • Slim Pickens *Gregory* • Michael Anderson Jr *Martin Hale* • Peter Breck *Hodges* • Robert McQueeny [Robert McQueeney] *Marcus* ■ *Dir* Arnold Laven • *Scr* Sam Peckinpah, from the novel *The Dice of God* by Hoffman Birney

The Glory Stompers ★

Action drama 1967 · US · Colour · 85mins

Violence erupts between warring bikers when Dennis Hopper's Black Souls beat up Stompers leader Jody McCrea and take his girlfriend to be sold in a Mexican white-slave market. Jock Mahoney rescues McCrea and joins his old friend on the manhunt south of the border. This is nothing more than a hippy western substituting cowboys with Hell's Angels, horses with choppers and campfire talk with a laughable love-in. Risible dialogue and mindless action puts this near the bottom of the rebel riders heap. AJ

Dennis Hopper *Chino* • Jody McCrea *Darryl* • Chris Noel *Chris* • Jock Mahoney *Smiley* • Saundra Gayle *Jo Ann* • Robert Tessier *Magoo* • Astrid Warner *Doreen* • Gary Wood *Pony* ■ *Dir* Anthony M Lanza • *Scr* James Gordon White, John Lawrence

The Glove ★★

Action adventure 1978 · US · Colour · 90mins

Escaped convict Roosevelt "Rosey" Grier is equipped with a custom-built steel glove that can smash through people and solid metal. Ex-cop turned bounty hunter John Saxon is offered $20,000 for his recapture. This is an odd, before-its-time combination of science-fiction, action and social issues that fails to make its mark in each area it tries to embrace. Bizarre, but entertaining by default. AJ

John Saxon *Sam Kellough* • Roosevelt Grier [Rosey Grier] *Victor Hale* • Joanna Cassidy *Sheila Michaels* • Joan Blondell *Mrs Fitzgerald* • Jack Carter *Walter Stratton* • Keenan Wynn *Bill Schwartz* • Aldo Ray *Prison guard* • Michael Pataki *Harry Iverson* ■ *Dir* Ross Hagen • *Scr* Hubert Smith, Julian Roffman

The Gnome-Mobile ★★★ U

Fantasy 1967 · US · Colour · 81mins

This whimsical fantasy in the Disney tradition of whiter-than-white family fun is packed with enchanting special effects and merry, if instantly forgettable, tunes. Matthew Garber and Karen Dotrice protect gnomes living in redwood forests from mindless lumber barons. This little-known live action feature deserves better attention; kids will love it. Veteran Walter Brennan is a standout in a dual role and there's a knockout car chase finale. RS DVD

Walter Brennan *DJ Mulrooney/Knobby* • Tom Lowell *Jasper* • Matthew Garber *Rodney Winthrop* • Ed Wynn *Rufus* • Karen Dotrice *Elizabeth Winthrop* • Richard Deacon *Ralph Yarby* • Sean McClory *Horatio Quaxton* • Jerome Cowan *Dr Conrad Ramsey* ■ *Dir* Robert Stevenson • *Scr* Ellis Kadison, from the novel *The Gnomobile: a Gnice Gnew Gnarrative With Gnonsense, But Gnothing Gnaughty* by Upton Sinclair

Go ★★★★ 18

Comedy crime drama
1999 · US · Colour · 98mins

Doug Liman's film intertwines three separate storylines to present a picture of mixed-up Los Angeles youth. It's Christmas Eve, and two supermarket checkout girls are trying to raise some rent money by rather dubious means. A colleague drives with his mates to Las Vegas, but their good-time gambling turns sour. In the meantime, two male soap stars become embroiled in a police sting. Katie Holmes, Sarah Polley, Jay Mohr and Scott Wolf are all on great form in an ensemble vision of 20-something angst that boasts a superb soundtrack. The result is original and hilarious. LH. Contains swearing, sex scenes and drug abuse. DVD

Katie Holmes *Claire Montgomery* • Sarah Polley *Ronna Martin* • Desmond Askew *Simon Baines* • Scott Wolf *Adam* • Jay Mohr *Zack* • Timothy Olyphant *Todd Gaines* • Jimmy Shubert *Victor Jr* • Nathan Bexton *Mannie* ■ *Dir* Doug Liman • *Scr* John August

The Go-Between ★★★★ PG

Period drama 1971 · UK · Colour · 111mins

Director Joseph Losey and writer Harold Pinter's wonderfully resonant adaptation of LP Hartley's classic Edwardian romance is a beautiful, beguiling and brilliant exposé of a repressive and manipulative class system. Julie Christie and Alan Bates excel as the upper-class girl and her farmer lover carrying on a clandestine relationship, unwittingly aided by young "postman" Dominic Guard, who delivers their letters. Gorgeously shot by Gerry Fisher on Norfolk locations, this is thought-provoking costume drama of the highest order. AJ

Julie Christie *Marian Maudsley* • Alan Bates *Ted Burgess* • Dominic Guard *Leo Colston* • Margaret Leighton *Mrs Maudsley* • Michael Redgrave *Leo, as an old man* • Michael Gough *Mr Maudsley* • Edward Fox *Hugh Trimingham* • Richard Gibson *Marcus Maudsley* ■ *Dir* Joseph Losey • *Scr* Harold Pinter, from the novel by LP Hartley

Go Chase Yourself ★★★ U

Comedy 1938 · US · BW · 70mins

Gullible bank clerk Joe Penner wins a posh caravan in a lottery and is subsequently hijacked by a trio of crooks. The ensuing ride increasingly careers out of control to create a crazy comic farrago that manages to include numerous characters and situations. A vehicle for Penner, a then popular comic star of American radio, this is one for fans of zany farce. RK

Joe Penner *Wilbur Meely* • Lucille Ball *Carol Meely* • June Travis *Judith Daniels* • Richard Lane *Nails* • Fritz Feld *Count Pierre de Louis-Louis* • Tom Kennedy *Ice-Box* • Jack Carson *Warren Miles* ■ *Dir* Edward F Cline [Edward Cline] • *Scr* Paul Yawitz, Bert Granet, from a story by Walter O'Keefe

Go Fish ★★★★ 18

Romantic drama 1994 · US · BW · 79mins

Unpretentious, inoffensive and very funny, this ultra low-budget festival hit, about finding true love in the lesbian community, effortlessly cruises between queer politics and hip funkiness. It's all about the very Woody Allen-esque things that happen when terminally single Guinevere Turner goes on a blind date with the neurotic VS Brody just to please her best mates. Arty yet wholly accessible, this monochrome marvel works on numerous levels, and is a genuinely hilarious heart-warmer. AJ. Contains swearing and nudity.

VS Brodie *Ely* • Guinevere Turner *Max* • T Wendy McMillan *Kia* • Migdalia Melendez *Evy* • Anastasia Sharp *Daria* • Mary Garvey *Student/Jury member* • Danielia Falcon *Student/Jury member* • Tracy Kimme *Student/Jury member* ■ *Dir* Rose Troche • *Scr* Rose Troche, Guinevere Turner

Go for a Take ★ U

Comedy 1972 · UK · Colour · 89mins

A British comedy with minimal laugh potential. Reg Varney and Norman Rossington are waiters on the run from debt collectors who take refuge in a film studio, a scenario which leads to some amazingly unfunny sequences. It's enough to make the *Carry On* films seem as witty as Oscar Wilde. TH

Reg Varney *Wilfrid Stone* • Norman Rossington *Jack Foster* • Sue Lloyd *Angel Montgomery* • Dennis Price *Dracula* • Julie Ege *April* • Patrick Newell *Generous Jim* • David Lodge *Graham* • Jack Haig *Security man* ■ *Dir* Harry Booth • *Scr* Alan Hackney, from a story by Alan Hackney, Harry Booth

Go for Broke! ★★

Second World War drama 1951 · US · BW · 90mins

The title was the war cry of the 442nd Regimental Combat Team, a unit made up of Japanese-Americans who fought alongside their fellow Americans against the Nazis. Van Johnson plays the lieutenant in charge of them, who overcomes his initial wariness when he sees how they fight in Italy. The cynical motivation behind this MGM effort was that, in the postwar era, Japan was becoming a major market for Hollywood movies, so a story like this was good publicity. But it's not an especially good drama. AT

Van Johnson *Lt Michael Grayson* • Lane Nakano *Sam* • George Miki *Chick* • Akira Fukunaga *Frank* • Ken K Okamoto *Kaz* • Henry Oyasato *O'Hara* • Harry Hamada *Masami* ■ *Dir/Scr* Robert Pirosh

Go into Your Dance ★★

Musical comedy drama 1935 · US · BW · 92mins

This was the only movie in which Al Jolson and his wife Ruby Keeler appeared together, and they pleasantly deliver some tuneful numbers by Harry Warren and Al Dubin (who appear briefly as themselves). The choreographer Bobby Connolly was no Busby Berkeley, but he does a reasonable job. The feeble plot attempted to combine two of Warners' specialities – the backstage musical and the gangster movie. RB

Al Jolson *Al Howard* • Ruby Keeler *Dorothy Wayne* • Glenda Farrell *Sadie Howard* • Helen Morgan (1) *Luana Bell* • Barton MacLane *The Duke* • Sharon Lynne *Blonde* • Patsy Kelly *Irma* • Benny Rubin ■ *Dir* Archie Mayo • *Scr* Earl Baldwin, from a story by Bradford Ropes

Go, Johnny, Go! ★★

Musical 1959 · US · BW · 75mins

Rock legend Chuck Berry and disc jockey Alan Freed (who also produced the film) beat up the soundtrack to this otherwise dull effort. The *Pygmalion*-like storyline involves the transformation of an orphan (Jimmy Clanton) into a rock 'n' roll hero. The highlights are the songs, such as *Little Queenie*, and Ritchie Valens hitting his strident form in his only film appearance. (Valens's life was well portrayed by Lou Diamond Phillips in the film *La Bamba* 27 years later.) TH

Alan Freed • Jimmy Clanton *Johnny* • Sandy Stewart *Julie Arnold* • Chuck Berry • Herb Vigran *Bill Barnett* • Frank Wilcox *Mr Arnold* • Barbara Woodell *Mrs Arnold* • Milton Frome *Mr Martin* • Richie Valens ■ *Dir* Paul Landres • *Scr* Gary Alexander

Go, Man, Go! ★★ U

Sports drama 1953 · US · BW · 83mins

One of two films directed by James Wong Howe, the Cantonese-born cinematographer whose credits include *The Prisoner of Zenda, Sweet Smell of Success* and *Hud* (for which he won his second Oscar). It's the story of Abe Saperstein (played by Dane Clark), the man who founded the world famous, all-black Harlem Globetrotters basketball team. Sidney Poitier appears, along with some bona fide Globetrotters, and the message about racism retains its power. AT

Dane Clark *Abe Saperstein* • Pat Breslin [Patricia Breslin] *Sylvia Saperstein* • Sidney Poitier *Inman Jackson* • Ruby Dee *Irma Jackson* • The Harlem Globetrotters • Edmon Ryan *Zack Leader* • Bram Nossen *James Willoughby* • Anatol Winogradoff *Papa Saperstein* ■ *Dir* James Wong Howe • *Scr* Arnold Becker (front for Alfred Palca)

Go Naked in the World ★★

Drama 1961 · US · Colour · 103mins

MGM embarked on a series of lavish melodramas in the 1960s. This tosh, in which Gina Lollobrigida is taken home to meet dad Ernest Borgnine by infatuated son Anthony Franciosa, is not the best example. There's no thrill at all when we discover that Borgnine, and most of the townsfolk, already know about Lollobrigida's shady background. Given an X certificate on its original release, the film looks pretty tame today. TS

Gina Lollobrigida *Giulietta Cameron* • Anthony Franciosa *Nick Stratton* • Ernest Borgnine *Pete Stratton* • Luana Patten *Yvonne Stratton* • Will Kuluva *Argus Diavolos* • Philip Ober *Josh Kebner* • John Kellogg *Cobby* • Nancy R Pollock *Mary Stratton* ■ *Dir* Ranald MacDougall • *Scr* Ranald MacDougall, from the novel by Tom T Chamales

Go Now ★★ 15

Drama romance 1995 · UK · Colour · 82mins

Michael Winterbottom tackles another gloomy subject in this grim drama. Robert Carlyle is in love with Juliet Aubrey, randy and raucous. His life turns sour when he discovers he has multiple sclerosis. The film chronicles his physical deterioration and how the inability to lead a normal life affects both Carlyle's morale and his relationship with Aubrey. Winterbottom's interpretation is unsentimental, though he remains sympathetic, but there is little hope on offer. LH. Contains sex scenes and some swearing.

Robert Carlyle *Nick Cameron* • Juliet Aubrey *Karen Walker* • James Nesbitt *Tony* • Sophie Okonedo *Paula* • John Brobbey *Geoff* • Darren Tighe *Dell* • Berwick Kaler *Sammy* • Sean McKenzie *George* ■ *Dir* Michael Winterbottom • *Scr* Paul Henry Powell, Jimmy McGovern

Go Tell It on the Mountain ★★★

Drama 1984 · US · Colour · 96mins

This is a stagey but engrossing rite-of-passage picture set initially during the mid-1930s. James Bond III gives a mature performance as a teenager trying to come to terms with both his sexuality and a hostile stepfather, before his conversion to the Temple of the Fire Baptised. Rosalind Cash and Alfre Woodard feature in a superb supporting cast, but it's Paul Winfield as the uncompromising Gabriel who holds the attention. Stan Lathan directs with a touch too much reverence for his material, but nevertheless provides a sobering insight into the black experience in pre-civil rights America. DP

Paul Winfield *Gabriel Grimes* • Rosalind Cash *Aunt Florence* • James Bond III *John Grimes* • Roderic Wimberly *Roy Grimes* • Olivia Cole *Elizabeth Grimes* • Ving Rhames *Young Gabriel* • Alfre Woodard *Esther* • CCH Pounder *Deborah* • Linda Hopkins *Sister McCandless* ■ *Dir* Stan Lathan • *Scr* Gus Edwards, Leslie Lee, from the novel by James Baldwin

Go Tell the Spartans ★★★ 15

War drama 1977 · US · Colour · 110mins

One of the few American movies to deal in depth with the morality of the Vietnam conflict, which officially started as "policing" action in 1964 – the year in which the film is set. It plays like a transplanted western, with veteran Burt Lancaster starring as a military adviser beset with doubts about his mission and its value. The screenplay is both clever and perceptive, and director Ted Post does what he can, but the scale is limited and the supporting cast lacks gravitas. Nevertheless, the film is surprisingly moving, peppered with witty lines spat out with relish by Lancaster. TS. Contains swearing.

Burt Lancaster *Major Asa Barker* • Craig Wasson *Corporal Stephen Courcey* • Jonathan Goldsmith *Sergeant Oleonowski* • Marc Singer *Captain Al Olivetti* • Joe Unger *Lt Raymond Hamilton* • Dennis Howard *Corporal Abraham Lincoln* • David Clennon *Lt Finley Wattsberg* • Evan Kim *Cowboy* ■ *Dir* Ted Post • *Scr* Wendell Mayes, from the novel *Incident at Muc Wa* by Daniel Ford

Go to Blazes ★★ U

Comedy 1961 · UK · Colour · 79mins

This substandard comedy caper is now mainly of interest for providing Maggie Smith with her second screen role. The story of some clottish crooks who train themselves up as firemen in order to use the engine they've bought as a getaway vehicle is both derivative and dull. Dave King and Daniel Massey generate few comic sparks, but there's a fun cameo from Robert Morley as an obliging arsonist. DP

Dave King *Bernard* • Robert Morley *"Arson" Eddie* • Daniel Massey *Harry* • Dennis Price *Withers* • Coral Browne *Colette* • Norman Rossington *Alfie* • Maggie Smith *Chantal* • Miles Malleson *Salesman* • Finlay Currie *Judge* ■ *Dir* Michael Truman • *Scr* Patrick Campbell, Vivienne Knight, from a story by Peter Myers, Ronald Cass

Go West ★★★★ U

Silent comedy 1925 · US · BW · 69mins

All the great comedians have headed in this direction at some time or another, and Buster Keaton may have been exceptional – but he was no exception. This is, perhaps, the only one of his silent movies which tries for a touch of Chaplin-esque sentiment: he's called Friendless and his touching way with a favourite cow – he places the milking pail beneath her hoping she will milk herself – achieves a gingerly-handled tenderness. There's a great stampede of cattle at the end which Buster tries to stop, though the cops don't believe his story. TH

Buster Keaton *Friendless, Homer Holiday* • Howard Truesdale *Thompson, owner of the Diamond Bar Ranch* • Kathleen Myers *Gloria, his daughter* • Ray Thompson *Foreman* • Joe Keaton *Man in barber chair* • Roscoe "Fatty" Arbuckle *Fat woman in store* • Babe London *Fat woman's daughter* • Erwin Connelly *Stockyard owner* ■ *Dir* Buster Keaton • *Scr* Raymond Cannon, from an idea by Buster Keaton

Go West ★★ U

Comedy 1940 · US · BW · 77mins

The fourth film the Marx Brothers made for MGM is one of their weakest vehicles, with too much time being spent in the company of John Carroll and Diana Lewis. Sorely missing the stately presence of Margaret Dumont and saddled with a mediocre script, they are forced to plunder that Buster Keaton masterpiece *The General* for the best scene in the picture. There are a couple of other worthwhile routines, but it's all rather hit and miss. DP DVD

Groucho Marx *S Quentin Quale* • Chico Marx *Joe Panello* • Harpo Marx *"Rusty"* • John Carroll *Terry Turner* • Diana Lewis *Eve Wilson* • Walter Woolf King *Beecher* ■ *Dir* Edward Buzzell • *Scr* Irving Brecher

Go West, Young Man ★★★

Comedy 1936 · US · BW · 79mins

The lines may not be as outrageous as in her earlier films, but Mae West is as physically suggestive as ever in her own adaptation of a Lawrence Riley play. Poking fun at herself, she plays a modern-day film star on tour to promote her new picture. She perks up at the sight of handsome Randolph Scott and decides to stay on and see what develops. AE

Mae West *Mavis Arden* • Warren William *Morgan* • Randolph Scott *Bud Norton* • Alice Brady *Mrs Struthers* • Elizabeth Patterson *Aunt Kate* • Lyle Talbot *Francis X Harrigan* • Isabel Jewell *Gladys* • Margaret Perry *Joyce* ■ *Dir* Henry Hathaway • *Scr* Mae West, from the play *Personal Appearance* by Lawrence Riley

The Goalkeeper's Fear of the Penalty Kick ★★★★ PG

Drama 1971 · Austria/W Ger · Colour · 96mins

In adapting his own novel for the screen, Peter Handke retains its existential aura of Camus, Sartre and Kafka. Yet, with goalkeeper Arthur Brauss exhibiting a passion for all things American, this is recognisably a Wim Wenders movie (indeed, it was the first to bring him international recognition). With its imagery focusing on vehicles and modes of communication, and a resolute refusal to justify Brauss's motives for killing a cinema cashier, this could be described as an existential thriller. Wenders invests seemingly inconsequential objects with an almost sinister significance to reflect his antihero's mental deterioration following that fateful spot kick. DP. In German with English subtitles.

Arthur Brauss *Joseph Bloch* • Kai Fischer *Hertha Gabler* • Erika Pluhar *Gloria* • Libgart Schwarz *Maid* • Marie Bardischewski *Maria* • Michael Toost *Salesman* • Bert Fortell *Customs official* • Edda Köchl *Girl in Vienna* ■ *Dir* Wim Wenders • *Scr* Wim Wenders, Peter Handke, from a novel by Peter Handke

GoBots: Battle of the Rocklords ★ U

Science-fiction animation 1986 · US · Colour · 70mins

Yet another kid's animation movie that is little more than an extended commercial for a new line of toys. Hanna-Barbera, home of *Yogi Bear* and *The Flintstones*, provides the less-than-inspired animation, while the Tonka corporation provides the product – a range of robots that can be transformed into vehicles and spaceships. This amounts to little more than an arcade game. RS

Margot Kidder *Solitaire* • Roddy McDowall *Nuggit* • Michael Nouri *Boulder* • Telly Savalas *Magmar* • Ike Eisenmann *Nick* • Bernard Erhard *Cy-Kill* • Marilyn Lightstone *Crasher* • Morgan Paull *Matt* ■ *Dir* Don Lusk, Alan Zaslove, Ray Patterson • *Scr* Jeff Segal

God Is My Co-Pilot ★★ U

Second World War drama
1945 · US · BW · 87mins

A wartime flag-waver extolling the heroism of Major General Channault's Flying Tigers outfit, which flew against the Japanese from Pearl Harbor to China. Chennault himself is played by Raymond Massey, but the lead role goes to Dennis Morgan who flies, prays to his co-pilot and survives to guide us through the flashbacks. These include him being shot down and surviving in enemy territory. AT

Dennis Morgan *Col Robert L Scott* • Dane Clark *Johnny Petach* • Raymond Massey *Maj Gen Chennault* • Alan Hale *"Big Mike" Harrigan* • Andrea King *Catherine Scott* • John Ridgely *Tex Hill* • Stanley Ridges *Col Meriam Cooper* • Craig Stevens *Ed Rector* ■ *Dir* Robert Florey • *Scr* Peter Milne, Abem Finkel, from the book by Col Robert L Scott

God Said, "Ha!" ★★

Comedy drama 1998 · US · Colour · 87mins

Julia Sweeney directs and stars in this recording of her self-penned one-woman stage show. Far from being lightweight stand-up comedy, this monologue takes us through her experience of temporarily losing her independence as she nursed her cancer-stricken brother. To add to the trauma of his slow death and an invasion by her parents, Sweeney then discovered that she had a rare form of cervical cancer. Utilising only the most basic of sets, it seems very theatrical and rough round the edges, but the emotional honesty is affecting. LH

Julia Sweeney ■ *Dir* Julia Sweeney • *Scr* Julia Sweeney, from her play

God Told Me to ★★

Horror thriller 1976 · US · Colour · 91mins

The title is a sniper's justification for climbing to the top of a water tower in New York, loading up a high velocity rifle and casually popping innocent people in the street. Larry Cohen's thriller (also known as *Demon*) spirals off into a weird world of sexual fantasy, religious fanaticism and even alien invasion. Lovers of movie schlock might well find their lusts satisfied, though audiences who value more prosaic things, such as decent photography, a script that makes sense and convincing performances, might find it somewhat lacking. AT

Tony LoBianco *Peter Nicholas* • Deborah Raffin *Casey Forster* • Sandy Dennis *Martha Nicholas* • Sylvia Sidney *Elizabeth Mullin* • Sam Levene *Everett Lukas* • Robert Drivas *David Morten* ■ *Dir/Scr* Larry Cohen

The Goddess ★★★

Drama 1958 · US · BW · 105mins

An excellent rendition of the "poor, working-class girl makes it in the movies" scenario, written with great depth and understanding by Paddy Chayefsky. Allegedly based on the life of Marilyn Monroe, and full of oblique references to abused childhoods and scenes of reckless pill-popping, this is nevertheless a serious attempt to explore the nature of female fame and sexual charisma. Kim Stanley turns in a fine performance as the ambitious starlet, who's part manipulative minx, part vulnerable victim, and she is ably supported by a fine cast. SH

Kim Stanley *Emily Ann Faulkner* • Betty Lou Holland *Mother* • Joan Copeland *Aunt* • Gerald Hiken *Uncle* • Burt Brinckerhoff *Boy* • Steven Hill *John Tower* • Gerald Petrarca *Minister* • Linda Soma *Bridesmaid* • Curt Conway *Writer* • Lloyd Bridges *Dutch Seymour* ■ *Dir* John Cromwell • *Scr* Paddy Chayefsky

The Godfather ★★★★★ 18

Crime drama 1972 · US · Colour · 168mins

Not only one of the all-time high watermarks of American cinema, the young Francis Ford Coppola's elegiac organised-crime saga also proves that an intelligent, sometimes slow-moving, drama with impeccable artistic credentials can also create queues around the block. Beginning after the end of the Second World War, it traces the handover within the Corleone family from the old world values of Don Vito (a heavily disguised but stately Marlon Brando) to his son, the "white sheep" Michael (Al Pacino, proving that his risky casting was inspired). The Mafia is never mentioned by name, but underneath all the slayings and sinister "offers you can't refuse", this is an immigrant family drama about assimilation, blood loyalty and honour, rich with subtle acting and blessed with stunning cinematography. AC. In English and Italian with subtitles. Contains violence, swearing and sex scenes. [video] DVD

Marlon Brando *Don Vito Corleone* • Al Pacino *Michael Corleone* • James Caan *Sonny Corleone* • Richard Castellano *Clemenza* • Robert Duvall *Tom Hagen* • Sterling Hayden *McCluskey* • John Marley *Jack Woltz* • Richard Conte *Barzini* • Diane Keaton *Kay Adams* ■ *Dir* Francis Ford Coppola • *Scr* Francis Ford Coppola, Mario Puzo, from the novel by Mario Puzo • *Cinematographer* Gordon Willis • *Production Designer* Dean Tavoularis • *Music* Nino Rota, Carmine Coppola

The Godfather, Part II ★★★★★ 18

Crime drama 1974 · US · Colour · 192mins

In *The Godfather*, Don Corleone's war hero son Michael (Al Pacino) turns into a man who orders death like room service. In *Part II*, Michael is a symbol of an America born of immigrant idealism and dying of corruption. Breathtaking in scope, this sequel shows the early life of the Don, brilliantly portrayed by Robert De Niro, as he flees Sicily and sails for New York. These sequences have the grandeur of a silent movie by DW Griffith or Erich von Stroheim; some later scenes, with Michael in Cuba, are clumsy and confusing, though the climax is as chilling as the look on Michael's face when he realises that even Family members can be rubbed out. Pacino gives a monumental performance and it was an equally monumental crime that he never won an Oscar for it. AT. In English and Italian with subtitles. Contains violence, swearing. [video] DVD

Al Pacino *Michael Corleone* • Robert Duvall *Tom Hagen* • Diane Keaton *Kay Corleone* • Robert De Niro *Vito Corleone* • Talia Shire *Connie* • John Cazale *Fredo Corleone* • Lee Strasberg *Hyman Roth* • Michael V Gazzo *Frank Pentangeli* ■ *Dir* Francis Ford Coppola • *Scr* Francis Ford Coppola, Mario Puzo, from characters created by Mario Puzo • *Cinematographer* Gordon Willis • *Production Designer* Dean Tavoularis • *Music* Nino Rota, Carmine Coppola

The Godfather Part III ★★★ 15

Crime drama 1990 · US · Colour · 163mins

The Godfather was a masterpiece and so, too, was its sequel. Yet this third picture is merely a distant relative and was made for purely mercenary reasons. Thanks to the badly bungled corkscrew plot, one is left with the basic theme of Michael Corleone (Al Pacino) unable to renounce crime and being slowly transformed into a martyr. Pacino has some fine moments and Andy Garcia is frequently electrifying as Sonny Corleone's bastard son Vincent Mancini, the new don on the block. However, Coppola's own daughter, Sofia, who took over at the last minute from Winona Ryder, is embarrassing as Michael's daughter Mary. AT. In English and Italian with subtitles. Contains violence and swearing. [video] DVD

Al Pacino *Michael Corleone* • Diane Keaton *Kay Adams* • Andy Garcia *Vincent Mancini* • Talia Shire *Connie Corleone Rizzi* • Eli Wallach *Don Altobello* • Joe Mantegna *Joey Zasa* • George Hamilton *BJ Harrison* • Bridget Fonda *Grace Hamilton* • Sofia Coppola *Mary Corleone* ■ *Dir* Francis Ford Coppola • *Scr* Francis Ford Coppola, Mario Puzo • *Cinematographer* Gordon Willis

Godmoney ★★★★ 18

Crime drama 1997 · US · Colour · 94mins

A powerful, striking American indie film, this probably deserved better than an unheralded video release. Using a cast of unknowns, first-time director Darren Doane transforms a predictable tale of drug dealing into an arresting and chilling portrait of moral apathy in American suburbia. Newcomer Rick Rodney (a dead ringer for John Malkovich) is the New York youngster who arrives in Los Angeles, determined to put his criminal past behind him. But when he loses his job and money runs short, a tempting offer from an ambitious local drug dealer proves difficult to pass up. JF [video] DVD

Rick Rodney *Nathan* • Bobby Field *Matthew* • Christi Allen *Dana* • Stewart Teggart *Jason* • Chad Nell *John* • Sean Atkins *Jeff* ■ *Dir* Darren Doane • *Scr* Sean Atkins, Darren Doane, Sean Christopher Nelson

Gods and Generals ★★ 12

Historical war drama
2002 · US · Colour · 209mins

The trouble with this painstakingly accurate account of the American Civil War is that most of the participants come across as walking waxworks. The second in a planned trilogy – the first being 1993's *Gettysburg* – by director Ronald F Maxwell, it sets up its lead characters – their names already heavy with history – with speeches that sound as if they have simply been culled from a catalogue of famous quotations, while the conflict's ostensible cause (to free the slaves) is given short shrift in minor exchanges. But the battlefield scenes are gorily impressive, and Robert Duvall gives real credence to his role as General Robert E Lee. TH [video] DVD

Jeff Daniels *Lt Col Joshua Lawrence Chamberlain* • Stephen Lang *Gen Thomas "Stonewall" Jackson* • Robert Duvall *Gen Robert E Lee* • Mira Sorvino *Fanny Chamberlain* • Kevin Conway *Sgt Buster Kilrain* • C Thomas Howell *Sgt Thomas Chamberlain* • Frankie Faison *Jim Lewis* ■ *Dir* Ronald F Maxwell • *Scr* Ronald F Maxwell, from the book by Jeffrey M Shaara • *Cinematographer* Kees Von Oostrum

Gods and Monsters ★★★★★ 15

Biographical drama
1998 · US/UK · Colour and BW · 105mins

Ian McKellen gives a brilliant performance as 1930s director James Whale – the "Father of Frankenstein" – in this inventive biographical fantasy. Set during Whale's twilight years, when he was ostracised by Hollywood for being a box-office failure and a homosexual to boot, this focuses on his infatuation with his hunky but heterosexual gardener (Brendan Fraser). Interspersed with the unfolding relationship are half-forgotten images from Whale's shadowy past, as well as occasional drug-addled sexual hallucinations. The result is a poignant and elegant masterpiece. AJ. Contains swearing, nudity, sex scene. [video] DVD

Ian McKellen *James Whale* • Brendan Fraser *Clayton Boone* • Lynn Redgrave *Hanna* • Lolita Davidovich *Betty* • Kevin J O'Connor *Harry* • David Dukes *David Lewis* • Brandon Kleyla *Young James Whale* • Pamela Salem *Sarah Whale* ■ *Dir* Bill Condon • *Scr* Bill Condon, from the novel *Father of Frankenstein* by Christopher Bram

God's Country ★★★★

Documentary 1985 · US · Colour · 90mins

Making his final foray into the documentary field, Louis Malle brought his trademark humanism to this study of the ultra-traditional farming community of Glencoe, Minnesota. The bulk of the action was filmed in 1979, when the aftershocks of Vietnam and Watergate could still be felt – even in this most isolated region, where patriarchy was synonymous with prejudice and a disconcerting lack of curiosity. Yet it's the closing segment, shot at the height of the Reagan era, that provides the most telling insights, as the fond-held hopes and schemes prove illusory. Touching and amusing, yet never patronising or cruel. DP

Louis Malle *Narrator* ■ *Dir* Louis Malle

God's Country and the Woman ★★ U

Drama 1937 · US · Colour · 85mins

It's hard to get excited when the woman of the title turns out to be minor Warner Bros actress Beverly Roberts, playing opposite George Brent instead of his regular co-star (and rumoured squeeze) Bette Davis. Brent plays a hunky lumberjack, but the real reason for watching is God's country itself, stunningly photographed in an early (and now forgotten) example of glorious Technicolor that almost justifies the daft plot and dialogue. TS

George Brent *Steve Russett* • Beverly Roberts *Jo Barton* • Barton MacLane *Bullhead* • Robert Barrat *Jefferson Russett* • Alan Hale *Bjorn Skalka* • Joseph King (1) *Red Munroe* ■ *Dir* William Keighley • *Scr* Norman Reilly Raine, from a story by Peter Milne, Charles Belden, from the novel *God's Country – and the Woman* by James Oliver Curwood • *Cinematographer* Tony Gaudio

God's Gift to Women ★

Romantic comedy 1931 · US · BW · 71mins

Parisian womaniser Frank Fay is irresistible to women, as evidenced by the numbers who pursue him. He sets his determined sights on American heiress Laura La Plante, but has difficulty persuading her that he's changed his ways. Fay, supported by a bevy of girls who include Joan Blondell and Louise Brooks, does his best with the thin, one-note material, as does director Michael Curtiz. But *Variety* got it right in 1931 when it observed that this was "no gift to audiences". RK

Frank Fay *Jacques Duryea/Toto* • Laura La Plante *Diane Churchill* • Joan Blondell *Fifi* • Charles Winninger *Mr Churchill* • Alan Mowbray *Auguste* • Louise Brooks *Florine* ■ *Dir* Michael Curtiz • *Scr* Joseph Jackson, Raymond Griffith, Frederick Hazlitt Brennan, from the play *The Devil Was Sick* by Jane Hinton

God's Gun ★★ 18

Western 1977 · Is/It · Colour · 92mins

Here's a little-seen novelty: an Italian-styled western produced in Israel and directed by that veteran of the spaghetti genre, Frank Kramer. It stars three actors old enough to know that sometimes you just take the money – Lee Van Cleef, Jack Palance and Richard Boone. Played with very little conviction, this is naff exploitation only made tolerable by its grizzled cast. TS. Contains violence, sex scenes. [video]

Lee Van Cleef *Father John/Lewis* • Jack Palance *Sam Clayton* • Richard Boone *The*

Sheriff • Sybil Danning *Jenny* • Leif Garrett *Johnny* • Cody Palance ■ *Dir* Frank Kramer [Gianfranco Parolini] • *Scr* Gianfranco Parolini, John Fonsecan

God's Little Acre ★★★

Melodrama 1958 · US · BW · 111mins

This is director Anthony Mann's version of Erskine Caldwell's steamy melodrama about a farmer in Georgia who thinks he's struck gold, except for that one acre he sets aside for the Almighty. What we have here is a giant metaphor, in which everyone is possessed by gold lust and just plain ordinary lust. As the farmer, Robert Ryan delivers a trademark performance of dignity unravelling as his family disintegrates. The picture lacks a decent female lead and is almost as pompous a family saga as, say, *Giant*, although it's not as elongated and the earth really does move. AT

Robert Ryan *Ty Ty Walden* • Aldo Ray *Will Thompson* • Tina Louise *Griselda* • Buddy Hackett *Pluto* • Jack Lord *Buck Walden* • Fay Spain *Darlin' Jill* • Vic Morrow *Shaw Walden* • Helen Westcott *Rosamund* ■ *Dir* Anthony Mann • *Scr* Philip Yordan (front for Ben Maddow), from the novel by Erskine Caldwell

The Gods Must Be Crazy ★★★ PG

Comedy
1980 · Botswana/S Afr · Colour · 108mins

There will be those who see this as inexcusably racist exploitation that mocks the traditions and expectations of the Kalahari bush tribe, whose peaceful existence is disturbed by a Coke bottle that drops from the sky. But others will applaud the barbed colonial satire that arises when N !xau ventures into civilisation to drop the contentious bottle off the edge of the world. Certainly audiences worldwide warmed to director Jamie Uys's slapstick style, turning this latter-day Keystone comedy into a cult smash. There are some crude laughs, but the juvenility is hard to ignore. DP. Contains violence and brief nudity. [VIDEO] DVD

Paddy O'Byrne *Narration* • N!xau *Xixo* • Marius Weyers *Andrew Steyn* • Sandra Prinsloo *Kate Thompson* • Nic De Jager *Jack Hind* • Louw Verwey *Sam Boga* • Michael Thys *Mpudi* • Fanyana Sidumo *First Card* • Joe Seakatsie *Second Card* ■ *Dir/Scr* Jamie Uys

The Gods Must Be Crazy II ★★★ PG

Comedy
1989 · US/Botswana/S Afr · Colour · 93mins

Considering his meagre resources, director Jamie Uys can hardly be blamed for the tackiness of the aerial effects in this sequel to his surprise box-office hit. He must also be commended for the patience with which he constructs his gags, several of which seem to take an age to pay off. However, the unsubtlety of his slapstick and the dubiousness of some of his cultural observation make this every bit as divisive a film as its predecessor. N!xau returns as the bushman confronting civilisation, this time after his children are accidentally abducted by poachers. Frantic fun or unforgivably offensive? DP [VIDEO] DVD

N!xau *Xixo* • Lena Ferugia *Dr Ann Taylor* • Hans Strydom *Dr Stephen Marshall* • Eiros *Xiri* • Nadies *Xisa* • Erick Bowen *Mateo* • Treasure Tshabalala *Timi* ■ *Dir/Scr* Jamie Uys

Gods of the Plague ★★★

Crime drama 1969 · W Ger · BW · 91mins

Rainer Werner Fassbinder's third feature, about a man released from prison who works his way back into the underworld, is a forceful homage to Hollywood *film noir*. However, despite the trenchcoats, trilbies and cigarette smoke, it is mainly a sombre meditation on the alienated postwar German generation. Fassbinder's cast, including Hanna Schygulla and future director Margarethe von Trotta, are exemplary. Fassbinder's lover of the time, Günther Kaufmann, the illegitimate son of a black GI and a Bavarian woman, plays a crook who dies whispering, "Life is so precious, even right now." RB. In German with English subtitles.

Harry Baer *Franz* • Hanna Schygulla *Joanna* • Margarethe von Trotta *Margarethe* • Günther Kaufmann *Günther* • Carla Aulaulu *Carla* • Ingrid Caven *Magdalena Fuller* • Jan George *Cop* • Marian Seidowski *Marian* • Rainer Werner Fassbinder *Porno buyer* ■ *Dir/Scr* Rainer Werner Fassbinder

God's Will ★★

Comedy 1989 · US · Colour · 100mins

With both mum and dad in the business, there was always a chance that Domenica Cameron-Scorsese was going to end up in movies. Here she bravely holds together her screenwriter mother Julia Cameron's directorial debut as the orphan who invokes the help of her dead, divorced parents to spare her the nightmare of living with their new spouses. Daniel Region and Laura Margolis also try hard as the squabbling showbiz luvvies, but the film never recovered from the theft of the soundtrack, as the dubbed dialogue sounds otherworldly. DP

Marge Kotlisky *God* • Daniel Region *Peter Potter* • Laura Margolis *Gillian Norwood* • Domenica Cameron-Scorsese *Victoria Potter* • Holly Fulger *Hedy* ■ *Dir/Scr* Julia Cameron

The Godsend ★ 15

Horror 1980 · UK · Colour · 82mins

A family discovers that their adopted daughter is really a demon out to murder them one by one in this tepid, ultra-slow and raggedly acted *Omen*-style fantasy borrowing most of its plot elements from that film but doing little of note with them. Although beautifully photographed, and accenting the psychologically scary side of the story more than the gruesome details, this low-key item is handled like a soporific soap opera. AJ [VIDEO]

Malcolm Stoddard *Alan Marlowe* • Cyd Hayman *Kate Marlowe* • Angela Pleasence *Stranger* • Patrick Barr *Dr Collins* • Wilhelmina Green *Bonnie* ■ *Dir* Gabrielle Beaumont • *Scr* Olaf Pooley, from the novel by Bernard Taylor • *Cinematographer* Norman Warwick

Godsend ★★ 15

Horror thriller
2003 · US/Can · Colour · 98mins

Robert De Niro revives the notorious old cliché of the mad scientist in this horror thriller. When the eight-year-old son (Cameron Bright) of Greg Kinnear and Rebecca Romijn-Stamos dies, De Niro's benign doctor offers to clone the dead boy at his Godsend Fertility Clinic. All goes well for a time, but then sinister cracks appear in the good doctor's façade, and the cloned child also begins to exhibit signs of evil. Apart from some neat shocks, the story is painfully predictable. TH. Contains swearing, violence. [VIDEO] DVD

Greg Kinnear *Paul Duncan* • Rebecca Romijn-Stamos *Jessie Duncan* • Robert De Niro *Dr Richard Wells* • Cameron Bright *Adam Duncan* • Marcia Bennett *Principal Hersch* • Zoie Palmer *Susan Pierce* • Janet Bailey *Cora Williams* • Devon Bostick *Zachary Clark Wells* ■ *Dir* Nick Hamm • *Scr* Mark Bomback

Godspell ★★★ U

Musical 1973 · US · Colour · 101mins

This New York-set reworking of the Gospel according to St Matthew following a famous off-Broadway production is an uneasy enchantment that's halfway between holy foolishness and hippy indulgence. Director David Greene's musical nevertheless has moments of infectious glee, as Gospel parables are narrated by a Christ figure (Victor Garber) in a Superman sweatshirt and workman's overalls. Though it won't make you turn on or drop out, it's worth tuning in. This innocent remnant of the flower-power era is far less calculated and mercenary than the same year's *Jesus Christ Superstar*. TH

Victor Garber *Jesus* • David Haskell *John/Judas* • Jerry Sroka *Jerry* • Lynne Thigpen *Lynne* • Katie Hanley *Katie* • Robin Lamont *Robin* • Gilmer McCormick *Gilmer* • Joanne Jonas *Joanne* • Jeffrey Mylett *Jeffrey* ■ *Dir* David Greene • *Scr* David Greene, John-Michael Tebelak, from the musical by John-Michael Tebelak, Stephen Schwartz

Godzilla ★★★★

Monster horror 1954 · Jpn/US · BW · 80mins

A gigantic dinosaur with radioactive breath is awakened by atomic testing and goes on a rampage, destroying Tokyo. The first, and best, of the long-running monster franchise from Toho Studios is sombre science fiction (in contrast to the kiddie-friendly sequels) and incorporates award-winning special effects by Eiji Tsuburaya into its nuclear-age allegory. Additional footage, directed by Terry Morse, featuring reporter Raymond Burr commenting on the manic mayhem, was spliced into a cut-down, dubbed version of the Japanese original. Director Ishiro Honda's 98-minute masterpiece makes a plea for peace and no more A-bomb testing. The 80-minute Americanised version doesn't. AJ.

Raymond Burr *Steve Martin* • Takashi Shimura *Dr Yamane* • Momoko Kochi *Emiko* • Akira Takarada *Ogata* • Akihiko Hirata *Dr Serizawa* • Sachio Sakai *Hagiwara* • Fuyuki Murakami *Dr Tabata* • Ren Yamamoto ■ *Dir* Terry Morse, Inoshiro Honda • *Scr* Takeo Murata, Inoshiro Honda, from the story *Godzilla, King of the Monsters* by Shigeru Kayama

Godzilla ★★ PG

Monster horror 1997 · US · Colour · 132mins

In this dreary American overhaul from *Independence Day* director Roland Emmerich, Japan's favourite giant lizard crawls out of radioactive waters in the South Pacific and heads for New York. Emmerich's blockbuster behemoth replaces man-in-suit special effects with dodgy computer digitals and sub-*Jurassic Park* thrills. What it doesn't replicate is the endearing charm the celebrated fire-breather had when he stomped through cardboard skyscrapers. The old Toho Studios' fantasy adventures may have had lower budgets, but even the cheapest shows more flair than this dismal monster mishmash. AJ [VIDEO] DVD

Matthew Broderick *Dr Niko Tatopoulos* • Jean Reno *Philippe Roaché* • Maria Pitillo *Audrey Timmonds* • Hank Azaria *Victor "Animal" Palotti* • Kevin Dunn *Colonel Hicks* • Michael Lerner *Mayor Ebert* • Harry Shearer *Charles Caiman* • Arabella Field *Lucy Palotti* ■ *Dir* Roland Emmerich • *Scr* Dean Devlin, Roland Emmerich, from a story by Ted Elliott, Terry Rossio, Dean Devlin, Roland Emmerich, from the character created by Toho Co Ltd

Godzilla Raids Again ★

Monster horror 1955 · Jpn/US · BW · 77mins

The first *Godzilla* sequel finds the giant lizard under an assumed name – Gigantis, because Warner Bros neglected to secure the rights to the name Godzilla – as he battles Angurus before stomping towards Tokyo and trashing Osaka en route. The usual shaky backdrops and hysterical civilian panic footage make less impact this time. It was eight years before Godzilla met King Kong to triumph again. AJ. A Japanese language film with both dubbed and subtitled versions.

Hiroshi Koizumi *Shoichi Tsukioka* • Setsuko Wakayama *Hedemi Yamaji* • Minoru Chiaki *Koji Kobayashi* ■ *Dir* Motoyoshi Oda • *Scr* Takeo Murata, Sigeaki Hidaka

Godzilla vs Gigan ★★★ PG

Monster horror 1972 · Jpn · Colour · 85mins

More totally bonkers fantasy mayhem from Japan's Toho Studios, as Godzilla makes another appearance to save the planet from intergalactic domination. This time alien cockroaches plan to occupy the Earth and summon Ghidorah, the three-headed dragon, and Gigan, a crimson-eyed metal bird, to fight the Monster Island duo of Godzilla and Anzilla at a children's amusement park. For the first time, the monsters talk to each other, and a note of contemporary relevance is struck as shots of Tokyo depict the aliens' dying world. AJ. Japanese dialogue dubbed into English. [VIDEO]

Haruo Nakajima *Godzilla* • Yukietsu Omiya *Angurus* • Kanta Ina *Ghidorah* • Kengo Nakayama • Hiroshi Ichikawa • Yuriko Hishimi ■ *Dir* Jun Fukuda • *Scr* Takeshi Kimura, Shinichi Skizawa

Godzilla vs King Ghidorah ★★★ PG

Monster horror 1991 · Jpn · Colour · 102mins

One of the best of the entire 22-strong Japanese *Godzilla* series, this also boasts one of the saga's most complex plots. It involves time travellers from the future intervening in the 1944 nuclear events, causing the monster lizard's birth and creating his three-headed flying nemesis Ghidorah to defeat Japan and stop it becoming a future world power. The time-warp elements do cause some confusion but are easy to forgive in such an imaginative story, which also neatly fills in details of Godzilla's humble beginnings. All the monster battles are epic and exciting. AJ. Japanese dialogue dubbed into English. [VIDEO]

Anna Nakagawa *Emmy Kano* • Kosuke Toyohara *Kenichiro Terasawa* • Megumi Odaka *Miki Saegusa* • Kiwako Harada *Chiaki Moriyuma* • Shoji Kobayashi *Yuzo Tsuchiashi* ■ *Dir/Scr* Kazuki Omori

Godzilla vs Mechagodzilla ★★ PG

Monster horror 1974 · Jpn · Colour · 79mins

You can't keep a good monster down, and for his 20th anniversary (and 14th film), Japan's Toho Studios created a worthy adversary for its money-making prehistoric lizard – a cyborg version of Godzilla himself! In this average entry in the variable series, Mechagodzilla is the secret weapon of ape-like aliens seeking world domination. Plenty of sparks fly in the extended cardboard battle scenes, and there are a couple of daft new creatures, but it's pretty much comic book stuff. AJ. In Japanese with English subtitles. [VIDEO]

Masaaki Daimon *Keisuke Shimizu* • Kazuya Aoyama *Masahiko Shimizu* ■ *Dir* Jun Fukuda • *Scr* Hiroyasu Yamamura, Jun Fukuda

Godzilla vs Megalon ★★★ PG

Monster horror 1973 · Jpn · Colour · 78mins

Megalon, a giant insect monster with drills for arms plus a death-ray head, and Gigan are teamed by the Seatopians to conquer the world in revenge for inflicting nuclear damage under the oceans. That's the cue for Godzilla to fight the monster menace and save Japan once more. Here Godzilla joins the brightly coloured Jet Jaguar robot for the barren desert battles, so part of the fun in watching cardboard model cities topple is

G

missing. But hilariously risible dubbed dialogue, more than makes up for the lack of stupid spectacle and the plot is interspersed with a sobering anti-pollution message. AJ. Japanese dialogue dubbed into English.

Katsuhiko Sasaki *Professor Goro Ibuki* • Hiroyuki Kawase *Rokuro Ibuki* ■ *Dir* Jun Fukuda • *Scr* Jun Fukuda, Shinichi Sekizawa, Takeshi Kimura

Godzilla vs Mothra ★★★ PG

Monster horror 1964 · Jpn · Colour · 102mins

Godzilla's fourth screen appearance, and Mothra's second, makes for an enjoyable romp through the odd conventions of Japanese monster moviedom. Mothra's giant egg is washed ashore by a hurricane and found by carnival promoters. When tiny twin guardians arrive to ask for its return to the giant moth's island home, the authorities beg for their help to get Mothra to fight Godzilla, who's once more embarking on a Tokyo attack. But the ageing Mothra isn't up to the battle royal, so the two hatching larvae move into silky-webbed action instead in a funny – both intentionally and otherwise – and reasonably exciting slice of zany mayhem. AJ. In Japanese with English subtitles.

Akira Takarada *News reporter* • Yuriko Hoshi *Girl photographer* • Hiroshi Koizumi *Scientist* • Yu Fujiki *Second reporter* • Emi Ito *One of twin girls* • Yumi Ito *One of twin girls* ■ *Dir* Inoshiro Honda • *Scr* Shinichi Sekizawa

Godzilla vs Mothra ★★★ PG

Monster horror 1992 · Jpn · Colour · 102mins

Thirty years after Toho first introduced Mothra, the studio virtually remade the same story in their attempt to modernise their monster dinosaur series for a new generation. It worked and this was a huge hit in Japan. Two tiny women, known as the Cosmos, summon up the creature Mothra to fight the evil Battra, who has been sent to destroy Earth. However, Godzilla appears and a three-way battle occurs in a fiery finale set in Tokyo. Good, colourful fun. AJ. Japanese dialogue dubbed into English.

Tetsuya Bessho *Takuya Fujita* • Akiji Kobayashi *Ryuzo Dobashi* • Satomi Kobayashi *Masako Tezuka* • Takehiro Murata *Kenji Ando* • Megumi Odaka *Miki Saegusa* ■ *Dir* Takao Okawara • *Scr* Kazuki Omori

Godzilla's Revenge ★

Monster horror 1969 · Jpn · Colour · 70mins

A bullied schoolboy realises his dream of going to Monster Island, where he meets Godzilla and his son, Minya, who teach him how to be brave. Stripped of the serious A-bomb underpinnings that made early entries in the Toho series so rich in irony, the tenth *Godzilla* movie is a very sad affair. Insult is added to injury by the inclusion of battle scenes from earlier adventures such as *Son of Godzilla* and *Ebirah, Horror of the Deep* to save money on special effects. AJ. In Japanese with English subtitles.

Kenji Sahara *Kenkichi Miki* • Tomonori Yazaki *Ichiro Miki* • Machiko Naka *Mrs Miki* • Sachio Sakai *Senbayashi* • Chotaro Togin *Assistant detective* ■ *Dir* Ishiro Honda [Inoshiro Honda] • *Scr* Shinichi Sekizawa

Gog ★★★

Science fiction 1954 · US · Colour · 82mins

Don't let the Z-grade title put you off – this is actually a decent little sci-fi techno shocker that predates *2001: a Space Odyssey* by more than a decade in its depiction of a computer programmed to kill. Richard Egan leads an undistinguished cast, with people being bumped off by two malevolent robots let loose in a subterranean laboratory in New Mexico. Originally released in 3-D, this combines great Saturday matinee thrills with Cold War tension and topical fears about all-powerful machines. RS

Richard Egan *David Sheppard* • Constance Dowling *Joanna Merritt* • Herbert Marshall *Dr Van Ness* • John Wengraf *Dr Zeltman* • Philip Van Zandt *Dr Elzevir* • Valerie Vernon *Madame Elzevir* • Stephen Roberts *Major Howard* • Byron Kane *Dr Carter* ■ *Dir* Herbert L Strock • *Scr* Tom Taggart, Richard G Taylor, from a story by Ivan Tors

Gohatto ★★★★ 15

Historical drama
1999 · Jpn/Fr/UK · Colour · 96mins

This is another variation on Herman Melville's allegorical novel *Billy Budd*, with its themes of authority, duty and homosexual repression in the military – here it's an elite samurai militia. Set in Kyoto in the mid-1860s and based on two semi-factual stories, this is ostensibly a murder mystery. But in a darkly comic and highly stylised tale, notions of loyalty and the implications of an era passing matter more than militia captain Takeshi Kitano's investigation into the sinister events that surround handsome but androgynous samurai Ryuhei Matsuda. Nagisa Oshima's film is less graphic than his celebrated sexual allegory *In the Realm of the Senses*, but it's every bit as assured. DP. In Japanese with English subtitles. Contains violence and brief nudity. DVD

"Beat" Takeshi [Takeshi Kitano] *Captain Toshizo Hijikata* • Ryuhei Matsuda *Sozaburo Kano, young samurai* • Shinji Takeda *Lieutenant Soji Okita* • Tadanobu Asano *Hyozo Tashiro* ■ *Dir* Nagisa Oshima • *Scr* Nagisa Oshima, from the stories *Shinsengumi Keppuroku* by Ryotaro Shiba • *Music* Ryuichi Sakamoto

Goin' Coconuts ★★

Comedy adventure
1978 · US · Colour · 93mins

The all-singing, all-dancing Osmond family were an international pop phenomenon in the 1970s. Two of the tribe, Donny and Marie Osmond, then graduated to their own TV show and – inevitably – a big-screen outing followed. This juvenile adventure finds the toothsome twosome under threat from villains in picturesque Hawaii, but the plot is of secondary importance as they deliver a clutch of songs before the obligatory happy ending. DF

Donny Osmond *Donny* • Marie Osmond *Marie* • Herb Edelman *Sid* • Kenneth Mars *Kruse* • Crystin Sinclaire *Tricia* • Ted Cassidy *Mickey* • Marc Lawrence (1) *Webster* • Khigh Dhiegh *Wong* • Harold Sakata *Ito* ■ *Dir* Howard Morris • *Scr* Raymond Harvey

Goin' South ★★★ PG

Western 1978 · US · Colour · 103mins

After making a respectable directorial debut in 1971 with *Drive, He Said*, Jack Nicholson planned a mystical western called *Moon Trap*. But the project didn't please the studios and Nicholson eventually turned to *Goin' South*, an amiable and wayward western in which he escapes the gallows and rides away with Mary Steenburgen. Steenburgen got the part after Jane Fonda turned it down – she felt it was another *Cat Ballou* – and after newcomers Jessica Lange and Meryl Streep were tested. It's easy to enjoy, even if his trademark leers are no substitute for real acting. The picture was a critical and commercial failure. AT DVD

Jack Nicholson *Henry Lloyd Moon* • Mary Steenburgen *Julia Tate* • Christopher Lloyd *Frank Towfield* • John Belushi *Hector* • Danny DeVito *Clyde/"Hog"* • Veronica Cartwright *Hermine* • Richard Bradford *Sheriff Andrew Kyle* • Jeff Morris *Big Abe* ■ *Dir* Jack Nicholson • *Scr* John Herman Shaner, Al Ramrus, Charles Shyer, Alan Mandel, from a story by John Herman Shaner

Goin' to Town ★★★

Musical comedy 1935 · US · BW · 74mins

Mae West writes herself another juicy role as a cattle baroness who makes a fortune from the timely acquisition of an oil field. Getting her man – in this case Paul Cavanagh – doesn't prove quite so easy, so Mae sets out to improve her social standing. She has a fine time mocking the hypocrisy of high society and memorably performs a song from the opera *Samson and Delilah* by Saint-Saëns. The weak line-up of male performers leaves Mae in full command of the proceedings. AE

Mae West *Cleo Borden* • Paul Cavanagh *Edward Carrington* • Gilbert Emery *Winslow* • Marjorie Gateson *Mrs Crane Brittony* • Tito Coral *Taho* • Ivan Lebedeff *Ivan Valadov* • Fred Kohler *Buck Gonzales* • Monroe Owsley *Fletcher Colton* ■ *Dir* Alexander Hall • *Scr* Mae West, from a story by Marion Morgan, George B Dowell

Going All the Way ★ 15

Drama 1997 · US · Colour · 98mins

A badly scripted, disappointing 1950s-set drama, this stars Jeremy Davies as the shy, nerdy photographer who makes friends with local jock Ben Affleck after they both return to their home town following service in the Korean War. Rose McGowan, Amy Locane and Rachel Weisz are the girls providing the glamour, but even this impressive young cast can't save the film from being clichéd, tediously plotted and ultimately irritating. JB. Contains swearing, sex scenes.

Jeremy Davies *Sonny Burns* • Ben Affleck *Gunner Casselman* • Amy Locane *Buddy Porter* • Rose McGowan *Gail Thayer* • Rachel Weisz *Marty Pilcher* • John Lordan *Elwood Burns* • Bob Swan *Luke* • Jill Clayburgh *Alma Burns* • Lesley Ann Warren *Nina Casselman* ■ *Dir* Mark Pellington • *Scr* Dan Wakefield, from his novel

Going Ape! ★ U

Comedy 1981 · US · Colour · 87mins

The hit TV comedy series *Taxi* was still running when stars Tony Danza and Danny DeVito took time out to appear in this big-screen outing about a guy (Danza) who stands to inherit a fortune if he can successfully look after his late father's orang-utans. Writer/director Jeremy Joe Kronsberg made a name for himself with his script for *Every Which Way but Loose*, which teamed Clint Eastwood with a lovable orang-utan. Kronsberg reached the logical (but erroneous) conclusion that if one orang-utan was funny, a whole bunch must be hilarious. DF

Tony Danza *Foster* • Jessica Walter *Fiona* • Stacey Nelkin *Cynthia* • Danny DeVito *Lazlo* • Art Metrano *Joey* • Frank Sivero *Bad Habit* • Rick Hurst *Brandon* • Howard Mann *Jules Cohen* ■ *Dir/Scr* Jeremy Joe Kronsberg

Going Berserk ★★ 15

Comedy 1983 · US/Can · Colour · 80mins

John Candy is reunited with some old chums from his Canadian TV days (Eugene Levy and Joe Flaherty) for this wildly erratic comedy. Candy plays a nice but dim driver engaged to the daughter of a politician who finds himself caught up in his prospective father-in-law's battle against a cult. Directed by David Steinberg, this is let down by a script with more misses than hits, but Candy is as effortlessly appealing as ever. JF

John Candy *John Bourgignon* • Joe Flaherty *Chick Leff* • Eugene Levy *Sal di Pasquale* • Alley Mills *Nancy Reese* • Pat Hingle *Ed Reese* • Ann Bronston *Patti Reese* • Eve Brent Ashe [Eve Brent] *Mrs Reese* • Elizabeth Kerr *Grandmother Reese* ■ *Dir* David Steinberg • *Scr* Dana Olsen, David Steinberg

Going Hollywood ★★ U

Musical comedy 1933 · US · BW · 77mins

Marion Davies and Bing Crosby co-star in this modest musical from MGM. The corny tale of a crooner, followed to Hollywood by a fan who poses as a French maid and supplants his current girlfriend and leading lady (Fifi D'Orsay), it provided Davies with an excellent showcase for her charm and her somewhat limited talents. It also disguises Crosby's lack of acting experience by letting him do what he did best – croon. RK

Bing Crosby *Bill Williams* • Marion Davies *Sylvia Bruce* • Fifi D'Orsay *Lili Yvonne* • Stuart Erwin *Ernest P Baker* • Patsy Kelly *Jill Barker* • Bobby Watson *Jack Thompson* • Three Radio Rogues *Film electricians* ■ *Dir* Raoul Walsh • *Scr* Donald Ogden Stewart, from a story by Frances Marion

Going Home ★★★

Drama 1971 · US · Colour · 97mins

Having murdered his wife some years previously, Robert Mitchum comes out of jail only to be tracked down by his vengeance-seeking son (Jan-Michael Vincent). Brenda Vaccaro plays the woman caught between them in Herbert B Leonard's sombre drama, which sank without trace at the American box office and was never released in Britain. However, it's worth watching for Mitchum's brooding performance as the violent hunk and Korean War veteran who feels the pain he inflicts on others. AT

Robert Mitchum *Harry K Graham* • Brenda Vaccaro *Jenny* • Jan-Michael Vincent *Jimmy Graham* • Jason Bernard *Jimmy at six* • Sally Kirkland *Ann Graham* • Josh Mostel *Bonelli* • George DiCenzo *Sergeant* ■ *Dir* Herbert B Leonard • *Scr* Lawrence B Marcus

Going in Style ★★★ PG

Comedy 1979 · US · Colour · 94mins

This touching and very funny movie was part of the great second career coming of George Burns. This teams him with fellow veterans Art Carney and Lee Strasberg, father of the American Method school of acting, as three old-timers who decide to relieve their boredom by robbing a bank. This was the second feature directed by the talented Martin Brest, a film-maker whose films (including *Beverly Hills Cop, Midnight Run* and *Scent of a Woman*) are inexplicably better known than he is. TS. Contains swearing.

George Burns *Joe* • Art Carney *Al* • Lee Strasberg *Willie* • Charles Hallahan *Pete* • Pamela Payton-Wright *Kathy* • Siobhan Keegan *Colleen* • Brian Neville *Kevin* • Constantine Hartofolis *Boy in park* ■ *Dir* Martin Brest • *Scr* Martin Brest, from a story by Edward Cannon

Going My Way ★★★★ U

Musical drama 1944 · US · BW · 120mins

Although writer/producer/director Leo McCarey bagged three Oscars for this effortless piece of Catholic whimsy, its enduring charm rests with the Oscar-winning performances of Bing Crosby and Barry Fitzgerald (the last performer to be nominated in both acting categories for the same role). The sequences in which the inner-city urchins are transformed into angelic choirboys beggar belief, but the brisk by-play between the streetwise Father Crosby and the peppery Father Fitzgerald more than compensates. Crosby was later rewarded for his positive portrayal with a private audience at the Vatican. DP

Bing Crosby *Father "Chuck" O'Malley* • Risë Stevens *Genevieve Linden* • Barry Fitzgerald *Father Fitzgibbon* • Frank McHugh *Father*

Timothy O'Dowd • James Brown (1) *Ted Haines Jr* • Gene Lockhart *Ted Haines Sr* • Jean Heather *Carol James* • Porter Hall *Mr Belknap* ■ *Dir* Leo McCarey • *Scr* Frank Butler, Frank Cavett, from a story by Leo McCarey

Going Off, Big Time ★★ 18

Crime comedy drama
2000 · UK · Colour · 83mins

Yet another British thriller that tries to be both cool and funny but rarely succeeds. Neil Fitzmaurice, who also wrote the script, stars as a young lad who ends up in jail by accident, only to emerge as a gangster-in-the-making four years later thanks to the tutelage of old codger Bernard Hill. Most of the clichés you'd expect are here, but it's made slightly more palatable by Fitzmaurice's nice performance and snappy direction from Jim Doyle. JB. Contains violence, swearing and drug abuse. [video] DVD

Neil Fitzmaurice *Mark Clayton* • Dominic Carter *Ozzi Shepherd* • Sarah Alexander *Stacey Bannerman* • Nick Lamont [Nicholas Lamont] *Paul* • Gabbi Barr *Natasha* • Nick Moss *Charlie* • Bernard Hill *Murray* • Stan Boardman *Arthur McCann* ■ *Dir* Jim Doyle • *Scr* Neil Fitzmaurice

Going Places ★★★

Musical comedy 1938 · US · BW · 84mins

This piece of horse nonsense has Dick Powell masquerading as a famous jockey in order to drum up more business for his employers. Trouble is, he finds himself riding a temperamental horse who can only be soothed by the trumpet playing of Louis Armstrong. His antics do, however, impress the lovely Anita Louise. Enjoy the great "Satchmo" in one of his rare featured roles and a musical cameo from the Dandridge sisters (Vivian and Dorothy). RB

Dick Powell *Peter Mason/Peter Randall* • Anita Louise *Ellen Parker* • Allen Jenkins *Droopy* • Ronald Reagan *Jack Withering* • Walter Catlett *Franklin Dexter* • Harold Huber *Maxie* • Larry Williams (1) *Frank* • Louis Armstrong *Gabe* ■ *Dir* Ray Enright • *Scr* Sig Herzig, Jerry Wald, Maurice Leo, Earl Baldwin, from the play *The Hottentot* by Victor Mapes, William Collier Sr

Going Under ★ PG

Comedy 1990 · US · Colour · 77mins

The best joke in this mix of lame lampoons and slapstick pratfalls is the fact that captain Bill Pullman's submarine is called *Standard*. It centres on the incompetence of Pullman's crew, purposely assembled by corrupt admiral Ned Beatty, and the craft's appearance as a whale after it is refitted. Genuinely substandard. DP [video]

Bill Pullman *Captain Biff Banner* • Wendy Schaal *Jan Michaels* • Ned Beatty *Admiral Malice* • Robert Vaughn *Wedgewood* • Roddy McDowall *The Secretary of Defense/Mr Neighbor* • Bud Cort *Randy McNally* ■ *Dir* Mark W Travis • *Scr* Darryl Zarubica, Randolph Davis

Goke, Bodysnatcher from Hell ★★★ 12

Science fiction horror
1968 · Jpn · Colour · 83mins

After an airplane passes through a strange cloud and crashes, Hideo Ko becomes a blood-sucking maniac and turns most of the other passengers into space vampires. Once again it's all down to aliens planning to invade Earth. Grisly and inventive make-up effects make Hajime Sato's gory and lurid pulp shocker a livelier effort than usual. AJ. In Japanese with English subtitles. [video] DVD

Hideo Ko *Hijacker* • Teruo Yoshida *Sugisaka* • Tomomi Sato *Kuzumi* • Eizo Kitamura *Mano* ■ *Dir* Hajime Sato • *Scr* Kyuzo Kobayashi, Susumu Takaku

Gold ★★★ 12

Adventure 1974 · UK · Colour · 118mins

This adventure was Britain's contribution to the 1970s rash of disaster movies. Shot in South Africa (to the fury of anti-apartheid groups and various trade unions), the film oversimplifies its themes of racism and exploitation, but as an action-packed thriller it delivers the goods. Seeking to prevent the sabotage that will send the price of gold soaring, Roger Moore is as wooden as a pit prop, but Bradford Dillman is a splendid villain and Susannah York invites sympathy as his duped wife. DP. Contains violence. [video]

Roger Moore *Rod Slater* • Susannah York *Terry Steyner* • Ray Milland *Hurry Hirschfeld* • Bradford Dillman *Manfred Steyner* • John Gielgud *Farrell* • Tony Beckley *Stephen Marais* • Simon Sabela *Big King* • Bernard Horsfall *Kowalski* ■ *Dir* Peter Hunt • *Scr* Wilbur Smith, Stanley Price, from the novel *Goldmine* by Wilbur Smith

The Gold and Glory ★ 15

Drama 1984 · Aus · Colour · 97mins

The naive premise at the centre of this intelligence-insulting story is that music is for sissies, while real men pound across unforgiving terrain and win both the admiration of their tough-as-nails fathers and the hearts of sensitive young girls. Quite what talented actors like Colin Friels and Nick Tate are doing in this kind of macho nonsense is anybody's guess. Run a mile rather than watch it. DP [video]

Joss McWilliam *Steve Lucas* • Nick Tate *Joe Lucas* • Josephine Smulders *Kerri Dean* • Robyn Nevin *Robyn Lucas* • Colin Friels *Adam Lucas* • Grant Kenny • Melanie Day *Gilda* • Melissa Jaffer *Ballet teacher* ■ *Dir* Igor Auzins • *Scr* Peter Schreck

Gold Diggers ★★

Musical 1983 · UK · BW · 95mins

Made by an all-female crew with everyone, including star Julie Christie, receiving the same daily wage, Sally Potter's debut feature is a bold statement on behalf of the cinematic sisterhood. Her monochrome deconstruction of the Hollywood musical is less laudable, however. Although Potter neatly reproduces such genre standards as the production number and the dream sequence, the symbolism is often so dense and self-satisfied that the viewer's response is more likely to be polite admiration than wholehearted enthusiasm. DP

Julie Christie *Ruby* • Colette Laffont *Celeste* • Hilary Westlake *Ruby's mother* • David Gale *Expert* • Tom Osborn *Expert's assistant* • Jacky Lansley *Tap dancer* • George Yiasoumi *Stage manager* ■ *Dir* Sally Potter • *Scr* Lindsay Cooper, Rose English, Sally Potter

Gold Diggers in Paris ★★

Musical 1938 · US · BW · 98mins

"Forget the ballet, whether Paris likes it or not we're going to do it our way." It's these words and sentiments that lead to the typically lavish Busby Berkeley number, which is the highlight here. This last, and rarest, in the *Gold Diggers* series has the accent on comedy and music, rather than story, but fans of the girls may need no further recommendation. RT

Rudy Vallee *Terry Moore* • Rosemary Lane *Kay Morrow* • Hugh Herbert *Maurice Giraud* • Allen Jenkins *Duke Dennis* • Gloria Dickson *Mona* • Melville Cooper *Pierre LeBrec* • Mabel Todd *Leticia* • Fritz Feld *Luis Leoni* ■ *Dir* Ray Enright • *Scr* Earl Baldwin, Warren Duff, from a story by Jerry Wald, Richard Macaulay, Maurice Leo, Jerry Horwin, James Seymour

Gold Diggers of Broadway ★★★

Musical 1929 · US · Colour · 105mins

This early talkie no longer exists in its entirety. Some years ago, however, the British Film Institute found the final reel, which makes for nine minutes of fascinating viewing. Filmed in early two-strip Technicolor, it starts with a brief plot-wrapping scene between Nancy Welford and Conway Tearle. After a dazzling overhead shot of backstage activity, it launches into a climactic revue section. Lavishly staged against an impressionistic Parisian backdrop and enthusiastically performed by an array of speciality dance and acrobatic acts, even what little remains clearly indicates why the film was such a huge success on its initial release. TV

Nancy Welford *Jerry* • Conway Tearle *Stephen Lee* • Winnie Lightner *Mable* • Ann Pennington *Ann Collins* • Lilyan Tashman *Eleanor* • William Bakewell *Wally* ■ *Dir* Roy Del Ruth • *Scr* Robert Lord, from the play by Avery Hopwood • *Choreography* Larry Ceballos

Gold Diggers of 1933 ★★★★

Musical 1933 · US · BW · 97mins

Some of the most powerful musical routines ever filmed are featured in this cracking Warner Bros opus, the first of the Busby Berkeley-choreographed series that followed his superb *42nd Street*. Ignore the Ruby Keeler/Dick Powell Broadway plot (though cherish the snappy dialogue) and concentrate on a real rarity, with song-and-dance direction that reflects the climate of the times. This is a movie of the Depression, mirroring the emotions of an audience tired of breadlines, Prohibition and worthless currency. This is a vital, venerable classic and Berkeley's ground-breaking kaleidoscopic is a revelation. TS

Warren William *J Lawrence Bradford* • Joan Blondell *Carol King* • Aline MacMahon *Trixie Lorraine* • Ruby Keeler *Polly Parker* • Dick Powell *Brad Roberts* • Guy Kibbee *Peabody* • Ned Sparks *Barney Hopkins* • Ginger Rogers *Fay Fortune* ■ *Dir* Mervyn LeRoy • *Scr* Erwin Gelsey, James Seymour, David Boehm, Ben Markson, from the play *Gold Diggers of Broadway* by Avery Hopwood

Gold Diggers of 1935 ★★★ U

Musical comedy 1935 · US · BW · 90mins

This virtually plotless tale, one of the first to be directed by Busby Berkeley, has student Dick Powell falling for millionaire's daughter Gloria Stuart. The dance numbers live up to expectations, leading up to the memorable climax of Oscar-winning song *Lullaby of Broadway*. Powell and Stuart are colourless leads, but the real star is Berkeley's amazing choreography. TS [video]

Dick Powell *Dick Curtis* • Gloria Stuart *Amy Prentiss* • Adolphe Menjou *Nicoleff* • Glenda Farrell *Betty Hawes* • Grant Mitchell *Louis Lamson* • Dorothy Dare *Arline Davis* • Alice Brady *Mrs Mathilda Prentiss* • Winifred Shaw *Winny* ■ *Dir* Busby Berkeley • *Scr* Manuel Seff, Peter Milne, from a story by Peter Milne, Robert Lord

Gold Diggers of 1937 ★★★ U

Musical comedy 1936 · US · BW · 102mins

The advent of film censorship placed a terrible burden on Warner Bros's potent *Gold Diggers* series. Not only was the generic title now highly suspect, but choreographer Busby Berkeley's use of semi-naked cavorting chorus girls also had to be curtailed. Consequently the production numbers in this film suffer from a lack of excitement, as well as from an obvious lack of budget. Nevertheless, the cast is likeable, even if baby-faced Dick Powell is beginning to grow tiresome in these sappy roles. This at least provides intelligent dialogue and a semi-decent plot. TS

Dick Powell *Rosmer Peek* • Joan Blondell *Norma Parry* • Glenda Farrell *Genevieve Larkin* • Victor Moore *JJ Hobart* • Lee Dixon *Boop Oglethorpe* • Osgood Perkins *Mory Wethered* • Charles D Brown *John Huge* ■ *Dir* Lloyd Bacon • *Scr* Warren Duff, from the play *Sweet Mystery of Life* by Richard Maibaum, Michael Wallace, George Haight

Gold Diggers: the Secret of Bear Mountain ★★ PG

Adventure 1995 · US · Colour · 89mins

Moving from LA with her mother, Christina Ricci is lonely and lost until she befriends fellow outcast and tomboy Anna Chlumsky. The two friends determine to run away and track down legendary gold in the caves beneath Bear Mountain. This is an utterly formulaic, Disney-esque tale, with stereotypes aplenty; its only redeeming features are the touching friendship between the two girls and Christina's inimitable charm. LH [video]

Christina Ricci *Beth Easton* • Anna Chlumsky *Jody Salerno* • Polly Draper *Kate Easton* • Brian Kerwin *Matt Hollinger* • Diana Scarwid *Lynette Salerno* • David Keith *Ray Karnisak* • Gillian Barber *Grace Briggs* ■ *Dir* Kevin James Dobson • *Scr* Barry Glasser

The Gold Express ★

Comedy crime drama
1955 · UK · BW · 58mins

In the 1930s, Gaumont British was one of the jewels of the domestic industry. Alas, beneath the Rank umbrella, it fell on such hard times that this dismal quickie was par for its course. A poor imitation of *The Lady Vanishes*, this train-bound comedy thriller is devoid of thrills and utterly lacking in eccentricity – despite the presence of May Hallat and Ivy St Helier as a couple of dotty whodunnit writers. The screwball by-play between honeymooning reporters Vernon Gray and Ann Walford is equally bogus. DP

Vernon Gray *Bob Wright* • Ann Walford *Mary Wright* • May Hallatt *Agatha Merton* • Ivy St Helier *Emma Merton* • Patrick Boxill *Mr Rover* • Charles Rolfe *George Phillips* • John Serret *Luke Dubois* • Delphi Lawrence *Pearl* ■ *Dir* Guy Fergusson • *Scr* Jackson Budd

Gold for the Caesars ★★ U

Adventure 1964 · Fr/It · Colour · 85mins

This stagey sword-and-sandal adventure was directed by Sabatino Ciuffini and Riccardo Freda under the supervision of Hollywood veteran, Andre De Toth. The ancient Roman settings reek of studio artifice and the plot is short on surprises. But Jeffrey Hunter is statuesque as the slave-cum-architect, who is sent on a perilous mission to find the titular gold by treacherous Massimo Girotti. A tolerable time-passer. DP. Italian dialogue dubbed into English.

Jeffrey Hunter *Lacer* • Mylène Demongeot *Penelope* • Ron Randell *Rufus* • Massimo Girotti *Maximus* • Giulio Bosetti *Scipio* • Ettore Manni *Luna* • Georges Lycan *Malendi* ■ *Dir* Andre De Toth, Sabatino Ciuffini, Riccardo Freda • *Scr* Arnold Perl, Sabatino Ciuffini, from the novel by Florence A Seward

Gold in the Streets ★ 15

Drama 1996 · UK/Ire · Colour · 93mins

The immensely talented Aidan Gillen and Ian Hart co-star with James Belushi in this substandard tale of Irish illegal immigrants in New York. Screenwriter Noel Pearson and debut director Elizabeth Gill have sadly failed here on all fronts. This is a clichéd, glossy nostalgia piece at the expense of the Irish community. Belushi as bar-owner Mario, the main employer of the immigrants, holds his own, as does Hart, but the remaining cast are all one-dimensional stereotypes who missed out on accent coaching. One to be missed. LH. Contains swearing.

Karl Geary *Liam* • James Belushi *Mario* • Ian Hart *Des* • Jared Harris *Owen* • Aidan Gillen *Paddy* • Louise Lombard *Mary* • Tom Hickey *Mr Costello* • Andrea Irvine *Breda* • Lorraine Pilkington *Rose* ■ *Dir* Elizabeth Gill (2) • *Scr* Janet Noble, Noel Pearson, from the play *Away Alone* by Janet Noble

Gold Is Where You Find It ★★★ U

Western 1938 · US · Colour · 95mins

Gold-miners and wheat farmers argue it out in the Sacramento valley in this Technicolored slice of hokum, knocked off in three weeks by director Michael Curtiz. Warners toplined George Brent, who's rather a forgotten star nowadays. His moustachioed gallantry graced many an action pic and in real life he married as often as Henry VIII. His romantic sparring partner is Olivia de Havilland who's married to that inveterate scene-stealer, Claude Rains. Brent is a mining engineer who falls for de Havilland, who is a farmer's daughter. AT

George Brent *Jared Whitney* • Olivia de Havilland *Serena Ferris* • Claude Rains *Col Ferris* • Margaret Lindsay *Rosanne Ferris* • John Litel *Ralph Ferris* • Tim Holt *Lanceford Ferris* • Barton MacLane *Slag Minton* ■ *Dir* Michael Curtiz • *Scr* Warren Duff, Robert Buckner, from the story by Clements Ripley

Gold of Naples ★★★★

Comedy drama 1954 · It · BW · 112mins

Here are four stories for the price of one, as great Italian director (and co-writer) Vittorio De Sica illustrates scenes of working-class life in Naples. Sophia Loren makes an early appearance as a philandering wife; Silvana Mangano plays a prostitute; Toto has problems with an unwanted house guest; and De Sica finds himself upstaged by a kid in a tale about a very unsuccessful gambler. The kind of wholesome sentimentality that's good for what ails you. TH. In Italian with English subtitles.

Toto *The husband* • Lianella Carrell *His wife* • Pasquale Cennamo *The racketeer* • Sophia Loren *Sofia, the wife* • Giacomo Furia *Rosario, the husband* • Alberto Farnese *Alfredo, the lover* • Vittorio De Sica *The Count* • Mario Passante *His valet* • Silvana Mangano *Theresa* ■ *Dir* Vittorio De Sica • *Scr* Cesare Zavattini, Vittorio De Sica, Giuseppe Marotta, from the novel by Giuseppe Marotta

Gold of the Seven Saints ★★ U

Western 1961 · US · BW · 88mins

Clint Walker and Roger Moore, stars of the western TV series *Cheyenne* and *Maverick* respectively, are here relocated to scenic Utah. They play fur trappers who strike it rich when they find the eponymous gold in this moderately entertaining retread of *The Treasure of the Sierra Madre*. Walker and Moore's couch potato fans were used to seeing them in colour, but Warners saved money by having the film shot in black and white. AT

Clint Walker *Jim Rainbolt* • Roger Moore *Shaun Garrett* • Leticia Roman *Tita* • Robert Middleton *Gondora* • Chill Wills *Doc Gates* • Gene Evans *McCracken* • Roberto Contreras *Armanderez* • Jack C Williams *Ames* • Art Stewart *Ricca* ■ *Dir* Gordon Douglas • *Scr* Leigh Brackett, Leonard Freeman, from the novel *Desert Guns* by Steve Frazee

The Gold Rush ★★★★★ U

Silent comedy 1925 · US · BW · 71mins

Charlie Chaplin allowed the copyright for this, the most light-hearted of his great features, to lapse in 1953 so that it passed into the public domain – a gift for audiences. As a prospector in the ice-bound gold fields – an outsider even in a world of outcasts – he falls for a contemptuous Georgia Hale, but finally claims the girl and the gold. The comedy dazzles (in scenes such as the dance of the bread rolls) and darkens (his starving comrade hallucinates that Charlie is a very edible chicken), but the ending is wonderfully affirmative, a fact that he couldn't help mocking. For the final embrace, shipboard photographers shout: "You've spoiled the picture!" Marvellously, though, he hadn't. TH DVD

Charles Chaplin *Lone prospector* • Mack Swain *Big Jim McKay* • Tom Murray *Black Larson* • Georgia Hale *Georgia* • Betty Morrissey *Georgia's friend* ■ *Dir/Scr* Charles Chaplin • *Cinematographer* Rollie Totheroh

The Golden Age of Buster Keaton ★★★★ U

Compilation 1975 · US · BW · 96mins

The genius of the most cinematic of all the silent clowns is celebrated in this hugely entertaining compilation. Director Jay Ward deserves a pat on the back for including rarely-seen footage from the early Fatty Arbuckle shorts in which Keaton began his film career, even though they seem to be playing on fast forward. In addition to classic scenes from such shorts as *The Playhouse* and *The Electric House*, there are more sustained sequences from Keaton's features that demonstrate not only his balletic skill and mastery of props, but also his unrivalled ability to develop a gag and his immaculate comic timing. DP

Buster Keaton ■ *Dir* Jay Ward

The Golden Age of Comedy ★★★★

Compilation 1958 · US · BW · 70mins

Containing material from both the Mack Sennett and Hal Roach archives, this was the first of Robert Youngson's slapstick compilations and it did much to restore Laurel and Hardy's then flagging reputation. Although there are clips featuring such clowns as Harry Langdon, Ben Turpin and Charley Chase, it's the Stan and Ollie excerpts that command the most attention. Two-reelers such as *The Second Hundred Years*, *You're Darn Tootin'*, *Two Tars* and *Double Whoopee* had scarcely been seen since the silent era, but not even their hilarity could match the anarchic brilliance of the pie fight from *The Battle of the Century*. DP

Dwight Weist *Narrator* • Ward Wilson *Narrator* ■ • *Scr* Robert Youngson • *Producer* Robert Youngson • *Music* George Steiner

Golden Balls ★★★ 18

Comedy 1993 · Sp · Colour · 88mins

The middle section of director Bigas Luna's "Iberian passion" trilogy (completed by *Jamon Jamon* and *The Tit and the Moon*) continues his bawdy contemplation on greed, food and sex. In another brazen performance, Spanish heart-throb Javier Bardem is a horny young buck who wants to erect a skyscraper in honour of himself and sees everyone as potential rungs towards that goal. He's also obsessed with stealing bidets, Julio Iglesias, Rolex watches and Salvador Dali in this fascinating study of sun-drenched selfishness and stubbornness. Sexually explicit and packed with unforgettable images. AJ. In Spanish with English subtitles. DVD

Javier Bardem *Benito Gonzalez* • Maria de Medeiros *Marta* • Maribel Verdú *Claudia* • Elisa Touati *Rita* • Raquel Bianca *Ana the maneater* • Alessandro Gassman *Melilla's friend* • Benicio Del Toro *Bob the friend from Miami* • Francesco Ma Dominedo *Mosca* ■ *Dir* Bigas Luna • *Scr* Bigas Luna, Cuca Canals

The Golden Blade ★★ U

Adventure fantasy
1953 · US · Colour · 79mins

Universal went in for camp and colourful exotic adventures, with simple good vs evil plots. Rock Hudson is Harun, the handsome and noble hero, George Macready (hiss!) is the nasty Grand Vizier, and Piper Laurie the Princess of Baghdad, the damsel in distress. More formulaic than most, it's still pleasantly escapist. RB

Rock Hudson *Harun* • Piper Laurie *Princess Khairuzan* • Gene Evans *Hadi* • Kathleen Hughes *Bakhamra* • George Macready *Jafar* • Steven Geray *Barcus* • Edgar Barrier *Caliph* ■ *Dir* Nathan Juran • *Scr* John Rich

The Golden Bowl ★★★★ 12

Period drama
2000 · UK/Fr/US · Colour · 124mins

This dazzling dramatisation of Henry James's tale of love and treachery marks a return to form for the film-making team of Ismail Merchant, James Ivory and Ruth Prawer Jhabvala. Kate Beckinsale is superb as Maggie Verver, daughter of millionaire Nick Nolte and new wife of impoverished Italian prince Jeremy Northam, whose Cornetto accent undermines the rest of the acting on show here. Her lack of guile is offset by manipulative Uma Thurman who, jilted by Northam, marries Nolte in an attempt to stay near him. As infidelity rears its ugly head, the four protagonists struggle to maintain their status within respectable society. Elegant, eloquent and imbued with turn-of-the-century opulence and social mores, the movie still has enough emotional clout to give it universal appeal. LH DVD

Uma Thurman *Charlotte Stant* • Kate Beckinsale *Maggie Verver* • Jeremy Northam *Prince Amerigo* • Nick Nolte *Adam Verver* • Anjelica Huston *Fanny Assingham* • James Fox *Colonel Bob Assingham* • Madeleine Potter *Lady Castledean* • Nicholas Day *Lord Castledean* ■ *Dir* James Ivory • *Scr* Ruth Prawer Jhabvala, from the novel by Henry James

Golden Boy ★★

Drama 1939 · US · BW · 99mins

The story of a violinist who also boxes was once considered a daringly left wing and extremely courageous work, bringing acclaim to its author Clifford Odets. But, in this watered-down movie version, the play's sting is largely missing and the New York tenement setting is sanitised. Lee J Cobb's performance as William Holden's dad is one of the worst pieces of character overacting in movie history. The film is cliché-ridden and very dated, and the only real reasons for watching now are the leads, with Barbara Stanwyck showing the ropes to an innocent Holden in the role that made him a star. TS.

Barbara Stanwyck *Lorna Moon* • William Holden (2) *Joe Bonaparte* • Adolphe Menjou *Tom Moody* • Lee J Cobb *Mr Bonaparte* • Joseph Calleia *Eddie Fuseli* • Sam Levene *Siggie* • Edward S Brophy [Edward Brophy] *Roxy Lewis* ■ *Dir* Rouben Mamoulian • *Scr* Lewis Meltzer, Daniel Taradash, Sara Y Mason, Victor Heerman, from the play by Clifford Odets

Golden Braid ★★★★ 15

Drama 1991 · Aus · Colour · 87mins

Dutch-born director Paul Cox is one of the unsung heroes of Australian cinema. His slow-moving but intense films always draw you into their core and bind you into the troubled lives of his characters. This subtly powerful drama is based on a story by Guy de Maupassant, although Cox has changed the ending to suggest that madness is not the only escape from the agony of isolation. As the clock repairer who becomes infatuated with a lock of hair, Chris Haywood manages to be both sinister and sympathetic. A truly compelling picture. DP

Chris Haywood *Bernard Simon* • Gosia Dubrowolska *Terese* • Paul Chubb *Joseph* • Norman Kaye *Psychiatrist* • Marion Heathfield *Housekeeper* • Monica Maughan *Antique-shop owner* • Robert Menzies *Ernst* • Jo Kennedy *Ernst's wife* • Paul Cox *Priest* ■ *Dir* Paul Cox • *Scr* Paul Cox, Barry Dickins, from the story *La Chevelure* by Guy de Maupassant

The Golden Child ★ PG

Action comedy 1986 · US · Colour · 89mins

Not even Eddie Murphy could save this horribly misconceived comedy adventure, in which he is cast rather improbably as a social worker who is asked to track down a Tibetan youngster (the "Golden Child") who holds the key to the world's survival. Murphy's quick-fire quips fall flat and Michael Ritchie's direction is best described as indifferent, while Charles Dance mugs away terribly as the baddie of the piece. JF. Contains some violence and swearing. DVD

Eddie Murphy *Chandler Jarrell* • Charles Dance *Sardo Numspa* • Charlotte Lewis *Kee Nang* • Victor Wong (2) *Old man* • JL Reate *Golden Child* • Randall "Tex" Cobb *Til* • James Hong *Dr Hong* • Shakti *Kala* ■ *Dir* Michael Ritchie • *Scr* Dennis Feldman

The Golden Coach ★★★★ U

Period drama
1953 · Fr/Ital · Colour · 105mins

Despite a contrived storyline, this vibrant costume drama succeeds mainly because of Claude Renoir's stunning Technicolor photography. Suggesting both the untouched beauty of 18th-century Peru and the fabulous dream world of the stage, the imagery mirrors the radiance of Anna Magnani. She's the star of a touring *commedia dell'arte* troupe torn between a love for her art and the dictates of her heart. Director Jean Renoir continued to explore the contrasts between drama and life in the rest of his unofficial "theatre" trilogy, *French Cancan* and *Elena et les Hommes*. DP

Anna Magnani *Camilla* • Odoardo Spadaro *Don Antonio* • Nada Fiorelli *Isabella* • Dante Rino *Harlequin* • Duncan Lamont *Viceroy* • George Higgins *Martinez* • Ralph Truman *Duke* ■ *Dir* Jean Renoir • *Scr* Jean Renoir, Renzo Avanzo, Jack Kirkland, Giulio Macchi, from the play *Le Carosse du Saint-Sacrement* by Prosper Mérimée

The Golden Disc ★ U

Musical 1958 · UK · BW · 77mins

The coffee bar was the only place to be seen in the early rock 'n' roll years, but it is almost impossible to see how they became teen meccas from this risible British pop picture. In the very worst "it's trad, dad" manner, it shows how Lee Patterson and Mary Steele jazz up her aunt's coffee shop with a record booth and the singing talents of odd-jobman Terry Dene. Well worth missing. DP

Lee Patterson *Harry Blair* • Mary Steele *Joan Farmer* • Terry Dene • Linda Gray (1) *Aunt Sarah* • Ronald Adam *Mr Dryden* • Peter Dyneley *Mr Washington* • David Jacobs • David Williams *Recording engineer* ■ *Dir* Don Sharp • *Scr* Don Sharp, Don Nicholl, from a story by Gee Nicholl

Golden Earrings ★★

Spy drama 1947 · US · BW · 94mins

British intelligence agent Ray Milland, on a mission to get his hands on a secret Nazi formula for poison gas, is helped by exotic gypsy Marlene Dietrich, in whose caravan he finds sanctuary and romance. Despite stylish direction from Mitchell Leisen and the heavyweight (if not exactly harmonious) pairing of Milland and Dietrich, the ridiculous plot manages to be both camp and humourless. This drivel proved Dietrich's glory days with von Sternberg were well and truly over. Not the best of comebacks. RK

Ray Milland *Col Ralph Denistoun* • Marlene Dietrich *Lydia* • Murvyn Vye *Zoltan* • Bruce Lester *Byrd* • Dennis Hoey *Hoff* • Quentin Reynolds • Reinhold Schünzel *Prof Krosigk* ■ *Dir* Mitchell Leisen • *Scr* Abraham Polonsky, Frank Butler, Helen Deutsch, from the novel by Yolanda Foldes

Golden Eighties ★★★

Musical drama
1986 · Fr/Be/Swi · Colour · 96mins

In the 1970s, the feminist Belgian director Chantal Akerman was known for her rather glum and static minimalist films. So it came as a surprise when Akerman turned her hand to a somewhat kitsch musical, in which the themes of love, sex and commerce are closely linked. Most of the small-scale, bittersweet film takes place in a shopping mall and revolves around a clothes boutique and a hair salon, where the characters play out their destinies to the accompaniment of an eclectic score and witty, sometimes raunchy lyrics. At its centre is the exquisite Delphine Seyrig, who tragically died four years later aged 58. RB. In French with English subtitles.

Delphine Seyrig *Jeanne Schwartz* • Myriam Boyer *Sylvie* • Fanny Cottençon *Lili* • Lio *Mado* • Pascale Salkin *Pascale* • Charles Denner *Monsieur Schwartz* • Jean-François Balmer *Monsieur Jean* • John Berry *Eli* • Nicolas Tronc *Robert Schwartz* ■ *Dir* Chantal Akerman • *Scr* Chantal Akerman, Leora Barish, Henry Bean, Pascal Bonitzer, Jean Gruault

Golden Gate ★★ 15

Crime drama 1994 · US · Colour · 86mins

Anyone who thinks that Matt Dillon is a one-trick actor should take a look at this moody period piece. Unfortunately, his astute performance as an eager law graduate discovering that working for the FBI doesn't automatically put him on the side of the good guys is rather wasted on such a disjointed and ultimately disappointing film. The un-American paranoia of the early 1950s is well captured, but the scenes set during the 1960s are lazily melodramatic. DP. Contains swearing. [video]

Matt Dillon *Kevin Walker* • Joan Chen *Marilyn Song* • Bruno Kirby *Ron Pirelli* • Teri Polo *Cynthia* • Ma Tzi *Chen Jung Song* • Stan Egi *Bradley Ichiyasu* • Jack Shearer *FBI Chief* • Peter Murnik *Byrd* • George Guidall *Meisner* ■ *Dir* John Madden • *Scr* David Henry Hwang

Golden Girl ★★★ U

Musical drama 1951 · US · Colour · 108mins

Talented, chirpy Mitzi Gaynor is largely remembered today for her appearance as Nellie Forbush in the movie version of *South Pacific*, but she adorned a run of minor Technicolored musicals at 20th Century-Fox, of which this is fairly typical. Gaynor is Lotta Crabtree, a legendary and glamorous performer in the days of the Civil War, most noted for her popular song *Oh, Dem Golden Slippers*, which she sang all over the Old West before becoming the toast of New York. Gaynor is charming in the role, and Dale Robertson makes a laconically attractive leading man. TS

Mitzi Gaynor *Lotta Crabtree* • Dale Robertson *Tom Richmond* • Dennis Day *Mart* • James Barton *Mr Crabtree* • Una Merkel *Mrs Crabtree* • Raymond Walburn *Cornelius* • Gene Sheldon *Sam Jordan* • Carmen D'Antonio *Lola Montez* ■ *Dir* Lloyd Bacon • *Scr* Walter Bullock, Charles O'Neal, Gladys Lehman, from a story by Arthur Lewis,Albert Lewis, Edward Thompson

Golden Needles ★★

Martial arts action
1974 · US · Colour · 92mins

Soon after his ground-breaking collaboration with Bruce Lee, director Robert Clouse returned to Hong Kong for this so-so action adventure. The "golden needles" of the title make up a priceless artefact that is being hunted by a disparate group of people. Joe Don Baker, Burgess Meredith and Elizabeth Ashley top the cast but, although Clouse still stuffs the film with plenty of martial arts mayhem, the mix of laughs and action never gels. JF

Joe Don Baker *Dan* • Elizabeth Ashley *Felicity* • Jim Kelly *Jeff* • Burgess Meredith *Winters* • Ann Sothern *Finzie* • Roy Chiao *Lin Toa* • Frances Fong *Su Lin* ■ *Dir* Robert Clouse • *Scr* S Lee Pogostin, Sylvia Schneble

Golden Rendezvous ★ 15

Action thriller 1977 · US · Colour · 97mins

John Vernon leads a terrorist assault on a floating casino, hoping his threat to nuke the vessel and its passengers will make the president of the United States hand over a ship full of gold bullion. Richard Harris plays the officer who puts his life on the line (as the actor puts his talent on hold) to foil the plot. This amateurish caper, based on the novel by Alistair MacLean, is *Goldfinger* at sea – without 007, Pussy Galore or a decent villain. AT [video]

Richard Harris *John Carter* • Ann Turkel *Susan Beresford* • David Janssen *Charles Conway* • Burgess Meredith *Van Heurden* • John Vernon *Luis Carreras* • Gordon Jackson *Dr Marston* • Keith Baxter *Preston* • Dorothy Malone *Elizabeth Taubman* • John Carradine *Fairweather* ■ *Dir* Ashley Lazarus • *Scr* Stanley Price, from the novel by Alistair MacLean

Golden Salamander ★★ U

Adventure 1949 · UK · BW · 90mins

Trevor Howard, usually not a dull performer, was certainly the wrong side of interesting in this utterly predictable thriller about gunrunning in the North African desert. Usually a dab hand at this sort of thing, director Ronald Neame is content to cruise in low gear. The only compensations are wily Wilfrid Hyde White and 17-year-old Anouk Aimée, whose assured performance belies the fact that she was making only her third film. DP

Trevor Howard *David Redfern* • Anouk [Anouk Aimée] *Anna* • Herbert Lom *Rankl* • Miles Malleson *Douvet* • Walter Rilla *Serafis* • Jacques Sernas *Max* • Wilfrid Hyde White *Agno* • Peter Copley *Aribi* ■ *Dir* Ronald Neame • *Scr* Ronald Neame, Victor Canning, Lesley Storm, from a novel by Victor Canning

The Golden Seal ★★ PG

Adventure 1983 · US · Colour · 90mins

This is the kind of family-oriented outdoor adventure that seemed old-fashioned in the 1960s, yet which film-makers everywhere doggedly continue to make. Director Frank Zuniga makes the most of his rugged scenery on the Aleutian Islands, but he singularly fails to generate much suspense around the hissable Michael Beck's pursuit of the precious golden seal because he makes the animal's friendship with lonely boy Torquil Campbell so Lassie-esque that their plucky triumph is inevitable. DP [video]

Steve Railsback *Jim Lee* • Penelope Milford *Tania Lee* • Michael Beck *Crawford* • Torquil Campbell *Eric* • Sandra Seacat *Gladys* • Seth Sakai *Semeyon* • Richard Narita *Alexei* ■ *Dir* Frank Zuniga • *Scr* John Groves, from the novel *A River Ran Out of Eden* by James Vance Marshall

The Golden Voyage of Sinbad ★★★ U

Fantasy adventure
1973 · UK · Colour · 104mins

John Phillip Law takes over the role of the legendary seafarer from Kerwin Mathews, who'd impressed in *The 7th Voyage of Sinbad*. However, the actors and the plot once again end up playing second fiddle to the magnificent Dynamation sequences meticulously created by the godfather of special effects, Ray Harryhausen. Particularly memorable are the talking figurehead, the hideous centaur and the multi-armed statue that tests Sinbad's swordfighting skills. *Sinbad and the Eye of the Tiger* followed. DP [video] DVD

John Phillip Law *Sinbad* • Caroline Munro *Margiana* • Tom Baker *Koura* • Douglas Wilmer *Vizier* • Martin Shaw *Rachid* • Grégoire Aslan *Hakim* • Kurt Christian *Haroun* • Takis Emmanuel *Achmed* ■ *Dir* Gordon Hessler • *Scr* Brian Clemens, from a story by Brian Clemens, Ray Harryhausen

GoldenEye ★★★★ 12

Spy adventure
1995 · UK/US · Colour · 124mins

When "M" says to James Bond, "I think you're a sexist, misogynist dinosaur, a relic of the Cold War," who can disagree? To ram home the point, "M" is played by a woman (Judi Dench) and a key scene is set in a Russian park that is now a dumping ground for statues of redundant communist heroes. However, Pierce Brosnan, on his first mission as 007, quickly establishes himself as the best Bond since Sean Connery and makes a fetish out of the old-fashioned values of loyalty and patriotism. There are also splendid Bond girls, including Izabella Scorupco and feisty Famke Janssen, who kills by crushing her victims between her thighs. AT. Contains violence. [video] DVD

Pierce Brosnan *James Bond* • Sean Bean *Alec Trevelyan* • Izabella Scorupco *Natalya Simonova* • Famke Janssen *Xenia Onatopp* • Joe Don Baker *Jack Wade* • Judi Dench *"M"* • Robbie Coltrane *Valentin Zukovsky* • Tcheky Karyo *Dimitri Mishkin* • Desmond Llewelyn *"Q"* • Samantha Bond *Miss Moneypenny* ■ *Dir* Martin Campbell • *Scr* Jeffrey Caine, Bruce Feirstein, from a story by Michael France, from characters created by Ian Fleming

Goldengirl ★ 15

Drama sports 1979 · US · Colour · 100mins

Susan Anton is an American athlete who is brainwashed and tortured into becoming a gold medal winner at the 1980 Moscow Olympics. Electric shock treatment and mental torture are among the methods employed by her father, Curt Jurgens, and her shrink, Leslie Caron, while her agent, James Coburn, wants to get her into bed. The film looked especially stupid in 1980 after the USA boycotted the Moscow Olympics. Poor direction and a ridiculous script don't help. AT [video]

Susan Anton *Goldine Serafin* • James Coburn *Jack Dryden* • Curt Jurgens *Dr Serafin* • Leslie Caron *Dr Sammy Lee* • Robert Culp *Steve Esselton* • James A Watson Jr *Winters* • Harry Guardino *Valenti* • Ward Costello *Cobb* ■ *Dir* Joseph Sargent • *Scr* John Kohn, from the novel by Peter Lear

Goldfinger ★★★★★ PG

Spy adventure 1964 · UK · Colour · 105mins

The third big-screen outing for Ian Fleming's suave superspy ranks among the slickest of all Bond movies. Endlessly entertaining and effortlessly performed, it's packed with classic moments. There's Shirley Eaton's legendary gold-plated death; the duel with bowler-hatted sidekick Oddjob (Harold Sakata); the best name for any Bond girl in Pussy Galore (enthusiastically played by Honor Blackman); and the mid-air showdown with Gert Fröbe's brilliantly bizarre villain obsessed with gold. But what makes these individual facets so memorable is the way in which they're unshowily integrated into the gripping storyline by director Guy Hamilton, who even managed to revive Sean Connery's flagging interest in 007 to coax his best performance of the entire series. DP [video] DVD

Sean Connery *James Bond* • Honor Blackman *Pussy Galore* • Gert Frobe [Gert Fröbe] *Auric Goldfinger* • Shirley Eaton *Jill Masterson* • Tania Mallett *Tilly Masterson* • Harold Sakata *Oddjob* • Bernard Lee *"M"* • Martin Benson *Solo* • Cec Linder *Felix Leiter* • Desmond Llewelyn *"Q"* • Lois Maxwell *Miss Moneypenny* ■ *Dir* Guy Hamilton • *Scr* Richard Maibaum, Paul Dehn, from the novel by Ian Fleming • *Music* John Barry (1) • *Production Designer* Ken Adam

Goldfish Memory ★★ 15

Romantic comedy
2003 · Ire/UK · Colour · 87mins

Dubliners look for love in this light-hearted romantic comedy from writer/director Liz Gill. Lecherous lecturer Sean Campion, cynical courier Keith McErlean and opportunistic bisexual Fiona O'Shaughnessy are just some of the characters who trade off partners with alarming frequency. The story is simplistic and clichéd, but this look at modern love still manages to raise the odd smile. KK. Contains swearing and sex scenes.

Sean Campion *Tom* • Flora Montgomery *Angie* • Jean Butler *Renee* • Peter Gaynor *David* • Fiona Glascott *Isolde* • Fiona O'Shaughnessy *Clara* • Keith McErlean *Red* • Justine Mitchell *Kate* ■ *Dir/Scr* Liz Gill [Elizabeth Gill (2)]

Goldstein ★★

Black comedy 1963 · US · BW · 82mins

This "far out" movie marked the directing debut of Philip Kaufman, who later wrote *The Outlaw Josey Wales* and *Raiders of the Lost Ark* and directed *The Right Stuff*. It's a very 1960s satire with biblical overtones – it's actually based on the story of the prophet Elijah. Lou Gilbert plays the tramp who rises from Lake Michigan, shuffles around Chicago, clashes with abortionists, sculptors and other wacky people, and then sinks again. AT

Lou Gilbert *Old man/Father* • Thomas Erhart *Sculptor* • Ellen Madison *Sally* • Benito Carruthers [Ben Carruthers] *Jay* • Charles Fischer *Mr Nice* • Nelson Algren ■ *Dir/Scr* Philip Kaufman, Benjamin Manaster

The Goldwyn Follies ★★ U

Musical comedy 1938 · US · Colour · 110mins

This might have been an unwatchable prize clunker, but for a few memorable touches. Not least of these is the fact that it contains the last song ever written by the great George Gershwin, the hypnotically beautiful *Love Walked In*. However, it's performed unmercifully by the graceless tenor Kenny Baker, whose warbling is a matter of taste. Taste does not apply to the antics of the Ritz Brothers, nor to Edgar Bergen and his dummy Charlie McCarthy. All are astoundingly awful. TS [video]

Adolphe Menjou *Oliver Merlin* • The Ritz Brothers [Al Ritz] • The Ritz Brothers [Jimmy Ritz] • The Ritz Brothers [Harry Ritz] • Vera Zorina *Olga Samara* • Kenny Baker (1) *Danny Beecher* • Andrea Leeds *Hazel Dawes* • Edgar Bergen • Helen Jepson *Leona Jerome* • Phil Baker *Michael Day* • Alan Ladd *Auditioning singer* ■ *Dir* George Marshall • *Scr* Ben Hecht, Sam Perrin, Arthur Phillips, from a story by Ben Hecht

The Golem ★★★★ PG

Silent horror classic 1920 · Ger · BW · 84mins

This is the most eye-catching of the several versions of the ancient Jewish legend, mainly because of the Expressionist sets by Hans Poelzig, and the use of chiaroscuro to create a Gothic effect. Paul Wegener, who co-directed with Carl Boese, plays the clay monster created by a rabbi to help his people fight against the Emperor's expulsion of the Jews from the ghetto in 16th-century Prague. Wegener's lumbering gait was imitated by Boris Karloff in James Whale's *Frankenstein*. RB DVD

Paul Wegener *The Golem* • Albert Steinrück *Rabbi Loew* • Lyda Salmonova *Miriam* • Ernst Deutsch *Famulus* • Hanns Sturm *Old rabbi* • Otto Gebühr *Emperor* • Lothar Müthel *Florian* • Loni Nest *Child* ■ *Dir* Paul Wegener, Carl Boese • *Scr* Paul Wegener, Henrik Galeen, from the novel *Der Golem* by Gustav Meyrinck • *Cinematographer* Karl Freund

G

The Golem ★★★

Horror 1936 · Cz/Fr · BW · 83mins

Julien Duvivier's sound version of this classic horror story was shot in Prague, where the Jewish folk legend was said to have originated. Harry Baur is Emperor Rudolf II, whose persecution of the Jews causes the clay monster (the Golem) to reanimate and punish the oppressors. Ironically, Baur's own Jewish wife was arrested by the Nazis during the Second World War. Despite a good French cast, this lacks the atmosphere and narrative drive of Paul Wegener's 1920 film. However, those unfamiliar with the story will still find this scary and may also see parallels with Boris Karloff's more celebrated Monster. RB. In French with English subtitles.

Harry Baur *Emperor Rudolf II* • Roger Karl *Chancellor Lang* • Germaine Aussey *Countess Strada* • Jany Holt *Rachel* • Charles Dorat *Rabbi Jacob* • Roger Duchesne *de Trignac* • Aimos [Raymond Aimos] *Toussaint* • Ferdinand Hart *The Golem* ■ *Dir* Julien Duvivier • *Scr* Julien Duvivier, André-Paul Antoine, JD Antoine, from the novel *Der Golem* by Gustav Meyrinck

Golem, the Spirit of Exile ★★

Drama 1992 · Ger/Fr · Colour · 105mins

With Hanna Schygulla assuming a variety of ethereal disguises, and cinematographer Henri Alekan producing his customarily sublime images, this treatise on the plight of the displaced has more in common with *Wings of Desire* than the silent, Expressionist versions of the old Jewish Golem myth. Unfortunately, writer/director Amos Gitai surrounds the travails of Ophrah Shemesh's family with so many obscure references that it's almost impossible to identify with her problems. For all its sincerity, and cameos from directors Samuel Fuller and Bernardo Bertolucci, this is heavy going. DP. In French with English subtitles.

Hanna Schygulla *Naomi* • Vittorio Mezzogiorno • Ophrah Shemesh ■ *Dir/Scr* Amos Gitai

Goliath and the Barbarians ★★ [15]

Period adventure 1959 · It · Colour · 81mins

It's AD 568 and dastardly barbarians are on the rampage, raping and pillaging in downtown Verona. But Steve Reeves stands in their way, all rippling muscles and flashing teeth, keen to play tug of war with cart horses. Mr Reeves was a minor Arnold Schwarzenegger of his day, a former Mr Universe who enjoyed brief stardom in a series of deliriously awful epics that cost twice as much to publicise as they did to produce. The English dubbing, the cardboard sets and the lack of any technical proficiency make this peculiarly endearing. AT. Italian dialogue dubbed into English.

Steve Reeves *Emiliano* • Chelo Alonso *Londo* • Bruce Cabot *Alboyna* • Giulia Rubini *Sabina* • Livio Lorenzon *Igor* • Luciano Marin *Svevo* • Arturo Dominici *Delfo* • Furio Meniconi *Marco* ■ *Dir* Carlo Campogalliani • *Scr* Carlo Campogalliani, Gino Mangini, Nino Stresa, Giuseppe Taffarel, from a story by Emimmo Salvi, Gino Mangini

Gone Are the Days ★★★

Comedy drama 1963 · US · BW · 97mins

Actor Ossie Davis turns his heartfelt play *Purlie Victorious* into a screen vehicle for himself and his wife Ruby Dee. Davis plays a self-styled preacher who returns to his little Southern home town in order to start his own church. Great performances from the committed cast make the most of the somewhat dated humour, pertinently used to underscore the racist thrust of the plot. Alan Alda makes his film debut as one of the more liberal-thinking white characters. AJ

Ossie Davis *Purlie Victorious* • Ruby Dee *Lutiebelle* • Sorrell Booke *Capt Cotchipee* • Godfrey Cambridge *Gitlow* • Hilda Haynes *Missy* • Alan Alda *Charlie Cotchipee* • Beah Richards *Idella* • Charles Welch *Sheriff* ■ *Dir* Nicholas Webster • *Scr* Ossie Davis, from his play *Purlie Victorious*

Gone Fishin' ★ [PG]

Comedy 1997 · US · Colour · 90mins

A misguided and truly abysmal comedy vehicle for Joe Pesci and Danny Glover, who play a couple of disaster-prone chums on a fishing trip. Along the way the bumbling duo end up with a map to a missing fortune. As a result, they are pursued by a lethal conman (Nick Brimble) and the two women on his trail (Rosanna Arquette and Lynn Whitfield). Two hours of unsuccessful fly fishing would provide more entertainment. JF DVD

Joe Pesci *Joe Waters* • Danny Glover *Gus Green* • Rosanna Arquette *Rita* • Lynn Whitfield *Angie* • Willie Nelson *Billy "Catch" Pooler* • Nick Brimble *Dekker Massey* • Gary Grubbs *Phil Beasly* • Carol Kane *Donna Waters* ■ *Dir* Christopher Cain • *Scr* Jill Mazursky Cody [Jill Mazursky], Jeffrey Abrams

Gone in 60 Seconds ★★★ [15]

Action crime drama
1974 · US · Colour · 93mins

The versatile HB Halicki not only wrote, directed and starred in this grandaddy of the car-chase movie; he also supplied the vehicles, 93 of which ended up demolished. Influencing a range of films from *The Cannonball Run* to *Death Race 2000*, Halicki's story of a ring of professional car thieves culminates in the now classic 40-minute chase sequence. It was enough of a cult hit to warrant a sequel in 1989, during the filming of which Halicki was tragically killed performing a stunt. RS DVD

HB Halicki *Maindrian Pace* • Marion Busia *Pumpkin Chase* • Jerry Daugirda *Eugene Chase* • James McIntyre *Stanley Chase* • George Cole *Atlee Jackson* • Ronald Halicki *Corlis Pace* ■ *Dir/Scr* HB Halicki

Gone in Sixty Seconds ★★ [15]

Action crime drama
2000 · US · Colour · 117mins

The car's the star in this boys-and-their-toys action drama that, unfortunately, has too little action to cover for the absence of plot. Nicolas Cage is a reformed car thief who agrees to pull off an impossible job – steal 50 top-of-the-range cars in four nights – for bad guy Christopher Eccleston, in return for brother Giovanni Ribisi's life. Cage ropes in his old crew – including Angelina Jolie and Vinnie Jones – but it's over an hour before we get any stealing or crashing of any description. JB DVD

Nicolas Cage *Randall "Memphis" Raines* • Angelina Jolie *Sara "Sway" Wayland* • Giovanni Ribisi *Kip Raines* • Delroy Lindo *Det Roland Castlebeck* • Will Patton *Atley Jackson* • Christopher Eccleston *Raymond Calitri* • Chi McBride *Donny Astricky* • Robert Duvall *Otto Halliwell* ■ *Dir* Dominic Sena • *Scr* Scott Rosenberg, from the 1974 film

Gone to Earth ★★★★ [PG]

Period romantic drama
1950 · UK · Colour · 110mins

Michael Powell and Emeric Pressburger's weirdly compelling film about a Shropshire lass who communes with nature and is at odds with the local community. Produced by Alexander Korda and David O Selznick, who saw it as a showcase for his wife, Jennifer Jones, it's a full-blooded melodrama, a piece of Celtic chemistry dominated by the unearthly beauty of Miss Jones. When Selznick saw the finished film he cut 30 minutes, retitled it *The Wild Heart* and ordered new scenes by director Rouben Mamoulian. Naturally it flopped everywhere, but has lately been restored and revalued. AT DVD

Jennifer Jones *Hazel Woodus* • David Farrar *Jack Reddin* • Cyril Cusack *Edward Marston* • Esmond Knight *Abel Woodus* • Sybil Thorndike *Mrs Marston* • Hugh Griffith *Andrew Vessons* • Edward Chapman *Mr James* • Beatrice Varley *Aunt Prowde* • George Cole *Albert* ■ *Dir* Michael Powell, Emeric Pressburger • *Scr* Michael Powell, Emeric Pressburger, from the novel by Mary Webb

Gone with the Wind ★★★★★ [PG]

Period romantic drama
1939 · US · Colour · 224mins

At four hours and at least three directors, David O Selznick's epic American Civil War romance is less a film, more a way of life. Forever falling in and out of favour with critical consensus, it will remain an audience favourite for all time. A war movie with a beating female heart, thanks to the bestselling source novel by Margaret Mitchell, this was, in 1939, the most expensive film ever made: $4 million, and the money is up there on the screen in impressive set pieces such as the burning of Atlanta. But the key is Vivien Leigh's Scarlett O'Hara, a tragic but resourceful southern heroine, yet destined for comeuppance at the hands of Clark Gable's Rhett Butler. No mention of slavery, but this is not a history lesson, it's a love story – one of the best. AC DVD

Vivien Leigh *Scarlett O'Hara* • Clark Gable *Rhett Butler* • Leslie Howard *Ashley Wilkes* • Olivia de Havilland *Melanie Hamilton* • Hattie McDaniel *Mammy* • Thomas Mitchell *Gerald O'Hara* • Barbara O'Neil *Ellen O'Hara* • Laura Hope Crews *Aunt "Pittypat" Hamilton* • Ona Munson *Belle Watling* • Butterfly McQueen *Prissy* ■ *Dir* Victor Fleming • *Scr* Sidney Howard, Ben Hecht (uncredited), Jo Swerling (uncredited), Oliver HP Garrett (uncredited), from the novel by Margaret Mitchell • *Producer* David O Selznick • *Cinematographer* Ernest Haller, Lee Garmes, Ray Rennahan • *Editor* Hal C Kern, James E Newcom • *Music* Max Steiner • *Production Designer* William Cameron Menzies

Gonks Go Beat ★ [U]

Science-fiction comedy musical
1965 · UK · BW · 87mins

This tedious slice of 1960s nonsense stars Kenneth Connor as the Martian mediator in the war between Beatland and Balladisle – we all know rockin' hepcats and lounge lizards are mortal enemies, right? With the theat of exile to the planet Gonk hanging over the proceedings, a *Romeo and Juliet*-style romance between the factions is arranged, providing the excuse for an endless parade of forgettable songs. JF

Kenneth Connor *Wilco Roger* • Frank Thornton *Mister A&R* • Barbara Brown *Helen* • Ian Gregory *Steve* • Terry Scott *PM* • Lulu • Ginger Baker ■ *Dir* Robert Hartford-Davis • *Scr* Jimmy Watson

Good Advice ★★★ [15]

Romantic comedy
2001 · US · Colour · 88mins

In this good-natured romantic comedy high flying stockbroker Charlie Sheen disgraces himself professionally, loses his job, his reputation and his girlfriend (Denise Richards), who is a less than successful agony aunt. Desperate for money, Sheen decides to keep Richards's departure a secret and poses as the woman and ghost-writes her local newspaper column. But complications arise when the mysteriously invigorated advice page becomes a nationwide sensation. SF DVD

Charlie Sheen *Ryan Turner* • Angie Harmon *Paige Henson* • Denise Richards *Cindy Styne* • Barry Newman *Donald Simpson* • Estelle Harris *Iris* • Jon Lovitz *Barry Sherman* • Rosanna Arquette *Cathy Sherman* ■ *Dir* Steve Rash • *Scr* Robert Horn, Daniel Margosis

Good Boy! ★★ [U]

Fantasy action comedy
2003 · US · Colour · 84mins

It may lack the imagination usually associated with the Jim Henson production studio, but this dogs-from-outer-space caper is affable enough. Pitching its laughs squarely at younger kids, the story centres on lonely 12-year-old Liam Aiken, who is shocked to discover his new pooch, Hubble (voiced by Matthew Broderick), is actually an alien scout from the Dog Star, Sirius. What follows is a predictable lesson in friendship and loyalty, in which comedy is ultimately buried by weak acting and sentimentality. SF DVD

Molly Shannon *Mrs Baker* • Liam Aiken *Owen Baker* • Kevin Nealon *Mr Baker* • Brittany Moldowan *Connie Fleming* • Hunter Elliot *Frankie* • Mikhael Speidel *Fred* • Matthew Broderick *Hubble/Canid 3942* • Delta Burke *Barbara Ann* • Vanessa Redgrave *The Greater Dane* • Carl Reiner *Shep* ■ *Dir* John Hoffman • *Scr* John Hoffman, from a story by John Hoffman, Zeke Richardson, from the story *Dogs from Outer Space* by Zeke Richardson

Good Burger ★ [PG]

Comedy 1997 · US · Colour · 91mins

Young fans of TV channel Nickelodeon stars Kenan and Kel are about the only ones who will be remotely amused by this misjudged comedy. The duo work in a burger bar called, you guessed it, Good Burger. The pair mug at every available opportunity while trying to save their little burger bar from being taken over by corporate bad guys. Parents be warned: it does include some adult themes and occasionally cruel humour. JB

Kenan Thompson *Dexter Reed* • Kel Mitchell *Ed* • Abe Vigoda *Otis* • Sinbad *Mr Wheat* • Shar Jackson *Monique* • Dan Schneider *Mr Bailey* • Jan Schwieterman *Kurt Bozwell* • Ron Lester *Spatch* ■ *Dir* Brian Robbins • *Scr* Dan Schneider, Kevin Kopelow, Heath Siefert, from their characters

The Good Companions ★★★★ [U]

Musical comedy 1933 · UK · BW · 112mins

Bet you didn't know this was the first talkie seen by a reigning British monarch. Adapted from the celebrated novel and play by JB Priestley, this charming musical comedy is full of surprises, not least of which is John Gielgud's facility for song and dance. Victor Saville directs with a light touch and strings together the many episodes with deceptive ease, conveying both the atmosphere of the

Depression and the relief the Dinky Doos touring troupe brings to everyone. While Jessie Matthews is superb in the role that established her as an international star, Edmund Gwenn steals every scene he's in. DP

Jessie Matthews *Susie Dean* • Edmund Gwenn *Jess Oakroyd* • John Gielgud *Inigo Jolifant* • Mary Glynne *Miss Trant* • Percy Parsons *Morton Mitcham* • AW Baskcomb *Jimmy Nunn* • Dennis Hoey *Joe Brundit* ■ *Dir* Victor Saville • *Scr* WP Lipscomb, Angus MacPhail, Ian Dalrymple, from the novel and play by JB Priestley

The Good Companions ★★★ U

Musical comedy 1956 · UK · Colour · 107mins

JB Priestley's 1929 novel was first filmed in 1933 with John Gielgud and Jessie Matthews. This remake has a glittering array of female talent, although the men are less showy, but this still proves how British movies of the time could cast in depth without having to offer roles to the acting knights of the realm. The story, about a concert party, has dated, and it's all a bit too polite, but the cast makes it well worth watching. AT

Eric Portman *Jess Oakroyd* • Celia Johnson *Miss Trant* • Janette Scott *Susie Dean* • John Fraser *Inigo Jolifant* • Hugh Griffith *Morton Mitcham* • Rachel Roberts (1) *Elsie Longstaff/ Effie Longstaff* • Thora Hird *Mrs Oakroyd* • Alec McCowen *Albert* • Joyce Grenfell *Lady Parlitt* • Anthony Newley *Mulbrau* ■ *Dir* J Lee Thompson • *Scr* TJ Morrison, JL Hodgson, John Whiting, from the novel and play by JB Priestley

Good Cop, Bad Cop ★★ 18

Crime thriller 1993 · US · Colour · 88mins

Notable mainly for giving Pamela Anderson an early opportunity to show her ability to wear very few clothes, this is an entertaining if erratic comedy thriller. Robert Hays is the hapless executive who is forced to go on the run when he gets implicated in the murder of a powerful man's daughter. Anderson plays a prostitute who may or may not be an ally. The tone veers all over the place, but it's always watchable. JF. Contains swearing, violence and sex scenes.

David Keith *Mace* • Robert Hays *Mitch* • Pamela Anderson *Sarah* • Charles Napier *Mayor Stiles* • Stacy Keach *Bob Jenkins* • Leo Rossi *Detective Atkins* ■ *Dir/Scr* David A Prior

Good Day for a Hanging ★★ U

Western 1958 · US · Colour · 85mins

The debonair but lightweight Fred MacMurray made a surprisingly believable western star at a low point in his career, before *The Shaggy Dog* and other Disney comedies revived it. Here he's the town marshal who thinks he's captured the sheriff's killer, played by a charismatic Robert Vaughn. Intending to carry out the execution he meets almost universal opposition – no one believes that such a charmer could be guilty. AE

Fred MacMurray *Ben Cutler* • Maggie Hayes [Margaret Hayes] *Ruth Granger* • Robert Vaughn *The Kid* • Joan Blackman *Laurie Cutler* • James Drury *Paul Ridgely* • Wendell Holmes *Tallant Joslin* • Edmon Ryan *William Selby* ■ *Dir* Nathan Juran • *Scr* Daniel B Ullman, Maurice Zimm, from a story by John Reese

The Good Die First ★★ 15

Spaghetti western
1967 · It/W Ger · BW · 106mins

It's the details that make this routine and rather anaemic Spaghetti western moderate fun. Lee Van Cleef plays a bandit who undergoes a miraculous change of heart when he becomes the sheriff of a one-horse town, while Gordon Mitchell is the villain who comes up against his ex-partner when he tries to rob the local mine of its payroll. AJ. Italian dialogue dubbed into English.

Lee Van Cleef *Cudlipp* • Gordon Mitchell (1) *Burton* • Antonio Sabato *Ben Novack* • Lionel Stander *Preacher* • Graziella Granata *Sally* • Ann Smyrner *Lola* ■ *Dir* Giorgio Stegani • *Scr* Warren Kiefer [Lorenzo Sabatini], Fernando Di Leo, Mino Roli, Giorgio Stegani, from a story by Warren Kiefer [Lorenzo Sabatini]

The Good Die Young ★★★ PG

Crime drama 1954 · UK · BW · 93mins

This well-crafted British heist thriller, atmospherically directed by Lewis Gilbert, stars Laurence Harvey as the leader of a quartet of ne'er-do-wells who team up to pull off a robbery that goes wrong. The talented cast also includes Gloria Grahame, Joan Collins, Stanley Baker, Robert Morley and Margaret Leighton, whose second husband was Harvey. PF DVD

Laurence Harvey *Miles "Rave" Ravenscourt* • Gloria Grahame *Denise* • Richard Basehart *Joe* • Joan Collins *Mary* • John Ireland *Eddie* • René Ray *Angela* • Stanley Baker *Mike* • Margaret Leighton *Eve Ravenscourt* • Robert Morley *Sir Francis Ravenscourt* ■ *Dir* Lewis Gilbert • *Scr* Lewis Gilbert, Vernon Harris, from a novel by Richard Macauley

The Good Earth ★★★

Drama 1937 · US · Sepia · 137mins

This saga about Chinese peasants won the second of two Oscars on the trot for MGM's Austrian import, Luise Rainer. It's a bit long and worthy, but is redeemed by Rainer's moving portrayal and by a cleverly filmed plague of locusts. The few location shots of China were made in 1934 for another project by director George Hill, who then committed suicide. AT

Paul Muni *Wang Lung* • Luise Rainer *O-Lan* • Walter Connolly *Uncle* • Tilly Losch *Lotus* • Charley Grapewin *Old father* • Jessie Ralph *Cuckoo* • Soo Yong *Aunt* • Keye Luke *Elder son* ■ *Dir* Sidney Franklin • *Scr* Talbot Jennings, Tess Schlesinger, Claudine West, Francis Marion, from the novel by Pearl S Buck • *Cinematographer* Karl Freund

The Good Fairy ★★★★

Comedy 1935 · US · BW · 100mins

This delightful comedy stars Margaret Sullavan at her least cloying as the "good fairy" who's released from an asylum and bursts into the life of Herbert Marshall's prickly, unsuccessful Budapest lawyer, liberating him from his dreary existence. The inventive script by Preston Sturges abounds in slapstick, misunderstandings and verbal tomfoolery, while William Wyler's direction doesn't miss a trick. The good supporting cast includes that splendid character actor Eric Blore, who went on to appear in several Preston Sturges films. AE

Margaret Sullavan *Luisa "Lu" Ginglebusher* • Herbert Marshall *Dr Max Sporum* • Frank Morgan *Konrad* • Reginald Owen *Detlaff* • Alan Hale *Maurice Schlapkohl* • Beulah Bondi *Dr Schultz* • Cesar Romero *Joe* • Eric Blore *Doctor Metz* ■ *Dir* William Wyler • *Scr* Preston Sturges, from the play by Ferenc Molnar

The Good Father ★★★★ 15

Drama 1986 · UK · Colour · 86mins

Oscar-winner Anthony Hopkins gives another moving and impressive performance – this time as a bitter man dealing with his separation from his wife. Director Mike Newell and writer Christopher Hampton touch on a sensitive subject and handle it admirably. Hopkins's character feels he is a man with no rights – he sees his son only once a week. So he embarks on a crusade to help another wronged man (Jim Broadbent), whose ex-wife has decided to emigrate to Australia with their child. Hopkins handles the rage and the calm of his character with precision, and it remains hard to believe that it took until 1991's *The Silence of the Lambs* for him to be recognised as one of the world's finest screen actors. JB

Anthony Hopkins *Bill Hooper* • Jim Broadbent *Roger Miles* • Harriet Walter *Emmy Hooper* • Frances Viner *Cheryl Langford* • Simon Callow *Mark Varda* • Joanne Whalley *Mary Hall* • Miriam Margolyes *Jane Powell* • Stephen Fry *Creighton* ■ *Dir* Mike Newell • *Scr* Christopher Hampton, from the novel by Peter Prince

The Good Girl ★★★ 15

Comedy drama
2001 · US/Ger/Neth · Colour · 89mins

Small-town America comes in for another indie lashing in this patchy, pathos-packed comedy. Jennifer Aniston will surprise many as the shopgirl whose infatuation with wannabe writer Jake Gyllenhaal sends ripples through her insular Texan community. But it's the peripheral characters who bring some much-needed colour to the occasionally predictable proceedings, most notably born-again security guard Mike White and mischievous makeover clerk Zooey Deschanel. Engaging and enjoyable, but lacking edge. DP DVD

Jennifer Aniston *Justine Last* • Jake Gyllenhaal *Holden Worther* • John C Reilly *Phil Last* • Tim Blake Nelson *Bubba* • Zooey Deschanel *Cheryl* • Mike White *Corny* ■ *Dir* Miguel Arteta • *Scr* Mike White

The Good Guys and the Bad Guys ★★

Comedy western 1969 · US · Colour · 90mins

Despite the stirring presence of Robert Mitchum and a useful support cast, director Burt Kennedy completely fails to carry off this *Ride the High Country* clone for several reasons. Co-star George Kennedy is a talented character actor but he lacks the starpower to be a convincing adversary for Mitchum. There is also an uncomfortable sense of period, as cars and horses jostle in a ludicrous finale, and the comedic tone is uncertain. TS

Robert Mitchum *Marshal Flagg* • George Kennedy *Big John McKay* • Martin Balsam *Mayor Wilker* • David Carradine *Waco* • Lois Nettleton *Mary* • Tina Louise *Carmel* • John Davis Chandler *Deuce* • John Carradine *Ticker* ■ *Dir* Burt Kennedy • *Scr* Ronald M Cohen, Dennis Shryack

Good Guys Wear Black ★★ 15

Action thriller 1977 · US · Colour · 91mins

Another slick, monotonously violent starring vehicle for the perpetually wooden Chuck Norris, who was a video star before the term was even invented. Inevitably, he's a Vietnam veteran, this time facing an enemy closer to home when he discovers that his old unit are being bumped off one by one and he's next on the hit list. Director Ted Post's efforts here are no more than workmanlike and the acting is all over the place. JF DVD

Chuck Norris *John T Booker* • Anne Archer *Margaret* • Lloyd Haynes *Murray Saunders* • James Franciscus *Conrad Morgan* • Dana Andrews *Edgar Harolds, Government man* • Jim Backus *Doorman* • Larry Casey [Lawrence P Casey] *Mike Potter* • Anthony Mannino *Gordie Jones* ■ *Dir* Ted Post • *Scr* Bruce Cohn, Mark Medoff, from a story by Joseph Fraley

Good Luck ★★★

Comedy drama 1996 · US · Colour · 98mins

Paraplegic Gregory Hines teams up with bitter ex-pro football star Vincent D'Onofrio, who lost his sight in an accident, to compete in a white-water rafting race. With elements of both the buddy pic and the road movie, this comedy is all about people achieving their dreams and realising that disability needn't be a handicap to life. Some might find it a little too heavy on the schmaltz, but Richard LaBrie directs with a sure hand and he's helped by the strong rapport between the two leads, sharp dialogue and amusing doses of black comedy. RS

Gregory Hines *Bernard "Bern" Lemley* • Vincent D'Onofrio *Tony "Ole" Olezniak* • James Earl Jones *James Bing* • Max Gail *Farmer John* • Joe Theismann • Roy Firestone • Robert O'Reilly *Bartender* • Jack Rader *Drag queen* ■ *Dir* Richard LaBrie • *Scr* Bob Comfort

Good Luck, Miss Wyckoff ★★ 18

Drama 1979 · US · Colour · 86mins

Anne Heywood, a repressed single schoolteacher, is raped by a young black janitor in Kansas in 1956. Despite her initially shocked reaction, she eventually gives in to the relationship, complicating her struggle to come to grips with her own sexuality. A grim and controversial portrayal of human sexuality that, despite a strong cast, many viewers may find offensive rather than insightful. AJ

Anne Heywood *Evelyn Wyckoff* • Donald Pleasence *Dr Steiner* • Robert Vaughn *Dr Neal* • Carolyn Jones *Beth* • Dorothy Malone *Mildred* • Ronee Blakley *Betsy* • Dana Elcar *Mr Havermeyer* • Doris Roberts *Rene* ■ *Dir* Marvin J Chomsky • *Scr* Polly Platt, from the novel by William Inge

A Good Man in Africa ★★ 15

Comedy drama 1993 · US · Colour · 90mins

This tale of consular shenanigans in a small African republic is a sad misfire from Bruce Beresford. William Boyd's screenplay, from his own novel, has casanova diplomat Colin Friels blackmailed into "persuading" doctor Sean Connery to support president elect Lou Gossett Jr's building project. Ponderous and completely devoid of humour, it's saved only by Connery. AJ. Contains swearing, sex scenes and nudity.

Colin Friels *Morgan* • Sean Connery *Dr Murray* • Joanne Whalley-Kilmer [Joanne Whalley] *Celia* • Louis Gossett Jr *Adekunle* • John Lithgow *Fanshawe* • Diana Rigg *Chloe* • Sarah-Jane Fenton *Priscilla* • Jeremy Crutchley *Dalmire* ■ *Dir* Bruce Beresford • *Scr* William Boyd, from his novel

Good Morning... and Goodbye ★★ 18

Satirical sex melodrama
1967 · US · Colour · 78mins

This is one of exploitation maverick Russ Meyer's best sex morality fables, although devotees may be disappointed by the minimal nudity. Meyer lifts the seamy lid on rustic sexual desires, wants and shortcomings, as sexually frustrated Alaina Capri cheats on her rich farmer husband Stuart Lancaster with construction worker Patrick Wright. A forest trip to meet sorceress Haji puts the lead back in Lancaster's pencil and sorts out the muddled affairs. The film is wild, melodramatic and portentous in Meyer's trademark "kitsch-and-think" way. AJ DVD

Alaina Capri *Angel* • Stuart Lancaster *Burt* • Patrick Wright *Stone* • Haji *Sorceress* • Karen Ciral *Lana* • Don Johnson *Ray* • Tom Howland *Herb* ■ *Dir* Russ Meyer • *Scr* John E Moran [Jack Moran], from a story by Russ Meyer

Good Morning, Babylon
★★★★ 15

Period drama
1987 · It/Fr/US · Colour · 112mins

A deeply affecting and beautifully shot, if rather coolly observed tale of two Italian stonemason brothers who find they can no longer make a living restoring cathedrals in their native Tuscany. Arrriving in America around the time of the First World War, they end up working for DW Griffith on his epic *Intolerance*. In their first English language film, directors Paolo and Vittorio Taviani have created a deeply symbolic story, shot through with autobiographical resonance. If this sounds a touch heavy – it is. At the same time, the film is imbued with such a lyrical love of film-making and sterling performances that you find yourself drawn into its web. SH. In English and Italian with subtitles.

Vincent Spano *Nicola Bonnano* • Joaquim de Almeida *Andrea Bonnano* • Greta Scacchi *Edna* • Désirée Becker *Mabel* • Omero Antonutti *Bonnano* • Charles Dance *DW Griffith* • Bérangère Bonvoisin *Mrs Griffith* ■ *Dir* Paolo Taviani, Vittorio Taviani • *Scr* Tonino Guerra, Vittorio Taviani, Paolo Taviani, from an idea by Lloyd Fonvielle

Good Morning, Boys
★★★★ U

Comedy 1937 · UK · BW · 74mins

Will Hay returns to his celebrated music-hall persona of the cynically incompetent schoolmaster in the first of several films he made with French director Marcel Varnel. Having to bluff furiously to remain one step ahead of a class that contains the ever-mischievous Graham Moffat, Hay is close to his peak as he lectures to educationalists, flirts with chanteuse Lilli Palmer and helps prevent the theft of the *Mona Lisa*. DP DVD

Will Hay *Dr Benjamin Twist* • Martita Hunt *Lady Bagshott* • Peter Gawthorne *Col Willoughby-Gore* • Graham Moffatt *Albert* • Fewlass Llewellyn *Dean* • Mark Daly *Arty Jones* • Peter Godfrey *Cliquot* • C Denier Warren *Henri Duval* • Lilli Palmer *Yvette* ■ *Dir* Marcel Varnel • *Scr* Val Guest, Leslie Arliss, Marriott Edgar, Anthony Kimmins, from a story by Anthony Kimmins

Good Morning, Miss Dove
★★ U

Drama 1955 · US · Colour · 107mins

Director Henry Koster had the biggest hit of his career with the first movie released in CinemaScope, *The Robe*, but prior to that he was better known as a purveyor of schmaltzy films. This is an ideal subject for Koster, a warm-hearted tale (told in flashback) of how a small town feels about its spinster schoolmarm and how she affects the lives of everybody who crosses her path. Koster brings it off effectively, but star Jennifer Jones seems ill-cast as the prissy Miss Dove. TS

Jennifer Jones *Miss Dove* • Robert Stack *Tom Baker* • Kipp Hamilton *Jincey Baker* • Robert Douglas *Mr Porter* • Peggy Knudsen *Billie Jean* • Marshall Thompson *Mr Pendleton* • Chuck Connors *Bill Holloway* • Biff Elliot *Alex Burnham* • Jerry Paris *Maurice* ■ *Dir* Henry Koster • *Scr* Eleanore Griffin, from the novel by Frances Gray Patton

Good Morning, Night
★★★★ 15

Crime drama based on a true story
2003 · It · Colour · 102mins

Director Marco Bellocchio examines Italy's turbulent political situation in the late 1970s in this intense reconstruction of the kidnap and murder of Aldo Moro. Robert Herlitzka plays the former prime minister with patient dignity, as he attempts to reason with Luigi Lo Cascio, the hot-headed Red Brigade leader whose motives and methods are increasingly questioned by Maya Sansa, who comes to feel like a victim herself, despite having a civil service job to allay the suspicions of the gang's Roman neighbours. Ideologically provocative, but also a deeply moving human drama. DP. In Italian with English subtitles. DVD

Maya Sansa *Chiara* • Luigi Lo Cascio *Mariano* • Pier Giorgio Bellocchio [Piergiorgio Bellocchio] *Ernesto* • Giovanni Calcagno *Primo* • Paolo Briguglia *Enzo* • Roberto Herlitzka *Aldo Moro* ■ *Dir/Scr* Marco Bellocchio

Good Morning, Vietnam
★★★ 15

Biographical comedy drama
1987 · US · Colour · 116mins

Robin Williams received an Oscar nomination for giving here what is essentially a stand-up comedy performance. He plays a motor-mouth disc jockey sent to Vietnam to entertain the GIs, and adds rather more salt, pepper and hot sauce to the place than the military brass would have liked. Based on the case of a real US armed forces DJ, the film is distinctive for being Hollywood's first Vietnam comedy and among the first movies to treat the Vietnamese themselves as real people. The action loses its way, however, whenever the film tries to get serious, but when Williams is behind the studio mike, it offers a decent showcase for his virtuoso talents. PF. Contains violence and swearing. DVD

Robin Williams *Airman Adrian Cronauer* • Forest Whitaker *Private Edward Garlick* • Tran Tung Thanh *Tuan* • Chintara Sukapatana *Trinh* • Bruno Kirby *Lieutenant Steven Hauk* • Robert Wuhl *Marty Lee Dreiwitz* • JT Walsh *Sergeant-Major Dickerson* ■ *Dir* Barry Levinson • *Scr* Mitch Markowitz

Good Neighbor Sam
★★★

Comedy 1964 · US · Colour · 130mins

A very funny, though overlong, Jack Lemmon farce, this has a familiar plot that involves him pretending to be married to sexy Romy Schneider in order to help her come into a small fortune. Slight enough, but spun out with a lot of 1960s fripperies, including a high degree of risqué – for then – gags and jokes about advertising and consumerism. Under-rated director David Swift directs the glossy farrago with aplomb. TS

Jack Lemmon *Sam Bissel* • Edward G Robinson *Simon Nurdlinger* • Romy Schneider *Janet Lagerlof* • Dorothy Provine *Minerva Bissel* • Michael Connors [Mike Connors] *Howard Ebbets* • Anne Seymour *Irene Krump* • Charles Lane (2) *Jack Bailey* ■ *Dir* David Swift • *Scr* James Fritzell, Everett Greenbaum, David Swift, from the novel by Jack Finney

Good News
★★★★ U

Musical comedy 1947 · US · Colour · 89mins

One of the most delightful of the MGM musicals from a golden period, this college romp marked the directorial debut of *Meet Me in St Louis* choreographer Charles Walters, who would follow this movie with such greats as *Easter Parade* and *High Society*. Here, despite the presence of rather over-age students June Allyson and Peter Lawford, Walters injects real verve and genuine *joie de vivre* into such numbers as *Billion Dollar Baby* and *My Blue Heaven*. A real treat for fans of musicals. TS

June Allyson *Connie Lane* • Peter Lawford *Tommy Marlowe* • Patricia Marshall *Pat McClellan* • Joan McCracken *Babe Doolittle* • Ray McDonald *Bobby Turner* • Mel Tormé *Danny* • Robert Strickland [Robert E Strickland] *Peter Van Dyne III* • Donald MacBride *Coach Johnson* ■ *Dir* Charles Walters • *Scr* Betty Comden, Adolph Green, from the musical by Lawrence Schwab, Frank Mandel, BG De Sylva, Lew Brown, Ray Henderson

The Good Old Naughty Days
★★★

Documentary 2002 · Fr · BW · 71mins

Compiled from a stash of some 300 "smokers" found in a French attic, this quaint, but nevertheless explicit selection of silent smut suggests that tastes in pornography haven't altered much since early last century. Filmed between 1905 and 1930, the shorts have a technical polish that suggests the guiding hand of moonlighting studio hacks. Moreover, they contain a surprising amount of penetrative action, as well as a brief sequence of bestiality. But, overall, a peek-a-boo tone prevails, with the antics of the voluptuous participants (many of whom were prostitutes) appearing much more natural than the choreographed gyratings of today's sexploitation stars. DP. In French with English subtitles.

Dir Michel Reilhac

Good Sam
★★ U

Comedy drama 1948 · US · BW · 114mins

Store manager Gary Cooper is such a soft touch that his marriage to Ann Sheridan suffers. After all his good deeds, the day finally arrives when Cooper needs to be bailed out of his financial troubles. But will anyone come to his rescue? This suffers from being contrived and drawn out. Coop's good Samaritan is so exasperatingly stupid at times that it's hard to feel much sympathy for him. AE

Gary Cooper *Sam Clayton* • Ann Sheridan *Lu Clayton* • Ray Collins *Rev Daniels* • Edmund Lowe *HC Borden* • Joan Lorring *Shirley Mae* • Clinton Sundberg *Nelson* • Minerva Urecal *Mrs Nelson* • Louise Beavers *Chloe* ■ *Dir* Leo McCarey • *Scr* Ken Englund, from a story by Leo McCarey, John Klorer

The Good Son
★★★ 18

Drama 1993 · US · Colour · 82mins

Macaulay Culkin plays an outwardly friendly youngster who takes a murderous dislike to his cousin (Elijah Wood), who comes to stay when his mother dies and his father is away on business. Sadly, despite its controversial subject matter – the UK video release was delayed because of the tragic Jamie Bulger murder case – there's little attempt to explain Culkin's psychopathic behaviour. However, Wood is superb and director Joseph Ruben lays on some slickly scary moments. JF DVD

Macaulay Culkin *Henry Evans* • Elijah Wood *Mark Evans* • Wendy Crewson *Susan Evans* • David Morse *Jack Evans* • Daniel Hugh-Kelly *Wallace* • Jacqueline Brookes *Alice Davenport* • Quinn Culkin *Connie Evans* • Ashley Crow *Janice* ■ *Dir* Joseph Ruben • *Scr* Ian McEwan

The Good, the Bad and the Ugly
★★★★★ 18

Classic spaghetti western
1966 · It/Sp · Colour · 155mins

The concluding part of the "Dollars" trilogy (that began in 1964 with *A Fistful of Dollars*) is not only the most graphically violent of the three, but also surpasses the compassion and dark humour of its predecessors. There's nothing particularly new about a plotline involving buried treasure, but that's partly the point, as Leone is paying homage to the Hollywood western while revising its cherished traditions. He dexterously interweaves strands of communal and individual drama, which he throws into shocking relief against the bloody futility of the American Civil War. The genre had never witnessed such stylised violence, yet, while Lee Van Cleef and Eli Wallach unflinchingly accept it, Clint Eastwood can still spare some humanity for a dying soldier. And it's all superbly scored by Ennio Morricone. DP DVD

Clint Eastwood *"Joe"/"Blondie"* • Eli Wallach *Tuco* • Lee Van Cleef *Setenza/"Angel Eyes"* ■ *Dir* Sergio Leone • *Scr* Sergio Leone, Luciano Vincenzoni, from a story by Age-Scarpelli [Agenore Incrocci, Furio Scarpelli], Luciano Vincenzoni, Sergio Leone • *Music* Ennio Morricone • *Cinematographer* Tonino Delli Colli

The Good Thief
★★★ 15

Crime caper thriller
2002 · UK/Ire/Fr · Colour · 104mins

Nick Nolte's American in Nice is a thief, heroin addict and professional gambler, the charming but morally dubious hero of Neil Jordan's remake of the classic French thriller *Bob Le Flambeur*. Nolte rescues a young Eastern European immigrant from a life of prostitution and then goes cold turkey in order to orchestrate a big casino heist. Unfortunately, Jordan overcomplicates proceedings with too many characters and too many rival heist plots, which detract from the towering central performance of Nolte. BP. Contains violence, swearing and drug abuse. DVD

Nick Nolte *Bob Montagnet* • Tcheky Karyo *Roger* • Saïd Taghmaoui *Paulo* • Gérard Darmon *Raoul* • Emir Kusturica *Vladimir* • Marc Lavoine *Remi* ■ *Dir* Neil Jordan • *Scr* Neil Jordan, from the 1955 film *Bob Le Flambeur* by Jean-Pierre Melville, Auguste Le Breton

Good Time Girl
★★

Crime drama 1948 · UK · BW · 92mins

As the reform school rebel who hooks up with a gang of American crooks, Jean Kent created a screen image that she was never totally able to shake in this moody melodrama. Kent's sneering, sultry performance must have seemed very daring in those dank postwar days, but nowadays her petulance seems more like posturing. Director David MacDonald allows the plot to meander in order to make the most obvious social observations. DP

Jean Kent *Gwen Rawlings* • Dennis Price *Red* • Herbert Lom *Max* • Bonar Colleano *American* • Peter Glenville *Jimmy the waiter* • Flora Robson *Chairman of juvenile court* • Diana Dors *Lyla Lawrence* • George Carney *Mr Rawlings* ■ *Dir* David MacDonald • *Scr* Muriel Box, Sydney Box, Ted Willis, from the novel *Night Darkens the Streets* by Arthur la Bern

Good Times
★★ PG

Musical 1967 · US · Colour · 91mins

William Friedkin, director of *The French Connection* and *The Exorcist*, made his feature debut with this silly but amusing piece of wish-fulfilment, which stars the then-married pop duo, Sonny and Cher. Although it has dated badly, this potted history of Hollywood movie styles is, in its own small way, quite a clever satire, at the expense of both Tinseltown and the audiences who'll watch any old rubbish. Naturally, Sonny and Cher get to sing *I Got You Babe*, even though it has absolutely nothing to do with the plot. George Sanders puts in a rather shamefaced guest appearance. DP DVD

Sonny Bono • Cher • George Sanders *Mordicus* • Norman Alden *Warren* ■ *Dir* William Friedkin • *Scr* Tony Barrett

Good to Go
★★ 15

Musical drama 1986 · US · Colour · 86mins

Singer Art Garfunkel plays a journalist investigating the go-go music scene in Washington, in the wake of a gang rape and murder. The police turn out to be pursuing their own agenda and Art ends up on the side of the music-loving gang. Sadly, Garfunkel is less than convincing and the music peppering the plot is annoying rather than enjoyable. JB

Art Garfunkel *SD Blass* • Robert DoQui *Max* • Harris Yulin *Harrigan* • Reginald Daughtry *Little Beats* • Richard Brooks *Chemist* • Paula Davis *Evette* • Richard Bauer *Editor* • Michael White *Gil Colton* ■ *Dir/Scr* Blaine Novak

The Good Wife ★★★ 15

Drama 1986 · Aus · Colour · 93mins

In this moral tale of small-town lust, set in 1930s Australia, Rachel Ward yearns to break free from her dreary home life and indifferent husband Bryan Brown. After a brief tumble with her brother-in-law, the good wife goes bad and hits town looking for romance and sex. Enter Sam Neill. This erotic fandango may not exactly be *Madame Bovary*, but Ward and Neill act up a storm, while Brown demonstrates why a nice girl might consider adultery. NF. Contains swearing.

Rachel Ward *Marge Hills* • Bryan Brown *Sonny Hills* • Sam Neill *Neville Gifford* • Steven Vidler *Sugar Hills* • Jennifer Claire *Daisy* • Bruce Barry *Archie* • Clarissa Kaye-Mason [Clarissa Kaye] *Mrs Jackson* • Carole Skinner *Mrs Gibson* ■ *Dir* Ken Cameron • *Scr* Peter Kenna

Good Will Hunting ★★★★ 15

Drama 1997 · US · Colour · 121mins

Matt Damon and Ben Affleck wrote and starred in this moving drama directed by Gus Van Sant. Damon is Will, a wrong-side-of-the-tracks janitor at top college MIT who has an exceptional mind, and whose mathematical genius is discovered by professor Stellan Skarsgård. Damon, however, is an emotionally troubled young man, so psychologist Robin Williams is brought in to help him. Skilfully directed and beautifully performed by Damon, Williams, Skarsgård, Affleck and Minnie Driver (as Damon's intellectual girlfriend), this won Oscars for Damon and Affleck's screenplay as well as for Williams's subtle performance. JB. Contains swearing. DVD

Matt Damon *Will Hunting* • Robin Williams *Sean McGuire* • Ben Affleck *Chuckie* • Minnie Driver *Skylar* • Stellan Skarsgård *Lambeau* • John Mighton *Tom* • Rachel Majorowski *Krystyn* • Colleen McCauley *Cathy* ■ *Dir* Gus Van Sant • *Scr* Matt Damon, Ben Affleck

A Good Woman ★★★ PG

Period comedy drama
2004 · UK/It/Sp/US · Colour · 92mins

Oscar Wilde's waspish morality tale *Lady Windermere's Fan* gets both a fresh 1930s setting and a significant US slant. Mark Umbers and a stilted Scarlett Johansson play American newlyweds, who set society tongues wagging in a resort on Italy's beautiful Amalfi coast when Umbers is spotted apparently becoming intimate with notorious New York gold-digger Helen Hunt. The intricate web of secrets and lies that emerges as the scandal spreads is a tad contrived but it's still a highly agreeable movie, thanks to delicious dialogue and some spirited performances. SF

Helen Hunt *Mrs Erlynne* • Scarlett Johansson *Meg Windermere* • Tom Wilkinson *Tuppy* • Stephen Campbell Moore *Lord Darlington* • Mark Umbers *Robert Windermere* • Milena Vukotic *Contessa Lucchino* • Diana Hardcastle *Lady Plymdale* • John Standing *Dumby* ■ *Dir* Mike Barker • *Scr* Howard Himelstein, from the play *Lady Windermere's Fan* by Oscar Wilde

The Good Woman of Bangkok ★★★

Documentary 1991 · Aus · Colour · 82mins

While director Gough Lewis refused to reveal on screen that he slept with his subject during the making of *Sex: the Annabel Chong Story*, Dennis O'Rourke makes an open secret of his physical liaison with Thai prostitute Yaowalak Chonchanakun in this relentlessly uncomfortable pseudo-documentary. Shot over nine months on Super 8, the action alternates between interviews with the often exhausted (or possibly drug-addled) girl and discreetly filmed footage of the Bangkok sex industry in action. Any insights O'Rourke gains about the nature of love are buried beneath his sense of guilt at exploiting Yaowalak and acquiescing in the system that enslaves her. DP

Dir/Scr Dennis O'Rourke

Goodbye Again ★★★

Romantic drama 1961 · US · BW · 119mins

This is the film version of the book *Aimez-Vous Brahms* (the movie's French title) by once-fashionable, controversial novelist Françoise Sagan. It's sensitively but rather boringly directed by director Anatole Litvak. Ingrid Bergman is loved by toy boy Anthony Perkins while really harbouring a deep passion for playboy Yves Montand. Perkins picked up an acting award at Cannes for his performance and the Paris locations are attractive. But the running time stretches a very slight tale a long way. TS

Ingrid Bergman *Paula Tessier* • Yves Montand *Roger Demarest* • Anthony Perkins *Philip Van Der Besh* • Jessie Royce Landis *Mrs Van Der Besh* • Jackie Lane [Jocelyn Lane] *Maisie I* • Jean Clarke *Maisie II* • Michèle Mercier *Maisie III* • Pierre Dux *Maître Fleury* ■ *Dir* Anatole Litvak • *Scr* Samuel Taylor, from the novel *Aimez-Vous Brahms* by Françoise Sagan

Goodbye Charlie ★★

Fantasy comedy 1964 · US · Colour · 116mins

Despite stylish direction from Vincente Minnelli, the presence of Debbie Reynolds and Tony Curtis, and stalwart support from Pat Boone and Walter Matthau, this film still comes a cropper. This witless heaven-and-earth tale has Reynolds struggling manfully to portray a writer who, having been murdered by a jealous husband (Matthau), returns to Earth as a beautiful girl. Reynolds consorts with his/her best friend (Curtis) and is courted by Boone, to the discomfort of everyone – including the audience. RK

Tony Curtis *George Tracy* • Debbie Reynolds *Charlie Sorel/The Woman* • Pat Boone *Bruce Minton* • Joanna Barnes *Janie* • Ellen McRae [Ellen Burstyn] *Franny* • Laura Devon *Rusty* • Martin Gabel *Morton Craft* • Roger C Carmel *Inspector* • Walter Matthau *Sir Leopold Sartori* ■ *Dir* Vincente Minnelli • *Scr* Harry Kurnitz, from a play by George Axelrod

Goodbye Charlie Bright ★★★ 18

Drama 2000 · UK · Colour · 83mins

A rite-of-passage yarn about a bunch of lifelong mates on a south London council estate and the last long, hot summer that they spend together before circumstances send them off on separate ways. The film charts their close but volatile kinship against a backdrop of the usual "laddish" behaviour. While the script and direction are erratic, the film benefits enormously from the authenticity of location filming and from credible performances by a young cast. A very bright start for writer/director Nick Love. DA DVD

Paul Nicholls *Charlie Bright* • Roland Manookian *Justin* • Phil Daniels *Eddie* • Jamie Foreman *Tony* • Danny Dyer *Francis* • Dani Behr *Blondie* • David Thewlis *Dad* ■ *Dir* Nick Love • *Scr* Nick Love, Dominic Eames, from a story by Nick Love

Goodbye, Columbus ★★★

Comedy 1969 · US · Colour · 101mins

This adaptation of Philip Roth's novella stars Richard Benjamin as a librarian who woos pretty rich girl Ali MacGraw. Set in the affluent Jewish community of New York and the swanky Florida resort of Boca Raton, it's a comedy that spins on MacGraw's parents (Jack Klugman and Nan Martin) who dislike Benjamin because he's penniless. The rest of the plot revolves around MacGraw's birth control method, or lack of it. Pretty daring for 1969, it seems pretty pointless now. Even so, it's nicely acted and cleverly observed. AT. Contains some swearing, brief nudity and sex scenes.

Richard Benjamin *Neil Klugman* • Ali MacGraw *Brenda Patimkin* • Jack Klugman *Mr Patimkin* • Nan Martin *Mrs Patimkin* • Michael Meyers *Ron* • Lori Shelle *Julie Patimkin* • Royce Wallace *Carlotta* • Sylvie Strauss *Aunt Gladys* ■ *Dir* Larry Peerce • *Scr* Arnold Schulman, from the novella by Philip Roth

Goodbye, Dragon Inn ★★★

Comedy drama 2003 · Tai · Colour · 82mins

In this, one of director Tsai Ming-liang more accessible films, a classic Chinese action movie screens in a dilapidated, barely populated cinema. There's far more going on in the movie-within-the-movie, Hu King's 1966 flick *Dragon Inn*, which is watched in near silence by a handful of lonely customers, including two elderly gentlemen played by actors from Hu's original movie, who just may or may not be ghosts. Barely a word is spoken throughout while the rain comes down outside and a cashier (Chen Shiang-chyi) goes about her business on what emerges as the picture house's last night. But the film gives off sense of melancholy that gets in your bones like damp and stays with you. LF. A Mandarin/Taiwanese language film.

Lee Kang-sheng *Projectionist* • Chen Shiang-chyi [Chen Xiangqi] *Ticket woman* • Kiyonobu Mitamura *Japanese tourist* • Chun Shih • Miao Tien ■ *Dir/Scr* Tsai Ming-liang

Goodbye Emmanuelle ★★ 18

Erotic drama 1977 · Fr · Colour · 94mins

Sylvia Kristel packs her suitcase for another suitably exotic location (the Seychelles) in this aimless retread through another thin story idea, which as usual is just a pretext for lots of soft-focus disrobing. Given that she has to do little but take her clothes off, it's probably best to gloss over the limitations of Kristel's acting, although the film still possesses a touch more class than the formulaic erotic thrillers on offer nowadays. *Emmanuelle 4* followed in 1985. JF. French dialogue dubbed into English. Contains sex scenes and nudity. DVD

Sylvia Kristel *Emmanuelle* • Umberto Orsini *Jean* • Jean-Pierre Bouvier *Grégory* • Charlotte Alexandra *Chloë* • Jacques Doniol-Valcroze *Michel Cordier* • Olga Georges-Picot *Florence Cordier* ■ *Dir* François Leterrier • *Scr* François Leterrier, Monique Lange, from the characters created by Emmanuelle Arsan

The Goodbye Girl ★★★★ PG

Romantic comedy
1977 · US · Colour · 105mins

A Neil Simon script, Mike Nichols wielding the megaphone and Robert De Niro to star. It seemed nothing could stop *Bogart Slept Here* from becoming the movie of the year. But two weeks into production, the director and his star were at odds over everything from Method acting to comic timing. De Niro was sacked and went off to make *Taxi Driver*, leaving Nichols to shut down the picture. Two years later, Richard Dreyfuss took the lead in what was now *The Goodbye Girl*, and Neil Simon's winter of discontent was made glorious summer by this unprepossessing son of New York. Dreyfuss is inspired, his gay Richard III the highlight of a wisecracking romantic comedy that barely pauses for breath, and he's ably matched by Marsha Mason. Dreyfuss won an Oscar, a success De Niro still regards as the one that got away. DP

Richard Dreyfuss *Elliott Garfield* • Marsha Mason *Paula McFadden* • Quinn Cummings *Lucy McFadden* • Paul Benedict *Mark Morgenweiss* • Barbara Rhoades *Donna Douglas* • Theresa Merritt *Mrs Crosby* ■ *Dir* Herbert Ross • *Scr* Neil Simon

Good Bye Lenin! ★★★ 15

Comedy drama 2003 · Ger · Colour · 116mins

The fall of the Berlin Wall and the reunification of Germany is less than obvious material for a comedy, but director Wolfgang Becker's critical and commercial smash illustrates the "before" and "after" from a quirky and amusing perspective. Katrin Sass plays a staunch socialist who lapses into a coma for eight months, during which time the seeds of change are planted in Berlin. When she finally wakes, doctors warn her devoted son (Daniel Brühl) that any shocks could kill her, so he sets about hiding all traces of reunification. There are some big laughs and the social comment is nicely done, but the subplots are integrated with less skill. JC. In German with English subtitles. DVD

Daniel Brühl *Alex Kerner* • Katrin Sass *Christiane Kerner, Alex's mother* • Chulpan Khamatova *Lara* • Maria Simon *Ariane Kerner, Alex's sister* • Florian Lukas *Denis* • Alexander Beyer *Rainer* • Burghart Klaussner *Robert Kerner, Alex's father* ■ *Dir* Wolfgang Becker • *Scr* Bernd Lichtenberg, Wolfgang Becker

Goodbye Lover ★★ 18

Comedy crime thriller
1997 · US · Colour · 96mins

Director Roland Joffé tries to make this revenge comedy amusing but fails. In the end, it's saved by the performances of Don Johnson and Ellen DeGeneres. Johnson plays the rich businessman who is pushed over a balcony by his useless brother (Dermot Mulroney) and the sister-in-law (Patricia Arquette) with whom he was having an affair. DeGeneres's cop gets the only good lines and delivers them with aplomb. JB DVD

Patricia Arquette *Sandra Dunmore* • Dermot Mulroney *Jake Dunmore* • Ellen DeGeneres *Sgt Rita Pompano* • Mary-Louise Parker *Peggy Blaine* • Don Johnson *Ben Dunmore* • Ray McKinnon *Rollins* • Alex Rocco *Detective Crowley* ■ *Dir* Roland Joffé • *Scr* Ron Peer, Joel Cohen, Alec Sokolow

Goodbye, Mr Chips ★★★★★ U

Drama 1939 · UK/US · BW · 109mins

British star Robert Donat pipped Clark Gable to the best actor Oscar the year *Gone with the Wind* swept the awards with his marvellous portrayal of author James Hilton's crusty pedagogue. Donat ages throughout the film in a subtle and worldly-wise manner, and he's not overly reliant on movie make-up to do so. This is a warm-hearted, humanitarian work, beautifully filmed in England by MGM and is a fine example of that great studio at its peak. Immaculately directed by the under-rated Sam Wood, the film introduced world audiences to Greer Garson, who replaced Norma Shearer overnight to become first lady of the MGM lot. This finely crafted tale continues to work its magic and even the most cynical viewer won't fail to be moved. TS DVD

Robert Donat *Charles Chipping* • Greer Garson *Katherine Ellis* • Terry Kilburn *John Colley/*

Peter Colley • John Mills *Peter Colley as a young man* • Paul Henreid *Max Staefel* • Judith Furse *Flora* • Lyn Harding *Dr Wetherby* • Milton Rosmer *Charteris* ■ *Dir* Sam Wood • *Scr* RC Sherriff, Claudine West, Eric Maschwitz, Sidney Franklin, from the novella by James Hilton, serialised in *British Weekly* • *Cinematographer* FA Young [Freddie Young] • *Art Director* Alfred Junge

Goodbye, Mr Chips ★ PG

Musical drama
1969 · US/UK · Colour · 152mins

Rex Harrison and Richard Burton both had the sense to send Terence Rattigan's script back, and not even an Oscar nomination can hide the fact that this is one of Peter O'Toole's least distinguished performances. The fact that John Williams and Leslie Bricusse were also nominated for best score is preposterous, as the songs in this adaptation of James Hilton's delightful novel are shocking. DP

Peter O'Toole *Arthur "Chips" Chipping* • Petula Clark *Katherine Bridges* • Michael Redgrave *Headmaster* • George Baker *Lord Sutterwick* • Sian Phillips *Ursula Mossbank* • Michael Bryant *Max Staefel* • Patricia Hayes *Miss Honeybun* ■ *Dir* Herbert Ross • *Scr* Terence Rattigan, from the novella by James Hilton, serialised in *British Weekly*

Goodbye, My Fancy ★★★ U

Romantic drama 1951 · US · BW · 107mins

This is hardly the film for which Joan Crawford will be remembered. It is, however, a fascinating example of how miscasting can ruin an otherwise engaging story. Crawford plays a congresswoman caught up in a romantic triangle while revisiting her old school to receive an honorary degree. Even her stellar power failed to make the picture play at the box office and her presence overbalances what was a pretty flimsy comedy in the first place. Robert Young and Frank Lovejoy are the love rivals but they can do nothing to repair the damage. DP

Joan Crawford *Agatha Reed* • Robert Young (1) *Dr James Merrill* • Frank Lovejoy *Matt Cole* • Eve Arden *Woody* • Janice Rule *Virginia Merrill* • Lurene Tuttle *Ellen Griswold* • Howard St John *Claude Griswold* • Viola Roache *Miss Shackleford* ■ *Dir* Vincent Sherman • *Scr* Ivan Goff, Ben Roberts, from the play by Fay Kanin

Good-bye, My Lady ★★ U

Adventure drama 1956 · US · BW · 95mins

Brandon de Wilde, the wide-eyed youngster from *Shane*, stars in this cute but engaging story about an orphan boy who lives in the Mississippi swamps and befriends a dog with unusual gifts as a hunter. Turns out that the dog is a rare breed and its owner wants it back. Veteran director William A Wellman makes a tidy job of things, and it's far less syrupy than the Disney equivalent *Old Yeller*. AT

Walter Brennan *Uncle Jesse* • Phil Harris *Cash* • Brandon de Wilde *Skeeter* • Sidney Poitier *Gates* • William Hopper *Grover* • Louise Beavers *Bonnie* • Vivian Vance *Wife* ■ *Dir* William A Wellman • *Scr* Sid Fleischman, from a novel by James Street

Goodbye New York ★★ 15

Comedy 1984 · US · Colour · 90mins

A year before she starred in the hysterically funny *Lost in America* with Albert Brooks, Julie Hagerty made this pale precursor (which could have been subtitled *Lost in Israel*). After oversleeping on a Paris flight, Hagerty finds herself stranded in Israel. Instead of getting the first plane back like any normal person, she ends up living on a kibbutz and falling in love with soldier Amos Kollek (who also directs). Hagerty, whose brand of kooky comedy could brighten up the dullest movie, is funny to watch, but this material doesn't match her talents. JB

Julie Hagerty *Nancy Callaghan* • Amos Kollek *David* • Shmuel Shiloh *Moishe* • Aviva Ger *Ilana* • David Topaz *Albert* • Jennifer Babtist *Lisa* • Christopher Goutman *Jack* • Hanan Goldblat *Avi* ■ *Dir/Scr* Amos Kollek

Goodbye, Norma Jean ★★ 18

Biographical drama
1976 · US/Aus · Colour · 93mins

A sleazy, sensationalist biopic of Norma Jean Baker, the young brunette who reinvented herself as that ultimate blonde screen icon, Marilyn Monroe. Misty Rowe plays Marilyn, and does an OK job. But she has never come close to matching Monroe's screen success and, after spending the 1980s appearing in broad teen comedies, she returned to the role of Monroe in a 1989 sequel *Goodnight, Sweet Marilyn*. DA

Misty Rowe *Norman Jean Baker* • Terrence Locke *Ralph Johnson* • Patch Mackenzie *Ruth Latimer* • Preston Hanson *Hal James* • Marty Zagon *Irving Olbach* • Andre Philippe *Sam Dunn* ■ *Dir* Larry Buchanan • *Scr* Larry Buchanan, Lynn Shubert

The Goodbye People ★★

Comedy 1984 · US · Colour · 104mins

It's hard to understand how Herb Gardner came to make his directorial debut with this adaptation of his own stage play, nearly 20 years after it flopped on Broadway. Sentimentality drips off this indigestible mush like the ketchup oozing out of the hot dogs sold by Martin Balsam's retired Coney Island vendor. Both he and disgruntled toy maker Judd Hirsch try to cut down on the corn, but Gardner piles it on with relish. DP

Judd Hirsch *Arthur Korman* • Martin Balsam *Max Silverman* • Pamela Reed *Nancie "Shirley" Scot* • Ron Silver *Eddie Bergson* • Michael Tucker *Michael Silverman* • Gene Saks *Marcus Soloway* ■ *Dir* Herb Gardner • *Scr* Herb Gardner, from his play

Goodbye Pork Pie ★★ 18

Road movie 1981 · NZ · Colour · 102mins

The first New Zealand feature to recoup its costs at the domestic box office is a road movie in the good old counterculture tradition. Indeed, there's a real coming-of-age feel as unlikely buddies Tony Barry and Kelly Johnson learn about life, love and responsibility on a cross-country trek that's littered with eccentric characters and angry lawmen. It's dated in places, the sexism is unforgiveable and the episodic structure stops it building up a real head of steam, but first-time writer/director/producer Geoff Murphy does pack the picture with plenty of action and offbeat humour. DP. Contains swearing. DVD

Tony Barry *John* • Kelly Johnson *Gerry Austin* • Claire Oberman *Shirl* • Shirley Gruar *Sue* • Jackie Lowitt *Leslie Morris* • Don Selwyn *Kaitaia policeman* • Shirley Dunn *Car rental girl* • Paki Cherrington *Taxi driver* ■ *Dir* Geoff Murphy • *Scr* Geoff Murphy, Ian Mune

GoodFellas ★★★★★ 18

Crime drama 1990 · US · Colour · 145mins

Martin Scorsese's unflinching depiction of the attraction and the brutal reality of the Mafia lifestyle is a masterwork on every artistic level. Direction, script – based on Nicholas Pileggi's non-fiction book *Wiseguy* – photography, ensemble acting (Joe Pesci won a deserved Oscar, but he's matched by Robert De Niro and Ray Liotta) and driving pop and rock soundtrack seamlessly combine to dazzling effect in this instant classic. Crackling with raw energy, Scorsese's fascinating new take on themes explored in his earlier *Mean Streets* enthrals from the first violent frames to the stunning final sequence. Be prepared to be completely bowled over by a director in full control of top-notch material at the peak of his talents. AJ. Contains drug abuse, swearing, violence. DVD

Robert De Niro *James Conway* • Ray Liotta *Henry Hill* • Joe Pesci *Tommy DeVito* • Lorraine Bracco *Karen Hill* • Paul Sorvino *Paul Cicero* • Frank Sivero *Frankie Carbone* • Tony Darrow *Sonny Bunz* • Mike Starr *Frenchy* ■ *Dir* Martin Scorsese • *Scr* Nicholas Pileggi, Martin Scorsese, from the book *Wiseguy* by Nicholas Pileggi • *Cinematographer* Michael Ballhaus • *Editor* Thelma Schoonmaker

A Goofy Movie ★★ U

Animated comedy
1995 · US · Colour · 74mins

Mickey Mouse's pal Goofy gets his own movie, but fans of the original short cartoons in which he was a co-star may be shocked to discover that Goofy is now a dad, and not a cool one either, preferring to drag his son off fishing rather than let him chat up girls. The story is rather ordinary and the bland computer animation looks less interesting than anything kids can catch nowadays on TV. JB DVD

Bill Farmer *Goofy* • Jason Marsden *Max* • Jim Cummings *Pete* • Kellie Martin *Roxanne* • Rob Paulsen *PJ* • Wallace Shawn *Principal Mazur* • Frank Welker *Bigfoot* • Kevin Lima *Lester* • Florence Stanley *Waitress* ■ *Dir* Kevin Lima • *Scr* Jymn Magon, Chris Matheson, Brian Pimental, from a story by Jymn Magon

The Goonies ★★★ PG

Adventure 1985 · US · Colour · 108mins

Before making it big directing *Home Alone*, Chris Columbus wrote the screenplay from a story by Steven Spielberg for this good-natured romp, in which a gang of children tackles pirates while searching for missing treasure. The tale rattles along like a juvenile *Raiders of the Lost Ark* and the young leads are likeable enough. There's also some nice hamming from villains Anne Ramsey, Joe Pantoliano and Robert Davi. JF. Contains some swearing and violence. DVD

Sean Astin *Mikey* • Josh Brolin *Brand* • Jeff Cohen *Chunk* • Corey Feldman *Mouth* • Kerri Green *Andy* • Martha Plimpton *Stef* • Ke Huy Quan *Data* • John Matuszak *Sloth* • Robert Davi *Jake* • Joe Pantoliano *Francis* • Anne Ramsey *Mama Fratelli* ■ *Dir* Richard Donner • *Scr* Chris Columbus, from a story by Steven Spielberg

The Goose Steps Out ★★★★ U

Second World War comedy
1942 · UK · BW · 66mins

A wonderful comedy in which Will Hay is sent to a Nazi academy to get hold of Frank Pettingell's plans for a gas bomb. As usual, Hay's academic shortcomings are soon exposed, this time by a class of Hitler Youth that includes Peter Ustinov, Charles Hawtrey and Barry Morse, but he still manages to insult Hitler at every turn, steal a sample bomb casing and pass on some bogus invasion plans before heading back to Blighty. The script is packed with morale-boosting jokes that still seem pretty fresh, and Hay is in prime form. DP

Will Hay *William Potts/Muller* • Frank Pettingell *Professor Hoffman* • Julien Mitchell *General Von Glotz* • Charles Hawtrey *Max* • Peter Croft *Hans* • Anne Firth *Lena* • Leslie Harcourt *Vagel* ■ *Dir* Will Hay, Basil Dearden • *Scr* Angus MacPhail, John Dighton, from a story by Bernard Miles, Reginald Groves

The Goose Woman ★★★

Silent drama 1925 · US · BW

One of the *grand dames* of silent Hollywood, Louise Dresser, gives an impassioned performance in this emphatic adaptation of a Rex Beach story that was itself inspired by the infamous Hall-Mills or "Pig Woman" case. As the former diva who hopes to restore lost celebrity by claiming to have witnessed a killing near her humble abode, Dresser ably conveys the shabby grandeur of the faded icon, whose deception backfires when she learns her only son is implicated in the crime. This old-fangled melodrama is directed with customary gravitas by Clarence Brown. DP

Louise Dresser *Mary Holmes/Marie de Nardi* • Jack Pickford *Gerald Holmes* • Constance Bennett *Hazel Woods* • James O Barrows *Jacob Riggs* • Spottiswoode Aitken *Jacob Riggs* ■ *Dir* Clarence Brown • *Scr* Melville Brown, Dwinelle Benthall (titles), from the story by Rex Beach

Gor ★ 15

Action fantasy 1987 · US · Colour · 90mins

The sword-and-sorcery genre had well and truly run its course by the time Fritz Kiersch's lame-brained effort saw the light of day. Urbano Barberini is a nerdy professor transported to a distant planet where he sets about freeing its people from the tyrannical slavery of their overlord, played by the under-used Oliver Reed. All the staple ingredients are present – sword duels, scenes of torture, pastiche erotica – but any attempt at humour fails. Jack Palance turns up at the end to introduce himself as the villain of the sequel, *Outlaw of Gor*. RS

Urbano Barberini *Cabot* • Rebecca Ferratti *Talena* • Paul L Smith [Paul Smith] *Surbus* • Oliver Reed *Sarm* • Jack Palance *Xenos* ■ *Dir* Fritz Kiersch • *Scr* Rick Marx, Peter Welbeck [Harry Alan Towers], from the novel *Tarnsman of Gor* by John Norman

GORA ★★★ 15

Science-fiction comedy
2004 · Tur · Colour · 127mins

Omer Faruk Sorak's raucous and colourful sci-fi spoof piles on both jokes and adventure. Cem Yilmaz plays Arif, a none-too-smart conman and producer of fake UFO pictures, who is kidnapped by aliens and imprisoned on the planet of Gora. Once there, he must prove his bravery and cunning to have any hope of getting back to Earth. Coming from a country not internationally known for its science fiction or comedy output, this is an entertaining enterprise, despite its modest budget. KK. In Turkish with English subtitles. Contains swearing.

Cem Yilmaz *Arif/Commander Logar/Ersan Kuneri/Commander Kubar* • Ozge Ozberk *Ceku* • Ozan Guven *216 Robot-2* • Safak Sezer *Kuna* • Rasim Oztekin *Bob Marley Faruk* • Ozkan Ugur *Garavel* • Idil Firat *Mulu* ■ *Dir* Omer Faruk Sorak • *Scr* Cem Yilmaz

The Gorbals Story ★★

Drama 1949 · UK · BW · 74mins

This is a grim affair in which Glaswegian artist Howard Connell recalls the tough tenement existence that not only shaped his talent, but almost drove him to murder. Adapted by director David MacKane from Robert McLeish's play, the film strives valiantly for authenticity, but the social message is badly fumbled and the performances highly theatrical. DP

Howard Connell *Willie Mutrie* • Betty Henderson *Peggie Anderson* • Russell Hunter *Johnnie Martin* • Majorie Thomson *Jean Mutrie* • Roddy McMillan *Hector* • Isobel Campbell *Nora Reilly* • Jack Stewart *Peter Reilly* • Archie Duncan *Bull* ■ *Dir* David MacKane • *Scr* David MacKane, from the play by Robert McLeish

Gordon the Black Pirate ★★ U

Swashbuckling adventure
1961 · It · Colour · 82mins

Like many Italian swashbucklers of the period, the action here is brisk but predictable, while the tawdry surface opulence can't disguise the cheapness of the production. (Ricardo Montalban's pirate ship was actually a fishing boat.) However, Vincent Price – who apparently only agreed to star in the picture because it allowed him to go art hunting – has a hissably good time as the governor's secretary with a nasty sideline in slavery. DP

Ricardo Montalban *Gordon, the Black Buckaneer* • Vincent Price *Romero* • Giulia Rubini *Manuela* • Liana Orfei *Luana* • Mario Feliciani *Tortuga* ■ *Dir* Mario Costa • *Scr* John Byrne, Ottavio Poggi

Gordon's War ★★

Blaxploitation crime drama
1973 · US · Colour · 89mins

Vietnam veteran Paul Winfield returns home to Harlem and has to cope with his wife's death from a drug overdose. Declaring war on the ghetto underworld, he organises a strike force to rid the neighbourhood of pushers. This is a slickly packaged blaxploitation vigilante drama, shot on gritty locations and with more credible action and less comic-strip violence than most of its ilk. AJ

Paul Winfield *Gordon* • Carl Lee *Bee* • David Downing *Otis* • Tony King *Roy* • Gilbert Lewis *Spanish Harry* • Carl Gordon *Luther the Pimp* • Nathan C Heard *Big Pink* • Grace Jones *Mary* • Adam Wade *Hustler* ■ *Dir* Ossie Davis • *Scr* Howard Friedlander, Ed Spielman

Gordy ★ U

Comedy adventure
1994 · US · Colour · 86mins

This excruciating children's drama about a talking pig was released a year before *Babe* made eating bacon a capital crime. Cute to the point of nausea, *Gordy* includes every barnyard cliché in the book as he escapes the slaughterhouse, tries to find his folks and saves the young heir to a corporation from drowning. Its saving grace, for those who like that sort of thing, is a country and western soundtrack with stars such as Boxcar Willie and Roy Clark. FL DVD

Michael Roescher *Hanky Royce* • Doug Stone *Luke MacAllister* • Kristy Young *Jinnie Sue MacAllister* • Deborah Hobart *Jessica Royce* • Tom Lester *Cousin Jake* • Tom Key *Brinks* • Ted Manson *Henry Royce* • Justin Garms *Gordy* ■ *Dir* Mark Lewis (1) • *Scr* Leslie Stevens, from a story by Jay Sommers, Dick Chevillat

The Gore-Gore Girls ★ 18

Detective horror 1972 · US · Colour · 80mins

This is just as boring, amateur and stupid as splatter pioneer Herschell Gordon Lewis's previous snooze-fests. Private detective Frank Kress tries to solve a series of stripper murders at comedian Henny Youngman's club with the help of local reporter Amy Farrell. If you can stay awake long enough, the close-up mutilations may offend. One of the first movies given an American X certificate for violence. AJ DVD

Frank Kress *Abraham Gentry* • Amy Farrell *Nancy Weston* • Hedda Lubin *Marlene* • Henny Youngman *Marzdone Mobilie* ■ *Dir* Herschell Gordon Lewis • *Scr* Alan J Dachman

Gorgeous ★★ PG

Romantic comedy
1999 · HK · Colour · 95mins

Both Jackie Chan and Tony Leung Chiu-Wai strike against type in this unconvincing blend of chop socky and romantic comedy. Yet the central character is Qi Shu, who plays a naive dreamer from a Taiwanese fishing village, who flies to Hong Kong in response to a message in a bottle. Undeterred by the fact its sender is Leung's gay make-up artist, she tilts her cap at Chan. DP. In Cantonese with English subtitles. DVD

Jackie Chan *CN Chan* • Qi Shu *Bu* • Tony Leung Chiu-Wai [Tony Leung (2)] *Albert* • Emil Chow *LW Lo* • Jen Hsien-Chi *Bu's suitor* ■ *Dir* Vincent Kok • *Scr* Vincent Kok, Jackie Chan, Lo Yiu-Fai, from a story by Ivy Ho

The Gorgeous Hussy ★★

Historical romantic drama
1936 · US · BW · 103mins

Joan Crawford scandalises Washington society as the innkeeper's daughter who becomes President Andrew Jackson's bit-on-the-side. Crawford wanted the part because she rather resented Norma Shearer getting all the juicy historical roles MGM had to offer. Audiences were apathetic, though, and Franchot Tone comes off badly. AT

Joan Crawford *Margaret "Peggy" O'Neal Eaton* • Robert Taylor (1) *"Bow" Timberlake* • Lionel Barrymore *Andrew Jackson* • Franchot Tone *John Eaton* • Melvyn Douglas *John Randolph* • James Stewart *"Rowdy" Dow* • Alison Skipworth *Mrs Beal* • Beulah Bondi *Rachel Jackson* • Louis Calhern *Sunderland* ■ *Dir* Clarence Brown • *Scr* Ainsworth Morgan, Stephen Morehouse Avery, from the novel by Samuel Hopkins Adams

Gorgo ★★★ PG

Monster adventure
1961 · UK · Colour · 73mins

This highly derivative film has borrowed from so many other monster movies that it is almost as much fun spotting the swipes as it is watching the picture itself. Special effects boffin Tom Howard's creatures are the sweetest rampaging dinosaurs you will ever see, and the model London landmarks trampled by Mrs Gorgo are risible. Bill Travers and William Sylvester keep straight faces as this enjoyable tosh unfolds around them. DP

Bill Travers *Joe Ryan* • William Sylvester *Sam Slade* • Vincent Winter *Sean* • Bruce Seton *Professor Flaherty* • Joseph O'Conor *Professor Hendricks* • Martin Benson *Dorkin* • Christopher Rhodes *McCartin* • Maurice Kaufmann *Radio reporter* ■ *Dir* Eugène Lourié • *Scr* John Loring [Robert L Richards], Daniel Hyatt [Daniel James], from their story

The Gorgon ★★★ 15

Horror 1964 · UK · Colour · 79mins

Barbara Shelley, Hammer's best ever *femme fatale*, is possessed by the snake-tressed, stone-gazing spirit of the Greek mythological creature in director Terence Fisher's most poetic and under-rated fearful fairy tale. Totally unclassifiable, it relies less on its absurd story and more on provocative imagery. But, while it may fall short of the monstrous mark, the period atmosphere is powerfully evoked and it's made headier by the peerless Peter Cushing and Christopher Lee at the height of their dramatic authority. AJ

Peter Cushing *Namaroff* • Christopher Lee *Prof Carl Meister* • Richard Pasco *Paul Heitz* • Barbara Shelley *Carla Hoffman* • Michael Goodliffe *Professor Heitz* • Patrick Troughton *Kanof* • Jack Watson *Ratoff* • Jeremy Longhurst *Bruno Heitz* ■ *Dir* Terence Fisher • *Scr* John Gilling, from a story by J Llewellyn Devine

Gorilla at Large ★★★

Thriller 1954 · US · Colour · 81mins

An above-average chiller, though probably not a film that star Anne Bancroft would regard as one of her career highlights. She still cuts a fine figure in her trapeze artist catsuit, in this tale of bizarre killings seemingly linked to fellow amusement park employee Cameron Mitchell (resplendent in a crummy gorilla costume). Director Harmon Jones swells the story with a superb supporting cast. This was originally released in 3-D, so things hurtle at you for no apparent reason. RS

Cameron Mitchell *Joey Matthews* • Anne Bancroft *Laverne Miller* • Lee J Cobb *Detective Sergeant Garrison* • Raymond Burr *Cyrus Miller* • Charlotte Austin *Audrey Baxter* • Peter Whitney *Kovacs* • Lee Marvin *Shaughnessy* • Warren Stevens *Mack* ■ *Dir* Harmon Jones • *Scr* Leonard Praskins, Barney Slater

Gorillas in the Mist ★★★★ 12

Biographical drama
1988 · US · Colour · 123mins

Sigourney Weaver gives a tour-de-force performance in this fascinating account of Dian Fossey's ground-breaking research into the closed world of the gorilla. She admirably presents a warts-and-all portrait of the woman who slowly gained access to a tribe of remote primates facing extinction; according to Michael Apted's biographical drama, Fossey's passion for her gorillas was offset by her coldness as a human being and a commitment to her work that bordered on obsession. Apted's direction is sympathetic and he makes the most of the stunning jungle location, while Bryan Brown is good as Weaver's lover. JF. Contains violence and swearing. DVD

Sigourney Weaver *Dian Fossey* • Bryan Brown *Bob Campbell* • Julie Harris *Roz Carr* • John Omirah Miluwi *Sembagare* • Iain Cuthbertson *Dr Louis Leakey* • Constantin Alexandrov *Van Vecten* • Waigwa Wachira *Mukara* • Iain Glen *Brendan* • David Lansbury *Larry* ■ *Dir* Michael Apted • *Scr* Anna Hamilton Phelan, from a story by Anna Hamilton Phelan, Tab Murphy, from the book by Dian Fossey and an article by Harold TP Hayes

Gorky Park ★★★ 15

Spy thriller 1983 · US · Colour · 123mins

Moscow cop William Hurt – looking pained and acting sincere – investigates the case of three faceless corpses. Are the deaths due to Lee Marvin's business operation or are they a result of spy games? Dennis Potter's screenplay is a bit ponderous, but Michael Apted's direction makes the most of the plot convolutions and locations (with Helsinki standing in for Moscow). TH DVD

William Hurt *Arkady Renko* • Lee Marvin *Jack Osborne* • Brian Dennehy *William Kirwill* • Ian Bannen *Iamskoy* • Joanna Pacula *Irina Asanova* • Michael Elphick *Pasha Pavlovich* • Richard Griffiths *Anton* • Rikki Fulton *Major Pribluda* • Alexei Sayle *Golodkin* ■ *Dir* Michael Apted • *Scr* Dennis Potter, from the novel by Martin Cruz Smith

GORP ★

Comedy 1980 · US · Colour · 90mins

Director Joseph Ruben was an adept practitioner of good-natured exploitation fluff, often set in a high school milieu. But this crudely unfunny summer camp comedy about Jewish jocks trying to get laid is the worst and most lightweight of the lot. Michael Lembeck and Dennis Quaid drown under an interminable onslaught of sexist gags and macho posturing. AJ

Michael Lembeck *Kavell* • Dennis Quaid *Mad Grossman* • Philip Casnoff *Bergman* • Fran Drescher *Evie* • David Huddleston *Walrus Wallman* • Robert Trebor *Rabbi Blowitz* • Lou Wagner *Federman* ■ *Dir* Joseph Ruben • *Scr* Jeffrey Konvitz, from a story by Martin Zweiback, Jeffrey Konvitz

Gosford Park ★★★★ 15

Period murder mystery
2001 · US/UK · Colour · 131mins

Maverick director Robert Altman takes the English country-house murder mystery and turns it on its head. A huge cast of mostly British thespians flesh out the part whodunnit, part *Upstairs, Downstairs* satire, while Altman assuredly presents the 1930s-set drama from the servants' perspective. The opening of the piece – when the guests and their maids and valets arrive at Gosford Park – is as good as anything Altman's done in 30 years: multi-layered and impeccably choreographed. Meanwhile, the dramatic pace is maintained thanks to some sparkling dialogue – the Oscar-winning acidic script is by *Monarch of the Glen* actor Julian Fellowes – and fine performances. It has all the makings of a classic but then Stephen Fry's bumbling detective arrives and a surfeit of irony defuses the exquisitely-constructed mood. AC. Contains swearing and a sex scene. DVD

Maggie Smith *Constance, Countess of Trentham* • Michael Gambon *Sir William McCordle* • Kristin Scott Thomas *Lady Sylvia McCordle* • Emily Watson *Elsie* • Kelly Macdonald *Mary Maceachran* • Clive Owen *Robert Parks* • Helen Mirren *Mrs Wilson* • Eileen Atkins *Mrs Croft* • Alan Bates *Jennings* • Derek Jacobi *Probert* • Bob Balaban *Morris Weissman* • Jeremy Northam *Ivor Novello* • Ryan Phillippe *Henry Denton* • Richard E Grant *George* • Stephen Fry *Inspector Thompson* • Charles Dance *Raymond, Lord Stockbridge* ■ *Dir* Robert Altman • *Scr* Julian Fellowes, from an idea by Robert Altman, Bob Balaban

Gospa ★★★

Drama based on a true story
1995 · Can/Cro/US · Colour · 121mins

With its title deriving from the Croat for "Our Lady", this is a reverential account of the events that followed the Marian apparition to six children in the Bosnian hill town of Medjugorje in 1981. While it's not always easy to accept Morgan Fairchild as a nun, Martin Sheen gives a dignified performance as the parish priest who was prosecuted by the state for incitement to insurrection after he failed to prevent the shrine from becoming a place of pilgrimage. DP

Martin Sheen *Father Jozo Zovko* • Michael York *Milan Vikovic* • Morgan Fairchild *Sister Fafijana Zovko* • Frank Finlay *Monsignor* ■ *Dir* Jakov Sedlar • *Scr* Ivan Aralica, Paul Gronseth

The Gospel According to St Matthew ★★★★★ U

Biblical drama 1964 · It/Fr · BW · 129mins

Eschewing the crowd-pleasing grandeur of other biblical dramas, Pier Paolo Pasolini employed a neorealist approach to reaffirm the immediate social significance of Christ's teaching. This collaboration between a Marxist director and the Catholic Church (which contributed to the budget) is remarkable not only for the power of its message, but also for the gentle conviction of Enrique Irazoqui's Jesus, as he rails against injustice and works miracles with a compassion that is absent from the more reverential Hollywood testaments. With the sublime classical score underpinning the rugged beauty of Calabria, this is one of the most relevant religious films ever made. DP. Italian dialogue dubbed into English. DVD

Enrique Irazoqui *Jesus Christ* • Margherita Caruso *Mary, as a girl* • Susanna Pasolini *Mary, as a woman* • Marcello Morante *Joseph* • Mario Socrate *John the Baptist* • Settimo Di Porto *Peter* • Otello Sestili *Judas* • Ferruccio Nuzzo *Matthew* ■ *Dir/Scr* Pier Paolo Pasolini • *Cinematographer* Tonino Delli Colli

Gossip ★★ 15

Thriller 1999 · US · Colour · 90mins

Three college students start a rumour about a prudish fellow student having sex at a party. It gets out of hand, leading to an accusation of rape and an innocent man's arrest. The gossip-mongers are then caught in the middle as they fight about whether to come clean. The film has striking visuals, but never fully capitalises on the dramatic potential of its premise, while the young cast gives shallow performances. ST. Contains violence, swearing and sex scenes. [VIDEO] DVD

James Marsden *Derrick* • Lena Headey *Cathy Jones* • Norman Reedus *Travis* • Kate Hudson *Naomi* • Joshua Jackson *Beau* • Marisa Coughlan *Sheila* • Edward James Olmos *Det Curtis* • Sharon Lawrence *Det Kelly* • Eric Bogosian *Professor Goodwin* ■ *Dir* Davis Guggenheim • *Scr* Theresa Rebeck, Gregory Poirier, from a story by Gregory Poirier

Gösta Berlings Saga ★★★★

Silent drama 1924 · Swe · BW · 183mins

Widely acclaimed as Mauritz Stiller's finest film (which it isn't), this adaptation of Selma Lagerlöf's period novel is best known for bringing Greta Garbo to international attention. As the Italian countess who is delivered from the Gothic nightmare of Ekeby Hall by defrocked priest Lars Hanson, she is so lovingly lit by Stiller and cameraman Julius Jaenzon that it's little wonder studio boss Louis B Mayer was sufficiently entranced to invite her to Hollywood. Bafflingly, the film itself, with its multifarious melodramatic situations, was less enthusiastically received and Stiller was forced to prune several scenes to the detriment of its sprawling episodic logic. DP

Lars Hanson *Gösta Berlings* • Gerda Lundequist *Margaretha Samzelius, born Celsing* • Hilda Forsslund *Margaretha's mother* • Otto Elg-Lundberg *Major Samzelius* • Sixten Malmerfelt *Melchior Sinclaire* ■ *Dir* Mauritz Stiller • *Scr* Mauritz Stiller, Ragnar Hyltén-Cavallius, from the novel by Selma Lagerlöf

Gotcha! ★★★ 15

Comedy spy drama
1985 · US · Colour · 96mins

A youthful Anthony Edwards impresses as a shy college kid who embarks upon a European vacation and gets involved with a spy ring, while Linda Fiorentino's turn as a sultry spy leaves one pondering why it took so long for her to blossom into a star. Director Jeff Kanew offers plenty of frantic scurrying about and sharp one-liners to paper over the elements of *déjà vu*, if little in the way of actual danger and suspense. RS [VIDEO]

Anthony Edwards *Jonathan Moore* • Linda Fiorentino *Sasha Banicek/Cheryl Brewster* • Nick Corri *Manolo* • Alex Rocco *Al* • Marla Adams *Maria* • Klaus Loewitsch [Klaus Löwitsch] *Vlad* • Christopher Rydell *Bob Jensen* • Christie Claridge *Girl student* ■ *Dir* Jeff Kanew • *Scr* Dan Gordon, from a story by Paul G Hensler, Dan Gordon

Gothic ★★★ 18

Horror 1986 · UK · Colour · 83mins

Ken Russell's talent to abuse past icons goes wondrously berserk here, as he resurrects the notorious 19th-century literary booze-up of Byron, Shelley, Mary Godwin and Polidori at the Villa Diodati on the shores of Lake Geneva. It's this incestuous, laudanum-quaffing occasion that led to the writing of *Frankenstein* and, while Gabriel Byrne, Julian Sands and Natasha Richardson take it seriously enough, Russell keeps undermining them with overwrought visual decadence. TH. Contains swearing, violence, sex scenes. [VIDEO] DVD

Julian Sands *Percy Bysshe Shelley* • Natasha Richardson *Mary Godwin* • Gabriel Byrne *Lord Byron* • Myriam Cyr *Claire* • Timothy Spall *Dr John Polidori* • Dexter Fletcher *Rushton* • Andreas Wisniewski *Fletcher* • Alec Mango *Murray* ■ *Dir* Ken Russell • *Scr* Stephen Volk

Gothika ★★ 15

Supernatural horror thriller
2003 · US · Colour · 94mins

For this overblown horror effort, director Mathieu Kassovitz deploys every cliché in the book – and then moves on to volume two. Halle Berry plays a psychiatrist who, after a car crash, finds herself incarcerated in her own asylum accused of the murder of her husband. She has no memory of these events and, to make matters worse, is haunted by ghostly images of a young girl. The result is – with the exception of a couple of cynically engineered jolts – resolutely unscary. AS. Contains violence. [VIDEO] DVD

Halle Berry *Dr Miranda Grey* • Robert Downey Jr *Dr Pete Graham* • Charles S Dutton *Dr Doug Grey* • John Carroll Lynch *Sheriff Ryan* • Bernard Hill *Phil Parsons* • Penélope Cruz *Chloe Sava* • Dorian Harewood *Teddy Howard* ■ *Dir* Mathieu Kassovitz • *Scr* Sebastian Gutierrez

Goto, l'Ile d'Amour ★★★★ 15

Fantasy drama
1968 · Fr · Colour and BW · 89mins

The surreal poetry that characterised Walerian Borowczyk's animation is clearly evident in his first live-action feature. Shot through with moments of extravagant colour, which lend a certain sinister enchantment to the cruel fairy-tale world of Goto, the heavily stylised visuals make the characters seem as insignificant as the array of symbolic objects (such as music boxes and phonographs) littered around the residence of Pierre Brasseur's cuckolded dictator. With its flycatchers, duels and acts of self-sacrifice, there's an operatic feel to the storyline, which is reinforced by the sublime Handel organ concerto and the theatricality of the performances. DP. In French with English subtitles. [VIDEO]

Pierre Brasseur *Goto III* • Ligia Branice *Glossia* • Ginette Leclerc *Gonasta* • René Dary *Gomor* • Jean-Pierre Andréani *Gono* • Michel Charrel *Grymp* ■ *Dir/Scr* Walerian Borowczyk • *Cinematographer* Paul Coteret

Le Goût des Autres ★★★★ 15

Comedy 1999 · Fr · Colour · 112mins

Agnès Jaoui makes her directorial debut with this astute comedy of socio-cultural manners, which she wrote with co-star Jean-Pierre Bacri. A Woody Allenesque air pervades proceedings, as we follow the efforts of Bacri's boorish businessman to impress amateur actress Anne Alvaro. The subplots involving a drug-dealing barmaid and designer-dominated wife lack focus, but Bacri and Alvaro make a delightful odd couple and helped the film garner a best foreign film Oscar nomination and a raft of domestic awards. DP. In French with English subtitles. Contains swearing, drug abuse and sex scenes. [VIDEO] DVD

Anne Alvaro *Clara Davaux* • Jean-Pierre Bacri *Jean-Jacques Castella* • Brigitte Catillon *Béatrice* • Alain Chabat *Bruno Deschamps* • Agnès Jaoui *Manie* • Gérard Lanvin *Franck Moreno* ■ *Dir* Agnès Jaoui • *Scr* Agnès Jaoui, Jean-Pierre Bacri

The Governess ★★ 15

Period drama 1997 · UK/Fr · Colour · 109mins

Someone laced the corsets far too tight for this rigid drama set in the mid-19th century, in which Jewish girl Minnie Driver pretends to be a gentile so she can earn money for her family working as a governess, taking a job on a remote Scottish island. It's not long, of course, before she embarks on an affair with her stiff-upper-lipped, married employer Tom Wilkinson. Writer/director Sandra Goldbacher never manages to convey any feeling of sensuality between the mismatched pair. JB [VIDEO] DVD

Minnie Driver *Rosina DaSilva/Mary Blackchurch* • Tom Wilkinson *Mr Charles Cavendish* • Florence Hoath *Clementina Cavendish* • Jonathan Rhys Meyers *Henry Cavendish* • Harriet Walter *Mrs Cavendish* • Arlene Cockburn *Lily Milk* • Emma Bird *Rebecca* ■ *Dir/Scr* Sandra Goldbacher

Government Girl ★★★ U

Second World War comedy
1943 · US · BW · 93mins

This simple but affecting tale of love among the armaments stars Sonny Tufts and Olivia de Havilland and follows the understated 1940s tradition of slipping a spot of satire in among standard wartime propaganda. The two main stars give us a lively, knockabout relationship (Tufts is a production expert and de Havilland a Washington secretary), but beneath the gloss and wisecracks is a heavier message about the stifling nature of government bureaucracy. SH

Olivia de Havilland *Smokey* • Sonny Tufts *Ed Browne* • Agnes Moorehead *Mrs Wright* • Anne Shirley *May* • Jess Barker *Dana* • James Dunn *Sergeant Joe* • Paul Stewart *Branch* • Harry Davenport *Senator MacVickers* ■ *Dir* Dudley Nichols • *Scr* Dudley Nichols, from a story by Adela Rogers St John

Goya in Bordeaux ★★★★ 15

Biographical drama
1999 · Sp/It · Colour · 104mins

Realising a long-cherished project, Carlos Saura has impeccably captured the increasingly tormented vision of the Spanish painter, who spent his declining years in French exile. The re-creation of the sombre canvases, which reflected the impact of both Goya's Napoleonic trauma and his insulating deafness, is achieved with imaginative authenticity by Vittorio Storaro, with the tableaux sequence depicting the "Disasters of War" engravings making the most impact. As the ageing Goya, Francisco Rabal excels. However, with a mastery of sound and dance complementing the beauty, the glory belongs to Saura. DP. In Spanish with English subtitles.

Francisco Rabal *Goya* • Maribel Verdú *Duchess of Alba* • Jose Coronado *Goya as a young man* • Dafne Fernandez *Rosario* • Eulalia Ramón *Leocadia* • Joaquín Climent *Moratin* • Cristina Espinosa *Pepita Tudo* • José Maria Pou *Godoy* ■ *Dir/Scr* Carlos Saura

Gozu ★★ 18

Black comedy horror
2003 · Jpn · Colour · 129mins

Hideki Sone is sent to execute his fellow mobster Sho Aikawa, after their gang boss decides his violent outbursts are getting too erratic. What follows is an eccentric and largely inexplicable black comedy, laced with surreal horror as cult director Takashi Miike's bizarre imagination runs riot to sometimes questionable effect. SF. In Japanese with English subtitles. Contains violence and sex scenes. [VIDEO] DVD

Hideki Sone *Minami* • Sho Aikawa *Ozaki* • Kimika Yoshino *Female Ozaki* • Shohei Hino *Nose* • Keiko Tomita *Innkeeper' sister* • Harumi Sone *Kazu, autistic innkeeper* • Renji Ishibashi *Boss* ■ *Dir* Takashi Miike • *Scr* Sakichi Sato

Grace and Glorie ★★★

Drama 1998 · US · Colour · 98mins

There's a whiff of *Fried Green Tomatoes* permeating this TV movie, with Gena Rowlands assuming the role of a testy nursing-home inmate who decides to use her experience to help someone in greater pain than herself. Diane Lane plays the woman trying to rebuild her own life who decides to take care of the terminally ill Rowlands. Unashamedly sentimental, but Rowlands adds some class. DP

Gena Rowlands *Grace Stiles* • Diane Lane *Glorie* • Neal McDonough *David* • Chris Beetem *Roy* • Carrie Preston *Charlene* ■ *Dir* Arthur Allan Seidelman • *Scr* Grace McKeaney, from a play by Tom Ziegler

The Grace of God ★★★ PG

Documentary drama
1998 · Can · Colour · 70mins

Ten years in the making, this is an ambitious investigation into both society's evolving attitude to homosexuality and the film-making process itself. Adopting a docudrama approach, the film chronicles a young man's gradual appreciation of his sexuality and the difficulty he experiences in explaining his preference to family and friends. But director Gerald L'Ecuyer also builds in something approximating an audience response, as he includes interviews with the cast and crew to examine their opinions on both their individual contributions to the project and the social and emotional issues it raises. However, it's a meditative journey that is never quite as compelling or revealing as it should be. DP [VIDEO]

Michael Riley • David Bolt • David Cronenberg ■ *Dir/Scr* Gerald L'Ecuyer

Grace of My Heart ★★★★ 15

Romantic musical drama
1996 · US · Colour · 111mins

Smart and hip, director Allison Anders's affectionate hymn to those 1960s songwriters who made New York's Brill Building the place to be rarely misses a beat. Illeana Douglas touchingly plays a thinly disguised Carole King, anxious for fame as a singer rather than composer of girl group classics, whose string of failed relationships includes one with "surf pop" genius Matt Dillon. John Turturro's turn as a shadowy Phil Spector-like figure is absolutely brilliant, there's strong support from Bridget Fonda, and the songs written expressly for the movie by Burt Bacharach, Lesley Gore and Elvis Costello are convincing. AJ. Contains swearing and sex scenes. [VIDEO]

Illeana Douglas *Denise Waverly/Edna Buxton* • Matt Dillon *Jay Phillips* • Eric Stoltz *Howard Caszatt* • Bruce Davison *John Murray* • Patsy Kensit *Cheryl Steed* • Jennifer Leigh Warren *Doris Shelly* • John Turturro *Joel Millner* • Chris Isaak *Matthew Lewis* • Bridget Fonda *Kelly Porter* ■ *Dir/Scr* Allison Anders

Grace Quigley ★★★ 15

Black comedy 1984 · US · Colour · 87mins

After seeing him murder her landlord, elderly widow Katharine Hepburn hires hitman Nick Nolte to kill aged friends and neighbours who would benefit from euthanasia. Anthony Harvey's comedy is certainly ebony-hued, but the two stars carry it off in sprightly fashion. In the end, though, it all gets rather sentimental – a result, it appears, of being mauled by distributors prior to release. The film's original title was *The Ultimate Solution of Grace Quigley* – solutions don't get much more ultimate than this one. TH [VIDEO] DVD

Katharine Hepburn *Grace Quigley* • Nick Nolte *Seymour Flint* • Kit Le Fever *Muriel* • Chip Zien *Dr Herman* • William Duell *Mr Jenkins* • Elizabeth Wilson *Emily Watkins* ■ *Dir* Anthony Harvey • *Scr* A Martin Zweiback

The Gracie Allen Murder Case ★★

Detective comedy mystery
1939 · US · BW · 75mins

Philo Vance creator SS Van Dine had always been a fan of George Burns and Gracie Allen. So he was as disappointed as anyone when Paramount decided to drop Burns from this tailor-made Philo Vance mystery. The ditzy Gracie concentrates on driving Warren William crazy as he

U = SUITABLE FOR ALL Uc = SUITABLE FOR ALL, ESPECIALLY FOR YOUNG CHILDREN (VIDEO ONLY) PG = PARENTAL GUIDANCE

attempts to clear Kent Taylor of the murder of an escaped convict. More a burlesque than a mystery, the focus is firmly on Allen, as she mangles words and muddles clues. DP

Gracie Allen • Warren William *Philo Vance* • Ellen Drew *Ann Wilson* • Kent Taylor *Bill Brown* • Jed Prouty *Uncle Ambrose Martin* • Jerome Cowan *Daniel Mirche* ■ *Dir* Alfred E Green • *Scr* Nat Perrin, from the story by SS Van Dine

The Graduate ★★★★★ 15

Satirical comedy drama
1967 · US · Colour · 101mins

This landmark satire on America's bourgeoisie thrust the unknown Dustin Hoffman into the limelight and won a best director Oscar for Mike Nichols. In his film debut, Hoffman is sensational as the innocent college graduate seduced by older married woman Anne Bancroft and then falling for her daughter Katharine Ross. The humour in Calder Willingham and Buck Henry's screenplay has the bite of a dry martini, Robert Surtees's stunning, innovative camerawork contributes telling visual ironies and the Simon and Garfunkel soundtrack perfectly captures the mood of disaffected youth seething beneath the laid-back exterior of 1960s California. Nichols's Oscar launched him into the top rank of Hollywood directors. TH. Contains sex scenes and nudity. [VIDEO] DVD

Dustin Hoffman *Benjamin Braddock* • Anne Bancroft *Mrs Robinson* • Katharine Ross *Elaine Robinson* • William Daniels *Mr Braddock* • Elizabeth Wilson *Mrs Braddock* • Murray Hamilton *Mr Robinson* • Brian Avery (1) *Carl Smith* • Walter Brooke *Mr Maguire* ■ *Dir* Mike Nichols • *Scr* Calder Willingham, Buck Henry, from the novel by Charles Webb • *Editor* Sam O'Steen • *Production Designer* Richard Sylbert

Graffiti Bridge ★★ 15

Musical 1990 · US · Colour · 86mins

After *Purple Rain*, this is the best film from the artist who was still then known as Prince. It's a sequel of sorts, which finds him once again basically playing Prince, aka the Kid. His old nemesis from *Purple Rain*, Morris Day, and his band the Times return – this time they are warring nightclub owners – and once again steal the show. But despite an impressive array of musical talent, the tunes aren't memorable, and as a film director, Prince is a brilliant musician. JF [VIDEO]

Prince *The Kid* • Ingrid Chavez *Aura* • Morris Day • Jerome Benton *Jerome* • Michael Bland • Damon Dickson • Mavis Staples *Melody Cool* • George Clinton ■ *Dir/Scr* Prince

Grand Canyon ★★★★ 15

Drama 1991 · US · Colour · 128mins

After the critical mauling he received for his ill-judged black comedy *I Love You to Death*, writer/director Lawrence Kasdan returned to the ensemble territory of *The Big Chill*. However, the warm nostalgia of the latter is largely absent this time as Kasdan attempts to come to grips with the fear and violence afflicting modern-day Los Angeles. It's an ambitious task, and at times the script strays toward sentimental melodrama, but Kasdan's direction is as assured as ever. He is rewarded with excellent performances, including a scene-stealing role for Steve Martin, who plays an arrogant film producer reportedly modelled on action master Joel Silver of *Lethal Weapon* fame. JF [VIDEO] DVD

Danny Glover *Simon* • Steve Martin *Davis* • Kevin Kline *Mack* • Mary McDonnell *Claire* • Mary-Louise Parker *Dee* • Alfre Woodard *Jane* • Jeremy Sisto *Roberto* • Tina Lifford *Deborah* ■ *Dir* Lawrence Kasdan • *Scr* Lawrence Kasdan, Meg Kasdan

Grand Central Murder ★★

Mystery drama 1942 · US · BW · 73mins

The reliable, if slightly dog-eared Van Heflin stars as a private detective and Patricia Dane is a Broadway star whose downfall is charted in flashbacks. The settings for this acceptable low-budget B-thriller are the railway sidings and the underground passages of New York's Grand Central Station, a dramatic location that has always attracted film-makers. AT

Van Heflin *"Rocky" Custer* • Patricia Dane *Mida King* • Cecilia Parker *Constance Furness* • Virginia Grey *Sue Custer* • Sam Levene *Inspector Gunther* • Samuel S Hinds *Roger Furness* ■ *Dir* S Sylvan Simon • *Scr* Peter Rurie, from a novel by Sue MacVeigh

Le Grand Chemin ★★★★ 15

Drama 1987 · Fr · Colour · 106mins

A sugary confection with a hard centre may not be to everyone's taste, but the crunches in this charming rite-of-passage picture make the melting moments all the more sweet. Anémone and Richard Bohringer both won Césars (the French equivalent of an Oscar) for their performances as a grief-stricken couple whose care of a nine-year-old Parisian boy results in a bitter tug of war for his affections. Young Antoine Hubert is endearingly wide-eyed throughout his introduction to the ways of grown-ups and Vanessa Guedj is quite wonderful as the knowing tomboy who acts as his guide. DP. In French with English subtitles.

Anémone *Marcelle* • Richard Bohringer *Pelo* • Antoine Hubert *Louis* • Vanessa Guedj *Martine* • Christine Pascal *Claire* • Raoul Billerey *Priest* • Pascale Roberts *Yvonne* • Marie Matheron *Solange* ■ *Dir/Scr* Jean-Loup Hubert

Grand Hotel ★★★★★ U

Drama 1932 · US · BW · 107mins

This star-filled melodrama became a blueprint for almost every glossy Hollywood soap opera that followed it. Greta Garbo, John and Lionel Barrymore, Joan Crawford and Wallace Beery vie for screen time as the various residents of the Berlin hotel, but it is art director Cedric Gibbons who deserves the plaudits for the luscious look of the film. One of the biggest projects in Hollywood at the time, the all-star cast caused MGM numerous problems as far as billing was concerned. In the end, the word "Garbo" appeared at the top of the bill to honour a clause stating she would have top billing, while the other actors were billed in alphabetical order below. JB [VIDEO] DVD

Greta Garbo *Grusinskaya* • John Barrymore *The Baron Felix Benvenuto Frihern Von Gaigern* • Joan Crawford *Flaemmchen* • Wallace Beery *General Director Preysing* • Lionel Barrymore *Otto Kringelein* • Jean Hersholt *Senf* ■ *Dir* Edmund Goulding • *Scr* William A Drake, from his play, from the play *Menschen im Hotel* by Vicki Baum • *Cinematographer* William Daniels [William H Daniels] • *Costume Designer* Adrian

Le Grand Jeu ★★★

Erotic romantic drama
1933 · Fr · BW · 115mins

Pierre-Richard Willm flees to Morocco to forget the Parisian society woman who has spurned him. His plan backfires when he meets a cabaret singer who is her double. Marie Bell (in a dual role) co-stars in this French excursion into romantic melodrama that is somewhat fantastical, but is directed in fine style with loads of exotic and erotic atmosphere by Jacques Feyder and Marcel Carné. RK. A French language film.

Marie Bell *Florence/Irma* • Pierre-Richard Willm *Pierre Martel* • Charles Vanel *Clément* • George Pitoeff *Nicolas* • Françoise Rosay *Blanche* ■ *Dir* Jacques Feyder, Marcel Carné • *Scr* Jacques Feyder, Charles Spaak

Grand Jury ★★

Crime drama 1976 · US · Colour · 100mins

This feeble drama finds Leslie Nielson, before his comedy career renaissance in the early 1980s, in decidedly unfunny mode. Bruce Davison and Meredith MacRae are the naive young couple whose involvement in an insurance scam has disastrous consequences. Director Christopher Cain went on to make *Young Guns*. TH

Leslie Nielsen *John Williams* • Bruce Davison *Bobby Allen* • Meredith MacRae *Nancy Williams* • Larry Barton *Parking lot owner* • Myron Griffin *Inspector Hanes* • Alice Reinheart *Jury foreman* • Michael Rougas *Jimmy* ■ *Dir/Scr* Christopher Cain

Grand National Night ★★★

Crime drama 1953 · UK · BW · 77mins

Having been a hit on stage and then as a radio serial, Dorothy and Campbell Christie's play is ably brought to the screen. It's very much in the Edgar Wallace tradition, with Nigel Patrick's friends in the racing fraternity standing by him after his bitchy wife, Moira Lister, is accidentally killed during a drunken squabble. The means by which the corpse arrives in Liverpool and the final twist strain the credibility slightly. But the cat-and-mouse game involving Michael Hordern (who excels as the dogged detective determined to nail Patrick) is teased out with mischievous ingenuity. DP

Nigel Patrick *Gerald Coates* • Moira Lister *Babs Coates* • Beatrice Campbell *Joyce Penrose* • Betty Ann Davies *Pinkie Collins* • Michael Hordern *Inspector Ayling* • Noel Purcell *Philip Balfour* ■ *Dir* Bob McNaught • *Scr* Bob McNaught, Val Valentine, from the play by Campbell Christie, Dorothy Christie

Le Grand Pardon ★★★

Crime drama 1981 · Fr · Colour · 125mins

Alexandre Arcady scored a big hit with this second feature. Inspired by actual events, it explores the tensions that exist between the Arab and Jewish gangsters who compete for influence in the Parisian underworld. There's no shortage of imposing performances, most notably from Roger Hanin, as the racketeer who takes his family and heritage as seriously as his empire, and Bernard Giraudeau, who stirs up a turf war with racial, as well as criminal implications. However, the action sequences lack invention, although the film is vastly superior to the 1992 Miami sequel, *Day of Atonement*. DP. In French and English with subtitles.

Roger Hanin *Raymond Bettoun* • Jean-Louis Trintignant *Commissionaire Duché* • Bernard Giraudeau *Pascal Villars* • Richard Berry *Maurice Bettoun* • Clio Goldsmith *Viviane* • Anny Duperey *Carole* • Richard Bohringer *The Sexton* • Robert Hossein *Manuel Carreras* ■ *Dir* Alexandre Arcady • *Scr* Alexandre Arcady, Daniel Saint-Hamont, Alain Le Henry

Grand Prix ★★★ PG

Sports action drama
1966 · US · Colour · 162mins

One of the best motor-racing films ever made, filmed in Cinerama-SuperPanavision – the Bugatti of screen ratios. Racing fans will adore the glimpses of Graham Hill, the banking at Monza and the 1960s speed machines, which seem so flimsy compared to the cars that race today. There are spectacular stunts, of course, but the human pile-ups between the races scrape the bottom of the drama cliché barrel. AT [VIDEO]

James Garner *Pete Aron* • Eva Marie Saint *Louise Frederickson* • Yves Montand *Jean-Pierre Sarti* • Toshiro Mifune *Izo Yamura* • Brian Bedford *Scott Stoddard* • Jessica Walter *Pat* • Antonio Sabato *Nino Barlini* • Françoise Hardy *Lisa* ■ *Dir* John Frankenheimer • *Scr* Robert Alan Aurthur, from his story • *Editor* Fredric Steinkamp, Henry Berman, Stewart Linder, Frank Santillo

Grand Slam ★★★

Crime thriller
1967 · It/Sp/W Ger · Colour · 119mins

This *Rififi*-style heist movie should have been a corker. Edward G. Robinson is the brains of the operation, while Klaus Kinski and Janet Leigh co-star as a former Nazi with a hair-trigger temper and the ice-cool secretary with the key to a fabulous gem collection. There's even the added bonus of the Rio backdrop and a twist ending. Yet, somehow this thriller doesn't quite come off, as Robinson and gang boss Adolfo Celi are given too little to do, Kinski over-indulges in his trademark neuroses and gigolo Robert Hoffmann's attempted seduction of Leigh lacks wit and charm. DP

Janet Leigh *Mary Ann* • Robert Hoffmann *Jean-Paul Audry* • Edward G Robinson *Prof James Anders* • Adolfo Celi *Mark Milford* • Klaus Kinski *Erich Weiss* • Georges Rigaud *Gregg* • Riccardo Cucciolla *Agostino* ■ *Dir* Giuliano Montaldo • *Scr* Mino Roli, Marcello Fondato, Antonio de la Loma, Augusto Caminito, from a story by Mino Roli, Augusto Caminito, Bianchini

Grand Theft Auto ★★ PG

Action comedy 1977 · US · Colour · 80mins

Ron Howard's full-length feature directing debut is very much a family affair. Made under the aegis of that canny judge of film talent Roger Corman, this was co-written by Howard's father Rance (who also appears) and offers a role for brother Clint. The film itself is little more than than an extended *Dukes of Hazzard* adventure. JF [VIDEO] DVD

Ron Howard *Sam Freeman* • Nancy Morgan *Paula Powers* • Marion Ross *Vivian Hedgeworth* • Peter Isacksen *Sparky* • Barry Cahill *Digby Powers* • Hoke Howell *Preacher* • Lew Brown (2) *Jack Clepper* • Elizabeth Rogers *Priscilla Powers* ■ *Dir* Ron Howard • *Scr* Ron Howard, Rance Howard

Grand Theft Parsons ★★★★ 12

Black comedy based on a true story
2003 · US/UK · Colour · 84mins

Jackass stunt-show star Johnny Knoxville plays his first leading role in this spirited film charting the bizarre road trip one man took in the name of friendship. Knoxville plays Phil Kaufman, the maverick road manager of cult 1970s US country singer Gram Parsons. Having made a pact with Parsons prior to the performer's untimely death, Kaufman steals the coffin to cremate the corpse according to his buddy's final wishes. Michael Shannon is hilarious as a hippy hearse-owner, while a bitchy Christina Applegate adds sass as a fictional gold-digging ex of Parsons. Wittily scripted and lovingly directed. SF DVD

Johnny Knoxville *Phil Kaufman* • Christina Applegate *Barbara Mansfield* • Michael Shannon *Larry Oster-Berg* • Marley Shelton *Susie* • Robert Forster *Stanley Parsons* • Phil Kaufman *Handcuffed felon* ■ *Dir* David Caffrey • *Scr* Jeremy Drysdale

La Grande Bouffe ★★★ 18

Satirical comedy 1973 · Fr · Colour · 124mins

Marco Ferreri's satire is like Buñuel's *The Discreet Charm of the Bourgeoisie* in reverse: where Buñuel's characters never quite get to their waiting feast, Ferreri's gather in a villa and gorge themselves on food, wine and women. This is not a picture for bulimics or the obese; nor is it as subversively funny as it might have been. Nevertheless, there are some great scenes – notably

G

the moment when the ample buttocks of Andréa Ferréol are used to mould a vast slab of *mousse de foie gras*. AT. In French with English subtitles.

Marcello Mastroianni *Pilot* • Ugo Tognazzi *Chef* • Michel Piccoli *TV producer* • Philippe Noiret *Judge* • Andréa Ferréol *Teacher* • Monique Chaumette *Madeleine* • Florence Giorgetti *Anne* • Rita Scherrer *Anulka* ■ *Dir* Marco Ferreri • *Scr* Marco Ferreri, Rafael Arcona

La Grande Illusion ★★★★★ U

Classic First World War drama
1937 · Fr · BW · 108mins

Critics vie to heap superlatives on Renoir's masterpiece and landmark of world cinema, but one of the film's highest accolades of all came from Nazi propaganda boss Josef Goebbels, who classified it as "Cinematographic Enemy No 1". Made on the eve of the Second World War but set in a German PoW camp during the First World War, it has also been called the ultimate anti-war film – no small claim since it does not contain a single battle scene, making its point with dialogue rather than action. Though not an easy film, it's worth the effort. PF. In French with English subtitles. DVD

Jean Gabin *Maréchal* • Erich von Stroheim *Von Rauffenstein* • Pierre Fresnay *Capt De Boeldieu* • Dalio [Marcel Dalio] *Rosenthal* • Dita Parlo *Peasant woman* • Julien Carette *Actor* • Gaston Modot *Engineer* • Jean Dasté *Schoolteacher* • Georges Peclet *French soldier* ■ *Dir* Jean Renoir • *Scr* Charles Spaak, Jean Renoir • *Cinematographer* Christian Matras • *Art Director* Lourié [Eugène Lourié]

Les Grandes Manoeuvres ★★★★ U

Romantic comedy
1955 · Fr/It · Colour · 102mins

One of the pioneers of French silent and early sound cinema, René Clair's critical fortunes had dipped dramatically by the time he made his first colour feature. Yet this is one of the glories of a career studded with delights. Combining wit and grace with comic impudence, Clair concocts a frothy comedy that turns into a poignant drama, as dragoon Gérard Philipe realises that his reputation as a gadabout has thwarted his one chance of true love with Michèle Morgan whom he wagered his comrades he could seduce. DP. In French with English subtitles. DVD

Michèle Morgan *Marie Louise Riviere* • Gérard Philipe *Lt Armand de la Verne* • Brigitte Bardot *Lucie* • Yves Robert *Felix* • Jean Desailly *Victor Duverger* • Pierre Dux *Colonel* • Jacques François *Rudolph* • Lise Delamare *Jeanne* • Jacqueline Maillan *Juliette* ■ *Dir* René Clair • *Scr* René Clair, Jerome Geronimi, Jean Marsan, from a story by Courteline

Grandeur et Décadence d'un Petit Commerce de Cinéma ★★★

Drama 1986 · Fr · Colour · 90mins

Originally made for French TV, this took former New Wave icon Jean-Luc Godard's determined bid to demythologise the movie-making process to a higher plain. Ostensibly seeking to greenlight an adaptation of a James Hadley Chase novel, failed auteur Jean-Pierre Léaud and producer Jean-Pierre Mocky end up ogling the auditioning starlets, while spouting theories and dropping the touchstone names of those ensconced in the cinematic pantheon. With Godard himself interrupting these rambling discourses to denounce everything from pretentiousness to Polanski, this is a scathing exposé of the commercial considerations underpinning even the most chaste art house project. DP. A French language film.

Jean-Pierre Léaud *Gaspar Bazin* • Jean-Pierre Mocky *Jean Almereyda* • Marie Valéra *Eurydice* ■ *Dir* Jean-Luc Godard • *Scr* Jean-Luc Godard, from a novel by James Hadley Chase

Grandview, USA ★★ 15

Drama 1984 · US · Colour · 97mins

The cast may be a who's who of future stars, but the plot of this teen angst drama is right out of yesteryear. Set in the Midwest of the mid-1980s, the film follows Jamie Lee Curtis's bid to keep her father's demolition derby in business, while sidestepping the adoring advances of star driver Patrick Swayze. C Thomas Howell is also involved, but the smartest acting comes from veterans Troy Donahue and M Emmet Walsh. DP

Jamie Lee Curtis *Michelle "Mike" Cody* • C Thomas Howell *Tim Pearson* • Patrick Swayze *Ernie "Slam" Webster* • Troy Donahue *Donny Vinton* • Jennifer Jason Leigh *Candy Webster* • William Windom *Bob Cody* • Carole Cook *Betty Welles* • M Emmet Walsh *Mr Clark* ■ *Dir* Randal Kleiser • *Scr* Ken Hixon

The Grapes of Wrath ★★★★★ PG

Drama 1940 · US · BW · 129mins

In this magnificent adaptation of John Steinbeck's Depression-era novel, Henry Fonda plays the farmer who leads his family from the dust bowl of Oklahoma to the promised land of California. The scene when their home is bulldozed is heart-rending and their fate as migrant workers has lasting power. But the film also has some weaknesses, notably a corny religious symbolism in place of Steinbeck's raw politics. It's stupendously photographed by Gregg Toland, but the Oscars went to director John Ford and Jane Darwell, who's unforgettable as Ma Joad. AT DVD

Henry Fonda *Tom Joad* • Jane Darwell *Ma Joad* • John Carradine *Casey* • Charley Grapewin *Grandpa Joad* • Dorris Bowdon *Rosaharn* • Russell Simpson *Pa Joad* • OZ Whitehead *Al* • John Qualen *Muley* • Eddie Quillan *Connie* • Zeffie Tilbury *Grandma Joad* • Frank Sully *Noah* ■ *Dir* John Ford • *Scr* Nunnally Johnson, from the novel by John Steinbeck • *Music* Alfred Newman • *Art Director* Richard Day, Mark-Lee Kirk

Grass ★★★★ 15

Documentary
1999 · Can · Colour and BW · 78mins

In the 1940s, New York's Mayor Fiorello La Guardia commissioned a report that discredited accepted views on the medical, psychological and social impact of marijuana. Yet its possession remains a criminal offence and documentarist Ron Mann here sets out to discover why. Although it's narrated by hemp advocate Woody Harrelson and utilises clips from famously alarmist movies such as *Reefer Madness* and *Marijuana: Assassin of Youth*, this superbly researched film isn't just a pot-head's plea for tolerance. Mann also explores the racist history of US drug laws and the way Harry J Anslinger, director of the Federal Bureau of Narcotics from 1930–67, used them to further his own career. DP DVD

Woody Harrelson *Narrator* ■ *Dir* Ron Mann • *Scr* Solomon Vesta

Grass: a Nation's Battle for Life ★★★★

Silent documentary 1925 · US · BW · 70mins

Although they are best remembered for *King Kong*, Merian C Cooper and Ernest B Schoedsack were renowned travel chroniclers during the silent era. The film is full of spectacular set pieces, such as the perilous crossing of the torrential Karun river and the final barefoot ascent. But there's a troublingly civilised arrogance about the possibility that, like their mentor, Robert Flaherty, the pair manipulated the action by urging 50,000 Bakhtiari nomads to take the most treacherous (and, thus, most cinematic) route across the Zardeh Kuh mountains in search of grazing land. DP

Dir Merian Cooper [Merian C Cooper], Ernest B Schoedsack, Marguerite Harrison

The Grass Harp ★★★ PG

Drama 1995 · US · Colour · 102mins

Charles Matthau's film based on Truman Capote's autobiographical novel may be old-fashioned, but it also has the polish that used to make studio pictures so irresistible. The exceptional ensemble cast gives this memoir of a Deep South childhood in the late 1930s its charm. As the chalk-and-cheese sisters who raise orphan Edward Furlong, Piper Laurie and Sissy Spacek bind together the episodic narrative. They also give it a credibility that makes Jack Lemmon and Walter Matthau's more outrageous turns delightful rather than damaging. DP. Contains some swearing. DVD

Piper Laurie *Dolly Talbo* • Sissy Spacek *Verena Talbo* • Walter Matthau *Judge Charlie Cool* • Edward Furlong *Collin Fenwick* • Nell Carter *Catherine Creek* • Jack Lemmon *Dr Morris Ritz* • Mary Steenburgen *Sister Ida* • Sean Patrick Flanery *Riley Henderson* ■ *Dir* Charles Matthau • *Scr* Stirling Silliphant, Kirk Ellis, from the novel by Truman Capote

The Grass Is Greener ★★ PG

Romantic comedy
1960 · UK · Colour · 100mins

Too much talk, too little action and a miscast Robert Mitchum contribute to this disappointing screen adaptation of the West End hit. The plot rests on the romantic complications that ensue when American multi-millionaire Mitchum takes a tour of English earl Cary Grant's stately home and falls for his wife, played by Deborah Kerr. Director Stanley Donen, usually at home with soufflé-light comedy romance, fails to rescue this one from its all-too-evident stage origins and a leaden script. RK

Cary Grant *Victor Rhyall* • Deborah Kerr *Hilary Rhyall* • Robert Mitchum *Charles Delacro* • Jean Simmons *Hattie Durrant* • Moray Watson *Sellers* ■ *Dir* Stanley Donen • *Scr* Hugh Williams, Margaret Williams, from their play

The Grasshopper ★

Drama 1970 · US · Colour · 95mins

Bored with her small-town life in British Columbia, Jacqueline Bisset becomes a Las Vegas showgirl and pop star's girlfriend. Then she moves to Los Angeles, gets beaten up and learns the meaning of life. Produced and scripted by Garry Marshall and Jerry Belson, the team behind the sitcoms *Happy Days* and *Mork and Mindy*, this is a flashily directed "message movie" dressed up with lots of sex and violence. AT. Contains swearing and scenes of violence.

Jacqueline Bisset *Christine Adams* • Jim Brown *Tommy Marcott* • Joseph Cotten *Richard Morgan* • Corbett Monica *Danny Raymond* • Ramon Bieri *Roosevelt Dekker* • Christopher Stone *Jay Rigney* • Roger Garrett *Buck Brown* • Stanley Adams *Buddy Miller* ■ *Dir* Jerry Paris • *Scr* Jerry Belson, Garry Marshall, from the novel *The Passing of Evil* by Mark McShane

Grateful Dawg ★★ 12

Music documentary
2000 · US · Colour · 78mins

Grateful Dead frontman Jerry Garcia and mandolin-playing musicologist David Grisman met at a concert in the mid-1960s and bonded over their shared love of bluegrass music. The pair lost touch after their short-lived band Old & In the Way split up in the late 1970s and this respectful documentary records the artistic consequences of their reunion some dozen years later. Unfortunately, director Gillian Grisman (daughter of David) is clearly too over-awed by her subjects to pry into the darker corners of their relationship. DP. Contains swearing. DVD

Dir Gillian Grisman

Gravesend ★★★ 18

Drama 1995 · US · Colour · 81mins

A madcap adventure for a quartet of Brooklyn buddies becomes a dead-end nightmare. This breathless "stash the stiff" opus frantically blends voiceovers, flashbacks, character profiles and graveyard humour. Salvatore Stabile's feature debut – made for just $5,000 when he was only 19 – so impressed Steven Spielberg that he offered him a contract at DreamWorks. DP. Contains swearing, violence.

Thomas Brandise *Mikey* • Tom Malloy *Chicken* • Michael Parducci *Ray* • Tony Tucci *Zane* • Sean Quinn *Mark* • Carmel Altomare *Zane's mother* • Teresa Spinelli *Zane's grandmother* ■ *Dir/Scr* Salvatore Stabile

Graveyard Shift ★★★ 18

Supernatural horror
1986 · US/Can · Colour · 82mins

An intriguing modern-dress vampire movie that plays rather like *Taxi Driver* with a screenplay by Bram Stoker. Its bloodsucker hero, credibly brought to life (after death) by Silvio Oliviero, works nights as a New York cabbie – a great way to meet potential supper guests. Director Gerard Ciccoritti shows great flair for fetishist images though his rock video-style technique ultimately grates. But the urban night-time setting is neatly evoked, and it was followed by an underwhelming sequel, *The Understudy: Graveyard Shift II*. RS DVD

Silvio Oliviero *Stephen Tsepes* • Helen Papas *Michelle* • Cliff Stoker *Eric Hayden* • Dorin Ferber *Gilda* ■ *Dir* Gerard Ciccoritti [Jerry Ciccoritti] • *Scr* Gérard Ciccoritti

Graveyard Shift ★★ 18

Horror 1990 · US · Colour · 82mins

Adapted from the Stephen King short story, this substandard chiller could just about be seen as an anti-capitalist parable. Essentially, it's an excuse to trot out all the clichés of the splatter-movie genre, with a giant man-eating rodent as the central menace. David Andrews is a bloodless hero and director Ralph S Singleton's acquiescence to racial and physical stereotypes is regrettable. Watch for Brad Dourif's demented cameo. DP. Contains violence and swearing.

David Andrews *John Hall* • Kelly Wolf *Jane Wisconsky* • Stephen Macht *Warwick* • Brad Dourif *Tucker Cleveland* • Andrew Divoff *Danson* ■ *Dir* Ralph S Singleton • *Scr* John Esposito, from the short story *Graveyard Shift* from the book *Night Shift* by Stephen King

The Gravy Train ★★

Action comedy 1974 · US · Colour · 95mins

Stacy Keach and Frederic Forrest are brothers, both no-hopers and low-lifes, who join up with Barry Primus and rob an armoured car. When Primus runs away with all the money and Margot Kidder, he provides an ample excuse for an hour or so of vengeful bloodletting, as well as some social comments about the nightmare of the American Dream. AT

Stacy Keach *Calvin Dion* • Frederic Forrest *Russell Dion* • Margot Kidder *Margie* • Barry Primus *Tony* • Richard Romanus *Carlo* •

U = SUITABLE FOR ALL Uc = SUITABLE FOR ALL, ESPECIALLY FOR YOUNG CHILDREN (VIDEO ONLY) PG = PARENTAL GUIDANCE

Denny Miller *Rex* • Jack Starrett *Rancher* ■ *Dir* Jack Starrett • *Scr* Bill Kerby, David Whitney [Terrence Malick]

Gray Lady Down ★★★ PG

Disaster movie 1978 · US · Colour · 105mins

A flurry of clichés almost engulfs this aquatic thriller about a Charlton Heston-commanded nuclear submarine stuck on the edge of an ocean canyon and awaiting a Stacy Keach-commanded rescue mission. Everything that can happen does happen, from ramming by a Norwegian freighter to earth slides, but David Greene's direction transcends banalities with pace and panache, while Heston's authority is the sort that could walk on water. TH

Charlton Heston *Captain Paul Blanchard* • David Carradine *Captain Gates* • Stacy Keach *Captain Bennett* • Ned Beatty *Mickey* • Stephen McHattie *Murphy* • Ronny Cox *Commander Samuelson* • Dorian Harewood *Fowler* • Rosemary Forsyth *Vickie* ■ *Dir* David Greene • *Scr* Howard Sackler, James Whittaker, Frank P Rosenberg (adaptation), from the novel *Event 1000* by David Lavallee

Grayeagle ★★ PG

Western 1977 · US · Colour · 99mins

Independent film-maker Charles B Pierce attempts a low-rent version of John Ford's classic *The Searchers*, this time telling the story from the Indians' point of view, with Ben Johnson in the lead and Natalie Wood's sister Lana as the girl kidnapped by the Cheyenne. With a cast that also includes Jack Elam, this isn't unwatchable, but its aspirations to worthiness soon become tiresome. TS

Ben Johnson *John Colter* • Iron Eyes Cody *Standing Bear* • Lana Wood *Beth Colter* • Jack Elam *Trapper Willis* • Paul Fix *Running Wolf* • Alex Cord *Grayeagle* • Jacob Daniels *Scar* • Jimmy Clem *Abe Stoud* • Charles B Pierce *Bugler* ■ *Dir/Scr* Charles B Pierce

Gray's Anatomy ★★★

Comedy 1996 · US/UK · Colour · 80mins

The writer and actor Spalding Gray is probably best known for his filmed monologue *Swimming to Cambodia*, inspired by his experiences as a minor cast member of *The Killing Fields*. This is another such monologue, this time starting from Gray's discovery of a sight defect that required some drastic surgery. Director Steven Soderbergh films Gray at a desk, circling him and presenting a strange assortment of backdrops to the diverting and wildly discursive talk. Readers are warned that the film begins with some shocking images of eye injuries. AT. Contains swearing.

Spalding Gray ■ *Dir* Steven Soderbergh • *Scr* Spalding Gray, Renée Shafransky, from their performance piece

Grease ★★★★ PG

Musical romance
1978 · US · Colour · 105mins

Fresh from *Saturday Night Fever*, John Travolta was the biggest movie star in the world when he teamed up with Olivia Newton-John to help turn one of Broadway's biggest hits into one of Hollywood's most successful musicals. The film aims to evoke nostalgia for a time before most of its audience would have been born – 1950s America – where Rydell High is the setting for a rather slender tale of teenage love and pre-Vietnam innocence. It succeeds in the task, thanks to some toe-tapping numbers, sprightly hoofing and slick performances. PF DVD

John Travolta *Danny Zucco* • Olivia Newton-John *Sandy Olsson* • Stockard Channing *Betty Rizzo* • Jeff Conaway *Kenickie* • Barry Pearl *Doody* • Michael Tucci *Sonny* • Kelly Ward *Putzie* ■ *Dir* Randal Kleiser • *Scr* Bronte Woodard, Allan Carr, from the musical by Warren Casey, Jim Jacobs

Grease 2 ★★ PG

Musical 1982 · US · Colour · 109mins

An unprepossessing sequel to the massive hit, this is notable for a great title song by the Four Tops and a then-unknown Michelle Pfeiffer in a clinging short skirt. This is the story of Rydell High some years on from those halcyon days of drainpipe trousers and stiff petticoats. The problem is that director and choreographer Patricia Birch tries to bring those high steppin' innocent production values to an altogether grittier era of emerging 1960s liberalism. SH DVD

Michelle Pfeiffer *Stephanie* • Maxwell Caulfield *Michael* • Didi Conn *Frenchy* • Eve Arden *Ms McGee* • Sid Caesar *Coach Calhoun* • Adrian Zmed *Johnny Nogerilli* • Christopher McDonald *Goose* • Peter Frechette *Lou DiMucci* • Lorna Luft *Paulette Rebchuck* ■ *Dir* Patricia Birch • *Scr* Ken Finkleman

Greased Lightning ★★ PG

Biographical comedy drama
1977 · US · Colour · 92mins

Richard Pryor never really looks comfortable in this story of the America's first black stock-car racing driver, Wendell Scott, who battled prejudice to reach the top of his chosen profession. It's a fascinating story, but the main problem is that it never makes up its mind whether it is a straightforward biopic or a comedy. However, the supporting cast can't be faulted, and there's some strong racing footage. JF

Richard Pryor *Wendell Scott* • Beau Bridges *Hutch* • Pam Grier *Mary Jones* • Cleavon Little *Peewee* • Vincent Gardenia *Sheriff Cotton* • Richie Havens *Woodrow* • Julian Bond *Russell* • Earl Hindman *Beau Welles* ■ *Dir* Michael Schultz • *Scr* Kenneth Voze, Lawrence DuKore, Melvin Van Peebles, Leon Capetanos

Greaser's Palace ★★

Satirical western drama
1972 · US · Colour · 91mins

Ostensibly a western parody, this plotless comedy extravaganza from film-maker Robert Downey chronicles the exploits of a Christ-like figure called Zoot Suit (Allan Arbus) who descends upon an unsuspecting town en route to becoming a singer. Its audacious, nutball approach is finally its undoing, becoming a technically proficient slice of allegorical pretentiousness. RS

Allan Arbus *Zoot Suit* • Albert Henderson *Seaweedhead Greaser* • Michael Sullivan *Lamy Greaser* • Luana Anders *Cholera Greaser* • James Antonio *Vernon* • George Morgan *Coo Coo* • Ron Nealy *Ghost/Card Man* • Larry Moyer *Captain Good* ■ *Dir/Scr* Robert Downey Sr

The Great Adventure ★★★ U

Adventure 1953 · Swe · BW · 73mins

This internationally acclaimed drama from film-maker Arne Sucksdorff won a prize at the Cannes film festival in 1954. Set in Sweden, it tells the simple story of two boys who secretly befriend an otter over one winter's season but then find that the animal wants to return to the wild. Visually striking, this showed nature without any hint of Disney-esque sentiment. Veteran documentary film-maker Sucksdorff not only directed the film but also wrote, produced, edited, photographed and acted in it. AE. In Swedish with English subtitles.

Anders Norborg *Anders* • Kjell Sucksdorff *Kjell* • Arne Sucksdorff *Father* • Norman Shelley *Narrator* • Gunnar Sjöberg *Narrator* ■ *Dir/Scr* Arne Sucksdorff

The Great American Broadcast ★★★ U

Musical drama 1941 · US · BW · 91mins

A cheerfully fictionalised account of the early days of American radio, culminating in the first coast-to-coast hook-up of stations. This breezy Fox musical casts Jack Oakie and John Payne as ambitious entrepreneurs and Alice Faye as their singing star, with the trio going through the usual break-ups and reconciliations. With some catchy songs (by Mack Gordon and Harry Warren) and cameos by such wireless celebrities as Jack Benny and Rudy Vallee, it's a generous measure of relaxing entertainment. AE

Alice Faye *Vicki Adams* • Jack Oakie *Chuck Hadley* • John Payne *Rix Martin* • Cesar Romero *Bruce Chadwick* • James Newill *Singer* ■ *Dir* Archie Mayo • *Scr* Don Ettlinger, Edwin Blum, Robert Ellis, Helen Logan

The Great American Cowboy ★★★

Documentary 1973 · US · Colour · 90mins

This Oscar-winning documentary takes an inside look at rodeo as a professional sport. Spending months on the road with the riders travelling from one prize contest to the next, director Kieth Merrill and writer Douglas Kent Hall focus on a veteran star (Larry Mahan) and his younger rival (Phil Lyne). Subjective camerawork involves the audience in the thrills and spills of the arena, while slow-motion dissects the high-speed action. Overlong for all but rodeo devotees, it has the bonus of warm narration by retired cowboy star Joel McCrea. AE

Joel McCrea *Narrator* ■ *Dir* Kieth Merrill • *Scr* Douglas Kent Hall

The Great Balloon Adventure ★★

Adventure 1978 · US · Colour · 83mins

Katharine Hepburn waited two years for director Richard A Colla to finance this amiable adventure, and then refused to take a penny in payment. When asked why she took on the role of a junk dealer who helps a couple of boys rebuild their grandfather's balloon and re-create his circus act, she confessed that it fulfilled a long-standing ambition to fly in a hot-air balloon. DP

Katharine Hepburn *Miss Pudd* • Kevin McKenzie *Alby* • Dennis Dimster *Chris* • Obie *Joshua* ■ *Dir* Richard A Colla • *Scr* Eugene Poinc, from a story by Maria L de Ossio, Eugene Poinc, Richard A Colla

Great Balls of Fire! ★★★ 15

Musical biography
1989 · US · Colour · 107mins

There's a whole lotta shakin' goin' on in *The Big Easy* director Jim McBride's bright rock 'n' roll biography of Jerry Lee Lewis, played with style and flash by Dennis Quaid. It's an entertaining romp, following Jerry Lee's life in the 1950s up to his fall from grace in London after he married his 13-year-old cousin Myra (sweetly played by Winona Ryder). It's Quaid's on-the-edge performance and the music that makes this so much fun, plus the able support from Ryder, Alec Baldwin and Trey Wilson. JB. Contains swearing and sex scenes. DVD

Dennis Quaid *Jerry Lee Lewis* • Winona Ryder *Myra Gale Lewis* • John Doe *JW Brown* • Stephen Tobolowsky *John Phillips* • Trey Wilson *Sam Phillips* • Alec Baldwin *Jimmy Swaggart* • Joe Bob Briggs [John Bloom (2)] *Dewey "Daddy-O" Phillips* ■ *Dir* Jim McBride • *Scr* Jim McBride, Jack Baran, from the non-fiction book by Myra Lewis, Murray Silver

The Great Bank Robbery ★★ U

Comedy western 1969 · US · Colour · 97mins

The idea of robbing a bank so safe that it's where the likes of Jesse James keep their loot is an amusing one, but a leaden screenplay from *The Exorcist's* William Peter Blatty and the desperately uneven direction of Hy Averback defeat the best efforts of the eclectic cast to bring the premise to life. Zero Mostel is disastrously miscast as a phoney evangelist, while "wooden" is too kind an adjective to describe the performances of Clint Walker and Kim Novak. TS

Zero Mostel *Reverend Pious Blue* • Kim Novak *Lyda Kabanov* • Clint Walker *Ben Quick* • Claude Akins *Slade* • Akim Tamiroff *Papa Pedro* • Larry Storch *Juan* • John Anderson *Kincaid* • Sam Jaffe *Brother Lilac* • Mako *Secret service agent Eliot Fong* • Elisha Cook Jr *Jeb* • Ruth Warrick *Mrs Applebee* ■ *Dir* Hy Averback • *Scr* William Peter Blatty, from the novel by Frank O'Rourke

The Great Barrier ★★ U

Historical drama 1937 · UK/US · BW · 84mins

Considering the state of the British film industry in 1937, this rugged account of the building of the Canadian-Pacific railroad was ambitious in the extreme. It was shot on location in Alberta and British Columbia by former silent star Milton Rosmer, who was still a relatively inexperienced director. The safety net was Hollywood import Richard Arlen. However, not even his brawny turn as a reformed gambler who averts a strike could overcome the pioneering platitudes. DP

Richard Arlen *Hickey* • Lilli Palmer *Lou* • Antoinette Cellier *Mary Moody* • Barry Mackay *Steve* ■ *Dir* Milton Rosmer, Geoffrey Barkas • *Scr* Michael Barringer, Milton Rosmer, Ralph Spence, from the novel *The Great Divide* by Alan Sullivan

The Great British Train Robbery ★★★

Crime drama 1966 · W Ger · BW · 104mins

This German movie is a surprisingly effective reconstruction of the audacious raid on a Royal Mail train that resulted in the theft of £2.6 million. Capturing the atmosphere of 1960s London with sharp black-and-white photography, directors John Olden and Claus Peter Witt adopt a brisk, workmanlike style befitting the pseudo-documentary approach to the planning and execution of the robbery. The gang turn in unfussy performances and there is an end-of-career part for Isa Miranda. DP. German dialogue dubbed into English.

Horst Tappert *Michael Donegan* • Hans Cossy *Patrick Kinsey* • Karl Heinz Hess *Geoffrey Black* • Günther Neutze *Archibald Arrow* • Hans Reiser *Thomas Webster* • Rolf Nagel *Gerald Williams* • Harry Engel *George Slowfoot* • Isa Miranda *Mona* ■ *Dir* John Olden, Claus Peter Witt • *Scr* Henry Kolarz, Robert Muller, from the book *The Robbers' Tale: the Real Story of the Great Train Robbery* by Peta Fordham

The Great Caruso ★★★★ U

Musical biography
1951 · US · Colour · 104mins

A popular and sentimentalised biopic of the legendary tenor, a role MGM's own lyric tenor Mario Lanza was born to play. The ramshackle screenplay doesn't really matter as Lanza performs such full-blooded arias as *La Donna e Mobile*, *Celeste Aida* and *Vesti la Giubba* in that remarkable golden voice, although the actual hit song from the movie was *The Loveliest Night of the Year*, sung by Lanza's co-star, Ann Blyth. This was Lanza's biggest success in an all-too-short career that ended with his early death at the age of 38. TS

G

Mario Lanza *Enrico Caruso* • Ann Blyth *Dorothy Benjamin* • Dorothy Kirsten *Louise Heggar* • Jarmila Novotna *Maria Selka* • Richard Hageman *Carlo Santi* • Carl Benton Reid *Park Benjamin* ■ *Dir* Richard Thorpe • *Scr* Sonia Levien, William Ludwig, from a story by Dorothy Caruso

Great Catherine ★ U

Historical comedy
1968 · UK · Colour · 98mins

This farrago about the romantic life of the Empress of Russia is more like a *Carry On* movie transferred to St Petersburg. Peter O'Toole breezes through it all as an English Light Dragoons captain who finds himself in the Empress's bedchamber, while art house heroine Jeanne Moreau is hopelessly miscast as Catherine. The jokes are constantly telegraphed, and the flashy, tricksy direction roots the film in the Swinging Sixties. AT

Peter O'Toole *Captain Edstaston* • Zero Mostel *Patiomkin* • Jeanne Moreau *Catherine* • Jack Hawkins *Sir George Gorse* • Akim Tamiroff *Sergeant* • Marie Lohr *Dowager Lady Gorse* • Kenneth Griffith *Naryshkin* ■ *Dir* Gordon Flemyng • *Scr* Hugh Leonard, from the play *Great Catherine Whom Glory Still Adores* by George Bernard Shaw

The Great Chase ★★★

Documentary 1961 · US · BW · 91mins

The chase sequence put the movement into moving pictures and this documentary, put together by Harvey Cort, is a splendid celebration of those breakneck pursuits that proved an invaluable fall-back for dramatic and comic directors alike. The clips range from the horseback raid on a steam train in Edwin S Porter's *The Great Train Robbery* (1903) to Buster Keaton's classic railroad dash in *The General* (1927). There's also a chance to relive some of Pearl White's brushes with death in the peerless serial *The Perils of Pauline* (1914), Lillian Gish's ice floe encounter in *Way Down East* (1920) and Douglas Fairbanks's swashbuckling antics in *The Mark of Zorro* (1920). DP

Dir Harvey Cort • *Music* Larry Adler

Great Day ★ U

Drama 1944 · UK · BW · 79mins

As the village of Denley prepares to welcome First Lady Eleanor Roosevelt, alcoholic First World War veteran Eric Portman disgraces himself by stealing from a lady's purse. His daughter, Sheila Sim, dithers over whether she should marry her boss, while his wife, Flora Robson, dedicates herself to the Womens' Guild. This American-financed aberration feels like an episode of *Mrs Dale's Diary* and would have been better suited to the radio. AT

Eric Portman *Captain Ellis* • Flora Robson *Mrs Ellis* • Sheila Sim *Margaret Ellis* • Isabel Jeans *Lady Mott* • Walter Fitzgerald *John Tyndale* • Philip Friend *Geoffrey Winthrop* • Marjorie Rhodes *Mrs Mumford* ■ *Dir* Lance Comfort • *Scr* Wolfgang Wilhelm, John Davenport, from a play by Lesley Storm

A Great Day in Harlem ★★★★★ U

Music documentary
1994 · US · BW and Colour · 59mins

A famous photograph of 57 jazz musicians and a club owner outside a Harlem brownstone is the starting point for this stunningly inventive documentary. The shot covers every jazz generation up to 1958 and includes Dizzy Gillespie and Sonny Rollins. Director Jean Bach splices together voiceovers, snappy interviews, promotional films and home movies to unearth not just the spontaneity and uncertainty of jazz life, but also to home in on its passion, sensitivity and morality. Incidentally, it was *Kramer vs Kramer* director Robert Benton, then art director at *Esquire*, who commissioned the photograph. JM

Quincy Jones *Narrator* ■ *Dir* Jean Bach • *Scr* Jean Bach, Susan Peehl, Matthew Seig

Great Day in the Morning ★★★

Western 1956 · US · Colour · 91mins

Strikingly shot by William Snyder against the jaw-dropping landscape of the Colorado Territory, this eve-of-Civil-War western features a redoubtable performance by Robert Stack as a southern maverick forced to choose between patriotism and his pocket. Competing for his attention are wealthy Virginia Mayo and saloon entertainer Ruth Roman. The dialogue in the literate script is sharp-tongued, the action is serviceably staged and the villainy of Raymond Burr and Alex Nicol is impressive. Unfortunately, Jacques Tourneur's direction is uninspired. DP

Robert Stack *Owen Pentecost* • Virginia Mayo *Ann Merry Alaine* • Ruth Roman *Boston Grant* • Alex Nicol *Stephen Kirby* • Raymond Burr *Jumbo Means* • Leo Gordon *Zeff Masterson* ■ *Dir* Jacques Tourneur • *Scr* Lesser Samuels, from the novel by Robert Hardy Andrews • *Cinematographer* William Snyder

The Great Diamond Robbery ★★ PG

Comedy crime 1953 · US · BW · 87mins

Red Skelton was one of the great American clowns. A vaudevillian, he became a radio favourite in the 1940s. But it was in film and television that his particular brand of slapstick really made its mark. He was already well established by the time he played a gullible diamond cutter conned by crooks, in what proved to be a disappointing end to his MGM career. Fortunately the comedian continued to enjoy huge success on the small screen where his own TV show ran for more than 20 years. DF

Red Skelton *Ambrose C Park* • Cara Williams *Maggie Drumman* • James Whitmore *Remlick* • Kurt Kasznar *Tony* • Dorothy Stickney *Emily Drumman* • George Mathews *Duke Fargoh* ■ *Dir* Robert Z Leonard • *Scr* Laslo Vadnay, Martin Rackin, from a story by Laslo Vadnay

The Great Dictator ★★★★★ U

Satirical comedy 1940 · US · BW · 124mins

Hitler didn't see the joke but he got the point. Charlie Chaplin's first dialogue feature was brilliant satire on the anti-Semitic Nazi regime, with Chaplin in the dual role of a Jewish barber and dictator Adenoid Hynkel. This features some of Chaplin's greatest comic moments – the glories of the barber shaving a customer in time to a Hungarian dance by Brahms, contrasting with Hynkel's solo ballet with a globe of the world. Bliss, even though Chaplin said that, if he had known of the Nazis' real horror, he would never have made such a burlesque, and the final speech, pleading for universal tolerance when the barber takes over from Hynkel, is passionate but mawkish. TH DVD

Charles Chaplin *Jewish barber/Hynkel, dictator of Tomania* • Paulette Goddard *Hannah* • Jack Oakie *Napaloni, dictator of Bacteria* • Reginald Gardiner *Schultz* • Henry Daniell *Garbitsch* • Billy Gilbert *Herring* • Grace Hayle *Madame Napaloni* • Carter DeHaven (1) *Bacterian ambassador* ■ *Dir/Scr* Charles Chaplin

The Great Escape ★★★★★ PG

Classic Second World War adventure
1963 · US · Colour · 172mins

One of the all time great war movies from director John Sturges, who'd already pulled off this populist ensemble trick for with the western *The Magnificent Seven*. Once again, Elmer Bernstein supplies a theme people still hum today, and three of the Seven are reunited – Steve McQueen, Charles Bronson and James Coburn. It's the ultimate *Boy's Own* PoW escape yarn, with collapsing tunnels, probing searchlights and British pluck upon which clichés have been built. It's impossible not to get caught up in the escape party's plans, as led by Richard Attenborough, assisted by the aforementioned, plus Donald Pleasence and James Garner, each escapee with his own speciality. AC DVD

Steve McQueen *Hilts, "The Cooler King"* • James Garner *Hendley, "The Scrounger"* • Richard Attenborough *Bartlett, "Big X"* • Charles Bronson *Danny Velinski, "Tunnel King"* • Donald Pleasence *Blythe, "The Forger"* • James Donald *Ramsey, "The SBO"* • James Coburn *Sedgwick, "Manufacturer"* • John Leyton *Willie, "Tunneler"* • Gordon Jackson *MacDonald, "Intelligence"* • David McCallum *Ashley-Pitt, "Dispersal"* ■ *Dir* John Sturges • *Scr* James Clavell, WR Burnett, from a book by Paul Brickhill

Great Expectations ★★★★★ PG

Classic period drama
1946 · UK · BW · 113mins

David Lean black-and-white adaptation of the Charles Dickens novel is a master in its literary field. It is the tale of orphaned Pip (played as a boy by Anthony Wager and as an adult by John Mills) who comes into an unexpected fortune. From the opening sequence on the Kentish marshes, when the young Pip encounters Finlay Currie's terrifying escaped convict, through his love for Estella (played by Jean Simmons as a child and Valerie Hobson as an adult), the fine cast fleshes out a carefully pruned version of the book, which excises entire characters but retains the magical Dickens spirit. It looks sumptuous and earned Oscars for cinematography and design. AC DVD

John Mills *Pip as an adult* • Valerie Hobson *Estella as an adult* • Bernard Miles *Joe Gargery* • Francis L Sullivan *Jaggers* • Martita Hunt *Miss Havisham* • Finlay Currie *Abel Magwitch* • Alec Guinness *Herbert Pocket* • Ivor Barnard *Wemmick* • Anthony Wager *Pip as a child* • Jean Simmons *Estella as a child* ■ *Dir* David Lean • *Scr* David Lean, Ronald Neame, Anthony Havelock-Allan, Cecil McGivern, Kay Walsh, from the novel by Charles Dickens • *Cinematographer* Guy Green • *Editor* Jack Harris • *Art Director* John Bryan, Wilfrid Shingleton

Great Expectations ★★ U

Period drama
1974 · US/UK · Colour · 118mins

Following the success of Carol Reed's *Oliver Twist*, it was only a matter of time before someone suggested another musical Dickens. Mercifully the songs were out. What's left is a retelling of Pip's progress in which the scenes seem to be staged solely for the benefit of the big production number that never arrives. This superbly crafted story becomes simplistic, and only Margaret Leighton's Miss Havisham rings true. DP DVD

Michael York *Pip* • Sarah Miles *Estella* • Margaret Leighton *Miss Havisham* • James Mason *Magwitch* • Anthony Quayle *Jaggers* • Robert Morley *Pumblechook* • Joss Ackland *Joe Gargery* ■ *Dir* Joseph Hardy • *Scr* Sherman Yellen, from the novel by Charles Dickens

Great Expectations ★★★ U

Animated drama 1985 · Aus · Colour · 69mins

One of a series of animated Dickens adaptations, this is a useful introduction for younger viewers to one of the author's most popular novels. Even taking into account the sensibilities of its audience, the film still wastes such key scenes as Pip's meeting with Magwitch in the marshes and the visits to Miss Havisham's creepy house. However, director Jean Tych does succeed in making London seem a far less inviting place than Joe Gargery's forge. DP

Bill Kerr • Phillip Hinton • Simon Hinton • Barbara Hawley ■ *Dir* Jean Tych • *Scr* from the novel by Charles Dickens

Great Expectations ★★★ 15

Romantic drama
1997 · US · Colour · 106mins

After the minor miracle he worked with *A Little Princess*, Alfonso Cuarón rather lost the plot with this Dickens update. He opted for a loose retelling centred on the eerie Everglades and the New York art scene. But while he lashes on the style, he fumbles the book's underlying themes. He's also ill-served by his leads, with Ethan Hawke consumed by sensitivity and Gwyneth Paltrow too shallow to be a worthy object of obsession. So it's left to a gleefully deranged Anne Bancroft and a caringly criminal Robert De Niro to provide the substance. DP. Contains swearing and some violence. DVD

Ethan Hawke *Finnegan "Finn" Bell* • Gwyneth Paltrow *Estella* • Hank Azaria *Walter Plane* • Chris Cooper *Joe* • Anne Bancroft *Nora Diggers Dinsmoor* • Robert De Niro *Lustig* • Josh Mostel *Jerry Ragno* • Kim Dickens *Maggie* ■ *Dir* Alfonso Cuarón • *Scr* Mitch Glazer, from the novel by Charles Dickens

The Great Flamarion ★★★

Film noir 1945 · US · BW · 78mins

In this imaginative low-budget *film noir*, the great Erich von Stroheim (then past his peak) teamed up with talented young director, Anthony Mann. Von Stroheim has the title role of the vaudeville sharpshooter who, despite an unhappy history with women, makes the mistake of falling for his alluring young assistant, played by Mary Beth Hughes. Of course this is very bad news for Hughes's husband, played by Dan Duryea. The film was made on such a shoestring that a park scene had to be faked on a soundstage with just a bench, a lamp and thick fog. AE

Erich von Stroheim *Flamarion* • Mary Beth Hughes *Connie Wallace* • Dan Duryea *Al Wallace* • Steve Barclay [Stephen Barclay] *Eddie* • Lester Allen *Tony* ■ *Dir* Anthony Mann • *Scr* Anne Wighton, Heinz Herald, Richard Weil, from the story *Big Shot* by Vicki Baum

The Great Gabbo ★★★

Musical drama 1929 · US · BW · 92mins

Erich von Stroheim gives an outstanding performance as the egomaniacal ventriloquist who allows his dummy to speak the words of his heart. Based on a story by Ben Hecht and directed with no little style by James Cruze, the film slows slightly in the second half to accommodate a number of vaudeville acts (which were originally shown in somewhat blurred colour). But it's impossible to take your eyes off von Stroheim DP

Erich von Stroheim *Gabbo* • Betty Compson *Mary* • Don Douglas *Frank* • Margie "Babe" Kane [Marjorie Kane] *Babe* ■ *Dir* James Cruze • *Scr* Hugh Herbert, from the story *The Rival Dummy* by Ben Hecht

The Great Garrick ★★★ U

Comedy 1937 · UK · BW · 90mins

Brian Aherne is the famous 18th-century actor David Garrick, who tells his London audience that he's been invited to perform at the Comédie Française and intends to give the French a lesson in acting. Hearing this, French actors hatch a plot to discredit Garrick as he spends a night in Calais.

This is a bright and breezy affair, although it amounts to little more than a charade. Aherne's future sister-in-law, Olivia de Havilland, adds to the fun, plus, in her second featured role, Lana Turner. The stylish direction is by James Whale. AT

Brian Aherne *David Garrick* • Olivia de Havilland *Germaine De Le Corbe* • Edward Everett Horton *Tubby* • Melville Cooper *M Picard* • Luis Alberni *Basset* • Lionel Atwill *Beaumarchais* • Marie Wilson *Nicolle* • Lana Turner *Auber* ■ *Dir* James Whale • *Scr* Ernest Vadja, from his play *Ladies and Gentleman*

The Great Gatsby ★★ U

Romantic drama 1949 · US · BW · 91mins

F Scott Fitzgerald's novel provides plenty of plot for a screenwriter to work with, but his silky style simply refuses to translate to the screen. Alan Ladd's limited acting technique almost accidentally conveys some of the mystery of the millionaire who becomes the toast of Long Island society. But while he valiantly attempts to look enigmatic, Betty Field blows the whole illusion with a gauche interpretation of Daisy Buchanan. Elliott Nugent directs with some *noirish* touches, but can't counter the script's verbosity. DP

Alan Ladd *Jay Gatsby* • Betty Field *Daisy Buchanan* • Macdonald Carey *Nick Carraway* • Ruth Hussey *Jordan Baker* • Barry Sullivan *Tom Buchanan* • Howard Da Silva *Wilson* • Shelley Winters *Murtle Wilson* • Henry Hull *Dan Cody* • Carole Mathews *Ella Cody* ■ *Dir* Elliott Nugent • *Scr* Cyril Hume, Richard Maibaum, from the play by Owen Davis, from the novel by F Scott Fitzgerald

The Great Gatsby ★★★ PG

Romantic drama
1974 · US · Colour · 135mins

This was Paramount's third stab at bringing F Scott Fitzgerald's jazz-age classic to the screen. Robert Redford is unquestionably more handsome than Alan Ladd, but he's no more demonstrative or credible as the millionaire with a dark past. Mia Farrow, meanwhile, is better cast than Betty Field, though her Daisy Buchanan is more skittishly irresponsible than irresistibly infatuating. While Jack Clayton's direction is suitably languid, the lush imagery only reinforces the superficiality of Francis Ford Coppola's reverential script. DP [video]

Robert Redford *Jay Gatsby* • Mia Farrow *Daisy Buchanan* • Bruce Dern *Tom Buchanan* • Karen Black *Myrtle Wilson* • Scott Wilson *George Wilson* • Sam Waterston *Nick Carraway* • Lois Chiles *Jordan Baker* ■ *Dir* Jack Clayton • *Scr* Francis Ford Coppola, from the novel by F Scott Fitzgerald

The Great Georgia Bank Hoax ★★★

Comedy 1977 · US · Colour · 93mins

The Watergate scandal was still haunting the US when this satire about corruption in a Georgia bank was released. The lightweight plot was given added resonance by the (intentional) Watergate references, as one case of embezzlement leads to an even bigger scam by the bank's boss, Burgess Meredith. Richard Basehart and the always reliable Ned Beatty add a touch of class to proceedings. DF

Burgess Meredith *Jack* • Richard Basehart *Emanuel* • Ned Beatty *Julius* • Charlene Dallas *Cathy* • Paul Sand *Richard* • Michael Murphy *Manigma* • Constance Forslund *Patricia* ■ *Dir/Scr* Joseph Jacoby

Great Guns ★★ PG

Comedy 1941 · US · BW · 70mins

Laurel and Hardy's first feature for 20th Century-Fox is a plodding army comedy with echoes of their own *Pack Up Your Troubles* and the Abbott and Costello hit *Buck Privates*, which had been released earlier the same year. Directed by Monty Banks, the film has sadly too little Stan and Ollie and far too much of a romance between Sheila Ryan and Dick Nelson. It's hardly vintage, so savour the laughs when they come. DP [video]

Stan Laurel *Stan* • Oliver Hardy *Ollie* • Sheila Ryan *Ginger Hammond* • Dick Nelson *Dan Forrester* • Edmund MacDonald *Hippo* • Charles Trowbridge *Colonel Ridley* • Ludwig Stossel *Dr Schickel* • Kane Richmond *Captain Baker* ■ *Dir* Monty Banks • *Scr* Lou Breslow

Great Guy ★★

Crime drama 1936 · US · BW · 73mins

James Cagney was in dispute with his regular employer, Warner Bros, when he appeared in this movie for minor studio, Grand National. This weak crime drama lacked the Warners gloss, but Cagney makes a point of abandoning his tough-guy image, playing an incorruptible weights-and-measures inspector who exposes a food scam to cheat customers. There is less than the usual violence, and he even allows himself to be bossed around by Mae Clarke, the actress who received his celebrated grapefruit massage in *The Public Enemy*. AE

James Cagney *Johnny Cave* • Mae Clarke *Janet Henry* • James Burke *Pat Haley* • Edward Brophy *Pete Reilly* • Henry Kolker *Conning* • Bernadene Hayes *Hazel Scott* ■ *Dir* John G Blystone • *Scr* Henry McCarty, Horace McCoy, Henry Johnson, Henry Ruskin, from the stories by James Edward Grant

The Great Impostor ★★ U

Biographical comedy adventure
1960 · US · BW · 112mins

By the time he made this biopic of Ferdinand Waldo Demara Jr, a notorious real-life impostor, Tony Curtis had proved that he wasn't just a pretty face. But even his considerable comic gifts were not enough to sustain this episodic, mildly amusing comedy, in which he masquerades as a professor, a Trappist monk, a navy surgeon and a prison administrator who forestalls a riot. It's a pity that in this potentially interesting case history, the character's motivations are never sufficiently explained. RB

Tony Curtis *Ferdinand Waldo Demara Jr* • Edmond O'Brien *Captain Glover* • Arthur O'Connell *Warden Chandler* • Gary Merrill *Pa Demara* • Joan Blackman *Catherine Lacey* • Robert Middleton *Brown* • Doodles Weaver *Farmer* ■ *Dir* Robert Mulligan • *Scr* Liam O'Brien, from the book by Robert Crichton

The Great Jewel Robber ★★

Crime drama based on a true story
1950 · US · BW · 91mins

David Brian, probably best known today for his starring role in the popular TV series *Mr District Attorney*, parades his burly talents on the other side of the law as the titular criminal of this efficient programme filler. The director is the under-rated British expatriate Peter Godfrey, who was beginning his decline from Warner Bros features through credits like this to work on TV series. This is pleasing enough, but nothing special. TS

David Brian *Gerard Dennis* • Marjorie Reynolds *Martha* • Jacqueline de Wit *Mrs Vinson* • Alice Talton [Alix Talton] *Brenda* • John Archer *Sampter* • Perdita Chandler *Peggy* • Robert B Williams *Captain Ryan* ■ *Dir* Peter Godfrey • *Scr* Borden Chase, from the story *The Life of Gerard Graham Dennis* by Borden Chase, GG Dennis

The Great John L ★

Biographical sports drama
1945 · US · BW · 96mins

Bing Crosby turned producer with this lumbering biopic of a heavyweight boxer who marries a vaudeville star, turns to drink and sinks ever lower from there. Crosby snapped hunky Greg McClure from a small theatre in Los Angeles to play the title role and tied him to a multi-picture contract. It's a demanding role, and McClure clearly isn't up to it. But worst of all, the story, telling of the boxer's loss of self respect and sudden rehabilitation, has that Crosby overlay of schmaltz. AT

Greg McClure *John L Sullivan* • Linda Darnell *Anne Livinstone* • Barbara Britton *Kathy Harkness* • Lee Sullivan *Mickey* • Otto Kruger *Richard Martin* • Wallace Ford *McManus* • George Mathews *John Flood* • Robert Barrat *Billy Muldoon* ■ *Dir* Frank Tuttle • *Scr* James Edward Grant

Great Land of the Small ★★★ U

Fantasy 1987 · Can · Colour · 87mins

This children's fantasy genuinely conveys the imagination and innocence of childhood by creating a credible child's world. It pulls no emotional punches as it tells the fetching tale of two kids from the city who learn all about invisible creatures and rainbows from their grandmother in the country. They then encounter a hobbit-like creature and help him in his quest for his missing gold dust. JM [video]

Karen Elkin *Jenny* • Michael Blouin *David* • Michael J Anderson *Fritz* • Ken Roberts *Flannigan* • Lorraine Desmarais *Mother* ■ *Dir* Vojtech Jasny • *Scr* David Sigmund

The Great Lie ★★★★

Romantic melodrama
1941 · US · BW · 107mins

This is one of the greatest films Bette Davis made at Warner Bros. Once termed "women's pictures", they are now recognised as being among the finest products of the studio system. Here Davis is given more than a run for her money by co-star Mary Astor, who collected the best supporting actress Oscar as Davis's rival in love for handsome George Brent, allegedly Davis's lover in real life. The titular lie involves the "ownership" of Brent's child, and both female stars pull out all the stops. TS

Bette Davis *Maggie* • Mary Astor *Sandra* • George Brent *Pete Van Allen* • Lucile Watson *Aunt Ada* • Hattie McDaniel *Violet* • Grant Mitchell *Joshua Mason* • Jerome Cowan *Jock Thompson* • Charles Trowbridge *Senator Greenfield* ■ *Dir* Edmund Goulding • *Scr* Lenore Coffee, from the novel *January Heights* by Polan Blanks

The Great Locomotive Chase ★★ U

Wartime action adventure
1956 · US · Colour · 71mins

Davy Crockett star Fess Parker features in this folksy American Civil War action adventure. Jeffrey Hunter's Confederate railroader is up against Parker's Union spy, on a mission to destroy enemy supply lines. Hunter is tireless in pursuit of the gang that stole his train, but Parker is the hero of the piece and his audacious escape makes for a resounding finale, which partly compensates for the otherwise ponderous storytelling. DP [video]

Fess Parker *James J Andrews* • Jeffrey Hunter *William A Fuller* • Jeff York *William Campbell* • John Lupton *William Pittenger* • Eddie Firestone *Robert Buffum* • Kenneth Tobey *Anthony Murphy* • Slim Pickens *Pete Bracken* ■ *Dir* Francis D Lyon • *Scr* Lawrence Edward Watkin

The Great Lover ★★★

Comedy 1949 · US · BW · 80mins

One of Bob Hope's better vehicles casts him as a scoutmaster trying to cope with a group of dedicated "child foresters" on a transatlantic liner. The diversions include the beautiful daughter (Rhonda Fleming) of a penniless duke, and a cardsharp who is murdering passengers. The risible script makes room for a brief but splendid cameo by Jack Benny, and Richard Lyon plays one of the youths, urging the unwilling Hope to give up cigarettes and women. "A boy forester never makes a mistake," he tells Hope, who replies: "Too bad your parents weren't foresters." TV

Bob Hope *Freddie Hunter* • Rhonda Fleming *Duchess Alexandria* • Roland Young *CJ Dabney* • Roland Culver *Grand Duke Maximillian* • Richard Lyon *Stanley* • Jim Backus *Higgins* ■ *Dir* Alexander Hall • *Scr* Edmund Beloin, Melville Shavelson, Jack Rose

The Great Madcap ★★★

Comedy 1949 · Mex · BW · 90mins

The second film of Luis Buñuel's Mexican comeback began as a jobbing assignment, but ended up dictating the way the master surrealist would work for the remainder of his career, by teaching him the value of meticulous pre-planning. Some have sought anti-bourgeois satire in drunken patriarch Fernando Soler's revenge on the worthless family that tried to trick him into believing he had squandered his fortune. But the storyline of this gentle comedy is pure Hollywood, as hard work brings out the best in those previously content to exploit. DP. In Spanish with English subtitles.

Fernando Soler *Ramiro* • Rosario Granados *Virginia* • Andres Soler *Ladislao* ■ *Dir* Luis Buñuel, Fernando Soler • *Scr* Luis Alcoriza, Janet Alcoriza, from a play by Adolfo Torrado

The Great Man ★★★

Drama 1956 · US · BW · 92mins

This hollow, cynical drama has a media personality's shining reputation tarnished during the preparation of a tribute. Impressing more as co-writer and director than as star, José Ferrer can do little about the predictable manner in which skeletons tumble out of various closets, but he draws wonderfully embittered performances from his expert cast. Ed Wynn is outstanding as the radio boss who discovered the "Studio King", though Julie London's abused singer, Dean Jagger's network boss and Keenan Wynn's self-seeking executive are also strong. Slick and satirical, but lacking the depth to be truly satisfying. DP

José Ferrer *Joe Harris* • Dean Jagger *Philip Carleton* • Keenan Wynn *Sid Moore* • Julie London *Carol Larson* • Joanne Gilbert *Ginny* • Ed Wynn *Paul Beaseley* • Jim Backus *Nick Cellantano* • Russ Morgan *Eddie Brand* ■ *Dir* José Ferrer • *Scr* Al Morgan, José Ferrer, from the novel by Al Morgan

The Great Man Votes ★★ U

Drama 1939 · US · BW · 71mins

Sharpish political satire about floating voter John Barrymore whose personal problems – widower, drunkard, two kids to raise – make him the target of spin doctors. This is a showcase for Barrymore's bloated talent, though by this time he was several years and several bottles past his prime. AT

John Barrymore *Gregory Vance* • Peter Holden *Donald Vance* • Virginia Weidler *Joan Vance* • Katherine Alexander *Miss Billow* • Donald MacBride *Iron Hat McCarthy* • Bennie Bartlett *Dave McCarthy* • Brandon Tynan *Chester Ainslee* • Elisabeth Risdon *Phoebe Ainslee* ■ *Dir* Garson Kanin • *Scr* John Twist, from a story by Gordon Malherbe Hillman

The Great Man's Lady ★★★

Western 1942 · US · BW · 90mins

A melodramatic western epic, told in flashback and featuring Barbara Stanwyck made-up as a 100-year-old woman. It tells the saga of how Stanwyck backed husband Joel McCrea

G

in forging a town out of the wilderness, only to disagree about the eventual coming of the railroad. Director William A Wellman is at home with this kind of material, and much of the staging is impressive despite the slow pace. TS

Barbara Stanwyck *Hannah Sempler* • Joel McCrea *Ethan Hoyt* • Brian Donlevy *Steely Edwards* • Katharine Stevens [KT Stevens] *Girl biographer* • Thurston Hall *Mr Sempler* • Lloyd Corrigan *Mr Cadwallader* • Etta McDaniel *Delilah* • Frank M Thomas *Senator Knobs* ■ *Dir* William A Wellman • *Scr* WL River, Adela Rogers St John, Seena Owen, from the story *The Human Side* by Vina Delmar

The Great McGinty ★★★★

Comedy 1940 · US · BW · 83mins

Don't be put off just because this is a comedy about American politics with no star names. Writer Preston Sturges persuaded Paramount to let him make his directing debut for a ten-dollar fee, and the result is this delicious study in comic irony. It's the story of an Irishman who rises through a corrupt party machine to become governor of a state, then is ruined in a crazy minute of honesty. Proving as brilliant a director as he was a writer, Sturges won the Oscar for best original screenplay and opened the doors for other writers such as Billy Wilder to direct their work. Brian Donlevy attacks his role with gusto, while supporting players shine in every scene. AE

Brian Donlevy *Dan McGinty* • Muriel Angelus *Catherine McGinty* • Akim Tamiroff *Boss* • Allyn Joslyn *George* • William Demarest *Politician* • Louis Jean Heydt *Thompson* • Arthur Hoyt *Mayor Tillinghast* ■ *Dir/Scr* Preston Sturges

The Great McGonagall ★ 15

Comedy 1974 · UK · Colour · 84mins

Whatever the shortcomings of the Victorian versifier – the unemployed Scot who was determined to be the Queen's laureate – he didn't deserve this snide, incoherent jeering. Comedians Spike Milligan and Peter Sellers lead with the machetes, carving fun out of a simple-minded man whose verses didn't scan and whose thoughts were banal, but it's the mutual admiration society of the principals that scores its own goal. TH

Spike Milligan *William McGonagall* • Peter Sellers *Queen Victoria* • Julia Foster *Mrs McGonagall* ■ *Dir* Joseph McGrath • *Scr* Spike Milligan, Joseph McGrath

The Great Mr Handel ★★★ U

Biographical drama
1942 · UK · Colour · 98mins

Clearly intended as a treatise on patriotism at the height of the Second World War, this handsome biopic explores how someone of German extraction could become a true Briton. Heading a capable supporting cast, Wilfrid Lawson is imposing in the title role as he atones for his squabbles with both Church and State by composing *The Messiah*. DP

Wilfrid Lawson *George Frideric Handel* • Elizabeth Allan *Mrs Cibber* • Malcolm Keen *Lord Chesterfield* • Michael Shepley *Sir Charles Marsham* • Max Kirby *Frederick, Prince of Wales* • Hay Petrie *Phineas* ■ *Dir* Norman Walter • *Scr* L DuGarde Peach, Gerald Elliott, Victor MacClure [Victor McClure]

The Great Moment ★★★★

Biographical drama 1944 · US · BW · 80mins

How do you make an entertaining tribute to the forgotten dentist who first discovered the anaesthetic? The great comedy writer/director Preston Sturges had the answer, but audiences didn't want to know, giving him his one flop among a string of hits. Without sacrificing scientific detail, Sturges embellishes the situations with valid slapstick humour, conveying the horror of an amputation before anaesthesia through the fainting of an unprepared onlooker (William Demarest). According to Sturges, the great moment in the life of the dentist, sensitively portrayed by Joel McCrea, is not his discovery, but a gesture of great humanity which ends the film on an upbeat note. AE

Joel McCrea *WTG Morton* • Betty Field *Elizabeth Morton* • Harry Carey *Prof Warren* • William Demarest *Eben Frost* • Louis Jean Heydt *Dr Horace Wells* • Julius Tannen *Dr Jackson* • Edwin Maxwell *VP medical society* • Porter Hall *President Pierce* ■ *Dir* Preston Sturges • *Scr* Preston Sturges, from a biography by Rene Fulop-Miller

The Great Muppet Caper ★★★ U

Musical comedy 1981 · US · Colour · 97mins

Although crammed full of big names, this second Muppet movie is something of a disappointment. The parodies of the Busby Berkeley-esque production numbers are artfully staged and the byplay between Charles Grodin and Miss Piggy is charged with comic eroticism. But there are too many scenes that seem to be merely passing the time until the plot is ready to resume rolling. Kermit, Fozzie and Gonzo are particularly ill-served as the reporters investigating the theft of Diana Rigg's diamond. DP

Jim Henson *Kermit the Frog/Rowlf/Dr Teeth/Waldorf* • Frank Oz *Miss Piggy/Fozzie Bear/Animal* • Dave Goelz *Gonzo/Chester Rat/Bill the Frog/Zoot* • Diana Rigg *Lady Holiday* • Charles Grodin *Nicky Holiday* • John Cleese *Neville* • Robert Morley *British gentleman* • Peter Ustinov *Truck driver* • Jack Warden *Editor* • Peter Falk *Tramp* ■ *Dir* Jim Henson • *Scr* Tom Patchett, Jay Tarses, Jerry Juhl, Jack Rose

The Great Northfield Minnesota Raid ★★★

Western 1972 · US · Colour · 91mins

Yet another foray into American folk-hero territory, in this case the bank heist by the Jesse James gang. It lacks pace but looks so purposefully authentic that you expect the brown-hued edges to curl like ancient photographs. Directed by Philip Kaufman, the film boasts Robert Duvall and Cliff Robertson in the leading roles of Jesse James and Cole Younger. Robertson's moody antiheroism is at one with the rain-soaked Northfield town in this, one of the first of the revisionist westerns. TH. Contains violence, swearing and nudity.

Cliff Robertson *Cole Younger* • Robert Duvall *Jesse James* • Luke Askew *Jim Younger* • RG Armstrong *Clell Miller* • Dana Elcar *Allen* • Donald Moffat *Manning* • John Pearce *Frank James* ■ *Dir/Scr* Philip Kaufman

The Great O'Malley ★

Drama 1937 · US · BW · 71mins

Humphrey Bogart received his first star billing for this terrible Warner Bros programmer, a grotesquely sentimentalised crime melodrama in which slum-dweller Bogart is forced into criminality because his daughter is crippled. Pat O'Brien is the Irish cop on Bogart's case. Bogart's daughter is played by a scene-stealing Sybill Jason, who also becomes a victim of O'Brien's intractability. AT

Pat O'Brien *James Aloysius O'Malley* • Humphrey Bogart *John Phillips* • Frieda Inescort *Mrs Phillips* • Henry O'Neill *Attorney for defence* • Hobart Cavanaugh *Pinky Holden* • Mary Gordon *Mrs O'Malley* • Sybil Jason *Barbara Phillips* ■ *Dir* William Dieterle • *Scr* Milton Krims, Tom Reed, from the story *The Making of O'Malley* by Gerald Beaumont

The Great Outdoors ★★ PG

Comedy 1988 · US · Colour · 86mins

John Hughes's attempt to re-create the success of the previous year's adult comedy *Planes, Trains and Automobiles* backfires with this routine outing. John Candy, the obnoxious one in the aforementioned *Planes*, gets to be the nice guy this time around, finding himself stuck on vacation with his appalling brother-in-law Dan Aykroyd. Hughes's script is a mechanical retread of past glories and director Howard Deutch fails to bring much inspiration to the slapstick. Look out for a pre-stardom Annette Bening in a supporting role. JF DVD

Dan Aykroyd *Roman Craig* • John Candy *Chet Ripley* • Stephanie Faracy *Connie Ripley* • Annette Bening *Kate Craig* • Chris Young *Buck Ripley* • Ian Giatti *Ben Ripley* • Hilary Gordon *Cara Craig* • Rebecca Gordon *Mara Craig* ■ *Dir* Howard Deutch • *Scr* John Hughes

The Great Race ★★★★ U

Comedy 1965 · US · Colour · 153mins

Jack Lemmon sports one of the most dastardly moustaches this side of a Victorian melodrama to compete against clean-cut good guy Tony Curtis in a 1908 automobile race from New York to Paris. Director Blake Edwards pays homage to the cartoon characterisation and slapstick wackiness of silent comedies in this stylised and overlong, but lavish and entertaining comedy extravaganza. Lemmon overplays to particular comic effect as the hiss-worthy villain, and the score is by Henry Mancini. PF

Tony Curtis *The Great Leslie* • Jack Lemmon *Professor Fate/Prince Hapnik* • Natalie Wood *Maggie DuBois* • Peter Falk *Max* • Keenan Wynn *Hezekiah* • Arthur O'Connell *Henry Goodbody* • Vivian Vance *Hester Goodbody* • Dorothy Provine *Lily Olay* ■ *Dir* Blake Edwards • *Scr* Arthur Ross, from a story by Arthur Ross, Blake Edwards

The Great Rock 'n' Roll Swindle ★★★★ 18

Drama documentary
1979 · UK · Colour · 100mins

The rise and fall of the Sex Pistols is charted in director Julien Temple's docu-fiction account of the punk era in all its anarchic glory. Using backstage interviews, concert clips, newsreels, staged sequences and animation footage from their aborted vehicle *Who Killed Bambi?* (which "King Leer" Russ Meyer was set to direct), a fascinating and remarkably honest slice of rock history emerges from the swirling mass of material. All the relevant bases are touched on including *God Save the Queen*, the jaunt to Rio to visit Great Train Robber Ronnie Biggs, Nancy Spungen's manslaughter and Sid Vicious's death, with manager guru Malcolm McLaren shown as the ultimate manipulator of the masses and, on the evidence here, fully earning the title "King Con". AJ

Malcolm McLaren *The Embezzler* • Sid Vicious *The Gimmick* • Johnny Rotten [John Lydon] *The Collaborator* • Steve Jones *The Crook* • Paul Cook *The Tea-maker* • Ronald Biggs *The Exile* ■ *Dir/Scr* Julien Temple

The Great St Louis Bank Robbery ★★

Crime 1959 · US · BW · 89mins

Only the name of its leading actor rescues this minor hold-up picture from obscurity. The rest of the cast and crew on this production, based on the story of a real heist, never made it to the big time. The young Steve McQueen, pre-Hollywood stardom, shows his mettle as the youngster driving the getaway car for three professional criminals. The build-up to the robbery is rather protracted, but the climax is effectively handled. AE

Steve McQueen *George Fowler* • David Clarke *Gino* • Crahan Denton *John Egan* • Molly McCarthy *Ann* ■ *Dir* Charles Guggenheim, John Stix • *Scr* Richard T Heffron

The Great St Trinian's Train Robbery ★★ U

Comedy 1966 · UK · Colour · 90mins

Although Frank Launder couldn't resist the temptation of returning to his old stamping ground in 1980's *The Wildcats of St Trinian's*, this should have been the last in the film series (that began with *The Belles of St Trinian's*) based on Ronald Searle's ghoulish schoolgirls, as it had clearly run out of steam. Frankie Howerd's limitations as a film actor are all too apparent in this mix of vulgar comedy and Swinging Sixties satire. DP

Frankie Howerd *Alphonse Askett* • Reg Varney *Gilbert* • Desmond Walter-Ellis *Leonard Edwards* • Cyril Chamberlain *Maxie* • Stratford Johns *The Voice* • Richard Wattis *Bassett* • Dora Bryan *Amber Spottiswood* • George Cole *Flash Harry* ■ *Dir* Frank Launder, Sidney Gilliat • *Scr* Frank Launder, Ivor Herbert, from the drawings by Ronald Searle

The Great Santini ★★★ PG

Drama 1979 · US · Colour · 110mins

This adaptation of Pat Conroy's novel has a title that suggests a story about an escapologist or a racing driver is in the offing. In fact, it tells of a retired fighter pilot called Bull Meechum (nicknamed "Santini"), whose drunkenness makes life a misery for his wife (Blythe Danner) and children. Like *The Prince of Tides*, also based on a Conroy original, it's a thick slice of Deep South angst and sour mash philosophy in which drink turns dialogue into poetry. But Robert Duvall is magnificent in the lead role and earned an Oscar nomination for his pains, as did Michael O'Keefe. AT

Robert Duvall *Bull Meechum* • Blythe Danner *Lillian Meechum* • Michael O'Keefe *Ben Meechum* • Stan Shaw *Toomer Smalls* • Lisa Jane Persky *Mary Anne Meechum* • Julie Anne Haddock *Karen Meechum* • Brian Andrews *Matthew Meechum* • Theresa Merritt *Arrabelle Smalls* ■ *Dir* Lewis John Carlino • *Scr* Lewis John Carlino, from the novel by Pat Conroy

The Great Scout & Cathouse Thursday ★★

Comedy western
1976 · US · Colour · 105mins

Set in Colorado in 1908, this is a coarse, crass and calamitous misjudgement. Yet it's worth watching to witness the battle of wills between Lee Marvin and Oliver Reed, in which the former strains every sinew to stop himself lapsing into caricatured mugging, while the latter tempts him to stray with an exhibition of unabashed showboating. Caught in the middle are Robert Culp, as the politician who once gypped the feuding duo, and Kay Lenz, as the hooker who takes a fancy to Marvin. DP. Contains violence and swearing.

Lee Marvin *Sam Longwood* • Oliver Reed *Joe Knox* • Robert Culp *Jack Colby* • Elizabeth Ashley *Nancy Sue* • Strother Martin *Billy* • Sylvia Miles *Mike* • Kay Lenz *Thursday* ■ *Dir* Don Taylor • *Scr* Richard Shapiro

The Great Silence ★★★ 15

Spaghetti western
1967 · It/Fr · Colour · 100mins

What do you get when you cross an Italian director with a German villain and a French hero? The answer is a thumping good spaghetti western from director Sergio Corbucci. Klaus Kinski stars as a bounty hunter waiting to pick off the outlaws hiding in the Sierra Madre as the severe winter of 1896

U = SUITABLE FOR ALL Uc = SUITABLE FOR ALL, ESPECIALLY FOR YOUNG CHILDREN (VIDEO ONLY) PG = PARENTAL GUIDANCE

drives them into the border villages. Mute gunfighter Jean-Louis Trintignant stands in his way, amid stunning shots of the snow-covered mountains. DP. Italian dialogue dubbed into English. Contains violence. DVD

Jean-Louis Trintignant *Silenzio* • Klaus Kinski *Tigrero* • Vonetta McGee *Pauline* ■ *Dir* Sergio Corbucci • *Scr* Sergio Corbucci, Vittoriano Petrilli, Mario Amendola, Bruno Corbucci • *Music* Ennio Morricone

The Great Sinner ★★

Romantic drama 1949 · US · BW · 109mins

Fyodor Dostoyevsky's *The Gambler* has defeated many a film-maker this side of the Russian border. In MGM's lushly upholstered version of the tale, two of the world's best-looking stars, Gregory Peck and Ava Gardner, are seemingly without a clue as to what they're supposed to be thinking or doing under the heavy hand of director Robert Siodmak. Peck looks none too comfortable in the period clothes, though Gardner's aristocrat is ravishing, sumptuously gowned and photographed. Hardly watchable. TS

Gregory Peck *Fyodor Dostoyevsky* • Ava Gardner *Pauline Ostrovski* • Melvyn Douglas *Armand Le Glasse* • Walter Huston *General Ostrovski* • Ethel Barrymore *Granny* • Frank Morgan *Aristide Pitard* • Agnes Moorehead *Emma Getzel* • Ludwig Stossel *Hotel manager* ■ *Dir* Robert Siodmak • *Scr* Ladislas Fodor, Christopher Isherwood, from a story by Ladislas Fodor, Rene Fulop-Miller, from the story *The Gambler* by Fyodor Dostoyevsky

The Great Sioux Massacre ★★ U

Historical western
1965 · US · Colour · 92mins

Sidney Salkow directs this virtual remake of his own *Sitting Bull*, made in 1954. One of the cinema's periodic examinations of Custer's Last Stand, this B western re-creates the famous Battle of the Little Bighorn. Philip Carey plays Custer as an idealist who is initially outspoken in his defence of north American Indian rights. Later he is forced to compromise these ideals in order to further his political ambitions in Washington. AT

Joseph Cotten *Major Reno* • Darren McGavin *Captain Benton* • Philip Carey *Col George Armstrong Custer* • Julie Sommars *Caroline Reno* • Nancy Kovack *Libbie Custer* • John Matthews *Dakota* • Michael Pate *Sitting Bull* • Iron Eyes Cody *Crazy Horse* ■ *Dir* Sidney Salkow • *Scr* Fred C Dobbs, from a story by Sidney Salkow, Marvin Gluck

The Great Sioux Uprising ★★ U

Western 1953 · US · Colour · 80mins

This western brings a fresh perspective to a familiar horse-rustling scenario. Jeff Chandler plays a new veterinarian in town, who discovers that prominent horse trader Lyle Bettger is stealing animals from the Sioux and selling them to the army. Chandler finds himself caught between the tribe and the local ranchers, while female lead Faith Domergue looks on. Don't be misled by the title: there's an attempt to rouse the Sioux, but no great uprising. AE

Jeff Chandler *Jonathan Westgate* • Faith Domergue *Joan Britton* • Lyle Bettger *Stephen Cook* • John War Eagle *Red Cloud* • Stephen Chase (1) *Major McKay* • Stacy Harris *Uriah* ■ *Dir* Lloyd Bacon • *Scr* Melvin Levy, J Robert Bren, Gladys Atwater, from a story by J Robert Bren, Gladys Atwater

The Great Smokey Roadblock ★★ 15

Action adventure 1977 · US · Colour · 85mins

Hard on the wheels of *Smokey and the Bandit* came this clapped-out vehicle for Henry Fonda, in which he's an ageing trucker making one last bid at a journey before being overtaken by his finance company. The oddballs rolling along with him hold some interest (a load of evicted prostitutes and Robert Englund out of *A Nightmare on Elm Street* make-up), but the decrepit pace eventually makes this a vehicle only a scrapyard could love. TH [video]

Henry Fonda *Elegant John* • Eileen Brennan *Penelope* • Robert Englund *Beebo* • John Byner *Disc Jockey* • Austin Pendleton *Guido* • Susan Sarandon *Ginny* • Melanie Mayron *Lulu* • Marya Small *Alice* ■ *Dir/Scr* John Leone

The Great Texas Dynamite Chase ★★★

Crime drama 1976 · US · Colour · 88mins

Director Michael Pressman made his feature debut with this typically raucous offering (originally entitled *Dynamite Women*) from Roger Corman's New World company. Former *Playboy* model Claudia Jennings's feisty fugitive and Jocelyn Jones's bored bankteller are the prototype Thelma and Louise, but audiences will be divided about the validity of the "can't beat 'em, join 'em" morality, especially when the comic capers take on a darker tone. DP

Claudia Jennings *Candy Morgan* • Jocelyn Jones *Ellie Jo Turner* • Johnny Crawford *Slim* • Chris Pennock [Christopher Pennock] *Jake* • Tara Strohmeier *Pam Morgan* ■ *Dir* Michael Pressman • *Scr* David Kirkpatrick, Mark Rosin

The Great Train Robbery ★★★

Silent crime western 1903 · US · BW · 12mins

Often hailed as the cornerstone of the western genre, Edwin S Porter's 13-sequence adaptation of Scott Marble's heist thriller is also one of the most significant films in the development of screen storytelling. Among its many initiatives was the use of a screenplay, descriptive captions, panning shots and back-projected footage. But it's most important contribution to film grammar was the introduction of continuity editing, in which the action cross-cuts between parallel events to increase the narrative tension. Moreover, it also culminated in the iconic shot of bandit George Barnes firing his gun directly at the camera. A pivotal picture in cinema history. DP

George Barnes *Bandit* • Gilbert M Anderson *Bandit* • Frank Hanaway *Bandit* • Tom London *Engineer* • Mary Snow *Little girl* • AC Abadie *Sheriff* • Walter Cameron *Sheriff* ■ *Dir* Edwin S Porter • *Scr* Edwin S Porter, from a story by Scott Marble

The Great Waldo Pepper ★★★ PG

Drama 1975 · US · Colour · 102mins

Scripted by William Goldman, the story of the former First World War pilot who lives on false deeds and reckless stunts should have provided biting insights into the nature of heroism and Hollywood's shameless predilection for myth-making. Instead, we get a self-pitying tale of a dreamer who has out-lived both his times and his usefulness. Robert Redford effortlessly portrays Pepper's superficial charm, but lacks the depth to convey his torment. A missed opportunity, though the aerial sequences are stunning. DP [video]

Robert Redford *Waldo Pepper* • Bo Svenson *Axel Olsson* • Bo Brundin *Ernst Kessler* • Susan Sarandon *Mary Beth* • Geoffrey Lewis *Newton Potts* • Edward Herrmann *Ezra Stiles* ■ *Dir* George Roy Hill • *Scr* William Goldman, from a story by George Roy Hill

A Great Wall ★★★ PG

Drama 1985 · US/Chi · Colour · 95mins

Peter Wang caught the eye in Wayne Wang's *Chan Is Missing*. It's hardly surprising, therefore, that his debut as actor/director should share so many of the themes of his namesake's delightful *Dim Sum*. But instead of exploring how Chinese emigrants cope with life in America, this film focuses on the culture shock experienced by a family of first generation American Chinese during a visit to the old country. Avoiding controversial issues, this is essentially a guided tour of Beijing with some gentle drama thrown in. DP. In English and Mandarin with subtitles. [video]

Wang Xiao *Liu Yida* • Li Qinqin *Lili Chao* • Xiu Jian *Yu* • Sharon Iwai *Grace Fang* • Peter Wang *Leo Fang* ■ *Dir* Peter Wang • *Scr* Peter Wang, Shirley Sun

The Great Waltz ★★★★ U

Biographical drama 1938 · US · BW · 103mins

In this splendid MGM retelling of the life of Johann Strauss, romantic charmer Fernand Gravet stars as Strauss, with the composer here neglecting his wife (portrayed by the regrettably forgotten double Oscar-winner Luise Rainer) for an opera singer played by Miliza Korjus. Style is everything here, and cameraman Joseph Ruttenberg won the Oscar for best cinematography. But who directed this opulent extravaganza? The movie is credited to Frenchman Julien Duvivier, but he left about halfway through, and others, including WS Van Dyke II and Victor Fleming, replaced him. Josef von Sternberg took charge for the sumptuous finale. TS

Luise Rainer *Poldi Vogelhuber* • Fernand Gravet *Johann Strauss* • Miliza Korjus *Carla Donner* • Hugh Herbert *Hofbauer* • Lionel Atwill *Count Hohenfried* • Curt Bois *Kienzl* • Leonid Kinskey *Dudelman* ■ *Dir* Julien Duvivier • *Scr* Samuel Hoffenstein, Walter Reisch, from a story by Gottfried Reinhardt

The Great Waltz ★★ U

Musical 1972 · US · Colour · 133mins

Andrew L Stone followed up his Grieg biopic *Song of Norway* with a retread of the familiar saga of Johann Strauss. This version benefits from colour, Panavision and – predictably – some of the most beautiful waltzes this side of heaven. Horst Buchholz makes a valiant effort as young Johann, and there's a welcome on-screen appearance by Mary Costa, the singing voice of Princess Aurora in Walt Disney's animated *Sleeping Beauty*. TS

Horst Buchholz *Johann Strauss Jr* • Mary Costa *Jetty Treffz* • Rossano Brazzi *Baron Tedesco* • Nigel Patrick *Johann Strauss Sr* • Yvonne Mitchell *Anna Strauss* • James Faulkner *Josef Strauss* • Vicki Woolf *Lili Weyl* ■ *Dir/Scr* Andrew L Stone

The Great War ★★★★

First World War comedy drama
1959 · Fr/It · BW · 118mins

Alberto Sordi appeared in a number of films in 1959, but none as entertaining as this tragicomic Italian variation on that old Hollywood favourite, *What Price Glory?* Winning both the Golden Lion at Venice and the best director award for Mario Monicelli, this irreverent romp follows Sordi and fellow conscript Vittorio Gassman as they seek to distance themselves from the living hell of the trenches during the First World War. But whether squabbling over prostitute Silvana Mangano or enduring bungling officers, they make an irresistible team. DP. An Italian language film.

Vittorio Gassman *Giovanni Busacca* • Alberto Sordi *Oreste Jacovacci* • Silvana Mangano *Constantina* • Folco Lulli *Bordin* • Bernard Blier *Capitano Castelli* • Romolo Valli *Tenente Gallina* • Vittorio Sanipoli *Maggiore Venturi* • Nicola Arigliano *Giardino* • Mario Valdemarin *Aspirante Loquenzi* ■ *Dir* Mario Monicelli • *Scr* Mario Monicelli, Luciano Vincenzoni, Agenore Incrocci, Furio Scarpelli, from a story by Luciano Vincenzoni

The Great White Hope ★★★ 15

Biographical drama
1970 · US · Colour · 98mins

This heavyweight boxing fable, based on the real-life decline and fall of turn-of-the-century black champion Jack Johnson, has a knockout performance by James Earl Jones, but it only just gets by on points as drama and is undermined by an early form of political correctness. Director Martin Ritt wears his conscience too obviously on his sleeve in showing the bigotry that destroys Jones when he falls for a white woman (Jane Alexander), but all is forgiven with Jones's endearing mix of rage and gullibility. TH [video]

James Earl Jones *Jack Jefferson* • Jane Alexander *Eleanor* • Lou Gilbert *Goldie* • Joel Fluellen *Tick* • Chester Morris *Pop Weaver* • Robert Webber *Dixon* • Marlene Warfield *Clara* • RG Armstrong *Cap'n Dan* • Hal Holbrook *Cameron* ■ *Dir* Martin Ritt • *Scr* Howard Sackler, from his play

The Great White Hype ★★★ 15

Sports comedy drama
1996 · US · Colour · 86mins

This boxing comedy – a brave attempt at satirising the unsatirisable – boasts a heavy-hitting cast that includes boisterous Damon Wayans, sinister Samuel L Jackson and a typically oddball Jeff Goldblum. Wayans is the black heavyweight champion of the world, who has beaten all there is to beat and is seeking new opponents. Step forward fair-skinned rocker Terry Conklin, who once beat Wayans as an amateur, but has since given up the fight game. Jackson persuades him to go back into training again. There are some sharp observations among the many slapstick moments. JF [video] DVD

Samuel L Jackson *Reverend Fred Sultan* • Jeff Goldblum *Mitchell Kane* • Peter Berg *Terry Conklin* • Jon Lovitz *Sol* • Damon Wayans *James "the Grim Reaper" Roper* • Corbin Bernsen *Peter Prince* • Richard "Cheech" Marin *Julio Escobar* ■ *Dir* Reginald Hudlin • *Scr* Tony Hendra, Ron Shelton

The Great Ziegfeld ★★★★ U

Musical 1936 · US · BW · 168mins

This sumptuously mounted MGM musical biography of Broadway's most flamboyant showman is perhaps slightly too long for today's tastes, but it thrilled cinema-goers at the time and won the best film Oscar. Luise Rainer also won the first of two successive Academy Awards as best actress for her performance here as Ziegfeld's wife, Anna Held (she won the following year for *The Good Earth*), and her famous telephone scene is a lesson in screen acting. Suave William Powell is the Great Flo, a role he reprised eight years later in *Ziegfeld Follies*. TS DVD

William Powell *Florenz Ziegfeld* • Luise Rainer *Anna Held* • Myrna Loy *Billie Burke* • Frank Morgan *Billings* • Reginald Owen *Sampston* • Nat Pendleton *Sandow* • Virginia Bruce *Audrey Lane* • Ernest Cossart *Sidney* ■ *Dir* Robert Z Leonard • *Scr* William Anthony McGuire

The Greatest ★★★ PG

Biographical drama
1977 · US/UK · Colour · 97mins

Who else but Muhammad Ali could have starred in this biopic? The charismatic boxer takes to the screen with ease, dancing through his early life as Cassius Clay before reliving the 1975 "Rumble in the Jungle" when he regained his world heavyweight title by

G

defeating George Forman. Ali's induction into the Nation of Islam, his controversial evasion of the Vietnam draft and his ban from the ring is also given lengthy, if not objective treatment. Rather than restaging the fights, the film sensibly uses archive footage. AT DVD

Muhammad Ali • Ernest Borgnine *Angelo Dundee* • John Marley *Dr Pacheco* • Lloyd Haynes *Herbert Muhammad* • Robert Duvall *Bill McDonald* • Ben Johnson *Hollis* • James Earl Jones *Malcolm X* ■ *Dir* Tom Gries • *Scr* Ring Lardner Jr, from the book *The Greatest: My Own Story* by Muhammad Ali, Herbert Muhammad, Richard Durham

The Greatest Show on Earth ★★★★ U

Epic drama 1952 · US · Colour · 146mins

This is, perhaps, not as great as its title would have us believe, though it did win director Cecil B DeMille an Oscar. On display is a jumbo-sized package of all the clichés that money can buy, as circus owner Charlton Heston strives to control the untamed emotions of Betty Hutton, Cornel Wilde and Gloria Grahame. James Stewart gives the most original performance, playing a clown who never takes off his make-up. As usual, DeMille megaphones his direction, but this is still marvellous entertainment. TH

Charlton Heston *Brad* • James Stewart *Buttons, a clown* • Betty Hutton *Holly* • Dorothy Lamour *Phyllis* • Cornel Wilde *Sebastian* • Gloria Grahame *Angel* • Lyle Bettger *Klaus* • Lawrence Tierney *Henderson* • Henry Wilcoxon *Detective* • John Kellogg *Harry* • Rosemary Dvorak *Rosemary* • Bob Hope *Spectator* • Bing Crosby *Spectator* ■ *Dir* Cecil B DeMille • *Scr* Fredric M Frank, Barré Lyndon, Theodore St John, from a story by Theodore St John, Fredric M Frank, Frank Cavett

The Greatest Story Ever Told ★★★ U

Biblical drama 1965 · US · Colour · 190mins

George Stevens's epic re-telling of the life of Christ is a monumental achievement, given tremendous power by Max von Sydow's masterful portrayal of Jesus. Unfortunately, the film is fatally compromised by its cumbersome length and the casting of key players in every role. While the likes of Carroll Baker and Sidney Poitier work well, the inclusion of Pat Boone and John Wayne damages the fabric. It's a remarkable movie nonetheless, considering the fact that Stevens fell ill and the great David Lean took over. TS DVD

Max von Sydow *Jesus* • Dorothy McGuire *Mary* • José Ferrer *Herod Antipas* • Charlton Heston *John the Baptist* • Sidney Poitier *Simon of Cyrene* • Telly Savalas *Pontius Pilate* • John Wayne *Centurion* • Shelley Winters *Woman of no name* • Martin Landau *Caiaphas* • Claude Rains *Herod the Great* • Carroll Baker *Veronica* • David McCallum *Judas Iscariot* • Robert Loggia *Joseph* • Roddy McDowall *Matthew* • Angela Lansbury *Claudia* • Donald Pleasence *Dark hermit* • Sal Mineo *Uriah* • Pat Boone *Young man at the tomb* ■ *Dir* George Stevens • *Scr* George Stevens, James Lee Barrett, from the book by Fulton Oursler and radio scripts by Henry Denker

Greed ★★★★★ PG

Classic silent drama
1925 · US · BW · 134mins

This is the epic that ensured that director Erich von Stroheim was, ever after, seen as a genius who could not be trusted. Made over two years, this was planned to last ten hours, but MGM executives took it away from its creator and cut it down to a more commercial size. As an exercise in vicious irony, it tells the story of an unqualified dentist (Gibson Gowland), engaged to ZaSu Pitts, who becomes a lottery winner but then refuses to spend any of the money. For von Stroheim, human beings were just predatory animals and the moral squalor is never more evident than in the wedding scenes. His obsession with realistic detail reached its zenith during the final scenes in Death Valley, where the actors suffered hugely for the director's art. TH

Gibson Gowland *McTeague* • ZaSu Pitts *Trina* • Jean Hersholt *Marcus Schouler* • Chester Conklin *Mr Sieppe* • Sylvia Ashton *Mrs Sieppe* • Oscar Gottell *Sieppe Twin* • Otto Gottell *Sieppe Twin* • Frank Hayes *Old Grannis* ■ *Dir* Erich von Stroheim • *Scr* Erich von Stroheim, June Mathis, from the novel *McTeague* by Frank Norris • *Cinematographer* William Daniels [William H Daniels], Ben F Reynolds

The Greed of William Hart ★★

Crime melodrama 1948 · UK · BW · 74mins

Tod Slaughter gives another of his outrageously over-the-top performances in this low-budget British horror picture, based on the real-life exploits of the infamous 19th-century grave-robbers, Burke and Hare. Henry Oscar is equally larger-than-life as his partner in crime. The melodramatic style of the piece verges on the comical nowadays, but, taken on its own terms, the sum of the parts verges on the adequate. PF

Tod Slaughter *William Hart* • Henry Oscar *Mr Moore* • Jenny Lynn *Helen Moore* • Winifred Melville *Meg Hart* • Patrick Addison *Hugh Alston* • Arnold Bell *Doctor Cox* ■ *Dir* Oswald Mitchell • *Scr* John Gilling

Greedy ★★★ 12

Comedy 1994 · US · Colour · 107mins

In this slightly black comedy, the money-grabbing relatives of ailing millionaire Kirk Douglas become apprehensive when the old boy hires a sexy nurse. Michael J Fox and Nancy Travis are among the vultures awaiting their inheritance, but British director Jonathan Lynn's jibes are neither heartless nor hectic enough to gain a full complement of laughs. Movie buffs will note that the family name is McTeague after Erich von Stroheim's 1925 silent classic *Greed*. TH. Contains swearing and brief nudity.

Michael J Fox *Daniel McTeague* • Kirk Douglas *Uncle Joe McTeague* • Nancy Travis *Robin Hunter* • Olivia D'Abo *Molly Richardson* • Phil Hartman *Frank* • Ed Begley Jr *Carl* • Jere Burns *Glen* ■ *Dir* Jonathan Lynn • *Scr* Lowell Ganz, Babaloo Mandel

The Greek Tycoon ★★ 15

Drama 1978 · US · Colour · 111mins

Glossy tosh of a kind that the TV mini-series has made infamous, this is about the romance between a Greek shipping magnate and an American president's wife – Aristotle Onassis and Jackie Kennedy by any other name. Anthony Quinn and Jacqueline Bisset fill in the characters as best they can, but it's the lush staging that wins the day. British helmer J Lee Thompson directs this sumptuous rubbish. TH. Contains swearing.

Anthony Quinn *Theo Tomasis* • Jacqueline Bisset *Liz Cassidy* • Raf Vallone *Spyros Tomasis* • Edward Albert *Nico Tomasis* • James Franciscus *James Cassidy* • Charles Durning *Michael Russell* ■ *Dir* J Lee Thompson • *Scr* Mort Fine, from a story by Mort Fine, Nico Mastorakis, Win Wells

The Green Berets ★★ PG

War drama 1968 · US · Colour · 136mins

Most of the films made about the American involvement in Vietnam are highly critical and were produced long after the American withdrawal from that shameful conflict. John Wayne, however, saw Vietnam as a new Alamo, staunch Republican that he was, and both starred in and co-directed this flag-waving action adventure, a unique example of auteurism going nowhere. There's no denying the epic sweep of the action scenes, but even for Duke fans this is heavy-going, thick-eared nonsense. TS. Contains violence. DVD

John Wayne *Colonel Mike Kirby* • David Janssen *George Beckworth* • Jim Hutton *Sergeant Petersen* • Aldo Ray *Sergeant Muldoon* • Raymond St Jacques *Doc McGee* • Bruce Cabot *Colonel Morgan* • George Takei *Captain Nim* • Luke Askew *Sergeant Provo* ■ *Dir* John Wayne, Ray Kellogg • *Scr* James Lee Barrett, from the novel by Robin Moore

The Green Butchers ★★★★

Black comedy 2003 · Den · Colour · 95mins

A freak accident sets off an outrageous chain of events in this jet-black Danish comedy. Mads Mikkelsen and Nikolaj Lie Kaas star as mistreated butcher's shop underlings whose decision to establish their own meat emporium seems destined for failure, until they start selling a delicious new type of "chicken". However in true Sweeney Todd-style the succulent cuts have an unlikely source, posing a huge problem for the duo when eager customers demand more. The feature is brilliantly composed, skilfully mining life's cruel absurdities for maximum effect. The leads deliver such appealing performances that their murderous activities are surreal rather than shocking. SF. In Danish with English subtitles.

Mads Mikkelsen *Svend* • Nikolaj Lie Kaas *Bjarne/Eigil* • Line Kruse *Astrid* • Bodil Jorgensen *Tina* • Ole Thestrup *Holger* • Nicolas Bro *Hus Hans* ■ *Dir/Scr* Anders Thomas Jensen

Green Card ★★★ 15

Romantic comedy
1990 · Aus/Fr · Colour · 102mins

Despite being unoriginal, improbable and not as funny as it should be, Gérard Depardieu's much-anticipated English language debut is still an easy-going comedy. Directed by Peter Weir, it has undeniable charm and features two thoroughly engaging performances, with Andie MacDowell winning you over to her initially cold, calculating Manhattanite. Weir is a little heavy-handed with the comic set pieces, but he develops the romance with some care and turns the immigration inquiry into a nail-biting tear-jerker. DP. Contains swearing. DVD

Gérard Depardieu *George Faure* • Andie MacDowell *Brontë Parrish* • Bebe Neuwirth *Lauren Adler* • Gregg Edelman *Phil* • Robert Prosky *Brontë's lawyer* • Jessie Keosian *Mrs Bird* • Ethan Phillips *Gorsky* • Mary Louise Wilson *Mrs Sheehan* ■ *Dir/Scr* Peter Weir

The Green Cockatoo ★

Crime drama 1937 · UK · BW · 63mins

Sometimes even the greatest of talents don't add up to a successful movie. In this case the original story was by Graham Greene, the director was the great production designer William Cameron Menzies and the film was produced by noted director William K Howard. John Mills is miscast as a singer who sets out to avenge the murder of his brother (Robert Newton). A contrived and episodic imitation of a Hollywood gangster melodrama, set during one dark night in Soho. AE

John Mills *Jim Connor* • René Ray *Eileen* • Robert Newton *Dave Connor* • Charles Oliver *Terrell* • Bruce Seton *Madison* • Julian Vedey *Steve* • Allan Jeayes *Inspector* • Frank Atkinson *Butler* ■ *Dir* William Cameron Menzies • *Scr* Edward O Berkman, Arthur Wimperis, from a story by Graham Greene

Green Dolphin Street ★★

Adventure drama 1947 · US · BW · 141mins

Despite its Oscar-winning earthquake, this romantic drama is a dreary and overlong tale of the dark-haired Lana Turner travelling from the Channel Islands to New Zealand to marry businessman Richard Hart, who really desires her sister, played by Donna Reed. Van Heflin is Hart's partner who secretly covets Turner. AE

Lana Turner *Marianne Patourel* • Van Heflin *Timothy Haslam* • Donna Reed *Marguerite Patourel* • Richard Hart *William Ozanne* • Frank Morgan *Dr Edmund* • Edmund Gwenn *Octavius Patourel* • Dame May Whitty *Mother Superior* • Reginald Owen *Captain O'Hara* ■ *Dir* Victor Saville • *Scr* Samson Raphaelson, from a novel by Elizabeth Goudge

Green Fields ★★★

Comedy drama 1937 · US · BW · 105mins

This adaptation of a Yiddish play proved a huge success, despite a lacklustre performance from Michael Goldstein as the scholar who abandons the synagogue in search of truth. Instead, he finds love in the form of Helen Beverly, whose family are feuding with their neighbours over the privilege of hosting a city slicker in their humble home. Noted for its broad comedy, homespun wisdom and pastoral realism, this ranks among the finer non-English-language films produced in the US. DP. In Yiddish with English subtitles.

Michael Goldstein *Levy Yitzchok* • Helen Beverly *Tzineh* • Izidor Casher [Isidore Cashier] *David Noich* • Anna Appel *Rochel* • Max Vodnoy *Alkuneh* ■ *Dir* Edgar G Ulmer, Jacob Ben-Ami • *Scr* Peretz Hirshbein [Peretz Hirschbein], George G Moskov, from the play *Grine Felder* by Peretz Hirshbein [Peretz Hirschbein]

Green Fire ★★★ U

Romantic drama
1954 · US · Colour · 100mins

This glossy MGM adventure co-stars tanned Stewart Granger and sleek Grace Kelly, who were arguably the best-looking couple in movies since Vivien Leigh and Robert Taylor in *Waterloo Bridge*. In its day, this romp was accused of wasting Kelly's talents, but she's actually well cast as the plantation owner who falls for tough emerald miner Granger, and their love scenes together sizzle. The plot's a load of old hokum about slimy Murvyn Vye trying to steal Granger's emeralds, but there are some fine set pieces. TS

Stewart Granger *Rian Mitchell* • Grace Kelly *Catherine Knowland* • Paul Douglas *Vic Leonard* • John Ericson *Donald Knowland* • Murvyn Vye *El Moro* • José Torvay *Manuel* • Robert Tafur *Father Ripero* ■ *Dir* Andrew Marton • *Scr* Ivan Goff, Ben Roberts

Green for Danger ★★★★

Comedy thriller 1946 · UK · BW · 90mins

This is the kind of brisk, bright and thoroughly engaging entertainment that the British film industry has, sadly, forgotten how to make. But, then again, there are no more Alastair Sims to transform a passage of jovial banter into a moment of nail-biting suspense simply by slowing that melancholy Scottish accent and lowering those expressive oyster eyes. Gone, too, are such expert character actors as Leo Genn, whose ability to portray heroes and villains alike deepened the mystery in whodunnits such as this one, in which a patient is murdered on the operating table. Sidney Gilliat directs with a deliciously dark wit. DP

Alastair Sim *Inspector Cockrill* • Sally Gray *Nurse Linley* • Trevor Howard *Dr Barney Barnes* • Rosamund John *Nurse Esther Sanson* • Leo Genn *Mr Eden* • Judy Campbell *Sister Marion Bates* • Megs Jenkins *Nurse*

Woods • Moore Marriott *Joe Higgins* ■ *Dir* Sidney Gilliat • *Scr* Sidney Gilliat, Claude Guerney, from a novel by Christianna Brand

The Green Goddess ★

Adventure 1930 · US · BW · 80mins

George Arliss portrays a wily Rajah with a grudge against the British, who holds three Brits captive after they are fortunate enough to survive a plane crash. In its time, this was well received and hugely successful – Arliss gained a best actor Academy Award nomination (and won that same year for his performance in *Disraeli*). Be warned, though: the restrictions of early sound film-making, the stilted acting and the hoary melodramatic plot make this virtually unwatchable. AE

George Arliss *The Rajah* • HB Warner *Maj Crespin* • Alice Joyce *Lucilla Crespin* • Ralph Forbes *Doctor Traherne* • David Tearle *High temple priest* • Reginald Sheffield *Lt Cardew* ■ *Dir* Alfred E Green • *Scr* Julien Josephson, from the play by William Archer

Green Grass of Wyoming ★★ U

Drama 1948 · US · Colour · 84mins

Winding up the Flicka trilogy, this is yet another "how to do it" horsey picture, this time offering an insider's view of the highly competitive sport of trotting. Even though cinematographer Charles Clarke was nominated for an Oscar, it is comfortably the weakest of the series, eschewing wide-eyed innocence for a *Romeo and Juliet*-style romance between Peggy Cummins and Robert Arthur, respectively niece and son of implacable trotting rivals Charles Coburn and Lloyd Nolan. DP

Peggy Cummins *Carey Greenway* • Charles Coburn *Beaver* • Robert Arthur *Ken* • Lloyd Nolan *Rob McLaughlin* • Burl Ives *Gus* • Robert Adler *Joe* • Will Wright *Jake* ■ *Dir* Louis King • *Scr* Martin Berkeley, from the novel by Mary O'Hara

Green Grow the Rushes ★★ U

Comedy 1951 · UK · BW · 88mins

In his last home-grown picture before joining 20th Century-Fox, Richard Burton plays the leader of a gang of brandy smugglers in a nondescript and shameless reworking of Ealing's *Whisky Galore!* It was hardly a memorable parting gift: Burton was never an accomplished comedian and he struggles to make anything of his thin ration of jokes. Roger Livesey fares little better as the skipper whose activities have attracted the attention of three less-than-wise men from the ministry. DP

Roger Livesey *Captain Biddle* • Honor Blackman *Meg* • Richard Burton *Hammond* • Frederick Leister *Colonel Gill* • John Salew *Finch* • Colin Gordon *Fisherwick* • Geoffrey Keen *Prudhoe* • Cyril Smith *Hewitt* • Vida Hope *Polly* • Eliot Makeham *Urquhart* ■ *Dir* Derek Twist • *Scr* Howard Clewes, Derek Twist, from a novel by Howard Clewes

Green Hell ★

Adventure 1939 · US · BW · 84mins

There's a good half hour of hilarity to be had in this famously ludicrous jungle melodrama before tedium takes over. Although capably staged in studio sets by James Whale and well enough cast, it is made unendurable by the dialogue and situations. As Vincent Price once said, "About five of the worst pictures ever made are all in this one picture." AE

Douglas Fairbanks Jr *Keith Brandon* • Joan Bennett *Stephanie Richardson* • John Howard (1) *Hal Scott* • George Sanders *Forrester* • Vincent Price *David Richardson* • Alan Hale *Dr Loren* • George Bancroft *Tex Morgan* • Ray Mala *Mala* ■ *Dir* James Whale • *Scr* Frances Marion, Harry Hervey, from a story by Frances Marion

The Green Helmet ★★ U

Sports drama 1960 · US · BW · 88mins

Motor sport continues to be a frustratingly elusive subject for film-makers. Thus, a cameo from three-time champion Jack Brabham is the main reason for watching this undistinguished horse-power opera. The gradual disintegration of second-rate racer Bill Travers rarely gets out of low gear thanks to Michael Forlong's pedestrian direction. DP

Bill Travers *Greg Rafferty* • Ed Begley *Bartell* • Sidney James *Richie Launder* • Nancy Walters *Diane Bartell* • Ursula Jeans *Mrs Rafferty* • Megs Jenkins *Kitty Launder* • Sean Kelly *Taz Rafferty* • Jack Brabham ■ *Dir* Michael Forlong • *Scr* Jon Cleary, from his novel

The Green Horizon ★★

Drama 1981 · Jpn · Colour · 120mins

Noted for introducing *cinéma vérité* realism into his fictional features, director Susumu Hani spent much of the 1970s making wildlife documentaries for Japanese television. He combines both preoccupations in this mediocre melodrama, which looks superb but makes few emotional or intellectual demands. In what proved to be his final big-screen appearance, James Stewart is wasted as the owner of an African animal sanctuary whose peaceful idyll is disrupted when pilot Philip Sayer crash-lands in the jungle and falls in love with Stewart's granddaughter. DP

James Stewart *Old Man* • Philip Sayer *Man* • Kathy *Girl* ■ *Dir* Susumu Hani, Simon Trevor • *Scr* Shintaro Tsuji, from a story by Shuji Terayama

Green Ice ★★ 15

Crime caper 1981 · UK · Colour · 104mins

One of those films that doesn't realise the offence it is causing by making comedy thrills out of a national tragedy. Ryan O'Neal and Anne Archer are fine as the couple involved in a risky heist of gems to fill rebel coffers in Colombia, and Omar Sharif is an entertaining enough villain, but the general light-heartedness of tone sits awkwardly on a story involving torture and armed struggle. Perhaps that's taking it too seriously, but caper movies shouldn't be made of such stern stuff. TH

Ryan O'Neal *Joseph Wiley* • Anne Archer *Holbrook* • Omar Sharif *Meno Argenti* • Domingo Ambriz *Miguel* • John Larroquette *Claude* • Philip Stone *Kellerman* • Michael Sheard *Jaap* • Enrique Lucero *Lucho* ■ *Dir* Ernest Day • *Scr* Edward Anhalt, Ray Hassett, Anthony Simmons, Robert De Laurentis, from the book by Gerald Browne

Green Light ★★

Medical drama 1937 · US · BW · 84mins

This torrid tear-jerker stars Errol Flynn as a surgeon who takes the blame when a patient dies on the operating table. Flynn then finds religion, uses his own body to experiment with a new vaccine and falls in love with the dead patient's daughter. It's sanctimony all the way, and pretty daft it is, too. Made by Warner Bros to placate its restless star who was feeling trapped as an action hero, this co-stars Anita Louise and was directed by the master of cringe, Frank Borzage. AT

Errol Flynn *Dr Newell Paige* • Anita Louise *Phyllis Dexter* • Margaret Lindsay *Frances Ogilvie* • Cedric Hardwicke *Dean George Harcourt* • Walter Abel *Dr John Stafford* • Henry O'Neill *Dr Endicott* • Spring Byington *Mrs Dexter* • Erin O'Brien-Moore *Pat Arlen* ■ *Dir* Frank Borzage • *Scr* Milton Krims, Paul Green (uncredited), from the novel by Lloyd C Douglas

The Green Man ★★★★ PG

Comedy 1956 · UK · BW · 76mins

If you ever doubted that Alastair Sim was the finest British screen comedian of the sound era, then here's the proof of his immense talent. As the assassin with the mournful smile, he gives a performance of rare genius that more than makes amends for the longueurs in the script. The sequence in which he persuades three old dears to cease their recital so that his radio bomb can finish off politician Raymond Huntley is a masterclass in the lost art of farce. Huntley also excels as the pompous target, but George Cole is overly bumbling as the vacuum-cleaner salesman who uncovers the plot. DP

DVD

Alastair Sim *Hawkins* • George Cole *William Blake* • Jill Adams *Ann Vincent* • Avril Angers *Marigold* • Terry-Thomas *Boughtflower* • John Chandos *McKecknie* • Raymond Huntley *Sir Gregory Upshoot* ■ *Dir* Robert Day • *Scr* Sidney Gilliat, Frank Launder, from their play *Meet a Body*

Green Mansions ★★ U

Romantic adventure
1959 · US · Colour · 104mins

Audrey Hepburn stars a mystical "Bird Girl", communing with nature and winning the heart of Anthony Perkins in the Venezuelan jungle. Alas, the film (directed by the star's then husband, actor Mel Ferrer) is misconceived. A poor screenplay fails to capture the elusive magic of the fantasy novel from which it was adapted, and the whole thing is photographed in unattractive shades of green. However, the doe-like beauty of Hepburn, followed around by a lookalike young deer, and an equally youthful Perkins, afford some fleeting pleasure. RK

Audrey Hepburn *Rima* • Anthony Perkins *Abel* • Lee J Cobb *Nuflo* • Sessue Hayakawa *Runi* • Henry Silva *Kua-Ko* • Nehemiah Persoff *Don Panta* • Michael Pate *Priest* ■ *Dir* Mel Ferrer • *Scr* Dorothy Kingsley, from the novel by William Henry Hudson

The Green Mile ★★★ 18

Fantasy prison drama
1999 · US · Colour · 180mins

Set in a Louisiana prison in 1935, this overblown, sentimental fantasy starsTom Hanks as a warden who forms a life-affirming relationship with a black prisoner, on death row for the murder of two little girls. Suspension of disbelief is essential if you're to enjoy Frank Darabont's reverential adaptation of Stephen King's 1996 novel. All the wardens are angels, bar one, while giant-sized newcomer Michael Clarke Duncan is too gentle to convince as a convicted child-killer. Yet Darabont manipulates our emotions masterfully, and only the very hard-hearted will remain unshocked by the harrowing execution scenes. DM. Contains violence, swearing. DVD

Tom Hanks *Paul Edgecomb* • David Morse *Brutus "Brutal" Howell* • Bonnie Hunt *Jan Edgecomb* • Michael Clarke Duncan *John Coffey* • James Cromwell *Warden Hal Moores* • Michael Jeter *Eduard Delacroix* • Graham Greene (2) *Arlen Bitterbuck* • Doug Hutchison *Percy Wetmore* • Sam Rockwell *"Wild Bill" Wharton* • Harry Dean Stanton *Toot-Toot* ■ *Dir* Frank Darabont • *Scr* Frank Darabont, from the novel by Stephen King

The Green Pastures ★★★ U

Religious drama 1936 · US · BW · 91mins

Warner Bros's faithful screen version of playwright Marc Connelly's Pulitzer Prize-winning smash hit re-tells the Old Testament in terms of a Saturday night fishfry. Today this interpretation may irritate some, but in fact this all-black production works as effectively now as it did in its time, making the Bible accessible and giving work to many black artists. Rex Ingram plays De Lawd, and Eddie "Rochester" Anderson is a memorable Noah. TS

Rex Ingram (2) *De Lawd/Adam/Hezdrel* • Oscar Polk *Gabriel* • Eddie "Rochester" Anderson *Noah* • Frank Wilson *Moses* • George Reed *Mr Deshee* • Abraham Gleaves *Archangel* • Myrtle Anderson *Eve* • Al Stokes *Cain* • Edna M Harris *Zeba* ■ *Dir* Marc Connelly, William Keighley • *Scr* Marc Connelly, Sheridan Gibney, from the play by Marc Connelly, suggested by the collection of stories *Ol' Man Adam an' His Chillun* by Roark Bradford

The Green Ray ★★★★ PG

Comedy drama 1986 · Fr · Colour · 94mins

Unlike Eric Rohmer's previous films, the dialogue of this comedy of manners was almost entirely improvised by the actors. How one reacts to the film may depend on how one reacts to the character of the overly fastidious Delphine, played superbly by Marie Rivière. Not knowing what to do on her holidays, she goes to Cherbourg, then the mountains and then Biarritz, but is bored and depressed everywhere until she meets the man of her dreams. The title, taken from the Jules Verne novel, refers to the last ray of sunset, the green of which is supposed to make observers more aware of the feelings of others. Rohmer's films have much the same effect. RB. In French with English subtitles. DVD

Marie Rivière *Delphine* • Vincent Gauthier *Jacques* • Béatrice Romand *Béatrice* • Sylvie Richez *Sylvie* • Basile Gervaise *Grandfather* ■ *Dir/Scr* Eric Rohmer

G

The Green Room ★★★

Drama 1978 · Fr · Colour · 94mins

Alfred Hitchcock's *Vertigo* haunts this film, inspired by the works of Henry James. Director/co-writer François Truffaut also stars as the obituarist whose life is devoted to the memory of his beloved wife and the victims of the First World War. Such is the totality of his grief that even when he befriends Nathalie Baye, the best he can offer her is a chance to become a fellow mourner at his vigil. Peering through cinematographer Nestor Almendros's gloomy interiors, it's easy to see just how personal a project this was, but it's harder to share in Truffaut's obsessions. DP. In French with English subtitles.

François Truffaut *Julien Davenne* • Nathalie Baye *Cecilia Mandel* • Jean Dasté *Bernard Humbert* • Jean-Pierre Moulin *Gérard Mazet* • Antoine Vitez *Bishop's secretary* • Jane Lobre *Madame Rambaud* • Monique Dury *Editorial secretary* ■ *Dir* François Truffaut • *Scr* François Truffaut, Jean Gruault, from the works of Henry James

The Green Scarf ★★

Mystery 1954 · UK · BW · 88mins

This murky murder mystery is set in Paris with an oh-so-British cast as French characters. Michael Redgrave is a lawyer defending a blind, deaf and dumb murder suspect (Kieron Moore) who, thinking his wife (Ann Todd) had killed her lover, confesses to the crime. Courtroom dramas seldom fail to hold the attention and this is no exception, despite the mechanical performances, lame script and uninspiring direction. RB

Michael Redgrave *Deliot* • Ann Todd *Solange* • Leo Genn *Rodelec* • Kieron Moore *Jacques* • Richard O'Sullivan *Jacques as a child* • Jane Lamb *Solange as a child* • Ella Milne *Louise* • Jane Griffiths *Danielle* ■ *Dir* George More O'Ferrall • *Scr* Gordon Wellesley, from the novel *The Brute* by Guy des Cars

The Green Slime ★★

Science-fiction horror
1968 · US/Jpn · Colour · 90mins

The first official Japanese/American co-production mixes the worst of both industries in this blah monster confection. After successfully thwarting an earthbound asteroid, astronauts unknowingly take on board a cargo of native green cells. Will Richard Jaeckel and rocket pilot Robert Horton ever stop fighting over mini-skirted Luciana Paluzzi long enough to notice the growing alien threat? While initially intriguing, all interest evaporates once the silly protoplasmic squids become visible. AJ

Robert Horton *Jack Rankin* • Richard Jaeckel *Vince Elliot* • Luciana Paluzzi *Lisa Benson* • Bud Widom *Jonathan Thompson* • Ted Gunther *Dr Halvorsen* • Robert Dunham *Captain Martin* • David Yorston *Lt Curtis* ■ *Dir* Kinji Fukasaku • *Scr* Charles Sinclair, William Finger, Tom Rowe, from a story by Ivan Reiner

G

The Green Years ★★★

Drama 1946 · US · BW · 126mins

MGM didn't need top stars to have a huge box-office success with its film adaptation of AJ Cronin's popular novel. Set in Scotland, it's capably directed by Britain's Victor Saville. In his first major role, nine-year-old Dean Stockwell shines as the boy growing up in a hostile family environment and forging a close relationship with his extraordinary great-grandfather. A bearded Charles Coburn plays the alcoholic old codger so engagingly that he received his third Oscar nomination for best supporting actor. AE

Charles Coburn *Alexander Gow* • Tom Drake *Robert Shannon* • Beverly Tyler *Alison Keith* • Hume Cronyn *Papa Leckie* • Gladys Cooper *Grandma Leckie* • Dean Stockwell *Robert Shannon as a child* • Selena Royle *Mama Leckie* • Jessica Tandy *Kate Leckie* ■ *Dir* Victor Saville • *Scr* Robert Ardrey, Sonya Levien, from the novel by AJ Cronin

Greenfingers ★★★ 15

Comedy drama
2000 · UK/US · Colour · 86mins

Clive Owen stars as the no-hope convict who's transferred to an open prison. An incident with a packet of African violet seeds means he's commanded by the governor to create a garden. His patch attracts the attention of gardening guru Helen Mirren and soon Owen's team are doing out-reach work and entering the Hampton Court Palace show. Based on a true story, this is desperately sweet, particularly with regard the burgeoning romance between Owen and Natasha Little as Mirren's daughter. The end result is hardly earth-shattering, but it's entertaining. LH [video] DVD

Clive Owen *Colin Briggs* • Helen Mirren *Georgina Woodhouse* • David Kelly *Fergus Wilks* • Warren Clarke *Governor Hodge* • Danny Dyer *Tony* • Adam Fogerty *Raw* • Paterson Joseph *Jimmy* • Natasha Little *Primrose Woodhouse* ■ *Dir/Scr* Joel Hershman

The Greengage Summer ★★★ PG

Romantic drama 1961 · UK · Colour · 95mins

Charmingly capturing the brilliance of youth and the beauty of the champagne country, director Lewis Gilbert's adaptation of Rumer Godden's novel suffers only from a disappointingly trite ending. As the 16-year-old forced to take charge of her siblings when their mother falls ill, Susannah York radiates the innocent's new-found lust for life and, whether getting tipsy for the first time or suffering from the initial pangs of love, she is truly captivating. As the mystery man who steals her heart, Kenneth More allows her the space to mature, while also revealing a more cynical side in his dealings with his landlady lover, Danielle Darrieux. DP [video]

Kenneth More *Eliot* • Danielle Darrieux *Madame Zizi* • Susannah York *Joss Grey* • Claude Nollier *Madame Corbet* • Jane Asher *Hester Grey* • Elizabeth Dear *Vicky Grey* • Richard Williams *Willmouse Grey* • David Saire *Paul* ■ *Dir* Lewis Gilbert • *Scr* Howard Koch, from the novel by Rumer Godden

Greenwich Village ★★★ U

Musical 1944 · US · Colour · 78mins

Jolly enjoyable Technicolor 20th Century-Fox musical, ostensibly set in the titular artists' quarter of New York City in the Roaring Twenties. But, since the speakeasy run by proprietor William Bendix features the fabulous Carmen Miranda and vivacious Vivian Blaine, we're clearly in the mid-1940s, which means superb musical arrangements and the skimpiest of plots on which to hang them. Don Ameche is the hick composer hired by Bendix to write a show, but keep your eyes sharply peeled for a glimpse of the legendary Judy Holliday. TS

Carmen Miranda *Princess Querida* • Don Ameche *Kenneth Harvey* • William Bendix *Danny O'Mara* • Vivian Blaine *Bonnie Watson* • Felix Bressart *Moger* • Tony De Marco • Sally De Marco • BS Pully *Brophy* ■ *Dir* Walter Lang • *Scr* Earl Baldwin, Walter Bullock, Michael Fessier (adaptation), Ernest B Pagano (adaptation), from a story by Fred Hazlitt Brennan [Frederick Hazlitt Brennan]

Greetings ★★★ 18

Satirical comedy 1968 · US · Colour · 87mins

Brian De Palma's early experimental feature follows the efforts of two men (Robert De Niro and Gerrit Graham) to get their best friend rejected for the army draft. The slight story is a mere springboard to attack such political targets as Lyndon Johnson, the Vietnam War and the Warren Commission report on the assassination of John F Kennedy, using *cinéma vérité*, sexual obsession and voyeurism. Slapdash, vulgar and smug, it was a huge youth culture hit, caused an explosion in the independent underground in the US and spawned the sequel *Hi, Mom!*. AJ. Contains nudity, swearing. [video] DVD

Jonathan Warden *Paul Shaw* • Robert De Niro *Jon Rubin* • Gerrit Graham *Lloyd Clay* • Richard Hamilton *Pop artist* • Megan McCormick *Marina* • Alan Garfield [Allen Garfield] *Smut peddler* ■ *Dir* Brian De Palma • *Scr* Charles Hirsch, Brian De Palma

Grégoire Moulin ★★★ 15

Comedy 2001 · Fr · Colour · 90mins

Resembling Buster Keaton with his deadpan stone face, first-time feature director and star Artus de Penguern can't be accused of holding back in his portrayal of the office nobody trying to return a purse to the girl of his dreams – *Madame Bovary*-obsessed ballet teacher Pascale Arbillot. But the comedy's spiralling descent into farce as he encounters a series of increasingly belligerent eccentrics, never quite manages the right balance between slapstick and insight. A frantic, but wildly inconsistent comedy. DP. In French with English subtitles.

Artus de Penguern *Grégoire Moulin* • Pascale Arbillot *Odile Bonheur/Emma in Madame Bovary* • Didier Bénureau *Jean-François* • Marie-Armelle Deguy *Solange* • Antoine Duléry *Emmanuel Lacarrière* • Serge Riaboukine *Taxi driver* ■ *Dir* Artus de Penguern • *Scr* Artus de Penguern, Jérôme L'Hotsky

Gregory's Girl ★★★★ 12

Romantic comedy
1980 · UK · Colour · 87mins

This is a case of near faultless film-making from Bill Forsyth, who latterly hasn't fulfilled this early promise under the auspices of Hollywood. As director, he keeps a wry eye on the triangle linking school goalkeeper John Gordon-Sinclair, centre forward Dee Hepburn and her pal Clare Grogan. But it is as scriptwriter that he excels, capturing the anxieties and insecurities of teen love and the language of the playground with consummate skill. He also creates a glorious array of secondary characters, including Robert Buchanan and William Greenlees as Sinclair's lovelorn mates and Chic Murray as the laconic headmaster. DP. Contains swearing. [video] DVD

Gordon John Sinclair [John Gordon-Sinclair] *Gregory* • Dee Hepburn *Dorothy* • Jake D'Arcy *Phil Menzies* • Clare Grogan *Susan* • Robert Buchanan *Andy* • William Greenlees [Billy Greenlees] *Steve* • Chic Murray *Headmaster* • Alex Norton *Alec* ■ *Dir/Scr* Bill Forsyth

Gregory's Two Girls ★★ 15

Comedy 1999 · UK/Ger · Colour · 111mins

A strong anti-American flavour laces this sequel to Bill Forsyth's best-known film. There's still plenty of his quirky observational humour, though, which provides the perfect platform for John Gordon-Sinclair to give a genial performance of political awareness, social ineptitude and sexual timidity. Now a teacher at his old school, Gregory wavers between a crush on fifth-former Carly McKinnon and the advances of hot-blooded colleague, Maria Doyle Kennedy. Alas, the plot to expose local industrialist Dougray Scott's part in Third World repression is barely credible. DP [video] DVD

John Gordon-Sinclair *Gregory Underwood* • Dougray Scott *Fraser Rowan* • Maria Doyle Kennedy *Bel* • Carly McKinnon *Frances* • Hugh McCue *Douglas* • Kevin Anderson *Jon* • Fiona Bell *Maddy Underwood* • Martin Schwab *Dimitri* ■ *Dir/Scr* Bill Forsyth

Gremlins ★★★★ 15

Black comedy horror
1984 · US · Colour · 101mins

This wonderfully anarchic affair is probably one of Hollywood's blackest mainstream hits. Zach Galligan is the teenager who is given a cuddly exotic pet mogwai called Gizmo, but through carelessness unwittingly unleashes a viciously murderous swarm of little gremlins. There's no doubt whose side director Joe Dante is on and he gleefully trashes the view of small-town America portrayed by feel-good movies such as *It's a Wonderful Life* (which is being screened on TV throughout the tale). Film buffs will delight in all the in-jokes and the cameos. JF. Contains violence and swearing. [video] DVD

Zach Galligan *Billy Peltzer* • Phoebe Cates *Kate* • Hoyt Axton *Rand Peltzer* • Frances Lee McCain *Lynn Peltzer* • Polly Holliday *Mrs Deagle* • Keye Luke *Grandfather* • John Louie *Chinese boy* • Dick Miller *Mr Futterman* ■ *Dir* Joe Dante • *Scr* Chris Columbus • *Executive Producer* Steven Spielberg

Gremlins 2: the New Batch ★★★ 15

Black comedy horror
1990 · US · Colour · 102mins

Joe Dante's anarchic view of life is given full rein in this chaotic but cracking sequel. The action is transplanted to a skyscraper in New York where mad scientist Christopher Lee inadvertently lets the evil gremlins loose to take over the entire building. As with the original, Dante bombards the screen with a never-ending stream of movie spoofs, slapstick violence and sly little treats for film buffs. JF. Contains violence, swearing. [video]

Zach Galligan *Billy Peltzer* • Phoebe Cates *Kate Beringer* • John Glover *Daniel Clamp* • Robert Prosky *Grandpa Fred* • Howie Mandel *Gizmo* • Tony Randall *"Brain" Gremlin* • Robert Picardo *Forster* • Christopher Lee *Dr Catheter* • Dick Miller *Murray Futterman* ■ *Dir* Joe Dante • *Scr* Charlie Haas, from characters created by Chris Columbus

Gremloids ★★★ PG

Science-fiction comedy
1990 · US · Colour · 86mins

In this reasonably successful low-budget *Star Wars* spoof, a navigation mistake lands cosmic bad guy Buckethead on Earth instead of in a galaxy far, far away. He's in hot pursuit of a princess who's run off with some secret radio transmissions. Buckethead (and indeed he does have a bucket on his head!) is the Darth Vader of director Todd Durham's refreshing piece, which doesn't set its satirical sights too high and hits more targets dead on as a result. AJ [video]

Paula Poundstone *Karen* • Chris Elliott *Hopper* • Alan Marx *Max* ■ *Dir/Scr* Todd Durham

Grendel, Grendel, Grendel ★★★

Animated adventure
1981 · Aus · Colour · 88mins

Briefly popular with the chattering classes, John Gardner's reworking of the legend of Beowulf was an ambitious choice for an animated feature. The graphics are bold and colourful, the songs (apart from the trite theme tune) slyly apposite and the voices packed with character – particularly impressive is Peter Ustinov's reading of the monster, transforming him from the scourge of Hrothgar's kingdom into the hapless victim of its superstition and intolerance. But, lacking either the intellectual weight of its source or the levity to make it child friendly, the film failed to find an audience. DP

Peter Ustinov *Grendel* • Keith Michell *Shaper* • Arthur Dignam *Beowolf* • Ed Rosser *King* ■ *Dir* Alexander Stitt • *Scr* Alexander Stitt, from the novel *Grendel* by John Gardner

The Grey Fox ★★★★ PG

Western 1982 · Can · Colour · 87mins

Richard Farnsworth gives a marvellous performance in this low-budget Canadian picture. Emerging in 1901 after 33 years in jail, Farnsworth tries to pick up where he left off as one of the Old West's most notorious outlaws – but those days are long gone. Shot in pseudo-documentary style, which gives the film the flavour of old photographs, this is a real charmer in the tradition of *The Wild Bunch* and *Butch Cassidy*. AT [video]

Richard Farnsworth *Bill Miner/George Edwards* • Jackie Burroughs *Kate Flynn* • Wayne Robson *William "Shorty" Dunn* • Timothy Webber *Sergeant Fernie* • Ken Pogue *Jack Budd* • Gary Reineke *Detective Seavey* ■ *Dir* Phillip Borsos • *Scr* John Hunter

Grey Gardens ★★★

Documentary 1975 · US · Colour · 95mins

Edith Bouvier Beale (79) and daughter Edie (56) – aunt and cousin of Jacqueline Onassis – were filmed by David and Albert Maysles over a few weeks in their squalid, decaying 28-room Long Island mansion, which was officially declared a health hazard. An intriguing, rather voyeuristic "non-fiction feature" on the lives of two eccentric women, who may or may not be giving performances for the ever present camera, it raises questions about the unvarnished "truth" which the Maysles brothers' "Direct Cinema" claimed to represent. The result is curious, but a bit unnerving. RB

Dir Ellen Hovde, Muffie Meyer, David Maysles, Albert Maysles

Grey Owl ★★★ PG

Biographical drama
1999 · UK/Can · Colour · 113mins

Pierce Brosnan stars as the eponymous hero of this worthy biography about one of the first eco-warriors, who became a celebrated conservationist in the 1930s. As Archie Grey Owl, trapper Brosnan flutters the heart of a young Iroquois woman (Annie Galipeau). He gives up the cruelty of snares and works as a guide and naturalist before his memoirs make him famous. Director Richard Attenborough certainly conveys the magnificence of the wilderness settings, but fails to capture the essence of his potentially fascinating protagonist. TH [video] DVD

Pierce Brosnan *Archibald Belaney/Grey Owl* • Annie Galipeau *Anahareo/Pony* • Renée Asherson *Carrie Belaney* • Stephanie Cole *Ada Belaney* • Nathaniel Arcand *Ned White Bear* • Stewart Bick *Cyrus Finney* • Vlasta Vrana *Harry Champlin* ■ *Dir* Richard Attenborough • *Scr* William Nicholson

Greyfriars Bobby ★★★★ U

Comedy drama based on a true story
1961 · US/UK · Colour · 86mins

Forget the accents and the shabby sets, this is Disney at its best. The true story of the Skye terrier who refuses to desert its master after his burial in an Edinburgh kirkyard is irresistible, and never maudlin or tacky. Laurence Naismith, Donald Crisp and Kay Walsh judge their performances to perfection and director Don Chaffey does well to restrain the enthusiasm of the youngsters. But no one's eyes will be anywhere other than on the little dog. Don't be ashamed to cheer when he's granted the freedom of the city. DP [video] DVD

Donald Crisp *John Brown* • Laurence Naismith *Mr Traill* • Alex Mackenzie *Old Jock* • Kay Walsh *Mrs Brown* • Duncan Macrae *Constable Maclean* • Andrew Cruickshank *Lord Provost* • Gordon Jackson *Farmer* • Rosalie Crutchley *Farmer's wife* • Joyce Carey *First lady* ■ *Dir* Don Chaffey • *Scr* Robert Westerby, from the story by Eleanor Atkinson

Greystoke: the Legend of Tarzan, Lord of the Apes ★★★ PG

Adventure 1984 · UK/US · Colour · 131mins

This claims to be the definitive screen version of Edgar Rice Burroughs's tale. The early scenes in the primate colony are moving and deftly handled, but once the action leaves the jungle, the film begins noticeably to sag. Christopher Lambert looks the part, but is not a skilful enough actor to carry off the complexities of Tarzan's plight in this decidedly adult version of the tale. However, Ralph Richardson injects some much-needed warmth and fun, and the film also looks glorious. Although the direction may sometimes lose its way, this still adds up to stirring entertainment. SH. Contains brief nudity. [video] DVD

Christopher Lambert *John Clayton, Tarzan* • Ralph Richardson *Earl of Greystoke* • Ian Holm *Captain Phillippe D'Arnot* • James Fox *Lord Esker* • Andie MacDowell *Jane Porter* • Cheryl Campbell *Lady Alice Clayton* • John Wells *Sir Evelyn Blount* • Nigel Davenport *Major Jack Downing* • Ian Charleson *Jeffson Brown* • Richard Griffiths *Captain Billings* ■ *Dir* Hugh Hudson • *Scr* PH Vazak [Robert Towne], Michael Austin, from the novel *Tarzan of the Apes* by Edgar Rice Burroughs • *Cinematographer* John Alcott • *Make-up* Rick Baker • *Production Designer* Stuart Craig

Gribouille ★★★

Drama 1937 · Fr · BW · 86mins

French character actor Raimu, renowned for his association with Marcel Pagnol, here finds his generous nature gets him into trouble. As a jury member, he takes pity on accused killer Michèle Morgan and takes her into his home. Directed by Marc Allégret, this was the third film appearance of Morgan, then 17, who would mature into one of France's most accomplished actresses. An American version of the story, *The Lady in Question*, was made in 1940 with Brian Aherne and Rita Hayworth. RK. In French with English subtitles.

Raimu *Camille* • Jeanne Provost *Louise* • Michèle Morgan *Natalie* • Gilbert Gil *Claude* • Jean Worms *Presiding judge* • Carette [Julien Carette] *Lurette* ■ *Dir* Marc Allégret • *Scr* Marcel Achard, HG Lustig, from a story by Marcel Achard

Gridlock'd ★★★ 18

Black comedy
1996 · US/UK · Colour · 87mins

In Vondie Curtis-Hall's engaging look at inner city life, Tim Roth and Tupac Shakur (who was killed while the movie was in post production) play jazz musicians trying to kick heroin. The comedy builds up from the way they are shunted between civic centres and red-tape nightmares. Despite the depressing subject matter, the angry sadness that underscores the outwardly comic playing gives this some neat twists. AJ [video] DVD

Tim Roth *Stretch* • Tupac Shakur *Spoon* • Thandie Newton *Cookie* • Vondie Curtis-Hall *D-Reper* • Charles Fleischer *Mr Woodson* • Howard Hesseman *Blind man* • John Sayles *First cop* • Eric Payne *Second cop* ■ *Dir/Scr* Vondie Curtis-Hall

Il Grido ★★

Drama 1957 · US/It · BW · 116mins

Also known as *The Outcry*, this is a typically neorealist effort from Italian writer/director Michelangelo Antonioni. A factory worker and his child are abandoned by the mother and wander the industrialised Po Valley. Antonioni's use of a rugged-looking but bad American actor (Steve Cochran) in the lead was a mistake, though it was typical of Italian movies at the time. (They never recorded live sound or bothered about accents.) A minor work from a major director who hit his stride with his next film, *L'Avventura*. AT

Steve Cochran *Aldo* • Alida Valli *Irma* • Betsy Blair *Elvia* • Dorian Gray *Virginia* • Lyn Shaw *Andreina* • Gabriella Pallotta *Edera* ■ *Dir* Michelangelo Antonioni • *Scr* Michelangelo Antonioni, Elio Bartolini, Ennio De Concini, from a story by Michelangelo Antonioni

Grief ★★ 18

Comedy drama 1993 · US · Colour · 82mins

Five crazy days in the life of a TV company producing *The Love Judge* soap opera come under the spotlight in director Richard Glatzer's cheap but cheerful tale. Gay story editor Craig Chester is at the centre of the action, still mourning the Aids-related death of his lover while fancying seemingly heterosexual writer Alexis Arquette. Throw in the fact that his boss is played by Jackie Beat (in post-Divine mode) and it becomes clear this mildly amusing spoof of American pop culture is working on a reasonably diverting level of its own. AJ. Contains swearing, sex scenes and nudity. [video]

Craig Chester *Mark* • Jackie Beat *Jo* • Illeana Douglas *Leslie* • Lucy Gutteridge *Paula* • Alexis Arquette *Bill* • Carlton Wilborn *Jeremy* • Robin Swid *Kelly* ■ *Dir/Scr* Richard Glatzer

Grievous Bodily Harm ★★★ 18

Thriller 1987 · Aus · Colour · 96mins

This rattling thriller from director Mark Joffe takes no prisoners. The bruising action never lets up, from the moment when crusading crime reporter Colin Friels discovers that a teacher's dead wife was a secret blue movie actress. Add a touch of corruption and a conspiracy theory to the brew and you have a highly potent picture, helped along by the gutsy performances of Friels, John Waters as the morbidly obsessed widower and Bruno Lawrence as a bent cop. DP. Contains swearing, brief nudity. [video]

Colin Friels *Tom Stewart* • Bruno Lawrence *Det Sgt Ray Birch* • John Waters (3) *Morris Martin* • Joy Bell *Claudine* • Chris Stalker *Allen* • Kim Gyngell *Mick* • Shane Briant *Stephen Enderby* ■ *Dir* Mark Joffe • *Scr* Warwick Hind

The Grifters ★★★★ 18

Crime drama 1990 · US · Colour · 105mins

It's not quite a contradiction in terms to describe this dramatisation of Jim Thompson's novel as a highly colourful *film noir*. Director Stephen Frears neatly shifts between the audacious scams executed by a trio of con artists, sudden moments of calculated violence and the intense rivalry that develops among expert bet chiseller Anjelica Huston, her ambitious son John Cusack and his scheming girlfriend Annette Bening. Cusack gives a lightweight performance, but the powerhouse playing of his Oscar-nominated co-stars grabs the attention through every twist and turn. DP. Contains violence, swearing and nudity. [video]

Anjelica Huston *Lilly Dillon* • John Cusack *Roy Dillon* • Annette Bening *Myra Langtry* • Pat Hingle *Bobo Justus* • Henry Jones *Simms* • JT Walsh *Cole* • Martin Scorsese *Narrator* ■ *Dir* Stephen Frears • *Scr* Donald E Westlake, from the novel by Jim Thompson

Grim Prairie Tales ★★★

Horror western 1990 · US · Colour · 86mins

A collection of stories grouped together by one theme, told by a city traveller and a mountain man (Brad Dourif and James Earl Jones) who meet on the desolate plains one night. The stories – a mixture of horror, western and comedy – are entertainingly performed by Marc McClure, William Atherton and Scott Paulin, but the real plaudits once again belong to Jones. JB

Brad Dourif *Farley* • James Earl Jones *Morrison* • Will Hare *Lee* • Marc McClure *Tom* • William Atherton *Arthur* • Lisa Eichhorn *Maureen* • Michelle Joyner *Jenny* • Wendy Cooke *Eva* • Scott Paulin *Martin* • Bruce M Fischer *Colochez* ■ *Dir/Scr* Wayne Coe

The Grinch ★★★★ PG

Comedy fantasy
2000 · US/Ger · Colour · 100mins

Dr Seuss's cult children's favourite *How the Grinch Stole Christmas!* gets the big-budget Hollywood treatment in this seasonal spectacular from director Ron Howard. Starring an irrepressible and almost unrecognisable Jim Carrey, it's the magical and visually splendid tale of a miserable, green-furred mountain-dweller who's out to wreck the extravagant festive celebrations in the kooky town of Whoville below. A vivacious delight capable of charming the most Scrooge-like viewer, this fantasy frolic is a heart-warmer. However, parents should be warned that the often dark humour and Carrey's madcap excesses may be too much for the very young. SF [video] DVD

Jim Carrey *Grinch* • Jeffrey Tambor *Mayor Augustus May Who* • Christine Baranski *Martha May Whovier* • Bill Irwin *Lou Lou Who* • Molly Shannon *Betty Lou Who* • Clint Howard *Whobris* • Taylor Momsen *Cindy Lou Who* • Anthony Hopkins *Narrator* ■ *Dir* Ron Howard • *Scr* Jeffrey Price, Peter S Seaman, from the book by Dr Seuss • *Art Director* Michael Corenblith • *Set Designer* Merideth Boswell • *Costume Designer* Rita Ryack • *Make-up effects* Rick Baker

Grip of the Strangler ★★

Mystery horror 1958 · US · BW · 81mins

Studying the 20-year-old murders of the "Haymarket Strangler", writer Boris Karloff becomes gruesomely possessed by the maniac responsible. Why? Because he *was* the maniac responsible! Karloff merely shuts one eye and bites his lower lip to become the madman in this pale Jekyll and Hyde clone. But while he shows his gift for changing personalities with the simplest shift of expression, whipping up minor scares in the process, the obvious low budget and simplistic script fail to give him much support. AJ

Boris Karloff *James Rankin* • Jean Kent *Cora Seth* • Elizabeth Allan *Barbara Rankin* • Anthony Dawson *Detective Superintendent Burk* • Vera Day *Pearl* • Tim Turner *Kenneth McColl* ■ *Dir* Robert Day • *Scr* Jan Read, John C Cooper, from a story by Jan Read

The Grissom Gang ★★★ 15

Crime thriller 1971 · US · Colour · 123mins

This is a thoroughly brutish and violent reworking of a notorious original, directed by Robert Aldrich, a major talent with a dark imagination. Disturbingly overlong, this sombre epic remains relentlessly watchable thanks to a superb central performance from Kim Darby as the kidnapped heiress at the centre of the drama. The thugs are comic-book creations, buffoonish and degenerate, and Aldrich can't decide whether the movie is a comedy, a thriller or something in between. TS. Contains violence, swearing. [video] DVD

Kim Darby *Barbara Blandish* • Tony Musante *Eddie Hagan* • Scott Wilson *Slim Grissom* • Irene Dailey *Ma Grissom* • Robert Lansing *Dave Fenner* ■ *Dir* Robert Aldrich • *Scr* Leon Griffiths, from the novel *No Orchids for Miss Blandish* by James Hadley Chase

Grizzly ★ 15

Adventure 1976 · US · Colour · 87mins

One of many *Jaws* rip-offs, this replaces the shark with a very angry, hungry grizzly bear who gets his kicks snacking off the visitors to a nature reserve. As the body count rises, park ranger Christopher George is joined in his pursuit by pilot Andrew Prine and naturalist Richard Jaeckel. You'll root for the bear. AT [video]

Christopher George *Ranger* • Andrew Prine *Helicopter pilot* • Richard Jaeckel *Naturalist* • Joan McCall *Photographer* ■ *Dir* William Girdler • *Scr* Harvey Flaxman, David Sheldon

Grizzly Falls ★★★ PG

Adventure 1999 · Can/UK · Colour · 90mins

Narrated in flashback by Richard Harris, this outdoor adventure combines an acute sense of place, a sure understanding of childhood and a pronounced empathy with the animal kingdom. Bryan Brown is the nominal lead, as a hunter seeking the son kidnapped by a vengeful grizzly. Director Stewart Raffill occasionally allows the pace to slacken, but the wolf attack and the showdown with trapper Oliver Tobias add excitement to the furry feel-good. DP [video] DVD

Bryan Brown *Tyrone Bankston* • Tom Jackson *Joshua* • Oliver Tobias *Genet* • Richard Harris *Old Harry* • Daniel Clark *Young Harry* ■ *Dir* Stewart Raffill • *Scr* Richard Beattie, Stuart Margolin

Grizzly Mountain ★★

Adventure 1997 · US · Colour · 96mins

Although the title and the presence of Grizzly Adams himself, Dan Haggerty, imply it, this lame backwoods tale is no relation to the movie (*The Life and Times of Grizzly Adams*) and TV series that brought former animal trainer Haggerty his fame. Here, the time-travelling story finds jaded city kids

Dylan Haggerty (Dan's son) and Nicole Lund being whisked back in time to the Wild West for some adventures with Haggerty Sr. The scenery is nice, but the plotting and performances leave a lot to be desired. JF

Dan Haggerty *Jeremiah* • Kim Morgan Greene *Betty* • Nicole Lund *Nicole Marks* • Martin Kove *Marshall Jackson* • Perry Stephens *Burt "Boss Man" Mann* • Dylan Haggerty *Dylan Marks* • Megan Haggerty *Megan Marks* ■ *Dir* Jeremy Haft • *Scr* Jeremy Haft, Peter White, from a story by Eric Parkinson

Groove ★★★ 18

Drama 2000 · US · Colour · 80mins

In this low-budget independent film, not even a police raid stops a party of San Francisco ravers from dancing 'til dawn. First-time director Greg Harrison makes things difficult for himself, setting the repetitive scenario almost entirely in a disused warehouse. But he succeeds in capturing the sweaty intensity of dance culture and maintaining our interest in the shallow characters. Hamish Linklater is utterly convincing as a strait-laced Midwesterner whose life is transformed by his initiation into the drug-fuelled urban dance scene. DM DVD

MacKenzie Firgens *Harmony Stitts* • Lola Glaudini *Leyla Heydel* • Denny Kirkwood *Colin Turner* • Hamish Linklater *David Turner* • Rachel True *Beth Anderson* • Steve Van Wormer *Ernie Townsend* ■ *Dir/Scr* Greg Harrison

The Groove Tube ★★★ 18

Comedy satire 1974 · US · Colour · 72mins

This saucy upstart of a movie pokes fun at all aspects of US TV. A spin-off from the similarly themed theatrical production, it consists of a series of sketches satirising such small-screen fare as children's programmes, sports broadcasts and adverts. It is inconsistent, but its scatalogical approach means it does occasionally hit some worthwhile targets. With its X-rated, bad-taste style this can be seen as the forerunner to later shock comedies. DF

Buzzy Linhart *The Hitchhiker* • Richmond Baier *The Girl* • Christine Nazareth *Theatre Girl* • Chevy Chase *The Fingers/Geritan/"Four Leaf Clover"* • Jennifer Welles *Geritan* • Ken Shapiro *Koko the Clown/Kramp TV Kitchen/ The Dealer/Newscaster/"Just You, Just Me"* • Richard Belzer *President* ■ *Dir* Ken Shapiro • *Scr* Ken Shapiro, Lane Sarasohn

Grosse Pointe Blank ★★★★ 15

Black comedy drama
1997 · US · Colour · 102mins

Hitman John Cusack returns to his home town for an assassination, an assignment that coincides with his high-school reunion. Named in tribute to John Boorman's cult thriller *Point Blank*, this sharp and witty black comedy from director George Armitage has the assassin bumping into old flame Minnie Driver, whom he jilted on prom night ten years before. Armitage's direction only really goes into overdrive for the final stretch, when Cusack discovers conventional free-marketeers just as ruthless as he is. The star is as charismatic as ever, while the rest of the cast, including Dan Aykroyd and Cusack's older sister Joan, are really superior. TH DVD

John Cusack *Martin Q Blank* • Minnie Driver *Debi Newberry* • Alan Arkin *Dr Oatman* • Dan Aykroyd *Mr Grocer* • Joan Cusack *Marcella* • Hank Azaria *Lardner* • K Todd Freeman *McCullers* • Mitchell Ryan *Mr Newberry* ■ *Dir* George Armitage • *Scr* Tom Jankiewicz, DV DeVincentis, Steve Pink, John Cusack, from a story by Tom Jankiewicz

The Grotesque ★ 18

Black comedy 1995 · UK · Colour · 93mins

Want to know how to turn a witty and original novel into a hackneyed bore in one easy lesson? Just watch director John-Paul Davidson's lamentable black comedy based on author Patrick McGrath's wildly acerbic tale about the class struggle in 1940s England. The story of what happens when new butler Sting arrives at the house of eccentric explorer Alan Bates is stunningly conventional. AJ

Alan Bates *Sir Hugo Coal* • Sting *Fledge* • Theresa Russell *Lady Harriet Coal* • Lena Headey *Cleo Coal* • Steven Mackintosh *Sidney Giblet* • Anna Massey *Mrs Giblet* • Timothy Kightley *Harbottle* • Jim Carter *George Lecky* ■ *Dir* John-Paul Davidson • *Scr* Patrick McGrath, from his novel

Ground Zero ★★★ 15

Thriller 1987 · Aus · Colour · 96mins

Although we're used to the way governments keep us in the dark, this political thriller from Australia still manages to shock with its story, based on fact, about a man seeking reasons for his father's death during British A-bomb testing in the outback in the 1950s. Colin Friels and Jack Thompson put genuine feeling into their roles as they lift the lid on past moral meltdown, but Donald Pleasence, playing the hermit-like survivor of those nuclear trials, who steals every scene he's in. TH. Contains violence and swearing.

Colin Friels *Harvey Denton* • Jack Thompson *Trebilcock* • Donald Pleasence *Prosper Gaffney* • Natalie Bate *Pat Denton* • Simon Chilvers *Commission president* • Neil Fitzpatrick *Hooking* • Bob Maza *Wallemare* ■ *Dir* Michael Pattinson, Bruce Myles • *Scr* Jan Sardi, Mac Gudgeon

Groundhog Day ★★★★★ PG

Comedy fantasy 1993 · US · Colour · 96mins

Hollywood once produced three or four classic comedies each year. Nowadays we're lucky to get one a decade and this is a contender for the 1990s. Bill Murray gives one of the best performances of his career as Phil Connors, the weatherman with attitude, trapped in a day he will remember for the rest of his life because, unless he can find some answers, it will *be* the rest of his life. Director Harold Ramis uses every cinematic trick in the book to keep what is essentially a one-gag movie brimming with life and fresh ideas. Stephen Tobolowsky is superb as a nerdy insurance salesman and, as Murray's TV producer, Andie MacDowell has never been better. DP. Contains swearing. DVD

Bill Murray *Phil Connors* • Andie MacDowell *Rita Hanson* • Chris Elliott *Larry* • Stephen Tobolowsky *Ned* • Brian Doyle-Murray *Buster* • Marita Geraghty *Nancy* • Angela Paton *Mrs Lancaster* • Rick Ducommun *Gus* ■ *Dir* Harold Ramis • *Scr* Danny Rubin, Harold Ramis, from a story by Danny Rubin

The Groundstar Conspiracy ★★

Drama 1972 · Can · Colour · 95mins

This effective thriller about spies in the space programme is really one of those high-gloss flicks Universal made to show off its contract players, in this case George Peppard and Michael Sarrazin. Director Lamont Johnson handles the suspense well and, though the script could have been tighter and the leading lady (Christine Belford) more distinguished, the Vancouver locations look splendid. TS

George Peppard *Tuxan* • Michael Sarrazin *Welles* • Christine Belford *Nicole* • Cliff Potts *Mosely* • James Olson *Stanton* • Tim O'Connor *Gossage* • James McEachin *Bender* • Alan Oppenheimer *Hackett* ■ *Dir* Lamont Johnson • *Scr* Matthew Howard, from the novel *The Alien* by LP Davies

The Group ★★★★

Drama 1966 · US · Colour · 146mins

Notable as one of the first films to show the emotional development of women as individuals and not just as lost souls awaiting salvation by men, this glitzy, glossy and extremely good drama is based on the iconoclastic blockbuster by Mary McCarthy. It is beautifully played by the likes of Candice Bergen, Jessica Walter and, particularly, Joan Hackett, whose ultimate fate is skilfully drawn. SH

Candice Bergen *Elinor "Lakey" Eastlake* • Joan Hackett *Dorothy "Dottie" Renfrew* • Elizabeth Hartman *Priss Hartshorn* • Shirley Knight *Polly Andrews* • Joanna Pettet *Kay Strong* • Mary-Robin Redd *Pokey Prothero* • Jessica Walter *Libby MacAusland* • Larry Hagman *Harald Peterson* • Hal Holbrook *Gus Leroy* • Richard Mulligan *Dick Brown* ■ *Dir* Sidney Lumet • *Scr* Sidney Buchman, from the novel by Mary McCarthy

The Grudge ★★ 15

Horror thriller 2004 · US · Colour · 87mins

Takashi Shimizu directs this English-language remake of his cult horror, but adds little to the genre. Essentially a haunted-house story, it begins with student social worker Sarah Michelle Gellar making a house call and encountering some seriously spooky goings-on – the house is home to a demon and anyone who enters its walls is cursed. This chiller has installed many superfluous tricks of the horror movie trade, designed to make the film more accessible to a western audience. KK DVD

Sarah Michelle Gellar *Karen* • Jason Behr *Doug* • Clea DuVall *Jennifer Williams* • William Mapother *Matthew Williams* • KaDee Strickland *Susan Williams* • Bill Pullman *Peter* • Rosa Blasi *Maria* • Grace Zabriskie *Emma* ■ *Dir* Takashi Shimizu • *Scr* Stephen Susco, from the film *Ju-On: the Grudge* by Takashi Shimizu

The Grudge 2 ★★★

Horror thriller 2003 · Jpn · Colour · 100mins

Japanese writer/director Takashi Shimizu continued to mine his *Ju-On* horror franchise with this atmospheric sequel to 2003's *The Grudge: Ju-On*. Creepier than its predecessor though never genuinely scary, the feature sees the cast and crew of a TV special fall victim to a lethal curse after filming in the original's spooky suburban residence. While Shimuzu again employs a non-linear narrative style, this time it's less confusing, thanks to more fully-fleshed characters and greater plot exposition. SF. In Japanese with English subtitles.

Noriko Sakai *Kyoko Harase* • Chiharu Niyama *Tomoko Miura* • Yui Ichikawa *Chiharu* • Takako Fuji *Kayako* • Yuya Ozeki *Toshio* ■ *Dir/Scr* Takashi Shimizu

The Grudge: Ju-On ★★ 15

Horror thriller 2003 · Jpn · Colour · 88mins

This haunted house chiller lacks the eerie originality of much recent Japanese horror. This is partly due to the fact that Takashi Shimizu was remaking his own 2000 direct-to-video offering. The flashbacking story never regains the sense of foreboding that pervades careworker Megumi Okina's first visit to the abode possessed by a ghostly boy. Disconcerting, but short on terror. DP. In Japanese with English subtitles. Contains violence. DVD

Megumi Okina *Rika Nishina* • Misaki Ito *Hitomi Tokunaga* • Misa Uehara (2) *Izumi Toyama* • Kanji Tsuda *Katsuya Tokunaga* • Shuri Matsuda *Kazumi Tokunaga* • Takako Fuji *Kayako* • Yuya Ozeki *Toshio* • Yui Ichikawa *Chiharu* • Kayoko Shibata *Mariko* • Yukako Kukuri *Miyuki* ■ *Dir/Scr* Takashi Shimizu

The Gruesome Twosome ★★ 18

Horror 1967 · US · Colour · 71mins

From its bizarre puppet-slaying opening, Herschell Gordon Lewis's schlock fest has only one item on its agenda. Like the B-movie date sequence, this is hilariously subversive, while also more than a little disquieting. The Wizard of Gore can never be accused of excessive proficiency, but he is certainly very proficient at serving up an excess of entrails and lashings of red goo. The plot involves murderous efforts of a devoted son to supply his mother's wig shop with plenty of genuine hair. Riotously third-rate, it's a textbook chunk of drive-in Gothic. DP DVD

Elizabeth Davis • Chris Martell • Gretchen Welles • Rodney Bedell ■ *Dir* Herschell Gordon Lewis • *Scr* Louise Downe

Grumpier Old Men ★★ 12

Comedy 1996 · US · Colour · 96mins

Old stagers Walter Matthau and Jack Lemmon cruise through this unaccountably popular sequel. Ann-Margret also returns from the first film, while Sophia Loren turns up as a much-married interloper who stirs up the boys' bile by buying their beloved bait shop and turning it into a restaurant. The grumpy pair forget their incessant feuding to wage war on the restaurant. They all deserve better material. JF

Jack Lemmon *John Gustafson* • Walter Matthau *Max Goldman* • Ann-Margret *Ariel Gustafson* • Sophia Loren *Maria Ragetti* • Burgess Meredith *Grandpa Gustafson* • Daryl Hannah *Melanie Gustafson* • Kevin Pollak *Jacob Goldman* ■ *Dir* Howard Deutch • *Scr* Mark Steven Johnson, from his characters

Grumpy ★★

Mystery drama 1930 · US · BW · 74mins

George Cukor's debut film-directing credit (albeit shared with Cyril Gardner) was this musty, dusty screen version of a long-running play, popular on both sides of the Atlantic in the 1920s. It stars veteran actor Cyril Maude, reprising his stage role of "Grumpy", a white-haired, fragile-looking retired lawyer who is both lovable and irascible. He gets to grips with solving a small mystery concerning a diamond acquired by his granddaughter's boyfriend. Cosy, and rather boring. RK

Cyril Maude *"Grumpy" Bullivant* • Phillips Holmes *Ernest Heron* • Frances Dade *Virginia* • Paul Lukas *Berci* • Halliwell Hobbes *Ruddick* ■ *Dir* George Cukor, Cyril Gardner • *Scr* Doris Anderson, from the play *Grumpy, a Play in Four Acts* by Horace Hodges, Thomas Wigney Percyval

Grumpy Old Men ★★★ 12

Comedy drama 1993 · US · Colour · 99mins

Jack Lemmon and Walter Matthau are one of the all-time great partnerships and this engaging comedy marked their seventh screen collaboration. In this high-concept tale, they are warring senior citizens whose feuding escalates as they battle for the hand of Ann-Margret. Although the script isn't quite as strong as it could be, the chemistry between the two stars is irresistible and they are matched by an equally strong supporting cast. JF. Contains some swearing.

Jack Lemmon *John Gustafson* • Walter Matthau *Max Goldman* • Ann-Margret *Ariel Truax* • Burgess Meredith *Grandpa Gustafson* • Daryl Hannah *Melanie Gustafson* • Kevin Pollak *Jacob Goldman* • Ossie Davis *Chuck* • Buck Henry *Elliott Snyder* ■ *Dir* Donald Petrie • *Scr* Mark Steven Johnson

Guadalcanal Diary ★★★★ PG

Second World War action drama
1943 · US · BW · 89mins

Richard Tregaskis's novel, an "I was there" account of the struggle to recapture the South Pacific island of Guadalcanal from the Japanese during the Second World War, was difficult to film without resorting to cliché. Nevertheless, 20th Century-Fox pulls out all the stops in the authenticity stakes here, with superbly staged action sequences. Richard Jaeckel is exceptionally fine, and there's solid back-up from stars such as William Bendix, Anthony Quinn and Lloyd Nolan. Preston Foster offers some unusually unsentimental homilies as the padre and, overall, the movie contains a rare honesty. SH DVD

Preston Foster *Father Donnelly* • Lloyd Nolan *Hook Malone* • William Bendix *Taxi Potts* • Richard Conte *Captain Davis* • Anthony Quinn *Jesus "Soose" Alvarez* • Richard Jaeckel *Private Johnny Anderson* • Roy Roberts *Captain Cross* • Lionel Stander *Butch* ■ *Dir* Lewis Seiler • *Scr* Lamar Trotti, Jerry Cady [Jerome Cady], from the diary by Richard Tregaskis

Guantanamera ★★ 15

Drama 1995 · Sp /Cu/Ger · Colour · 101mins

This road movie – the last project completed by Tomás Gutiérrez Alea, Cuba's best-known director – has too many echoes of Alea's own *Death of a Bureaucrat* for comfort. The passing of a famous singer's funeral cortege across the island should have inspired some seething satire, but the swipes are merely passing blows at easy targets. There's simply not enough tension in the developing romance between one-time lecturer Mirtha Ibarra and her gone-to-bad student Jorge Perugorria to hold our attention. A disappointing swansong. DP

Carlos Cruz *Adolfo* • Mirtha Ibarra [Mirta Ibarra] *Georgina* • Raul Eguren *Candido* • Jorge Perugorria *Mariano* • Pedro Fernandez *Ramon* • Luis Alberto Garcia *Tony* • Conchita Brando *Yoyita* ■ *Dir* Tomás Gutiérrez Alea, Juan Carlos Tabio • *Scr* Eliseo Alberto Diego, Tomás Gutiérrez Alea, Juan Carlos Tabio

The Guardian ★★★ 18

Supernatural horror
1990 · US · Colour · 88mins

There's much pleasure to be had in this offering from William Friedkin, mainly from watching leading lady Jenny Seagrove in her first American starring role. The part is virtually unplayable, but, as the demonic nanny, Seagrove really makes us believe she's on nodding terms with hell. It could have been a lot more scary, but that's a minor quibble in a generally satisfying tale of the supernatural. TS. Contains swearing and violence. [video]

Jenny Seagrove *Camilla* • Dwier Brown *Phil* • Carey Lowell *Kate* • Brad Hall *Ned Runcie* • Miguel Ferrer *Ralph Hess* • Natalia Nogulich [Natalija Nogulich] *Molly Sheridan* ■ *Dir* William Friedkin • *Scr* Stephen Volk, William Friedkin, Dan Greenburg, from the novel *The Nanny* by Dan Greenburg

Guardian ★★ 15

Horror thriller 2000 · US · Colour · 86mins

The proliferation of a dangerous new drug convinces Gulf War veteran-turned-cop Mario Van Peebles that he has to protect a "special" child from the evil spirit Telal. This demonology thriller blithely blags ideas from any number of uninspired forebears. John Terlesky directs with brisk efficiency, but that's hardly a recommendation. DP [video] DVD

Mario Van Peebles *John Kross* • James Remar *Carpenter* • Ice-T *Max* • Stacy Oversier *Selene* • Daniel Hugh Kelly *Agent Taylor* • Steve Zad *David Lichtmann* ■ *Dir* John Terlesky • *Scr* John Terlesky, Gary J Tunnicliffe, Jeff Yagher

Guardian Angels ★★

Comedy 1995 · Fr · Colour · 110mins

Director Jean-Marie Poiré followed up his blockbusting time-travel fantasy, *Les Visiteurs*, with this patchy comedy. A mix of character comedy and perilous slapstick, the action centres on the shady-dealing Gérard Depardieu, who encounters his guardian angel while trying to protect a friend's son from the Triads and recover $14 million in stolen loot. Depardieu is in rollicking form, but Christian Clavier, whose naive priest has a thoroughly resistible guardian angel of his own, steals the show. DP. A French language film.

Gérard Depardieu *Antoine Carco* • Christian Clavier *Père Tarain* • Eva Grimaldi *Regina Podium* ■ *Dir* Jean-Marie Poiré • *Scr* Jean-Marie Poiré, Christian Clavier

Guarding Tess ★★★ 12

Comedy drama 1994 · US · Colour · 91mins

Shirley MacLaine does almost too good a job of playing cantankerous president's widow Tess Carlisle – a former First Lady from hell. MacLaine is so believable in the leading role she's almost unendurable to watch, while Nicolas Cage, as long-suffering secret service minder Doug Chesnic, displays the same sure comic touch he brought to 1998's *City of Angels*. It's attractively staged by *Police Academy* director Hugh Wilson and remains entertaining until it finally lurches into melodrama. TH. Contains violence and swearing. [video] DVD

Shirley MacLaine *Tess Carlisle* • Nicolas Cage *Doug Chesnic* • Austin Pendleton *Earl* • Edward Albert *Barry Carlisle* • James Rebhorn *Howard Shaeffer* • Richard Griffiths *Frederick* • John Roselius *Tom Bahlor* ■ *Dir* Hugh Wilson • *Scr* Hugh Wilson, Peter Torokvei

The Guardsman ★★★★

Romantic comedy 1931 · US · BW · 81mins

The celebrated husband-and-wife acting team of Lynn Fontanne and Alfred Lunt repeated their stage roles in this screen version of Ferenc Molnar's romantic comedy. Tormented by jealousy, the husband tests his wife by disguising himself as a Russian officer and attempting to seduce her. Although very theatrical, the film survives as a cherishable testament to the couple's exceptional skills. The story was remade as the musical *The Chocolate Soldier* in 1941. RK

Alfred Lunt *The Actor* • Lynn Fontanne *The Actress* • Roland Young *The Critic* • ZaSu Pitts *Liesl* • Maude Eburne *Mama* • Herman Bing *A Creditor* ■ *Dir* Sidney Franklin • *Scr* Ernst Vajda [Ernest Vajda], Claudine West, from the play by Ferenc Molnar

Guelwaar ★★★★

Political satire
1992 · Sen/Fr · Colour · 115mins

One of the best-known of black African film-makers, Ousmane Sembene forged his reputation with the searing satire of Senegalese life, *Xala*. He is no less scathing in this supremely controlled study of the conflicts of politics, language, religion and custom that divide a state proud of its independence and yet still reliant on overseas aid. The disappearance of a political dissident's corpse exposes all manner of contradictions as Catholic priests and Muslim imams feud over the burial, while the mayor and his chief of police fight to keep the truth about his death a secret. Third World cinema close to its best. DP. In French with English subtitles.

Omar Seck *Gora* • Ndiawar Diop *Barthelemy* • Mame Ndoumbe Diop *Nogoy Marie Thioune* • Isseu Niang *Veronique* • Myriam Niang *Helene* ■ *Dir/Scr* Ousmane Sembene

La Guerre Est Finie ★★★★ 15

Political drama 1966 · Fr/Swe · BW · 116mins

Typically overlapping the present, memory and imagination, Alain Resnais here offers a troubling study of the gulf between passive commitment and direct action. Written by the exiled Spanish author Jorge Semprun, the film focuses on the three days in which middle-aged revolutionary Yves Montand comes to recognise that his unswerving allegiance to the cause of overthrowing Franco is faltering. Montand gives a performance of great solemnity, and he is well supported by Ingrid Thulin as his loyal mistress and Geneviève Bujold as the student with whom he has a brief affair. DP. In French with English subtitles. [video]

Yves Montand *Diego* • Ingrid Thulin *Marianne* • Geneviève Bujold *Nadine Sallanches* • Jean Dasté *Chief* • Jorge Semprun *Narrator* • Dominique Rozan *Jude* • Michel Piccoli *First customs inspector* ■ *Dir* Alain Resnais • *Scr* Jorge Semprun

Guerrilla: the Taking of Patty Hearst ★★★ 12A

Documentary 2003 · US/UK · Colour · 89mins

Robert Stone's meticulously researched, compelling documentary sheds new light on the 1974 kidnapping of heiress Patty Hearst by the Symbionese Liberation Army, and her apparent conversion to their cause. Director Stone uses archive footage plus interviews with surviving SLA members to investigate the events. He deliberately avoids the obvious – and possibly unanswerable – question that divided America at the time: was Hearst brainwashed or a willing collaborator with the group? Instead, the film concentrates on the equally fascinating relationship between the terrorists and the mass media that reported – and some might argue, abetted – their crimes. AS. Contains swearing.

Dir Robert Stone

Guess What Happened to Count Dracula ★

Horror 1970 · US · Colour · 80mins

Not a lot actually. The Transylvanian vampire apparently changed his name to Count Adrian (Des Roberts) and took to hanging around a mod Sunset Strip disco called Dracula's Castle. Well, that's according to this atrocious exploitation quickie directed and written by Laurence Merrick. AJ

Des Roberts *Count Dracula* • Claudia Barron *Angelica* • John Landon *Guy* • Robert Branche *Dr Harris* • Frank Donato *Imp* • Sharon Beverly *Vamp* ■ *Dir/Scr* Laurence Merrick

Guess Who ★★ 12A

Romantic comedy
2005 · US · Colour · 105mins

Bernie Mac stars as a suspicious, intimidating potential father-in-law in this race-reversed comic homage to the 1967 classic *Guess Who's Coming to Dinner*. Mac is mortified when his eldest daughter (Zoë Saldana) comes home for his wedding anniversary party with white boyfriend Ashton Kutcher in tow. Mac's quick-fire delivery complements Kutcher's clownish physical comedy and though the knockabout laughs are too in-your-face, they do have a crude appeal. SF

Bernie Mac *Percy Jones* • Ashton Kutcher *Simon Green* • Zoë Saldana *Theresa Jones* • Judith Scott *Marilyn Jones* • Hal Williams *Howard Jones* • Kellee Stewart *Keisha Jones* • Robert Curtis Brown *Dante* • RonReaco Lee *Reggie* ■ *Dir* Kevin Rodney Sullivan • *Scr* David Ronn, Jay Scherick, Peter Tolan, from a story by David Ronn, Jay Scherick

Guess Who's Coming to Dinner ★★★★ PG

Comedy drama 1967 · US · Colour · 103mins

In their last movie together, Spencer Tracy and Katharine Hepburn play a rich couple whose liberal principles are tested by the proposed marriage of their daughter to a black doctor. As he is Sidney Poitier, all intellectual politesse, there's never any doubt about the outcome. The film may have a foregone conclusion, but it's worth watching as the acting is so good. Tracy and an Oscar-winning Hepburn were a deceptively rare cinema double-act, who seemed genuinely fond of each other both on and off screen. This is an outstanding swan song. TH. Contains swearing. [video] DVD

Spencer Tracy *Matthew Drayton* • Sidney Poitier *John Prentice* • Katharine Hepburn *Christina Drayton* • Katharine Houghton *Joey Drayton* • Cecil Kellaway *Monsignor Ryan* • Beah Richards *Mrs Prentice* • Roy E Glenn Sr [Roy Glenn] *Mr Prentice* • Isabell Sanford [Isabel Sanford] *Tillie* ■ *Dir* Stanley Kramer • *Scr* William Rose

Guest House Paradiso ★ 15

Comedy 1999 · UK · Colour · 86mins

This is a big-screen version of the TV series *Bottom*, with slightly better sets and plenty of cartoon violence. Stars Rik Mayall and Adrian Edmondson have no one to blame but themselves for this puerile farce: Edmondson directs, from a script he co-wrote with Mayall. The story, for what it's worth, finds sociopaths Richie and Eddie running a revolting hotel in the shadow of a nuclear power plant. JF [video]

Rik Mayall *Richie Twat* • Adrian Edmondson *Eddie Elizabeth Ndingobaba* • Vincent Cassel *Gino Bolognese* • Hélène Mahieu *Gina Carbonara* • Bill Nighy *Mr Johnson* • Simon Pegg *Mr Nice* • Fenella Fielding *Mrs Foxfur* ■ *Dir* Adrian Edmondson • *Scr* Adrian Edmondson, Rik Mayall

Guest in the House ★★

Drama 1944 · US · BW · 120mins

Anne Baxter stars as a mentally disturbed but beautiful young woman who falls for her doctor's brother (Ralph Bellamy). Baxter doesn't allow Bellamy's marriage or her own relationship with the doctor (Scott McKay) to stand in her way. Directed by John Brahm with lots of atmosphere and an excellent cast, this overlong drivel is all the more depressing because it compels one to keep watching. AJ

Anne Baxter *Evelyn Heath* • Ralph Bellamy *Douglas Proctor* • Aline MacMahon *Aunt Martha* • Ruth Warrick *Ann Proctor* • Scott McKay *Dan Proctor* • Jerome Cowan *Mr Hackett* • Marie McDonald *Miriam* ■ *Dir* John Brahm • *Scr* Ketti Frings, from the play *Dear Evelyn* by Hagar Wilde, Dale Eunson

Guest Wife ★★ U

Comedy 1945 · US · BW · 84mins

A comedy variation on the eternal triangle theme – bachelor foreign correspondent must play married to keep his job, borrows banker friend's wife, inevitable complications ensue – is unfortunately short on intended laughs. An increasingly chaotic and unconvincing farce, directed with too heavy a hand by Sam Wood, in which only Claudette Colbert, at her sparkling best as the "borrowed" wife, rises above the material. RK [video]

Claudette Colbert *Mary Price* • Don Ameche *Joe Parker* • Richard Foran [Dick Foran] *Christopher Price* • Charles Dingle *AT Worth* •

G

Grant Mitchell *Detective* • Wilma Francis *Susy* ■ *Dir* Sam Wood • *Scr* Bruce Manning, John Klorer

A Guide for the Married Man ★★★ PG

Comedy 1967 · US · Colour · 87mins

Walter Matthau, married for years, suddenly breaks one of the Ten Commandments: he covets his neighbour's wife. Fortunately, his best friend, Robert Morse, is a philanderer himself, and more than willing to teach Matthau the art of having an affair and getting away with it. This is, clearly, a variation on *The Seven Year Itch*, for which Matthau, by the way, was first choice. There's plenty to enjoy in this comedy of sexual mores, which is most notable for its glorious gallery of guest spots including Lucille Ball, Jack Benny, Jayne Mansfield, Phil Silvers and Terry-Thomas. AT

Walter Matthau *Paul Manning* • Robert Morse *Ed Stander* • Inger Stevens *Ruth Manning* • Sue Anne Langdon [Sue Ane Langdon] *Irma Johnson* • Jackie Russell *Miss Harris* • Claire Kelly *Harriet Stander* • Linda Harrison *Miss Stardust* • Elaine Devry *Jocelyn Montgomery* ■ *Dir* Gene Kelly • *Scr* Frank Tarloff, from his book

G

The Guilt of Janet Ames ★★★

Psychological drama 1947 · US · BW · 81mins

Psychiatry was very much in fashion in stage and screen drama when this offbeat drama was made. Its fascinating premise also tapped into postwar guilt and paranoia, with Rosalind Russell as a woman whose husband was killed in the war when he threw himself on a grenade to save five comrades. She sets out to trace the men whose lives were spared to see if they were worthy of her husband's sacrifice. TV

Rosalind Russell *Janet Ames* • Melvyn Douglas *Smithfield Cobb* • Sid Caesar *Sammy Weaver* • Betsy Blair *Katie* • Nina Foch *Susie Pierson* • Charles Cane *Walker* • Harry Von Zell *Carter* ■ *Dir* Henry Levin • *Scr* Louella MacFarlane, Allen Rivkin, Devery Freeman, from a story by Lenore Coffee

Guilty? ★★

Crime mystery 1956 · UK · BW · 94mins

This might have been an enthralling thriller had director Edmond T Gréville had a more original plot to work with. There's certainly enough incident, as sleuthing attorney John Justin heads to Avignon to unearth the evidence that will clear Resistance heroine Andrée Debar of the murder of the lover whose wartime betrayal resulted in her incarceration in a concentration camp. But, instead of delving into the guilty secrets of France under the Nazi occupation, the story develops a more straightforward strand, involving an undercover agent Barbara Laage. DP

John Justin *Nap Rumbold* • Barbara Laage *Jacqueline Delbois* • Donald Wolfit *Judge* • Stephen Murray *Summers* • Norman Wooland *Pelton* • Frank Villard *Pierre Lemaire* • Andrée Debar *Vicki Martin* • Betty Stockfeld *Mrs Roper* ■ *Dir* Edmond T Gréville • *Scr* Maurice J Wilson, Ernest Dudley, from the novel *Death Has Deep Roots* by Michael Gilbert

The Guilty ★★ 15

Crime thriller
2000 · Can/UK/US · Colour · 107mins

Bill Pullman puts in an unusually reptilian performance as a sleazy, high-flying lawyer prepared to go to any extremes to save his career in this join-the-dots thriller. Engaging to watch and nicely shot, it's hampered by the fact that every plot twist is neon-signposted, while many characters are hammy stereotypes. Consequently what begins as a fast-paced, contemporary *film noir* soon plunges into melodrama, despite a strong turn from Gabrielle Anwar. SF. Contains swearing and violence. DVD

Bill Pullman *Callum Crane* • Devon Sawa *Nathan Corrigan* • Gabrielle Anwar *Sophie Lennon* • Angela Featherstone *Tanya Duncan* • Joanne Whalley *Natalie Crane* • Darcy Belsher *Dennis* • Jaimz Woolvett *Leo* ■ *Dir* Anthony Waller • *Scr* William Davies, from the TV serial by Simon Burke

Guilty as Charged ★★★ 18

Black comedy 1991 · US · Colour · 91mins

Rod Steiger revisits his homicidal persona from *No Way to Treat a Lady* in this black comedy. He's at his scenery-chewing best as mad religious tycoon Ben Kallin, dispatching criminals in his home-made electric chair. *South Park*'s Chef, Isaac Hayes, is one of Steiger's little helpers. It's all a shocker of some voltage, with Lauren Hutton looking aghast and director Sam Irvin making it stylish, if not plausible. TH DVD

Rod Steiger *Ben Kallin* • Lauren Hutton *Liz Stanford* • Heather Graham *Kimberly* • Lyman Ward *Mark Stanford* • Isaac Hayes *Aloysius* • Zelda Rubenstein *Edna* • Erwin Keyes *Deek* ■ *Dir* Sam Irvin • *Scr* Charles Gale

Guilty as Sin ★★★ 15

Thriller 1993 · US · Colour · 102mins

Ever since his masterpiece *12 Angry Men*, director Sidney Lumet has had a taste for legal thrillers. And before it topples from high mystery to low melodrama, this film cops a plea for craftsmanship at least, with Rebecca De Mornay as the slick lawyer defending wife-killer Don Johnson, whose lethal duplicity involves the death of more than one woman. Larry Cohen's script is far more serrated than the *Jagged Edge* it resembles and so, prior to his succumbing to clichés, is Lumet's handling of some suspenseful legal scenes. TH. Contains violence, swearing. DVD

Rebecca De Mornay *Jennifer Haines* • Don Johnson *David Greenhill* • Stephen Lang *Phil Garson* • Jack Warden *Moe Plimpton* • Dana Ivey *Judge Tompkins* • Ron White *Diangelo* ■ *Dir* Sidney Lumet • *Scr* Larry Cohen

Guilty by Suspicion ★★★ 15

Drama 1990 · US · Colour · 100mins

The investigation of the House Un-American Activities Committee into communism in Hollywood is one of the most shameful episodes in movie history. But the film folk whose careers were destroyed by the infamous blacklist deserve a better memorial than Irwin Winkler's well-intentioned but underachieving picture. Set at the height of the 1951 witch-hunt, the action centres on film-maker Robert De Niro's dilemma – lose everything he's worked for or betray the "fellow travellers" among his friends. The film fails to generate the requisite atmosphere of fear and suspicion. DP. Contains swearing. DVD

Robert De Niro *David Merrill* • Annette Bening *Ruth Merrill* • George Wendt *Bunny Baxter* • Patricia Wettig *Dorothy Nolan* • Sam Wanamaker *Felix Graff* • Luke Edwards *Paulie Merrill* • Chris Cooper *Larry Nolan* • Ben Piazza *Darryl F Zanuck* • Martin Scorsese *Joe Lesser* ■ *Dir/Scr* Irwin Winkler

Guilty Bystander ★★

Film noir 1950 · US · BW · 91mins

Zachary Scott finds himself in familiar thriller territory as an ex-cop with a drink problem, a crummy job and a failed marriage. His problems escalate when his son is kidnapped and the convoluted storyline throws in smuggling for good measure. The supporting cast lends strength to the flimsy plot. TS

Zachary Scott *Max Thursday* • Faye Emerson *Georgia* • Mary Boland *Smitty* • Sam Levene *Capt Tonetti* • J Edward Bromberg *Varkas* • Kay Medford *Angel* • Jed Prouty *Dr Elder* • Harry Landers *Bert* ■ *Dir* Joseph Lerner • *Scr* Don Ettlinger, from a novel by Wade Miller

Guilty Conscience ★★★★

Thriller 1985 · US · Colour · 104mins

The writing partnership of Richard Levinson and William Link was responsible for some of the most popular shows in recent TV history. They also penned dozens of TV movies, but few surpassed this taut drama in which Anthony Hopkins gives a bravura performance as a lawyer who cross-examines his alter ego to concoct the perfect plan to murder his wife. But while he is scheming and dreaming of a future with his mistress, other plots are being hatched behind his back. Blythe Danner and Swoosie Kurtz match Hopkins every step of the way in a chatty but clever thriller. DP

Anthony Hopkins *Arthur Jamison* • Blythe Danner *Louise Jamison* • Swoosie Kurtz *Jackie Willis* • Wiley Harker *Older man* • Ruth Manning *Older woman* ■ *Dir* David Greene • *Scr* Richard Levinson, William Link

Guilty Hands ★★★

Crime drama 1931 · US · BW · 60mins

Deliciously inventive, this crime drama stars Lionel Barrymore as the former district attorney attempting to commit the perfect murder to prevent his daughter from marrying a playboy bounder. More usually a comic snob, Alan Mowbray must have been flattered to play the scoundrel, with no less a figure than Kay Francis as his mistress. Bayard Veiller's original screenplay comes up with an unforgettable way for Mowbray to settle the score, while WS Van Dyke's direction is visually accomplished. AE

Lionel Barrymore *Richard Grant* • Kay Francis *Marjorie West* • Madge Evans *Barbara Grant* • William Bakewell *Tommy Osgood* • C Aubrey Smith *Rev Hastings* • Polly Moran *Aunt Maggie* • Alan Mowbray *Gordon Rich* • Forrester Harvey *Spencer Wilson* ■ *Dir* WS Van Dyke • *Scr* Bayard Veiller, from his story

The Guinea Pig ★★ U

Drama 1948 · UK · BW · 93mins

Richard Attenborough makes light of his 20-odd years to play a boy half his age in this class-barrier melodrama. Accepted by a top public school as part of an educational experiment, working-class Attenborough endures the raillery of classmates and family with practised angst as he passes from victim to insider with the help of teacher Robert Flemyng. Wallowing in the clichés of establishment privilege, director Roy Boulting makes few demands of a cast that almost sleepwalks through familiar characterisations. DP

Richard Attenborough *Jack Read* • Sheila Sim *Lynne Hartley* • Bernard Miles *Mr Read* • Cecil Trouncer *Mr Hartley, housemaster* • Robert Flemyng *Nigel Lorraine* • Edith Sharpe *Mrs Hartley* • Joan Hickson *Mrs Read* • Peter Reynolds *Grimmett* ■ *Dir* Roy Boulting • *Scr* Warren Chetham Strode, Bernard Miles, from the play by Warren Chetham Strode

Guinevere ★★★

Romantic drama
1999 · US · Colour · 104mins

A knock-out performance from Sarah Polley is the main reason for seeing this insightful, if sentimental coming-of-age saga. Polley plays an affection-starved 21-year-old, who meets middle-aged photographer Stephen Rea at her sister's wedding. Attracted by his bohemian charisma, she becomes his apprentice and lover. This familiar May-December romance contains as many deft strokes as it does missteps. AJ

Stephen Rea *Connie Fitzpatrick* • Sarah Polley *Harper Sloane* • Jean Smart *Deborah Sloane* • Gina Gershon *Billie* • Jasmine Guy *Linda* • Francis Guinan *Alan Sloane* • Paul Dooley *Walter* ■ *Dir/Scr* Audrey Wells

Gulliver's Travels ★★ U

Animated fantasy 1939 · US · Colour · 76mins

An age in production, this animated version of Jonathan Swift's timeless satire owes more to the imagination of the Fleischer brothers than it does to the venerable Dublin dean's. The most serious failing is the time it takes for Gulliver to embark on his Lilliputian adventures, with far too long being devoted to the pointless feud between kings Little of Lilliput and Bombo of Blefescu. Stylistic inconsistencies in the artwork also irritate. DP DVD

Dir Dave Fleischer • *Scr* Dan Gordon, Ted Pierce, Izzy Sparber, Edmond Seward, from a story by Edmond Seward, from the novel by Jonathan Swift • *Producer* Max Fleischer

Gulliver's Travels ★ U

Part-animated satirical fantasy
1977 · UK/Bel · Colour · 76mins

This is a dismal combination of dire songs, unutterable dialogue and one of the worst mergers of animated and live-action footage ever committed to celluloid. Richard Harris looks like a man enduring a nightmare as he attempts desperately to interact with his clumsily drawn co-stars. DP

Richard Harris *Gulliver* • Catherine Schell *Girl* • Norman Shelley *Father* • Meredith Edwards *Uncle* ■ *Dir* Peter Hunt • *Scr* Don Black, from the novel by Jonathan Swift

Gulliver's Travels ★★

Animated fantasy adventure
1983 · Sp · Colour · 80mins

Spanish animator Cruz Delgado elects here to focus on the Brobdingnag element of Jonathan Swift's celebrated satire. The colourful graphics are firmly aimed at a younger audience, as is the simplified storyline, with Lemuel Gulliver's encounters with a mammoth crab, a ravenous feline and a furious hornet taking precedence over political events at the court of Prince Fleenap. However, he does make the jealous jester a suitably hissable nemesis. DP. Spanish dialogue dubbed into English.

Nelson Modlin *Gulliver* • Alexa Bates *Glundalich* • Jack Taylor *Prince Flinap* • Leon Liberman *Bufo* ■ *Dir* Cruz Delgado • *Scr* from the novel by Jonathan Swift

Gumball 3000: the Movie ★★★ 18

Documentary 2003 · US/UK · Colour · 97mins

Lasting six days and spanning 3000 miles of occasionally treacherous terrain, the Gumball Rally may seem like just another excuse for a bunch of minor celebrities, extreme sports stars and everyday opportunists to see their name in the headlines. But Steven Green's documentary reveals high levels of both competitive spirit and cameraderie, as the likes of supermodel Jodie Kidd, the *Jackass* duo Ryan Dunn and Tony Hawk, and hip-hop comics the Cuban Brothers negotiate the route from San Francisco to Miami and the various cops they encounter along it. Burt Reynolds provides the genially sardonic commentary. DP. Contains swearing. DVD

Burt Reynolds *Narrator* ■ *Dir* Steven Green

The Gumball Rally ★★★ PG

Comedy adventure
1976 · US · Colour · 102mins

A precursor to such frantic cross-country races as *The Cannonball Run* and *Smokey and the Bandit*, this is a reasonable example of the genre, unhindered by a serious plot and full of tyre-squealing action. It's directed and produced by stuntman Chuck Bail and, though the actors are constantly upstaged by the customised autos, Michael Sarrazin and rival Tim McIntire do raise a few smiles as bungling cop Normann Burton desperately tries to stop their contest. Watch out for Raul Julia in a small role. TH

Michael Sarrazin *Michael Bannon* • Normann Burton [Norman Burton] *Roscoe* • Gary Busey *Gibson* • John Durren *Preston* • Susan Flannery *Alice* • Harvey Jason *Lapchick* • Tim McIntire *Steve Smith* • Raul Julia *Franco* ■ *Dir* Chuck Bail • *Scr* Leon Capetanos, from a story by Leon Capetanos, Chuck Bail

Gumby: the Movie ★★

Animated fantasy adventure
1995 · US · Colour · 90mins

Having first demonstrated his genius for claymation with the abstract jazz fantasy, *Gumbasia*, Art Clokey became something of an institution on American television in the 1950s with the adventures of a pliable green blob. The star of this heavy-handed show, Gumby, joins with his old pals to confound the attempt of their great rivals, the Blockheads, to replace his invaluable dog, Lowbelly, with an android hound. DP

Charles Farrington *Gumby/Claybert/Fatbuckle/Kapp* • Art Clokey *Pokey/Prickle/Gumbo* • Gloria Clokey *Goo* • Manny LaCarruba *Thinbuckle* • Alice Young *Ginger* • Janet MacDuff *Gumba* ■ *Dir* Art Clokey • *Scr* Art Clokey, Gloria Clokey, from characters created by Art Clokey

Gummo ★★★★ 18

Drama 1997 · US · Colour · 85mins

Abandoning any pretence of linear narrative, director Harmony Korine – writer of the highly controversial *kids* – presents an impressionistic collection of grim insights into a neighbourhood recovering from a destructive tornado. Using a variety of techniques, including hand-held camerawork, this follows two geeky adolescents, Jacob Reynolds and Nick Sutton, as they sniff glue, torture cats and gross out the locals. This extraordinary investigation into the tarnished American Dream is repulsive, shocking and definitely not for the faint-hearted. AJ. Contains violence, swearing, sex scenes, drug abuse and nudity.

Jacob Reynolds *Solomon* • Nick Sutton *Tummler* • Jacob Sewell *Bunny Boy* • Lara Tosh *Girl in car* • Darby Dougherty *Darby* • Chloë Sevigny *Dot* • Carisa Glucksman *Helen* • Jason Guzak *Skinhead* • Casey Guzak *Skinhead* ■ *Dir/Scr* Harmony Korine

Gumshoe ★★★★ 15

Crime comedy 1971 · UK · Colour · 82mins

Director Stephen Frears made his feature debut with this wonderfully understated homage to *film noir*. Albert Finney excels as the bingo caller who has dreams of writing like Dashiell Hammett and acting like Humphrey Bogart. Following the example of Woody Allen in *Play It Again, Sam*, screenwriter Neville Smith blends fond parody with an original story that has an undeniable charm of its own. But this also has an unexpectedly hard edge, thanks to its tough themes of drugs and gunrunning and Frears's astute snapshots of Liverpool. DP. Contains swearing and violence.

Albert Finney *Eddie Ginley* • Billie Whitelaw *Ellen* • Frank Finlay *William* • Janice Rule *Mrs Blankerscoon* • Carolyn Seymour *Alison Wyatt* • Fulton Mackay *John Straker* • George Innes *Bookshop proprietor* • Wendy Richard *Anne Scott* • Maureen Lipman *Naomi* ■ *Dir* Stephen Frears • *Scr* Neville Smith

The Gumshoe Kid ★

Comedy 1990 · US · Colour · 98mins

This goofy leftover from the 1980s somehow got released in 1990 as a last gasp of "madcap" comedy before the plethora of movies made from *Saturday Night Live* sketches hit their mark. Cash-strapped amateur sleuth Jay Underwood is foisted on his private detective uncle Vince Edwards, but he is unwilling to trust the teenager with anything too taxing. Through a series of stupid coincidences, Underwood ends up on the run from murderers with a woman (Tracy Scoggins) he was assigned to watch. ST

Jay Underwood *Jeff Sherman* • Tracy Scoggins *Rita Benson* • Vince Edwards *Ben Sherman* • Arlene Golonka *Gracie Sherman* ■ *Dir* Joseph Manduke • *Scr* Victor Bardack

Gun Crazy ★★★★

Film noir 1949 · US · BW · 87mins

This unsung minor masterpiece influenced everything from the work of Jean-Luc Godard to *Bonnie and Clyde* and *Natural Born Killers*. A stylish *film noir* from director Joseph H Lewis, it's about a smouldering *femme fatale* (Peggy Cummins in the role of her life) who leads the psychotic, gun-fixated John Dall astray. Originally based on a *Saturday Evening Post* short story by MacKinlay Kantor, the taut screenplay is the work of Kantor and the blacklisted Dalton Trumbo (here credited as Millard Kaufman). The plot was reworked less effectively for 1992's *Guncrazy*. TS

John Dall *Bart Tare* • Peggy Cummins *Annie Laurie Starr* • Berry Kroeger *Packett* • Annabel Shaw [Anabel Shaw] *Ruby Tare* • Harry Lewis *Clyde Boston* • Morris Carnovsky *Judge Willoughby* • Stanley Praeger [Stanley Prager] *Bluey-Bluey* • Nedrick Young *Dave Allister* ■ *Dir* Joseph H Lewis • *Scr* MacKinlay Kantor, Millard Kaufman [Dalton Trumbo], from a story by MacKinlay Kantor in *The Saturday Evening Post*

Gun Duel in Durango ★★ U

Western 1957 · US · BW · 73mins

Rugged George Montgomery spent most of the 1950s appearing as the hero of short and snappy minor westerns. This time he's the leader of a band of outlaws who decides it's time to change for the better. Before he can marry sweetheart Ann Robinson he has to prove himself, but his old gang have ways of persuading him to join them in another raid. Comfortably predictable – naturally, there is a final showdown – it is directed competently enough to please genre fans. RB

George Montgomery *Dan* • Ann Robinson *Judy* • Steve Brodie *Dunston* • Bobby Clark *Robbie* • Frank Ferguson *Sheriff Howard* • Donald Barry *Larry* • Denver Pyle *Ranger captain* ■ *Dir* Sidney Salkow • *Scr* Louis Stevens

Gun for a Coward ★★ U

Western 1957 · US · Colour · 88mins

This interesting western is from that period in the 1950s when juvenile delinquency was the byword and all Hollywood youths were crazy mixed-up kids. Jeffrey Hunter and Dean Stockwell are both excellent as the troubled teens coping with the death of their father, watched over by their older sibling, the reliable Fred MacMurray. Promises more than it delivers. TS

Fred MacMurray *Will Keough* • Jeffrey Hunter *Bless Keough* • Janice Rule *Aud Niven* • Chill Wills *Loving* • Dean Stockwell *Hade Keough* • Josephine Hutchinson *Mrs Keough* • Betty Lynn *Claire* • Iron Eyes Cody *Chief* ■ *Dir* Abner Biberman • *Scr* R Wright Campbell

Gun Fury ★★★ U

Western 1953 · US · Colour · 78mins

Rock Hudson gives an adequate performance as a rancher whose fiancée Donna Reed is abducted. The film boasts a moody plot that pits the gauche, honest and upright Hudson against psychotic baddie Phil Carey (who's outstanding) and his gang, including Lee Marvin and Neville Brand. Originally filmed in the novelty of 3-D, this exciting psychological western was directed by Raoul Walsh, who appears to have encouraged inexperienced star Hudson to overact. TS

Rock Hudson *Ben Warren* • Donna Reed *Jennifer Ballard* • Phil Carey [Philip Carey] *Frank Slayton* • Roberta Haynes *Estella Morales* • Lee Marvin *Blinky* • Leo Gordon *"Jess Burgess"* • Neville Brand *Brazos* • Ray Thomas *Doc* ■ *Dir* Raoul Walsh • *Scr* Irving Wallace, Roy Huggins, from the novel *Ten against Caesar* by Kathleen B George, Robert A Granger

Gun Glory ★★ U

Western 1957 · US · Colour · 88mins

This last film British-born actor Stewart Granger made under his seven-year contract with MGM was a farewell without much glory. Granger, who was best as a swashbuckling hero, seems ill-at-ease as a gunfighter returning home to his ranch after some years away, to find that his wife has died and his teenage son is bitter towards him. Director Roy Rowland commits the cardinal casting sin of putting his plainly inadequate son Steve in the role of Granger's son. But the plot and the lovely Rhonda Fleming make this CinemaScope western watchable. RB

Stewart Granger *Tom Early* • Rhonda Fleming *Jo* • Chill Wills *Preacher* • Steve Rowland *Young Tom Early* • James Gregory *Grimsell* • Jacques Aubuchon *Sam Winscott* • Arch Johnson *Gunn* • William Fawcett *Martin* ■ *Dir* Roy Rowland • *Scr* William Ludwig, Philip Yordan (front for Ben Maddow), from the novel *Man of the West* by Philip Yordan

The Gun in Betty Lou's Handbag ★★★ 15

Comedy 1992 · US · Colour · 84mins

Director Allan Moyle might seem a curious choice for this comic slice of small-town life, considering he is best known for those celebrations of teenage angst, *Pump Up the Volume* and *Empire Records*. However, he keeps this preposterous story ticking along nicely and coaxes an engaging performance out of Penelope Ann Miller as the timid librarian who finds a murder weapon and confesses to the crime to spice up her life. DP. Contains swearing. DVD

Penelope Ann Miller *Betty Lou Perkins* • Eric Thal *Alex Perkins* • Alfre Woodard *Ann* • Julianne Moore *Elinor* • Andy Romano *Herrick* • Ray McKinnon *Frank* • William Forsythe *Beaudeen* • Cathy Moriarty *Reba* ■ *Dir* Allan Moyle • *Scr* Grace Cary Bickley

The Gun Runners ★★★

Crime adventure 1958 · US · Colour · 82mins

This cheaply-made version of Ernest Hemingway's *To Have and Have Not* is creditably close to Howard Hawks's adaptation in 1944 and Michael Curtiz's *The Breaking Point* in 1950. Director Don Siegel draws a persuasive performance from Audie Murphy as the hard-up fishing boat captain. Patricia Owens is good as his caring wife, Everett Sloane excellent as his drunken assistant, and Eddie Albert outstanding as the treacherous gunrunner who hires his boat. AE

Audie Murphy *Sam Martin* • Eddie Albert *Hanagan* • Patricia Owens *Lucy Martin* • Everett Sloane *Harvey* • Richard Jaeckel *Buzurki* • Jack Elam *Arnold* ■ *Dir* Don Siegel • *Scr* Daniel Mainwaring, Paul Monash, from the novel *To Have and Have Not* by Ernest Hemingway

Gun Shy ★ 15

Romantic crime comedy
2000 · US · Colour · 97mins

Sandra Bullock is to blame here, for it was she who decided she just *had* to make this uneven and almost humour-free comedy. Liam Neeson is woefully miscast as an undercover agent who is suffering from nerves and a very dodgy stomach, leading him to seek bowel advice from a nurse (Bullock). The movie's only saving grace is Oliver Platt (surely one of the funniest actors in movies today) as the Mafia hood Neeson is supposed to be bringing to justice. But even he can't stop this from hurtling towards the bin marked "avoid". JB DVD

Liam Neeson *Charlie* • Oliver Platt *Fulvio Nesstra* • Sandra Bullock *Judy Tipp* • José Zuniga *Fidel Vaillar* • Richard Schiff *Elliott* • Mary McCormack *Gloria Nesstra* ■ *Dir/Scr* Eric Blakeney

G

Gun Smoke ★★★

Western 1931 · US · BW · 63mins

A truly unusual western that features rugged *Wings* star Richard Arlen in the leading role, but is better remembered for the performance of William "Stage" Boyd, stealing Arlen's thunder as a villainous deranged mobster out west. This Boyd was a star of the Broadway theatre (hence "Stage" to differentiate him from former Cecil B DeMille star William "Hopalong Cassidy" Boyd), whose career was given a boost by his performance in this film. In fact, this movie also began a short trend where machine guns vied with six-guns on the range. TS

Richard Arlen *Brad Farley* • William "Stage" Boyd *Kedge Darvis* • Mary Brian *Sue Vancey* • Eugene Pallette *Stub Wallack* • Charles Winninger *Tack Gillup* • Louise Fazenda *Hampsey Dell* • Brooks Benedict *Spot Skee* ■ *Dir* Edward Sloman • *Scr* Grover Jones, William McNutt

Gunbus ★ PG

Adventure 1986 · UK · Colour · 88mins

Scott McGinnis and Jeff Osterhage try valiantly to drum up some knockabout bonhomie here as Wild West outlaws enrolled in a British fighter squadron during the First World War, but everything from the stereotypical characters to the risible banter is against them. The aerial action is so inept that it only emphasises the shortcomings of this disappointing buddy movie. DP. Contains some violent scenes.

Scott McGinnis *Barney* • Jeff Osterhage *Luke* • Ronald Lacey *Fritz* • Miles Anderson *Bannock* • Valerie Steffen *Yvette* • Ingrid Held *Mitsou* • Keith Buckley *Commander von Schlussel* • Terence Harvey *Colonel Canning* ■ *Dir* Zoran Perisic • *Scr* Thom Keyes

Guncrazy ★★★ 15

Crime drama 1992 · US · Colour · 92mins

Director Tamra Davis here does a solid job with this tale of teenager Drew Barrymore who falls for an ex-con. This occasionally tries to be a 1990s version of the much more subtle *Badlands*, as the pair go on the run, firing guns aplenty, but Barrymore and co-stars James LeGros and Billy Drago keep their performances realistic. The plot is a reworking of the 1949's *Gun Crazy*. JB. Contains violence, swearing. DVD

Drew Barrymore *Anita Minteer* • James LeGros *Howard Hickock* • Michael Ironside *Kincaid* • Ione Skye *Joy* • Billy Drago *Hank* • Joe Dallesandro *Rooney* ■ *Dir* Tamra Davis • *Scr* Matthew Bright

A Gunfight ★★★

Western 1971 · US · Colour · 89mins

In this offbeat western Kirk Douglas and Johnny Cash give excellent performances as two ageing gunfighters who have fallen on hard times. In response to speculation in the town, Douglas proposes that they should stage a gun duel and charge admission so that the survivor can make a fresh start. Tension mounts under Lamont Johnson's sharp direction of Harold Jack Bloom's screenplay, as we don't want either man to die. But the handling of the outcome is not entirely satisfactory. AE

Kirk Douglas *Will Tenneray* • Johnny Cash *Abe Cross* • Jane Alexander *Nora Tenneray* • Raf Vallone *Francisco Alvarez* • Karen Black *Jenny Simms* • Eric Douglas *Bud Tenneray* ■ *Dir* Lamont Johnson • *Scr* Harold Jack Bloom

Gunfight at Comanche Creek ★★ U

Western 1964 · US · Colour · 90mins

Audie Murphy follows in the footsteps of George Montgomery in a remake of the 1957 western *Last of the Badmen*. In this hybrid of a 1940s-style detective movie and the traditional western, detective Murphy poses as an outlaw to infiltrate a particularly ruthless gang of robbers. Their cunning plan involves using escaped convicts to commit further crimes, and then killing them so they can collect the bounty. Murphy's lightweight style undermines the suspense. AE

Audie Murphy *Bob Gifford* • Ben Cooper *Carter* • Colleen Miller *Abbie Stevens* • DeForest Kelley *Troop* • Jan Merlin *Nielson* • John Hubbard *Marshal Shearer* • Damian O'Flynn *Winton* • Susan Seaforth *Janie* ■ *Dir* Frank McDonald • *Scr* Edward Bernds

The Gunfight at Dodge City ★★ U

Western 1959 · US · Colour · 80mins

Joseph M Newman allows this Dodge City encounter to meander to its inevitable showdown between reformed outlaw Joel McCrea and his old gang. However, sheriff McCrea seems to have more on his mind than law and order, as both widowed saloon owner Nancy Gates and minister's daughter Julie Adams tug on his heart strings. Snarling unconvincingly, Richard Anderson leads the assorted desperadoes. DP

Joel McCrea *Bat Masterson* • Julie Adams *Pauline* • John McIntire *Doc* • Nancy Gates *Lily* • Richard Anderson *Dave* • James Westerfield *Rev Howard* ■ *Dir* Joseph M Newman • *Scr* Martin Goldsmith, Dan Ullman [Daniel B Ullman], from a story by Dan Ullman [Daniel B Ullman]

Gunfight at the OK Corral ★★★★ PG

Western 1957 · US · Colour · 117mins

Wyatt Earp and Doc Holliday were never better portrayed on screen than here, played by movie giants Burt Lancaster and Kirk Douglas respectively. The Leon Uris screenplay may veer towards the turgid in setting up the action, but once the gunplay starts the screen positively ignites: director John Sturges's shoot-out finale is a mesmerisingly fine piece of cinema, brilliantly photographed and edited. There's also a soaring, nostalgic title ballad by Frankie Laine, and a marvellously etched supporting performance from Jo Van Fleet as Holliday's woman. TS

Burt Lancaster *Wyatt Earp* • Kirk Douglas *John H "Doc" Holliday* • Rhonda Fleming *Laura Denbow* • Jo Van Fleet *Kate Fisher* • John Ireland *Johnny Ringo* • Frank Faylen *Cotton Wilson* • Earl Holliman *Charles Bassett* • Lyle Bettger *Ike Clanton* • Dennis Hopper *Billy Clanton* • DeForest Kelley *Morgan Earp* • Lee Van Cleef *Ed Bailey* ■ *Dir* John Sturges • *Scr* Leon Uris, from the article *The Killer* by George Scullin • *Music* Dmitri Tiomkin

Gunfight in Abilene ★★

Western 1967 · US · Colour · 85mins

Teen idol Bobby Darin heads a cast that includes Michael Sarrazin and a pre-*Airplane!* Leslie Nielsen in this very routine Universal western. Darin gives a capable performance as the disillusioned American Civil War veteran who's reluctantly recruited as the sheriff of Abilene by cattle baron Nielsen, but co-star Emily Banks is an unconvincing heroine and William Hale's direction is leaden. A remake of 1956's *Showdown at Abiline*. TS

Bobby Darin *Cal Wayne* • Emily Banks *Amy Martin* • Leslie Nielsen *Grant Evers* • Donnelly Rhodes *Joe Slade* • Don Galloway *Ward Kent* • Michael Sarrazin *Cord Decker* • Barbara Werle *Leann* ■ *Dir* William Hale • *Scr* Berne Giler, John DF Black, from the novel *Gun Shy* by Clarence Upson Young

The Gunfighter ★★★★ U

Western 1950 · US · BW · 81mins

Gregory Peck gives a performance of characteristic dignity and grit in this simmering western about the stark realities of frontier life. Having been forced to go for his gun by a bar-room braggart, gunslinger Peck rides off to a neighbouring town to visit his estranged wife and son, only to find his presence resented by the locals and his life threatened by the brothers of his latest victim. Veteran director Henry King expertly strips away the glamour of the gunfighter to reveal a man who regrets his past, but knows killing is his only future. DP DVD

Gregory Peck *Jimmy Ringo* • Helen Westcott *Peggy Walsh* • Millard Mitchell *Sheriff Mark Strett* • Jean Parker *Molly* • Karl Malden *Mac* • Skip Homeier *Hunt Bromley* • Anthony Ross *Charlie* • Verna Felton *Mrs Pennyfeather* ■ *Dir* Henry King • *Scr* William Bowers, William Sellers, Nunnally Johnson, from a story by William Bowers, Andre De Toth

Gung Ho! ★★★ PG

Second World War drama
1943 · US · BW · 82mins

This drama was a huge wartime hit for Universal with its rousing fictionalised re-creation of a highly successful August 1942 attack in which a battalion of specially picked marine raiders took a Pacific island back from the Japanese. The force's motto is "gung ho", a Chinese expression for working in harmony. Randolph Scott is suitably heroic as the tough commander, and a young Robert Mitchum also appears. AE DVD

Randolph Scott *Col Thorwald* • Grace McDonald *Kathleen Corrigan* • Alan Curtis *John Harbison* • Noah Beery Jr *Kurt Richter* • J Carrol Naish *Lt Cristoforos* • Bob Mitchum [Robert Mitchum] *"Pig-Iron" Matthews* ■ *Dir* Ray Enright • *Scr* Lucien Hubbard, from a story by Capt WS LeFrançois

Gung Ho ★★★ 15

Comedy 1986 · US · Colour · 107mins

Ron Howard directs this small but often enjoyable comedy. Michael Keaton is the car factory foreman trying to create peace between the workers and the new Japanese owners of the plant, who, of course, want their employees to be punctual, correct and up at six in the morning doing exercises in the parking lot. Keaton is a deft hand at comedy, and he is capably supported by George Wendt (*Cheers*) and Coen Brothers regular John Turturro. JB DVD

Michael Keaton *Hunt Stevenson* • Mimi Rogers *Audrey* • George Wendt *Buster* • Gedde Watanabe *Kazihiro* • John Turturro *Willie* • Soh Yamamura [So Yamamura] *Mr Sakamoto* ■ *Dir* Ron Howard • *Scr* Lowell Ganz, Babaloo Mandel, from a story by Edwin Blum, Lowell Ganz, Babaloo Mandel

Gunga Din ★★★★★ U

Adventure 1939 · US · BW · 112mins

This absolutely spiffing action adventure, probably the best of its kind, is loosely based on the imperialist poem by Rudyard Kipling. However, it actually takes its plot premise from the Broadway classic *The Front Page*, and it's no surprise that both the play and this story were written by the same team, Ben Hecht and Charles MacArthur. Casting couldn't be bettered, as Cary Grant, Douglas Fairbanks Jr and Victor McLaglen swashbuckle their way across the 19th-century Indian frontier, only to be rescued ultimately by water boy Sam Jaffe. George Stevens makes a superb job of handling the rumbustious squaddies in his biggest budget movie. This immensely enjoyable epic is timeless. TS

Cary Grant *Cutter* • Victor McLaglen *MacChesney* • Douglas Fairbanks Jr *Ballantine* • Sam Jaffe *Gunga Din* • Joan Fontaine *Emmy* • Eduardo Ciannelli *Guru* • Montagu Love *Colonel Weed* ■ *Dir* George Stevens • *Scr* Joel Sayre, Fred Guiol, from a story by Ben Hecht, Charles MacArthur, from the poem by Rudyard Kipling

Gunhed ★★★ 12

Science-fiction action
1989 · Jpn · Colour · 96mins

In 2025, the super computer Kyron-5 began hostilities with mankind. By 2083, fearless techno-bounty hunters assault the computer's island HQ initiating the great Robot War. The only hope for man's future lies in fabled fighting machine Unit 507, the last of the Gunheds. Can this bio-droid penetrate the island's dizzying battle levels for victory over the machine? A smash hit in Japan, director Masato Harada's dark vision is an exciting helter-skelter action adventure, with few pauses for breath. AJ. Japanese dialogue dubbed into English.

Landy Leyes *Gunhed* • Masahiro Takashima *Brooklyn* • Brenda Bakke *Sergeant Nim* • Yujin Harada *Steven* • Kaori Mizushima *Eleven* • Aya Enyoji *Bebe* • Mickey Curtis *Bancho* • James B Thompson *Balba* ■ *Dir* Masato Harada • *Scr* Masato Harada, James Bannon

Gunman's Walk ★★★

Western 1958 · US · Colour · 94mins

Although he spent most of his career directing low-budget movies, Phil Karlson was one of the shrewdest of his breed. His ability to draw symbolic significance from the landscape is just one of the ways in which he hauls this pseudo-biblical western up a notch. Another is the subtle manner in which Karlson lets Tab Hunter exhibit his natural tendency to over-act, making Hunter's role as the hothead son of former gunslinger Van Heflin one of his best. Kathryn Grant also does well as the mixed-race girl who captures the heart of Heflin's clean-living younger son, James Darren. DP

Van Heflin *Lee Hackett* • Tab Hunter *Ed Hackett* • Kathryn Grant *Clee Chouard* • James Darren *Davy Hackett* • Mickey Shaughnessy *Will Motely* • Robert F Simon *Harry Brill* ■ *Dir* Phil Karlson • *Scr* Frank S Nugent, from a story by Ric Hardman

Gunmen ★★★ 18

Action adventure 1994 · US · Colour · 90mins

Eclectic casting lifts what is basically a trashy and gory B-movie thriller out of the ordinary. Christopher Lambert and Mario Van Peebles play a mismatched duo forced to team up to locate a boat that holds millions of dollars stolen from drugs lord Patrick Stewart; Denis Leary and an army of swarthy bandits are also hot on their trail. The two stars spark off each other nicely and director Deran Sarafian stages some enjoyably ludicrous action set pieces. JF. Contains violence, swearing, drug abuse and nudity.

Christopher Lambert *Dani Servigo* • Mario Van Peebles *Cole Parker* • Denis Leary *Armor O'Malley* • Patrick Stewart *Loomis* • Kadeem Hardison *Izzy* • Sally Kirkland *Bennett* ■ *Dir* Deran Sarafian • *Scr* Stephen Sommers

Gunn ★★

Detective drama 1967 · US · Colour · 94mins

Blake Edwards's successful TV series of the early 1960s, *Peter Gunn*, comes to the big screen with Craig Stevens reprising his role as the private investigator. The story involves Mafia treachery, offshore bordellos and exploding yachts, with Stevens waltzing through it with a girl on each arm. At times Edwards creates a lovely pastiche of 1940s Hollywood but for the most part this is just slick. A 1989 TV movie, also directed by Edwards, starred an uncharismatic Peter Strauss in the title role. AT

Craig Stevens *Peter Gunn* • Laura Devon *Edie* • Edward Asner *Jacoby* • Sherry Jackson *Samantha* • Helen Traubel *Mother* • Albert Paulsen *Fusco* • MT Marshall [Marion Marshall] *Daisy Jane* • J Pat O'Malley *Tinker* • Regis Toomey *"The Bishop"* ■ *Dir* Blake Edwards • *Scr* Blake Edwards, William Peter Blatty, from a story and characters created by Blake Edwards

Gunnar Hede's Saga ★★★★

Silent drama 1922 · Swe · BW · 70mins

One of the Swedish masterworks of director Mauritz Stiller, based on a novel by Selma Lagerlöf, this is the tale of an introspective young man who is cast off the family estate for befriending a young female violinist. He seeks to emulate his grandfather by bringing a vast herd of reindeer down from the snowy north but suffers a serious accident during the journey. This drive, with its stampede, puts the film in the epic class, but it is also concerned with dreams, hallucinations and the power of memory. AE

Einar Hanson *Gunnar Hede* • Pauline Brunius *Gunnar's mother* • Mary Johnson *Ingrid* • Adolf Olchansky *Mr Blomgren* • Stina Berg *Mrs Blomgren* • Hugo Björne *Gunnar's father* • Theckla Ahlander *Miss Stava* ■ *Dir* Mauritz Stiller • *Scr* Mauritz Stiller, from the novel *En Herrgårdssägen* by Selma Lagerlöf

Gunpoint ★★ PG

Western 1966 · US · Colour · 82mins

A late Audie Murphy vehicle, with the ageing baby-faced war hero playing a sheriff trying to capture a gang of train robbers who have taken a saloon girl hostage. Murphy is always watchable and there's expert support from grizzled western veterans Denver Pyle and Edgar Buchanan, but this unoriginal movie is little better than TV fodder. Director Earl Bellamy makes good use of his locations, but the low budget is very evident. TS

Audie Murphy *Chad Lucas* • Joan Stanley *Uvalde* • Warren Stevens *Nate Harlan* • Edgar Buchanan *Bull* • Denver Pyle *Cap Hold* • Royal Dano *Ode* • Nick Dennis *Nicos* • William Bramley *Hoag* ■ *Dir* Earl Bellamy • *Scr* Willard Willingham, Mary Willingham

Gunpowder ★ PG

Comedy thriller 1985 · UK · Colour · 81mins

Hopelessly dated spy thriller, complete with evil master criminals, suave agents and girls with suggestive names. There are plenty of familiar British faces in the cast, including David Gilliam and Gordon Jackson, but the movie raises more unintentional laughs than thrills. JF

David Gilliam *Mike Gunn* • Martin Potter *Charles Powder* • Gordon Jackson *Sir Anthony Phelps* • Debra Burton *Coffee Carradine* • David Miller *Dr Vache* • Susan Rutherford

Penny Keynes • Anthony Schaeffer *Lovell* • Rachel Laurence *Miss Belt* ■ *Dir* Norman J Warren • *Scr* Rory H MacLean

The Gunrunner ★★ 15

Crime drama
1984 · Can/US · Colour · 78mins

Had Kevin Costner not found fame, this early outing may have remained in the obscurity it deserves. Set in the 1920s, it opens with Costner vowing to run guns for some Chinese rebels. But back in Montreal, his purpose is blunted by the fact his family has not only fallen on hard times, but has also become involved with the Mob. DP

Kevin Costner *Ted Beaubien* • Sara Botsford *Maude* • Paul Soles *Lochman* • Gerard Parkes *Wilson* • Ron Lea *George* ■ *Dir* Nardo Castillo • *Scr* Arnie Gelbart

Guns at Batasi ★★★★

Drama 1964 · UK · BW · 104mins

Overlooked in 1964 as a routine piece of stiff-upper-lip-manship, this film is a fascinating epitaph for the British Empire and a whole slew of movies about Imperial derring-do. Set in an Africa well brushed by what Harold Macmillan called "the wind of change", it's the story of insurrection in a newly independent state and what the resident British army does about it. Staunchly traditional, it's also subversive and satirical, with a standout performance by Richard Attenborough as the apoplectic RSM Lauderdale. AT

Richard Attenborough *RSM Lauderdale* • Mia Farrow *Karen Ericksson* • Jack Hawkins *Lt Col Deal* • Flora Robson *Miss Barker-Wise* • John Leyton *Pte Wilkes* • Errol John *Lt Boniface* • Earl Cameron *Capt Abraham* ■ *Dir* John Guillermin • *Scr* Robert Holles, from his novel *The Siege of Battersea*

Guns for San Sebastian ★★ PG

Western
1968 · US/Fr/Mex/It · Colour · 106mins

This uncomfortable blend of social theology, coarse comedy and bruising action is made all the more intolerable by the sloppy dubbing. This adaptation is full of bombastic pronouncements and glib posturings, with Anthony Quinn at full throttle as a mid-18th-century Mexican drifter posing as a priest. There's a brooding dignity about Charles Bronson's misguided loyalty, Henri Verneuil handles the fighting with aplomb, and Ennio Morricone's score helps, too. DP. French dialogue dubbed into English.

Anthony Quinn *León Alastray* • Anjanette Comer *Kinita* • Charles Bronson *Teclo* • Sam Jaffe *Father Joseph* • Silvia Pinal *Felicia* • Jorge Martinez DeHoyos *Cayetano* • Jaime Fernandez *Golden Lance* • Rosa Furman *Agueda* ■ *Dir* Henri Verneuil • *Scr* James R Webb, from the novel *A Wall for San Sebastian* by William Barby Faherty

Guns in the Heather ★★ U

Spy adventure 1969 · US · Colour · 85mins

Disney decamped to Ireland for this so-so adventure, also known as *The Secret of Boyne Castle* and *Spy Busters*. Kurt Russell stars as a student who helps his brother, a CIA agent, prevent a defecting scientist from falling into the clutches of communist agents. The 18-year-old Russell gives the impression that the material is beneath him and the routine round of sanitised set pieces and narrow squeaks hardly makes for gripping viewing. DP

Glenn Corbett *Tom Evans* • Alfred Burke *Kersner* • Kurt Russell *Rich Evans* • Patrick Dawson *Sean O'Connor* • Patrick Barr *Lord Boyne* • Hugh McDermott *Carleton* • Patrick Westwood *Levick* ■ *Dir* Robert Butler • *Scr* Herman Groves, Charles Frend, from a novel by Lockhart Amerman

The Guns of August ★★★

First World War documentary
1964 · US · BW · 100mins

Governments on either side were slow to recognise the value of propaganda at the outbreak of the First World War. To his credit, producer/director Nathan Kroll was able to uncover a wealth of archive material, much of it previously unseen, for his adaptation of Barbara Tuchman's acclaimed, Pulitzer Prize-winning study of Europe on the precipice. Chronicling events from the funeral of Edward VII in 1910 to the armistice in 1918, the film presents an indelible image of what was meant to be the war to end all wars. DP

Fritz Weaver *Narrator* ■ *Dir* Nathan Kroll • *Scr* from the non-fiction work by Barbara W Tuchman

Guns of Darkness ★★★

Drama 1962 · UK · BW · 102mins

A minor film from director Anthony Asquith, but extremely interesting nonetheless, despite the all-too-obvious overuse of Elstree interiors, doubling for a swampy South America where pacifist planter David Niven and pregnant wife Leslie Caron find themselves aiding revolutionaries. This promises more intellectually than it delivers cinematically: Niven's motivation seems unclear, and his character's boorishness makes him hard to like, let alone understand, while Caron's part is seriously underwritten. There's excellent support, though, from David Opatoshu and James Robertson-Justice. TS

David Niven *Tom Jordan* • Leslie Caron *Claire Jordan* • James Robertson-Justice *Hugo Bryant* • David Opatoshu *President Rivera* • Derek Godfrey *Hernandez* • Richard Pearson *Bastian* • Eleanor Summerfield *Mrs Bastian* • Ian Hunter *Dr Swann* ■ *Dir* Anthony Asquith • *Scr* John Mortimer, from the novel *Act of Mercy* by Francis Clifford

Guns of Fort Petticoat ★★★

Western 1957 · US · Colour · 81mins

Audie Murphy launched his own production company with this intriguing slant on the western siege theme. Branded a coward for refusing to participate in the Sand Creek massacre, Murphy heads for Texas to forge a band of seemingly defenceless women into a fighting force. It's steadily directed by George Marshall and the Indian attack on the fortified mission should keep action fans happy. But Walter Doniger's screenplay is keener to explore the unsung heroism of the frontierswoman. DP

Audie Murphy *Lieutenant Frank Hewitt* • Kathryn Grant *Ann Martin* • Hope Emerson *Hannah Lacey* • Jeff Donnell *Mary Wheeler* • Jeanette Nolan *Cora Melavan* ■ *Dir* George Marshall • *Scr* Walter Doniger, from a story by C William Harrison

Guns of Hate ★★

Western 1948 · US · BW · 61mins

Tim Holt had an extraordinary career, appearing in two of the greatest westerns ever, John Ford's *Stagecoach* and *My Darling Clementine*. He chose to reject conventional Hollywood stardom to ride the movie range in a series of programme fillers and to work with the horses he loved. In this very ordinary RKO B-western he sets out to find the killers of Jason Robards. It's distinguished only by terrific performances from Tony Barrett and Steve Brodie as the villains. TS

Tim Holt *Bob* • Nan Leslie *Judy* • Richard Martin (1) *Chito* • Steve Brodie *Morgan* • Myrna Dell *Dixie* • Tony Barrett *Wyatt* • Jason Robards [Jason Robards Sr] *Ben Jason* ■ *Dir* Lesley Selander • *Scr* Norman Houston, Ed Earl Repp

The Guns of Navarone ★★★★ PG

Second World War adventure
1961 · UK/US · Colour · 150mins

This classic wartime adventure is based on Alistair MacLean's bestselling novel about a daring commando raid on two enormous German guns that are threatening British naval operations. Grim-faced Gregory Peck is handed the task of leading the mission when things begin to go wrong, and he's well supported by Anthony Quinn – on familiar territory playing a Greek. However, the acting honours are stolen by David Niven as the cynical, cowardly explosives expert. A belated follow-up, *Force 10 from Navarone*, was released 17 years later. AT DVD

Gregory Peck *Capt Mallory* • David Niven *Cpl Miller* • Anthony Quinn *Andrea Stavros* • Stanley Baker *CPO Brown* • Anthony Quayle *Maj Franklin* • James Darren *Pappadimos* • Irene Papas *Maria* • Gia Scala *Anna* • James Robertson-Justice *Jensen* • Richard Harris *Barnsby* • Bryan Forbes *Cohn* ■ *Dir* J Lee Thompson • *Scr* Carl Foreman, Alistair MacLean, from the novel by Alistair MacLean

Guns of the Magnificent Seven ★★ PG

Western 1969 · US · Colour · 101mins

This second sequel (after 1966's *Return of the Seven*) to a great original wisely retains the majestic Elmer Bernstein score. This time out, Yul Brynner relinquishes his role of mercenary gunman to George Kennedy, and the Mexican-set locations were actually filmed in Spain. Thankfully, this movie neither looks nor feels like a European western, despite the fact that it was made at the height of the spaghetti western's popularity. A touch of class is provided by Fernando Rey as the revolutionary leader in need of rescue by Kennedy's gang. The third and final sequel is 1972's *The Magnificent Seven Ride!* TS. Contains violence. DVD

George Kennedy *Chris* • James Whitmore *Levi Morgan* • Monte Markham *Keno* • Bernie Casey *Cassie* • Joe Don Baker *Slater* • Scott Thomas *PJ* • Fernando Rey *Quintero* ■ *Dir* Paul Wendkos • *Scr* Herman Hoffman

Guns of the Timberland ★ U

Western 1960 · US · Colour · 91mins

Alan Ladd is as wooden as the scenery in this feeble logging drama produced by Aaron Spelling (*Dynasty*). Although cliché-ridden, it does raise worthwhile environmental considerations, as Ladd and his team of lumberjacks want to remove forest cover that protects the inhabitants of a valley from huge mudslides. Frankie Avalon supplies the pop music interludes and the supporting cast includes Ladd's daughter, Alana. AE

Alan Ladd *Jim Hadley* • Jeanne Crain *Laura Riley* • Gilbert Roland *Monty Walker* • Frankie Avalon *Bert Harvey* • Lyle Bettger *Clay Bell* • Noah Beery Jr *Blackie* • Verna Felton *Aunt Sarah* • Alana Ladd *Jane Peterson* ■ *Dir* Robert D Webb • *Scr* Aaron Spelling, Joseph Petracca, from the novel by Louis L'Amour

Gunsight Ridge ★★ U

Western 1957 · US · BW · 85mins

A western starring Joel McCrea and containing a secret piano-playing villain called Velvet Clark can't be all bad, although it comes pretty close. The middle-aged McCrea is an undercover agent who rides a well-worn trail to track down the aforementioned Velvet (Mark Stevens), currently operating under the guise of a mine owner. Director Francis D Lyon fails to breathe new life into this plot. RB

Joel McCrea *Mike* • Mark Stevens *Velvet Clark* • Joan Weldon *Molly* • Darlene Fields *Rosa* • Addison Richards *Sheriff Jones* • Carolyn Craig *Girl* • Robert Griffin *Babcock* • Slim Pickens *Hank Moss* ■ *Dir* Francis D Lyon • *Scr* Talbot Jennings, Elizabeth Jennings

The Gunslinger ★★ PG

Western 1956 · US · Colour · 74mins

This early Roger Corman venture is a fitfully entertaining camp western featuring two female adversaries and giving more emphasis to sex and violence than was customary at the time. Curvaceous Beverly Garland is the town marshal's widow who straps on his guns and badge after he's gunned down. Equally curvaceous Allison Hayes is the saloon-keeper who hires John Ireland's gunslinger to kill Garland. The film's microbudget shows up in a saloon chorus line made up of only three girls. AE

John Ireland *Cane Miro* • Beverly Garland *Rose Hood* • Allison Hayes *Erica Page* • Martin Kingsley *Gideon Polk* • Jonathan Haze *Jack Hays* • Chris Alcaide *Joshua Tate* • Richard Miller [Dick Miller] *Jimmy Tonto* • Bruno VeSota *Zebelon Tabb* ■ *Dir* Roger Corman • *Scr* Charles B Griffith, Mark Hanna

G

Gunsmoke ★★ U

Western 1953 · US · Colour · 79mins

This routine western stars Audie Murphy as a gunslinger who has a change of heart when he's hired by a landowner to kill a rancher. The result is nothing special, but it does offer a chance to see Susan Cabot before she became a Roger Corman cult heroine. The film has nothing to do with the TV series of the same name. TS

Audie Murphy *Reb Kittredge* • Susan Cabot *Rita Saxon* • Paul Kelly (1) *Dan Saxon* • Charles Drake *Johnny Lake* • Mary Castle *Cora DuFrayne* • Jack Kelly *Curly Mather* • Jesse White *Professor* • William Reynolds *Brazos* ■ *Dir* Nathan Juran • *Scr* DD Beauchamp, from the novel *Roughshod* by Norman A Fox

The Guru ★★ U

Satirical drama
1969 · US/Ind · Colour · 111mins

Made shortly after the Beatles sat at the feet of the Maharishi at Rishikesh, this heavy-handed satire on colliding cultures suffers from the fact that James Ivory appears to have little sympathy for any of the characters. Michael York's pop star is portrayed as shallow, while Rita Tushingham's hippy is an opportunistic groupie. Only sitar master and spiritual mentor Utpal Dutt is permitted any depth, but the subtle blend of humility and egotism owes more to his own canny delivery than the mocking bombast of the script. DP

Utpal Dutt *Ustad Zafar Khan* • Michael York *Tom Pickle* • Rita Tushingham *Jenny* • Aparna Sen *Ghazala* • Madhur Jaffrey *Begum Sahiba* • Barry Foster *Chris* ■ *Dir* James Ivory • *Scr* Ruth Prawer Jhabvala, James Ivory

The Guru ★★★ 15

Romantic comedy
2002 · US/UK/Fr/Ger · Colour · 90mins

This appealing romantic comedy marked the first leading role for British actor Jimi Mistry, who more than holds his own alongside Hollywood actresses Heather Graham and Marisa Tomei. Mistry plays an amiable dance instructor who moves from India to New York in search of Broadway success. His bubble quickly bursts, but he stumbles into a career as a guru to gullible socialite Tomei, dispensing second-hand sex advice gleaned from porn actress friend Graham. There's a winning sweetness to Mistry's character and the film is bright and amusing. JC. Contains swearing and sex scenes. DVD

Heather Graham *Sharonna* • Marisa Tomei *Lexi* • Jimi Mistry *Ramu Chandra Gupta* • Christine Baranski *Chantal* • Michael McKean

Dwain • Malachy McCourt *Father Flannagan* • Rob Morrow *Josh* • Sanjeev Bhaskar *Cook* ■ *Dir* Daisy von Scherler Mayer • *Scr* Tracey Jackson, from an idea by Shekhar Kapur

Guru in Seven ★★ 18

Comedy 1997 · UK · Colour · 102mins

Made for a mere £33,000, this is essentially an Asian *Alfie*. Rebelling against the prejudices of his parents, artist Nitin Chandra Ganatra bets his friends that he can bed a week's worth of women following his split from the love of his life, Ernestina Quarcoo. Director Shani Grewal takes this as an excuse to savage everything from Bollywood musicals to Punjabi economic expectation, but he fails in his bid to show older subcontinentals to be every bit as suburban as the rest of Britain's bourgeoisie. DP. Contains swearing. DVD

Saeed Jaffrey *Mr Walia* • Jacqueline Pearce *Joan* • Nitin Chandra Ganatra *Sanjay* • Lea Rochelle *Nora* • Lynne Michelle *Candy* • Elle Lewis *Holly* • Amanda Pointer *Gaynor* • Ernestina Quarcoo *Jill* ■ *Dir/Scr* Shani Grewal [Shani S Grewal]

G

Gus ★★ U

Comedy 1976 · US · Colour · 92mins

Disney family films of this cosily low-budget kind were an endangered species even when this was made. Younger viewers may still enjoy the gentle humour of this story about a football team taking on a mule which can kick a ball one hundred yards. Ed Asner and Don Knotts are the two-legged heroes. TH

Ed Asner [Edward Asner] *Hank Cooper* • Don Knotts *Coach Venner* • Gary Grimes *Andy Petrovic* • Tim Conway *Crankcase* • Liberty Williams *Debbie Kovac* • Dick Van Patten *Cal Wilson* • Ronnie Schell *Joe Barnsdale* • Bob Crane *Pepper* ■ *Dir* Vincent McEveety • *Scr* Arthur Alsberg, Don Nelson, from a story by Ted Key

Guy ★★★ 18

Drama 1996 · UK /Ger · Colour · 90mins

Covering the same sort of territory as *The Truman Show* and *Edtv*, Michael Lindsay-Hogg's psychological thriller steers the subject matter into much darker territory. Hope Davis is the aspiring film-maker who decides to make an ordinary stranger (Vincent D'Onofrio) the star of her new movie, provoking a complex battle of wills in which the lines between the subject and the film-maker become increasingly blurred. A small-scale but intriguing study of voyeurism. JF

Vincent D'Onofrio *Guy* • Hope Davis *"The Camera"* • Kimber Riddle *Veronica* • Diane Salinger *Gail* • Richard Portnow *Al* • Valente Rodriguez *Low Rider* • Michael Massee *Mark* • John O'Donohue *Detective* • Lucy Liu *Woman at newstand* ■ *Dir* Michael Lindsay-Hogg • *Scr* Kirby Dick

A Guy Named Joe ★★★

Wartime romantic drama
1944 · US · BW · 119mins

A supernatural morale-booster for wartime, this is an MGM glossy with all that great studio's polish. Spencer Tracy stars as an air force pilot who is killed on a mission. He returns in spirit to help the living – in particular his former girlfriend Irene Dunne and her admirer, new pilot Van Johnson. Victor Fleming directed the unification of the two with splendid aplomb, and fans of the film included Steven Spielberg, who remade it as *Always* (1989). TH

Spencer Tracy *Pete Sandidge* • Irene Dunne *Dorinda Durston* • Van Johnson *Ted Randall* • Ward Bond *Al Yackey* • James Gleason *Col "Nails" Kilpatrick* • Lionel Barrymore *The General* • Barry Nelson *Dick Rumney* • Esther Williams *Ellen Bright* • Irving Bacon *Corporal* ■ *Dir* Victor Fleming • *Scr* Dalton Trumbo, from a story by Chandler Sprague, David Boehm, Frederick H Brennan

A Guy Thing ★★ 12

Romantic comedy
2002 · US · Colour · 97mins

It appears that men can be saved from making grave marital mistakes by kooky free spirits who wake up in their beds after the bachelor party and alert them to the possibility of a new life. If you can swallow that, you may enjoy this flimsy feature in which the stars do the comedy equivalent of tap-dancing so quickly, you don't notice the scenery's coming down around them. Jason Lee, Selma Blair and Julia Stiles earn their pay as groom, bride and spanner in the works respectively. Energetic, but underwritten. RT DVD

Jason Lee *Paul* • Julia Stiles *Becky* • Selma Blair *Karen* • James Brolin *Ken* • Shawn Hatosy *Jim* • Lochlyn Munro *Ray* • Diana Scarwid *Sandra* ■ *Dir* Chris Koch • *Scr* Greg Glienna, Pete Schwaba, Matt Tarses, Bill Wrubel, from the story by Greg Glienna

Guys and Dolls ★★★★ U

Musical comedy 1955 · US · Colour · 143mins

When producer Sam Goldwyn set about filming this great Broadway musical, he went after the best dancer he could find, his ideal Sky Masterson, Gene Kelly. Louis B Mayer wouldn't release Kelly to his rival, however, so Goldwyn went for the best actor in the movies. That's how Marlon Brando became the definitive Masterson, singing the Frank Loesser songs himself, cleverly choreographed by Michael Kidd, whose depiction of Broadway is one of the film's highlights. With Jean Simmons waking up to love with *If I Were a Bell*, and Frank Sinatra and Vivian Blaine as Nathan Detroit and his ever-lovin' Miss Adelaide, what more could you want? TS DVD

Marlon Brando *Sky Masterson* • Jean Simmons *Sarah Brown* • Frank Sinatra *Nathan Detroit* • Vivian Blaine *Miss Adelaide* • Robert Keith (1) *Lieutenant Brannigan* • Stubby Kaye *Nicely-Nicely Johnson* • BS Pully *Big Jule* • Sheldon Leonard *Harry the Horse* • Regis Toomey *Arvide Abernathy* • Johnny Silver *Benny Southstreet* ■ *Dir* Joseph L Mankiewicz • *Scr* Joseph L Mankiewicz, from a musical by Abe Burrows, Jo Swerling, from short stories by Damon Runyon

The Guyver ★★ 15

Science-fiction action
1991 · US · Colour · 84mins

One day you're saving the universe as Luke Skywalker in *Star Wars*, the next you're playing a CIA agent who turns into a cockroach. Such is the fate of Mark Hamill in this unintentionally hilarious movie based on a popular Japanese comic book. Co-directors Steve Wang and Joji Tani handle the action well in this tale of a college student who becomes an armour-plated superhero, courtesy of the titular device, and takes on monster-changing bad guys. Unfortunately, characterisation and dialogue play second-fiddle to a series of hilariously rubbery monsters. RS

Mark Hamill *Max* • Vivian Wu *Mizky* • Jack Armstrong *Sean* • David Gale *Balcus* • Michael Berryman *Lisker* • Jimmie Walker *Striker* • Spice Williams *Weber* • Peter Spellos *Ramsey* ■ *Dir* Steve Wang, Screaming Mad George [Joji Tani] • *Scr* Jon Purdy, from characters created by Yoshiki Takaya

Guyver 2: Dark Hero ★★★ 15

Science-fiction action
1994 · US · Colour · 95mins

The same mix of science fiction, martial arts and weird creatures as the Japanese comic book-inspired original, director Steve Wang's rousing sequel is even more lunatic and action-packed. David Hayter takes over from Jack Armstrong as the armour-plated hero. This time he's after the Zoanoid aliens responsible for double-crossing archaeologist Kathy Christopherson as she unearths a cave-bound spaceship. Lots of acrobatic monster-bashing ensues with just enough eye-opening plot to keep the mind similarly amused. AJ DVD

David Hayter *Sean Barker* • Kathy Christopherson *Cori* • Christopher Michael *Atkins* • Bruno Giannotta *Crane* • Stuart Weiss *Marcus* ■ *Dir* Steve Wang • *Scr* Nathan Long, from a story by Steve Wang, from characters created by Yoshiki Takaya

Gymkata ★ 18

Action adventure 1985 · US · Colour · 85mins

Former Olympic gymnast Kurt Thomas has the misfortune to find himself in the lead of this shambolic martial arts action adventure that attempts to retell the Robin Hood legend in the style of *The Arabian Nights*. Sent by a secret government agency to prevent the overthrow of the ruler of an almost medieval kingdom, he's soon up to his eyeballs in spies and crooked officials and, of course, head over heels in love with a kung fu fighting princess. DP. Contains swearing and violence.

Kurt Thomas *Jonathan Cabot* • Tetchie Agbayani *Princess Rubali* • Richard Norton *Zamir* • Edward Bell *Paley* • John Barrett *Gomez* • Conan Lee *Hao* • Bob Schott *Thorg* • Buck Kartalian *The Khan* ■ *Dir* Robert Clouse • *Scr* Charles Robert Carnes, from the novel *The Terrible Game* by Dan Tyler Moore

Gypsy ★★★★ PG

Musical biography
1962 · US · Colour · 137mins

Rosalind Russell stars as the fabulous Rose Hovick, the mother of real-life stripper Gypsy Rose Lee, in this marvellous presentation of the great Broadway show. Some songs are missing and Mervyn LeRoy's direction is possibly too "theatrical", but this is a bright, dazzling and above all entertaining movie. It contains a fabulous array of colourful showbiz characters and a performance by Russell that will knock your socks off. There are other great moments, too: Natalie Wood's tender, touching *Little Lamb* and her final triumphant striptease. TS

Rosalind Russell *Rose* • Natalie Wood *Louise "Gypsy"* • Karl Malden *Herbie Sommers* • Paul Wallace *Tulsa* • Betty Bruce *Tessie Tura* • Parley Baer *Mr Kringelein* • Harry Shannon *Grandpa* ■ *Dir* Mervyn LeRoy • *Scr* Leonard Spigelgass, from the musical by Arthur Laurents, from the memoirs by Gypsy Rose Lee [Rose Louise Hovick] • *Music* Jule Styne • *Lyrics* Stephen Sondheim

Gypsy ★★★ PG

Musical biography
1993 · US · Colour · 136mins

Filmed in 1962 with the splendid Rosalind Russell in the role of the most monstrous showbusiness mother of them all, this re-creation was made for US television. The score survives, and the great Jerome Robbins's choreography is faithfully duplicated by Bonnie Walker. Most things work, especially a touching performance from Cynthia Gibb as young Louise, but the whole founders on the central casting of Bette Midler. She looks fine, but all the technique in the world can't conceal that she's not a skilled actress. TS

Bette Midler *Rose Hovick* • Peter Riegert *Herbie* • Cynthia Gibb *Louise Hovick* • Jennifer Beck *June Hovick* • Ed Asner [Edward Asner] *Rose's father* ■ *Dir* Emile Ardolino • *Scr* Arthur Laurents, from his musical, from the memoirs by Gypsy Rose Lee [Rose Louise Hovick] • *Music* Jule Styne • *Lyrics* Stephen Sondheim

The Gypsy and the Gentleman ★★

Period drama 1958 · UK · Colour · 107mins

This is hardly the sort of potboiler you would expect from a film-maker of Joseph Losey's calibre. By attempting to re-ceate the look of contemporary art, however, he brings some undeserved sophistication to this otherwise garish adaptation. Melina Mercouri roars through this Regency bodice-ripper with a demented glee that totally swamps Keith Michell's brooding aristocrat. DP

Melina Mercouri *Belle* • Keith Michell *Deverill* • Patrick McGoohan *Jess* • June Laverick *Sarah* • Flora Robson *Mrs Haggard* • Lyndon Brook *John* • Clare Austin *Vanessa* • Helen Haye *Lady Ayrton* • Newton Blick *Ruddock* ■ *Dir* Joseph Losey • *Scr* Janet Green, from the novel *Darkness I Love You* by Nina Warner Hooke

Gypsy Colt ★★★ U

Drama 1954 · US · Colour · 71mins

Is there a 13-year-old horse-mad daughter in the house? If so, get those tissues at the ready for this endearing if rather treacly tale, which reworks *Lassie Come Home* for the equine fan. A young horse owner is reduced to despair by her parents' decision to sell her much-loved pet to a racing stables, but love will out, even when it's on four sturdy legs. This highly professional film presses all the right emotional buttons. SH

Donna Corcoran *Meg MacWade* • Ward Bond *Frank MacWade* • Frances Dee *Em MacWade* • Lee Van Cleef *Hank* • Larry Keating *Wade Y Gerald* • Bobby Hyatt *Phil Gerald* • Nacho Galindo *Pancho* • Rodolfo Hoyos Jr [Rodolfo Hoyos] *Rodolfo* ■ *Dir* Andrew Marton • *Scr* Martin Berkeley, from a story by Eric Knight

The Gypsy Moths ★★★ 15

Drama 1969 · US · Colour · 102mins

Steve McQueen was to have starred in this gripping, if resolutely sombre romance, but then director John Frankenheimer cast Burt Lancaster and Deborah Kerr, reuniting the stars of *From Here to Eternity*. Lancaster is one of three skydivers who arrive in Kansas to perform their death-defying stunts. Thrilling in the air and depressing on the ground, it's a study of nobodies going nowhere, with Lancaster silently morose for most of the time while Kerr simmers. Gene Hackman, Sheree North and Bonnie Bedelia, in her screen debut, add to the general mood of listlessness. AT

Burt Lancaster *Mike Rettig* • Deborah Kerr *Elizabeth Brandon* • Gene Hackman *Joe Browdy* • Scott Wilson *Malcolm Webson* • William Windom *V John Brandon* • Bonnie Bedelia *Annie Burke* • Sheree North *Waitress* ■ *Dir* John Frankenheimer • *Scr* William Hanley, from the novel by James Drought

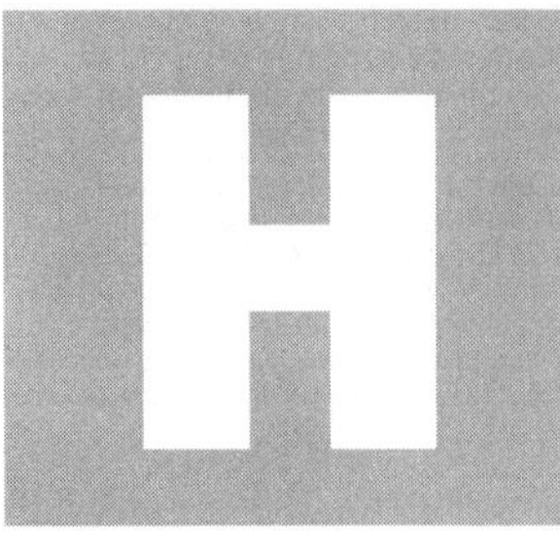

HM Pulham Esq ★★★★ U

Drama 1941 · US · BW · 119mins

Director King Vidor makes a memorable and moving film about a stuffy Bostonian who played safe and in old age regrets not marrying the love of his life. Robert Young showed new depths as the wistful Harry Pulham, while Hedy Lamarr demonstrated that she could be more than just a glamour figure as the advertising copywriter in New York who tries to liberate him from his stifling background of wealth and privilege. Vidor also wrote the script with his wife, Elizabeth Hill, and there's an uncredited walk-on part from Ava Gardner. AE

Hedy Lamarr *Marvin Myles* • Robert Young (1) *HM Pulham Esq* • Ruth Hussey *Kay Motford* • Charles Coburn *Pulham Sr* • Fay Holden *Mrs Pulham* • Van Heflin *Bill King* • Leif Erickson *Rodney "Bo-Jo" Brown* ■ *Dir* King Vidor • *Scr* King Vidor, Elizabeth Hill, from the novel by John P Marquand • *Art Director* Cedric Gibbons

HMS Defiant ★★★ PG

Period adventure
1962 · UK · Colour · 100mins

Director Lewis Gilbert told virtually the same tale (albeit set in a different war) in *Sink the Bismarck!* as he does here in this entertaining seafaring adventure. This richly coloured romp benefits immensely from the experienced playing of Dirk Bogarde, Alec Guinness and an underused Anthony Quayle, all of whom are clearly enjoying themselves as they swash buckles in the Napoleonic wars. It's hard to keep your eyes off the young Bogarde, who's absolutely splendid as a demented martinet. Also known as *Damn the Defiant!* TS. Contains violence. [video] DVD

Alec Guinness *Captain Crawford* • Dirk Bogarde *Lieutenant Scott-Padget* • Anthony Quayle *Vizard* • Tom Bell *Evans* • Maurice Denham *Surgeon Goss* • Walter Fitzgerald *Admiral Jackson* • Victor Maddern *Dawlish* • Murray Melvin *Wagstaffe* • Nigel Stock *Senior Midshipman Kilpatrick* • Richard Carpenter *Lieutenant Ponsonby* ■ *Dir* Lewis Gilbert • *Scr* Nigel Kneale, Edmund H North, from the novel *Mutiny* by Frank Tilsley

The H-Man ★★★

Science fiction 1954 · Jpn · Colour · 78mins

Taking time out from his *Godzilla/Rodan* industry, director Inoshiro Honda came up with one of his best movies. Men turning into oozing green slime after being exposed to a nuclear test zone. Rain washes some of the gelatinous residue into the Tokyo sewers where it proliferates to attack the population. Flame throwers set the city sewage system alight in a spectacular climax to an engaging fantasy chock-full of hallucinatory images and impressive visual effects. Honda's semi-sequel *The Human Vapor* (1964) failed to match the same extraordinary weirdness. AJ. Japanese dialogue dubbed into English.

Yumi Shirakawa *Girl* • Kenji Sahara *Detective* • Akihiko Hirata *Scientist* • Eitaro Ozawa *Inspector Tominaga* • Koreya Senda *Dr Maki* • Mitsuru Sato *Uchida* ■ *Dir* Inoshiro Honda • *Scr* Takeshi Kimura, Hideo Kaijo

Habit ★★★

Horror 1995 · US · Colour · 112mins

A New York alcoholic, played by writer/director Larry Fessenden with his front tooth missing, meets mysterious Meredith Snaider at a Halloween party and immediately starts having terrifying dreams, with the odd bite appearing on his body. Incredibly, Fessenden accomplishes something new with very familiar vampire material, combining creepy camerawork, scary atmospherics and mesmerising performances. AJ

Larry Fessenden *Sam* • Meredith Snaider *Anna* • Aaron Beall *Nick* • Patricia Coleman *Rae* • Heather Woodbury *Liza* • Jesse Hartman *Lenny* ■ *Dir/Scr* Larry Fessenden

Hackers ★★★ 12

Thriller 1995 · US · Colour · 100mins

Teenage hackers uncover a massive computer fraud in this adventure that's set against the intriguing backdrop of New York's cyber-culture. It's little more than a standard industrial espionage chase thriller, given a stylish patina by its digital-age atmosphere, complete with often bewildering technical data and imaginative journeys down the information super-highway. New mouse on the mat Jonny Lee Miller and tough net surfer Angelina Jolie interface well as the console-crossed lovers. AJ. Contains swearing and brief nudity. [video] DVD

Jonny Lee Miller *Dade Murphy* • Angelina Jolie *Kate* • Jesse Bradford *Joey* • Matthew Lillard *Cereal Killer* • Laurence Mason *Nikon* • Renoly Santiago *Phantom Phreak* • Fisher Stevens *The Plague* • Wendell Pierce *Agent Dick Gill* ■ *Dir* Iain Softley • *Scr* Rafael Moreu

Hadley's Rebellion ★★

Drama 1984 · US · Colour · 96mins

A young boy moves from Georgia to California, only to find his prep-school classmates are less than friendly. That is, until he takes up wrestling. Shallow, predictable and very much in the *Rocky* mould, the only redeeming feature seems to be the chemistry between Griffin O'Neal as Hadley and William Devane as his coach. FL

Griffin O'Neal *Hadley Hickman* • William Devane *Coach Ball* • Adam Baldwin *Bobo McKenzie* • Lisa Lucas *Linda Johnson* • Eric Boles *Mr Stevens* • Israel Juarbe *Manuel Hernandez* • Chad McQueen *Rick Stanton* ■ *Dir/Scr* Fred Walton

Hail Caesar ★

Comedy 1994 · US · Colour · 93mins

The most appalling thing about this is that it marks a low point in the career of Samuel L Jackson: he plays the postman who repeatedly suffers at the hands of the main character's dog. This unrepentantly awful film has Anthony Michael Hall directing himself as a too-cool rock 'n' roll wannabe who must prove himself to his girlfriend's father by working in dad's eraser factory. ST

Anthony Michael Hall *Julius Caesar MacGruder* • Robert Downey Jr *Jerry* • Judd Nelson *Prisoner One* • Samuel L Jackson *Mailman* • Frank Gorshin *Mr Dewitt* • Nicholas Pryor *Mr Bidwell* • Leslie Danon *Annie* ■ *Dir* Anthony Michael Hall • *Scr* Robert Mittenthal, from a story by Mark Twain

Hail! Hail! Rock 'n' Roll! ★★★★ U

Music documentary
1987 · US · Colour · 115mins

Normally pop documentaries veer from on-stage electricity and dressing-room silliness to the rambling of band members posing as philosophers. *This Is Spinal Tap* did a superb spoof on all this. Now, avoiding all the pitfalls and pratfalls of the genre, comes one of the screen's most accomplished pop biographies ever, easily on a par with *The Last Waltz*. Making no attempt to gloss over Chuck Berry's brittle personality, his arrogance and petulance, it also brings out the racism Chuck experienced in his youth and examines the nature of his unique guitar sound. Telling comments by the likes of Little Richard and Bo Diddley are joined to a big-blast concert at the Fox Theatre, St Louis, to celebrate Chuck's 60th birthday. TH [video]

Roy Orbison ■ *Dir* Taylor Hackford

Hail, Hero! ★★★

Drama 1969 · US · Colour · 87mins

Michael Douglas's screen debut benefits from the direction of David Miller. Something of a radical in his youth, Douglas Jr brings an authenticity to this tale about a boy who drops out of college to enlist for Vietnam, not because he believes in the war – he doesn't – but because of his hawkish parents, played by Arthur Kennedy and Teresa Wright. The pacifist message is often awkward and cringe-inducing, but one admires the film's ambition and honesty. AT

Michael Douglas *Carl Dixon* • Arthur Kennedy *Albert Dixon* • Teresa Wright *Santha Dixon* • John Larch *Mr Conklin* • Charles Drake *Senator Murchiston* • Mercer Harris *Jimmy* • Peter Strauss *Frank Dixon* ■ *Dir* David Miller • *Scr* David Manber, from the novel by John Weston • *Music/lyrics* Gordon Lightfoot

Hail the Conquering Hero ★★★★★ U

Comedy 1944 · US · BW · 96mins

This extraordinarily daring wartime comedy stars Eddie Bracken as the dejected son of a dead First World War hero, prevented by hay fever from serving in the current conflict. When some battle veterans persuade him to return home and masquerade as a valiant marine to please his dear old mother, he receives a hero's welcome from the entire town. Writer/director Preston Sturges handles the mounting complications with dazzling dexterity and draws delightful performances from his favourite character actors, most notably William Demarest as the hard-boiled sergeant and Raymond Walburn as the pompous windbag of a mayor. Ella Raines also sparkles under Sturges's encouragement. AE DVD

Eddie Bracken *Woodrow Truesmith* • Ella Raines *Libby* • Bill Edwards *Forrest Noble* • Raymond Walburn *Mayor Noble* • William Demarest *Sergeant* ■ *Dir/Scr* Preston Sturges

La Haine ★★★★ 15

Drama 1995 · Fr · BW · 97mins

Responsible for causing a scandal on its domestic release, this bruising portrait of disaffected youth confirmed its writer/director Mathieu Kassovitz as the *wunderkind* of French cinema. Presenting the housing schemes on the outskirts of Paris as hotbeds of racial hatred and social unrest, the film follows three lads from different ethnic backgrounds and explores how they spend their endless spare time. Vincent Cassel is outstanding as the Jewish skinhead, but it's Kassovitz's restless camerawork and a script as funny as it is hard-hitting that make this such an impressive and important work. DP. In French with English subtitles. Contains violence, swearing and drug abuse. [video] DVD

Vincent Cassel *Vinz* • Hubert Kounde *Hubert* • Saïd Taghmaoui *Saïd* • Karim Belkhadra *Samir* • Edouard Montoute *Darty* • François Levantal *Astérix* • Solo Dicko *Santo* • Marc Duret *Inspector "Notre Dame"* • Héloïse Rauth *Sarah* ■ *Dir/Scr* Mathieu Kassovitz

Hair ★★ 15

Musical 1979 · US · Colour · 116mins

If ever a musical is caught firmly in its time, then it's *Hair*. In this film version, director Milos Forman fails to capture the enormous energy of the original stage show, which was a celebrated load of old nonsense even back in the mid-1960s. Anyone who had any pretensions to hippydom at the time will find their toes curling at the memory, and those born since will be quite bemused at all the fuss. Apart from Treat Williams's table-top dance, the leads have little to be proud of. SH. Contains nudity. [video] DVD

John Savage *Claude* • Treat Williams *Berger* • Beverly D'Angelo *Sheila* • Annie Golden *Jeannie* • Dorsey Wright *Hud* • Don Dacus *Woof* • Cheryl Barnes *Hud's fiancée* • Nicholas Ray *General* ■ *Dir* Milos Forman • *Scr* Michael Weller, from the musical by Gerome Ragni, James Rado, Galt MacDermot

The Hairdresser's Husband ★★★★ 15

Drama 1990 · Fr · Colour · 78mins

French director Patrice Leconte has never been a great respecter of political correctness, and this eccentric comedy sees him at his most dubious. If you can overcome his attitude to both women and Arabic culture then there are some utterly charming moments, as the wonderful Jean Rochefort delights in the delicate hands of hairdresser Anna Galiena. The scenes of a seaside childhood and the sudden tragic twist remain longest in the mind, along with Rochefort's marvellously impish performance. AJ. In French with English subtitles. Contains sex scenes. [video] DVD

Jean Rochefort *Antoine* • Anna Galiena *Mathilde* • Roland Bertin *Antoine's father* • Maurice Chevit *Agopian* • Philippe Clevenot *Morvoisieux* • Jacques Mathou *Monsieur Chardon* • Claude Aufaure *Customer* • Albert Delpy *Donecker* ■ *Dir* Patrice Leconte • *Scr* Claude Klotz, Patrice Leconte

Hairspray ★★★★ PG

Satirical musical comedy
1988 · US · Colour · 87mins

These days Ricki Lake has to deal with more than her fair share of eccentrics on her chat show, but she probably still hasn't come across anyone weirder than John Waters, who launched her into stardom with this kitsch classic. Waters tones down his usual excesses, but his mischievous black sense of humour is still very much to the fore in this affectionate salute to those Z-grade teen movies. Lake is the fun-loving Tracy Turnblad, who becomes the new teen dancing queen much to the horror of wealthy snobs Debbie Harry and Sonny Bono, who want their daughter to shine. The soundtrack is a constant delight, as is the eclectic cast. JF [video]

Ricki Lake *Tracy Turnblad* • Divine *Edna Turnblad/Arvin Hodgepile* • Sonny Bono *Franklin von Tussle* • Ruth Brown *Motormouth Maybell* • Colleen Fitzpatrick *Amber von Tussle* • Debbie Harry [Deborah Harry] *Velma von Tussle* • Michael St Gerard *Link Larkin* • Leslie Ann Powers *Penny Pingleton* • Jerry Stiller *Wilbur Turnblad* • Pia Zadora *Beatnik girl* ■ *Dir/Scr* John Waters (2)

The Hairy Ape ★★

Drama 1944 · US · BW · 91mins

Many liberties are taken with Eugene O'Neill's 1920s' play about dockyard politics, mainly to dilute its fairly blatant communism. The plot is further twisted into wartime flagwaver, with William Bendix as the "hairy ape", a resentful stoker on a ship that runs refugees from Lisbon to America. On-board lovers are snotty heiress Susan Hayward and ship's engineer John Loder, who clash when Hayward insists on being shown the boiler room and is horrified by the sight of Bendix. AT

William Bendix *Hank Smith* • Susan Hayward *Mildred Douglas* • John Loder *2nd Engineer Tony Lazar* • Dorothy Comingore *Helen Parker* • Roman Bohnen *Paddy* ■ *Dir* Alfred Santell • *Scr* Robert D Andrews, Decla Dunning, from the play by Eugene O'Neill

Half a Sixpence ★★★★ U

Musical 1967 · UK · Colour · 139mins

Based on HG Wells's minor classic *Kipps*, this is one of the very few British musicals that doesn't have you squirming in your seat with embarrassment, for which we have to thank veteran Hollywood director George Sidney. Admittedly, the story drags once Tommy Steele and Julia Foster's relationship hits the rocks, but so much of what has gone on before is slickly staged and joyously played that you should forgive it this pause for breath. Rattling through David Heneker's catchy songs and hurling himself into Gillian Lynne's energetic dance routines, Steele has never been better on screen. DP

Tommy Steele *Arthur Kipps* • Julia Foster *Ann* • Cyril Ritchard *Harry Chitterlow* • Penelope Horner *Helen Walsingham* • Elaine Taylor *Kate* • Grover Dale *Pearce* • Hilton Edwards *Shalford* ■ *Dir* George Sidney (2) • *Scr* Beverley Cross, from the novel *Kipps* by HG Wells

Half Angel ★★ U

Comedy 1951 · US · Colour · 75mins

Robert Riskin penned some of Frank Capra's most popular films, but he was sadly off form with this slight romantic frippery. Loretta Young lacks the frivolity to carry off the part of a starchy nurse whose true character only emerges during her frequent bouts of sleepwalking. There's little for Joseph Cotten and John Ridgely (as the suitors in love with the different aspects of her personality) to do but look on adoringly. Director Richard Sale was out of his depth. DP

Loretta Young *Nora* • Joseph Cotten *John Raymond* • Cecil Kellaway *Mr Gilpin* • Basil Ruysdael *Dr Jackson* • Jim Backus *Michael Hogan* • Irene Ryan *Kay* • John Ridgely *Tim* • Therese Lyon *Mrs McCarey* ■ *Dir* Richard Sale • *Scr* Robert Riskin, from a story by George Carleton Brown

Half-Baked ★ 18

Comedy 1998 · US · Colour · 78mins

An unwise and utterly unfunny attempt to resurrect a genre we'd hoped had disappeared into a cultural black hole along with flared trousers – the 1970s drug comedy as typified by Cheech and Chong. Comedian Dave Chappelle stars as one of a gang of pothead pals dreaming up crazy schemes to spring a friend from prison. There are occasional lapses into amusement, but all too often it hits the obvious button. RS. Contains violence, drug abuse, nudity and swearing.

Dave Chappelle *Thurgood/Sir Smoka Lot* • Jim Breuer *Brian* • Guillermo Diaz *Scarface* • Harland Williams *Kenny* • Rachel True *Mary Jane* • Snoop Doggy Dogg [Snoop Dogg] *Scavenger Smoker* • Clarence Williams III *Samson Simpson* • Tommy Chong *Squirrel Master* • Willie Nelson *Historian Smoker* ■ *Dir* Tamra Davis • *Scr* Dave Chappelle, Neal Brennan

The Half-Breed ★★ U

Western 1952 · US · Colour · 81mins

A very minor contribution to the cycle of films beginning with *Broken Arrow* in 1950, which challenged the usual western stereotypes favoured by Hollywood. Here the white villain wants the Apache reservation cleared of its inhabitants as there's gold for the taking. Robert Young, giving his usual polished performance as a gambler, helps Jack Buetel's eponymous hero defuse the situation, conveniently saving RKO the expense of staging a big battle scene, but disappointing fans eager for some rousing action. AE

Robert Young (1) *Dan Craig* • Janis Carter *Helen* • Jack Buetel *Charlie Wolf* • Barton MacLane *Marshal* • Reed Hadley *Crawford* • Connie Gilchrist *Ma Higgins* • Damian O'Flynn *Captain Jackson* ■ *Dir* Stuart Gilmore • *Scr* Harold Shumate and Richard Wormser, from a story by Robert Hardy Andrews

Half Moon Street ★★★ 18

Political thriller 1986 · UK · Colour · 85mins

This eagerly awaited next movie from director Bob Swaim (*La Balance*) failed miserably at the theatrical box office, but it's hard to see why. Based on Paul Theroux's novel *Doctor Slaughter*, here's the ultra-sexy Sigourney Weaver as a prim Middle East scholar in the daytime and a call girl by night, while Michael Caine is Lord Bulbeck, the British diplomat who favours her favours. Adult and certainly different, there's a grim topicality about Arab wheelings and dealings in the Mayfair byway of the title, and the film's subsequent reputation will lead you to believe that it's a dog. It isn't. TS

Sigourney Weaver *Dr Lauren Slaughter* • Michael Caine *Lord Bulbeck* • Patrick Kavanagh *General Sir George Newhouse* • Faith Kent *Lady Newhouse* • Ram John Holder *Lindsay Walker* • Keith Buckley *Hugo Van Arkady* • Annie Hanson *Mrs Van Arkady* • Patrick Newman *Julian Shuttle* • Niall O'Brien *Captain Twilley* • Nadim Sawalha *Karim Hatami* ■ *Dir* Bob Swaim • *Scr* Edward Behr, Bob Swaim, from the novel *Doctor Slaughter* by Paul Theroux

The Half Naked Truth ★★★★

Comedy 1932 · US · BW · 77mins

The now almost forgotten Lee Tracy, a wonderfully fast-talking, sour-looking, wisecracking star of the 1930s, is here at the top of his form as an unscrupulous publicity man. This delectable comedy, classily directed by Gregory La Cava, has Tracy scheming to make fiery Lupe Velez into an instant celebrity by blackmailing neurotic producer Frank Morgan. Velez, known as the "Mexican Spitfire", soon to marry Johnny "Tarzan" Weissmuller, committed suicide in 1944. RB

Lee Tracy *Bates* • Lupe Velez *Teresita* • Eugene Pallette *Achilles* • Frank Morgan *Farrell* • Robert McKenzie *Col Munday* • Franklin Pangborn *Hotel manager* ■ *Dir* Gregory La Cava • *Scr* Gregory La Cava, Corey Ford, from a story by Ben Markson, HN Swanson, from the novel *Phantom Fame* by David Freedman, Bartlett Cormack

Half Past Dead ★★ 12

Action crime thriller
2002 · US · Colour · 94mins

Steven Seagal fails to convince here as an undercover FBI agent sent to the "New Alcatraz". Once in the hi-tech prison, Seagal finds himself at the centre of a hostage situation when a group called the "49ers" break in so they can interrogate a death-row inmate regarding the whereabouts of $200 million in gold. Writer/director Don Michael Paul overloads the film with action to compensate for the lack of style or coherence. TH. Contains violence and swearing. DVD

Steven Seagal *Sascha Petrosevitch* • Morris Chestnut *Donny/49er One* • Ja Rule *Nick Frazier* • Nia Peeples *49er Six* • Tony Plana *The warden, El Fuego* • Kurupt *Twitch* • Michael "Bear" Taliferro *Little Joe* • Claudia Christian *EZ Williams* ■ *Dir/Scr* Don Michael Paul

Half Shot at Sunrise ★★★ U

Comedy 1930 · US · BW · 78mins

The first to admit that their films were never on a par with their stage shows, Bert Wheeler and Robert Woolsey deserve better than the anonymity in which they now languish. Their wisecracking interchanges were littered with risqué puns and their slapstick had plenty of zip. They were top-billed for the first time in this lively comedy about a couple of First World War soldiers who keep out of the clutches of the military police to sample the delights of Paris. Some of the gags miss the mark and the musical moments are an intrusion, but it's mostly sparky stuff. DP

Bert Wheeler *Tommy* • Robert Woolsey *Gilbert* • John Rutherford *MP Sergeant* • George MacFarlane *Col Marshall* • Roberta Robinson *Eileen* • Edna May Oliver *Mrs Marshall* ■ *Dir* Paul Sloane [Paul H Sloane] • *Scr* James Ashman Creelman, Anne Caldwell, Ralph Spence, from a story by James Ashman Creelman

The Halfway House ★★★

Portmanteau drama 1943 · UK · BW · 95mins

Produced by Michael Balcon and directed by Basil Dearden, this is a halfway decent stab at the difficult art of the portmanteau picture – a selection of short stories linked by a common theme. In an admirable all-star cast, Mervyn and Glynis Johns are splendid as the ghostly hosts at a Welsh inn, where the guests are given the chance to re-evaluate their lives and make a more positive contribution to the war effort. Cowardice, black marketeering, family unity and the thorny issue of Irish neutrality are all explored in an intelligent piece of propaganda that still makes for optimistic entertainment. DP

Françoise Rosay *Alice Meadows* • Tom Walls *Captain Harry Meadows* • Mervyn Johns *Rhys* • Glynis Johns *Gwyneth* • Alfred Drayton *Oakley* • Esmond Knight *David Davies* • Richard Bird *Sub-lieutenant Richard French* • Philippa Hiatt *Margaret* • Sally Ann Howes *Joanna French* ■ *Dir* Basil Dearden • *Scr* Angus MacPhail, Diana Morgan, from the play *The Peaceful Inn* by Denis Ogden

Hallelujah ★★ U

Drama 1929 · US · BW · 105mins

Although plainly hampered by the primitive sound techniques, King Vidor received an Oscar nomination for this ground-breaking talkie. However, today it's impossible to escape the period racism in the tale of cotton-picker Daniel L Haynes, who twice finds redemption following a crime. Although MGM made much of the all-black cast, this was more to mollify white audiences than make a social statement, and the colour prejudice is clearly evident. DP

Daniel L Haynes *Zeke* • Nina Mae McKinney *Chick* • William E Fountaine *Hot Shot* • Harry Gray *Parson* • Fannie Belle DeKnight *Mammy* • Everett McGarrity *Spunk* • Victoria Spivey *Missy Rose* ■ *Dir* King Vidor • *Scr* Wanda Tuchock, Ransom Rideout, from a story by King Vidor • *Music/lyrics* Irving Berlin

Hallelujah, I'm a Bum ★★★ U

Musical comedy 1933 · US · BW · 84mins

With its rhyming dialogue and witty songs by Rodgers and Hart, this Depression-set musical doesn't quite come off (director Lewis Milestone was really happier with tougher material), but is a brave attempt with some fine moments. Al Jolson is a hobo living in Central Park (with his sidekick Egghead, played by famed silent comic Harry Langdon) who falls in love with the girlfriend of the mayor (Frank Morgan) and tries to change his ways. SN Behrman's script, based on a story by Ben Hecht, is amusing and incisive, but the title song had to be filmed twice, the word "bum" being replaced by "tramp" for British audiences. TV

Al Jolson *Bumper* • Madge Evans *June Marcher* • Frank Morgan *Mayor Hastings* • Harry Langdon *Egghead* • Chester Conklin *Sunday* • Tyler Brooke *Mayor's secretary* ■ *Dir* Lewis Milestone • *Scr* SN Behrman, from a story by Ben Hecht • *Music/lyrics* Richard Rogers, Lorenz Hart • *Music* Alfred Newman

The Hallelujah Trail ★★★ U

Comedy western
1965 · US · Colour · 139mins

Beleaguered cavalry commander Burt Lancaster is under attack from a bizarre collection of pressure groups in this comedy western. Lee Remick leads a brigade of temperance women trying to stop a shipment of whiskey from reaching Denver, while local Indians are equally eager to divert the barrels. Director John Sturges is free with the wagon-trail clichés, not always to great effect, but the film's worth a look, if only for Martin Landau's performance. TH DVD

Burt Lancaster *Col Thadeus Gearhart* • Lee Remick *Cora Templeton Massingale* • Jim Hutton *Capt Paul Slater* • Pamela Tiffin *Louise Gearhart* • Donald Pleasence *Oracle Jones* • Brian Keith *Frank Wallingham* • Martin Landau *Chief Walks-Stooped-Over* • John Anderson *Sergeant Buell* ■ *Dir* John Sturges • *Scr* John Gay, from the novel *Hallelujah Train* by Bill Gulick

The Halliday Brand ★★

Western 1957 · US · BW · 77mins

A rather dreary psychological western from cult director Joseph H Lewis that bears all the hallmarks of a quick, cheap shoot and a poorly thought-through sub-Freudian screenplay. Having said that, Lewis fans may still find much to enjoy in this picture. In a short running time, sterling work is done by the classy lead quartet of Joseph Cotten, Ward Bond, Viveca Lindfors and Betsy Blair, but it's all very intense and brooding. TS

Joseph Cotten *Daniel* • Viveca Lindfors *Aleta* • Betsy Blair *Martha* • Ward Bond *Big Dan* • Bill Williams *Clay* • Jay C Flippen *Chad Burris* • Christopher Dark *Jivaro* • Jeanette Nolan *Nante* ■ *Dir* Joseph H Lewis • *Scr* George W George, George S Slavin

Halloween ★★★★★ 18

Horror 1978 · US · Colour · 87mins

Simple but horribly effective, John Carpenter practically patented the slasher genre with this low-budget suburban horror, in the process launching Jamie Lee Curtis as a new scream queen. Michael Myers is the six-year-old boy who murders his sister on Halloween and is institutionalised until his escape 15 years later. He returns in a plain, white mask to cause murderous mayhem, despite the intervention of his equally spooky psychiatrist (Donald Pleasence, in a career-reviving turn). The film is expertly plotted, beginning in broad daylight and building to a series of bloody crescendos as licentious babysitters and boyfriends are picked off. Its power to grip and jolt has never diminished, thanks in part to Carpenter's own pulsing score. AJ. Contains violence, swearing, sex scenes, drug abuse, nudity. DVD

Donald Pleasence *Dr Sam Loomis* • Jamie Lee Curtis *Laurie Strode* • Nancy Loomis *Annie* • PJ Soles *Lynda* • Charles Cyphers *Brackett* • Kyle Richards *Lindsey* • Brian Andrews *Tommy* • John Michael Graham *Bob* • Nancy Stephens *Marion* • Arthur Malet *Graveyard keeper* • Mickey Yablans *Richie* • Brent Le Page *Lonnie* • Tony Moran *Michael aged 21* ■ *Dir* John Carpenter • *Scr* Debra Hill, John Carpenter

Halloween II ★★ 18

Horror 1981 · US · Colour · 87mins

With the exception of *H20*, the sequels to John Carpenter's 1978 horror masterpiece have been universally awful. However, like that film, this was the only one to feature the original star Jamie Lee Curtis, and is better for it. This takes up where the original finished, with Curtis being taken to hospital still in shock, but before long her indestructible nemesis is stalking her around the wards. Carpenter had a hand in the script, but this is a by-the-numbers retread and the direction lacks flair. JF [video] DVD

Jamie Lee Curtis *Laurie Strode* • Donald Pleasence *Dr Sam Loomis* • Charles Cyphers *Leigh Brackett* • Jeffrey Kramer *Graham* • Lance Guest *Jimmy* • Pamela Susan Shoop [Pamela Shoop] *Karen* • Hunter Von Leer *Gary Hunt* ■ *Dir* Rick Rosenthal • *Scr* John Carpenter, Debra Hill, from their characters

Halloween III: Season of the Witch ★ 15

Science-fiction horror
1982 · US · Colour · 91mins

This deserves a star for being the most original of all the *Halloween* sequels – the problem is that it's also one of the worst. Dumping the Michael Myers storyline, the film has mad toy mogul Dan O'Herlihy supplying children with lethal Halloween masks. Tom Atkins plays the father who stumbles across O'Herlihy's evil plan. There are a few good gory bits, but the story is daft and the direction from Tommy Lee Wallace is disappointing. JF. Contains swearing and violence. [video] DVD

Tom Atkins *Dr Dan Challis* • Stacey Nelkia *Ellie* • Dan O'Herlihy *Conal* • Ralph Strait *Buddy* • Michael Currie *Rafferty* • Jadeen Barbor *Betty* • Bradley Schachter *Little Buddy* ■ *Dir/Scr* Tommy Lee Wallace

Halloween 4: the Return of Michael Myers ★★ 18

Horror 1988 · US · Colour · 88mins

After the misguided, Michael Myers-less *Halloween III*, it's back-to-basics time and the result is a competent, but yawningly empty, slasher thriller. Danielle Harris steps into the Jamie Lee Curtis role, playing one of the last surviving relatives of the caged psycho, who once again escapes and heads back to his home turf for some more blood-letting. Donald Pleasence reprises his role as Dr Loomis from the first two films, but by now any genuine menace was seeping away fast. JF [video] DVD

Donald Pleasence *Dr Loomis* • Ellie Cornell *Rachel Carruthers* • Danielle Harris *Jamie Lloyd* • George P Wilbur *Michael Myers* • Michael Pataki *Dr Hoffman* ■ *Dir* Dwight H Little • *Scr* Alan B McElroy, from a story by Dhani Lipsius, Larry Rattner, Benjamin Ruffner, Alan B McElroy, from the characters created by Debra Hill, John Carpenter

Halloween 5: the Revenge of Michael Myers ★★ 18

Horror 1989 · US · Colour · 96mins

More slashing by numbers, as Danielle Harris once again dodges nasty Uncle Michael Myers, who, surprise surprise, managed to survive this film's predecessor. Shot back to back with Part 4, the only link with John Carpenter's original is Donald Pleasence as the barking psychiatrist Dr Sam Loomis, named after a character in *Psycho*. Otherwise, it's business as usual. JF [video] DVD

Donald Pleasence *Dr Loomis* • Ellie Cornell *Rachel* • Beau Starr *Meeker* • Danielle Harris *Jamie* • Wendy Kaplan *Tina* • Donald L Shanks [Don Shanks] *Michael Myers* ■ *Dir* Dominique Othenin-Girard • *Scr* Michael Jacobs, Dominique Otherin-Girard, Shem Bitterman, from the characters created by Debra Hill, John Carpenter

Halloween 6: the Curse of Michael Myers ★ 18

Horror 1995 · US · Colour · 84mins

The worst of the series so far. Director Joe Chappelle tries to give menace by proxy to the laughable awfulness, reviving Carpenter's original *Halloween* score as a backdrop. It doesn't work, and neither do the revelations intended to explain Michael Myers's years of murder and mayhem. Donald Pleasence gives his usual reliable performance, but sadly the line, "Not dead. Just very much retired", proved to be his epitaph: he died shortly after shooting. AJ. Contains swearing, violence, nudity. [video] DVD

Donald Pleasence *Dr Loomis* • Mitch Ryan [Mitchell Ryan] *Dr Wynn* • Marianne Hagan *Kara Strode* • Paul Rudd *Tommy Doyle* • Mariah O'Brien *Beth* • Kim Darby *Debra Strode* • George P Wilbur *Mike Myers* ■ *Dir* Joe Chappelle • *Scr* Daniel Farrands, from the characters created by Debra Hill, John Carpenter

Halloween: Resurrection ★ 15

Horror 2002 · US · Colour · 78mins

In this seventh sequel, six students are chosen by the Dangertainment Network to spend Halloween night in the old Myers house, which has been fitted with cameras for a live internet broadcast. Given the set-up, it doesn't come as a total surprise when Michael – still not dead despite having been decapitated in *H20* – arrives to turn things bloody for the benefit of online viewers who think it's all a charade. The stale "Big Brother" plot sinks into a morass of clichéd shocks and messy camerawork. AJ [video] DVD

Busta Rhymes *Freddie Harris* • Brad Loree *Michael "The Shape" Myers* • Jamie Lee Curtis *Laurie Strode* • Bianca Kajlich *Sara Moyer* • Sean Patrick Thomas *Rudy* • Daisy McCrackin *Donna* • Katee Sackhoff *Jen* ■ *Dir* Rick Rosenthal • *Scr* Larry Brand, Sean Hood, from a story by Brand, from characters created by Debra Hill, John Carpenter

Halloween H20: 20 Years Later ★★★ 18

Horror 1998 · US · Colour · 82mins

John Carpenter's classic 1978 chiller gets a 1990s makeover, although in the hands of director Steve Miner, a veteran of horror franchises such as *Friday the 13th* and *House*, the emphasis is still firmly on frights rather than in-jokes. Jamie Lee Curtis, back in the role that made her name, is now a recovering alcoholic and headteacher at an exclusive school. The problem is that the murderous Michael is keen to celebrate the 20th anniversary of his first massacre. Curtis steals the show from the teenage TV pin-ups, but Miner's direction is merely efficient, rather than scary. JF. Contains violence and swearing, with some sexual references. [video] DVD

Jamie Lee Curtis *Laurie Strode/Keri Tate* • Michelle Williams *Molly* • Joseph Gordon-Levitt *Jimmy* • Josh Hartnett *John* • Adam Arkin *Will Brennan* • LL Cool J *Ronny* • Jodi Lyn O'Keefe *Sarah* • Adam Hann-Byrd *Charlie* • Janet Leigh *Norma* ■ *Dir* Steve Miner • *Scr* Robert Zappia, Matt Greenberg, from a story by Robert Zappia, from characters created by Debra Hill, John Carpenter

The Halloween Tree ★★★★ U

Animated fantasy 1993 · US · Colour · 69mins

Ray Bradbury's children's novel is superbly brought to the screen in this top-notch animation feature made for television by the Hanna-Barbera studio. Four children, who desperately want to help a sick friend, embark on a journey through the multicultural and religious history of All Hallows' Eve. Guided by Mr Moundshroud (voiced by Leonard Nimoy) they learn a 4,000-year history and moral lesson en route to a gallant sacrifice. Brilliantly adapted by Bradbury, the combination of traditional Halloween imagery with the less globally well-known ones is as inventive as *Tim Burton's The Nightmare before Christmas*. AJ [video]

Leonard Nimoy *Mr Moundshroud* ■ *Dir* Mario Piluso • *Scr* Ray Bradbury, from his novel

Halls of Anger ★★

Drama 1970 · US · Colour · 98mins

Formula film about a school riven with racial violence. The production boasts a certain class, but there's no lesson to be learned here that hasn't been taught in a dozen other movies with similar plots and settings. Some interest resides, though, in the cast – not leads Calvin Lockhart or Janet MacLachlan, but look further and you'll spot the likes of Rob Reiner, Ed Asner and a very young Jeff Bridges. DA

Calvin Lockhart *Quincy Davis* • Janet MacLachlan *Lorraine Nash* • James A Watson Jr *JT Watson* • Jeff Bridges *Douglas Falk* • Rob Reiner *Leaky Couloris* • DeWayne Jessie *Lerone Johnson* • Patricia Stich *Sherry Vaughn* • Edward Asner *Ernie McKay* ■ *Dir* Paul Bogart • *Scr* John Shaner, Al Ramrus

Halls of Montezuma ★★★ U

Second World War action drama
1950 · US · Colour · 108mins

A big-budget, ferociously patriotic 20th Century-Fox Second World War movie, directed by one of the all-time greats of the genre, Lewis Milestone. The action isn't of the highest standard, but this is enjoyable, largely thanks to an excellent cast headed by Richard Widmark, and backed up by Jack Palance, a pre-*Dragnet* Jack Webb and Robert Wagner as the youngster of the outfit. The Technicolor photography is quite outstanding, and there's no unnecessary romance. TS [video] DVD

Richard Widmark *Lt Anderson* • Walter (Jack) Palance [Jack Palance] *Pigeon Lane* • Reginald Gardiner *Sgt Johnson* • Robert Wagner *Coffman* • Karl Malden *Doc* • Richard Hylton *Cpl Stuart Conroy* • Richard Boone *Lt Col Gilfilan* • Skip Homeier *Pretty Boy* • Don Hicks *Lt Butterfield* • Jack Webb *Correspondent Dickerman* ■ *Dir* Lewis Milestone • *Scr* Michael Blankfort • *Cinematographer* Winton C Hoch, Harry Jackson

Hamam: the Turkish Bath ★★★ 15

Drama 1996 · It/Tur/Sp · Colour · 98mins

This atmospheric drama slowly draws you into the back streets of Istanbul and even more deeply into the lives of their inhabitants. The Turkish cast is admirable, but the focus falls firmly on Alessandro Gassman, as the Italian businessman who inherits a bath-house from an aunt and whose independent lifestyle eventually leads to tragedy. Director Ferzan Ozpetek's sunny cityscapes are striking, but it's the evocative interiors with their haunting light and architectural beauty that give this search for cultural and sexual identity its extraordinary sense of serenity and fulfilment. DP. In Italian and Turkish with English subtitles. Contains swearing, nudity. [video] DVD

Alessandro Gassman *Francesco* • Francesca D'Aloja *Marta* • Mehmet Gunsur *Mehmet* • Carlo Cecchi *Oscar* • Halil Ergun *Osman* ■ *Dir* Ferzan Ozpetek • *Scr* Ferzan Ozpetek, Stefano Tummolini

Hambone and Hillie ★★★ PG

Comedy drama 1984 · US · Colour · 86mins

Heroic canines have always been popular with moviegoers, but few tales of four-pawed adventure have been as brutal as this cross-country epic, which includes an escaped convict's horrific assault on a pregnant woman and a dog's gruesome death. Thankfully there are more wholesome episodes, such as Hambone's friendships with a lonely paraplegic. As the grandmother hoping her lost hound will find his way home, the venerable Lillian Gish is adorable. DP [video]

Lillian Gish *Hillie Radcliffe* • Timothy Bottoms *Michael Radcliffe* • Candy Clark *Nancy Rollins* • OJ Simpson *Tucker* • Robert Walker [Robert Walker Jr] *Wanderer* • Jack Carter *Lester Burns* • Alan Hale [Alan Hale Jr] *McVickers* • Anne Lockhart *Roberta Radcliffe* ■ *Dir* Roy Watts • *Scr* Sandra K Bailey, Michael Murphey, Joel Soisson, from a story by Ken Barnett

Hamburger Hill ★★★★ 18

War drama 1987 · US · Colour · 104mins

Unjustly overshadowed by Oliver Stone's *Platoon* and Stanley Kubrick's *Full Metal Jacket*, John Irvin's *Hamburger Hill* is almost their equal. The story has the classic simplicity of a past era of war movies: troops of the 101st Airborne Division attack Hill 937 in the Ashau Valley, Vietnam, and after ten days and 11 assaults, when everyone has been put through the meat grinder, the hill is renamed after America's favourite fast food. Reducing the Vietnam war to the level of symbol is an efficient means of conveying the pointless sacrifice, and Irvin does the messy job superbly. Not for the lily-livered. AT. Contains violence, swearing and brief nudity. [video] DVD

Anthony Barrile *Languilli* • Michael Patrick Boatman [Michael Boatman] *Motown* • Don Cheadle *Washburn* • Michael Dolan *Murphy* • Don James *McDaniel* • Dylan McDermott *Sergeant Frantz* • MA Nickles *Galvan* ■ *Dir* John Irvin • *Scr* James Carabatsos

Hamilton ★★★

Spy thriller 1998 · Swe · Colour · 127mins

Jan Guillou's Carl Hamilton is apparently the Scandinavian answer to Tom Clancy's Jack Ryan, and his bestsellers have been filmed a number of times and this is one of the most successful adaptions. *Fargo* star Peter Stormare enjoys the opportunity to be the eponymous hero who, along with sidekick Mats Langbacka, is on the trail of a Russian gang trying to unload a nuclear missile. There are also good supporting roles for Lena Olin and Mark Hamill, and award-winning commercials director Harald Zwart keeps the action racing along. JF. In Swedish with English subtitles.

Mark Hamill *Mike Hawkins* • Lena Olin *Tessie* • Peter Stormare *Carl Hamilton* • Mats Langbacka *Ake Stalhandske* • Madeleine Elfstrand *Anna* • Thomas Hedengran *Gustavsson* • Mikael Ahlberg *Andersson* ■ *Dir* Harald Zwart • *Scr* Jonas Cornell, William Aldridge, from novels by Jan Guillou

Hamlet ★★★★★ U

Classic tragedy 1948 · UK · BW · 147mins

Laurence Olivier directed himself in this astonishing Shakespeare adaptation, which won five Academy Awards. Desmond Dickinson's camerawork adds mood to the moment as Larry's blond-headed Prince Hamlet wanders around Elsinore Castle, ambiguously pursuing Ophelia (Jean Simmons), berating his mother Eileen Herlie and stalking his new stepfather Basil Sydney. (Olivier also played the ghost of Hamlet's father, to eerie effect.) For the sake of pace – and the film certainly has that! – adapter Alan Dent removes the supporting characters Rosencrantz and Guildenstern, while William Walton's music adds atmospheric lustre. Despite all the cuts, this is a very great Dane. TH DVD

Laurence Olivier *Hamlet* • Eileen Herlie *Gertrude* • Basil Sydney *Claudius* • Norman Wooland *Horatio* • Felix Aylmer *Polonius* • Terence Morgan *Laertes* • Jean Simmons *Ophelia* • Peter Cushing *Osric* • Stanley Holloway *Gravedigger* • Anthony Quayle *Marcellus* ■ *Dir* Laurence Olivier • *Scr* Alan Dent, from the play by William Shakespeare • *Costume Designer* Roger K Furse • *Art Director* Roger K Furse, Carmen Dillon

Hamlet ★★★★

Tragedy 1964 · USSR · BW · 150mins

The Russian version of Shakespeare's most famous tragedy was filmed by veteran director Grigori Kozintsev to commemorate the 400th anniversary of the playwright's birth. His treatment is a study of medieval state machinations, and is set in an Elsinore whose inhabitants are contained by an impressive fortress of stone and iron. It may lack the depth of other film versions, but the images, enriched by the dramatic Shostokovich music, are bold and powerful – as is the great Russian actor Innokenti Smoktunovsky, whose Prince of Denmark is a man of action, not a brooding dreamer. RB. A Russian language film.

Innokenti Smoktunovsky *Hamlet* • Mikhail Nazvanov *King* • Elsa Radzin *Queen* • Yuri Tolubeyev *Polonius* • Anastasia Vertinskaya *Ophelia* • Vladimir Erenberg *Horatio* • C Olesenko *Laertes* • Vadim Medvedev *Guildenstern* • Igor Dmitriev *Rosencrantz* ■ *Dir* Grigori Kozintsev • *Scr* Grigori Kozintsev, Boris Pasternak, from the play by William Shakespeare

Hamlet ★★★

Tragedy 1964 · US · BW · 186mins

When Richard Burton played the title role in John Gielgud's production of *Hamlet* on Broadway in 1964, he was the most famous young actor in the world. Fortunately his performance was captured (over two nights) using a short-lived multi-camera system, Electronovision. Dismissed at the time as poor, both picture and sound quality are in fact perfectly acceptable; indeed, the 15 cameras pick up nuances of which the theatre audience would have been unaware. The stage production, done in modern dress on crude rostra, would today be dismissed as cheap, but Burton is revealed as a technical actor in the Olivier mould, and his showy performance makes him the funniest screen Hamlet. DM

Richard Burton *Hamlet* • Hume Cronyn *Polonius* • Alfred Drake *Claudius* • Eileen Herlie *Gertrude* • William Redfield *Guildenstern* • Linda Marsh *Ophelia* • Robert Milli *Horatio* ■ *Dir* Bill Colleran, John Gielgud • *Scr* from the play by William Shakespeare

Hamlet ★★★ U

Tragedy 1969 · UK · Colour · 112mins

While Kenneth Branagh shot his 1996 version of the play on lavish, expansive sets, here star Nicol Williamson and director Tony Richardson opted for extreme close-ups. While it might have made those in the back row feel part of the proceedings, Williamson's booming performance sits uncomfortably on the small screen. Compensations come from Roger Livesey's dual role as Lucianus and the Player King and Anthony Hopkins's Claudius. DP

Nicol Williamson *Hamlet* • Gordon Jackson *Horatio* • Anthony Hopkins *Claudius* • Judy Parfitt *Gertrude* • Mark Dignam *Polonius* • Michael Pennington *Laertes* • Marianne Faithfull *Ophelia* • Ben Aris *Rosencrantz* • Clive Graham *Guildenstern* • Peter Gale *Osric* • Roger Livesey *Lucianus/Player King* • Michael Elphick *Captain* • Anjelica Huston *Court lady* ■ *Dir* Tony Richardson • *Scr* from the play by William Shakespeare

Hamlet ★★★★ PG

Tragedy 1990 · US · Colour · 128mins

Franco Zeffirelli directs this surprisingly vigorous rendition of a play essentially about indecision and hesitancy. Mel Gibson is the screen's most muscular Prince of Denmark, but he gives a good account of himself, as does Helena Bonham Carter as the abused Ophelia – yet it's Alan Bates who most impresses as the villainous Claudius. Not one for the purists, but a laudable attempt to introduce Shakespeare to the blockbuster generation. DP. Contains nudity.

Mel Gibson *Hamlet* • Glenn Close *Queen Gertrude* • Alan Bates *Claudius* • Paul Scofield *Ghost* • Ian Holm *Polonius* • Helena Bonham Carter *Ophelia* • Stephen Dillane *Horatio* • Nathaniel Parker *Laertes* • Sean Murray (1) *Guildenstern* • Michael Maloney *Rosencrantz* • Trevor Peacock *Gravedigger* • John McEnery *Osric* ■ *Dir* Franco Zeffirelli • *Scr* Franco Zeffirelli, Christopher De Vore, from the play by William Shakespeare

Hamlet ★★★★ PG

Tragedy 1996 · US · Colour · 232mins

This monumental full-length, unabridged version of the play has Kenneth Branagh directing himself as the Prince. Admirable, and challenging, this is a very showbizzy staging – in addition to the leading players (such as Kate Winslet as Ophelia, Julie Christie's Gertrude, Derek Jacobi as Claudius), there is a veritable galaxy of star appearances to tweak the interest. While some critics might say this is not so much a movie as a chorus-line of talents, Branagh has to be admired for the ambition of this ravishingly beautiful staging. TH

Kenneth Branagh *Hamlet* • Derek Jacobi *Claudius* • Julie Christie *Gertrude* • Richard Briers *Polonius* • Kate Winslet *Ophelia* • Nicholas Farrell *Horatio* • Michael Maloney *Laertes* • Brian Blessed *Ghost* • Gérard Depardieu *Reynaldo* • Jack Lemmon *Marcellus* • Charlton Heston *Player King* • Rufus Sewell *Fortinbras* • Richard Attenborough *English Ambassador* • Timothy Spall *Rosencrantz* • Reece Dinsdale *Guildenstern* • John Gielgud *Priam* • Judi Dench *Hecuba* ■ *Dir* Kenneth Branagh • *Scr* Kenneth Branagh, from the play by William Shakespeare • *Production Designer* Tim Harvey • *Art Director* Desmond Crowe

Hamlet ★★★ 12

Tragedy 2000 · US · Colour · 106mins

Writer/director Michael Almereyda's distinctive new take on Shakespeare's famous tragedy retains the Bard's language but timewarps the story into a contemporary setting. Radical re-interpretations don't always come off, but Almereyda's marriage of 16th-century words and 21st-century visuals works well. So, too, does the reinvention of Elsinore as a dodgy multinational corporation, with Hamlet a paranoid pawn caught up in the struggle for its control. Ethan Hawke is an uncharismatic lead, but there are some sparky supporting turns. DA. Contains violence. DVD

Ethan Hawke *Hamlet* • Kyle MacLachlan *Claudius* • Diane Venora *Gertrude* • Sam Shepard *Ghost* • Bill Murray *Polonius* • Liev Schreiber *Laertes* • Julia Stiles *Ophelia* • Karl Geary *Horatio* • Steve Zahn *Rosencrantz* • Dechen Thurman *Guildenstern* ■ *Dir* Michael Almereyda • *Scr* Michael Almereyda, from the play by William Shakespeare

Hamlet Goes Business ★★★★ PG

Comedy drama 1987 · Fin · BW · 85mins

Only Aki Kaurismäki could turn Shakespeare's most complex play into an offbeat drama about the rubber duck business. Transferring the action from Elsinore to a modern Finnish boardroom, the writer/director also shifts the thematic emphasis away from insanity and the inability to act and places it on cruelty and a wilful defiance of progress. Seeking revenge for the murder of his father, Pirkka-Pekka Petelius is like a character from a *film noir*, an impression reinforced by Timo Salminen's shadowy monochrome photography. All the *dramatis personae* are wickedly reinvented, as are the Bard's famous quotations. Add a stunning score, and the result is a palpable hit. DP. In Finnish with English subtitles.

Pirkka-Pekka Petelius *Hamlet* • Esko Salminen *Klaus* • Kati Outinen *Ophelia* • Elina Salo *Gertrud* • Esko Nikkari *Polonius* • Kari Vaananen *Lauri Polonius* • Hannu Valtonen *Simo* • Mari Rantasila *Helena* • Turo Pajala *Rosencrantz* • Aake Kalliala *Guildenstern* • Pentii Auer *Father/Ghost* ■ *Dir* Aki Kaurismäki • *Scr* Aki Kaurismäki, from the play by William Shakespeare

Hammer ★★

Crime drama 1972 · US · Colour · 92mins

Tough guy Fred Williamson's breakthrough movie was this below average blaxploitation crime thriller produced by drive-in movie king Al Adamson. Williamson plays a dock worker-turned-prizefighting boxer whose Mafia manager wants him to start throwing bouts. Williamson based his character on Muhammad Ali and even copies his moves in the ring which is the only interesting thing to cling on to as the tedium increases in this formulaic potboiler. AJ

Fred Williamson *BJ Hammer* • Bernie Hamilton *Davis* • Vonetta McGee *Lois* • William Smith *Brenner* • Charles Lampkin *Big Sid* • Elizabeth Harding *Rhoda* ■ *Dir* Bruce D Clark [Bruce Clark] • *Scr* Charles Johnson

Hammers over the Anvil ★★ 15

Period drama based on a true story
1992 · Aus · Colour · 97mins

This is the dull tale of a young crippled boy (Alexander Outhred) in the Australian outback and his hero worship of the rugged Russell Crowe, who seems to spend his time either with his horses (naked and clothed) or shagging a married woman (Charlotte Rampling) who's come to town seemingly for that reason alone. Notable for Russell Crowe riding naked across a field. JB DVD

Russell Crowe *East Driscoll* • Charlotte Rampling *Grace McAllister* • Alexander Outhred *Alan Marshall* • Frankie J Holden *Bushman* ■ *Dir* Ann Turner • *Scr* Peter Hepworth, Ann Turner, from the journals by Alan Marshall

Hammersmith Is Out ★★

Drama 1972 · US · Colour · 114mins

Peter Ustinov's reputation may now rest on his skill as a raconteur, but he was once considered to be the British film industry's great white hope as a director. This makes it hard to see why. It's a bizarre story about madman Richard Burton escaping a mental hospital – run by a language-mangling Ustinov – to become a tycoon, with Elizabeth Taylor in tow. It may have been intended as a spoof, but it comes across as an indulgence. TH

Elizabeth Taylor *Jimmie Jean Jackson* • Richard Burton *Hammersmith* • Peter Ustinov *Doctor* • Beau Bridges *Billy Breedlove* • Leon Ames *General Sam Pembroke* • George Raft *Guido Scartucci* • Jose Espinoza *Duke* ■ *Dir* Peter Ustinov • *Scr* Stanford Whitmore

Hammett ★★★

Crime drama 1982 · US · Colour · 97mins

Wim Wenders's first Hollywood movie is a flawed but fascinating crime drama. In this fictionalised tale, Frederic Forrest plays the legendary novelist Dashiell Hammett, down on his luck and entangled in corruption and blackmail involving a Chinese prostitute. The under-rated Forrest is quite superb and there are strong supporting turns from the likes of Peter Boyle and Marilu Henner. The tone is uneven, but Wenders still succeeds in summoning up an authentic *film noir* atmosphere. JF

Frederic Forrest *Hammett* • Peter Boyle *Jimmy Ryan* • Marilu Henner *Kit Conger/Sue Alabama* • Roy Kinnear *English Eddie Hagedorn* • Elisha Cook Jr *Eli the taxi driver* • Lydia Lei *Crystal Ling* • RG Armstrong *Lieutenant O'Mara* • Richard Bradford *Detective Bradford* ■ *Dir* Wim Wenders • *Scr* Ross Thomas, Dennis O'Flaherty, Thomas Pope, from the novel by Joe Gores

Hamsun ★★★

Biographical drama
1996 · Den/Swe/Nor/Ger · Colour · 158mins

Cutting a Lear-like figure as a man who has outlived his times, Max von Sydow dominates this controversial study of the Nobel laureate whose admiration for Hitler led to him being branded a traitor after the liberation of Norway. However, as Jan Troell is keen to point out, Knut Hamsun was more concerned with denouncing British imperialism and advancing the cause of Norwegian independence than bolstering the hated regime of Vidkun Quisling. This is a fascinating study and Hamsun's meeting with Hitler is riveting. DP. A Swedish language film.

Max von Sydow *Knut Hamsun* • Ghita Norby *Marie Hamsun* • Sverre Anker Ousdal *Vidkun Quisling* • Eindride Eidsvold *Tore Hamsun* • Gard B Eidsvold *Arild Hamsun* • Anette Hoff *Ellinor Hamsun* • Asa Soderling *Cecilia Hamsun* • Svein Erik Brodal *Holmboe* • Ernst Jacobi *Adolf Hitler* ■ *Dir* Jan Troell • *Scr* Per Olov Enquist, from the non-fiction book *Prosessen mot Hamsun* by Thorkild Hansen

Hana-Bi ★★★★ 18

Crime drama 1997 · Jpn · Colour · 98mins

With its fragmentary structure intended to resemble the "fireworks" (the literal translation of *Hana-Bi*) of the title, this is definitely a detective film with a difference. Winner of the Golden Lion at Venice, it's a lyrical, compassionate tale as ex-cop Takeshi "Beat" Kitano (who also directs) seeks to care for both his dying wife and his partner, disabled while chasing a criminal. To counteract the grim reality of Kitano's problems back in the city, there are lengthy passages of contemplative silence and pastoral vistas, as well as symbolic paintings commenting on the action. Although there are still explosive sequences of gun-play, this is a far cry from earlier Kitano films such as *Sonatine*. DP. In Japanese with English subtitles. Contains violence and some swearing. DVD

Takeshi Kitano *Yoshitika Nishi* • Kayoko Kishimoto *Miyuki (Nishi's wife)* • Ren Osugi *Horibe* • Susumu Terajima *Detective Nakamura* • Tetsu Watanabe *Tesuka (junkyard owner)* ■ *Dir/Scr* Takeshi Kitano

The Hand ★★★ 18

Horror 1981 · US · Colour and BW · 99mins

Oliver Stone's second directorial effort was this fine psychological horror tale about cartoonist Michael Caine losing his hand in a freak car accident and the severed limb seeking violent revenge on all his enemies. Or is Caine committing the murders and simply hallucinating? What makes this dark fantasy more than just an angry, depressing and gory remake of the classic *The Beast with Five Fingers* is Stone's multi-dimensional and thoughtful script that explores the many facets of madness. AJ. Contains violence, swearing and nudity. [VIDEO]

Michael Caine *Jon Lansdale* • Andrea Marcovicci *Anne Lansdale* • Annie McEnroe *Stella Roche* • Bruce McGill *Brian Ferguson* • Viveca Lindfors *Doctor* • Rosemary Murphy *Karen Wagner* • Mara Hobel *Lizzie Lansdale* ■ *Dir* Oliver Stone • *Scr* Oliver Stone, from the novel *The Lizard's Tale* by Marc Brandel • *Cinematographer* King Baggott

Hand Gun ★★ 18

Crime thriller 1994 · US · Colour · 85mins

Treat Williams plays a small-time crook who, with brother Paul Shulze, gets in over his head when his equally crooked father (Seymour Cassel) does a runner with the takings of a bank robbery. The cast features colourful character actors, but the writing lacks focus and the direction is overheated. JF. Contains swearing, violence, sex scenes and nudity. [VIDEO]

Treat Williams *George McCallister* • Seymour Cassel *Jack McCallister* • Paul Schulze *Michael McCallister* • Frank Vincent *Earl* • Anna Thomson [Anna Levine] *Laura* • Michael Imperioli *Benny* • Michael Rapaport *Lenny* • Star Jasper *Sally* ■ *Dir/Scr* Whitney Ransick

The Hand of Night ★

Horror 1966 · UK · Colour · 89mins

Hapless William Sylvester visits Morocco and is enticed into a den of vampires by beautiful Moorish princess Alizia Gur. Awkwardly combining the Dracula myth with middle-eastern mummy motifs, but bringing nothing of its own to the terror table except exotic locations, this tedious sub-Hammer horror filler is further eroded by bland performances. AJ

William Sylvester *Paul Carver* • Diane Clare *Chantal* • Alizia Gur *Marisa* • Edward Underdown *Gunther* • Terence de Marney *Omar* • William Dexter *Leclerc* ■ *Dir* Frederic Goode • *Scr* Bruce Stewart

The Hand That Rocks the Cradle ★★★★ 15

Thriller 1992 · US · Colour · 105mins

Cool, Teutonic-looking Rebecca De Mornay plays the "Nanny from Hell", wreaking havoc on the sunny designer family life of Annabella Sciorra and Matt McCoy, in this nerve-racking psychological thriller. Director Curtis Hanson successfully plugs into every deep-seated fear of middle-class parents, with De Mornay doing a neat turn in icy malevolence wrapped up in the guise of responsible carer. This is pure hokum, of course, but extremely effective until the last 30 minutes, when the plot rapidly self-destructs. SH. Contains violence, swearing and nudity. [VIDEO] DVD

Annabella Sciorra *Claire Bartel* • Rebecca De Mornay *Mrs Mott/"Peyton Flanders"* • Matt McCoy *Michael Bartel* • Ernie Hudson *Solomon* • Julianne Moore *Marlene* • Madeline Zima *Emma Bartel* • John de Lancie *Doctor Mott* • Mitchell Laurance *Lawyer* ■ *Dir* Curtis Hanson • *Scr* Amanda Silver

A Handful of Dust ★★★★ PG

Period drama 1987 · UK · Colour · 114mins

In this glossily depressing adaptation of Evelyn Waugh's satire on the between-wars aristocracy, James Wilby stars as the dull, duty-bound estate owner cuckolded by his adulterous wife Kristin Scott Thomas and man-about-town Rupert Graves. Directed by Charles Sturridge with the same impeccable detail he brought to his TV adaptation of *Brideshead Revisited*, the impressive performances can't lighten a cynicism which tries to persuade us that the wages of goodness are death. TH [VIDEO] DVD

James Wilby *Tony Last* • Kristin Scott Thomas *Brenda Last* • Rupert Graves *John Beaver* • Anjelica Huston *Mrs Rattery* • Judi Dench *Mrs Beaver* • Alec Guinness *Mr Todd* • Richard Beale *Ben* • Jackson Kyle *John Andrew* ■ *Dir* Charles Sturridge • *Scr* Charles Sturridge, Tim Sullivan, Derek Granger, from the novel by Evelyn Waugh

Handgun ★★★★ 18

Thriller 1983 · UK/US · Colour · 95mins

An intriguing if only partially successful attempt by British director Tony Garnett to redress the balance in favour of the female victim of male violence. Karen Young is excellent as the passive young woman whose experiences at the hands of Texan brute Clayton Day (another finely etched performance) turn her into a marauding vigilante. On the plus side, there are a great sense of menace and tension, good supporting performances and an intelligent, sensitive handling of tricky issues. The minus is Garnett's overall thesis that the way to handle violence is to strike back. However, this is still a minor classic. SH. Contains violence, swearing and nudity. [VIDEO]

Karen Young *Kathleen Sullivan* • Clayton Day *Larry Keeler* • Suzie Humphreys *Nancy* • Helena Humann *Miss Davis* • Ben Jones *Chuck* ■ *Dir/Scr* Tony Garnett

Handle with Care ★★ U

Drama 1958 · US · BW · 82mins

Dean Jones, that stalwart of Disney features during the 1960s and 1970s makes an earlier career stab at teen-idoldom in this undistinguished drama. As law student Zachary Davis, Jones investigates small-town crime in a legal process that allows such pupils to take on mock grand-jury work. Sincere, but boring. TH

Dean Jones *Zachary Davis* • Joan O'Brien *Mary Judson* • Thomas Mitchell *Mayor Dick Williston* • John Smith *Bill Reeves* • Walter Abel *Professor Bowdin* • Burt Douglas *Ray Crowder* ■ *Dir* David Friedkin • *Scr* David Friedkin, Morton Fine, from the teleplay *Mock Trial* by Samuel Grafton, Edith Grafton

The Handmaid's Tale ★★★ 18

Futuristic drama
1990 · US · Colour · 103mins

Adapted from the Margaret Atwood bestseller, this dystopian drama has Natasha Richardson living in a born-again America run on puritanical lines in a polluted future. As one of the few fertile women around, she's ordered to bear Robert Duvall a child for wife Faye Dunaway. The republic's religious rites and oppression of women echo some of today's theocratic fanaticisms, but it's a story that never gets its act or acting together, although Duvall is a formidable presence in this feminist protest. TH. Contains violence, swearing and sex scenes. [VIDEO]

Natasha Richardson *Kate* • Faye Dunaway *Serena Joy* • Aidan Quinn *Nick* • Elizabeth McGovern *Moira* • Victoria Tennant *Aunt Lydia* • Robert Duvall *Commander* • Blanche Baker *Ofglen* • Traci Lind *Ofwarren/Janine* ■ *Dir* Volker Schlöndorff • *Scr* Harold Pinter, from the novel by Margaret Atwood

Hands across the Table ★★★★

Screwball comedy 1935 · US · BW · 79mins

A manicurist and a penniless playboy, each determined to marry money and betrothed to dull but appropriately wealthy partners, meet, fall in love, and break off their engagements. The simple plot services a superior romantic comedy: sparkling, witty and marvellously played by Carole Lombard and Fred MacMurray, both of whose progress into top stardom was hastened by the film's box-office success. Ralph Bellamy and Astrid Allwyn are the future spouses who are thrown over, and Mitchell Leisen directs with the lightness of touch you would expect from a Paramount production of the period. RK

Carole Lombard *Regi Allen* • Fred MacMurray *Theodore Drew III* • Ralph Bellamy *Allen Macklyn* • Astrid Allwyn *Vivian Snowden* • Ruth Donnelly *Laura* • Marie Prevost *Nona* • Joseph Tozer *Peter* • William Demarest *Natty* ■ *Dir* Mitchell Leisen • *Scr* Herbert Fields, Norman Krasna, Vincent Lawrence, from the story *Bracelets* by Viña Delmar [Vina Delmar]

Hands of Orlac ★★★

Silent crime horror
1924 · Austria · BW · 90mins

Robert Wiene's adaptation of Maurice Renard's sensationalist novel suffers from an uncertainty of tone. For the most part, the action is staged in a realistic manner, thus making the moments of expressionist stylisation all the more incongruous. However, Conrad Veidt is mesmerising as the concert pianist living on his nerves after his shattered hands are replaced with those of a murderer. Equally compelling is Fritz Kortner's blackmailer, but not even he's prepared for the final twist. DP

Conrad Veidt *Orlac* • Fritz Kortner *Nera* • Carmen Cartellieri *Regine* • Paul Adkonas *Diener* ■ *Dir* Robert Wiene • *Scr* Louis Nerz, from the novel by Maurice Renard

The Hands of Orlac ★★★★

Horror 1960 · UK/Fr · BW · 101mins

Filmed twice before (most notably as *Mad Love* in 1935), this elegant version of Maurice Renard's psychological case study of murderous obsession still exerts a morbid fascination. Mel Ferrer is a little lightweight as the pianist given a convicted strangler's hands after a plane crash, but Christopher Lee is a remorseless revelation as the sadistic magician tormenting him, ensuring the chilling tension is maintained right up until the final surprise twist. AJ

Mel Ferrer *Steven Orlac* • Christopher Lee *Nero* • Dany Carrel *Li-Lang* • Felix Aylmer *Dr Cochrane* • Basil Sydney *Siedelman* • Lucile Saint-Simon *Louise Cochrane* • Donald Wolfit *Prof Volcheff* • Donald Pleasence *Coates* ■ *Dir* Edmond T Gréville • *Scr* John Baines, Donald Taylor, Edmond T Gréville, from the novel by Maurice Renard

Hands of the Ripper ★★★ 15

Horror 1971 · UK · Colour · 81mins

This entertaining piece of nonsense from Hammer is about Jack the Ripper's daughter who, having watched her dad dismember mama, goes barmy whenever she gets kissed in a flickering light. Cue therapist Eric Porter, who tries to cure her but then starts covering up her murders. Porter is too serious for these proceedings, but Angharad Rees is a swell Ms Ripper. TS [VIDEO] DVD

Eric Porter *Dr John Pritchard* • Angharad Rees *Anna* • Jane Merrow *Laura* • Keith Bell *Michael Pritchard* • Derek Godfrey *Dysart* • Dora Bryan *Mrs Golding* • Marjorie Rhodes *Mrs Bryant* • Lynda Baron *Long Liz* • Marjorie Lawrence *Dolly* ■ *Dir* Peter Sasdy • *Scr* LW Davidson, from a story by Edward Spencer Shew

Hands over the City ★★★ U

Political drama 1963 · It · Colour · 99mins

Italian director Francesco Rosi imported American actor Rod Steiger to give weighty menace to the role of a property tycoon who manipulates civic politicians to let him develop his land, despite the effect on the people living there. Steiger gives a suitably overbearing performance as the ruthless millionaire in whom fascism has not died, but the film is too angry to articulate its arguments properly. It's still great dramatic entertainment, though. TH. An Italian language film.

Salvo Randone *De Angeli* • Rod Steiger *Nottola* • Guido Alberti *Maglione* ■ *Dir* Francesco Rosi • *Scr* Francesco Rosi, Raffaele La Capria, Enzo Provenzale, Enzo Forcella

Hands Up! ★★★

Silent comedy 1926 · US · BW · 50mins

Raymond Griffith, the debonair silent comedian who specialised in take-offs of traditional Hollywood fare, comes close to matching the best of Harold Lloyd and Buster Keaton in this delightfully brisk parody of the American Civil War. As a Confederate spy sent out west, Griffith displays considerable ingenuity in surviving firing squads and hostile tribes as he tracks down a stagecoach carrying gold to the Union side. He even finds a way of living happily ever after with both of his lady loves, played by Marion Nixon and Virginia Lee Corbin. AE

Raymond Griffith *Confederate spy* • Marion Nixon [Marian Nixon] *The girl he loves* • Virginia Lee Corbin *The other girl he loves* • Mack Swain *Mine owner* • Montague Love [Montagu Love] *Union general* • George Billings *Abraham Lincoln* • Noble Johnson *Sitting Bull* ■ *Dir* Clarence Badger • *Scr* Monty Brice, Lloyd Corrigan, from a story by Reginald Morris

Hang 'Em High ★★★ 18

Western 1968 · US · Colour · 114mins

Clint Eastwood is once again a man of few words but many bullets in the first western he made back in America after Sergio Leone had virtually invented him – as a film star and a distinctive screen character – in the spaghetti westerns they made together. Eastwood does the strong, silent stuff with characteristic efficiency in a tale of revenge and justice for all, which is perhaps more memorable as a staging post in Eastwood's career than as a landmark in the history of the western. PF. Contains violence. [VIDEO] DVD

Clint Eastwood *Jed Cooper* • Inger Stevens *Rachel* • Ed Begley *Cap'n Wilson* • Pat Hingle *Judge Adam Fenton* • Arlene Golonka *Jennifer* • James MacArthur *Preacher* • Ruth White *Madam Peaches Sophie* • Bruce Dern *Miller* • Alan Hale Jr *Stone* • James Westerfield *Prisoner* • Dennis Hopper *Prophet* • Ben Johnson *Sheriff Dave Bliss* ■ *Dir* Ted Post • *Scr* Leonard Freeman, Mel Goldberg

Hangar 18 ★ PG

Science-fiction drama
1980 · US · Colour · 96mins

Two space shuttle astronauts witness a collision with a UFO that crash-lands in Texas. When the White House hides the wreck in a remote air base hangar, astronaut Gary Collins tries to uncover the conspiracy over the accident for which he is being blamed. Any resemblance to *Close Encounters* and the "Roswell incident" are purely intentional in another sluggish and slapdash slice of speculative science-fiction from the notorious Sunn Classics outfit, who exclusively made drive-in exploitation fare. AJ [VIDEO]

Darren McGavin *Harry Forbes* • Robert Vaughn *Gordon Cain* • Gary Collins *Steve Bancroft* • Joseph Campanella *Frank Lafferty* • Pamela Bellwood *Sarah Michaels* ■ *Dir* James L Conway • *Scr* Steven Thornley, James L Conway, Tom Chapman, from a novel by Robert Weverka

Hangfire ★★ 18

Action drama 1991 · US · Colour · 85mins

Efficient but unremarkable action film about a hostage crisis that starts when a group of escaped prisoners take over a small community in New Mexico. Chief escapee is Lee DeBroux, who's plausibly dangerous, while Jan-Michael Vincent represents the National Guard which arrives in force. Not to be outwitted, though, is the local sheriff, played by Brad Davis, who died shortly after the film was completed. AT

Brad Davis *Sheriff Ike Slayton* • Kim Delaney *Maria* • Ken Foree *Billy* • Lee DeBroux *Kuttner* • Jan-Michael Vincent *Johnson* • James Tolkan *Patch* • George Kennedy *Warden* • Yaphet Kotto *Lieutenant* • Lou Ferrigno *Smitty* ■ *Dir* Peter Maris • *Scr* Brian D Jeffries

Hangin' with the Homeboys ★★★★ 15

Comedy drama 1991 · US · Colour · 85mins

Among the last films to be released in the 'hood sequence of urban black American movies that took US cinema by storm in the early 1990s, this is the only one to focus on the interaction between black and Hispanic youths. Writer/director Joseph B Vasquez's third feature explores some overly familiar situations, but there is a real sense of life as it is lived in his depiction of a night in the lives of four friends from the Bronx. Much of this freshness is due to the fact that the young cast was encouraged to improvise. Stand-up comics Doug E Doug and Mario Joyner clearly relish the opportunity, but John Leguizamo and Nestor Serrano give the more rounded performances. DP. Contains violence, swearing and nudity.

Doug E Doug *Willie* • Mario Joyner *Tom* • John Leguizamo *Johnny* • Nestor Serrano *Vinny* • Kimberly Russell *Vanessa* • Mary B Ward *Luna* • Reggie Montgomery *Rasta* • Christine Claravall *Daria* • Rosemarie Jackson [Rose Jackson] *Lila* ■ *Dir/Scr* Joseph B Vasquez

The Hanging Garden ★★★ 15

Drama 1997 · Can/UK · Colour · 91mins

A heavy-duty Canadian drama about a once fat and troubled teen who returns to the family home after ten years away. He's now fit, well adjusted and happily gay, but his homecoming prompts hauntings of his past and memories of his miserable adolescence. The leading role is taken by the unknown Chris Leavins, but watch out for Kerry Fox and *The Sweet Hereafter's* Sarah Polley among the supports. This is a tough watch, but an emotional drama worth persevering with nevertheless. DA

Chris Leavins *Sweet William* • Troy Veinotte *Sweet William, teenager* • Kerry Fox *Rosemary* • Sarah Polley *Rosemary, teenager* • Seana McKenna *Iris* • Peter MacNeill *Whiskey Mac* ■ *Dir/Scr* Thom Fitzgerald

The Hanging Tree ★★★★ PG

Western 1959 · US · Colour · 102mins

This is a superb western, set in and around a wild mining community, that climaxes in a moving demonstration of the power of love. Gary Cooper gives a magnificent performance as the spiritually wounded doctor who cares for Maria Schell's temporarily blind and abandoned Swiss immigrant. The lascivious attentions of Karl Malden add spice to the scenario and George C Scott, in his screen debut, also makes an impact as a fanatical healer. Director Delmer Daves does a wonderful job of evoking the frontier atmosphere with the able assistance of cameraman Ted McCord. AE

Gary Cooper *Doc Joe Frail* • Maria Schell *Elizabeth Mahler* • Karl Malden *Frenchy Plante* • Ben Piazza *Rune* • George C Scott *Dr George Grubb* • Karl Swenson *Mr Flaunce* • Virginia Gregg *Mrs Flaunce* • John Dierkes *Society Red* ■ *Dir* Delmer Daves • *Scr* Wendell Mayes, Halsted Welles, from the novella by Dorothy M Johnson

Hanging Up ★★ 15

Comedy melodrama
2000 · US · Colour · 90mins

Delia Ephron's novel about three sisters dealing with their senile father (Walter Matthau) is translated to the screen by director Diane Keaton, who also stars as the eldest sibling. However, Keaton and her co-star Lisa Kudrow get very little screen time compared to Meg Ryan, the daughter who is usually responsible for dear old dad. The trio spend little time together, so the film ends up a lifeless and clichéd tale about Ryan's relationship with Matthau. JB DVD

Meg Ryan *Eve* • Diane Keaton *Georgia* • Lisa Kudrow *Maddy* • Walter Matthau *Lou* • Adam Arkin *Joe* • Duke Moosekian *Omar Kunundar* • Ann Bortolotti *Ogmed Kunundar* ■ *Dir* Diane Keaton • *Scr* Delia Ephron, Nora Ephron, from the novel by Delia Ephron

The Hangman ★★ U

Western 1959 · US · BW · 86mins

The writer of *Stagecoach* and one of Hollywood's most reliable directors team up for a psychological western in which Robert Taylor plays a marshal with a reputation for stringing people up. Jack Lord is Taylor's current quarry, though he's apparently gone straight and has a family. Then Taylor gets a lesson in humanity from local sheriff Fess Parker. Those looking for bursts of action and spectacular scenery should search elsewhere, but others might appreciate this low-key study of a psychotic peace officer. AT

Robert Taylor (1) *Mackenzie Bovard* • Fess Parker *Sheriff Buck Weston* • Tina Louise *Selah Jennison* • Jack Lord *Johnny Bishop* • Shirley Harmer *Kitty Bishop* • Gene Evans *Big Murph* ■ *Dir* Michael Curtiz • *Scr* Dudley Nichols, from a story by Luke Short

Hangman ★★ 18

Detective thriller
2000 · US/Can · Colour · 91mins

A serial killer uses the game of Hangman to torture his victims in this low-budget thriller. Mädchen Amick is the psychiatrist who is somehow linked to each of the crimes, Lou Diamond Phillips the cop assigned to the case, and Dan Lauria gives his usual gruff performance as the police chief. Unfortunately, less attention was paid to the script than to the performances, and anyone who sits through until the end will be annoyed by this TV movie's weak resolution. JB DVD

Lou Diamond Phillips *Det Nick Roos* • Mädchen Amick *Grace* • Vincent Corazza *Joe Little* • Robert Haley *Dr Henry Mitchell* • Dan Lauria *Capt Gil Roemer* ■ *Dir* Ken Girotti • *Scr* Vladimir Nemirovsky

Hangman's House ★★

Silent melodrama 1928 · US · BW · 72mins

One of John Ford's earlier essays on his beloved Ireland, this late silent production features one of the master director's favourite actors, Victor McLaglen, as the Irish patriot who kills a drunken wastrel in a duel, freeing his widow for the man she had always loved. However, the stars – June Collyer, Larry Kent, Earle Foxe – mean little and the story drags. The film's highlight these days is the glimpse of a very young John Wayne as an excited horse race spectator. AE

June Collyer *Connaught O'Brien* • Larry Kent *Dermott McDermott* • Earle Foxe *John Darcy* • Victor McLaglen *Citizen Hogan* • Hobart Bosworth *Lord Chief Justice O'Brien* • John Wayne ■ *Dir* John Ford • *Scr* Marion Orth, Philip Klein, from the novel by Brian Oswald Donn-Byrne

Hangman's Knot ★★★

Western 1952 · US · Colour · 80mins

Roy Huggins, legendary creator of television series including *The Fugitive* and *Maverick*, also wrote films and directed just one – this successful drama set at the end of the American Civil War. Here Randolph Scott plays an officer leading a group of Confederate soldiers who steals a Union gold shipment unaware that the war has been over for a month. Regarded as common criminals, they take refuge in a stagecoach station, where the claustrophobic action erupts. A tense chamber western that deserves reappraisal. BB

Randolph Scott *Matt Stewart* • Donna Reed *Molly Hull* • Claude Jarman Jr *Jamie Groves* • Frank Faylen *Cass Browne* • Lee Marvin *Ralph Bainter* ■ *Dir/Scr* Roy Huggins

Hangmen Also Die ★★★

Second World War drama
1943 · US · BW · 138mins

A powerful piece of wartime propaganda begins in occupied Czechoslovakia with the assassination of notorious Nazi butcher Reinhard Heydrich. This is a consummate piece of committed film-making – devised by Bertolt Brecht and the film's director, Fritz Lang – in which the Nazis are portrayed as brutal but intelligent enemies who systematically murder Czech citizens until the perpetrator is delivered to them by the underground. It may take a while to accept Hollywood actors Brian Donlevy, Walter Brennan and Dennis O'Keefe as Czechs, but the effort is worth it. AE

Brian Donlevy *Dr Franz Svoboda* • Walter Brennan *Prof Novotny* • Anna Lee *Mascha Novotny* • Gene Lockhart *Emil Czaka* • Dennis O'Keefe *Jan Horek* • Alexander Granach *Alois Gruber* • Margaret Wycherly *Aunt Ludmilla Novotny* ■ *Dir* Fritz Lang • *Scr* John Wexley, from a story by Fritz Lang, Bertolt Brecht

Hangover Square ★★★

Horror 1945 · US · BW · 77mins

Following his successful collaboration with director John Brahm and screenwriter Barré Lyndon on *The Lodger*, Laird Cregar again takes the role of a psychopathic killer haunting the fog-bound streets of London. Here the burly star plays a young composer who turns nasty whenever he hears harsh sounds. Linda Darnell and George Sanders (as singer and psychologist respectively) co-star in this melodrama. The score by the great Bernard Herrmann stands out. AE

Laird Cregar *George Harvey Bone* • Linda Darnell *Netta Longdon* • George Sanders *Dr Allan Middleton* • Glenn Langan *Carstairs* ■ *Dir* John Brahm • *Scr* Barré Lyndon, from the novel by Patrick Hamilton

Hangup ★★

Crime drama 1973 · US · Colour · 92mins

Also known as *Super Dude*, this was veteran director Henry Hathaway's last film – and, possibly, his worst. Black policeman William Elliott saves a young heroin addict (Marki Bey) from herself and her dependency, but then leaves her when he finds out she was a hooker. A very unsympathetic hero, and a curious sense of moral outrage, make this a surly sort of thriller and Hathaway's usual action can't divert us from this unpleasantness. TH

William Elliott *Ken* • Marki Bey *Julie* • Cliff Potts *Lou* • Michael Lerner *Richards* • Wally Taylor *Sergeant Becker* ■ *Dir* Henry Hathaway • *Scr* Albert Maltz, Lee Lazich, from the novel *The Face of Night* by Bernard Brunner

Hanky Panky ★★ 15

Comedy thriller 1982 · US · Colour · 102mins

After the success of *Stir Crazy*, you could understand Gene Wilder and director Sidney Poitier wanting to reunite with Richard Pryor. When he pulled out, however, it might have been more advisable to cast an actor in the same comic mould rather than rewrite the role in a romantic vein for Gilda Radner. The script gives Wilder and Radner, who married shortly afterwards, nothing to feed off and the endless round of coincidences and bad Hitchcock parodies soon become wearisome. DP DVD

Gene Wilder *Michael Jordon* • Gilda Radner *Kate Hellman* • Kathleen Quinlan *Janet Dunn* • Richard Widmark *Ransom* • Robert Prosky *Hiram Calder* • Josef Sommer *Adrian Pruitt* ■ *Dir* Sidney Poitier • *Scr* Henry Rosenbaum, David Taylor

Hannah and Her Sisters ★★★★★ 15

Comedy drama 1986 · US · Colour · 106mins

Having apparently peaked with Annie Hall and Manhattan, Woody Allen returned to familiar territory and struck gold with this warmer, multi-stranded, near-nepotistic family saga, whose happy ending is a pleasant surprise after the usual awkward dates, clandestine meetings and failed marriages. Allen's neurotic TV producer has some memorable comic scenes revolving around a cancer scare, but the maestro ultimately cedes centre stage to the siblings of the title, Mia Farrow's straight-laced Hannah, Barbara Hershey's adulterous Lee and Dianne Weist's kooky Holly. Scoring Max von Sydow from his beloved Ingmar Bergman's repertory company is a coup for Allen, but the surprise hit is an urbane, coquettish Michael Caine as Farrow's straying husband. AC. Contains swearing. DVD

Woody Allen *Mickey Sachs* • Michael Caine *Elliot* • Mia Farrow *Hannah* • Carrie Fisher *April* • Barbara Hershey *Lee* • Max von Sydow *Frederick* • Dianne Wiest *Holly* • Lloyd Nolan *Evan* • Maureen O'Sullivan *Norma* • Daniel Stern *Dusty* • Sam Waterston *David* • Tony Roberts *Mickey's ex-partner* • Julie Kavner *Gail* ■ *Dir/Scr* Woody Allen

Hanna's War ★★ 15

Biographical war drama
1988 · US · Colour · 143mins

Menahem Golan's biopic of the Hungarian poet Hanna Senesh is undermined by a crusty script and unsubtle characterisation. Recruited by squadron leader Anthony Andrews for a vital Balkan mission, Maruschka Detmers settles for a kind of designer heroism as she battles behind the lines before suffering at the hands of Donald Pleasence's sadistic torturer. His villainy and Ellen Burstyn's cameo are the best things in this muddled melodrama. DP

Ellen Burstyn *Katalin Senesh* • Maruschka Detmers *Hanna Senesh* • Anthony Andrews *Squadron Leader McCormack* • Donald Pleasence *Rosza Gabor* • David Warner *Captain Julian Simon* ■ *Dir* Menahem Golan • *Scr* Menahem Golan, Stanley Mann, from *The Diaries of Hanna Senesh* by Hanna Senesh, from the non-fiction book *A Great Wind Cometh* by Yoel Palgi

Hannibal ★ U

Historical adventure
1959 · It · Colour · 104mins

In this grotty historical epic, Victor Mature crosses the Alps to smash the Roman Empire, pausing along the way for a dalliance with Rita Gam. The pace is sluggish, the acting is wooden, the scenery looks painted on and the battles are staged with about six extras and a few circus elephants. AT. Italian dialogue dubbed into English.

Victor Mature *Hannibal* • Rita Gam *Sylvia* • Milly Vitale *Danila* • Rik Battaglia *Hasdrubal* • Franco Silva *Maharbal* • Mario Girotti [Terence Hill] *Quintilius* • Mirko Ellis *Mago* ■ *Dir* Edgar G Ulmer • *Scr* Mortimer Braus, from an idea by Allesandro Continenza, from a story by Ottavio Poggi

Hannibal ★★★ 18

Horror thriller 2001 · US · Colour · 125mins

In this long-awaited sequel to *The Silence of the Lambs*, Anthony Hopkins reprises his Oscar-winning role, this time with his tongue set firmly in his cheek. Top FBI agent Clarice Starling (creditably played by Julianne Moore) is sent to the house of one of Hopkins's former victims, Gary Oldman (an extraordinary performance), who hopes to revitilise her search for his attacker. This lacks mystery, suspense and psychological resonance, but there's plenty of gory action and black humour. The superior prequel, *Red Dragon* followed in 2002. JA. Contains swearing, violence and nudity. [VIDEO] DVD

Anthony Hopkins *Hannibal Lecter* • Julianne Moore *Clarice Starling* • Gary Oldman *Mason Verger* • Ray Liotta *Paul Krendler* • Frankie R Faison [Frankie Faison] *Barney the orderly* • Giancarlo Giannini *Rinaldo Pazzi* • Francesca Neri *Allegra Pazzi* ■ *Dir* Ridley Scott • *Scr* David Mamet, Steven Zaillian, from the novel by Thomas Harris

Hannibal Brooks ★★ U

Second World War comedy drama
1968 · UK · Colour · 101mins

If you were trying to escape from the Germans in the Second World War, surely the last thing you'd want is an elephant tagging along to slow things down. Yet that's what happens here, as PoW Oliver Reed tries to cross the Alps via pachyderm in Michael Winner's tepid stab at war comedy. Michael J Pollard and John Alderton join the antics, but the tale's extremely hard to swallow. NF

Oliver Reed *Hannibal Brooks* • Michael J Pollard *Packy* • Wolfgang Preiss *Colonel Von Haller* • Helmut Lohner *Willi* • Karin Baal *Vronia* • Peter Karsten *Kurt* • John Alderton *Bernard* ■ *Dir* Michael Winner • *Scr* Dick Clement, Ian La Frenais, from a story by Michael Winner, Tom Wright

Hannie Caulder ★★ 15

Western 1971 · UK · Colour · 81mins

It should have been a major feminist work, a mystic western about a raped and widowed frontierswoman taught to shoot by a lone bounty hunter. Trouble is, this is that rare anomaly, the British western, shot in Spain with all the associated problems of realism, not the least of which is the casting of Raquel Welch in the title role. The photography is handsome, but the pace is slack, and the violence unpleasant. TS [VIDEO]

Raquel Welch *Hannie Caulder* • Robert Culp *Thomas Luther Price* • Ernest Borgnine *Emmett Clemens* • Strother Martin *Rufus Clemens* • Jack Elam *Frank Clemens* • Christopher Lee *Bailey* • Diana Dors *Madame* ■ *Dir* Burt Kennedy • *Scr* ZX Jones [David Haft Kennedy], from a story by Peter Cooper, from characters created by Ian Quicke, Bob Richards • *Cinematographer* Edward Scaife

Hanoi Hilton ★★ 15

War drama 1987 · US · Colour · 120mins

The Hanoi Hilton was the name given by the American inmates of Hoa Lo Prison in Hanoi, North Vietnam, during the war. Set far from the paddy fields and rivers of the usual Vietnam war movie, this drama covers ten years and many mini-dramas as PoWs arrive and discuss their experiences. Written directly for the screen, it has the talkiness of a play, but this is no liberal piece: the politics are Rambo's. Stunted and uninvolving. AT [VIDEO]

Michael Moriarty *Williamson* • John Edwin Shaw *Mason* • Ken Wright *Kennedy* • Paul Le Mat *Hubman* • David Soul *Oldham* • Stephen Davies *Miles* • Lawrence Pressman *Cathcart* ■ *Dir/Scr* Lionel Chetwynd

Hanover Street ★★ PG

Romantic Second World War drama
1979 · UK/US · Colour · 104mins

Director Peter Hyams is more at home with battle sequences than romantic clinches, as is his star, Harrison Ford, who often looks distinctly uncomfortable as an American pilot whose air-raid encounter with nurse Lesley-Anne Down leads to trouble with her husband, Christopher Plummer. Apart from some lovely photography, it was all done much better in the 1940 Vivien Leigh/Robert Taylor vehicle, *Waterloo Bridge*. DP. Contains swearing and nudity. [VIDEO] DVD

Harrison Ford *David Halloran* • Lesley-Anne Down *Margaret Sellinger* • Christopher Plummer *Paul Sellinger* • Alec McCowen *Major Trumbo* • Richard Masur *Lt Jerry Cimino* • Michael Sacks *Lt Martin Hyer* • Patsy Kensit *Sarah Sellinger* • Max Wall *Harry Pike* • Shane Rimmer *Col Ronald Bart* • Keith Buckley *Lt Wells* • Sherrie Hewson *Phyllis* • John Ratzenberger *Sgt John Lucas* ■ *Dir/Scr* Peter Hyams • *Cinematographer* David Watkin

Hans Christian Andersen ★★★★ U

Musical drama 1952 · US · Colour · 107mins

Children should enjoy this sentimental Hollywood fabrication of the life of the great storyteller, and sophisticated adults will appreciate the superb Frank Loesser songs, notably the charming *Inchworm*, the unforgettable *Ugly Duckling* and the rollicking *Wonderful Copenhagen*. They're all performed by star Danny Kaye, in possibly his best screen performance, a role that became identified with him. A big hit in its day, it's worthwhile recalling the anti-Semitism which erupted in Scandinavia back in the 1950s over the Jewish Kaye playing Denmark's treasured raconteur. TS [VIDEO] DVD

Danny Kaye *Hans Christian Andersen* • Farley Granger *Niels* • Jeanmaire [Zizi Jeanmaire] *Doro* • Joey Walsh [Joseph Walsh] *Peter* • Philip Tonge *Otto* • Erik Bruhn *The Hussar* • Roland Petit *The Prince* • John Brown *Schoolmaster* • John Qualen *Burgomaster* ■ *Dir* Charles Vidor • *Scr* Moss Hart, from a story by Myles Connolly

Hanussen ★★★★ 15

Drama 1988 · Hun/W Ger · Colour · 111mins

This film is the last and marginally least effective of the "stranger in his homeland" trilogy directed by István Szabó and starring Klaus Maria Brandauer. Here, the character vaunted and then victimised by a frightened regime is a war-wounded clairvoyant, whose fame is tarnished when he predicts the formation of the Third Reich. The period detail is flawless, the ensemble playing impeccable and Brandauer's performance mesmerising, but it lacks the subtle imagery and insight of its predecessors. DP. In German with English subtitles. Contains violence, swearing and nudity. [VIDEO]

Klaus Maria Brandauer *Klaus Schneider/"Erik-Jan Hanussen"* • Erland Josephson *Dr Bettelheim* • Ildiko Bansagi *Sister Betty* • Walter Schmidinger *Propaganda minister* • Karoly Eperjes *Captain Tibor Nowotny* • Grazyna Szapolowska *Valery de la Meer* • Colette Pilz-Warren *Dagma* ■ *Dir* István Szabó • *Scr* István Szabó, Peter Dobai

The Happening ★★

Comedy 1967 · US · Colour · 91mins

Very much of its hippy period, it is indicative of the quality of this film that the title song by the Supremes has survived longer in popular culture than the movie it originates from. Anthony Quinn is his usual gruff self as a kidnapped gangster, and the period cast of George Maharis, Michael Parks and Robert Walker Jr is pleasantly supported by a young Faye Dunaway in her screen debut. It's forgettable stuff, except for a startling, unpleasant change of tone at the end. TS. Contains violence, swearing, nudity.

Anthony Quinn *Roc Delmonico* • George Maharis *Taurus* • Michael Parks *Sureshot* • Robert Walker Jr *Herby* • Martha Hyer *Monica Delmonico* • Faye Dunaway *Sandy* • Milton Berle *Fred* • Oscar Homolka *Sam* ■ *Dir* Elliot Silverstein • *Scr* Frank R Pierson, James D Buchanan, Ronald Austin, from a story by James D Buchanan, Ronald Austin

The Happiest Days of Your Life ★★★★ U

Comedy 1950 · UK · BW · 78mins

You can almost smell the school dinners in this wonderful comedy, adapted by John Dighton and Frank Launder from Dighton's play and directed by Launder (for once without longtime partner Sidney Gilliat). The bones of contention that arise when Margaret Rutherford's academy for young ladies is accidentally evacuated to a building already occupied by Alastair Sim's boys' school are beautifully observed, but the comic highlight is the precision with which the pupils scurry around the school to avoid groups of visiting VIPs. DP [VIDEO]

Alastair Sim *Wetherby Pond* • Margaret Rutherford *Miss Whitchurch* • Joyce Grenfell *Miss Gossage* • Richard Wattis *Arnold Billings* • John Bentley *Richard Tassell* • Bernadette O'Farrell *Miss Harper* • Guy Middleton *Victor Hyde-Brown* • Edward Rigby *Rainbow* ■ *Dir* Frank Launder • *Scr* Frank Launder, John Dighton, from the play by John Dighton

The Happiest Millionaire ★★★ U

Musical 1967 · US · Colour · 158mins

This film has its place in history as the last one personally produced by Walt Disney. Yet why he felt this polished but hardly glittering picture should last over two and a half hours is anyone's guess, as it's far too long. The songs by the Sherman brothers aren't up to much, while the Romeo and Juliet story never catches light, in spite of the presence of Fred MacMurray, Greer Garson, Geraldine Page and Tommy Steele, making his Hollywood debut as a Buttons-like matchmaker. DP

Fred MacMurray *Anthony J Drexel Biddle* • Tommy Steele *John Lawless* • Greer Garson *Mrs Cordelia Biddle* • Geraldine Page *Mrs Duke* • Gladys Cooper *Aunt Mary Drexel* • Hermione Baddeley *Mrs Worth* • Lesley Ann Warren *Cordy Biddle* • John Davidson *Angie Duke* • Paul Peterson *Tony Biddle* • Eddie Hodges *Livingston Biddle* ■ *Dir* Norman Tokar • *Scr* AJ Carothers, from the play by Kyle Crichton, from the book *My Philadelphia Father* by Kyle Crichton, Cordelia Drexel Biddle

Happily Ever After ★★ U

Animation 1990 · US · Colour · 71mins

While the animation is competent, what lets down this stubbornly unmagical fairy tale is the laboured plot, in which Snow White is aided by the seven dwarfs' cousins after her prince is snatched away by the wicked queen's vengeful brother Lord Maliss. The one bright spot, however, are the voiceovers, with Malcolm McDowell sneerily villainous as Maliss, Irene Cara tunefully vulnerable as Snow White and Tracey Ullman delightfully winsome as Moonbeam. DP [VIDEO]

Dom DeLuise *Looking Glass* • Phyllis Diller *Mother Nature* • Zsa Zsa Gabor *Blossom* • Edward Asner *Scowl* • Sally Kellerman *Sunburn* • Irene Cara *Snow White* • Carol Channing *Muddy* • Tracey Ullman *Moonbeam/Thunderella* • Michael Horton *Prince* • Malcolm McDowell *Lord Maliss* ■ *Dir* John Howley • *Scr* Martha Moran, Robby London

Happiness ★★★★★ 18

Black comedy drama
1998 · US · Colour · 139mins

Todd Solondz's stunningly acted and brilliantly scripted film looks at the extraordinary lives of a group of men and women who engage in shocking antisocial behaviour, including obscene phone calls, murder and paedophilia. What's so amazing about this tragicomedy is its lack of moral judgement – the viewers are left to make up their own minds about the events – and its pungent humour that emerges from the sickest of circumstances. You may even feel pity for these people and get drawn into their lives – though the film's most controversial scene (the frankest of discussions between an unlikely child molester and his inquisitive son) will play on your mind for days. JC. Contains sex scenes, strong sexual references and swearing. [VIDEO] DVD

Jane Adams (2) *Joy Jordan* • Jon Lovitz *Andy Kornbluth* • Philip Seymour Hoffman *Allen* • Dylan Baker *Bill Maplewood* • Lara Flynn Boyle *Helen Jordan* • Louise Lasser *Mona Jordan* • Ben Gazzara *Lenny Jordan* • Jared Harris *Vlad* • Marla Maples *Ann Chambeau* • Elizabeth Ashley *Diane Freed* ■ *Dir/Scr* Todd Solondz

The Happiness of the Katakuris ★★★★ 15

Musical black comedy horror
2001 · Jpn · Colour · 112mins

Forget the schlock grotesqueries that have become Takeshi Miike's trademark and instead revel in the colourful kitsch of this hilarious zombie musical. The tale of a family whose dream of running a rural retreat is confounded by the guests' unfortunate habit of dying, is packed with quirky characters, macabre comedy and song-and-dance routines that succeed in revealing emotion while cranking up the camp quotient. There are even flights of claymation fantasy that evoke the surrealism of Czech master, Jan Svankmajer. The cast is sporting to the extreme and Akio Nomura's photography is exhilarating, but paramount is Miike's outrageous sense of mischief . DP. In Japanese with English subtitles. [VIDEO] DVD

Kenji Sawada *Masao Katakuri* • Keiko Matsuzaka *Terue Katakuri* • Shinji Takeda *Masayuki Katakuri* • Naomi Nishida *Shizue Katakuri* • Tetsuro Tanba [Tetsuro Tamba] *Nihei Katakuri* • Naoto Takenaka *Reporter/singer on TV* • Tamaki Miyazaki *Yurie Katakuri* ■ *Dir* Takashi Miike • *Scr* Kikumi Yamagishi, from the film *The Quiet Family* by Kim Ji-woon

Happy ★★ U

Comedy musical 1933 · US · BW · 83mins

Rarely seen comic musical about boffin and hard-up musician Stanley Lupino and his attempts to find a market for his new invention. The star – whose daughter Ida would go on to Hollywood fame in later years – had a hand in the script as well so it's pretty much his show, and he delivers the goods with some lively playing from co-stars Laddie Cliff and Will Fyffe. JF

Stanley Lupino *Frank Brown* • Laddie Cliff *George* • Will Fyffe *Simmy* • Dorothy Hyson *Lillian* • Harry Tate *Dupont* • Renee Gadd *Pauline* • Gus McNaughton *Waller* ■ *Dir* Fred Zelnik • *Scr* Austin Melford, Arthur Woods, Frank Launder, Stanley Lupino, from the play *Es War Einmal ein Musikus* by Karl Notl, Jacques Bachrach, Alfred Hahm

Happy Anniversary ★★

Comedy 1959 · US · BW · 82mins

Made in the days when television was a burgeoning rival to the cinema's ability to pull in mass audiences, this comedy has David Niven and Mitzi Gaynor as a happily married couple whose daughter (Patty Duke) reveals her father's past life on a children's TV show. Topical jokes for the time, but not now in these days of multi-media revolution. TH

David Niven *Chris Walters* • Mitzi Gaynor *Alice Walters* • Carl Reiner *Bud* • Loring Smith *Mr Gans* • Monique Van Vooren *Jeanette* • Phyllis Povah *Mrs Gans* • Patty Duke *Debbie Walters* ■ *Dir* David Miller • *Scr* Joseph Fields, Jerome Chodorov, from the play *Anniversary Waltz* by Jerome Chodorov

Happy Birthday, Gemini ★★

Comedy drama 1980 · US · Colour · 107mins

Director Richard Benner scored a notable hit in 1977 with the Canadian gay/drag movie *Outrageous*, which spawned an equally successful sequel *Too Outrageous* ten years later. In between Benner delivered this adaptation of Albert Innaurato's hit Broadway comedy about a man coming to terms with his sexuality. The stage play had drawn accusations of homophobia for some of its more extreme moments but the film avoided all such problems. The late Madeline Kahn does some of her best work here but she is somewhat swamped by the overall dullness of the piece. DF

Madeline Kahn *Bunny Weinberger* • Rita Moreno *Lucille Pompi* • Robert Viharo *Nick Geminiani* • Alan Rosenberg *Francis Geminiani* • Sarah Holcomb *Judith Hastings* • David Marshall Grant *Randy Hastings* ■ *Dir* Richard Benner • *Scr* Richard Benner, from the play *Gemini* by Albert Innaurato

Happy Birthday to Me ★★ 15

Horror 1981 · Can · Colour · 106mins

J Lee Thompson directed this stalk-and-slash horror, but no amount of high-tone style, technical expertise or lavish production values can make this outrageously contrived and overly complicated shocker any less lacklustre. Is college student Melissa Sue Anderson killing snobby sorority members during blackouts caused by a near-fatal car crash? A ludicrous bombardment of twists and turns includes "six of the most bizarre murders you'll ever see." AJ. Contains violence, swearing, nudity. DVD

Melissa Sue Anderson *Virginia* • Glenn Ford *Dr Faraday* • Lawrence Dane *Hal* • Sharon Acker *Estelle* • Frances Hyland (2) *Mrs Patterson* • Tracey Bregman [Tracy Bregman] *Ann* • Jack Blum *Alfred* • Matt Craven *Steve* ■ *Dir* J Lee Thompson • *Scr* Timothy Bond, Peter Jobin, John Saxton, John Beaird, from a story by John Saxton

Happy Birthday, Wanda June ★★

Comedy 1971 · US · Colour · 105mins

When big-game hunter Rod Steiger returns from eight years in the Amazonian wilds, he finds his bimbo wife Susannah York educated, liberated and about to marry again – to either a pacifist doctor (George Grizzard) or a vacuum cleaner salesman (Don Murray). Kurt Vonnegut Jr's screenplay, based on his off-Broadway play about the modern world's need for heroes, is stuck in a theatrical mire, in which style and content collide. TH

Rod Steiger *Harold Ryan* • Susannah York *Penelope Ryan* • George Grizzard *Dr Norbert Woodley* • Don Murray *Herb Shuttle* • William Hickey *Looseleaf Harper* • Steven Paul *Paul Ryan* • Pamelyn Ferdin *Wanda June* • Pamela Saunders *Mildred Ryan* ■ *Dir* Mark Robson • *Scr* Kurt Vonnegut Jr, from his play

The Happy Ending ★★

Melodrama 1969 · US · Colour · 111mins

An old-style women's melodrama – one of the last of the breed – made by tough-guy director Richard Brooks and starring his real-life wife, Jean Simmons, whose fine performance earned her Oscar and Golden Globe nominations. Bored with her husband of 16 years, Simmons drinks, watches movies on TV, then suddenly ups for the Bahamas and has a fling with a gigolo. This is a film that strains for significance: "They're more alive then we are," Simmons tells husband John Forsythe after watching Bogart and Bergman in a re-run of *Casablanca*. AT

Jean Simmons *Mary Wilson* • John Forsythe *Fred Wilson* • Shirley Jones *Flo* • Lloyd Bridges *Sam* • Teresa Wright *Mrs Spencer* • Dick Shawn *Harry Bricker* • Nanette Fabray *Agnes* • Robert Darin [Bobby Darin] *Franco* • Tina Louise *Helen Bricker* ■ *Dir/Scr* Richard Brooks

Happy Ever After ★★ U

Comedy 1954 · UK · Colour · 84mins

David Niven got so little practice at playing cads that you can almost forgive him for being so bad here, as the gruff English landlord whose new regime drives his tenants to the point of murder. This underachieving film cries out for black comedy as the locals draw lots to see who will do the dirty deed. Would-be assassins George Cole, Joseph Tomelty and Michael Shepley mug like crazy to raise a laugh. DP

David Niven *Jasper O'Leary* • Yvonne De Carlo *Serena McGlusky* • Barry Fitzgerald *Thady O'Heggarty* • George Cole *Terence* • AE Matthews *General O'Leary* • Noelle Middleton *Kathy McGlusky* • Robert Urquhart *Dr Michael Flynn* • Michael Shepley *Major McGlusky* • Joseph Tomelty *Dooley* • Eddie Byrne *Lannigan* ■ *Dir* Mario Zampi • *Scr* Jack Davies, Michael Pertwee, LAG Strong

Happy Face Murders ★★★ 18

Crime thriller based on a true story 1999 · US · Colour · 94mins

Where would tele-moviedom be without stranger-than-fiction stories culled from the tabloids? Marg Helgenberger and Henry Thomas acquit themselves admirably as the cops investigating the brutal murder of a young woman. But the acting honours go to Ann-Margret, who is virtually unrecognisable as a dowdy grandmother, whose obsession with TV detective shows enables her to rig the clues to implicate her younger lover in the crime. Surprisingly suspenseful. DP

Ann-Margret *Lorraine Petrovich* • Marg Helgenberger *Jen Powell* • Henry Thomas *Dylan McCarthy* • Nicholas Campbell *Rusty Zuvic* ■ *Dir* Brian Trenchard-Smith • *Scr* John Pielmeier

The Happy Family ★★★ U

Comedy 1952 · UK · BW · 88mins

One of those "they don't make 'em like this any more" comic capers in which Stanley Holloway and Kathleen Harrison star as a shop-keeping couple refusing to move from their humble dwelling to accommodate the 1951 Festival of Britain. This is an innocent, gentle lark, harking back to an infinitely preferable if somewhat mythically rosy era when officialdom was bumptious but owlishly benign, and the "great unwashed" behaved like a troupe of good-hearted medieval tumblers. Watch out for a youthful George Cole. SH

Stanley Holloway *Henry Lord* • Kathleen Harrison *Lillian Lord* • Naunton Wayne *Mr Filch* • Dandy Nichols *Ada* • John Stratton *David* • Eileen Moore *Joan* • Shirley Mitchell *Marina* • Margaret Barton *Anne* • George Cole *Cyril* ■ *Dir* Muriel Box • *Scr* Muriel Box, Sydney Box, from the play by Michael Clayton Hutton

Happy Gilmore ★★ 12

Sports comedy 1996 · US · Colour · 92mins

Adam Sandler has come on a bit since he made this knockabout comedy in which he stars as a second-rate ice hockey player whose thuggish tactics are the only thing keeping him on the team. When his slap-shot is turned into a golfer's drive, Sandler sees a way of earning enough cash on the fairway to save his granny's home from the IRS. Typical no-brainer fare. JF. Contains swearing, violence. DVD

Adam Sandler *Happy Gilmore* • Christopher McDonald *Shooter* • Julie Bowen *Virginia* • Frances Bay *Grandma* • Carl Weathers *Chubbs* • Alan Covert [Allen Covert] *Otto* • Robert Smigel *IRS agent* • Bob Barker • Richard Kiel *Mr Larson* • Dennis Dugan *Doug Thompson* • Lee Trevino ■ *Dir* Dennis Dugan • *Scr* Tim Herlihy, Adam Sandler

Happy Go Lovely ★★ U

Musical 1950 · UK · Colour · 93mins

This lacklustre musical was shot in Britain with Hollywood journeyman Bruce Humberstone directing. Cesar Romero and Vera-Ellen were also imported to sugar the pill for American audiences, and they give polished performances as the down-at-heel producer and his protégée, although David Niven is less at home as the millionaire conned into financing their Edinburgh Festival show. DP DVD

David Niven *BG Bruno* • Vera-Ellen *Janet Jones* • Cesar Romero *John Frost* • Bobby Howes *Charlie* • Diane Hart *Mae* • Gordon Jackson *Paul Tracey* • John Laurie *Jonskill* ■ *Dir* Bruce Humberstone [H Bruce Humberstone] • *Scr* Val Guest, Arthur Macrae, from a story by F Dammann, H Rosenfeld

Happy Go Lucky ★★ U

Musical romantic comedy 1943 · US · Colour · 81mins

New Yorker Mary Martin uses her savings for a trip to the Caribbean in search of a rich husband. She finds a suitable candidate in an eccentric millionaire (former crooner Rudy Vallee), but loses her heart to beachcomber Dick Powell. Martin and Powell are the nominal stars of this slimline escapist musical, but it's "incendiary blonde" Betty Hutton, also chasing a man (Eddie Bracken) in what passes for plot, who walks away with it. Curtis Bernhardt, taking time out from melodrama, directs. RK

Mary Martin *Marjory Stuart* • Dick Powell *Pete Hamilton* • Betty Hutton *Bubbles Hennessy* • Eddie Bracken *Wally Case* • Rudy Vallee *Alfred Monroe* • Mabel Paige *Mrs Smith* ■ *Dir* Curtis Bernhardt • *Scr* Walter DeLeon, Norman Panama, Melvin Frank, from a story by John Jacoby, Michael Uris • *Music/lyrics* Frank Loesser, Jimmy McHugh, Henry J Sayers

The Happy Hooker ★★ 18

Comedy 1975 · US · Colour · 93mins

Liberally sprinkled with sex, satire and no little savvy, Xaviera Hollander's memoirs made her the toast of New York. However, this screen adaptation has reduced her bestselling insights to a series of cheap conquests in a battle of the sexes. Playing the Big Apple's most famous madam, Lynn Redgrave does a splendid job, but, Jean-Pierre Aumont aside, she gets little help from the rest of the cast. DP. Contains swearing and nudity.

Lynn Redgrave *Xaviera Hollander* • Jean-Pierre Aumont *Yves St Jacques* • Lovelady Powell *Madelaine* • Nicholas Pryor *Carl Gordon* • Elizabeth Wilson *Mrs Gordon* • Tom Poston *J Arthur Conrad* • Conrad Janis *Fred* • Richard Lynch *Cop* ■ *Dir* Nicholas Sgarro • *Scr* William Richert, from the book by Xaviera Hollander, Robin Moore, Yvonne Dunleavy

The Happy Hooker Goes to Hollywood ★

Comedy 1980 · US · Colour · 85mins

Probably the raciest in the series (although that's not saying much) – but definitely the most hopeless – this boasts a new Xaviera Hollander in Martine Beswick, who this time decides to put her talents to use helping a film company facing extinction. The likes of Adam West and Phil Silvers should have known better, and it's neither steamy nor funny. JF

Martine Beswick *Xaviera Hollander* • Adam West • Phil Silvers • Richard Deacon • Edie Adams ■ *Dir* Alan Roberts • *Scr* Devi Goldenberg

The Happy Hooker Goes to Washington ★ 18

Comedy 1977 · US · Colour · 84mins

The original *Happy Hooker* was a pretty tame affair, and this too suffers from a surprising prudishness. Joey Heatherton steps into Lynn Redgrave's high heels and sexy outfits as the now-famous madam, who gets involved in national politics when she is called to Capitol Hill. Few laughs. JF

Joey Heatherton *Xaviera Hollander* • George Hamilton *Ward Thompson* • Ray Walston *Senator Sturges* • Jack Carter *Senator Caruso* ■ *Dir* William A Levey • *Scr* Robert Kaufman

Happy Hour ★ PG

Comedy 1987 · US · Colour · 83mins

Ever wonder what happened to Jamie Farr after *MASH?* He ended up in this execrable comedy about a secret ingredient that makes beer drinkers up their consumption. The result is chaos as beer sales jump and beer is foisted on the young ("Mom, can I have some more in my cereal?") Scientists decide the formula must be destroyed, which would have been good advice for this as well. ST

Richard Gilliland *Blake Teegarden* • Jamie Farr *Crummy Fred* • Tawny Kitaen *Misty Roberts* • Ty Henderson *Bill* • Rich Little *Mr X* ■ *Dir* John De Bello • *Scr* John De Bello, Constantine Dillon, J Stephen Peace

Happy Is the Bride ★★★ U

Comedy 1957 · UK · BW · 84mins

Directed by co-scriptwriter Roy Boulting, this remake of *Quiet Wedding* (one of the most fondly remembered British comedies of the Second World War) hasn't the polish of Anthony Asquith's version, but what it lacks in style it almost makes up for in verve, as such practised *farceurs* as Cecil Parker, Terry-Thomas and Joyce Grenfell do their level best to complicate the arrangements for Ian Carmichael and Janette Scott's nuptials. Yet the plaudits must go to Athene Seyler, who steals the show in the same role she played in the original. DP

Ian Carmichael *David Chaytor* • Janette Scott *Janet Royd* • Cecil Parker *Arthur Royd* • Terry-Thomas *Policeman* • Joyce Grenfell *Aunt Florence* • Eric Barker *Vicar* • Edith Sharpe *Mildred Royd* • Elvi Hale *Petula* • John Le Mesurier *Chaytor* • Nicholas Parsons *John Royd* • Athene Seyler *Aunt Harriet* ■ *Dir* Roy Boulting • *Scr* Roy Boulting, Jeffrey Dell, from the play *Quiet Wedding* by Esther McCracken

Happy Land ★★ U

Drama 1943 · US · BW · 75mins

Don Ameche stars as an Iowa shopkeeper who loses his son in the Second World War and is consoled by the ghost of his own father, a veteran of the First World War. Intended to convince the bereaved that their loved ones have not died in vain, it's a fairly creepy and decidedly sudsy experience as Ameche is shown what a good life both he and his son have had. AT

Don Ameche *Lew Marsh* • Frances Dee *Agnes* • Harry Carey *Gramp* • Ann Rutherford *Lenore Prentiss* • Cara Williams *Gretchen Barry* • Richard Crane *Rusty* • Henry Morgan [Harry Morgan] *Tony Cavrek* ■ *Dir* Irving Pichel • *Scr* Kathryn Scola, Julien Josephson, from the novel by MacKinlay Kantor

Happy Landing ★★★ U

Comedy musical 1938 · US · BW · 101mins

Norwegian Olympic Champion ice skater Sonja Henie was a petite blonde who rapidly became one of Hollywood's highest-ranking movie stars after her first two films struck gold for 20th Century-Fox. Here, the winsome Henie enjoys the company of two men and a nothing plot about a bandleader's plane landing near Henie's house in a very Hollywood Norway, hence the title. But plots don't matter when Sonja skates, Ethel Merman sings and the two guys are amiable Don Ameche and handsome Cesar Romero. TS

Sonja Henie *Trudy Erickson* • Don Ameche *Jimmy Hall* • Jean Hersholt *Herr Erickson* • Ethel Merman *Flo Kelly* • Cesar Romero *Duke Sargent* • Billy Gilbert *Counter man* • Wally Vernon *Al Mahoney* ■ *Dir* Roy Del Ruth • *Scr* Milton Sperling, Boris Ingster

Happy Man ★★★

Drama 2000 · Pol · Colour · 84mins

The influence of fellow Polish director Krzysztof Kieslowski is evident throughout Malgorzata Szumowska's solemn but understated story of Piotr Jankowski, an aspiring but indolent writer in his late 20s, who still lives with his mother. When she's diagnosed with cancer, he seeks to make her happy by finding a wife, quickly settling on factory worker and single mother Malgorzata Chajewska-Krzysztofik. With industrial sites, monasteries and tenements providing an evocative backdrop, this is a social treatise with a spiritual heart. DP. In Polish with English subtitles.

Jadwiga Jankowska-Cieslak *Mother* • Piotr Jankowski *Janek* • Malgorzata Chajewska-Krzysztofik *Marta* • Roman Gancarczyk *Rudy* ■ *Dir/Scr* Malgorzata Szumowska • *Cinematographer* Michal Englert, Marek Gajczak

Happy Mother's Day... Love, George ★★★

Mystery thriller 1973 · US · Colour · 90mins

Actor Darren McGavin's directorial debut was the last movie lounge singer Bobby Darin made before his untimely death. Darin is part of a solid cast in a very strange horror soap opera about Ron Howard returning to his boyhood Nova Scotia home to discover the identity of his father. His investigations uncover a twisted family tree and some gruesome murders as he traces his roots in the tranquil community. Striking visuals combine with the offbeat story to unusual effect and create an unusual genre item. AJ

Patricia Neal *Cara* • Cloris Leachman *Ronda* • Bobby Darin *Eddie* • Tessa Dahl *Celia* • Ron Howard *Johnny* • Kathie Browne *Crystal* • Joseph Mascolo *Piccolo* • Simon Oakland *Ron Howard* ■ *Dir* Darren McGavin • *Scr* Robert Clouse • *Cinematographer* Walter Lassally

Happy New Year ★★

Crime caper 1974 · Fr/It · Colour · 114mins

Claude Lelouch would be a much better film-maker were he not such a fan of his own work. This tired treatise on the attraction of opposites is so self-satisfied that it even begins with a clip from *Une Homme et une Femme*, the opus that forged the director's international reputation. This glossy but empty picture focuses on the unlikely romance between rugged jewel thief Lino Ventura and Riviera sophisticate Françoise Fabian. The opening heist has its moments, but the rest is bogus bohemianism. DP. In French with English subtitles.

Lino Ventura *Simon* • Françoise Fabian *Françoise* • Charles Gérard *Charles* • Silvano Tranquilli *Italian lover* ■ *Dir* Claude Lelouch • *Scr* Claude Lelouch, Pierre Uytterhoeven

Happy New Year ★★★ 15

Comedy 1987 · US · Colour · 84mins

This engaging cross between a comedy, love story, heist picture and buddy movie is an undeservedly neglected American remake of Claude Lelouch's 1974 film. It boasts winning performances by Charles Durning and Peter Falk as two old partners in crime, planning the robbery of a Palm Beach jewellery store. Lelouch himself makes a brief early appearance, but the movie ultimately belongs to Falk, who dons a series of brilliant disguises, including one as an old woman – based on his own mum – that sees him turn in one of Hollywood's finest drag acts since Dustin Hoffman's in *Tootsie*. PF [video]

Peter Falk *Nick* • Charles Durning *Charlie* • Wendy Hughes *Carolyn Benedict* • Tom Courtenay *Edward Sanders* • Tracy Brooks Swope *Nina* • Joan Copeland *Sunny* • Daniel Gerroll *Curator* • Bruce Malmuth *Police lieutenant* ■ *Dir* John G Avildsen • *Scr* Warren Lane [Nancy Dowd], from the 1974 film

The Happy Road ★★ U

Comedy drama 1956 · US · BW · 99mins

Gene Kelly's second movie of the seven he directed solo was filmed on location in France. In it, he stars as an American widower who is drawn to a French divorcée when their kids run away from their Swiss school and head for Paris. The children are not without charm, but the situations are predictable, and the view of the French is a bit too patronising. RB

Gene Kelly *Mike Andrews* • Barbara Laage *Suzanne Duval* • Michael Redgrave *General Medworth* • Bobby Clark *Danny Andrews* • Brigitte Fossey *Janine Duval* • Roger Treville *Dr Solaise* ■ *Dir* Gene Kelly • *Scr* Arthur Julian, Joseph Morhaim, Harry Kurnitz, from a story by Arthur Julian, Harry Kurnitz

Happy, Texas ★★★★ 12

Comedy 1999 · US · Colour · 94mins

This comedy of errors is an unexpected revelation, in which Jeremy Northam stars as a convict who escapes from an overturned prison van with fellow prisoner Steve Zahn. They end up in the Texas town of Happy where they are mistaken for two homosexual carnival organisers who've been hired to help with a beauty contest for five year olds. The local (male) sheriff takes a shine to Northam, while Zahn falls for schoolteacher Illeana Douglas ("That whole gay thing is more of a hobby, really"). A small comic gem from director/co-writer Mark Illsley. TH. Contains swearing, violence. [video] DVD

Jeremy Northam *Harry Sawyer* • Steve Zahn *Wayne Wayne Wayne Jr* • Ally Walker *Josephine "Joe" McLintock* • Illeana Douglas *Ms Schaefer* • William H Macy *Sheriff Chappy Dent* • MC Gainey *Bob Maslow* • Ron Perlman *Nalhober* ■ *Dir* Mark Illsley • *Scr* Ed Stone, Mark Illsley, Phil Reeves

The Happy Thieves ★

Comedy crime drama
1962 · US · BW · 89mins

Richard Condon's first novel *The Oldest Confession* was an entertaining yarn which provided the basis for this unentertaining yawn. The cause lay in the fatigued direction by George Marshall and the full-of-holes script. Nor are matters helped by the uneasy pairing of Rex Harrison and Rita Hayworth as two art thieves attempting to steal a Goya from the Prado in Madrid. Needless to say, the robbery, like the film, fails to come off. RB

Rex Harrison *Jim Bourne* • Rita Hayworth *Eve Lewis* • Joseph Wiseman *Jean Marie Calbert* • Grégoire Aslan *Dr Munoz* • Alida Valli *Duchess Blanca* • Brita Ekman [Britt Ekland] *Mrs Pickett* ■ *Dir* George Marshall • *Scr* John Gay, from the novel *The Oldest Confession* by Richard Condon

The Happy Time ★★★

Period comedy 1952 · US · BW · 93mins

The screen version of a hugely successful Broadway play, set in the 1920s, concerns itself with a French-Canadian family headed by Charles Boyer and Marsha Hunt. The central focus, though, is on the growing pains and awakening sexuality of their adolescent son, Bobby Driscoll. The theme is a well-worn one now, but this is still a gentle and loving evocation of family life and teenage anxieties, as viewed in a more innocent and subtle age than our own. RK

Charles Boyer *Jacques Bonnard* • Louis Jourdan *Uncle Desmonde* • Marsha Hunt *Susan Bonnard* • Kurt Kasznar *Uncle Louis* • Linda Christian *Mignonette Chappuis* • Bobby Driscoll *Bibi* ■ *Dir* Richard Fleischer • *Scr* Earl Felton, from the play by Sam A Taylor, from the novel by Robert Fontaine

Happy Times ★★★ PG

Comedy 2001 · Chi · Colour · 98mins

Zhang Yimou directs this charming comedy of inner-city manners. Exploring the shift in morality and reduction in privacy that have attended economic reform, this tale centres on Zhao Benshan, a middle-aged huckster, whose attempts to impress his gold-digging fiancée result in him befriending her blind, teenage stepdaughter, Dong Jie. Often shooting with hidden cameras, and deftly avoiding lapses of tone and taste, Zhang concentrates on the everyday lives of these marginalised characters, while also staging some droll set pieces. DP. In Mandarin with English subtitles. [video] DVD

Zhao Benshan *Old Zhao* • Dong Jie *Wu Ying, blind girl* • Dong Lihua *Chunky mama* • Fu Biao *Little Fu* • Leng Qibin *Little fatty* • Li Xuejian *Old Li* ■ *Dir* Zhang Yimou • *Scr* Gui Zi, from the story *Shifu Yue Lai Yue Youmo* by Mo Yan

Happy Together ★★★ 15

Romantic comedy
1989 · US · Colour · 98mins

A sweet but slight comedy about a shy young writer (Patrick Dempsey) and a brash, aspiring actress (Helen Slater) who, owing to a mix-up, end up as roommates in an all-male college dormitory. Both leads are fine, but they don't have much to work with in what is an entertaining if made-by-numbers comedy romance. Look for Brad Pitt in an early role. JB. Contains swearing, sexual references, brief nudity. [video]

Patrick Dempsey *Christopher Wooden* • Helen Slater *Alexandra "Alex" Page* • Dan Schneider *Gooseflesh* • Kevin Hardesty *Slash* • Marius Weyers *Denny Dollenbacher* • Barbara Babcock *Ruth Carpenter* • Gloria Hayes *Luisa Dellacova* • Brad Pitt *Brian* • Aaron Harnick *Wally* • Ron Sterling *Trevor* ■ *Dir* Mel Damski • *Scr* Craig J Nevius

Happy Together ★★ 15

Romantic drama
1997 · HK · Colour and BW · 92mins

Director Wong Kar-Wai's reputation rests on his genius for combining audacious imagery with human stories, but this adaptation is his least coherent or convincing film. The relationship between Leslie Cheung and Tony Leung, Hong Kong lovers on holiday in Argentina, is so destructive it's hard to empathise with either character when their conversations are so accusatory and their actions so self-interested. Christopher Doyle's photography is sumptuous, but Wong's direction is over-indulgent. DP. In Spanish, Cantonese and Mandarin with English subtitles. Contains swearing, sex scenes, violence. [video] DVD

Leslie Kwok-Wing Cheung [Leslie Cheung] *Ho Po-Wing* • Tony Chiu-Wai Leung [Tony Leung (2)] *Lai Yiu-Fai* • Chang Chen *Chang* ■ *Dir* Wong Kar-Wai • *Scr* Wong Kar-Wai, from the novel *The Buenos Aires Affair* by Manuel Puig

Happy We ★★★

Drama 1983 · Swe · Colour · 111mins

This comedy drama about the reunion of three university pals closely preceded Swedish director Lasse Hallström's breakthrough hit *My Life as a Dog*. They recall old times, re-enact the sketches they had performed in college revues and catch up on the disappointments and broken dreams of adulthood. Coaxing pleasing performances from his cast, Hallstrom treads the fine line between pertinence and sentiment with some skill. DP. In Swedish with English subtitles.

Brasse Brännström *Thomas Bengtsson* • Ivan Oljelund *Erik Bengtsson* • Magnus Härenstam *Klasse Wallin* • Pia Green *Anna Wallin* • Lars Amble *Fredrik Wahlgren* ■ *Dir* Lasse Hallström • *Scr* Brasse Brännström, Lasse Hallström, Magnus Härenstam

The Happy Years ★★★ U

Period comedy 1950 · US · Colour · 109mins

Set at the dawn of the 20th century, this gently humorous exercise in nostalgia stars Dean Stockwell as a precocious and trouble-prone American schoolboy in the small town of Lawrenceville. Based on the then popular magazine stories, the movie centres on the japes and scrapes of Stockwell and his young friends and the despair he causes to the stalwart schoolmaster and his long-suffering parents. Hardly life as it's lived now, but a pleasant enough movie, nicely cast and well directed. RK

Dean Stockwell *John Humperdink Stover* • Darryl Hickman *Tough McCarthy* • Scotty Beckett *Tennessee Shad* • Leon Ames *Samuel H Stover Sr* • Margalo Gillmore *Mrs Stover* • Leo G Carroll *The old Roman* • Robert Wagner ■ *Dir* William A Wellman • *Scr* Harry Ruskin, from Owen Johnson's stories *The Lawrenceville School*

Hara-Kiri ★★★

Silent drama 1928 · Fr · BW · 87mins

Although the history books tend to concentrate on the experiments of the impressionist and surrealist avant-garde, French commercial cinema in the late silent era was also capable of producing pictures of stunning visual beauty. This Oriental melodrama from director/star Marie-Louise Iribe is a case in point. However, the story of the wife who leaves her academic husband for a shogun's son was also rather daring, especially as she elects to die by her own hand to rejoin him in the afterlife, after he is killed trying to rescue a maiden from a ravine. DP

Marie-Louise Iribe *Nicole Daomi* • Constant Rémy *Professor Daomi Samura* • André Berley *Police inspector* • Liao Szi-Jen *Prince Fujiwara* • Labusquière *Ambassador* • Michaud *Guide* • Wuriu *Fujiwara's brother* • Toshi Komori *Marquis Awaji* ■ *Dir* Marie-Louise Iribe • *Scr* Pierre Lestringuez

Harakiri ★★★★

Period drama 1962 · Jpn · BW · 134mins

Masaki Kobayashi's extraordinary samurai drama is far darker than anything Akira Kurosawa made, which explains why it is not as immediately accessible. Shot in black-and-white widescreen, this epic explores and challenges the militaristic cult of the

H

samurai who, by 1630, have been reduced to beggars and are disembowelling themselves. Since the film's premiere at Cannes in 1963, a legend grew about its violence on account of a scene where a young samurai commits ritual suicide using a bamboo sword. An unblinking and majestic piece of film-making. AT. A Japanese language film.

Tatsuya Nakadai *Hanshiro Tsugumo* • Shima Iwashita *Miho Tsugumo* • Akira Ishihama *Motome Chijiiwa* • Yoshio Inaba *Jinai Chijiiwa* • Rentaro Mikuni *Kageyu Saito* ■ *Dir* Masaki Kobayashi • *Scr* Shinobu Hashimoto, from the novel by Yasuhiko Takiguchi • *Cinematographer* Yoshio Miyajima

Hard-Boiled ★★★★ 18

Action crime drama
1992 · HK · Colour · 122mins

Although *A Better Tomorrow* and *The Killer* caught the eye of the film buffs, this was the first film that really launched Hong Kong maestro John Woo in the UK. The plot is formulaic: mismatched cops Chow Yun-Fat and Tony Leung join forces to track down a ruthless gunrunner. However, the sensuous flair Woo brings to the many stunning action sequences remains vibrantly fresh today, while the melodramatic playing and plotting brings an odd but touching humanity to the piece. JF. In Cantonese with English subtitles. Contains violence and swearing. DVD

Chow Yun-Fat *Inspector Yuen ("Tequila")* • Tony Chiu-Wai Leung [Tony Leung (2)] *Tony* • Teresa Mo *Teresa* • Philip Chan *Superintendent Pang* • Anthony Wong (1) *Johnny Wong* • Bowie Lam *Yuen's partner* • Kwan Hoi-Shan *Mr Hoi* ■ *Dir* John Woo • *Scr* Barry Wong, from a story by John Woo

Hard Choices ★★★ 18

Crime drama 1984 · US · Colour · 86mins

This strange amalgam of teenage crime and taboo romance is one of those surprising animals – a film that becomes less predictable as it unfolds. Beginning as a straightforward action thriller, it follows the troubles of 15-year-old Bobby (Gary McCleery) after he is caught driving a getaway car for his two brothers in a robbery that ends with the murder of a policeman. Margaret Klenck plays a worker with juvenile offenders who tries to help the boy, while actor/director John Sayles co-stars as a drug-pushing pal who comes to her aid. FL

Margaret Klenck *Laura Stephens* • Gary McCleery *Bobby Lipscomb* • John Seitz *Sheriff Mavis Johnson* • John Sayles *Don* • John Snyder *Ben* • Martin Donovan (2) *Josh* • JT Walsh *Deputy Anderson* • Spalding Gray *Terry Norfolk* ■ *Dir* Rick King • *Scr* Rick King, from a story by Robert Mickelson, Rick King

Hard Contract ★★

Crime drama 1969 · US · Colour · 105mins

A philosophically soft-centred morality play, with stone-faced James Coburn playing a professional killer at large in Europe, on the trail of three people he has agreed to kill for mysterious client Burgess Meredith. Coburn also has sexual hang-ups about the women (Lilli Palmer, Lee Remick) he encounters. Writer/director S Lee Pogostin takes what could have been a James Bond-style thriller and throttles it with too much chat, despite the fine cast. TH

James Coburn *John Cunningham* • Lee Remick *Sheila Metcalfe* • Lilli Palmer *Adrianne* • Burgess Meredith *Ramsey Williams* • Patrick Magee *Alexi* • Sterling Hayden *Michael Carlson* • Claude Dauphin *Maurice* • Helen Cherry *Evelyn Carlson* • Karen Black *Ellen* ■ *Dir/Scr* S Lee Pogostin

Hard Country ★★

Romantic drama
1981 · US · Colour · 104mins

The title of this drama could refer to the difficulties in making it in country music or it could refer to the tough life of small-town Texas. In the end, the plot revolves around Jan-Michael Vincent, who labours away at a factory by day and shakes his thing down at the saloon by night. His girlfriend Kim Basinger (in her movie debut) has to choose between settling down with Vincent or following her friend and role model (real-life country star Tanya Tucker) to the bright lights of California and a recording career. Predictable, but still watchable. FL

Jan-Michael Vincent *Kyle Richardson* • Kim Basinger *Jodie Lynn Palmer* • Michael Parks *Royce Richardson* • Gailard Sartain *Johnny Bob* • Tanya Tucker *Caroline Peters* • Daryl Hannah *Loretta Palmer* ■ *Dir* David Greene • *Scr* Michael Kane, from a story by Michael Kane, Michael Martin Murphey

A Hard Day's Night ★★★★★ U

Musical comedy 1964 · UK · BW · 89mins

At a time when Elvis and Cliff were still making old-style musicals, this progenitor of the modern music video smashed the mould. Satirising the endless round of banal inquisition, petty regulation and screaming adoration to which the Fab Four were subjected, this musical odyssey enabled them to mock authority and shirk duty without allowing such anti-establishment rebelliousness to detract from the working-class respectability of their "Mop Top" image. However, Richard Lester's film is not just a homage to Buster Keaton-style slapstick and Busby Berkeley spectacle; it's also a handbook of new wave film techniques, from Fellini and the *nouvelle vague* to Free Cinema and the Czech Film Miracle. DP DVD

John Lennon • Paul McCartney • George Harrison • Ringo Starr • Wilfrid Brambell *Grandfather* • Norman Rossington *Norm* • Victor Spinetti *TV director* • John Junkin *Shake* • Deryck Guyler *Police inspector* • Anna Quayle *Millie* • Kenneth Haigh *Simon* • Richard Vernon *Man on train* • Eddie Malin *Hotel waiter* • Robin Ray *TV floor manager* • Lionel Blair *TV choreographer* ■ *Dir* Richard Lester • *Scr* Alun Owen • *Cinematographer* Gilbert Taylor

Hard Eight ★★★ 18

Crime drama 1996 · US · Colour · 97mins

The feature debut from Paul Thomas Anderson, director of *Boogie Nights*, is a minimally plotted mood piece featuring a magnetic central performance from Philip Baker Hall. He plays the sweetly bumbling elderly professional gambler who takes dim-witted John C Reilly under his wing to teach him some of the tricks of the Las Vegas casino trade. All's well until Reilly falls for hooker Gwyneth Paltrow and she takes a client hostage. Despite the somewhat lethargic pace, this is a cool, sharply observed thriller that knows its own strengths and makes the most of them. AJ

Philip Baker Hall *Sydney* • John C Reilly *John* • Gwyneth Paltrow *Clementine* • Samuel L Jackson *Jimmy* • F William Parker *Hostage* • Philip Seymour Hoffman *Young craps player* ■ *Dir/Scr* Paul Thomas Anderson

Hard Evidence ★★★ 15

Thriller based on a true story
1994 · US · Colour · 90mins

Since the glossy inanities of *Charlie's Angels*, Kate Jackson has carved herself a nice little niche by appearing in worthy true-life TV dramas, and this is a typically competent example. Jackson plays a single mother who takes a job with the Georgia Labor Department, only to discover that the bureaucracy is riddled with corruption. Dean Stockwell scores as Jackson's villainous boss, but Jan Egleson's direction is a touch pedestrian. JF. Contains violence. DVD

Kate Jackson *Sandra Clayton* • John Shea *Tommy Marchant* • Dean Stockwell *Sam Caldwell* • Terry O'Quinn *Harris Wiley* • Beth Broderick *Melissa Brewer* ■ *Dir* Jan Egleson • *Scr* Richard Rashke, from his articles in the *Georgia Gazette*

Hard, Fast and Beautiful ★★ U

Drama 1951 · US · BW · 78mins

This was an early Ida Lupino venture as a director for her own independent production company. Claire Trevor gives a spot-on portrayal of a frustrated woman who pins all her hopes of worldly success on the tennis-playing skills of her daughter. Sally Forrest is competent enough as the youngster propelled into becoming a champion, but the film is a little too relentless in its dramatic agenda. AE

Claire Trevor *Milly Farley* • Sally Forrest *Florence Farley* • Carleton Young *Fletcher Locke* • Robert Clarke *Gordon McKay* ■ *Dir* Ida Lupino • *Scr* Martha Wilkerson, from a novel by John R Tunis

Hard Feelings ★★★ 15

Drama 1981 · Can · Colour · 100mins

A quietly rewarding coming-of-age drama set in early 1960s' America and featuring believable performances from a largely unknown cast. Carl Marotte is the confused adolescent who is getting to grips with his impending adulthood and social (and racial divides). Directed with low-key affection by Daryl Duke and co-written by John Herzfeld, who went on to make the fine black comedy *Two Days in the Valley*. JF

Carl Marotte *Bernie Hergruter* • Charlaine Woodard [Charlayne Woodard] *Winona Lockhart* • Vincent Bufano *Russell Linwood* • Grand Bush [Grand L Bush] *Lathom Lockhart* ■ *Dir* Daryl Duke • *Scr* WD Richter, John Herzfeld, from the novel by Don Bredes

Hard Goodbyes: My Father ★★★

Drama 2002 · Gr/Ger · Colour · 108mins

Set in Athens against the backdrop of the Apollo moon programme in the late 1960s, this gentle study of childhood grief rather drifts towards its life-affirming conclusion. First-time director Penny Panayotopoulou delightfully conveys the mix of emotions racing through young Yorgos Karayannis's lively imagination after his beloved father is killed in a car crash. She also catches the boy's contrasting relationships with his mother, Ioanna Tsirigouli, and senile grandma, Despo Diamantidou. The gentle humour adroitly keeps mawkishness at bay; minor, but moving. DP. In Greek with English subtitles.

Yorgos Karayannis *Elias* • Stelios Mainas *Elias's father* • Ioanna Tsirigouli *Elias's mother* • Hristos Bouyotas *Aris* • Despo Diamantidou *Elias's grandmother* ■ *Dir/Scr* Penny Panayotopoulou

Hard Knocks ★★★

Drama 1980 · Aus · Colour · 85mins

Tracy Mann won an Australian Film Institute award as best actress for her superb performance in this affecting drama, which focuses on her attempts to leave her criminal past behind and start over again. Her subtle performance is well backed up by familiar Australian character actors Bill Hunter, Max Cullen and Tony Barry, while the believable script from director Don McLennan and Hilton Bonner (who has a supporting role) was also nominated for an award. JF

Tracy Mann *Sam* • Bill Hunter *Brady* • Max Cullen *Newman* • Tony Barry *Barry* ■ *Dir* Don McLennan • *Scr* Don McLennan, Hilton Bonner

Hard Men ★★★ 18

Crime drama
1996 · UK/Fr · Colour and sepia · 83mins

This oddly compelling and amusing journey through the greasy spoon cafés and sleazy brothels of Soho is trashy pulp fiction, boldly executed by first-time writer/director JK Amalou. It follows the fortunes of three violent gangsters who run a London numbers racket for Kray-inspired mobster Pops (played by real-life ex-con "Mad" Frankie Fraser). But one (Vincent Regan) wants out of the crooked game – family life beckons – so Pops orders his two remaining stooges to cut off the traitor's hand and have it on his desk by the next morning. Lee Ross is great as the drug freak Speed. AJ. Contains violence, swearing, drug abuse and nudity. DVD

Vincent Regan *Tone* • Ross Boatman *Bear* • Lee Ross *Speed* • "Mad" Frankie Fraser *Pops Den* • Ken Campbell *Mr Ross* • Mirella D'Angelo *Chantal* • Irene Ng *Suki* • Robyn Lewis *Leila* ■ *Dir/Scr* JK Amalou

Hard Promises ★★ PG

Romantic comedy
1991 · US · Colour · 91mins

This forgettable comedy is made slightly less so by an experienced cast. William Petersen is Sissy Spacek's ex-husband, who is invited to her upcoming wedding and is determined to disrupt the ceremony. Petersen overpowers the rest of the cast with his relentless sliminess, which leaves you to wonder why Spacek's character married him in the first place. Populated with clichés instead of supporting characters. JB

Sissy Spacek *Chris Coalter* • William L Petersen *Joey Coalter* • Brian Kerwin *Walter Humphrey* • Mare Winningham *Dawn* • Jeff Perry *Pinky* • Olivia Burnette *Beth Coalter* • Peter MacNicol *Stuart Coalter* • Rip Torn ■ *Dir* Martin Davidson • *Scr* Jule Selbo

Hard Rain ★★★ 15

Action thriller
1997 · US/UK/Jpn/Ger/Den · Colour · 92mins

Christian Slater and Minnie Driver battle the elements in this slim, waterlogged but fast-paced adventure that throws bad guys together with the forces of nature after a flood envelops a small town on the same night a daring robbery takes place. Utterly preposterous in places, this nonetheless zips along merrily and offers some impressively tongue-in-cheek performances from Morgan Freeman and Randy Quaid. JB. Contains violence, swearing. DVD

Morgan Freeman *Jim* • Christian Slater *Tom* • Randy Quaid *Sheriff* • Minnie Driver *Karen* • Edward Asner *Charlie* • Richard Dysart *Henry* • Betty White *Doreen* • Michael Goorjian *Kenny* ■ *Dir* Mikael Salomon • *Scr* Graham Yost

The Hard Ride ★

Action drama 1971 · US · Colour · 92mins

A dismal *Easy Rider* rip-off with Robert Fuller as the Vietnam veteran bringing his buddy's dead body home and finding that he has inherited a motorcycle. Fuller doesn't really know one end of a bike from another but, hey man, he's soon riding the highway and getting to know native Americans, while the soundtrack offers endless songs about peace and love. AT

Robert Fuller *Phil* • Sherry Bain *Sheryl* • Tony Russel *Big Red* • William Bonner *Grady* • Marshall Reed *Father Tom* • Mikel Angel *Ralls* ■ *Dir/Scr* Burt Topper

Hard Target ★★★ 18

Action thriller 1993 · US · Colour · 91mins

Cult Hong Kong director John Woo's Hollywood debut was regarded as a major disappointment by his die-hard fans, but it still remains leaps ahead of most American action fodder. It is also easily Jean-Claude Van Damme's best movie, even if Woo doesn't quite achieve the impossible and coax a performance out of him. Van Damme plays an unemployed sailor who spoils the human hunting games of some wealthy millionaires when he fights back. The plotting is minimal, but Lance Henriksen and Arnold Vosloo make for terrific baddies and Woo orchestrates some stunning action set pieces with panache. JF. Contains swearing and violence. [VIDEO] DVD

Jean-Claude Van Damme *Chance Boudreaux* • Lance Henriksen *Emil Fouchon* • Yancy Butler *Natasha "Nat" Binder* • Wilford Brimley *Uncle Douvee* • Kasi Lemmons *Carmine Mitchell* • Arnold Vosloo *Pik Van Cleaf* • Bob Apisa *Mr Lopacki* • Chuck Pfarrer *Douglas Binder* ■ *Dir* John Woo • *Scr* Chuck Pfarrer

Hard Time ★★ 12

Crime drama 1998 · US · Colour · 87mins

In this TV movie, Burt Reynolds (also directing) plays an unstable cop who is framed for murder when a police drugs bust goes wrong. The strong supporting cast includes old sparring partner Charles Durning, but while the handling of Reynolds the director is assured, his action-man lead performance is less convincing. Two sequels followed. JF [VIDEO] DVD

Burt Reynolds *Logan McQueen* • Charles Durning *Duffy* • Robert Loggia *Martin* • Billy Dee Williams *Barker* • Mia Sara *Susan Myler* • Michael Buie *Higgs* ■ *Dir* Burt Reynolds • *Scr* David S Cass Sr, Steve Wesley

Hard Times ★★★★ 15

Period action drama
1975 · US · Colour · 89mins

This marvellously evocative tough-as-nails Depression era drama has a sanguine James Coburn managing unsmiling brute Charles Bronson, who's well cast as a slugger of mythical dimensions. Debut director Walter Hill takes an elliptical, almost existential, route in telling his story, which means that the overall impact is dissipated quite early on. Nevertheless, there's much to admire, particularly the combination of cinematographer Phil Lathrop's Panavision photography and editor Roger Spottiswoode's handling of the fight sequences. TS [VIDEO] DVD

Charles Bronson *Chaney* • James Coburn *Spencer "Speed" Weed* • Jill Ireland *Lucy Simpson* • Strother Martin *Poe* • Maggie Blye *Gayleen Schoonover* • Michael McGuire *Gandil* • Robert Tessier *Jim Henry* ■ *Dir* Walter Hill • *Scr* Walter Hill, Bryan Gindorff, Bruce Henstell • *Cinematographer* Philip Lathrop • *Editor* Roger Spottiswoode

Hard to Get ★★★ U

Comedy 1938 · US · BW · 78mins

Yes, this is the *You Must Have Been a Beautiful Baby* movie, with crooner Dick Powell serenading the young and lovely Olivia de Havilland in a wacky screwball comedy from Warner Bros. She's rich, he's poor, and they're supported by a great cast of hand-picked eccentrics. Penny Singleton is charming as a kooky maid, and Charles Winninger, as Olivia's rich dad, is hysterically funny. Skilled and under-rated director Ray Enright keeps up the necessary pace. TS

Dick Powell *Bill Davis* • Olivia de Havilland *Margaret Richards* • Charles Winninger *Big Ben Richards* • Allen Jenkins *Roscoe* • Bonita Granville *Connie Richards* • Penny Singleton *Hattie* • Grady Sutton *Stanley Potter* ■ *Dir* Ray Enright • *Scr* Jerry Wald, Maurice Lee, Richard Macauley, from a screen story by Wally Klein, Joseph Schrank, from the story *Classified* by Stephen Morehouse Avery

Hard to Handle ★★★

Comedy 1933 · US · BW · 82mins

The original title *A Bad Boy* was dropped by Warner Bros, who feared audiences would expect a gangster movie. But, in this pacey Depression-era drama, James Cagney still fires on all cylinders as an entrepreneur and wittily refers back to his 1931 role in *The Public Enemy* by promoting grapefruit rather than squashing one into the face of his girlfriend (Mary Brian). Director Mervyn LeRoy orchestrates some fine period trappings, including the sort of dance marathon later featured in *They Shoot Horses, Don't They?*. AT

James Cagney *Lefty Merrill* • Mary Brian *Ruth Waters* • Ruth Donnelly *Lil Waters* • Allen Jenkins *Radio announcer* • Claire Dodd *Marlene Reeves* • Gavin Gordon *John Hayden* ■ *Dir* Mervyn LeRoy • *Scr* Wilson Mizner, Robert Lord, from a story by Houston Branch

Hard to Hold ★ 15

Musical drama 1984 · US · Colour · 88mins

Pop sensation Rick Springfield made an ill-advised career move when he decided to appear in this humdrum vehicle tailored to his limited talents. He plays a spoilt teen idol who falls in love with feisty Janet Eilber, mainly because she hasn't got a clue that he's a big star. Poorly written, directed and acted, this cynical cash-in is totally unbelievable because of the lack of any chemistry between the two supposed lovers. AJ [VIDEO]

Rick Springfield *James Roberts* • Janet Eilber *Diana Lawson* • Patti Hansen *Nicky Nides* • Albert Salmi *Johnny Lawson* ■ *Dir* Larry Peerce • *Scr* Thomas Hedley, from a story by Richard Rothstein, Thomas Hedley

Hard to Kill ★★★ 18

Action thriller 1989 · US · Colour · 91mins

This was the movie that set action superstar Steven Seagal on his monosyllabic road to riches. He plays a cop who is grievously wounded when a gang invades his marital bedroom and sprays it with gunfire. Seagal survives, though his wife isn't so lucky. It takes seven years to recover from the ordeal, but he emerges stronger than ever and, after the usual period of fearsome solo martial arts training, wreaks a terrible revenge on his attackers. JF [VIDEO] DVD

Steven Seagal *Mason Storm* • Kelly LeBrock *Andy Stewart* • Bill Sadler [William Sadler] *Vernon Trent* • Frederick Coffin *Kevin O'Malley* • Bonnie Burroughs *Felicia Storm* • Andrew Bloch *Captain Dan Hulland* • Zachary Rosencrantz *Sonny Storm* • Dean Norris *Detective Sergeant Goodhart* ■ *Dir* Bruce Malmuth • *Scr* Steven McKay, Steven Pressfield, Ronald Shusett

Hard Traveling ★★ PG

Period courtroom drama
1985 · US · Colour · 93mins

A very slow and laborious tale which relies on far too many flashbacks. Centred around the court case of JE Freeman in Depression America, the film explains how an ordinary, gentle man finds the love of his life but is driven to robbery and murder in order to survive and provide for her. Based on the background of director Dan Bessie and the novel *Bread and a Stone* written by his father, this well-meaning project has substance but little style. LH [VIDEO]

JE Freeman *Ed Sloan* • Ellen Geer *Norah Sloan* • Barry Corbin *Frank Burton* • James Gammon *Sergeant Slattery* • Jim Haynie *Lieutenant Fisher* ■ *Dir* Dan Bessie • *Scr* Dan Bessie, from the novel *Bread and a Stone* by Alvah Bessie

The Hard Way ★★★

Melodrama 1942 · US · BW · 109mins

This was Ida Lupino's chance to carry a Warner Bros melodrama, and she does the job splendidly as the tough dame from the industrial slums who ruthlessly propels talented younger sister Joan Leslie to showbiz stardom. Incisively written by Daniel Fuchs and Peter Viertel, it is visually powerful thanks to ace cameraman James Wong Howe's strong influence on director Vincent Sherman. AE

Ida Lupino *Helen Chernen* • Joan Leslie *Katherine Chernen* • Dennis Morgan *Paul Collins* • Jack Carson *Albert Runkel* • Gladys George *Lily Emery* • Faye Emerson *Waitress* • Paul Cavanagh *John Shagrue* ■ *Dir* Vincent Sherman • *Scr* Daniel Fuchs, Peter Viertel, from a story by Jerry Wald

The Hard Way ★★★★ 15

Action comedy 1991 · US · Colour · 106mins

Michael J Fox and James Woods have a wonderful time sending up their established screen personae in this cheerful comedy thriller. Fox is the pampered film star who wants to ditch his lightweight image with a grittier new role as a hard-nosed detective – and who better to teach him the ropes than real-life hard-nosed detective Woods? The two reluctant partners then get caught up in the hunt for a serial killer (an over-the-top Stephen Lang). Action specialist John Badham piles on the mayhem with explosive set pieces, but the real joy comes from the two stars, as Woods is nearly driven mad by Fox's determination to live his life. JF. Contains swearing and violence. [VIDEO] DVD

Michael J Fox *Nick Lang* • James Woods *John Moss* • Stephen Lang *"Party Crasher"* • Annabella Sciorra *Susan* • Delroy Lindo *Captain Brix* • Luis Guzman *Pooley* • Mary Mara *China* • LL Cool J *Billy* • John Capodice *Grainy* • Christina Ricci *Bonnie* • Penny Marshall *Angie* ■ *Dir* John Badham • *Scr* Daniel Pyne, Lem Dobbs, from a story by Lem Dobbs, Michael Kozoll

The Hard Word ★★★ 18

Crime comedy drama
2002 · Aus/UK · Colour · 99mins

Aussie writer/director Scott Roberts's gritty debut feature is a hot-blooded crime drama that practically oozes sleazy chic. Visually stark and unsentimental, it has a brooding, muscular intensity, off-set by the darkest black comedy. Pony-tailed Guy Pearce is the leader of a trio of bank-robbing brothers who are released early from an Australian prison so they can pull off a multi-million dollar heist for their corrupt lawyer. The events that follow are scarcely original, but they're executed with precision, wit and force. SF [VIDEO] DVD

Guy Pearce *Dale Twentyman* • Rachel Griffiths *Carol Twentyman* • Robert Taylor (4) *Frank Malone* • Joel Edgerton *Shane Twentyman* • Damien Richardson *Mal Twentyman* • Rhondda Findleton *Jane Moore* • Kate Atkinson *Pamela* • Vince Colosimo *Det Mick Kelly* ■ *Dir/Scr* Scott Roberts

Hardball ★★★ 12

Sports drama
2001 · US/Ger · Colour · 101mins

Keanu Reeves is a drifter who agrees to coach a Little League team of boys from a tough housing project in Chicago. In an atmosphere where guns speak louder than words, and war paint is real blood, the kids learn that what matters in life is turning up, even if you don't win. The coach is taught his own lessons of redemption, to live up to the principles of teacher Diane Lane. Despite his charm, Keanu Reeves hasn't the authority to carry it through, and his performance only underlines the clichés. TH. Contains violence and swearing. [VIDEO] DVD

Keanu Reeves *Conor O'Neill* • Diane Lane *Elizabeth Wilkes* • John Hawkes *Ticky Tobin* • DB Sweeney *Matt Hyland* • Mike McGlone *Jimmy Fleming* • Sterling Brim *Sterling* • Michael Jordan *Jamal* ■ *Dir* Brian Robbins • *Scr* John Gatins, from the book *Hardball: a Season in the Projects* by Daniel Coyle

Hardcore ★ 18

Sex comedy 1977 · UK · Colour · 79mins

Fiona Richmond, once Britain's number one sex symbol, plays a woman called Fiona in this bizarre sex comedy. Wrapped around the flimsiest of plots (a woman arrives at a friend's villa to find someone taking away the furniture) is a catalogue of sexual adventures, which must have included every fumbling cliché writer/director James Kenelm Clarke had ever come across. DM. Contains swearing, sex scenes and nudity. [VIDEO]

Fiona Richmond *Fiona* • Anthony Steel *Robert* • Victor Spinetti *Duncan* • Ronald Fraser *Marty* • Graham Stark *Inspector Flaubert* • Graham Crowden *Lord Yardarm* ■ *Dir* James Kenelm Clarke • *Scr* James Kenelm Clarke, Michael Robson

H

Hardcore ★★★ 18

Drama 1979 · US · Colour · 103mins

George C Scott stars as a Michigan Calvinist searching for his errant daughter who has become a porn actress in Los Angeles. Scott's search leads him through a warren of massage parlours, nude encounters and snuff movies, but he maintains a chilly aloofness, nursing his bigotry and heading towards that inevitable explosion of violence. Written and directed by Michigan Calvinist Paul Schrader, this flawed but generally impressive transposition of *The Searchers* inhabits the same sleazy yet redemptive world as Schrader's script for *Taxi Driver*. AT [VIDEO]

George C Scott *Jake Van Dorn* • Peter Boyle *Andy Mast* • Season Hubley *Niki* • Dick Sargent *Wes DeJong* • Leonard Gaines *Ramada* ■ *Dir/Scr* Paul Schrader

The Harder They Come ★★★ 15

Crime drama 1972 · Jam · Colour · 103mins

Jamaica's first indigenous feature became something of a cult hit and made a huge star of Jimmy Cliff, whose own experiences, to a degree, inform the plot. After a hard-hitting opening, in which keenly observed documentary detail captures both the exotic and ugly sides of Kingston, this reggae reworking of the old rags-to-riches story disappointingly descends into banal blaxploitation. The struggle to make it in the music business is convincingly depicted, but director Perry Henzell loses his way when Cliff resorts to cop killing to boost his record sales. Whatever the film's shortcomings, though, the music is superb. DP. With subtitles. [VIDEO] DVD

Jimmy Cliff *Ivan* • Carl Bradshaw *José* • Basil Keane *Preacher* • Janet Bartley *Elsa* • Winston Stona *Police detective* • Bobby Charlton *Record company manager* • Ras Daniel Hartman *Pedro* ■ *Dir* Perry Henzell • *Scr* Perry Henzell, Trevor Rhone [Trevor D Rhone]

The Harder They Fall ★★★ 15

Sports drama 1956 · US · BW · 104mins

This riveting exposé of corruption in professional boxing is given added poignancy by the fact that the star is Humphrey Bogart in his last role, aged, mellowed and dying. He gives a terrific performance as the washed-up sports columnist forced to work for boxing promoter Rod Steiger, and what a joy it is to revel in their contrasting acting styles: Bogie so casual and effortless, Steiger so Method and explosive. Director Mark Robson attempts rugged realism, but this is full-blooded melodrama. TS DVD

Humphrey Bogart *Eddie Willis* • Rod Steiger *Nick Benko* • Jan Sterling *Beth Willis* • Mike Lane *Toro Moreno* • Max Baer *Buddy Brannen* • Jersey Joe Walcott *George* • Edward Andrews *Jim Weyerhause* • Harold J Stone *Art Leavitt* • Carlos Montalban *Luis Agrandi* ■ *Dir* Mark Robson • *Scr* Philip Yordan, from the novel by Budd Schulberg

Hardly Working ★★

Comedy 1981 · US · Colour · 91mins

Jerry Lewis produced this "comeback" comedy which should be marked "return to sender". Directed by Lewis to recoup his fortunes after his spell out of the limelight, it's about an unemployed circus clown who bumbles around looking for work and sympathy. Some good moments, but generally this is too self-pitying for comfort. TH

Jerry Lewis *Bo Hooper* • Susan Oliver *Claire Trent* • Roger C Carmel *Robert Trent* • Deanna Lund *Millie* • Harold J Stone *Frank Loucazi* ■ *Dir* Jerry Lewis • *Scr* Michael Janover, Jerry Lewis, from a story by Michael Janover

Hardware ★★★★ 18

Science-fiction horror
1990 · UK · Colour · 89mins

Sex, drugs and rock 'n' roll are the components greasing the splatter-punk engine of director Richard Stanley's impressive debut. Twenty-first century soldier of fortune Dylan McDermott gives his estranged sculptress girlfriend Stacey Travis a junked robot so she can weld the spare parts into surreal artwork. Neither know that the cyborg is really a scrapped prototype developed for future military warfare to kill without mercy – until it reconstructs itself and goes on the bloody rampage. A purposely trashy shock to the system, this is meant to disturb, and does so without apology. AJ

Dylan McDermott *Mo* • Stacey Travis *Jill* • John Lynch *Shades* • William Hootkins *Lincoln* • Iggy Pop *Angry Bob* • Mark Northover *Alvy* ■ *Dir* Richard Stanley • *Scr* Richard Stanley, Mike Fallon, from the story *Shok!* from the comic book *Fleetway Comics 2000 AD* by Steve McManus, Kevin O'Neill

The Hardys Ride High ★★ U

Comedy 1939 · US · BW · 80mins

The sixth in the long saga of the Hardy family. This time Mickey Rooney, Lewis Stone and company come into a $2 million inheritance and move to Detroit. The moral is that money and luxuries are no substitute for the small-town values and everyday joys of the Hardys' home town of Carvel. Rooney, now 16, starts smoking and falls for a gold-digging chorus girl. Problem is, Rooney was actually 19 at the time, but looked about nine. AT

Mickey Rooney *Andy Hardy* • Lewis Stone *Judge James K Hardy* • Cecilia Parker *Marian Hardy* • Fay Holden *Mrs Emily Hardy* • Ann Rutherford *Polly Benedict* ■ *Dir* George B Seitz • *Scr* Kay Van Riper, Agnes C Johnson, William Ludwig, from characters created by Aurania Rouverol

Harem ★★ 15

Romantic drama 1985 · Fr · Colour · 93mins

Obsession usually makes for good drama, but not this time. The kidnapping of Wall Street stockbroker Nastassja Kinski by enthralled Arab prince Ben Kingsley is an upmarket white-slave story that looks ravishing, though nobody really gets ravished. The trouble is, the prince is too sensitive for his own good or for his victim's bad. Rudolph Valentino in *The Sheik* wouldn't have stood for such nonsense. It all fizzles out in a welter of silly talk and a supposedly ironic ending – an ending that can't come soon enough. TH

Nastassja Kinski *Diane* • Ben Kingsley *Selim* • Dennis Goldson *Massoud* • Zohra Segal *Affaf* • Michel Robin *Monsieur Raoul* • Julette Simpson *Zelide* • Karen Bowen *Mrs Green* ■ *Dir* Arthur Joffé • *Scr* Arthur Joffé, Tom Rayfiel, from a story by Arthur Joffé, Richard Prieur, Antonio B Hernandez

Harem Suare ★★★

Historical drama
1999 · It/Fr/Tur · Colour · 106mins

Revisiting many of the themes from *The Turkish Bath* – forbidden love, ritual cleansing and the passage of long-established tradition – Ferzan Ozpetek here explores the political manoeuvrings occurring within the Sultan's palace against the backdrop of the Ottoman eclipse during the early 20th century. Marie Gillain gives a spirited performance as the favoured courtesan whose doomed love for trusted servant Alex Descas comes to mirror her master's growing political impotence. DP. In French, Turkish and Italian with English subtitles.

Marie Gillain *Safiye* • Alex Descas *Nadir* • Lucia Bosé *Old Safiye* • Valeria Golino *Anita* • Malick Bowens *Midhat* • Christophe Aquilon *Sumbul* • Serra Yilmaz *Gulfidan* • Haluk Bilginer *Abdulhamit* ■ *Dir* Ferzan Ozpetek • *Scr* Gianni Romilo, Ferzan Ozpetek

Harlan County, USA ★★★

Documentary 1976 · US · Colour · 103mins

Barbara Kopple's Oscar-winning documentary, which was years in the making, is a powerful and compelling record of the strike called at the Brookside colliery in Kentucky after management refused to recognise the workers' union status. It's a shrewdly compiled piece, but in spite of the expert manipulation, what emerges is a portrait of a community bursting with initiative, intelligence, camaraderie and a real sense of justice and self-worth. Exploring every aspect of Harlan life, Kopple gives particular attention to the miners' wives as they stand by their husbands on the picket line. DP

Dir/Scr Barbara Kopple

Harlem Nights ★★ 18

Period crime comedy
1989 · US · Colour · 110mins

Eddie Murphy's directing debut and star vehicle hits engine trouble early on and conks out completely long before the home straight. The plan was to make a latter-day version of a 1930s' gangster movie; the result has some nifty costumes, luscious sets and neat music, but, on almost every other count, it's a mess. PF. Contains swearing and violence. DVD

Eddie Murphy *Quick* • Richard Pryor *Sugar Ray* • Danny Aiello *Sergeant Phil Cantone* • Michael Lerner *Bugsy Calhoune* • Della Reese *Vera* • Redd Foxx *Bennie Wilson* • Berlinda Tolbert *Annie* • Stan Shaw *Jack Jenkins* • Jasmine Guy *Dominique La Rue* • Arsenio Hall *Crying man* ■ *Dir/Scr* Eddie Murphy • *Cinematographer* Woody Omens • *Production Designer* Lawrence G Paull • *Costume Designer* Joe I Tompkins

Harlequin ★★ 15

Drama 1980 · Aus · Colour · 88mins

Director Simon Wincer's second feature is an odd attempt to update the story of Rasputin to 1980s Australia. Robert Powell plays a charismatic healer who convinces senator David Hemmings and his wife that he can cure their son's leukaemia. This is typical of the kind of curio that Hemmings opted for as his once-glittering career went into a steep decline, and Wincer piles on the mystery without really developing the story. Hollywood veteran Broderick Crawford pops up as Hemmings's spin doctor. JF DVD

Robert Powell *Gregory Wolfe* • David Hemmings *Senator Nick Rast* • Carmen Duncan *Sandra Rast* • Broderick Crawford *Doc Wheelan* • Gus Mercurio *Mr Bergier* • Alan Cassell *Mr Porter* • Mark Spain *Alex Rast* ■ *Dir* Simon Wincer • *Scr* Everett De Roche

Harley Davidson and the Marlboro Man ★ 15

Action adventure 1991 · US · Colour · 94mins

A blatant, dispiriting plug for leather and lung cancer with Mickey Rourke and Don Johnson as bikers who in 1996 (for some reason this is a futuristic thing) are mistaken for drug runners instead of the slimeballs they really are. Lacking the energy and exploitation thrills of the 1960s' biker movies it tries to emulate, this is more like a retread of those dreadful *Cannonball Run* movies. AT DVD

Mickey Rourke *Harley Davidson* • Don Johnson *Marlboro* • Chelsea Field *Virginia Slim* • Daniel Baldwin *Alexander* • Giancarlo Esposito *Jimmy Jiles* • Vanessa Williams [Vanessa L Williams] *Lulu Daniels* • Robert Ginty *Thom* • Tia Carrere *Kimiko* ■ *Dir* Simon Wincer • *Scr* Don Michael Paul

Harlow ★★

Biographical drama
1965 · US · Colour · 124mins

This not altogether believable biopic of the platinum blonde bombshell views Jean Harlow as an unhappy innocent trying to become a star in 1930s Hollywood while dodging the ever-present casting couch. The film did well at the box office, and Carroll Baker, Red Buttons (as Harlow's agent) and Angela Lansbury (as Harlow's mother) rise above the limitations of the script. JG

Carroll Baker *Jean Harlow* • Martin Balsam *Everett Redman* • Red Buttons *Arthur Landau* • Mike Connors *Jack Harrison* • Angela Lansbury *Mama Jean Bello* • Peter Lawford *Paul Bern* • Leslie Nielsen *Richard Manley* ■ *Dir* Gordon Douglas • *Scr* John Michael Hayes, from the non-fiction book *An Intimate Biography* by Irving Shulman, Arthur Landau

Harlow ★

Biographical drama 1965 · US · BW · 107mins

Made the same year as the marginally better biopic starring Carroll Baker as Harlow, this exploitative film cashes in sad, sorry life of the Hollywood starlet. Carol Lynley isn't up to the role and Ginger Rogers (who play's Jean's mother) really should have known better. The producers rushed to get this out before the Paramount film using the Electronovision process, and the sloppiness shows. RT

Carol Lynley *Jean Harlow* • Efrem Zimbalist Jr *William Mansfield* • Barry Sullivan *Marino Bello* • Ginger Rogers *Mama Jean* • Hurd Hatfield *Paul Bern* • Hermione Baddeley *Marie Dressler* • Lloyd Bochner *Marc Peters* • Audrey Totter *Marilyn* • John Williams *Jonathan Martin* • Jack Kruschen *Louis B Mayer* • Celia Lovsky *Maria Ouspenskaya* • Robert Strauss *Hank* • Sonny Liston *First fighter* ■ *Dir* Alex Segal • *Scr* Karl Tunberg

The Harness ★★★★

Romantic drama
1971 · US · Colour · 120mins

An excellent version of a heart-warming John Steinbeck story, offering a leading role to under-rated Lorne Greene, the Canadian actor best known as Ben Cartwright in *Bonanza*. Here he plays a farmer whose life is dominated by his sick wife until the arrival of two newcomers at his ranch. The rich photography is from one of the all-time Hollywood camera maestros, Russell Metty, and this is a TV movie of distinction from Universal, who pioneered films specifically made for the small screen. TS

Lorne Greene *Peter Randall* • Julie Sommars *Jennifer Shagaras* • Murray Hamilton *Roy Kern* • Lee H Montgomery [Lee Montgomery] *Tor Shagaras* • Louise Latham *Emma Randall* • Henry Beckman *Doc Marn* • Joan Tompkins *Millie Chappel* ■ *Dir* Boris Sagal • *Scr* Leon Tokatyan, Edward Hume, from the short story by John Steinbeck

Harold & Kumar Get the Munchies ★★★ 15

Comedy 2004 · US/Can · Colour · 84mins

If the phrase "from the director of *Dude, Where's My Car?*" sends shivers down your spine, then you may be surprised by this likeable comedy from Danny Leiner. Affable young stoners John Cho and Kal Penn hit the road in search of White Castle burgers to satisfy their post-pot hunger pains. What follows is an exuberant, offbeat road movie that is a minor delight, thanks to its surprising warmth and some inspired comic riffs. IF. Contains swearing, sexual references and drug abuse. DVD

John Cho *Harold Lee* • Kal Penn *Kumar Patel* • Paula Garcés *Maria* • Neil Patrick Harris • David Krumholtz *Goldstein* • Eddie Kaye Thomas *Rosenberg* • Christopher Meloni *Freakshow* ■ *Dir* Danny Leiner • *Scr* Hayden Schlossberg, Jon Hurwitz

Harold and Maude ★★★★ 15

Black comedy drama
1972 · US · Colour · 87mins

Rarely has such a strange love affair been presented so charmingly as the one here between morbid young Harold (Bud Cort) and 79-year-old concentration camp survivor Maude (Ruth Gordon). Depressed by life, and rejected by his wealthy mother Vivian Pickles, the death-fascinated Harold drives a hearse to funerals, meets the skittish Maude and falls in love. A cult classic, the film started life as a graduate thesis by Colin Higgins, whose landlady helped him to set it up for direction by Hal Ashby. The performances are a delightful bonus in a movie that, for all its eccentricities, likes people. TH DVD

Ruth Gordon *Maude* • Bud Cort *Harold* • Vivian Pickles *Mrs Chasen* • Cyril Cusack *Glaucus* • Charles Tyner *Uncle Victor* • Ellen Geer *Sunshine Dore* • Eric Christmas *Priest* • G Wood *Psychiatrist* ■ *Dir* Hal Ashby • *Scr* Colin Higgins • *Music* Cat Stevens

Harper ★★★★ 12

Detective thriller
1966 · US · Colour · 115mins

Also known as *The Moving Target*, this features an early script by screenwriting guru William Goldman. Paul Newman is a Chandleresque private eye in the missing persons business, and Lauren Bacall the wealthy client who hires him to find her spouse. From the moment Newman recycles coffee for his breakfast beverage, we know the territory: a detective, with only honour to sustain him, up against the idle rich with time on their hands and murder on their minds. Goldman's pungent script, Jack Smight's pacy direction and Newman's confident portrayal make this a classy thriller. A sequel, *The Drowning Pool*, followed nine years later. TH

Paul Newman *Lew Harper* • Lauren Bacall *Mrs Sampson* • Julie Harris *Betty Fraley* • Arthur Hill *Albert Graves* • Janet Leigh *Susan Harper* • Pamela Tiffin *Miranda Sampson* • Robert Wagner *Alan Taggert* • Robert Webber *Dwight Troy* • Shelley Winters *Fay Estabrook* ■ *Dir* Jack Smight • *Scr* William Goldman, from the novel by Ross MacDonald

Harper Valley PTA ★★★

Comedy 1978 · US · Colour · 101mins

Ode to Billy Joe demonstrated the potential for pop ballads to inspire movies and this spicy comedy, based on Jeannie C Riley's song about small-town hypocrisy, continued the trend. Barbara Eden takes the lead as a sexy widow whose lifestyle offends the uptight members of the local Parent-Teachers Association, but turns the tables on them by exposing their own foibles. A moderate hit theatrically, this was turned into a TV series with Eden re-creating her sassy role. DF

Barbara Eden *Stella Johnson* • Ronny Cox *Willis Newton* • Nanette Fabray *Alice Finely* • Susan Swift *Dee Johnson* • Louis Nye *Kirby Baker* • Pat Paulsen *Otis Harper Jr* ■ *Dir* Richard Bennett • *Scr* George Edwards, Barry Schneider, from the song by Tom T Hall

The Harrad Experiment ★ 15

Drama 1973 · US · Colour · 91mins

James Whitmore and Tippi Hedren are a learned married couple who run Harrad College, a bastion of libertarian values where young people are obliged to live with each other and work out their sexual hang-ups. Doubtless Hollywood felt it was being terribly grown-up to tackle such a story, but it's relentlessly tedious and hardly likely to raise anything more than a smile, despite some rather coy nudity and dirty dialogue. AT DVD

James Whitmore *Philip Tenhausen* • Tippi Hedren *Margaret Tenhausen* • Don Johnson *Stanley* • B Kirby Jr [Bruno Kirby] *Harry* • Laurie Walters *Sheila* • Melanie Griffith ■ *Dir* Ted Post • *Scr* Michael Werner, Ted Cassedy, from the novel by Robert H Rimmer

The Harrad Summer ★ 15

Drama 1974 · US · Colour · 100mins

Too much experience is less than a good thing, as this indifferent sequel to *The Harrad Experiment* about students at a sex-education college demonstrates. When the students return to their communities, they take their extra-curricular "homework" with them. Leads Robert Reiser and Laurie Walters don't take any acting honours with this, while director Steven Hilliard Stern's name is more distinguished than his talents. TH

Robert Reiser *Stanley Kolasukas* • Laurie Walters *Sheila Grove* • Richard Doran *Harry Schacht* • Victoria Thompson *Beth Hillyer* • Emmaline Henry *Margaret Tonhausen* • Bill Dana *Jack Schacht* ■ *Dir* Steven Hilliard Stern • *Scr* Morth Thaw, Steve Zacharias

Harriet Craig ★★★

Psychological drama 1950 · US · BW · 94mins

This is a rip-roaring vehicle for Joan Crawford, who ably demonstrates on screen all those "qualities" so vividly documented in *Mommie Dearest*. Crawford, as ever, tends to chew the scenery to achieve effect, in contrast to the superb Rosalind Russell in the earlier talkie version of the play on which this was based. Nevertheless, the star breathes life into this hoary old chestnut about a woman more taken by her possessions than by her family, and makes the whole dated premise a mesmerising experience. TS

Joan Crawford *Harriet Craig* • Wendell Corey *Walter Craig* • Lucile Watson *Celia Fenwick* • Allyn Joslyn *Billy Birkmire* • William Bishop *Wes Miller* • KT Stevens *Clare Raymond* • Raymond Greenleaf *Henry Fenwick* • Ellen Corby *Lottie* ■ *Dir* Vincent Sherman • *Scr* Anne Froelick, James Gunn, from the play *Craig's Wife* by George Kelly

Harriet the Spy ★★★ PG

Comedy 1996 · US · Colour · 97mins

Harriet (Michelle Trachtenberg) is the schoolgirl who spies on her friends and family, making copious observations about them in her secret notebook. It's hardly a surprise that, when the book falls into the wrong hands and Harriet's scribblings are read out, her subjects are none too pleased. While not as colourful or zippily paced as popular children's source novel, this is a quirky film that benefits from a great group of kids and a warm adult performance from Rosie O'Donnell as Harriet's nanny. JB DVD

Michelle Trachtenberg *Harriet* • Gregory Smith *Sport* • Vanessa Lee Chester *Janie Gibbs* • Rosie O'Donnell *Ole Golly* • J Smith-Cameron *Mrs Welsch* • Robert Joy *Mr Welsch* • Eartha Kitt *Agatha K Plummer* ■ *Dir* Bronwen Hughes • *Scr* Douglas Petrie, Theresa Rebeck, from the novel by Louise Fitzhugh, adapted by Greg Taylor, Julie Talen

Harrison's Flowers ★★ 15

War drama 2000 · Fr · Colour · 126mins

The internecine slaughter in the former Yugoslavia provides little more than a heart-tugging backdrop for Elie Chouraqui's real story: worried Andie MacDowell's selfless search for missing photojournalist husband David Strathairn. Adopting a US-centric world view, this achingly sincere (and, in MacDowell's case, seriously miscast) picture seems to intimate that a calamity isn't legitimate unless it's appeared in *Newsweek*. DP DVD

Andie MacDowell *Sarah* • David Strathairn *Harrison* • Elias Koteas *Yeager* • Adrien Brody *Kyle* • Brendan Gleeson *Stevenson* • Alun Armstrong *Samuel Brubeck* ■ *Dir* Elie Chouraqui • *Scr* Elie Chouraqui, Isabel Ellsen, Michael Katims, Didier Le Pêcheur

Harry and Son ★★ 15

Drama 1984 · US · Colour · 111mins

Paul Newman here stars, directs, co-writes and co-produces in a one-man band attempt to create a meaningful family melodrama. What we get is an awful lot of breast-beating, home truths and hysterical outbursts, but not much true understanding of why a father (Newman) and son (Robby Benson) find each other such fraught company in the first place. The members of a stellar cast (Joanne Woodward, Morgan Freeman, Ellen Barkin) stand around a lot, wringing their hands on the edge of the bear pit. Someone badly needed to divest Newman of one of his hats, but presumably nobody dared. SH. Contains swearing and nudity.

Paul Newman *Harry Keach* • Robby Benson *Howard Keach* • Ellen Barkin *Katie* • Wilford Brimley *Tom* • Judith Ivey *Sally* • Ossie Davis *Raymond* • Morgan Freeman *Siemanowski* • Maury Chaykin *Lawrence* • Joanne Woodward *Lilly* ■ *Dir* Paul Newman • *Scr* Paul Newman, Ronald L Buck, from the novel *A Lost King* by Raymond DeCapite

Harry and Tonto ★★★★

Comedy 1974 · US · Colour · 115mins

Art Carney strikes a blow for the older generation – and won an Oscar in the process – with this story of a widower in his 70s who, after being evicted from his New York apartment, sets off on an odyssey across America with his cat Tonto. Intending to call on his grown-up children along the way, he ends up discarding a few prejudices. Paul Mazursky directs with a keen eye for characters, including Ellen Burstyn as a daughter who finds Harry's charm a bit too much, and Larry Hagman as a son forced to confront his own failure. Hitch-hiker Melanie Mayron puts in a teenage flourish, but it's Carney's last hurrah which compels attention. TH

Art Carney *Harry* • Ellen Burstyn *Shirley* • Chief Dan George *Sam Two Feathers* • Geraldine Fitzgerald *Jessie* • Larry Hagman *Eddie* • Arthur Hunnicutt *Wade* • Melanie Mayron *Ginger* ■ *Dir* Paul Mazursky • *Scr* Paul Mazursky, Josh Greenfeld

Harry and Walter Go to New York ★★ U

Crime caper 1976 · US · Colour · 106mins

Vaguely influenced by the success of *The Sting*, this box-office dud admittedly has an attractive cast: James Caan and Elliott Gould as song-and-dance men turned safecrackers, Michael Caine as a sort of Mabuse-like mastermind and Diane Keaton as their ditzy confederate in an elaborate bank heist. Although money has been lavished on the re-creation of the New York of 1890, the script isn't nearly clever or funny enough. AT

James Caan *Harry Dighby* • Elliott Gould *Walter Hill* • Michael Caine *Adam Worth* • Diane Keaton *Lissa Chestnut* • Charles Durning *Rufus T Crisp* • Lesley Ann Warren *Gloria Fontaine* ■ *Dir* Mark Rydell • *Scr* John Byrum, Robert Kaufman

Harry Black and the Tiger ★★ U

Adventure 1958 · UK · Colour · 116mins

One-legged hunter (Stewart Granger) is employed to kill a man-eating Bengal tiger that is terrorising an Indian village. With him on his mission are an old flame, her son and her husband (Anthony Steel), whose wartime cowardice caused the hunter's crippling injury. Director Hugo Fregonese makes the best of the love triangle situation, but this is still weak, although Indian locations and CinemaScope colour photography keep things interesting to look at. BB

Stewart Granger *Harry Black* • Barbara Rush *Christian Tanner* • Anthony Steel *Desmond Tanner* • IS Johar *Bapu* • Martin Stephens *Michael Tanner* • Frank Olegario *Dr Chowdhury* ■ *Dir* Hugo Fregonese • *Scr* Sydney Boehm, from the novel *Harry Black* by David Walker

Harry, He's Here to Help ★★★ 15

Black comedy 2000 · Fr · Colour · 111mins

Good intentions go horribly awry in Dominik Moll's darkly comic and disturbingly ambiguous study of male malice. Laurent Lucas plays a harassed family man on holiday who encounters Sergi Lopez, a former schoolfriend made good. There's something instantly sinister about Lopez's generosity towards Lucas; it establishes a tension that is shattered with chillingly twisted logic. Turning the isolated Swiss locations to his atmospheric advantage, Moll depicts Lopez's brutally efficient crimes with restraint. DP. In French with English subtitles. Contains violence, swearing and nudity. DVD

Laurent Lucas *Michel* • Sergi Lopez *Harry Balestrero* • Mathilde Seigner *Claire* • Sophie Guillemin *Prune* • Liliane Rovère *Mother* • Domnique Rozan *Father* ■ *Dir* Dominik Moll • *Scr* Dominik Moll, Gilles Marchand

Harry in Your Pocket ★★★

Crime drama 1973 · US · Colour · 102mins

This is a film that boasts sleight-of-hand performing artist Tony Giorgio as its technical adviser (he also appears on-screen as a detective) and a plot concerning young Michael Sarrazin and Trish Van Devere learning how to pick a pocket or two. The stars find themselves under the tutelage of veteran pickpockets James Coburn, perfectly cast as a smoothie, and Walter Pidgeon, as a sleazy sophisticate, in one of the latter's better later roles. This heartfelt one-off is the only major credit of producer/director Bruce Geller, unless you count his 1976 TV movie *The Savage Bees*. TS. Contains some strong language.

James Coburn *Harry* • Michael Sarrazin *Ray Houlihan* • Trish Van Devere *Sandy Coletto* • Walter Pidgeon *Casey* • Michael C Gwynne *Fence* • Tony Giorgio *First detective* ■ *Dir* Bruce Geller • *Scr* Ron Austin, James David Buchanan

Harry Potter and the Chamber of Secrets ★★★★ PG

Fantasy adventure 2002 · US/UK/Ger · Colour, sepia · 154mins

Those who love the bestselling work of fantasy author JK Rowling will find this sequel even more to their taste, with the mood darker and more scary. Here, predatory spiders stalk Harry (an audibly older Daniel Radcliffe) through the Forbidden Forest, there's a mandrake root with an ear-splitting scream and Harry even exchanges a kiss with Hermione (Emma Watson). Director Chris Columbus has allowed some mechanical repetition to creep in, but overall this is ingenious as well as faithful. Among the adult performers, Kenneth Branagh stands out as the egotistical new teacher Gilderoy Lockhart, upstaging even the special effects. TH DVD

Daniel Radcliffe *Harry Potter* • Rupert Grint *Ron Weasley* • Emma Watson *Hermione Granger* • Richard Harris *Prof Albus Dumbledore* • Maggie Smith *Prof Minerva McGonagall* • Kenneth Branagh *Gilderoy Lockhart* • Robbie Coltrane *Rubeus Hagrid* • Alan Rickman *Prof Severus Snape* • Julie Walters *Mrs Molly Weasley* • Mark Williams *Mr Arthur Weasley* • Shirley Henderson *Moaning Myrtle* • Jason Isaacs *Lucius Malfoy* • Richard Griffiths *Uncle Vernon Dursley* • Fiona Shaw *Aunt Petunia Dursley* • Miriam Margolyes *Professor Sprout* • John Cleese *Nearly Headless Nick* • Tom Felton *Draco Malfoy* • Bonnie Wright *Ginny Weasley* • Toby Jones *Dobby, the house elf* ■ *Dir* Chris Columbus • *Scr* Steve Kloves, from the novel by JK Rowling

Harry Potter and the Philosopher's Stone ★★★★ PG

Fantasy adventure 2001 · US · Colour · 146mins

With millions of Harry Potter books sold around the world, this is more than just a big-budget movie adaptation – it's a cultural phenomenon. Twelve-year-old Daniel Radcliffe makes a likeable Harry – the boy wizard who's whisked off to Hogwarts School of Witchcraft and Wizardry. A scene-stealing Robbie Coltrane is among a host of familiar adult faces who breathe life into JK Rowling's charming characters. To criticise at all feels like an act of isolationism and yet there is a lack of emotional core – Harry's orphan status fails to move – and, at two and a half hours in length, the movie is perhaps too long for the younger fidgets. However, this faithful rendition of the inaugural Harry Potter book demonstrates that the franchise is in safe, sensible hands. AC DVD

Daniel Radcliffe *Harry Potter* • Rupert Grint *Ron Weasley* • Emma Watson *Hermione Granger* • Robbie Coltrane *Rubeus Hagrid* • Maggie Smith *Prof Minerva McGonagall* • Alan Rickman *Prof Severus Snape* • Richard Harris *Prof Albus Dumbledore* • Ian Hart *Prof Quirrell* • Richard Griffiths *Uncle Vernon Dursley* • Fiona Shaw *Aunt Petunia Dursley* • John Cleese *Nearly Headless Nick* • Zoë Wanamaker *Madame Hooch* • John Hurt *Mr Ollivander* • Julie Walters *Mrs Molly Weasley* • David Bradley (3) *Mr Angus Filch* • Tom Felton *Draco Malfoy* • Leslie Phillips *The sorting hat (voice)* ■ *Dir* Chris Columbus • *Scr* Steve Kloves, from the novel by JK Rowling

Harry Potter and the Prisoner of Azkaban ★★★★ PG

Fantasy adventure 2004 · US · Colour · 135mins

Mexican director Alfonso Cuarón brings a darker, edgier, scarier feel to this third instalment, which has boy wizard Harry (Daniel Radcliffe) contending not only with Gary Oldman's escaped convict, but also the difficulties involved with turning teen. But there's still plenty of fun to be had, with ghosts, ghouls and gadgets galore, the most striking gizmo being a shape-shifting triple-decker bus. David Thewlis, Emma Thompson and Timothy Spall join the list of cameoing celebrities, while the young leads are all growing into their roles. The film has the odd dull patch, but, by and large, this adventure is on a par with its predecessors. DA DVD

Daniel Radcliffe *Harry Potter* • Rupert Grint *Ron Weasley* • Emma Watson *Hermione Granger* • Michael Gambon *Prof Albus Dumbledore* • Maggie Smith *Prof Minerva McGonagall* • Robbie Coltrane *Rubeus Hagrid* • Alan Rickman *Prof Severus Snape* • David Thewlis *Prof Lupin* • Emma Thompson *Prof Sybill Trelawney* • Gary Oldman *Sirius Black* • Julie Walters *Mrs Molly Weasley* • Timothy Spall *Peter Pettigrew* ■ *Dir* Alfonso Cuarón • *Scr* Steve Kloves, from the novel by JK Rowling

H

Harry's War ★★★

Comedy 1981 · US · Colour · 98mins

Edward Herrmann here plays nicely against type as the postman who takes a stand against the Internal Revenue Service after it erroneously demands huge back taxes from his aunt, Geraldine Page. Writer/director Kieth Merrill is over-earnest in his celebration of small-town values, but this is pleasantly uplifting entertainment. DP

Edward Herrmann *Harry Johnson* • Geraldine Page *Beverly Payne* • Karen Grassle *Kathy Johnson* • David Ogden Stiers *Ernie Scelera* • Salome Jens *Wilda Crawley* • Elisha Cook Jr *Sergeant Billy* ■ *Dir/Scr* Kieth Merrill

Hart's War ★★★ 15

Second World War courtroom drama 2002 · US · Colour · 119mins

Colin Farrell impresses as he defends a black pilot from a trumped-up murder charge in this workmanlike adaptation of John Katzenbach's novel set in a German PoW camp. Dispensing with combat action after the compelling cross-country opening, director Gregory Hoblit laudably concentrates on exposing the pernicious racism that existed within the US armed services during the Second World War, with the emphasis on courtroom drama rather than the escape subplot. Nominal star Bruce Willis is undertaxed as the senior American officer and his characterisation pales significantly beside Marcel Iures's cultured Nazi commandant. DP DVD

Bruce Willis *Col William A McNamara* • Colin Farrell (2) *Lt Thomas W Hart* • Terrence Howard *Lt Lincoln A Scott* • Cole Hauser *Staff Sgt Vic W Bedford* • Marcel Iures *Col Werner Visser* • Linus Roache *Capt Peter A Ross* • Rory Cochrane *Sgt Carl S Webb* ■ *Dir* Gregory Hoblit • *Scr* Billy Ray, Terry George, from the novel by John Katzenbach

Harum Scarum ★★ U

Musical comedy 1965 · US · Colour · 82mins

Another sub-standard entry in the screen career of Elvis Presley. Here he plays a movie star who travels to the Middle East to attend the premiere of his latest film and gets caught up in a plot to assassinate a local ruler. The exotic locations add a *frisson* of interest to the usual formula, but this is negated by the lacklustre plot and forgettable songs. DF DVD

Elvis Presley *Johnny Tyronne* • Mary Ann Mobley *Princess Shalimar* • Fran Jeffries *Aishah* • Michael Ansara *Prince Dragna* • Jay Novello *Zacha* • Philip Reed *King Toranshah* • Theo Marcuse *Sinan* • Billy Barty *Baba* ■ *Dir* Gene Nelson • *Scr* Gerald Drayson Adams

The Harvest ★★ 18

Thriller 1993 · US · Colour · 93mins

The illegal trade in body parts stands as a metaphor for the exploitative nature of Hollywood film-making in this flashy thriller from debut director David Marconi. Playing fast and loose with traditional narrative structures, Marconi throws in flashbacks, dream sequences and episodes that could equally be real or simply part of wannabe writer Miguel Ferrer's latest screenplay. However, too little attention is paid to either theme or characterisation. DP. Contains violence, sex scenes, nudity and swearing. DVD

Miguel Ferrer *Charlie Pope* • Leilani Sarelle Ferrer [Leilani Ferrer] *Natalie Caldwell* • Henry Silva *Detective Topo* • Tim Thomerson *Steve Mobley* • Harvey Fierstein *Bob Lakin* • Anthony John Denison *Noel Guzmann* ■ *Dir/Scr* David Marconi

Harvey ★★★★★ U

Comedy 1950 · US · BW · 107mins

James Stewart gives a knockout performance in a classic comic fantasy about tipsy Elwood P Dowd and his unusual friendship with Harvey, an invisible 6ft tall white rabbit. This is superb whimsy about the fine line between sanity and insanity, and Henry Koster directs this loving tribute to eccentricity and bar-room philosophy with a deft touch. Alongside the satiric misunderstandings, character mix-ups and revitalised clichés come poignant comments about humanity's lack of communication, which touch both the funny bone and the heart. Guaranteed to leave you with a smile on your face for ages afterwards. AJ DVD

James Stewart *Elwood P Dowd* • Josephine Hull *Veta Louise Simmons* • Peggy Dow *Miss Kelly* • Charles Drake *Dr Sanderson* • Cecil Kellaway *Dr Chumley* • Victoria Horne *Myrtle Mae* • Jesse White *Wilson* • William Lynn *Judge Gaffney* • Wallace Ford *Lofgren* ■ *Dir* Henry Koster • *Scr* Mary Chase, Oscar Brodney, from the play by Mary Chase • *Cinematographer* William Daniels [William H Daniels]

The Harvey Girls ★★★ U

Musical comedy 1946 · US · Colour · 96mins

Once intended as a vehicle for Lana Turner, this Technicolored musical comedy became one of Judy Garland's greatest personal triumphs. She plays a mail-order bride who joins up with waitresses sent out west by restaurateur Fred Harvey to serve the passengers on the new cross-country railroads. The plot is as cardboard as the scenery, and John Hodiak is a totally inadequate and lacklustre leading man. There's good work from Angela Lansbury and Ray Bolger, though, but the film belongs to Garland, and she is wonderful. TS

Judy Garland *Susan Bradley* • John Hodiak *Ned Trent* • Ray Bolger *Chris Maule* • Preston Foster *Judge Sam Purvis* • Virginia O'Brien *Alma* • Angela Lansbury *Em* • Marjorie Main *Sonora Cassidy* • Chill Wills *HH Hartsey* • Kenny Baker (1) *Terry O'Halloran* • Cyd Charisse *Deborah* ■ *Dir* George Sidney (2) • *Scr* Edmund Beloin, Nathaniel Curtis, Harry Crane, James O'Hanlon, Samson Raphaelson, from a story by Eleanore Griffin, William Rankin, from a novel by Samuel Hopkins Adams • *Music Director* Lennie Hayton • *Choreographer* Robert Alton

Harvey Middleman, Fireman ★★★

Comedy drama 1965 · US · Colour · 75mins

Ernest Pintoff made some very droll short cartoons, including *The Critic*, which won an Oscar. *Harvey Middleman, Fireman* was the first of his few features, starring the then (as now) unknown Gene Troobnick as a New York fireman. Troobnick is a happily married father of two, with a happy-go-lucky view of life. Until, that is, he rescues an attractive young woman from a fire, kisses her and then falls madly in love. Suddenly in turmoil, he even goes to a shrink, played by the monstrously hammy Hermione Gingold. It's a small, slight, charmingly cranky movie. AT

Gene Troobnick [Eugene Troobnick] *Harvey Middleman* • Hermione Gingold *Mrs Koogleman* • Patricia Harty *Lois* • Arlene Golonka *Harriet* • Will Mackenzie *Dinny* • Ruth Jaroslow *The mother* • Charles Durning *Dooley* ■ *Dir/Scr* Ernest Pintoff

Has Anybody Seen My Gal? ★★★

Musical comedy 1952 · US · Colour · 88mins

Millionaire Charles Coburn decides to check whether the family of the woman he loved many years ago, but who turned down his marriage proposal, is worthy of inheriting his fortune. Masquerading as an eccentric artist and taking a job as a soda jerk, he rents a room in the family house, arranges an anonymous gift of money for them, and gleefully watches the results. Breezily directed by Douglas Sirk, with a cast that includes Rock Hudson and Piper Laurie (and with James Dean in a bit part), this beguiling comedy owes much of its appeal to Coburn's performance. RK

Charles Coburn *Samuel Fulton* • Rock Hudson *Dan Stebbins* • Piper Laurie *Millicent Blaisdell* • Gigi Perreau *Roberta Blaisdell* • Lynn Bari *Harriet Blaisdell* • Larry Gates *Charles Blaisdell* • William Reynolds *Howard Blaisdell* • Skip Homeier *Carl Pennock* • James Dean *Youth* ■ *Dir* Douglas Sirk • *Scr* Joseph Hoffman, from a story by Eleanor H Porter

The Hasty Heart ★★★ U

Second World War drama 1949 · UK · BW · 102mins

In transferring John Patrick's hit play to the screen, Vincent Sherman remained faithful to the text, but neglected his duty as a film director by failing to challenge the eye as well as the ear. In an overblown but Oscar-nominated performance, Richard Todd dominates the action as a self-pitying Scot who makes life unbearable for his fellow patients in a Burmese field hospital. Patricia Neal also overdoes her angel of mercy act, but there is the compensation of seeing Ronald Reagan give one of his best performances. DP

Ronald Reagan *Yank* • Patricia Neal *Sister Margaret* • Richard Todd *Corporal Lachlan McLachlan* • Anthony Nicholls *Lt Col Dunn* • Howard Marion-Crawford *Tommy* • Ralph Michael *Kiwi* • Alfie Bass *Orderly* ■ *Dir* Vincent Sherman • *Scr* Ranald MacDougall, from the play by John Patrick

Hatari! ★★★★ U

Adventure 1962 · US · Colour · 151mins

Howard Hawks's amiable safari romp, which he shot in East Africa, is ecologically sound, almost plotless and so long that you can wander in and out of it with no sense of missing anything. But if you did, you would lose out on a wonderful roller-coaster ride of fun and adventure, plus the sort of camaraderie between star John Wayne, director Hawks and writer Leigh Brackett that only long-term collaboration can produce. The movie also contains the best setting-a-dislocated-shoulder-by-hand scene ever. TS DVD

John Wayne *Sean Mercer* • Elsa Martinelli *Dallas* • Hardy Kruger *Kurt* • Red Buttons *Pockets* • Gérard Blain *Chip Maurey* • Michèle Girardon *Brandy* • Bruce Cabot *Indian* ■ *Dir* Howard Hawks • *Scr* Leigh Brackett, from a story by Harry Kurnitz

Hatchet for the Honeymoon ★★★ 15

Horror thriller 1969 · It/Sp · Colour · 84mins

Mario Bava's darkly comic and elegant shocker stars Italian 1960s staple Stephen Forsyth as a bridal gown salon owner driven to murdering his models on their wedding nights. It's when he starts wearing white veils himself to kill his wife (Laura Betti) that the real twisted trouble begins. Revealing the killer's identity from the outset is unusual for the *giallo* (Italian thriller) genre, but Bava's ironic chiller pushes rich visual delirium to both macabre and mischievous limits. AJ. Italian dialogue dubbed into English. Contains violence. DVD

Stephen Forsyth *John Harrington* • Dagmar Lassander *Helen Wood* • Laura Betti *Mildred Harrington* • Jesus Puente *Inspector Russell* • Femi Benussi *Alice Norton* • Antonia Mas *Louise* ■ *Dir* Mario Bava • *Scr* Mario Bava, Santiago Moncado, Mario Musy, from a story by Santiago Moncado

The Hatchet Man ★★

Crime melodrama 1932 · US · BW · 74mins

Edward G Robinson stars here as an Oriental gangster. Loretta Young is in Chinese make-up, too, as Robinson's ward and eventual bride, an event that causes the hatchets to come out. Sundry subplots and a trip to China, where J Carroll Naish is naturally a big cheese, fill in the screen time. The flabby romance and unusually slow direction by William A Wellman produces a disappointing result. AT

Edward G Robinson *Wong Low Get* • Loretta Young *Toya San* • Dudley Digges *Nag Hong Fah* • Leslie Fenton *Harry En Hai* • Edmund Breese *Yu Chang* • Tully Marshall *Long Sen Yat* • J Carroll Naish *Sun Yat Sen* ■ *Dir* William Wellman [William A Wellman] • *Scr* JG Alexander, from the play *The Honorable Mr Wong* by Achmed Abdullah, David Belasco

A Hatful of Rain ★★★

Drama 1957 · US · BW · 108mins

Don Murray stars as a Korean war veteran who keeps his heroin addiction a secret from his pregnant wife Eva Marie Saint. Described by director Fred Zinnemann as "the grimmest of all the films I ever made," this pioneering study of drug addiction remains a powerful experience, gaining enormously from the moody black-and-white CinemaScope photography of New York, its documentary detail and from Bernard Herrmann's music. AT

Eva Marie Saint *Celia Pope* • Don Murray *Johnny Pope* • Anthony Franciosa *Polo* • Lloyd Nolan *John Pope Sr* • Henry Silva *Mother* • Gerald O'Loughlin [Gerald S O'Loughlin] *Chuck* • William Hickey *Apples* ■ *Dir* Fred Zinnemann • *Scr* Michael Vincent Gazzo, Alfred Hayes, Carl Foreman (uncredited), from the play by Michael Vincent Gazzo • *Cinematographer* Joe MacDonald

Hatter's Castle ★★★

Period drama 1941 · UK · BW · 103mins

Although certain liberties were taken with AJ Cronin's novel, this is nevertheless an enthralling melodrama that combines an oppressive Gothic atmosphere with some untethered Victorian bombast. Overshadowing such stars in the making as Deborah Kerr and James Mason, Robert Newton gnaws at the exquisitely designed scenery as the Glasgow hatter who drives his family to the verge of madness in order to line his pockets and juggle his love life. DP

Robert Newton *James Brodie* • Deborah Kerr *Mary Brodie* • Beatrice Varley *Mrs Brodie* • James Mason *Dr Renwick* • Emlyn Williams *Dennis* • Henry Oscar *Grierson* • Enid Stamp-Taylor *Nancy* ■ *Dir* Lance Comfort, James Carter • *Scr* Rodney Ackland, from the novel by AJ Cronin

Haunted ★★★ 15

Supernatural thriller
1995 · UK/US · Colour · 103mins

Right from the Edwardian prologue, a palpable air of malevolence hangs over this tale of murder, madness and memory. As the sceptic whose tragic past catches up with him as he investigates the supernatural at a Sussex stately home, Aidan Quinn gives a performance of substance and subtlety that perfectly complements the quirkier cameos of his co-stars. Kate Beckinsale makes a suitably creepy coquette and Anthony Andrews revels in his eccentricity, but topping the lot is Anna Massey's deliciously Danvers-esque nanny. DP. Contains a sex scene and nudity.

Aidan Quinn *David Ash* • Kate Beckinsale *Christina Mariell* • Anthony Andrews *Robert Mariell* • John Gielgud *Dr Doyle* • Anna Massey *Nanny Tess Webb* • Alex Lowe *Simon Mariell* • Geraldine Somerville *Kate* • Liz Smith *Old gypsy woman* ■ *Dir* Lewis Gilbert • *Scr* Tim Prager, Lewis Gilbert, Bob Kellet, from the novel by James Herbert

The Haunted Heart ★ 15

Horror 1995 · US · Colour · 91mins

This dire psycho-thriller stars Diane Ladd as a doting mother who murders anyone who suggests to her son Morgan Weisser that it's time for him to leave home and make his own way in the world. Limp slaughter matches the lame script in a forgettable bust. AJ

Diane Ladd *Olivia Hendrix* • Olympia Dukakis *Mrs Jay* • Morgan Weisser *Tom* • Ele Keats *Audrey* • Matt Clark *Ben Wilson* ■ *Dir* Frank LaLoggia • *Scr* Michael Angelella

Haunted Honeymoon ★ PG

Comedy horror 1986 · US · Colour · 79mins

While a funny actor, Gene Wilder is weighed down here by his own directorial incompetence. His attempt to emulate earlier haunted-house scare movies fails because he borrows too heavily from them. Noise wins over wit in this second-rate entry in the genre. Even Dom DeLuise can't save the day. JM

Gene Wilder *Larry Abbot* • Gilda Radner *Vickie Pearle* • Dom DeLuise *Aunt Kate* • Jonathan Pryce *Charles Abbot* • Paul L Smith [Paul Smith] *Dr Paul Abbot* • Peter Vaughan *Francis Sr* • Bryan Pringle *Pfister* • Roger Ashton-Griffiths *Francis Jr* • Jim Carter *Montego* • Eve Ferret *Sylvia* ■ *Dir* Gene Wilder • *Scr* Gene Wilder, Terence Marsh

The Haunted House of Horror ★★ 15

Horror 1969 · UK · Colour · 87mins

A psycho killer murders a Swinging Sixties' fashion victim at a happening in a suburban London mansion. Which of the 30-something actors playing teen revellers (including Frankie Avalon on a *Beach Party* vacation) is the crazed culprit? An effective shocker in its day – partly owing to some subtle gay overtones in the whodunnit aspects of the plot, but the only screams of terror this elicits now come from the trendy outfits. AJ DVD

Frankie Avalon *Chris* • Jill Haworth *Sheila* • Richard O'Sullivan *Peter* • Veronica Doran *Madge* • Julian Barnes *Richard* • Robin Stewart *Henry* • Mark Wynter *Gary* • Gina Warwick *Sylvia* • Clifford Earl *Police sergeant* ■ *Dir* Michael Armstrong • *Scr* Michael Armstrong, Peter Marcus

The Haunted Mansion ★★ PG

Comedy horror 2003 · US · Colour · 84mins

Another Disney theme-park-ride-derived movie, this saga can't escape the limitations of its funfair origins. Eddie Murphy plays a workaholic estate agent who interrupts the family holiday for a visit to a potential sale – a vast mansion that turns out to be haunted by a lovelorn ghost. If sumptuous photography and lavish production design were all a family-friendly horror comedy needed to get by, this would qualify as an inoffensive hit. However, it's an uninspired catalogue of fright-less genre clichés. AJ DVD

Eddie Murphy *Jim Evers* • Terence Stamp *Ramsley* • Nathaniel Parker *Master Edward Gracey* • Marsha Thomason *Sara Evers* • Jennifer Tilly *Madame Leota* • Wallace Shawn *Ezra* • Dina Waters *Emma* • Marc John Jefferies *Michael* • Aree Davis *Megan* ■ *Dir* Rob Minkoff • *Scr* David Berenbaum, from the Disney theme-park ride

The Haunted Palace ★★★ 18

Horror 1963 · US · Colour · 83mins

Enjoy a double dose of horror from the guru of ghoul, Vincent Price, who plays two characters in Roger Corman's creepy tale of curses; although the title is borrowed from an Edgar Allan Poe poem, the tale is based on an HP Lovecraft story. Price is at his deliciously evil best, wreaking terrible revenge on a local community. Horror veteran Lon Chaney Jr is also on hand to give his customary chilling support, playing Price's faithful servant. NF

Vincent Price *Charles Dexter Ward/Joseph Curwen* • Debra Paget *Ann Ward* • Lon Chaney Jr *Simon Orne* • Frank Maxwell *Dr Marinus Willet* • Leo Gordon *Edgar Weeden* • Elisha Cook [Elisha Cook Jr] *Peter Smith* ■ *Dir* Roger Corman • *Scr* Charles Beaumont, from the story *The Case of Charles Dexter Ward* by HP Lovecraft

Haunted Summer ★★ 18

Historical romantic drama
1988 · US · Colour · 102mins

Yet another treatment of the meeting between poets Byron and Shelley, writer Mary Godwin and Dr Polidori in Italy in 1816. Despite the acting efforts of Philip Anglim, Laura Dern, Alice Krige and Eric Stoltz, this tale makes unconvincing history. Director Ivan Passer seems determined to lower the drama just as Ken Russell, with the similarly themed *Gothic*, upped it. TH

Eric Stoltz *Percy Shelley* • Philip Anglim *Lord Byron* • Alice Krige *Mary Godwin* • Laura Dern *Claire Clairmont* • Alex Winter *John Polidori* • Peter Berling *Maurice* • Don Hodson *Rushton* ■ *Dir* Ivan Passer • *Scr* Lewis John Carlino, from the novel by Anne Edwards

The Haunting ★★★★★ 12

Horror 1963 · US/UK · BW · 107mins

This is one of the best supernatural chillers ever made. Richard Johnson plays the psychic researcher who brings along two mediums to help him investigate a monstrously haunted mansion steeped in spectral phenomena. All the more effective for keeping its horrors unseen, director Robert Wise's masterful adaptation of Shirley Jackson's *The Haunting of Hill House* is an exercise in invisible terror; all you see are pulsating walls and all you hear are loud pounding noises. Julie Harris shines as the spinster worst affected by the poltergeist events, whose psychological state is cleverly kept in question. AJ DVD

Julie Harris *Eleanor Vance* • Claire Bloom *Theodora* • Richard Johnson *Dr John Markway* • Russ Tamblyn *Luke Sanderson* • Fay Compton *Mrs Sanderson* • Rosalie Crutchley *Mrs Dudley* • Lois Maxwell *Grace Markway* • Valentine Dyall *Mr Dudley* • Diane Clare *Carrie Fredericks* ■ *Dir* Robert Wise • *Scr* Nelson Gidding, from the novel *The Haunting of Hill House* by Shirley Jackson

The Haunting ★★ 12

Supernatural horror
1999 · US · Colour · 107mins

Director Jan De Bont's remake of Robert Wise's 1963 classic is a frightless wonder, which isn't the least bit scary despite using computer-generated animation to show all the poltergeist activity (effectively unseen in the original, but yawningly overblown here). Hokey in the extreme, with a daft script and numerous unintentional laughs, only the beautifully designed baroque sets impress in this shallow spookfest. AJ DVD

Liam Neeson *Dr David Marrow* • Catherine Zeta-Jones *Theo* • Owen Wilson *Luke Sanderson* • Lili Taylor *Eleanor "Nell" Vance* • Bruce Dern *Mr Dudley* • Marian Seldes *Mrs Dudley* • Virginia Madsen *Jane* ■ *Dir* Jan De Bont • *Scr* David Self, from the novel *The Haunting of Hill House* by Shirley Jackson • *Production Designer* Eugenio Zanetti

Haunting Fear ★ 18

Horror drama 1990 · US · Colour · 84mins

A Poe-faced horror romp, loosely based on Edgar Allan's *The Premature Burial*, about a husband and mistress conniving to drive his wife (video "scream queen" Brinke Stevens) round the twist. Jan-Michael Vincent and Karen Black star in this schlocky horror picture show from B-movie master Fred Olen Ray, and you may recognise the faces of many fright stalwarts. DA

Jan-Michael Vincent *Lt James Trent* • Karen Black *Dr Julia Harcourt* • Jay Richardson *Terry Monroe* • Michael Berryman *Mortician* • Brinke Stevens *Victoria Monroe* • Robert Quarry *Visconti* ■ *Dir* Fred Olen Ray • *Scr* Sherman Scott [Sam Newfield], from the short story *The Premature Burial* by Edgar Allan Poe

The Haunting of Helen Walker ★★★ 15

Supernatural period drama
1995 · US · Colour · 87mins

Valerie Bertinelli looks somewhat out of place in this adaptation of Henry James's classic tale *The Turn of the Screw*. As you would expect of the prolific British TV dramatist Hugh Whitemore, this version includes a polished screenplay, but it lacks the palpable menace of Jack Clayton's 1961 version, *The Innocents*. Diana Rigg, Michael Gough and Paul Rhys add a touch of class beyond the dreams of most TV movies. DP

Valerie Bertinelli *Helen Walker* • Diana Rigg *Mrs Grose* • Florence Hoath *Flora Goffe* • Michael Gough *Barnaby* • Aled Roberts *Miles Goffe* • Paul Rhys *Edward Goffe* • Christopher Guard *Peter Quint* • Elizabeth Morton *Miss Jessel* ■ *Dir* Tom McLoughlin • *Scr* Hugh Whitemore, from the novel *The Turn of the Screw* by Henry James

The Haunting of Morella ★★★

Horror 1990 · US · Colour · 87mins

Roger Corman recaptures the energy and essence of his own Poe series from the 1960s in this production for his New Horizons company directed by Jim Wynorski. David McCallum lends great authority to his role as a blind New England recluse whose witch wife was burned at the stake. Unfortunately, her spirit returns in the body of her grown-up daughter and a new reign of terror begins. Tarted up with modish gore, lesbianism and grisly violence, this entertaining neo-Gothic romp is packed with cheap thrills and blood-letting. AJ. Contains violence, sex scenes and nudity.

David McCallum *Gideon* • Nicole Eggert *Morella/Lenora* • Christopher Halsted *Guy* • Lana Clarkson *Coel Deveroux* • Maria Ford *Diane* • Jonathan Farwell *Doctor Gault* ■ *Dir* Jim Wynorski • *Scr* RJ Robertson, from the story by Edgar Allan Poe

Hav Plenty ★★ 15

Romantic comedy
1998 · US · Colour · 83mins

Newcomer Christopher Scott Cherot writes, directs and stars in this gauche romantic comedy. Lee Plenty (Cherot) is an aspiring writer who is suffering from writer's block and living in his car until his rich friend Havilland Savage (Chenoa Maxwell) invites him to Washington DC for New Year's Eve. That Hav and Plenty will make a lovely couple is a truth that seems to evade everyone except Hav's gran and, of course, the audience. FL. Contains swearing and sex scenes.

Christopher Scott Cherot *Lee Plenty* • Chenoa Maxwell *Havilland Savage* • Hill Harper *Michael Simmons* • Tammi Katherine Jones *Caroline Gooden* • Robinne Lee *Leigh Darling* ■ *Dir/Scr* Christopher Scott Cherot

Havana ★★★ 15

Romantic thriller
1990 · US · Colour · 138mins

Robert Redford's seventh collaboration with director Sydney Pollack was one of the box-office bombs of the 1990s. But this *Casablanca* clone makes for polished, if occasionally pedestrian, entertainment. As there's surprisingly little passion between Redford and his co-star Lena Olin, the main interest here lies in the excellence of the supporting cast, with Alan Arkin typically assured as a shady casino boss, Raul Julia convincing as Olin's pro-Communist husband and Tomas Milian truly unnerving as the brutal police chief. DP. Contains swearing, violence and sex scenes. DVD

Robert Redford *Jack Weil* • Lena Olin *Roberta "Bobby" Duran* • Alan Arkin *Joe Volpi* • Tomas Milian *Menocal* • Daniel Davis *Marion Chigwell* • Tony Plana *Julio Ramos* • Betsy Brantley *Diane* • Lise Cutter *Patty* • Raul Julia *Arturo Duran* • Mark Rydell *Meyer Lansky* ■ *Dir* Sydney Pollack • *Scr* Judith Rascoe, David Rayfiel, from a story by Judith Rascoe

Havana Widows ★★

Comedy 1933 · US · BW · 63mins

In most respects this is a *Gold Diggers* movie with Joan Blondell, but one misses the songs and those suggestive Busby Berkeley dance routines. Blondell and Glenda Farrell play unemployed chorus girls on the loose in Cuba and looking for sugardaddies after they borrow some cash from their gangster friends. Fans of this sort of movie will find it funny and charmingly raffish. AT

Joan Blondell *Mae Knight* • Glenda Farrell *Sadie Appleby* • Guy Kibbee *Deacon Jones* • Lyle Talbot *Bob Jones* • Allen Jenkins *Herman Brody* ■ *Dir* Ray Enright • *Scr* Earl Baldwin

Have Rocket, Will Travel ★★ U

Science-fiction comedy
1959 · US · BW · 76mins

As their movie contract with Columbia came to an end, the Three Stooges thought their careers were over, but this juvenile romp in outer space put them back on top as firm family favourites. The trio (with new Stooge Joe De Rita) play cleaners at a rocket base who accidentally send themselves to Venus, where they encounter a talking unicorn, a brain machine, a flame-throwing giant spider and doppelgangers of themselves. This silly, aimless fun substitutes painful sight gags and weird sound effects for wit and invention. AJ

Moe Howard *Moe* • Larry Fine *Larry* • Joe De Rita *Curley Joe* • Jerome Cowan *JP Morse* • Anna-Lisa *Dr Ingrid Naarveg* • Bob Colbert [Robert Colbert] *Dr Ted Benson* ■ *Dir* David Lowell Rich • *Scr* Raphael Hayes

Having Wonderful Time ★★★

Romance 1938 · US · BW · 69mins

Arthur Kober's satirical play about Jewish New Yorkers on holiday in the Catskills lost much of its nuance in this movie version – despite being adapted by Kober himself – but it certainly benefited from a sparkling RKO cast, headed by the marvellous Ginger Rogers and Lucille Ball. The film is a veritable treasure trove for fans of the period: that's Dean Jagger as Ginger's brother, plus Eve Arden and Ann Miller among the holidaymakers. Red Skelton, billed as Richard, makes an impressive feature debut, and most of the folks at Camp Kare-Free, for that matter, will seem like old buddies. TS

Ginger Rogers *Teddy Shaw* • Douglas Fairbanks Jr *Chick Kirkland* • Peggy Conklin *Fay Coleman* • Lucille Ball *Miriam* • Lee Bowman *Buzzy Armbuster* • Eve Arden *Henrietta* • Dorothea Kent *Maxine* • Richard Skelton [Red Skelton] *Itchy Faulkner* • Dean Jagger *Charlie* ■ *Dir* Alfred Santell • *Scr* Arthur Kober, from his play

H

Hawa ★★★ 15

Supernatural mystery thriller
2003 · Ind · Colour · 127mins

This supernatural chiller transfers the supposedly fact-based action of the 1981 sleeper *The Entity* to an Indian hill station where a divorced mother of two helps run the family antique shop. Tabu occasionally struggles to convince as the woman whose life begins to unravel after she claims to have been raped by an unseen force, but director Guddu Dhanoa sustains the sinister atmosphere to disconcerting effect. DP. A Hindi language film. DVD

Tabu *Sanjana* • Shahbaaz Khan *Doctor* • Mukesh Tiwari *Psychiatrist* • Imran Khan *Sanjana's brother* • Grusha Kapoor *Pooja* ■ *Dir* Guddu Dhanoa • *Scr* Sutanu Gupta, from his story

Hawaii ★★★ PG

Period drama 1966 · US · Colour · 181mins

The fact that this adaptation of James Michener's novel was nominated for seven Oscars and won none is a clue that here is a big empty movie which middlebrow Hollywood felt had something significant to say. Packed with tempestuous love affairs, natural disasters, culture clashes and slick action sequences, the film does little more than transfer the familiar western pioneering theme to the Pacific island. This meander through 20 years of the 19th century would be intolerably dull without the towering performance of Max von Sydow, who almost makes his unyielding missionary sympathetic in spite of his monstrous views. DP

Max von Sydow *Abner Hale* • Julie Andrews *Jerusha Bromley* • Richard Harris *Rafer Hoxworth* • Carroll O'Connor *Charles Bromley* • Elizabeth Cole *Abigail Bromley* • Diane Sherry *Charity Bromley* • Heather Menzies *Mercy Bromley* • Torin Thatcher *Reverend Thorn* • Gene Hackman *John Whipple* ■ *Dir* George Roy Hill • *Scr* Dalton Trumbo, Daniel Taradash, from the novel by James Michener

The Hawaiians ★

Period drama 1970 · US · Colour · 133mins

This bland family saga is unenlivened by location shooting and the reuniting of the star (Charlton Heston) and director (Tom Gries) of the classic western *Will Penny*. For its UK premier (under the title *Master of the Islands*), a huge cardboard cut-out of Heston stood outside the London Pavilion. Today, that cardboard figure seems to symbolise the movie, and the publicity stunt was certainly far more entertaining than the film itself. TS

Charlton Heston *Whip Hoxworth* • Geraldine Chaplin *Purity Hoxworth* • John Phillip Law *Noel Hoxworth* • Tina Chen *Nyuk Tsin* • Alec McCowen *Micah Hale* • Mako *Mun Ki* • Don Knight *Milton Overpeck* ■ *Dir* Tom Gries • *Scr* James R Webb, from the novel *Hawaii* by James A Michener

The Hawk ★★★ 15

Thriller 1992 · UK · Colour · 83mins

Rumour has it that this intriguing home-grown movie was inspired by the Yorkshire Ripper investigation of the late 1970s and early 80s. Helen Mirren stars as the North East housewife who begins to suspect that there's a link between a series of murders and her husband's business trips, but her fragile mental health means that no one will believe her. The quality of the performances gives this overly bleak and murky thriller some much needed depth and spark. SH. Contains swearing, violence, nudity and drug abuse. DVD

Helen Mirren *Annie Marsh* • George Costigan *Stephen Marsh* • Rosemary Leach *Mrs Marsh* • Melanie Hill *Norma* • Owen Teale *Ken Marsh* • Clive Russell *Chief Inspector Daybury* • Christopher Madin *Matthew Marsh* • Marie Hamer *Jackie Marsh* • David Harewood *Sergeant Streete* • Pooky Quesnel *WPC Clarke* • Caroline Paterson *Jan* • John Duttine *John* • Nadim Sawalha *Bahnu* ■ *Dir* David Hayman • *Scr* Peter Ransley, from his novel

Hawk the Slayer ★ PG

Fantasy adventure
1980 · UK · Colour · 89mins

Not so much swords and sorcery as rubber rapiers and woeful witchcraft, as good brother John Terry battles with bad brother Jack Palance for possession of a mystic blade. Gimmicky direction by Terry Marcel can't hide the low budget of this production, debased by trite ideas and a banal approach. TH DVD

Jack Palance *Voltan* • John Terry *Hawk* • Bernard Bresslaw *Gort* • Ray Charleson *Crow* • Peter O'Farrell *Baldin* • Morgan Sheppard *Ranulf* • Cheryl Campbell *Sister Monica* • Annette Crosbie *Abbess* • Roy Kinnear *Innkeeper* • Warren Clarke *Scar* ■ *Dir* Terry Marcel • *Scr* Harry Robertson, Terry Marcel

Hawken's Breed ★★

Western 1989 · US · Colour · 93mins

Low-budget western that looks like it was shot in someone's back garden. The main interest resides in its always watchable star, Peter Fonda, sadly reduced to making B-movies like this during his "wilderness" years. Veteran cowboy actor Jack Elam also appears. Director Charles B Pierce specialises in such genre no-budgeters. DA

Peter Fonda *Hawken* • Jack Elam *Tackett* • Bill Thurman *Jeb Kline* • Serene Hedin *Spirit* • Chuck Pierce Jr *Noel Hickman* • Sue Anne Langdon [Sue Ane Langdon] *Holly Clawson* • Dennis Fimple *Crawley* ■ *Dir/Scr* Charles B Pierce

Hawks ★★★ 15

Black comedy drama
1988 · UK · Colour · 105mins

Timothy Dalton stars in this modest little black comedy set in London and the Netherlands. He's a charismatic lawyer stricken with cancer, who lifts fellow sufferer Anthony Edwards out of his gloom and whisks him away to Amsterdam for one final fling. Sentimentality is never far from the surface, but the enthusiastic playing of the two stars overcomes the more mawkish moments, and there are refreshing turns from Camille Coduri and Janet McTeer as the two English girls they meet on the continent. JF. Contains swearing.

Timothy Dalton *Bancroft* • Anthony Edwards *Deckermensky, "Decker"* • Janet McTeer *Hazel* • Camille Coduri *Maureen* • Julie T Wallace *Ward sister* • Connie Booth *Nurse Jarvis* • Robert Lang *Walter Bancroft* • Jill Bennett *Vivian Bancroft* • Sheila Hancock *Regina* • Caroline Langrishe *Carol* ■ *Dir* Robert Ellis Miller • *Scr* Roy Clarke, from an idea by Barry Gibb, David English

Hawks and Sparrows ★★★★ PG

Fantasy 1966 · It · BW · 84mins

Working for the last time in monochrome, Pier Paolo Pasolini conceived this allegorical fantasy as a showcase for the legendary comic actor, Toto, and newcomer Ninetto Davoli. In addition to playing a couple of modern-day vagabonds, they also appear in a parable related by a talking crow, in which a pair of 12th-century monks are detailed by St Francis of Assisi to convert the birds to Christianity. Their lack of success in the parable is reflected back in the present day as Pasolini parodies Fellini, Rossellini and himself, and in so doing rejects Marxism, Catholicism and neorealism as the answer to Italy's problems. With excellent music from Ennio Morricone, this is one of the controversial director's more humorous offerings. DP. Italian dialogue dubbed into English.

Toto *Innocenti Toto/Brother Ciccillo* • Ninetto Davoli *Innocenti Ninetto/Brother Ninetto* • Femi Benussi *Luna* • Rossana Di Rocco *Ninetto's friend* • Lena Lin Solaro *Urganda la Sconosciuta* ■ *Dir/Scr* Pier Paolo Pasolini

Hawmps ★★ PG

Comedy western
1976 · US · Colour · 113mins

Sounds funny: a cavalry troop switching to camels for transport. Despite being based on a true incident, the camel corps idea is not enough to sustain a film, and it shows. Slim Pickens, who rode the bomb to destruction in *Dr Strangelove*, joins the slapstick. How long can you watch before getting the hump? NF

James Hampton *Howard Clemmons* • Christopher Connelly *Uriah Tibbs* • Slim Pickens *Naman Tucker* • Denver Pyle *Colonel Seymour Hawkins* • Gene Conforti *Hi Jolly* • Mimi Maynard *Jennifer Hawkins* • Jack Elam *Bad Jack Cutter* ■ *Dir* Joe Camp • *Scr* William Bickley, Michael Warren, from a story by Joe Camp, William Bickley, Michael Warren

Häxan ★★★★ 15

Silent horror documentary
1921 · Swe · BW · 87mins

Danish director Benjamin Christensen's documentary-style investigation into *Witchcraft through the Ages* (the English title) employs an array of cinematic devices, with etchings, manuscripts and re-enacted episodes (in which Christensen himself plays the Devil). Three years in the making, the film sees the witch as a harmless victim of a superstitious and repressive Church. This illuminating, frightening and amusing film was banned in some countries at the time, ostensibly because of its violence and nudity, but its anticlericalism might have weighed more heavily with the censors. It was Christensen's most famous film; he subsequently directed a few minor horror films in Hollywood in the late 1920s. RB

Benjamin Christensen *The Devil/The fashionable doctor* • Ella La Cour *Karna, the witch* • Emmy Schönfeld *Karna's collaborator* • Kate Fabian *Lovesick maiden* ■ *Dir/Scr* Benjamin Christensen

The Hazing ★ 15

Drama 1977 · US · Colour · 84mins

Imagine *National Lampoon's Animal House* without the jokes or a decent director. That's this dud, which sounds like a horror film but isn't, although it does use the stalk-and-slash plot staple of a college fraternity initiation prank that goes wrong, killing a student. Douglas Curtis makes his directing debut with this hazily executed melodrama. AJ

Charlie Martin Smith [Charles Martin Smith] *Barney* • Jeff East *Craig* • Brad David *Rod* • Kelly Moran *Wendy* • David Hayward *Carl* ■ *Dir* Douglas Curtis • *Scr* Bruce Shelley, David Ketchum

He Got Game ★★★★ 15

Sports drama 1998 · US · Colour · 130mins

This superb sports drama from writer/director Spike Lee sets out to prove that basketball is not just a game, but rather an essential part of the American way of life. From the opening shots of young men at obsessive play, set to music by Aaron Copland, Lee sets the tone of a world in which Jake Shuttlesworth (a powerful portrayal by Denzel Washington) is allowed out of prison – where he's serving a term for his wife's manslaughter – to talk his son Jesus (real-life pro Ray Allen), into becoming part of the prison warden's old college basketball team, and get himself paroled into the bargain. The confrontations feel real, the games have tension and the underlying message is universally scathing – sport is no longer for kudos, but purely for the money. TH. Contains swearing, sex scenes and violence.

Denzel Washington *Jake Shuttlesworth* • Ray Allen *Jesus Shuttlesworth* • Milla Jovovich *Dakota Burns* • Rosario Dawson *Lala Bonilla* • Hill Harper *Coleman "Booger" Sykes* • Ned Beatty *Warden Wyatt* • Jim Brown *Spivey* • Bill Nunn *Uncle Bubba* • John Turturro *Coach Billy Sunday* • Lonette McKee *Martha Shuttlesworth* ■ *Dir/Scr* Spike Lee

He Knows You're Alone ★★ 18

Thriller 1981 · US · Colour · 89mins

Recycling an idea from the Bela Lugosi shocker *The Corpse Vanishes* in 1942, this predictably heavy-handed slasher movie has a killer stalking brides-to-be, terrorising them with increasingly ugly games of cat-and-mouse. No real surprises here, unless you count the fact that the director Armand Mastroianni is the late Marcello's cousin, and a young Tom Hanks makes his film acting debut. AJ. Contains violence.

Don Scardino *Marvin* • Caitlin O'Heaney *Amy Jensen* • Elizabeth Kemp *Nancy* • Tom Rolfing *Killer* • Lewis Arlt *Len Gamble* • Patsy Pease *Joyce* • James Rebhorn *Carl* • Tom Hanks *Elliot* • Paul Gleason *Daley* ■ *Dir* Armand Mastroianni • *Scr* Scott Parker

He Laughed Last ★★

Comedy 1956 · US · Colour · 76mins

Blake Edwards's second outing as a writer/director is a satire on the gangster movie. Recording star Frankie Laine plays a nightclub owner whose employee Lucy Marlow is a dancer and hostess who inherits a mobster's fortune, much to the dismay of her policeman boyfriend. There are musical numbers, fun with gangster conventions and Marlow is a dish, but it doesn't disguise the fact that this is a dime-budget offering. AT

Frankie Laine *Gino Lupo* • Lucy Marlow *Rosemary Lebeau* • Anthony Dexter *Dominic* • Dick Long [Richard Long] *Jimmy Murphy* • Alan Reed *Big Dan Hennessy* ■ *Dir* Blake Edwards • *Scr* Blake Edwards, from a story by Blake Edwards, Richard Quine

He Loves Me... He Loves Me Not ★★★ 12

Romantic thriller 2002 · Fr · Colour · 92mins

French director Laetitia Colombani's beautifully crafted debut is a romantic thriller split into interconnected halves. In the first segment, Audrey Tautou edges towards *Fatal Attraction* territory, as her apparent affair with married cardiologist Samuel Le Bihan starts to sour. However, in the second segment, the story is replayed, this time from Le Bihan's viewpoint, and previously innocuous events take on a very different and unexpected meaning. Anchored by two strong central performances, this tightly coiled treat is a chilling mass of contradictions and surprises. SF. In French with English subtitles. DVD

Audrey Tautou *Angélique* • Samuel Le Bihan *Loïc* • Isabelle Carré *Rachel* • Clément Sibony *David* • Sophie Guillemin *Héloïse* • Eric Savin *Julien* • Michèle Garay *Claire Belmont* • Elodie Navarre *Anita* ■ *Dir* Laetitia Colombani • *Scr* Laetitia Colombani, Caroline Thivel

He Ran All the Way ★★★

Crime drama 1951 · US · BW · 77mins

John Garfield's final role saw him give a typically intense performance as a thug on the run after a payroll robbery. Life seems to be improving when he (briefly) finds sanctuary with Shelley Winters. Then Garfield's tendency to panic leaves Winters to choose between her father and her lover. A happy ending seems unlikely, however, as was the case with the actor, whose career suffered during the Communist witch-hunts in 1950s' Hollywood. JM

John Garfield *Nick* • Shelley Winters *Peg* • Wallace Ford *Mr Dobbs* • Selena Royle *Mrs Dobbs* • Gladys George *Mrs Robey* • Norman Lloyd *Al Molin* • Bobby Hyatt *Tommy Dobbs* ■ *Dir* John Berry • *Scr* Guy Endore, Hugo Butler, from the novel by Sam Ross

He Rides Tall ★★

Western 1964 · US · BW · 83mins

Tony Young was an American TV star in a violent (for its time) western series called *Gunslinger*, and Universal released two vehicles for him theatrically: this one, a stark, grim story that was X-rated in the UK, and a companion piece called *Taggart*. This is the (marginally) better of the two, but Young simply didn't have what it takes to be a movie star. TS

Tony Young *Marshal Morg Rocklin* • Dan Duryea *Bart Thorne* • Jo Morrow *Kate McCloud* • Madlyn Rhue *Ellie Daniels* • RG Armstrong *Josh McCloud* ■ *Dir* RG Springsteen • *Scr* Charles W Irwin, Robert Creighton Williams [Bob Williams], from a story by Charles W Irwin

He Said, She Said ★★★ 15

Comedy 1991 · US · Colour · 110mins

Two warring TV talk show hosts (Kevin Bacon and Elizabeth Perkins) carry on their relationship both in front of and behind the cameras. The film is split into two halves (one directed by Ken Kwapis, the other by his wife Marisa Silver) so you see the romance from each point of view. Both Bacon and Perkins are attractively amiable, but neither manages to sustain the comedy and, after part one, it does get a bit tedious. JB. Contains some swearing. DVD

Kevin Bacon *Dan Hanson* • Elizabeth Perkins *Lorie Bryer* • Sharon Stone *Linda* • Nathan Lane *Wally Thurman* • Anthony LaPaglia *Mark* • Stanley Anderson *Mr Weller* • Brad Pitt ■ *Dir* Ken Kwapis, Marisa Silver • *Scr* Brian Hohlfeld, from his story

He Walked by Night ★★★ PG

Thriller 1948 · US · BW · 78mins

One of those economic miracles – a B-thriller made for peanuts which manages to create some vivid images and a high degree of tension. Its success is mainly owing to ace cameraman John Alton, a master of black-and-white moodiness, while Anthony Mann is thought to have given credited director Alfred Werker a hand. Richard Basehart stars as a thief who kills a cop and is tracked down by the Los Angeles police. Much emphasis is placed on detection methods and on Basehart's personality in a compelling character study that also delivers in terms of action. AT

Richard Basehart *Davis Morgan* • Scott Brady *Sergeant Marty Brennan* • Roy Roberts *Captain Breen* • James Cardwell *Chuck Jones* • Whit Bissell *Reeves* ■ *Dir* Alfred Werker • *Scr* John C Higgins, Crane Wilbur, Harry Essex, from a story by Crane Wilbur • *Cinematographer* John Alton

He Was Her Man ★★★

Crime drama 1934 · US · BW · 70mins

Snappy, exuberant, Roaring Twenties-like thriller, with James Cagney as the safecracker who gives up a life of crime to scare off rivals who've been trying to put him inside. Joan Blondell is the wisecracker who stands by him and pulls him through, while Lloyd Bacon directs in the tradition of machine-gun macho. TH

James Cagney *Flicker Hayes* • Joan Blondell *Rose Lawrence* • Victor Jory *Nick Gardella* • Frank Craven *Pop Sims* • Harold Huber *JC Ward* • Russell Hopton *Monk* • Ralf Harolde *Red Deering* • Sarah Padden *Mrs Gardella* ■ *Dir* Lloyd Bacon • *Scr* Tom Buckingham, Niven Busch, from a story by Robert Lord

He Who Gets Slapped ★★★★★

Silent drama 1924 · US · BW · 72mins

Lon Chaney Sr gives one of his best performances in the film version of Leonid Andreyev's Broadway success. The Man of a Thousand Faces plays a disillusioned scientist whose professional disappointments force him to alter his appearance and join the circus as a clown. But instead of finding happiness and freedom in a world of total make-believe, he soon discovers a different grief lies hidden beneath the greasepaint and tinsel. Beautifully told, and flawlessly directed by Victor Sjöström (making his second film in the US), this is a poetic silent masterpiece. AJ

Lon Chaney *Paul Beaumont/"He Who Gets Slapped"* • Norma Shearer *Consuelo* • John Gilbert (1) *Bezano* • Tully Marshall *Count Mancini* • Marc MacDermott *Baron Regnard* • Ford Sterling *Tricaud* ■ *Dir* Victor Seastrom [Victor Sjöström] • *Scr* Carey Wilson, Victor Seastrom [Victor Sjöström], from the play *He, the One Who Gets Slapped* by Leonid Andreyev, translated by Gregory Zilboorg

He Who Rides a Tiger ★★

Crime drama 1965 · UK · BW · 102mins

This crime melodrama is a "kitchen sink" tale – overflowing with soap – that's as unpredictable as its cat burglar protagonist, played by Tom Bell. One moment he's soft on orphans and the eager Judi Dench; the next he's stealing jewels from stately homes and erupting into demented violence. Bell admirably combines both personality traits in his performance, but the shifts from realism to romanticism in Trevor Peacock's script are less credible. DP

Tom Bell *Peter Rayston* • Judi Dench *Joanne* • Paul Rogers *Superintendent Taylor* • Kay Walsh *Mrs Woodley* • Ray McAnally *Orphanage superintendent* • Jeremy Spenser *The Panda* • Peter Madden *Peepers Woodley* ■ *Dir* Charles Crichton • *Scr* Trevor Peacock

Head ★★★★ PG

Musical comedy 1968 · US · Colour · 85mins

Bob Rafelson had been the brains behind the Monkees, the American pop group formed in the image of the Beatles specifically for an NBC TV series. With the band's popularity on the wane, he and co-writer Jack Nicholson fashioned this psychedelic romp that beefed up the usual bubblegum slapstick with Vietnam footage and old movie clips. It went over the heads of most fans in 1968, but it's essential viewing for anyone who knows all the words to the Monkees' theme tune. DP DVD

Annette Funicello *Minnie* • Timothy Carey *Lord Highn'Low* • Logan Ramsey *Officer Faye Lapid* • Abraham Sofaer *Swami* • Sonny Liston • Carol Doda *Sally Silicone* • Frank Zappa *Critic* • June Fairchild *Jumper* • Victor Mature *Big Victor* • Teri Garr *Testy True* • Peter Tork • David Jones [Davy Jones] *David Jones* • Micky Dolenz • Michael Nesmith ■ *Dir* Bob Rafelson • *Scr* Jack Nicholson, Bob Rafelson

Head above Water ★ 15

Comedy mystery thriller
1996 · US/UK · Colour · 88mins

Jim Wilson, producer of Kevin Costner hits such as *The Bodyguard* and *Dances with Wolves*, came a cropper with this modest but thoroughly unfunny black comedy, a remake of a little known Norwegian film. Harvey Keitel and Cameron Diaz are the mismatched newlyweds who fast fall out when the latter's ex (Billy Zane) turns up. Wilson never gets a handle on the underwritten script, and the talented performers are reduced to unfunny mugging. JF

Harvey Keitel *George* • Cameron Diaz *Nathalie* • Craig Sheffer *Lance* • Billy Zane *Kent* • Shay Duffin *Policeman* • Mo *Mo, the bird* ■ *Dir* Jim Wilson (2) • *Scr* Theresa Marie, from the film *Hodet over Vannet* by Geir Eriksen, Eirik Ildahl

Head of State ★★ 12

Comedy 2003 · US · Colour · 91mins

In this political satire, Chris Rock stars as a black presidential candidate deliberately handpicked to bolster opposition votes. He also makes his directorial debut, co-writes and produces. There's no subtlety as he saturates the strength-through-adversity storyline with patronising stereotypes, repetitive sight gags and his customary quick-fire retorts. Though his concise observations on social decay are wryly amusing, the humour overall is clumsy. SF. Contains swearing. DVD

Chris Rock *Mays Gilliam* • Bernie Mac *Mitch Gilliam* • Dylan Baker *Martin Geller* • Nick Searcy *Brian Lewis* • Lynn Whitfield *Debra Lassiter* • Robin Givens *Kim* • Tamala Jones *Lisa Clark* • James Rebhorn *Senator Bill Arnot* • Keith David *Bernard Cooper* ■ *Dir* Chris Rock • *Scr* Ali LeRoi, Chris Rock

Head Office ★ 15

Comedy 1986 · US · Colour · 87mins

In this trite comedy Judge Reinhold plays an inept bod, inveigled into a job in a top multinational company where he is used and abused, but still falls for his company director's daughter Lori-Nan Engler. Sadly Reinhold fails to be funny enough to carry the movie and the only sparky moments are down to support characters Don Novello and Richard Masur. Both Rick Moranis and Danny DeVito are killed off in the first 20 minutes, which is one of the movie's many mistakes. LH

Eddie Albert *Helmes* • Danny DeVito *Stedman* • Lori-Nan Engler *Rachael* • Don King • Don Novello *Sal* • Judge Reinhold *Jack Issel* • Jane Seymour (2) *Jane* • Wallace Shawn *Hoover* • Rick Moranis *Gross* ■ *Dir/Scr* Ken Finkleman

Head On ★★★

Comedy drama 1980 · Can · Colour · 86mins

Sally Kellerman and Stephen Lack star in this bizarre but sometimes intriguing drama about two drivers who are involved in a head-on crash and then become lovers. Both like playing dangerous games, both sexual and otherwise, and soon the stakes begin to rise as the film flits between tension and comedy. Originally known as *Fatal Attraction*, this is an interestingly quirky movie lent weight by the lead performances and the supporting cast, which includes John Huston. JB

Sally Kellerman *Michelle Keys* • Stephen Lack *Peter Hill* • John Huston *Clarke Hill* • Lawrence Dane *Frank Keys* • John Peter Linton *Gad Bernstein* • Hadley Kay *Stanley* • Robert Silverman *Michelle's analyst* • Maxwell Moffett *Henry* ■ *Dir* Michael Grant • *Scr* James Sanderson, Paul Illidge

Head On ★★ 18

Drama 1997 · Aus · Colour · 99mins

It's hard to see how writer/director Ana Kokkinos could have made her raw study of being young, gay and Greek in Melbourne any more abrasive. She and actor Alex Dimitriades deserve credit for making the central character so antiheroic, as he spurns cultural identity and social stability for a nihilistic diet of drugs and rough trade. DP. In English and Greek with subtitles. Contains drug abuse, sex scenes, swearing. DVD

Alex Dimitriades *Ari* • Paul Capsis *Johnny, "Toula"* • Julian Garner *Sean* • Elena Mandalis *Betty* • Tony Nikolakopoulos *Dimitri* • Damien Fotiou *Joe* • Eugenia Fragos *Sofia* • Dora Kaskanis *Dina* ■ *Dir* Ana Kokkinos • *Scr* Andrew Bovell, Ana Kokkinos, Mira Robertson, from the novel *Loaded* by Christos Tsiolkas

Head-On ★★★★ 18

Romantic drama
2003 · Ger/Tur · Colour · 121mins

Fatih Akin's award-winning marital drama explores the extent to which Germany's Turkish population retains its national identity. Making evocative use of both Hamburg and Istanbul, Akin creates a genuine sense of community, as hard-drinking 40-something Birol Unel and parentally repressed Sibel Kekilli contract a marriage of convenience that initially suits both parties. But as Unel becomes increasingly jealous of the liberated Kekilli's string of lovers, they come to view the relationship in very different terms. The leads are excellent, with the debuting Kekilli particularly impressive. DP. In German, Turkish and English with subtitles. Contains swearing, sex scenes and drug abuse.

Birol Unel *Cahit Tomruk* • Sibel Kekilli *Sibel Guner* • Catrin Striebeck *Maren* • Guven Kirac *Seref* • Meltem Cumbul *Selma* • Cem Akin *Yilmaz Guner* • Aysel Iscan *Birsen Guner* • Demir Gokgol *Yunus Guner* ■ *Dir/Scr* Fatih Akin

Head over Heels ★★ 12

Romantic comedy
2000 · US · Colour · 82mins

Teen heart-throb Freddie Prinze Jr co-stars here with Monica Potter in a romantic comedy that starts off amusingly but sinks into mediocrity. Potter plays an unlucky-in-love art curator who moves into a luxury New York flat with four supermodels. It's not long before she then falls for neighbour Prinze Jr, that is until she sees him apparently club someone to death. Misunderstandings and nods to *Rear Window* run roughshod through what is left of the plot. LH DVD

Monica Potter *Amanda* • Freddie Prinze Jr *Jim Winston* • China Chow *Lisa* • Shalom Harlow *Jade* • Ivana Milicevic *Roxana* • Sarah O'Hare *Candi* ■ *Dir* Mark S Waters [Mark Waters] • *Scr* Ron Burch, David Kidd, from a story by Ron Burch, David Kidd, John J Strauss, Ed Decter

Head over Heels in Love ★★★ U

Musical 1937 · UK · BW · 78mins

Having made her movie name under the direction of Victor Saville, Jessie Matthews went to work for her four-time co-star and then husband Sonnie Hale, whose first outing behind the camera this was. The story centres on Jessie's inability to make up her mind between suitors Robert Flemyng and Louis Borell. Unfortunately, neither comes across as anyone to lose sleep over, and Hale's inexperience shows away from the musical numbers. Alfred Junge's sets give the film a sophistication too often missing from British musicals of the period. DP

Jessie Matthews *Jeanne* • Robert Flemyng *Pierre* • Louis Borell *Marcel* • Romney Brent *Matty* • Helen Whitney Bourne *Norma* • Paul Leyssac *Max* • Eliot Makeham *Martin* ■ *Dir* Sonnie Hale • *Scr* Fred Thompson, Dwight Taylor, Marjorie Gaffney, from the play *Pierre ou Jac* by François de Crosset

HEALTH ★★★

Satirical comedy
1980 · US · Colour · 102mins

One of director Robert Altman's social comedies, which exemplifies the maxim that they shall have muesli wherever they go. It's set at a health food convention as its members try to elect a new president, though political corruption is Altman's target for satire. Among the wild and wacky women of whom Altman seems very fond are Glenda Jackson, Lauren Bacall – playing an 83-year-old virgin – and Carol Burnett. James Garner is engagingly macho in contrast. The pile-up of off-the-wall jokes does get a bit tiresome by the end, however. TH

Glenda Jackson *Isabella Garnell* • Carol Burnett *Gloria Burbank* • James Garner *Harry Wolff* • Lauren Bacall *Esther Brill* • Dick Cavett • Paul Dooley *Dr Gil Gainey* • Henry Gibson *Bobby Hammer* • Alfre Woodard *Hotel manager* ■ *Dir* Robert Altman • *Scr* Frank Barhydt, Paul Dooley, Robert Altman

H

Hear My Song ★★★★ 15

Comedy drama 1991 · UK · Colour · 109mins

Just when you think they don't make 'em like that any more, debutant director Peter Chelsom comes along and proves that they most certainly do. This is a delicious confection, with just the right amounts of "Oirish" whimsy, Scouse nous, bittersweet romance and broad comedy. Adrian Dunbar is the personification of impudent charm as the club owner seeking the tax-exiled tenor Josef Locke (played with gruff amiability by Ned Beatty). The Irish sequences get the nod over those set in Liverpool; how could a run-in with a mystery singer hope to compete with a runaway cow? A treat. DP. Contains some violence, swearing, nudity.

Ned Beatty *Josef Locke* • Adrian Dunbar *Micky O'Neill* • Shirley Anne Field *Cathleen Doyle* • Tara FitzGerald *Nancy Doyle* • William Hootkins *Mr X* • Harold Berens *Benny Rose* • David McCallum *Jim Abbott* • John Dair *Derek* • Norman Vaughan • James Nesbitt *Fintan O'Donnell* ■ *Dir* Peter Chelsom • *Scr* Peter Chelsom, Adrian Dunbar, from a story by Peter Chelsom

Hear No Evil ★ 15

Thriller 1993 · US · Colour · 92mins

This dismal stalker thriller has deaf personal trainer Marlee Matlin being pursued by cop Martin Sheen and a creepy man in black. Both of them want to get their hands on a rare coin she doesn't even know she has. It's tedious and annoying fare, packed with every cliché imaginable but little else of interest. JB. Contains violence and swearing.

Marlee Matlin *Jillian Shanahan* • DB Sweeney *Ben Kendall* • Martin Sheen *Lieutenant Philip Brock* • John C McGinley *Mickey O'Malley* ■ *Dir* Robert Greenwald • *Scr* RM Badat [Randall Badat], Kathleen Rowell, from a story by Danny Rubin, RM Badat [Randall Badat]

The Hearse ★★ 15

Horror 1980 · US · Colour · 95mins

Trish Van Devere inherits a house from an aunt that turns out to be haunted by a witch who looks exactly like her. The plot is thickened by a hearse that drives itself and Joseph Cotten as the local estate agent. Tthis wouldn't make a grasshopper jump, but it's nicely made and features Cotten in his last major role. AT DVD

Trish Van Devere *Jane Hardy* • Joseph Cotten *Walter Pritchard* • David Gautreaux *Tom Sullivan* • Donald Hotton *Rev Winston* • Med Flory *Sheriff* ■ *Dir* George Bowers • *Scr* Bill Bleich, from an idea by Mark Tenser

Heart ★ 15

Sports drama 1987 · US · Colour · 90mins

As a weary retread of one of the best boxing movies ever – Robert Wise's 1949 film *The Set-Up* – this has lost all grip. A pallid imitation of a vivid original, Brad Davis is the retired pugilist tricked into a comeback by slimy manager Steve Buscemi, while girlfriend Frances Fisher looks on aghast. As well she might: despite Buscemi's performance, this low-budget film never even begins to be a contender. TH DVD

Brad Davis *Eddie Brennan* • Frances Fisher *Jeannie* • Steve Buscemi *Nicky* • Robinson Frank Adu *Buddy* • Jesse Doran *Diddy* • Sam Gray *Leo* ■ *Dir* James Lemmo • *Scr* James Lemmo, Randy Jurgensen

Heart ★★★ 18

Psychological thriller
1997 · UK · Colour · 81mins

A gripping and unusual psychological thriller from the pen of ace TV scriptwriter Jimmy McGovern. In the *Cracker* creator's first work written expressly for the big screen, a devastated Saskia Reeves allows the heart of her beloved son, killed in an accident, to be given to Christopher Eccleston. It's when Reeves strikes up an uneasy relationship with Eccleston to ensure he is a worthy recipient that the really startling aspect of the story begins to take shape. For those not put off by some truly shocking twists or the graphic blood-letting and surgical detail, director Charles McDougall's dark passion play crackles with style, black humour and energy. AJ. Contains swearing, violence and sex scenes.

Christopher Eccleston *Gary Ellis* • Saskia Reeves *Marie Ann McCardle* • Kate Hardie *Tess Ellis* • Rhys Ifans *Alex Madden* • Anna Chancellor *Nicola Farmer* • Bill Paterson *Mr Kreitman* • Matthew Rhys *Sean McCardle* • Jack Deam *Policeman* ■ *Dir* Charles McDougall • *Scr* Jimmy McGovern

Heart and Souls ★★★ PG

Fantasy drama 1993 · US · Colour · 99mins

Four ghosts get the chance to tie up loose ends in their lives by taking over the body of uptight yuppie Robert Downey Jr, in director Ron Underwood's touching flight of comedy fantasy. Once over the far-too-elaborate set-up, this becomes a cosy whimsical fable with fewer signposted twists than initially anticipated. Endearing and sentimental, the highlight is Downey Jr's fabulously funny and versatile performance, with Tom Sizemore, Alfre Woodard, Kyra Sedgwick and Charles Grodin adding sparkling support as the spirits. AJ

Robert Downey Jr *Thomas Reilly* • Charles Grodin *Harrison Winslow* • Alfre Woodard *Penny Washington* • Kyra Sedgwick *Julia* • Tom Sizemore *Milo Peck* • David Paymer *Hal, the bus driver* • Elisabeth Shue *Anne* ■ *Dir* Ron Underwood • *Scr* Brent Maddock, SS Wilson, from a story by Brent Maddock, SS Wilson, from a screenplay (unproduced) by Eric Hansen, Gregory Hansen

Heart Beat ★★

Biographical drama
1979 · US · Colour · 108mins

Ambitious but ultimately doomed attempt to shed light on the stars of the Beat Generation, despite some extraordinary performances from the talented cast. This loosely biographical tale focuses on the strange relationship between Jack Kerouac (John Heard) and the Cassadys (Nick Nolte and Sissy Spacek), but although all three have rarely been better, director John Byrum seems at a loss to know where to develop the story. JF

Nick Nolte *Neal Cassady* • Sissy Spacek *Carolyn Cassady* • John Heard *Jack Kerouac* • Ray Sharkey *Ira* • Ann Dusenberry *Stevie* • Margaret Fairchild *Mrs Kerouac* • Tony Bill *Dick* ■ *Dir* John Byrum • *Scr* John Byrum, from memoirs by Carolyn Cassady

Heart Condition ★★★ 15

Action comedy 1990 · US · Colour · 95mins

Bob Hoskins and Denzel Washington star in this paranormal buddy movie as the mismatched pair – one alive, one a ghost. Hoskins, with the transplanted heart of Washington inside him, investigates the latter's death. Writer/director James D Parriott doesn't quite pull off the invisibility gags, nor does he allow his talented stars enough space to fill their characters. Despite its flaws, its sentimental heart is in the right place, if slightly out of condition. A pleasant enough time-waster. AJ. Contains swearing and violence.

Bob Hoskins *Jack Moony* • Denzel Washington *Napoleon Stone* • Chloe Webb *Crystal Gerrity* • Roger E Mosley *Captain Wendt* • Ja'net DuBois *Mrs Stone* • Alan Rachins *Dr Posner* • Ray Baker *Harry Zara* • Jeffrey Meek *John Graham* ■ *Dir/Scr* James D Parriott

The Heart Is a Lonely Hunter ★★★★ PG

Drama 1968 · US · Colour · 118mins

Set in a small Southern town, this is a compelling version of novelist Carson McCullers's acute study of the anxieties and aspirations of a disparate group of troubled characters. Alan Arkin gives an Oscar-nominated performance as the deaf-mute who tries to bring peace and consolation to a fellow mute, an impotent café owner, an adolescent tomboy (Sondra Locke), an alcoholic Marxist and a black doctor battling against injustice. Director Robert Ellis Miller makes the novel's points without heavy-handedness and debutants Stacy Keach and Locke (also nominated for an Academy Award) hold their own in a splendid supporting cast. DP

Alan Arkin *John Singer* • Laurinda Barrett *Mrs Kelly* • Stacy Keach *Blount* • Chuck McCann *Antonapoulos* • Biff McGuire *Mr Kelly* • Sondra Locke *Mick Kelly* • Percy Rodriguez *Dr Copeland* • Cicely Tyson *Portia* • Jackie Marlowe *Bubber Kelly* • Johnny Popwell *Willie* • Wayne Smith *Harry* ■ *Dir* Robert Ellis Miller • *Scr* Thomas C Ryan, from the novel by Carson McCullers

The Heart Is Deceitful above All Things ★★★ 15

Drama 2004 · US · Colour · 98mins

This haunting drama traces the mutually dependent relationship between truck-stop prostitute Sarah (portrayed by director Asia Argento herself) and her son Jeremiah (Jimmy Bennett). Removing the youngster from his foster parents at the age of seven, Sarah initiates him into an itinerant life of poverty, violence and abuse. The raw horror of events is impossible to escape, and Argento's passion oozes from every frame, but her closeness to the material sometimes means there's insufficient plot exposition and this plays like a series of emotionally-charged vignettes. SF. Contains swearing and drug abuse.

Asia Argento *Sarah* • Jimmy Bennett *Young Jeremiah* • Peter Fonda *Grandfather* • Ben Foster *Fleshy boy* • Ornella Muti *Grandmother* • Kip Pardue *Luther* • Michael Pitt *Buddy* • Jeremy Renner *Emerson* • Cole Sprouse *Older Jeremiah* • Dylan Sprouse *Older Jeremiah* • Winona Ryder *Psychologist* ■ *Dir* Asia Argento • *Scr* Asia Argento, Alessandro Magania, from the short story collection by JT LeRoy

Heart like a Wheel ★★★ PG

Biographical drama
1983 · US · Colour · 108mins

Shirley Muldowney is often described as the world's first woman racing driver, though because she drives hot-rods and dragsters she isn't recognised as such in Europe. This greasy, gutsy biopic covers a span of 25 years and gives Bonnie Bedelia an acting challenge she passes with flying colours. Marriage, divorce and romance with her manager Beau Bridges are just some of the pitstops on the way to winning the world championship three times. AT

Bonnie Bedelia *Shirley Muldowney* • Beau Bridges *Connie Kalitta* • Leo Rossi *Jack Muldowney* • Hoyt Axton *Tex Roque* • Bill McKinney *Don "Big Daddy" Garlits* • Anthony Edwards *John Muldowney (age 15–23)* • Dean Paul Martin *Sonny Rigotti* ■ *Dir* Jonathan Kaplan • *Scr* Ken Friedman

Heart of a Child ★★★ 12

Drama based on a true story
1994 · US · Colour · 88mins

The subject of this TV movie kept the Canadian tabloids occupied for a couple of months as two mothers-to-be on opposite sides of the country learn that the only way one of their unborn babies can survive is by receiving the heart of the other. As the women facing the agonising decision, Michele Green and Ann Jillian give solid performances, while the versatile Rip Torn does well as the doctor advising them. DP DVD

Ann Jillian *Alice Holc* • Michele Greene *Karen Schouten* • Terry O'Quinn *Gordon Holc* • Bruce Greenwood *Fred Schouten* • Rip Torn *Dr Leonard Bailey* • Andrew Wheeler *Dr Cramer* • Cindy Girling *Dr Cynthia Adler* • Ric Reid *Terry Waterhouse* • William B Davis *Vern* ■ *Dir* Sandor Stern • *Scr* Susan Nanus

The Heart of a Man ★★ U

Musical 1959 · UK · BW · 92mins

Veteran director Herbert Wilcox bowed out of films with this undistinguished and wholly unconvincing slice-of-life drama, which was produced by his actress wife Anna Neagle. Frankie Vaughan stars as the homecoming sailor who is offered £1,000 reward by an eccentric tramp if he can honestly earn £100 within a week. Following stints as a bouncer, a boxer and a commissionaire, he finally makes good as a singer and meets sultry chanteuse Anne Heywood. DP

Frankie Vaughan *Frankie* • Anne Heywood *Julie* • Tony Britton *Tony* • Peter Sinclair *Bud* • Michael Medwin *Sid* • Anthony Newley *Johnny* ■ *Dir* Herbert Wilcox • *Scr* Jack Trevor Story, Pamela Bower, from a story by Rex North

Heart of Dixie ★ 15

Drama 1989 · US · Colour · 91mins

Starring Ally Sheedy, Virginia Madsen and Phoebe Cates, this is 1950s-style melodrama of the worst order. The girls are at college in the Deep South and are at odds with the racism and sexism of where they live. Romances ensue, consciousness is raised and the film improves briefly towards the end with the arrival of the first black student on campus. LH

Ally Sheedy *Maggie* • Virginia Madsen *Delia* • Phoebe Cates *Aiken* • Treat Williams *Hoyt* • Don Michael Paul *Boots* • Kyle Secor *Tuck* •

Francesca Roberts *Keefi* ■ *Dir* Martin Davidson • *Scr* Tom McCown, from the novel *Heartbreak Hotel* by Ann Rivers Siddons

Heart of Glass ★★★★ PG

Period drama 1976 · W Ger · Colour · 90mins

An allegorical treatise on the nature of the Germanic character, Werner Herzog's audacious tale of a 19th-century Bavarian town being cast into despondency by the death of its patron (who alone knows the secret of its trademark ruby glass) is best known for the fact its cast reportedly delivered its somnambulist performances under the influence of hypnosis. Herzog's part-mythical, part-prophetic vision of desolation and dependence (reinforced by the extraordinary blend of the Gothic and the Wagnerian in Henning von Gierke and Cornelius Siegel's stylised settings) gives this film a power that surpasses its novelty. DP. In German with English subtitles. DVD

Josef Bierbichler *Hias* • Stefan Güttler *Huttenbesitzer* • Clemens Scheitz *Adalbert* • Sepp Müller • Volker Prechtel ■ *Dir* Werner Herzog • *Scr* Werner Herzog, Herbert Achternbusch

The Heart of Justice ★★★★ 12

Mystery thriller 1992 · US · Colour · 87mins

Director Bruno Barreto would work again with Dennis Hopper in the romantic drama *Acts of Love*, but this earlier, made-for-TV collaboration is a classier affair, with Eric Stoltz as a journalist who sets out to unravel the mysterious murder of well-known novelist Hopper. Barreto secures a clutch of superb portrayals from the likes of William H Macy, Bradford Dillman, Jennifer Connelly and Joanna Miles, and look out, too, for a delightful cameo from Vincent Price. JF. Contains some swearing, violence and sexual references.

Jennifer Connelly *Emma Burgess* • Bradford Dillman *Mr Burgess* • Dermot Mulroney *Elliot Burgess* • Dennis Hopper *Austin Blair* • Vincent Price *Shaw* • Eric Stoltz *David Leader* • William H Macy *Booth* • Joanna Miles *Mrs Burgess* • Harris Yulin *Keneally* • Keith Reddin *Simon* ■ *Dir* Bruno Barreto • *Scr* Keith Reddin

The Heart of Me ★★★ 15

Period romantic drama
2002 · UK · Colour · 91mins

Director Thaddeus O'Sullivan has given this period tale of adultery and redemption a bittersweet piquancy – memorably enhanced by the actors – while Nicholas Hooper's original score underlines its discreet romanticism. Scriptwriter Lucinda Coxon has lost some of the affecting sensibility of Rosamond Lehmann's novel about two sisters who are in love with the same man by relying too much on emotional clichés. Nevertheless, Paul Bettany, Olivia Williams and Helena Bonham Carter do make an engaging *ménage à trois*, entangled in the class restrictions of the 1930s as well as their own lusts. TH DVD

Helena Bonham Carter *Dinah* • Olivia Williams *Madeleine* • Paul Bettany *Rickie* • Eleanor Bron *Mrs Burkett* • Luke Newberry *Anthony* • Tom Ward *Jack* • Gillian Hanna *Betty* • Andrew Havill *Charles* • Rosie Bonham Carter *Clarissa* ■ *Dir* Thaddeus O'Sullivan • *Scr* Lucinda Coxon, from the novel *The Echoing Grove* by Rosamond Lehmann

Heart of Midnight ★ 18

Horror thriller
1988 · US · Colour and BW · 106mins

A sick fantasy that's neither sick nor fantastic enough, director Matthew Chapman's degrading attempt to be meaningful in a horror thriller context is a pretentiously arty bore. Jennifer Jason Leigh is the woman on the verge of a nervous breakdown who inherits a tacky LA nightclub-cum-brothel from a debauched uncle. Only a cameo from the fabulous Brenda Vaccaro saves this daft psychodrama from being a complete write-off. AJ DVD

Jennifer Jason Leigh *Carol Rivers* • Peter Coyote *Sharpe/Larry* • Gale Mayron *Sonny* • Sam Schact *Uncle Fletcher* • Denise Dummont *Mariana* • Frank Stallone *Ledray* • Steve Buscemi *Eddy* • Brenda Vaccaro *Betty Rivers* ■ *Dir* Matthew Chapman • *Scr* Matthew Chapman, Everett DeRoche

The Heart of the Matter ★★★

Drama 1953 · UK · BW · 105mins

Graham Greene's tale of wartime infidelity and tortured conscience in Sierra Leone has, like its protagonist, not been faithful to its source. The religious and moral dilemma facing the adulterous police commissioner Scobie has been downplayed to concentrate on the human tragedy of a doomed love triangle. With the innocent intensity of her emotions clearly displayed, Maria Schell gives the best performance of the three leads, contrasting with the over-indulgent tantrums of Elizabeth Allan and the muted angst of Trevor Howard. DP

Trevor Howard *Harry Scobie* • Elizabeth Allan *Louise Scobie* • Maria Schell *Helen* • Denholm Elliott *Wilson* • Peter Finch *Father Rank* • Gérard Oury *Yusef* • George Coulouris *Portuguese captain* ■ *Dir* George More O'Ferrall • *Scr* Ian Dalrymple, Lesley Storm, from the novel by Graham Greene

Heartaches ★★ 15

Comedy 1981 · Can · Colour · 88mins

Pregnant Annie Potts decides to walk out on her husband Robert Carradine rather than face up to the reality of the baby's paternity. She teams up with kooky Margot Kidder for a series of misadventures, in a well-played if slightly predictable comic tale of gals doing it for themselves. JB

Margot Kidder *Rita Harris* • Annie Potts *Bonnie Howard* • Robert Carradine *Stanley Howard* • Winston Rekert *Marcello Di Stassi* • Guy Sanvido *Aldo* • Arnie Achtman *Alvin* ■ *Dir* Donald Shebib • *Scr* Terence Heffernan

Heartbeat ★★

Romantic comedy 1946 · US · BW · 101mins

In 1942 Ginger Rogers, aged 30, played a 12-year-old girl for laughs in *The Major and the Minor*. Four years later, it was no laughing matter when she attempted to convince as a teenage French escapee from a reform school who becomes a pickpocket. In a film that strains vainly for charm, only Basil Rathbone – as Ginger's mentor in the art of picking pockets – provides any. RB

Ginger Rogers *Arlette* • Jean-Pierre Aumont *Pierre* • Adolphe Menjou *Ambassador* • Basil Rathbone *Prof Aristide* • Melville Cooper *Roland Medeville* • Mikhail Rasumny *Yves Cadubert* ■ *Dir* Sam Wood • *Scr* Morrie Ryskind, Roland Leigh, from the film *Battement de Coeur* by Hans Wilhelm, Max Kolpé, Michel Duran

Heartbeeps ★★★ U

Science-fiction comedy
1981 · US · Colour · 74mins

This under-rated sci-fi comedy features a rare screen performance from cult *Taxi* star Andy Kaufman (immortalised by Jim Carrey in *Man on the Moon*) and a welcome movie outing for Broadway diva Bernadette Peters. Set in 1995, they play servant robots who meet in a factory, fall in love, run away and hide out in a junkyard where they have a robot baby. Full of charming details and honest sentiment, Stan Winston's mechanical makeovers were deservedly Oscar-nominated. AJ

Andy Kaufman *Val* • Bernadette Peters *Aqua* • Randy Quaid *Charlie* • Kenneth McMillan *Max* • Melanie Mayron *Susan* • Christopher Guest *Calvin* • Dick Miller *Watchman* ■ *Dir* Allan Arkush • *Scr* John Hill • *Music* John Williams

Heartbreak Hotel ★★ 15

Fantasy drama 1988 · US · Colour · 96mins

A fistful of movies have sought to evoke the spirit of Elvis Presley, including films such as Jim Jarmusch's *Mystery Train* and even Tony Scott's Quentin Tarantino-scripted *True Romance*. Here, youngster Charlie Schlatter drags Elvis home to cheer up mom Tuesday Weld. Unfortunately, David Keith as Elvis neither looks nor moves remotely like the man, and the whole flimsy premise is quick to collapse. TS. Contains violence and swearing.

David Keith *Elvis Presley* • Tuesday Weld *Marie Wolfe* • Charlie Schlatter *Johnny Wolfe* • Angela Goethals *Pam Wolfe* • Jacque Lynn Colton *Rosie Pantangellio* • Chris Mulkey *Steve Ayres* ■ *Dir/Scr* Chris Columbus

The Heartbreak Kid ★★★ PG

Comedy 1972 · US · Colour · 101mins

This marvellously witty and genuinely disturbing black comedy is given extra potency by the casting of director Elaine May's own daughter Jeannie Berlin as the Jewish wife jettisoned for a blonde "shikse" on her honeymoon. As the husband, Charles Grodin is brilliant and Cybill Shepherd is well cast as the other woman, while veteran Eddie Albert is the very antagonistic father. The acid cruelty of the first part of the film is not, alas, sustained throughout, and, frankly, neither is the plotline, which fails to reach any kind of climax. But there's more than enough left to satisfy sophisticated audiences. TS

Charles Grodin *Lenny Cantrow* • Cybill Shepherd *Kelly Corcoran* • Jeannie Berlin *Lila Kolodny* • Eddie Albert *Mr Corcoran* • Audra Lindley *Mrs Corcoran* • William Prince *Colorado Man* • Augusta Dabney *Colorado Woman* • Mitchell Jason *Cousin Ralph* ■ *Dir* Elaine May • *Scr* Neil Simon, from the story *A Change of Plan* by Bruce Jay Friedman

The Heartbreak Kid ★★★

Romantic drama 1993 · Aus · Colour · 91mins

This Australian rites-of-passage drama explores the prejudices against age-gap romances. Claudia Karvan and Alex Dimitriades give convincing performances as the middle-class teacher and the teenage student for whom she breaks her close family ties. Director Michael Jenkins makes clever use of a handheld camera to disguise the material's stage origins and makes several telling points about Melbourne's Greek community and their place in Australian society. DP

Claudia Karvan *Christina* • Alex Dimitriades *Nick* • Nico Lathouris *George* • Steve Bastoni *Dimitri* • Doris Younane *Evdokia* • George Vidalis *Vasili* • Louis Mandylor *Eleni* • William McInnes *Southgate* ■ *Dir* Michael Jenkins • *Scr* Michael Jenkins, Richard Barrett

Heartbreak Ridge ★★★ 15

War drama 1986 · US · Colour · 124mins

Clint Eastwood struts his stern stuff in this typically hard-nosed war epic, playing a grizzled gunnery sergeant training a batch of rookie soldiers. He's the main reason to watch a by-the-numbers drama, which recycles many vintage clichés of the genre, from the misfit recruit gaining dignity and the old, die-hard veteran versus the modern major, to the virgin platoon's first bitter taste of battle on the beaches of Grenada. It's a movie the US Department of Defense openly condemned – "drill sergeants are not permitted by regulations to swear at recruits". AJ. Contains violence and swearing. DVD

Clint Eastwood *Sergeant Thomas Highway* • Marsha Mason *Aggie* • Everett McGill *Major Powers* • Moses Gunn *Sergeant Webster* • Eileen Heckart *Little Mary* • Bo Svenson *Roy Jennings* • Boyd Gaines *Lieutenant Ring* • Mario Van Peebles *"Stitch" Jones* • Arlen Dean Snyder *Master Sergeant Choozoo* ■ *Dir* Clint Eastwood • *Scr* James Carabatsos

Heartbreakers ★★★ 18

Romantic comedy
1984 · US · Colour · 94mins

Although it provides in passing a snapshot of Reagan's America, this perceptive drama concentrates more on wounded individuals than prevailing social trends. It's about the corners that artist Peter Coyote and businessman Nick Mancuso have painted themselves into. However, good as they are as the self-obsessed 30-somethings who can't commit to anything that might impinge upon their precious personal freedom, it's gallery clerk Carole Laure and model Carol Wayne who hold the piece together. An impressive debut from writer/director Bobby Roth. DP. Contains swearing and sex scenes.

Peter Coyote *Blue* • Nick Mancuso *Eli* • Carole Laure *Liliane* • Max Gail *King* • Kathryn Harrold *Cyd* • Carol Wayne *Candy* • James Laurenson *Terry Ray* • Jamie Rose *Libby* ■ *Dir/Scr* Bobby Roth

Heartbreakers ★★★ 15

Comedy 2001 · US · Colour · 123mins

This complex, smart-talking con-trick comedy revolves around the appeal of mother-and-daughter grifters Sigourney Weaver and Jennifer Love Hewitt. Weaver marries a man of means, while Hewitt seduces him before consummation, resulting in a nice big divorce settlement. It's well cast, with Ray Liotta as an earlier victim and Gene Hackman in fine WC Fields mode as the duo's latest patsy, a wheezing tobacco baron. Weaver and Hewitt's man-eating appeal is entirely credible but ultimately the men are funnier than the women. The key problem with this multilayered farce is that it is 20 minutes too long. AC DVD

Sigourney Weaver *Angela Nardino/Max Conners/Ulga Yevanova* • Jennifer Love Hewitt *Wendy/Page Conners/Jane Helstrom* • Ray Liotta *Dean Cumanno/Vinny Staggliano* • Jason Lee *Jack Withrowe* • Anne Bancroft *Gloria Vogal/Barbara* • Jeffrey Jones *Mr Appel* • Gene Hackman *William B Tensy* • Carrie Fisher *Mrs Surpin* ■ *Dir* David Mirkin • *Scr* Robert Dunn (2), Paul Guay, Stephen Mazur

Heartburn ★★★ 15

Comedy drama 1986 · US · Colour · 104mins

Based on the bestselling novel by *When Harry Met Sally...* scriptwriter Nora Ephron about her tempestuous marriage to Watergate journalist Carl Bernstein, this has Meryl Streep as the cookery writer who marries columnist Jack Nicholson, only to discover that life isn't always happy ever after when he has an affair while she's pregnant. Nicholson gets all the best lines and does well with what is essentially a rather shallow part with few redeeming features, but Streep is somewhat at sea with the humorous side of her role and ends up as a rather unsympathetic character. JB DVD

Meryl Streep *Rachel Samstat* • Jack Nicholson *Mark Forman* • Jeff Daniels *Richard* • Maureen Stapleton *Vera* • Stockard Channing *Julie* • Richard Masur *Arthur* • Catherine O'Hara *Betty* • Steven Hill *Harry* • Milos Forman *Dmitri* • Natalie Stern *Annie* • Karen Akers *Thelma Rice* ■ *Dir* Mike Nichols • *Scr* Nora Ephron, from her autobiographical novel

H

Heartland ★★★★

Historical western
1979 · US · Colour · 95mins

Based on the memoirs of Elinore Randall Stewart, this portrait of pioneer life on the Wyoming frontier circa 1910 is perhaps the cinema's truest reflection of the female experience of the west. Bringing the wealth of historical detail to vibrant life is Conchata Ferrell as a widow who progresses from housekeeper to wife as she comes to understand the terse determination of rancher Rip Torn. Never flinching from the grim realities of the daily grind, former documentarist Richard Pearce manages to find moments of raw joy amid the hardships. DP

Rip Torn *Clyde Stewart* • Conchata Ferrell *Elinore Randall* • Barry Primus *Jack* • Lilia Skala *Grandma Landauer* • Megan Folsom *Jerrine* • Amy Wright *Clara Jane* • Jerry Hardin *Cattle buyer* • Mary Boylan *Ma Gillis* ■ *Dir* Richard Pearce • *Scr* Beth Ferris, from the books and papers by Elinore Randall Stewart

H

Heartlands ★★★ 12

Comedy drama
2002 · UK/US · Colour · 87mins

Michael Sheen is a mild-mannered, darts-playing newsagent who lives in a dull Midlands town where men still get Kevin Keegan-style perms. His unexciting little world collapses when his wife runs off to Blackpool with the captain of the darts team, so Sheen hops on his scooter in not-particularly-hot pursuit. Director Damien O'Donnell again demonstrates the knack for blending comedy and tragedy he exhibited with *East Is East*, and produces a film that's both entertaining and a wry comment on an England that other film-makers have largely ignored. BP DVD

Michael Sheen *Colin* • Mark Addy *Ron* • Jim Carter *Geoff* • Celia Imrie *Sonja* • Ruth Jones *Mandy* • Philippa Peak *Sarah* • Jane Robbins *Sandra* • Paul Shane *Zippy* • Mark Strong *Ian* ■ *Dir* Damien O'Donnell • *Scr* Paul Fraser, from a story by Paul Fraser, Richard Jobson, Andrew Keyte, from an idea by Paul Fraser

Hearts and Minds ★★★★

Documentary 1974 · US · Colour · 111mins

America's failure of arms in Vietnam is still a running sore in the hearts and minds of the US military and the American people. Director Peter Davis's Oscar-winning documentary twists the knife again, trying to unravel why the Americans became involved with the whole bloody business, and its honesty and full-frontal recording of experiences made it a hot potato for distributors at the time. That it can now be seen shows just how far times and politics can change. TH

Dir Peter Davis

Heart's Desire ★★

Musical 1935 · UK · BW · 79mins

Grace Moore, Lily Pons and Richard Tauber were just three operatic luminaries who found their vocal skills were in demand with film-makers seeking some serious culture. Here Tauber plays a Viennese beer-garden singer who is persuaded to leave home and love to perform on the London stage, but then finds himself attracted to a glamorous socialite. Obviously, acting did not come naturally, but there is no denying the quality of the tenor's voice even though the songs and arias are presented without a flicker of flair. DP

Richard Tauber *Joseph Steidler* • Leonora Corbett *Frances Wilson* • Kathleen Kelly *Anna* • Paul Graetz *Florian* • Carl Harbord *Oliver Desmond* • George Graves *Granville Wilson* • Diana Napier *Diana Sheraton* • Frank Vosper *Van Straaten* ■ *Dir* Paul Stein [Paul L Stein] • *Scr* Bruno Frank, L Du Garde Peach, Roger Burford, Jack Davies Jr, Clifford Grey, from a story by Lioni Pickard

Hearts in Atlantis ★★ 12

Supernatural drama
2001 · US/Aus · Colour · 96mins

Adapting two stories from the eponymous collection by Stephen King, William Goldman's uneven script spins a rose-tinted tale of coming-of-age in 1960s America that sits uneasily beside a nebulous conspiracy subplot. In a small New England town, neglected 11-year-old Anton Yelchin strikes up a meaningful friendship with mysterious neighbour Anthony Hopkins, who is soon revealed to have the power to read minds, attracting the attention of sinister government figures who want to exploit his ability. Blandly directed, this is poorly paced and charmless. AJ DVD

Anthony Hopkins *Ted Brautigan* • Anton Yelchin *Bobby Garfield* • Hope Davis *Liz Garfield* • Mika Boorem *Carol Gerber* • David Morse *Robert Garfield* ■ *Dir* Scott Hicks • *Scr* William Goldman, from short story collection *Hearts in Atlantis* by Stephen King

Hearts of Darkness: a Film-Maker's Apocalypse ★★★★★ 15

Documentary 1991 · US · Colour · 91mins

An enthralling documentary about the making of Francis Ford Coppola's Vietnam drama *Apocalypse Now*. Using new interviews and footage shot on location by Coppola's wife, Eleanor, this is a catalogue of madness and inspiration in the jungles of the Philippines that ranges from an overweight and unprepared Marlon Brando, the firing of Harvey Keitel, Martin Sheen's heart attack, previously unseen footage (a superb sequence in a French plantation house which Coppola foolishly cut), to crises such as typhoons and President Marcos withdrawing his helicopters to fight a real war. With contributions from Coppola, screenwriter John Milius, and a characteristically incoherent Dennis Hopper, this is an unmissable treat for fans of the movie and, indeed, for anyone interested in the cinema. AT. Contains swearing.

Dir/Scr Fax Bahr, George Hickenlooper

Hearts of Fire ★ 15

Drama 1987 · US · Colour · 91mins

This hilariously bad rock movie was an unfortunate swan song for the talented director Richard Marquand (*Jagged Edge*). Fiona Flanagan plays the aspiring young musician torn between a woefully miscast Rupert Everett and a monosyllabic Bob Dylan. There's no respite in the bland soundtrack. JF. Contains swearing.

Rupert Everett *James Colt* • Bob Dylan *Billy Parker* • Fiona Flanagan *Molly McGuire* • Ian Dury *Bones* • Richie Havens *Pepper Ward* • Julian Glover *Alfred* • Suzanne Bertish *Anne Ashton* ■ *Dir* Richard Marquand • *Scr* Scott Richardson, Joe Eszterhas

Hearts of the West ★★★★ PG

Comedy drama 1975 · US · Colour · 102mins

Inspired by the experiences of writer Zane Grey and shot in the style of a 1930s western series, this is a wonderfully inventive and richly nostalgic picture. Jeff Bridges stars as an unpublished writer of western stories who discovers he's being conned by gangsters. By chance he falls in with a film crew, becoming a stuntman and, briefly, a star. Bridges is excellent in the lead, but he's almost upstaged by Andy Griffith's performance as a fellow stuntman. The likeable result is sure to appeal to fans of B-westerns. AT

Jeff Bridges *Lewis Tater* • Andy Griffith *Howard Pike* • Donald Pleasence *AJ Nietz* • Blythe Danner *Miss Trout* • Alan Arkin *Kessler* • Richard B Shull *Stout crook* • Herbert Edelman [Herb Edelman] *Eddie Polo* • Alex Rocco *Earl* ■ *Dir* Howard Zieff • *Scr* Rob Thompson

Hearts of the World ★★★

Silent First World War drama
1918 · US · BW · 152mins

After making his epic *Intolerance*, DW Griffith wrote, produced and directed this picture as a contribution to the war effort in 1918, incorporating documentary footage and scenes shot at the Front. It stars Lillian Gish and Robert Harron as two lovers and shows the devastating effect of the war on one small French village. Griffith's feeling for his characters overcomes the contrivances of the plot and moments of sentimentality. Technical adviser Erich von Stroheim is also seen as a Prussian officer, while making his first screen appearance as the teenager with a wheelbarrow is a young Noël Coward. AE

Adolphe Lestina *Grandfather* • Josephine Crowell *Mother* • Lillian Gish *Girl* • Robert Harron *Boy* • Dorothy Gish *Little Disturber* • Erich von Stroheim *German soldier* • Noël Coward *Boy with wheelbarrow* ■ *Dir* DW Griffith • *Scr* M Gaston de Tolignac [DW Griffith], Capt Victor Marier [DW Griffith]

Heat ★★ 18

Cult drama 1972 · US · Colour · 96mins

Underground icon Joe Dallesandro plays a former child actor-turned-hustler, with Sylvia Miles as a fading minor movie star, in director Paul Morrissey's *Sunset Boulevard* revisited which is given the usual tacky Andy Warhol spin. Andrea Feldman adds further bizarre twists and trashy turns to the "Hollyweird" parody as Miles's daughter. Sometimes hilariously camp, sometimes just very ordinary, this was the most commercially successful of Warhol's bad taste trilogy, which also featured *Flesh* and *Trash*. AJ DVD

Sylvia Miles *Sally* • Joe Dallesandro *Joe* • Pat Ast *Motel Owner* • Andrea Feldman *Jessica* • Ray Vestal *Movie Producer* • PJ Lester *Sally's former husband* ■ *Dir* Paul Morrissey • *Scr* Paul Morrissey, John Hollowell

Heat ★ 18

Crime drama 1987 · US · Colour · 96mins

Once the world's biggest box office draw, poor Burt Reynolds was reduced to the status of "Burt who?" until *Boogie Nights* revived his name. His fall from grace isn't difficult to comprehend on the evidence of this drab, squalid action movie. Reynolds, relying on his trademark toughie-with-a-heart-of-gold persona, plays a freelance bodyguard who's up against Las Vegas slimeballs, but dreams of one day retiring. A muddled, violent and humourless experience. RS

Burt Reynolds *Mex* • Karen Young *Holly* • Peter MacNicol *Cyrus Kinnick* • Howard Hesseman *Pinchus Zion* • Neill Barry *Danny DeMarco* • Diana Scarwid *Cassie* • Joseph Mascolo *Baby* ■ *Dir* Dick Richards • *Scr* William Goldman, from his novel

Heat ★★★★ 15

Crime thriller 1995 · US · Colour · 163mins

Directed by Michael Mann, this crime thriller about a cop (Al Pacino) and a robber (Robert De Niro) is epic in scale and in length. Though punctuated by bursts of virtuoso action, including a running battle in downtown LA that ranks as one of the best action scenes ever filmed, it is the unusual emphasis on the characters that impresses most, especially De Niro as the calm, methodical loner whose life is arranged so that he can abandon everything in 30 seconds when the heat is on. Pacino, by contrast, is more of a cliché: angst-ridden and on his third marriage. We catch Pacino acting all the time, and it's also a pity that after so much brilliance Mann should succumb to a derivative ending. AT DVD

Al Pacino *Vincent Hanna* • Robert De Niro *Neil McCauley* • Val Kilmer *Chris Shiherlis* • Jon Voight *Nate* • Tom Sizemore *Michael Cheritto* • Diane Venora *Justine* • Amy Brenneman *Eady* • Ashley Judd *Charlene* • Mykelti Williamson *Drucker* • Wes Studi *Casals* • Natalie Portman *Lauren* ■ *Dir/Scr* Michael Mann • *Cinematographer* Dante Spinotti

Heat and Dust ★★★ 15

Drama 1982 · UK · Colour · 124mins

Ex-BBC researcher Julie Christie travels to India to investigate her late great-aunt Olivia (Greta Scacchi) who caused a scandal in the 1920s – and it doesn't take long for us to guess that she became rather too familiar with an Indian. Adapting her own novel, Ruth Prawer Jhabvala produces a new twist on EM Forster's *A Passage to India*, using two characters and separate time zones to express similar ideas about cultural collision. It's arty and exotic, with Christie and Scacchi refusing to be upstaged by the ravishing scenery. AT DVD

Julie Christie *Anne* • Christopher Cazenove *Douglas* • Greta Scacchi *Olivia Rivers* • Julian Glover *Mr Crawford* • Susan Fleetwood *Mrs Crawford* • Shashi Kapoor *The Nawab* • Madhur Jaffrey *The Begum* • Nickolas Grace *Harry* • Zakir Hussain *Inder Lal* • Barry Foster *Major Minnies* • Amanda Walker *Lady Mackleworth* • Patrick Godfrey *Dr Saunders* ■ *Dir* James Ivory • *Scr* Ruth Prawer Jhabvala, from her novel

Heat and Sunlight ★★

Drama 1988 · US · BW · 98mins

In his feature *Signal 7*, Rob Nilsson not only employed a purely improvisational technique, but also pioneered the method of shooting on video before transferring the results to celluloid. He repeats the trick in this disappointing follow-up, which is atmospherically scored by David Byrne and Brian Eno. However, the lack of a coherent screenplay means the action is too often allowed to ramble, although there is tension when Nilsson's pathologically jealous photographer is consumed by violent rages directed at Consuelo Faust, with whom he's been having an affair. DP

Rob Nilsson *Mel Hurley* • Consuelo Faust *Carmen* • Don Bajema *Mitch* • Ernie Fosselius *Bobby* ■ *Dir/Scr* Rob Nilsson • *Music/lyrics* David Byrne, Brian Eno, Mark Adler, David Schickele, Michael Small

Heat Wave ★★★★

Drama based on a true story
1990 · US · Colour · 92mins

This Emmy award-winning TV movie is based on actual events that occurred during the civil rights riots that turned the Watts district of Los Angeles into a battleground in the summer of 1965. As an ambitious journalist who is branded a race traitor for his coverage of the story, Blair Underwood gives a performance of dignity and integrity that invites comparisons with Sidney Poitier. Cicely Tyson and James Earl Jones are typically impressive, while director Kevin Hooks assuredly blends discussion of the social issues with explosive action. DP

Cicely Tyson *Ruthana Richardson/Motherdear* • Blair Underwood *Robert Richardson* • James Earl Jones *Junius Johnson* • Sally Kirkland *Mrs Canfield* • Margaret Avery (2) *Roxie Turpin* • Vondie Curtis-Hall *Clifford Turpin* ■ *Dir* Kevin Hooks • *Scr* Michael Lazarou

Heathers ★★★★★ 18

Black comedy 1989 · US · Colour · 98mins

Don't allow the fact that Michael Lehmann directed *Hudson Hawk* to put you off his stunning debut with this movie about an all-girl high-school clique terrorising fellow students. Their actions prompt Winona Ryder and Christian Slater to engineer a rash of deaths to break the clique's hold on their schoolmates. Beneath the hip, lip-glossed surface of this devastatingly witty black comedy lurks a serious satire on peer-group pretensions and other teen movies. But the message never gets in the way of the snappy dialogue or on-target jabs at the in-crowd lunacy of high-school life. AJ. Contains violence, swearing and sex scenes. [video] DVD

Winona Ryder *Veronica Sawyer* • Christian Slater *Jason "JD" Dean* • Shannen Doherty *Heather Duke* • Lisanne Falk *Heather McNamara* • Kim Walker *Heather Chandler* • Penelope Milford *Pauline Fleming* • Glenn Shadix *Father Ripper* • Lance Fenton *Kurt Kelly* • Patrick Labyorteaux *Ram Sweeney* ■ *Dir* Michael Lehmann • *Scr* Daniel Waters

The Heat's On ★★ U

Musical comedy 1943 · US · BW · 78mins

After her lively sparring match with WC Fields in *My Little Chickadee*, Mae West was off-screen for nearly four years until producer/director Gregory Ratoff persuaded her to return in this musical comedy. West herself was in fine shape but the script wasn't, especially after she had rewritten her part to make it more sympathetic. In fact, her role as a Broadway sex siren seems out of date and her time on screen is quite limited. AE

Mae West *Fay Lawrence* • Victor Moore *Hubert Bainbridge* • William Gaxton *Tony Ferris* • Lester Allen *Mouse Beller* • Mary Roche *Janey Bainbridge* • Almira Sessions *Hannah Bainbridge* • Hazel Scott • Alan Dinehart *Forrest Stanton* • Lloyd Bridges *Andy Walker* ■ *Dir* Gregory Ratoff • *Scr* Fitzroy Davis, George S George, Fred Schiller, from a story by Boris Ingster, Lou Breslow

Heatwave ★★★ 15

Thriller based on a true story
1981 · Aus · Colour · 90mins

Militant liberal Judy Davis protests the crime-related gentrification of downtown Sydney, only to get caught up in political intrigue and romance with an ambitious architect (Richard Moir). Davis gives a typically fine performance, while director Phillip Noyce expertly tightens the suspense screws to produce a memorably disturbing finish. Set against a sultry Christmas backdrop, this is a jet-black thriller. AJ [video]

Judy Davis *Kate Dean* • Richard Moir *Steven West* • Chris Haywood *Peter Hauseman* • Bill Hunter *Robert Duncan* • John Gregg *Phillip Lawson* • Anna Jemison *Victoria West* • John Meillon *Freddy Dwyer* • Dennis Miller *Mick Davies* ■ *Dir* Phillip Noyce • *Scr* Phillip Noyce, Phillip Noyce, Marc Rosenberg, Mark Stiles, Tim Gooding

Heaven ★★ 18

Documentary 1987 · US · Colour · 59mins

Actress Diane Keaton's first film as director is a sweet idea gone sour. A variety of ordinary people – boxing promoter Don King being an exception – are interviewed and asked to explain their views on death and a possible afterlife. However, despite some intriguing old film clips, Keaton's patronising narration and ludicrously affected camera angles deflate the airy bubble of an idea that needed a more light-handed touch. TH [video]

Dir Diane Keaton • *Cinematographer* Joe Kelly, Frederick Elmes

Heaven ★★

Thriller 1998 · NZ/US · Colour · 102mins

The built-in bonus about films involving clairvoyants is that the director can flit between flashbacks and prophecies and bemuse the viewer into thinking something significant is going on. Scott Reynolds is partly guilty of such manipulative chicanery; however, the convoluted tale is so slickly edited that it's hard to avoid wondering how transvestite stripper Danny Edwards's visions are going to affect architect Martin Donovan in his confrontations with gambling boss Richard Schiff and embittered ex-wife Joanna Going. Patrick Malahide also appears as a shady shrink. DP. Contains violence, swearing and nudity.

Martin Donovan (2) *Robert Marling* • Joanna Going *Jennifer Marling* • Richard Schiff *Stanner* • Patrick Malahide *Dr Melrose* • Danny Edwards *Heaven* • Karl Urban *Sweeper* ■ *Dir* Scott Reynolds • *Scr* Scott Reynolds, from a novel by Chad Taylor

Heaven ★★★ 15

Romantic thriller
2002 · US/UK/Fr/Ger/It · Colour · 92mins

German director Tom Tykwer's English-language debut falls between mainstream thriller and art house character study. There's little sense of connection between Cate Blanchett's accidental terrorist and Giovanni Ribisi's Italian cop, who helps her escape when a plan to blow up a drug-dealing tycoon backfires. Blanchett is excellent as the widowed English teacher, stripped of reason by her need for revenge, but the conclusion is unpersuasive and exposes Tykwer's discomfort with cerebral rather than visceral material. DP. In English and Italian with subtitles. [video] DVD

Cate Blanchett *Philippa* • Giovanni Ribisi *Filippo* • Remo Girone *Filippo's father* • Stefania Rocca *Regina* • Mattia Sbragia *Major Pini* ■ *Dir* Tom Tykwer • *Scr* Krzysztof Kieslowski, Krzysztof Piesiewicz

Heaven and Earth ★★★★ 15

War drama 1993 · US · Colour · 134mins

After *Platoon* and *Born on the Fourth of July*, Oliver Stone turns his attention to the Vietnamese themselves, in particular a village girl named Le Ly (Hiep Thi Le) who endures the horrors of the war only to marry a psychotic American soldier (Tommy Lee Jones) who takes her to California. Unjustly slated by the critics, the picture shows all of Stone's brilliance in creating scenes of unusual vividness – it's horrifying, beautiful, ugly and moving all at the same time. It is also, at times, an unsettling black comedy about cultural and religious rituals that switches from Buddhist shrines in rice paddies to consumerist shrines in supermarkets. AT. Contains violence and swearing. [video] DVD

Tommy Lee Jones *Sergeant Steve Butler* • Joan Chen *Mama* • Haing S Ngor *Papa* • Hiep Thi Le *Le Ly* • Debbie Reynolds *Eugenia* ■ *Dir* Oliver Stone • *Scr* Oliver Stone, from the non-fiction books *When Heaven and Earth Changed Places* by Le Ly Hayslip, Jay Wurts and *Child of War, Woman of Peace* by Le Ly Hayslip, James Hayslip

Heaven Can Wait ★★★★★

Fantasy comedy 1943 · US · Colour · 112mins

A witty satire masquerading as a Fox family saga, this movie gets its title from the prologue where the Devil (Laird Cregar) sits in judgement on Don Ameche's Henry Van Cleve. This is as good as Ameche gets; not only is he perfectly cast, but also brilliantly directed by the comic genius Ernst Lubitsch, working in colour for the first time. The film has great warmth, charm and honesty, and grows on you until, at the end, you're sorry to leave. Gene Tierney has never looked lovelier –and that's *really* saying something– nor *The Merry Widow* used more emotively. Each viewing confirms this film's growing status as a classic. TS

Gene Tierney *Martha* • Don Ameche *Henry Van Cleve* • Charles Coburn *Hugo Van Cleve* • Marjorie Main *Mrs Strabel* • Laird Cregar *His Excellency, the Devil* • Spring Byington *Bertha Van Cleve* • Allyn Joslyn *Albert Van Cleve* ■ *Dir* Ernst Lubitsch • *Scr* Samson Raphaelson, from the play *Birthdays* by Lazlo Bus-Fekete • *Cinematographer* Edward Cronjager

Heaven Can Wait ★★★★ PG

Fantasy comedy 1978 · US · Colour · 96mins

An updated version of the 1941 film *Here Comes Mr Jordan*, this is one of the few remakes that is almost as good as the original. Warren Beatty co-directs and stars as the football player accidentally selected to die after a car accident. Realising he has been called before his time, Beatty bargains with celestial James Mason and gets the chance to live again but in someone else's body, that of a wealthy businessman whose wife is plotting to kill him. Well played, well written (by Beatty and Elaine May) and well directed, this is one of the highlights of Beatty's career. JB [video] DVD

Warren Beatty *Joe Pendleton* • Julie Christie *Betty Logan* • James Mason *Mr Jordan* • Jack Warden *Max Corkle* • Charles Grodin *Tony Abbott* • Dyan Cannon *Julia Farnsworth* • Buck Henry *Escort* • Vincent Gardenia *Krim* ■ *Dir* Warren Beatty, Buck Henry • *Scr* Elaine May, Warren Beatty, from the play by Harry Segall

Heaven Is a Playground ★★ 15

Sports drama 1991 · US · Colour · 102mins

No sporting cliché is left unturned for this well-cast but disappointing basketball drama. DB Sweeney is the idealistic lawyer who helps equally idealistic coach Michael Warren with a talented but troublesome cadre of players from the ghetto and protect them from sleazy sports shark Richard Jordan. There's no faulting the playing, but the script and direction of Randall Fried lack focus. JF [video]

DB Sweeney *Zack* • Michael Warren *Byron* • Richard Jordan *Racine* • Victor Love *Truth* • Bo Kimble *Matthew* • Janet Julian *Dalton* ■ *Dir* Randall Fried • *Scr* Randall Fried, from the non-fiction book by Rick Telander

Heaven Knows, Mr Allison ★★★★ PG

Second World War drama
1957 · US · Colour · 101mins

This is a rare gem, a marvellously touching two-hander, beautifully acted by the sublime duo of Robert Mitchum and Deborah Kerr in their prime. The tale is simplicity itself: she's a nun and he's a marine, and they're stranded on a Japanese-occupied Pacific island during the Second World War. Director John Huston wisely lets the stars bring their magic touch to the clever screenplay. This is an early 20th Century-Fox CinemaScope feature, and the compositions and locations are superbly handled by the great English cameraman Ossie Morris, while Russell Lloyd's editing is dynamic, especially in Mitchum's exciting raids into enemy territory. TS DVD

Deborah Kerr *Sister Angela* • Robert Mitchum *Mr Allison* ■ *Dir* John Huston • *Scr* John Huston, John Lee Mahin

Heaven Only Knows ★★

Western fantasy 1947 · US · BW · 98mins

An angel descends from heaven to the Wild West to attend to the soul of a psychotic saloon keeper and get him married to a demure schoolteacher. The bar owner, also a ruthless killer, arrived on Earth without a soul and the angel tries to put this right. Robert Cummings makes a relatively human angel in this western fantasy, whose more mawkish elements are tempered by a vague sense of humour. AT

Robert Cummings *Mike* • Brian Donlevy *Duke* • Marjorie Reynolds *Ginger* • Jorja Cartwright *Drusilla* • Bill Goodwin *Plumber* • Stuart Erwin *Sheriff* • John Litel *Reverend* • Peter Miles *Speck O'Donnell* ■ *Dir* Albert S Rogell • *Scr* Art Arthur, Ernest Haycox, Rowland Leigh, from the story by Aubrey Wisberg

Heaven Tonight ★★ 15

Musical drama 1990 · Aus · Colour · 93mins

Guy Pearce makes his feature film debut in this familiar tale of a young man falling out with his family when he embarks on a musical career. The twist this time is that the biggest obstacle is his father John Waters, a 1960s rock legend who is less than enamoured by the fact that his boy is now getting all the attention. The two leads are fine, but the machinations of the music business lack realism and the songs are awful. JF [video]

John Waters (3) *Johnny Dysart* • Rebecca Gilling *Annie Dysart* • Guy Pearce *Paul Dysart* • Kim Gyngell *Baz Schultz* ■ *Dir* Pino Amenta • *Scr* Frank Howson, Alister Webb

Heavenly Bodies ★★ 15

Musical drama 1985 · Can · Colour · 85mins

A rather bizarre attempt to cash in on the aerobics explosion of the early 1980s. The story is set around a dance studio, where the young owner finds herself in all sorts of difficulty when she rebuffs the charms of an egocentric rival. It's pretty risible stuff, leadenly directed by Lawrence Dane, and a clutch of distinctly forgettable tunes hardly helps matters. JF. Contains swearing and nudity. [video]

Cynthia Dale *Samantha* • Richard Rebiere *Steve* • Walter George Alton *Jack* • Laura Henry *Debbie* • Stuart Stone *Joel* • Patricia Idlette *KC* • Pam Henry *Patty* • Linda Sorenson *TV producer* ■ *Dir* Lawrence Dane • *Scr* Lawrence Dane, Ron Base

The Heavenly Body ★★

Romantic comedy 1943 · US · BW · 94mins

The title not only refers to Hedy Lamarr, making her first attempt at light comedy, but also the heavens above in this contrived wartime comedy. William Powell exercises his perfectly honed comedy skills to little avail as the eccentric astronomer whose nocturnal gazing causes him to neglect Lamarr as his wife. After she takes up astrology, the predicted arrival of a tall, dark stranger duly occurs when James Craig comes knocking at the door. AE

William Powell *William B Whitley* • Hedy Lamarr *Vicky Whitley* • James Craig *Lloyd X Hunter* • Fay Bainter *Margaret Sibyll* • Henry O'Neill *Professor Stone* • Spring Byington *Nancy Potter* ■ *Dir* Alexander Hall • *Scr* Michael Arlen, Walter Reisch, Harry Kurnitz, from a story by Jacques Thery

Heavenly Creatures ★★★★★ 18

Psychological drama based on a true story
1994 · NZ · Colour · 97mins

This is the film that launched the career of Kate Winslet, who within three years of appearing in this fact-based New Zealand drama was starring in *Titanic*. It also transformed the fortunes of director Peter Jackson, who went from making ingenious schlock horrors to directing the *Lord of the Rings* trilogy. The real star of this masterly mix of nostalgia, innocence and menace, however, is Melanie Lynskey, who is mesmerising as the matricidal half of the teenage duo who scandalised a nation in the early 1950s. Although Winslet and Lynskey

H

dominate the film, they are splendidly supported by Diana Kent and Clive Merrison as Winslet's parents, and by Sarah Peirse as Lynskey's ill-fated mother. DP. Contains violence and swearing. DVD

Melanie Lynskey *Pauline Parker* • Kate Winslet *Juliet Hulme* • Sarah Peirse *Honora Parker* • Diana Kent *Hilda Hulme* • Clive Merrison *Henry Hulme* • Simon O'Connor *Herbert Reiper* ■ *Dir* Peter Jackson • *Scr* Peter Jackson, Frances Walsh

The Heavenly Kid ★★ 15

Comedy fantasy 1985 · US · Colour · 87mins

A dim teenage spin on *Heaven Can Wait*, which finds 1950s rock 'n' roll rebel Lewis Smith earning his chance to book a place in Heaven if he helps out confused 1980s teenager Jason Gedrick. Richard Mulligan fares the best in a lightweight cast, but all are let down by the lazy script. JF

Lewis Smith *Bobby* • Jason Gedrick *Lenny* • Jane Kaczmarek *Emily* • Richard Mulligan *Rafferty* • Mark Metcalf *Joe* • Beau Dremann *Bill* ■ *Dir* Cary Medoway • *Scr* Cary Medoway, Martin Copeland

Heavenly Pursuits ★★★ 15

Satirical comedy 1986 · UK · Colour · 86mins

A delightful British film about miracles and religion, sharply written and directed by Charles Gormley. Tom Conti is the teacher at a Glasgow Catholic school who gets caught up in possible miraculous goings-on and then finds himself at the mercy of his colleagues and the media in this well-realised satire. Odd and often hilarious, this treat of a movie features terrific performances from a cast which includes David Hayman, Helen Mirren and Ewen Bremner. JB

Tom Conti *Vic Mathews* • Helen Mirren *Ruth Chancellor* • David Hayman *Jeff Jeffries* • Brian Pettifer *Father Cobb* • Jennifer Black *Sister* • Dave Anderson *Headmaster* • Tom Busby *Monseigneur Brusse* • Ewen Bremner *Stevie Deans* ■ *Dir/Scr* Charles Gormley

Heavens Above! ★★ PG

Comedy 1963 · UK · BW · 113mins

This is only a minor entry on the CVs of both Peter Sellers and the Boulting brothers. The satire at the expense of the Church of England is too gentle, the resolution is beyond contrivance and the church-goers are clumsy stereotypes. As a prison chaplain ministering to the well heeled, Sellers wallows in whimsy, leaving centre stage to Irene Handl and Eric Sykes's gypsy family. DP

Peter Sellers *Reverend John Smallwood* • Cecil Parker *Archdeacon Aspinall* • Isabel Jeans *Lady Despard* • Eric Sykes *Harry Smith* • Bernard Miles *Simpson* • Brock Peters *Matthew* • Ian Carmichael *The Other Smallwood* • Irene Handl *Rene Smith* ■ *Dir* John Boulting • *Scr* John Boulting, Frank Harvey, from an idea by Malcolm Muggeridge

Heaven's Burning ★★★★ 18

Road movie thriller
1997 · Aus/Jpn · Colour · 95mins

After cracking Hollywood with his charismatic turn in *LA Confidential*, Russell Crowe headed Down Under for this stunning but criminally overlooked Australian thriller. He plays a getaway driver with a conscience who forms an odd relationship with Youki Kudoh, an unhappy Japanese woman trying to dump her possessive husband. The pair are forced to go on the run, pursued by the cops, Crowe's psychopathic ex-colleagues and Kudoh's even crazier spouse. Director Craig Lahiff makes stunning use of Australian locations and fashions a moving, melancholic romance that is peppered with shocking bursts of violence. JF. Contains violence, swearing and nudity.

Russell Crowe *Colin O'Brien* • Youki Kudoh *Midori Takada* • Kenji Isomura *Yukio Takada* • Ray Barrett *Cam O'Brien* • Robert Mammone *Mahood* • Petru Gheorghiu *Boorjan* ■ *Dir* Craig Lahiff • *Scr* Louis Nowra

Heaven's Gate ★★★ 18

Western 1980 · US · Colour · 207mins

Michael Cimino's notorious western soared over budget and was so trashed by the New York critics that the bankrupted studio, United Artists, withdrew the film and cut it by an hour. Sadly, this is the version usually seen today. While some of the director's ambition still shines through – notably the wondrous photography, the set-piece battle and the roller-skating dance – the story, about a Wyoming range war between cattlemen and persecuted immigrants, makes little sense. The full version, however, is a superb, five-star achievement. AT. Contains violence, swearing, sex scenes and nudity. DVD

Kris Kristofferson *James Averill* • Christopher Walken *Nathan D Champion* • John Hurt *Billy Irvine* • Sam Waterston *Frank Canton* • Brad Dourif *Mr Eggleston* • Isabelle Huppert *Ella Watson* • Joseph Cotten *Reverend Doctor* • Jeff Bridges *John H Bridges* • Richard Masur *Cully* • Terry O'Quinn *Captain Minardi* • Mickey Rourke *Nick Ray* ■ *Dir/Scr* Michael Cimino • *Cinematographer* Vilmos Zsigmond

Heaven's Prisoners ★★★ 15

Thriller 1996 · US · Colour · 126mins

Alec Baldwin stars as ex-New Orleans cop Dave Robicheaux, a man at odds with himself over his alcoholism, loss of faith and love of violence. Adapted from the second in a series of crime novels by James Lee Burke, this has Robicheaux rescuing a small girl from a lagoon air-crash and thinking he's spiritually saved, only to find he's up to his neck in drug smuggling and murder. Baldwin is a little too engaging in the lead, and the plot becomes a rather routine tale of vengeance, but director Phil Joanou keeps a good deal of the novel's sinister atmosphere. TH. Contains violence, swearing, sex scenes and nudity. DVD

Alec Baldwin *Dave Robicheaux* • Kelly Lynch *Annie Robicheaux* • Mary Stuart Masterson *Robin Gaddis* • Eric Roberts *Bubba Rocque* • Teri Hatcher *Claudette Rocque* • Vondie Curtis-Hall *Minos P Dautrieve* • Badja Djola *Batist* • Samantha Lagpacan *Alafair* • Joe Viterelli *Didi Giancano* ■ *Dir* Phil Joanou • *Scr* Harley Peyton, Scott Frank, from the novel by James Lee Burke

Heavy ★★★★ 15

Drama 1995 · US · Colour · 100mins

The coming of age of an overweight, 30-something pizza chef may not seem like a very promising viewing experience, but writer/director James Mangold's marvellous feature debut has a ring of truth few real-life dramas manage. Pruitt Taylor Vince is exceptional as the withdrawn gentle giant who must cross emotional thresholds he never dared acknowledge. The drama is set in motion when Vince's imperious mother (Shelley Winters) decides to match him with new waitress Liv Tyler. Often unbearably poignant, the attention to small details pays heartfelt dividends in this sensitive and low-key triumph. AJ. Contains swearing.

Pruitt Taylor Vince *Victor* • Liv Tyler *Callie* • Shelley Winters *Dolly* • Deborah Harry *Delores* • Joe Grifasi *Leo* • Evan Dando *Jeff* • David Patrick Kelly *Grey man in hospital* • Marian Quinn *Darlene* ■ *Dir/Scr* James Mangold

Heavy Metal ★★ 15

Animated science-fiction fantasy
1981 · US · Colour · 86mins

This cult favourite from the 1980s, based on an American comic book, now looks a tad dated. A mix of mythical imagery and X-rated animation, this compendium of stories was eagerly lapped up by American teens, but it pales in comparison to the amoral savagery of 1990s Japanese *animé*, while the AOR rock soundtrack is quaint rather than subversive. Nevertheless, the animation is still striking and a talented cast of American comics provide voices. JF DVD

Richard Romanus *Harry Canyon* • Susan Roman *Girl/Satellite* • John Candy *Desk sergeant* • Marilyn Lightstone *Queen/Whore* • Jackie Burroughs *Katherine* • George Touliatos *Pilot* • Harold Ramis *Zeke* ■ *Dir* Gerald Potterton • *Scr* Dan Goldberg, Len Blum, from the comic magazine by Richard Corben, Angus McKie, Dan O'Bannon, Thomas Warkentin, Berni Wrightson • *Music* Elmer Bernstein

Heavy Petting ★★ 15

Documentary 1988 · US · Colour · 71mins

As hard as it would seem to make a boring documentary about sex, director Obie Benz and his conceptual collaborator, Pierce Rafferty, have done just that. This supposedly humorous look at American sexual mores uses newsreel footage, school education shorts, film and television clips as well as personal reminiscences about dating and masturbation, from such personalities as Spalding Gray, Allen Ginsberg, William Burroughs and Sandra Bernhard, all to extremely dull effect. Scenes from feature films mingle with 1950s sitcom clips and pop songs with little rhyme, reason or amusement. Remarkably facile, kitsch and uninformative, this is far too safe for a sex documentary. AJ

Dir Obie Benz • *Scr* Suzanne Fenn, Lianne Halfron, from an idea by Pierce Rafferty

Heavyweights ★ PG

Comedy 1995 · US · Colour · 93mins

This sickly teen movie from Disney is about health farm Camp Hope, where overweight kids go to diet. The camp is taken over by a maniacal fitness guru who forces the inmates to endure humiliation, starvation and abuse. Buried deep beneath the cringe-inducing sequences is a satire about commercialism, since the kids are to become part of a wider merchandising scheme. Avoid if possible. AT DVD

Tom McGowan *Pat* • Aaron Schwartz *Gerry* • Shaun Weiss *Josh* • Tom Hodges *Lars* • Leah Lail *Julie* • Paul Feig *Tim* • Kenan Thompson *Roy* • David Bowe *Chris Donelly* ■ *Dir* Steven Brill • *Scr* Judd Apatow, Steven Brill

Hedd Wyn ★★★ 12

Biographical drama
1992 · UK · Colour · 114mins

The first film in Welsh to receive an Oscar nomination, Paul Turner's biopic has a typically British period polish. Huw Garmon gives a respectful performance as Ellis Evans, the teenage poet who wrote under the name of "Hedd Wyn" before dying in the First World War. The war scenes give the film a power and poignancy to rival that of the trench poem *Yr Arwr* (*The Hero*) which posthumously won Evans the Chair at the National Eisteddfod, a prize he'd always coveted. DP. In Welsh with English subtitles. Contains some strong language.

Huw Garmon *Ellis Evans/Hedd Wyn* • Sue Roderick *Lizzie Roberts* • Judith Humphreys *Jini Owen* • Nia Dryhurst *Mary Catherine Hughes* • Grey Evans *Evan Evans* ■ *Dir* Paul Turner • *Scr* Alan Llwyd

Hedda ★★★★ PG

Drama 1975 · UK · Colour · 102mins

Glenda Jackson earned her fourth and final Oscar nomination in this filmed record of her RSC triumph as Ibsen's heroine, the bored and pregnant wife of an egghead several rungs down from her on the social ladder. Jackson gives a powerful interpretation of the role, making it very much a part of the then-emerging women's movement, as does Trevor Nunn's own adaptation. Directing his first film for the cinema (he directed *Anthony and Cleopatra* for TV in 1974), Nunn commendably resists the chance to "open up" the play by keeping the action mostly within the gloomy brown walls of the Tesman drawing room. AT

Glenda Jackson *Hedda* • Peter Eyre *George Tesman* • Timothy West *Judge Brack* • Jennie Linden *Thea Elvsted* • Patrick Stewart *Ejlert Lovborg* • Constance Chapman *Julie* • Pam St Clement *Bertha* ■ • *Scr* Trevor Nunn, from the play *Hedda Gabler* by Henrik Ibsen

Hedwig and the Angry Inch ★★ 15

Musical comedy 2001 · US · Colour · 87mins

Writer/director John Cameron Mitchell adapts his successful off-Broadway rock musical and has a game try at opening up this erratic "rags to bitches" biography of a fictional German transsexual singer (played by Mitchell himself). Using surreal flashbacks, camp humour, crude animation and glam rock songs, Hedwig is introduced as a young boy called Hansel living in East Berlin before the Wall came down. Having a sex-change operation to marry a GI and escape to America, Hedwig then has her music and lyrics ripped off by pop sensation Michael Pitt. Very much a love it or hate it experience. AJ DVD

John Cameron Mitchell *Hedwig/Hansel Schmidt* • Alberta Watson *Mother* • Michael Pitt *Tommy Gnosis* • Andrea Martin *Phyllis Stein* • Maurice Dean Wint *Sergeant Luther Robinson* • Miriam Shor *Yitzhak* • Stephen Trask *Skszp* ■ *Dir* John Cameron Mitchell • *Scr* John Cameron Mitchell, from the play by John Cameron Mitchell, Stephen Trask

Heidi ★★★ U

Drama 1937 · US · BW · 84mins

One of Shirley Temple's most popular films, expertly directed by tough veteran Allan Dwan, on a relatively big budget that allows for expansive Christmas settings and a sleigh chase in the snow. Temple is excellent as the orphan nobody wants and, despite her awkward interpretation of a Dutch girl in one particular musical number, her Swiss miss is convincing. Of course, some may find themselves feeling rather nauseous as Heidi helps a distressed sick girl to walk, causes butler Arthur Treacher to lose his dignity and clowns with an organ-grinder's monkey. TS DVD

Shirley Temple *Heidi* • Jean Hersholt *Adolph Kramer* • Arthur Treacher *Andrews* • Helen Westley *Blind Anna* • Pauline Moore *Elsa* • Thomas Beck *Pastor Schultz* • Mary Nash *Fraulein Rottenmeier* • Sig Rumann [Sig Ruman] *Police captain* ■ *Dir* Allan Dwan • *Scr* Walter Ferris, Julien Josephson, from the novel by Johanna Spyri

Heidi ★★★

Drama 1965 · Austria/W Ger · Colour · 94mins

One of the most-filmed children's classics is given a colourful makeover by Werner Jacobs in this lively German-language version. Defiantly resisting the example of such twee predecessors as Shirley Temple, Eva Maria Singhammer radiates homely vivacity as the little Alpine girl who is kidnapped from her beloved grandfather (Gustav Knuth) so she can rally the flagging spirits of disabled Gertraud Mittermayr in Frankfurt. Starting off rather like a junior rustic idyll, the central city segment of Johanna Spyri's tale is given some much-needed melodramatic steel by Margot Trooger's frosty governess. DP. German dialogue dubbed into English.

Eva Maria Singhammer *Heidi* • Gertraud Mittermayr *Klara* • Gustav Knuth *Alp-Oehi* • Lotte Ledl *Dete* • Ernst Schröder *Sesemann* • Margot Trooger *Miss Rottenmeier* • Rolf Moebius *Dr Klassen* • Rudolf Vogel *Sebastian* ■ *Dir* Werner Jacobs • *Scr* Richard Schweizer, Michael Hallen (adaptation), from the novel by Johanna Spyri

Heidi's Song ★★ U

Animated musical
1982 · US · Colour · 90mins

After numerous live-action versions, Johanna Spyri's much-loved classic gets the cartoon treatment in this sugary, critter-strewn offering. This was a rare feature outing for the Hanna-Barbera studio, which had concentrated on TV shows such as *The Flintstones* and *Top Cat* after its production of countless Tom and Jerry shorts. But little of the old magic is evident in this lacklustre adaptation, which is not helped by the abundance of substandard songs from the usually reliable Sammy Cahn and Burton Lane. Margery Gray does what she can as Heidi, while Sammy Davis Jr adds a little pizzazz as Head Ratte. DP [VIDEO]

Lorne Greene *Grandfather* • Margery Gray *Heidi* • Sammy Davis Jr *Head Ratte* • Peter Cullen *Gruffle* • Roger DeWitt *Peter* • Richard Erdman *Herr Sessmann* • Fritz Feld *Sebastian* ■ *Dir* Robert Taylor (3) • *Scr* Joseph Barbera, Robert Taylor, Jameson Brewer, from the novel by Johanna Spyri

Heimat ★★★★★ 15

Epic drama
1984 · W Ger · BW and Colour · 923mins

It took over five years to shoot the 923 minutes that make up this monumental mosaic of 20th-century German history, and it was worth every second. Set in a village in the Hunsrück uplands, Edgar Reitz's masterpiece chronicles the life of the farming family into which Marita Breuer marries in 1919, paying as much attention to local detail as to the great events that shaped the nation's destiny. Wrongly dismissed in some quarters as high-class soap opera, the story not only eschews cheap melodramatics, but also meticulously develops its characters, who are played with uniform excellence by the huge cast. Also shown in 11 parts on TV, this is a stunningly photographed epic, with monochrome being tantalisingly embossed with patches of colour. DP. In German with English subtitles. DVD

Michael Lesch *Paul Simon* • Marita Breuer *Maria Wiegand* • Gertrud Bredel *Katharina Simon* • Willi Burger *Mathias Simon* • Rüdiger Weigang *Eduard Simon* • Karin Kienzler *Pauline Simon* • Arno Lang *Robert Krober* ■ *Dir* Edgar Reitz • *Scr* Edgar Reitz, Peter Steinbach • *Cinematographer* Gernat Roll

Heimat 2 ★★★★★ 15

Epic drama
1992 · Ger · BW and Colour · 1509mins

The sequel to Edgar Reitz's magisterial 1984 film is officially the longest feature in screen history. But not one second of its 1500-plus minutes is wasted, as Reitz chronicles the social, cultural and political experiences of a group of friends at the Munich conservatoire in the 1960s. The prime focus is on country boy Henry Arnold and his passion for his elusive musical muse, Salome Kammer. But, amazingly (considering there are 71 principal characters), Reitz handles each episode with so much historical, psychological and intellectual integrity that even the most minor subplot has an affecting intimacy. A monumental masterpiece. DP DVD

Henry Arnold *Hermann Simon* • Eva Maria Bayerwaltes *Aunt Pauline* • Edith Behleit *Mother Lichtblau* • Johanna Bittenbinder *Erika* • Martin Maria Blau *Jean-Marie Weber* • Marinus Georg Brand *Herr Gross* • Hannes Demming *Father Aufschrey* • Veroncia Ferres *Dorli* • Salome Kammer *Clarissa Lichtblau* ■ *Dir/Scr* Edgar Reitz

Heimat 3: a Chronicle of Endings and Beginnings ★★★★★ 12A 15

Epic drama 2004 · Ger/UK · Colour · 678mins

Edgar Reitz concludes his remarkable history of one German family's experience of the 20th century with this compelling six-part feature. Reuniting as the Berlin Wall tumbles, composer Henry Arnold and avant-garde singer Salome Kammer agree to resume their star-crossed romance and employ workers from the former East Germany to renovate their dream house on the Rhine. As before, the accumulation of personal and period details draws us into the lives of characters whose all-too-human foibles make them all the more intriguing. Superbly directed and spiritedly played, this is a fitting finale to the most intelligent and sophisticated soap opera in cinema history. DP. In German with English subtitles.

Salome Kammer *Clarissa Lichtblau* • Henry Arnold *Hermann Simon* • Uwe Steimle *Gunnar* • Tom Quaas *Udo* • Peter Schneider *Tillmann* • Heiko Senst *Tobi* • Michael Kausch *Ernst Simon* • Matthias Kniesbeck *Anton* • Karen Hempel *Petra* • Peter Götz *Reinhold* • Julia Prochnow *Moni* • Antje Brauner *Jana* ■ *Dir* Edgar Reitz • *Scr* Edgar Reitz, Thomas Brussig

Heimkehr ★★★★

Silent romantic drama
1928 · Ger · BW · 110mins

Joe May pioneered the German movie serial and directed numerous feature films, as well as launching the career of Fritz Lang, before creating what many regard as his masterpiece. This tragic melodrama, which bears the hallmark of both UFA (the German national production body) stylisation and Hollywood gloss, has more in common with FW Murnau's *Sunrise* than May's own follow-up, the grittily realistic street drama, *Asphalt*. A tale of doomed wartime romance sees Dita Parlo caught between Gustav Fröhlich and Lars Hanson. Produced by Erich Pommer, it's expertly photographed by Gunther Rittau. DP

Lars Hanson *Richard* • Dita Parlo *Anna* • Gustav Fröhlich *Karl* ■ *Dir* Joe May • *Scr* Fred Majo, Dr Fritz Wendhauser, from the novel *Karl und Anna* by Leonhard Franck

The Heiress ★★★★★ U

Period drama 1949 · US · BW · 114mins

An immaculately cast and brilliantly directed movie adaptation of Henry James's novel *Washington Square*. Olivia de Havilland quite rightly won her second Academy Award as the plain spinster seeking affection from fortune hunter Montgomery Clift. Clift also gives a finely controlled performance of great subtlety and, though both he and de Havilland are too good-looking for their roles, it is this quintessential Hollywood factor that keeps you riveted to the screen. As de Havilland's autocratic father, Ralph Richardson delivers arguably his finest screen work, and these flawless casting choices contribute to what is surely the most satisfying screen adaptation of James's original story. TS

Olivia de Havilland *Catherine Sloper* • Montgomery Clift *Morris Townsend* • Ralph Richardson *Dr Austin Sloper* • Miriam Hopkins *Lavinia Penniman* • Vanessa Brown *Maria* • Mona Freeman *Marian Almond* • Selena Royle *Elizabeth Almond* • Ray Collins *Jefferson Almond* • Betty Linley *Mrs Montgomery* ■ *Dir* William Wyler • *Scr* Ruth Goetz, Augustus Goetz, from their play, from the novel *Washington Square* by Henry James • *Music* Aaron Copland • *Costume Designer* Edith Head, Gile Steele • *Art Director* John Meehan

Heist ★★★★ 15

Heist drama
2001 · US/Can · Colour · 104mins

Writer/director David Mamet cranks up the suspense with his crack at a genre picture: the one-last-job heist. Gene Hackman is the boat-building master thief planning retirement with moll Rebecca Pidgeon. Typically, caper organiser Danny DeVito foists nervy nephew Sam Rockwell on Hackman's regular crew and the seemingly infinite double-crosses start rolling from there. As ever, Mamet's overcooked dialogue crackles, especially when delivered by Hackman, DeVito and fellow thief Delroy Lindo, and his eye for plot detail is acute. AC [VIDEO] DVD

Gene Hackman *Joe Moore* • Danny DeVito *Mickey Bergman* • Delroy Lindo *Bobby Blane* • Sam Rockwell *Jimmy Silk* • Rebecca Pidgeon *Fran* • Patti LuPone *Betty Croft* ■ *Dir/Scr* David Mamet

Hejar ★★★ PG

Drama 2001 · Tur/Gr/Hun · Colour · 119mins

Sentiment dilutes the political potency of this earnest melodrama, which was banned by the Turkish authorities for "promoting Kurdish nationalism" and "presenting the police in a negative light". Sukran Gungor plays the retired judge who is forced to abandon his isolationism when his Kurdish neighbours are killed by the police and their five-year-old daughter (Dilan Ercetin) seeks refuge with him. Director Handan Ipekci chooses to concentrate on the battle of wills between the petulant innocent and the curmudgeonly nationalist. DP. In Turkish and Kurdish with English subtitles.

Sukran Gungor *Rifat Bey* • Dilan Ercetin *Hejar* • Fusun Demirel *Sakine* • Ismail Hakki Sen *Abdulkadir Evdo* • Yildiz Kenter *Muzeyyen Hanim* ■ *Dir/Scr* Handan Ipekci

Hélas pour Moi ★★

Drama 1993 · Fr/Swi · Colour · 85mins

The English title is *Oh, Woe Is Me* and it's a reworking of the ancient Greek myth of Alcmene and Amphitryon. Gérard Depardieu drifts around a rainy Swiss lakeside village soliciting opinions on everything from love to the war in Bosnia. His body is then borrowed by God. It looks slapped together in a day or so, with Depardieu appearing as if in homage to Godard's earlier achievements. Wonderful music by Beethoven, Bach and Shostakovich gives the illusion of beauty. AT. A French language film.

Gérard Depardieu *Simon Donnadieu* • Laurence Masliah *Rachel Donnadieu* • Bernard Verley *Abraham Klimt* • Jean-Louis Loca *Max Mercure* • François Germond *Pastor* • Jean-Pierre Miquel *Other Pastor* ■ *Dir* Jean-Luc Godard • *Scr* Jean-Luc Godard, from the play *Amphitryon 38* by Jean Giraudoux

Held Up ★ PG

Crime comedy 1999 · US · Colour · 85mins

Jamie Foxx plays the out-of-towner who gets caught up in a convenience store robbery after being dumped by his fiancée (Nia Long) for spending their house savings on a vintage car. This crass comedy of errors a stereotyped affair from top to bottom, with Foxx's performance a long, long way behind his winning turns in *Collateral* and *Ray*. DP. Contains some violence and swearing. [VIDEO]

Jamie Foxx *Michael Dawson* • Nia Long *Rae* • Barry Corbin *Pembry* • John Cullum *Jack* • Jake Busey *Beaumont* • Michael Shamus Wiles *Biker* • Eduardo Yanez *Rodrigo* ■ *Dir* Steve Rash • *Scr* Erik Fleming, Jeff Eastin

The Helen Morgan Story ★★★

Musical biography 1957 · US · BW · 118mins

Although Ann Blyth bears no resemblance to Helen Morgan and doesn't sing (Gogi Grant does the dubbing), she gives a sincere and effective performance as the great torch singer. This biopic plays fast and loose with the facts of Morgan's tumultuous life, but has considerable Prohibition-era atmosphere through the moody black-and-white photography of Ted McCord allied to the fast-paced direction of Michael Curtiz. Paul Newman scores as the opportunist who weaves in and out of her life. AE

Ann Blyth *Helen Morgan* • Paul Newman *Larry* • Richard Carlson *Wade* • Gene Evans *Whitey Krause* • Alan King *Ben* • Cara Williams *Dolly* ■ *Dir* Michael Curtiz • *Scr* Oscar Saul, Dean Reisner, Stephen Longstreet, Nelson Gidding

H

Helen of Troy ★★★ U

Epic adventure
1955 · US/It · Colour · 115mins

Filmed in Italy by Robert Wise, the future director of *West Side Story* and *The Sound of Music*, this excursion into Greek myth boasts a weird cast: Jacques Sernas as Paris and Rossana Podesta as Helen are a lacklustre romantic couple, while Stanley Baker's Achilles is a real heel. Janette Scott and even Brigitte Bardot add support, but it's a bit of a slog until the wooden horse lumbers into view and starts the sacking of Troy. AT DVD

Rossana Podesta *Helen* • Jacques Sernas *Paris* • Cedric Hardwicke *Priam* • Stanley Baker *Achilles* • Niall MacGinnis *Menelaus* • Nora Swinburne *Hecuba* • Harry Andrews *Hector* • Brigitte Bardot *Andraste* ■ *Dir* Robert Wise • *Scr* John Twist, Hugh Gray

The Helicopter Spies ★★ PG

Spy adventure 1968 · US · Colour · 91mins

The hilarious staccato-speak and all-action breeziness of *The Man from UNCLE* are handled with flair by David McCallum and Robert Vaughn in this feature that has been skilfully plucked from an episode of the comic-book TV series. Even the ham-fisted clichés are part of the fun. Still, no amount of action can disguise the creakiness of the presentation. JM DVD

Robert Vaughn *Napoleon Solo* • David McCallum *Illya Kuryakin* • Carol Lynley *Annie* • Bradford Dillman *Luther Sebastian* • Lola Albright *Azalea* • John Dehner *Dr Kharmusi* • Leo G Carroll *Mr Waverly* ■ *Dir* Boris Sagal • *Scr* Dean Hargrove

Hell and High Water ★★★ U

Action spy drama
1954 · US · Colour · 102mins

A splendid submarine movie starring Richard Widmark that makes the best of the confined surroundings to pump up the atmosphere. Twentieth Century-Fox boss Darryl F Zanuck didn't want to spend too much time on this one, so he entrusted it to jobbing director Samuel Fuller. The film became yet another heady Fuller brew, full of action, espionage, romance and cardboard characterisation. The result is, of course, immensely enjoyable and a feast for Fuller fans. The supporting cast helps hide the fact that the female lead (Bella Darvi, Zanuck's mistress at the time) can't act. TS

Richard Widmark *Adam Jones* • Bella Darvi *Denise* • Victor Francen *Professor Montel* • Cameron Mitchell *"Ski" Brodski* • Gene Evans *Chief Holter* • David Wayne *Dugboat Walker* • Stephen Bekassy *Neuman* ■ *Dir* Samuel

Fuller • *Scr* Jesse L Lasky Jr [Jesse Lasky Jr], Samuel Fuller, from a story by David Hempstead

Hell below Zero ★★★ U

Adventure 1954 · UK · Colour · 86mins

Alan Ladd took advantage of the tax break that helped US stars if they spent 18 months in Europe by making a series of British movies aimed at the international market, including this action adventure based on the Hammond Innes novel *The White South*. It's smoothly directed by another American, the excellent and under-rated Mark Robson, and Ladd is terrific pitted against grim-faced whalers in the Antarctic wastes. TS

Alan Ladd *Duncan Craig* • Joan Tetzel *Judie Nordahl* • Basil Sydney *Bland* • Stanley Baker *Erik Bland* • Joseph Tomelty *Captain McPhee* • Niall MacGinnis *Dr Howe* • Jill Bennett *Gerda Peterson* • Peter Dyneley *Miller* ■ *Dir* Mark Robson • *Scr* Alec Coppel, Max Trell, Richard Maibaum, from the novel *The White South* by Hammond Innes

H

Hell Bent for Glory ★★

First World War drama
1957 · US · BW · 91mins

Also known as *Lafayette Escadrille*, this First World War saga was a deeply personal project for director William Wellman, who had himself been an ace fighter pilot with the Lafayette Flying Corps. Wellman's high hopes were dashed, however, when Paul Newman dropped out. He was replaced by blond Malibu lifeguard Tab Hunter, who really doesn't cut it as a war hero. Clint Eastwood gets an early featured role as one of Wellman's flying chums, and Wellman himself is played by his son. AT

Tab Hunter *Thad Walker* • Etchika Choureau *Renee* • Marcel Dalio *Drillmaster* • David Janssen *Duke Sinclaire* • Paul Fix *US General* • Veola Vonn *The Madam* • Will Hutchins *Dave Putnam* • Clint Eastwood *George Moseley* • Bill Wellman Jr [William Wellman Jr] *Bill Wellman* ■ *Dir* William A Wellman • *Scr* AS Fleischman, from the story *C'est la Guerre* by William A Wellman

Hell Bent for Leather ★★ U

Western 1960 · US · Colour · 81mins

This uninspired Audie Murphy western is given a novel moral twist by the fact that evil marshal Stephen McNally keeps pursuing our baby-faced hero even though he knows he's innocent. Felicia Farr is the girl Murphy enlists to help him, and there are some mean hombres in tow. It also gains from being filmed in CinemaScope, and from the presence of old-time western hero Bob Steele. TS

Audie Murphy *Clay* • Felicia Farr *Janet* • Stephen McNally *Deckett* • Robert Middleton *Ambrose* • Rad Fulton *Moon* • Jan Merlin *Travers* • Bob Steele *Jared* ■ *Dir* George Sherman • *Scr* Christopher Knopf, from a novel by Ray Hogan

Hell Boats ★

Wartime drama
1970 · UK/US · Colour · 95mins

A feeble Second World War drama, made for peanuts and with a poor cast. James Franciscus is an American lieutenant commander in the Royal Navy, who arrives in the Mediterranean to find an undisciplined rabble and a lonely wife, played by Elizabeth Shepherd. Things blow up (German supply dumps) and things break down (actors' accents and relationships) via wobbly back projection. AT

James Franciscus *Lt Commander Tom Jeffords* • Elizabeth Shepherd *Alison Ashurst* • Ronald Allen *Commander Roger Ashurst* • Reuven Bar Yotam *CPO Yacov* • Mark Hawkins *Lt Barlow* ■ *Dir* Paul Wendkos • *Scr* Anthony Spinner, Donald Ford, Derek Ford, from a story by SS Schweitzer

Hell Camp ★★ 18

Action drama 1986 · US · Colour · 95mins

This disappointing slice of straight-to-video fodder – released in the States as *Opposing Force* – fails to deliver on an intriguing premise. Tom Skerritt and Lisa Eichhorn are among the military guinea pigs undergoing tests in the field to see how they stand up to being prisoners of war. The problem is that bonkers camp boss Anthony Zerbe starts taking the experiments a little too seriously. JF. Contains violence, swearing and nudity.

Tom Skerritt *Major Logan* • Lisa Eichhorn *Lt Casey* • Anthony Zerbe *Becker* • Richard Roundtree *Sgt Stafford* • Robert Wightman *Gen McGowan* • John Considine *Gen MacDonald* ■ *Dir* Eric Karson • *Scr* Gil Cowan

Hell Comes to Frogtown ★ 15

Science-fiction action adventure
1988 · US · Colour · 82mins

This is almost the ultimate in dumb movie plotlines. Professional wrestler "Rowdy" Roddy Piper stars as Sam Hell, the last potent man alive, who is chosen to rescue and impregnate various buxom maidens held captive by mutant frog folk. The directors never allow anything as trivial as common sense to get in the way of the fun, with most of the *Carry On*-style jokes focusing on Piper's "below the belt" equipment. Bad enough to be beyond criticism: how can you hate a movie which includes such immortal lines as "Eat lead, froggies!" RS

Roddy Piper *Sam Hell* • Sandahl Bergman *Spangle* • Cec Verrell *Centinella* • William Smith *Captain Devlin/Count Sodom* • Rory Calhoun *Looney Tunes* • Nicholas Worth *Bull* • Kristi Somers *Arabella* ■ *Dir* RJ Kizer, Donald G Jackson • *Scr* Randall Frakes, from a story by Donald G Jackson, Randall Frakes

Hell Divers ★★ U

Action drama 1932 · US · BW · 108mins

This overlong action drama casts Clark Gable and Wallace Beery as a pair of tough officers in the US Navy. Dorothy Jordan is the woman who comes between them, though their rivalry is resolved when Beery sacrifices all to save Gable's life. The narrative mostly consists of endless flying missions that get less impressive the further the film progresses. Director George Hill, best known for his silent drama *The Big House*, later shot himself while making *The Good Earth*. AT

Clark Gable *Steve* • Wallace Beery *Windy* • Conrad Nagel *Duke* • Dorothy Jordan *Ann* • Marjorie Rambeau *Mame Kelsey* • Marie Prevost *Lulu* • Cliff Edwards *Baldy* • Robert Young (1) *Young officer* ■ *Dir* George Hill • *Scr* Harvey Gates, Malcolm Stuart Boylan, JK McGuinness, Ralph Graves, from a story by Lt Cdr Frank Wead

Hell Drivers ★★★★ PG

Thriller 1957 · UK · BW · 103mins

This gripping British thriller is given a cutting edge of social reality by former Hollywood director Cy Endfield (billed here as C Raker Endfield). Stanley Baker stars as the ex-con given the job of driving lorries at perilous speeds to meet the deadlines of a haulage company, who uncovers a racket run by his unprincipled manager. There's a splendid performance from Patrick McGoohan as a lethal rival driver and a marvellous co-starring role for Herbert Lom. Watch out, too, for a young, pre-Bond Sean Connery. TH DVD

Stanley Baker *Tom Yately* • Herbert Lom *Gino* • Peggy Cummins *Lucy* • Patrick McGoohan *Red* • William Hartnell *Cartley* • Wilfrid Lawson *Ed* • Sidney James *Dusty* • Jill Ireland *Jill* • Alfie Bass *Tinker* • Gordon Jackson *Scottie* • David McCallum *Jimmy Yately* • Sean Connery *Johnny* ■ *Dir* C Raker Endfield [Cy Endfield] • *Scr* John Kruse, C Raker Endfield [Cy Endfield]

Hell in the Pacific ★★★★ PG

Second World War drama
1968 · US · Colour · 97mins

Director John Boorman touches the primitive nerve of mankind at odds with itself and nature (anticipating his masterpiece, *Deliverance*, four years later) in this story of an American pilot and a Japanese sailor marooned on an island in wartime. The catchpenny title masks the solidly psychological nature of the action, as Lee Marvin displays a dramatic complexity rarely seen in his other works, while Toshiro Mifune exhibits honour as a sword that cuts both ways. The dynamics of the pair having to share their lives makes for compelling viewing. TH DVD

Lee Marvin *US marine pilot* • Toshiro Mifune *Japanese naval officer* ■ *Dir* John Boorman • *Scr* Alexander Jacobs, Eric Bercovici, from a story by Reuben Bercovitch

Hell Is a City ★★★ PG

Thriller 1959 · UK · BW · 91mins

Made when Hammer wasn't just a house of horror, this brisk crime thriller was filmed on location in Manchester. Stanley Baker bristles with northern grit as the inspector out to nab the escaped convict whose crimes include murder and robbing bookie Donald Pleasence. Director Val Guest demonstrates a flair for realism and no-nonsense pacing. DP

Stanley Baker *Inspector Martineau* • John Crawford *Don Starling* • Donald Pleasence *Gus Hawkins* • Maxine Audley *Julia Martineau* • Billie Whitelaw *Chloe Hawkins* • Joseph Tomelty *Furnisher Steele* • George A Cooper *Doug Savage* ■ *Dir* Val Guest • *Scr* Val Guest, from a novel by Maurice Proctor

Hell Is for Heroes ★★★ 15

Second World War adventure
1962 · US · BW · 86mins

Having already won a screenwriting Oscar for *Battleground* (1949), Robert Pirosh here came up with an even more uncompromising insight into the terrifying uncertainty of frontline life. Director Don Siegel builds steadily towards the pitiless battle sequences by allowing us to get to know the members of the small unit ordered to overpower a German pillbox, whose only hope of survival is to mislead the Germans into believing they are a much more substantial force. Steve McQueen is overly intense and Bob Newhart's comic monologue a mite ill-judged, but the rest of the cast is superb. DP DVD

Steve McQueen *Reese* • Bobby Darin *Private Corby* • Fess Parker *Sergeant Pike* • Harry Guardino *Sergeant Larkin* • James Coburn *Corporal Henshaw* • Mike Kellin *Private Kolinsky* • Joseph Hoover *Captain Loomis* • Bill Mullikin *Private Cumberly* • LQ Jones *Sergeant Frazer* • Bob Newhart *Private Driscoll* ■ *Dir* Don Siegel • *Scr* Robert Pirosh, Richard Carr, from a story by Robert Pirosh

Hell Night ★★ 18

Horror 1981 · US · Colour · 101mins

Producer Irwin Yablans's poor attempt to do for the haunted house genre what *Halloween* did for the psycho slasher, sees four teens on a fraternity initiation, locked overnight in an old dark house where a deranged madman axed his deformed family to death 12 years earlier. Former adult film-maker Tom DeSimone directs with a distinctly unpleasant edge, but Linda Blair acts as if she's in a different film from the rest of the average cast. AJ DVD

Linda Blair *Marti* • Vincent Van Patten *Seth* • Peter Barton *Jeff* • Kevin Brophy *Peter* • Jenny Neumann *May* • Suki Goodwin *Denise* ■ *Dir* Tom DeSimone • *Scr* Randolph Feldman

Hell on Frisco Bay ★★

Crime thriller 1955 · US · Colour · 98mins

Alan Ladd stars as the former cop framed and jailed on a manslaughter charge, who is seeking revenge on the violent racketeer responsible, played by Edward G Robinson. Ladd is aided by a first-rate cast, including Joanne Dru as his wife, Fay Wray as a faded film star and Paul Stewart as her lover and Robinson's right-hand man. Jayne Mansfield has a bit in a nightclub and Rod Taylor makes an early appearance. AE

Alan Ladd *Steve Rollins* • Edward G Robinson *Victor Amato* • Joanne Dru *Marcia Rollins* • William Demarest *Dan Bianco* • Nestor Paiva *Lou Fiaschetti* • Perry Lopez *Mario Amato* • Paul Stewart *Joe Lye* • Fay Wray *Kay Stanley* • Jayne Mansfield *Blonde* • Stanley Adams *Hammy* • Rodney Taylor [Rod Taylor] *Brodie Evans* ■ *Dir* Frank Tuttle • *Scr* Sydney Boehm, Martin Rackin, from the magazine serial *The Darkest Hour* by William P McGivern

Hell Ship Mutiny ★ U

Adventure drama 1957 · US · BW · 66mins

In the 1940s, the well built Jon Hall was a kind of male Dorothy Lamour, only instead of a sarong, he was mostly seen in a loincloth. Though still handsome here, Hall remains fully clothed, despite the South Seas setting, in this rather dire low-budget Republic adventure. He's a ship's captain helping a princess rid her island of thieves. RB

Jon Hall *Captain Knight* • John Carradine *Malone* • Peter Lorre *Lamouet* • Roberta Haynes *Mareva* • Mike Mazurki *Ross* • Charles Mauu *Tula* ■ *Dir* Lee Sholem, Elmo Williams • *Scr* DeVallon Scott, Wells Root

Hell to Eternity ★★★

Biographical Second World War drama
1960 · US · BW · 133mins

Based on a true story of Second World War hero Guy Gabaldon, the film presents a slightly different angle on the war: how the Californian Japanese community was affected by the bombing of Pearl Harbor. Most of the movie, however, is the usual slam-bang battle stuff, until Jeffrey Hunter – with divided loyalties due to his upbringing by Japanese foster parents – uses his knowledge of his adopted tongue to get an enemy battalion to surrender. RB

Jeffrey Hunter *Guy Gabaldon* • David Janssen *Bill* • Vic Damone *Pete* • Patricia Owens *Sheila* • Miiko Taka *Ester* • Sessue Hayakawa *General Matsui* • George Takei *George* ■ *Dir* Phil Karlson • *Scr* Ted Sherdeman, Walter Roeber Schmidt, from a story by Gil Doud

Hell Town ★★ U

Western 1937 · US · BW · 55mins

Zane Grey's novel *Born to the West* was first filmed in 1926 and plenty of silent footage resurfaces in this Paramount remake, which was originally released under that title. But the main interest lies in the performance of a pre-fame John Wayne, as a drifter whose dalliance with Marsha Hunt incurs the wrath of his Wyoming rancher cousin, Johnny Mack Brown. Unfortunately, Wayne is easily upstaged by his co-stars, with Monte Blue taking the honours as the scheming saloon owner intent on cheating Duke out of Brown's prized herd. DP DVD

John Wayne *Dare Rudd* • Marsha Hunt *Judy* • Johnny Mack Brown *Tom Fillmore* • Monte Blue *Bart Hammond* • Syd Saylor *Dinkey Hooley* • Alan Ladd *Inspector* ■ *Dir* Charles Barton • *Scr* Stuart Anthony, Robert Yost, from the novel *Born to the West* by Zane Grey

Hell Up in Harlem ★ 18

Crime drama 1973 · US · Colour · 90mins

The weak sequel to *Black Caesar* finds Fred Williamson fighting both his father and the mob for control of Harlem. When the Mafia kidnap his children, he leads a posse of frogmen against mob headquarters in the Florida Keys. Plenty of double-crossing mayhem and hand-held camera action fail to enliven the usually reliable director Larry Cohen's blaxploitation caper. AJ

Fred Williamson *Tommy Gibbs* • Julius Harris *Papa Gibbs* • Gloria Hendry *Helen Bradley* • Margaret Avery (2) *Sister Jennifer* • D'Urville Martin *Reverend Rufus* • Tony King *Zach* ■ *Dir/Scr* Larry Cohen

The Hell with Heroes ★

Crime drama 1968 · US · Colour · 101mins

Eminently missable, this features Rod Taylor and Peter Duel trying to make a dishonest buck after the Second World War by smuggling contraband. Harry Guardino plays Mr Big and Claudia Cardinale his mistress, a thankless role with which she looks suitably bored. TV director Joseph Sargent made his big-screen debut here. AT

Rod Taylor *Brynie MacKay* • Claudia Cardinale *Elena* • Harry Guardino *Lee Harris* • Kevin McCarthy *Colonel Wilson* • Pete Duel *Mike Brewer* • William Marshall (2) *Al Poland* • Don Knight *Pepper* ■ *Dir* Joseph Sargent • *Scr* Halsted Welles, Harold Livingston, from a story by Harold Livingston

Hellborn ★

Crime drama 1961 · US · Colour · 75mins

An undercover cop in drag, a judge warning the audience of the dangers of pornography and a beauty queen cornered by a sadistic psycho killer – what else could this be but another poverty row, sexploitation quickie from Ed Wood Jr, famously acknowledged as the world's worst director? The last film directed by the cult auteur of *Plan 9 for Outer Space* has Dino Fantini going berserk watching a stag movie and turning into a sex maniac. AJ

Kenne Duncan *Lt Matt Carson* • James "Duke" Moore [Duke Moore] *Sgt Randy Stone* • Jean Fontaine *Gloria Henderson* • Carl Anthony *Johnny Ryde* • Dino Fantini *Dirk Williams* • Jeanne Willardson *Mary Smith* ■ *Dir/Scr* Edward D Wood Jr

Hellbound: Hellraiser II

★★ 18

Horror 1988 · UK · Colour · 89mins

Allegory is replaced by the just plain gory in the first sequel to Clive Barker's ground-breaking macabre masochistic myth about the dark angels of hell and their Faustian bargains. Kenneth Cranham is the demented doctor anxious to meet the Cenobite messengers, while asylum inmate Ashley Laurence (still recovering from *Hellraiser* events) is forced to fight the invoked demons for her father's soul. Routinely directed by Tony Randel, some disturbing eeriness is conjured up between the blood-soaked illogicalities and outlandish inconsistencies. AJ. Contains violence, swearing and nudity. DVD

Ashley Laurence *Kirsty Cotton* • Clare Higgins *Julia* • Kenneth Cranham *Dr Channard* • Imogen Boorman *Tiffany* • William Hope *Kyle Macrae* • Oliver Smith *Browning* • Sean Chapman *Uncle Frank* • Doug Bradley *Pinhead* ■ *Dir* Tony Randel • *Scr* Peter Atkins, from a story by Clive Barker

Hellboy ★★★ 12

Horror action adventure
2004 · US · Colour · 116mins

Blade II director Guillermo del Toro tackles another comic-book adaptation with this faithful take on Mike Mignola's unlikely superhero, Hellboy. A visually appealing marriage of action, horror and romance, it's both intelligent and fun. In a wry and often poignant performance, Ron Perlman brings unusual depth to the titular character, a cigar-chomping demon intended by the Nazis for acts of evil, but instead raised by the Allies to be an agent of good. From his arch-enemy Rasputin (Karel Roden) to his pyrokinetic love interest (Selma Blair), every aspect of Hellboy's world is exotic and exciting. Though the film loses momentum towards the end, it's still a strong example of its genre. SF. Contains violence. DVD

Ron Perlman *Hellboy* • John Hurt *Professor Trevor "Broom" Bruttenholm* • Selma Blair *Liz Sherman* • Jeffrey Tambor *Tom Manning* • Karel Roden *Grigori Rasputin* • Rupert Evans *John Myers* • Doug Jones *Abe Sapien* • Ladislav Beran *Kroenen* ■ *Dir* Guillermo del Toro • *Scr* Guillermo del Toro, from a story by Guillermo del Toro, Peter Briggs, from the comic book by Mike Mignola

Hellcats of the Navy ★★ U

Second World War drama
1957 · US · BW · 77mins

This barely average war movie is filled with phoney back-projected battles and an equally phoney performance from Ronald Reagan as a submarine commander who offers moral homilies to his crew on a mission to look for Japanese mines. After a skirmish, Reagan is forced to leave one of his men behind, while a crass romance with comely nurse Nancy Davis (his real-life wife and the future First Lady) complicates matters. This was the only time they acted together. AT

Ronald Reagan *Commander Casey Abbott* • Nancy Davis *Helen Blair* • Arthur Franz *Lieutenant Commander Don Landon* • Robert Arthur *Freddy Warren* • William Leslie *Lieutenant Paul Prentice* • William Phillips [William "Bill" Phillips] *Carroll* • Harry Lauter *Wes Barton* ■ *Dir* Nathan Juran • *Scr* David Lang, Raymond T Marcus [Bernard Gordon], from a story by David Lang, from the book *Hellcats of the Sea* by Charles A Lockwood, Hans Christian

Heller in Pink Tights ★★★

Western 1960 · US · Colour · 100mins

George Cukor, renowned as a woman's director in Hollywood, might seem an unlikely choice to direct a western, but this is an unlikely example of the genre, dealing as it does with a group of travelling theatricals, led by stunning Sophia Loren. Anthony Quinn and Steve Forrest flex their emotions as rivals for La Loren, but the real star is Cukor's skill as a film-maker. The production design is superb, and Loren and her troupe, whether on-stage or off-stage, look great in Technicolor. TS

Sophia Loren *Angela Rossini* • Anthony Quinn *Tom Healy* • Margaret O'Brien *Della Southby* • Steve Forrest *Clint Mabry* • Eileen Heckart *Lorna Hathaway* • Edmund Lowe *Manfred "Doc" Montague* • Ramon Novarro *De Leon* • George Mathews *Sam Pierce* ■ *Dir* George Cukor • *Scr* Dudley Nichols, Walter Bernstein, from the novel *Heller with a Gun* by Louis L'Amour • *Art Director* Hal Pereira

Hellfighters ★★ PG

Adventure 1969 · US · Colour · 115mins

John Wayne douses oilfield fires while trying to dampen the passion his daughter (Katharine Ross) feels for his young partner (Jim Hutton). Based on the exploits of firefighter Red Adair, the film's technical adviser, this old-style action movie hardly sets the world alight with its perfunctory action and tacked-on romance. Vera Miles, who was Wayne's love interest in *The Man Who Shot Liberty Valance*, here plays his ex-wife, while buffs will spot the similarities between this and the 1998 asteroid epic, *Armageddon*. AT

John Wayne *Chance Buckman* • Katharine Ross *Tish Buckman* • Jim Hutton *Greg Parker* • Vera Miles *Madelyn Buckman* • Jay C Flippen *Jack Lomax* • Bruce Cabot *Joe Horn* • Edward Faulkner *George Harris* ■ *Dir* Andrew V McLaglen • *Scr* Clair Huffaker

The Hellfire Club ★★ U

Historical adventure
1961 · UK · Colour · 93mins

Depravity, debauchery and devil worship? There's nothing of the sort in this would-be horror flick, in which such sins are sadly bleached of any lurid content. Keith Michell stars as the dispossessed son who returns to claim his degenerate father's estate, only to be challenged by his cousin Peter Arne, who's up to all kinds of dirty tricks by virtue of his Hellfire Club membership. The club was, in fact, a group of 18th-century aristocrats bent on the violation of local maidens while praying to Satan and all his works, but any relationship between the real story and this hokum is coincidental. TH

Keith Michell *Jason* • Adrienne Corri *Isobel* • Peter Cushing *Merryweather* • Kai Fischer *Yvonne* • Peter Arne *Thomas* • David Lodge *Timothy* • Bill Owen *Martin* • Miles Malleson *Judge* ■ *Dir* Robert S Baker, Monty Berman • *Scr* Leon Griffiths, Jimmy Sangster, from a story by Jimmy Sangster

Hellgate ★★ U

Western 1952 · US · Colour · 87mins

Hellgate is a remote prison in New Mexico where the brutal regime in the 1860s is made worse by the desert heat. Sterling Hayden plays the wrongly imprisoned veterinary surgeon, persecuted by the harsh and embittered commandant portrayed by Ward Bond, in this unremittingly grim production. AE

Sterling Hayden *Gil Hanley* • Joan Leslie *Ellen Hanley* • Ward Bond *Lt Tod Vorhees* • Jim Arness [James Arness] *George Redfield* • Marshall Bradford *Doctor Pelham* • Peter Coe *Jumper Hall* • Richard Paxton *George Nye* • John Pickard *Gundy Boyd* ■ *Dir* Charles Marquis Warren • *Scr* Charles Marquis Warren, from a story by Charles Marquis Warren, John C Champion

Hello Again ★★★ PG

Black comedy 1987 · US · Colour · 96mins

Making it to the big screen from TV's *Cheers*, Shelley Long is rather small-time in one of those supernatural plots that were popular after *Ghostbusters*. She's a plastic surgeon's plastic wife, who chokes to death and returns to a much-altered life thanks to her medium sister. Long's brittle vivacity crumples under an overload of whimsy, though Judith Ivey, as the spaced-out, hippy sister, tunes us in to the cosmos to some comical effect. TH. Contains some swearing. DVD

Shelley Long *Lucy Chadman* • Gabriel Byrne *Kevin Scanlon* • Judith Ivey *Zelda* • Corbin Bernsen *Jason Chadman* • Sela Ward *Kim Lacey* • Austin Pendleton *Junior Lacey* ■ *Dir* Frank Perry • *Scr* Susan Isaacs

Hello, Dolly! ★★★★ U

Musical 1969 · US · Colour · 139mins

Despite Barbra Streisand's underaged Dolly Levi, this lavish 20th Century-Fox movie version of the long-running Broadway hit is a wondrous treat under Gene Kelly's expert direction, and now looks like the virtual last gasp of the great era of costly Hollywood musicals. Among the twinkling, shining stars are Britain's own Michael Crawford and the man who had taken the title song to number one in the US charts five years earlier, Louis "Satchmo" Armstrong himself. The design, use of colour and, particularly, the marvellous score are quite breathtaking, and the film won three Oscars. TS DVD

Barbra Streisand *Dolly Gallagher Levi* • Walter Matthau *Horace Vandergelder* • Michael Crawford *Cornelius Hackl* • Louis Armstrong *Orchestra leader* • Marianne McAndrew *Irene Molloy* • EJ Peaker *Minnie Fay* • Danny Lockin *Barnaby Tucker* • Joyce Ames *Ermengarde* ■ *Dir* Gene Kelly • *Scr* Ernest Lehman, from the musical *Hello, Dolly!* by Jerry Herman, Michael Stewart, from the play *The Matchmaker* by Thornton Wilder • *Cinematographer* Harry Stradling • *Music* Lenny Hayton, Lionel Newman • *Production Designer* John De Cuir

Hello Down There ★★ U

Comedy 1969 · US · Colour · 97mins

This would-be comedy comes across as a sort of underwater *Swiss Family Robinson*, with Tony Randall as the designer of a submersible house who agrees to test it out on his wife and children. The plethora of generation gap jokes soon grates on the nerves, as do the bratty adolescent cast members, including a young Richard Dreyfuss, but there's no denying an ingenious premise that should dazzle the youngsters. RS

Tony Randall *Fred Miller* • Janet Leigh *Vivian Miller* • Jim Backus *TR Hollister* • Roddy McDowall *Nate Ashbury* • Merv Griffin • Ken Berry *Mel Cheever* • Kay Cole *Lorrie Miller* • Richard Dreyfuss *Harold Webster* • Harvey Lembeck *Sonarman* ■ *Dir* Jack Arnold • *Scr* Frank Telford, John McGreevey, from a story by Ivan Tors, Art Arthur

H

Hello, Frisco, Hello ★★ U

Period musical 1943 · US · Colour · 98mins

After time off for motherhood, Alice Faye returned in another Fox period musical with her regular co-stars of the time, John Payne and Jack Oakie. The script is routine stuff about Payne's impresario making a singing star out of Faye on the turn-of-the-century Barbary Coast and how she repays the debt when he's down on his luck. To supplement the period numbers, Mack Gordon and Harry Warren wrote *You'll Never Know*, an Oscar-winning song about separated lovers with a wartime relevance that helped the film to box-office success. AE

Alice Faye *Trudy Evans* • John Payne *Johnny Cornell* • Jack Oakie *Dan Daley* • Lynn Bari *Bernice Croft* • Laird Cregar *Sam Weaver* • June Havoc *Beulah Clancy* • Ward Bond *Sharkey* ■ *Dir* H Bruce Humberstone • *Scr* Robert Ellis, Helen Logan, Richard Macauley

Hello – Goodbye ★

Comedy 1970 · US/UK · Colour · 100mins

Michael Crawford plays Harry England, a man obsessed with luxury cars, an interest which embroils him in a love affair while on a trip to France. Only later does he discover the object of his affection is actually the wife of the wealthy baron who employs him. A meandering romantic comedy which is more like a Skoda than a Bentley. DF

Michael Crawford *Harry England* • Geneviève Gilles *Dany* • Curt Jurgens *Baron De Choisis* • Ira Fürstenberg [Ira von Fürstenberg] *Evelyne* • Lon Satton *Cole* • Peter Myers *Bentley* • Mike Marshall *Paul* ■ *Dir* Jean Negulesco • *Scr* Roger Marshall

Hello, Hemingway ★★★

Drama 1990 · Cub · Colour · 88mins

Set in the pre-Castro Cuba that played host to the exiled Ernest Hemingway (whose elusive presence lingers just off screen), this rites-of-passage drama draws its inspiration from the author's Pulitzer prize-winning masterpiece, *The Old Man and the Sea*. However, director Fernando Perez doesn't overdo the parallels between the obsessive fisherman's battles with the elements and Elvis-besotted teenager Laura de la Uz's bid to land the scholarship in the States that will enable her to break away from her impoverished family and increasingly politicised boyfriend. DP. In Spanish with English subtitles.

Laura de la Uz *Larita* • Raul Paz *Victor* • Herminia Sanchez *Josefa* • Caridad Hernandez *Rosenda* • Enrique Molina *Manolo* • Maria Isabel Diaz *Flora* • Micheline Calvert *Miss Amalia* • Marta Del Rio *Doctor Martinez* ■ *Dir* Fernando Perez • *Scr* Maydo Royero

Hello Sister! ★★★

Drama 1933 · US · BW · 55mins

It is a sad fact that most of the nine movies directed by Erich von Stroheim were subject to a great deal of interference. He completed *Walking Down Broadway*, his first and last sound film, on time and within budget. Yet 20th Century-Fox, with some reshoots and re-editing, released it under the crass title of *Hello Sister!* Pity, because there are enough bizarre touches in this uncharacteristically simple tale of boy meets girl on Broadway, to display von Stroheim's touch. He removed his name from the credits, spent the rest of his life as an actor, and never directed again. RB

ZaSu Pitts *Millie* • Boots Mallory *Peggy* • James Dunn *Jimmy* • Terrance Ray *Mac* • Minna Gombell *Mona* • Hattie McDaniel *Black woman in apartment house* ■ *Dir* Erich von Stroheim • *Scr* Erich von Stroheim, Leonard Spigelgass, Geraldine Nomis, Harry Ruskin, Maurine Watkins, from the play *Walking Down Broadway* by Dawn Powell • *Cinematographer* James Wong Howe

Hellraiser ★★★ 18

Horror 1987 · UK · Colour · 89mins

Popular horror writer Clive Barker transferred his trademark perverse chills visually intact to the screen in his directorial debut. A surreal, claustrophobic and graphic shocker about the consequences of opening a Chinese puzzle box, the film allows Barker to introduce a dark new mythology to the genre as well as the Cenobites, leather-clad, disfigured angels from hell with intriguing concepts of dimensional pleasure and pain. Despite his uneven direction and the odd Cricklewood locations, this absorbing sadomasochistic chiller really delivers the gruesome goods. A first sequel, *Hellbound: Hellraiser II*, followed in 1988. AJ. Contains violence and swearing. DVD

Andrew Robinson *Larry Cotton* • Clare Higgins *Julia Cotton* • Ashley Laurence *Kirsty Swanson* • Sean Chapman *Frank Cotton* • Oliver Smith *Frank the Monster* • Doug Bradley *Lead Cenobite* ■ *Dir* Clive Barker • *Scr* Clive Barker, from his novella *The Hellbound Heart*

Hellraiser III: Hell on Earth ★★★ 18

Horror 1992 · US · Colour · 89mins

Pinhead, the Cenobite superstar of author Clive Barker's bloody brainchild, tempts new disciples down the path of perverse pleasure in this distinct improvement on *Hellbound: Hellraiser II*. Here, director Anthony Hickox's high-energy horror comic strip is hot-wired by a keen visual sense and big dipper drive. More a supernatural sadomasochistic action thriller than the murky Gothic nightmares of the previous two episodes, this is funny, original and unpredictable. AJ. Contains violence, swearing, sex scenes, drug abuse, nudity. DVD

Terry Farrell *Joey Summerskill* • Doug Bradley *Pinhead/Elliott Spencer* • Paula Marshall *Terri* • Kevin Bernhardt *JP Monroe* • Ken Carpenter *Doc/Camerahead* • Peter Boynton *Joey's father* • Aimee Leigh *Sandy* ■ *Dir* Anthony Hickox • *Scr* Peter Atkins, from a story by Peter Atkins, Tony Randel, from characters created by Clive Barker

Hellraiser: Bloodline ★★★ 18

Horror 1996 · US · Colour · 81mins

Showing clear signs of the studio tinkering that made director Kevin Yagher take his name off the credits, the ragged third sequel to author Clive Barker's Cenobite saga still does the blood-drenched business. Exploring the evil origins of the lament configuration box (the key to unlocking the pleasures of Hell), genre icon Pinhead (Doug Bradley) takes sadomasochism into space in this audacious episode. Not the disaster it's made out to be. A forgettable fourth sequel, subtitled *Inferno*, followed in 2001. AJ. Contains swearing and violence. DVD

Bruce Ramsay *Phillipe Lemarchand/John Merchant/Paul Merchant* • Valentina Vargas *Angelique* • Doug Bradley *Pinhead* ■ *Dir* Alan Smithee [Kevin Yagher] • *Scr* Peter Atkins

Hellriders ★

Action drama 1983 · US · Colour · 83mins

Adam (*Batman*) West stars as a jogging-mad doctor taking on the nastiest biker gang on the road when they ride into his desert town. Boringly endless Harley Davidson footage and lacklustre stunts take up most of the running time. Tina Louise plays a woman-in-rape-peril after her car breaks down nearby and was clearly going through the same arid unemployment spell as West. AJ

Adam West *Dr Dave Stanley* • Tina Louise *Claire Delancey* • Renee Harmon *Dutch* ■ *Dir* James Bryan • *Scr* Renee Harmon, James Bryan

Hell's Angels ★★★ PG

First World War drama
1930 · US · BW and Colour · 126mins

Howard Hughes's legendary air epic was almost completed as a silent movie, then virtually remade as a talkie. After sacking several directors, Hughes finally directed it himself and, despite good reviews and huge queues, the film cost too much to show a profit. The First World War aerial combat scenes remain spectacular and are the reason why Hughes made the film in the first place. Jean Harlow is still sexy down the decades, but Ben Lyon and James Hall are stilted as the brothers who fight the war, and for Harlow. AT DVD

Ben Lyon *Monte Rutledge* • James Hall *Roy Rutledge* • Jean Harlow *Helen* • John Darrow *Karl Arnstedt* • Lucien Prival *Baron von Kranz* • Frank Clarke *Lt von Bruen* • Roy Wilson *Baldy* • Douglas Gilmore *Capt Redfield* ■ *Dir* Howard Hughes, Marshall Neilan, Luther Reed • *Scr* Joseph Moncure March, Harry Behn (adaptation), Howard Estabrook (adaptation), from a story by Marshall Neilan, Joseph Moncure March

Hell's Angels on Wheels ★★★ 18

Action drama 1967 · US · Colour · 79mins

A cult biker movie, originally banned by the British censors and full of carnage and copulation. Jack Nicholson plays a character called Poet (as characters were called in those days) who falls in with Adam Roarke's gang. As with his later film *The Stunt Man*, director Richard Rush uses a barrage of camera tricks, frenzied cutting and other "look at me" gimmicks which here help to enhance the boy-meets-biker girl story. AT DVD

Jack Nicholson *Poet* • Adam Roarke *Buddy* • Sabrina Scharf *Shill* • Jana Taylor *Abigale* • John Garwood *Jock* • Richard Anders *Bull* • Mimi Machu *Pearl* • James Oliver *Gypsy* ■ *Dir* Richard Rush • *Scr* R Wright Campbell

Hell's Half Acre ★★

Crime drama 1954 · US · BW · 90mins

In this complicated crime drama, Wendell Corey is the reformed racketeer in Honolulu, involved in murder and blackmail, who hides out in the tough slum district of the city that gives the film its title. Evelyn Keyes is a further complication as the long abandoned wife who comes looking for him. Some skilful location shooting and the efforts of a good cast keep it moderately interesting. AE

Wendell Corey *Chet Chester* • Evelyn Keyes *Dona Williams* • Elsa Lanchester *Lida O'Reilly* • Marie Windsor *Rose* • Nancy Gates *Sally Lee* • Leonard Strong *Ippy* • Jesse White *Tubby Otis* • Keye Luke *Chief Dan* • Philip Ahn *Roger Kong* ■ *Dir* John H Auer • *Scr* Steve Fisher • *Cinematographer* John L Russell

Hell's Highway ★★★

Drama 1932 · US · BW · 60mins

A hard-hitting exposé of life in an American prison camp in the South, this is one of three notable films that writer Rowland Brown managed to direct in a career blighted by a reputation for truculence. This little-known rival to *I Was a Fugitive from a Chain Gang* has a hackneyed storyline, but the powerful performances from Richard Dix (convict) and C Henry Gordon (sadistic chief guard), its stark atmosphere and some of the incidents (such as the death of a deaf-mute who does not hear the posse demanding his surrender) stick in the mind. AE

Richard Dix *Frank "Duke" Ellis* • Tom Brown *Johnny Ellis* • Louise Carter *Mrs Ellis* • Rochelle Hudson *Mary Ellen* • C Henry Gordon *Blacksnake Skinner* • Warner Richmond *Pop-Eye Jackson* • Sandy Roth *Blind Maxie* ■ *Dir* Rowland Brown • *Scr* Samuel Ornitz, Robert Tasker, Rowland Brown

Hell's House ★★ PG

Crime 1932 · US · BW · 71mins

This strictly lower-order B-picture fare concerns a youth (Junior Durkin) whose association with a racketeer (Pat O'Brien) lands him, though innocent of a crime, in a reform school run by abusive overseers. Junior's girlfriend is played by Bette Davis in one of the many inferior roles visited on her during her Warner Bros contract. Made with no real flair, the movie is an undemanding time-filler. RK DVD

Junior Durkin *Jimmy Mason* • Pat O'Brien *Kelly* • Bette Davis *Peggy Gardner* • Junior Coghlan *Shorty* • Charley Grapewin *Uncle Henry* • Emma Dunn *Aunt Emma* • Morgan Wallace *Frank Gebhardt* ■ *Dir* Howard Higgin • *Scr* Paul Gangelin, B Harrison Orkow, from the story by Howard Higgin

Hell's Island ★★

Crime 1955 · US · Colour · 84mins

With its rather shabby hero (a DA sacked because of a drink problem who becomes a bouncer), an overweight mastermind, a shady lady and a missing, priceless jewel, you realise rather quickly that this is a rehash of *The Maltese Falcon*. Set on a Caribbean island, where these B-list adventurers search for a big chunk of ruby which might have been lost in a place crash, it crams in a lot of sidebar plots and VistaVision scenery, all efficiently, if anonymously directed by Phil Karlson. AT

John Payne *Mike Cormack* • Mary Murphy *Janet Martin* • Francis L Sullivan *Barzland* • Eduardo Noriega (1) *Inspector Pena* • Arnold Moss *Paul Armand* • Walter Reed *Lawrence* ■ *Dir* Phil Karlson • *Scr* Maxwell Shane, from a story by Jack Leonard, Martin M Goldsmith

Hell's Kitchen ★★★

Crime drama 1939 · US · BW · 79mins

This Dead End Kid's film was considered so provocative that later movies became less violent. A brutal depiction of life in a New York shelter school for boys, the story involves a superintendent (Grant Mitchell) imposing intolerable hardship on the youngsters, while stealing school funds. When one boy dies, after being locked in a freezer, the others hold a mock trial condemning the man to death. BB

Billy Halop *Tony Marco* • Bobby Jordan *Joey Richards* • Leo Gorcey *Gyp Haller* • Huntz Hall *Bingo* • Gabriel Dell *Ace* • Margaret Lindsay *Beth Avery* • Ronald Reagan *Jim Donahue* • Grant Mitchell *Hiram Crispin* ■ *Dir* Lewis Seiler, EA Dupont • *Scr* Crane Wilbur, Fred Niblo Jr, from a story by Crane Wilbur

The Hellstrom Chronicle ★★★

Drama documentary
1971 · US · Colour · 89mins

The microscopic action and doom-laden predictions contained in this stylised documentary reveal a sinister side to the insect antics of *Microcosmos*. Yes, the deadly purpose behind Walon Green's film is to warn us that bugs will eventually rule the planet, as they have an evolutionary durability that we can only dream of. However, it would be easier to take this unpalatable message more seriously were it not delivered by such a flagrantly bogus expert. Lawrence Pressman's performance as Nils Hellstrom is just irritatingly smug and distracts from the excellence of the photography, which clearly won this undeserving curio its Oscar. DP

Lawrence Pressman *Professor Hellstrom* ■ *Dir* Walon Green • *Scr* David Seltzer • *Music* Lalo Schifrin • *Cinematographer* Helmuth Barth, Walon Green, Vilis Lapenieks, Ken Middleham, Heinz Sielmann

Hellzapoppin' ★★★★ U

Comedy 1941 · US · BW · 80mins

This surreal, almost plotless film version of vaudevillians Ole Olsen and Chic Johnson's famous long-running Broadway hit is a genuine one-off. Of course, it's virtually impossible to re-create characters on screen who wreak havoc in the theatre, so a number of cinematic devices have been incorporated to hilarious effect – the actual projectionist showing the movie is turned into an on-screen character (almost). Some of these gags work on TV, but many don't, and the place to revel in this forerunner of *The Goon Show* and Monty Python is really in the cinema, where it approaches comic masterpiece status. TS

Ole Olsen *Ole* • Chic Johnson *Chic* • Martha Raye *Betty* • Hugh Herbert *Quimby* • Jane Frazee *Kitty* • Robert Paige *Jeff* • Mischa Auer *Pepi* • Richard Lane *The director* • Elisha Cook Jr *Selby* ■ *Dir* HC Potter • *Scr* Warren Wilson, Nat Perrin, Alex Gottlieb, from a story by Nat Perrin, from the play by Ole Olsen, Chic Johnson • *Music/lyrics* Sammy Fain, Charles Tobias

Help! ★★★★ U

Musical comedy 1965 · UK · Colour · 91mins

A disappointment after the exhilarating *A Hard Day's Night*, the second Beatles feature is still hugely enjoyable. Sweeping John, George, Paul and Ringo from Swiss ski-slopes to the beaches of the Bahamas, this extremely silly story follows the attempts of an Eastern cult (led by Leo McKern and Eleanor Bron) to recover a ceremonial ring that has ended up on Ringo's finger. Pop classics (*Ticket to Ride* and the title song) abound and there are plenty of sharp one-liners. Nevertheless, the grander scale and the needs of the story prevent director Richard Lester from repeating the wisecracking familiarity of the first Fab Four film. DP

John Lennon *John* • Paul McCartney *Paul* • Ringo Starr *Ringo* • George Harrison *George* • Leo McKern *Clang* • Eleanor Bron *Ahme* • Victor Spinetti *Foot* • Roy Kinnear *Algernon* ■ *Dir* Richard Lester • *Scr* Marc Behm, Charles Wood, from a story by Marc Behm

Help, I'm a Fish! ★★★ U

Animated adventure
2000 · Den/Ger/Ire · Colour · 76mins

Younger children will enjoy this Danish-made cartoon, voiced in its English version by, among others, Alan Rickman and Terry Jones. The easy-to-follow plot has a small child accidentally swallowing a nutty professor's fish formula, which turns her into a starfish. Her friends swallow the same potion, and follow her into the sea to give her the antidote. The animation features some neat visual touches, and the young heroes are cute, but not too cute. Even the songs are OK. Nicest of all, though, is the film's general reliance on traditional animation techniques, rather than hi-tech wizardry. DA [video] DVD

Alan Rickman *Joe* • Terry Jones *Prof HO MacKrill* • Aaron Poul *Chuck* • Jeff Pace *Fly* • Michelle Westerson *Stella* • Louise Fribo *Sasha* • David Bateson *Crab/Shark* ■ *Dir* Stefan Fjeldmark, Michael Hegner • *Scr* Stefan Fjeldmark, Karsten Kiilerich, John Stefan Olsen, from a story by Stefan Fjeldmark, Karsten Kiilerich

Hemingway's Adventures of a Young Man ★★

Adventure drama
1962 · US · Colour · 142mins

Loosely assembled from ten of the autobiographical Nick Adams stories and the Italian segment of *A Farewell to Arms*, this is an ill-judged, miscast odyssey that seeks to combine the artistry of Ernest Hemingway's fiction with the macho posturing of his private life. As the titular seeker-after-experience, Richard Beymer's struggle to impose his personality on the proceedings is hampered by a script containing too many opportunities for scene-stealing cameos. DP

Richard Beymer *Nick Adams* • Diane Baker *Carolyn* • Corinne Calvet *Contessa* • Fred Clark *Mr Turner* • Dan Dailey *Billy Campbell* • James Dunn *Telegrapher* • Juano Hernandez *Bugs* • Arthur Kennedy *Dr Adams* • Ricardo Montalban *Major Padula* • Paul Newman *Ad Francis* • Susan Strasberg *Rosanna* • Jessica Tandy *Mrs Adams* • Eli Wallach *John* ■ *Dir* Martin Ritt • *Scr* AE Hotchner, from stories by Ernest Hemingway

Hemoglobin ★★★ 18

Horror 1997 · US/Can · Colour · 88mins

Troubled Roy Dupuis and his wife visit a remote North American island in an attempt to find descendants of his twin ancestors who had lived there hundreds of years before. There they meet a clan of strange mutants with rather unsavoury eating habits. This is a slick and sick story of hereditary horror from Dan O'Bannon and Ron Shusett, the scriptwriters of *Alien*. Romance, vampirism and incest are all touched on in this bizarre stomach-churner with Rutger Hauer's performance keeping a tight rein on the scare tactics. AJ. Contains graphic violence and sex scenes. [video]

Rutger Hauer *Dr Marlowe* • Roy Dupuis *John Strauss* • Kristin Lehman *Kathleen Strauss* • Jackie Burroughs *Lexie Krongold* • Joanna Noyes *Byrde* • Felicia Shulman *Yolanda* ■ *Dir* Peter Svatek • *Scr* Charles Adair, Dan O'Bannon, Ronald Shusett

Hen in the Wind ★★★

Melodrama 1948 · Jpn · BW · 90mins

The tale of a wife who is forced into prostitution to pay her son's hospital bills while her husband fights at the front sounds more suitable for Kenji Mizoguchi than Yasujiro Ozu. However, while this allegorical study of postwar Japan may not be thematically typical of Ozu's work, it certainly bears his stylistic imprint. Spurning reliance on symbolic close-ups, the imagery is notable for its compositional precision and the use of cutting to establish spatial relationships. DP. In Japanese with English subtitles.

Kinuyo Tanaka *Tokiko* • Shuji Sano *Shuichi Amamiya* • Chishu Ryu *Kazuichiro Satake* • Takeshi Sakamoto *Hikozo Sakai* • Kuniko Miyake • Chieko Murata *Akiko Ida* • Eijiro Tono • Koji Mitsuo ■ *Dir* Yasujiro Ozu • *Scr* Yasujiro Ozu, Ryosuke Saito

Henna ★★★ PG

Drama 1990 · Ind/Pak · Colour · 180mins

An epic Indian tale of love that crosses the borders between India and Pakistan. Just before his marriage, Rishi Kapoor is swept away at sea and wakes up in the care of a young girl, Henna (Zeba). He finds that he has no memory of his past life. A storm on their wedding night returns Kapoor's memory and he realises he must go back to India, though he's now wanted by the police as a spy. The traditional virtues of the Indian cinema are readily apparent (songs, costumes and sparkle) and the film is put together with charm. DP. In Hindi and Urdu with English subtitles. [video] DVD

Zeba *Henna* • Rishi Kapoor *Chandra Prakash* • Ashwini Bhave *Chandni* • Saeed Jaffrey ■ *Dir* Randhir Kapoor • *Scr* Jainendra Jain, from a story by Khodzhi Ahmad Abbas, J Sathe

Hennessy ★★★★ 15

Political thriller 1975 · UK · Colour · 99mins

Controversial in its time – because it showed the Royal Family under threat – this 1970s drama still has a full charge of suspense, with Rod Steiger as the embittered Belfast man intent on blowing up the state opening of Parliament to avenge the accidental slaughter of his family. Actor Richard Johnson (on whose story the film is based) is working with Trevor Howard to bring down this lone terrorist on behalf of MI5, while the IRA's Eric Porter is in pursuit as well. After a lifetime of hackery, director Don Sharp turns in his best movie, while Steiger gives a consummate portrayal of a righteously vengeful man. TH [video]

Rod Steiger *Hennessy* • Lee Remick *Kate Brooke* • Richard Johnson *Inspector Hollis* • Trevor Howard *Commander Rice* • Eric Porter *Tobin, IRA Leader* • Peter Egan *Williams* • Ian Hogg *Gerry* ■ *Dir* Don Sharp • *Scr* John Gay, from a story by Richard Johnson

Henry & June ★★★ 18

Biographical erotic drama
1990 · US · Colour · 136mins

Director Philip Kaufman followed up *The Unbearable Lightness of Being* with this intellectually erotic depiction of the bizarre relationship between author Henry Miller (Fred Ward), his wife June (Uma Thurman) and the writer Anaïs Nin (Maria de Medeiros). Based on Nin's diaries, it's a rather slow and stilted film whose main interest now lies in its cast, which, as well as a young Thurman, includes Richard E Grant as Nin's bland husband and Kevin Spacey as Henry's friend. Nowhere near as sexy as the original publicity led viewers to believe, it became notorious more for its subject matter than for what actually appears on screen. JB [video] DVD

Fred Ward *Henry Miller* • Uma Thurman *June Miller* • Maria de Medeiros *Anaïs Nin* • Richard E Grant *Hugo* • Kevin Spacey *Osborn* • Jean-Philippe Ecoffey *Eduardo* • Bruce Myers *Jack* • Jean-Louis Buñuel *Publisher/Editor* ■ *Dir* Philip Kaufman • *Scr* Philip Kaufman, Rose Kaufman, from the diaries of Anaïs Nin

Henry Fool ★★★★ 18

Comedy drama 1997 · US · Colour · 131mins

Writer/director Hal Hartley is one of the quirkiest and most original of independent film-makers, and in this effort, the winner of the best screenplay at Cannes, he is on fine form. It's about a shy garbage collector and his promiscuous sister whose humdrum lives are changed for ever by the arrival of the charismatic rogue, Henry Fool (Thomas Jay Ryan), who moves into the basement of their house with the apparent intention of putting the finishing touches to his memoirs. The end product is a strangely compelling and, at times, hysterically funny fable, with a cast that does justice to the director's talent for discovering high drama in even the humblest of characters. TH. Contains swearing, sexual references and some violence. [video]

Thomas Jay Ryan *Henry Fool* • James Urbaniak *Simon Grim* • Parker Posey *Fay* • Maria Porter *Mary* • James Saito *Mr Deng* • Kevin Corrigan *Warren* • Liam Aiken *Ned* • Camille Paglia ■ *Dir/Scr* Hal Hartley

Henry: Portrait of a Serial Killer ★★★★★ 18

Psychological horror
1986 · US · Colour · 79mins

Instead of portraying a cultured, super-intelligent serial killer such as Hannibal Lecter, John McNaughton's disturbing directorial debut offers us a piece of poor white trash (Michael Rooker) who drifts anonymously from city to city, murdering at random. No one knows he is a mass murderer until he lets flatmate and fellow ex-con Tom Towles in on his gruesome hobby. McNaughton's rough, non-judgemental direction gives the film a stylishly chilling documentary feel, while the killer's use of a camcorder asks some challengingly uncomfortable questions about voyeurism and the nature of screen violence. This is a true modern classic. JF [video] DVD

Michael Rooker *Henry* • Tom Towles *Otis* • Tracy Arnold *Becky* • Mary Demas *Dead Woman/Dead Prostitute/Hooker* • Anne Bartoletti *Waitress* ■ *Dir* John McNaughton • *Scr* Richard Fire, John McNaughton

Henry: Portrait of a Serial Killer, Part II ★★ 18

Psychological horror
1996 · US · Colour · 84mins

With director John McNaughton and actor Michael Rooker gone, this sequel immediately has two strikes against it, though it does end up being somewhat better than one might think. Neil Giuntoli takes over as Henry, continuing his travels around the country until he finds menial work in one location. When he finds out his boss is a professional arsonist, they start exchanging trade secrets and help each other out. KB [video]

Neil Giuntoli *Henry* • Rich Komenich *Kai* • Kate Walsh *Cricket* • Carri Levinson *Louisa* • Daniel Allar *Rooter* • Penelope Milford *Woman in woods* ■ *Dir/Scr* Charles Parello

Henry VIII and His Six Wives ★★★ PG

Historical drama
1972 · UK · Colour · 120mins

As one has the right to expect, the costumes and locations for this film version of the acclaimed BBC TV series *The Six Wives of Henry VIII* are superb. However, the story suffers from being compressed into just over two hours (the series ran for six 90-minute episodes), and, while it is understandable to focus on Anne Boleyn and the break with Rome, it overbalances the action to the detriment of the later wives. Keith Michell gives a textbook portrayal of Henry, but he is outshone by Bernard Hepton as Cranmer and Donald Pleasence as Cromwell. DP [video]

Keith Michell *King Henry VIII* • Frances Cuka *Catherine of Aragon* • Charlotte Rampling *Anne Boleyn* • Jane Asher *Jane Seymour* • Jenny Bos *Anne of Cleves* • Lynne Frederick *Catherine Howard* • Barbara Leigh-Hunt *Catherine Parr* • Donald Pleasence *Thomas Cromwell* • Michael Gough *Norfolk* • Brian Blessed *Suffolk* • Bernard Hepton *Archbishop Cranmer* • Michael Goodliffe *Thomas More* ■ *Dir* Waris Hussein • *Scr* Ian Thorne

Henry V ★★★★★ U

Classic historical drama
1944 · UK · Colour · 131mins

Having failed to secure the services of William Wyler or Carol Reed, Laurence Olivier embarked on his directorial debut with some misgivings. David O Selznick had already refused to allow Olivier's wife Vivien Leigh to play Katharine as he didn't want his star in a bit part, and the war had necessitated the shooting of the Agincourt scenes in Ireland to find enough extras. Dislocating his ankle while filming the ambush scene, Olivier still handled the battle sequences with a skill that belied his inexperience. Released to great acclaim with victory over Hitler in sight, the film chimed in with the nation's ebullience and it remains a colourful and rousing spectacle. DP [video] DVD

Laurence Olivier *King Henry V* • Robert Newton *Ancient Pistol* • Leslie Banks *Chorus* • Renée Asherson *Princess Katharine* • Esmond Knight *Fluellen* • Leo Genn *Constable of France* • Ralph Truman *Montjoy, a French herald* • Harcourt Williams *King Charles VI of France* ■ *Dir* Laurence Olivier • *Scr* Laurence Olivier, Alan Dent, from the play by William Shakespeare • *Cinematographer* Robert Krasker • *Art Director* Paul Sheriff • *Costume Designer* Roger Furse [Roger K Furse]

Henry V ★★★★ PG

Historical drama
1989 · UK · Colour · 131mins

It's hard to recall the furore that greeted this film on its original release. Almost everyone compared first-time director Kenneth Branagh with Laurence Olivier, who made his own debut behind the camera with the same play 45 years earlier. The knives were clearly out for the pretender to Olivier's throne, yet he produced a version that was as much of its time as Olivier's had been. Instead of the booming patriotism befitting the wartime flag-waver that was served up by Olivier, Branagh decided to focus on the savagery and futility of war. He thoroughly merited his best actor Oscar nomination, though his inclusion in the direction category was more than a little flattering. DP [video] DVD

Kenneth Branagh *Henry V* • Derek Jacobi *Chorus* • Brian Blessed *Exeter* • Ian Holm *Captain Fluellen* • Paul Scofield *French King* • Michael Maloney *Dauphin* • Alec McCowen *Ely* • Emma Thompson *Katherine* • Richard Briers *Bardolph* • Robert Stephens *Pistol* • Robbie Coltrane *Sir John Falstaff* • Judi Dench *Mistress Quickly* ■ *Dir* Kenneth Branagh • *Scr* Kenneth Branagh, from the play by William Shakespeare

Her Alibi ★★ PG

Comedy thriller 1989 · US · Colour · 90mins

Bruce Beresford directs this uneven comedy thriller. Designed to continue Tom Selleck's rise in the movies after his success in *Three Men and a Baby*, it's a rather ludicrous tale that needs more than just a well-known actor and an actress model (Paulina Porizkova) in the lead roles. A talented cast, a decent script and something more than the "I think my girlfriend's going to kill me" plot would also have made a big difference. JB. Contains swearing. [video]

Tom Selleck *Phil Blackwood* • Paulina Porizkova *Nina Ionescu* • William Daniels *Sam* • James Farentino *Frank Polito* • Hurd Hatfield *Troppa* • Patrick Wayne *Gary Blackwood* • Tess Harper *Sally Blackwood* ■ *Dir* Bruce Beresford • *Scr* Charlie Peters

Her Best Friend's Husband ★★

Romantic drama 2002 · Can · Colour · 95mins

Widowed lawyer Cheryl Ladd tries to save the marriage of her best friend (Bess Armstrong) and ends up falling for her husband (William R Moses). This TV movie is proficiently acted and director Waris Hussein adds the occasional twist, but this is still a very tame and utterly predictable affair. DP

Cheryl Ladd *Jane Thornton* • Bess Armstrong *Mandy Roberts* • William R Moses *Will Roberts* • Lindy Booth *Kelly Roberts* • John Ralston *Elliott* • Meg Hogarth *Evelyn* ■ *Dir* Waris Hussein • *Scr* Duane Poole, from a story by Jean Abounader

Her Cardboard Lover ★ U

Romantic drama 1942 · US · Colour · 92mins

Robert Taylor and Norma Shearer, under George Cukor's direction, co-star as a penniless songwriter in love with a millionairess who hires him as a secretary-cum-bodyguard to inflame the jealousy of her on-again/off-again lover, George Sanders. Despite its illustrious stars and director, this is a candidate for one of the worst films ever made. Taylor smiles a lot, Shearer – in her final film – sobs and twitters and Sanders looks uncomfortable, as well he might. To call the script witless is an understatement. RK

Norma Shearer *Consuelo Croyden* • Robert Taylor (1) *Terry Trindale* • George Sanders *Tony Barling* • Frank McHugh *Chappie Champagne* • Elizabeth Patterson *Eva* • Chill Wills *Judge* ■ *Dir* George Cukor • *Scr* John Collier, Anthony Veiller, William H Wright, Jacques Deval, from the play *Her Cardboard Lover* by Valerie Wyngate, PG Wodehouse, from the play *Dans Sa Cadeur Naïve* by Jacques Deval

Her Husband's Affairs ★★★

Screwball comedy 1947 · US · BW · 83mins

The witty team of Ben Hecht and Charles Lederer provided better and worse screenplays than this screwball comedy with the misleading title. The "affairs" indicated are actually business ventures involving advertising man Franchot Tone, in which his wife, Lucille Ball, interferes. The comedy comes from an unlikely source – the quest to create the perfect embalming fluid – but it's Edward Everett Horton who provides most of the fun in yet another film that pokes fun at the world of advertising. RB

Lucille Ball *Margaret Weldon* • Franchot Tone *William Weldon* • Edward Everett Horton *JB Cruikshank* • Mikhail Rasumny *Prof Glinka* • Gene Lockhart *Peter Winterbottom* • Nana Bryant *Mrs Winterbottom* • Jonathan Hale *Governor Fox* ■ *Dir* S Sylvan Simon • *Scr* Ben Hecht, Charles Lederer

Her Majesty Love ★★★

Musical comedy 1931 · US · BW · 75mins

The presence of the inimitable WC Fields (for once minus the bibulous cynicism) enlivens this lightweight musical comedy, which marked the official Hollywood debut of William Dieterle, who'd spent the previous year making German-language versions of US box-office hits. Demonstrating the juggling genius that sustained his vaudeville career, Fields upstages Broadway star Marilyn Miller, whose marriage prospects are dashed when he reveals to her beau's ennobled family that he is a barber and she's a barmaid at a Berlin cabaret. An amiable frippery. DP

Marilyn Miller *Lia Toerrek* • Ben Lyon *Fred von Wellingen* • WC Fields *Lia's father* • Ford Sterling *Otmar* • Leon Errol *Baron von Schwarzdorf* • Chester Conklin *Emil* • Harry Stubbs *Hanneman* • Maude Eburne *Aunt Harriette* ■ *Dir* William Dieterle • *Scr* Robert Lord, Arthur Caesar, Henry Blanke, Joseph Jackson, from a play by R Bernauer, R Oesterreicher

Her Man ★★

Drama 1930 · US · BW · 85mins

This unconvincing, wearying waterfront melodrama has little to recommend it. Helen Twelvetrees plays a café hostess whose brief encounter with sailor Ricardo Cortez reaches its inevitable happy ending after his bout of fisticuffs with her brutal boss. James Gleason and his barroom cronies provide a few lighter moments and the lovers' day out has a certain charm. But director Tay Garnett can do little to rescue this stilted affair that has the look of a silent and the creaky dialogue of an early talkie. DP

Helen Twelvetrees *Frankie* • Marjorie Rambeau *Annie* • Ricardo Cortez *Johnnie* • Phillips Holmes *Dan* • James Gleason *Steve* • Franklin Pangborn *Sport* • Harry Sweet *Eddie* ■ *Dir* Tay Garnett • *Scr* Tom Buckingham, from a story by Howard Higgin, Tay Garnett

Her Own Rules ★★ PG

Romantic drama 1998 · US · Colour · 86mins

This frothy confection was made for American TV, set in England and filmed in Ireland, though that's hardly likely to bother Barbara Taylor Bradford's legion of fans. Melissa Gilbert exchanges the Little House on the Prairie for a string of luxury hotels as a wealthy woman who's seeking the truth about her traumatic past. Jean Simmons leads a distinguished supporting cast in this soapy melodrama. JF [video] DVD

Melissa Gilbert *Meredith Sanders* • Jean Simmons *Katherine Stratten* • Jeremy Sheffield *Lucas Kent* • Britta Smith *Mrs Mattingly* ■ *Dir* Bobby Roth • *Scr* Cathleen Young, from the novel by Barbara Taylor Bradford

Her Twelve Men ★★

Comedy 1954 · US · BW · 90mins

After several years of mediocre vehicles and with age creeping up on her, Greer Garson's swansong came with this glutinously sentimental but otherwise inoffensive film about a schoolteacher whose patience and sweet nature has the desired effect on a bunch of difficult young schoolboys. Robert Ryan and Barry Sullivan co-star with the gracious Garson under the experienced control of Robert Z Leonard, once one of the studio's premier directors of women. RK

Greer Garson *Jan Stewart* • Robert Ryan *Joe Hargrave* • Barry Sullivan *Richard Y Oliver Sr* • Richard Haydn *Dr Avord Barrett* • Barbara Lawrence *Barbara Dunning* • James Arness *Ralph Munsey* • Rex Thompson *Homer Curtis* • Tim Considine *Richard Y Oliver Jr* ■ *Dir* Robert Z Leonard • *Scr* William Roberts, from the story *Miss Baker's Dozen* by Louise Baker

Her Wedding Night ★★

Comedy 1930 · US · BW · 78mins

Director Frank Tuttle concocts a frenzied farce, in which Clara Bow, the original It Girl, plays a movie star whose stay in an Italian riviera town results in a ride on a romantic merry-go-round with a composer of sentimental ditties. The pair end up mistakenly getting married while checking into what they think is a hotel. Although Bow is clearly uncomfortable with dialogue, this still has its fun moments. DP

Clara Bow *Norma Martin* • Ralph Forbes *Larry Charters* • Charlie Ruggles [Charles Ruggles] *Bertie Bird* • Richard "Skeets" Gallagher *Bob Talmadge* • Geneva Mitchell *Marshall* • Rosita Moreno *Lulu* • Natalie Kingston *Eva* ■ *Dir* Frank Tuttle • *Scr* Henry Myers, from the play *Little Miss Bluebeard* by Avery Hopwood

Herbie Goes Bananas ★★ U

Comedy 1980 · US · Colour · 89mins

This fourth film about Herbie the Love Bug was the one that finally put the skids under the series. The novelty of having a VW Beetle with a mind of its own was already showing signs of wearing off in *Herbie Goes to Monte Carlo*, when an "exotic" location was used to cover the holes in the plot. However, the sights of South America are not enough to distract us from the flimsiness of this story, as Herbie rubs bumpers with a gang of smugglers on his way to Brazil. DP [video] DVD

Cloris Leachman *Aunt Louise* • Charles Martin Smith *Davie Johns* • John Vernon *Prindle* • Stephan W Burns *Pete Stanchek* • Elyssa Davalos *Melissa* • Joaquin Garay III *Paco* • Harvey Korman *Captain Blythe* • Richard Jaeckel *Shepard* • Alex Rocco *Quinn* ■ *Dir* Vincent McEveety • *Scr* Don Tait, from characters created by Gordon Buford

Herbie Goes to Monte Carlo ★★★ U

Comedy 1977 · US · Colour · 100mins

The third in Disney's series about the "Love Bug" VW Beetle with a mind of its own is rather predictable, though still entertaining. This time out, Herbie is reunited with driver Dean Jones and falls for a powder-blue Lancia (driven by Julie Sommars) during the Paris to Monte Carlo rally. Putting a headstrong intelligence under the bonnet of a car has been a winning formula, but there are only a few touches here that rise above the mechanical. TH [video] DVD

Dean Jones *Jim Douglas* • Don Knotts *Wheely Applegate* • Julie Sommars *Diane Darcy* • Jacques Marin *Inspector Bouchet* • Roy Kinnear *Quincey* ■ *Dir* Vincent McEveety • *Scr* Arthur Alsberg, Don Nelson, from characters created by Gordon Buford

Herbie Rides Again ★★★ U

Comedy 1974 · US · Colour · 84mins

The sequel to Disney's smash hit *The Love Bug*, this is the second of four films featuring the Volkswagen Beetle with a mind of its own. Director Robert Stevenson and scriptwriter/producer Bill Walsh return to ensure the action remains fast, furious and very funny. The original cast may have departed, but in its place are such seasoned veterans as Keenan Wynn and Helen Hayes, who are tremendous value as the tycoon determined to build an enormous skyscraper and the dotty dear who won't leave the old homestead. The effects may have dated somewhat, but the film is still in perfect working order. DP [video] DVD

Helen Hayes *Mrs Steinmetz* • Stefanie Powers *Nicole Harris* • Ken Berry *Willoughby Whitfield* • John McIntire *Mr Judson* • Keenan Wynn *Alonzo Hawk* • Huntz Hall *Judge* ■ *Dir* Robert Stevenson • *Scr* Bill Walsh, from a story by Gordon Buford

Hercules ★★★ U

Fantasy adventure 1957 · It · Colour · 98mins

This film launched the immensely popular Italian film genre known as "peplum", although it is better known worldwide as the "sword and sandal" cycle. Ex-Mr Universe Steve Reeves cuts an imposing figure in the title role, though there was more to him than just bulging biceps. In lesser hands, the scenes in which he longs to become mortal might have induced giggling, and there is a definite spark between him and Sylva Koscina as his beloved, Iole. DP. Italian dialogue dubbed into English. [video]

Steve Reeves *Hercules* • Sylva Koscina *Iole* • Gianna Maria Canale *Antea* • Fabrizio Mioni *Jason* • Ivo Garrani *Pelias* • Arturo Dominici *Eurysteus* ■ *Dir* Pietro Francisci • *Scr* Pietro Francisci, Ennio de Concini, Gaio Frattini, from a story by Pietro Francisci

Hercules ★ PG

Adventure fantasy
1983 · US · Colour · 99mins

A bizarre, misguided throwback to those dubbed monstrosities of the 1950s and 1960s, this would-be epic attempts to cash in on the brief craze for sword-and-sorcery nonsense in the early 1980s. Lou Ferrigno (*The Incredible Hulk*) gets to wear slightly more clothing than in his old TV show. Unfortunately he has more dialogue as well, while the effects are ropey. JF

Lou Ferrigno *Hercules* • Mirella D'Angelo *Circe* • Sybil Danning *Arianna* • Ingrid Anderson *Cassiopea* • William Berger *King Minos* • Brad Harris *King Augeas* ■ *Dir/Scr* Lewis Coates [Luigi Cozzi]

Hercules ★★★ U

Animated musical
1997 · US · Colour · 91mins

As a dumbed-down version of the Greek myth this Disney animation has its moments, but few that will appeal to students of legend. Here Hercules, son of almighty Zeus, is brought up as a mortal, thanks to the machinations of Underworld ruler Hades, and has to pass tests to prove both his manhood and his godhood. Some of the draughtsmanship of the animation is wonderful, as are the voiceovers of James Woods and Danny DeVito, but the powerful original idea is sapped by the need to make it a teenage comic strip cartoon. TH [video]

Charlton Heston *Narrator* • Tate Donovan *Hercules* • Danny DeVito *Phil* • James Woods *Hades* • Susan Egan *Meg* • Rip Torn *Zeus* • Samantha Eggar *Hera* ■ *Dir* John Musker, Ron Clements • *Scr* Ron Clements, John Musker, Donald McEnery, Bob Shaw, Irene Mecchi, from an idea by Joe Haidar • *Production Designer* Gerald Scarfe

Hercules II ★ 15

Action adventure fantasy
1983 · US · Colour · 88mins

The second misbegotten attempt by Italian hack director Luigi Cozzi to marry *Star Wars*-style fantasy with sword-and-sandal epic is no better than the first. Made at the same time as the original *Hercules* but released two years later, this time the task of strongman Lou Ferrigno is to find some lost thunderbolts hidden among a welter of lousy special effects. AJ

Lou Ferrigno *Hercules* • Milly Carlucci *Urania* • Sonia Viviani *Glaucia* • William Berger *King Minos* • Carlotta Green *Athena* • Claudio Cassinelli *Zeus* ■ *Dir* Lewis Coates [Luigi Cozzi] • *Scr* Lewis Coates [Luigi Cozzi]

Hercules in New York ★★ PG

Fantasy comedy adventure
1969 · US · Colour · 87mins

Expelled from Mount Olympus by jealous dad Zeus, Hercules ends up in New York during the psychedelic 1960s. This one-joke spectacle was conceived as a pastiche of cheap sword-and-sandal epics, and would have been quickly forgotten had it not starred one Arnold Strong (real name Schwarzenegger) in his first film role. Arnie is stripped of his voice (through bad dubbing), his clothes and all dignity. DP [video] DVD

Arnold Stang *Pretzie* • Arnold Strong [Arnold Schwarzenegger] *Hercules* • Deborah Loomis *Helen* • James Karen *The Professor* • Ernest Graves *Zeus* • Tanny McDonald *Juno* • Taina Elg *Nemesis* • Michael Lipton *Pluto* ■ *Dir* Arthur A Seidelman [Arthur Allan Seidelman] • *Scr* Aubrey Wisberg

Hercules Returns ★★★ 15

Comedy 1993 · Aus · Colour · 76mins

A one-joke film – but a joke that's so good it just about sustains the whole running time of the film. David Argue, Bruce Spence and Mary Coustas are battling to reopen a classic cinema, much to opposition of slimy businessman Michael Carman, who plots to destroy their opening night by providing them with an Italian version of an old Hercules epic. It falls to the intrepid trio to provide all the voices themselves. The plotting is tenuous, but the redubbed beefcake epic is a constant delight. JF

David Argue *Brad McBain* • Michael Carman *Sir Michael Kent* • Mary Coustas *Lisa* • Bruce Spence *Sprocket* • Brendon Suhr *King* ■ *Dir* David Parker • *Scr* Des Mangan, from his live show *Double Take Meet Hercules*

Hercules, Samson and Ulysses ★★ U

Fantasy action adventure
1963 · It · Colour · 85mins

While this suffers from a paucity of ideas and a shortage of funds, it offers considerably more humour than the majority of sword-and-sandal pictures. This is because Ulysses (Enrico Cerusico) finds the macho posturing of Hercules (Kirk Morris) and Samson (Richard Lloyd) so derisory. However, he's still a team player and his brain directs their brawn in a showdown with a force of Philistines. DP. Italian dialogue dubbed into English.

Kirk Morris *Hercules* • Richard Lloyd *Samson* • Liana Orfei *Delilah* • Enzo Cerusico *Ulysses* • Aldo Giuffre *Seren* ■ *Dir/Scr* Pietro Francisci

Hercules Unchained ★★ U

Fantasy adventure
1959 · It/Fr · Colour · 92mins

Photographed by future horror director Mario Bava, this was the first of many sequels to the sword-and-sandal epic that made one-time Mr Universe, Steve Reeves, a movie star. Here he is reunited with Sylva Koscina, only to be parted from her again when she is abducted by a Theban giant (played by former boxing champion Primo Carnera). It's action all the way, campily staged with disastrous dubbing. DP. Italian dialogue dubbed into English.

Steve Reeves *Hercules* • Sylva Koscina *Iole* • Sylvia Lopez *Omphale, Queen of Lydia* • Primo Carnera *Antaeus* • Patrizia Della Rovere *Penelope* ■ *Dir* Pietro Francisci • *Scr* Pietro Francisci, Ennio De Concini

The Herd ★★★★

Political drama 1978 · Tur · Colour · 118mins

Contrasting the traditional methods of simple, superstitious shepherds and the entrenched rivalry between their nomadic tribes with the corruption, injustice and inhumanity of contemporary consumer society, this calamitous odyssey from the plains of Anatolia to the backstreets of Ankara is an unflinchingly scathing portrait of modern Turkey. Written in prison (where he was serving 19 years for killing a magistrate in a café brawl), this was the picture that brought the nation's most important film-maker, Yilmaz Guney, to international attention. Like its successor, *The Enemy*, it was directed by Zeki Okten in exact accordance with its author's exhaustively detailed notes. DP. In Turkish with English subtitles.

Tarik Akan *Sirvan* • Melike Demirag *Berivan* • Tuncel Kurtiz *Hamo* ■ *Dir* Zeki Okten • *Scr* Yilmaz Guney • *Cinematographer* Izzet Akay

Here Come the Co-Eds ★★★ U

Musical comedy 1945 · US · BW · 90mins

Bud Abbott and Lou Costello as two incident-prone nincompoops who get jobs as caretakers at a staid girls school. The pair create their normal slapstick mayhem and the snobbish atmosphere of the school crumbles before them. Well established by this time, they breeze through this well constructed vehicle, which is zany even by their own wacky standards. Horror star Lon Chaney Jr can also be spotted down the cast in a slightly less ghoulish role than normal. DF

Bud Abbott *Slats McCarthy* • Lou Costello *Oliver Quackenbush* • Peggy Ryan *Patty* • Martha O'Driscoll *Molly McCarthy* • June Vincent *Diane Kirkland* • Lon Chaney Jr *"Strangler" Johnson* • Donald Cook *Larry Benson* ■ *Dir* Jean Yarbrough • *Scr* Arthur T Horman, John Grant, from a story by Edmund L Hartmann

Here Come the Girls ★★★

Musical comedy 1953 · US · Colour · 77mins

A terrific musical comedy, as Bob Hope, "the oldest chorus boy in the business", gets his big break standing in for star crooner Tony Martin, whom one "Jack the Slasher" is threatening to kill. The central premise is not fully realised by director Claude Binyon, but the turn-of-the-century setting is attractive, the Technicolor is luscious, and there's a funny turn from Fred Clark as an irascible impresario. TS

Bob Hope *Stanley Snodgrass* • Tony Martin *Allen Trent* • Arlene Dahl *Irene Bailey* • Rosemary Clooney *Daisy Crockett* • Millard Mitchell *Albert Snodgrass* • William Demarest *Dennis Logan* • Fred Clark *Harry Fraser* • Robert Strauss *Jack the Slasher* ■ *Dir* Claude Binyon • *Scr* Edmund Hartmann [Edmund L Hartmann], Hal Kanter, from a story by Edmund Hartmann [Edmund L Hartmann] • *Cinematographer* Lionel Lindon

Here Come the Huggetts ★★★

Comedy 1948 · UK · BW · 92mins

Following the success of 1947's *Holiday Camp*, Jack Warner and Kathleen Harrison's Huggett clan were given a picture of their own by the Rank front office. Directed by Ken Annakin with such a keen eye for the everyday that the film almost has sociological value, this prototype soap is enlivened by the antics of Diana Dors, the blonde bombshell niece who disrupts the placid suburban household. Peter Rogers (who produced the *Carry On* series) is one of the scriptwriting quintet, so the drama is liberally sprinkled with laughs. *Vote for Huggett* and *The Huggetts Abroad* quickly followed. DP

Jack Warner *Joe Huggett* • Kathleen Harrison *Ethel Huggett* • Jane Hylton *Jane Huggett* • Susan Shaw *Susan Huggett* • Petula Clark *Pat Huggett* • Diana Dors *Diana Hopkins* • Jimmy Hanley *Jimmy* • David Tomlinson *Harold Hinchley* ■ *Dir* Ken Annakin • *Scr* Mabel Constanduros, Denis Constanduros, Peter Rogers, Muriel Box, Sydney Box, from characters created by Godfrey Winn

Here Come the Waves ★★ U

Second World War musical comedy
1944 · US · BW · 99mins

One among too many disposable musicals springing from the war effort, this one offers two Betty Huttons for the price of one. Bing Crosby is a crooner who joins the navy with heroic aims, but only sees action in the entertainment unit where he must handle shows put on by the navy's distaff side, including twin sisters both played by Hutton. The movie's main claim to fame is the Oscar-nominated song, *Accentuate the Positive*. RK

Bing Crosby *Johnny Cabot* • Betty Hutton *Susan Allison/Rosemary Allison* • Sonny Tufts *Windy* • Ann Doran *Ruth* • Gwen Crawford *Tex* • Noel Neill *Dorothy* • Catherine Craig *Lieutenant Townsend* ■ *Dir* Mark Sandrich • *Scr* Allan Scott, Ken Englund, Zion Myers • *Music* Harold Arlen • *Lyrics* Johnny Mercer

Here Comes Mr Jordan ★★★★ U

Screwball comedy fantasy
1941 · US · BW · 89mins

A clever, charming and ingenious fantasy that was a popular hit in its day, starring a slightly miscast but nevertheless excellent Robert Montgomery. Following an air crash, boxer Montgomery is accidentally rushed to heaven before his allotted due date, and has to be found a new body until his official time is up. The preposterous plot is brilliantly constructed and charmingly performed, with character actor James Gleason in a career-best role as the fighter's manager. Claude Rains (as the eponymous Mr Jordan) and Edward Everett Horton keep the whimsical whole effortlessly down-to-earth. TS

Robert Montgomery *Joe Pendleton* • Evelyn Keyes *Bette Logan* • Claude Rains *Mr Jordan* • Rita Johnson *Julia Farnsworth* • Edward Everett Horton *Messenger No 7013* • James Gleason *Max Corkle* ■ *Dir* Alexander Hall • *Scr* Sidney Buchman, Seton I Miller, from the play *Heaven Can Wait* by Harry Segall

Here Comes the Groom ★★ U

Comedy 1951 · US · BW · 113mins

Despite a fine cast headed by Bing Crosby, Jane Wyman and Franchot Tone, this Frank Capra comedy about a newsman who imports two war orphans in order to win back a former fiancée is a disappointment. Capra's leaden approach betrays his lack of confidence in the material. TV

Bing Crosby *Pete* • Jane Wyman *Emmadel Jones* • Alexis Smith *Winifred Stanley* • Franchot Tone *Wilbur Stanley* • James Barton *Pa Jones* • Louis Armstrong • Dorothy Lamour ■ *Dir* Frank Capra • *Scr* Virginia Van Upp, Liam O'Brien, Myles Connolly, from a story by Robert Riskin, Liam O'Brien

Here Comes the Navy ★★ U

Adventure comedy 1934 · US · BW · 88mins

In effect, this is little more than a recruitment poster for the US Navy, with James Cagney pressed into heroic peacetime service by a studio worried about his image as a racketeer or sociopath. Cagney is also paired for the first time with Pat O'Brien, who steals Cagney's girl; Cagney joins the navy and woos O'Brien's sister, played by Gloria Stuart. There are a few songs to boot, and the whole forgettable thing is smoothly packaged. AT

James Cagney *Chesty O'Connor* • Pat O'Brien *Biff Martin* • Gloria Stuart *Dorothy Martin* • Frank McHugh *Droopy* • Dorothy Tree *Gladys* ■ *Dir* Lloyd Bacon • *Scr* Ben Markson, Earl Baldwin, from a story by Ben Markson

Here Comes the Sun ★★ U

Musical comedy 1945 · UK · BW · 83mins

Director John Baxter made his name with such gritty working-class dramas as *Love on the Dole*. Yet he supplies exactly the required lightness of touch for this amiable musical comedy. What makes the film particularly interesting is that it marked the last screen teaming for more than a decade of those Crazy Gang stalwarts, Bud Flanagan and Chesney Allen, who dropped from the limelight the following year because of Allen's arthritis. The plot is confusing, revolving around a newspaper owner's forged will, but the stars' charming routines ably compensate. DP

Bud Flanagan *Corona Flanagan* • Chesney Allen *Ches Allen* • Elsa Tee *Helen Blare* • Joss Ambler *Bradshaw* • Dick Francis *Governor* • John Dodsworth *Roy Lucas* ■ *Dir* John Baxter • *Scr* Geoffrey Orme, from a story by Bud Flanagan, Reginald Purdell

Here on Earth ★★

Drama 1993 · Por · Colour · 105mins

This is not an easy watch, with its central theme that misery is not the preserve of any one particular group of people. There's too little to draw you in to either the story of a rich man whose world falls apart after the death of his father or that of a couple of hard-up lovers who are driven to murder. Portuguese director Joao Botelho is a unique talent, but this isn't perhaps the best introduction for those coming fresh to his work. DP. In Portuguese with English subtitles. Contains swearing.

Luis Miguel Cintra *Miguel Chagas* • Jessica Weiss *Isabel* • Pedro Hestnes *Antonio* • Rita Dias *Cecilia* • Isabel De Castro *Miguel's mother* • Laura Soveral *Governess* • Iñes de Medeiros *Prostitute* • Henrique Viana *Inspector* ■ *Dir/Scr* Joao Botelho

H

Here on Earth ★★ PG

Romantic drama 2000 · US · Colour · 92mins

Leelee Sobieski stars in this saccharine high-school romance as a small town girl torn between rich kid Chris Klein and farm boy Josh Hartnett. Sobieski and Klein approach their roles with dewy-eyed earnestness, while Hartnett gives the film its only solid performance. Director Mark Piznarski too often uses pop music to intensify the drama rather than trust his actors with the task. ST DVD

Leelee Sobieski *Samantha* • Chris Klein *Kelley* • Josh Hartnett *Jasper* • Michael Rooker *Malcolm Arnold* • Annie Corley *Betsy Arnold* • Bruce Greenwood *Earl Cavanaugh* • Annette O'Toole *Jo Cavanaugh* ■ *Dir* Mark Piznarski • *Scr* Michael Seitzman

Here We Go Again ★★ U

Comedy 1942 · US · BW · 76mins

Unlikely though the concept sounds, ventriloquism was really big on the wireless in the 1940s. In the US, Edgar Bergen and his cheeky rascal Charlie McCarthy graduated from their own radio show to appear in a clutch of movies in the 1930s and 1940s. This one features fellow radio favourites Fibber and Molly McGee (Jim and Marian Jordan) who are celebrating their 20th anniversary with a second honeymoon. DF

Edgar Bergen • Jim Jordan *Fibber McGee* • Marian Jordan *Molly McGee* • Harold Peary *Gildersleeve* • Ginny Simms *Jean* • Bill Thompson *Wimple* • Gale Gordon *Caldwalder* ■ *Dir* Allan Dwan • *Scr* Paul Gerard Smith, Joe Bigelow, from a story by Paul Gerard Smith, from the radio series *Fibber McGee and Molly* by Don Quinn

Here We Go round the Mulberry Bush ★★

Comedy 1967 · UK · Colour · 96mins

One of those Swinging Sixties curios that abound with white boots, sooty eyes, pelmet skirts and *Thunderbirds*-style dancing. Originally a rather slight but charming novel by Hunter Davies about a young bloke who longs to acquire his very own dolly bird, it has been turned into an English Tourist Board commercial, extolling the delights of fab young Britain. The book's teeth have been firmly extracted and replaced instead by the soft gums of nonstop swingdom. SH

Barry Evans *Jamie McGregor* • Judy Geeson *Mary Gloucester* • Angela Scoular *Caroline Beauchamp* • Sheila White *Paula* • Adrienne Posta *Linda* • Vanessa Howard *Audrey* • Diane Keen *Claire* • Denholm Elliott *Mr Beauchamp* • Christopher Timothy *Spike* ■ *Dir* Clive

Donner • *Scr* Hunter Davies, Larry Kramer, from the novel *Here We Go round the Mulberry Bush* by Hunter Davies

Hero ★★★ U

Documentary
1987 · UK/Mex · Colour · 82mins

In 1986, Mexico became the first nation to host the World Cup twice. Although it's best remembered here for the "Hand of God" incident that took Argentina into the semi-finals, this was Diego Maradona's tournament for all the right reasons, too, most notably the mesmeric solo efforts against England and Belgium. But while these are included in Tony Maylam's official record, too many other key moments are omitted because he elected to follow ten key players rather than cover each match. Nevertheless, it remains a passable memoir for fans. DP

Michael Caine *Narrator* ■ *Dir* Tony Maylam • *Music* Rick Wakeman

Hero ★★★★★ 12

Martial arts fantasy
2002 · HK/Chi/US · Colour · 95mins

Chinese master Zhang Yimou's first foray into *wu xia* (heroic martial arts) will inevitably invite comparisons with Ang Lee's *Crouching Tiger, Hidden Dragon* but *Hero* could be judged as superior on a number of levels. A nameless warrior (Jet Li) has apparently risked all to slay a group of assassins intent on killing a powerful warlord, but while the story is diverting, it's the visuals that dazzle. Each sequence seemingly surpasses the last, both in inventiveness and beauty. Christopher Doyle's gorgeous, colour-saturated cinematography complements the gripping tale, though western viewers may be surprised at the film's ultimate theme: a defence of totalitarianism against the chaos and insecurity of freedom. AS. In Mandarin with English subtitles. Contains violence. DVD

Jet Li *Nameless* • Tony Leung Chiu-Wai [Tony Leung (2)] *Broken Sword* • Maggie Cheung Man-Yuk [Maggie Cheung] *Flying Snow* • Zhang Ziyi *Moon* • Chen Dao Ming *King* • Donnie Yen *Sky* ■ *Dir* Zhang Yimou • *Scr* Zhang Yimou, Li Feng, Wang Bin, from their story

A Hero Ain't Nothin' but a Sandwich ★★

Drama
1978 · US · Colour · 107mins

Ralph Nelson directs this honest, well-mounted film about the travails of a black teenage boy (Larry B Scott) drawn into drug addiction, and the effect on his caring parents (Cicely Tyson, Paul Winfield) and concerned white schoolteacher (David Groh). He produced an admirable attempt to address the social and educational problems of black urban society, which was happily devoid of sensationalism. However, the film is also talky, earnest and disappointingly dull. RK

Cicely Tyson *Sweets* • Paul Winfield *Butler* • Larry B Scott *Benjie* • Helen Martin *Mrs Bell* • Glynn Turman *Nigeria* • David Groh *Cohen* • Kevin Hooks *Tiger* ■ *Dir* Ralph Nelson • *Scr* Alice Childress, from her novel

Hero and the Terror ★ 15

Action thriller
1988 · US · Colour · 92mins

Chuck Norris plays a softer hero here – a troubled cop still traumatised from his experience capturing a serial killer (Jack O'Halloran) in his past, while dealing with the upcoming birth of his girlfriend's child. The stress increases when "the Terror", as he's known, escapes and resumes his savage spree. While Norris is to be applauded for trying something different, it comes at the expense of a boring and mostly uneventful story. KB DVD

Chuck Norris *O'Brien* • Brynn Thayer *Kay* • Steve James (1) *Robinson* • Jack O'Halloran *Simon Moon* • Jeffrey Kramer *Dwight* • Ron O'Neal *Mayor* ■ *Dir* William Tannen (2) • *Scr* Dennis Shryack, Michael Blodgett, from the novel by Michael Blodgett

Hero at Large ★★★ PG

Comedy
1980 · US · Colour · 93mins

This daft but occasionally funny comedy has amiable John Ritter becoming a real-life hero after foiling a crime while dressed up as superhero Captain Avenger. What is more interesting than the quick-fire action on screen is the cast, which includes a pre-stardom Anne Archer and the excellent Kevin Bacon, who found fame four years later with *Footloose*. JB

John Ritter *Steve Nichols* • Anne Archer *J Marsh* • Bert Convy *Walter Reeves* • Kevin McCarthy *Calvin Donnelly* • Harry Bellaver *Eddie* • Anita Dangler *Mrs Havacheck* • Jane Hallaren *Gloria* • Kevin Bacon ■ *Dir* Martin Davidson • *Scr* AJ Carothers

Hero of Babylon ★★

Period adventure
1963 · It · Colour · 98mins

The *Goliath* series was just one of the many sword-and-sandal cycles that kept the world's musclemen and the Italian film industry busy in the early 1960s. Also known as *Goliath, King of Slaves*, this all-action adventure stars Gordon Scott as the rippling renegade fighting injustice and tyranny in the ancient city of Babylon. Having already played such superheroes as Tarzan, Maciste and Hercules, Scott made a suitable successor to ex-Mr Universe Steve Reeves. Laughably bad in places, but then that's part of the fun. DP. In Italian with English subtitles.

Gordon Scott • Michael Lane [Mike Lane] • Geneviève Grad • Moira Orfei • Piero Lulli ■ *Dir* Siro Marcellini • *Scr* Gianpaolo Callegari, Siro Marcellini, Albert Valentin

The Heroes ★★★

Adventure
1968 · US/Iran · Colour · 96mins

The alternative title of this US-Iranian co-production, *The Invincible Six*, gives the clue to its origins. It's a rehash of *The Magnificent Seven*, with Stuart Whitman leading a band of renegade mercenaries who take pity on a village at the mercy of bandits. Veteran director Jean Negulesco puts urgency into the action and, although it's in no way the equal of the illustrious western classic, it's still tense enough. TH

Stuart Whitman *Tex* • Elke Sommer *Zari* • Curt Jurgens *The Baron* • Ian Ogilvy *Ronald* • Behrooz Vosugi *Jahan* • Lon Satton *Mike* • Isarco Ravaioli *Giorgio* • James Mitchum *Nazar* ■ *Dir* Jean Negulesco • *Scr* Guy Elmes, Chester Erskine, from the novel *The Heroes of Yucca* by Michael Barrett

The Heroes ★★

Adventure
1972 · It/Fr/Sp · Colour · 110mins

Rod Steiger leads a band of post-Second World War misfits in pursuit of some loot stolen by former hooker Rosanna Schiaffino in this lacklustre Italian movie. The cast is interesting but director Duccio Tessari doesn't know what to do with them except have them spout clichés in North African locations. TH. Italian dialogue dubbed into English.

Rod Steiger *Günther von Lutz* • Rosanna Schiaffino *Katrin* • Rod Taylor *Bob Robson* • Claude Brasseur *Raphael Tibaudet* • Terry-Thomas *John Cooper* • Gianni Garko *Schreiber* • Aldo Giuffre *Spartaco* ■ *Dir* Duccio Tessari • *Scr* Luciano Vincenzoni, Sergio Donati, from a novel by Albert Kantof

Heroes ★★ 15

Comedy drama
1977 · US · Colour · 107mins

Henry Winkler was the star of the TV show *Happy Days* when he was given the role of a traumatised Vietnam veteran who escapes from hospital with dreams of running a worm farm in California. On the road he meets Sally Field, herself a TV star on the rise. Written by Vietnam veteran James Carabatsos, it's a late straggler in the long run of counterculture movies that never delivers either as a comedy or a drama. The main interest now is the supporting role by Harrison Ford. AT

Henry Winkler *Jack Dunne* • Sally Field *Carol Bell* • Harrison Ford *Kenny Boyd* • Val Avery *Bus Driver* • Olivia Cole *Jane Adcox* • Hector Elias *Dr Elias* • Dennis Burkley *Gus* • Tony Burton *Chef* ■ *Dir* Jeremy Paul Kagan • *Scr* James Carabatsos

Heroes for Sale ★★★

Drama
1933 · US · BW · 71mins

In the 1930s, Warners prided itself on being the moviegoer's social conscience. But producer Hal Wallis tried to pack too many issues into this Depression melodrama, for no sooner has war veteran Richard Barthelmess conquered his morphine addiction than he's riding the rails in search of work. Even when he pals up with Robert Barrat, whose revolutionary washing machine sets him up for life, his troubles aren't over. Luckily, William Wellman concentrates on pace and people, and avoids preaching. DP

Richard Barthelmess *Tom Holmes* • Aline MacMahon *Mary Dennis* • Loretta Young *Ruth Holmes* • Gordon Westcott *Roger Winston* • Robert Barrat *Max* • Berton Churchill *Mr Winston* ■ *Dir* William A Wellman • *Scr* Robert Lord, Wilson Mizner

The Heroes of Telemark ★★★ U

Second World War thriller
1965 · UK · Colour · 123mins

Reluctant scientist Kirk Douglas and fiery resistance fighter Richard Harris have to overcome their hatred of each other, as well as the Germans, to sabotage an atomic bomb project in this brawny war story set in Norway in 1942. Director Anthony Mann sustains a nail-biting tension throughout the daredevil mission. The night sequences are particularly striking, although Robert Krasker's photography throughout will have you positively pining for the fjords. DP DVD

Kirk Douglas *Dr Rolf Pedersen* • Richard Harris *Knut Straud* • Ulla Jacobsson *Anna* • Michael Redgrave *Uncle* • David Weston *Arne* • Anton Diffring *Major Frick* • Eric Porter *Terboven* • Mervyn Johns *Colonel Wilkinson* • Jennifer Hilary *Sigrid* ■ *Dir* Anthony Mann • *Scr* Ivan Moffat, Ben Barzman

Heroes Stand Alone ★★ 18

War drama
1989 · US · Colour · 79mins

This little-seen war drama from the Roger Corman stable has Chad Everett leading a team of mercenaries to pick up survivors from an American plane that has crashed during an illegal flight over a war-torn Central American country. Mark Griffiths's film is critical of American involvement in the region and portrays interfering Cubans and Russians in a favourable light. The Peruvian locations are attractive, as is Elsa Olivero. AE

Chad Everett *Zack Duncan* • Bradford Dillman *Walt Simmons* • Rick Dean *Willie* • Michael Chieffo *Killer* • Elsa Olivero *Rosa* ■ *Dir* Mark Griffiths • *Scr* Thomas McKelvey Cleaver

The Heroic Trio ★★★ 18

Action fantasy
1992 · HK · Colour · 83mins

A massive box office hit in its home country, this Hong Kong action fantasy still packs a visual punch thanks to the larger than life presence of stars Maggie Cheung, Michelle Yeoh and Anita Mui. Blessed with comic book-style super powers, the strikingly-clad trio take on an evil sorcerer who's masterminding the abduction of male babies as part of a plot for world domination. Though not as cutting edge as it once was, this remains riotously entertaining, with some great, theatrical fight sequences and plenty of dark, slapstick humour. A sequel, *Heroic Trio 2: Executioners*, followed. SF. In Cantonese with English subtitles.

Anita Mui *Tung/Wonder Woman* • Maggie Cheung *Chat/The Thief Catcher* • Michelle Yeoh *Ching/Invisible Woman* • Damian Lau *Inspector Lau* • James Pak *Inventor* • Anthony Wong (1) *Kau* ■ *Dir* Johnny To • *Scr* Sandy Shaw, Susanne Chan

Heroines of Evil ★★★

Drama
1979 · Fr · Colour · 88mins

This is another trio of immoral tales from Walerian Borowczyk, although he seems more preoccupied this time with the luxuriant look of the film than the moral implications of his taboo-riven anecdotes. Set in Renaissance Rome, *Margherita* focuses on the murder of a prominent banker and the painter Raphael by the latter's model lover. But this tale of lust and greed has nothing on the bestial insinuation of both *Marceline* (in which a girl exacts the ultimate revenge on the parents who killed her pet rabbit) and *Marie* (in which a kidnap victim is rescued by her trusty hound). DP. In French with English subtitles.

Marina Pierro *Margherita Luti* • François Guétary *Raphael Sanzio* • Jean-Claude Dreyfus *Bini* • Jean Martinelli *Pope* • Pierre Benedetti *Mad painter* • Philippe Desboeuf *Doctor* • Gaëlle Legrand *Marceline Cain* • Pascale Christophe *Marie* ■ *Dir* Walerian Borowczyk • *Scr* Walerian Borowczyk, from the short story *Le Sang et l'Agneau* by Andre Pieyre de Mandiargues and the non-fiction book *Promenades dans Rome* by Stendhal

Hero's Island ★★★

Action drama
1962 · US · Colour · 94mins

A rather weird historical movie, part children's film and part symbolic drama, set on an island off the coast of the Carolinas in the early 1700s. Two former slaves and their children go to live on the island, but the father is murdered by marauding fishermen. Castaway James Mason offers his help but because the woman is deeply religious he agrees to non-violence until there's no other alternative. Big themes bump into each other – religion, pacificism – but none are fully developed in a typically flawed effort from writer/director Leslie Stevens. AT

James Mason *Jacob Webber* • Kate Manx *Devon Mainwaring* • Neville Brand *Kingstree* • Rip Torn *Nicholas* • Warren Oates *Wayte* • Robert Sampson *Enoch* • Harry Dean Stanton *Dixey* ■ *Dir/Scr* Leslie Stevens (1)

Hers to Hold ★★★

Romance
1943 · US · BW · 93mins

Having reached her 20s, Deanna Durbin was successfully relaunched as a young adult, playing a society figure in this romantic comedy which boosted the war effort with its scenes in a real aircraft factory. In this second sequel to *Three Smart Girls*, she sings the very popular *Say a Prayer for the Boys Over There* as well as Cole Porter's *Begin the Beguine* and a song from Bizet's *Carmen*. Joseph Cotten is her rather mature romantic interest, while Charles Winninger and Nella Walker play her parents for the third time. AE

Deanna Durbin *Penelope Craig* • Joseph Cotten *Bill Morley* • Charles Winninger *Judson Craig* • Evelyn Ankers *Flo Simpson* • Gus Schilling *Rosey Blake* • Nella Walker *Dorothy Craig* • Ludwig Stossel *Binns* • Samuel S Hinds *Dr Crane* ■ *Dir* Frank Ryan • *Scr* Lewis R Foster, from a story by John D Klorer

He's My Girl ★★ 15

Romantic comedy
1987 · US · Colour · 99mins

This cross-dressing farce should be called "Some Like It Tepid". TK Carter plays Reggie who, pretending to be his best mate David Hallyday, wins a trip to Hollywood. The problem is the winners need to be a couple. Cue Reggie becoming Regina and the two friends getting into a *Twelfth Night* set of misunderstandings on holiday. The only aspect of interest is Jennifer Tilly as a rather lovely waitress – the rest is just plain silly. LH

TK Carter *Reggie/Regina* • David Hallyday *Bryan* • David Clennon *Mason Morgan* • Misha McK *Tasha* • Jennifer Tilly *Lisa* • Warwick Sims *Simon Sledge* ■ *Dir* Gabrielle Beaumont • *Scr* Charles Bohl, Taylor Ames, from a story by Taylor Ames

Hester Street ★★★★ PG

Period drama 1975 · US · BW · 89mins

This marvellously evocative study of Jewish immigrant life in turn-of-the-century New York, mainly told in delightfully subtitled Yiddish, features an outstanding lead performance from the Oscar-nominated Carol Kane. She plays the wife of Steven Keats, summoned from the old country after he has been in America for a dangerous few years. Unsurprisingly she finds him a changed man, so she sets out to make her own way in the New World. Electing to film in black-and-white, director Joan Micklin Silver creates a world so real you can smell the herrings. TS. In English and Yiddish with subtitles.

Steven Keats *Jake* • Carol Kane *Gitl* • Mel Howard *Bernstein* • Dorrie Kavanaugh *Mamie* • Doris Roberts *Kavarsky* • Stephen Strimpell *Peltner* • Lauren Frost *Fanny* • Paul Freedman *Joey* ■ *Dir* Joan Micklin Silver • *Scr* Joan Micklin Silver, from the story *Yekl* by Abraham Cahan • *Cinematographer* Kenneth Van Sickle

Hexed ★★ 15

Comedy thriller 1993 · US · Colour · 88mins

his early attempt to send up the *Fatal Attraction/Basic Instinct* genre is a patchy affair that's enlivened by the enthusiastic playing of the cast. Arye Gross is a compulsive liar working at a hotel whose fantasy world is interrupted when he gets mixed up with murderous *femme fatale* Claudia Christian. Director Alan Spencer produced the TV spoof *Sledge Hammer!*, but he struggles to bring the brainless charm of that series to this big-screen outing. JF

Arye Gross *Matthew Welsh* • Claudia Christian *Hexina* • Adrienne Shelly *Gloria O'Connor* • Ray Baker *Victor Thummell* • R Lee Ermey *Detective Ferguson* • Michael E Knight *Simon Littlefield* ■ *Dir/Scr* Alan Spencer

Hey Arnold! the Movie ★★★ U

Animated comedy
2002 · US · Colour · 72mins

Arnold is not the most attractive of cartoon heroes, with a head shaped like an elongated rugby ball and bushy hair parted like the Red Sea. However, his heart is in the right place and when he learns that a greedy land developer called Sheck is about to bulldoze his downtown neighbourhood, he determines to save it, with the help of best friend Gerald and love-hate interest Helga. Derived from the popular TV series, the film is a bit rough round the animated edges, but regular viewers will enjoy seeing their favourite characters up on the big screen. TH DVD

Spencer Klein *Arnold* • Francesca Marie Smith *Helga/Deep Voice* • Jamil Walker Smith *Gerald/Rasta guy* • Dan Castellaneta *Grandpa/Nick Vermicelli* • Tress MacNeille *Grandma/Mayor Dixie/Red* • Paul Sorvino *Scheck* • Jennifer Jason Leigh *Bridget* • Christopher Lloyd *Coroner* • Vincent Schiavelli *Mr Bailey* ■ *Dir* Tuck Tucker • *Scr* Craig Bartlett, Steve Viksten, from characters created by Craig Bartlett

Hey Babu Riba ★★★

Romantic drama
1986 · Yug · Colour · 109mins

Flashing back from the funeral of the girl who epitomised the innocence of 1950s Yugoslavia, this is a film of laboured symbolism and clumsy nostalgia. Yet, while the violation of the teenage Gala Videnovic by a swaggering Party activist might lack subtlety, the exuberant fun she has with the four Belgrade lads who made up her rowing team is slyly staged by director Jovan Acin. He cleverly contrasts the fact that the promises of freedom made in the music and movies flooding in from America were just as empty as those peddled by the communists. DP. In Serbo-Croat with English subtitles.

Gala Videnovic *Miriana Zivkovic/"Esther"* • Relja Bacic *Glen* • Nebojsa Bakocevic *Young Glen* • Marko Todorovic *Sacha* • Dragan Bjelogrlic *Young Sacha* • Srdjan Todorovic *Young Kicha* ■ *Dir/Scr* Jovan Acin

Hey Boy! Hey Girl! ★ U

Musical 1959 · US · BW · 80mins

Hey Rubbish! This is one of those inane zero-budget musicals with singer Keely Smith emotionally blackmailing Louis Prima and his band, the Witnesses. She's only going to sing with them if they'll play at the church fête with which she's associated. The result is pretty lacklustre and, considering Prima and Smith were married and working together at the time, you'd expect better. TH

Louis Prima • Keely Smith *Dorothy Spencer* • James Gregory *Father Burton* • Henry Slate *Marty Moran* • Kim Charney *Buzz* • Barbara Heller *Grace Dawson* ■ *Dir* David Lowell Rich • *Scr* Raphael Hayes, James West

Hey! Hey! USA ★★ U

Comedy 1938 · UK · BW · 88mins

Made without the assistance of his regular stooges, Moore Marriott and Graham Moffat, this is one of Will Hay's least memorable outings. Removed from his familiar milieu, he seems uncomfortable with the material and strives too hard for laughs. The film casts him as a stowaway on board a transatlantic liner who poses as a famous history professor to stop gangsters Edgar Kennedy and David Burns kidnapping a millionaire's son. DP DVD

Will Hay *Benjamin Twist* • Edgar Kennedy *Bugs Leary* • David Burns *Tony Ricardo* • Eddie Ryan *Ace Marco* • Fred Duprez *Cyrus Schultz* • Paddy Reynolds *Mrs Schultz* • Tommy Bupp *Bertie Schultz* • Arthur Goullet *Gloves Johnson* ■ *Dir* Marcel Varnel • *Scr* Marriott Edgar, Val Guest, JOC Orton

Hey, Let's Twist! ★★★ U

Musical 1961 · US · BW · 78mins

Who remembers Joey Dee? When this film was made he was one of the hottest names in pop music, having introduced, with his group the Starliters, the Twist at the Peppermint Lounge in New York. An energetic, pint-sized performer, Dee made two films (the other was *Two Tickets to Paris*) which are fascinating sociological time capsules capturing the start of the Swinging Sixties. TV

Joey Dee • Teddy Randazzo *Rickey Dee* • Kay Armen *Angie* • Zohra Lampert *Sharon* • Dino Di Luca *Papa* ■ *Dir* Greg Garrison • *Scr* Hal Hackady

Hi, Gang! ★★ U

Second World War comedy
1941 · UK · BW · 96mins

Married Hollywood film stars Bebe Daniels and Ben Lyon were hugely popular in Britain, particularly during the Second World War, when they stayed in England to entertain the public and the troops, rather than escape to the safety of the US. This film was a spin-off from their famous radio series, a spirited romp featuring Bebe and Ben as radio personalities for rival broadcasting companies. DF

Bebe Daniels *The Victory Girl* • Ben Lyon *Her Other Half* • Vic Oliver *Nuisance with the ideas* • Moore Marriott *Uncle Jerry* • Graham Moffatt *Albert* • Felix Aylmer *Lord Amersham* ■ *Dir* Marcel Varnel • *Scr* Val Guest, Marriott Edgar, JOC Orton, Howard Irving Young, from the radio series by Bebe Daniels, Ben Lyon

The Hi-Jackers ★★

Crime drama 1963 · UK · BW · 69mins

This low-budget crime thriller from the Butcher's studio is set in the rough-and-ready world of trucking. However, British lorry drivers don't have the cinematic glamour of their American counterparts, so identifying the familiar British faces – Anthony Booth (Tony Blair's father-in-law), Patrick Cargill, Glynn Edwards – is the main point of interest in this very dated movie. JF

Anthony Booth *Terry McKinley* • Jacqueline Ellis *Shirley* • Derek Francis *Jack Carter* • Patrick Cargill *Inspector Grayson* • Glynn Edwards *Bluey* • David Gregory *Pete* • Harold Goodwin (2) *Scouse* • Anthony Wager *Smithy* • Arthur English *Bert* ■ *Dir/Scr* Jim O'Connolly

Hi-Life ★★ 15

Comedy drama 1998 · US · Colour · 81mins

Sadly, despite a good cast of young American actors, this ordinary comedy-drama plays more like a soap than a serious big-screen picture. Actor Eric Stoltz owes $900 to vicious bookie Charles Durning after the dosh. He borrows the money from girlfriend Moira Kelly, telling her it's to pay for sister Daryl Hannah's abortion. Kelly's brother, bartender Campbell Scott, is drawn into the whole confusing affair as the net begins to close around Stoltz's elaborate deceit. LH

Campbell Scott *Ray* • Eric Stoltz *Jimmy* • Daryl Hannah *Maggie* • Moira Kelly *Susan* • Katrin Cartlidge *April* • Charles Durning *Fatty* • Peter Riegert *Miner* ■ *Dir/Scr* Roger Hedden

The Hi-Lo Country ★★★ 15

Western drama 1998 · US · Colour · 109mins

Woody Harrelson and the impressive Billy Crudup are bosom-buddy cowboys who run a ranch together in the American west after the Second World War. Their friendship becomes sorely tested when Harrelson begins an affair with the object of Crudup's desire, Patricia Arquette. This is a sumptuous, sprawling western from director Stephen Frears and producer Martin Scorsese, who last collaborated on *The Grifters*. But, while beautifully shot, there is little new here in a familiar tale of best friends clashing over love. Both female leads – Arquette and Penélope Cruz – are two-dimensional; often a flaw in the traditional western, but inexcusable in a 1990s take on the genre. LH. Contains violence and sex scenes.

Woody Harrelson *Big Boy Matson* • Billy Crudup *Pete Calder* • Patricia Arquette *Mona Birk* • Cole Hauser *Little Boy Matson* • Penélope Cruz *Josepha O'Neil* • Enrique Castillo *Levi Gomez* • Darren Burrows *Billy Harte* • Sam Elliott *Jim Ed Love* ■ *Dir* Stephen Frears • *Scr* Walon Green, from the novel by Max Evans • *Cinematographer* Oliver Stapleton

Hi, Mom! ★★★★ 18

Satirical comedy
1970 · US · BW and Colour · 86mins

In director Brian De Palma's sex-fixated, counterculture satire, Robert De Niro's character from *Greetings* returns to make a semi-pornographic film about his neighbours and bomb a laudromat in the name of revolutionary politics. Meanwhile his best friend (Gerrit Graham) gets involved with a radical theatre troupe. The final reel is given over to a brilliantly extended sequence of said troupe's confrontational play, *Be Black, Baby*, where fact, fiction, theatre and film merge with stunning docudrama realism. De Niro reveals the charismatic form that would mark his later career. AJ DVD

Robert De Niro *Jon Rubin* • Jennifer Salt *Judy Bishop* • Lara Parker *Jeannie Mitchell* • Gerrit Graham *Gerrit Wood* • Nelson Peltz *Playboy* • Charles Durnham [Charles Durning] *Superintendent* • Allen Garfield *Joe Banner* ■ *Dir* Brian De Palma • *Scr* Brian De Palma, from a story by Charles Hirsch, Brian De Palma

Hi, Nellie! ★★★

Crime comedy 1934 · US · BW · 75mins

Paul Muni takes a contemporary role for a change, as a tough newspaper editor demoted to the lonely-hearts column, in a terrific example of the tough, fast-paced, beautifully-made newspaper movie that Warner Bros did so well. And who could resist a cast that boasts wisecracking Glenda Farrell (as Muni's ex) and cynical comedian Ned Sparks? Skilled Mervyn LeRoy directs with style and verve. TS

Paul Muni *Bradshaw* • Glenda Farrell *Gerry* • Douglass Dumbrille *Harvey Dawes* • Robert Barrat *Brownell* • Ned Sparks *Shammy* • Hobart Cavanaugh *Fullerton* • Pat Wing *Sue* ■ *Dir* Mervyn LeRoy • *Scr* Sidney Sutherland, Abem Finkel, from a story by Roy Chanslor

Hickey and Boggs ★★★ 15

Thriller 1972 · US · Colour · 106mins

Re-enacting their cynical, laconic roles as rundown private eyes from the *I Spy* TV series, Bill Cosby and Robert Culp extend the concept without losing pace or interest as they stumble upon a lethal *femme fatale* while searching for the proceeds of a Pittsburgh bank robbery. Walter Hill's first venture into feature scriptwriting, allied with Culp's own direction, keep this as crisp as a cracker, though some plot points are annoyingly mysterious. Look out for James Woods in an early role. TH. Contains violence and swearing.

Bill Cosby *Al Hickey* • Robert Culp *Frank Boggs* • Rosalind Cash *Nyona* • Sheila Sullivan *Edith Boggs* • Isabel Sanford *Nyona's mother* • Ta-Ronce Allen *Nyona's daughter* • Lou Frizzell *Lawyer* • James Woods *Lt Wyatt* ■ *Dir* Robert Culp • *Scr* Walter Hill

Hidalgo ★★ 12

Epic adventure based on a true story
2003 · US · Colour · 130mins

This sprawling "underdog" epic has Viggo Mortensen playing real-life cowboy Frank T Hopkins, a specialist in endurance horse races. Hopkins and mustang Hidalgo are challenged to compete in the Ocean of Fire, a 3,000-mile race across the Arabian Desert. Man and mustang are soon facing sandstorms, dastardly rivals, attractive *femmes fatales* and Omar Sharif's inevitably noble sheikh. This is big and clumsy, but quite watchable. DA. Contains violence. DVD

Viggo Mortensen *Frank T Hopkins* • Omar Sharif *Sheikh Riyadh* • Zuleikha Robinson *Jazira* • Saïd Taghmaoui *Prince Bin Al Reeh* • Louise Lombard *Lady Anne Davenport* • Adam Alexi-Malle *Aziz* • Silas Carson *Katib* ■ *Dir* Joe Johnston • *Scr* John Fusco

The Hidden ★★★★ 18

Science-fiction horror
1987 · US · Colour · 92mins

A rip-roaring buddy movie with an extraterrestrial twist. LAPD cop Michael Nouri and his alien partner Kyle MacLachlan investigate a series of weird crimes, and find the culprit responsible is a renegade slug-like creature from MacLachlan's home planet which invades earthly bodies and makes them commit nasty mayhem. Beginning in frantic top gear, director Jack Sholder keeps the high-energy proceedings rattling along, yet still manages to find time for sharp and meaningful character interplay between the fun-packed, gross-out special effects. A minor gem. AJ

Michael Nouri *Tom Beck* • Kyle MacLachlan *Lloyd Gallagher* • Ed O'Ross *Cliff Willis* • William Boyett *Jonathan Miller* • Clu Gulager *Lieutenant Ed Flynn* • Claudia Christian *Brenda Lee Van Buren* • Clarence Felder *Lieutenant John Masterson* • Richard Brooks *Sanchez* ■ *Dir* Jack Sholder • *Scr* Bob Hunt

The Hidden II ★★ 18

Science-fiction horror
1993 · US · Colour · 89mins

This hopelessly second-rate sequel to the brilliant 1987 original, set 15 years later, finds Raphael Sbarge taking on the Kyle MacLachlan benevolent alien role. This time he searches out the daughter (Kate Hodge) of the Michael Nouri character to help him defeat the shape-shifting slug-like alien menace organising a mass spawning at a warehouse rave. Very talky, ineptly comic and shamelessly using the best footage from the first film, this soon falls into formula chase theatrics. AJ

Raphael Sbarge *MacLachlan* • Kate Hodge *Juliet* • Michael Nouri *Detective Beck* ■ *Dir/Scr* Seth Pinsker

Hidden Agenda ★★★ 15

Political thriller 1990 · UK · Colour · 106mins

Ken Loach's movies tend to be rather preachy, but the better ones, including this investigation into a murdered American civil rights activist in Northern Ireland, engage both the mind and the heart. American activist Frances McDormand teams up with British cop Brian Cox to get at the truth and uncover a huge conspiracy. This is a tense depiction of the Troubles during the 1980s; Loach brings a keen sense of time and place to the issues he raises, while McDormand and Cox strike just the right acting notes. AJ. Contains violence, swearing, nudity. DVD

Frances McDormand *Ingrid Jessner* • Brian Cox *Peter Kerrigan* • Brad Dourif *Paul Sullivan* • Mai Zetterling *Moa* • Bernard Bloch *Henri* • John Benfield *Maxwell* • Jim Norton *Brodie* ■ *Dir* Ken Loach • *Scr* Jim Allen

Hidden Agenda ★★ 18

Action thriller 2001 · Can · Colour · 90mins

Aficionados of ornate garden statuary might want to look away during the ballistic finale of this over-elaborate, under-financed espionage thriller from Marc S Grenier. They won't miss much, although Dolph Lundgren does all that's expected of him as the former FBI agent who helps the government spirit away the witness protection programme's most endangered members. DP DVD

Dolph Lundgren *Jason Price* • Maxim Roy *Renee Brooks* • Serge Houde *Paul Elkert* • Alan Fawcett *Sam Turgesen* • Ted Whittall *Sonny Mathis* ■ *Dir* Marc S Grenier • *Scr* Les Weldon

Hidden City ★★ 15

Thriller 1987 · UK · Colour and BW · 107mins

Stephen Poliakoff's first feature as director is weighed down by confusion. It follows the search by sociologist Charles Dance and obsessive Cassie Stuart for a piece of government film which may contain a sinister secret. Formidably filled with menace, there are just too many plotlines, which prevent this debut achieving high status. However, Poliakoff's script goes some way to removing the audience's objections to these implausibilities, creating a menacing and seedy vision of London. TH

Charles Dance *James Richards* • Cassie Stuart *Sharon Newton* • Bill Paterson *Anthony* • Richard E Grant *Brewster* • Alex Norton *Hillcombe* • Tusse Silberg *Barbara* • Richard Ireson *Schoolmaster* • Saul Jephcott *Curtis* ■ *Dir/Scr* Stephen Poliakoff

The Hidden Eye ★★

Crime mystery 1945 · US · BW · 69mins

Edward Arnold stars as the blind detective, Captain Duncan Maclain, whose guide dog, a German shepherd named Friday, helps solve a trio of slayings and prevents a fourth. The clue common to all the murders is a perfume which the dog recognises. Arnold's character, plus dog, first appeared in director Fred Zinnemann's second feature *Eyes in the Night*, but this sequel, directed by Richard Whorf, fails to realise its potential. AT

Edward Arnold *Captain Duncan Maclain* • Frances Rafferty *Jean Hampton* • William "Bill" Phillips *Marty Corbell* • Ray Collins *Philip Treadway* • Paul Langton *Harry Gifford* ■ *Dir* Richard Whorf • *Scr* George Harmon Coxe, Harry Ruskin, from characters created by Baynard Kendrick

Hidden Fear ★★

Crime drama 1957 · US · BW · 83mins

Directed by the now-fashionable Andre De Toth, this B-picture is about the hunt for a killer in Copenhagen. Benefiting from on-location filming, it's interesting only because it features so many stars – John Payne, Alexander Knox, Conrad Nagel – who had lost their glimmer by this time. Fox musical regular Payne only made three more features before his death in 1989. TH

John Payne *Mike Brent* • Alexander Knox *Hartman* • Conrad Nagel *Arthur Miller* • Natalie Norwick *Susan Brent* • Anne Neyland *Virginia Kelly* ■ *Dir* Andre De Toth • *Scr* Andre De Toth, John Ward Hawkins

Hidden Fears ★★

Psychological thriller
1993 · US · Colour · 90mins

Years after the public, brutal and unsolved murder of her husband by two ruffians, Meg Foster learns the identity of the murderers – just as the eyewitnesses begin to die. Foster tries to warn the remaining bystanders, but her TV appeal to flush out the two redneck brothers only serves to put them on her trail. Though the hillbillies are too cartoon-like, solid acting performances and a nice twist ending make this thriller worth a look. ST

Meg Foster *Maureen Dietz* • Frederic Forrest *Mike* • Bever-Leigh Banfield *Helen* • Marc Macaulay *Marty Van Beeber* • Patrick Cherry *Calvin Van Beeber* ■ *Dir* Jean Bodon • *Scr* Stuart Kaminsky, from the novel *Exercise in Terror* by Stuart Kaminsky

The Hidden Fortress ★★★★★ PG

Adventure 1958 · Jpn · BW · 138mins

The *chambara* (or swordplay film) had long been a favourite with Japanese audiences before Akira Kurosawa popularised it in the West. Kurosawa always regarded this rousing adventure as his favourite project, and George Lucas cited as a major influence on *Star Wars*. Indeed, it's easy to recognise characters from a galaxy far, far away, as imperilled princess Misa Uehara, her bodyguard Toshiro Mifune, and prattling peasants Minoru Chiaki and Kamatari Fujiwara seek to smuggle gold through enemy territory. But Kurosawa's own debt to the westerns of John Ford is readily evident in both his use of CinemaScope (this was Japan's first widescreen feature) and his expert blend of action and comedy. Spectacular, amusing and exciting. DP. In Japanese with English subtitles. Contains violence. DVD

Toshiro Mifune *Rokurota* • Misa Uehara (1) *Lady Yukihime* • Minoru Chiaki *Tahei* • Kamatari Fujiwara *Matashichi* • Susumu Fujita *Hyoe Tadokoro* • Takashi Shimura *Izumi* ■ *Dir* Akira Kurosawa • *Scr* Ryuzo Kikushima, Hideo Oguni, Shinobu Hashimoto, Akira Kurosawa

Hidden Homicide ★ U

Murder mystery 1958 · UK · BW · 81mins

This bargain-basement thriller would have worked as a TV episode. Spun out to feature length, however, the gaping holes in the narrative logic become glaringly apparent. Director Tony Young badly fumbles this story of a writer who is so convinced by the circumstantial evidence surrounding his uncle's death, he begins to consider himself a suspect. Griffith Jones lacks the vulnerability to convince in the lead. DP

Griffith Jones *Michael Cornforth* • Patricia Laffan *Jean* • James Kenney *Oswald Castellan* • Bruce Seton *Bill Dodd* • Maya Koumani *Marian* • Robert Raglan *Ashbury* • Richard Shaw *Wright* • Charles Farrell *Mungo Peddey* ■ *Dir* Tony Young • *Scr* Tony Young, Bill Luckwell, from the novel *Murder at Shinglestrand* by Paul Capon

Hide and Seek ★★ U

Comedy thriller 1963 · UK · Colour · 92mins

After a decade top-lining some of the wittiest social satires ever made in the UK, Ian Carmichael's fortunes were on the wane by the time he starred in this leaden comedy thriller. Director Cy Endfield mishandles the jokier aspects of the plot, in which a scientist working on a top secret project is presumed to have defected when, in actuality, he's been kidnapped. DP

Ian Carmichael *David Garrett* • Janet Munro *Maggie* • Curt Jurgens *Hubert Marek* • George Pravda *Frank Melnicker* • Kieron Moore *Paul* • Hugh Griffith *Wilkins* • Derek Tansley *Chambers* • Judy Parfitt *Chauffeur* ■ *Dir* Cy Endfield • *Scr* David Stone, Robert Foshko, from a story by Harold Greene

Hide and Seek ★★ 18

Thriller 2000 · US · Colour · 95mins

Clearly this hostage drama was designed to arouse chattering-class indignation by laying siege to the bounds of decency. But, instead, it's little more than a smugly contentious "scandal the week" movie. Ever prone to excess, Jennifer Tilly gives a hysterical performance as the childless woman who joins fertility specialist Vincent Gallo in kidnapping mother-to-be Daryl Hannah in order to steal her baby. The dangerously offbeat approach requires a director with considerably more finesse than Sidney J Furie. DP DVD

Daryl Hannah *Anne White* • Jennifer Tilly *Helen* • Bruce Greenwood *Jack White* • Vincent Gallo *Frank* ■ *Dir* Sidney J Furie • *Scr* Joel Hladecek, Yas Takata

Hide and Seek ★★ 15

Psychological horror thriller
2005 · Ger/US · Colour · 96mins

Director John Polson demonstrates how not to make a suspense thriller with this weak tale of terror. It follows young Dakota Fanning as she invents a new playmate to help her cope with her mother's suicide. But her games with "Charlie" soon assume a more malevolent tone, much to the distress of her psychologist father (Robert De Niro). Although Fanning is customarily good, she's let down by De Niro, who starts off sleepwalking and ends up chewing the scenery. SF. Contains violence. DVD

Robert De Niro *David Callaway* • Dakota Fanning *Emily Callaway* • Famke Janssen *Katherine* • Elisabeth Shue *Elizabeth* • Amy Irving *Alison Callaway* • Dylan Baker *Sheriff Hafferty* • Melissa Leo *Laura* • Robert John Burke [Robert Burke] *Steven* ■ *Dir* John Polson • *Scr* Ari Schlossberg

Hide in Plain Sight ★★★★ PG

Crime drama 1980 · US · Colour · 87mins

Actor James Caan made an impressive directorial debut with this gutsy, unfussily acted account of a father who goes in search of his children after his wife (who is now involved with a renegade gangster) becomes part of the witness protection programme. Based on actual events, the action is shrewdly paced to reflect the painfully slow progress made by Caan's untutored factory worker in attempting to glean information from an uncaring, jobsworthing system. Yet, in striving to convey his character's frustration, Caan places more emphasis on his socio-political message than on the human interest angle. DP

James Caan *Thomas Hacklin Jr* • Jill Eikenberry *Alisa Hacklin* • Robert Viharo *Jack Scolese* • Joe Grifasi *Matty Stanek* • Barbra Rae *Ruthie Hacklin Scolese* • Kenneth McMillan *Sam Marzetta* • Josef Sommer *Jason R Reid* • Danny Aiello *Sal Carvello* ■ *Dir* James Caan • *Scr* Spencer Eastman, from a book by Leslie Waller

Hideaway ★★ 18

Horror thriller 1995 · US · Colour · 102mins

After a near-death experience in a car crash, antiques dealer Jeff Goldblum develops a psychic link to a satanist serial killer in this confusing psychological horror thriller. It's devoid of any real terror or suspense, though good computer-generated visual effects go a long way in maintaining the interest. However, the dispassionate Goldblum prevents any empathy with his quandary and the low-key approach of director Brett Leonard flattens any rich potential the premise might have had. AJ. Contains violence, swearing and nudity. DVD

Jeff Goldblum *Hatch Harrison* • Christine Lahti *Lindsey Harrison* • Alicia Silverstone *Regina Harrison* • Jeremy Sisto *Vassago* • Alfred Molina *Dr Jonas Nyeborn* • Rae Dawn Chong *Rose Orwetto* ■ *Dir* Brett Leonard • *Scr* Andrew Kevin Walker, Neal Jimenez, from the novel *Hideaway* by Dean R Koontz

The Hideaways ★★ U

Drama 1973 · US · Colour · 105mins

Originally released under the cumbersome title *From the Mixed-Up Files of Mrs Basil E Frankweiler*, this was heavily touted as the comeback, after three years, of Ingrid Bergman. It's a flimsy tale about two children who have the run of New York's Metropolitan Museum and wonder if a Michelangelo sculpture is a fake or not. Bergman plays a white-haired eccentric who may have a clue to the sculpture's origin. Lauren Bacall played the same role in a 1995 TV-movie under the original title. AT

Ingrid Bergman *Mrs Frankweiler* • Sally Prager *Claudia* • Johnny Doran *Jamie* • George Rose *Saxonburg* • Richard Mulligan *Mr Kincaid* • Georgann Johnson *Mrs Kincaid* • Madeline Kahn *Schoolteacher* ■ *Dir* Fielder Cook • *Scr*

Blanche Hanalis, from the novel *From The Mixed-Up Files of Mrs Basil E Frankweiler* by EL Konigsburg

Hideous Kinky ★★★ 15

Drama 1998 · UK/Fr · Colour · 94mins

Kate Winslet followed her headline-grabbing role in the blockbuster *Titanic* with the lead in this lower-profile film, based on the book by Esther Freud. She plays Julia, who decides to uproot her two young daughters and seek adventure and possibly romance in the Morocco of 1972. While Julia's journey is quite interesting and full of colour, the tale of expatriate life in Marrakesh is often repetitive. Both mother and older daughter Bea (Bella Riza) come off as two selfish children, leaving the heart of the film to the younger child, played with skill by Carrie Mullan. JB [video] DVD

Kate Winslet *Julia* • Saïd Taghmaoui *Bilal* • Bella Riza *Bea* • Carrie Mullan *Lucy* • Pierre Clémenti *Santoni* • Abigail Cruttenden *Charlotte* ■ *Dir* Gillies MacKinnon • *Scr* Billy MacKinnon, from the novel by Esther Freud

Hideous Sun Demon ★ PG

Science-fiction horror
1959 · US · BW · 71mins

Scientist Robert Clarke is exposed to nuclear radiation and turns into a scaly lizard-like monster when exposed to the sun's rays. Wordy dialogue, hopeless acting, wonky photography and a soundtrack that later turned up in *Night of the Living Dead* have made this farcical science-fiction fantasy a cult hit in the *Plan 9 from Outer Space* so-bad-it's-funny tradition. AJ [video]

Robert Clarke *Dr Gilbert McKenna* • Patricia Manning *Ann Russell* • Nan Peterson *Trudy Osborne* • Patrick Whyte *Dr Frederick Buckell* • Fred LaPorta *Dr Jacob Hoffman* ■ *Dir* Robert Clarke, Tom Boutross, Thomas Cassarino • *Scr* ES Seeley Jr, Doane Hoag, from the story *Strange Pursuit* by Robert Clarke, Phil Hiner

Hider in the House ★★ 18

Thriller 1989 · US · Colour · 103mins

Until it breaks down the believability barrier, director Matthew Patrick's unusual psycho thriller is tightly constructed and grippingly written. Former mental institution inmate Gary Busey hides in the home of well-to-do Mimi Rogers and Michael McKean, obsessively spies on them and eventually intervenes in their personal affairs. When he's found out the all-too-familiar maelstrom of mayhem begins. Yet Busey and Rogers raise enormous empathy before the plot degenerates into a stock shocker. AJ. Contains violence, swearing, sex scenes and nudity. [video]

Gary Busey *Tom Sykes* • Mimi Rogers *Julie Dryer* • Michael McKean *Phil Dryer* • Kurt Christopher Kinder *Neil Dryer* • Candy Hutson [Candace Hutson] *Holly Dryer* • Bruce Glover *Gary Hufford* ■ *Dir* Matthew Patrick • *Scr* Lem Dobbs

Hiding Out ★★ 15

Comedy thriller 1987 · US · Colour · 98mins

Jon Cryer has rarely found the right vehicle for his comedic talents and, although this provides him with a rare starring role, it founders on a lame, unconvincing script. He plays a stockbroker who, finding himself on the run from the Mob, decides to hide out as a college student. Given that he looks far too young as a bearded adult, this charade works wonders, but complications ensue when a fellow student (Annabeth Gish) falls for him. Director Bob Giraldi seems unsure whether this is a teen comedy or a light-hearted thriller. JF. Contains some violence and swearing. [video]

Jon Cryer *Andrew Morenski* • Keith Coogan *Patrick Morenski* • Annabeth Gish *Ryan Campbell* • Gretchen Cryer *Aunt Lucy* • Oliver Cotton *Killer* • Claude Brooks *Clinton* • Lou Walker *Ezzard* ■ *Dir* Bob Giraldi • *Scr* Joe Menosky, Jeff Rothberg

The Hiding Place ★★

Second World War drama
1975 · US · Colour · 146mins

Produced by Billy Graham's Evangelistic Association, this rather flat story of Dutch Christians giving shelter to persecuted Jews during the Second World War, wears its heart, but not its art, on its sleeve. Julie Harris and Arthur O'Connell – in his final film role – are just too well-scrubbed to pass for wartime citizens, despite the quality of their performances. This is certainly a moving experience, but it never really gets anywhere. TH

Julie Harris *Betsie ten Boom* • Eileen Heckart *Katje* • Arthur O'Connell *Casper ten Boom* • Jeannette Clift *Corrie ten Boom* • Robert Rietty *Willem ten Boom* • Pamela Sholto *Tine* • Paul Henley *Peter ten Boom* ■ *Dir* James F Collier • *Scr* Allan Sloane, Lawrence Holben, from the non-fiction book by Corrie Ten Boom, John Sherrill, Elizabeth Sherrill

High and Low ★★★★ 12

Crime drama
1963 · Jpn · BW and Colour · 143mins

Akira Kurosawa's genius for literary adaptation also included hard-boiled pulp, as he proves with this reworking of Ed McBain's *King's Ransom*. It begins on a single set, as Toshiro Mifune's corrupt tycoon debates whether to pay the ransom demanded for the chauffeur's son, who was mistakenly kidnapped instead of his own offspring. But then the action opens out to follow the police on their desperate hunt around the seedier parts of town. Displaying a masterly control of mood and visual style, Kurosawa is more concerned with the morality of the case than its safe solution. However, this is still a riveting and tense thriller. DP. In Japanese with English subtitles. [video] DVD

Toshiro Mifune *Kingo Gondo* • Kyoko Kagawa *Reiko, Gondo's wife* • Tatsuya Mihashi *Kawanishi* • Yutaka Sada *Aoki, the chauffeur* • Tatsuya Nakadai *Inspector Tokuro* • Takashi Shimura *Director* ■ *Dir* Akira Kurosawa • *Scr* Akira Kurosawa, Ryuzo Kikushima, Hideo Oguni, Eijiro Hisaita, from the novel *King's Ransom* by Ed McBain [Evan Hunter]

The High and the Mighty ★★ U

Drama 1954 · US · Colour · 146mins

As a crippled airplane flies through the sky, having passed the point of no return, it is up to washed-up pilot John Wayne to save the day. Director William A Wellman seems restrained by the CinemaScope format, and Ernest K Gann, adapting his novel to the screen, writes mundane flashbacks which dissipate the tension. Shallow characterisation doesn't help, either. A big hit in its day, this gained Oscar nominations for Wellman and supporting actresses Claire Trevor and Jan Sterling, while Dimitri Tiomkin won for his dramatic score. AE

John Wayne *Dan Roman* • Claire Trevor *May Holst* • Laraine Day *Lydia Rice* • Robert Stack *Sullivan* • Jan Sterling *Sally McKee* • Phil Harris *Ed Joseph* • Robert Newton *Gustave Pardee* • David Brian *Ken Childs* • Paul Kelly (1) *Flaherty* ■ *Dir* William A Wellman • *Scr* Ernest K Gann, from his novel

High Anxiety ★★★ 15

Parody 1977 · US · Colour · 93mins

This parody of Alfred Hitchcock's greatest hits rather sums up the strengths and weaknesses of Mel Brooks's films. By opting for the best known scenes in *Spellbound*, *Vertigo*, *North by Northwest* and *Psycho*, he settles for easy laughs and thus misses the chance to kid around with the real aficionados. Moreover, not enough thought has gone into the non-spoof scenes, many of which run out of steam. There are many funny moments, but perhaps Hitch was just too self-mocking to be spoofable. AJ. Contains swearing. [video]

Mel Brooks *Richard H Thorndyke* • Madeline Kahn *Victoria Brisbane* • Cloris Leachman *Nurse Diesel* • Harvey Korman *Doctor Charles Montague* • Ron Carey *Brophy* • Howard Morris *Professor Lilloman* • Dick Van Patten *Doctor Wentworth* • Jack Riley *Desk clerk* ■ *Dir* Mel Brooks • *Scr* Mel Brooks, Ron Clark, Rudy DeLuca, Barry Levinson

High Art ★★★★ 18

Drama 1998 · US · Colour · 97mins

This is an intimate, skilfully observed study of the complex relationship between two neighbours, one a previously famous photographer (Ally Sheedy), the other an assistant editor of a photography magazine (Radha Mitchell). Despite its themes of drug abuse and lesbianism, this is far from being a sensationalist drama, while the gradual deepening of the ambitious, strong-willed Mitchell's attraction to and fascination with the drained, almost lifeless Sheedy is given credibility by the thoughtful script and stripped-bare performances. DP. Contains swearing, sex scenes and drug abuse. [video]

Ally Sheedy *Lucy Berliner* • Radha Mitchell *Syd* • Patricia Clarkson *Greta Krauss* • Gabriel Mann *James, Syd's boyfriend* • Bill Sage *Arnie* • Ahn Duong *Dominique, "Frame" editor* • Tammy Grimes *Vera, Lucy's mother* • David Thornton *Harry, Syd's boss* ■ *Dir/Scr* Lisa Cholodenko

High-ballin' ★★ 15

Action 1978 · US/Can · Colour · 98mins

This low-budget trucking epic followed in the wake of Burt Reynolds's *Smokey and the Bandit* and went head-to-head with Sam Peckinpah's *Convoy*. Jerry Reed is joined by biker Peter Fonda and female trucker Helen Shaver. The real star, though, is the massive rig that bowls down the freeway causing mayhem while our three heroes resist various hijackers, bootleggers and the corrupt trucking boss played by Chris Wiggins. AT [video]

Peter Fonda *Rane* • Jerry Reed *Duke* • Helen Shaver *Pickup* • Chris Wiggins *King Carroll* • Michael Ironside *Butch* ■ *Dir* Peter Carter • *Scr* Paul Edwards, from a story by Richard Robinson, Stephen Schneck

High Barbaree ★★

Second World War drama
1947 · US · BW · 90mins

In this Second World War yarn, Van Johnson steers his downed navy seaplane towards High Barbaree, a fabled Pacific island his uncle once told him about. Co-pilot Cameron Mitchell keeps him company while he tells his story, which leads to flashbacks re-creating Johnson's life back home with sweetheart June Allyson. This is less a war movie than a soupy romance. AT

Van Johnson *Alec Brooke* • June Allyson *Nancy Fraser* • Thomas Mitchell *Capt Thad Vail* • Marilyn Maxwell *Diana Case* • Henry Hull *Dr Brooke* • Claude Jarman Jr *Alec, age 14* • Cameron Mitchell *Lt Moore* ■ *Dir* Jack Conway • *Scr* Anne Morrison Chaplin, Whitfield Cook, Cyril Hume, from the novel by Charles Nordhoff, James Norman Hall

High Boot Benny ★★★★ 15

Thriller 1993 · Ire · Colour · 78mins

In keeping with the principles of the non-sectarian school at the centre of his controversial drama, writer/director Joe Comerford tries to be even-handed, and he avoids many of the situations inherent in films about the Troubles. Frances Tomelty does well as the idealistic matron, as does Marc O'Shea as the confused teenager from Northern Ireland who seeks refuge south of the border. The tarring and feathering scene and the brutal army reprisal will chill to the marrow. DP [video]

Marc O'Shea *Benny* • Frances Tomelty *Matron* • Alan Devlin *Manley* • Annie Farr *Dorothy* • Seamus Ball *Father Bergin* • Fiona Nicholas *Orphan* ■ *Dir/Scr* Joe Comerford

The High Bright Sun ★★ PG

Wartime drama 1965 · UK · Colour · 109mins

This attempt to make emotional drama (army officer Dirk Bogarde's love for archaeology student Susan Strasberg) out of a national crisis (the Cypriot struggle against British occupation) results in one of the most stilted and wooden movies that Bogarde ever made for Rank. Director Ralph Thomas hammers away at the obvious and rapidly loses credibility, while Ian Stuart Black's dialogue is awesomely improbable. Bogarde, though, pulls the film up by its bootstraps. TH. Contains some swearing and violence. [video]

Dirk Bogarde *Major McGuire* • George Chakiris *Haghios* • Susan Strasberg *Juno Kozani* • Denholm Elliott *Baker* • Grégoire Aslan *Skyros* • Colin Campbell *Emile* • Joseph Furst *Dr Andros* • Katherine Kath *Mrs Andros* ■ *Dir* Ralph Thomas • *Scr* Ian Stuart Black, Bryan Forbes, from the novel by Ian Stuart Black

The High Cost of Loving ★★ U

Comedy 1958 · US · BW · 87mins

That splendid actress Gena Rowlands, who found fame in husband John Cassavetes's powerful films, made an inauspicious screen debut in this tame domestic comedy directed by and co-starring José Ferrer. A celebrated stage and screen actor, Ferrer also directed seven so-so films. His fifth effort tells of a husband who thinks he is losing his office job, and whose wife fails to tell him she's expecting a baby. RB

José Ferrer *Jim Fry* • Gena Rowlands *Virginia Fry* • Joanne Gilbert *Syd Heyward* • Jim Backus *Paul Mason* • Bobby Troup *Steve Heyward* • Philip Ober *Herb Zorn* • Edward Platt *Eli Cave* • Charles Watts *Boylin* ■ *Dir* José Ferrer • *Scr* Rip Van Ronkel, from a story by Milo Frank Jr, Rip Van Ronkel

The High Country ★ PG

Romantic adventure
1981 · Can · Colour · 91mins

After winning rave reviews for his role in *The Last Picture Show*, Timothy Bottoms was reduced to making tedious dramas such as this. He plays an escaped prisoner dragging Linda Purl through the mountains in what is an excuse for director Harvey Hart to film lots of impressive Canadian scenery in between the mediocre chase scenes. JB [video]

Timothy Bottoms *Jim* • Linda Purl *Kathy* • George Sims *Larry* • Jim Lawrence *Casey* • Bill Berry *Carter* • Walter Mills *Clem* • Paul Jolicoeur [Paul Coeur] *Red* • Dick Butler *Herbie* ■ *Dir* Harvey Hart • *Scr* Bud Townsend

High Crimes ★★ 12

Courtroom thriller
2002 · US · Colour · 110mins

Carl Franklin's military-themed legal thriller squanders its quality cast on the most formulaic of scripts. Ashley Judd plays a successful attorney whose life is thrown into chaos when her husband (Jim Caviezel) is exposed as a former soldier accused of the murder of eight civilians during the civil war in El Salvador. Morgan Freeman is thoroughly wasted as the alcoholic lawyer who educates Judd in the peculiarities of military law. This trundles along without ever reaching the dramatic peaks one would expect.

H

JC. Contains violence and sexual references. DVD

Ashley Judd *Claire Kubik* • Morgan Freeman *Charlie Grimes* • Jim Caviezel *Tom Kubik* • Amanda Peet *Jackie* • Tom Bower *Mullins* • Adam Scott *Lieutenant Embry* • Bruce Davison *Brigadier General Marks* • Juan Carlos Hernandez *Major Hernandez* ■ *Dir* Carl Franklin • *Scr* Yuri Zeltser, Cary Bickley, from the novel by Joseph Binder

High Fidelity ★★★★ 15

Comedy drama
2000 · US/UK · Colour · 108mins

Stephen Frears transposes Nick Hornby's novel from north London to downtown Chicago, but this slickly scripted, knowingly played and comedy stands, on its merits, as an *Alfie* for the millennial generation. As the owner of a failing vinyl emporium, John Cusack combines reluctant self-awareness with genuine delusion as he attempts to reconcile the loss of girlfriend Iben Hjejle to lusty neighbour Tim Robbins by dating singer Lisa Bonet. However, it's when directly addressing the viewer or compulsively compiling Top Five lists that Cusack, and the film, come alive. DP. Contains swearing, a sex scene, brief nudity. DVD

John Cusack *Rob Gordon* • Iben Hjejle *Laura* • Todd Louiso *Dick* • Jack Black *Barry* • Lisa Bonet *Marie De Salle* • Catherine Zeta-Jones *Charlie* • Joan Cusack *Liz* • Tim Robbins *Ian* • Lili Taylor *Sarah* • Natasha Gregson Wagner *Caroline* ■ *Dir* Stephen Frears • *Scr* DV DeVincentis, Steve Pink, John Cusack, Scott Rosenberg, from the novel by Nick Hornby

High Flight ★★ U

Action drama 1957 · UK · Colour · 105mins

The training of jet pilots in peacetime makes for a dull subject, despite some capably-staged midair crises. For dramatic take-off, therefore, this British-made film relies on the tense relationship between Ray Milland's commanding officer and Kenneth Haigh's rebellious young cadet. Haigh must have seemed ideal casting, having just made his name on stage as Jimmy Porter in *Look Back in Anger*, but he lacks screen presence. AE

Ray Milland *Wing Commander David Rudge* • Bernard Lee *Flight Sergeant Harris* • Kenneth Haigh *Tony Winchester* • Anthony Newley *Rodger Endicott* • Kenneth Fortescue *John Fletcher* • Sean Kelly *Cadet Day* • Helen Cherry *Louise* • Leslie Phillips *Squadron Leader Blake* • John Le Mesurier *Commandant* ■ *Dir* John Gilling • *Scr* Joseph Landon, Ken Hughes, from a story by Jack Davies

High Heels ★★ 18

Black comedy 1991 · Sp · Colour · 108mins

After a string of cult hits, it was inevitable that Pedro Almodóvar would eventually take a false step. Abandoning his trademark Euro-trash style, he attempts to tackle more serious themes in this disconcerting melodrama. He is so hell-bent on presenting a weighty treatise on families, the media and the price of fame that he allows too many scenes to become morose. The performances of Marisa Paredes and Victoria Abril just about save the day. DP. In Spanish with English subtitles.

Victoria Abril *Rebecca* • Marisa Paredes *Becky del Paramo* • Miguel Bose *Judge Dominguez/Femme Letal/Hugo* • Pedro Diez del Corral *Alberto* • Feodor Atkine *Manuel* • Ana Lizaran [Anna Lizaran] *Margarita* • Rocio Munoz *Little Rebecca* • Mairata O'Wisiedo *Judge's mother* ■ *Dir/Scr* Pedro Almodóvar

High Heels and Low Lifes ★★ 15

Crime comedy 2001 · UK · Colour · 82mins

Mel Smith's noble directorial ambitions are ill-served by this lumpy comic script about a nurse and an actress (Minnie Driver and Mary McCormack) who get tangled up with London gangsters. Driver completely outacts and "out-charismas" McCormack, thus unbalancing the *Thelma & Louise* double act, and only a cameo from Michael Gambon as a camp villain truly lights up the screen. AC. Contains swearing, violence, nudity. DVD

Minnie Driver *Shannon* • Michael Gambon *Kerrigan* • Mary McCormack *Frances* • Kevin McNally *Mason* • Mark Williams *Tremaine* • Danny Dyer *Danny* • Kevin Eldon *McGill* • Darren Boyd *Ray* • John Sessions *Director* ■ *Dir* Mel Smith • *Scr* Kim Fuller, from a story by Kim Fuller, from a story by Georgia Pritchett

High Hell ★★

Action adventure 1957 · US · BW · 85mins

One of those cheaply-made thrillers that always sound more enticingly full of menace than they really are. This one is all about a mine-owner's wife who takes a fancy to her husband's partner. The problems start when all three find themselves trapped in a snowbound hut high up in the Canadian Rockies. John Derek stars alongside familiar British faces Patrick Allen and Jerold Wells. TH

John Derek *Craig Rhodes* • Elaine Stewart *Lenore Davidson* • Patrick Allen *Luke Fulgham* • Jerold Wells *Charlie Spence* • Al Mulock *Frank Davidson* • Rodney Burke *Danny Rhodes* • Colin Croft *Dell Malverne* ■ *Dir* Burt Balaban • *Scr* Irve Tunick, from the novel *High Cage* by Steve Frazee

High Hopes ★★★★ 15

Comedy drama 1988 · UK · Colour · 107mins

After making *Bleak Moments*, Mike Leigh waited 17 years before directing this, his next feature. It's an amusing and affecting, if sometimes grim, look at the lives of six people in Thatcher's Britain: a working-class couple with counter-cultural pretensions, an obnoxious up-market twosome, and a pair of consumerist vulgarians. The characters may be caricatures, while the plot is slender and the film overlong, yet Leigh's unique blend of improvisation, invention and satire – what might be called misanthropy with a comic twist – combine to distinctive and telling effect. PF. Contains swearing and sex scenes.

Philip Davis *Cyril Bender* • Ruth Sheen *Shirley* • Edna Doré *Mrs Bender* • Philip Jackson *Martin Burke* • Heather Tobias *Valerie Burke* • Lesley Manville *Laetitia Boothe-Braine* • David Bamber *Rupert Boothe-Braine* • Jason Watkins *Wayne* ■ *Dir/Scr* Mike Leigh

High Lonesome ★★ U

Western 1950 · US · Colour · 81mins

This is a sociologically interesting cross between a western and a juvenile problem picture, with the snarling, brooding John Barrymore Jr, son of "the Great Profile", as a teenager with a conscience. It's directed by Alan LeMay, who is, alas, no cinematic craftsman. TS

John Barrymore Jr [John Drew Barrymore] *Cooncat* • Chill Wills *Boatwhistle* • John Archer *Pat Farrell* • Lois Butler *Meagan Davis* • Kristine Miller *Abbey Davis* • Basil Ruysdael *Horse Davis* • Jack Elam *Smiling Man* • Dave Kashner *Roper* ■ *Dir/Scr* Alan LeMay

High Lonesome ★★★ 12

Music documentary
1993 · US · Colour and BW · 89mins

Fans of Kentucky's special brand of music will enjoy this documentary. The main focus is on 82-year-old Bill Monroe, "the father of bluegrass", who fused local hillbilly music with Scots-Irish traditions brought by immigrants to the Kentucky coal fields. The music then developed and led to its acceptance at Nashville's Grand Ole Opry. The postwar period concentrates on the legendary Flatt and Scruggs, and the use of TV in spreading their music. AT

Dir Rachel Liebling • *Scr* Rachel Liebling

High Noon ★★★★★ U

Classic western 1952 · US · BW · 84mins

This is the film that put director Fred Zinnemann on the Hollywood A-list, revived the career of Gary Cooper and made Grace Kelly a star. If that's not enough, this multiple Oscar-winner was also one of the first psychological westerns, breaking the mould of the gun-toting tales that had dominated the genre since the early silent era. It was also a highly controversial film, being seen as an attack on those who deserted their colleagues during the communist witch-hunts that turned Hollywood into a place of fear between 1947 and 1951. DP DVD

Gary Cooper *Will Kane* • Grace Kelly *Amy Kane* • Thomas Mitchell *Jonas Henderson* • Lloyd Bridges *Harvey Pell* • Katy Jurado *Helen Ramirez* • Otto Kruger *Percy Mettrick* • Lon Chaney Jr *Martin Howe* • Henry Morgan [Harry Morgan] *William Fuller* • Lee Van Cleef *Jack Colby* ■ *Dir* Fred Zinnemann • *Scr* Carl Foreman, from the story *The Tin Star* by John W Cunningham • *Cinematographer* Floyd Crosby • *Music* Dmitri Tiomkin • *Editor* Elmo Williams, Harry Gerstad

High Plains Drifter ★★★★ 18

Western 1973 · US · Colour · 100mins

Sex, sadism and the supernatural are loosely bundled in Clint Eastwood's stylishly self-conscious western: man-with-no-name satire or fable of mystic revenge, take your pick. Eastwood looms out of the desert, a mirage of retribution on a town's inhabitants who stood by while their honest sheriff was whipped to death. Eastwood seems, not altogether successfully, to be paying off debts to his former mentor, Sergio Leone – gratitude he can only express obliquely via the occult references in this distinctive variation on the spaghetti western. TH. Contains violence and swearing. DVD

Clint Eastwood *The Stranger* • Verna Bloom *Sarah Belding* • Mariana Hill [Marianna Hill] *Callie Travers* • Mitchell Ryan *Dave Drake* • Jack Ging *Morgan Allen* • Stefan Gierasch *Mayor Jason Hobart* • Ted Hartley *Lewis Belding* ■ *Dir* Clint Eastwood • *Scr* Ernest Tidyman • *Cinematographer* Bruce Surtees

High Pressure ★★

Comedy 1932 · US · BW · 72mins

William Powell stars as a racketeer who falls for an inventor's scheme to convert sewage into artificial rubber. He sets up a corporation and sells stocks to raise some cash, romancing Evelyn Brent along the way. Powell breezes through this nonsense, which is not quite a gangster picture and not quite good enough for director Mervyn LeRoy. AT

William Powell *Gar Evans* • Evelyn Brent *Francine* • George Sidney (1) *Colonel Ginsburg* • Frank McHugh *Mike Donoghey* • Guy Kibbee *Clifford Gray* • Evalyn Knapp *Helen* • Ben Alexander *Geoffrey* • Harry Beresford *Dr Rudolph* ■ *Dir* Mervyn LeRoy • *Scr* Joseph Jackson, from the story *Hot Money* by SJ Peters and the play by Aben Kandell

High Risk ★★

Action adventure 1981 · US · Colour · 91mins

Laughable action adventure about four chums who decide that the solution to their money woes is a quick trip to Colombia to lift a fortune from a drugs kingpin. Naturally, things don't go quite according to plan. It boasts a pretty good cast – James Coburn, James Brolin, Anthony Quinn, Lindsay Wagner – but the sheer implausibility of the tale makes it hard to feel involved. JF

James Brolin *Stone* • Cleavon Little *Rockney* • Bruce Davison *Dan* • Chick Vennera *Tony* • Anthony Quinn *Mariano* • Lindsay Wagner *Olivia* • James Coburn *Serrano* • Ernest Borgnine *Clint* ■ *Dir/Scr* Stewart Raffill

High Road to China ★★★ PG

Action adventure
1983 · US · Colour · 100mins

Tom Selleck was offered the lead in *Raiders of the Lost Ark*, but had to refuse because he was contracted to the TV show *Magnum PI*. Instead he starred in this *Raiders* wannabe, playing a First World War flying ace who helps spoiled rich girl Bess Armstrong track down her missing father. While low on special effects, thanks to zippy direction from Brian G Hutton this romps along merrily in the style of 1940s Saturday matinées, while Selleck cuts quite a dash as the suave, wise-cracking hero. JB

Tom Selleck *O'Malley* • Bess Armstrong *Eve Tozer* • Jack Weston *Struts* • Wilford Brimley *Bradley Tozer* • Robert Morley *Bentik* • Brian Blessed *Suleiman Khan* • Cassandra Gava *Alessa* ■ *Dir* Brian G Hutton • *Scr* Sandra Weintraub Roland, S Lee Pogostin, from the novel by Jon Cleary

High School ★★★

Documentary 1968 · US · BW · 75mins

For over three decades, Fred Wiseman, a leading exponent of Direct Cinema or *cinéma vérité*, has entered various institutions with his hand-held camera, shot a vast amount of footage, and edited it down dispassionately, being careful not to make a subjective point. However, in his second documentary (the first, *Titicut Follies*, was set in an insane asylum), he eavesdrops on a middle-class school in Philadelphia and seems to be exposing the deadly conformity of the place. Concentrating mostly on student-teacher relationships, it has too narrow a focus, but is still fascinating. RB

Dir/Scr Frederick Wiseman • *Cinematographer* Richard Leiterman • *Editor* Frederick Wiseman

High School Confidential ★★★

Cult drama 1958 · US · BW · 85mins

The patriotic and paternalistic Louis B Mayer would have turned in his grave had he seen this deeply subversive, hugely exploitative MGM offering about school kids getting high on marijuana. It also packs in gang warfare, hot-rod racing, alcoholism, plenty of sex and a note of seriousness when lead delinquent, Russ Tamblyn, turns out to be a narcotics agent. Jan Sterling plays an English teacher and that 1950s icon, Mamie Van Doren, turns up as Tamblyn's lascivious aunt. Rock star Jerry Lee Lewis has a cameo appearance as himself. AT

Russ Tamblyn *Tony Baker* • Jan Sterling *Arlene Williams* • John Drew Barrymore *JI Coleridge* • Mamie Van Doren *Gwen Dulaine* • Diane Jergens *Joan Staples* • Jerry Lee Lewis ■ *Dir* Jack Arnold • *Scr* Lewis Meltzer, Robert Blees, from a story by Robert Blees

High School High ★★ 15

Comedy 1996 · US · Colour · 81mins

This misfiring spoof is chiefly aimed at the Michelle Pfeiffer hit *Dangerous Minds*, but also takes drive-by shots at all and sundry. Jon Lovitz is the idealistic teacher determined to make a difference at a school so crime-ridden the headmistress has to appeal at assembly for the return of kidnapped tutors. It's good to see perennial sidekick Lovitz in a lead role, but both the script and the supporting performances are patchy. JF. Contains some violence, swearing, drug abuse and nudity.

Jon Lovitz *Richard Clark* • Tia Carrere *Victoria Chappell* • Louise Fletcher *Mrs Doyle* • Mekhi Phifer *Griff* • Malinda Williams *Natalie* • Guillermo Diaz *Paco* • Lexie Bigham *Two Bags* • Gil Espinoza *Alonzo* ■ *Dir* Hart Bochner • *Scr* David Zucker, Robert LoCash, Pat Proft

High Season ★★ 15

Satirical drama 1987 · UK · Colour · 90mins

Oddly old-fashioned, romantic fluff, with Jacqueline Bisset as a photographer on the Greek island of Rhodes. Clare Peploe's film chronicles her encounters with all manner of people who need shooting – though not necessarily with a camera – including obnoxious tourists, spies and an egocentric ex-hubby. The main interest lies in the picture-postcard views of both the island and Bisset, and in a classy supporting cast. DA [video] DVD

Jacqueline Bisset *Katherine* • James Fox *Patrick* • Irene Papas *Penelope* • Sebastian Shaw *Basil Sharp* • Kenneth Branagh *Rick Lamb* • Lesley Manville *Carol Lamb* • Robert Stephens *Konstantinis* ■ *Dir* Clare Peploe • *Scr* Clare Peploe, Mark Peploe

High Sierra ★★★ PG

Crime thriller 1941 · US · BW · 95mins

This is the film that turned character actor Humphrey Bogart into a fully-fledged star. Bogie, in a role turned down by George Raft, plays melancholic gangster "Mad Dog" Roy Earle, making his last stand from a log cabin in the landscape of the title. The plot's actually a bit daft, and there's some risible nonsense with a disabled girl (the excellent Joan Leslie) and a dog. But screenwriters John Huston and WR Burnett have, on the whole, fashioned a pacy melodrama. Remade in 1955 as *I Died a Thousand Times*. TS [video] DVD

Humphrey Bogart *"Mad Dog" Roy Earle* • Ida Lupino *Marie Garson* • Alan Curtis *Babe Kozak* • Arthur Kennedy *Red Hattery* • Joan Leslie *Velma* • Henry Hull *"Doc" Banton* • Barton MacLane *Jake Kranmer* • Henry Travers *Pa* ■ *Dir* Raoul Walsh • *Scr* John Huston, WR Burnett, from the novel by WR Burnett

High Society ★★★★ U

Musical romantic comedy
1956 · US · Colour · 102mins

This musical remake of the 1940 film *The Philadelphia Story* was a smash hit. It's cleverly under-directed by the brilliant Charles Walters and offers many joys, notably the teaming of crooners Crosby and Frank Sinatra for the brilliantly witty Cole Porter number *Well, Did You Evah?*, and the delightful Grace Kelly in a role she plays perfectly, that of a spoiled rich brat. Sinatra and Celeste Holm make a snappy pair of journalists (and bring that snap to another Porter classic, *Who Wants to be a Millionaire?*), but Crosby seems somewhat ill at ease, and jazz great Louis Armstrong is reduced to the chorus and stooge to Crosby. TS [video] DVD

Bing Crosby *CK Dexter-Haven* • Grace Kelly *Tracy Samantha Lord* • Frank Sinatra *Mike Connor* • Celeste Holm *Liz Imbrie* • John Lund *George Kittredge* • Louis Calhern *Uncle Willie* • Sidney Blackmer *Seth Lord* • Louis Armstrong ■ *Dir* Charles Walters • *Scr* John Patrick, from the play *The Philadelphia Story* by Philip Barry • *Music* Johnny Green (1), Saul Chaplin

High Spirits ★★★ 15

Supernatural comedy
1988 · US · Colour · 93mins

Neil Jordan's boil-in-the-bag *Beetle Juice* goes for Ealing whimsy and easy laughs and, incredibly, manages both in spite of such a slender plot. Peter O'Toole hits the right note of craziness as a "haunted" castle owner whose staff of fake spectres battle real poltergeists during the American tourist season, with suitably madcap results. However, too many desperate characters veer off into so many disparate subplots that complete satisfaction is never achieved. AJ [video]

Peter O'Toole *Peter Plunkett* • Daryl Hannah *Mary Plunkett* • Steve Guttenberg *Jack* • Beverly D'Angelo *Sharon* • Liam Neeson *Martin Brogan* • Ray McAnally *Plunkett Senior* • Liz Smith *Mrs Plunkett* • Jennifer Tilly *Miranda* • Peter Gallagher *Brother Tony* • Connie Booth *Marge* ■ *Dir/Scr* Neil Jordan

High Stakes ★★ 18

Romantic thriller 1989 · US · Colour · 82mins

Sally Kirkland, as a New York prostitute, gives a superbly sensitive performance and almost redeems this story of her attempt to rescue her daughter from the Mob, while falling in love with a Wall Street operator. Not particularly thrilling material, though Kirkland puts in a portrayal beyond the call of duty. Any other interest is provided by an early appearance from Sarah Michelle Gellar, plus a pre-*Misery* role for Kathy Bates. TH [video]

Sally Kirkland *Melanie "Bambi" Rose* • Robert LuPone *John Stratton* • Richard Lynch *Slim* • Sarah Gellar [Sarah Michelle Gellar] *Karen* • Kathy Bates *Jill* • WT Martin *Bob* • Eddie Earl Hatch *Earl* ■ *Dir/Scr* Amos Kollek

High Tide ★★★ 15

Drama 1987 · Aus · Colour · 101mins

This bleak tale of a woman who unexpectedly discovers her long-abandoned daughter is saved by the stirring, emotionally loaded central performance of Judy Davis, one of the most fascinating and adventurous actors working today, whose well-documented eccentricity has prevented her achieving major star status. This often thoughtful, intelligent film shows us once again what a charismatic celluloid presence she can be. SH. Contains swearing. [video]

Judy Davis *Lilli* • Jan Adele *Bet* • Claudia Karvan *Ally* • Colin Friels *Mick* • John Clayton *Col* • Frankie J Holden *Lester* • Monica Trapaga *Tracey* • Mark Hembrow *Mechanic* ■ *Dir* Gillian Armstrong • *Scr* Laura Jones

High Tide at Noon ★★

Drama 1957 · UK · BW · 110mins

Since his graduation to features in the early 1950s, one-time documentarist Philip Leacock had mostly impressed, yet he came unstuck with this *Romeo and Juliet* story set alongside the Nova Scotia fishing banks. Leacock surveys the local scenery with a keen eye, but his handling of the melodramatic ructions caused by Betta St John's rejection of Patrick McGoohan and Michael Craig in favour of outsider William Sylvester is less sure. DP

Betta St John *Joanna MacKenzie* • William Sylvester *Alec Douglas* • Michael Craig *Nils* • Patrick McGoohan *Simon Breck* • Flora Robson *Donna* • Alexander Knox *Stephen* ■ *Dir* Philip Leacock • *Scr* Neil Paterson, from the novel by Elizabeth Ogilvie

High Time ★★ U

Musical comedy 1960 · US · Colour · 102mins

Sammy Cahn and Jimmy Van Heusen picked up an Oscar nomination for their song *The Second Time Around*, but that's the only bright spot in Blake Edwards's twee comedy. Bing Crosby ladles on the charm as the millionaire widower who heads back to college for some long overdue education. Crosby gets to romance pouting professor Nicole Maurey, but he's clearly aware the script is ludicrously lightweight. Fabian and Tuesday Weld play his unhip fellow students. DP

Bing Crosby *Harvey Howard* • Fabian *Gil Sparrow* • Tuesday Weld *Joy Elder* • Nicole Maurey *Helene Gauthier* • Richard Beymer *Bob Bannerman* • Yvonne Craig *Randy Pruitt* • Patrick Adiarte *TJ Padmanagham* ■ *Dir* Blake Edwards • *Scr* Tom Waldman, Frank Waldman, from a story by Garson Kanin

High Velocity ★

Action drama 1977 · US · Colour · 105mins

This is exploitation movie-making at its crassest. Both Ben Gazzara and Paul Winfield are utterly wasted as hard-boiled Vietnam vets hired to rescue corporate tycoon Keenan Wynn kidnapped by a guerrilla force. Amid the substandard action scenes director Remi Kramer tries to make a point about foreign businesses in Third World countries corrupting officials, but offers no genuine insight. RS

Ben Gazzara *Clifford Baumgartner* • Britt Ekland *Mrs Andersen* • Paul Winfield *Watson* • Keenan Wynn *Mr Andersen* • Alejandro Rey *Alejandro Martel* ■ *Dir* Remi Kramer • *Scr* Remi Kramer, Michael J Parsons

High Voltage ★ U

Drama 1929 · US · BW · 63mins

Even if given leeway for being made in the 1920s, this terminally dull tale of a snow-bound group of bus passengers sheltering in a remote church is still unimaginatively shot with appallingly little plot development. Only future screwball comedian Carole Lombard (billed as Carol) shows any spirit, playing the smart-talking, bad girl equal to mysterious tough guy William Boyd. The action is practically static, with ludicrous dialogue doing nothing to perk up events. SF DVD

William Boyd (1) *Bill the boy* • Owen Moore *Detective Dan Egan* • Carol Lombard [Carole Lombard] *Billie Davis* • Diane Ellis *The kid* • Billy Bevan *Gus, the driver* • Phillips Smalley *Banker Henderson* ■ *Dir* Howard Higgin • *Scr* Elliott Clawson, James Gleason

High Voltage ★★ 18

Action crime thriller
1998 · US · Colour · 92mins

The presence of Bruce Lee's daughter Shannon Lee will perk up the interest among martial arts buffs, but this is strictly second-division material. Antonio Sabato Jr plays the head of a gang of small-time crooks who inadvertently rob a bank managed by Lee. However, in reality, it's controlled by Asian crime boss George Cheung, who proceeds to exact a bloody revenge. There's no shortage of gunplay and explosions but the martial arts on show are pretty passé. JF [video]

Antonio Sabato Jr *Johnny Clay* • William Zabka *Bulldog* • Lochlyn Munro *Larry* • George Kee Cheung *Victor Phan* • Shannon Lee *Jane* • Amy Smart *Molly* ■ *Dir* Isaac Florentine • *Scr* Mike Mains

High Wall ★★★

Crime drama 1947 · US · BW · 98mins

Stylish, angst-ridden *film noir* with Robert Taylor as the traumatised war veteran and possible wife killer who falls in love with his psychiatrist, Audrey Totter. She recommends brain surgery and truth-drugs; Taylor realises that if he has the surgery he will be judged sane and tried for murder. As the flashbacks roll past, we realise everyone has a sexual hang-up that the war just made worse. Taylor looks convincingly ravaged throughout, and Herbert Marshall makes a splendidly shady character. AT

Robert Taylor (1) *Steven Kenet* • Audrey Totter *Dr Ann Lorrison* • Herbert Marshall *Willard I Whitcombe* • Dorothy Patrick *Helen Kenet* • HB Warner *Mr Slocum* • Warner Anderson *Dr George Poward* • Moroni Olsen *Dr Phillip Dunlap* ■ *Dir* Curtis Bernhardt • *Scr* Sydney Boehm, Lester Cole, from the novel and play by Alan R Clark, Bradbury Foote

High, Wide and Handsome ★★★★ U

Western musical 1937 · US · BW · 110mins

Offbeat but entertaining, this epic period musical dramatises the efforts of prospectors, led by Randolph Scott, to exploit oil under their land. The astonishing climax, in which a pipeline is constructed over a hill in Pennsylvania, involves an entire circus and its elephants thwarting a band of saboteurs. A screen original by Oscar Hammerstein II, who wrote lyrics to some wonderful songs with music by Jerome Kern, it has inventive direction by Rouben Mamoulian. Memorable performances are drawn from Irene Dunne as the medicine show singer and Akim Tamiroff as the wily saloon keeper. AE

Irene Dunne *Sally Watterson* • Randolph Scott *Peter Cortlandt* • Dorothy Lamour *Molly Fuller* • Elizabeth Patterson *Grandma Cortlandt* • Raymond Walburn *Doc Watterson* • Charles Bickford *Red Scanlon* • Akim Tamiroff *Joe Varese* ■ *Dir* Rouben Mamoulian • *Scr* Oscar Hammerstein II, George O'Neil

A High Wind in Jamaica ★★★

Swashbuckling adventure
1965 · UK · Colour · 105mins

Alexander Mackendrick's penultimate picture is a solidly crafted adaptation of Richard Hughes's bestseller about a gnarled pirate who finds himself playing nursemaid to a group of young stowaways. Although occasionally becalmed during its more melodramatic passages, it is still marvellous entertainment. Anthony Quinn is fine in the action sequences but doesn't always convince, but James Coburn is on top form as his first mate and cinematographer Douglas Slocombe's seascapes are often very beautiful. DP

Anthony Quinn *Juan Chavez* • James Coburn *Zac* • Benito Carruthers [Ben Carruthers] *Alberto* • Lila Kedrova *Rosa* • Deborah Baxter *Emily Thornton* • Viviane Ventura *Margaret Fernandez* • Martin Amis *John Thornton* • Roberta Tovey *Rachel Thornton* • Gert Frobe [Gert Fröbe] *Dutch captain* ■ *Dir* Alexander Mackendrick • *Scr* Stanley Mann, Ronald Harwood, Denis Cannan, from the novel by Richard Hughes

Higher and Higher ★★★ U

Musical 1943 · US · BW · 86mins

French import Michèle Morgan was top-billed in this bright adaptation of the Broadway hit, but it's best remembered now as Frank Sinatra's first starring vehicle after becoming America's most popular teenage crooner. There's accomplished support from Jack Haley, who re-creates his Broadway role; less memorable are Mel Tormé and Victor Borge, neither of whom really cut it as movie players. Veteran director Tim Whelan doesn't get in the way. TS [video]

Michèle Morgan *Millie* • Frank Sinatra *Frank* • Jack Haley *Mike* • Leon Errol *Drake* • Marcy McGuire *Mickey* • Victor Borge *Sir Victor Fitzroy Victor* • Mary Wickes *Sandy* • Elisabeth Risdon *Mrs Keating* • Barbara Hale *Katherine* • Mel Tormé *Marty* ■ *Dir* Tim Whelan • *Scr* Jay Dratler, Ralph Spence, William Bowers, Howard Harris, from the play by Gladys Hurlbut, Joshua Logan

Higher Learning ★★★ 15

Drama 1995 · US · Colour · 123mins

Director John Singleton's third feature depicts a university campus as social microcosm. In a place where race and peer pressure matter more than intelligence and individuality, only professor Laurence Fishburne seems capable of thinking for himself. However, his idealistic belief seems curiously naive alongside the terrified eagerness with which freshmen

H

Michael Rapaport, Omar Epps and Kristy Swanson seek to fit into their new environment. Cole Hauser is chillingly effective as the white supremacist skinhead who reveals Rapaport's potential for violence, while Jennifer Connelly gives the most adult performance. DP. Contains swearing, violence and drug abuse. DVD

Jennifer Connelly *Taryn* • Ice Cube *Fudge* • Laurence Fishburne *Professor Maurice Phipps* • Omar Epps *Malik Williams* • Kristy Swanson *Kristen Connor* • Michael Rapaport *Remy* • Tyra Banks *Deja* • Cole Hauser *Scott Moss* ■ *Dir/Scr* John Singleton

Highlander ★★★ 15

Action adventure fantasy
1986 · US/UK · Colour · 111mins

So confused as to be hilariously watchable, director Russell Mulcahy's cult fantasy wavers between sci-fi, horror flick and music video as 16th-century Scottish clansman Christopher Lambert is schooled in being an immortal swordsman by Sean Connery for eternal battles with the evil Clancy Brown. There are some great sword-lunging duels (the best, in fact, is in a Madison Square Garden garage at the beginning) but the plot itself is never as pointedly directed. TH. Contains violence, swearing, nudity. DVD

Christopher Lambert *Connor MacLeod* • Roxanne Hart *Brenda Wyatt* • Clancy Brown *Kurgan* • Sean Connery *Ramirez* • Beatie Edney *Heather* • Alan North *Lieutenant Frank Moran* • Sheila Gish *Rachel Ellenstein* ■ *Dir* Russell Mulcahy • *Scr* Gregory Widen, Peter Bellwood, Larry Ferguson, from a story by Gregory Widen

Highlander II: the Quickening ★★ 15

Action adventure fantasy
1990 · US · Colour · 85mins

Despite some absurdly silly casting (Christopher Lambert as a Scotsman?), the first *Highlander* was a worldwide smash and hoots of fun into the bargain. This time around it just doesn't click, even though both Lambert and Sean Connery return from the original. The two leads once again exude charisma, but there's not enough flash to cover the lack of substance. JF. Contains swearing and violence. DVD

Christopher Lambert *Connor MacLeod* • Sean Connery *Juan Villa-Lobos Ramirez* • Virginia Madsen *Louise Marcus* • Michael Ironside *General Katana* • Allan Rich *Alan Neyman* • John C McGinley *Blake* ■ *Dir* Russell Mulcahy • *Scr* Peter Bellwood, from a story by Brian Clemens, William N Panzer, from characters created by Gregory Widen

Highlander III: the Sorcerer ★ 15

Action adventure fantasy
1995 · Can/Fr/UK · Colour · 93mins

Just when you thought the *Highlander* saga couldn't sink any further into diluted caricature and empty rock video flash, along comes this terminally dreary second sequel. This time immortal Christopher Lambert must battle Mario Van Peebles over the fate of his adopted son in a flaccid fantasy that makes a lot of noise but not a lot of sense. AJ. Contains swearing, violence and sex scenes. DVD

Christopher Lambert *Connor MacLeod/Russell Nash* • Mario Van Peebles *Kane* • Deborah Unger [Deborah Kara Unger] *Alex Johnson/Sarah* • Mako *Nakano* • Raoul Trujillo *1st warrior* • Jean-Pierre Pérusse *2nd warrior* • Martin Neufeld *Stenn* ■ *Dir* Andy Morahan [Andrew Morahan] • *Scr* Paul Ohl, from a story by William N Panzer, Brad Mirman, from characters created by Gregory Widen

Highlander: Endgame ★ 18

Action adventure fantasy
2000 · US · Colour · 96mins

The fourth instalment in the variable series is a mass of chaotic action searching for a plot among the remnants of badly directed pop promos. Christopher Lambert's Connor MacLeod character joins forces with Adrian Paul's Duncan MacLeod from the TV series to fight killer Bruce Payne. Jerkily whizzing between centuries and countries for maximum audience bewilderment, this cobbled together farrago is a complete write-off. AJ DVD

Christopher Lambert *Connor MacLeod* • Adrian Paul *Duncan MacLeod* • Bruce Payne *Jacob Kell* • Lisa Barbuscia *Faith/Kate* • Donnie Yen *Jin Ke* • Jim Byrnes *Dawson* • Beatie Edney *Heather* • Sheila Gish *Rachel Ellenstein* ■ *Dir* Douglas Aarniokoski • *Scr* Joel Soisson, from a story by Eric Bernt, Gillian Horvath, William Panzer [William N Panzer], from characters created by Gregory Widen

Highly Dangerous ★★★ U

Comedy thriller 1950 · UK · BW · 88mins

Eric Ambler's playful script is the main reason for watching this lively espionage adventure, although there's also some wonderful character acting from Wilfrid Hyde White and Michael Hordern. Margaret Lockwood is particularly sprightly as an entomologist caught up in intrigue behind the Iron Curtain by reporter Dane Clark. Director Roy Ward Baker imparts a jaunty mix of thrills and comedy, but he doesn't always succeed in persuading American actor Clark (making his British screen debut) to drop the Hollywood pizzazz. DP

Margaret Lockwood *Frances Gray* • Dane Clark *Bill Casey* • Marius Goring *Anton Razinski* • Naunton Wayne *Hedgerley* • Wilfrid Hyde White *Luke* • Eugene Deckers *Alf* • Olaf Pooley *Assistant* • Michael Hordern *Rawlings* ■ *Dir* Roy Ward Baker • *Scr* Eric Ambler

Highpoint ★★ PG

Thriller 1979 · Can · Colour · 86mins

Richard Harris takes a job with Christopher Plummer, who has stolen $10 million and is now being pursued by both the Mafia and the CIA. The high point of this muddled thriller is a climactic tussle on top of a Toronto skyscraper. It's exciting enough but hardly worth enduring the rest of this routine film for. Kate Reid and Beverly D'Angelo complete a cast that's rather classier than the movie merits. DA

Richard Harris *Louis Kinney* • Christopher Plummer *James Hatcher* • Beverly D'Angelo *Lise Hatcher* • Kate Reid *Rachel Hatcher* • Peter Donat *Don Maranzella* • Robin Gammell *Banner* • Saul Rubinek *Centino* ■ *Dir* Peter Carter • *Scr* Richard Guttman, Ian Sutherland

Highway Patrolman ★★★ 15

Crime thriller 1991 · Mex · Colour · 100mins

English director Alex Cox does his cult reputation no harm at all with this evocative Spanish language thriller, filmed in Mexico where he now resides. Well-known Latin American actor Roberto Sosa plays an idealistic cop who learns that his new job is not quite the noble career he had in mind. How disillusionment leads to corruption and worse is the prime concern of Cox's morality tale, filmed extensively with a hand-held camera using long single takes. AJ. In Spanish with English subtitles. Contains violence, swearing, sex scenes.

Roberto Sosa *Pedro Rojas* • Bruno Bichir *Anibal* • Zaide Silvia Gutierrez *Griselda* • Vanessa Bauche *Maribel* • Pedro Armendáriz Jr *Sgt Barreras* • Malena Doria *Abuela* ■ *Dir* Alex Cox • *Scr* Lorenzo O'Brien

Highway 61 ★★★

Road movie 1992 · Can · Colour · 110mins

This offbeat comedy hasn't the same raw edge as the director and leads' thriller *Roadkill*, but it's dark enough, as rock 'n' roll roadie Valerie Buhagiar persuades good-natured barber Don McKellar to drive her brother's coffin across the Canadian border and down to New Orleans. Everyone along the road has "eccentric" written into their job description, but none of them is quite as weird as Earl Pastko who, as "Satan". Sparky, quirky and fun. DP. Contains violence, swearing, sex scenes, drug abuse and nudity.

Valerie Buhagiar *Jackie Bangs* • Don McKellar *Pokey Jones* • Earl Pastko *Mr Skin/"Satan"* • Peter Breck *Mr Watson* • Art Bergmann *Otto* • Johnny Askwith *Claude* ■ *Dir* Bruce McDonald • *Scr* Don McKellar, from a story by Don McKellar, Bruce McDonald, Allan Magee

Highway to Hell ★★★ 15

Horror comedy 1992 · US · Colour · 90mins

This oddball horror comedy pits the hordes of hell against a young eloping couple. An uneven contest you might think, but not when it's Chad Lowe whose fiancée is kidnapped by a cop from hell and who has just 24 hours to spring her from the underworld. Sounds daft, but director Ate De Jong delivers enough inventive visuals, including a three-headed dog and literal "hand" cuffs, to keep you decently entertained. Ben Stiller turns up dressed, bizarrely, as Attila the Hun. It's that kind of movie. RS

Patrick Bergin *Beezle* • Chad Lowe *Charlie Sykes* • Kristy Swanson *Rachel Clark* • Adam Storke *Royce* • Pamela Gidley *Clara* • Richard Farnsworth *Sam* • Jarrett Lennon *Adam* • Ben Stiller *Cook/Attila the Hun* ■ *Dir* Ate De Jong • *Scr* Brian Helgeland

The Highwayman ★★ 18

Black comedy road movie thriller
1999 · Can/US · Colour · 89mins

The chief point of interest in this black road movie is an almost unrecognisable Jason Priestley shooting his image to pieces as a psychotic bank robber. Along with sidekicks Bernie Coulson and Laura Harris, he heads to Canada to locate Stephen McHattie, whom Harris insists is her long lost father. There's little logic to the plotting and an unneccessarily high body count. JF

Laura Harris *Ziggy* • Stephen McHattie *Frank Drake* • Jason Priestley *Breakfast* • Bernie Coulson *Panda* • Gordon Michael Woolvett *Walter* • Louis Gossett Jr *Phil Bishop* ■ *Dir* Keoni Waxman • *Scr* Richard Beattie

Highwaymen ★★ 18

Crime thriller 2003 · US · Colour · 77mins

Jim Caviezel stars as a vengeful widower stalking the killer of his wife along dusty highways. His quarry (played by Colm Feore) kills women by running over them with his customised Cadillac El Dorado, as he is too severly disabled to carry out the killings with his own hands. The story begins well enough but then just trots out all the usual serial-killer clichés. The mayhem is more bloodthirsty than chilling, while the vicious tone and tired execution of the film are a turn-off. TH DVD

Jim Caviezel *Rennie Cray* • Rhona Mitra *Molly Poole* • Frankie Faison *Will Macklin* • Colm Feore *James Fargo* • Andrea Roth *Alexandra Farrow* • Gordon Currie *Ray Boone* ■ *Dir* Robert Harmon • *Scr* Craig Mitchell, Hans Bauer

La Hija del Engaño ★★★

Drama 1951 · Mex · BW · 80mins

Luis Buñuel virtually disowned the four features he produced in Spain for Filmofono. Indeed, he dubbed them "abominable cinema". Yet, having rejuvenated his career with *Los Olvidados*, he returned to one of this neglected quartet for a crowd-pleasing follow-up. Based on Carlos Arniches's stage musical, this Madrileño melodrama is not noticeably superior to the 1935 version, which Buñuel had all but directed because of Luis Marquina's inexperience. However, Fernando Soler impresses as the bourgeois salesman who gives away the baby daughter he discovers is not his own, only to be reunited, years later, at his seedy nightclub. DP. A Spanish language film.

Fernando Soler *Don Quintín* • Alicia Caro *Marta* • Ruben Rojo *Paco* • Nacho Contra *Jonron* ■ *Dir* Luis Buñuel • *Scr* Luis Alcoriza, Raquel Rojas, from the play *Don Quintín el Amargao* by Carlos Arniches

Hijack Stories ★★ 15

Crime drama
2000 · Ger/UK/Fr · Colour · 90mins

Having made such a positive impression with *Mapantsula*, Oliver Schmitz comes undone with this clumsily unfeasible Soweto crime drama. It's unlikely enough that black Jo'burg actor Tony Kgoroge should be so readily accepted into the fold by childhood buddy-turned-street hood Rapulana Seiphemo. But that he should then be transformed into the type of character he wishes to play in an upcoming TV series strains credibility too far. The asides on class and race in the new South Africa and the way the media perpetuates stereotypes are shrewd enough, but they lack bite. DP DVD

Tony Kgoroge *Sox* • Rapulana Seiphemo *Zama* • Percy Matsemela *Fly* • Makhaola Ndebele *Joe* • Moshidi Motshegwa *Grace* ■ *Dir* Oliver Schmitz • *Scr* Oliver Schmitz, Lesego Rampolokeng, from their story

Hijacking Hollywood ★★★

Comedy 1997 · US · Colour · 93mins

This satire about movie-making has Henry Thomas as a starstruck newcomer who turns up in Hollywood to try to get work from distant relative Mark Metcalf, a major producer. However, fed up with an endless number of menial chores, mostly associated with the new blockbuster *Moby Dick 2: Ahab's Revenge*, Thomas decides to hold the production to ransom by stealing essential master footage. Constantly amusing, this is an independent comedy that deserves greater exposure. DF

Henry Thomas *Kevin Conroy* • Scott Thompson *Russell* • Mark Metcalf *Michael Lawrence* • Neil Mandt *Tad* • Nicole Gian *Sarah Lawrence* • Helen Duffy *Mother* ■ *Dir* Neil Mandt • *Scr* Neil Mandt, Jim Rossow

Hilary and Jackie ★★★★ 15

Biographical drama
1998 · UK · Colour · 117mins

Emily Watson excels at portraying the often difficult, selfish and driven cellist Jaqueline du Pré in this controversial biopic of the unusual relationship between her and sister Hilary (Rachel Griffiths). The film is a fascinating, no-holds-barred account of Jackie's musical career and private life. While many column inches have been devoted to the incident when Jackie asks Hilary whether she can sleep with her husband, and then does so, the film – thanks to Watson's mesmerising performance – should be lauded for its fascinating realisation of Jackie's talent and almost destructive personality. JB. Contains swearing and sex scenes. DVD

Emily Watson *Jacqueline "Jackie" du Pré* • Rachel Griffiths *Hilary du Pré* • David Morrissey *Kiffer Finzi* • James Frain *Daniel Barenboim* • Charles Dance *Derek du Pré* • Celia Imrie *Iris du Pré* • Rupert Penry-Jones *Piers du Pré* • Bill Paterson *Cello teacher* ■

U = SUITABLE FOR ALL Uc = SUITABLE FOR ALL, ESPECIALLY FOR YOUNG CHILDREN (VIDEO ONLY) PG = PARENTAL GUIDANCE

Dir Anand Tucker • *Scr* Frank Cottrell Boyce, from the non-fiction book *A Genius in the Family* by Hilary du Pré, Piers du Pré

Hilda Crane ★

Melodrama 1956 · US · Colour · 87mins

Free-thinking Hilda (Jean Simmons), who escaped the suffocating clutches of her unloving, rigidly conventional family, returns from New York to her small home town two marriages and several men later. Broke, disillusioned and unhappy, she makes a third "respectable" marriage, plunging herself into further disaster. A really dismal "woman's picture", paralysed by a combination of cliché and cop-out. Simmons struggles, with some success, in her showy role. RK

Jean Simmons *Hilda Crane* • Guy Madison *Russell Burns* • Jean-Pierre Aumont *Jacques de Lisle* • Judith Evelyn *Mrs Crane* • Evelyn Varden *Mrs Burns* • Peggy Knudsen *Nell Bromley* • Gregg Palmer *Dink* • Richard Garrick *Dr Francis* ■ *Dir* Philip Dunne • *Scr* Philip Dunne, from a play by Samuel Raphaelson

The Hill ★★★★ 12

Prison drama 1965 · UK · BW · 118mins

When director Sidney Lumet cast Sean Connery in *The Hill*, the former 007 cast his fake hair to the wind for the first time. It's a terse, tough picture about an army prison in North Africa where the inmates are forced to march up and down a phoney hill. It's the Greek myth of Sisyphus with a vengeance, an impudent symbol for British colonial impotence in the 1960s, though it's set during the Second World War. AT. Contains some strong language and violence. [VIDEO]

Sean Connery *Joe Roberts* • Harry Andrews *Sergeant Major Wilson* • Ian Bannen *Harris* • Roy Kinnear *Monty Bartlett* • Ian Hendry *Staff Sergeant Williams* • Michael Redgrave *Medical officer* • Alfred Lynch *George Stevens* • Ossie Davis *Jacko King* • Jack Watson *Jock McGrath* • Norman Bird *Commandant* ■ *Dir* Sidney Lumet • *Scr* Ray Rigby, RS Allen, from their play

A Hill in Korea ★★ PG

War drama 1956 · UK · BW · 68mins

A British patrol is caught behind enemy lines during the Korean War – a conflict given hardly a moment's thought by the British cinema. Badly made on Portuguese locations and containing reams of sermonising dialogue, it's nevertheless made watchable by the presence of future stars Robert Shaw and Michael Caine, who actually spent his national service in Korea and was the film's largely ignored military adviser. AT [VIDEO]

George Baker *Lieutenant Butler* • Harry Andrews *Sergeant Payne* • Stanley Baker *Corporal Ryker* • Michael Medwin *Private Docker* • Ronald Lewis *Private Wyatt* • Robert Shaw *Lance-Corporal Hodge* • Michael Caine *Private Lockyer* ■ *Dir* Julian Amyes • *Scr* Ian Dalrymple, Anthony Squire

Hill's Angels ★ U

Comedy 1979 · US · Colour · 95mins

This slow-moving tale, released in the US as *The North Avenue Irregulars*, is typical of the poor product that Disney came up with during the 1970s. The story, in which naive young priest Edward Herrmann organises his women parishioners to combat organised crime after one of them loses the church funds at the racetrack, is a poorly realised excuse for a string of madcap chase scenes. At least the cast is sensible enough not to take it seriously. SH [VIDEO]

Edward Herrmann *Michael Hill* • Barbara Harris *Vickie* • Susan Clark *Anne* • Karen Valentine *Jane* • Michael Constantine *Marv* • Cloris Leachman *Claire* • Patsy Kelly *Rose Rafferty* ■ *Dir* Bruce Bilson • *Scr* Don Tait, from the book *The North Avenue Irregulars* by Rev Albert Fay Hill

The Hills Have Eyes ★★★★ 18

Horror 1977 · US · Colour · 89mins

Drawing inspiration from the myth of Sawney Bean and his Scottish cannibal clan, director Wes Craven crafted the best of his early low-budget horror epics. Brutal desert dwellers lay murderous siege to stranded innocent campers in the *Scream* maestro's exploration of depravity and the survival instinct. Using mirror images of two families at the opposing extremes of humanity, Craven's sharp sense of suspense and his willingness to take shock images to their limits carries a potent charge. AJ. Contains violence, swearing, nudity. [VIDEO] DVD

Susan Lanier *Brenda Carter* • Robert Houston *Bobby Carter* • Martin Speer *Doug Wood* • Russ Grieve *Big Bob Carter* • Dee Wallace [Dee Wallace Stone] *Lynne Wood* • Virginia Vincent *Ethel Carter* • James Whitworth *Jupiter* • Michael Berryman *Pluto* • John Steadman *Fred* • Janus Blythe *Ruby* • Lance Gordon *Mars* • Arthur King [Peter Locke] *Mercury* ■ *Dir/Scr* Wes Craven

The Hills Have Eyes Part II ★ 18

Horror 1985 · US · Colour · 86mins

Lightning doesn't strike twice for director Wes Craven, who ill-advisedly goes back to the desert cannibals versus middle-class Americans theme for his hack sequel. This time a busload of youths break down in the Yucca Valley en route to a motorcycle rally and are forced to battle the homicidal barbarians from the first film. Consign this one to the sequel scrapheap. AJ [VIDEO]

Michael Berryman *Pluto* • Tamara Stafford *Cass* • Kevin Spirtas *Kevin Blair* • Janus Blythe *Ruby* ■ *Dir/Scr* Wes Craven

The Hills of Donegal ★★

Musical romantic drama
1947 · UK · BW · 85mins

If Irish eyes are still smiling at the end of this melodramatic tarradiddle, it'll have more to do with the black stuff than the quality of John F Argyle's picture. A few sentimental songs enliven the opening segment, as Dinah Sheridan bids farewell to the stage to marry her singing partner's cousin. But no sooner have she and John Bentley settled in Donegal than he's forced to take drastic steps to prevent the tempestuous Tamara Desni from raking up an old affair. DP

Dinah Sheridan *Eileen Hannay* • James Etherington *Michael O'Keefe* • Moore Marriott *Old Jake* • John Bentley *Terry O'Keefe* • Irene Handl *Mrs Mactavish* • Tamara Desni *Carole Wells* ■ *Dir* John F Argyle [John Argyle] • *Scr* John Dryden

Hills of Home ★★★ U

Adventure 1948 · US · Colour · 96mins

Marvellous Lassie vehicle, in which the world's most famous collie stars in a reworking of the canine classic *Greyfriars Bobby*, itself a source for the following year's *Challenge to Lassie*. Edmund Gwenn is the kindly Scottish doctor who tries to cure our heroine of her aversion to water, veteran Donald Crisp plays his friend, and Janet Leigh is simply lovely to look at. TS

Edmund Gwenn *Dr William MacLure* • Donald Crisp *Drumsheugh* • Tom Drake *Tammas Milton* • Janet Leigh *Margit Mitchell* • Rhys Williams *Mr Milton* • Reginald Owen *Hopps* ■ *Dir* Fred Wilcox [Fred M Wilcox] • *Scr* William Ludwig, from the sketches *Doctor of the Old School* by Ian MacLaren

Hills of Kentucky ★★★

Silent adventure 1927 · US · BW

One-time prop boy, director Howard Bretherton was credited with over 100 features during his career, including several B-westerns with William "Hopalong" Boyd and Buck Jones. This Rin-Tin-Tin adventure was only his second outing and his inexperience occasionally shows through. Yet the action sequences are thrilling, particularly the legendary plunge into the waterfall by the dog star to rescue Dorothy Dwan from certain death. DP

Jason Robards [Jason Robards Sr] *Steve Harley* • Dorothy Dwan *Janet* • Tom Santschi *Ben Harley* • Nanette ■ *Dir* Howard Bretherton • *Scr* Edward Clark, from the story *The Untamed Heart* by Dorothy Yost

The Hillside Strangler ★★ 18

Horror thriller based on a true story
2004 · US/UK · Colour · 93mins

C Thomas Howell and Nicholas Turturro get their aspiring pimp attitudes exactly right as cousins Kenneth Bianchi and Angelo Buono who collectively became known as "The Hillside Strangler" for their series of murders in Hollywood in the late 1970s. Little else in director Chuck Parello's depressingly crude case history makes this tedious trawl through the sleazy underbelly of Tinseltown worthwhile. The murders are depicted clinically, and the viewer must decide if this is a fair factual representation or just tasteless censor baiting. AJ DVD

C Thomas Howell *Kenneth Bianchi* • Nicholas Turturro *Angelo Buono* • Allison Lange *Claire Shelton* • Lin Shaye *Jenny Buono* • Kent Masters-King *Gabrielle* • Cletus Young *Charlie Lloyd* • Roz Witt *Frances Bianchi* ■ *Dir* Chuck Parello [Charles Parello] • *Scr* Stephen Johnston, Chuck Parello [Charles Parello]

Himalaya ★★★ PG

Adventure drama
1999 · Nep/Swi/Fr/UK · Tinted · 104mins

Travel writer Eric Valli made his feature debut with this Oscar-nominated ethnographical odyssey, which was released in the States as *Caravan*. Drawing on his own experiences, the wizened Thilen Lhondup gives a supremely naturalistic performance as the Nepalese salt trader who relies on traditional wisdom to get his yak herd to market across some of the world's most inhospitable terrain. Yet, for all Thilen's simple courage and the visual splendour of the widescreen mountainscapes, this poetic tribute to the hardy spirit of a remarkable people is short on dramatic incident. DP. In Tibetan with English subtitles. [VIDEO]

Thilen Lhondup *Tinlé* • Lhakpa Tsamchoe *Péma* • Gurgon Kyap *Karma* • Karma Tensing Nyima Lama *Norbou* • Karma Wangiel *Passang* ■ *Dir* Eric Valli • *Scr* Nathalie Azoulai, Olivier Dazat, Louis Gardel, Jean-Claude Guillebaud, Jacques Perrin • *Cinematographer* Eric Guichard, Jean-Paul Meurisse

The Hindenburg ★★ PG

Disaster drama
1975 · US · Colour and BW · 109mins

The 1970s cycle of disaster movies came crashing down amid the debris of this box-office bomb that has all the pace and substance of the famous German airship itself. In trying to combine their sabotage theory with the kind of soap-opera characterisation established in *Airport*, scriptwriters Nelson Gidding, Richard A Levinson and William Link have succeeded only in producing a bore. However, the mix of actual newsreel with new footage at the climax is well done. DP [VIDEO]

George C Scott *Colonel Ritter* • Anne Bancroft *The Countess* • William Atherton *Boerth* • Roy Thinnes *Martin Vogel* • Gig Young *Edward Douglas* • Burgess Meredith *Emilio Pajetta* • Charles Durning *Capt Pruss* ■ *Dir* Robert Wise • *Scr* Nelson Gidding, Richard A Levinson, William Link, from the book by Michael M Mooney

Hindle Wakes ★★★ U

Silent drama 1927 · UK · BW · 115mins

Estelle Brody excels in this adaptation of the stage hit, as the mill girl seduced by a tycoon's son on the works' outing to Blackpool. With its homespun morality echoing FW Murnau's *Sunrise* and its pert heroine resembling Clara Bow in *It*, Maurice Elvey's class-conscious drama is very much in keeping with the cinematic and societal trends of 1927. It lacks the sophistication of any of the above, but it marks a major advance on silent technique and presages the docudramatic realism that would continue to characterise British movies. DP [VIDEO]

Estelle Brody *Fanny Hawthorne* • Norman McKinnel *Nathaniel Jeffcoate* • Humberston Wright *Chris Hawthorne* • Marie Ault *Mrs Hawthorne* • John Stuart *Alan Jeffcoate* • Irene Rooke *Mrs Jeffcoate* ■ *Dir* Maurice Elvey • *Scr* Victor Saville, from the play by Stanley Houghton

Hindle Wakes ★★★ PG

Romantic drama 1931 · UK · BW · 70mins

Having twice been adapted for the silent screen, Stanley Houghton's play was accorded its talkie debut in this solid, but visually conservative presentation. Making only her second picture, Belle Chrystall turns in a remarkably mature performance as the Lancashire mill lass who defies convention by refusing to marry the boss's son after a scandalous holiday romance. John Stuart ably reprises the caddish role he'd played in Maurice Elvey's 1927 version, while Sybil Thorndike and Edmund Gwenn provide practised support. DP [VIDEO]

Belle Chrystall *Fanny Hawthorne* • Sybil Thorndike *Mrs Hawthorne* • John Stuart *Alan Jeffcoate* • Muriel Angelus *Beatrice Farrar* • Edmund Gwenn *Chris Hawthorne* • Mary Clare *Mrs Jeffcoate* • Norman McKinnel *Nat Jeffcoate* ■ *Dir* Victor Saville • *Scr* Victor Saville, Angus MacPhail, from the play *Hindle Wakes* by Stanley Houghton

Hindle Wakes ★★

Romantic melodrama
1952 · UK · BW · 87mins

A weak adaptation of Stanley Houghton's theatrical warhorse about cross-class love in the early years of the last century. The story of a Lancashire mill lass who refuses to marry the boss's son after spending her summer factory holiday with him at Blackpool is hardly likely to raise the eyebrows of the prudish or the pulse rate of the thrill-seeker. DP

Lisa Daniely *Jenny Hawthorne* • Leslie Dwyer *Chris Hawthorne* • Brian Worth *Alan Jeffcoate* • Sandra Dorne *Mary Hollins* • Ronald Adam *Nat Jeffcoate* • Joan Hickson *Mrs Hawthorne* • Bill Travers *Bob* ■ *Dir* Arthur Crabtree • *Scr* John Baines, from the play by Stanley Houghton

Hindustan Ki Kasam ★★ PG

Drama 1999 · Ind · Colour · 153mins

Despite being a box-office smash, the critics found little to applaud in this overwrought melodrama set during the 1971 Indo-Pakistani war. Even stars of the calibre of Amitabh Bachchan and Prem Chopra are out of sorts. Considering writer/director Veeru Devgan was supposedly intent on fostering better relations between the feuding neighbours, he takes a pronouncedly anti-Pakistani stance in relating the tale of the novelist who is mistaken for his twin brother, who happens to be a nationalist assassin.

DP. A Hindi language film. Contains some mild violence and swearing.

Amitabh Bachchan • Ajay Devgan • Manisha Koirala • Prem Chopra ■ *Dir* Veeru Devgan • *Scr* Hriday-Janak, Tanveer Khan

The Hired Gun ★★ U

Western 1957 · US · BW · 63mins

It makes a bit of a change to find a western in which a female plays the key role, and Anne Francis makes the most of her opportunity as the woman, wrongly convicted of murder, who cheats the hangman by escaping across the border into Mexico. Co-star Rory Calhoun is the gunman hired to bring her back, who comes to believe in her innocence and sets about proving it. Calhoun formed his own production company to make this picture but seemingly forgot to tell veteran director Ray Nazarro that he wasn't shooting another B-western. AE

Rory Calhoun *Gil McCord* • Anne Francis *Ellen Beldon* • Vince Edwards *Kell Beldon* • John Litel *Mace Beldon* • Chuck Connors *Judd Farrow* • Robert Burton *Nathan Conroy* ■ *Dir* Ray Nazarro • *Scr* David Lang, Buckley Angell

The Hired Hand ★★★★ 15

Western 1971 · US · Colour · 86mins

Peter Fonda had some clout in Hollywood when this post-hippy western was made, having produced and starred as "Captain America" in the cult hit *Easy Rider* two years earlier. In addition to starring here, Fonda also makes a fine job of directing this cold, almost existential western about a wife (the superb Verna Bloom) torn between two drifters, her husband Fonda and the older Warren Oates. This has all the clever bleakness and cyclical sense of destiny now associated with its writer, Alan Sharp, and is richly rewarding in its portrayal of the tough reality of frontier life. TS DVD

Peter Fonda *Harry Collings* • Warren Oates *Arch Harris* • Verna Bloom *Hannah Collings* • Robert Pratt *Dan Griffin* • Severn Darden *McVey* • Ted Markland *Luke* • Owen Orr *Mace* ■ *Dir* Peter Fonda • *Scr* Alan Sharp

Hired to Kill ★ 18

Action adventure 1990 · US · Colour · 92mins

Brian Thompson is cast as a soldier of fortune whose mission to overthrow a tinpot island dictator involves disguising himself as a gay fashion designer with a hit squad of female mercenaries all dressed as fashion models. Happens everyday, right? Stalwarts Oliver Reed – relishing his role as a sadistic secret police chief – and George Kennedy were somehow persuaded to appear. RS

Brian Thompson *Frank Ryan* • Oliver Reed *Michael Bartos* • José Ferrer *Rallis* • George Kennedy *Thomas* • Michelle Moffett *Ana* ■ *Dir* Nico Mastorakis, Peter Rader • *Scr* Nico Mastorakis, Kirk Ellis, Fred C Perry, from a story by Nico Mastorakis

Hired Wife ★★★

Comedy drama 1940 · US · BW · 95mins

Indispensable, caring, efficient secretary Rosalind Russell proposes a marriage of convenience to her boss, Brian Aherne, so that his tax situation can benefit by putting his property in his wife's name. He's preoccupied with advertising model Virginia Bruce, but when she disappears into the arms of John Carroll, Aherne accepts Russell's offer. What follows is comfortingly predictable in this slimly plotted romantic comedy, elevated into delightful froth by Aherne's charm and Russell's splendid performance. RK

Rosalind Russell *Kendal Browning* • Brian Aherne *Stephen Dexter* • Virginia Bruce *Phyllis Walden* • Robert Benchley *Roger Van Horn* • John Carroll *Jose* ■ *Dir* William A Seiter • *Scr* Richard Connell, Gladys Lehman, from a story by George Beck

The Hireling ★★★ PG

Period drama 1973 · UK · Colour · 103mins

Set in the socially divided Britain of 1923, this adaptation of an LP Hartley novel makes up in elegance and ideas for what it lacks in drama. Neurotic, upper-class Sarah Miles hires the services of chauffeur Robert Shaw, and their working relationship helps to restore some balance in her fraught existence. However, his adoration for his mistress soon adds a touch of agitation to the mix. Director Alan Bridges's period piece has a topical relevance about who is really in the driving seat, but the drama is too crass to be affecting. TH

Robert Shaw *Leadbetter* • Sarah Miles *Lady Franklin* • Peter Egan *Captain Hugh Cantrip* • Elizabeth Sellars *Lady Franklin's mother* • Caroline Mortimer *Connie* • Patricia Lawrence *Mrs Hansen* ■ *Dir* Alan Bridges • *Scr* Wolf Mankowitz, from the novel by LP Hartley

Hiroshima, Mon Amour ★★★★ PG

Drama 1959 · Fr · BW · 100mins

Alain Resnais's first feature stunned audiences in 1959, and together with Jean-Luc Godard's *A Bout de Souffle* and François Truffaut's *The 400 Blows* it heralded the French New Wave. The story tells of a French actress who has an affair in Hiroshima with a Japanese architect while recalling an earlier, wartime affair with a German soldier. Marguerite Duras's script is about collaboration as well as reconciliation, while Resnais weaves time zones, silence and sound, and juxtaposes lush images of seduction with shocking documentary footage of survivors of the atomic bomb. AT. In French with English subtitles. DVD

Emmanuelle Riva *Elle* • Eiji Okada *Lui* • Bernard Fresson *L'Allemand* • Stella Dassas *La Mère* • Pierre Barbaud *Le Père* ■ *Dir* Alain Resnais • *Scr* Marguerite Duras

His and Hers ★ U

Satire 1960 · UK · BW · 91mins

Probably the main amusement for viewers of this comedy will be in spotting the familiar faces in the cast, not least Oliver Reed as a poet and Kenneth Williams as an unlikely policeman. The under-nourished screenplay has Terry-Thomas as a writer who transforms from silly ass to recognisable human being when forced to confront reality during a research trip on Bedouins in the desert. BB

Terry-Thomas *Reggie Blake* • Janette Scott *Fran Blake* • Wilfrid Hyde White *Charles Dunton* • Nicole Maurey *Simone Rolfe* • Joan Sims *Hortense* • Kenneth Connor *Harold* • Kenneth Williams *Policeman* • Oliver Reed *Poet* ■ *Dir* Brian Desmond Hurst • *Scr* Stanley Mann, Jan Lowell, Mark Lowell

His Brother's Wife ★★★

Melodrama 1936 · US · BW · 91mins

When Robert Taylor's medical scientist goes off to the jungle to find a cure for spotted fever, Barbara Stanwyck, with whom he has had a whirlwind romance, is so enraged that she takes revenge by marrying his brother. Eventually, of course, she repents and turns up in the tropics to assist her true love, whereupon the melodrama escalates into situations so absurd and dialogue so risible as to become treasurable. The stars, whose real-life romance was news (they would marry in 1939), play this hokum for all its worth. RK

Barbara Stanwyck *Rita Wilson Claybourne* • Robert Taylor (1) *Chris Claybourne* • Jean Hersholt *Professor "Pop" Fahrenheim* • Joseph Calleia *"Fish-Eye"* • John Eldredge *Tom Claybourne* • Samuel S Hinds *Dr Claybourne* ■ *Dir* WS Van Dyke • *Scr* Leon Gordon, John Meehan, from a story by George Auerbach

His Butler's Sister ★★ U

Musical comedy 1943 · US · BW · 93mins

Deanna Durbin stars as a small-town girl with ambitions to be a great singer. She goes to New York to seek the help of composer Franchot Tone, only to be put to work as a maid by his butler, Pat O'Brien. Complications ensue before the inevitable resolution. The star gets to sing several numbers (including *Nessun Dorma*) in this delightful nonsense, which Frank Borzage directs in the right spirit. RK

Deanna Durbin *Ann Carter* • Franchot Tone *Charles Gerard* • Pat O'Brien *Martin* • Akim Tamiroff *Popoff* • Walter Catlett *Kalb* • Elsa Janssen *Severina* ■ *Dir* Frank Borzage • *Scr* Samuel Hoffenstein, Betty Reinhardt

His Double Life ★★

Comedy drama 1933 · US · BW · 63mins

Delightfully fussy character actor Roland Young is the reclusive painter who adopts the identity of his dead valet, and former silent star Lillian Gish makes an isolated comeback as the woman who weds the already-married Young under his assumed identity. However, the best version of this oft-filmed story is unquestionably *Holy Matrimony* with Monty Woolley and Gracie Fields. AE

Roland Young *Priam Farrel* • Lillian Gish *Alice* • Montague Love [Montagu Love] *Duncan Farrel* • Lumsden Hare *Oxford* • Lucy Beaumont *Mrs Leek* ■ *Dir* Arthur Hopkins • *Scr* Arthur Hopkins, Clara Beranger, from the play *The Great Adventure* by Arnold Bennett, from his novel *Buried Alive*

His Girl Friday ★★★★★ U

Classic comedy 1939 · US · BW · 91mins

The fastest-talking comedy in the history of Hollywood, this brilliant reworking of the classic newspaper play *The Front Page* by director Howard Hawks is the perfect vehicle for Cary Grant (never better) and Rosalind Russell (never tougher) and is still achingly funny today. Limited for most of the time to two sets (the newspaper office and the pressroom at the jail), the film's great strength is the interplay between the two leads, as former spouses who are having a tough time remaining apart. It also boasts one of the blackest comedy situations ever, as a small-time loser finds himself up against city corruption and imminent execution. Clever, witty and extremely satisfying. TS DVD

Cary Grant *Walter Burns* • Rosalind Russell *Hildy Johnson* • Ralph Bellamy *Bruce Baldwin* • Gene Lockhart *Sheriff Peter B Hartwell* • Porter Hall *Murphy* • Ernest Truex *Roy B Bensinger* • Cliff Edwards *Endicott* • Clarence Kolb *Mayor* • Billy Gilbert *Joe Pettibone* ■ *Dir* Howard Hawks • *Scr* Charles Lederer, from the play *The Front Page* by Ben Hecht, Charles MacArthur

His Kind of Woman ★★★ 12

Film noir 1951 · US · BW · 114mins

An interesting and enjoyably overheated melodrama from the Howard Hughes regime at RKO, this overlong, unwieldy movie shows signs of the great one's tinkerings: scenes don't make sense, obvious exteriors were filmed indoors, cast members come and go and Robert Mitchum looks bored. However, the whole is still entertaining, with a fine sense of parody that has won the movie quite a cult following. Mitchum's relationship with Jane Russell is genuinely provocative, but the movie is hijacked by Vincent Price at his posturing best. TS. Contains some violence.

Robert Mitchum *Dan Milner* • Jane Russell *Lenore Brent* • Vincent Price *Mark Cardigan* • Tim Holt *Bill Lusk* • Charles McGraw *Thompson* • Raymond Burr *Nick Ferraro* ■ *Dir* John Farrow • *Scr* Frank Fenton, Jack Leonard, from the story *Star Sapphire* by Gerald Drayson Adams

His Lordship ★★★ U

Crime drama 1936 · UK · BW · 68mins

Character star George Arliss's great days were behind him when he returned to his native England to take on a dual role in this political potboiler, which is only held together by the sheer strength of his presence. The film's stage derivation seeps through the whole enterprise, and the combination of *Boys' Own* heroics and the politics of war is as hard to take today as it probably was then. But Arliss was undeniably a star, and those who only know his historical roles may enjoy seeing him in a contemporary part. TS

George Arliss *Richard/Lord Dunchester* • Romilly Lunge *Bill Howard* • René Ray *Vera* • Jessie Winter *Lady Dunchester* • John Ford *Ibrahim* ■ *Dir* Herbert Mason • *Scr* Maude T Howell, L du Garde Peach, Edwin Greenwood, from the play *The Nelson Touch* by Neil Grant

His Majesty O'Keefe ★★★ U

Swashbuckling adventure 1953 · US · Colour · 89mins

Burt Lancaster is in fine, devil-may-care form as a sea captain teaching islanders how to be enterprising and beat off pirates, while he himself picks up a Polynesian girl (Joan Rice) to be queen to his king. Its colonial message – naive natives ruled by intrepid white man – is dubiously patronising, but its good-natured breeziness defies serious criticism. TH

Burt Lancaster *Captain David O'Keefe* • Joan Rice *Dalabo* • André Morell *Alfred Tetins* • Abraham Sofaer *Fatumak* • Archie Savage *Boogulroo* • Benson Fong *Mr Chou* • Teresa Prendergast *Kakofel* ■ *Dir* Byron Haskin • *Scr* Borden Chase, James Hill, from a novel by Lawrence Klingman, Gerald Green

His New Job ★★★

Silent comedy 1915 · US · BW · 32mins

In this uncharacteristic Chaplin short, his first for the Essanay studio, he disregarded the company's highly organised working methods and improvised a comedy about film-making based on what he saw around him. It shows Charlie seeking a job at a studio, quashing competition from cross-eyed Ben Turpin, and creating mayhem on the set of a costume film where Gloria Swanson (uncredited) is among the extras. This was Chaplin's first collaboration with cameraman Rollie Totheroh, with whom he worked regularly for the next 30 years. AE

Charles Chaplin *Film Extra* • Ben Turpin *Film Extra* • Charlotte Mineau *Actress* • Leo White • Gloria Swanson ■ *Dir/Scr* Charles Chaplin

His Woman ★★

Drama 1931 · US · BW · 76mins

Gary Cooper, the unlikely captain of a tramp steamer, rescues a baby from a drifting vessel at sea and decides to keep it. Advertising for female help on the return journey to America, he gets Claudette Colbert, a girl with a shady past. The script it mediocre, as is the direction, while Cooper is at his most expressionless. Colbert, though, gives it everything, as usual. RK

Gary Cooper *Captain Sam Whalan* • Claudette Colbert *Sally Clark* • Averell Harris *Mate Gatson* • Richard Spiro *Sammy the baby* • Hamtree Harrington *Aloysius* • Sidney Easton *Mark* • Douglass Dumbrille *Alisandroe* • Raquel Davido *Maria Estella* ■ *Dir* Edward Sloman • *Scr* Adelaide Heilbron, Melville Baker, from the novel *The Sentimentalists* by Dale Collins

Histoire de Marie et Julien ★★★★ 15

Romantic drama
2003 · Fr/It · Colour · 144mins

Jacques Rivette abandoned his *Scenes from the Parallel Life* quartet having only completed *Duelle* (1975) and *Noroît* (1976). But this reworking of the third instalment owes as much to *film noir* and classic horror as it does to its predecessors. Chronicling the romance between clock-repairer Jerzy Radziwilowicz and the mysterious Emmanuelle Béart, this is as formally and intellectually challenging as Rivette's best work. But what is most noteworthy is the intensity of the performances and the sophisticated manner in which Béart's distracted ethereality and Radziwilowicz's relationship with antique dealer Anne Brochet are established. DP. In French with English subtitles. DVD

Emmanuelle Béart *Marie* • Jerzy Radziwilowicz *Julien* • Anne Brochet *Madame X* • Bettina Kee *Adrienne* • Olivier Cruveileire *Editor* • Nicole Garcia *Friend* ■ *Dir* Jacques Rivette • *Scr* Jacques Rivette, Pascal Bonitzer, Christine Laurent • *Cinematographer* William Lubtchansky

Une Histoire Inventée ★★★

Comedy 1990 · Can · Colour · 100mins

Also known as *An Imaginary Tale*, this is an occasionally amusing, but mostly jumbled ensemble piece from French Canadian director André Forcier. The film focuses on a handful of disparate Montrealites, whose everyday lives are packed with more eccentric occurrences than most people could pack into a lifetime. The best moments are provided by the precious production of *Othello*, played before pensioners bussed in by a mobster, and the beauty who keeps countless ex-lovers at her beck and call. DP. In French with English subtitles.

Jean Lapointe *Gaston* • Louise Marleau *Florence* • Charlotte Laurier *Soledad* • Marc Messier *Lentaignes* • Jean-François Pichette *Tibo* • France Castel *Alys* ■ *Dir* André Forcier • *Scr* André Forcier, Jacques Marcotte

Une Histoire Simple ★★★

Drama 1978 · Fr · Colour · 107mins

Although this study of bourgeois foibles received an Oscar nomination for best foreign film, director Claude Sautet is rather guilty of revisiting old haunts without having anything particularly new to show us. However, no one depicts the suffocating ennui of a seemingly successful life with such surety, and here he's excellently served by Romy Schneider, who won a César for her portrayal of a liberated woman who aborts lover Claude Brasseur's baby only to become pregnant by ex-husband Bruno Cremer. DP. In French with English subtitles.

Romy Schneider *Marie* • Bruno Cremer *Georges* • Claude Brasseur *Serge* • Arlette Bonnard *Gabrielle* • Sophie Daumier *Esther* • Eva Darlan *Anna* • Francine Bergé *Francine* • Roger Pigaut *Jérôme* • Madeleine Robinson *Marie's mother* ■ *Dir* Claude Sautet • *Scr* Claude Sautet, Jean-Loup Dabadie

Histoires Extraordinaires ★★★★ 18

Portmanteau horror
1967 · Fr/It · Colour · 115mins

Out of the three episodes based on the macabre tales by Edgar Allan Poe, the third – the only modern-day one, directed by Federico Fellini – is far and away the best, though it's pretty familiar Fellini territory. It stars Terence Stamp as a British actor in Rome who bets his head he can escape having an accident. Louis Malle's telling of *William Wilson*, about a man (Alain Delon) who kills his doppelgänger, is handsome; while Roger Vadim saw to it that his wife Jane Fonda wore revealing clothes and caused an incestuous *frisson* by casting her brother Peter as her lover. RB [video]

Jane Fonda *Countess Frederica Metzengerstein* • Peter Fonda *Baron Wilhelm* • Alain Delon *William Wilson/His double* • Brigitte Bardot *Giuseppina* • Terence Stamp *Toby Dammit* • Vincent Price *Narrator* ■ *Dir* Roger Vadim, Louis Malle, Federico Fellini • *Scr* Roger Vadim, Pascal Cousin, from the story *Metzengerstein* ; Louis Malle, Daniel Boulanger, from the story *William Wilson* ; Federico Fellini, Bernardino Zapponi, from the story *Never Bet the Devil Your Head,; all by Edgar Allan Poe*

Historias Mínimas ★★★★ 15

Comedy drama
2002 · Arg/Sp · Colour · 87mins

More than a decade after missing his step with *Eversmile, New Jersey*, Argentinian Carlos Sorin regains his sense of direction with this beguiling road movie. Making evocative use of the sprawling Patagonian landscape, he interweaves a trio of intimate narratives that forces viewers to re-assess their priorities by reducing life to its essentials. Travelling salesman Javier Lombardo's bid to woo a widow with a birthday cake for her child and cash-strapped mother Javiera Bravo's game-show experience are droll and shrewd. But the film's compassionate humanity is best exhibited in myopic octogenarian Antonio Benedictis's journey of atonement in search of his missing dog. DP. In Spanish with English subtitles. DVD

Javier Lombardo *Roberto* • Antonio Benedictis *Don Justo* • Javiera Bravo *Mariá Flores* • Francis Sandoval *Mariá's daughter* ■ *Dir* Carlos Sorin • *Scr* Pablo Solarz

History Is Made at Night ★★★

Drama 1937 · US · BW · 97mins

This bizarre piece of fluff from melodrama maestro Frank Borzage finds Charles Boyer in good form as a waiter, jewel thief and restaurateur who saves Jean Arthur from her abusive marriage to shipping magnate Colin Clive. The story moves from Paris to New York, involves kidnapping and seduction, and ends rather darkly, on a sinking ship, with a confession of murder followed by a suicide. It's a lot to fit in one movie, which might explain the various loose ends – though this hardly seems to matter. AT

Charles Boyer *Paul Dumond* • Jean Arthur *Irene Vail* • Leo Carrillo *Cesare* • Colin Clive *Bruce Vail* • Ivan Lebedeff *Michael* • George Meeker *Norton* ■ *Dir* Frank Borzage • *Scr* Gene Towne, Graham Baker, from their story

History Is Made at Night ★

Spy comedy
1999 · UK /Fr/Ger/Fin · Colour · 94mins

It's hard to believe that the director of *Darkness in Tallinn* could have made this dismal spy caper. Ilkka Jarvilaturi's ill-conceived comedy manages the seemingly impossible feat of making Irène Jacob look incompetent. Besides disrobing at regular intervals, she overplays every situation, although she's not helped by her partner in ignominy, the usually reliable Bill Pullman, who resorts to mugging. DP

Bill Pullman *Harry* • Irène Jacob *Natasha* • Bruno Kirby *Max* • Glenn Plummer *Dave* • Udo Kier *Ivan* ■ *Dir* Ilkka Jarvilaturi • *Scr* Patrick Amos, from a story by Jean-Pierre Gorin, Patrick Amos

The History of Mr Polly ★★★★ U

Drama 1948 · UK · BW · 91mins

John Mills gives one of the finest performances of his career as the draper whose search for contentment involves him in an unhappy marriage and a feud at a country inn. The supporting cast is impeccable, with Betty Ann Davies neatly switching from giggling cousin to grousing wife, and Moore Marriott inch-perfect as wizened Uncle Pentstemon. The scenes with Sally Ann Howes on the wall don't quite come off, but the encounters with Mills's ghastly family and the duel with Finlay Currie are well staged. Enormously entertaining. DP [video]

John Mills *Alfred Polly* • Sally Ann Howes *Christabel* • Megs Jenkins *Plump woman* • Finlay Currie *Uncle Jim* • Diana Churchill *Annie* • Betty Ann Davies *Miriam* • Edward Chapman *Mr Johnson* • Shelagh Fraser *Minnie* • Moore Marriott *Uncle Pentstemon* ■ *Dir* Anthony Pelissier • *Scr* Anthony Pelissier, from the novel by HG Wells

History of the World Part 1 ★★★★ 15

Comedy 1981 · US · Colour · 88mins

Mel Brooks's full-frontal assault on how we got where we are today has something to offend everyone: Moses drops five of the original 15 commandments and Brooks, as a waiter at the Last Supper, asks: "Are you all together or is it separate cheques?" From a hilarious Spanish Inquisition number to a "Jews in space" routine, it's vaudeville at its most vulgar with broader strokes than Monty Python, but without the smugness. So what happened to *History of the World Part 2*? Don't ask. TH. Contains some swearing. [video]

Mel Brooks *Moses/Comicus/Torquemada/Jacques/King Louis XVI* • Dom DeLuise *Emperor Nero* • Madeline Kahn *Empress Nympho* • Harvey Korman *Count de Monet* • Cloris Leachman *Madame de Farge* • Ron Carey *Swiftus* • Gregory Hines *Josephus* • Pamela Stephenson *Mademoiselle Rimbaud* • Sid Caesar *Chief caveman* • Orson Welles *Narrator* ■ *Dir/Scr* Mel Brooks

A History of Violence ★★★★ 18

Thriller 2005 · US/Can · Colour · 95mins

Although he plays it surprisingly straight for once, director David Cronenberg nevertheless brings a dry wit and a satiric edge to this dark thriller. Life is sweet for local coffee-shop owner Viggo Mortensen and his wife Maria Bello. But when Mortensen becomes a media hero after preventing a hold-up, a disfigured thug (Ed Harris) surfaces with henchmen in tow. Insisting Mortensen is his old Mob buddy, he manages to cast doubt even in Bello's mind, creating a central "is-he-or-isn't-he" mystery that's deliciously teased out. Once that question is solved, the film sags slightly. LF. Contains swearing and violence.

Viggo Mortensen *Tom Stall* • Maria Bello *Edie Stall* • William Hurt *Richie Cusack* • Ashton Holmes *Jack Stall* • Stephen McHattie *Leland Jones* • Peter MacNeill *Sheriff Sam Carney* • Ed Harris *Carl Fogarty* • Greg Bryk *William "Billy" Orser* ■ *Dir* David Cronenberg • *Scr* Josh Olson, from the graphic novel by John Wagner, Vince Locke

Hit! ★★★

Crime drama 1973 · US · Colour · 134mins

One of the better blaxploitation thrillers directed by the frustratingly erratic Sidney J Furie. There are shades of *French Connection II* in the plotting, which finds lawman Billy Dee Williams taking on the Gallic gangsters he blames for his daughter's death. However, this more than stands up in its own right, with Williams's compelling turn well supported by Richard Pryor. It's a touch overlong, but riveting nevertheless. JF

Billy Dee Williams *Nick Allen* • Richard Pryor *Mike Willmer* • Paul Hampton *Barry Strong* • Gwen Welles *Sherry Nielson* • Warren Kemmerling *Dutch Schiller* • Janet Brandt *Ida* ■ *Dir* Sidney J Furie • *Scr* Alan R Trustman, David M Wolf

The Hit ★★★★ 18

Thriller 1984 · UK · Colour · 93mins

Twelve years after *Gumshoe*, his directing debut, Stephen Frears made his second big-screen outing with this surreal comedy thriller – a blend of cockney gorblimey characters with a dash of Buñuel and spaghetti western. Terence Stamp plays a supergrass, exiled in Spain, where hitmen John Hurt and Tim Roth track him down and abduct him. Stamp is cool about the whole thing and seems to accept his destiny, while the hoods are as jumpy as fleas. Charismatic acting, the seemingly endless road across the Spanish plains and the unexpected twist make for very stylish entertainment. AT [video]

John Hurt *Braddock* • Tim Roth *Myron* • Terence Stamp *Willie Parker* • Fernando Rey *Policeman* • Laura Del Sol *Maggie* • Bill Hunter *Harry* • Lennie Peters *Mr Corrigan* ■ *Dir* Stephen Frears • *Scr* Peter Prince

Hit and Run ★★★ PG

Drama 1999 · US · Colour · 88mins

Margaret Colin finds her life shattered when she accidentally hits a child with her car. After leaving the scene to call for help, she returns only to hear the outraged reaction from onlookers who believe it's a hit-and-run and decides to keep quiet. As her life falls apart she must wrestle with her conscience as well as the detective who suspects her. Writer Karen Stillman's thoughtful script and Colin's intense but restrained performance keep this TV tale of an innocent woman trapped by circumstance effective. MC [video] DVD

Margaret Colin *Joanna Kendall* • Drew Pillsbury *Doug Kendall* • Lisa Vidal *Meredith Reed* ■ *Dir* Dan Lerner • *Scr* Karen Stillman

Hit List ★★★

Thriller 1984 · Fr · Colour · 90mins

Annie Girardot and François Marthouret are best known in France as comedy players, which makes their performances in this bruising vigilante picture all the more commendable. The plot has Marthouret's kindly cop keeping his distance while grieving mother Girardot picks off the gangsters responsible for her daughter's death. Alain Bonnot's second feature rather revels in the violent nature of the revenge, but – thanks to Girardot's chillingly calculated portrayal – the film's power comes more from the ferocity of her hatred than the bloodiness of her retribution. DP. French dialogue dubbed into English.

Annie Girardot *Jeanne* • François Marthouret *Kalinsky* • Bernard Brieux *David* • Sandrine Dumas *Nathalie* • Pascal Tedes *Jacky* • Paul Crauchet *Pierre* ■ *Dir* Alain Bonnot • *Scr* Alain Bonnot, André G Brunelin, Marie-Thérèse Cuny, from the novel *Nathalie, ou la Punition* by Gérard Moreau

Hit List ★★ 18

Action thriller 1988 · US · Colour · 83mins

This is the epitome of the straight-to-video movie, a ragbag of formula thrills and recycled material from better films. William Lustig peppers his tale of a professional kidnapping gone wrong with bursts of unpleasant violence and, after a tight opening, allows the script to merely become an excuse for a succession of shoot-outs and chases. Lance Henriksen scores as the psychopathic hitman, but Jan-Michael Vincent gives a marvellous impersonation of an oak desk. RS [video]

Jan-Michael Vincent *Jack Collins* • Leo Rossi *Frank DeSalvo* • Lance Henriksen *Chris Caleek* • Charles Napier *Tom Mitchum* • Rip Torn *Vic Luca* • Jere Burns *Jared Riley* ■ *Dir* William Lustig • *Scr* John Goff, Peter Brosnan, from a story by Aubrey K Rattan

Hit Man ★★ 18

Crime thriller 1972 · US · Colour · 86mins

In this clumsy reworking of *Get Carter*, ex-pro Bernie Casey is fittingly cast as the footballer-turned-lawyer seeking revenge on the porn baron who killed the brother who was searching for his daughter's rapist. But he looks uncomfortable during his sex scenes, unlike Pam Grier whose abrasive femininity was about to make her a major star. Director George Armitage packs the picture with bloodily violent set pieces, but otherwise directs without much distinction. DP. Contains swearing, violence, sex scenes, nudity and drug abuse.

Bernie Casey *Tyrone Tackett* • Pam Grier *Gozelda* • Lisa Moore *Laural* • Bhetty Waldron *Irvelle* • Sam Laws *Sherwood* • Candy All *Rochelle Tackett* ■ *Dir* George Armitage • *Scr* George Armitage, from the novel *Jack's Return Home* by Ted Lewis

H

Hit the Deck ★★★★ U

Musical 1955 · US · Colour · 112mins

The sailors-on-shore-leave theme may be familiar, but this version of the 1927 stage hit (with a totally new story) is immensely entertaining. Though no *On the Town*, and made when MGM's musical department was winding down, it still has all the studio know-how and a delightful cast. Jane Powell, Vic Damone and Tony Martin do well by the melodies, and Debbie Reynolds and Russ Tamblyn romp through an inventive routine in a fun-house, and best of all there's the irrepressible Ann Miller getting every ounce of humour from the lively script and tapping out Hermes Pan's exuberant choreography. TV

Jane Powell *Susan Smith* • Tony Martin *Chief Boatswain's Mate William F Clark* • Debbie Reynolds *Carol Pace* • Walter Pidgeon *Rear Admiral Daniel Xavier Smith* • Vic Damone *Rico Ferrari* • Gene Raymond *Wendell Craig* • Ann Miller *Ginger* • Russ Tamblyn *Danny Xavier Smith* ■ *Dir* Roy Rowland • *Scr* Sonya Levien, William Ludwig, from the musical by Herbert Fields, from the play *Shore Leave* by Hubert Osborne

Hit the Dutchman ★

Crime drama
1992 · US/USSR · Colour · 116mins

This flat-footed gangster movie has Bruce Nozick as the Jewish bootlegger straight out of the pen and into the rackets. The cast is in the straight-to-video league, though director Menahem Golan first announced the project in 1974 to star George Segal. A major drawback is the location – this movie claims to be set in New York, but it was shot rouble-cheap in Moscow, which supposedly resembles Brooklyn in the 1920s. AT

Bruce Nozick *Dutch Shultz* • Christopher Bradley *Vincent "Mad Dog" Coll* • Eddie Bowz *Joey Noey* • Will Kempe *Legs Diamond* • Sally Kirkland *Emma, Dutch's mother* • Jeff Griggs *Peter Coll* ■ *Dir* Menahem Golan • *Scr* Joseph Goldman, from a story by Alex Simon

Hit the Ice ★★★ U

Musical comedy 1943 · US · BW · 82mins

This was made when the comedy team of Abbott and Costello were the top money-makers for Universal Studios, which gave them good production values, amusing tailor-made scripts and sterling musical support. Bud and Lou are press photographers who get involved with gangsters at a ski resort (cue some inventive slapstick on the ice rink). The crooks include two of Hollywood's finest villains, Sheldon Leonard and Marc Lawrence. TV

Bud Abbott *Flash Fulton* • Lou Costello *"Tubby" McCoy* • Ginny Simms *Marcia Manning* • Patric Knowles *Dr Bill Elliot* • Elyse Knox *Peggy Osborne* • Joe Sawyer *Buster* • Marc Lawrence (1) *Phil* • Sheldon Leonard *"Silky Fellowsby"* ■ *Dir* Charles Lamont • *Scr* Robert Lees, Frederic I Rinaldo, John Grant, from a story by True Boardman

Hit the Saddle ★

Western 1937 · US · BW · 61mins

This B-western from the initial batch of Republic's Three Mesquiteers series has leads Ray Corrigan and Robert Livingston fighting wild horse thieves and falling out over a disreputable saloon entertainer. Max Terhune is the third Mesquiteer, supplying comic relief with his ventriloquist act. This has added interest because the beer hall floozie is Rita Hayworth, back in the days when she was Rita Cansino. AE

Robert Livingston *Stony Brooke* • Ray "Crash" Corrigan *Tucson Smith* • Max Terhune *Lullaby Joslin* • Rita Cansino [Rita Hayworth] *Rita* • JP McGowan *Rance McGowan* • Edward Cassidy *Sheriff Miller* ■ *Dir* Mack V Wright • *Scr* Oliver Drake, from characters created by William Colt MacDonald

Hitch ★★★ 12

Romantic comedy
2005 · US · Colour · 113mins

Will Smith puts his easy charm to good use in this flimsy but appealing New York-set romantic comedy. He plays a professional "date doctor" who discreetly helps ordinary guys woo the women of their dreams. When talk of his success reaches the ears of gossip columnist Eva Mendes, she decides to unmask the anonymous cupid, unaware that he's also the mishap-prone suitor trying to win her heart. Initially, the film makes up for in laughs what it lacks in substance. Unfortunately, as the overlong tale hits its final third, it abruptly loses its spark. SF. Contains swearing and sexual references. DVD

Will Smith *Alex "Hitch" Hitchens* • Eva Mendes *Sara Melas* • Kevin James *Albert Brennaman* • Amber Valletta *Allegra Cole* • Julie Ann Emery *Casey* • Michael Rapaport *Ben* • Adam Arkin *Max Trundle* ■ *Dir* Andy Tennant • *Scr* Kevin Bisch

The Hitch-Hiker ★★★★

Film noir 1953 · US · BW · 71mins

Ida Lupino made history as the only woman to direct a *film noir* with this wilderness thriller, which was developed from a news story by Daniel Mainwaring (who was denied a credit by RKO president Howard Hughes because of his political radicalism). Making the desert seem every bit as threatening as the urban jungle, Lupino draws a performance of crackling malevolence from William Talman, as the serial killer physically and mentally scarred by his abusive childhood. Equally authentic is the impotent terror of weekend fishermen and hostages Edmond O'Brien and Frank Lovejoy. DP

Edmond O'Brien *Roy Collins* • Frank Lovejoy *Gilbert Bowen* • William Talman *Emmett Myers* • José Torvay *Captain Alvarado* • Sam Hayes *Sam* • Wendell Niles *Wendell* ■ *Dir* Ida Lupino • *Scr* Collier Young, Ida Lupino, Robert Joseph, from a story by Daniel Mainwaring (uncredited)

The Hitcher ★★★★ 18

Thriller 1986 · US · Colour · 93mins

C Thomas Howell picks up icy passenger Rutger Hauer in this feature debut from director Robert Harmon. As it turns out, Hauer is a serial killer who quickly embroils Howell in a harrowing desert intrigue by implicating him in his sick crimes. Jennifer Jason Leigh, as the waitress who believes Howell's story, adds humanity along the way. Despite the film's huge lapses in logic and moments of wild self-parody, the paranoiac plot twists and grim body count generate some gruesome suspense. It has become something of a cult film, thanks to its surreal style and Hauer's inimitable presence. Howell returned for an inferior straight-to-video sequel in 2003. AJ. Contains violence and swearing. DVD

Rutger Hauer *John Ryder* • C Thomas Howell *Jim Halsey* • Jennifer Jason Leigh *Nash* • Jeffrey DeMunn *Captain Esteridge* ■ *Dir* Robert Harmon • *Scr* Eric Red

The Hitchhiker's Guide to the Galaxy ★★★★ PG

Science-fiction comedy adventure
2005 · US/UK · Colour · 108mins

Douglas Adams's classic BBC radio series/book/TV series finally made it to the big screen without sacrificing any of its late creator's jovially lugubrious vision. Martin Freeman stars as put-upon everyman Arthur Dent who, in the company of extraterrestrial friend Ford Prefect (rapper Mos Def), escapes the Earth moments before it's demolished to make way for a hyperspace bypass. Armed with Ford's copy of the eponymous guide – a PDA travelogue voiced by Stephen Fry – Arthur tries to make sense of a universe while pondering the nature of existence. Although signs of Hollywood studio tampering are in evidence, director Garth Jennings stays true to the oddity at the heart of this quintessentially British space odyssey. JR

Martin Freeman *Arthur Dent* • Mos Def *Ford Prefect* • Sam Rockwell *Zaphod Beeblebrox* • Zooey Deschanel *Trish McMillan/Trillian* • Bill Nighy *Slartibartfast* • Anna Chancellor *Questular* • John Malkovich *Humma Kavula* • Alan Rickman *Marvin the Paranoid Android* • Stephen Fry *The Book* • Helen Mirren *Deep Thought* ■ *Dir* Garth Jennings • *Scr* Douglas Adams, Karey Kirkpatrick from the radio series, book and TV series by Douglas Adams

Hitler ★★

Biographical drama 1962 · US · BW · 102mins

According to this heavy-handed, often risible Freudian biopic of the Nazi dictator, the cause of the Second World War was Hitler's mother fixation. He is attracted to his niece and Eva Braun because of their resemblance to his mother. Richard Basehart brings a fair amount of intensity and hysteria to the title role, but most of the film is just sensationalist and phoney. RB

Richard Basehart *Adolf Hitler* • Cordula Trantow *Geli Raubal* • Maria Emo *Eva Braun* • Martin Kosleck *Joseph Goebbels* • John Banner *Gregor Strasser* • Martin Brandt *General Guderian* • John Wengraf *Dr Morell* • John Mitchum *Hermann Goering* ■ *Dir* Stuart Heisler • *Scr* Sam Neuman, E Charles Straus

Hitler: the Last Ten Days ★★ PG

Second World War drama
1973 · UK · Colour and BW · 100mins

Alec Guinness is Hitler trapped in his bunker while Berlin burns above him. It's a brave, incredibly detailed performance, but the film's Italian writer/director Ennio De Concini conspires against him, going for the obvious (cuts to black-and-white documentary footage). He also unwisely adds hindsight in Simon Ward's Hauptmann Hoffman, who not only invades the bunker armed with battalions of postwar guilt, but also plants political doubts in the mind of Eva Braun, played by German actress Doris Kunstmann. AT

Alec Guinness *Adolf Hitler* • Simon Ward *Hauptmann Hoffmann* • Adolfo Celi *General Krebs* • Diane Cilento *Hanna Reitsch* • Gabriele Ferzetti *Field Marshal Keitel* • Eric Porter *General Von Greim* • Doris Kunstmann *Eva Braun* • Joss Ackland *General Burgdorf* ■ *Dir* Ennio De Concini • *Scr* Ennio De Concini, Maria Pia Lenco, Wolfgang Reinhardt, Ivan Moffat, from the non-fiction book *The Last Days of the Chancellery* by Gerhard Boldt

Hitler's Children ★★★

Second World War drama
1943 · US · BW · 81mins

Edward Dmytryk's drama purports to show how the Nazi regime punished women for refusing to bear babies for the Third Reich. Sterilisation and public lashing are two of the penalties dished out in what is either outright exploitation or earnest education, depending on your point of view. Bonita Granville is one of the persecuted women, while Tim Holt plays her Nazi officer boyfriend who puts a stop to the floggings. This box-office goldmine is surely one of the weirdest propaganda movies ever made; a year later the same team produced a Japanese equivalent entitled *Behind the Rising Sun*. AT

Tim Holt *Karl* • Bonita Granville *Anna* • Kent Smith *Prof Nichols* • Otto Kruger *Colonel Henkel* • HB Warner *Bishop* • Lloyd Corrigan *Franz Erhart* ■ *Dir* Edward Dmytryk • *Scr* Emmett Lavery, from the non-fiction book *Education for Death* by Gregor Ziemer

Hitler's Madman ★★★

Second World War drama
1943 · US · BW · 83mins

The first Hollywood picture of melodrama king Douglas Sirk is a B-movie about the assassination of the Nazi, Reinhard Heydrich, and the savage reprisals which left the Czech village of Lidice razed to the ground. Made a short time after the actual events it depicted, the film has an urgency about it, if little of the director's later finesse. Sirk reputedly met Heydrich in Berlin in the 1920s and remembered his expressive face and Shakespearean style of declaiming – which may explain John Carradine's performance as the Nazi monster. AT

John Carradine *Heydrich* • Patricia Morison *Jarmila* • Alan Curtis *Karel* • Ralph Morgan *Hanka* • Howard Freeman *Himmler* • Ludwig Stossel *Mayor Bauer* • Edgar Kennedy *Nepomuk* • Ava Gardner *Katy Chotnik* ■ *Dir* Douglas Sirk • *Scr* Peretz Hirshbein, Melvin Levy, Doris Malloy, from a story by Emil Ludwig, Albrecht Joseph, from the story *Hangmen's Village* by Bart Lytton

The Hitman ★★ 18

Action thriller 1991 · US · Colour · 89mins

This vehicle for the ageing Chuck Norris at least benefits from significantly better direction than his other movies of the period, as brother Aaron Norris gives the proceedings a sharp, atmospheric look and a harder edge to the sporadic violence. Norris, however, as a cop who goes undercover into the Mafia after nearly being killed in the line of duty, is his usual bland self. KB

Chuck Norris *Cliff Garret/Danny Grogan* • Michael Parks *Ronny "Del" Delaney* • Al Waxman *Marco Luganni* • Alberta Watson *Christine De Vera* • Salim Grant *Tim Murphy* • Ken Pogue *Chambers* • Marcel Sabourin *Andre Lacombe* ■ *Dir* Aaron Norris • *Scr* Don Carmody, Robert Geoffrion

Hitman's Run ★★ 18

Crime thriller 1999 · US · Colour · 89mins

There's little spark evident in this weary action thriller. The ever-prolific Eric Roberts plays an ex-Mob assassin in the witness protection programme whose cover is blown by a teenage hacker who breaks into the FBI's security files. There is plenty of gunplay, but the direction is strictly by the numbers. JF

Eric Roberts *Tony Lazorka/John Dugan* • Esteban Powell *Brian Segal* • C Thomas Howell *Tom Holly* • Farrah Forke *Sarah* ■ *Dir* Mark L Lester • *Scr* Eric Barker

Ho! ★★

Crime drama 1968 · Fr · Colour · 110mins

In yet another flashy, trashy crime thriller from his 1960s period, Jean-Paul Belmondo is a former race car star turned getaway driver who gets involved in a gang power struggle. His decision to go it alone incurs the wrath of girlfriend Joanna Shimkus, as well as fellow gang members. Over-plotted doesn't start to describe the ridiculous round of arrests, escapes, press exposés, robberies and shoot-outs that follows. By failing to keep either events or the gregarious Belmondo in check, director Robert Enrico allows the film to descend into chaos. DP. French dialogue dubbed into English.

Jean-Paul Belmondo *Ho* • Joanna Shimkus *Benedite* • Sydney Chaplin *Canter* • Alain Mottet *Paul* • Paul Crauchet *Briand* ■ *Dir* Robert Enrico • *Scr* Pierre Pelegri, Lucienne Hamon, Robert Enrico, from the novel by José Giovanni

Hoa-Binh ★★★

War drama 1970 · Fr · Colour · 90mins

Famed as the New Wave's most inventive cinematographer, Raoul Coutard was also a veteran war cameraman, and he brought that experience to bear on his even-handed, Oscar-nominated directorial debut. Couched in melodramatic terms, this is nevertheless an uncompromisingly authentic account of the everyday ramifications of the American involvement in Vietnam. Forced to accept menial work to support his sister, young Phi San gives a dignified and determined performance, which is counterpointed by the senseless savagery of the war footage. DP

Phi San *Hung* • Xvar Ha Moi *Mother* • Le Qynh *Father* • Danièle Delorme *Nurse* ■ *Dir* Raoul Coutard • *Scr* Raoul Coutard, from the novel *La Colonne de Cendres* by Françoise Lorrain

Hobson's Choice ★★★★ U

Classic comedy 1953 · UK · BW · 102mins

Winner of the British Academy Award for best British film in 1954, this is a splendid adaptation of the celebrated Harold Brighouse play. The role of the Salford cobbler at war with his wilful daughter is tailor-made for Charles Laughton (who had previously enjoyed much stage success in the role of Henry Horatio Hobson), and he gives one of his very best performances. The slick by-play between the leads belies the fact that Laughton detested Brenda de Banzie as Maggie and resented John Mills for landing the son-in-law part he wanted to go to Robert Donat. Director David Lean handles cast and material with equal care, judging the moments of comedy and poignancy perfectly. DP [video] DVD

Charles Laughton *Henry Horatio Hobson* • John Mills *Willie Mossop* • Brenda de Banzie *Maggie Hobson* • Daphne Anderson *Alice Hobson* • Prunella Scales *Vicky Hobson* • Richard Wattis *Albert Prosser* • Derek Blomfield *Freddy Beenstock* • Helen Haye *Mrs Hepworth* • Joseph Tomelty *Jim Heeler* ■ *Dir* David Lean • *Scr* David Lean, Norman Spencer, Wynyard Browne, from the play by Harold Brighouse

Hockey Night ★★

Drama 1984 · Can · Colour · 74mins

Likeable comedy, less exploitative than it could have been, about a pretty girl who becomes the goalie of a boys' hockey team in a small Canadian town. The film is pitched at early teens, so don't expect too many jokes about scoring own goalies! Megan Follows stars, but the best-known name in the cast is Rick Moranis. DA

Megan Follows *Cathy Yarrow* • Rick Moranis *Coach Willy Leipert* • Sean McCann *Mr Kozak* • Gail Youngs *Alice Yarrow* • Yannick Bisson *Spear Kozak* • Henry Ramer *Bill Moss* ■ *Dir* Paul Shapiro • *Scr* Paul Shapiro, Jack Blum

Hocus Pocus ★★★ PG

Black comedy 1993 · US · Colour · 92mins

An unusually black comedy from Disney, this makes for patchy entertainment. Three witches – Bette Midler, Kathy Najimy and Sarah Jessica Parker – are resurrected by a group of youngsters on Halloween and proceed to cause mayhem as they plot their revenge against the community that condemned them to death three centuries earlier. The three stars are the best thing about this uneven movie, but the youngsters acquit themselves admirably. JF [video] DVD

Bette Midler *Winifred Sanderson* • Sarah Jessica Parker *Sarah Sanderson* • Kathy Najimy *Mary Sanderson* • Omri Katz *Max* • Thora Birch *Dani* • Vinessa Shaw *Allison* • Amanda Shepherd *Emily* ■ *Dir* Kenny Ortega • *Scr* Neil Cuthbert, Mick Garris, from a story by Mick Garris, David Kirschner

Hoffa ★★★ 15

Biographical drama
1992 · US · Colour · 134mins

Jimmy Hoffa was one of the most controversial figures in American trade union history, but Danny DeVito's portrayal seems to be a figment of screenwriter David Mamet's imagination, and too little light is shed on Hoffa's alleged involvement with the Mob. However, as a study of a man devoted to his cause, it is a powerful piece of drama, and DeVito directs with an impressive epic sweep. Jack Nicholson dominates the screen as the belligerent Teamsters' boss, and Kevin Anderson is magnificently vindictive as Robert Kennedy. Flawed but forceful. DP. Contains swearing, violence and nudity. [video] DVD

Jack Nicholson *James R Hoffa* • Danny DeVito *Bobby Ciaro* • Armand Assante *Carol D'Allesandro* • JT Walsh *Frank Fitzsimmons* • John C Reilly *Pete Connelly* • Frank Whaley *Young kid* • Kevin Anderson *Robert Kennedy* ■ *Dir* Danny DeVito • *Scr* David Mamet

Hoffman ★ 15

Sex comedy 1970 · UK · Colour · 106mins

Not even Peter Sellers can make this tale of middle-aged Hoffman, blackmailing Sinead Cusack to stay for a week in his apartment, anything other than tediously peculiar, if not downright perverse. Adapted by Ernest Gebler from his novel, it's a sex comedy that's neither very sexy nor very comic. TH [video] DVD

Peter Sellers *Benjamin Hoffman* • Sinead Cusack *Janet Smith* • Jeremy Bulloch *Tom Mitchell* • Ruth Dunning *Mrs Mitchell* • David Lodge *Foreman* ■ *Dir* Alvin Rakoff • *Scr* Ernest Gebler, from his novel

The Holcroft Covenant ★★ 15

Spy thriller 1985 · UK · Colour · 107mins

Michael Caine's chasing his father's Nazi legacy either to atone for or rebuild Hitler's empire. It's easy to blame once-talented director John Frankenheimer (*The Manchurian Candidate*) for making this farrago unwatchable, but the more likely obstacle is the source material: Robert Ludlum's thriller is cinematically intractable. The locations look good, Lilli Palmer is graceful, and Anthony Andrews manfully struggles with an impossible role as Caine's brother. TS [video]

Michael Caine *Noel Holcroft* • Anthony Andrews *Johann Tennyson von Tiebolt* • Victoria Tennant *Helden Tennyson von Tiebolt* • Lilli Palmer *Althene Holcroft* • Mario Adorf *Jurgen Maas/Erich Kessler* • Michael Lonsdale [Michel Lonsdale] *Manfredi* ■ *Dir* John Frankenheimer • *Scr* George Axelrod, Edward Anhalt, John Hopkins, from the novel by Robert Ludlum

Hold Back the Dawn ★★★★

Romantic comedy drama
1941 · US · BW · 116mins

A smashing comedy drama with Charles Boyer as a wartime refugee who marries schoolmarm Olivia de Havilland as a means of gaining entry into the US. Paulette Goddard is his partner in the deception and his chosen companion on his wedding night. Set largely on the US-Mexican border, in one of those fly-blown hotels filled with "characters", this is a very witty but also rather dark charade, written by Charles Brackett and Billy Wilder just before Wilder became a director himself. AT

Charles Boyer *Georges Iscovescu* • Olivia de Havilland *Emmy Brown* • Paulette Goddard *Anita Dixon* • Victor Francen *Van Den Luecken* • Walter Abel *Inspector Hammock* • Curt Bois *Bonbois* • Rosemary DeCamp *Berta Kurz* • Veronica Lake *Movie actress* ■ *Dir* Mitchell Leisen • *Scr* Charles Brackett, Billy Wilder, from a story by Ketti Frings

Hold Back the Night ★★★★ 15

Drama 1999 · UK/It · Colour · 99mins

A powerful little drama about a strong-willed teenager (Christine Tremarco) who, while fleeing an abusive father, hooks up with two similarly restless souls: a grungy environmental protester (Stuart Sinclair Blyth) and a terminally ill woman (Sheila Hancock) whose dying wish is to see the sunrise at Orkney's Ring of Brodgar. Strong performances, believable characters and a script that doesn't offer easy answers combine to create an affecting journey. Tremarco's defensive, aloof behaviour often makes her difficult to care for, but then this isn't a story which shies away from risks, and it's a brave film that favours psychological plausibility above easy audience engagement. JC. Contains violence and swearing. [video] DVD

Christine Tremarco *Charleen* • Stuart Sinclair Blyth *Declan* • Sheila Hancock *Vera* • Richard Platt *Michael* • Julie Ann Watson *Jackie* • Kenneth Colley *Bob* • Tommy Tiernan *John* ■ *Dir* Phil Davis [Philip Davis] • *Scr* Steve Chambers

Hold Me, Thrill Me, Kiss Me ★★★ 18

Comedy 1992 · US · Colour · 92mins

Legend has it independent writer/director Joel Hershman set out to make a movie as tasteless, tacky and vulgar as anything Hollywood could make, only for much less money. He succeeded. Adrienne Shelley, Max Parrish, Sean Young and Diane Ladd star in a quirky, sleazy comedy about a drifter who hooks up with a nymphomaniac stripper and her nice-as-spice sister, only to find depravity and violence coming at him from not such an unexpected quarter. Eccentrically watchable. DA. Contains swearing and sex scenes. [video]

Max Parrish *Eli/Bud/Fritz* • Adrienne Shelly *Dannie* • Sean Young *Twinkle* • Diane Ladd *Lucille* • Andrea Naschak [April Rayne] *Sabra* • Ania Suli *Olga* ■ *Dir/Scr* Joel Hershman

Hold My Hand ★★

Comedy 1938 · UK · BW · 76mins

Stanley Lupino takes the lead in the film version of his stage play. Lupino plays Eddie Marston, whose generous offer to risk money financing his ward's newspaper backfires on him when he's accused of embezzlement. There are the usual romantic entanglements in a short, sharp romp that's absolutely typical of its time. The great comedian Fred Emney, whose long career extended into the 1970s, appears as Lord Milchester. DF

Stanley Lupino *Eddie Marston* • Fred Emney *Lord Milchester* • Barbara Blair *Jane Howard* • Sally Gray *Helen* • Polly Ward *Paula Pond* • Bertha Belmore *Lady Milchester* • Jack Melford *Pop Currie* • John Wood *Bob Crane* ■ *Dir* Thornton Freeland • *Scr* Clifford Grey, Bert Lee, William Freshman, from the play by Stanley Lupino

Hold That Blonde ★★

Crime comedy 1945 · US · BW · 76mins

This patchy comedy is short on originality and cruelly exposes the limitations of Eddie Bracken, here playing a kleptomaniac intent on preventing Veronica Lake from pinching a priceless Romanov bracelet. Bracken throws himself into every double take and slapstick set piece, yet he's totally upstaged by the sinister duo of Albert Dekker and George Zucco. Director George Marshall makes the most of the breakneck chases, but not even Lake can make this a gem. DP

Veronica Lake *Sally Martin* • Eddie Bracken *Ogden Spencer Trulow III* • Albert Dekker *Inspector Callahan* • Frank Fenton *Mr Phillips* • George Zucco *Pavel Sorasky* • Donald MacBride *Mr Kratz* ■ *Dir* George Marshall • *Scr* Walter DeLeon, Earl Baldwin, E Edwin Moran, from the play by Paul Armstrong

Hold That Co-Ed ★★★

Musical comedy 1938 · US · BW · 80mins

The "Great Profile", John Barrymore, made some six movies in 1938. Four years later he was dead, a burnt-out alcoholic once regarded as the greatest stage performer, and his finest screen portrayals were in the days of silent cinema. However, his own need for cash never stopped the flamboyant Barrymore from working, and here he walks away with the movie as a bluff governor who sponsors a college football team to win votes. All jolly good fun, and the old ham is a delight to watch under George Marshall's fast-paced direction. TS

John Barrymore *Governor* • George Murphy *Rusty* • Marjorie Weaver *Marjorie* • Joan Davis *Lizzie* • Jack Haley *Wilbur* • George Barbier *Breckenridge* • Ruth Terry *Edie* • Donald Meek *Dean Thatcher* ■ *Dir* George Marshall • *Scr* Karl Tunberg, Don Ettinger, Jack Yellen, from a story by Karl Tunberg, Don Ettinger

Hold That Ghost ★★★

Comedy 1941 · US · BW · 86mins

A superior Abbott and Costello comedy that finds the zany duo inheriting a supposedly haunted mansion, thanks to a gangster's will. The heroes intend to turn the place into a restaurant, but once on the premises they encounter all sorts of spooky phenomena. Musical relief is provided by the boys' regular collaborators, the Andrews Sisters. Over the years this type of comedy chiller would provide the double act with some of their finest celluloid moments as the boys encountered Universal Pictures' full gallery of classic monsters. DF

Bud Abbott *Chuck Murray* • Lou Costello *Ferdinand Jones* • Richard Carlson *Dr Jackson* • Evelyn Ankers *Norma Lind* • Joan Davis *Camille Brewster* • Marc Lawrence (1) *Charlie Smith* ■ *Dir* Arthur Lubin • *Scr* Robert Lees, Frederic I Rinaldo, John Grant

Hold-Up ★★

Crime drama
1985 · Fr/Can · Colour · 114mins

Even a tightly focused performance by Jean-Paul Belmondo can't hide the grinding predictability of a film in which a trio of bank robbers have more trouble with themselves than the law. Belmondo's natural ease and early appearance in a clown suit (in order to rob the bank) might help you stay the distance. Female lead Kim Cattrall is better than her track record (*Police Academy*, *Porky's*) suggests. The film was later remade by Bill Murray under the title *Quick Change*. JM. French dialogue dubbed into English.

Jean-Paul Belmondo *Grimm* • Guy Marchand *Georges* • Kim Cattrall *Lise* • Jean-Pierre Marielle *Labrosse* • Tex Konig *Lasky* • Jacques Villeret *Cab driver* ■ *Dir* Alexandre Arcady • *Scr* Alexandre Arcady, Francis Veber, Daniel Saint-Harmont, from the novel *Quick Change* by Jay Cronley

Hold Your Man ★★★

Romantic comedy melodrama
1933 · US · BW · 88mins

Clark Gable and blonde bombshell Jean Harlow co-star as a charming, womanising petty gangster and a seemingly tough young woman who, after much fencing and wisecracking, fall in love. But things go wrong when he accidentally kills a man. Sam Wood directs this bizarre and unsettling mix of comedy, romance and melodrama, which strains credibility to the limit but is still satisfying entertainment. RK

Jean Harlow *Ruby Adams* • Clark Gable *Eddie Hall* • Stuart Erwin *Al Simpson* • Dorothy Burgess *Gypsy Angikon* • Muriel Kirkland *Bertha Dillian* • Garry Owen *Slim* • Barbara Barondess *Sadie Kline* ■ *Dir* Sam Wood • *Scr* Anita Loos, Howard Emmett Rogers, from a story by Anita Loos

H

The Hole ★★★

Drama 1998 · Tai/Fr · Colour · 90mins

Whereas in *The River*, director Tsai Ming-liang presented water as a cause of corruption and pain, here it ebbs back towards its traditional symbolism as a source of life and a force for good. Stranded in a Taipei gripped by a mystery millennial virus, Li Kangsheng becomes obsessed with his downstairs neighbour, Yang Kuei-Mei, after a clumsy plumber leaves a hole in his floor. Interspersed with musical reveries, performed by Yang in ironic tribute to the 1950s singer Grace Chang, this is a delightfully quirky film, in which the minimalism of ennui gives way to the gentle magic of romance. DP. In Mandarin with English subtitles.

Yang Kuei-Mei *Woman downstairs* • Li Kangsheng *Man upstairs* • Miao Tien *Salesman* • Tong Hsiang-Chu *Plumber* • Lin Hui-Chin *Neighbour* ■ *Dir* Tsai Ming-liang • *Scr* Tsai Ming-Liang, Yang Ping-Ying

The Hole ★★★ 15

Psychological thriller
2001 · UK/Fr · Colour · 98mins

Director Nick Hamm's adaptation of Guy Burt's cult novel is a mixed blessing. On the one hand, this sly study in teenage angst is a harrowing thriller raising some interesting questions about love-crazed students. On the other, it's a murky muddle of unbelievable motivations and shaggy-dog daftness. Yet the slow descent into sleight-of-hand suspense, virtually negating everything that has gone before, strains credulity to breaking point, as posh pupil Thora Birch suddenly reappears after going missing for 18 days and police psychologist Embeth Davidtz tries to find out where she's been and what happened to her three dead companions. AJ DVD

Thora Birch *Elizabeth "Liz" Dunn* • Desmond Harrington *Mike* • Daniel Brocklebank *Martin* • Laurence Fox *Geoff* • Keira Knightley *Frankie* • Steven Waddington *DCS Tom Howard* • Embeth Davidtz *Dr Philipa Norwood* ■ *Dir* Nick Hamm • *Scr* Ben Court, Caroline Ip, from the novel *After the Hole* by Guy Burt

A Hole in My Heart ★★ 18

Drama 2004 · Swe/Den · Colour · 93mins

This ferocious drama from director Lukas Moodysson is a film that's not so much experienced as endured. Thorsten Flinck plays a boorish porn director who's shooting a cheap hardcore flick in the front room of his shabby flat, while his reclusive son (Bjorn Almroth) hides himself away in his bedroom. Initially, corrosive humour and an atmosphere of unreal absurdity take the edge off the film's deeply unsettling style, but the cycle of shock becomes as monotonous as it is distasteful. SF. In Swedish with English subtitles. Contains violence, sex scenes and nudity. DVD

Thorsten Flinck *Rickard* • Bjorn Almroth *Eric* • Sanna Brading *Tess* • Goran Marjanovic *Geko* ■ *Dir/Scr* Lukas Moodysson

A Hole in the Head ★★ U

Comedy 1959 · US · Colour · 115mins

Set in Miami Beach, Frank Capra's penultimate film stars Frank Sinatra as a widower whose hotel, the Garden of Eden, is threatened with closure. Edward G Robinson is Sinatra's brother, while Eleanor Parker plays a wealthy widow who may be the answer to his prayers. It's crudely sentimental and desperately dated, as demonstrated by Carolyn Jones's irritating role as Sinatra's beatnik girlfriend. The high spot is Ol' Blue Eyes singing *High Hopes*. AT DVD

Frank Sinatra *Tony Manetta* • Edward G Robinson *Mario Manetta* • Eddie Hodges *Ally Manetta* • Eleanor Parker *Mrs Rogers* • Carolyn Jones *Shirl* ■ *Dir* Frank Capra • *Scr* Arnold Shulman, from his play

A Hole Lot of Trouble ★★

Comedy 1969 · UK · Colour · 27mins

Veteran producer/director Francis Searle ended his career with a number of comedy shorts (all about 30 minutes long) designed to accompany features in the dying days of the double bill. Such shorts took a simple idea and exploited the potential to the maximum – Eric Sykes's *The Plank* is arguably the perfect example. Here, Arthur Lowe and friends explore the comic potential surrounding a group of workman digging a hole. DF

Arthur Lowe *Whitehouse* • Bill Maynard *Bill* • Tim Barrett *Longbottom* • Victor Maddern *Percy* • Brian Weske *Digby* • Leslie Dwyer *Evangelist* • Ken Parry *Charles* • Hani Borelle *Fenella* ■ *Dir* Francis Searle • *Scr* Ian Flintoff

Holes ★★★ PG

Comedy drama adventure
2003 · US · Colour · 112mins

Based on the award-winning novel for young adults by Louis Sachar, this Disney adaptation is lighter and more bland than it should be. Shia LaBeouf is Stanley Yelnats, who believes that generations of his family were cursed long ago by Eartha Kitt. He's accused of theft and sentenced to a juvenile detention centre in the Texas desert. There Mr Sir (Jon Voight) makes the youngsters dig accurately-shaped holes "to build character" and is himself in awe of the Warden (Sigourney Weaver). Flashbacks to the past introduce outlaw Kissin' Kate Barlow (Patricia Arquette), while in the present LaBeouf discovers the real reason for the hole-digging and helps the mute Zero (Khleo Thomas) regain his voice. Director Andrew Davis's whimsical tone sugars the bitterness. TH DVD

Sigourney Weaver *The Warden* • Jon Voight *Mr Sir* • Patricia Arquette *Kissin' Kate Barlow* • Tim Blake Nelson *Dr Pendanski* • Dulé Hill *Sam* • Shia LaBeouf *Stanley Yelnats IV* • Henry Winkler *Stanley's father* • Nate Davis [Nathan Davis] *Stanley's grandpa* • Eartha Kitt *Madame Zeroni* • Khleo Thomas *Zero* ■ *Dir* Andrew Davis • *Scr* Louis Sachar, from his novel

Holiday ★★★

Romantic comedy 1930 · US · BW · 83mins

This is a capable filming of Philip Barry's hit Broadway comedy, with Robert Ames as the young nonconformist who rescues Ann Harding from an oppressive life in high society. Mary Astor is her sister, while Monroe Owsley is her weak brother drowning in drink. Under Edward H Griffith's direction, Ann Harding gained an Oscar nomination, though this adaptation has been eclipsed by George Cukor's definitive 1938 version with Katharine Hepburn. AE

Ann Harding *Linda Seton* • Mary Astor *Julia Seton* • Edward Everett Horton *Nick Potter* • Robert Ames *Johnny Case* • Hedda Hopper *Susan Potter* • Monroe Owsley *Ned Seton* • William Holden (1) *Edward Seton* ■ *Dir* Edward H Griffith • *Scr* Horace Jackson, from the play by Philip Barry

Holiday ★★★★★ U

Romantic comedy 1938 · US · BW · 91mins

This absolutely magical entertainment – an expert brew of comedy, pathos, romance and social comment – comes courtesy of the team which, two years later, would reunite to make *The Philadelphia Story*: screenwriter Donald Ogden Stewart, working from a play by Philip Barry; director George Cukor; and Cary Grant and Katharine Hepburn, he at his most thoughtful and charming, she never more beautiful or touching. Previously filmed in 1930, it's the tale of a man (Grant) who falls in love with a girl (Doris Nolan). When she turns out to be from the top drawer of mega-wealthy New York society, he finds himself enmeshed in more than he bargained for – especially after her sister (Hepburn) takes a shine to him. The stars sparkle in the midst of a superb supporting cast. RK DVD

Katharine Hepburn *Linda Seton* • Cary Grant *Johnny Case* • Doris Nolan *Julia Seton* • Lew Ayres *Ned Seton* • Edward Everett Horton *Nick Potter* • Henry Kolker *Edward Seton* • Binnie Barnes *Laura Cram* • Jean Dixon *Susan Elliott Potter* • Henry Daniell *Seton Cram* ■ *Dir* George Cukor • *Scr* Donald Ogden Stewart, Sidney Buchman, from the play by Philip Barry

Holiday Affair ★★★★ U

Seasonal romantic drama
1949 · US · BW · 86mins

In this absolutely charming yet little-known RKO Christmas movie, Janet Leigh plays a widowed single mother torn between Robert Mitchum and Wendell Corey (that's a contest?) and, not surprisingly, drawn to the one her son prefers. There's a sweet opening sequence and a nice sense of New York at Christmas. Mitchum reveals what a subtle actor he could be and Leigh proves yet again that she was one of the most delectable of cinematic charmers. Cynics should steer well clear, but if you're in the right mood this is delightful seasonal entertainment. TS

Robert Mitchum *Steve* • Janet Leigh *Connie* • Wendell Corey *Carl* • Gordon Gebert *Timmy* • Griff Barnett *Mr Ennis* • Esther Dale *Mrs Ennis* • Henry O'Neill *Mr Crowley* • Henry Morgan [Harry Morgan] *Police lieutenant* ■ *Dir* Don Hartman • *Scr* Isobel Lennart, from the story *Christmas Gift* by John D Weaver

Holiday Affair ★★★ U

Seasonal romance
1996 · US · Colour · 85mins

Get out the mistletoe, ignite the Yule log and wallow in Cynthia Gibb's romantic dilemma. In this TV remake of the 1949 film, Gibb is the widowed mother who finds herself torn between marriage to her financially secure lawyer boyfriend and a relationship with a handsome department store salesman. To add to her problems, one of her suitors is leaving town on New Year's Eve – for good. A cheerful holiday diversion. MC DVD

Cynthia Gibb *Jodie* • David James Elliott *Steve Mason* • Curtis Blanck *Timmy* • Tom Irwin *Paul Davis* • Al Waxman *Mr Crowley* ■ *Dir* Alan Myerson • *Scr* Ara Watson, Sam Blackwell, from the 1949 film

Holiday Camp ★★★ U

Comedy drama 1947 · UK · BW · 93mins

Directed by Ken Annakin, this compendium of interlinked stories was more notable for its scripting credits than for the quality of the writing. Ted Willis, Sydney and Muriel Box and Peter Rogers were among the contributors but, although many of the episodes are reasonably diverting, none of them gives the stars enough to chew on. What is fascinating, however, is the picture of camp life, which should keep *Hi-De-Hi!* fans entertained. Jack Warner and Kathleen Harrison steal the show as the Huggetts, who went on to feature in three more movies (beginning with *Here Come the Huggetts*) as well as their own radio show. DP

Flora Robson *Esther Harmon* • Dennis Price *Squadron Leader Hardwicke* • Jack Warner *Joe Huggett* • Kathleen Harrison *Ethel Huggett* • Hazel Court *Joan Martin* • Peter Hammond *Harry Huggett* • Yvonne Owen *Angela Kirby* • Jimmy Hanley *Jimmy Gardner* • Esma Cannon *Elsie Dawson* ■ *Dir* Ken Annakin • *Scr* Sidney Box, Peter Rogers, Denis Constanduros, Mabel Constanduros, Ted Willis, from a story by Godfrey Winn

Holiday for Lovers ★★ U

Romantic comedy
1959 · US · Colour · 102mins

At a time when B-movies were overrun with delinquent juveniles, this old-fashioned family comedy had nothing more to offer than a couple of hormonally zestful bobby-soxers. Screenwriter Luther Davis and director Henry Levin do nothing to drag Ronald Alexander's play into the rock 'n' roll era, preferring instead to dabble in coy innuendo as Jill St John and Carol Lynley chase the chaps during stuffy Clifton Webb and sensible Jane Wyman's South American vacation. DP

Clifton Webb *Robert Dean* • Jane Wyman *Mary Dean* • Jill St John *Meg Dean* • Carol Lynley *Betsy Dean* • Paul Henreid *Eduardo Barroso* • Gary Crosby *Paul Gattling* • Wally Brown *Joe* ■ *Dir* Henry Levin • *Scr* Luther Davis, from the play by Ronald Alexander

Holiday in Mexico ★★★ U

Musical 1946 · US · Colour · 127mins

Made to help cement America's Good Neighbour policy, this epic MGM musical actually never left the Culver City soundstages; the clever Hanna-Barbera animated title sequence establishes the only "authentic" Mexican flavour. Nevertheless, there's much to enjoy, despite the overlength that director George Sidney was prone to in the 1940s. It's effectively a vehicle for delightful ingénue Jane Powell, who (unbelievably) develops a crush on much older pianist José Iturbi. But there's also some knockout piano choreography, created by youngster Stanley Donen. TS

Walter Pidgeon *Jeffrey Evans* • José Iturbi • Roddy McDowall *Stanley Owen* • Ilona Massey *Toni Karpathy* • Xavier Cugat • Jane Powell *Christine Evans* • Hugo Haas *Angus* ■ *Dir* George Sidney (2) • *Scr* Isobel Lennart, from a story by William Kozlenko

Holiday in the Sun ★★ U

Comedy mystery 2001 · US · Colour · 89mins

Mary-Kate and Ashley Olsen hit adolescence in this flimsy Bahamian adventure, and the focus is squarely on boys. Unfortunately, their male counterparts are even less accomplished in the acting department than the twins. Steve Purcell's direction doesn't help, as he pads proceedings with so many MTV travelogue shots that he forgets to tackle the key plotline – which sees the Olsens turn detective to track down some antiques smugglers who have framed one of their beaus – until the last third. DP [VIDEO] DVD

Mary-Kate Olsen *Madison Stewart* • Ashley Olsen *Alex Stewart* • Austin Nichols *Griffen Grayson* • Ben Easter *Jordan Landers* • Ashley Hughes *Keegan Grayson* • Markus Flanigan [Markus Flanagan] *Harrison* ■ *Dir* Steve Purcell • *Scr* David T Wagner, Brent Goldberg

Holiday Inn ★★★★ U

Musical comedy 1942 · US · BW · 100mins

This much loved musical paired Crosby and Astaire for the first time, playing a song-and-dance team. The ingenious but wafer-thin plot sees Crosby split from the act to run an inn which only opens on public holidays, but this is basically a vehicle for some wonderful Irving Berlin songs and some magical Astaire dance routines. Most of the songs celebrate the aforementioned public holidays, but one in particular – Crosby's rendition of *White Christmas* – really caught the public imagination, making his version of the song one of the most successful recordings of all time. DF [VIDEO] DVD

Bing Crosby *Jim Hardy* • Fred Astaire *Ted Hanover* • Marjorie Reynolds *Linda Mason* • Virginia Dale *Lila Dixon* • Walter Abel *Danny Reid* • Louise Beavers *Mamie* • John Gallaudet *Parker* • James Bell *Dunbar* ■ *Dir* Mark Sandrich • *Scr* Claude Binyon, Elmer Rice, from an idea by Irving Berlin • *Choreographer* Danny Dare

Holiday on the Buses ★ PG

Comedy 1973 · UK · Colour · 82mins

After 1971's *On the Buses* and *Mutiny on the Buses* (1972), this third movie culled from the hit TV series is one of the worst films you'll ever see. Having been sacked from the bus depot, Stan and Jack fetch up at a Welsh holiday camp. The film's only achievement is the sheer amount of smutty sniggering it manages to cram into 85 minutes. Absolutely abysmal. DP [VIDEO] DVD

Reg Varney *Stan Butler* • Stephen Lewis *Inspector Blake* • Bob Grant *Jack* • Doris Hare *Mrs Butler* • Michael Robbins *Arthur* • Anna Karen *Olive* • Wilfrid Brambell *Bert* • Arthur Mullard *Wally Briggs* ■ *Dir* Bryan Izzard • *Scr* Ronald Wolfe, Ronald Chesney, from their TV series *On the Buses*

Holidays on the River Yarra ★★★

Drama 1991 · Aus · Colour · 88mins

This was part of the Melbourne urban cinema boom of the early 1990s, along with Geoffrey Wright's controversial *Romper Stomper*. Leo Berkeley's edgy drama portrays a city of unemployment, racial tension and disillusionment. Not content with voicing their views about various ethnic minorities at home, the lads here get involved in a far-fetched scheme to overthrow the reformist government of a small African island. While its realism is decidedly diminished by the doltishness of several minor characters, this is still a disturbing study of disaffection. DP

Craig Adams *Eddie* • Luke Elliot *Mick* • Alex Menglet *Big Mac* • Sheryl Munks *Valerie* • Kim Gyngell *Stewie* • Ian Scott *Frank* • Chris Askey *Eric* ■ *Dir/Scr* Leo Berkeley

Hollow Man ★★ 18

Science-fiction thriller
2000 · US/Ger · Colour · 107mins

In this updating of the *Invisible Man* tale, arrogant scientist Kevin Bacon makes himself invisible and promptly embarks on prattish schoolboy pranks. Challenged for much of a story, the film resorts to turning Bacon's laboratory into a haunted house, from where the see-through psychopath traps his colleagues to dispose of them one by one. Unlikely scientist Elisabeth Shue leads the fight back in an unambitious, predictable sci-fi thriller. AME. Contains violence, sex scenes, swearing, nudity. [VIDEO] DVD

Elisabeth Shue *Linda McKay* • Kevin Bacon *Sebastian Caine* • Josh Brolin *Matthew Kensington* • Kim Dickens *Sarah Kennedy* • Glen Grunberg *Carter Abbey* • Joey Slotnick *Frank Chase* • Mary Randle *Janice Walton* • William Devane *Doctor Kramer* ■ *Dir* Paul Verhoeven • *Scr* Andrew W Marlowe, from a story by Gary Scott Thompson, Andrew W Marlowe

Hollow Point ★★ 18

Crime comedy
1996 · US/Can · Colour · 98mins

Thomas Ian Griffith plays this "both guns blazing" adventure for laughs with the help of *Wayne's World* babe Tia Carrere. Sidney J Furie directs, but his camera trickery and Griffith's gun-toting prowess are overshadowed by the two more accomplished members of the cast, *Third Rock from the Sun's* John Lithgow and, with his tongue very firmly in his cheek, Donald Sutherland. JB. Contains violence, swearing and brief nudity. [VIDEO] DVD

Tia Carrere *Diane Norwood* • Thomas Ian Griffith *Max Perish* • Donald Sutherland *Garrett Lawton* • John Lithgow *Thomas Livingston* • David Hemblen *Oleg Krezinsky* • Carl Alacchi *Alberto Capucci* ■ *Dir* Sidney J Furie • *Scr* James H Stewart, Robert Geoffrion

Hollow Reed ★★★ 15

Drama 1995 · UK/Ger · Colour · 101mins

With a subject that's usually the preserve of the TV movie, this drama gains little from being made for the cinema, but the performances make it memorable. As directed by Angela Pope, the film is tensely moving when it concentrates on estranged gay doctor Martin Donovan, who is trying to save his son, Sam Bould, from what he believes are the attacks of ex-wife Joely Richardson's live-in lover, Jason Flemyng. However, the subsequent courtroom scenes become a gay rights manifesto during which genuine grievances over-ripen into dishonest special pleading. TH. Contains violence, swearing and nudity. [VIDEO]

Martin Donovan (2) *Martyn Wyatt* • Ian Hart *Tom Dixon* • Joely Richardson *Hannah Wyatt* • Sam Bould *Oliver Wyatt* • Jason Flemyng *Frank Donally* • Shaheen Khan *Dr Razmu* • Kelly Hunter *Jamie's mum* ■ *Dir* Angela Pope • *Scr* Paula Milne, from a story by Neville Bolt

Hollow Triumph ★★★ PG

Film noir 1948 · US · BW · 79mins

Producer/star Paul Henreid plays a gangster on the run from gamblers he's robbed. He murders a lookalike psychiatrist and assumes his identity, even inflicting a scar on his face to complete the resemblance. The story takes some swallowing but offers ingenious twists and, in true fatalistic *film noir* fashion, shows that no matter how hard you try, you can't escape your fate. The dramatic photography is the work of John Alton, one of the masters of *film noir*, who is given full rein by director Steve Sekely. AE [VIDEO]

Joan Bennett *Evelyn Hahn* • Paul Henreid *John Muller* • Eduard Franz *Frederick Muller* • Leslie Brooks *Virginia Taylor* • John Qualen *Swangron* ■ *Dir* Steve Sekely • *Scr* Daniel Fuchs, from the novel by Murray Forbes

The Holly and the Ivy ★★★ U

Seasonal drama 1952 · UK · BW · 83mins

The stage origins of this family drama are all too obvious. Vicar Ralph Richardson gathers his children around him at Christmas in his Norfolk rectory, only for the festive spirit to be dampened by a startling revelation. Celia Johnson is on hand like a thick cardigan to provide comfort, and, despite the clunky direction by George More O'Ferrall, the outcome is bleaker than you expect. TH

Ralph Richardson *Rev Martin Gregory* • Celia Johnson *Jenny Gregory* • Margaret Leighton *Margaret Gregory* • Denholm Elliott *Michael "Mick" Gregory* • John Gregson *David Patterson* • Hugh Williams *Richard Wyndham* ■ *Dir* George More O'Ferrall • *Scr* Anatole de Grunwald, from the play by Wynard Browne

Hollywood ★★ U

Silent comedy drama
1923 · US · BW · 30mins

One of the biggest productions of the silent period to exploit the insatiable appetite of picturegoers for glimpses of the film capital, this Paramount comedy put little-known players in the lead roles to contrast with the celebrities who appeared as themselves, including Cecil B DeMille, Mary Pickford, Gloria Swanson and Will Rogers. As the young would-be star from the Midwest who has no success in Hollywood while her entire family is offered work, Hope Drown was aptly named: she was never seen again. AE

Hope Drown *Angela Whitaker* • Luke Cosgrave *Joel Whitaker* • George K Arthur *Lem Lefferts* • Ruby Lafayette *Grandmother Whitaker* • Roscoe Arbuckle [Roscoe "Fatty" Arbuckle] *Fat man in casting director's office* • Gertrude Astor • Mary Astor • Charles Chaplin • Cecil B DeMille • Douglas Fairbanks • Mary Pickford • ZaSu Pitts • Will Rogers • Gloria Swanson ■ *Dir* James Cruze • *Scr* from a story by Frank Condon, Tom Geraghty

Hollywood Boulevard ★★★ 18

Comedy 1976 · US · Colour · 78mins

Roger Corman agreed to finance this parody of his own cash-strapped movie-making style, provided Allan Arkush and Joe Dante could complete it for less than $90,000. Ten days later (and $10,000 under budget), they submitted this patchy but often hilarious pastiche, in which New World (Corman's production company) becomes Miracle Pictures and Corman classics are given a whole new lease of life. Candice Rialson proves a good sport , while veterans such as Paul Bartel sieze the opportunity to send up the Corman canon. An inferior sequel followed in 1989. DP [VIDEO]

Candice Rialson *Candy Wednesday* • Mary Woronov *Mary McQueen* • Rita George *Bobbi Quackenbush* • Jeffrey Kramer *Patrick Hobby* • Dick Miller *Walter Paisley* • Richard Doran *Producer* • Paul Bartel *Erich Von Leppe* ■ *Dir* Joe Dante, Allan Arkush • *Scr* Patrick Hobby

Hollywood Canteen ★★★ U

Musical comedy 1944 · US · BW · 125mins

This Warner Bros contribution to the war effort was the studio's top-grossing hit of 1944, thanks to the cornucopia of stars who strut their stuff or play themselves. The line-up, to mention a mere few, includes the Andrews Sisters, Jack Benny, Joan Crawford, Bette Davis, Peter Lorre, Roy Rogers and Trigger, Barbara Stanwyck and Jimmy Dorsey and his Band. The plot? Soldiers Robert Hutton and Dane Clark spend their unforgettable leave at the Hollywood Canteen. Written and directed by Delmer Daves, it's a feeble excuse for what is a fascinating entertainment. RK

Robert Hutton *Slim* • Dane Clark *Sergeant* • Janis Paige *Angela* • Jonathan Hale *Mr Brodel* • Barbara Brown *Mrs Brodel* • Bette Davis • John Garfield • Joan Leslie • Jack Benny • Joan Crawford • Sydney Greenstreet • Peter Lorre • Barbara Stanwyck • Jane Wyman • Roy Rogers ■ *Dir/Scr* Delmer Daves

Hollywood Cavalcade ★★★ U

Drama 1939 · US · Colour · 88mins

Amiable and colourful slice of early Hollywood life, loosely based on the Mack and Mabel story (Mack Sennett, pioneer director, and Mabel Normand, early comedy superstar), pairing 20th Century-Fox's blonde Alice Faye and cheery Don Ameche, both coiffed and frocked totally, and shamefully, out of period. Still, the re-creations of silent movie days are fun, and the great Buster Keaton appears, as indeed does the real Mack Sennett (who also supervised the direction of the silent sequences). Al Jolson himself reprises his ground-breaking role from *The Jazz Singer*, so there's a fair amount of pleasure to be had. TS

Alice Faye *Molly Adair* • Don Ameche *Michael Linnett Connors* • J Edward Bromberg *Dave Spingold* • Alan Curtis *Nicky Hayden* • Stuart Erwin *Pete Tinney* • Jed Prouty *Chief of police* ■ *Dir* Irving Cummings • *Scr* Irving Pascal, from a story by Hilary Lynn, Brown Holmes, from an idea by Lou Breslow

Hollywood Ending ★★★

Comedy drama 2002 · US · Colour · 112mins

A stupendous pratfall, made all the more hilarious by its sheer unexpectedness, is the highlight of Woody Allen's gentle dig at the ethics and aesthetics of mainstream moviemaking. As ever, the ensemble is exemplary, with Téa Leoni particularly impressive as the estranged wife of Allen's washed-up director, who takes a chance on him for her Hollywood producing debut. But the central conceit that Allen is stricken psychosomatically blind just before shooting begins, yet still muddles through, strains to breaking point. DP

Woody Allen *Val Waxman* • Téa Leoni *Ellie* • George Hamilton *Ed* • Debra Messing *Lori* • Mark Rydell *Al Hack* • Tiffani Thiessen [Tiffani-Amber Thiessen] *Sharon Bates* • Treat Williams *Hal* ■ *Dir/Scr* Woody Allen

Hollywood Harry ★★

Crime 1985 · US · Colour · 96mins

The first (and so far) only film from cult favourite Robert Forster, whose career was revitalised by *Jackie Brown*. A warm salute to the classic gumshoe movies of the past, Forster also stars as the private eye of the title, hired to find a rich man's daughter who has disappeared into the seamier side of Hollywood. Forster's real-life daughter Kate pops up in a supporting role. JF

Robert Forster *Harry* • Kate Forster *Danielle* • Joe Spinell *Max* • Shannon Wilcox *Candy* • Pete Shrum *Clapper* • Redmond Gleeson *Skeeter* • Reed Morgan *Farmer* ■ *Dir* Robert Forster • *Scr* Curt Allen

Hollywood High ★

Comedy 1976 · US · Colour · 81mins

A forerunner to the teenage sex comedies of the 1980s, this still somehow manages to be even worse than what was to follow. Forget about the plot: the movie is basically a collection of vignettes concerning four loose-living teenage girls going from place to place and having (or trying) to have sex with their boyfriends. The only attempt at creating a character comes with a parody of Fonzie (called

H

the Fenz) from *Happy Days*, though he does nothing but blurt out lines like "Fenzi needs another beer!" KB

Marcy Albrecht *Bebe* • Sherry Hardin *Candy* • Rae Sperling *Monica* • Kevin Mead *The Fenz* • John Young *Mike* ■ *Dir* Patrick Wright

Hollywood Homicide ★★★ 12

Police comedy drama
2003 · US · Colour · 111mins

In this serviceable buddy movie, Harrison Ford plays a homicide detective who's busier moonlighting with his real-estate deals than solving crimes, while partner Josh Hartnett is an affable dimwit with a yen to take to the stage. The plot makes little sense, and it all degenerates into the inevitable car chase in the final act, but there's just enough wit in the script and chemistry between the likeable leads to offset much of the hoary genre's predictability. AS. Contains violence, swearing. DVD

Harrison Ford *Joe Gavilan* • Josh Hartnett *KC Calden* • Lena Olin *Ruby* • Bruce Greenwood *Lt Bennie Macko* • Isaiah Washington *Antoine Sartain* • Lolita Davidovich *Cleo Ricard* • Keith David *Leon* • Master P *Julius Armas* • Gladys Knight *Olivia Robidoux* • Lou Diamond Phillips *Wanda* • Dwight Yoakam *Leroy Wasley* • Martin Landau *Jerry Duran* ■ *Dir* Ron Shelton • *Scr* Robert Souza, Ron Shelton

Hollywood Hot Tubs ★★ 15

Sex comedy 1984 · US · Colour · 98mins

Not the worst of the teen sex comedies so popular in the 1980s, but don't take that as a recommendation. This tracks the adventures of a young teenager who gets an adolescent's dream job: fixing jacuzzis at the homes of rich Hollywood women. It's directed by prolific sex comedy maker Chuck Vincent. There's a sequel. JF

Donna McDaniel *Leslie Maynard* • Michael Andrew *Jeff* • Paul Gunning *Eddie* • Katt Shea [Katt Shea Ruben] *Dee Dee* • Edy Williams *Desire* • Jewel Shepard *Crystal* ■ *Dir* Chuck Vincent • *Scr* Mark Borde, Craig McDonnell

Hollywood Hotel ★★

Musical 1937 · US · BW · 100mins

Warner Bros musicals by 1937 had lost the big budgets and the vitality of such hits as *42nd Street* and *Dames*, even though Busby Berkeley was still directing and Dick Powell was still performing in them. This feeble story has Powell as a musician seeking success in Hollywood. Fortunately, it is rescued from complete mediocrity by the appearances of Benny Goodman and his orchestra and by fine Johnny Mercer–Richard Whiting songs. AE

Dick Powell *Ronnie Bowers* • Rosemary Lane *Virginia* • Lola Lane *Mona Marshall* • Hugh Herbert *Chester Marshall* • Ted Healy *Fuzzy* • Glenda Farrell *Jonesy* • Johnnie Davis *Georgia* • Benny Goodman • Susan Hayward *Starlet at table* • Ronald Reagan *Radio announcer* • Carole Landis *Hat check girl* ■ *Dir* Busby Berkeley • *Scr* Jerry Wald, Maurice Leo, Richard Macauley

Hollywood or Bust ★★★★ U

Comedy 1956 · US · Colour · 94mins

The 17th and last film teaming Dean Martin and Jerry Lewis shows no visible signs of the rapidly approaching on-set cracks in the relationship. Brilliant comic director Frank Tashlin indulges the duo and himself in a frantically stylised, often surreal, trek across the USA, ending in the movie capital of the title. This is a remarkably lavish and well-designed comedy, but the real highlight comes before the titles, as Lewis pays heartfelt tribute to movie fans around the world. Hard to believe, but this jape started life as a road movie for Humphrey Bogart and Shirley Booth called *Route 66*. TS

Dean Martin *Steve Wiley* • Jerry Lewis *Malcolm Smith* • Anita Ekberg • Pat Crowley *Terry Roberts* • Maxie Rosenbloom *"Bookie" Benny* ■ *Dir* Frank Tashlin • *Scr* Erna Lazarus, from her story *Beginner's Luck*

Hollywood Party ★★★ U

Musical comedy
1934 · US · BW and Colour · 65mins

Among the most gloriously miscalculated follies of the early sound era, this MGM extravaganza was originally intended to showcase the cream of the studio's star roster. Instead, it ended up being a manic montage of cockeyed comic cuts spinning off from fading movie icon Jimmy Durante's attempt to persuade Jack Pearl to sell him some lions for his next picture. Introduced by special guest Mickey Mouse, a Technicolor musical segment, *The Hot Chocolate Soldiers*, impressed contemporary audiences, but the hilarious tit-for-tat egg smashing sequence, featuring Lupe Velez and Laurel and Hardy, is the biggest highlight today. DP

Stan Laurel *Stan* • Oliver Hardy *Ollie* • Jimmy Durante *Schnarzan the Shouting Conqueror* • Mrs Jean Durante • Lupe Velez *Lupe Velez/ Jaguar Woman* • Ted Healy • Moe Howard *Moe* • Curly Howard *Curly* • Larry Fine *Larry* ■ *Dir* Richard Boleslawski, Allan Dwan, Roy Rowland • *Scr* Howard Dietz, Arthur Kober

Hollywood Revue ★★★★

Musical 1929 · US · BW · 114mins

Despite some now dated and rather tedious sequences, this Oscar-nominated movie is a historical document and a "must see" for anyone with a taste for early Hollywood, musicals, MGM stars and variety programmes. It was one of the first plotless revues to showcase a studio's stars. Lavishly staged under Charles Reisner's direction, the line-up of luminaries includes Lionel Barrymore, Joan Crawford, Buster Keaton, Laurel and Hardy, Bessie Love and Jack Benny. The range of acts embraces everything from Shakespeare to a variety of musical numbers of which the highlight is a spectacular treatment of "Singin' in the Rain", unveiled here 23 years before Gene Kelly performed it. RK

John Gilbert (1) • Norma Shearer • Joan Crawford • Bessie Love • Marion Davies • Lionel Barrymore • Ann Dvorak *Chorus girl* • Gus Edwards • Oliver Hardy • Jack Benny *Emcee* • Buster Keaton • Stan Laurel • Marie Dressler • Conrad Nagel *Emcee* ■ *Dir* Charles Reisner • *Scr* Al Boasberg, Robert E Hopkins

Hollywood Shuffle ★★★★ 15

Satire 1987 · US · Colour · 77mins

Shot for just $100,000, this spot-on satire slams Uncle Tom, Rochester and Superfly types alike as it swipes at the way in which Hollywood has (and continues to) miscast and misuse its African-American talent. Forgive it for falling flat occasionally, because hilarious scenes like the "act black" training school, the "boyz from the 'hood" review show and the great roles "done black" dream sequence all more than compensate with their razor-sharp wit and insight. The man to thank for this gem is co-writer/director Robert Townsend, who also shines as a struggling actor forced to choose between a part and his principles. DP. Contains swearing.

Robert Townsend *Bobby Taylor* • Anne-Marie Johnson *Lydia* • Starletta DuPois *Bobby's mother* • Helen Martin *Bobby's grandmother* • Craigus R Johnson *Stevie Taylor* • Ludie Washington *Tiny* • Keenen Ivory Wayans *Donald* ■ *Dir* Robert Townsend • *Scr* Keenen Ivory Wayans, Robert Townsend

Hollywood Vice Squad ★★ 18

Action comedy 1986 · US · Colour · 96mins

When Robin Wright runs away from home and into Hollywood's porn industry and prostitution racket, her mother (Trish Van Devere) solicits the help of police captain Ronny Cox. Pitched as a spoof, Penelope Spheeris's film has several additional casting in-jokes, notably Cox who basically repeats his role from the *Beverly Hills Cop* films. Carrie Fisher has fun with her role as a sort of "Dirty Harry in a dress" while John Travolta's brother Joey also makes a brief appearance. AT

Ronny Cox *Captain Jensen* • Frank Gorshin *Walsh* • Leon Isaac Kennedy *Hawkins* • Trish Van Devere *Pauline Stanton* • Carrie Fisher *Betty Melton* • Ben Frank *Daley* • Evan Kim *Chang* • Robin Wright [Robin Wright Penn] *Lori Stanton* • Joey Travolta *Stevens* ■ *Dir* Penelope Spheeris • *Scr* James J Docherty

Holocaust 2000 ★★★

Science-fiction horror
1977 · It/UK · Colour · 101mins

The coming of the Antichrist is the theme of Alberto De Martino's spaghetti horror film, in which Kirk Douglas flexes his sense of morality and does battle with the Devil. Meanwhile his cherub-faced son Simon Ward is committing obnoxious acts that are anything but angelic. Derivative of such supernatural successes as *The Omen*, its special effects only spark distaste, but not a few goosebumps. TH

Kirk Douglas *Robert Caine* • Agostina Belli *Sara Golan* • Simon Ward *Angel Caine* • Anthony Quayle *Professor Griffith* • Virginia McKenna *Eva Caine* • Alexander Knox *Meyer* ■ *Dir* Alberto De Martino • *Scr* Sergio Donati, Alberto De Martino, Michael Robson, from a story by Sergio Donati, Alberto De Martino

Holy Man ★★ PG

Comedy drama 1998 · US · Colour · 109mins

In this satire on consumerism, Eddie Murphy plays a wandering mystic who's hired by an ailing shopping channel to turn around its fortunes. As the ratings soar, Murphy also finds time to teach channel executive Jeff Goldblum and media analyst Kelly Preston the value of love. However, Murphy's holy innocent begins to grate, and what was intended to be a thought-provoking comedy ends up as another wearisome effort to distance Murphy from his *48 HRS* persona. TH. Contains some swearing. DVD

Eddie Murphy *"G"* • Jeff Goldblum *Ricky Hayman* • Kelly Preston *Kate Newell* • Robert Loggia *John McBainbridge* • Jon Cryer *Barry* • Eric McCormack *Scott Hawkes* • Morgan Fairchild • James Brown (2) *James Brown* ■ *Dir* Stephen Herek • *Scr* Tom Schulman

Holy Matrimony ★★★★ U

Comedy 1943 · US · BW · 85mins

This second talkie screen adaptation of Arnold Bennett's novel, *Buried Alive*, is far superior to the 1933 version, *His Double Life*. Monty Woolley excels as the gruff English painter who passes himself off as his dead butler to escape the unwanted attentions of the art world. He is ably supported by Gracie Fields, in her full Hollywood debut, as the no-nonsense wife who stands by him when the truth emerges. Weepie specialist John M Stahl simply has to point the camera, as much of his work has been done for him in Nunnally Johnson's literate and smoothly developed script. DP

Monty Woolley *Priam Farli* • Gracie Fields *Alice Challice* • Laird Cregar *Clive Oxford* • Una O'Connor *Mrs Leek* • Alan Mowbray *Mr Pennington* • Melville Cooper *Dr Caswell* ■ *Dir* John M Stahl • *Scr* Nunnally Johnson, from the novel *Buried Alive* by Arnold Bennett

Holy Matrimony ★ PG

Comedy 1994 · US · Colour · 89mins

This dire comedy from former *Star Trek* star Leonard Nimoy suffers from a clutch of one-note performances and unlikeable characters. After Patricia Arquette and Tate Donovan rob a county fair, they hide out in the Hutterite (like the Amish, only more conservative) community where Donovan grew up. When he dies, Hutterite tradition means that Arquette has to marry his younger brother (Joseph Gordon-Levitt) , even though he's just 12 years old. JB

Patricia Arquette *Havana* • Joseph Gordon-Levitt *Zeke* • Armin Mueller-Stahl *Uncle Wilhelm* • Tate Donovan *Peter* • John Schuck *Markowski* • Lois Smith *Orna* • Courtney B Vance *Cooper* ■ *Dir* Leonard Nimoy • *Scr* David Weisberg, Douglas S Cook

The Holy Mountain ★★★ U

Silent adventure drama
1926 · Ger · BW · 105mins

Trained in modern dance, Leni Riefenstahl made her acting debut in this "mountain film" by the genre's finest exponent, Arnold Fanck. But she also picked up a few directorial tips, as the presentation of her rhythmic routine and the glorification of human athleticism would influence the visual style of her 1938 masterpiece, *Olympiad*. The story of her tangled romance with mountaineers Luis Trenker and Ernst Petersen is pure melodrama, but Fanck's use of a moving camera and time-lapse photography to capture both the raw beauty of the scenery and the viewpoint of the sportsmen remains impressive. DP DVD

Leni Riefenstahl *Diotima* • Ernst Petersen *Vigo* • Luis Trenker *Vigo's friend* • Frida Richard *Diotima's mother* • Hannes Schneider *Mountain guide* • Friedrich Schneider *Colli* ■ *Dir* Arnold Fanck • *Scr* Arnold Fanck, Hans Schneeberger

The Holy Mountain ★★★★ 18

Surreal drama
1973 · US/Mex · Colour · 113mins

Alexandro Jodorowsky's follow-up to his cult classic, *El Topo*, is every bit as eccentric and challenging. Memorable images abound in the opening section, in which the messianic Horacio Salinas is saved by a limbless dwarf and witnesses an amphibian reconstruction of the crimes of the Conquistadores, before the tone shifts from mystical to comic inside the chimney lair of Jodorowsky's scheming alchemist. However, the catalogue of loopy vignettes itself soon gives way to a journey to the titular mountain where the worthies who rule the world are said to reside. Don't try searching for meaning, simply surrender to the experience. DP

Alexandro Jodorowsky *Alchemist* • Horacio Salinas *Christ figure* • Ramona Saunders *Written woman* ■ *Dir/Scr* Alexandro Jodorowsky

Holy Smoke ★★★ 18

Drama 1999 · US · Colour · 109mins

After the class-crossing passion of *Titanic* and her emergence as a star, Kate Winslet lets her hair down (and a lot more besides) in this lampoon on Australian bigotry from Jane Campion. Winslet plays the daughter of a white trash family from Sydney who becomes a disciple of an Indian guru. Fearful of his influence over her, Winslet's family hires an American "exit counsellor" and cult buster (Harvey Keitel), who takes her to the outback and tries to break her spirit. Both funny and dramatic. TH. Contains swearing, sex scenes and nudity. DVD

Kate Winslet *Ruth Barron* • Harvey Keitel *PJ Waters* • Julie Hamilton *Miriam* • Tim Robertson *Gilbert* • Sophie Lee *Yvonne* • Dan Wyllie *Robbie* • Pam Grier *Carol* ■ *Dir* Jane Campion • *Scr* Jane Campion, from the autobiographical work *My Guru and His Disciple* by Christopher Isherwood

Homage ★★★

Psychological thriller 1995 · US · Colour · 97mins

This slice of deep-fried Deep South melodrama, while it never really succeeds in throwing off its stage origins, still makes for entertainingly overheated viewing. Blythe Danner is the faded southern belle locked in a strange relationship with handyman Frank Whaley, until her actress daughter Sheryl Lee arrives to turn up the sexual tension another few degrees. The three stars are superb, and Mark Medoff does his best to open up his play. JF. Contains violence, sex scenes, swearing.

Blythe Danner *Katherine Samuel* • Frank Whaley *Archie Landrum* • Sheryl Lee *Lucy Samuel* • Bruce Davison *Joseph Smith* • Danny Nucci *Gilbert Tellez* ■ *Dir* Ross Kagan Marks • *Scr* Mark Medoff, from his play *The Homage That Follows*

Hombre ★★★★ PG

Western 1967 · US · Colour · 106mins

Paul Newman has said that his best movies all start with an "H", and this fine, grim western bears him out. This is a *Stagecoach* variation, assembling differing characters for a trek through Arizona, played by a very distinguished cast including veteran Fredric March and a gnarled Richard Boone. Only import Diane Cilento (Sean Connery's ex-wife) seems ill-at-ease in a pivotal role. The movie is beautifully shot by veteran photographer James Wong Howe, and Newman's piercing blue eyes have seldom been more prominently featured. The plot has many valid points to make about incipient racism, and the film is deeply rewarding. TS. Contains swearing. [VIDEO]

Paul Newman *John Russell* • Fredric March *Favor* • Richard Boone *Grimes* • Diane Cilento *Jessie* • Cameron Mitchell *Braden* • Barbara Rush *Adra Favor* • Martin Balsam *Mendez* ■ *Dir* Martin Ritt • *Scr* Irving Ravetch, Harriet Frank Jr, from the novel by Elmore Leonard

Hombre Mirando al Sudeste ★★★

Drama 1986 · Arg · Colour · 105mins

Argentinian director Eliseo Subiela enjoyed box-office success in the Americas with this, although it was little seen in Europe. Also known as *Man Looking Southeast*, it's a mystical political parable in which opposition to the state is equated with insanity, but it shifts from satire to sinister comment with some ease. There are fine performances from Hugo Soto as a Christ-like patient who claims to come from outer space and Lorenzo Quinteros as the doctor seeking to certify him. DP. In Spanish with English subtitles. Contains nudity.

Lorenzo Quinteros *Dr Dennis* • Hugo Soto *Rantes* • Ines Vernengo *Beatriz* • Cristina Scaramuzza *Nurse* • Rubens W Correa *Dr Prieto* ■ *Dir/Scr* Eliseo Subiela

Home Alone ★★★★ PG

Comedy 1990 · US · Colour · 98mins

This modest comedy became one of the highest grossing pictures of all time. Writer/producer John Hughes and director Chris Columbus tuned in to two key elements: the fantasy of Steven Spielberg's *ET*, with its children triumphing over adult adversity, and the perennial chase of Tom and Jerry cartoons. Thus Macaulay Culkin, then ten years old and already in his fifth picture, is the youngster left stranded by his parents who fly to Paris for the holiday. He pigs out on junk food, watches videos and then copes heroically with two burglars (Joe Pesci and Daniel Stern). Surprisingly violent in a cartoon-like way, it captured every child's heart. AT [VIDEO] DVD

Macaulay Culkin *Kevin McCallister* • Joe Pesci *Harry* • Daniel Stern *Marv* • John Heard *Peter* • Roberts Blossom *Marley* • Catherine O'Hara *Kate* • John Candy *Gus Polinski* ■ *Dir* Chris Columbus • *Scr* John Hughes

Home Alone 2: Lost in New York ★★★ PG

Comedy 1992 · US · Colour · 119mins

Yep, Kevin McCallister (Macaulay Culkin) has managed to ditch his family again, this time getting on the wrong plane and ending up alone in New York while they are heading for Florida. And, armed with Dad's wallet, he enjoys all of life's luxuries at the Plaza hotel until he runs into inept burglars Joe Pesci and Daniel Stern once again. What worked in the first film is not quite as entertaining here, but, as slapstick escapism goes, this is well engineered stuff. JB [VIDEO] DVD

Macaulay Culkin *Kevin McCallister* • Joe Pesci *Harry Lyme* • Daniel Stern *Marvin Murchins* • Catherine O'Hara *Kate McCallister* • John Heard *Peter McCallister* • Devin Ratray *Buzz* • Hillary Wolf *Megan* • Maureen Elisabeth Shay *Linnie* ■ *Dir* Chris Columbus • *Scr* John Hughes, from his characters

Home Alone 3 ★★★ PG

Comedy 1997 · US · Colour · 102mins

This time it's cute Alex D Linz whose befuddled parents have mistakenly left him on his own in the house, when an international espionage team come calling to steal back a top secret computer chip hidden in his new toy. Pity the hapless baddies as the plucky boy devises ingenious booby traps to foil them. Writer John Hughes's third neatly-plotted variation on the same theme is good knockabout fun. An unnecessary made-for-TV third sequel appeared in 2002. AME [VIDEO] DVD

Alex D Linz *Alex Pruitt* • Olek Krupa *Beaupre* • Rya Kihlstedt *Alice* • Lenny Von Dohlen *Jernigan* • David Thornton *Unger* • Haviland Morris *Karen Pruitt* • Kevin Kilner *Jack Pruitt* ■ *Dir* Raja Gosnell • *Scr* John Hughes

Home and Away ★ U

Comedy 1956 · UK · BW · 92mins

This a non-Huggett reunion for Jack Warner and Kathleen Harrison. Written and directed by Vernon Sewell, this contrived tale of a widow trying to cheat a fortune out of the pools is meant to be whimsical and slightly wicked. However, it ends up merely frantic and unfunny, with the Warner-Harrison partnership having one of its few off days. DP [VIDEO]

Jack Warner *George Knowles* • Kathleen Harrison *Elsie Harrison* • Lana Morris *Mary Knowles* • Charles Victor *Ted Groves* • Thora Hird *Margie Groves* • Leslie Henson *Uncle Tom* ■ *Dir* Vernon Sewell • *Scr* Vernon Sewell, RF Delderfield, from the play *Treble Trouble* by Heather McIntyre

The Home and the World ★★★★ U

Period drama 1984 · Ind · Colour · 139mins

Throughout his career, Indian director Satyajit Ray turned to the works of his mentor, Rabindranath Tagore, for inspiration. Victor Banerjee loses his wife (Swatilekha Chatterjee) after he breaks with the tradition of seclusion and introduces her to a dashing patriot (Soumitra Chatterjee) in this compelling conversation piece, based on Tagore's novel, exploring the dangers inherent in both repression and liberation. One of the few true auteurs of world cinema, Ray also wrote the script and composed the score. However, while the leads give immaculate performances and the director never used colour better, the film is not quite a masterwork. DP. In Bengali with English subtitles.

Soumitra Chatterjee *Sandip Mukherjee* • Victor Banerjee *Nikhilesh Choudhury* • Swatilekha Chatterjee *Bimala Choudhury* • Gopa Aich *Sister-in-law* • Jennifer Kapoor *Miss Gilby* ■ *Dir* Satyajit Ray • *Scr* Satyajit Ray, from a novel by Rabindranath Tagore

Home at Seven ★★★ U

Mystery 1952 · UK · BW · 81mins

This was Ralph Richardson's sole venture as a film director, and a pretty fair job he makes of it, too. He also re-creates his stage role as the timid bank clerk whose dose of amnesia coincides with a murder and a robbery. The strength of the picture is that you're never quite sure whether he's bluffing or baffled, and the secret is tightly kept right to the end. It's more than a mite stagey, though, with wife Margaret Leighton and doctor Jack Hawkins particularly guilty of overseasoning the ham. DP [VIDEO]

Ralph Richardson *David Preston* • Margaret Leighton *Janet Preston* • Jack Hawkins *Dr Sparling* • Frederick Piper *Mr Petherbridge* • Diana Beaumont *Ellen* • Meriel Forbes *Peggy Dobson* • Michael Shepley *Major Watson* • Margaret Withers *Mrs Watson* ■ *Dir* Ralph Richardson • *Scr* Anatole de Grunwald, from the play by RC Sherriff

A Home at the End of the World ★★★ 15

Drama 2004 · US · Colour · 96mins

Spanning three richly detailed decades from the 1960s onwards, this warm relationship drama explores the complex bonds of love and friendship between former childhood friends, played as adults by Colin Farrell and Dallas Roberts. Reunited in early 1980s New York, the duo form an unconventional family with free-spirited older woman Robin Wright Penn. In a trio of beautifully nuanced performances, the actors breathe life into Michael Cunningham's multilayered but meandering script. SF. Contains swearing, sex scenes and drug abuse.

Colin Farrell (2) *Bobby Morrow* • Robin Wright Penn *Clare* • Dallas Roberts *Jonathan Glover* • Sissy Spacek *Alice Glover* • Matt Frewer *Ned Glover* • Erik Smith *Bobby (1974)* • Harris Allan *Jonathan (1974)* • Andrew Chalmers *Bobby (1967)* ■ *Dir* Michael Mayer • *Scr* Michael Cunningham, from the novel by Michael Cunningham

Home before Dark ★★

Drama 1958 · US · BW · 136mins

Only Jean Simmons's most ardent fans will obtain any pleasure from this long-winded and bleak psychological drama. As the wife recovering from a mental breakdown, she returns to her unloving college professor husband (Dan O'Herlihy), a stepsister (Rhonda Fleming) in whom her husband is more interested and a domineering stepmother (Mabel Albertson). Reminiscent of those thrillers in which leading ladies were nearly driven insane for their wealth, this Mervyn LeRoy production tries to be more subtle but ends up merely dull. AE

Jean Simmons *Charlotte Bronn* • Dan O'Herlihy *Arnold Bronn* • Rhonda Fleming *Joan Carlisle* • Efrem Zimbalist Jr *Jake Diamond* • Mabel Albertson *Inez Winthrop* • Steve Dunne *Hamilton Gregory* • Joan Weldon *Frances Barrett* ■ *Dir* Mervyn LeRoy • *Scr* Robert Bassing, Eileen Bassing, from the novel *Home before Dark* by Eileen Bassing

Home for the Holidays ★★★ 15

Comedy drama 1995 · US · Colour · 98mins

Jodie Foster follows up her quirky directorial debut (*Little Man Tate*) with this uneven comedy drama about a group of grown-up kids returning to the family home for a Thanksgiving that, of course, is filled with romance, rows, misunderstandings and strange behaviour. Despite the occasional awkward switches between comedy and sentiment, this works most of the time thanks to the impressive cast. JB. Contains some swearing. [VIDEO]

Holly Hunter *Claudia Larson* • Robert Downey Jr *Tommy Larson* • Anne Bancroft *Adele Larson* • Charles Durning *Henry Larson* • Dylan McDermott *Leo Fish* • Geraldine Chaplin *Aunt Glady* • Steve Guttenberg *Walter Wedman* • Claire Danes *Kitt* ■ *Dir* Jodie Foster • *Scr* WD Richter, from a short story by Chris Radant

Home Free All ★

Comedy drama 1983 · US · Colour · 92mins

Stewart Bird's one and only feature is a depressing and incoherent mess about two childhood friends in New York City who meet again as adults and try to make sense out of their unproductive and neurotic lives. Predictably, they just end up making things worse as an ill-fated affair only creates more confusion. The action is punctuated with ethnic jokes that, were they really required in the film, should at least have been wittier. ST

Allan Nicholls *Barry Simon* • Roland Caccavo *Al* • Maura Ellyn *Cathy* • Shelley Wyant *Rita* • Lucille Rivin *Lynn* • Lorry Goldman *Marvin* • Janet Burnham *Chastity* • José Ramon Rosario *Custodian* • Chazz Palminteri *Hijacker* ■ *Dir/Scr* Stewart Bird

Home Fries ★ 12

Drama 1998 · US · Colour · 89mins

Drew Barrymore stars in this ill-conceived mix of romance, black humour and very little comedy. While her romance with Luke Wilson (she's a pregnant waitress, he's her Lamaze partner) works quite nicely, it's mixed in with a subplot (he and his brother scared their stepdad to death – literally) that doesn't work at all. Barrymore does her best, but there's little to work with. JB. Contains swearing, sexual references, violence. [VIDEO]

Drew Barrymore *Sally* • Jake Busey *Angus* • Catherine O'Hara *Mrs Lever* • Shelley Duvall *Mrs Jackson* • Luke Wilson *Dorian* • Kim Robillard *Billy* ■ *Dir* Dean Parisot • *Scr* Vince Gilligan

Home from the Hill ★★★

Melodrama 1960 · US · Colour · 149mins

A splendid MGM melodrama, lengthy but nevertheless totally engrossing. Robert Mitchum delivers one of his finest performances as the Texas patriarch whose sons turn his domestic life inside out. In its day this movie was notable for the star-making performances of two Georges (Peppard and Hamilton) as Mitch's offspring, one legitimate, the other not. This is from the same period in flamboyant director Vincente Minnelli's career as *Some Came Running*, and shares with it a loving use of CinemaScope and an intense use of colour. TS

Robert Mitchum *Captain Wade Hunnicutt* • Eleanor Parker *Hannah Hunnicutt* • George Peppard *Rafe Copley* • George Hamilton *Theron Hunnicutt* • Everett Sloane *Albert Halstead* • Luana Patten *Libby Halstead* ■ *Dir* Vincente Minnelli • *Scr* Irving Ravetch, Harriet Frank Jr, from the novel by William Humphrey

H

Home Front ★ PG

Comedy 1987 · US · Colour · 88mins

This is yet another entry on the CV of Alan Smithee, the "person" who carries the can when the disgruntled director who actually made the film removes his or her name from the credits. And you have to admit that removing their names was a wise move here on the part of co-directors Terry Winsor and Paul Aaron, for this teenage comedy is excruciatingly awful. Lynn Redgrave and Jon Cryer try to haul the crude story out of the gutter, but fail. DP. Contains swearing.

Jon Cryer *Morgan Stewart* • Lynn Redgrave *Nancy Stewart* • Nicholas Pryor *Senator Tom Stewart* • Viveka Davis *Emily* • Paul Gleason *Jay Springsteen* • Andrew Duncan *General Fenton* ■ *Dir* Alan Smithee [Terry Winsor], Alan Smithee [Paul Aaron] • *Scr* Ken Hixon, David Titcher

Home in Indiana ★★★ U

Drama 1944 · US · Colour · 103mins

A beguiling 20th Century-Fox horse-racing melodrama, beautifully shot by Edward Cronjager in glorious Technicolor. An unusually top-billed Walter Brennan seems to enjoy himself watching over two relative newcomers, Jeanne Crain and June Haver. Lon McCallister, who plays Brennan's young orphaned nephew, swiftly established himself as a star in this movie, but his film career only lasted another nine years. Director Henry Hathaway handles the climactic trotting race superbly, and, if it all seems familiar, Fox remade it in 1957 as the Pat Boone vehicle *April Love*. TS

Walter Brennan *JP "Thunder" Bolt* • Lon McCallister *Sparke Thorton* • Jeanne Crain *Char* • June Haver *Cri-Cri* • Charlotte Greenwood *Penny* • Ward Bond *Jed Bruce* • Charles Dingle *Godaw Boole* • Robert Condon *Gordon Bradley* ■ *Dir* Henry Hathaway • *Scr* Winston Miller, from the novel *The Phantom Filly* by George Agnew Chamberlain

Home Is Where the Hart Is ★

Comedy 1987 · US/Can · Colour · 94mins

Following his success in the *Airplane!* movies, Leslie Nielsen turned from playing straight roles to almost exclusively appearing in comedies. Unfortunately some of his choices reflected rather dubious judgement, and this is one such project. The story concerns a centenarian, Slim Hart (Joe Austin), and his conniving nurse, who has her eye on his inheritance. Funny man Martin Mull also appears but can't rescue this damp squib. DF

Valri Bromfield *Belle Haimes* • Stephen E Miller *Rex Haines* • Martin Mull *Carson Boundy* • Eric Christmas *Martin Hart* • Ted Stidder *Art Hart* • Deanne Henry *Selma Dodge* • Leslie Nielsen *Sheriff Nashville Schwartz* • Joe Austin *Slim "Pappy" Hart* ■ *Dir/Scr* Rex Bromfield • *Music/lyrics* Long John Baldry

Home Movies ★★★

Comedy 1979 · US · Colour · 90mins

Brian DePalma was teaching at New York's Sarah Lawrence College when he conceived the idea for this bold but misfiring comedy about a film-making guru who encourages his students to live as the stars of their own movies. Relishing the role of "the Maestro", Kirk Douglas turns in a devilish performance, made all the more effective by DePalma's neat tactic of shooting many of his scenes in the style of a self-aggrandising film diary. But the picture belongs to Keith Gordon as a nerd goaded into seizing editorial control of his sad existence by poaching his brother's fiancée. DP

Kirk Douglas *Dr Tuttle, "the Maestro"* • Nancy Allen *Kristina* • Keith Gordon *Denis* • Gerrit Graham *James* • Vincent Gardenia *Dr Byrd* ■ *Dir* Brian De Palma • *Scr* Robert Harders, Gloria Norris, Kim Ambler, Dana Edelman, Stephan LeMay, Charles Loventhal, from a story by Brian DePalma

A Home of Our Own ★★★ PG

Drama 1993 · US · Colour · 100mins

Oscar-winner Kathy Bates (*Misery*) gives another sterling performance, this time as a downtrodden mother determined to keep a roof over the heads of her children in this 1960s-set drama. Discovering that her eldest son Edward Furlong has turned to petty crime, she decides to uproot her brood from LA and ends up in Idaho, determined to find a home for her family without taking charity. It's an often depressing tale, bolstered by warm performances from Bates and Furlong and understated direction from Tony Bill, but it ultimately gets bogged down in its own relentlessness. JB

Kathy Bates *Frances Lacey* • Edward Furlong *Shayne Lacey* • Soon-Teck Oh *Mr Munimura* • Tony Campisi *Norman* • Amy Sakasitz *Annie Lacey* • Miles Feulner *Murray Lacey* • Clarissa Lassig *Lynn Lacey* • TJ Lowther *Craig Lacey* ■ *Dir* Tony Bill • *Scr* Patrick Duncan

Home of the Brave ★★★

Second World War drama
1949 · US · BW · 86mins

Is one form of racial discrimination as bad as another? Since anti-Semitism had received a wide airing in recent movies, producer Stanley Kramer, director Mark Robson and writer Carl Foreman changed the theme of Arthur Laurents's Second World War play to attack prejudice against black people instead. In this low-budget drama, set on a South Pacific island held by the Japanese, James Edwards is excellent as the black soldier whose biggest enemy is a bigoted corporal (Steve Brodie). When his best friend is killed, Edwards's legs become paralysed, and it is up to Jeff Corey's army psychiatrist to find a solution. AE

Douglas Dick *Maj Robinson* • Steve Brodie *Corporal TJ Everett* • Jeff Corey *Doctor* • Lloyd Bridges *Finch* • Frank Lovejoy *Mingo* • James Edwards *Peter Moss* ■ *Dir* Mark Robson • *Scr* Carl Foreman, from the play by Arthur Laurents

Home of the Brave ★★★ U

Experimental concert movie
1986 · US · Colour · 91mins

If you liked performance artist Laurie Andersen's 1981 Top Ten hit *O Superman*, you may find this multi-media concert film fascinating. If not, her unconventional warbling and post-hippy presentation will seem a pretentious bore. That said, Andersen's unorthodox music is mixed with a nice line in eccentric humour and accompanied by a well-staged array of colourful visuals, while cult author William S Burroughs adds to the rarefied feel. AJ

Dir/Scr Laurie Anderson

Home on the Range ★★ U

Animated comedy western
2004 · US · Colour · 73mins

Despite the impressive voice talent, Disney's old-fashioned, Wild West-set tale of three cows who try to save their farm from repossession is too weak and uninspiring to really charm. The animals need more depth and definition, particularly given the flimsy plotline and crudely rendered landscapes. The film has some nice moments, but this is a pedestrian affair. SF DVD

Roseanne Barr *Maggie* • Judi Dench *Mrs Caloway* • Jennifer Tilly *Grace* • Cuba Gooding Jr *Buck* • Randy Quaid *Alameda Slim* • Carole Cook *Pearl* • Richard Riehle *Sheriff Brown* • Charles Haid *Lucky Jack* • Steve Buscemi *Wesley* ■ *Dir* Will Finn, John Sanford (2) • *Scr* Will Finn, John Sanford (2), from a story by Will Finn, John Sanford (2), Michael Labash, Sam Levine, Mark Kennedy, Robert Lence

Home Page ★★★

Documentary 1998 · US · Colour · 99mins

Documentary-maker Doug Block turns his attention to the internet with this portrait of young "web guru" Justin Hall, whose homepage diary not only evangelises the Net creed, but also reveals his most intimate thoughts and actions. Just about everyone Hall encounters on his whistle-stop tour is a cybergeek in awe of his site status. But, having become hooked himself in the course of production, Block wisely avoids depicting these online obsessives as nerds in need of a life, and presents their enthusiasm and eccentricities with the baffled respect their expertise merits. DP

Dir Doug Block • *Scr* Doug Block, Deborah Rosenberg

Home, Sweet Home ★★★

Silent drama 1914 · US · BW · 62mins

This was the film that consolidated DW Griffith's reputation and established the cinema as a mature art form and supreme entertainment experience. Slight by the standards of what was to come, this heavily sentimentalised biopic of composer John Howard Payne (writer of the song that gives the film its title) features a marvellous line-up of most of Griffith's favourite stars. Henry B Walthall is Payne and the luminous Lillian Gish his long-suffering sweetheart. It looks quaint today, but parts were risible even then, especially the hell-to-heaven "flying" finale. However, it still makes fascinating cinema, with innovation and moments of superb playing. TS

Henry B Walthall *John Howard Payne* • Josephine Crowell *Mother* • Lillian Gish *Sweetheart* • Dorothy Gish *Sister* ■ *Dir* DW Griffith • *Scr* HE Aitken, DW Griffith, from the song by John Howard Payne

Home Sweet Home ★★

Musical comedy 1945 · UK · BW · 93mins

Both Nicolette Roeg and Tony Pendrell were making only their second big-screen appearances in this slight musical comedy, and their inexperience shows. Music-hall favourite Frank Randle was hardly more familiar with the camera; however, his slack-jawed clowning provides the only real interest in this backstage Cinderella story. DP

Nicolette Roeg *Jacqueline Chantry* • Frank Randle *Frank* • Tony Pendrell *Eric Wright* • HF Maltby *Colonel Wright* • Hilda Bayley *Mrs Wright* • Cecil Fredericks *Webster* • Stan Little *Young Herbert* • Bunty Meadows *Bunty* ■ *Dir* John E Blakeley • *Scr* Roney Parsons, Anthony Toner, Frank Randle

Home Sweet Homicide ★★★ U

Detective comedy drama
1946 · US · BW · 89mins

This is a typically enjoyable Lloyd Bacon offering. A domestic comedy, it has siblings Peggy Ann Garner, Dean Stockwell and Connie Marshall attempting to matchmake their widowed mother, Lynn Bari, with the eligible Randolph Scott. However, there's also a mystery element by dint of the fact that she's a whodunnit writer and he's a cop investigating the same murder that the kids want to solve. Neither scenario contains a scintilla of suspense, but it's nice to be reminded of what fun family entertainment used to be. DP

Peggy Ann Garner *Dinah Carstairs* • Randolph Scott *Lt Bill Smith* • Lynn Bari *Marian Carstairs* • Dean Stockwell *Archie Carstairs* • Connie Marshall *April Carstairs* • James Gleason *Sgt Dan O'Hare* ■ *Dir* Lloyd Bacon • *Scr* F Hugh Herbert, from the novel by Craig Rice

Home Team ★ PG

Sports comedy drama
1998 · Can · Colour · 91mins

Hollywood still hasn't got the hang of football (or soccer, as they insist on calling it), and this family-oriented frolic is decidedly minor league. As an ex-pro with gambling problems, Steve Guttenberg is sentenced to community service at a tough children's home, where the powers that be think that footie might be the best way to improve team spirit. DP DVD

Steve Guttenberg *Mr Butler* • Ryan Slater • Tyler Hynes *Chip* • Johnny Morina *Alex* ■ *Dir* Allan A Goldstein • *Scr* Pierce O'Donnell

Home to Danger ★★

Mystery 1951 · UK · BW · 67mins

Rona Anderson inherits an estate when her father commits suicide and is immediately attacked by a mysterious assailant. As the corpses mount up, so do the suspects in this standard whodunnit, directed by Terence Fisher, who later hit his stride with his pioneering Hammer horrors. AT

Guy Rolfe *Robert* • Rona Anderson *Barbara* • Francis Lister *Wainwright* • Alan Wheatley *Hughes* • Bruce Belfrage *Solicitor* • Stanley Baker *Willie Dougan* ■ *Dir* Terence Fisher • *Scr* John Temple-Smith, Francis Edge

Home Town Story ★★ U

Drama 1951 · US · BW · 61mins

Released during the Red Scare to reinforce confidence in corporate America, this was distributed by MGM, but supervised by John K Ford, the head of the General Motors film unit. The scenario couldn't be much more cynically corny, as small-town editor Jeffrey Lynn abandons his paper's anti-capitalist stance after his kid sister, Melinda Plowman, is rescued in the nick of time by machinery manufactured by Donald Crisp's conglomerate. However, the picture has been delivered from its deserved obscurity by the appearance of a young Marilyn Monroe. DP DVD

Jeffrey Lynn *Blake Washburn* • Donald Crisp *John MacFarland* • Marjorie Reynolds *Janice Hunt* • Alan Hale Jr *Slim Haskins* • Marilyn Monroe *Iris Martin* • Barbara Brown *Mrs Washburn* • Melinda Plowman *Katie Washburn* ■ *Dir/Scr* Arthur Pierson

Homeboy ★★ 15

Drama 1988 · US · Colour · 110mins

Touted as the new Brando, Mickey Rourke ended up making talent-wasting movies like this pet project about a boxer. Despite the presence of a scene-stealing Christopher Walken, it's Rourke's narcissism that dominates as he slouches into battle with an expressionless face and an intimidating faith in his ability to enthral and audience. It was a mistaken faith. TH

Mickey Rourke *Johnny Walker* • Christopher Walken *Wesley Pendergrass* • Debra Feuer *Ruby* • Thomas Quinn *Lou* • Kevin Conway *Grazziano* • Antony Alda *Ray* • Jon Polito *Moe Fingers* ■ *Dir* Michael Seresin • *Scr* Eddie Cook, from a story by Mickey Rourke

Homecoming ★★

Second World War medical romance
1948 · US · BW · 112mins

MGM knew it would be enough to put Clark Gable together with Lana Turner for the crowds to flock in and didn't try very hard to make a worthwhile picture. Gable is the smug society doctor, married to Anne Baxter, who joins the medical corps, falls in love with Lana Turner's nurse while serving overseas and comes to dedicate himself to helping others. Anne Baxter gives the sharpest performance on view, while the glossy, long-winded direction is by Mervyn LeRoy. AE

Clark Gable *Ulysses Delby Johnson* • Lana Turner *Lt Jane "Snapshot" McCall* • Anne Baxter *Penny Johnson* • John Hodiak *Dr Robert Sunday* • Ray Collins *Lt Col Avery Silver* • Gladys Cooper *Mrs Kirby* • Cameron Mitchell *Sgt Monkevickz* • Art Baker *Mr Williams* ■ *Dir* Mervyn LeRoy • *Scr* Paul Osborn, Jan Lustig, from the story *The Homecoming of Ulysses* by Sidney Kingsley

The Homecoming ★★★★ 12

Drama 1973 · US/UK · Colour · 109mins

One of theatrical director Peter Hall's rare forays into film, this adaptation of Harold Pinter's play is more an account of a performance than a breakout from the restraint of the stage. But it's still white hot with bitterness, resentment and rancid randiness as north London butcher Paul Rogers makes mincement of his family (Cyril Cusack, Ian Holm, Michael Jayston, Terence Rigby) while Vivien Merchant flaunts her high-tease power to stunning effect. Pinter's dialogue has never been so enigmatic, menacing or comic. TH DVD

Cyril Cusack *Sam* • Ian Holm *Lenny* • Michael Jayston *Teddy* • Vivien Merchant *Ruth* • Terence Rigby *Joey* • Paul Rogers *Max* ■ *Dir* Peter Hall • *Scr* Harold Pinter, from his play

Homecoming ★★★ U

Drama 1996 · US · Colour · 100mins

Distinguished actress Anne Bancroft won praise for her portrayal of a crotchety grandmother in this sentimental TV movie. When their mother abandons them in a strange city, teenager Kimberlee Peterson and her three younger siblings are forced to begin a difficult journey in search of a home. They embark on a 500-mile trek that leads them to the cantankerous grandmother they never knew. Up-and-coming star Peterson more than holds her own opposite the imposing Bancroft. MC DVD

Anne Bancroft *Abigail "Ab" Tillerman* • Kimberlee Peterson *Dicey Tillerman* • Trever O'Brien *James Tillerman* • Hanna Hall *Maybeth Tillerman* • William Greenblatt *Sammy Tillerman* • Bonnie Bedelia *Eunice* • Anna Louise Richardson *Liza Tillerman* ■ *Dir* Mark Jean • *Scr* Christopher Carlson, Mark Jean, from the novel by Cynthia Voigt

Homegrown ★★★ 18

Comedy drama 1998 · US · Colour · 97mins

A Cheech and Chong movie for the Tarantino generation? Not exactly, but this tale of reefer madness does have the same sharp turns from hilarity to horror, plus a starry, eclectic supporting cast who pop up with atypical characterisations. After the brutal murder of their drug dealer boss, drug harvesters Billy Bob Thornton, Hank Azaria and Ryan Phillippe decide to carry on as normal and keep the profits for themselves. The "Class A" cast and the ensuing twists and turns bring a lively buzz to proceedings. JC. Contains swearing and drug abuse. [video]

Billy Bob Thornton *Jack* • Hank Azaria *Carter* • Kelly Lynch *Lucy* • Ryan Phillippe *Harlan* • John Lithgow *Malcolm/Robert* • Jon Bon Jovi *Danny* • Jamie Lee Curtis *Sierra Kahan* • Judge Reinhold *Policeman* • Ted Danson *Gianni* ■ *Dir* Stephen Gyllenhaal • *Scr* Stephen Gyllenhaal, Nicholas Kazan, from a story by Stephen Gyllenhaal, Jonah Raskin

Homeless to Harvard: the Liz Murray Story ★★★

Drama based on a true story
2003 · US · Colour · 95mins

Thora Birch was nominated for an Emmy for her performance in this true-story drama. Born into an impoverished Bronx family, Liz Murray spent much of her early life in squalid housing or public hostels. Her father was a drug addict, and her mother was schizophrenic, legally blind and HIV-positive. However, at the age of 15, Murray turned her life around and eventually won a scholarship to Harvard. Director Peter Levin lays on the melodrama, but Birch manages to convey Murray's spirit, while Kelly Lynch impresses as her mother. DP. Contains drug abuse.

Thora Birch *Liz Murray* • Kelly Lynch *Jean Murray* • Michael Riley *Peter Murray* • Ellen Page *Young Lisa* • Liz Murray *Social worker* ■ *Dir* Peter Levin • *Scr* Ronni Kern

Homer ★★

Drama 1970 · US · Colour · 90mins

Liberal helpings of sex, drugs and rock 'n' roll – everything stereotypical of late 1960s America – is thrown into this jumble. All the themes had already been thoroughly explored by the time John Trent's film about the young generation was released, though there is a decent soundtrack which includes Led Zeppelin, Cream and the Byrds. NF

Don Scardino *Homer Edwards* • Alex Nicol *Mr Edwards* • Tisa Farrow *Laurie Grainger* • Lenka Peterson *Mrs Edwards* • Ralph Endersby *Hector* • Trudy Young *Sally* • Arch McDonnell *Mr Grainger* • Jan Campbell *Mrs Grainger* ■ *Dir* John Trent • *Scr* Claude Harz, from a story by Claude Harz, Matt Clark

Homer and Eddie ★★ 15

Road movie 1989 · US · Colour · 95mins

James Belushi co-stars with Whoopi Goldberg in this mediocre road movie, in which a con artist (Goldberg) who takes a mentally handicapped man (Belushi) across country so he can visit his dying father. In the right hands, this could have been so much better, but director Andrei Konchalovsky blunders at every turn. JB [video]

James Belushi *Homer Lanza* • Whoopi Goldberg *Eddie Cervi* • Anne Ramsey *Edna* • Karen Black *Belle* • Beah Richards *Linda Cervi* ■ *Dir* Andrei Konchalovsky • *Scr* Patrick Cirillo

Hometown USA ★★ 15

Comedy 1979 · US · Colour · 92mins

The son of a world heavyweight champion and known to millions as Jethro in *The Beverly Hillbillies*, Max Baer Jr made his third outing as a director with this predictable paean to the days when rebels didn't have causes and cars were used exclusively for parking and "chickie" runs. The period trappings may be overly familiar, the direction occasionally slipshod and the humour decidedly on the coarse side, but there are amusing moments along the way as David Wilson and Brian Kerwin try to help Gary Springer improve his luck with girls, only to end up dating them themselves. DP [video]

Gary Springer *Rodney C Duckworth* • David Wilson *Recil Calhoun* • Brian Kerwin *TJ Swackhammer* • Pat Delaney *Marilyn* ■ *Dir* Max Baer Jr • *Scr* Jesse Vint

Homeward Bound: the Incredible Journey ★★★ U

Adventure 1993 · US · Colour · 84mins

It seemed invidious to remake the 1963 Disney true-life adventure classic *The Incredible Journey*, especially with talking animals. But while the original remains the superior picture, this is still a treat for children, thanks to the astonishing performances of its animal cast. The vocal talents of Michael J Fox, Sally Field and Don Ameche certainly help pep up the pets' personalities, although you expect more of a screenwriter like Caroline Thompson than a series of playground-level wisecracks. Nevertheless, good family fare. DP [video] DVD

Michael J Fox *Chance* • Sally Field *Sassy* • Don Ameche *Shadow* • Kim Greist *Laura* • Robert Hays *Bob* • Benj Thall *Peter* • Veronica Lauren *Hope* • Kevin Chevalia *Jamie* ■ *Dir* Duwayne Dunham • *Scr* Caroline Thompson, Linda Wolverton, from the film *The Incredible Journey* by James Algar, from the novel by Sheila Burnford

Homeward Bound II: Lost in San Francisco ★★ U

Adventure 1996 · US · Colour · 85mins

This sequel opens with an airport mix-up resulting in an accidental abandonment. However, with Shadow and Sassy to help him, Chance isn't alone for long. Romance is in the air as our heroic trio are befriended by a pack of street dogs. Ralph Waite replaces the late Don Ameche as the sagacious Shadow, but not all the casting is as felicitous: the decision to have strays voiced by African-American actors has unfortunate racist overtones. DP [video] DVD

Michael J Fox *Chance* • Sally Field *Sassy* • Ralph Waite *Shadow* • Robert Hays *Bob* • Kim Greist *Laura* • Veronica Lauren *Hope* ■ *Dir* David R Ellis • *Scr* Chris Hauty, from a story by Chris Hauty, Julie Hickson, from characters created by Sheila Burnford

Homework ★★★★

Documentary 1989 · Iran · Colour · 85mins

This is a fascinating documentary insight into the workings of the Iranian education system from Abbas Kiarostami, the former illustrator who established the film department at Iran's Institute for the Intellectual Development of Children and Young Adults. There, he began a relationship with film and culture that has given rise to comparisons with Satyajit Ray and Eric Rohmer. Here, as various stressed schoolboys tell their stories, it becomes clear that Kiarostami has made an astute study into the nature of childhood, in a country where many parents are illiterate and children are forced to play their part in providing for the family. DP. In Farsi with English subtitles.

Dir Abbas Kiarostami

Homicidal ★★★ 12

Horror 1961 · US · BW · 87mins

William Castle's grisly gender-switch thriller was the first and most obvious *Psycho* clone (some contemporary critics even preferred it to the Hitchcock classic), taking transvestite terror to its illogical conclusion. A weird tale of decapitations, delirious dementia and dysfunctional drag, time has watered down Castle's sneaky surprises and tongue-in-cheek denouement. But, while you won't need his fun "Fright Break" – 45 seconds to leave the cinema if too nervous to cope with the climax – Castle's prowess at powerhouse panic still rustles up some scares. AJ [video]

Glenn Corbett *Karl* • Patricia Breslin *Miriam Webster* • Jean Arless [Joan Marshall] *Emily/Warren* • Eugenie Leontovich *Helga* • Alan Bunce *Dr Jonas* • Richard Rust *Jim Nesbitt* ■ *Dir* William Castle • *Scr* Robb White

Homicide ★★★★ 15

Crime thriller 1991 · US · Colour · 96mins

David Mamet's third outing as writer/director is a tough look at racial prejudice inside and outside the police force. Mamet's roots as a playwright are evident in some scenes, but there's no denying the power of the whole piece as Joe Mantegna's Jewish cop investigates murder and a drug cartel, and finds organised anti-Semitism and an underground Jewish resistance movement. Its conclusions are bleak, yet reaching them makes for absorbing viewing. AT. Contains violence and swearing. [video] DVD

Joe Mantegna *Bob Gold* • William H Macy *Tim Sullivan* • Natalija Nogulich *Chava* • Ving Rhames *Randolph* • Vincent Guastaferro *Lieutenant Senna* • Rebecca Pidgeon *Ms Klein* ■ *Dir/Scr* David Mamet

L'Homme de Ma Vie ★★★ 15

Drama 1992 · Fr/Can · Colour · 98mins

Many viewers will only have come across the Portuguese actress Maria de Medeiros in Philip Kaufman's *Henry and June* or Quentin Tarantino's *Pulp Fiction*. However, this amusing adult comedy from Jean-Charles Tacchella affords her the chance to demonstrate the talent that had long since established her as a top European star. As the flighty 20-something searching for the rich man of her dreams, she is both kittenish and capricious, greeting each heartbreak with a shrug and a new dress. The action sags briefly, but Tacchella mostly keeps things light. DP. In French with English subtitles. [video]

Maria de Medeiros *Aimée* • Thierry Fortineau *Maurice* • Jean-Pierre Bacri *Malcolm* • Anne Letourneau *Catherine* • Ginette Garcin *Arlette* ■ *Dir/Scr* Jean-Charles Tacchella

L'Homme du Train ★★★★ 12

Black comedy drama
2002 · Fr/UK/Ger/Jpn · Colour · 86mins

Male bonding has been a recurring theme throughout director Patrice Leconte's career, but he's never handled the subject with such wit, sensitivity and insight as in this superb two-hander. The key to its success is the easy rapport between Jean Rochefort's retired teacher and Johnny Hallyday's taciturn thief, as they contemplate heart surgery and a bank robbery, respectively. A whiff of chauvinism pervades the subplots, but mostly the atmosphere is one of late-life regret tinged with a wistful envy for each other's lifestyle. Rochefort is typically mischievous, but the revelation is Hallyday who lowers his guard of Gallic cool to reveal genuine vulnerability. DP. In French with English subtitles. [video] DVD

Jean Rochefort *Manesquier* • Johnny Hallyday *Milan* • Jean-François Stévenin *Luigi* • Charlie Nelson *Max* • Pascal Parmentier *Sadko* • Isabelle Petit-Jacques *Viviane* ■ *Dir* Patrice Leconte • *Scr* Claude Klotz

Un Homme et une Femme ★★★★ PG

Romantic drama
1966 · Fr · BW, Colour and Sepia · 103mins

Winner of the best foreign film Oscar and the Palme d'Or at Cannes, this teasing melodrama is one of the most famous examples of artistic triumph over adversity. The switches to sepia-tinted film stock were much applauded at the time (although they look rather flashy and trite today), but they were forced on director Claude Lelouch because he lacked the funds to shoot the picture in colour. Amid the chic cinematic trickery, Jean-Louis Trintignant and Anouk Aimée are splendid as the widowed couple teetering on the brink of romance. They would reunite in a sequel released in the UK as *A Man and a Woman: 20 Years Later*. DP. In French with English subtitles. [video] DVD

Jean-Louis Trintignant *Jean-Louis Duroc* • Anouk Aimée *Anne Gauthier* • Pierre Barouh *Pierre Gauthier* • Valérie Lagrange *Valerie Duroc* • Simone Paris *Headmistress* • Antoine Sire *Antoine Duroc* • Souad Amidou *Françoise Gauthier* • Henri Chemin *Jean-Louis's co-driver* ■ *Dir* Claude Lelouch • *Scr* Pierre Uytterhoeven, Claude Lelouch, from a story by Claude Lelouch • *Music* Francis Lai

H

Hondo ★★★ PG

Western 1953 · US · Colour · 79mins

This fine colourful western was originally made in 3-D, which explains the odd look of certain segments, notably the marvellous title sequence where John Wayne just keeps on walking off the screen and, supposedly, into the audience. Wayne, in his prime, plays a grim, buckskin-clad cavalry scout who comes across Oscar-nominated Geraldine Page and her son Lee Aaker and eventually helps them fend off some Indians. There is a strange tendency for some scenes to fade into black as though not fully completed by director John Farrow, yet this is still a mature, good-looking western. TS

John Wayne *Hondo Lane* • Geraldine Page *Angie Lowe* • Ward Bond *Buffalo* • Michael Pate *Vittoro* • James Arness *Lennie* • Rodolfo Acosta *Silva* • Leo Gordon *Ed Lowe* • Lee Aaker *Johnny* ■ *Dir* John Farrow • *Scr* James Edward Grant, from the story *The Gift of Cochise* by Louis L'Amour

H

Honest ★ 18

Crime caper 2000 · UK · Colour · 105mins

Directed by one half of the Eurythmics and starring three of the four members of All Saints, this crime caper is part vanity project, part nostalgic throwback to the kitsch excesses of the Swinging Sixties. Melanie Blatt and real-life siblings Natalie and Nicole Appleton play three East End sisters who support their stay-at-home dad (James Cosmo) by dressing up as fellas and robbing London's great and good. Atrociously acted, ineptly plotted and directed with little sense of pace, period or plausibility. NS DVD

Nicole Appleton *Gerry Chase* • Natalie Appleton *Mandy Chase* • Melanie Blatt *Jo Chase* • Peter Facinelli *Daniel Wheaton* • James Cosmo *Tommy Chase* • Jonathan Cake *Andrew Pryce-Stevens* • Corin Redgrave *Duggie Ord* ■ *Dir* David A Stewart • *Scr* David A Stewart, Dick Clement, Ian La Frenais

Honey ★★ PG

Dance drama 2003 · US · Colour · 90mins

Jessica Alba stars in this spirited urban drama, the debut feature of music-video director Bille Woodruff. Alba is the aspiring choreographer who's given a big break by a sleazy white video director, only to realise that her heart lies with the underprivileged kids she'd previously taught dance classes to. With cameos by top acts such as Tweet and Missy Elliott, there's plenty for fans of hip-hop/R&B to enjoy, even if the cautionary tale is as simplistic as it is idealistic. SF DVD

Jessica Alba *Honey Daniels* • Mekhi Phifer *Chaz* • Joy Bryant *Gina* • Lil' Romeo *Benny* • David Moscow *Michael Ellis* • Lonette McKee *Darlene Daniels* • Zachary Isaiah Williams *Raymond* ■ *Dir* Bille Woodruff • *Scr* Alonzo Brown, Kim Watson

Honey, I Blew Up the Kid ★★★ U

Comedy fantasy 1992 · US · Colour · 85mins

After nerdy scientist Rick Moranis accidentally pumps up his son into a 50ft giant, this film is reduced to a one-note romp that almost creaks to a halt. However, there is a well-sustained spirit of infectious enthusiasm, bug-eyed innocence and wild lunacy that harks back to the "creature features" of the 1950s. The central idea of a normally harmless child running amok in the adult world is strong, and Moranis is reliably goofy. JM DVD

Rick Moranis *Wayne Szalinski* • Marcia Strassman *Diane Szalinski* • Robert Oliveri *Nick Szalinski* • Daniel Shalikar *Adam Szalinski* • Joshua Shalikar *Adam Szalinski* • Lloyd Bridges *Clifford Sterling* • John Shea *Hendrickson* • Keri Russell *Mandy* • Amy O'Neill *Amy Szalinski* ■ *Dir* Randal Kleiser • *Scr* Thom Eberhardt, Peter Elbling, Garry Goodrow, from a story by Garry Goodrow, from characters created by Stuart Gordon, Brian Yuzna, Ed Naha

Honey, I Shrunk the Kids ★★★★ U

Comedy fantasy 1989 · US · Colour · 89mins

The Absent-Minded Professor meets *The Incredible Shrinking Man* in a joyous, innocuous and thrilling Walt Disney adventure that will appeal to both young and old. Rick Moranis makes you laugh long and loud as the wacky inventor whose molecular reducer shrinks his two kids, and the children next door, to the size of Tom Thumb's thumb. How they cope with giant insects and water sprinklers in their hazardous garden-turned-jungle makes for epic chills, doubling as a neat eco-learning quest in the best Disney tradition. Two sequels and a TV series followed. AJ DVD

Rick Moranis *Wayne Szalinski* • Matt Frewer *Big Russ Thompson* • Marcia Strassman *Diane Szalinski* • Kristine Sutherland *Mae Thompson* • Thomas Brown [Thomas Wilson Brown] *Little Russ Thompson* • Jared Rushton *Ron Thompson* ■ *Dir* Joe Johnston • *Scr* Ed Naha, Tom Schulman, from a story by Stuart Gordon, Brian Yuzna, Ed Naha

The Honey Pot ★★★

Comedy 1967 · UK/US/It · Colour · 150mins

Amusing if laboured, Joseph L Mankiewicz's reworking of Ben Jonson's *Volpone* came via Thomas Sterling's novel *The Evil of the Day* and Frederick Knott's play *Mr Fox of Venice*. The idea of having millionaire Rex Harrison test the loyalty of former lovers Edie Adams, Capucine and Susan Hayward by pretending to be dying is just as Jonson intended. But the intricate comedy could do without the contrived murder mystery that is unconvincingly tacked on here. Mankiewicz's dialogue has none of the original musicality and wit, yet Harrison valiantly tries to sparkle and Maggie Smith is fun as Hayward's nurse. DP

Rex Harrison *Cecil Fox* • Susan Hayward *Mrs Lone-Star Crockett Sheridan* • Cliff Robertson *William McFly* • Capucine *Princess Dominique* • Edie Adams *Merle McGill* • Maggie Smith *Sarah Watkins* • Adolfo Celi *Inspector Rizzi* ■ *Dir* Joseph L Mankiewicz • *Scr* Joseph L Mankiewicz, from the novel *The Evil of the Day* by Thomas Sterling, from the play *Mr Fox of Venice* by Frederick Knott

Honey, We Shrunk Ourselves ★★ PG

Science-fiction comedy
1997 · US · Colour · 71mins

Despite the presence of original star Rick Moranis, the concept was clearly running out of steam by the time Disney made this straight-to-video second sequel to *Honey, I Shrunk the Kids*. This time it's the adults who get downsized as Moranis, together with his wife, brother and sister-in-law, are miniaturised by his shrinking machine. The effects are fine, and director Dean Cundey (cinematographer on *Jurassic Park*), keeps the action bustling along, but it still feels old hat. JF DVD

Rick Moranis *Wayne Szalinski* • Eve Gordon *Diane Szalinski* • Robin Bartlett *Patty Szalinski* • Allison Mack *Jenny Szalinski* • Jake Richardson *Gordon Szalinski* • Bug Hall *Adam Szalinski* ■ *Dir* Dean Cundey • *Scr* Karey Kirkpatrick, Nell Scovell, Joel Hodgson, from characters created by Stuart Gordon, Brian Yuzna, Ed Naha

Honeymoon ★★

Romantic dance drama
1959 · Sp/UK · Colour · 90mins

A dancer (Ludmila Tcherina) who has sacrificed her career for marriage to a possessive husband (Anthony Steel), is drawn to return to the stage while honeymooning in Spain where the great Antonio dances. The innovative film-maker Michael Powell, unable to resist Antonio's invitation to make a film with him, came unstuck with this loosely scripted Anglo-Spanish co-production, which ends up as part travelogue, part dance film. Regarded as a rare disaster from the director of *The Red Shoes*, it nonetheless ravishes the eye and provides an opportunity to see Antonio perform his signature *zapateado*. RK

Anthony Steel *Kit* • Ludmilla Tcherina *Anna* • Antonio • Léonide Massine ■ *Dir* Michael Powell • *Scr* Michael Powell, Luis Escobar, Gregorio Martinez Sierra

Honeymoon Hotel ★★

Comedy 1964 · US · Colour · 88mins

A bachelor (Robert Morse) is stood up at the altar and decides to go on the Caribbean honeymoon anyway. In place of the bride, he takes his pal Robert Goulet (making his movie debut as a playboy salesman) and the usual romantic complications ensue. It could have been a sophisticated sex comedy in the hands of a Billy Wilder, but this farce never manages to grow up. Even Elsa Lanchester as a confused chambermaid can't save it. JG

Robert Goulet *Ross Kingsley* • Nancy Kwan *Lynn Hope* • Robert Morse *Jay Menlow* • Jill St John *Sherry* • Keenan Wynn *Mr Sampson* • Elsa Lanchester *Chambermaid* ■ *Dir* Henry Levin • *Scr* RS Allen, Harvey Bullock

Honeymoon in Vegas ★★★★ 15

Romantic comedy
1992 · US · Colour · 91mins

Nicolas Cage is in lovably dopey form here, as he finally proposes to his long-suffering girlfriend Sarah Jessica Parker (also excellent) only to see crooked gambler James Caan win her in a poker game. Director Andrew Bergman remains a much under-rated talent, and he expertly blends the classic elements of farce with a healthy dash of eccentricity to produce a delightful comedy. As Cage embarks on an epic journey to Hawaii and back to Las Vegas to reclaim his fiancée, who is gradually falling for the wealthy Caan, Bergman largely steers clear of the gloopy sentimentality that mars so many other romantic comedies. JF. Contains some swearing. DVD

Nicolas Cage *Jack Singer* • James Caan *Tommy Korman* • Sarah Jessica Parker *Betsy Nolan/Donna* • Pat Morita *Mahi* • Johnny Williams *Johnny Sandwich* • John Capodice *Sally Molars* • Anne Bancroft *Bea Singer* ■ *Dir/Scr* Andrew Bergman

The Honeymoon Killers ★★★★ 18

Crime drama based on a true story
1969 · US · BW · 102mins

A fat and lonely spinster from Alabama latches on to a Spanish-born gigolo. Posing as brother and sister, they murder elderly women for their money. Based on the real-life case of Martha Beck and Ray Fernandez, who were both executed in 1951, this cult, low-budget thriller immerses us not only in the psychology of the murderous pair, but also in the dreadful lives and trash culture of their victims. A chilling, utterly compelling picture, which François Truffaut named as one of his favourite films. AT DVD

Shirley Stoler *Martha Beck* • Tony LoBianco *Ray Fernandez* • Mary Jane Higby *Janet Fay* • Doris Roberts *Bunny* • Delphine Downing *Kip McArdle* ■ *Dir/Scr* Leonard Kastle

The Honeymoon Machine ★★ U

Comedy 1961 · US · Colour · 86mins

Naval lieutenant Steve McQueen misappropriates his ship's computer by using it to cheat at roulette in the Venice casino. However, there are three spanners in the works: admiral's daughter Brigid Bazlen, McQueen's former girlfriend Paula Prentiss and the Russians who think the Third World War is being launched. This is what passed in 1961 as a saucy Cold War comedy, but *Dr Strangelove* it isn't, and McQueen was never at his best in this sort of thing. AT

Steve McQueen *Lt Fergie Howard* • Brigid Bazlen *Julie Fitch* • Jim Hutton *Jason Eldridge* • Paula Prentiss *Pam Dunstan* • Dean Jagger *Admiral Fitch* • Jack Weston *Signalman Burford Taylor* ■ *Dir* Richard Thorpe • *Scr* George Wells, from the play *The Golden Fleecing* by Lorenzo Semple Jr

The Honeymooners ★★★★ 15

Romantic comedy
2003 · Ire/UK · Colour · 85mins

The debut feature of writer/director Karl Golden, this is a charming piece of Irish whisky-soaked whimsy that was shot on digital video in just 18 days. Jonathan Byrne plays the jilted bridegroom who flees the disaster of his wedding day and meets a waitress (Alex Reid) who is also on the run, from a relationship with a married man. Holed up in a rural retreat, their relationship begins as a frosty one, but begins to thaw even as their original partners come looking for them. The delight of this small-scale piece is in the naturalistic dialogue that plays up both comedy and character, as well as the delicately nuanced performances. TH. Contains swearing. DVD

Alex Reid *Claire* • Jonathan Byrne *David* • Justine Mitchell *Fiona* • Conor Mullen *Peter* • David Nolan *Ben* • Eamonn Hunt *Larry* • Briana Corrigan *Mary* ■ *Dir/Scr* Karl Golden

The Honeymooners ★

Comedy 2005 · US · Colour · 90mins

The classic 1950s American sitcom is updated here as an African-American comedy, and the result is a desperately feeble movie. Cedric the Entertainer plays bus-driver Ralph, who, along with his sewer-worker buddy Ed (Mike Epps), is constantly on the look out for the perfect get-rich-quick scheme. The plans always come to nothing, much to exasperation of their long suffering spouses (Gabrielle Union and Regina Hall). Featuring a very poor script, unimaginative performances and uninspiring direction, this is tedious in the extreme. GM

Cedric the Entertainer *Ralph Kramden* • Mike Epps *Ed Norton* • Gabrielle Union *Alice Kramden* • Regina Hall *Trixie Norton* • Eric Stoltz *William Davis* • Jon Polito *Kirby* • John Leguizamo *Dodge* • Carol Woods *Alice's mom* ■ *Dir* John Schultz • *Scr* Barry W Blaustein, Danny Jacobson, Don Rhymer, David Sheffield

Honeysuckle Rose ★★ 15

Drama 1980 · US · Colour · 114mins

Willie Nelson, the man who wrote *Crazy* for Patsy Cline in the 1960s, became better known in later years for his battles with the IRS over back taxes. By that time he had also embarked on a film career, and this low-key entry was an early effort. In a bold piece of casting, Nelson plays a country and western star whose love for his wife (Dyan Cannon) and son is jeopardised by his career and alcoholic excesses. A crisis looms when Amy Irving, the daughter of his friend Slim Pickens, takes up with him. FL

Willie Nelson *Buck* • Dyan Cannon *Viv* • Amy Irving *Lily* • Slim Pickens *Garland* • Joey Floyd

Jamie • Charles Levin *Sid* • Priscilla Pointer *Rosella* ■ *Dir* Jerry Schatzberg • *Scr* Carol Sobieski, William D Wittliff, John Binder, from the story *Intermezzo* by Gösta Steven, Gustaf Molander

The Honkers ★★★

Drama 1971 · US · Colour · 102mins

James Coburn plays an ageing rodeo rider who returns to his home town after a lengthy absence to discover his long-suffering wife has taken up with another man and wants a divorce. At first, Coburn approaches the theme as cautiously as if it were a bucking bronco, but eventually he comes to terms with the role and puts in a competent performance. Actor-turned-director Steve Ihnat, who died shortly after completing the film, intended it to be a thoughtful western, but his approach lacks adventure. TH. Contains swearing and drug abuse.

James Coburn *Lew Lathrop* • Lois Nettleton *Linda Lathrop* • Slim Pickens *Clete* • Anne Archer *Deborah Moon* • Richard Anderson *Royce* • Ted Eccles *Bobby Lathrop* • Ramon Bieri *Jack Ferguson* ■ *Dir* Steve Ihnat • *Scr* Steve Ihnat, Stephen Lodge

Honky Tonk ★★★

Romantic adventure
1941 · US · BW · 104mins

There was tangible on-screen chemistry between "king of the movies" Clark Gable and up-and-coming sexpot Lana Turner, and their scenes together here sizzle. The framework is an amiable adventure with Gable as a conman and Turner the judge's daughter he falls for. There's lively support from Claire Trevor and Marjorie Main, and Chill Wills is endearing as Gable's sidekick, but it all gets far too talky around the middle, and doesn't really recover. However, as a souvenir of two great Hollywood stars in their prime and as a reminder of what MGM was capable of, this will do nicely. TS

Clark Gable *Candy Johnson* • Lana Turner *Elizabeth Cotton* • Frank Morgan *Judge Cotton* • Claire Trevor *"Gold Dust" Nelson* • Marjorie Main *Mrs Varner* • Albert Dekker *Brazos Hearn* • Chill Wills *Sniper* ■ *Dir* Jack Conway • *Scr* Pandro S Berman, John Sanford

Honky Tonk Freeway ★ 15

Comedy 1981 · US · Colour · 102mins

This shambolic, unfunny farce concerns a small Florida town, desperately in need of trade, that goes to any lengths to ensure it's not to be bypassed by a new motorway. William Devane is the mayor orchestrating the tourist-catching antics, while Beau Bridges, Teri Garr and Jessica Tandy act like crazy as the trippers invade. Grotesque. TH [video]

Beau Bridges *Duane Hansen* • William Devane *Mayor Calo* • Hume Cronyn *Sherm* • Beverly D'Angelo *Carmen Shelby* • Teri Garr *Ericka* • Howard Hesseman *Snapper* • Geraldine Page *Sister Mary Clarise* • Jessica Tandy *Carol* ■ *Dir* John Schlesinger • *Scr* Edward Clinton

Honkytonk Man ★★ 15

Drama 1982 · US · Colour · 117mins

Clint Eastwood made this a family affair by featuring his son, Kyle, as the teenage nephew under the spell of an alcoholic country singer returned to rural roots. But that nepotism was as much of a mistake (Kyle's acting is not up to the demands of the role) as the idea that Eastwood himself could pass for a vocalist. He can do many things, such as produce and direct himself in this drama, but a singer he's not. This fatal flaw destabilises the whole movie. TH. Contains swearing and a sex scene. [video]

Clint Eastwood *Red Stovall* • Kyle Eastwood *Whit* • John McIntire *Grandpa* • Alexa Kenin *Marlene* • Verna Bloom *Emmy* • Matt Clark *Virgil* • Barry Corbin *Derwood Arnspriger* • Jerry Hardin *Snuffy* ■ *Dir* Clint Eastwood • *Scr* Clancy Carlile, from his novel

Honolulu ★★

Musical 1939 · US · BW · 82mins

A movie star (Robert Young) changes places with a plantation owner in Honolulu (also played by Young) and romances dancer Eleanor Powell whom he meets on board an ocean liner. Some great dancing from the accomplished Powell, a couple of lively numbers and the appearance of George Burns and Gracie Allen partially enliven this otherwise dead musical, with a forgettable score and pedestrian direction. RK

Eleanor Powell *Dorothy March* • Robert Young (1) *Brooks Mason/George Smith* • George Burns *Joe Duffy* • Gracie Allen *Millie de Grasse* • Clarence Kolb *Horace Grayson* • Jo Ann Sayers *Nurse* ■ *Dir* Edward Buzzell • *Scr* Herbert Fields, Frank Partos

Honor among Lovers ★★

Romantic comedy 1931 · US · BW · 75mins

A trifling romantic comedy, worth seeing for its always appealing stars: Claudette Colbert as the secretary wooed by playboy exec Fredric March but marrying Monroe Owlsey instead. March fires her and predicts her marriage will quickly dissolve, but changes his mind and offers them both a job. Made by Hollywood's foremost – indeed only – woman director at the time, Dorothy Arzner. AT

Claudette Colbert *Julia Traynor* • Fredric March *Jerry Stafford* • Monroe Owsley *Philip Craig* • Charles Ruggles *Monty Dunn* • Ginger Rogers *Doris Blake* • Avonne Taylor *Maybelle* • Pat O'Brien *Conroy* ■ *Dir* Dorothy Arzner • *Scr* Austin Parker, Gertrude Purcell, from the story by Austin Parker

The Honorary Consul ★★★ 18

Drama 1983 · UK · Colour · 99mins

Michael Caine gives what was hailed at the time as the performance of his life in this Graham Greene story about an alcoholic British consul in a corrupt South American backwater, who's mistakenly kidnapped only to find that nobody wants to pay the ransom for his return. Bob Hoskins makes the most of his role as a police chief, but Richard Gere, as a doctor looking for his missing father, battles with an English accent and loses. It could have been much better without John Mackenzie's stolid direction. TH. Contains swearing, sex scenes. [video]

Michael Caine *Charley Fortnum* • Richard Gere *Dr Eduardo Plarr* • Bob Hoskins *Colonel Perez* • Elpidia Carrillo *Clara* • Joaquim de Almeida *Leon* • A Martinez *Aquino* • Stephanie Cotsirilos *Marta* ■ *Dir* John Mackenzie • *Scr* Christopher Hampton, from the novel by Graham Greene

Honour among Thieves ★★★★

Crime drama 1954 · Fr/It · BW · 87mins

This brooding study of dishonour among thieves established the vogue for gangster films in 1950s France. Jean Gabin won the best actor prize at Venice for his performance as a world-weary hood on his last blag who is forced to make impossible choices when his longtime partner, René Dary, is held for ransom by ruthless rival, Lino Ventura. Director Jacques Becker stages the action efficiently enough, but his main interest lies in the dynamic that drives these luxury-loving mobsters to acts of clinical violence and guilt-free treachery. DP. In French with English subtitles.

Jean Gabin *Max* • René Dary *Riton* • Jeanne Moreau *Josy* • Dora Doll *Lola* • Lino Ventura *Angelo* • Paul Frankeur *Pierrot* ■ *Dir* Jacques Becker • *Scr* Jacques Becker, Albert Simonin, Maurice Griffe, from a novel by Albert Simonin

Hoodlum ★★ 18

Period crime drama
1997 · US · Colour · 124mins

Laurence Fishburne had a supporting role in 1984's *The Cotton Club*, as a black gangster fighting Dutch Schultz's attempts to take over the Harlem numbers racket. Here the same bloody story takes centre stage, with Fishburne again refusing to bow down to Schultz, played by Tim Roth in foul-mouthed, psychopathic form. Andy Garcia is crime boss Lucky Luciano, pondering which side of the fence to sit on. Fishburne is as charismatic as ever, but the script takes some swallowing, while director Bill Duke takes an age to get the action pumping. JF. Contains violence and some swearing. [video] DVD

Laurence Fishburne *Ellsworth "Bumpy" Johnson* • Tim Roth *Dutch Schultz* • Vanessa L Williams *Francine Hughes* • Andy Garcia *Lucky Luciano* • Cicely Tyson *Stephanie "Queen" St Clair* • Clarence Williams III *Bub Hewlett* ■ *Dir* Bill Duke • *Scr* Chris Brancato

Hoodlum Empire ★★

Crime drama 1952 · US · BW · 97mins

This nickel-and-dime gangster picture was knocked out quickly by Republic Studios following the 1950 report by the Senate Crime Investigating Committee. Chaired by Senator Este Kefauver, the report not only exposed organised crime, but also severely criticised Hollywood violence and its glamorisation of criminals. Accordingly, the film takes pains to establish its serious credentials and moral strength as Brian Donlevy digs deep into the syndicate's dark secrets. AT

Brian Donlevy *Senator Bill Stephens* • Forrest Tucker *Charley Pignatalli* • Claire Trevor *Connie Williams* • Vera Ralston *Marthe Dufour* • Luther Adler *Nick Mancani* • John Russell *Joe Gray* • Gene Lockhart *Senator Tower* • Grant Withers *Rev Andrews* ■ *Dir* Joseph Kane • *Scr* Bruce Manning, Bob Considine

The Hoodlum Priest ★★★

Drama 1961 · US · BW · 102mins

Don Murray produced and pseudonymously co-wrote this social problem picture and stars as the Jesuit priest who helps juvenile delinquents and ex-cons by establishing halfway houses for them. One of these rehabilitating hoodlums, Keir Dullea, does well until he gets trapped into robbery and murder. The blend of piety and profanity is often hard to take, though Dullea is excellent in his screen debut and Murray's commitment is obvious. AT

Don Murray *Rev Charles Dismas Clark* • Cindi Wood *Ellen Henley* • Larry Gates *Louis Rosen* • Keir Dullea *Billy Lee Jackson* • Logan Ramsey *George Hale* • Don Joslyn *Pio Gentile* • Sam Capuano *Mario Mazziotti* ■ *Dir* Irvin Kershner • *Scr* Don Deer [Don Murray], Joseph Landon

The Hoodlum Saint ★

Comedy drama 1946 · US · BW · 91mins

This disjointed comedy drama with a religious angle is one of the few real duds of William Powell's long stay at MGM. He appears as a disillusioned First World War veteran who carves out a fortune for himself but disappoints the girl he loves, played by Esther Williams (who should never have left the water). Powell tells old friends in need of help to appeal to St Dismas, the "hoodlum saint", but then his own luck runs out. AE

William Powell *Terry Ellerton O'Neill* • Esther Williams *May Lorrison* • Angela Lansbury *Dusty Millard* • James Gleason *Sharp* • Lewis Stone *Father Nolan* ■ *Dir* Norman Taurog • *Scr* Frank Wead, James Hill

The Hook ★★

War drama 1962 · US · Colour · 97mins

At the end of the Korean War, three GIs rescue a North Korean from the sea and are ordered to execute him. A thought-provoking situation – the ethics involved in the difference between soldiers killing on the battlefield and face-to-face execution – is weighed down by endless debate and contrived circumstances. But the performances from Kirk Douglas, Nick Adams and Robert Walker Jr (here making his screen debut) are suitably powerful. RB

Kirk Douglas *Sergeant PJ Briscoe* • Robert Walker Jr *Private OA Dennison* • Nick Adams *Private VR Hackett* • Enrique Magalona *"The gook", prisoner* • Nehemiah Persoff *Captain Van Ryn* ■ *Dir* George Seaton • *Scr* Henry Denker, from the novel *L'Hameçon* by Vahé Katcha

Hook ★★★ U

Fantasy adventure
1991 · US · Colour · 135mins

In Steven Spielberg's take on *Peter Pan*, Robin Williams is the grown-up Peter, a ruthless business pirate who has no time for his family and no memory of his magical past. That changes, however, when his children are kidnapped and he gets a visit from Tinkerbell (Julia Roberts). As good as Williams is, the film is stolen by an almost unrecognisable Dustin Hoffman, whose Hook is suitably pantomimic yet oddly sympathetic. Although the sentimentality gets a little sticky at times, this remains rousing entertainment. JF [video] DVD

Dustin Hoffman *Captain James Hook* • Robin Williams *Peter Banning/Peter Pan* • Julia Roberts *Tinkerbell* • Bob Hoskins *Smee* • Maggie Smith *Granny Wendy* • Caroline Goodall *Moira Banning* • Charlie Korsmo *Jack* • Phil Collins *Inspector Good* • Gwyneth Paltrow *Young Wendy* ■ *Dir* Steven Spielberg • *Scr* Jim V Hart, Malia Scotch Marmo, from a story by Jim V Hart, Nick Castle, from characters created by JM Barrie • *Music* John Williams • *Art Director* Norman Garwood • *Set Designer* Garrett Lewis • *Costume Designer* Anthony Powell

Hook, Line and Sinker ★★ U

Comedy 1969 · US · Colour · 87mins

Things turned sour for Jerry Lewis following the hit comedy *The Disorderly Orderly* (1964), as his later films were a motley bunch of misfires. *Hook, Line and Sinker* falls into this category. Lewis plays a man who finds out he is dying and goes on a globe-trotting spending spree, only to discover later that the diagnosis was wrong. Hugely in debt, he then decides to fake his own death. An unusually mean-spirited film that highlights the difficulty directors had in catching the Lewis genius. He was always at his best when directing himself. DF [video]

Jerry Lewis *Peter Ingersoll/Fred Dobbs* • Peter Lawford *Dr Scott Carter* • Anne Francis *Nancy Ingersoll* • Pedro Gonzalez-Gonzales *Perfecto* • Jimmy Miller *Jimmy* • Jennifer Edwards *Jennifer* ■ *Dir* George Marshall • *Scr* Rod Amateau, from a story by David Davis, Rod Amateau

Hoop Dreams ★★★★★ 12

Sports documentary
1994 · US · Colour · 171mins

American basketball films may not be the most riveting entertainment for the average British viewer. However, this three-hour documentary – cut down from 250 hours of footage – that follows the fortunes of two inner city Chicago kids whose only way out is through basketball, packs an enormous emotional punch. Film-maker

Steve James not only displays an impassioned commitment to these central characters and their desires but also lays them bare so that our empathy is fully engaged. An often simple subject which is full of riches. JM. Contains swearing. DVD

Dir Steve James (2) • *Scr* Steve James, Fred Marx, Peter Gilbert • *Cinematographer* Peter Gilbert

Hooper ★★★★ PG

Action comedy 1978 · US · Colour · 95mins

One of the best movies to exploit Burt Reynolds's brand of wise-guy charm, in which he's an over-the-hill stuntman determined to become a legend by completing a final outrageous feat – a record-breaking leap across a collapsed bridge in a jet-fuelled car. All this to convince young rival Jan-Michael Vincent, doubtful girlfriend Sally Field and obnoxious film-maker Robert Klein of his greatness. The director, Hal Needham, was himself a former stuntman, which may explain why there are so many chariot rides, helicopter jumps and barroom brawls. TH. Contains some swearing.

Burt Reynolds *Sonny Hooper* • Jan-Michael Vincent *Ski* • Sally Field *Gwen* • Brian Keith *Jocko* • John Marley *Max Berns* • Robert Klein *Roger Deal* • James Best *Cully* • Adam West *Adam* ■ *Dir* Hal Needham • *Scr* Thomas Rickman [Tom Rickman], Bill Kerby, from a story by Walt Green, Walter S Herndon

Hooray for Love ★★

Musical 1935 · US · BW · 75mins

This minor musical only really comes to life when Bill Robinson tapdances his way onto the screen supported by Fats Waller and others. Gene Raymond stars as the rich college kid who sinks all his wealth into a stage show starring the girl he loves, played by Ann Sothern. Lionel Stander is amusing as a Russian orchestra conductor while Thurston Hall is seen starting an active period as a Hollywood character actor after being off screen since the early 1920s. AE

Ann Sothern *Pat* • Gene Raymond *Doug* • Bill Robinson *Bill* • Thurston Hall *Commodore* • Pert Kelton *Trixie* • Georgia Caine *Duchess* • Lionel Stander *Chowsky* ■ *Dir* Walter Lang • *Scr* Lawrence Hazard, Ray Harris, from a story by Marc Lachmann

Hoosiers ★★★★ PG

Sports drama 1986 · US · Colour · 115mins

A story about a former army man, played with great swagger and insight by Gene Hackman, who is invited by a friend and high-school principal to train the school's basketball team. And while Hackman's turning the team around, he also gets to work on the town drunk, Dennis Hopper, and fellow teacher Barbara Hershey. Set in 1951, it's a finely drawn study of postwar American mores, evocatively scored by Jerry Goldsmith and sharply directed by first-timer David Anspaugh. Also known as *Best Shot* in the UK. AT DVD

Gene Hackman *Norman Dale* • Barbara Hershey *Myra Fleener* • Dennis Hopper *Shooter* • Sheb Wooley *Cletus Summers* • Fern Persons *Opal Fleener* • Maris Valainis *Jimmy Chitwood* • Brad Boyle *Whit* • Steve Hollar *Rade* • Brad Long *Buddy* ■ *Dir* David Anspaugh • *Scr* Angelo Pizzo

Hoover Street Revival ★★ 15

Documentary 2002 · UK/Fr · Colour · 99mins

Sophie Fiennes barely scratches the surface in this disappointing digi-video portrait of Bishop Noel Jones, the brother of actress-singer Grace Jones, whose charismatic ministry attracts a weekly congregation of more than a thousand to the Greater Bethany Community Church in the deprived Watts district of Los Angeles. Aerial shots of the sprawling neighbourhood offer little insight into the social problems endured by its inhabitants or how Jones and his pastoral team operate among them – other than to sell videos of his grandstanding sermons. Fiennes's fragmentary approach keeps her subject and his flock at a distance. DP DVD

Dir/Scr Sophie Fiennes

Hopalong Cassidy ★★

Western 1935 · US · BW · 60mins

The first of a series of westerns that ran for nearly 20 years on film and television in which former silent star William Boyd established a new career as Hopalong Cassidy, the silver-haired knight of the range. Bill Cassidy is shot in the leg during this bland story of feuding ranchers and rustlers and a nickname is born. Jimmy (later James) Ellison appears as his young screen partner for the first of eight times. AE

William Boyd (1) *Bill "Hopalong" Cassidy* • Jimmy Ellison [James Ellison] *Johnny Nelson* • Paula Stone *Mary Meeker* • Robert Warwick *Jim Meeker* • Charles Middleton *Buck Peters* • Frank McGlynn Jr *Red Connors* ■ *Dir* Howard Bretherton • *Scr* Doris Schroeder, Harrison Jacobs, from the novel by Clarence E Mulford

Hope and Glory ★★★★★ 15

Second World War drama 1987 · UK · Colour · 107mins

War may be hell if you're a grown-up, but it's a wheeze if you're nine years old and living in suburban London during the Blitz. Anyway, that's how it looks to the young hero of director John Boorman's whimsical, funny, nostalgic, semi-autobiographical memoir of family life in the Second World War. Sebastian Rice-Edwards gives an extraordinarily confident performance in the lead role, and he's matched by Geraldine Muir, playing his five-year-old sister. Sammi Davis as their rebellious elder sibling, meanwhile, gives a poignant portrayal of the teenager caught between sexual awakening and the savage truths of the day. The film is on the episodic side, and Sarah Miles and Ian Bannen might both have toned down their eccentric portrayals a notch, but these are minor quibbles in a delightful movie. PF. Contains swearing.

Sebastian Rice-Edwards *Bill Rohan* • Geraldine Muir *Sue Rohan* • Sarah Miles *Grace Rohan* • David Hayman *Clive Rohan* • Sammi Davis *Dawn Rohan* • Susan Wooldridge *Molly* • Jean-Marc Barr *Bruce* • Ian Bannen *Grandfather George* ■ *Dir/Scr* John Boorman • *Cinematographer* Philippe Rousselot

Hope Floats ★★ PG

Romance 1998 · US · Colour · 109mins

Sandra Bullock stars as Birdee, who finds out via a Ricki Lake-style talk show that her husband has been unfaithful. So she decides to return to the small home town where she was once a beauty queen to get over the pain, with her mother (a wonderful Gena Rowlands) and young daughter at her side. There's far too much moping and sobbing, but director Forest Whitaker makes the scenes of budding romance (with Harry Connick Jr) amusing. JB. Contains some swearing and sexual references. DVD

Sandra Bullock *Birdee Pruitt* • Harry Connick Jr *Justin Matisse* • Gena Rowlands *Ramona Calvert* • Mae Whitman *Bernice Pruitt* • Michael Paré *Bill Pruitt* • Cameron Finley *Travis* • Kathy Najimy *Toni Post* • Bill Cobbs *Nurse* • Rosanna Arquette *Connie* ■ *Dir* Forest Whitaker • *Scr* Steven Rogers

Hope Springs ★★ 12

Romantic comedy 2002 · UK/US · Colour · 88mins

Little Voice director Mark Herman takes a stab at a "traditional" relationship movie – and fails miserably – with this lazy and spark-free romantic comedy. A by-the-numbers exercise, this stars Colin Firth as a sensitive English artist who heads to the small US town of Hope to mend his broken heart after he is betrayed by brittle fiancée Minnie Driver. There he finds more than a shoulder to cry on in the shape of free-spirited nurse Heather Graham. The film simply shambles along, hampered by limp direction. SF DVD

Colin Firth *Colin Ware* • Heather Graham *Mandy* • Minnie Driver *Vera* • Oliver Platt *Doug Reed* • Frank Collison *Fisher* • Mary Steenburgen *Joanie Fisher* • Mary Black *Mrs Peterson* • Ken Kramer *Mr Peterson* ■ *Dir* Mark Herman • *Scr* Mark Herman, from the novel *New Cardiff* by Charles Webb

Hoppity Goes to Town ★★ Uc

Animated musical comedy 1941 · US · Colour · 74mins

Partially inspired by Frank Capra's *Mr Deeds Goes to Town*, this was one of the first animated features not to be based on a classic children's fable. However, the weakness in the storyline was to prove the film's undoing. Neither Hoppity the grasshopper's battle with the villainous C Bagley Beetle for the attentions of the drippy Honey Bee nor the insect colony's need to find new lodgings are enchanting enough to fire the imagination or hold the attention. The artwork is pleasing, but the voiceovers are as feeble as the songs. DP

Kenny Gardner *Dick* • Gwen Williams *Mary* • Jack Mercer *Mr Bumble/Swat the Fly* • Ted Pierce *C Bagley Beetle* • Stan Freed *Hoppity* • Pauline Loth *Honey Bee* • Guinn "Big Boy" Williams *Narrator* ■ *Dir* David Fleischer [Dave Fleischer] • *Scr* David Fleischer, Dan Gordon, Isidore Sparber, William Turner, Mike Meyer, Graham Place, Bob Wickersham, Cal Howard • *Music/lyrics* Hoagy Carmichael, Frank Loesser

Hopscotch ★★★ 15

Spy comedy 1980 · US · Colour · 100mins

CIA operative Walter Matthau takes revenge for being demoted to a desk job by leaking his memoirs, chapter by chapter, to other intelligence agencies. Of course, he has to be stopped, but not before leading ex-boss Ned Beatty on a merry chase around the world. There are some splendid performances – Glenda Jackson, Herbert Lom, Sam Waterston – but it's Matthau who carries it all with his brand of serene cynicism. TH

Walter Matthau *Miles Kendig* • Glenda Jackson *Isobel von Schmidt* • Sam Waterston *Cutter* • Ned Beatty *Myerson* • Herbert Lom *Mikhail Yaskov* • David Matthau *Ross* ■ *Dir* Ronald Neame • *Scr* Brian Garfield, Bryan Forbes, from the novel by Brian Garfield

Horizons West ★★

Western 1952 · US · Colour · 80mins

Cult director Budd Boetticher needed a much bigger budget, a far better script and another hour to do justice to this story of three brothers who become rivals after the Civil War. While Rock Hudson and James Arness are content to plough their parcels of land, Robert Ryan becomes a ruthless empire builder. Julia Adams, meanwhile, is the widow caught up in their sibling rivalry. Ryan gives a decent performance, but the film lacks the scorched visuals of Boetticher's best work. AT

Robert Ryan *Dan Hammond* • Julia Adams [Julie Adams] *Lorna Hardin* • Rock Hudson *Neal Hammond* • John McIntire *Ira Hammond* • Judith Braun *Sally* • Raymond Burr *Cord Hardin* • James Arness *Tiny* • Dennis Weaver *Dandy Taylor* ■ *Dir* Budd Boetticher • *Scr* Louis Stevens

The Horizontal Lieutenant ★ U

Second World War romantic comedy 1962 · US · Colour · 90mins

This fourth co-starring vehicle for Paula Prentiss and Jim Hutton in three years is also the weakest, largely thanks to the screenplay. Richard Thorpe directs them for the second time (after 1961's *The Honeymoon Machine*) but, nearing 70, after averaging four films a year for 40 years, he seems to be treading water. Set during the Second World War and located on a Pacific Island, this so-called comedy stems from the attempt to capture a Japanese guerrilla by Hutton, who is more interested in Prentiss. BB

Jim Hutton *2d Lt Merle Wye* • Paula Prentiss *Lt Molly Blue* • Jack Carter *Lt William Monck* • Jim Backus *Cmdr Jerry Hammerslag* • Charles McGraw *Col Charles Korotny* • Miyoshi Umeki *Akiko* ■ *Dir* Richard Thorpe • *Scr* George Wells, from the novel *The Bottletop Affair* by Gordon Cotler

The Horn Blows at Midnight ★★★

Comedy 1945 · US · BW · 77mins

On his subsequent radio and television shows, comedian Jack Benny got a good deal of comic mileage from mentioning this movie to its detriment. This film is by no means as bad as Benny would have you believe: it's certainly preposterous, and grossly whimsical, but its tale of a dopey trumpeter who dreams that he's an angel dispatched to Earth and able to destroy it with one blast of his horn, is not so absurd after all. Benny himself is excellent and there's fine support, particularly a cameo from camp hotel detective Franklin Pangborn. TS

Jack Benny *Athanael* • Alexis Smith *Elizabeth* • Dolores Moran *Fran* • Allyn Joslyn *Osidro* • Reginald Gardiner *Archie Dexter* • Guy Kibbee *The Chief* • John Alexander *Doremus* • Franklin Pangborn *Sloan* • Margaret Dumont *Miss Rodholder* • Bobby Blake [Robert Blake] *Junior* ■ *Dir* Raoul Walsh • *Scr* Sam Hellman, James V Kern, from an idea by Aubrey Wisberg

The Hornet's Nest ★★ U

Crime comedy 1955 · UK · BW · 64mins

This is a slight comedy from the days of double-bills when a second feature could be brief. June Thorburn and Marla Landi play Pat and Terry, two models who get more than they bargained for when they set up home on a barge. Unbeknown to them, a jewel thief has hidden his ill-gotten gains on board and is determined to get the goods back at all cost. DF

Paul Carpenter *Bob Bartlett* • June Thorburn *Pat* • Marla Landi *Terry Savarese* • Charles Farrell *Posh Peterson* • Larry Burns *Alfie* ■ *Dir* Charles Saunders • *Scr* Allan Mackinnon, from a story by John Roddick

Hornet's Nest ★★

Second World War drama 1970 · US · Colour · 109mins

Rock Hudson stars as an American paratrooper who leads a group of Italian children against a dam controlled by the Nazis. No bouncing bombs here, just layers of cuteness and a superfluous love interest in the shape of Italian sex siren Sylva Koscina who plays a German nurse. The idea that kids can become killers with a moral purpose hardly figures in the script, while the direction barely conceals the improbabilities. Nice scenery, though. AT

Rock Hudson *Captain Turner* • Sylva Koscina *Bianca* • Mark Colleano *Aldo* • Sergio Fantoni von Hecht • Jacques Sernas *Major Taussig* • Giacomo Rossi Stuart *Schwalberg* ■ *Dir* Phil Karlson • *Scr* SS Schweitzer, from a story by SS Schweitzer, Stanley Colbert

The Horrible Dr Hichcock ★★ 18

Horror 1962 · It · Colour · 83mins

One of two Italian horror films (the other is *The Spectre*) featuring the eponymous British surgeon. This one was originally released in the UK, heavily cut, as *The Terror of Dr Hichcock*. Reputedly in homage to Hammer, storms rage, mists swirl and doors creak as Dr H's new bride is haunted by the ghost of his first wife. The casual viewer will find it all preposterous, but cultists revere this as one of the most stylish works of director Riccardo Freda. DM. Italian dialogue dubbed into English. [video]

Robert Flemyng *Dr Bernard Hichcock* • Barbara Steele *Cynthia* • Teresa Fitzgerald [Maria Teresa Vianello] *Margaret* • Harriet White [Harriet Medin] *Martha* • Montgomery Glenn *Dr Kurt Lowe* ■ *Dir* Robert Hampton [Riccardo Freda] • *Scr* Julyan Perry [Ernesto Gastaldi]

Horror Express ★★★ 15

Horror 1972 · UK/Sp · Colour · 83mins

In this rattlingly good chiller set on the Trans-Siberian railway at the turn of the last century, what is believed to be a frozen Missing Link starts to revive in the presence of classic horror movie stars Peter Cushing and Christopher Lee, here playing rival anthropologists. The suspense is kept to a maximum by the clever and beautifully timed editing of Robert Dearberg. Director Eugenio (Gene) Martin is unable to control Telly Savalas, who chews the scenery as the leader of a group of Cossacks. Shame. TS [video] DVD

Christopher Lee *Prof Alexander Saxton* • Peter Cushing *Dr Wells* • Telly Savalas *Kazan* • Silvia Tortosa *Irina* • Alberto de Mendoza *Inspector* ■ *Dir* Eugenio Martin • *Scr* Armand D'Usseau, Julian Halevey [Julian Zimet], from a story by Eugenio Martin

Horror Hospital ★★ 18

Comedy horror 1973 · US · Colour · 88mins

Combining audience preoccupations with medicine and terror, director Antony Balch attempts to spoof the usual horror contents by taking them so far over the edge that they self-destruct. There's a Rolls-Royce with scythes, belligerent bikers and, of course, a burns-scarred mad scientist, plus Robin Askwith as an aspiring rock musician seeking a rest cure. The result is an almost unwatchable mess, but try to stay the course: the psychological subtext is fascinating. TH. Contains some swearing. [video]

Michael Gough *Dr Storm* • Robin Askwith *Jason Jones* • Vanessa Shaw *Judy Peters* • Ellen Pollock *Aunt Harris* • Skip Martin *Frederick* • Dennis Price *Mr Pollack* ■ *Dir* Antony Balch • *Scr* Antony Balch, Alan Watson

Horror of Dracula ★★★★★ 15

Classic horror 1958 · UK · Colour · 77mins

Bram Stoker's terrifying vampire creation becomes a modern classic in the adept hands of the House of Hammer. The film was epoch-making in its impact, due to the fabulous Gothic atmosphere, Terence Fisher's stylish direction and the fact that the undead tale was shot in vivd, gory colour for the first time. Christopher Lee's interpretation of Dracula is astonishingly fresh, heroic and powerful, while Peter Cushing makes an ideal Van Helsing. The latter's climactic battle with his blood-sucking nemesis is justly acclaimed as a magic movie moment in the history of the horror genre. AJ [video] DVD

Peter Cushing *Van Helsing* • Michael Gough *Arthur Holmwood* • Melissa Stribling *Mina Holmwood* • Christopher Lee *Count Dracula* • Carol Marsh *Lucy Holmwood* • John Van Eyssen *Jonathan Harker* • Miles Malleson *Marx, the undertaker* ■ *Dir* Terence Fisher • *Scr* Jimmy Sangster, from the novel by Bram Stoker

The Horror of Frankenstein ★★ 12

Horror 1970 · UK · Colour · 91mins

Ralph Bates is no substitute for Peter Cushing in Hammer's feeble attempt to remake their classic *The Curse of Frankenstein*. He overplays the doctor as ridiculously evil in this throwaway comic variation, while David Prowse is no replacement for Christopher Lee as the Monster. There's little subtlety, and the accent is on black humour in this very lowbrow entry. Happily, Cushing reprised his role in the series finale, 1973's *Frankenstein and the Monster from Hell*. AJ. [video] DVD

Ralph Bates *Victor Frankenstein* • Kate O'Mara *Alys* • Graham James *Wilhelm* • Veronica Carlson *Elizabeth* • Bernard Archard *Elizabeth's father* • Dennis Price *Grave robber* • Joan Rice *Grave robber's wife* • David Prowse [Dave Prowse] *Monster* ■ *Dir* Jimmy Sangster • *Scr* Jimmy Sangster, Jeremy Burnham, from characters created by Mary Shelley

Horrors of the Black Museum ★★★ 15

Horror 1959 · UK/US · Colour · 78mins

This infamously lurid horror begins with one of the most memorably vicious shocks of the 1950s fear-era – a girl unwrapping a gift of binoculars, looking through and having her eyes gouged by two spring-loaded metal spikes. Michael Gough stars as the arrogant crime book author who hypnotises his assistant into committing horrendous homicides to satisfy his readers' demands for gruesome detail. A tawdry catalogue of tortures, purple dialogue and risible acting (wooden Shirley Anne Field), this crudely effective melodrama is a British exploitation classic. AJ. Contains violence. [video] DVD

Michael Gough *Edmond Bancroft* • June Cunningham *Joan Berkley* • Graham Curnow *Rick* • Shirley Anne Field *Angela* • Geoffrey Keen *Superintendent Graham* • Gerald Andersen *Dr Ballan* • John Warwick *Inspector Lodge* • Beatrice Varley *Aggie* • Austin Trevor *Commissioner Wayne* ■ *Dir* Arthur Crabtree • *Scr* Aben Kandel, Herman Cohen

Hors la Vie ★★★★ 15

Biographical drama
1991 · Fr/It/Bel · Colour · 93mins

Based on the real-life experiences of Roger Auque, this compelling drama provides a graphic insight into the plight of the political hostage, with Hippolyte Girardot magnificent in the role of the abducted French photographer. Lebanese director Maroun Bagdadi expertly conveys the claustrophobia, uncertainty and sheer terror of being at the mercy of people willing to kill for their cause. Yet he wisely avoids presenting the captors as inhuman fanatics, while also resisting the temptation to justify their actions with long tracts of rhetorical propaganda. DP. In French and Arabic with English subtitles. [video]

Hippolyte Girardot *Patrick Perrault* • Rafic Ali Ahmad *Walid, "Chief"* • Hussein Sbeity *Omar* • Habib Hammoud *Ali, "Philippe"* • Magdi Machmouchi *Moustaph* ■ *Dir* Maroun Bagdadi • *Scr* Maroun Bagdadi, from the non-fiction book by Roger Auque, Patrick Forestier

Horse Feathers ★★★★★ U

Comedy 1932 · US · BW · 63mins

In their penultimate movie for Paramount Pictures Groucho, Chico, Harpo and, this time around, Zeppo, display a wonderful disarray of puns, slapstick and misunderstandings as Groucho becomes head of a college that needs to win a crucial football game. Chico operates out of a speakeasy in which speech is not at all easy, while dogcatcher Harpo strums a melancholy melody. A classic which is still unmissable. TH [video] DVD

Groucho Marx *Professor Wagstaff* • Harpo Marx *Pinky* • Chico Marx *Baravelli* • Zeppo Marx *Frank* • Thelma Todd *Connie Bailey* • David Landau *Jennings* • James Pierce *Mullens* • Nat Pendleton *McCarthy* ■ *Dir* Norman Z McLeod • *Scr* Bert Kalmar, Harry Ruby, SJ Perelman

The Horse in the Gray Flannel Suit ★★ U

Comedy drama 1968 · US · Colour · 112mins

The poster line "All's fair in love and woah" gives you some idea of the quality of this strained Disney offering. The ever-willing Dean Jones is back in harness for this silly story about an advertising executive who uses his daughter's pet nag to help sell a brand of stomach pill. Even reliable director Norman Tokar fails to get the pace above a canter. Look out for a young Kurt Russell. DP [video]

Dean Jones *Fred Bolton* • Diane Baker *Suzie Clemens* • Lloyd Bochner *Archer Madison* • Fred Clark *Tom Dugan* • Ellen Janov *Helen Bolton* • Morey Amsterdam *Charlie Blake* • Kurt Russell *Ronnie Gardner* ■ *Dir* Norman Tokar • *Scr* Louis Pelletier, from the novel *The Year of the Horse* by Eric Hatch

The Horse Soldiers ★★★ PG

War drama 1959 · US · Colour · 114mins

This stirring Civil War epic was not liked on its release by fans of the great western director John Ford: it's not really a western and it seemed dramatically unconvincing. Today, however, Ford's marvellous set pieces are genuinely thrilling, and there's nostalgic value in seeing two great movie stars (John Wayne and William Holden) teamed so cleverly. The film is based on a true incident (the 1863 Grierson raid deep into the South to cut supply lines to Vicksburg), and Ford tells the tale straight. TS [video] DVD

John Wayne *Colonel John Marlowe* • William Holden (2) *Major Henry Kendall* • Constance Towers *Hannah Hunter* • Althea Gibson *Lukey* • Hoot Gibson *Brown* • Anna Lee *Mrs Buford* ■ *Dir* John Ford • *Scr* John Lee Mahin, Rackin Martin, from the novel by Harold Sinclair

Horse Thief ★★★★ PG

Drama 1986 · Chi · Colour · 86mins

Tian Zhuangzhuang combines a preoccupation with cinematic technique and his reverence for the forbidding majesty of the Tibetan plains in this stunningly photographed study of life in one of China's most marginalised communities. Yet against the harsh conditions that force Rigzin Tseshang to steal horses in order to feed his family, the film tenders the consolation provided by Buddhism and its exquisitely mystical ceremonies. Employing a range of transitional and optical devices, Tian not only reveals the relevance of religion to these hardy people, but also the importance of the cultural continuity that Beijing is so determined to suppress. DP. In Mandarin with English subtitles.

Rigzin Tseshang *Norbu* • Dan Jiji *Dolma* • Jamco Jayang *Tashi* • Gao Ba *Nowre* ■ *Dir* Tian Zhuangzhuang • *Scr* Rui Zhang

The Horse Whisperer ★★★ PG

Romantic drama
1998 · US · Colour · 162mins

Robert Redford won the Hollywood bidding war over the movie rights to British author Nicholas Evans's bestseller about a Montana cowboy who cures traumatised horses. Directing himself for the first time, Redford fits the role as snugly as those faded denims, watched glowingly by Kristin Scott Thomas. She's a New Yorker with a daughter and a horse, both disabled in a road accident. So, leaving husband Sam Neill behind, they trot off to Montana to see horse shrink Redford. The story's blend of Disney wildlife film and adult romance is bizarre and, at nearly three hours, far too long, but the Montana scenery is stunning. AT [video] DVD

Robert Redford *Tom Booker* • Kristin Scott Thomas *Annie MacLean* • Sam Neill *Robert MacLean* • Dianne Wiest *Diane Booker* • Scarlett Johansson *Grace MacLean* • Chris Cooper *Frank Booker* ■ *Dir* Robert Redford • *Scr* Eric Roth, Richard LaGravenese, from the novel by Nicholas Evans

The Horseman on the Roof ★★ 15

Period drama 1995 · Fr · Colour · 130mins

At the time the most expensive film ever made in France, Jean-Paul Rappeneau's film was too burly for the costume crowd and too deep for the slam-bang brigade. This tale of 19th-century politics and plague is full of arresting set pieces, yet there is little narrative cohesion beside the predictable course of the romance between dashing revolutionary Olivier Martinez and Juliette Binoche, the loyal wife searching for her ageing husband. DP. In French with English subtitles. Contains violence and brief nudity. [video]

Juliette Binoche *Pauline De Théus* • Olivier Martinez *Angelo* • Laura Marioni *Carla* • Paul Chevillard *Giacomo* • Richard Sammel *Franz* • Claudio Amendola *Maggionari* • Gérard Depardieu *Police Commissioner* • Jean Yanne *Door to door salesman* ■ *Dir* Jean-Paul Rappeneau • *Scr* Jean-Paul Rappeneau, Nina Companeez, Jean-Claude Carrière, from the novel by Jean Giono • *Cinematographer* Thierry Arbogast

The Horsemen ★★

Drama 1971 · US · Colour · 100mins

Buzkashi is the Afghan sport in which a headless calf's carcass is kicked about by men on horses until either someone wins (according to rules seemingly made up on the spot) or no other player is left alive. It's a natural subject for John Frankenheimer, but the lack of a story proves to be a problem. Omar Sharif and Jack Palance are the buzkashi rivals, losing leg and face respectively. AT

Omar Sharif *Uraz* • Leigh Taylor-Young *Zereh* • Jack Palance *Tursen* • David De *Mukhi* • Peter Jeffrey *Hayatal* • Mohammed Shamsi *Osaman Bey* • Saeed Jaffrey *District Chief* ■ *Dir* John Frankenheimer • *Scr* Dalton Trumbo, from a novel by Joseph Kessel

Horses and Champions ★★ U

Sports drama 1994 · US · Colour · 90mins

Timothy Bottoms stars in this run-of-the-mill melodrama. Has there ever been a movie about horses in which the rank outsider doesn't win the day? Well this efficient, but one-paced picture wasn't about to change the winning formula. Indeed, it even boasted of being a cross between *National Velvet* and *Cinderella* in its advertising campaign. DP [video]

Timothy Bottoms *Ben Choice* • Christopher Boyer *Mr Smith* • Ramsay Midwood *Ferdie* • Linda L Miller *Mrs Loveridge* • Christopher Pettiet *Joe* ■ *Dir/Scr* Jonathan Tydor

The Horse's Mouth ★★★ U

Comedy 1958 · UK · BW · 94mins

Alec Guinness earned an Oscar nomination for his droll adaptation of Joyce Cary's celebrated novel. He also

H

turns in a solid performance as Gulley Jimson, the irascible, self-obsessed artist whose decision to paint a mural arouses the curiosity of friends and foes alike. John Bratby's paintings cleverly reflect the character's temperament and they have been beautifully shot by Arthur Ibbetson, whose use of colour is painterly indeed. The problem is that the focus is so firmly on Guinness that the other characters are left on the sideline. DP

Alec Guinness *Gulley Jimson* • Kay Walsh *Coker* • Renee Houston *Sarah* • Mike Morgan *Nosey* • Robert Coote *Sir William Beeder* ■ *Dir* Ronald Neame • *Scr* Alec Guinness, from the novel by Joyce Cary

The Hospital ★★ 15

Black comedy 1971 · US · Colour · 98mins

Paddy Chayefsky won an Oscar for his script for this manic black comedy, but it's hard to see why the Academy would be taken in by its heavy-handed satire, crude characterisation and undisciplined structure. Frankly, it's a mess and a more talented director than Arthur Hiller would have been pressed to make anything of it. However, towering above all of this is a sensational performance from George C Scott as the surgeon who conquers his midlife crisis while murder, magic and madness rage around him. DP

George C Scott *Dr Herbert Bock* • Diana Rigg *Barbara Drummond* • Barnard Hughes *Drummond* • Andrew Duncan *William Mead* • Nancy Marchand *Head Nurse Christie* • Stephen Elliott *Sundstrom* ■ *Dir* Arthur Hiller • *Scr* Paddy Chayefsky

The Hostage ★★★ 12

Thriller 1966 · US · Colour · 79mins

One of scores of independent features made in the 1960s, this has a dime budget, bleak locations, bags of energy, and John Carradine and Harry Dean Stanton in key roles. It's a crime story with a twist, about a six-year-old boy trapped in a removal van that contains a corpse. Shot in Iowa, it's tensely directed by Russell S Doughton and co-edited by Gary Kurtz, later the producer of *Star Wars*. AT. Contains violence. DVD

Don O'Kelly *Bull* • Harry Dean Stanton *Eddie* • John Carradine *Otis Lovelace* • Danny Martins *Davey Cleaves* • Ron Hagerthy *Steve Cleaves* ■ *Dir* Russell S Doughton • *Scr* Robert Laning, from the novel by Henry Farrell

Hostage ★★★ 18

Action spy drama 1992 · UK · Colour · 96mins

This British-made spy thriller about Machiavellian double dealing in Whitehall too often resembles John le Carré on speed. Sam Neill stars as a disgruntled agent sent to Argentina to rescue a British subject held captive by guerrillas, only to fall in love with former 007 girl Talisa Soto. A mildly diverting and topical international morality play from acclaimed television director Robert Young is enlivened by a solid supporting cast, while James Fox camps it up gloriously as a hypocritical Whitehall mandarin. RS DVD

Sam Neill *John Rennie* • Talisa Soto *Joanna* • James Fox *Hugo Paynter* • Art Malik *Kalim Said* • Cristina Higueras *Gabriella* • Michael Kitchen *Fredericks* ■ *Dir* Robert Young (2) • *Scr* Arthur Hopcraft, from the novel *No Place to Hide* by Ted Allbeury

Hostage ★★ 15

Crime action thriller
2004 · US/Ger · Colour · 113mins

A slickly made if preposterously plotted thriller, this has Bruce Willis in dour mode as an LAPD hostage negotiator who quits his job to become a small-town police chief after an assignment ends in tragedy. Willis's past catches up with him, however, when three teenagers break into the hi-tech home of businessman Kevin Pollak, taking Pollak and his kids hostage. All this is watchable enough, but lacks the trademark twinkle and smug self-confidence that Willis brought to the *Die Hard* series. DA. Contains swearing and violence.

Bruce Willis *Jeff Talley* • Kevin Pollak *Walter Smith* • Jonathan Tucker *Dennis Kelly* • Ben Foster *Mars* • Marshall Allman *Kevin Kelly* • Michelle Horn *Jennifer Smith* • Jimmy Bennett *Tommy Smith* • Jimmy "Jax" Pinchak *Sean Mack* • Kim Coates *The watchman* • Serena Scott Thomas *Jane Talley* ■ *Dir* Florent Siri [Florent Emilio Siri] • *Scr* Doug Richardson, from the novel by Robert Crais

Hostage: the Christine Maresch Story ★★ 18

Drama based on a true story
1982 · Aus · Colour · 88mins

This Australian production unashamedly employs melodramatic symbolism to emphasise the unbelievable truth of its true-life subject. Director Frank Shields secures a full-throttle performance from Ralph Schicha, as the brutal husband who not only subjects wife Kerry Mack to endless domestic violence, but also forces her to participate in the bank raids that sustain his neo-Nazi activities. DP

Kerry Mack *Christine Maresch* • Ralph Schicha *Walter Maresch* • Gabriella Barraket *Mandy* • Judy Nunn *Mrs Lewis* ■ *Dir* Frank Shields (2) • *Scr* Frank Shields, John Lind

Hostages ★★★

Second World War drama
1943 · US · BW · 87mins

Not a particularly good war movie, but a rare chance to see Luise Rainer, winner of consecutive best actress Oscars for *The Great Ziegfeld* and *The Good Earth*. She is superb, though the real revelation is bulky William Bendix as leader of the Czech Resistance. The rest of the imported cast seem to be having as much trouble with their accents as with the plot. Director Frank Tuttle later fell foul of the McCarthyite witch-hunt; he wasn't blacklisted, but his career was never the same. TS

Arturo de Cordova *Paul Breda* • Luise Rainer *Milada Pressinger* • William Bendix *Janoshik* • Roland Varno *Jan Pavel* • Oscar Homolka *Lev Pressinger* • Katina Paxinou *Maria* • Paul Lukas *Rheinhardt* • Fred Giermann *Captain Patzer* • Felix Basch *Doctor Wallerstein* ■ *Dir* Frank Tuttle • *Scr* Lester Cole, Frank Butler, from the novel by Stefan Heym

Hostages ★★★★

Documentary drama
1993 · US/UK · Colour · 105mins

This is a gruelling and uncompromising account of the five-year incarceration endured by western hostages Terry Anderson, Tom Sutherland, Frank Reed, John McCarthy, Terry Waite and Brian Keenan after they were abducted in the Lebanon by a group of Hezbollah fundamentalists. Although director David Wheatley also includes actuality footage and reconstructions of the families' frustrated efforts to secure the sextet's release, it's the scenes set in the Beirut hideout that make the biggest dramatic impact. Played with conviction by a superior cast, this is a worthy tribute to the courage and determination of all involved. DP

Harry Dean Stanton *Frank Reed* • Colin Firth *John McCarthy* • Josef Sommer *Tom Sutherland* • Ciaran Hinds *Brian Keenan* • Jay O Sanders *Terry Anderson* • Conrad Asquith *Terry Waite* • Kathy Bates *Peggy Say* • Natasha Richardson *Jill Morrell* ■ *Dir* David Wheatley • *Scr* Bernard MacLaverty

Hostile Guns ★★ U

Western 1967 · US · Colour · 91mins

This is a slightly superior outing in producer AC Lyles's western series based on the nostalgic appeal of veteran players. A strong and simple storyline helps, as does the presence of George Montgomery and Yvonne De Carlo, who both show plenty of life – he as the marshal, she as an old flame who's one of four prisoners he's transporting across the desert in a wagon. Close behind are the kinfolk (headed by John Russell) of one of the convicts, waiting for the right moment to rescue him. Tab Hunter, in his mid-30s, represents youth. AE

George Montgomery *Gid McCool* • Yvonne De Carlo *Laura Mannon* • Tab Hunter *Mike Reno* • Brian Donlevy *Marshal Willett* • John Russell *Aaron* • Leo Gordon *Hank Pleasant* • Robert Emhardt *RC Crawford* ■ *Dir* RG Springsteen • *Scr* Steve Fisher, Sloan Nibley, from a story by James Edward Grant, Sloan Nibley

Hostile Hostages ★★★ 15

Black comedy 1994 · US · Colour · 92mins

Stand-up comedian Denis Leary stars in this highly amusing attack on "relationship management", which takes effective side-swipes at the American class system. Leary plays a small-time thief holding a dysfunctional family hostage at Christmas, who ends up getting caught in the middle of their multiple feuds and neuroses. Judy Davis and Kevin Spacey's "couple from hell" give Leary solid support in director Ted Demme's bitingly dark comedy. Released on DVD under its US title, *The Ref*. AJ. Contains swearing. DVD

Denis Leary *Gus* • Judy Davis *Caroline* • Kevin Spacey *Lloyd* • Robert J Steinmiller Jr *Jesse* • Glynis Johns *Rose* • Raymond J Barry *Huff* • Christine Baranski *Connie* ■ *Dir* Ted Demme • *Scr* Richard LaGravenese, Marie Weiss, from a story by Marie Weiss

Hostile Intentions ★★ 18

Thriller 1995 · US · Colour · 85mins

Occasionally dubious in tone, this is nevertheless a lively slice of girl power. Tia Carrere, Tricia Leigh Fisher and Lisa Dean Ryan head down Mexico way for a wild weekend only to fall foul of the corrupt local cops. When one of them attempts to rape Fisher, the girls blast their way out of jail, sparking a violent cross-country race for the border. It belts along at a helter-skelter pace. JF. Contains violence, nudity, swearing and drug abuse.

Tia Carrere *Nora* • Tricia Leigh Fisher *Maureen* • Lisa Dean Ryan *Caroline* • Carlos Gomez *Juan* ■ *Dir/Scr* Catherine Cyran

Hostile Waters ★★★ PG

Thriller based on a true story
1996 · US/UK · Colour · 91mins

A heavyweight cast gives this real-life submarine disaster story a sheen of class. The setting is the Reagan era, when a Russian sub collided with an American one in the Caribbean. This film traces the heroic attempts of the Soviet crew to repair their badly damaged craft, while the US worries about a potential nuclear catastrophe. Rutger Hauer, Martin Sheen and Max von Sydow head the top-notch cast in this TV movie, and director David Drury keeps the tension high. JF

Rutger Hauer *Captain Britanov* • Martin Sheen *Aurora Skipper* • Max von Sydow *Admiral Chernavin* • Rob Campbell *Sergei Preminin* • Harris Yulin *Admiral Quinn* • Regina Taylor *Lieutenant Curtis* ■ *Dir* David Drury • *Scr* Troy Kennedy Martin, from research by Tom Mangold, Peter Huchthausen, William Cran

Hostile Witness ★★ U

Courtroom drama
1968 · UK · Colour · 100mins

Ray Milland directs and stars in this interesting, if disappointing tale of a barrister vowing revenge against the hit-and-run driver who killed his daughter. But he ends up questioning his own sanity when he finds himself in the dock for the murder of his neighbour. This was written for the screen by Jack Roffey from his own play, and it shows: the script reads as though it is meant for the stage and the actors emote as if they are playing to a live audience. JB

Ray Milland *Simon Crawford QC* • Sylvia Syms *Sheila Larkin* • Felix Aylmer *Mr Justice Osborne* • Raymond Huntley *John Naylor* • Geoffrey Lumsden *Major Hugh Maitland* • Norman Barrs *Charles Milburn* ■ *Dir* Ray Milland • *Scr* Jack Roffey, from his play

Hot Blood ★★★

Musical romance 1956 · US · Colour · 85mins

"Be there when Jane Russell shakes her tambourines!" the posters implored, and she certainly did, flaunting the gypsy stereotype in this overly heated Romany romance. Russell and Cornel Wilde are LA gypsies forced by their families into an arranged marriage. Naturally, they fight like crazy at first, until the predictable reconciliation. However, the risible aspects are compensated for by director Nicholas Ray's dramatic use of colour and expert use of the CinemaScope screen. Ray also gets animated performances from the usually wooden leads. RB

Jane Russell *Annie Caldash* • Cornel Wilde *Stephan Torino* • Luther Adler *Marco Torino* • Joseph Calleia *Papa Theodore* • Mikhail Rasumny *Old Johnny* • Nina Koshetz *Nita Johnny* • Helen Westcott *Velma* • Jamie Russell *Xano* ■ *Dir* Nicholas Ray • *Scr* Jesse Lasky Jr, from a story by Jean Evans

The Hot Box ★★ 18

War drama 1972 · US/Phil · Colour · 80mins

Jonathan Demme was something of a chicks-in-chains specialist in his days working for Roger Corman, most famously with *Caged Heat*. However, he gets a writing and executive producer credit on this Philippines-shot women-in-prison movie about four American nurses who find some revolutionary fervour while stationed in a repressive Latin American country. Again, Demme is fully on the side of the woman prisoners and in fact most of the movie is set outside the walls where the escaped convicts end up becoming partisans fighting the fascist government. Something of a politically-correct exploitation movie. JF

Andrea Cagan *Bunny* • Margaret Markov *Lynn* • Rickey Richardson *Ellie* • Laurie Rose *Sue* • Carmen Argenziano *Flavio* • Charles Dierkop *Garcia/Major Dubay* ■ *Dir* Joe Viola • *Scr* Jonathan Demme, Joe Viola

The Hot Chick ★★★ 12

Comedy 2002 · US · Colour · 100mins

Rob Schneider makes an enjoyable contribution to the "body-swap" sub-genre with this comedy, in which an ancient earring causes small-time crook Clive and high-school princess Jessica to get under each other's skin. Schneider plays up his feminine side with disarming conviction, especially in his bonding moments with Jessica's pretty best friend Anna Faris. However, the humour is frequently juvenile slapstick, with few opportunities for toilet humour being wasted. Executive producer Adam Sandler pops up in an amusing cameo. JC DVD

Rob Schneider *Clive/Jessica Spencer* • Anna Faris *April* • Matthew Lawrence *Billy* • Eric Christian Olsen *Jake* • Robert Davi *Stan* • Melora Hardin *Carol* • Alexandra Holden *Lulu* •

Rachel McAdams *Jessica Spencer/Clive* • Adam Sandler *Bongo player* ■ *Dir* Tom Brady • *Scr* Tom Brady, Rob Schneider

Hot Dog – The Movie ★ 18

Comedy 1984 · US · Colour · 94mins

Not a sausage or a bun in sight, yet this remains cinema's equivalent of fast food: indigestible and utterly unmemorable. This typically crude example of the 1980s party movie, distinguished by some eye-catching ski footage, stars David Naughton as one of many horny adolescents contesting the world freestyle championship. Blatantly sexist – Shannon Tweed and other similarly unclad ladies are there like so much tinsel on a Christmas tree – this plays like some tired old Hollywood executive's idea of what teens want to see. RS [video]

David Naughton *Dan* • Patrick Houser *Harkin* • Tracy N Smith *Sunny* • John Patrick Reger *Rudi Garmischt* • Frank Koppola *Squirrel* • James Saito *Kendo* • Shannon Tweed *Sylvia Fonda* ■ *Dir* Peter Markle • *Scr* Mike Marvin

Hot Enough for June ★★★

Spy satire 1963 · UK · Colour · 98mins

James Bond is dead! Long live Nicolas Whistler – or at least that's what this spy spoof would have us believe. Everything here is just on the unfunny side of clever; for instance, the American title *Agent 8* is a reference both to Federico Fellini's $8\frac{1}{2}$, released earlier the same year, and the fact that this was the eighth collaboration between director Ralph Thomas and Dirk Bogarde. Cheerfully sending up his own Rank image as much as that of Bond, Bogarde merely passes muster, for the real star of the show is Robert Morley as the spymaster who equates espionage with the Eton wall game. DP

Dirk Bogarde *Nicolas Whistler* • Sylva Koscina *Vlasta Simenova* • Robert Morley *Colonel Cunliffe* • Leo McKern *Simenova* • Roger Delgado *Josef* • John Le Mesurier *Allsop* • Richard Vernon *Roddinghead* ■ *Dir* Ralph Thomas • *Scr* Lukas Heller, from the novel *Night of Wenceslas* by Lionel Davidson

Hot Lead and Cold Feet ★★ U

Comedy western 1978 · US · Colour · 85mins

Jim Dale was snapped up by Disney for this kiddie western. He plays three parts: grumpy patriarch Jasper Bloodshy and his two sons, one nerdy and feeble, the other a gunslinger. Prepare, though, to wade through several tons of Disney treacle as Dale earns every cent of his fee. American TV comic Don Knotts must have been cast to assist box-office revenue. AT [video]

Jim Dale *Eli/Wild Billy/Jasper Bloodshy* • Karen Valentine *Jenny* • Don Knotts *Denver Kid* • Jack Elam *Rattlesnake* • John Williams *Mansfield* • Darren McGavin *Mayor Ragsdale* • Warren Vanders *Boss Snead* • Debbie Lytton *Roxanne* ■ *Dir* Robert Butler • *Scr* Joseph L McEveety, Arthur Alsberg, Don Nelson, from a story by Rod Piffath

Hot Millions ★★★ U

Comedy caper 1968 · UK · Colour · 106mins

A large, disparate cast of famous faces, from Maggie Smith to Bob Newhart, pulls out some moderately funny stops in this bubbly, engaging tale of manipulative Peter Ustinov parting a large multinational from a sizeable portion of its shekels. Ustinov is thankfully given a large, containing script to curb his worst excesses, the jokes come thick and relatively fast, and there is a charming jauntiness. The enterprise tends to run dangerously low on steam towards the end, but it grabs the attention with a considerable degree of style. SH

Peter Ustinov *Marcus Pendleton/Caesar Smith* • Maggie Smith *Patty Terwilliger* • Karl Malden *Carlton J Klemper* • Bob Newhart *Willard C Gnatpole* • Robert Morley *Caesar Smith* • Cesar Romero *Customs Officer* ■ *Dir* Eric Till • *Scr* Ira Wallach, Peter Ustinov

Hot Money ★★

Heist comedy 1979 · Can · Colour · 78mins

There are only a handful of performers in cinema history whose mere presence can raise the quality of a film by at least a couple of notches. Orson Welles is one of the few, and he alone makes this tepid Canadian heist comedy worth bothering with. Sadly, we see too little of him as the sheriff to crooked deputy Michael Murphy. It's contrived, unfunny and clear to see why the film was withheld for five years – but at least there's Orson. DP

Orson Welles *Sheriff* • Michael Murphy *Burt* ■ *Dir* Selig Usher • *Scr* Carl DeSantis, Phyllis Camesano, Joel Cohen, Neil Cohen

Hot Pursuit ★★ 15

Comedy 1987 · US · Colour · 88mins

John Cusack plays a college boy in pursuit of his girlfriend who has gone on holiday with her parents; as one might expect, his journey is beset with silly disasters. It's essentially an attempt to reprise the actor's first hit – Rob Reiner's *The Sure Thing* – but, although Cusack is always engaging to watch, this film has none of the wit of that delightful comedy. JB [video] DVD

John Cusack *Dan Bartlett* • Wendy Gazelle *Lori Cronenberg* • Monte Markham *Bill Cronenberg* • Shelley Fabares *Buffy Cronenberg* • Jerry Stiller *Victor Honeywell* • Ben Stiller *Chris Honeywell* • Robert Loggia *Mac MacLaren* ■ *Dir* Steven Lisberger • *Scr* Steven Lisberger, Steven Carabatsos [Steven W Carabatsos], from a story by Steven Lisberger

Hot Resort ★ 18

Comedy 1985 · US · Colour · 87mins

There's not much in the way of humour in this teen comedy concerning four American youths who get up to various sexual shenanigans while working at a Caribbean resort hotel. Poor old Frank Gorshin wanders in and out of the virtually plotless story, while Bronson Pinchot shows none of the comic talent that would later make him famous. Cannon Pictures basically used the same plot for the execrable *Hot Chili* in the very same year. KB [video]

Tom Parsekian *Marty* • Debra Kelly *Liza* • Bronson Pinchot *Brad* • Michael Berz *Kesey* • Dan Schneider *Chuck* • Samm-Art Williams *Bill Martin* • Marcy Walker *Franny* • Frank Gorshin *Mr Green* ■ *Dir* John Robins • *Scr* John Robins, Boaz Davidson, Norman Hudis, from a story by Paul Max Rubenstein

The Hot Rock ★★★★ U

Crime caper 1972 · US · Colour · 100mins

This caper movie, based on a novel by Donald E Westlake, is not without its flaws, but it boasts a sense of finesse and fun that other films in the genre sadly lack. Robert Redford and George Segal head a quartet of criminals bent on stealing a fabulous diamond from the Brooklyn Museum. Inevitably, their ineptitude at robbery is a reflection of their incompetence at living. Peter Yates, working from a William Goldman script that shouldn't have split the tale into four distinct parts, directs without momentum but achieves interest through his actors' considerable expertise. Hot stuff. TH

Robert Redford *John Dortmunder* • George Segal *Andrew Kelp* • Zero Mostel *Abe Greenberg* • Ron Leibman *Murch* • Paul Sand *Alan Greenberg* • Moses Gunn *Dr Amusa* ■ *Dir* Peter Yates • *Scr* William Goldman, from a novel by Donald E Westlake

Hot Shot ★★

Sports drama 1986 · US · Colour · 89mins

This run-of-the-mill American take on soccer provides more unintentional laughs than genuine drama. Pele, who obviously got the film bug during *Escape to Victory*, plays a football legend who is called to help a youngster embrace the greatest game. Look for early appearances by a pre-stardom Mario Van Peebles, Jimmy Smits and Billy Warlock. JF

Jim Youngs *Jimmy Kristidis* • Pelé *Santos* • David Groh *Jerry Norton* • Mario Van Peebles *Hoffman* • Billy Warlock *Vinnie Fortino* • Jimmy Smits *Stars team member* ■ *Dir* Rick King • *Scr* Rick King, Joe Sauter

Hot Shots! ★★★ PG

Spoof action 1991 · US · Colour · 81mins

If ever a movie was ripe for sending up, then *Top Gun* was it, and, although this lacks the charm of classic spoofs *Airplane!* and *The Naked Gun*, there are enough good gags on show to win over those who wished Tom Cruise had gone down in flames. This time director Jim Abrahams goes solo without the Zucker brothers, but he still displays the same cheerful lack of taste and subtlety. Charlie Sheen stars as the ludicrously macho fighter pilot hero, but Lloyd Bridges bags the most laughs as the untogether commanding officer. JF. Contains swearing. [video] DVD

Charlie Sheen *Sean "Topper" Harley/Rhett Butler/Superman* • Cary Elwes *Kent Gregory* • Valeria Golino *Ramada Thompson/Scarlett O'Hara/Lois Lane* • Lloyd Bridges *Admiral Benson* • Kevin Dunn *Lieutenant Commander Block* • William O'Leary *Pete "Dead Meat" Thompson* • Kristy Swanson *Kowalski* • Efrem Zimbalist Jr *Wilson* • Jon Cryer *Jim "Wash Out" Pfaffenbach* ■ *Dir* Jim Abrahams • *Scr* Pat Proft, Jim Abrahams

Hot Shots! Part Deux ★★ PG

Spoof action 1993 · US · Colour · 81mins

The law of diminishing laughs applies to Jim Abrahams and Pat Proft's self-conscious parody of the Rambo series, with Charlie Sheen reprising his role of the superhero with zero tolerance for the enemy. Lloyd Bridges also returns, this time as the US president, but this sequel is too reminiscent of its predecessor to be terribly amusing. Still, there are some laughs to be had and look out for a brief appearance by Rowan Atkinson. TH. Contains swearing. [video] DVD

Charlie Sheen *Topper Harley* • Lloyd Bridges *Tug Benson* • Valeria Golino *Ramada Rodham Hayman* • Richard Crenna *Colonel Denton Walters* • Brenda Bakke *Michelle Rodham Huddleston* • Miguel Ferrer *Harbinger* • Rowan Atkinson *Dexter Hayman* ■ *Dir* Jim Abrahams • *Scr* Jim Abrahams, Pat Proft

Hot Spell ★★★

Drama 1958 · US · BW · 88mins

This rather stagey family melodrama, set in New Orleans, was the last of the five films that Shirley Booth made before returning to the stage and TV. As in her first film, *Come Back, Little Sheba* in 1952, for which she won the best actress Oscar, Booth plays a distressed housewife dreaming of better days. Her sensitive performance is contrasted with Anthony Quinn's bombastic one as her philandering husband. Shirley MacLaine, on the verge of real stardom, is touching as the couple's daughter. Sub-Tennessee Williams it may be, but it offers a certain amount of pleasure. RB

Shirley Booth *Alma Duval* • Anthony Quinn *Jack Duval* • Shirley MacLaine *Virginia Duval* • Earl Holliman *Buddy Duval* • Eileen Heckart *Fan* • Clint Kimbrough *Billy Duval* • Warren Stevens *Wyatt* • Jody Lawrance *Dora May* ■ *Dir* Daniel Mann • *Scr* James Poe, from the play *Next of Kin* by Lonnie Coleman

The Hot Spot ★★★ 18

Black comedy thriller
1990 · US · Colour · 124mins

Don Johnson is the drifter, holed up in a small Texas town, who falls for bad girl Virginia Madsen and good girl Jennifer Connelly. Director Dennis Hopper turns in a faithful tribute to the *film noir* thrillers of old, but, this being the 1990s, he ups the sexual content a number of degrees. There are lots of fans, dust and people sweating, and Madsen smoulders away furiously to good effect. While not quite so convincing, Johnson is still suitably mean and brooding as the fall guy. JF. Contains violence, swearing, sex scenes and nudity. [video] DVD

Don Johnson *Harry Madox* • Virginia Madsen *Dolly Harshaw* • Jennifer Connelly *Gloria Harper* • Charles Martin Smith *Lon Gulik* • William Sadler *Frank Sutton* • Jerry Hardin *George Harshaw* • Barry Corbin *Sheriff* ■ *Dir* Dennis Hopper • *Scr* Nona Tyson, Charles Williams, from the novel *Hell Hath No Fury* by Charles Williams

Hot Stuff ★★ 15

Comedy 1979 · US · Colour · 87mins

In the 1970s US police established numerous undercover fencing set-ups which resulted in the recovery of over a billion dollars worth of stolen goods and led to thousands of arrests. This cop comedy takes that sting as its starting point and weaves around it a tale of double dealing involving the Mafia. Dom DeLuise directs and stars as a cop badly in need of some success. The sharp script and pacy style ensures interest is maintained, but it should have been better. DF [video]

Dom DeLuise *Ernie Fortunato* • Jerry Reed *Doug Van Horne* • Suzanne Pleshette *Louise Webster* • Luis Avalos *Ramon* • Ossie Davis *Captain Geibarger* • Marc Lawrence (1) *Carmine* • Richard Davalos *Charles* ■ *Dir* Dom DeLuise • *Scr* Michael Kane, Donald E Westlake

Hot Summer Night ★★

Crime drama 1957 · US · BW · 85mins

Experienced television director David Friedkin shot this tightly scripted drama in just nine days. Although it lacks the grit of other contemporary crime B-movies, there's an atypically anti-media slant to this tale of the ambitious reporter who risks the life of his wife in his efforts to further his career by interviewing the leader of a notorious bank gang. However, we're so used to seeing Leslie Nielsen parodying situations like these that some of the riper dialogue has an unintentionally comic ring. DP

Leslie Nielsen *William Joel Partain* • Colleen Miller *Irene Partain* • Edward Andrews *Lou Follett* • Jay C Flippen *Oren Kobble* • James Best *Kermit* • Paul Richards (1) *Elly Horn* • Robert Wilke [Robert J Wilke] *Tom Ellis* ■ *Dir* David Friedkin • *Scr* Morton Fine, David Friedkin, from a story by Edwin P Hicks

Hot Target ★★ 18

Crime thriller 1985 · NZ · Colour · 91mins

A rather predictable and ham-fisted attempt at a gripping thriller, this New Zealand film tries to cover its clichéd tracks with twists and turns aimed at confusing the viewer. Simone Griffeth is the wife planning to get rid of husband Bryan Marshall with the help of a lover, unaware that her accomplice is actually a thief setting her up. Are you still with us? A *film noir* that's more bland than black. JF. Contains swearing and nudity. [video]

Simone Griffeth *Christine Webber* • Steve Marachuk *Greg Sandford* • Bryan Marshall *Clive Webber* • Peter McCauley *Detective Inspector Nolan* ■ *Dir* Denis Lewiston • *Scr* Denis Lewiston, from a story by Gerry O'Hara

H

Hot Times ★ 18

Sex comedy 1974 · US · Colour · 71mins

Jim McBride directs this excruciating sex comedy. Gone were the invention and insight of *David Holzman's Diary*, and in their place came an endless stream of cheap gags at the expense of callow Henry Cory, who heads for New York after failing to lose his virginity at college and suddenly finds himself at the centre of a sexual Shangri-la. Unsurprisingly, McBride didn't secure funds for another feature for nine years, but then proceeded to prove his worth with *Breathless* and *The Big Easy*. DP

Henry Cory *Archie* • Gail Lorber *Ronnie* • Amy Farber *Bette* • Bob Lesser *Coach/Guru* • Steve Curry *Mughead* ■ *Dir/Scr* Jim McBride

Hot to Trot ★ PG

Comedy 1988 · US · Colour · 79mins

A confused and confusing comedy, this outdated tat has Bobcat Goldthwait getting tips from a talking horse (voiced by John Candy) and thinking he's on to a whinnying streak. Unsurprisingly, he's not. TH

Bobcat Goldthwait *Fred Chaney* • Dabney Coleman *Walter Sawyer* • Jim Metzler *Boyd Osborne* • Cindy Pickett *Victoria Peyton* • Virginia Madsen *Allison Rowe* • John Candy *Don* ■ *Dir* Michael Dinner • *Scr* Stephen Neigher, Hugo Gilbert, Charlie Peters, from a story by Stephen Neigher, Hugo Gilbert

The Hot Touch ★

Romantic thriller
1982 · Can/Fr · Colour · 92mins

Roger Vadim was once the *enfant terrible* of French cinema. Yet, by the early 1980s, he was reduced to accepting third-rate assignments across the Atlantic. This art-scam thriller is as bogus as the paintings churned out by Wayne Rogers for crooked dealer Patrick Macnee. Only the sinister commission from the psychopathic Lloyd Bochner – to replace a series of pictures lost in the war – has anything going for it. DP

Wayne Rogers *Danny Fairchild* • Marie-France Pisier *Dr Emillienne Simpson* • Lloyd Bochner *Severo* • Samantha Eggar *Samantha O'Brien* • Patrick Macnee *Vincent Reblack* • Melvyn Douglas *Max Reich* • Gloria Carlin *Kelly* • Allan Kolman *Lincoln Simpson* ■ *Dir* Roger Vadim • *Scr* Peter Dion, from a story by Peter Dion

Hot Water ★★★ U

Silent comedy 1924 · US · BW · 53mins

Harold Lloyd's previous comedy, *Girl Shy*, was eight reels long and had theatre owners complaining about the gaps between the pratfalls. Lloyd got the message and took the scissors to *Hot Water*, cutting out the intricate plotting and concentrating on his trademark stunts. The story is simple: Lloyd is a newly married man coping with shopping, traffic and, naturally, his mother-in-law. This isn't one of Lloyd's best films, though his bespectacled character always has charm and there's a brilliant scene in a traffic jam when he's encumbered by a turkey that he's won in a raffle. AT

Harold Lloyd *Hubby* • Jobyna Ralston *Wifey* • Josephine Crowell *Mother-in-law* • Charles Stevenson *Brother-in-law* • Pat Harmon *Straphanger* • Andy DeVilla *Cop* • Mickey McBan *Brother-in-law* ■ *Dir* Sam Taylor, Fred C Newmeyer • *Scr* Thomas J Gray, Tim Whelan, John Grey, Sam Taylor

Hotel ★★

Drama 1967 · US · Colour · 108mins

Rod Taylor and Kevin McCarthy play tycoons who fight for the ownership of a deluxe hotel, the St Gregory in New Orleans, as sundry guests, each with a personalised mini-drama, check in and out. Sadly, Taylor and McCarthy don't cut it as the business rivals and the film could have done with more glamour and big stars to do justice to Arthur Hailey's bestseller. AT

Rod Taylor *Peter McDermott* • Catherine Spaak *Jeanne* • Karl Malden *Keycase* • Melvyn Douglas *Trent* • Kevin McCarthy *O'Keefe* • Merle Oberon *Duchess* • Richard Conte *Dupere* • Michael Rennie *Duke of Lanbourne* • Carmen McRae *Christine, the singer* ■ *Dir* Richard Quine • *Scr* Wendell Mayes, from the novel by Arthur Hailey

Hotel ★★★ 18

Black comedy thriller
2001 · UK/It · Colour · 111mins

Director Mike Figgis confirmed his position as one of Britain's most visionary directors with this part-improvised film-making "exercise" – shot over a weekend in Venice using a cast as varied as David Schwimmer, Rhys Ifans and John Malkovich. The story, which unfolds in a decidedly obtuse and sketchy fashion, concerns the making of a movie of John Webster's *Duchess of Malfi*, against a background of murder and casual cannibalism. Salma Hayek is superbly irritating as an MTV-style documentary host, and when Burt Reynolds pops up as a financier, you know you're in weird waters. Odd, compelling and darkly funny. AC DVD

Rhys Ifans *Trent Stoken* • Saffron Burrows *Naomi/Duchess of Malfi* • David Schwimmer *Jonathan Danderfine* • Salma Hayek *Charlee Boux* • Burt Reynolds *Flamenco manager* • Julian Sands *O, tour guide* • Danny Huston *Hotel manager* • Lucy Liu *Kawika* • Chiara Mastroianni *Nurse* • John Malkovich *Omar Jonnson* ■ *Dir/Scr* Mike Figgis

Hotel Berlin ★★

Second World War drama
1945 · US · BW · 98mins

An updated, retitled adaptation of Vicki Baum's 1943 novel *Berlin Hotel*, which, like her more famous *Grand Hotel*, observes the comings and the goings of the guests in said hotel as the Allies close in. In this case, it's mainly a Nazi packing up at war's end and preparing to leave for South America with a plan to start another world war, and a Noble prize-winning scientist whose life has been destroyed by the Nazis. Warner Bros hoped they had another *Casablanca* on their hands; they didn't. AT

Helmut Dantine *Martin Richter* • Andrea King *Lisa Dorn* • Raymond Massey *Arnim Von Dahnwitz* • Faye Emerson *Tillie Weiler* • Peter Lorre *Johannes Koenig* • Alan Hale *Hermann Plottke* • George Coulouris *Joachim Helm* ■ *Dir* Peter Godfrey • *Scr* Jo Pagano, Alvah Bessie, from the novel *Berlin Hotel* by Vicki Baum

Hotel Colonial ★★ 15

Adventure thriller
1987 · US/It · Colour · 101mins

This beautifully shot but insubstantial melodrama is set in Latin America. John Savage plays an American out of his depth when he travels to Colombia to discover the truth behind his brother's reported death and comes up against the sinister Robert Duvall. Rachel Ward plays the love interest and all three produce capable performances, but the meandering script lacks gravitas. JF

John Savage *Marco Venieri* • Robert Duvall *Carrasco* • Rachel Ward *Irene Costa* • Massimo Troisi *Werner* ■ *Dir* Cinzia Torrini • *Scr* Enzo Monteleone, Cinzia Torrini, Ira R Barmak, Robert Katz, from a story by Enzo Monteleone • *Cinematographer* Giuseppe Rotunno

Hotel de Love ★★★ 15

Romantic comedy
1996 · Aus/US · Colour · 92mins

This unusually well-constructed Australian romantic comedy has much of the style of *Muriel's Wedding* and features British beauty Saffron Burrows, Pippa Grandison and old stager Ray Barrett. Twin brothers (Aden Young, Simmon Bossell) fall for high school goddess Melissa (Burrows), who leads them a merry dance before heading off to college. It's a lightweight affair, but it exudes a certain charm. JF

Aden Young *Rick Dunne* • Saffron Burrows *Melissa Morrison* • Simon Bossell *Stephen Dunne* • Pippa Grandison *Alison Leigh* • Ray Barrett *Jack Dunne* • Julia Blake *Edith Dunne* • Peter O'Brien (2) *Norman* • Belinda McClory *Janet* ■ *Dir/Scr* Craig Rosenberg

Hôtel du Nord ★★★

Drama 1938 · Fr · BW · 84mins

This brooding study may not be Marcel Carné's most accomplished work, but it's still undeniably affecting. Designer Alexandre Trauner reproduces the atmospheric settings that were essential to Carné's poetic realist style. Indeed, the tatty interiors and quaintly rundown canal landmarks are the real stars of a film that only comes fitfully to life. Doomed lovers Annabella and Jean-Pierre Aumont are just a touch too tragic, while Arletty and Louis Jouvet are a little too unbridled in their villainy. DP. In French with English subtitles.

Annabella *Renée* • Arletty *Raymonde* • Louis Jouvet *M Edmond* • Jean-Pierre Aumont *Pierre* • Jeanne Marken [Jane Marken] *Louise Lecouvreur* • André Brunot *Emile Lecouvreur* • Bernard Blier *Prosper* ■ *Dir* Marcel Carné • *Scr* Marcel Carné, Henri Jeanson, Jean Aurenche (adaptation), from the novel by Eugène Dabit

Hôtel du Paradis ★★★ 15

Drama 1986 · UK/Fr · Colour · 113mins

Jana Bokova's thoughtful study of isolation and thwarted ambition displays a maturity rare in debutante directors. In a poignant reference to his own career, Fernando Rey plays an actor taking one last stab at legitimacy after wasting his talent in escapist entertainments. His fellow residents – among them Fabrice Luchini's frustrated film-maker and Hugues Quester's penurious thespian – are no less acquainted with disappointment. The tone is melancholic, but attention to detail makes this affecting. DP. French dialogue dubbed into English.

Fernando Rey *Joseph* • Bérangère Bonvoisin • Hugues Quester *Maurice* • Marika Rivera *Marika* • Carola Regnier *Sarah* • Raul Gimenez *Emilio* • Michael Medwin *English producer* • Fabrice Luchini *Arthur* ■ *Dir/Scr* Jana Bokova

Hotel Imperial ★★★

Silent First World War drama
1927 · US · BW · 84mins

The noted Swedish director Mauritz Stiller arrived in Hollywood in 1925 with his protégée, Greta Garbo. He could not fit in with the studio system and only completed two pictures for Paramount in two and a half years, the first being this powerful drama of wartime espionage and romance. Visually striking with its vast hotel setting and beautifully paced, it stars Pola Negri in an unusually restrained performance as the hotel chambermaid who helps an Austrian officer trapped behind Russian lines. Billy Wilder updated the story to the Second World War for *Five Graves to Cairo*. AE

Pola Negri *Anna Sedlak* • James Hall *Lieutenant Paul Almasy* • George Siegmann *General Juschkiewitsch* • Max Davidson *Elias Butterman* • Michael Vavitch *Tabakowitsch* ■ *Dir* Mauritz Stiller • *Scr* Jules Furthman, from the play by Lajos Biró • *Cinematographer* Bert Glennon

The Hotel New Hampshire ★★★ 18

Comedy drama 1984 · US · Colour · 103mins

On its original release, there was anything but a critical consensus on this adaptation of John Irving's expansive novel. Many blamed the book for the film's episodic structure and the sensationalist nature of the fates that befall the central characters. Others praised writer/director Tony Richardson for the fidelity of his approach. The cast does its best, although the characters are a pretty hard bunch to sympathise with. David Watkin's photography is a bonus, however. DP. Contains swearing, sex scenes and violence. DVD

Rob Lowe *John Berry* • Jodie Foster *Franny Berry* • Paul McCrane *Frank Berry* • Beau Bridges *Win Berry* • Lisa Banes *Mary Berry* • Jennie Dundas *Lilly Berry* • Seth Green *Egg Berry* • Nastassja Kinski *Susie the Bear* • Wallace Shawn *Freud* • Wilford Brimley *"Iowa Bob" Berry* • Joely Richardson *Waitress* • Matthew Modine • Amanda Plummer ■ *Dir* Tony Richardson • *Scr* Tony Richardson, from the novel by John Irving

Hotel Paradiso ★★

Comedy 1966 · US/UK · Colour · 100mins

Adapted by producer/director Peter Glenville and Jean-Claude Carrière from Georges Feydeau and Maurice Desvallières's famous stage farce *L'Hôtel du Libre Echange*, this is a classic example of how what might be hilarious in the theatre can end up being a dead duck on the screen. The action is so flatly directed that not even that great editor Anne Coates can inject any pace into the endless round of bedroom toing and froing that should have been funnier. DP

Alec Guinness *Benedict Boniface* • Gina Lollobrigida *Marcelle Cot* • Robert Morley *Henri Cot* • Peggy Mount *Angelique Boniface* • Akim Tamiroff *Anniello* • Marie Bell *La Grande Antoinette* • Derek Fowldes [Derek Fowlds] *Maxime* ■ *Dir* Peter Glenville • *Scr* Jean-Claude Carrière, Peter Glenville, from the play *L'Hôtel du Libre Echange* by Georges Feydeau, Maurice Desvallières

Hotel Reserve ★★★ U

Thriller 1944 · UK · BW · 88mins

Jointly directed by Victor Hanbury, Lance Comfort and Max Greene, this subdued thriller, set just before the Second World War, is lifted by James Mason's performance as a "wronged man", in this case a refugee accused of being a spy. The plot has enough suspense and intrigue, but this movie only fitfully comes to life as Mason sets out discover the real villain. TH

James Mason *Peter Vadassy* • Lucie Mannheim *Madame Suzanne Koche* • Raymond Lovell *Monsieur Robert Duclos* • Julien Mitchell *Monsieur Beghin* • Clare Hamilton *Miss Mary Skelton* • Martin Miller *Herr Walter Vogel* • Herbert Lom *Monsieur André Roux* • Frederick Valk *Herr Emil Schimler* ■ *Dir* Victor Hanbury, Lance Comfort, Max Greene • *Scr* John Davenport, from the novel *Epitaph for a Spy* by Eric Ambler

Hotel Rwanda ★★★★ 12

Drama based on a true story
2004 · S Afr/UK/It · Colour · 116mins

Don Cheadle delivers the performance of his career in this gut-wrenching drama based on events in Rwanda in the mid-1990s. It's an inspirational and shame-inducing story of one man's courage in the face of genuine horror. Cheadle plays true-life hero Paul Rusesabagina, a hotel manager who saved the lives of more than 1200 refugees – the majority of them Tutsi – by sheltering them at his workplace. Cleanly shot with an acute sense of realism, the film focuses on the emotional interaction between its characters as they struggle to survive despite appalling indifference from the West. By homing in on just one element of the Hutu campaign of genocide, Terry George gives a human face to the shocking statistics. SF DVD

Don Cheadle *Paul Rusesabagina* • Sophie Okonedo *Tatiana Rusesabagina* • Nick Nolte *Colonel Oliver* • Joaquin Phoenix *Jack Daglish* • Desmond Dube *Dube* • David O'Hara *David* • Cara Seymour *Pat Archer* • Fana Mokoena *General Augustin Bizimungo* ■ *Dir* Terry George • *Scr* Terry George, Keir Pearson

Hotel Sahara ★★★ U

Second World War comedy
1951 · UK · BW · 87mins

A marvellous comedy idea: during the desert campaign in the Second World War, Peter Ustinov's hotel is utilised at various times by British, German, Italian and French forces. Naturally, proprietor Ustinov manages to accommodate them all, plus a few visiting Arabs as well. Very funny, and played at a fast and furious pace by a wonderful cast. TS

Yvonne De Carlo *Yasmin Pallas* • Peter Ustinov *Emad* • David Tomlinson *Captain "Puffin" Cheynie* • Roland Culver *Major Bill Randall* • Albert Lieven *Lt Gunther Von Heilicke* • Bill Owen *Private Binns* • Sidney Tafler [Sydney Tafler] *Corporal Pullar* • Eugene Deckers *French Spahi Officer* ■ *Dir* Ken Annakin • *Scr* Patrick Kirwan, George H Brown

Hotel Sorrento ★★ 15

Drama 1994 · Aus · Colour · 107mins

Family drama from Down Under about the ties that threaten to unbind when one of three sisters writes a tell-all book about life in their home town, the Aussie seaside resort of Sorrento. The book purports to be fiction, but the other two siblings reckon there's more than a few grains of uncomfortable truth in it. It's nicely acted by Joan Plowright, Caroline Goodall and Tara Morice, but the material is dull and the pace is plodding. DA

Caroline Goodall *Meg Moynihan* • Caroline Gillmer *Hilary Moynihan* • Tara Morice *Pippa Moynihan* • Joan Plowright *Marge Morrisey* • John Hargreaves *Dick Bennett* • Ray Barrett *Wal Moynihan* • Ben Thomas *Troy Moynihan* • Nicholas Bell *Edwin* ■ *Dir* Richard Franklin • *Scr* Richard Franklin, Peter Fitzpatrick, from the play by Hannie Rayson

Hotel Splendide ★★ 15

Comedy 1999 · UK/Fr · Colour · 98mins

Terence Gross's feature debut bears a calculated physical resemblance to the dark fables of Jean-Pierre Jeunet and Marc Caro. But this post-Thatcherite fairy tale is no *Delicatessen*, despite its metaphorical preoccupation with dietary fads and bodily functions. Apart from Katrin Cartlidge's melancholia, nothing convinces – whether it's the ease with which Toni Collette drives a wedge between simpering hotel manager Stephen Tompkinson and his chef brother, Daniel Craig, the facile jibes at the lingering matriarchal legacy or the palliative power of European cuisine. Dramatically wayward and symbolically gauche. DP

Toni Collette *Kath* • Daniel Craig *Ronald Blanche* • Katrin Cartlidge *Cora Blanche* • Stephen Tompkinson *Dezmond Blanche* • Hugh O'Conor *Stanley Smith* • Helen McCrory *Lorna Bull* ■ *Dir/Scr* Terence Gross

Hotel Terminus: the Life and Times of Klaus Barbie ★★★★★

Documentary
1987 · US/Fr · BW and Colour · 267mins

Having been denied an Oscar for *The Sorrow and the Pity*, Marcel Ophüls finally received his due reward for this damning study of the unholy alliance of political expediency and anti-Semitic corruption that allowed former Gestapo chief Klaus Barbie (the so-called "Butcher of Lyons") to spend over 30 contented years in Bolivia, in spite of the enormity of his crimes against humanity. In the course of interviews with victims, enemies, collaborators and others, it becomes clear that Barbie had many willing accomplices – and only some wore Nazi uniforms. This epic historical documentary is also a moral indictment of timeless resonance. DP. In English, French, German and Spanish with subtitles.

Jeanne Moreau *Narrator* ■ *Dir* Marcel Ophüls

Houdini ★★★ U

Biographical drama
1953 · US · Colour · 105mins

This is the first of five films real-life married couple Tony Curtis and Janet Leigh – the so-called "elite of the milkshake set" – made together. As the famous escapologist, Curtis is half-naked for most of the early scenes, a treat for his teenage fans at the time. When he finds Mrs Houdini, he pays the rent by dreaming up ever more ambitious stunts, leading to his fatal accident in 1926 when he drowned upside down in a locked water tank. The movie covers some 40 years, though Curtis and Leigh age no more than 40 minutes. An entertaining hagiography. AT

Tony Curtis *Houdini* • Janet Leigh *Bess* • Torin Thatcher *Otto* • Angela Clarke *Mrs Weiss* • Stefan Schnabel *Prosecuting attorney* • Ian Wolfe *Fante* • Sig Ruman *Schultz* • Michael Pate *Dooley* • Connie Gilchrist *Mrs Schultz* ■ *Dir* George Marshall • *Scr* Philip Yordan, from a biography by Harold Kellock

Hound Dog Man ★★★ U

Musical 1959 · US · Colour · 86mins

Before such singer/actors as Sting or Madonna, there was Fabian, a good-looking teen idol who charmingly acknowledged that, despite carefully constructed hit records, he couldn't sing. This movie marked his screen debut, straight into a leading role in an amiable, rustic near-western. The title is deliberately redolent of Elvis Presley, but actually means what it says: Fabian hangs around the farm with some dogs. Under talented director Don Siegel's watchful eye, this is a beautifully filmed drama, and Fabian acquits himself remarkably well. TS

Fabian *Clint* • Carol Lynley *Dony* • Stuart Whitman *Blackie Scantling* • Arthur O'Connell *Aaron Mckinney* • Dodie Stevens *Nita Stringer* ■ *Dir* Don Siegel • *Scr* Fred Gipson, Winston Miller, from the novel by Fred Gipson

The Hound of the Baskervilles ★★★★★ PG

Classic mystery 1939 · US · BW · 79mins

This must be the classiest Sherlock Holmes movie in the B-picture canon, even if Nigel Bruce's Watson is left spluttering behind Basil Rathbone's superb Holmes. The moors are scarved in fog as the intrepid sleuths follow the paw-prints of an enormous beast that's threatening the last of the Baskerville line. Surprisingly, for 1939, Holmes's final words are: "Quick, Watson, the needle!" – a reference to his drug addiction, but audiences of the time scarcely knew that. An exceptional, chilling joy. TH DVD

Richard Greene *Sir Henry Baskerville* • Basil Rathbone *Sherlock Holmes* • Wendy Barrie *Beryl Stapleton* • Nigel Bruce *Dr Watson* • Lionel Atwill *Dr James Mortimer* • John Carradine *Barryman* • Barlowe Borland *Frankland* • Beryl Mercer *Mrs Jenifer Mortimer* ■ *Dir* Sidney Lanfield • *Scr* Ernest Pascal, from the novel by Sir Arthur Conan Doyle

The Hound of the Baskervilles ★★★★★ PG

Classic mystery 1959 · UK · Colour · 83mins

In this atmospheric tour de force, thrilling Hammer horror and the fabulous logic of Sir Arthur Conan Doyle are the perfect match in what was the first Sherlock Holmes adventure after the Universal series featuring Basil Rathbone ended in 1946 with *Dressed to Kill*, and also the first in colour. It weaves a darkly romantic gothic spell around the dreaded hound from hell that stalks the foggy moors on the lookout for cursed Baskerville family members. Peter Cushing gives one of his finest performances as the unflappable Baker Street sleuth and Christopher Lee is on top form as Sir Henry. AJ DVD

Peter Cushing *Sherlock Holmes* • André Morell *Dr Watson* • Christopher Lee *Sir Henry* • Marla Landi *Cecile* • Ewen Solon *Stapleton* • Francis De Wolff *Dr Mortimer* • Miles Malleson *Bishop Frankland* • John Le Mesurier *Barrymore* • David Oxley *Sir Hugo Baskerville* ■ *Dir* Terence Fisher • *Scr* Peter Bryan, from the novel by Sir Arthur Conan Doyle

The Hound of the Baskervilles ★ PG

Parody 1977 · UK · Colour · 81mins

Paul Morrissey directs this woeful lampoon of Sir Arthur Conan Doyle's most celebrated story. Peter Cook takes on the role of Baker Street's finest, while Dudley Moore doubles up as the doggedly dim Watson and Holmes's mother. Never did the duo look so bereft of inspiration as they watch gag after gag refuse to respond to the ministrations of such comic geniuses as Spike Milligan, Kenneth Williams and Terry-Thomas. DP. Contains some swearing. DVD

Peter Cook *Sherlock Holmes* • Dudley Moore *Dr Watson/Mrs Holmes/Mrs Spiggott* • Denholm Elliott *Stapleton* • Joan Greenwood *Beryl Stapleton* • Terry-Thomas *Dr Mortimer* • Max Wall *Mr Barrymore* • Irene Handl *Mrs Barrymore* • Kenneth Williams *Sir Henry Baskerville* • Roy Kinnear *Seldon* • Prunella Scales *Glynis* • Penelope Keith *Massage parlour receptionist* • Spike Milligan *Baskerville police force* ■ *Dir* Paul Morrissey • *Scr* Peter Cook, Dudley Moore, Paul Morrissey, from the novel by Sir Arthur Conan Doyle

The Hound of the Baskervilles ★★★ 15

Detective mystery
1983 · UK · Colour · 95mins

There had already been one superb version of this classic Sherlock Holmes mystery with Basil Rathbone as Baker Street's finest. Indeed, there had even been an admirable one with Peter Cushing. Yet director Douglas Hickox still deemed it necessary to trek across Dartmoor for a further encounter with the accursed Baskervilles and their pesky pooch. Head and shoulders above a cast of familiar British faces, Ian Richardson goes for the sardonic approach as Holmes in this solid take on the tale. DP DVD

Ian Richardson *Sherlock Holmes* • Donald Churchill *Dr Watson* • Denholm Elliott *Dr Mortimer* • Nicholas Clay *Jack Stapleton* • Martin Shaw *Sir Henry Baskerville* • Glynis Barber *Beryl Stapleton* • Edward Judd *Mr Barrymore* • Eleanor Bron *Mrs Barrymore* • Brian Blessed *Geoffrey Lyons* • Connie Booth *Laura Lyons* • Ronald Lacey *Inspector Lestrade* ■ *Dir* Douglas Hickox • *Scr* Charles Pogue, from the novel by Sir Arthur Conan Doyle

The Hour before the Dawn ★★

Second World War spy drama
1944 · US · BW · 74mins

Franchot Tone is a pacifist English lord who weds his Austrian servant, sultry Veronica Lake, not realising she is a German spy helping the Nazis plan an invasion of England. It sounds like fun, but this propaganda piece, made at the height of the Second World War, is unremittingly earnest and none too convincing. Adapted from one of Somerset Maugham's lesser works, it puts too much strain on Lake's histrionic reserves, while Tone seems bemused by the whole business. TV

Franchot Tone *Jim Hetherton* • Veronica Lake *Dora Bruckmann* • John Sutton *Roger Hetherton* • Binnie Barnes *May Hetherton* • Henry Stephenson *Gen Hetherton* • Philip Merivale *Sir Leslie Buchannan* ■ *Dir* Frank Tuttle • *Scr* Michael Hogan, Lesser Samuels, from the novel by W Somerset Maugham

The Hour of Decision ★★

Mystery drama 1957 · UK · BW · 80mins

This tidy little whodunnit may not break the mould, but it packs in more than its fair share of surprises. Jeff Morrow plays a journalist discovering his wife is implicated in a murder because of an adulterous affair. Hazel Court seems a little distracted, though Morrow gets better support from Lionel Jeffries and Anthony Dawson. DP

Jeff Morrow *Joe Sanders* • Hazel Court *Peggy Sanders* • Lionel Jeffries *Elvin Main* • Anthony Dawson *Garry Bax* • Mary Laura Wood *Olive Bax* • Carl Bernard *Inspector Gower* • Vanda Godsell *Eileen Chadwick* ■ *Dir* C Pennington Richards • *Scr* Norman Hudis

H

Hour of the Assassin ★★★ 15

Political thriller 1987 · US · Colour · 88mins

This political thriller is directed by Luis Llosa, with Peru standing in for a mythical South American country. Erik Estrada is sent there to kill a newly-elected democratic president, while Robert Vaughn is the CIA agent whose orders are to stop the assassin at any cost. No subtleties here, but the film has an exciting Costa-Gavras flavour and has quite a few surprises in its cartridge belt. TH

Erik Estrada *Martin Fierro* • Robert Vaughn *Sam Merrick* • Alfredo Alvarez Calderon *Ortiz* • Orlando Sacha *Folco* • Reynaldo Arenas *Paladoro* • Lourdes Berninzon *Adriana* ■ *Dir* Luis Llosa • *Scr* Matt Leipzig

Hour of the Gun ★★★★

Western 1967 · US · Colour · 100mins

A superb follow-up to his own *Gunfight at the OK Corral* from director John Sturges, this film starts where the previous movie climaxed, and charts the moral decline of lawman Wyatt Earp from upright marshal to relentless avenger. He's portrayed brilliantly by a grim James Garner, in a far cry from his customary jolly screen image. Doc Holliday is also perfectly played by Jason Robards, providing a marvellous contrast to Garner's Earp. This movie, with its fine use of Panavision and its memorable Jerry Goldsmith score, prefigures the darker, anti-romantic westerns that were to come, notably those of director Sam Peckinpah. TS

James Garner *Wyatt Earp* • Jason Robards *Doc Holliday* • Robert Ryan *Ike Clanton* • Albert Salmi *Octavius Roy* • Charles Aidman *Horace Sullivan* • Steve Ihnat *Warshaw* • Jon Voight *Curly Bill Brocius* ■ *Dir* John Sturges • *Scr* Edward Anhalt • *Cinematographer* Lucien Ballard

The Hour of the Pig ★★★ 15

Comedy drama
1993 · UK/Fr · Colour · 107mins

British director Leslie Megahey here dares to be different to such a degree that the odd outbreak of perfunctory or off-target acting matters not one jot. He has successfully created a distinctive other world, specifically a medieval France which is defined by upper-class corruption, peasant superstition and ecclesiastical apathy. This ludicrous mixture of dark comedy and original thrills is revealed through the story of a smart Paris lawyer (Colin Firth) who has to defend a pig on a charge of murder. Though sometimes creaking under the burden of its own ideas, the film is still intelligent and wonderfully dotty. JM

Colin Firth *Richard Courtois* • Ian Holm *Albertus* • Donald Pleasence *Pincheon* • Amina Annabi *Samira* • Nicol Williamson *Seigneur Jehan d'Auferre* • Michael Gough *Magistrate Boniface* • Harriet Walter *Jeannine* • Jim Carter *Mathieu* • Lysette Anthony *Filette d'Auferre* ■ *Dir/Scr* Leslie Megahey

Hour of the Star ★★★★ 15

Drama 1985 · Bra · Colour · 95mins

Directed by a 52-year-old mother of nine, this debut stands as one of Third Cinema's most remarkable examples of magical neorealism. Suzana Amaral graphically depicts Sao Paolo's grinding poverty, while still investing her film with brave humour and touching humanity. Marcelia Cartaxo deservedly won the best actress prize at Berlin for her performance as the virginal typist, whose dreams of celebrity and romance are confounded as much by society's expectations as her own lack of self-esteem and the swaggering ignorance of her boorish boyfriend. DP. In Portuguese with English subtitles.

Marcelia Cartaxo *Macabea* • José Dumont *Olimpico* • Tamara Taxman *Gloria* • Fernanda Montenegro *Mme Carlotta* ■ *Dir* Suzana Amaral • *Scr* Suzana Amaral, Alfredo Oroz, from a novella by Claire Lispector

The Hour of the Wolf ★★★ 15

Psychological drama
1967 · Swe · BW · 83mins

This relentlessly ominous study of the price of artistic creativity comprises a series of gothic flashbacks inspired by Liv Ullmann's discovery of the diary belonging to her missing and much-tormented husband, Max von Sydow. With Sven Nykvist's camera surreally conjuring up expressionist horror, von Sydow is mocked by the ghoulish members of Erland Josephson's household and subjected to visions of demons and phantoms from his past. Nevertheless, we expect more of Bergman than eerie set pieces. DP. In Swedish with English subtitles.. Contains violence. DVD

Max von Sydow *Johan Borg* • Liv Ullmann *Alma Borg* • Erland Josephson *Baron von Merkens* • Ingrid Thulin *Veronica Vogler* ■ *Dir/Scr* Ingmar Bergman

The Hour of 13 ★★

Mystery thriller 1952 · UK · BW · 77mins

Whereas 1934 thriller, *The Mystery of Mr X*, unmasked the killer in the opening sequence, this remake plays its cards much closer to its chest. Set in Edwardian London, this stars Peter Lawford as a Raffles-like jewel thief who becomes Inspector Roland Culver's chief suspect when a purloined pendant is found beside the body of one of ten policemen murdered in identical fashion. Lawford makes an appealing hero, but the pleasure comes from watching the accomplished supporting cast. DP

Peter Lawford *Nicholas Revel* • Dawn Addams *Jane Frensham* • Roland Culver *Connor* • Derek Bond *Sir Christopher Lenhurst* • Leslie Dwyer *Ernie Perker* • Michael Hordern *Sir Herbert Frensham* ■ *Dir* Harold French • *Scr* Leon Gordon, Howard Emmett Rogers, from the novel *X v Rex* by Philip MacDonald

The Hours ★★★★ 12

Drama 2002 · US · Colour · 110mins

David Hare's magnificent screenplay is a poignant exploration of longing, desire and regret that interweaves the lives of three women from different eras. Nicole Kidman's neurosis-driven Virginia Woolf is the most developed and compelling character, but co-stars Julianne Moore and Meryl Streep are also interesting, as a stifled 1950s housewife and a present-day lesbian book editor respectively. Had Moore and Streep's scenarios been made weightier and less clichéd, the feature would have been a masterpiece. As it stands, it's a sophisticated and poetic triumph from director Stephen Daldry. SF. Contains swearing. DVD

Meryl Streep *Clarissa Vaughan* • Julianne Moore *Laura Brown* • Nicole Kidman *Virginia Woolf* • Ed Harris *Richard Brown* • Toni Collette *Kitty* • Claire Danes *Julia Vaughan* • Jeff Daniels *Louis Waters* • Stephen Dillane *Leonard Woolf* • Allison Janney *Sally Lester* • John C Reilly *Dan Brown* • Miranda Richardson *Vanessa Bell* ■ *Dir* Stephen Daldry • *Scr* David Hare, from the novel by Michael Cunningham

The Hours and Times ★★★★ 18

Drama 1992 · US · BW · 54mins

Shortly after the birth of his son Julian, and at the end of the 1963 UK tour that saw the start of Beatlemania around the country, John Lennon accompanied the band's manager, Brian Epstein, on a short holiday to Spain. This highly plausible, carefully written and superbly played film takes its starting point from rumours of what might have occurred during the trip. Ian Hart is magnificent as the cynical Lennon, who is torn between his affection for a man to whom he owed so much and his insatiable urge to mock. David Angus also impresses as the timid, homosexual Epstein, but the real credit goes to writer/director Christopher Münch. DP. Contains swearing, nudity.

David Angus *Brian Epstein* • Ian Hart *John Lennon* • Stephanie Pack *Marianne* • Robin McDonald *Quinones* • Sergio Moreno *Miguel* ■ *Dir/Scr* Christopher Münch

The Hours of the Day ★★★ 15

Drama 2003 · Sp · Colour · 98mins

With its grindingly authentic depiction of the mundane existence of a suburban Barcelona shopkeeper, Jaime Rosales's debut feature opens as a study of those trapped in the often ignored gap between poverty and comfort. But from the moment Alex Brendemühl strangles a female taxi driver on a deserted country road, the film becomes increasingly tense, as we wonder why he committed such a senseless crime and whether he will kill again. Moreover, it forces us to reconsider his relationships with his doting mother, ambitious girlfriend and loyal friend, whose wedding he conspires to ruin. DP. In Spanish with English subtitles. Contains swearing and violence. DVD

Alex Brendemühl *Abel* • Vincente Romero *Marcos* • María Antonia Martínez *Mother* • Agata Roca *Tere* • Pape Monsoriu *Trini* • Irene Belza *Carmen* ■ *Dir* Jaime Rosales • *Scr* Jaime Rosales, Enric Rufas

House ★★ 15

Horror comedy 1986 · US · Colour · 88mins

A straightforward haunted house chiller, furnished with effective fun-fuelled scares. Blocked author William Katt (playing a Stephen King clone) moves into a Gothic mansion previously owned by his nutty late aunt to work on his Vietnam memoirs. Soon strange phenomena and rubbery creatures from a sinister netherworld are roaming the floors. Director Steve Miner ably steers between broad humour and beastly visitations for tame shock value. AJ DVD

William Katt *Roger Cobb* • George Wendt *Harold Gorton* • Richard Moll *Big Ben* • Kay Lenz *Sandy* • Mary Stavin *Tanya* • Michael Ensign *Chet Parker* ■ *Dir* Steve Miner • *Scr* Ethan Wiley, from a story by Fred Dekker

House! ★★ 15

Comedy 2000 · UK · Colour · 85mins

A rundown seafront bingo hall faces closure due to the twin threats of a leaking roof and competition from a new superhall. The establishment's only hope lies in a lucrative national lotto game and an usherette's psychic ability to influence the way balls fall. Kelly Macdonald and Jason Hughes give spirited performances, as do Freddie Jones and Miriam Margolyes. But they're hogtied by a weak script and ham-fisted handling which fails to generate tension, even during the climactic big-game finale. DA DVD

Kelly Macdonald *Linda* • Jason Hughes *Gavin* • Freddie Jones *Mr Anzani* • Miriam Margolyes *Beth* • Mossie Smith *Kay* • Bruce Forsyth • Keith Chegwin ■ *Dir* Julian Kemp • *Scr* Jason Sutton, from an idea by Eric Styles

House II: the Second Story ★ 15

Horror comedy 1987 · US · Colour · 84mins

Director Ethan Wiley's dumb fright farce starts out as a bad John Hughes teen comedy and ends up like a demented episode of *Bonanza*. Arye Gross and Lar Park Lincoln move into their great-great-grandfather's property and dig up the legendary Old West outlaw for a crystal skull with magical properties. Zombie Gramps then leads the duo on a wild chase through endless alternate universes to battle an uninspired array of rubber creatures. AJ DVD

Arye Gross *Jesse McLaughlin* • Jonathan Stark *Charlie* • Royal Dano *Gramps* • Bill Maher *John* • John Ratzenberger *Bill Towner* • Lar Park Lincoln *Kate* • Amy Yasbeck *Lana* • Gregory Walcott *Sheriff* • Dwier Brown *Clarence* ■ *Dir/Scr* Ethan Wiley

House III: The Horror Show ★ 18

Horror 1989 · US · Colour · 91mins

This grisly tale of a mass murderer sent to the electric chair who returns after death to terrorise the cop who brought him to justice bears more than a cursory resemblance to the equally turgid Wes Craven vehicle *Shocker*, released the same year. Brion James plays the killer with his tongue firmly in his cheek, while director James Isaac delivers a jumbled movie that between the bouts of predictable action is a solid bore. Yet another sequel, *House IV: Home Deadly Home*, followed in 1992. RS DVD

Lance Henriksen *Lucas McCarthy* • Brion James *Max Jenke* • Rita Taggart *Donna McCarthy* • Dedee Pfeiffer *Bonnie McCarthy* • Aron Eisenberg *Scott McCarthy* • Thom Bray *Peter Campbell* ■ *Dir* James Isaac • *Scr* Allyn Warner, Leslie Bohem, Alan Smithee

The House across the Bay ★★

Crime drama 1940 · US · BW · 87mins

Joan Bennett marries likeable racketeer George Raft then shops him to the authorities for his own good. Unfortunately he gets sent to Alcatraz for longer than she anticipated, thanks to a double-cross by his lawyer Lloyd Nolan who wants Bennett all to himself. Then there's Walter Pidgeon's wealthy aviator as her third devotee. It must be the parade of jewellery and high fashion (26 changes of costume, according to publicity) that makes her, an otherwise dull character, such an attraction. Occasional expressionistic lighting is not enough to redeem a trite and absurd story. AE

George Raft *Steve Larwitt* • Joan Bennett *Brenda Bentley* • Lloyd Nolan *Slant Kolma* • Walter Pidgeon *Tim Nolan* • Gladys George *Mary Bogale* • Peggy Shannon *Alice* ■ *Dir* Archie Mayo • *Scr* Kathryn Scola, from a story by Myles Connolly

House Arrest ★★★ PG

Comedy 1996 · US · Colour · 104mins

This odd but surprisingly watchable comedy takes a fresh look at the impact of marital discord. Worried that their parents are about to get a divorce, Kyle Howard and Amy Sakasitz decide drastic action is required. So they lock them in the basement, together with their friend's bickering mum and dad. Pretty soon other pupils are queueing up for their unique marriage guidance programme. The performances of both adults and youngsters are uniformly strong and, although sentimentality isn't kept entirely at bay, this still makes for thoughtful entertainment. JF

Jamie Lee Curtis *Janet Beindorf* • Kevin Pollak *Ned Beindorf* • Kyle Howard *Grover Beindorf* • Russel Harper *TJ Krupp* • Amy Sakasitz *Stacy Beindorf* • Wallace Shawn *Vic Finley* • Jennifer Love Hewitt *Brooke Figler* • Jennifer Tilly *Cindy Figler* ■ *Dir* Harry Winer • *Scr* Michael Hitchcock

House by the Cemetery ★★★ 18

Horror 1981 · It · Colour · 75mins

A flesh-eating ghoul (Giovanni de Nari) inhabits the basement of a family's New England home and must continue his gruesomely bizarre surgical practices on them to remain a living dead zombie in Italian gore maestro Lucio Fulci's last great grisly horror movie before his work slid into the incoherent schlock gutter. Visually arresting, excessively nasty and building to a well-sustained climax of exciting Gothic melodrama, this is a highly effective *Grand Guignol* shocker and a favorite among Fulci aficionados. AJ. Italian dialogue dubbed into English. DVD

Catriona MacColl *Lucy Boyle* • Paolo Malco *Norman Boyle* • Ania Pieroni *Ann* • Silvia Collatina *Mae Freudstein* • Giovanni Frezza *Bob Boyle* • Giovanni de Nari *Dr Freudstein* ■ *Dir* Lucio Fulci • *Scr* Lucio Fulci, Giorgio Mariuzzo, from a story by Elisa Livia Briganti [Elisa Briganti]

House by the River ★★★

Film noir 1950 · US · BW · 87mins

This has been described as Fritz Lang's most Teutonic American picture. However, the surfeit of atmosphere can't atone for the lack of suspense in this tired treatise on the old adage, "murder will out". The byplay between evil novelist Louis Hayward and his envious, lame brother Lee Bowman is effective, but the romance between Bowman and his prissy sister-in-law (Jane Wyatt) is less convincing. Making moody use of light and shade, Lang involves us more deeply than the plot merits. DP

Louis Hayward *Stephen Byrne* • Lee Bowman *John Byrne* • Jane Wyatt *Marjorie Byrne* • Dorothy Patrick *Emily Gaunt* • Ann Shoemaker *Mrs Ambrose* • Jody Gilbert *Flora Bantam* • Sarah Padden *Mrs Beach* ■ *Dir* Fritz Lang • *Scr* Mel Dinelli, from the novel by AP Herbert

House Call ★★★ 18

Thriller 1996 · Neth · Colour · 100mins

Ben Verbong directs this eerie thriller with an effective blend of tension and shocking violence, taking what is essentially a TV-movie plot and investing it with splendidly unpredictable atmosphere. Divorced doctor Renée Soutendijk moves into a seaside condo with her young son, but ignores the warnings of her fellow residents and befriends copywriter Victor Löw. But it takes a series of obscene phone calls, the presence of a peeping tom and a brutal murder to make her finally question their relationship. DP. In Dutch with English subtitles. Contains swearing, violence and sex scenes.

Renée Soutendijk *Roos Hartman* • Victor Löw *Eric Coenen* • Hans Hoes *Jacy* • Jaimy Siebel *Davy* • Huib Rooymans *Erwin Nijkamp* • Peter Smits *Officer* ■ *Dir* Ben Verbong • *Scr* Jean van de Velde, from a idea by Gijs Versluys

House Calls ★★ PG

Comedy 1978 · US · Colour · 93mins

This hospital romance can't decide whether it wants to be a scorching screwball or a cosy sitcom. Making her Hollywood debut, Glenda Jackson is way below her *Touch of Class* form as a divorcee seeking commitment from Walter Matthau's newly footloose widower. But then, under Howard Zieff's lacklustre direction, no one emerges from this muddled comedy with much credit. DP

Walter Matthau *Dr Charley Nicholas* • Glenda Jackson *Ann Atkinson* • Art Carney *Dr Amos Willoughby* • Richard Benjamin *Dr Norman Soloman* • Candice Azzara [Candy Azzara] *Ellen Grady* • Dick O'Neill *Irwin Owett* ■ *Dir* Howard Zieff • *Scr* Julius J Epstein, Alan Mandel, Charles Shyer, Max Shulman, from a story by Max Shulman, Julius J Epstein

A House Divided ★★★ 15

Period drama based on a true story 2000 · US · Colour · 96mins

This TV drama is the tale of a woman who returns to her family's plantation at the end of the Civil War, only to have to fight for her birthright when it is revealed she is mixed race, raised by her father (Sam Waterston) as white, but also the daughter of a slave he raped. Jennifer Beals gives a terrific performance as the young woman caught between her white family and the prejudices of having a black mother. JB

Sam Waterston *David Dickson* • Jennifer Beals *Amanda Dickson* • Lisa Gay Hamilton *Julia* • Tim Daly [Timothy Daly] *Charles Dubose* • Shirley Douglas *Elizabeth Dickson* • Sean McCann *Rutherford* ■ *Dir* John Kent Harrison • *Scr* Paris Qualles, from the non-fiction book *Woman of Color, Daughter of Privilege: Amanda Dickson* by Kent Anderson Leslie

The House in Nightmare Park ★ PG

Comedy thriller 1973 · UK · Colour · 91mins

One of the few low points in comedian Frankie Howerd's career is this failed fright farce, which invites poor comparisons with Bob Hope's horror comedy classic *The Cat and the Canary*. Howerd, who aptly plays a ham actor, is invited to perform at Ray Milland's creepy stately home and discovers he's heir to the family fortune. As the corpses pile up, so do the lame gags. DP

Frankie Howerd *Foster Twelvetrees* • Ray Milland *Stewart Henderson* • Hugh Burden *Major Reginald Henderson* • Kenneth Griffith *Ernest Henderson* • John Bennett *Patel* • Rosalie Crutchley *Jessica Henderson* • Ruth Dunning *Agnes Henderson* • Elizabeth MacLennan *Verity* ■ *Dir* Peter Sykes • *Scr* Clive Exton, Terry Nation

House in the Woods ★★★

Thriller 1957 · UK · BW · 62mins

This is an unexpectedly tense British B-movie from little-known director Maxwell Munden. Playing a painter who many suspect of slaughtering his spouse, Ronald Howard reveals a flair for villainy as he lurks around the country hideaway he's leased to writer Michael Gough and wife Patricia Roc. Logic is not the strong suit of Munden's script, but he more than compensates with his eerie exploitation of both the cottage's shadowy interiors and its isolated setting. DP

Ronald Howard *Spencer Rowland* • Patricia Roc *Carol Carter* • Michael Gough *Geoffrey Carter* • Andrea Troubridge *Mrs Shellaby* • Bill Shine *Col Shellaby* • Norah Hammond *Mrs Bletchley* ■ *Dir* Maxwell Munden • *Scr* Maxwell Munden, from the short story *Prelude to Murder* by Walter C Brown

House of a Thousand Dolls ★★

Thriller 1967 · Sp/W Ger · Colour · 95mins

Vincent Price plays more of a supporting role in this tawdry and self-consciously titillating exposé of white slavery in Tangiers. As a villainous magician, he abducts young women in his famous disappearing act and passes them on to the mysterious "King of Hearts" who sets them to work in a local brothel. George Nader's investigation of the disappearances and the kingpin's real identity is the main – and boring – thrust of the story. Directed by Jeremy Summers, on typically low-brow form, this is surprisingly exploitative for its era. AJ

Vincent Price *Felix Manderville* • Martha Hyer *Rebecca* • George Nader *Stephen Armstrong* • Ann Smyrner *Marie Armstrong* • Wolfgang Kieling *Inspector Emil* ■ *Dir* Jeremy Summers • *Scr* Peter Welbeck [Harry Alan Towers], Carmen M Román

House of America ★★★ 15

Drama 1996 · UK/Neth · Colour and BW · 93mins

By combining stylised colour with sun-tinted monochrome, first-time director Marc Evans cleverly contrasts the post-industrial Welsh wilderness with the wide-open spaces of the American neverland described by Jack Kerouac. But the film – about three kids who grow up in a rundown mining village believing their father has found the good life across the Atlantic – quickly descends into tabloid caricature. DP. Contains swearing, sex scenes and some violence.

Sian Phillips *Mam* • Steven Mackintosh *Sid Lewis* • Lisa Palfrey *Gwenny Lewis* • Matthew Rhys *Boyo Lewis* • Richard Harrington *Cat* ■ *Dir* Marc Evans • *Scr* Edward Thomas, from his play

House of Angels ★★★★ 15

Comedy drama 1992 · Swe · Colour · 114mins

Scandinavian culture is littered with tales of respectable rural folk resisting devious city slickers. But Colin Nutley slyly inverts that scenario in this gentle satire, in which the entrenched prejudices of the countrysiders are held up to ridicule. Caricature is almost inevitable in the depiction of the locals, appalled by the fact that cabaret star Helena Bergström and her leather-clad biker buddy, Rikard Wolff, have decided to live on the farm inherited from her rich grandfather. Whimsically charming. DP. In Swedish with English subtitles. Contains sex scenes and swearing.

Helena Bergström *Fanny Zander* • Rikard Wolff *Zac* • Per Oscarsson *Erik Zander* • Sven Wollter *Axel Flogfält* • Viveka Seldhahl *Rut Flogfält* • Reine Brynolfsson *Fleming Collmert* • Jakob Eklund *Mårten Flogfält* • Ernst Günther *Gottfried Pettersson* ■ *Dir/Scr* Colin Nutley

House of Angels II: The Second Summer ★★

Comedy 1994 · Swe · Colour · 137mins

They say you should never go home, but that's exactly where director Colin Nutley should have allowed Helena Bergström and Rikard Wolff to go. Instead he sweeps them off to New York in this contrived sequel. Admittedly, their options were limited, their farmhouse having burned down while they were away on tour. But their adventures in the Big Apple with Tord Pettersson and his emigrant brother are less than riveting. DP. In Swedish with English subtitles.

Helena Bergström *Fanny* • Rikard Wolff *Zac* • Sven Wollter *Axel* • Ernst Günther *Gottfried* • Tord Pettersson *Ivar* • Reine Brynolfsson *Vicar* ■ *Dir/Scr* Colin Nutley

House of Bamboo ★★★

Crime drama 1955 · US · Colour · 98mins

Director Samuel Fuller was often described as a Hollywood maverick, but he functioned more than adequately as a house director of action movies at 20th Century-Fox, making tightly budgeted films look costly. This thick-ear crime drama is one of his better efforts, boasting good performances from three well-cast Hollywood leading men (Robert Ryan, Robert Stack, Cameron Mitchell) and some striking Tokyo photography from cameraman Joe MacDonald. TS

Robert Ryan *Sandy Dawson* • Robert Stack *Eddie Kenner/Spanier* • Shirley Yamaguchi *Mariko* • Cameron Mitchell *Griff* • Brad Dexter *Captain Hanson* • Sessue Hayakawa *Inspector Kita* ■ *Dir* Samuel Fuller • *Scr* Harry Kleiner, Samuel Fuller

The House of Bernarda Alba ★★★ 15

Drama 1987 · Sp · Colour · 103mins

While still laying the blame for Franco's tyranny on the prejudices of the bourgeoisie, Marcel Camus's adaptation of Federico Garcia Lorca's play places more emphasis on the melodramatic tensions that build up after a handsome suitor intrudes upon the solitary mourning which a widow imposes on her five daughters following their father's death. Opening out the action without diluting its intensity, Camus conjures up some evocative visuals and draws thoughtful performances from Irene Gutierrez Caba and her frustrated brood. DP. A Spanish language film.

Irene Gutierrez Caba *Bernarda Alba* • Ana Belén *Adela* • Florinda Chico *Poncia* • Enriqueta Carballeira *Angustias* • Vicky Peña *Martirio* • Aurora Pastor *Magdalena* • Mercedes Lezcano *Amelia* • Rosario Garcia-Ortega *Maria Josefa* ■ *Dir* Mario Camus • *Scr* Mario Camus, Antonio Larreta, from the play by Federico Garcia Lorca

House of Blackmail ★★ U

Crime drama 1953 · UK · BW · 71mins

Maurice Elvey was the most prolific director in British cinema history, making over 300 features after his debut in 1913. Unfortunately, this low-budget B-movie, in which a hitch-hiker finds himself in trouble after taking a lift from a woman who's being blackmailed, is not one of his best efforts. We could do with more surprises, but the pace is unrelenting and there are typically solid performances from Mary Germaine, William Sylvester and John Arnatt. DP

William Sylvester *Jimmy* • Mary Germaine *Carol Blane* • Alexander Gauge *John Markham* • John Arnatt *Peter Carter* • Dennis Shaw [Denis Shaw] *Bassett* • Ingeborg Wells *Emma* ■ *Dir* Maurice Elvey • *Scr* Allan MacKinnon

House of Cards ★★

Political thriller 1968 · US · Colour · 104mins

A lacklustre political thriller set in France, where a rich right-wing group who feel betrayed over Algerian independence are plotting to take over the country and execute De Gaulle. George Peppard is the innocent American in Paris who tumbles the plot, and Orson Welles is briefly imposing as the French publisher who is financing it. Sadly, the promising idea is rather undermined by some hammy acting and a tendency to stage scenes in front of some tourist location or other. AT

George Peppard *Reno Davis* • Inger Stevens *Anne de Villemont* • Orson Welles *Charles Leschenhaut* • Keith Michell *Hubert Morillon* • Ralph Michael *Claude de Gonde* • Maxine Audley *Matilde Vosiers* • William Job *Bernard Bourdon* • Peter Bayliss *Edmond Vosier* ■ *Dir* John Guillermin • *Scr* Irving Ravetch, Harriet Frank Jr, from a novel by Stanley Ellin

House of Cards ★ 15

Drama 1993 · US · Colour · 108mins

When Kathleen Turner's archaeologist husband falls to his death from a Mayan pyramid in Mexico, she packs up and returns to the States where her six-year-old daughter begins to behave very strangely. Child psychologist Tommy Lee Jones is brought in to help. At first, you think the little girl is going to take us into Stephen King territory; instead, it leads only to the usual clichéd drama. Sad to see Jones and Turner wasting their time. AT

Kathleen Turner *Ruth Matthews* • Tommy Lee Jones *Dr Jake Beerlander* • Asha Menina *Sally Matthews* • Shiloh Strong *Michael Matthews* • Esther Rolle *Adelle* ■ *Dir* Michael Lessac • *Scr* Michael Lessac, from a story by Michael Lessac, Robert Jay Litz

House of Dark Shadows ★★★★ 18

Gothic horror 1970 · US · Colour · 92mins

The first of two movie offshoots (along with *Night of Dark Shadows*) from the popular US daytime horror soap *Dark Shadows*, featuring a number of series regulars, is one of the best horror movies of the 1970s. Eighteenth-century vampire Barnabas Collins (Jonathan Frid) rises from his Maine grave to convert all the residents of the family mansion to his evil bloodsucking ways. Lavish production values, stunning photography, great special effects and moments of pure bone-chilling shock make this a resonant delight, exquisitely directed by series producer Dan Curtis. AJ

Jonathan Frid *Barnabas Collins* • Joan Bennett *Elizabeth Collins Stoddard* • Grayson Hall *Dr Julia Hoffman* • Kathryn Leigh Scott *Maggie Evans* • Roger Davis *Jeff Clark* • Nancy Barrett *Carolyn Stoddard* • John Karlen *Willie Loomis* • Thayer David *Prof T Eliot Stokes* • Louis Edmonds *Roger Collins* • Donald Briscoe *Todd Jennings* • David Henesy *David Collins* ■ *Dir* Dan Curtis • *Scr* Sam Hall, Gordon Russell, from the TV series created by Dan Curtis, Art Wallace • *Cinematographer* Arthur J Ornitz

House of Dracula ★★ PG

Horror 1945 · US · BW · 64mins

Not to be confused with *House of Frankenstein*, this sequel stars Glenn Strange as Frankenstein's monster, Lon Chaney Jr as the Wolf Man and, most impressively, the elegant John Carradine as Count Dracula. Needless to add, they are all splendid to watch under the famously copyrighted Universal make-up. It's the plot that's tiresome, as Onslow Stevens tries to "cure" the monsters of their evil qualities by resorting to science. Erle C Kenton's direction keeps things suitably murky, however, and that Universal house style always adds pleasure to the experience. TS

Lon Chaney Jr *Lawrence Talbot* • John Carradine *Count Dracula* • Martha O'Driscoll *Miliza Morell* • Lionel Atwill *Inspector Holtz* • Jane Adams (1) *Nina* • Onslow Stevens *Dr Edelman* • Ludwig Stossel *Ziegfried* • Glenn Strange *The Monster* ■ *Dir* Erle C Kenton • *Scr* Edward T Lowe

House of Evil ★ 15

Horror 1968 · Mex/US · Colour · 72mins

Boris Karloff wanders around a castle equipped with a torture dungeon in one of the four little-seen Mexican cheapies the master of the macabre made just prior to his death in 1969. The plot is very much in the vein of *The Old Dark House* with many of the cast coming to sticky ends. All the south of the border scenes were shot by director Juan Ibanez, while Jack Hill directed the Los Angeles-based interiors with Karloff. AJ

Boris Karloff *Mathias Morthevald* • Julissa *Lucy Durand* • Andres Garcia *Carlos Bisler* • Beatriz Baz *Cordelia Rush* • Quintin Bulnes *Dr Emerich Horvath* ■ *Dir* Juan Ibanez, Jack Hill • *Scr* Jack Hill, Luis Enrique Vergara, from the story *The Fall of the House of Usher* by Edgar Allan Poe

House of Evil ★★★ 18

Horror 1983 · US · Colour · 87mins

Although basically another *Friday the 13th* retread, the feature debut of Mark Rosman avoids most of the obvious pitfalls that plague the slasher genre to emerge as a skilfully-made shocker. An end-of-term slumber party turns into a bloody nightmare when a sorority group unlock the dark secret of their out-to-lunch housemother. Numerous innovative touches – Kathryn McNeil fighting off her unknown assailant while under drug-induced hallucinations – elevate this perceptive, low-gore entry above its contemporaries. AJ

Kathryn McNeil *Katherine* • Eileen Davidson *Vicki* • Janis Zido *Liz* • Robin Meloy *Jeanie* • Harley Kozak [Harley Jane Kozak] *Diane* • Jodie Draigie *Morgan* • Ellen Dorsher *Stevie* • Lois Kelso Hunt *Mrs Dorothy Slater* • Christopher Lawrence *Dr Nelson Beck* ■ *Dir* Mark Rosman • *Scr* Mark Rosman, Bobby Fine

The House of Fear ★★ U

Mystery 1944 · US · BW · 69mins

Not one of the best of the Basil Rathbone–Nigel Bruce forays into Sherlock Holmes territory, which is a shame because the finale could have been wonderfully surprising if it had been treated better. The members of the "Good Comrades Club" – a group of wealthy men living in a Scottish mansion – are being killed off one by one, and Watson himself is kidnapped when he joins Holmes to investigate. TH DVD

Basil Rathbone *Sherlock Holmes* • Nigel Bruce *Dr Watson* • Aubrey Mather *Alastair* • Dennis Hoey *Lestrade* • Paul Cavanagh *Simon Merrivale* • Holmes Herbert *Alan Cosgrave* ■ *Dir* Roy William Neill • *Scr* Roy Chanslor, from the story *The Adventures of the Five Orange Pips* by Sir Arthur Conan Doyle

House of Flying Daggers ★★★★ 15

Period martial arts drama
2004 · HK/Chi · Colour · 114mins

In 859 AD, the declining Tang dynasty faces revolt from a secret, Robin Hood-like society, known as House of Flying Daggers. Can the blind knife-throwing showgirl Zhang Ziyi guide undercover police captain Takeshi Kaneshiro to their mysterious new leader? Visually ravishing and artfully directed, Zhang Yimou's film suffers from too many drawn-out climaxes and a tepid romantic subplot. But the director's masterful panache, poetic finesse and gravity-bending fight choreography are a continual delight, even if Ziyi's acrobatic *femme fatale* steals the entire operatic show. AJ. In Mandarin with English subtitles. DVD

Takeshi Kaneshiro *Jin* • Andy Lau *Leo* • Zhang Ziyi *Mei* • Song Dandan *Yee* ■ *Dir* Zhang Yimou • *Scr* Zhang Yimou, Li Feng, Wang Bin, from a story by Zhang Yimou, Li Feng, Wang Bin

House of Fools ★★★ 15

Wartime black comedy drama
2002 · Rus/Fr · Colour · 104mins

This patchy but generally affecting film unfolds in a mental hospital on the Russian-Chechen border during the war of 1994-6. Chechen rebels commandeer the asylum, and patient Julia Vysotsky, who has delusions that she is engaged to popstar Bryan Adams, transfers her affections to Chechen Sultan Islamov. The scenes where Adams plays himself in honey-lit fantasy sequences are bizarre, and this is frequently sentimental and hackneyed, but director Andrei Konchalovsky somehow wrenches moments of genuine poignancy from the material. DP. In Russian with English subtitles. Contains violence, swearing, sex scenes, drug abuse, nudity. DVD

Bryan Adams • Julia Vysotsky *Janna* • Sultan Islamov *Ahmed* • Stanislav Varkki *Ali* • Vladas Bagdonas *Doctor* • Yevgeny Mironov [Yevgeni Mironov] *Soldier* • Elena Fomina *Lucy* • Marina Politseymako *Vika* ■ *Dir/Scr* Andrei Konchalovsky

House of Frankenstein ★★★

Horror 1944 · US · BW · 70mins

The sequel to *Frankenstein Meets the Wolf Man* adds John Carradine as Dracula into the engaging Universal monster mix. Mad doctor Boris Karloff escapes from prison after the building is struck by lightning and, with hunchback J Carrol Naish, seeks revenge on those who put him there. For this he enlists the help of the trio of vintage horror characters: Dracula, Frankenstein's monster and the Wolf Man. Glenn Strange plays the monster and Lon Chaney Jr the Wolf Man in a bundle of laughs and suspense. AJ

Boris Karloff *Dr Gustav Niemann* • Lon Chaney Jr *Lawrence Stewart Talbot* • J Carrol Naish *Daniel* • John Carradine *Count Dracula* • Anne Gwynne *Rita Hussman* • Peter Coe *Carl Hussman* • Lionel Atwill *Inspector Arnz* • Glenn Strange *The Monster* ■ *Dir* Erle C Kenton • *Scr* Edward T Lowe, from the story *The Devil's Brood* by Curt Siodmak

House of Games ★★★★ 15

Psychological thriller
1987 · US · Colour · 97mins

After several notable plays and screenplays, David Mamet became a director with this delectably clever parlour-game picture, which should delight connoisseurs of thrillers and cryptic crosswords. It's rather low on directorial flair, but high on literacy and performance values. Mamet's then-wife, Lindsay Crouse, plays a psychiatrist confronting the gambler (Joe Mantegna) who drove one of her patients to near-suicide. A card game results, with psychiatrist and gambler realising how similar their respective trades are. The joker in the pack is Mamet himself: this deck is well and truly stacked with bluff, double-bluff and a thrilling finale. AT. Contains violence and swearing. DVD

Lindsay Crouse *Margaret Ford* • Joe Mantegna *Mike* • Mike Nussbaum *Joey* • Lilia Skala *Dr Littauer* • JT Walsh *Businessman* ■ *Dir* David Mamet • *Scr* David Mamet, from a story by David Mamet, Jonathan Katz

The House of Mirth ★★ PG

Romantic drama
2000 · UK/US · Colour · 140mins

Edith Wharton's wonderful novel about a woman striving for financial and intellectual independence in a conservative, upper-crust society is faithfully brought to the screen by Terence Davies. Too faithfully, in fact: Davies directs at such a slow pace that much of the plot and characters seem rather lifeless. Gillian Anderson, from TV's *The X Files*, has a good shot at playing the heroine, though in the end she lacks the power required. Despite the budget limitations, the film's look is impressive. RB DVD

Gillian Anderson *Lily Bart* • Eric Stoltz *Lawrence Selden* • Anthony LaPaglia *Sim Rosedale* • Laura Linney *Bertha Dorset* • Terry Kinney *George Dorset* • Dan Aykroyd *Gus Trenor* • Elizabeth McGovern *Carry Fisher* • Eleanor Bron *Mrs Peniston* • Jodhi May *Grace Stepney* ■ *Dir* Terence Davies • *Scr* Terence Davies, from the novel by Edith Wharton

House of Mortal Sin ★★★ 15

Horror 1975 · UK · Colour · 99mins

This hugely under-rated shocker from cult director Pete Walker features Anthony Sharp, giving an extraordinary performance as a Catholic priest who sublimates his desires by violating the sanctity of the confessional and torturing his distressed victims with guilt. Anyone trying to stop his course of "divine justice" is murdered by such diverse means as incense burners and poisoned holy wafers. Walker stalwart Sheila Keith is on hand to give this warped morality tale its clever twist. AJ DVD

Anthony Sharp *Father Xavier Meldrum* • Susan Penhaligon *Jenny Welch* • Stephanie Beacham *Vanessa Welch* • Norman Eshley *Father Bernard Cutler* • Sheila Keith *Miss Brabazon* • Hilda Barry *Mrs Meldrum* • Stewart Bevan *Terry* ■ *Dir* Pete Walker • *Scr* David McGillivray

House of Mystery ★★★

Supernatural fantasy
1961 · UK · BW · 55mins

This is a neat little spine-tingler from Vernon Sewell, who was a dab hand at summoning up demons from beyond. There are plenty of uneasy moments in this haunting story, in which a couple of newlyweds learn the grim secret of their dream house from the resident spook himself. DP

Jane Hylton *Stella Lemming* • Peter Dyneley *Mark Lemming* • Nanette Newman *Joan Trevor* • Maurice Kaufmann *Henry Trevor* • Colin Gordon *Burdon* • Molly Urquhart *Mrs Bucknall* ■ *Dir* Vernon Sewell • *Scr* Vernon Sewell, from a play by Pierre Mills, C Vylars

House of Numbers ★★

Crime drama 1957 · US · BW · 91mins

Some of this implausible but quite ingenious thriller was shot in San Quentin prison, the eponymous house of the title. Behind bars is a bad guy, who is helped in his escape by his good twin brother. As both are played by Jack Palance, fans of the ever-watchable star get a double helping particularly as he effectively differentiates the two characters. RB

Jack Palance *Bill Judlow/Arnie Judlow* • Barbara Lang *Ruth Judlow* • Harold J Stone *Henry Nova* • Edward Platt *Warden* ■ *Dir* Russell Rouse • *Scr* Russell Rouse, Don Mankiewicz, from a novel by Jack Finney

House of 1000 Corpses ★★★ 18

Horror 2001 · US · Colour · 85mins

US rock star Rob Zombie is well known for his love of old horror films, so it's no surprise that his directorial debut takes a warped trip into the heart of B-movie-style terror. A homage to the so-called "grindhouse" shlockers of the 1970s, Zombie's self-penned story of two young couples falling victim to a sadistic family of inbred sickos is a low-budget nightmare with a big-budget feel. Derivative, yet darkly entertaining, the oddball feature makes up for an unfortunate lack of gore with inspired imagery, innovative cinematography and some fabulously freaky performances. Sadly, the overall tale is too incoherent to appeal much beyond its core horror audience. SF DVD

Sid Haig *Captain Spaulding* • Bill Moseley *Otis* • Sheri Moon *Baby* • Karen Black *Mother Firefly* • Chris Hardwick *Jerry Goldsmith* • Erin Daniels *Denise Willis* • Jennifer Jostyn *Mary Knowles* • Rainn Wilson *Bill Hudley* ■ *Dir/Scr* Rob Zombie

The House of Rothschild ★★★

Biographical drama 1934 · US · BW · 94mins

How the Rothschild dynasty rose from German ghetto obscurity to become the foremost banking house in Europe is a fascinating study of international monetary intrigue, early 19th century-style. Set against a lavishly mounted backdrop of the Napoleonic Wars, George Arliss plays two key roles – family patriarch Mayer and his son, Nathan – while Boris Karloff eschews monster make-up in this rather entertaining history lesson. AJ

George Arliss *Mayer Rothschild/Nathan Rothschild* • Boris Karloff *Count Ledrantz* • Loretta Young *Julie Rothschild* • Robert Young (1) *Captain Fitzroy* • C Aubrey Smith *Duke of Wellington* • Arthur Byron *Baring* • Reginald Owen *Herries* ■ *Dir* Alfred Werker • *Scr* Nunnally Johnson, from a play by George Humbert Westley

House of Sand and Fog ★★★★ 15

Drama 2003 · US/UK · Colour · 121mins

Revolving around a formidable Oscar-nominated turn by Ben Kingsley, the slow-burning film tells the story of a former Iranian colonel reduced to working menial jobs in the US. Desperate to return his family to the prosperity they once knew, he spends his life's savings on the repossessed home of recovering addict Jennifer Connelly, only to come into tragic confrontation with the woman over the property. First-time director Vadim Perelman paints a vivid and moving picture of cultural alienation and desperation. If Connelly looks too well groomed for her tortured role, it certainly doesn't spoil her overall strong performance, while Shohreh Aghdashloo and Jonathan Ahdout are wonderful as Kingsley's wife and son. SF. Contains swearing. DVD

Jennifer Connelly *Kathy Nicolo* • Ben Kingsley *Massoud Amir Behrani* • Ron Eldard *Lester Burdon* • Shohreh Aghdashloo *Nadi Behrani* • Jonathan Ahdout *Esmail* • Frances Fisher *Connie Walsh* • Kim Dickens *Carol* ■ *Dir* Vadim Perelman • *Scr* Vadim Perelman, Shawn Lawrence Otto, from the novel by Andre Dubus III

House of Secrets ★★

Thriller 1956 · UK · Colour · 97mins

A box-office sleeper in its day, this patchy thriller will probably seem threadbare to modern audiences, but director Guy Green uses Paris locations well and keeps the story ticking along. Groomed by Rank as the successor to Dirk Bogarde, Michael Craig never quite lived up to the reputation generated by the studio press office. However, as a naval officer impersonating his counterfeiting lookalike, he holds his own. DP

Michael Craig *Larry Ellis* • Julia Arnall *Diane* • Brenda de Banzie *Madame Ballu* • Barbara Bates *Judy* • David Kossoff *Van de Heide* • Gérard Oury *Pindar* • Geoffrey Keen *Burleigh* •

Anton Diffring *Lauderbache* ■ *Dir* Guy Green • *Scr* Robert Buckner, Bryan Forbes, from the novel *Storm over Paris* by Sterling Noel

The House of Seven Corpses ★★★

Horror 1973 · US · Colour · 90mins

An effective low-budget horror movie about making a low-budget horror movie. John Carradine is the creepy caretaker of a haunted house where a film crew is stalked by a real-life zombie while shooting an occult thriller. It's always enjoyable watching actors play actors, especially bad ones, and director Paul Harrison throws in some genuine scares and surprises to add to the cheap fun. He also sustains the tense atmosphere, until a truly horrific climax. AJ

John Ireland *Eric Hartman* • Faith Domergue *Gayle* • John Carradine *Mr Price* • Carole Wells *Anne* • Jerry Strickler *David* • Ron Foreman *Ron* ■ *Dir/Scr* Paul Harrison

House of Strangers ★★★

Crime drama 1949 · US · BW · 100mins

Famous for a prolonged wrangle over a screenwriting credit and a protest from the Bank of America, which funded most of Hollywood's studios, this crime drama features Edward G Robinson as a man who achieves the American Dream by becoming a successful banker but is then arrested for malpractice. Three of his sons take over and prevent him from resuming his responsibilities. Richard Conte's affair with Susan Hayward is a dramatic dead end and you feel the picture would have been better as a gangster thriller about the Mafia. Despite these flaws, Robinson's performance and the subversive theme make it well worth watching. AT

Edward G Robinson *Gino Monetti* • Susan Hayward *Irene Bennett* • Richard Conte *Max Monetti* • Luther Adler *Joe Monetti* • Paul Valentine *Pietro Monetti* • Efrem Zimbalist Jr *Tony* ■ *Dir* Joseph L Mankiewicz • *Scr* Philip Yordan, from the novel *I'll Never Go There Any More* by Jerome Weidman

House of the Dead ★★ 15

Horror thriller
2003 · US/Can/Ger · Colour · 86mins

This cartoonish, techno-driven splatter spectacular, based on a bestselling computer game, is a tedious tale about a group of over-sexed teens who arrive on an island for a rave party, only to discover the secluded paradise has been taken over by death-dealing cadavers. Taking refuge in an old dark house, they must use all their wits and any available weapon to survive the night and the relentless undead onslaught. A repetitive gore-fest. AJ. Contains violence, swearing.

Jonathan Cherry *Rudy* • Tyron Leitso *Simon* • Clint Howard *Salish* • Ona Grauer *Alicia* • Ellie Cornell *Casper* • Will Sanderson *Greg* • Enuka Okuma *Karma* • Jürgen Prochnow *Captain Kirk* ■ *Dir* Uwe Boll • *Scr* Mark A Altman, Dave Parker, from the story by Mark A Altman, Dan Bates, from the computer game

House of the Long Shadows ★★ 15

Horror 1983 · UK · Colour · 97mins

Vincent Price, Christopher Lee, Peter Cushing and John Carradine team up for the first and last time in this miscalculated update of the creaky horror classic *Seven Keys to Baldpate* from director Pete Walker. Desi Arnaz Jr is the author who bets publisher Richard Todd he can write a novel in 24 hours while holed up in an eerie Welsh mansion populated by the celebrated foursome. Tongue-in-cheek thrills and soft horror make little impact in a camp romp that wastes the talents of all involved. AJ

Vincent Price *Lionel* • Peter Cushing *Sebastian* • Christopher Lee *Corrigan* • Desi Arnaz Jr *Kenneth Magee* • Richard Todd *Sam Allison* • John Carradine *Lord Grisbane* • Julie Peasgood *Mary Norton* ■ *Dir* Pete Walker • *Scr* Michael Armstrong, from the novel *Seven Keys to Baldpate* by Earl Derr Biggers

The House of the Seven Gables ★★★

Period drama 1940 · US · BW · 88mins

One of the pioneers of the costume drama in German silent cinema, Joe May doesn't quite catch the American idiom in this adaptation of Nathaniel Hawthorne's 19th-century classic, which is more gothic than puritan in tone. George Sanders is, however, deliciously caddish as the scheming son who exploits a curse to consign brother Vincent Price to jail in a bid to take over the family mansion. DP

George Sanders *Jaffrey Pyncheon* • Margaret Lindsay *Hepzibah Pyncheon* • Vincent Price *Clifford Pyncheon* • Dick Foran *Matthew Holgrave/Matthew Maule* • Nan Grey *Phoebe Pyncheon* • Cecil Kellaway *Philip Barton* ■ *Dir* Joe May • *Scr* Lester Cole, Harold Greene, from the novel by Nathaniel Hawthorne

The House of the Seven Hawks ★★ U

Crime thriller 1959 · UK · BW · 91mins

Workhorse director Richard Thorpe had just completed some uncredited second unit work on MGM's epic *Ben-Hur* when he was sent by the studio to Britain and Holland to direct this bland B-movie. This story of a horde of Nazi diamonds lost since the war stars Robert Taylor, also slumming as the heroic ship's skipper who rumbles the plot. Everyone apart from Taylor speaks in thick European accents, while the cast includes that legendary actor/manager, Donald Wolfit. AT

Robert Taylor (1) *John Nordley* • Nicole Maurey *Constanta Sluiter* • Linda Christian *Elsa* • Donald Wolfit *Van Der Stoor* • David Kossoff *Wilhelm Dekker* ■ *Dir* Richard Thorpe • *Scr* Jo Eisinger, from the novel *The House of the Seven Flies* by Victor Canning

The House of the Spirits ★★ 15

Drama
1993 · Por/Den/Ger/US · Colour · 132mins

Isabel Allende's classic tale of dynastic rivalry and magic realism is one of those books that, for all the temptations, should have been left well alone. Danish director Bille August chose an impossibly difficult text for his first English-language film, and his own script (which takes monumental liberties with the original) is desperately pedestrian, but it's the casting that condemns this prestige project. DP. Contains violence, swearing and nudity.

Jeremy Irons *Esteban Trueba* • Meryl Streep *Clara Del Valle* • Glenn Close *Ferula* • Winona Ryder *Blanca* • Antonio Banderas *Pedro* • Vincent Gallo *Esteban Garcia* • Vanessa Redgrave *Nivea* • Maria Conchita Alonso *Transito* • Armin Mueller-Stahl *Severo* ■ *Dir* Bille August • *Scr* Bille August, from the novel by Isabel Allende

The House of Usher ★ 18

Horror 1988 · US · Colour · 87mins

A stupefying and sleazy modern-day redefinition of the doomed Usher family's desperate desire to continue their bloodline. Oliver Reed hams it up a storm as the super-sensitive Roderick Usher, while Donald Pleasence doesn't leave any of the cheap scenery unchewed. This is a depressing mixture of rape, murder, torture and severed body parts. AJ

Oliver Reed *Roderick Usher* • Romy Windsor *Molly McNulty* • Rufus Swart *Ryan Usher* • Norman Coombes *Mr Derrick* • Anne Stradi *Mrs Derrick* • Carole Farquhar *Gwen* • Philip Godewa *Dr Bailey* ■ *Dir* Alan Birkinshaw • *Scr* Michael J Murray, from the story *The Fall of the House of Usher* by Edgar Allan Poe

House of Wax ★★★★ PG

Period horror 1953 · US · Colour · 84mins

Director Andre De Toth's close remake of *The Mystery of the Wax Museum* (1933) is an exciting and diverting shocker that established Vincent Price as a major horror star. Price brilliantly portrays a mad masked sculptor – his mind and body deformed in a museum blaze staged by his insurance-hungry partner – who returns to dip human corpses in boiling wax for display in his chamber of horrors. Charles Bronson plays Price's mute assistant in this atmospheric *Grand Guignol* masterpiece, one of the most effective (and profitable) movies ever to use the 3-D gimmick. AJ DVD

Vincent Price *Professor Henry Jarrod* • Frank Lovejoy *Lieutenant Tom Brennan* • Phyllis Kirk *Sue Allen* • Carolyn Jones *Cathy Gray* • Paul Picerni *Scott Andrews* • Roy Roberts *Matthew Burke* • Charles Buchinsky [Charles Bronson] *Igor* ■ *Dir* Andre De Toth • *Scr* Crane Wilbur, from the play *The Mystery of the Wax Museum* by Charles Belden

House of Wax ★★★ 15

Horror 2004 · US/Aus · Colour · 112mins

Except for its central premise, this "re-imagining" of the 1953 classic has little in common with the Vincent Price movie. Debuting director Jaume Collet-Serra delivers a formulaic yet surprisingly effective horror. All the genre clichés are present and correct as Elisha Cuthbert and college pals (socialite Paris Hilton among them) fall prey to a sadistic killer in a remote town dominated by a mysterious wax museum. Though convention dictates they get picked off one by one, the enjoyment is in the imaginative and ultra-gory methods of dispatch. SF. Contains swearing and violence.

Elisha Cuthbert *Carly Jones* • Chad Michael Murray *Nick Jones* • Brian Van Holt *Bo/Vincent* • Paris Hilton *Paige* • Jared Padalecki *Wade* • Jon Abrahams *Dalton Chapman* • Robert Ri'chard *Blake* ■ *Dir* Jaume Collet-Serra • *Scr* Carey W Hayes, Chad Hayes, from the play *The Mystery of the Wax Museum* by Charles Belden

House of Whipcord ★★ 18

Horror 1974 · UK · Colour · 97mins

Dismayed by the permissive society, a dithery old judge and his stern mistress turn their home into a house of correction where girls of loose morals (and looser costumes) are imprisoned, chastised, flogged and finally hanged. Most newspaper critics who bothered to see this exploitation movie soundly rubbished it. However, a minority saw it as an allegory about censorship and the Mary Whitehouse brigade, and a satire on Britain's right wing who wished to see the return of capital punishment. AT DVD

Barbara Markham *Mrs Wakehurst* • Patrick Barr *Justice Bailey* • Ray Brooks *Tony* • Ann Michelle *Julia* • Penny Irving *Ann-Marie De Vernay* • Sheila Keith *Walker* • Dorothy Gordon *Bates* • Robert Tayman *Mark Dessart* • David McGillivray *Cavan* ■ *Dir* Pete Walker • *Scr* David McGillivray, from a story by Pete Walker

House of Women ★

Prison drama 1962 · US · BW · 85mins

A major studio like Warner Bros is much too strait-laced to produce an out-and-out exploitation movie, though that was the pitch for this story of women convicts. Chief among the women is Shirley Knight, sentenced to five years for robbery even though she's pregnant and just about as saintly as Mother Teresa or Mary Pickford. Compared to Jonathan Demme's *Caged Heat*, this is a Women's Institute tea party. AT

Shirley Knight *Erica* • Andrew Duggan *Warden Cole* • Constance Ford *Sophie Brice* • Barbara Nichols *Candy Kane* • Margaret Hayes *Zoe* ■ *Dir* Walter Doniger • *Scr* Crane Wilbur

The House of Yes ★★★

Comedy drama 1997 · US · Colour · 87mins

Another offbeat offering featuring indie film favourite Parker Posey. It's a black comedy set in Washington DC, in which Josh Hamilton stars as Posey's all-American twin brother, returning to his dysfunctional family home for Thanksgiving with his fiancée Tori Spelling. Posey – who is convinced that she is Jackie Onassis and loves her brother in more than just a filial way – is not pleased and decides to re-enact the JFK assassination, with real bullets. This witty walk on the wild side contains strong performances and an edgy sense of humour. LH

Parker Posey *Jackie-O* • Josh Hamilton *Marty* • Tori Spelling *Lesly* • Freddie Prinze Jr *Anthony* • Geneviève Bujold *Mrs Pascal* • Rachael Leigh Cook *Young Jackie-O* • David Love *Young Marty* ■ *Dir* Mark Waters • *Scr* Mark Waters, from the play by Wendy MacLeod

H

House on Bare Mountain ★★

Horror 1962 · US · Colour · 61mins

Nudies meet the nasties in the first topless monster flick from exploitation maestro Lee Frost (credited as RL Frost). Co-producer Bob Cresse (another sleaze icon) plays Granny Good, narrating the tale of the day her School for Good Girls was invaded by the Wolf Man, Frankenstein and Dracula. The undressed cast is clearly drunk as tepid scares punctuate the daily routine of nude art classes, bare sunbathing and naked jogging. A tacky and tawdry classic. AJ

Bob Cresse *Granny Good* • Hugh Cannon *Krakow* • Laura Eden *Prudence Bumgartner* • Warren Ames *The monster* • Jeffrey Smithers *Dracula* ■ *Dir* RL Frost [Lee Frost] • *Scr* Denver Scott

The House on Carroll Street ★★★ PG

Thriller 1987 · US · Colour · 96mins

A convincingly robust Kelly McGillis is the political activist in an slender plot about senator Mandy Patinkin smuggling Nazis into America. Hounded out of her job by the McCarthyite tendency, she takes work reading to Jessica Tandy and begins to notice strange goings-on across the way. Jeff Daniels ably plays the FBI agent she enlists to solve the mystery. Sub-Hitchcock it may be, but this is still enjoyable. TH DVD

Kelly McGillis *Emily Crane* • Jeff Daniels *Cochran* • Mandy Patinkin *Ray Salwen* • Jessica Tandy *Miss Venable* • Jonathan Hogan *Alan* • Remak Ramsay *Senator Byington* ■ *Dir* Peter Yates • *Scr* Walter Bernstein

House on Haunted Hill ★★★ 12

Horror 1958 · US · BW · 74mins

In terms of sheer silly spookiness, this William Castle production has never been equalled, as Vincent Price tries to scare overnight guests to death at a creepy mansion. Originally featuring "Emergo" – a plastic skeleton flown over people's heads in the audience – the script matches that gimmick in terms of subtlety. But Castle's directorial crassness does actually supply some genuinely frightening moments, and Price performs with zest. AJ DVD

Vincent Price *Frederick Loren* • Carol Ohmart *Annabelle Loren* • Richard Long *Lance Schroeder* • Alan Marshal *Dr David Trent* •

Carolyn Craig *Nora Manning* • Elisha Cook [Elisha Cook Jr] *Watson Pritchard* ■ *Dir* William Castle • *Scr* Robb White

House on Haunted Hill ★★★ 18

Horror 1999 · US · Colour · 88mins

Held together by stylish direction from William Malone, some genuinely nasty jolts and a keen sense of genre history, this big-budget remake of the 1958 film compares favourably with the original. The simple plot has theme park developer Geoffrey Rush (here doing a creditable Vincent Price impression) offering a group of strangers $1 million to spend the night in a supposedly spook-infested, Art Deco asylum. Malone captures the essence of the 1950s frightener while updating the shocks with computer effects and grisly gore. AJ DVD

Geoffrey Rush *Stephen Price* • Famke Janssen *Evelyn Price* • Taye Diggs *Eddie* • Peter Gallagher *Blackburn* • Chris Kattan *Pritchett* • Ali Larter *Sara* • Bridgette Wilson *Melissa Marr* ■ *Dir* William Malone • *Scr* Dick Beebe, from a story by Robb White

H

The House on 92nd Street ★★★★ U

Spy documentary drama
1945 · US · BW · 87mins

Produced by Louis de Rochemont – co-founder/producer of the influential American newsreel *The March of Time* – this semi-documentary espionage thriller started a trend in postwar Hollywood for true-life crime dramas notable for their realism, "voice of doom" narration and understated use of authentic locations. Readily taking to the documentary style, director Henry Hathaway sets a cracking pace as double agent William Eythe keeps federal agent Lloyd Nolan informed about the activities of a Nazi spy ring operated from New York by Signe Hasso and Gene Lockhart. DP

William Eythe *Bill Dietrich* • Lloyd Nolan *Inspector George A Briggs* • Signe Hasso *Elsa Gebhardt/Mr Christopher* • Gene Lockhart *Charles Ogden Roper* • Leo G Carroll *Colonel Hammersohn* ■ *Dir* Henry Hathaway • *Scr* Barre Lyndon, Charles G Booth, John Monks Jr, from a story by Charles G Booth

The House on Telegraph Hill ★★★★

Thriller 1951 · US · BW · 92mins

A richly layered *film noir*, starring Richard Basehart as the manipulative guardian of a young heir, and outwardly vulnerable but inwardly steely Valentina Cortese as the war refugee who enters the US on the purloined papers of the boy's dead mother. Basehart and Cortese interact splendidly, with little being said but much atmospherically hinted at, and the movie throbs with a dark subtext on human fallibility. SH

Richard Basehart *Alan Spender* • Valentina Cortese *Victoria Kowelska* • William Lundigan *Major Marc Anders* • Fay Baker *Margaret* • Gordon Gebert *Chris* ■ *Dir* Robert Wise • *Scr* Elick Moll, Frank Partos, from the novel *The Frightened Child* by Dana Lyon

The House on the Waterfront ★★

Crime adventure 1955 · Fr · Colour · 96mins

Not even Jean Gabin's brand of melancholic machismo could buoy this downbeat tale of the diver who discovers a woman's body and sets out to prevent the perpetrator from repeating his crime. The underwater sequences (directed by Louis Malle) are handled capably enough, but director Edmond T Gréville is much more comfortable with the affair between Gabin's partner, Henri Vidal, and Andrée Debar. DP. A French language film.

Jean Gabin *Le Captain Le Quévic* • Andrée Debar *Martine* • Henri Vidal *Michel* • Jean-Roger Caussimon *M Black* • Gaby Basset *The bistrot proprietor* • Robert Berri *L'Hercule* ■ *Dir* Edmond T Gréville • *Scr* Jacques Viot

The House on Trubnaya Square ★★★★★

Silent satirical comedy
1928 · USSR · BW · 81mins

Although this was the film that launched the great Vera Maretskaya's career, co-star Vladimir Fogel died only a year later. His knowing performance as a hairdresser with ideas above his station is one of the many pleasures of this glorious silent comedy. Whether craning down the side of the titular tenement or roving Moscow's streets, Yevgeni Alexeyev's camera picks up every delicious detail of the rustic Maretskaya's rebellion against her employer's refusal to let her join a housemaid's union. Visually vibrant, satirically astute and packed with wonderfully observed characters, this is Boris Barnet's finest hour. DP

Vera Maretskaya *Parasha Pitounova* • Vladimir Fogel *Golikov* • Yelena Tyapkina *Mrs Golikova* • Vladimir Batalov *Semyen Byvalov* ■ *Dir* Boris Barnet • *Scr* Boris Zorich, Anatoly Marienhof, Vadim Shershenevich, Victor Shklovsky, Nikolai Erdman

House Party ★★★★ 15

Comedy 1990 · US · Colour · 99mins

Acting as a lighter alternative to those hard, unsettling visions of modern black America from the likes of Spike Lee, this fresh comedy makes no attempt to pander to a more mainstream audience but remains a hugely enjoyable affair. Rap duo Kid 'n' Play (Christopher Reid and Christopher Martin) take the lead roles, the former playing a grounded high school student who will stop at nothing to get to a party at his best friend's house. Directed at a frenetic pace by Reginald Hudlin, this boasts a terrific soundtrack, cameos from a host of rap stars and a scene-stealing performance from Robin Harris. JF. Contains swearing.

Christopher Reid *Kid* • Christopher Martin *Play* • Robin Harris *Pop* • Martin Lawrence *Bilal* • Tisha Campbell *Sidney* • Adrienne-Joi Johnson *Sharane* • Paul Anthony *Stab* • Bowlegged Lou *Pee-Wee* ■ *Dir/Scr* Reginald Hudlin

House Party 2 ★★ 15

Comedy 1991 · US · Colour · 90mins

The original *House Party* was a surprise hit around the world, but this shallow sequel failed to recapture the same magic. Kid 'n' Play (Christopher Reid and Christopher Martin) return once again, but this time they're at college. To ease some financial worries, they decide to hold another massive party which is the cue for further hip-hop cameos. JF. Contains swearing. DVD

Christopher Reid *Kid* • Christopher Martin *Play* • Queen Latifah *Zora* • Iman *Sheila* • Eugene Allen *Groove* • George Anthony Bell *Reverend Simms* • Martin Lawrence *Bilal* ■ *Dir* George Jackson, Doug McHenry • *Scr* Rusty Cundlieff, Daryl G Nickens, from characters created by Reginald Hudlin

House Party 3 ★★ 15

Comedy 1994 · US · Colour · 89mins

Kid 'n' Play rap on through to another, third *House Party*, but by now the comedy beats are flagging. This time Kid (Christopher Reid) is ready to put his partying days behind him and marry his girlfriend (Tisha Campbell), much to the concern of long-time partner Play (Christopher Martin). Fans of the first two instalments won't be disappointed by the mix of rap and raunch, but the plotting and direction are haphazard and the tack factor high. JF

Christopher Reid *Kid* • Christopher Martin *Play* • David Edwards *Stinky* • Angela Means *Veda* • Tisha Campbell *Sydney* • Ketty Lester *Aunt Lacy* • Chris Tucker *Johnny Booze* ■ *Dir* Eric Meza • *Scr* Takashi Bufford, from a story by David Toney, Takashi Bufford, from characters created by Reginald Hudlin

The House That Dripped Blood ★★★ 12

Portmanteau horror
1971 · UK · Colour · 97mins

Directed with imaginative flair by Peter Duffell and featuring Christopher Lee and Peter Cushing in tailor-made roles as two of the four tenants of the menacing title abode, this is one of the best compendium films from Amicus (Hammer's main horror rival at the time). Robert Bloch's satisfying tales of terror involve possession, mysterious waxworks, voodoo and vampirism for an effective mix of spine-tingling sincerity, creepy atmospherics and witty send-ups of the genre. AJ. Contains violence. DVD

Denholm Elliott *Charles* • Joanna Dunham *Alice* • Peter Cushing *Philip* • Joss Ackland *Rogers* • Christopher Lee *Reid* • Nyree Dawn Porter *Ann* • Jon Pertwee *Paul* • Ingrid Pitt *Carla* • John Bennett *Holloway* • John Bryans *Stoker* ■ *Dir* Peter Duffell • *Scr* Robert Bloch

The House Where Evil Dwells ★ 18

Horror 1982 · US · Colour · 83mins

The 19th-century ghosts of a cuckolded Japanese samurai, his unfaithful wife and her lover terrorise a young couple when they move into their Kyoto haunted house. After US diplomat and old family friend Doug McClure arrives on the scene, the three are doomed to re-enact the spiritual love triangle. The soft-core sex, low-key gore and an attack by large crabs (!) do nothing to keep the boredom at bay. AJ

Edward Albert *Ted* • Susan George *Laura* • Doug McClure *Alex* • Amy Barrett *Amy* • Mako Hattori *Otami* • Toshiyuki Sasaki *Shugoro* • Toshiya Maruyama *Masanori* • Okajima Tsuyako *Witch* • Henry Mitowa *Zen Monk* ■ *Dir* Kevin Connor • *Scr* Robert Suhosky, from the novel by James Hardiman

Houseboat ★★★★ U

Romantic comedy drama
1958 · US · Colour · 105mins

This delightfully played, relatively unsophisticated comedy based on a slim but oh-so-romantic premise, as lovely Sophia Loren takes charge of lawyer Cary Grant's three children and, eventually of course, Grant himself. Beautifully photographed by Ray June, who made a similarly fabulous job of *Funny Face*, this is an easy-on-the-eye glamfest that also contains a fabulous supporting performance from Harry Guardino as a handyman in wolf's clothing. Needless to say, Grant sails through the movie with accomplished ease. TS DVD

Sophia Loren *Cinzia Zaccardi* • Cary Grant *Tom Winston* • Martha Hyer *Carolyn Gibson* • Harry Guardino *Angelo Donatello* • Eduardo Ciannelli *Arturo Zaccardi* • Murray Hamilton *Alan Wilson* ■ *Dir* Melville Shavelson • *Scr* Melville Shavelson, Jack Rose

Houseguest ★★ PG

Comedy 1995 · US · Colour · 104mins

This so-so vehicle for American comedy star Sinbad went straight to video this side of the pond. In this variation on a familiar theme, the nautically named comedian plays a petty con artist on the run from the Mob who, passing himself off as the long-lost chum of uptight lawyer Phil Hartman, moves in with his family. Sinbad's freewheeling style raises the odd giggle, and he works well with Hartman. However, the direction is uninspired, and the result is predictable. JF DVD

Sinbad *Kevin Franklin* • Phil Hartman *Gary Young* • Kim Greist *Emily Young* • Chauncey Leopardi *Jason Young* • Talia Seider *Sarah Young* ■ *Dir* Randall Miller • *Scr* Lawrence Gay, Michael DiGaetano

Household Saints ★★★

Comedy drama 1993 · US · Colour · 124mins

Executive produced by Jonathan Demme, this is a quirky tale of Italian-American Catholics in New York. Vincent D'Onofrio wins Tracey Ullman in a pinochle game and they marry. Though bullied by his mother (Judith Malina), she gives birth to a daughter (Lili Taylor). As Taylor grows, so do her love for Jesus and her obsession with her saintly namesake, St Teresa. Director Nancy Savoca portrays three generations of comic and tragic family life with tenderness and empathy. LH

Tracey Ullman *Catherine Falconetti* • Vincent D'Onofrio *Joseph Santangelo* • Lili Taylor *Teresa* • Judith Malina *Carmela Santangelo* • Michael Rispoli *Nicky Falconetti* • Victor Argo *Lino Falconetti* • Michael Imperioli *Leonard Villanova* • Rachael Bella *Young Teresa* ■ *Dir* Nancy Savoca • *Scr* Nancy Savoca, Richard Guay, from the novel by Francine Prose

The Householder ★★★ U

Comedy 1963 · US/Ind · BW · 96mins

Adapted from her own novel by Ruth Prawer Jhabvala and produced by Ismail Merchant, James Ivory's debut feature launched one of the most successful teams in cinema history. Bearing in mind that the production nearly collapsed through lack of funds, this account of mummy's boy Shashi Kapoor's troubled early marriage to Leela Naidu is admirably authentic. Yet it took some editing assistance from Satyajit Ray to give the narrative its sense of drama and pace. Rough edges remain, but the camerawork of Ray regular Subrata Mitra is deeply sensitive and the performances are touchingly honest. DP DVD

Shashi Kapoor *Prem Sagar* • Leela Naidu *Indu* • Harindranath Chattopadhyay *Mr Chadda* • Durga Khote *The Mother* • Pro Sen *Sohanlal* ■ *Dir* James Ivory • *Scr* Ruth Prawer Jhabvala, from her novel

The Housekeeper's Daughter ★★

Crime comedy 1939 · US · BW · 79mins

The only fireworks in this lowbrow murder farce come at the end when they're let off by drunken crime reporter Adolphe Menjou and press photographer William Gargan. It's one of many slapstick moments in this feature-length product from Hal Roach. Joan Bennett is the housekeeper's daughter with a past, and John Hubbard is the novice reporter up against Marc Lawrence's gang boss. Victor Mature makes his debut here. AE

Joan Bennett *Hilda* • Adolphe Menjou *Deakon Maxwell* • John Hubbard *Robert Randall* • William Gargan *Ed O'Malley* • George E Stone *Benny* • Peggy Wood *Olga* • Donald Meek *Editor Wilson* • Marc Lawrence (1) *Floyd* • Lilian Bond [Lillian Bond] *Gladys* • Victor Mature *Lefty* ■ *Dir* Hal Roach • *Scr* Rian James, Gordon Douglas, from a story by Donald Henderson Clarke

Housekeeping ★★★★ PG

Comedy drama 1987 · US · Colour · 111mins

Director Bill Forsyth has been sadly underused by the American film industry, particularly after his Robin Williams vehicle *Being Human* floundered because of creative differences. Yet it all started so well with this charming and superbly controlled study of the way in which children manage to survive even the most outrageous whims of the adults entrusted with their care. Sara Walker and Andrea Burchill are splendid as the young sisters who seem to have immunised themselves against the upheavals that periodically shatter their world, while Christine Lahti has never been better as the dippy aunt who appears to be their saviour. DP. Contains swearing.

Christine Lahti *Aunt Sylvie* • Sara Walker *Ruth* • Andrea Burchill *Lucille* • Anne Pitoniak *Lily* • Barbara Reese *Nona* • Bill Smillie *Sheriff* • Wayne Robson *Mr French* • Margot Pinvidic *Helen* ■ *Dir* Bill Forsyth • *Scr* Bill Forsyth, from the novel by Marilynne Robinson

Housemaster ★★★

Comedy drama 1938 · UK · BW · 95mins

This adaptation of an Ian Hay play brought actor Otto Kruger over from America for the role of his life, as the housemaster victimised by the school's head after disciplinary measures result in a revolt of the pupils. Director Herbert Brenon demonstrates his empathy with the nuances of the English class system. TS

Otto Kruger *Charles Donkin* • Diana Churchill *Rosemary Faringdon* • Phillips Holmes *Philip de Courville* • Joyce Barbour *Barbara Fane* • René Ray *Chris Faringdon* • Cecil Parker *Sir Berkeley Nightingale* • Jimmy Hanley *Travers* ■ *Dir* Herbert Brenon • *Scr* Dudley Leslie, Elizabeth Meehan, from the play *Bachelor Born* by Ian Hay

HouseSitter ★★★ PG

Romantic comedy
1992 · US · Colour · 101mins

Goldie Hawn is at her dippiest as the waitress who overturns the life of Steve Martin's staid architect in this likeable if somewhat silly movie. Martin is recovering from rejection by the love of his life (Dana Delany) when he meets Hawn, who decides to help his convalescence by moving into the dream house he has built but left empty after getting the elbow from his dream woman. When Hawn tells the neighbourhood that she's his new wife, the comic complications pile on, to generally amusing effect. DP. Contains swearing. DVD

Steve Martin *Newton Davis* • Goldie Hawn *Gwen* • Dana Delany *Becky* • Julie Harris *Edna Davis* • Donald Moffat *George Davis* • Peter MacNicol *Marty* • Richard B Shull *Ralph* ■ *Dir* Frank Oz • *Scr* Mark Stein, from a story by Mark Stein, Brian Grazer

How Do I Love Thee? ★★ PG

Comedy drama 1970 · US · Colour · 108mins

Jackie Gleason was perhaps not the most fortuitous choice to play an unrepentant atheist in keen debate with his philosophy professor son. Maureen O'Hara and Shelley Winters do little more than referee this talkathon, which is rarely worth listening to. DP

Jackie Gleason *Stanley Waltz* • Maureen O'Hara *Elsie Waltz* • Shelley Winters *Lena Mervin* • Rosemary Forsyth *Marion Waltz* ■ *Dir* Michael Gordon • *Scr* Everett Freeman, Karl Tunberg, from the novel *Let Me Count the Ways* by Peter DeVries

How Green Was My Valley ★★★★★ U

Drama 1941 · US · BW · 117mins

This magnificent Oscar-winning family saga may seem a trifle dated, with its superb, but phoney, studio re-creations of the valleys of South Wales. But there's no denying its power to move as well as entertain audiences, as director John Ford lovingly details life in the pits and valleys of the region. Ford rightly won the best director Oscar and the movie won best picture, but often overlooked is the sincerity of the film's hand-picked cast, notably sturdy Walter Pidgeon and fiery Ford regular Maureen O'Hara. The best supporting actor Oscar went to Donald Crisp's patriarch. This is precisely the kind of movie that gave Hollywood film-making supremacy in its heyday. TS DVD

Walter Pidgeon *Mr Gruffydd* • Maureen O'Hara *Angharad* • Donald Crisp *Mr Morgan* • Roddy McDowall *Huw* • Anna Lee *Bronwyn* • John Loder *Ianto* • Sara Allgood *Mrs Morgan* • Barry Fitzgerald *Cyfartha* ■ *Dir* John Ford • *Scr* Philip Dunne, from the novel by Richard Llewellyn • *Cinematographer* Arthur Miller

How I Got Into College ★★★ 15

Comedy 1989 · US · Colour · 83mins

This romantic teen comedy stars Corey Parker as a lovestruck, non-academic sort who plans to enrol in the same college as the girl he worships (Lara Flynn Boyle). The trouble is, he's not the college type. Luckily the college in question is about to launch a new initiative allowing some "ordinary" guys to enter their hallowed halls. Witty, and likeable juvenile fare, above average for the genre. DF

Anthony Edwards *Kip* • Corey Parker *Marlon* • Lara Flynn Boyle *Jessica* • Finn Carter *Nina* • Charles Rocket *Leo* • Christopher Rydell *Oliver* • Philip Baker Hall *Dean Patterson* ■ *Dir* Savage Steve Holland • *Scr* Terrel Seltzer

How I Spent My Summer Vacation ★★ U

Thriller 1967 · US · Colour · 89mins

Made as a TV movie of the week by Universal, who pioneered such things, this confused would-be thriller was renamed *Deadly Roulette* and released in cinemas here largely because of its extremely attractive cast. A boyish Robert Wagner stars as a former soldier who seeks revenge on sophisticated, wealthy Peter Lawford following an incident when Lawford humiliated him; others aboard for the ride include Lola Albright, Jill St John and a dapper Walter Pidgeon. TS

Robert Wagner *Jack Washington* • Peter Lawford *Ned Pine* • Lola Albright *Mrs Pine* • Walter Pidgeon *Lewis Gannet* • Jill St John *Nikki Pine* • Michael Ansara *Pucci* ■ *Dir* William Hale • *Scr* Gene Kearney

How I Won the War ★★★★ 12

Black comedy 1967 · UK · Colour · 105mins

John Lennon's decision to take a break from the Beatles and accept the part of Private Gripweed was the major talking point when this film was initially released. Based on Patrick Ryan's biting attack on the follies of war and brass-hat incompetence, Richard Lester's feature broadens the satire and throws in a little surrealism and slapstick to make the subtleties of the book suitably cinematic. Getting by with a little help from his friends, Michael Crawford is admirably gung ho as the head of the special cricket pitch unit. DP. Contains violence. DVD

Michael Crawford *Lt Ernest Goodbody* • John Lennon *Gripweed* • Roy Kinnear *Clapper* • Lee Montague *Sgt Transom* • Jack MacGowran *Juniper* • Michael Hordern *Grapple* • Jack Hedley *Melancholy musketeer* • Karl Michael Vogler *Odlebog* ■ *Dir* Richard Lester • *Scr* Charles Wood, from the novel by Patrick Ryan

How Stella Got Her Groove Back ★★★ 15

Romantic comedy drama
1998 · US · Colour · 119mins

Based on the novel by Terry McMillan, this is a companion piece to the earlier *Waiting to Exhale*, which also starred Angela Bassett. Here she plays single mother Stella, who is encouraged by her best friend (Whoopi Goldberg) to escape her downbeat existence for a holiday in Jamaica. It's there that she meets half-her-age hunk Taye Diggs, and the audience is treated to picture-postcard shots of both their romance and the island itself. You'll want to book a holiday to the Caribbean before the film is over, but you won't be as enchanted with the characters only briefly sketched. JB. Contains some swearing and sex scenes. DVD

Angela Bassett *Stella* • Whoopi Goldberg *Delilah* • Regina King *Vanessa* • Taye Diggs *Winston Shakespeare* • Suzzanne Douglas *Angela* • Michael J Pagan *Quincy* • Sicily *Chantel* • Richard Lawson *Jack* ■ *Dir* Kevin Rodney Sullivan • *Scr* Ronald Bass, Terry McMillan, from the novel by Terry McMillan

How Sweet It Is! ★

Comedy 1968 · US · Colour · 97mins

An unspeakably tasteless and witless comedy about two married Americans discovering sex in Europe, hoping to bring excitement to their marriage and maturity to their teenage offspring. Debbie Reynolds canoodles with Maurice Ronet at James Garner's expense, while Paul Lynde and Terry-Thomas share the few laughs on offer. Jerry Paris directs with a total lack of sophistication, allowing the usually reliable Garner to mug shamelessly. TS

James Garner *Grif Henderson* • Debbie Reynolds *Jenny Henderson* • Maurice Ronet *Philippe Maspere* • Terry-Thomas *Gilbert Tilly* • Paul Lynde *The Purser* • Marcel Dalio *Louis* ■ *Dir* Jerry Paris • *Scr* Garry Marshall, Jerry Belson, from the novel *The Girl in the Turquoise Bikini* by Muriel Resnik

How the West Was Won ★★★★ PG

Epic western 1962 · US · Colour · 157mins

One of only two narrative films made in three-camera Cinerama; if you look very carefully you can see the joins in its widescreen version, which are especially noticeable down the tree trunks. Of the three credited directors, Henry Hathaway shot the all-star Rivers, Plains and Outlaws sections, while George Marshall filmed that dangerous stunt-work on the railroad, and the great John Ford directed the splendid American Civil War sequence, beginning with a marvellous slice of widescreen action, as surgical tables are sluiced down, seeming to drown the audience. The majestic score is by Alfred Newman, and was used again to witty comic effect in 1984's *Romancing the Stone*. TS

James Stewart *Linus Rawlings* • John Wayne *General William T Sherman* • Gregory Peck *Cleve Van Valen* • Henry Fonda *Jethro Stuart* • Carroll Baker *Eve Prescott* • Lee J Cobb *Marshal Lou Ramsey* • Carolyn Jones *Julie Rawlings* • Karl Malden *Zebulon Prescott* • George Peppard *Zeb Rawlings* • Robert Preston *Roger Morgan* • Debbie Reynolds *Lilith Prescott* • Eli Wallach *Charlie Gant* • Richard Widmark *Mike King* • Walter Brennan *Colonel Hawkins* • Raymond Massey *Abraham Lincoln* • Agnes Moorehead *Rebecca Prescott* • Thelma Ritter *Agatha Clegg* • Spencer Tracy *Narrator* ■ *Dir* John Ford, Henry Hathaway, George Marshall • *Scr* James R Webb, from articles in *Life Magazine* • *Cinematographer* William Daniels [William H Daniels], Milton Krasner, Charles Lang Jr [Charles Lang], Joseph LaShelle

How to Be a Player ★★ 18

Sex comedy 1997 · US · Colour · 89mins

Wearing its politically incorrect badges with some pride this breezy sex comedy is still a lot of fun. MTV host and comic Bill Bellamy is the wonderfully conceited stud who takes time out to show his chums how to be a player – that is, how to keep all sorts of girls happy while still remaining in a long-term relationship. However, he has not reckoned on his sister (Natalie Desselle), who thinks it's time that this particular player got a red card. Subtlety doesn't come into it. JF. Contains swearing, sex scenes and sexual references.

Bill Bellamy *Drayton Jackson* • Natalie Desselle *Jenny Jackson* • Lark Voorhies *Lisa* • Mari Morrow *Katrina* • Pierre Edwards *David* • Jermaine "Big Hugg" Hopkins [Jermaine Hopkins] *Kilo* ■ *Dir* Lionel C Martin • *Scr* Mark Brown, Demetria Johnson, from a story by Mark Brown

How to Be a Woman and Not Die in the Attempt ★★★ 15

Comedy drama 1991 · Sp · Colour · 85mins

This wry and amusing comedy stars Carmen Maura as a working wife and mum who finally takes umbrage at her workaholic hubby's chauvinistic belief that she should not only bring home a wage, but also be solely responsible for bringing up their three kids. Waspishly written and beautifully acted, especially by Maura, this is proof that quality films from Spain don't have to have the name "Almodóvar" attached to them. DA. In Spanish with English subtitles. DVD

Carmen Maura *Carmen* • Antonio Resines *Antonio* ■ *Dir* Ana Belén • *Scr* Carmen Rico-Godoy, from her novel

How to Be Very, Very Popular ★★★ U

Musical comedy 1955 · US · Colour · 89mins

This musical saw Betty Grable bring down the curtain on a career in which she had been everything the title said. But the 38-year-old star is soundly upstaged in her swan song by Sheree North, a blond bombshell 16 years her junior making only her fourth feature. The film gave writer/producer/director Nunnally Johnson the excuse to keep his stars in the skimpiest of costumes. Not even that old scene stealer Charles Coburn could beat that sort of competition. DP

Betty Grable *Stormy* • Sheree North *Curly* • Robert Cummings *Wedgewood* • Charles Coburn *Tweed* • Tommy Noonan *Eddie* • Orson Bean *Toby* • Fred Clark *Mr Marshall* • Charlotte Austin *Midge* ■ *Dir* Nunnally Johnson • *Scr* Nunnally Johnson, from a play by Howard Lindsay, from a novel by Edward Hope and a play by Lyford Moore, Harlan Thompson

How to Beat the High Cost of Living ★★★ 15

Crime comedy 1980 · US · Colour · 104mins

Long before they got together on the small screen in the sitcom *Kate and Allie*, Susan Saint James and Jane Curtin teamed up on this appealing caper comedy. Along with Jessica Lange, they play old schoolfriends who find themselves in need of money, thanks to the incompetence of their menfolk. They hatch a plot to steal thousands from a giant plastic moneyball set up as a publicity stunt in the local shopping mall. DF

Susan Saint James *Jane* • Jane Curtin *Elaine* • Jessica Lange *Louise* • Richard Benjamin *Albert* • Eddie Albert *Max* • Cathryn Damon *Natalie* • Dabney Coleman *Jack Heintzel* • *Dir* Robert Scheerer • *Scr* Robert Kaufman, from a story by Leonora Thuna

How to Commit Marriage ★

Comedy 1969 · US · Colour · 95mins

In this self-conscious, dire comedy, Bob Hope and Jane Wyman play about-to-be-divorced parents. When their daughter Joanna Cameron brings home her fiancé, they try to pretend all is well. But the boy's father (Jackie Gleason) becomes suspicious, their charade is revealed and the wedding is called off. The kids then turn to an eastern mystic in an embarrassing attempt to cross the comedy of Hope and Gleason with the "anything goes" style of the Swinging Sixties. DF

Bob Hope *Frank Benson* • Jackie Gleason *Oliver Poe* • Jane Wyman *Elaine Benson* • Leslie Nielsen *Phil Fletcher* • Maureen Arthur *Lois Gray* • Joanna Cameron *Nancy Benson* • Tim Matheson *David Poe* ■ *Dir* Norman Panama • *Scr* Ben Starr, Michael Kanin

How to Fill a Wild Bikini ★ U

Musical comedy 1965 · US · Colour · 92mins

The fifth in AIP's beach party series is the biggest washout of the lot. With Frankie Avalon away on naval reserve duty, he's limited to a cameo role as the suspicious coastguard who calls on witch doctor Buster Keaton to ensure that Annette Funicello doesn't fall into the clutches of beefcake Dwayne Hickman. Boasting some of the worst song-and-dance routines ever committed to celluloid. DP

Annette Funicello *Dee Dee* • Dwayne Hickman *Ricky* • Brian Donlevy *BD* • Harvey Lembeck *Eric Von Zipper* • Beverly Adams *Cassandra* • Buster Keaton *Bwana* • Mickey Rooney *Peachy Keane* • Frankie Avalon *Frankie* • Brian Wilson *Beach boy* • Elizabeth Montgomery *Witches' witch* ■ *Dir* William Asher • *Scr* William Asher, Leo Townsend

H

How to Frame a Figg ★

Comedy 1971 · US · Colour · 103mins

This clumsy, unsubtle vehicle for American comedian Don Knotts has him typecast as a simple-minded fellow – the eponymous Mr Figg – who's batted back and forth between rival, crooked politicians. This won't mean much to British audiences; it didn't mean much to American audiences, either. TH

Don Knotts *Hollis Figg* • Joe Flynn *Kermit Sanderson* • Edward Andrews *Mayor Chisolm* • Elaine Joyce *Ema Lethakusic* • Yvonne Craig *Glorianna* • Frank Welker *Prentiss Gates* ■ *Dir* Alan Rafkin • *Scr* George Tibbles, from a story by Don Knotts, Edward J Montagne

How to Get Ahead in Advertising ★★★ 15

Satirical comedy 1989 · UK · Colour · 90mins

After the truly wonderful *Withnail and*, this comic follow-up, which reunited Richard E Grant with writer/director Bruce Robinson, proved something of a disappointment. Grant is the troubled advertising executive who develops an evil alter ego: a boil which can not only talk but is intent on taking over his whole body. There are some neat, surreal touches, another manic performance from Grant and a solid supporting cast, but the evil side of advertising is too broad and too obvious a target for Robinson to get his teeth into. JF. Contains swearing and some nudity.

Richard E Grant *Dennis Bagley* • Rachel Ward *Julia Bagley* • Richard Wilson *Bristol* • Jacqueline Tong *Penny Wheelstock* • John Shrapnel *Psychiatrist* • Susan Wooldridge *Monica* ■ *Dir/Scr* Bruce Robinson

How to Lose a Guy in 10 Days ★★ 12

Romantic comedy
2003 · US/Ger · Colour · 110mins

Kate Hudson's journalist is assigned a magazine feature for which she must snare a guy and then make him dump her, while her target, Matthew McConaughey, is involved in a bet to make a woman fall in love with him – and both have ten days to do it in. Despite the odd mildly amusing observation on the mating rituals of New Yorkers and some pretty cinematography, the contrived plot and leaden supporting cast smother any sign of light, fizzy wit. AS DVD

Kate Hudson *Andie Anderson* • Matthew McConaughey *Benjamin Barry* • Adam Goldberg *Tony* • Michael Michele *Spears* • Shalom Harlow *Green* • Bebe Neuwirth *Lana Jong* • Robert Klein *Phillip Warren* ■ *Dir* Donald Petrie • *Scr* Kristen Buckley, Brian Regan, Burr Steers

How to Make a Monster ★★ PG

Horror 1958 · US · BW and Colour · 73mins

When a Hollywood make-up effects man is told horror is passé, he applies special drugged cosmetics to the actors playing Frankenstein's creature and the Werewolf on his last movie so they'll think they really are monsters and murder the meddlesome moguls. Cue the re-use of old fright masks, props and veteran stars from AIP successes such as *I Was a Teenage Werewolf*, affectionately mocking the genre. A must for 1950s schlock fans. AJ DVD

Robert H Harris *Pete Dummond* • Paul Brinegar *Rivero* • Gary Conway *Tony Mantell* • Gary Clarke *Larry Drake* • Malcolm Atterbury *Richards* ■ *Dir* Herbert L Strock • *Scr* Kenneth Langtry, Herman Cohen

How to Make an American Quilt ★★★ 12

Drama 1995 · US · Colour · 111mins

This low-key but enjoyable film, based on the book by Whitney Otto and directed by Jocelyn Moorhouse, features moving performances from the female-dominated cast. Winona Ryder stars as the marriage-shy young woman who listens while her older relatives recount tales of love and disappointment as they add squares to a growing and symbolic quilt. Some of the episodic tales work better than others, but all are interesting and there are splendid characterisations from the cast. JB DVD

Winona Ryder *Finn* • Ellen Burstyn *Hy* • Anne Bancroft *Glady Joe* • Kate Capshaw *Sally* • Dermot Mulroney *Sam* • Maya Angelou *Anna* • Alfre Woodard *Marianna* • Jean Simmons *Em* • Kate Nelligan *Constance* • Rip Torn *Arthur* • Samantha Mathis *Young Sophia* • Adam Baldwin *Finn's father* • Claire Danes *Young Glady Joe* ■ *Dir* Jocelyn Moorhouse • *Scr* Jane Anderson, from the novel by Whitney Otto • *Music* Thomas Newman

How to Marry a Millionaire ★★★★ U

Comedy 1953 · US · Colour · 91mins

This is a fabulously cast and witty reworking of that much-filmed 20th Century-Fox standby, the one about the three gals seeking rich husbands, smartened up and photographed in Fox's stunning new screen process, CinemaScope. Marilyn Monroe, Betty Grable, and Lauren Bacall play the girls, so who could ask for more? This film was the first shot in Scope, though released after *The Robe*, and it's preceded by an introductory orchestral sequence specially designed to show off the wonders of the then new magnetic stereophonic sound, with Alfred Newman conducting *Street Scene*. TS DVD

Betty Grable *Loco* • Marilyn Monroe *Pola* • Lauren Bacall *Schatze Page* • David Wayne *Freddie Denmark* • Rory Calhoun *Eben* • Cameron Mitchell *Tom Brookman* • Alex D'Arcy *J Stewart Merrill* • Fred Clark *Waldo Brewster* • William Powell *JD Hanley* ■ *Dir* Jean Negulesco • *Scr* Nunnally Johnson, from the plays *The Greeks Had a Word for It* by Zoe Akins and *Loco* by Dale Eunson, Katherine Albert • *Music* Alfred Newman

How to Murder a Rich Uncle ★★★ U

Black comedy 1957 · UK · BW · 79mins

Glorious memories of *Kind Hearts and Coronets* are occasionally stirred by this black comedy about the English aristocracy. Nigel Patrick – who also directed with an uncredited Max Varnel – stars as Sir Henry Clitterburn, down on his uppers, who plots to murder visiting Canadian uncle Charles Coburn in order to inherit a bundle. His plans go awry, of course. There's lots to enjoy here, including a lovely gallery of English eccentrics and, making his second credited screen appearance, Michael Caine. AT

Nigel Patrick *Henry* • Charles Coburn *Uncle George* • Wendy Hiller *Edith* • Katie Johnson *Alice* • Anthony Newley *Edward* • Athene Seyler *Grannie* • Noel Hood *Aunt Marjorie* • Michael Caine *Gilrony* ■ *Dir* Nigel Patrick • *Scr* John Paxton, from the play *Il Faut Tuer Julie* by Didier Daix

How to Murder Your Wife ★★★★ PG

Comedy 1965 · US · Colour · 113mins

Confirmed bachelor Jack Lemmon wakes up after a night on the town married to luscious Virna Lisi, much to the dismay of his faithful butler Terry-Thomas, in director Richard Quine's brilliant politically incorrect comedy. Thereafter, strip-cartoonist Lemmon's action-man character Bash Brannigan becomes cosily domesticated. To placate his fans, who want Brannigan restored to bachelorhood, Lemmon kills off his cartoon hero's wife; but then Lisi disappears and Lemmon finds himself accused of murder. So many scenes to cherish. TH DVD

Jack Lemmon *Stanley Ford* • Virna Lisi *Mrs Ford* • Terry-Thomas *Charles* • Claire Trevor *Edna* • Eddie Mayehoff *Harold Lampson* • Sidney Blackmer *Judge Blackstone* • Max Showalter *Tobey Rawlins* • Jack Albertson *Dr Bentley* • Alan Hewitt *District attorney* ■ *Dir* Richard Quine • *Scr* George Axelrod

How to Save a Marriage and Ruin Your Life ★★

Comedy 1968 · US · Colour · 102mins

Dean Martin hits on a brilliant plan to save his friend's marriage in this convoluted comedy. Eli Wallach is cheating on his wife Katharine Bard, and Martin's rescue strategy involves seducing Wallach's mistress himself. Unfortunately he's got the wrong girl. From this one simple mix-up a muddle of gigantic proportions develops and the plot – hardly on an even keel from the beginning – lists hopelessly out of control. DF

Dean Martin *David Sloane* • Stella Stevens *Carol Corman* • Eli Wallach *Harry Hunter* • Anne Jackson *Muriel Laszlo* • Betty Field *Thelma* • Jack Albertson *Mr. Slotkin* • Katharine Bard *Mary Hunter* ■ *Dir* Fielder Cook • *Scr* Stanley Shapiro, Nate Monaster

How to Steal a Million ★★★ U

Crime comedy 1966 · US · Colour · 118mins

Audrey Hepburn hires Peter O'Toole to steal her father's fake Cellini Venus in this heist caper set in the Paris art world, which reunited Hepburn with her *Roman Holiday* director William Wyler for the third and final time. It's overlong and overwritten, and shows its age in the Swinging Sixties decor and the rather frantic mood. But there are compensations in the supporting cast, including greedy art collector Eli Wallach, the replacement for George C Scott, whom Wyler fired after only one day of shooting. AT DVD

Audrey Hepburn *Nicole Bonnet* • Peter O'Toole *Simon Dermott* • Eli Wallach *Davis Leland* • Hugh Griffith *Charles Bonnet* • Charles Boyer *De Solnay* • Fernand Gravey [Fernand Gravet] *Grammont* • Marcel Dalio *Senor Paravideo* • Jacques Marin *Chief guard* ■ *Dir* William Wyler • *Scr* Harry Kurnitz, from the story *Venus Rising* by George Bradshaw

How to Steal the World ★★ PG

Spy adventure 1968 · US · Colour · 86mins

Stretched to feature length from a couple of TV episodes, this was the last *Man from UNCLE* picture produced by MGM, with Robert Vaughn and David McCallum looking very bored after four years of tongue-in-cheek espionage. Barry Sullivan runs through all the tricks of arch-villainy as a rogue agent, but despite guests of the calibre of Eleanor Parker and Leslie Nielsen, the series ended on a distinctly flat note. DP DVD

Robert Vaughn *Napoleon Solo* • David McCallum *Illya Kuryakin* • Barry Sullivan *Robert Kingsley* • Leslie Nielsen *Gen Harmon* • Eleanor Parker *Margitta* ■ *Dir* Sutton Roley • *Scr* Norman Hudis

How to Succeed in Business without Really Trying ★★★★ U

Musical comedy 1967 · US · Colour · 116mins

A superb film re-creation of Frank Loesser and Abe Burrows's wonderfully acerbic stage musical, with all of Bob Fosse's original choreography preserved on film by Dale Moreda. Robert Morse repeats his Broadway role in a marvellously wicked, devastatingly funny part as a ruthless window cleaner who claws his way to the top of World Wide Wickets, the company run by, of all people, crooner Rudy Vallee. This also has to be the only musical where the hero sings the love song to himself. TS

Robert Morse *J Pierpont Finch* • Michele Lee *Rosemary Pilkington* • Rudy Vallee *JB Biggley* • Anthony Teague *Bud Frump* • Maureen Arthur *Hedy LaRue* • Murray Matheson *Benjamin Ovington* ■ *Dir* David Swift • *Scr* David Swift, from the musical by Abe Burrows, Willie Gilbert, Jack Weinstock, from the novel by Shepherd Mead • *Music/lyrics* Frank Loesser

How U Like Me Now ★★

Romantic comedy
1992 · US · Colour · 109mins

Darryl Roberts wrote, produced and directed this low-budget feature set in Chicago's African-American community. Darnell Williams is a smart guy bored with his nine-to-five job and at cross-purposes with his live-in lover Salli Richardson, who is more interested in social climbing. As the couple's relationship disintegrates their friends offer "battle of the sexes"-style counselling. In the end, though, this is all rather two-dimensional. LH

Darnell Williams *Thomas* • Salli Richardson *Valerie* • Daniel Gardner *Spoony* • Raymond Whitefield *Alex* • Debra Crable *Michelle* • Darryl Roberts *BJ* • Byron Stewart *Pierre* ■ *Dir/Scr* Darryl Roberts

Howard, a New Breed of Hero ★ PG

Comedy fantasy 1986 · US · Colour · 105mins

Marvel Comics meets George Lucas's Industrial Light and Magic, and an uneasy, bland alliance it is, too, with Howard T Duck transported to mid-1980s punkland. Howard takes to the dreadful music of the time and feisty chanteuse Lea Thompson, but fails to ignite any form of discernible plot line or audience response. The movie, a resounding flog on release, remains a tedious mess until the final few reels, when Mr Lucas's boys throw in some dynamic special effects. Execrable. SH. Contains mild swearing.

Lea Thompson *Beverly Switzler* • Tim Robbins *Phil Blumburtt* • Jeffrey Jones *Dr Jenning* • Paul Guilfoyle (2) *Lieutenant Welker* • Liz Sagal *Ronette* • Dominique Davalos *Cal* • Holly Robinson *K C* ■ *Dir* Willard Huyck • *Scr* Willard Huyck, Gloria Katz, from a character created by Steve Gerber

Howards End ★★★★★ PG

Period drama 1992 · UK · Colour · 142mins

This adaptation of EM Forster's novel is the best film made by the long-time team of director James Ivory, producer Ismail Merchant and writer Ruth Prawer Jhabvala, with an elegance that never hides grim insights into the upper middle-classes. Matriarchal Vanessa Redgrave dies after writing a letter bequeathing her country home, Howards End, to new friend Emma Thompson. But the note is destroyed by the family snobs-in-residence, whose head (Anthony Hopkins) then falls in love with Thompson. Meanwhile, the low expectations of the clerking classes are dismally exemplified by Samuel West, whose affair with Helena Bonham Carter leads to tragedy. From the clerk's dank lodgings to Howards End's cosy rurality, the perfect period detail allows Hopkins and Thompson to create extraordinarily convincing portraits. One of the finest conversions of a novel to cinema. TH [video] DVD

Anthony Hopkins *Henry Wilcox* • Emma Thompson *Margaret Schlegel* • Helena Bonham Carter *Helen Schlegel* • Vanessa Redgrave *Ruth Wilcox* • James Wilby *Charles Wilcox* • Samuel West *Leonard Bast* • Prunella Scales *Aunt Juley* • Jemma Redgrave *Evie Wilcox* • Nicola Duffett *Jacky Bast* ■ *Dir* James Ivory • *Scr* Ruth Prawer Jhabvala, from the novel by EM Forster

The Howards of Virginia ★★★ U

Historical epic 1940 · US · BW · 110mins

The clash between the forces of conservatism and the emergence of the American democratic spirit form the stuff of this historical epic. Set before and during the American Revolution, it also encompasses a love story between a progressive Virginian (Cary Grant) and the daughter (Martha Scott) of a wealthy reactionary (Cedric Hardwicke). Directed with confident sweep by Frank Lloyd, this handsomely mounted film is itself a cavalcade of events that includes the Boston Tea Party. Yet, for all its incident, political ideas and careful attention to period, it's less than compelling, and the debonair Grant is miscast. RK [video]

Cary Grant *Matt Howard* • Martha Scott *Jane Peyton Howard* • Sir Cedric Hardwicke [Cedric Hardwicke] *Fleetwood Peyton* • Alan Marshal *Roger Peyton* • Richard Carlson *Thomas Jefferson* • Paul Kelly (1) *Captain Jabez Allen* • Irving Bacon *Tom Norton* • Elisabeth Risdon *Aunt Clarissa* • Alan Ladd *Neighbour* ■ *Dir* Frank Lloyd • *Scr* Sidney Buchman, from the novel *The Tree of Liberty* by Elizabeth Page

The Howling ★★★★ 18

Horror comedy 1981 · US · Colour · 86mins

Co-writer John Sayles and director Joe Dante have huge fun turning werewolf clichés on their head in this rare beast – a horror film that gore fans and film buffs can enjoy. For the former, there is Rob Bottins's amazing make-up and a witty plot in which a sceptical TV journalist (Dee Wallace) uncovers a werewolf colony. For the latter, Dante touches his cap to monster greats of the past by naming key characters after cult horror directors such as Terry (Terence) Fisher and Fred (Freddie) Francis. JF. Contains violence, swearing and nudity. [video] DVD

Dee Wallace [Dee Wallace Stone] *Karen White* • Patrick Macnee *Dr George Waggner* • Dennis Dugan *Chris* • Christopher Stone *R William "Bill" Neill* • Belinda Balaski *Terry Fisher* • Kevin McCarthy *Fred Francis* • John Carradine *Erle Kenton* • Slim Pickens *Sam Newfield* • Elisabeth Brooks *Marsha* • Robert Picardo *Eddie* • Dick Miller *Walter Paisley* ■ *Dir* Joe Dante • *Scr* John Sayles, Terence H Winkless, from the novel by Gary Brandner

Howling II: Your Sister Is a Werewolf ★★ 18

Horror comedy 1984 · US · Colour · 86mins

After the sly wit of Joe Dante's 1981 original, director Philippe Mora opts for a very camp spin for the first of a number of sequels. The setting is Transylvania, with Reb Brown tracking down the werewolf queen (Sybil Danning). Even the presence of Christopher Lee fails to impress, though the mix of gore and clumsy parody exerts a bizarre charm. JF [video]

Christopher Lee *Stefan Crosscoe* • Annie McEnroe *Jenny Templeton* • Reb Brown *Ben White* • Sybil Danning *Stirba* • Marsha A Hunt *Mariana* • Judd Omen *Vlad* ■ *Dir* Philippe Mora • *Scr* Robert Sarno, Gary Brandner, from the novel *The Howling* by Gary Brandner

The Howling III ★★ 18

Horror comedy 1987 · Aus · Colour · 94mins

This entry is notable for being perhaps the daftest of all the sequels, and for that reason is almost watchable in a perverse sort of way. It's a sort of "Tie Me Werewolf Down Sport", with researcher Barry Otto investigating a marsupial branch of the lycanthropic family Down Under. For the most part, this is an erratic mess. JF. Contains violence and swearing. [video] DVD

Barry Otto *Professor Harry Beckmeyer* • Imogen Annesley *Jerboa* • Dasha Blahova *Olga Gorki* • Max Fairchild *Thylo* • Ralph Cotterill *Professor Sharp* • Leigh Biolos *Donny Martin* • Frank Thring *Jack Citron* • Barry Humphries *Dame Edna Everage* ■ *Dir* Philippe Mora • *Scr* Philippe Mora, from the novel by Gary Brandner

Howling IV ★★ 18

Horror 1988 · UK · Colour · 87mins

Director John Hough attempts to bring the werewolf franchise back on track after the daft excesses of Philippe Mora's first two loopy sequels. The story concerns writer Romy Windsor, who keeps having visions of a young nun and a wolf-like creature. Convinced they are the result of stress, she and her husband head for the countryside where they encounter a young nun. Hough manages to spring a few healthy shocks, but the story takes too long to get going. Still, three more sequels followed. JF [video] DVD

Romy Windsor *Marie* • Michael T Weiss *Richard* • Antony Hamilton *Tom* • Susanne Severeid *Janice* • Lamya Derval *Eleanor* • Norman Anstey *Sheriff* ■ *Dir* John Hough • *Scr* Clive Turner, Freddie Rowe, from a story by Clive Turner, from the novel *The Howling* by Gary Brandner

Huck and the King of Hearts ★★★

Adventure 1993 · US · Colour · 103mins

A very loose, modern adaptation of the classic Mark Twain story. In this appealing family tale, a cardsharp and his young pal Huck travel across America searching for Huck's grandfather. Director Michael Keusch's film gains much from its likeable cast, which includes *Dances with Wolves's* Graham Greene, Dee Wallace Stone and Chauncey Leopardi as Huck. JB

Chauncey Leopardi *Billy "Huck" Thomas* • Graham Greene (2) *Jim* • Dee Wallace Stone *Aunt Darlene* • Joe Piscopo *Max* • Gretchen Becker *Lisa* • Ed Trotta *Ed* • John Astin *Zach* ■ *Dir* Michael Keusch • *Scr* Christopher Sturgeon, from the novel *The Adventures of Huckleberry Finn* by Mark Twain

Huckleberry Finn ★★

Adventure drama 1931 · US · BW · 79mins

Jackie Coogan became a hugely popular child star after appearing with Chaplin in *The Kid* and Paramount had initial success in re-launching him in the early sound period in the title role of *Tom Sawyer* in 1930. Here he plays Tom again with Junior Durkin as Huck; together the duo save two young girls from falling into the hands of a pair of rascals. The film has some antiquated charm but Coogan can't match the pugnacity of Mickey Rooney in 1939's *The Adventures of Huckleberry Finn*. AE

Jackie Coogan *Tom Sawyer* • Mitzi Green *Becky Thatcher* • Junior Durkin *Huckleberry Finn* • Jackie Searl [Jackie Searle] *Sid Sawyer* • Clarence Muse *Jim* • Clara Blandick *Aunt Polly* ■ *Dir* Norman Taurog • *Scr* Grover Jones, William Slavens McNutt, from the novel *The Adventures of Huckleberry Finn* by Mark Twain

Huckleberry Finn ★★★ U

Musical period adventure
1974 · US · Colour · 109mins

Reader's Digest flirted with film production in the 1970s, and to its credit produced two very watchable Mark Twain movies, of which this is the second, continuing Jeff East's characterisation of Huckleberry Finn from 1973's *Tom Sawyer*. Both movies were shot on location and handsomely filmed in Panavision, and both had totally forgettable scores by the Sherman brothers, then coming off a roll with *Mary Poppins* and *The Jungle Book*. There's some clever casting in this one, but political correctness dilutes Paul Winfield's all-too-noble Jim. Veteran J Lee Thompson directs perfectly adequately, but the whole is without sparkle. TS [video]

Jeff East *Huckleberry Finn* • Paul Winfield *Jim* • Harvey Korman *King* • David Wayne *Duke* • Arthur O'Connell *Colonel Grangerford* • Gary Merrill *Pap* • Natalie Trundy *Mrs Loftus* • Lucille Benson *Widder Douglas* ■ *Dir* J Lee Thompson • *Scr* Robert B Sherman, Richard M Sherman, from the novel *The Adventures of Huckleberry Finn* by Mark Twain

The Hucksters ★★★ U

Drama 1947 · US · BW · 110mins

To launch Deborah Kerr's Hollywood career, MGM surrounded her with a mighty cast of stars: Clark Gable, Sydney Greenstreet, Adolphe Menjou and Ava Gardner. The story, about the sharp practices of Madison Avenue advertising types, has dated badly; MGM wasn't in the business of criticising big business, even something as symbolically trivial as Greenstreet's bathroom soap empire. Gable joins the firm and gets the job of persuading 25 society women to endorse the soap. As a star package it has still has bags of glamour and some sparkling wit. AT [video]

Clark Gable *Victor Albee Norman* • Deborah Kerr *Kay Dorrance* • Sydney Greenstreet *Evan Llewellyn Evans* • Adolphe Menjou *Mr Kimberly* • Ava Gardner *Jean Ogilvie* • Keenan Wynn *Buddy Hare* • Edward Arnold *Dave Lash* • Aubrey Mather *Valet* ■ *Dir* Jack Conway • *Scr* Luther Davis, Edward Chodorov, George Wells, from the novel by Frederic Wakeman

Hud ★★★★★ 12

Drama 1963 · US · BW · 107mins

In this powerhouse drama, Paul Newman gives his finest screen performance as the heedless, sexually aggressive rancher's son whose strained relationship with his idealistic father (Melvyn Douglas) comes to a head when disease infects their cattle. Echoing his role in *Shane*, Brandon de Wilde, as Newman's nephew, looks on with a mixture of horror and envy as his uncle trashes towns and relationships. The film was nominated for seven Oscars, winning three – best supporting actor for Douglas, best actress for Patricia Neal (as the housekeeper) and best black and white cinematography for James Wong Howe. Despite his charismatic portrayal, Newman lost out to Sidney Poitier in *Lilies of the Field*. AT [video] DVD

Paul Newman *Hud Bannon* • Patricia Neal *Alma Brown* • Melvyn Douglas *Homer Bannon* • Brandon de Wilde *Lon Bannon* • John Ashley *Hermy* • Whit Bissell *Burris* • Crahan Denton *Jesse* • Val Avery *Jose* ■ *Dir* Martin Ritt • *Scr* Irving Ravetch, Harriet Frank Jr, from the novel *Horseman, Pass By* by Larry McMurtry • *Cinematographer* James Wong Howe

Hudson Hawk ★★ 15

Action comedy 1991 · US · Colour · 95mins

Bruce Willis helped write the story and the title song of this so-called action comedy, in which he stars as a retired cat burglar who is persuaded to return to his criminal activities. There are some good action scenes, especially during the heist of a Leonardo da Vinci artefact, but Willis is not a strong enough screen presence to rise above the poor material. Meanwhile, Richard E Grant and Sandra Bernhard are awful as the villains. TH. Contains swearing and violence. [video] DVD

Bruce Willis *Hudson Hawk* • Danny Aiello *Tommy Five-Tone* • Andie MacDowell *Anna Baragli* • James Coburn *George Kaplan* • Richard E Grant *Darwin Mayflower* • Sandra Bernhard *Minerva Mayflower* • David Caruso *Kit Kat* ■ *Dir* Michael Lehmann • *Scr* Steven E de Souza, Daniel Waters, from a story by Bruce Willis, Robert Kraft

Hudson's Bay ★★★

Historical adventure 1940 · US · BW · 95mins

This rather spurious historical romance ended up as one of 20th Century-Fox's no-expense-spared backlot historical pageants. It features Fox's lovely contract star Gene Tierney and, on loan from Warner Bros, the distinguished and fashionable Paul Muni; they are surrounded by Fox's 1940s repertory company including Laird Cregar and Vincent Price. The trouble is that director Irving Pichel fails to bring some sense of scale to this saga of the founder of the Hudson's Bay Trading Company TS

Paul Muni *Pierre Radisson* • Gene Tierney *Barbara Hall* • Laird Cregar *Gooseberry* • John Sutton *Lord Edward Crew* • Virginia Field *Nell Gwynn* • Vincent Price *King Charles II* ■ *Dir* Irving Pichel • *Scr* Lamar Trotti

The Hudsucker Proxy ★★★★ PG

Comedy drama 1994 · US · Colour · 106mins

This is a throwback to the good old days of the screwball comedy. When Joel and Ethan Coen pay tribute to a period or a style of film-making, however, they never slavishly re-create. Here they marry the Art Deco designs of the 1930s with the go-get-'em attitudes of the 1950s to fashion a parable that might just have something to say about America in the 1990s. This is a classic "little man against the system" scenario, with Tim Robbins wonderfully ingenuous as the nobody who hits gold when he invents the Hula-Hoop. Paul Newman mistakes excessive for comic, unlike Jennifer Jason Leigh, whose impression of Rosalind Russell doing a Katharine Hepburn is a hoot. DP [video] DVD

Tim Robbins *Norville Barnes* • Jennifer Jason Leigh *Amy Archer* • Paul Newman *Sidney J Mussburger* • Charles Durning *Waring Hudsucker* • John Mahoney *Chief* • Jim True *Buzz* • William Cobbs [Bill Cobbs] *Moses* • Bruce Campbell *Smitty* ■ *Dir* Joel Coen • *Scr* Joel Coen, Ethan Coen, Sam Raimi

H

Hue and Cry ★★★★ U

Comedy 1947 · UK · BW · 78mins

After this early effort, director Charles Crichton went on to greater acclaim for making *The Lavender Hill Mob* and, more recently, *A Fish Called Wanda*. However there's much to enjoy in this slight but entertaining Ealing comedy caper – the first of the genre from the famous studio – as Alastair Sim and a gang of East End urchins set out to thwart some fiendish crooks. A fun frolic from a more innocent age, with some evocative location footage of postwar London . PF DVD

Alastair Sim *Felix H Wilkinson* • Harry Fowler *Joe Kirby* • Valerie White *Rhona* • Jack Warner *Jim Nightingale* • Frederick Piper *Mr Kirby* • Heather Delaine *Mrs Kirby* • Douglas Barr *Alec* ■ *Dir* Charles Crichton • *Scr* TEB Clarke

Huey Long ★★★

Documentary
1985 · US · Colour and BW · 88mins

A documentary portrait of Huey P Long, governor and senator of Louisiana from 1928 to 1935, when he was assassinated. Long's short career has few equals in modern America. He called himself "Kingfish" (he promised to make every man a king) and ran Louisiana as his private fiefdom. Directed by Ken Burns, this is a compelling portrait of a demagogue who inspired the 1949 feature film *All the King's Men*. Paul Newman played Long's brother, also a Louisiana governor, in the 1989 film *Blaze*. AT

David McCullough *Narrator* ■ *Dir* Ken Burns • *Scr* Geoffrey C Ward

The Huggetts Abroad ★ U

Comedy 1949 · UK · BW · 83mins

Having first encountered the Huggetts in *Holiday Camp*, it's somewhat apt that we should bid them farewell at the end of another sojourn. However, it's with relief not regret that we part company with Jack Warner, Kathleen Harrison et al, as this brief series that began in 1948 with *Here Come the Huggetts* had clearly run out of steam. It's one contrivance after another once Warner chucks his job and hauls the family off to South Africa. Unfunny and very dull. DP

Jack Warner *Joe Huggett* • Kathleen Harrison *Ethel Huggett* • Susan Shaw *Susan Huggett* • Petula Clark *Pet Huggett* • Dinah Sheridan *Jane Huggett* • Hugh McDermott *Bob McCoy* • Jimmy Hanley *Jimmy* ■ *Dir* Ken Annakin • *Scr* Mabel Constanduros, Denis Constanduros, Ted Willis, Gerard Bryant, from characters created by Godfrey Winn

Hugs and Kisses ★★★

Sex comedy 1967 · Swe · BW · 93mins

This charming but otherwise unexceptional Swedish sex comedy entered the history books by changing the obscenity law in the UK. It concerns a young married couple (Sven-Bertil Taube and Agneta Ekmanner), who invite the husband's male friend to stay in their house. The consequent jealousy and other friction is brightly played, but somewhat predictable. The BBFC wanted shots of Ekmanner naked removed. The press protested and eventually the film was passed uncut. Because there was no prosecution, the precedent that pubic hair was not in itself obscene was established. DM. A Swedish language film.

Agneta Ekmanner *Eva* • Sven-Bertil Taube *Max* • Håkan Serner *John* • Lena Granhagen *Hickan* ■ *Dir/Scr* Jonas Cornell

Hukkle ★★★ 12A

Crime mystery drama
2002 · Hun · Colour · 77mins

With a visual lyricism that recalls Russian director Alexander Dovzhenko and a sensitivity to the comic potential of sound that's reminiscent of Jacques Tati, Gyorgy Palfi's first feature is certainly technically accomplished. A sinister mystery lurks beneath this quirky depiction of the rhythms of rural Hungarian life and Palfi succeeds in luring us into its heart without ever quite revealing the reasons for a sudden spate of deaths. He occasionally succumbs to directorial excess, but the engaging characters and intriguing narrative make this a compelling allegory. DP. In Hungarian with English subtitles.

Jozsef Farkas *Police officer* • Ferenc Nagy *Bee-keeper* • Mihalyne Kiraly *Grandmother* • Edit Nagy *Shepherdess* • Istvan Barath *Pig owner* ■ *Dir/Scr* Gyorgy Palfi

Hulchul ★ PG

Romantic comedy
2004 · Ind · Colour · 166mins

Director Priyadarshan here produces a perfect example of Bollywood comedy at its mind-numbing worst. Amrish Puri is the rigidly principled patriarch of one household, who's pitted against the clan of matriarch Lakshmi from a neighbouring village. Akshaye Khanna and Kareena Kapoor play opposing members of each family who cunningly hatch a plan to pretend to fall in love. The cast mugs and grimaces while the juvenile slapstick shows a complete lack of wit or inspiration. OA. A Hindi language film. DVD

Akshaye Khanna *Jai* • Kareena Kapoor *Anjali* • Suniel Shetty [Sunil Shetty] *Veer* • Paresh Rawal *Kishen* • Jackie Shroff *Balram* • Arshad Warsi *Lucky* • Arbaaz Khan *Shakti* • Amrish Puri *Angaarchand* • Lakshmi *Lakshmidevi* ■ *Dir* Priyadarshan • *Scr* Neeraj Vora

Hulk ★★★ 12

Science-fiction action drama
2003 · US · Colour · 132mins

Ang Lee was hardly the obvious choice for a genre more noted for campy fun and destructive action than the subtleties of human relationships. What has emerged is a curate's egg of a movie that is unlikely to totally satisfy anyone. The childhood trauma that feeds Bruce Banner's rage is an oddly grim subplot, while the later action scenes feel tacked on despite their technical virtuosity. Matters aren't helped by Eric Bana's detached performance as Banner, but Nick Nolte injects a soupçon of fun as the older incarnation of his insane dad and Lee's use of editing – including split screens to suggest comic-strip frames – is quite innovative. AS. Contains violence. DVD

Eric Bana *Bruce Banner/Dr Bruce Krenzler/The Hulk* • Jennifer Connelly *Betty Ross* • Sam Elliott *General Ross* • Josh Lucas *Glenn Talbot* • Nick Nolte *David Banner* • Paul Kersey *Young David Banner* • Cara Buono *Edith Banner* • Stan Lee *Security guard* • Lou Ferrigno *Security guard* ■ *Dir* Ang Lee • *Scr* John Turman, Michael France, James Schamus, from a story by James Schamus, from the character created by Stan Lee, Jack Kirby

Hullabaloo over Georgie and Bonnie's Pictures ★★★ PG

Comedy 1979 · UK/Ind · Colour · 33mins

This Merchant Ivory production is an arch comedy of manners. Originally commissioned for television, it was shot without a completed script and occasionally loses its way. Centred around princes, palaces, *objets d'art* and those who would exploit them, this minor entry in an illustrious canon is as delicate as the miniatures that dealers Larry Pine and Peggy Ashcroft try to prize away from maharajah Victor Bannerjee and his sister, Aparna Sen. Playful, but still a worthwhile discussion of the value of art. DP

Peggy Ashcroft *Lady Gwyneth* • Victor Bannerjee [Victor Banerjee] *Georgie* • Aparna Sen *Bonnie* • Saeed Jaffrey *Sri Narain* • Jane Booker *Lynn* ■ *Dir* James Ivory • *Scr* Ruth Prawer Jhabvala

Hum ★★★ PG

Action drama 1991 · Ind · Colour · 176mins

Although age was catching up with him, Amitabh Bachchan confirmed his position as a Bollywood superstar with this action drama. It was made by Mukul S Anand, who was to die so tragically young in 1997. In the opening section, Bachchan's small-time racketeer finds himself caught up in a docklands gang war, while in the second (set several years later) he alternates between the battle against a terrorist organisation and Kimi Katkar's bid for stardom. The abrasive and suggestive nature of this film is typified by the blatant symbolism of the bar-room dance number. DP. In Hindi with English subtitles.

Amitabh Bachchan *Tiger* • Romesh Sharma *Gonsalves* • Danny Denzongpa *Bakhtawar* • Anupam Kher *Inspector Giridhar* • Kimi Katkar ■ *Dir* Mukul S Anand • *Scr* Ravi Kapoor, Mohan Kaul

Hum Dil De Chuke Sanam ★★★ PG

Romantic musical comedy
1999 · Ind · Colour · 180mins

Aishwarya Rai stars as the headstrong daughter of palace singer Vikram Gokhale, who is married off to lawyer Ajay Devgan despite her love for hedonistic musician Salman Khan. However, when her husband discovers the truth, he heads for Italy to deliver his bride to his rival. Packed with colourful ceremonials and shuttling between Europe and Rajasthan, this escapist masala is greatly enhanced by glossy photography and lively songs. DP. In Hindi with English subtitles.

Ajay Devgan *Vanraj* • Salman Khan *Sameer* • Aishwarya Rai *Nandini* • Vikram Gokhale *Pundit Darbar* ■ *Dir* Sanjay Leela Bhansali • *Scr* Sanjay Leela Bhansali, Kenneth Phillips, from a story by Pratap Karwat

Hum Tum ★★★ PG

Romantic comedy
2004 · Ind · Colour · 142mins

The Bollywood romantic comedy has never been more popular, but Kunal Kohli's globetrotting saga takes its inspiration from *When Harry Met Sally...* . Cartoonist Saif Ali Khan and Rani Mukerji spend a decade avoiding the obvious realisation that they're made for each other. The initial encounter in Amsterdam is probably the liveliest, as subsequently Kohli struggles to find convincing reasons for keeping the couple apart. The leads are well matched, but the storyline is a tad too familiar. DP. In Hindi with English subtitles. DVD

Saif Ali Khan *Karan Kapoor* • Rani Mukherjee [Rani Mukherji] *Rhea Prakash* • Rishi Kapoor • Rati Agnihotri • Kiron Kher • Jimmy Shergill • Abhishek Bachchan ■ *Dir* Kunal Kohli • *Scr* Kunal Kohli, Siddharth Raj Anand

Hum Tumhare Hain Sanam ★★★ U

Musical romantic drama
2000 · Ind · Colour · 174mins

Director KS Adiyaman's remake of his own Tamil hit was finally released after a protracted shoot spanning six years. What emerges is a typically convoluted story in which ageing Alok Nath is left to rear the orphaned children of his best friend as well as his own grandchildren. In time, his favourite grandchild Madhuri Dixit marries her devoted "stepbrother" Shah Rukh Khan. However, their happiness is short-lived. There's little in the way of subtle shading here but, with its impressive all-star cast and songs from some of India's leading composers, this is an enjoyable melodrama. DP. A Hindi language film. DVD

Shah Rukh Khan *Gopal* • Salman Khan *Suraj* • Madhuri Dixit *Radha* • Atul Agnihotri *Prashant* • Alok Nath *Devnarayan* ■ *Dir/Scr* KS Adiyaman

Human Cargo ★★

Romantic drama 1936 · US · BW · 87mins

This feeble romantic drama has Brian Donlevy and Claire Trevor as rival newshounds trying to unmask a gang smuggling aliens (the human variety) into the USA. Made by Fox, it lacks the tabloid, crusading spirit of the Warner Bros equivalents – *Five Star Final*, for instance – while the class difference between the two stars seems derived from *It Happened One Night*. Rita Hayworth, billed as Rita Cansino, makes an early appearance. AT

Claire Trevor *Bonnie Brewster* • Brian Donlevy *Packy Campbell* • Alan Dinehart *Lionel Crocker* • Ralph Morgan *District Attorney Cary* • Helen Troy *Susie* • Rita Cansino [Rita Hayworth] *Carmen Zoro* ■ *Dir* Allan Dwan • *Scr* Jefferson Parker, Doris Malloy, from the novel *I Will Be Faithful* by Kathleen Shepard

The Human Comedy ★★★★ U

Second World War drama
1943 · US · BW · 116mins

This beautifully realised adaptation of William Saroyan's novel looks at life in an American small town during the Second World War. Mickey Rooney gives a moving performance as the high school student turned telegraph boy around whom the everyday events revolve. Director Clarence Brown shamelessly pulls the heartstrings by leaning heavily on nostalgia, religion, family responsibility and patriotism, as he fills the screen with instantly recognisable characters everyone has met at one time or another. An emotionally engaging masterpiece of admirable simplicity. AJ

Mickey Rooney *Homer Macauley* • Frank Morgan *Willie Grogan* • James Craig *Tom Spangler* • Marsha Hunt *Diana Steed* • Fay Bainter *Mrs Macauley* • Ray Collins *Mr Macauley* • Van Johnson *Marcus Macauley* • Donna Reed *Bess Macauley* ■ *Dir* Clarence Brown • *Scr* Howard Estabrook, from the novel by William Saroyan

The Human Condition ★★★★★

Epic war drama 1958 · Jpn · BW · 579mins

Adapted from Gomikawa's six-part novel, Masaki Kobayashi's epic masterpiece reflects his own experiences as a pacifist in Japan during the Second World War. Four years in the making and running for a mammoth 579 minutes, Masaki Kobayashi's heart-rending antiwar trilogy was a controversial project; the Shochiku studio was reluctant to bankroll it, but was rewarded with a work of unparalleled power and poignancy. Sent to supervise a Manchurian copper mine, Tatsuya Nakadai attempts to curb brutal overseer Eitaro Ozawa's maltreatment of the enslaved Chinese workforce, only to find himself dispatched to the front without a chance to take leave of his wife, Michiyo Aratama. This harrowing exploration of the savage horror of combat is ambitious, shocking and unforgettable. DP. In Japanese with English subtitles.

Tatsuya Nakadai *Kaji* • Michiyo Aratama *Michiko* • Ineko Arima *Yang Chun Lan* • So Yamamura *Okishima* • Akira Ishihama *Chen* • Shinji Nambara *Kao* • Eitaro Ozawa *Okazaki* ■ *Dir* Masaki Kobayashi • *Scr* Zenzo Matsuyama, Masaki Kobayashi, from the novel *Ningen No Joken* by Jumpei Gomikawa

Human Desire ★★★

Film noir 1954 · US · BW · 90mins

Emile Zola's bleak novel about the murderous triangle that engulfs a train driver, a stationmaster and his wife seems tailor-made for the screen. But just as the powerful themes and images had confounded Jean Renoir in *La Bête Humaine* in 1938, so they eluded Fritz Lang in this *film noir* that was prevented from exploring the book's seamier side by the strictures of the Hollywood Production Code. Lang's preoccupation with the sights and symbolism of the railway yards too often leaves the characters stranded in the sidings. DP

Glenn Ford *Jeff Warren* • Gloria Grahame *Vicki Buckley* • Broderick Crawford *Carl Buckley* • Edgar Buchanan *Alec Simmons* • Kathleen Case *Ellen Simmons* • Peggy Maley *Jean* ■ *Dir* Fritz Lang • *Scr* Alfred Hayes, from the novel *La Bête Humaine* by Emile Zola • *Cinematographer* Burnett Guffey

The Human Factor ★★ 18

Action thriller 1975 · UK · Colour · 92mins

This action film aspires to the status of political conspiracy thriller, but it's really little more than *Death Wish* with a CIA subplot. George Kennedy is the NATO bigwig based in Naples whose family is wiped out by terrorists. Kennedy plays war games for a living, so he decides to put his theories into practice and hit the vengeance trail – with messy consequences. AT

George Kennedy *John Kinsdale* • John Mills *Mike McAllister* • Raf Vallone *Dr Lupo* • Arthur Franz *General Fuller* • Rita Tushingham *Janice Meredith* • Barry Sullivan *Edmonds* • Haydée Politoff *Pidgeon* ■ *Dir* Edward Dmytryk • *Scr* Tom Hunter, Peter Powell

The Human Factor ★★★ 15

Spy drama 1979 · UK/US · Colour · 110mins

Faithfully adapted by Tom Stoppard, this espionage thriller has all the complexities of characterisation and plot one expects from a Graham Greene "entertainment". But Otto Preminger (who completed the picture with his own cash after the backers withdrew) never really comes to terms with the notions of honour, isolation and Englishness that underpin the novel. The cast sustain the suspense, with Nicol Williamson admirable as the double agent whose favour for an old friend has dire consequences. DP

Nicol Williamson *Maurice Castle* • Richard Attenborough *Colonel John Daintry* • Joop Doderer *Cornelius Muller* • John Gielgud *Brigadier Tomlinson* • Derek Jacobi *Arthur Davis* • Robert Morley *Doctor Percival* • Ann Todd *Castle's mother* • Iman *Sarah* ■ *Dir* Otto Preminger • *Scr* Tom Stoppard, from the novel by Graham Greene

Human Highway ★ 12

Fantasy musical comedy
1982 · US · Colour · 83mins

Here's a painful lesson for studios – never allow pop stars the money to make their own films. What was hippy icon Neil Young thinking about when he dreamt up this abysmal anti-nuke comedy about a pair of gas station attendants (Young and Russ Tamblyn) working in the shadow of a nuclear power plant. This embarrassment includes a climactic musical number where the cast sing as they ascend toward heaven. Even Dennis Hopper as a truck stop restaurant cook can't save this one. RS

Neil Young *Lionel Switch* • Russ Tamblyn *Fred Kelly* • Dean Stockwell *Otto Quartz* • Dennis Hopper *Cracker* • Charlotte Stewart *Charlotte Goodnight* • Sally Kirkland *Katherine* • Geraldine Baron *Irene* ■ *Dir* Bernard Shakey [Neil Young], Dean Stockwell • *Scr* Bernard Shakey [Neil Young], Jeanne Fields, Dean Stockwell, Russ Tamblyn, James Beshears

The Human Jungle ★★ PG

Police drama 1954 · US · BW · 78mins

This unremarkable police drama, filmed in pseudo-documentary style, stars Gary Merrill, whose main claims to fame are as Bette Davis's husband and as an unsuccessful Senatorial candidate. Here he plays a police captain in charge of a tough neighbourhood and much of the running time is given over to police procedure, though Chuck Connors makes his mark as a killer. AT

Gary Merrill *Danforth* • Jan Sterling *Mary* • Paula Raymond *Pat Danforth* • Emile Meyer *Rowan* • Regis Toomey *Geddes* • Lamont Johnson *Lannigan* • Chuck Connors *Swados* ■ *Dir* Joseph M Newman • *Scr* William Sackheim, Daniel Fuchs, from a story by William Sackheim

Human Nature ★★★ 15

Comedy drama
2001 · Fr/US · Colour · 91mins

Charlie Kaufman can't quite recapture the eccentric glories of *Being John Malkovich* with this gleefully lewd screenplay. However, plucky performances from Patricia Arquette and Rhys Ifans (involving much nudity) keep promo wizard Michel Gondry's makeshift feature debut from collapsing under the weight of its percipient, but largely undeveloped ideas. The narrative involving Arquette, the lustily primitive Ifans and dullard scientist Tim Robbins exhausts its supply of laughs and logic and ends up wallowing in crass slapstick and cheerful smut. DP DVD

Tim Robbins *Nathan Bronfman* • Patricia Arquette *Lila Jute* • Rhys Ifans *Puff* • Miranda Otto *Gabrielle* • Robert Forster *Nathan's father* • Mary Kay Place *Nathan's mother* • Rosie Perez *Louise* ■ *Dir* Michel Gondry • *Scr* Charlie Kaufman

Human Resources ★★★

Drama 1999 · Fr/UK · Colour · 103mins

Class and family loyalties clash with so-called social advancement and economic expediency in Laurent Cantet's industrial drama. In this powerful directorial debut, Cantet describes the relationship between graduate trainee Jalil Lespert (the cast's sole professional) and, playing Lespert's father, factory machinist Jean-Claude Vallod, whose uncomplaining sacrifices have helped his son progress. Yet the handling of the strike that follows Lespert's naive involvement in the debate over a shorter working week is less assured. DP. In French with English subtitles.

Jalil Lespert *Franck* • Jean-Claude Vallod *Father* • Chantal Barré *Mother* • Véronique de Pandelaère *Sylvie* • Michel Begnez *Olivier* • Lucien Longueville *Boss* ■ *Dir* Laurent Cantet • *Scr* Laurent Cantet, Gilles Marchand

The Human Stain ★★ 18

Romantic drama
2003 · US · Colour · 101mins

With this stately adaptation, director Robert Benton struggles to retain the shocking power of author Philip Roth's angry meditation on race, class, sex and political correctness. Anthony Hopkins plays a university professor driven from his job after supposedly making a racial slur. Hopkins then enlists the help of a local author (Gary Sinise) to tell his story and begins a Viagra-fuelled affair with white trash janitor Nicole Kidman. This never convinces – Hopkins and Kidman are miscast, Sinise and Ed Harris are clichéd and the opening flash-forward dissipates any suspense. AJ. Contains swearing. DVD

Anthony Hopkins *Coleman Silk* • Nicole Kidman *Faunia Farley* • Ed Harris *Lester Farley* • Gary Sinise *Nathan Zuckerman* • Wentworth Miller *Young Coleman Silk* • Jacinda Barrett *Steena Paulsson* • Harry Lennix *Mr Silk* • Clark Gregg *Nelson Primus* ■ *Dir* Robert Benton • *Scr* Nicholas Meyer, from the novel by Philip Roth

Human Traffic ★★★ 18

Comedy drama
1999 · UK/Ire · Colour · 95mins

Director Justin Kerrigan's debut movie is a valiant attempt to put across the atmosphere of Britain's club scene. It follows the fortunes of five friends who go out on a lost, drug- and drink-fuelled weekend in the dance halls of Cardiff. John Simm can't get it together with girls and confides in friend Lorraine Pilkington as their night out turns into two days of frenzied rave-up. *Trainspotting* it isn't, but the spirited acting from the talented youngsters and the inspired visuals come out of the screen like a chemical rush. TH. Contains swearing, sexual references and drug abuse. DVD

John Simm *Jip* • Lorraine Pilkington *Lulu* • Shaun Parkes *Koop* • Danny Dyer *Moff* • Nicola Reynolds *Nina* • Dean Davies *Lee* • Jan Anderson *Karen Benson* • Jo Brand *Mrs Reality* • Howard Marks ■ *Dir/Scr* Justin Kerrigan • *Cinematographer* Dave Bennett

L'Humanité ★★★ 18

Crime drama 1999 · Fr · Colour · 141mins

Due to its frustrating lack of incident and pedestrian pacing, Bruno Dumont's film found little favour at Cannes, even though non-professionals Emmanuel Schotté and Severine Caneele took the main acting awards. Yet, this drawn-out investigation into the rape and murder of an 11-year-old girl exerts a macabre fascination, not least because of Schotté's eccentric turn as the thin-skinned cop whose methods are definitely unconventional. Dumont makes effective use of the Pas de Calais's soul-destroying landscape and draws a vigorously earthy performance from Caneele. DP. In French with English subtitles.

Emmanuel Schotté *Pharaon de Winter* • Severine Caneele *Domino* • Philippe Tullier *Joseph* • Ghislain Ghesquière *Police chief* ■ *Dir/Scr* Bruno Dumont

The Humanoid ★★ PG

Science fiction 1979 · It · Colour · 95mins

Mad scientist Arthur Kennedy and his girlfriend Barbar Bach want to conquer the universe but invincible humanoid Richard Kiel prevents him with the help of dwarf guru Marco Yeh and a robot dog. Gore-maestro Aldo Lado's leaden direction fluffs any outrageous pantomime enjoyment that could have been gleaned. Ennio Morricone's avant-garde electronic score is one of the composers most unusual. AJ

Richard Kiel *Golob* • Corinne Cléry *Barbara Gibson* • Leonard Mann *Nick* • Barbara Bach *Lady Agatha* • Arthur Kennedy *Kraspin* • Marco Yeh *Tom-Tom* ■ *Dir* George B Lewis [Aldo Lado] • *Scr* Adriano Bolzoni, Aldo Lado

Humoresque ★★★★ U

Melodrama 1946 · US · BW · 119mins

Wonderful Warner Bros tosh containing a fine performance from Joan Crawford as a rich, autocratic patron to intense violinist John Garfield. Based on a Fannie Hurst story, it contains some of the most riotously preposterous dialogue ever: check out Crawford's reply when asked if she likes classical music. Shades of *Golden Boy* abound, not surprisingly since the screenplay is co-written by Clifford Odets, on whose play that film was based; but this is better, and not just because Garfield's violin playing is dubbed by the great Isaac Stern. Lovers of melodrama will enjoy this immensely. TS

Joan Crawford *Helen Wright* • John Garfield *Paul Boray* • Oscar Levant *Sid Jeffers* • J Carrol Naish *Rudy Boray* • Joan Chandler *Gina* • Tom D'Andrea *Phil Boray* • Peggy Knudsen *Florence* • Ruth Nelson *Esther Boray* ■ *Dir* Jean Negulesco • *Scr* Clifford Odets, Zachary Gold, from a story by Fannie Hurst

The Hunchback of Notre Dame ★★★★ PG

Classic silent drama 1923 · US · BW · 86mins

The first film version of Victor Hugo's classic tale is a masterpiece of the silent era. It showcases magnificent sets and Lon Chaney's definitive take on deformed bell-ringer Quasimodo, with a secret infatuation for gypsy girl Esmeralda. From under a 72-pound rubber hump, and with his face covered by lumps of putty, the grotesque Chaney gives an eloquent performance, full of pathos and yearning, which dominates the screen despite all the other epic trappings. It's for his inimitable genius alone that this sprawling saga is now most fondly remembered. AJ DVD

Lon Chaney *Quasimodo* • Ernest Torrence *Clopin* • Patsy Ruth Miller *Esmeralda* • Norman Kerry *Phoebus* • Kate Lester *Mme De Gondelaurier* • Brandon Hurst *Jehan* • Raymond Hatton *Gringoire* • Tully Marshall *Louis XI* • Nigel de Brulier *Dom Claude* ■ *Dir* Wallace Worsley • *Scr* Edward T Lowe Jr, Perley Poore Sheehan, from the novel *Notre Dame de Paris* by Victor Hugo

The Hunchback of Notre Dame ★★★★★ PG

Classic gothic drama
1939 · US · BW · 116mins

For many, Charles Laughton is the cinema's definitive Quasimodo, and his poignant performance reveals more subtleties with every viewing. Laughton captures the tragic soul of Notre Dame's famous bell-ringer, and both his make-up and speech patterns are truly convincing. This is a splendidly full-blooded RKO enterprise, with spectacular crowd scenes and superb supporting performances, notably from a sensual Maureen O'Hara as Esmeralda the gypsy and a callow Edmond O'Brien as the youthful romantic lead. Thomas Mitchell – best known as Scarlett O'Hara's father in *Gone with the Wind* – is marvellous, too, as the king of the beggars. Two major future directors had a big hand in this epic – Jacques Tourneur handled the crowds and Robert Wise was the film editor. TS

Charles Laughton *Quasimodo* • Maureen O'Hara *Esmeralda* • Cedric Hardwicke *Frollo* • Thomas Mitchell *Clopin* • Edmond O'Brien *Gringoire* • Alan Marshal *Phoebus* • Walter Hampden *Claude* • Harry Davenport *Louis XI* ■ *Dir* William S Dieterle [William Dieterle] • *Scr* Sonya Levien, Bruno Frank, from the novel *Notre Dame de Paris* by Victor Hugo • *Cinematographer* Joseph August [Joseph H August] • *Art Director* Van Nest Polglase

The Hunchback of Notre Dame ★★

Gothic drama 1956 · Fr/It · Colour · 103mins

This sadly misbegotten version of the Victor Hugo classic features Anthony Quinn as Quasimodo under a ton of make-up and Gina Lollobrigida, as Esmeralda, struggling beneath the weight of her own inadequacy. At least the Technicolor and widescreen presentation makes the film an interesting visual experience. The unfortunate director was veteran Jean Delannoy, whose track record was more prestigious than this clumsy adaptation would have us believe. TH

Gina Lollobrigida *Esmeralda* • Anthony Quinn *Quasimodo* • Jean Danet *Capt Phoebus* • Alain Cuny *Claude Frollo* • Philippe Clay *Clopin Trouillefou* • Danielle Dumont *Fleur de Lys* • Robert Hirsch *Gringoire* • Jean Tissier *Louis XI* ■ *Dir* Jean Delannoy • *Scr* Jacques Prévert, Jean Aurenche, from the novel *Notre Dame de Paris* by Victor Hugo • *Cinematographer* Michel Kelber

The Hunchback of Notre Dame ★★★★ PG

Gothic drama 1982 · US · Colour · 97mins

One of the best adaptations, for television, of Victor Hugo's classic tale of the misshapen Parisian bell-ringer and his ill-fated love for the gypsy girl Esmeralda. A brilliant and authentically literate script by John Gay is seized on with relish by Anthony Hopkins and Derek Jacobi (playing Quasimodo and Dom Claude Frollo respectively) who both give their difficult characters a warmth and sympathy beyond their tragic and villainous dimensions. Wonderful period production values are the icing on the cake. AJ

Anthony Hopkins *Quasimodo* • Derek Jacobi *Dom Claude Frollo* • Lesley-Anne Down *Esmerelda* • John Gielgud *Charmolue* • Robert Powell *Phoebus* • David Suchet *Trouillefou* • Tim Pigott-Smith *Philippe* • Nigel Hawthorne *Esmerelda trial magistrate* ■ *Dir* Michael Tuchner • *Scr* John Gay, from the novel *Notre Dame de Paris* by Victor Hugo

H

The Hunchback of Notre Dame ★★★★ U

Animated musical drama
1996 · US · Colour · 96mins

This animated version of the Victor Hugo classic is one of the better of the 1990s Disney movies. As with previous versions, it's the tale of Quasimodo, the deformed keeper of the Notre Dame bells, and his unrequited love for Esmeralda, a gypsy whose actions lead to her persecution. It's darker and more adult than previous Disney animations, but there's still room for three mischievous and mobile gargoyles – Victor, Hugo and Laverne. Tom Hulce, Demi Moore and Kevin Kline provide voiceovers to match the poignancy of the drama. A typical straight-to-video sequel followed. TH DVD

Tom Hulce *Quasimodo* • Demi Moore *Esmeralda* • Kevin Kline *Phoebus* • Jason Alexander *Hugo* • Mary Kay Bergman *Quasimodo's mother* • Corey Burton *Brutish guard* ■ *Dir* Gary Trousdale, Kirk Wise • *Scr* Irene Mecchi, Bob Tzudiker, Noni White, Jonathan Roberts, Will Finn, Tab Murphy, from a story by Tab Murphy, from the novel *Notre Dame de Paris* by Victor Hugo

The Hundred Steps ★★★

Crime drama based on a true story
2000 · It · Colour · 104mins

A clarion call from Marco Tullio Giordana for all Sicilians to unite against civic corruption and Mob rule, this fact-based story lacks the dramatic impetus to match the director's passion. Luigi Lo Cascio gives an infectiously subversive performance as Peppino Impastato, the nephew of a Mafioso, who not only joins the Communist Party, but also establishes a radio station to denounce the crimes of his neighbour, Tano Badalamenti (Tony Sperandeo). DP. In Italian with English subtitles.

Luigi Lo Cascio *Peppino Impastato* • Luigi Maria Burruano *Father* • Lucia Sardo *Mother* • Paolo Briguglia *Giovanni* • Tony Sperandeo *Tano Badalamenti* ■ *Dir* Marco Tullio Giordana • *Scr* Marco Tullio Giordana, Monica Zapelli, Claudio Fava

A Hungarian Fairy Tale ★★★ PG

Surreal drama 1986 · Hun · BW · 97mins

This is an imaginative allegory based on the myth that a giant bird will descend on Hungary to rescue it in times of trouble. The nation appears here in the person of a small boy who is searching for the father he has never known. Beautifully shot in glowing monochrome, the film balances its precise socio-political commentary with moments of charming fantasy and black humour. DP. In Hungarian with English subtitles.

David Vermes *Andris* • Maria Varga *Maria* • Husak Frantisek *Antal Orban* • Pal Hetenyi *Hungarian voice* • Eszter Csakanyi *Young woman* • Peter Trokan *Teacher* • Szilvia Toth *Tunde* • Judit Pogany *Tunde's mother* • Geza Balkay *Tunde's stepfather* • Gabor Reviczky *Tunde's father* ■ *Dir* Gyula Gazdag • *Scr* Gyula Gazdag, Miklos Gyorffy, Kata Tolmer

Hunger ★★★★

Drama 1966 · Den/Nor/Swe · BW · 110mins

In adapting Knut Hamsun's first novel, Danish director Henning Carlsen has produced a compelling character study that delves into the mind of an artist on the verge of both physical and mental collapse. Per Oscarsson won the best actor prize at Cannes for his agonisingly truthful performance as a writer in turn-of-the-century Norway, whose poverty and creative anxiety are compounded by the callous indifference of an affluent flirt (a vibrantly coquettish Gunnel Lindblom) who humiliates him just as he has reason to hope for better times. DP. A Norwegian/Swedish language film.

Per Oscarsson *The Writer* • Gunnel Lindblom *Ylajali* • Sigrid Horne-Rasmussen *Landlady* • Osvald Helmuth *Pawnbroker* • Henki Kolstad *Editor* ■ *Dir* Henning Carlsen • *Scr* Henning Carlsen, Peter Seeberg, from the novel *Sult* by Knut Hamsun

The Hunger ★★★ 18

Horror 1983 · US · Colour · 92mins

Scientist Susan Sarandon replaces ageing David Bowie in vampire Catherine Deneuve's affections in director Tony Scott's visually sumptuous adaptation of Whitley Strieber's enigmatic bestseller. Set against a generally effective backdrop of immortal decadence, embodying several centuries of glossy fashion and culture, this MTV-influenced undead tale emphasises style over content, despite an understated mix of sly humour, sexual mystery and clever make-up illusion. AJ. Contains violence, swearing, nudity. DVD

Catherine Deneuve *Miriam* • David Bowie *John Blaylock* • Susan Sarandon *Sarah Roberts* • Cliff De Young *Tom Haver* • Beth Ehlers *Alice Cavender* • Dan Hedaya *Lieutenant Allegrezza* ■ *Dir* Tony Scott • *Scr* Ivan Davis, Michael Thomas, from the novel by Whitley Strieber

Hungry for You ★★

Erotic science-fiction thriller
1996 · US · Colour · 92mins

Rochelle Swanson stars in this decidedly unPC computer thriller. It's 2010 and sex has been outlawed everywhere in the United States except Nevada, with the result that everyone relies on the internet for visceral entertainment. However, it's still dangerous out on the wild, wild web and when an on-line punter is murdered, Swanson's virtual temptress is the prime suspect pursued by human detective Michael Phenicie. DP

Michael Phenicie *Rodney* • Rochelle Swanson *Viva* • Gary Wood *Brannagan* • Nancy Hochman *Val* • Ritchie Montgomery *Arnold* ■ *Dir* Dimitri Logothetis • *Scr* Terry Lennox

Hungry Hill ★★ PG

Period drama 1946 · UK · BW · 97mins

In this adaptation of du Maurier's novel about family rivalry in 19th-century Ireland, the plot-packed, melodramatic excesses of the book seem slightly ludicrous on screen. Margaret Lockwood admirably plays against type as the local firebrand tamed by the cruelty of the copper-mining family into which she marries. However, Brian Desmond Hurst's direction is typically florid and flabby, while the painted backdrops are just atrocious. DP

Margaret Lockwood *Fanny Ross* • Dennis Price *Greyhound John* • Cecil Parker *Copper John* • Michael Denison *Henry Brodrick* • Dermot Walsh *Wild Johnnie* • FJ McCormick *Old Tim* • Eileen Crowe *Bridget* • Jean Simmons *Jane Brodrick* ■ *Dir* Brian Desmond Hurst • *Scr* Daphne du Maurier, Terence Young, Francis Crowdy, from the novel by Daphne du Maurier • *Cinematographer* Desmond Dickinson

Hunk ★★★ PG

Comedy 1987 · US · Colour · 98mins

Computer nerd Steve Levitt makes a pact with Devil's emissary Deborah Shelton so he can become a beach bum with pecs appeal in this intermittently charming comedy fantasy. A pleasant enough time-waster, with gorgeous bodies of both sexes to ogle at, and James Coco puts in a fine turn as the time-travelling Satan with a neat line in amusing historical references. AJ

John Allen Nelson *Hunk Golden* • Steve Levitt *Bradley Brinkman* • Deborah Shelton *O'Brien* • Rebeccah Bush *Sunny* • James Coco *Dr D* • Robert Morse *Garrison Gaylord* ■ *Dir/Scr* Lawrence Bassoff

The Hunley ★★★ 12

War drama based on a true story
1999 · US · Colour · 90mins

John Gray brings history to life in this meticulous, made-for-TV reconstruction of a little-known naval engagement involving the CSS *Huntley*'s bid to break the Union's blockade of Confederacy ports. Made shortly after the submarine was raised off the coast of Charleston, the film exposes not only the bitter hatred that rent American society in the 1860s, but also the wanton barbarism this inspired. With Armand Assante heading a serviceable cast, this is both intelligent and accomplished. DP

Armand Assante *Lt George Dixon* • Donald Sutherland *Gen Pierre Beauregard* • Alex Jennings *Alexander* • Christopher Bauer [Chris Bauer] *Simkins* • Gerry Becker *Capt Pickering* ■ *Dir* John Gray • *Scr* John Gray, from a story by John Fasano, John Gray

The Hunt ★★★★★

Drama 1966 · Sp · BW · 88mins

Director Carlos Saura has fashioned a pitiless and scathing assault on a society and the attitudes that shaped it. His contempt scorches into the celluloid like the heat in which a trio of Civil War veterans go rabbit shooting on the arid site of a former battlefield. Equal scorn is poured on aristocratic and nouveau riche sensibilities, as a combination of vanity, snobbery, fiscal envy and politico-sexual repression drive the unrepentant Falangists to acts of savagery that leave their young companion rigid with indolent incomprehension. Deservedly, Saura's impeccable control of performance, pace and atmosphere earned him the best director prize at Berlin. DP. In Spanish with English subtitles.

Ismael Merlo *José* • Alfredo Mayo *Paco* • José Maria Prada *Luis* • Emilio Gutiérrez Caba *Enrique* • Fernando Sanchez Polack *Juan* • Violetta Garcia *Nina* ■ *Dir* Carlos Saura • *Scr* Angelino Fons, Carlos Saura, from a story by Carlos Saura

The Hunt for Red October ★★★★ PG

Thriller 1990 · US · Colour · 129mins

This submarine drama marks the first screen appearance of Jack Ryan, the US agent subsequently played by Harrison Ford in *Patriot Games* and *Clear and Present Danger* and most recently by Ben Affleck in *The Sum of All Fears*. Here, Alec Baldwin as Ryan plays second fiddle to Sean Connery, charismatic as ever as the Russian commander who sparks an international crisis when he starts heading his sub straight for the USA. As the superpowers engage in the usual round of accusations and denials, it's left to Baldwin to figure out whether Connery is defecting or preparing to attack. John McTiernan's no-frills direction ensures that the tension rarely slips below pressure-cooker level. JF DVD

Sean Connery *Captain Marko Ramius* • Alec Baldwin *Jack Ryan* • Scott Glenn *Captain Bart Mancuso* • Sam Neill *Captain Vasily Borodin* • James Earl Jones *Admiral James Greer* • Joss Ackland *Andrei Lysenko* • Richard Jordan *Jeffrey Pelt* • Peter Firth *Ivan Putin* • Tim Curry *Dr Petrov* • Courtney B Vance *Seaman Jones* • Stellan Skarsgård *Captain Tupolev* ■ *Dir* John McTiernan • *Scr* Larry Ferguson, Donald Stewart, from the novel by Tom Clancy

Hunted ★★ PG

Drama 1952 · UK · BW · 81mins

This cross-country adventure stop-starts too often to engross, but it benefits from the effortless rapport between Dirk Bogarde and Jon Whiteley as a pair of runaways whose friendship is forged in adversity. Fleeing after the murder of his wife's lover, Bogarde makes a credible fugitive, particularly when threatening his young companion, who thinks he's burned down his foster parents' home. Director Charles Crichton makes the most of the various locales, but there's a predictability about the round of encounters and escapes. DP

Dirk Bogarde *Chris Lloyd* • Jon Whiteley *Robbie* • Elizabeth Sellars *Magda Lloyd* • Kay Walsh *Mrs Sykes* • Frederick Piper *Mr Sykes* • Julian Somers *Jack Lloyd* • Jane Aird *Mrs Campbell* • Jack Stewart *Mr Campbell* • Geoffrey Keen *Detective Inspector Deakin* • Joe Linnane *Pawnbroker* ■ *Dir* Charles Crichton • *Scr* Jack Whittingham, from the story by Michael McCarthy

The Hunted ★★★ 18

Action thriller 1995 · US · Colour · 105mins

In this proficient action thriller, video favourite Christopher Lambert plays a businessman based in the Far East who becomes the target of a crazed ninja gang after accidentally witnessing a murder. Help comes in the form of a modern-day samurai warrior (Yoshio Harada), who's looking to settle a centuries-old feud. Director JF Lawton ensures there's plenty of swordsmanship and violent action scenes, while the performances are a cut above the norm for this sort of genre flick. JF. Contains violence, nudity and a sex scene. DVD

Christopher Lambert *Paul Racine* • John Lone *Kinjo* • Joan Chen *Kirina* • Yoshio Harada *Takeda* • Yoko Shimada *Mieko* • Mari Natsuki *Junko* ■ *Dir/Scr* JF Lawton

The Hunted ★★ 15

Thriller 1998 · US/Can · Colour · 91mins

This instantly forgettable TV adventure is constructed around a similar premise to the infinitely superior *A Simple Plan*. Mädchen Amick stars as an insurance investigator searching for a crashed plane carrying a stolen $12 million. Stranded in mountainous terrain after wrecking her jeep, her only ally appears to be recluse Harry Hamlin – but can he be trusted? It's adequately performed and directed, but low on surprises. JF. Contains violence and some mild swearing. [video] DVD

Harry Hamlin *Doc Kovac* • Mädchen Amick *Samantha "Sam" Clark* • Hannes Jaenicke *Jan Kroeger* • Enuka Okuma *Tracy* • Robert Moloney *Dorse* • Peter LaCroix *Ranger McNulty* • Fulvio Cecere *Detective Cuneo* • Peter Bryant (2) *Uniformed officer* ■ *Dir* Stuart Cooper • *Scr* Bennett Cohen, David Ives

The Hunted ★★★ 15

Action thriller 2002 · US · Colour · 90mins

This military thriller is far-fetched in the extreme, but luckily the action sequences have a terrific, visceral impact. A traumatised US veteran of the Kosovo conflict (Benicio Del Toro) is loose in the woods, dispatching game hunters with little more than a knife and brute strength, and the man who taught him how to kill (a typically gruff Tommy Lee Jones) is brought in to track him down. The two leads have a hard time bringing distinct personalities to their rather clichéd characters, though both have enough natural presence to partly overcome this. TH. Contains violence and swearing. [video] DVD

Tommy Lee Jones *LT Bonham* • Benicio Del Toro *Aaron Hallam* • Connie Nielsen *Special Agent Abby Durrell* • Leslie Stefanson *Irene Kravitz* • John Finn *Ted Chenoweth* • José Zuniga *Moret* • Ron Canada *Van Zandt* • Mark Pellegrino *Dale Hewitt* ■ *Dir* William Friedkin • *Scr* David Griffiths, Peter Griffiths, Art Monterastelli

The Hunter ★★ 15

Action thriller based on a true story
1980 · US · Colour · 98mins

Steve McQueen's final film is a badly muffed attempt to update the classic western bounty-hunter story. Known for his doggedness and unconventional methods, Ralph "Papa" Thorson brought thousands of fugitives to justice during his career, and McQueen was attracted to his all-action style and his offbeat personality. However, as directed by Buzz Kulik, the movie is not much more than a series of crash-bang pursuits with Thorson being the only rounded character. DP [video] DVD

Steve McQueen *Ralph "Papa" Thorson* • Eli Wallach *Ritchie Blumenthal* • Kathryn Harrold *Dotty* • Ben Johnson *Sheriff Strong* • Tracey Walter *Rocco Mason* • LeVar Burton *Tommy Price* • Richard Venture *Spota* ■ *Dir* Buzz Kulik • *Scr* Ted Leighton, Peter Hyams, from the non-fiction book by Christopher Keane

The Hunters ★★★ PG

War drama 1958 · US · Colour · 103mins

Robert Mitchum plays a fighter pilot in the Korean War who falls for the wife of his colleague. The final film to be produced and directed by the actor Dick Powell, this could be dismissed as a naive piece of anti-communist propaganda, were it not for Mitchum's characteristically mesmeric presence and for some splendidly orchestrated aerial action sequences. The two-timing wife is played by May Britt, a Swedish-born beauty of dubious talent who retired in 1960 after marrying Sammy Davis Jr. AT DVD

Robert Mitchum *Major Cleve Saville* • Robert Wagner *Lieutenant Ed Pell* • Richard Egan *Colonel "Dutch" Imil* • May Britt *Kristina* • Lee Philips *Lieutenant Carl Abbott* • John Gabriel *Lieutenant Corona* • Stacy Harris *Colonel "Monkey" Moncavage* ■ *Dir* Dick Powell • *Scr* Wendell Mayes, from the novel by James Salter

Hunting ★★★

Drama 1992 · Aus · Colour · 97mins

Atmospherically shot around Melbourne, this thriller keeps threatening to turn into something exceptional only to lapse back into mediocrity at all the wrong moments. John Savage seems to be in a different film from everyone else for the first third of the action as he arrives from the States to rescue his struggling business, but there's definitely a spark in the love scenes he shares with secretary Kerry Armstrong. Guy Pearce is a standout. DP. Contains violence, nudity, sex scenes.

John Savage *Michael Bergman* • Guy Pearce *Sharp* • Kerry Armstrong *Michelle Harris* • Rebecca Rigg *Debbie McCormack* • Jeffrey Thomas *Larry Harris* • Rhys McConnochie *Bill Stockton* ■ *Dir/Scr* Frank Howson

The Hunting Party ★ 18

Western 1971 · UK · Colour · 104mins

Not just tripe, but a production that is also lewd and crude. It is sad to see the great Gene Hackman slumming in this British-made, Spanish-shot western, as a vicious Texan tycoon hunting down Oliver Reed and his gang, who have kidnapped his wife, Candice Bergen. Hackman has a high-powered rifle on his side; all Reed has is a leering expression. TH. Contains violence and nudity. [video]

Oliver Reed *Frank Calder* • Candice Bergen *Melissa Ruger* • Gene Hackman *Brandt Ruger* • Simon Oakland *Matthew Gunn* • Mitchell Ryan *Doc Harrison* • LQ Jones *Hog Warren* • GD Spradlin *Sam Bayard* • William Watson *Loring* • Ronald Howard *Watt Nelson* ■ *Dir* Don Medford • *Scr* William Norton, Gilbert Alexander, Lou Morheim, from a story by Gilbert Alexander, Lou Morheim

Hurlyburly ★★ 18

Drama 1998 · US · Colour · 117mins

David Rabe's acclaimed, hard-hitting play about moral bankruptcy in Hollywood ends up on screen 14 years later as a dated bore. An outstanding cast makes the most of Rabe's razor-sharp dialogue, which covers all offensive bases from dark misogyny to cynical drug-taking. Alas, Anthony Drazan's static direction fails to lift the stagey material, and all attempts to open out this fear and self-loathing talkfest fail miserably. Kevin Spacey, giving a subtle performance, and Anna Paquin, in her first adult role, bolster Sean Penn's star turn. Overall, though, this is a draining and mind-numbing experience. AJ [video] DVD

Sean Penn *Eddie* • Kevin Spacey *Mickey* • Robin Wright Penn *Darlene* • Meg Ryan *Bonnie* • Chazz Palminteri *Phil* • Garry Shandling *Artie* • Anna Paquin *Donna* ■ *Dir* Anthony Drazan • *Scr* David Rabe, from his play

The Hurricane ★★★ PG

Disaster adventure 1937 · US · BW · 99mins

John Ford grudgingly took on this screen adaptation of Charles Nordhoff and James Norman Hall's South Seas yarn about a vendetta between a native sailor and the governor of Tahiti, whose problems are solved by the timely intervention of some spectacularly inclement weather. Raymond Massey, Mary Astor and Dorothy Lamour (most fetching in her trademark sarong) star, and the resulting melodrama offers solid entertainment. AT [video]

Dorothy Lamour *Marama* • Jon Hall *Terangi* • Mary Astor *Mme Germaine DeLaage* • C Aubrey Smith *Father Paul* • Thomas Mitchell *Dr Kersaint* • Raymond Massey *Gov Eugene DeLaage* • John Carradine *Warden* ■ *Dir* John Ford • *Scr* Dudley Nichols, Oliver HP Garrett, from the novel by Charles Nordhoff, James Norman Hall as serialised in *The Saturday Evening Post*

Hurricane ★ 15

Drama 1979 · US · Colour · 114mins

A dismal rehash of John Ford's 1937 movie, itself no great shakes, this has missionaries thumping their bibles while their daughters fornicate with native boys. To make this would-be epic, producer Dino De Laurentiis built the entire town of Pago Pago on the Polynesian island of Bora Bora, as well as a luxury hotel to house the cast and crew. Costing around $20 million, it was a mega-flop. AT [video]

Jason Robards *Captain Charles Bruckner* • Mia Farrow *Charlotte Bruckner* • Max von Sydow *Dr Bascomb* • Trevor Howard *Father Malone* • Timothy Bottoms *Jack Sanford* • James Keach *Sergeant Strang* ■ *Dir* Jan Troell • *Scr* Lorenzo Semple Jr, from the novel by Charles Nordhoff, James Norman Hall

The Hurricane ★★★★ 15

Biographical drama
1999 · US · Colour · 139mins

Veteran director Norman Jewison tackles bigotry and prejudice in this true story of racial injustice. Denzel Washington stars as Rubin "Hurricane" Carter, the boxer who was framed for three murders and sentenced to three life terms. Bob Dylan wrote a song about the case, and countless petitions were organised on his behalf. But it took a teenage boy named Lesra Martin (Vicellous Reon Shannon) to liberate Carter after 19 years of wrongful imprisonment. Washington's gradual progression from hate-filled loner to dignified role model is powerful. TH [video] DVD

Denzel Washington *Rubin "Hurricane" Carter* • Vicellous Reon Shannon *Lesra Martin* • Deborah Kara Unger *Lisa* • Liev Schreiber *Sam* • John Hannah *Terry* • Dan Hedaya *Vincent Della Pesca* • Debbi Morgan *Mae Thelma Carter* • Clancy Brown *Lt Jimmy Williams* • Rod Steiger *Judge Sarokin* ■ *Dir* Norman Jewison • *Scr* Armyan Bernstein, Dan Gordon, Christopher Cleveland, from the autobiography *The Sixteenth Round* by Rubin "Hurricane" Carter and the biography *Lazarus and the Hurricane* by Sam Chaiton, Terry Swinton • *Cinematographer* Roger Deakins

The Hurricane Express ★★ U

Action drama 1932 · US · BW · 76mins

As one chase and pile-up follows another, this may look like an old serial – which is exactly what it was originally. The storyline suffers in the condensation to feature length and, as the mysterious train-smashing Wrecker has the uncanny trick of wearing face masks that fool people into mistaking him for somebody else, the plot becomes more confusing than a railway timetable. A very young John Wayne is often woeful as the avenging hero. AE DVD

John Wayne *Larry Baker* • Shirley Grey *Gloria Martin/Gloria Stratton* • Conway Tearle *Stevens* • Tully Marshall *Mr Edwards* ■ *Dir* Armand Schaefer, JP McGowan • *Scr* George Morgan, JP McGowan, from a story by Colbert Clark, Barney A Sarecky, Wyndham Gittens

Hurricane Streets ★★★ 15

Drama 1997 · US · Colour · 84mins

A triple winner at the Sundance Film Festival (for best dramatic picture, director and cinematography), this is a gripping, gritty little drama. The impressively mature Brendan Sexton III stars as a 15-year-old petty thief with aspirations of a better life beyond the New York gang he belongs to. He carries the weight of the film as the tough teen hampered by a poor upbringing, severe asthma and his girlfriend's overprotective father. Writer/director Morgan J Freeman has a better grasp of urban dialogue and expressive camerawork than he does focused storytelling, but it's still a creditable debut. JC. Contains swearing, violence and drug abuse. [video]

Brendan Sexton III *Marcus* • Shawn Elliott *Paco* • José Zuniga *Kramer* • David Roland Frank *Chip* • Carlo Alban *Benny* • Antoine McLean *Harold* • Mtume Gant *Louis* • Lynn Cohen *Lucy* • Edie Falco *Joanna* ■ *Dir/Scr* Morgan J Freeman

Hurry Sundown ★

Drama 1967 · US · Colour · 145mins

Whoever would have thought that Otto Preminger could have turned out such a stinker as this? There's little pleasure in watching this overlong adaptation, which totally miscasts Michael Caine as a ruthless southerner, replete with menacing accent and surly scowl as he tries to buy up most of Georgia. A feisty Jane Fonda's along for the ride, John Phillip Law is vacant and wan, Faye Dunaway is blowsy and tiresome, Robert Hooks is noble and dull – and they've got the more interesting roles! TS

Michael Caine *Henry Warren* • Jane Fonda *Julie Ann Warren* • John Phillip Law *Rad McDowell* • Faye Dunaway *Lou McDowell* • Robert Hooks *Reeve Scott* • Beah Richards *Rose Scott* • George Kennedy *Sheriff Coombs* • Burgess Meredith *Judge Purcell* ■ *Dir* Otto Preminger • *Scr* Thomas C Ryan, Horton Foote, from the novel by KB Gilden

Hurry Up, or I'll Be 30 ★★ 15

Comedy 1973 · US · Colour · 83mins

In this extremely low-budget would-be comedy, John Lefkowitz tries to sort out his life in time for that ageist deadline, totally unaided by Brooklyn-born director Joseph Jacoby. This film's real (if any) interest today lies in the fact that hidden away in the cast list is pint-sized wonder Danny DeVito. Even in his tiny role here, DeVito's more interesting than leading man Lefkowitz could ever be. TS. Contains some swearing. [video]

John Lefkowitz *George Trapani* • Linda De Coff *Jackie Tice* • Ronald Anton *Vince Trapani* • Maureen Byrnes *Flo* • Danny DeVito *Petey* • David Kirk *Mr Trapani* • Frank Quinn *Mark Lossier* • Selma Rogoff *Mrs Trapani* ■ *Dir* Joseph Jacoby • *Scr* David Wiltse, Joseph Jacoby, from a story by Joseph Jacoby

Husbands ★

Drama 1970 · US · Colour · 141mins

There are few things more tedious in cinema than flailing improvisation. This self-indulgent wallow from John Cassavetes is disappointing. Coping with the death of their buddy through booze, nostalgia and sex, New Yorkers Cassavetes, Peter Falk and Ben Gazzara cut depressing figures of suburban manhood. But we could accept them more readily if they weren't so obviously three arrogant actors imposing their angst and art upon us. DP

Ben Gazzara *Harry* • Peter Falk *Archie* • John Cassavetes *Gus* • Jenny Runacre *Mary Tynan* • Jenny Lee Wright *Pearl Billingham* • Noelle Kao *Julie* • Leola Harlow *Leola* • Meta Shaw *Annie* ■ *Dir/Scr* John Cassavetes

Husbands and Wives ★★★★★ 15

Comedy drama 1992 · US · Colour · 103mins

Throughout this excellent enterprise, Woody Allen employs a hand-held camera to convey the intensity and instability of the key relationship on screen, that between himself and Mia Farrow as a successful but troubled media couple. This dissection of two relationships (the other is between Sydney Pollack and Judy Davis) is piled high with wit and vigour as it comments on the foibles of the artsy self-obsessed of midtown Manhattan. In a film released at the time of Woody and Mia's own troubles, rich ideas and strong performances abound. JM. Contains swearing. [video] DVD

Woody Allen *Gabe Roth* • Mia Farrow *Judy Roth* • Judy Davis *Sally* • Sydney Pollack *Jack*

H

• Juliette Lewis *Rain* • Lysette Anthony *Sam* • Liam Neeson *Michael* • Blythe Danner *Rain's mother* ■ *Dir/Scr* Woody Allen

Hush ★ 12

Thriller 1998 · US · Colour · 91mins

Don't let the classy cast (Jessica Lange, Gwyneth Paltrow) fool you: this is a truly awful film. Paltrow is the young woman who marries mummy's boy Johnathon Schaech, only to find when they visit the family home that mother (Lange) will do just about anything to keep her boy close at hand. This should have been played much more for laughs or scares, whereas instead it's just done ludicrously seriously. JB. Contains violence, swearing. DVD

Jessica Lange *Martha Baring* • Gwyneth Paltrow *Helen* • Johnathon Schaech *Jackson Baring* • Nina Foch *Alice Baring* • Debi Mazar *Lisa* • Kaiulani Lee *Sister O'Shaughnessy* • David Thornton *Gavin* • Hal Holbrook *Dr Hill* ■ *Dir* Jonathan Darby • *Scr* Jonathan Darby, Jane Rusconi, from a story by Jonathan Darby

Hush... Hush, Sweet Charlotte ★★★ 15

Gothic drama 1964 · US · BW · 132mins

Having revived the careers of Bette Davis and Joan Crawford in the Hollywood melodrama *What Ever Happened to Baby Jane?* director Robert Aldrich was anxious to recall them for *Hush... Hush, Sweet Charlotte*. While Davis readily agreed, sensing another triumph, Crawford cried off, so Aldrich cast Olivia de Havilland. The result is a delirious slice of American Gothic about two warring cousins and an inheritance. All the Deep South conventions are present – shadowy mansion, secrets in the closet – in a heady brew for fans of Hollywood's golden age. AT

Bette Davis *Charlotte* • Olivia de Havilland *Miriam* • Joseph Cotten *Drew* • Agnes Moorehead *Velma* • Cecil Kellaway *Harry* • Victor Buono *Big Sam* • Mary Astor *Jewel Mayhew* • Wesley Addy *Sheriff* • George Kennedy *Foreman* ■ *Dir* Robert Aldrich • *Scr* Henry Farrell, Lukas Heller

Hussy ★★ 18

Drama 1979 · UK · Colour · 90mins

Muddled melodrama, with Helen Mirren as a nightclub hostess and part-time prostitute who gets involved with drugs and gangsters, but who finally forges a new life for herself. Mirren does her best to transcend mediocre material, but can't work miracles. The best thing one can say about the film is that it re-creates well the seedy, druggy atmosphere of British nightclubs of the period. DA. Contains swearing, violence and sex scenes.

Helen Mirren *Beaty Simons* • John Shea *Emory* • Daniel Chasin *Billy Simons* • Murray Salem *Max* • Paul Angelis *Alex* • Jenny Runacre *Vere* • Patti Boulaye *Tama* • Marika Rivera *Nadine* ■ *Dir/Scr* Matthew Chapman

Hustle ★★★★ 15

Thriller 1975 · US · Colour · 114mins

Director Robert Aldrich gives this seedy story the same sense of corruption, depravity and urban alienation that made his 1955 masterpiece *Kiss Me Deadly* so memorable. Burt Reynolds stars as the world-weary detective who can barely rouse himself to mumble the sour asides contained in Steve Shagan's uncompromising script. Catherine Deneuve is less sure-footed, but Ben Johnson, Eddie Albert and Ernest Borgnine provide sinister support in this brooding thriller. DP. Contains swearing. DVD

Burt Reynolds *Lt Phil Gaines* • Catherine Deneuve *Nicole Britton* • Eddie Albert *Leo Sellers* • Ben Johnson *Marty Hollinger* • Eileen Brennan *Paula Hollinger* • Ernest Borgnine *Santoro* • Paul Winfield *Sgt Louis Belgrave* ■ *Dir* Robert Aldrich • *Scr* Steve Shagan

The Hustler ★★★★★ 15

Drama 1961 · US · BW · 129mins

This classic drama is showing its age nowadays: all that mock-poetic, soul-searching dialogue and the alcoholic heroine are firmly rooted in 1950s social realism. However, as a showcase for Paul Newman's best screen performance to date, this is still a masterpiece, with Newman, Jackie Gleason and George C Scott striking sparks in the perfectly captured pool-hall atmosphere. The picture is streets ahead of Martin Scorsese's flashy sequel, *The Color of Money*, for which Newman finally won his deserved Oscar. AT. Contains violence. DVD

Paul Newman *"Fast" Eddie Felson* • Jackie Gleason *Minnesota Fats* • Piper Laurie *Sarah Packard* • George C Scott *Bert Gordon* • Myron McCormick *Charlie Burns* • Murray Hamilton *Findlay* • Michael Constantine *Big John* ■ *Dir* Robert Rossen • *Scr* Sidney Carroll, Robert Rossen, from the novel by Walter Tevis • *Cinematographer* Eugen Schüfftan

Hustler White ★★ 18

Erotic comedy drama
1996 · US · Colour · 75mins

This is the closest that maverick actor/director Bruce LaBruce has come to mainstream cinema, although it is worth adding that previous works have included gay pornography, Super 8 shorts and features including *No Skin off My Ass*. Not then an ordinary film-maker. Co-directed with Rick Castro, the film relates how a pretentious German film director (played by LaBruce himself) who picks up a Santa Monica Boulevard hustler (Tony Ward) and is shown the underbelly of the Los Angeles gay scene. Intentionally outrageous, the film somehow remains unshocking in its depiction of perversity. Nevertheless, this is strictly for the cognoscenti. BB DVD

Tony Ward *Montgomery "Monti" Ward* • Bruce LaBruce *Jürgen Anger* • Kevin P Scott *Eigil Vesti* • Ivar Johnson *Piglet* • Ron Athey *Seymour Kasabian* • Miles H Wildecock II *Peter Festus* ■ *Dir/Scr* Bruce LaBruce, Rick Castro

Hyderabad Blues ★★★

Romantic comedy
1998 · Ind · Colour · 85mins

Made in just 17 days in the wake of the unprecedented commercial success of *English, August* , Nagesh Kukunoor's romantic comedy explores a side of India rarely seen in Bollywood's more shamelessly escapist entertainments. The director also stars as an exile who returns home after 12 years in the United States to feel as much an outsider in India as he does abroad. With effective support from Vikram Inamdar and Rajshri Nair, this remains enjoyable, while also questioning arranged marriages, the wisdom of upholding homeland traditions and India's role in the modern world. DP. In English, Hindi and Telugu with subtitles.

Nagesh Kukunoor *Varun Naidu* • Rajshri Nair *Ashwini* • Vikram Inamdar ■ *Dir/Scr* Nagesh Kukunoor

Hyènes ★★★

Drama 1992 · Sen · Colour · 113mins

A strain of indigenous magic realism has run through much sub-Saharan and west African cinema in the 1990s. The Senegalese director Djibril Diop Mambety employs it in this symbolic drama that focuses on the clash between progress and tradition and the blurred line between proud nationhood and post-colonial dependence. The story revolves around a returning wealthy woman who offers untold riches to her fellow villagers if they help her wreak vengeance on the former lover who once drove her into exile. It fails to deliver what it promises, but this is still challenging. DP. In French with English subtitles.

Mansour Diouf *Dramaan* • Ami Diakhate *Linguere* • Mahouredia Gueye *The Mayor* • Issa Ramagelissa Samb *The Professor* ■ *Dir* Djibril Diop Mambety • *Scr* Djibril Diop Mambety, from the play *The Visit* by Friedrich Durrenmatt

The Hypnotist ★★

Crime drama 1957 · UK · BW · 89mins

Irish-born director Montgomery Tully was one of the key figures in the British B-movie industry during the 1950s and 1960s. This is one of his better efforts, as psychiatrist Roland Culver attempts to frame disturbed test pilot Paul Carpenter for the murder of his wife. Culver does a nice line in evil manipulation and Patricia Roc is typically spirited as the girlfriend standing by her man, but poor old Carpenter probably needed to be hypnotised to give a decent performance. DP

Roland Culver *Dr Francis Pelham* • Patricia Roc *Mary Foster* • Paul Carpenter *Val Neal* • William Hartnell *Inspector Rose* • Kay Callard *Susie* • Ellen Pollock *Barbara Barton* • Gordon Needham *Sergeant Davies* • Martin Wyldeck *Dr Bradford* • Oliver Johnston *Dr Kenyon* ■ *Dir* Montgomery Tully • *Scr* Montgomery Tully, from a play by Falkland Cary

Hysteria ★★ 15

Mystery thriller 1964 · UK · BW · 81mins

Having presented Hammer with the sizeable hits, *Paranoiac* and *Nightmare*, Freddie Francis reteamed with screenwriter Jimmy Sangster to complete his psycho trilogy. Sadly, the bemusing experiences of amnesiac American tourist Robert Webber rarely set pulses racing, despite the menacing ministrations of nursing home shrink Anthony Newlands and a mysterious murder. Strewn with mind-bending visuals and preposterous dialogue, this is more mediocre than macabre. DP

Robert Webber *Chris Smith* • Anthony Newlands *Dr Keller* • Jennifer Jayne *Gina* • Maurice Denham *Hemmings* • Lelia Goldoni *Denise* • Sue Lloyd *French girl* ■ *Dir* Freddie Francis • *Scr* Jimmy Sangster

Hysterical Blindness ★★ 15

Drama 2002 · US · Colour · 98mins

Why Mira Nair chose this as the follow-up to *Monsoon Wedding* isn't obvious. She imparts no personality whatsoever to this resolutely downbeat and utterly contrived tale of female bonding, in which New Jersey 30-something Uma Thurman and best mate Juliette Lewis (both of whom overplay to the hilt) seek solace from their humdrum existence in booze binges and unsuitable blokes. Uninspired and garishly resistible. DP DVD

Uma Thurman *Debby* • Gena Rowlands *Virginia* • Juliette Lewis *Beth* • Justin Chamber *Rick* • Ben Gazzara *Nick* ■ *Dir* Mira Nair • *Scr* Laura Cahill, from her play

I

I Accuse! ★★★ U

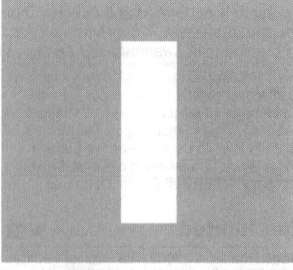

Historical drama 1958 · UK · BW · 99mins

José Ferrer directs and stars in this drama about the famous treason trial in France which saw Alfred Dreyfus framed and sentenced to life imprisonment on Devil's Island. Ferrer makes a compelling hero and he is supported by a fine cast of stalwarts. Gore Vidal's screenplay was intended, perhaps, as an allegory about the McCarthy era. The photography is by Freddie Young, who went on to win three Oscars for his work with David Lean. AT

José Ferrer *Alfred Dreyfus* • Anton Walbrook *Major Esterhazy* • Viveca Lindfors *Lucie Dreyfus* • Leo Genn *Major Picquart* • Emlyn Williams *Emile Zola* • David Farrar *Mathieu Dreyfus* • Donald Wolfit *General Mercier* • Herbert Lom *Major Dupaty De Clam* ■ *Dir* José Ferrer • *Scr* Gore Vidal, from the non-fiction book *Captain Dreyfus – a Story of Mass Hysteria* by Nicholas Halasz

I Aim at the Stars ★★ U

Biographical drama 1960 · US · BW · 106mins

Was it right for the Americans to employ a German scientist who had worked for Hitler on the US space programme? Was it possible for a man who invented the devastating V-2 rocket for the Nazis to have been apolitical? These are the compelling questions raised and then fudged in this tame biopic of rocket expert Wernher von Braun. Unfortunately, despite Curt Jurgens's earnest performance, we never learn much about the man's inner space. RB

Curt Jurgens *Wernher von Braun* • Victoria Shaw *Maria* • Herbert Lom *Anton Reger* • Gia Scala *Elizabeth Beyer* • James Daly *Major William Taggert* • Adrian Hoven *Mischke* ■ *Dir* J Lee Thompson • *Scr* Jay Dratler, from a story by George Froeschel, U Wolter, HW John

I Am a Camera ★★ 12

Comedy drama 1955 · UK · BW · 95mins

This is a hugely disappointing film adaptation of John Van Druten's stage version of Christopher Isherwood's celebrated Berlin tales. John Collier must shoulder most of the blame for his drab script that completely misses the decadence and sordid charm of the underside of pre-war German society. Laurence Harvey's lack of technique is cruelly exposed playing Isherwood, but Julie Harris makes a spirited Sally Bowles. DP DVD

Julie Harris *Sally Bowles* • Laurence Harvey *Christopher Isherwood* • Shelley Winters *Natalia Landauer* • Ron Randell *Clive* • Lea Seidl *Fraulein Schneider* • Anton Diffring *Fritz* ■ *Dir* Henry Cornelius • *Scr* John Collier, from the play *I Am a Camera* by John Van Druten, from the short story collection *The Berlin Stories* by Christopher Isherwood

I Am a Dancer ★★ U

Documentary 1972 · UK/Fr · Colour · 88mins

While ballet fans will rejoice at the prospect of seeing Rudolph Nureyev and Margot Fonteyn give a full performance as Armand and Marguerite, those hoping to learn more about the Russian maestro will be disappointed. Given the amount of access permitted director Pierre Jourdain, one might have expected more than a few rehearsal sequences. But, then, how could Jourdain have possibly provided an in-depth analysis when he clearly had difficulty keeping the leaping star in full shot? DP

Dir/Scr Pierre Jourdain

I Am a Fugitive from a Chain Gang ★★★★

Classic drama 1932 · US · BW · 93mins

The title tells all in terms of plot, but it gives no indication of the power generated by the Oscar-nominated performance of Paul Muni, as the war veteran framed for a hold-up and sentenced to work in a Georgia chain gang at the mercy of sadistic guards. One of the most forceful of Warner Bros's conscience-shaking cycle of movies in the 1930s, it exposed a pitiless regime. Director Mervyn LeRoy pushed audiences of the day to the limits of endurance. TH

Paul Muni *James Allen* • Glenda Farrell *Marie Woods* • Helen Vinson *Helen* • Noel Francis *Linda* • Preston Foster *Pete* • Allen Jenkins *Barney Sykes* • Berton Churchill *Judge* • Edward Ellis *Bomber Wells* • David Landau *Warden* ■ *Dir* Mervyn LeRoy • *Scr* Howard J Green, Brown Holmes, Sheridan Gibney, from the autobiography *I Am a Fugitive from a Georgia Chain Gang* by Robert E Burns

I Am a Nymphomaniac ★★ 18

Erotic drama 1971 · Fr · Colour · 91mins

Made with half an eye on the censors, this is more a romp than a porn pic, with Sandra Jullien's numerous close encounters being mostly of the soft-core kind. The premise is as cheap as the production, with Jullien's mundane life being transformed by an accident in a lift shaft. Thence, it's one conquest after another, although she does take time out to consult a priest and a doctor about her sudden shift in interests. DP. French dialogue dubbed into English. DVD

Sandra Jullien *Carole* • Janine Raynaud *Murielle* • Yves Vincent *Priest* • Patrick Verde *Michel* • Michel Lemoine *Hugo* ■ *Dir* Max Pécas • *Scr* Claude Mulot

I Am Cuba ★★★★

Propaganda drama
1964 · USSR/Cub · BW · 118mins

Resisting the temptations that floored Sergei Eisenstein in Mexico in the 1930s, Stalin's former cinema chief Mikhail Kalazatov not only captures the vibrancy of the people, but also the state of the nation in this propagandist paean to the Castro revolution, made in the aftermath of the Cuban Missile Crisis. The four stories dwell equally on the evils of the Batista regime and the benefits of Communism. But what distinguishes this from agitprop is the stunning cinematography of Sergei Urussevsky, whose "emotional camera" pulls off feats of technical audacity that are both political and artistic. DP. A Russian/Spanish/English language film.

Sergio Corrieri *Alberto* • José Gallardo *Pedro* • Raúl Garcia *Enrique* • Luz Maria Collazo *Maria/Betty* • Jean Bouise *Jim* ■ *Dir* Mikhail Kalatozov • *Scr* Yevgeni Yevtushenko, Enrique Pineda Barnet

I Am Curious – Yellow ★★★ 18

Erotic comedy drama
1967 · Swe · BW · 116mins

Although it played a key role in undermining US censorship rules, Vilgot Sjöman's mix of soft-core sex and political satire is merely a curio now that its power to shock has diminished. The vox pops that sociologist Lena Nyman conducts on the streets of Stockholm are quite revealing of mid-1960s Swedish attitudes, but the stylised couplings with boyfriend Sjöman and car salesman Börje Ahlstedt, while contextual, seem designed purely to titillate. The follow-up *I Am Curious – Blue* made less impact. DP. In Swedish with English subtitles. Contains sex scenes and nudity.

Lena Nyman *Lena* • Börje Ahlstedt *Börje* • Vilgot Sjöman *Director* • Peter Lindgren *Rune, Lena's father* • Chris Wahlström *Rune's friend* ■ *Dir/Scr* Vilgot Sjöman

I Am David ★★★ PG

Period adventure drama
2003 · US/UK · Colour · 91mins

Opening in a bleak Bulgarian labour camp in the early 1950s, this thoughtful film follows the resourceful young Ben Tibber as he makes a daring escape and heads for the safety of Denmark. The initial tension dissipates somewhat once David forgets his fears and increasingly comes to trust the strangers that he encounters en route. But Tibber's guarded performance sustains interest even when director Paul Feig allows the pace to slacken. DP

Ben Tibber *David* • Joan Plowright *Sophie* • Jim Caviezel *Johannes* • Maria Bonnevie *David's mother* • Viola Carinci *Maria* • Silvia de Santis *Elsa* • Francesco De Vito *Roberto* • Paco Reconti *Giovanni* ■ *Dir* Paul Feig • *Scr* Paul Feig, from the novel *North to Freedom* by Anne Holm

I Am Frigid... Why? ★★ 18

Erotic drama 1972 · Fr · Colour · 91mins

Also known as *She Should Have Stayed in Bed*, this soft-core trash centres on a gardener's daughter who experiments with boarding school lesbianism and high society prostitution in an effort to regain the sexual fervour lost after she was raped. All stylised fumble and tumble. DP. French dialogue dubbed into English. Contains sex scenes and nudity. DVD

Sandra Jullien [Sandra Julien] *Doris* • Marie-George Pascal *Carla Chambon* • Jean-Luc Terrade *Eric Chambon* • Anne Kerylen *Eva* • Thierry Murzeau *Luc* • Virginie Vignon *Patricia* ■ *Dir/Scr* Max Pécas

I Am Sam ★ 12

Comedy drama
2001 · US/Ger · Colour · 126mins

The emotionally manipulative story of a single parent (Sean Penn) with a mental age of seven, this focuses on a custody battle for his daughter, whose seventh birthday conveniently makes him an untenable parent. Quite apart from being an offensive, inaccurate and unhelpful portrait of mental illness (Penn's *Rain Man*-influenced autism comes and goes to suit the mawkish script), this is a blatant vanity project for Penn and a naive piece of schmaltz. AC DVD

Sean Penn *Sam Dawson* • Michelle Pfeiffer *Rita Harrison* • Dakota Fanning *Lucy Diamond Dawson* • Dianne Wiest *Annie* • Loretta Devine *Margaret Calgrove* • Richard Schiff *Turner* • Laura Dern *Randy Carpenter* • Mary Steenburgen *Dr Blake* ■ *Dir* Jessie Nelson • *Scr* Kristine Johnson, Jessie Nelson

I Am the Cheese ★★

Psychological thriller
1983 · US · Colour · 95mins

Make-up artist Robert Jiras goes behind the cameras for the first (and last time) for a respectful adaption of the novel by Robert Cormier (who also has a cameo). The story focuses on the attempt of psychiatrist Robert Wagner to unlock the long buried memories of traumatised adolescent Robert MacNaughton. The same source material would inspire the 1992 film *Lapse of Memory*. JF

Robert MacNaughton *Adam* • Hope Lange *Betty Farmer* • Don Murray *David Farmer* • Robert Wagner *Dr Brint* • Cynthia Nixon *Amy* ■ *Dir* Robert Jiras • *Scr* David Lange, Robert Jiras, from the novel by Robert Cormier

I Am the Law ★★★

Crime drama 1938 · US · BW · 83mins

Edward G Robinson stars as a law professor appointed as a special prosecutor to flush out urban racketeers, in one of those films where everyone who has information to deliver is bumped off before they can divulge it. The climax is truly weird as Robinson shows home movies and shots of the electric chair to his gathered suspects in a circus tent. Interestingly, New York's *Herald Tribune* found Robinson's moral rhetoric unconvincing at the time. TS

Edward G Robinson *John Lindsay* • Barbara O'Neil *Jerry Lindsay* • John Beal *Paul Ferguson* • Wendy Barrie *Frankie Ballou* • Otto Kruger *Eugene Ferguson* • Arthur Loft *Tom Ross* ■ *Dir* Alexander Hall • *Scr* Jo Swerling, from a story by Fred Allhoff

I Believe in You ★★★ U

Drama 1952 · UK · BW · 94mins

Michael Relph and Basil Dearden ladle on the good intentions in this unusual drama about the probation service, only to spoil everything by emphasising the patronising conceit that the proletariat will always be ignorant ne'er-do-wells without the guiding influence of the kindly middle classes. Cecil Parker turns from a bumbling do-gooder into a hard-nosed champion of the underprivileged as he helps Harry Fowler and Joan Collins to stumble back on to the straight and narrow. Incapable of giving a bad performance, Celia Johnson is sidelined once Parker finds his feet. DP

Celia Johnson *Matty* • Cecil Parker *Henry Phipps* • Godfrey Tearle *Mr Pyke* • Harry Fowler *Hooker* • George Relph *Mr Dove* • Joan Collins *Norma* • Laurence Harvey *Jordie* • Sidney James *Sergeant Brodie* ■ *Dir* Michael Relph, Basil Dearden • *Scr* Jack Whittingham, Nicholas Phipps, Michael Relph, Basil Dearden, from the novel *Court Circular* by Sewell Stokes

I Bought a Vampire Motorcycle ★★★ 18

Horror comedy 1989 · UK · Colour · 100mins

What TV director Dirk Campbell's homegrown horror spoof lacks in budget, finesse, genuine scares and acting, it more than makes up for in a wealth of clever ideas that gives a neat spin on formula undead mythology. After buying a possessed antique motorbike, which uses blood for petrol and won't kick-start during daylight hours, sleazy rider Neil Morrissey enlists the help of priest Anthony Daniels to exorcise the splatter machine. Cheesy gore, a garlic-breathed detective (Michael Elphick) and tasteless visual gags add to the lunatic fun in this unusually adventurous camp chiller. AJ

Neil Morrissey *Nick Oddie, "Noddy"* • Amanda Noar *Kim* • Michael Elphick *Inspector Cleaver* • Anthony Daniels *Priest* • Andrew Powell *Roach* • George Rossi *Chopper* • Midge Taylor *First Road Toad* • Daniel Peacock *Buzzer* • Burt Kwouk *Fu King owner* ■ *Dir* Dirk Campbell • *Scr* Mycal Miller, John Wolskel

I Can Get It for You Wholesale ★★★ U

Drama 1951 · US · BW · 88mins

A fairly tough adaptation of Jerome Weidman's colourful bestseller about the rag trade, toned down for the screen but providing a superb leading role for dynamic Susan Hayward. She's the gal who goes from seamstress to model to head of a fashion house, and still can't make up her mind whether she wants amiable Dan Dailey or suave George Sanders. This is the same tale that, in its musical incarnation on Broadway, featured a young unknown who brought the house down nightly – Barbra Streisand. TS

Susan Hayward *Harriet Boyd* • Dan Dailey *Teddy Sherman* • George Sanders *Noble* • Sam Jaffe *Cooper* • Randy Stuart *Marge* • Marvin Kaplan *Four Eyes* • Harry Von Zell *Savage* ■ *Dir* Michael Gordon • *Scr* Abraham Polonsky, Vera Caspary, from the novel by Jerome Weidman

I Capture the Castle ★★★★ PG

Period romantic drama
2002 · UK/S Afr · Colour · 108mins

Genteel poverty has never looked so enchanting, as the Mortmain family, headed by creatively blocked writer Bill Nighy, all lead lives of bohemian chaos in a dilapidated castle. Events are recorded by the 17-year-old diarist Cassandra (Romola Garai), whose interest in the opposite sex is awakened when two American brothers (Henry Thomas and Marc Blucas) stumble across the Mortmains on their way to an inherited estate. The 1930s period trappings are laid on a little too thickly, but this is a reassuringly solid and intelligent adaptation, beautifully photographed and expertly performed. TH DVD

Henry Thomas *Simon Cotton* • Marc Blucas *Neil Cotton* • Rose Byrne *Rose Mortmain* • Romola Garai *Cassandra Mortmain* • Bill Nighy *James Mortmain* • Tara FitzGerald *Topaz* • Henry Cavill *Stephen* • Sinead Cusack *Mrs Elspeth Cotton* • David Bamber *Vicar* ■ *Dir* Tim Fywell • *Scr* Heidi Thomas, from the novel by Dodie Smith

I Confess ★★★★ PG

Drama 1953 · US · BW · 90mins

Dismissed by the critics and shunned by the public, this is perhaps Alfred Hitchcock's most under-rated film. In many ways, it shares the transference-of-guilt theme he had explored in his previous movie, *Strangers on a Train*. But what alienated many audiences was an unfamiliarity with the codes of Catholicism that prevent a priest from betraying the secrets of the confessional. Seen today, this is a classic Hitchcock "wrong man" story, which makes marvellous use of its Quebec settings. Montgomery Clift's haunted look is ideal, but some of his Method mannerisms jar. Talky, serious and difficult, but long overdue for reappraisal. DP DVD

Montgomery Clift *Father Michael William Logan* • Anne Baxter *Ruth Grandfort* • Karl Malden *Inspector Larrue* • Brian Aherne *Willy Robertson* • OE Hasse *Otto Keller* • Dolly Haas *Alma Keller* • Roger Dann *Pierre Grandfort* • Charles Andre *Father Millais* ■ *Dir* Alfred Hitchcock • *Scr* George Tabori, William Archibald, from the play *Nos Deux Consciences* by Paul Anthelme

I Could Go On Singing ★★★ U

Musical drama 1963 · UK · Colour · 95mins

Judy Garland's last film, originally called *The Lonely Stage*, is a London-based melodrama attractively shot on location and co-starring Dirk Bogarde. Most of the movie is very average, pieced together when the star's illnesses made it necessary to finish the project in a hurry. However, what this picture does contain is arguably the finest example of improvisational screen acting ever: a single take set in a hospital where Garland and her character merge in a shattering moment of rare movie honesty. TS

Judy Garland *Jenny Bowman* • Dirk Bogarde *David Donne* • Jack Klugman *George Kogan* • Aline MacMahon *Ida* • Gregory Phillips *Matt* •

Pauline Jameson *Miss Plimpton* ■ *Dir* Ronald Neame • *Scr* Mayo Simon, from a story by Robert Dozier

I Could Read the Sky ★★★ 15

Drama 1999 · UK/Ire · Colour · 82mins

Nichola Bruce's debut feature is a lyrical evocation of an Irish exile's life as he looks back from his spartan London bedsit on his youth and his itinerant struggle to find work over the water. Although Stephen Rea and Maria Doyle Kennedy contribute telling cameos, Dermot Healy, as the regret-scarred narrator, dominates proceedings. Bruce re-creates the fragmentary imperfection of memory by superimposing events into an elliptical, almost abstract diary of a mind. DP DVD

Dermot Healy *The old man* • Stephen Rea *PJ* • Brendan Coyle *Francie* • Maria Doyle Kennedy *Maggie* ■ *Dir* Nichola Bruce • *Scr* Timothy O'Grady, Nichola Bruce, from the novel by Steve Pyke, Timothy O'Grady

I Cover the Waterfront ★★

Drama 1933 · US · BW · 75mins

Journalist Ben Lyon romances Claudette Colbert as a means to expose her father (Ernest Torrence, who died before the film's release), a suspected smuggler of Chinese immigrants. Smart-aleck dialogue between Lyon and Colbert vies with various seaborne chases, and there's a surprise appearance from a shark that carries off someone's leg. AT

Claudette Colbert *Julie Kirk* • Ben Lyon *Joseph Miller* • Ernest Torrence *Eli Kirk* • Hobart Cavanaugh *McCoy* • Maurice Black *Ortegus* • Harry Beresford *Old Chris* • Purnell Pratt *John Phelps* ■ *Dir* James Cruze • *Scr* Wells Root, Jack Jevne, from a novel by Max Miller

ID ★★★★ 18

Drama 1994 · UK/Ger · Colour · 107mins

This is a remarkable debut by director Philip Davis, also known as an actor in films such as *Quadrophenia* and *High Hopes*. Although some of the asides about racism in football ring a little hollow and not all of his extras resemble hardened thugs, Davis presents a highly credible picture of what anthropologist Desmond Morris has described as the soccer tribe defending its patch. Reece Dinsdale gives an eye-opening performance as the dedicated policeman who turns into a rabid hooligan, and the support from pub personnel Warren Clarke and Saskia Reeves and peaches-and-cream girlfriend Claire Skinner is also impressive. Riveting. DP. Contains violence, swearing, sex scenes.

Reece Dinsdale *John* • Richard Graham (2) *Trevor* • Claire Skinner *Marie* • Sean Pertwee *Martin* • Saskia Reeves *Lynda* • Warren Clarke *Bob* • Philip Glenister *Charlie* • Perry Fenwick *Eddie* ■ *Dir* Philip Davis • *Scr* Vincent O'Connell, from a story by James Bannon

I Didn't Do It ★★

Comedy thriller 1945 · UK · BW · 99mins

This was George Formby's penultimate picture, and the toothy grin, gormless heroism and the cheeky songs that had seen him through 18 features were now wearing more than a little thin. This eminently forgettable comedy whodunnit did little to reverse his box-office decline. This story in which he turns detective to prove his innocence after he is accused of the murder of an acrobat is too short on gags or clues to hold the attention. DP

George Formby *George Trotter* • Billy Caryll *Pa Tubbs* • Hilda Mundy *Ma Tubbs* • Gaston Palmer *Le Grand Gaston* • Jack Daly *Terry O'Rourke* • Carl Jaffe *Hilary Vance* • Ian Fleming *Inspector Twyning* ■ *Dir* Marcel Varnel • *Scr* Norman Lee, Howard Irving Young, Stephen Black, Peter Fraser, Michael Vaughan

I Died a Thousand Times ★★

Crime drama 1955 · US · Colour · 109mins

In this cheesy remake of *High Sierra*, Jack Palance steps into Humphrey Bogart's shoes as "Mad Dog" Earl, the hard-boiled gangster who wants to finish a lifetime of crime with a spectacular heist. It was a by-the-numbers story back in 1941 and it proves even more tired in this barely competent caper. Palance is certainly no Bogie, but the top-notch supporting cast is a movie buff's delight and well worth catching. AJ

Jack Palance *Roy Earle* • Shelley Winters *Marie Gibson* • Lori Nelson *Velma* • Lee Marvin *Babe* • Earl Holliman *Red* • Perry Lopez *Louis Mendoza* • Pedro Gonzalez [Pedro Gonzalez-Gonzales] *Chico* • Lon Chaney Jr *Big Mac* • Dennis Hopper *Joe* ■ *Dir* Stuart Heisler • *Scr* WR Burnett, from his novel *High Sierra*

I Dismember Mama ★ 18

Horror 1972 · US · Colour · 76mins

Filmed as *Poor Albert and Little Annie*, this low-grade slasher movie gained notoriety under its amusing but deceptive new title. Mother-hating Albert, played by the maniacal-looking Zooey Hall, escapes from an asylum, murders "impure" women, and abducts a nine-year-old girl called Annie. The poor direction here renders some scenes as totally incomprehensible. One of those films that turns out to be just a title and nothing else. DM

Zooey Hall *Albert* • Geri Reischl *Annie* • Joanne Moore Jordan *Mrs Robertson* • Greg Mullavey *Detective* • Marlene Tracy *Alice* ■ *Dir* Paul Leder • *Scr* William Norton

I Don't Buy Kisses Anymore ★★ PG

Romantic comedy
1992 · US · Colour · 107mins

Long-suffering *Seinfield* star Jason Alexander gets a rare leading role in this slender but warmly performed romantic comedy. He plays a shy bachelor who strikes up a friendship with smart student Nia Peeples, who unbeknown to him, sees him as perfect case study for her course. However, things get complicated when Alexander begins falling in love with her. While no laugh fest, it will leave you smiling. JF

Jason Alexander *Bernie Fishbine* • Nia Peeples *Theresa Garabaldi* • Lainie Kazan *Sarah Fishbine* • Lou Jacobi *Irving Fein/Gramps* • Eileen Brennan *Frieda* ■ *Dir* Robert Marcarelli • *Scr* Jonnie Lindsell

The I Don't Care Girl ★★★ U

Biographical musical drama
1952 · US · Colour · 77mins

An under-written but entertaining biopic of Broadway club sensation Eva Tanguay, portrayed zappily by talented 20th Century-Fox contract star Mitzi Gaynor. Best remembered today as Nellie Forbush in the movie of *South Pacific*, and still happily performing live across the USA, Mitzi's not bad at all, and she's certainly helped by some rich Technicolor and smart co-stars David Wayne and Oscar Levant. TS

Mitzi Gaynor *Eva Tanguay* • David Wayne *Ed McCoy* • Oscar Levant *Bennett* • Bob Graham *Larry* • Craig Hill *Keene* ■ *Dir* Lloyd Bacon • *Scr* Walter Bullock

I Don't Want to Be Born ★★ 18

Horror 1975 · UK · Colour · 89mins

Joan Collins is cursed by a dwarf and gives birth to a killer baby in this hilariously cheap British answer to *Rosemary's Baby*, which also goes under a number of intriguing titles, including *The Devil within Her*. Donald Pleasence delivers the tiny terror who begins childhood by drowning his nanny and then moves on to dunking dead mice in teacups. This bargain-basement Hammer is irresistible trash from sinister start to foolish finish. AJ

Joan Collins *Lucy Carlesi* • Eileen Atkins *Sister Albana* • Donald Pleasence *Dr Finch* • Ralph Bates *Gino Carlesi* • Caroline Munro *Mandy* • Hilary Mason *Mrs Hyde* ■ *Dir* Peter Sasdy • *Scr* Stanley Price, from a story by Nato De Angeles

I Dood It ★★★ U

Musical comedy 1943 · US · BW · 102mins

Astonishing to find that Vincente Minnelli (*Meet Me in St Louis*, *An American in Paris*) directed this awkwardly contrived semi-musical from MGM, with Red Skelton as the tailor's assistant wooing actress Eleanor Powell from afar, by wearing his clients' clothes and looking a desirable fashion-plate. The title comes from Skelton's radio catch-phrase and there are some bright spots among the grey. Basically, it's a retread of Buster Keaton's *Spite Marriage*. TH

Red Skelton *Joseph Rivington Renolds* • Eleanor Powell *Constance Shaw* • Richard Ainley *Larry West* • Patricia Dane *Surelia Brenton* • Sam Levene *Ed Jackson* • Thurston Hall *Kenneth Lawlor* ■ *Dir* Vincente Minnelli • *Scr* Sig Herzig, Fred Saidy

I Dream of Jeanie ★★ U

Biographical musical drama
1952 · US · Colour · 90mins

Republic picked on the work of the popular 19th-century songwriter Stephen Foster for this low-budget musical biopic, because it was in the public domain and wouldn't cost anything. Foster's life was so depressing that writer Alan LeMay concocted a lighter version in which the impractical dreamer is rescued from his financial problems by a wiser brother. Filmed in the studio's erratic Trucolor process, it is packed with Foster's works, with Eileen Christy pleasant as Foster's true love. AE

Ray Middleton *Edwin P Christy* • Bill Shirley *Stephen Foster* • Muriel Lawrence *Inez McDowell* • Eileen Christy *Jeanie McDowell* • Lynn Bari *Mrs McDowell* • Richard Simmons [Dick Simmons] *Dunning Foster* ■ *Dir* Allan Dwan • *Scr* Alan LeMay

I Dream Too Much ★★

Musical comedy 1935 · US · BW · 97mins

This RKO musical comedy was only Henry Fonda's third film, and he's badly miscast. He simply doesn't convince us he's the composer of Jerome Kern songs such as *I'm the Echo*, *The Jockey on the Carousel* and the title number. Hank's co-star is the French opera star Lily Pons, who made only two more films yet had a town in Maryland named after her. AT

Henry Fonda *Jonathan Street* • Lily Pons *Annette Street* • Eric Blore *Roger Briggs* • Osgood Perkins *Paul Darcy* • Lucien Littlefield *Mr Dilley* • Lucille Ball *Gwendolyn Dilley* • Mischa Auer *Pianist* ■ *Dir* John Cromwell • *Scr* James Gow, Edmund North, from a story by Elsie Finn, David G Wittels

I Dreamed of Africa ★★ 12

Biographical drama
2000 · US · Colour · 109mins

Although Kim Basinger valiantly holds her own as conservationist Kuki Gallmann, Hugh Hudson's direction sadly fails to support her efforts, never hammering home any political aspect beyond the stunning South African scenery. Basinger and husband Vincent Perez move from Italy to Kenya in the early 1970s, but end up arguing about the amount of time he spends away from home on hunting expeditions. LH DVD

Kim Basinger *Kuki Gallmann* • Vincent Perez *Paolo Gallmann* • Eva Marie Saint *Franca* • Daniel Craig *Declan Fielding* • Lance Reddick *Simon* • Connie Chiume *Wanjiku* ■ *Dir* Hugh Hudson • *Scr* Paula Milne, Susan Shilliday, from the memoirs by Kuki Gallmann

I Escaped from Devil's Island ★★

Prison drama 1973 · US · Colour · 86mins

Following hard on the heels of *Papillon* came this less self-important yarn in which Jim Brown leads a bunch of decidedly over-nourished men across the ocean and into the jungle. They leave behind the creature comforts of the French penal colony, journey on a raft made from animal skins, and encounter lepers, bare-breasted native girls and their own animal instincts. Made by Roger Corman's studio, it smacks its lips over the violence that exists in prison and outside. AT

Jim Brown *Le Bras* • Christopher George *Davert* • Rick Ely *Jo-Jo* • Richard Rust *Zamorra* ■ *Dir* William Witney • *Scr* Richard L Adams

I Even Met Happy Gypsies ★★★★

Drama 1967 · Yug · Colour · 90mins

Following his revisionist, Oscar-nominated war picture, *Three*, Aleksandar Petrovic received another best foreign film nomination for this docudramatic insight into the lifestyle of the gypsies of the Vojvodnia region, which also won the Special Jury Prize at Cannes. With a cast including non-professional performers speaking their own language (Serbo-Croat, Slovak and Romany), Petrovic illuminates the story of the feather trader who saves a girl from her abusive stepfather with a wealth of authentic detail. DP. With subtitles.

Bekim Fehmiu *Bora* • Olivera Vuco *Lence* • Bata Zivojinovic *Mirta* • Gordana Jovanovic *Tisa* • Mija Aleksic *Father Pavle* • Rahela Ferari *Nun* • Severin Bijelic *Religious peasant* • Etelka Filipovski *Bora's wife* • Milorad Jovanovic *Toni* ■ *Dir/Scr* Aleksandar Petrovic

I Found Stella Parish ★★

Melodrama 1935 · US · BW · 84mins

An unashamed assault on the tear ducts, this hoary melodrama rather went against the Warner Bros grain, substituting the customary hard-edged realism for a little soft-soap and glamour. Bedecked in gowns by the legendary costume designer Orry-Kelly and playing against cavernous sets, Kay Francis emotes for all she's worth as the stage diva prepared to sacrifice almost everything to prevent her daughter from learning of her misdeeds on the way to the top. Directing with earnestness, Mervyn LeRoy flatters Francis in every shot. DP

Kay Francis *Stella Parish* • Ian Hunter *Keith Lockridge* • Paul Lukas *Stephen Norman* • Sybil Jason *Gloria Parish* • Jessie Ralph *Nana* • Joseph Sawyer [Joe Sawyer] *Chuck* ■ *Dir* Mervyn LeRoy • *Scr* Casey Robinson, from the story by John Monk Saunders

I Got the Hook Up ★ 18

Comedy 1998 · US · Colour · 89mins

This dismal comedy is rapper Master P's second feature. He teams with AJ Johnson as a couple of hustlers whose discovery of a consignment of cell phones leads them into an anarchic series of misadventures. But, despite scrapes with dissatisfied customers and the FBI, there's little to laugh at here. Michael Martin's direction is clumsy, and there are crass attitudes to women and the disabled. Embarrassingly bad. DP

U = SUITABLE FOR ALL Uc = SUITABLE FOR ALL, ESPECIALLY FOR YOUNG CHILDREN (VIDEO ONLY) PG = PARENTAL GUIDANCE

Master P *Black* • AJ Johnson [Anthony Johnson] *Blue* • Gretchen Palmer *Sweet Lorraine* • Frantz Turner *Dalton* • Tommy "Tiny" Lister Jr [Tom "Tiny" Lister Jr] *T-Lay* • Anthony Boswell *Little Brother* • Ice Cube *Gun runner* • Snoop Doggy Dogg [Snoop Dogg] *Bar patron* ■ *Dir* Michael Martin • *Scr* Master P, from a story by Master P, Leroy Douglas, Carrie Mingo

I Heard the Owl Call My Name ★★★★ U

Drama 1973 · US · Colour · 74mins

Adapted without condescension or overt sentimentality by director Daryl Duke, this superior TV movie makes powerful use of the British Columbian coastscape to emphasise the grinding poverty of the native Indians who dwell there and the enormity of the task facing Tom Courtenay, as the inexperienced Anglican priest sent to minister to them. With humble support from Dean Jagger, as the bishop who sustains the novice's faith as isolation saps his morale, Courtenay achieves a sincerity and compassion that stands in stark contrast to his more cynical kitchen-sink persona. DP [video]

Tom Courtenay *Father Tark Brian* • Dean Jagger *Bishop* • Paul Stanley *Jim Wallace* • Marianne Jones *Keetah* • George Clutesi *George P Hudson* • Keith Pepper *Alan Spencer* ■ *Dir* Daryl Duke • *Scr* Gerald Di Pego, from the novel by Margaret Craven

I ♥ Huckabees ★★★★ 15

Black comedy drama
2004 · US/UK/Ger · Colour · 102mins

Director David O Russell's bravely weird film is a melange of cod-existential philosophy, Gen-X angst, corporate intrigue and slapstick comedy. Jason Schwartzman is an environmental activist whose "Open Spaces Coalition" is sponsored by the Huckabees superstore chain, represented by executive Jude Law. Troubled by a series of coincidences, Schwartzman employs existential detectives (played by the brilliantly wacky Dustin Hoffman and Lili Tomlin) to investigate his life, and through them meets firefighter Mark Wahlberg. Simultaneously odd, ambitious, pretentious and optimistic, this will irritate some viewers hugely while delighting others. AS. Contains swearing. [video] DVD

Jason Schwartzman *Albert Markovski* • Isabelle Huppert *Caterine Vauban* • Dustin Hoffman *Bernard Jaffe* • Lily Tomlin *Vivian Jaffe* • Jude Law *Brad Stand* • Mark Wahlberg *Tommy Corn* • Naomi Watts *Dawn Campbell* • Angela Grillo *Angela Franco* ■ *Dir* David O Russell • *Scr* David O Russell, Jeff Baena

I Hired a Contract Killer ★★★ 15

Comedy thriller
1990 · Fin/Swe · Colour · 74mins

Aki Kaurismäki made his English language debut with this doggedly downbeat slice of black comedy. Importing his inimitable sense of perspective and timing to London, the man many see as Finland's finest director transforms the city into a hostile urban wilderness. It's here that discarded civil servant Jean-Pierre Léaud seeks refuge from the hitman he no longer requires, having fallen for flowerseller Margi Clarke. Kaurismäki keeps the performances edgy with short scenes and minimalist dialogue, opting for a melancholic rather than a suspenseful air. DP [video]

Margi Clarke *Margaret* • Jean-Pierre Léaud *Henri Boulanger* • Kenneth Colley *Killer* • Trevor Bowen *Department head* • Imogen Claire *Secretary* • Nicky Tesco *Pete* • Charles Cork *Al* ■ *Dir/Scr* Aki Kaurismäki

The I Inside ★★ 15

Mystery thriller
2003 · UK/US · Colour · 87mins

Fragments of memory become pieces of a mind-bending jigsaw puzzle in this twisting thriller. Hospitalised heir Ryan Phillippe wakes up with amnesia following a near-death experience and finds he is inexplicably able to travel in time and uses his new gift to reconstruct his terrifying lost years. This is sleekly executed and visually handsome, with some engaging performances, but it's not as clever as it believes and the too-convenient conclusion is disappointing. SF. Contains swearing, violence. [video] DVD

Ryan Phillippe *Simon Cable* • Sarah Polley *Clair* • Piper Perabo *Anna* • Stephen Rea *Dr Newman* • Stephen Lang *Mr Travitt* • Robert Sean Leonard *Peter Cable* ■ *Dir* Roland Suso Richter • *Scr* Michael Cooney, Scott Bogart Timothy, from the play *Point of Death* by Michael Cooney

I Know What You Did Last Summer ★★★ 15

Horror thriller 1997 · US · Colour · 96mins

Director Jim Gillespie's stalk-and-slash saga gives *Scream* writer Kevin Williamson the chance to revive his favourite psycho-killer clichés. Four high-school graduates cover up a hit-and-run accident, only to have the dark tragedy rear its head a year later when a hook-wielding masked fisherman starts bumping them off. The beautiful photography makes this watchable, but Gillespie's chiller trades on outdated thrills all the way through to its creak-and-shriek showdown. A sequel, *I Still Know What You Did Last Summer*, followed in 1998. AJ [video] DVD

Jennifer Love Hewitt *Julie James* • Sarah Michelle Gellar *Helen Shivers* • Ryan Phillippe *Barry Cox* • Freddie Prinze Jr *Ray Bronson* • Muse Watson *Benjamin Willis* • Bridgette Wilson *Elsa Shivers* • Anne Heche *Melissa Egan* ■ *Dir* Jim Gillespie • *Scr* Kevin Williamson, from the novel by Lois Duncan

I Know Where I'm Going! ★★★★★ U

Romantic comedy 1945 · UK · BW · 89mins

Of all the classics produced by Michael Powell and Emeric Pressburger, this may be the most unsung but it's undoubtedly the most entrancing. As the headstrong young woman and the laird who distracts her from her stuffy fiancé, Wendy Hiller and Roger Livesey are superb, and there's knowing support from Pamela Brown, John Laurie and Finlay Currie. Erwin Hillier's photography is as beautiful as it is atmospheric, but it's the expert mix of romance and comedy, arresting use of the landscape and respectful fascination with the local culture that make this so compelling. DP [video] DVD

Wendy Hiller *Joan Webster* • Roger Livesey *Torquil* • Pamela Brown *Catriona Potts* • Nancy Price *Mrs Crozier* • John Laurie *John Campbell* • George Carney *Mr Webster* • Walter Hudd *Hunter* • Captain Duncan MacKechnie *Captain "Lochinvar"* • Petula Clark *Cheril* ■ *Dir/Scr* Michael Powell, Emeric Pressburger

I Like It like That ★★★ 15

Romantic comedy
1994 · US · Colour · 102mins

Written and directed by Spike Lee alumnus Darnell Martin, this is a rare look at the lives of the Latino population jostling for space in the Bronx. At the centre of this engaging film is Lauren Velez, who gets the chance to prove she's more than just a homebird when her husband is jailed and she lands a job with a record label. The racial mix is just a tad too cosy and the message that men are all the same no matter what their colour is stated too blandly. But Martin knows her patch and coaxes a lovely performance from the sassy Velez. DP. Contains violence, swearing, sex scenes, drug abuse and nudity. [video]

Lauren Velez *Lisette Linares* • Jon Seda *Chino Linares* • Tomas Melly *Li'l Chino Linares* • Desiree Casado *Minnie Linares* • Isaiah Garcia *Pee Wee Linares* • Jesse Borrego *Alexis* • Griffin Dunne *Stephen Price* ■ *Dir/Scr* Darnell Martin

I Live in Fear ★★★ PG

Drama 1955 · Jpn · BW · 98mins

Shot at the height of the Cold War and a mere decade after the atomic assault on Japan, Akira Kurosawa's drama about life under the shadow of the bomb was originally conceived as a satire and an uncertainty of tone fatally undermines its purpose. By having Toshiro Mifune descend into dementia, his desire to escape the holocaust by relocating his sneering family to a Brazilian hideaway can too easily be dismissed as senile paranoia instead of prescient warning. DP. In Japanese with English subtitles. [video] DVD

Toshiro Mifune *Kiichi Nakajima* • Eiko Miyoshi *Toyo Nakajima* • Haruko Togo *Yoshi* • Takashi Shimura *Harada* ■ *Dir* Akira Kurosawa • *Scr* Akira Kurosawa, Shinobu Hashimoto, Hideo Oguni • *Music* Fumio Hayasaka

I Live in Grosvenor Square ★ U

Romance 1945 · UK · BW · 114mins

This expensive, ridiculous and tedious romantic drama has Anna Neagle, a duke's granddaughter, switching her affections from Rex Harrison's army major to Dean Jagger's American sergeant. It's unbelievable that dull Jagger could oust charismatic Rex, or that Rex would be such a generous loser – but it's typical of the way the entire production panders to the American market, where it played as *A Yank in London*. AE

Anna Neagle *Lady Patricia Fairfax* • Rex Harrison *Maj David Bruce* • Dean Jagger *Sgt John Patterson* • Robert Morley *Duke of Exmoor* • Jane Darwell *Mrs Patterson* • Nancy Price *Mrs Wilson* ■ *Dir* Herbert Wilcox • *Scr* Nicholas Phipps, William D Bayles, from a story by Maurice Cowan

I Live My Life ★★

Romantic comedy 1935 · US · BW · 85mins

Animosity turns to amorousness (as you knew it would) when a rich, bored society girl and a humble archaeologist who disdains her friends and her lifestyle fall in love. Joan Crawford and Brian Aherne star in this desperately routine film, directed with a surprising lack of brio by WS Van Dyke. Designer clothes and sophisticated cocktail parties lend a fleeting and superficial gloss to the tepid screenplay. AJ

Joan Crawford *Kay* • Brian Aherne *Terry* • Frank Morgan *Bentley* • Aline MacMahon *Betty* • Eric Blore *Grove* ■ *Dir* WS Van Dyke • *Scr* Joseph L Mankiewicz, Gottfried Reinhardt, Ethel Borden, from the short story *Claustrophobia* by Abbie Carter Goodloe • *Music* Dimitri Tiomkin [Dmitri Tiomkin]

I Lived with You ★★

Romantic comedy 1933 · UK · BW · 100mins

Ivor Novello was once the pin-up boy of British stage and screen, but he was also a gifted tunesmith and playwright. Indeed, he penned the West End hit on which this old-fashioned romantic melodrama was based. Novello also stars, as the exiled Russian aristocrat who sews dissent in cockney Eliot Makeham's dour working-class household, and radiates an insouciant charm, especially in his dealings with the family's daughter, Ursula Jeans. It's all directed with a teasingly respectable salaciousness, but of much greater interest to most film fans will be the pre-fame performances of Jack Hawkins and Ida Lupino. RT

Ivor Novello *Prince Felix Lenieff* • Ursula Jeans *Gladys Wallis* • Ida Lupino *Ada Wallis* • Minnie Rayner *Mrs Wallis* • Eliot Makeham *Mr Wallis* • Jack Hawkins *Mort* ■ *Dir* Maurice Elvey • *Scr* H Fowler Mear, from the play *I Lived with You* by Ivor Novello

I Love a Man in Uniform ★★★ 18

Psychological thriller
1993 · Can · Colour · 94mins

Canadian director David Wellington's first feature divided audiences on its initial release, who couldn't decide whether it was merely provocative or just plain disturbing. Whatever your opinion, there is no denying that star Tom McCamus is mesmerising as the struggling actor who lands the role of a tough-talking cop on a TV show, only to find that reality and make-believe blur when he starts patrolling the streets in his uniform, passing himself off as a real policeman. JB. Contains violence and swearing. [video]

Tom McCamus *Henry Adler* • Brigitte Bako *Charlie Warner* • Kevin Tighe *Frank* • David Hemblen *Father* • Alex Karzis *Bruce* • Graham McPherson *Mr Pearson* • Daniel MacIvor *Director* • Wendy Hopkins *Casting director* ■ *Dir/Scr* David Wellington

I Love a Soldier ★★

Second World War romantic drama
1944 · US · BW · 106mins

Director Mark Sandrich must have longed for the good old days while handling this mediocre weepie for, while Paulette Goddard and Sonny Tufts may have looked good together, they were definitely no Fred and Ginger (whom he directed five times at RKO). The leads occasionally spark into life, as Tufts's dashing GI melts the hardened heart of Goddard's war-effort welder. DP

Paulette Goddard *Eva Morgan* • Sonny Tufts *Dan Gilgore* • Mary Treen *Cissy Grant* • Walter Sande *Stiff Banks* • Ann Doran *Jenny* • Beulah Bondi *Etta Lane* ■ *Dir* Mark Sandrich • *Scr* Allan Scott

I Love Melvin ★★★ U

Musical 1953 · US · Colour · 77mins

An undervalued little musical, with Donald O'Connor and Debbie Reynolds reunited after the success of the previous year's *Singin' in the Rain* and at the top of their form again here. O'Connor plays a photographer's assistant who cons Reynolds by telling her she's in line to be a cover girl. There are some charming duos – O'Connor's skating slides are a sight to behold – and plenty of zip. TH

Donald O'Connor *Melvin Hoover* • Debbie Reynolds *Judy LeRoy* • Una Merkel *Mom Schneider* • Richard Anderson *Harry Flack* • Allyn Joslyn *Pop Schneider* • Les Tremayne *Mr Hennenman* • Noreen Corcoran *Clarabelle* ■ *Dir* Don Weis • *Scr* George Wells, Ruth Brooks Flippen, from a story by Laslo Vadnay

I Love My... Wife ★★

Comedy 1970 · US · Colour · 95mins

A credit sequence charting Elliott Gould's progress from sexual novice to hopeful bridegroom gets this adult comedy off to a lively start. However, no sooner has disillusion set in than the inspiration dries up, and what might have been an amusing insight into the sexual insecurities of the post-sixties male becomes an assault on women in general. Writer Robert Kaufman's one-liners are as smugly predictable as his coarsely satirical observations. DP

Elliott Gould *Dr Richard Burrows* • Brenda Vaccaro *Jody Borrows* • Angel Tompkins

Helene Donnelly • Dabney Coleman *Frank Donnelly* • Joan Tompkins *Grandma Dennison* ■ *Dir* Mel Stuart • *Scr* Robert Kaufman

I Love Trouble ★★★ PG

Romantic comedy thriller
1994 · US · Colour · 117mins

If you can get your head round the idea of Julia Roberts as a ruthlessly ambitious newspaper reporter, then there's plenty to enjoy in this frivolous thriller. However, it's too long and too deliberate to fulfil its ambition of re-creating the "rat-a-tat" screwball style that made the 1930s battle-of-the-sexes comedies such a delight. Nick Nolte is closer to the mark as the cynical hack tinkering with old columns to lighten the load, but neither the rivalry nor the romance between the stars is convincing. DP DVD

Nick Nolte *Peter Brackett* • Julia Roberts *Sabrina Peterson* • Saul Rubinek *Sam Smotherman* • James Rebhorn *The Thin Man* • Robert Loggia *Matt Greenfield* • Kelly Rutherford *Kim* • Olympia Dukakis *Jeannie* • Marsha Mason *Senator Gayle Robbins* ■ *Dir* Charles Shyer • *Scr* Nancy Meyers, Charles Shyer

I Love You Again ★★★★

Screwball comedy 1940 · US · BW · 98mins

An absolutely hysterical MGM screwball comedy with super-sophisticates William Powell and Myrna Loy taking a break from their *Thin Man* series in an ingeniously written farce, in which amnesiac Powell spends the whole movie trying to persuade his wife, Loy, not to divorce him in order to marry her 1940s version of a toyboy. It's Powell's film, as he essays pratfalls and double takes with great *élan* in this superb comedic tour de force. TS

William Powell *Larry Wilson/George Carey* • Myrna Loy *Kay Wilson* • Frank McHugh *Doc Ryan* • Edmund Lowe *Duke Sheldon* • Donald Douglas [Don Douglas] *Herbert* • Nella Walker *Kay's mother* ■ *Dir* WS Van Dyke II [WS Van Dyke] • *Scr* Charles Lederer, George Oppenheimer, Harry Kurnitz, from a story by Leon Gordon, Maurine Watkins, from a novel by Octavus Roy Cohen

I Love You, Alice B Toklas ★★

Satirical comedy 1968 · US · Colour · 93mins

Even when Peter Sellers could seemingly do no wrong, director Hy Averback's satirical comedy was a dubious proposition. Despite promising early scenes in which asthmatic lawyer Sellers is at odds with his pushy girlfriend (the brilliant Joyce Van Patten), it all falls apart when Sellers eats marijuana-spiked cookies and becomes a hippy dropout. Very much of its time, this provided a Hollywood breakthrough for screenwriters Paul Mazursky and Larry Tucker. TH. Contains brief nudity.

Peter Sellers *Harold* • Jo Van Fleet *Mother* • Leigh Taylor-Young *Nancy* • Joyce Van Patten *Joyce* • David Arkin *Herbie* • Herb Edelman *Murray* • Louis Gottlieb *Guru* ■ *Dir* Hy Averback • *Scr* Paul Mazursky, Larry Tucker

I Love You, I Love You Not ★★ 15

Drama 1997 · US/UK · Colour · 88mins

Claire Danes stars as a withdrawn teenager, falling for the school jock Jude Law at her New York school. It all goes horribly wrong when her classmates discover her grandmother, Jean Moreau, is a Holocaust survivor and their anti-Semitism kicks in. Grandmother and granddaughter share their respective suffering – Danes playing Moreau in the flashback sequences in Germany. While the message is important, it's been better explored in better films. LH

Jeanne Moreau *Nana* • Claire Danes *Daisy* • Jude Law *Ethan* • Carrie Slaza *Jane* • Jerry Tanklow *Mr Gilman* • James Van Der Beek *Tony* ■ *Dir* Billy Hopkins • *Scr* Wendy Kesselman, from a play by Wendy Kesselman

I Love You to Death ★★ 15

Black comedy based on a true story
1990 · US · Colour · 93mins

One of those unfortunate efforts which looks a wow on paper – great plot, great director, grade-A comic cast – but which sinks like a celluloid *Titanic* under the weight of more ham than a butcher's shop. Based on a gift of a true story (woman tries desperately to kill unfaithful hubby, but he seems clottishly indestructible), yet everyone appears inexplicably hellbent on pressing the destruct button. A dreadful waste of all concerned. SH. Contains violence DVD

Kevin Kline *Joey Boca* • Tracey Ullman *Rosalie Boca* • Joan Plowright *Nadja* • River Phoenix *Devo* • William Hurt *Harlan James* • Keanu Reeves *Marlon James* • Miriam Margolyes *Joey's mother* ■ *Dir* Lawrence Kasdan • *Scr* John Kostmayer

I Married a Dead Man ★★★

Drama 1983 · Fr · Colour · 110mins

This drama of mistaken identity was previously filmed as *No Man of Her Own* in 1950 and, more recently, as *Mrs Winterbourne* in 1996. Nathalie Baye plays a pregnant woman who, after surviving a train crash, finds herself mistaken for one of its many victims. It is in the interests of her and the unborn child not to reveal the truth, but she soon finds herself in over her head. Baye is superb and the scenes with her and her newborn child bring tears to the eyes. LH. French dialogue dubbed into English.

Nathalie Baye *Helene/Patricia* • Francis Huster *Pierre* • Richard Bohringer *Frank* • Madeleine Robinson *Lena* • Guy Tréjan *Monsieur Meyrand* • Victoria Abril *Fifo* ■ *Dir* Robin Davis • *Scr* Robin Davis, Patrick Laurent, from the novel *I Married a Dead Man* by William Irish [Cornell Woolrich]

I Married a Monster from Outer Space ★★★

Science-fiction horror
1958 · US · BW · 77mins

Soon-to-be-wed Tom Tryon has his body taken over by a rhubarb-faced alien in Gene Fowler Jr's smartly directed paranoia classic: substitute Gloria Talbott's UFO-duplicated husband for a red in her bed and the true anti-Communist undercurrent becomes apparent. Fowler worked as an editor for Fritz Lang, and the German expressionist influence is evident in the use of shadows and weird angles to heighten the atmospheric tension. Intelligent and well packaged. AJ

Tom Tryon *Bill Farrell* • Gloria Talbott *Marge Farrell* • Peter Baldwin *Swanson* • Robert Ivers *Harry* • Chuck Wassil *Ted* • Valerie Allen *B Girl* • Ty Hungerford *Mac* • Ken Lynch *Dr Wayne* ■ *Dir* Gene Fowler Jr • *Scr* Louis Vittes

I Married a Strange Person ★★★

Animated comedy
1997 · US · Colour · 76mins

Acclaimed for the crayon-drawn *Your Face* and *One of Those Days*, Bill Plympton is revered by his fellow animators. It's easy to see why from this feature, which can be summed up in a single word – strange! Newlyweds Grant and Kerry Boyer seem blissfully happy until a pair of ducks fly into their satellite dish, transforming the TV into a malevolent machine that gives Grant the power to turn his fantasies into reality. Combining moments of mock horror (such as when a neighbour is attacked by his lawn) and surreal humour, this makes for perfect late-night escapism. DP

Charis Michaelson • Tom Larson • Richard Spore • Chris Cooke ■ *Dir* Bill Plympton • *Scr* Bill Plympton, PC Vey

I Married a Witch ★★★★

Romantic fantasy comedy
1942 · US · BW · 76mins

This was one of the films French director René Clair made in Hollywood during his wartime exile. It's a comedy about a witch who is reincarnated in order to persecute the descendant of the judge who condemned her to be burned at the stake 300 years earlier. The fact that the descendant, played by Fredric March, is running for political office is curiously prescient of the McCarthy witch-hunts that occurred some five years later. Veronica Lake was usually typecast as a sultry *femme fatale*, but as the witch she shows a real flair for whimsy. AT

Fredric March *Wallace Wooley/Jonathan Wooley/Nathaniel Wooley/Samuel Wooley* • Veronica Lake *Jennifer* • Robert Benchley *Dr Dudley White* • Susan Hayward *Estelle Masterson* • Cecil Kellaway *Daniel* • Elizabeth Patterson *Margaret* • Robert Warwick *JB Masterson* ■ *Dir* Rene Clair [René Clair] • *Scr* Robert Pirosh, Marc Connelly, Dalton Trumbo (uncredited), from the novel *The Passionate Witch* by Thorne Smith, as completed by Norman Matson

I Married a Woman ★★ U

Comedy 1958 · US · BW and Colour · 83mins

After a decade as the blonde bombshell of British cinema, Diana Dors graces this Hollywood comedy with her considerable assets – with mixed results. She does well enough as a pouting lovely who tries to put the pep back into her marriage, but co-star George Gobel, a top TV comedian, is an eminently resistible personality whose bungling wimp routine adds considerably to the burden of watching this desperately unfunny charade. DP

Diana Dors *Janice* • George Gobel *Marshall Briggs* • Adolphe Menjou *Sutton* • Jessie Royce Landis *Mother* • Nita Talbot *Miss Anderson* • William Redfield *Eddie* • Steve Dunne *Bob* • John McGiver *Girard* • John Wayne • Angie Dickinson *Screen wife* ■ *Dir* Hal Kanter • *Scr* Goodman Ace

I Married an Angel ★ U

Fantasy musical romance
1942 · US · BW · 83mins

This disastrous end to the Jeanette MacDonald/Nelson Eddy partnership is for die-hard devotees only. Mangling a hit Broadway musical by Richard Rodgers and Lorenz Hart, MGM miscast Eddy as a Budapest playboy while MacDonald fares little better, being restrained for most of the picture as an angel dreamed up by Eddy. A lighter, more satirical thrust might have improved matters, but director WS Van Dyke doesn't find much humour in Anita Loos's script. AE

Jeanette MacDonald *Anna Zador/Brigitta* • Nelson Eddy *Count Willie Palaffi* • Binnie Barnes *Peggy* • Edward Everett Horton *Peter* • Reginald Owen *Herman "Whiskers" Rothbart* ■ *Dir* WS Van Dyke • *Scr* Anita Loos, from the musical by Richard Rodgers, Lorenz Hart, from the play by Vaszary Janos

I Met Him in Paris ★★★

Romantic comedy 1937 · US · BW · 86mins

A formula vehicle for Claudette Colbert, this comedy finds her taking a well-earned vacation from a boring fiancée in a familiar Paramount-designed Paris. There she's courted by two more men, and ends up on the Swiss ski slopes with both. Will she choose morose and cynical playwright Melvyn Douglas or charming smoothie playboy Robert Young? En route to the answer, Claude Binyon's screenplay crackles with barbed wit, delivered in best high-comedy style by the trio. RK

Claudette Colbert *Kay Denham* • Melvyn Douglas *George Potter* • Robert Young (1) *Gene Anders* • Lee Bowman *Berk Sutter* • Mona Barrie *Helen Anders* • George Davis *Cutter driver* ■ *Dir* Wesley Ruggles • *Scr* Claude Binyon, from the story by Helen Meinardi

I Met My Love Again ★★★

Romantic drama 1938 · US · BW · 77mins

The romance of a youthful small-town couple is shattered when she is swept off her feet and elopes with a writer. Widowed ten years later, she returns home with her daughter and, to the disapproval of the over-protective townsfolk, tries to take up with her former love, now a college professor. This is basically soap opera elevated by a first-rate cast, with Henry Fonda and Joan Bennett as the lovers trying to resurrect their relationship. RK

Joan Bennett *Julie Wier Shaw* • Henry Fonda *Ives Towner* • Louise Platt *Brenda Lane* • Alan Marshal *Michael Shaw* • Dame May Whitty *Aunt William* • Alan Baxter *Tony* ■ *Dir* Arthur Ripley, Joshua Logan • *Scr* David Hertz, from the novel *Summer Lightning* by Allene Corliss • *Cinematographer* Hal Mohr

I, Monster ★★ 12

Horror 1971 · UK · Colour · 77mins

Dr Jekyll and Mr Hyde become Dr Marlowe and Mr Blake in a vapid attempt to give a Freudian psychological interpretation to the oft-told tale. Christopher Lee is convincing as the doctor meddling with a dangerous formula, and the Victorian London atmosphere is well captured, but director Stephen Weeks's inexperience means that any complex themes are quickly abandoned, and the end result is flatter than you might expect. AJ DVD

Christopher Lee *Dr Marlowe/Mr Blake* • Peter Cushing *Utterson* • Mike Raven *Enfield* • Richard Hurndall *Lanyan* • George Merritt *Poole* • Kenneth J Warren *Dean* • Susan Jameson *Diane* ■ *Dir* Stephen Weeks • *Scr* Milton Subotsky

I Never Promised You a Rose Garden ★★★★ 18

Drama 1977 · US · Colour · 88mins

Anthony Page's adaptation of Joanne Greenberg's semi-autobiographical bestseller never explores mental illness in any real depth, but is still a highly sympathetic study of someone facing up to its consequences. This Roger Corman production is steered away from any melodramatic pitfalls by Kathleen Quinlan's exemplary performance, as a teenage schizophrenic plagued by sexually charged fantasies and recurrent thoughts of suicide. Bibi Andersson is equally impressive as her intuitive psychiatrist. DP

Bibi Andersson *Dr Fried* • Kathleen Quinlan *Deborah Blake* • Ben Piazza *Mr Blake* • Lorraine Gary *Mrs Blake* • Darlene Craviotto *Carla* • Reni Santoni *Hobbs* • Susan Tyrrell *Lee* ■ *Dir* Anthony Page • *Scr* Lewis John Carlino, Gavin Lambert, from a novel by Hannah Green [Joanne Greenberg]

I Never Sang for My Father ★★★★

Drama 1969 · US · Colour · 92mins

This immensely moving screen version of Robert Anderson's sensitive play was scripted by the playwright himself, giving a superb career-best role to Melvyn Douglas as the ageing, domineering father. Gene Hackman, as the suffering adult son, and Estelle Parsons, as the daughter made an outcast because she married a Jew, are also outstanding. Gilbert Cates's direction manages to make this both depressing and uplifting at the same time, and, though resolutely theatrical, it remains compulsively watchable. TS

Melvyn Douglas *Tom Garrison* • Gene Hackman *Gene Garrison* • Dorothy Stickney *Margaret Garrison* • Estelle Parsons *Alice* • Elizabeth Hubbard *Peggy* • Lovelady Powell *Norma* ■ *Dir* Gilbert Cates • *Scr* Robert W Anderson, from his play

I Only Want You to Love Me ★★★

Drama based on a true story
1976 · W Ger · Colour · 104mins

Made for television during a creative crisis on *Satan's Brew*, this is one of Rainer Werner Fassbinder's most accessible films. This intellectually rigorous and expertly staged melodrama explores the modern tendency towards the breakdown of familial communication, and also the way in which material gestures have come to replace demonstrations of affection. Workaholic builder Vitus Zeplichal cuts a genuinely tragic figure as his emotional inarticulacy reduces him from doting son to crazed killer. DP. In German with English subtitles.

Vitus Zeplichal *Peter* • Elke Aberle *Erika* • Alexander Allerson *Father* • Erni Mangold *Mother* • Johanna Hofer *Erika's grandmother* • Wolfgang Hess *Building superintendent* ■ *Dir/Scr* Rainer Werner Fassbinder

I Ought to Be in Pictures ★★★★ 15

Comedy 1982 · US · Colour · 102mins

Neil Simon has adapted this all-laughing, all-crying drama from his own stage play. It comes complete with a performance by Dinah Manoff which avoids direct sentimentality – but which still involves us emotionally – as the Hollywood-struck girl. She travels to Tinseltown to track down her father (Walter Matthau) who's now living with a forgiving girlfriend (Ann-Margret). He used to be a screenwriter but these days seems interested mainly in drinking and gambling. Herbert Ross directs with level-headed cool, letting Simon's script do all the work. TH [video]

Walter Matthau *Herbert Tucker* • Ann-Margret *Stephanie* • Dinah Manoff *Libby* • Lance Guest *Gordon* • Lewis Smith *Soldier* • Martin Ferrero *Monte Del Rey* ■ *Dir* Herbert Ross • *Scr* Neil Simon, from his play

IP5 ★ 15

Drama 1992 · Fr · Colour · 114mins

The French cinema movement called *cinéma du look* came to a shuddering halt with this atrocious, self-referential road movie from Jean-Jacques Beineix. Sadly it was the swansong of Yves Montand, who died just days after "dying" in this film and whose gaunt expression is far more haunting than any of the director's stylised imagery. Half-baked social and ecological theories abound, as Montand joins graffiti artist Olivier Martinez and rapper Sekkou Sall in a search of the Island of Pachyderms. Alternately painful and embarrassing to watch. DP. In French with English subtitles. [video]

Yves Montand *Léon Marcel* • Olivier Martinez *Tony* • Sekkou Sall *Jockey* • Géraldine Pailhas *Gloria* • Colette Renard *Clarisse/Monique* ■ *Dir* Jean-Jacques Beineix • *Scr* Jean-Jacques Beineix, Jacques Forgeas, from a film by Jacques Forgeas

I – Proud to Be an Indian ★★★ 18

Drama 2003 · Ind/UK · Colour · 123mins

Director Puneet Sira makes his feature debut with this provocative call for British-based Asians to unite in the face of neo-Nazi racism. Skinhead Tim Lawrence allies with Pakistani exile Imran Ali Khan to drive Sohail's Indian family from its London neighbourhood. The romance between Sohail and Khan's sister, Heena Tasleem, smacks of Bollywood contrivance, but the discussion of the rise of supremacist intolerance in the UK and the impact of subcontinental tension on the diaspora is well-meaning. DP. In English and Hindi with subtitles. Contains violence, swearing. [video] DVD

Sohail Khan *I* • Kulbhushan Kharbanda *Father* • Tim Lawrence *Cain* • Imran Ali Khan *Aslam* • Heena Tasleem *Noor* ■ *Dir* Puneet Sira • *Scr* Vekeana Dhillon, Puneet Sira, Sohail Khan

IQ ★★★★ U

Romantic comedy
1994 · US · Colour · 91mins

When Meg Ryan pulls into Tim Robbins's garage, it's love at first sight for the mechanic. But this romantic tale has an added twist, for Ryan happens to be the niece of Albert Einstein (as portrayed by Walter Matthau). Since Ryan is engaged to the pompous Stephen Fry (an unlikely bit of casting), Matthau decides to use his grey cells in the match-making department and help Robbins win the affections of Ryan. It's immaculately set in the 1950s, and the stars are well supported by the likes of Gene Saks and Lou Jacobi. AT [video] DVD

Meg Ryan *Catherine Boyd* • Tim Robbins *Ed Walters* • Walter Matthau *Albert Einstein* • Lou Jacobi *Kurt Godel* • Gene Saks *Boris Podolsky* • Joseph Maher *Nathan Liebknecht* • Stephen Fry *James Moreland* • Tony Shalhoub *Bob Walters* ■ *Dir* Fred Schepisi • *Scr* Andy Breckman, Michael Leeson, from a story by Andy Breckman

I Remember Mama ★★★★ U

Drama 1948 · US · BW · 128mins

San Francisco in the early 20th century is the setting for this cosy story of a family of Norwegian immigrants and their struggles for survival. Irene Dunne brings her usual class and charm to the role of the matriarch who holds everyone together and Barbara Bel Geddes plays the daughter who records day-to-day life in her diary. Directed by George Stevens with a warm heart and a diverting way with a cliché, it also has a knockout performance by Cedric Hardwicke as a rundown old actor. TH [video]

Irene Dunne *Mama* • Barbara Bel Geddes *Katrin* • Oscar Homolka *Uncle Chris* • Philip Dorn *Papa* • Sir Cedric Hardwicke [Cedric Hardwicke] *Mr Hyde* • Edgar Bergen *Mr Thorkelson* • Rudy Vallee *Dr Johnson* • Ellen Corby *Aunt Trina* ■ *Dir* George Stevens • *Scr* DeWitt Bodeen, from a play by John Van Druten, from the novel *Mama's Bank Account* by Kathryn Forbes • *Cinematographer* Nicholas Musuraca

I, Robot ★★★★ 12

Science-fiction action thriller
2004 · US/Ger · Colour · 109mins

Sci-fi writer Isaac Asimov's stories provide the inspiration for this futuristic action thriller, set in Chicago in the year 2035 when robots have been fully integrated into society. When a top scientist from the US Robotics corporation turns up dead, detective Will Smith suspects the involvement of a prototype that may not be bound by the laws that govern its brethren. Smith gives a charismatic performance, and this blockbuster succeeds chiefly because of the use of CGI, blending the robots seamlessly into the human environment. Director Alex Proyas keeps the action racing along. TH. Contains violence. [video] DVD

Will Smith *Detective Del Spooner* • Bridget Moynahan *Dr Susan Calvin* • Bruce Greenwood *Lawrence Robertson* • James Cromwell *Dr Alfred Lanning* • Chi McBride *Lieutenant John Bergin* • Alan Tudyk *Sonny* • Adrian L Ricard [Adrian Ricard] *Granny* • Jerry Wasserman *Baldez* ■ *Dir* Alex Proyas • *Scr* Jeff Vintar, Akiva Goldsman, from a story by Jeff Vintar, suggested by the short story collection by Isaac Asimov

I Saw What You Did ★★

Thriller 1965 · US · BW · 81mins

Two teenage girls (Andi Garrett, Sarah Lane), alone one night in a large and fairly isolated house, play a prank on a number of strangers by phoning random numbers and announcing, "I saw what you did, I know who you are." When one of the calls is taken by a man who has just murdered his wife, the joke turns sour. Made by schlock-horror merchant William Castle, this has its moments, as the wife-killer (John Ireland) sets out to find the perpetrator of the threatening phone call. Joan Crawford is also on hand to emote as Ireland's demanding lover. Remade as a TV movie in 1988. RK

Joan Crawford *Amy Nelson* • John Ireland *Steve Marak* • Leif Erickson *Dave Mannering* • Patricia Breslin *Ellie Mannering* • Andi Garrett *Libby* • Sarah Lane *Kit* ■ *Dir* William Castle • *Scr* William P McGivern, from the novel *Out of the Dark* by Ursula Curtiss

I See a Dark Stranger ★★★ U

Second World War drama
1946 · UK · BW · 107mins

Having penned *The Lady Vanishes* for Alfred Hitchcock and *Night Train to Munich* for Carol Reed, Frank Launder and Sidney Gilliat struck out on their own for this tale of wartime treachery. Uncertain handling mars an otherwise diverting romp, in which Deborah Kerr's Irish republican sympathies lead her, unwittingly, to spy for the Nazis. Her feisty devotion to the cause carries the film through its more implausible moments, but she struggles to get much response from a taciturn Trevor Howard. A touch too clever for its own good, but rattling entertainment all the same. DP [video]

Deborah Kerr *Bridie Quilty* • Trevor Howard *Lieutenant David Bayne* • Raymond Huntley *Miller* • Liam Redmond *Timothy* • Michael Howard *Hawkins* ■ *Dir* Frank Launder • *Scr* Wolfgang Wilhelm, Sidney Gilliat, Frank Launder • *Producer* Sidney Gilliat

I See Ice ★★ U

Comedy 1938 · UK · BW · 78mins

This typical George Formby vehicle sees the Lancashire comedian cast as a property man in an ice ballet production who, in his spare time, is an obsessive amateur photographer. Sporting a bow tie that conceals a mini-camera, George sets forth to snap candid photos and gets in all sorts of comical messes. Fast-paced, British comedy with all the usual ingredients of the time: romance, gangsters, misunderstandings and buckets of slapstick. DF [video]

George Formby *George Bright* • Kay Walsh *Judy Gaye* • Betty Stockfeld *Mrs Hunter* • Cyril Ritchard *Paul Martine* • Garry Marsh *Galloway* ■ *Dir* Anthony Kimmins • *Scr* Anthony Kimmins, Austin Melford

I Shot Andy Warhol ★★★★ 18

Biographical drama
1995 · US/UK · Colour · 99mins

Valerie Solanas was famous for 15 minutes when she tried to assassinate Pop Art king Andy Warhol in 1968. Director Mary Harron's endlessly fascinating case history delves into the complex personality of the lesbian feminist author and finally makes sense of what tipped her over the edge into paranoid fantasy. Rarely do films capture a cultural era as precisely as this evocative saga, which does it masterfully with a sure, sophisticated style and with wit and drama to spare. AJ. Contains swearing, sex scenes and drug abuse. [video]

Lili Taylor *Valerie Solanas* • Jared Harris *Andy Warhol* • Stephen Dorff *Candy Darling* • Martha Plimpton *Stevie* • Danny Morgenstern *Jeremiah Newton* • Lothaire Bluteau *Maurice Girodias* • Tahnee Welch *Viva* ■ *Dir* Mary Harron • *Scr* Mary Harron, Daniel Minahan • *Music* John Cale

I Shot Jesse James ★★★ U

Western 1949 · US · BW · 72mins

Samuel Fuller gained his first directing opportunity with this low-budget western told in the emphatic, headline style for which he would become noted. His script takes a characteristically offbeat approach to a familiar situation – the assassination of Jesse James – by telling it from the point of view of Bob Ford, played by John Ireland. He was the "dirty little coward" of ballad fame who took advantage of Jesse's friendship and hospitality to shoot him in the back of the head. Fuller attempts to make it the tragedy of someone who has killed a man he loved, but such a flawed character evokes little concern. AE

Preston Foster *John Kelley* • Barbara Britton *Cynthy Waters* • John Ireland *Bob Ford* • Reed Hadley *Jesse James* • J Edward Bromberg *Kane* • Victor Kilian *Soapy* ■ *Dir* Samuel Fuller • *Scr* Samuel Fuller, from articles by Homer Croy

I Spy ★★ 12

Spy action comedy
2002 · US · Colour · 92mins

This routine reworking of the 1960s TV espionage series has US secret agent Owen Wilson going undercover as the assistant to boxing champion Eddie Murphy. Wilson uses Murphy to get close to billionaire industrialist Malcolm McDowell, who is intent on selling an invisible plane to the highest bidder. The laidback Wilson and the motormouthed Murphy have an engaging on-screen chemistry, but the likeable twosome are sold short by witless writing and predictable plotting. IF. Contains some violence. [video] DVD

Eddie Murphy *Kelly Robinson* • Owen Wilson *Alex Scott* • Famke Janssen *Rachel Wright* • Malcolm McDowell *Arnold Gundars* • Gary Cole *Carlos* • Phill Lewis *Jerry* • Viv Leacock *T J* ■ *Dir* Betty Thomas • *Scr* Marianne Wibberley, Cormac Wibberley, Jay Scherick, David Ronn, from a story by Marianne Wibberley, Cormac Wibberley, from characters created by Morton Fine, David Friedman

I Spy Returns ★★ PG

Spy adventure 1994 · US · Colour · 92mins

This TV movie reunites Bill Cosby and Robert Culp, the stars of the 1960s *I Spy* series that was notable for its pairing of a black and a white actor. Over a quarter of a century after the last show, Cosby and Culp return to secret service duty, as they babysit their offspring on their first assignment in Vienna. Director Jerry London makes the most of the city's stunning sights, while generating enough tension to offset the quips. Culp and Cosby reel back the years, but the joke does wear a little thin by the end. DP [video] DVD

Bill Cosby *Alexander "Scotty" Scott* • Robert Culp *Kelly Robinson* • George Newbern *Bennett Robinson* • Salli Richardson *Nicole Scott* • Jonathan Hyde *Baroodi* ■ *Dir* Jerry London • *Scr* Michael Norell, from characters created by Morton Fine, David Friedkin

I Start Counting ★★

Crime drama 1970 · UK · Colour · 107mins

Director David Greene taxes the patience with this manipulative whodunnit. There are so many dead ends in this adaptation that it soon becomes a matter of indifference whether Bryan Marshall is responsible for the series of sex attacks near his home. Much more intriguing, however, is the effect the slayings have on his foster sister, Jenny Agutter, whose hero worship is both disturbing and potentially deadly. DP

Jenny Agutter *Wynne* • Bryan Marshall *George* • Clare Sutcliffe *Corrine* • Simon Ward *Conductor* • Gregory Phillips *Len* • Lana Morris *Leonie* • Billy Russell *Grandad* ■ *Dir* David Greene • *Scr* Harris Richard, from a novel by Audrey Erskine Lindop

I Still Know What You Did Last Summer ★ 18

Horror 1998 · US/Ger · Colour · 96mins

Noisy, flashy and deadly dull, *Judge Dredd* director Danny Cannon's sequel to *I Know What You Did Last Summer* features the return of college beauty in peril Jennifer Love Hewitt, this time fighting off the masked fisherman during hurricane season in the Bahamas. Without the horror-nerd energy of writer Kevin Williamson's original script, this plotless slab of wet T-shirt terror drearily alternates between the sou'westered spectre freaking out his victims with fake scares and viciously hooking them by the throat. Dismal. AJ DVD

Jennifer Love Hewitt *Julie James* • Freddie Prinze Jr *Ray Bronson* • Brandy Norwood [Brandy] *Karla Wilson* • Mekhi Phifer *Tyrell* • Muse Watson *Ben Willis* • Bill Cobbs *Estes* ■ *Dir* Danny Cannon • *Scr* Trey Callaway, from characters created by Lois Duncan

I Take This Woman ★★

Romantic drama 1940 · US · BW · 97mins

Intended as a vehicle for MGM's latest acquisition, Hedy Lamarr, this quickly became one of those films notorious for its troubled production history. Initial director Josef von Sternberg was replaced by Frank Borzage, before the movie was almost completely remade by the competent but undistinguished W S Van Dyke. Lamarr is the suicidal girl who marries Spencer Tracy to forget her failed romance with Kent Taylor. Tracy, a physician committed to his work with the poor, now finds himself transformed into a fashionable doctor in order to provide his wife with luxuries. The two stars are excellent but the material is trite. AE

Spencer Tracy *Dr Karl Decker* • Hedy Lamarr *Georgi Gragore* • Verree Teasdale *Mme Marcesca* • Kent Taylor *Phil Mayberry* • Laraine Day *Linda Rodgers* • Mona Barrie *Sandra Mayberry* • Jack Carson *Joe* • Paul Cavanagh *Bill Rodgers* • Frances Drake *Lola Estermont* • Marjorie Main *Gertie* ■ *Dir* WS Van Dyke • *Scr* James Kevin McGuiness, from the story *A New York Cinderella* by Charles MacArthur

I Thank a Fool ★★

Drama 1962 · UK · Colour · 99mins

In this relishably hoary old melodrama, woman-with-a-past Susan Hayward becomes entangled with her old nemesis, barrister Peter Finch, and his mentally ill wife Diane Cilento. Euthanasia always provides a controversial plot point; the rest is murder/mystery from another age, with ripe dialogue by *Ben-Hur* writer Karl Tunberg. The stellar cast do their best in one of MGM's prestige British productions, but audiences were unimpressed. DM

Susan Hayward *Christine Allison* • Peter Finch *Stephen Dane* • Diane Cilento *Liane Dane* • Cyril Cusack *Captain Ferris* • Kieron Moore *Roscoe* • Athene Seyler *Aunt Heather* • Richard Wattis *Ebblington* • Peter Sallis *Sleazy doctor* • Joan Hickson *Landlady* ■ *Dir* Robert Stevens • *Scr* Karl Tunberg, from a novel by Audrey Erskine Lindop

I Thank You ★★ U

Musical comedy 1941 · UK · BW · 77mins

If there's one genre in which the British cinema has a tendency to fail, it's the musical comedy. Here, Marcel Varnel has an expert cast at his disposal, but not even Arthur Askey and Richard Murdoch, plus Will Hay old boys Moore Marriott and Graham Moffatt, can warm up this tepid "upstairs-downstairs" charade. DP

Arthur Askey *Arthur* • Richard Murdoch *Stinker* • Lily Morris *Lady Randall* • Moore Marriott *Pop Bennett* • Graham Moffatt *Albert* • Peter Gawthorne *Dr Pope* • Kathleen Harrison *Cook* • Felix Aylmer *Henry Potter* ■ *Dir* Marcel Varnel • *Scr* Val Guest, Marriott Edgar, from a story by Howard Irving Young

I, the Jury ★

Crime thriller 1953 · US · BW · 87mins

Mickey Spillane was a former trampoline artist and narcotics agent who turned to thriller writing in 1947 with *I, the Jury*. At the time, the novel's violence was shocking, as was the blinkered morality of its thuggish private eye Mike Hammer as he avenges his friend's murder. UA signed Spillane to a four-film deal. They may have lavished 3-D on the movie but the cast is barely adequate and the novel is watered down. It flopped, but Hammer's next cinematic exploit, *Kiss Me Deadly*, was a masterpiece. AT

Biff Elliot *Mike Hammer* • Preston Foster *Captain Pat Chambers* • Peggie Castle *Charlotte Manning* • Margaret Sheridan *Velda* • Alan Reed *George Kalecki* • Frances Osborne *Myrna* ■ *Dir* Harry Essex • *Scr* Harry Essex, from a novel by Mickey Spillane

I, the Jury ★★ 18

Crime thriller 1982 · US · Colour · 102mins

This updated remake of the first Mike Hammer movie, with Hammer's murdered friend now a Vietnam veteran, is closer to Mickey Spillane's original. With its sex and violence, the movie fittingly has the ambience of a penny dreadful and a trashy B-movie. As Hammer, Armand Assante also looks the part – menacing and thick – and the body count is high. The women in the cast seem simply required to get their clothes off as often as possible. AT

Armand Assante *Mike Hammer* • Barbara Carrera *Dr Charlotte Bennett* • Laurene Landon *Velda* • Alan King *Charles Kalecki* • Geoffrey Lewis *Joe Butler* • Paul Sorvino *Detective Pat Chambers* ■ *Dir* Richard T Heffron • *Scr* Larry Cohen, from the novel by Mickey Spillane

I, the Worst of All ★★★★

Historical drama
1990 · Arg · Colour · 105mins

Argentinian director Maria Luisa Bemberg is probably best known in this country for *Miss Mary*, a stylish period tale starring Julie Christie. This historical drama has none of the gloss of that film, yet with its stark and striking lighting designs, its symbolically lavish costumes and delicately nuanced performances, it is a deeply affecting study of Sister Juana Ines de la Cruz, one of the most important religious poets of the 17th century. A brave and beautiful film. DP. In Spanish with English subtitles.

Assumpta Serna *Sister Juana Ines de la Cruz* • Dominique Sanda *Vice-Reine Maria Luisa* • Héctor Alterio *Viceroy* • Lautaro Murua *Archbishop of Mexico* • Alberto Segado *Father Miranda* ■ *Dir* Maria Luisa Bemberg • *Scr* Maria Luisa Bemberg, Antonio Larreta, from the essay *The Traps of Faith* by Octavio Paz, from the book *Sor Juana: Her Life and Her World* by Octavio Paz

I Think I Do ★ 15

Romantic comedy
1997 · US · Colour · 89mins

In a film as wishy washy as its title, six university friends meet up again at a mutual pal's wedding. Firstly we are subjected to their unfortunate back stories in flashback, before the gang of Alexis Arquette, his boyfriend Tuc Watkins and the rest appear at girlfriend Lauren Velez's nuptials where their college habit of bed hopping is resurrected. As far as token gay drama goes, this is old-fashioned fare and unsupported by poor standards in almost every department. LH DVD

Alexis Arquette *Bob* • Guillermo Diaz *Eric* • Jamie Harrold *Matthew Edward Lynch* • Christian Maelen *Brendan* • Marni Nixon *Aunt Alice* • Lauren Velez *Carol Anita Gonzalez* ■ *Dir/Scr* Brian Sloan

I Wake Up Screaming ★★★★ PG

Film noir 1941 · US · BW · 78mins

In hindsight, this turned out to be one of 20th Century-Fox's key *films noirs*. It contains a quintessential plot about a beautiful murdered actress and a grab-bag of seedy unusual suspects, such as the tough sports promoter and the unseemly detective whose more-than-professional interest in the dead girl is enthralling. This is a clever and fast-moving atmospheric thriller with a sordid undertone that leaves you wanting more, and it contains a superb cast of 1940s icons. TS

Betty Grable *Jill Lynn* • Victor Mature *Frankie Christopher* • Carole Landis *Vicky Lynn* • Laird Cregar *Ed Cornell* • William Gargan *Jerry McDonald* • Alan Mowbray *Robin Ray* • Elisha Cook Jr *Harry Williams* ■ *Dir* H Bruce Humberstone • *Scr* Dwight Taylor, from the novel by Steve Fisher

I Walk Alone ★★★

Crime drama 1947 · US · BW · 97mins

Burt Lancaster and Kirk Douglas give solid performances in this bruising *film noir* about ex-bootleggers who fall out over their spoils. Wendell Corey also impresses as the spineless accountant, who is murdered after helping Douglas build his empire while Lancaster is doing time. The action is kept nicely on the boil by Byron Haskin, who handles the violent set pieces, the romantic interludes and the musical numbers with assurance. DP

Burt Lancaster *Frankie Madison* • Kirk Douglas *Noll Turner* • Lizabeth Scott *Kay Lawrence* • Wendell Corey *Dave* • Kristine Miller *Mrs Richardson* ■ *Dir* Byron Haskin • *Scr* Charles Schnee, Robert Smith, John Bright, from the play *Beggars Are Coming to Town* by Theodore Reeves

I Walk the Line ★★ 15

Crime thriller 1970 · US · Colour · 92mins

When upright Tennessee sheriff Gregory Peck falls for a white trash, in-bred moonshiner's daughter (Tuesday Weld), his career goes quickly on the skids. There's more than a touch of Tennessee Williams's *Baby Doll* to this torrid tale, but Peck seems badly miscast and that cripples the story from the beginning. On the plus side, there are some hokey country tunes from Johnny Cash, and director John Frankenheimer creates a convincing Deep South ambience. AT

Gregory Peck *Sheriff Henry Tawes* • Tuesday Weld *Alma McCain* • Estelle Parsons *Ellen Haney* • Ralph Meeker *Carl McCain* • Lonny Chapman *Bascomb* • Charles Durning *Hunnicutt* • Jeff Dalton *Clay McCain* ■ *Dir* John Frankenheimer • *Scr* Alvin Sargent, from the novel *An Exile* by Madison Jones

I Walked with a Zombie ★★★★ PG

Horror 1943 · US · BW · 65mins

Is the invalid wife of a Caribbean plantation owner (Tom Conway) really the victim of a voodoo curse? In her quest to find out, nurse Frances Dee uncovers dark family secrets in cult producer Val Lewton's ingenious reworking of *Jane Eyre*. Jacques Tourneur's direction creates palpable fear and tension in a typically low-key nightmare from the Lewton fright factory. The lighting, shadows, exotic setting and music all contribute to the immensely disturbing atmosphere, making this stunning piece of poetic horror a classic of the genre. AJ.

Tom Conway *Paul Holland* • Frances Dee *Betsy* • James Ellison *Wesley Rand* • Edith Barrett *Mrs Rand* • Christine Gordon *Jessica Holland* • James Bell *Dr Maxwell* • Richard Abrams *Clement* ■ *Dir* Jacques Tourneur • *Scr* Curt Siodmark, Ardel Wray, from a story by Inez Wallace • *Editor* Mark Robson

I Wanna Hold Your Hand ★★★

Comedy 1978 · US · Colour · 98mins

This gentle comedy, set in 1964, focuses on four New Jersey teenagers who are obsessed with meeting the Beatles, just as the Fab Four are about to make their debut on TV's *Ed Sullivan Show*. You don't get the Beatles of course, but there are lots of shots of winkle-pickered shoes and the movie has bags of ingenuity and charm. Steven Spielberg acted as executive producer. AT

Nancy Allen *Pam Mitchell* • Bobby DiCicco *Tony Smerko* • Marc McClure *Larry Dubois* • Susan Kendall Newman *Janis Goldman* • Theresa Saldana *Grace Corrigan* • Wendie Jo Sperber *Rosie Petrofsky* ■ *Dir* Robert Zemeckis • *Scr* Robert Zemeckis, Bob Gale • *Executive Producer* Steven Spielberg • *Music* The Beatles

I Want to Go Home ★

Satirical comedy 1989 · Fr · Colour · 110mins

Written by American cartoonist and humourist Jules Feiffer, it stars Adolph Green, co-writer of *On the Town*, *Singin' in the Rain* and *The Band Wagon*. Despite this obvious talent it really doesn't work at all, not even when Gérard Depardieu crops up as a university don. The involvement of Alain Resnais – one of the most deeply intellectual of French directors – is explained by his lifelong love of comics. AT

Adolph Green *Joey Wellman* • Gérard Depardieu *Christian Gauthier* • Linda Lavin *Lena Apthrop* • Micheline Presle *Isabelle Gauthier* • John Ashton *Harry Dempsey* ■ *Dir* Alain Resnais • *Scr* Jules Feiffer

I Want to Live! ★★★★ 15

Biographical crime melodrama
1958 · US · BW · 116mins

Four-time loser Susan Hayward finally won an Oscar for her riveting portrayal of Barbara Graham, whose wretched life saw her descend into prostitution, fraud, perjury and drug addiction before she was finally convicted of murder. She was framed, according to the stance taken here on the notorious 1955 case, reinforcing the anti-capital punishment argument of director Robert Wise's campaigning opus. It's the depiction of Graham's brave march to her gas chamber execution that won over Academy Award voters to Hayward's side. AJ DVD

Susan Hayward *Barbara Graham* • Simon Oakland *Ed Montgomery* • Virginia Vincent *Peg* • Theodore Bikel *Carl Palmberg* • Wesley Lau *Henry Graham* ■ *Dir* Robert Wise • *Scr* Nelson Gidding, Don Mankiewicz, from articles by Ed Montgomery, from letters by Barbara Graham

I Want What I Want ★

Drama 1971 · UK · Colour · 105mins

Is it strange for a film producer to cast his own wife as a man who has a sex change operation? You can judge for yourself after watching this movie, in which producer Raymond Stross finds such a role for his spouse Anne Heywood – a former beauty queen whose real name was Violet Pretty. Heywood starts out as a Roy and ends up as a Wendy but nothing – not even some hideous make-up, silly clothes and a deep voice – can disguise the fact that she's a woman from start to finish. Not a very helpful contribution to a little-understood subject. AT

Anne Heywood *Roy/Wendy* • Harry Andrews *Father* • Jill Bennett *Margaret Stevenson* • Paul Rogers *Mr Waites* • Michael Coles *Frank* ■ *Dir* John Dexter • *Scr* Gillian Freeman, from a novel by Geoff Brown

I Want You ★★★ U

Drama 1951 · US · BW · 97mins

Producer Samuel Goldwyn's attempt to follow up the critical and popular success of his seven Oscar-winning 1946 masterpiece *The Best Years of Our Lives* resulted in this similarly themed movie, this time portraying the effects of the Korean War on American small-town families. The screenplay by novelist Irwin Shaw is excellent, and the performances ring touching and true. This is very much a period artefact, fascinating to watch today and inspired by the induction of Goldwyn's own son. TS

Dana Andrews *Martin Greer* • Dorothy McGuire *Nancy Greer* • Farley Granger *Jack Greer* • Peggy Dow *Carrie Turner* • Robert Keith (1) *Thomas Greer* • Mildred Dunnock *Sarah Greer* ■ *Dir* Mark Robson • *Scr* Irwin Shaw, from stories by Edward Newhouse

I Want You ★ 18

Thriller 1998 · UK · Colour · 83mins

Michael Winterbottom's turgid sexual melodrama is meant to be a deep psychological study into erotic compulsion, manipulation, bitterness and betrayal, but the director misses every target by miles. After serving nine years for murder, Alessandro Nivola heads back to his home town to pursue ex-girlfriend Rachel Weisz. Something unspeakable connects them – but what? The answer is easy to guess, and it's not worth wading through all the empty emotions and dire dialogue to find out. AJ. Contains swearing and sex scenes.

Labina Mitevska *Smokey* • Rachel Weisz *Helen* • Alessandro Nivola *Martin* • Luka Petrusic *Honda* • Carmen Ejogo *Amber* • Ben Daniels *DJ Bob* ■ *Dir* Michael Winterbottom • *Scr* Eoin McNamee

I Wanted to See Angels ★★★

Drama 1992 · Rus · Colour · 83mins

Nothing could prepare you for the stark portrait of Moscow on the edge painted here by Sergei Bodrov. Essentially, this is a grim love story in which a disillusioned biker and a street kid cling together for survival in a place held hostage by the latest fad and by the forces of crime. But what is most striking about the film is Bodrov's gritty style and his determination to show the seediness and the hopelessness of Boris Yeltsin's Russia. DP. In Russian with English subtitles.

Alexei Baranov • Natasha Ginko • Lea Akeojakova • Alex Jarkov ■ *Dir* Sergei Bodrov • *Scr* Sergei Bodrov, Carolyn Cavallero

I Wanted Wings ★★

Action drama 1941 · US · BW · 133mins

Ray Milland, William Holden and Wayne Morris join the army air corps and head for Texas for their training as fighter pilots. The script is top-heavy with plot as the three men work out their romantic entanglements, learn to fly and bond in buddy-buddy fashion. Veronica Lake (billing herself as that for the first time, having changed her professional name from Constance Keane) is the beauty. Director Mitchell Leisen apparently thought she had no talent and bullied her. AT

Ray Milland *Jeff Young* • William Holden (2) *Al Ludlow* • Wayne Morris *Tom Cassidy* • Brian Donlevy *Capt Mercer* • Constance Moore *Carolyn Bartlett* • Veronica Lake *Sally Vaughn* ■ *Dir* Mitchell Leisen • *Scr* Richard Maibaum, Beirne Lay Jr, Sig Herzig, from a story by Eleanore Griffin, Frank Wead, from the non-fiction book by Beirne Lay Jr • *Special Effects* Gordon Jennings

I Was a Communist for the FBI ★★ U

Thriller 1951 · US · BW · 81mins

Although based on a *Saturday Evening Post* article given by undercover agent Matt Cvetic to journalist Pete Martin, this Red-baiting propaganda was clearly couched in fictional terms, thus making its Oscar nomination in the documentary feature category all the more puzzling. Shot as a *film noir*, it's too soused with political bile to be an effective thriller, no matter how much director Gordon Douglas cranks up the suspense. Frank Lovejoy stars as a steelworker recruited by the FBI to infiltrate his communist union. As an insight into the hysteria that gripped America in the early days of the Cold War, it's an invaluable document. DP

Frank Lovejoy *Matt Cvetic* • Dorothy Hart *Eve Merrick* • Philip Carey *Mason* • Dick Webb *Crowley* • James Millican *Jim Blandon* • Ron Hagerthy *Dick Cvetic* ■ *Dir* Gordon Douglas • *Scr* Crane Wilbur, from the article *I Posed as a Communist for the FBI* by Matt Cvetic, Pete Martin

I Was a Male War Bride ★★★★★ U

Screwball comedy 1949 · US · BW · 101mins

In this hilarious comedy of errors, French army officer Cary Grant marries American WAC Ann Sheridan and attempts to get to the States using the "war bride" bill. Director Howard Hawks wrings every ounce of humour from this bizarre situation, making splendid use of European locations (with interiors filmed at Shepperton Studios), and his cast could scarcely be improved upon. This is one of Grant's cleverest, most subtle performances, but the breezy Sheridan is more than a match for him: just watch that timing in the "sleeplessness in the guest house" sequence, and the increasing sense of frustration as an uncredited Lionel Murton tells Grant again and again, "you can't sleep here" (the film's British release title). TS DVD

Cary Grant *Captain Henri Rochard* • Ann Sheridan *Lieutenant Catherine Gates* • William Neff *Captain Jack Rumsey* • Marion Marshall *WAC* • Randy Stuart *WAC* • Eugene Gericke *Tony Jowitt* ■ *Dir* Howard Hawks • *Scr* Charles Lederer, Leonard Spigelgass, Hagar Wilde, from the article *Male War Bride Trial to Army* in the *Baltimore Sun* by Henri Rochard

I Was a Shoplifter ★★

Crime drama 1950 · US · BW · 74mins

A gang blackmails kleptomaniacs into becoming professional thieves in this moderately engaging drama. Scott Brady stars as an undercover cop, while Mona Freeman plays the judge's daughter who is recruited by the ring. The film was denounced as "a course in shoplifting" by a censor in Atlanta, who promptly banned it. Interest is added by the appearances of two future stars: Tony (here Anthony) Curtis as a lecherous killer, and Rock Hudson as a store detective. AE

Scott Brady *Jeff Andrews* • Mona Freeman *Faye Burton* • Andrea King *Ina Perdue* • Anthony Curtis [Tony Curtis] *Pepe* • Charles Drake *Herb Klaxon* • Gregg Martell *The champ* • Rock Hudson *Si Swanson* ■ *Dir* Charles Lamont • *Scr* Irwin Gielgud, from his story

I Was a Spy ★★ U

Spy drama 1934 · UK · BW · 86mins

Fans of vintage British cinema will enjoy this sprightly espionage yarn, set during the First World War and bearing a close resemblance to the Mata Hari legend. The lovely Madeleine Carroll plays a Belgian nurse who goes undercover with fellow spy Herbert Marshall and gets caught trying to sabotage a German munitions dump. Conrad Veidt, exiled from his homeland following the victory of the Nazis, plays a villainous German officer. AT

Madeleine Carroll *Martha Cnockhaert McKenna* • Conrad Veidt *Commandant Oberaertz* • Herbert Marshall *Stephan* • Gerald du Maurier *Doctor* • Edmund Gwenn *Burgomaster* • Nigel Bruce *Scotty* ■ *Dir* Victor Saville • *Scr* WP Lipscomb

I Was a Teenage Frankenstein ★★★ 15

Horror 1957 · US · BW and Colour · 73mins

If *I Was a Teenage Werewolf* has one of the most famous exploitation titles of all time, this quickie sequel contains some of the best-remembered dialogue: "Answer me, you have a civil tongue in your head. I know, I sewed it in there." As the resident evil scientist, horror dependable Whit Bissell swaps lucrative lycanthropy for ugly monster-making using car-crash cadavers. Immensely idiotic, naturally, but sometimes incredibly effective (especially the lively, colour climax), this lurid hokum has an unexpectedly neat line in self-parody. AJ

Whit Bissell *Professor Frankenstein* • Phyllis Coates *Margaret* • Robert Burton *Dr Karlton* • Gary Conway *Teenage Monster* • George Lynn *Sergeant Burns* • John Cliff *Sergeant McAffee* • Marshall Bradford *Dr Randolph* ■ *Dir* Herbert L Strock • *Scr* Kenneth Langtry

I Was a Teenage Werewolf ★★ 15

Horror 1957 · US · BW · 75mins

Rebel without a Cause meets *The Wolf Man* in a trend-setting cult classic, complete with rock 'n' roll, rumbles and teen traumas. Michael Landon (yes, Little Joe Cartwright from *Bonanza* himself) is the troubled student who tears his classmates to shreds after therapy administered by mad scientist Whit Bissell regresses him to his primal past. The suspense is minimal, the production values low, and the time-lapse special effects are hokey, but, even if this seminal shocker now only scrapes by on quaint nostalgia, its title will always be a part of horror history. AJ

Michael Landon *Tony* • Yvonne Lime *Arlene* • Whit Bissell *Dr Alfred Brandon* • Tony Marshall *Jimmy* • Dawn Richard *Theresa* • Barney Phillips *Detective Donovan* • Ken Miller *Vic* ■ *Dir* Gene Fowler Jr • *Scr* Ralph Thornton

I Was an Adventuress ★★★

Comedy drama 1940 · US · BW · 80mins

What fun this should have been, with scene-stealers Peter Lorre and Erich von Stroheim playing confidence tricksters who are abandoned by their partner-in-crime, seductive Vera Zorina, when she finds true love. The settings are lavish, and the pair's efforts to get the team back together generate enough twists to keep one watching. Alas, Gregory Ratoff's direction fails to add the necessary sparkle. Zorina's balletic skills are showcased in the final reel with an excerpt from *Swan Lake* choreographed by her husband, George Balanchine. TV

Zorina [Vera Zorina] *Countess Tanya Vronsky* • Richard Greene *Paul Vernay* • Erich von Stroheim *Andre Desormeaux* • Peter Lorre *Polo* • Sig Rumann [Sig Ruman] *Herr Protz* • Fritz Feld *Henri Gautier* • Cora Witherspoon *Aunt Cecile* ■ *Dir* Gregory Ratoff • *Scr* Karl Tunberg, Don Ettlinger, John O'Hara, from the film *J'Etais une Aventurière* by Jacques Companeez, Herbert Juttke, Hans Jacoby, Michael Duran

I Was Born, but... ★★★★★

Silent comedy drama 1932 · Jpn · BW · 100mins

Yasujiro Ozu established himself among Japan's greatest film-makers with this exemplary *shomin-geki* or lower-middle-class domestic movie. Coaxing wondrously natural performances from Hideo Sugawara and Tokkankozo, Ozu fashions a minutely observed silent comedy, in which the brothers' disgust at their father's subservience to his boss prompts them to go on hunger strike. The opening segment is played almost entirely in dumb show, although the captions used to explain the harsh realities of the adult world are never intrusive and reinforce the film's ironic take on childhood innocence and life's little injustices. DP

Hideo Sugawara *Older son, Ryoichi* • Tokkankozo *Younger son, Keiji* • Tatsu Saito *Father, Yoshi* • Mitsuko Yoshikawa *Mother* • Takeshi Sakamoto *Boss* • Seiji Nishimura *Schoolmaster* ■ *Dir* Yasujiro Ozu • *Scr* Akira Fushimi, James Maki [Yasujiro Ozu], Geibei Ibushiya • *Cinematographer* Hideo Shigehara

I Was Happy Here ★★★

Drama 1966 · UK · BW · 90mins

A bittersweet story of Irish disenchantment, this reminds us just how good Sarah Miles could be, even if she hasn't made many films of late. Here she is Cass, the girl who leaves her home and boyfriend in Ireland for the bright lights of London only to find an unhappy marriage with Julian Glover. When she next returns to own country, Cass has to confront her mixed feelings about her former home. Directed by Desmond Davis from a story by Edna O'Brien, the character's winsomeness can be a bit cloying, but Miles is impressive as the wide-eyed innocent who makes us sympathise with her contrary nature. TH

Sarah Miles *Cass* • Cyril Cusack *Hogan* • Julian Glover *Dr Matthew Langdon* • Sean Caffrey *Colin Foley* • Marie Kean *Barkeeper* • Eve Belton *Kate* • Cardew Robinson *Gravedigger* ■ *Dir* Desmond Davis • *Scr* Desmond Davis, Edna O'Brien, from the short story *A Woman by the Seaside* by Edna O'Brien

I Was Monty's Double ★★★★ U

Second World War drama 1958 · UK · BW · 96mins

The Second World War as fought on the pages of popular fiction is littered with doubles planted as decoys to divert the enemy away from a vital theatre of operation. But, as is so often the case, it is the truth that provides the best stories. John Guillermin's film gains credibility not only because the title role is played by General Montgomery's double himself, ME Clifton James, but also because his autobiography has been so skilfully adapted by Bryan Forbes. Astute, unassuming and slick. DP

John Mills *Major Harvey* • Cecil Parker *Colonel Logan* • Patrick Allen *Colonel Matthers* • ME Clifton James • Patrick Holt *Colonel Dawson* • Leslie Phillips *Major Tennant* • Michael Hordern *Governor of Gibraltar* • Marius Goring *Neilson* • Barbara Hicks *Hester* • Sidney James *YMCA porter* • Victor Maddern *Orderly*

Sergeant • Alfie Bass *Small man* • John Le Mesurier *Adjutant RAPC* ■ *Dir* John Guillermin • *Scr* Bryan Forbes, from a non-fiction book by ME Clifton James

I Was on Mars ★★ 15

Comedy 1991 · Ger/US/Swi · Colour · 83mins

This comedy misfire paints a decidedly unflattering picture of the flipside of the American Dream. Duped out of her savings almost as soon as she sets foot in New York and speaking nothing but her native Polish, Maria Schrader doggedly pursues petty conman Dani Levy out of a mixture of sheer desperation and inexplicable attraction. Their freewheeling romance is strewn with moments of melodrama, and the inventive use of angle and close-up adds a *frisson* to the low-budget proceedings. DP

Maria Schrader *Silva* • Dani Levy *Alio* • Mario Giacalone *Nic* • Antonia Rey *Mama* ■ *Dir* Dani Levy • *Scr* Dani Levy, Maria Schrader

I Went Down ★★★ 15

Crime comedy
1997 · Ire/UK/Sp · Colour · 102mins

Although the absurd is never far beneath its surface, this dark crime comedy also has plenty to say about loyalty, greed and the pitfalls of macho posturing. Writer Conor McPherson asks a great deal of director Paddy Breathnach by packing so much incident into his script and the cycle of revenge, kidnaps, escapes and double-crosses prevents the action from gaining much momentum. But the exchanges between doltish hitman Brendan Gleeson and his reluctant accomplice Peter McDonald are often splutteringly funny, and there's a nice turn from Peter Caffrey as their quarry. one. DP. Contains violence, swearing and a sex scene.

Brendan Gleeson *Bunny Kelly* • Peter McDonald *Git Hynes* • Peter Caffrey *Frank Grogan* • Antoine Byrne *Sabrina Bradley* • David Wilmot *Anto* • Michael McElhatton *Johnner Doyle* • Joe Gallagher *Steo Gannon* • Conor McPherson *Loser in nightclub* ■ *Dir* Paddy Breathnach • *Scr* Conor McPherson

I Will... I Will... for Now ★★ 15

Romantic comedy
1976 · US · Colour · 103mins

...well, no, perhaps not. The expected chemistry between Diane Keaton and Elliott Gould fails to spark in this cack-handed marital farce which climaxes in a sex-clinic for little reason other than the fact that, like Everest, it's there – and just as enormous a stereotype to scale. The supporting cast includes Victoria Principal. TH

Elliott Gould *Les Bingham* • Diane Keaton *Katie Bingham* • Paul Sorvino *Lou Springer* • Victoria Principal *Jackie Martin* • Robert Alda *Dr Magnus* ■ *Dir* Norman Panama • *Scr* Norman Panama, Albert E Lewin

I Woke Up Early the Day I Died ★★

Crime comedy 1998 · US · Colour · 89mins

After Tim Burton's mesmerising biopic of Edward D Wood, it probably made commercial sense to dust off one of Wood's supposedly lost screenplays and film it for a new generation. Alas, this semi-homage to the bargain basement style of film-making that was Wood's trademark fails to gel. Its slim tale of an escaped lunatic (Billy Zane) perpetrating a robbery only to lose all the cash is done in a Chaplin-esque silent movie way, heavy on the slapstick. The one point of interest is a veritable flood of cameos. RS

Billy Zane *The Thief* • Ron Perlman *Cemetary caretaker* • Tippi Hedren *Maylinda* • Andrew McCarthy *Cop* • Will Patton *Preacher* • Carel Struycken *Undertaker* ■ *Dir* Aris Iliopulos • *Scr* Edward D Wood Jr

I Wonder Who's Killing Her Now? ★★★

Comedy 1975 · US · Colour · 87mins

This amusing independent production was written by a former associate of Woody Allen, though its approach is closer to the zaniness of Mel Brooks's films. Estranged hubby Bob Dishy hires someone to murder his wife, in order to collect the insurance to pay off his debts. When the policy is cancelled, he tries to cancel the hit, but finds out the man hired someone to do the job... who hired someone else... who hired someone else... and so on. Dishy gives a hilarious performance, expertly handling his character's fast-talking, half-truths and outright lies. KB

Bob Dishy • Bill Dana • Joanna Barnes • Vito Scotti • Richard Libertini ■ *Dir* Steven Hilliard Stern • *Scr* Mickey Rose

I Wonder Who's Kissing Her Now ★★★ U

Biographical musical
1947 · US · Colour · 104mins

Agreeable, if not exactly memorable, film biography of Joe Howard, a vaudeville singer and tunesmith in the 1890s. Mark Stevens plays Howard, while Lenore Aubert is the European star who entices him with her charms. The beauty of making a movie about a hit songwriter is that you don't have to send out for any new tunes, and Howard's own, including the title song, make easy listening. PF

Mark Stevens *Joe Howard* • June Haver *Katie* • Martha Stewart *Lulu Madison* • Reginald Gardiner *Will Hough* • Lenore Aubert *Fritzi Barrington* • William Frawley *Jim Mason* • Gene Nelson *Tommy Yale* ■ *Dir* Lloyd Bacon • *Scr* Lewis R Foster, Marion Turk

Ice ★★ 18

Action crime thriller
1994 · US · Colour · 87mins

Former porn star Traci Lords had by this stage improved on her previously poor acting skills. Though not great, she is better than one might expect as a professional thief who teams up with her husband to relieve a Mafia hood of some diamonds. When her husband gets "iced" in the process, Lords's life gets very complicated. There are shoot-outs and broken glass enough for several movies. KB DVD

Traci Lords *Ellen Reed* • Zach Galligan *Rick* • Michael Bailey Smith *Courier* • Floyd Levine *Det Prine* • Jamie Alba *Det Little* • Jean Pflieger *Jeweller* • Phillip Troy *Charley* ■ *Dir* Brooke Yeaton • *Scr* Sean Dash

Ice Age ★★★ U

Animated adventure
2002 · US · Colour · 77mins

A moody mammoth, a slow-thinking sloth and a sinister sabre-toothed tiger team up during the Pleistocene era to return a lost human infant to his parents. It's wittily scripted with plenty of banter between the lead characters, voiced by John Leguizamo and Denis Leary among others. The style of the animation is boxy, sharp-edged and with a coldness fitting the sub-zero setting. SF DVD

Ray Romano *Manfred* • John Leguizamo *Sid* • Denis Leary *Diego* • Goran Visnjic *Soto* • Jack Black *Zeke* • Tara Strong [Tara Charendoff] *Roshan/Start* ■ *Dir* Chris Wedge, Carlos Saldanha • *Scr* Michael Berg, Michael J Wilson, Peter Ackerman, from a story by Michael J Wilson

Ice Bound ★★★

Drama based on a true story
2003 · Can/US · Colour · 95mins

A sterling performance from Susan Sarandon is the main reason to watch this frost-bitten TV biopic from director Roger Spottiswoode. It tells the incredible true story of Dr Jerri Nielsen, who successfully treated herself for breast cancer while marooned at a South Pole research station. Sarandon is commanding in the lead – the doctor's grit and wry humour seem to belong to the actress rather than the character – but she makes the extreme situation believable. RT

Susan Sarandon *Dr Jerri Nielsen* • Aidan Devine *Big John Penny* • Cynthia Mace *Claire "Fingers" Furinski* • Kathryn Zenna *Galley-Annie* ■ *Dir* Roger Spottiswoode • *Scr* Peter Pruce, Maria Nation, from the autobiography *Ice Bound: A Doctor's Incredible Battle for Survival at the South Pole* by Jerri Nielsen, Maryanne Vollers

Ice Castles ★★★ PG

Romantic sports drama
1978 · US · Colour · 104mins

Lynn-Holly Johnson emotes almost as well as she skates, and Donald Wrye's sentimental melodrama exercises a curious fascination. This owes much to Colleen Dewhurst's sharp performance as the Iowa skating coach who grooms her protégée for Olympic stardom. Tom Skerritt also impresses as Johnson's farmer father, though Robby Benson is something of an irritant as the boyfriend. DP

Robby Benson *Nick Peterson* • Lynn-Holly Johnson *Alexis Winston* • Colleen Dewhurst *Beulah Smith* • Tom Skerritt *Marcus Winston* • Jennifer Warren *Deborah Macland* • David Huffman *Brian Dockett* ■ *Dir* Donald Wrye • *Scr* Donald Wrye, Gary L Baim, from a story by Gary L Baim

Ice Cold in Alex ★★★★ PG

Second World War drama
1958 · UK · BW · 124mins

This is the film in which John Mills swigs the most famous glass of beer in movie history. And how well he's earned it, having steered clear of the bottle, Axis troops and a desert full of mines to bring an ambulance to safety after the fall of Tobruk in 1942. Onboard are second-in-command Harry Andrews, nurses Sylvia Sims and Diane Clare and Anthony Quayle's suspicious-acting South African, who bribes his way onto the ambulance with gin, threatening Mills's temper and temperance. This is a straightforward but never simplistic tale of battling the odds. Director J Lee Thompson keeps the action tense and every jolt felt in the vehicle's cabin will throw you to the edge of your armchair. DP DVD

John Mills *Captain Anson* • Sylvia Syms *Sister Diane Murdoch* • Anthony Quayle *Captain Van der Poel* • Harry Andrews *MSM Pugh* • Diane Clare *Sister Denise Norton* • Richard Leech *Captain Crosbie* ■ *Dir* J Lee Thompson • *Scr* Christopher Landon, TJ Morrison, from the novel by Christopher Landon

The Ice Follies of 1939 ★★★

Musical 1939 · US · BW and Colour · 83mins

The three-star rating is strictly for the ice-skating, some of it spectacularly executed by the dazzling International Ice Follies company, for which the rest of this movie is a thin excuse. The almost nonexistent plot has James Stewart as an ice-skater and Joan Crawford as his actress wife, suffering marital strife when she is offered a Hollywood contract. Neither the stars, nor the stalwart support of MGM character actors such as Lewis Stone can rescue the pathetic script. RK

Joan Crawford *Mary McKay* • James Stewart *Larry Hall* • Lew Ayres *Eddie Burgess* • Lewis Stone *Douglas Tolliver* • Lionel Stander *Mort Hodges* ■ *Dir* Reinhold Schünzel • *Scr* Leonard Praskins, Florence Ryerson, Edgar Allan Woolf, from a story by Leonard Praskins • *Music* Roger Edens

Ice Palace ★★

Drama 1960 · US · Colour · 143mins

Edna Ferber has had many of her novels turned into films, *Giant* (1956) being perhaps the most memorable. This is a markedly less successful saga about the social development of Alaska. Filtered through the friendship-become-enmity of pioneers Richard Burton and Robert Ryan, it's a a less than enthralling plod through the early years of the 20th century. TH

Richard Burton *Zeb Kennedy* • Robert Ryan *Thor Storm* • Carolyn Jones *Bridie Ballantyne* • Martha Hyer *Dorothy Kennedy* • Jim Backus *Dave Husack* • Ray Danton *Bay Husack* • Diane McBain *Christine Storm* • Karl Swenson *Scotty Ballantyne* • George Takei *Wang* ■ *Dir* Vincent Sherman • *Scr* Harry Kleiner, from a novel by Edna Ferber

The Ice Pirates ★★★ 15

Science-fiction adventure
1984 · US · Colour · 89mins

Although little more than an Errol Flynn-type intergalactic swashbuckler, this slight space opera is good inventive fun even if it does err on the crudely silly side. Space pirate Robert Urich searches the universe for the prized commodity of water, gets captured, falls in love with princess Mary Crosby and escapes with her to search for her father on a mysterious planet covered in water. Great art direction and neat special effects augment the constant stream of smart-aleck remarks and sexual innuendo. AJ

Robert Urich *Jason* • Mary Crosby *Princess Karina* • Anjelica Huston *Maida* • Michael D Roberts *Roscoe* • John Matuszak *Killjoy* • Ron Perlman *Zeno* • John Carradine *Supreme Commander* ■ *Dir* Stewart Raffill • *Scr* Stewart Raffill, Stanford Sherman

Ice Station Zebra ★★★ U

Adventure 1968 · US · Colour · 139mins

For a time, the action in this Cold War thriller is as frozen stiff as the title, as a far-off Polar outpost becomes a magnet for Russian and American forces out to recover some satellite photographs. Then it thaws into activity when Patrick McGoohan, as a British agent, arrives on the scene to stir Rock Hudson out of his slumber. Ernest Borgnine overacts, and the then popular though now rather clichéd Alistair MacLean original is given a steady treatment by director John Sturges. TH DVD

Rock Hudson *Commander James Ferraday* • Ernest Borgnine *Boris Vaslov* • Patrick McGoohan *David Jones* • Jim Brown *Captain Leslie Anders* • Tony Bill *Lt Russell Walker* • Lloyd Nolan *Admiral Garvey* • Alf Kjellin *Colonel Ostrovsky* ■ *Dir* John Sturges • *Scr* Douglas Heyes, from the story by Harry Julian Fink, from the novel by Alistair MacLean

The Ice Storm ★★★★★ 15

Drama 1997 · US · Colour · 107mins

Director Ang Lee's adaptation about two dysfunctional families in suburban New England is an accomplished ensemble drama. Set in 1973, the film focuses on the complicated relationships between two neighbouring families, with Nixon's unfolding Watergate disgrace as the backdrop. Kevin Kline is cheating on his wife Joan Allen with bored neighbour Sigourney Weaver, while their teenage children are experimenting with their own sexual desires. Cinematographer Frederick Elmes's beautifully realised ice storm draws the drama to a cathartic climax. Outstanding performances by Allen and Weaver as the wives are matched by those of the younger cast members. JB. Contains swearing. [VIDEO] DVD

Kevin Kline *Ben Hood* • Sigourney Weaver *Janey Carver* • Joan Allen *Elena Hood* • Tobey Maguire *Paul Hood* • Christina Ricci *Wendy Hood* • Henry Czerny *George Clair* • Elijah Wood *Mikey Carver* • Adam Hann-Byrd *Sandy Carver* • Katie Holmes *Libbets Casey* ■ *Dir* Ang Lee • *Scr* James Schamus, from the novel by Rick Moody

Iceman ★★★★ PG

Fantasy drama 1984 · US · Colour · 96mins

Two of Universal's most successful pictures are recalled in this fascinating sci-fi outing. With an opening that echoes *Frankenstein* and a plotline reminiscent of *ET*, Fred Schepisi's film couldn't have much better role models. While its subject matter is hardly new, the approach is refreshingly intelligent. John Lone gives a remarkable performance as the primitive man rescued from a 40,000-year incarceration in ice, registering fear, bewilderment, trust and curiosity with shifts of expression so subtle they cannot fail to convince. As the scientists monitoring his progress, Timothy Hutton and Lindsay Crouse also underplay to good effect. DP. Contains violence and swearing. [VIDEO]

Timothy Hutton *Dr Stanley Shephard* • Lindsay Crouse *Dr Diane Brady* • John Lone *Charlie* • Josef Sommer *Whitman* • David Strathairn *Dr Singe* • Philip Akin *Dr Vermeil* • Danny Glover *Loomis* • Amelia Hall *Mabel* ■ *Dir* Fred Schepisi • *Scr* Chip Proser, John Drimmer, from a story by John Drimmer

The Iceman Cometh ★★ PG

Drama 1973 · US · Colour · 171mins

Eugene O'Neill's massive play, first performed in 1946, is a gift for actors and a challenge for audiences: set in Harry Hope's bar – meeting and drinking place for drop-outs and other transients – it's one long talk-fest. If one swallows the implausibility of drunken hobos being both articulate and poetic, you will adore every minute and admire the performances of the powerhouse cast. AT DVD

Lee Marvin *Theodore "Hickey" Hickman* • Fredric March *Harry Hope* • Robert Ryan *Larry Slade* • Jeff Bridges *Don Parritt* • Bradford Dillman *Willie Oban* • Sorrell Booke *Hugo Kalmar* ■ *Dir* John Frankenheimer • *Scr* Thomas Quinn Curtiss, from the play by Eugene O'Neill

Ichi the Killer ★★★ 18

Crime thriller
2001 · Jpn/HK/S Kor · Colour · 120mins

Director Takashi Miike's adaptation of a *manga* serial is unrelenting, as sadomasochistic mobster Tadanobu Asano seeks to uncover the identity of a crazed leather-clad assassin who weeps openly as he dispatches his victims. Always frantic, occasionally surreal and often teetering on the brink of bad taste, the action revels in its depravity – although many will blench at the excessive gore and few will find much humour in the mean-spirited misogyny. But Miike's audacity, combined with the madcap and deadpan performances, render this revoltingly irresistible. DP. In Japanese and English with subtitles. DVD

Tadanobu Asano *Kakihara* • Nao Omori *Ichi* • Shinya Tsukamoto *Jijii* • Alien Sun *Karen* • Susumu Terajima *Suzuki* • Sabu [Hiroyuki Tanaka] *Kaneko* ■ *Dir* Takashi Miike • *Scr* Sakichi Sato, from the *manga* serial *Koroshiya 1* by Hideo Yamamoto

The Icicle Thief ★★★ PG

Satirical comedy
1989 · It · Colour and BW · 81mins

This astute satire on the ruin of cinema by television ends up being just a tad too clever for its own good. Co-writer/director Maurizio Nichetti gives a manic performance as the director who sees his homage to the postwar classic *Bicycle Thieves* being mixed up with some commercials during a special TV screening. While the interaction of the characters from these diametrically opposed fictional worlds amuses, it's the response of the typical Italian family that gives the film its cutting edge. DP. In Italian with English subtitles. [VIDEO]

Maurizio Nichetti *Antonio Piermattei/Maurizio Nichetti* • Caterina Sylos Labini *Maria Piermattei* • Federico Rizzo *Bruno Piermattei* • Matteo Augardi *Paolo Piermattei* • Renato Scarpa *Don Italo* ■ *Dir* Maurizio Nichetti • *Scr* Maurizio Nichetti, Mauro Monti

I'd Climb the Highest Mountain ★★★ U

Drama 1951 · US · Colour · 86mins

A clumsy and off-putting title for a charming slice of 20th Century-Fox period Americana. The slim plot in these movies seldom matters, and here a vivacious Susan Hayward narrates a series of vignettes about her marriage to a young minister (an undercast William Lundigan), all filmed in the Blue Ridge Mountains of Georgia where the original Corra Harris novel was set. The supporting cast is well chosen, with character actors Gene Lockhart, Ruth Donnelly and Alexander Knox most welcome, lending the film a spurious authenticity. TS

Susan Hayward *Mary Thompson/Narrator* • William Lundigan *William Thompson* • Rory Calhoun *Jack Stark* • Barbara Bates *Jenny Brock* • Gene Lockhart *Mr Brock* • Lynn Bari *Mrs Billywith* • Ruth Donnelly *Glory White* • Kathleen Lockhart *Mrs Brock* • Alexander Knox *Salter* ■ *Dir* Henry King • *Scr* Lamar Trotti, from the novel by Corra Harris

I'd Rather Be Rich ★★★ U

Romantic comedy
1964 · US · Colour · 95mins

To cheer up her ailing grandfather (Maurice Chevalier), Sandra Dee agrees to introduce him to her fiancé (Andy Williams). But when he's delayed, she asks Robert Goulet to impersonate him. Thoroughly likeable remake of the Charles Laughton/Deanna Durbin comedy, *It Started with Eve*. Surprisingly, given how engaging he is, this is Andy Williams's only screen performance to date. JG

Sandra Dee *Cynthia Dulaine* • Robert Goulet *Paul Benton* • Andy Williams *Warren Palmer* • Maurice Chevalier *Philip Dulaine* • Gene Raymond *Martin Wood* • Charles Ruggles *Dr Charles Crandall* • Hermione Gingold *Miss Grimshaw* ■ *Dir* Jack Smight • *Scr* Oscar Brodney, Norman Krasna, Leo Townsend

Idaho Transfer ★

Science fiction 1973 · US · Colour · 87mins

Director Peter Fonda was still in hippy *Easy Rider* message mode with this well-intentioned but ridiculous science-fiction parable. Some present day kids take part in an experiment with a time machine that "teleports" them to Idaho in 2044, where they plan to start a new civilisation. Anarchy soon rears its head as they become savages without leadership. Bleak, boring and unfocused. AJ

Kelley Bohanan *Karen* • Kevin Hearst *Ronald* • Caroline Hildebrand *Isa* • Keith Carradine *Arthur* • Dale Hopkins *Leslie* ■ *Dir* Peter Fonda • *Scr* Thomas Matthiesen

An Ideal Husband ★★★ U

Comedy 1947 · UK · Colour · 92mins

Oscar Wilde's clever writing is subtly interpreted here by Alexander Korda in this class production of one of his more famous drawing-room comedies. A stellar list of the day's witty players (Paulette Goddard, C Aubrey Smith, Michael Wilding) lends a dash of celluloid pizzazz to the stylish melting pot. The downside is the rather plodding pace that seems to handcuff the players and their words. SH [VIDEO]

Paulette Goddard *Mrs Cheveley* • Michael Wilding *Viscount Goring* • Hugh Williams *Sir Robert Chiltern* • Diana Wynyard *Lady Chiltern* • C Aubrey Smith *Earl of Caversham* • Glynis Johns *Mabel Chiltern* • Constance Collier *Lady Markby* • Christine Norden *Mrs Marchmont* • Harriette Johns *Lady Basildon* • Fred Groves *Phipps* ■ *Dir* Alexander Korda • *Scr* Lajos Biró, from the play by Oscar Wilde

An Ideal Husband ★★★★ PG

Comedy 1999 · UK/US · Colour · 93mins

While it shares the wit of Alexander Korda's 1947 version, writer/director Oliver Parker's adaptation of Oscar Wilde's 1895 play has the dual advantage of impeccable casting and, in the current climate of parliamentary sleaze, topicality. This British period piece is visually spot-on, but Parker's energetic opening out of the action occasionally seems a little excessive. What matters most, however, are the performances, with Rupert Everett a stand out. DP [VIDEO] DVD

Cate Blanchett *Lady Gertrude Chiltern* • Minnie Driver *Mabel Chiltern* • Rupert Everett *Arthur Goring* • Julianne Moore *Mrs Laura Cheveley* • Jeremy Northam *Sir Robert Chiltern* • John Wood *Lord Caversham* • Lindsay Duncan *Lady Markby* • Peter Vaughan *Phipps* • Jeroen Krabbé *Baron Arnheim* ■ *Dir* Oliver Parker • *Scr* Oliver Parker, from the play by Oscar Wilde

Identification of a Woman ★★★ 18

Drama 1982 · It · Colour · 122mins

Throughout his career Michelangelo Antonioni has been preoccupied with transient love and urban alienation, and this was clearly a retreat into familiar territory following the lukewarm reception that his video experiment, *The Oberwald Mystery*, received. Antonioni treats the artistic and romantic problems of director Tomas Milian with a knowing irony. However, as the sequences in the fog and backwaters of Venice suggest, this is also a genuine lament for the decline in meaningful communication both between people and between the film-maker and his audience. DP. In Italian with English subtitles. [VIDEO]

Tomas Milian *Niccolò* • Christine Boisson *Ida* • Daniela Silverio *Mavi* • Marcel Bozzuffi *Mario* • Lara Wendel *Girl at pool* • Veronica Lazar *Carla Farra* ■ *Dir* Michelangelo Antonioni • *Scr* Michelangelo Antonioni, Gérard Brach, Tonino Guerra, from a story by Michelangelo Antonioni

Identity ★★★ 15

Murder mystery thriller
2003 · US · Colour · 86mins

A classy cast is stranded at a remote motel in the Nevada desert on the proverbial dark and stormy night. The place is suspiciously reminiscent of another roadside hostelry (proprietor: N Bates), so it's no surprise when they find themselves being picked off one by one in increasingly bloody ways. The shocks are well staged, there are flashes of wit and the performances are sly without being too tongue-in-cheek. Unfortunately, director James Mangold can't sustain the atmosphere in the face of increasingly outlandish plot twists. AS. Contains violence and swearing. [VIDEO] DVD

John Cusack *Ed* • Ray Liotta *Rhodes* • Amanda Peet *Paris* • John Hawkes *Larry* • Rebecca DeMornay *Caroline Suzanne* • Alfred Molina *Doctor* • John C McGinley *George* • Clea DuVall *Ginny* • Jake Busey *Robert Maine* • William Lee Scott *Lou* • Leila Kenzle *Alice* • Pruitt Taylor Vince *Malcolm Rivers* • Carmen Argenziano *Defense lawyer* ■ *Dir* James Mangold • *Scr* Michael Cooney

The Idiot ★★

Drama 1951 · Jpn · BW · 165mins

Famous for his versions of Shakespeare's *Macbeth* (*Throne of Blood*, 1957) and *King Lear* (*Ran*, 1985), Kurosawa's attempt to adapt Dostoyevsky is far less successful. The story is updated and transposed to snowbound Okinawa where a prince and his emotionally unstable friend share a woman. Dostoyevsky's original novel was always difficult, but the Japanese version makes even stronger demands on its audience in terms of its weird performances and cultural context. AT. In Japanese with English subtitles.

Masayuki Mori *Kinji Kameda, the Idiot* • Toshiro Mifune *Denkichi Akama* • Setsuko Hara *Taeko Nasu* • Takashi Shimura *Ono, the father* • Yoshiko Kuga *Ayako Ono* ■ *Dir* Akira Kurosawa • *Scr* Eijiro Hisaita, Akira Kurosawa, from the novel by Feodor Mikhailovich Dostoyevsky

Idiot Box ★★★ 18

Comedy 1996 · Aus · Colour · 81mins

Writer/director David Caesar's throbbing comedy adopts the abrasive approach of *Trainspotting* to debunk the contention that the media scars the impressionable. It also launches an assault on the macho cult of superiority to which the Australian male still clings. Ben Mendelsohn and Jeremy Sims are outstanding as the Aussie answer to Beavis and Butt-head, whose indiscriminate viewing prompts them to attempt a doomed bank robbery. Often anarchically funny, the use of TV theme tunes to underscore the action is a masterstroke. DP. Contains swearing, violence. [VIDEO]

Ben Mendelsohn *Kev* • Jeremy Sims *Mick* • John Polson *Jonah* • Robyn Loau *Lani* • Graeme Blundell *Detective Eric* • Deborah Kennedy *Detective Loanne* • Stephen Rae *Colin* ■ *Dir/Scr* David Caesar

The Idiots ★★★★ 18

Comedy drama 1998 · Den · Colour · 109mins

The third film to emerge from the Dogme 95 collective (following director Lars von Trier's own *Breaking the Waves* and 1998's *Festen*), this utilises the group's complete rejection of film-making artifice to maximum effect and creates an unsettling experience. Von Trier thrusts his hand-held camera in the midst of a bunch of Danish dropouts, who test the waters of cultural acceptance by pretending to be mentally disabled in all manner of public places. Although uncomfortably comic in its portrayal of people feigning disability, the disturbing (and for a few seconds pornographic) content is balanced by mesmerising naturalistic performances and emotionally engaging situations. JC. In Danish with English subtitles. [VIDEO] DVD

Bodil Jorgensen *Karen* • Jens Albinus *Stoffer* • Anne Louise Hassing *Susanne* • Troels Lyby *Henrik* • Nikolaj Lie Kaas *Jeppe* • Louise Mieritz *Josephine* • Henrik Prip *Ped* • Luis Mesonero *Miguel* ■ *Dir/Scr* Lars von Trier • *Cinematographer* Lars von Trier

Idiot's Delight ★★★

Comedy 1939 · US · BW · 105mins

This now somewhat dated mix of romance, comedy, and antiwar flag waving, offers the treasurable sight of Clark Gable dancing on screen for the first and last time. He plays a hoofer who, with his all-girl dancing troupe, finds himself stranded in a European hotel as war threatens to break out. There, his old flame Norma Shearer turns up in the guise of a Russian countess, complete with foreign accent. Impeccably directed by Garbo's favourite, Clarence Brown. RK

Norma Shearer *Irene Fellara* • Clark Gable *Harry Van* • Edward Arnold *Achille Weber* • Charles Coburn *Dr Waldersee* • Joseph Schildkraut *Capt Kirvline* • Burgess Meredith *Quillery* ■ *Dir* Clarence Brown • *Scr* Robert E Sherwood, from his play

The Idle Class ★★★ U

Silent comedy drama
1921 · US · BW · 26mins

Charlie Chaplin has an early dig at the aristocracy and he's in fine comic form playing a dual role alongside Edna Purviance. The story revolves around various opportunities for Chaplin to play extremes of character – an arrogant, drunken, wealthy husband and an endearing, sensitive but, obviously, impoverished tramp – but he still manages to deliver observations on social inequalities with intelligence. TH DVD

Charles Chaplin *Tramp/Husband* • Edna Purviance *Wife* • Mack Swain *Father* • Henry Bergman *Tramp/Cop* • John Rand *Tramp/Guest* • Rex Storey *Robber/Guest* ■ *Dir/Scr* Charles Chaplin

Idle Hands ★★★ 18

Comedy horror 1999 · US · Colour · 88mins

The Beast with Five Fingers is given an energetic *Scream!* update in a delightful slasher flick casting a winking eye on genre clichés and cannily redefining them into first class popcorn entertainment. Lazy college kid Devon Sawa can't control his supernaturally possessed hand and ends up killing his best friends without knowing it. Director Rodman Flender, who accurately pushes the jump-scare button on numerous remarkable occasions and always hits the funny bone dead on. AJ. Contains violent scenes. DVD

Devon Sawa *Anton* • Seth Green *Mick* • Elden Henson *Pnub* • Jessica Alba *Molly* • Christopher Hart *The Hand* • Vivica A Fox *Debi* • Jack Noseworthy *Randy* • Katie Wright *Tanya* ■ *Dir* Rodman Flender • *Scr* Terri Hughes, Ron Milbauer

The Idol ★★

Drama 1966 · UK · BW · 109mins

This would-be profound psychological study centres on good-looking young American student Michael Parks who is drawn to the girlfriend of his pal John Leyton. Unfortunately, Leyton's mother (Jennifer Jones) also finds herself drawn to the young lothario. Enjoyable if you're in the right mood and John Dankworth's music is always worth listening to. JG

Jennifer Jones *Carol* • Michael Parks *Marco* • John Leyton *Timothy* • Jennifer Hilary *Sarah* • Guy Doleman *Martin Livesey* • Natasha Pyne *Rosalind* ■ *Dir* Daniel Petrie • *Scr* Millard Lampell, from a story by Ugo Liberatore

The Idolmaker ★★★★ 15

Drama 1980 · US · Colour · 113mins

This exposé of the American pop music industry of the late 1950s tears the dream to pieces mercilessly. Starring in a tale clearly inspired by the way singer Frankie Avalon was built up, only to be succeeded by Fabian, both Peter Gallagher and Paul Land are eagerly naive. They play youngsters at the mercy of Ray Sharkey, who is quite brilliant as an unscrupulous entrepreneur (based on Avalon and Fabian's real-life manager Bob Marcucci). First-time feature director Taylor Hackford gives it a sceptical shine and makes sure the facts never obscure the bitter-pill entertainment. TH. Contains swearing.

Ray Sharkey *Vincent Vacarri* • Tovah Feldshuh *Brenda Roberts* • Peter Gallagher *Guido, "Caesare"* • Paul Land *Tommy Dee* • Joe Pantoliano *Gino Pilato* • Maureen McCormick *Ellen Fields* • John Aprea *Paul Vacarri* • Olympia Dukakis *Mrs Vacarri* ■ *Dir* Taylor Hackford • *Scr* Edward Di Lorenzo

if.... ★★★★ 15

Drama 1968 · UK · BW and Colour · 111mins

Clearly indebted to Jean Vigo's *Zéro de Conduite*, this striking story of schoolboy revolt was originally offered to Nicholas Ray in the hope that he would produce a British equivalent to his classic *Rebel without a Cause*. With its surrealistic elements, it was something of a departure for *This Sporting Life* director Lindsay Anderson, but he succeeds in both capturing the atmosphere and absurdities of public school life and investing the satire with plenty of venom. Malcolm McDowell gives a blistering performance in what is a key film in British cinema history. DP. Contains violence, nudity.

Malcolm McDowell *Mick Travers* • David Wood *Johnny* • Richard Warwick *Wallace* • Christine Noonan *The Girl* • Rupert Webster *Bobby Philips* • Robert Swann *Rowntree* • Hugh Thomas *Denson* • Peter Jeffrey *Headmaster* • Mona Washbourne *Matron* • Arthur Lowe *Mr Kemp, housemaster* • Charles Sturridge *Markland* ■ *Dir* Lindsay Anderson • *Scr* David Sherwin, from the (unproduced) screenplay *Crusaders* by David Sherwin, John Howlett • *Cinematographer* Miroslav Ondricek

If a Man Answers ★★

Romantic comedy
1962 · US · Colour · 95mins

After *Gidget*, Sandra Dee went on to further stardom in the *Tammy* films for producer Ross Hunter. Here Hunter teamed her with real-life husband, teen heart-throb Bobby Darin. Dee is a Franco/American who marries Darin and soon feels neglected. Her mother's helpful advice for saving the marriage includes treating hubby like a pet dog, and then inventing an imaginary lover to make him jealous. Too cute for its own good perhaps, but on the whole harmless fun. DF

Sandra Dee *Chantal Stacey* • Bobby Darin *Eugene Wright* • Micheline Presle *Maman Stacey* • John Lund *John Stacey* • Cesar Romero *Robert Swan/Adam Wright* • Stefanie Powers *Tina* ■ *Dir* Henry Levin • *Scr* Richard Morris, from a novel by Winifred Wolfe

If I Had a Million ★★★

Comedy drama 1932 · US · BW · 88mins

Paramount put its top directors, writers and stars into this episodic film built around various people's reaction to being handed a cheque for one million dollars. Charles Laughton has the most memorable response as the humble office clerk resigning his position in style, while Charlie Ruggles and WC Fields are also handed memorable comic sequences. On the more sentimental side, Wynne Gibson scores as the prostitute who knows how to indulge herself. A sensibly short running time means the idea doesn't overstay its welcome. AE

Richard Bennett *John Glidden* • Charlie Ruggles [Charles Ruggles] *Henry Peabody* • Wynne Gibson *Violet Smith* • George Raft *Edward Jackson* • WC Fields *Rollo* • Alison Skipworth *Emily La Rue* • Gene Raymond *John Wallace* • Frances Dee *Mary Wallace* • Charles Laughton *Phineas V Lambert* • Gary Cooper *Steven Gallagher* • Jack Oakie *Mulligan* • May Robson *Mary Walker* • Blanche Frederici *Mrs Garvey* ■ *Dir* Stephen Roberts, James Cruze, Norman Z McLeod, Norman Taurog, H Bruce Humberstone, Ernst Lubitsch, William A Seiter, Lothar Mendes • *Scr* Claude Binyon, Malcolm Stuart Boylan, Harvey Gates, Joseph L Mankiewicz, Oliver HP Garrett, Grover Jones, William Slavens McNutt, Whitney Bolton, Robert Sparks, Joseph L Mankiewicz, Lawton Mackall, Robert Sparks, Joseph L Mankiewicz, from the novel *Windfall* by Robert D Andrews, Grover Jones, William Slavens McNutt

If I Were Free ★★

Romantic drama 1933 · US · BW · 65mins

London antique shop owner Irene Dunne, who has suffered an appalling marriage to Nils Asther, falls in love with lawyer Clive Brook, taking refuge in alcohol from his unhappy marriage to a wife who refuses to divorce him. This glum and plodding drama is directed by Elliott Nugent, more at home with comedy but with no room to raise a smile here. The journey to the happy ending, though slow, is mercifully short, and the stars (and supporting players) give impeccable performances. RK

Irene Dunne *Sarah Casanove* • Clive Brook *Gordon Evers* • Nils Asther *Tono Casanove* • Henry Stephenson *Hector Stribling* • Vivian Tobin *Jewel Stribling* ■ *Dir* Elliott Nugent • *Scr* Dwight Taylor, from the play *Behold, We Live!* by John Van Druten. • *Cinematographer* Edward Cronjager • *Music* Max Steiner

If I Were King ★★★★ U

Period adventure 1938 · US · BW · 100mins

A sparklingly witty and polished historical romp, this gives plum roles to Ronald Colman as the romantic poet and audacious rogue François Villon and to Basil Rathbone as the wily, cackling French monarch, Louis XI, who allows Villon to save him from losing his throne. Preston Sturges's screenplay provides dialogue that is a constant delight, and no one has declaimed poetry better on screen than Colman. Frank Lloyd's direction is admirably brisk and Ellen Drew shines as the ordinary girl who loves Villon without reservation. A rare delight. AE

Ronald Colman *François Villon* • Basil Rathbone *Louis XI* • Frances Dee *Katherine de Vaucelles* • Ellen Drew *Huguette* • CV France *Father Villon* • Henry Wilcoxon *Captain of the Watch* • Heather Thatcher *Queen* ■ *Dir* Frank Lloyd • *Scr* Preston Sturges, from the play by Justin Huntly McCarthy

If It's Tuesday, This Must Be Belgium ★★

Comedy 1969 · US · Colour · 98mins

A party of "oh, wow" Americans fly in to Heathrow for a whirlwind tour of Europe, taking in all the familiar sights. Their courier is chirpy cockney Ian McShane, whose eyes are on the female tourists rather than the cultural highspots, and the clichés are as thick as the accents. As a send-up of the package tour, it's mild-mannered and moderately amusing, with the best moments provided by a dizzying array of cameos from the likes of Joan Collins and the pop singer Donovan, who also composed the score. AT

Suzanne Pleshette *Samantha Perkins* • Ian McShane *Charlie* • Mildred Natwick *Jenny Grant* • Murray Hamilton *Fred Ferguson* • Sandy Baron *John Marino* • Michael Constantine *Jack Harmon* • Norman Fell *Harve Blakely* • Patricia Routledge *Mrs Featherstone* • Donovan • Anita Ekberg • Ben Gazzara • John Cassavetes • Robert Vaughn • Joan Collins ■ *Dir* Mel Stuart • *Scr* David Shaw, inspired by a cartoon in *The New Yorker*

If Lucy Fell ★★ 15

Romantic comedy
1996 · US · Colour · 88mins

Writer/director/star Eric Schaeffer overstretches himself somewhat with this uneven romantic comedy. It's about two friends (Schaeffer and Sarah Jessica Parker), who have made a pact to jump off the Brooklyn Bridge together if neither finds love before Parker's 30th birthday, which is now only a month away. Their attempts at finding the ideal partner include Ben Stiller and Elle Macpherson, but you can work out who their true soul mate will be well before the end of the movie. Sugary sweet and inexcusably predictable. JB. Contains some swearing and sexual references.

Sarah Jessica Parker *Lucy Ackerman* • Eric Schaeffer *Joe MacGonaughgill* • Ben Stiller *Bwick Elias* • Elle Macpherson *Jane Lindquist* • James Rebhorn *Simon Ackerman* • Robert John Burke [Robert Burke] *Handsome man* ■ *Dir* Eric Schaeffer • *Scr* Eric Schaeffer, from a story by Tony Spiridakis, Eric Schaeffer

If Only ★★★ 15

Romantic fantasy comedy
1998 · Sp/Fr/Can/UK/Lux · Colour · 90mins

In this 20-something romantic comedy Douglas Henshall stars as the "resting" actor who loses the love of his life, Lena Headey, after a stupid infidelity. Unwittingly encountering a means to turn back time, he returns to the past to try to rectify his mistake. But in spite of strong and convincing performances from Headey, Henshall and the lovely Penélope Cruz, the time travel device is a source of weakness and acts as an irritation to an otherwise entertaining movie. LH. Contains swearing. DVD

Lena Headey *Sylvia Weld* • Douglas Henshall *Victor Bukowski* • Penélope Cruz *Louise* • Gustavo Salmeron *Rafael* • Mark Strong *Dave Summers* • Charlotte Coleman *Alison Hayes* • Elizabeth McGovern *Diane* ■ *Dir* Maria Ripoll • *Scr* Rafa Russo

If These Walls Could Talk ★★★ 15

Portmanteau drama
1996 · US · Colour · 97mins

Cher and Demi Moore weigh in to the abortion debate with this surprisingly gritty compendium about the subject. The three tales in this film deal with unwanted pregnancies from the 1950s to the present. In the first story, Moore plays a woman taking desperate measures at a time when abortion was illegal; in the second, Sissy Spacek is the 1970s' mother and wife who divides her family when she contemplates abortion; and Cher takes centre stage and makes her directorial debut in the concluding story about a woman doctor facing the wrath of anti-abortionists. Although made for TV, this takes a measured, intelligent look at a controversial issue. JF DVD

Demi Moore *Claire Donnelly* • Shirley Knight *Mary Donnelly* • Catherine Keener *Becky* • Jason London *Kevin Donnelly* • CCH Pounder *Jenny Ford* • Sissy Spacek *Barbara Ryan Barrows* • Xander Berkeley *John Barrows* • Hedy Burress *Linda Barrows* • Janna Michaels *Sally Barrows* • Cher *Dr Beth Thompson* • Anne Heche *Christine Cullen* • Eileen Brennan *Tessie* • Jada Pinkett [Jada Pinkett Smith] *Patti* • Lindsay Crouse *Frances White* ■ *Dir* Nancy Savoca, Cher • *Scr* Nancy Savoca, from a story by Susan Nanus, Earl Wallace, from material by Stuart Kaplan (1952); Nancy Savoca, I Marlene King (1974); Nancy Savoca, Pamela Wallace, from a story by Pamela Wallace (1996)

If These Walls Could Talk 2 ★★ 15

Portmanteau drama
2000 · US · Colour · 92mins

Made for TV, these three intimate but uneven portraits of the lesbian experience in America cross over three different decades from the 1960s to the millennium. *1961* is the standout and features a daring performance by Vanessa Redgrave as the surviving member of a 50-year lesbian relationship. *1972* stars Chloë Sevigny in a provocative, semi-amusing piece about a group of gay college co-eds. Last and least is *2000*, produced and directed by then couple Anne Heche and Ellen DeGeneres. Even the presence of Sharon Stone can't save this wannabe comedy about two lesbians who want a baby. MC

Vanessa Redgrave *Edith* • Chloë Sevigny *Amy* • Sharon Stone *Fran* • Ellen DeGeneres *Kal* ■ *Dir* Jane Anderson, Martha Coolidge, Anne Heche • *Scr* Jane Anderson (1961), Sylvia Sichel, from her story (1972), Anne Heche (2000)

If Winter Comes ★★

Drama 1947 · US · BW · 96mins

This is an unashamedly sentimental adaptation about an outwardly respectable publisher suspected by his neighbours of driving a pregnant girl to suicide. As the only friend of waif Janet Leigh, Walter Pidgeon's husband is caught between his demanding wife (Angela Lansbury) and his passionate mistress (Deborah Kerr). For all the suffering and stiff upper lips on show, however, this is a thoroughly resistible melodrama, while Victor Saville's direction is unshaded. DP

Walter Pidgeon *Mark Sabre* • Deborah Kerr *Nona Tybar* • Angela Lansbury *Mabel Sabre* • Binnie Barnes *Natalie Bagshaw* • Janet Leigh *Effie Bright* • Dame May Whitty *Mrs Perch* ■ *Dir* Victor Saville • *Scr* Marguerite Roberts, Arthur Wimperis, from the novel by ASM Hutchinson

If You Could Only Cook ★★★★

Comedy 1935 · US · BW · 70mins

This screwball gem, directed by William A Seiter, stars Herbert Marshall and the bell-voiced Jean Arthur, posing as butler and cook in a mobster's house. The movie opened in London bearing the fraudulent legend "A Frank Capra Production" on the advertising. Bill Seiter's reaction to this ploy is unrecorded, but Capra was furious, and persuaded studio boss Harry Cohn to buy him the Broadway hit *You Can't Take It with You* in lieu of settlement. TS

Herbert Marshall *Jim Buchanan* • Jean Arthur *Joan Hawthorne* • Leo Carrillo *Mike Rossini* • Lionel Stander *Flash* • Alan Edwards *Bob Reynolds* • Frieda Inescort *Evelyn Fletcher* • Gene Morgan *Al* ■ *Dir* William A Seiter • *Scr* Howard J Green, Gertrude Purcell, from the story by F Hugh Herbert

If You Knew Susie ★★ U

Musical comedy 1948 · US · BW · 90mins

Eddie Cantor's last proper film performance (following this he only made cameo appearances) reunites him with Joan Davies, with whom he enjoyed a considerable hit in *Show Business*. Unfortunately he fails to repeat that success here, but the film does have its moments. Cantor and Davis are the retired song-and-dance act who discover, by chance, that the Government them a fortune. DF

Eddie Cantor *Sam Parker* • Joan Davis *Susie Parker* • Allyn Joslyn *Mike Garrett* • Charles Dingle *Mr Whitley* • Phil Brown *Joe Collins* ■ *Dir* Gordon M Douglas [Gordon Douglas] • *Scr* Warren Wilson, Oscar Brodney, Bud Pearson, Lester A White

Igby Goes Down ★★★ 15

Comedy drama
2002 · US/Ger · Colour · 93mins

Writer/director Burr Steers's bittersweet comedy takes the first of many strange turns in an uncomfortable opening sequence: the asphyxiation of Susan Sarandon by sons Kieran Culkin and Ryan Philippe. Dark moments such as these permeate this offbeat coming-of-age tale, with an acid-tongued Culkin often outshining his more experienced co-stars. It may take a while to tune in to the script's coldness of heart and the savage cynicism bursting from alienated teen protagonist Igby. Yet the film elicits sympathy via flashbacks to his unhappy childhood. Steer's amusing, barbed dialogue is another prime asset. JC

Kieran Culkin *Igby Slocumb* • Claire Danes *Sookie Sapperstein* • Jeff Goldblum *D H* • Amanda Peet *Rachel* • Ryan Phillippe *Oliver Slocumb* • Bill Pullman *Jason Slocumb* • Susan Sarandon *Mimi Slocumb* • Jared Harris *Russel* • Rory Culkin *Young Igby* • Cynthia Nixon *Mrs Piggee* ■ *Dir/Scr* Burr Steers

Ikinai ★★★★

Road movie 1998 · Jpn · Colour · 100mins

It soon becomes clear from watching Hiroshi Shimizu's directorial debut that he has learned a great deal from his mentor, Takeshi Kitano. Leavening the quirky comedy with poignant drama, this perfectly paced road movie concerns a group of world-weary men on a New Year bus tour that will culminate in the "accident" they hope will guarantee their dependents a healthy insurance payout. But the unscheduled arrival of a life-loving young woman prompts some to rethink their decision. Poking gentle fun at Japanese attitudes to tourism, duty and death, this is a constant delight and a masterclass in ensemble acting. DP. In Japanese with English subtitles.

Dankan *Aragaki* • Nanako Okouchi *Nakano* • Toshinori Omi *Kimura* • Ippei Soda *Ozawa* • Yoichi Nukumizu *Yashiro* • Great Gidayu *Nose* • Hiroyuki Kishi *Mochizuki* • Takashi Mitsuhashi *Komatsu* ■ *Dir* Hiroshi Shimizu • *Scr* Dankan, from the novel *Futeiki Basu no Kyaku* by Fumio Nakahara.

Ikingut ★★★

Period adventure
2000 · Ice/Nor/Den · Colour · 85mins

Set in northern Iceland several centuries ago and exploring the themes of friendship and superstition, this cautionary folk tale is ideal for younger viewers seeking something superior to the usual popcorn fodder. Unconvinced by his elders' assertion that an "ice demon" is threatening the community's livelihood, Hjalti Runar Jonsson saves an Inuit boy (Hans Tittus Nakinge) from the murderous prejudices of his neighbours. The two boys then band together to prevent the continuation of the hunt. Sigurdur Sverrir Palsson's crystal clear cinematography captures the forbidding beauty of the snowy wastes. DP. In Icelandic with English subtitles.

Hjalti Runar Jonsson *Boas* • Hans Tittus Nakinge *Ikingut* • Palmi Gestsson *Thorkell* • Magnus Ragnarsson *Father Jon* • Freydis Kirstofersdottir *Asa* ■ *Dir* Gisli Snaer Erlingsson • *Scr* Jon Steinar Ragnarsson

Ikiru ★★★★★ PG

Drama 1952 · Jpn · BW · 141mins

Many critics regard this contemporary drama as Akira Kurosawa's greatest achievement. The story would appear to have many pitfalls: a meek civil servant is told he has terminal cancer, so he gets drunk, confronts the emptiness of his life and finally makes amends by turning a derelict city area into a children's playground. This is almost the preserve of the American TV movie – crassly manipulative – but such is the delicacy of Kurosawa's direction, and the power of Takashi Shimura's performance, that you will be moved to tears. AT. In Japanese with English subtitles.

Takashi Shimura *Kanji Watanabe* • Nobuo Kaneko *Mitsuo Watanabe, Kanji's son* • Kyoko Seki *Kazue Watanabe, Mitsuo's wife* • Makoto Kobori *Kiichi Watanabe, Kanji's brother* • Kumeko Urabe *Tatsu Watanabe* ■ *Dir* Akira Kurosawa • *Scr* Akira Kurosawa, Shinobu Hashimoto, Hideo Oguni

I'll Be Home for Christmas ★★ PG

Seasonal comedy 1998 · US · Colour · 82mins

A vehicle for *Home Improvement* teen actor Jonathan Taylor Thomas, this is watchable enough if you're in a festive mood. He's the smart aleck college kid who finds himself stranded in the desert, wearing a Santa suit (don't ask), and facing a bizarre journey back to his family for the holidays. While the nightmare trip home has been done better, there are some laughs to be had. JB

Jonathan Taylor Thomas *Jake* • Jessica Biel *Allie* • Adam LaVorgna *Eddie* • Gary Cole *Jake's father* • Eve Gordon *Carolyn* • Lauren Maltby *Tracey* ■ *Dir* Arlene Sanford • *Scr* Harris Goldberg, Tom Nursall, from a story by Michael Allin

I'll Be Seeing You ★★ PG

Romantic drama 1944 · US · BW · 85mins

This over-egged schmaltz from the David O Selznick stable is professionally made, as you'd expect from a major movie of its period. Ginger Rogers is impossibly cast as the girl let out of jail for Christmas, who falls for disturbed, shell-shocked soldier Joseph Cotten. The tale is basically junk, despite the valiant efforts of the two leads. The title song is a lovely and evocative wartime ballad, and deserved better than being attached to this tosh. TS

Ginger Rogers *Mary Marshall* • Joseph Cotten *Zachary Morgan* • Shirley Temple *Barbara Marshall* • Spring Byington *Mrs Marshall* • Tom Tully *Mr Marshall* ■ *Dir* William Dieterle • *Scr* Marion Parsonnet, from the play *Double Furlough* by Charles Martin

I'll Be There ★★ 12

Romantic musical comedy
2003 · US/UK · Colour · 100mins

Young Welsh opera singer Charlotte Church tries to progress from diva to film star with this attempt at musical comedy. She shines through the story as the teenager who discovers her real father is a washed-up former pop star (Craig Ferguson). The latter finds a new direction in life when he comes across Church, a newspaper delivery girl in Cardiff, who is the result of a brief liaison he had with her mother Jemma Redgrave. Naturally he discovers that his long-lost daughter is a singing prodigy and sets about carving out a career for her. TH

Craig Ferguson *Paul Kerr* • Jemma Redgrave *Rebecca Edmonds* • Charlotte Church *Olivia* • Joss Ackland *Evil Edmonds* • Ralph Brown *Digger McQuade* • Ian McNeice *Graham* • Steve Noonan *Gordano* • Imelda Staunton *Dr Bridget* • Phyllida Law *Mrs Williams* ■ *Dir* Craig Ferguson • *Scr* Craig Ferguson, Philip McGrade

I'll Be Your Sweetheart ★★★

Musical 1945 · UK · BW · 104mins

Having cornered the market in costume dramas, Gainsborough had a tilt at period musicals with this passable imitation of glossy Fox fripperies. Unfortunately, Michael Rennie is too stolid to convince as a tunesmith stomping the streets of *fin de siècle* London to find a publisher for his ditties. More at home, however, are Garry Marsh, as an unscrupulous sheet music pirate, and Margaret Lockwood, as the blowsy music hall star who helps Rennie. Val Guest directs with brio, but the songs he's saddled with are second-rate. DP

Margaret Lockwood *Edie Storey* • Michael Rennie *Bob Fielding* • Vic Oliver *Sam Kahn* • Peter Graves (1) *Jim Knight* • Moore Marriott *George le Brunn* • Frederick Burtwell *Pacey* • Maudie Edwards *Mrs Jones* ■ *Dir* Val Guest • *Scr* Val Guest, Val Valentine

I'll Be Yours ★★ U

Comedy 1947 · US · BW · 89mins

Deanna Durbin sings four songs in the course of persuading meat-packer Adolphe Menjou to employ struggling lawyer Tom Drake, by pretending the young man is her jealous husband. The film is a remake of *The Good Fairy* (1935), which starred Margaret Sullavan. This time around, with the element of fantasy abandoned, the result is a lacklustre semi-musical, signalling the approaching end of Durbin's moneymaking film career. RK

Deanna Durbin *Louise Ginglebusher* • Tom Drake *George Prescott* • William Bendix *Wechsberg* • Adolphe Menjou *J Conrad Nelson* • Walter Catlett *Mr Buckingham* • Franklin Pangborn *Barber* ■ *Dir* William A Seiter • *Scr* Felix Jackson, from the film *The Good Fairy* by Preston Sturges, from the play *The Good Fairy* by Ferenc Molnar, from the adaptation and translation *The Good Fairy* by Jane Hinton

I'll Cry Tomorrow ★★★★

Biographical drama 1955 · US · BW · 118mins

Susan Hayward stars here in one of the two biographical roles most identified with her, the other being her Oscar-winning performance as condemned murderess Barbara Graham in *I Want to Live!* (1958). In this superior MGM biopic, Hayward plays the tormented actress and self-confessed dipsomaniac Lillian Roth – she starred with the Marx Brothers in *Animal Crackers*. Some may think that Hayward over-acts the drunk scenes, but most will find her performance to be vulnerable and honest: as an actress, she was certainly a great movie star. Helen Rose's superb costume design won an Oscar. TS

Susan Hayward *Lillian Roth* • Richard Conte *Tony Bardeman* • Eddie Albert *Burt McGuire* • Jo Van Fleet *Katie Roth* • Don Taylor *Wallie* • Ray Danton *David Tredman* • Margo *Selma* ■ *Dir* Daniel Mann • *Scr* Helen Deutsch and Jay Richard Kennedy, from the book by Lillian Roth, Mike Connolly, Gerold Frank

I'll Do Anything ★★★ 12

Comedy drama 1994 · US · Colour · 111mins

This swept-under-the-carpet folly was badly received, even though it's a reasonably well observed and often funny comedy about Hollywood, with Nick Nolte playing a struggling actor trying to juggle his career with single-parent duties. James L Brooks filmed the movie as a musical, but all the songs were cut out after preview audiences gave it the thumbs down. The end result holds up surprisingly well despite the obvious holes where the songs have been dropped. A real oddity that's well worth watching. AJ. Contains swearing and nudity.

Nick Nolte *Matt Hobbs* • Whittni Wright *Jeannie Hobbs* • Albert Brooks *Burke Adler* • Julie Kavner *Nan Mulhanney* • Joely Richardson *Cathy Breslow* • Tracey Ullman *Beth Hobbs* • Ian McKellen *John Earl McAlpine* ■ *Dir/Scr* James L Brooks

I'll Get You for This ★★

Crime drama 1950 · UK · BW · 89mins

George Raft in his mid-50s was no longer in demand for starring roles in Hollywood, so he worked for less money in Europe, beginning with this corny adaptation of a James Hadley Chase thriller set in Italy. Raft is convincing enough as an American gambler and dances as smoothly as ever with Coleen Gray's American tourist, but looks puffed out fleeing from a murder frame-up. AE

George Raft *Nick Cain* • Coleen Gray *Kay Wonderly* • Enzo Staiola *Toni* • Charles Goldner *Massine* • Walter Rilla *Mueller* • Martin Benson *Sperazza* • Peter Illing *Ceralde*

■ *Dir* Joseph M Newman • *Scr* George Callahan, William Rose, from the novel *I'll Get You for This* by James Hadley Chase

Ill Met by Moonlight ★★★★ U

Second World War drama
1956 · UK · BW · 100mins

Although Michael Powell and Emeric Pressburger's inimitable movies often had wartime settings, not many could be called simply war films. This, however, is a rare exception and a very satisfying example of the genre to boot. Loosely based on a real operation in the Second World War, the action finds Dirk Bogarde on stirring form as a British officer given the task of working with the partisans in occupied Crete to kidnap the local German commander (Marius Goring). Fine acting, rugged scenery and a trenchant score all add to the film's attractions. PF DVD

Dirk Bogarde *Major Paddy Leigh Fermor* • Marius Goring *General Karl Kreipe* • David Oxley *Captain Billy Stanley Moss* • Cyril Cusack *Sandy* • Laurence Payne *Manoli* • Wolfe Morris *George* • Michael Gough *Andoni Zoidakis* ■ *Dir* Michael Powell, Emeric Pressburger • *Scr* Michael Powell, Emeric Pressburger, from the book by W Stanley Moss • *Music* Mikis Theodorakis

I'll Never Forget What's 'Is Name ★★★

Comedy drama 1967 · UK · Colour · 98mins

After a string of Swinging Sixties satires, Michael Winner rather ran out of steam with this scathing look at the world of advertising. Substituting style for substance, the director allows the plot to ramble in places, although he redeems himself with a finale of triumphant vulgarity. Oliver Reed is moodily unconvincing as the commercials director with literary pretensions, but Orson Welles is corpulently corrupt as the man who leads him back down the path of transient achievement and empty glamour. Nearly spot-on, but frustratingly inconsequential. DP

Orson Welles *Jonathan Lute* • Oliver Reed *Andrew Quint* • Carol White *Georgina* • Harry Andrews *Gerald Slater* • Michael Hordern *Headmaster* • Wendy Craig *Louise Quint* • Marianne Faithfull *Josie* • Frank Finlay *Chaplain* • Edward Fox *Walter* ■ *Dir* Michael Winner • *Scr* Peter Draper

I'll Remember April ★★

Second World War drama
1999 · UK/US · Colour · 90mins

This cynical piece of family film-making duplicitously seeks to rewrite history by soft-pedalling American treatment of its Japanese citizens during the Second World War. Set on the California coast in early 1942, it tells how a scampish quartet of 10-year-olds hide castaway sailor Yuji Okumoto in a disused factory until they can plan his escape. Trevor Morgan is the lead, but most eyes will be on his co-star, Haley Joel Osment (*The Sixth Sense*). DP

Mark Harmon *John Cooper* • Trevor Morgan *Duke Cooper* • Pam Dawber *Barbara Cooper* • Pat Morita *Abe Tanaka* • Haley Joel Osment *Pee Wee* • Yuji Okumoto *Matsuo* ■ *Dir* Bob Clark • *Scr* Mark Sanderson

I'll See You in My Dreams ★★★ U

Musical biography 1951 · US · BW · 105mins

One of Doris Day's best vehicles, a rags-to-riches biopic based on the life of Gus Kahn, one of Tin Pan Alley's most popular songwriters. Kahn's played here by the likeable Danny Thomas, in one of his several attempts at movie stardom – he eventually found fame on American television. Day plays his wife, vying with Patrice Wymore for Thomas's charms. Michael Curtiz gives this film a warm, unpretentious style . TS

Doris Day *Grace LeBoy Kahn* • Danny Thomas *Gus Kahn* • Frank Lovejoy *Walter Donaldson* • Patrice Wymore *Gloria Knight* • James Gleason *Fred* • Mary Wickes *Anna* • Jim Backus *Sam Harris* ■ *Dir* Michael Curtiz • *Scr* Melville Shavelson, Jack Rose, from a story by Grace Kahn, Louis F Edelman

I'll Sleep When I'm Dead ★★ 15

Crime drama 2003 · UK/US · Colour · 98mins

This reunites Mike Hodges and Clive Owen and revisits territory Hodges explored so memorably with Michael Caine in *Get Carter* more than 30 years ago. As with *Carter*, the central character is a gangster out to investigate and avenge the death of a brother. Here, Owen has turned his back on crime when the suicide of his brother (Jonathan Rhys Meyers) forces him back. Despite the film's pedigree, an excellent cast and atmospheric camerawork, there are huge problems with the structure and woeful script. BP. Contains swearing, violence. DVD

Clive Owen *Will Graham* • Charlotte Rampling *Helen* • Jonathan Rhys Meyers *Davey Graham* • Jamie Foreman *Mickser* • Ken Stott *Turner* • Sylvia Syms *Mrs Bartz* • Malcolm McDowell *Boad* ■ *Dir* Mike Hodges • *Scr* Trevor Preston

I'll Take Romance ★★★

Musical 1937 · US · BW · 85mins

Billed on its original advertisements as "Her Greatest Romance!", this was the last American film and penultimate movie of the Metropolitan Opera's lyric soprano, Nashville-born Grace Moore. This is a pleasant enough trifle viewed today, one of those silly plots about a kidnapped opera star, but the story doesn't really matter, existing only as an excuse for Miss Moore to sing some arias and the particularly attractive title song. TS

Grace Moore *Elsa Terry* • Melvyn Douglas *James Guthrie* • Helen Westley *Madame Della* • Stuart Erwin *"Pancho" Brown* • Margaret Hamilton *Margot* • Walter Kingsford *William Kane* ■ *Dir* Edward H Griffith • *Scr* George Oppenheimer, Jane Murfin, from a story by Stephen Morehouse Avery

I'll Take Sweden ★★

Romantic comedy
1965 · US · Colour · 96mins

Set in the 1960s, when Sweden meant "S-E-X" to a generation of film-goers, this limp comedy has an effervescing Bob Hope sadly deflated by a weak script and inept direction. Hope is Tuesday Weld's father, desperate to break up her relationship with Frankie Avalon, so he decamps to Sweden with daughter in tow. New love blossoms, to limited comic effect, but you can listen to Frankie Avalon sing. TH

Bob Hope *Bob Holcomb* • Tuesday Weld *JoJo Holcomb* • Frankie Avalon *Kenny Klinger* • Dina Merrill *Karin Grandstedt* • Jeremy Slate *Erik Carlson* ■ *Dir* Frederick De Cordova • *Scr* Nat Perrin, Bob Fisher, Arthur Marx, from a story by Nat Perrin

Illegal ★★★

Crime thriller 1955 · US · BW · 87mins

A gripping thriller with Edward G Robinson as the DA who, after sending an innocent man to the chair, changes sides and becomes a lawyer, defending a racketeer. The story has some startling twists, and with its strong performances and tightly controlled bursts of violence, this is another low-budget miracle from Lewis Allen, who also directed that marvellous assassination thriller, *Suddenly*, in 1954. AT

Edward G Robinson *Victor Scott* • Nina Foch *Ellen Miles* • Hugh Marlowe *Ray Borden* • Jayne Mansfield *Angel O'Hara* • Albert Dekker *Frank Garland* • Howard St John *EA Smith* • Ellen Corby *Miss Hinkel* • DeForest Kelley *Clary* ■ *Dir* Lewis Allen • *Scr* WR Burnett, James R Webb, from the play *The Mouthpiece* by Frank J Collins

Illegally Yours ★ PG

Romantic comedy
1988 · US · Colour · 102mins

Rob Lowe revived his flagging career in the 1990s with tongue-in-cheek performances in *Wayne's World* and *Austin Powers: the Spy Who Shagged Me*, but he was still in a trough when he made this dreadful romantic comedy. Lowe finds himself serving on a jury that is trying his ex-girlfriend. Dire in the extreme. JB

Rob Lowe *Richard Dice* • Colleen Camp *Molly Gilbert* • Kenneth Mars *Hal B Keeler* • Harry Carey Jr *Wally Finnegan* ■ *Dir* Peter Bogdanovich • *Scr* MA Stewart, Max Dickens

Illicit ★★

Romantic drama 1931 · US · BW · 76mins

A glum and unmemorable weepie, this recounts the love affair and marriage of Barbara Stanwyck and James Rennie. Married life, however, spells the death of romance and the onset of boredom and infidelity. The future great star of melodrama does what she can with the material, which was given a controversial makeover two years later to become *Ex-Lady*, for another up-and-coming melodrama queen, Bette Davis. RK

Barbara Stanwyck *Anne Vincent* • James Rennie *Dick Ives* • Ricardo Cortez *Price Baines* • Natalie Moorhead *Margie True* • Charles Butterworth *Georgie Evans* • Joan Blondell *Helen "Duckie" Childers* ■ *Dir* Archie Mayo • *Scr* Harvey Thew, from the play by Edith Fitzgerald, Robert Riskin

illtown ★★★

Crime drama 1996 · US · Colour · 94mins

A disturbing, harrowing look at the reality of drug dealing, this excellent adaption of the novel *The Cocaine Kids* also works as a compellingly offbeat thriller. Michael Rapaport and Lili Taylor are superb as the nice couple from the suburbs who also co-ordinate a team of teenagers who supply drugs to clubbers. However, their amoral lifestyle is threatened by the arrival of former partner Adam Trese. JF

Michael Rapaport *Dante* • Lili Taylor *Micky* • Adam Trese *Gabriel* • Tony Danza *D'Avalon* • Isaac Hayes *George* • Saul Stein *Gunther* ■ *Dir* Nick Gomez • *Scr* Nick Gomez, from the book *The Cocaine Kids* by Terry Williams

Illumination ★★★★

Drama 1972 · Pol · Colour · 91mins

Krzysztof Zanussi's fourth feature chronicles the academic and sentimental education of a doctorate student, whose friends seem to live unquestioningly while he spends his time searching for answers in the physical laws of the universe. He passes such milestones as his first affair, the death of a friend, marriage, fatherhood, military service and the discovery that he has a fatal heart disease. The insertion of documentary passages and self-conscious stylisation affects the accessibility of Zanussi's contentions, but this is a bold attempt to say something serious about the human condition in a provocative and cinematic manner. DP. In Polish with English subtitles.

Stanislaw Latallo *Franciszek Retman* • Monika Denisiewicz-Olbrzychska *Agnieszka* • Malgorzata Pritulak *Malgosia* • Edward Zebrowski *Doctor* • Jan Skotnicki *Patient* ■ *Dir/Scr* Krzysztof Zanussi

Illusion of Blood ★★★ 15

Fantasy horror 1965 · Jpn · Colour · 104mins

Shiro Toyoda's adaptation of a frequently-filmed 19th-century kabuki play dispenses with any mitigating circumstances for the haunted samurai's crimes and makes him an outright villain. Left destitute by the death of his master, Tatsuya Nakadai falls under the spell of the scheming Junko Ikeuchi and brutally murders his wife to contract an advantageous marriage, but Mariko Okada's spirit refuses to rest in peace. Brimming with lust, greed, treachery, insanity and revenge, not to mention bloodshed, this is both shamelessly commercial and stylishly creative. DP. In Japanese with English subtitles. DVD

Tatsuya Nakadai *Iemon* • Mariko Okada *Oiwa* • Kanzaburo Nakamura *Naosuke* • Junko Ikeuchi *Osode* • Mayumi Ozora *Oume* • Masao Mishima *Takuetsu* • Keiko Awaji *Omaki* ■ *Dir* Shiro Toyoda • *Scr* Toshio Yasumi, from the play *Ghost Story of Yotsuya* by Nanboku Tsuruya

The Illustrated Man ★★★ 15

Science-fiction fantasy
1969 · US · Colour · 98mins

Despite Rod Steiger inventing dialogue as he goes along, and the original author, Ray Bradbury, being angered by the producers' refusal to let him in on filming, this fantasy fable from director Jack Smight works surprisingly well. Steiger is in moody mode as an Everyman whose futuristic adventures are depicted in tattoos over a large part of his body. Claire Bloom, then Steiger's real-life wife, shares the drama if not the star billing, which Steiger deserved if only for the gruelling daily make-up routine. TH. Contains violence and nudity.

Rod Steiger *Carl* • Claire Bloom *Felicia* • Robert Drivas *Willie* • Don Dubbins *Pickard* • Jason Evers *Simmons* • Tim Weldon *John* ■ *Dir* Jack Smight • *Scr* Howard B Kreitsek, from the book by Ray Bradbury

Illustrious Corpses ★★★★★

Political thriller 1976 · It · Colour · 120mins

A dazzling conspiracy thriller which begins with the assassination of a public prosecutor. There's a funeral, another assassination, then another before cop Lina Ventura – Italy's Robert Mitchum – gets on to the case, discovering that everything is rotten in the corridors of power. Inviting comparison with Hollywood movies such as *Executive Action* and *The Parallax View*, director Francesco Rosi's cynicism about Italian politics makes for a shocking and dispiriting denouement, while his preference for staging scenes amid architectural echoes of the Roman Empire implies that history teaches us nothing. AT. In Italian with English subtitles.

Lino Ventura *Inspector Rogas* • Alain Cuny *Judge Rasto* • Paolo Bonacelli *Dr Maxia* • Marcel Bozzuffi *Indolent Man* • Tina Aumont *Prostitute* • Max von Sydow *Chief Magistrate Riches* • Fernando Rey *Minister of Justice* ■ *Dir* Francesco Rosi • *Scr* Francesco Rosi, Tonino Guerra, Lino Jannuzzi, from the novel *Il Contesto* by Leonardo Sciascia

Ilya Muromets ★★★★ U

Fantasy adventure
1956 · USSR · Colour · 91mins

This glorious folktale from Mosfilm chronicles the deeds of farmer's son Boris Andreyev, who is miraculously delivered from lifelong paralysis to help the Prince of Kiev repel the Tartar hordes. Director Aleksandr Ptushko had a gift for capturing the young imagination, but he was also a master of spectacle, whose genius for devising enchanting effects is readily evident in this first Russian widescreen venture. His use of stop-motion animation is also inspired, as are his monsters – the wind demon, Nightingale the Robber, and the fire-breathing, three-headed dragon. DP. In Russian with English subtitles.

Boris Andreyev *Ilya* • Andrei Abrikosov *Prince Vladimir* • Natalya Medvedeva *Princess Apraksia* • Ninel Myshkova [Yelena Myshkova] *Vassilisa* • Alexander Shvorin *Sokolnichek* • Sergei Martinson *Traitor* ■ *Dir* Aleksandr Ptushko • *Scr* Mikhail Kochnev

I'm All Right Jack ★★★★★ U

Satirical comedy 1959 · UK · BW · 100mins

A Boulting Brothers' sparkling comedy of industrial manners, set in a factory, with Dennis Price and Richard Attenborough knee-deep in shady dealings and in need of naive Ian Carmichael to unwittingly carry them through. Terry-Thomas also appears, playing the personnel manager driven to distraction by Carmichael's incompetence. But stealing the entire show is Peter Sellers as the union official chained to the rule book, whose faith in communism is inspired by thoughts of "all them cornfields and ballet in the evenings". DP DVD

Ian Carmichael *Stanley Windrush* • Peter Sellers *Fred Kite* • Terry-Thomas *Major Hitchcock* • Richard Attenborough *Sidney de Vere Cox* • Dennis Price *Bertram Tracepurcel* • Margaret Rutherford *Aunt Dolly* • Irene Handl *Mrs Kite* • Liz Fraser *Cynthia Kite* • John Le Mesurier *Waters* ■ *Dir* John Boulting • *Scr* Frank Harvey, Alan Hackney, John Boulting, from the novel *Private Life* by Alan Hackney

I'm Dancing as Fast as I Can ★★★ 15

Drama 1982 · US · Colour · 101mins

A powerful drama, with Jill Clayburgh terrific as a pill-popping documentary film-maker who decides to go cold turkey and kick her habit. The film graphically portrays the physical and mental consequences of her gutsy decision. Unfortunately, the production is weaker than the performances – but what performances! And what a cast! In addition to Clayburgh, look out for powerhouse turns from Nicol Williamson, Daniel Stern, Dianne Wiest, Joe Pesci, John Lithgow and Geraldine Page. DA

Jill Clayburgh *Barbara Gordon* • Nicol Williamson *Derek Bauer* • Dianne Wiest *Julie Addison* • Joe Pesci *Roger* • Geraldine Page *Jean Martin* • Daniel Stern *Jim* • John Lithgow *Brunner* ■ *Dir* Jack Hofsiss • *Scr* David Rabe, from the novel by Barbara Gordon • *Cinematographer* Jan De Bont

I'm Going Home ★★★★ PG

Comedy drama
2001 · Fr/Por · Colour · 85mins

Now in his 90s, Portuguese director Manoel de Oliveira again demonstrates the grace and power of cerebral film-making with this wry treatise on the threat posed to the world's literary heritage by the increasingly commercialised and dumbed-down world of "entertainment". Michel Piccoli's acclaimed thespian contemplates quitting the boards to take on his most challenging role: surrogate parent to his orphaned grandson. The lengthy theatrical extracts from the works of Shakespeare, Eugene Ionesco and James Joyce may frustrate some of the audience, but the film's sly wit and well-versed wisdom make abundant reparation for such meanderings. DP. In French with English subtitles. DVD

Michel Piccoli *Piccoli, Michel* • Antoine Chappey *George* • Leonor Baldaque *Sylvia* • Leonor Silveira *Marie* • Catherine Deneuve *Marguerite* • John Malkovich *John Crawford, the director* ■ *Dir/Scr* Manoel de Oliveira

I'm Gonna Git You Sucka ★★★ 15

Blaxploitation spoof
1988 · US · Colour · 84mins

Sending up the blaxploitation movies of the 1970s is a hard thing to carry off since the originals now look pretty funny anyway. Keenen Ivory Wayans makes a fair attempt, as he writes, directs and stars in this daft tale about a man returning from the army to find his brother has overdosed on gold medallions. Of course, he must take revenge against Mr Big (John Vernon) who sold the chains to his sibling. The film features some of the best known blaxploitation stars, including Bernie Casey, Antonio Fargas and *Shaft* composer Isaac Hayes. JB. Contains swearing, violence, sex scenes and nudity. DVD

Keenen Ivory Wayans *Jack Spade* • Bernie Casey *John Slade* • Antonio Fargas *Flyguy* • Steve James (1) *Kung Fu Joe* • Isaac Hayes *Hammer* • Clu Gulager *Lieutenant Baker* ■ *Dir/Scr* Keenen Ivory Wayans

I'm Losing You ★★★ 18

Drama 1998 · US · Colour · 98mins

Writer/director Bruce Wagner adapts his own novel about a wealthy but misery-plagued Los Angeles family. Patriarch Frank Langella discovers he has terminal cancer but decides not to tell his family. Meanwhile son Andrew McCarthy, a "resting" actor, feuds with ex-wife Gina Gershon over their daughter. Langella's adopted daughter/niece Rosanna Arquette has just made a disturbing discovery about how her parents really died. Sharp scripting and a strong cast give this soapy film more depth than its soapy plot might suggest. LH DVD

Frank Langella *Perry Needham Krohn* • Amanda Donohoe *Mona Deware* • Rosanna Arquette *Rachel Krohn* • Buck Henry *Philip Dragom* • Elizabeth Perkins *Aubrey* • Andrew McCarthy *Bertie Krohn* • Gina Gershon *Lidia* • Ed Begley Jr *Zev* ■ *Dir* Bruce Wagner • *Scr* Bruce Wagner, from his novel

I'm No Angel ★★★★

Comedy 1933 · US · BW · 87mins

The third, best, and most profitable of Mae West's films (said to have hauled Paramount out of financial difficulties), in which the buxom, blonde vulgarian plays Tira, a carnival entertainer determined to climb the social ladder "wrong by wrong". In the course of the action, Mae gets acquitted of murder, sings several songs, does a lion-taming act, and sues Cary Grant, the object of her affections, for breach of promise. Wesley Ruggles directs the lively proceedings, which, thanks to the Legion of Decency having not yet been formed, are generously loaded with the star's *double entendres*. RK

Mae West *Tira* • Cary Grant *Jack Clayton* • Gregory Ratoff *Benny Pinkowitz* • Edward Arnold *Big Bill Barton* • Ralf Harolde *Slick Wiley* • Kent Taylor *Kirk Lawrence* • Gertrude Michael *Alicia Hatton* ■ *Dir* Wesley Ruggles • *Scr* Mae West, Harlan Thompson, from the (unproduced) screenplay *The Lady and the Lions* by Lowell Brentano

I'm Not Rappaport ★★★ 12

Comedy drama 1996 · US · Colour · 129mins

A park bench provides the setting for some stimulating verbal exchanges between Walter Matthau and Ossie Davis in this pleasing demonstration of "grey power". They play octogenarian pensioners who join forces to battle against the way relatives and institutions try to pigeonhole them because of their age. Written and directed by Herb Gardner, from his Broadway play, this is a fine example of stars lifting a drama out of the realm of cliché through a mix of pratfalls and poignancy. TH

Walter Matthau *Nat Moyer* • Ossie Davis *Midge Carter* • Amy Irving *Clara Gelber* • Craig T Nelson *The Cowboy* • Boyd Gaines *Pete Danforth* • Martha Plimpton *Laurie Campbell* • Guillermo Diaz *JC* • Elina Lowensohn *Clara Lemlich* • Ron Rifkin *Feigenbaum* ■ *Dir* Herb Gardner • *Scr* Herb Gardner, from his play • *Music* Gerry Mulligan

I'm Not Scared ★★★ 15

Thriller 2003 · It/Sp/UK · Colour · 96mins

Ten-year-old Michele (Giuseppe Cristiano) discovers a dark secret in an underground cellar at a ruined farmhouse. It is a boy, chained up and almost blinded by the light, whom Michele befriends. This starts off as an offbeat horror, contrasting the beauty of the southern Italian countryside and the innocence of its protagonist with a mood of genuine unease and foreboding. The early scenes are riveting, and the film evolves into something that is part thriller, part family drama and part rite of passage. Director Gabriele Salvatores just about holds it all together. BP. In Italian with English subtitles. Contains swearing. DVD

Aitana Sanchez-Gijon *Anna* • Dino Abbrescia *Pino* • Giorgio Careccia *Felice* • Riccardo Zinna *Pietro* • Michele Vasca *Candela* • Antonella Stefanucci *Assunta* • Diego Abatantuono *Sergio* • Giuseppe Cristiano *Michele* • Mattia Di Pierro *Filippo* ■ *Dir* Gabriele Salvatores • *Scr* Niccolò Ammaniti, Francesca Marciano, from the novel *Io Non Ho Paura* by Niccolò Ammaniti

I'm with Lucy ★★★ PG

Romantic comedy
2002 · US/Fr · Colour · 86mins

Monica Potter stars in this unusual but superficial romantic comedy. She plays a New York journalist who thinks she's with her dream partner until he abruptly dumps her. Potter then embarks on five blind dates that viewers learn early on result in a marriage. The fun is in guessing which one of the very different men Lucy actually chooses, as the impressively cast movie flits back and forth. Clichéd, but enjoyably frothy. SF DVD

Monica Potter *Lucy* • John Hannah *Doug* • Gael García Bernal *Gabriel* • Anthony LaPaglia *Bobby* • Henry Thomas *Barry* • David Boreanaz *Luke* • Julianne Nicholson *Jo* • Harold Ramis *Jack* • Julie Christie *Dori* • Craig Bierko *Peter* ■ *Dir* Jon Sherman • *Scr* Eric Pomerance

The Image ★★★★ 15

Drama 1990 · US · Colour · 89mins

An interesting and provocative look at TV journalism, with Albert Finney in fine form as the megalomaniac broadcaster who will do anything for good ratings. More hard-hitting than *Broadcast News*, and almost as impressive as *Network*, this cable-TV movie also boasts a fine cast including Kathy Baker, John Mahoney, Marsha Mason and Spalding Gray. Also watch out for a young Brad Pitt in one of his earlier (and smaller) roles. JB. Contains swearing and nudity.

Albert Finney *Jason Cromwell* • Marsha Mason *Jean Cromwell* • John Mahoney *Irv Mickelson* • Swoosie Kurtz *Joanne Winslow-Darvish* • Kathy Baker *Marcie Guilford* • Spalding Gray *Frank Goodrich* • Brad Pitt *Steve Black* ■ *Dir* Peter Werner • *Scr* Brian Rehak

The Imagemaker ★★ 15

Political comedy drama
1986 · US · Colour · 89mins

An American president's former spin doctor Michael Nouri finds himself in possession of an audio tape which could damage his former boss. Ostensibly about government corruption and media manipulation, this is a disappointing addition to the genre. Director Hal Weiner misses out on an opportunity to portray the intricacies of White House life. TH

Michael Nouri *Roger Blackwell* • Anne Twomey *Molly Grainger* • Jerry Orbach *Byron Caine* • Jessica Harper *Cynthia* • Farley Granger *Ambassador* ■ *Dir* Hal Weiner • *Scr* Dick Goldberg, Hal Weiner

Images ★★★★

Psychological drama
1972 · Ire · Colour · 103mins

Director Robert Altman is probably best known for weaving multiple plotlines round his ensemble casts in films such as *Nashville, Short Cuts* and *Prêt-à-Porter*. This disturbing portrait of the collision between fantasy and reality in the mind of schizophrenic Susannah York isn't his most accessible work but it's worth making the effort. York and husband René Auberjonois find their country weekend is disrupted by her violent hallucinations. York won the best actress award at the 1972 Cannes film festival for her stunning performance, which is complemented by Altman's innovative direction and Vilmos Zsigmond's photography. TH

Susannah York *Cathryn* • René Auberjonois *Hugh* • Marcel Bozzuffi *Rene* • Hugh Millais *Marcel* • Cathryn Harrison *Susannah* ■ *Dir* Robert Altman • *Scr* Robert Altman, from the story *In Search of Unicorns* by Susannah York

Imaginary Crimes ★★★ PG

Drama 1994 · US · Colour · 100mins

Harvey Keitel gives one of his most nuanced performances here as a single parent trying to support his family and raise two daughters in 1960s Oregon. Always on the verge of "something big" that will make his fortune, Keitel is slowly revealed to be a self-centred conman. Fairuza Balk is also a standout as his elder daughter, an aspiring writer, who relates the tale in flashback. These are great characters; shame about the soap-opera approach. AJ

Harvey Keitel *Ray Weiler* • Fairuza Balk *Sonya* • Kelly Lynch *Valery* • Vincent D'Onofrio *Mr Webster* • Diane Baker *Abigail Tate* • Chris Penn *Jarvis* • Amber Benson *Margaret* ■ *Dir* Anthony Drazan • *Scr* Kristine Johnson, Davia Nelson, from the novel by Sheila Ballantyne

Imaginary Heroes ★★ 18

Black comedy drama
2004 · US/Ger · Colour · 111mins

In this dark comedy drama, Sigourney plays the matriarch of a suburban family that falls apart when the elder son commits suicide. Weaver retreats into her hippy, pot-smoking past while hubby Jeff Daniels quits his job to spend way too much time sitting on park benches. Emile Hirsch is the neglected younger son who is left to not only cope with his own grief, but his developing sexuality as well. The movie is well made and very nicely acted, but nothing about it is particularly memorable. DA. Contains drug abuse.

Sigourney Weaver *Sandy Travis* • Emile Hirsch *Tim Travis* • Jeff Daniels *Ben Travis* • Michelle Williams *Penny Travis* • Kip Pardue *Matt Travis* • Deirdre O'Connell *Marge Dwyer* • Ryan Donowho *Kyle Dwyer* • Suzanne Santo *Steph Connors* *Dir/Scr* Dan Harris [Daniel P Harris]

Imagine: John Lennon ★★★ 15

Documentary
1988 · US · Colour and BW · 99mins

Employing a format similar to the one used in the *Anthology* series, this solidly crafted documentary traces the career of John Lennon before and after the Beatles. In addition to TV and archive footage, the film includes home-movie material from the 1970s, which is far more arresting than the familiar scenes of the Fab Four running through their hits before crowds of Beatlemaniacs. Soundbites from interviews given by Lennon from the early 1960s onwards have been deftly shaped into an informative narrative. Few new facts emerge, but it is still a must for fans. TS

John Lennon *Narrator* ■ *Dir* Andrew Solt • *Scr* Sam Egan, Andrew Solt

Imagining Argentina ★★ 15

Political drama
2003 · UK/Sp/US · Colour · 103mins

Christopher Hampton explores the theme that imagination can free people trapped in horrendous circumstances against the backdrop of Argentina's military dictatorship, but fluffs it badly. Antonio Banderas is a writer whose journalist wife Emma Thompson is arrested by the junta and becomes one of the "disappeared". Banderos discovers that he can psychically "see" the fates of these victims, though his wife's whereabouts remain a mystery. Banderas comes across like a politically-charged Doris Stokes and the denouement is bog-standard Hollywood mush. AS. Contains violence. DVD

Antonio Banderas *Carlos Rueda* • Emma Thompson *Cecilia Rueda* • Rubén Blades *Silvio Ayala* • María Canals [Maria Canals] *Esme Palomares* • Leticia Dolera *Teresa Rueda* • Kuno Becker *Gustavo Santos* • John Wood *Amos Sternberg* • Claire Bloom *Sara Sternberg* ■ *Dir* Christopher Hampton • *Scr* Christopher Hampton, from the novel by Lawrence Thornton

Imitation General ★★ U

War comedy 1958 · US · BW · 88mins

Sergeant Glenn Ford faces a dilemma when his commanding officer is killed in action. He decides to impersonate him, fearing that morale would decline if news of the general's death got around. Using his new authority, Ford issues various orders and advances the war effort by several months. It's pitched as a wartime comedy but lacks a sharp enough satirical bite to make the point that it's the uniform that counts, not the jerk inside it. AT

Glenn Ford *Master Sergeant Murphy Savage* • Red Buttons *Corporal Chan Derby* • Taina Elg *Simone* • Dean Jones *Corporal Terry Sellers* • Kent Smith *Brig Gen Charles Lane* ■ *Dir* George Marshall • *Scr* William Bowers, from a story by William Chamberlain

Imitation of Life ★★★★★

Melodrama 1934 · US · BW · 111mins

Masterfully directed by John M Stahl, this is an exemplary and irresistible contribution to the vein of melodrama known as "a woman's picture", and earned an Oscar nomination for best film. The versatile and accomplished Claudette Colbert stars as the struggling widow and mother of a small daughter who joins forces with her black maid (Louise Beavers), also the mother of a small daughter, to revitalise their lives and fortunes by opening a successful pancake business. Trouble strikes on all fronts when Beavers's light-skinned daughter grows up and sets out to pass for white with devastating consequences, and Colbert's teenage daughter falls in love with her mother's beau (Warren William). A superb weepie with a moral lesson about racism. RK

Claudette Colbert *Beatrice "Bes" Pullman* • Warren William *Stephen Archer* • Rochelle Hudson *Jessie Pullman* • Ned Sparks *Elmer Smith* • Louise Beavers *Delilah Johnson* • Fredi Washington *Peola Johnson* ■ *Dir* John M Stahl • *Scr* William Hurlbut, from a novel by Fannie Hurst

Imitation of Life ★★★★★ U

Melodrama 1959 · US · Colour · 123mins

Danish-born German émigré Douglas Sirk carved his Hollywood niche directing socially aware depictions of 1950s American bourgeois gentility. His swansong gem is a vehicle for an unconsciously self-parodying Lana Turner, starring as an ambitious actress oblivious to various domestic troubles, including her black maid's trauma at being tragically rejected by her lighter-skinned daughter on racial grounds. This was Sirk's and producer Ross Hunter's biggest box-office collaboration. A masterfully formalised and sumptuously decorated ten-hanky weepie, it also benefits from Turner's delirious, melodramatic mood swings and a gut-wrenching funeral song performed by international gospel star Mahalia Jackson. DO

Lana Turner *Lora Meredith* • John Gavin *Steve Archer* • Sandra Dee *Susie, age 16* • Dan O'Herlihy *David Edwards* • Susan Kohner *Sarah Jane, age 18* • Robert Alda *Allen Loomis* • Juanita Moore *Annie Johnson* ■ *Dir* Douglas Sirk • *Scr* Eleanore Griffin, Allan Scott, from a novel by Fannie Hurst • *Cinematographer* Russell Metty • *Costume Designer* Bill Thomas, Jean Louis

Immaculate Conception ★★★ 15

Drama 1991 · UK · Colour · 117mins

Melissa Leo is a wife desperate to get pregnant but who only succeeds after visit to a mystic Indian fertility sect. She rates it as a miracle and embraces both baby and religion to the exclusion of all else. Hubby James Wilby feels cold-shouldered as a result and jumps to the understandable conclusion that the conception may have been rather less immaculate than his wife let on. This is offbeat subject matter but it is handsomely mounted, with good performances from the two attractive leads. DA. In English and Urdu with subtitles.

James Wilby *Alister* • Melissa Leo *Hannah* • Ronny Jhutti *Kamal* • Shabana Azmi *Samira* ■ *Dir/Scr* Jamil Dehlavi

Immediate Family ★★★ 15

Drama 1989 · US · Colour · 95mins

This absorbing if schematic family drama is distinguished by an impressive cast. Glenn Close and James Woods play a wealthy childless couple who decide to adopt Mary Stuart Masterson's baby. But Masterson suddenly changes her mind, preferring to bring up the baby in near poverty with her boyfriend, Kevin Dillon. The script pushes all the expected buttons, while Jonathan Kaplan, who made *The Accused* and *Love Field*, directs. AT DVD

Glenn Close *Linda Spector* • James Woods *Michael Spector* • Mary Stuart Masterson *Lucy Moore* • Kevin Dillon *Sam* • Jane Greer *Michael's mother* ■ *Dir* Jonathan Kaplan • *Scr* Barbara Benedek

The Immigrant ★★★★★ U

Silent comedy drama
1917 · US · BW · 20mins

One of the funniest, and bleakest, of Charlie Chaplin's early silents, with the steel of his social comment supporting the humour as he enters America, penniless and only just recovering from seasickness. Images of exclusion abound – a shot of the Statue of Liberty is followed by the immigrants being herded like cattle. Chaplin's social concerns put him closer to the writings of Charles Dickens than to the work of his fellow comedians. There's underlying bitterness here, sweetened only by his love for Edna Purviance. Profoundly affecting. TH DVD

Charles Chaplin *An immigrant* • Edna Purviance *An immigrant* • Albert Austin *Russian immigrant/a diner* • Tiny Sanford *Gambler-thief* • Eric Campbell *Head waiter* ■ *Dir/Scr* Charles Chaplin

Immoral Mr Teas ★★ 18

Sex comedy 1959 · US · Colour · 62mins

The very first nudie-cutie movie from *Playboy* photographer-turned-cult director Russ Meyer is a landmark sexploitation classic. Before this coy tale of a delivery man (Meyer's army buddy Bill Teas) with the ability to see fully-clothed women naked appeared, the soft-core sex industry consisted of either pseudo-documentaries warning of the dangers of sexual activity or nudist colony romps. Meyer's silent farce, with a leering narration, changed all that and influenced an entire generation of smut peddlers. Badly dated, but a vital history lesson in the evolution of the sex film. AJ

Bill Teas *Mr Teas* • Ann Peters • Marily Wesley • Michele Roberts • Dawn Danielle • Edward J Lakso *Narrator* • Peter A DeCenzie ■ *Dir/Scr* Russ Meyer

Immoral Tales ★★★ 18

Erotic drama 1974 · Fr · Colour · 98mins

Using a visual style so sumptuous it's almost tactile, this collection is as much an exercise in artistic pastiche as erotic iconography. A different sexual taboo is tackled in each episode: the loss of virginity in *The Tide*; masturbation in *Thérèse, the Philosopher*; lesbianism in *Erzsebet Bathory*; and incest in *Lucrezia Borgia*. Yet director Walerian Borowczyk seems more interested in staging stylised tableaux than exploring either society's response to or the emotional make-up of his characters. DP. In French with English subtitles. DVD

Lise Danvers *Julie* • Fabrice Luchini *André* • Charlotte Alexandra *Thérèse* • Paloma Picasso *Erzsebet Bathory* • Pascale Christophe *Istvan* • Florence Bellamy *Lucrezia Borgia* • Lorenzo Berinizi *Casar Borgia* ■ *Dir* Walerian Borowczyk • *Scr* Walerian Borowczyk, from the story *La Marée* by André Pieyre de Mandiargues

Immortal Bachelor ★★

Comedy 1980 · It · Colour · 112mins

Often hilarious and frequently racy, this Neapolitan farce finds cleaning woman Monica Vitti on trial for murdering her philandering husband, Giancarlo Giannini. Meanwhile, jury member Claudia Cardinale fantasises about Vitti's predicament in relation to her own marriage to boring Vittorio Gassman. The quartet of fine Italian comedy stars help to move director Marcello Fondato's slight skit up a few entertainment notches. But only just... AJ. In Italian with English subtitles.

Claudia Cardinale *Gabriella Sansoni* • Vittorio Gassman *Andrea Sansoni* • Giancarlo Giannini *Gino Benacio* • Monica Vitti *Tina Candela* ■ *Dir* Marcello Fondato • *Scr* Marcello Fondato, Francesco Scardamaglia

Immortal Beloved ★★★★ 15

Biographical romantic drama
1994 · UK/US · Colour · 115mins

The director of gruesome horror flick *Candyman* might seem an unlikely biographer of Beethoven, but, in seeking to identify the "immortal beloved" addressed in the composer's will, Bernard Rose has produced a respectful and imaginative study. It's an audacious mixture of *Citizen Kane* and *Amadeus*, with some *Fantasia*-like musical sequences added. Cinema has rarely given classical music such a chance to weave its spell. Gary Oldman gives a bravura performance, although some scenes might have been played with a touch more moderato. DP. Contains nudity.

Gary Oldman *Ludwig van Beethoven* • Jeroen Krabbé *Anton Schindler* • Isabella Rossellini *Countess Anna Maria Erdody* • Johanna Ter Steege *Joanna van Beethoven* • Valeria Golino *Julia Guicciardi* • Miriam Margolyes *Frau Strelcher* ■ *Dir/Scr* Bernard Rose

The Immortal Sergeant ★★★

Second World War drama
1943 · US · BW · 90mins

Decent Second World War flagwaver, with soldier Henry Fonda and other platoon members lost in the desert wastes of Libya. It's a story of survival in which sergeant Thomas Mitchell has the homing instincts of a pigeon, if not the stamina of a camel, enabling Fonda to become a hero by leading his people to safety. Meanwhile, assorted airborne Germans are on hand to provide bursts of action, and Maureen O'Hara appears in flashback so as not to make this an all-boy affair. AT

Henry Fonda *Colin* • Maureen O'Hara *Valentine* • Thomas Mitchell *Sergeant Kelly* • Allyn Joslyn *Cassity* • Reginald Gardiner *Benedict* • Melville Cooper *Pilcher* • Bramwell Fletcher *Symes* ■ *Dir* John M Stahl • *Scr* Lamar Trotti, from the novel by John Brophy • *Cinematographer* Arthur Miller

The Immortal Story ★★★ 15

Drama 1968 · Fr · Colour · 54mins

This weird little Orson Welles movie was made for French TV. The parable-like story is by Karen Blixen (author of *Out of Africa*) and concerns a Macao trader who hires a young sailor to sleep with his "wife" – who isn't his wife at all, but a whore. Welles revels in the role of the trader. Jeanne Moreau is as good as one expects but Norman Eshley as the sailor has an impossible task – to be pretty and plausible at the same time. It's easy to be cynical about it, but it is atmospheric. AT. A French language film.

Orson Welles *Mr Clay* • Jeanne Moreau *Virginie Ducrot* • Roger Coggio *Elishama Levinsky–the Clerk* • Norman Eshley *Paul–the Sailor* • Fernando Rey *Merchant in Street* ■ *Dir* Orson Welles • *Scr* Orson Welles, Louise de Vilmorin, from the story by Isak Dinesen [Karen Blixen]

Impact ★★★

Crime melodrama 1949 · US · BW · 111mins

This is tough stuff, as Brian Donlevy's wife and lover plan on getting rid of him, but it's not quite as easy as it seems. There's a terrific supporting cast, including Charles Coburn, Anna May Wong and Mae Marsh, but you'll find yourself rooting for Donlevy, so often cast as the heavy earlier in his career. It's a clever movie that doesn't quite make it as an A-feature, but still has a good deal of class and style. TS

Brian Donlevy *Walter Williams* • Ella Raines *Marsha Peters* • Charles Coburn *Lieutenant Quincy* • Helen Walker *Irene Williams* • Anna May Wong *Su Lin* • Mae Marsh *Mrs Peters* ■ *Dir* Arthur Lubin • *Scr* Dorothy Reid, Jay Dratler

Impact ★★ U

Crime drama 1963 · UK · BW · 64mins

Co-written by star Conrad Phillips and director Peter Maxwell, this was produced in a matter of days on a shoestring budget and contains no surprises as ace reporter Phillips is set up as a train robber by vengeful club boss George Pastell. Maxwell just about keeps what action there is ticking over, but he is fighting a losing battle with a cast that is substandard, even for a B-movie. DP

Conrad Phillips *Jack Moir* • George Pastell *The Duke* • Ballard Berkeley *Bill Mackenzie* • Linda Marlowe *Diana* ■ *Dir* Peter Maxwell • *Scr* Peter Maxwell, Conrad Phillips

Impasse ★★

Adventure 1969 · US · Colour · 99mins

Filmed in the Philippines, Richard Benedict's film is a stale, derivative action tale about a crock of gold buried by four GIs during the Second World War. Burt Reynolds plays a shady trader based in Manila who persuades the soldiers to regroup and reclaim it. The result is a sort of *Treasure of the Sierra Madre*, minus the style and the great acting. AT

Burt Reynolds *Pat Morrison* • Anne Francis *Bobby Jones* • Lyle Bettger *Hansen* • Rodolfo Acosta *Draco* • Jeff Corey *Wombat* • Clarke Gordon *Trev Jones* • Miko Mayama *Mariko* ■ *Dir* Richard Benedict • *Scr* John C Higgins

The Impatient Maiden ★★★

Romantic drama 1932 · US · BW · 72mins

James Whale directed just 20 features and, justifiably, his reputation stands on four landmark horror movies. This early work blends comedy, romance and medical drama. The "maiden" of the title is 19-year-old Mae Clarke (who took over from Clara Bow), and is already suspicious of marriage – until she falls in love with doctor Lew Ayres. Whale's fluent camera, intelligent use of actors and quirky mix of pathos and humour make for a characteristically intriguing film. BB

Lew Ayres *Myron Brown* • Mae Clarke *Ruth Robbins* • Una Merkel *Betty Merrick* • Andy Devine *Clarence Howe* • John Halliday *Albert Hartman* ■ *Dir* James Whale • *Scr* Richard Schayer, Winifred Dunn, from the novel by Donald Henderson Clarke

Imperative ★★★

Drama
1982 · W Ger/Fr · BW and Colour · 96mins

Coming between his key Solidarity era, *The Contract* (1980), and the Golden Lion-winning *A Year of the Quiet Sun* (1984), this is one of Krzysztof Zanussi's least-known films. It follows the trials of disillusioned academic Robert Powell, whose search for elusive truths in religion makes for absorbing if rather bleak viewing. DP

Robert Powell *Augustin* • Brigitte Fossey *Yvonne* • Sigfrit Steiner *Professor* • Matthias Habich *Theologist* • Leslie Caron *Mother* ■ *Dir/Scr* Krzysztof Zanussi

The Imperfect Lady ★

Period drama 1947 · US · BW · 97mins

This lavishly mounted damp squib of a drama miscasts the essentially demure Teresa Wright as a music hall dancer of Victorian London. Ray Milland's aristocratic politician eventually persuades her to marry him but this coincides with a nasty scandal when Wright is the only alibi for accused murderer Anthony Quinn. Apparently Paulette Goddard was considered for the lead role – which might have made the picture worth watching. AE

Ray Milland *Clive Loring* • Teresa Wright *Millicent Hopkins* • Cedric Hardwicke *Lord Belmont* • Virginia Field *Rose Bridges* • Anthony Quinn *Jose Martinez* • Reginald Owen *Mr Hopkins* ■ *Dir* Lewis Allen • *Scr* Karl Tunberg, from a story by Ladislas Fodor

Imperial Venus ★★★

Historical drama
1963 · It/Fr · Colour · 140mins

This sweeping costume drama was clearly a jobbing assignment for Jean Delannoy, whose prospects had suffered greatly from comparisons with the young Turks of the New Wave. There's undeniable splendour in this account of the life and loves of Napoleon's sister, Paolina, but the absence of passion renders it a stilted and stuffy affair. Like many 1960s movies from the Continent, it was made in English alongside the foreign-language version. DP

Gina Lollobrigida *Paolina* • Stephen Boyd *Jules de Canouville* • Gabriele Ferzetti *Freron* • Raymond Pellegrin *Napoleon* • Micheline Presle *Josephine* • Massimo Girotti *Leclerc* • Giulio Bosetti *Camillo Borghese* ■ *Dir* Jean Delannoy • *Scr* Jean Delannoy, Jean Aurenche, Rodolphe M Arlaud, Leonardo Benvenuti [Leo Benvenuti], Piero De Bernardi, John Michael Hayes

The Impersonator ★★

Crime mystery 1962 · UK · BW · 63mins

Signing an American star for a British movie has always been considered a surefire way of attracting international attention. Back in the 1960s our cash-strapped companies had to make do with the likes of minor character actor John Crawford. To give him his due, he's the best thing in this unsettling study of insularity, playing an airman stationed near a sleepy country community who becomes the prime suspect when a number of women die in suspicious circumstances. DP

John Crawford *Jimmy Bradford* • Jane Griffiths *Ann Loring* • Patricia Burke *Mrs Lloyd* • John Salew *Harry Walker* • John Dare *Tommy Lloyd* ■ *Dir* Alfred Shaughnessy • *Scr* Alfred Shaughnessy, Kenneth Cavender

The Importance of Being Earnest ★★★★ U

Period comedy drama
1952 · UK · Colour · 91mins

Shot in sumptuous Technicolor, this respectful adaptation of Oscar Wilde's sparkling comedy of errors thankfully rarely breaks free of its theatrical origins. Anthony Asquith keeps Wilde's polished barbs and *bons mots* firmly to the fore and the film is an invaluable record of an expert cast at work. Michael Redgrave and Michael Denison are clipped and composed as the gentlemen of leisure, whose innocent deceptions imperil their romantic aspirations towards the coquettish Joan Greenwood and Dorothy Tutin. Upstaging them all is Dame Edith Evans as Lady Bracknell, whose quavering "A handbag" is one of British cinema's great moments. DP [video] DVD

Michael Redgrave *Jack Worthing* • Michael Denison *Algernon Moncrieff* • Edith Evans *Lady Bracknell* • Dorothy Tutin *Cecily Cardew* • Joan Greenwood *Gwendolen Fairfax* • Margaret Rutherford *Miss Prism* ■ *Dir* Anthony Asquith • *Scr* Anthony Asquith, from the play by Oscar Wilde • *Costume Designer* Beatrice Dawson

The Importance of Being Earnest ★★

Comedy drama 1992 · US · Colour · 123mins

This modern take on one of Oscar Wilde's most celebrated plays is set in London, but the period is contemporary and the African-American cast make no attempt to get their tongues round British accents. The film suffers from the usual problems of trying to "open up" a stage play, and the low-budget tape-to-film look doesn't help. This is an experiment that doesn't really work. JF

Brock Peters *Doctor Chausible* • CCH Pounder *Miss Prism* • Obba Babatunde *Lane* • Wren T Brown *Algernon* • Chris Calloway *Gwendolyn* • Lanei Chapman *Cecily* ■ *Dir* Kurt Baker • *Scr* Peter Andrews, Kurt Baker, from the play by Oscar Wilde

The Importance of Being Earnest ★★★ U

Period comedy drama
2002 · UK/US · Colour · 89mins

This adaptation of Oscar Wilde's famously witty play benefits from superb performances from Rupert Everett, Judi Dench and Colin Firth as Jack (who pretends to have a younger brother named Earnest, so he can escape his stuffy country home for wilder times in London). Beautifully filmed by Oliver Parker, this only falls down in the casting of Reese Witherspoon as Jack's young ward Cecily (sounding and looking too modern) and Frances O'Connor (again, looking far too contemporary) as Jack's intended Gwendolen. JB [video] DVD

Rupert Everett *Algernon "Algy" Moncrieff* • Colin Firth *Jack Worthing/"Earnest"* • Frances O'Connor *Gwendolen Fairfax* • Reese Witherspoon *Cecily Cardew* • Judi Dench *Lady Bracknell* • Tom Wilkinson *Dr Chasuble* • Anna Massey *Miss Prism* • Edward Fox *Lane* ■ *Dir* Oliver Parker • *Scr* Oliver Parker, from the play by Oscar Wilde

The Important Man ★★★★

Drama 1961 · Mex · BW · 100mins

Mexican director Ismael Rodriguez teamed with Japanese superstar Toshiro Mifune for this adaptation of the novel by Rogelio Barriga Rivas. Mifune excels as the coarse peasant, who, in spite of abusing his family and consorting with other women, has set his heart on being elected "chief for a day" in a forthcoming religious festival. Strikingly photographed by camera ace Gabriel Figueroa, this Oscar-nominated neorealist drama refuses either to sentimentalise the harsh rural conditions or excuse the boorish behaviour of its antiheroic protagonist. DP. A Spanish language film.

Toshiro Mifune *Animas Trujano* • Antonio Aguilar *Tadeo* • Columba Dominguez *Juana* • Flor Silvestre *Catalina* ■ *Dir* Ismael Rodriguez • *Scr* Ismael Rodriguez, Vincente Orona Brillas, Ricardo Garibay, from the novel *La Mayordomia* by Rogelio Barriga Rivas

The Impostor ★★★ U

Second World War drama
1944 · US · BW · 57mins

The Nazi invasion of France saves condemned murderer Jean Gabin from the guillotine when an air raid hits. He impersonates a French soldier and transforms himself into a resistance hero in North Africa, bravely launching an attack on an Italian desert base. Made by French wartime exiles in Hollywood, this is a relatively rare French flagwaver, with a charismatic performance by Gabin. AT

Jean Gabin *Clement* • Richard Whorf *Lt Varenne* • Allyn Joslyn *Bouteau* • Ellen Drew *Yvonne* • Peter Van Eyck *Hafner* • Ralph Morgan *Col De Bolvan* ■ *Dir* Julien Duvivier • *Scr* Julien Duvivier, Marc Connelly, Lynn Starling, Stephen Longstreet • *Music* Dimitri Tiomkin [Dmitri Tiomkin]

Impostor ★ 15

Science-fiction thriller
2001 · US · Colour · 91mins

It's 2079, and is weapons expert Gary Sinise really a synthetic robot programmed by an alien enemy to assassinate a leading politician? Or is he the same human being he's convinced he's always been? Bland Sinise races against time to prove his humanity. This B-movie staggers towards an irritating ending while making numerous pit stops at "Cliché Central" along the way. AJ [video] DVD

Gary Sinise *Spence Olham* • Madeleine Stowe *Maya Olham* • Vincent D'Onofrio *Major Hathaway* • Tony Shalhoub *Nelson Gittes* • Tim Guinee *Dr Carone* • Elizabeth Peña *Midwife* • Gary Dourdan *Captain Burke* • Lindsay Crouse *Chancellor* ■ *Dir* Gary Fleder • *Scr* Caroline Case, Ehren Kruger, David N Twohy [David Twohy], from the short story by Philip K Dick, adapted by Scott Rosenberg

The Impostors ★★★ 15

Period comedy 1998 · US · Colour · 96mins

Actor Stanley Tucci followed his critically acclaimed directorial debut, *Big Night*, with this farcical comedy, in which he and the under-rated Oliver Platt star as two out-of-work actors during the Depression who stow away on a luxury liner populated with eccentric passengers. A spoof on classics like *Grand Hotel*, the film features some rather old-fashioned slapstick, which often works well thanks to the timing skills of the eclectic cast. Enjoyable but uneven. JB. Contains some swearing. [video]

Oliver Platt *Maurice* • Stanley Tucci *Arthur* • Walker Jones *Maître d'* • Jessica Walling *Attractive woman* • David Lipman *Baker* • E Katherine Kerr *Gertrude* • George Guidall *Claudius* • William Hill *Bernardo* • Alfred Molina *Jeremy Burtom* • Lili Taylor *Lily* • Steve Buscemi *Happy Franks* • Isabella Rossellini *Queen (veiled woman)* • Billy Connolly *Sparks* • Hope Davis *Emily* • Campbell Scott *Meistrich* • Woody Allen ■ *Dir/Scr* Stanley Tucci

Impromptu ★★★ 15

Biographical romantic comedy
1991 · UK · Colour · 102mins

Hugh Grant is Chopin, Julian Sands is Liszt, but Judy Davis is superb as notorious female novelist George Sand, who flits from love affair to duel with a wondrous disregard for the conventions of 19th-century society. There's some splendid casting here, not least Ralph Brown of *Withnail and I* fame as Eugène Delacroix and Emma Thompson as the Duchess d'Antan. It's not exactly history, but still hugely enjoyable. DP [video]

Judy Davis *George Sand* • Hugh Grant *Frederic Chopin* • Mandy Patinkin *Alfred DeMusset* • Bernadette Peters *Marie d'Agoult* • Julian Sands *Franz Liszt* • Ralph Brown *Eugene Delacroix* • Georges Corraface *Felicien Mallefille* • Anton Rodgers *Duke d'Antan* • Emma Thompson *Duchess d'Antan* • Anna Massey *George Sand's mother* ■ *Dir* James Lapine • *Scr* Sarah Kernochan

Improper Channels ★★

Comedy 1981 · Can · Colour · 91mins

A comedy about child abuse? Rest assured, this Canadian screwball isn't as sinister as it sounds: five-year-old Sarah Stevens's injuries are merely the result of a scrape in her father's camper. Officious social worker Monica Parker thinks otherwise, however, and dad Alan Arkin has to reunite with his estranged wife, Mariette Hartley, to retrieve the tot from care. Director Eric Till accentuates the ridiculousness of the situation. Unfortunately, the screenplay's attempts to put a message across not only feel preachy, but also slow down the farce. DP

Alan Arkin *Jeffrey Martley* • Mariette Hartley *Diana Martley* • Monica Parker *Gloria Washburn* • Sarah Stevens *Nancy Martley* • Danny Higham *Jack* • Richard Farrell *Fraser* ■ *Dir* Eric Till • *Scr* Ian Sutherland, Adam Arkin, Morrie Ruvinsky, from a story by Morrie Ruvinsky

Improper Conduct ★★ 18

Erotic thriller 1994 · US · Colour · 91mins

Steven Bauer stars in this straight-to-video thriller, which, unconvincingly, also tries to provide a serious indictment of sexual harassment. Lee Ann Beaman plays a woman who sets out to avenge the hounding of her sister (Tahnee Welch, Raquel's daughter) who was driven out of her job after turning down the advances of the boss's son-in-law; Bauer is the lawyer friend who reluctantly helps her. JF. Contains violence, swearing and sex scenes. [video]

Steven Bauer *Sam* • Tahnee Welch *Ashley* • John Laughlin *Michael* • Nia Peeples *Bernadette* • Lee Anne Beaman *Kay* • Stuart Whitman *Mr Frost* ■ *Dir* Jag Mundhra • *Scr* Carl Austin, from a story by Jag Mundhra

An Impudent Girl ★★★★ 15

Drama 1985 · Fr · Colour · 92mins

This is a typically insightful study of burgeoning youth from director Claude

Miller. In only her third feature, Charlotte Gainsbourg is both rebellious and vulnerable as the teenager seeking an escape from her monotonous home life by hooking up with her idol, teenage pianist Clothilde Baudon. Their misadventures are more painful and revelatory than those featured in most rites-of-passage pictures, largely because the doubts and dreams the girls harbour are so normal. However, the film derives much of its honesty from the exceptional performance of Gainsbourg, whose expressions and emotions always ring true. DP. In French with English subtitles.

Charlotte Gainsbourg *Charlotte Castang* • Bernadette Lafont *Leone* • Jean-Claude Brialy *Sam* • Raoul Billerey *Antoine* • Clothilde Baudon *Clara Bauman* ■ *Dir* Claude Miller • *Scr* Claude Miller, Luc Béraud, Bernard Stora, Annie Miller

Impulse ★★

Crime thriller 1955 · UK · BW · 80mins

This is a routine British second-feature, although Arthur Kennedy is a cut above the average imported American lead. Kennedy has a fling with nightclub singer Constance Smith, who involves him in a crime. Screenwriter "Jonathan Roach" is actually Cy Endfield, taking refuge in the UK from the McCarthy witch-hunts, while Charles de Lautour took credit for Endfield as director. DM

Arthur Kennedy *Alan Curtis* • Constance Smith *Lila* • Joy Shelton *Elizabeth Curtis* • Jack Allen *Freddie* • James Carney *Jack Forrester* • Cyril Chamberlain *Gray* ■ *Dir* Charles de Lautour, Cy Endfield • *Scr* Lawrence Huntington, Jonathan Roach [Cy Endfield], John Gilling, from a story by Carl Nystrom, from a story by Robert S Baker

Impulse ★

Crime thriller 1975 · US · Colour · 89mins

Film historians seeking the quintessential ham performance by William Shatner would be advised to choose this mid-1970s effort. Ruth Roman's little girl can't convince her that her new boyfriend (guess who) is really a psychotic murderer. Shatner uses his famous stop/start enunciation to ludicrous extremes. His performance alone makes this a must for bad movie fans. KB

William Shatner *Matt Stone* • Ruth Roman *Julia Marstow* • Jennifer Bishop (1) *Ann Moy* • Kim Nicholas *Tina Moy* • Harold Sakata *Karate Pete* • James Dobson *Clarence* ■ *Dir* William Grefé • *Scr* Tony Crechales

Impulse ★★★ 18

Thriller 1984 · US · Colour · 86mins

This sharp, under-rated slice of horror manages to put a sly spin on a familiar scenario. In a typical small town, the residents are starting to behave a little oddly; there's nothing particularly outlandish in their actions, it is just that they seem to be giving in to their baser instincts. Tim Matheson is the outsider who begins to think that something is up, and he is well supported by relative newcomers Meg Tilly and Bill Paxton, plus scene-stealing veteran Hume Cronyn. JF

Tim Matheson *Stuart* • Meg Tilly *Jennifer* • Hume Cronyn *Dr Carr* • John Karlen *Bob Russell* • Bill Paxton *Eddie* • Amy Stryker *Margo* • Claude Earl Jones *Sheriff* • Robert Wightman *Howard* ■ *Dir* Graham Baker • *Scr* Bart Davis, Don Carlos Dunaway

Impulse ★★★ 18

Psychological thriller
1990 · US · Colour · 104mins

Actor-turned-director Sondra Locke is probably still best known for her acrimonious split from then-partner Clint Eastwood in the late 1980s. She brings a deft hand to this rather gloomy look at LA cops and hookers, and Theresa Russell gives one of her best film performances as a hard-boiled undercover cop. There is a lot that is very ordinary about this movie, but Russell's presence ensures that it succeeds. SH. Contains swearing, sex scenes, violence, nudity.

Theresa Russell *Lottie Mason* • Jeff Fahey *Stan Harris* • George Dzundza *Joe Morgan* • Alan Rosenberg *Charley Katz* • Nicholas Mele *Rossi* • Eli Danker *Dimarjian* ■ *Dir* Sondra Locke • *Scr* John De Marco, Leigh Chapman, from a story by John De Marco

In a Lonely Place ★★★★★ PG

Classic film noir 1950 · US · BW · 89mins

This dark, gripping *film noir* is one of the best dramas ever made about the movie industry. Humphrey Bogart stars as the jaded Hollywood screenwriter who becomes the prime suspect in the murder of hat-check girl Martha Stewart. In one of the roles of his career, Bogart is both sympathetic and sinister at the same time, a complex character teetering on the brink of destruction. His co-star and soulmate here is Gloria Grahame, then director Nicholas Ray's wife, though the part was specifically written for Bogart's wife, Lauren Bacall, whom Warner Bros refused to loan out. AT DVD

Humphrey Bogart *Dixon Steele* • Gloria Grahame *Laurel Gray* • Frank Lovejoy *Brub Nicolai* • Carl Benton Reid *Captain Lochner* • Art Smith *Mel Lippman* • Jeff Donnell *Sylvia Nicolai* • Martha Stewart *Mildred Atkinson* • Robert Warwick *Charlie Waterman* • Morris Ankrum *Lloyd Barnes* ■ *Dir* Nicholas Ray • *Scr* Andrew Solt, from a story by Edmund H North, from the novel by Dorothy B Hughes • *Cinematographer* Burnett Guffey

In a Shallow Grave ★★ 15

Romantic drama 1988 · US · Colour · 87mins

A worthy, if sometimes melodramatic tale from the respected American Playhouse team. Michael Biehn plays a bitter war hero who becomes fascinated with a young man (Patrick Dempsey) working for him. A study in class and sexual tension, it's beautifully acted, if directed at a slack pace. JF

Michael Biehn *Garnet Montrose* • Maureen Mueller *Georgina Rance* • Michael Beach *Quintas Pearch* • Patrick Dempsey *Potter Daventry* • Thomas Boyd Mason *Edgar Doust* ■ *Dir* Kenneth Bowser • *Scr* Kenneth Bowser, from the novel by James Purdy

In a Year of 13 Moons ★★★★ 18

Drama 1978 · W Ger · Colour · 119mins

Inspired by the suicide of his lover, Armin Meier, this was one of Rainer Werner Fassbinder's most personal statements: as well as writer/director, he acted as cinematographer, designer and editor. The film also ranks among his most uncompromising condemnations of conformity, with transsexual Volker Spengler's desire to find emotional and social acceptance a root cause of his/her misery. Fassbinder refuses to let us identify with the characters and employs harshly lit and cluttered visuals to distract from the dialogue. Jarring, pessimistic and played with terrifying candour, this is a unique and disconcerting experience. DP. In German with English subtitles.

Volker Spengler *Elvira Weishaupt* • Ingrid Caven *Red Zora* • Gottfried John *Anton Saitz* • Elisabeth Trissenaar *Irene* • Eva Mattes *Marie-Ann* ■ *Dir/Scr* Rainer Werner Fassbinder

In America ★★★★ 15

Drama 2003 · US/Ire/UK · Colour · 101mins

Co-written by director Jim Sheridan, along with his two daughters Naomi and Kirsten, the intimate story is seen through the eyes of an 11-year-old girl, living as an illegal immigrant in a run-down New York tenement building with her younger sister and Irish parents (Samantha Morton and Paddy Considine). Though the youngsters view the US as a place of wonder, past tragedy casts a dark shadow over the family, giving the picture a profound emotional resonance. Sheridan demonstrates remarkable versatility and sensitivity, shooting on video to create an ethereal, dream-like ambience. The performances are entrancing, with real-life sisters Sarah and Emma Bolger a revelation as the screen siblings. SF DVD

Samantha Morton *Sarah* • Paddy Considine *Johnny* • Sarah Bolger *Christy* • Emma Bolger *Ariel* • Djimon Hounsou *Mateo* ■ *Dir* Jim Sheridan • *Scr* Jim Sheridan, Naomi Sheridan, Kirsten Sheridan

In & Out ★★★★ 12

Comedy 1997 · US · Colour · 86mins

Kevin Kline stars as the soon-to-be-married small town teacher who is outed by an ex-pupil-turned-Hollywood-star (Matt Dillon) during his televised Oscar acceptance speech. Inspired by Tom Hanks' *Philadelphia* acceptance speech (in which he thanked his gay professor), this has some very funny moments as Kline, his wedding-obsessed mother (Debbie Reynolds) and surprised fiancée (Joan Cusack) struggle with the fact he may be gay, and there's a nice supporting turn from Tom Selleck as the openly gay reporter who comes to town to cover the story. Thanks to Kline's sharp but moving performance, what could have been a stereotypical or even camp role is actually a fleshed out and sensitive one. JB. Contains swearing. DVD

Kevin Kline *Howard Brackett* • Joan Cusack *Emily Montgomery* • Tom Selleck *Peter Malloy* • Matt Dillon *Cameron Drake* • Debbie Reynolds *Berniece Brackett* • Glenn Close • Whoopi Goldberg • Jay Leno ■ *Dir* Frank Oz • *Scr* Paul Rudnick

In Bed with Madonna ★★★ 15

Music documentary
1991 · US · BW and Colour · 113mins

Shot during the 1990 "Blond Ambition" tour and released as *Truth or Dare* in the States, this is hardly an intimate portrait of Madonna as she's so aware of the presence of the camera that it's performance all the way. The on-stage concert sequences, for all their colour and polish, are positively dull beside the monochrome backstage scenes, in which no one is spared the Ciccone wrath (even God gets His ear bent before every show). The shredding of Kevin Costner is a treat, but on the downside there's the rudeness to her childhood friend. Perhaps most revealing are the scenes with then boyfriend Warren Beatty. DP. Contains swearing. DVD

Dir Alek Keshishian

In Caliente ★★

Romantic musical 1935 · US · BW · 84mins

"The lady in red, the fellas adore the lady in red..." and that's about all there is to adore in this lacklustre Warner Bros romantic vehicle for star Dolores Del Rio. Despite routines from ace choreographer Busby Berkeley, this musical never really gets off Warner's backlot, and leading man Pat O'Brien lacks the requisite lightness for this type of fluff. TS

Dolores Del Rio *Rita Gomez* • Pat O'Brien *Larry MacArthur* • Leo Carrillo *Jose Gomez* • Edward Everett Horton *Harold Brandon* • Glenda Farrell *Clara* • Phil Regan *Pat Casey* ■ *Dir* Lloyd Bacon • *Scr* Jerry Wald, Julius Epstein [Julius J Epstein], Ralph Block, Warren Duff, from the story *Caliente* by Ralph Block, Warren Duff

In Casablanca Angels Don't Fly ★★★★ PG

Drama 2003 · Mor/It · Colour · 97mins

One-time producer Mohamed Asli makes an assured directorial debut with this moving treatise on the age-old clash between town and country mores. Home is very much where the heart is for waiter Rachid El Hazmir and cook Abdelaziz Essghyr, as each man dreams of what he has left behind in an isolated village in the Atlas Mountains. But for co-worker Abdessamed Miftah El Kheir, the city offers new riches, symbolised by his passion for a pair of designer shoes. Leavening his neorealist approach with the occasional technical flourish, Asli tells each story with a fond care that is even more apparent as each man sees his cherished wish soured by cruel caprice. DP. In Arabic and Berber with English subtitles.

Abdessamed Miftah El Kheir *Ismail* • Abderrazak El Badaoui *Restaurant owner* • Rachid El Hazmir *Said* • Leila El Ahyani *Aicha* • Abdelaziz Essghyr *Ottman* ■ *Dir* Mohamed Asli • *Scr* Siham Douguena

In Celebration ★★★

Drama 1974 · UK · Colour · 131mins

Director Lindsay Anderson reunites the cast of London's Royal Court production for this screen version of David Storey's play. Three sons (Alan Bates, James Bolam, Brian Cox) return to their northern roots for the 40th wedding anniversary celebrations of parents Bill Owen and Constance Chapman. While all three have exceeded the career achievements of their miner father, their homecoming brings the usual saga of angst, buried resentments and skeletons in the closet. While its stage origins do hinder the pace of the action, this is wryly observant and well acted. TH

Alan Bates *Andrew Shaw* • James Bolam *Colin Shaw* • Brian Cox *Steven Shaw* • Constance Chapman *Mrs Shaw* • Gabrielle Daye *Mrs Burnett* • Bill Owen *Mr Shaw* ■ *Dir* Lindsay Anderson • *Scr* David Storey, from his play

In Cold Blood ★★★★ 15

Crime drama based on a true story
1967 · US · BW · 128mins

Truman Capote's book about two young real-life murderers was a shocking bestseller in its day, and thought impossible to bring to the screen. Yet writer/director Richard Brooks did deliver this harrowing movie adaptation, remarkably faithful to its source and featuring two relatively unknown actors as the youngsters who wiped out a Kansas family during a robbery. The mood is properly dour and relentless, and the use of actual locations superb. The supporting cast is full of well-known Hollywood players, with the likes of John Forsythe, Will Geer and Paul Stewart ensuring that the grim subject matter remains resolutely unsensationalised. TS. Contains violence and swearing. DVD

Robert Blake *Perry Smith* • Scott Wilson *Dick Hickock* • John Forsythe *Alvin Dewey* • Paul Stewart *Reporter* • Gerald S O'Loughlin *Harold Nye* • Jeff Corey *Hickock's father* • John Gallaudet *Roy Church* • James Flavin *Clarence Duntz* • Charles McGraw *Perry's father* • Will Geer *Prosecuting attorney* ■ *Dir* Richard Brooks • *Scr* Richard Brooks, from the non-fiction book by Truman Capote • *Cinematographer* Conrad Hall

In Country ★★★ 15

Drama 1989 · US · Colour · 110mins

This was Bruce Willis's first real stab at proving himself a serious actor, and he delivers a credibly moody performance as a disturbed Vietnam veteran trying to piece his life together after the conflict. Emily Lloyd also emerges with honours in one of her first American roles. However, both are let down by a meandering script that never quite gets to grips with the subject matter and uneven direction from the usually reliable Norman Jewison (director of *Moonstruck* among other hits). JF. Contains violence. [video]

Bruce Willis *Emmett Smith* • Emily Lloyd *Samantha Hughes* • Joan Allen *Irene* • Kevin Anderson *Lonnie Malone* • Richard Hamilton *Grampaw* • Judith Ivey *Anita Stevens* ■ *Dir* Norman Jewison • *Scr* Frank Pierson, Cynthia Cidre, from the novel by Bobbie Ann Mason

The In Crowd ★★ PG

Romantic dance drama
1988 · US · Colour · 95mins

Donovan Leitch (son of Donovan and brother of Ione Skye) stars in this 1960s-set rock 'n' roll drama as the wannabe singer/dancer who becomes an overnight star. Good attention to period detail and a great R 'n' B soundtrack make this both instantly feel good and instantly forgettable. LH

Donovan Leitch *Del Green* • Joe Pantoliano *Perry Parker* • Jennifer Runyon *Vicky* • Wendy Gazelle *Gail* • Sean Gregory Sullivan *Popeye* • Bruno Kirby *Norris* ■ *Dir* Mark Rosenthal • *Scr* Lawrence Konner, Mark Rosenthal

The In Crowd ★★ 12

Thriller 2000 · US · Colour · 101mins

In an uneven career, Mary Lambert may have hit a new low with this trashy teen thriller. Swimming boldly against the postmodernist tide, she attempts to restore credence to those slasher clichés that no one can take seriously any more. Consequently, there isn't a moment's suspenseful doubt about what's really behind vixenish snob Susan Ward's interest in paroled mental patient Lori Heuring. The smug scripting and erratic performances scream "direct to video". JF. Contains some swearing and violence. [video] DVD

Susan Ward *Brittany Foster* • Lori Heuring *Adrien Williams* • Matthew Settle *Matt Curtis* • Nathan Bexton *Bobby* • Tess Harper *Dr Amanda Giles* • Ethan Erickson *Tom* ■ *Dir* Mary Lambert • *Scr* Mark Gibson, Philip Halprin

In Custody ★★ U

Drama 1993 · UK · Colour · 120mins

If only Ismail Merchant had kept this adaptation of Anita Desai's novel for his second outing as a director, we might have been talking four stars here instead of two. After 30 years as producer to James Ivory, he finally seized the directorial reins on a project that was obviously close to his heart, but simply lacked the experience to bring it fully to life. The story, about an academic seeking to record the work of a dissolute Urdu poet, is thought-provoking, touching and often very amusing, but the picture lacks pace and focus. DP. In Urdu with English subtitles. [video] DVD

Shashi Kapoor *Nur* • Sameer Mitha *Manu* • Neena Gupta *Sarla* • Rupinder Kaur *Mrs Bhalla* • Om Puri *Deven* • Shahid Masood *Dhanu* • Tiblu Khan *Student* ■ *Dir* Ismail Merchant • *Scr* Anita Desai, Shahrukh Husain, from the novel by Anita Desai

In Dreams ★★ 18

Psychological thriller
1998 · US · Colour · 95mins

Neil Jordan proves again what an inconsistent director he can be with this contrived chiller. The visuals are impressively stylised, as Jordan summons up the nightmare world in which New England resident Annette Bening becomes trapped as she finds her mind invaded by the thoughts of a serial killer. Yet his handling of the various flashbacks and reveries is haphazard, creating tension by sleight of hand rather than plot progression or sustained atmosphere. DP. Contains violence and swearing. [video] DVD

Annette Bening *Claire Cooper* • Katie Sagona *Rebecca Cooper* • Aidan Quinn *Paul Cooper* • Robert Downey Jr *Vivian Thompson* • Stephen Rea *Doctor Silverman* ■ *Dir* Neil Jordan • *Scr* Bruce Robinson, Neil Jordan, from the novel *Doll's Eyes* by Bari Wood

In Enemy Country ★★

Second World War drama
1968 · US · Colour · 106mins

This uninspired Second World War hokum from Universal utilised the studio's backlot when its TV series weren't in production. Still, star Tony Franciosa copes manfully, going undercover to dispose of a Nazi torpedo factory, while British interest centres on import Tom Bell and the very artificial European setting. Producer/director Harry Keller does a serviceable job, however, and scores some points for effort. TS

Tony Franciosa [Anthony Franciosa] *Colonel Charles Waslow-Carton* • Anjanette Comer *Denise Marchois* • Guy Stockwell *Lt Col Philip Braden* • Paul Hubschmid *Baron Frederich von Wittenberg* • Tom Bell *Captain Ian Peyton-Reid* ■ *Dir* Harry Keller • *Scr* Edward Anhalt, from a story by Sy Bartlett

In God We Trust ★ 15

Comedy 1980 · US · Colour · 92mins

Marty Feldman gets it horribly wrong as writer, director and star of this dismally unfunny comedy about a naive monk who receives a crash course in worldliness when he goes to Hollywood on a fundraising mission for his monastery. Blatant in its satire and inept in its characterisation, the film misses every one of its social and religious targets. Richard Pryor does himself no favours as God in a film that's beyond salvation. DP [video]

Marty Feldman *Brother Ambrose* • Peter Boyle *Dr Melmoth* • Louise Lasser *Mary* • Richard Pryor *God* • Andy Kaufman *Armageddon T Thunderbird* • Wilfrid Hyde White *Abbot Thelonius* • Severn Darden *Priest* ■ *Dir* Marty Feldman • *Scr* Marty Feldman, Chris Allen

In God's Hands ★★ 12

Sports adventure drama
1998 · US · Colour · 93mins

Soft-core director Zalman King takes a change of pace with this saga concerning three beach bum surfers (played by three real-life champion surfers) travelling halfway around the world looking for great waves. That sentence essentially covers the entire plot of the movie, which never has a clear direction or purpose except to show reels of surfing action. The footage is expertly photographed, but with little else going on, the movie literally becomes a lesser version of *The Endless Summer*. KB [video] DVD

Patrick Shane Dorian *Shane* • Matt George *Mickey* • Mathew Stephen "Matty" Liu *Keoni* • Shaun Thompson *Wyatt* ■ *Dir* Zalman King • *Scr* Zalman King, Matt George

In Good Company ★★★ PG

Comedy drama 2004 · US · Colour · 105mins

In the aftermath of a company takeover, young hotshot Topher Grace takes the job and the office of Dennis Quaid. As the displaced executive, Quaid manages to look both tough and tender – he's equally concerned for the future of his daughter Scarlett Johansson as he is for his fellow workers. These professional and personal lives collide when Grace and Johansson begin seeing each other, threatening to destroy the men's already unsteady alliance. Although there's a whiff of inevitability about it all, the fine cast still offer up plenty of surprises. KK [video] DVD

Dennis Quaid *Dan Foreman* • Scarlett Johansson *Alex Foreman* • Topher Grace *Carter Duryea* • Marg Helgenberger *Ann Foreman* • David Paymer *Morty* • Philip Baker Hall *Eugene Kalb* • Clark Gregg *Steckle* • Selma Blair *Kimberly Duryea* • Frankie Faison *Corwin* ■ *Dir/Scr* Paul Weitz

In Harm's Way ★★★★ PG

Second World War action drama
1965 · US · BW · 160mins

Producer/director Otto Preminger had a rough critical ride in the 1960s, not least for this marvellous Second World War epic, which begins with the Japanese attack on Pearl Harbour. The fine hand-picked cast includes John Wayne and Kirk Douglas as naval officers suffering mixed fortunes during and after the attack, and they are well supported by Patricia Neal, Brandon de Wilde and Dana Andrews. The main flaw is that the special effects in the later sea battles look unconvincing (they were shot using models). Nevertheless, the film has great scale (and a great score by Jerry Goldsmith), and, unusually, the characters aren't dwarfed by the canvas. TS [video] DVD

John Wayne *Captain Rockwell Torrey* • Kirk Douglas *Commander Paul Eddington* • Patricia Neal *Lieutenant Maggie Haynes* • Tom Tryon *Lieutenant William McConnel* • Paula Prentiss *Bev McConnel* • Brandon de Wilde *Ensign Jeremiah Torrey* • Jill Haworth *Ensign Annalee Dorne* • Dana Andrews *Admiral Broderick* • Stanley Holloway *Clayton Canfil* • Patrick O'Neal *Commander Neal O'Wynn* • Slim Pickens *Chief Petty Officer Culpepper* • George Kennedy *Colonel Gregory* • Henry Fonda *Cincpac Admiral* ■ *Dir* Otto Preminger • *Scr* Wendell Mayes, from the novel by James Bassett

In Her Defense ★★ 15

Thriller 1998 · Can · Colour · 93mins

Sidney J Furie just about keeps this courtroom thriller from collapsing under the weight of its clichés and contrivances. When deaf artist Marlee Matlin asks lawyer Michael Dudikoff to help her secure a divorce from her abusive millionaire husband, it's not long before they become lovers. But then Dudikoff kills the husband in self-defence and Matlin is arrested for the crime. Watchable and proficiently done, but predictable. DP. Contains swearing and sex scenes. [video]

Marlee Matlin *Jane Claire* • Michael Dudikoff *Andrew Garfield* • Sophie Lorain *Debra Turner* • Steven Morgan *John Danforth* • Maurice Arsenault *Serge Richard* • David Attis *Jeffrey Fishman* • John Ball *Mark Micka* ■ *Dir* Sidney J Furie • *Scr* Marc Lynn, Jeffrey M Rosenbaum

The In-Laws ★★★ PG

Comedy 1979 · US · Colour · 98mins

Arthur Hiller's frantic screwball variation on the buddy theme is never quite as funny as it thinks it is, but the laughs keep coming thanks to the inspired pairing of Alan Arkin and Peter Falk. Determined to stand by his daughter's prospective father-in-law, Arkin's New York dentist heads off to South America to help Falk's eccentric CIA agent recover some stolen Treasury plates. The fun lies in the way Falk lures Arkin into ever more ludicrous situations. DP [video] DVD

Peter Falk *Vince Ricardo* • Alan Arkin *Sheldon Kornpett* • Richard Libertini *General Garcia* • Nancy Dussault *Carol Kornpett* • Penny Peyser *Barbara Kornpett* • Arlene Golonka *Jean Ricardo* • Ed Begley Jr *Barry Lutz* ■ *Dir* Arthur Hiller • *Scr* Andrew Bergman

The In-Laws ★★ 12

Comedy 2003 · US/Ger/Can · Colour · 93mins

In this unnecessary reworking of the 1979 comedy, Michael Douglas and Albert Brooks take over as, respectively, a secret agent and a nervy medical professional who are united by the impending marriage of their offspring. Once Brooks has rumbled Douglas's true profession, he becomes involved in a madcap mission which involves nutty French arms dealer David Suchet. This underwritten and overplayed film relies solely on Douglas and Brooks for comic momentum, but the partnership cracks under the strain. TH [video] DVD

Michael Douglas *Steve Tobias* • Albert Brooks *Jerry Peyser* • Robin Tunney *Angela Harris* • Ryan Reynolds *Mark Tobias* • Candice Bergen *Judy Tobias* • David Suchet *Jean-Pierre Thibodoux* • Lindsay Sloane *Melissa Peyser* • Maria Ricossa *Katherine Peyser* • Russell Andrews *Agent Will Hutchins* ■ *Dir* Andrew Fleming • *Scr* Nat Mauldin, Ed Solomon, from the film by Andrew Bergman

In like Flint ★★ PG

Spy spoof 1967 · US · Colour · 109mins

This sub-James Bond adventure, a sequel to *Our Man Flint*, sees James Coburn return as the stone-faced spy. The plot concerns a group of women on the Virgin Islands planning to rule the world, hence the presence of a bevy of beauties, and plenty of insipid innuendo. It's often laughable, though Lee J Cobb does bring a touch of class to the crass proceedings. TH DVD

James Coburn *Derek Flint* • Lee J Cobb *Cramden* • Jean Hale *Lisa* • Andrew Duggan *President Trent* • Anna Lee *Elisabeth* • Hanna Landy *Helena* • Totty Ames *Claire* ■ *Dir* Gordon Douglas • *Scr* Hal Fimberg

In Love and War ★★★

Second World War drama
1958 · US · Colour · 104mins

This 20th Century-Fox film was designed to show off the studio's talented roster of contract. It's a pleasingly clichéd wartime melodrama, offering showy roles to Robert Wagner and Jeffrey Hunter, both looking far more 1950s than 1940s, though Bradford Dillman scores highest as the thoughtful member of a trio of marines experiencing both romance and conflict. The women – the splendid Dana Wynter, Hope Lange and Sheree North – emerge with credit. TS

Robert Wagner *Frankie O'Neill* • Dana Wynter *Sue Trumbell* • Jeffrey Hunter *Nico Kantaylis* • Hope Lange *Andrea Lenaine* • Bradford Dillman *Alan Newcombe* • Sheree North *Lorraine* • France Nuyen *Kalai Ducanne* ■ *Dir* Philip Dunne • *Scr* Edward Anhalt, from the novel *The Big War* by Anton Myrer

In Love and War ★★ 15

Biographical drama
1996 · US · Colour · 108mins

A typically humane but sadly uninvolving biographical drama from director Richard Attenborough. Set during the First World War, it centres on the romance between a young Ernest Hemingway, injured in combat, and the nurse who cares for him. One of the film's problems is the total lack of chemistry between its stars, Chris O'Donnell and Sandra Bullock, both hopelessly miscast. Despite some attractive location photography in Italy, the whole project seems curiously stillborn. AT [video] DVD

Chris O'Donnell *Ernest Hemingway* • Sandra Bullock *Agnes von Kurowsky* • Ingrid Lacey *Elsie "Mac" MacDonald* • MacKenzie Astin *Henry Villard* • Emilio Bonucci *Domenico Caracciolo* • Ian Kelly *Jimmy McBride* • Alan Bennett *Porter* ■ *Dir* Richard Attenborough • *Scr* Anna Hamilton Phelan, Clancy Sigal, Allan Scott, from a story by Allan Scott, Dimitri Villard, from the biography *Hemingway in Love and War* by Henry S Villard, James Nagel

In My Father's Den ★★★★ 15

Mystery drama
2004 · NZ/Ire/UK · Colour · 125mins

The desolate landscape of New Zealand's Central Otago region reflects the emotional heft of this powerful drama. Disillusioned war photographer Matthew MacFadyen returns home for his father's funeral, then finds himself drawn into a family mystery as he becomes attached to sullen teen Emily Barclay, the daughter of a former lover. Making the most of an evocative soundtrack, writer/director Brad McGann skilfully updates Maurice Gee's novel of bereavement and despair without losing sight of its stark emotional pull. Enthralling, adult and moving. JR

Matthew MacFadyen *Paul Prior* • Miranda Otto *Penny Prior* • Emily Barclay *Celia Steimer* • Colin Moy *Andrew Prior* • Jodie Rimmer *Jackie Steimer* • Jimmy Keen *Jonathan Prior* ■ *Dir* Brad McGann • *Scr* Brad McGann, from the novel by Maurice Gee

In My Skin ★★★ 18

Psychological drama
2002 · Fr · Colour · 85mins

Chilling in its depiction of self-mutilation, this lacks psychological insight into why so many women feel compelled to harm their bodies. Marina de Van's use of an unflinching camera and split screens to show the wounds her seemingly successful market researcher inflicts upon herself is relentlessly assured. But her fascination with the fragility of flesh becomes all-consuming and we don't see enough of the measures she takes to explain her injuries or the impact they have on her colleagues and anxious lover, Laurent Lucas. DP. In French with English subtitles. DVD

Marina de Van *Esther* • Laurent Lucas *Vincent* • Léa Drucker *Sandrine* • Thibault de Montalembert *Daniel* ■ *Dir/Scr* Marina de Van

In Name Only ★★★ U

Drama 1939 · US · BW · 90mins

A great cast in a superior soapy drama, as unhappily married Cary Grant falls for widow Carole Lombard and tries to free himself from the clutches of his social-climbing wife, Kay Francis. Of the extraordinary crop of films made in Hollywood in 1939, this conventional melodrama is often overlooked, but, despite rather slow-moving direction from John Cromwell, it's well worth a viewing. TS

Carole Lombard *Julie Eden* • Cary Grant *Alec Walker* • Kay Francis *Maida Walker* • Charles Coburn *Mr Walker* • Helen Vinson *Suzanne* • Katherine Alexander *Laura* • Jonathan Hale *Dr Gateson* • Maurice Moscovich *Dr Muller* • Nella Walker *Mrs Walker* ■ *Dir* John Cromwell • *Scr* Richard Sherman, from the novel *Memory of Love* by Bessie Brewer

In Old Arizona ★★★

Western 1929 · US · BW · 94mins

This big-budget first western talkie is the best screen representation of the Cisco Kid, the colourful creation of master storyteller O Henry. In an Oscar-winning performance, Warner Baxter plays the caballero with an infectious zest, all flashing teeth and flashing spurs, stealing hearts and stagecoach strongboxes with equal abandon, while Edmund Lowe plods behind as the lawman who can never quite get his man. In the best role of her career, Dorothy Burgess makes a spirited Mexican senorita, while the ending has a sharp O Henry-ish twist. Director Raoul Walsh lost an eye during the filming which was completed by Irving Cummings. AE

Edmund Lowe *Sgt Mickey Dunne* • Dorothy Burgess *Tonia Maria* • Warner Baxter *The Cisco Kid* • J Farrell MacDonald *Tad* ■ *Dir* Raoul Walsh, Irving Cummings • *Scr* Tom Barry, from a story by O Henry

In Old California ★★ PG

Western 1942 · US · BW · 87mins

In this very routine Republic western, John Wayne is rather oddly cast as a pharmacist who finds himself entangled in the evil schemes of a local gunman. To hold your interest, there's Binnie Barnes as a spirited saloon hostess and died-in-the-wool villain Albert Dekker. The film lacks a firm director's hand, so practised comic actors Patsy Kelly and Edgar Kennedy have plenty of opportunities to scene-steal. TS

John Wayne *Tom Craig* • Binnie Barnes *Lacey Miller* • Albert Dekker *Britt Dawson* • Helen Parrish *Ellen Sanford* • Patsy Kelly *Helga* ■ *Dir* William McGann • *Scr* Gertrude Purcell, Frances Hyland, from a story by J Robert Bren, Gladys Atwater

In Old Chicago ★★★ U

Historical disaster drama
1937 · US · BW · 91mins

Released a year after MGM's *San Francisco*, this film about the Chicago fire of 1871 is a storm in a teacup compared with MGM's stupendously filmed earthquake, and Tyrone Power is no Clark Gable. There is a lot of scene-setting and subplotting family virtues set beside political corruption before a cow kicks over a kerosene lamp and the special effects team makes the Windy City go up in smoke. AT

Tyrone Power *Dion O'Leary* • Alice Faye *Belle Fawcett* • Don Ameche *Jack O'Leary* • Alice Brady *Molly O'Leary* • Andy Devine *Pickle Bixby* ■ *Dir* Henry King • *Scr* Lamar Trotti, Sonya Levien, from the story *We the O'Learys* by Niven Busch

In Old Kentucky ★★★

Comedy 1935 · US · BW · 85mins

The homespun personality of Will Rogers made him one of the most popular stars of early talkies, and his amiable performance holds together this occasionally simple-minded tale of country folk and racehorse rivalries. Whether learning to tap-dance or trying to make a purchase at a fashion house, Rogers is always engaging. Sadly this was to be his last film: he was killed in a plane crash shortly after its completion. TV

Will Rogers *Steve Tapley* • Dorothy Wilson *Nancy Martingale* • Russell Hardie *Dr Lee Andrews* • Charles Sellon *Ezra Martingale* • Bill Robinson *Wash Jackson* ■ *Dir* George Marshall • *Scr* Sam Hellman, Gladys Lehman, from the play by Charles T Dazey

In Old Montana ★★

Western 1939 · US · BW · 61mins

Spectrum was a "poverty row" outfit churning out westerns as supporting fillers. This is a typical example, featuring singing cowboy Fred Scott. There's some action in this one, but unfortunately far too much plot. The sets and costumes, not to mention stories, were continuously reused in this material, and director Raymond K Johnson churned out 18 of these B westerns between 1931 and 1941 to little distinction. For fans only. TS

Fred Scott *Fred Dawson* • Jean Carmen *June Allison* • John Merton *Ed Brandt* • Harry Harvey *Doc Flanders* • Walter McGrail *Joe Allison* ■ *Dir* Raymond K Johnson • *Scr* Jackson Parks, Homer King Gordon, Raymond K Johnson, Barney Hutchinson

In Our Time ★★ U

Second World War drama
1944 · US · BW · 110mins

A belated tribute to the gallant Poles who confronted the Nazis in 1939, this Warner Bros melodrama suffers from the romanticised vision of European stoicism that blighted many a Hollywood flagwaver. Initially, it's a tale of pride and prejudice, as Paul Henreid's aristocratic family disapprove of his marriage to English tourist Ida Lupino. But once their farm has been razed to the ground, intolerance is transformed into indomitability as the resistance struggle begins. Henreid and Victor Francen (as his uncle) coast on auto-pilot, but Lupino looks decidedly ill at ease. DP

Ida Lupino *Jennifer Whittredge* • Paul Henreid *Count Stephan Orvid* • Nancy Coleman *Janina Orvid* • Mary Boland *Mrs Bromley* • Victor Francen *Count Pavel Orvid* ■ *Dir* Vincent Sherman • *Scr* Ellis St Joseph, Howard Koch

In Person ★★

Musical romantic comedy
1935 · US · BW · 87mins

Ginger Rogers took a break from Fred Astaire by co-starring with the non-dancing, non-singing and, some would say, non-acting George Brent. Rogers plays a temperamental film star escaping her fans by adopting a disguise and fleeing to a mountain resort in the company of Brent. Ginger has a couple of pleasant dance routines, which only serve to remind audiences of Fred's absence. RB

Ginger Rogers *Carol Corliss aka Miss Colfax* • George Brent *Emory Parks* • Alan Mowbray *Jay Holmes* • Grant Mitchell *Judge Thaddeus Parks* ■ *Dir* William A Seiter • *Scr* Allan Scott, from a novel by Samuel Hopkins Adams

In Praise of Older Women ★★ 18

Drama 1978 · Can · Colour · 105mins

This is soft-core smut dressed in a wispy veil of sophistication. The source material considered the socio-political situation that made the promiscuity of so many well-heeled Hungarians something more than mere lust. But Susan Strasberg's anti-Communist opinions matter less than the smouldering glances she gives Tom Berenger, whose character's sexual education began at the age of 12, when he pimped for prostitutes during the Second World War. Karen Black and Alexandra Stewart also rank among his many conquests, but they're undone by the anachronistic dialogue and George Kaczender's leering direction. DP

Tom Berenger *Andra Vayda* • Karen Black *Maya* • Susan Strasberg *Bobbie* • Helen Shaver *Ann MacDonald* • Marilyn Lightstone *Klari* • Alexandra Stewart *Paula* • Marianne McIsaac *Julika* • Alberta Watson *Mitzi* ■ *Dir* George Kaczender • *Scr* Paul Gottlieb, from the novel by Stephen Vizinczey

In Pursuit ★★ 15

Thriller 2000 · US · Colour · 87mins

The presence of super-model Claudia Schiffer will catch the eye of laddish video renters, but even they are likely to be disappointed with this dull *noirish* thriller. Daniel Baldwin is the lawyer who finds his cosy life upended when he finds himself the number one suspect in the murder of Schiffer's businessman husband. There are plenty of tortuous plot twists but none is believable and the result is another formulaic thriller. JF DVD

Daniel Baldwin *Rick Alvarez* • Claudia Schiffer *Catherine Wells* • Coolio *Carl Wright* • Dean Stockwell *Charles Welz* • Sarah Lassez *Abby Berkhoff* ■ *Dir* Peter Pistor • *Scr* John Penney, from a story by Peter Pistor

In Search of Famine ★★★★

Drama 1980 · Ind · Colour · 124mins

A Calcutta film crew arrives in a remote village to document the devastating 1943 famine, but is greeted with unexpected suspicion and hostility by the poverty-stricken villagers. Unable to bridge this gap of understanding, the visitors return home empty-handed. One of Indian cinema's most insightful recorders of the country's social fabric, Mrinal Sen has created a lively film, no less profound for revealing the underlying comedy springing from the cultural divide between the protagonists. An excellent piece, this won the special jury prize at Berlin. RB. A Bengali language film.

Dhritiman Chatterjee *Director* • Smita Patil *Actress* • Sreela Majumdar *Woman* • Gita Sen *Widow* • Dipankar Dey *Villager* ■ *Dir* Mrinal Sen • *Scr* Mrinal Sen

In Search of Gregory ★★

Psychological drama
1970 · UK/It · Colour · 89mins

Having co-written such seminal pictures as *L'Avventura* and *Blowup*, it's not surprising echoes of Michelangelo Antonioni abound in this cryptic tale from Tonino Guerra. Unfortunately, director Peter Wood doesn't have the master's genius for expressing emotion through landscape, so Julie Christie's Genevan odyssey is more maddening than enigmatic. Enchanted by her father Adolfo Celi's description of a handsome house guest, Christie imagines him to be the same man whose picture she sees at the airport (Michael Sarrazin). It's an intriguing idea but it needs firmer handling than this. DP

Julie Christie *Catherine* • Michael Sarrazin *Gregory* • John Hurt *Daniel* • Adolfo Celi *Max* • Roland Culver *Wardle* • Tony Selby *Taxi driver* • Jimmy Lynn *Air steward* ■ *Dir* Peter Wood • *Scr* Tonino Guerra, Lucile Laks

In Search of the Castaways ★★ U

Fantasy adventure
1961 · US/UK · Colour · 94mins

This was Disney's second dip into the works of Jules Verne, but it can't be compared with the splendid *20,000 Leagues under the Sea*. Hayley Mills stars as a tigerish teen who ropes Maurice Chevalier and Wilfrid Hyde White into helping search for her father. But, as the action moves from South America to Australia, director Robert Stevenson subjects his cast to all manner of natural disasters. The effects have dated badly and the meandering story rarely thrills. DP DVD

Maurice Chevalier *Professor Jacques Paganel* • Hayley Mills *Mary Grant* • George Sanders *Thomas Ayrton* • Wilfrid Hyde White *Lord Glenarvan* • Michael Anderson Jr *John Glenarvan* ■ *Dir* Robert Stevenson • *Scr* Lowell S Hawley, from the novel *Captain Grant's Children* by Jules Verne

In the Army Now ★ PG

Comedy 1994 · US · Colour · 88mins

Pauly Shore is something of an acquired taste, but he's got no chance of raising a laugh in this marvel of military mayhem, thanks to the eight writers who toiled on the lamentable script. Comedy seems to have been the last thing on their minds when they penned this barmy story about a doltish shop assistant who finds himself in the middle of a US mission against Libya. No satire, no farce, no wit. DP

Pauly Shore *Bones Conway* • Andy Dick *Jack Kaufman* • Lori Petty *Christine Jones* • David Alan Grier *Fred Ostroff* • Esai Morales *Sergeant Stern* ■ *Dir* Daniel Petrie Jr • *Scr* Daniel Petrie Jr, Fax Bahr, Adam Small, Ken Kaufman, Stu Krieger, from a story by Steve Zacharias, Jeff Buhai, Robbie Fox

In the Bedroom ★★★★ 15

Drama 2001 · US · Colour · 125mins

This is a film about grief that touches the heart and leaves a deep and lasting impression. Tom Wilkinson and Sissy Spacek are both excellent as the parents swamped by moral and psychological trauma after the murder of their son. Trapped in a claustrophobic community, they live in close proximity to their child's killer – and the woman whose involvement with their son indirectly led to his death – and their intense grief and outrage pushes them to breaking point. The movie's measured pace and elegance of observation complement the astounding confidence of actor/director Todd Field, whose handling of the delicately balanced material makes his feature debut a rare find. LH. Contains violence, swearing. [video] DVD

Sissy Spacek *Ruth Fowler* • Tom Wilkinson *Matt Fowler* • Nick Stahl *Frank Fowler* • Marisa Tomei *Natalie Strout* • William Mapother *Richard Strout* • William Wise *Willis Grinnel* • Celia Weston *Katie Grinnel* • Karen Allen *Marla Keyes* ■ *Dir* Todd Field • *Scr* Rob Festinger, Todd Field, from the story *Killing* by Andre Dubus

In the Belly of the Whale ★★★

Drama 1984 · W Ger · Colour · 97mins

Made a year before she scored an international hit with the sex comedy *Men...*, Doris Dörrie's second directorial outing is an assured melodrama in which cop Peter Sattmann is forced to join forces with his estranged wife when their daughter disappears. Dorrie challenges traditional assumptions about male-female relationships, but here she also manages to juggle satire and suspense as the bickering couple reluctantly agree to a truce in order to save the young girl's life. It takes a while to settle, but give it time. DP. German dialogue dubbed into English.

Janna Marangosoff *Carla* • Eisi Gulp *Rick* • Silvia Reize *Marta* • Peter Sattmann *Frank* ■ *Dir* Doris Dörrie • *Scr* Michael Juncker, Doris Dörrie

In the Bleak Midwinter ★★★ 15

Comedy drama 1995 · UK · BW · 94mins

After the grand-standing and faintly embarrassing excesses of *Mary Shelley's Frankenstein*, Kenneth Branagh returns to his roots for this gentle and modestly amusing dig at theatrical pretensions. With Branagh opting to remain behind the camera, the leading role goes to Michael Maloney, who plays a struggling actor attempting to stage a Christmas production of *Hamlet* with a bitchy, egocentric group of luvvies. Branagh regular Richard Briers has a ball with the material. However, the stunning black-and-white cinematography cannot disguise the slightness of the material. JF [video] DVD

Michael Maloney *Joe Harper* • Richard Briers *Henry Wakefield* • Hetta Charnley *Molly* • Joan Collins *Margaretta D'Arcy* • Nicholas Farrell *Tom Newman* • Celia Imrie *Fadge* • Jennifer Saunders *Nancy Crawford* • Julia Sawalha *Nina* • John Sessions *Terry Du Bois* ■ *Dir/Scr* Kenneth Branagh

In the Blink of an Eye ★★★ 12

Drama based on a true story
1996 · US · Colour · 85mins

Director Micki Dickoff's fine made-for-TV drama is based on her own experiences, with Veronica Hamel playing the campaigning film-maker who takes up the case of a childhood friend (Mimi Rogers) in prison for a murder she did not commit. The two female leads give commanding performances and Dickoff produces a tense and fiery examination of the iniquities of the American legal system. JF. Contains swearing and violence. [video] DVD

Veronica Hamel *Micki Dickoff* • Mimi Rogers *Sunny Jacobs* • Piper Laurie *Kay Trafero* • Polly Bergen *Murial* • Carlos Gomez *Jose Quinon* ■ *Dir* Micki Dickoff • *Scr* Rama Laurie Stagner, Dan Witt

In the Company of Men ★★★★★ 18

Black comedy drama
1997 · US · Colour · 93mins

Brave, hard-hitting and controversial, director Neil LaBute's pitch-black comedy detailing the complexities of office politics and male rivalry is a deliberately uncomfortable viewing experience. Aaron Eckhart and Matt Malloy are exceptional as the two white-collar workers betting on who can seduce the most vulnerable girl in their office – Stacy Edwards's deaf secretary – and then dump her as an exercise in revenge against the fair sex. LaBute indulges in blatant misogyny and painful honesty to put his acerbic points across in a provocative, compelling shocker. AJ. Contains swearing. [video]

Aaron Eckhart *Chad* • Stacy Edwards *Christine* • Matt Malloy *Howard* • Emily Cline *Suzanne* • Jason Dixie *Keith, intern* ■ *Dir/Scr* Neil LaBute

In the Company of Spies ★★★ 15

Spy thriller 1999 · US · Colour · 100mins

This CIA TV drama is written by Roger Towne, who writes a pacy actioner, and is helped by strong cast. Tom Berenger, a retired CIA agent now running a restaurant, is brought back in by his old boss Ron Silver to rescue an agent with important information who has been captured in North Korea. Well-researched and swift-moving, the script so pleased the real CIA that they allowed film-makers to use their headquarters in Langley, Virginia, as a location. JB [video]

Tom Berenger *Kevin Jefferson* • Alice Krige *Sarah Gold* • Ron Silver *Tom Lenahan* • Clancy Brown *Dale Beckham* ■ *Dir* Tim Matheson • *Scr* Roger Towne

In the Cool of the Day ★★

Drama 1963 · US · Colour · 91mins

Terminally ill New Yorker Jane Fonda runs off to Greece with her husband's business partner, Peter Finch, who in turn is fleeing from the wife he scarred in a car crash. This romantic tragedy aspires to the level of Greek myth but amounts to little more than Greek piffle. Worth watching, however, for the locations, such as the glorious ancient site of Delphi, all beautifully shot by cameraman Peter Newbrook. AT

Jane Fonda *Christine Bonner* • Peter Finch *Murray Logan* • Angela Lansbury *Sibyl Logan* • Arthur Hill *Sam Bonner* • Constance Cummings *Mrs Gellert* • Alexander Knox *Frederick Bonner* • Nigel Davenport *Leonard* • John Le Mesurier *Dr Arraman* ■ *Dir* Robert Stevens • *Scr* Meade Roberts, from the novel by Susan Ertz

In the Cut ★★★ 18

Thriller 2003 · US/Aus · Colour · 113mins

Susanna Moore's notoriously explicit novel gives director Jane Campion another opportunity to explore her favourite theme – the self-destructive elements of female desire. Meg Ryan stars as a New York teacher who falls for detective Mark Ruffalo. But he is enigmatic and is investigating a series of murders that he himself might have committed. Campion's trademark off-kilter camerawork matches the increasingly skewed world view of her protagonist and Ryan is a revelation. Ultimately, the film works as a study of sexual longing but fails as a thriller. StH [video] DVD

Meg Ryan *Frannie Avery* • Mark Ruffalo *Det James Malloy* • Jennifer Jason Leigh *Pauline* • Nick Damici *Det Richard Rodriguez* • Sharrieff Pugh *Cornelius Webb* • Kevin Bacon *John Graham* ■ *Dir* Jane Campion • *Scr* Jane Campion, Susanna Moore, from the novel by Susanna Moore

In the Deep Woods ★★ 18

Thriller 1992 · US · Colour · 91mins

Rosanna Arquette stars in this tepid TV thrillers. She plays an author of children's books who finds herself caught up in the investigation into a friend's murder. As you'd expect, Anthony Perkins (in his last film) features as someone who just might be a bit on the sinister side in this occasionally scary thriller. JB [video] DVD

Rosanna Arquette *Joanna Warren* • Anthony Perkins *Detective Paul Miller* • Will Patton *Agent Eric Gaines* • DW Moffett *Frank* • Chris Rydell [Christopher Rydell] *Tommy Warren* ■ *Dir* Charles Correll • *Scr* Robert Nathan, Robert Rosenblum, from the novel *In the Deep of the Woods* by Nicholas Conde

In the Doghouse ★★ U

Comedy 1961 · UK · BW · 93mins

Long before James Herriot, Alex Duncan appeared on the bestseller lists with *It's a Vet's Life*. Adapted by Michael Pertwee, the tale makes a fine vehicle for Leslie Phillips, who resorts to his trademark charm to atone for his misadventures in a new country practice. However, he also gets to reveal an unexpected action-man side as he thwarts a horse-smuggling ring run by his deadly rival (James Booth). This patchy film is perhaps most significant for bringing down the curtain on the career of Peggy Cummins. DP

Leslie Phillips *Jimmy Fox-Upton* • Peggy Cummins *Sally* • Hattie Jacques *Primrose Gudgeon* • James Booth *Bob Skeffington* • Dick Bentley *Mr Peddle* • Colin Gordon *Dean* • Joan Heal *Mrs Peddle* • Fenella Fielding *Miss Fordyce* ■ *Dir* Darcy Conyers • *Scr* Michael Pertwee, from the novel *It's a Vet's Life* by Alex Duncan

In the French Style ★★★

Romance 1963 · US/Fr · BW · 105mins

Seeing what an impact Jean Seberg made in *A Bout de Souffle*, Hollywood sent her back to Paris for this trend-chasing, slightly risqué movie based on two short stories by Irwin Shaw, who also produced here. As an American art student in Paris, Seberg has affairs with young student Philippe Forquet and journalist Stanley Baker before finally settling on someone else. Seberg is beautiful and convincing as the new independent woman, quite a contrast to a Hollywood still churning out Doris Day comedies. AT

Jean Seberg *Christina James* • Stanley Baker *Walter Beddoes* • Addison Powell *Mr James* • Jack Hedley *Bill* • Maurice Teynac *Baron* • James Leo Herlihy *Dr John Haislip* • Philippe Forquet *Guy* ■ *Dir* Robert Parrish • *Scr* Irwin Shaw, from his short stories *In the French Style* and *A Year to Learn the Language*

In the Gloaming ★★★★

Drama 1997 · US · Colour · 67mins

Disabled actor Christopher Reeve made his directorial debut with this short, but superbly realised, drama. Boasting a five-star cast, it centres on Aids patient Robert Sean Leonard's homecoming and the very different welcomes he receives from mother Glenn Close, father David Strathairn and sister Bridget Fonda. With a poignant cameo from Whoopi Goldberg as a live-in nurse, this is a painfully truthful study of a family facing tragedy and the need to express emotions before it's too late. DP

Glenn Close *Janet* • Robert Sean Leonard *Danny* • Bridget Fonda *Anne* • Whoopi Goldberg *Myrna* • David Strathairn *Martin* ■ *Dir* Christopher Reeve • *Scr* Will Scheffer, from the short story by Alice Elliott Dark

In the Good Old Summertime ★★★ U

Musical comedy 1949 · US · Colour · 102mins

This charming remake of romantic classic *The Shop around the Corner* provides a showcase for the great Judy Garland (she replaced a pregnant June Allyson). Garland is touching as the enamoured pen pal who doesn't realise that colleague Van Johnson is her secret letter lover, and there are some terrific moments where the plot takes a hiatus to let Garland perform in front of an on-screen audience. The child with Garland and Johnson in the closing sequence is Garland's real-life daughter, Liza Minnelli. TS

Judy Garland *Veronica Fisher* • Van Johnson *Andrew Larkin* • SZ "Cuddles" Sakall [SZ Sakall] *Otto Oberkugen* • Spring Byington *Nellie Burke* • Clinton Sundberg *Rudy Hansen* • Buster Keaton *Hickey* • Liza Minnelli ■ *Dir* Robert Z Leonard • *Scr* Samson Raphaelson, Frances Goodrich, Ivan Tors, Albert Hackett, from the play *The Shop around the Corner* by Miklos Laszlo

In the Heat of the Night ★★★★★ 15

Crime drama 1967 · US · Colour · 105mins

Winner of five Oscars, including best picture, this powerhouse drama about racial tension in the Deep South was released at the height of the civil rights movement and a year before the assassination of Martin Luther King. Sidney Poitier is the immaculately dressed Philadelphia cop who is wrongly arrested for murder while changing trains in a small town in Mississippi, ruled by Rod Steiger's rancid, bigoted police chief. The plot is a set-up, a stacked deck, yet the atmosphere is palpably unpleasant, and Poitier and Steiger have a field day. A major movie for its time, it spawned two further films featuring Poitier's character (*They Call Me Mr Tibbs* and *The Organization*) and a television series. AT. Contains swearing and violence. [video] DVD

Sidney Poitier *Virgil Tibbs* • Rod Steiger *Bill Gillespie* • Warren Oates *Sam Wood* • Quentin Dean *Dolores Purdy* • James Patterson *Purdy* • William Schallert *Webb Schubert* • Jack Teter *Philip Colbert* • Lee Grant *Mrs Leslie Colbert* ■ *Dir* Norman Jewison • *Scr* Stirling Silliphant, from the novel by John Ball • *Cinematographer* Haskell Wexler • *Editor* Hal Ashby • *Music* Quincy Jones

In the Line of Duty: Smoke Jumpers ★★ PG

Action drama based on a true story
1996 · US · Colour · 87mins

Despite its fascinating subject matter – the true story of daredevil parachuting firefighters – this is formulaic fare. Adam Baldwin plays the airborne fireman who is forced to re-evaluate his gung-ho career after falling for ex-firefighter and single mother Lindsay Frost. The action scenes are gripping enough, but veteran TV-movie director Dick Lowry spends too much time exploring domestic trials and tribulations. JF [video] DVD

Adam Baldwin *Don Mackey* • Lindsay Frost *Rene* • Timothy Carhart *Tom Classen* • Rob Youngblood *Timmerman* ■ *Dir* Dick Lowry • *Scr* Gy Waldron, Stephen Harrigan

In the Line of Fire ★★★★ 15

Thriller 1993 · US · Colour · 123mins

Clint Eastwood in tears (not many, but they're there) is just one of the novelties in this hugely enjoyable thriller in which Eastwood is a secret service agent who is not only visibly ageing – a fact that he admits to his younger lover, Rene Russo – but is also shamed by his past inability to save President Kennedy from assassination. That's why he's so obsessed with John Malkovich, would-be killer of the current First Executive. Eastwood reveals the same vulnerability that made his performance in *Unforgiven* so compelling, while the Oscar-nominated Malkovich makes an admirable adversary. TH. Contains swearing, violence and sex scenes. DVD

Clint Eastwood *Frank Horrigan* • John Malkovich *Mitch Leary* • Rene Russo *Lilly Raines* • Dylan McDermott *Al D'Andrea* • Gary Cole *Bill Watts* • Fred Dalton Thompson *Harry Sargent* • John Mahoney *Sam Campagna* ■ *Dir* Wolfgang Petersen • *Scr* Jeff Maguire • *Music* Ennio Morricone

In the Meantime, Darling ★★

Wartime comedy 1944 · US · BW · 71mins

The newly-wed young wife (Jeanne Crain) of an army officer (Frank Latimore), forced by army rules to live with other wives in a hotel near the military camp, kicks against the establishment and falls into misunderstandings with her husband before he is shipped overseas and she comes to terms with reality. This potentially interesting idea is dissipated by an uninspired, indecisive script. RK

Jeanne Crain *Maggie* • Frank Latimore *Lt Daniel Ferguson* • Eugene Pallette *HB Preston* • Mary Nash *Mrs Preston* • Stanley Prager *Lt Red Pianatowski* ■ *Dir* Otto Preminger • *Scr* Arthur Kober, Michael Uris

In the Mood for Love ★★★★ PG

Romantic drama
2000 · HK/Fr · Colour · 97mins

Hong Kong auteur Wong Kar-Wai returns to the more accessible narrative style of his earlier work with this ravishing romantic melodrama set in the early 1960s. Newspaper editor Tony Leung (who won the best actor prize at Cannes for his performance) moves into a noisy apartment at the same time as secretary Maggie Cheung takes possession of a flat down the hall. When they both realise their (unseen) partners are having an affair, they're drawn together by the sense of mutual humiliation and their own innocent courtship begins. This is a sumptuously shot, sensuous wade through the emotions of a repressed culture. AJ. In Cantonese with English subtitles. DVD

Cheung Man-Yuk [Maggie Cheung] *Mrs Chan, née Su Lizhen* • Tony Leung Chiu-Wai [Tony Leung (2)] *Chow Mo-Wan* • Rebecca Pan *Mrs Suen* • Lui Chun *Mr Ho* ■ *Dir* Wong Kar-Wai • *Scr* Wong Kar-Wai, incorporating quotations from the writings of Liu Yi-Chang

In the Mouth of Madness ★★★ 18

Horror 1994 · US · Colour · 91mins

Part homage to HP Lovecraft, part lampoon of Stephen King, John Carpenter's treatise on the psychological power of horror begins well, only to descend rapidly into genre cliché. The idea that a novel can turn its readers into demons might have been further developed, but screenwriter Michael De Luca is more interested in subjecting insurance fraud investigator Sam Neill to the bizarre goings-on in missing author Jürgen Prochnow's home town of Hobbs End. Many scenes are confidently handled, but bookend sequences in an asylum aren't enough to put this in the *Caligari* class. DP. Contains swearing and violence.

Sam Neill *John Trent* • Jürgen Prochnow *Sutter Cane* • Julie Carmen *Linda Styles* • Charlton Heston *Jackson Harglow* • David Warner *Dr Wrenn* • John Glover *Saperstein* ■ *Dir* John Carpenter • *Scr* Michael De Luca

In the Name of Buddha ★★★ 18

Documentary drama
2002 · UK/Sri L · Colour · 146mins

The UN estimates that over 60,000 Sri Lankans were killed and another 1.6 million displaced during the 20-year war between that nation's government and its Tamil population. Director Rajesh Touchriver conveys something of the scale of the tragedy in this ambitious attempt to expose the atrocities committed by both government forces and the Indian peacekeeping force. However, while his discussion of the way political leaders manipulate religious and cultural issues is calculatingly contentious, and his handling of the jungle setting and the relentlessly graphic combat sequences is impressive for a first-time film-maker. DP. In Tamil and Hindi with English subtitles.

Shiju *Siva* • Soniya *Geetha* • Jyothi Lal *Leader* • Amit *Mikara* ■ *Dir* Rajesh Touchriver • *Scr* Rajesh Touchriver, from a story by Sai George

In the Name of the Father ★★★★ 15

Biographical drama
1993 · Ire/UK/US · Colour · 127mins

This is a stirring and exceptionally well acted, though controversial, dramatisation of Gerry Conlon's book about the grave miscarriage of justice suffered by the Guildford Four. Daniel Day-Lewis is highly impressive as Conlon, a naive young Irishman who couldn't blow his own hat off, arrested by the police for terrorist bombings along with three equally unlikely friends. Directed by Jim Sheridan, the story packs an enormous dramatic punch. Pete Postlethwaite is brilliant as Conlon's bemused and hapless father, and the only false note is struck by Emma Thompson, hopelessly miscast (albeit Oscar-nominated) as the Four's solicitor. SH. Contains drug abuse, violence, swearing. DVD

Daniel Day-Lewis *Gerry Conlon* • Emma Thompson *Gareth Peirce* • Pete Postlethwaite *Guiseppe Conlon* • John Lynch *Paul Hill* • Mark Sheppard *Paddy Armstrong* • Beatie Edney *Carole Richardson* • Marie Jones *Sarah Conlon* • Britta Smith *Annie Maguire* • Corin Redgrave *Robert Dixon* ■ *Dir* Jim Sheridan • *Scr* Terry George, Jim Sheridan

In the Name of the Pope King ★★★★

Historical drama 1977 · It · Colour · 107mins

Set during the mid-19th century, this lavish historical drama focuses on the resistance of the Papal States to the cause of Italian unification. As the magistrate seeking to use his dwindling influence to save his son – an imprisoned member of Garibaldi's rebel army – Nino Manfredi gives a performance of abject despair. With his magisterial use of colour and attention to historical detail, Luigi Magni not only evokes the grandeur of the Vatican, but also makes accessible the intricate political and theological issues at stake. DP. In Italian with English subtitles.

Nino Manfredi *Don Colombo* • Danilo Mattei *Cesare Costa* • Carmen Scarpitta *Contessa Flaminia* • Giovanella Grifeo *Teresa* • Salvo Randone *Papa Nero* ■ *Dir/Scr* Luigi Magni

In the Navy ★★ U

Musical comedy 1941 · US · BW · 82mins

Abbott and Costello made such an impact as bumbling army recruits in *Buck Privates* that Universal immediately repeated the formula with another service comedy. Dick Powell plays a popular crooner who, fed up with the good life, enlists in the navy (under a false name) where he encounters misfit sailors Abbott and Costello. The Andrews Sisters (a big hit in *Buck Privates*) are on hand again, enlivening the proceedings with a few songs. DF

Bud Abbott *Smokey Adams* • Lou Costello *Pomeroy Watson* • Dick Powell *Tommy Halstead* • Claire Dodd *Dorothy Roberts* • Laverne Andrews • Maxene Andrews • Patty Andrews ■ *Dir* Arthur Lubin • *Scr* Arthur T Horman, John Grant, from the story *They're in the Navy Now* by Arthur T Horman

In the Presence of Mine Enemies ★★

Second World War drama
1997 · US · Colour · 96mins

Armin Mueller-Stahl stars in this heartfelt, but only partially successful, Second World War drama as a rabbi in the Warsaw ghetto who tries to keep himself and his Jewish community alive during the Nazi occupation. Charles Dance bravely takes on the role of the SS officer. The movie is directed by Joan Micklin Silver, best known for her two previous studies of Jewish life – *Hester Street* and *Crossing Delancey*. AT

Armin Mueller-Stahl *Rabbi Adam Heller* • Charles Dance *Captain Richter* • Elina Lowensohn *Rachel Heller* ■ *Dir* Joan Micklin Silver • *Scr* Joan Micklin Silver, from an original script by Rod Serling

In the Realm of the Senses ★★★★ 18

Erotic drama based on a true story
1976 · Fr/Jpn · Colour · 97mins

Based on a notorious murder case that scandalised Japan in the 1930s, Nagisa Oshima's tale of puissant passion is also a complex study of gender status and oppression. However, the eroticism is so hard-core it has invariably prevented a considered assessment of the writer/director's achievement. Laced with cultural and historical allusions and imagery as beautiful as it is powerful, the film follows geisha Eiko Matsuda and her lover Tatsuya Fuji as they willingly risk death in a bid to find ultimate sexual fulfilment in a militarist society. DP. In Japanese with English subtitles. DVD

Tatsuya Fuji *Kichi-zo* • Eiko Matsuda *Sada* • Aoi Nakajima *Toku* • Meika Seri *Maid Matsuko* • Taiji Tonoyama *Old beggar* ■ *Dir/Scr* Nagisa Oshima

In the Soup ★★

Comedy 1936 · UK · BW · 72mins

Director Henry Edwards does little to disguise the theatrical origins of this comic warhorse, which shows just how reliant Ralph Lynn was on his fellow Aldwych farceurs. Without Tom Walls's wiles and Robertson Hare's pomposity, Lynn's silly-ass antics have a third-rate Bertie Wooster feel as he and Judy Gunn pose as servants in order to prevent his old colonial uncle discovering their marriage and disinheriting them. That said, Ralph Lumley's play does throw up a couple of amusing set pieces. DP

Ralph Lynn *Horace* • Judy Gunn *Kitty* • Morton Selten *Abernathy Ruppershaw* • Nelson Keys *Emile Moppert* • Bertha Belmore *Madame Moppert* ■ *Dir* Henry Edwards • *Scr* H Fowler Mear, from a play by Ralph Lumley

In the Soup ★★★ 15

Comedy 1992 · US · Colour · 95mins

An unusual angle on the struggle to bring script to screen marks Alexandre Rockwell's larger-than-life comedy out from the many other indie films about indie films. The twist is that writer Steve Buscemi's pretentious 500-page epic is to be financed by hoodlum Seymour Cassel, who embarks on various criminal activities to raise the $250,000 budget. Good casting and some bright ideas, but the movie-making theme seems to fall by the wayside as Cassel pulls Buscemi into his unwholesome activities. As a result, the film loses its satirical edge. However, Cassel's energetic performance is a treat. JC DVD

Steve Buscemi *Aldolpho Rollo* • Seymour Cassel *Joe* • Jennifer Beals *Angelica* • Pat Moya *Dang* • Will Patton *Skippy* • Jim Jarmusch *Monty* • Carol Kane *Barbara* ■ *Dir* Alexandre Rockwell • *Scr* Alexandre Rockwell, Tim Kissell

In the Spirit ★★★ 18

Black comedy 1990 · US · Colour · 90mins

Screwball black comedy, with Peter Falk and Elaine May as houseguests of nutty new-age mystic Marlo Thomas. The couple need brass balls rather than crystal ones when unforeseen circumstances make them targets of a killer who's already polished off the prostitute next door. Great cast, but irritating material, and characters you're as likely to loathe as to love. Watch out for a single-scene cameo from Melanie Griffith as the not-so-happy hooker. DA

Jeannie Berlin *Crystal* • Marlo Thomas *Reva Prosky* • Elaine May *Marianne Flan* • Olympia Dukakis *Sue* • Peter Falk *Roger Flan* • Melanie Griffith *Lureen* ■ *Dir* Sandra Seacat • *Scr* Jeannie Berlin, Laurie Jones

In the White City ★★★★ 15

Drama 1983 · Swi/Por · Colour · 108mins

Duality lies at the heart of Alain Tanner's intriguing existential drama. Sailor Bruno Ganz loves two women in contrasting locations: his Swiss wife, Julia Vonderlinn, and Teresa Madruga, the chambermaid he meets in Lisbon. Even the footage is two-tone, as it juxtaposes traditional 35mm with the Super-8 home movies that Ganz shoots as he survives various misadventures. Superbly controlled and atmospherically scored, this is an endlessly questioning study of emotional disquiet. DP. In French with English subtitles.

Bruno Ganz *Paul* • Teresa Madruga *Rosa* • Julia Vonderlinn *Elisa* • Jose Carvalho *Bar proprietor* • Victor Costa *Bartender* ■ *Dir/Scr* Alain Tanner

In This Our Life ★★★

Melodrama 1942 · US · BW · 96mins

This rip-roaring Warner Bros melodrama, directed by then newcomer John Huston, has an excellent cast including (watch closely) a cameo from his father Walter as a bartender. The scenery is chewed to bits by Bette Davis, who manages to destroy the life of her sister Olivia de Havilland and then destroys herself. There's some amazing plotting, as the wonderfully nasty Davis is involved in a hit-and-run and tries to lay the blame on the son of her black cook. Super stuff, not to be taken at all seriously. TS

Bette Davis *Stanley Timberlake* • Olivia de Havilland *Roy Timberlake* • George Brent *Craig Fleming* • Dennis Morgan *Peter Kingsmill* • Charles Coburn *William Fitzroy* • Hattie McDaniel *Minerva Clay* • Walter Huston *Bartender* ■ *Dir* John Huston • *Scr* Howard Koch, John Huston, from the novel by Ellen Glasgow • *Cinematographer* Ernie Haller [Ernest Haller] • *Music* Max Steiner

In This World ★★★★ 15

Documentary drama
2002 · UK · Colour · 86mins

Director Michael Winterbottom's timely documentary-drama variation on the road movie won the Golden Bear at Berlin – as much for its humanity as its technical audacity and storyline. Shot on digital video and transferred to 35mm widescreen, this is an occasionally contrived exploration of the contentious and often overlapping issues of political asylum, economic migration and people-trafficking. En route from Afghanistan to London, the hardships of life for teenager Jamal Udin Torabi and his cousin Enayatullah, and for many of those they encounter on their journey, are arrestingly portrayed. The poverty, prejudice, exploitation, desperation and danger presented is sickeningly authentic; it's just a shame such brutal realism is compromised by a sentimental ending. DP. In English, Pashtu and Farsi with subtitles. DVD

Jamal Udin Torabi *Jamal* • Enayatullah *Enayat* • Wakeel Khan *Enayat's uncle* • Nabil Elouahabi *Yusif* ■ *Dir* Michael Winterbottom • *Scr* Tony Grisoni • *Cinematographer* Marcel Zyskind

In Too Deep ★★ 18

Erotic crime thriller 1990 · Aus · Colour · 101mins

This flawed thriller is set against the backdrop of the Melbourne music scene. The story focuses on Hugo Race, a small-time crook dreaming of a music career who has lucked into some evidence of government corruption. He attempts to stay one step ahead of the cops while resolving his relationship with jazz singer Samantha Press. Melbourne has never looked quite so exotic. JF

Hugo Race *Mack Donnelly* • Santha Press *Wendy Lyall* • Rebekah Elmaloglou *JoJo Lyall* • John Flaus *Miles* • Dominic Sweeney *Dinny* ■ *Dir* John Tatoulis, Colin South • *Scr* Deborah Parsons

In Too Deep ★★ 18

Action thriller 1999 · US · Colour · 92mins

This run-of-the-mill cops-and-robbers thriller is distinguished by strong performances from Omar Epps and rapper-turned-actor LL Cool J. Epps plays a young undercover cop who gets in over his head while investigating a charismatic drugs lord. He is soon torn between duty and their budding friendship. LL Cool J plays the likeable villain, an interesting combination of kindness and malice. Beyond the acting, however, this movie offers no surprises, and an unnecessary romance between Epps and Nia Long impedes the pace. ST DVD

Omar Epps *Jeff Cole/J Reid* • LL Cool J *Dwayne "God" Gittens* • Nia Long *Myra* • Pam Grier *Detective Angela Wilson* • Stanley Tucci *Preston Boyd* ■ *Dir* Michael Rymer • *Scr* Michael Henry Brown, Paul Aaron

In Which We Serve ★★★★★ U

Second World War drama 1942 · UK · BW · 109mins

This wartime propaganda film is a thinly disguised take on the maritime exploits of Lord Mountbatten. Co-directed by the debuting David Lean and Noël Coward, it has matured to become a paean to a lost world. Told in flashback, as a group of stranded sailors await rescue after the sinking of their ship, the film is immensely moving, and contains definitive performances from Coward himself (his speech about his ship, the HMS *Torrin*, is a classic) and Celia Johnson, all chintz, beauty and stoicism in her film debut. A box-office hit in its day, the film was awarded a special Oscar, to Coward for his "outstanding production achievement". TS DVD

Noël Coward *Captain "D"* • John Mills *O/S "Shorty" Blake* • Bernard Miles *CPO Walter Hardy* • Celia Johnson *Alix Kinross* • Joyce Carey *Mrs Hardy* • Kay Walsh *Freda Lewis* • Derek Elphinstone *Number One* • Frederick Piper *Edgecombe* • Geoffrey Hibbert *Joey Mackridge* • George Carney *Mr Blake* • Daniel Massey *Bobby Kinross* • Michael Wilding *"Flags"* • Richard Attenborough *Young stoker* ■ *Dir* Noël Coward, David Lean • *Scr* Noël Coward, from the experiences of Lord Louis Mountbatten

In Your Hands ★★★ 15

Prison drama 2004 · Den · Colour · 96mins

In this restrained Dogme 95 drama, Annette K Olesen attempts to explore the impact of crime and incarceration on the psyche and spirituality of a group of socially diverse women in a bleak Danish prison. Olesen focuses on chaplain Ann Eleonora Jorgensen's struggle to gain the trust of suspicious and damaged souls such as new inmate Trine Dyrholm, who appears to possess mystical powers. Subplots involving Jorgensen's longing for a baby and timid warden Nicolaj Kopernikus's tender friendship with Dyrholm are neatly used to consider the role of both women and religion in society. DP. In Danish with English subtitles. Contains swearing. DVD

Ann Eleonora Jorgensen *Anna* • Trine Dyrholm *Kate* • Nicolaj Kopernikus *Henrik* • Sonja Richter *Marion* • Lars Ranthe *Frank* • Henrik Prip *Doctor* • Jens Albinus *Carsten* ■ *Dir* Annette K Olesen • *Scr* Kim Fupz Aakeson, Annette K Olesen

Inadmissible Evidence ★★★

Drama 1968 · UK · BW · 95mins

Just because you're paranoid doesn't mean to say you don't have enemies. Nicol Williamson re-creates his role from John Osborne's stage play as the solicitor who fears he's being persecuted by everyone. The fact that he treats his wife (Eleanor Fazan), mistress (Jill Bennett) and colleagues with equal contempt seems to have escaped him. Williamson's tour de force of invective loses some of its impact on screen as director Anthony Page presents the speeches in fragmented form. TH

Nicol Williamson *Bill Maitland* • Eleanor Fazan *Anna Maitland* • Jill Bennett *Liz* • Peter Sallis *Hudson* • David Valla *Jones* • Eileen Atkins *Shirley* • Lindsay Anderson *Barrister* ■ *Dir* Anthony Page • *Scr* John Osborne, from his play

Inauguration of the Pleasure Dome ★★★ PG

Experimental movie 1954 · US · Colour · 36mins

Another of Kenneth Anger's medium-length ciné-poems expressing his vision of the occult. The film has gone through several incarnations – the first had a soundtrack by Harry Parch, the second uses Janacek's *Glagolithic Mass* to better effect. In 1966, Anger then added an opening reading of Coleridge's *Kubla Khan* accompanied by stills of Satanist guru Aleister Crowley and talismanic symbols, which became known as the *Sacred Mushroom Edition*. One does not have to share Anger's esoteric philosophy to relish his imagery, often outrageously camp and pretentious as it is. RB

Anaïs Nin *Astarte* • Curtis Harrington *Cesare the Somnambulist* ■ *Dir/Scr* Kenneth Anger • *Music* Leos Janacek

Inbetweeners ★★ 15

Comedy romance 2000 · UK · Colour · 90mins

Anyone who's been to university will recognise most of the situations in Darren Paul Fisher's debut. But observational comedy means more than merely stringing together a few truisms in a "year-in-the-life" format: the viewer needs something more to hang on to than an endless round of naff parties, transient romances and other cynically recalled memoirs. Fisher is to be applauded for bringing this digital video offering in for £30,000. But some juvenile dialogue and the drama club performances deserve censure for settling, at best, for mediocrity. DP DVD

Finlay Robertson *David Marshall* • Kate Loustau *Nicole Miles* • Lynn Edmonstone *Steph Thornhill* • Toby Walton *Jack Easterford* • Sarah Vandenbergh *Cassie Sanderson* • Alex Harcourt-Smith *Marc Bailey-Piper* • Johnny Ball *Lecturer* ■ *Dir/Scr* Darren Fisher

Incendiary Blonde ★★★

Biographical musical 1945 · US · Colour · 113mins

An explosive Technicolor musical biopic giving a somewhat selective account of the colourful life of Texas Guinan, infamous nightclub queen of the Prohibition era, whose famous catchprase was "Hello suckers!". Lavishly mounted by Paramount, the movie is lively and entertaining, jam-packed with songs, including *It Had to Be You*, and lots of incident involving bootlegging gangsters, one of whom (Arturo De Cordova) is Texas's lover. Betty Hutton's most significant role to date saw the star hurling herself at the material – both dramatic and musical – with the force of a neutron bomb. RK

Betty Hutton *Texas Guinan* • Arturo de Cordova *Bill Romero Kilgannon* • Charlie Ruggles [Charles Ruggles] *Cherokee Jim* • Albert Dekker *Joe Cadden* ■ *Dir* George Marshall • *Scr* Claude Binyon, Frank Butler, from the biography *Life of Texas Guinan* by Thomas Guinan, WD Guinan

Incense for the Damned ★★ 18

Horror 1970 · UK · Colour · 86mins

This oddity fails to surmount its production problems. The low budget ran out in Cyprus and planned re-shoots never happened, so it was hastily patched together and then disowned by horror maestro Robert Hartford-Davis. Yet flashes of imagination shine through as Patrick Macnee helps Madeline Hinde save her fiancé Patrick Mower from Greek satanists. Released on video and DVD under its US title, *Bloodsuckers*. AJ. Contains violence, sex scenes, drug abuse, nudity. DVD

Patrick Macnee *Major Derek Longbow* • Peter Cushing *Dr Goodrich* • Alex Davion [Alexander Davion] *Tony Seymour* • Johnny Sekka *Bob Kirby* • Madeline Hinde *Penelope* • Patrick Mower *Richard Fountain* • Imogen Hassall *Chriseis Constandindi* • Edward Woodward *Holmstrom* • David Lodge *Colonel* ■ *Dir* Michael Burrowes [Robert Hartford-Davis] • *Scr* Julian More, from the novel *Doctors Wear Scarlet* by Simon Raven

Inchon ★

War drama 1981 · S Kor · Colour · 140mins

Dollar for dollar and with adjustments for inflation, this is the biggest flop in the history of the cinema. Financed to the tune of $46 million by the Church of the Reverend Sung Myung Moon, it's a vast re-creation of a major battle in the Korean war. Laurence Olivier as Douglas MacArthur leads a peculiar cast, while ex-Bond director Terence Young juggles the explosions and romantic interludes. It opened briefly, received a critical mauling and has barely been seen again. AT

Laurence Olivier *General Douglas MacArthur* • Jacqueline Bisset *Barbara Hallsworth* • Ben Gazzara *Major Frank Hallsworth* • David Janssen *David Feld* ■ *Dir* Terence Young • *Scr* Robin Moore, Laird Koenig, from a story by Paul Savage, Robin Moore

The Incident ★★★

Drama 1967 · US · BW · 107mins

This neatly compressed drama began as a live TV play called *Ride with Terror* but the planned Hollywood version, to be produced by Joseph E Levine, never came off. Tony Musante and Martin Sheen (in his screen debut) play two New York delinquents who make life a misery for the passengers on a subway train, including GI Beau Bridges, pensioner Thelma Ritter and bullied wife Jan Sterling. This structure – the 16 passengers representing a cross section of life in the big smoke – is filmed with considerable attack as the thugs taunt and expose the flaws in everyone's characters. AT

Tony Musante *Joe Ferrone* • Martin Sheen *Artie Connors* • Beau Bridges *Private First Class Felix Teflinger* • Jack Gilford *Sam Beckerman* • Thelma Ritter *Bertha Beckerman* • Brock Peters *Arnold Robinson* • Ruby Dee *Joan Robinson* • Donna Mills *Alice Keenan* ■ *Dir* Larry Peerce • *Scr* Nicholas E Baehr, from his play *Ride with Terror*

Incident at Phantom Hill ★★ U

Western 1966 · US · Colour · 87mins

From a period when Universal was making co-features to support its "A" product, invariably starring or trying out contract artists or television names, this stars *Laramie's* Robert Fuller opposite veteran baddie Dan Duryea. The tale of stolen bullion, hostile Apaches and the like is decked out in Technicolor to very little avail. The director is former floor assistant Earl Bellamy, whose technique is strictly TV, but old-timers Duryea and *Rio Bravo's* Claude Akins keep it just about watchable. TS

Robert Fuller *Matt Martin* • Jocelyn Lane *Memphis* • Dan Duryea *Joe Barlow* • Tom Simcox *Adam Long* • Linden Chiles *Dr Hanneford* • Claude Akins *Krausman* ■ *Dir* Earl Bellamy • *Scr* Frank Nugent, Ken Pettus, from a story by Harry Tateleman

Incognito ★ 15

Thriller 1997 · US · Colour · 103mins

Director John Badham takes a good cast and a reasonably interesting concept and comes up with this deeply disappointing thriller. You can hardly blame stars like Rod Steiger, who literally phones in his brief role as the artist father of art forger Jason Patric. The plot involves Patric's decision to accept a fortune to fake a Rembrandt and the mayhem that ensues. Lovers of art and good movies should give this one a wide berth. TH. Contains some swearing.

Jason Patric *Harry Donovan* • Irène Jacob *Marieke Van Den Broeck* • Thomas Lockyer *Alistar Davies* • Ian Richardson *Turley, prosecutor* • Rod Steiger *Milton A Donovan* ■ *Dir* John Badham • *Scr* Jordan Katz

The Incredible Hulk ★★★ PG

Fantasy action adventure 1977 · US · Colour · 90mins

Based on the Marvel Comics cartoon, this pilot feature (released theatrically in the UK) spawned an 80-episode series. The show itself borrowed its formula from *The Fugitive*, but this TV movie is more of a sci-fi affair, with scientist Bill Bixby channelling the grief caused by his wife's death into an exploration of the link between stress, strength and gamma radiation. Former Mr Universe Lou Ferrigno became a cult figure as Bixby's hulking green alter ego. Another TV movie, *The Return of the Incredible Hulk* was screened shortly after this launch feature. DP. DVD

Bill Bixby *Dr David Bruce Banner* • Susan Sullivan *Dr Elaina Marks* • Jack Colvin *Jack McGee* • Lou Ferrigno *The Hulk* ■ *Dir* Kenneth Johnson • *Scr* Kenneth Johnson, Thomas E Szollosi, Richard Christian Matheson, from the comic books by Stan Lee, Jack Kirby

The Incredible Hulk Returns ★★ PG

Fantasy action adventure
1988 · US · Colour · 93mins

Bursting from the pages of Marvel Comics on to our TV screens in 1978, the Incredible Hulk was, briefly, essential viewing for teenagers everywhere. But, by the time this TV movie appeared a decade later, audiences had grown out of his superheroic exploits, in much the same way that Bill Bixby grew out of his clothes (and turned into snarling Lou Ferrigno) every time he had a temper tantrum. Another Marvel regular, the mighty Thor, provides the villainy. DP. DVD

Bill Bixby *David Banner* • Lou Ferrigno *The Incredible Hulk* • Lee Purcell *Maggie Shaw* • Tim Thomerson *Le Beau* • Eric Kramer [Eric Allan Kramer] *Thor* • Jack Colvin *Jack McGee* ■ *Dir* Nicholas Corea • *Scr* Nicholas Corea, from characters created by Stan Lee, Jack Kirby

The Incredible Journey ★★★★ U

Adventure 1963 · US · Colour · 76mins

Not only is this easily the best of Disney's true-life adventures, but it's also far superior to the studio's dumbed down 1993 remake, *Homeward Bound: the Incredible Journey*. Syn (as Tao the cat), Muffey (Bodger the bull terrier) and Rink (Luath the labrador) are outstanding as the abandoned pets who make their way across the treacherous Canadian wilderness to reunite with their owners. On the way they encounter danger in the form of bears, mountain lions and a disgruntled porcupine. Subtly narrated by Rex Allen, this is only slightly spoiled by the wooden performances of the humans in the cast. Compelling family viewing. DP

Rex Allen *Narrator* • Emile Genest *John Longridge* • John Drainie *Professor Jim Hunter* • Tommy Tweed *Hermit* • Sandra Scott *Mrs Hunter* • Syme Jago *Helvi Nurmi* • Marion Finlayson *Elizabeth Hunter* ■ *Dir* Fletcher Markle • *Scr* James Algar, from the novel by Sheila Burnford

The Incredible Melting Man ★★ 18

Horror 1977 · US · Colour · 82mins

Astronaut Alex Rebar returns from Saturn a changed man. His flesh is decomposing and he finds he's developed a taste for human meat. A deliberate throwback to cheap 1950s frights, William Sachs's film provides little of interest, apart from showcasing Oscar winner (*An American Werewolf in London*) Rick Baker's oozing, slimy and putrefying make-up to stunning effect. AJ DVD

Alex Rebar *Melting Man* • Burr DeBenning *Dr Ted Nelson* • Myron Healey *General Perry* • Michael Alldredge *Sheriff Blake* • Ann Sweeny *Judy Nelson* • Lisle Wilson *Dr Loring* • Jonathan Demme *Matt* ■ *Dir/Scr* William Sachs • *Make-up* Rick Baker

The Incredible Mr Limpet ★★

Part-animated fantasy comedy
1964 · US · Colour · 102mins

Don Knotts stars as meek clerk Henry Limpet, who's obsessed with fish, in this part live action, part animated wartime fantasy. When he is turned down for the navy because of his short-sightedness Knotts is despondent. Later, he falls off a dock into the ocean and is miraculously transformed into an animated fish. In his new guise, he finds fulfilment by guiding US vessels pursuing German U-boats. Sentimental sub-Disney. DF

Don Knotts *Henry Limpet* • Carole Cook *Bessie Limpet* • Jack Weston *Lt George Stickle* • Andrew Duggan *Adm Harlock* ■ *Dir* Arthur Lubin • *Scr* Jameson Brewer, John C Rose, Joe DiMona, from the novel *Mr Limpet* by Theodore Pratt

The Incredible Sarah ★★

Biographical drama
1976 · UK · Colour · 105mins

Oscar-winning British actress Glenda Jackson hams it up as famous French actress Sarah Bernhardt, in a performance that hardly hints at a great future in politics. Despite many obvious errors of judgement, director Richard Fleischer was clearly at the end of his creative tether with this humdrum *Reader's Digest*-backed look at Bernhardt's life, so all he can do is to provide some entertainment value. He only just succeeds. TH

Glenda Jackson *Sarah Bernhardt* • Daniel Massey *Sardou* • Yvonne Mitchell *Mam'selle* • Douglas Wilmer *Montigny* • David Langton *Duc De Morny* • Simon Williams *Henri De Ligne* ■ *Dir* Richard Fleischer • *Scr* Ruth Wolff

The Incredible Shrinking Man ★★★★★

Science fiction 1957 · US · BW · 91mins

A must-see classic, directed by the master of 1950s' science fiction, Jack Arnold, and derived from the thought-provoking novel by genre luminary Richard Matheson. Grant Williams slowly shrinks after passing through a radioactive cloud and, on the way down, sees his marriage disintegrate and is terrorised by the pet cat and a basement spider. A cogent comment on the plight of the "little man", Arnold's superlative thriller still retains its irony, shock and power. Williams gives a sensitive portrayal of a man hounded by the media and consigned to a freak's world, whose descent provides a memorable climax. AJ

Grant Williams *Scott Carey* • Randy Stuart *Louise Carey* • April Kent *Clarice* • Paul Langton *Charlie Carey* • Raymond Bailey *Dr Thomas Silver* • William Schallert *Dr Arthur Bramson* ■ *Dir* Jack Arnold • *Scr* Richard Matheson, from his novel *The Shrinking Man*

The Incredible Shrinking Woman ★★★

Science-fiction comedy
1981 · US · Colour · 88mins

A very odd spoof on the wonderful *The Incredible Shrinking Man*, brought bang up to date with some neat special effects but lacking the shock value of the original. Lily Tomlin is very funny as the housewife accidentally sprayed with a new perfume and ending up the size of the germs she tries so hard to eradicate in her home. This is a pleasing little jaunt through highly familiar territory, directed with flair and a light touch by Joel Schumacher. SH. Contains swearing.

Lily Tomlin *Pat Kramer/Judith Beasley* • Charles Grodin *Vance Kramer* • Ned Beatty *Dan Beame* • Henry Gibson *Dr Eugene Nortz* ■ *Dir* Joel Schumacher • *Scr* Jane Wagner, from the novel *The Shrinking Man* by Richard Matheson

The Incredible Two-Headed Transplant ★

Science-fiction horror
1971 · US · Colour · 87mins

This low-budget nonsense is so laughably bad as to have garnered a minor cult reputation among trash horror movie fans. Bruce Dern is perfectly cast as a deranged scientist who grafts the head of a murderer on to the body of a retarded giant who – predictably – goes on a Frankenstein-style rampage. Anthony M Lanza, unsurprisingly, never directed another film again, although acclaimed make-up effects artist Rick Baker was responsible for the gorilla suit. RS

Bruce Dern *Roger* • Pat Priest *Linda* • Casey Kasem *Ken* • Albert Cole *Cass* • John Bloom (1) *Danny* ■ *Dir* Anthony M Lanza • *Scr* James Gordon White, John Lawrence

The Incredibles ★★★★ U

Animated comedy adventure
2004 · US · Colour and BW · 110mins

Originally conceived as a hand-drawn project, this spectacular comic book-style adventure is another triumph for Pixar's brand of computer-animated magic. Mr Incredible (voiced by Craig T Nelson), once one of the world's foremost superheroes, is now an insurance agent living incognito in the suburbs (thanks to a super-litigious society having turned doing good deeds into an invitation for a lawsuit). But duty eventually calls and soon he's squeezing himself back into his old costume and fighting crime on the sly. Brad Bird instils his characters with genuine personalities, emotions and values. The film's slightly overlong, but its sophistication, wit and skill more than compensate. SF DVD

Craig T Nelson *Bob Parr/Mr Incredible* • Holly Hunter *Helen Parr/Elastigirl* • Samuel L Jackson *Lucius Best/Frozone* • Jason Lee *Buddy Pine/Syndrome* • Sarah Vowell *Violet Parr* • Spencer Fox *Dashiell "Dash" Parr* • Elizabeth Peña *Mirage* • Wallace Shawn *Gilbert Huph* • John Ratzenberger *The Underminer* • Brad Bird *Edna "E" Mode* ■ *Dir/Scr* Brad Bird

The Incredibly Strange Creatures Who Stopped Living and Became Mixed-up Zombies ★★

Horror comedy 1963 · US · Colour · 82mins

This legendary turkey was billed as the "First Monster Musical" and features such awful production numbers as *The Mixed-up Zombie Stomp*, complete with tacky striptease routines. Cash Flagg (director Ray Dennis Steckler's alter ego) falls under the sinister spell of a sideshow fortune-teller who throws acid in her patron's faces and then confines them to cages where they become rabid zombies ready to break loose when the rock songs begin. AJ

Cash Flagg [Ray Dennis Steckler] *Jerry* • Carolyn Brandt *Marge Neilson* • Brett O'Hara *Madame Estrella* • Atlas King *Harold* ■ *Dir* Ray Dennis Steckler • *Scr* Gene Pollock, Robert Silliphant, from a story by EM Kevke

The Incredibly True Adventures of Two Girls in Love ★★★ 15

Romantic comedy drama
1995 · US · Colour · 91mins

Likeable same-sex love story, about the romance between two girls from widely differing social and financial backgrounds. One is a working-class lesbian who lives with other lesbians, including her mum. The other is from a wealthy background, hugely popular, and complete with boyfriend. Burgeoning romance arouses wrath from both sets of friends and relatives. Engaging performances and sensitive plot-handling ensure you'll be rooting for the triumph of true love. And, of course, triumph it does. DA DVD

Laurel Holloman *Randy Dean* • Nicole Parker [Nicole Ari Parker] *Evie Roy* • Maggie Moore *Wendy* • Kate Stafford *Rebecca Dean* • Sabrina Artel *Vicky* • Toby Poser *Lena* ■ *Dir/Scr* Maria Maggenti

Incubus ★★★ 18

Horror 1965 · US · BW · 88mins

William Shatner speaking Esperanto and sharing screen time with someone calling himself Incubus. No, it's not a "lost" episode of *Star Trek* but a rare experimental art movie that was unavailable for years until a print belatedly became available. Best described as a kind of Swedish art movie filmed in California, this finds Shatner in the land of Nomen Tuum, where he's under threat from Allyson Ames's witch and the devil's little helper, Incubus. Shatner actually handles his part and the Esperanto dialogue well, and the black-and-white photography by Conrad Hall (Oscar winner for *Butch Cassidy*) is alternately stunning and haunting. KB. In Esperanto with English subtitles.

William Shatner *Marc* • Milos Milos *Incubus* • Allyson Ames *Kia* • Eloise Hardt *Amael* • Robert Fortier *Olin* ■ *Dir/Scr* Leslie Stevens (1)

Indecent Behavior ★★ 18

Erotic thriller 1993 · US · Colour · 94mins

Shannon Tweed is the undisputed queen of the erotic thriller and this proved to be one of her most popular films. The story is completely daft: Tweed plays an extremely unlikely sex therapist, under suspicion when one of her patients dies, who becomes involved with the detective investigating the case. The plot is largely an excuse for Tweed to get up to some ludicrously stylised sex sessions set to a sub-MTV soundtrack. It's actually pretty funny, but for all the wrong reasons. Three sequels followed. JF. Contains violence, sex scenes, swearing, nudity. DVD

Shannon Tweed *Rebecca Mathis* • Gary Hudson *Nick Sharkey* • Michelle Moffett *Carol Lefter* • Lawrence Hilton-Jacobs *Lou Parsons* • Jan-Michael Vincent *Tom Mathis* ■ *Dir* Lawrence Lanoff • *Scr* Rosalind Robinson

Indecent Proposal ★★★★ 15

Drama 1993 · US · Colour · 112mins

Would you pay $1 million to sleep with Demi Moore? Robert Redford thinks she's worth it, as he puts the proposal to Moore's husband Woody Harrelson after learning they need the money. The interesting "would *you* do it?" premise of Adrian Lyne's film goes slightly awry as the moral issues are dumped in favour of all three main characters simply showing how selfish they are. This is probably best seen as a good example of the excesses and emptiness of the early 1990s. But, with a cast like this, who are we to quibble? JB. Contains swearing, sex scenes and nudity. DVD

Robert Redford *John Gage* • Demi Moore *Diana Murphy* • Woody Harrelson *David Murphy* • Seymour Cassel *Mr Shackelford* • Oliver Platt *Jeremy* • Billy Connolly *Auction emcee* • Joel Brooks *Realtor* • Pierre Epstein *Van Buren* • Sheena Easton • Herbie Hancock ■ *Dir* Adrian Lyne • *Scr* Amy Holden Jones, from the novel by Jack Engelhard

Independence Day ★★★ 15

Drama 1983 · US · Colour · 109mins

A perfectly realised slice of small-town life from director Robert Mandel, who would later gain some cult credibility by directing the pilot for *The X Files*. Adapted by Alice Hoffman from her own novel, the story features Kathleen Quinlan as a bored young woman torn between making a new life for herself and her developing relationship with David Keith. Mandel's direction is unobtrusive and sympathetic. JF

Kathleen Quinlan *Mary Ann Taylor* • David Keith *Jack Parker* • Frances Sternhagen *Carla Taylor* • Cliff De Young *Les Morgan* • Dianne Wiest *Nancy Morgan* • Josef Sommer *Sam Taylor* • Richard Farnsworth *Evan* ■ *Dir* Robert Mandel • *Scr* Alice Hoffman

Independence Day ★★★★ 12

Science-fiction adventure
1996 · US · Colour · 138mins

No film had presented the destruction of the Earth on such an epic scale before this preposterously successful smash-hit sci-fi adventure came along. Of course, when we say Earth, we really mean the United States. The story is simple: gigantic alien spacecraft hover above major cities and set about destroying everything below, with mind-boggling set pieces of mass destruction. Will Smith, playing the wisecracking fighter pilot, is the big winner, with his charismatic performance making him one of the biggest box-office draws in the western world. Jeff Goldblum, Hollywood's most unlikely action star, delivers a variation of his boffin role in *Jurassic Park*. But this is, after all, a special effects, not an acting, showcase, and a darn entertaining one at that. JF. Contains violence and swearing. [video] DVD

Will Smith *Captain Steve Hiller* • Bill Pullman *President Thomas J Whitmore* • Jeff Goldblum *David Levinson* • Mary McDonnell *Marilyn Whitmore* • Judd Hirsch *Julius Levinson* • Robert Loggia *General William Grey* • Randy Quaid *Russell Casse* • Margaret Colin *Constance Spano* • Harvey Fierstein *Marty Gilbert* • Adam Baldwin *Major Mitchell* • Brent Spiner *Dr Brakish Okun* • Vivica A Fox *Jasmine Dubrow* ■ *Dir* Roland Emmerich • *Scr* Dean Devlin, Roland Emmerich

Indestructible Man ★★ PG

Science fiction 1956 · US · BW · 70mins

This revenge B-movie is saved by another patented display of dolour from Lon Chaney Jr. He's transformed into a Frankensteinian lug by a jolt of electricity, this time applied to his executed cadaver by cancer specialist Robert Shayne. Thenceforth it's stalk 'n'slash 1950s-style, as Chaney seeks to prevent crooked lawyer Ross Elliott from locating loot stashed in the LA sewer system. DP [video] DVD

Lon Chaney Jr *The Butcher* • Marian Carr *Eva Martin* • Robert Shayne *Prof Bradshaw* ■ *Dir* Jack Pollexfen • *Scr* Sue Bradford, Vi Russell

The Indian Fighter ★★★ PG

Western 1955 · US · Colour · 88mins

Kirk Douglas stars in this under-rated and beautifully made western, which was the first film to be produced by Douglas's own company, Bryna. Its classy eroticism is exemplified by the casting of Italian star Elsa Martinelli as Douglas's maid, though Diana Douglas (Kirk's ex-wife and Michael's mum) also appears as a settler with more than a passing interest in the leading man. He is in his buckskinned prime, full of virile derring-do as he leads an Oregon-bound wagon train through "Injun" territory. TS [video]

Kirk Douglas *Johnny Hawks* • Elsa Martinelli *Onahti* • Walter Abel *Captain Trask* • Walter Matthau *Wes Todd* • Diana Douglas *Susan Rogers* • Lon Chaney Jr *Chivington* ■ *Dir* Andre De Toth • *Scr* Frank Davis, Ben Hecht, from a story by Ben Kadish [Robert L Richards]

The Indian in the Cupboard ★★★★ PG

Fantasy adventure
1995 · US · Colour · 92mins

Wrapping culture-clash comedy up with *Honey, I Shrunk the Kids*-style special effects, director Frank Oz's assured, funny version of the Lynne Reid Banks novel is a low-key fantasy. A young boy discovers that an old cupboard given to him on his birthday can animate his playthings in this enchanting family fable. Ultimately he must learn responsibility when he brings his toy Indian (well played by rap artist Litefoot) to life and starts treating him like a human Action Man. Muppet maestro Oz and his screenwriter Melissa Mathison never get too heavy, condescending or cloying with their sweet-natured message. AJ [video] DVD

Hal Scardino *Omri* • Litefoot *Little Bear* • Lindsay Crouse *Jane* • Richard Jenkins *Victor* • Rishi Bhat *Patrick* • Steve Coogan *Tommy* ■ *Dir* Frank Oz • *Scr* Melissa Mathison, from the novel by Lynne Reid Banks

The Indian Runner ★★★ 15

Drama 1991 · US · Colour · 121mins

Sean Penn took everyone by surprise with this, his writing and directorial debut. It's a remarkably assured, mature drama, inspired by the Bruce Springsteen song *Highway Patrolman*, and follows the troubled relationship between David Morse and his disturbed younger brother (an electrifying Viggo Mortensen). The story is slight but Penn's commitment to his tragic characters shines through and his direction is pleasingly unflashy, aside from sudden jolts of violence. JF. Contains swearing. [video] DVD

David Morse *Joe Roberts* • Viggo Mortensen *Frank Roberts* • Valeria Golino *Maria Roberts* • Patricia Arquette *Dorothy* • Charles Bronson *Father* • Sandy Dennis *Mother* • Dennis Hopper *Caesar* • Jordan Rhodes *Randall* ■ *Dir* Sean Penn • *Scr* Sean Penn, from the song *Highway Patrolman* by Bruce Springsteen

Indian Summer ★★★★ 15

Comedy drama 1993 · US · Colour · 93mins

There is a wonderful sense of place and a bittersweet atmosphere of remembrance and regret generated by director Mike Binder, who also wrote the semi-autobiographical script. There is also the quality of the ensemble acting, in which no one tries to steal a march on any other member of the cast. However, Alan Arkin is particularly impressive as the camp director who invites his favourite guests to spend a final summer in the woods before he's closed down. DP. Contains swearing, sex scenes and drug abuse. [video] DVD

Alan Arkin *Uncle Lou* • Matt Craven *Jamie Ross* • Diane Lane *Beth Warden/Claire Everett* • Bill Paxton *Jack Belston* • Elizabeth Perkins *Jennifer Morton* • Kevin Pollak *Brad Berman* • Sam Raimi *Stick Coder* ■ *Dir/Scr* Mike Binder

The Indian Tomb ★★★

Adventure drama
1959 · W Ger/Fr/It · Colour · 95mins

The second half of Fritz Lang's two-part film (the first being *The Tiger of Eschnapur*) tells an exotic tale, evoking the world of silent serials. German architect Harald Berger and beautiful Indian dancer Seeta (unconvincingly played by Hollywood actress Debra Paget) face further perils as their romance is threatened by love rival Walter Reyer. Lang's straight-faced approach provides some unintentional laughs, but it has magical moments. RB. In German with English subtitles.

Debra Paget *Seeta* • Walter Reyer *Chandra* • Paul Hubschmid *Harald Berger* • Claus Holm *Dr Walter Rhode* • Sabine Bethmann *Irene Rhode* • Valery Inkijinoff *Yama* ■ *Dir* Fritz Lang • *Scr* Fritz Lang, Werner Jörg Lüddecke, Thea von Harbou, from an idea by Thea von Harbou, from a novel by Richard Eichberg

Indian Uprising ★ U

Western 1951 · US · Colour · 75mins

In a feeble roundup of the situations being explored in bigger and better westerns of the period, George Montgomery plays the cavalry captain who's temporarily stripped of his command while trying to keep the peace between settlers and Indians. Villains are after the gold on the Indian reservation and that stirs up Geronimo, as played by Miguel Inclan. AE

Eddy Waller *Sagebrush* • George Montgomery *Captain Case McCloud* • Audrey Long *Norma Clemson* • Carl Benton Reid *John Clemson* • Miguel Inclan *Geronimo* ■ *Dir* Ray Nazarro • *Scr* Kenneth Gamet, Richard Schayer, from a story by Richard Schayer

Indiana Jones and the Last Crusade ★★★★★ PG

Action adventure
1989 · US · Colour · 121mins

The Temple of Doom saw the Indiana Jones series lurch off the rails a little, but all was restored with this third movie. The masterstroke here was the introduction of Sean Connery as Indy's crotchety dad, and the snappy by-play between him and Harrison Ford adds a wonderful new twist to the adventure. The quest this time is for the Holy Grail, and finds Jones reunited with old chums, such as Denholm Elliott, and old enemies, namely the Nazis. As usual, the action is on an epic scale and delivered with breathless enthusiasm and much panache by director Steven Spielberg. There is also a neat framing sequence in the beginning with River Phoenix as the young Indy that explains such things as our hero's fear of snakes. JF. Contains swearing, violence. [video] DVD

Harrison Ford *Indiana Jones* • Sean Connery *Dr Henry Jones* • Denholm Elliott *Marcus Brody* • Alison Doody *Dr Elsa Schneider* • John Rhys-Davies *Sallah* • Julian Glover *Walter Donovan* • River Phoenix *Young Indy* • Alexei Sayle *Sultan* ■ *Dir* Steven Spielberg • *Scr* Jeffrey Boam, from a story by George Lucas, Menno Meyjes, from characters created by George Lucas, Philip Kaufman • *Music* John Williams • *Cinematographer* Douglas Slocombe

Indiana Jones and the Temple of Doom ★★★★ PG

Action adventure
1984 · US · Colour · 112mins

Steven Spielberg continued his homage to the classic cliffhanger serials of his youth with this follow-up to the rousing *Raiders of the Lost Ark*. It's a trifle overblown and unsubtle, but it still has great sets, fun performances and terrific action – the standout is a wild ride through an Indian mine. Harrison Ford is engaging as Indy and goes a long way in making up for the inferior story and often gruesome gags. AJ [video] DVD

Harrison Ford *Indiana Jones* • Kate Capshaw *Willie Scott* • Ke Huy Quan *Short Round* • Amrish Puri *Mola Ram* • Roshan Seth *Chatter Lal* • Philip Stone *Captain Blumburtt* • Roy Chiao *Lao Che* • David Yip *Wu Han* ■ *Dir* Steven Spielberg • *Scr* Willard Huyck, Gloria Katz, from a story by George Lucas, from characters created by George Lucas, Philip Kaufman

Indianapolis Speedway ★★

Action drama 1939 · US · BW · 85mins

Despite being a remake of the Jimmy Cagney/Howard Hawks hit *The Crowd Roars*, this car-racing drama fails on the first lap. As the champion driver who tries too hard to look after his kid brother, Pat O'Brien lacks Cagney's bravado and energy while director Lloyd Bacon displays none of Hawks's feeling for the material. John Payne is no more than adequate as the younger brother but Ann Sheridan shows why Warner Bros were promoting her as "the Oomph Girl". AE

Pat O'Brien *Joe Greer* • Ann Sheridan *Frankie Merrick* • John Payne *Eddie Greer* • Gale Page *Lee Mason* • Frank McHugh *Spud Connors* ■ *Dir* Lloyd Bacon • *Scr* Sig Herzig, Wally Klein, from the story *The Roar of the Crowd* by Howard Hawks, William Hawks • *Cinematographer* Sid Hickox

Indictment: the McMartin Trial ★★★★ 18

Courtroom drama based on a true story
1995 · US · Colour · 125mins

This starry made-for-TV production, executive produced by Oliver Stone, is based on a case in the US, in which a family that ran a private day care centre was accused of child abuse. James Woods is the lawyer assigned to defend one of the accused (Henry Thomas), while Mercedes Ruehl is the ruthless prosecutor. The A-list cast are uniformly superb but what distinguishes this drama is the way director Mick Jackson keeps the viewer guessing as to what actually happened to the children. JF [video]

James Woods *Danny Davis* • Mercedes Ruehl *Lael Rubin* • Henry Thomas *Ray Buckey* • Shirley Knight *Peggy Buckey* • Sada Thompson *Virginia McMartin* • Lolita Davidovich *Kee McFarlane* • Mark Blum *Wayne Satz* • Alison Elliott (2) *Peggy Ann Buckey* • Chelsea Field *Christine Johnson* ■ *Dir* Mick Jackson • *Scr* Abby Mann, Myra Mann

Indien ★★

Comedy drama
1993 · Austria · Colour · 90mins

One of the few Austrian pictures of recent times to gain any sort of international recognition, this sentimental comedy drama was widely tipped for a best foreign film Oscar. Directed by Paul Harather and co-scripted with his two stars, Josef Hader and Alfred Dorfer, the story chronicles the changing relationship between two government hotel inspectors as they sample the facilities in various establishments. In true *Odd Couple* fashion there's plenty of sparring from the ill-matched couple. DP. In German with English subtitles.

Josef Hader *Heinzi Bösel* • Alfred Dorfer *Kurt Fellner* ■ *Dir* Paul Harather • *Scr* Paul Harather, Josef Hader, Alfred Dorfer, from a play by Josef Hader, Alfred Dorfer

Indiscreet ★★★

Romantic comedy 1931 · US · BW · 92mins

One of Gloria Swanson's more successful attempts to extend her career into talkies, this comedy drama features her as the woman with a past who attempts to protect her younger sister (Barbara Kent) from the attentions of rakish Monroe Owsley. He's actually an ex-lover of Swanson's, and Kent is none too pleased when she finds out. Meanwhile Swanson has a budding romance with Ben Lyon's impulsive author. Largely scripted by the songwriting team of DeSylva, Brown and Henderson (who throw in a couple of lightweight numbers for Swanson to perform), this is a bright rehash of familiar situations, directed imaginatively by Leo McCarey. AE

Gloria Swanson *Geraldine Trent* • Ben Lyon *Tony Blake* • Monroe Owsley *Jim Woodward* • Barbara Kent *Joan Trent* • Arthur Lake *Buster Collins* • Maude Eburne *Aunt Kate* ■ *Dir* Leo McCarey • *Scr* BG DeSylva, Lew Brown, Ray Henderson, from their story *Obey That Impulse*

Indiscreet ★★★ PG

Romantic comedy
1958 · UK/US · Colour · 99mins

Two of the screen's most elegant stars provide much of the pleasure in this glossy romantic comedy, adapted by Norman Krasna from his play *Kind Sir*. The action has been transplanted from New York to foggy London (it was filmed at Elstree) with Ingrid Bergman as a famous actress looking for love and Cary Grant as the diplomat who's pretending he's married when he's not. Highlights include Grant dancing a superb Highland reel and a witty supporting performance as a chauffeur in disguise from the under-rated David Kossoff. It's nonsense, of course, but utterly charming. TS [video] DVD

Cary Grant *Philip Adams* • Ingrid Bergman *Anna Kalman* • Cecil Parker *Alfred Munson* • Phyllis Calvert *Margaret Munson* • David Kossoff *Carl Banks* ■ *Dir* Stanley Donen • *Scr* Norman Krasna, from his play *Kind Sir*

Indiscretion of an American Wife ★★★ U

Drama 1954 · US/It · BW · 63mins

Director Vittorio De Sica's claustrophobic study of the end of a brief encounter is brilliantly filmed in stark black and white in Rome's famous Stazione Terminale. The story brings together Jennifer Jones and Montgomery Clift as lovers who can't bear to make the final break. The stars are filmed in magnificent close-ups, their anxiety almost palpable. Jones's husband, David O Selznick, recut this movie considerably, but it has a raw truth about it that is still deeply moving. TS

Jennifer Jones *Mary Forbes* • Montgomery Clift *Giovanni Doria* • Gino Cervi *Commissioner* • Dick Beymer [Richard Beymer] *Paul, Mary's nephew* ■ *Dir* Vittorio De Sica • *Scr* Cesare Zavattini, Luigi Chiarini, Giorgio Prosperi, Truman Capote, from a story by Cesare Zavattini

Indochine ★★★★ 15

Period romance 1991 · Fr · Colour · 151mins

Winner of the Oscar for best foreign language film, this epic drama set in French Indochina in the 1930s also won five Césars, including best actress for the imperious Catherine Deneuve and best supporting actress for Dominique Blanc. Having hooked us on a melodramatic love triangle involving Deneuve, her teenage daughter and a handsome naval officer, the picture plunges us into a breathless adventure as the daughter encounters the brutal realities of French rule when she follows the officer to his far-flung base. DP. In French with English subtitles. Contains violence, swearing, sex scenes and drug abuse. DVD

Catherine Deneuve *Eliane* • Vincent Perez *Jean-Baptiste* • Linh Dan Pham *Camille* • Jean Yanne *Guy* • Dominique Blanc *Yvette* • Henri Marteau *Emile* • Carlo Brandt *Castellani* ■ *Dir* Régis Wargnier • *Scr* Régis Wargnier, Erik Orsenna, Louis Gardel, Catherine Cohen

Infernal Affairs ★★★★ 15

Crime drama 2002 · HK · Colour · 96mins

Andrew Lau directs this satisfyingly complex and simmeringly atmospheric crime drama. However, it's very much a team effort, with co-director Alan Mak and Felix Chong's taut screenplay bringing the best out of an impressive cast. Andy Lau plays a Hong Kong detective in the pay of Triad mobster Eric Tsang, who is being investigated by longtime undercover cop Tony Leung. The tension as both sides search for the moles betraying their plans often becomes unbearable and it's to directors Lau and Mak's credit that they refuse to allow the action to descend into clichéd showdown pyrotechnics. DP. In Cantonese with English subtitles. Contains violence and drug abuse. DVD

Tony Leung (2) *Chan Wing Yan* • Andy Lau *Inspector Lau Kin Ming* • Anthony Wong (1) *Superintendent Wong* • Eric Tsang *Sam* • Kelly Chen *Dr Lee Sum Yee* • Sammi Cheng *Mary* • Edison Chen *Young Lau Kin Ming* • Shawn Yue *Young Chan Wing Yan* • Chapman To *Keung* ■ *Dir* Andrew Lau, Alan Mak • *Scr* Alan Mak, Felix Chong

Infernal Affairs II ★★★ 15

Crime drama 2003 · HK · Colour · 114mins

Fleshing out the opening sequence of Andrew Lau and Alan Mak's original crime thriller, this is a satisfyingly complex prequel that expertly lays the ground for the entire *Infernal Affairs* trilogy. The action centres around Shawn Yue and Edison Chen, who are operating as moles in the triads and the Hong Kong police respectively. But their positions look likely to be compromised as Francis Ng conducts a gang war against his murdered father's henchmen. DP. In Cantonese with English subtitles. DVD

Edison Chen *Lau Kin Ming* • Shawn Yue *Chan Wing Yan* • Anthony Wong (1) *Superintendent Wong* • Francis Ng *Ngai Wing-Hau* • Eric Tsang *Sam* • Carina Lau *Mary* • Chapman To *Keung* • Andrew Lin *Ngai's brother* • Bey Logan *Inspector Calvin* ■ *Dir* Andrew Lau, Alan Mak • *Scr* Felix Chong, Alan Mak

Infernal Affairs 3 ★★★

Crime drama 2003 · HK · Colour · 118mins

The concluding part of this thrilling trilogy opens shortly after the climax of the original, with Hong Kong cop Andy Lau convinced that he's become a hero without being rumbled as a mole for triad boss Eric Tsang. However, his cover could still be blown if newcomer Leon Lai digs too deep – that is, providing his links with mobster Chen Dao Ming aren't exposed by Tony Leung, who is working undercover in Tsang's gang. The action becomes unnecessarily intricate, but the set pieces throb with explosive panache. DP. In Cantonese with English subtitles.

Andy Lau *Lau Kin Ming* • Tony Chiu-Wai Leung [Tony Leung (2)] *Chan Wing Yan* • Anthony Wong (1) *Superintendent Wong* • Eric Tsang *Sam* • Kelly Chen *Dr Lee Sum Yee* • Sammi Cheng *Mary* • Edison Chen *Young Lau Kin Ming* • Shawn Yue *Young Chan Wing Yan* • Leon Lai *Yeung* • Chen Dao Ming *Shen* ■ *Dir* Andrew Lau, Alan Mak • *Scr* Felix Chong, Andrew Lau

Inferno ★★★

Drama 1953 · US · Colour · 83mins

Sharply directed by Britain's Roy Ward Baker, this ingenious thriller rests securely on the performance of Robert Ryan as the millionaire playboy left to die in the desert with a broken leg by his wife and her lover. Most of the film covers Ryan's heroic efforts to survive the extremes of temperature, hunger and natural hazards. This was one of the most effective pictures ever made for showing in 3-D, which emphasised the vastness of the desert, but the avoidance of gimmicky effects means that it works as well shown flat. AE

Robert Ryan *Carson* • Rhonda Fleming *Geraldine Carson* • William Lundigan *Joseph Duncan* • Larry Keating *Emory* • Henry Hull *Sam Elby* • Carl Betz *Lieutenant Mark Platt* ■ *Dir* Roy Ward Baker • *Scr* Francis Cockrell • *Cinematographer* Lucien Ballard

Inferno ★★★ 18

Horror 1980 · It · Colour · 101mins

Italian director Dario Argento follows up *Suspiria* with this slightly demented but compulsive shocker. Student Leigh McCloskey returns to New York from Rome following the untimely demise of his girlfriend. His sister has discovered that her apartment building has some malevolent occupants whose supernatural powers result in a number of violent deaths. Argento creates enough striking moments to offset inconsistencies in the plot. TH. Italian dialogue dubbed into English.

Leigh McCloskey *Mark Elliot* • Irene Miracle *Rose Elliot* • Eleonora Giorgi *Sara* • Daria Nicolodi *Countess Elise* ■ *Dir* Dario Argento • *Scr* Dario Argento, from a story by Dario Argento • *Music* Keith Emerson

The Infiltrator ★★★ 18

Political thriller 1995 · US · Colour · 88mins

This intense TV thriller is based on the true story of Yaron Svoray, an Israeli-born reporter. Svoray (Oliver Platt) travels to Germany to investigate neo-Nazism and infiltrates a skinhead gang. As he gets closer to uncovering the leaders, the full horror of their violent, hate-mongering movement becomes clear. Platt's convincing performance is particularly effective in this powerful drama. MC. Contains swearing and violence, including a sexual assault. DVD

Oliver Platt *Yaron Svoray* • Arliss Howard *Eaton* • Peter Riegert *Rabbi Cooper* • Alan King *Rabbi Hier* • Tony Haygarth *Gunther* • Michael Byrne *Creutz* • Julian Glover *Bielert* • Alex Kingston *Anna* ■ *Dir* John Mackenzie • *Scr* Guy Andrews, from a story by Robert J Avrech, Guy Andrews, from the non-fiction book *In Hitler's Shadow: an Israeli's Amazing Journey inside Germany's Neo-Nazi Movement* by Yaron Svoray, Nick Taylor

Infinity ★★★

Biographical romantic drama 1996 · US · Colour · 119mins

Matthew Broderick both stars in and directs this feature about Nobel Prize-winning physicist Richard Feynman, who worked on the development of the atomic bomb. The opening half, where Broderick meets and romances Patricia Arquette in pre-Second World War New York, is both touching and powerful. It's an above average debut (scripted by Broderick's mother, Patricia) but viewers of a non-technical disposition might have preferred more emphasis on romance and less on science. LH

Matthew Broderick *Richard Feynman* • Patricia Arquette *Arline Greenbaum* • Peter Riegert *Mel Feynman* • Dori Brenner *Tutti Feynman* • Peter Michael Goetz *Dr Hellman* ■ *Dir* Matthew Broderick • *Scr* Patricia Broderick, from the memoirs *Surely You're Joking, Mr Feynman!* and *What Do You Care What Other People Think?* by Richard Feynman

Information Received ★★

Thriller 1962 · UK · BW · 77mins

Routine British crime movie in which Scotland Yard show rather more enterprise than usual, foiling an underworld gang by substituting an informer as the safe-cracker imported from America for a big job. The bogus one is played by William Sylvester, but top billing goes to Sabina Sesselmann, a starlet with an alluring name but not enough talent. AT

Sabina Sesselman *Sabina Farlow* • William Sylvester *Rick Hogan* • Hermione Baddeley *Maudie* • Edward Underdown *Drake* • Robert Raglan *Supt Jeffcote* • Frank Hawkins *Sgt Jarvie* ■ *Dir* Robert Lynn • *Scr* Paul Ryder, from a story by Berkely Mather • *Cinematographer* Nicolas Roeg

The Informer ★★★ PG

Drama 1935 · US · BW · 91mins

This screen version of Liam O'Flaherty's novel is an art film with a vengeance. Given a low budget, director John Ford had a free hand to film this grim story set in Dublin in 1922 during the Irish Civil War. Victor McLaglen, driven by poverty to inform against the IRA, is then racked by guilt as he faces inevitable retribution. Ford adopted a heavily stylised approach with overt symbolism and won an Academy Award along with leading actor McLaglen, screenwriter Dudley Nichols and composer Max Steiner. While Ford's less pretentious works are much to be preferred, this is still a powerful picture of great historic interest. AE

Victor McLaglen *Gypo Nolan* • Heather Angel *Mary McPhillip* • Preston Foster *Dan Gallagher* • Margot Grahame *Katie Madden* • Wallace Ford *Frankie McPhillip* ■ *Dir* John Ford • *Scr* Dudley Nichols, from the novel by Liam O'Flaherty

The Informers ★★ 12

Crime drama 1963 · UK · BW · 100mins

Nowadays British crime films of the 1950s and 1960s look rather quaint, with the dogged attempts of performers to either act tough and growl in East End argot as they plan their blags, or portray the clipped decency of the Scotland Yard flatfoot. While eminently watchable, this police procedural crime drama from director Ken Annakin is a case in point. Nigel Patrick is the archetypal inspector in a mac, while Frank Finlay is as brutal as a pantomime villain. DP

Nigel Patrick *Chief Insp Johnnoe* • Margaret Whiting *Maisie* • Colin Blakely *Charlie Ruskin* • Derren Nesbitt *Bertie Hoyle* • Frank Finlay *Leon Sale* • Catherine Woodville *Mary Johnnoe* • Harry Andrews *Supt Bestwick* • Allan Cuthbertson *Smythe* ■ *Dir* Ken Annakin • *Scr* Alun Falconer, Paul Durst, from the novel *Death of a Snout* by Douglas Warner

Inherit the Wind ★★★★ U

Courtroom drama 1960 · US · BW · 123mins

This is a stirring title for a gripping courtroom drama, inspired by the real-life trial in 1925 of a young Tennessee teacher charged with giving lessons on the Darwinian theory of evolution in a state school. Very much a drama of words and ideas, the film was a critical hit but a commercial flop in its day. Yes, the plot meanders and even drags at points, but ultimately it engrosses thanks to major-league performances from Spencer Tracy and Fredric March as the opposing lawyers in what became known as the "Scopes Monkey Trial". PF DVD

Fredric March *Matthew Harrison Brady* • Spencer Tracy *Henry Drummond* • Gene Kelly *EK Hornbeck* • Florence Eldridge *Mrs Brady* • Dick York *Bertram T Cates* • Donna Anderson *Rachel Brown* • Harry Morgan *Judge* • Elliott Reid *Davenport* ■ *Dir* Stanley Kramer • *Scr* Nathan E Douglas [Nedrick Young], Harold Jacob Smith, from the play by Jerome Lawrence, Robert E Lee • *Cinematographer* Ernest Laszlo • *Music* Ernest Gold

Inherit the Wind ★★★★

Courtroom drama
1999 · US · Colour · 127mins

An all-star line-up make this drama about the famous 1925 "Scopes Monkey Trial" compelling viewing. A schoolteacher – derided for expounding Darwinian theory – is arrested and tried in a case that soon generates national interest. A stocky courtroom drama ensues and forms the bulk of what was originally a stage play of the same name. Attention to 1920s period detail and heavyweight performances make this a well-above-average, made-for-television drama. LH

Jack Lemmon *Henry Drummond* • George C Scott *Matthew Harrison Brady* • Beau Bridges *EK Hornbeck* • Piper Laurie *Sarah Brady* • Lane Smith *Reverend Jeremiah Brown* ■ *Dir* Daniel Petrie Sr [Daniel Petrie] • *Scr* Nedrick Young, Harold Jacob Smith, from the play by Jerome Lawrence, Robert E Lee

The Inheritance ★★★ 18

Drama 1976 · It · Colour · 98mins

Dominique Sanda has a juicy role here as a social climber with her eyes on a fortune owned by one of Italy's grandest families. First she marries one of the sons; then she seduces his father, the lusty patriarch played by Anthony Quinn. Sadly, Quinn's life force soon runs dry as Sanda wears him out in bed. He does, though, bequeath her the entire estate, which doesn't make for harmonious family relations. Veteran director Mauro Bolognini directs this moral tale with his usual elegance and with more than a touch of the Viscontis. AT. Italian dialogue dubbed into English.

Anthony Quinn *Gregorio Ferramonti* • Fabio Testi *Mario Ferramonti* • Dominique Sanda *Irene* • Luigi Proietti *Pippo Ferramonti* • Adriana Asti *Teta Ferramonti* ■ *Dir* Mauro Bolognini • *Scr* Ugo Pirro, Sergio Bazzini

The Inheritance ★★★ 15

Drama
2003 · Den/Nor/Swe/UK · Colour · 110mins

Per Fly's film is a grittily engrossing mix of the plot machinations of a glitzy soap like *Dallas* and the grainy shooting style of Dogme95. Ulrich Thomsen excels as the prodigal son who passes from reluctant duty to ruthless obsession as he returns from exile in Sweden to run the family firm. However, he so dominates proceedings that both Ghita Norby and Lisa Werlinder are reduced to caricatures as his scheming mother and despairing wife. The corporate shenanigans are also a touch formulaic, but the film is still scripted and played with admirable spirit. DP. In Danish, Swedish, French with English subtitles. Contains violence. DVD

Ulrich Thomsen *Christoffer* • Lisa Werlinder *Maria* • Ghita Norby *Annelise* • Lars Brygmann *Ulrik* • Karina Skands *Benedikte* ■ *Dir* Per Fly • *Scr* Per Fly, Kim Leona, Mogens Rukov, Dorte Hogh

The Inheritor ★★

Thriller 1973 · Fr · Colour · 112mins

In this jet-setting political thriller, Jean-Paul Belmondo plays the heir to a business empire who suspects that his father's death in a plane crash was no accident. When he investigates further, with the help of a magazine journalist, he finds evidence of fascist activity close to home. There are the usual romantic sideshows complicating an already over-fussy plot, but this is as empty as a TV mini-series. DP. French dialogue dubbed into English.

Jean-Paul Belmondo *Cordell* • Carla Gravina *Liza* • Jean Rochefort *Berthier* • Charles Denner *David* • Maureen Kerwin *Lauren* • Michel Beaune *Lambert* ■ *Dir* Philippe Labro • *Scr* Philippe Labro, Jacques Lanzmann

The Inheritors ★★★ 15

Drama 1997 · Austria/Ger · Colour · 94mins

By combining the style of the Hollywood range war movie with that of the German *Heimat* (or homeland) film, Austrian director Stefan Ruzowitzky has come up with what he terms an " Alpine western". Set just after the First World War, the story centres on a group of peasants who defy their foreman by refusing to sell the land they've inherited to a rival farmer. The action errs towards the melodramatic and the acting is too determinedly rustic, yet the stylised realism is ideal for such a stark study of liberty. DP. In German with English subtitles.

Simon Schwarz *Lukas* • Sophie Rois *Emmy* • Lars Rudolph *Severin* • Julia Gschnitzer *Old Nane* • Ulrich Wildgruber *Danninger* ■ *Dir/Scr* Stefan Ruzowitzky • *Music* Erik Satie

L'Inhumaine ★★★★

Silent melodrama
1923 · Fr · BW and Tinted · 130mins

While not perhaps the most ambitious or accomplished experiment of the French Impressionist era, this is certainly the most artful. With a score by Darius Milhaud, exteriors designed by Robert Mallet-Stephens, a Cubist laboratory by Fernand Léger, and Georgette Leblanc's apartment given an Art Deco look by Alberto Cavalcanti, Marcel L'Herbier's silent (and in some prints tinted) melodrama has avant-garde written all over it. However, the tale of the singer who is saved from the clutches of maharajah Philippe Hériat by noble scientist Jaque Catelain is also notable for its audacious visual abstraction and the precision of its rapid cross-cutting. DP

Georgette Leblanc *Claire Lescot* • Jaque Catelain *Einar Norsen* • Marcelle Pradot *L'Innocente* • Philippe Hériat *Djorah de Manilha* • Léonid Walter de Malte *Kranine* ■ *Dir* Marcel L'Herbier • *Scr* Marcel L'Herbier, from a story by Pierre Mac Orlan [Pierre Dumarchais], Mme Georgette Leblanc-Maeterlink

The Initiation ★★ 18

Horror 1984 · US · Colour · 92mins

Daphne Zuniga is the amnesiac sorority sister up to her pretty neck in bad-taste college pranks in this tacky *Nightmare on Elm Street* clone. The "Repressed Desires" costume party has to be seen to be believed, but nothing else is worth the effort in this lame stalk-and-slash item, where most of the horror takes place off screen. Vera Miles adds a touch of class to the mayhem. AJ [video] DVD

Vera Miles *Frances Fairchild* • Clu Gulager *Dwight Fairchild* • Daphne Zuniga *Kelly Terry* • James Read *Peter* • Marilyn Kagan *Marcia* • Patti Heider *Nurse* • Robert Dowdell *Jason Randall* • Frances Peterson *Megan* ■ *Dir* Larry Stewart • *Scr* Charles Pratt Jr

Inn for Trouble ★★ U

Comedy 1960 · UK · BW · 98mins

This movie spin-off from *The Larkins*, the popular sitcom of the late 1950s, moved the family away from 66 Sycamore Street and into a country pub, and that's where the problems begin. One of the series' great strengths was its portrait of a typical urban neighbourhood, populated by familiar characters. A whole new world had to be created here, however, with only Pa and Ma (David Kossoff and Peggy Mount) and Eddie (Shaun O'Riordan) providing continuity. Even the presence of Leslie Phillips and Charles Hawtrey can't make up for the general lifelessness. DP

Peggy Mount *Ada Larkins* • David Kossoff *Alf Larkins* • Leslie Phillips *John Belcher* • Glyn Owen *Lord Bill Osborne* • Yvonne Monlaur *Yvette* • Charles Hawtrey *Silas* • AE Matthews *Sir Hector Gore-Blandish* • Shaun O'Riordan *Eddie Larkins* • Ronan O'Casey *Jeff Rogers* ■ *Dir* CM Pennington-Richards • *Scr* Fred Robinson, from his TV series *The Larkins*

The Inn of the Sixth Happiness ★★★★ PG

Biographical romantic drama
1958 · UK · Colour · 151mins

Ingrid Bergman's screen appeal was usually based on the vulnerability of her characters, so for her to present the tenacity and courage of Gladys Aylward, the domestic servant who set out to bring Christianity to the peasants of China, was a considerable challenge. It's a glamorised portrayal (and one with which Aylward was not completely satisfied), but it's also a gritty and completely sympathetic performance, backed by some exceptional support playing, notably from Athene Seyler. DP [video] DVD

Ingrid Bergman *Gladys Aylward* • Curt Jurgens *Captain Lin Nan* • Robert Donat *Mandarin* • Ronald Squire *Sir Francis Jamison* • Noel Hood *Miss Thompson* • Athene Seyler *Mrs Lawson* • Burt Kwouk *Li* ■ *Dir* Mark Robson • *Scr* Isobel Lennart, from the novel *The Small Woman* by Alan Burgess

The Inner Circle ★★★ 15

Drama 1991 · It/US · Colour · 131mins

While Nikita Mikhalkov remained in Russia and went on to win an Oscar for the sublime *Burnt by the Sun*, his brother Andrei Konchalovsky rather slipped into a cinematic backwater during his US exile. He returned home to shoot this muddled but nevertheless intriguing story about a nobody who allows delusions of grandeur to destroy his life after he is appointed as Stalin's projectionist. Tom Hulce gives an intelligent performance as Ivan, while Lolita Davidovich is truly touching as his wife, risking everything for the sake of a Jewish orphan. DP [video]

Tom Hulce *Ivan Sanshin* • Lolita Davidovich *Anastasia Sanshin* • Bob Hoskins *Beria* • Aleksandr Zbruev *Stalin* • Feodor Chaliapin Jr *Professor Bartnev* ■ *Dir* Andrei Konchalovsky • *Scr* Andrei Konchalovsky, Anatoli Usov

Innerspace ★★★ PG

Science-fiction comedy
1987 · US · Colour · 114mins

This attempt to update *Fantastic Voyage* doesn't measure up to director Joe Dante's best work, but it's still a notch above the usual Hollywood fodder. Dennis Quaid is the hotshot military man who is miniaturised and mistakenly pumped into the body of lowly supermarket clerk Martin Short. The effects are excellent and Dante's sly humour shines through occasionally, but it lacks the anarchy the director is noted for and Short's hysterics begin to grate. JF. Contains some swearing and violence. [video] DVD

Dennis Quaid *Lt Tuck Pendelton* • Martin Short *Jack Putter* • Meg Ryan *Lydia Maxwell* • Kevin McCarthy *Victor Scrimshaw* • Fiona Lewis *Dr Margaret Canker* • Vernon Wells *Mr Igoe* ■ *Dir* Joe Dante • *Scr* Jeffrey Boam, Chip Proser, from a story by Chip Proser

Innocence ★★★ 12

Romantic drama
2000 · Aus/Bel · Colour · 95mins

Paul Cox's gentle late-life romance cross-cuts between postwar Belgium and millennial Adelaide to prove that true love can never die. Julia Blake and Charles "Bud" Tingwell provide a truly touching insight into the depth of emotion that can still be stirred in old age, although Cox doesn't quite trust us to relate to their twilight canoodling and repeatedly flashes back to show their younger selves recklessly indulging their passion. With Terry Norris also ringing true as the husband who has long shared Blake's life, but not her bed, this is delicate without ever being patronising. DP

Julia Blake *Claire* • Charles "Bud" Tingwell [Charles Tingwell] *Andreas* • Terry Norris *John* • Robert Menzies *David* • Marta Dusseldorp *Monique* ■ *Dir/Scr* Paul Cox

Innocence ★★

Mystery drama
2004 · Fr/Bel/UK · Colour · 115mins

The symbolic female journey from childhood to adolescence is transformed into a dreamy and lyrical fairy tale. The film takes place in a mysterious, isolated girls' boarding school, where each new pupil arrives in a coffin and from then onwards is never permitted to leave the grounds. There's no explanation for any of the strangeness that unfolds, nor is there a particularly coherent plot. Instead, the picture offers a series of flowing, interlocking experiences, viewed largely through the eyes of the latest arrival (Zoé Auclair). Though the feature is extremely beautiful, for most viewers it's likely to be a case of style over baffling substance. SF. In French with English subtitles.

Zoé Auclar *Iris* • Marion Cotillard *Mademoiselle Eva* • Hélène de Fougerolles *Mademoiselle Edith* • Berangère Haubruges *Bianca* • Lea Bridarolli *Alice* ■ *Dir* Lucile Hadzihalilovic • *Scr* Lucile Hadzihalilovic, from the novella *Mine-Haha* by Frank Wedekind

Innocence Unprotected ★★★★ U

Drama 1968 · Yug · BW and Colour · 76mins

Consisting of fond flashbacks, gentle satire and an uplifting tribute to human indomitability, this unique film is an endless delight. Combining newsreel footage of the Nazi occupation, clips from Yugoslavia's second talkie, and interviews with surviving members of the cast and crew, director Dusan Makavejev enables us to appreciate both the historical importance of this hoary melodramatic film, and the pride of its makers in confounding the Gestapo to produce a heartfelt statement of national defiance. DP. In Serbian with English subtitles. [video]

Dragoljub Aleksic *Acrobat Aleksic* • Ana Milosavljevic *Nada the orphan* • Vera Jovanovic *Wicked Stepmother* • Bratoljub Gligorijevic *Mr Petrovic* • Ivan Zivkovic *Aleksic's brother* • Pera Milosavljevic *Servant* ■ *Dir/Scr* Dusan Makavejev

The Innocent ★★★ 15

Period drama 1984 · UK · Colour · 95mins

Set in the Yorkshire Dales, this coming-of-age saga takes place in the early 1930s against the backdrop of the Depression. The central character, Tim (Andrew Hawley), suffers from epilepsy, and his problems are compounded by his constantly arguing parents and the continuing affair between a family friend and a married woman. Certainly a change of pace for John MacKenzie, director of *The Long Good Friday*. His film also features early appearances from Liam Neeson and Miranda Richardson. AT

Andrew Hawley *Tim Dobson* • Kika Markham *Mrs Dobson* • Kate Foster *Win* • Liam Neeson *John Carns* • Patrick Daley *Eddie King* • Paul Askew *Stanley* • Tom Bell *Frank Dobson* • Miranda Richardson *Mary Turner* ■ *Dir* John Mackenzie • *Scr* Ray Jenkins, from the novel *The Aura and the Kingfisher* by Tom Hart

The Innocent ★★ 15

Thriller 1993 · UK/Ger · Colour · 113mins

Despite its impressive cast, this brooding, rather old-fashioned Cold War thriller never really grips. In an odd bit of casting, the always impressive American actor Campbell Scott plays an English technician in 1950s Berlin who gets caught up in a tortuous espionage plot instigated by CIA man Anthony Hopkins, here saddled with an unconvincing US accent. Isabella Rossellini supplies the glamour as the woman Scott falls for, but, while director John Schlesinger expertly captures the grey chill of the time and place, he gets lost in the detail. JF [video]

Anthony Hopkins *Bob Glass* • Isabella Rossellini *Maria* • Campbell Scott *Leonard Markham* • Ronald Nitschke *Otto* • Hart Bochner *Russell* • James Grant *MacNamee* • Jeremy Sinden *Captain Lofting* • Richard Durden *Black* ■ *Dir* John Schlesinger • *Scr* Ian McEwan, from his novel

Innocent Blood ★★★ 15

Comedy horror 1992 · US · Colour · 110mins

Blood flies everywhere as the horror movie and the gangster film collide head on in this atmospheric offering from John Landis. From the moment Anne Parillaud sinks her teeth into hoodlum Robert Loggia, it's clear that this isn't going to be your average vampire chiller. The whole production drips with style as Loggia chomps his way towards fulfilling his ambition of controlling the underworld by means of the undead. Parillaud slinks through the picture, falling for Anthony LaPaglia in the process, but it's the excesses of Loggia and crooked lawyer Don Rickles that command the attention. DP. Contains violence, swearing, sex scenes and nudity. [video]

Anne Parillaud *Marie* • Anthony LaPaglia *Joe Gennaro* • Robert Loggia *Sal "The Shark" Macelli* • David Proval *Lenny* • Rocco Sisto *Gilly* • Don Rickles *Emmanuel Bergman* • Chazz Palminteri *Tony* • Tony Sirico *Jacko* ■ *Dir* John Landis • *Scr* Michael Wolk

Innocent Bystanders ★★ 18

Spy thriller 1972 · UK · Colour · 106mins

We're in 007 territory again with this spy thriller from *The Italian Job* director Peter Collinson. This time our rather more fallible superhero is played by Stanley Baker, with boss Donald Pleasence sending him on a mission to locate a missing Russian scientist. A strong cast also includes Geraldine Chaplin and Dana Andrews, but those of a delicate disposition may find this defector drama leans too heavily on sadism and violence. TH

Stanley Baker *John Craig* • Geraldine Chaplin *Miriam Loman* • Donald Pleasence *Loomis* • Dana Andrews *Blake* • Sue Lloyd *Joanna Benson* • Derren Nesbitt *Andrew Royce* • Vladek Sheybal *Aaron Kaplan* • Warren Mitchell *Omar* ■ *Dir* Peter Collinson • *Scr* James Mitchell, from the novel by James Munro [James Mitchell]

Innocent Lies ★★ 18

Period crime mystery
1995 · UK/Fr · Colour · 84mins

Supposedly inspired by the country house whodunnits of Agatha Christie, Patrick Dewolf's period curio is much darker and far less well-constructed than anything concocted by the grand old lady of crime. Indeed, this is played at such a hysterical pitch that you could be forgiven for thinking it was a parody. As the cop investigating the death of his colleague, Adrian Dunbar behaves most peculiarly, especially in the presence of the deranged Gabrielle Anwar. Only Joanna Lumley emerges with any credit as her viciously snobby mother. DP. Contains sex scenes and violence.

Adrian Dunbar *Alan Cross* • Florence Hoath *Angela Cross* • Sophie Aubry *Solange Montfort* • Joanna Lumley *Lady Helena Graves* • Gabrielle Anwar *Celia Graves* • Alexis Denisof *Christopher Wood* • Stephen Dorff *Jeremy Graves* ■ *Dir* Patrick Dewolf • *Scr* Kerry Crabbe, Patrick Dewolf

An Innocent Man ★★★ 18

Crime thriller 1989 · US · Colour · 108mins

Tom Selleck attempted to toughen up his image with this hard-edged thriller, but it was only a partial success. He plays an airline mechanic who is framed by two bent cops and finds himself in prison, where he nurses a desire for revenge. Director Peter Yates is an old hand when it comes to this sort of thing, and he stages the action scenes with some panache. Selleck, however, isn't entirely convincing as the innocent man who is transformed from a nice middle-class chap to a hard-bitten inmate. JF. Contains violence, swearing. DVD

Tom Selleck *Jimmie Rainwood* • F Murray Abraham *Virgil Cane* • Laila Robins *Kate Rainwood* • David Rasche *Mike Parnell* • Richard Young *Danny Scalise* • Badja Djola *John Fitzgerald* • Todd Graff *Robby* ■ *Dir* Peter Yates • *Scr* Larry Brothers

Innocent Moves ★★★★ PG

Biographical drama
1993 · US · Colour · 105mins

Released in the US as *Searching for Bobby Fischer*, this marked the directorial debut of Steven Zaillian, who had just completed scriptwriting duties on *Schindler's List*. This true story not only reveals the ruthless side of competitive chess, but also explores the dangers of parents using children to fulfil their own ambitions. Conrad Hall's Oscar-nominated photography is as impressive as the acting, with young Max Pomeranc, himself a top-ranking player, upstaging the likes of Joe Mantegna and Ben Kingsley. DP DVD

Max Pomeranc *Josh Waitzkin* • Joe Mantegna *Fred Waitzkin* • Joan Allen *Bonnie Waitzkin* • Ben Kingsley *Bruce Pandolfini* • Laurence Fishburne *Vinnie* • Robert Stephens *Poe's teacher* • David Paymer *Kalev* ■ *Dir* Steven Zaillian • *Scr* Steven Zaillian, from the autobiographical novel by Fred Waitzkin

Innocent Sinners ★★ U

Drama 1957 · UK · BW · 95mins

The gentle talent of British director Philip Leacock was responsible for classic films about childhood, including *The Kidnappers* and racism, *Take a Giant Step*. This engaging film – based on a novel by Rumer Godden, another expert on youthful emotions – tells the slightly idealised story tells of a teenage girl who creates a garden in the ruins of a bombed church only to find herself in trouble with the authorities. Typically of the director, it is compassionate and nicely acted. BB

June Archer *Lovejoy Mason* • Flora Robson *Olivia Chesney* • David Kossoff *Mr Vincent* • Barbara Mullen *Mrs Vincent* • Catherine Lacey *Angela Chesney* • Susan Beaumont *Liz* ■ *Dir* Philip Leacock • *Scr* Neil Paterson, from the novel *An Episode of Sparrows* by Rumer Godden

The Innocent Sleep ★★★ 15

Mystery thriller 1995 · UK · Colour · 95mins

Rupert Graves plays a homeless man in this downbeat British thriller, set in London's Cardboard City. Graves is enjoying the five-star facilities of a warehouse underneath Tower Bridge when he realises that an assassination is in progress. He gets away but, when he goes to the police, he discovers that the detective heading the investigation was actually involved in the killing. Scott Michell's direction catches the downtrodden atmosphere of London's underworld, and he's helped by a good cast. TH

Annabella Sciorra *Billie Hayman* • Rupert Graves *Alan Terry* • Michael Gambon *Matheson* • Franco Nero *Cavani* • John Hannah *James* • Oliver Cotton *Lusano* • Tony Bluto *Thorn* • Paul Brightwell *Pelham* ■ *Dir* Scott Michell • *Scr* Ray Villis

L'Innocente ★★★★ 15

Period drama 1976 · It · Colour · 123mins

Luchino Visconti's last film is one of his best and was clearly the inspiration behind Martin Scorsese's *The Age of Innocence*. The film saw the baroque director returning to his favourite theme: the decline of turn-of-the-20th-century Italian aristocracy and its implications for today's society. Giancarlo Giannini plays the adulterous Sicilian gentleman who is mortified by his wife's own sexual misconduct, while Laura Antonelli is magnificent as the unfaithful spouse. A visually stunning meditation on mores and manners. AJ. In Italian with English subtitles. DVD

Giancarlo Giannini *Tullio Hermil* • Laura Antonelli *Giuliana Hermil* • Jennifer O'Neill *Teresa Raffo* • Rina Morelli *Tullio's mother* • Massimo Girotti *Count Stefano Egano* • Didier Haudepin *Federico Hermil* • Marie Dubois *Princess* ■ *Dir* Luchino Visconti • *Scr* Suso Cecchi D'Amico, Enrico Medioli, Luchino Visconti, from a novel by Gabriele D'Annunzio

The Innocents ★★★★

Horror 1961 · UK · BW · 99mins

As this terrifying but neglected picture proves, there was much more to British cinema in the early 1960s than angry young men. Truman Capote and John Mortimer both had a hand in the script for this adaptation of Henry James's *The Turn of the Screw*, and the film bristles with menace as it draws you inexorably towards its chilling conclusion. Rarely has horror looked so beautiful, with cinematographer Freddie Francis reinforcing the eerie atmosphere. Deborah Kerr is excellent as the haunted governess, Pamela Franklin and Martin Stephens send shivers down the spine as her sinister charges, and Peter Wyngarde as Quint is evil personified. DP

Deborah Kerr *Miss Giddens* • Michael Redgrave *Uncle* • Peter Wyngarde *Peter Quint* • Megs Jenkins *Mrs Grose* • Martin Stephens *Miles* • Pamela Franklin *Flora* • Clytie Jessop *Miss Jessel* • Isla Cameron *Anna* ■ *Dir* Jack Clayton • *Scr* William Archibald, Truman Capote, John Mortimer, from the novella *The Turn of the Screw* by Henry James

Les Innocents aux Mains Sales ★★ 18

Crime drama
1975 · Fr/It/W Ger · Colour · 120mins

This is one melodrama that Rod Steiger wanted to wash his hands of. In a faintly risible plot, he's the husband whose wife (Romy Schneider) and her lover (Paolo Giusti) conspire to murder for money. Director Claude Chabrol was nearly as bored with the idea as audiences (he played poker while making the film). Nevertheless, he manages to create some genuinely creepy moments, while Steiger puts together a professional performance. TH. A French language film.

Rod Steiger *Louis Wormser* • Romy Schneider *Julie Wormser* • Paolo Giusti *Jeff Marle* • Jean Rochefort *Lawyer legal* • François Maistre *Inspector Lamy* • Pierre Santini *Inspector Villon* • François Perrot *Georges Thorent* • Hans Christian Blech *Judge* ■ *Dir* Claude Chabrol • *Scr* Claude Chabrol, from the novel *Damned Innocents* by Richard Neely

Innocents in Paris ★★★

Comedy 1953 · UK · BW · 102mins

Considering the quality of the cast, this episodic British comedy could have been a great deal funnier than it is. Following a party of tourists on their weekend in Paris, Anatole de Grunwald's script has a pseudo-Ealing cosiness that prevents it from throwing caution to the wind and becoming downright comic. There are neat touches from Alastair Sim seeking to inebriate a Soviet politician and from Margaret Rutherford as an amateur artist at the Louvre, but the rest of the misadventures lack a vital spark. DP

Alastair Sim *Sir Norman Barker* • Margaret Rutherford *Gladys Inglott* • Ronald Shiner *Dicky Bird* • Claire Bloom *Susan Robbins* • Claude Dauphin *Max de Lorne* • Laurence Harvey *François* • Jimmy Edwards *Captain George Stilton* • James Copeland *Andy MacGregor* • Gaby Bruyere *Josette* ■ *Dir* Gordon Parry • *Scr* Anatole de Grunwald

Inseminoid ★★ 18

Science-fiction horror
1981 · UK · Colour · 88mins

The basic concepts of *Alien* are taken to the sleaziest and goriest extremes in director Norman J Warren's addition to the murderous space-creature genre. Shot entirely in Chiselhurst caves, it stars Judy Geeson and Stephanie Beacham as two members of an interstellar archaeological mission. Geeson is impregnated by a nasty ET and mutates into a killer, horrifically murdering anyone who threatens her impending motherhood. The pace is fast enough to cover the film's more ridiculous aspects. AJ

Judy Geeson *Sandy* • Robin Clarke *Mark* • Jennifer Ashley *Holly* • Stephanie Beacham *Kate* • Steven Grives *Gary* • Barrie Houghton *Karl* ■ *Dir* Norman J Warren • *Scr* Nick Maley, Gloria Maley

Inserts ★★★ 18

Period drama
1975 · UK/US · Colour · 111mins

This intriguing but ultimately disappointing drama looks at 1930s Hollywood, where has-been director Richard Dreyfuss is making a porno movie with a gay actor and a former silent movie queen. The decision to limit the picture to a small cast and a single interior set at a British studio may be in homage to Harold Pinter, or it may just betray a lack of finance. Even so, one sorely misses the soft light and the waving palms of Hollywood, and Bob Hoskins with an American accent doesn't help matters. Dreyfuss, though, is excellent, creating a richly complex character. AT

Richard Dreyfuss *Boy Wonder* • Jessica Harper *Cathy* • Stephen Davies *Rex* • Veronica Cartwright *Harlene* • Bob Hoskins *Big Mac* ■ *Dir/Scr* John Byrum

Inside Daisy Clover ★★ 15

Period drama 1965 · US · Colour · 123mins

Gavin Lambert's novel about the turbulent career of a precocious Hollywood musical star of the 1930s had potential to be a lot of fun. Unfortunately in the hands of director Robert Mulligan it treads an uncomfortable line between satire and drama, with disappointing results. Natalie Wood, by then a movie veteran of more than 20 years, is Daisy and Robert Redford plays her handsome husband, whose sexual orientation makes him less than an ideal spouse. The two stars reteamed soon after for *This Property Is Condemned*. TH

Natalie Wood *Daisy Clover* • Christopher Plummer *Raymond Swan* • Robert Redford *Wade Lewis* • Roddy McDowall *Walter Baines* • Ruth Gordon *The Dealer* • Katharine Bard *Melora Swan* ■ *Dir* Robert Mulligan • *Scr* Gavin Lambert, from his novel

Inside Deep Throat ★★ 18

Documentary 2005 · US · Colour · 89mins

Shot for $25,000 in 1972 by hairdresser-turned-director Gerard Damiano, *Deep Throat* became a $600-million phenomenon that brought pornography to mainstream America. The making of that notoriously amateur hardcore comedy, its acceptance as "porno-chic", the rise and fall of star Linda Lovelace and inevitable moral backlash are all brought together in this unfocused documentary. Directors Fenton Bailey and Randy Barbato ambitiously attempt to cover all bases in their efforts to put the landmark movie in historical context. Pop culturists will find it entertaining enough, if overlong and annoyingly superficial in key areas. AJ. Contains sex scenes and nudity.

Dennis Hopper *Narrator* ■ *Dir/Scr* Fenton Bailey, Randy Barbato

Inside Edge ★★ 18

Action crime thriller
1992 · US · Colour · 84mins

Michael Madsen isn't exactly cast against type in this clichéd crime flick. He plays a renegade cop, whose methods bring him into conflict with his department. Sexy siren Rosie Vela, working for local hood Richard Lynch seduces Madsen into working with her boss to advance his own career while eliminating the boss's competition. It follows all the usual conventions, from the crusty chief of police to the partner who is doomed from the moment he walks on screen, but there are a few surprises en route. ST

Michael Madsen *Richard Montana* • Richard Lynch *Mario Gio* • Rosie Vela *Lisa Zamora* • George Jenesky *Hip-Hop* • Tony Peck *Dan Nealy* ■ *Dir* Warren Clark • *Scr* Vincent Gutierrez, William Tannen, from a screenplay (unproduced) by Vincent Gutierrez

Inside I'm Dancing ★★★ 15

Comedy drama
2004 · UK/Ire/Ger · Colour · 99mins

This tragicomic tale of the odd-couple friendship that develops between two severely disabled young men could have ended up as a thoroughly mawkish affair. James McAvoy is the outgoing, rebellious patient with muscular dystrophy, whose arrival at a sleepy residential care home is a tonic for diffident youth Steven Robertson (whose character has cerebral palsy). Director Damien O'Donnell has come up with a worthwhile drama that may not tread any new ground, but at least goes over old territory with some skill and style. DA. Contains swearing. DVD

James McAvoy *Rory O'Shea* • Steven Robertson *Michael Connolly* • Romola Garai *Siobhan* • Gerard McSorley *Fergus Connolly* • Tom Hickey *Con O'Shea* • Brenda Fricker *Eileen* ■ *Dir* Damien O'Donnell • *Scr* Jeffrey Caine, from a story by Christian O'Reilly

The Inside Man ★★ 15

Political thriller
1984 · Swe/UK · Colour · 89mins

Two years before his career-reviving performance in David Lynch's *Blue Velvet*, Dennis Hopper turned up in this Anglo-Swedish co-production as a CIA agent assigned to track down a top-secret laser device stolen from a grounded Russian submarine. Actor-turned-director Tom Clegg cut his teeth on such homegrown crime yarns as *McVicar* and *Sweeney 2*. RT

Dennis Hopper *Miller* • Hardy Kruger *Mandell* • Gösta Ekman (2) *Larsson* • Kare Molder *Kallin* • David Wilson *Baxter* • Celia Gregory *Theresa* ■ *Dir* Tom Clegg • *Scr* Alan Plater, from a story by Tom Clegg, William Aldridge, from the novel *The Fighter* by Harry Kullman

Inside Moves: the Guys from Max's Bar ★★★

Drama 1980 · US · Colour · 112mins

This study of disability suffers from the same surfeit of sentiment that blights so many Hollywood attempts to be liberal and profound. Husband-and-wife team Valerie Curtin and Barry Levinson have scripted several eye-opening scenes, however, while director Richard Donner brings realism to proceedings by de-glamorising his Los Angeles locations. Diana Scarwid was nominated for a best supporting actress Oscar, but it's the relationship between failed suicide John Savage and would-be basketball star David Morse that provides the dramatic core. DP

John Savage *Roary* • David Morse *Jerry Maxwell* • Diana Scarwid *Louise* • Amy Wright *Ann* • Tony Burton *Lucius Porter* • Bill Henderson *Blue Lewis* • Steve Kahan *Burt* • Jack O'Leary *Max Willatowski* ■ *Dir* Richard Donner • *Scr* Valerie Curtin, Barry Levinson, from a novel by Todd Walton

Inside Out ★★ PG

Adventure comedy
1975 · UK · Colour · 93mins

Telly Savalas's popularity at the time as TV cop Kojak ensured this routine caper movie a modest audience in cinemas. It's a blatant rip-off of another Savalas picture, *The Dirty Dozen*, with several dubious types going after a stash of Nazi gold in the Cold War era. James Mason and Robert Culp bring some extra class to the proceedings. AT. Contains some violence and swearing.

Telly Savalas *Harry Morgan* • James Mason *Ernst Furben* • Robert Culp *Sly Wells* • Aldo Ray *Sergeant Prior* • Günter Meisner *Schmidt* • Adrian Hoven *Dr Maar* • Wolfgang Lukschy *Reinhard Holtz* ■ *Dir* Peter Duffell • *Scr* Judd Bernard, Stephen Schneck

Inside Straight ★★

Period drama 1951 · US · BW · 86mins

Set in San Francisco during the Comstock Lode financial crisis, the action is comprised of a series of flashbacks to the 1850s as a self-seeking tycoon looks back on his career and the romances that helped shape him. David Brian lacks the charisma to cut much of a figure, but Arlene Dahl and the scheming Mercedes McCambridge make more of an impression. DP

David Brian *Rip MacCool* • Arlene Dahl *Lily Douvane* • Barry Sullivan *Johnny Sanderson* • Mercedes McCambridge *Ada Stritch* • Lon Chaney Jr *Shocker* ■ *Dir* Gerald Mayer • *Scr* Guy Trosper

The Insider ★★★★★ 15

Drama based on a true story
1999 · US · Colour · 151mins

Big Tobacco comes under the spotlight in Michael Mann's virtuoso ethical drama, based on the true case of a whistle-blower whose life was ruined when he decided to tell all to *60 Minutes*. Russell Crowe plays Jeffrey Wigand, the sacked executive who went public with his firm's dark secrets, only to find his interview canned by network heads terrified of a potentially catastrophic law suit. Al Pacino sears the screen as Lowell Bergman, the producer who broke the story, while Christopher Plummer is superb as anchorman Mike Wallace. Mann has little interest in his female characters – Diane Venora is underused as Wigand's wife Liane – but this remains a dazzling exposé of money, morals and the media. NS. Contains swearing. DVD

Al Pacino *Lowell Bergman* • Russell Crowe *Jeffrey Wigand* • Christopher Plummer *Mike Wallace* • Diane Venora *Liane Wigand* • Philip Baker Hall *Don Hewitt* • Lindsay Crouse *Sharon Tiller* • Debi Mazar *Debbie De Luca* • Stephen Tobolowsky *Eric Kluster* • Gina Gershon *Helen Caperelli* • Michael Gambon *Thomas Sandefur* • Rip Torn *John Scanlon* ■ *Dir* Michael Mann • *Scr* Eric Roth, Michael Mann, from the article *The Man Who New Too Much* by Marie Brenner

Insignificance ★★★★ 15

Comedy drama 1985 · UK · Colour · 104mins

Director Nicolas Roeg's wild, wacky and wonderful chamber piece is an exploration of love, life and the whole damn thing. Set in a hotel room in 1954, Roeg assembles four characters who bear a striking resemblance to celebrities of that era. Theresa Russell is "Marilyn Monroe", whose interest in Michael Emil's "Einstein" extends beyond his theory of relativity. Tony Curtis is the Joe McCarthy clone, while Gary Busey is the Joe DiMaggio figure still pining for Marilyn. TH

Gary Busey *Ballplayer* • Tony Curtis *Senator* • Michael Emil *Professor* • Theresa Russell *Actress* • Will Sampson *Elevator attendant* • Patrick Kilpatrick *Driver* ■ *Dir* Nicolas Roeg • *Scr* Terry Johnson, from his play

Insomnia ★★★ 15

Psychological crime thriller
1997 · Nor · Colour · 92mins

Debutant director Erik Skjoldbjaerg pulls off something of a generic coup here, by staging a *film noir* in the relentless glare of the midnight sun. Set in an isolated town on the polar extremities, the action begins with a hunt for the killer of a teenage girl. But when city cop Stellan Skarsgård accidentally shoots his colleague during a bungled ambush, the emphasis shifts to his struggle to remain focused on the case while battling his suppressed sense of guilt. Dazzlingly photographed by Erling Thurmann-Andersen, this taut thriller stints on narrative complexity, but packs quite a psychological punch. DP. In Norwegian with English subtitles. Contains some sex scenes. DVD

Stellan Skarsgård *Jonas Engström* • Sverre Anker Ousdal *Erik Vik* • Bjørn Floberg *Jon Holt* • Gisken Armand *Hilde Hagen* • Maria Bonnevie *Ane* • Maria Mathiesen *Tanja Lorentzen* ■ *Dir* Erik Skjoldbjaerg • *Scr* Nikolaj Frobenius, Erik Skjoldbjaerg

Insomnia ★★★★★ 15

Psychological crime thriller
2002 · US · Colour · 113mins

Based on the 1997 Norwegian blockbuster of the same name, Christopher Nolan's masterfully directed psychodrama proves that hit European movies can be remade successfully. Intensely gripping throughout and set in Alaska, this *noir* nightmare has hard-boiled LAPD detective Al Pacino sent to a small fishing town to investigate a brutal murder. When he mistakenly kills his partner on a fudged stakeout and blames the hunted assassin (Robin Williams) who saw what he did, the killer blackmails him into pinning both deaths on someone else. And so a convoluted cat-and-mouse game begins with Pacino – terminally sleepless from the endless daylight – barely staying one step ahead in the evidence-planting conspiracy. Nolan's bitterly ironic and inventive thriller features Pacino on dynamite form. AJ. Contains violence, swearing, nudity. DVD

Al Pacino *Will Dormer* • Robin Williams *Walter Finch* • Hilary Swank *Ellie Burr* • Maura Tierney *Rachel Clement* • Martin Donovan (2) *Hap Eckhart* • Nicky Katt *Fred Duggar* • Jonathan Jackson *Randy Stetz* • Paul Dooley *Chief Charles Nyback* ■ *Dir* Christopher Nolan • *Scr* Hillary Seitz, from the 1997 film by Nikolaj Frobenius, Erik Skjoldbjaerg

Inspecteur Lavardin ★★★ 15

Crime mystery
1986 · Fr/Swi · Colour · 100mins

Chabrol's sequel to *Cop au Vin*, with Jean Poiret repeating his role as the unorthodox policeman. This time he investigates the murder of a famous Catholic writer whose naked body – with the word "pig" on a buttock – is found on a beach. Then Lavardin discovers that the victim's wife, Bernadette Lafont, is an ex-girlfriend of his and the chief suspect. What follows is often quite grisly, decked out with eccentric characters and a cast that includes Jean-Claude Brialy. AT. In French with English subtitles.

Jean Poiret *Inspector Jean Lavardin* • Bernadette Lafont *Hélène Mons* • Jean-Claude Brialy *Claude Alvarez* • Jacques Dacqmine *Raoul Mons* • Hermine Claire *Véronique Manguin* ■ *Dir* Claude Chabrol • *Scr* Claude Chabrol, Dominique Roulet

The Inspector ★★★

Drama 1962 · UK · Colour · 111mins

Having lost his Jewish fiancée to the Nazis, Dutch police inspector Stephen Boyd saves another Jewish girl (Dolores Hart) immediately after the war and attempts to smuggle her to Palestine. Bizarrely, they board a canal boat and end up in Morocco. The Americans pick them up in Tangier and ask the girl, who suffered in the death camps, to testify at the Nuremberg trials. A melodrama that doesn't quite obscure its more serious intentions, this is worth watching because of its impressive supporting cast. AT

Stephen Boyd *Peter Jongman* • Dolores Hart *Lisa Held* • Leo McKern *Brandt* • Hugh Griffith *Van der Pink* • Donald Pleasence *Sgt Wolters* • Harry Andrews *Ayoob* • Robert Stephens *Dickens* • Marius Goring *Thorens* • Finlay Currie *De Kooi* ■ *Dir* Philip Dunne • *Scr* Nelson Gidding, Jan de Hartog

An Inspector Calls ★★★★ PG

Drama 1954 · UK · BW · 76mins

It may be a gripping night out at the theatre, but JB Priestley's celebrated play loses some of its impact on screen. The revelations made by the unwelcome visitor seem so much less shocking away from the intimate confines of the stage, especially as the use of flashback to reveal the family's guilty secrets deprives us of their reactions as the truth emerges. Yet this is a highly polished production, made all the more irresistible by another superb performance from Alastair Sim. DP DVD

Alastair Sim *Inspector Poole* • Arthur Young *Arthur Birling* • Olga Lindo *Sybil Birling* • Eileen Moore *Sheila Birling* • Bryan Forbes *Eric Birling* • Brian Worth *Gerald Croft* • Jane Wenham *Eva Smith* ■ *Dir* Guy Hamilton • *Scr* Desmond Davis, from the play by JB Priestley

Inspector Clouseau ★★★ U

Comedy 1968 · UK · Colour · 91mins

Although Peter Sellers seemed to have the character copyright on the gauche, Gallic policeman, this oddity sees Alan Arkin accent-ing the more positive aspects of the role as Clouseau arrives in a tediously swinging London to investigate the aftermath of the Great Train Robbery. Arkin is certainly a better straight actor than Sellers was, but he doesn't have Sellers's sense of self-importance, which is so very necessary for laughs. Worth looking at for variety's sake. TH

Alan Arkin *Inspector Jacques Clouseau* • Frank Finlay *Superintendent Weaver* • Beryl Reid *Mrs Weaver* • Delia Boccardo *Lisa Morrel* • Patrick Cargill *Sir Charles Braithwaite* • Barry Foster *Addison Steele* ■ *Dir* Bud Yorkin • *Scr* Tom Waldman, Frank Waldman, from a character created by Blake Edwards, Maurice Richlin

Inspector Gadget ★ U

Comedy action adventure
1999 · US · Colour · 75mins

This screen version of the "cuddly cyborg" cartoon series is the most mindless Hollywood movie you're ever likely to find. Abandoning all plot after the first reel, it devotes its energies to beating us senseless with a succession of slapstick effects sequences. Matthew Broderick's performance as the computerised cop is so bland he barely exists, while the script is witless, ineptly structured and solely reliant on Gadget's extendable bits and bobs. Amazingly, there's a straight-to-video sequel. JC DVD

Matthew Broderick *Inspector Gadget/RoboGadget/John Brown* • Rupert Everett *Sanford Scolex* • Joely Fisher *Brenda/RoboBrenda* • Michelle Trachtenberg *Penny* ■ *Dir* David Kellogg • *Scr* Kerry Ehrin, Zak Penn, from a story by Dana Olsen, Kerry Ehrin, from characters created by Andy Heyward, Jean Chalopin, Bruno Bianchi

The Inspector General ★★★ U

Musical comedy 1949 · US · Colour · 101mins

This splendid Danny Kaye vehicle is ostensibly based on the Gogol play about a wandering buffoon mistaken for the visiting dignitary of the title. Warner Bros prepared this as a musical, importing Deanna Durbin's director Henry Koster, and giving Kaye free rein by commissioning songs from Mrs Kaye – the clever Sylvia Fine – and the brilliant Johnny Mercer. The numbers aren't particularly outstanding, but their tongue-twisting lyrics and use of romantic pathos served the star well. TS DVD

Danny Kaye *Georgi* • Walter Slezak *Yakov* • Barbara Bates *Leza* • Elsa Lanchester *Maria* • Gene Lockhart *The mayor* • Alan Hale *Kovatch* ■ *Dir* Henry Koster • *Scr* Philip Rapp, Harry Kurnitz, from the play by Nikolai Gogol

Inspiration ★★ U

Drama 1931 · US · BW · 73mins

Parisian artist's model Greta Garbo and trainee diplomat Robert Montgomery fall in love, but the relationship runs into trouble when he learns of her past lovers. The only inspired element in this turgid drivel is Garbo herself, whose luminous presence and exquisite suffering almost rise above the material. Garbo and Montgomery were never teamed again after this picture. RK

Greta Garbo *Yvonne* • Robert Montgomery *Andre Martel* • Lewis Stone *Delval* • Marjorie Rambeau *Lulu* • Judith Vosselli *Odette* • Beryl

Mercer *Marthe* • John Miljan *Coutant* • Edwin Maxwell *Julian Montell* • Oscar Apfel *Vignaud* ■ *Dir* Clarence Brown • *Scr* Gene Markey, from a treatment by James Forbes, from the novel *Sappho* by Alphonse Daudet

Instinct ★★ 15

Psychological drama
1999 · US · Colour · 118mins

What caused anthropologist Anthony Hopkins to go on a murderous rampage while studying gorillas in Rwanda? That's what idealistic psychiatrist Cuba Gooding Jr tries to find out when Hopkins is finally arrested and placed in a mental institution in this plodding treatise on animal-versus-human instincts. The film naturally features a fine performance from Hopkins, yet this is hardly riveting because it's mainly constructed as a series of prison interviews. AJ. Contains violence and swearing. DVD

Anthony Hopkins *Ethan Powell* • Cuba Gooding Jr *Theo Caulder* • Donald Sutherland *Ben Hillard* • Maura Tierney *Lyn Powell* • George Dzundza *Dr John Murray* • John Ashton *Guard Dacks* ■ *Dir* Jon Turteltaub • *Scr* Gerald DiPego, from his story, from the novel *Ishmael* by Daniel Quinn

Institute Benjamenta, or This Dream People Call Human Life ★★★ PG

Drama 1995 · UK · BW · 100mins

The first live-action film from the talented Brothers Quay animation team both confounds and intrigues. Mark Rylance is an aspiring butler who attends a mysterious school to learn the rituals of service, but soon finds his training consists of an endless repetition of one single lesson. Alternately fascinating and banal, this hotch-potch of ideas and images is a sub-Cocteau treatise on the meaning and futility of life. Boasting good performances, atmospheric direction and evocative Hampton Court locations, this is strangely hypnotic in a tedious way. AJ

Mark Rylance *Jakob von Gunten* • Alice Krige *Lisa Benjamenta* • Gottfried John *Johannes Benjamenta* • Daniel Smith *Kraus* • Joseph Alessi *Pepino* • Jonathan Stone *Hebling* ■ *Dir* Timothy Quay, Stephen Quay • *Scr* Alan Passes, Brothers Quay, from the novella *Jakob von Gunten,and other texts by Robert Walser*

Intacto ★★★ 15

Thriller 2001 · Sp · Colour · 104mins

Director Juan Carlos Fresnadillo makes a solid feature debut with this study of chance, survival, identity and greed. Strewn with imposing set pieces and tellingly intimate details, it's a film that puts plot and impact above characterisation. The premise that luck can be stolen is pursued with an unrelenting logic that brings unexpected twists, as gambler Eusebio Poncela exploits the gift for good fortune of petty thief and plane-crash survivor Leonardo Sbaraglia, in order to exact his revenge on casino boss Max von Sydow. Slick and superficial, but also intriguing. DP. In Spanish and English with subtitles. DVD

Max von Sydow *Samuel* • Leonardo Sbaraglia *Tomas* • Eusebio Poncela *Federico* • Mónica López *Sara* • Antonio Dechent *Alejandro* ■ *Dir* Juan Carlos Fresnadillo • *Scr* Juan Carlos Fresnadillo, Andrés Koppel

The Intelligence Men ★★ U

Comedy 1965 · UK · Colour · 98mins

Morecambe and Wise found the transition from TV celebrities to film stars a difficult one to make. They were not helped by the fact that, for their big-screen debut, Sid Green and Dick Hills (scriptwriters of their ITV series at the time) failed to marry the familiar Eric and Ernie characteristics that kept audiences in stitches week after week with the demands of what is, in all honesty, a fitfully entertaining spy spoof. DP

Eric Morecambe *Eric* • Ernie Wise *Ernie Sage* • William Franklyn *Colonel Grant* • April Olrich *Madame Petrovna* • Richard Vernon *Sir Edward Seabrook* • Gloria Paul *Gina Carlotti* • Jacqueline Jones *Karin* • Warren Mitchell *Prozoroff* ■ *Dir* Robert Asher • *Scr* SC Green, RM Hills, from a story by Peter Blackmore

Intent to Kill ★★

Thriller 1958 · UK · BW · 88mins

Cinematographer Jack Cardiff turned director with this B-thriller, set in Montreal. Critics at the time wondered why he bothered. Richard Todd plays a brain surgeon whose marital problems pale into insignificance when he's asked to operate on South American leader Herbert Lom who is the target for assassins. Forget about Lom's record on human rights – not the film's concern – and concentrate instead on the mechanics of thriller-making. AT

Richard Todd *Dr Bob McLaurin* • Betsy Drake *Nancy Ferguson* • Herbert Lom *Juan Menda* • Warren Stevens *Finch* • Carlo Justini *Francisco Flores* • Paul Carpenter *O'Brien* • Alexander Knox *Dr McNeil* • Lisa Gastoni *Carla Menda* • Peter Arne *Kral* ■ *Dir* Jack Cardiff • *Scr* Jimmy Sangster, from a novel by Michael Bryan

Intent to Kill ★ 18

Action thriller 1992 · US · Colour · 94mins

If you can believe in ex-porn star Traci Lords as a nonconformist policewoman going after a drug dealer who's trying to retrieve a lost dope shipment, you'll believe the rest of this predictable action thriller. Yaphet Kotto plays Traci's captain and wins all the acting honours, but Traci gets to wear the more alluring outfits when she poses as a hooker. Otherwise this formula B-movie is notable for its high quota of graphic violence. AJ. Contains violence, nudity and drug abuse. DVD

Traci Lords *Vicki Stewart* • Yaphet Kotto *Captain Jackson* • Scott Patterson *Al* • Angelo Tiffe *Salvador* ■ *Dir/Scr* Charles T Kanganis

Interiors ★★★ 15

Psychological melodrama
1978 · US · Colour · 87mins

Coming between Woody Allen's great comic masterpieces *Annie Hall* and *Manhattan*, this intense drama baffled fans and divided critics on its original release. The influence of Ingmar Bergman is unmistakeable, but there are also echoes of Chekhov and Eugene O'Neill in this story of a family thrown into turmoil. Allen's stylish compositions and his astute handling of the cast are impressive, but the script lacks weight and some of the more searching scenes topple over into melodrama. Oscar-nominated Geraldine Page dominates the proceedings as the mentally disturbed mother. DP DVD

Kristin Griffith *Flyn* • Mary Beth Hurt *Joey* • Richard Jordan *Frederick* • Diane Keaton *Renata* • EG Marshall *Arthur* • Geraldine Page *Eve* • Maureen Stapleton *Pearl* • Sam Waterston *Michael* ■ *Dir/Scr* Woody Allen • *Cinematographer* Gordon Willis

Interlude ★

Romantic drama 1957 · US · Colour · 88mins

This virtually unwatchable drama (a remake of 1939's *When Tomorrow Comes*) features a miscast June Allyson as a woman who falls for married conductor Rossano Brazzi in Munich. Instead of having a wonderful sensual adventure, she wastes time trying to decide between Brazzi and unappealing doctor Keith Andes. Douglas Sirk provides heavy-handed and humourless direction. TS

June Allyson *Helen Banning* • Rossano Brazzi *Tonio Fischer* • Marianne Cook *Reni* • Françoise Rosay *Countess Reinhart* • Keith Andes *Dr Morley Dwyer* ■ *Dir* Douglas Sirk • *Scr* Daniel Fuchs, Franklin Coen, Inez Cocke, from the film *When Tomorrow Comes* by Dwight Taylor, from the novel *Serenade* by James M Cain

Interlude ★★★ PG

Romantic drama
1968 · US · Colour · 108mins

A charming remake of that hoary old romance about a wide-eyed innocent abroad who falls for a sophisticated married musician, previously filmed (as *When Tomorrow Comes*) with Irene Dunne and Charles Boyer, and lugubriously with June Allyson and Rossano Brazzi. Here the casting is nearly perfect, with dashing intellectual Oskar Werner and Barbara Ferris as the reporter who becomes entranced by him. TS

Oskar Werner *Stefan Zelter* • Barbara Ferris *Sally* • Virginia Maskell *Antonia* • Donald Sutherland *Lawrence* • Nora Swinburne *Mary* • Alan Webb *Andrew* • Bernard Kay *George Selworth* • John Cleese ■ *Dir* Kevin Billington • *Scr* Lee Langley, Hugh Leonard

Intermezzo ★★★★

Romance 1936 · Swe · BW · 88mins

A famous violinist employs a young pianist to give his daughter lessons, but falls in love with her, leaves his wife, and embarks on a concert tour with the girl as his accompanist. Directed by one of Sweden's foremost film-makers of the period, Gustaf Molander, and starring that country's most distinguished leading man, Gösta Ekman, this classy bittersweet romantic drama is notable for instigating the international career of Ingrid Bergman. David Selznick saw the film and, two years later, invited the relative unknown to Hollywood to star in an English-language remake. The rest, as they say, is history. RK. In Swedish with English subtitles.

Gösta Ekman (1) *Holger Brandt* • Inga Tidblad *Margit Brandt* • Ingrid Bergman *Anita Hoffman* • Hasse Ekman *Ake Brandt* • Britt Hagman *Ann-Marie Brandt* ■ *Dir* Gustav Molander [Gustaf Molander] • *Scr* Gustav Molander, Gösta Stevens

Intermezzo ★★★★ PG

Romance 1939 · US · BW · 69mins

This was producer David O Selznick's remake of the Swedish movie which also starred Ingrid Bergman. Originally only intending to purchase the story, Selznick was persuaded to also import Miss Bergman, who here makes her American debut, and her natural beauty was the movie's initial sales gimmick. The tale of obsessive love is old hat, but is remarkably and touchingly well played by Bergman and Leslie Howard. The film was to have been directed by William Wyler, who Selznick allegedly fired in order to hire the Russian émigré Gregory Ratoff, who owed Selznick and could therefore forfeit his director's salary to pay off his gambling debt. TS DVD

Ingrid Bergman *Anita Hoffman* • Leslie Howard *Holger Brandt* • Edna Best *Margit Brandt* • John Halliday *Thomas Stenborg* • Cecil Kellaway *Charles Moler* • Enid Bennett *Greta Stenborg* • Ann E Todd *Ann Marie* • Douglas Scott *Eric Brandt* ■ *Dir* Gregory Ratoff • *Scr* George O'Neil, from the film by Gustav Molander, Gösta Stevens

interMission ★★★ 18

Crime comedy drama
2003 · Ire/UK/US · Colour · 101mins

For all its crudity and violence, this edgy slice-of-life tale remains compulsively addictive. Part grimy ensemble drama, part bruise-black comedy, it follows a group of interlinking characters doing whatever it takes to stay buoyant in a crime-ridden area of Dublin. At the centre of events is Cillian Murphy, a supermarket shelf-stacker who plots revenge after ex-girlfriend Kelly Macdonald shacks up with a middle-aged bank manager. While the protagonists may not be likeable, they're certainly absorbing. SF. Contains swearing, violence. DVD

Colin Farrell (2) *Lehiff* • Shirley Henderson *Sally* • Kelly Macdonald *Deirdre* • Colm Meaney *Det Jerry Lynch* • Cillian Murphy *John* • Ger Ryan *Maura* • Brian F O'Byrne *Mick* • Michael McElhatton *Sam* • Deirdre O'Kane *Noeleen* • David Wilmot *Oscar* ■ *Dir* John Crowley • *Scr* Mark O'Rowe

Internal Affairs ★★★★ 18

Crime thriller 1990 · US · Colour · 109mins

In this gripping thriller from *Leaving Las Vegas* director Mike Figgis, Andy Garcia stars as an Internal Affairs investigator who's determined to prove that fellow police officer Richard Gere is corrupt. Gere is especially good as the dishonest and often violent policeman, but, in the end, this film focuses more on Gere's general nastiness than the interesting vendetta between the pair that starts the movie. JB. Contains violence, swearing and sex scenes. DVD

Richard Gere *Dennis Peck* • Andy Garcia *Sergeant Raymond Avilla* • Nancy Travis *Kathleen Avilla* • Laurie Metcalf *Sergeant Amy Wallace* • Richard Bradford *Lieutenant Sergeant Grieb* • William Baldwin *Van Stretch* ■ *Dir* Mike Figgis • *Scr* Henry Bean

International House ★★★

Comedy 1933 · US · BW · 70mins

In this great, if paper-thin, antique comedy, WC Fields arrives by autogyro at a hotel in China where a giant television is about to be unveiled. Many popular radio performers of the day turn up to take part in the celebrations, including Rudy Vallee, George Burns and Gracie Allen, while Cab Calloway sings *Reefer Man*. Bela Lugosi appears as a Russian general in a rollicking good show that will appeal to nostalgia lovers. AJ

WC Fields *Professor Quail* • Bela Lugosi *General Petronovich* • Stuart Erwin *Tommy Nash* • Sari Maritza *Carol Fortescue* • George Burns *Dr Burns* • Gracie Allen *Nurse Allen* • Rudy Vallee • Cab Calloway ■ *Dir* Edward Sutherland [A Edward Sutherland] • *Scr* Frances Martin, Walter DeLeon, from a story by Lou Heifetz, Neil Brant

International Lady ★★ U

Second World War spy drama
1941 · US · BW · 102mins

Hungarian-born Ilona Massey, who enjoyed a brief career as an opera singer, is the "international lady" in this overlong piece of light-hearted wartime hokum. She's the spy who passes coded messages to the Nazis through the songs she broadcasts. George Brent's government agent and Basil Rathbone's Scotland Yard detective are both hot on her trail. AE

George Brent *Tim Hanley* • Ilona Massey *Carla Nillson* • Basil Rathbone *Reggie Oliver* • Gene Lockhart *Sidney Grenner* ■ *Dir* Tim Whelan • *Scr* Howard Estabrook, from a story by E Lloyd Sheldon, Jack DeWitt

International Settlement ★★ U

Thriller 1938 · US · BW · 70mins

With his long-standing enthusiasm for films torn from the day's headlines, Fox studio chief Darryl F Zanuck ordered one to exploit the Japanese invasion of China. He handed it to his B-feature unit as a "special" to star

Dolores Del Rio and George Sanders. Sanders is the adventurer in Shanghai's International Settlement district where he is first shot at, then saved by Del Rio's French nightclub singer. Newsreel footage of the bombing of Shanghai is incorporated into the climax. AE

George Sanders *Del Forbes* • Dolores Del Rio *Lenore Dixon* • June Lang *Joyce Parker* • Dick Baldwin *Wally Burton* • John Carradine *Murdock* • Keye Luke *Dr Wong* ■ *Dir* Eugene Forde • *Scr* Lou Breslow, John Patrick, from a story by Lynn Root, Frank Fenton

International Velvet ★★ PG

Drama 1978 · US/UK · Colour · 110mins

More than 30 years on from the MGM classic *National Velvet*, Elizabeth Taylor has grown into Nanette Newman, lives with Christopher Plummer and has ambitions for her niece, Tatum O'Neal, to win an Olympic equestrian title. Anthony Hopkins plays Tatum's coach. Bryan Forbes considered the title "puerile" and lost his fight to change it, but this movie, a concoction devised by a near-destitute MGM, was probably a lost cause anyway; everything is far too sugary. AT [video]

Tatum O'Neal *Sarah Brown* • Christopher Plummer *John Seaton* • Anthony Hopkins *Captain Johnny Johnson* • Nanette Newman *Velvet Brown* • Peter Barkworth *Pilot* • Dinsdale Landen *Mr Curtis* ■ *Dir* Bryan Forbes • *Scr* Bryan Forbes, suggested by the novel *National Velvet* by Enid Bagnold

The Internecine Project ★★ 15

Thriller 1974 · UK · Colour · 85mins

A selection of gravel-voiced actors including James Coburn and Keenan Wynn accompany actress Lee Grant in this lukewarm espionage thriller. Despite some awful dialogue, Coburn still manages to play the hard-edged plot with his tongue in his cheek, and he got his own back 17 years later when he parodied roles like this as a murder-happy spy in *Hudson Hawk*. JB. Contains violence and swearing. DVD

James Coburn *Robert Elliot* • Lee Grant *Jean Robertson* • Harry Andrews *Albert Parsons* • Ian Hendry *Alex Hellman* • Michael Jayston *David Baker* • Keenan Wynn *EJ Farnsworth* ■ *Dir* Ken Hughes • *Scr* Barry Levinson, Jonathan Lynn, from the novel *Internecine* by Mort W Elkind • *Cinematographer* Geoffrey Unsworth

Internes Can't Take Money ★★★

Medical drama 1937 · US · BW · 77mins

A young hospital doctor helps a gangster's widow find her missing child in a modest programme filler that stars Joel McCrea as the sympathetic medic and the wonderful Barbara Stanwyck as the mother. The film was an unexpected box-office hit for Paramount, but the studio badly missed the boat: it was MGM that picked up Max Brand's Dr Kildare character, cast Lew Ayres in the role and made a series of highly successful features over a nine-year period. RK

Barbara Stanwyck *Janet Haley* • Joel McCrea *James Kildare* • Lloyd Nolan *Hanlon* • Stanley Ridges *Innes* • Gaylord Pendleton [Steve Pendleton] *Interne Jones* • Lee Bowman *Interne Weeks* • Irving Bacon *Jeff* ■ *Dir* Alfred Santell • *Scr* Rian James, Theodore Reeves, from a story by Max Brand

The Interns ★★

Romantic drama 1962 · US · BW · 119mins

All sorts of sexual shenanigans go on behind the screens at a big American hospital when four newly-qualified doctors arrive for work. Clearly intended as the flipside of Doctor Kildare's squeaky-clean adventures, this movie was advertised at the time as being really adult and racy. It wasn't then and it isn't now, and the only reason to watch is the cast. A sequel, *The New Interns*, followed in 1964. AT

Michael Callan *Dr Considine* • Cliff Robertson *Dr John Paul Otis* • James MacArthur *Dr Lew Worship* • Nick Adams *Dr Sid Lackland* • Suzy Parker *Lisa Cardigan* • Haya Harareet *Mado* • Anne Helm *Mildred* • Stefanie Powers *Gloria* • Buddy Ebsen *Dr Sidney Wohl* • Telly Savalas *Dr Riccio* • Katharine Bard *Nurse Flynn* ■ *Dir* David Swift • *Scr* Walter Newman, David Swift, from a novel by Richard Frede

Interpol ★

Crime thriller 1957 · UK · BW · 91mins

Known as *Pickup Alley* in the US, this feeble thriller about tracking down a dope-peddling syndicate by the international police force boasted that it was filmed in London, Paris, Athens, Naples, Rome, Lisbon and New York. It looks as though they sometimes forgot to take the script with them. Trevor Howard obviously relishes acting the master villain for a change, though co-stars Victor Mature and Anita Ekberg don't try to act at all. AE

Victor Mature *Charles Sturgis* • Anita Ekberg *Gina Broger* • Trevor Howard *Frank McNally* • Bonar Colleano *Amalio* • Alec Mango *Salko* ■ *Dir* John Gilling • *Scr* John Paxton, from the novel by AJ Forrest

The Interpreter ★★★★ 12A

Political thriller
2005 · UK/US/Fr · Colour · 128mins

This engrossing thriller has the distinction of being the first movie to film inside the United Nations headquarters in New York. Nicole Kidman plays a translator who overhears a threat to murder an African head of state (Earl Cameron) in a dialect that few can understand. Recently bereaved Secret Service agent Sean Penn is then assigned to keep an eye on the imperilled interpreter, but the affair takes a distinctly sinister turn as Penn begins to suspect there is more to Kidman than meets the eye. Sydney Pollack's return to directing may be a little too worthy for its own good, but the performances of Kidman and Penn turn this into a tightly knit and intelligent film. KK. Contains violence.

Nicole Kidman *Silvia Broome* • Sean Penn *Tobin Keller* • Catherine Keener *Dot Woods* • Jesper Christensen *Nils Lud* • Yvan Attal *Philippe* • Earl Cameron *Edmund Zuwanie* • Michael Wright *Marcus* • George Harris (2) *Kuman-Kuman* ■ *Dir* Sydney Pollack • *Scr* Charles Randolph, Scott Frank, Steven Zaillian, from a story by Martin Stellman, Brian Ward

Interrogation ★★★★

Political drama 1982 · Pol · Colour · 118mins

Although set in the last days of Stalinism, the parallels with the Solidarity era meant that Ryszard Bugaski's harrowing drama was immediately banned on its release in Poland. When it was eventually reissued, Krystyna Janda won the best actress prize at Cannes in 1990 for her performance as the falsely accused cabaret artist, who is pitilessly tortured on account of her sexual liaison with a major implicated in anti-government activity. DP. In Polish with English subtitles.

Krystyna Janda *Antonia Dziwisz* • Adam Ferency *Morawsky* • Janusz Gajos *Zawada* • Agnieszka Holland *Witowska* • Olgierd Lukaszewicz ■ *Dir* Ryszard Bugajski • *Scr* Ryszard Bugajski, Janusz Dymek

The Interrupted Journey ★

Crime drama 1949 · UK · BW · 85mins

This tale of the unexpected plays so many tricks on the viewer that it soon becomes impossible to identify with the plight of novelist Richard Todd, whose inability to choose between wife Valerie Hobson and mistress Christine Norden spells disaster for his fellow passengers on a speeding express. Cheap production, gimmicky script. DP

Richard Todd *John North* • Valerie Hobson *Carol North* • Christine Norden *Susan Wilding* • Tom Walls *Mr Clayton* • Dora Bryan *Waitress* • Arnold Ridley *Saunders* ■ *Dir* Daniel Birt • *Scr* Michael Pertwee

Interrupted Melody ★★★★ U

Biographical drama
1955 · US · Colour · 105mins

This lush and expensive MGM biopic is about the Australian singer Marjorie Lawrence, who contracted polio at the peak of her career. It's marvellously played by under-rated redhead Eleanor Parker. The writers, William Ludwig and Sonya Levien, won an Oscar for best adapted screenplay. Glenn Ford is superb as the doctor who inspires the singer in her fight against the disease, and the supporting cast is led by Roger Moore. TS

Glenn Ford *Dr Thomas King* • Eleanor Parker *Marjorie Lawrence* • Roger Moore *Cyril Lawrence* • Cecil Kellaway *Bill Lawrence* • Eileen Farrell *Singing voice* ■ *Dir* Curtis Bernhardt • *Scr* William Ludwig, Sonya Levien, from the book by Marjorie Lawrence

Intersection ★★★ 15

Drama 1994 · US · Colour · 94mins

Few will remember the glossy French movie *The Things of Life*, of which this is an even glossier remake. Richard Gere is a well-groomed architect, married to Sharon Stone and having an affair with journalist Lolita Davidovich. The usual *ménage à trois*, then, with designer labels and capped teeth, all droolingly shot and written like a TV soap. The trick is to give Gere's dilemma (Sharon or Lolita?) some resonance, so a stunningly staged car smash takes centre stage and takes the decision out of his hands. AT. Contains swearing, sex scenes and brief nudity. [video] DVD

Richard Gere *Vincent Eastman* • Sharon Stone *Sally Eastman* • Lolita Davidovich *Olivia Marshak* • Martin Landau *Neal* • Jenny Morrison [Jennifer Morrison] *Meaghan Eastman* ■ *Dir* Mark Rydell • *Scr* David Rayfiel, Marshall Brickman, from the film *The Things of Life/Les Choses de la Vie* by Paul Guimard, Jean-Loup Dabadie, Claude Sautet, from the novel *Les Choses de la Vie* by Paul Guimard

Interstella 5555 ★★ PG

Animated science-fiction musical
2003 · Jpn/Fr · Colour · 68mins

Sniping at the inanity of designer pop, this futuristic animé was scripted and scored by electronica duo Daft Punk and realised by veteran Japanese creative artist Leiji Matsumoto. The story of a four-piece combo's abduction from its own planet to be reprogrammed and repackaged as the all-conquering Crescendolls by a malevolent tycoon is ably told without dialogue and includes some nimble montage sequences that expose and parody the excesses of the music business. But the soundtrack too often stands apart from comic-book action, which is bereft of sophistication and character depth. DP DVD

Dir Kazuhisa Takenouchi • *Scr* Thomas Bangalter, Cédric Hervet, Guy-Manuel De Homem-Christo • *Music* Daft Punk • *Visual supervisor* Leiji Matsumoto

Interval ★★★

Romantic drama
1973 · US/Mex · Colour · 85mins

Returning to the screen after six years, a well-preserved 62-year-old Merle Oberon starred in, produced and co-edited this soapy tale of a wealthy globetrotting woman on holiday in Mexico who meets and falls in love with a painter 20 years her junior. Her final film, directed stolidly in a colourful location by Daniel Mann, was a case of life imitating bad art, because Oberon, then living in Mexico, fell for her young co-star, Robert Wolders, who soon became her fourth husband. RB

Merle Oberon *Serena Moore* • Robert Wolders *Chris* • Claudio Brook *Armando Vertiz* • Russ Conway *Fraser* • Charles Bateman *Husband* ■ *Dir* Daniel Mann • *Scr* Gavin Lambert

Interview with the Vampire: the Vampire Chronicles ★★★ 18

Horror 1994 · US · Colour · 122mins

When the highly anticipated movie version of Anne Rice's cult novel finally came to the screen, it was a decidedly anaemic affair. All sumptuously dressed up with nowhere really interesting to go, director Neil Jordan's lavish adaptation is a stylised horror tale lacking the emotional depth and jet-black darkness of the doom-laden tome. Still, Tom Cruise is fine as the vampire Lestat, whose close relationship with handsome Brad Pitt forms an erotic twist on the Dracula legend. It's Antonio Banderas who gives the most full-blooded performance as the bisexual Armand in a beautifully mounted production, low on divine decadence but high on evocative elegance. AJ. Contains violence, swearing, nudity. [video] DVD

Tom Cruise *Lestat de Lioncourt* • Brad Pitt *Louis Pointe du Lac* • Antonio Banderas *Armand* • Stephen Rea *Santiago* • Christian Slater *Daniel Malloy* • Kirsten Dunst *Claudia* • Domiziana Giordano *Madeleine* ■ *Dir* Neil Jordan • *Scr* Anne Rice, from her novel

Intervista ★★★★ 15

Biographical documentary drama
1987 · It · Colour · 106mins

A breathless, brilliant insight into the vanities and inanities of the motion picture business from the inimitable Federico Fellini. A curio rather than a classic, it sweeps the viewer from the 1980s to the Cinecittà film studio of over 60 years ago, when a wide-eyed youth from Rimini came to Rome to make his name. Packed with clips from screen gems and blurring the line between past and present, studio reality and cinematic illusion, this climaxes with a wickedly staged reunion between Marcello Mastroianni and Anita Ekberg, the stars of Fellini's classic *La Dolce Vita*. DP. In Italian with English subtitles. [video]

Federico Fellini • Marcello Mastroianni • Anita Ekberg • Sergio Rubini *Reporter* • Maurizio Mein ■ *Dir* Federico Fellini • *Scr* Federico Fellini, Gianfranco Angelucci

Intimacy ★★★ 18

Drama 2000 · Fr/UK · Colour · 114mins

This controversial first English-language film from French director Patrice Chéreau depicts the sexual act in some of the most explicit scenes ever passed by the British Board of Film Classification. Estranged love rat Mark Rylance and bored paramour Kerry Fox indulge their desperate sexual passions every Wednesday afternoon at his sleazy flat. As their casual affair grows ever more compulsive, the anonymity Rylance thought he wanted starts to drive him so crazy that he begins to follow his nameless lover. This is an intriguing exploration of the dynamics between intimate love and physical sex, but it's also theatrical and wordy. AJ. Contains swearing, sex scenes and nudity. [video] DVD

Mark Rylance *Jay* • Kerry Fox *Claire* • Timothy Spall *Andy* • Alastair Galbraith *Victor* • Philippe Calvario *Ian* • Marianne Faithfull *Betty* •

Susannah Harker *Susan, Jay's wife* ■ *Dir* Patrice Chéreau • *Scr* Patrice Chéreau, Anne-Louise Trividic, from stories by Hanif Kureishi

Intimate Relations ★★★ 15

Black comedy drama based on a true story
1995 · UK/Can · Colour · 95mins

This 1950s-set drama lifts the lid on the lusty bedroom antics of the supposedly staid British. Rupert Graves is the sailor who takes a room as a boarder in the home of a seemingly normal family. It's not long before Julie Walters (a great, almost sinister turn) and her teenage daughter are vying for his affections, and hapless Graves finds himself out of his depth. Writer/director Philip Goodhew's debut feature is quirky and engrossing fare with a very dark edge. JB. Contains violence, swearing and a sex scene.

Julie Walters *Marjorie Beasley* • Rupert Graves *Harold Guppy* • Matthew Walker *Stanley Beasley* • Laura Sadler *Joyce Beasley* • Holly Aird *Deirdre* • Les Dennis *Maurice Guppy* ■ *Dir/Scr* Philip Goodhew

The Intimate Stranger ★★

Mystery drama 1956 · UK · BW · 95mins

This was the second film made in England by the blacklisted Hollywood director Joseph Losey, working under the pseudonym of Walton, which was his middle name. Blacklisted writer Howard Koch had written the script about an American film producer in London who is married to the daughter of the studio chief and is being blackmailed by a woman whose letters suggest she might be his mistress. It's a feeble effort with poor performances and cardboard sets, but the theme of the story – illusion, paranoia, guilt – are fascinating when set beside Losey's own predicament. AT

Richard Basehart *Reggie Wilson* • Mary Murphy *Evelyn Stewart* • Constance Cummings *Kay Wallace* • Roger Livesey *Ben Case* • Faith Brook *Lesley Wilson* • Mervyn Johns *Ernest Chapple* • Vernon Greeves *George Merns* • André Mikhelson *Steve Vadney* ■ *Dir* Joseph Walton [Joseph Losey] • *Scr* Peter Howard [Howard Koch], from the novel *Pay the Piper* by Paul Howard

Into the Arms of Strangers: Stories of the Kindertransport ★★★ PG

Documentary
2000 · US · BW and Colour · 112mins

Less penetrating than Mark Jonathan Harris's Oscar-winner, *The Long Way Home*, this is, nevertheless, a moving tribute to the 10,000 Jewish children who fled Europe in the desperate months before the outbreak of the Second World War. Adhering to the testimonial format favoured by Holocaust documentaries, the film commemorates the indomitability of the survivors of the *Kindertransport* exodus. It also recalls the selfless courage of the terrified parents, who often sacrificed everything to spare their children from the coming nightmare. Yet, disappointingly, it skirts such contentious issues as the anti-Semitism in Britain and the United States at the time. DP DVD

Judi Dench *Narrator* ■ *Dir/Scr* Mark Jonathan Harris

Into the Mirror ★★ 15

Supernatural horror
2003 · S Kor · Colour · 113mins

Although debuting director Kim Seong-ho pulls off some neat visual effects, this chiller lacks the character depth and psychological novelty to do more than mildly unnerve. Despite an intriguing opening, in which Kim Hye-na suggests that her deceased twin sister might be behind the apparent suicides at Gi Ju-bong's renovated department store, director Kim dwells too long on security guard Yu Ji-tae's self-pitying reflections. The outcome is as predictable as the set-piece shocks. DP. In Korean with English subtitles. Contains violence. DVD

Yu Ji-tae *Woo Yeong-min* • Kim Myeong-min *Heo Hyeon-su* • Kim Hye-na *Lee Ji-hyeon* • Gi Ju-bong *Jeong Ill-seong* • Kim Myeong-su *Choi Sang-gi* • Lee Young-jin *Choi Mi-jeong* ■ *Dir/Scr* Kim Seong-ho

Into the Night ★★ 15

Comedy thriller 1985 · US · Colour · 114mins

John Landis came a bit of a cropper with this lacklustre comedy caper, although it has aged better than some of his efforts. The then relatively unknown Jeff Goldblum and Michelle Pfeiffer take the lead roles: Goldblum the innocent bystander who inadvertently gets caught up with smuggler Pfeiffer and Arab terrorists. The action bustles along amusingly enough and Landis stuffs the pictures with cameos from everyone from David Bowie to Roger Vadim. JF DVD

Jeff Goldblum *Ed Okin* • Michelle Pfeiffer *Diana* • Stacey Pickren *Ellen Okin* • Bruce McGill *Charlie* • Kathryn Harrold *Christie* • Carl Perkins *Mr Williams* • David Bowie *Colin Morris* • Richard Farnsworth *Jack Caper* • John Landis *Savak 4* • Dan Aykroyd *Herb* • Roger Vadim *Monsieur Melville* ■ *Dir* John Landis • *Scr* Ron Koslow

Into the Sun ★★ 15

Action adventure 1992 · US · Colour · 96mins

Anthony Michael Hall's career started slipping the minute he started losing his geeky teenage looks, and this was one of his failed bids to relaunch himself as an action star. It's still worth a look, though, if only for a smarter-than-usual premise. Hall is the Hollywood star researching a new film role who is reluctantly taken under the wing of maverick air force ace Michael Paré. Soon the pair find themselves caught up in a real-life war. JF

Anthony Michael Hall *Tom Slade* • Michael Paré *Captain Paul Watkins* • Deborah Maria Moore [Deborah Moore] *Major Goode* • Terry Kiser *Mitchell Burton* • Brian Haley *Lieutenant DeCarlo* ■ *Dir* Fritz Kiersch • *Scr* John Brancato, Michael Ferris, from their story

Into the West ★★★ PG

Fantasy 1992 · Ire/UK · Colour · 102mins

A dark-hued fable about two children who run away to the wild Irish hills on a white stallion, pursued by their drunkard gypsy father (Gabriel Byrne) and Ellen Barkin. Set against some majestic scenery, this is partly a grim look at the hardships and discrimination suffered by travellers in Ireland, and partly an excursion into Gaelic myth, sensitively handled by Mike Newell. The two young leads (Ciaran Fitzgerald and Ruaidhri Conroy) are both outstanding in this poetic tale of belief and redemption. AT DVD

Gabriel Byrne *Papa Riley* • Ellen Barkin *Kathleen* • Ciaran Fitzgerald *Ossie Riley* • Ruaidhri Conroy *Tito Riley* • David Kelly *Grandpa Ward* • Johnny Murphy *Tracker* ■ *Dir* Mike Newell • *Scr* Jim Sheridan, from a story by Michael Pearce

Intolerable Cruelty ★★★ 12

Satirical romantic comedy
2003 · US · Colour · 95mins

This is by far Joel and Ethan Coen's most expensive film and also their first working from an existing script. That it turns out to be their weakest to date may not be unconnected. A slick, colourful screwball comedy, it follows the quest of ultra-successful divorce lawyer George Clooney to marry professional gold-digger Catherine Zeta-Jones using his own cast-iron "pre-nup". The film is populated with wonderful grotesque supporting characters, but these turns distract from rather than add to the central plot. Clooney works his socks off, but this lacks a hard centre and plot keeps racing ahead of character. AC DVD

George Clooney *Miles Longfellow Massey* • Catherine Zeta-Jones *Marylin Rexroth* • Geoffrey Rush *Donovan Donaly* • Cedric the Entertainer *Gus Petch* • Edward Herrmann *Rex Rexroth* • Paul Adelstein *Wrigley* • Richard Jenkins *Freddy Bender* • Billy Bob Thornton *Howard Drexler Doyle* • Julia Duffy *Sarah Batista O'Flanagan Sorkin* • Jonathan Hadary *Heinz, the Baron Krauss von Espy* ■ *Dir* Joel Coen • *Scr* Robert Ramsey, Matthew Stone, Ethan Coen, Joel Coen, from a story by Robert Ramsey, Matthew Stone, John Romano

Intolerance ★★★★★ PG

Classic silent drama
1916 · US · BW · 177mins

A magnificent and deeply significant achievement of early cinema, this sprawling multilayered epic helped define storytelling in the movies, with its early use of such devices as parallel action and the dramatic close-up. Made as a riposte by genius director DW Griffith to those who accused him of racism after his ground-breaking *The Birth of a Nation*, this analyses the effects of intolerance in four tales set throughout the ages, which are interspersed with the eternal image of a mother (Lillian Gish) and baby. The Babylonian sequences are as notorious as they are astounding, with gigantic sets almost dwarfing the rampant violence and nudity, but the contemporary tale is exciting and touching, too. Seen restored, this is one of the most satisfying films ever made. TS DVD

Lillian Gish *The woman who rocks the cradle* • Mae Marsh *The Dear One* • Fred Turner *Father* • Robert Harron *Boy* • Howard Gaye *Christ* • Lillian Langdon *Mary* • Olga Grey *Mary Magdalene* • Margery Wilson *Brown Eyes* • Frank Bennett (1) *Charles IX* • Josephine Crowell *Catherine de Midici* • Constance Talmadge *Mountain girl* • Alfred Paget *Belshazzar* • Seena Owen *Attarea* ■ *Dir/Scr* DW Griffith

Intrigue ★ PG

Adventure 1947 · US · BW · 86mins

In Shanghai after the Second World War, former tough-guy pilot George Raft finds himself working for a black-marketeering outfit. But when he discovers that the gang's food-price fixing is causing suffering to orphans, he sets out to remedy the situation. Edwin L Marin's direction has no discernible influence over the cliché-ridden and totally unbelievable plot, or the now ageing Raft's impassive performance. AJ

George Raft *Brad Dunham* • June Havoc *Tamara Baranoff* • Helena Carter *Linda Arnold* • Tom Tully *Marc Andrews* • Marvin Miller *Ramon* • Dan Seymour *Karidian* ■ *Dir* Edwin L Marin • *Scr* Barry Trivers, George Slavin, from a story by George Slavin

Introducing Dorothy Dandridge ★★★ 15

Biographical drama
1999 · US · Colour · 110mins

Halle Berry may have won Golden Globe for her performance, but there's a lingering feeling she was accoladed to atone for the shameful treatment meted out to the subject of Martha Coolidge's earnest, but unrevealing TV biopic. Too little is made of the institutionalised racism that blighted 1950s Tinseltown and transformed the Oscar-nominated star of *Carmen Jones* into a marginalised, pill-popping drunk. Despite the award, Berry is too slight a talent for the part and she's easily overshadowed by Klaus Maria Brandauer's imposing Otto Preminger. Released on video and DVD as *Face of an Angel*. DP DVD

Halle Berry *Dorothy Dandridge* • Brent Spiner *Earl Mills* • Obba Babatunde *Harold Nicholas* • Klaus Maria Brandauer *Otto Preminger* • Loretta Devine *Ruby Dandridge* • Cynda Williams *Vivian Dandridge* ■ *Dir* Martha Coolidge • *Scr* Shonda Rhimes, Scott Abbott, from the biography *Dorothy Dandridge* by Earl Mills

The Intruder ★★★ U

Drama 1953 · UK · BW · 81mins

An intriguing idea – why would a wartime hero become a peacetime thief? – is played out mechanically by director Guy Hamilton, but performed with some force by officer Jack Hawkins, who finds a former member of his regiment (Michael Medwin) burgling his home. Hamilton was still honing his craft here, but he went on to be a fine action director. TH

Jack Hawkins *Wolf Merton* • Hugh Williams *Tim Ross* • Michael Medwin *Ginger Edwards* • George Cole *John Summers* • Dennis Price *Leonard Perry* • George Baker *Adjutant* • Richard Wattis *Schoolmaster* • Dora Bryan *Dora Bee* ■ *Dir* Guy Hamilton • *Scr* Robin Maugham, John Hunter, Anthony Squire, from the novel *Line on Ginger* by Robin Maugham

The Intruder ★★★ 15

Drama 1961 · US · BW · 79mins

A remarkable one-off from horror producer/director Roger Corman, turning his hand to this stark tale of bigotry in the Deep South based on a controversial novel by screenwriter Charles Beaumont. William Shatner is the *agent provocateur* who incites racist riots in opposition to the then new US school integration. As Shatner's character's true motives are revealed, the film becomes particularly effective and genuinely unsettling. Not a success in its day, it has achieved a certain cult notoriety. TS

William Shatner *Adam Cramer* • Frank Maxwell *Tom McDaniel* • Beverly Lunsford *Ella McDaniel* • Robert Emhardt *Verne Shipman* • Jeanne Cooper *Vi Griffin* ■ *Dir* Roger Corman • *Scr* Charles Beaumont, from his novel

Intruder in the Dust ★★★

Drama 1949 · US · BW · 86mins

A solid adaptation of William Faulkner's novel about a black man (Juano Hernandez) who faces a lynch mob after he's accused of shooting a white man. He isn't guilty, of course, but his pride and obvious contempt for the justice system harm his case. Director Clarence Brown, best known for his work with Garbo, refuses to let hysteria invade the picture and he gets marvellous atmosphere from his location shooting in Oxford, Mississippi, Faulkner's home town. AT

David Brian *John Gavin Stevens* • Claude Jarman Jr *Chick Mallison* • Juano Hernandez *Lucas Beauchamp* • Porter Hall *Nub Gowrie* • Will Geer *Sheriff Hampton* ■ *Dir* Clarence Brown • *Scr* Ben Maddow, from the novel by William Faulkner

Invaders from Mars ★★★★ PG

Science-fiction drama
1953 · US · Colour · 77mins

William Cameron Menzies helped to design *Gone with the Wind* and directed *Things to Come*, and his Martian fairy tale has achieved cult status because of its distorted sets and abstract surrealism. Yes, you can see the zips on the aliens' suits, and, yes, the paranoia scares are strictly kids' stuff. But that's precisely why this pulp nightmare has built up a following. For it perfectly depicts, from a child's point of view, the ultimate horror of having no one to trust and nowhere to turn. AJ DVD

Helena Carter *Dr Pat Blake* • Arthur Franz *Dr Stuart Kelston* • Jimmy Hunt *David MacLean* • Leif Erickson *George MacLean* • Hillary Brooke *Mary MacLean* ■ *Dir* William Cameron Menzies • *Scr* William Cameron Menzies, Richard Blake, John Tucker Battle, from a story by John Tucker Battle

Invaders from Mars ★★★ PG

Science-fiction comedy
1986 · US · Colour · 94mins

Director Tobe Hooper, best known for *The Texas Chain Saw Massacre*, skirts a fine line between kitsch and spoof in his big-budget remake of the 1953 B-movie. Clinging closely to the original primal paranoia story of a young boy's neighbourhood suddenly being overrun by aliens, Hooper's deadpan sci-fi comedy provides good scares, great visual design and Stan Winston's wonderfully wild Martian monster special effects. AJ

Karen Black *Linda* • Hunter Carson *David Gardner* • Timothy Bottoms *George Gardner* • Laraine Newman *Ellen Gardner* • James Karen *General Wilson* • Louise Fletcher *Mrs McKeltch* ■ *Dir* Tobe Hooper • *Scr* Dan O'Bannon, Don Jakoby, Richard Blake

Invasion ★★ PG

Science-fiction thriller
1965 · UK · BW · 77mins

Aliens put an invisible force field around a secluded country hospital in this endearingly daffy British oddity, which must feature the cheapest alien takeover in history. Edward Judd is the scientist battling the extraterrestrial Oriental women in spacesuits, in an efficiently made and, yes, mildly exciting slice of cut-price science fiction. Director Alan Bridges imbues the Home Counties atmosphere with a peculiar ambience that's astonishingly heady at times, too. AJ

Edward Judd *Dr Vernon* • Yoko Tani *Lystrian leader* • Valerie Gearon *Dr Claire Harlan* • Lyndon Brook *Brian Carter* • Tsai Chin *Nurse Lim* ■ *Dir* Alan Bridges • *Scr* Roger Marshall, from a story by Robert Holmes

Invasion of the Astro-Monster ★★ U

Science-fiction adventure
1965 · Jpn · Colour · 90mins

This marked Godzilla's fifth film appearance and his change of status from Japan's evil enemy to much-loved national institution. Don't bother trying to work out incomprehensible plot is – something about Godzilla and Rodan being shipped off in space bubbles to Planet X so they can defeat three-headed Ghidrah – just enjoy the usual cheesy special effects, atrocious dubbing and Nick Adams trying to look as if his scenes weren't shot separately in the States. AJ. Japanese dialogue dubbed into English.

Nick Adams *Glenn* • Akira Takarada *Fuji* • Kumi Mizuno *Namikawa* • Keiko Sawai • Akira Kubo ■ *Dir* Inoshiro Honda • *Scr* Shinichi Sekizawa • *Special Effects* Eiji Tsuburaya

Invasion of the Body Snatchers ★★★★★ PG

Classic science-fiction thriller
1956 · US · BW · 80mins

Pods from outer space land in a small Californian town and start replicating the inhabitants, replacing them with unfeeling doubles, in director Don Siegel's chilling science-fiction tale. This classic of the genre (co-scripted by an uncredited Sam Peckinpah) reflects the blacklisting hysteria of the McCarthy era, as Siegel tersely piles on the nightmare with pulse-pounding briskness. Although expertly remade since (including 1993's *Body Snatchers*), the original is still the most striking, with a justly famous scalp-freezing ending. AJ

Kevin McCarthy *Miles Bennell* • Dana Wynter *Becky Driscoll* • Larry Gates *Danny* • King Donovan *Jack* • Carolyn Jones *Theodora* • Jean Willes *Sally* • Ralph Dumke *Nick* • Virginia Christine *Wilma* ■ *Dir* Don Siegel • *Scr* Daniel Mainwaring, Sam Peckinpah, from the novel *The Body Snatchers* by Jack Finney

Invasion of the Body Snatchers ★★★ 15

Science-fiction thriller
1978 · US · Colour · 110mins

It was always going to be hard to better Don Siegel's 1956 classic, and if director Philip Kaufman doesn't quite succeed, he does manage to summon up an equally chilling air of paranoia in this remake, set in a coldly impersonal San Francisco. Donald Sutherland stars as the health inspector who begins to worry that people are acting weirdly normal, and there is solid support from Brooke Adams and a young Jeff Goldblum, plus a creepy turn from Leonard Nimoy. JF. Contains swearing and brief nudity. DVD

Donald Sutherland *Matthew Bennell* • Brooke Adams *Elizabeth Driscoll* • Leonard Nimoy *Dr David Kibner* • Veronica Cartwright *Nancy Bellicec* • Jeff Goldblum *Jack Bellicec* • Art Hindle *Geoffrey* • Kevin McCarthy *Running man* • Robert Duvall *Priest on swing* • Don Siegel *Taxi driver* ■ *Dir* Philip Kaufman • *Scr* WD Richter, from the novel *The Body Snatchers* by Jack Finney

Invasion of the Saucer Men ★

Science-fiction comedy
1957 · US · BW · 69mins

A "so-bad-it's-almost-good" sci-fi quickie where aliens inject Hicksville teens with alcohol so they'll be arrested for drink driving. Well, it's one way to take over the world, but won't it take rather a long time? Fans of the 1960s TV series *Batman* will recognise Frank Gorshin (the Riddler) as the conman planning to keep a dead alien in his ice box. Wretched, and unintentionally funny. AJ

Steven Terrell *Johnny* • Gloria Castillo *Joan* • Frank Gorshin *Joe* • Raymond Hatton *Larkin* ■ *Dir* Edward L Cahn • *Scr* Robert J Gurney Jr, Al Martin, from a story by Paul Fairman

Invasion Quartet ★ U

Second World War comedy
1961 · UK · BW · 91mins

MGM's British department showed just how far its reputation had plummeted since the glory days of the late 1930s with this woeful wartime farrago. One might have had higher hopes for a script by Jack Trevor Story and John Briley, but what they serve up here is a preposterous tale about a ragtag outfit sent into Nazi-occupied France to knock out a gun aimed at Dover. DP

Bill Travers *Major Freddie Oppenheimer* • Spike Milligan *Lt Godfrey Pringle* • Grégoire Aslan *Major Pierre Debrie* • John Le Mesurier *Colonel* • Thorley Walters *Lt Commander Cummings* • Maurice Denham *Dr Barker* • Thelma Ruby *Matron* • Millicent Martin *Sister Kay Manning* • John Wood *Duty officer, War Office* • Eric Sykes *German band conductor* ■ *Dir* Jay Lewis • *Scr* Jack Trevor Story, John Briley, from a story by Norman Collins

Invasion USA ★

Drama 1952 · US · BW · 73mins

Patrons in a New York bar are hypnotised by a weird stranger (Dan O'Herlihy) into believing America has been attacked by communist nuclear weapons. The reason for this theme? To prove the nation must always be prepared for such an event. A laughable slice of Cold War hysteria, ineptly handled by director Alfred E Green, with cheap special effects and a reliance on newsreel footage, which makes it appear even shoddier. AJ

Gerald Mohr *Vince* • Peggie Castle *Carla* • Dan O'Herlihy *Mr Ohman* • Robert Bice *George Sylvester* • Tom Kennedy *Bartender* ■ *Dir* Alfred E Green • *Scr* Robert Smith, from the story by Robert Smith, Franz Spencer

Invasion USA ★ 18

Action adventure
1985 · US · Colour · 103mins

Cold War paranoia brings out the jingoistic worst in American hardman Chuck Norris, resulting in a prime slice of hammy action. Norris plays a retired CIA man who discovers a band of marauding Russian terrorists have invaded the United States and are killing innocent people and spreading panic all across Florida. Acting completely alone, Norris massacres entire divisions of Ruskies who have no answer to his warrior-like skills. Complete trash. JF DVD

Chuck Norris *Matt Hunter* • Richard Lynch *Rostov* • Melissa Prophet *McGuire* • Alexander Zale *Nikko* • Alex Colon *Tomas* ■ *Dir* Joseph Zito • *Scr* Chuck Norris, James Bruner, from a story by Aaron Norris, James Bruner

Inventing the Abbotts ★★★ 15

Romantic drama
1997 · US · Colour · 102mins

Pat O'Connor's follow-up to *Circle of Friends* isn't quite as enjoyable, but is a pleasant enough distraction. Joaquin Phoenix and Billy Crudup star as two working-class brothers in 1950s Illinois who share a fascination for the neighbouring wealthy Abbott family, and two of the daughters – Jennifer Connelly and Liv Tyler – in particular. While there is a tentative romance between Phoenix and Tyler, it's overshadowed by deception and resentment between the families, which ultimately gives the film a depressing tone. Nice performances, though. JB. Contains swearing. DVD

Joaquin Phoenix *Doug Holt* • Billy Crudup *Jacey Holt* • Liv Tyler *Pamela Abbott* • Will Patton *Lloyd Abbott* • Kathy Baker *Helen Holt* • Jennifer Connelly *Eleanor Abbott* • Michael Sutton *Steve* • Joanna Going *Alice Abbott* ■ *Dir* Pat O'Connor • *Scr* Ken Hixon, from the story by Sue Miller

Invention of Destruction ★★★★

Part-animated fantasy
1958 · Cz · BW · 95mins

Adapted from a Jules Verne novel, this ingenious fantasy (with its pirates, volcanos, submarines, underwater cycles, hidden laboratories and rocket cannon) also borrows liberally from *20,000 Leagues under the Sea* and *The Mysterious Island*. There's also a hint of Méliès in Karel Zeman's audacious blend of animation, puppetry, models, glass shots and live-action, which evokes the glorious 19th-century illustrations of the novel. The story of villainous aristocrat Miroslav Holub's attempt to steal the explosive developed by professor Arnost Navratil and his intrepid assistant, Lubor Tokos, is action-packed. DP. In Czech with English subtitles.

Arnost Navratil *Prof Roche* • Lubor Tokos *Simon Hart* • Miroslav Holub *Argitas* • Frantisek Slegr *Pirate captain* • Vaclav Kyzlink *Serke* • Hugh Downs *Narrator* ■ *Dir* Karel Zeman • *Scr* Karel Zeman, from the novel *Face au Drapeau* by Jules Verne

Investigation of a Citizen above Suspicion ★★★ 18

Crime drama 1970 · It · Colour · 109mins

This Kafkaesque drama, which won the 1970 Oscar for best foreign film, caused a storm of protest when it was released in its native Italy. Exploring the nation's fascist legacy, director Elio Petri pulls no punches in his depiction of a police chief who murders his mistress and then taunts his underlings with a string of clues. While Gian Maria Volonté is chilling as the contemptuous cop, Petri seems as pleased with the scam as his protagonist. He overloads the symbolism and drives home his political points when a craftiness commensurate with Ennio Morricone's score would have sufficed. DP. In Italian with English subtitles.

Gian Maria Volonté *Police Inspector* • Florinda Bolkan *Augusta Terzi* • Salvo Randone *Plumber* • Gianni Santuccio *Police commissioner* • Arturo Dominici *Mangani* ■ *Dir* Elio Petri • *Scr* Elio Petri, Ugo Pirro

Invincible ★★ 12

Historical drama
2001 · Ger/UK/Ire/US · Colour · 132mins

Werner Herzog's lumbering study of the Nazi-sympathising mesmerist Erik Jan Hanussen whose bogus accomplishments bewitched Weimar Germany never comes close to rivalling the complexity and intrigue of *Hanussen*, director István Szabó's 1988 treatment of the same story. Tim Roth delivers his lines in a near-hypnotic monotone, while the painfully uncomfortable performance of Jouko Ahola – as the Polish Jew roped in to play an Aryan strongman in Roth's act – fatally undermines the drama. DP

Tim Roth *Erik Jan Hanussen* • Jouko Ahola *Zishe* • Anna Gourari *Marta Farra* • Max Raabe *Master of ceremonies* • Jacob Wein *Benjamin* • Udo Kier *Count Helldorf* ■ *Dir/Scr* Werner Herzog

The Invisible Agent ★★★ U

Science-fiction spy drama
1942 · US · BW · 81mins

Frank Lloyd (who twice won the Best Director Oscar) directs this tenuously connected response to the 1933 Claude Rains classic. Once again the emphasis is on flag-waving escapism, with Jon Hall inheriting the evaporating talents of grandfather Rains, this time behind enemy lines in an attempt to confound the Axis. John P Fulton's Oscar-nominated special effects steal the show, but there are also some sterling supporting performances. DP

Ilona Massey *Maria Sorenson/Maria Goodrich* • Jon Hall *Frank Raymond/Frank Griffin* • Peter Lorre *Baron Ikito* • Sir Cedric Hardwicke [Cedric Hardwicke] *Conrad Stauffer* • J Edward Bromberg *Karl Heiser* ■ *Dir* Edwin L Marin • *Scr* Curtis Siodmak [Curt Siodmak], inspired by the novel *The Invisible Man* by HG Wells

The Invisible Boy ★★★ U

Science fiction 1957 · US · BW · 90mins

Edmund Cooper's original short story made no mention of a robot. But, following the success of *Forbidden Planet*, producer Nicholas Nayfack persuaded Cyril Hume to rework it as a vehicle for Robby the Robot. The parallel between young Richard Eyer being groomed for greatness by his scientist father Philip Abbott, and Robby's rebellion against a megalomanic supercomputer is neatly drawn. But younger viewers will be more interested in Robby and Eyer's invisible antics than any cornball moralising. DP

Richard Eyer *Timmie Merrinoe* • Philip Abbott *Dr Merrinoe* • Diane Brewster *Mary Merrinoe* • Harold J Stone *General Swayne* • Robert H Harris *Professor Allerton* ■ *Dir* Herman Hoffman • *Scr* Cyril Hume, from a story by Edmund Cooper

The Invisible Circus ★★ 15

Drama 2000 · US · Colour · 92mins

This is a beautiful travelogue saddled with an inconsequential story. Jordana Brewster heads for Europe to discover why her adored sister, Cameron Diaz, committed suicide. Amsterdam, Paris

I

and the Portuguese coastline look stunning, but the flashbacks to Diaz's transition from 1960s hippy to 1970s anarchist are totally unconvincing, as is Brewster's hesitant romance with her sister's old flame, Christopher Eccleston. Director Adam Brooks relies on dodgy fashions and bad wigs for period feel, without making us care about his characters. DP [video] DVD

Cameron Diaz *Faith O'Connor* • Jordana Brewster *Phoebe O'Connor* • Christopher Eccleston *Wolf* • Blythe Danner *Gail O'Connor* • Patrick Bergin *Gene* ■ *Dir* Adam Brooks • *Scr* Adam Brooks, from the novel by Jennifer Egan

Invisible Ghost ★ PG

Psychological mystery horror
1941 · US · BW · 60mins

With his old studio, Universal, pulling out of horror, Bela Lugosi signed with Poverty Row outfit Monogram. The first of several pictures he made for them, this is technically the best (director Joseph H Lewis went on to make several highly regarded *film noir* classics). But the plot, outlandish even by 1941 standards, now exhibits a naivety worthy of Ed Wood. Doctor Lugosi thinks he's under the spell of dead wife Betty Compson, and a series of murders ensues. DM [video] DVD

Bela Lugosi *Dr Charles Kessler* • Polly Ann Young *Virginia* • John McGuire *Ralph/Paul* • Clarence Muse *Evans* ■ *Dir* Joseph H Lewis • *Scr* Helen Martin, Al Martin

The Invisible Kid ★ 15

Science-fiction comedy
1988 · US · Colour · 92mins

Nerd student Jay Underwood stumbles onto an invisibility formula and uses it to wander into the girls' locker rooms and cause havoc. A juvenile fantasy laden with dumb jock gags and inane sexist humour. Karen Black, queen of the B-movie cameo, wastes her talents once more playing Underwood's air-head mother. AJ [video]

Jay Underwood *Grover Dunn* • Karen Black *Mom* • Wally Ward *Milton McClane* • Chynna Phillips *Cindy Moore* ■ *Dir/Scr* Avery Crounse

The Invisible Man ★★★★★ PG

Classic science-fiction horror
1933 · US · BW · 68mins

Claude Rains is one of the most undervalued stars of Hollywood's Golden Age. It's ironic that a familiar face that few could put a name to should have made his name in a film in which he spends most of the action swathed in bandages or invisible. In truth, the success of this superb adaptation of HG Wells's novel is down to John P Fulton and John J Mescall's pioneering special effects and the eerie atmosphere conjured up by horror maestro James Whale. When playful pranks give way to megalomania and murder, the hidden dangers of Rains's miraculous concoction begin to take effect. A classic. DP [video] DVD

Claude Rains *Jack Griffin, the Invisible Man* • Gloria Stuart *Flora Cranley* • William Harrigan *Dr Kemp* • Henry Travers *Dr Cranley* • Una O'Connor *Mrs Hall* ■ *Dir* James Whale • *Scr* RC Sherriff, Philip Wylie (uncredited), from the novel by HG Wells • *Cinematographer* Arthur Edeson • *Art Director* Charles D Hall

The Invisible Man Returns ★★★

Science-fiction thriller
1940 · US · BW · 81mins

The first sequel to the Claude Rains classic, while more modestly scaled than its predecessor, still receives a first-class treatment from director Joe May and, in many instances, surpasses the visual magic of the original. Vincent Price replaces Rains and gets his first starring role as a man condemned to hang for a murder he didn't commit. He persuades the brother of the man who created the invisible serum to give him a dose so he can find the real killer. Price's rich theatrical voice assures his invisible man has a credible presence. AJ

Vincent Price *Geoffrey Radcliffe* • Sir Cedric Hardwicke [Cedric Hardwicke] *Richard Cobb* • Nan Grey *Helen Manson* • John Sutton *Dr Frank Griffin* • Cecil Kellaway *Inspector Sampson* • Alan Napier *Willie Spears* ■ *Dir* Joe May • *Scr* Kurt Siodmak [Curt Siodmak], Lester Cole, from their story • *Cinematographer* Milton Krasner • *Special Effects* John Fulton

The Invisible Man's Revenge ★★ PG

Horror 1944 · US · BW · 74mins

Special effects maestro John P Fulton is (yet again) the saviour of this Universal programmer. Jon Hall (who'd headlined *The Invisible Agent* two years earlier) also returns, this time seeking retribution for his abandonment on a diamond-seeking safari by the aristocratic Lester Matthews and Gale Sondergaard. Scream queen Evelyn Ankers plays their daughter, whom Hall plans to seduce despite her romantic ties to newspaper reporter Alan Curtis. The inimitable John Carradine makes the most of his limited time as a reclusive, eccentric scientist. DP [video]

Jon Hall *Robert Griffin/Martin Field* • Leon Errol *Herbert Higgins* • John Carradine *Dr Peter Drury* • Alan Curtis *Mark Foster* • Evelyn Ankers *Julie Herrick* • Gale Sondergaard *Lady Irene Herrick* ■ *Dir* Ford Beebe • *Scr* Bertram Millhauser, suggested by the novel *The Invisible Man* by HG Wells

The Invisible Menace ★

Murder mystery 1938 · US · BW · 54mins

A dull B-feature murder mystery set in a remote military post, in which Boris Karloff is the prime suspect who, of course, cannot possibly be the guilty one. Eddie Craven repeats his role from the stage production on which this is based. The Broadway play was a flop so the real mystery was why Warner Bros wanted to film it not once but twice – the second time as *Murder on the Waterfront* in 1943. AE

Boris Karloff *Jevries/Dolman* • Marie Wilson *Sally Pratt* • Eddie Craven *Eddie Pratt* • Regis Toomey *Lieutenant Matthews* • Henry Kolker *Colonel Hackett* ■ *Dir* John Farrow • *Scr* Crane Wilbur, from the play *Without Warning* by Ralph Spencer Zink

The Invisible Ray ★★★

Science-fiction horror
1936 · US · BW · 82mins

The film that introduced Boris Karloff to a role he would visit throughout his career – that of a sympathetic scientist whose remarkable discovery makes him a threat to society. Here, he becomes contaminated by a radioactive meteor found in Africa and learns his touch means death. When he suspects Bela Lugosi of trying to take the credit for his discovery, the "Radium X" substance within the meteor causes him to go insane and seek vengeance. Innovative special effects for its era and the ever-dependable "gruesome twosome" supplying the thrills. AJ

Karloff [Boris Karloff] *Dr Janos Rukh* • Bela Lugosi *Dr Felix Benet* • Frances Drake *Diane Rukh Drake* • Frank Lawton *Ronald Drake* • Violet Kemble Cooper [Violet Kemble-Cooper] *Mother Rukh* • Walter Kingsford *Sir Francis Stevens* • Beulah Bondi *Lady Arabella Stevens* ■ *Dir* Lambert Hillyer • *Scr* John Colton, from a story by Howard Higgin, Douglas Hodges • *Special Effects* John P Fulton

Invisible Strangler ★

Horror 1976 · US · Colour · 85mins

Shot in 1976 as *The Astral Factor*, it's not hard to see why this confusing would-be chiller was kept on the shelf until 1984. A boy strangles his mother when she tells him she wishes she had had an abortion. Imprisoned in a mental asylum, he learns an ancient Buddhist technique for becoming invisible and escapes death row to murder all the people responsible for his sentence. A terrible script and amateur-hour direction condemn the viewer to hard labour as well. AJ

Robert Foxworth *Lieutenant Charles Barrett* • Stefanie Powers *Candy Barrett* • Elke Sommer *Chris* • Sue Lyon *Miss De Long* • Leslie Parrish *Coleen Hudson* ■ *Dir* John Florea • *Scr* Arthur C Pierce, from the story by Arthur C Pierce, Earle Lyon

Invisible Stripes ★★

Crime drama 1939 · US · BW · 81mins

A routine and deeply moralistic gangster story, in which George Raft is determined to go straight when he comes out of prison. The great William Holden, in his second significant screen role, plays Raft's volatile younger brother, and their mother is played by, of all people, Flora Robson – who was aged 37 at the time and wears rubber wrinkles. Humphrey Bogart is in it as well, as a trigger-happy killer. Director Lloyd Bacon keeps things moving. AT

George Raft *Cliff Taylor* • Jane Bryan *Peggy* • William Holden (2) *Tim Taylor* • Humphrey Bogart *Chuck Martin* • Flora Robson *Mrs Taylor* • Paul Kelly (1) *Ed Kruger* • Lee Patrick *Molly* ■ *Dir* Lloyd Bacon • *Scr* Warren Duff, from a story by Jonathan Finn, from the novel *Invisible Stripes* by Lewis E Lawes

The Invisible Woman ★★

Science-fiction comedy
1940 · US · BW · 72mins

It's hard to see how John P Fulton's special effects merited an Oscar nomination when the titular Virginia Bruce's shadow is often clearly visible, but that sums up this sloppy lampoon. Much merriment is to be had at Bruce's encounters with her abusive boss Charles Lane and hoodlum Oscar Homolka, while Margaret Hamilton and Charles Ruggles provide amusement as a couple of scandalised domestics. But the primary reason for catching this hackneyed comedy is John Barrymore's performance as the eccentric scientist. DP

John Barrymore *Prof Gibbs* • Virginia Bruce *Kitty Carroll* • John Howard (1) *Richard Russell* • Charlie Ruggles [Charles Ruggles] *George* • Oscar Homolka *Blackie* • Edward Brophy *Bill* • Margaret Hamilton *Mrs Jackson* ■ *Dir* A Edward Sutherland • *Scr* Robert Lees, Gertrude Purcell, Fred Rinaldo [Frederic I Rinaldo], from a story by Kurt Siodmak [Curt Siodmak], Joe May

The Invitation ★★★★

Comedy drama 1973 · Swi · Colour · 99mins

Demonstrating a narrative fluidity and a fondness for his characters, regardless of their foibles, director Claude Goretta evokes the great Jean Renoir with this gentle take on petty bourgeois values. As the penpusher who invites his workmates to a garden party at his newly acquired country house, Michel Robin is a study in gracious timidity. Ultimately, though, all his guests prove to be archetypes as the sun and wine lower their office defences. Flitting from benevolent boss to flighty secretary to boorish joker, Goretta deftly reveals the person behind the persona with the help of a fine ensemble cast. Slight but delectable. DP. In French with English subtitles.

Jean-Luc Bideau *Maurice* • Jean Champion *Alfred* • Pierre Collet *Pierre* • Jacques Rispal *Rene* • Cecile Vassort *Aline* • Rosine Rochette *Helene* ■ *Dir* Claude Goretta • *Scr* Claude Goretta, Michel Viala

Invitation to a Gunfighter ★★★★ U

Western 1964 · US · Colour · 88mins

George Segal is a Confederate soldier who returns from the war to find the Union townspeople have seized his farm and hired a gunfighter to kill him. Written and directed by Richard Wilson, an associate of Orson Welles back in the Mercury theatre and *Citizen Kane* days, it's an allegory about political exile and conformity that spends too much time in debate at the expense of action. Nevertheless, it's lifted by a knockout performance from Yul Brynner as the Creole gunfighter. AT [video]

Yul Brynner *Jules Gaspard D'Estaing* • Janice Rule *Ruth Adams* • Brad Dexter *Kenarsie* • Alfred Ryder *Doc Barker* • Mike Kellin *Tom* • George Segal *Matt Weaver* • Strother Martin *Fiddler* ■ *Dir* Richard Wilson • *Scr* Richard Wilson, Elizabeth Wilson, Alvin Sapinsley, from a story by Hal Goodman, Larry Klein

Invitation to Happiness ★★★

Sports drama 1939 · US · BW · 98mins

A well-bred society girl and an ambitious professional boxer fall in love and marry, but the clash of their different worlds and desires leads to several difficulties. A routine romantic drama, the film is lifted by the attractive star casting of Irene Dunne and Fred MacMurray, the characteristic Paramount gloss of the production and a comedy element injected by Charles Ruggles (brother of director Wesley). Polished performances, some ringside action and a satisfactory resolution complete the package. RK

Irene Dunne *Eleanor Wayne* • Fred MacMurray *Albert "King" Cole* • Charlie Ruggles [Charles Ruggles] *Pop Hardy* • Billy Cook *Albert Cole Jr* • William Collier Sr *Mr Wayne* ■ *Dir* Wesley Ruggles • *Scr* Claude Binyon, from a story by Mark Jerome

Invitation to the Dance ★★★

Dance musical 1956 · US · Colour · 93mins

Gene Kelly's personal and most ambitious undertaking is a pure dance film, which he conceived, choreographed and directed. It comprises three different ballets starring Kelly and an impressive assembly of American and European dancers. Of these, *Ring around the Rosy* (music by André Previn) is the most successful and entertaining segment, concerning a bracelet which passes through many hands before coming back to its original owner. The finale, *Sinbad the Sailor*, danced to Rimsky-Korsakov's *Scheherazade*, in which Kelly dances with animated cartoon characters (and Carol Haney's Scheherazade), is the most innovative and experimental. RK

Gene Kelly *The clown/The marine/Sinbad* • Igor Youskevitch *The lover/The artist* • Claire Sombert *The loved* • David Paltenghi *The husband* • Daphne Dale *The wife* • Carol Haney *Scheherazade* • Tamara Toumanova *Streetwalker* • Tommy Rall *Boyfriend* ■ *Dir/Scr* Gene Kelly • *Choreographer* Gene Kelly

Invitation to the Wedding ★ PG

Romantic comedy
1983 · UK · Colour · 88mins

A senile bishop (Ralph Richardson, indulging his real-life passion for motorbikes) mistakenly weds the daughter of an impoverished earl to a visiting American. The dull confusion is compounded by the arrival of a Texan evangelist played, astoundingly, by John Gielgud, whose self-confessed inability with accents is well demonstrated. Inept and unfunny. DM

Ralph Richardson *Bishop Willy* • John Gielgud *Clyde Ormiston* • Paul Nicholas *David Anderson* • Susan Brooks *Lady Anne* ■ *Dir/ Scr* Joseph Brooks

Invocation of My Demon Brother ★★★ 15

Experimental horror
1969 · US · Colour · 11mins

Underground film-maker Kenneth Anger described his 11-minute short as "the shadowing forth of Our Lord Lucifer as the Powers of Darkness gather at a midnight mass". A homage to Satanist guru Aleister Crowley, it uses dynamic montage to Mick Jagger's Moog synthesiser soundtrack, rejecting narrative. Anger himself plays the Magus, while Bobby Beausoleil is Lucifer, who appears at the climax. In between are shots of a Satanic ritual, a Rolling Stones concert and GIs leaping from helicopters in Vietnam. Only for those who are in tune with Anger's homoerotic sensibility and striking visual style. RB [video]

Speed Hacker *Wand-bearer* • Lenore Kandel *Deaconess* • William Beutel *Deacon* • Kenneth Anger *Magus* • Anton Szandor La Vey *His Satanic Majesty* • Bobby Beausoleil *Lucifer* ■ *Dir/Scr* Kenneth Anger

The Ipcress File ★★★★ PG

Spy thriller 1965 · UK · Colour · 102mins

Len Deighton's first spy novel had everything except a name for its off-the-peg hero. Producer Harry Saltzman decided on Harry Palmer and cast the virtually unknown Michael Caine. Designed as a counterpart to the Bond movies, which Saltzman also co-produced, the story uncovers KGB operatives in the British secret service. It's cunning, calculated and still works, thanks to some droll humour, John Barry's marvellously twangy score, Sidney J Furie's energetic direction and spot-on performances. Caine reprised the role in four further films, beginning with 1966's *Funeral in Berlin*. AT. Contains swearing. [video] DVD

Michael Caine *Harry Palmer* • Nigel Green *Dalby* • Guy Doleman *Colonel Ross* • Sue Lloyd *Jean Courtney* • Gordon Jackson *Jock Carswell* • Aubrey Richards *Radcliffe* • Frank Gatliff *Bluejay/Grantby* ■ *Dir* Sidney J Furie • *Scr* Bill Canaway, James Doran, from the novel by Len Deighton • *Cinematographer* Otto Heller • *Music* John Barry (1) • *Editor* Peter Hunt • *Art Director* Ken Adam

Iphigenia ★★★

Drama 1976 · Gr · Colour · 128mins

Having already made *Elektra* and *The Trojan Women*, Michael Cacoyannis completed his Euripidean trilogy with this Oscar-nominated adaptation of *Iphigenia in Aulis*. In spite of the fragmentary nature of the source, the story of the ill-fated Athenian expedition to rescue Helen of Troy still makes for compelling viewing. However, Cacoyannis's overindulgence in directorial flourishes undermines the efforts of a sterling cast. DP. In Greek with English subtitles.

Irene Papas *Clytemnestra* • Costa Kazakos *Agamemnon* • Costa Carras *Menelaus* • Tatiana Papamoskou *Iphigenia* • Christos Tsangas *Ulysses* • Panos Michalopoulos *Achilles* • Angelos Yannoulis *Servant* ■ *Dir* Michael Cacoyannis • *Scr* Michael Cacoyannis, from the play *Iphigenia in Aulis* by Euripides • *Editor* Michael Cacoyannis

Irene ★★ U

Musical comedy
1940 · US · BW and Colour · 81mins

RKO threw money at this slight confection that was bought as a vehicle for the Fred Astaire and Ginger Rogers before they parted company in 1939. The studio was rewarded with its third biggest hit of the year, but there was nothing remarkable about this Cinderella story. Indeed, the songs are a pretty sorry batch. Director Herbert Wilcox coaxes a reasonably frothy performance from his wife, Anna Neagle, but Ray Milland looks distinctly uncomfortable. DP [video]

Anna Neagle *Irene O'Dare* • Ray Milland *Don Marshall* • Billie Burke *Mrs Vincent* • Alan Marshal *Bob Vincent* • Arthur Treacher *Betherton* • Roland Young *Mr Smith* ■ *Dir* Herbert Wilcox • *Scr* Alice Duer Miller, from the musical comedy by James H Montgomery

Iris ★★★★ 15

Biographical drama
2001 · UK/US · Colour · 86mins

Richard Eyre's film succeeds on the strength of its performances alone in this biography of one of the 20th century's most talented female writers. Judi Dench *is* Iris Murdoch. Without her and the incredible support from Jim Broadbent as Murdoch's devoted husband John Bayley and Penelope Wilton as society hostess Janet Stone, this simply wouldn't have the required emotional impact. As it is, you're moved to many, many tears. Murdoch's sharp academic mind is established from the beginning but the story becomes really compelling once the parallel flashback encounters between the young Iris and John (Kate Winslet and Hugh Bonneville) run concurrently with the older writer's gradual deterioration from Alzheimer's disease. LH [video] DVD

Judi Dench *Iris Murdoch* • Jim Broadbent *John Bayley* • Kate Winslet *Young Iris* • Hugh Bonneville *Young John* • Penelope Wilton *Janet Stone* • Juliet Aubrey *Young Janet Stone* • Samuel West *Young Maurice* • Timothy West *Old Maurice* • Eleanor Bron *College principal* ■ *Dir* Richard Eyre • *Scr* Richard Eyre, Charles Wood, from the books *Iris: a Memoir* and *Elegy for Iris* by John Bayley

Irish Eyes Are Smiling ★★ U

Biographical musical comedy
1944 · US · Colour · 89mins

This musical comedy is based very loosely on the life of turn-of-the-century songwriter Ernest R Ball, who's played rather one-dimensionally by Dick Haymes. After its opening scenes in Cleveland, the story moves to New York as Ball searches for fame and fortune and falls in love with a burlesque entertainer (June Haver). Standard fare. SH

Monty Woolley *Edgar Brawley* • June Haver *Mary "Irish" O'Neill* • Dick Haymes *Ernest R Ball* • Anthony Quinn *Al Jackson* ■ *Dir* Gregory Ratoff • *Scr* Earl Baldwin, John Tucker Battle, from a story by EA Ellington

The Irish in Us ★★

Comedy 1935 · US · BW · 80mins

Response to this comedy depends on a tolerance towards sentimental family dramas with doses of Irish blarney. Still, there's no denying the quality of the cast, especially the enchanting Olivia de Havilland, then a newcomer to the studio treadmill. The story centres around the three O'Hara brothers (James Cagney, Pat O'Brien, Frank McHugh), who live in New York looked after by mother Mary Gordon. There's romantic rivalry between two of the brothers, family feuding and an unlikely boxing match finale. BB

James Cagney *Danny O'Hara* • Pat O'Brien *Pat O'Hara* • Olivia de Havilland *Lucille Jackson* • Frank McHugh *Mike O'Hara* • Allen Jenkins *Carbarn Hammerschlog* • Mary Gordon *Ma O'Hara* ■ *Dir* Lloyd Bacon • *Scr* Earl Baldwin, from a story idea by Frank Orsatti

The Irishman ★★★★

Drama 1978 · Aus · Colour · 108mins

British actor Michael Craig, so long under contract to Rank, had to emigrate to Australia to get a role as big and beefy as this. He's a teamster so resistant to change that he prefers his team of horses to anything mechanical. Stubborn and doomed he may be, but we're willing him to succeed through battles against progress and the sad skirmishes of a family at war with itself. Donald Crombie directs with a sharp eye for period detail (the 1920s) and Michael Craig does him proud. TH

Michael Craig *Paddy Doolan* • Robyn Nevin *Jenny Doolan* • Simon Burke *Michael Doolan* • Lou Brown *Will Doolan* • Bryan Brown *Eric Haywood* ■ *Dir* Donald Crombie • *Scr* Donald Crombie, from a novel by Elizabeth O'Conner

Irma la Douce ★★★★ 15

Comedy 1963 · US · Colour · 137mins

Billy Wilder took a hit Broadway musical, cut out all the songs and still came up trumps with this near-classic comedy. Jack Lemmon plays a priggish *gendarme* who dons a variety of improbable but hilarious disguises to save the soul (if not the virtue) of Shirley MacLaine's Parisian hooker. Set in and around the Les Halles food market, brilliantly re-created on a Hollywood sound stage by art director Alexander Trauner, it's a puzzle of a picture about morality and redemption, energetically performed by its two leads. Blink and you'll miss James Caan making his screen debut as one of MacLaine's clients. AT [video] DVD

Jack Lemmon *Nestor* • Shirley MacLaine *Irma La Douce* • Lou Jacobi *Moustache* • Bruce Yarnell *Hippolyte* • Herschel Bernardi *Inspector LeFevre* • Hope Holliday *Lolita* • Bill Bixby *Tattooed sailor* ■ *Dir* Billy Wilder • *Scr* Billy Wilder, IAL Diamond, from the play by Alexander Breffort, from the musical by Marguerite Monnot • *Music* André Previn • *Cinematographer* Joseph LaShelle

Irma Vep ★★★★ 15

Satirical comedy 1996 · Fr · Colour · 94mins

Part homage, part satire, this is a gleefully scattershot and largely improvised view of French cinema. Lured to Paris to headline in a remake of silent classic *Les Vampires*, Hong Kong film star Maggie Cheung finds herself at the mercy of a director on the verge of a nervous breakdown, a volatile crew member with amorous intentions and a mêlée of critics without an original thought to rub together. Sportingly sending up her own superstar status, Cheung is nevertheless overshadowed by Jean-Pierre Léaud, who slyly lampoons the type of tortured auteur with whom he made his name. DP. In English and French with subtitles. [video]

Maggie Cheung • Jean-Pierre Léaud *René Vidal* • Nathalie Richard *Zoé* • Bulle Ogier *Mireille* • Lou Castel *José Murano* ■ *Dir* Olivier Assayas • *Scr* Olivier Assayas

Iron and Silk ★★★

Biographical drama
1990 · US · Colour · 94mins

American college graduate Mark Salzman travelled to China in 1982 to teach English and learn the martial arts from the celebrated kung fu master Pan Qingfu. Both men play themselves in this pleasing adaptation of Salzman's bestselling book, which not only recounts his travels, but also his romantic encounter with a local girl (beautifully played by Vivian Wu). Blending gentle comedy with serious cultural observations, the film is directed with considerable care by Shirley Sun, and special mention should also be made of cinematographer James Hayman for his stunning images of Hangzhou. DP. In English and Mandarin with subtitles.

Mark Salzman *Teacher Mark* • Pan Qingfu *Teacher Pan* • Jeanette Lin Tsui *Teacher Hei* • Vivian Wu *Ming* • Sun Xudong *Sinbad* • Zheng Guo *Mr Song* • To Funglin *Old Sheep* ■ *Dir* Shirley Sun • *Scr* Shirley Sun, Mark Salzman, from the book by Mark Salzman

The Iron Curtain ★★

Spy drama 1948 · US · BW · 86mins

This early Cold War drama is a pseudo-documentary, its grave tone alerting us to imminent communist takeover if not for the efforts of Dana Andrews and Gene Tierney. It seems the Soviets are up to no good in Canada, where spies and atomic secrets lie thick on the ground. Andrews is a Soviet dissident who wants to defect with his wife Tierney. The story is based on fact, hence the low-key and, unfortunately, rather dull approach. AT

Dana Andrews *Igor Gouzenko* • Gene Tierney *Anna Gouzenko* • June Havoc *Karanova* • Berry Kroeger *Grubb* • Edna Best *Mrs Foster* • Stefan Schnabel *Ranev* • Nicholas Joy *Dr Norman* ■ *Dir* William A Wellman • *Scr* Milton Krims, from the memoirs of Igor Gouzenko

Iron Eagle ★★ 15

Action adventure
1985 · US · Colour · 111mins

One of the better *Top Gun* cash-ins, although it hardly deserved the long-running video franchise it grew into. Jason Gedrick plays the teenage flier who goes on a secret mission to rescue his father, a hostage in an unnamed Arab country ruled by nasty David Suchet. Louis Gossett Jr is the sympathetic serviceman who breaks the rules to help him by teaching him to fly and stealing a couple of F-16s. Utter tosh, of course, but the flying sequences are quite good. JF. Contains violence, swearing. [video] DVD

Louis Gossett Jr *"Chappy" Sinclair* • Jason Gedrick *Doug Masterson* • David Suchet *Minister of Defence* • Tim Thomerson *Ted Masterson* ■ *Dir* Sidney J Furie • *Scr* Sidney J Furie, Kevin Elders

Iron Eagle II ★★ PG

Action adventure
1988 · Can · Colour · 95mins

Despite being a sequel, this made a surprising impact at the box office. Produced in 1988, it gave a glimpse of political changes to come, with the Russians and Americans joining forces to combat a new threat from the Middle East. Plenty of airborne gung-ho action, but the performers fail to convince and the attempts at humour fall flat. A second sequel, *Aces: Iron Eagle III* followed in 1992. JF. Contains violence, swearing. [video]

Louis Gossett Jr *Brig Gen Charles "Chappy" Sinclair* • Mark Humphrey *Captain Matt Cooper* • Stuart Margolin *General Stillmore* • Alan Scarfe *Colonel Vladimir Vardovsky* ■ *Dir* Sidney J Furie • *Scr* Sidney J Furie, Kevin Elders

Iron Eagle IV ★★ 12

Action adventure
1995 · Can · Colour · 91mins

The *Iron Eagle* franchise struggled to number four on the back of Louis Gossett Jr's enduring popularity in the role of air-force general Chappy Sinclair (retired). He is now running an air school for young offenders and they discover the local air base is being used by criminals involved with toxic chemicals. The authorities don't believe them, so they take matters into their own hands. Only Gossett Jr is worth watching. JF [video] DVD

Louis Gossett Jr *Chappy Sinclair* • Al Waxman *General Kettle* • Jason Cadieux *Doug Masters* • Joanne Vannicola *Wheeler* ■ *Dir* Sidney J Furie • *Scr* Michael Stokes, from characters created by Kevin Elders, Sidney J Furie

The Iron Giant ★★★★ U

Animated science-fiction adventure
1999 · US · Colour · 82mins

This version of Ted Hughes's children's fable liberally borrows images from 1950s comic-book art and conventions from the era's science-fiction movies to stunning effect. To a soundtrack of *American Graffiti*-style hits, this heavy-metal *ET* tells the tale of nine-year-old Hogarth, the giant alien robot he saves from electrical overload, and the fiercely protective relationship that develops between them. But the real thrills begin when a Communist-hating FBI agent arrives who is convinced that the walking Meccano set poses a Cold War threat. With political allegory for the adults and excitement galore for the kids, this poignant fairy tale should appeal to both. AJ DVD

Jennifer Aniston *Annie Hughes* • Harry Connick Jr *Dean McCoppin* • Vin Diesel *The Iron Giant* • James Gammon *Marv Loach/Floyd Turbeaux* • Cloris Leachman *Mrs Tensedge* • Christopher McDonald *Kent Mansley* • John Mahoney *General Rogard* • Eli Marienthal *Hogarth Hughes* • M Emmet Walsh *Earl Stutz* ■ *Dir* Brad Bird • *Scr* Tim McCanlies, Andy Brent Forrester [Brent Forrester], from a story by Brad Bird, from the novel by Ted Hughes

The Iron Glove ★★ U

Period adventure 1954 · US · Colour · 76mins

Unless you're a Robert Stack fan, there's little to recommend this period tomfoolery about a young pretender to the throne of King George I. To be fair, Bob swashes a mean buckle; he also gets to romance the lovely Ursula Theiss, who later became Robert Taylor's second wife. The Technicolor's nice, the running time is mercifully short and Alan Hale Jr is on hand to remind audiences of his father, who he so uncannily resembled. TS

Robert Stack *Charles Wogan* • Ursula Thiess *Ann Brett* • Richard Stapley *James Stuart* • Charles Irwin *James O'Toole* • Alan Hale Jr *Patrick Gaydon* • Leslie Bradley *Duke of Somerfield* ■ *Dir* William Castle • *Scr* Jesse L Lasky Jr [Jesse Lasky Jr], DeVallon Scott, Douglas Heyes, from a story by Robert E Kent, from a story by Samuel J Jacoby

The Iron Horse ★★★★★ PG

Silent epic western 1924 · US · BW · 134mins

Already a veteran of more than 40 films by the tender age of 29, John Ford established himself as a major talent with this colossal tale of railroads, romance and revenge. The pioneering work on the first transcontinental railroad brings with it greed, villainy and murder as Davy Brandon's surveyor father is murdered, supposedly by Indians. The adult Davy (George O'Brien) later returns to discover the real culprit. Although brimming over with incident, it's the re-creation of the pioneering West that earns the film its place in cinema history. Twentieth Century-Fox spared no expense to give a ring of authenticity to the gaudy saloons, the dusty cattle drives and the murderous raids, but it's Ford's affinity for the period and its people that brings the scene to life. DP DVD

George O'Brien *Davy Brandon* • Madge Bellamy *Miriam Marsh* • Cyril Chadwick *Peter Jesson* • Fred Kohler *Bauman* • Gladys Hulette *Ruby* • James A Marcus *Judge Haller* ■ *Dir* John Ford • *Scr* Charles Kenyon, from a story by John Russell, Charles Kenyon

Iron Jawed Angels ★★★ 12

Period drama based on a true story
2004 · US · Colour · 118mins

Hilary Swank joins Frances O'Connor, Julia Ormond and Anjelica Huston in this interesting made-for-TV tale about women's suffrage in early 20th-century America. Swank, O'Connor and Ormond play frontline radicals in the fight for the establishment of the female vote, while Huston portrays the disapproving voice of the movement's "old guard". The inclusion of a cheesy romantic subplot is unnecessary, but the script, if a little on the wordy side, is smart and sassy, and the performances are uniformly excellent. DA

Hilary Swank *Alice Paul* • Frances O'Connor *Lucy Burns* • Julia Ormond *Inez Mulholland-Boissevain* • Anjelica Huston *Carrie Chapman Catt* • Molly Parker *Emily Leighton* • Patrick Dempsey *Ben Weissman* ■ *Dir* Katja von Garnier • *Scr* Sally Robinson, Eugenia Bostwick Singer [Eugenia Bostwick-Singer], Raymond Singer, Jennifer Friedes, from a story by Jennifer Friedes

The Iron Ladies ★★★ 15

Comedy based on a true story
2000 · Thai · Colour · 104mins

A huge hit in its native Thailand, this comedy hails from the *Cool Runnings* stable of strange-but-true sports stories. Had it simply been the tale of a cash-struck volleyball team which defies the odds to take the national championships by storm, it might have been entertaining. But the fact that the players are an assortment of gays, drag queens and ladyboys gives it a human diversity that ensures the triumphs over adversity aren't confined to the court. Blending sentiment, slapstick and lashings of high camp, director Yongyooth Thongkonthoon could never be accused of subtlety, but his film has honesty and zest. DP. In Thai with English subtitles.

Jesdaporn Pholdee *Chai* • Sashaparp Virakamin *Mon* • Aekkachai Buranaphanit *Wit* • Gokgorn Benjathikul *Pia* ■ *Dir* Yongyooth Thongkonthun • *Scr* Visuttichai Boonyakarnjana, Jira Maligool, Yongyooth Thongkonthun

The Iron Maiden ★★ U

Comedy 1962 · UK · Colour · 93mins

This largely misfiring British comedy attempts to marry *The Maggie* and *The Titfield Thunderbolt*, but fails to match either. Yet again we have grown men going weak at the knees over a piece of clapped-out machinery, but here it's a traction engine instead of a boat or a train and it strains for the same level of romance. Off to a slow start, the picture falls away towards the middle and finishes with a traction race that's hard not to like, even if it does steal every "aren't enthusiasts funny" joke that escaped being nailed down in *Genevieve*. DP

Michael Craig *Jack Hopkins* • Anne Helm *Kathy Fisher* • Jeff Donnell *Mrs Fisher* • Alan Hale Jr *Paul Fisher* • Noel Purcell *Admiral Sir Digby Trevelyan* ■ *Dir* Gerald Thomas • *Scr* Vivian A Cox, Leslie Bricusse, from a story by Harold Brooks, Kay Bannerman

The Iron Major ★★ U

Biographical drama 1943 · US · BW · 85mins

Pat O'Brien had played the famous football coach Knute Rockne in a highly successful 1940 biopic at Warner Bros. Three years later RKO Radio's executives had the brainwave of pitching him into this wartime propaganda piece about another real-life football coach, Frank Cavanaugh, who became a First World War hero. Nicknamed the Iron Major after he survived severe injuries received at the front, he returned to football until becoming blind. But O'Brien is too bland for leading roles. AE

Pat O'Brien *Frank Cavanaugh* • Ruth Warrick *Florence Ayres* • Robert Ryan *Father Donovan* • Leon Ames *Robert Stewart* • Russell Wade *Manning* • Bruce Edwards *Lt Jones* ■ *Dir* Ray Enright • *Scr* Aben Kandel, Warren Duff, from a book by Florence Cavanaugh

The Iron Man ★★

Sports drama 1931 · US · BW · 81mins

Tod Browning directs this conventional boxing drama about a lightweight on his way to the title. Playing the boxer is Lew Ayres, who must somehow cope with the demands of his manager as well as the duplicity of his wife, played by Jean Harlow. Critics weren't entirely enthusiastic about Harlow's performance, but her move to MGM a year later saw her brief but spectacular career really take off. AT

Lew Ayres *Young Mason* • Robert Armstrong *George Regan* • Jean Harlow *Rose Mason* • John Miljan *Paul H Lewis* • Eddie Dillon [Edward Dillon] *Jeff* • Mike Donlin *McNeil* ■ *Dir* Tod Browning • *Scr* Francis Edward Faragoh, from a novel by WR Burnett

Iron Man ★★

Sports drama 1951 · US · BW · 81mins

The action is clumsily choreographed in this boxing B-movie. Lumbering about the ring as though he's got a sack of coal on his back, ex-miner Jeff Chandler couldn't look any less like a potentially murderous pug. Which rather undermines the premise that he's being exploited by ruthless brother Stephen McNally, while hoping to raise the dough to open a radio shop with girlfriend Evelyn Keyes. Rockier than *Rocky V*. DP

Jeff Chandler *Coke Mason* • Evelyn Keyes *Rose Warren* • Stephen McNally *George Mason* • Rock Hudson *Tommy "Speed" O'Keefe* • Jim Backus *Max Watkins* • James Arness *Alex* ■ *Dir* Joseph Pevney • *Scr* Borden Chase, George Zuckerman, from the novel by WR Burnett

The Iron Mask ★★

Swashbuckling adventure
1929 · US · BW · 95mins

This fair swashbuckler has Douglas Fairbanks repeating his 1921 role as the noble swordsmith D'Artagnan in *The Three Musketeers*, and is done very much in the style of a silent picture. In fact, *The Iron Mask* was heavily touted as Fairbanks's first talkie, though the actor, who never really enjoyed an intimate relationship with a microphone, only spoke a brief prologue and an epilogue to appease the studio. Film historians have argued that Fairbanks himself had never used his own voice, citing as evidence the fact that his son, Douglas Fairbanks Jr, had revoiced the film for a 1940 re-issue. AT

Douglas Fairbanks *D'Artagnan* • Belle Bennett *The Queen Mother* • Marguerite de la Motte *Constance* • Dorothy Revier *Milady De Winter* • Vera Lewis *Mme Peronee* • Rolfe Sedan *Louis XIII* ■ *Dir* Allan Dwan • *Scr* Elton Thomas, from the novels *The Three Musketeers* and *The Viscount of Bragelonne* by Alexandre Dumas

Iron Maze ★★★ 15

Mystery thriller
1991 · US/Jpn · Colour · 97mins

Jeff Fahey gives one of his best performances in this moody, downbeat thriller, playing a blue-collar worker implicated in the attempted murder of a Japanese businessman bent on closing down a steelworks. The excellent JT Walsh is the sceptical cop investigating the crime, while Bridget Fonda is the interloper's American bride who may have been having an affair with Fahey. It's a little self-important for its own good, but director Hiroaki Yoshida accurately captures the bleakness of a small town dying. JF. Contains violence, swearing, sex scenes and nudity. DVD

Jeff Fahey *Barry* • Bridget Fonda *Chris* • Hiroaki Murakami *Junichi Sugita* • JT Walsh *Jack Ruhle* • Gabriel Damon *Mikey* • John Randolph *Mayor Peluso* • Peter Allas *Eddie* ■ *Dir* Hiroaki Yoshida • *Scr* Tim Metcalfe, from the short story *In The Grove* by Ryunosuke Akutagawa, from a story by Hiroaki Yoshida

The Iron Mistress ★★

Biographical adventure
1952 · US · Colour · 108mins

Steely-eyed Alan Ladd stars as Jim Bowie, famed inventor of the knife (the "iron mistress" that bears his name), in this would-be rip-roaring Warner Bros adventure. Trouble is, the screenplay isn't as sharp as the knife itself, and there's a fair bit of romantic padding holding up the action, as Ladd gets rejected by Virginia Mayo only to fall for Phyllis Kirk en route to his destiny at the Alamo. There's a distinct run-of-the-mill feeling to the tale. TS. Biopic of Jim Bowie starring Alan Ladd.

Alan Ladd *Jim Bowie* • Virginia Mayo *Judalon de Bornay* • Joseph Calleia *Juan Moreno* • Phyllis Kirk *Ursula de Veramendi* ■ *Dir* Gordon Douglas • *Scr* James R Webb, from a story by Paul I Wellman

Iron Monkey ★★★ 12

Period martial arts adventure
1993 · HK · Colour · 86mins

This assured blend of teenpic and Cantonese myth is proof positive that wire work was common in Hong Kong cinema long before dragons took to hiding. Determined to capture Yu Rong Guang, a 19th-century doctor who doubles as a masked champion of the oppressed, Qing Dynasty nasties kidnap martial arts master Donnie Yen's son to ensure his complicity. But the plan backfires. It's fun, but Yuen Woo-Ping is so preoccupied with his exhilarating stunt sequences that he does a disservice to the screenplay's sly political parallels to the present day. A sequel followed in 1996. DP. Cantonese dialogue dubbed into English. DVD

Yu Rong Guang *Dr Yang/Iron Monkey* • Donnie Yen *Wong Kei Ying* • Tsang Sze-man *Young Wong Fei-hung* • Jean Wang *Miss Orchid* ■ *Dir* Yuen Woo-Ping • *Scr* Cheung Tan, Lau Tai-muk, Tang Pik-yin, Tsui Hark

The Iron Petticoat ★★★★ U

Romantic comedy
1956 · UK · Colour · 90mins

...it's what's under the Iron Curtain! There's a fabulous chemistry between Katharine Hepburn as a Russian aviatrix and Bob Hope as an American serviceman that's a sheer joy to observe in this latter-day version of *Ninotchka*, filmed in England from a clever screenplay by Hollywood veteran Ben Hecht. A wonderful supporting cast excels under the direction of under-rated British great Ralph Thomas, and, with the Cold War long over, the attitudes expressed here now seem hilarious. TS DVD

Bob Hope *Chuck Lockwood* • Katharine Hepburn *Vinka Kovelenko* • James Robertson Justice [James Robertson-Justice] *Colonel Sklarnoff* • Robert Helpmann *Ivan Kropotkin* • David Kossoff *Dr Dubratz* • Sidney James *Paul* ■ *Dir* Ralph Thomas • *Scr* Ben Hecht, from a story by Harry Saltzman

The Iron Sheriff ★★★ U

Western 1957 · US · BW · 73mins

Another in a number of minor but competent westerns that were raised by the presence of Sterling Hayden's rugged looks. As a sheriff, Hayden sets out to prove that his son (Darryl Hickman) is innocent of robbery and murder, even though he has substantial evidence against him. What the film lacks in suspense, it makes up for in the playing and the intriguing moral dimension. RB

Sterling Hayden *Sheriff Galt* • Constance Ford *Claire* • John Dehner *Pollock* • Kent Taylor *Quincy* • Darryl Hickman *Benjie* ■ *Dir* Sidney Salkow • *Scr* Seeleg Lester

The Iron Triangle ★★★ 18

War action adventure
1988 · US · Colour · 86mins

One of a handful of American films which attempt to present all sides of the Vietnam war as fully developed characters. Political arguments are also largely ignored since this is a war between people who kill each other, take each other prisoner and sometimes find it hard to continue the killing. Narrator Beau Bridges plays an American captain who loathes the cruelty of his allies, the South Vietnamese, and is then taken prisoner; the Oscar-winner from *The Killing Fields*, Haing S Ngor, plays a North Vietnamese officer. AT [video]

Beau Bridges *Captain Keene* • Haing S Ngor *Captain Tuong* • Johnny Hallyday *Jacques* • James Ishida *Khoi* ■ *Dir* Eric Weston • *Scr* Eric Weston, John Bushelman, Larry Hilbrand

Iron Will ★★★ U

Period adventure
1994 · US · Colour · 104mins

Disney drew on a true story for this cracking piece of family entertainment. Set in 1917, it stars MacKenzie Astin as the South Dakota teenager who enters the world's toughest dog-sled marathon both to prevent the loss of the family farm following the death of his dad and to pay for his education. Naturally, all manner of dangers and disasters face him on the 522-mile trek from Canada to Minnesota. With action aplenty and a neat supporting turn from Kevin Spacey as a mythologising journalist, this should keep all amused. DP [video] DVD

MacKenzie Astin *Will Stoneman* • Kevin Spacey *Harry Kingsley* • David Ogden Stiers *JP Harper* • August Schellenberg *Ned Dodd* • Brian Cox *Angus McTeague* ■ *Dir* Charles Haid • *Scr* John Michael Hayes, Djordje Milicevic, Jeff Arch

Ironweed ★★★ 15

Drama 1987 · US · Colour · 136mins

Like a famished carnivore, Jack Nicholson sinks his teeth into this meaty role as a Depression-era alcoholic drifter. He is haunted by memories of the events that led to his current state of degradation – most tragically the accidental death of his baby son. Bag-lady Meryl Streep sees hope in his survival, but Hector Babenco's film is a grim odyssey with only the strong performances of Oscar-nominees Nicholson and Streep to sustain it. TH [video]

Jack Nicholson *Francis Phelan* • Meryl Streep *Helen Archer* • Carroll Baker *Annie Phelan* • Michael O'Keefe *Billy Phelan* • Diane Venora *Peg Phelan* • Fred Gwynne *Oscar Reo* • Tom Waits *Rudy* ■ *Dir* Hector Babenco • *Scr* Wiliam Kennedy, from his novel

Irreconcilable Differences ★★★★ 15

Comedy drama 1984 · US · Colour · 108mins

A highly engaging comedy about the way success changes everything, written by the *Baby Boom* team of Charles Shyer (also making his directorial debut) and Nancy Meyers. Ryan O'Neal and Shelley Long star as the bright young couple who lose sight of what's important as they prosper in Tinseltown – so much so, their nine-year-old daughter sues them for divorce. Way ahead of its time and full of sharp Hollywood satire, the entire bittersweet story is told in flashback as witness-stand testimony. AJ. Contains swearing and nudity. [video]

Ryan O'Neal *Albert Brodsky* • Shelley Long *Lucy Van Patten Brodsky* • Drew Barrymore *Casey Brodsky* • Sam Wanamaker *David Kessler* • Allen Garfield *Phil Hanner* • Sharon Stone *Blake Chandler* ■ *Dir* Charles Shyer • *Scr* Nancy Meyers, Charles Shyer

Irreversible ★★★★ 18

Drama 2002 · Fr · Colour · 93mins

Gaspar Noé's incendiary follow-up to *Seul contre Tous* is hard to watch and hard to forget. An intense and unflinching nightmare of rape and revenge, it is a haunting meditation on the fragility of life. Vincent Cassel and Monica Bellucci bare their souls magnificently as a middle-class couple who are plunged into a personal hell after Bellucci is raped and left for dead. Using inventive cinematography that tints every scene with acid-trip dementia, the film unfolds in reverse to embrace and deconstruct the whole spectrum of human emotion. It's distressing viewing that requires a strong stomach, yet, for all the feature's controversy, it never titillates. SF. In French with English subtitles. [video] DVD

Monica Bellucci *Alex* • Vincent Cassel *Marcus* • Albert Dupontel *Pierre* • Philippe Nahon *Philippe* • Jo Prestia *Le Ténia* ■ *Dir/Scr* Gaspar Noé

Is Anna Anderson Anastasia? ★★

Historical drama based on a true story
1956 · W Ger · Colour · 90mins

Swamped by the nostalgic tide that accompanied Ingrid Bergman's triumphant return to Hollywood in *Anastasia*, this German version shares its sympathy with the confused, but credible waif who became the hope of White Russian exiles clinging to any comfort after their defeat. Director Falk Harnack has no doubt she was a princess, not a Pole named Franziska Schanzkowksa, but he leaves Lilli Palmer's achingly vulnerable performance in a dramatic vacuum. DP. In German with English subtitles.

Lilli Palmer *Anna Anderson/Anastasia* • Ivan Desny *Gleb Botkin* • Suzanne von Almassy *Mrs Stevens* • Erika Dannhoff *Frau von Pleskau* • Berta Drews *Fraulein Peuthart* • Ellen Schwiers *Princess Katherine* ■ *Dir* Falk Harnack • *Scr* Herbert Reinecker

Is Paris Burning? ★★★

Second World War drama
1966 · US/Fr · BW · 165mins

"Is Paris burning?" asks Adolf Hitler as the French Resistance rattles the Nazi occupiers and prepares the city for liberation. Conceived on the same lines as *The Longest Day*, this black-and-white multilingual war epic boasts an all-star cast and contains some spectacular scenes of fighting along the boulevards of the eponymous capital. Maurice Jarre's jangly music maintains the momentum, while Gore Vidal and Francis Ford Coppola were just two of the writers who laboured on the episodic script. AT. A French/German/English language film.

Jean-Paul Belmondo *Morandat* • Yves Montand *Bizien* • Orson Welles *Nordling* • Charles Boyer *Monod* • Leslie Caron *Françoise Labe* • Jean-Pierre Cassel *Henri Karcher* • Alain Delon *Jacques Chaban-Delmas* • Kirk Douglas *Patton* • Glenn Ford *Bradley* • Robert Stack *Sibert* • Anthony Perkins *Warren* • Simone Signoret *Café proprietress* ■ *Dir* René Clément • *Scr* Francis Ford Coppola, Gore Vidal, Jean Aurenche, Pierre Bost, Claude Brule, Marcel Moussy, Beate von Molo, from the book by Larry Collins, Dominique LaPierre

Is There Sex after Death? ★★★

Comedy 1971 · US · Colour · 97mins

This is a series of skits, jokes and sketches, taking sex as their theme. Bawdier than Woody Allen's *Everything You Always Wanted Know about Sex*, this definitely deserved its R (Restricted) rating and would have been unmemorable if it wasn't for the wonderful performance by Buck Henry as Dr Manos, one of our guides to the weird and wonderful world of sex. This is an oddity worth seeking out for fans of vulgar and non-PC humour. DF

Buck Henry *Dr Manos* • Alan Abel *Dr Rogers* • Marshall Efron *Vince Domino* • Holly Woodlawn • Robert Downey Sr *Robert Downey* • Jim Moran *Dr Elevenike* • Rubin Carson ■ *Dir/Scr* Jeanne Abel, Alan Abel,

Isadora ★★★★

Biographical drama
1968 · UK · Colour · 138mins

Vanessa Redgrave superbly and insolently scandalises as Isadora Duncan, the improvisational and influential dancer whose life and career helped jazz up an earlier Jazz Age. She moves from James Fox to Jason Robards to Ivan Tchenko before her bizarre death – a broken neck caused by her scarf becoming entangled in the wheel of a sports car. Director Karel Reisz uses Isadora's life to celebrate a free-and-speakeasy era. Redgrave was Oscar-nominated for best actress but lost out to Barbra Streisand. TH

Vanessa Redgrave *Isadora Duncan* • James Fox *Gordon Craig* • Jason Robards *Paris Singer* • Ivan Tchenko *Sergei Essenin* • John Fraser *Roger* • Bessie Love *Mrs Duncan* ■ *Dir* Karel Reisz • *Scr* Melvyn Bragg, Clive Exton, from the autobiography *My Life* by Isadora Duncan, from the non-fiction book *Isadora Duncan: an Intimate Portrait* by Sewell Stokes

Ishtar ★ PG

Comedy 1987 · US · Colour · 107mins

Intended as a tribute to the Hope and Crosby *Road* movies, this has gone down in movie history as one of the grossest miscalculations of the blockbuster era. Even if you find it in yourself to accept the oddball casting of Warren Beatty and Dustin Hoffman as a couple of tone deaf songwriters, it's impossible to forgive the triteness and racial insensitivity of Elaine May's crass script. DP [video]

Warren Beatty *Lyle Rogers* • Dustin Hoffman *Chuck Clarke* • Isabelle Adjani *Shirra Assel* • Charles Grodin *Jim Harrison* • Jack Weston *Marty Freed* • Tess Harper *Willa* • Carol Kane *Carol* ■ *Dir/Scr* Elaine May

The Island ★★★★

Drama 1961 · Jpn · BW · 96mins

Already an established figure within Japanese cinema, Kenji Mizoguchi's protégé, Kaneto Shindo, garnered international acclaim for this austere study of the struggle for survival of a family farming a wild, isolated island. Always willing to experiment with theme and form, Shindo eliminated speech from this intense drama, as if to suggest both the couple's intuitive unity of purpose and the unjustifiable expenditure of effort when all their energies were needed to work the intractable land and fetch fresh water from the mainland. DP

Nobuko Otowa *Toyo* • Taiji Tonoyama *Senta* • Shinji Tanaka *Taro* • Masanori Horimoto *Jiro* ■ *Dir/Scr* Kaneto Shindo • *Cinematographer* Kiyoshi Kuroda

The Island ★★ 18

Adventure 1980 · US · Colour · 108mins

This isn't so much a comedown as a plunge to the depths for Peter Benchley, the author of *Jaws*, who adapted this quite ridiculous picture from his own novel. It beggars belief that legendary composer Ennio Morricone, the usually dependable Michael Caine and more than capable director Michael Ritchie frittered away their talents on this tale of 17th-century pirates caught in the Bermuda Triangle. It's not quite bad enough to be a bona fide turkey, but it's pretty awful all the same. DP [video]

Michael Caine *Blair Maynard* • David Warner *Jean-David Nau* • Angela Punch McGregor *Beth* • Frank Middlemass *Dr Windsor* • Don Henderson *Rollo* • Dudley Sutton *Dr Brazil* • Colin Jeavons *Hizzoner* ■ *Dir* Michael Ritchie • *Scr* Peter Benchley, from his novel

Island ★★

Psychological drama
1989 · Aus · Colour · 93mins

Dutch-born film-maker Paul Cox has emerged as a challenging Australian director, bringing a European slant to bear on a film industry primarily influenced by Hollywood. It's all the more disappointing, therefore, that this complex allegory, shot in Greece with an international cast, should fall so flat so often. Following the fortunes of three women on an island refuge, the film suffers from a pompous and paper-thin script, and a mishmash of acting styles that often makes it appear as if the characters are playing in completely different pictures. DP. Contains swearing.

Eva Sitta *Eva* • Irene Papas *Marquise* • Anoja Weerasinghe *Sahana* • Chris Haywood *Janis* • Norman Kaye *Henry* ■ *Dir/Scr* Paul Cox

The Island at the Top of the World ★★★ U

Adventure 1974 · US · Colour · 89mins

There's no question that this adventure falls below Disney's usual high standards, but it is not the unmitigated disaster that many critics considered it to be. Donald Sinden holds things together as an Edwardian explorer who sets out to rescue his son's Arctic expedition. Sinden's clash with a long lost Viking tribe stretches credibility, but the effects are pretty fair for their day, with the voyage by airship nicely done. DP [video] DVD

Donald Sinden *Sir Anthony Ross* • David Hartman *Professor Ivarsson* • Jacques Marin *Captain Brieux* • Mako *Oomiak* • David Gwillim *Donald Ross* ■ *Dir* Robert Stevenson • *Scr* John Whedon, from the novel *The Lost Ones* by Ian Cameron

Island in the Sky ★★ U

Action adventure 1953 · US · BW · 109mins

One of the chilliest films ever made. John Wayne is the pilot of a transport plane that makes an emergency landing on a frozen lake. He keeps the crew in shape while they endure six days of waiting to be rescued. The realism of the photography is dissipated by the clichéd characters, but Wayne is suitably heroic. AE

John Wayne *Captain Dooley* • Lloyd Nolan *Stutz* • Walter Abel *Colonel Fuller* • James Arness *McMullen* ■ *Dir* William A Wellman • *Scr* Ernest K Gann, from his novel

Island in the Sun ★★

Drama 1957 · US/UK · Colour · 119mins

Daring and critically abused in its day, this exotic concoction was former Fox head Darryl F Zanuck's first film as an independent producer, and he spared no expense: classy cast, fabulous locations, top director Robert Rossen, major source novel but, alas, not enough thought went into the script. Author Alec Waugh's tale of interracial sensuality deserved a more sensitive cinematic adaptation. Still, Harry Belafonte glowers at Joan Fontaine over a shared cocktail, James Mason goes suitably nuts as the crazed Maxwell Fleury, and Dorothy Dandridge and Joan Collins smoulder in the Caribbean heat. TS

James Mason *Maxwell Fleury* • Joan Fontaine *Mavis* • Joan Collins *Jocelyn* • Harry Belafonte *David Boyeur* • Dorothy Dandridge *Margot Seaton* ■ *Dir* Robert Rossen • *Scr* Alfred Hayes, from the novel by Alec Waugh

Island of Desire ★★

Second World War romantic drama
1952 · UK · Colour · 102mins

After their ship is torpedoed during the Second World War, a nurse and a marine are marooned on a tropical island, where their initial hostility blossoms into love. Enter an RAF pilot, who crash-lands, and is saved by the nurse, who amputates his arm. Steamy, sensuous Linda Darnell and wooden pretty-boy Tab Hunter are the unlikely starring couple, while genuinely one-armed Englishman Donald Gray plays the airman. The Jamaican locations are eye-catching, but the rest is such inept drivel as to become hilariously enjoyable. RK

Linda Darnell *Elizabeth Smythe* • Tab Hunter *Michael J "Chicken" Dugan* • Donald Gray *William Peck* • John Laurie *Grimshaw* • Sheila Chong *Tukua* ■ *Dir* Stuart Heisler • *Scr* Stephanie Nordli, from the novel *Saturday Island* by Hugh Brooke

The Island of Dr Moreau ★★★ 15

Science-fiction horror
1977 · US · Colour · 94mins

HG Wells's story about a mad scientist living on a remote island was filmed in 1932 with Charles Laughton as *Island of Lost Souls* and in 1996 with Marlon Brando. This stars Burt Lancaster as the lunatic who thinks he's sane, conducting genetic experiments for the sake of mankind. Michael York shows up, unwisely, as does Barbara Carrera. While never trying to be a classic, it's still a ripping yarn with a moral gloss and Lancaster's taciturn evil is often frightening. AT. Contains brief nudity.

Burt Lancaster *Dr Moreau* • Michael York *Andrew Braddock* • Nigel Davenport *Montgomery* • Barbara Carrera *Maria* • Richard Basehart *Sayer of the law* • Nick Cravat *M'Ling* • John Gillespie *Tigerman* ■ *Dir* Don Taylor • *Scr* John Herman Shaner, Al Ramrus, from the novel by HG Wells

The Island of Dr Moreau ★ 12

Science-fiction horror
1996 · US · Colour · 91mins

The third, and worst, version of the HG Wells classic fantasy about mad Doctor Moreau (here played by Marlon Brando) genetically reshaping the animal kingdom to form a new species of man in a remote tropical paradise. Badly miscast – David Thewlis, Val Kilmer and Marlon Brando all give lousy performances – and hopelessly directed by John Frankenheimer, this is a horrible miscalculation from start to finish. AJ. Contains violence and swearing. DVD

Marlon Brando *Dr Moreau* • Val Kilmer *Montgomery* • David Thewlis *Edward Douglas* • Fairuza Balk *Aissa Moreau* • Ron Perlman *Sayer of the Law* • Marco Hofschneider *M'Ling* • Temuera Morrison *Azazello* • Daniel Rigney *Hyena-Swine* ■ *Dir* John Frankenheimer • *Scr* Richard Stanley, Ron Hutchinson, from the novel by HG Wells

Island of Lost Souls ★★★★★ 12

Science-fiction horror
1932 · US · BW · 67mins

Banned in Britain for 21 years, the first, and best, version of HG Wells's provocative fantasy *The Island of Dr Moreau* is one of the best chillers ever made. Few horror films have as many terrifying facets or the harsh maturity of director Erle C Kenton. It's the uncompromising tale of doctor Charles Laughton grafting animals on to men in his tropical House of Pain to change evolution. Shot on beautiful sets, adding enormous atmospheric gloominess to the quite shocking and repellent imagery, Laughton turns in a memorably sadistic performance as the scarily mad scientist. Equally unforgettable is Bela Lugosi as the Sayer of the Law: "What is the law – are we not men!". AJ DVD

Charles Laughton *Dr Moreau* • Richard Arlen *Edward Parker* • Leila Hyams *Ruth Walker* • Bela Lugosi *Sayer of the Law* • Kathleen Burke *Lota, the panther woman* • Alan Ladd *Ape man* • Randolph Scott *Ape man* • Larry "Buster" Crabbe *Ape man* • Joe Bonomo *Ape man* ■ *Dir* Erle C Kenton • *Scr* Philip Wylie, Waldemar Young, from the novel *The Island of Dr Moreau* by HG Wells • *Cinematographer* Karl Struss

Island of Love ★★ U

Comedy 1963 · US · Colour · 100mins

This smutty and unfunny comedy was a non-starter from the word go, squandering the talents of Tony Randall and Walter Matthau, and leaving Warner Bros with egg on its face. It was a limp conclusion to a three-picture deal with the studio for stage director Morton Da Costa, who had brilliantly transferred *Auntie Mame* and *The Music Man* from stage to screen. Robert Preston gave a great performance as a confidence trickster in *The Music Man*, and he's a con artist here, too, but this time he's without good material. TS

Robert Preston *Steve Blair* • Tony Randall *Paul Ferris* • Georgia Moll [Giorgia Moll] *Elena Harakas* • Walter Matthau *Tony Dallas* • Betty Bruce *Cha Cha Miller* ■ *Dir* Morton Da Costa • *Scr* David R Schwartz, from a story by Leo Katcher

Island of Terror ★★ PG

Science-fiction horror
1966 · UK · Colour · 83mins

Bone marrow-sucking monsters are the by-product of cancer-cure research in this long-on-logic but high-on-hysteria cheapie, directed by Terence Fisher on a busman's holiday from Hammer Studios. Making the most of the isolated Irish setting and infusing the colourful carnage with a neat line in macabre humour, it's a reasonably tense offering, with the tentacled silicate creatures more fun than most of their B-feature sci-fi ilk. AJ

Peter Cushing *Dr Stanley* • Edward Judd *Dr David West* • Carole Gray *Toni Merrill* • Eddie Byrne *Dr Landers* • Sam Kydd *Constable Harris* ■ *Dir* Terence Fisher • *Scr* Edward Andrew Mann, Alan Ramsen

Island of the Blue Dolphins ★★★ U

Drama 1964 · US · Colour · 99mins

A Disney-style children's film about a native American girl forced to leave her home on an island off the California coast, after her father is murdered by white trappers. She goes back to save her brother but, when he falls prey to wild animals, she is left alone there with just a wild dog for company. Despite some weaknesses, this is well above average for its type. AT

Celia Kaye *Karana* • Larry Domasin *Ramo* • Ann Daniel *Tutok* • George Kennedy *Aleut captain* ■ *Dir* James B Clark • *Scr* Ted Sherdeman, Jane Klove, Robert B Radnitz, from the novel by Scott O'Dell

The Island on Bird Street ★★★

Wartime drama
1997 · Den/UK/Ger · Colour · 106mins

This adaptation of Uri Orlev's semi-autobiographical novel earned praise at the Berlin Film Festival not only for director Søren Kragh-Jacobsen , but also for composer Zbigniew Preisner and newcomer Jordan Kiziuk, who excels as the 11-year-old Jew who draws on the lessons of Robinson Crusoe to survive the isolation of a Polish ghetto during the Second World War. The multinational nature of the production occasionally undermines its authenticity, but it still manages to convey the resourcefulness of a child more aware of his father's promise to return than of any Nazi threat. DP

Patrick Bergin *Stefan* • Jordan Kiziuk *Alex* • Jack Warden *Boruch* • James Bolam *Dr Studjinsky* • Simon Gregor *Henryk* • Lee Ross *Freddy* • Michael Byrne *Bolek* ■ *Dir* Søren Kragh-Jacobsen • *Scr* John Goldsmith, Tony Grisoni, from the novel by Uri Orlev

Islands in the Stream ★★★

Drama 1976 · US · Colour · 115mins

With his grey beard, gravely voice and perpetual squint, George C Scott is ideally cast and riveting to watch here, playing a fisherman and sculptor who prefers to sit out the Second World War in the Bahamas. Based on Ernest Hemingway's posthumously published novel, this story of a curmudgeonly father who has a troubled relationship with his wife (Claire Bloom) and three sons is rather self-important. But the scenery is pretty to look at, and Jerry Goldsmith's score is one of his best. AT. Contains swearing.

George C Scott *Thomas Hudson* • David Hemmings *Eddy* • Gilbert Roland *Captain Ralph* • Susan Tyrrell *Lil* • Richard Evans *Willy* • Claire Bloom *Audrey* • Julius Harris *Joseph* • Hart Bochner *Tom* ■ *Dir* Franklin J Schaffner • *Scr* Denne Bart Petitclerc, from the novel by Ernest Hemingway

The Isle ★★★ 18

Psychological drama
2000 · S Kor · Colour · 88mins

Opening with a scene of lyrical tranquility, Kim Ki-Duk's fourth feature imperceptibly slides into a mêlée of pitiless cruelty and obsessive slaughter. With its latent sense of menace, the hesitant relationship between mute resort attendant Suh Jung and the suicidal Kim Yu-Seok promises much. But the use of shock tactics, particularly those involving fish hooks, deprives this visually ravishing but remorselessly sadistic melodrama of any allegorical intent it might have had. DP. In Korean with English subtitles. Contains swearing, sex scenes and violence. DVD

Suh Jung *Hee-Jin* • Kim Yu-Seok *Hyun-Shik* • Park Sung-Hee *Eun-A* • Cho Jae-Hyeon *Mang-Chee* • Jang Hang-Sun *Middle-aged man* ■ *Dir/Scr* Kim Ki-Duk

Isle of Fury ★★

Adventure drama 1936 · US · BW · 60mins

As an established star, Humphrey Bogart tended to gloss over his appearance in this film. Admittedly this adaptation isn't one of his image-making roles but it's not that bad either. Bogart is the fugitive who marries Margaret Lindsay and tries to start a new life on a South Seas island. Trouble arrives in the shape of detective Donald Woods who's come to track down Bogart and takes an unhealthy interest in his wife. TH

Humphrey Bogart *Val Stevens* • Margaret Lindsay *Lucille Gordon* • Donald Woods *Eric Blake* • EE Clive *Dr Hardy* • Paul Graetz *Capt Deever* ■ *Dir* Frank McDonald • *Scr* Robert Andrews, William Jacobs, from the novel *The Narrow Corner* by W Somerset Maugham

Isle of the Dead ★★★ 15

Horror 1945 · US · BW · 68mins

Quarantined on a Greek island during the 1912 Balkan war, General Boris Karloff is convinced the group he's looking after will succumb to the "vrykolaka", an ancient vitality-draining vampire. Director Mark Robson's film is creepy and claustrophobic, while intelligently raising issues about modern ideals versus pagan superstition. Karloff and Katherine Emery are both outstanding in this intense and imaginative miniature – another minor gem from cult producer Val Lewton's fright factory. AJ

Boris Karloff *General Ferides* • Ellen Drew *Thea* • Marc Cramer *Oliver* • Katherine Emery *Mrs St Aubyn* • Jason Robards [Jason Robards Sr] *Albrecht* ■ *Dir* Mark Robson • *Scr* Ardel Wray, Josef Mischel, inspired by the painting *The Isle of the Dead* by Arnold Boecklin

Isn't It Romantic ★★ U

Period comedy drama
1948 · US · BW · 72mins

Hearts are set a-flutter in the household of ex-Civil War officer Roland Culver, the father of three daughters (Veronica Lake, Mona Freeman, Mary Hatcher) when handsome smoothie Patric Knowles turns up on the doorstep, causing Veronica to jilt fiancé Billy De Wolfe. The most memorable thing about this innocuous semi-musical is the durable Rodgers and Hart title song. Lake, her famous "peek-a-boo" hairstyle necessarily abandoned for the period, was making her last appearance under her seven-year Paramount contract. RK

Veronica Lake *Candy* • Mona Freeman *Susie* • Mary Hatcher *Rose* • Billy De Wolfe *Horace Frazier* • Roland Culver *Major Euclid Cameron* • Patric Knowles *Richard "Rick" Brannon* ■ *Dir* Norman Z McLeod • *Scr* Josef Mischel, Richard L Breen, from the novel *Gather Ye Rosebuds* by Jeannette Covert Nolan

Isn't It Shocking? ★★★★

Black comedy thriller
1973 · US · Colour · 73mins

Made just a year after he started playing Hawkeye in *MASH*, this unconventional thriller was something of a change of pace for Alan Alda. That's not to say there isn't a vein of dark humour running throughout Lane Slate's teleplay, but there's little time for wisecracks as Alda's New England sheriff investigates the suspicious deaths of several elderly residents. With wonderfully eccentric support from Louise Lasser and Ruth Gordon, this is as much a study in small-town manners as it is a whodunnit. DP

Alan Alda *Sheriff Dan Barnes* • Louise Lasser *Blanche* • Edmond O'Brien *Justin Oates* • Ruth Gordon *Marge Savage* • Will Geer *Dr Lemuel Lovell* • Dorothy Tristan *Doc Lovell* ■ *Dir* John Badham • *Scr* Lane Slate

Isn't Life Wonderful ★★★

Silent romantic drama
1924 · US · BW · 90mins

Even with a phoney happy ending, the world wasn't interested in seeing a downbeat film that portrayed the wretched hunger and poverty in Germany after the First World War. Master film-maker DW Griffith lost his independence as a result of its failure, but it is a striking picture, shot on location in Germany with many local inhabitants as extras. Carol Dempster stars as a Polish refugee and Neil Hamilton is her lover, a soldier who returns ill from the front. AE

Carol Dempster *Inga* • Neil Hamilton *Paul* • Helen Lowell *Grandmother* • Erville Alderson *Professor* • Frank Puglia *Theodor* ■ *Dir* DW Griffith • *Scr* DW Griffith, from the short story *Isn't Life Wonderful!* by Maj Geoffrey Moss

Isn't Life Wonderful! ★★ U

Comedy 1952 · UK · Colour · 83mins

If your image of Donald Wolfit is all bluster and eyebrows, you won't recognise him in this whimsical comedy based on a once popular novel. There's something of the Clarence Day memoir *Life with Father* about this unremarkable period piece, as Cecil Parker presides over the antics of his underachieving kin. However, his grouchy snobbery quickly

U = SUITABLE FOR ALL Uc = SUITABLE FOR ALL, ESPECIALLY FOR YOUNG CHILDREN (VIDEO ONLY) PG = PARENTAL GUIDANCE

wears thin and there's precious little about his whimpering son Peter Asher, hopeless nephew Robert Urquhart or tipsy brother-in-law Wolfit to make us take their side. DP

Cecil Parker *Father* • Donald Wolfit *Uncle Willie* • Eileen Herlie *Mother* • Peter Asher *Charles* • Eleanor Summerfield *Aunt Kate* • Dianne Foster *Virginia* ■ *Dir* Harold French • *Scr* Brock Williams, from his novel *Uncle Willie and the Bicycle Shop*

Isn't She Great ★★ 15

Biographical comedy drama
1999 · US · Colour · 91mins

The incredible life of Jacqueline Susann, late author of the landmark bestseller *Valley of the Dolls*, gets short shrift in a trashy biography that reduces her achievements and personal tragedies to mere rags-to-riches anecdotes. Played by Bette Midler with theatrical mugging, Susann goes from lousy actress to celebrity writer thanks to the devotion of her press agent husband, Irving Mansfield (a miscast Nathan Lane). Aside from the neat period detail and camp support from Stockard Channing, this strangely affected showbiz saga veers from vapid farce to stale banality. AJ. Contains swearing. [VIDEO] DVD

Bette Midler *Jacqueline Susann* • Nathan Lane *Irving Mansfield* • Stockard Channing *Florence Maybelle* • David Hyde Pierce *Michael Hastings* • John Cleese *Henry Marcus* • Sarah Jessica Parker *Tira Gropman* ■ *Dir* Andrew Bergman • *Scr* Paul Rudnick, from the article *Wasn't She Great* by Michael Korda • *Music* Burt Bacharach

Istanbul ★★ U

Adventure drama 1957 · US · Colour · 84mins

Not even Errol Flynn's presence can redeem this adventure drama, a remake of the Fred MacMurray/Ava Gardner movie *Singapore* (1947). Flynn plays a rover who returns to the eponymous city to recover some loot, only to find that his wife has lost both her memory and the sought-after gems. Flynn described this later as "just one of those things", though at least we get Nat King Cole singing *When I Fall in Love*. TH

Errol Flynn *Jim Brennan* • Cornell Borchers *Stephanie Bauer/Karen Fielding* • John Bentley *Inspector Nural* • Torin Thatcher *Douglas Fielding* • Leif Erickson *Charlie Boyle* • Peggy Knudsen *Marge Boyle* • Nat King Cole *Danny Rice* ■ *Dir* Joseph Pevney • *Scr* Seton I Miller, Barbara Gray, Richard Alan Simmons, from a story by Seton I Miller

It ★★★ U

Silent comedy drama
1927 · US · BW · 76mins

Clara Bow became a major star as the "It Girl" in this delightful romantic comedy of the flapper age, directed by Clarence Badger (although Josef von Sternberg filled in while Badger was ill). "It" was a quality devised by the novelist Elinor Glyn that had most to do with sex appeal, which Bow had in abundance as part of her strikingly uninhibited acting style. The story is mild: Clara's the store clerk who makes a play for her boss, Antonio Moreno, because he has "it", but there is a striking subplot when she's suspected of being an unmarried mother. Handsome newcomer Gary Cooper can be seen in a bit role as a newspaper reporter. AE [VIDEO]

Clara Bow *Betty Lou* • Antonio Moreno *Cyrus Waltham* • William Austin *Monty* • Jacqueline Gadsdon *Adela Van Norman* • Gary Cooper *Newspaper reporter* • Elinor Glyn ■ *Dir* Clarence Badger • *Scr* Hope Loring, Louis D Lighton, Elinor Glyn, from the story by Elinor Glyn

It! ★★

Horror 1966 · UK · Colour · 95mins

Director Herbert J Leder made this dismal attempt to resurrect the legend of the Golem monster – most famously filmed in 1920 by Paul Wegener – for Swinging Sixties audiences. Roddy McDowall is an assistant museum curator, living with the mummified corpse of his mother (*Psycho* has a lot to answer for), who revives the original Golem to do his psychopathic bidding. A confused mix of black humour and horror, this is distinctly lacking in style, invention or (crucially) budget. RS

Roddy McDowall *Arthur Pimm* • Jill Haworth *Ellen Grove* • Paul Maxwell *Jim Perkins* • Aubrey Richards *Professor Weal* • Ernest Clark *Harold Grove* • Oliver Johnston *Trimingham* ■ *Dir/Scr* Herbert J Leder

It Ain't Hay ★★ U

Comedy 1943 · US · BW · 80mins

Damon Runyon's short story *Princess O'Hara* provides the basis for this Abbott and Costello comedy. Runyon, the great comic chronicler of show people, gossip columnists and gangsters, used a unique twisted vernacular in his writing, and such idiosyncracies have always proved difficult to translate to the screen. This time Bud and Lou must find a replacement race horse after a candy snack has fatal consequences. Originally made in 1935 (as *Princess O'Hara*) as a vehicle for veteran comedian Leon Errol. DF

Bud Abbott *Grover Mockridge* • Lou Costello *Wilbur Hoolihan* • Grace McDonald *Kitty McGloin* • Cecil Kellaway *King O'Hara* • Eugene Pallette *Gregory Warner* • Patsy O'Connor *Peggy, Princess O'Hara* ■ *Dir* Erle C Kenton • *Scr* Allen Boretz, John Grant, from the short story *Princess O'Hara* by Damon Runyon

It All Came True ★★★

Musical comedy 1940 · US · BW · 96mins

Why gangster Humphrey Bogart is hiding out in a boarding house whose tenants consist totally of hand-picked eccentric character actors is neither here nor there: the following year he would hit his stardom stride with *High Sierra* and *The Maltese Falcon*, and there would be no looking back. Top-billed over Bogie, and rightly so, is the simply magnificent Ann Sheridan. She just picks up this movie, rolls it up under her arms, and walks brazenly away with it. TS

Ann Sheridan *Sarah Jane Ryan* • Humphrey Bogart *Grasselli/Chips Maguire* • Jeffrey Lynn *Tommy Taylor* • ZaSu Pitts *Miss Flint* • Una O'Connor *Maggie Ryan* • Jessie Busley *Mrs Nora Taylor* • John Litel *Mr Roberts* ■ *Dir* Lewis Seiler • *Scr* Michael Fessier, Lawrence Kimble, from the short story *Better than Life* by Louis Bromfield in *Hearst's International-Cosmopolitan*

It Always Rains on Sunday ★★★★ PG

Crime drama 1947 · UK · BW · 87mins

This saga of interconnecting lives is one of Ealing's successful non-comedies. The drab city locale of Arthur La Bern's source novel is brilliantly re-created in the studio and the atmosphere is superbly captured by cameraman Douglas Slocombe. In a cast of well-known character actors, top-billed Googie Withers is particularly outstanding as the ex-lover of convict John McCallum, while Sydney Tafler and John Slater are the embodiment of East Enders. It is generally recognised today as a breakthrough movie in its portrayal of the English working class on screen and much of the credit should go to director and co-writer Robert Hamer. TS DVD

Googie Withers *Rose Sandigate* • Edward Chapman *George Sandigate* • Susan Shaw *Vi Sandigate* • John McCallum *Tommy Swann* • Patricia Plunkett *Doris Sandigate* • David Lines *Alfie Sandigate* • Sydney Tafler *Morry Hyams* • Betty Ann Davies *Sadie Hyams* • John Slater *Lou Hyams* • Jane Hylton *Bessie Hyams* ■ *Dir* Robert Hamer • *Scr* Angus MacPhail, Robert Hamer, Henry Cornelius, from the novel by Arthur La Bern

It Came from beneath the Sea ★★★ U

Science-fiction adventure
1955 · US · BW · 75mins

Careless atomic testing spawns a giant octopus in this classic monster flick, which includes stop-motion special effects from the great Ray Harryhausen. But radiation wasn't the cause of the suction-cup horror having a shortage of titanic tentacles – the ridiculously low budget saw to that! As the killer creature rampages through San Francisco to destroy the Golden Gate bridge, B-movie star Kenneth Tobey still finds time to battle biologist Donald Curtis for vampy Faith Domergue's charms. Predictable tosh, but good 1950s fun. AJ [VIDEO] DVD

Kenneth Tobey *Pete Mathews* • Faith Domergue *Lesley Joyce* • Ian Keith *Admiral Burns* • Donald Curtis *John Carter* • Dean Maddox Jr *Adam Norman* ■ *Dir* Robert Gordon • *Scr* George Worthing Yates, Hal Smith, from a story by George Worthing Yates

It Came from Outer Space ★★★★ PG

Science-fiction drama
1953 · US · BW · 76mins

Based on Ray Bradbury's short story *The Meteor*, this early 3-D classic was the first of many brilliant sci-fi films from director Jack Arnold, who went on to make *Tarantula* and *The Incredible Shrinking Man*. An alien spaceship lands in the Arizona desert, and its giant-eyed occupants adopt human identities while they repair their vessel. Astronomer Richard Carlson sees it happen, but no one believes him. Top heavy on eerie atmosphere and incorporating a neat plea for interracial tolerance, Arnold's tale uses stylish flourishes – including a fish-eye lens to simulate the aliens' point-of-view – resulting in a film that's as good as 1950s science fiction gets. AJ [VIDEO]

Richard Carlson *John Putnam* • Barbara Rush *Ellen Fields* • Charles Drake *Sheriff Matt Warren* • Russell Johnson *George* ■ *Dir* Jack Arnold • *Scr* Harry Essex, from the short story *The Meteor* by Ray Bradbury

It Conquered the World ★ PG

Science-fiction drama
1956 · US · BW · 68mins

Get ready to scream with laughter as a gravitationally-challenged, fanged carrot from Venus crawls around the Los Angeles countryside like a snail on Valium. It clearly couldn't conquer the world even if It tried! Hence it prepares to turn us dumb Earthlings into zombie slaves with the aid of what are supposed to be electronic bat-mites but which more closely resemble drunken boomerangs. One of quickie director Roger Corman's all-time worst films, yet cult fans will enjoy it for exactly that reason. AT [VIDEO]

Peter Graves (2) *Paul Nelson* • Beverly Garland *Claire Anderson* • Lee Van Cleef *Tom Anderson* • Sally Fraser *Joan Nelson* ■ *Dir* Roger Corman • *Scr* Lou Rusoff

It Could Happen to You ★★★ PG

Romantic comedy based on a true story
1994 · US · Colour · 97mins

With a title and a scenario worthy of Frank Capra, this cosy little romantic comedy is, incredibly, based on a true story. Nicolas Cage (reuniting with his *Honeymoon in Vegas* director, Andrew Bergman) plays a good-hearted cop. Rosie Perez gives one of her usual performances, shrieking the place down as she discovers hubby Cage has divided his lottery winnings with waitress Bridget Fonda. Cage, Perez and Fonda are on top form and the result is both charming and disarming. DP. Contains swearing. [VIDEO] DVD

Nicolas Cage *Charlie Lang* • Bridget Fonda *Yvonne Biasi* • Rosie Perez *Muriel Lang* • Wendell Pierce *Bo Williams* • Isaac Hayes *Angel* • Red Buttons *Zakuto* ■ *Dir* Andrew Bergman • *Scr* Jane Anderson

It Grows on Trees ★★ U

Fantasy comedy 1952 · US · BW · 84mins

Ditzy suburban housewife Irene Dunne, married to Dean Jagger, finds that two trees she had planted in her garden are sprouting dollar bills. The Treasury Department pronounces the money legal tender, and she embarks on a massive spending spree, only to discover that the bank notes, like leaves, fade and die. A whimsical and repetitive little fable, that falls somewhere between a feel-good movie and a simplistic moral tale. It was an unworthy final film for Dunne, who went into retirement after this. RK

Irene Dunne *Polly Baxter* • Dean Jagger *Phil Baxter* • Joan Evans *Diane Baxter* • Richard Crenna *Ralph Bowen* • Edith Meiser *Mrs Pryor* • Sandy Descher *Midge Baxter* ■ *Dir* Arthur Lubin • *Scr* Leonard Praskins, Barney Slater

It Had to Be You ★★ U

Romantic comedy 1947 · US · BW · 98mins

Although in characteristically sparky form, Ginger Rogers is unable to rescue this tired comedy romance with its psychological overtones. Ginger's a socialite suffering from serial desertion at the altar – she's the one who runs. Having abandoned three nearly husbands and set to try for a fourth (Ron Randell), she meets Cornel Wilde, her social inferior but her lifelong fantasy ideal made flesh. RK

Ginger Rogers *Victoria Stafford* • Cornel Wilde *"George"/Johnny Blaine* • Percy Waram *Mr Stafford* • Spring Byington *Mrs Stafford* • Ron Randell *Oliver HP Harrington* • Thurston Hall *Mr Harrington* • Charles Evans *Dr Parkinson* ■ *Dir* Don Hartman, Rudolph Maté • *Scr* Melvin Frank, Norman Panama, from a story by Allen Boretz, Don Hartman

It Happened at the World's Fair ★★★ PG

Musical 1962 · US · Colour · 100mins

This lightweight but enjoyable Elvis film was made in the wake of *Blue Hawaii's* box-office tidal wave. Here Elvis gets involved with a Chinese child, romances nurse Joan O'Brien and gets kicked in the shins by little Kurt Russell, who would grow up to portray Elvis himself on screen in the biopic *Elvis – the Movie*. And all this against the colourful background of the Seattle World's Fair. TS [VIDEO]

Elvis Presley *Mike Edwards* • Joan O'Brien *Diane Warren* • Gary Lockwood *Danny Burke* • Vicky Tiu *Sue-Lin* • Kurt Russell ■ *Dir* Norman Taurog • *Scr* Si Rose, Seaman Jacobs

It Happened Here ★★★★ PG

Drama 1963 · UK · BW · 96mins

A fascinating speculation on what might have happened if Hitler had successfully invaded Britain. It is also one of the most heroic films ever made, begun by teenagers Kevin Brownlow and Andrew Mollo in 1956 as a hobby. There are major flaws, naturally, mainly in the performances and the often naive writing, but forgive them. Instead, marvel at the provocative sight of the Third Reich goose-stepping down Whitehall and chill to the fascist overthrow of Little England. AT

Pauline Murray *Pauline* • Sebastian Shaw *Dr Richard Fletcher* • Fiona Leland *Helen Fletcher* • Honor Fehrson *Honor Hutton* • Percy Binns *Immediate Action Commandant* ■ *Dir* Kevin Brownlow, Andrew Mollo • *Scr* Kevin Brownlow, Andrew Mollo, from an idea by Kevin Brownlow

It Happened in Brooklyn ★★★ U

Musical 1947 · US · BW · 102mins

It happened to Frank Sinatra and Kathryn Grayson, reunited after *Anchors Aweigh* in as lightweight a piece of fluff as you're ever likely to see. The great Jimmy Durante virtually stops the show in a fabulous duet with Sinatra called *The Song's Gotta Come from the Heart*. The piano work is that of a very young André Previn, and Gloria Grahame's in there, too. All that was really needed was a decent director and Technicolor, but MGM was on one of its economy drives. As it is, it's just a jolly little musical movie. TS

Frank Sinatra *Danny Webson Miller* • Kathryn Grayson *Anne Fielding* • Jimmy Durante *Nick Lombardi* • Peter Lawford *Jamie Shellgrove* • Gloria Grahame *Nurse* ■ *Dir* Richard Whorf • *Scr* Isobel Lennart, from a story by John McGowan

It Happened in Rome ★★ U

Comedy 1956 · It · Colour · 95mins

Well, actually, some of it happened in Venice and Florence, as well. The trouble is, none of it is particularly interesting or original, as June Laverick, Isabelle Corey and Ingeborg Schoener city-hop in the hope of romance and adventure. The only truly significant feature of this tepid tourist advert is that it was co-written by the famous partnership of Age and Scarpelli, who penned some of the best films made by art house directors Mario Monicelli and Ettore Scola. DP

June Laverick *Margaret* • Isabelle Corey *Josette* • Ingeborg Schöner *Hilde* • Vittorio De Sica *The Count* • Isabel Jeans *Cynthia* • Massimo Girotti *Ugo Parenti* ■ *Dir* Antonio Pietrangeli • *Scr* Dario Fo, Antonio Pietrangeli, Agenore Incrocci, Furio Scarpelli

It Happened on Fifth Avenue ★

Musical comedy 1947 · US · BW · 114mins

Not a lot happens, in actual fact, in this interminable and rather juvenile comedy. A glib tramp and a bevy of his friends move into an empty New York mansion in which they all decide to play toffs until they are rumbled, but there is no discernible script to speak of, and the performances range from the banal to the execrable. SH

Don DeFore *Jim Bullock* • Gale Storm *Trudy O'Connor* • Charlie Ruggles [Charles Ruggles] *Michael O'Connor* • Victor Moore *McKeever* ■ *Dir* Roy Del Ruth • *Scr* Everett Freeman, Vick Knight, from a story by Herbert Clyde Lewis, Frederick Stephani

It Happened One Night ★★★★★ U

Romantic comedy 1934 · US · BW · 100mins

It started out as a minor film called *Night Bus* and MGM decided to punish its errant star Clark Gable by sending him over to Columbia to play the reporter. And what happened? As classy and charming a romantic comedy as you're ever likely to see, winning Oscars in all key departments – best film, director, stars, screenplay – thanks to whizzkid director Frank Capra and a marvellous foil to Gable in leading lady Claudette Colbert. The scene where runaway heiress Colbert hitches a lift and the infamous "Walls of Jericho" bedroom sequence have great charm, and confirm this standout movie's claims to classic status. Remade in 1956 as *You Can't Run Away from It*. TS DVD

Clark Gable *Peter Warne* • Claudette Colbert *Ellie Andrews* • Walter Connolly *Alexander Andrews* • Roscoe Karns *Oscar Shapeley* • Jameson Thomas *King Westley* • Alan Hale *Danker* • Arthur Hoyt *Zeke* • Blanche Frederici *Zeke's wife* ■ *Dir* Frank Capra • *Scr* Robert Riskin, from the story *Night Bus* by Samuel Hopkins Adams

It Happened to Jane ★★★ U

Comedy 1959 · US · Colour · 97mins

This bright and breezy comedy from the quirky, witty and under-rated director Richard Quine stars Doris Day as the "Jane from Maine" who becomes a national heroine when she sues Ernie Kovacs's grasping railroad boss for putting her lobster farm at risk. Jack Lemmon is on hand as Day's feckless lawyer, but the movie is stolen by Kovacs, whose performance, with hindsight, is clearly a caricature of legendary Columbia Studios head, Harry Cohn. (Did he get the joke?) TS

Doris Day *Jane Osgood* • Jack Lemmon *George Denham* • Ernie Kovacs *Harry Foster Malone* • Steve Forrest *Larry Hall* • Teddy Rooney *Billy Osgood* • Russ Brown *Uncle Otis* ■ *Dir* Richard Quine • *Scr* Norman Katkov, from a story by Max Wilk, Norman Katkov

It Happened Tomorrow ★★★★

Fantasy drama 1944 · US · BW · 85mins

A clever and very enjoyable fantasy, with a difficult theme handled expertly by French émigré director René Clair, who had demonstrated his understanding of American whimsy two years earlier with *I Married a Witch*. Reporter Dick Powell finds his career taking off when he's given the scoop on tomorrow's news – before it actually happens. Set in the 1890s, the strong cast includes veteran Jack Oakie as a mind-reader and Linda Darnell as Powell's girlfriend. The movie was Oscar-nominated for its score. TS

Dick Powell *Larry Stevens* • Linda Darnell *Sylvia* • Jack Oakie *Cigolini* • Edgar Kennedy *Inspector Mulrooney* • John Philliber *Pop Benson* • Edward Brophy *Jake Schomberg* ■ *Dir* René Clair • *Scr* René Clair, Dudley Nichols, Helene Fraenkel, from a story by Lord Dunsany, Hugh Wedlock, Howard Snyder, from the ideas of Lewis R Foster • *Music Director* Robert Stolz

It Happens Every Spring ★★★ U

Sports comedy 1949 · US · BW · 81mins

An original (if blinkered) little comedy about chemistry professor Ray Milland inventing a substance that causes baseballs to veer away from the bats. Obviously, he then gives up the distinguished groves of academe to become a star pitcher. This daffy nonsense is endearingly played by Milland and co-stars Jean Peters and Paul Douglas. The inventive screenplay is by Valentine Davies, who had just won an Oscar for his original story *Miracle on 34th Street*. TS

Ray Milland *Vernon Simpson* • Jean Peters *Deborah Greenleaf* • Paul Douglas *Monk Lanigan* • Ed Begley *Stone* • Ted De Corsia *Dolan* ■ *Dir* Lloyd Bacon • *Scr* Valentine Davies, from a story by Valentine Davies, from the short story *The Sprightly Adventures of Instructor Simpson* by Shirley W Smith

It Lives Again ★★★ 15

Horror 1978 · US · Colour · 86mins

Director Larry Cohen's sequel to his own cult classic *It's Alive* doesn't quite hit the same subversive targets as a forceful indictment of society's misuse of atomic power and drugs, but as a gory action thriller it certainly delivers. Frederic Forrest and Kathleen Lloyd are the expectant parents who get a shock when their offspring turns out to be a fanged and clawed mutant terror tot. Hardly subtle, but played with a winning conviction well above the call of duty. AJ. Contains violence and swearing. DVD

Frederic Forrest *Eugene Scott* • Kathleen Lloyd *Jody Scott* • John P Ryan *Frank Davis* • John Marley *Mallory* • Andrew Duggan *Dr Perry* • Eddie Constantine *Dr Forrest* • James Dixon *Detective Perkins* ■ *Dir/Scr* Larry Cohen

It Pays to Advertise ★★★

Comedy 1931 · US · BW · 63mins

Encouraged by secretary Carole Lombard and helped by advertising pal Skeets Gallagher, Norman Foster sets himself up in competition with his wealthy soap-manufacturer father with a number of unexpected commercial and personal consequences. An innocently amusing and enjoyable romantic comedy programmer to fill a spare hour, and one to please fans of Louise Brooks who appears in a featured supporting role. RK

Norman Foster *Rodney Martin* • Carole Lombard *Mary Grayson* • Skeets Gallagher [Richard "Skeets" Gallagher] *Ambrose Peale* • Eugene Pallette *Cyrus Martin* • Lucien Littlefield *Andrew Adams* • Louise Brooks *Thelma Temple* ■ *Dir* Frank Tuttle • *Scr* Arthur Kober, Ethel Doherty, from the play *It Pays to Advertise* by Roi Cooper Megrue, Walter Hackett

It Rains on Our Love ★★★

Romantic crime drama 1946 · Swe · BW · 95mins

Following the poor reception of *Crisis*, Ingmar Bergman turned independent for this adaptation of a play by Norwegian Oskar Braaten. Shades of Vigo and the French poetic realists colour this simple story, in which ex-jailbird Birger Malmsten and actress-turned-prostitute Barbro Kollberg receive a little help from umbrella-wielding fairy godfather Gosta Cederlund in their battle against the caprices of a hyprocritical, bureaucratic society. The action is never allowed to lapse into cheap melodrama and Bergman even manages to end on a note of unforced optimism. DP. In Swedish with English subtitles.

Barbro Kollberg *Maggi* • Birger Malmsten *David* • Gosta Cederlund *Gentleman with umbrella* • Julia Caesar *Mrs Ledin* • Gunnar Björnstrand ■ *Dir* Ingmar Bergman • *Scr* Herbert Grevenius, Ingmar Bergman

It Runs in the Family ★ PG

Comedy 1994 · US · Colour · 81mins

Despite the return of writer/narrator Jean Shepherd and director Bob Clark, this continuation of *A Christmas Story* (1983) is a big letdown. Though it's understandable that different actors had to be cast in the roles, the new additions have no sparkle, while Charles Grodin is grossly miscast as the Old Man. While the various vignettes were hilarious in Shepherd's books, they come across as flat and extremely rushed here. KB

Charles Grodin *Old Man* • Kieran Culkin *Ralphie Parker* • Mary Steenburgen *Mom* • Christian Culkin *Randy Parker* • Al Mancini *Zudoc* • Troy Evans *Gertz* ■ *Dir* Bob Clark • *Scr* Jean Shepherd, Leigh Brown, Bob Clark, from the novels *In God We Trust, All Others Pay Cash* and *Wanda Hickey's Night of Golden Memories and Other Disasters* by Jean Shepherd

It Runs in the Family ★★★ 12

Comedy drama 2002 · US · Colour · 104mins

Kirk Douglas here gives a major performance as a stroke victim, proving he is still a star of some power, overshadowing his son, Michael, and grandson, Cameron, in this sentimental comedy drama. Kirk, who has himself survived a disabling stroke, is the grand patriarch, a venerable attorney working with his son (Michael Douglas) who is married to a psychiatrist (Bernadette Peters). It's worth viewing, not particularly for the intricacies of narrative – there are none – but for seeing one of Hollywood's grandest clans in a family reunion. TH DVD

Michael Douglas *Alex Gromberg* • Kirk Douglas *Mitchell Gromberg* • Rory Culkin *Eli Gromberg* • Cameron Douglas *Asher Gromberg* • Diana Douglas *Evelyn Gromberg* • Michelle Monaghan *Peg Maloney* • Bernadette Peters *Rebecca Gromberg* • Geoffrey Arend *Malik* ■ *Dir* Fred Schepisi • *Scr* Jesse Wigutow

It Should Happen to You ★★★★ U

Romantic comedy 1954 · US · BW · 83mins

Two inimitable personalities and talents, *Born Yesterday's* Judy Holliday and, making his film debut, Jack Lemmon, are paired to delightful effect in this original, satirical romantic comedy, faultlessly directed by George Cukor. Holliday is small-town girl who arrives in the crowded anonymity of the Big Apple. Longing to be a "somebody", she hires a prominent billboard on which she has her name displayed. Soon the whole town's talking, among them businessman Peter Lawford, who covets Holliday's prime advertising site. The leads are superb, the movie just short of a perfect classic. RK DVD

Judy Holliday *Gladys Glover* • Peter Lawford *Evan Adams III* • Jack Lemmon *Pete Sheppard* • Michael O'Shea *Brod Clinton* • Vaughn Taylor *Entrikin* • Connie Gilchrist *Mrs Riker* ■ *Dir* George Cukor • *Scr* Garson Kanin

It Shouldn't Happen to a Dog ★★ U

Crime comedy 1946 · US · BW · 69mins

Doberman pinscher owners everywhere will be jealous of the skills displayed by this film's hero, an 85lb four-year-old called Rodney – but then he did share the same owners as Lassie. It's a pity that Rodney couldn't put more bite into this mild comedy in which he's mistakenly blamed for taking part in a hold-up, then helps his owner, an undercover policewoman (Carole Landis), and a reporter (Allyn Joslyn) round up a band of gangsters. AE

Carole Landis *Julia Andrews* • Allyn Joslyn *Henry Barton* • Margo Woode *Olive Stone* • Henry Morgan [Harry Morgan] *Gus Rivers* • Reed Hadley *Mike Valentine* ■ *Dir* Herbert I Leeds • *Scr* Eugene Ling, Frank Gabrielson, from the short story by Edwin Lanham

It Shouldn't Happen to a Vet ★★ U

Drama 1979 · UK · Colour · 88mins

Neither *All Creatures Great and Small* nor this amiable sequel were as successful as James Herriott's original memoirs or the long-running BBC television series. Yet this Yorkshire comedy is, nevertheless, a pleasingly unpretentious entertainment that can be enjoyed by the whole family. The formula of pre-war country cosiness, bawdy humour, folksy characterisation and animal emergency is meticulously repeated as John Alderton capably steps into the wellies vacated by Simon Ward, while Colin Blakely hammily takes over from Anthony Hopkins, leaving Lisa Harrow alone to return from the first venture. DP

John Alderton *James Herriot* • Colin Blakely *Siegfried Farnon* • Lisa Harrow *Helen Herriot* • Bill Maynard *Hinchcliffe* • Paul Shelley *Richard Carmody* • Richard Pearson *Granville* • Liz Smith *Mrs Dodds* ■ *Dir* Eric Till • *Scr* Alan Plater

It Started in Naples ★★

Romantic comedy
1960 · US · Colour · 99mins

Lawyer Clark Gable travels to Italy to settle his late brother's estate and runs into vengeful and hysterical Italians, Sophia Loren and lots of travelogue shots of Capri and the Amalfi coast. This is probably one of those movies where the cast and crew had more fun than the audience who watch their antics, and it's not a patch on Billy Wilder's similarly-themed *Avanti!*. Loren, however, is a vivacious delight in a role that was originally written for Capri's most famous resident, Gracie Fields. AT

Clark Gable *Mike Hamilton* • Sophia Loren *Lucia* • Marietto *Nando* • Vittorio De Sica *Mario Vitale* • Paolo Carlini *Renzo* ■ *Dir* Melville Shavelson • *Scr* Melville Shavelson, Jack Rose, Suso Cecchi D'Amico, from a story by Michael Pertwee, Jack Davies

It Started in Paradise ★★ U

Drama 1952 · UK · BW · 93mins

Opening in 1938, the story starts with ambitious designer Jane Hylton persuading her inspiration-blocked boss Martita Hunt that she needs a break from their London salon. But, no sooner has Hylton risen to the top than she becomes the target of fashion school graduate, Muriel Pavlow. Only a few sparks fly in Compton Bennett's competent blend of haut couture and low cunning, but Ronald Squire enjoys himself as a caustic critic. DP

Jane Hylton *Martha Watkins* • Ian Hunter *Arthur Turner* • Martita Hunt *Mme Alice* • Muriel Pavlow *Alison* • Brian Worth *Michael* • Terence Morgan *Edouard* • Ronald Squire *"Mary Jane"* • Kay Kendall *Lady Caroline* ■ *Dir* Compton Bennett • *Scr* Hugh Hastings, Marghanita Laski, from her story

It Started with a Kiss ★★★

Comedy 1959 · US · Colour · 103mins

When army sergeant Glenn Ford meets nightclub singer Debbie Reynolds, instant combustion leads to a hasty marriage. To test his affections she withholds sexual favours. Filmed on eye-catching Spanish locations, George Marshall's comedy relies on innuendo and double entendre for its laughs, with extra amusement provided by Eva Gabor as a marquesa lusting after Ford. Reynolds, pursued by a wealthy bullfighter, relishes the opportunity to escape her wholesome image in this slice of good, clean, dirty fun. RK

Glenn Ford *Sergeant Joe Fitzpatrick* • Debbie Reynolds *Maggie Putnam* • Eva Gabor *Marquesa de la Rey* • Gustavo Rojo *Antonio Soriano* • Fred Clark *General O'Connell* ■ *Dir* George Marshall • *Scr* Charles Lederer, from a story by Valentine Davies

It Started with Eve ★★★ U

Musical comedy 1941 · US · BW · 90mins

Deanna Durbin, everybody's ideal teenager, was blossoming into young womanhood when she starred opposite Charles Laughton in this delightful comedy. Laughton plays a crusty millionaire whose deathbed wish is to meet his son's fiancée. Son Robert Cummings picks up hat-check girl Durbin to impersonate his bride-to-be for a day. Naturally, Laughton takes a shine to her and recovers. Remade in 1964 as *I'd Rather Be Rich* starring Sandra Dee. RB

Deanna Durbin *Anne Terry* • Charles Laughton *Jonathon Reynolds* • Robert Cummings *J "Johnny" Reynolds Jr* • Guy Kibbee *Bishop* • Margaret Tallichet *Gloria Pennington* ■ *Dir* Henry Koster • *Scr* Norman Krasna, Leo Townsend, from the story *Almost an Angel* by Hans Kräly

It Takes Two ★★ U

Romantic comedy
1995 · US · Colour · 96mins

A bland twist on *The Parent Trap*, this story has two identical-in-appearance girls from opposite sides of the tracks (US TV stars Mary-Kate and Ashley Olsen) teaming up to bring their single parents (Kirstie Alley and Steve Guttenberg) together. So cute it will make your teeth ache. Very missable, unless you happen to be a little girl aged six. JB [video]

Kirstie Alley *Diane Barrows* • Steve Guttenberg *Roger Callaway* • Mary-Kate Olsen *Amanda Lemmon* • Ashley Olsen *Alyssa Callaway* • Philip Bosco *Vincenzo* ■ *Dir* Andy Tennant • *Scr* Deborah Dean Davis

It! The Terror from beyond Space ★★★

Science-fiction thriller
1958 · US · BW · 69mins

A rocket-ship crew returning from an interplanetary mission is menaced by a blood-drinking reptilian stowaway in this low-budget classic from science fiction's golden age. If the plot sounds familiar, it's because Edward L Cahn's briskly directed shocker is frequently cited as the blueprint for Ridley Scott's *Alien*. Ray "Crash" Corrigan wears the scaly rubber suit as the Martian monster, ably menacing Marshall Thompson and his fellow astronauts in a 1950s' relic that still delivers some decent scares. AJ

Marshall Thompson *Colonel Carruthers* • Shawn Smith *Ann Anderson* • Kim Spalding *Colonel Van Heusen* • Ann Doran *Mary Royce* • Dabbs Greer *Eric Royce* • Ray "Crash" Corrigan *"It"* ■ *Dir* Edward L Cahn • *Scr* Jerome Bixby

It Was an Accident ★ 18

Comedy drama
2000 · UK/Fr · Colour · 96mins

First-time director Metin Hüseyin doesn't romanticise a Walthamstow trapped between its mythologised gangland past and the present, in which petty crooks are as likely to resort to murder as the big boys. But Max Beesley's manic mobster reduces the proceedings to a shambles, and Chiwetel Ejiofor is cruelly exposed by the phoney slang of Oliver Parker's dismal screenplay. Thandie Newton is given even fewer favours as the girlfriend for whom small-time crook Ejiofor is reforming. Irredeemably crude and crass. DP [video] DVD

Chiwetel Ejiofor *Nicky Burkett* • Max Beesley *Mickey Cousins* • James Bolam *Fitch* • Nicola Stapleton *Kelly* • Neil Dudgeon *Holdsworth* • Hugh Quarshie *George Hurlock* • Thandie Newton *Noreen Hurlock* ■ *Dir* Metin Hüseyin • *Scr* Oliver Parker, from the novel by Jeremy Cameron

The Italian Connection ★★

Action crime thriller
1973 · US/It/W Ger · Colour · 87mins

This derivative Italian thriller is a curiously bloodless affair, despite the high body count. Director Fernando Di Leo, who worked with Sergio Leone on *A Fistful of Dollars*, directs this tale about Mafia inter-gang feuding with a breathless predictability. Luckily Mario Adorf is aggressively believable as a small-time thug framed for a six-million-dollar heroin heist and pursued by avenging hitmen. Stylistically flat, this is also clumsily dubbed. RS. Italian dialogue dubbed into English.

Mario Adorf *Luca Canali* • Henry Silva *Dave* • Woody Strode *Frank* • Adolfo Celi *Don Vito* • Luciana Paluzzi *Eva* • Sylva Koscina *Lucia* • Cyril Cusack *Corso* ■ *Dir* Fernando Di Leo • *Scr* Fernando Di Leo, Augusto Finocchi, Ingo Hermann, from a story by Fernando Di Leo

Italian for Beginners ★★★★ 15

Romantic comedy drama
2000 · Den · Colour · 107mins

If it wasn't for the admirably authentic visuals – shot on digital video using natural light – it would be easy to overlook the fact this genial suburban comedy has been accorded the Dogme seal of approval. Superbly served by a great ensemble cast, writer/director Lone Scherfig allows her tale of suburban Copenhagen lonely hearts to meander towards its satisfying, if shamelessly contrived, Venetian ending. But, behind the hesitant couplings of the diverse members of an ill-attended evening class, lie some potent yet subtly expressed ideas about how difficult it's becoming to communicate, trust and have faith in the modern world. DP. In Danish and Italian with English subtitles. DVD

Anders W Berthelsen *Andreas* • Anette Stovelbaek *Olympia* • Peter Gantzler *Jorgen Mortensen* • Ann Eleonora Jorgensen *Karen* • Lars Kaalund *Hal-Finn* • Sara Indrio Jensen *Giulia* ■ *Dir* Lone Scherfig • *Scr* Scherfig Lone • *Cinematographer* Jorgen Johannson

The Italian Job ★★★ PG

Comedy caper
1969 · UK/US · Colour · 95mins

Smashing vehicle stunt work distinguishes this Swinging Sixties romp. Unfortunately, despite a fine cast headed by criminals Michael Caine, Noël Coward and Benny Hill, the script doesn't quite come off. If the characters had been a little better developed and the director a little less flashy, this could have been a minor classic. That said, this is a mightily popular movie, helped by Quincy Jones's soundtrack and the marvellous Coward, who masterminds the whole wheeze from his prison cell. TS. Contains violence, swearing. [video] DVD

Michael Caine *Charlie Croker* • Noël Coward *Mr Bridger* • Benny Hill *Professor Simon Peach* • Raf Vallone *Altabani* • Tony Beckley *Freddie* • Rossano Brazzi *Beckerman* • Maggie Blye *Lorna* • Irene Handl *Miss Peach* • John Le Mesurier *Governor* ■ *Dir* Peter Collinson • *Scr* Troy Kennedy Martin • *Cinematographer* Douglas Slocombe • *Editor* John Trumper

The Italian Job ★★★ 12

Crime action thriller
2003 · US · Colour · 105mins

With a revised gold bullion robbery (now set in Venice and at the beginning of the film), F Gary Gray's supercharged direction and a smart script, this caper movie is just as enjoyable a ride as the British original. Mark Wahlberg carries plenty of easy-going charm in the Michael Caine role, heading a criminal gang that's revved up for revenge after associate Edward Norton has double-crossed them and absconded to Los Angeles with the booty. Norton's talents are wasted on such a sleazy, one-dimensional villain role, but Charlize Theron is beguiling as a sassy safecracker. JC. Contains swearing and violence. [video] DVD

Mark Wahlberg *Charlie Croker* • Charlize Theron *Stella Bridger* • Edward Norton *Steve* • Seth Green *Lyle* • Jason Statham *Handsome Rob* • Mos Def *Left Ear* • Franky G *Wrench* • Donald Sutherland *John Bridger* ■ *Dir* F Gary Gray • *Scr* Donna Powers, Wayne Powers, from the film by Troy Kennedy Martin

Italian Movie ★★★

Romantic comedy
1994 · US · Colour · 95mins

Fans of *Moonstruck* and *Big Night* could do worse than check out this lively romantic comedy from director Roberto Monticello. With more shrugs and hand gestures than the entire *Godfather* trilogy, the film follows Caprice Benedetti's frantic attempts to discover why husband Michael Dellafemina's sexual prowess is on the wane. Add some financial problems, in the form of creditor James Gandolfini, and you have a spicy dish that should appeal to most tastes. DP

Michael Dellafemina *Leonardo* • Caprice Benedetti *Anna* • Janet Sarno *Nina* • James Gandolfini *Angelo* • Rita Moreno *Isabella* ■ *Dir* Roberto Monticello • *Scr* Angela Scidurlo Rago, Eugenia Bone

An Italian Straw Hat ★★★★★

Silent comedy 1927 · Fr · BW · 60mins

The leading proponent of comic theory, Henri Bergson, considered this the near perfect film and, while others complained that its satirical assault on bourgeois sensibilities was lightweight, it's impossible not to be intoxicated by this balletic silent masterpiece. Taken at a pace to rival Mack Sennett, yet full of Chaplinesque subtlety, René Clair's adaptation bursts out on to the streets of Paris, as Albert Préjean meets with an unexpected problem en route to his wedding. His horse has eaten a lady's hat and he is now desperately seeking a replacement. The characters are mere pantomimic puppets, but the precision of their movement is a joy to behold. DP

Albert Préjean *Fadinard* • Olga Tchekowa *Anaïs de Beauperthuis* • Marise Maïa *The bride* • Alice Tissot *A cousin* • Jim Gérald *Beauperthuis* ■ *Dir* René Clair • *Scr* René Clair, from the play *Un Chapeau de Paille d'Italie* by Eugène Labiche, Marc Michel

It's a Big Country ★ U

Drama 1951 · US · BW · 88mins

MGM's flag-waving series of eight episodes intended to illustrate the richness and diversity of American life scores straight zeroes, except for Gary Cooper's monologue about Texas, directed by Clarence Brown, which is momentarily amusing. Yawn at the mawkish or pointless material in which stars like Fredric March and Gene Kelly appear. An obvious embarrassment before release, the picture was cut down to a standard running time. AE

Ethel Barrymore *Mrs Brian Patrick Riordan* • Keefe Brasselle *Sgt Maxie Klein* • Nancy Davis *Miss Coleman* • Van Johnson *Adam Burch* • Gene Kelly *Icarus Xenophon* • Janet Leigh *Rosa Szabo* • Fredric March *Papa Esposito* ■ *Dir* Richard Thorpe, John Sturges, Charles Vidor, Don Weis, Clarence Brown, William A Wellman, Don Hartman • *Scr* William Ludwig, Helen Deutsch, Isobel Lennart, Allen Rivkin, George Wells, Dore Schary, Dorothy Kingsley

It's a Boy ★★ U

Comedy 1933 · UK · BW · 77mins

America's most dapper farceur, Edward Everett Horton, was imported by producer Michael Balcon for this rather pedestrian adaptation of a long-running West End smash. Horton strikes the perfect note of manic fluster when his wedding to Wendy Barrie is disrupted by the arrival of a blackmailer posing as his illegitimate son. This should have been a highly amusing romp, but Tim Whelan's direction pays too much deference to the stage settings, and his comic timing is all to pot. DP [video]

Leslie Henson *James Skippett* • Edward Everett Horton *Dudley Leake* • Heather Thatcher *Anita Gunn* • Alfred Drayton *Eustace Bogle* ■ *Dir* Tim Whelan • *Scr* Austin Melford, Leslie Howard Gordon, John Paddy Carstairs, from the play by Austin Melford, Franz Arnold, Ernst Bach

It's a Date ★★★ U

Musical comedy 1940 · US · BW · 103mins

A famous actress (Kay Francis) has to face competition when a part she was hoping to get is offered instead to her ambitious daughter (Deanna Durbin). Love intervenes in the person of millionaire Walter Pidgeon, but will he choose Durbin or her mother? Now aged 19 and making her seventh feature film, Durbin reveals a more experienced grip on the art of acting, and some maturity in her singing of the usual rag-bag of songs that embellishes her films. Note the presence of SZ "Cuddles" Sakall, soon to become a Hollywood fixture with his fractured English and huggy-bear personality, here making his American debut. Remade as *Nancy Goes to Rio* in 1950. RK

Deanna Durbin *Pamela Drake* • Kay Francis *Georgia Drake* • Walter Pidgeon *John Arlen* • Eugene Pallette *Governor Allen* • Henry Stephenson *Captain Andrew* • Cecilia Loftus *Sarah Frankenstein* • Samuel S Hinds *Sidney Simpson* • SZ Sakall *Carl Ober* ■ *Dir* William A Seiter • *Scr* Norman Krasna, from a story by Jane Hall, Frederick Kohner, Ralph Block

It's a Dog's Life ★★ U

Period drama 1955 · US · Colour · 86mins

This MGM family pic displays all Hollywood's tackiest animal instincts. Highly sentimental, the action is narrated by a bull terrier named Wildfire, whose adventures take him from the Bowery slums to the lap of luxury. However, director Herman Hoffman allows himself to be distracted by Jeff Richards's romance with Jarma Lewis. Luckily, Edmund Gwenn and Dean Jagger provide some more interesting support. DP

Jeff Richards *Patch McGill* • Jarma Lewis *Mabel Maycroft* • Edmund Gwenn *Jeremiah Nolan* • Dean Jagger *Mr Wyndham* • Willard Sage *Tom Tattle* • Sally Fraser *Dorothy Wyndham* ■ *Dir* Herman Hoffman • *Scr* John Michael Hayes, from the story *The Bar Sinister* by Richard Harding Davis

It's a Gift ★★★★★

Classic comedy 1934 · US · BW · 71mins

Shades of Bacchus! It's the inimitable WC Fields in his most perfectly formed movie. Brilliantly conceived (by Fields himself, alias Charles Bogle), and beautifully structured (by director Norman Z McLeod), this is a milestone in screen comedy, and an emphatic must-see if you've decided you don't care for Fields or have never seen him before. The lengthy two-reel sequence on the porch is one of the funniest sustained sketches in sound cinema, and the store scene with Charles Sellon as blind Mr Muckle has to be seen to be believed. Kumquats will never be the same again. TS

WC Fields *Harold Bissonette* • Kathleen Howard *Amelia Bissonette* • Jean Rouverol *Mildred Bissonette* • Julian Madison *John Durston* • Tom Bupp [Tommy Bupp] *Norman Bissonette* • Baby LeRoy *Baby Dunk* • Charles Sellon *Mr Muckle* • Josephine Whittell *Mrs Dunk* ■ *Dir* Norman Z McLeod • *Scr* Jack Cunningham, from a story by Charles Bogle [WC Fields], from the play *The Comic Supplement (of American Life)* by JP McEvoy

It's a Grand Life ★★ U

Comedy 1953 · UK · BW · 106mins

If you have an aversion to music-hall stars on celluloid, give up, for vulgar Lancashire music-hall star Frank Randle has neither the wit of George Formby nor the warmth of Gracie Fields, and by the time this army caper was made he was looking tired and rather grubby. Still, the object of his fancy here is a young Diana Dors. TS

Frank Randle *Private Randle* • Diana Dors *Corporal Paula Clements* • Dan Young *Private Young* • Michael Brennan *Sergeant Major O'Reilly* • Jennifer Jayne *Private Desmond* ■ *Dir* John E Blakeley • *Scr* HF Maltby, Frank Randle, from a story by HF Maltby

It's a Great Day ★★ U

Comedy 1955 · UK · BW · 70mins

The Grove Family was one of BBC television's great popular successes, a series that today would be termed soap opera, but then was a compulsive, studio-bound rendering of the busy but uninvolving goings-on of a very average suburban family. The excellent Ruth Dunning and Edward Evans were Gladys and Bob Grove, and the acting honours, and the popularity stakes, were hijacked by formidable Nancy Roberts as Gran. This is a cheaply made feature version of the show, with the original cast, and now looks like a perfect period artefact. TS

Ruth Dunning *Gladys Grove* • Edward Evans *Bob Grove* • Sidney James *Harry Mason* • Vera Day *Blondie* • Sheila Sweet *Pat Grove* • Peter Bryant (1) *Jack Grove* • Nancy Roberts *Gran* ■ *Dir* John Warrington • *Scr* Roland Pertwee, Michael Pertwee, from their TV series *The Grove Family*

It's a Great Feeling ★★★ U

Musical comedy 1949 · US · Colour · 84mins

Just about everyone who happened to have been passing through the Warners lot seems to have been roped into this ever-so-gentle Tinseltown spoof. With Jack Carson and Dennis Morgan playing themselves as a couple of likely lads, there's much fun to be had with the whole idea of on-screen persona. However, it's Doris Day who shines as the waitress they trawl round the studio as the latest singing sensation. For all the star-spotting and backslapping aside, not a lot happens to hold the attention. DP

Doris Day *Judy Adams* • Dennis Morgan • Jack Carson • Bill Goodwin *Arthur Trent* • Gary Cooper • Joan Crawford • Errol Flynn *Jeffrey Bushfinkle* • Sydney Greenstreet • Danny Kaye • Patricia Neal • Eleanor Parker • Ronald Reagan • Edward G Robinson • Jane Wyman • Raoul Walsh • Michael Curtiz • King Vidor ■ *Dir* David Butler • *Scr* Jack Rose, Melville Shavelson, from a story by IAL Diamond

It's a Mad Mad Mad Mad World ★★★ U

Comedy 1963 · US · Colour · 148mins

Director/producer Stanley Kramer assembled the cream of Hollywood's comic talent for this monumental and mostly entertaining chase caper. The ever-versatile Spencer Tracy – in his penultimate film and clearly unwell – catches the eye as the henpecked detective at the front of the race to find a stash of stolen cash. It's rather ironic that the film was nominated for an editing Oscar, for, while the plethora of breakneck stunts undeniably have pace and precision, the action badly needed cutting by at least 80 minutes. DP [video] DVD

Spencer Tracy *Captain CG Culpeper* • Milton Berle *J Russell Finch* • Sid Caesar *Melville Crump* • Buddy Hackett *Benjy* • Ethel Merman *Mrs Marcus* • Mickey Rooney *Ding Bell* • Dick Shawn *Sylvester Marcus* • Phil Silvers *Otto Meyer* • Terry-Thomas *J Algernon Hawthorne* • Jonathan Winters *Lennie Pike* ■ *Dir* Stanley Kramer • *Scr* William Rose • *Cinematographer* Ernest Laszlo • *Music* Ernest Gold

It's a Pleasure ★★

Romantic drama 1945 · US · Colour · 89mins

Star ice-skating champion Sonja Henie here delivers the dazzling routines the fans had come to expect, further enhanced by an extravaganza of Technicolor. Unfortunately, whenever Henie, with her limited acting skills, leaves the ice to play out a romantic tale of woe with ice-hockey champ Michael O'Shea (also no actor), the movie collapses into a limp mess of clichés and embarrassing dialogue. The star rating is strictly for the "ice-capades". RK

Sonja Henie *Chris Linden* • Michael O'Shea *Don Martin* • Marie McDonald *Gail Fletcher* • Bill Johnson *Buzz Fletcher* • Gus Schilling *Bill Evans* • Iris Adrian *Wilma* ■ *Dir* William A Seiter • *Scr* Lynn Starling, Elliot Paul

It's a Very Merry Muppet Christmas Movie ★★ U

Seasonal comedy 2002 · US · Colour · 84mins

The Muppets lampoon the movies. When Joan Cusack threatens to close the Muppet Theatre, Kermit assumes the James Stewart role in *It's a Wonderful Life* and angel David Arquette shows him how life would have treated the likes of Fozzie and Miss Piggy had he never existed. The absence of most of the usual voice artists and the inclusion of some smutty innuendo compound this haphazard parody's overall mediocrity. DP [video] DVD

Steve Whitmire *Kermit/Rizzo the Rat/Beaker/Bean Bunny/Mr Poodlepants* • Dave Goelz *Gonzo the Great/Dr Bunsen Honeydew/Waldorf* • Bill Barretta *Pepe the Prawn/Dr Teeth/Rowlf the Dog/Swedish Chef/Johnny Fiama/Bobo the Bear/Howard/Lew Zealand* • Eric Jacobson *Miss Piggy/Fozzie Bear/Animal/Yoda* • David Arquette *Daniel* • Joan Cusack *Rachel Bitterman* • Whoopi Goldberg *Daniel's boss* • William H Macy *Glenn* ■ *Dir* Kirk R Thatcher • *Scr* Tom Martin, Jim Lewis

It's a Wonderful Life ★★★★★ U

Classic fantasy drama
1946 · US · BW · 130mins

This masterpiece from Frank Capra still has a lot to say about community spirit and is a film with much more to it than feel-good sentimentality. As the suicidal man who is shown the value of his life by his guardian angel, George Bailey is Mr Deeds, John Doe and Mr Smith rolled into one, and only James Stewart could have given him the self-doubt that gnaws away at his essential decency. As with all good morality tales, the villain has to be exceptional, too, and Lionel Barrymore is at the peak of his powers as the villainous Potter. The term Capra-esque is too often misapplied: forget the imitations and revel in the genuine article. DP [video] DVD

James Stewart *George Bailey* • Donna Reed *Mary Hatch* • Lionel Barrymore *Mr Potter* • Thomas Mitchell *Uncle Billy* • Henry Travers *Clarence Oddbody* • Beulah Bondi *Mrs Bailey* • Frank Faylen *Ernie* • Ward Bond *Bert* • Gloria Grahame *Violet Bick* • HB Warner *Mr Gower* ■ *Dir* Frank Capra • *Scr* Frances Goodrich, Albert Hackett, Frank Capra, Jo Swerling, Michael Wilson, from the short story *The Greatest Gift* by Philip Van Doren Stern • *Music* Dmitri Tiomkin

It's a Wonderful World ★★★★

Screwball comedy 1939 · US · BW · 85mins

This is a brilliantly funny but overlooked screwball comedy, nearly the last of its kind, in which James Stewart and wacky Claudette Colbert spend their time despising each other (until the final reel, that is). He's a private eye on the run, and she's a poet and they're looking for a killer, and… well, that's screwball enough. This is a screen original, written by the great Ben Hecht from his and Herman J Mankiewicz's story, and directed with skill and considerable pace by WS "Woody One-Take" Van Dyke II. TS

Claudette Colbert *Edwina Corday* • James Stewart *Guy Johnson* • Guy Kibbee *Captain Streeter* • Nat Pendleton *Sergeant Koretz* • Frances Drake *Vivian Tarbel* ■ *Dir* WS Van Dyke II [WS Van Dyke] • *Scr* Ben Hecht, from a story by Ben Hecht, Herman J Mankiewicz

It's a Wonderful World ★ U

Musical comedy 1956 · UK · Colour · 89mins

An anxious-to-please British musical comedy from director Val Guest. Set in the era before the advent of rock 'n' roll, the film follows the fortunes of composers Terence Morgan and George Cole, who, tired of being rejected in favour of more trendy music, pin their hopes of success on re-jigging a popular song. The music is not to everyone's taste, with Mylene Nicole's performance with Ted Heath's band striking the lowest note of all. DP

Terence Morgan *Ray Thompson* • George Cole *Ken Miller* • Kathleen Harrison *Miss Gilly* • Mylene Nicole [Mylène Demongeot] *Georgie Dubois* • James Hayter *Bert Fielding* • Harold Lang *Mervyn Wade* ■ *Dir/Scr* Val Guest

It's Alive ★★★ 18

Horror 1974 · US · Colour · 87mins

This breakthrough "mutant baby" movie marked the first time director Larry Cohen employed shock horror tactics to deal with serious social issues. Unsafe fertility drugs are blamed when Sharon Farrell's hideous newborn offspring, complete with claws and fangs, slaughters all the medics in the delivery room and embarks on a murder spree. Cohen's absorbing, grisly and cleverly written brainchild provides food for thought while still delivering the chilling goods. Oscar-winning make-up man Rick Baker designs the baby, and the movie features one of Bernard Herrmann's last scores. *It Lives Again* was the first of two sequels. AJ [video] DVD

John Ryan [John P Ryan] *Frank Davies* • Sharon Farrell *Lenore Davies* • Andrew Duggan *Professor* • Guy Stockwell *Clayton* • James Dixon *Lieutenant Perkins* ■ *Dir/Scr* Larry Cohen

It's Alive III: Island of the Alive ★★★ 18

Horror 1987 · US · Colour · 90mins

Topical issues, socially conscious humour and a great performance by Michael Moriarty (one of director Larry Cohen's rep company regulars) make this a worthy successor to the previous two killer mutant baby shockers. Moriarty plays a third-rate actor who deals with his mixed-up feelings about fathering one of the vicious tots by going to court to stop them being destroyed and getting them quarantined to a Florida island. A lively, absorbing and scary indictment crafted with Cohen's usual care and attention. AJ [video] DVD

Michael Moriarty *Stephen Jarvis* • Karen Black *Ellen Jarvis* • Laurene Landon *Sally* • Gerrit Graham *Ralston* • James Dixon *Dr Perkins* • Neal Israel *Dr Brewster* ■ *Dir/Scr* Larry Cohen • *Music* Laurie Johnson, Bernard Herrmann

It's All about Love ★★★ 15

Futuristic romantic drama
2002 · Den/UK/Swe/Neth · Colour · 100mins

Danish director Thomas Vinterberg turns his back on the stripped-down realism of Dogme 95 for his first English-language feature. The film is a lavishly created sci-fi love story in which Joaquin Phoenix and Claire Danes make handsome leads as a young married couple who decide to split after spending several years apart. But when Phoenix pays a flying visit to New York so that ice-skating superstar Danes can sign their divorce papers, he realises that his wife's celebrity lifestyle is not what it seems. Stylistically it looks gorgeous, but this cool sophistication comes at the expense of coherent plot development. Made with additional funding from Germany, Italy and Spain. SF. Contains swearing. [video] DVD

Joaquin Phoenix *John* • Claire Danes *Elena* • Douglas Henshall *Michael* • Alun Armstrong *David* • Margo Martindale *Betsy* • Mark Strong *Arthur* • Geoffrey Hutchings *Mr Morrison* • Sean Penn *Marciello* ■ *Dir* Thomas Vinterberg • *Scr* Thomas Vinterberg, Mogens Rukov

It's All Gone Pete Tong ★★ 15

Comedy drama
2004 · UK/Can · Colour · 92mins

Ibiza's rave scene is a fairly easy target for a few laughs in a mock documentary, but there are too few of them in Michael Dowse's story of a DJ who reaches the top only to discover he is going deaf. Paul Kaye delivers a credible performance as the disc jockey, but his substance-abusing character is initially so loathsome that the viewer is unlikely to care about him. The movie then shifts gear and generates some interest, thanks to the performances of Kaye and Beatriz Batarda, playing the woman who teaches him to lip-read. BP. Contains swearing and drug abuse.

Paul Kaye *Frankie Wilde* • Beatriz Batarda *Penelope Garcia* • Kate Magowan *Sonya Slowinski* • Mike Wilmot *Max Hagger* • Dave Lawrence [David Lawrence (2)] *Horst* • Paul J Spence *Alfonse* • Pete Tong ■ *Dir/Scr* Michael Dowse

It's All Happening ★★ U

Musical 1963 · UK · Colour · 96mins

Well, if it is, it's nothing to get excited about. This sentimental hokum feels like it was something Norman Wisdom rejected before being turned into a vehicle for Tommy Steele. With a cheeky grin never far from his face, Steele masterminds a talent show to raise funds for the local orphanage. The songs sound as though they were knocked out on a slow afternoon on Denmark Street, London's very own Tin Pan Alley. DP [video]

Tommy Steele *Billy Bowles* • Angela Douglas *Julie Singleton* • Michael Medwin *Max Catlin* • Jean Harvey (1) *Delia* • Bernard Bresslaw *Parsons* ■ *Dir* Don Sharp • *Scr* Leigh Vance

It's All True ★★★★

Political documentary drama
1993 · Fr/Bra · BW · 85mins

In 1942, the day after he shot the last scene of *The Magnificent Ambersons*, Orson Welles flew to Brazil to make a semi-documentary, *It's All True*, which was to be anti-Nazi propaganda financed by the State Department. The film was never finished; meanwhile, RKO cut *Ambersons* behind Welles's back, sacking him on his return and destroying his Hollywood career. This film mixes interviews, Welles's exhilarating footage of the Rio carnival and a reconstruction of one story in the intended documentary. It's a riveting piece of cinema archaeology, an unmissable treat for buffs and historians alike that also sheds new light on the *Ambersons* fiasco. AT

Dean Beville *Narration* • Miguel Ferrer *Narration* • Orson Welles • Joseph Biroc • Elizabeth Wilson • Richard Wilson ■ *Dir* Richard Wilson, Myron Meisel, Bill Krohn • *Scr* Bill Krohn, Richard Wilson, Myron Meisel, from a story by Robert J Flaherty • *Cinematographer* Gary Graver

It's Always Fair Weather ★★★★ U

Musical comedy 1955 · US · Colour · 101mins

Originally intended as a follow-up to *On the Town*, this wonderfully sardonic musical failed to find much critical approval or public acclaim on its original release. Now, in these more cynical times, we can appreciate this masterwork for what it is: a genuinely clever satire on all things American. Television is the main target here, but Madison Avenue advertising and the sports world take their fair share of knocks, as wartime buddies Gene Kelly, Dan Dailey and Michael Kidd plan a reunion, only to find they've nothing in common. TS

Gene Kelly *Ted Riley* • Dan Dailey *Doug Hallerton* • Cyd Charisse *Jackie Leighton* • Dolores Gray *Madeline Bradville* • Michael Kidd *Angie Valentine* • David Burns *Tim* ■ *Dir* Gene Kelly, Stanley Donen • *Scr* Betty Comden, Adolph Green

It's Great to Be Young ★★★★ U

Musical comedy 1956 · UK · Colour · 93mins

This light-hearted comedy has a remarkable level of energy and a superb sense of pace. John Mills stars as trumpet-playing, jazz-loving Mr Dingle, whose enforced resignation from Angel Hill School leads to a (very minor) revolution. The kids, led by Jeremy Spenser and Dorothy Bromiley, are charming, and, thanks to an excellent Ted Willis screenplay, the adults are utterly believable, as is the studio construction of the school. TS

John Mills *Dingle* • Cecil Parker *Frome* • John Salew *Routledge* • Elizabeth Kentish *Mrs Castle* • Mona Washbourne *Miss Morrow* • Mary Merrall *Miss Wyvern* • Jeremy Spenser *Nicky* • Dorothy Bromiley *Paulette* ■ *Dir* Cyril Frankel • *Scr* Ted Willis

It's Hard to Be Good ★★ U

Comedy 1948 · UK · BW · 100mins

A product of the Rank system, Jimmy Hanley had been in movies since the mid-1930s when he took the lead in this British comedy. The premise is interesting – making Hanley a war hero-turned-idealist whose every attempt to preach peace and goodwill backfires disastrously – but it needed a sharper touch from writer/director Jeffrey Dell. He merely repeats the basic idea instead of developing it, so that the situations become predictable, descending from satire to slapstick. AE

Jimmy Hanley *Capt James Gladstone Wedge* • Anne Crawford *Mary* • Raymond Huntley *Williams* • Geoffrey Keen *Sgt Todd* • Elwyn Brook-Jones *Budibent* • David Horne *Edward Beckett* ■ *Dir/Scr* Jeffrey Dell

It's in the Air ★★ U

Comedy 1938 · UK · BW · 83mins

George Formby's toothy grin, innuendo-laden songs and jaunty ukelele-strumming delighted UK audiences of the 1930s and 1940s. Underdog Formby would triumph against long odds and usually walk off with the girl. Some of his most popular vehicles found him dashing about on motorbikes or in uniform, and here these elements are combined, with Formby a motorcycle enthusiast who finds himself mistaken for an RAF pilot. DF [video]

George Formby *George Brown* • Polly Ward *Peggy* • Garry Marsh *Commanding officer* • Julien Mitchell *Sergeant-Major* • Jack Hobbs *Corporal Craig* • C Denier Warren *Sir Philip Bargrave* ■ *Dir/Scr* Anthony Kimmins

It's in the Bag ★★ U

Comedy 1945 · US · BW · 83mins

There's nothing quite like this idiosyncratic comedy, co-scripted by Alfred Hitchcock's wife, Alma Reville. It starts off with a clever Fred Allen voiceover mocking the credits and continues with various vaudeville-style sketches that are patchy fun, tending to overstay their welcome. The familiar link is a search for money hidden in one of five chairs. AE [video]

Fred Allen *Fred Floogle* • Jack Benny *Himself* • William Bendix *Himself* • Binnie Barnes *Eve Floogle* • Robert Benchley *Parker* • John Carradine *Pike* ■ *Dir* Richard Wallace • *Scr* Lewis R Foster, Fred Allen, Jay Dratler, Alma Reville

It's in the Water ★★★ 15

Comedy 1998 · US · Colour · 99mins

There's nothing new or particularly clever about debutant Kelli Herd's queer comedy. However, it does succeed in depicting lesbians and gays as everyday people rather than a misunderstood minority. Discontented housewife Keri Jo Chapman's romance with Teresa Garrett, a divorced nurse at an Aids hospice, more than compensates with its feel-good geniality, which is given satirical edge by standout supports from John Hallum and Barbara Lasater. DP [video] DVD

Keri Jo Chapman *Alex Stratton* • Teresa Garrett *Grace Miller* • Derrick Sanders *Mark Anderson* • Timothy Vahle *Tomas* • Barbara Lasater *Lily Talbott* • Nancy Chartier *Sloan* • John Hallum *Spencer* ■ *Dir/Scr* Kelli Herd

It's Love Again ★★★ U

Musical comedy 1936 · UK · BW · 80mins

The ever-delightful Jessie Matthews is in fine fettle in this frothy concoction that perfectly showcases both her musical talent and her vivacious comic personality. As a showgirl posing as a big-game-hunting socialite, she runs rings round columnist Robert Young. Lacking the glamour of a Hollywood musical (in spite of some impossibly chic Art Deco sets), this is still a pleasurable romp, with Sonnie Hale (Matthews's real-life husband at the time) amusing as the rival reporter responsible for the scam and Robb Wilton hilarious as a valet. DP [video]

Jessie Matthews *Elaine Bradford* • Robert Young (1) *Peter Carlton* • Sonnie Hale *Freddie Rathbone* • Ernest Milton *Archibald Raymond* • Robb Wilton *Boy* • Sara Allgood *Mrs Hopkins* ■ *Dir* Victor Saville • *Scr* Marion Dix, Lesser Samuels, Austin Melford

It's Love I'm After ★★★

Romantic comedy 1937 · US · BW · 90mins

This funny Bette Davis/Leslie Howard vehicle crackles with sophisticated one-liners, plus much histrionic raising of eyebrows and waving of hands, courtesy of a plot that revolves around a warring pair of famous Shakespearean actors. Davis shows us what an all-rounder she is, demonstrating a flair for deft comic timing, and even the normally lugubrious Howard joins in with verve and gusto. Olivia de Havilland is the perfect foil as Howard's besotted fan. SH

Leslie Howard *Basil Underwood* • Bette Davis *Joyce Arden* • Olivia de Havilland *Marcia West* • Eric Blore *Digges* • Patric Knowles *Henry Grant* ■ *Dir* Archie Mayo • *Scr* Casey Robinson, from the story *Gentleman after Midnight* by Maurice Hanline

It's My Party ★★ 15

Comedy drama 1996 · US · Colour · 105mins

Architect Eric Roberts learns he is about to lose his long battle against Aids and decides to throw a two-day pre-suicide farewell party surrounded by family and friends. But his guests are uncomfortable in the highly-charged atmosphere where opinions collide and secrets spill. Unsympathetic characters clash with heavy sentiment in director Randal Kleiser's well-meaning comedy drama, which quickly wears out its celebratory welcome. AJ [video]

Eric Roberts *Nick Stark* • George Segal *Paul Stark* • Marlee Matlin *Daphne Stark* • Roddy McDowall *Damian Knowles* • Olivia Newton-John *Lina Bingham* • Lee Grant *Amalia Stark* ■ *Dir/Scr* Randal Kleiser

It's My Turn ★★ 15

Romantic comedy
1980 · US · Colour · 86mins

An example of the disappointing career trajectory of leading lady Jill Clayburgh, who started the 1980s with this predictable romantic drama and is now guesting in TV's *Ally McBeal*. Clayburgh's in a relationship with Charles Grodin but then goes to a wedding and meets retired baseball player Michael Douglas. Difficult decisions lie ahead. While nicely performed, this never really gets going and ultimately offers no more depth than a TV soap. JB [video]

Jill Clayburgh *Kate Gunzinger* • Michael Douglas *Ben Lewin* • Charles Grodin *Homer* • Beverly Garland *Emma* • Steven Hill *Jacob* • Daniel Stern *Cooperman* • Dianne Wiest *Gail* ■ *Dir* Claudia Weill • *Scr* Eleanor Bergstein

It's Never Too Late ★★★ U

Comedy 1956 · UK · Colour · 95mins

An amiable comedy, with genteel Phyllis Calvert as a materfamilias whose scriptwriting talents are discovered by a Hollywood producer, but who finds she can only write when she's surrounded by her chaotic family. This is very much of its time, with its West End origins masked by skilful art direction, but the period cast is a British film fan's delight. Director Michael McCarthy whips up a fair old storm in this particular teacup, and, although nothing really happens, there's a great deal of pleasure to be had from watching Calvert attempt to rule over her unruly household. TS

Phyllis Calvert *Laura Hammond* • Patrick Barr *Charles Hammond* • Susan Stephen *Tessa Hammond* • Guy Rolfe *Stephen Hodgson* • Jean Taylor-Smith *Grannie* • Sarah Lawson *Anne* • Irene Handl • Shirley Anne Field ■ *Dir* Michael McCarthy • *Scr* Edward Dryhurst, from the play by Felicity Douglas

It's Never Too Late to Mend ★★

Melodrama 1937 · UK · BW · 95mins

Another over-ripe slice of melodrama for Tod Slaughter to sink his teeth into and, once again, he has a ball hamming things up. In this tale, he is a nasty aristocrat trying to get his evil way with a sweet young thing. To stand any chance he has to get rid of her lover, which he does by having him framed for a crime and incarcerated in a brutal prison. Don't expect any surprises and you won't be disappointed. JF

Tod Slaughter *Squire Meadows* • Marjorie Taylor *Susan Merton* • Jack Livesey *Tom Robinson* • Ian Colin *George Fielding* • Lawrence Hanray *Lawyer Crawley* • DJ Williams *Farmer Merton* • Roy Russell *Reverend Eden* • Johnny Singer *Joseph* ■ *Dir* David MacDonald • *Scr* HF Maltby, from a play by Charles Reade, Arthur Shirley

It's Not Cricket ★★★ U

Comedy 1948 · UK · BW · 71mins

Basil Radford and Naunton Wayne first displayed their passion for cricket as Charters and Caldicott in Alfred Hitchcock's sparkling spy thriller *The Lady Vanishes* in 1938. Here (in one of the last of their 11 features together) they play Bright and Early, who become private detectives after they are cashiered from the army for allowing Nazi Maurice Denham to slip through their fingers. The misadventures of the bungling double act are pleasing enough, but the humour has about as much depth as the England batting order. DP [video]

Basil Radford *Major Bright* • Naunton Wayne *Captain Early* • Susan Shaw *Primrose Brown* • Maurice Denham *Otto Fisch* • Alan Wheatley *Felix* • Diana Dors *Blonde* ■ *Dir* Alfred Roome, Roy Rich • *Scr* Bernard McNab, Gerard Bryant and Lyn Lockwood

It'$ Only Money ★★★ U

Comedy 1962 · US · BW · 83mins

It always proved difficult to capture the essential Jerry Lewis on film and, outside of France where he is regarded as a genius, the concensus is that he was a brilliant comic who never fully translated his skills to screen. Director Frank Tashlin worked a number of times with Lewis, with mixed results, and this is one of their better collaborations. Lewis plays Lester March, a TV repair man who yearns to be a detective and persuades a real detective to let him join an investigation into a missing heir. Less slapstick than usual but still with one or two standout comedy routines. DF

Jerry Lewis *Lester March* • Zachary Scott *Gregory DeWitt* • Joan O'Brien *Wanda Paxton* • Mae Questel *Cecilia Albright* • Jesse White *Pete Flint* • Jack Weston *Leopold* ■ *Dir* Frank Tashlin • *Scr* John Fenton Murray

It's That Man Again ★★ U

Comedy 1942 · UK · BW · 80mins

By the time Tommy Handley starred in this disappointing backstage vehicle, his radio show, *ITMA*, was attracting 40 million listeners each week, all desperate to laugh away their wartime blues. However, the comic's fast-talking style feels forced, and his weaknesses as a physical comedian restricted the type of business he was able to carry off. Thus, while casting him as the devious mayor of Foaming-at-the-Mouth seemed sound enough, the events that follow his acquisition of a bombed-out London theatre feel like so much padding. DP

Tommy Handley *Mayor Handley* • Greta Gynt *Stella Ferris* • Jack Train *Lefty/Funf* • Sidney Keith *Sam Scram* ■ *Dir* Walter Forde • *Scr* Howard Irving Young, Ted Kavanagh, from the radio series *ITMA* by Ted Kavanagh

It's the Old Army Game ★★★

Silent farce 1926 · US · BW · 70mins

Some of the best sequences from this WC Fields silent comedy were refined and re-used in his great 1934 talkie *It's a Gift*, where his raspy voice and the sound effects added considerably to the impact. Still, there's much merriment to be had here as a younger-looking, dark-haired Fields (as small-town pharmacist Elmer Prettywillie) attempts to obtain a decent night's sleep, and a family excursion to a Florida estate leads to general devastation. Plus there's the considerable bonus of the luminous Louise Brooks as his assistant. AE

WC Fields *Elmer Prettywillie* • Louise Brooks *Mildred Marshall* • Blanche Ring *Tessie Overholt* • William Gaxton *George Parker* ■ *Dir* Edward Sutherland [A Edward Sutherland] • *Scr* Tom J Geraghty [Tom Geraghty], J Clarkson Miller, from the play *It's the Old Army Game* by Joseph Patrick McEvoy, from theatrical sketches by Joseph Patrick McEvoy, WC Fields

It's Trad, Dad ★★★ U

Musical comedy 1961 · UK · BW · 73mins

Richard Lester had already worked with the anarchic Goons on television and on film, and thus was no stranger to madcap mayhem. This flair was on show in this film (also known as *Ring-a-Ding Rhythm*). It's a light-hearted musical romp with the simple message that rock 'n' roll is good for you. Soulful voiced Helen Shapiro and clean-cut Craig Douglas star as the kids trying to mount a music show, despite protests from the pompous mayor. Among the acts featured are rock 'n' roller Chubby Checker and teen idol Del Shannon. DF

Helen Shapiro *Helen* • Craig Douglas *Craig* • Felix Felton *Mayor* • Arthur Mullard *Police chief* • Timothy Bateson *Coffeeshop owner* • Derek Nimmo *Head waiter* ■ *Dir* Richard Lester • *Scr* Milton Subotsky

It's Turned Out Nice Again ★★★ U

Comedy 1941 · UK · BW · 77mins

George Formby's famous catch phrase was pressed into service for the title of this mischievous comedy, which proved to be his last assignment for Ealing Studios. Formby is a go-ahead ideas man at an underwear factory whose ambitious plans get his fellow knicker workers in a twist, but the action too often gets bogged down in a predictable subplot in which his smothering ma tries to break up his romance with Peggy Bryan. DP

George Formby *George Pearson* • Peggy Bryan *Lydia Pearson* • Edward Chapman *Uncle Arnold* • Elliot Mason *Mrs Pearson* • Wilfrid Hyde White *Removal man* ■ *Dir* Marcel Varnel • *Scr* Austin Melford, John Dighton, Basil Dearden, from the play *As You Were* by Hugh Mills, Wells Root

Ivan the Terrible, Part I ★★★★★ PG

Historical drama 1944 · USSR · BW · 94mins

Sergei Eisenstein's consummate work, this is an intense historical portrait of the life of the 16th century tsar who clashed with the Boyars and the Church and advanced Russia's position as an empire. Conceived as a trilogy and initially championed by Stalin, the project took a controversial turn over the changed depiction of the leader in *Part II*, and *Part III* was never made. *Part I* is an iconoclastic departure from the director's polemical, montage milestones with its exaggerated, expressionistic approach derived from the stylised artifice of opera, Kabuki theatre and shadow and puppet plays. In moving beyond his trademark staccato technique, Eisenstein created an absorbing and opulent work. DO. In Russian with English subtitles. DVD

Nikolai Cherkassov *Tsar Ivan IV* • Serafima Birman *The Boyarina Efrosinia Staritskaya, Tsar's Aunt* • Pavel Kadochnikov *Vladimir Andreyevich Staritsky* • Mikhail Zharov *Malyuta Skuratov* ■ *Dir/Scr* Sergei Eisenstein • *Cinematographer* Andrei Moskvin, Edouard Tissé • *Art Director* Isaac Shpinel

Ivan the Terrible, Part II ★★★★ PG

Historical drama 1946 · USSR · BW and Colour · 81mins

This second part of director Sergei Eisenstein's intended trilogy was completed in early 1946, by which time Eisenstein was recuperating from a heart attack. Emphasising the personal over the public aspect of the tsar's life, the film was shown to Eisenstein's ultimate boss, Stalin, who banned it because Ivan's bodyguard and the secret service were portrayed like the "Ku Klux Klan and Ivan himself was... weak and indecisive, somewhat like Hamlet." The film remained unshown until 1958, by which time Eisenstein had been dead for ten years. Admittedly less accessible than its predecessor, *Part II* is confined almost exclusively to dark interiors and even features a startling sequence that includes the director's only colour footage. DO. In Russian with English subtitles. DVD

Nikolai Cherkassov *Tsar Ivan IV* • Serafima Birman *The Boyarina Efrosinia Staritskaya, Tsar's Aunt* • Pavel Kadochnikov *Vladimir Andreyevich Staritsky* • Mikhail Zharov *Malyuta Skuratov* ■ *Dir/Scr* Sergei Eisenstein • *Music* Sergei Prokofiev

Ivanhoe ★★★★ U

Epic swashbuckling adventure
1952 · UK · Colour · 102mins

A justifiable box-office smash in what was, with hindsight, one of MGM's greatest years, this rollicking Technicolor swashbuckler remains the definitive screen version of Sir Walter Scott's memorable medieval classic. The cast and the action sequences are almost perfect; though suitably handsome, American Robert Taylor is a little dull as Sir Wilfred of Ivanhoe, but Elizabeth Taylor as Rebecca is at her loveliest, Emlyn Williams is wonderfully theatrical as Wamba, and villains George Sanders, Robert Douglas and, especially, lean and mean Guy Rolfe as Prince John are superb. Interestingly, Scott's sub-theme about anti-Semitism in 1190 England is not glossed over, making this one of the few 1950s movies to deal openly with such a tricky subject. TS

Robert Taylor (1) *Ivanhoe* • Elizabeth Taylor *Rebecca* • Joan Fontaine *Rowena* • George Sanders *De Bois-Guilbert* • Emlyn Williams *Wamba* • Robert Douglas *Sir Hugh De Bracy* ■ *Dir* Richard Thorpe • *Scr* Marguerite Roberts (uncredited), Noel Langley, from the novel by Sir Walter Scott, adapted by Aeneas MacKenzie

Ivan's Childhood ★★★★★ PG

Second World War drama
1962 · USSR · BW · 90mins

Winner of the Golden Lion at Venice, Andrei Tarkovsky's debut feature – about a 12-year-old boy (Kolya Burlyaev) who becomes a spy to take revenge on the Nazis who killed his family – may surprise those familiar only with his later philosophical treatises. The film would indistinguishable from many other examples of Soviet socialist realism, were it not for the chilling clarity of Vadim Yusov's photography and the visual flourishes that decorate the action. Even without these elements, however, this is still a shrewd insight into the reckless courage of youth and the grotesque poetry of combat. DP. In Russian with English subtitles. DVD

Kolya Burlyaev *Ivan* • Valentin Zubkov *Capt Kholin* • E Zharikov *Lt Galtsev* • S Krylov *Cpl Katasonych* ■ *Dir* Andrei Tarkovsky • *Scr* Vladimir Bogomolov, Mikhail Papava

ivansxtc. ★★★ 18

Satirical drama 1999 · US · Colour · 92mins

Illuminated by a charismatic lead performance from Danny Huston, this reworking of Leo Tolstoy's *The Death of Ivan Ilyich* charts the rapid rise and lonely downfall of a hotshot movie agent. Shot with High Definition digital cameras, Bernard Rose's arresting exposé of Hollywood dealing and hedonistic partying is more subjective than *The Player* and less cynical than *Swimming with Sharks*, though the overall emotional impact is lessened by a final section that aims for artful insight. Still, it's credible and wryly amusing. JC. Contains swearing, sex scenes, drug abuse, nudity. DVD

Danny Huston *Ivan Beckman* • Peter Weller *Don West* • Lisa Enos *Charlotte White* • Adam Krentzman *Barry Oaks* • Alex Butler *Brad East* • Morgan Vukovich *Lucy Lawrence* • Tiffani-Amber Thiessen *Marie Stein* ■ *Dir* Bernard Rose • *Scr* Lisa Enos, Bernard Rose, from the novel *The Death of Ivan Illyich* by Leo Tolstoy

I've Always Loved You ★★ U

Drama 1946 · US · Colour · 117mins

Hollywood's great early romanticist and first ever Oscar-winning director, Frank Borzage, came unstuck with this offering towards the end of his long career. It stars Philip Dorn as a brilliant concert conductor torn between love and jealousy of his latest protégée, Catherine McLeod – and that's about the size of the almost invisible plot, attached to a tedious script. The film does, however, offer a feast of musical interludes, and the off-screen piano playing of the great Artur Rubinstein. RK

Philip Dorn *Leopold Goronoff* • Catherine McLeod *Myra Hassman* • William Carter *George Sampter* • Maria Ouspenskaya *Mme Goronoff* • Felix Bressart *Frederick Hassman* • Fritz Feld *Nicholas* ■ *Dir* Frank Borzage • *Scr* Borden Chase, from the short story *Concerto* by Borden Chase

I've Been Watching You ★★ 15

Horror 2000 · US · Colour · 81mins

Ever since Dracula first clapped eyes on Jonathan Harker, a homoerotic undercurrent has simmered under the vampire story. Yet rarely has it been so close to the surface as in this frat boy offering from David DeCoteau. Arriving at university for his freshman year, jock Nathan Watkins is a natural for the Doma Tao Omega clique. But, what is it about president Bradley Stryker that he finds so irresistible? Elizabeth Bruderman is the nominal love interest, but she's a blood red herring. DP DVD

Nathan Watkins *Chris Chandler* • Josh Hammond *Dan* • Bradley Stryker *Devon* • Elizabth Bruderman *Megan* • Forrest Cochran *Barry* • Michael Lutz *Jordan* ■ *Dir* David DeCoteau • *Scr* B Louis Levy, Matthew Jason Walsh

I've Got You, Babe ★★ 12

Romantic comedy
1994 · HK · Colour · 92mins

Hong Kong's comedies haven't always travelled well, but it's not cultural considerations that hamstring this film, but director Cheung Chi-Sing's fussy use of flashbacks and his over-reliance on contrivances that unnecessarily complicate a relatively straightforward story. Lau Ching Wan stars as the confirmed bachelor who surprises himself by considering committing to Anita Yuen, only to have second thoughts after she announces she's pregnant and old flame Annabelle Lau Hiu-Tung re-appears on the scene. DP. A Cantonese language film.

Anita Yuen Wing-Yee [Anita Yuen] *Ron* • Lau Ching Wan *Charcoal* • Dayo Wong Chi Wah *Richard* • Annabelle Lau Hiu-Tung *Joyce* • Lai Mei Han *Ada Ho* ■ *Dir/Scr* Cheung Chi-Sing

I've Gotta Horse ★★ U

Musical comedy 1965 · UK · Colour · 92mins

Billy Fury, one of Britain's answers to Elvis back in the 1960s, deserved better than this dumb confection, which failed to do for him what similar threadbare flicks did for Cliff Richard. *Coronation Street* fans might enjoy watching Amanda Barrie in her movie heyday. However, nothing can take your mind off the terrible plot, as singer Fury misses rehearsals to watch his racehorse run in the Derby. TS

Billy Fury *Billy* • Amanda Barrie *Jo* • Michael Medwin *Hymie Campbell* • Marjorie Rhodes *Mrs Bartholemew* • Bill Fraser *Mr Bartholemew* • Peter Gilmore *Jock* • Jon Pertwee *Costumer's assistant* • Michael Cashman *Peter* ■ *Dir* Kenneth Hume • *Scr* Ronald Wolfe, Ronald Chesney, from a story by Kenneth Hume, Larry Parnes

I've Heard the Mermaids Singing ★★★ 15

Comedy drama 1987 · Can · Colour · 79mins

This modest movie competently tackles the hoary theme of a young woman's self-discovery. This is a very able first-time effort from writer/director Patricia Rozema and is notable for introducing Sheila McCarthy as the scatty lead who works in a deeply chic art gallery. McCarthy drew high critical acclaim for her strong, winning performance, but this initial praise failed to translate itself into further meaty roles. The movie has an unfortunate tendency to take itself too seriously at points but, overall, this is a laudable, enjoyable and often highly original movie. SH

Sheila McCarthy *Polly Vandersma* • Paule Baillargeon *Gabrielle St Peres* • Ann-Marie MacDonald *Mary Joseph* • John Evans *Warren* • Brenda Kamino *Japanese waitress* • Richard Monette *Clive* ■ *Dir/Scr* Patricia Rozema

Ivy ★★

Drama 1947 · US · BW · 98mins

You couldn't ask for a better mounted, more visually accomplished example of period melodrama set in Edwardian England than this account of Joan Fontaine as the determined Ivy. She poisons her husband Richard Ney and pins the blame on her lover Patric Knowles to clear the way for her conquest of Herbert Marshall's bachelor millionaire, but she reckons without Cedric Hardwicke's Scotland Yard inspector. Unfortunately, writer Charles Bennett and director Sam Wood fail to create any suspense and Ivy's ultimate fate is an irritating contrivance. AE

Joan Fontaine *Ivy Lexton* • Patric Knowles *Dr Roger Gretorex* • Herbert Marshall *Miles Rushworth* • Richard Ney *Jervis Lexton* • Sir Cedric Hardwicke [Cedric Hardwicke] *Inspector Orpington* ■ *Dir* Sam Wood • *Scr* Charles Bennett, from the novel *The Story of Ivy* by Marie Belloc Lowndes

JD's Revenge ★★ 18

Blaxploitation horror
1976 · US · Colour · 91mins

This cheap and cheerful horror chiller is neither good nor bad enough to become a true cult classic but it has its supporters. Glynn Turman is the college boy whose body becomes inhabited by a dead gangster from the Prohibition days who soon turns the unwilling lad into a ruthless killer. Lou Gossett pops up as a priest and delivers the film's best performance, and it's put together with confidence by Arthur Marks. JF

Glynn Turman *Ike* • Joan Pringle *Christella* • Louis Gossett Jr *Reverend Bliss* • Carl Crudup *Tony* • James Louis Watkins *Carl* • Alice Jubert *Roberta/Betty Jo* ■ *Dir* Arthur Marks • *Scr* Jaison Starkes

JFK ★★★★ 15

Historical thriller
1991 · US · Colour · 188mins

This is an overblown and factually shaky version of the events surrounding the assassination of John F Kennedy, and director Oliver Stone takes his self-appointed position as the chronicler of recent US history far too seriously to be objective or concise. Yet, decades after the event, the cover-up theory has lost none of its fascination. Whether you believe Lee Harvey Oswald acted alone on 22 November 1963 or whether you adhere to the accomplice theory, this is a compelling and persuasively staged conspiracy thriller. Stone deftly conveys a wealth of information and ensures every character makes an impact. The Oscar-winning photography and editing are superb, and the ensemble is a triumph of casting. DP. Contains drug abuse, swearing, violence. DVD

Kevin Costner *Jim Garrison* • Sissy Spacek *Liz Garrison* • Joe Pesci *David Ferrie* • Tommy Lee Jones *Clay Shaw* • Gary Oldman *Lee Harvey Oswald* • Jay O Sanders *Lou Ivon* • Michael Rooker *Bill Broussard* • Laurie Metcalf *Susie Cox* • Gary Grubbs *Al Oser* • John Candy *Dean Andrews* • Jack Lemmon *Jack Martin* • Walter Matthau *Senator Russell Long* • Ed Asner [Edward Asner] *Guy Bannister* • Donald Sutherland *Colonel X* • Kevin Bacon *Willie O'Keefe* • Brian Doyle-Murray *Jack Ruby* ■ *Dir* Oliver Stone • *Scr* Oliver Stone, Zachary Sklar, from the non-fiction book *On the Trail of the Assassins* by Jim Garrison, from the non-fiction book *Crossfire: the Plot That Killed Kennedy* by Jim Marrs • *Cinematographer* Robert Richardson • *Music* John Williams

JLG/JLG – Self Portrait in December ★★★

Experimental documentary
1994 · Fr/Swi · Colour · 65mins

Shot around his Swiss home on Lake Léman, this documentary is a self-portrait of the *enfant terrible* who once rocked cinema on its heels, only to be marginalised (albeit partly through his own connivance) by the art form he helped transform. Discussing his diverse sources of inspiration, Jean-Luc Godard appears secure in his reputation as a film-maker who has experimented with the moving image while making heartfelt and often controversial political and artistic statements. Referencing his own output and works that continue to influence him, this is an eloquent dissertation from one of cinema's few philosopher-poets DP. In French with English subtitles.

Dir/Scr Jean-Luc Godard

JW Coop ★★★

Drama 1971 · US · Colour · 112mins

After winning the best actor Oscar for *Charly*, Cliff Robertson used his clout to produce, direct, write and star in this story of a rodeo rider who, after spending ten years in jail, finds himself adrift in a more commercialised and cynical world. Robertson is excellent as the eponymous cowboy, but the film shows its age by confronting him with tiresome hippies. AT

Cliff Robertson *JW Coop* • Geraldine Page *Mama* • Cristina Ferrare *Bean* • RG Armstrong *Jim Sawyer* • RL Armstrong *Tooter Watson* ■ *Dir* Cliff Robertson • *Scr* Cliff Robertson, Gary Cartwright, Bud Shrake

Jab Pyaar Kisise Hota Hai ★★★ PG

Romantic comedy drama
1998 · Ind · Colour · 160mins

Salman Khan confirms his status as Bollywood's fastest rising star with this lively melodrama about coming to terms with the past and taking responsibility for one's actions. Khan plays an orphan who's allowed to mature into a self-centred waster by his doting grandfather Anupam Kher, until love forces him to mend his ways. Deepak Sereen, directs this tale with a lightness of tone and a seriousness of intent to good effect. DP. In Hindi with English subtitles.

Salman Khan *Suraj* • Twinkle Khanna *Komal* • Anupam Kher *Dhanrajgir, Suraj's grandfather* • Johny Lever [Johnny Lever] *Mahesh* ■ *Dir* Deepak Sareen • *Scr* Honey Irani, Javed Siddiqi, from a story by Honey Irani

Jabberwocky ★★ PG

Comedy fantasy 1977 · UK · Colour · 100mins

Terry Gilliam's debut feature is an uneven mix of medieval tomfoolery and crude *Monty Python* humour. Fellow Python Michael Palin plays the hero who, to prove his worth and win the hand of a fair maiden, sets out to kill the fearsome "manxome foe". The production design is stunning, and the look of the Jabberwock is based on the illustrations that Sir John Tenniel created for Carroll's original book. For all that, Gilliam's grim fantasy only occasionally raises itself above the tiresome. AJ DVD

Michael Palin *Dennis Cooper* • Max Wall *King Bruno the Questionable* • Deborah Fallender *Princess* • John Le Mesurier *Chamberlain* • Annette Badland *Griselda Fishfinger* • Warren Mitchell *Mr Fishfinger* • Brenda Cowling *Mrs Fishfinger* • Harry H Corbett *Squire* • Rodney Bewes *Other squire* • Bernard Bresslaw *Landlord* ■ *Dir* Terry Gilliam • *Scr* Terry Gilliam, Charles Alverson, from the poem *Jabberwocky* by Lewis Carroll

J'Accuse ★★★★

Silent war drama 1919 · Fr · BW · 150mins

Intercutting newreel footage and basing his intertitles on letters from the trenches, Abel Gance's silent drama brought home to audiences, who scarcely needed reminding, the imperative to prevent the recurrence of such barbarity. The rape and pregnancy of Marise Dauvray and the fury of her enlisted husband, Severin-Mars, were powerfully depicted. But nothing compares to the finale sequence, in which deranged poet Romuald Joubé summons the dead from their graves to reinforce the futility of war. Originally shown in three feature-length chapters, the film was reduced to around 150 minutes by the director, and the discarded footage was destroyed. DP

Romuald Joubé *Jean Diaz* • Severin-Mars *François Laurin* • Marise Dauvray *Edith Laurin* • Angèle Guys *Angèle* • Maxime Desjardins *Maria Lazare* ■ *Dir/Scr* Abel Gance

J'Accuse ★★★

War drama 1938 · Fr · BW · 95mins

As war loomed, Abel Gance reworked his 1919 classic to warn again of the follies of conflict. The poet is (over)played by Victor Francen, who vows to promote pacifism after surviving the slaughter of his trench patrol. However, his invention of unbreakable glass is misappropriated by the government and he is forced to summon the First World War dead from their graves to march across the country to persuade world leaders to outlaw fighting forever. Again the finale is the most moving and spectacular aspect of the picture, which is too often sidetracked by Francen's rivalry with Jean Max for Renée Devillers. DP. In French with English subtitles.

Victor Francen *Jean Diaz* • Jean Max *Henri Chimay* • Delaître *François Laurin* • Renée Devillers *Helene* • Line Noro *Edith* ■ *Dir* Abel Gance • *Scr* Abel Gance, Steve Passeur

Jack ★★★ PG

Comedy drama 1996 · US · Colour · 108mins

Robin Williams stars as a 10-year-old who looks like a 40-year-old, the result of an ageing disorder that has made his body mature at an incredible rate. Diane Lane and Brian Kerwin give subtle performances as Jack's confused parents, and there's a sweet contribution from Jennifer Lopez as his teacher. Unfortunately, Williams goes over the top again and his exuberance is unchecked by director Francis Ford Coppola. JB. Contains swearing. DVD

Robin Williams *Jack Powell* • Diane Lane *Karen Powell* • Brian Kerwin *Brian Powell* • Jennifer Lopez *Miss Marquez* • Bill Cosby *Lawrence Woodruff* • Fran Drescher *Dolores Durante* • Adam Zolotin *Louis Durante* • Michael McKean *Paulie* ■ *Dir* Francis Ford Coppola • *Scr* James DeMonaco, Gary Nadeau

Jack Ahoy! ★★★

Comedy 1934 · UK · BW · 70mins

This was a huge success in its day for jovial, lantern-jawed Jack Hulbert, and is one of a series of hits that still amuse today. Here, Hulbert sings *The Hat's on the Side of My Head* and gets kidnapped by Chinese revolutionaries! There's a nice pace and an easy-going air of geniality brought to this maritime caper by skilled director Walter Forde, and its breeziness is infectious. TS

Jack Hulbert *Jack Ponsonby* • Nancy O'Neil *Patricia Fraser* • Alfred Drayton *Admiral Fraser* • Tamara Desni *Conchita* • Henry Peterson *Larios* • Sam Wilkinson *Dodger* ■ *Dir* Walter Forde • *Scr* Jack Hulbert, Leslie Arliss, Gerard Fairlie, Austin Melford, from a story by Sidney Gilliat, JOC Orton

Jack & Sarah ★★★ 15

Romantic comedy drama
1995 · UK · Colour · 110mins

This is a refreshing spin on an ever-popular formula: men coping with babies. Richard E Grant is the lawyer who becomes a bumbling single father when his wife dies in childbirth; Samantha Mathis is the visiting American who is roped into being the child's nanny and falls for her employer. Grant and Mathis are appealing leads, but it is the classy hamming of Ian McKellen and Judi Dench that steals the show. Director Tim Sullivan just about keeps sentimentality at bay. JF. Contains swearing and brief nudity. DVD

Richard E Grant *Jack* • Samantha Mathis *Amy* • Judi Dench *Margaret* • Ian McKellen *William* • Cherie Lunghi *Anna* • Eileen Atkins *Phil* •

Imogen Stubbs *Sarah* • David Swift *Michael* • Laurent Grévill *Alain* • Kate Hardie *Pamela* ■ *Dir/Scr* Tim Sullivan

Jack and the Beanstalk ★★ U

Comedy
1952 · US · Colour and sepia · 82mins

Director Jean Yarbrough is currently being re-assessed as one of Hollywood's unsung journeymen, but this is the least of his five collaborations with Abbott and Costello, largely because there is no enchantment (let alone comedy) in the screenplay. The dreadful songs and the garish SuperCinecolor don't help much, either, making everything look fake instead of magical. However, Buddy Baer has fun as the Giant menacing Lou. DP DVD

Bud Abbott *Dinklepuss* • Lou Costello *Jack* • Buddy Baer *Sergeant Riley/Giant* • Dorothy Ford *Polly* • Barbara Brown *Mother* • David Stollery *Donald* ■ *Dir* Jean Yarbrough • *Scr* Nat Curtis, from a story by Pat Costello, Felix Adler

Jack Be Nimble ★★★ 18

Horror thriller 1992 · NZ · Colour · 91mins

This creepily gothic offering is a satisfyingly twisted affair. Alexis Arquette is Jack, a young man who embarks on a monstrous plan of revenge with the help of a hypnosis machine, after suffering years of abuse at the hands of brutal foster parents. Sarah Smuts-Kennedy plays his equally long-suffering – and now long lost – sister, while "Mr NZ Cinema" Bruno Lawrence makes one of his last appearances. It's an uneven ride but writer/director Garth Maxwell conjures up some disturbing imagery. JF

Alexis Arquette *Jack* • Sarah Smuts Kennedy *Dora* • Bruno Lawrence *Teddy* • Tony Barry *Clarrie* • Elizabeth Hawthorne *Clarrie's wife* • Brenda Simmons *Mrs Birch* • Gilbert Goldie *Mr Birch* • Tricia Phillips *Anne* • Paul Minifie *Kevin* ■ *Dir/Scr* Garth Maxwell

The Jack Bull ★★★★ 15

Western 1999 · US · Colour · 111mins

John Badham's unheralded but outstanding TV western was written by Dick Cusack and stars his son, John, as the horse dealer whose animals are mistreated by a neighbouring rancher. When the neighbour is backed up by the courts, Cusack launches an armed insurrection on the eve of Wyoming's bid for statehood. Cusack's Myrl Redding has the tragic overtones of a Thomas Hardy hero, a man to whom dreadful things happen, even in the best of times. This is a beautifully staged, unrelentingly sombre movie with satisfying political complexity. AT. Contains violence, swearing. DVD

John Cusack *Myrl Redding* • John Goodman *Judge Tolliver* • LQ Jones *Henry Ballard* • Miranda Otto *Cora* • John C McGinley *Woody* • John Savage *Slater* • Rodney A Grant *Billy* ■ *Dir* John Badham • *Scr* Dick Cusack, from the book *Michael Kohlhaas* by Heinrich Von Kleist

Jack Frost ★★ PG

Fantasy comedy drama
1998 · US · Colour · 97mins

In this charmless fantasy fable, a dead rock musician is resurrected as a snowman to watch over the son he neglected when he was alive. Michael Keaton as the sinister looking Frost-dad requires an energetic leap of imagination, and everything else is pretty unbelievable, too. If it had been played as broad farce it might have worked. Sadly, the four scriptwriters decided to aim for the emotional resonance of *Ghost*, coating this in sickly icing. JC DVD

Michael Keaton *Jack Frost* • Kelly Preston *Gabby Frost* • Joseph Cross *Charlie Frost* • Mark Addy *Mac* • Henry Rollins *Sid Gronic* • Dweezil Zappa *John Kaplan* ■ *Dir* Troy Miller • *Scr* Steve Bloom, Jonathan Roberts, Mark Steven Johnson, Jeff Cesario, from a story by Mark Steven Johnson

Jack London ★★

Biographical drama 1944 · US · BW · 93mins

This biopic of the novelist whose adventure stories have made many a movie stars Broadway actor Michael O'Shea. It's not ideal casting – you need someone like Clark Gable to pull off this globe-trotting, hard-drinking womaniser – while the film's emphasis on the Japanese-American conflict of 1904 is milked for its then contemporary relevance. Susan Hayward barely registers as London's wife. AT

Michael O'Shea *Jack London* • Susan Hayward *Charmain Kittredge* • Osa Massen *Freda Maloof* • Harry Davenport *Prof Hilliard* • Frank Craven *Old Tom* • Virginia Mayo *Mamie* • Ralph Morgan *George Brett* ■ *Dir* Alfred Santell • *Scr* Ernest Pascal, from the biography *The Book of Jack London* by Charmain London

Jack of Diamonds ★★★ U

Crime drama
1967 · US/W Ger · Colour · 107mins

A heist movie that – appropriately enough – steals its best ideas from earlier movies, specifically *Topkapi*, while George Hamilton's role as an elegant, sophisticated cat burglar harks back to Cary Grant in Hitchcock's *To Catch a Thief*. The result is a campy, quite amusing yarn about some dazzling diamonds and a robbery that doesn't go quite according to plan. Joseph Cotten plays Hamilton's mentor and there are three glamour queens playing themselves, draped in baubles: Carroll Baker, Zsa Zsa Gabor and Lilli Palmer. AT

George Hamilton *Jeff Hill* • Joseph Cotten *Ace of Diamonds* • Marie Laforêt *Olga* • Maurice Evans *Nicolai* • Alexander Hegarth *Brugger* • Carroll Baker • Zsa Zsa Gabor • Lilli Palmer ■ *Dir* Don Taylor • *Scr* Jack DeWitt, Sandy Howard, Robert L Joseph

Jack Reed: Badge of Honor ★★★ 15

Police drama 1993 · US · Colour · 89mins

Following the success of the mini-series *Shattered Promises* featuring Chicago cop Jack Reed, Brian Dennehy returns as the uncompromising lawman in this above average TV movie. Called in on what looks like an open-and-shut case of murder, Dennehy is blocked at every turn by the FBI because his chief suspect is its star witness in a vital arms smuggling trial. It's not all crime fighting, however, as Dennehy and his screen wife, Susan Ruttan also care for the murder victim's son. William Sadler does well as the x-ray technician with a decidedly dodgy past, but it's Dennehy who dominates the proceedings. DP DVD

Brian Dennehy *Jack Reed* • Susan Ruttan *Arlene Reed* • William Sadler *David Anatole* • Alice Krige *Joan Anatole* • RD Call *Lieutenant Lloyd Butler* ■ *Dir* Kevin Connor • *Scr* Andrew Laskos

Jack Reed: Death and Vengeance ★★ 15

Police drama 1996 · US · Colour · 86mins

This is another watchable entry in Brian Dennehy's successful made-for-TV Jack Reed franchise. Here Dennehy's bluff detective encounters murder and intrigue among the Russian émigré community in Chicago. Susan Ruttan returns as Reed's wife as does other series regular Charles S Dutton, while Dennehy handles all his chores – script, direction, performance – with his usual reliability. JF

Brian Dennehy *Jack Reed* • Charles Dutton [Charles S Dutton] *Charles Silvera* • Susan Ruttan *Arlene Reed* • Linda Carter *Roxanne* ■ *Dir* Brian Dennehy • *Scr* Bill Phillips, Brian Dennehy

Jack Reed: One of Our Own ★★ 15

Police drama 1995 · US · Colour · 87mins

Burly Brian Dennehy stars again as the veteran Chicago lawman. Dennehy also directed and co-scripted this brisk police procedural, in which a murder attempt on a young woman has ramifications closer to home after our hero uncovers a den of corruption at City Hall. Dennehy is an imposing presence and his partnership with Charles S Dutton is bruisingly effective. However, the plot in this TV movie is somewhat stale. DP

Brian Dennehy *Jack Reed* • Charles S Dutton *Lieutenant Charles Silvera* • Susan Ruttan *Arlene Reed* • Suki Kaiser *Sara Landry* • Justin Louis *Michael Quinn* • Michael Talbott *Eddie Dirkson* • Justin Burnette *John Jr* • CCH Pounder *Mrs Harris* ■ *Dir* Brian Dennehy • *Scr* Brian Dennehy, Bill Phillips

Jack Reed: a Search for Justice ★★★ 12

Police drama 1994 · US · Colour · 91mins

Hard-working Brian Dennehy is involved in just about every facet of this addition to the popular Jack Reed series, serving as star and director, as well as co-producer and co-writer. Here, he discovers that the nightclub owner he suspects of murdering a young employee has powerful friends in the local establishment. Dennehy is typically charismatic and there's able support from Charles S Dutton, Susan Ruttan and Miguel Ferrer. JF DVD

Brian Dennehy *Jack Reed* • Susan Ruttan *Arlene Reed* • Charles S Dutton *Charles Silvera* • Miguel Ferrer *Win Carter* • Charles Hallahan *Roy Galvin* ■ *Dir* Brian Dennehy • *Scr* Bill Phillips, Brian Dennehy

Jack the Bear ★★ 15

Drama 1993 · US · Colour · 94mins

The idea that real and imaginary terrors are often indistinguishable in the mind of a child is hardly an original one and this contrived tosh draws no startling conclusions, which is all the more disappointing as it's supposed to be a chiller. Danny DeVito hurls himself into the role of the widowed father, whose job as a horror show host does little to ease the fears of his son, who is impressively played by the film's major plus factor, Robert J Steinmiller Jr. DP

Danny DeVito *John Leary* • Robert J Steinmiller Jr *Jack Leary* • Miko Hughes *Dylan Leary* • Gary Sinise *Norman Strick* • Art LaFleur *Mr Festinger* • Stefan Gierasch *Grandpa Glickes* • Erica Yohn *Grandma Glickes* ■ *Dir* Marshall Herskovitz • *Scr* Steven Zaillian, from the novel *Jack the Bear* by Dan McCall

Jack the Giant Killer ★★★

Fantasy 1962 · US · Colour · 94mins

Having already made *Attack of the 50ft Woman*, former Oscar-winning art director Nathan "Jerry" Juran tried for the same heights, metaphorically speaking, with this charming and enjoyable children's fairy tale. Juran is reunited with Kerwin Mathews, his star in *The 7th Voyage of Sinbad*, and succeeds in creating a genuinely original romp for kids of all ages. Incidentally, on reissue the title lost its "Jack" and songs were bizarrely added to the soundtrack. TS

Kerwin Mathews *Jack* • Judi Meredith *Princess Elaine* • Torin Thatcher *Pendragon* • Walter Burke *Garna* • Roger Mobley *Peter* • Don Beddoe *Imp in bottle* ■ *Dir* Nathan Juran • *Scr* Orville H Hampton, Nathan Juran, from a story by Orville H Hampton

Jack the Ripper ★★★

Crime drama 1958 · UK · BW · 82mins

This likeable little shocker received "A" treatment on release, thus promoting "stars" Lee Patterson and Eddie Byrne to feature players, albeit very briefly. Canadian actor Patterson had quite a following in Britain during the late 1950s, thanks to a string of now forgotten programme fillers, and here his presence lends weight to the infamous tale. The film's stark title and its inevitable X certificate made it a box-office hit. The spooky atmosphere is well maintained, and the cheapness doesn't show. TS

Lee Patterson *Sam Lowry* • Eddie Byrne *Inspector O'Neill* • Betty McDowall *Anne Ford* • Ewen Solon *Sir David Rogers* • John Le Mesurier *Dr Tranter* • George Rose *Clarke* ■ *Dir* Robert S Baker, Monty Berman • *Scr* Jimmy Sangster, from a story by Peter Hammond, Colin Craig

The Jackal ★★★ 18

Action thriller 1997 · US · Colour · 119mins

Fred Zinnemann's *The Day of the Jackal* gets the Bruce Willis treatment here. The classic thriller about an assassin at large has been relocated to America and now comes equipped with all kinds of techno-props which add nothing at all to the original's ruthless efficiency. Willis supplants Edward Fox as the killer and, surprisingly, doesn't make too bad a job of it. Willis, Richard Gere (IRA terrorist) and Diane Venora (Russian intelligence officer) compete for the "Meryl Streep Most Authentic Foreign Accent" award. TH. Contains swearing and violence. DVD

Bruce Willis *The Jackal* • Richard Gere *Declan Mulqueen* • Sidney Poitier *FBI Deputy Director Carter Preston* • Diane Venora *Major Valentina Koslova* • Mathilda May *Isabella* • JK Simmons *Witherspoon* • Richard Lineback *McMurphy* • Leslie Phillips *Woolburton* ■ *Dir* Michael Caton-Jones • *Scr* Chuck Pfarrer, from the film *The Day of the Jackal* by Kenneth Ross

Jackass: the Movie ★★★ 18

Comedy 2002 · US · Colour · 85mins

Johnny Knoxville and his daredevil buddies take their eye-watering antics to new extremes in this feature-length version of the cult TV series. It builds on the group's MTV-spawned format, in which the modern-day clowns risk life and limb carrying out absurd, and often dangerous, stunts and pranks. It's far from subtle and definitely an acquired taste, but fans of the show won't be disappointed. Overall, this is spirited and darkly hilarious adults-only viewing. SF DVD

Johnny Knoxville • Bam Margera • Chris Pontius • Steve-O • Dave England • Ryan Dunn • Jason "Wee Man" Acuna ■ *Dir* Jeff Tremaine • *Scr* Jeff Tremaine, Spike Jonze, Johnny Knoxville, from their TV series

The Jacket ★★★ 15

Psychological thriller
2005 · US/UK/Ger · Colour · 102mins

Horrific sensory deprivation therapy gives Gulf War veteran Adrien Brody the ability to travel through time in this claustrophobic thriller. Brody plays a discharged marine with injury-related amnesia, who's committed to a mental institution after being tried for murder and found not guilty by reason of insanity. There, he falls into the clutches of doctor Kris Kristofferson (excellent), whose controversial treatment regimen inexplicably propels the soldier's disoriented mind into the future, where he meets a troubled young woman (Keira Knightley). This is the most accessible work to date from British director John Maybury, but, though gripping and disturbing, the overall plot has little substance. SF. Contains swearnig and violence.

Adrien Brody *Jack Starks* • Keira Knightley *Jackie Price* • Kris Kristofferson *Dr Becker* • Jennifer Jason Leigh *Dr Lorenson* • Kelly Lynch *Jean* • Brad Renfro *Stranger* • Daniel Craig *Mackenzie* • Steven Mackintosh *Dr Hopkins* • Fish *Jimmy Fleisher* ■ *Dir* John Maybury • *Scr* Massy Tadjedin, from a story by Tom Bleecker, Marc Rocco

Jackie Brown ★★★★ 15

Crime thriller 1997 · US · Colour · 147mins

Imaginatively dragging Elmore Leonard's bestseller *Rum Punch* into his own postmodern universe peppered with quirky dialogue and cinematic references, director Quentin Tarantino makes this re-energised crime thriller a homage to, and an updating of, 1970s pulp blaxploitation fiction. Black icon Pam Grier is great as the air hostess pressured into an entrapment scam after being arrested for cash smuggling, who uses her feminine wiles to outsmart everyone wanting to exploit or kill her. Tarantino draws maximum suspense from a superb cast and an array of visual techniques such as staging a key scene three times from three different points of view. Breathlessly exciting and cut to a fabulous array of funk classics. AJ. Contains swearing, violence, drug abuse, a sex scene. [VIDEO] DVD

Pam Grier *Jackie Brown* • Samuel L Jackson *Ordell Robbie* • Robert Forster *Max Cherry* • Bridget Fonda *Melanie* • Michael Keaton *Ray Nicolette* • Robert De Niro *Louis Gara* • Michael Bowen *Mark Dargus* • Lisa Gay Hamilton *Sheronda* • Tommy "Tiny" Lister Jr [Tom "Tiny" Lister Jr] *Winston* • Hattie Winston *Simone* • Denise Crosby *Public defender* ■ *Dir* Quentin Tarantino • *Scr* Quentin Tarantino, from the novel *Rum Punch* by Elmore Leonard

Jackie Chan's First Strike ★★ 12

Action thriller 1996 · HK/US · Colour · 80mins

Placing less emphasis on kung fu action and more on spectacular stunts, this Jackie Chan comedy thriller is a Bondesque romp shot on location all over the globe. A pretty idiotic plot sees Chan playing a Hong Kong cop who is hired by both the CIA and Russian intelligence to recover a stolen nuclear warhead. As ever, the storyline is a thin excuse to string together a series of breathtaking action sequences. JF. Cantonese dialogue dubbed into English. Contains violence. [VIDEO] DVD

Jackie Chan *Jackie* • Chen Chun Wu *Annie* • Jackson Lou *Tsui* • Bill Tung *Uncle Bill* • Jouri Petrov *Colonel Gregor Yegorov* ■ *Dir* Stanley Tong • *Scr* Stanley Tong, Nick Tramontane, Greg Mellot, Elliot Tong

Jackie Chan's Who Am I? ★★★★ 12

Martial arts action comedy
1998 · HK · Colour · 107mins

Jackie Chan's most sensational action scenes of the 1990s, impressive production values and super-slick direction illuminate this little-known movie. Although the plot doesn't bear close scrutiny (something about a top secret energy source, an African tribe and amnesia), the extraordinary set pieces – from a clog-assisted Rotterdam brawl, to a three-way rooftop battle – rival anything in a megabuck Hollywood blockbuster. Chan's trademark use of slapstick comedy at the height of the fighting works brilliantly, too. JC. Contains violence. [VIDEO] DVD

Jackie Chan *Jackie (aka Whoami)* • Michelle Ferre *Christine* • Mirai Yamamoto *Yuki* • Ron Smerczak *Morgan* • Ed Nelson *General Sherman* • Tom Pompert *CIA chairman* • Yanick Mbali *Baba* • Washington Sixolo *Village chief* ■ *Dir* Jackie Chan, Benny Chan • *Scr* Jackie Chan, Lee Reynolds, Susan Chan • *Stunt Co-ordinator* Jackie Chan

Jackie Stewart: Weekend of a Champion ★★★★

Documentary 1971 · UK · Colour · 80mins

Formula One fans musn't miss this excellent and sometimes quirky profile of Jackie Stewart as he prepares for the Monaco Grand Prix in 1971, the year he won his second World Championship. The film was produced by Roman Polanski – like Stewart, one of the smart set and a racing fanatic who wanders around the pits and the track, getting the inside story. Way above the standard of the usual sports documentary, it probes the mind and the frayed nervous system of a racing driver, and vividly captures the mad F1 circus at its most glamorous venue. AT

Dir/Scr Frank Simon

Jacknife ★★★ 15

Drama 1988 · US · Colour · 98mins

Robert De Niro returns to the traumas of Vietnam in this talky, yet engrossing, drama. He plays an ex-serviceman who has come to terms with the conflict, setting out to help his old friend Ed Harris, who is still deeply disturbed by his experiences of the war. Apart from a few, not entirely convincing, wartime flashbacks, director David Jones concentrates on the interplay between De Niro and Harris, and they both make the most of Stephen Metcalfe's perceptive script. A modest, rewarding experience. JF. Contains swearing. [VIDEO] DVD

Robert De Niro *Joseph "Megs" Megessey* • Ed Harris *Dave* • Kathy Baker *Martha* • Charles S Dutton *Jake* • Elizabeth Franz *Pru Buckman* • Tom Isbell *Bobby Buckman* • Loudon Wainwright III *Ferretti* • Sloane Shelton *Shirley* ■ *Dir* David Jones (3) • *Scr* Stephen Metcalfe, from his play *Strange Snow*

The Jackpot ★★★ U

Comedy 1950 · US · BW · 86mins

James Stewart wins a cash bonanza on a radio quiz show and finds that his life changes in many unexpected ways. To his dismay, he discovers he has to sell the prizes to pay the taxes on them. Lightweight comedy fluff, still timely in the National Lottery era, with Stewart turning on his effortless charm to lift the innocent fun up a few likeable notches. AJ

James Stewart *Bill Lawrence* • Barbara Hale *Amy Lawrence* • James Gleason *Harry Summers* • Fred Clark *Mr Woodruff* • Alan Mowbray *Leslie* • Patricia Medina *Hilda Jones* • Natalie Wood *Phyllis Lawrence* • Tommy Rettig *Tommy Lawrence* ■ *Dir* Walter Lang • *Scr* Phoebe Ephron, Henry Ephron, from an article by John McNulty

Jackpot ★★★

Drama 2001 · US · Colour · 100mins

From the Polish brothers, this – like its central protagonists – never quite gets going. Singer Jon Gries and manager Garrett Morris cruise the karaoke circuit hoping for fame and gain – turning in con tricks and zippy conversation. Gries has deserted his wife Daryl Hannah and child, sending home a weekly lottery ticket as child support. We've seen this all before in Bruce Paltrow's *Duets*, though this is less mainstream and more slick. LH

Jon Gries [Jonathan Gries] *Sunny Holiday* • Daryl Hannah *Bobbi* • Garrett Morris *Lester "Les" Irving* • Adam Baldwin *Mel James* • Peggy Lipton *Janice* • Mac Davis *Sammy Bones* ■ *Dir* Michael Polish • *Scr* Michael Polish, Mark Polish

Jack's Back ★★ 18

Mystery thriller 1988 · US · Colour · 92mins

James Spader enjoys himself in dual roles in this modern, nasty spin on the Jack the Ripper story. The setting is 1980s Los Angeles, where the Victorian serial killer's crimes are being visited upon a new generation. When suspicion falls on Spader, his twin brother (Spader again) sets out to prove the authorities wrong. The improbable plotting might raise some eyebrows, but director Rowdy Herrington summons up a fair amount of suspense. JF [VIDEO]

James Spader *John/Rick Wesford* • Cynthia Gibb *Christine Moscari* • Rod Loomis *Dr Sidney Tannerson* • Rex Ryon *Jack Pendler* • Robert Picardo *Dr Carlos Battera* • Jim Haynie *Sergeant Gabriel* • Wendell Wright *Captain Walter Prentis* ■ *Dir/Scr* Rowdy Herrington

Jackson County Jail ★★★★

Crime drama 1976 · US · Colour · 83mins

A stunning example of exploitation, artfully using the genre's stark conventions to make cogent comments on society. In one of her strongest roles, Yvette Mimieux plays an LA executive who has a disastrous encounter with southern "justice" after she is beaten up by hitch-hikers en route to New York. Michael Miller directs his gripping feminist B-movie with raw-edged grit and a clear eye for action, while co-star Tommy Lee Jones backs up Mimieux to the hilt. Upsetting, but highly recommended. AJ. Contains violence and swearing.

Yvette Mimieux *Dinah Hunter* • Tommy Lee Jones *Coley Blake* • Robert Carradine *Bobby Ray* • Frederic Cook *Hobie* • Severn Darden *Sheriff Dempsey* • Nan Martin *Allison* • Mary Woronov *Pearl* • Howard Hesseman *David* ■ *Dir* Michael Miller (2) • *Scr* Donald Stewart

Jacob ★★★ PG

Biblical drama
1994 · US/It/Ger · Colour · 90mins

Old Testament movies are invariably overwritten affairs in which reverence for the source stilts the drama. Here, screenwriter Lionel Chetwynd can't resist the grandiose language, but he makes a decent job of packing what is a sprawling and, at times, improbable tale into this TV movie. Filmed in Morocco, the story of Jacob's feud with his brother Esau, his complicated love life in exile and his eventual return and renaming, is directed with gravitas by Peter Hall. Matthew Modine brings charm to the title role. DP [VIDEO] DVD

Matthew Modine *Jacob* • Lara Flynn Boyle *Rachel* • Sean Bean *Esau* • Joss Ackland *Isaac* • Juliet Aubrey *Leah* • Irene Papas *Rebekah* • Giancarlo Giannini *Laban* ■ *Dir* Peter Hall • *Scr* Lionel Chetwynd

Jacob the Liar ★★★

Second World War comedy drama
1974 · E Ger · Colour · 95mins

Czech actor Vlastimil Brodsky received the 1975 Berlin Film Festival Silver Bear for his mesmerising performance in the title role of this moving film. It tells of a man who survives the nightmare of a Polish ghetto, helping others to do the same. Brodsky's dilemma stems from hearing news about a Russian advance via a Nazi radio. Fearful of telling about his clandestine spying, he pretends to have a radio, slowly building stories around his scant information to create the greatest commodity available to those in captivity – hope. Remade in 1999, with Robin Williams as Jakob. BB. In German with English subtitles.

Vlastimil Brodsky *Jacob* • Erwin Geschonneck *Kowalski* • Manuela Simon *Lina* • Henry Hübchen *Mischa* • Blanche Kommerell *Rosa* • Armin Mueller-Stahl *Roman Schtamm* ■ *Dir* Frank Beyer • *Scr* Jurek Becker, from his novel *Jakob der Lügner*

Jacob Two Two Meets the Hooded Fang ★★★

Fantasy 1999 · Can · Colour · 96mins

It was not going to be easy to translate a children's book, written in verse, to the screen (there was a previous attempt in 1977) but this is a nice attempt, made more enjoyable by an accomplished cast. Little Jacob (Max Morrow) who repeats everything twice, hence his nickname gets into trouble and is sent to the horrible children's prison island, which is ruled by the Hooded Fang (Gary Busey). It's a pantomime-style tale, and adults brought along for the ride will at least have fun spotting familiar actors in bizarre and silly roles. JB

Gary Busey *The Hooded Fang* • Miranda Richardson *Miss Fowl* • Ice-T *Justice Rough* • Mark McKinney *Mr Fish* • Max Morrow *Jacob Two Two* • Maury Chaykin *Louis Loser* ■ *Dir* George Bloomfield • *Scr* Tim Burns, from the novel *Jacob Two Two Meets the Hooded Fang* by Mordecai Richler

Jacob's Ladder ★★ 15

Horror thriller 1990 · US · Colour · 108mins

What's causing Vietnam veteran Tim Robbins's nightmare hallucinations as he wanders New York trying to figure out their mystical meaning? Although this assembly of horror clichés is tautly scripted by *Ghost* writer Bruce Joel Rubin, director Adrian Lyne orchestrates his satanic flashdance into a slightly pretentious mess of distorted *Platoon* images and Biblical red herrings. AJ. Contains violence, swearing and nudity. [VIDEO] DVD

Tim Robbins *Jacob Singer* • Elizabeth Peña *Jezzie* • Danny Aiello *Louis* • Matt Craven *Michael* • Pruitt Taylor Vince *Paul* • Jason Alexander *Donald Geary* • Macaulay Culkin *Gabe* • Eriq La Salle *Frank* ■ *Dir* Adrian Lyne • *Scr* Bruce Joel Rubin

Jacqueline ★★ U

Drama 1956 · UK · BW · 89mins

With good intentions endlessly lapsing into self-pity, John Gregson overdoes the pathos as the shipyard worker who is plunged into the depths of despair when he loses his job as a result of vertigo. There's a similar lack of restraint about Jacqueline Ryan (whose mother, Kathleen, co-stars) as the daughter who tries to land him a farm job. Although it was based on the novel *A Grand Man*, this mawkish melodrama owes more to the films of Shirley Temple than the imagination of Catherine Cookson. DP [VIDEO]

John Gregson *Mike McNeil* • Kathleen Ryan *Elizabeth McNeil* • Jacqueline Ryan *Jacqueline McNeil* • Noel Purcell *Mr Owen* • Cyril Cusack *Mr Flannagan* • Maureen Swanson *Maggie* • Tony Wright *Jack McBride* • Liam Redmond *Mr Lord* • Maureen Delaney *Mrs McBride* ■ *Dir* Roy Baker [Roy Ward Baker] • *Scr* Patrick Kirwan, Liam O'Flaherty, Patrick Campbell, Catherine Cookson, from the novel *A Grand Man* by Catherine Cookson

Jacquot de Nantes ★★★★★ PG

Biographical drama
1991 · Fr · Colour and BW · 114mins

Agnès Varda's tribute to her late husband, Jacques Demy, was considered too cosy and sentimental in some quarters. But this is a genuinely fond and often moving portrait of the film-maker as a young man. The sequences depicting how Demy painstakingly created his earliest animated efforts are compelling and superbly convey the nascent passion for cinema that would result in such classics as *The Umbrellas of Cherbourg*. It's to Varda's credit that the film works both as biography and drama, but perhaps her finest achievement is in coaxing such a charming performance out of the inexperienced Philippe Maron. DP. In French with English subtitles.

Philippe Maron *Jacquot 1* • Eduoard Joubeaud *Jacquot 2* • Laurent Monnier *Jacquot 3* • Brigitte De Villepoix *Marilou, Mother* • Daniel Dublet *Raymond, Father* • Clement Delaroche *Yvon 1* ■ *Dir* Agnès Varda • *Scr* Agnès Varda, from a story by Jacques Demy

Jade ★ 18

Erotic thriller 1995 · US · Colour · 91mins

William Friedkin's slick direction can't hide the trashy heart of this Joe Eszterhas scripted one-dimensional psycho thriller, which *NYPD Blue* TV actor David Caruso banked on to make him a star. No such luck. He's the assistant district attorney taking on the case of old flame Linda Fiorentino, a clinical psychologist who might be leading a double life as a murderous prostitute. Chazz Palminteri is the third part of a murky triangle. No one emerges with credit from this absurd farrago. AJ. Contains violence, sex scenes and swearing.

David Caruso *David Corelli* • Linda Fiorentino *Trina Gavin* • Chazz Palminteri *Matt Gavin* • Richard Crenna *Governor Edwards* • Michael Biehn *Bob Hargrove* • Donna Murphy *Karen Heller* ■ *Dir* William Friedkin • *Scr* Joe Eszterhas

The Jade Mask ★★ U

Mystery 1945 · US · BW · 63mins

Having previously provided stereotypical light relief, African-American stalwart Mantan Moreland finally became Sidney Toler's official chauffeur in the fourth of Monogram's cheaply proficient Charlie Chan mysteries. Edwin Luke, younger brother of Keye Luke, takes over as son Tommy, and is on hand as the Chinese sleuth investigates the murder of a much-detested scientist, who was conducting experiments into reinforced wood. This should have been a rattling good yarn, but director Phil Rosen permits too much comic schtick to sustain the tension. DP DVD

Sidney Toler *Charlie Chan* • Mantan Moreland *Birmingham Brown* • Edwin Luke *Tommy* • Janet Warren *Jean* • Edith Evanson *Louise* • Hardie Albright *Meeker* • Frank Reicher *Harper* ■ *Dir* Phil Rosen • *Scr* George Callahan, from characters created by Earl Derr Biggers

Jagged Edge ★★★★ 18

Thriller 1985 · US · Colour · 104mins

Because writer Joe Eszterhas has continually reworked the same basic formula (hero/heroine falls for murder suspect), it's easy to forget how startling the scenario was when it was first employed in this compelling thriller. Glenn Close is the defence attorney haunted by a case from her past when the wrong man went to jail, who falls in love with her client (Jeff Bridges), a charming publisher accused of brutally murdering his wife. Director Richard Marquand never misses a beat, gleefully tossing in red herrings and keeping the viewer constantly wondering whether Bridges is innocent or guilty. It remains an enthralling, if incredible, ride. JF. Contains violence, swearing and brief nudity. DVD

Jeff Bridges *Jack Forrester* • Glenn Close *Teddy Barnes* • Peter Coyote *Thomas Krasny* • Robert Loggia *Sam Ransom* • John Dehner *Judge Carrigan* • Lance Henriksen *Frank Martin* • Leigh Taylor-Young *Virginia Howell* • Marshall Colt *Bobby Slade* ■ *Dir* Richard Marquand • *Scr* Joe Eszterhas

Jaguar Lives! ★ 15

Martial arts action
1979 · US · Colour · 82mins

The kung fu craze had long since expired by the time this lacklustre 007 spoof hit cinemas. Falling into the "never-heard-of-him" category is Joe Lewis as Jaguar, an agent skilled in hand-to-hand combat who sets out to smash an international drug ring, while three former Bond villains – Donald Pleasence, Christopher Lee and Joseph Wiseman – ham it up. Director Ernest Pintoff was originally a cartoonist; it should be back to the drawing board for him. RS

Joe Lewis (1) *Jonathan Cross/Jaguar* • Christopher Lee *Adam Caine* • Donald Pleasence *General Villanova* • Barbara Bach *Anna* • Capucine *Zina Vanacore* • Joseph Wiseman *Ben Ashir* • Woody Strode *Sensei* ■ *Dir* Ernest Pintoff • *Scr* Yabo Yablonsky

Jail Bait ★★ PG

Crime 1954 · US · BW · 68mins

Despite the sexploitation title, schlockmeister Ed Wood Jr's follow-up to his legendary *Glen or Glenda* is an unusual crime melodrama with a surprise ending. Gangster Timothy Farrell coerces the plastic surgeon father of the accomplice he's killed to alter his face so he can avoid detection. Like every Wood film, the facts behind it are more entertaining than actually watching it: Bela Lugosi was too ill to play the surgeon so silent star Herbert Rawlinson took over only to die the day after filming, while future *Hercules* star Steve Reeves makes his feature debut. AJ

Lyle Talbot *Inspector Johns* • Dolores Fuller *Marilyn Gregor* • Steve Reeves *Lieutenant Bob Lawrence* • Herbert Rawlinson *Dr Boris Gregor* • Theodora Thurman *Loretta* • Timothy Farrell *Vic Brady* ■ *Dir* Edward D Wood Jr • *Scr* Alex Gordon, Edward D Wood Jr

Jail Bait ★★★

Drama 1972 · W Ger · Colour · 100mins

Franz-Xaver Kroetz so despised this adaptation of his play that he gained an injunction forcing director Rainer Werner Fassbinder to remove two scenes he felt particularly betrayed his characters. Ultimately, Fassbinder made a show of disowning it himself, but this flawed film (which was originally made for German television) is far from a failure.Teenage lust and the chasm between the generations are the central themes, but this is also a homage to Hollywood's rebellious youth pictures of the 1950s. A boy is sent to prison for a sexual relationship with an underage girl, but continues it on his release. The violence and treachery are shocking, but perhaps the most disturbing aspect is the ease with which fascist values were still being disseminated among the lower middle-classes of Germany at the time. DP. In German with English subtitles.

Eva Mattes *Hanni Schneider* • Harry Baer *Franz Bermeier* • Jorg von Liebenfels *Erwin Schneider, Hanni's father* • Ruth Drexel *Hilda Schneider, Hanni's mother* ■ *Dir* Rainer Werner Fassbinder • *Scr* Rainer Werner Fassbinder, from the play by Franz-Xaver Kroetz

Jail Busters ★★ U

Prison comedy 1955 · US · BW · 61mins

The Bowery Boys were getting a bit long in the tooth and their routines had grown beards, but that didn't stop them churning out four low-budget comedies a year with undiminished energy in the mid-1950s. Here, three of the team put themselves behind bars to help a reporter expose corruption. An attempt by the prison psychiatrist to interview Huntz Hall is predictably amusing. AE

Huntz Hall *Horace Debussy "Sach" Jones* • Leo Gorcey *Terrence Aloysius "Slip" Mahoney* • Bernard Gorcey *Louie Dumbrowski* • Barton MacLane *Guard Jenkins* • Anthony Caruso *Ed Lannigan* • Percy Helton *Warden BW Oswald* ■ *Dir* William Beaudine • *Scr* Edward Bernds, Elwood Ullman

Jailbreak ★★

Thriller 1997 · US · Colour · 89mins

Executive produced by Roger Corman, this lives up to his reputation for no-nonsense, fast-moving, low-budget entertainment. It also bears the Corman hallmark by virtue of the fact that it vaguely resembles his earlier *Jackson County Jail* (1976), in which the wrongfully arrested Yvette Mimieux went on the run with suspected killer Tommy Lee Jones. Ally Sheedy and David Carradine step into the roles for director Victoria Muspratt, who keeps the action brisk and bruising. DP. Contains violence, swearing and a sex scene.

Ally Sheedy *Susan Reed* • David Carradine *Coley* • Charles Napier *Sheriff Dempsey* • Todd Kimsey *Hobie* ■ *Dir* Victoria Muspratt • *Scr* Victoria Muspratt, Donald Stewart II [Donald E Stewart]

The Jailbreakers ★

Crime drama 1960 · US · BW · 63mins

This utterly predictable bargain-basement melodrama is something of a one-man effort, with Alex Grasshoff producing as well as directing from his own script, which pits Robert Hutton and Mary Castle against a gang of escaped convicts who have fetched up in a ghost town to search for their $400,000 stash. DP

Robert Hutton *Tom* • Mary Castle *June* • Michael O'Connell *Lake* • Gabe Delutri *Joe* • Anton Van Stralen *Steam* • Toby Hill *Karen* ■ *Dir/Scr* Alex Grasshoff

Jailhouse Rock ★★★★ U

Musical drama 1957 · US · BW · 97mins

This is Elvis Presley's glorious third movie, after *Love Me Tender* and *Loving You*, when the snarl and talent were for once harnessed to a suitable plot under the experienced direction of MGM veteran Richard Thorpe. Presley plays an ex-con whose subsequent Hollywood success goes to his head, causing former cellmate Mickey Shaughnessy to lay him flat with a blow to his money-spinning larynx. Elvis here reveals an acting talent on a par with that of James Dean, only previously hinted at in his first two movies. TS DVD

Elvis Presley *Vince Everett* • Judy Tyler *Peggy Van Alden* • Mickey Shaughnessy *Hunk Houghton* • Vaughn Taylor *Mr Shores* • Jennifer Holden *Sherry Wilson* • Dean Jones *Teddy Talbot* • Anne Neyland *Laury Jackson* • Mike Stoller *Pianist* ■ *Dir* Richard Thorpe • *Scr* Guy Trosper, from a story by Ned Young

Jake Speed ★★ 15

Comedy adventure
1986 · US · Colour · 100mins

This is a barely acceptable rip-off of *Romancing the Stone* and *Raiders of the Lost Ark*, with a girl who vanishes in Paris and the fictional, paperback detective who sets out to find her. While Karen Kopins as the girl's sister and Wayne Crawford are hardly a match for Kathleen Turner and Michael Douglas, the white-slave-trader villain gives John Hurt ample opportunity to go way over the top. No new clichés here, as Sam Goldwyn might have said, but a certain self-conscious style. AT

Wayne Crawford *Jake Speed* • Dennis Christopher *Desmond Floyd* • Karen Kopins *Margaret Winston* • John Hurt *Sid* • Leon Ames *Pop* ■ *Dir* Andrew Lane • *Scr* Wayne Crawford, Andrew Lane

Jakob the Liar ★★ 12

Second World War comedy drama
1999 · US · Colour · 116mins

The more Robin Williams lays on the schmaltz, the fewer tears we shed in response. As Jakob, a fantasist living in a Jewish ghetto in war-torn Poland, he pulls out all the emotional stops but the result falls far short of tragic resonance. Overhearing a suggestion that all is going badly on the German front, Jakob finds he has to keep feeding his eager compatriots morsels of hope. Such fine actors as Armin Mueller-Stahl and Alan Arkin are enmeshed in a web of optimistic deceit that soon becomes as unconvincing as Williams himself. TH. DVD

Robin Williams *Jakob Heym* • Alan Arkin *Frankfurter* • Bob Balaban *Kowalsky* • Hannah Taylor Gordon *Lina* • Michael Jeter *Avron* • Armin Mueller-Stahl *Professor Kirschbaum* • Liev Schreiber *Mischa* • Nina Siemaszko *Rosa Frankfurter* ■ *Dir* Peter Kassovitz • *Scr* Peter Kassovitz, Didier Decoin, from the book *Jakob der Lügner* by Jurek Becker

Jalopy ★★ U

Comedy 1953 · US · BW · 61mins

Another in the long line of Bowery Boys pictures, which offered cheap laughs and a few thrills. This time the streetwise "boys", now well into their 30s, led as usual by Leo Gorcey – a tough, pug-nosed, little punk – and the tall and gormless Huntz Hall, enter an auto race after discovering a type of super fuel. The Bowery Boys, who averaged four features a year, continued with this sort of harmless nonsense throughout the 1950s. RB

Leo Gorcey *Terrence Aloysius "Slip" Mahoney* • Huntz Hall *Horace Debussy "Sach" Jones* • Bernard Gorcey *Louie Dumbrowski* • Robert Lowery *Skid Wilson* • Leon Belasco *Professor Bosgood Elrod* • Richard Benedict *Tony Lango* ■ *Dir* William Beaudine • *Scr* Tim Ryan, Jack Crutcher, Edmond Seward Jr, Bert Lawrence, from a story by Tim Ryan, Jack Crutcher

Jamaica Inn ★★ PG

Period adventure 1939 · UK · BW · 94mins

Alfred Hitchcock's last picture before his departure for Hollywood is the least of his three Daphne du Maurier adaptations (*Rebecca* and *The Birds* being the others). Charles Laughton's self-indulgent performance as the piratical squire goes some way to explaining the film's failure, but Hitch's lack of interest in the character's dual nature is mostly to blame. It isn't a completely lost cause, however: Maureen O'Hara is spirited yet vulnerable, while art director Tom N Moraham's reconstruction of Regency Cornwall brings a touch of authenticity to an otherwise lacklustre production. DP DVD

Charles Laughton *Sir Humphrey Pengallan* • Maureen O'Hara *Mary Yelland* • Leslie Banks *Joss Merlyn* • Emlyn Williams *Harry the Peddler* • Robert Newton *Jem Trehearne* • Wylie Watson *Salvation Watkins* ■ *Dir* Alfred Hitchcock • *Scr* Sidney Gilliat, Joan Harrison, JB Priestley, Alma Reville, from the novel *Jamaica Inn* by Daphne du Maurier

Jamaica Run ★★ U

Adventure 1953 · US · Colour · 92mins

Ray Milland – who never quite cut it as an action-romantic hero – skippers a schooner in the Caribbean, courting Arlene Dahl whose family live in a great mansion on Jamaica. But it seems that the provenance of the estate is in doubt and may lie at the bottom of the sea, locked in a shipwreck. Pitched as a straightforward action film, it has some good points: location shooting, a competently handled underwater fight and a splendidly Gothic episode when the house erupts in flames. AT

Ray Milland *Patrick Fairlie* • Arlene Dahl *Ena Dacey* • Wendell Corey *Todd Dacey* • Patric Knowles *William Montague* • Laura Elliot *Janice Clayton* ■ *Dir* Lewis R Foster • *Scr* Lewis R Foster, from the novel *The Neat Little Corpse* by Max Murray

Jamboree ★★ U

Musical drama 1957 · US · BW · 85mins

Jerry Lee Lewis belting out *Great Balls of Fire* is the main reason to catch this clumsy attempt to cash in on the rock 'n' roll boom of the late 1950s. The pretence of a story a routine affair, with Kay Medford's would-be hip agent trying to break up pop hopefuls Paul Carr and Freda Holloway, as she thinks a double act would damage Carr's sex symbol prospects. The mixed-race nature of the guest list is noteworthy, with Count Basie and Fats Domino billed alongside Carl Perkins, Connie Francis and Frankie Avalon. DP

Kay Medford *Grace Shaw* • Bob Pastine *Lew Arthur* • Paul Carr *Pete Porter* • Freda Holloway *Honey Wynn* • David King-Wood *Warren Sykes* • Jean Martin *Cindy Styles* ■ *Dir* Roy Lockwood • *Scr* Leonard Kantor, Milton Subotsky • *Cinematographer* Jack Etra

James and the Giant Peach ★★★★ U

Animated fantasy adventure
1996 · US · Colour · 85mins

For a writer of children's stories, Roald Dahl undoubtedly had a dark imagination. Here, though, there will only be squeals of delight as James and his insect allies escape from a killer shark, skeleton pirates and a couple of awful aunts as they ride a giant peach to the city where dreams come true. It took three years to combine the live-action sequences with state-of-the-art model animation, and the latter is greatly assisted by the personality-packed voices of Susan Sarandon, Richard Dreyfuss, Simon Callow and David Thewlis. However, it's Joanna Lumley and Miriam Margolyes as the ghastly Spiker and Sponge who steal this wonderfully pantomimic show. DP DVD

Paul Terry *James* • Joanna Lumley *Aunt Spiker* • Miriam Margolyes *Aunt Sponge* • Pete Postlethwaite *Old Man* • Simon Callow *Grasshopper* • Richard Dreyfuss *Centipede* • Jane Leeves *Ladybug* • Susan Sarandon *Spider* • David Thewlis *Earthworm* ■ *Dir* Henry Selick • *Scr* Steven Bloom, Jonathan Roberts, from the novel by Roald Dahl

James Baldwin: the Price of the Ticket ★★★ PG

Documentary 1989 · US · Colour · 86mins

James Baldwin was born black, poor and homosexual, yet he became one of the most celebrated American writers and civil rights activists of his up-tight era. Combining his expressive and controversial public speeches with rare archive footage, home movies and the recollections of his close friends and family (including interviews with his brother David, and writers Maya Angelou and William Styron), director Karen Thorsen provides a powerful and moving document into his life, works and beliefs, which skilfully puts across his insightful mind and keen, irrepressible spirit. AJ

Dir Karen Thorsen

James Dean ★★★ 12

Biographical drama
2001 · US · Colour · 91mins

Brad Pitt, Johnny Depp and Leonardo DiCaprio were variously linked with this TV biopic of the ultimate troubled teen. But director Mark Rydell could not have chosen better than James Franco, who follows in the tragic star's Method footsteps and truly lives the part. Whether clashing with his father (Michael Moriarty) or pushing the boundaries of screen acting with Elia Kazan (Enrico Colantoni) and Nicholas Ray (Barry Primus), Franco captures the edginess that made Dean's highly personal style so unique. It's just a shame that the tone becomes increasingly gossipy. DP

James Franco *James Dean/Narrator* • Michael Moriarty *Winton Dean* • Valentina Cervi *Pier Angeli* • Enrico Colantoni *Elia Kazan* • Edward Herrmann *Raymond Massey* • Joanne Linville *Hedda Hopper* • Barry Primus *Nicholas Ray* ■ *Dir* Mark Rydell • *Scr* Israel Horovitz

The James Dean Story ★★ PG

Documentary 1957 · US · BW · 79mins

An early film from Robert Altman (co-directing with George W George) it relates the now familiar story of the 1950s star, who died too young after starring in only three movies. It makes use of archive material in a way that tries to inject drama into the documentary process – there's a stylised depiction of the fatal car crash – but because there's very little revelation, the overall effect is one of a boring whitewash. TH DVD

Martin Gabel *Narrator* ■ *Dir* George W George, Robert Altman • *Scr* Stewart Stern

James Dean – the First American Teenager ★★★ 15

Documentary 1975 · UK · Colour · 77mins

Writer/director Ray Connolly, who sprayed *Stardust* with sharp pop insights, here unravels the James Dean legend with an attractive mixture of objectivity and affection. Without resorting to cheap sentimentality, this documentary successfully deals with Dean's huge social impact and endurance as an icon, while also pinning down the facts of his life, and death. Interviews with colleagues and co-stars like Natalie Wood, Dennis Hopper and Sammy Davis Jr, as well as rare screen-test footage, provide added spice. JM

Stacy Keach *Narrator* ■ *Dir/Scr* Ray Connolly

The James Gang ★★ 15

Comedy drama
1997 · UK/Can · Colour · 94mins

A knowing soundtrack from Bernard Butler and gutsy performances from Helen McCrory and John Hannah are the only plus points in this willing, but otherwise sadly under-realised debut from director Mike Barker and screenwriter Stuart Hepburn. As the single mum who responds to a house fire by embarking on a hand-to-mouth crime spree, McCrory very nearly binds together the ramshackle sequence of stylised set pieces. DP. Contains swearing, nudity and sex scenes.

John Hannah *Spendlove James* • Helen McCrory *Bernadette James* • Jason Flemyng *Frank James* • Toni Collette *Julia Armstrong* • Darren Brownlie *Spendlove Jr* • David Brownlie *Spendlove Jr* • Lauren McMurray *Geraldine James* • Lauren McCracken *Jessica James* ■ *Dir* Mike Barker • *Scr* Stuart Hepburn, from an idea by Andrew Eaton, Paul Lee

Jamon Jamon ★★★★ 18

Erotic comedy drama
1992 · Sp · Colour · 90mins

Forget the over-hyped Pedro Almodóvar, director Bigas Luna represents the cutting edge of Spanish cinema with his witty exploration of flamenco love and desire. The first of a trilogy – completed by *Golden Balls* and *The Tit and the Moon* – Luna's frantic passion play rides a carnal carousel, with macho star discovery Javier Bardem posing in underwear, eating ham (*jamon*) and bullfighting in the nude. Call it paella porn or Andalucian art, it's entertaining and very hot stuff indeed. AJ. In Spanish with English subtitles. Contains violence, swearing and drug abuse DVD

Penélope Cruz *Silvia* • Anna Galiena *Carmen* • Javier Bardem *Raul* • Stefania Sandrelli *Conchita* • Juan Diego *Manuel* • Jordi Mollà *Jose Luis* ■ *Dir* Bigas Luna • *Scr* Cuca Canals, Bigas Luna

Jane and the Lost City ★ PG

Action adventure 1987 · UK · Colour · 88mins

The *Daily Mirror's* famous comic-strip heroine searches for lost diamonds, a lost city and a lost script somewhere in darkest Africa, in a painfully cheap comedy dredging the bottom of the *Carry On* barrel for its seaside postcard puns. Watching the accident-prone Jane lose her clothes in awkwardly telegraphed set-ups may keep some viewers attentive, but even Jasper Carrott, in no less than three unfunny roles, can't save this wretched effort from being anything other than a witless fiasco. AJ

Sam Jones *"Jungle Jack" Buck* • Maud Adams *Lola Pagola* • Jasper Carrott *Heinrich* • Kirsten Hughes *Jane* • Graham Stark *Tombs* • Robin Bailey *Colonel* • Ian Roberts *Carl Donner* ■ *Dir* Terry Marcel • *Scr* Mervyn Haisman, from a story by Mervyn Haisman, Terry Marcel, Harry Robertson, from characters in the *Jane* cartoon created by Norman Pettin in the *Daily Mirror*

Jane Austen in Manhattan ★★★ PG

Comedy 1980 · US/UK · Colour · 106mins

When an unknown playlet by Jane Austen is auctioned in New York, it's bought by a rich foundation and two directors fight for the right to produce it on stage – as an operetta or as a trendy piece of avant-garde. Never more than an arty contrivance, this James Ivory piece celebrates acting, performance and sheer eccentricity in a series of vignettes designed to indulge his cast. In this regard it's good to see Anne Baxter get probably her best role since *All about Eve*, in what was her final feature film. Meanwhile Sean Young makes her film debut as Ariadne Charlton. AT DVD

Anne Baxter *Lilianna Zorska* • Robert Powell *Pierre* • Michael Wager *George Midash* • Tim Choate *Jamie* • John Guerrasio *Gregory* • Katrina Hodiak *Katya* • Kurt R Johnson *Victor Charlton* • Sean Young *Ariadne Charlton* ■ *Dir* James Ivory • *Scr* Ruth Prawer Jhabvala, from the libretto *Sir Charles Grandison* by Jane Austen, Samuel Richardson • *Producer* Ismail Merchant

Jane Austen's Mafia ★★ 12

Spoof 1998 · US · Colour · 83mins

Jim Abrahams's Mafia spoof is in the same vein as his earlier hits *Airplane!* and *The Naked Gun*, with sadly similar jokes. That it works at all is only due to convincing performances from Olympia Dukakis, Jay Mohr, Christina Applegate and Lloyd Bridges, who plays a Don Corleone figure training his son (Mohr) to take over the family business. However, there comes a time when he's disposable, so fellow hoods send a temptress to woo Mohr away from his family and girlfriend (Applegate). LH . Contains swearing and some violence. DVD

Jay Mohr *Anthony Cortino* • Billy Burke *Joey Cortino* • Christina Applegate *Diane* • Pamela Gidley *Pepper Gianini* • Olympia Dukakis *Sophia* • Lloyd Bridges *Vincenzo Cortino* ■ *Dir* Jim Abrahams • *Scr* Jim Abrahams, Greg Norberg, Michael McManus

Jane Eyre ★★★★ PG

Period drama 1943 · US · BW · 96mins

British director Robert Stevenson has shown an unusual talent in his warmly sympathetic treatment of films about women. This typical 20th Century-Fox period melodrama is a fine example of his work, though many will persist in attributing the film's virtues to Orson Welles, who might have made a fine job of directing it, given the chance. Welles's Edward Rochester is suitably awesome, dominating his scenes (naturally), but, unfortunately, slowing the pace whenever he appears. Joan Fontaine is fine, though wan, in the title role. Watch for a young Elizabeth Taylor in a small but telling part early in the film. TS DVD

Orson Welles *Edward Rochester* • Joan Fontaine *Jane Eyre* • Margaret O'Brien *Adele* • Peggy Ann Garner *Jane, as a child* • John Sutton *Dr Rivers* • Sara Allgood *Bessie* • Henry Daniell *Brockelhurst* • Agnes Moorehead *Mrs Reed* • Elizabeth Taylor *Helen Burns* ■ *Dir* Robert Stevenson • *Scr* Aldous Huxley, Robert Stevenson, John Houseman, from the novel by Charlotte Brontë

Jane Eyre ★★★ PG

Period romantic drama
1996 · Fr/It/UK/US · Colour · 116mins

William Hurt's thoughtful, subdued interpretation of Mr Rochester makes its own gently neurotic contribution to the Brontë movie canon in Franco Zeffirelli's stylish and atmospheric take on the famous novel. Zeffirelli lays on sufficient simmering passion to make it interesting, yet at the same time brings the romantic longings of the two lead characters down to a more mundane, human level. Charlotte Gainsbourg was seen by some, however, as too fiery for the role of Jane. TH DVD

William Hurt *Rochester* • Charlotte Gainsbourg *Jane Eyre* • Joan Plowright *Mrs Fairfax* • Anna Paquin *Young Jane* • Geraldine Chaplin *Miss Scatcherd* • Billie Whitelaw *Grace Poole* • Maria Schneider *Mrs Rochester* • Fiona Shaw *Mrs Reed* • Elle Macpherson *Blanche Ingram* ■ *Dir* Franco Zeffirelli • *Scr* Hugh Whitemore, Franco Zeffirelli, from the novel by Charlotte Brontë

J

Janice Beard 45 WPM ★★★★ 15

Romantic comedy
1999 · UK · Colour · 77mins

Clare Kilner's highly impressive debut feature is quirky, original and extremely touching. Scottish newcomer Eileen Walsh stars as Janice, a plain Jane whose life revolves around her attempts to get her severely agoraphobic mother out the front door. In desperation, Janice heads for London and a temp job under the not-so-kind eye of a bitchy Patsy Kensit. There she develops a relationship with postboy Rhys Ifans and becomes unwittingly embroiled in a plot to steal vital documents from her company. The retro look, innovative cinematography and spot-on script combine to make a film brimming with humour and heart. LH DVD

Rhys Ifans *Sean* • Patsy Kensit *Julia* • David O'Hara *O'Brien* • Eileen Walsh *Janice Beard* • Sandra Voe *Mimi* • Frances Gray *Violet* • Zita Sattar *Jane* • Amelia Curtis *June* ■ *Dir* Clare Kilner • *Scr* Clare Kilner, Ben Hopkins

The January Man ★★★ 15

Crime thriller 1989 · US · Colour · 97mins

Kevin Kline is eminently watchable in this gritty thriller as the ex-New York cop brought back on to the force to track down a serial killer. Among the heavyweight supporting cast, Susan Sarandon stands out, and this even boasts a screenplay by Oscar-winning *Moonstruck* writer John Patrick Shanley. Given the talent at his disposal, director Pat O'Connor should have turned in a much better movie, but, even though this doesn't quite live up to its promise, it's still very entertaining. SH DVD

Kevin Kline *Nick Starkey* • Susan Sarandon *Christine Starkey* • Mary Elizabeth Mastrantonio *Bernadette Flynn* • Harvey Keitel *Frank Starkey* • Danny Aiello *Captain Vincent Alcoa* • Rod Steiger *Mayor Eamon Flynn* • Alan Rickman *Ed* • Faye Grant *Allison Hawkins* ■ *Dir* Pat O'Connor • *Scr* John Patrick Shanley

Japanese Story ★★★★ 15

Romantic drama
2003 · Aus/UK · Colour · 101mins

Sue Brooks's emotionally devastating film starts out as a relatively unpromising culture-clash romance, before becoming something unexpectedly profound. Geologist Toni Collette is saddled with an initially arrogant and cold Japanese businessman (Gotaro Tsunashima) for a research trip into the hostile Australian outback. Forced to survive a night in the freezing desert, an odd but tender relationship develops between the two. But then the drama suddenly shifts gear, forcing viewers to re-evaluate both their own basic assumptions and those of the characters. Carefully constructed, intelligent and well-acted. AS. Contains swearing and sex scenes. DVD

Toni Collette *Sandy Edwards* • Gotaro Tsunashima *Tachibana Hiromitsu* • Matthew Dyktynski *Bill Baird* • Lynette Curran *Mum* • Yumiko Tanaka *Yukiko Hiromitsu* • Kate Atkinson *Jackie* • Bill Young *Jimmy Smithers* ■ *Dir* Sue Brooks • *Scr* Alison Tilson

Japanese War Bride ★★

Drama 1952 · US · BW · 90mins

Shirley Yamaguchi plays the Japanese nurse who falls in love with Don Taylor, the American soldier she nurses back to health in Korea. Unfortunately, life at home in their Californian farming community isn't so harmonious, as Yamaguchi is almost destroyed by the hostility she faces. Although Marie Windsor is on her best vindictive form as the husband's jealous sister-in-law, this is a low pressure effort from director King Vidor. AE

Shirley Yamaguchi *Tae Shimizu* • Don Taylor *Jim Sterling* • Cameron Mitchell *Art Sterling* • Marie Windsor *Fran Sterling* • James Bell *Ed Sterling* • Louise Lorimer *Harriet Sterling* ■ *Dir* King Vidor • *Scr* Catherine Turney, from a story by Anson Bond

Japón ★★★ 18

Drama
2002 · Mex/Sp/Neth/Ger · Colour · 127mins

There is much to admire in writer/director Carlos Reygadas's debut feature, from the strikingly photographed landscapes to the considered exploration of both faith in modern Mexico and human frailty in isolation. The disparate elements don't quite coalesce into a satisfying story, but the relationship between widow Magdalena Flores and artist Alejandro Ferretis (who has ventured into the wilderness to commit suicide) is both touching and powerful in its simplicity, as she seeks to save his soul and he strives to prevent her grasping nephew from repossessing the hillside shack that's her world. DP. In Spanish with English subtitles. DVD

Alejandro Ferretis *The man* • Magdalena Flores *Ascen* • Yolanda Villa *Sabina* • Martin Serrano *Juan Luis* • Rolando Hernández *The judge* • Bernabé Pérez *The singer* • Fernando Benitez *Fernando* ■ *Dir/Scr* Carlos Reygadas

Jarrapellejos ★★★

Period drama 1987 · Sp · Colour · 107mins

For once including the all-too-human village priest among the oppressed, this is an involved and involving melodrama. Faithfully re-creating the atmosphere of rural Spain around 1910, Antonio Giménez-Rico weaves this story of aristocratic covetousness and corruption with a steady hand. Antonio Ferrandis gives a strutting performance as the lustful landowner willing to abuse the law and destroy reputations to satiate his lust and keep his reckless nephew out of trouble. Juan Diego is equally impressive as the artist/teacher, whose love for Aitana Sanchez-Gijon leads to her tragic and brutally depicted death. DP. In Spanish with English subtitles.

Antonio Ferrandis • Juan Diego • Lydia Bosch • Aitana Sanchez-Gijon ■ *Dir* Antonio Giménez-Rico • *Scr* Antonio Giménez-Rico, Manuel Gutierrez Aragon

Jason and the Argonauts ★★★ U

Fantasy adventure
1963 · UK · Colour · 99mins

In this lively adventure based on the Greek myth, a wooden Todd Armstrong sails in search of the Golden Fleece, encountering gods, demons and Honor Blackman playing chess with the destiny of men. Special-effects epics, masterminded by Ray Harryhausen, thrilled adults as well as children who were too young for Hammer horrors and Japanese monster movies. The tepid colour is a drawback, the stirring music by Bernard Herrmann a plus. AT DVD

Todd Armstrong *Jason* • Nancy Kovack *Medea* • Gary Raymond *Acastus* • Laurence Naismith *Argus* • Niall MacGinnis *Zeus* • Michael Gwynn *Hermes* • Jack Gwillim *King Aeëtes* • Honor Blackman *Hera* ■ *Dir* Don Chaffey • *Scr* Jan Reed, Beverly Cross

Jason Goes to Hell: the Final Friday ★★★ 18

Horror 1993 · US · Colour · 84mins

The spirit of Jason Voorhees is whisked back to Crystal Lake via a series of deadly soul transferences in director Adam Marcus's affectionate milking of *Friday the 13th* imagery, hewn from the past eight chapters and cleverly turned inside out for a new, improved joy ride. Affectionately witty, inventively shocking and shot through with a gleaming high-tone style, Marcus delivers the slasher goods and supplies edge-of-the-seat thrills on a par with the original film. A tenth instalment, *Jason X*, was released in 2002. AJ DVD

John D LeMay *Steven Freeman* • Kari Keegan *Jessica Kimble* • Kane Hodder *Jason Voorhees* • Steven Williams *Creighton Duke* • Steven Culp *Robert Campbell* • Erin Gray *Diana Kimble* • Rusty Schwimmer *Joey B* ■ *Dir* Adam Marcus • *Scr* Dean Lorey, Jay Huguely, from a story by Adam Marcus, Jay Huguely

Jason X ★★★ 15

Science-fiction action horror
2001 · US · Colour · 87mins

In 2455, student archaeologists return to the toxic wasteland of "Old Earth" and discover a hockey-masked body frozen in a cryogenic chamber. But on the journey back to "New Earth" with their find, Jason thaws out and returns to his old stalk-and-slash tricks aboard the spaceship. Director Jason Isaac's solid entry in the classic gore series is a treat for fans. AJ. Contains violence and swearing. DVD

Kane Hodder *Jason* • Lexa Doig *Rowan* • Lisa Ryder *KAY-EM 14* • Chuck Campbell *Tsunaron* • Jonathan Potts *Professor Lowe* • Peter Mensah *Sgt Brodski* • Melyssa Ade *Janessa* • Melody Johnson *Kinsa* • David Cronenberg *Dr Wimmer* ■ *Dir* Jim Isaac [James Isaac] • *Scr* Todd Farmer, from the character created by Victor Miller

Jason's Lyric ★★★ 18

Drama 1994 · US · Colour · 115mins

Directed by Doug McHenry, this curiously old-fashioned film attempts to put a new slant on the African-American experience. Although it revisits the familiar "going bad in the ghetto" theme, this feels more like a Hollywood problem picture of the late 1940s than an explosion of justifiable anger. This is mostly down to the fact that McHenry places as much emphasis on Allen Payne's sweet romance with Jada Pinkett as he does on his relationship with tearaway brother Bokeem Woodbine, who seems to have inherited the troubled mind of their dead father, played in flashback by Forest Whitaker. DP. Contains sex scenes, violence, swearing, nudity.

Allen Payne *Jason Alexander* • Jada Pinkett [Jada Pinkett Smith] *Lyric Greer* • Forest Whitaker *Maddog* • Bokeem Woodbine *Joshua Alexander* • Suzzanne Douglas *Gloria Alexander* • Anthony "Treach" Criss *Alonzo* ■ *Dir* Doug McHenry • *Scr* Bobby Smith Jr

Jassy ★★★ PG

Drama 1947 · UK · Colour · 97mins

Two years after she took the nation by storm in *The Wicked Lady*, Margaret Lockwood stars here as a woman with the gift of second sight. Of gypsy ancestry, she gets involved in the struggle to regain an inheritance. Lockwood's not all good, however, and murder is on the menu, but this time we are given hints of the heart beneath her wild exterior. This is by no means as silly as it sounds, even though the Gainsborough gang's all here, including Dennis Price hamming it up to the hilt. Great fun. SH

Margaret Lockwood *Jassy Woodroffe* • Patricia Roc *Dilys Helmar* • Dennis Price *Christopher Hatton* • Dermot Walsh *Barney Hatton* • Basil Sydney *Nick Helmar* • Nora Swinburne *Mrs Hatton* • John Laurie *Woodroffe* ■ *Dir* Bernard Knowles • *Scr* Dorothy Christie, Campbell Christie, Geoffrey Kerr, from the novel by Norah Lofts

Java Head ★★★

Romantic drama 1935 · UK · BW · 70mins

While one of two brothers (Ralph Richardson) settles down to marriage and is given the management of the fleet by his ship-owning father (Edmund Gwenn), the other (John Loder) seeks adventure in faraway climes. He returns with a Chinese bride (Anna May Wong), but the realisation that he still loves his childhood sweetheart (Elizabeth Allan), brings tragedy. This British-made combination of adventure, romance and melodrama, set in Bristol and at sea in the mid-19th century, boasts a fine cast. RK

Anna May Wong *Taou Yen* • Elizabeth Allan *Nettie Vollar* • John Loder *Gerrit Ammidon* • Edmund Gwenn *Jeremy Ammidon* • Ralph Richardson *William Ammidon* • Herbert Lomas *Barzil Dunsack* • George Curzon *Edward Dunsack* ■ *Dir* J Walter Ruben • *Scr* Martin Brown, Gordon Wellesley, from the novel by Joseph Hergesheimer

Jawbreaker ★★ 15

Black comedy 1999 · US · Colour · 83mins

This *Heathers*-style black comedy is about a trio of high school "It" girls, whose birthday prank on their best friend goes horribly wrong. Writer/director Darren Stein has a flair for striking cartoon visuals, but the plot soon runs out and the film's tone is excessively cold and cruel. Its strongest asset is the bright young cast, headed by Rose McGowan's malicious super-bitch and Judy Greer's convincing transformation from mousy nerd to sexy bombshell. JC. Contains swearing and sex scenes DVD

Rose McGowan *Courtney Shayne* • Rebecca Gayheart *Julie Freeman* • Julie Benz *Marcie Fox* • Judy Evans Greer [Judy Greer] *Fern Mayo* • Chad Christ *Zach Tartak* • Charlotte Roldan *Liz Purr* • Pam Grier *Detective Vera Cruz* • Carol Kane *Miss Sherwood* ■ *Dir/Scr* Darren Stein

Jaws ★★★★★ PG

Adventure thriller
1975 · US · Colour · 118mins

Peter Benchley's pulp bestseller is here turned into the scariest sea saga ever filmed, with Steven Spielberg creating maximum suspense in the first dark moments and then maintaining the momentum with brilliant sleight-of-hand direction. The tale of a great white shark terrorising a New England resort community and the modern-day Captain Ahab (Robert Shaw) employed to kill it is now a classic of the suspense thriller genre. John Williams's Oscar-winning music and the excellent performances of Roy Scheider and Richard Dreyfuss add to the ingeniously mounted tension that cleverly plays on all our deepest primeval fears. AJ. Contains violence, swearing and nudity. DVD

Roy Scheider *Brody* • Robert Shaw *Quint* • Richard Dreyfuss *Hooper* • Lorraine Gary *Ellen Brody* • Murray Hamilton *Vaughn* • Carl Gottlieb *Meadows* • Jeffrey C Kramer [Jeffrey Kramer] *Hendricks* • Susan Backlinie *Chrissie* • Jonathan Filley *Cassidy* ■ *Dir* Steven Spielberg • *Scr* Peter Benchley, Carl Gottlieb, Howard Sackler, from the novel by Peter Benchley • *Music* John Williams • *Editor* Verna Fields • *Cinematographer* Bill Butler • *Production Designer* Joe Alves

Jaws 2 ★★★ PG

Action adventure
1978 · US · Colour · 110mins

Three years after those infamous shark attacks, another great white swims into police chief Roy Scheider's resort town to cause more havoc in this shameless sequel. Director Jeannot Szwarc tries to ape Steven Spielberg's imaginative style and visceral terror, but any suspense he attempts to build comes unglued because it floats in all-too-familiar waters. Still, despite mayor Murray Hamilton not learning any lessons from previous events, stalwart Scheider is in full control of this follow-up that lacks the bite of the original classic. DP DVD

Roy Scheider *Police Chief Martin Brody* • Lorraine Gary *Ellen Brody* • Murray Hamilton *Mayor Larry Vaughan* • Joseph Mascolo *Len Peterson* • Jeffrey Kramer *Deputy Jeff Hendricks* • Collin Wilcox *Dr Lureen Elkins* • Ann Dusenberry *Tina Wilcox, Miss Amity* • Mark Gruner *Mike Brody* • Barry Coe *Andrews* ■ *Dir* Jeannot Szwarc • *Scr* Carl Gottlieb, Dorothy Tristan (uncredited), from characters created by Peter Benchley

Jaws III ★★ 12

Action adventure 1983 · US · Colour · 94mins

Originally called *Jaws 3-D*, once stripped of the gimmick that made it almost acceptable in theatres, this hapless opus stands as a testament to the law of diminishing returns. Director credit goes to Joe Alves, the production designer of Steven Spielberg's great original, but it's quite clear from this effort that he's no director, as a group of moderate talents act all at sea. TS DVD

Dennis Quaid *Mike Brody* • Louis Gossett Jr *Calvin Bouchard* • Bess Armstrong *Kathryn Morgan* • Simon MacCorkindale *Philip FitzRoyce* • John Putch *Sean Brody* • Lea Thompson *Kelly Ann Bukowski* • PH Moriarty *Jack Tate* ■ *Dir* Joe Alves • *Scr* Richard Matheson, Carl Gottlieb, from a story by Guerdon Trueblood, from characters created by Peter Benchley

Jaws of Satan ★

Horror 1979 · US · Colour · 92mins

A demon king cobra is sent from Hell to terrorise priest Fritz Weaver because of sins committed by his ancestors against Druids. The satanic serpent also commands others of its species to run amok while the local community idly stand by because they want their new dog track to open on schedule. This shoddy killer snake movie might have elicited some scares had the obvious glass panes protecting the actors not been visible in every stunt shot. Amateurish. AJ

Fritz Weaver *Father Farrow* • Gretchen Corbett *Dr Maggie Sheridan* • Jon Korkes *Paul Hendricks* • Norman Lloyd *Monsignor* ■ *Dir* Bob Claver • *Scr* Gerry Holland, from a story by James Callaway

Jaws the Revenge ★ 12

Action adventure 1987 · US · Colour · 86mins

This is the one where the big rubber shark gets to attack an aircraft, but that's not the only silly thing about this preposterous fourth entry in the series. Michael Caine makes the most of the summer weather in the Bahamas (the setting for most of the film) and delivers a cheerfully irrelevant cameo. Laughably inept. JF. Contains swearing and violence. [video] DVD

Lorraine Gary *Ellen Brody* • Lance Guest *Michael Brody* • Mario Van Peebles *Jake* • Karen Young *Carla Brody* • Michael Caine *Hoagie* • Judith Barsi *Thea Brody* ■ *Dir* Joseph Sargent • *Scr* Michael de Guzman, from characters created by Peter Benchley

Jay and Silent Bob Strike Back ★★★ 18

Satirical road movie
2001 · US · Colour · 100mins

Writer/director Kevin Smith's two recurring characters – dope-smoking, jive-talking Jay (Jason Mewes) and Silent Bob (Smith himself) – now have their own vehicle: an indulgent, dim-witted odyssey from Jersey to Hollywood where the two scatalogical scuzzballs plan to sabotage a movie based on comic-book alter egos Bluntman and Chronic. Unfortunately for an audience unfamiliar with Smith's oeuvre, the in-jokes come so fast that a detailed knowledge is required. Otherwise it's a fair-to-middling gross-out comedy elevated to high satire status by Ben Affleck, Matt Damon, Mark Hamill and many others sending themselves up. AC [video] DVD

Jason Mewes *Jay* • Kevin Smith (2) *Silent Bob* • Ben Affleck *Holden McNeil/Ben/Chuckie* • Matt Damon *Will Hunting/Matt Damon* • Chris Rock *Chaka* • Shannon Elizabeth *Justice the jewel thief* • Will Ferrell *Willenholly* • George Carlin *Hitchhiker* • Mark Hamill *Cock-knocker* • Carrie Fisher *Nun* • Shannen Doherty *Rene Mosier* • Seann William Scott *Brent* • Joey Lauren Adams *Alyssa Jones* • Alanis Morissette *The Woman* ■ *Dir/Scr* Kevin Smith (2)

Jaya Ganga ★★★ 15

Drama 1996 · Ind/Fr/US · Colour · 83mins

Working from his own novel, Vijay Singh makes an assured directorial debut with this lyrical dissertation on the mystical power of the goddess river, Ganges. Beautifully photographed and packed with ethnological detail, this is much more than an elegiac travelogue. Exiled novelist Asil Rais exploits his relationship with escaped courtesan Smitri Mishra to decipher his unresolved feelings for the Parisian lover who recently deserted him. But while their doomed romance provides the emotional core, this atmospheric odyssey is more concerned with the all-pervading influence of belief and superstition on modern India. DP. In Hindi and French with English subtitles.

Asil Rais *Nishant* • Smriti Mishra *Zehra* • Paola Klein [Paula Klein] *Jay/Nadja* • Jean-Claude Carrière *Professor* ■ *Dir* Vijay Singh • *Scr* Vijay Singh, from his novel *Jaya Ganga – In Search of the River Goddess* • *Cinematographer* Piyush Shah

The Jayhawkers ★★

Western 1959 · US · Colour · 103mins

This western pitches Jeff Chandler, as the leader of a private army of raiders called the Jayhawkers, against Fess Parker as the former jailbird who, for reasons of personal revenge, agrees to put a stop to Chandler's empire-building ambitions. With his Napoleon complex, a dislike for all women except his mother, and a strong affection for his adversary, Jeff Chandler is far more colourful than homespun Fess Parker. Although handsomely shot by Loyal Griggs and vigorously scored by Jerome Moross, this is long-winded and muddled. AE

Jeff Chandler *Luke Darcy* • Fess Parker *Cam Bleeker* • Nicole Maurey *Jeanne Dubois* • Herbert Rudley *Governor William Clayton* • Jimmy Carter *Paul* • Leo Gordon *Jake* ■ *Dir* Melvin Frank • *Scr* Melvin Frank, Joseph Petracca, Frank Fenton, Al Bezzerides

Jazz on a Summer's Day ★★★ U

Musical documentary
1959 · US · Colour · 87mins

Considering this is a record of the 1958 Newport Jazz Festival, it's telling that two of the most arresting sets come from rocker Chuck Berry and gospel singer Mahalia Jackson. However, you'll be equally enthralled by the performances of Anita O'Day and such jazz legends as Louis Armstrong, Thelonious Monk and Dinah Washington. Photographer Bert Stern's direction may be a touch self-serving, and Aram Avakian's editing takes in too many shots of the crowd and the nearby America's Cup trials, but they still capture the relaxed atmosphere of the gig and the evident enjoyment of the artists. DP [video] DVD

Dir Bert Stern

The Jazz Singer ★★★ U

Musical drama 1927 · US · BW · 84mins

In the autumn of 1927, a historic premiere took place in New York when Al Jolson spoke the prophetic words, "You ain't heard nothing yet!" in the first feature with spoken dialogue. Warner Bros had gambled everything on this "talker" that would transform cinema forever. Actually, there is very little dialogue in this crude and schmaltzy film about a cantor's son torn between a life in the theatre and the synagogue. It is Jolson's dynamic singing of *Toot, Toot, Tootsie* and *My Mammy*, recorded by the Vitaphone process on disc and synchronised to the action, that breathes life into a film whose pioneering aspect is its main interest. There were unnecessary remakes in 1952 (with Danny Thomas) and 1980 (with Neil Diamond). RB [video]

Al Jolson *Jakie Rabinowitz/Jack Robin* • May McAvoy *Mary Dale* • Warner Oland *Cantor Rabinowitz* • Eugenie Besserer *Sara Rabinowitz* • Bobby Gordon *Jakie at thirteen* • Otto Lederer *Moishe Yudelson* • Cantor Josef Rosenblatt • Richard Tucker *Harry Lee* • Myrna Loy *Chorus girl* • William Demarest *Buster Billings* ■ *Dir* Alan Crosland • *Scr* Alfred A Cohn, Jack Jarmuth, from the play *Day of Atonement* by Samson Raphaelson

The Jazz Singer ★★★ U

Musical drama 1952 · US · Colour · 106mins

This is an unnecessary, though likeable, updated remake of the oft-filmed story of the cantor's son who can't choose between showbiz and Yom Kippur. The main problem is Danny Thomas, who lacks the warmth the tale needs, while Peggy Lee – in one of her two feature leads (the other was in *Pete Kelly's Blues*, for which she was Oscar-nominated) – is anodyne. Not as bad, though, as the later version with Neil Diamond. TS

Danny Thomas *Jerry Golding* • Peggy Lee *Judy Lane* • Mildred Dunnock *Mrs Golding* • Eduard Franz *Cantor Golding* • Tom Tully *McGurney* • Alex Gerry *Uncle Louie* • Allyn Joslyn *George Miller* • Harold Gordon *Rabbi Roth* ■ *Dir* Michael Curtiz • *Scr* Frank Davis, Leonard Stern, Lewis Meltzer, from the play *Day of Atonement* by Samson Raphaelson

The Jazz Singer ★★ PG

Musical drama 1980 · US · Colour · 110mins

A "rocked-up" remake of the world's first talkie. *Cracklin' Rosie* man Neil Diamond updates the old Al Jolson role, playing a cantor's son who wants to make it big in the rock business. Laurence Olivier is his understandably dubious dad. Given the "rocky" nature of the film, the title now seems pretty meaningless. But, then, that description could be applied to the whole film which, though adequate, remains more a monument to the egomania of musicians than a significant contribution to world cinema. DA [video] DVD

Neil Diamond *Jess Robin/Yussel Rabinovitch* • Laurence Olivier *Cantor Rabinovitch* • Lucie Arnaz *Molly Bell* • Catlin Adams *Rivka Rabinovitch* • Franklyn Ajaye *Bubba* • Paul Nicholas *Keith Lennox* • Sully Boyar *Eddie Gibbs* ■ *Dir* Richard Fleischer • *Scr* Herbert Baker, Stephen H Foreman, from the play *Day of Atonement* by Samson Raphaelson

Je T'Aime, Je T'Aime ★★★

Science-fiction fantasy drama
1968 · Fr · Colour · 94mins

Returning to the subjects of lapsing time and unreliable memory that had informed all his earlier features, Alain Resnais harnessed that old sci-fi standby, the time machine, to bring an extra dimension to this intriguing study of lost happiness, despair and death. Unfortunately, as the suicide survivor dispatched to retrace his past, Claude Rich struggles to make an impact amid the fragmentary recollections of his affair with Olga Georges-Picot, for whose demise he may be responsible. DP. In French with English subtitles.

Claude Rich *Claude Ridder* • Olga Georges-Picot *Catrine* • Anouk Ferjac *Wiana Lust* • Annie Fargue *Agnès de Smet* • Bernard Fresson *Bernard Hannecart* • Marie-Blanche Vergne [Marie-Blanche Vergnes] *Marie-Noire Demoon* ■ *Dir* Alain Resnais • *Scr* Jacques Sternberg, Alain Resnais

Je, Tu, Il, Elle ★★★★

Drama 1974 · Bel · BW · 90mins

Compulsive eating and a craving for sex go hand in hand in this psychological drama from Chantal Akerman. The debuting director's decision to play the lead is not only courageous, but also reinforces her status as a symbol for universal womanhood, as she struggles to make the transition from adolescence into adulthood. The opening letter-writing sequence, in which she constantly munches sugar, is every bit as erotic as the encounters with trucker Niels Arestrup and her female lover, Claire Wauthion. This is a powerful, non-narrative study of anguish and identity. DP. In French with English subtitles.

Chantal Akerman *Julie* • Niels Arestrup *Truck-driver* • Claire Wauthion *Woman's lover* ■ *Dir/Scr* Chantal Akerman

Je Vous Aime ★★

Comedy 1980 · Fr · Colour · 105mins

Although this involved melodrama sets up Catherine Deneuve as an icon of independent womanhood, the men in her life are so weak that ditching them seems more like common sense than an act of female empowerment. Employing a complex network of flashbacks and excruciating exchanges, director Claude Berri shows how Deneuve assembled her entourage, demonstrating admirable control of his material, but makes Deneuve seem cold and strident rather than assuredly self-contained. DP. In French with English subtitles.

Catherine Deneuve *Alice* • Jean-Louis Trintignant *Julien* • Gérard Depardieu *Patrick* • Serge Gainsbourg *Simon* • Alain Souchon *Claude* • Christian Marquand *Victor* • Isabelle Lacamp *Dorothée* ■ *Dir* Claude Berri • *Scr* Claude Berri, Michel Grisolia

Je Vous Salue, Marie ★★★

Drama 1984 · Fr/Swi/UK · Colour · 86mins

In this impudent updating of the immaculate conception, Myriem Roussel, the daughter of a garage owner, discovers she is pregnant even though she has never slept with her boyfriend, cab driver Thierry Rode. Jean-Luc Godard's film was predictably condemned by the Pope, while various religious groups threatened cinemas and TV stations with blasphemy suits. But the picture itself is a charming, delicate and poetic piece about the mystery of Creation and the mystique of womankind, all set to heavenly music by Bach and Dvorak. AT. In French with English subtitles.

Myriem Roussel *Marie* • Thierry Rode *Joseph* • Philippe Lacoste *Angel Gabriel* • Manon Anderson *Girl* • Juliette Binoche *Juliette* • Malachi Jara Kohan *Jesus* • Johan Leysen *Professor* • Anne Gautier *Eva* ■ *Dir/Scr* Jean-Luc Godard

Jealousy, Italian Style ★★★★

Comedy drama 1970 · It · Colour · 106mins

Marcello Mastroianni won the Best Actor prize at Cannes for his work in this scattershot satire, which takes aim at just about every aspect of Italian social and cultural life. The plot is a hybrid of high opera and low Fellini: Mastroianni's doltish Communist bricklayer is a close cousin of that great clown, Toto, and Monica Vitti's flower-seller is a knowing parody of a neorealist waif. Caught between them is Giancarlo Giannini's pizza cook, who displays a glib charm. DP. Italian dialogue dubbed into English.

Marcello Mastroianni *Oreste* • Monica Vitti *Adelaide* • Giancarlo Giannini *Nello* • Manolo Zarzo *Uto* • Marisa Merlini *Silvana* • Hercules Cortez *Ambleto di Meo* • Josefina Serratosa *Antonia* ■ *Dir* Ettore Scola • *Scr* Furio Scarpelli, Age [Agenore Incrocci], Ettore Scola

Jean de Florette ★★★★★ PG

Period drama 1986 · Fr/It · Colour · 115mins

The first part of Claude Berri's adaptation of Marcel Pagnol's novel *L'Eau des Collines* is, quite simply, a tour de force. The screenplay (by Berri and Gérard Brach) is wholly cinematic, Bruno Nuytten's shimmering cinematography avoids mere pictorialism, while Berri's direction captures both the pace of the changing seasons and the unique atmosphere of Provence. The acting is also of the highest order. Gérard Depardieu is perhaps a little too insistent in asserting the worthiness of the hunchback, but Yves Montand and Daniel Auteuil are outstanding as the scheming Soubeyrans. The second part *Manon des Sources* continued the tale. DP. In French with English subtitles. Contains swearing and sexual references. [video] DVD

Yves Montand *César Soubeyran, Le Papet* • Gérard Depardieu *Jean de Florette [Cadoret]* • Daniel Auteuil *Ugolin Soubeyran, "Galignette"* • Elisabeth Depardieu *Aimée Cadoret* • Ernestine Mazurowna *Manon Cadoret* • Marcel Champel *Pique-Bouffigue* ■ *Dir* Claude Berri • *Scr* Gérard Brach, Claude Berri, from the novel *L'Eau des Collines* by Marcel Pagnol

Jeanne Dielman, 23 Quai du Commerce, 1080 Bruxelles ★★★★

Drama 1975 · Bel/Fr · Colour · 225mins

Chantal Akerman made her name with this audacious exploration of bourgeois feminism. Delphine Seyrig gives a studied display of dispassionate normalness as the widowed housewife

J

who makes ends meet by working afternoons as a prostitute. By shooting in long takes to capture each task in minute, real-time detail, Akerman renders the act of sleeping with a client just one more chore in Seyrig's daily routine. Yet, these rhythmic repetitions make the disrupted third day, with its climactic act of violence, all the more disturbing. DP. In French with English subtitles.

Delphine Seyrig *Jeanne Dielman* • Jan Decorte *Sylvain Dielman* • Henri Storck *First caller* • Jacques Doniol-Valcroze *Second caller* • Yves Bical *Third caller* • Chantal Akerman *Voice of neighbour* ■ *Dir/Scr* Chantal Akerman

Jeanne Eagels ★★

Biographical drama 1957 · US · BW · 108mins

Kim Novak does a good job of bringing out the anxieties of the 1920s stage (and screen) star Jeanne Eagels in this biopic. Three top screenwriters laboured on the dreary and contrived script but director George Sidney brings considerable visual flair to dramatic highlights – like the suicide of rival actress Elsie Desmond, played by Virginia Grey. Jeff Chandler supports as the carnival operator who pops in and out of Eagels's life. AE

Kim Novak *Jeanne Eagels* • Jeff Chandler *Sal Satori* • Agnes Moorehead *Madame Neilson* • Charles Drake *John Donahue* • Larry Gates *Al Brooks* • Virginia Grey *Elsie Desmond* • Gene Lockhart *Equity board president* • Joe De Santis *Frank Satori* ■ *Dir* George Sidney (2) • *Scr* Daniel Fuchs, Sonya Levien, John Fante, from a story by Daniel Fuchs

J

Jeanne la Pucelle ★★★★★ PG

Historical biographical drama
1994 · Fr · Colour · 237mins

Divided into two instalments – *Les Batailles* and *Les Prisons* – Jacques Rivette's sprawling account of Joan of Arc's rise and fall demonstrates once more his mastery of the epic form. Refusing to indulge in mere period pageantry or religious speculation, he has produced a cinematic portrait to rank alongside those of Carl Theodor Dreyer (*The Passion of Joan of Arc*, 1928) and Robert Bresson (*Le Procès de Jeanne d'Arc*, 1962). As the Maid of Orleans, Sandrine Bonnaire glows with the strength of her conviction, whether rallying the troops of Dauphin André Marcon or testifying to the heavenly nature of the voices that inspired her. Gaining in power throughout, this awesome achievement is both historically authentic and dramatically affecting. DP. In French with English subtitles.

Sandrine Bonnaire *Jeanne* • André Marcon *Charles, Dauphin of France* • Jean-Louis Richard *Le Tremoille* • Marcel Bozonnet *Regnault de Chartres* • Didier Sauvegrain *Raoul de Gaucourt* • Jean-Pierre Lorit *Jean d'Alencon* ■ *Dir* Jacques Rivette • *Scr* Pascal Bonitzer, Christine Laurent

Jeannie ★★★ U

Romantic comedy 1941 · UK · BW · 100mins

Known to millions as Janet in *Dr Finlay's Casebook*, Barbara Mullen made a hugely promising (but ultimately false) start to her film career in this charming comedy. As the bonny Scottish girl at the centre of a romantic tug-of-war between sales rep Michael Redgrave and wastrel Albert Lieven, she strikes a perfect balance between worldly innocence and innate sense. Redgrave revels in the chance to display his gift for comedy, while Lieven oozes smarmy charm. DP

Barbara Mullen *Jeannie McLean* • Michael Redgrave *Stanley Smith* • Wilfrid Lawson *James McLean* • Albert Lieven *Count Erich Von Wittgenstein* • Gus McNaughton *Angus Whitelaw* • Googie Withers *Laundry girl* ■ *Dir* Harold French • *Scr* Anatole de Grunwald, Roland Pertwee, Aimee Stuart, from a play by Aimee Stuart

Jeepers Creepers ★★★★ 15

Horror 2001 · US/Ger · Colour · 86mins

Victor Salva cleverly revitalises the slasher scenario by including an unknown ancient evil and fashioning the best nightmare avenue since Elm Street became a dead end. A routine road trip home becomes a waking nightmare for brother and sister students Justin Long and Gina Philips when they disturb a supernatural figure and its body-part-snatching business. Instantly suspenseful from the start and bolstered by tremendously believable performances from the two leads, Salva's unique flight of dark imagination is a terrific variation on the "psycho from hell" formula and a memorably gruesome horror fantasy. AJ. Contains violence. DVD

Gina Phillips [Gina Philips] *Trish Jenner* • Justin Long *Darry Jenner* • Jonathan Breck *The Creeper* • Patricia Belcher *Jezelle Gay Hartman* • Brandon Smith *Sgt Davis Tubbs* • Eileen Brennan *The Cat Lady* ■ *Dir/Scr* Victor Salva

Jeepers Creepers 2 ★★★ 15

Horror thriller
2003 · US/Neth · Colour · 99mins

In Victor Salva's campy sequel to his popular horror shocker, the flying flesh eater has got one more day to gorge on human body parts before his automatic hibernation cycle begins. What unfolds is a B-movie-style monster flick, as the creature disables a school bus and then starts picking off his chosen victims from the obnoxious teens within. The bickering youngsters provide plenty of tension as they try to formulate their escape, while the isolated, largely night-time setting adds to the overall sense of vulnerability and unease. Yet, for all its gory chills, the film is tongue-in-cheek and blackly comic. SF. Contains violence and swearing. DVD

Ray Wise *Jack Taggart* • Jonathan Breck *The Creeper* • Eric Nenninger *Scott Braddock* • Garikayi "G K" Mutambirwa [Garikayi Mutambirwa] *Deaundre "Double D" Davis* • Nicki Aycox [Nicki Lynn Aycox] *Minxie Hayes* • Drew Tyler Bell *Jonny Young* • Billy Aaron Brown *Andy "Bucky" Buck* • Kasan Butcher *Kimball "Big K" Ward* • Travis Schiffner *Izzy Bohen* ■ *Dir* Victor Salva • *Scr* Victor Salva, from his characters

Jefferson in Paris ★★★ 12

Period drama 1995 · US · Colour · 133mins

Nick Nolte bursts through the polite tapestry woven by director James Ivory and producer Ismail Merchant, in a study of the hypocrisy inherent in the life of US president-to-be Thomas Jefferson. He drafted the Declaration of Independence asserting that all men are created equal, yet had children by his household slave (Thandie Newton). While American ambassador to France in the late 18th century, he also had an affair with a married artist (Greta Scacchi). That Nolte makes the man at all tolerable is an indication of his acting skills, but he can't hide the fact that he is too modern a performer for this period role. TH. Contains brief nudity. DVD

Nick Nolte *Thomas Jefferson* • Greta Scacchi *Maria Cosway* • Jean-Pierre Aumont *D'Hancarville* • Simon Callow *Richard Cosway* • Seth Gilliam *James Hemings* • Thandie Newton *Sally Hemings* • James Earl Jones *Madison Hemings* • Michael Lonsdale [Michel Lonsdale] *Louis XVI* • Gwyneth Paltrow *Patsy Jefferson* • Estelle Eonnett *Polly Jefferson* ■ *Dir* James Ivory • *Scr* Ruth Prawer Jhabvala

Jeffrey ★★★★ 15

Romantic comedy
1995 · US · Colour · 89mins

Paranoid gay man Steven Weber turns celibate due to the Aids threat, and then meets the hunk of his dreams, Michael T Weiss, who is HIV-positive. Director Christopher Ashley's poignant adaptation is not only daring and sympathetic but extremely funny: a pitch-perfect look at New York gay society facing a common enemy with suitably mordant humour. Patrick Stewart is a knockout as the flamboyant queen who advises Weber to take a chance rather than opt out of life altogether. AJ DVD

Steven Weber *Jeffrey* • Michael T Weiss *Steve* • Irma St Paule *Mother Teresa* • Patrick Stewart *Sterling* • Robert Klein *Skip Winkley* • Christine Baranski *Ann Marwood Bartle* • Bryan Batt *Darius* • Sigourney Weaver *Debra Moorhouse* • Nathan Lane *Father Dan* • Olympia Dukakis *Mrs Marcangelo* ■ *Dir* Christopher Ashley • *Scr* Paul Rudnick, from the play by Paul Rudnick

Jekyll and Hyde... Together Again ★★ 18

Horror spoof 1982 · US · Colour · 83mins

The satirical comedy show *Saturday Night Live* was famous for spawning a number of careers and a host of film spin-offs. It also gave rise to a number of imitators, arguably the best of which was *Fridays*, a similarly trendy late-night mix of jokes and sketches. That show in turn gave rise to this spin-off, a movie designed to cash in on the popularity of Mark Blankfield's creation, a drug-crazed pharmacist. Here he plays a surgeon who changes personalities whenever he sniffs a strange powder. The transformation from small screen to big, however, wasn't so successful. DF

Mark Blankfield *Jekyll/Hyde* • Bess Armstrong *Mary* • Krista Errickson *Ivy* • Tim Thomerson *Dr Lanyon* • Michael McGuire *Dr Carew* ■ *Dir* Jerry Belson • *Scr* Monica Johnson, Harvey Miller, Jerry Belson, Michael Leeson, from the novel *The Strange Case of Dr Jekyll and Mr Hyde* by Robert Louis Stevenson

J'Embrasse Pas ★★★ 18

Drama 1991 · Fr · Colour · 110mins

Although they're always technically impeccable, the films of André Téchiné are invariably rather cold and detached. Consequently, it's hard to identify here with Manuel Blanc, the country mouse who comes to Paris hoping to make it in the movies and ends up on the streets as a rent boy. Clearly Blanc is faced with an impossible task in trying to salvage scenes from the excellent Philippe Noiret, but his own acting deficiencies don't help. Emmanuelle Béart provides some soul amid the degradation and desperation. DP. In French with English subtitles. Contains swearing.

Philippe Noiret *Romain* • Emmanuelle Béart *Ingrid* • Manuel Blanc *Pierre* • Hélène Vincent *Evelyne* • Yvan Desny [Ivan Desny] *Dimitri* • Christophe Bernard *Le Mac* ■ *Dir* André Téchiné • *Scr* André Techiné, Jacques Nolot, Michel Grisolia, from a story by Jacques Nolot

Jenifer ★★★

Drama 2001 · US/Can · Colour · 96mins

A co-founder of the Naked Angels theatre troupe and a driving force behind the establishment of the New York Women's Film Festival, Jenifer Estess had everything going for her. Then she contracted Amyotrophic Lateral Sclerosis, a degenerative cell condition better known as Lou Gehrig's Disease, and switched her energies to Project ALS, the charity she launched in the hope of finding a cure. Estess is played with great dignity by Laura San Giacomo in this heartfelt TV movie and director Jace Alexander keeps sentimentality firmly at bay. DP

Laura San Giacomo *Jenifer Estess* • Jane Kaczmarek *Valerie Estess* • Annabella Sciorra *Meredith Estess* • Jane Alexander *Marilyn Estess* • Maddie Corman *Julianne Hoffenberg* • Edie Falco *Wheelchair saleswoman* ■ *Dir* Jace Alexander • *Scr* David Marshall Grant, Geoffrey Nauffts, Patricia Resnick, from a story by Valerie Estess, Geoffrey Nauffts

Jennie Gerhardt ★★★

Melodrama 1933 · US · BW · 85mins

Romantic melodrama weepies involving a humble maid with a past and the son of the household seldom disappoint. This one, from a novel by Theodore Dreiser, stars Sylvia Sidney, who suffered so painfully in Dreiser's *An American Tragedy* and who once famously said of her career that she was "paid by the tear". She plays a victim of poverty, who falls pregnant but loses the father to an accident before they can marry. Finding work as a maidservant, she and Donald Cook fall in love, but her past presents an obstacle. Adequate direction, excellent supporting cast. RK

Sylvia Sidney *Jennie Gerhardt* • Donald Cook *Lester Kane* • Mary Astor *Letty Pace* • Edward Arnold *Senator Brander* • HB Warner *William Gerhardt* • Louise Carter *Mrs Gerhardt* ■ *Dir* Marion Gering • *Scr* SK Lauren, Frank Partos, from the novel by Theodore Dreiser

Jennifer ★★

Crime drama 1953 · US · BW · 70mins

The careers of married couple Ida Lupino and Howard Duff were at a low ebb when they made this slow-moving mystery in which Lupino, as a woman who has taken on the job of caretaker at a gloomy mansion, spends endless periods wandering the house in a quest to find out what happened to her predecessor, who mysteriously disappeared. The under-nourished sets, starkly lit for James Wong Howe's camera, betray the modest budget and the mystery's solution proves anti-climactic. TV

Ida Lupino *Agnes* • Howard Duff *Jim* • Robert Nichols *Orin* • Mary Shipp *Lorna* • Ned Glass *Grocery clerk* • Kitty McHugh *Landlady* • Russ Conway *Gardener* • Lorna Thayer *Grocery clerk* • Matt Dennis ■ *Dir* Joel Newton • *Scr* Virginia Myers

Jennifer ★ 15

Horror 1978 · US · Colour · 86mins

A terrible *Carrie* imitation with snakes substituted for telekinesis. Abused by her religious fanatic father Jeff Corey, withdrawn Lisa Pelikan also puts up with continual harassment from her high school classmates. It isn't long before she's using her supernatural power to call on the serpent gods to attack her tormentors. *Psycho*'s John Gavin, American game show host Bert Convey and Hollywood glamour queen Nina Foch are on hand to elicit scares, but fail miserably. AJ

Lisa Pelikan *Jennifer Baylor* • Bert Convy *Jeff Reed* • Nina Foch *Mrs Calley* • Amy Johnston *Sandra Tremayne* ■ *Dir* Brice Mack • *Scr* Kay Cousins Johnson, from a story by Steve Krantz

Jennifer Eight ★★★ 15

Thriller 1992 · US · Colour · 119mins

A thriller that disappeared without trace, despite the fact that the leads are Andy Garcia and star Uma Thurman. Thurman is effective as a blind woman who hears a murder and may be in danger herself, while Garcia gives his usual charismatic turn as the cop convinced the case is linked to one he fouled up years before. Some of the twists are far-fetched, but there's still plenty to keep followers of thrillers and fans of the two stars happy. JB. Contains swearing, violence and sex scenes. DVD

Andy Garcia *John Berlin* • Uma Thurman *Helena Robertson* • Lance Henriksen *Freddy Ross* • Kathy Baker *Margie Ross* • Graham Beckel *John Taylor* • Kevin Conway *Citrine* • John Malkovich *St Anne* • Perry Lang *Travis* ■ *Dir/Scr* Bruce Robinson

Jennifer on My Mind ★

Black comedy 1971 · US · Colour · 85mins

This ghastly drugs film was one of many made as the Summer of Love crashed and burned, with Michael Brandon and Tippy Walker as a rootless drifter and a rich girl who become pot-smoking partners when they meet up in Venice, then graduate to harder stuff when they get back home. The dire script is by Erich Segal, of *Love Story* fame, and is of interest solely because of an early small role for Robert De Niro. DA

Michael Brandon *Marcus* • Tippy Walker *Jenny* • Lou Gilbert *Max* • Steve Vinovich *Ornstein* • Robert De Niro *Gypsy cab driver* ■ *Dir* Noel Black • *Scr* Erich Segal, from the novel *Heir* by Roger L Simon

Jenny ★★ 12

Drama 1969 · US · Colour · 88mins

A young film-maker (Alan Alda) comes up with a novel way to dodge the draft, by proposing marriage to an unmarried pregnant woman (Marlo Thomas). Not unsurprisingly, their relationship of convenience begins to deepen. Thomas, as the eponymous Jenny, and Alda are pleasant leads as usual, but this is not quite the deep Vietnam-era drama it aspires to be. Harry Nilsson contributes a song. JG

Marlo Thomas *Jenny Marsh* • Alan Alda *Delano* • Marian Hailey *Kay* • Elizabeth Wilson *Mrs Marsh* • Vincent Gardenia *Mr Marsh* • Stephen Strimpell *Peter* • Fay Bernardi *Woman in bus* • Charlotte Rae *Bella Star* • Estelle Winwood • Fred Willard ■ *Dir* George Bloomfield • *Scr* George Bloomfield, from a story by Diana Gould

Jenny Kissed Me ★★★ 15

Drama 1984 · Aus · Colour · 99mins

Director Brian Trenchard-Smith here offers a sordid slice of Melbourne life. Ten-year-old Jenny, played by Tamsin West, has a close relationship with mother Deborra-Lee Furness's boyfriend, Ivar Kants. Although hardly creditable, the drama is just about held together by the director's uncompromising portrait of inner-city squalor and by Furness's compelling performance as she is driven into prostitution and drugs by despair. DP

Deborra-Lee Furness *Carol Grey* • Ivar Kants *Lindsay Fenton* • Tamsin West *Jenny Grey* • Paula Duncan *Gaynor Roberts* • Steven Grives *Mal Evans* ■ *Dir* Brian Trenchard-Smith • *Scr* Judith Colquhoun, Warwick Hind, Alan Lake

Jeopardy ★★★

Melodrama 1953 · US · BW · 68mins

This suspense melodrama was one of the last films John Sturges directed before he established his reputation with *Escape from Fort Bravo*. During a camping vacation on a remote Mexican beach, husband and father Barry Sullivan is pinioned in the water by fallen timber. With just four hours before the tide comes in, wife Barbara Stanwyck drives off to find assistance. Unfortunately, she runs into fleeing killer Ralph Meeker. Despite its slender running time, credibility flies out the window about halfway through. Until then, however, this is a taut and exciting little movie, with Stanwyck gutsy and subtle. RK

Barbara Stanwyck *Helen Stilwin* • Barry Sullivan *Doug Stilwin* • Ralph Meeker *Lawson* • Lee Aaker *Bobby Stilwin* • Bud Wolfe *Lieutenant's driver* • Saul Gorss *Captain's driver* • Bob Castro *Machine gunner* • Paul Fierro *Mexican lieutenant* ■ *Dir* John Sturges • *Scr* Mel Dinelli, from the radio play *A Question of Time* by Maurice Zimm

Jeremiah Johnson ★★★ PG

Western adventure
1972 · US · Colour · 111mins

A homogenised, ecologically sound and politically correct near-western about the real-life trapper "Liver-eatin' Johnson". It's a pretty but ultimately boring epic, in which a miscast (too young, too intelligent) Robert Redford struggles through a semi-allegorical screenplay, poorly fashioned by John Milius and Edward Anhalt. Despite sterling support from Will Geer and Allyn Ann McLerie, the movie simply doesn't jell, and Warner Bros delayed its release in favour of Redford's *The Candidate*. TS DVD

Robert Redford *Jeremiah Johnson* • Will Geer *Bear Claw* • Stefan Gierasch *Del Gue* • Allyn Ann McLerie *Crazy woman* • Charles Tyner *Robidoux* • Josh Albee *Caleb* • Joaquin Martinez *Paints His Shirt Red* • Paul Benedict *Reverend* ■ *Dir* Sydney Pollack • *Scr* John Milius, Edward Anhalt, from the novel *Mountain Man* by Vardis Fisher, from the story *Crow Killer* by Raymond W Thorp

Jeremy ★

Romance 1973 · US · Colour · 90mins

Dripping with sentimentality, this is *Love Story* without the style, and how it won writer/director Arthur Barron a prize at Cannes for Best First Feature is anybody's guess. Robby Benson and Glynnis O'Connor play a budding cellist and ballet student respectively whose burgeoning romance is threatened by parental intervention. What makes this so hard to watch with a straight face are the trite protestations and the achingly tasteful approach to sex. (The chess game seduction is a minor kitsch classic.) DP

Robby Benson *Jeremy* • Glynnis O'Connor *Susan* • Len Bari *Ralph* • Leonardo Cimino *Cello teacher* • Ned Wilson *Susan's father* • Chris Bohn *Jeremy's father* • Pat Wheel *Jeremy's mother* ■ *Dir/Scr* Arthur Barron

Jeremy Hardy versus the Israeli Army ★★★ 15

Documentary 2003 · UK · Colour · 74mins

Comedian Jeremy Hardy had the choice to spend his holiday with his in-laws in Florida or with the International Solidarity Movement in the West Bank. "Palestine won", he jokes. The ISM is a group involved in peaceful but direct protest, which means its members can often be found standing in front of Israeli tanks that are heading for Palestinian targets. Hardy was invited to join them by director and Palestinian exile, Leila Sansour. The deadpan humour for which Hardy is known serves him well here, undercutting the heroic and possibly foolhardy acts he participates in. The documentary itself is necessarily rough and ready – the technical difficulties and equipment shortages are part of its message – but it is a compelling piece of film-making whatever your political viewpoint. RT

Jeremy Hardy *Narrator* ■ *Dir* Leila Sansour • *Cinematographer* Leila Sansour, Katie Barlow

Jericho ★★★★

Drama 1991 · Ven · Colour · 90mins

Released to coincide with the celebrations marking the 500th anniversary of Columbus's voyage to the Americas, this revisionist Venezuelan drama could almost be considered an exercise in historical ethnography, such is the authenticity of its portrait of life among the native Indians. Particularly fascinating is the extended, untranslated sequence in which Dominican friar Cosme Cortazar is compelled to decipher the language and customs of the tribe that rescues him after he is separated from a murderous band of conquistadores. Strikingly photographed by Andrés Agustí, writer/director Luis Alberto Lamata's debut contrasts accepted notions of civilisation and savagery with unforced veracity. DP. In Spanish with English subtitles.

Cosme Cortazar *Santiago* ■ *Dir/Scr* Luis Alberto Lavata

The Jericho Mile ★★★★ 12

Prison drama 1979 · US · Colour · 97mins

This gripping if implausible movie – Michael Mann's debut as a director – stars Peter Strauss as a convicted murderer and loner who spends his time running around the prison perimeter fence. A warden notices his talent for running and organises a race against some Olympic hopefuls. Part *Cuckoo's Nest* (Strauss's character is called Murphy) and part *Loneliness of the Long Distance Runner*, it's a little fable about personal liberty that falls short of outright sentimentality. AT

Peter Strauss *Larry "Rain" Murphy* • Richard Lawson *RC Stiles* • Roger E Mosley *"Cotton" Crown* • Brian Dennehy *"Dr D"* • Billy Green Bush *Warden Earl Gulliver* • Ed Lauter *Jerry Beloit* ■ *Dir* Michael Mann • *Scr* Patrick J Nolan, Michael Mann, from a story by Patrick J Nolan

The Jerk ★★★★ 15

Comedy 1979 · US · Colour · 89mins

Has Steve Martin made a funnier film? Fans of this insist he hasn't, as Martin takes on the role of simple-minded and naive Navin Johnson, who suddenly discovers that his black parents aren't his natural kith and kin. He takes his dog and leaves the plantation to make his way in a world which is as loopy as him. There are some heavenly jokes (especially the one where he makes a fortune inventing an absurd nose support for spectacles), and Martin is in best "manic" mode. TH DVD

Steve Martin *Navin Johnson* • Bernadette Peters *Marie Kimball* • Catlin Adams *Patty Bernstein* • Mabel King *Mother* • Richard Ward *Father* • Dick Anthony Williams *Taj* • Bill Macy *Stan Fox* • M Emmet Walsh *Madman* • Dick O'Neill *Frosty* • Carl Reiner ■ *Dir* Carl Reiner • *Scr* Steve Martin, Carl Gottlieb, Michael Elias

The Jerky Boys ★

Comedy 1995 · US · Colour · 82mins

From the same bad-taste school as *Wayne's World*'s comes this TV sitcom, cartoon, comic book and platinum record-selling duo. Johnny Brennan and Kamal Ahmed play the moronic pair of phone pranksters, who use crank calls to be sociable and bluff their way into Mafia high society, incurring the wrath of New York crime boss Alan Arkin. This featherlight nonsense shows a distinct lack of comic inspiration. AJ

Johnny Brennan [John G Brennan] *Johnny Brennan* • Kamal Ahmed • Alan Arkin *Lazarro* • William Hickey *Uncle Freddy* • Alan North *Mickey* • Brad Sullivan *Worzic* • James Lorinz *Brett Weir* • Suzanne Shepherd *Mrs B* ■ *Dir* James Melkonian • *Scr* James Melkonian, Rich Wilkes, John G Brennan [Johnny Brennan], Kamal Ahmed

Jerry and Tom ★★★ 15

Black comedy 1998 · Can · Colour · 92mins

Actor-turned-director Saul Rubinek takes a stroll into Tarantino territory for this pleasingly black and quite stylish comedy. The film opens with two hitmen – Sam Rockwell and Joe Mantegna – waiting to complete their latest assignment with the desperately wisecracking Peter Riegert. We then go back in time to see how the two became partners. Rubinek seamlessly blends the flashbacks together and still finds time to put some flesh on the bones of the duo's victims. JF

Joe Mantegna *Tom* • Sam Rockwell *Jerry* • Charles Durning *Vic* • Maury Chaykin *Billy* • Peter Riegert *Stanley* • William H Macy *Karl* • Ted Danson *Guy who loved Vicki* ■ *Dir* Saul Rubinek • *Scr* Rick Cleveland

Jerry Maguire ★★★★ 15

Sports comedy romance
1996 · US · Colour · 133mins

Writer/director Cameron Crowe here balances one of the best performances of Tom Cruise's career with a clutch of superb supporting turns. Add a witty and tear-jerking script and the result is an unusual romantic comedy drama. Cruise is Jerry Maguire, a sports agent who, guilt-ridden one night about how he and his colleagues treat sport stars as commodities, writes a mission statement which effectively costs him his job. Cruise's relationships with his sole remaining client (a marvellous, Oscar-winning turn by Cuba Gooding Jr), the woman who stands by him (Renee Zellweger) and her adorable son (Jonathan Lipnicki) bring an infectious warmth to the film, which introduced the world to the catch phrase: "Show me the money!". JB. Contains swearing, a sex scene and brief nudity. DVD

Tom Cruise *Jerry Maguire* • Cuba Gooding Jr *Rod Tidwell* • Renee Zellweger *Dorothy Boyd* • Kelly Preston *Avery Bishop* • Jerry O'Connell *Frank Cushman* • Jay Mohr *Bob Sugar* • Bonnie Hunt *Laurel Boyd* • Regina King *Marcee Tidwell* • Jonathan Lipnicki *Ray Boyd* • Todd Louiso *Chad the nanny* • Eric Stoltz *Ethan Valhere* ■ *Dir/Scr* Cameron Crowe

Jersey Girl ★★ 15

Romantic comedy
1992 · US · Colour · 91mins

Jami Gertz stars as a girl from New Jersey who's looking for a way out of her mundane existence, and the opportunity arrives when she bumps into businessman Dylan McDermott at a Manhattan Mercedes showroom. Director David Burton Morris's bland movie falls down through lack of star power: Gertz comes across as a whining opportunist, and her scenes with McDermott lack chemistry. Some charm, but not enough to make it compelling viewing. JB

Jami Gertz *Toby Mastallone* • Dylan McDermott *Sal* • Sheryl Lee *Tara* • Joseph Bologna *Bennie Mastallone* • Joseph Mazzello *Jason* • Aida Turturro *Angie* • Molly Price *Cookie* ■ *Dir* David Burton Morris • *Scr* Gina Wendkos

Jersey Girl ★★★ 12

Comedy drama 2003 · US · Colour · 98mins

This reunites Ben Affleck with his *Chasing Amy* director Kevin Smith, and sees indie icon Smith going mainstream, and tough guy Affleck going mawkish. But the result, if slushy, isn't as bad as that might sound. In fact, this is probably Affleck's best performance in recent years. He plays a tough New York PR man who is literally left holding the baby when his wife (Jennifer Lopez) dies in childbirth. The film then follows the tough time he has balancing being a single dad with his career. Liv Tyler plays the new girl in his life, while George Carlin is his sage-like father. DA. Contains swearing. DVD

Ben Affleck *Ollie Trinke* • Raquel Castro *Gertie Trinke* • Liv Tyler *Maya* • George Carlin *Bart Trinke* • Jason Biggs *Arthur Brickman* • Jennifer Lopez *Gertrude Steiney* • Mike Starr *Block* • Stephen Root *Greenie* • Jason Lee *PR exec no 1* • Matt Damon *PR exec no 2* • Will Smith ■ *Dir/Scr* Kevin Smith (2)

Jerusalem ★★★

Period drama 1996 · Swe · Colour · 166mins

Bille August adapted this epic of rural discontent and religious fervour from the novel by Nobel Prize-winning author, Selma Lagerlöf, who had based her story on the actual 19th-century trek made by a group of Swedes to Jerusalem after they encountered the famed revivalist, Hellgum. Although Sven-Bertil Taube impresses as the impassioned preacher, it's the director's then wife, Pernilla August, who carries the drama as she feuds with Ulf Friberg for control of the family farm. This handsome period piece is occasionally sluggish. Made with funding from all the Scandinavian countries and Iceland. DP. In Swedish with English subtitles.

Ulf Friberg *Ingmar* • Maria Bonnevie *Gertrud* • Pernilla August *Karin* • Max von Sydow *Vicar* • Olympia Dukakis *Mrs Gordon* • Reine Brynolfsson *Tim* • Lena Endre *Barbro* • Jan Mybrand *Gabriel* • Sven-Bertil Taube *Hellgum* ■ *Dir* Bille August • *Scr* Bille August, from the novel by Selma Lagerlöf

The Jerusalem File ★ PG

Political thriller
1972 · US/Is · Colour · 92mins

John Flynn's second feature is a cynical slice of anti-Arab propaganda. Although it purports to steer a middle course, the script's sympathies clearly lie with the Israeli characters encountered by archaeology student Bruce Davison as he picks his way through the intricacies of the Middle Eastern situation in the aftermath of the Six Day War. Raoul Coutard's photography has an immediacy that perfectly complements the seriousness of the subject, but the sporadic outbursts of *Boys' Own* adventure sit uncomfortably with the political proselytising. DP

Bruce Davison *David* • Nicol Williamson *Lang* • Daria Halprin *Nurit* • Donald Pleasence *Samuels* • Ian Hendry *Mayers* • Koya Yair Rubin *Barak* ■ *Dir* John Flynn • *Scr* Troy Kennedy Martin • *Cinematographer* Raoul Coutard

Jesse James ★★★★ U

Classic western 1939 · US · Colour · 105mins

This western virtually canonises notorious outlaw Jesse James, here sympathetically portrayed by Tyrone Power as a glamorous Robin Hood-style figure of the Old West, riding out to right wrongs alongside his brother Frank, played by Henry Fonda. The rich 20th Century-Fox Technicolor is superb, and whether the real Jesse was as dashing or handsome as Power is irrelevant: this is stirring stuff, brilliantly directed by Henry King, one of the great masters of on-screen Americana. Nunnally Johnson's screenplay ignores most of the facts, but who cares? Henry Fonda reprised his role the following year in *The Return of Frank James*. TS

Tyrone Power *Jesse James* • Henry Fonda *Frank James* • Nancy Kelly *Zee* • Randolph Scott *Will Wright* • Henry Hull *Major Rufus Cobb* • Brian Donlevy *Barshee* • John Carradine *Bob Ford* • Jane Darwell *Mrs Samuels* ■ *Dir* Henry King • *Scr* Nunnally Johnson, from historical data asembled by Rosalind Schaeffer, Jo Frances James

Jesse James Meets Frankenstein's Daughter ★★ PG

Western horror 1966 · US · Colour · 79mins

Boasting the production values of an episode of TV's *Bonanza*, this profiles Frankenstein's "grand"daughter Narda Onyx, who carries on in the family tradition by transplanting a synthetic brain into Jesse James' s muscle-bound sidekick. The film's singular highlight is the over-ripe performance of Onyx. Like its same-year companion piece *Billy the Kid vs Dracula*, this has since achieved mind-boggling cult status. RS

John Lupton *Jesse James* • Cal Bolder *Hank Tracy/Igor* • Narda Onyx *Maria Frankenstein* • Steven Geray *Rudolph Frankenstein* • Felipe Turich *Manuel* ■ *Dir* William Beaudine • *Scr* Carl K Hittleman, from a story by Carl K Hittleman

Jessica ★ 18

Romantic comedy drama
1962 · US/It/Fr · Colour · 104mins

After her striking performance opposite John Wayne in *Rio Bravo*, Angie Dickinson deserved a major big-screen career. Instead, she ended up in films like this limp farce, playing the American midwife in a Sicilian village who prompts the jealous women into a love strike to get rid of her: no babies, no work. This was considered naughty enough in its day to be X-certificated for adults only. AE

Angie Dickinson *Jessica* • Maurice Chevalier *Father Antonio* • Noël-Noël *Old Crupi* • Gabriele Ferzetti *Edmondo Raumo* • Sylva Koscina *Nunzia Tuffi* • Agnes Moorehead *Maria Lombardo* ■ *Dir* Jean Negulesco • *Scr* Edith Sommer, from the novel *The Midwife of Pont Cléry* by Flora Sandstrom

Jesus ★★

Biblical drama 1979 · US · Colour · 121mins

Brian Deacon joins the pantheon of screen Christs, but this time it certainly isn't the greatest story ever told. Despite the compulsion of the title, this straightforward account of the life of Jesus Christ, narrated by Alexander Scourby, has little going for it apart from its enduring appeal to those of the Christian faith. Location filming does little to enhance the work of the undistinguished cast, while the producers were the biblically-named Genesis Project. TH

Alexander Scourby *Narrator* • Brian Deacon *Jesus* • Rivka Noiman *Mary* • Joseph Shiloah [Joseph Shiloach] *Joseph* ■ *Dir* Peter Sykes, John Kirsh • *Scr* Barnet Fishbein, from the Gospel of St Luke

Jesus Christ Superstar ★★ PG

Musical 1973 · US · Colour · 102mins

Andrew Lloyd Webber and Tim Rice's ground-breaking musical chronicling the last seven days of Jesus Christ works better on stage than screen, judging from director Norman Jewison's worthy adaptation. The score is brilliant, and Ted Neeley, Carl Anderson and Yvonne Elliman give great performances. However, they're undermined by Jewison's attempts to give the Passion Play a mod credibility. The result is a disappointment that would look less shallow without such a wrong-headed, anachronistic approach. AJ DVD

Ted Neeley *Jesus Christ* • Carl Anderson *Judas Iscariot* • Yvonne Elliman *Mary Magdalene* • Barry Dennen *Pontius Pilate* • Bob Bingham *Caiaphas* ■ *Dir* Norman Jewison • *Scr* Melvyn Bragg, Norman Jewison, from the musical by Tim Rice, Andrew Lloyd Webber • *Cinematographer* Douglas Slocombe

Jesus of Montreal ★★★★ 18

Satirical drama 1989 · Can · Colour · 114mins

Having charted *The Decline of the American Empire* in his previous picture, Québecois director Denys Arcand turned his attention to the Kingdom of God in this scathing satire. Mammon and the mores of the modern world also come in for denunciation as actor Lothaire Bluteau revives the spirit of Christ the Social Radical while revamping a long-running passion play. Touching on everything from religious hypocrisy and artistic integrity, to petty bureaucracy and the public's insatiable appetite for sensation, this compelling parable forces you to re-evaluate as you laugh. DP. In French with English subtitles. DVD

Lothaire Bluteau *Daniel* • Catherine Wilkening *Mireille* • Johanne-Marie Tremblay *Constance* • Rémy Girard *Martin* • Robert Lepage *René* • Gilles Pelletier *Father Leclerc* • Yves Jacques *Richard Cardinal* • Denys Arcand *The Judge* ■ *Dir/Scr* Denys Arcand

Jesus' Son ★★★ 18

Road movie
1999 · US/Can · Colour · 103mins

The hero of Alison Maclean's rambling but accomplished road movie is known merely as "FH". Suffice to say that this is not exactly a term of endearment – more an indication of Billy Crudup's cluelessness as he embarks on a drug-fuelled odyssey through 1970s America. Less a coherent drama than a collection of bizarre vignettes, the bitty narrative introduces a rogue's gallery of misfits whose unpredictable behaviour embroils Crudup in all manner of criminal activity. NS DVD

Billy Crudup *FH* • Samantha Morton *Michelle* • Greg Germann *Dr Shanis* • Denis Leary *Wayne* • Jack Black *Georgie* • Will Patton *John Smith* • Holly Hunter *Mira* • Dennis Hopper *Bill* ■ *Dir* Alison Maclean • *Scr* Elizabeth Cuthrell, David Urrutia, Oren Moverman, from a book of short stories by Denis Johnson

Jet Attack ★ U

War drama 1958 · US · BW · 68mins

One of the six B-programme-fillers director Edward L Cahn delivered in 1958, this is interesting chiefly for its use of faded names John Agar and Audrey Totter rather than its plot about a jet scientist whose plane is shot down over Korea. A Cahn season would reveal most of his films to be low-grade junk. This is no exception. TS

John Agar *Tom Arnett* • Audrey Totter *Tanya* • Gregory Walcott *Bill* • James Dobson *Sandy* • Leonard Strong *Major Wan* ■ *Dir* Edward L Cahn • *Scr* Orville H Hampton, from a story by Mark Hanna

Jet over the Atlantic ★★

Adventure thriller 1960 · US · BW · 92mins

A gas bomb on board a flight from Spain to New York threatens to asphyxiate all the passengers. As the back projected clouds float past, the cast get on with the business of holding their breath and praying for a miracle. Their unlikely saviour turns out to be convicted murderer, Guy Madison, a former pilot, who is in the custody of FBI agent George Raft. Also on board is reptilian George Macready as an English nobleman. AT

Guy Madison *Brett Matoon* • Virginia Mayo *Jean Gurney* • George Raft *Stafford* • Ilona Massey *Madame Galli-Cazetti* • George Macready *Lord Robert Leverett* • Anna Lee *Ursula Leverett* ■ *Dir* Byron Haskin • *Scr* Irving H Cooper

Jet Pilot ★★ U

Romantic drama
1957 · US · Colour · 108mins

Intended as a rehash of *Ninotchka*, this rubbishy airborne yarn has John Wayne as a US airman and Janet Leigh as a Russian pilot who wants to defect. Howard Hughes produced this mess of crass anti-communist propaganda and cringe-inducing romance. The film took 17 months to shoot and was completed around 1950; Hughes then delayed its release by a six years. AT

John Wayne *Colonel Shannon* • Janet Leigh *Anna* • Jay C Flippen *Maj Gen Black* • Paul Fix *Major Rexford* • Richard Rober *George Rivers* • Roland Winters *Colonel Sokolov* ■ *Dir* Josef von Sternberg • *Scr* Jules Furthman

Jet Storm ★★

Drama 1959 · UK · BW · 97mins

On a plane to New York, Richard Attenborough accuses a fellow passenger of killing his daughter in a hit-and-run accident. When Captain Stanley Baker investigates, it emerges that Attenborough has planted a bomb on board. Cue general hysteria. Despite the other passengers' mini-dramas – David Kossoff's Holocaust survivor, for instance – this is a star turn for Attenborough, who brings a convincing complexity to the role of bomber and bereft father. The film's moralising and eventual pay-off are hard to swallow, however. AT

Richard Attenborough *Ernest Tilley* • Stanley Baker *Captain Bardow* • Hermione Baddeley *Mrs Satterly* • Bernard Braden *Otis Randolf* • Diane Cilento *Angelica Como* • Barbara Kelly *Edwina Randolf* • David Kossoff *Dr Bergstein* • Virginia Maskell *Pam Leyton* • Harry Secombe *Binky Meadows* ■ *Dir* Cy Endfield • *Scr* Cy Endfield, Sigmund Miller, from a story by Sigmund Miller

La Jetée ★★★★★ PG

Classic science fiction
1962 · Fr · BW · 26mins

Composed almost exclusively of still photographs, Chris Marker's classic of post-apocalyptic science fiction makes for unforgettable viewing. Beginning with the childhood memory of a woman's face, the film traces Davos Hanich's efforts to uncover the meaning of this haunting image. Exploring many of the themes found in the *ciné-romans* of Alain Resnais, Marker uses photomontage to disturbing effect, but even more devastating is the one simple but indelible live-action sequence. A unique exploration of time, memory and vision. DP. In French with English subtitles. DVD

Hélène Chatelain *The woman* • Davos Hanich *The man* • Jacques Ledoux *The experimenter* • Jean Négroni *Narrator* ■ *Dir/Scr* Chris Marker • *Editor* Jean Ravel • *Music* Trevor Duncan

Jetsons: the Movie ★★★ U

Science-fiction animation
1990 · US · Colour · 78mins

Hanna-Barbera's less successful flipside of *The Flintstones* were the Space Age equivalent. Atom-powered ovens, robot vacuum cleaners, jet-propelled cars and flying saucer-shaped houses, the Jetson family has it all. What the film doesn't have is a strong story, just a thinly disguised environmental tract about furry space creatures losing their homes due to an asteroid mining operation. The songs are instantly forgettable, the ecology issue is no substitute for the original 1960s-themed whimsy, but the animation is colourful. AJ

George O'Hanlon *George Jetson* • Mel Blanc *Mr Spacely* • Penny Singleton *Jane Jetson* • Tiffany *Judy Jetson* • Patric Zimmerman *Elroy Jetson* • Don Messick *Astro* • Jean Vanderpyl *Rosie the Robot* ■ *Dir* William Hanna, Joseph Barbera • *Scr* Dennis Marks, additional dialogue Carl Sautter

Le Jeune Werther ★★★ 15

Drama 1992 · Fr · Colour · 90mins

There isn't an adult in sight in this canny updating of Goethe's novel, *The Sorrows of Young Werther*. Determined to know why their classmate committed suicide, Ismaël Jolé-Ménébhi and Thomas Brémond soon find themselves experiencing the same pangs of unrequited love for the elusive Miren Capello. True to the Romantic spirit of the original, yet echoing the argot and attitudes of 1990s French youth, Jacques Doillon's rite-of-passage picture captures the innocence of first love while remaining refreshingly free from corny sentiment. DP. In French with English subtitles.

Ismaël Jolé-Ménébhi *Ismael* • Marabelle Rousseau *Mirabelle* • Thomas Brémond *Theo* • Miren Capello *Miren* • Faye Anastasia *Faye* • Pierre Mezerette *Pierre* • Simon Clavière *Simon* ■ *Dir* Jacques Doillon • *Scr* Jacques Doillon, from the novel *The Sorrows of Young Werther* by JW von Goethe

Jeux Interdits ★★★★★

Drama 1953 · Fr · BW · 83mins

Named Best Foreign Language Film at the 1952 Oscars and awarded the Golden Lion at Venice, this is the most moving study of childhood innocence ever made. Delicately treading the line between insight and sentimentality, René Clément coaxes wondrous performances out of five-year-old Brigitte Fossey and 11-year-old Georges Poujouly (found in a camp for underprivileged kids) as the orphan and farmer's boy who cope with the traumas of the Nazi occupation by building a cemetery for animals, which they sanctify with totems taken from the neighbouring graveyard. Simple, poetic and painfully honest, this is one of the gems of French cinema. DP. In French with English subtitles.

Georges Poujouly *Michel Dolle* • Brigitte Fossey *Paulette* • Amédée *Francis Gouard* • Laurence Badie *Berthe Dolle* • Suzanne Courtal *Madame Dolle* • Lucien Hubert *Dolle, the father* • Jacques Marin *Georges Dolle* • Andre Wasley *Gouard, the father* ■ *Dir* René Clément • *Scr* René Clément, Jean Aurenche, Pierre Bost, Francois Boyer, from the novel *Les Jeux Inconnus* by Francois Boyer

Jew Süss ★★★

Period drama 1934 · UK · BW · 105mins

Lion Feuchtwanger's pro-Jewish 1925 novel was adapted for this comparatively lavish British production with an obvious regard to the rise of Fascism in Germany. Set in 18th-century Württemberg, Joseph "Jew Süss" Oppenheimer has risen to a position of power and influence in the Jewish community, but how will he react to the accusation that he is not really a Jew? The great German actor Conrad Veidt, exiled in England with his Jewish wife, is splendid in the title role, and the rest of the cast, including Cedric Hardwicke and Gerald du Maurier, are good. RB

Conrad Veidt *Joseph "Jew Süss" Oppenheimer* • Benita Hume *Marie Auguste* • Frank Vosper *Duke Karl Alexander* • Cedric Hardwicke *Rabbi Gabriel* • Gerald du Maurier *Wessensee* • Pamela Ostrer *Naomi Oppenheimer* • Paul Graetz *Landauer* ■ *Dir* Lothar Mendes • *Scr* Dorothy Farnum, AR Rawlinson, from the novel *Jud Süss* by Lion Feuchtwanger

The Jewel of the Nile ★★★★ PG

Action adventure
1985 · US · Colour · 101mins

The sequel to *Romancing the Stone* re-teams stars Michael Douglas, Kathleen Turner and Danny DeVito, and does so without falling into too many of the usual sequel pitfalls. Turner has become bored with all the lovey-dovey stuff and jumps at the chance of hitting the exploration trail once again, at odds with Douglas but determined to get even as he chases after a gem called the Jewel of the Nile, with DeVito in hot pursuit. The action and snappy one-liners come thick and fast, making this one of those rare sequels that's not too far short of the quality of the original. TH DVD

Michael Douglas *Jack Colton* • Kathleen Turner *Joan Wilder* • Danny DeVito *Ralph* • Spiros Focas *Omar* • Howard Jay Patterson *Barak* • Randall Edwin Nelson *Karak* • Samuel Ross Williams *Arak* • Timothy Daniel Furst *Sarak* • Hamid Fillali *Rachid* ■ *Dir* Lewis Teague • *Scr* Mark Rosenthal, Lawrence Konner, from characters created by Diane Thomas

Jewel Robbery ★★★

Romantic comedy 1932 · US · BW · 63mins

There's hardly time to catch your breath in this tight little Warner Bros movie from a period when the studio was at its height and pace was everything. Debonair Raffles-like gentleman burglar William Powell robs a jewellery store, locks up the proprietor and a smart customer, and starts making up to the latter's wife, the impossibly elegant Kay Francis who – wouldn't you guess? – longs for a little excitement in her bored life. It's not quite Lubitsch, but sophisticated and immensely enjoyable. TS

William Powell *Robber* • Kay Francis *Baroness Teri Von Horhenfels* • Hardie Albright *Paul* • André Luguet *Count André* • Henry Kolker *Baron Franz Von Horhenfels* • Spencer Charters *Johann Christian Lenz* ■ *Dir* William Dieterle • *Scr* Erwin Gelsey, from the play by Ladislaus Fodor [Ladislas Fodor]

Jezebel ★★★★ U

Romantic melodrama
1938 · US · BW · 100mins

This is an absolute cracker and contains, arguably, Bette Davis's best role – one which she fervently hoped would win her the part of Scarlett in the following year's *Gone with the Wind*. She had to settle for the consolation of a best actress Oscar for her role here as a beautiful but spoilt southern belle who goes completely over the top in her efforts to make her fiancé Henry Fonda jealous. This is a classic from the golden era of such overblown period blockbusters, directed by the incomparable William Wyler, with whom Davis was said to be infatuated. SR

Bette Davis *Julie Morrison* • Henry Fonda *Preston Dillard* • George Brent *Buck Cantrell* • Margaret Lindsay *Amy Bradford Dillard* • Fay Bainter *Aunt Belle Massey* • Richard Cromwell *Ted Dillard* • Donald Crisp *Dr Livingstone* • Henry O'Neill *General Theopholus Bogardus* ■ *Dir* William Wyler • *Scr* Clements Ripley, Abem Finkel, John Huston, Robert Bruckner, from the play by Owen Davis Sr [Owen Davis] • *Cinematographer* Ernest Haller • *Music* Max Steiner • *Costume Designer* Orry-Kelly

Jigsaw ★★

Crime drama 1949 · US · BW · 72mins

Franchot Tone is a crusading DA, fighting racketeers who have bumped off a journalist and who will rack up several further corpses before the end. The group, however, is prepared for Tone and sends a female operative to seduce him. This heavy-handed blend of violence and moralising is worth watching for some unbilled cameos from Henry Fonda, John Garfield and Marlene Dietrich, who did the film as a favour to her friend Mercedes McCambridge, the wife of the film's director, Fletcher Markle. AT

Franchot Tone *Howard Malloy* • Jean Wallace *Barbara Whitfield* • Myron McCormick *Charles Riggs* • Marc Lawrence (1) *Angelo Agostini* • Winifrid Lenihan *Mrs Hartley* • Betty Harper *Caroline Riggs* • Marlene Dietrich *Nightclub patron* • Henry Fonda *Nightclub waiter* • John Garfield *Street loiterer* ■ *Dir* Fletcher Markle • *Scr* Fletcher Markle, Vincent McConnor, from the story by John Roeburt

Jigsaw ★★★

Mystery drama 1962 · UK · BW · 108mins

This satisfying murder mystery benefits from the reassuring presence of Jack Warner as the detective on the case. Set in Brighton, director Val Guest adopts an unsensational, pseudo-documentary approach that concentrates on the often laborious details of police procedure as the identity of dead woman is ascertained and her killer is slowly unmasked. Among the cast of familiar British faces, American actress Yolande Donlan – Mrs Val Guest – is excellent as a spinster who narrowly misses being a murder victim. AT

Jack Warner *Det Insp Fellows* • Ronald Lewis *Det Sgt Wilks* • Yolande Donlan *Jean Sherman* • Michael Goodliffe *Clyde Burchard* • John Le Mesurier *Mr Simpson* • Moira Redmond *Joan Simpson* ■ *Dir* Val Guest • *Scr* Val Guest, from the novel *Sleep Long, My Love* by Hillary Waugh

Jigsaw ★

Mystery drama 1968 · US · Colour · 96mins

Spartacus author Howard Fast's novel *Fallen Angel* was filmed in 1965 as *Mirage*. It was an amnesia-based thriller that was hard to follow and easy to forget. This is a remake, reworked by Ranald MacDougall under the pseudonym Quentin Werty. There is one major change to the story: instead of amnesia, the hero's problem is an overdose of LSD which makes him unable to remember who was murdered, and why. AT

Harry Guardino *Arthur Belding* • Bradford Dillman *Jonathan Fields* • Hope Lange *Helen Atterbury* • Pat Hingle *Lew Haley* • Diana Hyland *Sarah* • Victor Jory *Dr Edward Arkroyd* • Paul Stewart *Dr Simon Joshua* • Susan Saint James *Ida* ■ *Dir* James Goldstone • *Scr* Quentin Werty [Ranald MacDougall], from the film *Mirage* by Peter Stone, from the novel *Fallen Angel* by Howard Fast

The Jigsaw Man ★★★ 15

Spy drama 1984 · UK · Colour · 90mins

Another outing for Laurence Olivier and Michael Caine, but this Cold War thriller is not a fraction as effective as their *Sleuth* 12 years before. The story, about a British traitor whose face is surgically altered by the Russians so that he can be sent back on a mission, doesn't convince and, like the most irritating of jigsaws, a lot of plot-pieces seem to be missing. TH. Contains swearing. DVD

Michael Caine *Sir Philip Kimberly* • Laurence Olivier *Admiral Sir Gerald Scaith* • Susan George *Penny* • Robert Powell *Jamie Frazer* • Charles Gray *Sir James Chorley* • Michael Medwin *Milroy* ■ *Dir* Terence Young • *Scr* Jo Eisinger, from the novel by Dorothea Bennet

Jill Rips ★★★ 18

Crime thriller 2000 · US · Colour · 90mins

A female serial killer is choosing her prey from the sleazy world of sadomasochism. When his brother becomes her latest victim, burnt-out ex-cop Dolph Lundgren investigates. This effective psycho-chiller ia directed with torrid verve and mature style by Anthony Hickox, evoking surprising sympathy for the maniac's motives. All this, plus the sight of Lundgren in bondage being walked on by a dominatrix clad in red leather! AJ

Dolph Lundgren *Matt* • Danielle Brett *Irene* • Charlie Seixas *Jim Conway* • Richard Fitzpatrick *Eddie* • Kristi Angus *Frances* ■ *Dir* Anthony Hickox • *Scr* Kevin Bernhardt, Gareth Wardell, from the novel by Frederick Lindsay

Jim Thorpe – All-American ★★ U

Sports biography 1951 · US · BW · 105mins

Jim Thorpe was often regarded as the finest all-round athlete America has ever produced. A native American Indian, he won a stack of Olympic gold medals in 1912, more than any other athlete had ever won, but was stripped of them because he had previously played professional baseball. He became a coach, a celebrity, a serial husband and a drunkard. As Thorpe, Burt Lancaster is ideally cast, but despite some fine support and an attempt not to sugar-coat the story, it's a conventional Hollywood biopic. AT

Burt Lancaster *Jim Thorpe* • Charles Bickford *Glenn S "Pop" Warner* • Steve Cochran *Peter Allendine* • Phyllis Thaxter *Margaret Miller* • Dick Wesson *Ed Guyac* • Jack Big Head *Little boy* ■ • *Scr* Frank Davis, Everett Freeman, from the story *Bright Path* by Douglas Morrow, Vincent X Flaherty, from a biography by Russell J Birdwell, James Thorpe

Jimi Hendrix ★★★★ 15

Documentary
1973 · US · BW and Colour · 97mins

Few burned as brightly or were extinguished as quickly as Jimi Hendrix. Made just three years after his untimely death, this documentary is a crucial insight into the guitarist's roots and the tremors he sent through 1960s pop with his electrifying blend of aggression, intensity and finesse. The live sequences, some culled from Woodstock and Monterey Pop, are priceless. But the interviews are also compelling, whether with his saxophone playing father Al, longtime girlfriend Fayne Pridgeon or fellow axe hero, Pete Townshend, who seemed to both fear and revere him. But let's not forget the Experience band members, Mitch Mitchell and Noel Redding, who somehow managed to keep up with him. DP

Dir Joe Boyd, John Head, Gary Weis • *Scr* Joe Boyd, John Head, Gary Weis • *Cinematographer* Leon Branton

J

Jimmy Hollywood ★★★ 15

Comedy drama 1994 · US · Colour · 104mins

Barry Levinson divides his time between intelligent, mainstream blockbusters such as *Sleepers* and *Rain Man*, and his more personal projects that remain best typified by *Diner*. This film falls into the latter category, a likeable enough little oddity. Joe Pesci stars as a struggling actor who becomes a vigilante when a thief snatches his car radio. Despite the farcical plot, there is a deep streak of melancholy running through the piece and, for all Pesci's bluster, the film is stolen by Christian Slater, who gives a beautifully understated performance as Pesci's slow-witted chum. JF. Contains violence and swearing.

Joe Pesci *Jimmy Alto* • Christian Slater *William* • Victoria Abril *Lorraine De La Pena* • Jason Beghe *Detective* • John Cothran Jr *Detective* • Harrison Ford ■ *Dir/Scr* Barry Levinson

Jimmy Neutron: Boy Genius ★★★ U

Animated comedy adventure
2001 · US · Colour · 79mins

Jimmy Neutron is a boy inventor living in the colourful community of Retroville, USA, who pilots his own rocketship and has a pet robot-dog called Goddard – after the rocket scientist Robert H Goddard, one of the cartoon's few nods to an adult audience. The communications satellite that Jimmy has fashioned out of a toaster alerts hostile aliens to the presence of his home town, and the Yookians spirit away all the grown-ups. Aimed at the very young, this lively cartoon adventure has less to keep adults amused. TH DVD

Debi Derryberry *Jimmy Neutron* • Patrick Stewart *King Goobot* • Martin Short *Ooblar* • Andrea Martin *Miss Fowl* • Megan Cavanagh *Mom/VOX* • Mark DeCarlo *Dad/Pilot/Arena guard* ■ *Dir* John A Davis • *Scr* John A Davis, Steve Oedekerk, David N Weiss, J David Stem

Jimmy the Gent ★★

Crime comedy 1934 · US · BW · 66mins

James Cagney and Bette Davis star in this romantic comedy about rival teams of con-artists who track down legatees left fortunes in unclaimed wills. Davis, appalled at her employer Cagney's behaviour, leaves him for another firm. It's a profitable racket and the story always hovers on the edge of the gangster movie. Sharply performed by the two stars and lasting barely over an hour, it doesn't stop for lunch. Surprisingly, Warners didn't team Cagney and Davis together again until *The Bride Came COD* in 1941. AT

James Cagney *Jimmy Corrigan* • Bette Davis *Joan Martin* • Alice White *Mabel* • Allen Jenkins *Louie* • Arthur Hohl *Joe Rector [Monty Barton]* • Alan Dinehart *James J Wallingham* • Philip Reed *Ronnie Gatson* ■ *Dir* Michael Curtiz • *Scr* Bertram Milhauser, from the story *Heir Chaser* by Laird Doyle, Ray Nazarro

Jimmy the Kid ★ PG

Comedy 1982 · US · Colour · 84mins

There are those who confuse acting with big movements, bulging eyes and exaggerated verbal delivery. Furthermore, noise is never a good substitute for wit. All of these irksome trifles are of no concern to Gary Coleman who plays a bored, bright rich kid enjoying his childhood in the company of his kidnappers. Clearly Walter Olkewicz, Paul Le Mat and Dee Wallace hold Coleman up as a role model, since they quickly descend to his level of inanity. JM

Gary Coleman *Jimmy Lovejoy* • Paul Le Mat *John Dortmunder* • Dee Wallace [Dee Wallace Stone] *May Dortmunder* • Don Adams *Harry Walker* • Walter Olkewicz *Andrew Kelp* • Ruth Gordon *Bernice Kelp* ■ *Dir* Gary Nelson • *Scr* Sam Bobrick, from the novel by Donald E Westlake

Jingle All the Way ★★ PG

Seasonal comedy 1996 · US · Colour · 85mins

Arnold Schwarzenegger is the overworked businessman who promises to buy the year's hottest toy – Turbo Man – for his neglected son. Alas, the doll sold out months previously, thus sparking a frantic hunt that sees Arnie crossing swords with an obsessed postman (Sinbad) and a crooked Santa (James Belushi). Schwarzenegger acquits himself well in the slapstick action sequences but he's a tad embarrassing during the cuddlier moments. Brian Levant's direction, meanwhile, could do with a harder edge. JF DVD

Arnold Schwarzenegger *Howard Langston* • Sinbad *Myron Larabee* • Phil Hartman *Ted Maltin* • Rita Wilson *Liz Langston* • Robert Conrad *Officer Hummell* • Martin Mull *DJ* • Jake Lloyd *Jamie Langston* • James Belushi *Mall Santa* ■ *Dir* Brian Levant • *Scr* Randy Kornfield

Jinnah ★★★

Biographical drama
1998 · Pak/UK · Colour · 110mins

Christopher Lee turns in a towering performance in this sincere tribute to Mohammed Ali Jinnah, the founder of Pakistan. Set either side of the Partition of India, it's a necessarily episodic biopic. But the decision to use a *Christmas Carol*-like conceit to link the story (in which Lee tours key moments in his life with celestial scholar Shashi Kapoor) is a preposterous miscalculation. Yet, director Jamil Dehlavi co-wrote the factually impeccable screenplay with Cambridge academic Akbar Ahmed. With James Fox stiffly uncomprehending as Mountbatten, this is less effusive, but also less impressive than *Gandhi*. DP

Christopher Lee *Quaid-e-Azam Mohammed Ali Jinnah* • James Fox *Lord "Dickie" Mountbatten* • Maria Aitken *Edwina Mountbatten* • Shashi Kapoor *Narrator* ■ *Dir* Jamil Dehlavi • *Scr* Jamil Dehlavi, Akbar Ahmed

Jinxed! ★ 15

Black comedy 1982 · US · Colour · 98mins

It was a disaster waiting to happen when Bette Midler, brashest of song-belters, teamed with Don Siegel, briskest of action directors. Off-screen squabbles didn't help this story of a lucky gambler's girl who ropes in Reno croupier Ken Wahl to make the game of blackjack a lethal deal for her partner. Rip Torn, as the gambler, offers a token portrait of sadistic seediness, but this goes sadly awry. TH. Contains violence, swearing.

Bette Midler *Bonita Friml* • Ken Wahl *Willie Brodax* • Rip Torn *Harold Benson* • Val Avery *Milt Hawkins* • Jack Elam *Otto* ■ *Dir* Don Siegel • *Scr* David Newman, Bert Blessing, from a story by Bert Blessing

Jit ★★★

Romantic comedy
1990 · Zim · Colour · 98mins

Director Michael Raeburn – though not himself a native Zimbabwean – has the privilege of making the nation's first wholly indigenous picture. Considering the inexperience of his largely non-professional cast, he packs this gentle love story with plenty of feel-good humour and even more foot-tapping *jit* jive. As the country boy who falls heavily for an independent city girl, Dominic Makuvachuma gives a relaxed display of charm as he disregards the warnings of his hard-drinking spirit ancestor Winnie Ndemera, to seek the "bride price" required to satisfy Sibongile Nene's grasping father. Slight and shaky, but amiable. DP

Dominic Makuvachuma *UK* • Sibongile Nene *Sofi* • Farai Sevenzo *Johnson* • Winnie Ndemera *Jukwa* • Oliver Mtukudzi *Oliver* • Lawrence Simbarashe *Chamba* • Kathy Kuleya *Nomsa* ■ *Dir/Scr* Michael Raeburn

Jitterbugs ★★ U

Comedy 1943 · US · BW · 74mins

Desperate for a hit after several disappointing outings, Laurel and Hardy revamped the 1933 programme filler *Arizona to Broadway*, with Ollie posing as a southern millionaire and Stan as a rich maiden aunt to help Vivian Blaine, whose mother has been swindled in a land deal. Even their devoted fans will admit that, for the most part, this is pretty feeble stuff, with the demands of the flimsy story getting in the way of the comedy. DP

Stan Laurel *Stan* • Oliver Hardy *Ollie* • Vivian Blaine *Susan Cowan* • Bob Bailey *Chester Wright* • Douglas Fowley *Malcolm Bennett* ■ *Dir* Mal St Clair [Malcolm St Clair] • *Scr* Scott Darling

Jivaro ★★

Adventure romance
1954 · US · Colour · 91mins

Fernando Lamas and Rhonda Fleming are adventurers seeking a cache of gold hidden in a region of the Amazon jungle populated by a tribe of headhunters, known as Jivaro. There's more life in the background foliage (shot on location) than in the leads in this lumbering yarn. RS

Fernando Lamas *Rio* • Rhonda Fleming *Alice Parker* • Brian Keith *Tony* • Lon Chaney Jr *Pedro* • Richard Denning *Jerry Russell* • Rita Moreno *Maroa* ■ *Dir* Edward Ludwig • *Scr* Winston Miller, from a story by David Duncan

Jiyan ★★★ 12A

Drama 2001 · Iraq/US · Colour · 99mins

In 1988, Iraqi planes bombarded the Kurdish town of Halabja with chemical and biological weapons in an assault that left 5,000 dead and a further 9,000 maimed. Bearing in mind the horror of that attack, it's understandable that director Jano Rosebiani errs on the emotional side in relating this inspiring story of the US-based expatriate businessman who returns home to build an orphanage for the victims. Yet, there's still a touching restraint in the portrayal of Kurdo Galali's optimistic relationship with traumatised child Jiyan (Pisheng Berzinji) and her protective cousin, Choman Hawrami. The overall tone is neorealist, but a humble poetry still shines through. DP. In Kurdish with English subtitles.

Kurdo Galali *Diyari Derbendikhari* • Pisheng Berzinji *Jiyan* • Choman Hawrami *Sherko* • Enwer Shexani *Salar* • Darya Qadir *Tavga* • Ehmed Sala *The Mayor* ■ *Dir/Scr* Jano Rosebiani

Jo Jo Dancer, Your Life Is Calling ★★ 18

Drama 1986 · US · Colour · 96mins

Richard Pryor directs himself as comedian Jo Jo Dancer in a story that bears an uncanny resemblance to his own colourful career, both on and offstage. It tells of his early days in showbusiness and of the effects of drug use and abuse, culminating in a stay in the hospital burns unit. The results are disappointing, given the dramatic possibilities offered by Pryor's life. TH

Richard Pryor *Jo Jo Dancer/Alter Ego* • Debbie Allen *Michelle* • Art Evans *Arturo* • Fay Hauser *Grace* • Barbara Williams (2) *Dawn* • Carmen McRae *Grandmother* • Billy Eckstine *Johnny Barnett* ■ *Dir* Richard Pryor • *Scr* Rocco Urbisci, Paul Mooney, Richard Pryor

Joan of Arc ★★ PG

Historical epic 1948 · US · Colour · 96mins

Brilliant and under-rated director Victor Fleming had a serious crush on Ingrid Bergman, and this costly farrago is effectively a Technicolored love letter to Bergman, who had played the role on stage. The result brought Fleming to an early grave, a comic-strip history lesson so dull and lengthy that it was trimmed down at each screening, its original 145-minute length mercifully eventually cut to around 100 minutes. A real endurance test. TS

Ingrid Bergman *Jeanne d'Arc* • José Ferrer *Dauphin, Charles VII* • Francis L Sullivan *Pierre Cauchon* • J Carrol Naish *Count John of Luxembourg* • Ward Bond *La Hire* • Shepperd Strudwick *Father Jean Massieu* • Gene Lockhart *Georges La Tremouille* • Leif Erickson *Jean Dunois* ■ *Dir* Victor Fleming • *Scr* Maxwell Anderson, Andrew Solt, from the play *Joan of Lorraine* by Maxwell Anderson • *Costume Designer* Dorothy Jeakins, Karinska

Joan of Arc ★★ 15

Historical biographical drama
1999 · Fr · Colour · 151mins

Kathryn Bigelow walked away from this project after refusing to cast Luc Besson's then-wife Milla Jovovich as the saint. Besson took over and cast Jovovich anyway. Sadly, she's the biggest problem in this epic story of the peasant girl who led the French to victory over the English. The prologue detailing Joan's childhood is dire, but the film does kick in after the entrance of John Malkovich as Charles VII, and there are some remarkable battle scenes before Joan's downfall. LH. Contains violence and swearing. DVD

Milla Jovovich *Joan of Arc* • John Malkovich *Charles VII* • Faye Dunaway *Yolande D'Aragon* • Dustin Hoffman *The Conscience* • Tcheky Karyo *Dunois* • Pascal Greggory *Duke of Alencon* • Vincent Cassel *Gilles de Rais* • Timothy West *Cauchon* • Gina McKee *Duchess of Bedford* ■ *Dir* Luc Besson • *Scr* Andrew Birkin, Luc Besson

Joan of Paris ★★ U

Second World War drama
1942 · US · BW · 91mins

Paul Henreid and Michèle Morgan made strong Hollywood debuts in this efficient slice of action, set in occupied France and briskly directed by Robert Stevenson. Morgan is the Joan of Paris, the brave barmaid who sidetracks Laird Cregar's Gestapo chief so that French pilot Paul Henreid and some downed RAF flyers can escape back to England. A pre-stardom Alan Ladd gains his first significant role as a wounded pilot nicknamed "Baby", while that worthy character actress May Robson, well into her 80s, makes her final screen appearance. AE

Paul Henreid *Paul Lavallier* • Michèle Morgan *Joan* • Thomas Mitchell *Father Antoine* • Laird Cregar *Herr Funk* • May Robson *Mlle Rosay* • Alexander Granach *Gestapo agent* • Alan Ladd *Baby* ■ *Dir* Robert Stevenson • *Scr* Charles Bennett, Ellis St Joseph, from a story by Jacques Thery, Georges Kessel

Joanna ★

Musical drama 1969 · UK · Colour · 112mins

Never have the Swinging Sixties seemed so ghastly as in this dismal "free love" fantasy from director Michael Sarne. Donald Sutherland makes the most of his passing role as a playboy who sweeps thrill-seeking art student Genevieve Waite off to North Africa before succumbing to leukaemia. Alas, the rest of the cast look uncomfortable as they contort to the music of Rod McKuen and get swept hither and thither by Waite's garish imagination. DP

Genevieve Waite *Joanna* • Christian Doermer *Hendrik Casson* • Calvin Lockhart *Gordon* • Donald Sutherland *Lord Peter Sanderson* • Glenna Forster-Jones *Beryl* • David Scheuer *Dominic Endersley* ■ *Dir/Scr* Michael Sarne

Jobman ★★★

Drama 1990 · S Afr · Colour · 97mins

Something of a companion piece to the powerful Australian picture by director Fred Schepisi *The Chant of Jimmie Blacksmith*, this bold, unblinkered film shows how a decent black man is driven outside the law by the pressures of racial prejudice. One of the first films tackling bigotry and its consequences to be made and shown in apartheid South Africa, it is, sadly, deprived of pace by director Darrell Roodt. Still, Kevin Smith gives a performance of dignity and power as the deaf-and-dumb Jobman. DP. Contains some swearing.

Kevin Smith (3) *Jobman* • Tertius Meintjes *Karel* • Lynn Gaines *Anna* • Marcel Van Heerden *Sergeant* • Goliath Davids *Pyp* • Josephine Liedeman *Petra* ■ *Dir* Darrell Roodt [Darrell James Roodt] • *Scr* Greg Latter, from a story by Achmat Dangor

Jock of the Bushveld ★★★ PG

Period adventure
1988 · S Afr · Colour · 93mins

Based on Percy Fitzpatrick's autobiographical account of life in the South African gold fields at the end of the last century, this is a stirring story that takes us from the depths of the earth to the great outdoors, via a crocodile-infested river. The hero of the title is a sort of White Fang of the velds, an ugly dog who becomes Fitzpatrick's companion and frequently his salvation. Action-packed, yet retaining a good grasp of period, this is a solid family adventure. DP

Jonathan Rands *Percy Fitzpatrick* • Jocelyn Broderick *Lilian Cubitt* • Olivier Ngwenya *Jim Makokel* • Gordon Mulholland *Tom Barnett* • Michael Brunner *Seedling* • Marloe Scott-Wilson *Maggie Maguire* ■ *Dir* Gray Hofmeyr • *Scr* John Cundill, from the book by Percy Fitzpatrick

Jocks ★ 15

Comedy 1986 · US · Colour · 90mins

Ever wondered when Christopher Lee's career reached its lowest point? It was probably in this comedy about college athletes, in which Lee plays the school president who is obsessed with winning. The school's only chance of winning a championship lies in tennis player Scott Strader – if he can stop partying long enough to play. ST

Scott Strader *The Kid* • Perry Lang *Jeff* • Richard Roundtree *Chip Williams* • RG Armstrong *Coach Beetlebom* • Christopher Lee *President White* ■ *Dir* Steve Carver • *Scr* Michael Lanahan, David Oas

Joe ★★★ 15

Drama 1970 · US · Colour · 92mins

Director John G Avildsen's violent "bigot-versus-counterculture" parable is very much a product of its conservative times, but its implausibility is tempered by strong performances. Peter Boyle became a star after playing the title character, a right-wing, blue-collar loud-mouth who forms a strange relationship with executive Dennis Patrick after the latter kills his wayward daughter's drug-pusher boyfriend. Shot on location in Greenwich Village with almost documentary-like precision, it's a creepy look at man's baser instincts, capped with a bloody massacre. Susan Sarandon makes her film debut here as Patrick's daughter. AJ

Peter Boyle *Joe Curran* • Susan Sarandon *Melissa Compton* • Patrick McDermott *Frank Russo* • Dennis Patrick *Bill Compton* • Audrey Caire *Joan Compton* ■ *Dir* John G Avildsen • *Scr* Norman Wexler

Joe Butterfly ★★ U

Comedy 1957 · US · Colour · 89mins

In this insipid comedy, Burgess Meredith does a capable job as Joe Butterfly, a wily local at the service of the American army occupying Japan. Fred Clark is splendid as a combustible colonel, but Audie Murphy is miscast as a brash photographer conducting a tentative romance with a local girl. Location filming in Japan only rubs in the falsity of the situations and the improbably cosy relationship between recent enemies. AE

Burgess Meredith *Joe Butterfly* • Audie Murphy *Private John Woodley* • George Nader *Sergeant Ed Kennedy* • Keenan Wynn *Henry Hathaway* • Keiko Shima *Cheiko* • Fred Clark *Colonel EE Fuller* ■ *Dir* Jesse Hibbs • *Scr* Sy Gomberg, Jack Sher, Marion Hargrove, from a play by Evan Wylie, Jack Ruge

Joe Dirt ★ 12

Comedy 2001 · US · Colour · 87mins

Is there no end to excrement jokes? Be warned, this is brimming with toilet humour and what remains is tasteless. David Spade is Joe Dirt, a white trash lost soul, whose cranium – split during childhood – is covered by the worst wig in cinema history. The film details Dirt's adventures since parental desertion at eight and explains his current conundrum – that he believes both a meteor and a nuclear bomb have fallen from the sky into his possession. LH. Contains swearing and sexual references. DVD

David Spade *Joe Dirt* • Brittany Daniel *Brandy* • Dennis Miller *Zander Kelly* • Adam Beach *Kicking Wing* • Christopher Walken *Clem* • Jaime Pressly *Jill* ■ *Dir* Dennie Gordon • *Scr* David Spade, Fred Wolf

Joe Hill ★★

Biographical drama
1971 · Swe/US · Colour · 114mins

Set in 1902 New York, this should have been a hard-hitting study of the part played by immigrants in the Industrial Workers of the World movement. But Bo Widerberg allows imagist lyricism to detract from the authenticity of his investigation of working-class struggle. As the folk singer whose political career is curtailed by a false murder rap, Thommy Berggren occasionally unleashes the fervour of the socialist zealot. But, apart from a few shrewd insights into the American psyche, this is a disappointing picture. DP

Thommy Berggren *Joe Hill* • Anja Schmidt *Lucia* • Kelvin Malave *Fox* • Evert Anderson *Blackie* • Cathy Smith *Cathy* • Hasse Persson *Paul* ■ *Dir* Bo Widerberg • *Scr* Bo Widerberg, Richard Weber, Steve Hopkins

Joe Kidd ★★ 15

Western 1972 · US · Colour · 83mins

The spaghetti western meets its classic American origins, but Clint Eastwood's potent "man with no name" persona conflicts with John Sturges's anonymous direction in this range war saga. Robert Duvall dispossessing Mexican-Americans of their land is the central thread of an indifferent effort scripted by Elmore Leonard. There's little to get excited about apart from one fun highlight, completely out of keeping with the rest of the film, where gunman Eastwood drives a train through a saloon to mow down the villains. AJ DVD

Clint Eastwood *Joe Kidd* • Robert Duvall *Frank Harlan* • John Saxon *Luis Chama* • Don Stroud *Lamarr* • Stella Garcia *Helen Sanchez* • James Wainwright *Mingo* • Paul Koslo *Roy* ■ *Dir* John Sturges • *Scr* Elmore Leonard

The Joe Louis Story ★★ U

Sports biography 1953 · US · BW · 88mins

Amateur pugilist Coley Wallace plays the boxing legend who emerged from the Chicago slums to become world champion in Robert Gordon's biography. The film follows Joe as he loses the title (and his wife) and wins it back before being crushed by Rocky Marciano in 1951. Wallace was picked because of his extraordinary physical resemblance to Louis, not for any real acting ability. On the positive side, many of the fight scenes include genuine archive footage which will delight boxing fans. AT

Coley Wallace *Joe Louis* • Paul Stewart *Tad McGeehan* • Hilda Simms *Marva Louis* • James Edwards *Chappie Blackburn* • John Marley *Mannie Seamon* • Dotts Johnson [Dots Johnson] *Julian Black* ■ *Dir* Robert Gordon • *Scr* Robert Sylvester

Joe Macbeth ★★★

Crime drama 1955 · UK · BW · 92mins

This interesting reworking of the "Scottish play" as gangster movie, set in the States but filmed in England, was directed with assurance at Shepperton by one of Britain's most talented film-makers, bohemian jazz freak and crime expert Ken Hughes. Americans Paul Douglas and Ruth Roman were imported to play the leads, and the support cast is perfect for its period, with an American-accented Sidney James as Banky, and Bonar Colleano as his revenge-seeking son Lennie. TS

Paul Douglas *Joe Macbeth* • Ruth Roman *Lily Macbeth* • Bonar Colleano *Lennie* • Grégoire Aslan *Duca* • Sidney James *Banky* • Nicholas Stuart *Duffy* • Robert Arden *Ross* • Minerva Pious *Rosie* ■ *Dir* Ken Hughes • *Scr* Phillip Yordan, from the play *Macbeth* by William Shakespeare

Joe Panther ★★

Drama 1976 · US · Colour · 110mins

Joe (Ray Tracey), a young Seminole Indian, feels like an outcast in a white man's world until he discovers a talent for professional alligator-wrestling. This is simplistic children's stuff that labours its messages as Joe struggles to find his way in life. The acting is wooden to say the least, and the music to the alligator battle is far too reminiscent of *Jaws*. TH

Ray Tracey *Joe Panther* • Brian Keith *Captain Harper* • Ricardo Montalban *Turtle George* • Alan Feinstein *Rocky* • Cliff Osmond *Rance* ■ *Dir* Paul Krasny • *Scr* Dale Eunson, from the novel by Zachary Ball

Joe Smith, American ★★

Second World War drama
1942 · US · BW · 63mins

Based on a Paul Gallico story, this propaganda thriller was the first of a number of "important low-budget pictures" assigned by MGM to executive producer Dore Schary, who later headed the studio. It tells of how aircraft factory worker Robert Young is kidnapped by Nazis but refuses to give them information. Made to help persuade the USA to enter the Second World War, the film cannot help but be dated, though it is directed with plenty of pace by Richard Thorpe. Watch out for Ava Gardner in a bit part in one of her earliest movies. RB

Robert Young (1) *Joe Smith* • Marsha Hunt *Mary Smith* • Harvey Stephens *Freddie Dunhill* • Darryl Hickman *Johnny Smith* • Jonathan Hale *Blake McKettrick* • Ava Gardner *Girl* ■ *Dir* Richard Thorpe • *Scr* Allen Rivkin, from a story by Paul Gallico

Joe Somebody ★★ PG

Romantic comedy drama
2001 · US · Colour · 94mins

There's a shrewd satirical intelligence at work in this contemporary take on the "conformity is contentment" rationale that made *Pleasantville* so effective. However, Tim Allen is too eager to please as the corporate video-maker who kicks against a system that has designated him a drone. Consequently, director John Pasquin's astutely conveyed community of spirit-sapping averageness is rapidly overturned by slapstick and schmaltz, as Allen has to choose between being the conqueror of bullying workmate Patrick Warburton or a good dad. Ultimately middlebrow mediocrity wins the day. DP DVD

Tim Allen *Joe Scheffer* • Julie Bowen *Meg Harper* • Kelly Lynch *Callie Scheffer* • Hayden Panettiere *Natalie Scheffer* • Jim Belushi [James Belushi] *Chuck Scarett* • Greg Germann *Jeremy* • Patrick Warburton *Mark McKinney* ■ *Dir* John Pasquin • *Scr* John Scott Shepherd

Joe the King ★

Drama 1999 · US · Colour · 101mins

Heavy-handed direction and a joyless script – both courtesy of actor Frank Whaley in his directorial debut – cripple this working-class melodrama about a lonely teenage boy who is coming of age. Noah Fleiss gives a sombre and vacant performance as Joe, while Val Kilmer is woefully miscast as his drunken father. ST

Noah Fleiss *Joe Henry* • Val Kilmer *Bob Henry* • Karen Young *Theresa* • Ethan Hawke *Len Coles* • John Leguizamo *Jorge* • Austin Pendleton *Winston* • Max Ligosh *Mike Henry* • James Costa *Ray* • Camryn Manheim *Mrs Basil* ■ *Dir/Scr* Frank Whaley

Joe versus the Volcano ★★★ PG

Comedy 1990 · US · Colour · 97mins

For his directorial debut, Oscar-winning *Moonstruck* screenwriter John Patrick Shanley came up with this flawed but still entertaining film. Tom Hanks is the downtrodden office worker who, on discovering that he has only a short time to live, accepts the proposition of shady millionaire Lloyd Bridges who offers him anything he wants for 20 days, after which he must throw himself into an active volcano on a remote island. Meg Ryan pops up playing three different women in Hanks's life. JF. Contains swearing.

Tom Hanks *Joe Banks* • Meg Ryan *DeDe/ Angelica/Patricia* • Lloyd Bridges *Graynamore* • Robert Stack *Dr Ellison* • Abe Vigoda *Waponis chief* • Dan Hedaya *Mr Waturi* • Amanda Plummer *Dagmar* • Ossie Davis *Marshall* ■ *Dir/Scr* John Patrick Shanley

Joe's Apartment ★★ 12

Comedy 1996 · US · Colour · 76mins

This was cable channel MTV's first movie production, a bid to turn the original 1992 live action/computer-animated short into a big screen hit. Jerry O'Connell is a jobless innocent who arrives in the Big Apple and finds that life is tough. Having conned his way into a rent-controlled apartment, he finds he shares it with about 50,000 singing, dancing and (luckily) friendly cockroaches. His new-found pals come to his aid when property magnate Robert Vaughn tries to kick him out. Laughs are fairly thin on the ground. JF. Contains swearing.

Jerry O'Connell *Joe* • Megan Ward *Lily* • Billy West *Ralph Roach* • Reginald Hudlin *Rodney Roach* • Jim Turner *Walter* • Robert Vaughn *Senator Dougherty* • Don Ho *Alberto Bianco* ■ *Dir/Scr* John Payson

Joey ★★

Comedy drama 1985 · US · Colour · 95mins

An 1980s movie, using an old-fashioned storytelling style, to put over its simple story of a music-obsessed teenager and his troubled relationship with his father. Aside from facing the usual problems of adolescence, Joey and his high school friends play in a rock 'n' roll band, and impress enough to get a once-in-a-lifetime opportunity to play at a prestigious doo-wop show. An obscure music movie memorable only because of the many original doo-wop stars making cameo appearances and singing their hits. DF

Neill Barry *Joey* • Elisa Heinsohn *Janie* • James Quinn *Joe Sr* • Linda Thorson *Principal O'Neill* • Ellen Hammill *Bobbie* • Rickey Ellis *John* • Dee Hourican *Bonnie* • Dan Grimaldi *Ted* • Frankie Lanz ■ *Dir/Scr* Joseph Ellison

Joey Boy ★ PG

Comedy 1965 · UK · BW · 87mins

Along with longtime collaborator Sidney Gilliat, Frank Launder was one of the bastions of British cinema in the 1940s and 1950s. But his brand of comedy had passed its sell-by date by the Swinging Sixties, as this awful film demonstrates only too well. Some TV sitcom stars are left with egg on their faces, none more so than Harry H Corbett as the brains behind a gang of petty crooks who join the army to avoid prison. DP

Harry H Corbett *"Joey Boy" Thompson* • Stanley Baxter *Benny "the Kid" Lindowski* • Bill Fraser *Sergeant Dobbs* • Percy Herbert *"Mad George" Long* • Lance Percival *Clarence Doubleday* • Reg Varney *"Rabbit" Malone* ■ *Dir* Frank Launder • *Scr* Frank Launder, Mike Watts, from the novel by Eddie Chapman

Joey Breaker ★★★

Drama 1993 · US · Colour · 92mins

Richard Edson is New York talent agent Joey, undergoing a *Jerry Maguire*-like crisis of conscience in this less well-known industry drama. Bob Marley's daughter Cedella plays Joey's girlfriend Cyan, who proves to be a much-needed humanising influence in his life. Writer/director Steven Starr obviously knows what he's talking about but, like our hero, we are left wondering why anyone would want to get involved in this amoral business in the first place. LH

Richard Edson *Joey Breaker* • Cedella Marley *Cyan Worthington* • Fred Fondren *Alfred Moore* • Erik King *Hip Hop Hank* • Gina Gershon *Jennie Chaser* • Philip Seymour Hoffman *Wiley McCall* • Mary Joy *Esther Trigliani* • Sam Coppola *Sid Kramer* ■ *Dir/Scr* Steven Starr

Jofroi ★★★★

Drama 1933 · Fr · BW · 55mins

The first of Marcel Pagnol's collaborations with writer Jean Giono, this featurette is an exquisite tribute to the director's beloved Provence. Filmed in his childhood home of La Treille and employing a relatively inexperienced cast, Pagnol tempered the corrosive humour of his "tragic burlesque" with rural lyricism and vibrant characterisation. Vincent Scotto is particularly memorable as the peasant who sells his land and then risks his life to prevent new owner Henri Poupon from cutting down too many trees. The passionate love for the land and wilful defiance of authority were to become recurrent themes, while the simple authenticity anticipated neorealism. DP. In French with English subtitles.

Vincent Scotto *Jofroi* • Henri Poupon *Fonse* • André Robert *The teacher* • Annie Toinon *Barbe* • Charles Blavette *Antonin* ■ *Dir* Marcel Pagnol • *Scr* Marcel Pagnol, from the story *Jofroi de la Maussan* by Jean Giono

J

John and Julie ★★ U

Comedy 1955 · UK · Colour · 82mins

This fantasy about the Queen's coronation arrived too late to catch the mood of national euphoria, but it's still a pleasing snapshot of 1950s Britain. Peter Sellers plays a policeman on the trail of Colin Gibson and Lesley Dudley, two little scamps who've run away from home in order to witness the pageantry. Even with such comic dependables as Wilfrid Hyde White and Sid James on hand, this is a pretty minor offering. DP

Colin Gibson *John* • Lesley Dudley *Julie* • Noelle Middleton *Miss Stokes* • Moira Lister *Dora* • Wilfrid Hyde White *Sir James* • Sidney James *Mr Pritchett* • Peter Sellers *PC Diamond* • Constance Cummings *Mrs Davidson* • Mona Washbourne *Miss Rendlesham* ■ *Dir/Scr* William Fairchild

John and Mary ★★

Drama 1969 · US · Colour · 92mins

A product of the Swinging Sixties, this drama of sexual mores was scripted by playwright John Mortimer and directed by Peter (*Bullitt*) Yates, but it remains conventionally stock-still in its attitudes. Icons of the time Dustin Hoffman and Mia Farrow play the eponymous couple who meet in a singles bar, make love and then spend an inordinate amount of time deciding what it all means. Not exactly compelling stuff. TH

Dustin Hoffman *John* • Mia Farrow *Mary* • Michael Tolan *James* • Sunny Griffin *Ruth* • Stanley Beck *Ernest* • Tyne Daly *Hilary* • Alix Elias *Jane* • Julie Garfield *Fran* • Olympia Dukakis *John's mother* ■ *Dir* Peter Yates • *Scr* John Mortimer, from a novel by Mervyn Jones • *Music* Quincy Jones

John Carpenter's Ghosts of Mars ★★ 15

Science-fiction action horror 2001 · US · Colour · 94mins

Set in the year 2176, the plot has cop Natasha Henstridge arrive at an isolated Martian mining town to transport notorious killer Ice Cube to a high-security prison. But the colonists are being possessed by the spooks of the title, and these Martian zombies swarm to defend their planet in a siege reminiscent of Carpenter's *Assault on Precinct 13*. There are moments of tension, but no real surprises. TH. Contains violence, swearing and drug abuse. VIDEO DVD

Ice Cube *James "Desolation" Williams* • Natasha Henstridge *Melanie Ballard* • Jason Statham *Jericho Butler* • Clea DuVall *Bashira Kincaid* • Pam Grier *Helena Braddock* • Joanna Cassidy *Whitlock* ■ *Dir* John Carpenter • *Scr* Larry Sulkis, John Carpenter • *Music* John Carpenter

John Goldfarb, Please Come Home ★

Comedy 1964 · US · Colour · 96mins

This is a lamentably unfunny satire about American colonialism. Peter Ustinov impersonates a Middle East potentate, King Fawz, who is being courted by the US which wants to build a military base in his country. Shirley MacLaine is a journalist doing a profile of him while Richard Crenna is Goldfarb, a spy plane pilot who is shot down and then co-opted into coaching Fawz's football team. None of the film's satirical scattershot hits its target. AT

Shirley MacLaine *Jenny Ericson* • Peter Ustinov *King Fawz* • Richard Crenna *John Goldfarb* • Jim Backus *Miles Whitepaper* • Scott Brady *Sakalakis* • Fred Clark *Heinous Overreach* • Wilfrid Hyde White *Guz* ■ *Dir* J Lee Thompson • *Scr* William Peter Blatty

John Grisham's The Rainmaker ★★★★ 15

Courtroom drama 1997 · US · Colour · 135mins

Francis Ford Coppola's riveting courtroom drama is an exceptionally well-crafted film that's a class above every other John Grisham adaptation. Matt Damon is excellent as the inexperienced lawyer thrown into the lion's den when he takes on the case of a young man dying of leukaemia, whose insurance company refuses to honour his claim. There's also a marvellous supporting cast including Jon Voight as the slimiest lawyer imaginable and Claire Danes as a battered wife sheltered by Damon. Courtroom cinema at its best. JC. Contains swearing, violence. VIDEO DVD

Matt Damon *Rudy Baylor* • Claire Danes *Kelly Riker* • Jon Voight *Leo F Drummond* • Mary Kay Place *Dot Black* • Mickey Rourke *Bruiser Stone* • Danny DeVito *Deck Shifflet* • Dean Stockwell *Judge Harvey Hale* • Teresa Wright *Miss Birdie* • Virginia Madsen *Jackie Lemanczyk* • Roy Scheider *Wilfred Keeley* • Danny Glover *Judge Tyrone Kipple*r ■ *Dir* Francis Ford Coppola • *Scr* Francis Ford Coppola, Michael Herr, from the novel by John Grisham

John Huston & The Dubliners ★★★

Documentary 1987 · US · Colour · 60mins

Having failed in the 1940s to bring *Ulysses* to the screen, John Huston finally got to adapt James Joyce in his last film, *The Dead*. Lilyan Sievernich's affectionate documentary reveals a man determined to make the most of his misfortunes – he was too ill to travel to Ireland and had to rely on Seamus Byrne's second unit to obtain the linking footage. He's seen barking orders from his wheelchair to ensure that a cast headed by his daughter, Anjelica, did justice to both the script penned by his son, Tony, and the spirit of Joyce's peerless prose. DP

Dir Lilyan Sievernich

John of the Fair ★★ U

Period adventure 1952 · UK · BW · 61mins

Shortly before embarking upon its series of Edgar Lustgarten true-crime cases, London production unit Merton Park made this rags-to-riches costume drama. Writer/director Michael McCarthy does a good job, on minimal resources, of re-creating the feel of an 18th-century English carnival. But once young John Charlesworth is revealed as the heir who stands between his wicked uncle and a fabulous estate, the action becomes more predictable. Rough and ready fare. DP

John Charlesworth *John Claydon* • Arthur Young *"Doc" Claydon* • Richard George *William Samuels* • Michael Mulcaster *Jasper Sly* • Hilda Barry *Ma Miggs* • Carol Wolveridge *Jill* • Sidney Bland *Gilroy* • David Garth *Sir Thomas Renton* ■ *Dir* Michael McCarthy • *Scr* Michael McCarthy, from the novel *John of the Fair* by Arthur William Groom

John Paul Jones ★★ U

Biographical drama 1959 · US · Colour · 125mins

Set during the American War of Independence, this historical drama is let down by an unappealing cast and a script which pours platitudes all over the Technirama screen. Robert Stack plays the eponymous hero, a Scottish lad who runs away to sea, becomes a captain and virtually invents the US navy. The film features a cameo from Bette Davis and a rousing score from Max Steiner, but the result is still a plodding effort. AT

Robert Stack *John Paul Jones* • Marisa Pavan *Aimee DeTellison* • Charles Coburn *Benjamin Franklin* • Erin O'Brien *Dorothea Danders* • Bette Davis *Catherine the Great* ■ *Dir* John Farrow • *Scr* John Farrow, Jesse Lasky Jr, from the story *Nor'wester* by Clements Ripley

John Q ★★★ 15

Action drama 2001 · US · Colour · 111mins

When his young son (Daniel E Smith) collapses after a game of baseball, decent Denzil Washington is informed by smarmy surgeon James Woods that he needs a heart transplant or he'll die. But Washington can't afford the operation and his insurance won't cover it. The answer? He takes the entire hospital emergency room hostage and demands treatment for his son. Unfortunately, it is then that the clichéd characters flood in like victims of an epidemic and seriously undermine the dramatic tension. What makes this work is Washington's fiercely committed performance as a man at the end of his tether. TH. Contains violence, swearing. VIDEO DVD

Denzel Washington *John Quincy Archibald* • Robert Duvall *Lt Frank Grimes* • James Woods *Dr Raymond Turner* • Anne Heche *Rebecca Payne* • Eddie Griffin *Lester* • Kimberly Elise *Denise Archibald* • Ray Liotta *Police Chief Monroe* • Daniel E Smith *Mike Archibald* ■ *Dir* Nick Cassavetes • *Scr* James Kearns

Johnny Allegro ★★

Crime drama 1949 · US · BW · 80mins

Having done a *Johnny Angel* in 1945, George Raft is now Johnny Allegro, an ex-criminal who agrees to help the Treasury Department. Their target is a villainous George Macready (did he ever play anyone nice?) who is masterminding a scheme to flood America with counterfeit money. AE

George Raft *Johnny Allegro* • Nina Foch *Glenda Chapman* • George Macready *Morgan Vallin* • Will Geer *Schultzy* • Gloria Henry *Addie* ■ *Dir* Ted Tetzlaff • *Scr* Karen De Wolf, Guy Endore, from a story by James Edward Grant

Johnny Angel ★★★★

Crime drama 1945 · US · BW · 79mins

Smoothie George Raft plays a sea captain out to find his father's killers in this tremendously entertaining melodrama, notable for a tangled flashback plot that remains wholly engrossing. The cast includes two stunning co-stars: Claire Trevor and Signe Hasso, the latter as the French girl who witnessed the murder. Hoagy Carmichael is a cab driver who rejoices in the name Celestial O'Brien, and he performs his (now classic) standard *Memphis in June*. With its tense direction from Edwin L Marin and superb, moody photography from Harry J Wild, the film deserves to be much better known. TS

George Raft *Johnny Angel* • Claire Trevor *Lilah* • Signe Hasso *Paulette* • Lowell Gilmore *Sam Jewell* • Hoagy Carmichael *Celestial O'Brien* • Marvin Miller *Gustafson* • Margaret Wycherly *Miss Drumm* ■ *Dir* Edwin L Marin • *Scr* Steve Fisher, Frank Gruber, from the novel *Mr Angel Comes Aboard* by Charles Gordon Booth

Johnny Apollo ★★★

Crime drama 1940 · US · BW · 94mins

Handsome matinée idol Tyrone Power got a chance to prove he was more than just a pretty face in this tough melodrama about the son of crooked financial scion Edward Arnold going to the bad. This is a very well acted and controlled movie, directed by talented 20th Century-Fox regular Henry Hathaway with just the right degree of understanding, and did wonders for Power's appeal at the box office. Also particularly effective is Dorothy Lamour as Ty's moll, and tough Lloyd Nolan as the rival hood. TS

Tyrone Power *Bob Cain/Johnny Apollo* • Dorothy Lamour *Mabel "Lucky" Dubarry* • Lloyd Nolan *Mickey Dwyer* • Edward Arnold *Robert Cain Sr* • Charley Grapewin *Judge Emmett T Brennan* • Lionel Atwill *Jim McLaughlin* • Marc Lawrence (1) *John Bates* ■ *Dir* Henry Hathaway • *Scr* Philip Dunne, Rowland Brown, from a story by Samuel G Engel, Hal Long

Johnny Be Good ★ 15

Sports comedy 1988 · US · Colour · 87mins

It's tough believing that Brat Pack geekmeister Anthony Michael Hall can even kick a ball, let alone be America's hottest football prospect in this sub-standard teen comedy posing as a cautionary tale. Hall just can't quite decide whether to take up numerous lucrative offers from talent scouts or drop the game to attend college with his sweetheart. This treats the ethics of signing young athletes as if it were merely another instalment of *Porky's*. RS VIDEO DVD

Anthony Michael Hall *Johnny Walker* • Paul Gleason *Coach Wayne Hisler* • Robert Downey Jr *Leo Wiggins* • Robert Downey Sr *NC AA Investigator* • Uma Thurman *Georgia Elkans* • Seymour Cassel *Wallace Gibson* • Steve James (1) *Coach Sanders* • Jennifer Tilly *Connie Hisler* ■ *Dir* Bud Smith • *Scr* Jeff Buhai, Steve Zacharias, David Obst

Johnny Belinda ★★★★

Drama 1948 · US · BW · 102mins

Jane Wyman won a well-deserved best actress Academy Award for her moving portrayal of the Nova Scotia deaf-mute rape victim in this fine Warner Bros film, which in director Jean Negulesco manages to combine outright melodrama with sensitive performances. Of course, either it works for you or it doesn't; in its day, it was a mighty popular and much parodied movie, but now the censor-circumventions make the whole thing seem as phoney as its sets, but the strength of the acting wins through. TS

Jane Wyman *Belinda McDonald* • Lew Ayres *Dr Robert Richardson* • Charles Bickford *Black McDonald* • Stephen McNally *Locky McCormick* • Jan Sterling *Stella McCormick* • Agnes Moorehead *Aggie McDonald* • Holmes Herbert *Judge* • Dan Seymour *Pacquet* ■ *Dir* Jean Negulesco • *Scr* Imgard von Cube, Allen Vincent, from the play *Johnny Belinda* by Elmer Harris • *Cinematographer* Ted McCord

Johnny Come Lately ★★★ U

Comedy drama 1943 · US · BW · 97mins

A strong performance from James Cagney and a fine supporting cast lift this otherwise unexceptional newspaper picture. Cagney plays a journalist who helps a widow keep her late's husband's newspaper running, despite the local politicians and businessmen who are trying to close it down. There's civic corruption, characters with shady pasts and a little romance, but mainly it's a story about integrity. AT

James Cagney *Tom Richards* • Grace George *Vinnie McLeod* • Marjorie Main *Gashouse Mary* • Marjorie Lord *Jane* • Hattie McDaniel *Aida* ■ *Dir* William K Howard • *Scr* John Van Druten, from the novel *McLeod's Folly* by Louis Bromfield

Johnny Concho ★★★

Western 1956 · US · BW · 85mins

Although an inexpensive western must have seemed a safe bet, it's strange that Frank Sinatra should have chosen this particular story for his producing debut. Strange because he's ideally cast as an obnoxious coward protected by his notorious gunslinger brother. After the brother is bumped off and his killers take over the town, It's predictable Sinatra should eventually summon up the courage to face them. Curiously, though, he never shakes off his odious earlier image. Sinatra's pal, former actor Don McGuire, co-wrote the script and made his directing debut with this very watchable drama. AE

Frank Sinatra *Johnny Concho* • Keenan Wynn *Barney Clark* • William Conrad *Tallman* • Phyllis Kirk *Mary Dark* • Wallace Ford *Albert Dark* • Dorothy Adams *Sarah Dark* ■ *Dir* Don McGuire • *Scr* David P Harmon, Don McGuire, from the story *The Man Who Owned the Town* by David P Harmon

Johnny Cool ★★★

Crime drama 1963 · US · BW · 101mins

Henry Silva plays the Sicilian hitman working overtime in America in this enjoyable gangster movie. At times the picture seems to be a parody of everything Mafioso; at others, the violence is quite shocking. The supporting cast is also a bizarre mix, while director William Asher (the man behind all those *Beach Party* movies) cleverly mixes and matches black comedy with *Naked City* realism. AT

Henry Silva *Johnny Cool/Giordano* • Elizabeth Montgomery *Dare Guiness* • Richard Anderson *Correspondent* • Jim Backus *Louis Murphy* • Joey Bishop *Used car salesman* • Brad Dexter *Lennart Crandall* • Telly Savalas *Mr Santangelo* • Sammy Davis Jr *"Educated"* ■ *Dir* William Asher • *Scr* Joseph Landon, from the novel *The Kingdom of Johnny Cool* by John McPartland

Johnny Dangerously ★★★ 15

Crime spoof 1984 · US · Colour · 86mins

Before donning the black cape for Tim Burton's *Batman*, Michael Keaton played for laughs in films such as *Mr Mom*, *Night Shift* and this spoof of 1930s gangster movies. He stars as a good-natured gangster whose brother is a crime-busting district attorney. It's enjoyably silly stuff and zips along at a fair old pace, peppered with some great one-liners. There's fun support from a cast that includes Joe Piscopo, Peter Boyle, Dom DeLuise and Maureen Stapleton, but the film belongs to Keaton, who once again shows his comedic talents to entertaining effect. JB DVD

Michael Keaton *Johnny Dangerously* • Marilu Henner *Lil* • Joe Piscopo *Vermin* • Danny DeVito *Burr* • Maureen Stapleton *Mom* • Griffin Dunne *Tommy* • Peter Boyle *Dundee* • Richard Dimitri *Maroni* • Glynnis O'Connor *Sally* • Byron Thames *Young Johnny* • Dom DeLuise *Pope* • Ray Walston *Vendor* ■ *Dir* Amy Heckerling • *Scr* Norman Steinberg, Bernie Kukoff, Harry Colomby, Jeff Harris

Johnny Dark ★★ U

Action drama 1954 · US · Colour · 85mins

Aimed at younger audiences and showcasing Universal's new breed of stars, this lightweight drama requires acceptance of Tony Curtis as an engineering genius who can design and drive a new racing car. The director, western veteran George Sherman, knows how to keep a film on the move and ensures that the thrills and spills of the racing scenes, particularly the climactic drive from the Canadian border to Mexico, are forcefully put over. Piper Laurie makes a pleasant leading lady. AE

Tony Curtis *Johnny Dark* • Piper Laurie *Liz Fielding* • Don Taylor *Duke Benson* • Paul Kelly (1) *Jim Scott* • Ilka Chase *Abbie Binns* • Sidney Blackmer *James Fielding* ■ *Dir* George Sherman • *Scr* Franklin Coen

Johnny Doesn't Live Here Anymore ★★ U

Comedy 1944 · US · BW · 73mins

The versatile Joe May was one of the directors who pulled German cinema up by its bootstraps in the aftermath of the First World War. Yet after he moved to Hollywood to escape the Nazi threat, his movies were, for the most part, routine. Simone Simon is typically charming as the career girl who suddenly finds her friend's flat being invaded by the pals to whom he's given keys. James Ellison might steal Simone's heart, but it's the laconic Robert Mitchum who steals the show in the final reel. Re-released as *And So They Were Married*. DP

Simone Simon *Kathie Aumont* • James Ellison *Mike O'Brien* • Robert Mitchum *CPO Jeff Daniels* • William Terry *Johnny Moore* • Minna Gombell *Mrs Collins* • Chick Chandler *Jack* ■ *Dir* Joe May • *Scr* Philip Yordan, John H Kafka, from a story by Alice Means Reeve

Johnny Eager ★★★

Crime drama 1941 · US · BW · 106mins

Robert Taylor is well cast as an unscrupulous racketeer, his virtually expressionless handsome features allowing an audience to read into his character all manner of evils. His co-star is sexy Lana Turner, then 21 years old and an instantly hot on-set item with the older Taylor. Acting honours, and the Oscar, went to Van Heflin as Taylor's self-pitying alcoholic friend, whose censor-circumventing role loosely implies a homosexual bond between the two men. A crisp, clever movie. TS

Robert Taylor (1) *Johnny Eager* • Lana Turner *Lisbeth Bard* • Edward Arnold *John Benson Farrell* • Van Heflin *Jeff Hartnett* • Robert Sterling *Jimmy Lanthrop* • Patricia Dane *Garnet* • Glenda Farrell *Mae Blythe* ■ *Dir* Mervyn LeRoy • *Scr* John Lee Mahin, James Edward Grant, from a story by Grant

Johnny English ★★ PG

Spy comedy adventure
2003 · UK/US/Fr · Colour · 83mins

Fans of Rowan Atkinson's rubbery-faced brand of physical comedy will know what to expect from this unassuming slice of slapstick. Based on a character portrayed by the *Mr Bean* star in a series of Barclaycard adverts, it sends up another home-grown institution – the James Bond-style super-spy. Atkinson plays the titular hero, an enthusiastic but bumbling intelligence agent appointed to track down those behind the theft of the crown jewels. Director Peter Howitt forgoes subtlety for youngster-friendly sight gags. SF DVD

Rowan Atkinson *Johnny English* • Natalie Imbruglia *Lorna Campbell* • Ben Miller *Bough* • John Malkovich *Pascal Sauvage* • Tim Pigott-Smith *Pegasus* • Kevin McNally *Prime Minister* • Oliver Ford Davies *Archbishop of Canterbury* • Greg Wise *Agent One* ■ *Dir* Peter Howitt • *Scr* Neal Purvis, Robert Wade, William Davies

Johnny Frenchman ★★★ U

Drama 1945 · UK · BW · 111mins

Among the few faults of the films produced at Ealing were their parochialism and their tendency to patronise in their depiction of the working classes. Screenwriter TEB Clarke's third film for the studio, this tale of the rivalry between Breton and Cornish fishing communities was intended to cement the *entente cordiale* in the latter days of the Second World War. It would have been a rather forgettable affair, but for the fact that it gave British audiences a rare chance to see the sublime French actress Françoise Rosay rising well above her capable co-stars and the level of her material. DP

Françoise Rosay *Lanec Florrie* • Tom Walls *Nat Pomeroy* • Patricia Roc *Sue Pomeroy* • Ralph Michael *Bob Tremayne* • Paul Dupuis *Yan Kervarec* • Frederick Piper *Zacky Penrose* ■ *Dir* Charles Frend • *Scr* TEB Clarke

Johnny Got His Gun ★ 12

Drama 1971 · US · Colour and BW · 106mins

Screenwriter Dalton Trumbo was imprisoned during the McCarthy witch-hunts yet won two Oscars under a pseudonym – for *Roman Holiday* and *The Brave One*. With this, Trumbo directed his own script from his own novel about a First World War soldier who has lost his arms, legs, face, sight, smell and hearing but is kept alive for medical research and experimentation. They think he's a vegetable but he isn't. It just drags on in its excruciating, cringe-inducing way. Simply awful. AT DVD

Jason Robards *Father* • Timothy Bottoms *Johnny/Joe Bonham* • Marsha Hunt *Mother* • Diane Varsi *Nurse* • Charles McGraw *Girl's father* ■ *Dir* Dalton Trumbo • *Scr* Dalton Trumbo, from his novel

Johnny Guitar ★★★★ PG

Cult western 1954 · US · Colour · 105mins

Although Nicholas Ray's simmering western subverts this notoriously conservative genre, the real purpose of his study in mob hysteria was to condemn the Communist witch-hunt then tearing Hollywood apart. Heavy with symbolism, Philip Yordan's script also crackles with repressed sexuality, as saloon owner Joan Crawford and cattle queen Mercedes McCambridge lock swords. Providing Crawford with one of her best roles and gloriously shot in Trucolor by Harry Stradling Jr, this baroque bonanza fascinates on so many levels that it demands to be repeatedly reviewed. DP DVD

Joan Crawford *Vienna* • Sterling Hayden *Johnny Guitar* • Mercedes McCambridge *Emma Small* • Scott Brady *Dancin' Kid* • Ward Bond *John McIvers* • Ben Cooper *Turkey Ralston* • John Carradine *Old Tom* • Ernest Borgnine *Bart Lonergan* ■ *Dir* Nicholas Ray • *Scr* Philip Yordan, from the novel by Ray Chanslor

Johnny Handsome ★★ 15

Crime drama 1989 · US · Colour · 89mins

One of the seemingly endless series of Mickey Rourke flops, director Walter Hill's downbeat glob of calculated nastiness shoehorns numerous genres together with scant success. Turning from latex monster to plastic surgeon's miracle, Rourke invests nil expression or thought into his role as a disfigured criminal who's given a new face in a prison hospital. Saved from total failure by a few energetically staged action sequences, this rancid movie also features a sleazy turn from Ellen Barkin. AJ. Contains violence, swearing. DVD

Mickey Rourke *John Sedley* • Ellen Barkin *Sunny Boyd* • Elizabeth McGovern *Donna McCarty* • Morgan Freeman *Lieutenant AZ Drones* • Forest Whitaker *Dr Steven Resher* • Lance Henriksen *Rafe Garrett* • Scott Wilson *Mikey Chalmette* ■ *Dir* Walter Hill • *Scr* Ken Friedman, from the novel *The Three Worlds of Johnny Handsome* by John Godey

Johnny Mnemonic ★ 15

Science-fiction thriller
1995 · Can/US · Colour · 92mins

Director Robert Longo's turgid sci-fi thriller, based on William Gibson's cyberpunk short story, is cyber junk. Keanu Reeves sleepwalks through the title role as a 21st-century hi-tech messenger who carries top-secret information thanks to a computer chip in his brain. Empty, flashy and incredibly dull, Longo's unpleasant movie is lamely tarted up with incomprehensible surf-cowboy jargon, gratuitous violence and second-rate special effects. AJ. Contains swearing, violence and nudity. DVD

Keanu Reeves *Johnny Mnemonic* • Dina Meyer *Jane* • Ice-T *J-Bone* • Takeshi [Takeshi Kitano] *Takahashi* • Denis Akiyama *Shinji* • Dolph Lundgren *Street Preacher* • Henry Rollins *Spider* ■ *Dir* Robert Longo • *Scr* William Gibson, from his short story

J

Johnny O'Clock ★★★

Film noir 1947 · US · BW · 95mins

Robert Rossen was that rarest of film-makers, a practising communist who managed to write social criticism into his screenplays before he was blacklisted. This under-rated *film noir* whodunnit marked his directorial debut, and is distinguished by superb Burnett Guffey photography – check out those expressionist angles – and a sharp and knowing screenplay, as Dick Powell's tough gambler and Lee J Cobb's policeman engage in terse exchanges over who killed the hat-check girl and the cop she fancied. TS

Dick Powell *Johnny O'Clock* • Evelyn Keyes *Nancy Hobbs* • Lee J Cobb *Inspector Koch* • Ellen Drew *Nelle Marchettis* • Nina Foch *Harriet Hobbs* • Thomas Gomez *Pete Marchettis* • John Kellogg *Charlie* ■ *Dir* Robert Rossen • *Scr* Robert Rossen, from a story by Milton Holmes

Johnny 100 Pesos ★★★ 15

Crime thriller based on a true story
1993 · Chil/Mex · Colour and BW · 90mins

The best bungled blag movies are invariably based on fact and this effectively contrasts the mounting concerns of the incompetent crooks with the overblown response of the authorities and the media. Set in post-Pinochet Santiago, the story of a schoolboy's attempt to rob a video store that serves as a front for a money laundering racket works well enough as a thriller. But the combination of Armando Araiza's ineptitude and ill-fortune presents Gustavo Graef-Marino with the opportunity to lace his black comedy with stinging political satire. DP. In Spanish with English subtitles.

Armando Araiza *Johnny Garcia* • Patricia Rivera *Gloria* • Willy Semler *Freddy* • Luis Gnecco *Don Alfonso* • Aldo Parodi *Loco* ■ *Dir* Gustavo Graef-Marino • *Scr* Gerardo Caceres, Gustavo Graef-Marino

Johnny Reno ★★

Western 1966 · US · Colour · 82mins

Dana Andrews is US marshal Johnny Reno, riding into serious trouble en route to Stone Junction. He ends up killing one would-be assassin and taking another prisoner, before coming up against Stone Junction's corrupt mayor Lyle Bettger. The story is slight, but what gives the film its modest appeal is the cast who are all much too old and experienced to have to prove anything any more. AT

Dana Andrews *Johnny Reno* • Jane Russell *Nona Williams* • Lon Chaney Jr *Sheriff Hodges* • John Agar *Ed Tomkins* • Lyle Bettger *Jess Yates* • Tom Drake *Joe Connors* ■ *Dir* RG Springsteen • *Scr* Steve Fisher, from a story by AC Lyles, Steve Fisher, Andrew Craddock

Johnny Stecchino ★★★ 18

Comedy 1991 · It · Colour · 115mins

Although it smashed box-office records at home, this anarchic comedy was little seen outside Roberto Benigni's native Italy. Miraculously pulling off slapstick gags that were stale even in the silent era, he coaxes you into siding with the naive bus driver who just happens to resemble a notorious Sicilian mobster. The comedy has a contentious edge, with some of the gags at the expense of the Mafia being daringly outspoken. With off-screen wife Nicoletta Braschi again winning the clown prince's heart, this frantic farce will either have you rolling on the carpet or scratching your head in puzzlement. DP. In Italian with English subtitles. DVD

Roberto Benigni *Dante/Johnny Stecchino* • Nicoletta Braschi *Maria* • Paolo Bonacelli *D'Agata* • Franco Volpi *Minister* • Ivano Marescotti *Dr Randazzo* • Alessandro De Santis *Lillo* ■ *Dir* Roberto Benigni • *Scr* Roberto Benigni, Vincenzo Cerami

Johnny Stool Pigeon ★★

Crime drama 1949 · US · BW · 76mins

This capable example of the semi-documentary crime film of the late 1940s, which comes complete with the usual voiceover narration, stars Dan Duryea as a gangster released from prison to help detective Howard Duff round up a drug-trafficking ring. The story is overly contrived, but director William Castle extracts strong performances from his leads. Taking a supporting role as a mute killer is a young contract player, Anthony (later Tony) Curtis. AE

Howard Duff *George Morton aka Mike Doyle/Narrator* • Shelley Winters *Terry Stewart* • Dan Duryea *Johnny Evans* • Anthony Curtis [Tony Curtis] *Joey Hyatt* • John McIntire *Nick Avery* • Gar Moore *Sam Harrison* • Leif Erickson *Pringle* ■ *Dir* William Castle • *Scr* Robert L Richards, from a story by Henry Jordan

Johnny Suede ★★★★ 15

Comedy fantasy 1991 · US · Colour · 93mins

With the rave reviews from *Thelma and Louise* still ringing in his ears, Brad Pitt further demonstrated his star quality as the bequiffed hero of this gentle tale, which marked the directorial debut of ex-cinematographer Tom DiCillo. Awash with pastel colours and dripping with style, this fantastical satire replaces the famous ruby slippers with a pair of suede shoes and the Great Oz with 1950s' pop idol Ricky Nelson. DiCillo's unerring eye for both the absurd and grim is complemented by his fine pacing and the tautness of his script. Pitt is superb and is well supported by Alison Moir and Catherine Keener. DP

Brad Pitt *Johnny Suede* • Richard Boes *Man in tuxedo* • Cheryl Costa *Woman in alley* • Michael Luciano *Mr Clepp* • Calvin Levels *Deke* • Nick Cave *Freak Storm* • Alison Moir *Darlette* • Catherine Keener *Yvonne* • Samuel L Jackson *B-Bop* ■ *Dir/Scr* Tom DiCillo • *Cinematographer* Joe DeSalvo

Johnny Tiger ★

Drama 1966 · US · Colour · 102mins

Robert Taylor's sensitive college professor goes to Florida to teach Seminole Indians, his three children in tow. However, his noble intentions are thwarted by a dying chief who wants his grandson (Chad Everett) to renounce contact with white people. The lack of dramatic tension and some inadequate performances (notably Everett in the title role) prove to be fatal weaknesses. AT

Robert Taylor (1) *George Dean* • Geraldine Brooks *Dr Leslie Frost* • Chad Everett *Johnny Tiger* • Brenda Scott *Barbara Dean* • Marc Lawrence (1) *William Billie* ■ *Dir* Paul Wendkos • *Scr* Paul Crabtree, Thomas Blackburn, Philip Wylie, R John Hugh, from the story *Tiger on the Outside* by R John Hugh

Johnny Tremain ★★★ U

Historical drama 1957 · US · Colour · 80mins

Covering a well-documented chapter of American history, this Disney film tells the story of Johnny, a former silversmith, who becomes committed to the revolutionary cause after being falsely accused of theft. Veteran director Robert Stevenson doesn't quite succeed in capturing the sights and sounds of the American colonial era but the kids will enjoy it. DP

Hal Stalmaster *Johnny Tremain* • Luana Patten *Cilla Lapham* • Jeff York *James Otis* • Sebastian Cabot *Jonathan Lyte* • Dick Beymer [Richard Beymer] *Rab Silsbee* • Walter Sande *Paul Revere* • Rusty Lane *Samuel Adams* • Whit Bissell *Josiah Quincy* ■ *Dir* Robert Stevenson • *Scr* Tom Blackburn, from the novel by Esther Forbes

Johnny Trouble ★★ U

Drama 1957 · US · BW · 79mins

This old-fashioned, sentimental drama marked the end of the overpowering Ethel Barrymore's career. She plays an elderly widow who stubbornly refuses to leave her apartment building after it is sold, and ends up with students for neighbours. She convinces herself that young delinquent Stuart Whitman is the offspring of her own, long-absent son. Both Whitman and Carolyn Jones as his girlfriend are rather good, given the circumstances. AE

Ethel Barrymore *Mrs Chandler* • Cecil Kellaway *Tom McKay* • Carolyn Jones *Julie* • Jesse White *Parsons* • Rand Harper *Phil* • Stuart Whitman *Johnny* • Paul Wallace *Paul* • Edward Byrnes [Edd Byrnes] *Elliott* ■ *Dir* John H Auer • *Scr* Charles O'Neal, David Lord, from the story *Prodigal's Mother* by Ben Ames Williams

Johns ★★★★ 18

Drama 1995 · US · Colour · 91mins

LA in all its sleazy glory is fascinatingly portrayed here by writer/director Scott Silver. David Arquette and Lukas Haas are both superb as two street hustlers determined to raise enough cash to fulfil Arquette's dream of spending Christmas Eve in a swish hotel suite. Many of the events that happen to them are based on true stories collected by Silver during his research. Very funny in places, as well as tragic and moving, this is one of those movies whose characters linger long in the memory. JB. Contains swearing and sex scenes. DVD

Lukas Haas *Donner* • David Arquette *John* • Arliss Howard *John Cardoza* • Keith David *Homeless John* • Christopher Gartin *Eli* • Josh Schaefer [Joshua Schaefer] *David* ■ *Dir/Scr* Scott Silver

Johnson Family Vacation ★ 12

Comedy road movie
2004 · US · Colour · 92mins

This dire comedy has so few laughs it barely warrants its genre description. In an unusually flat performance, Cedric the Entertainer plays a competitive sibling who takes his estranged wife (Vanessa Williams) and three children on a cross-country road trip to compete in his family's annual reunion contest. The mishaps that follow are lame and predictable, with the limpest slapstick and sight gags replacing genuine wit. SF. Contains swearing. DVD

Cedric the Entertainer *Nate Johnson/Uncle Earl* • Vanessa Williams [Vanessa L Williams] *Dorothy Johnson* • Solange Knowles *Nikki Johnson* • Bow Wow [Lil' Bow Wow] *DJ Johnson* • Gabby Soleil *Destiny Johnson* • Shannon Elizabeth *Chrishelle* • Steve Harvey *Mack Johnson* ■ *Dir* Christopher Erskin • *Scr* Todd R Jones, Earl Richey Jones

The Joke ★★★★

Drama 1968 · Cz · BW · 80mins

Jaromil Jires was the most stylistically audacious director of the Czech "new wave" of the early 1960s. However, he is more restrained in this studied adaptation of Milan Kundera's scathingly satirical novel. Josef Somr gives an exceptional performance as the student who is sentenced to a spell in one of the army's brutal black units after a political joke backfires. While the themes may be a little obscure, the hardships and humiliations Somr experiences often make excruciating viewing. DP. In Czech with English subtitles.

Josef Somr *Ludvik* • Jana Ditetova *Helena* • Ludek Munzar *Pavel* • Evald Schorm *Kosika* • Vera Kresadlova *Brozova* ■ *Dir* Jaromil Jires • *Scr* Jaromil Jires, from the novel *The Joke* by Milan Kundera

The Joker Is Wild ★★

Biographical drama 1957 · US · BW · 128mins

This workmanlike and overlong biography stars Frank Sinatra as comedian Joe E Lewis, whose vocal chords were seriously damaged by nightclub racketeers in the 1930s – which put paid to his original career as a singer. Lewis's stormy life and battle with alcoholism is not a lot of fun, though Jeanne Crain and Mitzi Gaynor add glamour as his two wives. TV

Frank Sinatra *Joe E Lewis* • Mitzi Gaynor *Martha Stewart* • Jeanne Crain *Letty Page* • Eddie Albert *Austin Mack* • Beverly Garland *Cassie Mack* • Jackie Coogan *Swifty Morgan* • Sophie Tucker ■ *Dir* Charles Vidor • *Scr* Oscar Saul, from the non-fiction book *Life of Joe E Lewis* by Art Cohn

The Jokers ★★★ U

Comedy thriller 1967 · UK · Colour · 95mins

A light-hearted romp, with Michael Crawford and Oliver Reed well cast as brothers who attempt to steal the Crown Jewels just for the heck of it. It's a quintessential "Swinging London" movie, full of nice locations and ever-so-British attitudes. The Dick Clement/Ian La Frenais screenplay was virtually director-proof and was entrusted to Michael Winner, who certainly does a decent job of it, making it seem regrettable that he ever veered away from comedy. TS

Michael Crawford *Michael Tremayne* • Oliver Reed *David Tremayne* • Harry Andrews *Inspector Marryatt* • James Donald *Colonel Gurney-Simms* • Daniel Massey *Riggs* • Michael Hordern *Sir Matthew* • Edward Fox *Lt Sprague* • Warren Mitchell *Lennie* • Frank Finlay *Harassed man* ■ *Dir* Michael Winner • *Scr* Dick Clement, Ian La Frenais, from a story by Michael Winner

Le Joli Mai ★★★★ U

Documentary 1962 · Fr · BW · 121mins

Chris Marker's fascinating documentary provides an invaluable snapshot of a city in transition. With its montage sequences, newsreel footage, narrated passages and probing interviews, it recalls the "city symphonies" made in the late silent era by the likes of Dziga Vertov, with Parisians of all classes and age groups proferring their views on everything from the nature of democracy to the state of French culture. With Yves Montand making an acerbic guide (the role is performed by Simone Signoret in the English version), this is *cinéma vérité* at its wittiest and most revealing. DP. A French language film.

Simone Signoret *Commentary* • Yves Montand *Commentary* ■ *Dir* Chris Marker • *Scr* Cathérine Varlin, Chris Marker

A Jolly Bad Fellow ★

Black comedy 1964 · UK · BW · 110mins

This is an ill-advised attempt by co-screenwriter Robert Hamer to recapture the glories of his 1949 Ealing classic *Kind Hearts and Coronets*. Leo McKern has the misfortune to play a university professor who uses his new undetectable poison to liquidate those he feels have no right to live. Don Chaffey took on the directorial chores after Hamer's death, but he was beaten before he started with this tasteless comedy. DP

Leo McKern *Professor Bowles-Ottery* • Janet Munro *Delia Brooks* • Maxine Audley *Clarinda Bowles-Ottery* • Duncan Macrae *Dr Brass* • Dennis Price *Professor Hughes* • Miles Malleson *Dr Woolley* • Leonard Rossiter *Dr Fisher* ■ *Dir* Don Chaffey • *Scr* Robert Hamer, Donald Taylor, from the novel *Down among the Dead Men* by CE Vulliamy

Jolson Sings Again ★★ U

Musical biography
1949 · US · Colour · 91mins

Made three years after the phenomenal success of *The Jolson Story*, this sequel suffers from the fact that the entertainer's later life was nowhere near as interesting as his rise to fame. Larry Parks produces another remarkable impersonation (backed by Jolson's own singing voice), particularly relishing the gag in which Parks (playing Jolson) meets Parks (playing himself) to discuss making the first film. Classic songs abound, but there's too little going on to give this anything but nostalgia value. DP DVD

Larry Parks *Al Jolson* • Barbara Hale *Ellen Clark* • William Demarest *Steve Martin* • Ludwig Donath *Cantor Yoelson* • Bill Goodwin *Tom Baron* • Myron McCormick *Col Ralph Bryant* ■ *Dir* Henry Levin • *Scr* Sidney Buchman • *Music Director* Morris Stoloff

The Jolson Story ★★★★★ U

Musical biography
1946 · US · Colour · 124mins

One of the most popular movies ever made, this biopic stars Larry Parks as the entertainer with the big ego and the even bigger talent. In re-recording his greatest hits for this movie, Al Jolson proved to be in finer, more mellow timbre than ever. These versions are therefore the definitive ones, and Parks totally convinces as he mimes his way through such landmarks as *April Showers*, *My Mammy* and *Toot Toot Tootsie Goodbye*. Okay, so the blacking-up is politically unfashionable these days, the lovable Jewish characters are mere caricatures, and the tale is appallingly fancified. Who cares? This is Hollywood entertainment on a grand scale, and you'll weep and cheer all the way to the uncompromising final curtain. TS DVD

Larry Parks *Al Jolson* • Evelyn Keyes *Julie Benson* • William Demarest *Steve Martin* • Bill Goodwin *Tom Baron* • Ludwig Donath *Cantor Yoelson* • Tamara Shayne *Mrs Yoelson* • John Alexander *Lew Dockstader* ■ *Dir* Alfred E Green • *Scr* Stephen Longstreet, Harry Chandlee, Andrew Solt

Jonah Who Will Be 25 in the Year 2000 ★★★★

Comedy
1976 · Swi/Fr · Colour and BW · 115mins

Seen from the virtually apolitical vantage point of a new millennium, Alain Tanner's right-on comedy might seem a muddle of wishy-washy notions and impossible dreams. But political radicalism had only recently died when he paid this tribute to the indomitability of the May 1968 veterans, who may have failed in their intentions, but who still had the courage to act. A magnificent ensemble cast endures life's buffeting with equanimity, while Tanner and co-screenwriter John Berger intertwine the diverging destinies with a dexterity that allows for revealing monochrome reveries (both brutal and fantastical). DP. In French with English subtitles.

Jean-Luc Bideau *Max Stigny* • Myriam Boyer *Mathilde Vernier* • Rufus *Mathieu Vernier* • Miou-Miou *Marie* • Jacques Denis *Marco Perly* • Dominique Labourier *Marguerite* • Roger Jendly *Marcel Certoux* • Myriam Mézières *Madeleine* ■ *Dir* Alain Tanner • *Scr* Alain Tanner, John Berger

Jonathan Livingston Seagull ★★★ U

Fantasy 1973 · US · Colour · 94mins

Despite its title, this philosophical oddity doesn't exactly soar into comprehension. Richard Bach's bestseller, very much of its time, is an "inspirational" parable about a seagull whose life parallels human existence – speed, contemplation, and finally redemption and resurrection. This intriguing existentialist idea is nearly flooded out by Neil Diamond's splashy score. TH [video]

James Franciscus *Jonathan Livingston Seagull* • Juliet Mills *Girl* • Hal Holbrook *Elder* • Philip Ahn *Chang* • David Ladd *Fletcher* • Kelly Harmon *Kimmy* ■ *Dir* Hall Bartlett • *Scr* Hall Bartlett, Richard Bach, from the novel by Richard Bach • *Music* Neil Diamond, Lee Holdridge

Jory ★★★ PG

Western 1972 · US · Colour · 92mins

An unusual western, with the emphasis less on the rootin', tootin' and shootin', and more on character development. Robby Benson, in his first film role, plays a teenager who's forced to fend for himself when his father and friends are murdered. The film has points to make about manhood and maleness as Benson is rapidly compelled to cast off his boyhood. But, if that makes it all sound rather tame, there's excitement and action, too. DA [video]

John Marley *Roy* • BJ Thomas *Jocko* • Robby Benson *Jory* • Brad Dexter *Jack* • Claudio Brook *Ethan* • Patricia Aspillaga *Carmelita* • Todd Martin *Barron* • Benny Baker *Mr Jordan* ■ *Dir* Jorge Fons • *Scr* Gerald Herman, Robert Irving, from a novel by Milton R Bass

Joseph Andrews ★★

Period comedy 1977 · UK · Colour · 103mins

Director Tony Richardson attempted to repeat the success of his Oscar-winning *Tom Jones* with another Fielding adaptation but falls flat on his farce. The bed-and-bawdy plot sees Peter Firth as the 18th-century footman involved in romantic adventures with the likes of Ann-Margret. It certainly looks good but Richardson fails to inject the necessary verve and pacing, opting for historical stereotypes and humour which is genteel at best. TH

Ann-Margret *Lady Booby* • Peter Firth *Joseph Andrews* • Michael Hordern *Parson Adams* • Beryl Reid *Mrs Slipslop* • Jim Dale *Pedlar* • Kenneth Cranham *Wicked Squire* • John Gielgud *Doctor* • Peggy Ashcroft *Lady Tattle* ■ *Dir* Tony Richardson • *Scr* Allan Scott, Chris Bryant, Tony Richardson, from the novel by Henry Fielding

Joseph: King of Dreams ★★ U

Animated musical drama
2000 · US · Colour · 71mins

DreamWorks's direct-to-video follow-up to *The Prince of Egypt* lacks the epic feel generated the first time around. The background art (some of it computer-generated) is acceptable, but the character design is not. The biggest problem is that the Biblical hero comes across here as shallow and a little smug, and it takes most of the movie before we can warm to him. KB [video] DVD

Ben Affleck *Joseph* • Mark Hamill *Judah* • Steven Weber *Simeon* • Jodi Benson *Asenath* • Maureen McGovern *Rachel* • Judith Light *Zuleika* ■ *Dir* Robert C Ramirez, Rob LaDuca • *Scr* Eugenia Bostwick-Singer, Raymond Singer, Joe Stillman, Marshall Goldberg

Josephine and Men ★★ U

Comedy 1955 · UK · Colour · 88mins

Josephine (pert, husky-voiced Glynis Johns) is one of those perverse women who is always drawn to the losers in life, her interest waning when their fortunes improve. Debonair Jack Buchanan plays her suave bachelor uncle who narrates her story in flashback. Josephine leaves her wealthy fiancé (Donald Sinden) for his friend (Peter Finch), an unsuccessful playwright – until their situations are reversed. Directed by Roy Boulting, this romantic comedy is pretty lightweight and not as funny as it could have been, but the cast is likeable. RB

Glynis Johns *Josephine Luton* • Jack Buchanan *Uncle Charles Luton* • Peter Finch *David Hewer* • Donald Sinden *Alan Hartley* • Ronald Squire *Frederick Luton* • William Hartnell *Inspector Parsons* ■ *Dir* Roy Boulting • *Scr* Roy Boulting, Frank Harvey, Nigel Balchin, from the story by Nigel Balchin

Josette ★★

Comedy 1938 · US · BW · 70mins

This slight romantic comedy features Don Ameche and Robert Young as two brothers on a mission to rescue their philandering father from the clutches of a singer. Of course they end up falling for her themselves – problem is they've picked on the wrong girl, played by Simone Simon. Joan Davis and Bert Lahr are prominent among the supporting players. This was Simon's last picture at 20th Century-Fox, and she temporarily returned to France before proving herself in Hollywood with *Cat People*. AE

Don Ameche *David Brossard Jr* • Simone Simon *Renee Le Blanc* • Robert Young (1) *Pierre Brossard* • Bert Lahr *Barney Barnaby* • Joan Davis *May Morris* • Paul Hurst *A Adolphus Heyman* • Lon Chaney Jr *Boatman* ■ *Dir* Allan Dwan • *Scr* James Edward Grant, from a play by Paul Frank, George Fraser, from a story by Ladislaus Vadnai

Josh and SAM ★ 12

Adventure 1993 · US · Colour · 93mins

In this unconvincing children's adventure, brothers Jacob Tierney and Noah Fleiss are miserably shuttled between their divorced parents until Tierney steals a car to embark on a road trip with his younger sibling. Meanwhile, Tierney has convinced Fleiss that he's not a little boy but in fact a Strategically Altered Mutant. Nonsensical fare that will annoy even the youngest viewers. JB [video]

Jacob Tierney *Josh* • Noah Fleiss *Sam* • Martha Plimpton *Alison* • Stephen Tobolowsky *Thom Whitney* • Joan Allen *Caroline* • Chris Penn *Derek Baxter* ■ *Dir* Billy Weber • *Scr* Frank Deese

Joshua Then and Now ★★

Comedy drama 1985 · Can · Colour · 127mins

Just as director Ted Kotcheff's earlier film of a Mordecai Richler novel *The Apprenticeship of Duddy Kravitz* gave Richard Dreyfuss a juicy role, this one gives James Woods the chance to show his combustible talent. He plays the son of a stripper and a pugilist-turned-convict who marries into London society in 1950 and then sees his life and career turned upside down when he returns to Canada in 1977. So much happens to Woods that this engrossing, if sketchy, drama might have made a better mini-series to give it more time with its admittedly interesting story. AT

James Woods *Joshua Shapiro* • Gabrielle Lazure *Pauline Shapiro* • Alan Arkin *Reuben Shapiro* • Michael Sarrazin *Kevin Hornby* • Linda Sorenson *Esther Shapiro* • Alan Scarfe *Jack Trimble* ■ *Dir* Ted Kotcheff • *Scr* Mordecai Richler, from his novel

Josie and the Pussycats ★★★ PG

Comedy 2001 · US · Colour · 94mins

Gleefully ridiculing fashion fads, disposable culture and product placement, writer/directors Harry Elfont and Deborah Kaplan denounce corporate greed without mocking the teenagers suckered in by pitiless exploitation. Pussycats Rachael Leigh Cook, Tara Reid and Rosario Dawson combine individuality with recognisable girlie traits, but the stars are Alan Cumming and Parker Posey, as record company executives seeking to sneak subliminal messages into the band's music. A hilariously perceptive satire on crass commercialism and public susceptibility to hype. DP [video] DVD

Rachael Leigh Cook *Josie McCoy* • Tara Reid *Melody Valentine* • Rosario Dawson *Valerie Brown* • Alan Cumming *Wyatt Frame* • Gabriel Mann *Alan M* • Parker Posey *Fiona* ■ *Dir* Harry Elfont, Deborah Kaplan • *Scr* Harry Elfont, Deborah Kaplan, from characters in *Archie Comics,created by John L Goldwater, Dan DeCarlo, Richard H Goldwater*

Jour de Fête ★★★★★ U

Comedy 1947 · Fr · Colour and BW · 77mins

If it hadn't been for modern technology, this comic masterpiece would have been permanently lost. Jacques Tati had hoped to shoot his debut feature in pioneering colour, but the stock was underdeveloped during processing and audiences had to make do with a black-and-white back-up copy until 1997, when a fully restored colour version (with a monochrome introduction) was released. Expanded from Tati's sublime 1947 short *L'Ecole des Facteurs*, the action chronicles the comic misadventures of village postman François as he tries to dispose of his letters at record speed in the style of the US mail service. There's a charming melancholy about some of the humour, but the slapstick is often frantic and balletic. Sheer genius. DP. In French with English subtitles. [video] DVD

Jacques Tati *François, the postman* • Guy Decomble *Roger, the showman* • Paul Frankeur *Marcel, the showman* • Maine Vallée *Jeannette* • Roger Rafal *Barber* ■ *Dir* Jacques Tati • *Scr* Jacques Tati, Henri Marquet

Le Jour Se Lève ★★★★ PG

Crime melodrama 1939 · Fr · BW · 85mins

Banned as demoralising by the Vichy government, following negative reviews, Marcel Carné's fatalistic drama is clearly symbolic of an entrapped nation awaiting its inevitable destruction. But it's also a heart-rending human drama, played against Alexandre Trauner's claustrophobic, yet painterly sets. Typically outstanding as the doomed, introspective hero, Jean Gabin is the epitome of existential despair, while Jules Berry's lecherous villain is as loathsome as Arletty's showgirl is worldly wise and Jacqueline Laurent's Françoise is innocent. Told mostly in flashback, the story perfectly illustrates Carné's mastery of poetic realism and Jacques Prévert's appreciation of the lyricism of everyday speech. DP. In French with English subtitles. [video]

Jean Gabin *François* • Jules Berry *M Valentin* • Jacqueline Laurent *Françoise* • Arletty *Clara* • René Génin *Concierge* • Mady Berry *Concierge's wife* • Bernard Blier *Gaston* • Marcel Peres *Paulo* ■ *Dir* Marcel Carné • *Scr* Jacques Prévert, Jacques Viot

Une Journée Tranquille ★★★ 15

Thriller 1999 · Fr · Colour · 71mins

This is a methodically told shaggy-dog story with a wicked twist in the tail. Written, produced and directed by Michael Jaffer, this is a thriller that seems consciously designed to stop you getting excited. Every task undertaken by birthday boy Christian Baltauss is downbeat and deliberate, whether intimidating petty crooks, setting up a major drug deal or bumping off a pimp who deals in underage innocents. However, this dour detachment somehow lends itself to a creeping fascination with both Baltauss and his fate. DP. In French with English subtitles.

Christian Baltauss *Man* • Jean-Jacques Benhamou *Friend* • Gilles Bellomi *Associate* • Georges Vaello *Pimp* • Alexandra Bonnet *Domino* ■ *Dir/Scr* Michael Jaffer

The Journey ★★

Political drama
1959 · US/Austria · Colour · 125mins

Yul Brynner and Deborah Kerr – who co-starred in *The King and I* – are reunited in this political drama about people trying to escape the Soviet invasion of Hungary in 1956. Brynner is a Soviet officer, while Kerr plays an Englishwoman trying to smuggle dissident Jason Robards over the border into Austria. The original script was set in China, but the location was changed to Hungary to give the film some topical relevance. Alas, the dramatic impact remains negligible. AT

Deborah Kerr *Lady Diana Ashmore* • Yul Brynner *Major Surov* • Jason Robards Jr [Jason Robards] *Paul Kedes/Flemying* • Robert Morley *Hugh Deverill* • EG Marshall *Harold Rhinelander* • David Kossoff *Simon Avron* • Anouk Aimée *Eva* • Ronny Howard [Ron Howard] *Billy Rhinelander* ■ *Dir* Anatole Litvak • *Scr* George Tabori

The Journey ★★★

Drama 1997 · US · Colour · 96mins

Although it constantly runs the risk of lapsing into stereotyping and culture-clash cliché, steady direction from Harish Saluja and discerning performances give this gentle drama its charm and poignancy. As the seasoned public school teacher retiring to his doctor son's Pittsburgh home, Roshan Seth exhibits both a reverence for tradition and stubborn insensitivity as he tries to educate his neglected granddaughter against the wishes of her American mother. DP

Roshan Seth *Kishan Singh* • Saeed Jaffrey *Ashok* • Carrie Preston *Laura Singh* • Antony Zaki *Raj Singh* • Betsy Zajko *Audrey* • Nora Bates *Jenny Singh* ■ *Dir* Harish Saluja • *Scr* Harish Saluja, Lisa Kirk Puchner

Journey back to Oz ★ U

Animated fantasy 1964 · US · Colour · 85mins

Liza Minnelli steps into her late mother's ruby slippers as the voice of Dorothy in this animated sequel to the much-loved Judy Garland classic.

J

Barely ringing any major changes from the evergreen original, Dorothy is transported over the rainbow again by another cyclone. There's no wizard this time (what a swizz!), just the Wicked Witch of the West's sister (voiced by Ethel Merman) to contend with. Lacklustre songs mark even more time and do little to keep boredom at bay. Made in 1964, but not released until a decade later. AJ

Liza Minnelli *Dorothy* • Mickey Rooney *Scarecrow* • Milton Berle *Cowardly Lion* • Danny Thomas *The Tin Man* • Ethel Merman *Mombi, the Bad Witch* ■ *Dir* Hal Sutherland • *Scr* Fred Ladd, Norm Prescott

Journey for Margaret ★★

Second World War drama
1942 · US · BW · 81mins

Like *Mrs Miniver*, this was one of MGM's efforts to convey to American audiences the effect of the Second World War on the British home front. In this tear-jerker, the emphasis is on homeless orphans of the Blitz for whom the best solution, it is suggested, is a new life in the United States. Robert Young plays the American journalist who befriends young William Severn who won't talk and little Margaret O'Brien who has retreated into a private world. Under the able coaxing of director WS Van Dyke II, it was the five-year-old O'Brien, in her first substantial role, who stole the picture. AE

Margaret O'Brien *Margaret* • Robert Young (1) *John Davis* • Laraine Day *Nora Davis* • Fay Bainter *Trudy Strauss* • Signe Hasso *Anya* • Nigel Bruce *Herbert V Allison* • William Severn *Peter Humphreys* ■ *Dir* WS Van Dyke II [WS Van Dyke] • *Scr* David Hertz, William Ludwig, from a book by William L White

Journey into Fear ★★★★ U

Spy drama 1942 · US · BW · 67mins

This is often identified as Orson Welles's third feature film, though he claimed to have acted only as co-writer (with star Joseph Cotten) and producer, with Norman Foster credited as sole director. Logic takes something of a back seat in this bewildering tale of arms smuggling in Turkey during the Second World War. Yet any narrative shortcomings are more than made up for by Welles's atmospheric camera angles and the gallery of disreputable characters. DP

Joseph Cotten *Howard Graham* • Orson Welles *Colonel Haki* • Dolores Del Rio *Josette Martel* • Ruth Warrick *Stephanie Graham* • Agnes Moorehead *Mrs Mathews* • Everett Sloane *Kopeikin* • Jack Moss *Banat* • Jack Durant *Gogo* ■ *Dir* Norman Foster • *Scr* Joseph Cotten, Orson Welles, from a novel by Eric Ambler • *Cinematographer* Karl Struss

The Journey of August King ★★★

Period drama 1995 · US · Colour · 95mins

Jason Patric and Thandie Newton star in this period drama directed by John Duigan. Newton plays a runaway slave in 19th-century North Carolina, who finds shelter with widowed farmer August King (Patric) and enters into a relationship with him. A beautiful looking film, this is severely limited by its sluggish pace and a lack of sexual tension between the two leads. LH

Jason Patric *August King* • Thandie Newton *Annalees Williamsburg* • Larry Drake *Olaf Singletary* • Sam Waterston *Mooney Wright* • Sara-Jane Wylde *Ida Wright* • Eric Mabius *Hal Wright* ■ *Dir* John Duigan • *Scr* John Ehle, from his novel • *Cinematographer* Slawomir Idziak

Journey of Hope ★★★★ PG

Drama based on a true story
1990 · Swi · Colour · 105mins

Although Xavier Koller's uncompromising feature won an Oscar for Best Foreign Film, its power derives from its basis in reality rather than the unsentimental solidity of his direction. Accompanied by his young son, Necmettin Cobanoglu travels from southern Turkey to Switzerland more in desperation than in hope, placing himself in the hands of guides who are every bit as treacherous as the forbidding mountain terrain they must cross. The physical perils are presented with a naturalism that makes them all the more terrifying, but it's the contrast between blind faith and pitiless greed that renders the action so harrowing. DP. In German with English subtitles.

Necmettin Cobanoglu *Haydar* • Nur Srer *Meryem* • Emin Sivas *Mehmet Ali* • Erdinc Akbas *Adana* • Yaman Okay *Türkmen* • Yasar Gner *Haci Baba* ■ *Dir* Xavier Koller • *Scr* Xavier Koller, Feride Cicekoglu, Heike Hubert

The Journey of Natty Gann ★★★ PG

Period adventure 1985 · US · Colour · 96mins

Set during the Depression, this Disney road movie is a kind of *Homeward Bound: the Incredible Journey* with people. Meredith Salenger is so good in the role of the 14-year-old who walks 2,000 miles in search of her lumberjack father that it beggars belief that she did not go on to become a star. John Cusack impresses here as a drifter convinced the open road is no place for a girl. There's plenty of action but the film scores best for its depiction of the hardships many faced in the 1930s. DP DVD

Meredith Salenger *Natty Gann* • John Cusack *Harry Slade* • Ray Wise *Sol Gann* • Lainie Kazan *Connie* • Scatman Crothers *Sherman* • Barry Miller *Parker* • Verna Bloom *Farm woman* ■ *Dir* Jeremy Kagan [Jeremy Paul Kagan] • *Scr* Jeanne Rosenberg

Journey through Rosebud ★★★

Drama 1972 · US · Colour · 91mins

Nothing to do with *Citizen Kane*, this is a heartfelt drama about the plight of the native American in modern society, living on reservations in conditions of Third World squalor. The message has been bottled in a rather contrived drama that seeks to draw parallels between the American Indians and the Vietnamese, with Kristoffer Tabori as the draft dodger who hides out on the Rosebud reservation in South Dakota. Robert Forster plays a Vietnam vet at the end of his tether and the direction is by Tom Gries who made the near-classic western *Will Penny*. AT

Robert Forster *Frank* • Kristoffer Tabori *Danny* • Victoria Racimo *Shirley* • Eddie Little Sky *Stanley Pike* • Roy Jenson *Park Ranger* • Wright King *Indian agent* ■ *Dir* Tom Gries • *Scr* Albert Ruben

Journey to Italy ★★★ PG

Romantic drama 1953 · It/Fr · BW · 81mins

After both *Stromboli* and *Europa '51* had met with a less than rapturous critical reception this Rossellini/Bergman collaboration saw their careers and their marriage at a low ebb. So this film – about an English couple (George Sanders and Ingrid Bergman), whose marriage is in crisis, travelling by car to Naples – could be seen as semi-autobiographical. On its release, the film was attacked for being clumsily made and sentimental but if one accepts the narrative simplicity and that the journey is both physical and spiritual, the film offers many rewards. Both English and Italian versions were filmed. RB DVD

Ingrid Bergman *Katherine Joyce* • George Sanders *Alexander Joyce* • Maria Mauban *Marie* • Paul Muller *Paul Dupont* • Leslie Daniels *Tony Burton* ■ *Dir* Roberto Rossellini • *Scr* Vitaliano Brancati, Roberto Rossellini

Journey to Shiloh ★★

War adventure 1967 · US · Colour · 101mins

More interesting today for its cast than its content, this dates from the period when Universal reverted to producing programme westerns to show off young talent. Here, James Caan gets a crack at a leading role, seeking Confederate glory but discovering only the horrors of civil war. The episodic, rambling narrative suggests some production interference along the way, and veteran TV director William Hale soon returned to the small screen. Keep your eyes peeled for novice Harrison Ford in an early movie role. TS

James Caan *Buck Burnett* • Michael Sarrazin *Miller Nalls* • Brenda Scott *Gabrielle DuPrey* • Don Stroud *Todo McLean* • Paul Peterson *JC Sutton* • Michael Burns *Eubie Bell* • Michael Vincent *Little Bit Lucket* • Harrison Ford *Willie Bill Bearden* ■ *Dir* William Hale • *Scr* Gene L Coon, from a novel by Will Henry

Journey to the Beginning of the World ★★★ U

Road movie 1997 · Por/Fr · Colour · 94mins

Nostalgia and regret are only to be expected when an 89-year-old film-maker takes a sentimental journey around his homeland. Manoel de Oliveira's wistful odyssey is made all the more poignant, though, by the fact that it contains Marcello Mastroianni's farewell performance as the director's alter ego. However, just as the reminiscences begin to weave their spell, the emphasis shifts on to Jean-Yves Gautier trying to persuade a long-lost aunt to overcome her xenophobia and accept him as family.This is a highly personal film, but fascinating all the same. DP. In French and Portuguese with English subtitles.

Marcello Mastroianni *Manoel* • Jean-Yves Gautier *Afonso* • Leonor Silveira *Judite* • Diogo Doria *Duarte* • Isabel de Castro *Maria Afonso* ■ *Dir/Scr* Manoel de Oliveira

Journey to the Center of the Earth ★★★★ U

Science-fiction adventure
1959 · US · Colour · 124mins

A lavish, well crafted adaptation of Jules Verne's classic tale, with James Mason leading an expedition into a volcano shaft and finding large mushrooms, giant lizards, an underground ocean and the lost city of Atlantis. Bernard Herrmann's fabulous music sets the mood for the spirited adventure, with the accent firmly on wholesome light-heartedness rather than vivid Verne danger. Singer Pat Boone adds his own brand of fantasy swashbuckling to the colourful proceedings, played out against some staggeringly imaginative subterranean sets. AJ DVD

Pat Boone *Alec McEwen* • James Mason *Professor Oliver Lindenbrook* • Arlene Dahl *Carla* • Diane Baker *Jenny* • Thayer David *Count Saknussemm* • Peter Ronson *Hans* ■ *Dir* Henry Levin • *Scr* Walter Reisch, Charles Brackett, from the novel *Voyage au Centre de la Terre* by Jules Verne • *Art Director* Lyle R Wheeler [Lyle Wheeler], Franz Bachelin, Herman A Blumenthal • *Set Designer* Walter M Scott, Joseph Kish

Journey to the Center of the Earth ★★ PG

Science-fiction adventure
1989 · US · Colour · 76mins

Bearing only a passing resemblance to the Jules Verne classic, this harmless family adventure relocates the action to Hawaii where a group of teens stumbles upon an alternative world while out exploring caves. The eclectic cast includes Nicola Cowper and Kathy Ireland, and, although Verne purists will be disgusted, it makes for blandly enjoyable entertainment. JF

Paul Carafotes *Richard* • Nicola Cowper *Chrystina* • Ilan Mitchell-Smith *Bryan* • Jeff Weston *Tola* • Jaclyn Bernstein *Sara* • Kathy Ireland *Wanda* ■ *Dir* Rusty Lemorande, Albert Pyun • *Scr* Rusty Lemorande, Debra Ricci, Regina Davis, Kitty Chalmers, from the novel *Voyage au Centre de la Terre* by Jules Verne

Journey to the Far Side of the Sun ★★★

Science-fiction drama
1969 · UK · Colour · 100mins

On the other side of the sun, astronaut Roy Thinnes finds a hidden planet mirroring Earth in every exact detail. Writer/producers Gerry and Sylvia Anderson, who created the cult puppet shows *Thunderbirds* and *Captain Scarlet*, as well as the live action series *UFO* and *Space 1999*, combine a clever concept with solid special effects. Add commendable direction from Robert Parrish and a memorable twist ending, and the result is a minor science-fiction gem. AJ

Ian Hendry *John Kane* • Roy Thinnes *Col Glenn Ross* • Patrick Wymark *Jason Webb* • Lynn Loring *Sharon Ross* • Loni von Friedl *Lise* • Herbert Lom *Dr Hassler* ■ *Dir* Robert Parrish • *Scr* Gerry Anderson, Sylvia Anderson, Donald James

Journey Together ★★★ U

Second World War drama documentary
1944 · UK · BW · 95mins

Richard Attenborough and Jack Watling train for Lancaster bombing missions, though their talents take them in different directions. Later the pair are shot down and bond in a life-raft in the middle of the North Sea. Designed to show the special relationship between Britain and America – Edward G Robinson waived his fee for playing a flying instructor – the film was directed for the RAF Film Unit by John Boulting. The script is based on a story written by Terence Rattigan to exorcise the shock of losing one of his closest friends in the war. AT

Richard Attenborough *David Wilton* • Jack Watling *John Aynesworth* • David Tomlinson *Smith* • Edward G Robinson *Dean McWilliams* • Sid Rider *Fitter* • Hugh Wakefield *Acting Lieutenant* ■ *Dir* John Boulting • *Scr* John Boulting, from a story by Terence Rattigan

Journey's End ★★★

First World War drama
1930 · US/UK · BW · 130mins

Gods and Monsters (1998), the excellent biopic of British-born Hollywood director James Whale, cast new light on Whale's first feature, an adaptation of RC Sherriff's First World War play. Whale, who served in the trenches, shot the picture in Hollywood because British studios were not yet fully equipped for sound. The film is a valuable record of the stage production, with the same splendidly stiff-upper-lip yet touching performances from the all-male cast and "simply topping" dialogue. Colin Clive is especially good as the captain breaking under the strain of war. RB

Colin Clive *Capt Stanhope* • Ian MacLaren *Lt Osborne* • David Manners *Second Lt Raleigh* • Billy Bevan *Second Lt Trotter* • Anthony Bushell *Second Lt Hibbert* • Robert A'Dair [Robert Adair] *Capt Hardy* ■ *Dir* James Whale • *Scr* Joseph Moncure March, from the play by RC Sherriff

Joy in the Morning ★★

Romantic drama
1965 · US · Colour · 101mins

Richard Chamberlain was nearing the end of his stint as TV's Doctor Kildare when he switched professions for this drab melodrama about the financial and marital difficulties of a law student in a small mid-western town in the late 1920s. Flatly directed, it forces you to take sides with either workaholic Chamberlain or his neglected bride, Yvette Mimieux, neither of whom are very sympathetic. DP

Richard Chamberlain *Carl Brown* • Yvette Mimieux *Annie McGairy* • Arthur Kennedy *Patrick Brown* • Oscar Homolka *Stan Pulaski* • Donald Davis *Anthony Byrd* • Joan Tetzel *Beverly Karter* • Sidney Blackmer *Dean James Darwent* • Virginia Gregg *Mrs Lorgan* ■ *Dir* Alex Segal • *Scr* Sally Benson, Alfred Hayes, Norman Lessing, from the novel *Joy in the Morning* by Betty Smith

The Joy Luck Club ★★★★ 15

Drama 1993 · US · Colour · 133mins

Faithfully adapted from Amy Tan's bestselling book, director Wayne Wang's moving yet witty melodrama mixes the stories of four Chinese-born mothers with those of their American-born daughters. Murder, suicide, betrayal and love are all captured in numerous three-hanky moments, beautifully (if sentimentally) played. Tan co-wrote the script with *Rain Man* scribe Ronald Bass and the result is a bit of a women's weepie, but it's an excellent one. JB [video] DVD

Kieu Chinh *Suyuan* • Tsai Chin *Lindo* • France Nuyen *Ying Ying* • Lisa Lu *An Mei* • Wen Ming-Na [Ming-Na] *June* • Tamlyn Tomita *Waverly* • Lauren Tom *Lena* ■ *Dir* Wayne Wang • *Scr* Amy Tan, Ronald Bass, from a novel by Amy Tan

Joy of Living ★★★

Screwball comedy 1938 · US · BW · 90mins

Irene Dunne was one of the great joys of 1930s Hollywood, both a talented singer and superb comedian. This screwball comedy with songs capitalises on those skills, and, as in Dunne's earlier musicals, the numbers were composed by Jerome Kern, including *You Couldn't Be Cuter*. She is cast as a wealthy Broadway star who escapes from her family of hangers-on and discovers a new lease of life with shipping magnate Douglas Fairbanks Jr. AE

Irene Dunne *Margaret* • Douglas Fairbanks Jr *Dannie* • Alice Brady *Minerva* • Guy Kibbee *Dennis* • Jean Dixon *Harrison* • Eric Blore *Potter* • Lucille Ball *Salina* ■ *Dir* Tay Garnett • *Scr* Gene Towne, Graham Baker, Allan Scott, from a story by Herbert Fields, Dorothy Fields

Joy of Madness ★★★★ PG

Documentary 2003 · Iran · Colour · 70mins

As those familiar with DVD extras will know, "Making of" documentaries rarely fulfil their promise. But 14-year-old Hana Makhmalbaf's record of her sister Samira's attempts to cast the acclaimed *At Five in the Afternoon* not only provides a unique insight into the pre-production process, but also reveals much about Afghan society in the wake of the Taliban. The devastation, fear and extreme poverty evident throughout Kabul are movingly conveyed. But even more telling are the contrasting attitudes of the mullah whom Samira auditions for the part of the father and Agheleh Rezaie, the teacher whose ambition is tempered by her uncertainty how far to assert women's rights in this paternalistic state. DP. In Farsi with English subtitles. DVD

Dir Hana Makhmalbaf • *Scr* Hana Makhmalbaf

Joy of Sex ★ 15

Sex comedy 1984 · US · Colour · 89mins

Using just the title of Alex Comfort's bestseller, and none of its factual content, this lame teenage sex comedy gives new meaning to the words dull, vulgar and pathetic. Michelle Meyrink mistakenly thinks she only has a few weeks left to live and embarks on a desperate, virginity-losing campaign. Distance has lent director Martha Coolidge's soporific erotic cabaret a certain campy 1980s nostalgia. AJ [video]

Cameron Dye *Alan Holt* • Michelle Meyrink *Leslie Hindenberg* • Charles Van Eman *Max Holt* • Lisa Langlois *Melanie* • Colleen Camp *Liz Sampson* ■ *Dir* Martha Coolidge • *Scr* Kathleen Rowell, JJ Salter

The Joyless Street ★★★★★

Silent drama 1925 · Ger · BW · 125mins

Unique in being the only film to boast Greta Garbo and Marlene Dietrich in its cast (the latter as an uncredited extra), this silent masterpiece is also significant for its development of the technique of "seamless" editing and for pioneering the style known as "street realism". Although staged on studio sets, there's an authenticity about the Vienna depicted in this study of middle-class desperation, as both Garbo (in her last pre-Hollywood picture) and Asta Nielsen have to sell more than their souls to feed their families, while those who profiteered from the First World War indulge themselves in every vice. DP

Asta Nielsen *Maria Lechner* • Greta Garbo *Greta Rumfort* • Werner Krauss *Joseph Gieringer/The Butcher of Melchior Street* • Valeska Gert *Mrs Greifer* • Marlene Dietrich ■ *Dir* GW Pabst • *Scr* Willy Haas, from a novel by Hugo Bettauer • *Cinematographer* Guido Seeber, Curt Oertel, Walter Robert Lach • *Editor* Hans Sohnle

Joyride ★★ 15

Crime drama 1977 · US · Colour · 89mins

Set in Alaska, this exploitation movie looks at four teenagers who get their kicks from sex and petty crime – until things get out of hand. Made for the teen market, the film is reasonably perceptive about life on the margins and has an interesting cast, in that all four leads are the children of established movie stars. Only Melanie Griffith (Tippi Hedren's daughter) went on to better things. AT [video]

Desi Arnaz Jr *Scott* • Robert Carradine *John* • Melanie Griffith *Susie* • Anne Lockhart *Cindy* • Tom Ligon *Sanders* ■ *Dir* Joseph Ruben • *Scr* Joseph Ruben, Peter Rainer

Joyriders ★★ 15

Road movie 1988 · UK · Colour · 92mins

In spite of the arresting opening, in which a frustrated Dubliner dumps her kids as left luggage, and some glorious Irish scenery, this drama is soon trapped within the confines of its limited budget, the underdeveloped script and the overcautious approach of debut director Aisling Walsh. Some of Patricia Kerrigan's scenes with daydreaming car thief Andrew Connolly are quite touching, but the pessimism and the narrowness of approach eventually underwhelm you. DP [video]

Patricia Kerrigan *Mary Flynn* • Andrew Connolly *Perky Rice* • Billie Whitelaw *Tammy O'Moore* • David Kelly *Daniel Tracey* • John Kavanagh *Hotel Manager* • Deirdre Donoghue *Dolores Flynn* • Tracy Peacock *Finbar Flynn* ■ *Dir* Aisling Walsh • *Scr* Andy Smith, from a story by Andy Smith, Aisling Walsh

The Joyriders ★★

Crime drama 1999 · US · Colour · 90mins

This overbearing melodrama is rendered almost unwatchable by a soundtrack strewn with purportedly inspirational songs. As the senior citizen who offers a trio of homeless delinquents a fresh start after they take him hostage with the gun he'd bought for his own suicide, Martin Landau does the job you expect of such a conscientious actor. But Bradley Battersby's feel-good direction is excuciating. DP

Martin Landau *Gordon Trout* • Kris Kristofferson *Eddie* • Heather McComb *Crystal* • Shawn Hatosy *Cam* • Elisabeth Moss *Jody* • Diane Venora *Celeste* ■ *Dir* Bradley Battersby • *Scr* Bradley Battersby, Jeff Spiegel

Ju Dou ★★★★★ 15

Drama 1990 · Chi/Jpn · Colour · 95mins

The first Chinese film to be nominated for an Oscar, this is one of the glories of Chinese cinema. Although superbly shot by Gu Changwei and Yang Lun, the primary credit for the film's visual splendours belongs to principal director Zhang Yimou, himself a former cinematographer, whose command of colour and camera angle complements his assured handling of this intense tale of illicit passion set in a cloth dyer's mill sometime in the 1920s. Gong Li gives a typically dynamic performance and this sly attack on China's elderly ruling elite is rightly considered by many to be Zhang's masterpiece. DP. In Mandarin with English subtitles. Contains violence, swearing and nudity. [video]

Li Wei *Yang Jinshan* • Gong Li *Ju Dou* • Li Baotian *Yang Tianqing* • Yi Zhang *Yang Tianbai as a child* • Jian Zheng *Yang Tianbai as a boy* ■ *Dir* Zhang Yimou, Yang Fengliang • *Scr* Liu Heng, from his story *Fuxi, Fuxi*

Juarez ★★★ U

Historical drama 1939 · US · BW · 116mins

In this epic about the French colonisation of Mexico, Paul Muni found a role that suited his stature, as Benito Pablo Juarez. This film was made in two halves, and then edited together, and it shows. Nevertheless, there is striking work on display here: Bette Davis's Empress Carlotta going mad is a highspot, and John Garfield brings an honest heartfelt intensity to the small role of Porfirio Diaz. But Brian Aherne is a stuffy Maximilian, and the plot is tortuously slow to unwind. Thank goodness for a splendid Erich Wolfgang Korngold score. TS [video]

Paul Muni *Benito Juarez* • Bette Davis *Carlotta* • Brian Aherne *Maximilian* • Claude Rains *Napoleon III* • Gale Sondergaard *Empress Eugenie* • John Garfield *Porfirio Diaz* • Donald Crisp *Marechal Bazaine* ■ *Dir* William Dieterle • *Scr* John Huston, Wolfgang Reinhardt, Aeneas MacKenzie, from the play *Juarez & Maximillian* by Franz Werfel, from the novel *The Phantom Crown* by Bertita Harding

Jubal ★★★★ PG

Western drama 1956 · US · Colour · 97mins

This adaptation of Paul I Wellman's novel *Jubal Troop* is a fine work with a magnificent, grim performance from Glenn Ford in the title role. But look closer and you'll recognise plot themes and motivations – yup, it's *Othello* out west, with Ernest Borgnine's rancher as the Moor and Rod Steiger cast in the Iago role. Loner Ford is an almost-Cassio, and the suspense is stretched tightly as you long for Ford and Steiger to settle the score. A brutal tale, well told by western maestro Delmer Daves, and magnificently photographed by Charles Lawton Jr. TS [video]

Glenn Ford *Jubal Troop* • Ernest Borgnine *Shep Horgan* • Rod Steiger *Pinky* • Valerie French *Mae Horgan* • Felicia Farr *Naomi Hoktor* • Basil Ruysdael *Shem Hoktor* • Noah Beery Jr *Sam* • Charles Bronson *Reb Haislipp* ■ *Dir* Delmer Daves • *Scr* Delmer Daves, Russell S Hughes, from the novel *Jubal Troop* by Paul I Wellman

Jubilee ★★★ 18

Black comedy 1978 · UK · Colour · 100mins

Queen Elizabeth I takes a trip into the future to witness "Anarchy in the UK" in Britain's first fully fledged punk movie. Director Derek Jarman, Ken Russell's former set designer, used the 1977 Silver Jubilee to comment on the disintegration of society, crafting a fiercely inventive experimental psycho-fantasy making ample use of New Wave music (Adam Ant, Chelsea, Siouxsie and the Banshees, the Slits) and the concerns of contemporary youth culture. Always more hip King's Road than hardcore street-cred, it remains an energetic and witty time capsule. AJ. Contains violence, swearing, sex scenes and nudity. [video]

Jenny Runacre *Bod/Queen Elizabeth I* • Little Nell *Crabs* • Toyah Willcox *Mad* • Jordan *Amyl Nitrite* • Hermine Demoriane *Chaos* • Ian Charleson *Angel* • Karl Johnson *Sphinx* • Linda Spurrier *Viv* • Neil Kennedy *Max* • Orlando [Jack Birkett] *Borgia Ginz* • Wayne County *Lounge Lizard* • Richard O'Brien *John Dee* • Adam Ant *Kid* ■ *Dir/Scr* Derek Jarman

Judas Kiss ★★★ 15

Crime thriller 1998 · US · Colour · 93mins

When a gang kidnaps a computer genius, a woman gets killed in the scrum. Turns out that she's the wife of a senator and then... well, that's just one twist in this strange thriller. Director Sebastian Gutierrez grafts the influence of Pedro Almodóvar onto Quentin Tarantino: the first few minutes are pornography, then it's a legit thriller, then it goes all weird again, and that's before Emma Thompson and Alan Rickman appear as New Orleans cops. She's tough and funny; he gives a creepily unreal performance. Made for cable TV, this could become a cult. AT [video] DVD

Carla Gugino *Coco Chavez* • Simon Baker-Denny *Junior Armstrong* • Gil Bellows *Lizard Browning* • Emma Thompson *Agent Sadie Hawkins* • Alan Rickman *Detective David Friedman* • Til Schweiger *Ruben Rubenbauer* • Greg Wise *Ben Dyson* ■ *Dir* Sebastian Gutierrez • *Scr* Sebastian Gutierrez, from a story by Deanna Fuller, Sebastian Gutierrez

J

Jude ★★★★ 15

Drama 1996 · UK · Colour and BW · 117mins

Co-produced by the BBC, this magnificent and appropriately distressing adaptation of Thomas Hardy's final novel did only fair business at British cinemas. As Jude, Christopher Eccleston has that haunted and naive look of a man buffeted by fate and destroyed by self-delusion, while Kate Winslet is perfect as Sue Bridehead, the fiery cousin whom Jude loves and whose vacillation drives the story along. Visually, the film is suitably gloomy and at two hours it's a brilliant distillation of a literary classic. AT. Contains some violence, nudity and sex scenes. [video] DVD

Christopher Eccleston *Jude Fawley* • Kate Winslet *Sue Bridehead* • Liam Cunningham *Phillotson* • Rachel Griffiths *Arabella* • June Whitfield *Aunt Drusilla* • Ross Colvin Turnbull *Little Jude* • James Daley *Jude as a boy* • Berwick Kaler *Farmer Troutham* ■ *Dir* Michael Winterbottom • *Scr* Hossein Amini, from the novel *Jude the Obscure* by Thomas Hardy

Judex ★★★

Classic silent adventure
1916 · Fr · BW · 270mins

Having thrilled audiences with *Les Vampires* and *Fantôas*, Louis Feuillade was denounced for the dark and dispiriting nature of his serials, celebrating the deeds of criminals. Consequently, this 12-part adventure is less compelling than its predecessors, although Feuillade continues to make atmospheric use of his locations and René Cresté cuts a dash as the count who assumes a crimefighting disguise to avenge the death of his father. DP

René Cresté *Judex* • Musidora *Diana Monti/ Mlle Verdier* • Yvette Andreyor *Jacqueline* • Marcel Levesque *Cocantin* • Louis Luebas *Favraux* ■ *Dir* Louis Feuillade • *Scr* Louis Feuillade, Arthur Bernède

Judex ★★★★

Mystery adventure 1963 · Fr/It · BW · 97mins

A glorious evocation of a bygone era, French director Georges Franju's tribute to the pioneering silent serials of fantasy writer Louis Feuillade is a thrilling combination of subversive derring-do and lyrical symbolism. The convoluted plot centres around the attempts of Channing Pollock's clandestine crusade to protect banker's daughter, Edith Scob, from the machinations of the diabolical Francine Bergé. From the enchanting opening at a masked ball, the battle of wits between real-life conjurer Pollock and the chameleon Bergé is endlessly entertaining. But it's the stylised, often surreal, quality of Marcel Fradetal's atmospheric photography that proves conclusively that pulp kitsch can, occasionally, touch poetry. DP

Channing Pollock *Judex/Vallieres* • Francine Bergé *Diana Monti/Marie Verdier* • Edith Scob *Jacqueline Favraux* • Michel Vitold *Favraux* ■ *Dir* Georges Franju • *Scr* Francis Lacassin, Jacques Champreux, from the 1916 film • *Cinematographer* Marcel Fradetal

Judge & Jury ★★★ 18

Action horror 1995 · US · Colour · 93mins

Following his execution, vicious murderer David Keith returns from the dead to take revenge on the two men he blames for his wife's death – disgraced detective Paul Koslo and over-the-hill American football player Martin Kove. A barnstorming performance from the ghostly Keith drives director John Eyres's *Shocker* retread, humorously blending chills and action for a fun, fright fix. Released on video/DVD in the UK as *From beyond the Grave*. AJ. Contains violence and swearing. DVD

David Keith *Joey* • Martin Kove *Michael Silvano* • Thomas Ian Nicholas *Alex Silvano* • Laura Johnson *Grace Silvano* • Kelly Perine *Roland* • Paul Koslo *Lockhart* • Robert Miranda *Coach Wagner* • Patricia Scanlon *Mary* ■ *Dir* John Eyres • *Scr* John Eyres, Amanda Kirpaul, John Cianetti

Judge Dredd ★★★★ 15

Science-fiction action adventure 1995 · US · Colour · 91mins

Director Danny Cannon's imaginatively over-the-top science-fiction rendering of the celebrated *2000 AD* comic-strip hero. In the future, the world has formed into densely populated Mega Cities with the Cursed Earth being the uninhabitable region lying between them. Law and order is maintained by a fleet of elite officers who are judge, jury and executioner all rolled into one, and Judge Dredd (Sylvester Stallone) is the most prolific of the brigade. Always exciting, this is an under-rated fantasy, full of flash, plenty of bang and packing a considerable wallop. AJ. Contains swearing, violence. DVD

Sylvester Stallone *Judge Dredd* • Armand Assante *Rico* • Rob Schneider *Fergie* • Jürgen Prochnow *Judge Griffin* • Max von Sydow *Judge Fargo* • Diane Lane *Judge Hershey* ■ *Dir* Danny Cannon • *Scr* William Wisher, Steven E de Souza, from a story by William Wisher, Michael DeLuca, from characters created by John Wagner, Carlos Ezquerra

Judge Hardy and Son ★★ U

Comedy crime 1939 · US · BW · 89mins

This is the eighth in the series that began in 1937 with *A Family Affair* and enshrines wholesome small-town values and smothers them in comedy. This entry has Andy (Mickey Rooney) doing some serious bonding with his dad, Judge Hardy (Lewis Stone), while also trying to win the school essay competition, as well as Ann Rutherford's pretty Polly. Then pneumonia strikes Andy's mum, and the relatives gather round her with Andy offering a prayer. This family wasn't named Hardy for nothing. AT

Lewis Stone *Judge James K Hardy* • Mickey Rooney *Andy Hardy* • Cecilia Parker *Marian Hardy* • Fay Holden *Mrs Emily Hardy* • Ann Rutherford *Polly Benedict* • Sara Haden *Aunt Milly* ■ *Dir* George B Seitz • *Scr* Carey Wilson, from characters created by Aurania Rouverol

Judge Hardy's Children ★★

Comedy drama 1938 · US · BW · 78mins

The third film in the series and the first to have the name "Hardy" in the title. The heavy political slant to this entry – the Hardys go to Washington DC and take part in a Supreme Court investigation into public utilities – is in direct response to Roosevelt's "New Deal". Lewis Stone, as Judge Hardy, has much to say about this but Mickey Rooney, as Andy, still gets to flirt with a succession of pretty young things, including teaching the daughter of the French ambassador how to dance. AT

Lewis Stone *Judge James K Hardy* • Mickey Rooney *Andy Hardy* • Cecilia Parker *Marian Hardy* • Fay Holden *Mrs Emily Hardy* • Ann Rutherford *Polly Benedict* • Betsy Ross Clarke [Betty Ross Clarke] *Aunt Milly* ■ *Dir* George B Seitz • *Scr* Kay Van Riper, from characters created by Aurania Rouverol

Judge Priest ★★★

Comedy drama 1934 · US · BW · 79mins

In the second of three films Will Rogers made for director John Ford, the folksy humorist portrays the sensible but lonely judge in 1890 Kentucky who quietly fights prejudice to see that justice is done and talks to his dead wife at her graveside. The treatment and appearance of a black character, Stepin Fetchit, accused of stealing some chickens, may seem racially offensive these days, but his character is regarded in an affectionate, if condescending, way and reflects attitudes at the time. AE

Stepin Fetchit *Jeff Poindexter* • Will Rogers *Judge William Pitman Priest* • Tom Brown *Jerome Priest* • Anita Louise *Ellie May Gillespie* • Henry B Walthall *Reverend Ashby Brand* • David Landau *Bob Gillis* • Hattie McDaniel *Aunt Dilsey* ■ *Dir* John Ford • *Scr* Dudley Nichols, Lamar Trotti, from a character created by Irvin S Cobb

The Judge Steps Out ★★★

Comedy 1949 · US · BW · 91mins

Canadian-born actor Alexander Knox was an under-rated figure in the cinema, despite receiving an Oscar nomination for his performance as Woodrow Wilson in *Wilson* (1944). In this movie he plays a man undergoing a midlife crisis – long before the term was fashionable. Knox also co-wrote his role as a judge who leaves the rat race, becomes a short-order cook and falls for Ann Sothern. This likeable movie wasn't a success, and Knox lapsed into supporting roles. TS

Alexander Knox *Judge Bailey* • Ann Sothern *Peggy* • George Tobias *Mike* • Sharyn Moffett *Nan* • Florence Bates *Chita* • Frieda Inescort *Evelyn Bailey* • Myrna Dell *Mrs Winthrop* ■ *Dir* Boris Ingster • *Scr* Boris Ingster, Alexander Knox, from a story by Boris Ingster

Judgement Deferred ★★

Crime thriller 1951 · UK · BW · 88mins

John Baxter forged a reputation in the early 1930s for social dramas and comedies notable for their sure grasp of character and locale. This is a remake of Baxter's own 1933 feature *Doss House*, much admired in its day for its gritty approach to poverty at a time when most producers were churning out glib escapism. Here, apart from some nice shots of Dorset, Bacter only manages to fashion a muddled melodrama that feels like sub-standard Frank Capra. DP

Hugh Sinclair *David Kennedy* • Helen Shingler *Kay Kennedy* • Abraham Sofaer *Chancellor* • Leslie Dwyer *Flowers* • Joan Collins *Lil Carter* • Harry Locke *Bert* ■ *Dir* John Baxter • *Scr* Geoffrey Orme, Barbara K Emary, Walter Meade, from a story by Herbert Ayres

A Judgement in Stone ★ 15

Thriller 1986 · Can · Colour · 100mins

A role only a Bette Davis, at full twitch, could love: a woman is enmeshed in murderous hysteria because of the dyslexia which has plagued her all her life. But it's Rita Tushingham who plays the "heroine" with camp and risible results. She eventually gets a job as housemaid with a middle-class American family but goes berserk when asked to compile a shopping list. This is directed – barely – by Tushingham's husband Ousama Rawi. TH

Rita Tushingham *Eunice Parchman* • Ross Petty *George Coverdale* • Shelley Peterson *Jackie Coverdale* • Jonathan Crombie *Bobby Coverdale* • Jessica Steen *Melinda Coverdale* • Aisha Tushingham *Young Eunice* ■ *Dir* Ousama Rawi • *Scr* Elaine Waisglass, from the novel by Ruth Rendell

Judgment at Nuremberg ★★★★ PG

Drama 1961 · US · BW · 178mins

The trial of the judges who enforced Hitler's laws allowing wartime atrocities to occur might not be obvious movie material, but in the hands of brilliant producer/director Stanley Kramer this three-hour saga is mesmerising. Kramer pulled out all the dramatic stops. As producer, he secured one of the great casts of all time, headed by Spencer Tracy as Allied judge Dan Haywood, with touching cameos by Oscar-nominated Judy Garland as Irene Hoffman and Montgomery Clift as Rudolph Petersen, both victims of Nazi tyranny. The film has great dignity, exemplified by Burt Lancaster's intellectual German Ernst Janning, and an Oscar-winning performance from Maximilian Schell. TS DVD

Spencer Tracy *Judge Dan Haywood* • Burt Lancaster *Ernst Janning* • Richard Widmark *Colonel Tad Lawson* • Marlene Dietrich *Madame Bertholt* • Maximilian Schell *Hans Rolfe* • Judy Garland *Irene Hoffman* • Montgomery Clift *Rudolph Petersen* • William Shatner *Captain Harrison Byers* ■ *Dir* Stanley Kramer • *Scr* Abby Mann

Judgment Day ★★★ 18

Action thriller 1999 · US · Colour · 85mins

This sci-fi thriller from director John Terlesky rises above its bargain-basement special effects, but suffers instead from a palpable lack of tension. As a giant meteor heads straight for Earth, FBI agent Suzy Amis and convict Ice-T go in search of academic Linden Ashby, who alone can prevent annihilation. Trouble is, he's been kidnapped by cult leader Mario Van Peebles, who believes the impending doom is God's will. Willing performances, sly humour and an effective (if inevitable) denouement place this just above the direct-to-video average. DP. Contains swearing, drug abuse and violence.

Ice-T *Reese* • Suzy Amis *Tyrell* • Mario Van Peebles *Payne* • Coolio *Luther* • Linden Ashby *Corbett* • Tom "Tiny" Lister Jr *Clarence* ■ *Dir* John Terlesky • *Scr* William Carson

Judgment in Berlin ★★★ PG

Courtroom drama 1988 · US · Colour · 92mins

Former Hollywood bad boy Sean Penn here proves his dramatic worth in a small part, playing the role of a key witness in the trial of two East Germans who in 1978 hijacked a Polish airliner in an attempt to escape to the west. It's an uneven but intriguing adaptation of Judge Herbert J Stern's account of the American trial of the escapees, over which he presided. Martin Sheen plays Stern with too much pomposity and Sean's father, Leon Penn, directs with cluttered symbolism. But, these flaws apart, it remains a fascinating remnant of the Cold War. TH. Contains swearing.

Martin Sheen *Herbert J Stern* • Sam Wanamaker *Bernard Hellring* • Max Gail *Judah Best* • Juergen Heinrich *Uri Andreyev* • Heinz Hoenig *Helmut Thiele* • Carl Lumbly *Edwin Palmer* • Sean Penn *Guenther X* ■ *Dir* Leo Penn • *Scr* Joshua Sinclair, Leo Penn, from the book by Herbert J Stern

Judgment Night ★★★ 18

Thriller 1993 · US · Colour · 105mins

This urban spin on the likes of *Deliverance* and *Southern Comfort* went straight to video here, but there are certainly far worse productions that get the big screen treatment. Stephen Hopkins has fashioned a sleek action thriller that is thoroughly implausible, but an exciting ride all the same. Emilio Estevez, Cuba Gooding Jr, Jeremy Piven and Stephen Dorff are the pampered suburbanites lost in the ghetto, who find themselves on the run from a ruthless gang when they witness a murder. Denis Leary is marvellously over the top as the psychopathic gang leader. JF

Emilio Estevez *Frank Wyatt* • Cuba Gooding Jr *Mike Peterson* • Denis Leary *Fallon* • Stephen Dorff *John Wyatt* • Jeremy Piven *Ray Cochran* • Peter Greene *Sykes* • Erik Schrody *Rhodes* ■ *Dir* Stephen Hopkins • *Scr* Lewis Colick, Jere Cunningham, Kevin Jarre, from their story

Judicial Consent ★★★ 18

Thriller 1995 · US · Colour · 95mins

Bonnie Bedelia stars in this above average straight-to-video thriller. She plays a judge who finds herself being drawn into a complex revenge plot designed to frame her for murder. The story defies belief but at least puts a fresh spin on the legal thriller format, and Bedelia delivers a typically gutsy performance. She is well supported by Billy Wirth, Will Patton and Dabney Coleman. JF. Contains violence, sex scenes, swearing, nudity. DVD

Bonnie Bedelia *Gwen Warwick* • Will Patton *Alan Warwick* • Dabney Coleman *Charles Mayron* • Billy Wirth *Martin* • Lisa Blount *District Attorney Theresa Lewis* ■ *Dir/Scr* William Bindley

Judith ★

War drama 1966 · US · Colour · 109mins

On the dockside in Palestine in 1947, a cargo ship unloads its packing cases and from one of these emerges Sophia Loren, fresh as a daisy. She rushes off to Peter Finch's kibbutz as an agent of the Jewish underground organisation, Haganah, to expose her former husband Hans Verner as a Nazi war criminal and a sponsor of Arab nationalism. But mostly she's there to make us crease up with laughter. This is a ludicrous action thriller that also serves as anti-Arab propaganda for Israel. The location photography is by Nicolas Roeg. AT

Sophia Loren *Judith* • Peter Finch *Aaron Stein* • Jack Hawkins *Major Lawton* • Hans Verner *Gustav Schiller* • Zharira Charifai *Dr Rachel* • Joseph Gross *Yaneck* • Terence Alexander *Carstairs* • Zipora Peled *Hannah* ■ *Dir* Daniel Mann • *Scr* John Michael Hayes, from a story by Lawrence Durrell

Judy Berlin ★★★★ 15

Comedy drama 1999 · US · BW · 93mins

This surreal portrait of suburban America charts the reaction of a community to a bizarre solar eclipse. As the neighbourhood is plunged into darkness, so the inhabitants wander through their own twilit inner worlds. Aaron Harnick has returned home to his parents after a failed foray to Hollywood. Glumly pacing his childhood turf, he encounters school friend Edie Falco, an aspiring and indefatigable actress, and a new-found intimacy unfolds. Eric Mendelsohn was voted best director at 1999's Sundance Festival for his efforts here, and the award is well deserved. Quirky, tender and honest. LH

Edie Falco *Judy Berlin* • Aaron Harnick *David Gold* • Bob Dishy *Arthur Gold* • Barbara Barrie *Sue Berlin* • Carlin Glynn *Maddie* • Bette Henritze *Dolores Engler* • Madeline Kahn *Alice Gold* • Julie Kavner *Marie* • Anne Meara *Bea* ■ *Dir/Scr* Eric Mendelsohn

Juggernaut ★★★ PG

Thriller 1974 · UK · Colour · 105mins

Director Richard Lester does his best with this solemn thriller about a luxury liner threatened by a mad bomber. It's the superb editing that carries the day, creating the required amount of tension. Female lead Shirley Knight is given little to do, existing simply as a romantic footnote to Omar Sharif's libido, and in the male-heavy cast, Richard Harris, David Hemmings and Anthony Hopkins provide the brains and brawn to save some pretty vacuous lives. TH [video] DVD

Richard Harris *Fallon* • Omar Sharif *Captain Brunel* • David Hemmings *Charlie Braddock* • Anthony Hopkins *Superintendent John McCleod* • Shirley Knight *Barbara Banister* • Ian Holm *Nicholas Porter* ■ *Dir* Richard Lester • *Scr* Richard DeKoker, Alan Plater • *Editor* Anthony Gibbs

The Juggler ★

Drama 1953 · US · BW · 85mins

A film of sledgehammer subtlety, with circus juggler Kirk Douglas as the Holocaust survivor who makes it to Israel where he searches for the wife he knows is dead and where, too, every Israeli soldier at the refugee camp is mistaken for a Nazi. A small boy helps him escape to Egypt where Douglas has friends he believes will help him. The film's maudlin sentimentality soars right off the scale and for Douglas, who devoted months to learning how to juggle, it's possibly the worst film of his career. AT

Kirk Douglas *Hans Muller* • Milly Vitale *Ya'El* • Paul Stewart *Detective Karni* • Joey Walsh [Joseph Walsh] *Yehoshua Bresler* • Alf Kjellin *Daniel* • Beverly Washburn *Susy* • Charles Lane (2) *Rosenberg* ■ *Dir* Edward Dmytryk • *Scr* Michael Blankfort, from his novel

Juha ★★★

Silent drama 1999 · Fin · BW · 77mins

The rural idyll of an adoring couple is shattered by a city slicker in Aki Kaurismäki's bold attempt to turn back the cinematic clock to the monochromed silent era. But, while Kaurismäki's fully conversant with the silent style, he succumbs to the temptation to punctuate the action with intrusive background sounds. Similarly, the cast struggles to reproduce the expressive posturing that dominated silent screen acting, with even the usually reliable Kati Outinen seeming out of sorts. DP

Sakari Kuosmanen *Juha* • Kati Outinen *Marja* • André Wilms *Shemeikka* • Markku Peltola *Driver* ■ *Dir* Aki Kaurismäki • *Scr* Aki Kaurismaki, from a novel by Juhani Aho

Juice ★★★ 15

Action drama 1991 · US · Colour · 90mins

A potent, if flawed, debut from Ernest R Dickerson, who earned his director's spurs after serving as cinematographer on some of Spike Lee's most incendiary works. Omar Epps gets top billing, playing a confused teenager who wants to be a DJ, but finds himself inexorably drawn into the world of crime when he reluctantly joins his pals on a store heist. Epps is impressive among a then largely unknown cast, although the late rapper Tupac Shakur steals the show in one of his first films. JF. Contains violence, swearing and sex scenes. [video]

Omar Epps *Quincy ("Q")* • Tupac Shakur *Bishop* • Jermaine Hopkins *Steel* • Khalil Kain *Raheem* • Cindy Herron *Yolanda* • Vincent Laresca *Radames* • Samuel L Jackson *Trip* • George O Gore [George Gore II] *Brian* ■ *Dir* Ernest R Dickerson • *Scr* Gerard Brown, Ernest R Dickerson, from a story by Ernest R Dickerson

Juke Box Rhythm ★★ U

Musical 1959 · US · BW · 82mins

If the thought of Johnny Otis performing *Willie and the Hand Jive* makes you misty, this is for you. There is amiable fun in watching a very young Jack Jones near the start of his career, as a singer helping an unknown designer (Hans Conried) convince a European princess visiting New York that he should design her coronation wardrobe. All just an excuse for Otis, the Nitwits, the Treniers and the Earl Grant Trio to render the sort of sounds that were making the charts in 1959. TV

Jo Morrow *Princess Ann* • Jack Jones (2) *Riff Manton* • Brian Donlevy *George Manton* • George Jessel • Hans Conried *Balenko* • Karin Booth *Leslie Anders* ■ *Dir* Arthur Dreifuss • *Scr* Mary C McCall Jr, Earl Baldwin, from a story by Lou Morheim

Jules et Jim ★★★★★ PG

Drama 1961 · Fr · BW · 101mins

Echoing the style of Jean Renoir while epitomising the exuberance of the *nouvelle vague*, this is a virtuoso technical performance from François Truffaut. He variously uses photographic stills, newsreel footage, freeze frames and undercranked, travelling and distorted imagery to capture both the era and the emotion described in Henri-Pierre Roché's semi-autobiographical tale. Embodying the complex contradictions of modern womanhood, Jeanne Moreau is enchanting, while, immune to her wilfulness, Oskar Werner and Henri Serre respond readily to her caprice. However, their failure to understand her motives and insecurities prevents them from detecting the incipient despair that will lead to tragedy. The masterpiece of a genius. DP. In French with English subtitles. [video] DVD

Jeanne Moreau *Catherine* • Oskar Werner *Jules* • Henri Serre *Jim* • Marie Dubois *Thérèse* • Vanna Urbino *Gilberte* • Sabine Haudepin *Sabine* • Boris Bassiak *Albert* ■ *Dir* François Truffaut • *Scr* Jean Grualt, François Truffaut, from a novel by Henri-Pierre Roché • *Cinematographer* Raoul Coutard • *Music* Georges Delerue

Jules Verne's Rocket to the Moon ★★ U

Science-fiction comedy
1967 · UK · Colour · 88mins

No prizes for guessing where the inspiration for the alternative title to this film, *Those Fantastic Flying Fools*, came from. But beware! These not-so-magnificent men in their rocketship to the Moon provide strictly routine science fantasy. A fabulous cast breathes life into an insipid Jules Verne concoction that has Burl Ives sending circus performers into Victorian orbit only to have them crash-land in tsarist Russia. Sadly, the comedy plummets even faster than the cheap special effects. AJ [video] DVD

Burl Ives *Phineas T Barnum* • Troy Donahue *Gaylord Sullivan* • Gert Frobe [Gert Fröbe] *Professor von Bulow* • Hermione Gingold *Angelica* • Lionel Jeffries *Sir Charles Dillworthy* • Terry-Thomas *Captain Sir Harry Washington-Smythe* • Jimmy Clitheroe *General Tom Thumb* ■ *Dir* Don Sharp • *Scr* Dave Freeman, from a story by Peter Welbeck [Harry Alan Towers], from the writings of Jules Verne

Julia ★★★★ PG

Drama 1977 · US · Colour · 112mins

Lillian Hellman's memoir provides the basis for Fred Zinnemann's sensitive movie about friendship, courage and the playwright's growing awareness of the Nazi menace during the early 1930s. Lillian (Jane Fonda) makes contact with her childhood friend Julia (Vanessa Redgrave), a committed anti-fascist. Later Lillian is persuaded to help smuggle money into Germany to aid in the fight against the Nazis. The film's strength lies not in complex plotting but in the excellent performances from Fonda, Oscar-winning Redgrave, and Jason Robards as Dashiell Hammett. Meryl Streep makes her feature debut. TH [video]

Jane Fonda *Lillian Hellman* • Vanessa Redgrave *Julia* • Jason Robards *Dashiell Hammett* • Maximilian Schell *Johann* • Hal Holbrook *Alan Campbell* • Rosemary Murphy *Dorothy Parker* • Meryl Streep *Anne Marie* ■ *Dir* Fred Zinnemann • *Scr* Alvin Sargent, from the memoirs *Pentimento* by Lillian Hellman

Julia and Julia ★★ 18

Drama 1987 · It · Colour · 97mins

Italian director Peter Del Monte's English debut is now primarily notable for being the first feature to be shot entirely using a high-definition video process, with the resulting footage being transferred to film for projection. However, the technique was still in its infancy and resists even master cinematographer Giuseppe Rotunno's efforts to create naturalistic visuals. The story proves equally unmalleable, as widowed travel agent Kathleen Turner seemingly enters a time warp that causes her to doubt whether Gabriel Byrne actually perished in a car smash on their honeymoon. DP [video]

Kathleen Turner *Julia* • Gabriele Ferzetti *Paolo's Father* • Gabriel Byrne *Paolo* • Sting *Daniel Osler* • Angela Goodwin *Paolo's Mother* ■ *Dir* Peter Del Monte • *Scr* Peter Del Monte, Silvia Napolitano, Sandro Petraglia, from a story by Peter Del Monte, Silvia Napolitano

Julia Has Two Lovers ★ 15

Drama 1990 · US · Colour · 82mins

Lucky old Julia (Daphna Kastner, who also wrote the script), especially as one of her two lovers is David Duchovny. Unfortunately, she's stuck in this tedious film, trying to decide whether to marry her boring lover (David Charles) or have an affair with the mysterious man who is attempting to seduce her over the phone. Badly written, acted and directed. JB [video]

Daphna Kastner *Julia* • David Duchovny *Daniel* • David Charles *Jack* • Tim Ray *Leo* • Martin Donovan (2) *Freddy* • Anita Olanick *Ursula* ■ *Dir* Bashar Shbib • *Scr* Bashar Shbib, Daphna Kastner, from a story by Daphna Kastner

Julia Misbehaves ★★

Comedy 1948 · US · BW · 99mins

With her long-lost daughter's romance about to progress to the altar, actress Julia Packett (Greer Garson) decides to go back to her conventional husband. Garson and Walter Pidgeon both flounder, especially Garson, who is called upon for some slapstick interludes in an attempt to enliven this flaccid romantic comedy. The heart-stoppingly lovely young Elizabeth Taylor plays the daughter and Peter Lawford is the man she really loves, but this is still disappointing. RK

Greer Garson *Julia Packett* • Walter Pidgeon *William Sylvester Packett* • Peter Lawford *Ritchie Lorgan* • Cesar Romero *Fred Gennochio* • Elizabeth Taylor *Susan Packett* • Lucile Watson *Mrs Packett* • Nigel Bruce *Col Willowbrook* ■ *Dir* Jack Conway • *Scr* William Ludwig, Harry Ruskin, Arthur Wimperis, from the novel *The Nutmeg Tree* by Margery Sharp

Julian Po ★★ 12

Comedy drama 1997 · US · Colour · 80mins

Christian Slater stars in this superficial drama about a young wanderer drifting into a small-town community. Initially treating him as an unwelcome stranger, the locals change their tune when they discover he's there for the sole purpose of committing suicide. Cue neighbours knocking on his door to unburden their hearts, offer advice and convince him life is worth it. Writer/director Alan Wade handles it all with aplomb, but his characters are little more than two-dimensional sketches. LH [video] DVD

Christian Slater *Julian Po* • Robin Tunney *Sarah* • Cherry Jones *Lucy* • Michael Parks *Vern* • Frankie Faison *Sheriff* • Harve Presnell *Mayor* ■ *Dir* Alan Wade • *Scr* Alan Wade, from the book *La Mort de Monsieur Golouja* by Branimir Scepanovic

J

Juliana ★★★

Drama 1988 · Peru · Colour · 97mins

Directors Fernando Espinoza and Alejandro Legaspi explore the topic of urban poverty with this naturalistic, but often warm and amusing tale, in which a young girl (Rosa Isabel Morfino) runs away from home to escape her abusive stepfather, Guillermo Esqueche. She then encounters the even more viciously exploitative Julio Vega, when she disguises herself as a boy in order to join the band of Lima street musicians that he manages. DP. In Spanish with English subtitles.

Rosa Isabel Morfino *Juliana* • Julio Vega *Don Pedro* • Guillermo Esqueche *Stepfather* • Edward Centeno *Clavito* • David Zuniga *Cobra* ■ *Dir* Fernando Espinoza, Alejandro Legaspi • *Scr* Rene Weber, Oswaldo Carpio, Stefan Kaspar, Fernando Espinoza, Alejandro Legaspi

Julie ★★★

Thriller 1956 · US · BW · 97mins

Doris Day suspects her husband Louis Jourdan is trying to kill her in director Andrew L Stone's tense thriller. Stone's speciality of filming dramas in real-life situations is put to good use here, and he certainly whips up the suspense even if the plot becomes rather implausible in places. Day is radiant and Jourdan very convincing, while Barry Sullivan and Frank Lovejoy give perfectly weighted supporting performances. TS

Doris Day *Julie Benton* • Louis Jourdan *Lyle Benton* • Barry Sullivan *Cliff Henderson* • Frank Lovejoy *Detective Captain Pringle* • John Gallaudet *Detective Cole* • Harlan Warde *Detective Pope* ■ *Dir/Scr* Andrew L Stone

Julie and the Cadillacs ★★ PG

Musical drama 1997 · UK · Colour · 106mins

This is less a film about making it in the pop business in the early 1960s than a homage to those corny "next stop the top" movies. Nigh on every scene is geared up to slipping in one of the 17 tunes on a soundtrack that seems to have been composed exclusively of B-side pastiches and comic ensemble routines. Despite the disappointing music, director Bryan Izzard's eagerly played film is spot-on in its tell-tale details, and provides a timely reminder that pop was once about talent, not just image. DP

Tina Russell *Julie Carr* • Toyah Willcox *Barbara Gifford* • Victor Spinetti *Cyril Wise* • Peter Polycarpou *Phil Green* • Thora Hird *Julie's grandmother* • James Grout *Mr Watkins* • Mike Berry *Mac MacDonald* ■ *Dir* Bryan Izzard • *Scr* John Dean • *Music/Lyrics* John Dean

julien donkey-boy ★★★★ 15

Drama 1999 · US · Colour · 99mins

Considering the downbeat realism of Harmony Korine's second feature *Gummo*, it wasn't a big step for the director to follow the Dogme ultra-realist style of film-making. However, there's greater narrative contrivance in this tale of the schizophrenic who finds solace from the tyranny of his abusive father by working in a school for the blind. Visionary German director Werner Herzog startles as the perversely dysfunctional parent, while Ewen Bremner excels as the interiorised outsider. Challenging, technically astute and inventive. DP. Contains swearing and sex scenes. [video] DVD

Ewen Bremner *Julien* • Chloë Sevigny *Pearl* • Werner Herzog *Father* • Evan Neumann *Chris* • Joyce Korine *Grandma* • Chrissy Kobylak *Chrissy* • Brian Fisk *Pond boy* • Alvin Law *Neighbour* ■ *Dir/Scr* Harmony Korine

J

Juliet of the Spirits ★★★ 15

Fantasy drama
1965 · Fr/It/W Ger · Colour · 120mins

Having explored his own fears and failings in $8\frac{1}{2}$, Federico Fellini here tries to do the same for his wife, Giulietta Masina, in this highly stylised daydream. In his first film in colour, the director employs bold hues to suggest the fantastical world in which Masina takes refuge from the even more artificial milieu into which her pretentious, philandering husband has plunged her. Determined to break from traditional storytelling techniques, Fellini strives for visual poetry, and while he succeeds in creating some memorable imagery, his ventures into Jungian psychology, spiritualism and astrology feel too much like dilettante dabbling. DP. In Italian with English subtitles. [video]

Giulietta Masina *Juliet* • Mario Pisu *Giorgio* • Sandra Milo *Susy/Fanny/Iris* • Caterina Boratto *Juliet's mother* • Luisa Della Noce *Adele* • Sylva Koscina *Sylva* ■ *Dir* Federico Fellini • *Scr* Federico Fellini, Tullio Pinelli, Brunello Rondi, Ennio Flaiano, from a story by Federico Fellini, Tullio Pinelli • *Cinematographer* Gianni Di Venanzo

Julius Caesar ★★★★★ U

Historical drama 1953 · US · BW · 116mins

Marlon Brando daringly took on the role of Mark Antony (with the help of some coaching from John Gielgud), in what was to become possibly the finest cinematic version of any of Shakespeare's plays. The cast assembled by MGM is mouthwatering. Brando is magnificent, his oration at Caesar's funeral the definitive delivery, while James Mason, as "the most noble Roman of them all" Brutus, is beautifully spoken. There's also no denying Gielgud makes a perfect "lean and hungry"-looking Cassius, Louis Calhern was clearly born to play Caesar himself, and Miklos Rosza's majestic score is mightily impressive. Director Joseph L Mankiewicz concentrates on the drama, not the spectacle, perhaps to disguise the fact that he was forced to use up the old *Quo Vadis* sets. TS [video]

James Mason *Brutus* • Marlon Brando *Mark Antony* • John Gielgud *Cassius* • Louis Calhern *Julius Caesar* • Edmond O'Brien *Casca* • Greer Garson *Calpurnia* • Deborah Kerr *Portia* • George Macready *Marullus* • Michael Pate *Flavius* • Richard Hale *Soothsayer* • Alan Napier *Cicero* ■ *Dir* Joseph L Mankiewicz • *Scr* Joseph L Mankiewicz, from the play by William Shakespeare • *Cinematographer* Joseph Ruttenberg • *Art Director* Cedric Gibbons, Edward Carfagno

Julius Caesar ★★ PG

Historical drama
1970 · UK · Colour · 111mins

This Shakespearean saga is particularly turgid, undermined by Stuart Burge's pedestrian direction and a surprisingly weak Brutus from Jason Robards. John Gielgud, who was Cassius in the far superior 1953 version, now plays Caesar, while Charlton Heston takes his second (though not his last) stab at playing Mark Antony on film. AT [video]

Charlton Heston *Mark Antony* • Jason Robards *Brutus* • John Gielgud *Julius Caesar* • Richard Johnson *Cassius* • Robert Vaughn *Casca* • Richard Chamberlain *Octavius Caesar* • Diana Rigg *Portia* • Jill Bennett *Calpurnia* ■ *Dir* Stuart Burge • *Scr* Robert Furnival, from the play by William Shakespeare

Jumanji ★★★★ PG

Fantasy adventure
1995 · US · Colour · 99mins

It was dismissed by many critics as a noisy, scary and worthless excuse for some ingenious computer effects, but as empty experiences go this fantasy adventure is absolutely exhilarating. Young audiences will be been held spellbound by the marauding wildlife that is unleashed when Kirsten Dunst and Bradley Pierce rescue Robin Williams from the sinister board game in which he's been trapped for 26 years. Any film where the action is determined by a roll of the dice is bound to be episodic, but this hardly detracts from the enjoyment as one spectacular set piece follows another. DP [video] DVD

Robin Williams *Alan Parrish* • Jonathan Hyde *Van Pelt/Sam Parrish* • Kirsten Dunst *Judy* • Bradley Pierce *Peter* • Bonnie Hunt *Sarah* • Bebe Neuwirth *Nora* • David Alan Grier *Bentley* • Patricia Clarkson *Carol Parrish* ■ *Dir* Joe Johnston • *Scr* Jonathan Hensleigh, Greg Taylor, Jim Strain, from a story by Greg Taylor, Jim Strain, Chris Van Allsburg, from the novel by Chris Van Allsburg

Jumbo ★★★★ U

Musical comedy 1962 · US · Colour · 123mins

A wonderfully warm-hearted MGM musical about circus rivalries, this is based on showman Billy Rose's Broadway extravaganza, which actually featured an elephant on stage. Star Doris Day is, sadly, too old and wise to play the ingénue here, but she delivers the lovely Rodgers and Hart songs superbly. Unlikely co-star Stephen Boyd, still hot from *Ben-Hur*, also acquits himself surprisingly well. However, the real joys are veterans Martha Raye and Jimmy Durante, whose "What elephant?" line from this movie has rightly become classic. TS

Doris Day *Kitty Wonder* • Stephen Boyd *Sam Rawlins* • Jimmy Durante *Pop Wonder* • Martha Raye *Lulu* • Dean Jagger *John Noble* • Joseph Waring *Harry* • Lynn Wood *Tina* • Charles Watts *Ellis* ■ *Dir* Charles Walters • *Scr* Sidney Sheldon, from the musical by Ben Hecht, Charles MacArthur • *Choreography* Busby Berkeley

Jump for Glory ★★

Crime drama 1937 · UK · BW · 75mins

What brought renowned action director Raoul Walsh to this side of the Atlantic is an open question. The Glory of the title is the opportunist "victim" (played by the elegant Valerie Hobson) of stylish thief Douglas Fairbanks Jr, who is mortified to discover that she's engaged to his blackmailing ex-partner in crime Alan Hale. Complications follow, before the inevitable contrived ending. Known as *When Thief Meets Thief* in the US, this is amiable but overcomplicated entertainment. BB

Douglas Fairbanks Jr *Ricky Morgan* • Valerie Hobson *Glory Howard* • Alan Hale *Jim Dial/Colonel Fane* • Jack Melford *Thompson* • Anthony Ireland *Sir Timothy Haddon* ■ *Dir* Raoul Walsh • *Scr* John Meehan, Harold French, from the novel by Gordon McDonnell

Jump the Gun ★★ 15

Drama 1996 · UK/S Afr · Colour · 108mins

The characters British director Les Blair sets down on the streets of Johannesburg could just as easily be found ducking and diving in London's East End. The cast, particularly Lionel Newton and Michele Burgers, works hard, but we've seen wannabe singers, dreamers, hustlers and prostitutes keep company so many times before. It's only the unusual locations and the occasional piece of inspired improvisation that make this more notable than a dozen other low-budget, lowlife dramas. DP. Contains swearing and sex scenes. [video]

Baby Cele *Gugu* • Lionel Newton *"Clint" Clinton* • Michele Burgers *Minnie* • Thulani Nyembe *Bazooka* • Rapulana Seiphemo *Thabo* • Danny Keogh *JJ* ■ *Dir/Scr* Les Blair

Jump Tomorrow ★★★★ PG

Romantic road movie
2001 · UK/US · Colour · 89mins

Joel Hopkins's first feature film is a feel-good road movie with an outsider's sense of place and a sensitive insight into the workings of the human heart. Essentially telling the story of a road trip from New York to Niagara Falls, Hopkins is aided enormously by a cosmopolitan and largely unknown cast. Lead actor Tunde Adebimpe excels as the timid Nigerian pen pusher, whose life is transformed on a meandering odyssey to his wedding day in the company of eccentric Frenchman Hippolyte Girardot, ravishing Spaniard Natalia Verbeke and her snooty English fiancé James Wilby. This is a film of rare subtlety and charm. DP [video] DVD

Tunde Adebimpe *George* • Hippolyte Girardot *Gérard* • Natalia Verbeke *Alicia* • Patricia Mauceri *Consuelo* • Isiah Whitlock Jr *George's uncle* • Kaili Vernoff *Heather Leather* • James Wilby *Nathan* ■ *Dir* Joel Hopkins • *Scr* Joel Hopkins, Nicola Usborne, Iain Tibbles

Jumpin' at the Boneyard ★★★ 15

Drama 1991 · US · Colour · 102mins

Tim Roth is mesmerising, both moving and effortlessly believable as a reformed small-time crook from the Bronx. Meeting up by chance with his brother (Alexis Arquette), he uncomfortably attempts to renew family ties and ensure that his sibling won't make the same mistakes he did. Roth's turn is matched by telling performances from Arquette and a pre-fame Samuel L Jackson, even though it makes for grim viewing. JF [video]

Tim Roth *Manny* • Alexis Arquette *Danny* • Danitra Vance *Jeanette* • Kathleen Chalfant *Mom* • Samuel L Jackson *Mr Simpson* • Luis Guzman *Taxi driver* • Elizabeth Bracco *Cathy* • Jeffrey Wright *Derek* ■ *Dir/Scr* Jeff Stanzler

Jumpin' Jack Flash ★★ 15

Comedy thriller 1986 · US · Colour · 100mins

Whoopi Goldberg's first major role following her debut in *The Color Purple* is a disappointment. She stars as a computer operator who inadvertently gets involved in international espionage when a message for help from a spy appears on her screen. Penny Marshall replaced Howard Zieff in the director's chair, the script went through several writers, and this raucous comedy certainly feels as if there were too many cooks. JB. Contains swearing. [video] DVD

Whoopi Goldberg *Terry Doolittle* • Stephen Collins *Marty Phillips* • John Wood *Jeremy Talbot* • Carol Kane *Cynthia* • Annie Potts *Liz Carlson* • Peter Michael Goetz *Mr Page* • Jim Belushi [James Belushi] *Sperry repairman* • Tracey Ullman *Fiona* ■ *Dir* Penny Marshall • *Scr* David H Franzoni, JW Melville, Patricia Irving, Christopher Thompson, from a story by David H Franzoni

Jumping for Joy ★★ U

Comedy 1955 · UK · BW · 84mins

Frankie Howerd was still best known as the headliner on radio's *Variety Bandbox* when he took his first real starring role in his third film outing. His famous nuances and grimaces were not really suited to the big screen and this tepid comedy about a racetrack dogsbody who finds himself protecting a champion greyhound from some dastardly crooks did not prove otherwise. Titter ye will not. DP [video]

Frankie Howerd *Willie Joy* • Stanley Holloway *"Captain" Jack Montague* • AE Matthews *Lord Cranfield* • Tony Wright *Vincent* • Alfie Bass *Blagg* • Joan Hickson *Lady Cranfield* • Lionel Jeffries *Bert Benton* ■ *Dir* John Paddy Carstairs • *Scr* Jack Davies, Henry E Blyth

Jumping Jacks ★★ U

Comedy 1952 · US · BW · 95mins

After impressing as comedy support in the *My Friend Irma* films, Dean Martin and Jerry Lewis were given their chance to become headliners and soon established themselves as huge box-office stars. As with much of the comedy talent of the time, the pair proved particularly popular in service comedies. In this one, they play up the slapstick as bumbling new recruits in a paratroop squad. Not as good as their earlier efforts. DF

Jerry Lewis *Hap Smith* • Dean Martin *Chick Allen* • Mona Freeman *Betty Carver* • Robert Strauss *Sgt McCluskey* ■ *Dir* Norman Taurog • *Scr* Robert Lees, Fred Rinaldo, Herbert Baker, James Allardice, Richard Weil, from a story by Brian Marlow

June Bride ★★★ U

Romantic comedy 1948 · US · BW · 96mins

Anything with Bette Davis in it is worth watching, but there are also some light, fluffy, witty moments to be savoured in this tale of two very spoilt hacks on a women's magazine who fall in love again while composing a daft feature on June weddings. Robert Montgomery is Davis's able co-star and he gives her a fair old run for her money in the scene-stealing stakes. Even if this profoundly inconsequential movie gives us little more than a few wry laughs, it does so with great style and touches of flair. Debbie Reynolds makes a fleeting film debut. SR

Bette Davis *Linda Gilman* • Robert Montgomery *Carey Jackson* • Fay Bainter *Paula Winthrop* • Betty Lynn *Boo Brinker* • Tom Tully *Mr Brinker* • Barbara Bates *Jeanne Brinker* • Debbie Reynolds *Boo's girl friend* ■ *Dir* Bretaigne Windust • *Scr* Ranald MacDougall, from the play *Feature for June* by Eileen Tighe, Graeme Lorimer

June Night ★★★

Drama 1940 · Swe · BW · 86mins

In the last film she made in Sweden before settling in America, Ingrid Bergman gives a performance to rival any of her early Hollywood assignments as a chemist whose affair with a sailor scandalises a quiet country town. As in so many Swedish films of the period, passions simmer beneath impassive surfaces and hypocritical citizens censure while secretly revelling in the sins of the accused. Bergman is quite captivating, and it's melodrama all the way, so get those hankies out. DP. In Swedish with English subtitles.

Ingrid Bergman *Kerstin Nordback/Sara Nordana* • Marianne Löfgren *Asa* • Lill-Tollie Zellman *Jane Jacobs* • Marianne Aminoff *Nickan* ■ *Dir* Per Lindberg • *Scr* Ragnar Hylten-Cavallius, Per Lindberg, from a story by Tora Nordstrom-Bonnier

Jungle Book ★★★ U

Adventure 1942 · US · Colour · 101mins

This is a starchy affair in which animal magic, preachy parable and jungle adventure have been loosely combined, missing the wisdom, drama and humour of Kipling's classic stories. Sabu stars as Mowgli, the child raised by wolves whose friends Baloo, Hathi and Bagheera protect him as he trails man-eating tiger Shere Khan and faces sundry human villains. Much of it seems rather stilted today, though the Technicolor jungle built in Los Angeles remains a captivating fantasy world. Heavy going for all its beauty. DP [video]

Sabu *Mowgli* • Joseph Calleia *Buldeo* • John Qualen *Barber* • Frank Puglia *Pundit* • Rosemary DeCamp *Messua* • Patricia O'Rourke *Mahala* • Ralph Byrd *Durga* • John Mather *Rao* • Faith Brook *English girl* ■ *Dir* Zoltan Korda • *Scr* Laurence Stallings, from the books by Rudyard Kipling

The Jungle Book ★★★★★ U

Classic animated adventure
1967 · US · Colour · 74mins

The last animated feature made under Walt Disney's personal supervision before his death, this barnstorming classic occupies a truly rewarding perch in the studio's history, repaying repeated releases in all formats, and ageing not a jot. Based on Rudyard Kipling's stories, it drops the "Man Cub" into a jungle at first perilous, then welcoming, then perilous, and so on. As with all the best Disneys, there is a terrific voice cast and many of the songs have become standards, such as *The Bare Necessities* and *I Wanna Be Like You*. The period's feathery drawing style abounds, and an all-round warmth pervades. AC [video] DVD

Phil Harris *Baloo the Bear* • Sebastian Cabot *Bagheera the Panther* • Louis Prima *King Louie of the Apes* • George Sanders *Shere Khan the Tiger* • Sterling Holloway *Kaa the Snake* • J Pat O'Malley *Colonel Hathi the Elephant* • Bruce Reitherman *Mowgli the Man Cub* • Verna Felton *Elephant* • Clint Howard *Elephant* • Chad Stuart *Vulture* • Lord Tim Hudson *Vulture* • John Abbott *Wolf* • Ben Wright (1) *Wolf* • Darleen Carr *Girl* ■ *Dir* Wolfgang Reitherman • *Scr* Larry Clemmons, Ralph Wright, Ken Anderson, Vance Gerry, from the books by Rudyard Kipling

The Jungle Book ★★★ PG

Period adventure
1994 · US · Colour · 119mins

This live-action version of the story of Mowgli, the boy brought up to adulthood by wolves, may lack the songs, but it is closer to Kipling's original tale than was the classic feature-length cartoon. Jason Scott Lee is effective battling villain Cary Elwes for the treasure buried beneath the lost city. The animal training is extraordinary, and John Cleese's regular appearances add a much-needed lightness to the tale: he even gets to mention "the bare necessities" without a glimmer of Pythonesque irony. TH [video]

Jason Scott Lee *Mowgli* • Cary Elwes *Captain Boone* • Lena Headey *Kitty Brydon* • Sam Neill *Major Brydon* • John Cleese *Doctor Plumford* • Jason Flemyng *Wilkins* ■ *Dir* Stephen Sommers • *Scr* Stephen Sommers, Ronald Yanover, Mark D Geldman, from a story by Ronald Yanover, Mark D Geldman, from the books by Rudyard Kipling

The Jungle Book 2 ★ U

Animated adventure
2003 · US · Colour · 69mins

Enticed back into the jungle by his friend Baloo the bear (voiced by John Goodman), bored man-cub Mowgli (Haley Joel Osment) battles old adversary Shere Kahn in Disney's lame assembly-line sequel to their much-loved 1967 animated classic. A thinly plotted, charmless rehash, rendered in cut-rate graphics, this is unremarkable, uninspired and unsatisfying. AJ [video] DVD

John Goodman *Baloo* • Haley Joel Osment *Mowgli* • Mae Whitman *Shanti* • Connor Funk *Ranjan* • Tony Jay *Shere Khan* • Jim Cummings *Kaa/Colonel Hathi/MC Monkey* • Bob Joles *Bagheera* • Phil Collins *Lucky* • John Rhys-Davies *Mowgli's father* ■ *Dir* Steve Trenbirth • *Scr* Karl Geurs

Jungle Cat ★★★★ U

Documentary 1959 · US · Colour · 69mins

Disney's superb *True-Life Adventures* series closed with this awe-inspiring portrait of the South American jaguar. The result of over two years in the Brazilian rainforest, this is the nature documentary at its best, as a couple of jaguars meet, mate and teach their kittens about the harsh realities of life. However, it's not all encounters with crocodiles and boa constrictors, as narrator Winston Hibler guides us through a history of the cat and plenty of other Amazonian animals get their moment in the spotlight. DP

Winston Hibler *Narrator* ■ *Dir* James Algar

Jungle Fever ★★★ 18

Drama 1991 · US · Colour · 126mins

Spike Lee's take on interracial romance is typically controversial, but lacks the visceral power that he brought to *Do the Right Thing*. Architect Wesley Snipes falls for his white temp Annabella Sciorra and decides to leave his wife for her. However, their relationship sees them swiftly ostracised by their family and friends. Lee's direction is wonderfully fluid and, as in most of his movies, he is superbly served by the striking cinematography of Ernest Dickerson and strong lead performances. JF. Contains swearing, sex scenes, drug abuse, nudity. [video] DVD

Wesley Snipes *Flipper Purify* • Annabella Sciorra *Angie Tucci* • Spike Lee *Cyrus* • Samuel L Jackson *Gator Purify* • Ossie Davis *The Good Reverend Doctor Purify* • Ruby Dee *Lucinda Purify* • Lonette McKee *Drew* • John Turturro *Paulie Carbone* • Anthony Quinn *Lou Carbone* • Frank Vincent *Mike Tucci* • Tim Robbins *Jerry* • Halle Berry *Vivian* • Brad Dourif *Leslie* ■ *Dir/Scr* Spike Lee

Jungle Gents ★★ U

Comedy 1954 · US · BW · 63mins

Another in the long running series of films featuring the Bowery Boys, a group of ageing New York urchins that themselves grew out of earlier film teams, namely the Dead End Kids and the East Side Kids. By 1954 the series (which had launched in 1946) was wearing thin and so were the plots. Here the gang go to Africa and overcome numerous obstacles before discovering a fortune in diamonds. DF

Leo Gorcey *Terrence Aloysius "Slip" Mahoney* • Huntz Hall *Horace Debussy "Sach" Jones* • Laurette Luez *Anatta* • Bernard Gorcey *Louie Dumbrowski* • David Condon [David Gorcey] *Chuck* • Bennie Bartlett *Butch* • Patrick O'Moore *Grimshaw* ■ *Dir* Edward Bernds • *Scr* Edward Bernds, Elwood Ullman

Jungle Jim ★★ U

Adventure 1948 · US · BW · 72mins

Retired Tarzan Johnny Weissmuller strides lumpenly through the bush protecting testy scientist Virginia Grey from hostile wildlife and ruthless treasure seeker George Reeves. So director William Berke wisely lavishes attention on JJ's pets who also distracted attention away from the cheap sets and the stock footage. Weissmuller would return as Jim for 12 sequels, plus a short-lived 1950s TV series. DP

Johnny Weissmuller *Jungle Jim* • Virginia Grey *Hilary Parker* • George Reeves *Bruce Edwards* • Lita Baron *Zia* ■ *Dir* William A Berke [William Berke] • *Scr* Carroll Young, from the comic strip by Alex Raymond

Jungle 2 Jungle ★★★ PG

Comedy adventure
1997 · US · Colour · 100mins

This junior version of *"Crocodile" Dundee* was another vehicle for *Home Improvement* star Tim Allen which failed to make much of dent on the UK market. Allen plays a New York financier who discovers he has a teenage son (Sam Huntington) who has been brought up by an Amazonian tribe. The kid's arrival in New York is the cue for the usual "fish out of water" gags. It's an amiable but predictable affair, and Martin Short is wasted in a silly Russian Mafia subplot. JF [video] DVD

Tim Allen *Michael* • Martin Short *Richard* • JoBeth Williams *Patricia* • Lolita Davidovich *Charlotte* • Sam Huntington *Mimi-Siku* • Valerie Mahaffey *Jan* • Leelee Sobieski *Karen* ■ *Dir* John Pasquin • *Scr* Bruce A Evans, Raynold Gideon, from the film *Un Indien dans la Ville* by Hervé Palud, Thierry Lhermitte, Igor Aptekman, Philippe Bruneau de la Salle

Junior ★★★ PG

Comedy 1994 · US · Colour · 105mins

Arnold Schwarzenegger reunites here with the *Twins* team of Danny DeVito and director Ivan Reitman for another comedy romp. Schwarzenegger and DeVito play struggling medical researchers working on a new fertility drug. When they lose their grant, in desperation Schwarzenegger injects himself with the experimental solution and ends up pregnant. It's pretty much a one-joke concept, but Reitman milks it for all it's worth, and only Emma Thompson as a fellow scientist and love interest looks out of place in an underwritten role. JF [video] DVD

Arnold Schwarzenegger *Dr Alexander Hesse* • Danny DeVito *Dr Larry Arbogast* • Emma Thompson *Dr Diana Reddin* • Frank Langella *Noah Banes* • Pamela Reed *Angela* • Judy Collins *Naomi* ■ *Dir* Ivan Reitman • *Scr* Kevin Wade, Chris Conrad

Junior Bonner ★★★★ PG

Drama 1972 · US · Colour · 100mins

Sam Peckinpah was one of the most talented movie directors ever. He could be tough in *The Wild Bunch* and he could be tender in *The Ballad of Cable Hogue*. Peckinpah was happiest among fellow professionals, and here he tells a tale of such a pro, the rodeo rider of the title, brilliantly played by Steve McQueen. As Junior tries to ride the unrideable, we watch his life pass by in the company of the superbly cast Robert Preston and Ida Lupino as his parents, and Joe Don Baker as his venal brother Curly. The Todd-AO widescreen compositions lose considerable impact on television, but the substance endures. TS [video] DVD

Steve McQueen *Junior Bonner* • Robert Preston *Ace Bonner* • Ida Lupino *Elvira Bonner* • Joe Don Baker *Curly Bonner* • Barbara Leigh *Charmagne* • Mary Murphy *Ruth Bonner* • Ben Johnson *Buck Roan* • Bill McKinney *Red Terwilliger* ■ *Dir* Sam Peckinpah • *Scr* Jeb Rosebrook • *Cinematographer* Lucien Ballard

Junior Miss ★★★ U

Comedy 1945 · US · BW · 57mins

One of those early and distinctly jaunty generation gap family tales in which a lively teenager (Peggy Ann Garner) exhibits such wildly rebellious behaviour as staying out past nine o'clock and wearing a natty ensemble that daringly reveals her shoulders. It all looks mind-bogglingly innocent today, but Garner gives concerned dad Allyn Joslyn a few nasty turns along the way. While undemanding, this is still entertaining. SR

Peggy Ann Garner *Judy Graves* • Allyn Joslyn *Harry Graves* • Michael Dunne [Steve Dunne] *Uncle Willis* • Faye Marlowe *Ellen Curtis* • Mona Freeman *Lois* • Sylvia Field *Grace Graves* ■ *Dir* George Seaton • *Scr* George Seaton, from the play by Jerome Chodorov, Joseph Fields

The Juniper Tree ★★★

Fantasy drama 1990 · US/Ice · BW · 80mins

This prize-winning film was inspired by a fairy tale by the Brothers Grimm. For most viewers, the lure will be the chance to see Icelandic pop star, Björk, in a rare acting role. But there's a genuine fascination in the way writer/director Nietzchka Keene combines the grim realism of the desolate, monochrome landscape with the enchantment of her fantastical fable, in which Bryndis Petra Bragadottir uses the witchcraft she learned from her mother to manipulate the emotions of a widowed farmer. DP

Björk Gudmundsdottir [Björk] *Margit* • Bryndis Petra Bragadottir *Katla* • Valdimar Orn Flygenring *Johann* • Gudrun Gisladottir *Mother* • Geirlaug Sunna Pormar *Jonas* ■ *Dir* Nietzchka Keene • *Scr* Nietzchka Keene, from a story by Wilhelm and Jacob Grimm

Junk Mail ★★★★ 15

Black comedy thriller
1997 · Nor/Den · Colour · 77mins

With a central character who resembles a cross between Charlie Chaplin and Buster Keaton, and deadpan humour reminiscent of Finnish film-maker Aki Kaurismäki, this comic hybrid is a delightfully offbeat accumulation of deft observations and sly coincidences. Robert Skjaestard is shambolically droll as the voyeuristic postman whose love for deaf blonde Andrine Saether prompts him to become the scourge of various bullies, slobs and thieves he encounters on his rounds. Director Pal Sletaune keeps his debut feature wonderfully lean and controlled, restricting himself to a couple of achingly funny set pieces. DP. In Norwegian with English subtitles. Contains violence, nudity and swearing. [video]

Robert Skjaerstad *Roy Amundsen* • Andrine Saether *Line Groberg* • Per Egil Aske *Georg Rheinhardsen* • Eli Anne Linnestad *Betsy* ■ *Dir* Pål Sletaune • *Scr* Pål Sletaune, Jonny Halberg

Juno and the Paycock ★★

Drama 1930 · UK · BW · 85mins

The constraints placed upon film-makers by the primitive nature of early sound recording equipment only partly explain Alfred Hitchcock's failure to transfer Sean O'Casey's celebrated play about the Irish Civil War successfully to the screen. Although an admirer of the material, which concerns an Irish family who think they have come into money, he found it stubbornly uncinematic and ended up staging the action in a calcified manner. However, Sara Allgood excels as Juno Boyle, thus creating the mould for every forbidding Hitchcock mother to come. DP

Sara Allgood *Juno Boyle* • Edward Chapman *Capt John "Paycock" Boyle* • Sydney Morgan *Joxer Daly* • John Longden *Chris Bentham* •

Kathleen O'Regan *Mary Boyle* • John Laurie *Johnny Boyle* ■ *Dir* Alfred Hitchcock • *Scr* Alfred Hitchcock, Alma Reville, from the play by Sean O'Casey

Junoon ★★★★ 15

Epic period drama
1978 · Ind · Colour · 121mins

This visually splendid epic drama sets a personal story of love and honour across racial and religious barriers against the historical backdrop of the Indian Mutiny. Shashi Kapoor's debut as a producer was billed as the first film to deal authentically with the Indian Mutiny. As the Pathan noble who rescues Anglo-Indian widow Jennifer Kendal and her daughter Nafisa Ali from a terrorist attack, Kapoor gives a larger-than-life performance that somewhat undermines Shyam Benegal's otherwise naturalistic direction. But with Shabana Azmi outstanding as his betrayed wife, this feature is always engrossing. DP. In Urdu with English subtitles.

Shashi Kapoor *Javed Khan* • Jennifer Kendal *Mariam Labadoor* • Nafisa Ali *Ruth Labadoor* • Shabana Azmi *Firdaus* • Naseeruddin Shah *Sarfraz Khan* • Kulbhushan Kharbanda *Ramjimal* • Tom Alter *Charles Labadoor* ■ *Dir/Scr* Shyam Benegal

Jupiter's Darling ★★★ U

Musical comedy 1955 · US · Colour · 96mins

An under-rated musical comedy about Hannibal and his elephants crossing the Alps to sack Rome. Esther Williams is in her Amazonian prime here, as she lures Howard Keel's Hannibal away from the Eternal City, and the two stars are superb together. Other pleasures include George Sanders and Richard Haydn as very English patricians, and the wonderful Marge and Gower Champion, who do a terrific song-and-dance number with painted elephants. TS

Esther Williams *Amytis* • Howard Keel *Hannibal* • Marge Champion *Meta* • Gower Champion *Varius* • George Sanders *Fabius Maximus* • Richard Haydn *Horatio* • William Demarest *Mago* ■ *Dir* George Sidney (2) • *Scr* Dorothy Kingsley, from the play *Road to Rome* by Robert Sherwood [Robert E Sherwood] • *Music* David Rose • *Choreographer* Hermes Pan

Jurassic Park ★★★★★ PG

Science-fiction adventure
1993 · US · Colour · 121mins

Steven Spielberg soared to new heights with this massively successful adventure. The world's ultimate theme park, featuring genetically re-created dinosaurs, is about to open and owner Richard Attenborough decides to give a sneak preview to a select few, including scientists Sam Neill and Laura Dern. However, all is not well in this new Garden of Eden, where T-Rex and his chums are the undoubted stars of the show. Spielberg orchestrates the action with effortless verve and, although it's a little too long and full of loose ends, only the most Scrooge-like viewer will fail to be transfixed by the thrilling action and the sheer scale of the director's vision. The dinosaurs returned in *The Lost World: Jurassic Park*. JF. Contains swearing and violence. DVD

Sam Neill *Dr Alan Grant* • Laura Dern *Dr Ellie Sattler* • Jeff Goldblum *Ian Malcolm* • Richard Attenborough *John Hammond* • Bob Peck *Robert Muldoon* • Martin Ferrero *Donald Gennaro* • BD Wong *Dr Wu* • Joseph Mazzello *Tim* • Ariana Richards *Lex* • Samuel L Jackson *Arnold* • Wayne Knight *Nedry* ■ *Dir* Steven Spielberg • *Scr* Michael Crichton, David Koepp, from the novel by Michael Crichton • *Cinematographer* Dean Cundey • *Visual Effects* Michael Lantieri, Dennis Muren, Phil Tippet, Stan Winston

Jurassic Park III ★★★ PG

Science-fiction adventure
2001 · US · Colour · 88mins

Jumanji director Joe Johnston takes the reins in this second sequel, and he's done a creditable job with what is basically a retread of the earlier films. We're back on Isla Sorna, where genetically engineered dinosaurs run wild, with another band of walking packed lunches: divorcees William H Macy and Téa Leoni looking for their lost 14-year-old son, paleontologist Sam Neill and his protégé Alessandro Nivola. It's familiar ground, but the set pieces are excellent. AC. Contains violence. DVD

Sam Neill *Dr Alan Grant* • William H Macy *Paul Kirby* • Téa Leoni *Amanda Kirby* • Alessandro Nivola *Billy Brennan* • Trevor Morgan *Eric Kirby* • Michael Jeter *Udesky* • John Diehl *Cooper* • Bruce A Young *Nash* • Laura Dern *Ellie Sattler* ■ *Dir* Joe Johnston • *Scr* Peter Buchman, Alexander Payne, Jim Taylor, from characters created by Michael Crichton

The Juror ★★ 18

Psychological thriller
1996 · US · Colour · 113mins

Demi Moore stars as the juror on a Mafia trial who is harassed, threatened and coerced by a Mob henchman Alec Baldwin to bring about a hung jury. Brian Gibson's film plods along predictably, with the only sparks of interest coming from the implausible plot twists. Still, thanks to a hilarious performance from Baldwin, it's marginally better than the similarly themed *Trial by Jury* with Joanne Whalley-Kilmer, which was made two years before. JB DVD

Demi Moore *Annie Laird* • Alec Baldwin *The Teacher* • Joseph Gordon-Levitt *Oliver* • Anne Heche *Juliet* • James Gandolfini *Eddie* • Lindsay Crouse *Tallow* • Tony LoBianco *Louie Boffano* • Michael Constantine *Judge Weitzel* ■ *Dir* Brian Gibson • *Scr* Ted Tally, from the novel by George Dawes Green

Jury Duty ★★ 12

Comedy 1995 · US · Colour · 84mins

Pauly Shore has never enjoyed the sort of profile over here that he holds in the US, although this enjoyably crass comedy is one his better flicks. In another variation on his lazy-slacker persona, he plays a layabout who gets himself on jury service and proceeds to create havoc at a sensational murder trial. There are good supporting turns from Stanley Tucci and Brian Doyle-Murray, and director John Fortenberry has fun sending up the courtroom-drama genre. JF

Pauly Shore *Tommy* • Tia Carrere *Monica* • Stanley Tucci *Frank* • Brian Doyle-Murray *Harry* • Abe Vigoda *Judge Powell* • Charles Napier *Jed* • Richard Edson *Skeets* ■ *Dir* John Fortenberry • *Scr* Neil Tolkin, Barbara Williams, Samantha Adams, from a story by Barbara Williams, Samantha Adams

Just a Gigolo ★★ 15

Period drama 1978 · W Ger · Colour · 88mins

Neither director David Hemmings nor a dream cast can do much with this lackadaisical look at how and why a disorientated Prussian war veteran become a gigolo in post-First World War Berlin. While this captures the disillusioned flavour of the era, its fragmented structure and an awkward performance from David Bowie in the lead leave much to be desired. Marlene Dietrich appears briefly to sing the title song; it was her last screen role. AJ. In English and German with subtitles.

David Bowie *Paul von Przygodsky* • Sydne Rome *Cilly* • Kim Novak *Helga* • David Hemmings *Captain Hermann Kraft* • Maria Schell *Mutti* • Curd Jürgens [Curt Jurgens] *Prince* • Marlene Dietrich *Baroness von Semering* ■ *Dir* David Hemmings • *Scr* Joshua Sinclair, Ennio De Concini

Just a Kiss ★★ 15

Romantic comedy
2002 · US · Colour · 86mins

Exploring how a single action, in this case an illicit kiss, can trigger off a chain of far-reaching events, this is a shallow relationship comedy laced with gallows humour. Performance-wise the film's nothing special, but it's the constant to-ing and fro-ing of timelines and the inappropriate flashes of "rotoscope" animation that are the picture's major downsides. They disturb the overall fluidity and make actor-turned-director Fisher Stevens look like he's trying way too hard to be hip and edgy. SF. Contains swearing and sex scenes. DVD

Ron Eldard *Dag* • Kyra Sedgwick *Halley* • Patrick Breen *Peter* • Marisa Tomei *Paula* • Marley Shelton *Rebecca* • Taye Diggs *Andre* • Sarita Choudhury *Colleen* ■ *Dir* Fisher Stevens • *Scr* Patrick Breen

Just Another Girl on the IRT ★★★ 18

Drama 1992 · US · Colour · 93mins

Terrific slice-of-life stuff, by turns funny and sad, with Ariyan Johnson excellent as an ordinary New York high-school student who's determined to better herself, but whose plans get back-burnered when she gets pregnant. Leslie Harris directs his first feature with real sensitivity. To our knowledge, and inexplicably, he hasn't made one since. The film's title refers to the New York subway system. DA

Ariyan Johnson *Chantel* • Kevin Thigpen *Tyrone* • Ebony Jerido *Natete* • Jerard Washington *Gerard* ■ *Dir/Scr* Leslie Harris

Just around the Corner ★★

Musical 1938 · US · BW · 70mins

Shirley Temple finds work for her architect father after befriending an eccentric old millionaire in this Depression-era fable directed by Irving Cummings. The little trouper was growing up and being given excessively mature dialogue, losing much of her bubbly charm. But she sings and dances with Bill Robinson for the fourth and last time, and that's pure magic. Joan Davis and Bert Lahr lend strong support. AE

Shirley Temple *Penny Hale* • Charles Farrell *Jeff Hale* • Joan Davis *Kitty* • Amanda Duff *Lola* • Bill Robinson *Corp Jones* • Bert Lahr *Gus* • Franklin Pangborn *Waters* • Cora Witherspoon *Aunt Julia Ramsby* • Claude Gillingwater Sr [Claude Gillingwater] *Samuel G Henshaw* ■ *Dir* Irving Cummings • *Scr* Ethel Hill, JP Mcevoy, Darrell Ware, from the novel *The Lucky Penny* by Paul Gerard Smith

Just Ask for Diamond ★★ U

Detective spoof 1988 · UK · Colour · 89mins

The original title of Anthony Horowitz's novel, *The Falcon's Malteser*, was dropped. Pity. For it gives some clues about what this whimsical take on *The Maltese Falcon* is trying to do – have fun. With characters such as the Fat Man and Lauren Bacardi to deal with, London-based private eye Tim Diamond (Dursley McLinden) and younger brother Nick (Colin Dale) get involved in a gem-quest. But instead of being endearing, this is slapdash and charmless. TH DVD

Dursley McLinden *Tim Diamond* • Colin Dale *Nick Diamond* • Susannah York *Lauren Bacardi* • Patricia Hodge *Brenda Von Falkenberg* • Michael Robbins *The Fat Man* • Roy Kinnear *Jack Splendide* • Jimmy Nail *Boyle* • Bill Paterson *Chief Inspector Snape* ■ *Dir* Stephen Bayly • *Scr* Anthony Horowitz, from his novel *The Falcon's Malteser*

Just before Dawn ★★★ 18

Horror 1980 · US · Colour · 86mins

This slasher, about a group of urban hikers sharing the Oregon wilderness with machete-wielding mountain men, is both derivative of *The Hills Have Eyes* and almost certainly an inspiration for *The Blair Witch Project*. Director Jeff Lieberman engineers a relentless build-up of suspense, culminating in an outrageous twist near the film's end. Actor Jack Lemmon's son, Chris, stars as one of the teenagers who ignore the warnings of forest ranger George Kennedy to not venture further. Haven't any of these people seen *Deliverance*? TH

George Kennedy *Roy McLean* • Mike Kellin *Ty* • Chris Lemmon *Jonathan* • Gregg Henry *Warren* • Deborah Benson *Constance* • Ralph Seymour *Daniel* ■ *Dir* Jeff Lieberman • *Scr* Mark Arywitz, Gregg Irving, from a story by Joseph Middleton

Just between Friends ★★★ 15

Drama 1986 · US · Colour · 106mins

Like that other 1960s' TV sitcom star Sally Field, Mary Tyler Moore moved in more serious circles in the 1980s and this moving drama certainly gave her a role to get her teeth into. She plays a bored California housewife, seemingly happily married to Ted Danson, whose life is turned on its head when she discovers that her husband has been cheating on her for years. Moore is good in the lead role, although the film is stolen by Christine Lahti, who is terrific as the other woman in a melodrama that packs a punch. JF. Contains swearing.

Mary Tyler Moore *Holly Davis* • Ted Danson *Chip Davis* • Christine Lahti *Sandy Dunlap* • Sam Waterston *Harry Crandall* • Susan Rinell *Kim Davis* ■ *Dir/Scr* Allan Burns

Just Can't Get Enough ★★ 18

Drama based on a true story
2001 · US · Colour · 90mins

This made-for-TV drama is based on the experiences of Dan Peterson, the business studies graduate who went to work for the legendary troupe of male strippers, the Chippendales. Jonathan Aube copes well with the descent into decadence, but he's upstaged by Shelley Malil as Steve Banerjee, the owner of Los Angeles nightclub whose business methods led to murder. Director Dave Payne catches the hedonistic 1980s air, but this never truly ignites. DP DVD

Jonathan Aube *Chad Patterson* • Shelley Malil *Steve Banerjee* • Paul Clark *Spencer Dabias* • John Paul Pitoc *Clayton* • Rebekah Ryan *Heather* ■ *Dir* David Payne [Dave Payne] • *Scr* Dave Payne

Just Cause ★★★ 18

Thriller 1995 · US · Colour · 97mins

In this entertaining thriller, Sean Connery plays a law professor called in to help Blair Underwood, who claims he has been wrongly convicted of the murder of a young child, partly because local cop Laurence Fishburne beat a confession out of him. Connery is as charismatic as ever in a story that, though a little uneven at times, manages some pleasing twists on the usual formula. Director Arne Glimcher throws in enough red herrings to keep viewers guessing right to the end and makes good use of the Everglades locations. JF. Contains swearing and violence. DVD

Sean Connery *Paul Armstrong* • Laurence Fishburne *Tanny Brown* • Kate Capshaw *Laurie Armstrong* • Blair Underwood *Bobby Earl* • Ed Harris *Blair Sullivan* • Christopher Murray *Wilcox* • Daniel J Travanti *Warden* •

Ned Beatty *McNair* ■ *Dir* Arne Glimcher • *Scr* Jeb Stuart, Peter Stone, from the novel by John Katzenbach

Just for You ★★★ U

Musical comedy 1952 · US · Colour · 104mins

Bing Crosby and Jane Wyman, who made such an agreeable duo in Frank Capra's *Here Comes the Groom* (1951), were teamed up again rather less successfully in this tale of Broadway producer Bing, who ignores his teenage children (Natalie Wood, Robert Arthur) until Jane puts him right. Ethel Barrymore is perfect as the headmistress of snooty girl's school, and Bing sings a lively Harry Warren/ Leo Robin song, *Zing a Little Zong*. RB

Bing Crosby *Jordan Blake* • Jane Wyman *Carolina Hill* • Ethel Barrymore *Allida de Bronkhart* • Robert Arthur *Jerry Blake* • Natalie Wood *Barbara Blake* • Cora Witherspoon *Mrs Angevine* ■ *Dir* Elliott Nugent • *Scr* Robert Carson, from the novel *Famous* by Stephen Vincent Benet

Just Imagine ★★ U

Science-fiction musical
1930 · US · BW · 104mins

In this misfiring film, it matters not that the songs are awful or that El Brendel is struck by lightning and projected to the New York of 1980, where he helps John Garrick wed Maureen O'Sullivan by his heroics on Mars. What is significant is the splendour of the Oscar-nominated cityscape and the accuracy of so many of the technological predictions (including test-tube babies and image phones). However, the film's poor box office persuaded the studios that sci-fi belonged in serials and B-pics. DP

El Brendel *Single O* • Maureen O'Sullivan *LN-18* • John Garrick *J-21* • Marjorie White *D-6* • Frank Albertson *RT-42* • Hobart Bosworth *Z-4* • Kenneth Thomson *MT-3* ■ *Dir* David Butler • *Scr* Lew Brown, David Butler, BG De Sylva, Ray Henderson • *Art Director* Stephen Goosson, Ralph Hammeras

Just like a Woman ★★

Comedy 1966 · UK · Colour · 89mins

Director Robert Fuest made his feature debut with this 1960s satire about a housewife (Wendy Craig) who rebels against her TV director husband (Francis Matthews). Craig here reveals the comic flair that enabled her to become the epitome of scatty domesticity in sitcoms such as *Not in Front of the Children* and *Butterflies*. Fuest's script strives too hard to be offbeat, however. DP

Wendy Craig *Scilla Alexander* • Francis Matthews *Lewis McKenzie* • John Wood *John Martin* • Dennis Price *Bathroom salesman* • Miriam Karlin *Ellen Newman* • Peter Jones *Saul Alexander* • Clive Dunn *Graff Von Fischer* ■ *Dir/Scr* Robert Fuest

Just like a Woman ★ 15

Comedy 1992 · UK · Colour · 101mins

Julie Walters is good value, but this comedy drama about transvestism is pretty worthless otherwise. Who is it aimed at? Closet cross-dressers? Ed Wood fanatics? Hard to tell, as it lurches from frilly farce to black-lace banality with sickly sentiment piled as high as the heels. Adrian Pasdar looks uncomfortable playing Gerald/ Geraldine, as will be those watching this curious frock opera that's as fake as his falsies. AJ [video] DVD

Julie Walters *Monica* • Adrian Pasdar *Gerald* • Paul Freeman *Miles Millichamp* • Susan Wooldridge *Louisa* • Gordon Kennedy *CJ* ■ *Dir* Christopher Monger • *Scr* Nick Evans, from the book *Geraldine, for the Love of a Transvestite* by Monica Jay

Just Married ★★ 12

Romantic comedy
2003 · US · Colour · 90mins

This banal offering aims for a teen twist on the romantic screwball comedy but the results are less than sparkling. Ashton Kutcher stars as the uncultured new husband of rich kid Brittany Murphy, whose wealthy parents disapprove of her choice of groom. During a disastrous honeymoon – no more than a series of slapstick vignettes performed in glamorous European locations – they begin to wonder if their marriage can really work. The stars are photogenic and enthusiastic, but this is brash and charmless. JC [video] DVD

Ashton Kutcher *Tom Leezak* • Brittany Murphy *Sarah McNerney* • Christian Kane *Peter Prentiss* • David Moscow *Kyle* • Monet Mazur *Lauren McNerney* • David Rasche *Mr McNerney* • Veronica Cartwright *Mrs McNerney* ■ *Dir* Shawn Levy • *Scr* Sam Harper

Just My Luck ★★ U

Comedy 1957 · UK · BW · 82mins

This horse-racing comedy is not a particularly distinguished Norman Wisdom movie, but is still a pleasant time-waster. On its original release, Rank realised the film's weaknesses and shored it up with a rock 'n' roll supporting feature. Today it's a brave viewer (or a devout fan of Wisdom) who'll watch, for the star's mawkish side is virtually given free rein as he tries to win enough money to buy a gift for Jill Dixon. TS [video] DVD

Norman Wisdom *Norman* • Margaret Rutherford *Mrs Dooley* • Jill Dixon *Anne* • Leslie Phillips *Hon Richard Lumb* • Delphi Lawrence *Miss Daviot* • Edward Chapman *Mr Stoneway* • Marjorie Rhodes *Mrs Hackett* • Joan Sims *Phoebe* ■ *Dir* John Paddy Carstairs • *Scr* Alfred Shaughnessy, Peter Blackmore

Just One of the Guys ★★★ 15

Comedy 1985 · US · Colour · 96mins

This energetic comedy, sort of *Tootsie* after a sex-change, is about a pretty high-school student (Joyce Hyser) who's convinced that her good looks have kept sexist male teachers from backing her entry in a citywide journalism competition. So she cross-dresses as a boy, and tries again at another school. The premise is slight and strained, but quirky performances elevate the film above the ordinary. Watch out for small roles from Sherilyn Fenn and Arye Gross. DA [video]

Joyce Hyser *Terry* • Clayton Rohner *Rick* • Billy Jacoby *Buddy* • William Zabka *Greg* • Toni Hudson *Denise* • Sherilyn Fenn *Sandy* • Deborah Goodrich *Deborah* • Arye Gross *Willie* ■ *Dir* Lisa Gottlieb • *Scr* Dennis Feldman, Jeff Franklin, from a story by Dennis Feldman

Just Tell Me What You Want ★★★

Comedy 1980 · US · Colour · 112mins

Alan King plays a spoilt and strident millionaire in this Sidney Lumet directed comedy. Married King is dallying with his longstanding mistress Ali MacGraw but failing to commit. Not surprisingly, MacGraw seeks solace with toy boy Peter Weller, prompting King to realise that he really really wants her. Adapted by Jay Presson Allen from her novel, this is a romantic comedy with an edge. King's performance has great gusto and watch out for Myrna Loy in her last and very notable performance as his long-suffering personal assistant. LH

Ali MacGraw *Bones Burton* • Alan King *Max Herschel* • Myrna Loy *Stella Liberti* • Keenan Wynn *Seymour Berger* • Tony Roberts *Mike Berger* • Peter Weller *Steven Routledge* • Sara Truslow *Cathy* ■ *Dir* Sidney Lumet • *Scr* Jay Presson Allen, from her novel

Just the Ticket ★★ 15

Romantic comedy drama
1998 · US · Colour · 110mins

The combination of star Andy Garcia and a script from director Richard Wenk that was ten years in the making should guarantee an interesting film. But, sadly, this is a lacklustre affair. Can a tale of a ticket tout selling illegal entry to the Pope's New York visit in order to retire and save his relationship really work? Garcia is all Italian charm to girlfriend Andie MacDowell's southern kookiness but, acceptable performances aside, rip-roaring romantic comedy this is not. LH. Contains swearing. [video] DVD

Andy Garcia *Gary Starke* • Andie MacDowell *Linda Paliski* • Richard Bradford *Benny Moran* • Fred Asparagus *Zeus* • Elizabeth Ashley *Mrs Paliski* • André B Blake *Casino* • Ron Leibman *Barry the Book* ■ *Dir/Scr* Richard Wenk

Just the Way You Are ★★ PG

Romantic comedy
1984 · US · Colour · 90mins

Offbeat, if a little slushy, comedy drama, in which Kristy McNichol plays a young woman who wears a leg brace following a childhood bout of polio. She hides her disability with a plaster cast on a skiing holiday in Europe and, while there, falls for Michael Ontkean, but will he still love her when he discovers the truth? It could have turned out to be quite a sob story, but, although the disparate elements don't quite meld together, it's nicely played by the cast. JF [video]

Kristy McNichol *Susan Berlanger* • Michael Ontkean *Peter Nichols* • Kaki Hunter *Lisa* • André Dussollier *François* • Catherine Salviat *Nicole* • Robert Carradine *Sam Carpenter* • Alexandra Paul *Bobbie* ■ *Dir* Edouard Molinaro • *Scr* Allan Burns

Just Us ★★★

Biographical drama
1986 · Aus · Colour · 95mins

A sincere, accomplished, but distinctly one-sided look at love across the prison grill. Australian journalist Gabrielle Carey, here renamed Jessica Taylor, and nicely played by Catherine McClements, wrote the original material based on her passionately felt, but ultimately doomed, affair with long-term prisoner Terry Haley (called Billy Carter in the movie). This is a gripping, pacily written, complex tale, marred only by a naivety of intent and the whiff of whitewash covering the convicted rapist's character. SR

Catherine McClements *Jessica Taylor* • Scott Burgess *Billy Carter* • Merfyn Owen • Gina Riley • Jay Mannering • Kim Gyngell ■ *Dir* Gordon Glenn • *Scr* Ted Roberts from the book by Gabrielle Carey

Just Visiting ★ PG

Comedy fantasy
2001 · Fr/US · Colour · 88mins

The time-travel farce *Les Visiteurs* became the highest grossing home-grown movie in French cinema history. The English-language remake from writer/director Jean-Marie Poiré relocates the action to America and increases the toilet-humour content at the expense of the original's rough charm. Tricked into poisoning his betrothed (Christina Applegate), 12th-century French nobleman Jean Reno gets wizard Malcolm McDowell to concoct a potion to send him back in time to avert the tragedy. But Reno and his idiot squire Christian Clavier end up in modern-day Chicago. A limp re-tread, this definitely loses something in the translation. AJ [video] DVD

Jean Reno *Thibault Malfete* • Christian Clavier *André* • Malcolm McDowell *Wizard* • Christina Applegate *Julia Malfete/Princess Rosalind* • Matt Ross *Hunter* • Tara Reid *Angelique* • George Plimpton *Dr Brady* ■ *Dir* Jean-Marie Gaubert [Jean-Marie Poiré] • *Scr* Jean-Marie Poiré, Christian Clavier, John Hughes, from the film *Les Visiteurs* by Jean-Marie Poiré, Christian Clavier

Just William ★★ U

Comedy 1939 · UK · BW · 74mins

Richmal Crompton's tousled terror made his screen debut in the excitable form of Dicky Lupino in this hectic adventure, co-written and directed by Graham Cutts, one of Britain's finest silent directors. Although he gets up to lots of mischief, William spends too much time on the trail of a conman and helping his father secure a seat on the council to be particularly funny. Lupino (the youngest member of that multi-talented showbiz family) hurtles around at full pelt, so it's left to Roddy McDowall to do the real acting as the hero's put-upon pal, Ginger. DP

Dicky Lupino *William Brown* • Fred Emney *Mr Brown* • Basil Radford *Mr Sidway* • Amy Veness *Mrs Bott* • Iris Hoey *Mrs Brown* • Roddy McDowall *Ginger* • Jenny Laird *Ethel Brown* • David Tree *Marmaduke Bott* ■ *Dir* Graham Cutts • *Scr* Doreen Montgomery, Ireland Wood, Graham Cutts, from the stories by Richmal Crompton

Just William's Luck ★★ U

Comedy 1947 · UK · BW · 92mins

Having concluded they need bikes to emulate the heroics of the Knights of the Round Table, William and his outlaws decide to marry off their older brothers and inherit their cast-off cycles. While William Graham captures something of the scruffy boisterousness of Richmal Crompton's timeless comic creation, director Val Guest's screenplay smoothes away the rougher edges to produce a sanitised tale of childhood mayhem. DP

William Graham *William Brown* • Garry Marsh *Mr Brown* • Jane Welsh *Mrs Brown* • Hugh Cross *Robert Brown* • Kathleen Stuart *Ethel Brown* • Leslie Bradley *Boss* • AE Matthews *Tramp* • Brian Roper *Ginger* • Audrey Manning *Violet Elizabeth Bott* ■ *Dir* Val Guest • *Scr* Val Guest, from the stories by Richmal Crompton

Just You and Me, Kid ★

Comedy 1979 · US · Colour · 94mins

Not even the pleasure of seeing George Burns trading wisecracks over a game of cards with fellow old-stagers Ray Bolger and Leon Ames can enliven this crass age-gap comedy. If only he'd spent more time with them and less with Brooke Shields, the runaway he discovers naked in the boot of his car after she goes on the run from a drug dealer. There is absolutely no spark between the leads, with his knowing drawl and her eager cuteness clashing in every exchange. Even less amusing is Burl Ives's demonstration of catatonia. Eminently missable. DP

George Burns *Bill* • Brooke Shields *Kate* • Burl Ives *Max* • Lorraine Gary *Shirl* • Nicolas Coster *Harris* • Keye Luke *Dr Device* ■ *Dir* Leonard B Stern • *Scr* Oliver Hailey, from a story by Tom Lazarus, Leonard B Stern

Just Your Luck ★ 15

Comedy thriller 1996 · US · Colour · 84mins

This slimly written tale begins in a café with a man dropping dead immediately after learning he's won six million dollars on the lottery. Virginia Madsen, Sean Patrick Flanery, Ernie Hudson and Jon Favreau are among the customers trying to convince the establishment's owner Jon Polito that they should cash in the ticket and keep the cash. Everyone in the group is so unlikeable that you won't care to sit through until the end to discover who ends up with the money. Witless and thin. JB. Contains swearing, and some violence and sexual references. [video]

J

Sean Patrick Flanery *Ray* • Virginia Madsen *Kim* • Ernie Hudson *Willie* • Alanna Ubach *Angela* • Vince Vaughn *Barry* • Jon Favreau *Straker* • Jon Polito *Nick* ■ *Dir* Gary Auerbach • *Scr* Todd Alcott, Gary Auerbach, from a story by Gary Auerbach

Juste avant la Nuit ★★★★

Thriller 1971 · Fr/It · Colour · 106mins

Claude Chabrol follows *La Femme Infidèle* and *Le Boucher* with another masterly thriller, in which Stéphane Audran (Mrs Chabrol) refuses to believe her husband – creepy Michel Bouquet – has intentionally murdered his mistress. The latter just happened to be married to their best friend; surely, Audran thinks, it was an accident? This little parable about guilt and bourgeois morality in the provinces amounts to as much or as little as you want to read into it. But few could resist the elegant way in which Chabrol tells the story or the immaculate acting of the cast. AT. A French language film.

Michel Bouquet *Charles* • Stéphane Audran *Helen* • François Périer *François* • Dominique Zardi *Prince* • Henri Attal *Cavanna* ■ *Dir* Claude Chabrol • *Scr* Claude Chabrol, from the novel *The Thin Line* by Edouard Atiyah

Justine ★ 15

Drama 1969 · US · Colour · 111mins

This catastrophic attempt to condense the four novels of Lawrence Durrell's celebrated *Alexandria Quartet* into a single film results in a messy farrago. Told in flashback by Justine's lover Darley (Michael York) it focuses on the influence and sexual exploits of the mysterious and beautiful Egyptian Jewess, played by French actress Anouk Aimée, who, with her banker husband, plans to send military aid to Palestine's Jews. It attempts to beef up the proceedings with sexual decadence, an international cast and some exotic atmosphere, but nothing helps. RK [video]

Anouk Aimée *Justine* • Dirk Bogarde *Pursewarden* • Robert Forster *Narouz* • Anna Karina *Melissa* • Philippe Noiret *Pombal* • Michael York *Darley* • George Baker *Mountolive* ■ *Dir* George Cukor • *Scr* Lawrence B Marcus, from the novels *The Alexandria Quartet* by Lawrence Durrell

Juwanna Mann ★ 12

Comedy 2002 · US · Colour · 87mins

A one gag movie that never threatens to raise a laugh, this cross-dressing basketball comedy is tantamount to *Tootsie* on testosterone. Miguel A Nunez Jr stars as a conceited hoop star who disguises himself as a woman to remain active during a suspension, but ends up learning a few home truths from Vivica A Fox and her team-mates. Clearly this isn't supposed to be a work of documentary realism, but too many aspects of Bradley Allenstein's screenplay go beyond credibility and actually insult the intelligence. DP [video] DVD

Miguel A Nunez Jr *Jamal Jeffries/Juwanna Mann* • Vivica A Fox *Michelle Langford* • Kevin Pollak *Lorne Daniels* • Tommy Davidson *Puff Smokey Smoke* • Kim Wayans *Latisha Jansen* • Jenifer Lewis *Aunt Ruby* ■ *Dir* Jesse Vaughan • *Scr* Bradley Allenstein

K-9 ★★ 15

Crime comedy 1989 · US · Colour · 97mins

Hollywood, desperately looking for new variations on the mismatched-cops scenario, briefly lit upon the concept of the buddy-doggy movie. This one has James Belushi as the detective who is reluctantly partnered with a surly canine in a bid to crack a drug smuggling ring. Belushi is as affable as ever, but even he looks a little embarrassed by the affair, particularly the mawkish ending. JF. Contains swearing and violence. [video] DVD

James Belushi *Thomas Dooley* • Mel Harris *Tracy* • Kevin Tighe *Lyman* • Ed O'Neill *Lt Brannigan* • James Handy *Lt Byers* • Daniel Davis *Halstead* • Cotter Smith *Gilliam* • John Snyder *Freddie* ■ *Dir* Rod Daniel • *Scr* Steven Siegel, Scott Myers

K-911 ★★ 12

Crime comedy 1999 · US · Colour · 87mins

This belated, video sequel to the canine cop comedy *K-9* was, improbably, a big rental hit at the end of the 1980s. James Belushi returns for this slight tale, in which he and his canine partner are helped out by fellow cop Christine Tucci and her Doberman to track down a mysterious mugger. Belushi coasts through the slight but amiable material. A further video sequel, *K-9 PI*, was released in 2002. JF. Contains swearing. [video] DVD

James Belushi *Thomas Dooley* • Christine Tucci *Welles* • James Handy *Captain Byers* • Wade Andrew Williams *Devon* • JJ Johnston *Fat Tommy* ■ *Dir* Charles T Kanganis • *Scr* Gary Scott Thompson, from characters created by Steven Siegel, Scott Myers

K-19: the Widowmaker ★★ 12

Action thriller based on a true story
2002 · US · Colour · 132mins

This workmanlike thriller is based on the true story of a Soviet nuclear submarine that sprung a radioactive leak and almost started the Third World War in 1961. Harrison Ford plays the captain at logger-heads with his second-in-command, Liam Neeson. After about an hour of these two locking horns, the nuclear reactor leaks and the film gets interesting. The horror of the radiation effects, the race against time, the claustrophobic tension – all of this works, but it's too late. StH. Contains violence. [video] DVD

Harrison Ford *Alexei Vostrikov* • Liam Neeson *Mikhail Polenin* • Peter Sarsgaard *Vadim Radtchenko* • Joss Ackland *Marshal Zelentstov* • John Shrapnel *Admiral Bratyeev* • Donald Sumpter *Dr Savran* • Tim Woodward *Partonov* ■ *Dir* Kathryn Bigelow • *Scr* Christopher Kyle, from a story by Louis Nowra

K-PAX ★★ 12

Science-fiction fantasy drama
2001 · US · Colour · 115mins

The prospect of class acts Kevin Spacey and Jeff Bridges going head-to-head is a delicious one, especially in what is essentially a talky two-hander about a mysterious stranger (Spacey) claiming to be a visitor from the planet K-Pax and the psychologist who attempts to crack his "delusional" state. Unfortunately, the story does not match their performances; once the seed of doubt has been sown in Bridges's mind that perhaps the zen-like Spacey really is from another planet, the film collapses in on itself. The final result is bloodless, touchy-feely schmaltz. AC. Contains violence and swearing. [video] DVD

Kevin Spacey *Prot* • Jeff Bridges *Dr Mark Powell* • Mary McCormack *Rachel Powell* • Alfre Woodard *Claudia Villars* • David Patrick Kelly *Howie* • Saul Williams *Ernie* ■ *Dir* Iain Softley • *Scr* Charles Leavitt, from a novel by Gene Brewer

K2 ★★★ 15

Adventure 1991 · US · Colour · 105mins

In this climbing epic, Michael Biehn is perfectly cast as a brash lawyer who lives life on the edge through his passion for mountaineering. This is largely *Boys' Own* stuff, with character development taking second place to macho heroics and bonding. However, director Franc Roddam responds by staging one exhilarating cliffside set piece after another, including a breathtaking avalanche sequence. JF. Contains swearing, nudity. [video] DVD

Michael Biehn *Taylor Brooks* • Matt Craven *Harold Jamieson* • Raymond J Barry *Phillip Claiborne* • Hiroshi Fujioka *Takane Shimuzu* • Luca Bercovici *Dallas Woolf* • Patricia Charbonneau *Jacki Metcalfe* • Julia Nickson-Soul *Cindy* • Jamal Shah *Malik* • Annie Grindlay *Lisa* • Elena Stiteler *Tracey* ■ *Dir* Franc Roddam • *Scr* Patrick Meyers, Scott Roberts, from the play by Patrick Meyers

Kaagaz Ke Phool ★★★★ U

Drama 1959 · Ind · BW · 139mins

Echoes of *Citizen Kane* and *A Star Is Born* ring around this Bollywood classic (the subcontinent's first in CinemaScope), which flopped on its original release. Guru Dutt excels as the director whose fortunes plummet after his star discovery, Waheeda Rehman, quits to avoid hurtful gossip. In his second role as this film's director, he also imbues the drama with a visual eloquence that conveys the "neverland" atmosphere of the movies, without losing sight of the human frailty afflicting even the most successful artists. DP. In Hindi with English subtitles. [video] DVD

Guru Dutt *Suresh Sinha* • Waheeda Rehman *Shanti* • Baby Naaz *Pummy* • Johnny Walker *Brother-in-law* • Mahesh Kaul *Father-in-law* ■ *Dir* Guru Dutt • *Scr* Abrar Alvi

Kaal ★★★ 15

Adventure thriller
2005 · Ind · Colour · 125mins

The problems facing tigers in India's wild jungles are at the heart of this adventure thriller from first-time writer/director Soham. John Abraham plays a well-respected conservationist working for *National Geographic* who is sent to Orbit Park (actually Jim Corbett National Park) in India to investigate a series of mysterious deaths, apparently caused by man-eating tigers. But what starts out as a routine mission soon turns into something more sinister. Soham's film has more vitality and genuine passion than many a big-budget Bollywood extravaganza, a sense of menace throughout. OA. In Hindi with English subtitles.

Ajay Devgan *Kali Pratap Singh* • John Abraham *Krish Thapar* • Esha Deol *Riya* • Vivek Oberoi *Dev* • Lara Dutta *Ishika* ■ *Dir/Scr* Soham [Soham Shah]

Kabhi Kabhie ★★ U

Romantic drama
1976 · Ind · Colour · 166mins

Director Yash Chopra is famed for introducing the psychopathic hero into Indian cinema. Here, however, he is on more traditional ground with a "masala melodrama" about arranged marriage set among the privileged classes: essentially a soap opera with a more than usually contrived plot. Amitabh Bachchan takes top billing, only to be upstaged by co-star Shashi Kapoor. DP. In Hindi and Urdu with English subtitles. [video] DVD

Amitabh Bachchan *Amit* • Raakhee Gulzar *Pooja* • Shashi Kapoor • Waheeda Rehman • Neetu Singh • Rishi Kapoor ■ *Dir* Yash Chopra • *Scr* Yash Chopra, Sagar Sarhadi

Kabhi Khushi Kabhie Gham... ★★★ PG

Drama 2001 · Ind · Colour · 210mins

This intense family saga is brought to life by some of Bollywood's biggest stars. Hrithik Roshan travels to London in the hope of uniting adopted sibling Shah Rukh Khan with Amitabh Bachchan, the proud father who disowned his youngest son after he married a chatty Punjabi shop owner, played by Kajol. With Jaya Bachchan piling on the piety as Amitabh's wife and Kareena Kapoor providing light relief as Kajol's mischievous sister, there are several shifts in mood and plenty of memorable musical moments. DP. In Hindi with English subtitles. [video] DVD

Amitabh Bachchan *Yashovardhan Raichand* • Jaya Bachchan *Nandini Raichand* • Shah Rukh Khan *Rahul* • Kajol *Anjali Sharma* • Hrithik Roshan *Rohan* • Kareena Kapoor *Pooja Sharma* ■ *Dir* Karan Johar • *Scr* Karan Johar, Sheena Parekh

Kadosh ★★★★ 15

Drama 1999 · Is/Fr · Colour · 116mins

As if the assault on the patriarchal nature of Hassidic Judaism wasn't controversial enough, Israeli director Amos Gitai chose an Arab (Yussef Abu Warda) to play the rabbi in this compelling Jerusalem-based drama. Indeed, Gitai compounds his audacity by viewing events from the perspective of his female protagonists. He remains studiously detached in depicting how Meital Barda refuses an arranged marriage, while her childless sister (Yael Abecassis) steps aside so her husband of ten years (Yoram Hattab) can obey the rabbinical dictate that he remarry to further his line. This is intelligently scripted, powerfully played and subtle in its subversion. DP. In Hebrew with English subtitles.

Yael Abecassis *Rivka* • Yoram Hattab *Meir* • Meital Barda *Malka* • Uri Ran Klauzner *Yossef* • Yussef Abu Warda *Rav Shimon* • Sami Hori *Yaakov* • Lea Koenig *Elisheva* • Rivka Michaeli *Gynaecologist* ■ *Dir* Amos Gitai • *Scr* Amos Gitai, Eliette Abecassis, Jacky Cukier

Kafka ★★★ 15

Psychological thriller
1991 · US/Fr · BW and Colour · 94mins

Steven Soderbergh's follow-up to *sex, lies, and videotape* is a far cry from that auspicious debut. Yet, with its stylish references to German expressionism and the great Universal horror films of the 1930s, this fantasy on the life of the Czech insurance-clerk-turned-novelist is possibly even bolder and more imaginative. Jeremy Irons acquits himself admirably in the title role, Alec Guinness and Ian Holm stand out in a splendid supporting cast, but the true stars are cinematographer Walt Lloyd and Gavin Bocquet's art department. DP. Contains violence. [video]

Jeremy Irons *Kafka* • Theresa Russell *Gabriela Rossman* • Joel Grey *Burgel* • Ian Holm *Dr Murnau* • Jeroen Krabbé *Bizzlebek* • Armin Mueller-Stahl *Inspector Grubach* • Alec Guinness *Chief clerk* • Brian Glover *Castle henchman* • Keith Allen *Assistant Ludwig* ■ *Dir* Steven Soderbergh • *Scr* Lem Dobbs

U = SUITABLE FOR ALL Uc = SUITABLE FOR ALL, ESPECIALLY FOR YOUNG CHILDREN (VIDEO ONLY) PG = PARENTAL GUIDANCE

Kagemusha ★★★★ PG

Period drama 1980 · Jpn · Colour · 152mins

Returning to direction after five years, the 70-year-old Akira Kurosawa proved that his powers hadn't diminished with this sprawling tale of court intrigue. Set during the civil wars of the 16th century, this is the most expensive picture ever made in Japan and won the Palme d'Or at Cannes. Admittedly, it could stand some judicious cutting and one or two of the set pieces smack of scale for spectacle's sake. But Tatsuya Nakadai is outstanding as the thief who becomes a puppet ruler, while Kurosawa's use of colour and his camera control are faultless. DP. In Japanese with English subtitles. [video] DVD

Tatsuya Nakadai *Shingen Takeda/Kagemusha* • Tsutomu Yamazaki *Nobukado Takeda* • Kenichi Hagiwara *Katsuyori Takeda* • Kota Yui *Takemaru Takeda* • Hideji Otaki *Masakage Yamagata* ■ *Dir* Akira Kurosawa • *Scr* Akira Kurosawa, Masato Ide

Kal Ho Naa Ho ★★★ 12

Romantic comedy
2003 · Ind · Colour · 187mins

Director Nikhil Advani clearly watched plenty of Hollywood romantic comedies before embarking on his debut feature. Yet it also retains a distinctive Bollywood flavour, despite the fact the action takes place in New York. Widow Jaya Bachchan wants to make at match between her plain daughter, Preity Zinta, and newly arrived do-gooder, Shah Rukh Khan. However, he's already agreed to help the womanising Saif Ali Khan woo Zinta. Tinkering with traditional storytelling tactics, Advani makes an impressive start, but the pace slackens. DP. In Hindi with English subtitles. [video] DVD

Shah Rukh Khan *Aman Mathur* • Saif Ali Khan *Rohit Patel* • Preity Zinta *Naina Catherine Kapur* • Jaya Bachchan *Jennifer Kapur* • Sonali Bendre *Doctor Priya* • Sushma Seth *Lajjo Kapur* • Dara Singh *Chaddha Uncle* ■ *Dir* Nikhil Advani • *Scr* Nikhil Advani, Karan Johar, Niranjan Iyengar

Kaleidoscope ★★★ U

Crime comedy drama
1966 · UK · Colour · 102mins

This 1960s caper is so swinging it almost comes off its hinges. Warren Beatty, not renowned at the time for his monkish life style, is strangely unconvincing as the cardsharp who literally marks winning cards, while hip chick Susannah York keeps his libido on the boil. The movie defies its dated trendiness with the sheer esprit of the performances. TH

Warren Beatty *Barney Lincoln* • Susannah York *Angel McGinnis* • Eric Porter *Harry Dominion* • Clive Revill *Inspector "Manny" McGinnis* • Murray Melvin *Aimes* • George Sewell *Billy* • Anthony Newlands *Leeds* • Jane Birkin *Exquisite Thing* ■ *Dir* Jack Smight • *Scr* Robert Carrington, Jane Howard Carrington

Kalifornia ★★ 18

Psychological thriller
1993 · US · Colour · 113mins

David Duchovny plays a writer researching serial killers for a book who gets rather too close to his subject in this so-so psycho teen road movie. A slow start builds to an explosive climax after Duchovny and his photographer girlfriend (Michelle Forbes) pick up two likely suspects as they travel from Kentucky to California. Brad Pitt does his mentally unbalanced act rather well, and Juliette Lewis is also good value as his trailer-trash, childlike sweetheart. Sadly, director Dominic Sena fails to develop an interesting scenario into anything other than empty attitude and annoying posturing. AJ. Contains violence, swearing and sex scenes. [video] DVD

Juliette Lewis *Adele Corners* • Brad Pitt *Early Grayce* • David Duchovny *Brian Kessler* • Michelle Forbes *Carrie Laughlin* • Sierra Pecheur *Mrs Musgrave* • Gregory "Mars" Martin *Walter Livesay* • David Milford *Driver* • Marisa Raper *Little girl* • Catherine Larson *Teenage girl* ■ *Dir* Dominic Sena • *Scr* Tim Metcalfe, from the story by Stephen Levy

Kama Sutra: a Tale of Love ★★★ 18

Erotic drama
1996 · Ind /UK/Jap/Ger · Colour · 109mins

"Kama Sutra" translates as "love lessons", and that's what princess Sarita Choudhury and royal servant girl Indira Varma learn in director Mira Nair's lavish historical romance. Varma's "sexual treachery" with Choudhury's betrothed, Naveen Andrews, gets her banished from court and puts her on the road to erotic self-awareness in a complex story mixing the mystical with the psychological. Oddly affecting and beautifully filmed. AJ . Contains violence, sex scenes, swearing, nudity. [video] DVD

Naveen Andrews *Raj Singh* • Sarita Choudhury *Tara* • Ramon Tikaram *Jai Kumar* • Rekha *Rasa Devi* • Indira Varma *Maya* • Pearl Padamsee *Maham Anga* • Arundhati Rao *Annabi* ■ *Dir* Mira Nair • *Scr* Helena Kriel, Mira Nair • *Cinematographer* Declan Quinn • *Music* Mychael Danna

Kameradschaft ★★★★★

Drama 1931 · Ger/Fr · BW · 83mins

A masterpiece of studio realism and an optimistic plea for peaceful co-existence, this is one of the few social tracts of the early sound era to retain its power in this more cynical age. Based on a 1906 mining disaster (although set in the immediate aftermath of the First World War), the story of the German workers who break through national boundaries to rescue their French comrades is loaded with idealistic symbolism. But, thanks to director GW Pabst's ingenious use of light and montage, it is also full of striking images designed to highlight the fragility of humanity and the futility of conflict. DP. In German and French with English subtitles.

Alexander Granach *Kaspar* • Fritz Kampers *Wilderer* • Daniel Mendaille *Pierre* • Ernst Busch *Kaplan* • Elisabeth Wendt *Françoise* • Gustav Püttjer *Jean* • Oskar Höcker *Emile* ■ *Dir* GW Pabst • *Scr* Ladislaus Vajda, Peter Martin Lampel, Karl Otten, Fritz Eckardt, from a story by Karl Otten • *Cinematographer* Fritz Arno Wagner, Robert Baberske

Kamikaze ★★★ 15

Satirical drama 1986 · Fr · Colour · 88mins

This is a classic example of the style of French films dubbed *cinéma du look* on account of their flashy visuals and throwaway narratives. It boasts a wonderfully over-the-top central performance from Michel Galabru as a mad scientist who invents a death ray that can zap anyone he takes a dislike to while watching TV. Great idea, but there is really only enough material in this satire on couch-potato culture for a razor-sharp sketch. DP. In French with English subtitles.

Richard Bohringer *Detective Romain* • Michel Galabru *Albert* • Dominique Lavanant *Laure Frontenac* • Riton Leibman *Olive* • Kim Massee *Léa* • Harry Cleven *Patrick* • Romane Bohringer *Julie* ■ *Dir* Didier Grousset • *Scr* Luc Besson, Didier Grousset, Michèle Halberstadt

Kamikaze 1989 ★★

Fantasy thriller
1983 · W Ger · Colour · 106mins

In the last major acting role of his eclectic career, Rainer Werner Fassbinder imbues his boozy, world-weary detective with a love of the law and a loathing of its guardians. He zealously pursues the bombers threatening an all-powerful media conglomerate. Unfortunately, director Wolf Gremm is unable to create a credible world of corruption and decadence to complement his star's self-referential performance. DP. In German with English subtitles.

Rainer Werner Fassbinder *Jansen* • Günther Kaufmann *Anton* • Boy Gobert *Blue Panther* • Arnold Marquis *Police chief* • Richy Müller *Nephew* • Nicole Heesters *Barbara* • Brigitte Mira *Personnel director* • Franco Nero *Weiss* ■ *Dir* Wolf Gremm • *Scr* Robert Katz, Wolf Gremm, from the novel *Murder on the 31st Floor* by Per Wahlöö

Kamouraska ★★★

Period romantic drama
1973 · Can/Fr · Colour · 124mins

This intense adaptation of Anne Hébert's novel was the most ambitious French-Canadian production to that date. It opens in a small Québecois village in 1839, as Geneviève Bujold nurses her second spouse, Marcel Cuvilier, and thinks back on her turbulent past.She recalls the brutal treatment meted out by her first husband, backwoodsman Philippe Léotard, and how she was helped to dispose of him by her lover, emigré American doctor Richard Jordan. The going is occasionally ponderous, but Bujold is outstanding. DP. In French and English with subtitles.

Geneviève Bujold *Elisabeth* • Richard Jordan *Nelson* • Philippe Léotard *Antoine* • Marcel Cuvelier *Jérôme* • Suzie Baillargeon *Aurélie* ■ *Dir* Claude Jutra • *Scr* Anne Hébert, Claude Jutra, from the novel *Kamouraska* by Anne Hébert

Kanal ★★★★ 12

Second World War tragedy
1957 · Pol · BW · 91mins

The second part of Andrzej Wajda's war trilogy, which won the Special Jury prize at Cannes, is a sobering re-creation of events that occurred during the 1944 Warsaw Uprising. Echoes of *Dante's Inferno* ring through the network of sewers where a resistance unit has taken refuge from the pursuing Nazis. The symbolism is occasionally overwrought, but there's no doubting the oppressive atmosphere of the cramped tunnels, or the simple heroism of the partisans as they attempt to suppress their growing desperation. DP. In Polish with English subtitles. Contains swearing and violence. [video]

Wienczylaw Glinski *Lt Zadra* • Tadeusz Janczar *Korab* • Teresa Izewska *Stokrotka* • Emil Karewicz *Madry* • Wladyslaw Sheybal [Vladek Sheybal] *Composer* • Tadeusz Gwiazdowski *Kula* ■ *Dir* Andrzej Wajda • *Scr* Jerzy Stefan Stawinski, from his short story

Kandahar ★★★★★ PG

Documentary drama
2001 · Iran/Fr · Colour · 81mins

This piercing insight into the plight of the Afghan people – and women in particular – under the Taliban regime is a must-see experience. It's impossible not to be moved and angered by Iranian director Mohsen Makhmalbaf's hybrid of documentary and road movie (loosely based on a real-life incident), in particular the sights exiled journalist Nelofer Pazira witnesses while trying to reach her suicidal sister in Kandahar. Yet this is less a condemnation of extreme patriarchy than an assertion that the spirit of sisterhood will somehow survive the monstrous repression. It's the toll of human misery caused by war that concerns Makhmalbaf, not political or religious correctness, and that's a salient lesson for us all. DP. In English and Farsi with subtitles. [video] DVD

Nelofer Pazira *Nafas* • Hassan Tantai *Tabib Sahid* • Sadou Teymouri *Khak* • Hayatalah Hakimi *Hayat* ■ *Dir/Scr* Mohsen Makhmalbaf

Kangaroo ★★

Romantic adventure
1952 · US · Colour · 84mins

Using frozen Australian earnings, 20th Century-Fox sent a full crew Down Under for this shoddy attempt to transpose a familiar western story to the outback. Australian players were relegated to minor parts, as Peter Lawford poses as the long-lost son of Finlay Currie's cattle king, who reforms after falling in love with the old man's daughter, Maureen O'Hara. Director Lewis Milestone used some of Sydney's historic landmarks to advantage, but there's little authentic local flavour to the story. AE

Maureen O'Hara *Dell McGuire* • Peter Lawford *Richard Connor* • Finlay Currie *Michael McGuire* • Richard Boone *Gamble* • Chips Rafferty *Trooper Leonard* • Letty Craydon *Kathleen* • Charles Tingwell *Matt* • Ron Whelan *Fenner* ■ *Dir* Lewis Milestone • *Scr* Harry Kleiner, from a story by Martin Berkeley

Kangaroo ★★★ 15

Drama 1986 · Aus · Colour · 99mins

The ever-excellent Judy Davis stars with her real-life husband Colin Friels as a couple who arrive in Sydney from Cornwall, and find themselves embroiled in an incipient socialist revolution. Literary to a point, though intelligent with it, but there is a lack of real character development. Friels, who doesn't quite have genuine star power, is very effective – charming and unsettling in equal doses – while Davis is a real treat to watch. TS [video]

Colin Friels *Richard Somers* • Judy Davis *Harriet Somers* • John Walton *Jack Calcott* • Julie Nihill *Vicki Calcott* • Hugh Keays-Byrne *Kangaroo* • Peter Hehir *Jaz* • Peter Cummins *Struthers* ■ *Dir* Tim Burstall • *Scr* Evan Jones, from the novel by DH Lawrence

Kangaroo Jack ★★ PG

Action comedy 2003 · US · Colour · 85mins

Calamity-prone friends Jerry O'Connell and Anthony Anderson are dispatched to Australia by O'Connell's mobster stepfather (Christopher Walken) to deliver $50,000 to a shady associate. When a wild kangaroo runs off with the cash, the duo set off across the outback in pursuit, assisted by wildlife conservationist Estella Warren. While too lightweight for most adults, its slapdash mixture of cheeky humour, speedily shot chase sequences and dim-witted monkey business should hold the attention of youngsters. SF [video] DVD

Jerry O'Connell *Charlie Carbone* • Anthony Anderson *Louis Fucci* • Estella Warren *Jessie* • Michael Shannon *Frankie the Vermin* • Christopher Walken *Sal* • Bill Hunter *Blue* • Marton Csokas *Mr Smith* • David Ngoombujarra *Mr Jimmy* ■ *Dir* David McNally • *Scr* Steve Bing, Scott Rosenberg, from a story by Steve Bing, Barry O'Brien

Kangchenjunga ★★★★

Drama 1962 · Ind · Colour · 102mins

Satyajit Ray's first venture into self-scripting and colour cinematography is also his most musical work, and fittingly he composed the score as well. Manipulative holidaying patriarch Chhabi Biswas meets his match in the form of Arun Mukherjee, the proud Darjeeling local who wishes to marry his younger daughter. A true dance to the music of time, this is both sly satire and compelling drama. DP. In Bengali with English subtitles.

Chhabi Biswas *Indranath Choudhuri* • Karuna Bannerji [Karuna Bannerjee] *Labanya* • Anil Chatterjee *Anil* • Anubha Gupta *Anima* • Subrata Sen *Shankar* • Indrani Singh *Tuklu* • Arun Mukherjee *Ashok* ■ *Dir/Scr* Satyajit Ray

K

Kanoon ★★★ PG

Courtroom drama 1960 · Ind · BW · 139mins

In addition to using cinema to highlight the key social, political and religious issues in Indian life, director BR Chopra also tried to introduce local audiences to the film styles popular in Hollywood. Essentially a treatise on capital punishment, this is a rare example of Indian *film noir*, with Rajendra Kumar starring as an ambitious lawyer who is forced to prosecute a thief for murder, even though he's sure the culprit is his new father-in-law – who turns out to be the judge trying the case. DP. In Hindi with English subtitles.

Ashok Kumar *Judge Badriprasad* • Nanda *Meena* • Rajendra Kumar *Public prosecutor* ■ *Dir* BR Chopra • *Scr* CJ Pavri

Kansas ★★ 15

Romantic melodrama
1988 · US · Colour · 105mins

A couple of young drifters (Matt Dillon and Andrew McCarthy) meet by chance when they steal a ride on a freight car. They become partners in crime before fate makes them bitter enemies. Australian director David Stevens follows both men's fortunes as their respective paths diverge. The detailed plot meanders, but the acting is appealing; Kyra Sedgwick is especially watchable as the trailer-trash tramp who hooks up with Dillon. AJ DVD

Matt Dillon *Doyle Kennedy* • Andrew McCarthy *Wade Corey* • Leslie Hope *Lori Bayles* • Kyra Sedgwick *Prostitute drifter* • Arlen Dean Snyder *George Bayles* • Alan Toy *Nordquist* • Harry Northup *Governor* ■ *Dir* David Stevens • *Scr* Spencer Eastman

Kansas City ★★★ 15

Period crime drama
1995 · US/Fr · Colour · 115mins

Some isolated felicities – Harry Belafonte as a ruthless gangster, some terrific jazz – elevate Robert Altman's semi-autobiographical tribute to the town of his birth, but *Kansas City* is not as spot-on as the writer/director's more successful work. A thief's wife (Jennifer Jason Leigh) kidnaps a politician's drug-addicted spouse (Miranda Richardson) in an attempt to free her husband (Dermot Mulroney) from the clutches of a mob. The 1930s' mood is beautifully evoked, but the film is too confused for its own good. TH. Contains swearing and some violence.

Jennifer Jason Leigh *Blondie O'Hara* • Miranda Richardson *Carolyn Stilton* • Harry Belafonte *Seldom Seen* • Michael Murphy *Henry Stilton* • Dermot Mulroney *Johnny O'Hara* • Steve Buscemi *Johnny Flynn* • Brooke Smith *Babe Flynn* • Jane Adams (2) *Nettie Bolt* • Gina Belafonte *Hey-Hey club hostess* ■ *Dir* Robert Altman • *Scr* Robert Altman, Frank Barhydt

Kansas City Bomber ★★★ 15

Sports drama 1972 · US · Colour · 94mins

The highs, lows and pitfalls of being a roller-derby queen are put under the spotlight in the defiantly unglamorous sleeper hit that proved Raquel Welch was a lot more than a pretty face. The former Hammer sex symbol is terrific as the roller-skating champion, juggling life as a single parent with her career when she joins an unfriendly new team. Top TV movie director Jerrold Freedman gives the picture a vital documentary feel and captures some hair-raising turns in the sporting sequences. Welch's daughter is played by a young Jodie Foster. AJ

Raquel Welch *Diane "KC" Carr* • Kevin McCarthy *Burt Henry* • Helena Kallianiotes *Jackie Burdette* • Norman Alden *Horrible Hank Hopkins* • Jeanne Cooper *Vivien* • Mary Kay Pass *Lovey* • Martine Bartlett *Mrs Carr* • Jodie Foster *Rita* ■ *Dir* Jerrold Freedman • *Scr* Thomas Rickman [Tom Rickman], Calvin Clements, from a story by Barry Sandler

Kansas City Confidential ★★★ 12

Film noir 1952 · US · BW · 99mins

Director Phil Karlson turned out a number of commendably gritty, modestly budgeted crime films, and this is a good example. Its ingenious story has John Payne's ex-convict become a detective to unearth an ex-policeman-turned-criminal mastermind. It features the innovative touch (taken from the 1950 Brink's hold-up) of bank robbers wearing grotesque masks to conceal their identities. AE DVD

John Payne *Joe Rolfe* • Coleen Gray *Helen* • Preston Foster *Timothy Foster* • Dona Drake *Teresa* • Jack Elam *Harris* • Neville Brand *Kane* • Lee Van Cleef *Tony* • Mario Siletti *Timaso* • Neville Brand *Kane* ■ *Dir* Phil Karlson • *Scr* George Bruce, Harry Essex, from a story by Harold R Greene, Rowland Brown

Kansas Raiders ★★★

Western 1950 · US · Colour · 80mins

Audie Murphy is well cast as the young Jesse James, playing the outlaw as a tortured teenager who joins forces with the notorious Quantrill's Raiders. Murphy is tremendously sympathetic in the role, and he has an experienced co-star in Brian Donlevy as the demented William Quantrill. This could be seen as a western precursor to the 1950s juvenile-delinquent cycle, but the glossy Technicolor softens the impact. TS

Audie Murphy *Jesse James* • Brian Donlevy *William Quantrill* • Marguerite Chapman *Kate Clarke* • Scott Brady *Bill Anderson* • Tony Curtis *Kit Dalton* • Richard Long *Frank James* • James Best *Cole Younger* • Dewey Martin *James Younger* • Richard Egan *First lieutenant* ■ *Dir* Ray Enright • *Scr* Robert L Richards, from his story

Kaos ★★★★

Period drama 1984 · It · Colour · 187mins

Italian siblings Paolo and Vittorio Taviani, who write and direct all their films together, have had an up-and-down career. One of their ups is this group of four folk tales by Luigi Pirandello about peasant life in Sicily at the turn of the 19th century – acted, in the main, by non-professionals. The misleading title is explained in the epilogue in which Pirandello is seen returning to his birthplace, the town of Kaos. Splendidly photographed landscapes (by Giuseppe Lanci) link the stories, which range from the tragic to the blackly comic, suiting the Tavianis' overcharged style. RB. In Italian with English subtitles.

Margarita Lozano *Mother* • Claudio Bigagli *Batà* • Ciccio Ingrassia *Don Lollò* • Franco Franchi *Zi' Diam* • Biagio Barone *Salvatore* • Salvatore Rossi *Patriarch* • Omero Antonutti *Luigi Pirandello* • Regina Bianchi *Mother* ■ *Dir* Paolo Taviani, Vittorio Taviani • *Scr* Paolo Taviani, Vittorio Taviani, Tonino Guerra, from the short story collection *Novelle per un Anno* by Luigi Pirandello

Kapo ★★★

Second World War drama
1959 · It/Fr · BW · 117mins

Oscar-nominated for best foreign film, this seeks to expose and excuse the desperate measures to which people resorted in order to survive the concentration camps. The opening episode, in which orphaned Jewish teenager Susan Strasberg is saved by a kindly doctor, is plausible enough, but the surfeit of stereotypes and clichéd situations undermines the authenticity of the Polish sequences when Strasberg's promotion to "kapo" – or prison-camp guard – induces megalomania. Strasberg's performance is as hysterical as the story is sentimental. DP. In English and Italian with subtitles.

Susan Strasberg *Edith/Nicole* • Laurent Terzieff *Sascha* • Emmanuelle Riva *Terese* • Didi Perego *Sofia* • Gianni Garko *German soldier* • Annabella Besi • Graziella Galvani • Mira Dinulovic ■ *Dir* Gillo Pontecorvo • *Scr* Gillo Pontecorvo, Franco Solinas

Karamurat, the Sultan's Warrior ★★★

Horror 1973 · Tur/It · Colour · 84mins

Although adapted from a popular series of comic books, Natuk Baytan's period chiller draws heavily from accounts of Vlad the Impaler, the notorious 15th-century ruler whose honorary title ("Dracula", meaning "son of the dragon") inspired Bram Stoker. So the tales of impaling and disembowling are all based on historical fact, as is the mission of Karamurat, the Sultan's janissary sent to deliver Transylvania from its terrifying tyrant. With as much flesh on display as gore, this is very much titillation Turkish style. DP. In Turkish with English subtitles.

Cuneyt Arkin *Karamurat* • Erol Tas *Mihal* • Meral Orhonsay • Melda Sozen ■ *Dir* Natuk Baytan

The Karate Kid ★★★ 15

Martial arts adventure
1984 · US · Colour · 121mins

This became a massive worldwide success, spawning a series of sequels and probably ruining Ralph Macchio's career in the process. The actor has struggled ever since to shake off the image of the kid, the bullied youngster who is taught the secrets of karate by wise old Pat Morita and turns the tables on his tormentors. It's a shame, because here Macchio rises above the trite script to deliver a sympathetic and believable performance. Morita is equally good and look out for Elisabeth Shue in an early role. JF. Contains some swearing and violence. DVD

Ralph Macchio *Daniel La Russo* • Noriyuki "Pat" Morita [Pat Morita] *Miyagi* • Elisabeth Shue *Ali* • Martin Kove *Kreese* • Randee Heller *Lucille La Russo* • William Zabka *Johnny* • Ron Thomas *Bobby* • Rob Garrison *Tommy* ■ *Dir* John G Avildsen • *Scr* Robert Mark Kamen

The Karate Kid Part II ★★ PG

Martial arts adventure
1986 · US · Colour · 108mins

This has been a perplexingly successful film series, especially given that all the usual clichés had been exhausted well before the end of the very first film. The only interesting aspect of this dull first sequel is that the action is set largely in Japan, but that aside it is an uninspired retread of the original. RT DVD

Ralph Macchio *Daniel La Russo* • Noriyuki "Pat" Morita [Pat Morita] *Miyagi* • Nobu McCarthy *Yukie* • Danny Kamekona *Sato* • Yuji Okumoto *Chozen* • Tamlyn Tomita *Kumiko* ■ *Dir* John G Avildsen • *Scr* Robert Mark Kamen, from characters created by Robert Mark Kamen

The Karate Kid III ★ PG

Martial arts adventure
1989 · US · Colour · 107mins

Here the "Kid" (27-year-old Ralph Macchio) has to defend his title and tackle the bad guys, initially without the help of his mentor Miyagi. The script takes leave of reality at an early stage, and it becomes increasingly daft and humourless with each scene. A third sequel, *The Next Karate Kid*, starring future Oscar-winner Hilary Swank, followed in 1995. JM. Contains swearing and violence. DVD

Ralph Macchio *Daniel La Russo* • Noriyuki "Pat" Morita [Pat Morita] *Mr Miyagi* • Robyn Lively *Jessica Andrews* • Thomas Ian Griffith *Terry Silver* • Martin L Kove [Martin Kove] *John Kreese* ■ *Dir* John G Avildsen • *Scr* Robert Mark Kamen, from characters created by Robert Mark Kamen

The Karate Killers ★★ PG

Spy adventure 1967 · US · Colour · 88mins

In this unfunny spy spoof, Napoleon Solo and Illya Kuryakin are dispatched to prevent the formula for turning sea water into gold from falling into the hands of a memorable, but woefully underused, rogues' gallery. *Man from UNCLE* regulars Robert Vaughn, David McCallum and Leo G Carroll cross swords with high-powered guest stars, but director Barry Shear's clumsy slapstick approach does no credit to the original TV series. DP DVD

Robert Vaughn *Napoleon Solo* • David McCallum *Illya Kuryakin* • Herbert Lom *Randolph* • Joan Crawford *Amanda True* • Curt Jurgens *Carl von Kesser* • Telly Savalas *Count de Franzini* • Terry-Thomas *Constable* ■ *Dir* Barry Shear • *Scr* Norman Hudis, from a story by Boris Ingster

Karmina ★★★

Romantic comedy horror
1996 · Can · Colour · 109mins

Accenting gothic romance and humor over shocks and gore, this horror trifle spins the engaging tale of young vampire Karmina (Isabelle Cyr) who leaves Transylvania for Québec to avoid an arranged marriage with the nasty Vlad (Robert Brouillette). There she falls in love with church organist Yves Pelletier. Beginning in lush bodice-ripping costume mode and providing some good laughs en route, this was enough of a homegrown hit to warrant the 2001 sequel, *Karmina 2: L'Enfer de Chabot*. AJ. In French with English subtitles.

Isabelle Cyr *Karmina* • Robert Brouillette *Philippe* • Yves Pelletier *Vlad* • France Castel *Esmeralda* • Gildor Roy *Ghislain Chabot* • Raymond Cloutier *Baron* • Sylvie Potvin *Baroness* ■ *Dir* Gabriel Pelletier • *Scr* Ann Burke, Yves Pelletier, Andrée Pelletier, Gabriel Pelletier

Karnaval ★★★

Drama 1998 · Fr/Bel/Swi · Colour · 88mins

Expertly exploiting an atmospheric locale, Thomas Vincent makes an impressive debut with this tale of adultery and racial intolerance set against the annual Dunkirk *karnaval* (carnival). Although the action opens with Amar Ben Abdallah's decision to quit his father's garage and head for Marseille, it's discontented wife Sylvie Testud who becomes the film's fulcrum. Trapped in a loveless marriage with boorish security guard Clovis Cornillac, her decision to romance the handsome stranger has unexpected repercussions. DP. A French language film.

Clovis Cornillac *Christian* • Sylvie Testud *Bea* • Amar Ben Abdallah *Larbi* • Dominique Baeyens *Doriane* ■ *Dir* Thomas Vincent • *Scr* Maxime Sassier, Thomas Vincent

Kaspar Hauser ★★★ 18

Historical drama
1993 · Ger · Colour · 133mins

While Werner Herzog explored the universal theme of corrupting civilisation in *The Enigma of Kaspar Hauser* (1974), Peter Sehr elects to speculate on the origins of the mystery man dumped in Nuremberg in 1828 after spending more than a decade of solitary confinement. Consequently, we are plunged into the politics of the Grand Duchy of Baden and left to fend for ourselves in much the same way as the sickly child who was exchanged for the Crown Prince by the Duke's scheming brother. It's a handsome film, but it only really comes to life during André Eisermann's rehabilitation under kindly professor Udo Samel. DP. In German with English subtitles.

André Eisermann *Kaspar Hauser* • Katharina Thalbach *Gräfin Hochberg* • Uwe Ochsenknecht *Ludwig von Baden* • Udo Samel *Daumer* • Jeremy Clyde *Stanhope* • Hansa Czypionka *Hennenhofer* • Hermann Beyer *Anselm Ritter von Feuerbach* • Cécile Paoli *Stefanie von Baden* ■ *Dir/Scr* Peter Sehr

Kate & Leopold ★★ 12

Romantic fantasy comedy
2002 · US · Colour · 113mins

Romantic comedy queen Meg Ryan plays cute again in this mediocre offering that attempts to freshen the usual formula by throwing a dippy time-travelling plot into the mix. It's a rather disastrous combination. Hugh Jackman plays Leopold, an Englishman abroad in 19th-century New York who falls through a time portal to the present day where he meets the overly quirky Ryan and woos her in the old-fashioned way. LH DVD

Meg Ryan *Kate McKay* • Hugh Jackman *Leopold, Duke of Albany* • Liev Schreiber *Stuart Bessler* • Breckin Meyer *Charlie McKay* • Natasha Lyonne *Darci* • Bradley Whitford *JJ Camden* • Spalding Gray *Dr Geisler* ■ *Dir* James Mangold • *Scr* James Mangold, Steven Rogers, from a story by Steven Rogers

Katia Ismailova ★★ 18

Crime drama 1994 · Rus/Fr · Colour · 94mins

Nikolai Leskov's classic 19th-century novel *Lady Macbeth of the Mtensk District* has here been updated and ruthlessly reworked by writer/director Valerii Todorovsky. Combining beauty with malice, Ingeborga Dapkunaite makes a marvellous *femme fatale*, but there's no real passion in her affair with carpenter Vladimir Mashkov or intrigue in her relationship with Yuri Kuznetsov's investigator. A bold attempt, but something of a misfire. DP. In Russian with English subtitles. Contains violence and sex scenes.

Ingeborga Dapkunaite *Katia* • Vladimir Mashkov *Sergei* • Alisa Freindlikh *Irina* • Aleksandr Feklistov *Mitia* • Yuri Kuznetsov *Romanov* ■ *Dir* Valerii Todorovsky • *Scr* Alla Krinitsyna, François Gérif, Cécile Vargaftig, from a story by Marina Sheptunova, Stanislav Govorukhin, from the novel *Lady Macbeth of the Mtensk District* by Nikolai Leskov

Katok i Skrypka ★★★

Drama 1961 · USSR · Colour · 55mins

Andrei Tarkovsky's diploma film from the Soviet State School of Cinema in Moscow (VGIK), is a medium-length feature that hints at the sort of director he would become. His rich pictorial sense, the leisurely contemplation of objects and his obsession with mirrors is already evident in this fable about a little boy who gets to drive a steamroller and demonstrate his skills on the violin. The message about the unity of workers and artists is somewhat crude, but the cinematography by Vadim Yusov, the cameraman on Tarkovsky's first three features, is striking. RB. A Russian language film.

Igor Fomchenko *Sasha* • V Zamansky [Vladimir Zamansky] *Sergey* • Marina Adzhubey *Mother* ■ *Dir* Andrei Tarkovsky • *Scr* Andrei Tarkovsky, Andrei Konchalovsky, from a story by S Bakhmetyeva

Kazaam ★★ 12

Fantasy comedy adventure
1996 · US · Colour · 89mins

An early film outing for basketball legend Shaquille O'Neal, this thinly entertaining family comedy sees the athlete playing an ancient genie who is reawakened from his boom box by bullied schoolboy Francis Capra. Problem is that his potential master doesn't believe in magic, and is reluctant to take up the three wishes offer. Actor-turned-director Paul Michael Glaser paces it nicely, but this is a kids-only affair. JF

Shaquille O'Neal *Kazaam* • Francis Capra *Max* • Ally Walker *Alice* • Marshall Manesh *Malik* • James Acheson *Nick* • Fawn Reed *Asia Moon* • John Costelloe *Travis* ■ *Dir* Paul Michael Glaser • *Scr* Christian Ford, Roger Soffer, from a story by Paul Michael Glaser

Keaton's Cop ★ 18

Crime thriller 1990 · US · Colour · 91mins

Grouchy cop Lee Majors teams up with former mobster Abe Vigoda to investigate several assassination attempts. Naturally, it's hate at first sight, but this artificial attempt to generate chemistry provides neither laughs nor action. The violence at times is so bloody and ghastly, most viewers will find it hard to even think of laughing later. KB

Abe Vigoda *Louie Keaton* • Lee Majors *Mike Gable* • Don Rickles *Jake Barber* • Tracy Brooks Swope *Susan Watson* ■ *Dir* Robert Burge • *Scr* Michael B Druxman

The Keep ★★★ 18

Horror 1983 · UK · Colour · 91mins

In one of the weirdest Second World War movies ever made, a bunch of German soldiers bivouac in an old Romanian castle and get gruesomely dispatched by some unseen, supernatural force. By turns chilling, stylish, portentous and just plain silly, Michael Mann's second feature was a box-office bomb that temporarily wrecked his cinema career. However, Gabriel Byrne as an SS officer with a serious haircut, and Ian McKellen as a mad professor, are worth the price of admission alone. AT

Scott Glenn *Glaeken Trismegestus* • Alberta Watson *Eva* • Jürgen Prochnow *Woermann* • Robert Prosky *Father Fonescu* • Gabriel Byrne *Raempffer* • Ian McKellen *Dr Cuza* • Morgan Sheppard *Alexandru* • Royston Tickner *Tomescu* ■ *Dir* Michael Mann • *Scr* Michael Mann, from a novel by F Paul Wilson

Keep Cool ★★★★

Comedy thriller
1997 · Chi/HK · Colour · 95mins

Deprived of official funding, Zhang Yimou shot this quirky urban comedy with little formal preparation and a great deal of ingenuity. The dizzyingly mobile, hand-held technique will surprise those expecting his trademark stateliness, but the frenetic movements are totally in keeping with hip bookseller Jiang Wen's foolhardy quest to avenge himself on the club-owning mobster who steals his girl. Capturing the bustle of Beijing, as well as sustaining the breathless comic pace, Zhang still finds time to comment on the growing influence of western fads and attitudes. DP. A Mandarin language film.

Jiang Wen *Xiao Shuai* • Li Baotian *Lao Zhang* • Qu Ying *An Hong* • Ge You *The policeman* • Zhang Yimou *The peddler* ■ *Dir* Zhang Yimou • *Scr* Ping Shu

Keep 'em Flying ★★ U

Comedy musical 1941 · US · BW · 86mins

Abbott and Costello join stunt pilot Dick Foran in the Air Corps for this feeble comedy that barely manages to taxi to the runway, let alone take off. There's plenty of plot, with Foran winning the battle for Carol Bruce's affections by helping her brother over his flying phobia. But the laughs are on wartime rations, with only Martha Raye amusing as the twin waitresses who have lovestruck Costello in a spin. DP

Bud Abbott *Blackie Benson* • Lou Costello *Heathcliff* • Martha Raye *Barbara Phelps/Gloria Phelps* • Dick Foran *Jinx Roberts* • Carol Bruce *Linda Joyce* • William Gargan *Craig Morrison* ■ *Dir* Arthur Lubin • *Scr* True Boardman, Nat Perrin, John Grant, from a story by Edmund L Hartmann

Keep Fit ★★★ U

Comedy 1937 · UK · BW · 78mins

It's hard now to imagine that a toothy-grinned, ukelele-strumming comic with a broad Lancashire accent could be a superstar – but George Formby certainly was. A huge box-office draw in Britain during the 1930s and 1940s, Formby's saucy wit and frantic comic style proved a great tonic to wartime audiences. This movie finds the star in fine form, belting out songs and throwing himself into comedy routines, as a weedy barber forced to compete with a more athletic rival. Add a dash of romance and the unmasking of a thief and you've got all the ingredients for a first-rate Formby film. DF

George Formby *George Green* • Kay Walsh *Joan Allen* • Guy Middleton *Hector Kent* • Gus McNaughton *Publicity man* • Edmund Breon *Sir Augustus Marks* • George Benson *Ernie Gill* • Evelyn Roberts *Barker* • C Denier Warren *Editor* ■ *Dir* Anthony Kimmins • *Scr* Anthony Kimmins, Austin Melford

Keep It Up Downstairs ★ 18

Period sex comedy
1976 · UK · Colour · 90mins

In the depths of its 1970s trough, British cinema relied heavily on sitcom spin-offs and smut. This dire tale of avarice, snobbery and seduction belongs firmly in the latter category. A sort of *Carry On Chatterley*, it might have been described as a costume comedy, had the cast kept its costumes on long enough. Just about everything's on view, but there's not a laugh in sight. DP. Contains sex scenes and nudity.

Diana Dors *Daisy Dureneck* • Jack Wild *Peregrine Cockshute* • William Rushton *Shuttleworth* • Aimi MacDonald *Actress* • Françoise Pascal *Mimi* • Simon Brent *Rogers* • Sue Longhurst *Lady Cockshute* ■ *Dir* Robert Young [Robert M Young] • *Scr* Hazel Adair

Keep the Aspidistra Flying ★★★ PG

Period romantic comedy
1997 · UK · Colour · 96mins

In director Robert Bierman's enjoyable adaptation of George Orwell's semi-autobiographical comedy, Richard E Grant is at his angst-ridden, edgy best as an advertising man who quits his job to pursue the life of a poet. Helena Bonham Carter provides a nice contrast as his very tolerant girlfriend, who loves him despite his many faults. The sharp dialogue and gently amusing tone lend appeal to a lightweight tale that's more of an appetiser than a main course. JC DVD

Richard E Grant *Gordon Comstock* • Helena Bonham Carter *Rosemary* • Julian Wadham *Ravelston* • Jim Carter *Erskine* • Harriet Walter *Julia Comstock* • Lesley Vickerage *Hermione* • Barbara Leigh-Hunt *Mrs Wisbeach* • Liz Smith *Mrs Meakin* ■ *Dir* Robert Bierman • *Scr* Alan Plater, from the novel by George Orwell

Keep Your Powder Dry ★★ U

Second World War drama
1945 · US · BW · 92mins

This is life in the Women's Army Corps as lived by new recruits Lana Turner, Laraine Day (locked in animosity both on screen and off) and Susan Peters, three girls from contrasting backgrounds. It's not exactly riveting, but the supporting cast boasts Agnes Moorehead. Sad footnote: Susan Peters was crippled in an accident after this and never walked again. RK

Lana Turner *Valerie Parks* • Laraine Day *Leigh Rand* • Susan Peters *Ann Darrison* • Agnes Moorehead *Lt Col Spottiswoode* • Bill Johnson *Capt Bill Barclay* • Natalie Schafer *Harriet Corwin* • Lee Patrick *Gladys Hopkins* • Marta Linden *Capt Sanders* ■ *Dir* Edward Buzzell • *Scr* Mary C McCall Jr, George Bruce

Keep Your Seats, Please ★★★ U

Comedy 1936 · UK · BW · 81mins

Ilya Ilf and Yevgeny Petrov's celebrated play *The Twelve Chairs* gets the George Formby treatment in this sprightly musical comedy. Taking time to intone such ukulele classics as *When I'm Cleaning Windows*, Formby exhibits a bit more nous than usual, as he and girlfriend Florence Desmond pursue a set of antique chairs, one of which contains the jewels bequeathed him by an eccentric aunt. Formby is upstaged in every scene that he shares with the lugubrious Alastair Sim, as the shady lawyer hired to track down the auctioned furniture. DP

George Formby *George* • Florence Desmond *Flo* • Gus McNaughton *Max* • Alastair Sim *Drayton* • Harry Tate *Auctioneer* • Hal Gordon *Sailor* ■ *Dir* Monty Banks • *Scr* Tom Geraghty, Ian Hay, Anthony Kimmins, from the play *The Twelve Chairs* by Ilya Ilf, Yevgeny Petrov

The Keeper ★★ 15

Horror 1976 · Can · Colour · 84mins

In this rarely seen horror thriller from Canadian child-actor-turned-director Tom Drake, asylum head Christopher Lee plans to insure his inmates, murder their heirs with a hypnosis machine and use the money to conquer the world. Drake strives for dotty weirdness, but his psychic melodrama hits rock bottom with a thud every time detective Tell Schreiber and inspector Ross Vezarian appear on screen. Their awful acting quickly grounds any hint of style or chilling ambience. AJ

Christopher Lee *The Keeper* • Tell Schrieber *Dick Driver* • Sally Gray *Mae B Jones* • Ross Vezarian *Inspector Clarke* • Ian Tracey *The Kid* • Jack Leavy *Mr Big* • Leo Leavy *Mr Big* ■ *Dir* Tom Drake • *Scr* Tom Drake, from a story by David Curnick, Donald Wilson

The Keeper ★★

Crime drama 1995 · US · Colour · 97mins

Prison guard Giancarlo Esposito takes under his protection – and even into his home – Haitian immigrant Isaach de Bankole, who swears he's been wrongly accused of rape. But doubts set in when Esposito becomes convinced Bankole has slept with his wife. Director Joe Brewster, using realistic dialogue and unobtrusive direction, is clearly more interested in the psychological aspects of the intimate piece and the contrasting value systems of each man, but blows it with the gathering soap operatics. AJ

Giancarlo Esposito *Paul Lamont* • Regina Taylor *Angela Lamont* • Isaach de Bankole *Jean Baptiste* • Ron Brice *Ross* • OL Duke *Baker* ■ *Dir/Scr* Joe Brewster

Keeper of the Flame ★★★ U

Drama 1942 · US · BW · 96mins

This was the second of Katharine Hepburn and Spencer Tracy's nine films together and their first with director George Cukor. It's not a comedy, though, but a protracted and rather hectoring piece of wartime propaganda, kept alive by the presence of the two stars. Hepburn is the proud widow of an American hero and journalist Tracy wants to write his biography. Tracy exudes his customary integrity and becomes a bit self-righteous as he unravels the man's secret life. Hepburn is radiant. AT

K

Spencer Tracy *Steven O'Malley* • Katharine Hepburn *Christine Forrest* • Richard Whorf *Clive Kerndon* • Margaret Wycherly *Mrs Forrest* • Donald Meek *Mr Arbuthnot* • Stephen McNally *Freddie Ridges* • Audrey Christie *Jane Harding* • Forrest Tucker *Geoffrey Midford* ■ *Dir* George Cukor • *Scr* Donald Ogden Stewart, from the novel by IAR Wylie

Keeping the Faith ★★★ 12

Romantic comedy
2000 · US · Colour · 123mins

This good-natured film has appealing actors, a few good laughs and some unpretentious insights into religion. First-time director Edward Norton also stars as a priest, while Ben Stiller plays his best friend, a rabbi. Their friendship is tested when they both fall in love with childhood friend Jenna Elfman. Norton's movie successfully blends romance, comedy and faith into a thoughtful and entertaining mix that benefits from wonderful chemistry between the leads and a strong supporting cast, including Anne Bancroft as Stiller's mother. ST. Contains swearing. DVD

Ben Stiller *Jake* • Edward Norton *Brian* • Jenna Elfman *Anna* • Anne Bancroft *Ruth* • Eli Wallach *Rabbi Lewis* • Ron Rifkin *Larry Friedman* • Milos Forman *Father Havel* • Holland Taylor *Bonnie Rose* • Lisa Edelstein *Ali Decker* ■ *Dir* Edward Norton • *Scr* Stuart Blumberg • *Music* Elmer Bernstein

Keeping Track ★★★ 15

Thriller 1986 · Can · Colour · 97mins

An interesting, suspenseful thriller with a fine pair of central performances from Michael Sarrazin and Margot Kidder as innocent bystanders who witness a major robbery and murder and find themselves thrown full pelt into saving their own necks. What lifts this film above the mundane is its concentration on the duo's burgeoning dependence on each other and issues of trust – the crash, bang, wallop come a very ordinary second. Worth catching. SH. Contains mild swearing.

Michael Sarrazin *Daniel Hawkins* • Margot Kidder *Claire Tremayne* • Alan Scarfe *Royle Wishert* • Ken Pogue *Captain McCullough* ■ *Dir* Robin Spry • *Scr* Jamie Brown, from a story by Jamie Brown, Robin Spry

Keetje Tippel ★★★ 18

Period biographical drama
1975 · Neth · Colour · 102mins

Paul Verhoeven's third feature is based on the memoirs of a Dutch woman who was born into poverty in the 1880s, became a prostitute, married twice and met Toulouse-Lautrec in Paris. From this material, Verhoeven creates a Dickensian view of Europe – the prostitution, workhouses, squalor and the social inequality – as Keetje rises up the social ladder. Rutger Hauer has a leading role, and the cameraman is Jan De Bont, later the director of *Speed* and *The Haunting*. AT. In Dutch with English subtitles. DVD

Monique van de Ven *Keetje* • Rutger Hauer *Hugo* • Eddie Brugman *Andre* • Hannah De Leeuwe *Mina* • Andrea Domburg *Keetje's mother* • Jan Blaaser *Keetje's father* ■ *Dir* Paul Verhoeven • *Scr* Gerard Soeteman, from the books by Neel Doff

Kelly's Heroes ★★★ PG

Second World War action adventure
1970 · US/Yug · Colour · 137mins

Clint Eastwood and Telly Savalas head the cast of this enjoyable, if occasionally slightly silly, adventure yarn about a group of maverick GIs who decide to fill a lull in the war by knocking off a hoard of German bullion in occupied France. Savalas and the eccentric Donald Sutherland set to their assignment with gusto, while Eastwood remains as cool as ever as half of Europe is blowing up around him. Despite many flaws, it's not dull by any means. PF. Contains some violence and swearing. DVD

Clint Eastwood *Kelly* • Telly Savalas *Big Joe* • Don Rickles *Crapgame* • Donald Sutherland *Oddball* • Carroll O'Connor *General Colt* • Hal Buckley *Maitland* • Stuart Margolin *Little Joe* • Fred Pearlman *Mitchell* ■ *Dir* Brian G Hutton • *Scr* Troy Kennedy Martin

Ken Park ★★★★

Drama 2002 · US/Neth/Fr · Colour · 96mins

Intensely shocking, hardcore explicit, ironically amusing, ultimately moving, tender and moral, Larry Clark's co-directed (with Ed Lachman) suburban Big Chill will polarise audiences. In its graphic depiction of provocative teenage sex, this heart-breaking satire is as controversial as they come in dealing matter-of-factly with child abuse, incest, autoeroticism and murder as Harmony Korine's script zeroes in on five stories revolving around the suicide of skateboarder Ken Park (Adam Chubbuck). The Clark debate – Smut Peddler or Artistic Genius – continues with this shattering wake-up call. AJ

James Ransome *Tate* • Tiffany Limos *Peaches* • Stephen Jasso *Claude* • James Bullard *Shawn* • Mike Apaletegui *Curtis* • Adam Chubbuck *Ken Park* • Wade Andrew Williams *Claude's father* • Amanda Plummer *Claude's mother* ■ *Dir* Larry Clark, Ed Lachman • *Scr* Harmony Korine

The Kennel Murder Case ★★★

Detective mystery 1933 · US · BW · 73mins

William Powell plays super-sleuth Philo Vance, looking into the murder of two brothers, both members of a Long Island kennel club. This doesn't faze our hero as he's also a dog fancier. Enjoyable and over in a flash – and so was Powell's four-film run as Vance, as Warner Bros replaced him with the serviceable Warren William. Powell then became Nick Charles in the *Thin Man* series. AT

William Powell *Philo Vance* • Mary Astor *Hilda Lake* • Eugene Pallette *Sgt Heath* • Ralph Morgan *Raymond Wrede* • Jack LaRue *Eduardo Grassi* • Helen Vinson *Doris Delafield* • Paul Cavanagh *Sir Bruce MacDonald* • Robert Barrat *Archer Coe* ■ *Dir* Michael Curtiz • *Scr* Robert N Lee, Peter Milne, Robert Presnell, from the novel *The Return of Philo Vance* by SS Van Dine

The Kentuckian ★★★ PG

Western 1955 · US · Colour · 99mins

Producer/star Burt Lancaster's only film as director is this marvellously photographed outdoor adventure. The main theme is Lancaster's relationship with his young son, touchingly portrayed by Donald MacDonald. The women are weakly cast, but there are a pair of prize villains: John Carradine as a travelling quack and, in his movie debut, nasty whip-wielding baddie Walter Matthau, whose main scene was hacked to ribbons by the UK censor before the film's original release. It has happily now been restored. The marvellous score is by Bernard Herrmann. TS DVD

Burt Lancaster *Big Eli* • Dianne Foster *Hannah* • Diana Lynn *Susie* • John McIntire *Zack* • Una Merkel *Sophie* • Walter Matthau *Bodine* • John Carradine *Fletcher* • Donald MacDonald *Little Eli* ■ *Dir* Burt Lancaster • *Scr* Ab Guthrie Jr, from the novel *The Gabriel Horn* by Felix Holt • *Cinematographer* Ernest Lazlo

Kentucky ★★★

Romantic drama 1938 · US · Colour · 95mins

The main interest today in this hoary old 20th Century-Fox horse-racing saga resides in two things: the splendid richness of the Technicolor and the Oscar-winning performance of veteran Walter Brennan (his second of three supporting actor Academy Awards). Loretta Young and Richard Greene are the impossibly good-looking young leads, and the bluegrass countryside has never looked more beguiling. The plot about feuding horse-breeding families owes as much to *Romeo and Juliet* as it does to the source novel by co-screenwriter John Taintor Foote. TS

Loretta Young *Sally Goodwin* • Richard Greene *Jack Dillon* • Walter Brennan *Peter Goodwin* • Douglass Dumbrille *John Dillon* • Karen Morley *Mrs Goodwin* • Moroni Olsen *John Dillon II* • Russell Hicks *Thad Goodwin Sr* • Willard Robertson *Bob Slocum* • Charles Waldron *Thad Goodwin* ■ *Dir* David Butler • *Scr* Lamar Trotti, John Taintor Foote, from the novel *The Look of Eagles* by John Taintor Foote

The Kentucky Fried Movie ★★★ 18

Comedy 1977 · US · Colour · 83mins

Director John Landis and scriptwriters Jerry Zucker, David Zucker and Jim Abrahams provide a consistently wacky collection of spoofs in a more hit-than-miss parody of TV commercials, B-movies, kung fu adventures and porno chic. A lot more vulgar than their later movies, which included *Airplane!* and *Naked Gun*, it's a breezy anthology of the sketches the trio had already presented on stage. A cheap, chucklesome time-waster that includes the star quality of Donald Sutherland and George Lazenby. AJ DVD

Colin Male *Spokesman* • Janice Kent *Barbara Duncan* • Michael Laurence (2) *Frank Bowman* • Larry Curan *Tom Leclair* • Richard A Baker [Rick Baker] *Dino (AM Today)* • David Zucker *Man/second technician/Grunwald* • Lenka Novak *Linda Chambers* • George Lazenby *Architect* • Donald Sutherland *Clumsy waiter* ■ *Dir* John Landis • *Scr* David Zucker, Jim Abrahams, Jerry Zucker

Kentucky Moonshine ★★★

Musical comedy 1938 · US · BW · 87mins

The zany comedy trio The Ritz Brothers are an acquired taste but this is probably their best film, with a funny script and a good supply of risible skits. As city slickers who, hearing that a radio show is looking for genuine hayseeds, pretend to be country bumkins, they dominate the film with their frantic mixture of slapstick, tomfoolery and musical clowning. Tony Martin is also on hand, playing it straight and singing the Lew Pollack–Sidney Mitchell songs. TV

Al Ritz • Harry Ritz • Jimmy Ritz • Tony Martin *Jerry Wade* • Marjorie Weaver *Caroline* • Slim Summerville *Hank Hatfield* • John Carradine *Reef Hatfield* • Wally Vernon *Gus Bryce* ■ *Dir* David Butler • *Scr* Art Arthur, MM Musselman, from the story by MM Musselman, Jack Lait Jr

Keoma ★★★ 15

Spaghetti western 1976 · It · Colour · 96mins

Originally despised, then admired for the elegance and poise of the camerawork, the spaghetti western is still one of the most watchable of all genres. This was released after the great days of the 1960s but hero Franco Nero still has plenty of the prerequisite man-alone spirit that Clint Eastwood originated. Director Enzo G Castellari attempts to fuse a popular theme – civil-rights protests – to the plot as Nero tries to clean up his town like a liberal activist. But the ruthless action is still the element of the film that works best. TH. Italian dialogue dubbed into English. DVD

Franco Nero *Keoma Shannon* • Woody Strode *George* • William Berger ■ *Dir* Enzo G Castellari • *Scr* Enzo G Castellari, Mino Roli, Nico Ducci, Luigi Montefiori

Kept Husbands ★★

Drama 1931 · US · BW · 76mins

Director Lloyd Bacon's creaky early talkie was promoted by RKO with the line "every inch a man – bought body and soul by his wife". This less-than-snappy slogan did nothing to drag them in off the streets at the time, and it's still not likely to set many pulses racing. However, star Joel McCrea rarely lets the side down, and he's easily the best thing in this melodrama about a steelworker who curbs the excesses of his frivolous wife Dorothy MacKaill, who just happens to be his boss's daughter. DP

Joel McCrea *Dick Brunton* • Dorothy MacKaill *Dorothy "Dot" Parker* • Robert McWade *Arthur Parker* • Florence Roberts *Mrs Henrietta Parker* • Clara Young *Mrs Post* • Mary Carr *Mrs Brunton* • Ned Sparks *Hughie* ■ *Dir* Lloyd Bacon • *Scr* Alfred Jackson, Forrest Halsey, from a story by Louis Sarecky

The Kerosene Seller's Wife ★★

Satirical drama
1989 · USSR · Colour · 101mins

Written and directed by Alexander Kaidanovsky, this is another of those *glasnost* assaults on the legacy of Stalinism. However, such is the density of the symbolism and the proliferation of dreams, flashbacks and surrealist interventions, that it's exceedingly difficult to keep up with the story of the doctor forced to become a kerosene salesman after he is betrayed to the authorities by his apparatchik twin brother. However, Alexander Bolyuev turns in a creditable performance, while Anna Myasoedova is suitably scheming as the spouse. DP. In Russian with English subtitles.

Vitautas Paukste *Yurgis Petravichus* • Alexander Bolyuev *Pavel Udaltsov/Sergei Udaltsov* • Anna Myasoedova *Olga* ■ *Dir/Scr* Alexander Kaidanovsky

Kes ★★★★★ PG

Drama 1969 · UK · Colour · 106mins

Ken Loach seems to acquire a surer mastery of his art with each picture, yet this, one of his earliest features, is still one of his best. Adapted from Barry Hines's "grim up North" novel, it has such a ring of authenticity that you can almost smell the chips. As ever, Loach coaxes remarkable performances, with Freddie Fletcher epitomising bullying big brotherhood and Brian Glover caricaturing every games teacher who never made it. Outstanding, however, is David Bradley as the teenager who finds solace – in a baby kestrel – from the pain of his dysfunctional family life and the torment of school. DP DVD

David Bradley (2) *Billy Casper* • Colin Welland *Mr Farthing* • Lynne Perrie *Mrs Casper* • Freddie Fletcher *Jud* • Brian Glover *Mr Sugden* • Bob Bowes *Mr Gryce* • Trevor Hasketh *Mr Crossley* • Eric Bolderson *Farmer* ■ *Dir* Ken Loach • *Scr* Ken Loach, Tony Garnett, Barry Hines, from the novel *A Kestrel for a Knave* by Barry Hines • *Cinematographer* Chris Menges

Kevin & Perry Go Large ★★★★ 15

Comedy 2000 · UK/US · Colour · 79mins

Harry Enfield takes his finest comic creations – the hormonally charged teenage boys Kevin and Perry (played by Enfield and Kathy Burke) – and successfully expands them from a sketch into a feature-length movie. Here the spotty twosome descend on an unsuspecting Ibiza, where they hope to become top DJs and, in doing so, attract loads of ladies. Ed Bye's film zips along thanks to Burke's hilarious leering and disgusting adventures that make *There's Something about Mary* look like *Mary*

Poppins. JB. Contains swearing and a sex scene. [VIDEO] DVD

Harry Enfield *Kevin* • Kathy Burke *Perry* • Rhys Ifans *Eye Ball Paul* • Laura Fraser *Candice* • James Fleet *Dad* • Louisa Rix *Mum* • Paul Whitehouse *Bouncer* • Steve McFadden *Bouncer* ■ *Dir* Ed Bye • *Scr* Harry Enfield, David Cummings, from characters created by Harry Enfield

The Key ★★

Political romantic drama
1934 · US · BW · 82mins

The rebellion against the British in Ireland forms the background to this drama. William Powell plays a British officer and concentrates more on his amorous career than the job in hand – namely the street fighting that one glimpses whenever the script starts to flag, based around the conflict between the Black and Tans and the Irish Revolutionaries. Colin Clive makes his mark as a British officer. AT

William Powell *Capt Tennant* • Edna Best *Norah Kerr* • Colin Clive *Andrew Kerr* • Halliwell Hobbes *General* • Hobart Cavanaugh *Homer* • Henry O'Neill *Dan* • Donald Crisp *Conlan* ■ *Dir* Michael Curtiz • *Scr* Laird Doyle, from a play by R Gore Browne, JL Hardy

The Key ★★★

Second World War drama
1958 · UK · BW · 138mins

Playing down her usual voluptuous glamour, Sophia Loren is heartbreakingly vulnerable here as the waterfront landlady who offers her favours to naval skippers. She is both a source of solace and disquiet, as few entrusted with her key survive for long. Instead of focusing on either her torment or her affair with the gruff William Holden, Carl Foreman's script spends too much time at sea. No matter how well director Carol Reed stages the action sequences, we're soon impatient for shore leave. DP

William Holden (2) *David Ross* • Sophia Loren *Stella* • Trevor Howard *Chris Ford* • Oscar Homolka *Captain Van Dam* • Kieron Moore *Kane* • Bernard Lee *Wadlow* • Beatrix Lehmann *Housekeeper* • Noel Purcell *Hotel porter* • Bryan Forbes *Weaver* • Michael Caine ■ *Dir* Carol Reed • *Scr* Carl Foreman, from the novel *Stella* by Jan De Hartog

The Key ★★★★

Erotic melodrama
1959 · Jpn · Colour · 96mins

Kon Ichikawa's darkly comic tale of spousal obedience and sexual prowess is also a sly satire on pornography and cinematic voyeurism. Adapted from the novel by Junichiro Tanizaki, the action stems from an ageing husband's hope that his wife's infidelity with a doctor will restore his potency. However, the liaison only sparks a tragic rivalry between his liberated wife and his ultra-traditional daughter. Compromised in its content by contemporary censorship strictures, this is still a daringly subversive picture, which benefits both from the subtly coloured widescreen lensing and the exemplary performance of Machiko Kyo. DP. In Japanese with English subtitles.

Ganjiro Nakamura *Mr Kenmochi* • Machiko Kyo *Ikuko Kenmochi* • Tatsuya Nakadai *Kimura* • Junko Kano *Toshiko Kenmochi* • Tanie Kitabayashi *Hana* ■ *Dir* Kon Ichikawa • *Scr* Natto Wada, Keiji Hasebe, Kon Ichikawa, from a novel by Junichiro Tanizaki • *Cinematographer* Kazuo Miyagawa

Key Exchange ★

Romantic comedy
1985 · US · Colour · 90mins

Brooke Adams stars in this farce as a TV producer with an unfaithful and commitment-shy boyfriend (Ben Masters). His lawyer friend Daniel Stern, recently married to an equally unfaithful partner, upsets the apple cart by making a play for Adams and the stage is set for a predictable scenario. Disastrous on all counts. LH

Ben Masters *Philip Bailey* • Brooke Adams *Lisa Simon* • Danny Aiello *Carabello* • Daniel Stern *Michael Fine* • Nancy Mette *April Fine* • Tony Roberts *David Slattery* • Seth Allen *Frank Mars* ■ *Dir* Barnet Kellman • *Scr* Kevin Scott, Paul Kurta, from the play by Kevin Wade

Key Largo ★★★ PG

Crime drama 1948 · US · BW · 96mins

A great Warner Bros cast was assembled for this screen version of Maxwell Anderson's steamy play, but, despite sterling work from movie icons Humphrey Bogart and Lauren Bacall (and, best of all, Edward G Robinson as a veteran gangster), the creaky theatrical origins show through, and the climactic Florida storms are as phoney as the allegorical plot devices. Nevertheless, Claire Trevor picked up an Oscar for playing Robinson's boozy floozy, and there's a fine feeling of postwar angst evoked by director John Huston. TS [VIDEO] DVD

Humphrey Bogart *Frank McCloud* • Edward G Robinson *Johnny Rocco* • Lauren Bacall *Nora Temple* • Lionel Barrymore *James Temple* • Claire Trevor *Gaye Dawn* • Thomas Gomez *Curley Hoff* • Harry Lewis *Toots Bass* • John Rodney *Deputy Clyde Sawyer* • Marc Lawrence (1) *Ziggy* ■ *Dir* John Huston • *Scr* John Huston, Richard Brooks, from the play by Maxwell Anderson • *Cinematographer* Karl Freund

Key to the City ★★

Romantic comedy 1950 · US · BW · 100mins

This breezy comedy stars Clark Gable and Loretta Young, who meet at a mayoral convention. He's the ex-docker-turned-politician and she's the more classy mayor of a tiny Maine town. Set in San Francisco, where Gable has to cope with several emergencies – as well as those sorts of misunderstandings that only happen in movies – it's a demonstration of staying power for Gable, who was nearing the end of his career at MGM. AT

Clark Gable *Steve Fisk* • Loretta Young *Clarissa Standish* • Frank Morgan *Fire chief Duggan* • Marilyn Maxwell *Sheila* • Raymond Burr *Les Taggart* • James Gleason *Sergeant Hogan* • Lewis Stone *Judge Silas Standish* • Raymond Walburn *Mayor Billy Butler* ■ *Dir* George Sidney (2) • *Scr* Robert Riley Crutcher, from a story by Albert Beich

Key Witness ★★★

Crime drama 1960 · US · BW · 82mins

A group of young thugs terrorise a youth and knife him to death. Only one man – Jeffrey Hunter – is prepared to tell the police what has happened even though dozens were witnesses. The story ropes in a lot of topical social concerns – drugs, racism, bike culture – and features Dennis Hopper as the leader of the ruffians. Tautly directed by B-movie maestro Phil Karlson, this was banned by the British censor, mainly because of the frequent use of flick-knives. AT

Jeffrey Hunter *Fred Morrow* • Pat Crowley *Ann Morrow* • Dennis Hopper *"Cowboy"* • Joby Baker *"Muggles"* • Susan Harrison *Ruby* • Johnny Nash *"Apple"* • Corey Allen *"Magician"* • Frank Silvera *Detective Rafael Torno* ■ *Dir* Phil Karlson • *Scr* Alfred Brenner, Sidney Michaels, from a novel by Frank Kane

The Keys of the Kingdom ★★

Drama 1944 · US · BW · 136mins

Gregory Peck, in only his second picture, gained a Best Actor Oscar nomination playing a saintly priest who runs a mission in 19th-century China. Directed by John M Stahl from a final script by Joseph L Mankiewicz, it's a long, talkative and rather undramatic picture (only a civil war injects much action), but its success saved Peck's career after the weak showing of his first movie, *Days of Glory*. AE

Gregory Peck *Father Francis Chisholm* • Thomas Mitchell *Dr Willie Tulloch* • Vincent Price *Rev Angus Mealy* • Rose Stradner *Mother Maria Veronica* • Roddy McDowall *Francis, as a boy* • Edmund Gwenn *Rev Hamish MacNabb* • Cedric Hardwicke *Monsignor Sleeth* ■ *Dir* John M Stahl • *Scr* Joseph L Mankiewicz, Nunnally Johnson, from the novel by AJ Cronin

The Keys to the House ★★★ PG

Drama
2004 · It/Ger/Fr/UK/Nor · Colour · 111mins

Deftly handling a delicate subject, this is a sensitively played and genuinely moving study of an absentee father's reconciliation with his disabled son. Italian director Gianni Amelio's life-affirming drama benefits from the joyful performance of teenager Andrea Rossi as the abandoned child. However, his naturalness sometimes contrasts sharply with the acting craft involved in Kim Rossi Stuart's otherwise admirable performance as the father. Unfortunately, the film loses its way when the pair head for Norway in search of teenager's pen pal. DP. In Italian with English subtitles.

Kim Rossi Stuart *Gianni* • Charlotte Rampling *Nicole* • Andrea Rossi *Paolo* • Alla Faerovich *Nadine* • Pierfrancesco Favino *Alberto* • Manuel Katzy *Taxi driver* • Michael Weiss *Andreas* ■ *Dir* Gianni Amelio • *Scr* Gianni Amelio, Sandro Petraglia, Stefano Rulli, from the autobiographical novel *Nati Due Volte (Born Twice)* by Giuseppe Pontiggia

Keys to Tulsa ★★ 18

Crime drama 1996 · US · Colour · 109mins

Don't raise your hopes about the quality of this film when you see the cool cast list – this is an interesting, if not exactly gripping, *film noir*. Eric Stoltz plays the prodigal son returning home to mum Mary Tyler Moore with the intention of straightening his life out. Lacking in tension and hindered by rather turgid direction, this is more of a well-played character piece than a taut thriller. JB [VIDEO] DVD

Eric Stoltz *Richter Boudreau* • Cameron Diaz *Trudy* • Randy Graff *Louise Brinkman* • Mary Tyler Moore *Cynthia Boudreau* • James Coburn *Harmon Shaw* • Deborah Kara Unger *Vicky Michaels Stovers* • Peter Strauss *Chip Carlson* • James Spader *Ronnie Stover* ■ *Dir* Leslie Greif • *Scr* Harley Peyton, from the novel by Brian Fair Berkey

Khakee ★★ 18

Police thriller 2003 · Ind · Colour · 171mins

In Rajkumar Santoshi's "prisoner and escort" thriller, the subcontinent's most wanted terrorist (Ajay Devgan) is guarded on the trip from Chandanghad to Mumbai by a team of lawmen – one of whom has a deadly mission to fulfil. The detectives are all caricatures, with Amitabh Bachchan's underachieving veteran being balanced by Akshay Kumar's short-fused maverick and Tusshar Kapoor's idealistic rookie. However, the performances are bullish and polished. DP. In Hindi with English subtitles. Contains violence. [VIDEO] DVD

Amitabh Bachchan *DCP Anant Shrivastav* • Ajay Devgan *Iqbal Ansari* • Akshay Kumar *Sr Inspector Shekhar Sachdev* • Tusshar Kapoor *Sub Inspector Ashwin Gupte* • Aishwarya Rai *Mahalaxmi* ■ *Dir* Rajkumar Santoshi • *Scr* Sridhar Raghavan, Rajkumar Santoshi

Khartoum ★★★ PG

Historical drama
1966 · UK · Colour · 122mins

Charlton Heston stars in this epic about General Gordon's last stand, when Sudanese warriors, led by the Mahdi, gave the British Empire a serious jolt. Heston's portrayal of Gordon is finely studied, suggesting a complexity that the script never quite comes to terms with. His performance contrasts with that of Laurence Olivier, whose Mahdi is all eye-rolling fanaticism. This boasts a fine supporting cast, and is often spectacular, but the direction is on the stodgy side. AT [VIDEO] DVD

Charlton Heston *General Charles Gordon* • Laurence Olivier *The Mahdi* • Richard Johnson *Colonel JDH Stewart* • Ralph Richardson *Mr Gladstone* • Alexander Knox *Sir Evelyn Baring* • Johnny Sekka *Khaleel* • Nigel Green *General Wolseley* • Michael Hordern *Lord Granville* • Zia Mohyeddin *Zobeir Pasha* ■ *Dir* Basil Dearden • *Scr* Robert Ardrey

Khrustaliov, My Car! ★★

Satirical comedy drama
1998 · Rus/Fr · BW · 137mins

Alexei German ended a 16-year hiatus as a director with this satire on Soviet society in the last days of Stalin. However, the break clearly sapped the insight and precision that made *My Friend Ivan Lapshin* so compelling. Instead, he delivers a rambling, often incoherent tale, in which the broad comedy of the opening Moscow section gives way to stylised realism inside the grim gulag to which Yuri Tsourilo's doctor is condemned. DP. A Russian language film.

Yuri Tsourilo *General Youri Glinski* • Nina Rouslanova *Wife* • Juri Jarvet *Swedish reporter* • M Dementiev *Son* • A Bachirov *Idiot* ■ *Dir* Alexei German • *Scr* Alexei German, Svetlana Karmalita

K

Khushi ★★ 12

Musical romantic drama
2002 · Ind · Colour · 162mins

Having already scored a Tamil hit with this tale of star-crossed lovers who take as much pleasure in squabbling as canoodling, director S J Surya made a Hindi version. The opening segment, in which the twosome are brought together in several chance situations from babyhood to adolescence, is rather neatly done. However, once the spirited Kareena Kapoor and rich boy Fardeen Khan become an item at college, their spats grow vexatious and tediously verbose. DP. In Hindi with English subtitles. [VIDEO] DVD

Fardeen Khan *Karan* • Kareena Kapoor *Khushi* • Amrish Puri • Johny Lever [Johnny Lever] • Navin Nischol • Beena ■ *Dir* SJ Surya • *Scr* SJ Surya, Aman Jafrey, Bholoo Khan, from the story by Surya

Khyber Patrol ★★★ U

Action drama 1954 · US · Colour · 72mins

Nicely paced and richly coloured shortish co-feature, following the trend set by Rock Hudson in *Bengal Brigade* and Tyrone Power in *King of the Khyber Rifles*. This time newcomer Richard Egan is offered a kickstart to stardom as he ruggedly romances lovely Dawn Addams and fights for the Empire on the Indian border, aided by pukka British actor Patric Knowles. TS

Richard Egan *Cameron* • Dawn Addams *Diana* • Raymond Burr *Ahmed* • Patric Knowles *Lieutenant Kennerly* • Paul Cavanagh *Melville* • Donald Randolph *Ishak Khan* • Philip Tonge *Colonel Rivington* • Patrick O'Moore *Brusard* ■ *Dir* Seymour Friedman • *Scr* Jack DeWitt, from a story by Richard Schayer

Kick! ★★

Comedy drama 1979 · US · Colour · 87mins

The name of Sean S Cunningham will forever be associated by horror fans with *Friday the 13th*. But just before he made that landmark in schlock horror, he was landed with this corny comedy that harks back to *Boys Town* and Bing Crosby's Father O'Malley movies such as *Going My Way*. Sadly, this story of a football team betting stolen money on themselves to help their coach to pay his gambling debts isn't on a par with any of the above. DP.

Jim Baker *Francis Xavier "Manny" Mansfield* • Malachy McCourt *Father Arch McCoy* • Chet Doherty *Dr Berryman* • Sel Skolnick *Mr Caputo* • Terry Vance *Amazing Grace* ■ *Dir* Sean S Cunningham • *Scr* Victor Miller, from a story by Stephen Miner

Kick ★★

Romantic drama 1999 · Aus · Colour · 92mins

This modest Aussie ballet comedy actually predates *Billy Elliot*. Real-life dancer Russell Page plays a school student who is a star of the rugby field but also has a secret passion and skill for the ballet. Inevitably his two very different worlds collide. Despite its similarities with the British film, this is actually closer in spirit to the Australian hit *Strictly Ballroom* and the latter's star Paul Mercurio also pops up here as Page's choreographer. JF

Russell Page *Matt Grant* • Rebecca Yates *Claire Andrews* • Paul Mercurio *David Knight* • Radha Mitchell *Tamara Spencer* • Martin Henderson *Tom Bradshaw* • Peter Gwynne *Dr Derrick* ■ *Dir* Lynda Heys • *Scr* Stuart Beattie

Kickboxer ★★★ 18

Martial arts adventure
1989 · US · Colour · 97mins

A key film in Jean-Claude Van Damme's career, this is the one that first gave an indication that the Muscles from Brussels could escape from straight-to-video hell and into the mainstream. Plot-wise, this is nothing special: Van Damme is the brother of an injured kickboxing champion who enters the ring seeking revenge. However, the fight sequences are staged with such élan that it is easy to ignore the hackneyed script and the rather wooden performances. The franchise spawned several sequels. JF. Contains swearing, violence and nudity. DVD

Jean-Claude Van Damme *Kurt Sloane* • Dennis Alexio *Eric Sloane* • Dennis Chan *Xian Chow* • Tong Po • Haskell Anderson *Winston Taylor* • Rochelle Ashana *Mylee* ■ *Dir* Mark DiSalle, David Worth • *Scr* Glen Bruce, from a story by Mark DiSalle, Jean-Claude Van Damme

Kickboxer 2: the Road Back ★★ 18

Martial arts adventure
1990 · US · Colour · 90mins

This explores much the same territory as its predecessor and the director is Hollywood journeyman Albert Pyun, whose name can be found on many a straight-to-video sleeve. The film stars Sasha Mitchell as the high-kicking hero who seeks revenge on the kung fu coward who killed his brother. You probably know the rest. JF. Contains violence and swearing.

Sasha Mitchell *David Sloan* • Peter Boyle *Justin Maciah* • Cary-Hiroyuki Tagawa *Mr Sangha* • Dennis Chan *Xian Chow* • Michel Qissi *Tong Po* • John Diehl *Morrison* ■ *Dir* Albert Pyun • *Scr* David S Goyer

Kickboxer III: the Art of War ★★ 18

Martial arts adventure
1992 · US · Colour · 91mins

Tinseltown never really came knocking for Sasha Mitchell, who bravely soldiers on in the role created by Jean-Claude Van Damme. The slimmest of plots (the hunt for a kidnapped girl) helps to link the numerous biffing sequences, which are competently, if unimaginatively, filmed. The fourth instalment in the series, subtitled *The Aggressor*, was originally rejected for video release in the UK. JF. Contains violence and swearing. DVD

Sasha Mitchell *David Sloan* • Dennis Chan *Xian Chow* • Richard Comar *Frank Lane* • Noah Verduzco *Marcos* • Ian Jacklin *Martine* ■ *Dir* Rick King • *Scr* Dennis Pratt

Kicked in the Head ★★

Black comedy thriller
1997 · US · Colour · 86mins

Self-pitying low-life Kevin Corrigan acts as a cocaine-delivery boy for his two-bit crook uncle James Woods, but things don't go as planned and he invokes the wrath of local crime boss Burt Young. Highly derivative, and populated by truly unlikeable characters, this forced black comedy thriller is neither dark nor amusing enough to perk any interest. An artificial dud, enlivened by the performances. AJ

Kevin Corrigan *Redmond* • Linda Fiorentino *Megan* • Michael Rapaport *Stretch* • James Woods *Uncle Sam* • Burt Young *Jack* • Lili Taylor *Happy* ■ *Dir* Matthew Harrison • *Scr* Kevin Corrigan, Matthew Harrison

Kicking and Screaming ★★★ 15

Comedy drama 1995 · US · Colour · 92mins

We're in "slacker" territory again, as a group of recent college grads (including Josh Hamilton and Olivia D'Abo) try to figure out what to do with their lives. Eric Stoltz plays the guy they don't want to become, a grad student who's been tending bar for the last ten years while he (allegedly) works on his dissertation. Everybody in this movie speaks in a painfully witty manner and it takes a while to go anywhere, but a lot of it is quite funny. ST

Josh Hamilton *Grover* • Olivia D'Abo *Jane* • Carlos Jacott *Otis* • Chris Eigeman *Max* • Eric Stoltz *Chet* • Jason Wiles *Skippy* • Parker Posey *Miami* • Cara Buono *Kate* • Elliott Gould *Grover's dad* • Sam Gould *Pete* ■ *Dir* Noah Baumbach • *Scr* Noah Baumbach, from a story by Oliver Berkman, Noah Baumbach

Kicking & Screaming ★★ PG

Sports comedy 2005 · US · Colour · 94mins

Will Ferrell stars as the put-upon son of a macho sports fanatic in this meek comedy. He attempts to prove himself to his intimidating father (Robert Duvall) by coaching a Little League soccer team that is stuck at the bottom of the table. Full of clichéd gags and flat improvisation, this unforgivably wastes the considerable talents of Robert Duvall as the bullying father. But, while unfocused, it is amiable and raises the occasional smile. GM

Will Ferrell *Phil Weston* • Robert Duvall *Buck Weston* • Kate Walsh *Barbara Weston* • Mike Ditka • Dylan McLaughlin *Sam Weston* • Josh Hutcherson *Bucky Weston* • Musetta Vander *Janice Weston* ■ *Dir* Jesse Dylan • *Scr* Leo Benvenuti, Steve Rudnick

The Kid ★★★★ U

Silent comedy drama
1921 · US · BW · 68mins

Charlie Chaplin's first feature as writer, director and star was something of a watershed in his career. From now on, slapstick would slowly be replaced by more observational comedy, while an increased emphasis would be placed on both social comment and pathos. Clearly recalling his own troubled childhood in Victorian London, the film is remarkable for the chemistry between the Tramp and moppet Jackie Coogan. Chaplin may try a touch too hard for tears in places, but the scenes in which he discovers the abandoned baby and the heaven sequence show just what a gifted film-maker he was. DP DVD

Charlie Chaplin [Charles Chaplin] *Tramp* • Carl Miller *Artist* • Edna Purviance *Mother* • Jackie Coogan *The Kid* • Tom Wilson *Policeman* ■ *Dir/Scr* Charles Chaplin

Kid ★★ 18

Thriller 1990 · US · Colour · 87mins

C Thomas Howell plays the Kid, a taciturn drifter in a long coat who comes back to his home town and makes out with the prettiest girl there. However, he also goes on a killing spree aimed at those who murdered his parents years before. Apart from the obvious nod to Clint Eastwood's laconic loner, Howell seems to be going for some kind of James Dean vibe here as well, but he's out of his league and the rest of the characters are mere stereotypes. Violent and derivative. ST

C Thomas Howell *Kid* • R Lee Ermey *Luke Clanton* • Dale Dye *Garvey* • Sarah Trigger *Kate* • Michael Bowen *Harlan* • Brian Austin Green *Metal Louie* • Damon Martin *Pete* • Lenore Kasdorf *Alice* ■ *Dir* John Mark Robinson • *Scr* Leslie Bohem

Kid Blue ★★★

Comedy western
1971 · US · Colour · 100mins

This seriously flakey comedy western – a sort of *Easy Rider* on horseback – has Dennis Hopper as a hopeless outlaw who goes straight and is hopeless at that as well. Hopper's outsider has a wayward charm, a hippy's glazed look and a talent for slapstick humour. Less a narrative than scenes glued randomly together, it's a mess, albeit an entertaining one. Completed in 1971 under its original title *Dime Box*, it was kept on the shelf for two years and retitled on release. AT

Dennis Hopper *Bickford Waner* • Warren Oates *Reese Ford* • Peter Boyle *Preacher Bob* • Ben Johnson *Sheriff "Mean John" Simpson* • Lee Purcell *Molly Ford* • Janice Rule *Janet Conforto* • Ralph Waite *Drummer* ■ *Dir* James Frawley • *Scr* Edwin Shrake

The Kid Brother ★★★★★ U

Silent comedy 1927 · US · BW · 82mins

The inventiveness of comedian Harold Lloyd has to be seen to be disbelieved in this comedy about the put-upon youngest of three sons and their widower father (Walter James). Ordered to close down a travelling show by his sheriff dad, Lloyd at last rebels against the constant bullying – because he's fallen in love with showgirl Jobyna Ralston – and triumphs over parental oppression. Some of the sight gags are brilliant, including the use of a butter churn as a way of wringing and hanging out clothes. The mechanisms of laughter-making don't come much better than this, and add up to one of the comedian's best movies. TH

Harold Lloyd *Harold Hickory* • Jobyna Ralston *Mary Powers* • Walter James *Sheriff Jim Hickory* • Leo Willis *Leo Hickory* • Olin Francis *Olin Hickory* • Constantine Romanoff *Sardoni* • Eddie Boland *"Flash" Farrell* • Frank Lanning *Sam Hooper* ■ *Dir* Ted Wilde, JA Howe, Lewis Milestone • *Scr* John Grey, Tom Crizer, Lex Neal, Howard Green, Ted Wilde

A Kid for Two Farthings ★★★ U

Comedy fantasy 1955 · UK · Colour · 91mins

Influenced by the neorealist fantasies of Italian director Vittorio De Sica, this is a delightful urban fairy tale set in London's East End in the harsh days after the Second World War. The story – of a small boy who finds a one-horned goat, which he is convinced is a miracle-working unicorn – is handled with a wonderfully light touch by director Carol Reed, and beautifully played by a cast in which Celia Johnson, Diana Dors and little Jonathan Ashmore stand out. Yet, for all its feel-good charm, the blend of realism and fantasy is not always convincing. DP

Celia Johnson *Joanne* • Diana Dors *Sonia* • David Kossoff *Kandinsky* • Joe Robinson *Sam* • Jonathan Ashmore *Joe* • Brenda de Banzie *"Lady" Ruby* • Vera Day *Mimi* • Primo Carnera *Python Macklin* • Sidney James *Ince Berg* • Irene Handl *Mrs Abramowitz* • Alfie Bass *Alf, the Bird Man* ■ *Dir* Carol Reed • *Scr* Wolf Mankowitz, from his novel

The Kid from Brooklyn ★★★ U

Musical comedy 1946 · US · Colour · 108mins

Based on Harold Lloyd's 1936 comedy *The Milky Way*, this is one of Danny Kaye's best vehicles, allowing the versatile comedian to strut his stuff as the milkman who becomes a boxing champ. If you're not a Kaye fan, this may be the movie that will make you change your mind, since it's relatively free of the sentimentality that mars so much of his later work. Producer Samuel Goldwyn surrounds his star with terrific character support and some super songs; the result is very pleasing. TS

Danny Kaye *Burleigh Sullivan* • Virginia Mayo *Polly Pringle* • Vera-Ellen *Susie Sullivan* • Walter Abel *Gabby Sloan* • Eve Arden *Ann Westley* • Steve Cochran *Speed Macfarlane* • Lionel Stander *Spider Schultz* • Fay Bainter *Mrs E Winthrop Lemoyne* ■ *Dir* Norman Z McLeod • *Scr* Don Hartman, Melville Shavelson, from the film *The Milky Way* by Grover Jones, Frank Butler, Richard Connell, from the play *The Milky Way* by Lynn Root, Harry Clork

The Kid from Left Field ★★ U

Comedy 1953 · US · BW · 80mins

Here's a cute baseball story in which Billy Chapin plays a nine-year-old kid who becomes manager of a baseball team after his advice takes it to the top of the league. In fact, it's Dan Dailey as the boy's father, a has-been player turned peanut seller, who's behind the tips. Well written by Jack Sher and directed by former editor Harmon Jones, this modest production has good support from Lloyd Bridges, Anne Bancroft and veteran Ray Collins as the club's owner. AE

Dan Dailey *Larry "Pop" Cooper* • Anne Bancroft *Marian* • Billy Chapin *Christy* • Lloyd Bridges *Pete Haines* • Ray Collins *Whacker* • Richard Egan *Billy Lorant* ■ *Dir* Harmon Jones • *Scr* Jack Sher

The Kid from Spain ★★★★ U

Musical comedy 1932 · US · BW · 91mins

This wonderfully insane Eddie Cantor vehicle has a wacky plot of confused identities, which climaxes when Cantor, mistaken for a great bullfighter, wears down an angry bull. Famed choreographer Busby Berkeley, not quite yet in his marvellous, tasteless stride, is responsible for the production numbers. Talented Leo McCarey also directed Laurel and Hardy and the Marx Brothers, and here he's aided by the cinematography of the great Gregg Toland. TS

Eddie Cantor *Eddie Williams* • Lyda Roberti *Rosalie* • Robert Young (1) *Ricardo* • Ruth Hall *Anita Gomez* • John Miljan *Pancho* • Noah Beery *Alonzo Gomez* • J Carrol Naish *Pedro* ■ *Dir* Leo McCarey • *Scr* William Anthony McGuire, Bert Kalmar, Harry Ruby

The Kid from Texas ★★ U

Western 1950 · US · Colour · 78mins

This is the film that made Audie Murphy a star. Here, America's most decorated Second World War hero plays Billy the Kid and gives a performance that completely overshadows Robert Taylor's earlier romanticised portrayal of the psychopathic killer. Murphy is riveting in a film that, frankly, is just an average Universal B-feature, given weight by its perfectly cast star and its distinguished supporting cast. TS

Audie Murphy *Billy the Kid* • Gale Storm *Irene Kain* • Albert Dekker *Alexander Kain* • Shepperd Strudwick *Jameson* • Will Geer *O'Fallon* ■ *Dir* Kurt Neumann • *Scr* Robert Hardy Andrews, Karl Kamb, from a story by Robert Hardy Andrews

Kid Galahad ★★★★ PG

Sports drama 1937 · US · BW · 97mins

Wayne Morris features as the chivalrous hotel porter in Warner Bros's fast-paced boxing saga, impeccably directed by Michael Curtiz, and teaming Edward G Robinson, Humphrey Bogart and Bette Davis. It's the mink-clad Davis, called "Fluff" who starts the action rolling, revealing sharp insights into prizefight manners and morals. Editor George Amy does a superb job in the cutting room, keeping the film on the move, and Humphrey Bogart, as a rival fight promoter, has seldom been meaner. Terrific stuff, cleverly handled and supremely entertaining. TS [video]

Edward G Robinson *Nick Donati* • Bette Davis *Louise "Fluff" Phillips* • Humphrey Bogart *Turkey Morgan* • Wayne Morris *"Kid Galahad"/Ward Guisenberry* • Jane Bryan *Marie Donati* • Harry Carey *Silver Jackson* ■ *Dir* Michael Curtiz • *Scr* Seton I Miller, from the novel by Francis Wallace

Kid Galahad ★★★ PG

Musical sports drama
1962 · US · Colour · 92mins

First filmed in 1937 with Edward G Robinson and Bette Davis, this boxing tale was considerably re-fashioned for Elvis Presley, playing the title character, a fighter who would rather be a garage mechanic. Much of the plotting was jettisoned to make way for Presley's musical interludes, and the film lacks the brittle excitement of the original, but a strong supporting cast and solid direction by Phil Karlson make this one of the singer's better movies. TV [video] DVD

Elvis Presley *Walter Gulick* • Gig Young *Willy Grogan* • Lola Albright *Dolly Fletcher* • Joan Blackman *Rose Grogan* • Charles Bronson *Lew Nyack* • Ned Glass *Lieberman* ■ *Dir* Phil Karlson • *Scr* William Fay, from the novel by Francis Wallace

Kid Glove Killer ★★★

Thriller 1942 · US · BW · 73mins

Director Fred Zinnemann's documentary background shines through here, as police laboratory workers Van Heflin and Marsha Hunt investigate the murder of the mayor. This was exactly the kind of movie that MGM made superbly, a B feature raised to A status with intelligent scripting, casting and direction. Heflin is impressive, but look closely at that stunning waitress with only two lines of dialogue – that's Ava Gardner. TS

Van Heflin *Gordon McKay* • Marsha Hunt *Jane Mitchell* • Lee Bowman *Gerald I Ladimer* • Samuel S Hinds *Mayor Daniels* • Cliff Clark *Captain Lynch* • Eddie Quillan *Eddie Wright* • Ava Gardner *Carhop* ■ *Dir* Fred Zinnemann • *Scr* Allen Rivkin, John C Higgins, from a story by John C Higgins

A Kid in Aladdin's Palace ★★

Fantasy adventure
1997 · US/Can · Colour · 89mins

This straight-to-video family film has an *Arabian Nights* setting, as a contemporary kid called Calvin gets whisked back to ancient Baghdad, magic-carpet style. There he encounters a bunch of story-tale characters: Aladdin, Ali Baba, Scheherazade and the like. A low budget means the film is a bit hit-and-myth, but less discriminating and younger kids should enjoy the genies and magic carpets. DA

Thomas Ian Nicholas *Calvin* • Rhona Mitra *Scheherazade* • Nicholas Irons *Ali Baba* • James Faulkner *Luxor* • Taylor Negron *Genie* • Aharon Ipale *Aladdin* ■ *Dir* Robert L Levy • *Scr* Michael Part, Robert L Levy, from characters created by Michael Part

Kid Millions ★★★ U

Musical comedy
1934 · US · BW and Colour · 86mins

Eddie Cantor is very much an acquired taste for modern audiences, but in his day the banjo-eyed comedian was a huge stage and screen star. The support cast is astounding: don't miss the great Nicholas Brothers dancing team, or a young Ethel Merman as a gangster's moll, or even Eve Sully as an Arab princess with a Brooklyn accent – treats indeed. The plot is one for collectors of the bizarre, as Eddie is left a fortune in Egypt. TS [video]

Eddie Cantor *Eddie Wilson Jr* • Ann Sothern *Joan Larrabee* • Ethel Merman *Dot Clark* • George Murphy *Jerry Lane* • Jesse Block *Ben Ali* • Eve Sully *Fanya* ■ *Dir* Roy Del Ruth, Willy Pogany • *Scr* Arthur Sheekman, Nat Perrin, Nunnally Johnson

Kid Nightingale ★★

Sports comedy 1939 · US · BW · 57mins

Those who don't find a boxing comedy a contradiction in terms may find this rather silly film enjoyable entertainment. John Payne plays a singing waiter who is persuaded by a promoter to become a singing boxer, Kid Nightingale. When his manager turns out to be less than honest, it's left to fiancée Jane Wyman to rescue him. There's mild comedy and a so-so song, *Who Told You I Cared?*. BB

John Payne *Steve Nelson* • Jane Wyman *Judy Craig* • Walter Catlett *Skip Davis* • Ed Brophy [Edward Brophy] *Mike Jordan* • Charles D Brown *Charles Paxton* • Max Hoffman Jr *Fitts* ■ *Dir* George Amy • *Scr* Charles Belden, Raymond Schrock, from a story by Lee Katz

Kid Rodelo ★ U

Western adventure
1966 · US/Sp · BW · 90mins

Horse opera hokum based on a Louis L'Amour tale. Ex-con Don Murray tries to retrieve some hidden gold, while staying a jump ahead of various villains – including Broderick Crawford – and the Indians. An uneasy Spanish/ US co-production, this suffers from a script crammed with clichés and fails to make the most of a good cast, which also includes Janet Leigh. JG

Don Murray *Kid Rodelo* • Janet Leigh *Nora* • Broderick Crawford *Joe Harbin* • Richard Carlson *Link* • José Nieto *Thomas Reese* ■ *Dir* Richard Carlson • *Scr* Jack Natteford, from a story by Louis L'Amour

The Kid Stays in the Picture ★★★ 15

Documentary 2001 · US · Colour · 89mins

Brett Morgen and Nanette Burstein's documentary on Robert Evans is much like the legendary US producer's movies themselves: bold, innovatively shot and highly entertaining. However, any dips it takes into life's dark side are sanitised with a brush of old Hollywood-style whitewash, usually dispensed by the man himself. The intimate story, which Evans narrates, unravels like a cautionary LA fairy tale. Crammed with priceless anecdotes about his cinematic achievements and bursting with juicy revelations about some of the movie industry's finest, it's scintillating viewing for anyone fascinated by the minutiae of celebrity life. Where this revelatory journey falls down is in the cleaning-up and rose-tinting of some events. SF [video] DVD

Robert Evans *Narrator* ■ *Dir* Brett Morgen, Nanette Burstein • *Scr* Brett Morgen, from the autobiography by Robert Evans

Kid Vengeance ★★ 15

Western 1977 · US · Colour · 86mins

This repellent revenge western teams genre veterans Lee Van Cleef and Jim Brown with 1970s teenage pop star Leif Garrett in some vain hope of snaring a gullible audience. Garrett plays a kid who goes after the killer of his parents (guess who?) and teams up with Brown's prospector whose gold has been stolen by the same man. Director Joseph Manduke pastes over the paucity of plot and simplicity of dialogue with violence and a number of savage deaths. This dispiriting affair marked Van Cleef's final foray into westerns. RS [video]

Lee Van Cleef *McClain* • Jim Brown *Isaac* • John Marley *Jesus* • Glynnis O'Connor *Lisa* • Leif Garrett *Tom* • Matt Clark *Grover* ■ *Dir* Joseph Manduke • *Scr* Bud Robbins, Jay Telfer, from a story by Ken Globus

Kidnapped ★

Adventure 1938 · US · BW · 93mins

It might have seemed a good idea at the time to team David Copperfield (Freddie Bartholomew) and the Cisco Kid (Warner Baxter) in Robert Louis Stevenson's classic action tale, but 20th Century-Fox should have also included a higher production budget and a better director than Alfred Werker. Sticking to the original story might have helped, too. This is a decidedly cheap and murky adaptation, and Baxter looks, and sounds, far too unathletic and American. TS

Warner Baxter *Alan Breck* • Freddie Bartholomew *David Balfour* • Arleen Whelan *Jean MacDonald* • C Aubrey Smith *Duke of Argyle* • Reginald Owen *Captain Hoseason* • John Carradine *Gordon* • Nigel Bruce *Neil MacDonald* • Miles Mander *Ebenezer Balfour* • Ralph Forbes *James* • HB Warner *Angus Rankeillor* ■ *Dir* Alfred Werker • *Scr* Sonya Levien, Eleanor Harris, Ernest Pascal, Edwin Blum, from the novels *Kidnapped* and *David Balfour* by Robert Louis Stevenson

Kidnapped ★ U

Adventure 1948 · US · BW · 81mins

Another weak screen version of Robert Louis Stevenson's yarn about a boy who claims an inheritance from his uncle, but is grabbed and sold into slavery. He escapes and sets off to reclaim his prize. Made by dime-budget Monogram Pictures, it stars Roddy McDowall as the young Scot saved by adventurer Alan Breck, played here by Dan O'Herlihy. McDowall's mother plays the wife of an innkeeper, her only film role. AT

Roddy McDowall *David Balfour* • Sue England *Aileen Fairlie* • Dan O'Herlihy *Alan Breck* • Roland Winters *Captain Hoseason* • Jeff Corey *Shuan* • Housley Stevenson [Houseley Stevenson] *Ebenezer* • Winefried McDowall *Innkeeper's wife* ■ *Dir* William Beaudine • *Scr* W Scott Darling, from the novel by Robert Louis Stevenson

Kidnapped ★★★ U

Adventure 1960 · US · Colour · 90mins

Robert Louis Stevenson's classic yarn is given the Walt Disney treatment, with James MacArthur playing the disinherited David Balfour and Peter Finch as the dashing Scottish loyalist who befriends him. Shot on beautiful Highland locations and with Peter O'Toole making an early screen appearance, this version of the tale is a decent enough romp. AT [video]

Peter Finch *Alan Breck* • James MacArthur *David Balfour* • Bernard Lee *Captain Hoseason* • Niall MacGinnis *Shuan* • John Laurie *Uncle Ebenezer* • Finlay Currie *Cluny MacPherson* • Peter O'Toole *Robin Oig MacGregor* • Miles Malleson *Mr Rankeillor* ■ *Dir* Robert Stevenson • *Scr* Robert Stevenson, from the novel by Robert Louis Stevenson

Kidnapped ★★★ U

Adventure 1971 · UK · Colour · 102mins

Michael Caine's witty swagger, in the role of outlaw Alan Breck, stirs some otherwise rather stiff porridge into life. Robert Louis Stevenson's stories have been filmed before, but this version is the one that is most faithful to the source, and it contains some strong performances: Trevor Howard as the Lord Advocate and Lawrence Douglas as young David keep the narrative moving along. TH [video] DVD

Michael Caine *Alan Breck* • Trevor Howard *Lord Grant* • Jack Hawkins *Captain Hoseason* • Donald Pleasence *Ebenezer Balfour* • Gordon Jackson *Charles Stewart* • Vivien Heilbron *Catriona* • Lawrence Douglas *David Balfour* ■ *Dir* Delbert Mann • *Scr* Jack Pulman, from the novel by Robert Louis Stevenson,

Kidnapped ★★★ PG

Crime drama based on a true story
1995 · US · Colour · 87mins

Dabney Coleman is one of the unsung heroes of Hollywood, equally at home in comedy or dramatic roles. In this gripping made-for-TV police thriller, he plays a serial abducter who begins a deadly cat-and-mouse game with frustrated FBI man Timothy Busfield. The two leads are backed up by strong supporting performances and no-nonsense direction from Bobby Roth. JF. Contains some violence. [video] DVD

Dabney Coleman *Arthur Milo* • Timothy Busfield *Agent Pete Honeycutt* • Lauren Tom *Lily Yee* • Tracey Walter *Oliver Tracy* • Barbara Williams (2) *Beth Honeycutt* ■ *Dir* Bobby Roth • *Scr* Thomas Baum

Kidnapped to Mystery Island ★★

Action adventure
1964 · It/W Ger · Colour · 89mins

Although this is supposed to be an all-action adventure, it is directed by Luigi Capuano with no sense of urgency and a disregard for the basics of scene-setting, which ensures that it rarely involves or convinces. It is one of the many pictures made in Italy with Guy Madison after his career had come to a virtual standstill in the US. However, he makes little impression in this thickheaded tale about the rescue of an English girl who has joined the "thugee" cult that kidnapped her some 15 years earlier. DP. Italian and German dialogue dubbed into English.

Guy Madison *Souyadhana* • Ingeborg Schöner *Edy* • Giacomo Rossi Stuart *Tremal-Naik* • Peter Van Eyck *Captain Macpherson* • Ivan Desny *Maciadi* • Giulia Rubini *Gundali* • Nando Poggi *Kammamuri* ■ *Dir* Luigi Capuano • *Scr* Arpad De Riso, Ottavio Poggi

The Kidnappers ★★★★ U

Drama 1953 · UK · BW · 89mins

Popular in its day and still charming, this drama tells the story of two Scottish orphans in turn-of-the-century Nova Scotia, who steal a baby when their stern grandfather won't let them have a dog. This slight tale is perfectly performed by two child actors, Jon Whiteley and Vincent Winter, and both youngsters received special Oscars as a result. Director Philip Leacock creates a realistic, almost documentary-like atmosphere of a closed-in, isolated community, and is helped by fine performances from Duncan Macrae and Jean Anderson as the grandparents. Charlton Heston starred in a TV movie remake, *The Little Kidnappers* (1990). TS [video]

Duncan Macrae *Granddaddy* • Jean Anderson *Grandma* • Adrienne Corri *Kirsty* • Theodore

K

Bikel *Willem Bloem* • Jon Whiteley *Harry* • Vincent Winter *Davy* • Francis De Wolff *Jan Hooft Sr* • James Sutherland *Arron McNab* • John Rae *Andrew McCleod* ■ *Dir* Philip Leacock • *Scr* Neil Paterson

The Kidnapping of the President ★★

Thriller 1980 · Can · Colour · 113mins

Terrorists kidnap President Hal Holbrook in Toronto, bundle him into a bomb-laden, booby-trapped truck and demand a hefty ransom for his release. Secret Service agent William Shatner – having beamed down from his intergalactic day job – goes to work, leaving the White House in the hands of Vice President Van Johnson and his wife Ava Gardner. AT

William Shatner *Jerry O'Connor* • Hal Holbrook *President Adam Scott* • Van Johnson *Vice President Ethan Richards* • Ava Gardner *Beth Richards* • Miguel Fernandes *Roberto Assanti* • Cindy Girling *Linda Steiner* ■ *Dir* George Mendeluk • *Scr* Richard Murphy, from a novel by Charles Templeton

kids ★★★★ 18

Drama 1995 · US · Colour · 90mins

Teenager Leo Fitzpatrick plays a self-styled "virgin surgeon", who spends his days beating up street trash, getting drunk and stoned and deflowering young girls. One of his conquests (Chloë Sevigny) tries to track him down to tell him he's HIV-positive while still dazed from her own diagnosis. Acerbically scripted by Harmony Korine and directed by influential underground photographer Larry Clark, this disturbingly explicit look at Generation X "skateboard culture" poses difficult questions and offers few easy answers. Deemed offensive exploitation by some, this is in fact highly moral and thought provoking. AJ. Contains swearing, sex scenes, drug abuse, nudity. DVD

Leo Fitzpatrick *Telly* • Justin Pierce *Casper* • Chloë Sevigny *Jennie* • Sarah Henderson *Girl* • Rosario Dawson *Ruby* • Harold Hunter *Harold* • Joseph Chan *Deli owner* ■ *Dir* Larry Clark • *Scr* Harmony Korine, from a story by Larry Clark, Jim Lewis

The Kids Are Alright ★★★ 15

Music documentary
1978 · UK · BW and Colour · 96mins

The value of this "rockumentary" trip through the highs and lows of The Who's career was increased by the death of the band's extrovert drummer Keith Moon in September 1978. However, fans will probably not want to dwell on the frankly depressing final concert footage, preferring to see Moon in classic 1960s action, when his hellraising was matched by his extraordinary on-stage energy. Director Jeff Stein occasionally errs into hagiography, but there's a generous sampling of hits (and the odd miss), interviews and rare archival material, as well as guest appearances by Steve Martin, Ringo Starr, Melvyn Bragg and Jeremy Paxman. DP DVD

Dir/Scr Jeff Stein

Kids in the Hall: Brain Candy ★★ 15

Comedy 1996 · Can/US · Colour · 84mins

Canada's answer to *Saturday Night Live* makes its first foray into the movies here. The all-male team's determination to play virtually every major role (as well as their penchant for dressing up in women's clothing) makes *Monty Python* a closer reference point, although they're not in the same league. However, this sketchy story of a young doctor who discovers a cure for depression has its moments. JF. Contains swearing and brief nudity.

Dave Foley *Marv/Psychiatrist/Suicidal businessman/New guy/Raymond* • Bruce McCulloch *Grivo/Alice/Cisco/Cop/White-trash man/Cancer boy* • Kevin McDonald *Chris Cooper/Chris's dad/Doreen* • Mark McKinney *Don Roritor/Simon/German patient/Nina Bedford/Cabbie/White-trash woman* • Scott Thompson *Wally Terzinsky/Mrs Hurdicure/ Baxter/Malek/Clemptor/The Queen* ■ *Dir* Kelly Makin • *Scr* Norm Hiscock, Bruce McCulloch, Kevin McDonald, Mark McKinney, Scott Thompson

Kids Return ★★★ 15

Crime comedy drama
1996 · Jpn · Colour · 107mins

This was the first feature director Takeshi Kitano completed after he fractured his skull in a near-fatal scooter accident. With two pals forming a stand-up comedy team, there's a strong sense of autobiography about this rites-of-passage picture. But the main focus falls on Masanobu Ando and Ken Kaneko, two schoolboys who leave the education system with little option but to drift into boxing and crime respectively. Cross-cutting with typical energy and invention, Kitano persuades us to warm to these underachievers. DP. In Japanese with English subtitles.

Masanobu Ando *Shinji Takagi* • Ken Kaneko *Masaru Miyawaki* • Leo Morimoto *Teacher* • Hatsuo Yamaya *Boxing club manager* • Mitsuko Oka *Coffee shop owner, Sachiko's mother* • Ryo Ishibashi *Local yakuza chief* ■ *Dir/Scr* Takeshi Kitano

Kids World ★★★

Comedy adventure
2001 · NZ/US · Colour · 96mins

This jolly comedy is bound to appeal to any pre-teen tired of being bossed around by either grown-ups or their senior siblings. Bullied at school and virtually invisible at home, 12-year-old Blake Foster's so-called life is transformed when he stumbles across a native American wishing glass and casts his elders into oblivion. However, the resulting kiddie utopia comes with an *Logan's Run*-style catch. Foster carries the picture with surprising aplomb, although Christopher Lloyd can't resist stealing the odd scene. DP

Christopher Lloyd *Leo* • Blake Foster *Ryan* • Michael Purvis *Twinkie* • Anton Tennet *Stu* ■ *Dir* Dale G Bradley • *Scr* Michael Lach

Kika ★★ 18

Comedy 1993 · Sp · Colour · 109mins

This offers up a familiar diet of sexual deviance, rape, murder and the media from Pedro Almodóvar, famous for his absurd irony and outrageous imagination. A master at creating, then tying up, the most convoluted plots, this is from his lacklustre middle period and focuses on shallow make-up artist Veronica Forqué, who makes up a dead body as a favour for a serial-killing author. But the stiff of said novelist's stepson's lesbian maid's psychologically disturbed porno-star brother suddenly comes back to life! A pointless charade. AJ. In Spanish with English subtitles.

Verónica Forqué *Kika* • Peter Coyote *Nicholas* • Victoria Abril *Andrea Caracortada* • Alex Casanovas *Ramón* • Rossy de Palma *Juana* • Santiago Lajusticia *Pablo* • Anabel Alonso *Amparo* • Bibi Andersen *Susana* ■ *Dir/Scr* Pedro Almodóvar

Kikuchi ★★★

Drama 1990 · Jpn · Colour · 68mins

Disconcerting in its depiction of tedious routine, yet bristling with a sense of latent violence, this brooding study of voyeurism and the dehumanising effect of modern city life marked the directorial debut of one-time *manga* artist Kenchi Iwamoto. Considering its relatively short length, the film is so successful in conveying the stupefyingly dull nature of Jiro Yoshimura's laundry job that his obsessional pursuit of checkout girl Misa Fukuma almost becomes understandable. Almost. DP. In Japanese with English subtitles.

Jiro Yoshimura *Kikuchi* • Yasuhiro Oka *Man* • Misa Fukuma *Woman* ■ *Dir/Scr* Kenchi Iwamoto

Kikujiro ★★★★★ 12

Comedy drama 1999 · Jpn · Colour · 116mins

With the violence that has characterised so many of his films toned down to slapstick socko, this is Takeshi Kitano's offbeat homage to *The Wizard of Oz*. As the amoral yakuza who accompanies nine-year-old Yusuke Sekiguchi on a cross-country mission to find his mother, Kitano gives an inspired demonstration of muddle-headed, short-fused deadpan. The duo meanders from racetrack to fairground, encountering en route a paedophile, a rude hotel clerk and a couple of soft-centred bikers. There are no deep messages here, just dream sequences, unexpected revelations and several achingly funny set pieces. A gem from a genius. DP. In Japanese with English subtitles. DVD

"Beat" Takeshi [Takeshi Kitano] *Kikujiro* • Kayoko Kishimoto *Miki, Kikujiro's wife* • Yusuke Sekiguchi *Masao* • Akaji Maro *Paedophile* • Yuko Daike *Masao's mother* ■ *Dir/Scr* Takeshi Kitano

Kill! ★

Thriller
1972 · Fr/It/Sp/W Ger · Colour · 102mins

Celebrated novelist Romain Gary directs this paper-thin co-production with little demonstrable understanding of the mechanics of movie-making. By allowing his tale of drug smuggling and porn peddling to quickly sprawl out of control, he sheds vital clues to the identity of the master criminal with such abandon that the solution is apparent almost from the outset. James Mason looks glum as the man from Interpol, but beside Jean Seberg as his wife he seems exhilarated. DP

James Mason *Alan* • Jean Seberg *Emily* • Stephen Boyd *Killian* • Curt Jurgens *Chief* • Daniel Emilfork *Inspector* • Henri Garcin *Lawyer* ■ *Dir* Herb Shriner • *Scr* Romain Gary

Kill a Dragon ★

Martial arts action adventure
1967 · US · Colour · 97mins

Rarely seen and largely unlamented, this muddled adventure with Jack Palance finds him in China to battle crime lord Fernando Lamas. The other familiar face in the cast is screen veteran Aldo Ray, but all three leads can do little with the preposterous, haphazard plotting. JF

Jack Palance *Rick* • Fernando Lamas *Patrai* • Aldo Ray *Vigo* • Alizia Gur *Tisa* • Tong Kam *Win Lim* ■ *Dir* Michael Moore (1) • *Scr* George Schenck, William Marks

Kill and Kill Again ★★★ 15

Martial arts action
1981 · US · Colour · 94mins

James Ryan is a world-famous martial artist, recruited by Anneline Kriel to save her father – a scientist who can make fuel out of potatoes – from an evil dictator. To do this, Ryan recruits guys with names like the Fly, Gorilla and Hotdog. Probably the best karate film ever made in South Africa, though that's not much of a recommendation. Lovers of cult movies will be in seventh heaven, however. ST

James Ryan *Steve Chase* • Anneline Kriel *Kandy Kane* • Ken Gampu *Gorilla* • Norman Robinson *Gypsy Billy* • Stan Schmidt *The Fly* • Bill Flynn *Hotdog* • Michael Mayer *Marduk* ■ *Dir* Ivan Hall • *Scr* John Crowther

Kill and Pray ★★★ 15

Spaghetti western
1967 · It/W Ger · Colour · 102mins

In the grand tradition of *A Bullet for the General*, director Carlo Lizzani's political western finds Lou Castel's hero Requiescant helping rebel bandits in their struggle against foreign financiers who are propping up a counter-revolutionary federal government. The Italian director Pier Paolo Pasolini was so impressed with the radical script of this spaghetti western with a difference that he agreed to appear in it as a revolutionary priest. Film scholar Lizzani wrote a full-length study of Italian cinema in the 1950s. TH. Italian dialogue dubbed into English.

Lou Castel *Requiescant* • Mark Damon *Ferguson* • Barbara Frey *Princy* • Pier Paolo Pasolini *Don Juan* • Franco Citti *Burt* ■ *Dir* Carlo Lizzani

Kill Bill Vol 1 ★★★★ 18

Part-animated martial arts drama
2003 · US · Colour and BW · 106mins

Quentin Tarantino marshals a bewildering number of multi-genre references into a hypnotically entertaining whole in this violent martial arts revenge drama. Giving a searing performance, Uma Thurman plays one of the Deadly Vipers, a crack assassination squad led by the eponymous Bill (David Carradine). Left for dead on her wedding day, she falls into a coma, only to awaken four years later swearing revenge on her traitorous co-workers. *Vol 1* deals with two members on her Death List Five: Vernita Green (Vivica A Fox) and O-Ren Ishii (Lucy Liu). Dripping with bloody ultra-violence and using startling flashbacks, knowingly fake dubbing and a quite brilliant *animé* section, this is both a daring experiment in sampled cinematic language and scrounged style, and a gloriously enchanting work of neo-art in itself. AJ. In English and Japanese with subtitles. Contains violence and swearing. DVD

Uma Thurman *The Bride/"Black Mamba"* • David Carradine *Bill* • Lucy Liu *O-Ren Ishii/ "Cottonmouth"* • Daryl Hannah *Elle Driver/ "California Mountain Snake"* • Vivica A Fox *Vernita Green/"Copperhead"* • Michael Madsen *Budd/"Sidewinder"* • Michael Parks *Sheriff* • Sonny Chiba *Hattori Hanzo* • Chiaki Kuriyama *Go Go Yubari* • Julie Dreyfus *Sofie Fatale* ■ *Dir* Quentin Tarantino • *Scr* Quentin Tarantino, from the character created by Q & U [Quentin Tarantino, Uma Thurman]

Kill Bill Vol 2 ★★★ 18

Martial arts drama
2003 · US · Colour and BW · 131mins

Long-winded, overly self-indulgent and talky, director Quentin Tarantino's wrap-up of his bloody revenge saga is something of an anti-climax. Detailing how the Bride (Uma Thurman) tracks down Deadly Viper assassins Budd (Michael Madsen) and Elle Driver (Daryl Hannah), before facing Bill (David Carradine) and an unexpected "adversary", it's the same mix as before except less visually dynamic and with a lot more unnecessary exposition. Yet the borrowed style, plus all the usual obscure genre references, still make this compressed exploitation-cinema history lesson into a buff treat. AJ. In English, Japanese and Mandarin with subtitles. Contains violence. DVD

Uma Thurman *Beatrix Kiddo/The Bride/"Black Mamba"/Mommy* • David Carradine *Bill/ "Snake Charmer"* • Daryl Hannah *Elle Driver/ "California Mountain Snake"* • Michael Madsen *Budd/"Sidewinder"* • Michael Parks *Earl McGraw/Esteban Vihaio* • Gordon Liu

Johnny Mo/Pai Mei • Samuel L Jackson *Rufus* • Bo Svenson *Reverend Harmony* ■ *Dir* Quentin Tarantino • *Scr* Quentin Tarantino, from the character created by Q & U [Quentin Tarantino, Uma Thurman]

Kill Me Again ★★★ 18

Crime thriller 1989 · US · Colour · 92mins

Marking John Dahl's directorial debut, this is far from flawless, but Dahl (*The Last Seduction*) demonstrates an already instinctive touch for *femmes fatales* and flawed heroes in a typically convoluted story about private detective Val Kilmer who is persuaded by beautiful Joanne Whalley-Kilmer to help her fake her death. Notable for providing an early psycho role for *Reservoir Dogs's* Michael Madsen, the main problem here is the two leads, who fail to convince. JF. Contains sex scenes, violence, swearing. [video] DVD

Joanne Whalley-Kilmer [Joanne Whalley] *Fay Forrester* • Val Kilmer *Jack Andrews* • Michael Madsen *Vince Miller* • Jonathan Gries *Alan Swayzie* • Pat Mulligan *Sammy* ■ *Dir* John Dahl • *Scr* David W Warfield, John Dahl

Kill Me If You Can ★★★★

Drama based on a true story
1977 · US · Colour · 100mins

In one of his most accomplished TV-movie roles, Alan Alda is riveting in the true story of Caryl Chessman, the notorious "Red Light Bandit", who served 12 years on death row before being executed in 1960. As the erudite Chessman, Alda veers between rage and serene determination with mesmerising power, and his performance was rewarded with an Emmy nomination. TV movies rarely come this stark or involving. AJ

Alan Alda *Caryl Chessman* • Talia Shire *Rosalie Asher* • John Hillerman *George Davis* • Barnard Hughes *Judge Fricke* ■ *Dir* Buzz Kulik • *Scr* John Gay

Kill Me Later ★★★ 15

Romantic comedy drama
2001 · US · Colour · 85mins

This offbeat, if patchy, comedy drama gets by on the charm of its two leads. Selma Blair is the depressed bank worker whose suicide bid is interrupted by would-be robber Max Beesley. She agrees to be his hostage on the condition that he kill her later. The sketchiness of the material occasionally shows through, and Dana Lustig's direction is also a little too tricksy for its own good. Blair and Beesley, however, make for a charming couple. JF [video]

Selma Blair *Shawn Holloway* • Max Beesley *Charlie Anders* • O'Neal Compton *Agent McGinley* • Lochlyn Munro *Agent Reed* • DW Moffett *Matthew Richmond* • Billy Fehr *Billy* ■ *Dir* Dana Lustig • *Scr* Annette Goliti Gutierrez, Dana Lustig

Kill Me Tomorrow ★★ U

Crime drama 1957 · UK · BW · 80mins

Warner Bros rarely pushed lead roles Pat O'Brien's way. Even so, it's hard to fathom why he crossed the Atlantic for the starring role in this far-fetched B-movie. You might expect an impoverished father trying to fund his son's eye operation to resort to some pretty desperate tactics – but confessing to a murder in order to raise the money? Terence Fisher directs with little enthusiasm, but it's worth hanging in there to catch the debut of Tommy Steele. DP

Pat O'Brien *Bart Crosbie* • Lois Maxwell *Jill Brook* • George Coulouris *Heinz Webber* • Wensley Pithey *Inspector Lane* • Freddie Mills *Waxy* • Ronald Adam *Brook* • Tommy Steele ■ *Dir* Terence Fisher • *Scr* Manning O'Brine, Robert Falconer

The Kill-Off ★★★ 18

Thriller 1989 · US · Colour · 93mins

The bleakness contained in Jim Thompson's hard-boiled novels has been a notoriously difficult tone to pull off in movie adaptations of his work, but director Maggie Greenwald's bitter little thriller does a better job than most. Loretta Gross stands out in the no-name ensemble cast as the vicious gossip-monger in a small American town, whose acid tongue is feared by every local resident. So they decide to do something to silence her. Not a great advert for human nature, but an engaging mood piece that's both grim and grimy. AJ. Contains swearing, drug abuse and nudity. [video]

Loretta Gross *Luane Devore* • Jackson Sims *Pete Pavlov* • Steve Monroe *Ralph* • Andrew Lee Barrett *Bobbie Ashton* • Cathy Haase *Danny Lee* • Jorjan Fox [Jorja Fox] *Myra Pavlov* ■ *Dir* Maggie Greenwald • *Scr* Maggie Greenwald, from a novel by Jim Thompson

Kill or Cure ★ U

Comedy mystery 1962 · UK · BW · 88mins

This is the kind of comedy that could have killed off the British film industry, despite its domestic star-power and the usually reliable writing team of David Pursall and Jack Seddon. When bumbling private detective Terry-Thomas tries to investigate a murder at a posh spa, the only interest is in seeing him lock comedy horns with Eric Sykes and Lionel Jeffries. Unfortunately, it is to little effect. TH

Terry-Thomas *J Barker-Rynde* • Eric Sykes *Rumbelow* • Dennis Price *Dr Crossley* • Lionel Jeffries *Inspector Hook* • Moira Redmond *Frances Reitman* • Ronnie Barker *Burton* ■ *Dir* George Pollock • *Scr* David Pursall, Jack Seddon

The Killer ★★★★ 18

Action thriller 1989 · HK · Colour · 106mins

A Hong Kong gangster movie that's directed with such over-the-top verve by John Woo you're transfixed by its audacity, despite several stomach-churning scenes of violence. Chow Yun-Fat plays the assassin who decides to quit his profession after accidentally blinding a singer (Sally Yeh) during a hit in a nightclub. When he learns that her sight could be restored through an operation, he decides to fund it by doing just one more job. Of its amoral kind it's great bullet-dodging fun, but it's definitely not for the faint-hearted. TH. In Cantonese with English subtitles. Contains violence, nudity. [video] DVD

Chow Yun-Fat *Jeff* • Danny Lee *Inspector "Eagle" Lee* • Sally Yeh *Jennie* • Kong Chu *Sydney Fung* • Kenneth Tsang *Sergeant Randy Chung* • Chung Lam *Willie Tsang* • Shing Fui-on *Johnny Weng* ■ *Dir/Scr* John Woo

Killer ★★ 18

Crime thriller 1994 · US · Colour · 93mins

Gangland hitman Anthony LaPaglia meets his match when he's assigned *femme fatale* Mimi Rogers as his last kill; the twist in director Mark Malone's contemporary *film noir* is that Rogers knows she's due to die and intends to make the heartless killer feel as guilty as possible. Is she his saviour, or his downfall? That's the central enigma of this pretentious look at the human condition. The stars deliver strong performances, but it's percolating with unfulfilled promise. AJ. Contains sex scenes, swearing, violence. [video]

Anthony LaPaglia *Mick* • Mimi Rogers *Fiona* • Matt Craven *Archie* • Peter Boyle *George* • Monika Schnarre *Laura* • Joseph Maher *Dr Alstricht* ■ *Dir* Mark Malone • *Scr* Gordon Melbourne, from a story by Mark Malone

Killer: a Journal of Murder ★★★ 18

Biographical prison drama
1995 · US · Colour and BW · 87mins

This violent drama is carried along by the intensity of James Woods's performance as Carl Panzram, who, having confessed to murdering 21 people, had the dubious "honour" of being one of America's first recognised serial killers. Robert Sean Leonard plays Henry Lesser, a liberal prison guard who sees the value in Panzram writing down his story for future reference. Leonard's approach contrasts with that of Robert John Burke, who plays a hard-line warden. An absorbing, if violent, case history. AJ. Contains swearing, violence. [video]

James Woods *Carl Panzram* • Robert Sean Leonard *Henry Lesser* • Ellen Greene *Elizabeth Wyatt* • Cara Buono *Esther Lesser* • Robert John Burke [Robert Burke] *RG Greiser* • Steve Forrest *Warden Charles Casey* • Jeffrey DeMunn *Sam Lesser* ■ *Dir* Tim Metcalfe • *Scr* Tim Metcalfe, from the non-fiction book by Thomas E Gaddis, James O Long

Killer Calibre 32 ★★

Spaghetti western 1967 · It · Colour

A spaghetti western that owes more to Saturday matinée series than to the grand designs of Sergio Leone. Peter Lee Lawrence stars as a dandified bounty hunter, hired to uncover the true identities of the seven masked men who have been repeatedly robbing the Carson City stagecoach. At least director Alfonso Brescia has the sense to realise that this has to be played tongue in cheek, and keeps the action moving at a fair lick. DP. Italian dialogue dubbed into English.

Peter Lee Lawrence *Silver* • Cole Kitosch *Averell* • Sherill Morgan ■ *Dir* Alfonso Brescia • *Scr* Gicca Lorenzo Palli

The Killer Elite ★★★ 18

Action thriller 1975 · US · Colour · 118mins

When the picture he wanted to make – *The Insurance Company* – was abruptly cancelled by the studio, Sam Peckinpah went straight on to direct this, which was already written, cast and ready to go. As a result, Peckinpah had nothing but contempt for this San Francisco-based thriller. *Godfather* co-stars James Caan and Robert Duvall are reunited in this tale of CIA spooks, car chases, martial artistry and bloody shoot-outs. The result is both quite exciting and instantly forgettable. AT [video] DVD

James Caan *Mike Locken* • Robert Duvall *George Hansen* • Arthur Hill *Cap Collis* • Bo Hopkins *Jerome Miller* • Mako *Yuen Chung* • Burt Young *Mac* • Gig Young *Laurence Weyburn* • Tom Clancy *O'Leary* ■ *Dir* Sam Peckinpah • *Scr* Marc Norman, Stirling Silliphant, from the novel *Monkey in the Middle* by Robert Rostand

Killer Fish ★★ 15

Adventure thriller
1978 · It/Bra · Colour · 96mins

In this interestingly cast co-production, a selected handful of near-stars enjoy an exotic Brazilian location shoot while pretending to hunt for purloined jewels in a lake full of piranha. Margaux Hemingway and Marisa Berenson feature, although there's a serious warning here to models who attempt acting careers. But it's still the best cast director Antonio Margheriti, purveyor of spaghetti western and horror, ever assembled. TS [video]

Lee Majors *Robert Lasky* • Karen Black *Kate Neville* • James Franciscus *Paul Diller* • Margaux Hemingway *Gabrielle* • Marisa Berenson *Ann* • Gary Collins *Tom* • Roy Brocksmith *Ollie* • Dan Pastorini *Hans* ■ *Dir* Anthony M Dawson [Antonio Margheriti] • *Scr* Michael Rogers

Killer Force ★★

Action thriller
1975 · Swi/Ire · Colour · 98mins

This thriller concerns a plot to rob a diamond mine in South Africa. Chief of security Telly Savalas teams up with Peter Fonda to foil the scheme. Director Val Guest's film features some impressive location footage; unfortunately, it also contains some tiresome philosophising. Maud Adams, as Fonda's girlfriend, seems bored rigid, while Christopher Lee appears as a disaffected British soldier. AT

Telly Savalas *Harry Webb* • Peter Fonda *Mike Bradley* • Christopher Lee *Chilton* • OJ Simpson *"Bopper" Alexander* • Maud Adams *Clare Chambers* • Hugh O'Brian *Lewis* ■ *Dir* Val Guest • *Scr* Val Guest, Michael Winder, Gerald Sanford

The Killer inside Me ★★ 18

Thriller 1975 · US · Colour · 91mins

Adapted from a novel by Jim Thompson, a classy purveyor of cult pulp fiction, this never quite convinces as it attempts to show the disintegration of well-respected deputy sheriff Stacy Keach into uncontrollable mania. Keach is one of those risk-all actors who can do many things; one thing he can't do, though, is to stand up to the clunkingly obvious direction of Burt Kennedy. TH [video]

Stacy Keach *Lou Ford* • Susan Tyrrell *Joyce Lakeland* • Tisha Sterling *Amy Stanton* • Keenan Wynn *Chester Conway* • Don Stroud *Elmer Conway* • Charles McGraw *Howard Hendricks* • John Dehner *Bob Maples* • John Carradine *Dr Smith* ■ *Dir* Burt Kennedy • *Scr* Edward Mann, Robert Chamblee, from the novel by Jim Thompson

The Killer Is Loose ★★★

Crime drama 1956 · US · BW · 73mins

A perceptive critic described Budd Boetticher's films as "small, glittering morality plays". In this neglected thriller, Wendell Corey stars as a bank clerk, involved in a robbery, whose wife is accidentally killed during the subsequent arrest. The seemingly mild-mannered clerk is sent to prison, escaping after three years. Now psychotic and revengeful he embarks on eye-for-an-eye retribution against the cop (Joseph Cotten) who shot his wife. This was Boetticher's first significant urban-set movie, directed with characteristic economy and building to a stunning climax. BB

Joseph Cotten *Sam Wagner* • Rhonda Fleming *Lila Wagner* • Wendell Corey *Leon "Foggy" Poole* • Alan Hale Jr *Denny* ■ *Dir* Budd Boetticher • *Scr* Harold Medford, from a story by John Hawkins, Ward Hawkins

Killer Klowns from Outer Space ★★★ 15

Science-fiction horror comedy
1988 · US · Colour · 82mins

Combining inspired amateur brashness, delightful *Loony Tunes* design and a winningly bizarre unreality, this engagingly cheap affair from effects wizards Stephen and Charles Chiodo is an infantile and vicious delight. Alien clowns invade Earth in a spacecraft masquerading as a circus tent; they intend to cocoon the local population in candy floss and suck out their life juices, unless two teens and a cop can stop them. This cleverly pays homage to 1950s' schlock, but with its acid custard pies, homicidal Jack in the Boxes and malevolent Punch and Judy shows, this is definitely not for children. AJ [video]

Grant Cramer *Mike* • Suzanne Snyder *Debbie* • John Allen Nelson *Officer Dave Hanson* • Royal Dano *Farmer Green* • John Vernon *Officer Mooney* ■ *Dir* Stephen Chiodo • *Scr* Stephen Chiodo, Charles Chiodo

K

Killer McCoy ★★

Sports drama 1947 · US · BW · 103mins

In this so-called "adult drama", designed to show he wasn't just able to play Andy Hardy, Mickey Rooney is cast as the son of a drunken entertainer who accidentally kills his best friend and takes over as a lightweight boxing champion. It's as implausible as only MGM can make it, and much emphasis is put on the pain that Rooney has endured to get there and keeps enduring when being punched senseless in the ring. AT

Mickey Rooney *Tommy McCoy* • Brian Donlevy *Jim Caighn* • Ann Blyth *Sheila Carrson* • James Dunn *Brian McCoy* • Tom Tully *Cecil Y Walsh* • Sam Levene *Happy* • Walter Sande *Bill Thorne* ■ *Dir* Roy Rowland • *Scr* Frederick Hazlitt Brennan, from the 1938 film *The Crowd Roars* by Thomas Lennon, George Bruce, George Oppenheimer • *Music/lyrics* Stanley Donen

Killer Nun ★★★ 18

Cult horror 1978 · It · Colour · 80mins

Morphine addiction, lesbianism, gore, scandal and Catholic guilt: it's all here in a gleefully demented Italian schlock cocktail that wallows in nasty sleaze while adopting an inappropriate and hilariously pious attitude. Anita Ekberg plays a paranoid nun who isn't sure if her homicidal nightmares are the real thing or not in trash merchant Giulio Berruti's bad-taste shocker, packed with sinful sex sessions and hard-edged violence. Andy Warhol icon Joe Dallesandro as a doctor and *The Third Man* beauty Alida Valli as the mother superior add extra cult value. AJ. In Italian with English subtitles.

Anita Ekberg *Sister Gertrud* • Joe Dallesandro *Dr Rowland* • Lou Castel *Peter* • Alida Valli *Mother Superior* ■ *Dir* Giulio Berruti • *Scr* Giulio Berruti, Alberto Tarallo

Killer Party ★★ 18

Horror 1986 · US · Colour · 87mins

It's April Fool's Day in this standard dead-teens-on-campus slasher tale involving lethal fraternity hi-jinks and a vengeful killer wearing a diver's suit. After a promising start, involving a film-within-a-rock-video-within-a-film sucker-punch, and despite some creative modes of murder, this good-looking nonsense drifts into a repetitive groove of laughs and scares. However, the late cult director Paul Bartel is as delightful as always, playing a stuffy professor. AJ

Martin Hewitt *Blake* • Ralph Seymour *Martin* • Elaine Wilkes *Phoebe* • Paul Bartel *Professor Zito* ■ *Dir* William Fruet • *Scr* Barney Cohen

The Killer Shrews ★ PG

Science-fiction horror
1959 · US · BW · 68mins

For sheer nerve the makers ought to have grabbed an Oscar for attempting to demonise an animal not much bigger than a mouse. However these are not just ordinary shrews, but the rampaging and flesh-eating side effects of genetic research carried out by bonkers scientist Baruch Lumet (father of noted director Sidney Lumet). The film boasts inept special effects and bargain-basement production values, contributing to its status today as a cult bad movie. RS

James Best *Thorne Sherman* • Ingrid Goude *Ann Craigis* • Baruch Lumet *Dr Craigis* • Ken Curtis *Jerry Lacer* • Gordon McLendon *Radford Baines* • Alfredo DeSoto *Mario* ■ *Dir* Ray Kellogg • *Scr* Jay Simms

Killer Tongue ★ 18

Horror 1996 · Sp/UK · Colour · 94mins

This sloppy made-in-Spain venture is a mixture of horror and humour posing as camp genre pastiche. Following her close encounter with an alien meteorite, amoral bank robber Melinda Clarke inexplicably grows an 18ft-long tongue which commits all manner of stupidly gory crimes on nuns, escaped prisoners and other lust-crazed victims. A tacky collage of hammy performances and shaky special effects. Spainful! AJ

Melinda Clarke *Candy* • Jason Durr *Johnny* • Mapi Galán *Rita* • Mabel Karr *Old nun* • Robert Englund *Chief screw* • Alicia Borrachero *Reporter* • Doug Bradley *Wig* • Michael Cule *Frank* ■ *Dir/Scr* Alberto Sciamma

The Killers ★★★★★ PG

Classic film noir 1946 · US · BW · 98mins

One of the most powerful and influential thrillers ever made, with director Robert Siodmak's bleak and pessimistic tone virtually defining the term *film noir*. Based on a short story of remarkable power by Ernest Hemingway, the movie broadens the tale superbly with intricate flashbacks and features a stunning film debut from Burt Lancaster, all coiled anger as the fall guy, and there's also a career-defining role for Ava Gardner as the *femme fatale*. The design is clearly influenced by cult artist Edward Hopper; Miklos Rosza's superb score that was made even more memorable when it was used again for TV's *Dragnet*. The Don Siegel version with Lee Marvin and Ronald Reagan is good, but don't miss this marvellous original. TS

Burt Lancaster *Ole "Swede" Anderson/Pete Lunn* • Ava Gardner *Kitty Collins* • Edmond O'Brien *Jim Reardon* • Albert Dekker *Big Jim Colfax* • Sam Levene *Lieutenant Sam Lubinsky* • Charles D Brown *Packy Robinson* • Donald MacBride *Kenyon* • Phil Brown *Nick Adams* • Charles McGraw *Al* • William Conrad *Max* • Vince Barnett *Charleston* ■ *Dir* Robert Siodmak • *Scr* Anthony Veiller, John Huston, from a short story by Ernest Hemingway • *Cinematographer* Elwood Bredell • *Set Designer* Jack Otterson, Martin Obzina • *Editor* Arthur Hilton

The Killers ★★★ 18

Crime thriller 1964 · US · Colour · 90mins

Ernest Hemingway's short story had already inspired a movie in 1946; this film was not a remake but a separate version of the tale. John Cassavetes is killed by hitmen Lee Marvin and Clu Gulager, who join forces to find out why the contract was ordered in the first place. Marvin exudes his usual power and menace in a dry run for his *Point Blank* character, and Ronald Reagan makes his last screen appearance before moving into politics. This was originally made for TV but released in cinemas because of its violent content. AT

Lee Marvin *Charlie Strom* • John Cassavetes *Johnny North* • Angie Dickinson *Sheila Farr* • Ronald Reagan *Jack Browning* • Clu Gulager *Lee* • Claude Akins *Earl Sylvester* • Norman Fell *Mickey Farmer* ■ *Dir* Donald Siegel [Don Siegel] • *Scr* Gene L Coon, from a short story by Ernest Hemingway

Killer's Kiss ★★★ 12

Crime drama 1955 · US · BW · 64mins

With films such as *Dr Strangelove*, *2001* and *A Clockwork Orange*, Stanley Kubrick became one of the world's most famous directors, but he began with low-budget thrillers. *Killer's Kiss*, his second film and a boxing-gangland story, has that streak of fatalism and cynicism that marks his later work. There is a terrific climax, when hero and villain have a fight surrounded by mannequins, plus a spurious ballet sequence featuring Kubrick's second wife Ruth Sobotka. It's a fascinating work, albeit weakly acted and rough at the edges. AT DVD

Frank Silvera *Vincent Rapallo* • Jamie Smith *Davy Gordon* • Irene Kane *Gloria Price* • Jerry Jarret *Albert* • Mike Dana *Hoodlum* • Felice Orlandi *Hoodlum* • Ralph Roberts *Hoodlum* • Phil Stevenson *Hoodlum* ■ *Dir* Stanley Kubrick • *Scr* Howard O Sackler, Stanley Kubrick, from a story by Stanley Kubrick

Killers of Kilimanjaro ★★ PG

Adventure 1960 · UK · Colour · 87mins

A typically schlocky outdoor adventure produced by Albert Broccoli, co-written by Richard Maibaum and shot by Ted Moore before they all hit gold with the Bond movies. Robert Taylor, a pricey Hollywood import, plays an engineer who is building a railroad and looking for some missing persons who may or may not have been kidnapped. Lions and natives play the part of bad guys if this is regarded as an African western, which it is. AT

Robert Taylor (1) *Robert Adamson* • Anne Aubrey *Jane Carlton* • John Dimech *Pasha* • Grégoire Aslan *Ben Ahmed* • Anthony Newley *Hooky Hook* • Donald Pleasence *Captain* ■ *Dir* Richard Thorpe • *Scr* John Gilling, Earl Felton, Richard Maibaum, Cyril Hume, from the book *African Bush Adventures* by JA Hunter, Daniel P Mannix

The Killing ★★★★ PG

Thriller 1956 · US · BW · 80mins

Stanley Kubrick's third feature is a thriller about a racetrack robbery, but he scrambles the time sequence and follows separate strands of the plot, detailing the planning, the robbery itself and the disastrous aftermath. Kubrick turns a familiar story into a masterly display of technique and a moving study of desperate characters who are in thrall to fate. Kirk Douglas was so impressed by the film that he agreed to star in Kubrick's next project, *Paths of Glory*, the success of which set the seal on Kubrick's reputation. AT DVD

Sterling Hayden *Johnny Clay* • Coleen Gray *Fay* • Marie Windsor *Sherry Peatty* • Elisha Cook Jr *George Peatty* • Jay C Flippen *Marvin Unger* • Vince Edwards *Val Cannon* • Ted De Corsia *Randy Kennan* ■ *Dir* Stanley Kubrick • *Scr* Jim Thompson, Stanley Kubrick, from the novel *Clean Break* by Lionel White

A Killing Affair ★★★

Psychological crime thriller
1985 · US · Colour · 100mins

This tale of Southern intrigue concerns the murder of Kathy Baker's fickle husband and the arrival of a mysterious stranger (Peter Weller). Is he the one responsible for the deed? Directing for the first time, David Saperstein's everyday story of backward folk in the backwoods has enough surprising twists and turns to keep you guessing. TH

Peter Weller *Baston Morris* • Kathy Baker *Maggie Gresham* • John Glover *Maggie's brother* • Bill Smitrovich *Pink Gresham* ■ *Dir* David Saperstein • *Scr* David Saperstein, from the novel *Monday, Tuesday, Wednesday* by Robert Houston

Killing Box ★★★ 18

Horror thriller 1993 · US · Colour · 78mins

An evil African force turns massacred Civil War soldiers into bloodthirsty zombies, who then go on a cannibalistic and crucifixion rampage. This highly unusual art house horror is too intense for the audience it's aimed at, yet too anaemic for gore fans. Nevertheless, director George Hickenlooper's grainy, documentary-style mood piece is a skilful work of hypnotic power. AJ

Corbin Bernsen *Colonel Nehemiah Strayn* • Adrian Pasdar *Captain John Harling* • Cynda Williams *Rebecca* • Ray Wise *Colonel George Thalman* • Martin Sheen *General Haworth* • Jefferson Mays *Martin Bradley* • Billy Bob Thornton *Langston* • David Arquette *Murphy* • Matt LeBlanc *Terhune* ■ *Dir* George Hickenlooper • *Scr* Matt Greenberg

Killing Cars ★★ 15

Mystery thriller
1986 · W Ger · Colour · 96mins

A disappointing early venture from the director of *The Nasty Girl*. As soon as he patents a non-polluting automobile, inventor Jürgen Prochnow becomes the target of international financiers and oil magnates, who fear the collapse of their empires if it's a success. A decent array of familar faces compete for close-ups, but the camera is more interested in Verhoeven's wife, Senta Berger. This never gets out of low gear. DP. German dialogue dubbed into English.

Jürgen Prochnow *Ralph Korda* • Senta Berger *Marie* • Agnes Soral *Violet* • Daniel Gélin *Kellermann* • William Conrad *Mahoney* ■ *Dir/Scr* Michael Verhoeven

Killing Dad ★ PG

Comedy 1989 · UK · Colour · 88mins

This singularly unimpressive film from Michael Austin fails in its attempts at black comedy. Denholm Elliott plays a depressive drunk returning home to the wife (Anna Massey) and son (Richard E Grant) he deserted 23 years ago. Instead of welcoming his father back with open arms, Grant, also a hopeless case, spends the remainder of the film plotting to kill him. Embarrassing for all concerned – including Julie Walters as Elliott's tarty girlfriend – this sank without a trace of laughter. LH DVD

Denholm Elliott *Nathy Berg* • Julie Walters *Judith* • Richard E Grant *Alistair Berg* • Anna Massey *Edith Berg* • Laura Del Sol *Luisa* • Ann Way *Margot* • Jonathan Phillips *Terry* ■ *Dir* Michael Austin • *Scr* Michael Austin, from the novel *Berg* by Ann Quinn

Killing 'em Softly ★ 15

Romantic crime comedy
1982 · Can/US · Colour · 86mins

Considering the title, this film could be mourning for the demise of George Segal's talent, if only temporarily, in this dull thriller in which he's a down-on-his luck musician who kills a rock manager and falls for singer Irene Cara, whose boyfriend is promptly framed for the murder. Segal's usual urbanity of manner is absent, and he looks panicky – as though he's realised the mess in which he's plunged himself. TH

George Segal *Jimmy Skinner* • Irene Cara *Janes Flores* • Clark Johnson *Michael* • Nicholas Campbell *Clifford* • Joyce Gordon *Poppy Mellinger* ■ *Dir* Max Fischer • *Scr* Leila Basen, from a story by Max Fischer, from a book by Laird Koenig

The Killing Fields ★★★★★ 15

Biographical war drama
1984 · UK · Colour · 135mins

Few feature films have captured a nation's agony more dramatically than Roland Joffé's *The Killing Fields*. It tells the story of Cambodia's Year Zero, when Pol Pot's Khmer Rouge entered the capital Phnom Penh, emptied it, turned the population into serfs and slaughtered nearly three million of them. To tell the story of this genocide, the picture has one conventional aspect – the perspective of American journalist Sidney Schanberg (Sam Waterston) – and one less so: the experiences of his Cambodian stringer Dith Pran (played by Haing S Ngor, a Cambodian doctor whose own suffering at the time was, if anything, even worse than that depicted in the film). The picture has scale and humanity; the evacuation of the capital is stunning, Ngor's suffering has great emotional force, while Waterston's complex mixture of shame and ambition is compelling. One of the greatest pictures of the

1980s. AT. Contains violence and swearing. [video] DVD

Sam Waterston *Sydney Schanberg* • Haing S Ngor *Dith Pran* • John Malkovich *Al Rockoff* • Julian Sands *Jon Swain* • Craig T Nelson *Military attaché* • Spalding Gray *US consul* • Bill Paterson *Dr MacEntire* • Athol Fugard *Dr Sundesval* • Graham Kennedy *Dougal* ■ *Dir* Roland Joffé • *Scr* Bruce Robinson, from the article *The Death and Life of Dith Pran* by Sydney Schanberg

The Killing Floor ★★★ PG

Historical drama
1984 · US · Colour and BW · 117mins

Bill Duke makes an excellent directorial debut with this impassioned drama of union and racial tension. It tells the story of a group of black workers fighting for their rights in a Chicago abattoir during the First World War. The then largely unknown cast – which includes Moses Gunn and Alfre Woodard – delivers believable performances, and Duke brings an air of gritty realism to the tale. JF. Contains some violence and swearing.

Damien Leake *Frank Custer* • Alfre Woodard *Mattie Custer* • Clarence Felder *Bill Bremer* • Moses Gunn *Heavy Williams* • Jason Green *Frank Custer Jr* • Jamarr Johnson *Lionel Custer* • Micaeh Johnson *Sarah Custer* • Ernest Rayford *Thomas Joshua* • Stephen Henderson *James Cheeks* • Dennis Farina *Harry Brennan* ■ *Dir* Bill Duke • *Scr* Leslie Lee, from a story by Elsa Rassback, adapted by Ron Milner

The Killing Grounds ★★

Thriller 1997 · US · Colour · 93mins

Backpackers turn back-stabbers when they stumble on a cache of gold bullion in a nihilistic riff on *Treasure of the Sierra Madre*. Further murderous complications occur when the real "owners" of the fortune turn up and are in no mood for sharing their ill-gotten gains. A sadistic thriller, with many gruesome moments as the cast die one by one. AJ

Priscilla Barnes *Della Desordo* • Rodney A Grant *Ned Stillwater* • Anthony Michael Hall *Art Styles* • Charles Rocket *Mel Delsordo* • Mike Michaud *Pilot* • Richard Brandes *Pilot number two* • James Jude Courtney *Craig* • Scott Brick *Deputy* ■ *Dir* Kurt Anderson • *Scr* Thomas Ritz, from the story by Richard Brandes, Kurt Anderson

The Killing Kind ★★

Psychological crime drama
1973 · US · Colour · 95mins

In Curtis Harrington's study of disturbed mother–son relationships, John Savage returns home after a spell in prison for a rape he didn't commit and falls into the doting arms of his overbearing mother (Ann Sothern). Unfortunately, her loving care is so suffocating it drives him to take violent revenge on the lawyer (Ruth Roman) responsible for his incarceration and the girl whose evidence put him away. Good performances elevate the familiar *Psycho* shadings in a seldom seen, lethargically paced suspense shocker. AJ

Ann Sothern *Thelma* • John Savage *Terry* • Ruth Roman *Rhea* • Luana Anders *Librarian* • Cindy Williams *Roomer* ■ *Dir* Curtis Harrington • *Scr* Lony Crechales, George Edwards

Killing Me Softly ★ 18

Erotic thriller 2001 · US/UK · Colour · 96mins

The English-language debut of acclaimed Chinese director Chen Kaige is more laughable than most late-night erotic thrillers. Joseph Fiennes is the stock "mysterious stranger" with whom shrewish Heather Graham falls passionately in love after a glance at a pelican crossing. Their explicit lovemaking was clearly intended as a selling point but, like the whole of this unlikely whodunnit involving dark secrets, incest and mountaineering (no, really), it's utterly fictional. One can only assume that, dazzled by some deeper symbolism, Chen simply wasn't aware how clangingly awful the dialogue was. AC [video] DVD

Heather Graham *Alice Loudon* • Joseph Fiennes *Adam Tallis* • Natascha McElhone *Deborah Tallis* • Ulrich Thomsen *Klaus* • Ian Hart *Daniel, senior police officer* • Jason Hughes *Jake* • Kika Markham *Mrs Blanchard* ■ *Dir* Chen Kaige • *Scr* Kara Lindstrom, from the novel *Killing Me Softly* by Nicci French [Sean French, Nicci Gerrard]

Killing Obsession ★★

Horror thriller 1994 · US · Colour · 95mins

This by-the-numbers psycho thriller has murderer John Savage convincing the authorities that he is now a reformed character and should be let out of prison. Of course, he promptly sets off after Kimberly Chase, the grown-up daughter of his last victim. John Saxon has a supporting role, but everything about the movie screams routine. JF

John Savage *Albert* • John Saxon *Dr Sachs* • Kimberly Chase *Annie* • Bernard White *Lt Jackson* ■ *Dir/Scr* Paul Leder

The Killing of a Chinese Bookie ★★★★ 15

Crime thriller 1976 · US · Colour · 104mins

A powerful performance from Ben Gazzara dominates this convoluted but compelling contemporary *film noir* by John Cassavetes. Los Angeles nightclub owner Gazzara is in debt to the Mob and agrees to dispatch a troublesome bookie (Soto Joe Hugh). The overlong narrative occasionally stumbles over the improvisational techniques Cassavetes used to increase the realism of the piece, and Timothy Agoglia Carey's assassin is far too over the top. However, there is a convincing atmosphere of gangster menace. TH [video]

Ben Gazzara *Cosmo Vitelli* • Timothy Agoglia Carey [Timothy Carey] *Flo* • Azizi Johari *Rachel* • Meade Roberts *Mr Sophistication* • Seymour Cassel *Mort Weil* • Alice Friedland *Sherry* • Donna Gordon *Margo* • Robert Phillips *Phil* • Morgan Woodward *John the boss* • Virginia Carrington *Betty the Mother* • Soto Joe Hugh [Hugh Soto] *Chinese bookie* ■ *Dir/Scr* John Cassavetes

The Killing of Angel Street ★★★

Drama 1981 · Aus · Colour · 101mins

Loosely based on actual events, this well-intentioned drama combines populist realism with clichés and corrupt stereotypes. Yet, for all its failings, Donald Crombie's film brings you onside at the outset, and keeps you rooting for Alexander Archdale and then, after his mysterious death, his feisty daughter Elizabeth Alexander. Particularly impressive is the way Crombie introduces elements of tension to the story that are more typical of a thriller, without losing sight of the human-interest angle. Efficient and engrossing. DP

Elizabeth Alexander *Jessica* • John Hargreaves *Elliot* • Alexander Archdale *BC Simmonds* • Reg Lye *Riley* • Gordon McDougall *Sir Arthur Wadham* • David Downer *Alan* • Ric Herbert *Ben* ■ *Dir* Donald Crombie • *Scr* Evan Jones, Cecil Holmes, Michael Craig, from a story by Michael Craig

The Killing of Satan ★★★

Horror fantasy 1983 · Phil · Colour · 95mins

Horror icon Ramon Revilla stars in this rousing story, playing the ne'er-do-well who takes on a self-styled Prince of Magic, who's wreaking havoc with the lives of his island subjects. Director Efren C Pinon could never be accused of subtlety, and in this gore-fest Revilla is confronted by snake women, laser-shooting henchmen and, finally, Satan himself. Yet, from its eerie Easter opening, this low-budget chiller provides a fascinating insight into the way in which Catholicism and local myths have combined to form the Philippines' unique sense of the supernatural. DP

Ramon Revilla *Lando San Miguel* • Elizabeth Oropesa *Lagring San Miguel* • Cecile Castillo *Luisa* • Charlie Davao *Satan* • Paquito Diaz *Pito* ■ *Dir* Efren C Pinon • *Scr* Joe Mari Avellana

The Killing of Sister George ★★★ 18

Drama 1968 · UK · Colour · 139mins

An ageing actress is fired arbitrarily and her character killed off from a TV serial. She takes to the bottle as her young female friend (Susannah York) is seduced from her by a rival. Frank Marcus's touching play is not so much touched as bruised by Robert Aldrich's heavy-handed direction, which alienated the actresses during shooting and was disliked. However, this is still a fascinating if flawed look at relationships so close they're weirdly sympathetic. TH [video] DVD

Beryl Reid *June Buckridge/"Sister George"* • Susannah York *Alice "Childie" McNaught* • Coral Browne *Mercy Croft* • Ronald Fraser *Leo Lockhart* • Patricia Medina *Betty Thaxter* • Hugh Paddick *Freddie* • Cyril Delevanti *Ted Baker* ■ *Dir* Robert Aldrich • *Scr* Lukas Heller, from the play by Frank Marcus

The Killing Time ★ 15

Crime thriller 1987 · US · Colour · 88mins

Slack morals, easy murder and brooding visuals are the very essence of classic and modern *film noir*. It's sad to see here, then, that little-known director Rick King – who was probably asked to walk west of California as a result of this effort – has made only a feeble gesture to the genre. As it is, the combination of Kiefer Sutherland, Beau Bridges, deceit and murder produces a film that comes across as too empty and confused to be of any real dramatic or entertainment value. JM. Contains swearing, violence. [video]

Beau Bridges *Sheriff Sam Wayburn* • Kiefer Sutherland *"Brian Mars"* • Wayne Rogers *Jake Winslow* • Joe Don Baker *Sheriff Carl Cunningham* • Michael Madsen *Stu* ■ *Dir* Rick King • *Scr* Don Bohlinger, James Nathan, Bruce Franklin Singer

Killing Time ★ 18

Thriller 1998 · UK · Colour · 85mins

A lame attempt at transferring Quentin Tarantino-style violence to the north of England. Kendra Torgan plays a super-cool Italian hit-woman, waiting for her target to arrive at a Sunderland hotel and assassinating anyone who gets in her way. Two police inspectors, including Craig Fairbrass, arrive to survey the damage. An exploitative, repetitive and pointless thriller, with the occasional suspenseful moment thrown in for good measure. AJ. Contains swearing, violence. [video] DVD

Craig Fairbrass *Bryant* • Kendra Torgan *Maria – the assassin* • Peter Harding *Madison* • Neil Armstrong *John* • Ian McLaughlin *George* • Stephen D Thirkeld *Charlie* ■ *Dir* Bharat Nalluri • *Scr* Neil Marshall, Fleur Costello, Caspar Berry

Killing Zoe ★★ 18

Crime drama 1993 · US · Colour · 91mins

Roger Avary co-wrote *Pulp Fiction* with Quentin Tarantino, and his debut feature as a director deals with many of the same themes. Eric Stoltz is a safecracker visiting his old friend Jean-Hugues Anglade in Paris; before you can say *Reservoir Dogs*, Anglade attempts to hold up a bank while high on booze and drugs. Avary gives his predictable heist tale a fresher edge than normal with some neat camerawork and a smattering of good jokes among the unflinching splatter. Julie Delpy adds a nice twist as a good-hearted prostitute. AJ [video] DVD

Eric Stoltz *Zed* • Julie Delpy *Zoe* • Jean-Hugues Anglade *Eric* • Tai Thai *François* • Bruce Ramsay *Ricardo* • Kario Salem *Jean* • Salvator Xuereb *Claude* • Gary Kemp *Oliver* ■ *Dir/Scr* Roger Avary

The Killing Zone ★★ 18

Thriller 1998 · UK · Colour · 92mins

Director Ian David Diaz worked miracles to get this ultra-low-budget British thriller made. Padraig Casey is the ultra-cool, saxophone-playing professional hitman who fancies himself as Michael Caine in his Harry Palmer period. He agrees to take one last job, but finds his enemies may be closer to him than he originally thought. Its biggest problem is that it actually feels like three different films, linked together very tenuously. Still, there are enough witty touches to suggest that Diaz may be a director to watch in the future. JF [video] DVD

Padraig Casey *Matthew Palmer* • Oliver Young *Lucas Finn* • Mark Bowden (2) *Lance Nash* • Richard Banks *Parry Fenton* • Giles Ward *Mr "Mad Dog" McCann* • Julian Boote *Mr Frazer* ■ *Dir/Scr* Ian David Diaz

Kim ★★★ U

Adventure 1950 · US · Colour · 112mins

In this colourful version of Rudyard Kipling's tale about "the little friend of all the world", Errol Flynn is splendidly tongue-in-cheek as young Kim's idol, Mahbub Ali, the swashbuckling Red Beard. A very American Dean Stockwell is the boy in question, and he does well, with Kim's "game" excellently brought to life by British director Victor Saville. Unfortunately, Saville's plodding pace and Flynn's lack of screen time don't help the heroics. Flaws apart, boys of all ages should enjoy this. TS

Errol Flynn *Mahbub Ali, the Red Beard* • Dean Stockwell *Kim* • Paul Lukas *Lama* • Robert Douglas *Colonel Creighton* • Thomas Gomez *Emissary* • Cecil Kellaway *Hurree Chunder* • Arnold Moss *Lurgan Sahib* • Reginald Owen *Father Victor* ■ *Dir* Victor Saville • *Scr* Leon Gordon, Richard Schayer, from the novel by Rudyard Kipling

Kim ★★★ PG

Adventure 1984 · US · Colour · 135mins

An ambitious but successful bid to adapt for TV Rudyard Kipling's classic story about a youngster used by British Intelligence in colonial India. Originally filmed in 1950 by Victor Saville, this entertaining remake features Peter O'Toole, excellent as a Buddhist monk, and there's a fine debut from Ravi Sheth as Kim. NF [video] DVD

Peter O'Toole *Lama* • Bryan Brown *Mahbub Ali* • Ravi Sheth *Kim* • John Rhys-Davies *Babu* • Julian Glover *Colonel Creighton* • Lee Montague *Kozelski* • Alfred Burke *Lurgan* ■ *Dir* John Davies • *Scr* James Brabazon, from the novel by Rudyard Kipling

Kin ★★ 15

Drama 2000 · S Afr/UK · Colour · 90mins

While there's much to admire in Amelia Vincent's stunning widescreen photography, this blend of intimate drama and eco-crusade never escapes from its multitude of contrivances. Miranda Otto plays the game reserve worker whose bid to protect the elephants in the Namibian bush is sidetracked by the demands made by her clergyman brother, Chris Chameleon, and visiting African-American lawyer, Isaiah Washington. DP

K

Miranda Otto *Anna* • Isaiah Washington *Stone* • Chris Chameleon *Marius* • Moses Kandjoze *Naniserri* • Ndondoro Hevita *Old man* • Susan Coetzer *Katinka* ■ *Dir/Scr* Elaine Proctor

Kind Hearts and Coronets

★★★★★ U

Classic black comedy
1949 · UK · BW · 101mins

Arguably the finest of the Ealing comedies, Robert Hamer's superb *comédie noire* has a deliciously witty script that slips smoothly between dastardly deaths in the guise of a self-satisfied memoir. However, the picture is elevated to greatness by the quality of its playing. Obviously, Alec Guinness, who essays the eight doomed D'Ascoynes, merits every superlative lavished on a performance of astounding versatility and virtuosity. But let's not forget Dennis Price as the ceaselessly inventive killer, and Joan Greenwood and Valerie Hobson as the vamp and the vestal in his life, who are singularly brilliant. DP DVD

Dennis Price *Louis Mazzini/Narrator* • Valerie Hobson *Edith D'Ascoyne* • Joan Greenwood *Sibella* • Alec Guinness *Duke/Banker/Parson/General/Admiral/Young Ascoyne D'Ascoyne/Young Henry/Lady Agatha D'Ascoyne* • Audrey Fildes *Mama* • Miles Malleson *Hangman* • Clive Morton *Prison governor* • John Penrose *Lionel* • Cecil Ramage *Crown counsel* • Hugh Griffith *Lord High Steward* ■ *Dir* Robert Hamer • *Scr* Robert Hamer, John Dighton, from a novel by Roy Horniman • *Producer* Michael Balcon

K

Kind Lady

★★

Drama 1935 · US · BW · 76mins

That accomplished supporting actress Aline MacMahon, then in her mid-30s, here plays the title role of a wealthy London spinster. She takes pity on a homeless artist, played with roguish charm by Basil Rathbone, only to have him invade her mansion with his cronies and seek to obtain her assets. Only adequately directed by George B Seitz. AE

Aline MacMahon *Mary Herries* • Basil Rathbone *Henry Abbott* • Mary Carlisle *Phyllis* • Frank Albertson *Peter* • Dudley Digges *Mr Edwards* • Doris Lloyd *Lucy Weston* ■ *Dir* George B Seitz • *Scr* Bernard Schubert, from the play by Edward Chodorov, from the story *The Silver Casket* by Hugh Walpole

Kind Lady

★★

Period drama 1951 · US · BW · 77mins

This remake of the 1935 film is here turned into an Edwardian costume drama, scripted by a trio that included Edward Chodorov, author of the original Broadway play. More glossy than its predecessor and directed by John Sturges with a keener sense of tension, it stars Ethel Barrymore as the elderly woman who is unwittingly preyed upon for her wealth. Unfortunately, classical actor Maurice Evans lacks the smooth and persuasive looks and personality of Basil Rathbone, but the movie is nonetheless moderately effective. RK

Ethel Barrymore *Mary Herries* • Maurice Evans *Henry Elcott* • Angela Lansbury *Mrs Edwards* • Keenan Wynn *Edwards* • John Williams *Mr Foster* • Doris Lloyd *Rose* • Betsy Blair *Ada Elcott* ■ *Dir* John Sturges • *Scr* Jerry Davis, Edward Chodorov, Charles Bennett, from the play by Edward Chodorov, from the story *The Silver Casket* by Hugh Walpole

A Kind of Hush

★★★ 15

Drama 1998 · UK · Colour · 91mins

Theatre director Brian Stirner makes his screen debut with this uncompromising study of child abuse and its consequences. While the action deals with the revenge wrought by a bunch of teenagers on their persecutors, the story is as much about the indomitability of the human spirit as it is about justifying vengeance. The performances of the inexperienced cast bristle with anger, but it's the wiser counsel of Roy Hudd that allows them to salvage some dignity from their indignation. DP. Contains sexual references and swearing.

Harley Smith *Stu* • Marcella Plunkett *Kathleen* • Ben Roberts *Simon* • Paul Williams *Mick* • Nathan Constance *Tony* • Peter Saunders *Wivva* • Mike Fibbens *Fish* • Roy Hudd *Chef* ■ *Dir* Brian Stirner • *Scr* Brian Stirner, from the novel *Getting Even* by Richard Johnson

A Kind of Loving

★★★★ 15

Drama 1962 · UK · BW · 107mins

Unlike the majority of other "grim up North" dramas that found critical favour during the social realist or "kitchen sink" phase of British film-making, John Schlesinger's debut feature is about making the most of life rather than carping on about the colour of the grass on the other side of the fence. Crisply adapted by Keith Waterhouse and Willis Hall, the film is like a scrapbook of typical human experience, with Schlesinger's eye for detail and his persuasive storytelling style creating characters who could have lived next door to you. Alan Bates and June Ritchie are excellent, but Thora Hird is exceptional. DP. Contains nudity. DVD

Alan Bates *Vic Brown* • June Ritchie *Ingrid Rothwell* • Thora Hird *Mrs Rothwell* • Bert Palmer *Mr Brown* • Gwen Nelson *Mrs Brown* • Malcolm Patton *Jim Brown* • Pat Keen *Christine* • David Mahlowe *David* • Jack Smethurst *Conroy* • James Bolam *Jeff* • Michael Deacon *Les* ■ *Dir* John Schlesinger • *Scr* Willis Hall, Keith Waterhouse, from the novel by Stan Barstow

Kindergarten Cop

★★★ 15

Action comedy 1990 · US · Colour · 106mins

This undemanding picture proves that Arnold Schwarzenegger can do comedy, providing he doesn't try too hard. As the cop forced to teach toddlers while searching for a crook's missing son, Arnie is at his best jousting with the little tykes. The romance with Penelope Ann Miller is less convincing, but not over-intrusive. Richard Tyson and Carroll Baker make almost pantomimic baddies, but this isn't really a children's film. DP. Contains some violence and swearing. DVD

Arnold Schwarzenegger *Detective John Kimble* • Penelope Ann Miller *Joyce* • Pamela Reed *Phoebe O'Hara* • Linda Hunt *Miss Scholwski* • Richard Tyson *Cullen Crisp* • Carroll Baker *Eleanor Crisp* • Cathy Moriarty *Sylvester's mother* ■ *Dir* Ivan Reitman • *Scr* Murray Salem, Herschel Weingrod, Timothy Harris, from a story by Murray Salem

The Kindred

★ 18

Science-fiction horror thriller
1986 · US · Colour · 88mins

Once hailed as one of America's greatest actors, Rod Steiger suffered a career breakdown in the mid-1980s, appearing in straight-to-video horror trash, of which this is fairly typical. The man who shared screen time with Brando in *On the Waterfront* is here reduced to hamming it up as a mad scientist in a fright wig, whose experiments result in the inevitable things in the cellar. Totally uninvolving from start to finish. RS

David Allen Brooks *John Hollins* • Amanda Pays *Melissa Leftridge* • Talia Balsam *Sharon Raymond* • Kim Hunter *Amanda Hollins* • Rod Steiger *Dr Phillip Lloyd* ■ *Dir* Jeffrey Obrow, Stephen Carpenter • *Scr* Stephen Carpenter, Jeffrey Obrow, John Penney, Earl Ghaffari, Joseph Stefano

King: a Filmed Record... Montgomery to Memphis

★★★

Biographical documentary
1970 · US · BW · 177mins

Fine documentary about Martin Luther King, co-directed by Hollywood heavyweights Joseph L Mankiewicz and Sidney Lumet. Using quality archive news footage, the film looks at the latter part of King's life, from his frontline civil rights activism of the mid-1950s, right through to his assassination in April 1968. The linking sequences are narrated by a host of film luminaries and admirers of King, including Paul Newman, Joanne Woodward, James Earl Jones and Sidney Poitier. There's no question who the real star is, though. DA

Paul Newman *Narrator* • Joanne Woodward *Narrator* • Ruby Dee *Narrator* • James Earl Jones *Narrator* • Clarence Williams III *Narrator* • Burt Lancaster *Narrator* • Ben Gazzara *Narrator* • Charlton Heston *Narrator* • Harry Belafonte *Narrator* • Sidney Poitier *Narrator* ■ *Dir* Sidney Lumet, Joseph L Mankiewicz

King and Country

★★★ PG

First World War drama
1964 · UK · BW · 82mins

Tom Courtenay is a hapless private who has had enough of trench warfare and walks away from his post. Naturally he's caught, and Dirk Bogarde is ordered to defend him at his court martial. This moving – if sometimes pompous – tale is really an allegory about the British class system, bearing a striking resemblance to Stanley Kubrick's *Paths of Glory* (1957). AT DVD

Dirk Bogarde *Captain Hargreaves* • Tom Courtenay *Private Arthur Hamp* • Leo McKern *Captain O'Sullivan* • Barry Foster *Lieutenant Webb* • James Villiers *Captain Midgley* • Peter Copley *Colonel* • Barry Justice *Lieutenant Prescott* ■ *Dir* Joseph Losey • *Scr* Evan Jones, from the play *Hamp* by John Wilson, from a story by James Lansdale Hodson

The King and Four Queens

★★

Western 1956 · US · Colour · 83mins

The King, of course, is Clark Gable, looking vaguely lost after MGM failed to renew his contract two years earlier. He plays a drifter who wanders into a near-deserted town, inhabited by Jo Van Fleet, a woman gunfighter with four daughters-in-law (including shady Eleanor Parker) and buried loot to protect. In some respects, this weird western owes much to Nicholas Ray's offbeat cult hit *Johnny Guitar*, though Gable barely perceives the subversive opportunities and director Raoul Walsh is only interested in the tough-guy stuff. A considerable rarity. AT

Clark Gable *Dan Kehoe* • Eleanor Parker *Sabina* • Jo Van Fleet *Ma McDade* • Jean Willes *Ruby* • Barbara Nichols *Birdie* • Sara Shane *Oralie* ■ *Dir* Raoul Walsh • *Scr* Margaret Fitts, Richard Simmons, from a story by Margaret Fitts

The King and I

★★★★ U

Musical 1956 · US · Colour · 127mins

Yul Brynner re-created his Broadway King for posterity in this faithful adaptation of Rodgers and Hammerstein's marvellous musical success about English governess Anna Leonowens and her sexless romance with the King of Siam. Brynner is magnificent and he deservedly picked up a best actor Oscar for what is unquestionably a great performance. As Mrs Anna, Deborah Kerr is both resolute and touching, with an unbilled Marni Nixon dubbing her singing voice. Unfortunately, 20th Century-Fox's use of its own DeLuxe Color lets down the production design, and a stronger director than Walter Lang would have been beneficial. TS DVD

Deborah Kerr *Anna Leonowens* • Yul Brynner *The King* • Rita Moreno *Tuptim* • Martin Benson *Kralahome* • Terry Saunders *Lady Thiang* • Rex Thompson *Louis Leonowens* • Carlos Rivas *Lun Tha* • Patrick Adiarte *Prince Chulalongkorn* • Alan Mowbray *British ambassador* • Geoffrey Toone *Ramsay* ■ *Dir* Walter Lang • *Scr* Ernest Lehman, from the musical by Oscar Hammerstein II, Richard Rodgers, from the book *Anna and the King of Siam* by Margaret Landon • *Cinematographer* Leon Shamroy • *Costume Designer* Irene Sharaff

The King and I

★★ U

Animated musical
1999 · US · Colour · 85mins

This breezy cartoon version of Rodgers and Hammerstein's musical may be no threat to Yul Brynner and Deborah Kerr in the original, but it introduces youngsters to some classic tunes. In an effort to make the complex plot more accessible to younger viewers, the film is rather dubiously enlivened by some new personalities – a black panther, a fire-breathing dragon and chubby Master Little. TH

Miranda Richardson *Anna* • Christiane Noll *Anna Leonowens (singing)* • Martin Vidnovic *King of Siam* • Ian Richardson *Kralahome* • Darrell Hammond *Master Little* • Allen D Hong *Prince Chululongkorn* • David Burnham *Prince Chulalongkorn (singing)* • Armi Arabe *Tuptim* ■ *Dir* Richard Rich • *Scr* Peter Bakalian, David Seidler, Jacqueline Feather, Arthur Rankin [Arthur Rankin Jr], from the musical by Richard Rodgers, Oscar Hammerstein II

The King and the Chorus Girl

★★★

Comedy 1937 · US · BW · 95mins

Hollywood's Belgian import Fernand Gravet co-stars with Joan Blondell in a tale about a European aristocrat who falls madly in love with an American chorus girl from the Folies Bergère. Helping to press his cause are Jane Wyman and Edward Everett Horton. A romantic comedy, adapted by Norman Krasna and Groucho Marx from their story *Grand Passion* and efficiently produced and directed by Mervyn LeRoy, there's nothing particularly grand or passionate about the movie, but it's enjoyable. RK

Fernand Gravet *Alfred* • Joan Blondell *Dorothy* • Edward Everett Horton *Count Humbert* • Alan Mowbray *Donald* • Jane Wyman *Babette* • Mary Nash *Duchess Anna* ■ *Dir* Mervyn LeRoy • *Scr* Norman Krasna, Groucho Marx, from their story *Grand Passion*

King Arthur

★★★ 12

Period action adventure
2004 · US/Ire/UK · Colour · 120mins

Antoine Fuqua's film is less a re-imagining of the Arthurian legend and more a Dark Ages-set remake of *The Magnificent Seven*. Most of the traditional elements are missing – no wizardry, no Camelot, no love triangle – and instead we get Arthur (a subdued Clive Owen) recast as a Roman captain posted to Hadrian's Wall and Guinevere (Keira Knightley) as a Boadicea-like warrior. The rousing death-or-glory speeches and the obligatory love scene fall flat, and it's also a shame the mystical nature of the original myth is dismissed. But there's still much pleasure to be had in the company of the charismatic knights and from the convincingly staged battles. GM. Contains violence and sex scenes. DVD

Clive Owen *Arthur* • Keira Knightley *Guinevere* • Stellan Skarsgård *Cerdic* • Stephen Dillane *Merlin* • Ray Winstone *Bors* • Hugh Dancy *Galahad* • Til Schweiger *Cynric* • Ioan Gruffudd *Lancelot* ■ *Dir* Antoine Fuqua • *Scr* David Franzoni

King Arthur Was a Gentleman ★★ U

Comedy 1942 · UK · BW · 94mins

It was once said that the Nazis thought they would win the Second World War because Britain's most effective men of action were nitwit comedians like Will Hay and George Formby. Over 50 years on, it's not easy to see how such tepid capers could have boosted morale. Yet this is as likeable as any flag-waving comedy, with Arthur Askey as the cheery Tommy who is convinced he has found King Arthur's sword Excalibur and is, therefore, invincible. The film could have done with fewer songs and more gags. DP

Arthur Askey *Arthur King* • Evelyn Dall *Susan Ashley* • Anne Shelton *Gwen Duncannon* • Max Bacon *Maxie* • Jack Train *Jack* • Peter Graves (1) *Lance* ■ *Dir* Marcel Varnel • *Scr* Val Guest, Marriott Edgar

King Cobra ★ 15

Science-fiction horror
1999 · US · Colour · 89mins

Scientists genetically create a giant snake in order to test a formula that will increase aggression without causing harmful side effects. It goes without saying that the snake escapes from the lab, re-appearing in a small town just before its annual beer festival is about to begin. The collection of very familiar characters may not have immediately doomed the film, but the scenes involving the snake do. The animatronic creation is so unconvincing that it's hardly surprising the snake does most of its business off-screen. KB DVD

Pat Morita *Nick Hashimoto* • Scott Brandon [Scott Hillenbrand] *Dr Brad Kagan* • Kasey Fallo *Deputy Jo Biddle* • Hoyt Axton *Mayor Ed Biddle* • Joseph Ruskin *Dr Irwin Burns* • Courtney Gains *Dr McConnell* • Eric Lawson *Sheriff Ben Lowry* • Erik Estrada *Bernie Alvarez* ■ *Dir/Scr* David Hillenbrand, Scott Hillenbrand

King Creole ★★★★ PG

Musical 1958 · US · BW · 110mins

This is arguably Elvis Presley's best film, and certainly his best acting performance. It's a tough New Orleans-set crime drama directed by Hollywood maestro Michael Curtiz, who invests the nightclub scenes with the kind of élan that turned the not dissimilar *Casablanca* into a classic. Elvis has tremendous support from a terrific back-up cast, notably from Walter Matthau as a reptilian villain, and from Carolyn Jones as a long-suffering moll. The songs are knockouts too, especially the Dixie-influenced title number. Don't miss. TS DVD

Elvis Presley *Danny Fisher* • Carolyn Jones *Ronnie* • Dolores Hart *Nellie* • Dean Jagger *Mr Fisher* • Liliane Montevecchi *"Forty" Nina* • Walter Matthau *Maxie Fields* • Jan Shepard *Mimi Fisher* • Paul Stewart *Charlie LeGrand* • Vic Morrow *Shark* ■ *Dir* Michael Curtiz • *Scr* Herbert Baker, Michael Vincente Gazzo, from the novel *A Stone for Danny Fisher* by Harold Robbins • *Music* Walter Scharf

King David ★★ PG

Biblical epic 1985 · US · Colour · 109mins

Lavish visuals and sonorous music (by Carl Davis) – both designed to match the grandeur of the subject – are badly wasted by director Bruce Beresford. In his hands, and after a promising canter through David's childhood, the spectacle quickly gets bogged down in tedious dialogue and, as the narrative begins to falter, Richard Gere (as the hero) is reduced to acting by gesture. Yet Edward Woodward, in the role of King Saul, transcends these flaws with charisma and substance. JM

Richard Gere *David* • Edward Woodward *Saul* • Alice Krige *Bathsheba* • Denis Quilley *Samuel* • Niall Buggy *Nathan* • Cherie Lunghi *Michal* • Hurd Hatfield *Ahimilech* ■ *Dir* Bruce Beresford • *Scr* Andrew Birkin, James Costigan, from a story by James Costigan

A King in New York ★★★ U

Satirical comedy 1957 · UK · BW · 100mins

An embittered Charles Chaplin all but abdicates as the king of comedy for his penultimate film, mirroring the loathing he felt for the way America had treated him in real life. As the deposed monarch of Estrovia he seeks sanctuary in the United States, where he finds himself at the mercy of both the House Un-American Activities Committee and advertising executive Dawn Addams. Made in Britain (the film's New York setting is unconvincing), there are some occasionally shrewd insights, but the scenes using a young boy to mouth Chaplin's own disgust with the USA are totally embarrassing. TH DVD

Charles Chaplin *King Shadhov* • Dawn Addams *Ann Kay* • Oliver Johnston *The Ambassador* • Maxine Audley *Queen Irene* • Harry Green *Lawyer Green* • Phil Brown *Headmaster* • John McLaren *Macabee Senior* • Sidney James *Mr Johnson* ■ *Dir/Scr* Charles Chaplin

The King Is Alive ★★ 15

Drama 2000 · Den/US · Colour · 105mins

Making several radical departures from the supposedly sacrosanct "vow of chastity", the fourth Dogme feature lacks the dramatic spark to match its audiovisual audacity. By working in English and outside Denmark, director Kristian Levring demonstrates a willingness to take chances. But the tale of a busload of passengers stranded in the African wilderness, who agree to enact *King Lear* while waiting for help, is as predictable as a disaster movie, with each caricatured character eventually revealing their inevitable flaw. Jennifer Jason Leigh works the hardest to achieve the least within a committed ensemble, all of whom come to resemble specimens in a cinematic laboratory. DP DVD

David Bradley (3) *Henry* • Jennifer Jason Leigh *Gina* • Janet McTeer *Liz* • Miles Anderson *Jack* • Romane Bohringer *Catherine* • Bruce Davison *Ray* • Lia Williams *Amanda* ■ *Dir* Kristian Levring • *Scr* Kristian Levring, Anders Thomas Jensen

King Kong ★★★★★ PG

Classic fantasy adventure
1933 · US · BW · 100mins

Arguably *the* monster movie of all time, this abiding take on *Beauty and the Beast* has a mythic power that belies its years. At its heart is the amazing ape (and dinosaur) animation of Willis O'Brien, his cutting-edge model work the CGI of its day, but it's the tragic story that stays etched on the memory. Robert Armstrong's Hollywood film-maker imperils starlet Fay Wray on a prehistoric island in his bid to turn a local legend into a hit on celluloid. Taking the giant gorilla Kong back to civilisation for entrepreneurial gain is bad for all concerned, not least the captive creature who ends his life atop the Empire State Building in one cinema's greatest climaxes. This thrilling adventure offers an early eco-message. AC DVD

Fay Wray *Ann Darrow* • Robert Armstrong *Carl Denham* • Bruce Cabot *John Driscoll* • Frank Reicher *Capt Englehorn* • Sam Hardy *Charles Weston* • Noble Johnson *Native chief* ■ *Dir* Merian C Cooper, Ernest B Schoedsack • *Scr* James Creelman, Ruth Rose, from an idea by Merian C Cooper, Edgar Wallace • *Cinematographer* Eddie Linden, Vernon Walker, JO Taylor • *Music* Max Steiner • *Special Effects* Willis O'Brien • *Sound Effects* Murray Spivack

King Kong ★ PG

Fantasy adventure
1976 · US · Colour · 129mins

This leaden and over-budgeted remake of the classic fantasy abandoned all the exotic mystery of the 1933 masterpiece in favour of glossy high camp and atrocious satire. A man in a monkey suit and pathetic giant models replaced the wonderful stop-motion techniques, pioneered by Willis O'Brien for the original, in this epic bomb. How Jessica Lange's career survived her debut in such a turkey ("put me down, you male chauvinist ape!") is a cinematic miracle. AJ. Younger children may find it frightening. DVD

Jessica Lange *Dwan* • Jeff Bridges *Jack Prescott* • Charles Grodin *Fred Wilson* • John Randolph *Captain Ross* • René Auberjonois *Bagley* • Ed Lauter *Carnahan* • Rick Baker *King Kong* ■ *Dir* John Guillermin • *Scr* Lorenzo Semple Jr, from the 1933 film • *Music* John Barry (1)

King Kong Lives ★ PG

Fantasy adventure
1986 · US · Colour · 100mins

As if the 1976 remake wasn't bad enough, producer Dino de Laurentiis and director John Guillermin sink to even more ludicrous depths with this awful sequel. The giant ape didn't die when he fell off the World Trade Centre ten years earlier, and now Linda Hamilton leads a surgical team attempting to revive him with a giant artificial heart. Meanwhile, back in the jungle, Brian Kerwin has discovered a female Kong. This couldn't be any worse. AJ DVD

Brian Kerwin *Hank Mitchell* • Linda Hamilton *Amy Franklin* • Peter Elliot *King Kong* • George Yiasoumi *Lady Kong* • John Ashton *Colonel Nevitt* ■ *Dir* John Guillermin • *Scr* Steven Pressfield, Ronald Shusett, from characters created by Merian C Cooper, Edgar Wallace

King Kong vs Godzilla ★★★ PG

Monster horror 1962 · Jpn · Colour · 87mins

Based on an early draft script by *King Kong* creator Willis O'Brien, and completely rewritten by the Japanese as a co-starring vehicle for their own monster hero Godzilla, director Inoshiro Honda's clash of the pop culture titans works more as an engagingly silly comedy more than a fully-fledged fantasy. After defeating a giant octopus threatening Japanese fishermen, Kong is drugged with narcotic berries and flown to Tokyo. Meanwhile Godzilla is woken up from frozen hibernation by an atomic sub and heads for the capital, where he battles Kong at Mount Fuji. Additional footage, starring Michael Keith and others, was directed by Thomas Montgomery for the American market. AJ. A Japanese language film.

Michael Keith *Eric Carter* • James Yagi *Yataka Omura* • Tadao Takashima *O Sakurai* • Mie Hama *Fumiko Sakurai* • Yu Fujiki *Kinzaburo Furue* ■ *Dir* Inoshiro Honda • *Scr* Bruce Howard, Paul Mason, Shinichi Sekizawa, from a story by Willis O'Brien

King Lear ★★ PG

Tragedy 1970 · UK/Den · BW · 131mins

If this sole attempt is anything to go by, Peter Brook's concept of filming Shakespeare was to de-emphasise the text by burying it within a phalanx of frantic camera movements and abrupt close-ups. Fortunately, Paul Scofield gives an astonishingly insightful and intense performance. Indeed, it's so good that it almost makes you forget the forbidding Danish backdrops and the directorial eccentricities. The supporting cast also strives to rescue this from the stylised carnage. DP

Paul Scofield *King Lear* • Irene Worth *Goneril* • Annelise Gabold *Cordelia* • Susan Engel *Regan* • Alan Webb *Duke of Gloucester* • Patrick Magee *Duke of Cornwall* • Cyril Cusack *Duke of Albany* • Jack MacGowran *The Fool* ■ *Dir* Peter Brook • *Scr* Peter Brook, from the play by William Shakespeare

King Lear ★★★★

Tragedy 1970 · USSR · BW · 139mins

Six years after his extraordinary adaptation of *Hamlet*, (and, ironically, the same year that Peter Brook released his own version of the play), Grigori Kozintsev returned to Shakespeare for this dark tale of misplaced trust and filial treachery. Working from Boris Pasternak's translation (which is lost in the Bardic subtitles), Kozintsev conceived a visually arresting drama that's shot through with political folly and human suffering. To that end, he's superbly served by Juri Jarvet, who plays Lear less as a crumbling wreck than an intemperate tyrant, supported only by Oleg Dal's truly touching Fool against Elsa Radzinya and Galina Volchek's vicious termagants. DP. In Russian with English subtitles.

Juri Jarvet *Lear* • Elsa Radzinya [Elsa Radzin] *Goneril* • Galina Volchek *Regan* • Valentina Shendrikova *Cordelia* • Karl Sebris *Earl of Gloucester* • Regimantis Adomaitis *Edmund* • Oleg Dal *Fool* ■ *Dir* Grigori Kozintsev • *Scr* Grigori Kozintsev, from the Russian translation of William Shakespeare's play by Boris Pasternak

K

King Lear – Fear and Loathing ★ 15

Experimental drama
1987 · US/Fr · Colour · 90mins

This isn't William Shakespeare's *King Lear*, or even Jean-Luc Godard's *King Lear*. It's just a self-indulgent mess about the idea of making a movie of *King Lear*. The project started out years before, scripted by Norman Mailer and starring Marlon Brando as a Mafia leader named Lear and Woody Allen as his Fool. Lee Marvin, Orson Welles and Dustin Hoffman were all involved at some point. By the time Godard got around to making it, he still had the clout to lure some very impressive names. AT

Burgess Meredith *Don Learo* • Peter Sellars *William Shakespeare Jr, the Fifth* • Molly Ringwald *Cordelia* • Jean-Luc Godard *Professor* • Woody Allen *Mr Alien* • Norman Mailer • Kate Mailer • Léos Carax *Edgar* ■ *Dir* Jean-Luc Godard • *Scr* Jean-Luc Godard, from the play *King Lear* by William Shakespeare

King of Alcatraz ★★

Comedy drama 1938 · US · BW · 55mins

J Carroll Naish escapes from Alcatraz, joins up with his old gang and hijacks a ship to Panama in a creaky old B-movie from Paramount. On board are two supposedly witty radio operators: Robert Preston (in his screen debut) and Lloyd Nolan, who gets shot early on. Luckily nurse Gail Patrick is on hand to operate following instructions from a doctor on the radio. The rest of the cast might hold your interest. AT

Gail Patrick *Dale Borden* • Lloyd Nolan *Raymond Grayson* • Harry Carey *Captain Glennan* • J Carrol Naish *Steve Murkil* • Robert Preston *Robert MacArthur* • Anthony Quinn *Lou Gedney* ■ *Dir* Robert Florey • *Scr* Irving Reis

King of Burlesque ★★★

Musical comedy 1936 · US · BW · 85mins

A rousing vehicle that couples two great 1930s stars at differing stages of their careers: Warner Baxter, top-billed as the titular monarch, and 20th Century-Fox's newest blonde star Alice Faye, singing her way to success with such terrific numbers as *I'm Shooting High*. The plot is familiar as Baxter marries socialite Mona Barrie and finds that burlesque, Faye and Park Avenue don't mix, but who cares when it's all done with such spit and polish? There's some really sharp dialogue, but best of all is a rare appearance in features from the great Fats Waller. TS

Warner Baxter *Kerry Bolton* • Alice Faye *Pat Doran* • Jack Oakie *Joe Cooney* • Arline Judge *Connie* • Mona Barrie *Rosalind Cleve* • Fats Waller *Ben* ■ *Dir* Sidney Lanfield • *Scr* Gene Markey, Harry Tugend, James Seymour, from a story by Vina Delmar

The King of Comedy ★★★★★ PG

Comedy drama 1983 · US · Colour · 104mins

Though a box-office failure, Martin Scorsese's black comedy is now considered by many to be his unsung masterpiece. Of all the director's outings with sparring partner Robert De Niro, this is the strangest. De Niro is an aspiring stand-up comedian and stalker-in-waiting who dreams of fronting his own TV show, rehearses for this moment of glory in his mother's basement and spends half his life waiting, symbolically, in reception. It's a powerful, complex performance, one that carries the story from farce into tragedy with ease, while Jerry Lewis is magnificent as the chilly old pro and chat-show king. AC. Contains swearing. DVD

Robert De Niro *Rupert Pupkin* • Jerry Lewis *Jerry Langford* • Diahnne Abbott *Rita* • Sandra Bernhard *Masha* • Cathy Scorsese *Dolores* • Catherine Scorsese *Mrs Pupkin* • Leslie Levinson *Roberta Posner* • Martin Scorsese *TV director* • Ed Herlihy • Liza Minnelli • Victor Borge • Tony Randall ■ *Dir* Martin Scorsese • *Scr* Paul D Zimmerman

King of Hearts ★★★★

First World War comedy drama
1966 · Fr/It · Colour · 101mins

One of the lesser luminaries of the French New Wave, Philippe de Broca scored a cult hit with this atmospheric black comedy set during the First World War. Alan Bates is superb as the Scot who comes across a small town earmarked for blanket bombing. The satirical swipes at monarchy, patriotism and war are played down in favour of whimsical – if occasionally anarchic – comedy, as the townsfolk, each one a former asylum patient, urge Bates to become their king. The French cast is exceptional. DP. Some French and German dialogue with English subtitles.

Alan Bates *Private Charles Plumpick* • Pierre Brasseur *General Geranium* • Jean-Claude Brialy *The Duke aka Le Duc de Trèfle* • Geneviève Bujold *Coquelicot* • Françoise Christophe *Duchess* • Julien Guiomar *Bishop Daisy aka Monseigneur Marguerite* • Michel Serrault *Crazy barber* ■ *Dir* Philippe de Broca • *Scr* Daniel Boulanger, from an idea by Maurice Bessy

The King of Jazz ★★★

Musical revue 1930 · US · Colour · 93mins

Considering the array of talent involved and the fact the film was shot in the expensive two-tone Technicolor process – including the first Technicolor animation – it's amazing that Universal entrusted this prestige project to debutant director John Murray Anderson, the only film he ever directed. However, he produces a stylish revue, showcasing the talents of songwriters Jack Yellen and Milton Ager, bandleader Paul Whiteman and first-timer Bing Crosby as a singer. It was still a spectacular flop. DP

John Boles • Laura La Plante • Jeanette Loff • Walter Brennan • Bing Crosby ■ *Dir* John Murray Anderson • *Scr* Charles MacArthur, Harry Ruskin, Edward T Lowe Jr • *Animation* Walter Lantz, Bill Nolan

The King of Kings ★★★★

Silent biblical drama
1927 · US · BW and Colour · 115mins

Complete with bookend sections in Technicolor (a lavish extravagance at the time), this is pure Cecil B DeMille. Not since his own version of *The Ten Commandments* had a biblical story been told on such a scale as this awesome retelling of the life of Christ. HB Warner might not have had the presence of Jeffrey Hunter (who would play the role in Nicholas Ray's 1961 remake), but he looks suitably spiritual, particularly during the harrowing Crucifixion scenes. Ernest Torrence impresses as Peter and Joseph Schildkraut is outstanding as Judas. Typically excessive, but truly reverential, this is a monument to the splendour of silent film. DP

HB Warner *Jesus, the Christ* • Dorothy Cumming *Mary, the Mother* • Ernest Torrence *Peter* • Joseph Schildkraut *Judas* • James Neill *James* • Joseph Striker *John* • Robert Edeson *Matthew* • Sidney D'Albrook *Thomas* • David Imboden *Andrew* • Jacqueline Logan *Mary Magdalene* ■ *Dir* Cecil B DeMille • *Scr* Jeanie Macpherson

King of Kings ★★★★ U

Biblical epic 1961 · US · Colour · 153mins

Films that feature portrayals of Jesus Christ generally have a bad reputation. This is an exception, despite the idiotic hype that flowed when it was made. Jeffrey Hunter, who plays Jesus, was forbidden to give interviews, his chest and armpits were shaved and the film was dubbed "I Was a Teenage Jesus", because Nicholas Ray had also directed James Dean in *Rebel without a Cause*. To compensate for some weak performances and for some lapses into high camp (notably Frank Thring's pouting Herod Antipas), there is a marvellous score, Orson Welles's narration and the lavish design that one associates with producer Samuel Bronston, who also made *El Cid* and *The Fall of the Roman Empire*. AT

Jeffrey Hunter *Jesus Christ* • Siobhan McKenna *Mary, Mother of Jesus* • Robert Ryan *John the Baptist* • Hurd Hatfield *Pontius Pilate* • Ron Randell *Lucius, the Centurion* • Viveca Lindfors *Claudia* • Rita Gam *Herodias* • Carmen Sevilla *Mary Magdalene* • Brigid Bazlen *Salome* • Harry Guardino *Barabbas* • Rip Torn *Judas* • Frank Thring *Herod Antipas* • Orson Welles *Narrator* • Grégoire Aslan *King Herod* ■ *Dir* Nicholas Ray • *Scr* Philip Yordan • *Set Designer* Georges Wakhevitch • *Music* Miklos Rozsa

The King of Marvin Gardens ★★★★

Crime drama 1972 · US · Colour · 104mins

Jack Nicholson and director Bob Rafelson's follow-up to *Five Easy Pieces* was this often pretentious yet absorbing study of two brothers. Nicholson is a radio presenter, intellectual and withdrawn; his brother, Bruce Dern, is an aspiring property developer, brash, married to Ellen Burstyn and living in a hopeless dream world. Set in a windy, charmless Atlantic City, its original title was *The Philosopher King*, and the final title derives from the American version of Monopoly. Some rate Nicholson's performance as a career best, and his wistful monologues on the radio are indeed brilliant; others may find the cerebral atmosphere easy to resist. AT. Contains violence, swearing.

Jack Nicholson *David Staebler* • Bruce Dern *Jason Staebler* • Ellen Burstyn *Sally* • Julia Anne Robinson *Jessica* • Benjamin "Scatman" Crothers [Scatman Crothers] *Lewis* • Charles Lavine *Grandfather* ■ *Dir* Bob Rafelson • *Scr* Jacob Brackman, from a story by Jacob Brackman, Bob Rafelson

King of New York ★★★★ 18

Crime thriller 1989 · US · Colour · 99mins

A cult grew quickly around Abel Ferrara, director of those notorious "video nasties" *Driller Killer* and *Ms 45*, as well as 1992's *Bad Lieutenant* with Harvey Keitel. This is similarly sordid and blood-soaked, the tale of a New York drug trafficker, played with appalling brilliance by a reptilian Christopher Walken. Ferrara has Sergio Leone's eye for a location – his dark, brooding view of the city is impressive – but what some will regard as gripping and apocalyptic, others will find repellent. AT. Contains violence, drug abuse, swearing, nudity. DVD

Christopher Walken *Frank White* • David Caruso *Dennis Gilley* • Larry Fishburne [Laurence Fishburne] *Jimmy Jump* • Victor Argo *Lieutenant Roy Bishop* • Wesley Snipes *Thomas Flanigan* • Janet Julian *Jennifer Poe* • Joey Chin *Larry Wong* • Giancarlo Esposito *Lance* • Paul Calderon *Joey Dalesio* • Steve Buscemi *Test Tube* ■ *Dir* Abel Ferrara • *Scr* Nicholas St John

The King of Paris ★★ 12

Romantic drama
1995 · Fr/UK · Colour · 102mins

A throwback to the literate films made in the 1930s, this is both sustained and undermined by its old-fashioned style. Expertly adopting the grand stage style, Philippe Noiret holds the piece together, even though his character's world is falling apart. Hungarian exile Veronika Varga exploits their romance to further her career before dumping him. Polished, yes, but also ponderous. DP. In French with English subtitles.

Philippe Noiret *Victor Derval* • Veronika Varga *Lisa Lanska* • Jacques Roman *Romain Coste* • Manuel Blanc *Paul Derval* • Michel Aumont *Marquis de Castellac* ■ *Dir* Dominique Maillet • *Scr* Jacques Fieschi, Jérôme Tonnerre, Bernard Minoret, Dominique Maillet

King of the Ants ★★ 18

Crime horror 2003 · US · Colour · 97mins

It's hard to believe that Charlie Higson from TV's *The Fast Show* wrote the script for this dark chiller based on his own novel. An intense and claustrophobic tale, it examines the cold-blooded horror that unfolds when young drifter Chris McKenna agrees to carry out a murder for corrupt building contractor Daniel Baldwin. This has its moments, making up for a shaky plot with scenes of calm and twisted brutality. SF. Contains swearing, sex scenes, nudity, violence. DVD

Chris McKenna *Sean Crawley* • Kari Wuhrer *Susan Gatley* • Daniel Baldwin *Ray Mathews* • George Wendt *Duke* • Timm Sharp *George* • Ron Livingston *Eric Gatley* ■ *Dir* Stuart Gordon • *Scr* Charlie Higson, from his novel

King of the Children ★★★★

Drama 1987 · Chi · Colour · 106mins

Chen Kaige explores the nature and value of education in this quietly combative inquiry into indoctrination and the unvanquishable curiosity of the individual. Set in the latter days of the Cultural Revolution, the story chronicles the conversion of Xie Yuan, a farm labourer who is ordered to supervise the local school, only for him to realise that freedom of expression and an appreciation of the world at large provide a better grounding in life than any Maoist platitude. This is a densely allegorical film, but it's also mesmerising and inspirational. DP. In Mandarin with English subtitles.

Xie Yuan *Lao Gan* • Yang Xuewen *Wang Fu* • Chen Shaohua *Headmaster Chen* ■ *Dir* Chen Kaige • *Scr* Chen Kaige, Wan Zhi, from a short story by Ah Cheng

King of the Damned ★★

Prison drama 1935 · UK · BW · 81mins

Critics of the time regarded Walter Forde's film as a dry-land version of *Mutiny on the Bounty*. The setting is a prison island where the methods used by governor CM Hallard are so harsh that a rebellion ensues, led by Conrad Veidt and Noah Beery. Since the convicts can't escape, they turn the island into a collective run on communist lines. Of course, there's a spot of romance as well between Veidt and the deposed governor's daughter (Helen Vinson). AT

Conrad Veidt *Convict 83* • Helen Vinson *Anna Courvin* • Noah Beery *Mooche* • Cecil Ramage *Ramon Montez* • Percy Walsh *Captain Perez* • Peter Croft *"Boy" convict* • CM Hallard *Commandant Courvin* ■ *Dir* Walter Forde • *Scr* Charles Bennett, Sidney Gilliat, AR Rawlinson, from a play by John Chancellor

King of the Grizzlies ★★★ U

Adventure drama
1969 · US/Can · Colour · 93mins

This family film benefits from producer Winston Hibler's extensive experience on Disney nature pictures. With Canada standing in for the Wild West, this action-packed adventure chronicles the friendship between native American John Yesno and a bear he cares for as a cub and later encounters as a hungry 10ft menace threatening Chris Wiggins's farm. Hibler's narration brings an educational angle to this beautifully photographed film. DP

John Yesno *Moki* • Chris Wiggins *Colonel Pierson* • Hugh Webster *Shorty* • Jack Van Evera *Slim* • Winston Hibler *Narrator* ■ *Dir* Ron Kelly • *Scr* Jack Spiers, Rod Peterson, Norman Wright, from the book *The Biography of a Grizzly* by Ernest Thompson Seton • *Cinematographer* Reginald Morris

King of the Gypsies ★★★

Drama 1978 · US · Colour · 111mins

Sterling Hayden stars as the dying gypsy leader who disinherits his son in favour of his grandson who, in turn, rejects his birthright. Critics weren't quite sure whether to expect a musical like *Fiddler on the Roof* or a bloody dynastic saga like *The Godfather*. They were disappointed on both counts, but this does offer an impressive cast, with Eric Roberts in his debut as the heir apparent, caught between loyalty to his gypsy ancestry and the attractions of the modern world. The intimidating Hayden is like a less-mannered Anthony Quinn. AT

Sterling Hayden *King Zharko Stepanowicz* • Shelley Winters *Queen Rachel* • Susan Sarandon *Rose* • Judd Hirsch *Groffo* • Eric Roberts *Dave* • Brooke Shields *Tita* ■ *Dir* Frank Pierson • *Scr* Frank Pierson, from the book by Peter Maas

King of the Hill ★★★★ PG

Drama 1993 · US · Colour · 90mins

Writer/director Steven Soderbergh's richly detailed and carefully controlled coming-of-age saga follows the adventures of a 12-year-old boy left to fend for himself in a St Louis hotel during the Depression. It's a sparkling gem, wonderfully acted by Jesse Bradford as the resourceful tyke who strides with an unsentimental confidence through every real or imagined threat to his existence. A rewarding drama from the *Sex, Lies, and Videotape* director, full of quirky characters and deeply satisfying quiet moments. AJ. Contains swearing.

Jesse Bradford *Aaron* • Jeroen Krabbé *Mr Kurlander* • Lisa Eichhorn *Mrs Kurlander* • Joseph Chrest *Ben* • Spalding Gray *Mr Mungo* • Elizabeth McGovern *Lydia* • Karen Allen *Miss Mathey* • Chris Samples *Billy Thompson* ■ *Dir* Steven Soderbergh • *Scr* Steven Soderbergh, from the memoirs of AE Hotchner

King of the Khyber Rifles ★★ U

Adventure 1953 · US · Colour · 99mins

Twentieth Century-Fox lavished Technicolor and its biggest star, Tyrone Power, on this *Boys' Own* yarn set in the subcontinent's North-West Frontier. As a half-Indian, half-British officer who falls for the general's daughter, Power is despised by his fellow officers, but still manages to galvanise the locals against the rebels. Solid direction from Henry King and some decent heroics are let down by a weak heroine (Terry Moore) and unconvincing American locations, which stand in for Peshawar. AT

Tyrone Power *Captain Alan King* • Terry Moore *Susan Maitland* • Michael Rennie *Brigadier General Maitland* • Guy Rolfe *Karram Khan* • John Justin *Lieutenant Heath* • Richard Stapley *Lieutenant Baird* ■ *Dir* Henry King • *Scr* Ivan Goff, Ben Roberts, from the novel by Talbot Mundy

King of the Mountain ★★

Drama 1981 · US · Colour · 90mins

Ever wonder what came between the hippies and slackers? You'll find out in this strangely pretentious movie about Californian gearheads. Harry Hamlin plays a guy who loves to drag race along Mulholland Drive with his friends, but has to reconsider his lifestyle when he gets serious about a girl. Dennis Hopper, as a burned-out racer, steals the show by spouting lines such as "he's drunk with the greed of his youth!", in his inimitable fashion. Sadly, it's not enough to spare us from the clichés on parade. ST

Harry Hamlin *Steve* • Joseph Bottoms *Buddy* • Deborah Van Valkenburgh *Tina* • Richard Cox *Roger* • Dennis Hopper *Cal* • Dan Haggerty *Rick* ■ *Dir* Noel Nosseck • *Scr* HR Christian, from the article *Thunder Road* by David Barry

King of the Roaring 20s – the Story of Arnold Rothstein ★★

Biographical drama 1961 · US · BW · 106mins

Like its companion piece *The George Raft Story*, which was also directed by Joseph M Newman, this marks a fascinating return to the gangster era. David Janssen makes a seductively likeable Rothstein, the infamous 1920s gambler, and since audiences had barely heard of him, let alone remembered that he was fat and squat, Janssen gets away with it. The supporting cast is notable, featuring Mickey Rooney and Diana Dors, near the end of her ill-advised Hollywood experience. TS

David Janssen *Arnold Rothstein* • Dianne Foster *Carolyn Green* • Mickey Rooney *Johnny Burke* • Jack Carson *"Big Tim" O'Brien* • Diana Dors *Madge* • Dan O'Herlihy *Phil Butler* • Keenan Wynn *Tom Fowler* ■ *Dir* Joseph M Newman • *Scr* Jo Swerling, from the book *The Big Bankroll: the Life and Times of Arnold Rothstein* by Leo Katcher

King of the Turf ★★

Drama 1939 · US · BW · 88mins

This racetrack story stars Adolphe Menjou as a former horse owner who has drifted into booze and general decline. Then he meets a kid, Roger Daniel, who lifts his heart and soul and inspires him to put his life back on track. Then the boy's mother (Dolores Costello) arrives with a fateful secret... Audiences who sobbed through *The Champ* got another dose of sentimental claptrap from this one, but cynics among today's audiences will find it virtually unwatchable. AT

Adolphe Menjou *Jim Mason* • Roger Daniel *Goldie* • Dolores Costello *Mrs Eve Barnes* • Walter Abel *Mr Barnes* ■ *Dir* Alfred E Green • *Scr* George Bruce

King of the Underworld ★★

Crime drama 1939 · US · BW · 69mins

A remake of the 1935 melodrama *Dr Socrates*, it features Kay Francis as a female doctor out for revenge. Gangster Humphrey Bogart is the object of her retribution after he killed her surgeon husband in an earlier incident. A feeble, risible effort that only earns a second star for having the benefit of a snarling Bogart. TH

Humphrey Bogart *Joe Gurney* • Kay Francis *Dr Carol Nelson* • James Stephenson *Bill Stevens* • John Eldredge *Dr Niles Nelson* ■ *Dir* Lewis Seiler • *Scr* Vincent Sherman, George Bricker, from the story *Dr Socrates* by WR Burnett

King of the Wind ★★★ U

Adventure 1989 · US · Colour · 101mins

This is a must-see for all keen young members of the pony set, albeit a rather dubious proposition for cynical grown-ups who regard horse racing as a short cut to bankruptcy. Despite that, this story of a legendary Arab horse and the teenage groom (Navin Chowdhry) who accompanies him from North Africa to England has some splendid photography and is a chance to see a remarkable cast of mainly British actors. TH

Frank Finlay *Edward Coke* • Jenny Agutter *Hannah Coke* • Nigel Hawthorne *Achmet* • Navin Chowdhry *Agba* • Ralph Bates *Leduc* • Neil Dickson *Earl of Godolphin* • Barry Foster *Mr Williams* • Jill Gascoine *Mrs Williams* • Joan Hickson *Duchess of Marlborough* • Anthony Quayle *Lord Granville* • Ian Richardson *Bey of Tunis* • Peter Vaughan *Captain* • Richard Harris *King George II* • Glenda Jackson *Queen Caroline* ■ *Dir* Peter Duffell • *Scr* Phil Frey, from the novel by Marguerite Henry, adapted by Leslie Sayle • *Cinematographer* Brian Morgan

King, Queen, Knave ★★★★

Comedy 1972 · US/W Ger · Colour · 91mins

A bold, intermittently successful attempt by Polish director Jerzy Skolimowski to bring Vladimir Nabokov's intensely literary black comedy to the screen. Gauche orphan John Moulder-Brown goes to stay with his uncle David Niven, only to be seduced by the latter's wife (Gina Lollobrigida) and asked to kill her husband. None of Nabokov's wordplay survives, but there are some startling moments of cold-hearted humour. TH

David Niven *Charles Dreyer* • Gina Lollobrigida *Martha Dreyer* • John Moulder-Brown *Frank* • Mario Adorf *Prof Ritter* ■ *Dir* Jerzy Skolimowski • *Scr* David Seltzer, David Shaw, from a novel by Vladimir Nabokov

King Ralph ★★ PG

Comedy 1991 · US · Colour · 92mins

Even the slobbish charm of John Goodman can't save this horribly misconceived comedy of palace shenanigans. When the entire British royal family is wiped out in a freak photography accident, the unlikely successor turns out to be a Las Vegas entertainer (Goodman), who proceeds to bumble his way through the affairs of state with the assistance of adviser Peter O'Toole. The latter, and John Hurt as a scheming courtier, look to be having a hugely enjoyable time, but the talented cast is let down by writer/director David S Ward's dim script. JF. Contains swearing, nudity.

John Goodman *Ralph Jones* • Peter O'Toole *Cedric Willingham* • John Hurt *Lord Graves* • Camille Coduri *Miranda* • Richard Griffiths *Phipps* • Leslie Phillips *Gordon* • James Villiers *Hale* • Joely Richardson *Princess Anna* • Julian Glover *King Gustav* ■ *Dir* David S Ward • *Scr* David S Ward, from the novel *Headlong* by Emlyn Williams

King Rat ★★★★ PG

Second World War prison drama 1965 · US · BW · 128mins

Set in a Japanese PoW camp, this stars George Segal as an opportunist and arch-manipulator, custodian of everything valuable from coffee to rats. It's a great performance – he is the sole American amid the pukka English accents and class warfare of James Fox and Denholm Elliott. Directed by Bryan Forbes from James Clavell's novel, and shot in Hollywood (not that you'd notice), this is a gripping if overlong drama, notable also for one of John Barry's finest scores. AT

George Segal *Corporal King* • Tom Courtenay *Lt Grey* • James Fox *Flight Lieutenant Marlowe* • Patrick O'Neal *Max* • Denholm Elliott *Lt Colonel Denholm Larkin* • James Donald *Dr Kennedy* • Todd Armstrong *Tex* • John Mills *Col Smedley-Taylor* • Gerald Sim *Col Jones* • Leonard Rossiter *Major McCoy* • John Standing *Capt Daven* • Alan Webb *Col Brant* ■ *Dir* Bryan Forbes • *Scr* Bryan Forbes, from the novel by James Clavell

King Richard and the Crusaders ★★ U

Historical epic 1954 · US · Colour · 113mins

Sir Walter Scott's novel *The Talisman* gets a Hollywood makeover courtesy of director David Butler. Rex Harrison blacks up to play the Muslim leader Saladin, who goes up against European powers led by Richard Lionheart (George Sanders). Laurence Harvey is the pretty juvenile lead, but it's Virginia Mayo who falls for sexy Saladin and gets the best line of dialogue: "War, war, that's all you think of, Dick Plantagenet!" AT

Rex Harrison *Saladin* • Virginia Mayo *Lady Edith* • George Sanders *King Richard I* • Laurence Harvey *Sir Kenneth* • Robert Douglas *Sir Giles Amaury* ■ *Dir* David Butler • *Scr* John Twist, from the novel *The Talisman* by Sir Walter Scott

King-Size Canary ★★★★★

Animated comedy 1947 · US · Colour · 8mins

Director Tex Avery made many brilliant short cartoons during his heyday at MGM, but this is arguably the purest, with a determined, nightmarish logic. Practically every gag is in the service of the plot in which a cat, a canary and a dog battle over a bottle of plant feed when they discover it turns them into giants.The deliberately cynical ending in which the bloated animals decide to end the picture because they have run out of "the stuff" underscores the futility of their power struggle. Serious or not, all of this is sublimated beneath a characteristic landslide of gags delivered at the usual break-neck pace and cheerful near-contempt for the genre that is still shockingly refreshing. CLP

Dir Tex Avery • *Scr* Heck Allen

King Solomon's Mines ★★★ U

Adventure 1937 · UK · BW · 76mins

The first of several adaptations of H Rider Haggard's tale, with Paul Robeson as the noble African who leads a party of British treasure hunters across the desert and through the jungles to the mythical diamond mine. Inevitably, Robeson often breaks the journey by launching into song – great voice, pity about the loss of narrative momentum. Cedric Hardwicke plays the traditional white hunter, Roland Young offers a sense of humour, while John Loder and Anna Lee embark on a gooey romance. This is an old-fashioned adventure, spiced up by a certain jungle mystery. AT

Paul Robeson *Umbopa* • Cedric Hardwicke *Allan Quatermain* • Roland Young *Commander Good* • John Loder *Henry Curtis* • Anna Lee *Kathy O'Brien* • Sydney Fairbrother *Gagool* ■ *Dir* Robert Stevenson • *Scr* Roland Pertwee, Michael Hogan, AR Rawlinson, Charles Bennett, (uncredited) Ralph Spence, from the novel *King Solomon's Mines* by H Rider Haggard

King Solomon's Mines ★★★ PG

Adventure 1950 · US · Colour · 98mins

Stewart Granger and Deborah Kerr star in this stirring adaptation of Sir Henry Rider Haggard's 1885 novel about the search for a lost city, the resting place of Solomon's royal booty. It's full of animal action, frenzied natives and sentimental love scenes, with Compton Bennett directing the static bits and Andrew Marton handling the African exteriors. The novel was an immediate success, but, curiously, it was not filmed until 1937. This remake won Oscars for its colour photography and editing. AT

Deborah Kerr *Elizabeth Curtis* • Stewart Granger *Allan Quatermain* • Richard Carlson *John Goode* • Hugo Haas *Van Brun* • Lowell Gilmore *Eric Masters* • Siriaque *Umbopa* ■ *Dir* Compton Bennett, Andrew Marton • *Scr* Helen Deutsch, from the novel by H Rider Haggard • *Cinematographer* Robert Surtees • *Editor* Ralph E Winters, Conrad A Nervig

King Solomon's Mines ★★ PG

Adventure 1985 · US · Colour · 95mins

Richard Chamberlain and Sharon Stone head off into the crocodile- and snake-infested jungle in search of buried treasure and something of the flair of Steven Spielberg's *Raiders of the Lost Ark*. Any similarity between their adventures and H Rider Haggard's source novel is probably accidental, but there's an old-fashioned charm to the enterprise that makes us overlook its faults. This was Sharon Stone's first starring role and it's obvious she was going places. A sequel, *Allan Quartermain and the Lost City of Gold*, followed in 1987. AT DVD

Richard Chamberlain *Allan Quatermain* • Sharon Stone *Jessie Huston* • Herbert Lom *Colonel Bockner* • John Rhys-Davies *Dogati* • Ken Gampu *Umbopa* ■ *Dir* J Lee Thompson • *Scr* Gene Quintano, James R Silke, from the novel by H Rider Haggard

King Solomon's Treasure ★★ PG

Adventure 1977 · Can/UK · Colour · 84mins

Allan Quartermain has been portrayed by such leading players as Cedric Hardwicke, Stewart Granger and Richard Chamberlain. John Colicos isn't exactly in their league, so any interest that this Anglo-Canadian co-production possesses lies in its teaming of ex-*Man from UNCLE* David McCallum with *Avengers* stalwart Patrick Macnee. Former Bond girl Britt Ekland co-stars as the curiously named Queen Nypeptha. RT

John Colicos *Allan Quatermain* • David McCallum *Sir Henry Curtis* • Patrick Macnee *Captain Good RN* • Britt Ekland *Queen Nypeptha* • Wilfrid Hyde White *Oldest club member* ■ *Dir* Alvin Rakoff • *Scr* Colin Turner, Allan Prior, from the novel *Allan Quatermain* by H Rider Haggard

The King Steps Out ★★★

Musical romance 1936 · US · BW · 85mins

Opera soprano Grace Moore shines in this adaptation of an operetta by the Marischka brothers, expertly transferred to the screen by the great director Josef von Sternberg. The plot's slight, but Moore and co-star Franchot Tone are both charming in their roles of princess and emperor. Moore was to make only three more features, her weight problem – glimpsed here but kept at bay – seriously interfering with

K

her casting, and she died in an air crash in 1947. TS

Miss Grace Moore [Grace Moore] *Elizabeth/ "Cissy"* • Franchot Tone *Emperor Franz Josef* • Walter Connolly *Maximilian, Duke of Bavaria* • Raymond Walburn *Von Kempen* • Elisabeth Risdon *Sofia* • Nana Bryant *Louise* • Herman Bing *Pretzelberger* ■ *Dir* Josef von Sternberg • *Scr* Sidney Buchman, from the operetta *Sissy* by Hubert Marischka, Ernst Marischka, from the play *Sissy's Brautfahrt* by Ernest Decsay, Gustav Hohn

The Kingdom ★★★★ 18

Black comedy horror thriller
1994 · Den/Swe/Ger · Colour · 239mins

This lengthy but eerily engrossing movie comprises the first four episodes of Lars von Trier's 13-part Danish TV series, a supernatural soap about the bizarre doctors, nurses, patients and restless spirits in a Copenhagen hospital. Shot with a visual style that mirrors the colour of bodily fluids, and filled with an incredible gallery of eccentric characters, von Trier's opus is darkly humorous and extremely creepy. After nearly four hours, though, those seeking a neat resolution might be a bit miffed. JC. In Danish and Swedish with English subtitles. Contains some violence. DVD

Ernst-Hugo Jaregard *Stig Helmer* • Kirsten Rolffes *Mrs Drusse* • Ghita Norby *Rigmor* • Soren Pilmark *Krogen* • Holger Juul Hansen *Dr Moesgaard* • Annevig Schelde Ebbe *Mary* • Jens Okking *Bulder* ■ *Dir* Lars von Trier • *Scr* Tomas Gislason, Lars von Trier, from a story by Lars von Trier, Niels Vorsel

Kingdom of Heaven ★★★★ 15

Epic historical drama
2005 · US/UK/Sp/Ger · Colour · 144mins

Director Ridley Scott once again finds inspiration in the past with this exciting mix of action, adventure and history lesson. At the outset, Orlando Bloom is just a 12th-century French blacksmith, but within minutes he has lost his family and been invited to the Holy Land by a Crusader father (Liam Neeson) previously unknown to him. The uneasy peace in Jerusalem between the Christians, under King Baldwin IV (Edward Norton), and the neighbouring Muslim forces of Saladin (a wonderful Ghassan Massoud) is threatened by fanatics, prompting Bloom to defend the city against overwhelming odds. While Bloom is rather unconvincing as a leader of men, the siege is breathtaking, the characters colourful, and the dialogue intelligent. BP. In English and Arabic with subtitles. Contains violence.

Orlando Bloom *Balian* • Eva Green *Sibylla* • Jeremy Irons *Tiberias* • David Thewlis *Hospitaler* • Brendan Gleeson *Reynald de Chatillon* • Marton Csokas *Guy de Lusignan* • Liam Neeson *Godfrey of Ibelin* • Ghassan Massoud *Saladin* • Edward Norton *King Baldwin IV* • Alexander Siddig *Imad* • Michael Sheen *Priest* • Kevin McKidd *English Sergeant* • Jon Finch *Patriarch of Jerusalem* • Iain Glen *Richard Coeur de Lion* ■ *Dir* Ridley Scott • *Scr* William Monahan

Kingdom of the Spiders ★★★ PG

Horror 1977 · US · Colour · 90mins

Angered by pesticides, swarms of tarantulas attack an Arizona town in this neat low-budget chiller, directed by dependable B-movie veteran John "Bud" Cardos. William Shatner, in one of his better non-*Star Trek* roles, plays a veterinarian who joins forces with insect expert Tiffany Bolling to ascertain why nature has run amok. The creepiness is made more credible by an above-average script and some admirable staging. AJ

William Shatner *Rack Hansen* • Tiffany Bolling *Diane Ashley* • Woody Strode *Walter Colby* • Lieux Dressler *Emma Washburn* • David McLean *Sheriff Gene Smith* • Altovise Davis *Birch Colby* ■ *Dir* John "Bud" Cardos • *Scr* Richard Robinson, Alan Caillou, from a story by Jeffrey M Sneller, Stephen Lodge

Kingpin ★★ 12

Sports comedy 1996 · US · Colour · 108mins

A typically vulgar tale from the Farrelly brothers, it lacks the soft centre that sweetened the taste of their later hit *There's Something about Mary.* Humour-wise, it's a very mixed bag, populated by the most irredeemably unpleasant characters. Ex-bowling prodigy Woody Harrelson's detachable rubber hand is overused to the point of annoyance, but there are some very funny moments involving Randy Quaid's *Forrest Gump*-like naivety, but Bill Murray's flamboyant villain gains the most laughs. JC. Contains some violence and swearing. DVD

Woody Harrelson *Roy Munson* • Randy Quaid *Ishmael Boorg* • Vanessa Angel *Claudia* • Bill Murray *Ernie McCracken* • Chris Elliott *The gambler* • William Jordan *Mr Boorg* • Richard Tyson *Owner of Stiffy's* ■ *Dir* Peter Farrelly, Bobby Farrelly • *Scr* Barry Fanaro, Mort Nathan

Kings and Desperate Men ★ 15

Drama 1981 · Can · Colour · 118mins

The presence of Margaret Trudeau is the only noteworthy aspect of this sloppy kidnap drama. But the former Canadian prime minister's ex-wife takes a back seat as her husband (Patrick McGoohan) is held hostage on his talk radio show by a gang of rookie terrorists. Fleetingly, at the start of the siege, this threatens to become gripping. Then McGoohan begins chomping on the scenery, and the dual ineptitude of Alexis Kanner's acting and direction becomes clear. DP

Patrick McGoohan *John Kingsley* • Alexis Kanner *Lucas Miller* • Andrea Marcovicci *Girl* • Margaret Trudeau *Elizabeth Kingsley* • August Schellenberg *Aldini* ■ *Dir* Alexis Kanner • *Scr* Edmund Ward, Alexis Kanner

Kings & Queen ★★★★ 15

Comedy drama 2004 · Fr · Colour · 152mins

Mathieu Amalric won a César for his performance as a neurotic viola player in Arnaud Desplechin's astute study of emotional self-delusion. Emmanuelle Devos is perhaps even more impressive as his obsessional ex-wife, who asks him to adopt the child of her first marriage to facilitate the success of her impending third. Desplechin employs an array of flashbacks, reveries and confessions to chronicle this bizarre relationship. Equally effective are the intimate encounters between Amalric and ten-year-old Valentin Lelong, and Devos and her novelist father (Maurice Garrel). DP. In French, English and German with subtitles. Contains swearing.

Emmanuelle Devos *Nora* • Mathieu Amalric *Ismaël* • Catherine Deneuve *Madame Vasset* • Maurice Garrel *Louis Jenssens* • Nathalie Boutefeu *Chloé Jenssens* • Jean-Paul Roussillon *Abel Vuillard* • Magali Woch *Arielle* • Hippolyte Girardot *M Mamanne* • Valentin Lelong *Elias* ■ *Dir* Arnaud Desplechin • *Scr* Roger Bohbot, Arnaud Desplechin

Kings Go Forth ★★ PG

Second World War drama
1958 · US · BW · 108mins

In this strange blend of war adventure and racial drama, Frank Sinatra and Tony Curtis star as two soldiers whose friendship is tested when the former falls for Natalie Wood, playing a girl of African descent. But it's Curtis who makes a move on Wood before dumping. Delmer Daves's film is very much part of the liberalisation of Hollywood movies that took place in the mid-1950s, but it's weighed down by plot contrivances and by its own self-importance. AT DVD

Frank Sinatra *Sam Loggins* • Tony Curtis *Britt Harris* • Natalie Wood *Monique Blair* • Leora Dana *Mrs Blair* • Karl Swenson *Colonel* ■ *Dir* Delmer Daves • *Scr* Merle Miller, from the novel by Joe David Brown

Kings of the Road ★★★★ 18

Road movie 1976 · W Ger · BW · 168mins

This is an elegiac epic as much about American cultural imperialism as the forgotten border country between East and West Germany. Making evocative use of rock music and touching on topics as diverse as exile, communication and the decline of the national film industry, the action is void of contrived incident and conventional characterisation. They are barely missed, however, as Wenders demonstrates his mastery of the long take and the visual metaphor, exploiting Robbie Müller's stylish monochrome photography to locate the poetry in a desolate landscape. DP. In German with English subtitles.

Rüdiger Vogler *Bruno Winter* • Hanns Zischler *Robert Lander* • Lisa Kreuzer *Cashier* • Rudolf Schündler *Robert's father* • Marquard Bohm *Man who has lost his wife* ■ *Dir/Scr* Wim Wenders

Kings of the Sun ★★★ U

Adventure 1963 · US · Colour · 107mins

This is one of Hollywood's rare excursions into Meso-American history, with George Chakiris (*West Side Story*) looking convincingly Mayan and virile even when addressing characters with names like Ixzubin and Ah Zok. It's all faintly ridiculous, but there are some spectacular scenes in authentic Mayan sites like Chichen Itza. The Mayans were keen on human sacrifice, but don't hold that against them: according to this story, they also built the first permanent settlement in Texas. AT

Yul Brynner *Black Eagle* • George Chakiris *Balam* • Shirley Anne Field *Ixchel* • Brad Dexter *Ah Haleb* • Barry Morse *Ah Zok* • Armando Silvestre *Isatai* • Leo Gordon *Hunac Ceel* • Victoria Vetri *Ixzubin* ■ *Dir* J Lee Thompson • *Scr* Elliott Arnold, James R Webb, from a story by Elliott Arnold

The King's Pirate ★★ U

Swashbuckling adventure
1967 · US · Colour · 99mins

Just what the movie world didn't need in the Swinging Sixties: a low-budget remake of the Errol Flynn/Maureen O'Hara swashbuckler *Against All Flags*, with TV star Doug McClure gauche and inadequate in the Flynn role. However, McClure's co-stars Jill St John and Guy Stockwell (Dean's brother), who both have some style and look comfortable in period costume, make amends. If you look closely you'll see an awful lot of the original film on display, with the new material cleverly shot around the footage by talented director Don Weis. TS

Doug McClure *Lt Brian Fleming* • Jill St John *Jessica Stephens* • Guy Stockwell *John Avery* • Mary Ann Mobley *Princess Patma* • Kurt Kasznar *Zucco* ■ *Dir* Don Weis • *Scr* Paul Wayne, Aeneas MacKenzie, Joseph Hoffman, from a story by Aeneas MacKenzie

King's Rhapsody ★★ U

Romantic drama 1955 · UK · Colour · 92mins

It was a sad sight to watch the great swashbuckler Errol Flynn in his two British movies for Herbert Wilcox. Clearly paunchy and slightly raddled, he managed to retain that twinkle in the eye but conveyed a general sense of slumming as he played opposite Mrs Wilcox, Anna Neagle. This is a sorry, tawdry affair, a Ruritanian romance that was past its sell-by date even as a play on the London stage. Flynn looks clearly the worse for drink in the many sequences where dialogue is played off him. Of course, that in itself is a reason for watching and enjoying this antiquated romp. TS

Anna Neagle *Marta Karillos* • Errol Flynn *King Richard of Laurentia* • Patrice Wymore *Princess Christiane* • Martita Hunt *Queen Mother* • Finlay Currie *King Paul* • Francis De Wolff *Prime Minister* • Joan Benham *Countess Astrid* ■ *Dir* Herbert Wilcox • *Scr* Pamela Bower, Christopher Hassall, AP Herbert, from the play by Ivor Novello

Kings Row ★★★★

Melodrama 1942 · US · BW · 126mins

Henry Bellamann's bestseller was the *Peyton Place* of its day, a steamy study of small-town mentality. Warner Bros did it full justice on the screen, subtly circumventing the censor and delivering a complex adult movie, with notable scenes and impeccable performances, offering career best opportunities to future US president Ronald Reagan ("where's the rest of me?" he shrieks after a wanton and unnerving amputation) and Ann Sheridan, the girl from the wrong side of the tracks. Only weak lead Robert Cummings is uncomfortably cast. Erich Wolfgang Korngold's music is a model of its kind, his main theme superb and stunningly melodic. Strong, intelligent entertainment. TS

Ann Sheridan *Randy Monaghan* • Robert Cummings *Parris Mitchell* • Ronald Reagan *Drake McHugh* • Betty Field *Cassandra Tower* • Charles Coburn *Dr Henry Gordon* • Claude Rains *Dr Alexander Tower* • Judith Anderson *Mrs Harriet Gordon* • Nancy Coleman *Louise Gordon* ■ *Dir* Sam Wood • *Scr* Casey Robinson, Henry Bellamann, from a novel by Henry Bellamann

The King's Thief ★ U

Period adventure 1955 · US · Colour · 78mins

David Niven is cast against type in this frightful Restoration melodrama as the villainous first minister of George Sanders (shamelessly overacting in his second turn as Charles II), intent on bumping off enemies. But plucky Ann Blyth, who enlists the help of highwayman Edmund Purdom, helps expose the nasty Niven. The "swashbuckless" plot limps along, with drab colour, indifferent performances and slack direction. DP

David Niven *Duke of Brampton* • Ann Blyth *Lady Mary* • Edmund Purdom *Michael Dermott* • George Sanders *Charles II* • Roger Moore *Jack* • John Dehner *Captain Herrick* • Sean McClory *Sheldon* • Tudor Owen *Simon* • Melville Cooper *Henry Wynch* ■ *Dir* Robert Z Leonard • *Scr* Christopher Knopf, from a story by Robert Hardy Andrews

The King's Trial ★★★

Historical drama
1990 · Fr/Por/W Ger/It · Colour · 91mins

The costumes and trappings of mid-17th-century Portugal have been lavishly re-created, but what makes this film stand out is its compelling tale of intrigue, lust and ambition. The overthrow of Alfonso VI by his brother Pedro and his wife Dona Maria is one of the darkest episodes in Portuguese history, and director Joao Mario Grilo recalls it with evident fascination and some relish. Carlos Daniel is fine as the feeble-minded king, but is outshone by Antonino Solmer and Aurelle Doazan as the schemers. DP. In Portuguese with English subtitles.

Carlos Daniel *King Alfonso VI* • Aurelle Doazan *Dona Maria* • Gerard Hardy *Preyssac* • Antonino Solmer *Pedro II* ■ *Dir* Joao Mario Grilo • *Scr* Jean-Pierre Theilladde, Daniel Arasse, Joao Mario Grilo

The King's Vacation ★★

Romantic comedy 1933 · US · BW · 60mins

Even in his heyday, the British born thespian George Arliss was something of an acquired taste. This Ruritanian comedy finds him playing a long-reigning monarch, who grows weary of court cant and abdicates. He then goes in search of the morganatic spouse he abandoned in order to ascend to the throne. However, Marjorie Gateson has turned into just the kind of snooty ninny he despises, so he heads back to his spurned queen to live in idyllic poverty. Hardly a piercing social tract, this is, nevertheless, an amiable fable. DP

George Arliss *Phillip the King* • Marjorie Gateson *Helen* • Dudley Digges *Lord Chamberlain* • Patricia Ellis *Millicent* • Florence Arliss *Margaret* • Dick Powell *John Kent* ■ *Dir* John G Adolfi • *Scr* Ernest Pascal, Maude T Howell, from a story by Ernest Pascal

The King's Whore ★★★ 15

Historical romantic drama
1990 · Fr/UK/Austria/It · Colour · 89mins

Timothy Dalton's theatrical background serves him well in the role of an Italian king who takes a shine to the wife of a French count. She doesn't fancy him, however, and the king's passion leads him to declare war on France. Director Axel Corti evidently admires *Barry Lyndon* and has a clear view of what the 17th century looked, sounded and smelt like. It's a lavish movie, though there are the usual Europudding lumps: a mishmash of a cast and an uneven script written by many hands. AT [video]

Timothy Dalton *King Vittorio Amadeo* • Valeria Golino *Jeanne de Luynes* • Robin Renucci *Charles de Luynes* • Stéphane Freiss *Count di Verua* • Feodor Chaliapin [Feodor Chaliapin Jr] *Scaglia* • Paul Crauchet *Duke of Luynes* • Margaret Tyzack *Dowager Countess* ■ *Dir* Axel Corti • *Scr* Axel Corti, Frederic Raphael, Daniel Vigne, from the novel *Jeanne de Luynes, comtesse de Verue* by Jacques Tournier • *Cinematographer* Gernot Roll

Kini and Adams ★★★

Drama 1997 · UK/Fr/Zim · Colour · 93mins

Burkina Faso's best-known director, Idrissa Ouedraogo, made his English-language debut with this investigation into the impact of industrialisation on rural Africa. Vusi Kunene and David Mohloki impress as the longtime buddies who fall out over the former's relationship with quarry foreman John Kani and gold-digging prostitute Netsayi Chigwendere. Although slightly muddled, this drama is still revealing in its discussion of women and their place in what is still, primarily, a patriarchal society. Made with additional backing from Switzerland and Ouedrago's home country. DP

Vusi Kunene *Kini* • David Mohloki *Adams* • John Kani *Ben* • Nthati Moshesh *Aida* • Netsayi Chigwendere *Binja* ■ *Dir* Idrissa Ouedraogo • *Scr* Idrissa Ouedraogo, Olivier Lorelle, Santiago Amigorena

Kinjite: Forbidden Subjects ★ 18

Action crime thriller
1989 · US · Colour · 93mins

Another Charles Bronson vehicle which you need a cast-iron gut to endure. This time the vigilante's friend plays an LA vice cop who teams up with a Japanese businessman whose daughter has been kidnapped by a gang who enslave children in the sex trade. This utterly repellent premise is handled by regular Bronson director J Lee Thompson as if it were merely an episode of *Kojak*. RS [video]

Charles Bronson *Lieutenant Crowe* • Perry Lopez *Eddie Rios* • Juan Fernandez *Duke* • Sy Richardson *Lavonne* • Peggy Lipton *Kathleen Crowe* • Nicole Eggert *DeeDee* • Bill McKinney *Father Burke* • James Pax *Hiroshi Hada* ■ *Dir* J Lee Thompson • *Scr* Harold Nebenzal

Kinsey ★★★★ 15

Biographical drama
2004 · US · Colour and BW · 113mins

Most people will find it difficult to imagine the level of sexual ignorance prevalent in 1948 when Alfred Kinsey published his ground-breaking book *Sexual Behaviour in the Human Male*. Director Bill Condon's excellent biopic charts the life of the academic (Liam Neeson) from his repressive religious childhood, when he is bullied by his moralistic father (John Lithgow), through his unsatisfactory first attempt at lovemaking with his wife (Laura Linney), which provokes his desire to research – and educate others about – human sexuality. Neeson has never been better, and there's also a fantastic performance from Peter Sarsgaard as a researcher and sexual adventurist. AS [video] DVD

Liam Neeson *Alfred Charles Kinsey* • Laura Linney *Clara Bracken McMillen* • Chris O'Donnell *Wardell Pomeroy* • Peter Sarsgaard *Clyde Martin* • Timothy Hutton *Paul Gebhard* • John Lithgow *Alfred Seguine Kinsey* • Tim Curry *Thurman Rice* • Oliver Platt *Herman Wells* • Dylan Baker *Alan Gregg* • Julianne Nicholson *Alice Martin* ■ *Dir/Scr* Bill Condon

Kipps ★★★ U

Comedy 1941 · UK · BW · 112mins

Critics were divided on the release of Carol Reed's adaptation of HG Wells's novel about the draper's clerk who discovers that, when it comes to social climbing, he has no head for heights. Some detected a certain detachment in Reed's direction, allowing Frank Launder and Sidney Gilliat's script to meander and supporting players to overact. But others claimed the film was stuffed with sly Wellsian satire, expertly staged set pieces and top-class acting from Michael Redgrave in the title role. While there is much to enjoy here, there are some interminable moments. DP

Michael Redgrave *Arthur Kipps* • Phyllis Calvert *Ann Pornick* • Diana Wynyard *Helen Walshingham* • Phillip Frost *Arthur as a boy* • Diana Calderwood *Ann as a girl* • Arthur Riscoe *Chitterlow* • Max Adrian *Chester Coote* • Helen Haye *Mrs Walshingham* • Michael Wilding *Ronnie Walshingham* ■ *Dir* Carol Reed • *Scr* Frank Launder, Sidney Gilliat, from the novel by HG Wells

Kippur ★★★

War drama based on a true story
2000 · Fr/It/Is · Colour · 118mins

This is a semi-autobiographical account of the ordeal experienced by seven members of a helicopter rescue unit, following the 1973 Day of Atonement attack on Israel by Syrian and Egyptian troops. Doubts have been raised about both the slowness of the opening scenes, as reservists Liron Levo and Tomer Ruso are diverted from the Golan Heights to the field hospital at Ramat David, and the repetitive nature of the various recovery missions. But Amos Gitai is seeking to show how the incessant carnage affects the morale of these hardly committed men, while also emphasising the human toll of this intractable struggle. DP. In Hebrew with English subtitles.

Liron Levo *Weinraub* • Tomer Ruso *Ruso* • Uri Ran Klauzner *Dr Klauzner* • Yoram Hattab *Pilot* • Juliano Merr *Captain* ■ *Dir* Amos Gitai • *Scr* Amos Gitai, Marie-Jose Sanselme

Kirikou and the Sorceress ★★★★ U

Animated fantasy adventure
1998 · Fr/Bel/Lux · Colour · 70mins

With a story inspired by a West African fable, graphics gleaned from indigenous art and a score by Senegalese star Youssou N'Dour, this is a glorious escape from the bland correctness and commercial cynicism of mainstream animation. Michel Ocelet's film challenges youngsters both to question social hierarchies and respect traditional values. But the infant Kirikou's quest to discover why the sorceress Karaba eats the local menfolk and surrounds herself with mischievous fetishes will also seize their imagination. DP. French dialogue dubbed into English. [video] DVD

Doudou Gueye Thiaw *Kirikou* • Maimouna Ndiaye *Kirikou's mother* • Awa Sene Sarr *Karaba the sorceress* • Robert Lionsol *Wise man of the mountain* • William Nadylam-Yotnda Sebastien Hébrant *Kirikou as a young man* • Tshilombo Lubambu *Kirikou's uncle* ■ *Dir* Michel Ocelot • *Scr* Michel Ocelot, Raymond Burlet

The Kirlian Witness ★★

Science-fiction mystery
1978 · US · Colour · 91mins

A very odd fantasy thriller made by one-time workers in the hardcore porn industry. A plant is the sole witness to a murder and Nancy Snyder, the victim's sister, uses her telepathic powers and sensitivity to flora to unmask the killer. Kirlian photography, capturing the aura around a living object, is used to solve the case. Slow, moody and just plain weird. AJ

Nancy Snyder *Rilla* • Ted Laplat *Dusty* • Joel Colodner *Robert* • Nancy Boykin *Laurie* • Lawrence Tierney *Detective* • Maia Danziger *Claire* ■ *Dir* Jonathan Sarno • *Scr* Jonathan Sarno, Lamar Sanders, from a story by Jonathan Sarno

Kismet ★★★ U

Fantasy adventure
1944 · US · Colour · 99mins

Arabian Nights-style tales were seldom the stuff of A-features, least of all at opulent MGM, but this adaptation of Edward Knoblock's play about the beggar–magician who aspires to royalty gets the full gloss treatment, with top stars Ronald Colman and Marlene Dietrich looking glamorous but ill at ease in this version of an oft-told hokey tale. The real value of this is by way of comparison to the 1955 musical version. Oh, and, of course, Dietrich. TS

Ronald Colman *Hafiz* • Marlene Dietrich *Jamilla* • James Craig *Caliph* • Edward Arnold *Mansur the Grand Vizier* • Hugh Herbert *Feisal* • Joy Ann Page [Joy Page] *Marsinah* • Florence Bates *Karsha* • Harry Davenport *Agha* ■ *Dir* William Dieterle • *Scr* John Meehan, from the play by Edward Knoblock • *Music* Herbert Stothat

Kismet ★★★ U

Fantasy musical 1955 · US · Colour · 108mins

Maligned in its day, this *Arabian Nights* farrago has much to recommend it now, notably muscular baritone Howard Keel having the time of his life. He plays Haaj – the beggar whose daughter has fallen for a caliph – with enormous energy, filling the screen with his worthy and under-rated performance. The rest of the cast also works hard, particularly the raunchy Dolores Gray, and Ann Blyth and Vic Damone make a perfectly acceptable pair of lovebirds and get all the best songs, especially the hit *Stranger in Paradise*. TS [video]

Howard Keel *Haaj, the Poet* • Ann Blyth *Marsinah* • Dolores Gray *Lalume* • Vic Damone *Caliph* • Monty Woolley *Omar* • Sebastian Cabot *Wazir* • Jay C Flippen *Jawan* • Mike Mazurki *Chief policeman* • Jack Elam *Hassan-Ben* ■ *Dir* Vincente Minnelli • *Scr* Charles Lederer, Luther Davis, from the play by Edward Knoblock • *Music/lyrics* George Forrest, Robert Wright

Kisna – the Warrior Poet ★★★ PG

Romantic adventure
2004 · Ind · Colour · 162mins

Cinematography and music combine to stirring effect in director Subhash Ghai's entertaining adventure. Vivek Oberoi stars as Kisna, the son of a stable boy, who gets caught between two cultures when he falls for Katherine (Antonia Bernarth), a British deputy commissioner's daughter. Set in pre-independence India, Ghai's epic melodrama contains moments of triumph and tragedy as the lovers struggle to stay together. Oberoi brings a wealth of melancholy to the role of Kisna, but surrenders centre stage to Bernath, who gives a very impressive performance. OA. In Hindi and English with subtitles. [video] DVD

Vivek Oberoi *Kisna* • Isha Sharwani *Laxmi* • Antonia Bernath *Katherine Beckett* • Polly Adams *Lady Katherine* • Rajat Kapoor *Prince Raghuraj* • Caroline Langrishe *Jennifer Beckett* • Michael Maloney *Peter Beckett* • Amrish Puri *Bhairo Singh* • Om Puri *Jumman Kisti* ■ *Dir* Subhash Ghai • *Scr* Sachin Bhowmick, Farrukh Dhondy, Subhash Ghai, Margaret Glover

The Kiss ★★★

Silent drama 1929 · US · Colour · 64mins

In provincial France Greta Garbo is tried for the murder of her husband Anders Randolf who, in a jealous fit, tried to kill the handsome Lew Ayres, who is infatuated with her. Defence lawyer Conrad Nagel is her own former lover. This thin melodrama is elevated by the silent but eloquent presence of Garbo, starring in a silent movie for the last time. Directed by France's Jacques Feyder, imported for the occasion, it was also MGM's final silent production, and marked the impressive debut of Ayres, soon to be a star of the talkies. RK

Greta Garbo *Irene* • Conrad Nagel *André* • Anders Randolf *Guarry* • Holmes Herbert *Lassalle* • Lew Ayres *Pierre* • George Davis *Durant* ■ *Dir* Jacques Feyder • *Scr* Hans Kräly, from a story by George M Saville

The Kiss ★★ 18

Thriller 1988 · US/Can · Colour · 93mins

Zombie cats, mutilation by escalator, supernatural mumbo jumbo and African demons are all to be found in this ludicrous chiller about an ancient witch (Joanna Pacula) who wants to pass on the secret of eternal youth via a kiss to her young niece (Meredith Salenger). Inane trash would be the best way to describe the directing debut of Pen Densham. Yet for all its faults, this stilted shocker is packed with enough gratuitous incident and hokey action to rivet the viewer. AJ [video]

Joanna Pacula *Felice* • Meredith Salenger *Amy* • Mimi Kuzyk *Brenda* • Nicholas Kilbertus *Jack* • Jan Rubes *Tobin* ■ *Dir* Pen Densham • *Scr* Stephen Volk, Tom Ropelewski, from a story by Stephen Volk

Kiss and Make-Up ★★

Romantic comedy 1934 · US · BW · 70mins

Cary Grant stars here as a top Parisian beauty consultant who falls for his client Genevieve Tobin. He soon discovers her charms are only skin deep and it's really his secretary Helen Mack he loves, but she's about to marry the flighty Tobin's ex-husband... Thin as lip gloss, but a sprinkling of witty cracks, the always expert Tobin and the incomparably polished Grant make this a watchable diversion. RK

Cary Grant *Dr Maurice Lamar* • Genevieve Tobin *Eve Caron* • Helen Mack *Annie* • Edward Everett Horton *Marcel Caron* • Lucien Littlefield *Max Pascal* • Mona Maris *Countess Rita* • Clara Lou Sheridan [Ann Sheridan] *Beauty operator* ■ *Dir* Harlan Thompson • *Scr*

K

George Marion Jr, Harlan Thompson, from the play *Kozmetika* by Istvan Bekeffi, adapted by Jane Hinton

Kiss and Tell ★★★

Romantic comedy 1945 · US · BW · 90mins

Once the world's biggest and smallest star, Shirley Temple was just another pretty teenage actress in the 1940s. This is one of her better later vehicles, thought quite shocking at the time. The mildly amusing comedy had the 17-year-old Temple pretending to be pregnant in order to divert attention from her brother's secret marriage. The film produced a sequel, *A Kiss for Corliss* in 1949, the year Temple retired from the movies. RB

Shirley Temple *Corliss Archer* • Jerome Courtland *Dexter Franklin* • Walter Abel *Mr Archer* • Katharine Alexander [Katherine Alexander] *Mrs Archer* • Robert Benchley *Uncle George Archer* • Porter Hall *Mr Franklin* • Virginia Welles *Mildred Pringle* • Tom Tully *Mr Pringle* • Darryl Hickman *Raymond Pringle* ■ *Dir* Richard Wallace • *Scr* F Hugh Herbert, from his play

A Kiss before Dying ★★★ 12

Crime drama 1956 · US · Colour · 93mins

A fine adaptation of author Ira Levin's dark tale about a social climber who kills his wealthy girlfriend when her pregnancy threatens her inheritance. It stars a cast-against-type Robert Wagner, cleverly made-up as a villain and relishing the kind of role he seldom played again. This *film noir* is actually shot in bright daylight colours by cinematographer Lucien Ballard, who makes excellent use of locations. A young Joanne Woodward plays the victim and a superb Mary Astor is Wagner's mother. AT DVD

Robert Wagner *Bud Corliss* • Jeffrey Hunter *Gordon Grant* • Virginia Leith *Ellen Kingship* • Joanne Woodward *Dorothy Kingship* • Mary Astor *Mrs Corliss* • George Macready *Leo Kingship* ■ *Dir* Gerd Oswald • *Scr* Lawrence Roman, from the novel by Ira Levin

A Kiss before Dying ★★★ 18

Thriller 1991 · US · Colour · 89mins

Despite a chilling performance from Matt Dillon, this attempt to update Ira Levin's novel for the 1990s doesn't quite get there. Dillon makes for a thoroughly charming psychopath, killing his way to the top of the corporate ladder by romancing twin wealthy heiresses, both played unconvincingly by Sean Young, and director James Dearden stages some effective, if derivative, set pieces. JF. Contains violence, swearing and nudity.

Matt Dillon *Jonathan Corliss* • Sean Young *Ellen/Dorothy Carlsson* • Max von Sydow *Thor Carlsson* • Jim Fyfe *Terry Dieter* • Ben Browder *Tommy Roussell* • Diane Ladd *Mrs Corliss* • Martha Gehman *Patricia Farren* • Shane Rimmer *Commissioner Mallet* • James Russo *Dan Corelli* ■ *Dir* James Dearden • *Scr* James Dearden, from the novel by Ira Levin

The Kiss before the Mirror ★★★

Crime drama 1933 · US · BW · 67mins

James Whale directed this atmospheric adaption of Ladislas Fodor's stage play, and also the 1938 remake, *Wives under Suspicion*. However, the enforcement of the Production Code in 1934 ensured that this is a much racier version that wallows in the lurid details of adultery and criminal passion. Paul Lukas turns in a solid performance, as a Viennese lawyer who admits to murdering his cheating wife. But he's well matched by Frank Morgan, as the defending attorney who comes to suspect spouse Nancy Carroll of deception as the case preys on his mind. DP

Nancy Carroll *Maria Held* • Frank Morgan *Dr Paul Held* • Paul Lukas *Dr Walter Bernsdorf* • Gloria Stuart *Frau Lucie Bernsdorf* • Jean Dixon *Hilda Frey* • Walter Pidgeon *Bachelor* • Charley Grapewin *Mr Schultz* • Donald Cook *Maria's lover* ■ *Dir* James Whale • *Scr* William Anthony McGuire, from the play by Ladislas Fodor

Kiss Daddy Good Night ★★★ 15

Psychological crime thriller 1987 · US · Colour · 78mins

The intriguing debut of Uma Thurman is an oddball affair. Playing a precocious young vamp, she picks up wealthy men in order to rob them. Unfortunately for the young "Poison Ivy", someone then begins to stalk her. It's untidily made, but Thurman has real presence and Steve Buscemi pops up in an early role. TH. Contains swearing and violence. DVD

Uma Thurman *Laura* • Paul Dillon *Sid* • Paul Richards (2) *William B Tilden* • Steve Buscemi *Johnny* • Annabelle Gurwitch *Sue* • David Brisbin *Nelson Blitz* ■ *Dir* Peter Ily Huemer • *Scr* Peter Ily Huemer, Michael Gabrieli, from a story by Peter Ily Huemer

A Kiss for Corliss ★

Comedy 1949 · US · BW · 87mins

No displays of affection were shown for this limp comedy, a sad end to the phenomenal career of Shirley Temple. Four years earlier she had starred as irrepressible teenager Corliss Archer in *Kiss and Tell*. In this sequel – in which Corliss is suspected of having spent the night with a playboy (David Niven) – the same director (Richard Wallace) guided her, sometimes ill-advisedly. As the plot's implausibilities increase, even the usually reliable Niven resorts to desperate mugging. TV

Shirley Temple *Corliss Archer* • David Niven *Kenneth Marquis* • Tom Tully *Harry Archer* • Virginia Welles *Mildred Pringle* • Darryl Hickman *Dexter Franklin* ■ *Dir* Richard Wallace • *Scr* Howard Dimsdale, from a story by Howard Dimsdale, from characters created by F Hugh Herbert

A Kiss in the Dark ★★

Romantic comedy 1949 · US · BW · 88mins

Concert pianist David Niven inherits an apartment block and becomes involved with his disparate collection of tenants, including photographic model Jane Wyman, with whom he falls in love. Niven's flair for comedy, and the confident presence of Wyman only just keep this afloat. Director Delmer Daves does his best, but the flat-footed script is under-stocked with laughs. RK

David Niven *Eric Phillips* • Jane Wyman *Polly Haines* • Victor Moore *Horace Willoughby* • Wayne Morris *Bruce Arnold* • Broderick Crawford *Mr Botts* • Joseph Buloff *Peter Danilo* • Maria Ouspenskaya *Madame Karina* ■ *Dir* Delmer Daves • *Scr* Harry Kurnitz, from a story by Everett Freeman, Devery Freeman

Kiss Kiss (Bang Bang) ★★

Comedy thriller 2001 · UK · Colour · 97mins

Chris Penn and Stellan Skarsgård star along with some familiar British faces (Paul Bettany, Allan Corduner, Martine McCutcheon) in this disappointing comedy thriller. Writer/director Stewart Sugg seems to be aiming for *Rain Man* territory but doesn't really succeed, as an over-the-hill hitman (Skarsgård) learns a few things from the mentally disabled son (Penn) of a friend. RT

Stellan Skarsgård *Felix* • Chris Penn *Bubba* • Paul Bettany *Jimmy* • Sienna Guillory *Kat* • Allan Corduner *Big Bob* • Ashley Artus *Mick Foot* • Martine McCutcheon *Mia* • Jacqueline McKenzie *Sherry* • Peter Vaughan *Daddy Zoo* ■ *Dir/Scr* Stewart Sugg

Kiss Me Again ★★★

Silent comedy 1925 · US · BW

This sophisticated romantic comedy was made by director Ernst Lubitsch during his Warner Bros days, and concerns a classic love triangle featuring a bored wife (Marie Prevost), her husband (Monte Blue), and her lover (John Roche). As handled by the masterly Lubitsch, displaying the "touch" and high style for which he would become famous at Paramount during the 1930s, the simple plot is transformed into an exercise in wit, depth and intelligence. The "It" Girl, Clara Bow, features in support. RK

Marie Prevost *Loulou Fleury* • Monte Blue *Gaston Fleury* • John Roche *Maurice Ferriere* • Clara Bow *Grizette, Dubois's secretary* • Willard Louis *Avocat Dubois* ■ *Dir* Ernst Lubitsch • *Scr* Hans Kräly, from the play *Divorçons* by Victorien Sardou, Emile de Najac

Kiss Me Deadly ★★★★★ 12

Classic film noir 1955 · US · BW · 100mins

One of the greatest examples of *film noir*, this early feature by director Robert Aldrich made him a name in arty circles (the critics of the French magazine *Cahiers du Cinéma* loved him and the film) and a formidable presence in cinema. He took a piece of Mickey Spillane pulp fiction and turned it into an astonishing fable, with Pandora's Box transformed into a nuclear furnace. The look is stylish and the tension builds to a climax that is near-apocalyptic. Spillane's detective Mike Hammer (Ralph Meeker) is a flawed antihero who, after picking up a girl on the run, finds himself in over his head in events beyond his control. Albert Dekker is a classily obnoxious villain, but it's the women you have to watch. As the title suggests, their embrace is lethal. TH DVD

Ralph Meeker *Mike Hammer* • Albert Dekker *Dr Soberin* • Paul Stewart *Carl Evello* • Maxine Cooper *Velda* • Gaby Rodgers *Gabrielle/Lily Carver* • Wesley Addy *Pat Chambers* • Juano Hernandez *Eddie Yeager* • Nick Dennis *Nick* • Cloris Leachman *Christina Bailey/Berga Torn* ■ *Dir* Robert Aldrich • *Scr* Al Bezzerides, from the novel by Mickey Spillane • *Cinematographer* Ernest Laszlo

Kiss Me Goodbye ★★★ PG

Romantic comedy 1982 · US · Colour · 101mins

Sally Field stars in this nicely played romantic fantasy as the widow rebuilding her life with hunky fiancé Jeff Bridges, only for her happy new existence to be complicated by the ghostly arrival of her late husband (James Caan), who is intent on stopping the wedding. Caan – whose deft comic touch has stolen the show in films such as *Mickey Blue Eyes* and *Honeymoon in Vegas* – is deliciously enjoyable as the interfering apparition, while Field and Bridges have fun with their romantic roles. JB

Sally Field *Kay Villano* • James Caan *Jolly Villano* • Jeff Bridges *Rupert Baines* • Paul Dooley *Kendall* • Claire Trevor *Charlotte Banning* • Mildred Natwick *Mrs Reilly* • Dorothy Fielding *Emily* • William Prince *Reverend Hollis* ■ *Dir* Robert Mulligan • *Scr* Charlie Peters, from the film *Dona Flor and Her Two Husbands* by Bruno Barreto, from the novel *Dona Flor and Her Two Husbands* by Jorge Amado

Kiss Me, Guido ★★ 15

Comedy 1997 · US/UK · Colour · 85mins

Heterosexual pizza chef Nick Scotti misunderstands a Manhattan apartment advertisement and moves in with gay choreographer Anthony Barrile, with the expected culture-clash fall-out. When wannabe actor Scotti takes over Barrile's camp role in an off-Broadway play, things get even more farcical. Tony Vitale's first feature borders on the amateurish and indulges in strained humour as Italian-American stereotypes get pitted against gay ones. Luckily, the likeable performances and classic disco soundtrack paper over the not-so-wisecracks. AJ. Contains swearing, violence, a sex scene, nudity.

Nick Scotti *Frankie* • Anthony Barrile *Warren* • Anthony DeSando *Pino* • Molly Price *Meryl* • Craig Chester *Terry* • Christopher Lawford *Dakota* ■ *Dir/Scr* Tony Vitale

Kiss Me Kate ★★★★ U

Musical comedy 1953 · US · Colour · 105mins

A splendid MGM version of Cole Porter's smash-hit Broadway show, originally filmed in 3-D, hence all those shots where Ann Miller and Howard Keel chuck things at the audience, including themselves. Director George Sidney utilises fabulous, cleverly disguised long takes in his filming of Keel, never better than as Fred Graham-cum-Petruchio, and Kathryn Grayson, playing difficult diva Lilli Vanessi, alias Shakespeare's tamed shrew Kate. Miller nearly steals the show with *Too Darn Hot*, and straight men Keenan Wynn and James Whitmore are wonderful in *Brush Up Your Shakespeare*. TS DVD

Kathryn Grayson *Lilli Vanessi, "Katherine"* • Howard Keel *Fred Graham, "Petruchio"* • Ann Miller *Lois Lane, "Bianca"* • Keenan Wynn *Lippy* • Bobby Van *"Gremio"* • Tommy Rall *Bill Calhoun, "Lucentio"* • James Whitmore *Slug* • Kurt Kasznar *"Baptista"* • Bob Fosse *"Hortensio"* • Ron Randell *Cole Porter* ■ *Dir* George Sidney (2) • *Scr* Dorothy Kingsley, from the play by Cole Porter, Samuel Spewack, Bella Spewack, from the play *The Taming of the Shrew* by William Shakespeare

Kiss Me, Stupid ★★★ PG

Comedy 1964 · US · BW · 121mins

Dean Martin is certainly an acquired taste: if you're a fan, then Billy Wilder's rather obvious satire on personal ambition and sexual manipulation sees the court jester of the Rat Pack on full throttle. He plays a sex-obsessed bar-room warbler, with Kim Novak as a hooker and Ray Walston as the amateur songwriter desperate to keep Martin's greasy paws off his wife. It's Wilder, so almost by definition it's smart and sharp, but if you have a single feminist bone in your body, prepare to blow a gasket. SH DVD

Dean Martin *Dino* • Kim Novak *Polly the Pistol* • Ray Walston *Orville J Spooner* • Felicia Farr *Zelda Spooner* • Cliff Osmond *Barney Millsap* • Barbara Pepper *Big Bertha* ■ *Dir* Billy Wilder • *Scr* Billy Wilder, IAL Diamond, from the play *L'Ora della Fantasia* by Anna Bonacci

Kiss of Death ★★★★

Film noir 1947 · US · BW · 98mins

Nothing in today's cinema of violence is as menacing as Richard Widmark's demented chuckle in this super-tough *film noir* thriller from ace director Henry Hathaway. Widmark's screen debut has passed into screen legend, most notably for the scene in which he shoves an elderly lady in a wheelchair down a flight of stairs in a fit of pique. The scene was thought too horrific for British audiences and was cut on UK release by a squeamish British censor. Shot in gritty style on authentic New York locations, the film features a surprisingly fine and sympathetic leading performance from the usually derided Victor Mature. An adult and involving crime drama with a truly tragic dimension. TS

Victor Mature *Nick Bianco* • Brian Donlevy *D'Angelo* • Coleen Gray *Nettie* • Richard Widmark *Tom Udo* • Karl Malden *Sergeant William Cullen* • Taylor Holmes *Earl Howser* • Howard Smith *Warden* • Anthony Ross

Williams ■ *Dir* Henry Hathaway • *Scr* Ben Hecht, Charles Lederer, from a story by Eleazar Lipsky

Kiss of Death ★★★ 18

Crime thriller 1994 · US · Colour · 96mins

Few screen debuts were as chilling as Richard Widmark's in the 1947 original, though in this remake Nicolas Cage is agreeably nasty, with a goatee beard and bulging biceps to complement a serious streak of social irresponsibility. The plot has been thoroughly made over, though it's still about an ex-con (David Caruso) who is determined to go straight, but is forced into becoming an informer for nasty cop Samuel L Jackson. A gripping effort, laced with black humour and directed by Barbet Schroeder with a sharp eye for the hell-holes of New York. AT. Contains swearing, violence and brief nudity. [VIDEO] DVD

David Caruso *Jimmy Kilmartin* • Samuel L Jackson *Calvin* • Nicolas Cage *Little Junior* • Helen Hunt *Bev* • Kathryn Erbe *Rosie* • Stanley Tucci *Frank Zioli* • Michael Rapaport *Ronnie* • Ving Rhames *Omar* • Philip Baker Hall *Big Junior* ■ *Dir* Barbet Schroeder • *Scr* Richard Price, from a story by Eleazar Lipsky, from the 1947 film

Kiss of Fire ★★ U

Period romantic drama
1955 · US · Colour · 87mins

A minor costume drama, set in the 18th century, in which pretty Barbara Rush, as pretender to the Spanish throne, has to make a hazardous journey from Sante Fe to Monterey, in order to get a ship to Spain. A little excitement is engendered by a few villains, Indians on the warpath, and a bit of swashbuckling, but the direction and dialogue are rather soggy. RB

Jack Palance *El Tigre* • Barbara Rush *Princess Lucia* • Rex Reason *Duke of Montera* • Martha Hyer *Felicia* • Alan Reed *Diego* • Leslie Bradley *Vega* ■ *Dir* Joseph M Newman • *Scr* Franklin Coen, Richard Collins, from the novel *The Rose and the Flame* by Jonreed Lauritzen

Kiss of Life ★★ 12

Fantasy drama
2003 · UK/Fr/Can · Colour · 83mins

British debutante director Emily Young's training in Poland is evident throughout this meditation on love and loss, in which the spirit of an accident victim returns to her London home and is confused to find that her children can't see her. Ingeborga Dapkunaite lacks the emotional resources to convey the feelings and frustrations that family life gives rise to. And as the husband (an overseas aid worker played by Peter Mullan) tries to get home for her birthday, his homeward trek through Eastern European squalor features encounters that are either too slight or too consciously symbolic to be of interest. DP. An English/Serb-Croat language film. [VIDEO] DVD

Ingeborga Dapkunaite *Helen* • Peter Mullan *John* • David Warner *Pap* • Millie Findlay *Kate* • James E Martin *Telly* • Ivan Bijuk *Old man* ■ *Dir/Scr* Emily Young

Kiss of the Dragon ★★★★ 18

Martial arts action thriller
2001 · Fr/US · Colour · 97mins

This furiously kinetic film combines the fighting talents of Asian superstar Jet Li with the canny genre production and scripting know-how of French auteur Luc Besson. Outrageously violent, hard-edged and constantly exciting, the film has Li as a Chinese intelligence officer sent to Paris on an undercover assignment, who becomes embroiled in a drug cartel conspiracy. Helped by hooker Bridget Fonda and hindered by super-nasty corrupt cop Tcheky Karyo, Li must use his amazing skills to see justice done. The breathtaking array of dazzling martial arts sequences are superb. AJ. Contains violence, sex scenes, swearing, drug abuse. [VIDEO] DVD

Jet Li *Liu Jiuan* • Bridget Fonda *Jessica* • Tcheky Karyo *Jean-Pierre Richard* • Ric Young *Mr Big* • Burt Kwouk *Uncle Tai* • Laurence Ashley *Aja* ■ *Dir* Chris Nahon • *Scr* Luc Besson, Robert Mark Kamen, from a story by Jet Li

Kiss of the Spider Woman ★★★★ 15

Drama
1985 · US/Bra · BW and Colour · 115mins

This is an unusual, intimate tale of two very different prisoners – a flamboyant gay man (William Hurt) and a reactionary political prisoner (Raul Julia) – who share a cell in a South American jail. (The *Spider Woman* of the title refers to an old movie plot Hurt lovingly recounts to Julia.) Hector Babenco's film hinges on the believability of their relationship and the way the vast gap between their opposing beliefs and attitudes slowly begins to narrow. The leads are top-notch, and the juxtaposition of dream-like monochrome fantasy with harsh, squalid reality is wonderfully conceived. JC [VIDEO]

William Hurt *Molina* • Raul Julia *Valentin* • Sonia Braga *Leni Lamaison/Marta/Spider Woman* • José Lewgoy *Warden* • Nuno Leal Maia *Gabriel* • Antonio Petrim *Clubfoot* ■ *Dir* Hector Babenco • *Scr* Leonard Schrader, from a novel by Manuel Puig

Kiss or Kill ★★ 18

Crime thriller 1997 · Aus · Colour · 92mins

This thriller opens brilliantly with a crime of harrowing intensity, but disappointingly ends up as a daftly-plotted chase movie in which a thieving couple are pursued by cops and a sportsman from whom they've stolen an incriminating videotape. The artsy and obtrusive jump cuts are misjudged, as is the film's denouement. JC. Contains swearing, sex scenes and some violence. [VIDEO]

Frances O'Connor *Nikki* • Matt Day *Al* • Chris Haywood *Detective Hummer* • Barry Otto *Adler Jones* • Andrew S Gilbert *Detective Crean* • Barry Langrishe *Zipper Doyle* • Max Cullen *Stan* ■ *Dir/Scr* Bill Bennett

Kiss the Boys Goodbye ★★★ U

Musical comedy 1941 · US · BW · 84mins

Claire Boothe's Broadway satire on Hollywood's search for an actress to play Scarlett O'Hara loses its caustic edge in the transformation into a musical comedy film. The hunt is on for a southern belle to star in a New York show, and Mary Martin heads south and ropes in her aunt and uncle to help her gain an audition and become the discovery of Don Ameche's director and Oscar Levant's composer. Not as sharp or topical as the play, but still a lot of fun. AE

Mary Martin *Cindy Lou Bethany* • Don Ameche *Lloyd Lloyd* • Oscar Levant *Dick Rayburn* • Virginia Dale *Gwen Abbott* • Barbara Jo Allen *Myra Stanhope* • Raymond Walburn *Top Rumson* • Elizabeth Patterson *Aunt Lilly Lou* • Jerome Cowan *Bert Fisher* ■ *Dir* Victor Schertzinger • *Scr* Harry Tugend, Dwight Taylor, from a play by Clare Boothe [Luce] • *Music Director* Victor Young

Kiss the Girls ★★★ 18

Detective thriller
1997 · US · Colour · 110mins

All surface gloss with little real substance, this gets by thanks to the atmospheric photography and great performances from Morgan Freeman and Ashley Judd. Freeman is a forensic psychologist whose niece has been abducted by a serial kidnapper known as "Casanova"; Judd is the only woman to have escaped from the villain's secret lair. Can Judd guide Freeman to the culprit? If all logic and credibility completely disappear as the conclusion nears, it's still a compelling enough thriller. AJ. Contains swearing and violence. [VIDEO] DVD

Morgan Freeman *Alex Cross* • Ashley Judd *Kate McTiernan* • Cary Elwes *Nick Ruskin* • Alex McArthur *Sikes* • Tony Goldwyn *Will Rudolph* • Jay O Sanders *Kyle Craig* • Bill Nunn *Sampson* • Brian Cox *Chief Hatfield* ■ *Dir* Gary Fleder • *Scr* David Klass, from the novel by James Patterson • *Cinematographer* Aaron Schneider

Kiss Them for Me ★★ U

Wartime comedy drama
1957 · US · Colour · 98mins

Oh dear. The combined talents of star Cary Grant and director Stanley Donen, so successful in both *Indiscreet* and *Charade*, fail miserably here, in a remake of that old perennial "three sailors on the town" plot (a veritable Donen classic), this time set in San Francisco during the Second World War and based loosely on the novel *Shore Leave*. The movie never really catches fire, and is worth viewing now only as a 1950s period piece. TS DVD

Cary Grant *Crewson* • Jayne Mansfield *Alice* • Suzy Parker *Gwenneth* • Leif Erickson *Eddie Turnbill* • Ray Walston *Lieutenant "Mac" McCann* • Larry Blyden *Mississip* • Nathaniel Frey *Chief Petty Officer Ruddle* • Werner Klemperer *Commander Wallace* ■ *Dir* Stanley Donen • *Scr* Julius Epstein, from the play by Luther Davis, from the novel *Shore Leave* by Frederic Wakeman

Kiss Tomorrow Goodbye ★★★★

Crime drama 1950 · US · BW · 102mins

James Cagney plays tough and mean in his *White Heat* mode in this cracking Warner Bros crime drama. The pace never lets up, and there's not a key character on show who displays any kind of morals or ethics whatsoever – even the cops are bent. Especially notable are Luther Adler as a phoney lawyer with a cheap line in philosophy and producer William Cagney as – surprise! – Cagney's screen brother. Under-rated when it first appeared, this movie's sheer constant venality gives it a very contemporary sheen. TS

James Cagney *Ralph Cotter* • Barbara Payton *Holiday Carleton* • Helena Carter *Margaret Dobson* • Ward Bond *Inspector Weber* • Luther Adler *Cherokee Mandon* • William Cagney *Ralph's brother* ■ *Dir* Gordon Douglas • *Scr* Harry Brown, from the novel by Horace McCoy

Kiss Tomorrow Goodbye ★★

Thriller 2000 · US · Colour · 85mins

Beverly Hills 90210 star Jason Priestley makes his directorial debut with this dark TV thriller. Nicholas Lea is suitably smug as the Hollywood producer who wakes from a wild night's partying on a Pacific beach next to a dead girl. Drifter Holt McCallany then informs Lea that he witnessed him killing the girl. This is very much McCallany's movie, as he blackmails his way into Lea's perfect life and gleefully begins to dismantle it. Undemanding entertainment. DP. Contains sex scenes.

Nicholas Lea *Dustin Yarma* • Kari Wuhrer *Darcy* • Jason Priestley *Jarred* • Holt McCallany *Minnow* • Jennifer Blanc *Sage* • Philip Casnoff *Mackey* ■ *Dir* Jason Priestley • *Scr* Ossie Cheek

Kissed ★★★ 18

Romantic drama 1996 · Can · Colour · 75mins

Director Lynne Stopkewich's exploration of the taboo of necrophilia will divide opinion. Molly Parker plays a young woman so fascinated by death she goes to work as a mortician in a funeral parlour. There she indulges her sexual fantasies with the deceased until a living, breathing boyfriend appears. But can he measure up to the safe embraces of her former lovers? It sounds completely nauseating, but, although the script is insultingly naive in places, the subject is tackled with discretion and the film makes its mark, thanks to Parker's sensitive performance. AJ. Contains swearing, sex scenes. [VIDEO]

Molly Parker *Sandra Larson* • Peter Outerbridge *Matt* • Jay Brazeau *Mr Wallis* • Natasha Morley *Young Sandra* • Jessie Winter Mudie *Carol* • James Timmons *Jan* • Joe Maffei *Biology teacher* • Robert Thurston *Detective* ■ *Dir* Lynne Stopkewich • *Scr* Lynne Stopkewich, Angus Fraser, from the story *We So Seldom Look on Love* by Barbara Gowdy

Kisses for My President ★★ U

Comedy 1964 · US · BW · 113mins

Polly Bergen stars as the first woman president of the United States in this thunderingly mawkish pre-feminist tract. A lot of talent that should have known better appears alongside Bergen, including the Fred MacMurray (as the protocol-cursed "First Man"), but everyone seems to be struggling with the material. Director Curtis Bernhardt fails to find the right screwball tone, and the result is surprisingly witless and cloying. The sets look cheap, too. TS

Fred MacMurray *Thad McCloud* • Polly Bergen *Leslie McCloud* • Arlene Dahl *Doris Reid* • Edward Andrews *Senator Walsh* • Eli Wallach *Valdez* • Donald May *John O'Connor* • Harry Holcombe *Bill Richards* • Anna Capri [Ahna Capri] *Gloria McCloud* ■ *Dir* Curtis Bernhardt • *Scr* Claude Binyon, Robert G Kane

Kissin' Cousins ★★ U

Musical 1964 · US · Colour · 87mins

Most of Presley's movie vehicles arouse the suspicion that their makers thought cheapness and speed more important than quality, but this double-trouble romantic comedy is a pleasant way to pass the time. Elvis plays the two leads: a (blond!) hillbilly, resisting the US Air Force's plan to build a missile base on his family's land, as well as the lieutenant cousin whose job it is to persuade them. JG [VIDEO]

Elvis Presley *Josh Morgan/Jodie Tatum* • Arthur O'Connell *Pappy Tatum* • Glenda Farrell *Ma Tatum* • Jack Albertson *Capt Robert Salbo* • Pam Austin [Pamela Austin] *Selena Tatum* • Cynthia Pepper *Midge* • Yvonne Craig *Azalea Tatum* ■ *Dir* Gene Nelson • *Scr* Gerald Drayson Adams, Gene Nelson, from a story by Gerald Drayson Adams, Gene Nelson

Kissing a Fool ★★ 15

Romantic comedy
1998 · US · Colour · 89mins

David Schwimmer tries to shrug off his nice-guy image to play a self-centred sports journalist, who tests his girlfriend's fidelity by asking his best friend Jason Lee to seduce her. Told in flashback at the girlfriend's wedding to one of the men (but which one?), this has good performances from Lee and Mili Avital, but a miscast Schwimmer struggles to convince as the sleazy rogue in this only moderately enjoyable effort. JC . Contains swearing and sexual references. [VIDEO]

David Schwimmer *Max Abbitt* • Jason Lee *Jay Murphy* • Mili Avital *Samantha Andrews* • Bonnie Hunt *Linda* • Vanessa Angel *Natasha* • Kari Wuhrer *Dara* ■ *Dir* Doug Ellin • *Scr* Doug Ellin, James Frey, from a story by James Frey

K

The Kissing Bandit ★★

Musical comedy 1949 · US · Colour · 102mins

A major flop on its first release, this film became famous because its star, Frank Sinatra, would constantly joke about it being the low point of his career. The idea of casting the then-puny actor as the son of a desperado noted for his female conquests probably seemed amusing at the time, but the star is palpably uneasy, the direction by Laslo Benedek (his first film) too stolid and the score mostly mundane. TV

Frank Sinatra *Ricardo* • Kathryn Grayson *Teresa* • J Carrol Naish *Chico* • Mildred Natwick *Isabella* • Ricardo Montalban *Fiesta dancer* • Ann Miller *Fiesta dancer* • Cyd Charisse *Fiesta dancer* ■ *Dir* Laslo Benedek • *Scr* Isobel Lennart, John Briard Harding

Kissing Jessica Stein ★★★ 15

Romantic comedy
2001 · US · Colour · 92mins

Two unknowns, Jennifer Westfeldt and Heather Juergensen, wrote an off-Broadway play about female sexuality and two women who attempt a lesbian affair. A few years later and they're both starring in the spin-off film – a witty, quirky, original New York story about a straight Jewish journalist (Westfeldt) who responds to a singles ad and ends up on a date with the also straight "but willing to experiment" Juergensen. As the women walk the Sapphic way, they have to deal with the shock waves this sends through family and friends. A sparklingly funny gem. LH [subtitles] DVD

Jennifer Westfeldt *Jessica Stein* • Heather Juergensen *Helen Cooper* • Scott Cohen *Josh Meyers* • Tovah Feldshuh *Judy Stein* • Jackie Hoffman *Joan* • Michael Mastro *Martin* ■ *Dir* Charles Herman-Wurmfeld • *Scr* Heather Juergensen, Jennifer Westfeldt, from their play *Lipschtick*

Kit Carson ★★★ U

Western 1940 · US · BW · 96mins

There was a time when Kit Carson and Buffalo Bill were the heroes of schoolboys everywhere, with their (largely fictional) achievements celebrated in comics. This is the definitive biopic of frontier scout Carson's adventurous life. Jon Hall makes a solid enough Carson as he tangles with expedition leader Dana Andrews for the love of Lynn Bari, but the script doesn't allow for much character depth. Since much of Carson's life was fictionalised in his own lifetime via dime novels, who could blame Hollywood for turning history into a rattling adventure? TS

Jon Hall *Kit Carson* • Lynn Bari *Dolores Murphy* • Dana Andrews *Captain John C Fremont* • Harold Huber *Lopez* • Ward Bond *Ape* • Renie Riano *Miss Genevieve Pilchard* ■ *Dir* George B Seitz • *Scr* George Bruce

The Kitchen ★★★ PG

Drama 1961 · UK · BW · 70mins

Dramatist Arnold Wesker drew on his experience as a pastrycook when he wrote his play, *The Kitchen*, here filmed with some of the cast from the original London stage production. Virtually plotless, the action records one day of hard work and thwarted ambition in a restaurant kitchen. The long, philosophical conversations do not adapt well to the screen, but the sequences showing food being churned out factory-style to the detriment of the workers' mental and physical health have a manic intensity. In its day, the play was regarded as an allegory of life's struggle. DM [subtitles]

Carl Mohner *Peter* • Mary Yeomans *Monica* • Brian Phelan *Kevin* • Tom Bell *Paul* • Howard Greene *Raymond* • Eric Pohlmann *Mr Marango* • James Bolam *Michael* ■ *Dir* James Hill • *Scr* Sidney Cole

Kitchen ★★★ 15

Romantic drama
1997 · HK/Jpn · Colour · 120mins

Employing various distancing devices, director Ho Yim studiously chronicles the relationship between the timid Yasuko Tomita and hairdresser Jordan Chan and the impact it has on his transsexual mother, Law Kar-Ying. While this strategy occasionally makes it difficult to identify with the characters, the tone shifts deftly between tenderness and eroticism, and there is a pleasing hesitancy about the romance. The result is an admirable, if not always engrossing drama. DP. In Cantonese with English subtitles. Contains some violence, swearing and nudity. [subtitles]

Jordan Chan *Louie* • Yasuko Tomita *Aggie* • Law Kar-Ying *Emma* • Karen Mok *Jenny* • Lau Siu-Ming *Mr Chiu* • Lo Koon-Lan *Chika* ■ *Dir* Ho Yim • *Scr* Ho Yim, from the novella by Banana Yoshimoto

Kitchen Stories ★★★★ PG

Comedy 2003 · Nor/Swe · Colour · 90mins

In this charming 1950s comedy, Bent Hamer concentrates on the slow-burning relationship between curmudgeonly Norwegian farmer Joachim Calmeyer and Tomas Norstrom, the jobsworthy representative of a Swedish furnishing institute detailed to record Calmeyer's kitchen habits. The initial series of near-wordless encounters is paced to perfection, but the humour becomes more personal and affecting once the bachelors break the rules of the exercise and begin communicating. The performances are a joy, especially once the duo begin to revel in their minor acts of rebellion. DP. In Norwegian with English subtitles. DVD

Joachim Calmeyer *Isak Bjorvik* • Tomas Norstrom *Folke Nilsson* • Reine Brynolfsson *Malmberg* • Bjørn Floberg *Grant* ■ *Dir* Bent Hamer • *Scr* Bent Hamer, Jorgen Bergmark

The Kitchen Toto ★★ 15

Drama 1987 · UK · Colour · 91mins

Bob Peck gives one of his all too rare film performances as the British Chief of Police handling unrest in Kenya during the 1950s. The tale is told through the eyes of Edwin Mahinda, a young Kikuyu boy whose loyalties are torn between the Mau Mau, his tribe's rebel group (the killers of his minister father) and the British whose service he is in. Director Harry Hook as a native Kenyan obviously understands the issues here, but does a poor job in making them comprehensible to your average viewer. LH [subtitles]

Edwin Mahinda *Mwangi* • Bob Peck *John Graham* • Phyllis Logan *Janet Graham* • Nicholas Charles *Mugo* • Ronald Pirie *Edward Graham* • Robert Urquhart *DC McKinnon* • Kirsten Hughes *Mary McKinnon* • Edward Judd *Dick Luis* ■ *Dir/Scr* Harry Hook

Kitne Door... Kitne Paas ★★★ PG

Romantic road movie
2001 · Ind · Colour · 146mins

Director Mehul Kumar makes a tidy job of this romantic road movie, which comes across as a Bollywood blend of *It Happened One Night* and *Planes, Trains and Automobiles.* Fardeen Khan and Amrita Arora star as two young Gujuratis who return to India for their respective arranged marriages after working in the United States, only to fall in love on the nightmare journey home. Glossing over the realities of life in the Indian countryside, this is escapism pure and simple, with the emphasis being on the lover's decreasingly tempestuous relationship rather than the clash between tradition and progress. DP. In Hindi with English subtitles. [subtitles] DVD

Fardeen Khan *Jatin* • Amrita Arora *Karishma* • Govind Namdev *Karishma's father* • Shama Deshpande *Karishma's mother* • Beena *Jatin's mother* ■ *Dir* Mehul Kumar • *Scr* Imtiaz Patel, Yunus Sejawal, Mehul Kumar, from a story by Mehul Kumar

Kitten with a Whip ★★

Thriller 1964 · US · BW · 83mins

Ann-Margret stars in this low-budget exploitation thriller about a juvenile delinquent who escapes from a detention centre and forces her way into the home of politician John Forsythe. Refusing to leave, she threatens to call the police and implicate him in a sex scandal. Then she calls in a pair of thugs who provide some mildly titillating thrills and purely gratuitous violence. This veers between the sub-standard and the subversive. AT

Ann-Margret *Jody Dvorak* • John Forsythe *David Patton* • Peter Brown *Ron* • Patricia Barry *Vera* • Richard Anderson *Grant* • James Ward *Buck* • Diane Sayer *Midge* • Ann Doran *Mavis Varden* • Patrick Whyte *Philip Varden* ■ *Dir* Douglas Heyes • *Scr* Douglas Heyes, from the novel by Wade Miller

Kitty ★

Wartime melodrama 1928 · UK · BW · 92mins

Directed by the admired Victor Saville, this silent melodrama had some spoken dialogue later tacked on to some sequences, making it officially Britain's first sound film. However, these awkward and pointless scenes only make worse what comes before in the tale of a possessive mother (Dorothy Cumming), whose vicious bad-mouthing of her RAF pilot son's fiancée causes him to crash and become paralysed. How the lovers, John Stuart and Estelle Brody, overcome Cumming's efforts to keep them apart, constitutes the plot of this ludicrously unconvincing tearjerker. RK

Estelle Brody *Kitty Greenwood* • John Stuart *Alex St George* • Marie Ault *Sarah Greenwood* • Dorothy Cumming *Mrs St George* • Winter Hall *John Furnival* • Olaf Hytten *Leaper* ■ *Dir* Victor Saville • *Scr* Violet E Powell, Benn W Levy, from the novel by Warwick Deeping

Kitty ★★★★

Period drama 1945 · US · BW · 103mins

Paulette Goddard is the cockney waif plucked from the streets of 18th-century London to be tutored for marriage into high society in this sumptuously mounted drama. Beautifully acted, well photographed and brilliantly directed, this is a harsh variation of *Pygmalion* with Goddard being forced into two unsuitable marriages. Ray Milland is his dependable self as the nobleman pulling the strings, Constance Collier is a dissipated aunt and Sara Allgood a Hogarthian wreck, but the real scene-stealing is done by Reginald Owen as a lecherous old duke. AE

Paulette Goddard *Kitty* • Ray Milland *Sir Hugh Marcy* • Patric Knowles *Brett Hardwood, the Earl of Carstairs* • Reginald Owen *Duke of Malmunster* • Cecil Kellaway *Thomas Gainsborough* • Constance Collier *Lady Susan Dewitt* • Dennis Hoey *Jonathan Selby* • Sara Allgood *Old Meg* ■ *Dir* Mitchell Leisen • *Scr* Darrell Ware, Karl Tunberg, from a novel by Rosamund Marshall • *Cinematographer* Daniel L Fapp • *Music* Victor Young • *Art Director* Hans Dreier, Walter Tyler

Kitty and the Bagman ★★

Period comedy drama
1982 · Aus · Colour · 95mins

With a rollicking blend of colourful characterisation and serio-comic drama, this Australian period picture piles mismanagement upon misjudgement. Catfights, bar-room brawls and bawdy brothel banter are the order of the day, as Donald Crombie attempts to re-create the coarse, corrupt atmosphere of 1920s Sydney. But while Liddy Clark and John Stanton turn in spirited performances as the feisty madam and bent cop caught up in a gang war, too much emphasis is placed on tone and tempo and not enough on substance. DP

Liddy Clark *Kitty O'Rourke* • John Stanton *Bagman* • Val Lehman *Lil Delaney* • Gerard Maguire *Cyril Vikkers* • Collette Mann *Doris de Salle* • Reg Evans *Chicka Delaney* • Kylie Foster *Sarah Jones* ■ *Dir* Donald Crombie • *Scr* John Burney, Philip Cornford

Kitty Foyle ★★★

Drama 1940 · US · BW · 106mins

Ginger Rogers won her best actress Oscar for this melodrama, which proved that she had a career outside her partnership with Fred Astaire. What Rogers was particularly good at was portraying the common, not to say vulgar, shop girl, and that is what Kitty Foyle is: a shop girl who can't make up her mind which man to choose – doctor James Craig or playboy Dennis Morgan? Viewed today, even Ginger fans might find this hard going. TS

Ginger Rogers *Kitty Foyle* • Dennis Morgan *Wyn Strafford* • James Craig *Mark* • Eduardo Ciannelli *Giono* • Ernest Cossart *Pop* • Gladys Cooper *Mrs Strafford* ■ *Dir* Sam Wood • *Scr* Dalton Trumbo, Donald Ogden Stewart, from the novel by Christopher Morley

The Klansman ★★

Drama 1974 · US · Colour · 107mins

In a small southern town, sheriff Lee Marvin fails to keep the lid on simmering racial tensions between civil rights activists and active members of the Ku Klux Klan. Vilified by most American critics, this potboiler didn't do much for the careers of either Marvin or Richard Burton, here cast as a dotty landowner who spits out philosophical bubble gum and gives sanctuary to local blacks. Cult director Samuel Fuller wrote the original script as a typically forthright overhaul of American race relations. AT

Lee Marvin *Sheriff Bascomb* • Richard Burton *Breck Stancill* • Cameron Mitchell *Deputy Butt Cut Cates* • Lola Falana *Loretta Sykes* • Luciana Paluzzi *Trixie* • David Huddleston *Mayor Hardy* • Linda Evans *Nancy Poteet* • OJ Simpson *Garth* ■ *Dir* Terence Young • *Scr* Millard Kaufman, Samuel Fuller, from the novel by William Bradford Huie

Klondike Annie ★★★

Musical comedy drama
1936 · US · BW · 78mins

Even in her later pictures, Mae West refused to be tamed, provoking the usual fierce attacks from the forces of righteousness. In this picture, they objected to her being the mistress of an Oriental, a murderess who then masquerades as a missionary, and a performer of songs such as *I'm an Occidental Woman in an Oriental Mood for Love.* Mae wrote the script and typically cast as the men in her life lumpish actors who wouldn't steal any of her limelight. Audiences loved it then, and it's still good fun. AE

Mae West *"The Frisco Doll", Rose Carlton* • Victor McLaglen *Capt Bull Brackett* • Philip Reed *Inspector Jack Forrest* • Helen Jerome Eddy *Sister Annie Alden* • Harry Beresford *Brother Bowser* • Harold Huber *Chan Lo* ■ *Dir* Raoul Walsh • *Scr* Mae West

Klute ★★★★★ 18

Thriller 1971 · US · Colour · 107mins

Jane Fonda deservedly won the best actress Oscar for her remarkably cool walk on the wild side as a call girl stalked by a homicidal maniac. But Donald Sutherland is on top form, too, playing the gentle small-town detective who teaches her the difference between love and sex as he closes in on the killer. A quite exceptional adult thriller, given a striking immediacy by Alan J Pakula's highly atmospheric direction and the nail-biting suspense. AJ. Contains swearing and nudity.

Jane Fonda *Bree Daniels* • Donald Sutherland *John Klute* • Charles Cioffi *Peter Cable* • Nathan George *Lieutenant Trask* • Roy R Scheider [Roy Scheider] *Frank Ligourin* • Dorothy Tristan *Arlyn Page* • Rita Gam *Trina* • Vivian Nathan *Psychiatrist* ■ *Dir* Alan J Pakula • *Scr* Andy Lewis, Dave Lewis • *Cinematographer* Gordon Willis

The Knack... and How to Get It ★★★ 15

Comedy 1965 · UK · BW · 85mins

This Palme d'Or-winning comedy is an energetic example of Richard Lester's fascination with the more manic methods of the French New Wave. In opening out Ann Jellicoe's stage play, he makes dizzying use of swinging London, as timid teacher Michael Crawford wheels home the brass bed that his womanising tenant Ray Brooks has assured him will transform his romantic fortunes. Although perfectly in tune with its time, the film is now hard to watch without wincing at the incessant stream of sexist witticisms and the painfully eager performances of Crawford and Brooks. DP DVD

Rita Tushingham *Nancy Jones* • Ray Brooks *Tolen* • Michael Crawford *Colin* • Donal Donnelly *Tom* • John Bluthal *Angry father* • Wensley Pithey *Teacher* • William Dexter *Dress shop owner* • Peter Copley *Picture owner* ■ *Dir* Richard Lester • *Scr* Charles Wood, from the play by Ann Jellicoe

Knave of Hearts ★★★★

Romantic drama
1954 · Fr/UK · BW · 109mins

Gallic heart-throb Gérard Philipe was destined for a tragically early death but he made a charming philanderer in this ironic romantic drama. In the episodic story, set and shot on location in London (by cinematographer Oswald Morris), Philipe, though married to Valerie Hobson, still finds himself attracted to Natasha Parry. Directed and co-written by René Clément, the film offers a refreshing view of England and English women as seen through French eyes. RB

Gérard Philipe *Andre Ripois* • Valerie Hobson *Catherine* • Joan Greenwood *Norah* • Margaret Johnston *Anne* • Natasha Parry *Patricia* • Germaine Montero *Marcelle* • Diana Decker *Diana* • Percy Marmont *Catherine's father* ■ *Dir* René Clément • *Scr* Hugh Mills, René Clément, Hugh Queneau, from the novel *Lovers, Happy Lovers!* by Louis Hemon

Knickerbocker Holiday ★★ U

Musical comedy drama
1944 · US · BW · 85mins

Originally a heavyweight and unappealingly heavy-handed musical, here this makes for a lightweight, and equally unappealing, film. Stripped of most of Kurt Weill's songs (and with its politics watered down) what is left is a tedious period piece, set in New York during the Pieter Stuyvesant era, about a romance between a subversive journalist (Nelson Eddy) and the daughter (Constance Dowling) of a Dutch councillor. RK

Nelson Eddy *Brom Broeck* • Charles Coburn *Pieter Stuyvesant* • Constance Dowling *Tina Tienhoven* • Ernest Cossart *Tienhoven* • Johnnie "Scat" Davis [Johnnie Davis] *Ten Pin* • Richard Hale *Tammany* • Shelley Winters *Ulda Tienhoven* • Glenn Strange *Big Muscle* ■ *Dir* Harry Joe Brown • *Scr* David Boehm, Roland Leigh, Harold Goldman, Thomas Lennon, from the musical by Kurt Weill, Maxwell Anderson

Knife Edge ★★ 15

Thriller 1990 · US · Colour · 85mins

Brad Dourif, who made such an impact in John Huston's *Wise Blood* (1979), is seen to much less effect in this bizarre story of an artist and his sexy sister (MK Harris and Sammi Davis) who move in on the life of a reclusive parolee (Dourif), changing all their lives. Kurt Voss directs as if he knew what it all symbolised, but audiences won't really care. TH

Brad Dourif *Bud Cowan* • Sammi Davis *Randi* • MK Harris [Michael Harris (2)] *Matthew* • Vic Tayback *George Samsa* • Max Perlich *Kid* ■ *Dir* Kurt Voss • *Scr* Kurt Voss, Larry Rattner, David Birke

Knife in the Head ★★★★

Political thriller
1978 · W Ger · Colour · 112mins

Chillingly suggesting that the West Germany of the 1970s was on the brink of a new form of totalitarianism, this multilayered film is at once a socialist tract, an uncompromising thriller and a downbeat human drama. Severely wounded after he is unwittingly caught up in a police raid, scientist Bruno Ganz (giving a quietly heroic performance) has to rebuild his life from scratch, inadvertently becoming a political pawn in the process. Shot with calculated detachment by director Reinhard Hauff, the action has an allegorical significance that is now primarily of historical importance. DP. A German language film.

Bruno Ganz *Dr Berthold Hoffmann* • Angela Winkler *Ann Hoffmann* • Hans Christian Blech *Scholz* • Udo Samel *Schurig* • Eike Gallwitz *Dr Groeske* • Carla Egerer *Nurse Angelika Mueller* ■ *Dir* Reinhard Hauff • *Scr* Peter Schneider

Knife in the Water ★★★★ PG

Drama 1962 · Pol · BW · 90mins

Nominated for the best foreign language film Oscar, the only feature completed by Roman Polanski in his native Poland is a lean, calculated study of male posturing and the hostilities that reinforce the generation gap. Shot in a steely black and white that intensifies both the film's chilling atmosphere and the crackling charge of sexual electricity that courses between the protagonists, the action is given an unbearable tension by its claustrophobic setting on board a yacht during a weekend cruise. The cast is superb, with the non-professional Zygmunt Malanowicz judging his swaggering brio to perfection. DP. In Polish with English subtitles. DVD

Leon Niemczyk *Andrzej* • Jolanta Umecka *Christine* • Zygmunt Malanowicz *Young man* ■ *Dir* Roman Polanski • *Scr* Jerzy Skolimowski, Jakub Goldberg, Roman Polanski • *Cinematographer* Jerzy Lipman

A Knight in Camelot ★★ PG

Fantasy comedy adventure
1998 · US · Colour · 84mins

Whoopi Goldberg brings her wacky comic sensibilities to this updated TV-movie version of Mark Twain's *A Connecticut Yankee in King Arthur's Court*. A computer researcher accidentally transports herself back to medieval times. Taken for a witch, Goldberg is thrown into a dungeon, but her laptop computer gets her out of trouble when she's able to predict a solar eclipse – proving to King Arthur (Michael York) and the jealous wizard Merlin (Ian Richardson) that she has magical powers. Preachy. MC DVD

Whoopi Goldberg *Vivien Morgan* • Michael York *King Arthur* • Amanda Donohoe *Queen Guinevere* • Ian Richardson *Merlin* • James Coombes *Sir Lancelot* • Robert Addie *Sir Sagramour* ■ *Dir* Roger Young • *Scr* Joe Wiesenfeld, from the novel *A Connecticut Yankee in King Arthur's Court* by Mark Twain

Knight Moves ★★★ 18

Thriller 1992 · US/Ger · Colour · 111mins

This is a lively thriller starring Christopher Lambert as a chess master whose bid to win a major tournament takes an unexpected turn when his lover ends up murdered. As corpses start piling up like captured pieces, cop Tom Skerritt and psychologist Diane Lane start whittling away at Lambert's defence. Solid performances, especially from the suitably intense-looking Lambert, and some decent plot twists keep the picture on the boil sufficiently to delight thriller fans as well as chess players. AT. Contains swearing and violence. DVD

Christopher Lambert *Peter Sanderson* • Diane Lane *Kathy Sheppard* • Tom Skerritt *Frank Sedman* • Daniel Baldwin *Andy Wagner* • Charles Bailey-Gates *David Willerman* • Arthur Brauss *Viktor Yurilivich* • Katherine Isobel *Erica Sanderson* • Ferdinand Mayne [Ferdy Mayne] *Jeremy Edmonds* • Don Thompson *Father* ■ *Dir* Carl Schenkel • *Scr* Brad Mirman

Knight of the Plains ★★ U

Western 1939 · US · BW · 62mins

Probably the most interesting fact about this B-western for viewers today is that it was co-produced by the great comedian Stan Laurel. It's a very average tale, featuring former opera singer-turned-singing cowboy Fred Scott, who's aided in his battle against villain John Merton by comic sidekick Al St John. Laurel's involvement seems to have been purely financial, and this is no different from other Scott star vehicles: mercifully short with a sort of period charm. TS

Fred Scott *Fred "Melody" Brent* • Al St John *"Fuzzy"* • Marion Weldon *Gail Rand* • Richard Cramer *Clem Peterson* • John Merton *Dan Carson/Pedro De Cordova* • Frank Larue *JC Rand* ■ *Dir* Sam Newfield • *Scr* Fred Myton

Knight without Armour ★★★ U

First World War spy romance
1937 · UK · BW · 103mins

In 1937 Marlene Dietrich, the highest paid actress in Hollywood, accepted a modest $350,000 to star in this lavish, British-made Alexander Korda production. This story of the First World War, Russian Revolution, rebelling peasantry and espionage, became a decent critical and commercial hit. Dietrich, who looks like Garbo in *Anna Karenina*, is radiant throughout, while love interest appears in the shape of spy Robert Donat, who wears heroism on his sleeve and what looks like a dead yak on his head. The script is pure drivel, but Jacques Feyder's direction has a real sheen. AT

Marlene Dietrich *Alexandra Adraxine, nee Vladinoff* • Robert Donat *AJ Fothergill/Peter Ouranoff* • Irene Vanbrugh *Duchess of Zorin* • Herbert Lomas *General Gregor Vladinoff* • Austin Trevor *Colonel Adraxine* • Basil Gill *Axelstein* • David Tree *Maronin* ■ *Dir* Jacques Feyder • *Scr* Lajos Biró, Arthur Wimperis, Frances Marion, from the novel *Without Armour* by James Hilton

Knightriders ★★★ 15

Drama 1981 · US · Colour · 140mins

A captivating left-field departure from zombie horror king George Romero. A travelling commune of motorcyclists try to live their lives according to the doctrine of King Arthur and the knights of the round table by organising medieval-style fairs, complete with jousting competitions. But self-styled monarch Ed Harris finds his Hell's Angels Camelot and his efforts to uphold a chivalrous code under threat from bickering and money problems. An unusual adventure fable. AJ

Ed Harris *Billy* • Tom Savini *Morgan* • Gary Lahti *Alan* • Amy Ingersoll *Linet* • Patricia Tallman *Julie* • Christine Forrest *Angie* • Warner Shook *Pippin* • Stephen King ■ *Dir/Scr* George A Romero

Knights and Emeralds ★ PG

Comedy drama 1986 · UK · Colour · 86mins

The regional film has been one of the least successful of British genres, with only the kitchen-sink dramas of the 1960s making any real impact on audiences at home, let alone abroad. This small-scale comedy is typical of the lack of ambition that blights these pictures. Set in the Midlands, it's a slight story about racism and the rivalry between black and white marching bands. DP

Christopher Wild *Kevin Brimble* • 1 [Beverly Hills] *Melissa* • Warren Mitchell *Mr Kirkpatrick* • Bill Leadbitter *Enoch* • Rachel Davies *Mrs Fontain* • Tracie Bennett *Tina* • Nadim Sawalha *Bindu* ■ *Dir/Scr* Ian Emes

Knights of the Round Table ★★★ PG

Period adventure
1953 · US · Colour · 111mins

This 1950s Hollywood retelling of the Arthurian legend finds Lancelot being given the red card by Arthur for his, shall we say, inappropriate affection for Guinevere, but galloping back to rescue the day by overcoming the wicked Mordred. Shot in Britain, as MGM's first CinemaScope movie, and starring the good-looking but passionless Robert Taylor and Ava Gardner as the doomed lovers, the finished product is long on pomp and pageantry, though sadly not as stirring as it sounds or should be. PF

Robert Taylor (1) *Sir Lancelot* • Ava Gardner *Queen Guinevere* • Mel Ferrer *King Arthur* • Stanley Baker *Sir Modred* • Anne Crawford *Morgan Le Fay* • Felix Aylmer *Merlin* • Maureen Swanson *Elaine* • Robert Urquhart *Sir Gawaine* ■ *Dir* Richard Thorpe • *Scr* Talbot Jennings, Jan Lustig, Noel Langley, from the prose romance *Le Mort d'Arthur* by Sir Thomas Malory

A Knight's Tale ★★★★ PG

Romantic period adventure
2001 · US · Colour · 126mins

This irreverent medieval caper sets out its stall right at the start, when Queen's anthemic *We Will Rock You* thuds on to the soundtrack at a joust. So far, so anachronistic. But the real twist is that the 14th-century spectators join in and clap in time. It's that kind of film, full of such cheeky flourishes – jousting fans sing rock songs, emcees talk up contestants like it's WWF wrestling, and dancers at a royal banquet groove to David Bowie's *Golden Years*. Writer/director Brian Helgeland certainly enjoys himself here, as do the cast. Heart-throb-in-waiting Heath Ledger dreams of being a knight, and so impersonates one with the help of sidekicks Mark Addy, Alan Tudyk and Paul Bettany (who casually steals the film with his portrayal of writer Geoffrey Chaucer). Tremendous, infectious fun. AC. Contains violence, nudity. DVD

Heath Ledger *William Thatcher/Sir Ulric of Liechtenstein* • Rufus Sewell *Count Adhemar* • Mark Addy *Roland* • Paul Bettany *Geoffrey Chaucer* • Shannyn Sossamon *Lady Jocelyn* • Alan Tudyk *Wat* • Laura Fraser *Kate* • Christopher Cazenove *John Thatcher* ■ *Dir/Scr* Brian Helgeland

K

Knock Off ★★ 18

Action thriller 1998 · HK/US · Colour · 87mins

This Jean-Claude Van Damme vehicle is another superficially authentic but ultimately fake Hong Kong thriller. True, director Tsui Hark has all the right credentials but, as with their previous project *Double Team*, this just isn't the real thing. Played more for laughs than that collaboration, this tale finds reformed counterfeiter Van Damme and partner Rob Schneider caught up in a plot to send miniature bombs all over the world, and Tsui stages some imaginatively destructive action set pieces. JF. Contains swearing and violence. DVD

Jean-Claude Van Damme *Marcus Ray* • Rob Schneider *Tommy Hendricks* • Lela Rochon *Karen* • Paul Sorvino *Johansson* • Carmen Lee *Ling Ho* • Wyman Wong *Eddie* • Glen Chin *Skinny* • Michael Miller (3) *Tickler* • Steve Brettingham *Hawkeye* • Mark Haughton *Bear* ■ *Dir* Tsui Hark • *Scr* Steven E de Souza

Knock on Any Door ★★★

Crime drama 1949 · US · BW · 99mins

Nicholas Ray's sympathy for the disadvantaged young – he would direct *Rebel without a Cause* six years later – is well to the fore in this sincerely meant but now very dated drama. John Derek stars as a slum youth who turns to crime and is charged with murder, while Humphrey Bogart plays his understanding, albeit powerless, attorney. A belated sequel, *Let No Man Write My Epitaph*, followed in 1960. TH

Humphrey Bogart *Andrew Morton* • John Derek *Nick Romano* • George Macready *District Attorney Kerman* • Allene Roberts *Emma* • Mickey Knox *Vito* • Barry Kelley *Judge Drake* • Cara Williams *Nelly* • Jimmy Conlin *Kid Fingers* ■ *Dir* Nicholas Ray • *Scr* Daniel Taradash, John Monks Jr, from a novel by Willard Motley

Knock on Wood ★★★ U

Musical comedy 1954 · US · Colour · 103mins

Comedy writers/directors Melvin Frank and Norman Panama earned themselves a best story and screenplay Oscar nomination for this crack-a-minute showcase for the talents of Danny Kaye. The breathless delivery, facial contortions and crowded gallery of eccentric characterisations that made him one of the finest cabaret performers of his generation never fitted entirely comfortably into a film narrative, with the action too often stalling to enable him to rattle through yet another of his patter routines. DP

Danny Kaye *Jerry Morgan* • Mai Zetterling *Ilse Nordstrom* • Torin Thatcher *Godfrey Langston* • David Burns *Marty Brown* • Leon Askin *Gromek* • Abner Biberman *Papinek* ■ *Dir/Scr* Norman Panama, Melvin Frank

Knockaround Guys ★★ 15

Crime comedy 2001 · US · Colour · 87mins

The retrieval of a stolen bag of Mob money sees low-level gangsters Barry Pepper, Vin Diesel and a couple of less intimidating associates exerting their muscle on a corrupt small-town sheriff. This downbeat, plodding drama gets some mileage out of its superior cast, but film-makers Brian Koppelman and David Levien are undeserving of this line-up, since their dialogue is mechanical and co-direction lifeless. Clint Mansell's moody score does enhance the atmosphere, but it's a dreary journey to reach the climactic shoot-out. JC DVD

Barry Pepper *Matty Demaret* • Vin Diesel *Taylor Reese* • Seth Green *Johnny Marbles* • Dennis Hopper *Benny "Chains" Demaret* • John Malkovich *Teddy Deserve* • Andrew Davoli *Chris Scarpa* • Tom Noonan *Sheriff* ■ *Dir/Scr* Brian Koppelman, David Levien

Knockin' on Heaven's Door ★★★

Road movie comedy
1997 · Ger · Colour · 100mins

Continuing the German love affair with the road movie, this odd-couple caper marked Til Schweiger's transition to superstardom. Together with fellow cancer victim Jan Josef Liefers, he refuses to wallow in institutionalised self-pity and hits the road in search of the adventure his life has been missing. However, a couple of cops and two hoods desperate to recover their stolen loot hardly make for ideal travelling companions. Thomas Jahn's compositional sense and judgement of tempo are remarkable for only a second-time director, but it's the spark between the leads that really makes the picture. DP. In German with English subtitles.

Til Schweiger *Martin Brest* • Jan Josef Liefers *Rudi Wurlitzer* • Moritz Bleibtreu *Abdul* • Thierry Van Werveke *Henk* • Leonard Lansink *Commissar Schneider* • Ralph Herforth *Assistant Keller* ■ *Dir* Thomas Jahn • *Scr* Thomas Jahn, Til Schweiger, from a story by Thomas Jahn

Knocks at My Door ★★★

Political drama
1991 · Ven/Arg/Cub/UK · Colour · 105mins

Based on Juan Carlos Gene's acclaimed play, this Venezuelan drama features the playwright himself as the mayor of an unnamed town who intercedes when nuns who have been sheltering a rebel soldier are brought before a military tribunal. Steadily directed by Alejandro Saderman, this earnest picture sheds some light on the uneasy relationship between church, army and state that exists in many South American countries. It might never escape its stage shackles, but it's thought-provoking and powerfully played. DP. In Spanish with English subtitles.

Veronica Oddo *Ana* • Elba Escobar *Ursula* • Juan Carlos Gene *Mayor Cerone* • José Antonio Rodriguez *Monsignor* • Ana Castell *Severa* • Frank Spano *Pablo the Fugitive* ■ *Dir* Alejandro Saderman • *Scr* Juan Carlos Gene, Alejandro Saderman, from the play *Golpes a Mi Puerta* by Juan Carlos Gene

The Knowledge of Healing ★★★ PG

Documentary 1996 · Swi · Colour · 93mins

Swiss director Franz Reichle seeks to explore the techniques of Tibetan medicine and prove their scientific validity in this intelligent but rather airless documentary. The Dalai Lama's own doctor, Tenzin Choedrak, guides us through the complex relationship between the body's spiritual and physical energies, as well as describing the numerous natural ingredients used in his pharmacy. But while the theoretical aspects are admirably illustrated with examples from age-old scrolls, it's the doctor's encounters with his patients that prove more intriguing, particularly his treatment of a Buddhist nun, who'd been beaten in reprisal for her anti-Chinese sentiments. DP. In Tibetan/Russian/German/Buryatian/ English/Romansch with subtitles.

Dir/Scr Franz Reichle

Knute Rockne – All American ★★ U

Biographical drama 1940 · US · BW · 97mins

In this biopic of the Norwegian-born American football coach – a national hero who died prematurely in a plane crash – Rockne is played by Pat O'Brien, who performs to the gallery and still seems to be wearing the dog collar from all those Cagney gangster pictures. But the movie is now more famous for Ronald Reagan in his favourite role as "The Gipper", Rockne's star player George Gipp, who died young of pneumonia. "Win one for the Gipper" is the well-known line which Reagan reprised on his presidential campaign trail, recalling not only his film role but also an age of patriotic achievement. AT

Pat O'Brien *Knute Rockne* • Ronald Reagan *George Gipp* • Gale Page *Bonnie Skilles Rockne* • Donald Crisp *Father Callahan* • Albert Basserman *Father Julius Nieuwland* ■ *Dir* Lloyd Bacon • *Scr* Robert Buckner, from the private papers of Mrs Knute Rockne

Koi Mere Dil Se Pooche ★★ 15

Romantic musical drama
2001 · Ind · Colour · 145mins

Until a flashback transforms it into a fever-pitch thriller, this had the makings of an entertaining romantic comedy. Sadly, the debuting Esha Deol lacks the poise to carry the conceit, as she rebuffs the attentions of fashion student Aftab Shivdasani because of the humiliations suffered at the hands of her supposedly deceased husband, Sanjay Kapoor. DP. In Hindi with English subtitles. DVD

Esha Deol *Aisha* • Jaya Bachchan *Mansi Devi* • Aftab Shivdasani *Aman* • Sanjay Kapoor *Dushyant* ■ *Dir/Scr* Vinay Shukla

Koi... Mil Gaya ★★★ 12

Science-fiction romantic drama
2003 · Ind · Colour · 156mins

Director Rakesh Roshan has wisely entrusted the special effects for this sci-fi film to James Colmer, who worked on the likes of *Independence Day*. But while the technology is cutting edge, the narrative owes more to the Cold War allegories of the 1950s when extraterrestrials came to Earth to urge us to get along despite our differences. Mentally handicapped Hrithik Roshan accidentally makes contact with a spaceship using his inventor father's equipment. It's slick, sentimental entertainment, although the songs will probably alienate sci-fi aficionados. DP. In Hindi with English subtitles. DVD

Rekha *Sonia Mehra* • Hrithik Roshan *Rohit Mehra* • Preity Zinta *Nisha* • Prem Chopra *Harbans Saxena* • Rajat Bedi *Raj Saxena* • Johnny Lever *Chelaram Sukhwani* ■ *Dir* Rakesh Roshan • *Scr* Sachin Bhowmick, Honey Irani, Robin Bhatt, Rakesh Roshan, Javed Siddiqui

Kokoda Crescent ★★

Comedy drama 1989 · Aus · Colour · 83mins

This tale of elderly suburban commandos went straight to video in its native Australia, but the presence of TV's Alf Garnett himself, Warren Mitchell, may attract the curious over here. Mitchell, Bill Kerr and Martin Vaughan play Second World War veterans who, with their equally gung-ho wives, take on the drug dealers and corrupt coppers who have infested the Sydney estate where they live. Director Ted Robinson conveys his message in sledgehammer terms, but his emphasis is firmly on the comic. DP. Contains violence and swearing.

Warren Mitchell *Stan* • Bill Kerr *Russ* • Ruth Cracknell *Alice* • Madge Ryan *Margaret* • Martin Vaughan *Eric* • Patrick Thompson *Brett* • Steve Jacobs *Policeman* ■ *Dir* Ted Robinson • *Scr* Patrick Cook

Kolobos ★ 18

Horror 1999 · US · Colour · 82mins

Five people sign up for a free holiday in return for participating in an experimental film. The catch? Once they are all locked in a deserted house and the video cameras are switched on, they are successively killed in increasingly violent ways. The characters are laughably stock, the dialogue inane and the effects are rendered so cheaply even rabid gore-hounds will feel cheated. AJ DVD

Amy Weber *Kyra* • Donny Terranova *Tom* • Nichole Pelerine *Erica* • John Fairlie *Gary* • Promise LaMarco *Tina* ■ *Dir* Daniel Liatowitsch, David Todd Ocvirk • *Scr* Nne Ebong, Daniel Liatowitsch, David Todd Ocvirk

Kolya ★★★★ 12

Comedy drama
1996 · Cz Rep/UK/Fr · Colour · 100mins

The winner of the Oscar for best foreign film, this is a delightful odd-couple story set in Prague during the last days of Communism. The director's father, Zdenek Sverak (who also scripted), is superb as the former Philharmonic cellist who takes custody of five-year-old Andrej Chalimon after his mother (a Russian interpreter with whom the impoverished musician had contracted a marriage of convenience) flits to the west. With no political axe to grind, Jan Sverak goes for the human interest angle and produces a joyous film, which provokes more than its fair share of smiles and surreptitious dabs of the eyes. DP. In Czech with English subtitles. Contains some swearing. DVD

Zdenek Sverak *Frantisek Louka* • Andrej Chalimon *Kolya* • Libuse Safrankova *Klara* • Ondrej Vetchy *Mr Broz* • Stella Zazvorkova *Mother* • Ladislav Smoljak *Mr Houdek* • Irena Livanova *Nadezda* • Lilian Mankina *Aunt Tamara* ■ *Dir* Jan Sverak • *Scr* Zdenek Sverak, from a story by Pavel Taussig

Komitas ★★★★

Biographical drama
1988 · W Ger · BW and Colour · 96mins

The influence of two very different Soviet directors pervades this poetic portrait of the monk and musician who lost his reason during the onslaught that decimated the Ottoman empire's Armenian population during the period around 1915. Director Don Askarian's atmospheric use of landscape and interiors gives this episodic film its unique audiovisual lyricism. Samuel Ovasapian excels as Komitas, who spent the last 20 years of his life in various mental institutions, tormented by his memories and imaginings. DP. A German language film.

Samuel Ovasapian *Komitas* • Onig Saadetian *Terlomesian* • Margarita Woskanjan *Pupil* • Reverend Yegishe Mangikian *Katholikos* ■ *Dir/Scr* Don Askarian

Komodo ★★ 12

Fantasy thriller 1999 · US · Colour · 85mins

In this undernourished eco-horror, a teenager is taken back to the island off the coast of the US where his parents were eaten by Komodo dragons, because his psychiatrist Jill Hennessey thinks it will cure his traumatic amnesia. Other potential victims for the ravenous lizards include evil hunters hired by an oil company to eradicate the slithering menace so they can drill the place dry. The ridiculous premise is given routine direction by special-effects artist Michael Lantieri, explaining why the computer graphic effects are of a higher standard than usual. AJ DVD

Jill Hennessy *Victoria* • Billy Burke *Oates* • Kevin Zegers *Patrick Connelly* • Paul Gleeson *Denby* • Nina Landis *Annie* ■ *Dir* Michael Lantieri • *Scr* Hans Bauer, Craig Mitchell

Kona Coast ★★

Adventure drama 1968 · US · Colour · 80mins

Set on Hawaii, this colourful melodrama features rugged Richard Boone, a tough guy who never quite made it as a major movie star but always had great screen presence. Here he's a fisherman whose daughter is murdered, possibly by a local racketeer who has also smashed up Boone's boat. Lots of action in front of majestic scenery ensues, but it all looks and sounds like an old studio picture from the 1930s. AT

Richard Boone *Sam Moran* • Vera Miles *Melissa Hyde* • Joan Blondell *Kittibelle Lightfoot* • Steve Ihnat *Kryder* • Chips Rafferty *Lightfoot* • Kent Smith *Akamai* ■ *Dir* Lamont Johnson • *Scr* Gil Ralston, from the story *Bimini Gall* by John D MacDonald

Konga ★★ PG

Science-fiction horror
1960 · UK · Colour · 85mins

Michael Gough as a botanist inventing a growth serum, a ratty zip-up gorilla suit, Margo Johns as a comely housekeeper, a miniature cardboard Big Ben and pop star Jess Conrad – what more could you want in a cheap and cheerful British *King Kong* imitation originally titled *I Was a Teenage Gorilla*? With its crude horror always verging on the farcical, the entertainment value stems from the sheer incompetence on full view. Enjoyably terrible and filmed on location in Croydon High Street. AJ [VIDEO]

Michael Gough *Dr Charles Decker* • Margo Johns *Margaret* • Jess Conrad *Bob Kenton* • Claire Gordon *Sandra Banks* • Austin Trevor *Dean Foster* • Jack Watson *Superintendent Brown* ■ *Dir* John Lemont • *Scr* Herman Cohen, Aben Kandel

Königsmark ★★★

Romantic drama 1935 · Fr · BW · 114mins

Silent master Maurice Tourneur directs this Ruritanian melodrama with all the visual majesty you would expect of someone who once worked as an assistant to the sculptor Auguste Rodin. It's a tantalising tale of romance and revenge, as princess Elissa Landi teams with Pierre Fresnay to avenge the murder of her husband. Amid the lavish trappings and grand posturings, Landi gives a splendid performance, echoing the tragedy of *Hamlet* (the clear inspiration for Pierre Benoit's source novel) after she guns down a spying maid. DP. A French language film.

Elissa Landi *Princess Aurore* • Pierre Fresnay *Raoul Vignerte* • John Lodge *Grand Duke Frederick* • Frank Vosper *Major Baron de Boise* • Marcelle Rogez *Countess Melusine* • Allan Jeayes *Grand Duke Rodolphe* • Romilly Lunge *Lieutenant de Hagen* • Cecil Humphreys *de Marçais* ■ *Dir* Maurice Tourneur • *Scr* from the novel by Pierre Benoit

Kontroll ★★★ 15

Thriller 2003 · Hun · Colour · 106mins

Nimrod Antal's directorial debut is both a simmering study of despised outcasts and an understated murder mystery that makes atmospheric use of its Budapest Metro setting. As the leader of a crew of apathetic ticket inspectors, Sandor Csanyi is impressively intense, contemplating unexplained anxieties that are only relieved by his crush on kooky Eszter Balla. However, Antal wisely lightens the mood with some bleakly comic encounters with fare-dodging passengers that allow the bullish supporting cast to shine. DP. In Hungarian with English subtitles. Contains swearing and violence. DVD

Sandor Csanyi *Bulcsu* • Zoltan Mucsi *Professor* • Csaba Pindroch *Muki* • Sandor Badar *Lecso* • Zsolt Nagy *Tibi* • Bence Matyassy *Bootsie* • Eszter Balla *Sofie* ■ *Dir* Nimrod Antal • *Scr* Jim Adler, Antal Nimrod

Korczak ★★★ PG

Historical drama
1990 · Pol/W Ger/Fr/UK · BW · 117mins

Scripted by Agnieszka Holland and shot in sombre monochrome by Robby Müller, this is an earnest attempt to portray the atrocities of the Holocaust without undue sentiment or sensationalism. Indeed, this is such a determinedly sensitive study that it's often hard to recognise it as the work of Andrzej Wajda, whose "war trilogy" was so full of anger at the loss of a generation. Tracing real-life events from 1936 to 1942, the film benefits from a dignified performance from Wojtek Pszoniak as Janusz Korczak, the doctor who ministered to the children of the Warsaw ghetto. DP. In Polish with English subtitles.

Wojtek Pszoniak [Wojciech Pszoniak] *Dr Janusz Korczak* • Ewa Dalkowska *Stefa* • Piotr Kozlowski *Heniek* ■ *Dir* Andrzej Wajda • *Scr* Agnieszka Holland

Korea ★★★

Period drama 1995 · Ire · Colour · 87mins

Although the lakeside community in County Cavan is receiving electricity, the biggest sparks come between Donal Donnelly and his sworn enemy Vass Anderson, especially when it's discovered their children have fallen in love. Set in the early 1950s, the spectre of the Korean conflict hangs over the proceedings in this thoughtful film, played with great conviction by a solid ensemble cast. DP. An English/ Gaelic language film.

Donal Donnelly *John Doyle* • Andrew Scott *Eamon Doyle* • Fiona Molony *Una Moran* • Vass Anderson *Ben Moran* • Christopher Callery ■ *Dir* Cathal Black • *Scr* Joe O'Byrne, from a story by John McGahern

Kotch ★★★ PG

Comedy drama 1971 · US · Colour · 114mins

We always knew that Walter Matthau and Jack Lemmon had their communal heart in the right place. But here it's worn a bit too strenuously on the frayed sleeve of Matthau, as an unwanted old man who walks out on his impatient son and daughter-in-law, and befriends a pregnant teenager. Lemmon, as debut director, accords his friend a leisurely pace and some great close-ups. The film's sentimentality veers into schmaltz, but what do you expect from this wonderfully odd couple? TH [VIDEO] DVD

Walter Matthau *Joseph P Kotcher* • Deborah Winters *Erica Herzenstiel* • Felicia Farr *Wilma Kotcher* • Charles Aidman *Gerald Kotcher* • Ellen Geer *Vera Kotcher* • Darrell Larson *Vincent Perrin* ■ *Dir* Jack Lemmon • *Scr* John Paxton, from the novel by Katherine Topkins

Koyaanisqatsi ★★★ U

Experimental documentary
1982 · US · Colour · 84mins

An offbeat documentary-cum-meditation about the decline of western civilisation, using the difference between the untamed American wilderness and hysterical, rush-hour Manhattan as its crux. Director Godfrey Reggio shuns narration in favour of powerful, repetitive music by minimalist composer Philip Glass to match his striking visuals. Made in the early 1980s when ecological warnings were starting to take hold, it was, for all its vacuity, a surprising success. The title is a Hopi Indian word meaning "life out of balance". Followed in 1988 by *Powaqqatsi*. TH [VIDEO] DVD

Dir Godfrey Reggio • *Scr* Ron Fricke, Michael Hoenig, Alton Walpole, Godfrey Reggio • *Producer* Godfrey Reggio, Francis Coppola [Francis Ford Coppola] • *Cinematographer* Ron Fricke • *Music Director* Michael Hoenig

Krakatoa, East of Java ★★ PG

Disaster movie 1969 · US · Colour · 121mins

Everyone knows that the Indonesian island of Krakatoa blew its top in 1883, killing 40,000 people and creating a tidal wave of such strength that ripples were felt off Bognor Regis. Everyone knows, too, that Krakatoa lies west of Java, not east, though that would have made for a less exotic title. Problem is, as with most disaster movies, it's a long haul before nature intrudes into the human dramas being enacted before back-projected images of the smoking volcano. AT [VIDEO] DVD

Maximilian Schell *Captain Chris Hanson* • Diane Baker *Laura Travis* • Barbara Werle *Charley* • Brian Keith *Connerly* • Rossano Brazzi *Giovanni Borghese* • Sal Mineo *Leoncavallo Borghese* • John Leyton *Douglas Rigby* • JD Cannon *Danzig* • Jacqui Chan *Toshi* ■ *Dir* Bernard L Kowalski • *Scr* Clifford Newton Gould, Bernard Gordon

Kramer vs Kramer ★★★★ PG

Drama 1979 · US · Colour · 100mins

Winner of the Oscar for best picture and scooping best actor and supporting actress statuettes for Dustin Hoffman and Meryl Streep, this runaway success now looks a little overwrought in places, but it is still an involving, moving and discerning study of the suffering endured by all embroiled in a divorce. You could cut the tension in the courtroom sequences with a knife, but writer/ director Robert Benton deserves greatest credit for the truth and restraint of the scenes in which Hoffman tries to win over six-year-old son Justin Henry, which could so easily have become false. DP [VIDEO] DVD

Dustin Hoffman *Ted Kramer* • Meryl Streep *Joanna Kramer* • Jane Alexander *Margaret Phelps* • Justin Henry *Billy Kramer* • Howard Duff *John Shaunessy* • George Coe *Jim O'Connor* • JoBeth Williams *Phyllis Bernard* • Bill Moor *Gressen* • Howland Chamberlain [Howland Chamberlin] *Judge Atkins* ■ *Dir* Robert Benton • *Scr* Robert Benton, from the novel by Avery Corman

Krámpack ★★★★ 15

Drama 2000 · Sp · Colour · 90mins

Older film-makers often mistakenly assume that teenagers are invariably desperate and obsessive about that all-important "first experience". Something much closer to the truth is suggested in this Spanish coming-of-age movie, in which everything is casual, experiments and mistakes are made, but ultimately nothing really matters. Two teenage boys, Fernando Ramallo and Jordi Vilches, spend the summer in Ramallo's parents' house by the seaside. By the end of the holiday, their sexualities have been determined. The source material has been intelligently opened out by director Cesc Gay, and the entire cast is good, with the boys outstanding. DM. In Spanish with English subtitles. [VIDEO] DVD

Fernando Ramallo *Dani* • Jordi Vilches *Nico* • Marieta Orozco *Elena* • Esther Nubiola *Berta* • Chisco Amado *Julian* • Ana Gracia *Sonia* • Myriam Mézières *Marianne* ■ *Dir* Cesc Gay • *Scr* Cesc Gay, Tomás Aragay, from the play by Jordi Sánchez

The Krays ★★★★ 18

Biographical crime drama
1990 · UK · Colour · 114mins

This is an intelligent biopic of Britain's most famous gangsters, the twin bruvvers who made life safe for East Enders when they weren't running protection rackets or inflicting gangland punishments on rival mobsters. To be fair, writer Philip Ridley and director Peter Medak largely avoid glamorising the violent world of Reggie and Ronnie, and are more interested in unravelling their complex personalities. They are helped by surprisingly convincing lead performances from Martin and Gary Kemp, although Billie Whitelaw effortlessly rises above everybody else in the star-studded cast as the boys' best friend, their mum. JF. Contains swearing, violence, nudity. [VIDEO] DVD

Gary Kemp *Ronnie Kray* • Martin Kemp *Reggie Kray* • Billie Whitelaw *Violet Kray* • Tom Bell *Jack "The Hat" McVitie* • Susan Fleetwood *Rose* • Charlotte Cornwell *May* • Kate Hardie *Frances* • Avis Bunnage *Helen* • Gary Love *Steve* • Steven Berkoff *George Cornell* • Jimmy Jewel *"Cannonball" Lee* • Barbara Ferris *Mrs Lawson* • Victor Spinetti *Mr Lawson* ■ *Dir* Peter Medak • *Scr* Philip Ridley

The Kremlin Letter ★★ 18

Spy thriller 1970 · US · Colour · 115mins

The letter in question goes from Moscow to Washington and proposes the annihilation of Red China. Warren Beatty turned this Cold War saga down; the studio, 20th Century-Fox, then vetoed Robert Redford, believing the film he had just made for them, *Butch Cassidy and the Sundance Kid*, was going to flop. So director John Huston hired Patrick O'Neal and backed him up with Hollywood exiles Orson Welles and George Sanders, here playing a transvestite. Hard to follow and gimmicky. AT [VIDEO]

Patrick O'Neal *Charles Rone* • Richard Boone *Ward* • Orson Welles *Bresnavitch* • Barbara Parkins *BA* • Max von Sydow *Col Kosnov* • George Sanders *"Warlock"* • Dean Jagger *"Highwayman"* • Bibi Andersson *Erika Boeck* • Ronald Radd *Potkin* ■ *Dir* John Huston • *Scr* John Huston, Gladys Hill, from a novel by Noel Behn

K

The Kreutzer Sonata ★★★★★ 15

Drama 1987 · USSR · Colour · 135mins

One of the truly great Russian films of the 1980s and a "must see" on all counts. Tolstoy's stifling, gripping tale of a dramatic, violent relationship between a man and his virtuoso musician wife is done great service by deep, multilayered direction and the searing performance of Oleg Yankovsky, who tells his story in flashback. Yankovsky's portrayal of jealousy erupting into hate is a cinematic triumph; the movie never lets its vice-like grip on the audience's emotions slacken. SH. In Russian with English subtitles. [VIDEO]

Oleg Yankovsky *Vasili Pozdnyshev* • Aleksandr Trofimov *Pozdnyshev's fellow traveller* • Irina Seleznyova *Lisa Pozdnyshev* • Dmitri Pokrovsky *Trukhachevsky* ■ *Dir* Mikhail Schweitzer, Sofia Milkina • *Scr* Mikhail Schweitzer, from the novel by Leo Tolstoy

Krippendorf's Tribe ★★ 12

Comedy 1998 · US · Colour · 90mins

Richard Dreyfuss plays an anthropologist whose tribe-seeking mission in New Guinea was a failure, forcing him to fabricate footage of a new tribe concocted from the names of his three kids. Not exactly a great comedy premise in the first place and it runs out of ideas (and laughs) well before the halfway mark. On this occasion, Dreyfuss's screen spark seems to have been "shorted", although Jenna Elfman has an appealingly kooky comic flair. Hardly worth seeking out. JC [VIDEO]

Richard Dreyfuss *James Krippendorf* • Jenna Elfman *Veronica Micelli* • Natasha Lyonne *Shelly* • Lily Tomlin *Ruth Allen* • Gregory Smith *Mickey* • Carl Michael Lindner *Edmund* • David Ogden Stiers *Henry Spivey* ■ *Dir* Todd Holland • *Scr* Charlie Peters, from the novel by Frank Parkin

Kristin Lavransdatter ★★★

Period drama
1995 · Ger/Nor/Swe · Colour · 180mins

Adapted from Sigrid Undset's Pulitzer Prize-winning novel, Liv Ullmann's film possesses all the beauty of a medieval tapestry, yet its length and inertia often make this epic seem more like a book of hours. Elizabeth Matheson's statuesque performance makes it difficult to sympathise with the landowner's daughter caught between duty and passion. However, neither she nor her less-than-gallant lover, Björn Skagestad, is given much assistance from either Ullmann's hoary script or her hesitant pacing. Fortunately, Sven Nykvist's photography is a delight and the colour, simplicity and sheer arduousness of rural life are admirably conveyed. DP. A Norwegian language film.

Lena Endre *Eline Ormsdatter* • Erland Josephson *Broder Edvin* • Elisabeth Matheson *Kristin Lavransdatter* • Sverre Anker Ousdal *Lavrans* • Björn Skagestad *Erlend* ■ *Dir* Liv Ullmann • *Scr* Liv Ullmann, from the novel by Sigrid Undset

Kronos ★★★

Science fiction 1957 · US · BW · 78mins

An enormous alien robot lands off the California coast and tramples on everything in sight as it advances towards Los Angeles on an energy-sucking spree. Despite its reliance on stock footage, cost-cutting special effects (mainly large-size props) and average direction, this unusually slanted invasion thriller is a perfect example of engagingly deranged 1950s B-movie-making. A minor classic. AJ

Jeff Morrow *Dr Leslie Gaskell* • Barbara Lawrence *Vera Hunter* • John Emery *Dr Eliot* • George O'Hanlon *Dr Arnie Culver* • Morris Ankrum *Dr Albert R Stern* • Kenneth Alton *McCrary* ■ *Dir* Kurt Neumann • *Scr* Lawrence Louis Goldman, from a story by Irving Block

Krull ★★★ PG

Fantasy adventure
1983 · UK/US · Colour · 120mins

Engaging without ever being enthralling, this fantasy performed badly at the box office and Columbia saw little return on its $27 million investment. Yet this maligned movie has many moments to enjoy, as Ken Marshall's prince seeks to release princess Lysette Anthony from the clutches of the Beast. The special effects may fall far short of spectacular, but they help to create a charming neverland and add considerably to the excitement of the quest. The acting honours go to Bernard Bresslaw as a cyclops and Freddie Jones as a seer. DP [video] DVD

Ken Marshall *Prince Colwyn* • Lysette Anthony *Princess Lyssa* • Freddie Jones *Ynyr* • Francesca Annis *Widow of the Web* • Alun Armstrong *Torquil* • David Battley *Ergo* • Bernard Bresslaw *Cyclops* • Liam Neeson *Kegan* • Todd Carty *Oswyn* • Robbie Coltrane *Rhun* • John Welsh *Seer* ■ *Dir* Peter Yates • *Scr* Stanford Sherman

Kuch Kuch Hota Hai ★★ U

Romantic drama
1998 · Ind · Colour · 176mins

Karan Johar's directorial debut offers little to distinguish it from the average Bollywood melodrama. Young Sana Saeed follows the instructions given in the letters she receives each birthday from her mother, Rani Mukherji, who died in childbirth. They set Saeed on a quest to find her mother's best friend, Kajol, who still holds a candle for Saeed's father, Shah Rukh Khan. Potboiling pulp. DP. In Hindi with English subtitles. [video]

Shahrukh Khan [Shah Rukh Khan] *Rahul* • Rani Mukherji *Tina* • Kajol *Anjali Sharma* • Sana Saeed *Anjali Khanna* • Salman Khan *Aman* • Reema Lagoo *Mrs Sharma* ■ *Dir/Scr* Karan Johar

Kuch Naa Kaho ★★★ U

Musical romantic comedy
2003 · Ind · Colour · 168mins

Veteran director Ramesh Sippy acts as producer on his son Rohan's debut feature, which piles one romantic comedy cliché upon another yet still manages to amuse. Abhishek Bachchan (himself the son of a Bollywood legend) stars as an Indian-American who returns to Mumbai for a family wedding only to find himself ensnared in his mother Suhasini Mulay's plot to find him a bride. However, he inevitably falls for the one woman who isn't interested in him, matchmaker Aishwarya Rai. DP. In Hindi with English subtitles. [video] DVD

Aishwarya Rai *Namrata* • Abhishek Bachchan *Raj* • Satish Shah *Rakesh* • Suhasini Mulay *Dr Malhotra* ■ *Dir* Rohan Sippy • *Scr* Neeraj Vora, Naushil Mehta, Nidhi Tuli, from a story by Rohena Gera

Kuffs ★★ 15

Comedy thriller 1991 · US · Colour · 97mins

An odd mix of comedy and action which only Christian Slater devotees will warm to. He plays the dropout whose brother – the owner of a privately funded San Francisco police franchise – is murdered in front of him. Slater is forced to shape up when he takes over the franchise in an attempt to find the killer. With Slater's smug smart-aleck asides to the camera and with silly sound effects throughout, this is pure trash with just enough flash to make it a mildly watchable potboiler. AJ. Contains violence, swearing. [video]

Christian Slater *George Kuffs* • Milla Jovovich *Maya Carlton* • Tony Goldwyn *Ted Bukovsky* • Bruce Boxleitner *Brad Kuffs* • Troy Evans *Captain Morino* • George De La Pena *Sam Jones* • Craig Benton *Paint store owner* • Ashley Judd *Paint store owner's wife* ■ *Dir* Bruce A Evans • *Scr* Bruce A Evans, Raynold Gideon

Kühle Wampe ★★★★ PG

Drama 1931 · Germany · BW · 68mins

Evicted from a Berlin tenement, Hertha Thiele's family makes the most of life in a camp for the dispossessed, despite the suicide of her son. Condemning big business and positing all sorts of social alternatives, Bertolt Brecht's Marxist manifesto may not sound the stuff of entertainment but the only film he didn't disown is anything but a dry political tract. It is often riotously funny, but the over-riding impression it leaves is of a lost age of innocence and a tragically missed opportunity to create a fairer world. DP. In German with English subtitles. [video]

Hertha Thiele *Annie Bönike* • Ernst Busch *Fritz* • Martha Wolter ■ *Dir* Slatan Dudow • *Scr* Bertolt Brecht, Ernst Ottwald

Kull the Conqueror ★★ 12

Fantasy action adventure
1997 · US · Colour · 91mins

Hercules star Kevin Sorbo made the switch from television to the big screen with this sword-and-sorcery epic, based on characters created by Robert E Howard of *Conan* fame. Sorbo becomes King of Valusia, but his attempts to free his people put him up against shape-shifting sorceress Tia Carrere.The disjointed proceedings deal with the clichéd *good versus evil* conventions of the genre, but with a darker hue and edgier atmosphere than normal. AJ [video]

Kevin Sorbo *Kull* • Tia Carrere *Akivasha* • Thomas Ian Griffith *Taligaro* • Litefoot *Ascalante* • Roy Brocksmith *Tu* • Harvey Fierstein *Juba* • Karina Lombard *Zareta* • Edward Tudor-Pole *Enaros* • Douglas Henshall *Ducalon* ■ *Dir* John Nicolella • *Scr* Charles Edward Pogue, from the Marvel Comics character created by Robert E Howard

Kundun ★★ 12

Religious biographical drama
1997 · US · Colour · 128mins

Emerging from his usual gangster-ridden mean streets, director Martin Scorsese sets his sights higher to the wide-open Himalayan spaces for this biography of the Dalai Lama. Scorsese's epic follows the Tibetan leader from his supposed reincarnation as the son of a humble family, through his investiture and his attempts to build a working relationship with – and eventual rejection of – Chinese socialism to his exile. Trouble is, the screenplay (by Melissa Mathison, who also wrote the script for *ET*) paints too rosy a picture of Buddhism, never questioning a country in which priests and poor are set so far apart. Roger Deakin's photography, though, is as luminous as a halo. TH [video] DVD

Tenzin Tsarong Thuthob *Dalai Lama as an adult* • Tencho Gyalpo *Dalai Lama's mother* • Tsewang Migyur Khangsar *Dalai Lama's father* ■ *Dir* Martin Scorsese • *Scr* Melissa Mathison

Kung Fu Hustle ★★★★ 15

Period martial arts comedy
2004 · HK/Chi · Colour · 98mins

As in his previous film *Shaolin Soccer*, writer/director/star Stephen Chow casts himself as the hapless, idiotic hero – here, a poor, weedy guy who wants to be a member of the infamous Axe Gang that terrorises 1940s Shanghai. In the middle of a homage to Scorsese's *Gangs of New York*, a hilariously impressive martial arts battle begins, with the exemplary fight scenes. Featuring more action than most action films, more comedy than most comedies and certainly more "nonsense" than most films in general, this is a dazzling and outrageous movie. KK. In Cantonese/ Mandarin with English subtitles. Contains violence.

Stephen Chow *Sing* • Yuen Wah *Landlord* • Leung Siu-lung *The Beast* • Dong Zhi-hua *Donut* • Chiu Chi-ling *Tailor* • Xing Yu *Coolie* • Chan Kwok-kwan *Brother Sum* • Lam Tze-chung *Sing's sidekick* ■ *Dir* Stephen Chow • *Scr* Stephen Chow, Tsang Kan-Cheong [Tsang Kan-Cheung], Lola Huo, Chan Man-keung

Kung-Fu Master ★★★

Romantic drama 1987 · Fr · Colour · 80mins

Agnès Varda was taking a risk in producing this potentially scandalous love story involving a 40-something woman and a 15-year-old boy. But this is not a film about physical desire. It's a considered study of the continued existence of the poetic values of courtly love (ingeniously symbolised by the arcade kung fu game that encapsulates chivalric heroism) and whether any idealised emotions can endure in the face of everyday reality. It's not always credible, but that it works at all is down to the sensitivity of Jane Birkin and the director's own son, Mathieu Demy. DP. In French and English with subtitles.

Jane Birkin *Mary-Jane* • Mathieu Demy *Julien* • Charlotte Gainsbourg *Lucy* ■ *Dir* Agnès Varda • *Scr* Agnès Varda, from an idea by Jane Birkin

Kung Phooey! ★★ 12

Martial arts spoof
2003 · US · Colour · 87mins

Darryl Fong seeks to explode a few myths with this martial arts spoof. But the staleness of the plot and the lameness of the gags means that this coarse satire doesn't succeed. Michael Chow stars as a monk who arrives Stateside to help uncle Wallace Choy recover an enchanted peach from monosodium glutamate smuggler Joyce Thi Brew. But Chow's ineptitude and Brew's pantomimic villainy become tiresome as the screenplay runs out of steam. DP DVD

Michael Chow *Art Chew* • Joyce Thi Brew *Helen Hu* • Colman Domingo *Roy Lee* • Darryl Fong *Waymon* • Karena Davis *Sue Shee* • Wallace Choy *Uncle Wong* ■ *Dir/Scr* Darryl Fong

Kurosawa ★★★

Documentary
2001 · US/UK/Jpn · Colour · 115mins

Frequently hailed as the most western of all Japanese directors, Akira Kurosawa was certainly responsible for introducing his country's rich cinematic heritage to the rest of the world. This reverential, but informed documentary traces his life from his traumatic early years, through his wartime apprenticeship and rise to international eminence with *Rashomon* and *Seven Samurai*, to his later masterpieces, which offered a judicious blend of the literary and the original, the historical and the contemporary, the epic and the intimate. Punctuated with apposite clips and revealing interviews, it's a worthy tribute to one of the few genuine masters of the art. DP. In English and Japanese with subtitles.

Sam Shepard *Narrator* • Paul Scofield *Reader* ■ *Dir/Scr* Adam Low

Kurt & Courtney ★★★ 15

Documentary 1997 · UK · Colour · 94mins

Documentarist Nick Broomfield has always employed a blend of charm and innocence to expose the frailties of his subjects. But here that tactic somewhat backfires because the people he meets in seeking to establish the facts about the death of grunge rock star Kurt Cobain have much darker agendas than his own idle curiosity. Cobain's widow Courtney Love certainly comes across as a difficult character (an impression compounded by her campaign to block the film's screening at the Sundance festival), but at least she is devoid of the bile and envy that motivates most of the others in the film. DP. Contains swearing. [video] DVD

Dir Nick Broomfield • *Editor* Mark Atkins • *Cinematographer* Joan Churchill, Alex Vendler

Kwaidan ★★★ PG

Portmanteau fantasy
1964 · Jpn · Colour · 154mins

A portmanteau film of four ghost stories, perhaps best viewed as separate films – one episode was originally cut to shorten the running time. One story concerns a samurai haunted by the beauty of his first wife; another is an ingenious tale about a man who drinks not only a cup of tea but also the man reflected on the surface of the drink. Viewers expecting a compendium of horror will be disappointed, for these tales are gentle, ironic and sad. All are stunningly photographed and exquisitely designed. AT. In Japanese with English subtitles. [video]

Rentaro Mikuni *Samurai* • Michiyo Aratama *1st wife* • Misako Watanabe *2nd wife* • Keiko Kishi *The woman* • Tatsuya Nakadai *Minokichi* • Katsuo Nakamura *Hoichi* • Rentaro Mikuni *Samurai* ■ *Dir* Masaki Kobayashi • *Scr* Yoko Mizuki, from stories by Lafcadio Hearn

Kyun! Ho Gaya Na ... ★★★ U

Romantic drama
2004 · Ind · Colour · 172mins

It should be easy enough to detect the chemistry between Aishwarya Rai and Vivek Oberoi in this amiable drama, as rumours of a romance between them was the talking point of the production. This centres on that old Bollywood standby, the class and culture clash, as Rai leaves her widowed father Tinnu Anand in the coffee-plantation town of Coorg and heads for Mumbai to work in Amitabh Bachchan's orphanage. However, her good intentions are sidetracked by the free-spirited Oberoi, while staying with his parents, Om Puri and Rati Agnihotri. DP. In Hindi with English subtitles.

Amitabh Bachchan *Raj Chauhan* • Aishwarya Rai *Diya* • Vivek Oberoi *Arjun* • Om Puri *Mr Khanna* • Tinnu Anand *Malhotra* ■ *Dir* Samir Karnik • *Scr* Samir Karnik, Rajesh Soni • *Music/Lyrics* Javed Akhtar

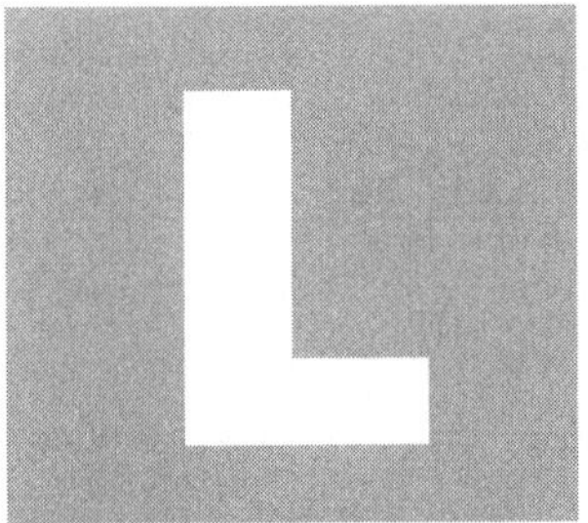

LA Confidential ★★★★★ 18

Crime drama 1997 · US · Colour · 132mins

Curtis Hanson's superlative filming of James Ellroy's complex 1950s detective story fuses period authenticity, fluid direction and searing, full-blooded performances. From the apparently open-and-shut case of a diner bloodbath, the sleazy scenario takes a trio of cops – ambitious rookie Guy Pearce, smooth TV adviser Kevin Spacey and hard man Russell Crowe – down a corpse-strewn path of crime, corruption and celebrity lookalikes. The roles fit the actors like tightly stitched gloves, and the film's brutality is amplified by the absence of clear-cut heroes, with the police characters as morally dubious as the film's villains. The excellent script won an Oscar, as did Kim Basinger for her hard-edged vamp, but the picture really deserved a hatful. JC. Contains swearing, violence, sex scenes. [VIDEO] DVD

Kevin Spacey *Jack Vincennes* • Russell Crowe *Bud White* • Guy Pearce *Edmund "Ed" Exley* • James Cromwell *Captain Dudley Smith* • Kim Basinger *Lynn Bracken* • Danny DeVito *Sid Hudgens* • David Strathairn *Pierce Patchett* • Ron Rifkin *District Attorney Ellis Loew* • Matt McCoy *"Badge of Honor" star Brett Chase* • Paul Guilfoyle (2) *Mickey Cohen* ■ *Dir* Curtis Hanson • *Scr* Curtis Hanson, Brian Helgeland, from the novel by James Ellroy • *Cinematographer* Dante Spinotti • *Music* Jerry Goldsmith

LA Story ★★★★ 15

Romantic comedy
1991 · US · Colour · 90mins

This warm-hearted salute to Los Angeles pretensions is a romantic comedy that boasts just enough quirkiness to satify the fans of Steve Martin who were worried that he might be selling out and abandoning his "wild and crazy" persona. He plays a weatherman, who falls for visiting British journalist Victoria Tennant while undergoing a mild midlife crisis. Martin as writer has fun sending up some of the crazier aspects of LA life and stages some lovely comic set pieces; if anything, a sniff of sentimentality is the film's failing. JF. Contains swearing and brief nudity. [VIDEO] DVD

Steve Martin *Harris K Telemacher* • Victoria Tennant *Sara McDowel* • Richard E Grant *Roland* • Marilu Henner *Trudi* • Sarah Jessica Parker *SanDeE** • Susan Forristal *Ariel* • Kevin Pollak *Frank Swan* • Sam McMurray *Morris Frost* • Patrick Stewart *Maître d' at L'Idiot* ■ *Dir* Mick Jackson • *Scr* Steve Martin

LA without a Map ★★★ 15

Romantic comedy
1998 · UK/Fr/Fin/Lux · Colour · 107mins

Mika Kaurismäki's film is a sharp comedy stab at Los Angeles, in which David Tennant plays the Englishman abroad – a Bradford undertaker who leaves his rain-swept, gloomy existence to track down beautiful American Vinessa Shaw to sunny Hollywood after spotting her in his local graveyard. Of course, everything which can go wrong once he gets there invariably does, but it's fun, unpredictable stuff, peppered with some fantastic supporting turns from Julie Delpy, Vincent Gallo and, playing himself in a deliciously tongue-in-cheek manner, Johnny Depp. JB

David Tennant *Richard Tennant* • Vinessa Shaw *Barbara* • Julie Delpy *Julie* • Vincent Gallo *Moss* • Cameron Bancroft *Patterson* • Joe Dallesandro *Michael* • Anouk Aimée • Saskia Reeves *Joy* • Johnny Depp ■ *Dir* Mika Kaurismäki • *Scr* Richard Rayner, Mika Kaurismäki, from the novel by Richard Rayner

LIE ★★★★ 18

Drama 2001 · US · Colour · 97mins

Paedophilia is given a chillingly benevolent face in director Michael Cuesta's emotive debut. The film lays bare the cycle of abuse that tarnishes the lives of a group of delinquent boys from Long Island, New York. Standing out among them is Howie (Paul Franklin Dano), a 15-year-old struggling to cope with his mother's death, whose innocence attracts the local paedophile, Big John (Brian Cox). This makes for gloomy and unsettling viewing. Though the film controversially questions the nature of all adult/child relationships, it's not explicit and doesn't resort to shock tactics. Instead, Cuesta combines intelligence with restraint, leaving the astonishingly moving performances of his cast to speak for themselves. SF [VIDEO] DVD

Brian Cox *Big John Harrigan* • Paul Franklin Dano [Paul Dano] *Howie Blitzer* • Billy Kay *Gary Terrio* • Bruce Altman *Marty Blitzer* • James Costa *Kevin Cole* • Tony Donnelly *Brian* • Walter Masterson *Scott* ■ *Dir* Michael Cuesta • *Scr* Stephen M Ryder, Michael Cuesta, Gerald Cuesta

LOC Kargil ★★ 18

War drama based on a true story
2003 · Ind · Colour · 247mins

In April 1999, Indian forces at Kargil in Kashmir mounted a campaign against 3,000 infiltrators from the Pakistani zone. Islamabad denied involvement in the incursion, which it blamed on regional rebels seeking independence from Delhi. Ultimately, "Operation Vijay" claimed over 1,000 lives on both sides. But there's no doubting where director J P Dutta's sympathies lie in this manipulative four-hour epic. Dutta focuses firmly on the heroics of the defenders, who are played by various matinée icons. Propaganda of the least subtle kind. DP. In Hindi with English subtitles. [VIDEO] DVD

Sanjay Dutt *Lt Col YK Joshi* • Abhishek Bachchan *Captain Vikram Batra* • Ajay Devgan *Lt Manoj Pandey* • Saif Ali Khan *Captain Anuj Nayyar* • Akshaye Khanna *Lt Balwan Singh* ■ *Dir/Scr* JP Dutta

The L-Shaped Room ★★★★ 15

Drama 1962 · UK · BW · 120mins

This was an angry young film in its day, which comes to life under the sensitive direction of Bryan Forbes. Set in shabby bedsit land, it features Leslie Caron in an Oscar-nominated role as the unmarried, pregnant girl with a decision to make. Wonderful performances – by Tom Bell, Brock Peters, Bernard Lee and music-hall veteran Cicely Courtneidge – make the tenement in which the L-shaped abode is situated a place of vitality, concern and eventual affirmation. TH [VIDEO] DVD

Leslie Caron *Jane Fosset* • Tom Bell *Toby* • Brock Peters *Johnny* • Cicely Courtneidge *Mavis* • Bernard Lee *Charlie* • Avis Bunnage *Doris* • Patricia Phoenix *Sonia* • Emlyn Williams *Dr Weaver* • Anthony Booth *Youth in street* ■ *Dir* Bryan Forbes • *Scr* Bryan Forbes, from the novel by Lynne Reid Banks

L.627 ★★★★ 15

Crime drama 1992 · Fr · Colour · 139mins

This ultra-realistic police drama is one of versatile director Bertrand Tavernier's finest achievements. Witten by ex-policeman Michel Alexandre, it follows Didier Bezace's narcotics unit as it pursues a gang of drug traffickers in Paris. Whether exploring the links between drugs and racism or revealing the prejudices and inadequacies of the force, Tavernier retains an admirable objectivity, which actually adds to the steel of the picture rather than tempering it. A sobering film that should be seen. DP. In French with English subtitles. Contains violence, swearing, drug abuse and nudity. [VIDEO]

Didier Bezace *Lucien "Lulu" Marguet* • Charlotte Kady *Marie* • Philippe Torreton *Antoine* • Nils Tavernier *Vincent* • Jean-Paul Comart *Dominique "Dodo" Cantoni* • Jean-Roger Milo *Manuel* • Lara Guirao *Cécile* ■ *Dir* Bertrand Tavernier • *Scr* Michel Alexandre

Labyrinth ★★★ U

Fantasy adventure
1986 · US · Colour · 97mins

The Muppet team go into *Alice in Wonderland* territory as baby-sitter Jennifer Connelly wishes her younger brother into the Goblin King's clutches and has only hours to rescue him from a castle maze. With plenty of fuzzball gremlins, cute sugar plum fairies and clumsy Hoggle the dwarf to keep the children amused (adults will laugh at David Bowie's Tina Turner wig for entirely different reasons!), Jim Henson's panto *Monty Python* (written by clan member Terry Jones) is weak on suspense and thrills, but is still firm fantasy fun. AJ [VIDEO] DVD

David Bowie *Jareth, King of the Goblins* • Jennifer Connelly *Sarah* • Toby Froud *Toby* • Shelley Thompson *Stepmother* • Christopher Malcolm *Father* • Natalie Finland *Fairy* • Brian Henson *Hoggle* • Michael Hordern *Wiseman* ■ *Dir* Jim Henson • *Scr* Terry Jones, from a story by Dennis Less, Jim Henson

L

Labyrinth ★★★

Drama documentary
1991 · Ger · Colour and BW · 86mins

A leading member of the Czech New Wave, Jaromil Jires had garnered little international attention since his 1968 adaptation of Milan Kundera's *The Joke*. This was his first feature to gain foreign distribution after the Velvet Revolution, and its blend of dramatic re-creation and archival footage reveals his powers to be undiminished. Maximilian Schell stars as a director whose research for a film on the writer is sidetracked by a sudden obsession with the historical persecution of the Jews. With Charlie Chaplin's son, Christopher, cameoing as Kafka, this is both stylish and provocative. DP. In German with English subtitles.

Maximilian Schell *The Director* • Christopher Chaplin *Franz Kafka* • Milos Kopecky *Rabbi Low* • Otto Sevcik *SS Gunther* ■ *Dir* Jaromil Jires • *Scr* Jaromil Jires, Alex Koenigsmark, Hans-Jorg Weyhmuller

Labyrinth of Passion ★★★ 18

Comedy 1982 · Sp · Colour · 94mins

This was the second full-length internationally-released feature from Spanish cult director Pedro Almodóvar, and it marked the first appearance of future Hollywood superstar Antonio Banderas. A freewheeling, pop culture screwball comedy, the frenetic action revolves around numerous love affairs between nymphomaniacs, analysts, visiting royalty and Islamic extremists in Madrid. It's much the same uneven gay/bisexual mix Almódovar camp followers expect and adore. AJ. In Spanish with English subtitles. [VIDEO]

Cecilia Roth *Sexilia* • Imanol Arias *Riza Niro* • Helga Liné *Toraya* • Marta Fernandez-Muro *Queti* ■ *Dir/Scr* Pedro Almodóvar

The Lacemaker ★★★★ 15

Romantic drama 1977 · Fr · Colour · 102mins

This is an agonisingly acute study of incompatability from Swiss director

Claude Goretta. Isabelle Huppert gives one of her finest performances as the shy hairdresser whose life falls apart when her romance with student Yves Beneyton brings on an inferiority complex. By giving the couple's early scenes a joyous feel, tinged with a sense of innocent excitement, Goretta makes the struggle to preserve their relationship all the more unbearable, although the Parisian segment strives too deliberately to achieve its effect. The final shot is one of the most gut-wrenching ever filmed. DP. In French with English subtitles.

Isabelle Huppert *Béatrice (Pomme)* • Yves Beneyton *François Beligne* • Florence Giorgetti *Marylène Thorent* • Anne-Marie Düringer [Annemarie Düringer] *Pomme's mother* ■ *Dir* Claude Goretta • *Scr* Pascal Lainé, Claude Goretta, from a novel by Pascal Lainé

Lacombe Lucien ★★★★ 12

Second World War drama
1974 · Fr · Colour · 132mins

Louis Malle's absorbing and provocative film about the Nazi occupation of France features Pierre Blaise as the loutish young peasant who, shunned by the Resistance, joins the Gestapo and terrorises the Jewish family he moves in with. It's a moral quagmire of a movie, charting a peasant's road to fascism and redemption; Malle's clinical depiction of torture and other crimes, and his refusal to condemn his "hero" caused the film to be vilified by some in France. Beautifully made and disturbingly acted by the non-professional Blaise, it remains one of the few major films about the issue of collaboration. AT. In French with English subtitles.

Pierre Blaise *Lucien* • Aurore Clément *France* • Holger Lowenadler *Albert Horn* • Thérèse Giehse *Bella Horn* • Stéphane Bouy *Jean Bernard* • Loumi Iacobesco *Betty Beaulieu* • René Bouloc *Faure* ■ *Dir* Louis Malle • *Scr* Louis Malle, Patrick Modiano • *Cinematographer* Tonino Delli Colli

The Lad ★★

Thriller 1935 · UK · BW · 72mins

Gordon Harker was such a favourite of crime writer Edgar Wallace that he frequently had material especially tailored for him. It's hardly surprising, therefore, that the actor is totally at home in this serviceable adaptation of one of Wallace's most popular thrillers. Posing as a detective to gain entrance to a country house, Harker soon realises he's not alone in having designs on a fabled family necklace. The action is brisk, but the performances are stiff. DP

Gordon Harker *Bill Shane* • Betty Stockfeld *Lady Fandon* • Jane Carr (1) *Pauline* • Gerald Barry *Lord Fandon* • Geraldine Fitzgerald *Joan* • Barbara Everest *Mrs Lorraine* • John Turnbull *Inspector Martin* ■ *Dir* Henry Edwards • *Scr* Gerard Fairlie, from the novel by Edgar Wallace

Ladder 49 ★★ 12

Action drama 2004 · US · Colour · 110mins

In this intended tribute to American firefighters, Joaquin Phoenix plays the raw recruit who earns his stripes under the auspices of father figure John Travolta and goes on to become a firehouse legend. His progress through life is recounted in flashback as he lies trapped in a burning building. This predictable story doesn't shy away from emotion – in fact it heads straight for it as if answering an alarm. Though stirring at times, this melodrama fails to live up to its laudable intention. KK. Contains swearing. DVD

Joaquin Phoenix *Jack Morrison* • John Travolta *Mike Kennedy* • Jacinda Barrett *Linda Morrison* • Robert Patrick *Lenny Richter* • Morris Chestnut *Tommy Drake* • Billy Burke *Dennis Gauquin* • Balthazar Getty *Ray Gauquin* • Tim Guinee *Tony Corrigan* ■ *Dir* Jay Russell • *Scr* Lewis Colick

Ladder of Swords ★★ 15

Thriller 1988 · UK · Colour · 94mins

Martin Shaw, cashing in on his TV celebrity, appeared in this little-known thriller. He plays a circus performer who finds himself suspected of murder when his troubled wife (Eleanor David) disappears. Bob Peck is the policeman who doggedly pursues him through the byways and alleyways of Big Top shenanigans. Director Norman Hull conveys some of the atmosphere and imagery of the circus, but animal lovers may be distressed by the fate of Shaw's other companion – Daley the bear. TH

Martin Shaw *Don Demarco* • Eleanor David *Denise Demarco* • Juliet Stevenson *Alice Howard* • Bob Peck *Detective Inspector Atherton* • Simon Molloy *Sergeant Bilby* • Pearce Quigley *Constable Lowe* • Anthony Benson *Grumpy Gun* ■ *Dir/Scr* Norman Hull

Ladies and Gentlemen, the Fabulous Stains ★★

Musical comedy drama
1981 · US · Colour · 87mins

Director Lou Adler produced *The Rocky Horror Picture Show* and clearly thought he was crafting another cult item with this determinedly offbeat tale of the rise and fall, and rise again, of an all-girl punk band named the Fabulous Stains. Instead it languished on the shelf for years. What makes it worth watching is the cast: the Tubes' Fee Waybill (in a great cameo), Ray Winstone, Sex Pistols' Steve Jones and Paul Cook, and the Clash's Paul Simonon. Supposedly a music business satire, the whole concept rings hollow and wears out its initial welcome pretty quickly. AJ

Diane Lane *Corinne Burns* • Ray Winstone *Billy* • Peter Donat *Harley Dennis* • David Clennon *Dave Robell–the Agent* • John Lehne *Stu McGrath* • Cynthia Sikes *Alicia Meeker* • Laura Dern *Jessica McNeil* • Marin Kanter *Tracy Burns* • Paul Cook *Danny* • Steve Jones *Steve* • Paul Simonon *Johnny* • John "Fee" Waybill *Lou Corpse* • Christine Lahti *Aunt Linda* ■ *Dir* Lou Adler • *Scr* Rob Morton

Ladies and Gentlemen, the Rolling Stones ★★

Music documentary
1974 · US · Colour · 82mins

How do you make the Rolling Stones look boring? Make a documentary about their 1972 US tour as dull as this one, in which Mick Jagger and company give all they've got, but the director (Rollin Binzer) can't seem to deliver. It would help if the cameras were in the right place at the right time. This is depressing stuff, especially for fans. TH

Dir Rollin Binzer

The Ladies Club ★★★

Action drama 1986 · US · Colour · 90mins

Advertised with the tagline "Men who attack woman have two big problems. The Ladies Club is about to remove them both!" this could so easily have fallen into the trap of sick exploitation. However, director Janet Greek handles her revenge tale with an assurance that keeps such formula vigilantism at bay. There are some good, low-key performances from the largely female cast playing rape victims who band together to give justice-evading criminals their just desserts. RS

Karen Austin *Joan Taylor* • Diana Scarwid *Lucy Bricker* • Christine Belford *Dr Constance Lewis* • Bruce Davison *Richard Harrison* • Shera Danese *Eva* • Beverly Todd *Georgiane* • Marilyn Kagan *Rosalie* • Kit McDonough *Carol* ■ *Dir* AK Allen [Janet Greek] • *Scr* Paul Mason, Fran Lewis Ebeling, from the novel *Sisterhood* by Betty Black, by Casey Bishop

Ladies' Day ★★ U

Romantic comedy 1943 · US · BW · 62mins

When the star pitcher of a baseball team becomes involved in a hot love affair, to the detriment of his performance on the field, his teammates, their manager, and even some of their wives set about trying to break up the romance. An occasionally diverting comedy, the movie stars Eddie Albert as the lovesick ball player and the raucous "Mexican spitfire" Lupe Velez as the girl. Leslie Goodwins directs the proceedings, squeezing what laughs he can out of the somewhat repetitive situation. RK

Lupe Velez *Pepita Zorita* • Eddie Albert *Wacky Waters* • Patsy Kelly *Hazel* • Max Baer *Hippo* • Jerome Cowan *Updyke* • Iris Adrian *Kitty* • Joan Barclay *Joan* ■ *Dir* Leslie Goodwins • *Scr* Charles E Roberts, Dane Lussier, from a play by Robert Considine, Edward Clark Lilley, Bertrand Robinson

Ladies in Lavender ★★★ 12

Period drama 2004 · UK · Colour · 99mins

The almost idyllic daily existence of two elderly sisters (played by the excellent Judi Dench and Maggie Smith) in mid-1930s Cornwall is thrown into upheaval when a handsome young man (Daniel Brühl) who can't speak English washes up on a nearby beach. Charles Dance, in his directorial debut, steers the story into unexpectedly subtle emotional regions that rely on character evolution and deft performances from the fine cast. This is a lively tale brimming with insight and a plot twist or two. KK. DVD

Judi Dench *Ursula Widdington* • Maggie Smith *Janet Widdington* • Daniel Brühl *Andrea Marowski* • Miriam Margolyes *Dorcas* • Natascha McElhone *Olga Danilof* • David Warner *Dr Francis Mead* • Freddie Jones *Jan Pendered* • Clive Russell *Adam Penruddocke* ■ *Dir* Charles Dance • *Scr* Charles Dance, from a short story by William J Locke

Ladies in Love ★★★

Romantic comedy 1936 · US · BW · 97mins

Three young lovelies (including Janet Gaynor and Loretta Young) rent a luxury apartment in Budapest in the hope of attracting their dream husbands. One of their beaus is played by Tyrone Power in a very early role that hints at his charismatic screen presence. There is no deep subtext involved – what you see is a huge chunk of good old-fashioned entertainment. Who cares if it all seems rather chauvinistic and fey for our modern palate? It works. SH

Janet Gaynor *Martha Kerenye* • Loretta Young *Susie Schmidt* • Constance Bennett *Yoli Haydn* • Simone Simon *Marie Armand* • Don Ameche *Dr Rudi Imre* • Paul Lukas *John Barta* • Tyrone Power Jr [Tyrone Power] *Karl Lanyi* ■ *Dir* Edward H Griffith • *Scr* Melville Baker, from a play by Ladislaus Bus-Fekete

Ladies in Retirement ★★★

Crime melodrama 1941 · US · BW · 91mins

Ida Lupino is at her most dramatically wild-eyed as the housekeeper to a retired actress (Isobel Elsom) who hatches a plot to help her two sisters (Elsa Lanchester and Edith Barrett). With Louis Hayward as the suspicious relative who uncovers the crime, there's an artificial symmetry which betrays the film's stage origins. It transfixes you with a purposeful expertise, though, mainly because Lupino can gain your sympathy while doing the most dastardly things. She can also imbue the act of washing-up with a menace you wouldn't believe. Remade in 1969 as *The Mad Room* with Stella Stevens. TH

Ida Lupino *Ellen Creed* • Louis Hayward *Albert Feather* • Evelyn Keyes *Lucy* • Elsa Lanchester *Emily Creed* • Edith Barrett *Louisa Creed* • Isobel Elsom *Leonora Fiske* ■ *Dir* Charles Vidor • *Scr* Garrett Fort, Reginald Denham, from the play by Reginald Denham, Edward Percy

Ladies' Man ★★★ U

Comedy drama 1931 · US · BW · 76mins

Smoothly amoral high-society man-about-town William Powell is loved by Kay Francis and lusted after by several society matrons whom he is happy to "escort" in return for their lavish tokens of gratitude. When, however, Carole Lombard, the daughter of one of his ladies, falls for him, disaster strikes. A highly sophisticated and brittle comedy of Park Avenue manners, the film boasts a sharp script by Herman J Mankiewicz that manages to combine wit with a penetrating exposé of the milieu in which it is set. RK

William Powell *Jamie Darricott* • Kay Francis *Norma Page* • Carole Lombard *Rachel Fendley* • Gilbert Emery *Horace Fendley* • Olive Tell *Mrs Fendley* • Martin Burton *Anthony Fendley* • John Holland *Peyton Waldon* • Frank Atkinson *Valet* ■ *Dir* Lothar Mendes • *Scr* Herman J Mankiewicz, from a story by Rupert Hughes

The Ladies' Man ★★★★ U

Comedy 1961 · US · Colour · 91mins

This is perhaps the most inventive and wittiest movie written, starring and directed by Jerry Lewis, one of the great clowns in the history of cinema. Playing a bitter, jilted man in a house full of women, Lewis proves himself a master of comic cinema, playing with the medium itself in a remarkable series of spirited gags in a marvellously constructed and elaborate set. Handyman Jerry is handsomely supported by viragos Helen Traubel and Kathleen Freeman, and there is a cameo from George Raft. TS DVD

Jerry Lewis *Herbert H Heebert* • Helen Traubel *Helen Welenmelon* • Pat Stanley *Fay* • Kathleen Freeman *Katie* • George Raft ■ *Dir* Jerry Lewis • *Scr* Jerry Lewis, Bill Richmond

The Ladies Man ★★ 15

Comedy 2000 · US · Colour · 80mins

Tim Meadows stars as a randy radio "love doctor" who talks twaddle to the lovelorn but is inexplicably a turn-on to the tuned-in. Derived from Meadows's regular slot on cult American comedy show *Saturday Night Live*, this big-screen treatment has him facing the twin problems of finding a wealthy but anonymous former flame while avoiding an angry posse of hubbies whose wives he's bedded. If this daft dollop of double entendres could do with the occasional dose of Viagra, at least Meadows's endearingly awful alter ego maintains a level of fun. DA DVD

Tim Meadows *Leon Phelps* • Karyn Parsons *Julie Simmons* • Billy Dee Williams *Lester* • Tiffani Thiessen [Tiffani-Amber Thiessen] *Honey DeLune* • Lee Evans *Barney* • Will Ferrell *Lance DeLune* ■ *Dir* Reginald Hudlin • *Scr* Tim Meadows, Dennis McNicholas

Ladies of Leisure ★★★

Romantic drama 1930 · US · BW · 98mins

The glorious combination of director Frank Capra and leading lady Barbara Stanwyck makes this whiskered plot worth watching. Stanwyck stars as a reformed gold-digger who falls for would-be artist Ralph Graves, but nobody believes her capable of true lurv. Well, would you? Capra's delicate soufflé touch gives the script the bounce and pace it needs and, of course, Stanwyck is stunning. SH

Barbara Stanwyck *Kay Arnold* • Ralph Graves *Jerry Strange* • Lowell Sherman *Bill Standish* •

Marie Prevost *Dot Lamar* • Nance O'Neil *Mrs Strange* • George Fawcett *Mr Strange* ■ *Dir* Frank Capra • *Scr* Jo Swerling, from the play *Ladies of the Evening* by Milton Herbert Gropper

Ladies of the Chorus ★ U

Romantic musical 1949 · US · BW · 57mins

A chorus girl in burlesque on Broadway steps out of her class, as did her mother before her, and falls in love with a smooth socialite. Directed by Phil Karlson from a monumentally feeble script, this dire but mercifully short musical programme-filler marks the less than notable first leading role for Marilyn Monroe. She is adequate to the undemanding task without giving any hint of the screen goddess she would become. RK

Marilyn Monroe *Peggy Martin* • Adele Jergens *May Martin* • Rand Brooks *Randy Carroll* • Nana Bryant *Mrs Adele Carroll* • Eddie Carr *Billy Mackay* ■ *Dir* Phil Karlson • *Scr* Harry Sauber, Joseph Carol, from the story by Harry Sauber

Ladies Should Listen ★★

Romantic comedy 1934 · US · BW · 62mins

Cary Grant stars in this romantic comedy about a man-about-town whose switchboard operator Frances Drake is secretly in love with him. She involves herself in his affairs, business and otherwise, leading to inevitable complications. It's not surprising that this title hardly springs to mind when considering the films of the incomparable Grant. Directed by Frank Tuttle, and with a reliable supporting cast of character players, it's no more than a passing entertainment, with a lazily superficial script. RK

Cary Grant *Julian de Lussac* • Frances Drake *Anna Mirelle* • Edward Everett Horton *Paul Vernet* • Nydia Westman *Susi Flamberg* • Clara Lou Sheridan [Ann Sheridan] *Adele* ■ *Dir* Frank Tuttle • *Scr* Guy Bolton, Claude Binyon, Frank Butler, from the play by Guy Bolton, from the play *La Demoiselle de Passy* by Alfred Savoir

Ladies They Talk About ★★★

Prison drama 1933 · US · BW · 64mins

Gang moll Barbara Stanwyck is sent to San Quentin through the efforts of powerful crime-fighting evangelist Preston Foster, who puts principle before love. Five years and several dramatic incidents later they are reunited. An entertaining crime melodrama, making a sincere attempt to portray life in a women's prison, this sometimes resembles a social gathering. The highly unlikely plot is much enlivened by acid comedy (despite some Hays Office objections), and Stanwyck's cool performance. RK

Barbara Stanwyck *Nan Taylor* • Preston S Foster [Preston Foster] *David Slade* • Lyle Talbot *Don* • Dorothy Burgess *Susie* • Lillian Roth *Linda* • Maude Eburne *Aunt Maggie* ■ *Dir* Howard Bretherton, William Keighley • *Scr* Brown Holmes, William McGrath, Sidney Sutherland, from the play by Dorothy Mackaye, Carlton Miles

Ladies Who Do ★★ U

Comedy 1963 · UK · BW · 81mins

A firm favourite in such TV series as *The Larkins* and *George and the Dragon*, Peggy Mount found films harder to come by. In the sixth of her ten pictures, she's joined by those other sitcom stalwarts Miriam Karlin and Dandy Nichols, as a trio of charladies who make a killing on the stock market through the tips they find among the office rubbish. With Harry H Corbett in support, this should have been quite amusing, but the ponderous script and the flat direction make it a one-joke bore. DP

Peggy Mount *Mrs Cragg* • Robert Morley *Colonel Whitforth* • Harry H Corbett *James Ryder* • Miriam Karlin *Mrs Higgins* • Avril Elgar *Emily Parish* • Dandy Nichols *Mrs Merryweather* • Jon Pertwee *Mr Tait* • Nigel Davenport *Mr Strang* • Graham Stark *Foreman* • Ron Moody *Inspector* ■ *Dir* CM Pennington-Richards • *Scr* Michael Pertwee, from an idea by John Bignell

The Lady & the Duke ★★★★ PG

Historical drama
2001 · Fr/Ger · Colour · 123mins

Eric Rohmer here creates a compelling study of quiet courage in the face of ever-present danger during the French Revolution. The story of royalist Scot Grace Elliott's (Lucy Russell) friendship with a radical sympathiser, the Duke of Orléans (Jean-Claude Dreyfus), is played out against Jean-Baptiste Marot's stunning canvasses, based on paintings and street maps of the period and brought to vivid life through the selective use of computer animation. The tender relationship between the ex-lovers is elegantly expressed through the literate dialogue, yet Rohmer imparts plenty of suspense into the proceedings as well. DP. In French with English subtitles. Contains violence. DVD

Lucy Russell *Grace Elliott* • Jean-Claude Dreyfus *Le Duc d'Orléans* • François Marthouret *Dumouriez* • Léonard Cobiant *Marquis de Champcenetz* • Caroline Morin *Nanon* • Alain Libolt *Duc de Biron* ■ *Dir* Eric Rohmer • *Scr* Eric Rohmer, from the memoir *Journal of My Life during the French Revolution* by Grace Elliott

The Lady and the Monster ★★

Science-fiction horror
1944 · US · BW · 86mins

The first of several adaptations of Curt Siodmak's cult novel *Donovan's Brain* was brought to the screen by Republic boss Herbert Yates as a change of pace for Vera Hruba Ralston, the Czech figure skater he would eventually marry. However, the only memorable thing about this laboured romp are the disconcerting expressionist images and Erich von Stroheim's gleefully deranged showboating. Sadly, Ralston's approximation of terror, as her lover Richard Arlen is possessed by the brain's malignant spirit and goes on a killing spree, is remembered only for its ineptitude. Re-edited and re-released in 1949 as *The Tiger Man*. DP

Vera Hruba Ralston [Vera Ralston] *Janice Farrell* • Richard Arlen *Patrick Cory* • Erich von Stroheim *Prof Franz Mueller* • Helen Vinson *Chloe Donovan* • Mary Nash *Mrs Fame* • Sidney Blackmer *Eugene Fulton* ■ *Dir* George Sherman • *Scr* Frederick Kohner, Dane Lussier, from the novel *Donovan's Brain* by Curt Siodmak

Lady and the Tramp ★★★★★ U

Animated musical adventure
1955 · US · Colour · 73mins

The Disney studio's first venture into CinemaScope remains one of its most enduring favourites. Ending a sequence of fairy-tale adaptations, it returned to the animal world of *Dumbo* and *Bambi* to create a cast of charming creatures, headed by a pampered cocker spaniel called Lady and a spaghetti-munching mongrel called Tramp. In addition to voicing Lady's mistress and Siamese cats Si and Am, Peggy Lee also co-composed the unforgettable songs (with Sonny Burke). A joy for children and romantics alike. DP DVD

Peggy Lee *Darling/Peg/Si/Am* • Barbara Luddy *Lady* • Larry Roberts *Tramp* • Bill Thompson *Jock/Bull/Dachsie* • Bill Baucon *Trusty* • Stan Freberg *Beaver* • Verna Felton *Aunt Sarah* ■ *Dir* Hamilton Luske, Clyde Geronimi, Wilfred Jackson • *Scr* Erdman Penner, Joe Rinaldi, Ralph Wright, Don DaGradi, from the novel *Lady* by Ward Greene

Lady and the Tramp II: Scamp's Adventure ★★ U

Animated musical adventure
2000 · US/Aus · Colour · 66mins

One of the longest delayed sequels in screen history will disappoint those with fond memories of the 1955 original. The highly conformist message will jar with those remember Tramp as a kind of canine James Dean. Scott Wolf voices Scamp with puppyish enthusiasm, lending excitement to his adventures and vulnerability to his clash with Chazz Palminteri's junkyard bruiser. There's even a little canoodling over the pasta with a pooch named Angel (Alyssa Milano). Fun, but not a patch on its predecessor. DP DVD

Scott Wolf *Scamp* • Alyssa Milano *Angel* • Chazz Palminteri *Buster* • Jeff Bennett *Tramp/ Jock/Dogcatcher* • Jodi Benson *Lady* • Bill Fagerbakke *Mooch* ■ *Dir* Darrell Rooney • *Scr* Jeannine Roussel, Bill Motz, Bob Roth, from characters created in the 1955 film

Lady Be Good ★★ U

Musical 1941 · US · BW · 111mins

This is a musical of two halves: a weak, badly-written and boring plot (the several acrimonious partings and tearful reconciliations of songwriting duo Robert Young and Ann Sothern), and a series of good songs, dazzling tap dancing from Eleanor Powell, and a fabulous finale staged by Busby Berkeley. The standout song is Jerome Kern's Oscar winner, *The Last Time I Saw Paris*, sung by Ann Sothern, and the rest of the wasted talents include Lionel Barrymore and Dan Dailey. RK

Eleanor Powell *Marilyn Marsh* • Ann Sothern *Dixie Donegan* • Robert Young (1) *Eddie Crane* • Lionel Barrymore *Judge Murdock* • John Carroll *Buddy Crawford* • Red Skelton *Joe "Red" Willet* • Virginia O'Brien *Lull* • Tom Conway *Mr Blanton* • Dan Dailey Jr [Dan Dailey] *Bill Pattison* • Phil Silvers *MC* ■ *Dir* Norman Z McLeod • *Scr* Jack McGowan, Kay Van Riper, John McClain, from a story by Jack McGowan • *Costume Designer* Adrian

Lady Beware ★★ 18

Thriller 1987 · US · Colour · 103mins

The story is familiar enough, but this slick straight-to-video thriller is still worth a look. Diane Lane gives one of her best performances as a department store window dresser whose mannequin displays attract the unwelcome attentions of a disturbed secret admirer (Michael Woods, brother of James). Director Karen Arthur succeeds in generating a creepy sense of menace. JF

Diane Lane *Katya Yarno* • Michael Woods *Jack Price* • Cotter Smith *Mac Odell* • Tyra Ferrell *Nan* • Peter Nevargic *Lionel* • Edward Penn *Thayer* ■ *Dir* Karen Arthur • *Scr* Susan Miller, Charles Zev Cohen

Lady by Choice ★★★

Comedy 1934 · US · BW · 74mins

An entertaining, if duller-edged, follow-up to Frank Capra's wonderful *Lady for a Day*, but here directed by David Burton with a rather more plodding hand. May Robson reprises a role similar to that of her scruffy fruit vendor Apple Annie (with a faint hint of *ennui*), this time given a major wash and brush-up à la *Pygmalion* by hoofer Carole Lombard. The latter, whose career was so tragically cut short, is always a joy to watch and this big-hearted, bouncy little movie shows her gift for *bons mots* to good advantage. But overall, this is short on pizzazz. SH

Carole Lombard *"Alabam" Georgia Lee* • May Robson *Patsy Patterson* • Roger Pryor *John Mills* • Walter Connolly *Judge Daly* • Arthur Hohl *Charlie Kendall* • Raymond Walburn *Front O'Malley* • James Burke *Sergeant Brannigan* • Mariska Aldrich *Lucretia* • William Faversham *Malone* • John Boyle *Walsh* ■ *Dir* David Burton • *Scr* Jo Swerling, from a story by Dwight Taylor

Lady Caroline Lamb ★★★ 15

Historical drama
1972 · UK/It · Colour · 117mins

Robert Bolt turned writer/director and wrote this historical drama for his wife, Sarah Miles. Lady Caroline Lamb was married to a future Prime Minister, had a celebrated affair with Lord Byron and generally scandalised Regency society. Miles plays the part to the hilt, appearing in some bizarre costumes and exploiting her own natural talent and extrovert character to advantage, being by turns ravishing, captivating, infuriating and pathetic. Laurence Olivier plays a camp Wellington with a false nose, Jon Finch is quietly authoritative as William Lamb/Lord Melbourne and Richard Chamberlain is perfectly pompous as Byron. Done in the rather flat style of a 1950s costume drama. AT

Sarah Miles *Lady Caroline Lamb* • Jon Finch *William Lamb* • Richard Chamberlain *Lord Byron* • John Mills *Canning* • Margaret Leighton *Lady Melbourne* • Pamela Brown *Lady Bessborough* • Ralph Richardson *The King* • Laurence Olivier *Duke of Wellington* ■ *Dir/Scr* Robert Bolt

Lady Chatterley's Lover ★ 18

Erotic drama 1981 · Fr/UK · Colour · 99mins

Sylvia Kristel's acting deficiencies were barely noticeable in the *Emmanuelle* pictures that made her name. Here, though, she is required to do more, and she is found severely wanting. Not that Nicholas Clay has anything to be proud of in his performance as the gamekeeper. Lots of period trappings, and Robert Fraisse's photography manages to be both nostalgic and pornographic. Poor DH Lawrence scarcely gets a look-in. DP DVD

Sylvia Kristel *Lady Constance Chatterley* • Nicholas Clay *Oliver Mellors* • Shane Briant *Sir Clifford Chatterley* • Ann Mitchell *Mrs Bolton* • Elizabeth Spriggs *Lady Eva* • Pascale Rivault *Hilda* • Anthony Head *Anton* • Bessie Love *Flora* ■ *Dir* Just Jaeckin • *Scr* Christopher Wicking, Just Jaeckin, from the novel *Lady Chatterley's Lover* by DH Lawrence

The Lady Cop ★★★

Detective drama 1979 · Fr · Colour · 103mins

Director Yves Boisset lifts the lid on provincial life in this simmering study of injustice and iniquitous influence. Demoted for linking the mayor to a gay scandal, Parisian detective Miou-Miou soon discovers that the drama group in a small northern town is behind the staging of some less than innocent entertainments. Miou-Miou is gutsily efficient, but the standout here is comedian Jean-Marc Thibault, who reveals a darker side as her boss. DP. French dialogue dubbed into English.

Miou-Miou *Inspecteur Corinne Levasseur* • Jean-Marc Thibault *Commissaire Porel* • Leny Escudero *Diego Cortez* • Jean-Pierre Kalfon *Backmann* ■ *Dir* Yves Boisset • *Scr* Yves Boisset, Claude Veillot

The Lady Eve ★★★★★ U

Classic screwball comedy
1941 · US · BW · 93mins

This wonderfully witty masterpiece, written and directed by the inimitable Preston Sturges, gives a couple of near career-best roles to two of Hollywood's finest players, who are perfectly cast here. Henry Fonda, a wealthy young man obsessed by snakes, lays himself wide open to the schemes of professional con artist Charles Coburn and his daughter,

L

Barbara Stanwyck. Fonda's buddy William Demarest intervenes, but Stanwyck, undeterred, later reappears in disguise at his palatial manse. Naturally, the assured sexual opportunist falls for the gauche brewer's son who has spent a year up the Amazon, resulting in a sparkling combination of romance and screwball comedy. TS DVD

Barbara Stanwyck *Jean Harrington/Lady Eve Sidwich* • Henry Fonda *Charles Poncefort Pike* • Charles Coburn *"Colonel" Harrington* • Eugene Pallette *Mr Pike* • William Demarest *Muggsy* • Eric Blore *Sir Alfred McGlennan Keith/"Pearly"* • Melville Cooper *Gerald* • Martha O'Driscoll *Martha* • Janet Beecher *Mrs Pike* • Robert Greig *Burrows* • Wilson Benge *Butler* ■ *Dir* Preston Sturges • *Scr* Preston Sturges, from the story *The Faithful Heart* by Monckton Hoffe

Lady for a Day ★★★★ U

Comedy 1933 · US · BW · 95mins

A wonderful screen version of Damon Runyon's tale of Apple Annie, the Times Square fruit seller who brings so much luck to Dave the Dude that, when her daughter arrives from Europe with an aristocratic fiancé, he puts her up in a hotel and turns her into the titular madam. A fabulous cast incarnates Runyon's street characters, but none is more impressive than Australian-born May Robson in the leading role, the performance of a lifetime which rightly won her an Oscar nomination. Columbia's whizzkid Frank Capra – he also directed the 1961 remake *Pocketful of Miracles* – also secured Academy nominations for best picture and best director. TS

Warren William *Dave the Dude* • May Robson *Apple Annie* • Guy Kibbee *Judge Blake* • Glenda Farrell *Missouri Martin* • Ned Sparks *Happy McGuire* • Walter Connolly *Count Romero* • Jean Parker *Louise* • Nat Pendleton *Shakespeare* • Barry Norton *Carlos* ■ *Dir* Frank Capra • *Scr* Robert Riskin, from the story *Madame la Gimp* by Damon Runyon

Lady for a Night ★★ U

Period melodrama 1942 · US · BW · 87mins

Great idea from Republic, shame about the execution. At one of the big studios, this riverboat romantic drama could have been done properly with a decent budget and possibly colour. As it is, John Wayne is awkwardly cast alongside top-billed Joan Blondell in a murder-driven plot. Director Leigh Jason wasn't the right choice to make all this back projection work, and the result is very average indeed. TS

Joan Blondell *Jenny Blake* • John Wayne *Jack Morgan* • Philip Merivale *Stephen Alderson* • Blanche Yurka *Julia Alderson* • Ray Middleton *Alan Alderson* • Edith Barrett *Katherine Alderson* • Leonid Kinskey *Boris* ■ *Dir* Leigh Jason • *Scr* Isabel Dawn, Boyce DeGaw, from a story by Garrett Fort

Lady from Louisiana ★★ PG

Drama 1941 · US · BW · 82mins

John Wayne considered himself too big a star to be landed with the part of a young lawyer in this bog-standard Republic programmer. Certainly, there is nothing remarkable about this tale of a crooked lottery in New Orleans. Ona Munson could be forgiven for sharing her co-star's disappointment, as her own career had failed to take off in spite of a splendid performance in *Gone with the Wind*. There is little chemistry between the pair and the spectacular storm finale is all too long in coming. DP

John Wayne *John Reynolds* • Ona Munson *Julie Mirbeau* • Ray Middleton *Blackie Williams* • Henry Stephenson *General Mirbeau* • Helen Westley *Mrs Brunot* • Jack Pennick *Cuffy* • Dorothy Dandridge *Felice* ■ *Dir* Bernard Vorhaus • *Scr* Vera Caspary, Michael Hogan, Guy Endore, from a story by Edward James, Francis Faragoh

The Lady from Shanghai ★★★★ PG

Romantic crime drama
1948 · US · BW · 83mins

This is a marvellous murky film with *noir* touches from arguably the American cinema's greatest director, Orson Welles (though cutting his beloved Rita Hayworth's hair short and dyeing it platinum for her role here was perhaps not one of his better ideas). Even stranger was his decision to play his own part with a bizarre Irish accent. Nevertheless, Everett Sloane as Hayworth's disabled husband is even better than he was in *Citizen Kane*, and the climactic hall of mirrors sequence is magnificently shot, and justly famed. TS DVD

Rita Hayworth *Elsa Bannister* • Orson Welles *Michael O'Hara* • Everett Sloane *Arthur Bannister* • Glenn Anders *George Grisby* • Ted De Corsia *Sidney Broome* • Erskine Sanford *Judge* • Gus Schilling *Goldie* • Carl Frank *District Attorney* • Louis Merrill *Jake* • Evelyn Ellis *Bessie* ■ *Dir* Orson Welles • *Scr* Orson Welles, from the novel *If I Die Before I Wake* by Sherwood King

The Lady from the Shanghai Cinema ★★ 15

Crime drama 1987 · Bra · Colour · 116mins

The visual ambience of this Brazilian misfire is impressive, but writer/director Guilherme De Almeida Prado misses the sardonic wit and complexity of the hard-boiled *films noirs* he seeks to emulate. The meeting of the dupe and the *femme fatale* is neatly achieved, but from the moment Maité Proença and her sinister husband begin reeling in boxer turned estate agent Antonio Fagundes, proceedings become bogged down. DP. In Portuguese with English subtitles.

Antonio Fagundes *Lucas* • Maité Proença *Suzana* • José Lewgoy *Linus* • Jorge Doria *Velho* • José Mayer *Bolivar* • Miguel Falabella *Lana* • Paulo Villaça *Walter Desdino* • Sergio Mamberti *Stan* ■ *Dir/Scr* Guilherme De Almeida Prado

The Lady Gambles ★★★

Melodrama 1949 · US · BW · 98mins

A happily married couple (Barbara Stanwyck, Robert Preston) take a trip to Las Vegas where the warm, wonderful, well-balanced wife develops a gambling addiction that drives her husband away and propels her into the most desperate of conditions. Directed by Michael Gordon, this is melodrama in capitals and italics, played for all its worth by the great Stanwyck. In her harrowing descent to the gutter she suffers with such conviction that fans both of the star and of soap opera can easily overlook the fact that this is perfunctorily written hokum. RK

Barbara Stanwyck *Joan Boothe* • Robert Preston *David Boothe* • Stephen McNally *Corrigan* • Edith Barrett *Ruth Phillips* • John Hoyt *Dr Rojac* • Elliott Sullivan *Barky* • Houseley Stevenson *Pawnbroker* • Peter Leeds *Hotel Clerk* • Don Beddoe *Mr Sutherland* • Anthony Curtis [Tony Curtis] *Bellboy* ■ *Dir* Michael Gordon • *Scr* Roy Huggins, Halsted Welles, from a story by Lewis Meltzer, Oscar Saul

Lady Godiva ★ U

Historical drama 1955 · US · Colour · 89mins

Maureen O'Hara, wrapped in yards of red hair to hide her nakedness, rides through 11th-century Coventry in this tedious, cardboard piece, obviously filmed on the Universal backlot. She is the Saxon bride of Saxon nobleman George Nader, determined to thwart plans for an alliance with the Normans. Cast as First Saxon is 25-year-old Clint Eastwood. RB

Maureen O'Hara *Lady Godiva* • George Nader *Lord Leofric* • Eduard Franz *King Edward* • Leslie Bradley *Count Eustace* • Victor McLaglen *Grimald* • Torin Thatcher *Lord Godwin* • Clint Eastwood *1st Saxon* ■ *Dir* Arthur Lubin • *Scr* Oscar Brodney, Harry Ruskin, from a story by Oscar Brodney

Lady Godiva Rides Again ★★

Comedy 1951 · UK · BW · 97mins

Apart from a wonderful speech by Alastair Sim's world-weary producer about the errant ways of the British film industry, this is a hugely disappointing satire from the usually reliable pairing of Frank Launder and Sidney Gilliat. It was cruelly ironic that Pauline Stroud's real-life flirtation with movie fame should turn out to be as brief as that of the pageant queen she plays here, but she's not helped by a script so thin it wouldn't hide Godiva's blushes. Although the supporting cast reads like a who's who of 1950s comedy, no one is around long enough to make much of an impact. DP

Dennis Price *Simon Abbott* • John McCallum *Larry Burns* • Stanley Holloway *Mr Clark* • Pauline Stroud *Marjorie Clark* • Gladys Henson *Mrs Clark* • Bernadette O'Farrell *Janie* • George Cole *Johnny* • Diana Dors *Dolores August* • Eddie Byrne *Eddie Mooney* • Kay Kendall *Sylvie* • Renee Houston *Beattie* • Dora Bryan *Publicity Woman* • Sidney James *Lew Beeson* • Joan Collins *Beauty Contestant* • Alastair Sim *Murington* ■ *Dir* Frank Launder • *Scr* Frank Lauder, Val Valentine

Lady Ice ★★

Crime drama 1973 · US · Colour · 91mins

In this misfiring caper movie Donald Sutherland rehashes his role in *Klute* as a strangely obsessive, slightly spooky insurance investigator attempting to recover stolen diamonds. It's hard to follow at times, impossible at others, and one is grateful for the few crumbs of enjoyment tossed at us by the strong cast. AT

Donald Sutherland *Andy Hammond* • Jennifer O'Neill *Paula Booth* • Robert Duvall *Ford Pierce* • Patrick Magee *Paul Booth* • Eric Braeden *Peter Brinker* • Jon Cypher *Eddy Stell* ■ *Dir* Tom Gries • *Scr* Alan Trustman, Harold Clemens, from a story by Alan Trustman • *Cinematographer* Lucien Ballard

Lady in a Cage ★★★ 18

Drama 1964 · US · BW · 94mins

This exercise in sadism and mental torture was banned outright in Britain and the fact that it stars Olivia de Havilland and is from the director of *633 Squadron* makes that all the more surprising. De Havilland plays a rich invalid who is trapped in her mechanical lift – the cage of the title – and is then systematically terrorised by a drunk, a prostitute and three thugs, one of whom is played by James Caan. It's an allegory about the beast in man and woman and has a surprise twist regarding de Havilland's past life. AT DVD

Olivia de Havilland *Mrs Hilyard* • Ann Sothern *Sade* • Jeff Corey *Wino* • James Caan *Randall* • Jennifer Billingsley *Elaine* • Rafael Campos *Essie* • William Swan *Malcolm Hilyard* ■ *Dir* Walter Grauman • *Scr* Luther Davis

Lady in a Jam ★★

Comedy 1942 · US · BW · 78mins

Irene Dunne is the eponymous character, a harebrained heiress who loses all her money while indulging her obsession for numerology, and whose behaviour has her kept under observation by psychiatrist Patric Knowles, posing as a chauffeur. A feeble romantic comedy that dredges the bottom of the barrel for its sprinkling of laughs, it squanders the star's superior gifts and the talent of director Gregory La Cava. RK

Irene Dunne *Jane Palmer* • Patric Knowles *Dr Enright* • Ralph Bellamy *Stanley Gardner* • Eugene Pallette *Billingsley* • Samuel S Hinds *Dr Brewster* • Queenie Vassar *Cactus Kate Palmer* ■ *Dir* Gregory La Cava • *Scr* Eugene Thackrey, Frank Cockrell, Otho Lovering • *Cinematographer* Hal Mohr

Lady in Cement ★★ 15

Crime drama 1968 · US · Colour · 89mins

A great title for the second of two movies starring Frank Sinatra as world-weary private detective Tony Rome. However, the film itself is not quite as effective as the first one (*Tony Rome*). Both Sinatra and skilled director Gordon Douglas seem merely to be going through the paces, but there is excellent support from Dan Blocker and comedian Joe E Lewis. Thick-eared and not as tough as it thinks it is, this does at least give us a glimpse of Raquel Welch in her heyday. TS. Contains violence, brief nudity. DVD

Frank Sinatra *Tony Rome* • Raquel Welch *Kit Forrest* • Richard Conte *Lieutenant Santini* • Martin Gabel *Al Mungar* • Lainie Kazan *Maria Baretto* • Pat Henry *Rubin* • Steve Peck *Paul Mungar* • Dan Blocker *Gronsky* ■ *Dir* Gordon Douglas • *Scr* Marvin H Albert, Jack Guss, from the novel by Marvin H Albert

The Lady in Question ★★★

Melodrama 1940 · US · BW · 79mins

Six years before their sensational pairing in Charles Vidor's erotically charged *Gilda* brought them stardom, a still youthful Rita Hayworth and Glenn Ford appeared in this reworking of the French classic, *Gribouille*. Brian Aherne stars as a kind-hearted French family man who, called to jury duty, takes pity on the accused (Hayworth). He gives her a job and lodging in his home, causing numerous upheavals and complications involving his wife (Irene Rich) and son (Ford). A curious, occasionally irritating, but entertaining mix of bluff domestic comedy and near tragedy, with Hayworth ravishingly lovely and quite touching. RK

Brian Aherne *André Morestan* • Rita Hayworth *Natalie Roguin* • Glenn Ford *Pierre Morestan* • Irene Rich *Michèle Morestan* • George Coulouris *Defense attorney* • Lloyd Corrigan *Prosecuting attorney* • Evelyn Keyes *Françoise Morestan* ■ *Dir* Charles Vidor • *Scr* Lewis Meltzer, from the film *Gribouille* by HG Lustig, Marcel Archard

The Lady in Question ★★★

Period murder mystery
1999 · US · Colour · 100mins

Having received favourable reviews for *Murder in a Small Town*, Gene Wilder reprises the role of theatre impresario-turned-detective Larry "Cash" Carter in this satisfying murder mystery TV sequel. Again set in Stamford, Connecticut, in the late 1930s, the tale hinges on the murder of Claire Bloom's anti-Nazi activist. Having established the period charm, director Joyce Chopra is largely content to let Wilder (who also co-scripted) take over. Overall, this is knotty, nostalgic and nicely judged. DP

Gene Wilder *Larry "Cash" Carter* • Mike Starr *Tony Rossini* • Cherry Jones *Mimi Barnes* • Michael Cumpsty *Klaus Gruber* • Claire Bloom *Emma Sachs* • Barbara Sukowa *Rachel Singer* ■ *Dir* Joyce Chopra • *Scr* Gene Wilder, Gilbert Pearlman

The Lady in Red ★★★★ 18

Period crime drama
1979 · US · Colour · 83mins

Produced on a slimline budget by Roger Corman's studio, this splendid retro gangster movie was shot in about a month by Lewis Teague from a script by John Sayles. Pamela Sue Martin plays a star-struck country girl who hopes to be a Hollywood star but gets caught up in Chicago's vice rings, working for madame Louise Fletcher and spending time in prison. On release she falls in love with gangster John Dillinger (Robert Conrad). Sayles's script does an impressive sweep of Chicago's underworld, social strata and economy in the 1930s and has in Martin a fiery, attractive heroine whom the press call "the lady in red". And as it's a Corman picture, there's a lot of sex and bullets, too. AT

Pamela Sue Martin *Polly Franklin* • Robert Conrad *John Dillinger* • Louise Fletcher *Anna Sage* • Robert Hogan *Jake Lingle* • Laurie Heineman *Rose Shimkus* • Glenn Withrow *Eddie* • Rod Gist *Pinetop* • Peter Hobbs *Pops Geissler* • Christopher Lloyd *Frognose* ■ *Dir* Lewis Teague • *Scr* John Sayles

The Lady in the Car with Glasses and a Gun ★★

Thriller 1970 · US/Fr · Colour · 105mins

This weird little thriller, hatched by Columbia to waste some funds locked in France, gave a starring role to British actress Samantha Eggar. She plays the secretary to businessman Oliver Reed; when she drives his car to Paris, various strangers claim they saw her the previous day. Is she deranged? Or is she the victim of some dark murder plot? Some genuinely creepy moments should keep you watching. AT

Samantha Eggar *Dany Lang* • Oliver Reed *Michael Caldwell* • John McEnery *Philippe* • Stéphane Audran *Anita Caldwell* • Billie Dixon *Secretary* • Bernard Fresson *Jean* ■ *Dir* Anatole Litvak • *Scr* Richard Harris, Eleanor Perry, from the novel *La Dame dans l'Auto avec des Lunettes et un Fusil* by Sébastien Japrisot • *Cinematographer* Claude Renoir

Lady in the Dark ★★★ U

Musical 1944 · US · Colour · 99mins

Fashion magazine editor Ginger Rogers, fearing for her mental health because of conflicts with three men in her life (Ray Milland, Warner Baxter, Jon Hall), consults psychiatrist Barry Sullivan, to whom she relates her dreams. These provide the basis for the film's production numbers, lavishly staged and extravagantly dressed. A major Broadway musical hit three years earlier, Paramount spared no expense in bringing it to the screen with a gold-plated design and production team and Mitchell Leisen directing. The public loved it, but it lost Danny Kaye (replaced by Mischa Auer) and much of its brilliant original score in the transfer and got a critical thumbs-down. RK

Ginger Rogers *Liza Elliott* • Ray Milland *Charley Johnson* • Jon Hall *Randy Curtis* • Warner Baxter *Kendall Nesbitt* • Barry Sullivan *Dr Brooks* • Mischa Auer *Russell Paxton* ■ *Dir* Mitchell Leisen • *Scr* Frances Goodrich, Albert Hackett, from the musical by Moss Hart, Kurt Weill, Ira Gershwin • *Costume Designer* Raoul Pene du Bois, Edith Head

Lady in the Lake ★★★★

Film noir 1947 · US · BW · 102mins

Robert Montgomery stars and directs himself as Philip Marlowe. Made only a year after Humphrey Bogart played Marlowe in *The Big Sleep*, Montgomery was looking for an offbeat approach that would surprise audiences and lessen the problems of directing himself while increasing the pressure on his co-stars. Just as Raymond Chandler's novels are written in the first person, so *Lady in the Lake* is a film in the first person: the camera is Marlowe and we only see what he would see, glimpsing Montgomery's face only in brief opening and closing sequences and when Marlowe looks in the mirror. Meanwhile, the camera smokes, gets kissed (by Audrey Totter) and punched (by various heavies). A gimmick, but it works. AT

Robert Montgomery *Philip Marlowe* • Lloyd Nolan *Lieutenant DeGarmot* • Audrey Totter *Adrienne Fromsett* • Tom Tully *Captain Kane* • Leon Ames *Derace Kingsby* • Jayne Meadows *Mildred Havelend* • Morris Ankrum *Eugene Grayson* • Lila Leeds *Receptionist* • Richard Simmons [Dick Simmons] *Chris Lavery* ■ *Dir* Robert Montgomery • *Scr* Steve Fisher, Raymond Chandler (uncredited), from the novel by Raymond Chandler

Lady in White ★★★★ 15

Supernatural thriller
1988 · US · Colour · 108mins

Frank LaLoggia's ghost story brings a wonderful sense of magical euphoria back to the genre. This highly romanticised, sentimental chiller puts Stephen King's brand of dark and violent suspense and Frank Capra's emotional fantasy into a Norman Rockwell setting with enthralling results. Lukas Haas is fantastic as the key holder to a past Halloween tragedy still haunting his sleepy community, in an evocative mini-masterpiece, jam-packed with dreamy atmosphere and incandescent supernatural enchantment. AJ. Contains violence and swearing.

Lukas Haas *Frankie Scarlatti* • Len Cariou *Phil* • Alex Rocco *Angelo Scarlatti* • Katherine Helmond *Amanda Harper* • Jason Presson *Gino Scarlatti* • Renata Vanni *Mama Assunta* • Angelo Bertolini *Papa Charlie* • Jared Rushton *Donald* ■ *Dir/Scr* Frank LaLoggia

The Lady Is Willing ★

Comedy 1942 · US · BW · 90mins

A glamorous stage star (Marlene Dietrich) finds an abandoned toddler in Manhattan and, in order to adopt him, undertakes a marriage of convenience with paediatrician Fred MacMurray. This leaden nonsense has nothing to recommend it other than the bizarre fascination of watching its *femme fatale* star attempting to play maternal in an uneasy mix of soap opera and romantic comedy. RK

Marlene Dietrich *Elizabeth Madden* • Fred MacMurray *Dr Corey McBain* • Aline MacMahon *Buddy* • Stanley Ridges *Kenneth Hanline* • Arline Judge *Frances* • Roger Clark *Victor* ■ *Dir* Mitchell Leisen • *Scr* James Edward Grant, Albert McCleery, from a story by James Edward Grant

Lady Jane ★★★ PG

Historical drama
1985 · UK · Colour · 135mins

Historical biopics are notoriously difficult to do well. It's easy enough to establish the correct period look, but the action is invariably hamstrung by the need to provide background information on each character and episode. Trevor Nunn's account of the events that culminated in the brief reign of Lady Jane Grey falls into the familiar traps, with the romance between Jane and the dissolute Guildford Dudley being couched in terms more befitting a Molly Ringwald movie. However Helena Bonham Carter plays Jane with admirable earnestness and she is well supported by Patrick Stewart as her father. DP DVD

Helena Bonham Carter *Lady Jane Grey* • Cary Elwes *Guilford Dudley* • John Wood *John Dudley, Duke of Northumberland* • Michael Hordern *Dr Feckenham* • Jill Bennett *Mrs Ellen* • Jane Lapotaire *Princess Mary* • Sara Kestelman *Frances Grey, Duchess of Suffolk* • Patrick Stewart *Henry Grey, Duke of Suffolk* • Warren Saire *King Edward VI* • Joss Ackland *Sir John Bridges* • Ian Hogg *Sir John Gates* ■ *Dir* Trevor Nunn • *Scr* David Edgar, from a story by Chris Bryant

Lady Killer ★★★★

Comedy thriller 1933 · US · BW · 76mins

James Cagney's rat-a-tat delivery and the film's pell-mell propulsion make this a joyous Warner Bros sideswipe at Hollywood itself. Cagney is the cinema usher who graduates to gangsterdom, ending up as a film star writing fan letters to himself. He co-stars again with Mae Clarke from *Public Enemy*, only this time he pulls her out of bed by her hair instead of filling her face with grapefruit. The legend is that it's based on the rise and rise of George Raft, but who cares? The fast-paced action and Cagney's mesmeric energy make this so worthwhile. TH

James Cagney *Dan Quigley* • Leslie Fenton *Duke* • Margaret Lindsay *Lois Underwood* • Henry O'Neill *Ramick* • Willard Robertson *Conroy* • Douglas Cosgrove *Jones* • Raymond Hatton *Pete* • Russell Hopton *Smiley* ■ *Dir* Roy Del Ruth • *Scr* Ben Markson, Lillie Hayward, from the story *The Finger Man* by Rosalind Keating Shaffer

Lady L ★★★★

Period comedy 1965 · Fr/It · Colour · 123mins

Like its writer and director, Peter Ustinov, this is an immense charmer. Set at the turn of the last century, it's about laundress Sophia Loren whose amorous adventures, told in flashback, take her downstairs and then upstairs in the class system. Though involved with anarchist Paul Newman, she still marries eccentric aristocrat David Niven. The elegant dazzle and elaborate sets may be there to blind us to the lack of real substance but with an impressive cast, who cares? It's a stylish diversion to make us regret that Ustinov left film-making. TH

Sophia Loren *Lady L* • Paul Newman *Armand* • David Niven *Lord Lendale* • Claude Dauphin *Inspector Mercier* • Philippe Noiret *Gérôme* • Michel Piccoli *Lecoeur* • Cecil Parker *Sir Percy* • Jean Wiener *Krajewski* • Daniel Emilfork *Kobeleff* • Peter Ustinov *Prince Otto* ■ *Dir* Peter Ustinov • *Scr* Peter Ustinov, from the novel by Romain Gary

Lady Liberty ★★

Comedy 1971 · It/Fr · Colour · 95mins

The original Italian title of this frolic is *La Mortadella* – the name of Italy's fattest sausage. The plot has Sophia Loren arriving in New York clutching this huge sausage, which sends the US customs officials first into a dither, and then into lip-smacking mode. Like the sausage itself, this comedy was made for the Italian market and racked up few export sales. The English version was written by Ring Lardner Jr, a blacklisted screenwriter who won an Oscar for *MASH*. AT

Sophia Loren *Maddalena Ciarrapico* • William Devane *Jock Fenner* • Luigi Proietti *Michele Bruni* • Beeson Carroll *Dominic* • Bill Deprato *Pasquale* • Danny DeVito *Mancuso* • Susan Sarandon *Sally* ■ *Dir* Mario Monicelli • *Scr* Leonard Melfi, Suso Cecchi D'Amico, Don Carlos Dunaway, RW Spera, Mario Monicelli, Ring Lardner Jr, from a story by Leonard Melfi, from an idea by RW Spera

Lady Luck ★★

Comedy 1946 · US · BW · 97mins

Robert Young plays a gambler whom Barbara Hale won't marry until he breaks his habit, because her dad – lovable Frank Morgan – comes from a long line of inveterate gamblers. Films like this are pleasant enough time-wasters, but they didn't give Young box-office clout. He eventually achieved international popularity in two TV series, *Father Knows Best* (1954-60) and *Marcus Welby, MD* (1969-76). TS

Robert Young (1) *Larry Scott* • Barbara Hale *Mary Audrey* • Frank Morgan *William Audrey* • James Gleason *Sacramento Sam* • Don Rice *Eddie* • Harry Davenport *Judge Martin* ■ *Dir* Edwin L Marin • *Scr* Lynn Root, Frank Fenton, from the story by Herbert Clyde Lewis

A Lady Mislaid ★★ U

Comedy thriller 1958 · UK · BW · 59mins

A policeman arrives at the country cottage of two spinster sisters to look for the body of the previous tenant's wife and duly unearths a skeleton in the chicken-coop. But whose skeleton is it? Phyllis Calvert and Gillian Owen play the sisters, Thorley Walters the husband under suspicion in this thriller-farce, directed by David MacDonald. A quaint idea and a decent cast make perfectly respectable entertainment out of an hour-long British programmer. RK

Phyllis Calvert *Esther Williams* • Alan White *Sgt Bullock* • Thorley Walters *Smith* • Gillian Owen *Jennifer Williams* • Richard Leech *George* • Constance Fraser *Mrs Small* ■ *Dir* David MacDonald • *Scr* Frederick Gotfurt, from a play by Kenneth Horne

Lady of Burlesque ★★★

Comedy mystery 1943 · US · BW · 91mins

When a chorus girl is strangled with a G-string, the show's star, Barbara Stanwyck, teams up with Michael O'Shea, the comic whose advances she has been spurning, to find the killer. Based on a novel written by America's most famous stripper, Gypsy Rose Lee, the movie has the perfect star in Stanwyck. Directed by William A Wellman and Oscar-nominated for its music (by Arthur Lange), it's a cracking little drama (released as *Striptease Lady* in the UK) that combines suspense and comedy with an authentic smell of the greasepaint. RK

Barbara Stanwyck *Dixie Daisy* • Michael O'Shea *Biff Brannigan* • J Edward Bromberg *SB Foss* • Iris Adrian *Gee Gee Graham* • Gloria Dickson *Dolly Baxter* • Charles Dingle *Inspector Harrigan* ■ *Dir* William A Wellman • *Scr* James Gunn, from the novel *The G-String Murders* by Gypsy Rose Lee • *Music* Arthur Lange

L

Lady of Deceit ★★★

Film noir 1947 · US · BW · 92mins

This is a smashing hard-bitten *film noir* from that great postwar period when weak men fell headlong for tough *femmes fatales*, and destiny took no hostages. Lawrence Tierney – better-known today for masterminding those pesky *Reservoir Dogs* – is married to pretty Audrey Long but head-over-heels in love with her divorced sister, sultry Claire Trevor; you just know no good can come of this. TS

Lawrence Tierney *Sam Wild* • Claire Trevor *Helen Trent* • Walter Slezak *Arnett* • Phillip Terry *Fred* • Audrey Long *Georgia Staples* • Elisha Cook Jr *Marty* • Isabel Jewell *Laury Palmer* • Esther Howard *Mrs Kraft* ■ *Dir* Robert Wise • *Scr* Richard Macaulay, Eve Green, from the novel *Deadlier Than the Male* by James Gunn

The Lady of Musashino ★★★ PG

Drama 1951 · Jpn · BW · 84mins

Following the critical and commercial disappointment of *Miss Oyu*, Kenji Mizoguchi similarly failed to catch the national mood with this downbeat assessment of postwar society. The story centres on a suburban housewife whose despair at the spread of progressive attitudes and her husband's philanderings drives her to dependence on a like-minded neighbour, who eventually betrays her trust. Kinuyo Tanaka excels in the lead role and her contrast with cousin-in-law Yukiko Todoroki is as striking as that between the Musashino Plain and downtown Tokyo. DP. In Japanese with English subtitles. DVD

Kinuyo Tanaka *Michiko* • Masayuki Mori *Tadao* • So Yamamura *Eiji* • Yukiko Todoroki *Tomiko* • Minako Nakamura *Yukiko Ono* ■ *Dir* Kenji Mizoguchi • *Scr* Yoshikata Yoda, from the novel *Musashino Fujin* by Shohei Ooka

Lady of the Tropics ★★★

Melodrama 1939 · US · BW · 91mins

An aimless, penniless New Yorker (Robert Taylor), cruising the Far East with his intended fiancée's wealthy family, falls in love with a girl of mixed race (Hedy Lamarr) in Saigon. He abandons everything to marry her, but with tragic consequences. The film, directed by Jack Conway, does full justice to Lamarr's fabled beauty, which, together with a superbly polished and sinister performance from Joseph Schildkraut as the villain of the piece, makes this nonsensical melodrama very watchable. RK

Robert Taylor (1) *Bill Carey* • Hedy Lamarr *Manon De Vargnes* • Joseph Schildkraut *Pierre Delaroch* • Gloria Franklin *Nina* • Ernest Cossart *Father Antoine* • Natalie Moorhead *Mrs Hazlitt* ■ *Dir* Jack Conway • *Scr* Ben Hecht

Lady on a Train ★★★ U

Crime comedy 1945 · US · BW · 90mins

With a licence to trill, opera singer Deanna Durbin's cinematic singing career was one of the most remarkable success stories of the 1930s and 1940s. This movie backed up her vocal talents with a better story than usual when, in the style of Agatha Christie, she sees a murder being committed on a passing train – and then has to try to convince the police. Her singing of *Night and Day* is the high-note of the movie. TH DVD

Deanna Durbin *Nikki Collins* • Ralph Bellamy *Jonathan* • Edward Everett Horton *Mr Haskell* • George Coulouris *Mr Saunders* • Allen Jenkins *Danny* • Dan Duryea *Arnold* ■ *Dir* Charles David • *Scr* Edmund Beloin, Robert O'Brien, from a story by Leslie Charteris • *Music* Miklos Rozsa

The Lady Pays Off ★

Comedy drama 1951 · US · BW · 80mins

"Teacher of the Year" Linda Darnell faces something of an image crisis after she runs up gambling debts of $7,000 in Stephen McNally's Reno casino. McNally gives her an ultimatum: she has to coach his daughter or face exposure. That's quite a clever premise for a plot, but then things get unbelievably tacky, with Darnell faking romantic interest in McNally, only to be redeemed by the awfully cute little girl. Douglas Sirk once said, "I have no feeling for this picture at all" and neither will most viewers. AT

Linda Darnell *Evelyn Warren* • Stephen McNally *Matt Braddock* • Gigi Perreau *Diana Braddock* • Virginia Field *Kay Stoddard* ■ *Dir* Douglas Sirk • *Scr* Frank Gill Jr, Albert J Cohen

Lady Sings the Blues ★★★★

Musical biography
1972 · US · Colour · 143mins

A biopic of jazz legend Billie Holliday, solely financed by Berry Gordy's Tamla Motown record label and starring Diana Ross in her screen debut. Like all Hollywood biopics, it's a typical rollercoaster ride, with Holliday suffering highs, lows, marriage, divorce, drug addiction, adulation and an early death. Ross is required to age some 20 years and gives a rich, compelling performance that only occasionally shouts "Gimme an Oscar". (She got a nomination, but lost out to Liza Minnelli in *Cabaret*). The 1930s ambience, nightclubs and drug culture are superbly evoked. AT

Diana Ross *Billie Holiday* • Billy Dee Williams *Louis McKay* • Richard Pryor *"Piano Man"* • James Callahan *Reg Hanley* • Paul Hampton *Harry* • Sid Melton *Jerry* • Virginia Capers *Mama Holiday* ■ *Dir* Sidney J Furie • *Scr* Terence McCloy, Chris Clark, Suzanne De Passe, from the autobiography by Billie Holiday, William Dufty

Lady Snowblood ★★★ 18

Period martial arts drama
1973 · Jpn · Colour · 97mins

Already a cult figure, Meiko Kaji acquired star status in this blood-geysering Meiji period action drama. Much of the opening segment focuses on her mother's desperate bid to have a child to avenge the murder of her husband. But once Kaji begins training for her mission, the emphasis shifts to the barbaric, as she seeks out the surviving trio on her chopping list.The film gains kudos by the co-starring turn of Akira Kurosawa's son, Toshio. A sequel followed in 1974. DP. In Japanese with English subtitles. DVD

Meiko Kaji *Yuki* • Toshio Kurosawa ■ *Dir* Toshiya Fujita • *Scr* Kazuo Uemura, Kazuo Koike, from a comic book by Kazuo Koike

A Lady Takes a Chance ★★★ U

Romantic comedy 1943 · US · BW · 82mins

A nicely packaged star vehicle for Jean Arthur, successfully paired with John Wayne in a romantic comedy about a rodeo star and a city gal. Arthur's second husband, the former singer Frank Ross, was the producer and surrounded her with talent: especially watchable is funny Phil Silvers as a tour guide. Director William A Seiter was one of Hollywood's unsung craftsmen. In this slight but engaging comedy, he cleverly keeps the romance bubbling. TS DVD

Jean Arthur *Mollie Truesdale* • John Wayne *Duke Hudkins* • Phil Silvers *Smiley Lambert* • Mary Field *Florrie Bendix* • Don Costello (1) *Drunk* • Grady Sutton *Malcolm* • Grant Withers *Bob* • Hans Conried *Gregg* ■ *Dir* William A Seiter • *Scr* Robert Ardrey, Garson Kanin (uncredited), from a story by Jo Swerling

The Lady Takes a Flyer ★★

Drama 1958 · US · Colour · 94mins

Jack Arnold, who made his name directing some of the best sci-fi pictures of the 1950s, such as *It Came from Outer Space* and *The Incredible Shrinking Man*, subsequently had an incredibly shrinking career. This predictable confection starred blonde Lana Turner and white-haired Jeff Chandler as a squabbling married couple – both are pilots – each with rivals for their affections. RB

Lana Turner *Maggie Colby* • Jeff Chandler *Mike Dandridge* • Richard Denning *Al Reynolds* • Andra Martin *Nikki Taylor* • Chuck Connors *Phil Donahue* • Reta Shaw *Nurse Kennedy* ■ *Dir* Jack Arnold • *Scr* Danny Arnold, from the story by Edmund H North

The Lady Vanishes ★★★★★ U

Classic thriller 1938 · UK · BW · 91mins

A close second behind *The 39 Steps* as the best film of Alfred Hitchcock's British period, this sublime comedy thriller was co-scripted by Alma Reville (Mrs Hitchcock) with Frank Launder and Sidney Gilliat. There isn't a wasted frame, as Michael Redgrave and Margaret Lockwood search a Balkan express for dotty Dame May Whitty. Basil Radford and Naunton Wayne drew all the plaudits as the cricket-mad Charters and Caldicott, but the support playing of Paul Lukas, Mary Clare and Cecil Parker is also first class. Hitchcock cameo fans should keep their eyes peeled during the London station scene. DP DVD

Margaret Lockwood *Iris Henderson* • Michael Redgrave *Gilbert Redman* • Paul Lukas *Dr Hartz* • Dame May Whitty *Miss Froy* • Cecil Parker *Eric Todhunter* • Linden Travers *"Mrs" Todhunter* • Naunton Wayne *Caldicott* • Basil Radford *Charters* • Mary Clare *Baroness* • Googie Withers *Blanche* ■ *Dir* Alfred Hitchcock • *Scr* Sidney Gilliat, Frank Launder, Alma Reville, from the novel *The Wheel Spins* by Ethel Lina White

The Lady Vanishes ★★ PG

Thriller 1979 · UK · Colour · 95mins

A pointless but watchable remake of the much-loved Hitchcock classic of 1938. It's slicker than the original – gone are the amateur model shots – but it lacks its charm, and has none of the atmosphere of impending war that gave the Hitchcock film so much of its meaning. But Miss Froy (Angela Lansbury in high camp mode) still goes missing on a train, leaving Elliott Gould and Cybill Shepherd (both miscast) flitting from one compartment to the next. AT DVD

Elliott Gould *Robert Condon* • Cybill Shepherd *Amanda Kelly* • Angela Lansbury *Miss Froy* • Herbert Lom *Dr Hartz* • Arthur Lowe *Charters* • Ian Carmichael *Caldicott* • Gerald Harper *Mr Todhunter* • Jean Anderson *Baroness Kisling* ■ *Dir* Anthony Page • *Scr* George Axelrod, from the 1938 film

The Lady Wants Mink ★★ U

Comedy 1953 · US · Colour · 92mins

You must leave your contemporary prejudices aside to enjoy this teaming of two of the most acerbic women in Hollywood history: Ruth Hussey and the redoubtable Eve Arden, who could make any line sound witty. Hussey stars as the wife breeding minks so she can own a fur coat. Husband Dennis O'Keefe has no chance of competing with Hussey, let alone Arden, but veterans William Demarest and Gene Lockhart do what they can with the feeble material. TS

Dennis O'Keefe *Jim Connors* • Ruth Hussey *Nora Connors* • Eve Arden *Gladys Jones* • William Demarest *Harvey Jones* • Gene Lockhart *Mr Heggie* • Hope Emerson *Mrs Hoxie* ■ *Dir* William A Seiter • *Scr* Dane Lussier, Richard Alan Simmons, from a story by Leonard Neubauer, Lou Schor

Lady Windermere's Fan ★★★

Silent drama 1916 · UK · BW · 65mins

Fred Paul's 1916 adaptation of Oscar Wilde's play is a rare surviving example of British *film d'art*. There's nothing particularly cinematic about the fixed-camera staging. But the sets are lovingly decorated and the playing is much less gesticulatory than the period norm. However, what will interest Wilde scholars is the way screenwriter Benedict James shifts the emphasis of the play by revealing at the outset the true identity of Mrs Erlynne. Thus, instead of being a jezebel, she is portrayed as a woman wronged by snobbery who is prepared to risk her newly regained reputation to save her daughter's honour. DP

Milton Rosmer *Lord Windermere* • Netta Westcott *Lady Windermere* • Nigel Playfair *Lord Augustus Lorton* • Irene Rooke *Mrs Erlynne* • Arthur Wontner *Lord Darlington* ■ *Dir* Fred Paul • *Scr* Benedict James, from the play by Oscar Wilde

Lady Windermere's Fan ★★★★

Silent drama 1925 · US · BW · 94mins

The Lubitsch touch – the ironic, risque style of director Ernst Lubitsch – was never more blatant in the way he lightens up one of Oscar Wilde's most judgemental plays, when adventuress Mrs Erlynne intrudes on the great and the good and threatens scandal. Ronald Colman, May McAvoy and Irene Rich look aghast in one of Lubitsch's best silent movies. TH

Ronald Colman *Lord Darlington* • Irene Rich *Mrs Erlynne* • May McAvoy *Lady Windermere* • Bert Lytell *Lord Windermere* • Edward Martindel *Lord Augustus* ■ *Dir* Ernst Lubitsch • *Scr* Julien Josephson, from the play by Oscar Wilde

Lady with a Past ★★★★

Romantic comedy 1932 · US · BW · 70mins

The delightful Constance Bennett (older sister of Joan), briefly the highest paid female star in Hollywood in the 1930s, was seen at her best in sophisticated, slightly risqué comedies. Here she is a good little rich girl, who discovers that she is much more popular with men if they think she's bad. Naturally, it all takes place in a chic and naughty Paris. Ben Lyon wittily plays Bennett's paid escort. Handsome David Manners is perfect as the young man who falls for her new self. RB

Constance Bennett *Venice Muir* • Ben Lyon *Guy Bryson* • David Manners *Donnie Wainwright* • Don Alvarado *The Argentine* • Albert Conti *René* • Merna Kennedy *Ann Duryea* ■ *Dir* Edward H Griffith • *Scr* Horace Jackson, from the story by Harriet Henry

The Lady with Red Boots ★★★

Fantasy drama
1974 · Fr/It/Sp · Colour · 92mins

Juan Buñuel, son of the legendary Spanish director, called on two of his father's best known stars, Catherine Deneuve and Fernando Rey, for this psychological thriller in which the cruel tricks played by writer Deneuve on manipulative millionaire Rey end in tragedy. Exploring the relationship between life and art, this highly stylised picture has all the hallmarks of a Buñuel film. However Juan lacks the control that characterised his father's use of satire and realism, and the outcome is confusing. DP. In French with English subtitles.

Catherine Deneuve *Françoise* • Fernando Rey *Perrot* • Adalberto Maria Merli *Man* • Jacques Weber *Painter* ■ *Dir* Juan Buñuel • *Scr* Juan Buñuel, Roberto Bodegas (dialogue)

The Lady with the Lamp ★★ U

Biographical drama 1951 · UK · BW · 99mins

Anna Neagle dons a simple cloth cap in this reverential biopic of Florence Nightingale. Once again under the tutelage of husband Herbert Wilcox, she gives an imperious performance as the daughter of a Hampshire landowner who reformed nursing and became a national icon during the Crimean War. To placate movie audiences, a disproportionate amount of time is devoted to the romance with Michael Wilding. DP

Anna Neagle *Florence Nightingale* • Michael Wilding *Sidney Herbert* • Gladys Young *Mrs Bracebridge* • Felix Aylmer *Lord Palmerston* • Julian D'Albie *Mr Bracebridge* • Arthur Young *WE Gladstone* • Edwin Styles *Mr Nightingale* • Helen Shingler *Parthenope Nightingale* • Helena Pickard *Queen Victoria* ■ *Dir* Herbert Wilcox • *Scr* Warren Chetham Strode, from the play by Reginald Berkeley

The Lady with the Little Dog ★★★★

Drama 1960 · USSR · BW · 88mins

This remains one of the most admired film adaptations of Anton Chekhov. The sensitive direction subtly evokes the prose of Chekhov's short love story, reflecting the lovers' psychology. The contrast between the seaside resort of Yalta in summer, where the two unhappily married people meet and fall in love, and Moscow in winter, is vividly portrayed. Iya Savvina gives a beautiful performance in the title role. RB. In Russian with English subtitles.

Iya Savvina *Anna Sergeyevna* • Alexei Batalov *Dmitri Gurov* • Nina Alisova *Madame Gurov* ■ *Dir* Josef Heifitz • *Scr* Josef Heifitz, from the story *Dama s Sobachkoy* by Anton Chekhov

A Lady without Passport ★★★

Crime drama 1950 · US · BW · 73mins

Director Joseph H Lewis was acknowledged as the great stylist of the Hollywood B-picture, but his touch was not noticeable in this *film noir* thriller about illegal aliens – which include glamorous Hedy Lamarr – trying to enter the United States. The focus of attention is so ambigious it comes across as confused, without any of the expected thrills. TH

Hedy Lamarr *Marianne Lorress* • John Hodiak *Pete Karczag* • James Craig *Frank Westlake* • George Macready *Palinov* • Steven Geray *Frenchman* • Bruce Cowling *Archer Delby James* ■ *Dir* Joseph H Lewis • *Scr* Howard Dimsdale, Cyril Hume, from a story by Lawrence Taylor

Ladybird Ladybird ★★★★ 18

Drama 1994 · UK · Colour · 97mins

Stand-up comic Crissy Rock won a Silver Bear at the Berlin Film Festival for her gutsy, warts-and-all performance in this harrowing drama from Ken Loach that will leave you emotionally exhausted. She hurls herself into the part of a mouthy Merseysider, whose string of abusive relationships results in her children being taken by the social services, and is simply but effectively supported by Vladimir Vega as a Paraguayan refugee who becomes her lover. Loach expertly prevents the endless crises from slipping into hysterical melodrama. DP. Contains violence, swearing and nudity. [VIDEO]

Crissy Rock *Maggie* • Vladimir Vega *Jorge* • Sandie Lavelle *Mairead* • Mauricio Venegas *Adrian* • Ray Winstone *Simon* • Clare Perkins *Jill* • Jason Stracey *Sean* ■ *Dir* Ken Loach • *Scr* Rona Munro

Ladybug, Ladybug ★★★

Drama 1963 · US · BW · 81mins

This is one of the American film industry's odder responses to the Cold War and the possibility of nuclear oblivion. Made for $350,000 by the husband and wife team of Frank and Eleanor Perry, it's set in an ordinary school in Ordinaryville, USA, and shows what happens when the head teacher has to prepare the school and its pupils for a nuclear blast. Vaguely resembling Peter Watkins's banned BBC film *The War Game*, the Perrys produce a weird blend of public information, corny melodrama and *Lord of the Flies*. A very arty relic. AT

June Connell *Mrs Maxton* • William Daniels *Mr Calkins* • James Frawley *Truck driver* • Richard Hamilton *JoAnn's father* • Kathryn Hays *Mrs Forbes* • Jane Hoffman *Mrs Hayworth* ■ *Dir* Frank Perry • *Scr* Eleanor Perry, from an article by Lois Dickert

Ladybugs ★★ PG

Comedy 1992 · US · Colour · 84mins

In this raucous Rodney Dangerfield comedy, the burly comic, whose abrasive style has never really found a niche in film, blusters in typical fashion as a salesman whose only chance of promotion lies in turning the company's girls' soccer team into champions. Naturally, it requires a lad in drag to act as playmaker and there is a record attempt at cramming the most locker-room gags into a single picture. Sadly the laughs are in short supply – until, that is, you see Hollywood's idea of a football match. DP. Contains some swearing. [VIDEO]

Rodney Dangerfield *Chester Lee* • Jackée *Julie Benson* • Jonathan Brandis *Matthew/Martha* • Ilene Graff *Bess* • Vinessa Shaw *Kimberly Mullen* • Tom Parks *Dave Mullen* • Jeannetta Arnette [Jeanetta Arnette] *Glynnis Mullen* ■ *Dir* Sidney J Furie • *Scr* Curtis Burch

Ladyhawke ★★★★ PG

Fantasy adventure
1985 · US · Colour · 118mins

Michelle Pfeiffer as the title's pretty predator and Rutger Hauer as a legendary lycanthrope give human poignancy to this medieval fairy tale of lovers cursed to shape-change into animals. Richard Donner proves to have an elegant eye for ancient as well as everyday fables, and it's all ravishingly filmed in Italy. Leo McKern dispels the dark from the Dark Ages with a comic turn as a Friar Tuck-ish priest, and Matthew Broderick makes an appealing young hero. TH. Contains some violence. [VIDEO] DVD

Matthew Broderick *Phillipe Gaston* • Rutger Hauer *Etienne Of Navarre* • Michelle Pfeiffer *Isabeau Of Anjou* • Leo McKern *Father Imperius* • John Wood *Bishop* • Ken Hutchison *Captain Marquet* • Alfred Molina *Cezar* ■ *Dir* Richard Donner • *Scr* Edward Khmara, Michael Thomas, Tom Mankiewicz, from a story by Edward Khmara • *Cinematographer* Vittorio Storaro

The Ladykillers ★★★★★ U

Classic comedy 1955 · UK · Colour · 86mins

A supreme blend of the seedy and the sinister, this was Ealing's last post on the comedy front. Directed with a mischievous glint by Alexander Mackendrick, the picture loses its way momentarily in the middle, when the stock scenario of a gang of ruthless thugs being stymied by a dotty innocent (the marvellous Katie Johnson as their landlady) wears a little thin. Nevertheless, this is British comedy at its best, with eccentric characters never for a second seeming out of place in the most everyday locations. Alec Guinness and his minions, among them Herbert Lom and Peter Sellers, are a marvellous collection of misfits, but they lose every scene to the Bafta-winning Johnson. DP [VIDEO] DVD

Alec Guinness *Professor Marcus* • Cecil Parker *Major Courtney* • Herbert Lom *Louis* • Peter Sellers *Harry* • Danny Green *One-Round* • Katie Johnson *Mrs Wilberforce* • Jack Warner *Police superintendent* • Philip Stainton *Police sergeant* • Frankie Howerd *Barrow boy* • Kenneth Connor *Cab driver* • Edie Martin *Lettice* ■ *Dir* Alexander Mackendrick • *Scr* William Rose, from his story

The Ladykillers ★★★ 15

Black comedy 2004 · US · Colour · 99mins

The Coen brothers (with Ethan gaining his first credit as co-director) have audaciously transplanted the premise of the delightful Ealing original (widow innocently lets rooms to a motley gang of criminals) from a dank north London suburb to the Deep South bible belt. Tom Hanks takes on the Guinness part of criminal mastermind, with Irma P Hall playing an anti-smoking Baptist who's not averse to face-slapping when she hears bad language. Hanks performs admirably as the eccentric professor, whose every utterance reeks of pompous southern verbosity. But the siblings' renowned quirkiness somehow seems at odds with the original offbeat masterpiece. TH. Contains swearing. [VIDEO] DVD

Tom Hanks *Prof Goldthwait Higginson Dorr III* • Irma P Hall *Mrs Marva Munson* • Marlon Wayans *Gawain MacSam* • JK Simmons *Garth Pancake* • Ma Tzi *The General* • Ryan Hurst *Lump* ■ *Dir* Joel Coen, Ethan Coen • *Scr* Joel Coen, Ethan Coen, from the film by William Rose

A Lady's Morals ★★★

Musical romance 1930 · US · BW · 86mins

The first of eight films made by talented Metropolitan Opera soprano Grace Moore before she was tragically killed in a plane crash in 1947. Moore stars as the famous opera singer Jenny Lind, the "Swedish Nightingale", in this highly fanciful treatment of what purports to be a complicated romantic relationship in Lind's life. An awesome hotch-potch of styles – it begins like a comic operetta and progresses to tragic romantic melodrama – it is nonetheless very charming. RK

Grace Moore *Jenny Lind* • Reginald Denny *Paul Brandt* • Wallace Beery *Barnum* • Gus Shy *Olaf* • Gilbert Emery *Broughm* ■ *Dir* Sidney Franklin • *Scr* Hans Kràly, Claudine West, John Meehan, Arthur Richman, from a story by Dorothy Farnum

Lagaan: Once upon a Time in India ★★★ PG

Romantic musical drama
2001 · Ind · Colour · 215mins

This sprawling historical masala is the most expensive picture ever produced in Bollywood. Set in the 1890s, its main thrust concerns the resistance mounted by peasants of the arid Bhuj region to an unjust agricultural tax. But the focus ultimately falls on the love triangle that forms between Gracy Singh, protest leader Aamir Khan and Rachel Shelley, the Raj rose who offers to teach the locals to beat a British XI at cricket and thus half the levy. With broad comedy, glossy dance routines and romantic tension, it's epic entertainment. DP. In Hindi, Bhojpuri and English with subtitles. [VIDEO] DVD

Aamir Khan *Bhuvan* • Gracy Singh *Guari* • Rachel Shelley *Elizabeth Russell* • Paul Blackthorne *Captain Andrew Russell* • AK Hangal *Shambukaka* • Suhasini Mulay *Yashodamai* • Kulbhushan Kharbanda *Rajah Puran Singh* • Raghuveer Yadav [Raghuvir Yadav] *Bhura* ■ *Dir* Ashutosh Gowariker • *Scr* Ashutosh Gowariker, Kumar Dave, Sanjay Dayma, from a story by Ashutosh Gowariker

The Lair of the White Worm ★★★ 18

Horror 1988 · UK · Colour · 89mins

Nude nuns, lesbian catfights and snake-cult rituals; what else could this be but a Ken Russell fantasy sextravaganza? Based on Bram Stoker's least famous novel, and starring a then unknown Hugh Grant, this Christianity versus Paganism tract is a delirious hoot from start to finish, so serious horror fans had better look elsewhere. Those in the mood for side-splitting nonsense – the kind that has reptilian Amanda Donohoe nakedly writhing through her country mansion to snake-charming music – are on the right track. AJ. Contains violence, swearing and sex scenes. [VIDEO]

Amanda Donohoe *Lady Sylvia Marsh* • Hugh Grant *Lord James D'Ampton* • Catherine Oxenberg *Eve Trent* • Peter Capaldi *Angus Flint* • Sammi Davis *Mary Trent* • Stratford Johns *Peters* • Paul Brooke *PC Erny* • Imogen Claire *Dorothy Trent* • Chris Pitt *Kevin* • Gina McKee *Nurse Gladwell* ■ *Dir* Ken Russell • *Scr* Ken Russell, from the novel by Bram Stoker

Laissez-passer ★★★ 12

War drama based on a true story
2001 · Fr/Ger/Sp · Colour · 163mins

Bertrand Tavernier's memoir of French film-making during the German Occupation caused a predictable storm in a country still scarred by its unresolved past. However, those unfamiliar with the Nazi-controlled Continental Films and the struggle for free artistic expression may decide that too much specialised knowledge is required to appreciate fully this sprawling account of the parallel careers of assistant director Jean Devaivre (Jacques Gamblin) and screenwriter Jean Aurenche (Denis Podalydès). The insight into studio politics is fascinating, but the domestic and espionage strands are less convincing. DP. In French with English subtitles. [VIDEO] DVD

Jacques Gamblin *Jean Devaivre* • Denis Podalydès *Jean Aurenche* • Marie Gillain *Olga* • Charlotte Kady *Suzanne Raymond* • Marie Desgranges *Simone Devaivre* • Maria Pitarresi *Reine Sorignal* • Ged Marlon *Jean-Paul Le Chanois* • Philippe Morier-Genoud *Maurice Tourneur* ■ *Dir* Bertrand Tavernier • *Scr* Jean Cosmos, Bertrand Tavernier, from the remembrances of Jean Aurenche, Jean Devaivre

Lake Consequence ★★ 18

Erotic melodrama 1992 · US · Colour · 86mins

Joan Severance plays a repressed housewife with a loving husband and son, whose temperature is raised by free-spirited gardener Billy Zane. Rope in the latter's girlfriend (May Karasun), a diabolical script and a hot-tub built for three, and you have a top-shelf title of little distinction. JC [VIDEO]

Joan Severance *Irene* • Billy Zane *Billy* • Whip Hubley *Jim* • May Karasun *Grace* • Courtland Mead *Christopher* ■ *Dir* Rafael Eisenman • *Scr* Zalman King, Melanie Finn, Henry Cobbold, from a story by MacGregor Douglas

Lake Placid ★★★ 15

Adventure thriller 1999 · US · Colour · 78mins

Writer/producer David E Kelley here turns his hand to a daft creature feature that will tickle fans of *Tremors*. There's something under the surface of Black Lake that's making monster munchies out of visitors, so warden Bill Pullman, paleontologist Bridget Fonda and nutty millionaire Oliver Platt decide to hunt down the critter before any other bits of semi-digested locals pop to the surface. Fonda and Pullman play it for laughs, but the show is stolen by Platt, one of the funniest supporting actors on film. JB [VIDEO] DVD

Bill Pullman *Jack Wells* • Bridget Fonda *Kelly Scott* • Oliver Platt *Hector Cyr* • Brendan Gleeson *Sheriff Hank Keough* • Betty White *Mrs Delores Bickerman* ■ *Dir* Steve Miner • *Scr* David E Kelley

Lakshya ★★★ 12

War drama 2004 · Ind · Colour · 288mins

Director Farhan Akhtar brought his famous father, Javed Akhtar, out of semi-retirement to script this epic tale of a spoilt brat's discovery of his true self on the field of combat. Wastrel Hrithik Roshan is persuaded by journalist girlfriend Preity Zinta to seek a purpose in life and enrol as an army cadet under colonel Amitabh Bachchan. A full-throttled adventure that makes spectacular use of the mountain scenery around Ladakh. DP. In Hindi with English subtitles. DVD

Hrithik Roshan *Karan Shergill* • Amitabh Bachchan *Col Sunil Damle* • Preity Zinta *Romila Dutta* • Om Puri *Major Pritam Singh* • Sushant Singh *Captain Jalal Akbar* • Sharad Kapoor *Major Binod Sengupta* ■ *Dir* Farhan Akhtar • *Scr* Javed Akhtar

Lamb ★★★★ 15

Drama 1985 · UK · Colour · 105mins

Although the central characters are a Christian Brother and one of his unruly students, this is one of the most sensitive "father and son" studies since *Bicycle Thieves*. Liam Neeson gives a dedicated performance as the religious teacher who finds a new vocation when he "kidnaps" epileptic Hugh O'Conor to spare him from the vindictive violence of headmaster Ian Bannen. Bernard MacLaverty adapts his own novel with care and genuine concern for his characters, without letting the action get bogged down in either spirituality or sentimentality. Director Colin Gregg makes London look disturbingly unwelcoming and handles the tragic conclusion with delicacy and truth. DP [VIDEO] DVD

Liam Neeson *Brother Sebastian, Michael Lamb* • Harry Towb *Priest* • Hugh O'Conor *Owen Kane* • Frances Tomelty *Mrs Kane* • Ian

L

Bannen *Brother Benedict* • Ronan Wilmot *Brother Fintan* • Denis Carey *Mr Lamb* ■ *Dir* Colin Gregg • *Scr* Bernard MacLaverty, from his novel

Lambada ★★ 15

Drama 1990 · US · Colour · 99mins

Remember the lambada, that dance fad that lasted about as long as an episode of *Come Dancing*? Well, this is the movie-of-the-dance as directed by Joel Silberg, who did a similar service to break-dancing in *Breakin'*. The plot is extremely unlikely (J Eddie Peck, maths teacher by day, dancer by night, teaches dropouts in the backroom of the dance club) and the dancing scenes are filmed as if they were soft porn, but Peck and his co-stars do their best with what's left. JB

J Eddie Peck *Kevin Laird* • Melora Hardin *Sandy* • Shabba-Doo *Raone* • Ricky Paull Goldin *Dean* • Basil Hoffman *Superintendent Leland* • Dennis Burkley *Uncle Big* • Keene Curtis *Principal Singleton* ■ *Dir* Joel Silberg • *Scr* Sheldon Renan, Joel Silberg, from a story by Joel Silberg

Lambada! The Forbidden Dance ★ 15

Drama 1990 · US · Colour · 93mins

One of two Lambada movies released at the same time to cash in on the dance craze. Here, the hip-swivelling Latin dance is merely a subplot to spice up the dire tale of a Brazilian princess who goes to America to campaign on behalf of the rainforest and ends up strutting her funky stuff on TV. A ludicrous premise if ever there was one and it's not helped by the casting of former Miss USA Laura Herring in the lead and 1980s' popsters Kid Creole and the Coconuts, who supply some of the music. JB

Laura Herring [Laura Harring] *Nisa* • Jeff James *Jason* • Sid Haig *Joa* • Richard Lynch *Benjamin Maxwell* • Barbra Brighton *Ashley* • Angela Moya *Carmen* ■ *Dir* Greydon Clark • *Scr* Roy Langsdon, John Platt

Lamerica ★★★

Drama 1994 · Fr/It · Colour · 116mins

This edgy drama is set in Albania just after the fall of communism. Two Italian capitalists aim to exploit a system in crisis by setting up a business front and pocketing all the proceeds. Looking for a fall guy they stumble on the wrong man, a recently liberated political prisoner. The Italians, initially ruthless, are forced to question their values. This is a politically poignant and powerful examination of how a country in turmoil causes personal crises. LH. In Italian with English subtitles.

Enrico Lo Verso *Gino* • Michele Placido *Fiore* • Carmelo Di Mazzarelli *Spiro* • Piro Milkani *Selimi* • Elida Janushi *Selimi's Cousin* ■ *Dir* Gianni Amelio • *Scr* Gianni Amelio, Andrea Porporati, Alessandro Sermoneta

The Lamp ★ 18

Horror 1987 · US · Colour · 85mins

This daft horror was one of several in the last two decades to raid folklore for under-exploited evil spirits. In this case, a genie released from its lamp goes berserk and kills most of the young unknowns who make up the cast. A promising idea, which in more creative hands could have developed into the likes of *Gremlins*, is frittered away through uninspired writing and direction. DM DVD

Deborah Winters *Eve Farrell* • James Huston *Dr Al Wallace* • Andra St Ivanyi *Alex Wallace* • Scott Bankston *Ted Pinson* • Mark Mitchell *Mike Daley* ■ *Dir* Tom Daley • *Scr* Warren Chaney

The Lamp Still Burns ★★

Drama 1943 · UK · BW · 90mins

Few actresses could suffer with the style and dignity of Rosamund John. In the third and last of the films she made for Leslie Howard (here producing his final picture), she plays a trainee nurse learning that gentility gets you nowhere in a crisis. Every hospital cliché has been scrubbed down and pressed into service – the cold efficient matron, the cantankerous patient and the handsome young doctor – and the wartime references give the film a home-front heroism that now makes the whole thing seem as stiff as a starched uniform. DP

Rosamund John *Hilary Clarke* • Stewart Granger *Larry Rains* • Godfrey Tearle *Sir Marshall Frayne* • Sophie Stewart *Christine Morris* • John Laurie *Mr Hervey* • Margaret Vyner *Pamela Siddell* • Cathleen Nesbitt *Matron* • Eric Micklewood *Dr Trevor* • Joyce Grenfell *Dr Barratt* ■ *Dir* Maurice Elvey • *Scr* Elizabeth Baron, Roland Pertwee, Major Neilson, from the novel *One Pair of Feet* by Monica Dickens

Lana in Love ★★★

Comedy 1991 · Can · Colour · 85mins

Having been spoilt for choice in *Julia Has Two Lovers*, Daphna Kastner experiences the pain of loneliness and the uncertainty of the lonely hearts columns in this reunion with director Bashar Shbib (with whom she'd co-written *Julia*). As the journalist whose busy life has left her little room for love, Kastner convincingly veers between the excitement of attraction and the nagging paranoia of self-doubt after she begins dating the seemingly suitable Clark Gregg. DP

Daphna Kastner *Lana* • Clark Gregg *Marty* • Ivan E Roth • Michael Gillis ■ *Dir* Bashar Shbib • *Scr* Bashar Shbib, Daphna Kastner

Lancelot and Guinevere ★★

Adventure drama
1963 · UK · Colour · 116mins

Real-life married couple Cornel Wilde and Jean Wallace play Lancelot and Guinevere, whose lingering love for each other almost destroys King Arthur's Camelot. The supporting cast is second-string British, the interiors were shot at Pinewood; Yugoslavia's army gets to dress up in medieval armour and run all over Ye Olde England. In other words, it's a cheapo that manages to look reasonably well-nourished. Wilde directs with dash and sometimes startling style. Sometimes the film shows signs of heavy cutting; the original plan was for a three-hour epic with an intermission. AT

Cornel Wilde *Sir Lancelot* • Jean Wallace *Queen Guinevere* • Brian Aherne *King Arthur* • George Baker *Sir Gawaine* • Archie Duncan *Sir Lamorak* ■ *Dir* Cornel Wilde • *Scr* Richard Schayer, Jefferson Pascal, from the prose romance *La Morte d'Arthur* by Sir Thomas Malory

Lancelot du Lac ★★★ PG

Period drama 1974 · Fr/It · Colour · 79mins

In his most expensive movie, director Robert Bresson manages to re-create the rich tapestry that is the timeworn world of King Arthur, his Knights and the Round Table code. Lancelot (Luc Simon) returns with fellow knights after a fruitless attempt to unearth the Holy Grail. All are suffering from a tremendous loss of faith, which drives Lancelot straight back into the arms of Arthur's Gueniêvre (Laura Duke Condominas). Instead of a straightforward moody swashbuckler, Bresson's skill lies in his ability here to make the film about crisis of belief and it is a fascinating study. LH. In French with English subtitles.

Luc Simon *Lancelot du Lac* • Laura Duke Condominas *Gueniêvre* • Humbert Balsan *Gawain* • Vladimir Antolek-Oresek *Artus* • Patrick Bernard *Mordred* • Arthur De Montalembert *Lionel* ■ *Dir/Scr* Robert Bresson • *Cinematographer* Pasqualino De Santis

Lancer Spy ★★★

Spy drama 1937 · US · BW · 84mins

In this atypical 20th Century-Fox 1930s melodrama, the urbane George Sanders has a rare meaty double role, starring as both a Prussian baron and the British officer sent out to replace him, only to find himself enmeshed in the caresses of cabaret singer Dolores Del Rio. The first half is very exciting, with a cast full of wonderfully sinister faces, including Peter Lorre and Lionel Atwill. But director Gregory Ratoff seems to tire of the romp, and the film grows lacklustre. Not as swashbuckling as it ought to have been. TS

Dolores Del Rio *Dolores Daria* • George Sanders *Lieutenant Bruce/Baron Von Rohback* • Peter Lorre *Major Sigfried Gruning* • Virginia Field *Joan Bruce* • Sig Rumann [Sig Ruman] *Lt Col Gottfried Hollen* • Joseph Schildkraut *Prince Ferdi Zu Schwarzwald* • Maurice Moscovich *General Von Meinhardt* • Lionel Atwill *Colonel Fenwick* ■ *Dir* Gregory Ratoff • *Scr* Philip Dunne, from the story by Marthe McKenna

Land and Freedom ★★★★ 15

Wartime drama
1995 · UK/Sp/Ger · Colour · 104mins

While the Spanish Civil War seemed an obvious choice of subject for Ken Loach, it was also quite a stretch in terms of action and scale after such domestic dramas as *Family Life* and *Raining Stones*. That he handles the combat scenes and period detail with such confidence adds to his reputation as one of Britain's most vital film-makers. Ian Hart's fallible unemployed Liverpudlian is our "guide" to the conflict as he signs up to fight against Franco. Some have criticised the film for speechmaking and didacticism, but this is all part of Loach's bid to open up the sometimes awkward politics of the time. Its full-bodied performances and courage to question make it rich and thought provoking. AC. In English, Spanish and Catalan with subtitles. DVD

Ian Hart *David Carne* • Rosana Pastor *Blanca* • Iciar Bollain *Maite* • Tom Gilroy *Gene Lawrence* • Marc Martinez *Vidal* • Frédéric Pierrot *Bernard* • Suzanne Maddock *Kim* • Mandy Walsh *Dot* • Angela Clarke *Kitty* ■ *Dir* Ken Loach • *Scr* Jim Allen

The Land before Time ★★★★ U

Animated adventure
1988 · US · Colour · 65mins

If your little dinosaur lovers are still a bit young for *Jurassic Park*, then this charming cartoon should have them in raptures. Directed by Don Bluth, it's a prehistoric reworking of his own *An American Tail*, with a displaced young brontosaurus called Littlefoot and his four dino-tot companions setting out across a strange and dangerous land in search of their families. Their adventures are pretty hair-raising as they encounter not only deadly predators, but also all manner of environmental hazards. Youngsters will love the adorable critters. Nine sequels (to date) followed in this popular kids' franchise. DP

Fred Gwynne *Narrator* • Gabriel Damon *Littlefoot* • Helen Shaver *Littlefoot's mother* • Bill Erwin *Grandfather* • Candice Houston *Cera* • Pat Hingle *Rooter* ■ *Dir* Don Bluth • *Scr* Stu Krieger, from a story by Judy Freudberg, Tony Geiss

The Land Girls ★★ 12

Period drama 1997 · UK/Fr · Colour · 110mins

Life on the home front is given a distinctly rosy glow in this naffly nostalgic adaptation of Angela Huth's novel. Anna Friel's randy northerner, Rachel Weisz's sheltered blue-stocking and Catherine McCormack's bourgeois prude are surely the most stereotypical volunteers in the history of the Women's Land Army. Consequently, from the moment these urban interlopers arrive at Tom Georgeson's Dorset farm, there isn't a single scene that ends unexpectedly. DP. Contains sexual references. DVD

Catherine McCormack *Stella* • Rachel Weisz *Ag* • Anna Friel *Prue* • Steven Mackintosh *Joe Lawrence* • Tom Georgeson *Mr Lawrence* • Maureen O'Brien *Mrs Lawrence* ■ *Dir* David Leland • *Scr* David Leland, Keith Dewhurst, from the novel by Angela Huth

Land of the Pharaohs ★★★ U

Historical epic 1955 · US · Colour · 103mins

The stiff dialogue in parts of this Hollywood epic about pyramid building and palace intrigue in ancient Egypt prompts the conclusion that co-writer William Faulkner would have been better off sticking to novels. But director Howard Hawks, the master storyteller, found it hard to make a bad movie and, all in all, this is a handsome and very serviceable historical melodrama, conceived and realised on the grand scale. Joan Collins is deliciously villainous as Princess Nellifer. PF

Jack Hawkins *Pharaoh* • Joan Collins *Princess Nellifer* • Dewey Martin *Senta* • Alexis Minotis *Hamar* • James Robertson-Justice *Vashtar* • Luisa Boni *Kyra* • Sydney Chaplin *Treneh* • James Hayter *Vashtar's servant* ■ *Dir* Howard Hawks • *Scr* William Faulkner, Harry Kurnitz, Harold Jack Bloom

Land Raiders ★★

Western 1969 · US · Colour · 101mins

An undistinguished western with a truly motley cast that makes this worth watching. Telly Savalas and *Route 66*'s George Maharis are surely the most unlikely brothers, but not quite as unlikely as the latter's Mexican accent. Also along for the bleak and dusty ride are stunning redhead Arlene Dahl and the girl Janet Landgard. Connoisseurs of the ludicrous will also enjoy finding Guy Rolfe and George Coulouris among the dross. It's sadistic, too. TS

Telly Savalas *Vince Carden* • George Maharis *Paul Cardenas* • Arlene Dahl *Martha Carden* • Janet Landgard *Kate Mayfield* • Jocelyn Lane *Luisa Rojas* • George Coulouris *Cardenas* ■ *Dir* Nathan H Juran [Nathan Juran] • *Scr* Ken Pettus, from a story by Ken Pettus, Jesse Lasky Jr, Pat Silver

The Land That Time Forgot ★★ PG

Fantasy adventure
1974 · UK · Colour · 86mins

The first, and worst, of the trilogy of Edgar Rice Burroughs lost world adventures produced by Amicus, despite the fact that it was co-scripted by sci-fi giant Michael Moorcock. In director Kevin Connor's excessively fake and slipshod saga, a First World War submarine discovers an uncharted haven for dinosaurs, cavemen and volcanoes. Doug McClure is out of his depth as the heroic lead, and the puppet monsters are just as weak. *At the Earth's Core* (1976) and *The People That Time Forgot* (1977) followed. AJ DVD

Doug McClure *Bowen Tyler* • John McEnery *Captain Von Schoenvorts* • Susan Penhaligon *Lisa Clayton* • Keith Barron *Bradley* • Anthony Ainley *Dietz* • Godfrey James *Borg* • Bobby Farr *Ahm* • Declan Mulholland *Olson* ■ *Dir*

Kevin Connor • *Scr* James Cawthorn, Michael Moorcock, from the novel by Edgar Rice Burroughs

The Land Unknown ★★

Fantasy adventure 1957 · US · BW · 78mins

A really cheesy sci-fi drama with Jock Mahoney down in the frozen wastes of Antarctica where dinosaurs frolic around a hot water oasis, apparently discovered in 1947. This is *The Lost World* on ice, with an entire menagerie of monsters, including the pantomime villain T-Rex as well as the flying pterodactyl which brings down our hero's helicopter in the opening scenes. Shawn Smith adds some romantic interest as a newshound whose clothes become more sparse, while Henry Brandon is the man who's been this way before and clearly left his marbles behind. AT

Jock Mahoney *Commander Hal Roberts* • Shawn Smith *Margaret Hathaway* • William Reynolds *Lieutenant Jack Carmen* • Henry Brandon *Hunter* • Phil Harvey *Steve Miller* • Douglas Kennedy *Captain Burnham* ■ *Dir* Virgil Vogel [Virgil W Vogel] • *Scr* Laszlo Gorog, from a story by Charles Palmer

Land without Bread ★★★★★

Documentary 1933 · Sp · BW · 29mins

An extraordinary documentary by the great surrealist director, Luis Buñuel, about a poverty-blighted region of north Spain, hemmed in by mountains. In-breeding between inhabitants has resulted in a race of grotesque dwarfs, and the final scene of contrast is the interior of a gold-encrusted Catholic church opposed to the dreadful misery of its context. One of Buñuel's most formidable anti-clerical swipes, it's still as angry as when it was made. Its images may be hideous, but they are true. TH. A Spanish language film.

Abel Jacquin *Narrator* ■ *Dir/Scr* Luis Buñuel

Land without Music ★★

Musical 1936 · UK · BW · 80mins

Walter Forde was a highly versatile director, but, on the evidence of this frippery, light opera was definitely not his forte. The story is paper-thin, as famous tenor Richard Tauber returns to his homeland to lead a melodic revolution against princess Diana Napier (Tauber's real-life wife), who has outlawed music. There are few memorable moments, and most of them are provided by the watchable Jimmy Durante, as a journalist with a song in his heart. DP

Richard Tauber *Mario Carlini* • Jimmy Durante *Jonah J Whistler* • Diana Napier *Princess Regent* • June Clyde *Sadie Whistler* • Derrick de Marney *Rudolpho Strozzi* • Esme Percy *Austrian Ambassador* • George "Gabby" Hayes *Captain Strozzi* • John Hepworth *Pedro* ■ *Dir* Walter Forde • *Scr* Rudolph Bernauer, Marian Dix, L DuGarde Peach, from a story by Fritz Koselka, Armin Robinson

Landfall ★★ U

Second World War drama
1949 · UK · BW · 88mins

Fighter pilot Michael Denison, poor chap, thinks he has sunk a British submarine while patrolling the skies over the English Channel. The court thinks so, too, and he gets transferred to desk duties and unburdens his guilt to barmaid Patricia Plunkett who decides to prove he actually sunk a German sub. Laurence Harvey can also be glimpsed in this dainty item from a vanished era of British war movies. AT

Michael Denison *Rick* • Patricia Plunkett *Mona* • Edith Sharpe *Rick's mother* • Sebastian Shaw *Wing-Cdr Dickens* • Maurice Denham *Wing-Cdr Hewitt* • Laurence Harvey *P/O Weaver* ■ *Dir* Ken Annakin • *Scr* Talbot Jennings, Gilbert Gunn, Anne Burnaby, from the novel by Nevil Shute

The Landlord ★★★★

Comedy drama 1970 · US · Colour · 109mins

Former editor Hal Ashby made a terrific debut as director with this comedy drama, featuring a superb Beau Bridges as the wealthy scion who learns about humanity and the African-American experience in New York from his tenants. Pearl Bailey and Diana Sands shine, and there's good work too from Robert Klein and Lee Grant. Fans of Ashby's subsequent cult classic *Harold and Maude* should check this out. TS

Beau Bridges *Elgar Enders* • Pearl Bailey *Marge* • Marki Bey *Lanie* • Diana Sands *Fanny* • Louis Gossett [Louis Gossett Jr] *Copee* • Douglas Grant *Walter Gee* • Melvin Stewart *Professor Duboise* • Lee Grant *Mrs Enders* • Robert Klein *Peter* ■ *Dir* Hal Ashby • *Scr* William Gunn [Bill Gunn], from the novel by Kristin Hunter

Landscape after Battle ★★★★ 12

Second World War drama
1970 · Pol · Colour · 104mins

As much a treatise on Polish anti-Semitism as a denunciation of the Nazis, Andrzej Wajda's grimly stylised picture is based on the writings of Tadeusz Borowski, a Holocaust survivor who committed suicide in 1959 at the age of 29. Wajda sends his restless camera in search of the grotesque ironies of life in a camp for displaced persons. Yet he also employs a lyrical expressionism to chronicle the romance between Daniel Olbrychski's writer and Stanislawa Celinska's terrified refugee. Both visually and intellectually disconcerting, this is a film of brutal poetic power. DP. A Polish language film. [VIDEO]

Daniel Olbrychski *Tadeusz* • Stanislawa Celinska *Nina* • Aleksander Bardini *Professor* ■ *Dir* Andrzej Wajda • *Scr* Andrzej Brzozowski, Andrzej Wajda, from the short stories by Tadeusz Borowski

Landscape in the Mist ★★★ 15

Road movie drama
1988 · Gr/Fr/It · Colour · 124mins

Convinced that their father resides in Germany, Greek children Tania Palaiologou and Michalis Zeke set out to find him on an odyssey that is littered with symbolic incidents and totemic characters. Despite Giorgos Arvanitis's moody photography, it's a gruelling experience, with only circus performer Stratos Tzortzoglou sympathising with their plight. But while the human story is relentlessly bleak, Theo Angelopoulos succeeds in depicting a nation obsessed with its past, by combining contemporary settings with countless allusions to ancient history and mythology. DP. In Greek with English subtitles.

Michalis Zeke *Alexander* • Tania Palaiologou *Voula* • Stratos Tzortzoglou *Orestes* ■ *Dir* Theo Angelopoulos • *Scr* Theo Angelopoulos, Tonino Guerra, Thanassis Valtinos

Lansky ★★ 15

Biographical crime drama
1999 · US · Colour · 111mins

A mumbling, whiny performance from Richard Dreyfuss undermines this cradle-to-grave TV biopic of gangster Meyer Lansky, associate of the equally notorious Bugsy Siegel. A Jewish immigrant, Lansky rises from the impoverished streets of New York's Lower East Side at the turn of the century and embarks on a life of crime. Lansky's life is unfortunately dramatised in cool, detached strokes by distinguished playwright David Mamet. MC [VIDEO] DVD

Richard Dreyfuss *Meyer Lansky* • Eric Roberts *Ben "Bugsy" Siegel* • Anthony LaPaglia *Charles "Lucky" Luciano* • Beverly D'Angelo *Teddy Lansky* • Illeana Douglas *Anna Lansky* ■ *Dir* John McNaughton • *Scr* David Mamet, from the biography *Meyer Lansky: Mogul of the Mob* by Uri Dan, Dennis Eisenberg, Eli Landau

Lantana ★★★★ 15

Thriller 2001 · Aus/Ger · Colour · 115mins

Ray Lawrence belies his roots in commercials with this engrossing adaptation of Andrew Bovell's play. It's a supremely controlled ensemble piece, in which chance and coincidence increase the tension of what is, ostensibly, a suburban thriller. But, as the mesh of interweaving relationships becomes increasingly complex, the identity and fate of a missing woman become less important than the resolution of the domestic crises involving psychiatrist Barbara Hershey and husband Geoffrey Rush, world-weary cop Anthony LaPaglia and the unhappy souls who inhabit the fringes of their lives. DP [VIDEO] DVD

Anthony LaPaglia *Leon Zat* • Geoffrey Rush *John Knox* • Barbara Hershey *Dr Valerie Somers* • Kerry Armstrong *Sonja Zat* • Rachael Blake *Jane O'May* • Glenn Robbins *Pete O'May* • Vince Colosimo *Nik Daniels* • Daniella Farinacci *Paula Daniels* ■ *Dir* Ray Lawrence • *Scr* Andrew Bovell, from his play *Speaking in Tongues*

Lapse of Memory ★★ PG

Thriller 1992 · Can/Fr · Colour · 81mins

Originally made in 1983 as the little seen *I Am the Cheese*, this is one of those repressed memory thrillers in which a sudden recollection spells danger for a previously contented amnesiac. Teenager Mathew Mackay struggles valiantly with the realisation that adoptive parents John Hurt and Marthe Keller are on the run from the Mob, but there's nothing that hasn't been done better in several similar scenarios. DP [VIDEO]

John Hurt *Conrad Farmer* • Marthe Keller *Linda Farmer* • Mathew Mackay *Bruce Farmer* • Kathleen Robertson *"Patrick"* • Marion Peterson *Dr Lauren Brint* ■ *Dir* Patrick Dewolf • *Scr* Patrick Dewolf, Philippe Le Guay, from the novel *I Am the Cheese* by Robert Cormier

Lara Croft: Tomb Raider ★ 12

Action adventure
2001 · US/Ger/UK/Jpn · Colour · 100mins

Angelina Jolie makes a credible enough Lara – athletic, somewhat top-heavy and with an English accent borrowed from Liz Hurley (rumoured to be an early contender for the role). The story is unsatisfying – a two-act yarn about finding two halves of an artefact in Cambodia and Siberia – and Simon West's direction does nothing to whip up any momentum as Lara joins forces with the apparent villains (led by Iain Glen). A boring dud. AC. Contains nudity and violence. [VIDEO] DVD

Angelina Jolie *Lara Croft* • Jon Voight *Lord Croft* • Noah Taylor *Bryce* • Iain Glen *Manfried Powell* • Daniel Craig *Alex West* • Christopher Barrie [Chris Barrie] *Hillary* • Leslie Phillips *Wilson* ■ *Dir* Simon West • *Scr* Patrick Massett, John Zinman, Simon West, from a story by Sara B Cooper, Mike Werb, Michael Colleary, from the computer game *Tomb Raider* by Core Design

Lara Croft Tomb Raider: the Cradle of Life ★ 12

Action adventure
2003 · US/UK/Ger/Jpn · Colour · 112mins

Director Jan De Bont does nothing in this sequel to refresh the franchise, nor untangle it from panic-led editing. This is unconvincing, witless, pancake-flat stuff. Teamed with disgraced former agent Gerard Butler, Angelina Jolie searches for the fabled Pandora's Box. Ciaran Hinds gives it his pantomime-all as the evil scientist, but the plot makes little sense and the set pieces are ho-hum. AC [VIDEO] DVD

Angelina Jolie *Lara Croft* • Gerard Butler *Terry Sheridan* • Ciaran Hinds *Jonathan Reiss* • Christopher Barrie [Chris Barrie] *Hillary* • Noah Taylor *Bryce* • Djimon Hounsou *Kosa* ■ *Dir* Jan De Bont • *Scr* Dean Georgaris, from a story by Steven E de Souza, James V Hart, from the computer game *Tomb Raider* by Core Design

The Laramie Project ★★★ 15

Drama based on a true story
2002 · US · Colour · 91mins

Adapted by director Moises Kaufman from his own play, which was itself based on testimony from the citizens of Laramie, Wyoming, this is a sobering account of the savage murder of HIV-positive student Matthew Shepard in 1998. However, Kaufman dissipates the impact of his exposure of homophobia in small-town America by studding the flashbacking action with cameos from well-meaning stars. Worthy, but flawed. DP [VIDEO] DVD

Christina Ricci *Romaine Patterson* • Steve Buscemi *Doc O'Conner* • Laura Linney *Sherry Johnson* • Summer Phoenix *Jen Malskog* • Clea DuVall *Amanda Gronich* • Peter Fonda *Dr Cantway* • Janeane Garofalo *Catherine Connolly* ■ *Dir* Moises Kaufman • *Scr* Moises Kaufman, from the play by Moises Kaufman and members of the Tectonic Theater Project

Larceny, Inc ★★

Crime comedy 1942 · US · BW · 95mins

Under cover of a smart luggage store, a gang of crooks plan to tunnel their way into the bank vault next door. However, the shop is so successful their plot is thwarted. Based on a Broadway show by husband and wife team SJ and Laura Perelman, this comedy boasts an enticing cast led by Edward G Robinson and featuring Anthony Quinn as one of the mobsters. Unfortunately, there aren't many laughs. Perhaps Warner Bros should have cast comedians as heavies rather than the other way around. AT

Edward G Robinson *J Chalmers "Pressure" Maxwell* • Jane Wyman *Denny Costello* • Broderick Crawford *Jug Martin* • Jack Carson *Jeff Randolph* • Anthony Quinn *Leo Dexter* • Edward S Brophy [Edward Brophy] *Weepy Davis* • Jackie Gleason *Hobart* ■ *Dir* Lloyd Bacon • *Scr* Everett Freeman, Edwin Gilbert, from the play *The Night Before Christmas* by Laura Perelman, SJ Perelman

Large ★ 15

Comedy 2000 · UK · Colour · 78mins

The Birmingham-set plot revolves around teenage slacker Luke de Woolfson who must turn over a new leaf before his 18th birthday so he can inherit the fortune of his dead rock star father. However, his mates and a grasping stepmother have other ideas. Debuting writer/director Justin Edgar throws in taste-free comic clichés and a bunch of relatively unknown actors cast as one-dimensional grotesques, and the result is appalling and amateurish. JC [VIDEO] DVD

Luke de Woolfson *Jason Mouseley* • Melanie Gutteridge *Sophie* • Simon Lowe *Rob* • Lee Oakes *Ian* • Mirren Delaney *Lisa Gates* • Emma Catherwood *Rachel "Measley" Beasley* • Les Dennis *Steve* ■ *Dir* Justin Edgar • *Scr* Justin Edgar, Michael Dent

Larger than Life ★★ PG

Comedy 1996 · US · Colour · 89mins

Bill Murray fans will have their allegiance tested by this extremely lightweight comedy about a motivational speaker who inherits an elephant from his estranged circus clown dad. Their cross-country journey to the animal's California destination is filled with calamitous incidents, but the laughs are spread thinly and this

L

only just about gets by on the star's cynical charm. JC DVD

Bill Murray *Jack Corcoran* • Janeane Garofalo *Mo* • Matthew McConaughey *Tip Tucker* • Linda Fiorentino *Terry* • Anita Gillette *Mom* ■ *Dir* Howard Franklin • *Scr* Roy Blount Jr, from the story by Pen Densham, Garry Williams

Larks on a String ★★★★

Satire 1969 · Cz · Colour · 90mins

Made towards the end of the period of creativity known as the "Czech Film Miracle", this caustic comedy was banned "for ever" by the authorities and director Jirí Menzel – co-writer/director of the Oscar-winning *Closely Observed Trains* – was prevented from filming for several years. Finally reaching cinema screens in 1990, after the Velvet Revolution, it justly shared the Golden Bear at the Berlin Film Festival that year. Set in a scrap-metal yard populated with discarded intellectuals and waiters, it is a sniping, eminently watchable romantic satire which, in keeping with many films of the time, sought to show how the Communist Party had failed the Czech working classes. DP. In Czechoslovakian with English subtitles.

Jitka Zelenohorska *Jitka* • Vaclav Neckar *Pavel* • Leos Sucharipa *Public prosecutor* • Jaroslav Satoransky *Angel* ■ *Dir* Jirí Menzel • *Scr* Jirí Menzel, from a novel by Bohumil Hrabal

Larry ★★★

Drama based on a true story 1974 · US · Colour · 80mins

David Seltzer, best known for his work on *The Omen*, wrote the screenplay for this affecting TV movie. Frederic Forrest gives an inspirational performance as a man discovered to have wrongly spent the first 26 years of his life in a mental institution, trying to come to terms with life outside the place that has been both his prison and his sanctuary. Veteran TV director William A Graham ably steers the action away from mawkish sentimentality, although his fascination with Forrest means several supporting characters are reduced to ciphers. DP

Frederic Forrest *Larry Herman* • Tyne Daly *Nancy Hockworth* • Michael McGuire *Dr McCabe* • Robert Walden *Tom Corman* • Katherine Helmond *Maureen Whitten* ■ *Dir* William A Graham • *Scr* David Seltzer, from the novel *Larry: Case History of a Mistake* by Dr Robert McQueen

Las Vegas Shakedown ★

Crime drama 1955 · US · BW · 79mins

B-movie actor Dennis O'Keefe is in his element in this clichéd thriller about a casino owner whose life is threatened by an ex-con, played with menace and a limp by Thomas Gomez. Coleen Gray, as a demure local schoolteacher, seems carried away by all the excitement. Although set in Las Vegas, it might as well be Dodge City 70 years earlier. AT

Dennis O'Keefe *Joe Barnes* • Coleen Gray *Julia Rae* • Charles Winninger *Mr Raff* • Thomas Gomez *Sirago* ■ *Dir* Sidney Salkow • *Scr* Steve Fisher

The Las Vegas Story ★★

Crime drama 1952 · US · BW · 88mins

There's no real chemistry between Jane Russell and former flame Victor Mature in this routine RKO drama, which involves a phoney murder plot set in a patently studio-bound Las Vegas. Russell performs as though there's no tomorrow, while troupers Vincent Price and Hoagy Carmichael provide professional support, but there's no denying that this film is far from their best. Director Robert Stevenson does what he can with the resolutely substandard screenplay. TS

Jane Russell *Linda Rollins* • Victor Mature *Dave Andrews* • Vincent Price *Lloyd Rollins* • Hoagy Carmichael *Happy* • Brad Dexter *Thomas Hubler* • Gordon Oliver *Drucker* • Jay C Flippen *Harris* ■ *Dir* Robert Stevenson • *Scr* Earl Felton, Harry Essex, Paul Jarrico (uncredited), from a story by Jay Dratler

Laserblast ★

Science-fiction fantasy 1978 · US · Colour · 80mins

This low-budget sci-fi drama appears to have been shot in director Michael Rae's back garden and living room. When teenager Kim Milford finds a laser gun left behind by visiting aliens he decides to wreak vengeance on those who have been making his life a misery. Not as interesting as it sounds, and executed with little imagination or feeling for the genre. RS

Kim Milford *Billy Duncan* • Cheryl Smith *Kathy Farley* • Gianni Russo *Tony Craig* • Ron Masak *Sheriff* • Keenan Wynn *Colonel Farley* • Roddy McDowall *Dr Mellon* ■ *Dir* Michael Rae • *Scr* Franne Schacht, Frank Ray Perilli

Laserhawk ★★ 12

Science-fiction adventure 1997 · Can · Colour · 101mins

Poor old Mark Hamill. Here, in what amounts to little more than a cameo, he lends some doubtful marquee value to a dire sci-fi thriller about a couple of teens who could be the unlikely saviours of Earth, facing an alien invasion. It was a confused and troubled production from day one and it certainly shows on the screen; it doesn't help that the all important effects are pretty ho-hum, too. JF

Jason James Richter *Zach* • Mark Hamill *Bob* • Melissa Galianos *Cara* • Gordon Currie *MK Ultra* ■ *Dir* Jean Pellerin • *Scr* John A Curtis

The Laserman ★★★

Comedy 1988 · US/HK · Colour · 93mins

Mixing sci-fi spoof with a sermon about the proliferation of weapons, this is a hit-and-miss affair from writer/director Peter Wang. Wang also appears as a New York cop, whose scientist friend Marc Hayashi gets embroiled in a sinister plot involving his laser gun project. There are some neat cultural insights and, fittingly, as Wang is on Woody Allen's Manhattan stomping ground, there is an interfering Jewish mother. DP. Contains brief nudity, swearing.

Marc Hayashi *Arthur Weiss* • Maryann Urbano *Jane Cosby* • Tony Kar-Fai Leung [Tony Leung (1)] *Joey Chung* • Peter Wang *Lieutenant Lu* • Joan Copeland *Ruth Weiss* • George Bartenieff *Hanson* • David Chang *Jimmy Weiss* • Sally Yeh *Susu* • Neva Small *Martha Weiss Chung* ■ *Dir/Scr* Peter Wang

Lassie: a New Generation ★★ U

Adventure 1994 · US · Colour · 91mins

Awesomely sentimental updating of the classic family film about the world's most intelligent canine. This time around Jon Tenney and Helen Slater are the city folk finding their feet in the country who are lucky enough to fall under the protective paw of the lovable collie. JF DVD

Jon Tenney *Steve Turner* • Helen Slater *Laura Turner* • Brittany Boyd *Jennifer Turner* • Frederic Forrest *Sam Garland* ■ *Dir* Daniel Petrie • *Scr* Matthew Jacobs, Gary Ross, Elizabeth Anderson

Lassie Come Home ★★★★★ U

Adventure 1943 · US · Colour · 88mins

This is the first and best of the canine capers featuring the lovable collie, whose popularity never waned even though she was actually played by a male dog called Pal. Here, Roddy McDowall is heartbroken when his pet is sold to the local squire, who then moves to Scotland with his granddaughter Elizabeth Taylor. But Lassie takes the high road back to her young master, while everyone dissolves into tears of happiness. Taylor never looked lovelier and Britain glows through MGM-tinted eyes. Of its kind, this is an absolute delight. TH

Roddy McDowall *Joe Carraclough* • Donald Crisp *Sam Carraclough* • Edmund Gwenn *Rowlie* • Dame May Whitty *Dolly* • Nigel Bruce *Duke of Rudling* • Elsa Lanchester *Mrs Carraclough* • Elizabeth Taylor *Priscilla* ■ *Dir* Fred M Wilcox • *Scr* Hugo Butler, from the novel by Eric Knight

Lassie's Great Adventure ★★★ U

Adventure 1963 · US · Colour · 102mins

The intrepid collie finds herself adrift in a balloon with Jon Provost in this outdoor survival story. Lassie and her master trek across the wilds, ward off a ferocious boar, negotiate raging rapids and befriend a native American trapper – all while Provost's parents await news from mountain rescue teams and Mountie patrols. The youngster's ingenuity is utterly unbelievable, but the scenery is fabulous and the dog magnificent. DP

June Lockhart *Ruth Martin* • Hugh Reilly *Paul Martin* • Jon Provost *Timmy* • Robert Howard *Sgt Sprague* • Will J White *Constable MacDonald* • Richard Kiel *Chinook Pete* • Walter Stocker *John Stanley* ■ *Dir* William Beaudine • *Scr* Monroe Manning, Charles O'Neal, from a story by Sumner Arthur Long

Lassiter ★★ 18

Period action adventure 1984 · US · Colour · 95mins

The modestly amiable Tom Selleck never fully recovered from the career blow of losing out on the Indiana Jones role, and this poorly conceived star vehicle did him no favours either. Set in 1934 he plays a London-based American jewel thief blackmailed by Bob Hoskins of the Yard into nabbing a cache of diamonds held in the German embassy. This is let down by an erratic script that doesn't know when to quit with the double-crosses, shaky period atmosphere and uninspired direction. RS

Tom Selleck *Lassiter* • Jane Seymour (2) *Sara* • Lauren Hutton *Kari* • Bob Hoskins *Becker* • Joe Regalbuto *Breeze* • Ed Lauter *Smoke* • Warren Clarke *Max Hofer* ■ *Dir* Roger Young • *Scr* David Taylor

Last Action Hero ★★★★ 15

Comedy action adventure 1993 · US · Colour · 125mins

This is a smart, funny blockbuster that gives director John McTiernan the opportunity to send up not only Arnold Schwarzenegger's heroic image, but also the action genre itself. The story centres around youngster Austin O'Brien, who finds himself sucked into the celluloid world of his biggest hero (Schwarzenegger), as he tracks bad guys Charles Dance and Anthony Quinn in his new film. Things become complicated when the fictional characters take the chance to escape into the real world. Schwarzenegger has rarely been better, and although McTiernan has fun spoofing the conventions of the action genre, he still manages to slip in some spectacular set pieces. JF. Contains swearing and violence. DVD

Arnold Schwarzenegger *Jack Slater* • F Murray Abraham *John Practice* • Art Carney *Frank* • Charles Dance *Benedict* • Frank McRae *Dekker* • Tom Noonan *Ripper* • Robert Prosky *Nick* • Anthony Quinn *Vivaldi* • Mercedes Ruehl *Mom* • Austin O'Brien *Danny Madigan* • Ian McKellen *Death* ■ *Dir* John McTiernan • *Scr* Shane Black, David Arnott, from a story by Zak Penn, Adam Leff

The Last Adventurers ★★

Romantic melodrama 1937 · UK · BW · 77mins

It's a pity there's not much entertainment value to be had from this wonderful curio about a twice-shipwrecked castaway saved by a sea captain whose daughter he then falls in love with, much to the old tar's displeasure. What is fascinating about Roy Kellino's adventure is that it was edited, with greater tautness than it deserves, by director-in-waiting David Lean. The casting is also noteworthy, including future *Carry On* star Esma Cannon in a rare glamour role. DP

Niall MacGinnis *Jeremy Bowker* • Roy Emerton *John Arkell* • Linden Travers *Ann Arkell* • Peter Gawthorne *Fergus Arkell* • Katie Johnson *Susan Arkell* • Kay Walsh *Margaret Arkell* • Johnnie Schofield *Stalky* • Norah Howard *Mary Allen* • Ballard Berkeley *Fred Delvin* • Esma Cannon *Polly Shepherd* • Tony Wylde *Glory Be* ■ *Dir* Roy Kellino • *Scr* Denison Clift

The Last American Hero ★★★★

Biographical drama 1973 · US · Colour · 94mins

While everyone writes about the American cinema in the early 1970s in terms of hotshot talents such as Coppola, Scorsese, Bogdanovich and Friedkin, a lot of other fine movies were being made, lower-key affairs such as this immensely likeable picture directed by Lamont Johnson. The excellent Jeff Bridges stars as a moonshiner's son, who begins a career in stock car racing in order to pay the legal fees of his imprisoned father. By no means an action movie or demolition derby, this is a funky character piece, written with insight and celebrating the survival of the pioneer spirit in modern America. AT

Jeff Bridges *Junior Jackson* • Valerie Perrine *Marge* • Geraldine Fitzgerald *Mrs Jackson* • Ned Beatty *Hackel* • Art Lund *Elroy Jackson Sr* • Gary Busey *Wayne Jackson* • William Smith II [William Smith] *Kyle Kingman* • Ed Lauter *Burton Colt* ■ *Dir* Lamont Johnson • *Scr* William Roberts, from articles by Tom Wolfe

The Last Angry Man ★★★ U

Drama 1959 · US · BW · 99mins

Paul Muni's last Hollywood film (and his first in over a decade) gave him the kind of worthy character he relished portraying: a dedicated doctor working among the Brooklyn poor who has to choose between appearing in a live television tribute and helping a patient in trouble with the police. Muni retained the knack of letting you know you were seeing great acting, and he duly picked up his fifth Oscar nomination as best actor. (His tricks included removing his false teeth to look haggard after a heart attack.) The character could have done with a few faults, but Muni still wins you over and his death scene is very moving. AE

Paul Muni *Dr Sam Abelman* • David Wayne *Woodrow Wilson Thrasher* • Betsy Palmer *Anne Thrasher* • Luther Adler *Dr Max Vogel* • Joby Baker *Myron Malkin* • Joanna Moore *Alice Taggert* • Nancy R Pollock *Sarah Abelman* • Billy Dee Williams *Josh Quincy* ■ *Dir* Daniel Mann • *Scr* Gerald Green, Richard Murphy, from the novel by Gerald Green

The Last Battle ★★★★ 15

Science fiction 1983 · Fr · BW · 88mins

With his first feature – an arresting poetic vision of post-apocalyptic Paris after an unspecified cataclysm has reduced the Earth to a desolate wasteland – director Luc Besson laid the groundwork for *The Fifth Element* and began his long relationship with actor Jean Reno. Four survivors battle for the future of mankind in this stark alternative to *Mad Max*, which conveys its raw emotions in carefully orchestrated, black-and-white visuals without any dialogue (poisonous gases having rendered the characters' vocal chords useless). It's a remarkable achievement that deals with hackneyed holocaust clichés on a compelling, humanistic plane. AJ [VIDEO] DVD

Pierre Jolivet *Young man* • Jean Bouise *Old doctor* • Fritz Wepper *Gang leader* • Jean Reno *Swordsman* ■ *Dir* Luc Besson • *Scr* Luc Besson, Pierre Jolivet

The Last Big Thing ★

Comedy drama 1996 · US · Colour · 98mins

Written, directed by and starring Dan Zukovic – so everyone knows who to blame – this pretentious would-be comedy is a vanity home movie purportedly laying bare America's warped love affair with trashy pop culture. Zukovic decides to attack his target by interviewing C-grade celebrities for *The Next Big Thing*, a fictitious magazine. So begins a steady stream of bogus interviews with empty-headed actors, lousy rock bands, supermodels and trips to stand-up comic venues. A mess. AJ

Dan Zukovic *Simon Geist* • Susan Heimbinder *Darla* • Mark Ruffalo *Brent* • Pamela Dickerson *Tedra* • Andrew Falk *Chris* ■ *Dir/Scr* Dan Zukovic

The Last Blitzkrieg ★

Second World War drama
1958 · US · BW · 84mins

Looking around for a Hollywood actor to play the English-speaking son of a top Nazi general, producer Sam Katzman should never have settled for Van Johnson, whose lightweight presence destroys the picture. Although this was filmed in Holland and uses some local players and crew, the obvious reliance on stock battle footage undermines credibility. AE

Van Johnson *Sergeant Richardson Kroner* • Kerwin Mathews *Wilitz* • Dick York *Sergeant Ludwig* • Larry Storch *Private First Class* • Lise Bourdin *Monique* ■ *Dir* Arthur Dreifuss • *Scr* Lou Morheim

The Last Boy Scout ★★★ 18

Action thriller 1991 · US · Colour · 105mins

The mismatched buddy movie reaches an apotheosis of sorts here in director Tony Scott's flashy, foul-mouthed and formula no-brainer, which forsakes plot for overblown shoot-outs and endless car chases. Lifting it marginally above the thick-ear realm is the engaging chemistry between seedy gumshoe Bruce Willis and ex-footballer Damon Wayans. Both actors let humour spring effortlessly from their own personalities as well as from their screen characters, and the snappy put-downs make the epic mindlessness bearable. AJ. Contains violence, drug abuse, swearing, nudity. [VIDEO] DVD

Bruce Willis *Joe Hallenbeck* • Damon Wayans *Jimmy Dix* • Chelsea Field *Sarah Hallenbeck* • Noble Willingham *Sheldon Marcone* • Taylor Negron *Milo* • Danielle Harris *Darian Hallenbeck* • Halle Berry *Cory* • Bruce McGill *Mike Matthews* • Chelcie Ross *Senator Baynard* ■ *Dir* Tony Scott • *Scr* Shane Black, from a story by Shane Black, Greg Hicks

The Last Bridge ★★★

Drama 1954 · Austria/Yug · BW · 108mins

During the 1950s, Maria Schell (elder sister to Maximilian) enjoyed great international acclaim, receiving a special mention award at the Cannes Festival for this antiwar movie. A rather melancholy demeanour suited her role here as a German doctor forced by Yugoslav patriots to help nurse their wounded, during the Second World War. The moral of the film is that nationality and barriers are irrelevant. Simple perhaps, but movingly told without undue histrionics. BB. A German language film.

Maria Schell *Helga Reinbeck* • Bernhard Wicki *Boro* • Barbara Rutting *Militza* • Carl Mohner *Sergeant Martin Berger* • Horst Haechler *Lieutenant Scherer* • Pable Mincie *Momcillo* ■ *Dir* Helmut Kautner [Helmut Käutner] • *Scr* Helmut Kautner [Helmut Käutner], Norbert Kunze

The Last Broadcast ★★★ 18

Horror 1998 · US · Colour · 87mins

A documentary crew disappears after going into the woods to make a film about a local legend. Sounds familiar? This shoestring documentary-style horror movie was actually made before *The Blair Witch Project*, though it didn't have the same impact. More formally structured than *Blair Witch*, this is about as scary and offers further proof of how easy it is for film-makers to manipulate fiction into a convincing form of "fact". DA [VIDEO] DVD

David Beard *David Leigh, the film-maker* • James Seward *Jim Suerd, the accused* • Stefan Avalos *Steven Avkast, "Fact or Fiction" host* • Lance Weiler *Locus Wheeler, "Fact or Fiction" host* ■ *Dir/Scr* Stefan Avalos, Lance Weiler

The Last Bus Home ★★ 15

Musical comedy drama
1997 · Ire · Colour · 90mins

Rather optimistically pitched as the punk version of *The Commitments*, this low-budget Irish effort remains an entertainingly rough and ready tale of the music business. Set at the end of the 1970s, Annie Ryan and Brian F O'Byrne are the idealistic punks determined to take the music world by storm with their band Dead Patriots. Slick it ain't, but maybe that was the point, and old New Wavers and punks will love the attitude and the vintage soundtrack . JF [VIDEO] DVD

Annie Ryan *Reena* • Brian F O'Byrne *Jessop* • John Cronin *Petie* • Barry Comerford *Joe* • Anthony Brophy *Billy* • Gemma Craven *Reena's mother* • Donal O'Kelly *Richie* • Brendan Coyle *Steve Burkett* ■ *Dir/Scr* Johnny Gogan

The Last Butterfly ★★

Second World War drama
1990 · Fr/Cz/UK · Colour · 110mins

An obscure entry into the Holocaust genre, shot in Czechoslovakia. Tom Courtenay stars as a French mime artist who is duped by the Nazis into performing at a town set aside for Jews. Only when Courtenay arrives does he tumble the fact that his act is purely to impress visiting Red Cross officials; when they are gone the Jews will be shipped to the death camps. Courtenay's mime act, a version of *Hansel and Gretel*, is the highlight in a worthy effort that never quite delivers its promised impact. AT

Tom Courtenay *Antoine Moreau* • Brigitte Fossey *Vera* • Ingrid Held *Michele* • Freddie Jones *Rheinberg* • Milan Knazko *Gruber* ■ *Dir* Karel Kachyna • *Scr* Karel Kachyna, Ota Hofman, from the novel *Les Enfants de Terezin* by Michael Jacot, Alex North

The Last Castle ★★★ 15

Prison thriller 2001 · US · Colour · 125mins

Robert Redford plays a court-martialled three-star general who's sent to a military jail, where he becomes embroiled in an acrimonious battle of wills with martinet warden James Gandolfini (of *Sopranos* fame). However, despite trying to produce a character study rather than an action melodrama, director Rod Lurie offers up a fairly generic prison flick. The pedestrian approach aside, this is still entertaining. TH. Contains violence and swearing. [VIDEO] DVD

Robert Redford *Lieutenant General Eugene R Irwin* • James Gandolfini *Colonel Winter* • Mark Ruffalo *Clifford Yates* • Clifton Collins Jr *Corporal Ramon Aguilar* • Delroy Lindo *General James "Jim" Wheeler* • Steve Burton *Captain Peretz* ■ *Dir* Rod Lurie • *Scr* David Scarpa, Graham Yost, from a story by David Scarpa

The Last Challenge ★★★

Western 1967 · US · Colour · 95mins

Here's a western which satisfyingly refreshes some stock characters and situations. It also has assured performances from Glenn Ford as the gunfighter turned lawman, Angie Dickinson as the saloon keeper who loves him, and Chad Everett as the young gunslinger who wants to kill him to build a reputation. On the strength of performances like the one he gives here, Everett deserved to become a big star; elsewhere, Jack Elam has a straight role as a hired gun. Richard Thorpe's slack direction lets the strong script (by John Sherry and Robert Emmett Ginna) carry the picture. AE

Glenn Ford *Marshal Dan Blaine* • Angie Dickinson *Lisa Denton* • Chad Everett *Lot McGuire* • Gary Merrill *Squint Calloway* • Jack Elam *Ernest Scarnes* • Delphi Lawrence *Marie Webster* ■ *Dir* Richard Thorpe • *Scr* John Sherry, Robert Emmett Ginna, from the novel *Pistolero's Progress* by John Sherry

The Last Chase ★★

Science fiction 1981 · US · Colour · 101mins

A hymn to that most American of institutions: the car. Set in the near future, this reactionary riposte to the green movement has Lee Majors achieving heroic status when he defies the authorities by driving his banned gas-guzzler across the country. Burgess Meredith is the wily pilot detailed to stop him. Hugely funny, though for all the wrong reasons. JF

Lee Majors *Frank Hart* • Burgess Meredith *Captain Williams* • Chris Makepeace *Ring* • Alexandra Stewart *Eudora* ■ *Dir* Martyn Burke • *Scr* CR O'Christopher, Taylor Sutherland, Martyn Burke, from the story by CR O'Christopher

The Last Command ★★★★★

Silent drama 1928 · US · BW · 87mins

The love-hate relationship between moody actor Emil Jannings and archetypal tyrant-director Josef von Sternberg created this masterpiece with its story of a Tsarist general (Jannings) working for peanuts as a bit-player in Hollywood. The extended flashback takes in his life in revolutionary Russia – including his seduction of a Communist actress (Evelyn Brent) – and his feud with a radical theatrical director who becomes his grudging benefactor in Tinseltown. Jannings is satisfyingly arrogant to the point of dementia, while von Sternberg's visuals have a poetic lyricism to offset the sour nature of the characters and story. A remarkable portrait of Russia and Hollywood at the height of their powers. TH

Emil Jannings *Gen Dolgorucki/Grand Duke Sergius Alexander* • Evelyn Brent *Natascha Dobrowa* • William Powell *Leo Andreiev* • Nicholas Soussanin *Adjutant* ■ *Dir* Josef von Sternberg • *Scr* John F Goodrich, Herman J mankiewicz (titles), from the story by Lajos Biró • *Cinematographer* Bert Glennon

The Last Command ★★★ PG

Historical western
1955 · US · Colour · 105mins

This recounting of the story of the Alamo is directed by veteran Frank Lloyd on what must have been Republic Studios' highest-ever budget. The tale is well told, with star Sterling Hayden making a most impressive Jim Bowie and veteran character actor Arthur Hunnicutt portraying a grizzled and probably accurate Davy Crockett. There's a healthy air of historical accuracy and it's enjoyable, although lacking in stature. TS [VIDEO]

Sterling Hayden *James Bowie* • Anna Maria Alberghetti *Consuela* • Richard Carlson *William Travis* • Arthur Hunnicutt *Davy Crockett* • Ernest Borgnine *Mike Radin* • J Carrol Naish *Santa Anna* ■ *Dir* Frank Lloyd • *Scr* Warren Duff, from a story by Sy Bartlett

The Last Contract ★★★

Crime drama
1998 · Swe/Nor/Fin · Colour · 114mins

The publication of John W Grow's pseudonymous novel about the murder of prime minister Olof Palme sent shockwaves through Sweden. However, Kjell Sundvall's thriller refuses to repeat the book's controversial accusations, settling instead for a flashback reconstruction of events leading up to the assassination. Echoes of *The Day of the Jackal* continuously reverberate as cop Mikael Persbrandt dogs the steps of international hitman Michael Kitchen. The action is suspenseful enough to sustain the interest. DP. A Swedish language film.

Pernilla August *Roger's ex-wife* • Michael Kitchen *Killer* • Mikael Persbrandt *Roger* • Reine Brynolfsson *Bo Ekman* • Bjørn Floberg *Tom Nielsen* • Jacqueline Ramel *Helene Salonen* ■ *Dir* Kjell Sundvall • *Scr* Borje Hansson, Mats Aréhn, Johan Bogaeus, from the novel *Sista kontraktet* by John W Grow

Last Dance ★★★ 18

Crime drama 1996 · US · Colour · 98mins

This prison drama has Sharon Stone languishing on death row for a dozen years, condemned to die for murdering two teenagers. Rob Morrow and Randy Quaid are the parole officers who oppose capital punishment, while flashbacks gradually reveal the true nature of Stone's crime. Stone's performance as the teenage social outcast now grown up is generally impressive and Bruce Beresford's direction is typically elegant and controlled, though the ending is a bit of a cop-out. AT. Contains swearing and violence. [VIDEO] DVD

Sharon Stone *Cindy Liggett* • Rob Morrow *Rick Hayes* • Randy Quaid *Sam Burns* • Peter Gallagher *John Hayes* • Jack Thompson *The Governor* • Jayne Brook *Jill* • Pamela Tyson *Legal aid attorney* • Skeet Ulrich *Billy* ■ *Dir* Bruce Beresford • *Scr* Ron Koslow, from a story by Ron Koslow, Steven Haft

The Last Days ★★★★ PG

Documentary
1998 · US · Colour and BW · 87mins

Steven Spielberg's obsession with the Holocaust continues with this remarkable documentary, in which five elderly survivors of the concentration camps return to compare then with now. The *Schindler's List* director executive-produced the film with the Shoah Foundation. Such was the Nazis' hatred for the Jews that, even though they knew they were defeated, they still set out to destroy them in Hungary during the "last days" of the Second World War. James Moll has assembled some poignant archive material which, combined with the survivors' testimony, makes piteously compelling viewing. However, the conclusion manages to be uplifting by showing the children and grandchildren who surround the survivors in their personal last days. TH

Dir/Scr James Moll

Last Days ★★★

Drama 2005 · US · Colour · 96mins

Gus Van Sant uses the 1994 suicide of Nirvana frontman Kurt Cobain to

L

explore death and loneliness. A rangy Cobain lookalike, Michael Pitt essays rocker-in-exile Blake as muttering and paranoid, stumbling around an unheated mansion and adjacent woods in search of a release from his demons. For the most part we must accept the "genius" that attracts parasitic hangers on. But through two songs, written and played by Pitt, we finally see the incoherent Blake communicate. Van Sant's single-angle shots, jarring sound design and disjointed, repetitive, impressionistic style will irritate some, but haunt others. AC

Michael Pitt *Blake* • Lukas Haas *Luke* • Asia Argento *Asia* • Scott Green *Scott* • Nicole Vicius *Nicole* • Ricky Jay *Detective* • Ryan Orion *Donovan* • Harmony Korine *Guy in club* ■ *Dir/Scr* Gus Van Sant

The Last Days of Chez Nous ★★★ 15

Drama 1992 · Aus · Colour · 92mins

Although she is becoming increasingly known for her costume dramas, Australian director Gillian Armstrong made her name with a series of documentaries about three working-class Adelaide women. Her experience of capturing the rhythms of everyday speech and making the most of confined spaces serves her well in this chatty character study, in which novelist Lisa Harrow reassesses her relationships with her husband Bruno Ganz and every member of her less-than-predictable family. Unfortunately, Harrow is the weakest link in a strong cast, with Kerry Fox typically arresting as the sister who makes a move on Ganz, and Bill Hunter excellent as their bluff father. DP DVD

Lisa Harrow *Beth* • Bruno Ganz *JP* • Kerry Fox *Vicki* • Miranda Otto *Annie* • Kiri Paramore *Tim* • Bill Hunter *Beth's father* • Lex Marinos *Angelo* • Mickey Camilleri *Sally* ■ *Dir* Gillian Armstrong • *Scr* Helen Garner

The Last Days of Disco ★★★ 15

Comedy drama 1998 · US · Colour · 108mins

Writer/director Whit Stillman captures – not completely successfully – the lives of the bright young things in the early 1980s who work by day and boogie on down at night before the death knell sounded for disco. Kate Beckinsale and Chloë Sevigny are overly mannered as the two girls who use an exclusive disco to meet rich kids, while Matt Keeslar and Robert Sean Leonard are among the male yuppie types who hook up with them. None of the characters in Stillman's sharply scripted world are remotely engaging, so just enjoy the disco music. JB. Contains violence, swearing, drug abuse, nudity.

Chloë Sevigny *Alice* • Kate Beckinsale *Charlotte* • Chris Eigeman *Des* • MacKenzie Astin *Jimmy* • Matt Keeslar *Josh* • Robert Sean Leonard *Tom* • Jennifer Beals *Nina* ■ *Dir/Scr* Whit Stillman

The Last Days of Dolwyn ★★ U

Drama 1949 · UK · BW · 95mins

Freely adapted from a historical incident, this is a classic example of how to squeeze all the life out of an intriguing situation by coating it with a thick layer of significance. The flooding of a Welsh valley, the refusal of an old woman to leave her home and the attempts of a murderer to conceal his crime should add up to a compelling drama. But Emlyn Williams spoils everything with a stagey approach, which sees everyone speaking in deliberate tones that owe nothing to real life. Richard Burton impresses in his debut, but the film belongs squarely to Dame Edith Evans. DP

Dame Edith Evans [Edith Evans] *Merri* • Emlyn Williams *Rob* • Richard Burton *Gareth* • Anthony James *Dafydd* • Barbara Couper *Lady Dolwyn* • Alan Aynesworth *Lord Lancashire* • Andrea Lea *Margaret* • Hugh Griffith *Minister* ■ *Dir/Scr* Emlyn Williams

The Last Days of Frankie the Fly ★★ 18

Crime drama 1996 · US · Colour · 91mins

Quentin Tarantino has a lot to answer for. If he hadn't cast Michael Madsen as the sadistic Mr Blonde in *Reservoir Dogs* we might never have been able to enjoy his performance as a Mob boss in this black comedy drama. Dennis Hopper is Madsen's luckless henchman who gets bitten by the movie-making bug and an insane desire to showcase the acting talents of Daryl Hannah. A game cast try to add punchy humour to the movie satire and acerbic resonance to the violent traits, but fails. AJ. Contains swearing, sexual references, violence. DVD

Dennis Hopper *Frankie* • Daryl Hannah *Margaret* • Kiefer Sutherland *Joey* • Michael Madsen *Sal* • Dayton Callie *Vic* ■ *Dir* Peter Markle • *Scr* Dayton Callie

The Last Days of Mussolini ★★★★

Second World War drama
1974 · It · Colour · 126mins

Rod Steiger contributes his own personal portrayal of the Fascist tyrant in an Italian film that allows the man to have a certain amount of vulnerability. Carlo Lizzani's drama shows him on the run – with mistress Lisa Gastoni – in the days before his own people caught him and strung him upside down from a lamp post. Steiger is tremendous as Mussolini, whom he would play again seven years later in *Lion of the Desert*. TH

Rod Steiger *Benito Mussolini* • Lisa Gastoni *Clara Petacci* • Henry Fonda *Cardinal Schuster* • Franco Nero *Col Valerio* • Lino Capolicchio *Pedro* ■ *Dir* Carlo Lizzani • *Scr* Carlo Lizzani, Fabio Pittorru • *Music* Ennio Morricone

The Last Days of Pompeii ★★★

Period drama 1935 · US · BW · 94mins

After trashing much of Manhattan in *King Kong*, producer Merian C Cooper and director Ernest B Schoedsack turned their attention to ancient Rome's most famous natural disaster. Basil Rathbone gives a fine performance as Pontius Pilate and Preston Foster is adequate in the lead role as a young blacksmith who becomes an amoral gladiator. If you can ignore the piety, this is a rousing yarn, with some good arena scenes and the best special effects money could buy at the time. AT

Preston Foster *Marcus* • Basil Rathbone *Pontius Pilate* • Alan Hale *Burbix* • John Wood *Flavius (as a man)* • Louis Calhern *Prefect* ■ *Dir* Ernest B Schoedsack • *Scr* Ruth Rose, Boris Ingster, from a story by James Ashmore Creelman, Melville Baker

The Last Days of Pompeii ★★

Period adventure 1960 · It · Colour · 94mins

Steve Reeves, the uncrowned king of the muscleman epic, is gladiator Glaucus, searching downtown Pompeii for the people who murdered his father. At first it looks like the Christians but then an insurrectionist plot is traced back to the temple priests and an Egyptian princess. Just when things seems to get sorted, Vesuvius blows its top! AT. Italian dialogue dubbed into English.

Steve Reeves *Glaucus* • Christine Kaufmann *Ione* • Barbara Carroll *Nydia* • Anne-Marie Baumann *Julia* • Mimmo Palmara *Gallinus* • Fernando Rey *High priest* ■ *Dir* Mario Bonnard • *Scr* Ennio De Concini, Sergio Leone, Duccio Tessari, Sergio Corbucci

The Last Debate ★★★ 15

Drama 2000 · US · Colour · 95mins

Director John Badham is best known for his no-nonsense action thrillers but he acquits himself pretty well with this absorbing TV movie about political skulduggery and media ethics. It focuses on a televised political debate in which journalists roast a candidate over a supposed scandal in his past. However, the interviewers find themselves in the firing line when another reporter (Peter Gallagher) questions the motives of those posing the questions. Venerable James Garner steals the show as the veteran panel moderator. JF

James Garner *Mike Howley* • Peter Gallagher *Tom Chapman* • Audra McDonald *Barbara Manning* • Donna Murphy *Joan Naylor* ■ *Dir* John Badham • *Scr* Jon Maas, from the novel by Jim Lehrer

The Last Detail ★★★★ 18

Drama 1973 · US · Colour · 99mins

Back in the early 1970s, star Jack Nicholson, writer Robert Towne and director Hal Ashby were the hippest team in Hollywood. Nicholson and Towne went on to *Chinatown* and Ashby and Towne to *Shampoo*; they could do no wrong and this earlier effort still has a combustible power. It's a story of two naval petty officers (Nicholson, Otis Young) and the pathetic young criminal (Randy Quaid) they have to escort to jail. Towne's script consists almost entirely of profanities and justifiably so, considering the characters aren't exactly choirboys. TH DVD

Jack Nicholson *Billy "Bad Ass" Buddusky* • Otis Young *"Mule" Mulhall* • Randy Quaid *Larry Meadows* • Clifton James *Chief master-at-arms* • Michael Moriarty *Marine duty officer* • Carol Kane *Young whore* ■ *Dir* Hal Ashby • *Scr* Robert Towne, from the novel by Darryl Ponicsan

The Last Dragon ★★ 15

Martial arts adventure
1985 · US · Colour · 106mins

Martial arts comes to Harlem in a kung fu adventure, which not surprisingly has an element of homage to Bruce Lee. With Motown guru Berry Gordy backing the project, there are plenty of musical interludes as well. Director Michael Schultz tries hard but can't quite tie the varied elements of action, romance, comedy and musical video together, though, as entertainment, this is engaging enough. NF. Contains swearing.

Taimak *Leroy Green* • Vanity *Laura Charles* • Christopher Murney *Eddie Arcadian* • Julius J Carry III *Sho'nuff* • Faith Prince *Angela* • Leo O'Brien *Richie* • Mike Starr *Rock* • Keshia Pulliam [Keshia Knight Pulliam] *Sophia* ■ *Dir* Michael Schultz • *Scr* Louis Venosta

Last Embrace ★★★★ 18

Thriller 1979 · US · Colour · 97mins

Jonathan Demme's early work shows some debt to Hitchcock. As Roy Scheider convincingly plays an agent being used for target practice with a riveting mix of bleakness, determination and paranoia, Demme never loses his grip, piling on the unsettling Hitch-style claustrophobia. The suspense is aided enormously by Tak Fujimoto's atmospheric camerawork and Miklos Rosza's thoughtful, vibrant score. JM. Contains swearing and nudity.

Roy Scheider *Harry Hannan* • Janet Margolin *Ellie Fabian* • John Glover *Richard Peabody* • Sam Levene *Sam Urdell* • Charles Napier *Dave Quittle* • Christopher Walken *Eckart* • Jacqueline Brookes *Dr Coopersmith* • Mandy Patinkin *Commuter* ■ *Dir* Jonathan Demme • *Scr* David Shaber, from the novel *The Thirteenth Man* by Murray Teigh Bloom

The Last Emperor ★★★★ 15

Epic biographical drama
1987 · It/UK/Ch · Colour · 209mins

The first western production to be allowed to film inside Beijing's Forbidden City and the winner of nine Oscars, Bernardo Bertolucci's majestic epic is one of the most visually arresting pictures of its time.The design beautifully juxtaposes the pre- and post-revolutionary Chinese worlds, and the red and yellow trappings of the simple uniforms of Mao's republic are stunningly displayed. However, the glorious images distance the viewer from the momentous events that overtook 20th-century China and, in spite of a multifaceted performance from John Lone, Emperor Pu Yi remains a stranger, even at the end of the film. DP. Contains swearing and brief nudity. DVD

John Lone *Aisin-Gioro "Henry" Pu Yi, as an adult* • Joan Chen *Elizabeth* • Peter O'Toole *Reginald Johnston, "RJ"* • Ying Ruocheng *Governor* • Victor Wong (2) *Chen Pao Shen* • Dennis Dun *Big Li* • Ryuichi Sakamoto *Masahiko Amakasu* • Maggie Han *Eastern Jewel* • Ric Young *Interrogator* ■ *Dir* Bernardo Bertolucci • *Scr* Bernardo Bertolucci, Mark Peploe, Enzo Ungari • *Cinematographer* Vittorio Storaro

The Last Escape ★★ U

Second World War drama
1970 · US · Colour · 90mins

United Artists had a pair of big hits in the 1960s with two war movies – *The Great Escape* and *633 Squadron*, both terrific action movies with knockout music scores. Having secured an audience for this type of subject, UA then worked the subject of the Second World War into the ground with films such as this one. It isn't any good, and smells of catchpenny picture-making, but Margit Saad looks nice and Stuart Whitman is amiable. TS

Stuart Whitman *Captain Lee Mitchell* • John Collin *Sgt Henry McBee* • Pinkas Braun *Von Heinken* • Martin Jarvis *Lt Donald Wilcox* • Günther Neutze *Major Hessel* • Margit Saad *Karen Gerhardt* • Patrick Jordan *Major Griggs* • Johnny Briggs *Corporal O'Connell* ■ *Dir* Walter E Grauman [Walter Grauman] • *Scr* Herman Hoffman, from a story by John C Champion, Barry Trivers

Last Exit to Brooklyn ★★★ 18

Drama 1989 · W Ger · Colour · 98mins

Director Uli Edel's hard-hitting adaptation is as depressing a film as you'll ever see. That's not to say it isn't an accomplished movie, but its brutal early-1950s Brooklyn backdrop, plus the gallery of abusive lowlifes, make for very uncomfortable viewing, especially during the climactic drunken gang bang involving prostitute Jennifer Jason Leigh. Artistically shot and lit by cinematographer Stefan Czapsky, the film also benefits from some strong acting and a moody score from Mark Knopfler. JC. Contains swearing, sex scenes, violence, nudity and drug abuse. DVD

Stephen Lang *Harry Black* • Jennifer Jason Leigh *Tralala* • Burt Young *Big Joe* • Peter Dobson *Vinnie* • Jerry Orbach *Boyce* • Stephen Baldwin *Sal* • Jason Andrews *Tony* • Ricki Lake *Donna* • Hubert Selby Jr *Cab driver* ■ *Dir* Ulrich Edel [Uli Edel] • *Scr* Desmond Nakano, from the short story collection by Hubert Selby Jr

The Last Flight ★★★

Drama 1931 · US · BW · 80mins

A fascinating early talkie, one of the few key films to deal with the legendary "lost generation", those American expatriates who found themselves in Paris or Madrid in the 1920s, characters beloved by authors F Scott Fitzgerald (who coined the phrase) and Ernest Hemingway. Former silent screen matinée idol Richard Barthelmess plays a flying ace and today's audiences may find his performance a little mannered, though his face remains tenderly expressive. The film marks the Hollywood debut of German émigré director Wilhelm Dieterle, later to distinguish himself with a series of Paul Muni biopics. TS

Richard Barthelmess *Cary Lockwood* • John Mack Brown [Johnny Mack Brown] *Bill Talbot* • Helen Chandler *Nikki* • David Manners *Shep Lambert* • Elliott Nugent *Francis* • Walter Byron *Frink* ■ *Dir* Wilhelm Dieterle [William Dieterle] • *Scr* John Monk Saunders, from the novel *Single Lady* by John Monk Saunders

The Last Flight of Noah's Ark ★ U

Adventure 1980 · US · Colour · 93mins

Quite what Disney hoped to achieve with this anaemic adventure is anyone's guess. Director Charles Jarrott seemed to think he could thrill youngsters with a plane crash, a storm at sea, a pair of young stowaways and some scene-stealing animals, while amusing the grown-ups with the *African Queen*-like banter between pilot Elliott Gould and missionary Geneviève Bujold. Wrong. DP [video]

Elliott Gould *Noah Dugan* • Geneviève Bujold *Bernadette Lafleur* • Ricky Schroder [Rick Schroder] *Bobby* • Tammy Lauren *Julie* • Vincent Gardenia *Stoney* • John Fujioka *Cleveland* • Yuki Shimoda *Hiro* ■ *Dir* Charles Jarrott • *Scr* Steven W Carabatsos, Sandy Glass, George Arthur Bloom, from the story by Ernest K Gann

The Last Frontier ★★★

Western 1955 · US · Colour · 98mins

A majestic and brooding western from director Anthony Mann, set mostly at night. In the story of three fur trappers who take jobs as cavalry scouts after losing their pelts to Indians, Mann's use of early CinemaScope is exemplary, with splendid tracking and panning shots, and there's some fascinating political commentary about the civilising of noble savage Victor Mature. Robert Preston is excellent as a single-minded military martinet, while the young Anne Bancroft shows early promise as his wife. TS

Victor Mature *Jed* • Guy Madison *Captain Riordan* • Robert Preston *Colonel Frank Marston* • James Whitmore *Gus* • Anne Bancroft *Corinna Marston* • Russell Collins *Captain Clark* • Peter Whitney *Sergeant Major Decker* • Pat Hogan *Mungo* ■ *Dir* Anthony Mann • *Scr* Philip Yordan, Russell S Hughes, from the novel *The Gilded Rooster* by Richard Emery Roberts

The Last Gangster ★★★

Crime drama 1937 · US · BW · 81mins

Edward G Robinson turns on the menace in the title role of what was among the last products of the golden age of 1930s' gangster movies. Some critics rated his portrayal of a pathological hood out for revenge as highly as his famed performance seven years earlier in *Little Caesar*. Taut direction, snappy writing and a talented supporting cast, including James Stewart, add to the value of an engrossing melodrama, only let down by a soppy ending. PF

Edward G Robinson *Joe Krozac* • James Stewart *Paul North* • Rose Stradner *Talva Krozac* • Lionel Stander *Curly* • Douglas Scott *Paul North Jr* • John Carradine *Casper* • Sidney Blackmer *San Francisco editor* • Edward Brophy *"Fats" Garvey* ■ *Dir* Edward Ludwig • *Scr* John Lee Mahin, from a story by William A Wellman, Robert Carson

Last Gasp ★★ 18

Thriller 1995 · US · Colour · 88mins

Ruthless real estate developer Robert Patrick slaughters a tribe of Mexican Indians for their land, only to become possessed by one of their spirits. Turning into a homicidal maniac with a painted face, he will stop at nothing to guard the ancient territory. Joanna Pacula is the concerned wife of one of his victims who tries to uncover the secret behind her husband's disappearance.The unrelieved grimness makes it more depressing than creepy. AJ [video] DVD

Robert Patrick *Leslie Chase* • Joanna Pacula *Nora Weeks* • Vyto Ruginis *Ray Tattinger* • Mimi Craven *Goldie* • Alexander Enberg *Duane* ■ *Dir* Scott McGinnis • *Scr* Pierce Milestone, Stanley Isaacs, David N Twohy [David Twohy]

The Last Gentleman ★

Comedy drama 1934 · US · BW · 78mins

Desperately dated comedy about an 80-year-old millionaire (George Arliss) who spends the whole film dying while his relatives descend like vultures waiting for him to expire. Panned by critics on release as being stagey and slow-paced, this musty old comedy will seem interminable – the constant ticking and chiming of Arliss's collection of 106 clocks don't help either. However, Arliss's dwindling army of admirers may enjoy it and the climax is ingenious. AT

George Arliss *Cabot Barr* • Edna May Oliver *Augusta* • Janet Beecher *Helen* • Charlotte Henry *Marjorie* • Frank Albertson *Allan* • Rafaela Ottiano *Retta* • Ralph Morgan *Loring* • Edward Ellis *Claude* ■ *Dir* Sidney Lanfield • *Scr* Leonard Praskins, from the play *The Head of the Family* by Katharine Clugston

The Last Good Time ★★

Romantic drama 1994 · US · Colour · 90mins

This is a restrained romance, about an ageing violinist who starts making beautiful music with a young girl who's fleeing an abusive boyfriend. Although the film strives for the Euro feel of Louis Malle's *Atlantic City USA*, it never quite achieves it, despite sterling performances from the leads Armin Mueller-Stahl and Olivia D'Abo. While it hits many of the right notes, it needs to have projected more. DA

Armin Mueller-Stahl *Joseph Kopple* • Olivia D'Abo *Charlotte Zwicki* • Maureen Stapleton *Ida Cutler* • Lionel Stander *Howard Singer* • Adrian Pasdar *Eddie* • Kevin Corrigan *Frank* • Zohra Lampert *Barbara* ■ *Dir* Bob Balaban • *Scr* Bob Balaban, John J McLaughlin, from the novel by Richard Bausch

The Last Great Wilderness ★★★ 18

Road movie comedy thriller 2002 · UK/Den · Colour · 92mins

Alastair Mackenzie stars in this offbeat drama directed by his brother David. Mackenzie plays Charlie, who's on his way to Skye to burn down the house of the pop star who ran off with his wife. On the road he meets Vincente (Jonny Phillips), who's on the run from thugs employed by a cuckolded husband, and they stumble across an isolated retreat, where the residents include a sex addict and a paedophile. Though hampered by budgetary restrictions, this is nevetheless a brave venture that taps into the spirit of *The Wicker Man*, but ultimately defies categorisation. BP [video] DVD

Alastair Mackenzie (2) *Charlie* • Jonny Phillips *Vincente* • Ewan Stewart *Magnus* • David Hayman *Ruaridh* • Victoria Smurfit *Claire* • Louise Irwin *Morag* • Jane Stenson *Flora* • John Comerford *Paul* ■ *Dir* David Mackenzie • *Scr* Michael Tait, Alastair Mackenzie, Gillian Berrie, David Mackenzie

The Last Grenade ★★

Action drama 1970 · UK · Colour · 93mins

Stanley Baker never quite attained the heady heights his obvious talents deserved and by the 1970s was the forgotten star of British cinema. Films like this only accelerated his decline, a predictable revenge drama with plenty of explosions and fights but little cranial activity. Baker plays a tough mercenary who vows retribution against a traitorous ex-colleague. Along the way he falls for the charms of Honor Blackman in a ludicrous subplot riddled with the kind of dialogue even soap operas would reject. RS

Stanley Baker *Major Harry Grigsby* • Alex Cord *Kip Thompson* • Honor Blackman *Mrs Katherine Whiteley* • Richard Attenborough *General Charles Whiteley* • Rafer Johnson *Joe Jackson* • Andrew Keir *Gordon Mackenzie* • Ray Brooks *Lieutenant David Coulson* • Julian Glover *Andy Royal* • John Thaw *Terry Mitchell* ■ *Dir* Gordon Flemyng • *Scr* Kenneth Ware, John Sherlock, James Mitchell, from the novel *The Ordeal of Major Grigsby* by John Sherlock

The Last Hard Men ★

Western 1976 · US · Colour · 97mins

You expect a lot better than this violent, sadistic revenge western from a picture starring Charlton Heston and James Coburn. The latter is the villain whose plan for getting back at former lawman Heston includes kidnapping his virginal daughter (played by Barbara Hershey) and having her raped within his sight. Director Andrew V McLaglen copies Sam Peckinpah's use of slow motion for key moments but misses the relentless intensity. Nasty. AE

Charlton Heston *Sam Burgade* • James Coburn *Zach Provo* • Barbara Hershey *Susan Burgade* • Jorge Rivero *Cesar Menendez* • Michael Parks *Sheriff Noel Nye* • Larry Wilcox *Mike Shelby* ■ *Dir* Andrew V McLaglen • *Scr* Guerdon Trueblood, from the novel *Gun Down* by Brian Garfield

Last Holiday ★★★ U

Comedy drama 1950 · UK · BW · 88mins

An amiable ensemble affair, Alec Guinness holds centre stage, as a stuffed shirt who, having been diagnosed with a fatal illness, discovers all-too-late that he's been missing out on the finer things in life. It's the supporting cast, however, that gives the film the animated gentility that is so achingly British. Kay Walsh, Wilfrid Hyde White, Sid James and Ernest Thesiger stand out among the eccentrics and everyday folk who populate JB Priestley's heart-warming script. Corny, perhaps, but nice. DP

Alec Guinness *George Bird* • Beatrice Campbell *Sheila Rockingham* • Kay Walsh *Mrs Poole* • Bernard Lee *Inspector Wilton* • Wilfrid Hyde White *Chalfont* • Muriel George *Lady Oswington* • Sidney James *Joe Clarence* ■ *Dir* Henry Cass • *Scr* JB Priestley

The Last Horror Movie ★★ 18

Horror thriller 2003 · UK · Colour · 78mins

This thriller is no doubt meant to be provocative and controversial, but it just tries too hard. The film follows the "exploits" of serial killer Kevin Howarth, who interrupts *vérité* video footage of his appallingly brutal crimes with speeches delivered to camera, attempting to explain his nihilist motives while challenging the audience for continuing to watch. Its pseudo-intellectual overtones sit uneasily with its more avowed exploitation elements and the extreme violence will certainly be too much for some audiences. AS

Kevin Howarth *Max Parry* • Mark Stevenson *Assistant* • Antonia Beamish *Petra* • Christabel Muir *Sam* • Jonathan Coote *John* • Rita Davies *Grandma* • John Berlyne *Phil* • Jim Bywater *Bill* ■ *Dir* Julian Richards • *Scr* James Handel, from an idea by Julian Richards

Last House on the Left ★★★ 18

Horror 1972 · US · Colour · 80mins

This was the legendary graphic shocker which put director Wes Craven on the road to horror fame. Inspired by Ingmar Bergman's *The Virgin Spring*, and infused by a repellent Vietnam sensibility, two girls are kidnapped on the way to a rock concert by four sadistic convicts and are subjected to humiliating rape, torture and death. Their parents then mete out an equally horrific revenge when the foursome conveniently turn up on their doorstep. This hard-to-watch and highly controversial cult film gains enormous power from its low-budget trappings and *cinéma vérité* approach. A benchmark in the annals of cinematic offensiveness. AJ [video] DVD

David A Hess [David Hess] *Krug* • Lucy Grantham *Phyllis* • Sandra Cassel *Mari Collingwood* • Marc Sheffler *Junior* ■ *Dir/Scr* Wes Craven

The Last Hunt ★★★★

Western 1956 · US · Colour · 108mins

Robert Taylor plays against his heroic, matinée idol image as a crazed, racist buffalo hunter who slaughters animals, tribesmen and anything else that comes close in an early "anti-western". Stewart Granger is another hunter, not quite in Taylor's league, who finally becomes disillusioned and steals pretty native American woman Debra Paget away from his partner. This remains an unsentimental movie, with muscular direction from Richard Brooks who achieves much authenticity by staging the action in Custer State Park, South Dakota, during the annual cull of the buffalo herd. AT

Robert Taylor (1) *Charles Gilson* • Stewart Granger *Sandy McKenzie* • Lloyd Nolan *Woodfoot* • Debra Paget *Indian girl* • Russ Tamblyn *Jimmy* • Constance Ford *Peg* ■ *Dir* Richard Brooks • *Scr* Richard Brooks, from the novel by Milton Lott

The Last Hurrah ★★★ U

Political drama 1958 · US · BW · 120mins

Spencer Tracy stars as an old-time political operator standing for mayor one last time and observed with wide-eyed approval by his nephew, Jeffrey Hunter. This is a great part for Tracy and he runs and runs with it, turning on the Irish-American blarney when it suits him, showing expediency and iron-hard calculation when he thinks no one is looking. As so often with John Ford's films, there's also a flabby sentimentality even when he's dealing with the cut-throat electoral process, but the film's optimism anticipated the defeat of Nixon and the triumph of Kennedy in 1961. AT

Spencer Tracy *Frank Skeffington* • Jeffrey Hunter *Adam Caulfield* • Dianne Foster *Maeve Caulfield* • Pat O'Brien *John Gorman* • Basil Rathbone *Norman Cass Sr* • Donald Crisp *The Cardinal* • James Gleason *Cuke Gillen* • Edward Brophy *Ditto Boland* ■ *Dir* John Ford • *Scr* Frank Nugent, from the novel by Edwin O'Conner

Last Images of the Shipwreck ★★★ 15

Drama 1989 · Arg/Sp · Colour · 122mins

Although it provides an unflinching glimpse of Buenos Aires lowlife, Eliseo Subiela's second feature is primarily concerned with the relationship between life and art. Trapped in both his marriage and his job, insurance salesman Lorenzo Quinteros becomes convinced that he has found the subject for his much-stalled novel after he encounters prostitute Noemi Frenkel and her three bizarre brothers. The pacing is occasionally ponderous and the fantasy elements incongruous, but the performances are first-rate. DP. In Spanish with English subtitles.

Lorenzo Quinteros *Roberto* • Noemi Frenkel *Estela* • Hugo Soto *Claudio* • Pablo Brichta *Jose* • Sara Benitez *Mother* • Andres Tiengo *Mario* ■ *Dir/Scr* Eliseo Subiela

The Last Island ★★★★

Drama 1990 · Neth · Colour · 115mins

A superior screenplay, telling characterisation and strong ensemble acting are the qualities that make this tale about the survivors of an airline crash marooned on a desert island into an engrossing and distinctive drama. Sharp direction by noted film-maker Marleen Gorris also helps expose the brutish realities that lie beneath the biscuit-thin veneer of what we like to think of as civilisation. Almost an adult version of *Lord of the Flies*. PF. In English and Dutch with subtitles. Contains swearing.

Patricia Hayes *Mrs Godame* • Paul Freeman *Sean* • Shelagh McLeod *Joanna* • Ian Tracey *Jack* • Marc Berman *Pierre* • Kenneth Colley *Nick* • Mark Hembrow *Frank* ■ *Dir/Scr* Marleen Gorris

The Last Journey ★★★ U

Drama 1936 · UK · BW · 62mins

By turns thrilling, ludicrous, tense and just plain naff, this British B-movie is well worth seeking out. Julian Mitchell plays a train driver who is forced into retirement and is so consumed by jealousy over his fireman's dalliance with his wife that he decides his last journey will end in disaster. After he forces the fireman to stoke the engine up to dangerously high speed, passenger and brain specialist Godfrey Tearle starts his heroic clamber along the speeding train to do his "there there, old chap, let's all have a nice cup of tea" speech. AT

Godfrey Tearle *Specialist* • Hugh Williams *Man* • Judy Gunn *Girl* • Mickey Brantford *Boy* • Julien Mitchell *Driver* • Olga Lindo *Wife* • Michael Hogan (1) *Fireman* ■ *Dir* Bernard Vorhaus • *Scr* John Soutar, H Fowler Mear, from the story *The Last Journey* by J Jefferson Farjeon

The Last Kiss ★★★ 15

Romantic comedy
2001 · It · Colour · 118mins

Exploring both the fear of commitment of a late 20-something male and the gnawing disappointment of his prospective mother-in-law, Gabriele Muccino's engaging ensemble piece also succeeds in alternating between romantic comedy and soap opera without becoming quaint or melodramatic. Much of this has to do with the screenplay's calculated intricacy and the accomplished performances of Stefano Accorsi and Stefania Sandrelli. Warm and witty. DP. In Italian with English subtitles.

Stefano Accorsi *Carlo* • Giovanna Mezzogiorno *Giulia* • Stefania Sandrelli *Anna* • Claudio Santamaria *Paolo* • Marco Cocci *Alberto* • Pierfrancesco Favino *Marco* • Sabrina Impacciatore *Livia* ■ *Dir* Gabriele Muccino • *Scr* Gabriele Muccino

The Last Known Address ★★★

Drama 1969 · Fr · Colour · 95mins

Written and directed by José Giovanni, this uncompromising police procedural questions whether the end ever really justifies the means. Bringing a dour purpose to the part of the veteran inspector demoted to a provincial beat after killing a murder suspect, Lino Ventura dominates proceedings as he seeks to persuade a reluctant witness to testify. Grittily shot by Étienne Becker, this is abrasive stuff. DP. French dialogue dubbed into English.

Lino Ventura *Inspector* • Marlène Jobert *Assistant* • Michel Constantin *Hood* • Alain Mottet *Chief* ■ *Dir/Scr* José Giovanni • *Cinematographer* Etienne Becker

The Last Laugh ★★★★★ U

Classic silent drama
1924 · Ger · BW · 90mins

FW Murnau, who had made an impact with his expressionist masterpiece, *Nosferatu, a Symphony of Horrors* (1922), here moved closer to the *Kammerspielfilm* (chamber film), which dealt with ordinary people and events with an element of social criticism. The imposing Emil Jannings plays an elderly doorman at a luxury hotel, proud of his work and uniform, who is reduced to becoming a lavatory attendant. Murnau's *mise en scène* and the brilliant camerawork allow the story to be told without the use of intertitles, except for one that introduces the epilogue. The happy ending, tacked on at the insistence of the producer, can also be accepted as the man's dream. RB DVD

Emil Jannings *Doorman* • Maly Delschaft *His daughter* • Max Hiller *Her fiancé* • Emilie Kurz *His aunt* • Hans Unterkircher *Hotel manager* ■ *Dir* FW Murnau • *Scr* Carl Mayer • *Cinematographer* Karl Freund

Last Life in the Universe ★★★★ 15

Comedy thriller
2003 · Thai/Neth/HK/UK · Colour · 103mins

Beautifully photographed by Christopher Doyle, Pen-ek Ratanaruang's enigmatic character study owes less to traditional Thai melodrama than the steely stylisation of the new wave of Japanese film-makers. The main focus falls on the unlikely relationship between meticulous librarian Tadanobu Asano and slapdash bar-girl Sinitta Boonyasak, whose sister's traffic death postponed one of Asano's frequent attempted suicides. Drily witty and occasionally truly magical, this is a slow-burning and deeply seductive story. DP. In Thai, Japanese and English with subtitles. Contains sex scenes, swearing, violence. DVD

Tadanobu Asano *Kenji* • Sinitta Boonyasak *Noi* • Laila Boonyasak *Nid* • Yutaka Matsushige *Yukio* • Takashi Miike *Yakuza* ■ *Dir* Pen-ek Ratanaruang • *Scr* Prabda Yoon, Pen-ek Ratanaruang

Last Light ★★★ 18

Prison drama 1993 · US · Colour · 100mins

Kiefer Sutherland made an impressive debut behind the camera with this bleak prison TV drama. He also takes the starring role as the brutalised prisoner on death row who forms a cautious and unlikely friendship with sensitive guard Forest Whitaker. Sutherland puts in one of his best performances, and he is matched by Whitaker, while there are also fine supporting turns from Amanda Plummer and Kathleen Quinlan. Despite its grim subject matter, this is gripping. JF DVD

Kiefer Sutherland *Denver Bayliss* • Forest Whitaker *Fred Whitmore* • Amanda Plummer *Lillian Burke* • Kathleen Quinlan *Kathy Rubicek* • Lynne Moody *Hope Whitmore* • Clancy Brown *Lionel McMannis* ■ *Dir* Kiefer Sutherland • *Scr* Robert Eisele

The Last Man on Earth ★★★

Horror 1964 · It/US · BW · 85mins

Based on Richard Matheson's classic horror novel *I Am Legend* (as was *The Omega Man* in 1971), directors Ubaldo Ragona (Italian version) and Sidney Salkow's (US version) atmospheric shocker pits Vincent Price against people infected with a mysterious plague that has turned them into vampires. Shot on stark Rome locations (standing in for Los Angeles), Price delivers one of his more restrained performances in this engrossing slice of futuristic horror. AJ

Vincent Price *Robert Morgan* • Franca Bettoja *Ruth* • Emma Danieli *Virginia* • Giacomo Rossi-Stuart [Giacomo Rossi Stuart] *Ben Cortman* ■ *Dir* Ubaldo Ragona, Sidney Salkow • *Scr* William P Leicester, Logan Swanson, from the novel *I Am Legend* by Richard Matheson

Last Man Standing ★ 18

Period crime drama
1996 · US · Colour · 96mins

Gun-for-hire Bruce Willis arrives in a small Texas town and gets involved in a gang war over bootleg alcohol in director Walter Hill's weak Prohibition-era remake of the Japanese classic *Yojimbo*. Every cliché in the Sergio Leone catalogue is dragged out and used to minor effect in this ham-fisted action thriller that's given an unattractive dusty look with uniformly weak performances to match. AJ. Contains violence, swearing, sex scenes and nudity. DVD

Bruce Willis *John Smith* • Christopher Walken *Hickey* • Alexandra Powers *Lucy Kalinski* • David Patrick Kelly *Doyle* • William Sanderson *Joe Monday* • Karina Lombard *Felina* • Ned Eisenberg *Fredo Strozzi* • Michael Imperioli *Giorgio Carmonte* ■ *Dir* Walter Hill • *Scr* Walter Hill, from the film *Yojimbo* by Akira Kurosawa, Ryuzo Kikushima, Hideo Oguni, from the novel *Red Harvest* by Dashiell Hammett

The Last Married Couple in America ★★

Comedy 1980 · US · Colour · 102mins

This last gasp of the 1970s fashion for marital comedies dealing in the sexual "liberation" of middle-class couples stars Natalie Wood and George Segal. They're a husband and wife who endeavour to deal with a surfeit of divorces among their friends. Despite the more than usual utterance of expletives, the competent direction of Gilbert Cates, a bunch of "swinging" couples paying for the wages of sin, and Richard Benjamin in neurotic mode, it was always superficial and is now old hat. RK

George Segal *Jeff Thomson* • Natalie Wood *Mari Thomson* • Richard Benjamin *Marv Cooper* • Arlene Golonka *Sally Cooper* • Allan Arbus *Al Squib* • Marilyn Sokol *Alice Squib* • Dom DeLuise *Walter Holmes* • Valerie Harper *Barbara* ■ *Dir* Gilbert Cates • *Scr* John Herman Shaner

The Last Marshal ★ 18

Action thriller 1999 · US · Colour · 97mins

Stuntman Mike Kirton made his directorial debut with this bruising cop flick. So it's no surprise that a couple of the action sequences, notably the chase involving a speedboat and a motorbike, are slickly accomplished. But the remainder is strewn with racist and misogynist slurs that are spewed out by Scott Glenn with all the meat-headed macho he can muster. As the Texas lawman in Miami, Glen pursues a gang of drug smugglers with pitiless violence. DP. Contains swearing, violence and nudity. DVD

Scott Glenn *Cole McClary* • Constance Marie *Rosa* • Randall Batinkoff *Jamie* • Vincent Castellanos *Toeres* ■ *Dir* Mike Kirton • *Scr* Scott Wiper, Mike Kirton

The Last Metro ★★★ PG

Wartime drama 1980 · Fr · Colour · 125mins

Considering he'd always wanted to make a film about the Occupation, François Truffaut largely ignores its hideous realities in this nostalgic tribute to the theatre. The dynamic between the members of Jewish manager Heinz Bennent's company is well sustained, as is the mystery of whether Bennent's wife Catherine Deneuve prefers him to actor/Resistance fighter Gérard Depardieu. But the life of this enclosed ensemble is too divorced from history to make the movie anything more than just a handsomely mounted, meticulously performed fantasy. DP. In French with English subtitles. DVD

Catherine Deneuve *Marion Steiner* • Gérard Depardieu *Bernard Granger* • Jean Poiret *Jean-Loup Cottins* • Heinz Bennent *Lucas Steiner* • Andréa Ferréol *Arlette Guillaume* • Paulette Dubost *Germaine Fabre* • Sabine Haudepin *Nadine Marsac* • Jean-Louis Richard *Daxiat* ■ *Dir* François Truffaut • *Scr* François Truffaut, Suzanne Schiffman, Jean-Claude Grumberg, from a story by François Truffaut, Suzanne Schiffman

The Last Mile ★★

Crime drama 1959 · US · BW · 82mins

The title is the term given to the walk from a death row cell to the electric chair, and is also the title of the play through which Spencer Tracy and Clark Gable won Hollywood contracts. In contrast, Mickey Rooney's reputation had long been established when he took the part of a vicious convict who organises a prison riot. The claim in the prologue that such things no longer happen in US prisons is as unconvincing as much of this clichéd but lively film. RB

Mickey Rooney *"Killer" John Mears* • Alan Bunce *Warden* • Frank Conroy *O'Flaherty (Guard)* • Leon Janney *Callahan (Guard)* • Frank Overton *Father O'Connors* • Clifford David *Convict Richard Walters* • Harry Millard *Convict Fred Mayor* • Ford Rainey *Convict "Red" Kirby* ■ *Dir* Howard W Koch • *Scr* Milton Subotsky, Seton I Miller, from the play by John Wexley

The Last Mitterrand ★★★ PG

Biographical drama
2005 · Fr · Colour · 116mins

As President François Mitterrand (Michel Bouquet) engages in his final battle with cancer, an ideological journalist (Jalil Lespert) endeavours to extract his memoirs and life lessons for a biography. Director Robert Guédiguian's semi-fictional look at Mitterrand's career attempts to contrast his socialist dream alternative with global capitalism to raise pertinent questions about both. A more than passing knowledge of French politics and Mitterrand's personal history is vital to glean maximum enjoyment from this conversation-based relationship between a writer searching for certainties and a statesman unsure of his legacy. AJ. In French with English subtitles.

Michel Bouquet *The President* • Jalil Lespert *Antoine Moreau* • Philippe Fretun *Dr Jeantot* • Anne Cantineau *Jeanne* • Sarah Grappin *Judith* • Catherine Salviat *Mado* • Jean-Claude Frissung *René* • Philippe Lemercier *Fleury, the bodyguard* ■ *Dir* Robert Guédiguian • *Scr* Georges-Marc Benamou, Gilles Taurand, from the book *Le Dernier Mitterrand* by Georges-Marc Benamou

The Last Movie ★

Experimental drama
1971 · US · Colour · 107mins

After the huge success of *Easy Rider* (1969), director Dennis Hopper could have made any movie he wanted. Sadly he did just that, and the resulting fiasco is one of the all-time classics of pretentiously

U = SUITABLE FOR ALL Uc = SUITABLE FOR ALL, ESPECIALLY FOR YOUNG CHILDREN (VIDEO ONLY) PG = PARENTAL GUIDANCE

incomprehensible cinema. Outlining the hippy antics of a film crew in South America aiming to shoot a western, Hopper uses movie-making as a metaphor for imperialism in this mess of over-indulgent allegory and mind-numbing ranting. AJ

Dennis Hopper *Kansas* • Stella Garcia *Maria* • Samuel Fuller *Director* • Daniel Ades *Thomas Mercado* • Tomas Milian *Priest* • Don Gordon *Neville* • Julie Adams *Mrs Anderson* • Peter Fonda *Sheriff* • Kris Kristofferson *Minstrel Wrangler* • Henry Jaglom *Minister's son* • Michelle Phillips *Banker's daughter* • Dean Stockwell *Billy* • Russ Tamblyn *Member of Billy's gang* ■ *Dir* Dennis Hopper • *Scr* Stewart Stern, from a story by Stewart Stern, Dennis Hopper

Last Night ★★★★ 15

Drama 1998 · Can/Fr · Colour · 90mins

"A small film that is really a big film" is how David Cronenberg, best known as a director but acting here, describes director Don McKellar's deeply moving tale. Set against the countdown to an unexplained Armageddon, this captivating ensemble piece makes imminent oblivion seem life-affirming. As McKellar reneges on a nostalgic family Christmas, old school pal Callum Keith Rennie completes his sexual wish-list, teacher Geneviève Bujold revisits her favourite students and Sandra Oh attempts to cross town to fulfil her suicide pact with husband Cronenberg. Poignant, provocative and visually striking. DP. Contains sex scenes, swearing, violence. [VIDEO]

Don McKellar *Patrick Wheeler* • Sandra Oh *Sandra* • Callum Keith Rennie *Craig Zwiller* • Sarah Polley *Jennifer Wheeler* • David Cronenberg *Duncan* • Robin Gammell *Mr Wheeler* • Roberta Maxwell *Mrs Wheeler* • Tracy Wright *Donna* • Geneviève Bujold *Mrs Carlton* ■ *Dir/Scr* Don McKellar • *Cinematographer* Douglas Koch

The Last of England ★ 18

Drama 1987 · UK · Colour and BW · 87mins

Director Derek Jarman's angry polemic on the state of Britain in the mid-1980s is one for his die-hard fans only. Scattershot images of inner-city decay and violent paramilitaries collide with clips from Jarman's own home movies as actor Nigel Terry gives voice to concerns about the urban plight invading the collective unconsciousness. Jarman experiments with technique in a boring melange of images jazzed up with deliberately confrontational material. Redundant and old-fashioned. AJ [VIDEO] DVD

Spring • Gerrard McArthur • Tilda Swinton • Nigel Terry ■ *Dir/Scr* Derek Jarman • *Music* Simon Fisher Turner

The Last of Mrs Cheyney ★★★

Comedy 1929 · US · BW · 94mins

MGM's favourite actress – after she married studio boss Irving Thalberg – Norma Shearer gives gloss, but not much conviction to the role of the eponymous Mrs Cheyney. Playing an adventuress let loose in English high society, she wreaks moral havoc with Basil Rathbone and Hedda Hopper (who went on to be a feared gossip columnist). Adapted from an oft-filmed stage play by Frederick Lonsdale it already seemed dated at the time it was released, but its social nuances are still fascinating. TH

Norma Shearer *Mrs Cheyney* • Basil Rathbone *Lord Arthur Dilling* • George Barraud *Charles* • Herbert Bunston *Lord Elton* • Hedda Hopper *Lady Maria* • Moon Carroll *Joan* • Madeleine Seymour *Mrs Wynton* • Cyril Chadwick *Willie Wynton* ■ *Dir* Sidney Franklin • *Scr* Hans Kräly, Claudine West, from the play by Frederick Lonsdale • *Art Director* Cedric Gibbons

The Last of Mrs Cheyney ★★★

Comedy drama 1937 · US · BW · 98mins

This Frederick Lonsdale theatrical chestnut has always attracted great female stars to its showy, creaky title role. The 1929 Norma Shearer version is rarely shown, but movie fans have the consolation of the 1951 remake called *The Law and the Lady* with a Cecil Beaton-dressed Greer Garson, and this rather slow, dated but still glossy and engaging Joan Crawford version from MGM's golden age. TS

Joan Crawford *Fay Cheyney* • William Powell *Charles* • Robert Montgomery *Lord Arthur Dilling* • Frank Morgan *Lord Kelton* • Jessie Ralph *Duchess* • Nigel Bruce *Sir William* • Benita Hume *Kitty* • Colleen Clare *Joan* • Ralph Forbes *Cousin John* ■ *Dir* Richard Boleslawski • *Scr* Leon Gordon, Samson Raphaelson, Monckton Hoffe, from the play by Frederick Lonsdale

The Last of Sheila ★★★

Murder mystery 1973 · US · Colour · 123mins

Sharing a liking for whodunnits and word games, composer Stephen Sondheim and actor Anthony Perkins joined forces to write this murder mystery movie. Set aboard a luxury yacht, widowed Hollywood producer James Coburn gets his friends and colleagues to play a Cluedo-like game, the result of which will reveal the killer of Coburn's wife. A conceit from start to finish, it should delight connoisseurs of camp, though few critics at the time appreciated the joke. AT

James Coburn *Clinton* • James Mason *Philip* • Raquel Welch *Alice* • Richard Benjamin *Tom* • Joan Hackett *Lee* • Ian McShane *Anthony* • Dyan Cannon *Christine* ■ *Dir* Herbert Ross • *Scr* Anthony Perkins, Stephen Sondheim • *Production Designer* Ken Adam

Last of the Badmen ★★

Western 1957 · US · Colour · 79mins

This western has a cracking premise: a gang springs outlaws from jail, uses them for hold-ups until the price on their head increases, then turns in their corpses and collects the reward. Unfortunately, George Montgomery is wooden as the detective who goes undercover to investigate the racket, and the intriguing plotline is inadequately realised thanks to the paucity of the budget. The story was used again in 1964 for *Gunfight at Comanche Creek*. TS

George Montgomery *Dan Barton* • James Best *Ted Hamilton* • Meg Randall *Lila* • Douglas Kennedy *Hawkins* • Michael Ansara *Kramer* • Keith Larsen *Roberts* • Robert Foulk *Taylor* • Willis Bouchley *Marshal Parker* ■ *Dir* Paul Landres • *Scr* Daniel B Ullman, David Chantler, from the story by Daniel B Ullman

Last of the Comanches ★★

Western 1952 · US · Colour · 85mins

Broderick Crawford is not the most charismatic of western stars but he's effectively cast as the burly cavalry sergeant fleeing across the desert from an Indian massacre with a handful of fellow soldiers. They pick up others en route and keep the Comanches at bay from an abandoned mission. The long siege is moderately suspenseful under director Andre De Toth's handling, while the excellent photography and score deserve a better picture. AE

Broderick Crawford *Sgt Matt Trainor* • Barbara Hale *Julia Lanning* • Johnny Stewart *Little Knife* • Lloyd Bridges *Jim Starbuck* • Mickey Shaughnessy *Rusty Potter* • George Mathews *Romany O'Rattigan* ■ *Dir* Andre De Toth • *Scr* Kenneth Gamet • *Cinematographer* Ray Cory, Charles Lawton Jr • *Music* George Duning

Last of the Dogmen ★★ PG

Romantic western adventure
1995 · US · Colour · 112mins

In this dumb modern western, a bounty hunter (Tom Berenger) on the trail of escaped convicts discovers a tribe of Cheyenne Indians living undisturbed in the Rocky Mountains. It's a pedestrian copy of *Dances with Wolves*, with native bonding and a spiky relationship between Berenger and a professor of Indian anthropology who's conveniently both female and attractive (Barbara Hershey). Throwing various other genre clichés into the soup, this has some decent work from Berenger, but the script isn't sharp enough to overcome the implausible premise. JC [VIDEO] DVD

Tom Berenger *Lewis Gates* • Barbara Hershey *Professor Lillian Sloan* • Kurtwood Smith *Sheriff Deegan* • Andrew Miller *Briggs* • Steve Reevis *Yellow Wolf* • Wilford Brimley *Narrator* ■ *Dir/Scr* Tab Murphy

The Last of the Fast Guns ★★★

Western 1958 · US · Colour · 82mins

Veteran director George Sherman brings his eye for environment and sureness of touch to this lively western. Hired by Carl Benton Reid to find his missing brother Eduard Franz, Jock Mahoney struts through northern Mexico with admirable purpose, countering the threat posed by Reid's grasping partner, Gilbert Roland (who stands to assume sole control of their business if Mahoney fails), with square-jawed efficiency. DP

Jock Mahoney *Brad Ellison* • Gilbert Roland *Miles Lang* • Linda Cristal *Maria O'Reilly* • Eduard Franz *Padre Jose* • Lorne Greene *Michael O'Reilly* • Carl Benton Reid *John Forbes* ■ *Dir* George Sherman • *Scr* David P Harmon

The Last of the Good Old Days ★★★★

Comedy 1989 · Cz · Colour · 97mins

With a blend of bedroom farce and socio-political allegory that recalls Jean Renoir's *La Règle du Jeu*, this is a deliciously barbed satire on the Czech ruling elite. With aristocrats and their domestics siding against the bourgeoisie and the bureaucrats, this inter-war country house comedy bristles with class conflict as self-made slob Marian Labuda tries to keep his innocent daughter away from indolent duke Josef Abrham. Wittily scripted by Jirí Blazek and shot in autumnal hues to suggest the passage of an era, this superbly acted period piece is hugely enjoyable. DP. A Czech language film.

Josef Abrham *Duke Alexei* • Marian Labuda *Josef Stoklasa* • Jaromir Hanzlik *Bernard Spera, the Librarian* • Rudolf Hrusinsky *Jakub Lhota* ■ *Dir* Jirí Menzel • *Scr* Jiri Blazek, from a novel by Vladislav Vancura

Last of the High Kings ★★ 15

Comedy drama
1996 · Ire/UK/Den · Colour · 100mins

This pleasant, if unremarkable, rites of passage drama revolves around the growing pains of Dublin lad Jared Leto as he tries to cope with being a descendant of Celtic Kings. His wacky family includes an overly political mother and a virtually unseen father (Gabriel Byrne) who communicates from America in Shakespearean couplets. When Christina Ricci arrives for the summer holidays, virginity-loss becomes a top agenda item. Set in the 1970s, Leto overdoes the cute confusion while the film is stolen by Stephen Rea in a small cameo as a know-it-all taxi driver. AJ. Contains some swearing and a sex scene. [VIDEO]

Catherine O'Hara *Cathleen* • Jared Leto *Frankie Griffin* • Christina Ricci *Erin* • Gabriel Byrne *Jack Griffin* • Stephen Rea *Cab driver* • Colm Meaney *Jim Davern* • Lorraine Pilkington *Jayne Wayne* • Emily Mortimer *Romy* ■ *Dir* David Keating • *Scr* David Keating, Gabriel Byrne, from the novel by Ferdia MacAnna

Last of the Mobile Hot-Shots ★★

Drama 1970 · US · Colour · 107mins

One of Sidney Lumet's lesser-known works, this trip into Tennessee Williams territory ultimately fails to live up to its promise. However, it is still worth a look for the talent alone. The script, based on Williams's play *The Seven Descents of Myrtle*, was co-written by Gore Vidal, while the interesting cast is headed up by James Coburn and Lynn Redgrave. (Released in the UK as *Blood Kin*.) JF

Lynn Redgrave *Myrtle* • Robert Hooks *Chicken* • Perry Hayes *George* • Reggie King *Rube* • James Coburn *Jeb* ■ *Dir* Sidney Lumet • *Scr* Gore Vidal, Mark Valenti, from the play *The Seven Descents of Myrtle* by Tennessee Williams

The Last of the Mohicans ★★★★★

Silent period adventure
1920 · US · BW · 74mins

This silent adaptation of James Fenimore Cooper's famous story was the masterpiece of Maurice Tourneur, the French-born director and father of Jacques who worked for MGM until a violent disagreement made him return to Europe. It has visuals to die for and some of the most ferocious massacre scenes ever filmed. Yet human values are never sacrificed in this story of an Indian scout, the last surivivor of the Mohican tribe, escorting two girls through perilous territory. The picture has a ruggedness to make pulses beat faster and a poignancy that touches the heart, while the ending is starkly tragic. Tourneur makes this special – despite being forced by an accident to share directorial duties with Clarence Brown. Watch for Boris Karloff in an early role as a marauding tribesman. TH

Wallace Beery *Magua* • Barbara Bedford *Cora Munro* • Albert Roscoe *Uncas* • Lillian Hall *Alice Munro* • Henry Woodward *Major Heyward* • James Gordon *Colonel Munro* • George Hackathorne *Captain Randolph* • Nelson McDowell *David Gamut* • Boris Karloff *Marauding Indian* ■ *Dir* Maurice Tourneur, Clarence Brown • *Scr* Robert A Dillon, from the novel by James Fenimore Copper

The Last of the Mohicans ★★★

Period adventure 1936 · US · BW · 91mins

Though not a patch on the 1920 or 1992 versions, this is an honest attempt at filming the James Fenimore Cooper classic. Randolph Scott makes a strapping Hawkeye, but Robert Barrat is ill-cast as Chingachgook, the native American of the title. The action sequences are remarkably well-staged by director George B Seitz. TS

Randolph Scott *Hawkeye* • Binnie Barnes *Alice Munro* • Heather Angel *Cora Munro* • Hugh Buckler *Colonel Munro* • Henry Wilcoxon *Major Duncan Heyward* • Robert Barrat *Chingachgook* ■ *Dir* George B Seitz • *Scr* Philip Dunne, John Balderston, Paul Perez, Daniel Moore, from the novel by James Fenimore Cooper

The Last of the Mohicans ★★★★ 15

Period adventure
1992 · US · Colour · 107mins

This exciting mix of high adventure, romance and history lesson is wonderfully presented in a colossal, glossy package. Daniel Day-Lewis is Hawkeye, the frontiersman raised by Mohicans, who gets caught between

L

two cultures when he falls for Madeleine Stowe, a British army officer's daughter. In the ensuing and, it must be said, often confusing bloody battles involving the French, the British and American Indians (the scalpings, by the way, are very realistic) he refuses to give up his adopted tribe's cause, or his love. The well staged action sequences and director Michael Mann's grandiose sense of scale combine to produce an epic that harks back to the good old-fashioned adventure films of Hollywood's heyday. AJ. Contains violence. DVD

Daniel Day-Lewis *Hawkeye* • Madeleine Stowe *Cora Munro* • Russell Means *Chingachgook* • Eric Schweig *Uncas* • Jodhi May *Alice Munro* • Steven Waddington *Major Duncan Heyward* • Wes Studi *Magua* • Maurice Roëves *Colonel Edmund Munro* • Patrice Chéreau *General Montcalm* • Mark A Baker *Colonial man* ■ *Dir* Michael Mann • *Scr* Michael Mann, Christopher Crowe, from the 1936 film, from the novel by James Fenimore Cooper • *Cinematographer* Dante Spinotti

Last of the Pony Riders ★★ U

Western 1953 · US · BW · 59mins

This innocuous story of the last days of the Pony Express was the last of the Gene Autry B-westerns as the two-fisted warbler moved his exploits to the small screen. A declining market had led to shorter running times and fewer songs (two in this one) for his last dozen pictures, while Autry himself was looking heavier and older. It's very much business as usual here with nothing very special. AE

Gene Autry • Smiley Burnette • Kathleen Case *Katie McEwen* • Dick Jones [Dickie Jones] *Johnny Blair* • John Downey *Tom McEwen* ■ *Dir* George Archainbaud • *Scr* Ruth Woodman

The Last of the Red Hot Lovers ★★

Comedy 1972 · US · Colour · 92mins

Happily married for more than 20 years, Alan Arkin craves to have just one extramarital affair, as if to prove his manhood and romantic worth. Neil Simon's script, based on his Broadway hit, was probably dated the day it opened, with its lazy one-liners and raunchiness. As Cashman, Alan Arkin brings his trademark tics and seediness, while Sally Kellerman, Paula Prentiss and Renee Taylor frustrate his longings AT

Alan Arkin *Barney Cashman* • Sally Kellerman *Elaine* • Paula Prentiss *Bobbi Michele* • Renee Taylor *Jeanette* • Bella Bruck *Cashier* ■ *Dir* Gene Saks • *Scr* Neil Simon, from his play

The Last of the Secret Agents ★★ U

Spy comedy 1966 · US · Colour · 76mins

US double act Marty Allen and Steve Rossi bungle their bid to be the new Abbott and Costello as recently recruited spies out to thwart international art thieves. Theo Marcuse has fun as the head of evil empire THEM, possessor of the lost arms of the Venus de Milo statue and desperate to bag the rest of her, but writer/director Norman Abbott of *Get Smart* and *The Munsters* TV fame offers us mere crumbs of comedy amid a stale series of slapstick routines. RS

Marty Allen *Marty Johnson* • Steve Rossi *Steve Donovan* • John Williams *J Frederick Duval* • Nancy Sinatra *Micheline* • Lou Jacobi *Papa Leo* ■ *Dir* Norman Abbott • *Scr* Mel Tolkin, from the story *Don Juan, Ole* by Norman Abbott, Mel Tolkin

Last Orders ★★★★ 15

Drama 2001 · UK/Ger · Colour · 105mins

A meditative Booker Prize-winning novel (by Graham Swift) told through multiple interior monologues should have been a tough one to adapt for the screen. But Australian writer/director Fred Schepisi has done a sterling job, assembling a dream cast to flesh out this deceptively simple, 1980s-set tale of four friends – Bob Hoskins, Ray Winstone, Tom Courtenay, David Hemmings, all on peak form – heading from London to Margate to scatter the ashes of a fifth (Michael Caine, seen in intelligently interwoven flashback). Not only is *Last Orders* a touching and perceptive drama about the war generation, it's also a moving and funny road movie about friendship, deceit and loss. AC. Contains swearing. DVD

Michael Caine *Jack Dodds* • Bob Hoskins *Ray "Lucky" Johnson* • Tom Courtenay *Vic Tucker* • David Hemmings *Lenny Tate* • Ray Winstone *Vince Dodds* • Helen Mirren *Amy* ■ *Dir* Fred Schepisi • *Scr* Fred Schepisi, from the novel by Graham Swift

The Last Outlaw ★★★

Western 1936 · US · BW · 72mins

The great John Ford directed a short, silent version of this story in 1919 and his screenplay forms the basis of director Christy Cabanne's lively comedy western. Ford's influence further pervades the work as it stars his favourite actor, Harry Carey, as the eponymous bank robber. He plays an old-time outlaw who's been in prison for 25 years and, unsurprisingly, has trouble in adjusting to the modern West when he returns home to see a daughter he's never met. BB

Harry Carey *Dean Payton* • Hoot Gibson *Chuck Wilson* • Tom Tyler *Al Goss* • Henry B Walthall *Under Sheriff Calvin Yates* • Margaret Callahan *Sally Mason* ■ *Dir* Christy Cabanne • *Scr* John Twist, Jack Townley, from a story by John Ford, E Murray Campbell

The Last Outlaw ★★ 15

Western 1993 · US · Colour · 89mins

Kiwi director Geoff Murphy followed up the success of *Young Guns II* with another stab at the western genre. A ridiculously coiffeured Mickey Rourke is left for dead by his gang of outlaws, so he hooks up with the local sheriff to gain his revenge. Rourke's performance is as outlandish as his hair, but the rest of the cast is a tad more convincing, while Murphy's no-nonsense direction keeps things bounding along at a rollicking pace. JF DVD

Mickey Rourke *Graff* • Dermot Mulroney *Eustis* • Ted Levine *Potts* • John C McGinley *Wills* • Steve Buscemi *Philo* • Keith David *Lovecraft* ■ *Dir* Geoff Murphy • *Scr* Eric Red

The Last Outpost ★★

First World War drama
1935 · US · BW · 70mins

This teaming of Cary Grant and Claude Rains is a far cry from their later brilliance in Hitchcock's *Notorious*, although in both films Grant is in love with Rains's wife. Set in Africa during the First World War, this earlier movie combines action scenes with amorous rivalry that drives Rains to plot Grant's murder. Gertrude Michael plays the woman in the triangle. It was originally directed by Louis Gasnier, then largely reshot by Charles Barton. AE

Cary Grant *Michael Andrews* • Gertrude Michael *Rosemary Haydon* • Claude Rains *John Stevenson* • Margaret Swope *Nurse Rowland* • Jameson Thomas *Cullen* • Colin Tapley *Lieutenant Prescott* • Akim Tamiroff *Mirov* ■ *Dir* Louis Gasnier, Charles Barton • *Scr* Philip MacDonald, from the short story *The Drum* by F Britten Austen, adapted by Frank Partos, Charles Brackett

The Last Page ★★

Crime 1952 · UK · BW · 84mins

Before it latched on to horror, Hammer made a deal with a minor American outfit to co-produce thrillers in Britain with lesser Hollywood stars. This ponderous drama was the first; it also marked Terence Fisher's directorial debut at the studio. It features stolid George Brent as the London bookshop manager who is blackmailed for a momentary indiscretion by his busty young assistant, Diana Dors, at the instigation of her evil boyfriend, Peter Reynolds. He and Dors bring some life to the picture, and she more than justifies its US title, *Man Bait*. AE

George Brent *John Harman* • Marguerite Chapman *Stella* • Raymond Huntley *Clive* • Peter Reynolds *Jeff* • Diana Dors *Ruby* • Eleanor Summerfield *Vi* • Meredith Edwards *Dale* • Conrad Phillips *Todd* ■ *Dir* Terence Fisher • *Scr* Frederick Knott, from a story by James Hadley Chase

The Last Party ★★★

Documentary 1993 · US · Colour · 96mins

Most definitely not your typical Robert Downey Jr film. Downey is the host for a heavily satirical documentary that takes a tongue-in-cheek look at the 1992 race for the US Presidency. And one suspects he may have used his heavy-duty Hollywood clout to rope in the famous names and faces who help him trawl his non-comprehending way through the complex workings of the Republican and Democratic conventions. Unrated and little seen, probably because America is a little sensitive to its politicians being slyly sent-up like this. A follow-up, *Last Party 2000*, appeared in 2001. DA

Robert Downey Jr *Host* ■ *Dir* Mark Benjamin, Marc Levin • *Scr* Marc Levin, Josh Richman, Donovan Leitch, Mark Benjamin

The Last Picture Show ★★★★★ 15

Classic drama 1971 · US · BW · 114mins

Beautifully adapted by director Peter Bogdanovich and Larry McMurtry (from the latter's novel), this is a masterclass in how to create fully rounded characters and then give them real lives to lead. While the nostalgic elements of this memoir of small-town Texas in the 1950s are lovingly realised (a miraculous blend of John Ford and Howard Hawks), it's the re-creation of that long-lost sense of community, in which everyone knew and respected one another, that makes this such a rewarding experience. Jeff Bridges and Cybill Shepherd stand out, but it's the playing of Timothy Bottoms, Ben Johnson and Cloris Leachman that gives the film its authenticity. A sequel, *Texasville*, eventually followed in 1990. DP DVD

Timothy Bottoms *Sonny Crawford* • Jeff Bridges *Duane Jackson* • Cybill Shepherd *Jacy Farrow* • Ben Johnson *Sam the Lion* • Cloris Leachman *Ruth Popper* • Ellen Burstyn *Lois Farrow* • Eileen Brennan *Genevieve* • Clu Gulager *Abilene* • Sam Bottoms *Billy* • Randy Quaid *Lester Marlow* ■ *Dir* Peter Bogdanovich • *Scr* Larry McMurtry, Peter Bogdanovich, from the novel by Larry McMurtry

Last Plane Out ★★

War drama 1983 · US · Colour · 92mins

Low on budget, production values and even a modicum of balance, this political thriller is mere anti-Sandinista propaganda. Produced by Jack Cox and based on his journalistic assignment to Nicaragua during the Somoza regime, it comes to something when the most sympathetic character is Somoza himself. A love affair with a Sandinista rebel (Julie Carmen) is also fashioned into this particularly unpersuasive tale. Check out *Under Fire* for a more interesting treatment of the times. TH

Jan-Michael Vincent *Jack Cox* • Julie Carmen *Maria Cardena* • Mary Crosby *Liz Rush* • David Huffman *Jim Corley* • William Windom *James Caldwell* • Lloyd Battista *Anastasio Somoza* ■ *Dir* David Nelson • *Scr* Ernest Tidyman

The Last Posse ★★ U

Western 1953 · US · BW · 72mins

This unusual western is more concerned with mystery and suspense, with the pieces of the sombre story told in flashbacks. What really happened to the posse that went after three men accused of theft and came back with a mortally wounded sheriff? Broderick Crawford is the lawman, and Charles Bickford co-stars as a ruthless rancher; John Derek is the latter's adopted son. Though ably directed by Alfred Werker, the film's structure becomes a little tiresome. AE

Broderick Crawford *Sheriff Frazier* • John Derek *Jed Clayton* • Charles Bickford *Sampson Drune* • Wanda Hendrix *Deborah Morley* • Warner Anderson *Robert Emerson* • Henry Hull *Stokely* ■ *Dir* Alfred Werker • *Scr* Seymour Bennett, Connie Lee Bennett, Kenneth Gamet, from the story by Seymour Bennett, Connie Lee Bennett

The Last Producer ★★ 15

Drama 2000 · US · Colour · 85mins

Burt Reynolds mugs his way through this Tinseltown tat. A poor relation of *Get Shorty*, the story revolves around Reynolds's has-been producer, who lands himself in hot water with loan sharks and insurance crooks in a bid to secure the rights to a screenplay he's confidant will put him back on top. Yet it's the supporting cast that catches the eye, with old stagers such as Charles Durning, Rod Steiger and Ann-Margret jostling for the limelight. DP DVD

Burt Reynolds *Sonny Wexler* • Ann-Margret *Mira Wexler* • Benjamin Bratt *Damon Black* • Charles Durning *Syd Wolf* • Greg Germann *Reuben Tallridge* • Rod Steiger *Sherri Ganse* • Lauren Holly *Frances Chadway* • Sean Astin *Bo Pomerants* ■ *Dir* Burt Reynolds • *Scr* Clyde Hayes

The Last Rebel ★

Western 1971 · US · Colour · 90mins

Sports star Joe Namath had tried acting before, but he still appears distinctly uncomfortable swapping a football for a pistol in this post-Civil War western. A muddled script and clumsy direction by the little-known Denys McCoy leave him looking either sheepish or grinning. At least there's polished support from Jack Elam as a friend turned enemy, Woody Strode as a black saved from lynching and Ty Hardin as a man with a badge. AE

Joe Namath *Burnside Hollis* • Jack Elam *Matt Graves* • Woody Strode *Duncan* • Ty Hardin *Sheriff* • Victoria George *Pearl* • Renato Romano *Virgil* ■ *Dir* Denys McCoy • *Scr* Warren Kiefer

The Last Remake of Beau Geste ★★★ PG

Comedy 1977 · US · Colour · 80mins

A scrappy but good-natured send-up of the oft-filmed desert yarn, directed by and starring the goggle-eyed, surrealist comedian Marty Feldman whose TV series and appearances in several Mel Brooks movies led to this project. As a director, Feldman is ramshackle, and there are certain Python elements in the spoof that casts him with Michael York as brothers who search the Sahara for Ann-Margret and a missing diamond. Some of it works and a lot of it doesn't, but it's worth seeing for the virtual who's who of British comedy. Film buffs will especially like the liberty taken with the Universal logo, and the sudden appearance of Feldman in the 1939 version with Gary Cooper. AT

Ann-Margret *Flavia Geste* • Marty Feldman *Digby Geste* • Michael York *Beau Geste* •

Peter Ustinov *Sergeant Markov* • James Earl Jones *Sheikh Abdul* • Trevor Howard *Sir Hector Geste* • Henry Gibson *General Pecheur* • Roy Kinnear *Corporal Boldini* • Spike Milligan *Crumble* • Terry-Thomas *Prison governor* • Irene Handl *Miss Wormwood* • Sinead Cusack *Isabel Geste* ■ *Dir* Marty Feldman • *Scr* Marty Feldman, Chris Allen, from a story by Sam Bobrick, from the novel by PC Wren

Last Resort ★★★★ 15

Drama 2000 · UK · Colour · 73mins

Documentarist Pawel Pawlikowski thoroughly merited his Bafta for this second foray into fictional film following *The Stringer* (1997). Not that he's abandoned authenticity altogether, as it's the gnawing sense of realism here that makes Russian emigrant Dina Korzun's plight all the more distressing. Arriving in the UK, she's detained in a holding centre, after being disowned by her fiancé. Korzun is equally misused by bureaucrats and internet pornographers as she tries to build a new life for herself and son, Artiom Strelnikov. With amusement arcade attendant Paddy Considine providing humour and humanity, and cinematographer Ryszard Lenczewski capturing seaside Britain's bleak beauty, this is a powerful indictment of political hypocrisy and everyday indifference. DP [video] DVD

Dina Korzun *Tanya* • Paddy Considine *Alfie* • Artiom Strelnikov *Artiom* • Lindsey Honey *Les* • Perry Benson *Immigration officer* • Katie Drinkwater *Katie* ■ *Dir* Pawel Pawlikowski • *Scr* Pawel Pawlikowski, Rowan Joffe • *Cinematographer* Ryszard Lenczewski

Last Rites ★ 18

Thriller 1988 · US · Colour · 103mins

This misfiring thriller marks one of the lowest points in Tom Berenger's career. He stars as a Catholic priest caught up in a totally bewildering plot revolving around murder and the Mafia. Poor writing, direction and acting must have left Berenger (Oscar-nominated for his role in Oliver Stone's *Platoon* two years earlier) wondering how he got talked into this one. NF. Contains violence and swearing. [video]

Tom Berenger *Father Michael Pace* • Daphne Zuniga *Angela* • Chick Vennera *Nuzo* • Anne Twomey *Zena Pace* • Dane Clark *Carlo Pace* • Paul Dooley *Father Freddie* ■ *Dir/Scr* Donald P Bellisario

Last Rites ★★★ 15

Psychological thriller
1998 · US · Colour · 83mins

Randy Quaid turns on the chilling charm in this smart made-for-TV thriller. He plays a killer on death row who survives his date with death, thanks to a timely bolt of lightning striking the prison. Awaking the next morning, he has no memory of his murderous past and it is up to shrink Embeth Davidtz to work out whether he is telling the truth and whether his newly-acquired "psychic" powers are genuine. Director Kevin Dowling has fun spinning out the mind games and the result is gripping. JF [video]

Randy Quaid *Jeremy Dillon* • Embeth Davidtz *Dr Lauren Riggs* • A Martinez *Matt* • Clarence Williams III *Warden Pierce* • Paul Benjamin *Fez* • Jack Coleman *Gary Blake* ■ *Dir* Kevin Dowling • *Scr* Tim Frost, from a story by Richard Outten

The Last Run ★★★★ 18

Crime drama 1971 · US · Colour · 91mins

John Huston started this thriller but quit after three weeks; a natural emnity between him and George C Scott and an awful lot of booze led to him being replaced by Richard Fleischer. The result, though, is marvellous, with Scott playing a lonely, burned-out gangster who agrees to do one last job – driving Spain's most wanted man and his girlfriend to the border, with the Mob and the police in pursuit. It's a riveting, Hemingway-style story with Scott playing to perfection a man staring fate straight between the eyes. The Spanish landscape is superbly captured, and the score is particularly haunting. AT [video]

George C Scott *Harry Garmes* • Tony Musante *Paul Ricard* • Colleen Dewhurst *Monique* ■ *Dir* Richard Fleischer • *Scr* Alan Sharp • *Cinematographer* Sven Nykvist • *Music* Jerry Goldsmith

The Last Safari ★★

Action adventure
1967 · UK · Colour · 110mins

Stewart Granger, recalling his heyday in *King Solomon's Mines*, is a former white hunter who loathes the tourists he shows around the bush. One such tourist is top-billed Kaz Garas (plucked from American TV) and his mistress, Gabriella Licudi, who discover that Stewart is haunted by the death of his best pal under the feet of an elephant. Shot in Kenya and full of travelogue sequences, it squanders any drama in the story, while the location photography is undermined by some eye-jarring process shots. AT

Kaz Garas *Casey* • Stewart Granger *Miles Gilchrist* • Gabriella Licudi *Grant* • Johnny Sekka *Jama* • Liam Redmond *Alec Beaumont* ■ *Dir* Henry Hathaway • *Scr* John Gay, from the novel *Gilligan's Last Elephant* by Gerald Hanley

The Last Samurai ★★★★ 15

Period action drama
2003 · US · Colour · 147mins

Edward Zwick's sweeping action drama set in the 19th century charts a poignant personal odyssey prompted by the clash of old and new cultures. Tom Cruise plays a disillusioned US captain hired by the young Japanese emperor to train the country's first modern, conscript army. After leading an inadequate campaign against the samurai warriors, the military man is captured by these alleged national enemies who teach him to reassess his beliefs and values. An epic movie in every way, the beautifully shot tale features a strong storyline, robust performances and spine-tingling, violent battle sequences. It suffers only from being overly idealistic and occasionally stereotypical. SF. In English and Japanese with subtitles. Contains violence. [video] DVD

Tom Cruise *Captain Nathan Algren* • Timothy Spall *Simon Graham* • Billy Connolly *Sergeant Zebulon Gant* • Tony Goldwyn *Colonel Benjamin Bagley* • Ken Watanabe *Katsumoto* • Hiroyuki Sanada *Ujio* • Koyuki *Taka* • Shichinosuke Nakamura *Emperor Meiji* ■ *Dir* Edward Zwick • *Scr* John Logan, Marshall Herskovitz, Edward Zwick, from the story by John Logan

The Last Seduction ★★★★ 18

Thriller 1993 · US · Colour · 105mins

John Dahl secured his reputation as one of the hottest directors of the 1990s with this cool-as-ice, wantonly playful, bitter-and-twisted excursion into neon-shaded contemporary *film noir*. At its commanding centre is sizzling and smouldering Linda Fiorentino in a star-making role as the man-eating *femme fatale* from hell. A gorgeous go-getter, she swaps dirty talk for dirty deeds when she cons husband Bill Pullman into doing a big drug deal, only to run off with the money. Hiding out in a small town, the manipulative mantrap changes identity, gets a new job and seduces besotted insurance agent Peter Berg into carrying out her every whim. This sassy and superior suspense thriller is a must-see – pulp fiction rarely comes as well appointed or as absorbingly clever. AJ [video] DVD

Linda Fiorentino *Bridget Gregory* • Peter Berg *Mike Swale* • Bill Pullman *Clay Gregory* • JT Walsh *Frank Griffith* • Bill Nunn *Harlan* • Herb Mitchell *Bob Trotter* • Brien Varady *Chris* • Dean Norris *Shep* • Donna Wilson *Stacy* ■ *Dir* John Dahl • *Scr* Steve Barancik

The Last Seduction 2 ★★ 18

Romantic crime thriller
1998 · UK/US · Colour · 94mins

This dull, irrelevant sequel follows one of the hippest, sexiest *films noirs* of the last three decades. Joan Severance steps into Linda Fiorentino's stilletos as the murderous ice maiden, who, finding the US too hot for her, heads for Barcelona and sets her sights on violent Irish crook Con O'Neill. However, on her tail is private eye Beth Goddard, who is not above using her own femine wiles to nab her prey. JF. Contains swearing, sex scenes and violence. [video] DVD

Joan Severance *Bridget Gregory* • Beth Goddard *Murphy* • Con O'Neill *Troy Fenton* • Rocky Taylor *Gabriel* • Dean Williamson *Earl McLaughlin* ■ *Dir* Terry Marcel • *Scr* Dave Cummings

The Last September ★★★ 15

Period drama
1999 · UK/Ire/Fr · Colour · 98mins

Theatre director Deborah Warner has rounded up a company of stellar British talent for this stylised depiction of the decline of English power in Ireland after the 1916 Easter rising. Maggie Smith and Michael Gambon are superlatively arch as aristocrats hosting relentless house parties and family gatherings despite the unrest, while Keeley Hawes plays the wayward niece whose rejection of an English soldier in favour of an Irish anarchist ultimately leads to tragedy. Slow and studied, Warner's film debut shows flashes of inspiration despite an innate theatricality that at times appears ridiculous and unreal. LH [video]

Maggie Smith *Lady Myra* • Michael Gambon *Sir Richard Naylor* • Jane Birkin *Francie Montmorency* • Fiona Shaw *Marda Norton* • Lambert Wilson *Hugo Montmorency* • David Tennant *Captain Gerald Colthurst* • Richard Roxburgh *Daventry* • Keeley Hawes *Lois Farquar* ■ *Dir* Deborah Warner • *Scr* John Banville, from a novel by Elizabeth Bowen

The Last Shot ★★

Crime drama 1969 · Fr · Colour · 105mins

Robert Hossein plays a gangster who has risen to the top of the public enemy list. Yet who should be on his tail but childhood buddy Charles Aznavour, now a top-ranking drug squad cop? Having made his directorial debut at the age of 22, Sergio Gobbi shook up the popular *policier* genre with an explosively tough brand of urban action that shocked 1960s cineastes. Here, however, he spends too much time on the romantic tug of war involving Virna Lisi. DP. French dialogue dubbed into English.

Robert Hossein *Robert Dillinger* • Charles Aznavour *Kramer* • Virna Lisi *Stella* ■ *Dir* Sergio Gobbi • *Scr* Sergio Gobbi, André Tabet

The Last Stage ★★★★

War drama based on a true story
1947 · Pol · BW · 105mins

One of the first postwar films made about the Holocaust, Wanda Jakubowska's masterpiece is all the more arresting because of its studied naturalism. As both the director and her co-scenarist, Gerda Schneider, had survived the horrors of Auschwitz, there's a dreadful authenticity to this memoir of a hospital interpreter who ministered to so many women during the final hours of their lives. This is a film devoid of easy emotion and cheap correctness. Instead, events are presented with a chilling normality that suggests the sort of detachment that enabled prisoners to bear the enormity of living with genocide. DP. In Polish with English subtitles.

Barbara Drapinska *Marthe* • Wanda Bartowna *Helene* • Tatiana Gorecka *Eugenie* • Antonina Gorecka *Anna* • Huguette Faget *Michele* • Alina Janowska *Dessa* ■ *Dir* Wanda Jakubowska • *Scr* Wanda Jakubowska, Gerda Schneider

Last Stand at Saber River ★★★ 12

Western 1997 · US · Colour · 90mins

Anyone who thinks Elmore Leonard only writes crime novels would do well to catch this handsomely mounted dramatisation of his 1959 American Civil War western. Tom Selleck seems to the stetson born as the Confederate trooper who reunites with his wife Suzy Amis to reclaim his Arizona homestead. But Dick Lowry's rousing TV movie is given additional interest by the teaming of David and Keith Carradine as the siblings caught up in Selleck's dispute. DP. Contains some swearing and violence. [video] DVD

Tom Selleck *Cable* • Suzy Amis *Martha* • Rachel Duncan *Clare* • Haley Joel Osment *Davis* • Keith Carradine *Vern Kidston* • David Carradine *Duane Kidston* • Tracey Needham *Lorraine* ■ *Dir* Dick Lowry • *Scr* Ronald M Cohen, from the novel by Elmore Leonard

The Last Starfighter ★★★ PG

Science-fiction adventure
1984 · US · Colour · 96mins

Lance Guest's prowess at video games is monitored by emissaries from the Star League of the future, who recruit him to defend the universe from evil invaders in this glossy, space-age fairy tale. While highly derivative *Star Trek*-like aliens mix with *Star Wars*-inspired dog-fights against a computer-graphic backdrop, the sensitive love story between Guest and Catherine Mary Stewart cuts through the cuteness and gives the intergalactic adventures a boost. AJ. Contains violence and swearing. [video]

Lance Guest *Alex Rogan* • Dan O'Herlihy *Grig* • Catherine Mary Stewart *Maggie Gordon* • Barbara Bosson *Jane Rogan* • Norman Snow *Xur* • Robert Preston *Centauri* • Kay E Kuter *Enduran* • Chris Hebert *Louis Rogan* ■ *Dir* Nick Castle • *Scr* Jonathan Betuel

Last Stop Paradise ★★★

Drama 1998 · Fr/Rom · Colour · 99mins

Romania's best-known film-maker, Lucian Pintilie, demonstrates an enviable talent for disconcerting development and quirky characterisation in this offbeat drama. Opening with a bizarre chase through Bucharest, the film settles down to concentrate on the tentative relationship between Costel Cascaval, a pig farmer about to embark on his national service, and Dorina Chiriac, a waitress engaged to the ageing owner of a mobile sausage stand. The impressive performances and Pintilie's unobtrusive camerawork keep the action edgy and unexpected. DP

Costel Cascaval *Mitou* • Dorina Chiriac *Norica* • Gheorghe Visu *Vatasescu* • Victor Rebengiuc *Grigore Cafanu* • Razvan Vasilescu *Burci* ■ *Dir* Lucian Pintilie • *Scr* Lucian Pintilie, Ravsan Popescu, Radu Aldulescu

Last Summer ★★★★

Psychological drama
1969 · US · Colour · 96mins

Unheralded for the substantial talent he was, film-maker Frank Perry will probably be best remembered for *Mommie Dearest* instead of tender, emotive movies such as this unnerving teenage odyssey, which contains some of the finest youth performances in American film. Barbara Hershey excels as the sadistic young tease, ultimately responsible for creating a jealousy with brutal and tragic consequences, and the performances Perry elicited from the boys Richard Thomas and Bruce Davison helped them to sterling careers after this movie. Oscar-nominated Catherine Burns proved harder to cast later on, but her brilliant acting illuminates this film. A brave, unsentimental, ultimately callous rites-of-passage movie. TS

Barbara Hershey *Sandy* • Richard Thomas *Peter* • Bruce Davison *Dan* • Cathy Burns [Catherine Burns] *Rhoda* • Ernesto Gonzalez *Anibal* • Ralph Waite *Peter's father* • Peter Turgeon *Mr Caudell* ■ *Dir* Frank Perry • *Scr* Eleanor Perry, from the novel by Evan Hunter

Last Summer in the Hamptons ★★★ 15

Comedy drama 1995 · US · Colour · 107mins

A bittersweet comedy in which a matriarch gathers together her theatrical family for a swansong retreat at their doomed Long Island summer house. Independent writer/director Henry Jaglom's talkfest indulges three generations of thespian intellectuals motivated by an undiluted need to articulate neurosis, self-doubt and desire, and the result is very entertaining, depending on one's taste for this kind of conspicuous, home-movie-like display of personal expression. While Jaglom lacks the visual wit and cheeky detachment of Woody Allen, he still concocts a steady stream of tickling episodes. DO. Contains swearing.

Victoria Foyt *Oona Hart* • Viveca Lindfors *Helena Mora* • Jon Robin Baitz *Jake Axelrod* • Melissa Leo *Trish Axelrod* • Martha Plimpton *Chloe Garfield* • Holland Taylor *Davis Mora Axelrod* • Ron Rifkin *Eli Garfield* • Roddy McDowall *Thomas* • Roscoe Lee Browne *Freddy* • André Gregory [Andre Gregory] *Ivan Axelrod* • Henry Jaglom *Max Berger* ■ *Dir* Henry Jaglom • *Scr* Henry Jaglom, Victoria Foyt

L

The Last Sunset ★★★

Western 1961 · US · Colour · 111mins

Multilayered and superbly cast, this incorporates themes not usually found in westerns, or in many other American movies of the period, notably incest and suicide. Under the heavy hand of *Dirty Dozen* director Robert Aldrich, this Freud-on-the-range saga doesn't quite come off, but the magnificent cast ensures that the film is not just for fans of the genre – Rock Hudson and Kirk Douglas are at ease in the saddle and a joy to watch. The brunt of the movie, however, is borne by Carol Lynley, excellent as a gal brought up on a savage frontier. TS

Rock Hudson *Dana Stribling* • Kirk Douglas *Brendan O'Malley* • Dorothy Malone *Belle Breckenridge* • Joseph Cotten *John Breckenridge* • Carol Lynley *Missy Breckenridge* • Neville Brand *Frank Hobbs* • Regis Toomey *Milton Wing* • Rad Fulton *Julesburg Kid* ■ *Dir* Robert Aldrich • *Scr* Dalton Trumbo, from the novel *Sundown at Crazy Horse* by Howard Rigsby

The Last Supper ★★★

Religious drama
1976 · Cub · Colour · 112mins

This allegory of "Christian liberalism", as the Cuban director Tomás Gutiérrez Alea describes it, has much in common with Luis Buñuel's *Viridiana* in its context and caustic wit. A plantation owner decides to re-create the Last Supper, casting 12 of his slaves as the Apostles, but the situation turns nasty. Filmed in muted colours with a powerful black cast, the picture belabours its message. RB. In Spanish with English subtitles.

Nelson Villagra *Count* • Silvano Rey *Chaplain* • Luis Alberto Garcia *Don Manuel* • José Antonio Rodriguez *Don Gaspar* • Samuel Claxton *Sebastian* • Mario Balmaseda *Martin Sanchez* ■ *Dir* Tomás Gutiérrez Alea • *Scr* Tomás Gutiérrez Alea, Tomás Gonzalez, Maria Eugenia Haya

The Last Supper ★★★ 15

Black comedy 1995 · US · Colour · 87mins

Five liberal students serve poisoned alcohol to a collection of bigoted extremists in this entertaining but insubstantial black comedy. It could be an intriguing, double-edged premise – are Cameron Diaz, Ron Eldard and the rest any less twisted than their victims? – but Dan Rosen's script presents the culinary vigilantes in purely one-dimensional terms. By far the movie's strongest features are its various dinner guests, particularly racist trucker Bill Paxton (the first victim), male chauvinist Mark Harmon and homophobic priest Charles Durning. JC. Contains violence, swearing and sex scenes. DVD

Cameron Diaz *Jude* • Ron Eldard *Pete* • Annabeth Gish *Paulie* • Jonathan Penner *Marc* • Courtney B Vance *Luke* • Jason Alexander *Anti-environmentalist* • Nora Dunn *Sheriff Stanley* • Charles Durning *Reverend Gerald Hutchens* • Mark Harmon *Dominant Male* • Bill Paxton *Zack* ■ *Dir* Stacy Title • *Scr* Dan Rosen

Last Tango in Paris ★★★★★ 18

Drama 1972 · It/Fr · Colour · 123mins

Bernardo Bertolucci's still controversial psychodrama blazed new cinematic frontiers in the way sex was treated on screen. Artfully shot, it's the steamy and thought-provoking tale of the intense love affair that ignites between two strangers. Marlon Brando is trying to get over his wife's suicide, Maria Schneider is about to marry, and both cling to their anonymous liaisons in order to separate their sexual desires from their oppressive daily realities. More existential than erotic, this brilliant study of a broken, tortured man allows Brando to deliver a devastating performance. Gato Barbieri's marvellous jazz score creates a delirious atmosphere, conducive to the breaking of taboos. AJ. In English and French with subtitles. Contains swearing, sex scenes and nudity. DVD

Marlon Brando *Paul* • Maria Schneider *Jeanne* • Jean-Pierre Léaud *Tom* • Catherine Allégret *Catherine* ■ *Dir* Bernardo Bertolucci • *Scr* Bernardo Bertolucci, Franco Arcalli • *Cinematographer* Vittorio Storaro

The Last Temptation of Christ ★★★★ 18

Religious drama 1988 · US · Colour · 156mins

Ignore all the controversy and see Martin Scorsese's moving adaptation of Nikos Kazantzakis's novel for what it is – a challenging essay on the life of Jesus had he ignored his divine destiny and chosen to pursue human aims instead. Certainly neither blasphemous nor offensive, Scorsese's re-creation of the biblical milieu is highly evocative and the all-star performances are welcome modern reinterpretations of scripture stereotypes. It's slightly too long, and Scorsese does pull some punches in deference to the subject matter, but these are minor criticisms of what is a contentious but sincere work. AJ DVD

Willem Dafoe *Jesus Christ* • Harvey Keitel *Judas Iscariot* • Barbara Hershey *Mary Magdalene* • Harry Dean Stanton *Saul/Paul* • David Bowie *Pontius Pilate* • Verna Bloom *Mary, mother of Jesus* • Andre Gregory *John the Baptist* • Juliette Caton *Girl angel* • Roberts Blossom *Aged master* • Irvin Kershner *Zebedee* ■ *Dir* Martin Scorsese • *Scr* Paul Schrader, from the novel *The Last Temptation* by Nikos Kazantzakis

The Last Time I Committed Suicide ★★★ 15

Biographical drama
1996 · US · Colour · 93mins

An artful glimpse into the early life of Beat Generation figure Neal Cassady, a restless spirit who provided friendship and inspiration to cultural icons Jack Kerouac and Ken Kesey. Thomas Jane captures Cassady's cool edginess and his sharp, self-aware narration adds much spirit to the rather laid-back, low-key story. This film's sticking point is the miscasting of Keanu Reeves, who is unconvincing as his persuasive, doggedly irresponsible best friend. That said, director Stephen Kay's evocative, dimly-lit ambience and the jazzy soundtrack gives the film a stylish vibe. JC. Contains some swearing and sexual references. DVD

Thomas Jane *Neal Cassady* • Keanu Reeves *Harry* • Pat McNamara *Father Fletcher* • Kate Williamson *Nurse Waring* • Claire Forlani *Joan* • Gretchen Mol *Cherry Mary* ■ *Dir/Scr* Stephen Kay

The Last Time I Saw Archie ★★ U

Comedy 1961 · US · BW · 98mins

Robert Mitchum is inveterate conman Archie Hall, who joins the army, is mistaken for a general in disguise, tricks everyone into believing his girlfriend is a Japanese agent and gets away with it. This sort of service comedy was a staple for the likes of Bob Hope and the Bilko of Phil Silvers, but Mitchum doesn't really have the light touch, though he's supported by a cast of established laughmeisters. AT

Robert Mitchum *Archie Hall* • Jack Webb *Bill Bowers* • Martha Hyer *Peggy Kramer* • France Nuyen *Cindy Hamilton* • Joe Flynn *Pte Russell Drexel* • James Lydon *Pte Billy Simpson* • Del Moore *Pte Frank Ostrow* • Louis Nye *Pte Sam Beacham* • Richard Arlen *Col Martin* • Don Knotts *Captain Little* ■ *Dir* Jack Webb • *Scr* William Bowers

The Last Time I Saw Paris ★★★ U

Romantic drama
1954 · US · Colour · 115mins

In the hands of talented writer/director Richard Brooks this version of F Scott Fitzgerald's *Babylon Revisited* is remarkably faithful to the original's style and tone. It's also beautifully cast, with Elizabeth Taylor in her sublime prime as the tragic love of alcoholic writer Van Johnson. MGM bought this property from Paramount as a vehicle for Taylor and lavished the best available talent on her (photography by Joseph Ruttenberg, gowns by Helen Rose, music by Conrad Salinger). Fitzgerald's vision of Paris's "lost generation" is well captured, and, although the second half reveals the weaknesses of the original, this is still intelligent and glossy film-making. TS DVD

Elizabeth Taylor *Helen Ellswirth* • Van Johnson *Charles Wills* • Walter Pidgeon *James Ellswirth* • Donna Reed *Marion Ellswirth* • Eva Gabor *Lorraine Quarl* • Kurt Kasznar *Maurice* • Roger Moore *Paul* ■ *Dir* Richard Brooks • *Scr* Philip G Epstein, Julius J Epstein, Richard Brooks, from the story *Babylon Revisited* by F Scott Fitzgerald

The Last Train ★★

Drama 1972 · Fr · Colour · 95mins

A drama set during the Nazi invasion of France, with Jean-Louis Trintignant mislaying his wife in the rush to get the last train from Paris and then helping Romy Schneider by posing as her husband. They fall in love, and then Trintignant's real wife shows up with their child. This is a solidly made story, based on a Georges Simenon novel, that trades heavily on the then commercial appeal of its two glamorous stars. AT

Romy Schneider *Anna* • Jean-Louis Trintignant *Julien* • Maurice Biraud *Deserter* • Régine *Large woman* • Serge Marquand *Man* ■ *Dir* Pierre Granier-Deferre • *Scr* Pascal Jardin, from a novel by Georges Simenon

Last Train from Bombay ★

Adventure 1952 · US · BW · 73mins

Jon Hall washes up in India for this B-movie, produced with every expense spared by Columbia. Hall plays an American diplomat whose friend (Douglas Kennedy) turns out to be a member of an insurrectionist group who plant bombs on trains. Shots of India are sort of glued into the picture, as is the sense that the former British colony needs help from America to stop it slipping into anarchy. AT

Jon Hall *Martin Viking* • Christine Larson *Mary Anne Palmer* • Lisa Ferraday *Charlane* • Douglas Kennedy *Kevin O'Hara* • Michael Fox *Captain Tamil* • Donna Martell *Nawob's daughter* • Matthew Boulton *Col Palmer* ■ *Dir* Fred F Sears • *Scr* Robert Libott

Last Train from Gun Hill ★★★★ 15

Western 1959 · US · Colour · 90mins

A very fine adult western, made by the same team (including director John Sturges and producer Hal Wallis) that worked on *Gunfight at the OK Corral*, with Kirk Douglas again in a starring role. Here, Douglas is at his most intense as a man seeking revenge following the rape and murder of his wife. Anthony Quinn makes a tough adversary, and the rich Technicolor and VistaVision photography is exemplary. Intelligent, finely wrought and exceptionally well cast. TS DVD

Kirk Douglas *Matt Morgan* • Anthony Quinn *Craig Belden* • Carolyn Jones *Linda* • Earl Holliman *Rick Belden* • Ziva Rodann *Catherine Morgan* • Brad Dexter *Beero* • Brian Hutton *Lee* ■ *Dir* John Sturges • *Scr* James Poe, from the story *Showdown* by Les Crutchfield

The Last Train from Madrid ★★★

Period war drama 1937 · US · BW · 85mins

One of the first Hollywood movies to use the Spanish Civil War as background, it avoided taking sides, and was really an excuse to get a number of Paramount contract players together to tell various, rather feeble, stories. But for those who like train movies, an almost vanished genre, there is much to enjoy. Dorothy Lamour, in one of her few dramatic roles, heads a good cast including Lew Ayres, who was to become a conscientious objector during the war, an action which ruined his career. RB

Dorothy Lamour *Carmelita Castillo* • Lew Ayres *Bill Dexter* • Gilbert Roland *Eduardo De Soto* • Karen Morley *Helene Rafitte* • Lionel Atwill *Colonel Vigo* • Helen Mack *Lola* • Robert Cummings *Juan Ramos* ■ *Dir* James Hogan • *Scr* Louis Stevens, Robert Wyler, from a story by Paul Harvey Fox, Elsie Fox

The Last Tycoon ★★★★ 15

Drama 1976 · US · Colour · 117mins

F Scott Fitzgerald's unfinished novel about Hollywood shows a studio boss, Monroe Stahr, in love with a young actress he spots on a film set. Stahr was based on MGM's Irving Thalberg and Robert De Niro plays him with all the personality of a paper cup, only coming alive when he's talking pictures, while the girl, Ingrid Boulting, is catatonic throughout. Yet this is all deliberate, allowing director Elia Kazan and scriptwriter Harold Pinter to explore the schism between the fantasy on the screen and the void in our lives. This approach led the film to critical and box-office doom. A pity, as it's a class act, with the strong cast bringing the edges of the story to vivid life. AT. Contains swearing. [video]

Robert De Niro *Monroe Stahr* • Tony Curtis *Rodriguez* • Robert Mitchum *Pat Brady* • Jeanne Moreau *Didi* • Jack Nicholson *Brimmer* • Donald Pleasence *Boxley* • Ingrid Boulting *Kathleen Moore* • Ray Milland *Fleishacker* • Dana Andrews *Red Ridingwood* • Theresa Russell *Cecilia Brady* • Peter Strauss *Wylie* • John Carradine *Guide* • Anjelica Huston *Edna* ■ *Dir* Elia Kazan • *Scr* Harold Pinter, from the novel by F Scott Fitzgerald

The Last Unicorn ★★ U

Animated adventure
1980 · US · Colour · 88mins

If it weren't for the lacklustre artwork, this animated fantasy might have been quite enchanting. The voices are top-notch and there's little wrong with Peter S Beagle's story, in which a brainy butterfly, a pirate cat, an apprentice wizard and a handsome prince join with a unicorn to help rescue her species. Younger viewers will probably forgive the flat animation, but the grown-ups are going to hate the tacky songs. DP [video] DVD

Alan Arkin *Schmendrick the Magician* • Jeff Bridges *Prince Lir* • Mia Farrow *The Last Unicorn/Lady Amalthea* • Tammy Grimes *Molly Grue* • Robert Klein *The Butterfly* • Angela Lansbury *Mommy Fortuna* • Christopher Lee *King Haggard* • Keenan Wynn *Captain Cully* ■ *Dir* Arthur Rankin Jr, Jules Bass • *Scr* Peter S Beagle, from his novel

The Last Valley ★★★★ 15

Period drama 1971 · UK · Colour · 119mins

A strange, ambitious and fascinating historical epic – one for the connoisseurs – in which mercenary soldier Michael Caine and scholar Omar Sharif discover a peaceful, hidden valley that's managed to avoid being ensnared in the Thirty Years War. What ensues in this Shangri-la is a debate about war, religion, the nature of the soul and the value of society – until something snaps when the swords come out to play and the stake is readied for a burning. Beautifully shot in Austria in 70mm, it contains one of Caine's very finest performances, a script that sidesteps pomposity and a marvellous score by John Barry. AT [video] DVD

Michael Caine *The Captain* • Omar Sharif *Vogel* • Florinda Bolkan *Erica* • Nigel Davenport *Gruber* • Per Oscarsson *Father Sebastian* • Arthur O'Connell *Hoffman* • Madeline Hinde *Inge* • Yorgo Voyagis *Pirelli* • Christian Roberts *Andreas* ■ *Dir* James Clavell • *Scr* James Clavell, from the novel by JB Pick • *Cinematographer* John Wilcox

The Last Victory ★★★ PG

Documentary
2004 · Neth/Aus/Fin/Sp · Colour · 89mins

The Palio is an annual horse racing event that culminates in a bareback race run round the central square of the Italian city of Siena. Director John Appel's documentary traces the pre-Palio preparations of the residents of Civetta, one of the competing Sienese districts. Some details of the race's long history wouldn't have gone amiss, but this colourful film still conveys the passions and partisanships of the Palio, which consolidates community pride in a way that we in Britain can only envy. A thoroughbred piece of work. DA. In Italian with English subtitles.

Dir/Scr John Appel

The Last Voyage ★★★

Drama 1960 · US · Colour · 91mins

Writer/director Andrew L Stone's speciality was filming on location; for this exciting melodrama, he purchased the liner *Ile de France* and put his stellar cast through its paces on her partially scuppered decks. It's exciting and well shot, with no visible studio footage at all. Robert Stack and Dorothy Malone head the cast, while George Sanders is excellent as the troubled captain. TS

Robert Stack *Cliff Henderson* • Dorothy Malone *Laurie Henderson* • George Sanders *Captain Robert Adams* • Edmond O'Brien *Second Engineer Walsh* • Woody Strode *Hank Lawson* • Jack Kruschen *Chief Engineer Pringle* • Tammy Marihugh *Jill Henderson* ■ *Dir/Scr* Andrew L Stone

The Last Wagon ★★★★

Western 1956 · US · Colour · 99mins

A smashing CinemaScope western that deserves to be better known, directed by one of the relatively unsung masters of the genre, Delmer Daves. The ever-excellent Richard Widmark plays trapper Todd, a renegade forced to help wagon train survivors through hostile Apache territory, and he hardly speaks a word for the first half-hour of the movie. Daves's use of landscape is exemplary, with opening sequence crane shots that deserve to be ranked among the cinema's finest. TS

Richard Widmark *Todd* • Felicia Farr *Jenny* • Susan Kohner *Jolie* • Tommy Rettig *Billy* • Stephanie Griffin *Valinda* • Ray Stricklyn *Clint* • Nick Adams *Ridge* • Carl Benton Reid *General Howard* ■ *Dir* Delmer Daves • *Scr* James Edward Grant, Delmer Daves, Gwen Bagni Gielgud, from a story by Gwen Bagni Gielgud

The Last Waltz ★★★★★ U

Documentary 1978 · US · Colour · 111mins

Having been one of the supervising editors of the remarkable rockumentary *Woodstock*, Martin Scorsese was the perfect choice of director for this stunning movie of the Band's farewell gig on Thanksgiving Day 1976. Taking a break from shooting *New York, New York*, he nevertheless planned this film to the last detail during rehearsals and was well served by seven cameramen, including Michael Chapman, Vilmos Zsigmond and Laszlo Kovacs, whose pinpoint shots allow you to concentrate on the performances and the brilliant music. The guests are a *Who's Who* of electric folk and R&B, making this not only an unmissable slice of nostalgia, but also a masterpiece of pop cinema. DP [video] DVD

Dir Martin Scorsese

The Last Warning ★★★

Silent mystery melodrama
1928 · US · BW · 87mins

This part-talkie lacks the eerie atmosphere of Paul Leni's earlier hit *The Cat and the Canary*. Using a theatre set originally designed for Rupert Julian's 1925 version of *The Phantom of the Opera*, it relieves the occasionally histrionic acting with some shadowy photography and a couple of quaint effects. Leading lady Laura La Plante, understudy John Boles and producer Roy D'Arcy are the prime suspects among a troupe reuniting to perform a play, which, five years earlier, witnessed the death of the play's star. DP

Laura La Plante *Doris* • Montague Love [Montagu Love] *McHugh* • Roy D'Arcy *Carlton* • Margaret Livingston *Evalinda* • John Boles *Qualie* • Burr McIntosh *Josiah* ■ *Dir* Paul Leni • *Scr* Alfred A Cohn, Robert F Hill, JG Hawks, Tom Reed (titles), from the story *House of Fear* by Wadsworth Camp, from the play *The Last Warning; a Melodrama in Three Acts* by Thomas F Fallon

The Last Wave ★★★★

Supernatural drama
1977 · Aus · Colour · 105mins

Peter Weir was inspired to make this film after he found a piece of broken statue on a Tunisian beach. Although Richard Chamberlain is clearly out of his depth in the lead, this is a mesmerising supernatural drama, in which a dramatic change in the weather and a series of troubling dreams prompt a Sydney lawyer to venture into the city's aboriginal underworld. Aboriginal pressure groups felt Weir had debased their mythology, but David Gulpilil and the other indigenous cast members obviously felt otherwise. DP

Richard Chamberlain *David Burton* • Olivia Hamnett *Annie Burton* • Gulpilil [David Gulpilil] *Chris Lee* • Frederick Parslow *Reverend Burton* • Vivean Gray *Dr Whitburn* ■ *Dir* Peter Weir • *Scr* Peter Weir, Tony Morphett, Petru Popescu

The Last Winter ★★★

Drama 1989 · Can · Colour · 115mins

An atmospheric film about a young country boy's coming of age in the Canadian Prairie. The open landscape and the punishing winters shape the mood of this semi-autobiographical work, written and directed by Aaron Kim Johnston. Joshua Murray gives a superior performance as the ten-year-old farm lad with a crush on his cousin, whose vivid fantasy life centres on a white stallion that gallops across the wintry scene. PF

Gerard Parkes *Grampa Jack* • Joshua Murray *William Jamieson* • David Ferry *Ross Jamieson* • Wanda Cannon *Audrey Jamieson* • Nathaniel Moreau *John Jamieson* • Kate Murray [Katharine Isabelle] *Winnie Jamieson* ■ *Dir/Scr* Aaron Kim Johnston

The Last Woman on Earth ★

Science fiction 1960 · US · Colour · 64mins

Crooks Anthony Carbone and Ed Wain fight over Betsy Jones-Moreland when they turn out to be the only survivors of a nuclear war in Puerto Rico. Not one of cult director Roger Corman's best efforts, this sci-fi *ménage à trois* tale is cheap, dull and unappealing. "Ed Wain" is the pseudonym of future Oscar-winning screenwriter Robert Towne, who hadn't finished the script (his first) in time and was brought along to complete it on location. Ever the cost-cutter, Corman then had Towne play the second lead, even though he'd never acted before. AJ

Antony Carbone *Harold* • Betsy Jones-Moreland *Evelyn* • Edward Wain [Robert Towne] *Martin* ■ *Dir* Roger Corman • *Scr* Edward Wain [Robert Towne]

Last Year at Marienbad ★★★★★ U

Drama 1961 · Fr/It · BW · 90mins

Written by modernist novelist Alain Robbe-Grillet, this is a complex cinematic riddle without an answer. Are Delphine Seyrig and Giorgio Albertazzi really reuniting a year after their first meeting? Or was she killed by her jealous husband, Sacha Pitoeff? Does the film take place in Albertazzi's memory, or is it simply an erotic fantasy on Seyrig's part? The winner of the Golden Lion at the Venice film festival, Alain Resnais' film is a triumph of camera movement, symbolic decor, abstract structure and stylised playing. A veritable masterpiece, but beware: it is as likely to irritate as it is to mesmerise. DP. In French with English subtitles. [video] DVD

Delphine Seyrig *A/Woman* • Giorgio Albertazzi *X/Stranger* • Sacha Pitoeff *M/Man/Husband or Lover* ■ *Dir* Alain Resnais • *Scr* Alain Robbe-Grillet • *Cinematographer* Sacha Vierny

The Last Yellow ★★ 15

Comedy drama
1999 · UK/Ger · Colour · 89mins

A promising cast can't disguise the stage origins of Julian Farino's dark comedy. The setting is Leicester, where bespectacled nerd Charlie Creed-Miles hires lodger Mark Addy to wreak revenge on the thug who gave his brother brain damage. The relationship between the two hapless avengers is well-drawn, but the intriguing preamble gives way to a disappointingly theatrical three-hander between the duo and their intended victim's trashy girlfriend (Samantha Morton). NS. Contains swearing and violence. [video] DVD

Mark Addy *Frank* • Charlie Creed-Miles *Kenny* • Samantha Morton *Jackie* • Kenneth Cranham *Len* • Alan Atherall *Donut* ■ *Dir* Julian Farino • *Scr* Paul Tucker, from his play

Latcho Drom ★★★★

Music documentary
1993 · Fr · Colour · 103mins

This is the second of Tony Gatlif's trilogy, which includes *Les Princes* (1982) and *Gadjo Dilo* (1997). Following the Romanies from their homelands in northern India across Africa and middle Europe to Spain, Gatlif's abstract odyssey is more a celebration of human indomitability and cultural vivacity than a protest against centuries of prejudice and injustice. What is so fascinating about this graceful musical tribute, is not just how the lyrics become increasingly bitter in countries where the persecution of the Romany peoples has been most vicious, but also how the music has both influenced and embraced the indigenous folk sound. DP. A French/Romany language film.

Dir/Scr Tony Gatlif

Late August, Early September ★★ 15

Drama 1998 · Fr · Colour · 106mins

Although the circle of friends around novelist François Cluzet chatter endlessly, they fail to interest us in either their personalities or their problems. Only Jeanne Balibar's intense misery at losing noncommittal literary editor Mathieu Amalric to designer Virginie Ledoyen strikes a chord. Employing tired New Wave techniques to achieve its multi-perspective structure, Olivier Assayas's trite picture is also guilty of some regrettable gender stereotyping. DP. In French with English subtitles. Contains swearing and sex scenes. [video]

Virginie Ledoyen *Anne Rosenwald* • Mathieu Amalric *Gabriel Deshays* • François Cluzet *Adrien Willer* • Jeanne Balibar *Jenny* • Alex Decas *Jérémie* ■ *Dir/Scr* Olivier Assayas

Late Autumn ★★★★

Drama 1960 · Jpn · Colour · 129mins

Coming towards the end of his illustrious 35-year career, Yasujiro Ozu had a little fun at his own expense with this gently comic, petit bourgeois drama. Confounding stylistic expectations, he experiments with a variety of transitional devices while structuring the narrative around blocks of diegetically linked scenes. His third film on the subject of arranged marriage is also one of his most slyly satirical, with the triumvirate of businessmen trying to find partners for widow Setsuko Hara and her independent daughter, Yoko Tsukasa, being ridiculed both for their insufferable interference and their smug acquiescence in postwar Japan's socio-political status quo. DP. In Japanese with English subtitles.

Setsuko Hara *Akiko Miwa* • Yoko Tsukasa *Ayako* • Mariko Okada *Yuriko Sasaki* • Keiji Sada *Shotaro Goto* • Chishu Ryu *Shukichi Miwa* ■ *Dir* Yasujiro Ozu • *Scr* Yasujiro Ozu, Kogo Noda

Late Bloomers ★★★ 15

Comedy drama 1995 · US · Colour · 107mins

This engaging lesbian comedy drama explores an extraordinary situation

L

through the eyes of everyday people. Neither basketball coach Connie Nelson nor school secretary and mother of two, Dee Hennigan, expect to fall in love. So, there's something charming about the way in which they see each other through the inevitable merry-go-round of confusion and derision that attends their romance. The homophobic reaction of their conservative neighbours is a touch formulaic, but this is offset by the nicely handled relationship with incomprehending teenage daughter Lisa Peterson. DP

Connie Nelson *Dinah Groshardt* • Dee Hennigan *Carly Lumpkin* • Gary Carter *Rom Lumpkin* • Lisa Peterson *Val Lumpkin* • Esteban Powell *Jamie Hooper* • Joe Nemmers *Rick Musso* ■ *Dir* Julia Dyer • *Scr* Gretchen Dyer

The Late Edwina Black ★

Crime mystery 1951 · UK · BW · 82mins

Apart from questioning how closely they read the script when they were offered their parts, the first duty here is to exonerate the actors of any responsibility for this feeble Victorian whodunnit. You could give director Maurice Elvey a ticking off for not trying a little harder to find ways of keeping the killer's identity a secret, but then what can he do with a story that was intent on giving the game away almost before it started? DP

David Farrar *Gregory Black* • Geraldine Fitzgerald *Elizabeth* • Roland Culver *Inspector* • Jean Cadell *Ellen the housekeeper* • Mary Merrall *Lady Southdale* • Harcourt Williams *Doctor Prendergast* ■ *Dir* Maurice Elvey • *Scr* Charles Frank, David Evans, from the play by William Dinner, William Morum

L

Late for Dinner ★★ PG

Comedy 1991 · US · Colour · 88mins

Brian Wimmer and Peter Berg show why they are fully paid-up members of the "straight-to-video club" as two fugitives who emerge from a 29-year suspended animation experiment to find that (you'll never guess it) the world has moved on since 1962 and they are slightly out of place. DP

Brian Wimmer *Willie Husband* • Peter Berg *Frank Lovegren* • Marcia Gay Harden *Joy Husband* • Colleen Flynn *Jessica Husband* • Kyle Secor *Leland Shakes* • Michael Beach *Dr David Arrington* • Bo Brundin *Dr Dan Chilblains* • Peter Gallagher *Bob Freeman* ■ *Dir* WD Richter • *Scr* Mark Andrus

The Late George Apley ★★★

Satirical comedy 1947 · US · BW · 98mins

John P Marquand's novel in diary form about the rigidities of Boston patrician existence at the turn of the century was brought to the screen by director Joseph L Mankiewicz and contains exemplary performances from British actors Ronald Colman and Peggy Cummins. Although lacking the barbs of the book, and minus the epilogue that gives the work its title, the movie is witty and stylish. TS

Ronald Colman *George Apley* • Peggy Cummins *Eleanor Apley* • Vanessa Brown *Agnes* • Richard Haydn *Horatio Willing* • Charles Russell *Howard Boulder* • Richard Ney *John Apley* • Percy Waram *Roger Newcombe* • Mildred Natwick *Amelia Newcombe* ■ *Dir* Joseph L Mankiewicz • *Scr* Philip Dunne, from the play by John P Marquand, George S Kaufman, from the novel by John P Marquand,

The Late Liz ★★

Religious drama 1971 · US · Colour · 119mins

Hollywood veterans Anne Baxter and Steve Forrest star in this rum drama about an alcoholic who goes on the wagon when she finds religion. The film has its heart in the right place, but it's not helped by the melodramatic direction and ripe acting, which give an unintentionally kitsch air to the proceedings. Like many such "battle with the bottle" movies, one feels an overwhelming urge afterwards to head down to the nearest boozer. DA

Anne Baxter *Liz Addams Hatch* • Steve Forrest *Jim Hatch* • James Gregory *Sam Burns* • Coleen Gray *Sue Webb* • Joan Hotchkis *Sally* • Jack Albertson *Reverend Rogers* ■ *Dir* Dick Ross • *Scr* Bill Rega, from an autobiography by Gert Behanna

Late Marriage ★★★

Comedy drama
2001 · Is/Fr · Colour · 102mins

The clash between tradition and progress dominates this Tel Aviv-based tale of family division. Much of the dispute between 30-something academic Lior Louie Ashkenazi and his Georgian-Jewish parents is darkly comic. He's secretly in love with a passionate Moroccan divorcee and single mum (Ronit Elkabetz) whereas his doting mother and father expect him to marry a nice young virgin. However, the scene in which the parents confront their son's lover in her own home is disturbingly dramatic while emphasising the cultural and generational rifts that run throughout Israeli society. Debuting director Dover Kosashvili handles cast and theme with equal aplomb. DP. In Hebrew and Georgian with English subtitles.

Lior Louie Ashkenazi *Zaza* • Ronit Elkabetz *Judith* • Moni Moshonov *Yasha* • Lili Kosashvili *Lili* ■ *Dir/Scr* Dover Kosashvili

Late Night Shopping ★★★ 15

Comedy 2001 · UK/Ger · Colour · 87mins

Regardless of the quality of this spirited sub-slacker comedy, debutant director Saul Metzstein is to be applauded for his casting and choice of cinematographer. Brian Tufano brings the same exemplary sense of place that elevated *Trainspotting*, *East Is East* and *Billy Elliot* to this tangled tale of four flailing friends. Occasional episodes sit uneasily, but such is the pace and perception of Jack Lothian's script and the unforced affability of Metzstein's direction that the *Friends* clichés and easy resolutions can be readily forgiven. DP DVD

Luke de Woolfson *Sean* • James Lance *Vincent* • Kate Ashfield *Jody* • Enzo Cilenti *Lenny* • Heike Makatsch *Madeline* • Shauna MacDonald *Gail* • Sienna Guillory *Susie* ■ *Dir* Saul Metzstein • *Scr* Jack Lothian • *Cinematographer* Brian Tufano

The Late Shift ★★★★

Comedy drama based on a true story
1996 · US · Colour · 90mins

British TV fans may not recognise the protagonists in this true-life drama about the battle of the talk show hosts, but it's still interesting to see the behind-the-scenes intrigue of American TV, *Larry Sanders* style. When Johnny Carson, king of the late night talkshow, announced his retirement from the *Tonight Show*, a battle began for his coveted job, with David Letterman and Jay Leno (played here by dead-ringers John Michael Higgins and Daniel Roebuck) the two main contenders. It was Leno's tough-as-nails manager Helen Kushnick (Kathy Bates) who was credited with getting Leno the job, but this TV movie delves into all the political manouevres on both sides. Director Betty Thomas injects the fascinating story – a riveting battle of egos – with nice touches of humour. JB

Kathy Bates *Helen Kushnick* • John Michael Higgins *David Letterman* • Daniel Roebuck *Jay Leno* • Bob Balaban *Warren Littlefield* • Ed Begley Jr *Rod Perth* ■ *Dir* Betty Thomas • *Scr* George Armitage, from the non-fiction bestseller by Bob Carter

The Late Show ★★★ 15

Comedy 1977 · US · Colour · 89mins

This is a patchy Robert Benton-directed homage to those old homburg-and-raincoat private eye movies which flourished in the 1940s. Art Carney and Lily Tomlin overact wildly as the curmudgeonly old PI and the neurotic object of his attentions, and the ensuing plot convolutions are so tangled as to be incomprehensible. Benton's crisp direction and a neat suburban atmosphere save the day, but this fails to hit the target. SH

Art Carney *Ira Wells* • Lily Tomlin *Margo* • Bill Macy *Charlie Hatter* • Eugene Roche *Ron Birdwell* • Joanna Cassidy *Laura Birdwell* ■ *Dir/Scr* Robert Benton

Late Spring ★★★★

Drama 1949 · Jpn · BW · 108mins

Yasujiro Ozu began to exhibit here the stylistic and thematic tropes that would sustain him for the remainder of his career: the "pillow shots" between scenes offering poetic digressions from the main action; the low-angle, almost static camerawork; and the preoccupation with lower-middle-class attitudes and the need to progress. Often ranked alongside *Tokyo Story*, the tale of professor Chishu Ryu's attempts to marry off Setsuko Hara, the daughter on whom he depends, remained one of the director's favourites. With its harmony of composition, tone and performance, it's easy to see why. DP. In Japanese with English subtitles.

Chishu Ryu *Professor Shukichi Somiya* • Setsuko Hara *Noriko, Somiya's daughter* • Yumeji Tsukioka *Aya Kitagawa* • Haruko Sugimura *Masa Taguchi, Noriko's aunt* • Hohi Aoki *Katsuyochi Taguchi* ■ *Dir* Yasujiro Ozu • *Scr* Kogo Noda, from the novel *Chichi to Musume (Father and Daughter)* by Kazuo Hirotsu • *Cinematographer* Yuharu Atsuta [Yushun Atsuta]

The Late Twentieth ★ 18

Thriller 2002 · UK · Colour · 79mins

Debutant director Hadi Hajaig deserves great credit for getting his film made and distributed, but the same cannot be said for the content of this abysmal London-set thriller. The encounter between John Webber's guilt-fuelled asylum escapee and drug-dealing killer Justin Allder is an utter shambles, with the action veering across time frames and plotlines without any credible motivation for the violent and improbable incidents. DP. Contains violence, swearing and drug abuse.

John Webber *The Man/Ali* • Justin Allder *Tom* • Sam Loggin *Jane* • Hannah Watkins *Emma* • Camilla Heaney *Margaret* • Markus Napier *Dave* • Paula Jennings *Eve* ■ *Dir/Scr* Hadi Hajaig

The Lathe of Heaven ★★★

Science-fiction drama
1979 · US · Colour · 105mins

Bruce Davison's dreams have the power to change reality in a classy adaptation of Ursula K LeGuin's popular novel. Can psychologist Kevin Conway manipulate him into dreaming a better world? Taking on lofty Kafka-esque subtexts, and using Texas landscapes to suggest the future, this subtle fantasy raises pertinent questions about individualism and the march of progress. A disappointing TV movie remake appeared in 2002, starring James Caan. AJ

Bruce Davison *George Orr* • Kevin Conway *Dr William Haber* • Margaret Avery (2) *Heather LeLache* • Peyton Park *Mannie Ahrens* • Niki Flacks *Penny Crouch* • Vandi Clark *Aunth Ethel* ■ *Dir* David Loxton, Fred Barzyk • *Scr* Roger E Swaybill, Diane English, from the novel by Ursula K LeGuin

Latin Boys Go to Hell ★★★ 18

Comedy drama
1997 · US/Ger/Sp/Jpn · Colour · 69mins

Ela Troyano's first feature is a cheap, cheerful and endearingly clumsy melodrama. Gay-and-proud-of-it Alexis Artiles is incensed when his hard-body lover Mike Ruiz picks up Manhattan teenager Irwin Ossa. Further romantic complications occur when Ossa develops a crush on his cousin John Bryant Davila while Artiles's closeness to heterosexual photographer Annie Iobst gets in the way of his own relationship. Sometimes funny, sometimes puerile, Latino machismo clichés are neatly subverted with remarkable style in this camp stew of betrayal and madness. AJ

Irwin Ossa *Justin Vega* • John Bryant Davila *Angel, Justin's cousin* • Alexis Artiles *Braulio* • Mike Ruiz *Carlos* • Jenifer Lee Simard *Andrea* ■ *Dir* Ela Troyano • *Scr* Ela Troyano, Andre Salas, from a novel by Andre Salas

Latin Lovers ★★ U

Musical comedy 1953 · US · Colour · 104mins

Multi-millionairess Lana Turner, on vacation in Rio and hungry to be loved for herself rather than her money, has problems deciding whether to choose rich John Lund or less rich but glamorous "Latin Lover" Ricardo Montalban. This hoary old romantic drivel, written by Isobel Lennart with an attempt at wit which occasionally succeeds, is directed on automatic pilot by Mervyn LeRoy. Leaden, but periodically enlivened by a song, and Lana and Ricardo dancing the samba. RK

Lana Turner *Nora Taylor* • Ricardo Montalban *Roberto Santos* • John Lund *Paul Chevron* • Louis Calhern *Grandfather Santos* • Jean Hagen *Anne Kellwood* • Eduard Franz *Dr Lionel Y Newman* • Beulah Bondi *Analyst* ■ *Dir* Mervyn LeRoy • *Scr* Isobel Lennart

Latino ★★ 15

Drama 1985 · US · Colour · 103mins

A former Green Beret and Vietnam veteran is sent to Honduras to help the CIA-backed Contras overthrow the Marxist government of neighbouring Nicaragua. But faced with the brutality of the Contras, our hero changes sides. Directed by the gifted cinematographer Haskell Wexler, this delivers the sort of emotionally top-heavy propaganda that once poured out of Uncle Joe Stalin's studios. It was filmed in Nicaragua with government endorsement, and back in America that well-known radical, George Lucas, co-financed it and helped with the editing. AT

Robert Beltran *Eddie Guerrero* • Annette Cardona *Marlena* • Tony Plana *Ruben Trevino* • Ricardo Lopez *Attila* • Luis Torrentes *Luis* ■ *Dir/Scr* Haskell Wexler

Latitude Zero ★★★

Science fiction
1969 · Jpn/US · Colour · 104mins

The *Godzilla* team of director Inoshiro Honda and special effects genius Eiji Tsuburaya inhabit Jules Verne territory in this absurdly enjoyable underwater fantasy mixing monsters and morality. Submarine commander Joseph Cotton ferries scientists to the underwater city of Latitude Zero, where radiation-immunisation research is being carried out. Cesar Romero is the evil genius who experiments with human brain transplants in animals and whose mission it is to destroy the undersea complex because of its good works. Delightfully campy. AJ

Joseph Cotten *Capt Craig McKenzie* • Cesar Romero *Malic* • Richard Jaeckel *Perry Lawton* • Patricia Medina *Lucretia* • Linda Haynes *Dr Anne Barton* • Akira Takarada *Dr Ken Tashiro* • Mari Nakayama *"Tsuroko" Okada* ■ *Dir* Ishiro Honda [Inoshiro Honda] • *Scr* Shinichi Sekizawa, Ted Sherdeman, from stories by Ted Sherdeman

Laugh and Get Rich ★★

Comedy 1931 · US · BW · 75mins

Gregory La Cava would go on to make funnier and faster films in the 1930s than this tale of a landlady having to put up with her lazy husband's crazy get-rich-quick schemes. That they are played by horse-faced Edna May Oliver and fidgety Hugh Herbert does help matters slightly, but the title originally mooted for the film, *Room and Bored*, might have been more appropriate. RB

Hugh Herbert *Joe Austin* • Edna May Oliver *Sarah Austin* • Dorothy Lee *Alice Austin* • John Harron *Hepburn* • Robert Emmett Keane *Phelps* ■ *Dir* Gregory La Cava • *Scr* Gregory La Cava, Ralph Spence, from a story by Douglas MacLean

Laugh, Clown, Laugh ★★★

Silent romantic drama
1928 · US · BW · 65mins

Lon Chaney does the noble thing by Loretta Young in Herbert Brenon's silent take on David Belasco and Tom Cushing's stage play. As the clown who persuades his partner Bernard Siegel to care for an abandoned waif, Chaney is both avuncular and vulnerable, as he realises that Young's heart belongs to dashing nobleman, Nils Asther. In her first starring role, the 15-year-old Young is enchantingly natural, but it's Chaney's command of mime that makes this moving. DP

Lon Chaney *Tito* • Bernard Siegel *Simon* • Loretta Young *Simonette* • Cissy Fitz-Gerald *Giacinta* • Nils Asther *Luigi* • Gwen Lee *Lucretia* ■ *Dir* Herbert Brenon • *Scr* Joseph Farnham (titles), Elizabeth Meehan (adaptation), from a play by David Belasco, Tom Cushing

Laughing at Life ★★

Drama 1933 · US · BW · 72mins

Made for a pittance and looking cheaper, this drama marks director Ford Beebe's second feature. Yet, already, the brisk, no-nonsense style that would characterise his work is clearly evident, as Victor McLaglen's mercenary departs for Latin America and runs into his long-lost son while mixed up with a gun-running racket. DP

Victor McLaglen *Dennis P McHale* • Conchita Montenegro *Panchita* • [William "Stage" Boyd] *Mason* • Lois Wilson *Mrs McHale* • Henry B Walthall *President Valenzuela* • Regis Toomey *Pat Collins* ■ *Dir* Ford Beebe • *Scr* Prescott Chaplin, Thomas Dugan, from a story by Ford Beebe

The Laughing Policeman ★★

Thriller 1973 · US · Colour · 111mins

Walter Matthau stars as the veteran cop investigating a mass slaughter on a public bus. The trail leads to the gay underworld and a lot of closet doors. Like Eastwood's Harry Callahan, Matthau has to cut through miles of red tape that favours the criminal and makes the cops look like SS stormtroopers. San Francisco is the slightly over-familiar backdrop to all this and it ends, predictably, with a bus journey along those up-and-down, bouncy-bouncy streets. AT

Walter Matthau *Jake Martin* • Bruce Dern *Leo Larsen* • Lou Gossett [Louis Gossett Jr] *Larrimore* • Albert Paulsen *Camerero* • Anthony Zerbe *Lt Steiner* • Val Avery *Pappas* • Cathy Lee Crosby *Kay Butler* ■ *Dir* Stuart Rosenberg • *Scr* Thomas Rickman [Tom Rickman], from the novel by Per Wahloo, Maj Sjowall

Laughing Sinners ★★

Melodrama 1931 · US · BW · 72mins

The Joan Crawford-Clark Gable duo would have better outings than this one in which Salvation Army officer Gable saves unhappy nightclub entertainer Crawford from herself after she's dumped by the slick cad (Neil Hamilton) she worships. Nonetheless, it starts well enough, and is a must for Crawford fans who will enjoy being reminded that she was once very pretty, a good dancer, and more talented than many of her later scenery-chewing roles allowed. RK

Joan Crawford *Ivy Stevens* • Neil Hamilton *Howard Palmer* • Clark Gable *Carl Loomis* • Marjorie Rambeau *Ruby* • Guy Kibbee *Cass Wheeler* • Cliff Edwards *Mike* ■ *Dir* Harry Beaumont • *Scr* Bess Meredyth, Martin Flavin, Edith Fitzgerald, from the play *Torch Song* by Kenyon Nicholson

Laughter ★★★

Comedy drama 1930 · US · BW · 85mins

This lively precursor of screwball comedy boasts ingratiating performances from Fredric March as an uninhibited composer and Nancy Carroll as his old girlfriend, who marries Frank Morgan for his money. Their conduct is shameless but great fun, as Carroll soon finds her new life empty and can't resist March's charms. Only Glenn Anders – overacting as a sourpuss romantic rival – spoils the atmosphere of sparkling jollity set up by little remembered director, Harry d'Abbadie D'Arrast. AE

Fredric March *Paul Lockridge* • Nancy Carroll *Peggy Gibson* • Frank Morgan *C Mortimer Gibson* • Glenn Anders *Ralph Le Saint* • Diane Ellis *Marjorie Gibson* • Leonard Carey *Benham* • Ollie Burgoyne *Pearl* ■ *Dir* Harry d'Abbadie D'Arrast • *Scr* Donald Ogden Stewart, from a story by Harry D'Abbadie D'Arrast, Douglas Doty

Laughter in Paradise ★★★★ U

Comedy 1951 · UK · BW · 92mins

Films made up of interwoven stories are notoriously difficult to do well, as it's all too easy either to lose the threads of the difficult episodes or to become impatient with the obviously makeweight ones. That director Mario Zampi nearly brings off the trick here is down almost entirely to the fantastic performance of Alastair Sim as the henpecked thriller writer whose inheritance depends on him receiving a 28-day jail sentence. The scene in which he tries to shoplift is one of the funniest in a career overladen with choice comic moments. DP [video]

Alastair Sim *Deniston Russell* • Fay Compton *Agnes Russell* • Beatrice Campbell *Lucille Grayson* • Veronica Hurst *Joan Webb* • Guy Middleton *Simon Russell* • George Cole *Herbert Russell* • AE Matthews *Sir Charles Robson* • Joyce Grenfell *Elizabeth Robson* • Anthony Steel *Roger Godfrey* • John Laurie *Gordon Webb* • Michael Pertwee *Stuart* • Audrey Hepburn *Cigarette girl* ■ *Dir* Mario Zampi • *Scr* Michael Pertwee, Jack Davies

Laughter in the Dark ★★★

Drama 1969 · UK · Colour · 106mins

Vladimir Nabokov's novel, set in 1930s Germany, is a study in sexual psychopathy and sadism. It's about an art dealer who is blinded in a car crash and whose wife, an usherette at a cinema, gets her lover to move in with them, taunting the disabled husband until he can take no more humiliation. Updated to the London art world in the 1960s, with further scenes set in Majorca, this is a gripping drama that's flawed only because everyone in it – even the blind husband – is unpleasant. Anna Karina is the wife-usherette, but everyone is eclipsed by the powerhouse Nicol Williamson. AT

Nicol Williamson *Sir Edward More* • Anna Karina *Margot* • Jean-Claude Drouot *Herve Tourace* • Peter Bowles *Paul* • Sian Phillips *Lady Elizabeth More* • Sebastian Breaks *Brian* • Kate O'Toole *Amelia More* ■ *Dir* Tony Richardson • *Scr* Edward Bond, from the novel by Vladimir Nabokov

Laughter on the 23rd Floor ★★★ 15

Comedy 2000 · US · Colour · 98mins

Mark Linn-Baker plays a comedy writer in this made-for-cable, Neil Simon memoir of his own days on the legendary weekly programme, *Your Show of Shows* with Sid Caesar. Richard Benjamin directs this adaptation, where quips fly faster than arrows (and do more damage) and everyone is so wrapped up in hitting deadlines that no one notices that frontman Nathan Lane is slowly going down the pan. Slick, smart and poignantly witty. DP [video]

Nathan Lane *Max Prince* • Mark Linn-Baker *Val* • Victor Garber *Kenny* • Saul Rubinek *Ira* • Peri Gilpin *Carol* • Dan Castellaneta *Milt* • Richard Portnow *Harry* ■ *Dir* Richard Benjamin • *Scr* Neil Simon, from his play

Laughterhouse ★★ PG

Comedy 1984 · UK · Colour · 88mins

When farmer Ian Holm faces a strike by his workforce, he decides to walk his Christmas-fattened geese from Norfolk to London's Smithfield market and the slaughterhouse. Actor Brian Glover's script incorporates union-bashing and media-lashing, but can't make the human characters very likeable, although Bill Owen does appear as one of the accompanying vocal yokels. A rather tame goose chase. TH [video]

Ian Holm *Ben Singleton* • Penelope Wilton *Alice Singleton* • Bill Owen *Amos* • Richard Hope *Hubert* • Stephen Moore *Howard* • Rosemary Martin *Continuity girl* ■ *Dir* Richard Eyre • *Scr* Brian Glover

Laura ★★★★★ PG

Classic film noir 1944 · US · BW · 83mins

"I shall never forget the night Laura died ..." begins the narrator, and neither will you. This taut, romantic mystery in which New York detective Dana Andrews falls in love with an image encapsulates what *film noir* is all about. Otto Preminger's moody, stark direction is greatly helped by the casting of beautiful Gene Tierney in the title role, a southern-accented Vincent Price as a smarmy gigolo and the incomparable Clifton Webb as a columnist. The David Raksin score is, quite simply, matchless. If you've never seen it, don't miss, and don't be put off by the film's now classic status – it's a rattling good thriller and bears watching time and time again. TS [video]

Gene Tierney *Laura Hunt* • Dana Andrews *Det Mark McPherson* • Clifton Webb *Waldo Lydecker* • Vincent Price *Shelby Carpenter* • Judith Anderson *Ann Treadwell* • Dorothy Adams *Bessie Clary* • James Flavin *McAvity* • Clyde Fillmore *Bullitt* • Ralph Dunn *Fred Callahan* • Grant Mitchell *Corey* • Kathleen Howard *Louise* • Lee Tung Foo *Servant* • Cy Kendall *Inspector* ■ *Dir* Otto Preminger • *Scr* Jay Dratler, Samuel Hoffenstein, Betty Reinhardt, Jerome Cady, from the novel by Vera Caspary • *Cinematographer* Joseph LaShelle, Lucien Ballard

Laura's Star ★★ U

Animated fantasy
2004 · Ger/Hun · Colour · 80mins

A little girl befriends a fallen star in this animated tale based on the children's book by Klaus Baumgart. Dubbed into English from German, the film takes what would be a decent premise for a short and drags it out to feature length. As sweet as it often is, there's not much to excite the imagination, as seven-year-old Laura struggles to settle into her new home in the city after moving from the country. Her salvation comes when she finds the injured star. Though the very young will enjoy the movie's picture-book simplicity, there's practically zero appeal for adults. SF. German dialogue dubbed into English.

Clemmie Hooton *Laura* • Anthony Da Silva *Tommy* • Matthew Thomas-Davis *Max* • Rebecca Vere *Mother/Sun* • Nick Saich *Father/Moon* • Mirko Nontschew *Robot cat/Bear* ■ *Dir* Piet de Rycker, Thilo Graf Rothkirch • *Scr* Piet de Rycker, from the illustrated book by Klaus Baumgart

Laurel and Hardy's Laughing 20s ★★★★ U

Comedy compilation 1965 · US · BW · 86mins

Robert Youngson's Laurel and Hardy compilation was advertised with a sworn statement from a research company that promised 253 laughs, "the record for laugh content of any comedy we have measured in our 30 years of experience". This collection lives up to that hype and is a treat for enthusiasts. The majority of the scenes are taken from Stan and Ollie's silent shorts, among them *Putting Pants on Philip, From Soup to Nuts, Wrong Again, The Finishing Touch* and *Liberty*. However, there is also a rare opportunity to see some of the other comics in the Hal Roach stable in action, among them the dapper Charley Chase and the scowling Edgar Kennedy. DP [video]

Stan Laurel *Stan* • Oliver Hardy *Ollie* • Charley Chase • Edgar Kennedy • James Finlayson • Jay Jackson *Narrator* ■ *Dir/Scr* Robert Youngson

Laurel Canyon ★★★ 18

Drama 2002 · US · Colour · 98mins

This is an engaging and skilfully observed drama, depicting the moth-to-a-flame effect of radically divergent personalities. Conservative couple Christian Bale and Kate Beckinsale find their relationship threatened by 1960s-style bohemianism, when they move in with his LA music-biz mother, Frances McDormand. McDormand delivers a strong performance, but disappointingly writer/director Lisa Cholodenko only scratches the surface of her libertine lifestyle, failing to explain Bale and Beckinsale's extreme reactions. SF. Contains swearing, drug abuse and nudity. [video] DVD

Frances McDormand *Jane* • Christian Bale *Sam* • Kate Beckinsale *Alex* • Natascha McElhone *Sara* • Alessandro Nivola *Ian* • Louis Knox Barlow *Fripp* • Russell Pollard *Rowan* • Imaad Wasif *Dean* ■ *Dir/Scr* Lisa Cholodenko

Lautrec ★★

Biographical drama
1998 · Fr/Sp · Colour · 127mins

Director Roger Planchon aims to depict the vibrancy of the environment that inspired Impressionist painter Henri de Toulouse-Lautrec. With many tableaux consciously staged to recall posters and canvases, this superbly designed film is a joy to behold. But the endless bohemian bonhomie often feels forced, and even the tempestuous relationship with Suzanne Valadon (Elsa Zylberstein) is devoid of passion. Régis Royer's portrait of Lautrec is lifelike, but this has all the emotional authenticity of a Hollywood biopic. DP. In French with English subtitles.

Régis Royer *Henri de Toulouse-Lautrec* • Elsa Zylberstein *Suzanne Valadon* • Anémone *Adèle de Toulouse-Lautrec* • Claude Rich *Alphonse de Toulouse-Lautrec* ■ *Dir/Scr* Roger Planchon

L

Lava ★★ 18

Black comedy crime thriller
2000 · UK · Colour · 95mins

Prompted by the true-life event that he witnessed which also inspired his brother Paul's screenplay for *The Last Yellow*, writer/director Joe Tucker's film is a tale of spiralling violence within the confines of a Notting Hill flat. Tucker also takes the lead role as a militaristic headcase who offers to avenge an assault that left his friend's (James Holmes) brother in a near-vegetative state. But as the body count increases, the film becomes more reliant on the bleak comedy generated by Tucker's macho posturing and Holmes's nerdy timidity. Nicola Stapleton fizzes as a thug's foul-mouthed girlfriend. DP DVD

Joe Tucker *Smiggy* • Nicola Stapleton *Julie* • James Holmes *Phillip* • Grahame Fox *Darrel* • Mark Leadbetter *Neville* • Tameke Empson *Maxine* • Leslie Grantham *Mr Aladdin* • Tom Bell *Eric* ■ *Dir/Scr* Joe Tucker

The Lavender Hill Mob ★★★★★ U

Classic crime comedy
1951 · UK · BW · 77mins

In this superb and subtle crime-film spoof, the inimitable Alec Guinness stars as the mild-mannered bank agent who discovers he has a devious criminal mind, and decides to steal £1-million-worth of gold bullion. Guinness is well supported by the impressive Stanley Holloway, Alfie Bass and Sid James as members of the gang he recruits. Watch out too for a couple of blink-and-miss-them walk-ons from James (billed as William) Fox and Audrey Hepburn. TEB Clarke deservedly won an Oscar for his beautifully constructed story and screenplay. Guinness lost out to Gary Cooper in *High Noon* in the best actor category. DP DVD

Alec Guinness *Henry Holland* • Stanley Holloway *Pendlebury* • Sidney James *Lackery* • Alfie Bass *Shorty* • Marjorie Fielding *Mrs Chalk* • John Gregson *Farrow* • Edie Martin *Miss Evesham* • Clive Morton *Station sergeant* • John Salew *Parkin* • Ronald Adam *Turner* • Arthur Hambling *Wallis* • Gibb McLaughlin *Godwin* • Audrey Hepburn *Chiquita* • William Fox [James Fox] *Gregory* ■ *Dir* Charles Crichton • *Scr* TEB Clarke

Law and Disorder ★★★ U

Comedy 1958 · UK · BW · 72mins

This is a smashing little comedy from the *Lavender Hill Mob* pairing of director Charles Crichton and co-writer TEB Clarke. Michael Redgrave is on sparkling form as a minor league crook whose detentions at Her Majesty's pleasure are explained away to his son as missionary excursions to Africa. The plot slows slightly after the son becomes judge Robert Morley's assistant and Redgrave slips into retirement. But normal service is resumed with the smuggling episodes and the hilarious divorce trial, staged to delay Redgrave's day in court. DP

Michael Redgrave *Percy Brand* • Robert Morley *Judge Crichton* • Ronald Squire *Colonel Masters* • Elizabeth Sellars *Gina Lasalle* • Joan Hickson *Aunt Florence* • Lionel Jeffries *Major Proudfoot* • Jeremy Burnham *Colin Brand* • Brenda Bruce *Mary Cooper* • George Coulouris *Bennie* • John Le Mesurier *Sir Humphrey Pomfret* ■ *Dir* Charles Crichton • *Scr* TEB Clarke, Patrick Campbell, Vivienne Knight, from the novel *Smuggler's Circuit* by Denys Roberts

Law and Disorder ★★★ 18

Comedy drama 1974 · US · Colour · 97mins

Exiled Czech director Ivan Passer's second American film was this uneven satire on the decline of neighbourhood life. When Carroll O'Connor and Ernest Borgnine set about organising a vigilante force to combat the rising tide of crime, the film is both insightful and amusing, but it never recovers from the sudden change in tone once they realise the enormity of their undertaking. Karen Black is superb as a chirpy hairdresser, while the leads have an unexpected chemistry. DP

Carroll O'Connor *Willie* • Ernest Borgnine *Cy* • Ann Wedgeworth *Sally* • Anita Dangler *Irene* • Leslie Ackerman *Karen* • Karen Black *Gloria* • Jack Kehoe *Elliott* • David Spielberg *Bobby* ■ *Dir* Ivan Passer • *Scr* Ivan Passer, William Richert, Kenneth Harris Fishman

The Law and Jake Wade ★★★★ U

Western 1958 · US · Colour · 86mins

Robert Taylor and Richard Widmark star as adversaries in this handsomely mounted western directed by that master of the genre, John Sturges. It's the tale of two outlaws who once rode together, but now the evil Widmark is back and trying to coerce a reformed Taylor into revealing where their ill-gotten loot is buried. Robert Surtees's photography is often breathtaking, while the clever, laconic screenplay by William Bowers tends to be under-rated, as was this fine, tense western. TS

Robert Taylor (1) *Jake Wade* • Richard Widmark *Clint Hollister* • Patricia Owens *Peggy Carter* • Robert Middleton *Ortero* • Henry Silva *Rennie* • DeForest Kelley *Wexler* • Burt Douglas *Lieutenant* • Eddie Firestone *Burke* ■ *Dir* John Sturges • *Scr* William Bowers, from the novel by Marvin H Albert

Law and Order ★★★★

Western 1932 · US · BW · 70mins

Terrific version of the Wyatt Earp legend, with the names changed since some of the participants in the tale were still alive at the time of this movie. (Earp himself had only been dead four years.) Co-scripter Huston's father Walter is superb as the town-taming marshal, and the great western star Harry Carey is cleverly cast as his tortured crony. The tone is rightly sombre, and the infamous shoot-out at the OK Corral is quite brilliantly directed, surprising since this is the A-feature debut of Edward L Cahn, whose career plummeted hereafter. TS

Walter Huston *Frame Johnson* • Harry Carey *Ed Brant* • Raymond Hatton *Deadwood* • Russell Simpson *Judge Williams* • Russell Hopton *Luther Johnson* • Ralph Ince *Poe Northrup* • Harry Woods *Walt Northrup* • Richard Alexander *Kurt Northrup* • Walter Brennan *Lanky Smith* ■ *Dir* Edward L Cahn • *Scr* John Huston, Tom Reed, from the story *Saint Johnson* by WR Burnett

Law and Order ★★★

Western 1936 · US · BW · 59mins

This low-budget western was released, somewhat aptly, by a production company named Reliable, because it contains just about everything you could possibly want from a Wild West matinée. Tom Tyler and Rex Lease play the Texas Rangers who romance Margaret Nearing while tackling Alan Bridge and his band of smugglers. The plot has several nice touches and the camerawork is above average. DP

Tom Tyler *Tom* • Rex Lease *Jimmy* • Margaret Nearing *Joan* • Alan Bridge [Al Bridge] *Travis* • Bill Gould *Drummond* ■ *Dir* Henri Samuels [Harry S Webb] • *Scr* Jay J Bryan, Rose Gordon, Carl Krusada

Law and Order ★★ U

Western 1940 · US · BW · 57mins

Released in this country as *Lucky Ralston*, this is one of several screen adaptations of WR Burnett's novel *Saint Johnson*. It may not have the star wattage of the 1932 version, but it's still a lively oater, with Johnny Mack Brown suitably square-jawed as the retired lawman who has to pin on the tin star one last time in order to deal with Harry Cording and his band of desperadoes. DP

Johnny Mack Brown *Bill Ralston* • Fuzzy Knight *Deadwood* • Nell O'Day *Sally Dixon* • James Craig *Brant* • Harry Cording *Poe Daggett* ■ *Dir* Ray Taylor • *Scr* Sherman Lowe, Victor McLeod, from the novel *Saint Johnson* by WR Burnett

Law and Order ★★ U

Western 1953 · US · Colour · 79mins

Town marshal Ronald Reagan plans to retire when he gets married, but, almost inevitably, is called on to fight one more battle against the bad guys. The theme recalls *High Noon*, and, like Gary Cooper, Reagan is the silent, brooding type. However, that's where the comparisons end in this remake of the superior 1932 original starring Walter Huston. AT

Ronald Reagan *Frame Johnson* • Dorothy Malone *Jeannie Bristow* • Alex Nicol *Lute Johnson* • Preston Foster *Kurt Durling* • Russell Johnson *Jimmy Johnson* • Barry Kelley *Fin Elder* • Ruth Hampton *Maria* • Chubby Johnson *Denver Cahoon* • Dennis Weaver *Frank Durling* • Jack Kelly *Jed* ■ *Dir* Nathan Juran • *Scr* John Bagni, Gwen Bagni, DD Beauchamp, from the novel *Saint Johnson* by WR Burnett

The Law and the Lady ★★

Period crime comedy
1951 · US · BW · 104mins

The Last of Mrs Cheyney, a slick, sophisticated and successful 1920s play by Frederick Lonsdale, had been twice filmed with Norma Shearer in 1929 and Joan Crawford in 1937. This third version, set at the turn of the 19th century and offering the odd amusing moment and an occasional burst of sharp repartee, is an otherwise pointless and inferior remake. A miscast Greer Garson and an unimpressive Michael Wilding play the sacked housemaid and the ne-er-do-well who team up to con wealthy high society. Overlong and erratic. RK

Greer Garson *Jane Hoskins* • Michael Wilding *Nigel Duxbury/Lord Minden* • Fernando Lamas *Juan Dinas* • Marjorie Main *Mrs Wortin* • Hayden Rorke *Tracy* ■ *Dir* Edwin H Knopf • *Scr* Leonard Spigelgass, Karl Tunberg, from the play *The Last of Mrs Cheyney* by Frederick Lonsdale

The Law of Desire ★★★ 18

Black comedy drama
1987 · Sp · Colour · 97mins

Released the year before *Women on the Verge of a Nervous Breakdown* catapulted Pedro Almódovar to international fame, this is a typically tangled, relationship comedy-drama centring on a homosexual love triangle between a film director and his two lovers and the film-maker's really strange family. Items that can be ticked-off on the Almodóvar checklist include early regulars Antonio Banderas and Carmen Maura (delivering a knockout performance), an off-kilter representation of romance, explicit sex, the unexpected murder of one of the central characters and truly outrageous plot twists. Not one of his very best, but still an absurdly funny and touching tale. JC. In Spanish with English subtitles. DVD

Eusebio Poncela *Pablo Quintero* • Carmen Maura *Tina Quintero* • Antonio Banderas *Antonio Benitez* • Miguel Molina *Juan Bermudez* ■ *Dir/Scr* Pedro Almodóvar

Law of the Underworld ★★

Crime drama 1938 · US · BW · 58mins

Two young lovers are framed for a robbery that culminates in murder in this undemanding B-movie starring Chester Morris as a gang leader with a soft centre. Anne Shirley and Richard Bond are the couple accused of the crime, their plight bringing out the best in the crook. Its fanciful but predictable course is given little vigour by Lew Landers's routine direction and the inexpressive performance of Morris. TV

Chester Morris *Gene Fillmore* • Anne Shirley *Annabelle* • Eduardo Ciannelli *Rockey* • Walter Abel *Rogers* • Richard Bond *Tommy* • Lee Patrick *Dorothy* • Paul Guilfoyle (1) *Batsy* • Frank M Thomas *Capt Gargan* • Eddie Acuff *Bill* • Jack Arnold *Eddie* • Jack Carson *Johnny* ■ *Dir* Lew Landers • *Scr* Bert Granet, Edmund L Hartmann, from the play *Crime* by John B Hymer, Samuel Shipman

The Law West of Tombstone ★★

Comedy western 1938 · US · BW · 72mins

Here's a programme filler that manages to cram into one short movie three key western plot figures, thinly-disguised caricatures of no less than Billy the Kid, Judge Roy Bean, and even ole' Ike Clanton and the boys! In his last RKO western, Harry Carey plays the Judge, while youngster Tim Holt (son of cowboy veteran Jack Holt) makes his RKO debut out west. TS

Harry Carey *Bill Parker* • Tim Holt *The Tonto Kid* • Evelyn Brent *Clara Martinez* • Jean Rouverol *Nitta Moseby* • Clarence Kolb *Sam Kent* • Allan Lane *Danny* • Esther Muir *Mme Mustache* • Bradley Page *Doc Howard* • Kermit Maynard ■ *Dir* Glenn Tryon • *Scr* John Twist, Clarence Upson Young, from the story by Clarence Upson Young

The Lawless ★★★

Drama 1950 · US · BW · 79mins

This pungent low-budget drama was one of the best films that Joseph Losey directed in Hollywood. Gaining a sense of realism from being largely filmed on location with locals as extras, it focuses on the prejudice suffered by Mexican "fruit tramps", itinerant workers who harvested crops in California. The scenes of a manhunt and mob violence have considerable force. This kind of film-making, presenting a bad image of American society, contributed to Losey's blacklisting and flight to Europe. AE

Macdonald Carey *Larry Wilder* • Gail Russell *Sunny Garcia* • John Sands [Johnny Sands] *Joe Ferguson* • Lee Patrick *Jan Dawson* • John Hoyt *Ed Ferguson* • Lalo Rios *Paul Rodriguez* ■ *Dir* Joseph Losey • *Scr* Geoffrey Homes [Daniel Mainwaring], from his novel *The Voice of Stephen Wilder*

The Lawless Breed ★★★

Biographical western
1952 · US · Colour · 82mins

In this splendidly titled biopic, notorious western outlaw John Wesley Hardin is sensitively portrayed by Rock Hudson in a star-making role that was to lift him out of the "beefcake" stakes for ever. It's directed by the veteran who first cast Hudson in a movie, the great Raoul Walsh. Hudson excels here, eliciting sympathy for a character who was clearly no good, and the flashback structure allows for an almost Thomas Hardy-like sense of life controlled by destiny. Better than the average B-feature. TS

Rock Hudson *John Wesley Hardin* • Julia Adams [Julie Adams] *Rosie* • Mary Castle *Jane Brown* • John McIntire *JG Hardin/John Clements* • Hugh O'Brian *Ike Hanley* • Dennis Weaver *Jim Clements* • Lee Van Cleef *Dirk Hanley* ■ *Dir* Raoul Walsh • *Scr* Bernard Gordon, from a story by William Alland

The Lawless Frontier ★★ U

Western 1935 · US · BW · 47mins

Another mediocre John Wayne programme filler from that period before his rescue from B-movies by director John Ford with the role of the

"Ringo Kid" in 1939's *Stagecoach*. This has one of the most standard of all plots: Wayne is avenging the murder of his parents in under an hour's running time. Little else of interest here to anyone other than fans of Wayne. TS [video] DVD

John Wayne *John Tobin* • Sheila Terry *Ruby* • George Hayes [George "Gabby" Hayes] *Dusty* • Earl Dwire *Zanti* • Yakima Canutt *Joe* ■ *Dir/Scr* Robert N Bradbury

The Lawless Heart ★★★ 15

Comedy drama
2001 · UK/US · Colour · 95mins

Gentle, wry humour illuminates the subtleties of modern relationships in this unassuming but poignant British comedy. The film examines how the sudden death of a mutual friend forces a trio of men to reassess their own lives and desires. Told from three different perspectives, each intricately crafted segment adds essential pieces to an emotional jigsaw of love, lust and questioned loyalties. Douglas Henshall is the least convincing, but Bill Nighy and Tom Hollander's understated performances bring quiet dignity to a mature and sharply observant tale. SF [video] DVD

Bill Nighy *Dan* • Douglas Henshall *Tim Marsh* • Tom Hollander *Nick* • Clémentine Célarié *Corinne* • Josephine Butler *Leah* ■ *Dir/Scr* Neil Hunter, Tom Hunsinger

A Lawless Street ★★ U

Western 1955 · US · Colour · 78mins

This routine Randolph Scott western is uninspiringly directed by Joseph H Lewis who fails to secure a satisfactory conclusion to the tale, which results in a soppy ending. Co-star Angela Lansbury was on her way up, between an MGM contract and Broadway revivalism, and a darn fine western heroine she makes. TS

Randolph Scott *Calem Ware* • Angela Lansbury *Tally Dickinson* • Warner Anderson *Hamer Thorne* • Jean Parker *Cora Dean* • Wallace Ford *Dr Amos Wynn* • John Emery *Cody Clark* • James Bell *Asaph Dean* • Ruth Donnelly *Molly Higgins* ■ *Dir* Joseph H Lewis • *Scr* Kenneth Gamet, from the novel *Marshal of Medicine Bend* by Brad Ward

Lawman ★★ 15

Western 1971 · US · Colour · 94mins

As a producer Michael Winner is capable of assembling major players in promising material, but as a director he's no great shakes, sabotaging his own films by doing his own editing and by relying too much on the zoom lens. This is an authentic-looking, tough western, filmed in situ in Durango, with a distinguished cast and a fine screenplay by Gerald Wilson, but it is totally destroyed by inept timing and a clumsy, ugly visual style. TS [video] DVD

Burt Lancaster *Jered Maddox* • Robert Ryan *Cotton Ryan* • Lee J Cobb *Vincent Bronson* • Sheree North *Laura Shelby* • Joseph Wiseman *Lucas* • Robert Duvall *Vernon Adams* • Albert Salmi *Harvey Stenbaugh* ■ *Dir* Michael Winner • *Scr* Gerald Wilson

Lawn Dogs ★★★★ 15

Drama 1997 · UK · Colour · 96mins

Fairy-tale themes embellish a starkly contemporary story in director John Duigan's masterful tale of helpless innocence abroad. Sam Rockwell is a lawnmower man for the exclusive Kentucky suburb Camelot Gardens, who strikes up a friendship with Mischa Barton, a new kid on the block recovering from a heart operation. How people misconstrue the relationship between the "lawn dog" and the vibrantly imaginative youngster makes for a witty and warm film. Duigan's visual trump card is his clever coupling of the deformed American Dream with the potent power of Eastern European fable, and his magical mystery tour through the childhood psyche is a quality diversion oozing with taste and class. AJ. Contains violence, swearing, a sex scene, brief nudity. [video] DVD

Mischa Barton *Devon* • Sam Rockwell *Trent* • Kathleen Quinlan *Clare* • Christopher McDonald *Morton* • Bruce McGill *Nash* • Eric Mabius *Sean* • David Barry Gray *Brett* ■ *Dir* John Duigan • *Scr* Naomi Wallace

The Lawnmower Man ★★★ 15

Science-fiction thriller
1992 · UK/US · Colour · 108mins

Eye-popping special effects are the star of this science-fiction tale, vaguely based on a Stephen King short story, but otherwise notable only for crossing a variation on the Frankenstein theme with the cinematic opportunities offered by "virtual reality". Pierce Brosnan plays a misguided scientist who selects his simple-minded gardener (Jeff Fahey) as a guinea pig for his experiments with hi-tech teaching aids and intelligence-boosting drugs. The film boasts cinema's first known cybersex scene. PF. Contains violence, nudity, swearing. [video] DVD

Jeff Fahey *Jobe Smith* • Pierce Brosnan *Dr Lawrence Angelo* • Jenny Wright *Marnie Burke* • Mark Bringleson *Sebastian Timms* • Geoffrey Lewis *Terry McKeen* • Jeremy Slate *Father McKeen* • Dean Norris *Director* • Colleen Coffey *Caroline Angelo* ■ *Dir* Brett Leonard • *Scr* Brett Leonard, Gimel Everett, from the short story by Stephen King

Lawnmower Man 2: Beyond Cyberspace ★ 12

Science fiction 1995 · US · Colour · 89mins

Stephen King's name is nowhere to be seen, nor are any of his clever plot concepts, in this thin sequel to the surprise hit. What remains is a tedious slice of confusing science fiction, as Matt Frewer attempts to take over the world through cyberspace. Scientist Patrick Bergin must stop him, aided by three computer whizzkids, with only a barrage of special effects to call on for help in director Farhad Mann's virtual unreality jumble. AJ. Contains violence and swearing. [video] DVD

Patrick Bergin *Dr Benjamin Trace* • Matt Frewer *Jobe* • Austin O'Brien *Peter* • Ely Pouget *Dr Cori Platt* • Kevin Conway *Walker* • Trever O'Brien *Young Peter* • Camille Cooper *Jennifer* ■ *Dir* Farhad Mann • *Scr* Farhad Mann, from a story by Michael Miner, Farhad Mann, from the film *The Lawnmower Man* by Brett Leonard, Gimel Envett

Lawrence of Arabia ★★★★★ PG

Historical epic adventure
1962 · UK · Colour · 209mins

Director David Lean's magisterial portrayal of one of Britain's most enigmatic yet charismatic heroes, TE Lawrence, whose precise role in the Arab revolt against the Turks during the First World War still perplexes military historians. Peter O'Toole's flamboyant performance hints at every aspect of Lawrence's complex character (including his masochism), while Robert Bolt and Michael Wilson's script develops into a withering satire on the ball-and-socket mentality of Lawrence's superiors. Taking 15 months to shoot in Saudi Arabia, Morocco, Spain and England, Lean's obsession with the desert mirrors Lawrence's own, via some awesomely beautiful images, notably the mirage that introduced the world to a new star, Omar Sharif. Winner of seven Oscars and restored to its original version in 1989, this is movie-making on the grandest scale. AT [video] DVD

Peter O'Toole *TE Lawrence* • Alec Guinness *Prince Feisal* • Anthony Quinn *Auda Abu Tayi* • Jack Hawkins *General Allenby* • José Ferrer *Turkish Bey* • Anthony Quayle *Colonel Harry Brighton* • Claude Rains *Mr Dryden* • Arthur Kennedy *Jackson Bentley* • Donald Wolfit *General Murray* • Omar Sharif *Sherif Ali Ibn El Kharish* ■ *Dir* David Lean • *Scr* Robert Bolt, Michael Wilson (uncredited), from the book *The Seven Pillars of Wisdom* by TE Lawrence • *Cinematographer* Freddie Young • *Music* Maurice Jarre • *Art Director* John Box

Laws of Attraction ★★ 12

Romantic comedy
2003 · UK/Ire/Ger · Colour · 90mins

Pierce Brosnan and Julianne Moore star here as rival divorce lawyers who fall in love after they get married. The leads do their best, but unfortunately lack any real chemistry or the effortless ease that Spencer Tracy and Katharine Hepburn would have brought to the roles. Overall, the film is neither as sharp nor as funny as it should be, and the best lines go to Frances Fisher, as Moore's mum. Watchable in an undemanding way. DA [video] DVD

Pierce Brosnan *Daniel Rafferty* • Julianne Moore *Audrey Woods* • Parker Posey *Serena* • Michael Sheen *Thorne Jamison* • Frances Fisher *Sara Miller* • Nora Dunn *Judge Abramovitz* ■ *Dir* Peter Howitt • *Scr* Aline Brosh McKenna, Robert Harling, from a story by Aline Brosh McKenna

Laws of Gravity ★★★★ 18

Drama 1992 · US · Colour · 94mins

One of the most impressive directorial debuts of the decade, this sassily-scripted drama cost 29-year-old Nick Gomez a mere $38,000. Shot with twitchy handheld energy by documentary veteran Jean de Segonzac, the action so reeks of those familiar Brooklyn streets that, while comparisons with Martin Scorsese's *Mean Streets* are inevitable, they are in no way unflattering. Adam Trese gives a hair-trigger performance as the small-time hood whose misdemeanours bring Peter Greene's gang into dispute with gun dealer Paul Schulze. But every bit as impressive is Edie Falco as Greene's feisty girlfriend. DP. Contains swearing, violence. [video]

Peter Greene *Jimmy* • Edie Falco *Denise* • Paul Schulze *Frankie* • Tony Fernandez *Tommy* • James McCauley *Kenny* • Anibal Lierras *Ray* • Miguel Sierra *Vasquez* • Adam Trese *Jon* ■ *Dir/Scr* Nick Gomez

The Lawyer ★★★

Courtroom drama
1969 · US · Colour · 119mins

Sidney J Furie's moderate courtroom drama was loosely based on the true story of Dr Sam Sheppard, whose arrest in 1954 for the alleged murder of his wife attracted the kind of media storm that gathered over the OJ Simpson affair. Barry Newman plays the lawyer defending a client who refuses to co-operate, whose family doubts his innocence and whose notoriety may prejudice a fair hearing. Too much time is spent in the company of Newman and his wife Diana Muldaur, but the formula worked well enough to resurface in the TV series *Petrocelli*. DP

Barry Newman *Tony Petrocelli* • Harold Gould *Eric P Scott* • Diana Muldaur *Ruth Petrocelli* • Robert Colbert *Jack Harrison* • Kathleen Crowley *Alice Fiske* • Warren Kemmerling *Sergeant Moran* • Booth Colman *Judge Crawford* ■ *Dir* Sidney J Furie • *Scr* Sidney J Furie, Harold Buchman

Lawyer Man ★★★

Drama 1932 · US · BW · 72mins

William Powell stars as the lawyer of the title, a socially conscious do-gooder with a shabby office on the Lower East Side of New York, an eye for the ladies, and a devoted, wisecracking secretary (Joan Blondell). Things come unstuck when he is seduced into partnership with a smart uptown lawyer and overreaches himself. This cynical look at legal ethics and political corruption, decently played and directed, holds the attention, as does Powell, despite the loss of plot credibility about two-thirds of the way through. RK

William Powell *Anton Adam* • Joan Blondell *Olga Michaels* • Helen Vinson *Barbara Bentley* • Alan Dinehart *Granville Bentley* • Allen Jenkins *Issy Levine* • David Landau *John Gilmurry* • Claire Dodd *Virginia St Johns* • Sheila Terry *Flo* • Kenneth Thomson *Dr Frank Gresham* ■ *Dir* William Dieterle • *Scr* Rian James, James Seymour, from the novel by Max Trell

Laxdale Hall ★★ U

Comedy 1953 · UK · BW · 75mins

The huge success of director Alexander Mackendrick's *Whisky Galore!* meant it was inevitable that film-makers would cast around for more stories of wily Scots running rings around the stiff-necked English. However, lightning didn't strike twice and this tale of the battle between Whitehall and a tiny Hebridean island, whose inhabitants won't pay a road tax, lacks the magic sparkle of Mackendrick's classic. JF

Ronald Squire *General Matheson* • Kathleen Ryan *Catriona Matheson* • Raymond Huntley *Samuel Pettigrew MP* • Sebastian Shaw *Hugh Marvell MP* • Fulton Mackay *Andrew Flett* • Jean Colin *Lucy Pettigrew* • Jameson Clark *Roderick McLeod* • Prunella Scales *Morag McLeod* ■ *Dir* John Eldridge • *Scr* Alfred Shaughnessy, John Eldridge, from the novel by Eric Linklater

Layer Cake ★★★ 15

Crime thriller
2004 · UK/US · Colour · 101mins

Daniel Craig plays a rising young drug dealer whose ambition is to make some quick money and then retire early to enjoy it. His plans – involving a massive shipment of ecstasy – are complicated by drugs lord Kenneth Cranham, who asks him to find the missing wayward daughter of an associate (dodgy businessman Michael Gambon). The performances are good, and Matthew Vaughn directs with assuredness and aplomb, but there's an over-familiarity about the subject matter. DA [video] DVD

Daniel Craig *XXXX* • Colm Meaney *Gene* • Kenneth Cranham *Jimmy Price* • George Harris (2) *Morty* • Jamie Foreman *JD, "The Duke"* • Michael Gambon *Eddie Temple* • Marcel Iures *Slavo* • Tom Hardy *Clarkie* • Ben Whishaw *Sidney* • Sienna Miller *Tammy* ■ *Dir* Matthew Vaughn • *Scr* JJ Connolly, from his novel

Layla Ma Raison ★★

Drama 1989 · Tun · Colour · 90mins

This film by Tunisian Taieb Louhichi is based on a 7th-century Arab legend about the doomed love between a poet and his beloved. The star-crossed lovers are separated by Layla's harsh father who feels his daughter has been dishonoured by the poet by enumerating her virtues in public. The biblical atmosphere and some splendid desert vistas almost overcome the weaknesses in the acting and the often obscure screenplay. RB. In Arabic with English subtitles.

Safy Boutella *Qays* • Anca Nicola *Layla* • Abderrahmane Al Rachi *Layla's Father* ■ *Dir* Taieb Louhichi

Layover ★★

Erotic thriller 2000 · US · Colour · 97mins

David Hasselhoff's presence in this contrived erotic thriller keeps it from falling through one of its many cavernous plot holes. The set-up is faintly ridiculous, as Hasselhoff leaves behind his own domestic difficulties to stumble into the troubled marriage of

Gregg Henry and his flirtatious wife Yvonne Scio. Everything from Hasselhoff and Henry's chauvinistic discourse on infidelity to the furtive fumbling in the lost-luggage office and the revelation of Scio's identity should be labelled "blatantly obvious". DP

David Hasselhoff *Dan Morrison* • Gregg Henry *Roy Dennis* • Yvonne Scio *Vicki* • Sherri Alexander *Allayne* ■ *Dir/Scr* Alan B McElroy

Lazybones ★★

Romantic comedy 1935 · UK · BW · 65mins

This early studio-based, Michael Powell-directed romantic comedy casts Ian Hunter as an extremely idle baronet who is also completely penniless. Seeking a solution to his lack of solvency, Hunter pursues American heiress Claire Luce, only to discover that she's been swindled by her advisers and is overdrawn as well. The plot is predictable, but the film nevertheless displays the first hints of Powell's inimitable style. LH

Claire Luce *Kitty McCarthy* • Ian Hunter *Sir Reginald Ford* • Sara Allgood *Bridget* • Bernard Nedell *Mike McCarthy* • Michael Shepley *Hildebrand Pope* • Bobbie Comber *Kemp* • Denys Blakelock *Hugh Ford* ■ *Dir* Michael Powell • *Scr* Gerard Fairlie, from a play by Ernest Denny

Le Mans ★★★ PG

Sports drama 1971 · US · Colour · 104mins

Steve McQueen's pet project about France's 24-hour car race was started by director John Sturges, who soon clashed with the star and was replaced by up-and-coming TV director Lee H Katzin. Unlike John Frankenheimer's similar *Grand Prix*, (1966) there's a minimum of detail concerning the emotional lives of the drivers. Instead there's the star looking charismatic and some of the most beautiful racing footage ever filmed. For fans of McQueen and auto racing that's probably sufficient. AT DVD

Steve McQueen *Michael Delaney* • Siegfried Rauch *Erich Stahler* • Elga Andersen *Lisa Belgetti* • Ronald Leigh-Hunt *David Townsend* • Fred Haltiner *Johann Ritter* • Luc Merenda *Claude Aurac* • Christopher Waite *Larry Wilson* • Louise Edlind *Anna Ritter* ■ *Dir* Lee H Katzin • *Scr* Harry Kleiner

Leadbelly ★★★

Musical biography
1976 · US · Colour · 126mins

Roger E Mosley stars as the famous rough 'n' tough American folk singer Huddie Ledbetter, known as Leadbelly, the traumas of whose eventful life included serving time on a chain gang. Made by Gordon Parks, the first black director of major Hollywood features (including *Shaft*), this is a technically proficient biopic, boasting excellent cinematography from Bruce Surtees, as well as all-round excellent performances. RK

Roger E Mosley *Huddie "Leadbelly" Ledbetter* • Paul Benjamin *Wes Ledbetter* • Madge Sinclair *Miss Eula* • Alan Manson *Chief Prison Guard* • Albert P Hall [Albert Hall] *Dicklicker* • Art Evans *Blind Lemon Jefferson* ■ *Dir* Gordon Parks • *Scr* Ernest Kinoy

The Leading Man ★★★ 15

Romantic comedy drama
1996 · UK · Colour · 95mins

Set in theatrical London, this perceptive adult comedy drama from director John Duigan involves the amorous encounters of a writer, his actress-mistress, his wife and a famous Hollywood hunk who's decided to tread the boards and is happy to provide a "distraction" to the playwright's extramarital activities. Although the thespian backdrop and central characters are a little underdeveloped, the bright, eclectic cast makes the romantic complications ring true. JC DVD

Jon Bon Jovi *Robin Grange* • Lambert Wilson *Felix Webb* • Anna Galiena *Elena Webb* • Thandie Newton *Hilary Rule* • Barry Humphries *Humphrey Beal* • David Warner *Tod* • Patricia Hodge *Delvene* • Diana Quick *Susan* ■ *Dir* John Duigan • *Scr* Virginia Duigan

The League of Extraordinary Gentlemen ★★★ 12

Period fantasy adventure
2003 · US/Ger · Colour · 105mins

Blade director Stephen Norrington tackles another comic-book adaptation with this ambitious take on Alan Moore's Victorian superhero fantasy. It springs from a fabulous concept, in which fictional adventurer Allan Quatermain (a charismatic Sean Connery) is teamed up with fellow 19th-century literary icons to save the world from megalomaniac madman, The Fantom. Although the special effects can be extremely ropey at times, the fast pace, quick-witted dialogue and overall spectacle help compensate for such shortcomings. SF. Contains some violence. DVD

Sean Connery *Allan Quatermain* • Shane West *Agent Tom Sawyer* • Stuart Townsend *Dorian Gray* • Peta Wilson *Mina Harker* • Jason Flemyng *Dr Henry Jekyll/Mr Edward Hyde* • Naseeruddin Shah *Captain Nemo* • Tony Curran *Rodney Skinner, the invisible man* • David Hemmings *Nigel* ■ *Dir* Stephen Norrington • *Scr* James Dale Robinson [James Robinson], from the graphic novel by Alan Moore, Kevin O'Neill

The League of Frightened Men ★★

Murder mystery 1937 · US · BW · 71mins

A group of Harvard graduates hires detective Nero Wolfe to find out how and why three of their number have died in mysterious circumstances. Having brought Rex Stout's famously sedentary and epicurean detective to the screen the previous year (in *Meet Nero Wolf*), with a very well-cast Edward Arnold, Columbia seemed poised for series. However, this serviceable but static second outing, with Walter Connolly taking over the role of Wolfe, proved the last, probably because an armchair-bound hero limited the possibilities for action. RK

Walter Connolly *Nero Wolfe* • Lionel Stander *Archie Goodwin* • Eduardo Ciannelli *Paul Chapin* • Irene Hervey *Evelyn Hibbard* • Victor Killian [Victor Kilian] *Pitney Scott* • Nana Bryant *Agnes Burton* ■ *Dir* Alfred E Green • *Scr* Eugene Solow, Guy Endore, from the novel by Rex Stout

The League of Gentlemen ★★★★ PG

Crime comedy 1960 · UK · BW · 108mins

This was the first feature from the Allied Film Makers company, with most of its founder members – producer Michael Relph, director Basil Dearden, screenwriter Bryan Forbes and actors Jack Hawkins and Richard Attenborough – making solid contributions to this rousing crime caper. Dating from a time when every third word a crook said didn't begin with an "f", this distant ancestor of such bungled heist pics as *Reservoir Dogs* gets off to a rather stodgy start, but, once Hawkins has assembled his far from magnificent seven and his intricate plan begins to unravel, the action really hots up. DP DVD

Jack Hawkins *Lt Col Hyde* • Nigel Patrick *Peter Graham Race* • Roger Livesey *Mycroft* • Richard Attenborough *Edward Lexy* • Bryan Forbes *Martin Porthill* • Kieron Moore *Stevens* • Robert Coote *Bunny Warren* • Terence Alexander *Rupert Rutland-Smith* ■ *Dir* Basil Dearden • *Scr* Bryan Forbes, from a novel by John Boland

The League of Gentlemen's Apocalypse ★★★ 15

Black comedy
2005 · UK/Ire · Colour · 91mins

This is a feature-length spin-off from the cult TV series about the twisted world of Royston Vasey. The sketch-show style of the programme means that the screenplay can concentrate on gags rather than character development. The plot itself is all but impossible to describe – suffice to say a trio of (fictional) characters break through into the real world to confront the show's writers. It's unlikely to win over any new converts, but fans will no doubt revel in its gleeful weirdness. AS. Contains swearing, sexual references and violence.

Mark Gatiss *Matthew Chinnery/Hilary Briss/ Mickey/Mark Gatiss/Sir Nicholas Sheet-Lightning* • Steve Pemberton *Tubbs Tattsyrup/ Pauline/Herr Lipp/Steve Pemberton/Lemuel Blizzard* • Reece Shearsmith *Edward Tattsyrup/Papa Lazarou/Geoff Tipps/The Rev Bernice Woodall/Reece Shearsmith/Father Halfhearte/Red Devil* • Michael Sheen *Jimmy Dyson* • David Warner *Dr Erasmus Pea* • Victoria Wood *Queen Mary II* • Bernard Hill *King William III* ■ *Dir* Steve Bendelack • *Scr* Jeremy Dyson, Mark Gatiss, Steve Pemberton, Reece Shearsmith

A League of Their Own ★★★ PG

Period sports comedy drama
1992 · US · Colour · 122mins

Before he won a couple of Oscars for more serious fare, Tom Hanks provided the laughs as the alcoholic ex-professional hired to coach a women's baseball team during the Second World War. The assembled players include Geena Davis and Lori Petty as sisters, Madonna as the team floozy and comedian Rosie O'Donnell as her best friend. Penny Marshall, who also directed Hanks in *Big*, has put together a somewhat uneven film, but any roughness is smoothed over by the talented cast and a great deal of affection for the era. JB DVD

Tom Hanks *Jimmy Dugan* • Geena Davis *Dottie Hinson* • Lori Petty *Kit Keller* • Madonna *Mae Mordabito* • Rosie O'Donnell *Doris Murphy* • Megan Cavanagh *Marla Hooch* • Tracy Reiner *Betty Horn* • Bitty Schram *Evelyn Gardner* • Ann Cusack *Shirley Baker* ■ *Dir* Penny Marshall • *Scr* Lowell Ganz, Babaloo Mandel, from a story by Kim Wilson, Kelly Candaele

Lean on Me ★★★ 15

Drama based on a true story
1989 · US · Colour · 103mins

Morgan Freeman takes over as principal of a problem New Jersey high school and eventually wins the hearts of his students after a rigorous clean-up campaign. The tough-love formula works like a charm thanks to Freeman's engaging central performance, and energetic direction by John G Avildsen who brings some of the grit he displayed in *Rocky*. AJ

Morgan Freeman *Joe Clark* • Robert Guillaume *Dr Frank Napier* • Beverly Todd *Ms Levias* • Lynne Thigpen *Leona Barrett* • Jermaine Hopkins *Thomas Sams* • Karen Malina White *Keneesha Carter* • Alan North *Mayor Don Bottman* • Ethan Phillips *Mr Rosenberg* ■ *Dir* John G Avildsen • *Scr* Michael Schiffer

Leap of Faith ★★★ PG

Satirical drama 1992 · US · Colour · 103mins

Steve Martin takes on the role of a cynical bogus evangelist who runs a travelling gospel show in a film that can't make up its mind whether it wants to be a comedy or a straight drama. When Martin and his team arrive at a poor Kansas town to fleece the residents, they find their consciences pricked as they get to know the townspeople. The interesting cast performs well, but the film loses its way as the plot becomes tangled with miracles and saccharine twists. JB DVD

Steve Martin *Jonas Nightengale* • Debra Winger *Jane* • Liam Neeson *Will* • Lolita Davidovich *Marva* • Lukas Haas *Boyd* • Meat Loaf *Hoover* • Philip Seymour Hoffman *Matt* • MC Gainey *Tiny* ■ *Dir* Richard Pearce • *Scr* Janus Cercone

The Learning Tree ★★★

Period drama 1969 · US · Colour · 106mins

Best known for his film about the black private eye *Shaft*, novelist, photographer, poet, composer and film-maker Gordon Parks was a one-man cultural phenomenon. One of the godfathers of independent African-American cinema, he based his feature debut on his autobiographical novel about a young man coming of age in 1920s Kansas. While he and cinematographer Burnett Guffey lovingly re-create the look and feel of the period, Parks struggles to animate the inexperienced cast. Historically important, but overly determined to be both authentic and significant. DP. Contains violence, swearing, nudity.

Kyle Johnson *Newt Winger* • Alex Clarke *Marcus Savage* • Estelle Evans *Sarah Winger* • Dana Elcar *Sheriff Kirky* • Mira Waters *Arcella Jefferson* • Joel Fluellen *Uncle Rob* • Malcolm Atterbury *Silas Newhall* • Richard Ward *Booker Savage* ■ *Dir* Gordon Parks • *Scr* Gordon Parks, from his novel

Lease of Life ★★★ U

Drama 1954 · UK · Colour · 90mins

Robert Donat is always unfairly overlooked in discussions of great British screen actors. An Oscar winner for *Goodbye, Mr Chips*, he fought chronic asthma throughout his life to give several moving and convincing performances, which usually belied the quality of the material. This tale of a Yorkshire vicar with only a year to live is a case in point. Thriller specialist Eric Ambler makes a mawkish mess of what is essentially a domestic drama but, through the gentle fidelity of his performance, Donat creates a decent and dignified character. DP

Robert Donat *William Thorne* • Kay Walsh *Vera Thorne* • Adrienne Corri *Susan Thorne* • Denholm Elliott *Martin Blake* • Walter Fitzgerald *Dean* • Cyril Raymond *Headmaster* • Reginald Beckwith *Foley* ■ *Dir* Charles Frend • *Scr* Eric Ambler, from a story by Frank Baker, Patrick Jenkins

The Leather Boys ★★★ 15

Drama 1963 · UK · BW · 107mins

Nearly 40 years on, it's almost impossible to see why this was once regarded as an unacceptably frank insight into the gay lifestyle. Colin Campbell is so hopelessly out of his depth as the young newlywed wrestling with his sexual identity that not even the excellence of Rita Tushingham and Dudley Sutton can salvage what were intended to be powerful scenes. Sidney J Furie's film is now something of a quaint period piece, full of techniques borrowed from the French New Wave. The end result is fussy and flash, but the wedding and the Butlin's sequences are priceless relics of 1960s life. DP

Rita Tushingham *Dot* • Colin Campbell *Reggie* • Dudley Sutton *Pete* • Gladys Henson *Gran* • Avice Landone *Reggie's mother* • Lockwood West *Reggie's father* • Betty Marsden *Dot's mother* ■ *Dir* Sidney J Furie • *Scr* Gillian Freeman, from the novel by Eliot George [Eliot Freeman]

Leather Jackets ★★★ 18

Crime drama 1991 · US · Colour · 90mins

English actor Cary Elwes is almost unrecognisable in this brooding, underrated crime drama, which also provided an early starring role for Bridget Fonda. The story focuses on the complicated relationships between reformed crook DB Sweeney, his fiancée (Fonda) and his best friend (Elwes), who is on the run from Asian mobsters. Director Lee Drysdale captures the bleakness of small-town life and is rewarded with fine performances from his young leads. JF

DB Sweeney *Mickey* • Bridget Fonda *Claudi* • Cary Elwes *Dobbs* • Christopher Penn [Chris Penn] *Big Steve* • Jon Polito *Fat Jack* • Craig Ng *Tron* • Marshall Bell *Stranger* • James LeGros *Carl* • Ginger Lynn Allen *Bree* ■ *Dir/Scr* Lee Drysdale

Leatherface: the Texas Chainsaw Massacre III

★★★ 18

Horror 1990 · US · Colour · 85mins

Gory, graphic and gruesome, director Jeff Burr's second sequel to Tobe Hooper's classic gut-wrencher combines the suffocating atmosphere of the original with the razor-sharp black comedy of Hooper's second reworking. Kate Hodge and William Butler are the ingenuous tourists who this time take a backwoods detour and end up being prospective sausage filler thanks to Leatherface and his splatter happy family of cannibals. More provocative and taboo-busting than the first two entries in the censor-upsetting series. The final sequel was *Texas Chainsaw Massacre: the Next Generation*. AJ DVD

Kate Hodge *Michelle* • William Butler *Ryan* • Viggo Mortensen *Tex* • Ken Foree *Benny* • Joe Unger *Tinker* • Tom Everett *Alfredo* • Toni Hudson *Sara* • Miriam Byrd-Nethery *Mama* • RA Mihailoff *Leatherface* ■ *Dir* Jeff Burr • *Scr* David J Schow, from characters created by Kim Henkel, Tobe Hooper

The Leatherneck ★★

Drama 1929 · US · BW · 76mins

Set in the aftermath of the First World War, William Boyd is defending himslf against charges of murder and desertion. This undernourished drama with moments of romance is notable only for what became of its stars – William Boyd turned cowboy and carved out a lucrative career as Hopalong Cassidy, while Alan Hale picked up a contract wih Warner Bros and became a character-stalwart with the studio. TH

William Boyd (1) *Joseph Hanlon* • Alan Hale *Otto Schmidt* • Robert Armstrong *William Calhoun* • Fred Kohler *Heckla* ■ *Dir* Howard Higgin • *Scr* Elliott Clawson, John W Krafft

Leave All Fair ★★★

Biographical drama
1985 · NZ · Colour · 88mins

A subtle, elegantly told story about the New Zealand writer Katherine Mansfield who died in 1923 and is recalled decades later by her husband (the literary critic John Middleton Murry) while visiting a publisher in Paris. Financed in New Zealand but shot entirely in France, the film's chief virtues are the superb performances by John Gielgud as the husband and Jane Birkin (an unusual casting choice) in a dual role as Mansfield and a woman who resembles the writer. Birkin adds layers of nuance to an otherwise conventional storyline. AT

John Gielgud *John Middleton Murry* • Jane Birkin *Marie Taylor/Katherine Mansfield* • Feodor Atkine *André de Sarry* • Simon Ward *Young John* ■ *Dir* John Reid • *Scr* Stanley Harper, Maurice Pons, John Reid

Leave 'em Laughing

★★★★ U

Drama 1981 · US · Colour · 103mins

Mickey Rooney turns in a standout performance as the real-life New York comedian Jack Thum who, with wife Anne Jackson, cared for dozens of homeless youngster, despite the rigours of the comedy circuit – and cancer. A TV movie that plucks hard on the heart-strings, it's redeemed by Rooney's brisk, no-nonsense take on the situation, helped by similar direction from Jackie Cooper, whose own childhood was spent in the *Our Gang* children's movies. TH

Mickey Rooney *Jack Thum* • Anne Jackson *Shirlee Thum* • [Allen Garfield] *Dr Arthur Abrams* • Elisha Cook [Elisha Cook Jr] *Jetter* • Michael LeClair *Tom* • William Windom *Smiley Jenkins* • Red Buttons *Roland Green* ■ *Dir* Jackie Cooper • *Scr* Cynthia W Mandelberg, from a story by Peggy Chantler-Dick

Leave Her to Heaven

★★★★ U

Crime melodrama
1945 · US · Colour · 105mins

Here's a wonderful chunk of 20th Century-Fox tosh in the most glowing Oscar-winning Technicolor you're ever likely to see. The sublimely beautiful Gene Tierney drops overacting Vincent Price to go off with dull but handsome author Cornel Wilde, and lets her pretty foster sister Jeanne Crain and Wilde take the blame for murder. This is glorious melodrama that knows no bounds. TS DVD

Gene Tierney *Ellen Berent* • Cornel Wilde *Richard Harland* • Jeanne Crain *Ruth Berent* • Vincent Price *Russell Quinton* • Mary Phillips [Mary Philips] *Mrs Berent* • Ray Collins *Glen Robie* • Gene Lockhart *Dr Saunders* ■ *Dir* John M Stahl • *Scr* Jo Swerling, from the novel *Leave Her to Heaven* by Ben Ames Williams • *Cinematographer* Leon Shamroy

Leave It to Beaver ★★ PG

Comedy 1997 · US · Colour · 84mins

The popular 1950s sitcom gets a modern big-screen update, but this forgettable family movie is only really of interest for fans or the easily amused. Unlike the enjoyably daft *Brady Bunch* movies, little or no concession has been made for contemporary audiences, aside from mild swearing and the occasional satirical moment. Saddled with a pedestrian script, stars Janine Turner and Christopher McDonald look far from comfy in their parental roles, although young Cameron Finley has a certain cute appeal. JC

Christopher McDonald *Ward Cleaver* • Janine Turner *June Cleaver* • Cameron Finley *Theodore "Beaver" Cleaver* • Erik Von Detten *Wally Cleaver* • Adam Zolotin *Eddie Haskell* • Barbara Billingsley *Aunt Martha* • Ken Osmond *Eddie Sr* ■ *Dir* Andy Cadiff • *Scr* Brian Levant, Lon Diamond, from the TV series by Bob Mosher, Joe Connelly

Leave of Absence ★★★ 12

Drama 1994 · US · Colour · 87mins

The ever-reliable Brian Dennehy delivers one of his most subtle and touching performances in this thoughtful drama. He plays a successful career man who falls for Jacqueline Bisset while married to Blythe Danner, then pushes his marriage to the edge by caring for Bisset when she falls victim to a terminal disease. It's made for TV, but it's in a different league from the usual small-screen fodder. JF DVD

Brian Dennehy *Sam Mercer* • Jacqueline Bisset *Nell Bergen* • Blythe Danner *Eliza Mercer* • Jessica Walter *Bess Kaufman* • Noelle Parker *Zoey Mercer* • Polly Bergen *Janet* • Grayce Spence *Phyllis* • Tonea Stewart *Cora Winsor* ■ *Dir* Tom McLoughlin • *Scr* Betty Goldberg, from a story by Polly Bergen

Leaves from Satan's Book

★★★

Silent religious drama
1919 · Den · BW · 110mins

This chronicle of evil through the ages was Carl Th Dreyer's second feature and gives notice of the thematic preoccupations that would concern him throughout his career. The satanic Helge Nissen poses as a New Testament Pharisee, a Spanish Inquisitor, a French revolutionary spy and a monk caught up in the 1918 Russo-Finnish War. But Dreyer is less interested in sin per se than in exploring the strength of faith exhibited by those facing temptation. The finale is easily the most accomplished cinematically, with Clara Pontoppidan's suicide being a moving montage of meticulously matched close-ups. DP

Helge Nissen *Satan* • Halvard Hoff *Jesus* • Jacob Texiere *Judas* • Erling Hansson *John* • Hallander Hellermann *Don Gomez* • Ebon Strandin *Isabella, his daughter* • Tenna Kraft *Marie Antoinette* • Emma Wiehe *Contesse de Chambord* • Carlo Wieth *Paavo Ralya* • Clara Pontoppidan *Siri* ■ *Dir* Carl Th Dreyer • *Scr* Carl Th Dreyer, Edgar Höyer, from the novel *Satans Sorger* by Marie Corelli

Leaving Las Vegas ★★★★ 18

Drama 1995 · US · Colour · 107mins

Mike Figgis's agonising study of alcoholic self-destruction impresses with its uncompromising honesty and exceptional performances. Nicolas Cage won a well-deserved Oscar for his portrayal of a failed Hollywood screenwriter who goes to Vegas to drink himself to death. Just as memorable is Oscar-nominated Elisabeth Shue as the prostitute who befriends him. Shooting in Super 16mm, Figgis strips away the gaudy glamour of Nevada's temptation capital, revealing it to a tawdry, neon-lit tourist trap. This is downbeat all the way, but the sensitivity of the direction and the authenticity of the acting also give it a redemptive feel. DP. Contains violence, swearing, nudity and drug abuse. DVD

Nicolas Cage *Ben Sanderson* • Elisabeth Shue *Sera* • Julian Sands *Yuri* • Richard Lewis *Peter* • Valeria Golino *Terri* • Steven Weber *Marc Nussbaum* • Kim Adams *Sheila* • Laurie Metcalf *Landlady* • Julian Lennon *Bartender in biker bar* ■ *Dir* Mike Figgis • *Scr* Mike Figgis, from the novel by John O'Brien

Leaving Lenin ★★★ 12

Comedy drama 1993 · UK · Colour · 89mins

A far cry from the wild things in *Twin Town*, the teens on this school trip have a comfortable life and much to look forward to. But they still have plenty to find out about themselves, and St Petersburg in the post-Communist era turns out to be the perfect scene for self-discovery. Shooting with an enthusiastic eye for the sights of the city and the naturalism of his young cast, director Endaf Emlyn makes the most of a rather contrived situation. DP. In Welsh with English subtitles.

Sharon Morgan *Eileen* • Wyn Bowen Harries *Mostyn* • Ifan Huw Dafydd *Mervyn* • Steffan Trevor *Spike* • Catrin Mai *Rhian* • Ivan Shvedov *Sasha* • Richard Harrington *Charlie* • Shelley Rees *Sharon* ■ *Dir* Endaf Emlyn • *Scr* Endaf Emlyn, Sion Eiri

Leaving Normal ★★★ 15

Comedy drama 1992 · US · Colour · 105mins

A kind of sub-*Thelma and Louise*, with *The Big Chill's* Meg Tilly as a bored housewife departing her second failed marriage and *Chicago Hope's* Emmy award-winning Christine Lahti as a world-weary waitress. The two meet at a bus stop in the town of Normal, Wyoming, and decide to head for the wilds of Alaska, where Lahti has inherited a house. Sentimental stuff from director Edward Zwick that owes much to his previous TV work on the acclaimed *Thirtysomething*. JB. Contains swearing and nudity.

Christine Lahti *Darly* • Meg Tilly *Marianne* • Patrika Darbo *66* • Lenny Von Dohlen *Harry* • Maury Chaykin *Leon* • Brett Cullen *Kurt* • James Gammon *Walt* • Eve Gordon *Emily* ■ *Dir* Edward Zwick • *Scr* Edward Solomon

La Lectrice ★★★★ 18

Erotic comedy 1988 · Fr · Colour · 94mins

Miou-Miou gives a beautifully judged performance as a professional reader in this wry erotic comedy from Michel Deville. This is the sort of French film that Hollywood thinks it can remake, but there's no one on the current A-list capable of reproducing Miou-Miou's subtle shifts from intellectual to companion, revolutionary to temptress, to suit the needs of her clients. Co-written by the director and his wife, Rosalinde, the script is a wonderful advertisement for books and the pleasures of reading. DP. In French with English subtitles. DVD

Miou-Miou *Constance/Marie* • Régis Royer *Eric* • Christian Ruché *Jean/Philippe* • Charlotte Farran *Coralie* • Brigitte Catillon *Eric's mother/Jocelyne* ■ *Dir* Michel Deville • *Scr* Rosalinde Deville, Michel Deville, from the novel by Raymond Jean, from a short story by Raymond Jean

The Leech Woman ★★

Horror 1960 · US · BW · 77mins

Scientist Coleen Gray goes to Africa in search of eternal youth and learns from a strange tribe that the ageing process can be reversed by drinking secretions from the pineal gland of sacrificial male victims. Her husband is the first dupe to provide the youth serum, but when it wears off she resorts to further murder to top up her supply. A workman-like potboiler. AJ

Phillip Terry *Dr Paul Talbott* • Coleen Gray *June* • Grant Williams *Neil Foster* • Gloria Talbott *Sally* • John Van Dreelen *Bertram Garvay* ■ *Dir* Edward Dein • *Scr* David Duncan, from a story by Ben Pivar, Francis Rosenwald

The Left Hand of God ★★

Romantic wartime adventure
1955 · US · Colour · 87mins

This 20th Century-Fox film, made in CinemaScope, has a miscast and extremely uncomfortable-looking (he was ill at the time) Humphrey Bogart posing as a priest in China in 1947, dallying with the lovely Gene Tierney and coping with warlord Lee J Cobb, complete with Hollywood oriental make-up. William E Barrett's original novel offered some provocative views on how a priest's mantle affects the man who wears it, but Bogart fails to convince as a tortured soul, and the screenplay simplifies the mental torment. TS

Humphrey Bogart *Jim Carmody* • Gene Tierney *Ann Scott* • Lee J Cobb *Mieh Yang* • Agnes Moorehead *Beryl Sigman* • EG Marshall *Dr Sigman* • Jean Porter *Mary Yin* ■ *Dir* Edward Dmytryk • *Scr* Alfred Hayes, from the novel by William E Barrett

The Left Handed Gun

★★★★ PG

Western 1958 · US · BW · 98mins

Paul Newman stepped into the role earmarked for James Dean and delivers a brilliant, Brando-esque screen portrayal of outlaw Billy the Kid as envisaged by writer Gore Vidal. In this terrific movie debut from director Arthur Penn, character actor John Dehner got the break of his life co-starring as Pat Garrett, while casting Hurd Hatfield as a nervous chronicler of the times was a clever touch. The

L

film was heavily truncated on its UK cinema release. TS

Paul Newman *Billy Bonney* • Lita Milan *Celsa* • John Dehner *Pat Garrett* • Hurd Hatfield *Moultrie* • James Congdon *Charlie Boudre* • James Best *Tom Folliard* ■ *Dir* Arthur Penn • *Scr* Leslie Stevens, from the teleplay *The Death of Billy the Kid* by Gore Vidal • *Editor* Folmar Blangsted

Left Luggage ★★ PG

Drama 1997 · Neth/Bel/US · Colour · 96mins

Set in 1970s Antwerp, Jeroen Krabbé's first feature as director settles for cheap sentiment when it might have more profitably explored the challenges faced by a strict, patriarchal culture confronted with a changing world. All the characters – from David Bradley's bigoted concierge to Isabella Rossellini's dutiful Hassidic wife – are one-dimensional, with even Laura Fraser's questioning student-cum-nanny governed more by her emotions than her reason. Earnest but shallow. DP. Contains some strong language.

Isabella Rossellini *Mrs Kalman* • Maximilian Schell *Chaja's father* • Marianne Sägebrecht *Chaja's mother* • Chaim Topol [Topol] *Mr Apfelshnitt* • Laura Fraser *Chaja* • Jeroen Krabbé *Mr Kalman* • Adam Monty *Simcha Kalman* • David Bradley (3) *Concierge* ■ *Dir* Jeroen Krabbé • *Scr* Jeroen Krabbe, Edwin de Vries, from the novel *The Shovel and the Loom* by Carl Friedman

Left, Right and Centre ★★ U

Comedy 1959 · UK · BW · 88mins

A spoof on the effect that television has on persuading voters where to put their X. Playing another in a long line of silly asses, Ian Carmichael is spot on as the TV pundit who runs for the Conservatives in a local election. It's hardly a searing satire, but director and co-writer Sidney Gilliat scores a few points at the expense of both the media and the establishment. Stealing everyone's thunder, however, is Alastair Sim as Carmichael's impoverished uncle seeking ways to maintain his stately pile. DP

Ian Carmichael *Robert Wilcot* • Patricia Bredin *Stella Stoker* • Alastair Sim *Lord Wilcot* • Eric Barker *Bert Glimmer* • Richard Wattis *Harding-Pratt* • Gordon Harker *Hardy* • Jack Hedley *Bill Hemingway* • Leslie Dwyer *Alf Stoker* ■ *Dir* Sidney Gilliat • *Scr* Sidney Gilliat, from the story by Sidney Gilliat, Val Valentine

The Legacy ★★ 18

Horror 1978 · UK · Colour · 94mins

This modern variation on *The Old Dark House* formula finds Californians Katharine Ross and Sam Elliott stranded with a group of strangers – the Who's Roger Daltrey among them – in an English country mansion. As the guests are bumped off one by one, a Satanism subplot is introduced into the already unfocused proceedings to add extra suspense – it doesn't. A botched supernatural thriller with only some fiendishly clever death scenes to commend it. AJ DVD

Katharine Ross *Maggie Walsh* • Sam Elliott *Pete Danner* • John Standing *Jason Mountolive* • Ian Hogg *Harry* • Margaret Tyzack *Nurse Adams* • Charles Gray *Karl Liebknecht* • Lee Montague *Jacques Grandier* • Hildegard Neil *Barbara Kirstenburg* • Roger Daltrey *Clive Jackson* ■ *Dir* Richard Marquand • *Scr* Jimmy Sangster, Patrick Tilley, Paul Wheeler, from the story by Jimmy Sangster

Legal Eagles ★★★ PG

Comedy thriller 1986 · US · Colour · 110mins

This high-gloss courtroom comedy thriller was director Ivan Reitman's next movie after his mega-hit *Ghostbusters*. Robert Redford and Debra Winger star as attorneys involved in the unusual case of an artist (Daryl Hannah) accused of stealing a painting by her late father. It's not long before district attorney Redford has hopped over the fence to help defence lawyer Winger get to the bottom of the conspiracy behind the case. There's plenty of star appeal and sexual chemistry, but the script tends towards flabbiness. PF DVD

Robert Redford *Tom Logan* • Debra Winger *Laura Kelly* • Daryl Hannah *Chelsea Deardon* • Brian Dennehy *Cavanaugh* • Terence Stamp *Victor Taft* • Steven Hill *Bower* • David Clennon *Blanchard* • John McMartin *Forrester* ■ *Dir* Ivan Reitman • *Scr* Jim Cash, Jack Epps Jr, from a story by Jim Cash, Ivan Reitman

Legalese ★★★

Satirical courtroom drama
1998 · US · Colour · 92mins

Veteran James Garner lends his unique charm to this satirical TV drama that once again exposes the failings of the legal profession. As sleazy lawyer Norman Keane, Garner takes on the case of actress Gina Gershon, who is charged with murder. There's nothing new or shocking here, but it's fun to watch old pro Garner at work, and there's good support from Kathleen Turner as a talk-show host. MC

James Garner *Norman Keane* • Kathleen Turner *Brenda Whitlass* • Gina Gershon *Angela Beale* • Mary-Louise Parker *Rica Martin* • Edward Kerr *Roy Guyton* • Brian Doyle-Murray *Harley Guyton* ■ *Dir* Glenn Jordan • *Scr* Billy Ray

Legally Blonde ★★★ 12

Comedy 2001 · US · Colour · 92mins

Reese Witherspoon tries – and generally succeeds – to be a grown-up version of Alicia Silverstone's character from *Clueless* in this entertaining comedy. She plays a sorority queen who's dumped by her rich boyfriend Matthew Davis before he goes to Harvard Law School, as he thinks she's not smart enough to be his wife. The Valley Girl follows him there to prove him wrong and get him back. It's all desperately silly, but the sight of a pink-clad Witherspoon tottering on stilettos through Harvard's revered halls is hilarious, and the star is perfect as the girl whose specialist subjects are *Cosmopolitan* and manicures. JB DVD

Reese Witherspoon *Elle Woods* • Luke Wilson *Emmett Richmond* • Selma Blair *Vivian Kensington* • Matthew Davis *Warner Huntington* • Victor Garber *Professor Callahan* • Jennifer Coolidge *Paulette* • Holland Taylor *Professor Stromwell* • Ali Larter *Brooke Taylor-Windham* • Raquel Welch *Mrs Windham Vandermark* ■ *Dir* Robert Luketic • *Scr* Karen McCullah Lutz, Kirsten Smith, from a novel by Amanda Brown

Legally Blonde 2: Red, White & Blonde ★★ PG

Comedy 2003 · US · Colour · 90mins

Reese Witherspoon returns as ditzy blonde socialite Elle Woods in this frothy but dumb sequel to the 2001 hit comedy. Having graduated from Harvard, the pink-clad cutie is now a rising young lawyer, intent on legally ending the animal experimentation that's keeping her beloved dog's mother locked up in a cosmetics lab. Without Witherspoon, however, the film would be a mess – some of the scenes are toe-curlingly embarrassing, while the plotline is beyond preposterous. SF DVD

Reese Witherspoon *Elle Woods* • Sally Field *Congresswoman Rudd* • Regina King *Grace Rossiter* • Jennifer Coolidge *Paulette Parcelle* • Bruce McGill *Stanford Marks* • Dana Ivey *Libby Hauser* • Bob Newhart *Sid Post* • Luke Wilson *Emmett Richmond* ■ *Dir* Charles Herman-Wurmfeld • *Scr* Kate Kondell, from a story by Eve Ahlert, Dennis Drake, Kate Kondell, from characters created by Amanda Brown

Legend ★★ PG

Fantasy adventure
1985 · US · Colour · 89mins

This is probably one of the few films on director Ridley Scott's CV he would prefer to forget. It's a daft fairy tale filled with all manner of goblins, elves and pixies, as well as Tom Cruise as a young peasant who falls in love with princess Mia Sara. He takes her to see the last surviving unicorns, little knowing that the Lord of Darkness (Tim Curry) has his own evil plan for the mythical creatures. Curry is certainly the best thing in the film, which surprisingly did nothing to dim Cruise's rising star. JB. DVD

Tom Cruise *Jack* • Tim Curry *Darkness* • Mia Sara *Lili* • David Bennent *Gump* • Alice Playten *Blix* • Billy Barty *Screwball* • Cork Hubbert *Brown Tom* • Peter O'Farrell *Pox* • Robert Picardo *Meg Mucklebones* ■ *Dir* Ridley Scott • *Scr* William Hjortsberg

The Legend ★★★ 15

Martial arts comedy
1993 · HK · Colour · 91mins

After several outings as Wong Fei-Hong, the exciting Jet Li plays another character from Chinese legend in this hugely entertaining adventure that recalls the kind of knockabout costume dramas on which the Hong Kong film industry was founded. The lively blend of action and comedy is typified by the pantomimic contest to reach the top of a wooden tower defended by the athletic Sibelle Hu. This is also an excellent vehicle for one of Hong Kong's top female stars, Josephine Siao. DP. In Cantonese with English subtitles. DVD

Jet Li *Fong Sai-Yuk* • Li Jai-Xing *Ting Ting* • Josephine Siao *Mother Fong* • Chu Kong *Father Fong* • Chan Sung-Yun *"Tiger" Lei* • Sibelle Hu *Lei Siu-Huan* ■ *Dir* Yuen Kwai [Corey Yuen] • *Scr* Chai Kung-Yung, Chang Jiang-Chung, Ji Ang

The Legend II ★★ 15

Martial arts comedy
1993 · HK · Colour · 96mins

You'll remember from the first movie that, after completing his tower-climbing exertions, Fong Sai-Yuk sided with the Red Flower Society in its battle against the corrupt ruling dynasty. Well, this sequel concentrates on that rebellion, while providing only the briefest of history lessons to help us get by. This has all the hallmarks of a hurried cash-in, with Jet Li allowing his temper to land him in the unlikeliest of situations. DP. Cantonese dialogue dubbed into English. DVD

Jet Li *Fong Sai-Yuk* • Josephine Siao *Mother Fong* • Li Jai-Xing *Ting Ting* • Adam Cheng *Mr Chen* ■ *Dir* Yuen Kwai [Corey Yuen] • *Scr* Chan Kin Chung, Jay On

The Legend of Bagger Vance ★★★ PG

Period sports drama
2000 · US · Colour · 121mins

Will Smith transcends his blockbuster image with a performance of real tenderness and integrity as a golfing guru in director Robert Redford's 1930s-set drama. With her late father's resort facing ruin, Charlize Theron launches a big-name golf tournament in Savannah. Lining up against golfing legends is local boy Matt Damon, an emotionally scarred First World War veteran. Damon has taken to the bottle, and is struggling to regain control of his swing and his life, until caddy Bagger Vance (Smith) provides the healing touch. As old-fashioned tale of love and redemption, it rings true. TH DVD

Will Smith *Bagger Vance* • Matt Damon *Rannulph Junuh* • Charlize Theron *Adele Invergordon* • Bruce McGill *Walter Hagen* • Joel Gretsch *Bobby Jones* • J Michael Moncrief *Hardy Greaves* ■ *Dir* Robert Redford • *Scr* Jeremy Leven, from the novel by Steven Pressfield

The Legend of Billie Jean ★★ 15

Drama 1985 · US · Colour · 91mins

After making her name a year earlier with *Supergirl*, Helen Slater opted for a more modest heroic role with this well-meaning if muddled teen thriller. She plays a young girl who, along with her brother and some friends, inadvertently become an 1980s' version of Bonnie and Clyde's gang. There's no faulting the feisty performances from the youngsters or the grown-ups, but the "kids good, adults bad" message is trite and clumsily handled. JF

Helen Slater *Billie Jean* • Christian Slater *Binx* • Keith Gordon *Lloyd* • Richard Bradford *Pyatt* • Martha Gehman *Ophelia* • Yeardley Smith *Putter* • Barry Tubb *Hubie* • Dean Stockwell *Muldaur* • Peter Coyote *Ringwald* ■ *Dir* Matthew Robbins • *Scr* Mark Rosenthal, Lawrence Konner

The Legend of Boggy Creek ★★

Horror documentary drama
1972 · US · Colour · 90mins

Long before *The Blair Witch Project* put Burkittsville on the map, this horror docudrama featured encounters with a hairy Bigfoot-type monster supposedly prowling the environs of Fouke, Arkansas. Producer/director Charles B Pierce captures a quality of folk legend and the panic, fear and terror the fabled creature has created in the small town thanks to candid interviews with local residents who claim to have seen the mysterious beast. The obtrusive pop songs are a mistake, and so are the mocked-up monster shots, but despite the leisurely pace, it's never static enough to become arty, or slow enough to be dull. AJ

Vern Stearman *Narration* ■ *Dir* Charles B Pierce • *Scr* Earl E Smith

The Legend of Grizzly Adams ★★★ U

Adventure 1990 · US · Colour · 73mins

Although Dan Haggerty made the role of Grizzly Adams his own on TV, Gene Edwards stepped into the mountain man's shoes for this amiable family adventure. Plagued by shooting problems, with director Ken Kennedy replacing Don Shanks part-way through production, the film has Grizzly leave the wilderness to come to the rescue of an old banker friend. It's not much of a plot, but Grizzly's forest pets will keep the youngsters happy. DP

Gene Edwards *Grizzly Adams* • Link Wyler *Trapper* • Wayne Brennan *Horace Carson* • Red West *Bodine* • LQ Jones *Reno* • Anthony Caruso *Don Carlos* • Acquanetta *Maria* • Carla Kay Tedrow *Carla Townly* ■ *Dir* Ken Kennedy • *Scr* Ken Kennedy, from a novel by Richard Dillon

The Legend of Hell House ★★★ 15

Horror 1973 · UK · Colour · 93mins

Richard Matheson's adaptation of his own novel is long on theory and short on terror. Dying millionaire Roland Culver offers a handsome reward to scientist Clive Revill and psychics Pamela Franklin and Roddy McDowall if they can discover the secret of the afterlife in a house with a history of violent hauntings. Although director John Hough makes atmospheric use of the eerie sets, he is too content to send shivers rather than shock, and thus dilutes the efforts of a cast that has valiantly entered into the spirit of the thing. DP. Contains a sex scene, swearing, nudity. DVD

Pamela Franklin *Florence Tanner* • Roddy McDowall *Ben Fischer* • Clive Revill *Dr Chris Barrett* • Gayle Hunnicutt *Ann Barrett* • Roland Culver *Rudolph Deutsch* • Peter Bowles *Hanley* • Michael Gough *Corpse* ■ *Dir* John Hough • *Scr* Richard Matheson, from his novel *Hell House*

The Legend of Lylah Clare ★★★

Drama 1968 · US · Colour · 129mins

This overlong melodrama is notoriously fascinating for movie cultists, dealing as it does with a sublimely silly plot involving a long-dead movie star about to have her life story filmed by her husband. Kim Novak incarnates Lylah and her lookalike, and Peter Finch is the demonic director. Both pull out all the stops (well, Kim pulls out her one) and the film topples over into unavoidable absurdity, a sort of wannabe *Sunset Boulevard*. The unique mixture of tormented sexuality and outright sadism here makes this a very peculiar experience. TS

Kim Novak *Lylah Clare/Elsa Brinkmann* • Peter Finch *Lewis Zarkan* • Ernest Borgnine *Barney Sheean* • Milton Selzer *Bart Langner* • Rossella Falk *Rossella* • Gabriele Tinti *Paolo* • Valentina Cortese *Countess Bozo Bedoni* • Jean Carroll *Becky Langner* ■ *Dir* Robert Aldrich • *Scr* Hugo Butler, Jean Rouverol, from the screenplay (unproduced) by Robert Thom, Edward DeBlasio

The Legend of 1900 ★★★★ 15

Epic period drama
1999 · It · Colour · 119mins

Every bit as lush, nostalgic and romantic as his *Cinema Paradiso*, director Giuseppe Tornatore's English language debut is a dreamy cross between *Life Is Beautiful* and *Titanic*. While about as plausible as the former and slightly less spectacular than the latter, this epic rumination on the human condition is still an engaging fable, delicately shot through with keen emotions and stunning visuals. It tells the strange tale of orphan Tim Roth, born on a cruise liner at the beginning of the 20th century, who becomes a star piano prodigy during the Roaring Twenties. Told in melancholy flashback by trumpet player Pruitt Taylor Vince, this bittersweet mood piece is packed with stunning images, all choreographed to another masterly Ennio Morricone score. Unusual and haunting. AJ [video] DVD

Tim Roth *Danny Boodman TD Lemon Novecento* • Pruitt Taylor Vince *Max Tooney* • Mélanie Thierry *The girl* • Bill Nunn *Danny Boodman* • Peter Vaughan *Music shop owner* • Niall O'Brien *Plymouth harbour master* • Gabriele Lavia *Farmer* • Alberto Vásquez *Mexican stoker* ■ *Dir* Giuseppe Tornatore • *Scr* Giuseppe Tornatore, from the stage monologue *Novecento* by Alessandro Baricco • *Cinematographer* Lajos Koltai

The Legend of the Holy Drinker ★★★★ PG

Drama 1988 · It/Fr · Colour · 122mins

This magical, generous-of-spirit film has Rutger Hauer turning in one of his finest performances, as a tramp in Paris who is given a life-saving donation by a stranger on condition that he repay it to a shrine of St Theresa. But the new life the money helps him attain diverts him from his quest to pay off the debt. Italian director Ermanno Olmi has created a film from Joseph Roth's novella which, while not pressing the religious nerve too painfully, still tackles the idea of "legend" with lyricism, evoking a magnificent Paris in the process. TH [video]

Rutger Hauer *Andreas Kartak* • Anthony Quayle *Distinguished gentleman* • Sandrine Dumas *Gabby* • Dominique Pinon *Woitech* • Sophie Segalen *Karoline* ■ *Dir* Ermanno Olmi • *Scr* Tullio Kezich, Ermanno Olmi, from the novella *Die Legende des beiligen Trinkers* by Joseph Roth

The Legend of the Lone Ranger ★★★ PG

Western 1981 · US · Colour · 92mins

This self-conscious attempt to bring back to the big screen the noble masked western avenger must be counted a failure largely owing to under-casting. Yet this Panavisioned retelling of the origins of the blue-clad hero and his Indian sidekick Tonto is not without a certain grandeur, and director and erstwhile cinematographer William A Fraker creates some dazzling imagery and scenic splendour, though he is terribly hampered by the plot provided. Totally unknown Klinton Spilsbury (allegedly revoiced by *Dallas* star Ken Kercheval, though some claim Stacy Keach did it) looks fine in costume, but lacks the necessary charisma and solidity that Clayton Moore brought to the role. TS [video]

Klinton Spilsbury *John Reid (the Lone Ranger)* • Michael Horse *Tonto* • Christopher Lloyd *Cavendish* • Jason Robards *President Grant* • Matt Clark *Sheriff Wiatt* • Juanin Clay *Amy Striker* • John Hart *Lucas Striker* • Richard Farnsworth *Wild Bill Hickok* • Ted Flicker [Theodore J Flicker] *Buffalo Bill Cody* ■ *Dir* William A Fraker • *Scr* Ivan Goff, Ben Roberts, Michael Kane, William Roberts, Jerry Berloshan, from characters created by George W Trendle

Legend of the Lost ★★ U

Adventure 1957 · US · Colour · 104mins

Big John Wayne stars as hard-drinking Joe January, not out west this time, but engaged as a guide by explorer Rossano Brazzi to search for Saharan treasure. Sophia Loren provides the love interest as a street girl looking for adventure. Unfortunately, what should have been a romp is taken far too seriously, and the Libyan locations are the main reasons for watching this languid travelogue. TS [video]

John Wayne *Joe January* • Sophia Loren *Dita* • Rossano Brazzi *Paul Bonnard* • Kurt Kasznar *Prefect Dukas* • Sonia Moser *Girl* • Angela Portaluri *Girl* • Ibrahim El Hadish *Galli Galli* ■ *Dir* Henry Hathaway • *Scr* Robert Presnell Jr, Ben Hecht • *Cinematographer* Jack Cardiff

The Legend of the 7 Golden Vampires ★★★ 15

Martial arts horror
1974 · UK/HK · Colour · 85mins

In its waning years, Hammer tried to make imaginative changes to the old favourites and this east-meets-west tale was one of the studio's better attempts to update the vampire formula. Peter Cushing's Van Helsing treks to China to take on his long-standing enemy Dracula with the help of a martial arts clan in this highly entertaining and surprisingly thoughtful kung fu horror movie. It sounds ludicrous, but it works, mainly thanks to excellent fight choreography and rousing direction from horror veteran Roy Ward Baker. AJ [video] DVD

Peter Cushing *Professor Lawrence Van Helsing* • David Chiang *Hsi Ching* • Julie Ege *Vanessa Buren* • Robin Stewart *Leyland Van Helsing* • Szu Shih *Mai Kwei* • John Forbes-Robertson *Dracula* • Robert Hanna *British consul* ■ *Dir* Roy Ward Baker • *Scr* Don Houghton

The Legend of the Suram Fortress ★★★ U

Fantasy drama 1984 · USSR · Colour · 83mins

After a 15-year hiatus, during which time he was twice jailed by the Soviet authorities, Sergei Paradjanov returned to directing with this beguiling allegory on the malingering disintegration of the USSR. The narrative concerns the revenge of a fortune-teller, who convinces a young man that he must be walled up inside a medieval Georgian fortress to save it from collapse. But such is the density of the symbolic and cultural references that western audiences would be advised simply to surrender themselves to the glorious visuals, composed with a uniquely painterly eye by Paradjanov and his star and co-director, Dodo Abashidze. DP. In Georgian with English subtitles. [video]

Venerik'o Andzhaparidze • Dodo Abashidze ■ *Dir* Dodo Abashidze, Sergei Paradjanov • *Scr* Vazha Ghigashvili

Legend of the Werewolf ★★ 18

Horror 1974 · UK · Colour · 86mins

David Rintoul plays a lycanthropic zoo keeper in a Paris-based slice of cod Hammer horror directed by Freddie Francis for Tyburn, his son Kevin's company. Although he offers little in the way of new ideas or situations, Francis does summon up a Gothic moodiness between the few scares. Loyal Peter Cushing fans will want to check out his usual top-notch performance as the coroner pursuing the snarling Rintoul. AJ [video]

Peter Cushing *Paul Cataflanque* • Ron Moody *Zoo keeper* • Hugh Griffith *Maestro Pamponi* • David Rintoul *Etoile* • Stefan Gryff *Max Gerard* • Lynn Dalby *Christine* • Renee Houston *Chou-Chou* • Marjorie Yates *Madame Tellier* • Roy Castle *Photographer* • Michael Ripper *Sewerman* ■ *Dir* Freddie Francis • *Scr* John Elder [Anthony Hinds]

Legend of the White Horse ★ PG

Fantasy adventure
1985 · US/Pol · Colour · 87mins

Billed as a family film, this preposterous fantasy could be a scary outing for the under-12s. Geologist father Christopher Lloyd goes to a fictitious country on an environmental "dig" and finds his plans interrupted, not to say stopped, by a white horse which turns into a dragon and several other menaces. A Polish-American production, this is a farrago hardly worth retrieving. TH [video]

Christopher Lloyd *Jim Martin* • Dee Wallace Stone *Alta* • Allison Balson *Jewel* ■ *Dir* Jerzy Domaradzki, Janusz Morgenstern • *Scr* Robert C Fleet

The Legend of Tom Dooley ★★★ U

Western 1959 · US · BW · 79mins

Inspired by folk group the Kingston Trio's hit song (which they perform on the soundtrack here) this Civil War western follows the lyrics all the way to their downbeat conclusion and turns out to be an unexpectedly resonant little picture. Michael Landon and Richard Rust are excellent as two of the Confederate soldiers who, not realising that the war is over, rob a Union stage and have to go on the run. Jo Morrow is good as the northern girl with whom Landon attempts to elope. Writer/producer Stan Shpetner deserves credit for an intelligent script, and director Ted Post handles his young cast well. AE

Michael Landon *Tom Dooley* • Jo Morrow *Laura* • Jack Hogan *Charlie Grayson* • Richard Rust *Country Boy* • Dee Pollock *Abel* • Ken Lynch *Father* • Howard Wright *Sheriff* • Ralph Moody *Doc Henry* ■ *Dir* Ted Post • *Scr* Stanley Shpetner

The Legend of Young Dick Turpin ★ U

Action adventure 1965 · US · Colour · 89mins

One of England's most famous, home-grown outlaws, Dick Turpin didn't have the headline notoriety of Jesse James, but his country-long ride still has a substantial interest. Unfortunately this movie, with David Weston and George Cole, is lumpen and packed with clichés. TH [video]

David Weston *Dick Turpin* • George Cole *Mr Evans* • Bernard Lee *Jeremiah* • Maurice Denham *Mr Fielding* ■ *Dir* James Neilson • *Scr* Robert Westerby

The Legends of Rita ★★★

Drama 2000 · Ger · Colour · 103mins

Bibiana Beglau and Nadja Uhl shared the best actress prize at Berlin for their work in this film which marks Volker Schlöndorff's return to the period that saw him in the vanguard of New German Cinema. Co-scripted by former DEFA stalwart, Wolfgang Kohlhaase, this memoir of life in the old East Germany eschews prejudiced western notions of repression and shortages. Yet it's undoubtedly the banality of her existence with Stasi officer Martin Wuttke that helps drive Beglau's one-time terrorist into the arms of the hard-drinking Uhl. DP. In German with English subtitles.

Bibiana Beglau *Rita Vogt* • Martin Wuttke *Erwin Hull* • Nadja Uhl *Tatjana* • Harald Schrott *Andi* • Alexander Beyer *Jochen* ■ *Dir* Volker Schlöndorff • *Scr* Wolfgang Kohlhaase, Volker Schlöndorff

Legends of the Fall ★★★★ 15

Epic drama 1994 · US · Colour · 127mins

In this fabulous throwback to the epic dramas of old, Anthony Hopkins is a stern patriarch whose disgust at the actions of his own government during the Indian Wars leads him to bring up his three sons (Brad Pitt, Aidan Quinn and Henry Thomas) on a remote ranch in the Montana mountains. However, their idyllic life is thrown into turmoil by outside events and by the arrival of the beautiful Julia Ormond. Edward Zwick fashions a poetic hymn to values of loyalty and family ties, which only occasionally slips into melodramatic cliché, while John Toll's Oscar-winning cinematography is equally at home with the stunning beauty of the mountainous terrain and the killing fields of war-torn France. JF. Contains violence, swearing, sex scenes and nudity. [video] DVD

Brad Pitt *Tristan* • Anthony Hopkins *Ludlow* • Aidan Quinn *Alfred* • Julia Ormond *Susannah* • Henry Thomas *Samuel* • Karina Lombard *Isabel Two* • Tantoo Cardinal *Pet* • Gordon Tootoosis *One Stab* • Paul Desmond *Decker* • Christina Pickles *Isabel* ■ *Dir* Edward Zwick • *Scr* Susan Shilliday, Bill Wittliff, from the novella by Jim Harrison

Legion of Iron ★ 18

Science-fiction action drama
1990 · US · Colour · 85mins

The story takes place deep under the surface of the Earth, where the negative of this clumsy and appallingly cheap movie should be hidden. It promises ample sex and violence – male athletes are kidnapped and forced to fight gladiator-style in a secret underground arena, with sexual rewards for the victors – but fails to deliver. KB [video]

Kevin T Walsh *Billy Hamilton* • Erika Nann *Diana* • Camille Carrigan *Allison* • Reggie De Morton *Lyle Wagner* ■ *Dir* Yakov Bentsvi • *Scr* Rueben Gordon, Steven Schoenberg, from a story by Edward Hunt

Legionnaire ★★ 15

Period action adventure
1998 · US · Colour · 94mins

Jean-Claude Van Damme plays a boxer heading for Morocco to avoid some disgruntled punters in Paris. Riddled with implausibilities and acted with metronomic rigidity, it's notable for only one thing – Van Damme's isn't the worst performance on display. That honour goes to Steven Berkoff, whose extravagant posturing almost gives the film a cockeyed kudos. On the plus side, the training sequences and the battles with the Berbers are competently handled by director Peter MacDonald, but he has little success in the scenes where his actors are required to talk. DP DVD

Jean-Claude Van Damme *Alain Lefevre* • Adewale Akinnuoye-Agbaje *Luther* • Steven Berkoff *Steinkampf* • Nicholas Farrell *Mackintosh* • Jim Carter *Lucien Galgani* ■ *Dir* Peter MacDonald • *Scr* Sheldon Lettich, Rebecca Morrison, by Sheldon Lettich, by Jean-Claude Van Damme

The Lemon Drop Kid ★★★

Drama 1934 · US · BW · 71mins

An early adaptation of the Damon Runyon fable better known for the Bob Hope version made in 1951. This is tougher and more serious, closer in tone to Runyan's original, with Lee Tracy as the racetrack tipster who gets entangled with both the law and the underworld. Talented Tracy, a half-forgotten actor today, was a past-master at this sort of fast-talking, energetic role, and director Marshall Neilan keeps things moving and vividly captures Runyon's world of offbeat Broadway denizens. TV

Lee Tracy *Wally Brooks* • Helen Mack *Alice Deering* • William Frawley *The professor* • Minna Gombell *Maizie* • Baby LeRoy *The baby* • Robert McWade *Mr Griggsby* • Henry B Walthall *Jonas Deering* • Clarence H Wilson [Clarence Wilson] *Martin Potter* ■ *Dir* Marshall Neilan • *Scr* Howard J Green, JP McEvoy, from the short story by Damon Runyon

L

The Lemon Drop Kid ★★★

Musical comedy 1951 · US · BW · 91mins

Bob Hope was no stranger to Damon Runyon's world of idiosyncratic, kind-hearted Broadway characters, having starred in *Sorrowful Jones*, one of many versions of *Little Miss Marker*. Here, he's a horse-racing tipster in debt to a gang boss, who has his pals dress up as Father Christmas to raise the money he needs on the pretext of collecting for elderly "dolls". Hope himself even appears in drag as an old dear. It may not be real Runyon but it has enough bright quips and inventive moments to be good Hope. AE

Bob Hope *Lemon Drop Kid* • Marilyn Maxwell *Brainey Baxter* • Lloyd Nolan *Charlie* • Jane Darwell *Nellie Thursday* • Andrea King *Stella* • Fred Clark *Moose Moran* • Jay C Flippen *Straight Flush* • William Frawley *Gloomy Willie* ■ *Dir* Sidney Lanfield • *Scr* Edmund Hartmann [Edmund L Hartmann], Frank Tashlin, Robert O'Brien, from a story by Edmund Beloin, from the short story by Damon Runyon

Lemon Popsicle ★★★

Drama 1978 · Is · Colour · 95mins

One of the biggest grossing films ever made in Israel, Boaz Davidson's nostalgic comedy was more risqué than many of the rites-of-passage teen pictures being made in Hollywood at the same time. With every song on the radio echoing their adolescent pangs, Yiftach Katzur, Jonathan Segal and Zachi Noy resort to an ageing nymphomaniac and a diseased prostitute to satiate their rampaging urges. At least until Anat Atzmon appears on the scene. Brisk, bawdy and handled with a genuine fondness for the period and the characters, it breaks every rule in the PC handbook, but spawned four sequels. DP. In Hebrew with English subtitles.

Yiftach Katzur *Bentzi* • Anat Atzmon *Nili* • Jonathan Segal *Momo* • Zachi Noy *Yuda'leh* ■ *Dir* Boaz Davidson • *Scr* Boaz Davidson, Eli Tavor

The Lemon Sisters ★ 15

Comedy 1989 · US · Colour · 88mins

Diane Keaton dropped her name as producer from the credits of this comedy drama, which shows she recognised it as the lemon it is. The story of three Atlantic City girlfriends – Keaton, Carol Kane and Kathryn Grody – trying to put their voices together as a singing group is a series of sorry sequences that are as banal as they are boring. Sourly reviewed when it first appeared, it was then shelved for a year before a brief release. TH

Diane Keaton *Eloise Hamer* • Carol Kane *Franki D'Angelo* • Kathryn Grody *Nola Frank* • Elliott Gould *Fred Frank* • Rubén Blades *CW* • Aidan Quinn *Frankie McGuinness* • Estelle Parsons *Mrs Kupchak* • Richard Libertini *Nicholas Panas* • Sully Boyar *Baxter O'Neil* ■ *Dir* Joyce Chopra • *Scr* Jeremy Pikser

Lemony Snicket's A Series of Unfortunate Events ★★★ PG

Fantasy comedy adventure 2004 · US/Ger · Colour · 103mins

This visually inspired adaptation combines the first three titles in Lemony Snicket's bestselling series. A darkly humorous gothic fantasy, it unfolds like a Grimm fairy tale as imagined by Tim Burton. In another of his wildly over-the-top performances, Jim Carrey is the evil Count Olaf, an actor and master of disguise who's on a murderous mission to swindle three orphaned siblings out of their family fortune. The children are fabulous and, as they encounter everything from man-eating leeches to falling fridges, demonstrate real talent and charm. Although flawed, thanks to its quirkiness and whimsical Victorian styling, the film's still an enjoyable affair. SF DVD

Jim Carrey *Count Olaf* • Meryl Streep *Aunt Josephine* • Jude Law *Lemony Snicket* • Emily Browning *Violet Baudelaire* • Liam Aiken *Klaus Baudelaire* • Kara Hoffman *Sunny Baudelaire* • Shelby Hoffman *Sunny Baudelaire* • Timothy Spall *Mr Poe* • Billy Connolly *Uncle Monty* ■ *Dir* Brad Silberling • *Scr* Robert Gordon, from the books by Lemony Snicket

Lena: My 100 Children ★★★★ U

Drama based on a true story 1987 · US · Colour · 94mins

This much-lauded TV movie is based on the true and deeply moving story of Lena Kuchler-Silberman, the extraordinary Polish Jew who risked her life to ensure a hundred Jewish children escaped from Poland to the Middle East just after the Second World War. The central role is wonderfully played by Linda Lavin who received many plaudits on the film's first transmission in 1987, the year Kuchler-Silberman died. A double-hanky movie. SH DVD

Linda Lavin *Lena Kuchler-Silberman* • Leonore Harris *Bella* • Cynthia Wilde *Rhea* • George Touliatos *Polonski* • John Evans *Sani* • Sam Malkin *Stefan* ■ *Dir* Ed Sherin [Edwin Sherin] • *Scr* Jonathan B Rintels Jr, Yabo Yablonsky, Maurice Hurley, from the non-fiction book *My Hundred Children* by Lena Kuchler-Silberman

Lena's Holiday ★★★

Comedy drama 1990 · US · Colour · 100mins

Hollywood has an unwritten law about luggage. If a suitcase gets accidentally switched, the replacement absolutely has to contain something stolen and the original's owner *must* endure all manner of dangers (comic or otherwise) before they, and their inevitable new-found love, retrieve their property and wave off the villains as they depart in a police car. But this tired old tale is lifted here by some perky performances, with Felicity Waterman and Chris Lemmon (son of Jack) clicking nicely as her cabbie accomplice. DP

Felicity Waterman *Lena* • Chris Lemmon *Mike Camden* • Nick Mancuso *Corey Flynn* • Michael Sarrazin *Jan Mackenzie* • Noriyuki "Pat" Morita [Pat Morita] *Fred* ■ *Dir* Michael Keusch • *Scr* Michael Keusch, Deborah Tilton

Lenin in October ★★★

Historical drama 1937 · USSR · BW · 114mins

Completed in just three months, to mark the 20th anniversary of the October Revolution, this propagandist biopic was designed less to celebrate historical fact than to reinforce the "cult of personality" that had been erected around the Bolshevik leader, VI Lenin. Yet, even this hagiographic purpose was of secondary consequence to extolling the part played by Stalin, not only in the overthrow of Tsarism, but also in helping Lenin secure power. BV Shchukin's amazing physical impersonation was based on hours of studying agit-prop newsreels. DP. In Russian with English subtitles.

BV Shchukin *VI Lenin* • NP Okhlopkov [Nikolai P Okhlopkov] *Vasily* • Vasili Vanin *Factory manager* ■ *Dir* Mikhail Romm • *Scr* Aleksei Kapler

Leningrad Cowboys Go America ★★★★ 15

Satirical comedy 1989 · Fin · Colour · 75mins

Proudly sporting the influence of Jim Jarmusch on his sleeve, Finnish director Aki Kaurismäki broke out of the art house ghetto and achieved cult status with this scattershot road movie. With their dead bassist travelling in his coffin and their Cadillac brimful of beer cans, the Leningrad Cowboys (whose hairstyles are more pointed than their winklepickers) fulfil their reputation as the world's worst rock band, as they lurch between disastrous Stateside gigs before finally landing in Mexico. Yet, this isn't a *Spinal Tap*-type of picture, as it isn't the Cowboys that are under the microscope, but the deliriously ordinary folk they meet en route. DP. In English and Finnish with subtitles.

Matti Pellonpaa *Vladimir* • Kari Vaananen *Igor* • Nicky Tesco *Lost cousin* • Jim Jarmusch *Car salesman* ■ *Dir/Scr* Aki Kaurismäki

Leningrad Cowboys Meet Moses ★★

Comedy 1993 · Fin/Fr/Ger · Colour · 94mins

What a busy year 1993 was for the fictional "worst rock'n'roll band in the world". In addition to this sequel to *Leningrad Cowboys Go America*, they also fronted *These Boots*, Aki Kaurismäki's five-minute history of Finland from 1950 to 1969. Unfortunately, neither film was as amusing as the original, although there are laughs in this trek from Mexico (where the Cowboys had enjoyed unexpected chart success), in the company of manager, Matti Pellonpaa. DP. In Finnish with English subtitles.

Kirsi Tykkylainen *Singer* • Matti Pellonpaa *Vladimir "Moses"* • Kari Vaananen *Igor* ■ *Dir/Scr* Aki Kaurismäki

Lenny ★★★ 18

Biographical drama 1974 · US · BW · 106mins

Whether you consider controversial American stand-up comedian Lenny Bruce a lost comic genius or a self-destructive chancer who caught the countercultural mood of the late 1950s and early 60s will dictate how much you enjoy Bob Fosse's mockumentary-styled biopic. Dustin Hoffman really comes alive during Bruce's improvised, convention-baiting routines (so much so that more people will have seen Hoffman than pre-video-age Bruce himself). Valerie Perrine is convincing, too, as his stripper wife. Fosse brilliantly captures Bruce's jazz-inflected style, and if the film, told in interlocking flashbacks, lacks a strong narrative arc, it more than compensates in style. AC. Contains swearing and nudity. DVD

Dustin Hoffman *Lenny Bruce* • Valerie Perrine *Honey Bruce* • Jan Miner *Sally Marr* • Stanley Beck *Artie Silver* • Gary Morton *Sherman Hart* ■ *Dir* Bob Fosse • *Scr* Julian Barry, from his play • *Cinematographer* Bruce Surtees

Lensman ★★ PG

Animated science-fiction adventure 1984 · Jpn · Colour · 107mins

Edward E "Doc" Smith's pulp sci-fi novels were among the inspirations behind *Star Wars*. This tale, set in the 25th century, features a young "lensman" who is endowed with mysterious powers to aid him in the fight against the forces of evil. Unfortunately, it's an uninspired amalgam of sci-fi clichés, redeemed only by the animation, which combines traditional hand-drawn artwork with state-of-the-art computer graphics. The American dubbed version was released in 1991. RS. Japanese dialogue dubbed into English.

Dir Yoshiaki Kawajiri, Kazuyuki Hirokawa • *Scr* Soji Yoshikawa, from a novel by Edward E "Doc" Smith

Leo ★★ 15

Drama 2002 · US/UK · Colour · 103mins

Director Mehdi Norowzian pursues two apparently separate stories: one of a young boy watching his mother descend into alcoholism after a family tragedy, while the other has a man (Joseph Fiennes) coming out of prison and attempting to rebuild his life. As the stories flash forwards and back, the identities of the characters and continuity of the plot become – a little – clearer. It's competently acted, moody, and often beautifully shot, but the fractured structure makes it impossible to engage emotionally with this sporadically intriguing curio. AS

Joseph Fiennes *Stephen* • Elisabeth Shue *Mary Bloom* • Justin Chambers *Ryan* • Deborah Kara Unger *Caroline* • Dennis Hopper *Horace* • Sam Shepard *Vic* • Jake Weber *Ben Bloom* • Mary Stuart Masterson *Brynne* ■ *Dir* Mehdi Norowzian • *Scr* Massy Tadjedin, Amir Tadjedin

Leo the Last ★★

Drama 1970 · UK · Colour · 103mins

Although British director John Boorman won the best director award at Cannes for this calculatingly arty docu-fantasy. It's all too contrived for comfort as convalescent aristocrat Leo (Marcello Mastroianni) sets up home in London's Notting Hill and gets to know the poverty-stricken residents who live there and who rent his properties. As an attempt at parable, it's obviously "let's-love-everyone" propaganda and comes out looking very banal. TH

Marcello Mastroianni *Leo* • Billie Whitelaw *Margaret* • Calvin Lockhart *Roscoe* • Glenna Forster-Jones *Salambo* • Graham Crowden *Max* • Gwen Ffrangcon-Davies *Hilda* • David De Keyser *David* ■ *Dir* John Boorman • *Scr* John Boorman, William Stair, from the play *The Prince* by George Tabori

Léolo ★★★★ 18

Comedy drama 1992 · Can/Fr · Colour · 102mins

It reveals much about this unconventional but curiously convincing take on childhood that its young hero considers himself to have been conceived during his mother's encounter with a sperm-filled Sicilian tomato. Despite this, Maxime Collin is clearly the sanest member of his family, bearing in mind the sinister antics of his father and siblings, the lasciviousness of his grandfather and the general household obsession with bowel movements. Employing expressionist tactics to give Collin's escapist and sexual fantasies a shoddy magic, Québecois director Jean-Claude Lauzon seemed a talent to be reckoned with. Tragically, he was killed in a plane crash in 1997. DP. In French with English subtitles.

Gilbert Sicotte *Narrator* • Maxime Collin *Leo, aka Léolo* • Ginette Reno *Mother* • Julien Guiomar *Grandfather* • Pierre Bourgault *The Word Tamer* • Giudetta Del Vecchio *Bianca* • Denys Arcand *Career counsellor* ■ *Dir/Scr* Jean-Claude Lauzon

Leon ★★★★★ 18

Thriller 1994 · Fr · Colour · 110mins

French director Luc Besson followed his international hit *Nikita* with his first American-set movie, a haunting and compulsive thriller that explores the relationship between the emotionally stunted hitman of the title and his 12-year-old neighbour Natalie Portman. Jean Reno is reluctantly forced to befriend and protect the girl after her family is wiped out in a horrific drugs operation led by Gary Oldman. Reno ends up teaching Portman the tricks of his trade so that she can take revenge on the deranged cop. The two masterly central performances intelligently convey how the hitman's carefully constructed, reclusive existence falls apart as he lets feelings enter his life for the very first time. But it's the ultra-stylish action scenes that propel this into the suspense stratosphere as Besson redefines the action genre with a series of totally breathtaking set pieces. AJ. Contains violence and swearing. DVD

Jean Reno *Leon* • Gary Oldman *Stansfield* • Natalie Portman *Mathilda* • Danny Aiello *Tony* • Michael Badalucco *Mathilda's father* • Peter Appel *Malky* • Ellen Greene *Mathilda's mother* ■ *Dir/Scr* Luc Besson

Léon Morin, Priest ★★★★ PG

Second World War drama 1961 · Fr/It · BW · 115mins

Few French film-makers have been as forthcoming about the Occupation as Jean-Pierre Melville. If his Resistance tribute, *L'Armée des Ombres*, is akin to *film noir*, this insight into the overpowering nature of love and faith recalls the restrained character studies of Robert Bresson. Reining in his natural exuberance, Jean-Paul Belmondo is holy yet human as the small-town priest whose ministrations elicit both spiritual and sexual responses from the previously agnostic Emmanuelle Riva. Utterly convincing in its period detail, this is a potent study of the mysteries of divine intervention. DP. A French language film. DVD

Jean-Paul Belmondo *Léon Morin* • Emmanuelle Riva *Barny* • Irène Tunc *Christine* • Nicole Mirel *Sabine* • Marco Behar *Edelman* ■ *Dir* Jean-Pierre Melville • *Scr* Jean-Pierre Melville, from a novel by Beatrice Beck

Leon the Pig Farmer ★★★ 15

Comedy 1992 · UK · Colour · 99mins

As a prime piece of crackling, this low-budget British comedy from Vadim Jean and Gary Sinyor isn't as hilarious as it thinks it is, but the story of a Jewish estate agent (Mark Frankel) discovering – shock! horror! – that his real father is a Yorkshire pig-breeder does have flashes of comic illumination to light up religious bigotry. The fantasy of a kosher pig is laboured, but there's still plenty of crisped flesh worth flossing for, especially Brian Glover as the breeder. TH. Contains swearing. DVD

Mark Frankel *Leon Geller* • Janet Suzman *Judith Geller* • Brian Glover *Brian Chadwick* • Connie Booth *Yvonne Chadwick* • David De Keyser *Sidney Geller* • Maryam D'Abo *Madeleine* • Gina Bellman *Lisa* • Vincenzo Ricotta *Elliot Cohen* • Jean Anderson *Mrs Samuels* • John Woodvine *Vitelli* • Annette Crosbie *Doctor Johnson* • Burt Kwouk *Art Collector* • Sean Pertwee *Keith Chadwick* ■ *Dir* Vadim Jean, Gary Sinyor • *Scr* Gary Sinyor, Michael Normand

Leonard, Part 6 ★ PG

Comedy 1987 · US · Colour · 81mins

It's never a good sign when the star of a movie – in this case comedian Bill Cosby – warned audiences to give it a wide berth. Cosby is the ex-CIA man who comes out of retirement to find out why his former colleagues, counter-agents, are being assassinated by killer animals. Paul Weiland directed this lame, would-be Bond send-up, but to no great effect. TH

Bill Cosby *Leonard* • Tom Courtenay *Frayn* • Joe Don Baker *Snyderburn* • Gloria Foster *Medusa* • Moses Gunn *Giorgio* • Pat Colbert *Allison* • Victoria Rowell *Joan* • David Maier *Man Ray* • Grace Zabriskie *Jefferson* • Jane Fonda ■ *Dir* Paul Weiland • *Scr* Jonathan Reynolds, from a story by Bill Cosby

The Leopard ★★★★★ PG

Period drama 1962 · It · Colour · 180mins

Beautifully photographed by master cameraman Giuseppe Rotunno, this opulent period classic sees director Luchino Visconti revisit the Risorgimento of the 1860s that he had previously explored in *Senso* (1954). Burt Lancaster is in tremendous form as the scion of a noble Italian family about to be brought down by a republican movement in this contemplation of Italian history and Visconti's own role – as an aristocratic Marxist – in it. The casting is splendid and some moments – such as the elaborate ballroom scene – are awash with visual splendour. The film, which deservedly won the Palme D'Or at Cannes, was dubbed and shortened for its American release. Visconti died in 1976, but Rotunno went on to supervise the film's restoration in the 1990s and this new print can now be seen in all its sumptuous widescreen glory. JA. In Italian with English subtitles. DVD

Burt Lancaster *Don Fabrizio, Prince of Salina* • Alain Delon *Tancredi, the Prince's nephew* • Claudia Cardinale *Angelica Sedara* • Paolo Stoppa *Don Calogero Sedara* • Rina Morelli *Maria Stella, wife of the Prince* • Romolo Valli *Father Pirrone* • Serge Reggiani *Don Ciccio Tumeo* • Leslie French *Cavalier Chevally* • Mario Girotti [Terence Hill] *Count Cavriaghi* ■ *Dir* Luchino Visconti • *Scr* Luchino Visconti, Suso Cecchi D'Amico, Pasquale Festa Campanile, Enrico Medioli, Massimo Franciosa, from the novel *Il Gattopardo* by Giuseppe Tomasi di Lampedusa • *Music* Nino Rota

The Leopard Man ★★★★

Thriller 1943 · US · BW · 66mins

This unconventionally haunting masterpiece of "quiet horror", produced by B-movie auteur Val Lewton, is set in a small New Mexico town. A nightclub dancer attempts to upstage her rival by bringing a live leopard to the show, but the spooked animal escapes into the night and, soon after, mauled bodies begin to appear. All is not what it seems, however, in this splendidly old-school chiller that boasts some unforgettable scenes. Director Jacques Tourneur never bettered the moment in which a young girl's blood trickles under a locked door as she is attacked by an unseen force, and this also features the best trapped-in-a-cemetery sequence ever. AJ

Dennis O'Keefe *Jerry Manning* • Jean Brooks *Kiki Walker* • Margo *Clo-Clo* • Isabel Jewell *Maria* • James Bell *Dr Galbraith* • Margaret Landry *Teresa Delgado* ■ *Dir* Jacques Tourneur • *Scr* Ardel Wray, Edward Dein, from the novel *Black Alibi* by Cornell Woolrich • *Producer* Val Lewton

Lepke ★★★ 18

Biographical crime drama 1975 · US · Colour · 104mins

This crime drama was designed to cash in on the gangster boom following the success of *The Godfather* and harked back to the golden age of James Cagney and Humphrey Bogart. Louis "Lepke" Buchalter was the Jewish hoodlum whose reign as the head of Murder Inc ended in the electric chair in 1944. Although he occasionally chews the scenery, Tony Curtis brings a disturbingly convincing megalomaniacal brutality to the title role, and he's well supported by Anjanette Cromer as his put-upon wife and Milton Berle, in a rare non-comic role, as his father-in-law. DP

Tony Curtis *Louis "Lepke" Buchalter* • Anjanette Comer *Bernice Meyer* • Michael Callan *Robert Kane* • Warren Berlinger *Gurrah Shapiro* • Gianni Russo *Albert Anastasia* • Vic Tayback *Lucky Luciano* • Mary Wilcox *Marion* • Milton Berle *Mr Meyer* ■ *Dir* Menahem Golan • *Scr* Wesley Lau, Tamar Hoffs, from a story by Wesley Lau

Leprechaun ★ 15

Horror 1992 · US · Colour · 87mins

This tacky debasement of a charming Irish legend is too juvenile for adult tastes and too gruesome for children. Three teenagers free nasty leprechaun (Warwick Davis) who's been trapped in a crate in a farmhouse for ten years and he then goes on the gory search for his stolen pot of gold. Made up of nothing but low points, the unfunny repartee, forced whimsicality and endless running around with characters shrieking "Gimme back my gold!" add shoddy insult to blarney injury. Sadly, four sequels followed. AJ DVD

Warwick Davis *The Leprechaun* • Jennifer Aniston *Tory* • Ken Olandt *Nathan* • Mark Holton *Ozzie* • Robert Gorman [Robert Hy Gorman] *Alex* • John Sanderford *JD* ■ *Dir/Scr* Mark Jones (2)

Les Patterson Saves the World ★ 15

Comedy 1987 · Aus · Colour · 85mins

Barry Humphries makes us laugh as Dame Edna Everage and as Australia's cultural attaché Sir Les Patterson, but this cinema outing is a catalogue of misfired jokes and rock bottom tastelessness. The beer-swilling Patterson racks up the sort of infantile puns that even the *Carry On* team would have thrown out. The plot about international espionage implies a sort of Bond send-up but to call it racist is to dignify it. Easily a candidate for the worst movie ever made. AT DVD

Barry Humphries *Sir Les Patterson/Dame Edna Everage* • Pamela Stephenson *Veronique Crudite* • Thaao Penghlis *Colonel Richard Godowni* • Andrew Clarke *Neville Thonge* • Henri Szeps *Dr Charles Herpes/Desiree* • Hugh Keays-Byrne *Inspector Farouk* • Garth Meade *Mustafa Toul* ■ *Dir* George Miller (1) • *Scr* Barry Humphries, Diane Millstead

Less than Zero ★★ 18

Drama 1987 · US · Colour · 94mins

The "Brat Pack" gets hedonistic in an overly glossy filming of Bret Easton Ellis's novel about rich kids living the wild life in Los Angeles. Robert Downey Jr is very convincing as a wealthy, charming cocaine addict on a slippery slope to rock bottom, and you'll struggle to find a sadder example of life imitating art. Andrew McCarthy and Jami Gertz are too lightweight for this material, though, and there's a lack of emotional involvement in what amounts to a pretty pop video about the perils of excess. RS DVD

Andrew McCarthy *Clay* • Jami Gertz *Blair* • Robert Downey Jr *Julian* • James Spader *Rip* • Tony Bill *Bradford Easton* • Nicholas Pryor *Benjamin Wells* • Donna Mitchell *Elaine Easton* • Michael Bowen *Hop* ■ *Dir* Marek Kanievska • *Scr* Harley Peyton, from the novel by Bret Easton Ellis

A Lesson Before Dying ★★★

Period drama 1999 · US · Colour · 101mins

Don Cheadle is the teacher attempting to restore dignity to a condemned man in this Emmy-winning TV movie set in rural 1940s Louisiana. Cheadle reluctantly visits a young African-American (Mekhi Phifer) due to be executed for a murder he did not commit. Unlike most movies in this genre, this is not about the search for an 11th-hour reprieve but rather an attempt to reconcile Phifer to his fate, however undeserved. The solid script, thoughtful direction and a first-rate cast, including veteran Cicely Tyson, make this memorable. MC

Don Cheadle *Grant Wiggins* • Cicely Tyson *Tante Lou* • Mekhi Phifer *Jefferson* • Irma P Hall *Miss Emma* • Brent Jennings *Reverend Ambrose* ■ *Dir* Joseph Sargent • *Scr* Ann Peacock, from the novel by Ernest J Gaines

Lesson in Love ★★★ PG

Comedy 1954 · Swe · BW · 91mins

Considering it was scripted within months of Ingmar Bergman divorcing his third wife, this is a surprisingly sprightly comedy of marital manners. However, it's the performances of Gunnar Björnstrand and Eva Dahlbeck, rather than the writing, that supply the sparkle in this story of the emotionally immature gynaecologist, who abandons a mistress to pursue his ex-wife to Copenhagen to witness her wedding to the sculptor she'd jilted at the altar once before. A minor charmer. DP. In Swedish with English subtitles. DVD

Gunnar Björnstrand *David Erneman* • Eva Dahlbeck *Marianne Erneman* • Yvonne Lombard *Suzanne* • Harriet Andersson *Nix* ■ *Dir/Scr* Ingmar Bergman

Let 'Em Have It ★

Crime drama 1935 · US · BW · 98mins

This cheap and plodding independent low-budget production was made simultaneously with James Cagney's much superior *"G" Men* in a new cycle that sought to glorify America's crime busters. Its demonstrations of the latest methods of scientific detection no longer enthral and Richard Arlen's federal agent is nowhere near as vital as Bruce Cabot's public enemy. AE

Richard Arlen *Mal Stevens* • Virginia Bruce *Eleanor Spencer* • Alice Brady *Aunt Ethel* • Bruce Cabot *Joe Keefer* • Harvey Stephens *Van Rensseler* • Eric Linden *Buddy Spencer* ■ *Dir* Sam Wood • *Scr* from a story by Joseph Moncure March, Elmer Harris

Let George Do It ★★★ U

Comedy 1940 · UK · BW · 79mins

One of the best George Formby comedies, with Basil Dearden producing and co-scripting and Ronald Neame behind the camera. On screen, Formby is supported by Phyllis Calvert, as the homely girl who falls for his toothy charm, and Coral Browne, as a wicked seductress, as well as villain supreme Torin Thatcher. The story sees Formby do his first bit for the war effort, as he fetches up in Bergen instead of Blackpool and finds himself on the trail of Quislings and the Gestapo. Never a dull moment. DP

George Formby *George* • Phyllis Calvert *Mary* • Garry Marsh *Mendez* • Romney Brent *Slim* • Bernard Lee *Nelson* • Coral Browne *Ivy* • Diana Beaumont *Greta* ■ *Dir* Marcel Varnel • *Scr* John Dighton, Austin Melford, Angus MacPhail, Basil Dearden

Let Him Have It ★★★★ 15

Biographical crime drama
1991 · UK · Colour · 115mins

Director Peter Medak followed his crime biopic *The Krays* with another *cause célèbre* torn from past headlines. The Derek Bentley case remains as much a classic crusading appeal against capital punishment today as it was back in 1952 when the mentally disabled teenage epileptic stood accused of inciting the shooting of a cop after a bungled factory burglary. With drab-chic production, Christopher Eccleston's marvellous central performance and a pop nostalgia soundtrack, the odious miscarriage of justice comes vividly to life to scandalise anew those unfamiliar with the true facts. AJ DVD

Chris Eccleston [Christopher Eccleston] *Derek Bentley* • Paul Reynolds *Chris Craig* • Tom Courtenay *William Bentley* • Tom Bell *Fairfax* • Eileen Atkins *Lilian Bentley* • Clare Holman *Iris Bentley* • Mark McGann *Niven Craig* • Michael Gough *Lord Goddard* • Serena Scott Thomas *Stella* • Ronald Fraser *Niven's judge* • Michael Elphick *Jack, the warder* ■ *Dir* Peter Medak • *Scr* Neal Purvis, Robert Wade

Let It Be ★★★★ U

Musical biography
1970 · UK · Colour · 80mins

Originally arranged as rehearsals for a one-off live show, the "Get Back" sessions proved to be the most directionless and destructive of the Beatles' career. With all four already pursuing personal projects, the tensions that would cause the final split were in evidence from the start. Yet, as Michael Lindsay-Hogg's *cinéma-vérité* record proves, the band was still capable of producing classical pop music, with the impromptu back-to-basics performance on the roof of the Apple building being the highlight. Astonishingly honest in its revelations, this under-rated – and Oscar-winning – film provides a saddening insight into the end of a dream. DP

Dir Michael Lindsay-Hogg • *Executive Producer* John Lennon, Paul McCartney, George Harrison, Ringo Starr

Let It Be Me ★ 12

Romantic drama 1995 · US · Colour · 91mins

This is a dance movie that fails to cut a rug. Campbell Scott wants to learn how to dance so he can impress his fiancée Jennifer Beals (of *Flashdance* fame). However, complications set in when both go to the same dancing instructor (Leslie Caron). An interesting supporting cast isn't enough to redeem this misfiring romance. FL. Contains swearing.

Jennifer Beals *Emily* • Campbell Scott *Gabriel* • Yancy Butler *Corinne* • Jamie Goodwin *Bud* • Leslie Caron *Marguerite* • Patrick Stewart *John* • Elliott Gould *Sam* • Erika Burke *Meg* ■ *Dir/Scr* Eleanor Bergstein

Let It Ride ★★ 15

Comedy 1989 · US · Colour · 86mins

Gamblers may recognise the twitches of anguish exhibited by Richard Dreyfuss as the symptoms of a compulsive chancer whose life depends on a long shot at a Florida racetrack. Others may recognise the twitches as symptoms of overacting. Those with supporting roles, such as Teri Garr, are more in control, but it's a very dislocated sort of movie. Screenwriter Nancy Dowd saw it, decided that all bets were off and insisted on a pseudonym. TH

Richard Dreyfuss *Joe Trotter* • Teri Garr *Pam* • David Johansen *Looney* • Jennifer Tilly *Vicki* • Allen Garfield *Greenberg* • Ed Walsh [Edward Walsh] *Marty* • Robbie Coltrane *Bookie* ■ *Dir* Joe Pytka • *Scr* Ernest Morton [Nancy Dowd], from the novel *Good Vibes* by Jay Cronley

Let No Man Write My Epitaph ★★★

Drama 1960 · US · BW · 105mins

Adapted from the novel by Willard Motley, this sturdy social drama is the sequel to the same author's *Knock on Any Door*, filmed by Nicholas Ray in 1949. Set in Chicago's deprived South Side, it stars teenage idol James Darren struggling to better himself, but getting involved with gangsters. British-born director Philip Leacock, whose Hollywood movies tackled strong themes, gets powerful performances from Burl Ives as a judge, and Shelley Winters as Darren's drug-addicted mother. Ella Fitzgerald not only gets to sing but also does a spot of acting. RB

Burl Ives *Judge Bruce Mallory* • Shelley Winters *Nellie Romano* • James Darren *Nick Romano* • Jean Seberg *Barbara Holloway* • Ricardo Montalban *Louie Ramponi* • Ella Fitzgerald *Flora* • Rodolfo Acosta *Max* ■ *Dir* Philip Leacock • *Scr* Robert Presnell Jr, from the novel by Willard Motley

Let the Devil Wear Black ★★ 18

Thriller 1999 · US · Colour · 91mins

Stacy Title, who directed the wickedly funny *The Last Supper*, falters in this atmospheric but mannered crime tale, very loosely based on *Hamlet*. Title's husband Joseph Penner, who also co-wrote the script, is the young man haunted by his father's death who begins to take a closer interest in the dodgy family business. The cast can't be faulted, and Title's visuals evoke some brooding menace. However, the allusions are mannered and only serve to show up the deficiencies in the script. JF DVD

Jonathan Penner *Jack Lyne* • Jacqueline Bisset *Jack's mother* • Mary-Louise Parker *Julia* • Jamey Sheridan *Uncle Carl* • Philip Baker Hall *Saul Hirsch* ■ *Dir* Stacy Title • *Scr* Stacy Title, Jonathan Penner

Let the Good Times Roll ★★★★

Music documentary
1973 · US · Colour · 100mins

An exhilarating blend of archive clips, fond memories and concert footage, this will prove irresistible to anyone who's ever tied on a blue suede shoe. Directors Robert Abel and Sid Levin frequently employ split screens to contrast "then" and "now", but the acts on display have lost none of the old hunger. Easy listeners will delight in The Five Satins and The Coasters, but hardcore rockers will be bouncing off the walls as Fats Domino, Chubby Checker, Bill Haley and Little Richard let rip. However, the highlight is Chuck Berry and Bo Diddley's rendition of *Johnny B Goode*. DP

Dir Sidney Levin, Robert Abel

Lethal Tender ★★ 15

Action thriller 1996 · Can · Colour · 89mins

Two of straight-to-video's finest, Gary Busey and Jeff Fahey, team up for this sly thriller that sensibly doesn't take itself too seriously while still delivering the goods on the action front. This time Fahey is the good-guy policeman who is conveniently visiting a dam when it is taken over by a gang of terrorists, led by Busey, who intend holding a city's water supply to ransom. Enjoyable enough. JF

Jeff Fahey *David Chase* • Kim Coates *Montessi* • Carrie-Anne Moss *Melissa Wilkins* • Gary Busey *Mr Turner* ■ *Dir* John Bradshaw • *Scr* Tony Johnston

Lethal Weapon ★★★★ 18

Action thriller 1987 · US · Colour · 112mins

In this action-romp *par excellence*, each overblown set piece becomes ever more ludicrous – implausibility is, after all, a large part of the fun here. The basic buddy-buddy situation is very familiar, but stylishly delivered. Mel Gibson plays the reckless detective whose disregard for danger makes him a walking time bomb for criminals and colleagues alike. Mature family man Danny Glover is his by-the-book, ever-fretful partner. The pair investigate a drugs ring, and bring a great deal of spirit to the mindless mayhem. JM. Contains violence, swearing, nudity. DVD

Mel Gibson *Martin Riggs* • Danny Glover *Roger Murtaugh* • Gary Busey *Joshua* • Mitchell Ryan *General McAllister* • Tom Atkins *Michael Hunsaker* • Darlene Love *Trish Murtaugh* • Traci Wolfe *Rianne Murtaugh* • Jackie Swanson *Amanda Hunsaker* • Damon Hines *Nick Murtaugh* • Ebonie Smith *Carrie Murtaugh* • Steve Kahan *Captain Ed Murphy* ■ *Dir* Richard Donner • *Scr* Shane Black

Lethal Weapon 2 ★★★ 18

Action thriller 1989 · US · Colour · 112mins

Let down by a tiresomely inconsistent script about South African drug runners and their crooked accountant, director Richard Donner here accents humour rather than explosive action. The result is an oddly toned, cartoon-like adventure with the comedy elements making the nasty violence seem even more gratuitous. However, Gibson and Glover's evident rapport continues to delight, as does Joe Pesci's fun turn. AJ. Contains violence, swearing and nudity. DVD

Mel Gibson *Martin Riggs* • Danny Glover *Roger Murtaugh* • Joe Pesci *Leo Getz* • Joss Ackland *Arjen Rudd* • Derrick O'Connor *Pieter Vorstedt* • Patsy Kensit *Rika van den Haas* • Darlene Love *Trish Murtaugh* • Traci Wolfe *Rianne Murtaugh* • Steve Kahan *Captain Murphy* • Mark Rolston *Hans* ■ *Dir* Richard Donner • *Scr* Jeffrey Boam, from a story by Shane Black, Warren Murphy, from characters created by Shane Black

Lethal Weapon 3 ★★★ 15

Action comedy thriller
1992 · US · Colour · 115mins

Mindless mayhem doesn't come slicker than in these action extravaganzas, and, even though the law of diminishing returns is starting to have an effect, the sheer scale of the set pieces will keep fans of the first two movies satisfied. This time around, Mel Gibson gets a girl after his own heart (cop Rene Russo), soon-to-retire partner Danny Glover looks more worried than ever, and Joe Pesci is the butt of the duo's jokes. JF. Contains violence and swearing. DVD

Mel Gibson *Martin Riggs* • Danny Glover *Roger Murtaugh* • Joe Pesci *Leo Getz* • Rene Russo *Lorna Cole* • Stuart Wilson (1) *Jack Travis* • Steve Kahan *Captain Murphy* • Darlene Love *Trish Murtaugh* • Traci Wolfe *Rianne Murtaugh* • Damon Hines *Nick Murtaugh* ■ *Dir* Richard Donner • *Scr* Jeffrey Boam, Robert Mark Kamen, from a story by Jeffrey Boam, from characters created by Shane Black

Lethal Weapon 4 ★★★ 15

Action comedy thriller
1998 · US · Colour · 120mins

The fourth instalment in the action series has a "going through the motions" feel to it all. Mel Gibson and Danny Glover continue to bicker away amicably, Joe Pesci remains the butt of most of their jokes, while the pregnant Rene Russo is stuck largely on the sidelines. Chris Rock also jumps aboard the franchise, but the most notable addition is Jet Li, the Hong Kong action star whose awesome fighting skills leave the rest of the cast looking bemused. JF. Contains swearing, violence, sex scenes, drug abuse. DVD

Mel Gibson *Martin Riggs* • Danny Glover *Roger Murtaugh* • Joe Pesci *Leo Getz* • Rene Russo *Lorna Cole* • Chris Rock *Lee Butters* • Jet Li *Wah Sing Ku* • Steve Kahan *Captain Murphy* • Kim Chan *Uncle Benny* • Darlene Love *Trish Murtaugh* • Traci Wolfe *Rianne* ■ *Dir* Richard Donner • *Scr* Channing Gibson, from a story by Jonathan Lemkin, Alfred Gough, Miles Millar, from characters created by Shane Black

Let's Be Famous ★

Comedy 1939 · UK · BW · 83mins

The chance to see *Coronation Street's* Betty Driver as a movie heroine is the only reason to catch this piffling Ealing comedy. Caught between the ambitions of her music-hall mother and strict chorister father, she catches the eye of Jimmy O'Dea, a chirpy Irish know-all who hopes to find fame on a radio programme. Only in 1930s Britain would anyone think that a spelling bee could be a source of hilarity. DP

Jimmy O'Dea *Jimmy Houlihan* • Betty Driver *Betty Pinbright* • Sonnie Hale *Finch* • Patrick Barr *Johnnie Blake* • Basil Radford *Watson* ■ *Dir* Walter Forde • *Scr* Roger MacDougal, Allan Mackinnon

Let's Dance ★★ U

Musical comedy 1950 · US · Colour · 112mins

One of Fred Astaire's minor movies, in which the maestro is inexplicably second-billed to the studio's blonde bombshell, Betty Hutton. Their styles simply don't mesh: a cowboy dance routine is particularly embarrassing, with Hutton firing on all cylinders and the suave Astaire reduced to mere background. The plot's a nothing about a war widow and her son, but enjoy the Frank Loesser score and some nice Technicolor. TS

Betty Hutton *Kitty McNeil* • Fred Astaire *Donald Elwood* • Roland Young *Mr Edmund Pohlwhistle* • Lucile Watson *Serena Everett* • Ruth Warrick *Carola Everett* • Gregory Moffett *Richard "Richie" Everett* • Barton MacLane *Larry Channock* • Shepperd Strudwick *Timothy Bryant* • Melville Cooper *Mr Charles Wagstaffe* ■ *Dir* Norman Z McLeod • *Scr* Allan Scott, Dane Lussier, from the story *Little Boy Blue* by Maurice Zolotow

Let's Do It Again ★★★

Musical comedy 1953 · US · Colour · 94mins

Columbia indulged in a little nostalgia with this musical remake of it's 1937 hit, *The Awful Truth*. Jane Wyman and Ray Milland are no Irene Dunne and Cary Grant, however, and their gallant attempts to whip up Mary Loos and Richard Sale's script into a frothy, light confection aren't helped by Ned Washington's decidedly uninspired songs. As the couple who divorce only to discover they were never so much in love, Wyman and Milland don't have the necessary lightness of touch. DP

Jane Wyman *Constance Stuart* • Ray Milland *Gary Stuart* • Aldo Ray *Frank McGraw* • Leon Ames *Chet Stuart* • Valerie Bettis *Lilly Adair* ■ *Dir* Alexander Hall • *Scr* Mary Loos, Richard Sale, from the play *The Awful Truth* by Arthur Richman • *Music/lyrics* Ned Washington

Let's Do It Again ★★★ U

Comedy 1975 · US · Colour · 112mins

This hysterically funny follow-up to *Uptown Saturday Night* again teams Sidney Poitier and Bill Cosby (under Poitier's direction) as the two lodge brothers who hypnotise a puny pugilist into becoming a dynamite boxer in order to make a quick fortune in bets. The not-very-original plot's really a series of loosely tied sketches, accompanied by a terrific Curtis Mayfield soundtrack. The third film in this series was *A Piece of the Action*, but this is easily the best. TS

Sidney Poitier *Clyde Williams* • Bill Cosby *Billy Foster* • Calvin Lockhart *Biggie Smalls* • John Amos *Kansas City Mack* • Denise Nicholas *Beth Foster* • Lee Chamberlin *Dee Dee Williams* • Mel Stewart *Ellison* ■ *Dir* Sidney Poitier • *Scr* Richard Wesley, from a story by Timothy March

Let's Face It ★★ U

Musical comedy 1943 · US · BW · 76mins

Fast-talking soldier Bob Hope lines up with loud-talking Betty Hutton in a farcical comedy of cheating husbands and fed-up wives. As a trawl of old jokes and lazy predictabilities, it's the sort of cannon fodder Paramount Studios turned out for troops' relaxation. But why, as it began life as a Cole Porter musical, are so few of his songs included? TH

Bob Hope *Jerry Walker* • Betty Hutton *Winnie Potter* • ZaSu Pitts *Cornelia Pidgeon* • Phyllis Povah *Nancy Collister* • Dave Willock *Barney Hilliard* • Eve Arden *Maggie Watson* ■ *Dir* Sidney Lanfield • *Scr* Harry Tugend, from the musical play by Dorothy Firelds, Herbert Fields, Cole Porter, from the play *Cradle Snatchers* by Norma Mitchell, Russell G Medcraft

Let's Get Harry ★★ 18

Action adventure 1986 · US · Colour · 98mins

The name of the fictitious "Alan Smithee" on the credits alerts everyone (well, movie buffs anyway) that the real director of a film chose to have his name taken off it. In this case it was Stuart Rosenberg who quit this thriller about South American drug dealers who kidnap some US oil workers. Robert Duvall plays a mercenary hired to release the hostages when the American government refuses to negotiate. Duvall gives the movie some class, but for the most part it's just a thick-ear adventure yarn that could easily have starred Chuck Norris. AT [video]

Robert Duvall *Norman Shrike* • Michael Schoeffling *Corey Burck* • Tom Wilson [Thomas F Wilson] *Pachowski* • Glenn Frey *Spence* • Rick Rossovich *Kurt Klein* • Ben Johnson *Mr Burck Sr* • Mark Harmon *Harry Burck* • Gary Busey *Jack* ■ *Dir* Alan Smithee [Stuart Rosenberg] • *Scr* Charles Robert Carner, from a story by Mark Feldberg, Samuel Fuller

Let's Get Laid ★★ 18

Sex comedy 1977 · UK · Colour · 92mins

Also known as *Love Trap*, this was Robin Askwith's farewell to the world of soft-core comedy. When you've been reduced to playing characters called Gordon Laid, it's easy to see how the novelty might have worn thin. The director is James Kenelm Clarke, whose involvement with the genre came after directing a BBC documentary on pornography. DP [video]

Fiona Richmond *Maxine Lupercal* • Robin Askwith *Gordon Laid* • Anthony Steel *Moncrieff Dovecraft* • Graham Stark *Inspector Nugent* • Linda Hayden *Gloria* ■ *Dir* James Kenelm Clarke • *Scr* Michael Robson

Let's Get Lost ★★★ 15

Documentary 1988 · US · BW · 114mins

Fashion photographer Bruce Weber produced and directed this documentary about the life and hard-drug times of jazz trumpeter Chet Baker. Because of his hard-living lifestyle Baker was described as the "James Dean of jazz". The talking-heads interviews with other musicians and lovers are interspersed with terrific jam sessions by the man whose edgy bouncy music belied his inner tribulations; this is one of the most elegant biopics of a musical world all unto itself. TH [video]

Dir Bruce Weber • *Scr* Susan Stribling

Let's Get Married ★★

Comedy 1960 · UK · BW · 90mins

This was a risqué (for its day) romance featuring Anthony Newley as a timid trainee doctor. The nervy Newley marries beautiful – but pregnant – model Anne Aubrey and finally overcomes his own lack of courage when he is called upon to deliver her baby. The main enjoyment comes from the array of British comedy talent in the supporting cast. DF

Anthony Newley *Dickie Bird* • Anne Aubrey *Anne Linton* • Bernie Winters *Bernie* • Hermione Baddeley *Mrs O'Grady* • James Booth *Photographer* • Lionel Jeffries *Marsh* • Diane Clare *Glad* • John Le Mesurier *Dean* • Victor Maddern *Works Manager* • Joyce Carey *Miss Finch* • Sydney Tafler *Pendle* • Betty Marsden *Miss Kaplan* • Cardew Robinson *Salesman* ■ *Dir* Peter Graham Scott • *Scr* Ken Taylor, from his novel *Confessions of a Kept Woman*

Let's Hope It's a Girl ★★★ 15

Comedy 1985 · Fr/It · Colour · 119mins

After his comic heist movie *Big Deal On Madonna Street* in 1958, it took Italian director Mario Monicelli almost 30 years to gain another world-wide success. This rather sprawling but entertaining semi-comic family saga with feminist undertones was helped by an excellent international cast, led by Sweden's Liv Ullmann. She plays an impoverished countess struggling to keep the family's decaying property. When the film sags occasionally, there is always the beautiful Catherine Deneuve and the ravishing Tuscan settings to distract one. RB. In French and Italian with English subtitles.

Liv Ullmann *Elena Leonardo* • Catherine Deneuve *Claudia* • Philippe Noiret *Count Leonardo* • Giuliana De Sio *Franca* ■ *Dir* Mario Monicelli • *Scr* Leo Benvenuti, Piero De Bernadi, Suso Cecchi D'Amico, Tullio Pinelli, Mario Monicelli

Let's Live a Little ★★

Comedy 1948 · US · BW · 85mins

This is the kind of frothy comedy that cries out for the likes of William Powell and Myrna Loy, but instead has to settle for Robert Cummings and Hedy Lamarr. Cummings seems more at home than his co-star with the endless round of misunderstandings and petty feuds, but the film suffers from a touch of the verbals whenever psychiatrist Lamarr gets to try out her couch-side manner on Cummings's neurotic advertising executive. Short on pace but fun. DP

Hedy Lamarr *Dr JO Loring* • Robert Cummings *Duke Crawford* • Anna Sten *Michele Bennett* • Robert Shayne *Dr Richard Field* • Mary Treen *Miss Adams* • Harry Antrim *James Montgomery* ■ *Dir* Richard Wallace • *Scr* Howard Irving Young, Edmund Hartmann [Edmund L Hartmann], Albert J Cohen, from a story by Albert J Cohen, Jack Harvey

Let's Make It Legal ★★ U

Comedy 1951 · US · BW · 73mins

Richard Sale directs this marital comedy about a couple (Claudette Colbert and Macdonald Carey) who decide to part after 20 years of wedded bliss. When, with divorce proceedings well under way, her old boyfriend from the distant past (Zachary Scott) turns up, her husband has second thoughts. A well-characterised screenplay and decent performances make for a proficient and mildly amusing film, in which starlet Marilyn Monroe flits through in a bathing suit. However, it's an autumnal echo of Colbert's glittering earlier outings in the genre, and the soufflé only rises half-way. RK

Claudette Colbert *Miriam* • Macdonald Carey *Hugh* • Zachary Scott *Victor* • Barbara Bates *Barbara Denham* • Robert Wagner *Jerry Denham* • Marilyn Monroe *Joyce* • Frank Cady *Ferguson* • Jim Hayward *Gardener* ■ *Dir* Richard Sale • *Scr* F Hugh Herbert, IAL Diamond, from the story by Mortimer Braus

Let's Make Love ★★★★ U

Romantic comedy
1960 · US · Colour · 113mins

Marilyn Monroe's penultimate film has always been under-rated by both critics and Monroe fans alike, but this musical actually contains some fabulous routines from the star. The lightweight plot – a trifle about a slumming billionaire – was originally created with Gregory Peck in mind. In the sophisticated hands of "woman's" director George Cukor, it becomes a fascinating study of Monroe's sexuality, helped by the fact that she and Peck's replacement, French heart-throb Yves Montand, were amorously involved in real life at the time. A delightful streak of contemporary satire runs through the film. TS [video] DVD

Marilyn Monroe *Amanda* • Yves Montand *Jean-Marc Clement* • Tony Randall *Howard Coffman* • Frankie Vaughan *Tony Danton* • Wilfrid Hyde White *John Wales* • David Burns *Oliver Burton* • Michael David *Dave Kerry* • Bing Crosby • Gene Kelly • Milton Berle ■ *Dir* George Cukor • *Scr* Norman Krasna, Hal Kanter

Let's Make Music ★★ U

Musical 1940 · US · BW · 80mins

Elderly spinster schoolteacher Elisabeth Risdon writes a song which is taken up by Bob Crosby, becomes a hit, and gives her a new lease of life as a star on the musical entertainment circuit. Leslie Goodwins directs this inane and implausible diversion, designed as a showcase for Bing's younger brother, who makes a respectable job of playing himself. RK

Bob Crosby • Jean Rogers *Abby Adams* • Elisabeth Risdon *Malvina Adams* • Joseph Buloff *Joe Bellah* • Joyce Compton *Betty* • Bennie Bartlett *Tommy* • Louis Jean Heydt *Mr Stevens* ■ *Dir* Leslie Goodwins • *Scr* Nathanael West

Let's Scare Jessica to Death ★★★★

Horror 1971 · US · Colour · 88mins

In this nail-biting must-see, director John Hancock cranks up the tension with a series of terrifying sequences and elicits an utterly convincing leading performance from Zohra Lampert. Lampert is recovering from mental illness and hopes to start over again with her husband in a seemingly quiet rural community. Alas, it isn't long before her neighbours begin to look like extras from a corny Hammer horror movie, and she discovers that a young squatter who is staying with her resembles a Victorian girl who drowned in a nearby lake. RS

Zohra Lampert *Jessica* • Barton Heyman *Duncan* • Kevin O'Connor *Woody* • Gretchen Corbett *Girl* • Alan Manson *Dorker* • Mariclare Costello *Emily* ■ *Dir* John Hancock • *Scr* Norman Jonas, Ralph Rose

Let's Spend the Night Together ★★ 15

Music documentary
1982 · US · Colour · 86mins

You would not have expected Hal Ashby, the director responsible for the rich eccentricity of *Harold and Maude* and the poignancy of *Coming Home*, to have steered his career towards blandness, especially with a film about the Rolling Stones. How could he have resisted making witty or punchy comments on the five highly distinctive band members? Instead, he settles for the mundane, filming the Stones playing their hits in American arenas so vast that the energy is sapped by the size. Only *Honky Tonk Woman* and a handful of helicopter shots reach across the divide. JM [video]

Dir Hal Ashby

Let's Talk about Sex ★

Comedy drama 1998 · US · Colour · 82mins

A lamentable attempt at a semi-erotic "women's film" written by, directed and starring the not-so-talented Troy Beyer. Beyer, a journalist, attempts to make it into television by cutting a video in which her friends and various outspoken women discuss their sex lives and fantasies. Somehow she manages to lose all her footage and stomps around cleaning her flat and crying. Combine the documentary-style "confessions" with a dreadful subplot about Beyer's own sex life, and you have a film for the shredder. Dire. LH

Troy Beyer *Jazz* • Randi Ingerman *Lena* • Paget Brewster *Michelle* • Joseph C Phillips *Michael* • Michaline Babich *Morgan* • Tina Nguyen *Drew* ■ *Dir/Scr* Troy Beyer

Let's Talk About Women ★★

Portmanteau comedy
1964 · Fr/It · BW · 110mins

Having already forged his reputation as a screenwriter, Ettore Scola made his directorial debut with this episodic comedy, which showcased the versatility of Vittorio Gassman. He takes a different role in each of the eight vignettes, which were intended to explore the many facets of womankind. But such is his dominance of the proceedings that there's little room for co-stars of the calibre of Sylva Koscina and Antonella Lualdi to make much of an impact. Patchy and dated. DP. An Italian language film.

Vittorio Gassman *Stranger/Practical joker/Client/Lover/Impatient lover/Waiter/Timid brother/Ragman/Prisoner* • Sylva Koscina *Reluctant girl* • Antonella Lualdi *Fiancée* • Walter Chiari *Philanderer* • Eleonora Rossi-Drago *Indolent lady* ■ *Dir* Ettore Scola • *Scr* Ettore Scola, Ruggero Maccari

The Letter ★★★

Drama 1929 · US · BW · 62mins

The legendary Broadway star who died of a drug overdose in 1929, Jeanne Eagels – the subject of the 1957 biopic with Kim Novak – plays a murderous middle-class wife in Malaya, who pleads self-defence to cover up her killing of a would-be lover, in the first of several adaptations of W Somerset Maugham's play. The later film starring Bette Davis may be better, but it's worth seeing this version because of the curiosity value. TH

Jeanne Eagels *Leslie Crosbie* • OP Heggie *Joyce* • Reginald Owen *Robert Crosbie* • Herbert Marshall *Geoffry Hammond* • Irene Browne *Mrs Joyce* ■ *Dir* Jean de Limur • *Scr* Garrett Fort, Monta Bell, Jean de Limur, from the play by W Somerset Maugham

The Letter ★★★★ PG

Drama 1940 · US · BW · 91mins

As well as its startling opening sequence, this vehicle for Bette Davis also contains one of her best performances. The film is superbly controlled by director William Wyler, who also guided Davis to her *Jezebel* Oscar, not to mention having an ongoing relationship with the star. The original W Somerset Maugham tale of repressed passions in Malaya is melodrama, pure and simple, but Davis uses her talent for turning tosh into art magnificently, and persuades us that this is a tragedy of untold dimensions rather than a formula product of the studio system. She is aided by atmospheric photography, an evocative and cleverly melodic score and excellent support from a sinister Gale Sondergaard. TS

Bette Davis *Leslie Crosbie* • Herbert Marshall *Robert Crosbie* • James Stephenson *Howard Joyce* • Gale Sondergaard *Mrs Hammond* • Bruce Lester *John Withers* • Elizabeth Earl (1) *Adele Ainsworth* • Victor Sen Yung *Ong Chi Seng* • Doris Lloyd *Mrs Cooper* ■ *Dir* William Wyler • *Scr* Howard Koch, from the play by W Somerset Maugham • *Cinematographer* Tony Gaudio • *Music* Max Steiner

Letter from an Unknown Woman ★★★★ U

Romantic melodrama
1948 · US · BW · 83mins

After one of the most tragic romantic openings in all movie history ("By the time you finish reading this letter I'll be dead"), this develops into a marvellously bittersweet tale. It's hauntingly played by Joan Fontaine and Louis Jourdan, and brilliantly and economically dramatised from Stefan Zweig's novel by émigré director Max Ophüls, who delivers that rare beast, a Hollywood art movie. For Ophüls, style was everything, but here the Zweig story harnesses his Viennese sensibility to a very real tale of an unrequited love so painful it tears at your heartstrings. It's very Viennese and very wonderful. TS

Joan Fontaine *Lisa Berndle* • Louis Jourdan *Stefan Brand* • Mady Christians *Frau Berndle* • Marcel Journet *Johann Stauffer* • Art Smith *John* • Howard Freeman *Herr Kastner* • John Good *Lt Leopold von Kaltnegger* ■ *Dir* Max Ophüls • *Scr* Howard Koch, from the novel *Brief Einer Unbekannten* by Stefan Zweig

Letter of Introduction ★★★

Comedy drama 1938 · US · BW · 100mins

John M Stahl produces and directs this enjoyable but slight comedy drama set in the world of theatre. It stars Adolphe Menjou as an ageing matinée idol who won't admit that aspiring young actress Andrea Leeds is actually his daughter. Adding to the pleasure are Ann Sheridan, wise-cracking Eve Arden, and ventriloquist Edgar Bergen (Candice's father) and his celebrated dummy Charlie McCarthy. RB

Adolphe Menjou *John Mannering* • Andrea Leeds *Kay Martin* • George Murphy *Barry Paige* • Rita Johnson *Honey* • Ann Sheridan *Lydia Hoyt* • Eve Arden *Cora* ■ *Dir* John M Stahl • *Scr* Sheridan Gibney, Leonard Spigelgass, from a story by Bernice Boone

Letter to Brezhnev ★★★★ 15

Comedy 1985 · UK · Colour · 91mins

An endearingly wayward comedy, a sort of *On the Town* reworked for Liverpool, with the Beatles replacing Leonard Bernstein and Leonid Brezhnev replacing Miss Turnstiles. Frank Clarke's ingenious and surely ad-libbed script starts when a Soviet ship docks in Liverpool and decants two sailors (Alfred Molina and Peter Firth) for shore leave. Two scouse girls (Margi Clarke and Alexandra Pigg) pick them up, have a good time and one of them falls in love, prompting the letter to the Kremlin. It's clever, vibrant, sexy and energetically performed. AT. Contains swearing and nudity. DVD

Alfred Molina *Sergei* • Peter Firth *Peter* • Margi Clarke *Teresa King* • Alexandra Pigg *Elaine Spencer* • Susan Dempsey *Girl In Yellow Pedal Pushers* • Ted Wood *Mick* • Ken Campbell *Reporter* ■ *Dir* Chris Bernard • *Scr* Frank Clarke

A Letter to Three Wives ★★★★ U

Drama 1949 · US · BW · 98mins

This is a witty and sophisticated, though perhaps a shade too literary, slice of entertainment from writer/director Joseph L Mankiewicz, double Oscar winner (best director, best screenplay) for this movie. Today, the clever framing device may seem a little arch, but there's no denying the strength of the central idea of three women receiving a letter from the town floosie, who claims to have absconded with one of their husbands. You never see her, but her beautifully undulating voice is that of Celeste Holm. The plot carries you along in this intelligent, almost anti-Hollywood movie. Paul Douglas makes a fine film debut, and the other Douglas, Kirk, demonstrates his star potential, but the movie is stolen by clever Thelma Ritter. There was an unnecessary TV remake in 1985. TS DVD

Jeanne Crain *Deborah Bishop* • Linda Darnell *Lora May Hollingsway* • Ann Sothern *Rita Phipps* • Kirk Douglas *George Phipps* • Paul Douglas *Porter Hollingsway* • Barbara Lawrence *Babe* • Jeffrey Lynn *Brad Bishop* • Connie Gilchrist *Mrs Finney* • Florence Bates *Mrs Manleigh* • Hobart Cavanaugh *Mr Manleigh* • Celeste Holm *Addie Ross* ■ *Dir* Joseph L Mankiewicz • *Scr* Joseph L Mankiewicz, from the adaptation by Vera Caspary of the novel by John Klempner

Letters from the East ★★

Political drama
1995 · UK/Ger/Swe/Fin · Colour · 105mins

Uncertain handling undermines intriguing material in this rare cinematic sortie into the Baltic republic of Estonia. Writer/director Andrew Grieve seeks to draw comparisons between the final days of the Nazi Occupation and the rising tide of nationalism that prompted the collapse of Communism. But, while powerful, the flashbacks to the terror that presaged the Red Army "liberation" slot uncomfortably into his tale of the British-raised woman who discovers that the mother she thought dead may have survived the war after all. DP

Ewa Fröling *Anna* • Mark Womack *Rein* • Ingeborga Dapkunaite *Marie, mother 1944* • Nicholas Le Prevost *Alan* • Rein Oja *Hans, father 1944* ■ *Dir/Scr* Andrew Grieve

Letters to an Unknown Lover ★★

Crime drama 1985 · UK/Fr · Colour · 101mins

This slow-burning wartime thriller was adapted from a novel by Pierre Boileau and Thomas Narcejac, the duo responsible for *Vertigo*. Director Peter Duffell struggles to capture the brooding sense of menace that envelopes fleeing PoWs Yves Beneyton and Ralph Bates when they are ensared by scheming sisters Cherie Lunghi and Mathilda May. DP

Cherie Lunghi *Helene* • Mathilda May *Agnes* • Yves Beneyton *Gervais* • Ralph Bates *Bernard* • Andréa Ferréol *Julia* ■ *Dir* Peter Duffell • *Scr* Pierre Boileau, Thomas Narcejac, from their novel *Les Louves*

Leviathan ★★★ 18

Science fiction 1989 · US/It · Colour · 93mins

As trashy and outstandingly stupid as this underwater *Alien* is, director George Pan Cosmatos does a great job of disguising its huge credibility gaps with a diverting fast pace and superior production design. A team of deep-sea miners discover a Russian shipwreck containing a stash of vodka laced with a genetically-mutated virus which progressively turns them into tentacled half-man, half-fish aqua-Draculas. An enjoyable monster scare. AJ

Peter Weller *Beck* • Richard Crenna *Doc* • Amanda Pays *Willie* • Daniel Stern *Sixpack* • Ernie Hudson *Jones* • Michael Carmine *DeJesus* • Lisa Eilbacher *Bowman* • Hector Elizondo *Cobb* • Meg Foster *Martin* ■ *Dir* George Pan Cosmatos • *Scr* David Webb Peoples, Jeb Stuart, from a story by David Webb Peoples

Levity ★★★ 15

Drama 2002 · US/Fr · Colour · 96mins

This sombre, low-key drama is a reflective film that treats its themes of redemption and forgiveness with almost pompous respect. In a performance as slow and plodding as the tale itself, Billy Bob Thornton plays a convicted killer who's released from prison after 22 years inside. Haunted by his crime, he tries to make amends by befriending his victim's sister (Holly Hunter). With its gentle stillness and muted visuals, the story skilfully conveys the quiet emotion at the heart of Thornton's spiritual quest. Although events occasionally feel contrived, the largely understated acting is appealing, and there's some surprisingly wry dialogue. SF. Contains swearing and sex scenes. DVD

Billy Bob Thornton *Manual Jordan* • Morgan Freeman *Miles Evans* • Holly Hunter *Adele Easley* • Kirsten Dunst *Sofia Mellinger* • Dorian Harewood *Mackie Whittaker* • Geoffrey Wigdor *Abner Easley* • Luke Robertson *Young Abner Easley* • Billoah Greene *Don* ■ *Dir/Scr* Ed Solomon

Lewis & Clark & George ★★ 18

Road movie 1996 · US · Colour · 82mins

Two convicts go on the run and head for the Mexican border in search of the map to a gold mine. When one of them hooks up with Rose McGowan, who's travelling in a stolen car with a snake for company, their plans start to unravel. A low-wattage mixture of neo-Sergio Leone western, road movie and *The Treasure of the Sierra Madre*, this is visually impressive, with energetic performances from the three leads, but it tries too hard to be hip and cool and fails. AJ. Contains swearing, sex scenes and violence.

Salvator Xuereb *Lewis* • Dan Gunther *Clark* • Rose McGowan *George* ■ *Dir/Scr* Rod McCall

Une Liaison Pornographique ★★★★ 15

Romantic drama
1999 · Fr/Bel/Swi · Colour · 77mins

Nathalie Baye won the best actress prize at Venice for her work in this intriguing, intelligent study of modern sexual manners. Director Frédéric Fonteyne contrives to lock us out of the hotel room as Baye and Sergi Lopez engage in the fantasy she outlined in a lonely hearts ad. However, as feelings begin to creep into their coupling, we are permitted to become emotional voyeurs. The linking interview sequences are a touch intrusive, but the veracity of the performances makes the characters' parting a source of genuine regret. DP. In French with English subtitles.

Nathalie Baye *Her* • Sergi Lopez *Him* ■ *Dir* Frédéric Fonteyne • *Scr* Philippe Blasband

Les Liaisons Dangereuses ★★★ 15

Drama 1959 · Fr · BW · 104mins

Roger Vadim directed (and co-wrote) this updated adaptation of Choderlos de Laclos's 18th-century epistolary novel. It coolly and poisonously exposes a very particular level of upper-class degeneracy in the sexual behaviour of Valmont and – in this version – his wife. Gérard Philipe (sadly nearing his premature death) and Jeanne Moreau co-star as the couple colluding in dangerous sexual adventures. Made with a measure of restraint and a nice feeling of irony by the generally showy Vadim. RK. In French with English subtitles.

Gérard Philipe *Valmont de Merteuil* • Jeanne Moreau *Juliette de Merteuil* • Jeanne Valerie *Cecile Volanges* • Annette Vadim *Marianne Tourvel* • Simone Renant *Madame Volanges* • Jean-Louis Trintignant *Danceny* ■ *Dir* Roger Vadim • *Scr* Roger Vadim, Roger Vailland, Claude Brule, from the novel by Choderlos De Laclos

Liam ★★ 15

Period drama
2000 · UK/Ger/It · Colour · 81mins

Directed by Stephen Frears, this is a familiar story of growing up poor and Catholic in the 1930s, as seen through the eyes of stuttering seven-year-old Liam (cheeky-faced newcomer Anthony Borrows). At times this seems like a compendium of scenes familiar from every other period film about working-class childhood. Similarly, the boy's world seems to be populated by stereotypes, such as his strident mum, the martinet schoolmarm and the over-zealous priest. Director Frears and the actors are simply ploughing a familiar furrow. DA DVD

Ian Hart *Dad Tom Sullivan* • Claire Hackett *Mam Sullivan* • Anne Reid *Mrs Abernathy* • Anthony Borrows *Liam Sullivan* • Megan Burns *Teresa Sullivan* • David Hart *Con Sullivan* ■ *Dir* Stephen Frears • *Scr* Jimmy McGovern, from the novel *The Back Crack Boy* by Joseph McKeown • *Cinematographer* Andrew Dunn

Lianna ★★ 18

Drama 1983 · US · Colour · 112mins

This is a low-key drama about the wife of a philandering university professor who returns to college to regain some confidence, and finds herself drifting into a lesbian affair with a teacher. Ignored by her husband and generally messed about by her lover, Linda Griffiths is overloaded with hang-ups. It's all a mite pat, with the script a bit of a shopping list of socio-sexual problems. AT

Linda Griffiths *Lianna* • Jane Hallaren *Ruth* • Jon DeVries *Dick* • Jo Henderson *Sandy* • Jessica Wight MacDonald *Theda* • Jesse Solomon *Spencer* • John Sayles *Jerry* • Stephen Mendillo *Bob* ■ *Dir/Scr* John Sayles

Liar ★★ 18

Thriller 1997 · US · Colour · 97mins

This game of psychological warfare isn't half as smart as it thinks it is. Tim Roth heads a fairly strong cast in a narratively fractured tale of two cops (Chris Penn and Michael Rooker) who are trying to pin a murder on their sole suspect. The film is intense and sharply directed by the Pate brothers, but Roth isn't credible as the playboy who may be a killer, and the flurry of contrivances that cast suspicion on everyone are equally difficult to swallow. JC. Contains violence and swearing DVD

Tim Roth *Wayland* • Chris Penn *Braxton* • Michael Rooker *Kennesaw* • Renee Zellweger *Elizabeth* • Ellen Burstyn *Mook* • Rosanna Arquette *Mrs Kennesaw* • Michael Parks *Doctor Banyard* ■ *Dir* Josh Pate, Jonas Pate • *Scr* Jonas Pate, Josh Pate

Liar Liar ★★★★ 12

Comedy 1997 · US · Colour · 82mins

Jim Carrey stars as a ruthless lawyer and compulsive liar, who misses his son's birthday party and is "cursed" to tell the truth for 24 hours. Carrey's frenzied physical and vocal contortions provide lots of amusing comic moments, as well as a few riotous ones, in a role that's not only tailor-made for his rubber-faced antics but also gives him an opportunity to show a more human side. His bravura performance is one of his funniest to date. JC. Contains some violence and swearing. [VIDEO] DVD

Jim Carrey *Fletcher Reede* • Maura Tierney *Audrey Reede* • Justin Cooper *Max Reede* • Cary Elwes *Jerry* • Anne Haney *Greta* • Jennifer Tilly *Samantha Cole* • Amanda Donohoe *Miranda* • Jason Bernard *Judge Marshall Stevens* • Swoosie Kurtz *Dana Appleton* • Mitchell Ryan *Mr Allan* ■ *Dir* Tom Shadyac • *Scr* Paul Guay, Stephen Mazur

Liar's Moon ★★ 15

Romantic drama
1982 · US · Colour · 100mins

A young Matt Dillon stars in this endearingly dumb romantic drama – crammed with clichés, woodenly acted, and generally cornier than Kansas in August, September *and* October. Dillon and Cindy Fisher play eloped newlyweds, who find their relationship haunted by a family secret from the past. As a gimmick, the film was originally released with alternative endings – one happy, one sad. Nowadays, it's usually seen with just the happy one. Soapy tosh. DA [VIDEO]

Matt Dillon *Jack Duncan* • Cindy Fisher *Ginny Peterson* • Christopher Connelly *Alex Peterson* • Yvonne De Carlo *Jeanene Dubois* • Hoyt Axton *Cecil Duncan* • Maggie Blye *Ellen "Babs" Duncan* • Broderick Crawford *Colonel Tubman* • Susan Tyrrell *Lora Mae Bouvier* ■ *Dir* David Fisher • *Scr* David Fisher, from the story by Janice Thompson, Billy Hanna

Libel ★★★

Drama 1959 · UK · BW · 98mins

This is one of Dirk Bogarde's better movies from the 1950s, when critics of the time were hoisting him into the Alec Guinness class. Bringing a libel action to clear his name against the man who doubts if he really was the prisoner of war he claims to have been, Bogarde's role is the teasing centre of a clever narrative. The context is artificial, but it's Bogarde you'll be watching, not those on the sidelines. Compelling, if stagey. TH

Dirk Bogarde *Sir Mark Loddon/Frank Welney/ Number Fifteen* • Olivia de Havilland *Lady Maggie Loddon* • Paul Massie *Jeffrey Buckenham* • Robert Morley *Sir Wilfred* • Wilfrid Hyde White *Hubert Foxley* • Anthony Dawson *Gerald Loddon* • Richard Wattis *Judge* • Richard Dimbleby • Martin Miller *Dr Schrott* • Millicent Martin *Maisie* ■ *Dir* Anthony Asquith • *Scr* Anatole de Grunwald, Karl Tunberg, from the play by Edward Wooll

Libeled Lady ★★★★

Screwball comedy 1936 · US · BW · 98mins

This marvellous comedy employs four great stars who play together with ease and show consummate professionalism in a wonderfully contrived farce. Spencer Tracy is the newspaper editor who can't concentrate on fiancée Jean Harlow while heiress Myrna Loy holds a libel action over him, so he uses smoothie William Powell in a counterplot. This is witty, sophisticated stuff, with the stars at their peaks. In real life, Harlow and Powell were an item, and their playing together is a joy to watch, while director Jack Conway maintains a terrific pace and the MGM gloss adds a quality finish. Remade in 1946 as *Easy to Wed*. TS

William Powell *Bill Chandler* • Myrna Loy *Connie Allenbury* • Jean Harlow *Gladys Benton* • Spencer Tracy *Warren Haggerty* • Walter Connolly *James B Allenbury* • Charley Grapewin *Hollis Bane* • Cora Witherspoon *Mrs Burns-Norvell* • EE Clive *Evans* ■ *Dir* Jack Conway • *Scr* Maurine Watkins, Howard Emmett Rogers, George Oppenheimer, from a story by Wallace Sullivan

The Liberation of LB Jones ★★★★

Drama 1970 · US · Colour · 102mins

Directed by William Wyler, this story of racism in the American South tells of a black undertaker whose wife is sleeping with one of the town's racist cops. Divorce proceedings backfire, and the story ends in chilling violence and little glimmer of hope. It's far more radical and disturbing than *In The Heat of the Night* – Stirling Silliphant wrote both – but lacks the showy drama that turned *Heat* into an Oscar-winner. Despite its intensity, this flopped and Wyler never made another film. AT

Lee J Cobb *Oman Hedgepath* • Anthony Zerbe *Willie Joe Worth* • Roscoe Lee Browne *Lord Byron Jones* • Lola Falana *Emma Jones* • Lee Majors *Steve Mundine* • Barbara Hershey *Nella Mundine* • Yaphet Kotto *Sonny Boy Mosby* • Chill Wills *Mr Ike* ■ *Dir* William Wyler • *Scr* Stirling Silliphant, Jesse Hill Ford, from the novel *The Liberation of Lord Byron Jones* by Jesse Hill Ford

Le Libertin ★★★ 15

Period comedy 2000 · Fr · Colour · 102mins

Adapted with delicious romp and circumstance, this fragment from the life of 18th-century encyclopaedist Denis Diderot is both a classic French farce and a biting snipe at the hypocrisy of the Establishment. Director Gabriel Aghion's eye for a bawdy set piece ensures the encounter between the decadent Diderot (Vincent Perez), an ultra-conservative cardinal (Michel Serrault) and a sultry artist (Fanny Ardant) has its fair share of knockabout antics. However, the screenplay's epigrammatic quality is disappointing. DP. In French with English subtitles.

Vincent Perez *Denis Diderot* • Fanny Ardant *Madame Therbouche* • Josiane Balasko *Baroness d'Holbach* • Michel Serrault *Cardinal* • Arielle Dombasle *Marquise de Jerfeuil* • Christian Charmetant *Marquis de Jerfeuil* • Françoise Lépine *Antoinette Diderot* ■ *Dir* Gabriel Aghion • *Scr* Gabriel Aghion, Eric-Emmanuel Schmitt, from a play by Eric-Emmanuel Schmitt

The Libertine ★★★★

Period biographical drama
2004 · UK/US · Colour · 130mins

Johnny Depp gives another remarkable performances as John Wilmot, second Earl of Rochester, the 17th-century poet who drank and debauched his way to an early grave only to earn posthumous critical acclaim for his life's work. Samantha Morton is marvellous as the girl embroiled in the Earl's life, while John Malkovich is an ambiguous King Charles II. Debuting director Laurence Dunmore gives the whole a simplicity of mood, enhanced by the music of Michael Nyman. But this is Johnny Depp's movie in that he eloquently and emotionally portrays the man who died at the age of 33, having exhausted what there was of his life. TH. Contains swearing, nudity and sex scenes.

Johnny Depp *John Wilmot, Second Earl of Rochester* • Samantha Morton *Elizabeth Barry* • John Malkovich *King Charles II* • Rupert Friend *Billy Downs* • Tom Hollander *George Etherege* • Shane MacGowan *17th-century bard* • Rosamund Pike *Elizabeth Malet* ■ *Dir* Laurence Dunmore • *Scr* Stephen Jeffreys, from his play

Liberty Heights ★★★★ 15

Period drama 1999 · US · Colour · 122mins

Barry Levinson has directed his share of large-scale productions, but he has always seemed happiest handling smaller, more personal films such as *Avalon* and this. The setting is Levinson's home town of Baltimore in the mid-1950s, when blacks, Jews and Gentiles led separate lives of mutual intolerance. The plot traces the family conflict caused when one of two Jewish brothers falls for a wealthy Protestant girl, while the other tentatively courts an African-American. Beautifully acted and crafted with a terrific eye for period detail, this is warm and uplifting. DA [VIDEO] DVD

Adrien Brody *Van Kurtzman* • Ben Foster *Ben Kurtzman* • Orlando Jones *Little Melvin* • Bebe Neuwirth *Ada Kurtzman* • Joe Mantegna *Nate Kurtzman* ■ *Dir/Scr* Barry Levinson

Liberty Stands Still ★★ 15

Thriller 2002 · Can/Ger · Colour · 92mins

Anyone who has seen the superior *Phone Booth* will be more than familiar with the execution and storyline of this tedious thriller. Centred around a single mobile phone call, it's another sniper revenge picture, only here it's bereaved father Wesley Snipes who's getting even for his daughter's fatal shooting. Snipes delivers a credible enough performance, but Linda Fiorentino is as ineffectual as the trapped character. For a race-against-time tale, the feature plods. SF. Revenge thriller starring Wesley Snipes. [VIDEO] DVD

Linda Fiorentino *Liberty Wallace* • Wesley Snipes *Joe* • Oliver Platt *Victor Wallace* • Martin Cummins *Russell Williams* • Jonathan Scarfe *Bill Tollman* • Hart Bochner *Hank Wilford* ■ *Dir/Scr* Kari Skogland

Licence to Kill ★★ 15

Spy adventure 1989 · US · Colour · 126mins

As hero James Bond turns his attentions to big-time drug barons, Timothy Dalton phones in his performance and there's a spectacular chase with an oil tanker. The title was to have been *Licence Revoked* until market research implied that Americans didn't know what "revoked" meant. Anyway, when 007 does get his licence revoked, he's asked to hand over his gun. "Then it's a farewell to arms," he says to "M" in the garden of Hemingway's home in Key West. It's a rare moment of style in a jaded effort. AT. Contains violence and swearing. [VIDEO] DVD

Timothy Dalton *James Bond* • Carey Lowell *Pam Bouvier* • Robert Davi *Franz Sanchez* • Talisa Soto *Lupe Lamora* • Anthony Zerbe *Milton Krest* • Frank McRae *Sharkey* • Everett McGill *Killifer* • Wayne Newton *Professor Joe Butcher* • Benicio Del Toro *Dario* • Desmond Llewelyn *"Q"* • Robert Brown *"M"* • Caroline Bliss *Miss Moneypenny* ■ *Dir* John Glen • *Scr* Michael G Wilson, Richard Maibaum, from characters created by Ian Fleming

License to Drive ★★ PG

Comedy 1988 · US · Colour · 86mins

Corey Haim and Corey Feldman team up to make this dippy comedy about a teenager (Haim) who fails his driving test but continues cruising, and has no end of mishaps. There are some laughs to be had and the Coreys are fine, although it's clear that they were relying here more on their looks than their talent. JB. Contains swearing. [VIDEO]

Corey Haim *Les* • Corey Feldman *Dean* • Carol Kane *Les's mother* • Richard Masur *Les's father* • Heather Graham *Mercedes* • Helen Hanft *Miss Heilberg* ■ *Dir* Greg Beeman • *Scr* Neil Tolkin

License to Live ★★★

Comedy drama 1999 · Jpn · Colour · 107mins

This was something of a departure for Japanese director Kiyoshi Kurosawa, better known for his cult horror flicks. Yet there's a darkly comic undercurrent running through this wryly observed family drama, in which Hidetoshi Nishijima awakes from a decade-long coma to learn from gruff fish farmer Koji Yakusho that his idyllic childhood has been overtaken by dysfunction and decay. Eschewing easy gags and paying oblique homage to Yasujiro Ozu with his restraint, Kurosawa explores such intriging themes as identity, loyalty and mortality without ever taking himself too seriously. DP. In Japanese with English subtitles.

Hidetoshi Nishijima *Yutaka* • Koji Yakusho *Fujimori* • Shun Sugata *Shinichiro* ■ *Dir/Scr* Kiyoshi Kurosawa

Licensed to Kill ★★

Spy spoof 1965 · UK · Colour · 96mins

Tom Adams is Charles Vine, the "Second Best Secret Agent in the Whole Wide World". Part send-up of the Bond ethos and part B-thriller, it's about a plot to assassinate some Euro-boffin who has invented an anti-gravity machine to which the British government wants exclusive rights. While Vine isn't in Bond's league as a Romeo, he's quite convincing in the guns and fists department. Adams reprised the role in 1966's *Where Bullets Fly* and in 1967's *Somebody's Stolen Our Russian Spy*. AT

Tom Adams *Charles Vine* • Karel Stepanek *Henrik Jacobsen* • Veronica Hurst *Julia Lindberg* • Peter Bull *Masterman* • John Arnatt *Rockwell* • Francis De Wolff *Walter Pickering* ■ *Dir* Lindsay Shonteff • *Scr* Lindsay Shonteff, Howard Griffiths

The Lie ★★★★ 18

Drama 1992 · Fr · Colour · 92mins

Following in the footsteps of many a key figure in French film history, François Margolin worked as a critic before taking his place behind the camera. In this, his debut feature, he explores the heartbreaking plight of innocents who become infected with the HIV virus through the irresponsibility of others. It's a subject that forces the viewer into taking sides, but Margolin might have allowed a few grey areas in the interests of both drama and truth. As the victim, Nathalie Baye gives a powerful performance. DP. A French film with English subtitles. [VIDEO]

Nathalie Baye *Emma* • Didier Sandre *Charles* • Hélène Lapiower *Louise* • Marc Citti *Louis* • Dominique Besnéhard *Rozenberg* ■ *Dir* François Margolin • *Scr* Denis Saada, François Margolin, from an idea by Denis Saada

Liebelei ★★★ U

Romantic drama 1932 · Ger · BW · 82mins

Max Ophüls bade farewell to his native Germany with this bittersweet confection. Clearly still delighting in the novelty of sound and the gliding mobility of Franz Planer's camera, he settles for froth rather than dwelling on the text's ironic observations on the impermanence of love and the unendurable scars it leaves. Thus, the giddy whirl of imperial Viennese society is captured with subtle effervescence, as Magda Schneider falls for dashing lieutenant Wolfgang Liebeneiner. But it's not all romantic sleigh rides, as cuckolded baron Gustaf Gründgens comes seeking revenge. DP. A German language film. [VIDEO]

Magda Schneider *Christine* • Wolfgang Liebeneiner *Fritz* • Luise Ullrich *Mitzi* • Olga Tschechowa *Baroness* • Gustaf Gründgens *Baron Eggerdorff* ■ *Dir* Max Ophüls • *Scr* Kurt Alexander, Hans Wilhelm, from the play by Arthur Schnitzler, adapted by Felix Salten

Liebestraum ★★★ 18

Mystery drama 1991 · US · Colour · 108mins

When architectural journalist Kevin Anderson is called to the deathbed of the mother he never knew (Kim Novak), a chance encounter with an old college friend (Bill Pullman) provides an opportunity to study the site of a unique, soon-to-be-demolished department store. As passion flares between Anderson and Pullman's wife (Pamela Gidley), Novak's increasingly feverish reminiscences point to a dark secret contained within the condemned building's walls. The plot spirals out of sight, but still has a dizzying compulsion, and both the direction and cinematography are relentlessly atmospheric. TH. Contains swearing, sex scenes and nudity. DVD

Kevin Anderson *Nick Kaminsky* • Pamela Gidley *Jane Kessler* • Bill Pullman *Paul Kessler* • Kim Novak *Mrs Anderssen* • Graham Beckel *Sheriff Ricker* • Zach Grenier *Barnett Ralston IV* • Thomas Kopache *Dr Parker* ■ *Dir/Scr* Mike Figgis

Lies ★★ 18

Erotic drama 1999 · S Kor · Colour · 107mins

It was the political undertones that caused Jang Jung Il's novel, *Tell Me a Lie*, to be banned in South Korea, but it's the scenes of sado-masochism and coprophilia that have earned this stark study of obsession its notoriety. The film opens with non-professionals Lee Sang Hyun and Kim Tae Yeon discussing the problems of playing their roles, and director Jang Sun Woo might have more profitably pursued this line of inquiry instead of graphically depicting the beatings given to a 30-something sculptor by his once-innocent teenage lover. This may be a provocative picture, but its content obscures its purpose. DP. In Korean with English subtitles.

Lee Sang Hyun *J* • Kim Tae Yeon *Y* • Jeon Hye Jin *Woori* ■ *Dir* Jang Sun Woo • *Scr* Sun Woo Jang, from the novel *Tell Me a Lie* by Jang Jung Il

L

The Lies Boys Tell ★★★ PG

Drama 1994 · US · Colour · 87mins

Writer Ernest Thompson won an Oscar for *On Golden Pond* and he transfers its theme of child-parent reconciliation to the open road in this entertaining TV movie. Kirk Douglas revels in the role of the retired travelling salesman who decides to embark on one last adventure before he dies. Craig T Nelson, who digs deep to convince as the wayward son who goes along for the ride, prevents Douglas from dominating the film. Funny, provocative and touching. DP DVD

Kirk Douglas *Ed Reece* • Craig T Nelson *Larry Reece* • Eileen Brennan *Sada* • Bess Armstrong *Connie* • Bonnie Bartlett *Sylvia Reece* • Richard Gilliland *Russ Reece* • Ernest Thompson *Cal* ■ *Dir* Tom McLoughlin • *Scr* Ernest Thompson, from the novel by Lamar Herrin

Lies My Father Told Me ★★★

Period drama 1975 · Can · Colour · 102mins

This screen version of writer Ted Allan's autobiographical opus about his early childhood is sympathetically directed by Czech émigré Jan Kadar. Benefitting hugely from a wonderfully warm performance from Yiddish actor Yossi Yadin as the young hero's grandfather, this Canadian film also features Allan himself (who wrote the script) playing old Mr Baumgarten. TS

Yossi Yadin *Zaida* • Len Birman *Harry Herman* • Marilyn Lightstone *Annie Herman* • Jeffrey Lynas *David Herman* • Ted Allan *Mr Baumgarten* • Barbara Chilcott *Mrs Tannenbaum* ■ *Dir* Jan Kadar • *Scr* Ted Allan, from his autobiography

Lt Robin Crusoe, USN ★★ U

Comedy adventure
1966 · US · Colour · 108mins

This pretty feeble Dick Van Dyke vehicle for Disney, ostensibly a comic update of the Robinson Crusoe story, was made when the studio had seemingly lost touch with contemporary audiences. Fortunately, Disney bounced back, but movies such as this one, featuring a chimp from outer space, didn't help. TS

Dick Van Dyke *Lieutenant Robin Crusoe* • Nancy Kwan *Wednesday* • Akim Tamiroff *Tanamashu* • Arthur Malet *Umbrella Man* • Tyler McVey *Captain* ■ *Dir* Byron Paul • *Scr* Bill Walsh, Donald DaGradi, from a story by Retlaw Yensid [Walt Disney]

The Lieutenant Wore Skirts ★★ U

Comedy 1956 · US · Colour · 98mins

Brash but lively fun, this is one of writer/director Frank Tashlin's lesser efforts. It's role-reversal time with glamorous Sheree North joining the Air Force and hubbie Tom Ewell reluctantly tagging along to carry out the household chores as the only civilian male at her base camp in Honolulu. His various schemes to have her discharged form the basis of the often tasteless humour. AE

Tom Ewell *Gregory Whitcomb* • Sheree North *Katy Whitcomb* • Rita Moreno *Sandra Gaxton* • Rick Jason *Capt Barney Sloan* • Les Tremayne *Henry Gaxton* • Alice Reinheart *Capt Briggs* • Gregory Walcott *Lt Sweeney* ■ *Dir* Frank Tashlin • *Scr* Albert Beich, Frank Tashlin, from a story by Albert Beich

Life ★★ 15

Prison comedy 1999 · US · Colour · 104mins

It's sad to see Eddie Murphy so completely unfunny in this cross between *The Shawshank Redemption* and *The Odd Couple*. Street-smart Murphy and bank clerk Martin Lawrence are framed by a Deep South sheriff for murder and sent to a Mississippi jail for life. Initially racist and brutal, the regime lightens up when warden Ned Beatty takes over and makes the pair his house-servants. The necessary chemistry between chalk-and-cheese Murphy and Lawrence is absent, so their banter is simply unpleasant. TH. Contains swearing and violence. DVD

Eddie Murphy *Rayford Gibson* • Martin Lawrence *Claude Banks* • Obba Babatundé [Obba Babatunde] *Willie Long* • Ned Beatty *Dexter Wilkins* • Bernie Mac *Jangle Leg* • Miguel A Nunez [Miguel A Nunez Jr] *Biscuit* • Clarence Williams III *Winston Hancock* • Bokeem Woodbine *Can't Get Right* ■ *Dir* Ted Demme • *Scr* Robert Ramsey, Matthew Stone

The Life and Death of Colonel Blimp ★★★★★ U

Period drama 1943 · UK · Colour · 156mins

Winston Churchill ordered this film to be banned from exportation during the Second World War in case it gave the wrong impression of the British fighting man. Based on the comic-strip character created by David Low, Michael Powell and Emeric Pressburger's film does indeed take a pop at the complacency of the top brass, yet, thanks to Roger Livesey's astonishing performance in the lead, it is also a tribute to the more laudable peculiarities of the British character – honour, loyalty and a genius for making the most of a bad lot. Anton Walbrook also excels as Livesey's Prussian nemesis who becomes a lifelong friend, while a young Deborah Kerr makes her mark playing the three women in Livesey's life. One of British cinema's masterpieces. DP DVD

Roger Livesey *Clive Candy* • Deborah Kerr *Edith Hunter/Barbara Wyn/Johnny Cannon* • Anton Walbrook *Theo Kretschmar-Schuldorff* • James McKechnie *Spud Wilson* • Neville Mapp *Stuffy Graves* • Roland Culver *Colonel Betteridge* • David Hutcheson *Hoppy* • Spencer Trevor *Period Blimp* • AE Matthews *President Of The Tribunal* ■ *Dir/Scr* Michael Powell, Emeric Pressburger

The Life and Death of Peter Sellers ★★★ 15

Biographical drama
2003 · US/UK · Colour · 121mins

The fact that this biopic about one of British cinema's most familiar figures is so engaging owes much to an Oscar-worthy performance by Geoffrey Rush, who plays Peter Sellers as a volatile and selfish man struggling for a personality beyond his comic creations. The film begins with Sellers already at the height of his radio success with The Goons and concentrates on his relationship with his put-upon first wife Anne (Emily Watson) and a stormy second marriage to Britt Ekland (Charlize Theron). BP DVD

Geoffrey Rush *Peter Sellers* • Emily Watson *Anne Sellers* • Charlize Theron *Britt Ekland* • Miriam Margolyes *Peg Sellers* • John Lithgow *Blake Edwards* • Stephen Fry *Maurice Woodruff* • Stanley Tucci *Stanley Kubrick* • Peter Vaughan *Bill Sellers* • Sonia Aquino *Sophia Loren* • Nigel Havers *David Niven* ■ *Dir* Stephen Hopkins • *Scr* Christopher Markus, Stephen McFeely, from the book by Roger Lewis

Life and Debt ★★★ PG

Documentary 2001 · US · Colour · 82mins

It's impossible to watch this documentary about the impact of globalisation on Jamaica without a rising sense of dismay. Director Stephanie Black refuses to pull her punches, and why should she, when she's got so much damning evidence at her disposal? Yet for all the eloquence of former Prime Minister Michael Manley and the local labourers betrayed by faceless multinational fat cats and the International Monetary Fund, it's the extracts from Jamaica Kincaid's book, *A Small Place*, that make the most telling impact. Angry agitprop this may be, but it's irresistibly persuasive. DP DVD

Belinda Becker *Narrator* ■ *Dir* Stephanie Black • *Scr* Jamaica Kincaid, from her book *A Small Place*

The Life and Extraordinary Adventures of Private Ivan Chonkin ★★★ 15

Drama
1994 · Cz Rep/UK/Fr/Rus · Colour · 110mins

Jirí Menzel, one of the key figures in the Czech film miracle of the 1960s, comes rather unstuck with this rough-and-ready adaptation of Russian writer Vladimir Voinovich's cult novel. A far cry from Menzel's slyly satirical masterpiece *Closely Observed Trains*, this tale set just before the Second World War is so broad in its comedy, it often borders on farce. Paying scant regard to the themes of repression and resistance and missing the opportunity for some colourful character comedy, Menzel opts for a hectic pace and vulgar caricature. It's played with great vigour and is hugely entertaining, but it's not one of the director's best. DP. In Czech with English subtitles.

Gennadiy Nazarov *Ivan Chonkin* • Zoya Buryak *Nyura* • Vladimir Ilyin *Golubev* • Valeriy Dubrovin *Kilin* • Alexei Zharkov *Gladyshev* • Yuriy Dubrovin *Volkov* ■ *Dir* Jirí Menzel • *Scr* Zdenek Sverak, Vladimir Voinovich, from the novel by Vladimir Voinovich

Life and Nothing But ★★★★ PG

Drama 1989 · Fr · Colour · 130mins

Philippe Noiret gives one of his most memorable performances as a major in charge of the identification of shell-shocked survivors of the First World War. As well as helping the bereaved, the authorities have charged him with the task of finding a suitable Unknown Soldier. Shot in muted colours by Bruno De Keyzer, the film's atmosphere of loss and despair is deeply moving. Sabine Azéma and Pascale Vignal also impress as they search for missing lovers. DP. In French with English subtitles.

Philippe Noiret *Dellaplane* • Sabine Azéma *Irène* • Pascale Vignal *Alice* • Maurice Barrier *Mercadot* • François Perrot *Perrin* ■ *Dir* Bertrand Tavernier • *Scr* Bertrand Tavernier, Jean Cosmos

The Life and Times of Grizzly Adams ★★ U

Adventure 1974 · US · Colour · 93mins

Dan Haggerty had once been an animal trainer, and it was his ease with bears that won him the role of Grizzly Adams in this wilderness adventure about a fur trapper who takes to the mountains when he is accused of a crime that he did not commit. Haggerty would later reprise the part in the popular TV series and the 1982 sequel, *The Capture of Grizzly Adams*. RT

Dan Haggerty *James "Grizzly" Adams* • Don Shanks *Indian Brave* • Lisa Jones *Young Peg* • Marjorie Harper *Adult Peg* ■ *Dir* Richard Friedenberg • *Scr* Larry Dobkin

The Life and Times of Judge Roy Bean ★★★ 15

Comedy western
1972 · US · Colour · 118mins

Although this is very much a vehicle for star Paul Newman, he nevertheless seems a little ill at ease as the titular Mr Bean. Despite help from a notable supporting cast, director John Huston's rambling, incident-packed movie is overlong and actually rather dull. However, its wry humour and surreal moments can't help but endear this to most audiences. Casting has seldom been more appropriate than Ava Gardner, in her late prime, as the embodiment of Lily Langtry, the object of the judge's affections. TS. Contains violence.

Paul Newman *Judge Roy Bean* • Jacqueline Bisset *Rose Bean* • Ava Gardner *Lily Langtry* • Tab Hunter *Sam Dodd* • John Huston *Grizzly Adams* • Stacy Keach *Bad Bob* • Roddy McDowall *Frank Gass* • Anthony Perkins *Reverend Lasalle* • Victoria Principal *Marie Elena* • Ned Beatty *Tector Crites* ■ *Dir* John Huston • *Scr* John Milius

The Life and Times of Rosie the Riveter ★★★

Second World War documentary
1980 · US · Colour and BW · 60mins

Forget the sham nostalgia of *Swing Shift*, as there was nothing romantic about working in America's munitions factories during the Second World War. Millions of women answered the call in 1941 and, for many of them, it was their first experience of full-time employment. Yet, rather than being welcomed with open arms by their male colleagues, they were patronised, marginalised and harassed. By shrewdly contrasting morale-boosting newsreel footage with whistleblowing personal testimonies, Connie Field is able to expose the conditions to which the "Rosies" were subjected without detracting from the scale of their achievement or their pride in it. DP

Dir/Scr Connie Field

The Life Aquatic with Steve Zissou ★★★ 15

Fantasy comedy drama
2004 · US · Colour · 113mins

Director Wes Anderson's odd drama is centred on famous oceanographer Steve Zissou (played by Bill Murray and obviously inspired by marine pioneer Jacques Cousteau), who embarks on a Moby Dick-style quest to hunt and kill the mysterious sea creature that ate

U = SUITABLE FOR ALL Uc = SUITABLE FOR ALL, ESPECIALLY FOR YOUNG CHILDREN (VIDEO ONLY) PG = PARENTAL GUIDANCE

his best friend. Murray is so laid-back he sometimes seems to be asleep, but there's great support from Owen Wilson as Zissou's (apparently) long-lost son and Jeff Goldblum as a richer, better-equipped rival oceanographer. For some, Anderson's world is too strange to be affecting; for others, there's an irresistible charm to his eccentric characters. AS. In English, Italian and Tagalog with subtitles. Contains swearing. DVD

Bill Murray *Steve Zissou* • Owen Wilson *Ned Plimpton* • Cate Blanchett *Jane Winslett-Richardson* • Anjelica Huston *Eleanor Zissou* • Willem Dafoe *Klaus Daimler* • Jeff Goldblum *Alistair Hennessey* • Michael Gambon *Oseary Drakoulias* • Bud Cort *Bill Ubell* • Seu Jorge *Pelé dos Santos* • Noah Taylor *Vladimir Wolodarsky* • Seymour Cassel *Esteban du Plantier* ■ *Dir* Wes Anderson • *Scr* Wes Anderson, Noah Baumbach

Life as a House ★★ 15

Drama 2001 · US/Ger · Colour · 120mins

Kevin Kline is a model-maker for an architectural firm who gets fired and informed he is dying in pretty short order. Kline then decides to spend his remaining months tearing down the shack his hated father left him, building his dream house on the same spot and patching things up with ex-wife Kristin Scott Thomas and wayward son Hayden Christensen. This clumsy drama oozes schmaltz and has as much insight in its title as in the whole of its running time. DP [video] DVD

Kevin Kline *George Monroe* • Kristin Scott Thomas *Robin Kimball* • Hayden Christensen *Sam* • Jamey Sheridan *Peter* • Sam Robards *David Dokos* • Scott Bakula *Kurt Walker* • Mary Steenburgen *Coleen Beck* ■ *Dir* Irwin Winkler • *Scr* Mark Andrus

Life at the Top ★★

Drama 1965 · UK · BW · 117mins

Having ridden roughshod over the citizens of Warnley in *Room at the Top*, Laurence Harvey leaves Yorkshire in search of the beautiful south in this hugely disappointing sequel. Mordecai Richler's adaptation and Ted Kotcheff's direction capture little of the spirit of swinging London, let alone the actions and emotions of a ruthlessly ambitious "angry young man". Harvey fails to rekindle the fire of his Oscar-nominated performance in the first film, and Jean Simmons is shamefully wasted as his put-upon wife. DP

Laurence Harvey *Joe Lampton* • Jean Simmons *Susan Lampton* • Honor Blackman *Norah Hauxley* • Michael Craig *Mark* • Donald Wolfit *Abe Brown* • Robert Morley *Tiffield* ■ *Dir* Ted Kotcheff • *Scr* Mordecai Richler, from the novel by John Braine

The Life before This ★★★ 15

Drama 1999 · Can · Colour · 87mins

A sombre meditation on fate, this Canadian drama is not without its faults, but is still well worth a look. The film opens with a shoot-out at a café in which innocent customers get caught in the crossfire. It then rewinds itself back to the beginning of the day and examines the interlinking stories of the individuals who by chance will find themselves at the coffee shop later that evening. The ensemble cast is superb, and although it is a tad too contrived for its own good, director Jerry Ciccoritti skilfully weaves together the various story strands. JF [video]

Catherine O'Hara *Sheena* • Stephen Rea *Brian* • Sarah Polley *Connie* • Joe Pantoliano *Jake Maclean* • Martha Burns *Gwen Maclean* • Emily Hampshire *Maggie* • Callum Keith Rennie *Martin Maclean* ■ *Dir* Jerry Ciccoritti • *Scr* Semi Chellas

Life Begins ★★

Drama 1932 · US · BW · 72mins

Covering the events of a night in a maternity ward, this features among other mothers-about-to-be the lovely Loretta Young, as a woman serving a life sentence for murder. However it's excellent character actress Aline MacMahon as the head nurse, both controlling and compassionate, who holds the rather fragmentary action together. Respectable, but downbeat. RK

Loretta Young *Grace Sutton* • Eric Linden *Jed Sutton* • Aline MacMahon *Miss Bowers* • Glenda Farrell *Florette* • Gilbert Roland *Tony* ■ *Dir* James Flood, Elliott Nugent • *Scr* Earl Baldwin, from the play by Mary M Axelson

Life Begins at 8.30 ★★

Comedy drama 1942 · US · BW · 84mins

Ida Lupino sacrifices herself to care for her father, alcoholic actor Monty Woolley, until dashing composer Cornel Wilde arrives on cue to nurse him through a production of *King Lear*. Everything really depends on the charisma of Woolley and his ability to be actorly, grand and tragic at the same time, a man described as "a god on stage but a rat off". Woolley acquits himself reasonably well, given an overwritten script and leaden direction from Irving Pichel. AT

Monty Woolley *Madden Thomas* • Ida Lupino *Kathi Thomas* • Cornel Wilde *Robert* • Sara Allgood *Mrs Lothian* • Melville Cooper *Barty* • J Edward Bromberg *Gordon* • William Demarest *Officer* ■ *Dir* Irving Pichel • *Scr* Nunnally Johnson, from the play *The Light Of The Heart* by Emlyn Williams

Life Begins at 40 ★★★

Comedy 1935 · US · BW · 73mins

A charmingly folksy Will Rogers vehicle in which the garrulous movie star-cum-philosopher is given acidic lines aplenty on the American way of life, though his well-practised lazy drawl seems deliberately to remove the sting in the barbs. This is one of his best pictures, with the star as a newspaper editor (Rogers contributed to a daily newspaper column and radio broadcasts in real life) bent on clearing an innocent young man's name. Director George Marshall manages to keep the sentiment at bay in this satisfying effort. ST

Will Rogers *Kenesaw H Clark* • Rochelle Hudson *Adele Anderson* • Richard Cromwell *Lee Austin* • George Barbier *Colonel Joseph Abercrombie* • Jane Darwell *Ida Harris* • Slim Summerville *T Watterson Meriwether* • Sterling Holloway *Chris* ■ *Dir* George Marshall • *Scr* Lamar Trotti, Robert Quillen, Dudley Nichols, William M Conselman, from the novel by Walter B Pitkin

Life Begins for Andy Hardy ★★★ U

Comedy drama 1941 · US · BW · 101mins

After ten episodes, MGM decided that Andy needed to grow up a bit. His country needed him but, no, he didn't go off to Guadalcanal, he has to decide between getting a job or going to college. He has a chat with dad and decides to go and "find himself" in New York, where he meets girlfriend Judy Garland. She drops into Andyworld for the third and last time, though MGM deleted her song from the final cut. Andy gets a job on a paltry salary, and Garland decides it's time to give dad a call. Working as a smart satire on big city business ethics, this is easily one of the best of the *Andy Hardy* series. AT

Mickey Rooney *Andy Hardy* • Lewis Stone *Judge James K Hardy* • Judy Garland *Betsy Booth* • Fay Holden *Mrs Emily Hardy* • Ann Rutherford *Polly Benedict* • Sara Haden *Aunt Milly* • Patricia Dane *Jennitt Hicks* • Ray McDonald *Jimmy Frobisher* ■ *Dir* George B Seitz • *Scr* Agnes Christine Johnston, from characters created by Aurania Rouverol

Life Begins in College ★★★ U

Comedy 1937 · US · BW · 93mins

Joan Davis co-stars with that blandest of crooners Tony Martin, in one of those college romps where all the students look old enough to draw pensions. The zany Ritz Brothers are along for the ride, helping the college football team. Gloria Stuart is a charming ingénue, and Nat Pendleton gets much mileage as an Indian at college, though some may find it tasteless today. Originally released in the UK as *The Joy Parade*. TS

The Ritz Brothers [Al Ritz] *Ritz Brother* • The Ritz Brothers [Jimmy Ritz] *Ritz Brother* • The Ritz Brothers [Harry Ritz] *Ritz Brother* • Joan Davis *Inez* • Tony Martin *Band Leader* • Gloria Stuart *Janet O'Hara* • Fred Stone *Coach O'Hara* • Nat Pendleton *George Black* • Dick Baldwin *Bob Hayner* ■ *Dir* William A Seiter • *Scr* Karl Tunberg, Don Ettlinger, Sidney Kuller, Ray Golden, Samuel Pokrass, from the stories by Darrell Ware

Life for Ruth ★★

Drama 1962 · UK · BW · 91mins

Following *Sapphire* (on racism) and *Victim* (on homosexuality), Basil Dearden turned his attention to religious conviction in another of the social realism pictures he made at the turn of the 1960s. The story of a father with deep-seated religious beliefs who refuses to consent to the blood transfusion that will save his daughter's life is often too contrived to make the weighty impact that Dearden intends. The nationwide scandal whipped up by doctor Patrick McGoohan spoils the intricately developed and delicately played feud between the girl's parents (Michael Craig and Janet Munro). DP

Michael Craig *John Harris* • Patrick McGoohan *Dr Jim Brown* • Janet Munro *Pat Harris* • Paul Rogers *Hart Jacobs* • Megs Jenkins *Mrs Gordon* • John Barrie *Mr Gordon* • Malcolm Keen *Mr Harris Sr* • Lynne Taylor *Ruth Harris* ■ *Dir* Basil Dearden • *Scr* Janet Green, John McCormick, from the play *Walk in the Shadow* by Janet Green

Life in Danger ★★

Thriller 1959 · UK · BW · 62mins

As Alfred Hitchcock repeatedly demonstrated in films such as *The Wrong Man*, there is nothing more terrifying for the innocent than finding the evidence in a murder case irrefutably piling up against them while all attempts at establishing an alibi founder on the most unlikely caprices of fate. This is the situation confronting Derren Nesbitt in this passable low-budget drama, which is made even more alarming by its picturesque country setting. DP

Derren Nesbitt *The Man* • Julie Hopkins *Hazel Ashley* • Howard Marion-Crawford *Major Peters* • Victor Brooks *Tom Baldwin* • Jack Allen *Jack Ashley* • Christopher Witty *Johnny Ashley* • Carmel McSharry *Mrs Ashley* • Mary Manson *Jill Shadwell* • Bruce Seton *Landlord* ■ *Dir* Terry Bishop • *Scr* Malcolm Hulke, Eric Paice

Life in Emergency Ward 10 ★ U

Drama 1959 · UK · BW · 82mins

Two years after taking the nation by storm, ITV's soap smash made it to the big screen. And what a disappointment it must have been. The characters find themselves caught up in the round of romantic entanglements and medical emergencies that were old hat at the time of MGM's *Dr Kildare* series. Michael Craig is dreadful as the Oxbridge General new boy playing fast and loose with the hearts of his patients and a colleague's neglected wife, and even the usually reliable Wilfrid Hyde White is off colour. DP [video]

Michael Craig *Dr Stephen Russell* • Wilfrid Hyde White *Professor Bourne-Evans* • Dorothy Alison *Sister Janet Fraser* • Glyn Owen *Dr Paddy O'Meara* • Rosemary Miller *Nurse Pat Roberts* • Charles Tingwell *Dr Alan Dawson* • Frederick Bartman *Dr Simon Forrester* • Joan Sims *Mrs Pryor* ■ *Dir* Robert Day • *Scr* Tessa Diamond, Hazel Adair, from the TV series

A Life in the Balance ★★★

Thriller 1955 · US · BW · 71mins

After *The Big Heat* and *The Wild One*, Lee Marvin was well established as a screen heavy when he made this thriller in Mexico City. It's a portrait of life in the slums, spiced up by the odd Buñuelian moment and the hunt for a serial killer with a religious fixation, played by Marvin. Ricardo Montalban plays the wrongly accused man, while Anne Bancroft is the love interest. AT

Ricardo Montalban *Antonio Gomez* • Anne Bancroft *Maria Ibinia* • Lee Marvin *The Murderer* • José Perez (1) *Paco Gomez* • Rodolfo Acosta *Lt Fernando* ■ *Dir* Harry Horner • *Scr* Robert Presnell Jr, Leo Townsend, from a story by Georges Simenon

Life in the Balance ★★

Thriller 2001 · US · Colour · 105mins

If you can accept the casting of Bo Derek as an alcoholic superstar lawyer, then you'll be able to swallow this far-fetched farrago. She throws herself into the case of a school textbook salesman (Bruce Boxleitner), who is on death row for murdering his wife and kids. Failing to convince with a single utterance, Derek relies heavily on forensics expert Tim Post. DP

Bo Derek *Kathryn Garr* • Stewart Bick *Jason Garr* • Bruce Boxleitner *Eric Johnson* • Jonathan Higgins *William Hockman* • Tim Post *Randall Innis* ■ *Dir* Adam Weissman • *Scr* Paul Koval

A Life in the Theater ★★★★

Drama 1993 · US · Colour · 90mins

As the veteran actor coming to the end of his career, that consummate professional Jack Lemmon savours every line of David Mamet's inspired dialogue in Gregory Mosher's version of Mamet's acclaimed play. It speaks volumes for Matthew Broderick that he stays the distance in his role as the promising newcomer who isn't simply prepared to listen and learn. The discussions on how certain scenes should be played are fascinating, but thanks to the passion of the performances they never become inaccessible. A touch highbrow, perhaps, but you don't often get to see acting of this calibre. DP

Jack Lemmon *Robert* • Matthew Broderick *John* ■ *Dir* Gregory Mosher • *Scr* David Mamet, from his play

Life Is a Bed of Roses ★★★★ PG

Fantasy 1983 · Fr · Colour · 111mins

The perfectibility of human existence is the awesome theme of director Alain Resnais's magical fable, structured in three parts. The first covers Ruggero Raimondi's pre-First World War project to create a "temple to happiness". In the second part (set in the present), a seminar examines the feasibility of creating Utopia. Finally, a medieval struggle between good and evil is played out through the imaginations of some children. Vittorio Gassman, Raimondi and Geraldine Chaplin set up the proposition with dramatic ardour, but some may find this intellectual puzzle rather heavy going. TH. In French with English subtitles.

L

Vittorio Gassman *Walter Guarini* • Ruggero Raimondi *Count Michel Forbek* • Geraldine Chaplin *Nora Winkle* • Fanny Ardant *Livia Cerasquier* • Sabine Azéma *Elisabeth Rousseau* ■ *Dir* Alain Resnais • *Scr* Jean Gruault

Life Is a Circus ★★ U

Comedy 1958 · UK · BW · 91mins

The Crazy Gang were a British institution: an informal collection of comedy acts brought together to enjoy a long career of comic surrealism. Their mix of zany slapstick, wacky doubletalk and sentimental humour may seem dated now but was massively popular in its day. This movie is a late entry in their canon, and it shows. The creaky storyline has the gang coming to the aid of an ailing circus and putting it back on its feet with some help from a magic lamp. DF

Bud Flanagan *Bud* • Teddy Knox *Sebastian* • Jimmy Nervo *Cecil* • Jimmy Gold *Goldie* • Charlie Naughton *Charlie* • Eddie Gray *Eddie* • Chesney Allen *Ches* • Michael Holliday *Carl Rickenbeck* • Lionel Jeffries *Genie* • Shirley Eaton *Shirley Winter* ■ *Dir* Val Guest • *Scr* Val Guest, John Warren, Len Heath

Life Is a Long Quiet River ★★★★ 15

Satirical comedy 1988 · Fr · Colour · 87mins

A breaker of box-office records and the winner of a clutch of Césars (the French Oscars), this offbeat and often hilarious debut feature seems a prime candidate for a Hollywood makeover. That it has been spared such a fate is primarily due to the subtleties underlying the blackly comic surface, which would confound even the most astute American director. These acerbic asides on class, education and parental expectations superbly complement the broader humour about mixed-at-birth babies. However, like the river of the title, the initial sparkle and freshness gives way to rather too much meandering. DP. In French with English subtitles.

Benoît Magimel *Momo* • Valerie Lalande *Bernadette* • Tara Romer *Million* • Jérôme Floc'h *Toc-Toc* • Sylvie Cubertafon *Ghislaine* • Emmanuel Cendrier *Pierre* ■ *Dir* Etienne Chatiliez • *Scr* Florence Quentin, Etienne Chatiliez

Life Is a Miracle ★★★ 15

Black comedy drama
2004 · Fr/Serb/Montenegro · Col · 154m

No one unearths the absurdity in political tragedy with such melancholic vigour as Emir Kusturica. This frantic take on the Bosnian civil war stars Slavko Stimac as a Serbian railway engineer whose life is disrupted when his opera-singing wife leaves him and his soccer-mad son (Vuk Kostic) is conscripted into the army. After Kostic is captured, Stimac intends to use Muslim nurse Natasa Solak as a bargaining chip for his son's return, but he falls in love with her. This is acerbic human drama, but it's almost a sideshow to the glorious set pieces. DP. In Serbian, German, Hungarian and English with subtitles. Contains swearing, nudity, drug abuse.

Slavko Stimac *Luka* • Natasa Solak *Sabaha* • Vesna Trivalic *Jadranka* • Vuk Kostic *Milos* • Aleksandar Bercek *Veljo* • Stribor Kusturica *Captain Aleksic* • Nikola Kojo *Filipovic* ■ *Dir* Emir Kusturica • *Scr* Emir Kusturica, Ranko Bozic

Life Is All You Get ★★★ 18

Drama 1998 · Ger · Colour · 115mins

This slice-of-life drama is an extended metaphor for Germany in the late Kohl era. Abandoning his blood kin, Jürgen Vogel opens his house to a disparate family of dispossessed outsiders, while enduring a romantic angst that represents the difficulty of attaining unification in the face of conflicting ideologies. Similar symbols abound – Vogel works in an abattoir, fears he may be HIV-positive, meets his girlfriend in a riot and is best mates with a Buddy Holly impersonator. But this gritty, often blackly comic picture is never as dense or affected as it sounds. DP. A German language film. Contains sex scenes.

Jürgen Vogel *Jan Nebel* • Christiane Paul *Vera* • Ricky Tomlinson *Buddy* • Armin Rohde *Harri* • Martina Gedeck *Lilo Nebel* ■ *Dir* Wolfgang Becker • *Scr* Wolfgang Becker, Tom Tykwer

Life Is Beautiful ★★★ PG

Second World War comedy drama
1997 · It · Colour · 111mins

Is this a glowing tribute to humanity *in extremis*, or an ill-judged trivialisation of pitiless barbarism? Both verdicts have been passed on Roberto Benigni's multi-award-winning film. The opening section, charting Benigni's courtship of the imperious Nicoletta Braschi, is delightful. It also serves as a poignant backdrop for the nightmare to follow, as Benigni tries to shelter his son from the bitterest of truths. The result is courageous, humanistic film-making, but only a qualified success. DP. In Italian with English subtitles. Contains violence. DVD

Roberto Benigni *Guido* • Nicoletta Braschi *Dora* • Giorgio Cantarini *Giosué* • Giustino Durano *Uncle* • Sergio Bustric *Ferruccio* • Marisa Paredes *Dora's mother* • Horst Buchholz *Dr Lessing* ■ *Dir* Roberto Benigni • *Scr* Roberto Benigni, Vincenzo Cerami, from their story • *Cinematographer* Tonino Delli Colli

Life Is Cheap... but Toilet Paper Is Expensive ★★★ 18

Comedy thriller 1990 · US · Colour · 86mins

Wayne Wang, the director of such light dramas as *Dim Sum*, *The Joy Luck Club* and *Smoke*, shows the darker side of his cinematic sensibilities in an offbeat, graphically violent Hong Kong tour of some really nasty tourist sights. Wang's world is one of on-screen defecation, severed hands and dead ducks, but the nastiness is made more palatable by some humorous touches (the film's courier hero is modelled on Clint Eastwood's "Man with No Name"). Considerably less warm than the director's American movies, this is an attention-grabbing film that deliberately sets out to shock. JC

Chan Kim Wan *Duck Killer* • Spencer Nakasako *Man With No Name* • Victor Wong (2) *Blind Man* • Cheng Kwan Min *Uncle Cheng* • Cora Miao *Money* • Chung Lam *Red Guard* • Allen Fong *Taxi Driver* ■ *Dir* Wayne Wang • *Scr* Spencer Nakasako

Life Is Sweet ★★★★★ 15

Black comedy 1990 · UK · Colour · 98mins

Writer/director Mike Leigh is on top form in this superbly observed satire on late-Thatcherite Britain. The wincingly funny and socially astute script touches on such issues as bulimia, free enterprise and social ambition without ever labouring the point. Alison Steadman and Jim Broadbent are outstanding as the thoroughly decent working-class couple, who watch their daughters develop with a mixture of pride and regret. Jane Horrocks does Essex slacker teen with great conviction, while Claire Skinner impresses as her tomboy sister, and Timothy Spall is sweatily repellent as a wannabe restaurateur. DP. Contains swearing, sex scenes and nudity. DVD

Alison Steadman *Wendy* • Jim Broadbent *Andy* • Jane Horrocks *Nicola* • Claire Skinner *Natalie* • Stephen Rea *Patsy* • Timothy Spall *Aubrey* • David Thewlis *Nicola's lover* • Moya Brady *Paula* • David Neilson *Steve* ■ *Dir/Scr* Mike Leigh

A Life Less Ordinary ★★ 15

Romantic comedy
1997 · UK/US · Colour · 99mins

Third time unlucky for the director, producer, writer and star quartet of *Shallow Grave* and *Trainspotting*. Desperate to regain his menial job in a giant American corporation, Ewan McGregor kidnaps his former boss's daughter, rich bitch Cameron Diaz. As the two go on the run, a pair of celestial cops (miscast Holly Hunter and Delroy Lindo) embark on a quest to make the unlikely duo fall in love. McGregor and Diaz are in good form, but this comes unstuck as the feel-good whimsy gets increasingly piled on. AJ DVD

Ewan McGregor *Robert* • Cameron Diaz *Celine Naville* • Holly Hunter *O'Reilly* • Delroy Lindo *Jackson* • Dan Hedaya *Gabriel* • Ian McNeice *Mayhew* • Frank Kanig *Ted* • Mel Winkler *Frank* ■ *Dir* Danny Boyle • *Scr* John Hodge

Life, Love and Tears ★★★

Drama 1984 · USSR · Colour · 103mins

A respected actor/director of stage and screen, Nikolay Gubenko played a major role in the reorganisation of the Soviet cinema in the era of *perestroika*, first as a film-maker and then as minister of culture. This is a solid enough example of the *bytovye*, a genre of films dealing with the darker side of everyday life that would have been unthinkable in less enlightened times. Although packed with allegorical references to Mikhail Gorbachev's removal of the old Communist guard, this fascinating drama is anything but an unquestioning tribute. DP. In Russian with English subtitles.

Zhanna Bolotova • Elena Fadeeva ■ *Dir/Scr* Nikolay Gubenko

The Life of David Gale ★★★ 15

Mystery drama
2003 · US/UK/Ger · Colour · 124mins

Director Alan Parker's film about the fictional David Gale, a respected academic and opponent of the death penalty who's awaiting execution never quite catches fire. It does, however, benefit from the astute casting of Kevin Spacey as the intellectual on death row who agrees to give an exclusive interview to tenacious reporter Kate Winslet. Audiences are more likely to enjoy the climactic twists and turns than the bulk of the movie, which fails to provide the tension or high drama we'd expect from this talented cast and director. JC. Contains violence, swearing, drug abuse, sex scenes, nudity. DVD

Kevin Spacey *David Gale* • Kate Winslet *Elizabeth "Bitsey" Bloom* • Laura Linney *Constance Harraway* • Gabriel Mann *Zack* • Matt Craven *Dusty* • Rhona Mitra *Berlin* • Leon Rippy *Braxton Belyeu* • Elizabeth Gast *Sharon Gale* ■ *Dir* Alan Parker • *Scr* Charles Randolph

The Life of Emile Zola ★★★★

Biographical drama 1937 · US · BW · 123mins

This is one of a remarkable series of Warner Bros melodramatic biopics whose central performances were once considered prime examples of cinematic acting. Like Lon Chaney before him, Mr Paul Muni (as he liked to be billed), a former Yiddish Art Theater star, was never more convincing than when disguised with make-up and wigs, and here he makes a very creditable Zola in a distinguished movie that has only dated in its earnestness. Giving Muni a run for the acting honours, and collecting a best supporting actor Oscar, is Joseph Schildkraut as Captain Alfred Dreyfus. In its courageous exposé of anti-Semitism, this film can be seen today as part of the Warners social tradition, though interestingly the word "Jew" is never spoken. Both picture and screenplay also rightly won Oscars. TS

Paul Muni *Emile Zola* • Gale Sondergaard *Lucie Dreyfus* • Joseph Schildkraut *Captain Alfred Dreyfus* • Gloria Holden *Alexandrine Zola* • Donald Crisp *Maître Labori* • Erin O'Brien-Moore *Nana* • Robert Barrat *Major Walsin-Esterhazy* ■ *Dir* William Dieterle • *Scr* Norman Reilly Raine, Heinz Herald, Geza Herczeg

A Life of Her Own ★★

Drama 1950 · US · BW · 108mins

Lana Turner, appropriately cast as an innocent from the Midwest who becomes a top-flight fashion model, suffers nobly in this archetypal "woman's magazine" tearjerker that can hardly be called original. George Cukor directs from a script that has Turner in love with married man Ray Milland, whose wife is crippled. The familiar territory is also inhabited by Tom Ewell as the model agency head, Louis Calhern as Milland's friend and lawyer and, best of all, Ann Dvorak as a model for whom things go badly wrong – as does the movie. RK

Lana Turner *Lily Brannel James* • Ray Milland *Steve Harleigh* • Tom Ewell *Tom Caraway* • Louis Calhern *Jim Leversoe* • Ann Dvorak *Mary Ashlon* • Barry Sullivan *Lee Gorrance* • Margaret Phillips *Nora Harleigh* • Jean Hagen *Maggie Collins* ■ *Dir* George Cukor • *Scr* Isobel Lennart, from the story *Abiding Vision* by Rebecca West

The Life of Oharu ★★★★★ PG

Period melodrama 1952 · Jpn · BW · 130mins

One of the great works from the greatest of Japanese directors, this episodic, tragic melodrama traces the life of a woman living under the severe moral code of the Genroku era in late 17th-century Japan. Played by Kinuyo Tanaka (who appeared in 11 Mizoguchi films and later became the first woman to direct a Japanese film), Oharu suffers a catalogue of injustices, most of them arbitrary and accidental, others of her own doing. The film, which won the Silver Lion at Venice in 1952, is informed by a Buddhist view of the world that acknowledges the impermanence of everything, especially happiness. Shot in long, beautiful takes, it is more devastating than depressing. DO. In Japanese with English subtitles. DVD

Kinuyo Tanaka *Oharu* • Toshiro Mifune *Katsunosuke* • Masao Shimizu *Kikuoji* • Ichiro Sugai *Shinzaemon* • Tsukue Matsuura *Tomo, mother* • Kiyoko Tsuji *Landlady of an inn* ■ *Dir* Kenji Mizoguchi • *Scr* Yoda Yoshikata, from the novel *Koshoku Ichidai Onna* by Saikaku Ihara • *Cinematographer* Yoshimi Hirano

The Life of Stuff ★★

Drama 1997 · UK · Colour · 87mins

A strong British cast has a nasty night out in this shallow, static study of a Glasgow criminal holding a party for select friends and colleagues to celebrate the demise of a rival boss. Jason Flemyng, Ciaran Hinds, Gina McKee and Ewen Bremner try their hardest, but the characters aren't fleshed out and the incidents are so meaningless that they soon lose your attention. JC. Contains violence, swearing and drug abuse.

Ewen Bremner *Fraser* • Liam Cunningham *Alec Sneddon* • Jason Flemyng *Willie Dobie* • Ciaran Hinds *David Arbogast* • Gina McKee *Janice* • Stuart McQuarrie *Leonard* ■ *Dir* Simon Donald • *Scr* Simon Donald, from his play

Life on a String ★★★★ PG

Drama 1991 · Chi/Ger/UK · Colour · 102mins

Alighting on such themes as spirituality and sensuality, discipline and independence, salvation and delusion, this is Chen Kaige's least regarded picture. Yet, his almost avant-garde use of the forbidding rural landscape and the haunting soundtrack delicately underscore the enigmatic story of the musician and his disciple who overcome physical blindness to master their art. As the old man clinging to his mentor's promise that his sight will be restored when he breaks the thousandth string on his sanxian, Liu Zhongyuan displays an affecting trust that contrasts sharply with the impetuosity of Huang Lei, whose love for a village girl shatters their partnership. DP. In Mandarin with English subtitles. [video]

Liu Zhongyuan *The Old Master* • Huang Lei *Shitou* • Xu Qing *Lanxiu* ■ *Dir* Chen Kaige • *Scr* Chen Kaige, from a short story by Shi Tiesheng

Life or Something like It ★ 12

Romantic comedy drama
2002 · US · Colour · 99mins

This would-be romantic comedy serves as further evidence of Angelina Jolie's post-Oscar career slide. Here she plays a has-it-all Seattle TV reporter (great job, great boyfriend, great big hair) who is informed by a tramp known as Prophet Jack (Tony Shalhoub) that she has a week to live. Cue much re-evaluating of life goals and cod-philosophical musings. Sadly, Jolie gives her character such a brittle, vain and shallow edge that it's impossible to care. AR [video] DVD

Angelina Jolie *Lanie Kerrigan* • Edward Burns *Pete* • Tony Shalhoub *Prophet Jack* • Christian Kane *Cal Cooper* • Melissa Errico *Andrea* • James Gammon *Lanie's father* • Stockard Channing *Deborah Connors* • Lisa Thornhill *Gwen* ■ *Dir* Stephen Herek • *Scr* John Scott Shepherd, Dana Stevens, from a story by John Scott Shepherd

Life-Size ★★ U

Fantasy comedy 2000 · US · Colour · 84mins

Neglected by her father Jere Burns, who's become a workaholic following the death of his wife, young Lindsay Lohan hopes a book of spells will enable her to resurrect her mother. However, she succeeds only in animating her fashion doll, played by Tyra Banks, who is intent on enjoying herself. This Disney TV movie throws out so many intriguing themes, it's disappointing to see it settle for the usual feel-good resolution. DP DVD

Lindsay Lohan *Casey* • Tyra Banks *Eve* • Jere Burns *Ben* • Anne Marie Loder *Drew* • Garwin Sanford *Richie* ■ *Dir* Mark Rosman • *Scr* Mark Rosman, Stephanie Moore, from a story by Stephanie Moore

Life Stinks ★ PG

Comedy 1991 · US · Colour · 91mins

The title tells all: the film stinks, as Mel Brooks tries to be Charlie Chaplin and fails miserably. As a billionaire, erecting a business monument to himself even if it means getting rid of a shantytown of vagrants, he's as callous and crass as expected. Then he succumbs to a bet that he can't live as a derelict and the plot falls apart while Brooks babbles for our sympathy as a put-upon everyman. TH. Contains swearing and drug abuse. [video]

Mel Brooks *Goddard Bolt* • Lesley Ann Warren *Molly* • Jeffrey Tambor *Vance Crasswell* • Stuart Pankin *Pritchard* • Howard Morris *Sailor* • Rudy DeLuca *J Paul Getty* • Teddy Wilson *Fumes* • Michael Ensign *Knowles* • Matthew Faison *Stevens* • Billy Barty *Willy* • Brian Thompson *Mean Victor* • Raymond O'Connor *Yo* • Carmine Caridi *Flophouse Owner* • Sammy Shore *Reverend At Wedding* ■ *Dir* Mel Brooks • *Scr* Mel Brooks, Rudy DeLuca, Steve Haberman, from a story by Ron Clark, Mel Brooks, Rudy DeLuca, Steve Haberman

Life Upside Down ★★★★

Drama 1964 · Fr · BW · 94mins

Alain Jessua made his feature debut with this piercing social critique, which dexterously combines experimental techniques with a self-deprecating sense of irony. Ultimately, it's hard to disagree with 30-something estate agent Charles Denner's desire to withdraw from his banal life and begin existing within himself. One sympathises with his frustrated fiancée Anna Gaylor, especially when she resorts to drastic measures to provoke a return to normalcy. But Jessua and Denner make the rejection of the rat race and the logic of emotional self-sufficiency seem like a viable alternative to the increasingly dehumanising experience of urban living. A curio, but compelling. DP. In French with English subtitles.

Charles Denner *Jacques Valin* • Anna Gaylor *Viviane* • Guy Saint-Jean *Fernand* • Nicole Guedon *Nicole* • Jean Yanne *Kerbel* ■ *Dir/Scr* Alain Jessua

Life with Father ★★★★ U

Comedy 1947 · US · Colour · 117mins

Warner Bros's movie version of the long-running Broadway hit is a rare charmer, beautifully directed by *Casablanca's* Michael Curtiz. If the whole seems slight and rather deliberately echoes MGM's 1944 hit *Meet Me in St Louis*, well, that's no bad thing. Watch for star-to-be Elizabeth Taylor (on loan to Warner Bros from MGM and looking radiant), and lovely support from Edmund Gwenn and ZaSu Pitts. Author Clarence Day Jr couldn't have wished for a better screen rendering of his reminiscences of family life in late-19th century New York. TS [video] DVD

William Powell *Clarence Day Sr* • Irene Dunne *Vinnie Day* • Elizabeth Taylor *Mary* • ZaSu Pitts *Cora* • Edmund Gwenn *Rev Dr Lloyd* • Jimmy Lydon [James Lydon] *Clarence Day Jr* • Martin Milner *John* • Derek Scott *Harlan* • Johnny Calkins *Whitney* • Emma Dunn *Margaret* ■ *Dir* Michael Curtiz • *Scr* Donald Ogden Stewart, from the play by Howard Lindsay, Russel Crouse, from the book by Clarence Day Jr

Life with Mikey ★★★ PG

Comedy 1993 · US · Colour · 91mins

This is a perfect vehicle for the charms of Michael J Fox, who's on to every trick as the thespian who turns agent after the public stops finding him cute. What makes his performance particularly good is the grace with which he accepts the fact he's been set up to lose every scene to Christina Vidal, as the little urchin he steers to stardom. Their relationship is great fun to watch, but the jabs at celebrity are delivered without any real conviction. Originally released in the UK as *Give Me a Break*. DP [video] DVD

Michael J Fox *Michael Chapman* • Christina Vidal *Angie Vega* • Nathan Lane *Ed Chapman* • Cyndi Lauper *Geena Briganti* • David Krumholtz *Barry Corman* • Christine Baranski *Carol* ■ *Dir* James Lapine • *Scr* Marc Lawrence

Life with the Lyons ★★ U

Comedy 1953 · UK · BW · 61mins

Based on the second long-running radio show made in Britain by the American stars Ben Lyon and Bebe Daniels (after *Hi Gang!* in 1941), this is a lightweight domestic comedy whose cosy appeal has been attenuated by the passage of time. The characters familiar to millions in the mid-1950s are total strangers to most viewers now, and they lack the spark and credibility of the other film family of the time, the Huggetts. As neither star had appeared in a movie in over a decade, it is perhaps not surprising that their playing looks laboured, although the marshmallow script about a reluctant landlord doesn't help the cause. DP [video] DVD

Bebe Daniels *Bebe* • Ben Lyon *Ben* • Barbara Lyon *Barbara* • Richard Lyon *Richard* • Horace Percival *Mr Wimple* • Molly Weir *Aggie* ■ *Dir* Val Guest • *Scr* Robert Dunbar, Val Guest, from the radio series by Bebe Daniels, Bob Block, Bill Harding

Lifeboat ★★★★ PG

Second World War drama
1944 · US · BW · 96mins

Alfred Hitchcock's tense drama has the distinction of being shot on what looks like the smallest ever film set. The action takes place exclusively on board a lifeboat after a liner is torpedoed by a Nazi sub. As so often in Hitchcock's films, the suspense lies not in the audience being kept in the dark about the identity of the villain, but in making us watch and wait while the characters find it out for themselves. Tallulah Bankhead is the pick of an exceptional cast, but it's all about Hitch's matchless ability to create, shatter and re-create tension until our nerves are frayed. DP. In English and German. [video]

Tallulah Bankhead *Connie Porter* • William Bendix *Gus* • Walter Slezak *Willy, U-boat captain* • Mary Anderson *Alice* • John Hodiak *Kovak* • Henry Hull *Rittenhouse* • Heather Angel *Mrs Higgins* • Hume Cronyn *Stanley Garrett* • Canada Lee *George "Joe" Spencer* ■ *Dir* Alfred Hitchcock • *Scr* Jo Swerling, from the story by John Steinbeck

Lifeforce ★ 18

Science-fiction horror
1985 · UK · Colour · 97mins

It's hard to believe that Tobe Hooper, director of the influential *The Texas Chain Saw Massacre*, came up with this laughably bad adaptation. Steve Railsback stars as one of a team of astronauts that discovers parasitic energy suckers on an invasion course for Earth in a strange craft lurking in the tail of Halley's Comet. Rather than the homage to vintage Hammer horror that Hooper wanted to make, this is more a cruel parody. AJ. Contains violence, swearing, nudity. [video] DVD

Steve Railsback *Colonel Tom Carlsen* • Peter Firth *Colonel Colin Caine* • Frank Finlay *Dr Hans Fallada* • Mathilda May *Space girl* • Patrick Stewart *Dr Armstrong* • Michael Gothard *Bukovsky* • Nicholas Ball *Derebridge* ■ *Dir* Tobe Hooper • *Scr* Dan O'Bannon, Don Jakoby, from the novel *The Space Vampires* by Colin Wilson

Lifeform ★★

Science-fiction action
1996 · US · Colour · 90mins

This low-budget sci-fi movie has its rewards, but falls just short of being a good movie. The emphasis here is not on the special effects, but an intriguing script that doesn't telegraph the plot twists. Essentially, the movie is a take on *Alien*, with an alien loose in a military compound, and the scientists and soldiers on the base trying to stop the menace. Much fun comes with unexpected situations forcing the viewer to reassess what he has just seen. Overall cheap production values, and a truly bad ending stop this from reaching sleeper status. KB

Cotter Smith *Case Montgomery* • Deirdre O'Connell *Dr Gracia Scott* • Ryan Phillippe *Private Ryan* • Raoul O'Connell *Private Jeffers* ■ *Dir/Scr* Mark H Baker

Lifeguard ★★ 15

Drama 1976 · US · Colour · 92mins

Sam Elliott is the wrong side of 30 and he's still a lifeguard on a California beach. What on earth is he gonna do when he grows up? Elliott is the sort of knucklehead you want to slap, though his girlfriend Anne Archer is urging him to do something really rewarding, like sell second-hand cars, which in California is almost a vocation. AT [video]

Sam Elliott *Rick Carlson* • Anne Archer *Cathy* • Stephen Young *Larry* • Parker Stevenson *Chris* • Kathleen Quinlan *Wendy* • Steve Burns *Machine Gun* • Sharon Weber *Tina* ■ *Dir* Daniel Petrie • *Scr* Ron Koslow

Lifespan ★★★ 18

Science fiction
1975 · US/Neth · Colour · 77mins

This shoestring thriller posits an intriguing contrast between humanitarian hopes for the elimination of disease and the sinister medical experimentation undertaken by the Nazis. Representing enlightened science is Hiram Keller, who discovers that a dead colleague may have concocted an elixir for eternal life, while the forces of darkness summon up Klaus Kinski, as the deranged industrialist sponsoring the unnatural project. Writer/director Alexander Whitelaw makes atmospheric use of both his Amsterdam locations and the antiseptic interiors that contrast so tellingly with the gloriously Gothic labs of expressionist horror. DP [video]

Hiram Keller *Dr Ben Land* • Tina Aumont *Anna* • Klaus Kinski *Nicholas Ulrich* ■ *Dir* Alexander Whitelaw • *Scr* Alexander Whitelaw, Judith Rascoe, Alva Ruben

The Lift ★★★ 15

Science fiction 1983 · Neth · Colour · 94mins

A lift with a mind of its own is the baffling culprit in a series of bizarre office block "accidents" in this rare example of Dutch horror exploitation. Maintenance man Huub Stapel can't find any mechanical fault but – in between soap opera interludes of domestic strife, which diffuse the claustrophobic suspense – eventually uncovers the alarming, if silly, truth. Writer/director Dick Maas extracts every ounce of menace in the final confrontation between man and machine and, appalling dubbing aside, this shocks without a single drop of blood being spilt. Less successfully, Maas remade the film in the US as *Down* (2001). AJ. Dutch dialogue dubbed into English. [video]

Huub Stapel *Felix Adelbaar* • Willeke Van Ammelrooy *Mieke de Beer* • Josine Van Dalsum *Saskia Adelaar* • Piet Romer *Manager* ■ *Dir/Scr* Dick Maas

Lift to the Scaffold ★★★★ PG

Crime thriller 1957 · Fr · BW · 87mins

Louis Malle made his feature directorial debut with this assured thriller, which recalled both the poetic realism of Marcel Carné and the brooding menace of American *films noirs*. In addition to making a star of Jeanne Moreau and giving a generation a phobia about elevators, the film also had a considerable influence on the nascent French New Wave through the moody naturalism of Henri Decaë's black-and-white photography. The sublime jazz score was improvised by Miles Davis and a band of European musicians while the film played on a screen before them. DP. In French with English subtitles. [video]

Jeanne Moreau *Florence Carala* • Maurice Ronet *Julien Tavernier* • Georges Poujouly *Louis* • Yori Bertin *Véronique* • Jean Wall

L

Simon Carala ■ *Dir* Louis Malle • *Scr* Louis Malle, from the novel *Ascenseur pour l'Echafaud* by Noël Calef

The Light across the Street ★★★

Drama 1956 · Fr · BW · 98mins

Early in her career Brigitte Bardot created a stir on the art house circuit with her smouldering performance in this cheerless tale of repressed passion. However, the real acting here comes from Raymond Pellegrin, as the disabled husband who is prevented from consummating the marriage and has to watch with growing indignation as his bride succumbs to the muscular charms of garage owner Roger Pigaut. With its fetid atmosphere, this may be *noir lite*, but is compelling nonetheless. DP. In French with English subtitles.

Brigitte Bardot *Olivia Marceau* • Raymond Pellegrin *Georges Marceau* • Roger Pigaut *Pietri* • Claude Romain *Barbette* ■ *Dir* Georges Lacombe • *Scr* Louis Chavance, René Masson, René Lefèvre, from the story *La Lumière d'en Face* by Jean-Claude Aurel

The Light at the Edge of the World ★

Adventure
1971 · US/Sp/Liech · Colour · 125mins

Some movies are just so awful you wonder how they could have been conceived in the first place. This overlong adaptation of a Jules Verne novel about a lighthouse that is beset by pirates is pathetic, geared for neither adults nor children, and has grievous trouble finding both style and tone. Star Kirk Douglas, villain Yul Brynner and female lead Samantha Eggar look uncomfortable, while director Kevin Billington seems out of his depth. TS. Contains violence.

Kirk Douglas *Will Denton* • Yul Brynner *Jonathan Kongre* • Samantha Eggar *Arabella* • Jean-Claude Drouot *Virgilio* • Fernando Rey *Captain Moriz* ■ *Dir* Kevin Billington • *Scr* Tom Rowe, Rachel Billington, Bertha Dominguez, from the novel by Jules Verne

The Light in the Forest ★★★ U

Period drama 1958 · US · Colour · 88mins

This intriguing period drama, which originated on Disney's *The Wonderful World of Color* series, should appeal to older children. James MacArthur stars as a white boy who, having been captured and raised by the Delaware Indians, is forced to go and live with a racist guardian under the terms of a 1764 peace treaty. Wendell Corey is utterly loathsome in an unusually unsympathetic role, while Carol Lynley makes an impressive film debut as his kindly servant. DP

James MacArthur *Johnny Butler/True Son* • Carol Lynley *Shenandoe* • Fess Parker *Del Hardy* • Wendell Corey *Wilse Owens* • Joanne Dru *Milly Elder* • Jessica Tandy *Myra Butler* • Joseph Calleia *Chief Cuyloga* • John McIntire *John Elder* ■ *Dir* Herschel Daugherty • *Scr* Lawrence Edward Watkin, from a novel by Conrad Richter

Light in the Piazza ★★★

Drama 1961 · US · Colour · 101mins

A splendid late MGM melodrama sumptuously produced in Europe, largely on Italian locations. It's based on a novel by Elizabeth Spencer about a mother caring for her mentally disabled daughter. As the daughter, Yvette Mimeux gives a performance of great subtlety under the direction of the still under-rated British cameraman-turned-director Guy Green, and Olivia de Havilland is perfectly cast as the mother. George Hamilton makes a suave suitor, but the film's delicate tone is disrupted by the silly antics of Rossano Brazzi and Barry Sullivan. TS

Olivia de Havilland *Margaret Johnson* • Rossano Brazzi *Signor Naccarelli* • Yvette Mimieux *Clara Johnson* • George Hamilton *Farizio Naccarelli* • Barry Sullivan *Noel Johnson* • Isabel Dean *Miss Hawtree* ■ *Dir* Guy Green • *Scr* Julius J Epstein, from the novella *The Light in the Piazza* by Elizabeth Spencer

Light It Up ★★ 15

Drama 1999 · US · Colour · 95mins

Picture *The Breakfast Club* in a *Dangerous Minds* kind of inner-city school against the backdrop of a *Dog Day Afternoon* siege and you've some idea of what to expect from this confrontational drama. Director Craig Bolotin strains to point out the latent militancy in today's "don't care" kids – providing they've got something to fight for. The reinstatement of popular teacher Judd Nelson proves to be such a cause. DP

Usher Raymond *Lester Dewitt* • Forest Whitaker *Officer Dante Jackson* • Rosario Dawson *Stephanie Williams* • Robert Ri'chard *Zacharias "Ziggy" Malone* • Judd Nelson *Ken Knowles* • Fredro Starr *Rodney J Templeton* • Sara Gilbert *Lynn Sabatini* • Clifton Collins Jr *Robert "Rivers" Tremont* ■ *Dir* Craig Bolotin • *Scr* Craig Bolotin, Druann Carlson

Light of Day ★★ PG

Drama 1987 · US · Colour · 102mins

Writer/director Paul Schrader's attempt to graft his favourite theme of moral redemption on to a story of rock 'n' roll gets hopelessly bogged down in soul-searching and family strife. To make things worse, Michael J Fox is badly miscast as a factory worker-cum-rock singer who must console a confused sister (Joan Jett), a religous mother (Gena Rowlands) and a father who has given up on all of them. Set in small-time, working-class Cleveland, the film stumbles towards that most wretched of movie clichés – the terminal disease. AT. Contains swearing.

Michael J Fox *Joe Rasnick* • Gena Rowlands *Jeanette Rasnick* • Joan Jett *Patti Rasnick* • Michael McKean *Bu Montgomery* • Thomas G Waites *Smittie* • Cherry Jones *Cindy Montgomery* • Michael Dolan *Gene Bodine* • Paul J Harkins *Billy Tettore* • Billy Sullivan [Billy L Sullivan] *Benji Rasnick* • Jason Miller *Benjamin Rasnick* • Tom Irwin *Reverend John Ansley* ■ *Dir/Scr* Paul Schrader

Light Sleeper ★★★ 15

Thriller 1991 · US · Colour · 98mins

One of director Paul Schrader's more successful examinations of down-and-outs on society's fringe, this film features a top-notch performance from Willem Dafoe as a middle-league, middle-aged drug supplier who's come to a crossroads in his life. The "fun" era of designer drugs is over, crack and the cops have moved into his Manhattan manor, and he wants out. So, too, does his upper-class boss Susan Sarandon (equally excellent) to whom he looks to solve his career dilemma. Violent redemption awaits both in Schrader's leisurely paced, rewarding study of terminal addiction. AJ. Contains swearing, violence, sex scenes and nudity. DVD

Willem Dafoe *John LeTour* • Susan Sarandon *Ann* • Dana Delany *Marianne* • David Clennon *Robert* • Mary Beth Hurt *Teresa Aranow* • Victor Garber *Tis* • Jane Adams (2) *Randi* ■ *Dir/Scr* Paul Schrader

The Light That Failed ★★★

Drama 1939 · US · BW · 87mins

Ronald Colman is impeccably cast as the former soldier-turned-artist who, going blind from a war wound, is determined to finish his masterpiece – a portrait of his turbulent cockney model (Ida Lupino). Under the restrained and expert direction of William A Wellman, an excellent supporting cast, headed by Walter Huston as Colman's friend, reflects the quality of the leading performances and Robert Carson's screenplay, to make for a moving drama. RK

Ronald Colman *Dick Heldar* • Walter Huston *Terpenhow* • Muriel Angelus *Maisie* • Ida Lupino *Bessie Broke* • Dudley Digges *The Nilghai* • Ernest Cossart *Beeton* ■ *Dir* William A Wellman • *Scr* Robert Carson, from the story by Rudyard Kipling

The Light Touch ★★

Crime drama 1951 · US · BW · 106mins

Writer/director Richard Brooks fails to bring a light touch to this predictable bag of clichés, which stars Pier Angeli as a young artist working for suave art dealer George Sanders. Sanders turns out not to be what he seems and, before she can say "palette-knife", the innocent girl finds herself involved with Stewart Granger (also not what he seems), with whom she falls in love. The locations are rather more worthy of attention than the plot, which gets her mixed up with international art-thieving. RK

Stewart Granger *Sam Conride* • Pier Angeli *Anna Vasarri* • George Sanders *Felix Guignol* • Kurt Kasznar *Mr Aramescu* • Joseph Calleia *Lt Massiro* • Larry Keating *Mr RF Hawkley* ■ *Dir* Richard Brooks • *Scr* Richard Brooks, from a story by Jed Harris, Tom Reed

Light Up the Sky ★ PG

Second World War comedy drama
1960 · UK · BW · 85mins

In this hackneyed theatrical hand-me-down Victor Maddern heads a plane-spotting detail during the Second World War. His crew comprises Sydney Tafler who's mourning his son, Harry Locke who's short of money, lovesick Johnny Briggs and Tommy Steele, who, in addition to going AWOL to do music-hall turns with Benny Hill, has made his mistress pregnant. Little relieves the incessant chat. DP

Ian Carmichael *Lieutenant Ogleby* • Tommy Steele *Eric McCaffey* • Benny Hill *Syd McCaffey* • Sydney Tafler *Ted Green* • Victor Maddern *Lance Bombardier Tomlinson* • Harry Locke *Roland Kenyon* • Johnny Briggs *Leslie Smith* • Cyril Smith *"Spinner" Rice* • Dick Emery *Harry the Driver* • Cardew Robinson *Compere* • Sheila Hancock *Theatre act* ■ *Dir* Lewis Gilbert • *Scr* Vernon Harris, from the play *Touch It Light* by Robert Storey

Light Years ★★

Animated science-fiction
1988 · Fr · Colour · 83mins

This space fantasy from French director René Laloux is a disappointingly weak attempt to blend adult science-fiction with children's fables. The *Heavy Metal* magazine-inspired animation is highly stylised and imaginative, but this tale of a young hero defending a Utopian land from destruction is too static and laboriously talky. Miramax's Harvey Weinstein directed the American version of the French original, which was scripted by Isaac Asimov. RS

Glenn Close *Ambisextra* • Christopher Plummer *Metamorphis* • Earl Hammond *Blaminhor* • Jennifer Grey *Airelle* • John Shea *Sylvain* • Bridget Fonda *Historian/Head* ■ *Dir* René Laloux, Harvey Weinstein • *Scr* Raphael Cluzel, Isaac Asimov (American version), from the novel *Robots Against Gandahar* by Jean-Pierre Andrevan, adapted by René Laloux

Light Years Away ★★★

Science fiction drama
1981 · Swi/Fr · Colour · 106mins

With its evocative Irish landscapes and its essentially two-handed approach to the drama, there's a touch of Samuel Beckett about Alain Tanner's reworking of the Daedalus/Icarus myth. Garage owner Trevor Howard takes on the mantle of the ancient Athenian whose son perished while flying too close to the sun, while Mick Ford plays the drifter who becomes his apprentice in the hope of learning the reality of Howard's closely guarded dream. This is more a study of eccentricity and ambition than science fiction, with Jean-François Robin's photography lending an element of fantasy. DP

Trevor Howard *Yoshka* • Mick Ford *Jonas* • Bernice Stegers *Betty* • Henri Virlojeux *Lawyer* • Odile Schmitt *Dancer* • Louis Samier *Trucker* ■ *Dir* Alain Tanner • *Scr* Alain Tanner, from the novel *La Voie Sauvage* by Daniel Odier

The Lighthorsemen ★★★ PG

First World War drama
1987 · Aus · Colour · 110mins

The misuse of Australian soldiers by their British commanders during the First World War had been well chronicled by Peter Weir in *Gallipoli*. But Simon Wincer adds a new dimension to the cannon-fodder theme by examining the horrors endured by the horses roped into service during the same conflict. The cavalry charge essential to Anthony Andrews's cunning plan to seize a Turkish water supply is both exhilarating and disturbing, as classical and modern warfare clash head on. Wincer makes the most of both animals and scenery. DP. Contains swearing.

Peter Phelps *Dave Mitchell* • Tony Bonner *Colonel Bourchier* • Gary Sweet *Frank* • John Walton *Tas* • Tim McKenzie *Chiller* • Jon Blake *Scotty* • Sigrid Thornton *Anne* • Anthony Andrews *Major Meinertzhagen* ■ *Dir* Simon Wincer • *Scr* Ian Jones

Lighthouse ★★★ 15

Horror 1999 · UK · Colour · 91mins

This low-budget horror is a surprising gem. Set in an isolated island lighthouse, it follows an escaped serial killer hunting down survivors of a wrecked prison ship. Although the film is ambitious, it never exceeds its capabilities. Instead, it relies largely on atmosphere and old-fashioned suspense techniques to deliver a highly effective spinetingler. Shooting entirely at night, director Simon Hunter makes full use of shadows and gloom, creating some wonderful finger-chewing set pieces. Show-stealer Chris Adamson oozes menace as the head-lopping psycho. SF DVD

James Purefoy *Richard Spader* • Rachel Shelley *Dr Kirsty McCloud* • Chris Adamson [Christopher Adamson] *Leo Rook* • Paul Brooke *Captain Campbell* • Don Warrington *Prison Officer Ian Goslet* • Chris Dunne *Chief Prison Officer O'Neil* • Bob Goody *Weevil* ■ *Dir/Scr* Simon Hunter

Lightning Jack ★★ PG

Comedy western 1994 · Aus · Colour · 93mins

Paul Hogan managed to raise the funds to make this spoof western via the Australian Stock Exchange. If only he could have raised some laughs as well! There's very little return on the gag investment in this only moderately entertaining comedy about a legendary gunslinger teaching the tricks of his trade to mute misfit and aspiring outlaw Cuba Gooding Jr. AJ. Contains violence, swearing.

Paul Hogan *Lightning Jack Kane* • Cuba Gooding Jr *Ben Doyle* • Beverly D'Angelo *Lana* • Kamala Dawson *Pilar* • Pat Hingle *Marshall Kurtz* • Richard Riehle *Reporter* • Frank McRae *Mr Doyle* • Roger Daltrey *John T Coles* • LQ Jones *Local sheriff* ■ *Dir* Simon Wincer • *Scr* Paul Hogan

Lightning over Water ★★★

Documentary drama
1980 · W Ger/Swe · Colour · 90mins

Nicholas Ray's his mesmerising screen debut, *They Live By Night* (1948), heralded a dozen productive years which saw him make a dozen good, often great, movies. This final film, shown posthumously and co-directed with friend and colleague Wim Wenders, is therefore doubly painful to watch as we recall a tense, tall, energetic director now withering away on screen, succumbing to lung cancer. The film is not about his proposed fictional story of a dying painter, but about family, friendship and a last ditch attempt to resurrect a style of cinema that began to decline alongside Ray's career in the 1960s. BB

Dir/Scr Nicholas Ray, Wim Wenders

Lightning Strikes Twice ★★

Mystery drama 1951 · US · BW · 91mins

A turgid Warner Bros melodrama from director King Vidor, who has trouble sorting out the plot. Richard Todd, in one of his first Hollywood movies, is cleared of murdering his wife but is still seen as guilty by his friends and neighbours, so he sets out to find the real killer with the help of new love Ruth Roman. It's neither *film noir* nor romance; Todd is excellent, as are Zachary Scott and Mercedes McCambridge, but Roman offers little in the crucial co-starring role. TS

Richard Todd *Richard Trevelyan* • Ruth Roman *Shelley Carnes* • Mercedes McCambridge *Liza McStringer* • Zachary Scott *Harvey Turner* • Frank Conroy *JD Nolan* • Kathryn Givney *Myra Nolan* • Rhys Williams *Father Paul* • Darryl Hickman *String* ■ *Dir* King Vidor • *Scr* Lenore Coffee, from the novel *A Man without Friends* by Margaret Echard

Lightning the White Stallion ★ U

Adventure 1986 · US · Colour · 87mins

Trading on his success in such earlier horse dramas as *National Velvet* and *The Black Stallion*, Mickey Rooney trots out every scene-stealing trick in the book as the impoverished breeder who unites with a couple of kids to recover the champion who's been stolen by a stablehand. Sentimental, sloppy and disappointing. DP [VIDEO]

Mickey Rooney *Barney Ingram* • Isabel Lorca *Stephanie Ward* • Susan George *Madame Rene* • Billy Wesley *Lucas* ■ *Dir* William A Levey • *Scr* Peter Welbeck [Harry Alan Towers], Rick Marx

Lights of New York ★★

Crime drama 1928 · US · BW · 57mins

Billed by Warner Bros as "the first 100 per cent all-talking picture" – *The Jazz Singer* was only partly sound – they really should have spent more on voice coaching for the many vaudeville stars (Helene Costello, Cullen Landis) hired to make this gangster movie more viable and entertaining. Directed by Bryan Foy, with Gladys Brockwell as the gangster's moll and Robert Elliott as the tough detective, the story flits from small-town integrity to "Great White Way" shenanigans, with sets dwarfing everyone and very few participants knowing how to project any kind of conviction. Still, it does have a certain novelty value. TH

Helene Costello *Kitty Lewis* • Cullen Landis *Eddie Morgan* • Gladys Brockwell *Molly Thompson* • Mary Carr *Mrs Morgan* • Wheeler Oakman *Hawk Miller* • Eugene Pallette *Gene* • Robert Elliott *Detective Crosby* • Tom Dugan *Sam* ■ *Dir* Bryan Foy • *Scr* Hugh Herbert, Murray Roth, from a story by Charles R Gaskill

Lights of Variety ★★★★ PG

Drama 1950 · It · BW · 92mins

Although Alberto Lattuada was credited with blocking the action for the camera, Federico Fellini's influence on the content of this "act of humility towards life" is clearly evident. Breaking with the neorealist tradition of locating characters within their environment, Fellini delights in revealing the human face behind the social mask, just as he exposes the tawdriness of the supposedly glamorous showbiz life endured by the stage-struck Carla Del Poggio until she abandons clown-manager Peppino De Filippo's itinerant band of misfits. Fellini's debut is one to savour. DP. In Italian with English subtitles. [VIDEO]

Peppino De Filippo *Checco Dal Monte* • Carla Del Poggio *Liliana Antonelli* • Giulietta Masina *Melina Amour* • Folco Lulli *Adelmo Conti* • Dante Maggio *Remo* ■ *Dir* Alberto Lattuada, Federico Fellini • *Scr* Federico Fellini, Alberto Lattuada, Tullio Pinelli, Ennio Flajano, from a story by Federico Fellini

The Lightship ★★ 15

Psychological thriller
1985 · US · Colour · 84mins

After the success of films as diverse as *Mephisto* and *Out of Africa*, Austrian actor Klaus Maria Brandauer looked set to become an international star. But he chose not wisely with this overt allegory in which Robert Duvall leads psychos aboard Captain Brandauer's rustbucket lightship. The trouble is the captain's role is as passive as his pacifism and it's Duvall who steers the action to the compass of his violence. TH. Contains violence and swearing. [VIDEO]

Robert Duvall *Caspary* • Klaus Maria Brandauer *Captain Miller* • Tom Bower *Coop* • Robert Costanzo *Stump* • Badja Djola *Nate* • William Forsythe *Gene* • Arliss Howard *Eddie* ■ *Dir* Jerzy Skolimowski • *Scr* William Mai, David Taylor, from the novel *Das Feuerschiff* by Siegfried Lenz

Like Father ★★★ 15

Drama 2001 · UK · Colour · 97mins

A young Durham boy finds himself marginalised by his adult relations as social and domestic issues collide head on in this well-meaning portrait of a proud region in uneasy transition. Produced by the Amber film collective, this is an occasionally naive melodrama, which settles for an overly cosy resolution. Discarded miner Joe Armstrong drifts apart from wife Anna Gascoigne in seeking to rebuild his career as a club entertainer, while falling out his dad, Ned Kelly, over a plan to redevelop the land on which his pigeon loft is located. DP

Ned Kelly *Arthur Elliott* • Joe Armstrong *Joe Elliott* • Jonathon Dent *Michael Elliott* • Anna Gascoigne *Carol Elliott* ■ • *Scr* Amber Films

Like Father, like Son ★★★ 15

Comedy 1987 · US · Colour · 95mins

Apart from running out of funny things for Dudley Moore and son Kirk Cameron to do once they have traded places, this first of several late-1980s body-swap comedies is surprisingly good value. Giggling and scurrying for all he is worth, Moore whoops it up as the surgeon reliving his teens, and his performance is not a million miles behind the one that won Tom Hanks an Oscar nomination in *Big*. DP. Contains swearing. [VIDEO] DVD

Dudley Moore *Dr Jack Hammond* • Kirk Cameron *Chris Hammond* • Margaret Colin *Ginnie Armbruster* • Catherine Hicks *Dr Amy Larkin* • Patrick O'Neal *Dr Armbruster* • Sean Astin *Trigger* • Cami Cooper [Camille Cooper] *Lori Beaumont* ■ *Dir* Rod Daniel • *Scr* Lorne Cameron, Steven L Bloom, from a story by Lorne Cameron

Like Grains of Sand ★★★ 15

Drama 1995 · Jpn · Colour · 123mins

Sprawling when it might have been intimate, Ryosuke Hashiguchi's second feature still has far more to say about sexual identity and the pain of adolescence than any number of Hollywood teenage dramas. There's no holding back the emotions in this romantic triangle, yet the members of the inexperienced cast never stray into caricature or melodramatics, even though their situation initially seems more than a little contrived and becomes increasingly tortuous. Yoshinori Okada is particularly impressive as the sensitive gay student who repays the loyalty of his best friend, Kota Kusano, by trying to help him win the trust of traumatised rape victim, Ayumi Hamazaki. DP. In Japanese with English subtitles. Contains swearing. [VIDEO]

Yoshinori Okada *Shuji Ito* • Kota Kusano *Hiroyuki Yoshida* • Koji Yamaguchi *Touru Kanbara* • Ayumi Hamazaki *Kasane Aihara* ■ *Dir/Scr* Ryosuke Hashiguchi

Like It Is ★★★ 18

Comedy drama 1997 · UK · Colour · 95mins

A young boxer from Blackpool (played by British amateur featherweight champion Steve Bell) finds love and disillusionment in London's gay clubland in first-time director Paul Oremland's good-natured production. Ian Rose is the record producer Bell follows to Soho after a one night stand, only to face harsh realities in the big city. Roger Daltrey is Rose's predatory boss and Dani Behr Daltrey's latest singing discovery, and both see Bell as a threat. Slightly awkward, yet avoiding the cliché traps that often handicap gay dramas, this is done with a naturalistic charm. AJ. Contains violence, swearing, sex scenes. [VIDEO] DVD

Steve Bell *Craig* • Roger Daltrey *Pop mogul* • Dani Behr *Paula* • Ian Rose *Matt* ■ *Dir* Paul Oremland • *Scr* Robert Cray

Like Mike ★★★ PG

Sports fantasy comedy
2002 · US · Colour · 95mins

Pubescent rapper Lil' Bow Wow stars as an orphan who longs to be a basketball star. When the pair of trainers he is wearing (that he believes once belonged to Michael Jordan) are struck by a handy bolt of lightning, he's transformed into an on-court whizz. As Lil' Bow Wow sets off on the road to NBA stardom, the film piles on the clichés, with his evil guardian (a typically offbeat Crispin Glover) seeking to exploit him. The movie redeems itself, however, with its light, playful tone and a winning central turn from Lil' Bow Wow. IF [VIDEO] DVD

Lil' Bow Wow *Calvin Cambridge* • Morris Chestnut *Tracy Reynolds* • Jonathan Lipnicki *Murph* • Brenda Song *Reg Stevens* • Jesse Plemons *Ox* • Julius Charles Ritter *Marlon* • Crispin Glover *Stan Bittleman* • Anne Meara *Sister Theresa* ■ *Dir* John Schultz • *Scr* Michael Elliot, Jordan Moffet, from a story by Michael Elliot

Like Water for Chocolate ★★★★ 15

Romantic fantasy
1993 · Mex · Colour · 109mins

The combination of culinary art and magic realism that made Laura Esquivel's bestseller so distinctive is very much to the fore in husband Alfonso Arau's acclaimed adaptation. Set in Mexico at the turn of the century, this epic of a forbidden love consummated only through food has a sizzling story and committed performances, but Arau's direction is naively over-emphatic, with scenes of great erotic intensity sometimes missing their mark. DP. In English and Spanish with subtitles. [VIDEO] DVD

Marco Leonardi *Pedro* • Lumi Cavazos *Tita* • Regina Torne *Mama Elena* • Mario Ivan Martinez *John Brown* • Ada Carrasco *Nacha* • Yareli Arizmendi *Rosaura* • Claudette Maille *Gertrudis* • Pilar Aranda *Chencha* ■ *Dir* Alfonso Arau • *Scr* Laura Esquivel, from her novel *Como Agua para Chocolate*

The Likely Lads ★★ PG

Comedy 1976 · UK · Colour · 86mins

This is a long way short of the standard of their TV series, with writers Dick Clement and Ian La Frenais falling into the trap of misusing film freedom to turn their material blue. However, Rodney Bewes and James Bolam are as engaging as ever as Bob and Terry, and their tour of the North East coast contains plenty of the wallowing and lamenting that gave the show its appeal. DP [VIDEO] DVD

Rodney Bewes *Bob Ferris* • James Bolam *Terry Collier* • Brigit Forsyth *Thelma Ferris* • Mary Tamm *Christina* • Sheila Fearn *Audrey* • Zena Walker *Laura* ■ *Dir* Michael Tuchner • *Scr* Dick Clement, Ian La Frenais

Li'l Abner ★★★★ U

Musical comedy 1959 · US · Colour · 75mins

This is a terrific adaptation of the brash and sassy Broadway show, highly stylised and superbly photographed by Daniel L Fapp (*West Side Story*) in eye-popping Technicolor and VistaVision – both sexy and witty to boot. The plot imposed on Al Capp's cartoon *Dogpatch* is classically simple: being the most worthless place in America the government wants to use it for nuclear testing. Cue for terrific songs, exhilarating dancing (choreography by Michael Kidd and Dee Dee Wood) and a wonderful cast, including Stella Stevens as Apassionata Von Climax and Julie Newmar as Stupefyin' Jones. TS

Peter Palmer *Li'l Abner* • Leslie Parrish *Daisy Mae* • Stubby Kaye *Marryin' Sam* • Howard St John *General Bullmoose* • Julie Newmar *Stupefyin' Jones* • Stella Stevens *Appassionata Von Climax* • Alan Carney *Mayor Dawgmeat* • Jerry Lewis *Frank* ■ *Dir* Melvin Frank • *Scr* Norman Panama, Melvin Frank, from their musical, from characters in the comic strip *Dogpatch, created by Al Capp*

Lilac Time ★★★

Silent First World War drama
1928 · US · BW · 79mins

Misunderstandings bloom, along with the flowers, in this vastly romantic, hugely successful crowd-pleaser set in the First World War. French girl Colleen Moore endures the usual wartime romantic tribulations as she waits for dashing English pilot Gary Cooper to keep his promise to return to her. It's a theme that has survived in many guises throughout the years because it basically lives up to its optimistic alternative title of *Love Never Dies*. TH

Colleen Moore *Jeannine Berthelot* • Gary Cooper *Capt Philip Blythe* • Burr McIntosh *Gen Blythe* • George Cooper *Mechanic's helper* ■ *Dir* George Fitzmaurice • *Scr* Carey Wilson, Willis Goldbeck, from the play by Jane Cowl, Jane Murfin

Lilacs in the Spring ★★ U

Fantasy 1955 · UK · Colour · 99mins

Unconscious as a result of a bomb explosion during the Blitz, a young entertainer with a boyfriend dilemma dreams of herself as Nell Gwynne, as Queen Victoria and as her own actress mother, who was killed en route to a reconciliation with her famous actor husband. A piece of romantic whimsy, produced and directed in Trucolor by Herbert Wilcox as a vehicle for his wife, Anna Neagle, who acquits herself well. Errol Flynn appears as her mother's estranged husband. RK

Anna Neagle *Carole Beaumont/Lillian Grey/Queen Victoria/Nell Gwyn* • Errol Flynn *John Beaumont* • David Farrar *Charles King/King Charles* • Kathleen Harrison *Kate* • Peter Graves (2) *Albert Gutman/Prince Albert* • Helen Haye *Lady Drayton* • Sean Connery ■ *Dir* Herbert Wilcox • *Scr* Harold Purcell, from the play *The Glorious Days* by Robert Nesbitt

Lili ★★★★ U

Romantic musical drama
1953 · US · Colour · 80mins

Gamine Leslie Caron stars as a waif who joins a carnival, while Mel Ferrer, in his most sympathetic role, is a self-pitying puppeteer who provides some of the film's most memorable moments. The score won an Oscar, and there's also a marvellously rich fantasy ballet sequence. Director Charles Walters makes superb use of MGM's French village set, beautifully photographed in Technicolor by Robert Planck, but children of all ages will gasp at the magic tricks performed by Jean-Pierre Aumont and his assistant Zsa Zsa Gabor. This is an absolute charmer. TS

Leslie Caron *Lili Daurier* • Mel Ferrer *Paul Berthalet* • Jean-Pierre Aumont *Marc* • Zsa Zsa Gabor *Rosalie* • Kurt Kasznar *Jacquot* • Amanda Blake *Peach Lips* ■ *Dir* Charles Walters • *Scr* Helen Deutsch, from the story by Paul Gallico • *Music* Bronislau Kaper

Lili Marleen ★★ 15

Second World War drama
1980 · W Ger · Colour · 111mins

Rainer Werner Fassbinder intended this wartime weepie to be both a homage to the Hollywood romance and an assault on the lingering influence of Nazi gloss on modern German cinema. However, his evident lack of interest in the project meant that his most expensive picture was also among his worst. Hanna Schygulla is off-key as the second-rate chanteuse who risks her status within the Reich to help smuggle her Jewish beloved, composer Giancarlo Giannini, to safety. Garishly designed and lazily directed. DP [VIDEO]

Hanna Schygulla *Wilkie Bunterberg* • Giancarlo Giannini *Robert Mendelssohn* • Mel Ferrer *David Mendelssohn* • Karl-Heinz von Hassel *Hans Henkel* • Erik Schumann *Von Strehlow* • Hark Bohm *Taschner* • Udo Kier *Drewitz* ■ *Dir* Rainer Werner Fassbinder • *Scr* Manfred Purzer, Joshua Sinclair, Rainer Werner Fassbinder, from the novel *Der Himmel Hat Viele Farben* by Lale Andersen

Lilies ★★ 15

Drama 1996 · Can · Colour · 91mins

It's easy to spot that this tale of lingering bitterness and repressed sexuality was adapted from a play. But while the seamless shifts between past and present might have impressed on stage, they appear here as stilted as Michel Marc Bouchard's dialogue. The tactic of using theatrics to prick a hardened conscience clearly derives from *Hamlet*. But the cross-dressing teen re-enactment of the death of St Sebastian simply heaps artifice upon contrivance. The juvenile cast impresses, but, cinematically, this is a disappointment. DP [VIDEO] DVD

Brent Carver *Countess Marie Laure de Tilly* • Marcel Sabourin *Bishop Jean Bilodeau* • Matthew Ferguson *Young Jean Bilodeau* • Danny Gilmore *Count Vallier de Tilly* • Alexander Chapman *Lydie-Anne de Rozier* • Aubert Pallascio *Old Simon Doucet* ■ *Dir* John Greyson • *Scr* Michel Marc Bouchard, from his play *Les Feluettes ou La Répétition d'un Drame Romantique*

Lilies of the Field ★★★★ U

Drama 1963 · US · BW · 90mins

Sidney Poitier won only the second Oscar for a black actor in 24 years – the first went to Hattie McDaniel in *Gone with the Wind* – for his role here as an itinerant handyman helping German nuns build a chapel on barren Arizona land. James Poe's simplistic screenplay might have become sluggishly sentimental without Ralph Nelson's discerning direction and Poitier's sharp humour, and the film also benefits from the distinguished performance of Lilia Skala as the mother superior. TH [VIDEO] DVD

Sidney Poitier *Homer Smith* • Lilia Skala *Mother Maria* • Lisa Mann *Sister Gertrude* • Isa Crino *Sister Agnes* • Francesca Jarvis *Sister Albertine* • Pamela Branch *Sister Elizabeth* • Stanley Adams *Juan* • Dan Frazer *Father Murphy* • Ralph Nelson *Mr Ashton* ■ *Dir* Ralph Nelson • *Scr* James Poe, from the novel by William E Barrett

Lilith ★★★★

Drama 1964 · US · BW · 113mins

This is a disturbing and poetic study of mental illness, with Warren Beatty as the therapist who becomes drawn to patient Jean Seberg. Shot in lustrous black and white, and the last film to be directed by Robert Rossen, this is a hypnotic experience, a movie which simmers suggestively but never comes fully to the boil. Trashed by most critics on release, and a predictable box-office bomb, its reputation has grown over the years. AT

Warren Beatty *Vincent Bruce* • Jean Seberg *Lilith Arthur* • Peter Fonda *Stephen Evshevsky* • Kim Hunter *Bea Brice* • Anne Meacham *Yvonne Meaghan* • James Patterson *Dr Lavrier* • Jessica Walter *Laura* • Gene Hackman *Norman* • Robert Reilly *Bob Clayfield* • René Auberjonois *Howie* ■ *Dir* Robert Rossen • *Scr* Robert Rossen, from the novel by JR Salamanca

Lillian Russell ★★ U

Biographical musical
1940 · US · BW · 127mins

Alice Faye takes the title role in this plodding biopic of a famous and colourful entertainer. Starting in the 1880s, the movie is lavishly mounted and costumed – it was Oscar-nominated for best interior decoration – and includes a clutch of pleasingly appropriate songs. But aside from some production number highlights, the dreary, cliché-strewn script, combined with the otherwise alluring Faye's lack of acting talent, sinks the enterprise. RK

Alice Faye *Lillian Russell* • Don Ameche *Edward Solomon* • Henry Fonda *Alexander Moore* • Edward Arnold *Diamond Jim Brady* • Warren William *Jesse Lewisohn* • Leo Carrillo *Tony Pastor* • Helen Westley *Grandma Leonard* • Dorothy Peterson *Cynthia Leonard* • Una O'Connor *Marie* ■ *Dir* Irving Cummings • *Scr* William Anthony McGuire • *Cinematographer* Leon Shamroy • *Costume Designer* Travis Banton • *Set Decorator* Thomas Little

Lilo & Stitch ★★★★ U

Animated science-fiction comedy
2002 · US · Colour · 81mins

An innovative and quirky mix of comedy, family drama and fast-paced action, this Disney fantasy is as lush and lovely as its Hawaiian setting. Accompanied by a foot-tapping Elvis Presley soundtrack, the film pushes a message of multicultural equality and tolerance so all-encompassing that it even embraces extraterrestrials. In doing so, it turns lonely youngster Lilo's friendship with cute but naughty alien fugitive Stitch into a candy-coloured morality tale. Yet, whether it's Lilo's older sister fighting to keep her sibling out of care, or badly behaved Stitch learning the values of a tidy bedroom, the life lessons are sweet and easy to swallow. Followed by a straight-to-video spin-off, *Stitch! The Movie* (2003) and a TV series. SF [VIDEO] DVD

Daveigh Chase *Lilo* • Christopher Michael Sanders [Chris Sanders] *Stitch* • Tia Carrere *Nani* • David Ogden Stiers *Jumba* • Kevin McDonald *Pleakley* • Ving Rhames *Cobra Bubbles* • Zoe Caldwell *Grand Councilwoman* • Jason Scott Lee *David Kawena* ■ *Dir/Scr* Chris Sanders, Dean DeBlois

Lily in Love ★★ 15

Comedy 1985 · Hun/US · Colour · 102mins

Despite bullish performances from Christopher Plummer and Maggie Smith, the idea that a wife would not recognise her husband beneath some risibly unconvincing greasepaint, requires a suspension of disbelief that this stodgy film's smugness fails to persuade us to make. As the stage ham desperate to land the part of an Italian blonde in his screenwriter wife's new movie, Plummer sportingly debunks his own reputation. DP [VIDEO] DVD

Christopher Plummer *Fitzroy Wynn/Roberto Terranova* • Maggie Smith *Lily Wynn* • Elke Sommer *Alice Braun* • Adolph Green *Jerry Silber* • Szabo Sander *Teodor* ■ *Dir* Karoly Makk • *Scr* Frank Cucci, from the play *The Guardsman* by Ferenc Molnar

Lilya 4-Ever ★★★★ 18

Drama 2002 · Swe/Den · Colour · 104mins

Teenager Oksana Akinishina excels in this sobering study of life on the bottom rung. As the eponymous Lilya, her naive vulnerability is readily evident whether she's being cheeky to the Russian mother who abandons her to emigrate to the United States, exchanging insults with the classmates who think she's turned to prostitution, swooning over the stranger who promises her the moon or enduring the exploitation of the grotesques who populate her nightmare existence in Malmo. But it's in the company of the 14-year-old Volodya (Artiom Bogucharskij), a substance-abusing runaway, that the film finds the flicker of human warmth that makes its uncompromising realism all the more tragic. DP. In Russian, English and Swedish with subtitles. DVD

Oksana Akinishina *Lilya* • Artiom Bogucharskij *Volodya* • Elina Benenson *Natasha* • Lilia Sinkarjova *Aunt Anna* • Pavel Ponomarjov *Andrei* • Tomas Neumann *Witek* • Ljubov Agapova *Lilya's mother* ■ *Dir/Scr* Lukas Moodysson

Limbo ★★★

Drama 1972 · US · Colour · 111mins

Kate Jackson was married for only two weeks before her husband went to Vietnam and now she thinks he's dead and has fallen in love again; Kathleen Nolan has four children and believes her husband is a prisoner of the Vietcong; Katherine Justice refuses to believe her husband was killed in action. All three get flashbacks as they drive to the airport where one man is coming home. Written by two directors – Joan Micklin Silver and James Bridges – and stylishly made by the veteran Mark Robson, it soft-peddles the politics but puts its foot down for emotional impact. AT

Kate Jackson *Sandy Lawton* • Katherine Justice *Sharon Dornbeck* • Stuart Margolin *Phil Garrett* • Hazel Medina *Jane York* • Kathleen Nolan *Mary Kay Buell* • Russell Wiggins *Alan Weber* • Joan Murphy *Margaret Holroyd* ■ *Dir* Mark Robson • *Scr* Joan Micklin Silver, James Bridges

Limbo ★★ 15

Drama 1999 · US · Colour · 121mins

John Sayles is both a pivotal indie director and mainstream screenwriter for hire, and the two sides are evident in this jarring blend of social study and outdoor adventure. When exploring the conflicting relationships within a small Alaskan coastal community, the film brims with life. However, contrivance takes over once former fisherman David Strathairn, torch singer Mary Elizabeth Mastrantonio and her troubled teenage daughter Vanessa Martinez are stranded on a remote island. The film's hard-won sense of spirituality is no substitute for the engrossing melodrama that precedes it. DP. Contains swearing. [VIDEO] DVD

Mary Elizabeth Mastrantonio *Donna De Angelo* • David Strathairn *Joe Gastineau* • Vanessa Martinez *Noelle De Angelo* • Kris Kristofferson *Smilin' Jack* • Casey Siemaszko *Bobby Gastineau* ■ *Dir/Scr* John Sayles

Limelight ★★

Musical 1936 · UK · BW · 65mins

This British musical co-stars Arthur Tracy, popular on radio and record as the "Street Singer" but proving himself woefully inadequate as an actor, and Anna Neagle. Lavishly mounted by director Herbert Wilcox, the tale concerns a chorus girl (Neagle) who, in love with a busker (Tracy), helps him to success in the theatre, but complications ensue when he falls for a socialite. A syrupy and very British backstage drama. RK

Anna Neagle *Marjorie Kaye* • Arthur Tracy *Bob Grant* • Jane Winton *Ray Madison* • Ellis Jeffreys *Lady Madeleine* • Muriel George *Mrs Kaye* • Alexander Field *Alf Sparkes* • Antony Holles *Impresario* • William Freshman *Joe* ■ *Dir* Herbert Wilcox • *Scr* Laura Whetter

Limelight ★★★★ U

Comedy drama 1952 · US · BW · 136mins

Meant as a summation of his life and art, Charles Chaplin's last American film has some stunning set pieces of vaudeville comedy – one featuring his great rival, Buster Keaton – but an inordinate degree of self-pity. As a drunken has-been entertainer, Chaplin saves young dancer Claire Bloom from suicide and nurses her to success, though his own comeback is doomed by a world which has no place for pantomime. Featuring five of his children, it's a very personal indulgence that works best as a celebration of British music hall, not as an exposé of Chaplin's own grievances. TH [VIDEO] DVD

Charles Chaplin *Calvero* • Claire Bloom *Terry* • Nigel Bruce *Postant* • Buster Keaton *Piano accompanist* • Sydney Chaplin *Neville* • Norman Lloyd *Bodalink* • Andre Eglevsky *Harlequin* • Melissa Hayden *Columbine* • Charles Chaplin Jr *Clown* • Wheeler Dryden *Clown* • Marjorie Bennett *Mrs Alsop* • Geraldine Chaplin *Street urchin* • Michael Chaplin *Street urchin* • Josephine Chaplin *Street urchin* ■ *Dir/Scr* Charles Chaplin • *Music* Charles Chaplin

The Limey ★★★★ 18

Thriller 1999 · US · Colour · 85mins

The past lives of Terence Stamp and Peter Fonda underline and illuminate this Steven Soderbergh thriller. Stamp plays Wilson, an English ex-con out for revenge, while Fonda is Valentine, a millionaire record producer whom Wilson thinks caused the death of his daughter. The former is shown as a much younger man in flashbacks taken from Ken Loach's *Poor Cow* (1967), while Fonda is now of an age when he has to hire minders to do his dirty work for him. With its Chandleresque dialogue and machine gun resonance, this requiem for the hard man is in the top flight of gangster movies. TH. Contains violence, swearing. [VIDEO] DVD

Terence Stamp *Wilson* • Peter Fonda *Terry Valentine* • Lesley Ann Warren *Elaine* • Melissa George *Jennifer "Jenny" Wilson* • Luis Guzman *Ed* • Barry Newman *Jim Avery* • Joe Dallesandro *Uncle John* • Nicky Katt *Stacy* ■ *Dir* Steven Soderbergh • *Scr* Lem Dobbs

Limit Up ★★ PG

Comedy 1989 · US · Colour · 83mins

This is an uneven Faustian comedy, set against the backdrop of the modern-day stock market. Nancy Allen is the broker, continually passed over by her male colleagues, who strikes a pact with the Devil via emissary Danitra Vance but soon has second thoughts. A good supporting cast, which includes Dean Stockwell, Sally Kellerman and blues legend Ray Charles, is wasted, and the script and direction are toothless. JF

Nancy Allen *Casey Falls* • Brad Hall *Marty Callahan* • Rance Howard *Chuck Feeney* • Danitra Vance *Nike* • Ray Charles *Julius* • Dean Stockwell *Peter Oak* • Luana Anders *Teacher* • Sally Kellerman *Nightclub singer* ■ *Dir* Richard Martini • *Scr* Luana Anders, Richard Martini, from a story by Richard Martini

The Limping Man ★★

Crime drama 1953 · UK · BW · 76mins

Basically this is just another of those 1950s British B-thrillers in which an American visitor to England finds himself up to his neck in trouble from the moment he lands. This time Lloyd Bridges is the minor Hollywood star whose casting ensured an American release. An implausible story of murder and mystery unfolds, redeemed by a "twist" ending. The blacklisted Cy Endfield was reduced to working on films like this without credit alongside the named director, Charles de Lautour. AE

Lloyd Bridges *Frank Prior* • Moira Lister *Pauline* • Helene Cordet *Helene* • Leslie Phillips *Cameron* • Alan Wheatley *Inspector Braddock* • Bruce Beeby *Kendal Brown* ■ *Dir* Charles de Lautour, Cy Endfield • *Scr* Ian Stuart, Reginald Long, from a story by Anthony Verney

Linda Lovelace for President ★★

Sex comedy 1975 · US · Colour · 100mins

Infamous porn star Linda Lovelace had become a blue movie icon following her performance in *Deep Throat*, so there was no shortage of people keen to cash in on her notoriety. Director Claudio Guzmán cast the star as a version of herself in this sex fantasy in which the porn queen runs for President of the United State. A broad comedy brimming with racial insults, painful double entendres and suggestive situations. DF

Linda Lovelace • Fuddie Bagley *Abdul Ali Umagooma* • Val Bisoglio *Rev Billy Easter* • Jack DeLeon *Captain Neldor* • Mickey Dolenz [Micky Dolenz] *Le Fenwick* ■ *Dir* Claudio Guzmán • *Scr* Jack S Margolis

The Lindbergh Kidnapping Case ★★★

Drama based on a true story
1976 · US · Colour · 148mins

Anthony Hopkins won an Emmy for his portrayal of Bruno Hauptmann, the man convicted of and executed for the kidnapping of aviator Charles Lindbergh's infant son. Director Buzz Kulik sets the scene well in this involving TV movie, outlining how Lindbergh (played by Cliff De Young) became a national hero and how the whole of America was appalled by the abduction. Yet, Kulik's approach to the investigation of the case is less sure-footed, as he adopts the official line in accepting the evidence without bothering to question its circumstantial nature. DP

Anthony Hopkins *Bruno Richard Hauptmann* • Joseph Cotten *Dr Joseph Francis Condon* • Cliff De Young *Charles Lindbergh* • Sian Barbara Allen *Anne Morrow Lindbergh* • Martin Balsam *Edward J Reilly* • Denise Alexander *Violet Sharpe* • Keenan Wynn *Fred Huisache* • Walter Pidgeon *Judge Trenchard* ■ *Dir* Buzz Kulik • *Scr* JP Miller

The Lineup ★★★

Crime drama 1958 · US · BW · 86mins

This riveting low-budget thriller, shot on location in San Francisco, was completely overlooked on its original release, being taken for a ripoff of a TV series to which it is only loosely connected. It teams Eli Wallach with veteran character actor Robert Keith, as two ruthless killers carrying on didactic conversations while tracking down passengers from a boat who have been unwitting heroin-carriers. Cleverly written by Stirling Silliphant and brilliantly staged by action director Don Siegel, the film is notable for its tense car chase along the uncompleted elevated freeway. AE

Eli Wallach *Dancer* • Robert Keith (1) *Julian* • Warner Anderson *Lieutenant Guthrie* • Richard Jaeckel *Sandy McLain* • Mary LaRoche *Dorothy Bradshaw* • William Leslie *Larry Warner* • Emile Meyer *Inspector Al Quine* • Marshall Reed *Inspector Fred Asher* • Raymond Bailey *Philip Dressler* ■ *Dir* Don Siegel • *Scr* Stirling Silliphant

The Linguini Incident ★★ 15

Comedy drama 1991 · US · Colour · 104mins

A designer restaurant called Dali is the setting for this bizarre and ultimately unsuccessful comedy. Bartender David Bowie, elegant as ever, is paired with a more quirky than usual Rosanna Arquette, who works as a waitress. Romance does blossom eventually, but not before cash-strapped Bowie has masterminded a robbery at the restaurant. Combine this with Arquette's Houdini-like desire to truss herself up in a tank full of water, and you have a plot as unappealing as a bowl of soggy pasta. LH

Rosanna Arquette *Lucy* • David Bowie *Monte* • Eszter Balint *Vivian* • Andre Gregory *Dante* • Buck Henry *Cecil* • Viveca Lindfors *Miracle* • Marlee Matlin *Jeanette* • Lewis Arquette *Texas Joe* • Iman *Dali guest* ■ *Dir* Richard Shepard • *Scr* Richard Shepard, Tamara Brott

Link ★ 15

Horror thriller 1986 · UK · Colour · 99mins

Ever wondered what a horror movie would look like made as PG Tips commercial? The answer lies here in this oddity, in which American zoologist Elisabeth Shue arrives at professor Terence Stamp's remote house-cum-laboratory to work on his revolutionary simian theories. On the brink of a major breakthrough, he mysteriously disappears, and Shue is left in charge of three gifted chimpanzees. Her wards gradually revert to the laws of the jungle and start a campaign of ludicrous menace. AJ

Terence Stamp *Dr Steven Phillip* • Elisabeth Shue *Jane Chase* • Steven Pinner *David* • Richard Garnett *Dennis* • David O'Hara *Tom* • Kevin Lloyd *Bailey* • Locke *Link* ■ *Dir* Richard Franklin • *Scr* Everett DeRoche, from the story by Lee Zlotoff, Tom Ackerman

The Lion ★★ U

Drama 1962 · UK · Colour · 95mins

Concocted to indulge William Holden's love of Africa and its wildlife (he had his own private game ranch and co-owned the luxurious Mount Kenya Safari Lodge), this movie also indulges its star's interest in the actress Capucine. She plays his ex-wife, now married to white hunter Trevor Howard; there is also a heavily symbolic lion named "King" who struts around and befriends Holden's daughter. AT

William Holden (2) *Robert Hayward* • Trevor Howard *John Bullitt* • Capucine *Christine* • Pamela Franklin *Tina* ■ *Dir* Jack Cardiff • *Scr* Louis Kamp, Irene Kamp, from a novel by Joseph Kessel

The Lion Has Wings ★★★ U

Second World War documentary drama
1939 · UK · BW · 72mins

Produced with foresight by Alexander Korda, and hustled into cinemas a mere eight weeks after it started shooting, this propagandist feature attempts to predict what would happen if war broke out. The film falls into two halves. The first, brilliantly edited (by William Hornbeck) documentary section contrasts peaceful England with a Germany arming for war; the second, frankly, ludicrous fictional section has Merle Oberon (Mrs Korda) fretting over RAF hubby Ralph Richardson. Still interesting to see today. TS

Merle Oberon *Mrs Richardson* • Ralph Richardson *Wing Commander Richardson* • June Duprez *June* • Robert Douglas *Briefing Officer* ■ *Dir* Michael Powell, Brian Desmond Hurst, Adrian Brunel • *Scr* Adrian Brunel, EVH Emmett, from a story by Ian Dalrymple

The Lion in Winter ★★★★★ 15

Historical drama
1968 · UK · Colour · 128mins

Katharine Hepburn is on Oscar-winning form and sparring verbally with Oscar-nominated Peter O'Toole in this adaptation of James Goldman's play about Henry II and Eleanor of Aquitaine. Set mostly within the austere castle ramparts over the Christmas festival, it's a story of a family squabble that has geopolitical import, a medieval dynastic war. While the script and the performances are simply dazzling, it is notable, too, for the screen debuts of Timothy Dalton and Anthony Hopkins who, like O'Toole, was a protégé of Hepburn's. John Barry's beautiful, melancholic score won an Oscar. AT DVD

Peter O'Toole *King Henry II* • Katharine Hepburn *Queen Eleanor* • Jane Merrow *Princess Alais* • John Castle *Prince Geoffrey* • Timothy Dalton *King Philip of France* • Anthony Hopkins *Prince Richard* • Nigel Stock *William Marshall* • Nigel Terry *Prince John* ■ *Dir* Anthony Harvey • *Scr* James Goldman, from his play • *Cinematographer* Douglas Slocombe

A Lion Is in the Streets ★★★

Drama 1953 · US · Colour · 88mins

James Cagney had a few run-ins with the guardians of the Hollywood Production Code before he managed to get the green light to adapt Adria Locke Langley's novel about political corruption in the Deep South. Loosely based on the life of Louisiana governor Huey Long, the film had to depart from the ending in the book to satisfy Hollywood's vision of the American Way. Cagney and director Raoul Walsh were old sparring partners, but this picture lacks the punch and pace of earlier outings, a fact attributable to Luther Davis's pedestrian script. DP

James Cagney *Hank Martin* • Barbara Hale *Verity Wade* • Anne Francis *Flamingo* • Warner Anderson *Jules Bolduc* • John McIntire *Jeb Brown* • Jeanne Cagney *Jennie Brown* • Lon Chaney Jr *Spurge* • Frank McHugh *Rector* ■ *Dir* Raoul Walsh • *Scr* Luther Davis, from the novel by Adria Locke Langley

The Lion King ★★★★ U

Animated musical adventure
1994 · US · Colour · 84mins

This crowd-pleasing cartoon musical from Walt Disney had enormous box-office appeal, and proved so popular that it was adapted as a spectacular stage show. For the children there's the story of how a lion cub, exiled by his wicked uncle, achieves his destiny; for grown-ups there's a visual feast of exciting animation work and some good Elton John songs. Voices range from Whoopi Goldberg to Rowan Atkinson, with Jeremy Irons a vocal standout as the evil uncle Scar. Two straight-to-video sequels (*The Lion King: Simba's Pride, The Lion King 3: Hakuna Matata*) followed. TH DVD

Jonathan Taylor Thomas *Young Simba* • Matthew Broderick *Adult Simba* • James Earl Jones *Mufasa* • Jeremy Irons *Scar* • Moira Kelly *Adult Nala* • Niketa Calame *Young Nala* • Ernie Sabella *Pumbaa* • Nathan Lane *Timon* • Robert Guillaume *Rafiki* • Rowan Atkinson *Zazu* • Madge Sinclair *Sarabi* • Whoopi Goldberg *Shenzi the Hyena* • Richard "Cheech" Marin *Banzai the Hyena* • Jim Cummings *Ed the Hyena* ■ *Dir* Roger Allers, Rob Minkoff • *Scr* Irene Mecchi, Jonathan Roberts, Linda Woolverton

Lion of Oz ★★ U

Animated adventure
2000 · Can · Colour · 74mins

This animated adventure – billed as a prequel to the events of *The Wizard of Oz* – suffers from an excess of contrivance. Yet the vocal talents on duty are impressive. Jason Priestley voices the heroic circus lion who becomes increasingly cowardly on his travels, while Jane Horrocks plays the little girl who helps him resist the wiles of Lynn Redgrave's Wicked Witch of the East. Tim Curry, Don DeLuise and Bob Goldthwait add to the fun. But don't expect the cartoon equivalent of *The Wizard of Oz*; this is much flimsier in its construction. DP DVD

Jason Priestley *The Lion* • Lynn Redgrave *The Witch* • Tim Curry *Captain Fitzgerald* • Kathy Griffin *Caroline* • Jane Horrocks *Wimsik* • Bob Goldthwait [Bobcat Goldthwait] *Silly Ozbul* • Dom DeLuise *Oscar Diggs* ■ *Dir* Tim Deacon • *Scr* Elana Lesser, Cliff Ruby, from the novel *The Lion of Oz and the Badge of Courage* by Roger S Baum

Lion of the Desert ★★★★ 15

War adventure 1981 · UK · Colour · 156mins

Financed by Colonel Gaddafi, this paean to Libya's national hero, Omar Mukhtar, is often stirring stuff, shot in stunning desert scenery and with hordes of extras not seen since the days of *Lawrence of Arabia*. Mukhtar was a fervent nationalist and Bedouin peasant who resisted Mussolini's annexation of Libya in the 1930s. As Mukhtar, Anthony Quinn is predictable but believable. Rod Steiger is very Rod Steiger as Mussolini, while Oliver Reed is often chilling as Musso's muscle man. There's a silly love interest patched in, but overall this is a fine film that must have been a nightmare to make. AT DVD

Anthony Quinn *Omar Mukhtar* • Oliver Reed *General Rodolfo Graziani* • Irene Papas *Mabrouka* • Raf Vallone *Colonel Diodiece* • Rod Steiger *Benito Mussolini* • John Gielgud *Sharif El Gariani* • Andrew Keir *Salem* ■ *Dir* Moustapha Akkad • *Scr* HAL Craig

Lionheart ★★ PG

Fantasy adventure
1986 · US · Colour · 100mins

A curious drama that attempts to interest younger viewers in a little medieval history. Sadly, neither director Franklin J Schaffner nor his star Eric Stoltz has any idea how to pitch the story of a knight who interrupts his quest to join King Richard in the Holy Land to help a gang of bedraggled kids from being sold into slavery by Gabriel Byrne. The result is a sort of live-action cartoon, but with none of the charm. DP

Eric Stoltz *Robert Nerra* • Gabriel Byrne *Black Prince* • Nicola Cowper *Blanche* • Dexter Fletcher *Michael* • Deborah Barrymore *Mathilda* • Nicholas Clay *Charles De Montfort* • Bruce Purchase *Simon Nerra* • Neil Dickson *King Richard* • Chris Pitt *Odo* ■ *Dir* Franklin J Schaffner • *Scr* Menno Meyjes, Richard Outten, from a story by Menno Meyjes

L

Lions Love ★

Comedy 1969 · US · Colour · 115mins

Irritating beyond belief, this will be totally unwatchable and incomprehensible to anyone who wasn't around in the 1960s and the American underground at that time. Directed by Agnès Varda, it's a skew-eyed looked at Hollywood in which American indie director Shirley Clarke arrives to make a movie. She hangs out with some actors, gets turned down by a producer, nearly commits suicide in an avant garde sort of way, watches a tape of the Kennedy assassination... AT

Viva *Harlow* • Richard Bright *Billy the Kid* • James Rado • Carlos Clarens • Billie Dixon ■ *Dir/Scr* Agnès Varda

Lips of Blood ★★★ 18

Erotic horror 1975 · Fr · Colour · 86mins

Jean Rollin is at his best when combining erotica and horror, but there's surprisingly little explicit action in this atmospheric tale of obsessive desire, in which Jean-Lou Philippe's desire to recall the significance of a castle he sees in a photograph results in his opening the graves of Montmartre and unleashing a bevy of female vampires. Anne Brilland's performance as the woman in white who haunts Philippe's dreams is ethereal and gives this intense, if occasionally over-indulgent picture its melancholic air. DP. In French with English subtitles. Contains nudity, violence. DVD

Jean-Lou Philippe *Young man* • Annie Brilland [Annie Belle] *Young woman* • Nathalie Perrey • Martine Grimaud • Catherine Castel *Twin vampire* • Marie-Pierre Castel *Twin vampire* • Paul Bisciglia *Psychiatrist* ■ *Dir* Jean Rollin • *Scr* Jean-Lou Philippe, Jean Rollin

L

Lipstick ★★★ 18

Drama 1976 · US · Colour · 82mins

This purported to be a serious drama about the crime of rape but is actually just an up-market exploitation movie, glossily directed by Lamont Johnson and featuring an eye-catching screen debut by Ernest Hemingway's grand-daughter, Margaux. She plays a fashion model who is raped by apparently nice music teacher Chris Sarandon. Margaux's sister, Mariel, also makes her screen debut as one of Sarandon's pupils and Anne Bancroft plays Margaux's lawyer who takes the case to court. A schlocky resolution turns Margaux into Charles Bronson. AT

Margaux Hemingway *Chris McCormick* • Chris Sarandon *Gordon Stuart* • Perry King *Steve Edison* • Anne Bancroft *Carla Bondi* • John Bennett Perry *Martin McCormick* • Mariel Hemingway *Kathy McCormick* • Robin Gammell *Nathan Cartwright* ■ *Dir* Lamont Johnson • *Scr* David Rayfiel

Liquid Sky ★★ 18

Science-fiction fantasy
1982 · US · Colour · 107mins

A dirty, funny, perverse and pretentiously over-long look at New York's punk-chic drug culture. An alien spacecraft lands on a Manhattan skyscraper and its inhabitants quickly get hooked on the powdered and sexual thrills indulged in by everyone populating the sordid landscape. Anne Carlisle, playing both male and female leads (don't ask, it's art!), then uses the aliens to vaporise her enemies. Indulgent and stylistically over the top to a distracting degree. AJ

Anne Carlisle *Margaret/Jimmy* • Paula Sheppard *Adrian* • Bob Brady *Owen* • Susan Doukas *Sylvia* • Otto von Wernherr *Johann* • Elaine C Grove *Katherine* ■ *Dir* Slava Tsukerman • *Scr* Slava Tsukerman, Nina V Kerova, Anne Carlisle

The Liquidator ★★ PG

Spy drama 1966 · UK · Colour · 104mins

One of dozens of Bond ripoffs, right down to Shirley Bassey belting out the title number. Aussie actor Rod Taylor plays a hitman and former soldier who is hired by MI6, in the person of Trevor Howard, to do some liquidating. Taylor, currently a waiter in a Paris bistro, sub-contracts the work out, leading to various complications, including the near assassination of Prince Philip. Very swinging 1960s in tone, with jet-set locations, snazzy cartoon titles and willing ladies in mini-skirts. AT

Rod Taylor *Boysie Oakes* • Trevor Howard *Mostyn* • Jill St John *Iris MacIntosh* • Wilfrid Hyde White *Chief* • David Tomlinson *Quadrant* • Eric Sykes *Griffen* • Akim Tamiroff *Sheriek* • Derek Nimmo *Fly* • Jeremy Lloyd *Young man* ■ *Dir* Jack Cardiff • *Scr* Peter Yeldham, from the novel by John Gardner

Lisa and the Devil ★★★ 18

Horror 1976 · It · Colour · 91mins

Mario Bava's subtle and sophisticated spellbinder is his most personal movie, one putting into focus his own dark obsessions and fears of manipulation. But for years the only available version of this movie was titled *The House of Exorcism* – the jumbled concoction it became when it was extensively recut and new footage added in a post-*Exorcist* frenzy. (Hence the Mickey Lion pseudonym Bava insisted on.) Yet Elke Sommer gives one of her most endearing performances as the tourist stumbling into a house filled with all manner of depravity, in this demonic possession case history. AJ DVD

Telly Savalas *Leandro* • Elke Sommer *Lisa Reiner/Elena* • Sylva Koscina *Sophia Lehar* • Alida Valli *Max's mother* ■ *Dir* Mickey Lion [Mario Bava] • *Scr* Alfredo Leone, Cecilio Paniagua

Lisboa ★★★

Road movie thriller
1999 · Sp/Arg · Colour · 99mins

Set along the Hispano-Portuguese border, Antonio Hernández's road thriller gets off to an arresting start, with Sergi Lopez's video salesman and Carmen Maura's runaway wife instantly developing a rapport that's every bit as intriguing as her seemingly implausible tale of financial misdeeds and callous assassinations. But as various members of her family (each one a sly Mafia caricature) catch up with them and mischievously muddy the water, the tension seeps away to be replaced by a more sinister tone. Diverting but underdeveloped. DP. In Spanish with English subtitles.

Carmen Maura *Berta* • Sergi Lopez *Joao* • Federico Luppi *Jose Luis* • Laia Marull *Veronica* • Antonio Birabent *Carlos* • Saturnino Garcia *Bruno* ■ *Dir* Antonio Hernández • *Scr* Antonio Hernández, Enrique Braso

Lisbon ★★★ PG

Thriller 1956 · US · Colour · 86mins

Republic sent star/producer/director Ray Milland to Portugal to unlock frozen funds and shoot this slack but enjoyable melodrama that made early use of the studio's own variant of CinemaScope, a process called Naturama. Milland chose Maureen O'Hara and suave Claude Rains as his co-stars, but it's a pity the story – a scheming O'Hara uses Milland through Rains to "rescue" her elderly husband from behind the Iron Curtain – isn't stronger. Nelson Riddle's adaptation of a Portuguese number for the title music is catchy. AE

Ray Milland *Captain Robert John Evans* • Maureen O'Hara *Sylvia Merrill* • Claude Rains *Aristides Mavros* • Yvonne Furneaux *Maria Maddalena Masanet* • Francis Lederer *Serafim* • Percy Marmont *Lloyd Merrill* • Jay Novello *Joao Casimiro Fonseca* ■ *Dir* R Milland [Ray Milland] • *Scr* John Tucker Battle, from a story by Martin Rackin

Lisbon Story ★★

Drama
1994 · Ger/Por · BW and Colour · 105mins

Wim Wenders directs this movie about a sound editor who receives a postcard begging him to help his director friend Patrick Bauchau complete his movie in Portugal. Editor Rüdiger Vogler heads south in his battered car only to find the director's flat empty. He wanders through Lisbon, filming it and involving himself in the city's wonderful music. Bauchau eventually surfaces and they complete the film. A shaggy dog story minus incident, directed without humour or vitality. BB. In English, German and Portuguese with subtitles.

Rüdiger Vogler *Phillip Winter* • Patrick Bauchau *Friedrich Monroe* • Teresa Salgueiro *Teresa* • Manoel de Oliveira ■ *Dir/Scr* Wim Wenders

The List ★★ 18

Thriller 2000 · Can · Colour · 88mins

Never the most persuasive of performers, Ryan O'Neal got by on boyish charm. But now in his 60s, he's left somewhat exposed by projects that call for more than a modicum of talent. He's not helped here by the sheer implausibility of director Sylvain Guy's screenplay, in which a respected judge thinks nothing of appropriating a key piece of evidence in the trial of a high-class hooker who is threatening to reveal the contents of her little black book. However, he appears the master of nuance beside Mädchen Amick. DP

Ryan O'Neal *Richard Miller* • Roc Lafortune *Dom Roselli* • Mädchen Amick *Gabrielle Mitchell* • Ben Gazzara *DA Bernard Salman* • Catherine Blythe *Elizabeth Miller* ■ *Dir/Scr* Sylvain Guy

The List of Adrian Messenger ★★★

Murder mystery 1963 · US · BW · 97mins

John Huston's bizarre take on *Kinds Hearts and Coronets* – with stars such as Burt Lancaster, Robert Mitchum, Tony Curtis and Frank Sinatra behind make-up for cameo roles – is a gleeful black comedy for most of its running time. An unknown killer begins to eliminate 11 men who knew him as a wartime traitor, and is planning to kill the boy who is the only obstacle to his acquisition of a huge fortune. As the plot wobbles into self-indulgence, it becomes more of a hoot for the cast than the audience. TH

George C Scott *Anthony Gethryn* • Dana Wynter *Lady Jocelyn Bruttenholm* • Clive Brook *Marquis of Gleneyre* • Herbert Marshall *Sir Wilfred Lucas* • Jacques Roux *Raoul LeBorg* • Bernard Archard *Inspector Pike* • Gladys Cooper *Mrs Karoudjian* • Walter Anthony Huston [Tony Huston] *Derek* • John Merivale *Adrian Messenger* • Marcel Dalio *Max* • John Huston *Huntsman* • Kirk Douglas *George Brougham* • Tony Curtis *Italian* • Burt Lancaster *Woman* • Robert Mitchum *Jim Slattery* • Frank Sinatra *Gypsy stableman* ■ *Dir* John Huston • *Scr* Anthony Veiller, from the novel by Philip MacDonald

Listen ★★

Erotic thriller 1996 · US · Colour · 101mins

This kinky concoction is hardly the most complicated of whodunnits, but Brooke Langton gives a spirited performance as the interior designer who suspects that the killer who's been preying on callers to an erotic chat line may live in her building. Joel Wyner provides some glamour as her hunky neighbour, but the real fireworks come from Sarah G Buxton as her one-time lesbian lover. DP. Contains sex scenes, swearing, violence, nudity.

Brooke Langton *Sarah Ross* • Sarah G Buxton [Sarah Buxton] *Krista Barron* • Gordon Currie *Jake Taft* • Andy Romano *Detective Sam Steinmann* • Joel Wyner *Randy Wilkes* • Evan Taylor *Detective Louis Penny* ■ *Dir* Gavin Wilding • *Scr* Jonas Quastel, Michael Bafaro

Listen, Darling ★★★

Romantic comedy 1938 · US · BW · 72mins

Mary Astor is a widowed mother struggling to support her children is tempted to marry a pompous, unattractive banker. Daughter Judy Garland and pal Freddie Bartholomew kidnap her in the family trailer to go in search of a more suitable match, and find two possibilities in devil-may-care Walter Pidgeon and kindly millionaire Alan Hale. Fresh and charming, this comedy has a reliable adult cast and terrific performances from Garland, Bartholomew and little Scotty Beckett as the incorrigible small brother. RK

Judy Garland *Pinkie Wingate* • Freddie Bartholomew *Buzz Mitchell* • Mary Astor *Dottie Wingate* • Walter Pidgeon *Richard Thurlow* • Alan Hale *JJ Slattery* • Scotty Beckett *Billie Wingate* • Barnett Parker *Abercrombie* • Gene Lockhart *Mr Drubbs* • Charles Grapewin [Charley Grapewin] *Uncle Joe* ■ *Dir* Edwin L Marin • *Scr* Elaine Ryan, Anne Morrison Chapin, from a story by Katherine Brush

Listen to Me ★ 15

Drama 1989 · US · Colour · 105mins

Roy Scheider oversees a bunch of squabbling students in a convoluted tale concerning a college debating competition. The final debate – on the morality of abortion – is due to be argued in front of Supreme Court judges, but this takes a back seat to the tribulations of the kids. Director Douglas Day Stewart fails to convey the passion and intellectual excitement of the debate in this cliché-ridden movie. LH

Kirk Cameron *Tucker Muldowney* • Jami Gertz *Monica Tomanski* • Roy Scheider *Charlie Nichols* • Amanda Peterson *Donna Lumis* • Tim Quill *Garson McKellar* • George Wyner *Dean Schwimmer* • Anthony Zerbe *Senator McKellar* • Christopher Atkins *Bruce Arlington* ■ *Dir/Scr* Douglas Day Stewart

Listen Up: the Lives of Quincy Jones ★★★ 15

Music documentary
1990 · US · Colour · 110mins

The first black composer to score mainstream Hollywood movies and the recipient of countless Grammys and six Oscar nominations, Quincy Jones has spent his career at the top. The same can't be said for his personal life. Deprived of his mother's love because of her mental illness, he has rarely enjoyed harmonious relationships with women, while he has twice required brain surgery. Ellen Weissbrod's documentary reveals Jones as a man of regrets behind the cheery façade. But, as fascinating as he is, the film lacks focus, meandering between recollections and tributes like a musical mystery tour. DP. Contains swearing.

Dir Ellen Weissbrod

Lisztomania ★ 18

Biographical fantasy
1975 · UK · Colour · 98mins

With *The Devils*, *The Music Lovers*, *Mahler* and *Tommy*, Ken Russell created a very powerful style that intimidated producers and divided the critics. However, he came a cropper with this ugly, migraine-inducing and mind-numbing bore. Liszt is here portrayed by pop idol Roger Daltrey of the Who; Paul Nicholas plays Richard Wagner, while Ringo Starr is a natural as the Pope. The result is an epic of self-loathing, self-parody and self-destruction. AT [VIDEO]

Roger Daltrey *Franz Liszt* • Sara Kestelman *Princess Carolyn* • Paul Nicholas *Richard Wagner* • Fiona Lewis *Countess Marie* • Veronica Quilligan *Cosima* • Nell Campbell *Olga* • Andrew Reilly *Hans von Bulow* • Ringo Starr *Pope* ■ *Dir/Scr* Ken Russell • *Producer* Roy Baird, David Puttnam

Little Annie Rooney ★★★

Silent comedy drama
1925 · US · BW · 93mins

A characteristic Mary Pickford picture, this piece of Irish-American whimsy presents her, at age 32, as the resourceful, impish, curly-headed 12-year-old who looks after her brother and her widowed father, a cop. When the latter is killed, little Annie and her band of neighbourhood ragamuffins capture the villains, while Annie gives blood to save the life of a wounded ruffian, played by William Haines. Under William Beaudine's directorial guidance, Pickford had another hit that condemned her to remain in curls. AE

Mary Pickford *Little Annie Rooney* • William Haines *Joe Kelly* • Walter James *Officer Rooney* • Gordon Griffith *Tim Rooney* ■ *Dir* William Beaudine • *Scr* Hope Loring, Louis D Lighton, from the story by Katherine Hennessey

The Little Ark ★★★

Adventure 1971 · Neth · Colour · 85mins

James B Clark wound down his 36-year career with this arduous Dutch adventure. Something of an animal expert, having previously handled *The Sad Horse*, *The Dog of Flanders* and *Flipper*, Clark was the ideal choice for this adaptation, in which several barnyard animals face the perils of a rampaging flood, together with their plucky owners, Philip Frame and Genevieve Ambas. With Theodore Bikel grumpily amiable as the old skipper who turns his houseboat into an ark, this should appeal to the discriminating pre-teen. DP

Theodore Bikel *Captain* • Philip Frame *Jan* • Genevieve Ambas *Adinda* • Max Croiset *Father Grijpma* • Johan De Slaa *Cook, "UK 516"* ■ *Dir* James B Clark • *Scr* Joanna Crawford, from the novel by Jan De Hartog

Little Big League ★★★ PG

Sports comedy 1994 · US · Colour · 115mins

This amiable wish-fulfilment comedy is about a 12-year-old kid (Luke Edwards) who inherits a Minnesota baseball team and decides he could do a better job than their current manager. If you can accept that grown sportsmen would take orders from a little pipsqueak, then the film will touch a few bases. Edwards conveys a real passion for the game and the script has more time for character development than your average slice of sporting life. JC [VIDEO]

Luke Edwards *Billy Heywood* • Timothy Busfield *Lou Collins* • John Ashton *Mac MacNally* • Ashley Crow *Jenny Heywood* • Kevin Dunn *Arthur Goslin* • Billy L Sullivan *Chuck Lobert* • Miles Feulner *Joey Smith* • Jonathan Silverman *Jim Bowers* • Dennis Farina *George O'Farrell* • Jason Robards *Thomas Heywood* ■ *Dir* Andrew Scheinman • *Scr* Gregory K Pincus, Adam Scheinman, from a story by Gregory K Pincus

Little Big Man ★★★★ 15

Epic western 1970 · US · Colour · 133mins

Having presented an alternative view of the gangster era in *Bonnie and Clyde*, director Arthur Penn re-examined some of the most cherished myths of the Old West in this sprawling, handsome and ceaselessly sly tragicomedy. While Dustin Hoffman dominates the film as the 121-year-old who claims to be the sole survivor of Custer's last stand at the Little Bighorn, the dignified, Oscar-nominated performance of Chief Dan George is equally noteworthy. One or two of Hoffman's encounters with the mavericks, hypocrites and fools of the frontier hang heavy, but this is an ambitious, offbeat and thoroughly provocative picture. DP [VIDEO] DVD

Dustin Hoffman *Jack Crabb* • Faye Dunaway *Mrs Pendrake* • Martin Balsam *Allardyce T Merriweather* • Richard Mulligan *General George A Custer* • Chief Dan George *Old Lodge Skins* • Jeff Corey *Wild Bill Hickok* • Amy Eccles [Aimee Eccles] *Sunshine* • Kelly Jean Peters *Olga* ■ *Dir* Arthur Penn • *Scr* Calder Willingham, from the novel by Thomas Berger

Little Bigfoot ★★ PG

Fantasy adventure
1995 · US · Colour · 92mins

A cheap and cheerful cash-in on *Bigfoot and the Hendersons*, with director Art Camacho upping the cuteness stakes by making the creature a baby. Ross Malinger plays the child who makes friends with Bigfoot Jr as the pair attempt to thwart the plans of a ruthless businessman. There are some reliable supporting turns from grown-ups such as PJ Soles and Matt McCoy, and children will love the cuddly creature. JF [VIDEO]

Ross Malinger *Payton Shoemaker* • PJ Soles *Carolyn Shoemaker* • Kenneth Tigar *Mr Largo* • Joseph Gritto *Little Bigfoot* • Matt McCoy *Sheriff Cliffton* • Caitlin Barrett *Maggie Shoemaker* ■ *Dir* Art Camacho • *Scr* Richard Preston Jr, from a story by Scott McAboy

Little Black Book ★★ 12

Romantic comedy
2004 · US · Colour · 102mins

If you can believe Brittany Murphy as the associate producer on a daytime talk show, you'll swallow any of this far-fetched nonsense. Murphy plays a dizzy 20-something who is egged on by her co-worker (Holly Hunter) to delve into the secrets held within her boyfriend's electronic organiser. Murphy's clumsy charm is engaging, while the role of self-serving confidante showcases Hunter's underused aptitude for comedy. But what starts off as a cute, if dumb, exploration of female insecurities soon becomes increasingly cringeworthy. SF. Contains sexual references. DVD

Brittany Murphy *Stacy Holt* • Holly Hunter *Barb* • Ron Livingston *Derek* • Julianne Nicholson *Joyce* • Kathy Bates *Kippie Kann* • Stephen Tobolowsky *Carl* • Kevin Sussman *Ira* ■ *Dir* Nick Hurran • *Scr* Melissa Carter, Elisa Bell, from a story by Melissa Carter

Little Boy Lost ★★★ U

Drama 1953 · US · BW · 94mins

Bing Crosby acquits himself admirably in this non-musical (though he does perform a handful of songs) in one of his few dramatic roles. He plays an American news reporter who returns to France after the Second World War to find his "lost" son. Crosby is well supported by a splendid French cast, including Nicole Maurey and little Christian Fourcade, as the boy he finds in an orphanage and hopes is his son. Made in France, the film is a pleasant, but modest, tear-jerker. RB

Bing Crosby *Bill Wainwright* • Claude Dauphin *Pierre Verdier* • Christian Fourçade *Jean* • Gabrielle Dorziat *Mother Superior* • Nicole Maurey *Lisa Garret* • Collette Dereal *Nelly* • Georgette Anys *Madame Quilleboeuf* ■ *Dir* George Seaton • *Scr* George Seaton, from the novel by Marghanita Laski

Little Buddha ★★★ PG

Religious drama
1993 · Fr/UK · Colour · 117mins

Buddhism has in recent years attracted the attention of big-name directors, with Martin Scorsese's 1997 homage to the Dalai Lama in *Kundun* preceded by this hymn to the faith from Bernardo Bertolucci. The drama comprises two parallel stories set 2,500 years apart: in one, Keanu Reeves plays Prince Siddhartha, who became the Buddha. In the other, an American boy is chosen as one of three children who could be the reincarnation of a lama. Although the contrast between the old and new cultures is handled well and Bertolucci's movie looks stunning, Reeves is horribly miscast in the pivotal role and Bridget Fonda is wasted in the uninspiring modern-day part of the tale. TH [VIDEO]

Keanu Reeves *Prince Siddhartha* • Ying Ruocheng *Lama Norbu* • Chris Isaak *Dean Conrad* • Bridget Fonda *Lisa Conrad* • Alex Weisendanger *Jesse Conrad* • Raju Lal *Raju* ■ *Dir* Bernardo Bertolucci • *Scr* Rudy Wurlitzer, Mark Peploe, from a story by Bernardo Bertolucci • *Cinematographer* Vittorio Storaro • *Music* Ryuichi Sakamoto

Little Caesar ★★★★ PG

Crime drama 1931 · US · BW · 75mins

This classic gangster picture established the legendary Edward G Robinson as one of the most unlikely movie stars, in a role based on real-life mobster Al Capone. This tough-as-nails crime melodrama consolidated the movie-making style begun by James Cagney's *The Public Enemy* the same year at Warner Bros, the studio that specialised in such tales. Robinson is so scene-stealingly good that one tends to forget the excellence of the rest of the cast, particularly carefree Douglas Fairbanks Jr and caustic Glenda Farrell. But nobody will ever forget the finale: "Mother of God, is this the end of Rico?" TS [VIDEO] DVD

Edward G Robinson *Cesare Enrico Bandello* • Douglas Fairbanks Jr *Joe Massara* • Glenda Farrell *Olga Strassoff* • William Collier Jr *Tony Passa* • Ralph Ince *Diamond Pete Montana* • George E Stone *Otero* • Thomas Jackson [Thomas E Jackson] *Lieutenant Tom Flaherty* • Stanley Fields *Sam Vettori* ■ *Dir* Mervyn LeRoy • *Scr* Francis Edward Faragoh, Robert N Lee, from the novel by WR Burnett

Little City ★★★ 15

Romantic comedy drama
1997 · US · Colour · 86mins

Set in San Francisco instead of Manhattan, it's one of those easy-on-the-eye and easier-on-the-brain tales of couples breaking up and getting together that you imagine Woody Allen would write if he had had a frontal lobotomy. Jon Bon Jovi is cute as the guy sleeping with Annabella Sciorra, while she also sees his best friend (Josh Charles), and Penelope Ann Miller, Joanna Going and JoBeth Williams are just some of the other people entangled in this relationship confusion. JB [VIDEO]

Jon Bon Jovi *Kevin* • Josh Charles *Adam* • Joanna Going *Kate* • Annabella Sciorra *Nina* • Penelope Ann Miller *Rebecca* • JoBeth Williams *Anne* ■ *Dir/Scr* Roberto Benabib

The Little Colonel ★★★ U

Musical drama
1935 · US · BW and Colour · 82mins

Talented moppet Shirley Temple was a huge star when this glutinous confection was made, the first of four movies she released the same year. Temple herself is the "Little Colonel" of the title, having won the heart of a regiment. It's a hard heart that won't be moved by Temple bringing together crusty old Lionel Barrymore and sweet Evelyn Venable. TS

Shirley Temple *Lloyd Sherman, The Little Colonel* • Lionel Barrymore *Colonel Lloyd* • Evelyn Venable *Elizabeth Lloyd Sherman* • John Lodge *Jack Sherman* • Sidney Blackmer *Swazey* • Alden Chase *Hull* • William Burress *Dr Scott* • David O'Brien [Dave O'Brien] *Frank Randolph* • Hattie McDaniel *Mom Beck* • Geneva Williams *Maria* ■ *Dir* David Butler • *Scr* William Conselman, from the story by Annie Fellows Johnston

The Little Convict ★★ U

Part-animated adventure
1980 · Aus · Colour · 76mins

Inspired by the real-life re-created location of Old Sydney Town, Australia, director Yoram Gross commissioned his *Dot and the Kangaroo* writer John Palmer to come up with this animated original. The amiable tale involves a group of convict deportees, a teenage lad and their adventures. Rolf Harris links all this, singing period songs such as *Seth Davey* and *The Wild Colonial Boy*, and appears as the on-screen narrator (live, not animated). TS [VIDEO]

Rolf Harris *Grandpa* ■ *Dir* Yoram Gross • *Scr* John Palmer

Little Darlings ★★★ 15

Drama 1980 · US · Colour · 90mins

At summer camp, streetwise tough Kristy McNichol and rich brat Tatum O'Neal bet on who can lose her virginity first. McNichol sets her sights on mumbling Matt Dillon while O'Neal tries to seduce Armand Assante, one of the camp instructors. Director Ronald F Maxwell's teen box-office hit veers from crude humour to cute sentimentality with such breathless aplomb that it takes the edge off what could have become merely exploitative material in less dextrous hands. Worth watching for McNichol alone who is funny and sensitive. AJ [VIDEO]

Tatum O'Neal *Ferris Whitney* • Kristy McNichol *Angel Bright* • Armand Assante *Gary Callahan* • Matt Dillon *Randy* • Krista Errickson *Cinder* ■ *Dir* Ronald F Maxwell • *Scr* Kimi Peck, Dalene Young, from a story by Kimi Peck

Little Dieter Needs to Fly ★★★

Documentary
1997 · Fr/UK/Ger · Colour · 80mins

Werner Herzog's personality always dominates his documentaries. Consequently, his curiosity is as much to the fore as Dieter Dengler's memory in this biographical study that will outrage the purists with its unconventional approach to truth. Raised in poverty in post-Nazi Germany, Dengler emigrated to the United States aged 18 to fulfil his flying ambitions. However, his stint in the USAF resulted in him being shot down over Laos and tortured by his captors before he managed to escape. Some of the reconstructions may seem extreme, but Dengler seems to trust the director implicitly and, moreover, they chime in with Herzog's perennial fixation with obsession. DP. In English and German with subtitles.

Werner Herzog *Narrator* ■ *Dir/Scr* Werner Herzog

Little Dorrit ★★★★★ U

Period drama 1987 · UK · Colour · 343mins

Running nearly six hours, this monumental reworking of Dickens is divided into two parts – *Nobody's Fault* and *Little Dorrit's Story* – with much of the action of the first half being repeated in the second, so that we see the unfolding drama from the different perspectives of its two main protagonists, the bashful Arthur Clennam and Little Dorrit herself, who has been raised by her father in the Marshalsea debtors' prison. Christine Edzard not only directed and scripted the film, but she also made many of the costumes and, along with her husband Richard Goodwin, built the sets at the warehouse in London's Rotherhithe that is both their home and their studio. The huge cast is

L

superb, with Derek Jacobi, Sarah Pickering and Alec Guinness outstanding. DP

Derek Jacobi *Arthur Clennam* • Alec Guinness *William Dorrit* • Sarah Pickering *Little Dorrit* • Cyril Cusack *Frederick Dorrit* • Joan Greenwood *Mrs Clennam* • Max Wall *Flintwinch* • Patricia Hayes *Affery* • Miriam Margolyes *Flora Finching* • Roshan Seth *Mr Pancks* ■ *Dir* Christine Edzard • *Scr* Christine Edzard, from the novel by Charles Dickens

The Little Drummer Girl ★★★ 15

Spy drama 1984 · US · Colour · 124mins

Diane Keaton is still in eye-flutteringly winsome mode seven years after Woody Allen's *Annie Hall*, so she never quite convinces here as the politically-correct actress who's recruited by Israeli Intelligence to infiltrate a Palestinian terrorist group. John le Carré's bestseller, from which this is adapted, has many different character shades, but director George Roy Hill opts for broader strokes of near caricature that suit Klaus Kinski's strident performance as the Israeli agent in charge of Keaton's enrolment. Too much talk slows the pace from urgency to languor. TH

Diane Keaton *Charlie* • Klaus Kinski *Kurtz* • Yorgo Voyagis *Joseph* • Sami Frey *Khalil* • David Suchet *Mesterbein* • Eli Danker *Litvak* • Ben Levine *Dimitri* • Michael Cristofer *Tayeh* • Bill Nighy *Al* • Anna Massey *Chairwoman* ■ *Dir* George Roy Hill • *Scr* Loring Mandel, from the novel by John le Carré

Little Fauss and Big Halsy ★★ 15

Action drama 1970 · US · Colour · 94mins

Robert Redford is the blondly handsome motorbike racer who swaggers sexually in tight jeans, brazenly exploits his plug-ugly mechanic Michael J Pollard (who drools at him) and gets ex-drug addict Lauren Hutton pregnant. Beyond this is a depiction of America's counterculture of druggies, drop-outs and groupies ready for sex with the racers. AT

Robert Redford *Big Halsy* • Michael J Pollard *Little Fauss* • Lauren Hutton *Rita Nebraska* • Noah Beery Jr *Seally Fauss* • Lucille Benson *Mom Fauss* • Linda Gaye Scott *Mometh* • Ray Ballard *Photographer* ■ *Dir* Sidney J Furie • *Scr* Charles Eastman

The Little Foxes ★★★★ PG

Period drama 1941 · US · BW · 111mins

It may have been something to do with the fact that director William Wyler and star Bette Davis were romantically involved that gave their many celluloid collaborations such an exciting buzz. This is a splendid example of Davis at the height of her powers as the deeply nasty Regina, the power-hungry schemer of a once wealthy southern clan. The critics always said of Wyler that he "understood women"; they meant that he was not afraid to give a talent like Davis's full flight while also managing to contain her worst histrionic excesses. The result here is a quite magnificent movie. SR

Bette Davis *Regina Hubbard Giddens* • Herbert Marshall *Horace Giddens* • Teresa Wright *Alexandra Giddens* • Richard Carlson *David Hewitt* • Patricia Collinge *Birdie Hubbard* • Dan Duryea *Leo Hubbard* • Charles Dingle *Ben Hubbard* • Carl Benton Reid *Oscar Hubbard* ■ *Dir* William Wyler • *Scr* Lillian Hellman, Arthur Kober, Dorothy Parker, Alan Campbell, from the play by Lillian Hellman

The Little Fugitive ★★ U

Drama 1953 · US · BW · 75mins

This independent production, winner of a Silver Lion at the Venice Film Festival, was made in New York by a team of three directors – Ray Ashley, Morris Engel, and Ruth Orkin – who were also responsible for writing, photography and editing. It's the slight story of a seven-year-old boy who is conned by his older brother into believing that he has committed a murder. The boy then runs away to savour the amusements at Coney Island. Peasant enough, but ultimately insubstantial. AE

Richie Andrusco *Joey Norton* • Rickie Brewster *Lennie Norton* • Winifred Cushing *Mother Norton* • Jay Williams *Pony Ride Man* • Will Lee *Photographer* ■ *Dir/Scr* Ray Ashley, Morris Engel, Ruth Orkin

The Little Giant ★★

Crime comedy 1933 · US · BW · 70mins

In one of the first gangster comedies, Edward G Robinson plays beer baron "Bugs" Ahearn, who at the end of Prohibition tries to establish himself as a respectable figure out west. Hiring Mary Astor's estate agent as his social adviser, he finds high society to be as full of crooks as the Chicago he left behind. Although briskly directed by Roy Del Duth, this is small beer compared to Robinson's later send-ups of his tough-guy image (*A Slight Case of Murder*, *Brother Orchid*). AE

Edward G Robinson *James Francis "Bugs" Ahearn* • Mary Astor *Ruth Wayburn* • Helen Vinson *Polly Cass* • Russell Hopton *Al Daniels* • Kenneth Thomson *John Stanley* • Shirley Grey *Edith Merriam* • Berton Churchill *Donald Hadley Cass* • Donald Dillaway *Gordon Cass* • Louise Mackintosh *Mrs Cass* ■ *Dir* Roy Del Ruth • *Scr* Wilson Mizner, Robert Lord

Little Giant ★★

Comedy 1946 · US · BW · 91mins

On this occasion, Abbott and Costello take a radical departure from their usual routine of playing pals who find themselves in all sorts of hot water. Here they perform separately rather than as a double act. Costello plays a country bumpkin who leaves for the big city to make enough money to marry his sweetheart. Abbott, in a double role, hires him on as a vacuum cleaner salesman. There's plenty of slapstick action in this film and it also features appearances from Lou's brother Pat and former Marx Brothers straight woman Margaret Dumont. DF

Bud Abbott *Mr EL Morrison/Tom Chandler* • Lou Costello *Benny Miller* • Brenda Joyce *Ruby* • Jacqueline de Wit *Hazel Temple* • George Cleveland *Uncle Clarence Goodring* • Elena Verdugo *Martha Hill* • Mary Gordon *Anna Miller* • Pierre Watkin *President PS Van Loon* • Margaret Dumont *Mrs Hendrickson* ■ *Dir* William A Seiter • *Scr* Walter DeLeon, from a story by Paul Jarrico, from Richard Collins

Little Giants ★★ PG

Sports comedy drama
1994 · US · Colour · 101mins

Yet again, another story of misfit kids who defy all the odds to trounce the champions. The one twist this utterly predictable American football comedy has going for it is that the side has been assembled to give a girl the chance to parade her skills against some boneheaded boys. As the girl in question, Shawna Waldron gives a good account of herself. However, the same can't be said of Rick Moranis as her gormless dad. DP

Rick Moranis *Danny O'Shea* • Ed O'Neill *Kevin O'Shea* • Sam Horrigan *Spike Hammers* • Shawna Waldron *Becky O'Shea* • Mary Ellen Trainor *Karen O'Shea* • Devon Sawa *Junior Floyd* • Susanna Thompson *Patty Floyd* ■ *Dir* Duwayne Dunham, Brian Levant • *Scr* James Ferguson, Robert Shallcross, Tommy Swerdlow, Michael Goldberg, from a story by James Ferguson, Robert Shallcross

Little Girl from Hanoi ★★★

War drama 1974 · Viet · BW

Whereas American pictures made during the Vietnam War concentrated on gung-ho heroics, Nguyen Hai Ninh's Vietnamese drama focuses on the human cost of the conflict, as a 12 year-old girl goes looking for her family during the Christmas air raids on Hanoi, only to meet a kindly soldier, to whom she confides her memories of happier times. As all Vietnamese pictures were made in black and white until the mid-1980s, the action has a newsreel feel to it, which reinforces its propaganda value. DP. In Vietnamese with English subtitles.

Dir Nguyen Hai Ninh • *Scr* Hoang Tich Chi, Nguyen Hai Ninh, Vuong Dan Hoang

The Little Girl Who Lives Down the Lane ★★★

Thriller 1976 · Can/Fr · Colour · 93mins

This chilling oddity – a psychological thriller exploring serious themes – features an intuitive performance from 13-year-old Jodie Foster that hints at what was to come. Grief-stricken Foster murders her mother when her father commits suicide and then buries both corpses in the cellar. Unfortunately, her suspicious actions arouse the curiosity of landlady Alexis Smith and – worse – the interest of her child-molesting, psychopathic son (a startling turn by Martin Sheen). This macabre fairy tale becomes a captivating experience under Nicolas Gessner's sensitive direction. AJ

Jodie Foster *Rynn Jacobs* • Martin Sheen *Frank Hallet* • Alexis Smith *Mrs Hallet* • Mort Shuman *Officer Miglioriti* • Scott Jacoby *Mario Podesta* ■ *Dir* Nicolas Gessner • *Scr* Laird Koenig, from his novel

The Little Hut ★

Comedy 1957 · US · Colour · 96mins

There's nothing more tedious than Hollywood tease, as director Mark Robson attempts to film a French sex farce in the days when censorship permitted only talk and no action. Shipwrecked together on a deserted South Pacific island are Stewart Granger as a neglectful husband, Ava Gardner as his love-starved wife, David Niven as his best friend and her would-be lover. Gardner hated the picture and only took it to be near her current beau, Walter Chiari, who turns up as the randy ship's chef. AE

Ava Gardner *Susan* • Stewart Granger *Sir Philip Ashlow* • David Niven *Henry Brittingham-Brett* • Walter Chiari *Mario* • Finlay Currie *Reverend Brittingham-Brett* • Jean Cadell *Mrs Brittingham-Brett* ■ *Dir* Mark Robson • *Scr* F Hugh Herbert, from a play by André Roussin, Nancy Mitford

Little Lord Fauntleroy ★★★

Silent drama 1921 · US · BW · 111mins

One of Mary Pickford's biggest box-office successes – and one of her own personal favourites – was this over-long version of Frances Hodgson Burnett's maudlin Victorian tale. As her own producer, Pickford elected to play both the widowed mother and her son, Cedric, whom she surrenders to an English castle for preparation to become the next Lord Fauntleroy. Under Alfred E Green's direction (with some help from Pickford's brother, Jack), Mary excelled both in another of her child roles, and as the mother forced to live apart from her precious son. The immaculate trick photography of the two together was quite an achievement at the time, and the vast castle set is memorable. AE

Mary Pickford *Cedric, Little Lord Fauntleroy/Dearest, Cedric's mother* • Claude Gillingwater *The Earl of Dorincourt* • Joseph Dowling *Haversham, the Earl's Counsel* • James A Marcus *Hobbs, the grocer* • Frances Marion *Her son, the pretender* ■ *Dir* Alfred E Green, Jack Pickford • *Scr* Bernard McConville, from the novel by Frances Hodgson Burnett • *Cinematographer* Charles Rosher

Little Lord Fauntleroy ★★★

Drama 1936 · US · BW · 98mins

David O Selznick proved the sceptics wrong when he chose this Victorian chestnut for his first independent production and had a critical and box-office success. He borrowed child star Freddie Bartholomew from MGM to portray the Brooklyn youngster who becomes a British lord and persuaded Dolores Costello to make a comeback, displaying radiant charm as the mother he calls "Dearest". Under John Cromwell's smooth direction, with C Aubrey Smith as the irritable earl who can't abide his American daughter-in-law, the sentimental story of the boy's arrival in England to take up his title is as well told as it possibly could be. AE

Freddie Bartholomew *Ceddie Errol* • Dolores Costello Barrymore [Dolores Costello] *"Dearest", Mrs Errol* • C Aubrey Smith *Earl of Dorincourt* • Guy Kibbee *Mr Hobbs* • Henry Stephenson *Havisham* • Mickey Rooney *Dick* ■ *Dir* John Cromwell • *Scr* Hugh Walpole, from the novel by Frances Hodgson Burnett

Little Malcolm and His Struggle Against the Eunuchs ★★

Comedy drama 1974 · UK · Colour · 109mins

Beatle George Harrison began his career as a movie producer with this messy political satire in which art student John Hurt forms a revolutionary group, the "Party of Dynamic Erection", and plans to launch a coup against the government. In fact, the group is a mask for Hurt's sexual incompetence and a metaphor for the fascism of the state. Lots of serious ideas go bang and whoosh in a display of verbal fireworks. AT

John Hurt *Malcolm Scrawdyke* • John McEnery *Wick Blagdon* • Raymond Platt *Irwin Ingham* • Rosalind Ayres *Ann Gedge* • David Warner *Dennis Charles Nipple* ■ *Dir* Stuart Cooper • *Scr* Derek Woodward, from the play by David Halliwell

Little Man Tate ★★★★ PG

Drama 1991 · US · Colour · 95mins

Jodie Foster made an impressive directorial debut with this touching drama about a young mother (played by Foster) who is determined to get the best for her exceptionally gifted six-year-old son (an enjoyable performance from Adam Hann-Byrd). While it has its clichéd moments, this is moving without being cloying. The film also features some nice supporting performances, notably from Dianne Wiest as a child psychologist, and from musician/actor Harry Connick Jr. JB. Contains some swearing. DVD

Jodie Foster *Dede Tate* • Dianne Wiest *Dr Jane Grierson* • Adam Hann-Byrd *Fred Tate* • Harry Connick Jr *Eddie* • David Pierce [David Hyde Pierce] *Garth* • Debi Mazar *Gina* • PJ Ochlan *Damon Wells* • George Plimpton *Winston F Buckner* ■ *Dir* Jodie Foster • *Scr* Scott Frank

Little Man, What Now? ★★★

Drama 1934 · US · BW · 91mins

With poverty and unemployment rife in Germany after the First World War, newlywed Douglass Montgomery loses his job, plunging himself and his pregnant wife Margaret Sullavan into a series of catastrophes. Sullavan glows at the centre of director Frank Borzage's film, rich in atmosphere and fascinating as a social document of the period. Viewed with hindsight, one is haunted by the knowledge of the Nazi regime to come. However, on the whole, this once popular and well-regarded film has dated badly, overdosing on sentimentality and with a rather weak hero. RK

Margaret Sullavan *Lammchen* • Douglass Montgomery *Hans Pinneberg* • Alan Hale *Holger Jachman* • Catherine Doucet *Mia Pinneberg* • DeWitt Jennings *Emil Kleinholtz* • Muriel Kirkland *Marie Kleinholz* ■ *Dir* Frank Borzage • *Scr* William Anthony McGuire, Rudolph Ditzen [Hans Fallada]

The Little Mermaid ★★★

Adventure 1976 · USSR · Colour · 81mins

Vladimir Bychkov's live-action version of Hans Christian Andersen's celebrated story has a certain charm, reminiscent of that Eastern bloc TV classic, *The Singing Ringing Tree*. He unfussily extracts a little fairy-tale magic from the stylised backdrops against which unfolds the story of prince Valentin Nikulin, who falls in love with Vika Novikova, the mermaid who delivered him from the wiles of her singing sisters. The downbeat ending won't please everyone, but at least Bychkov has remained true to his source. DP. A Russian language film.

Vika Novikova *The Little Mermaid* • Valentin Nikouline *Troubador* • Galina Artemova *Princess* • Yuri Senkevitch *Prince* • Galina Volchek *Witch* ■ *Dir* Vladimir Bychkov • *Scr* Victor Vitkovich, Grigory Lagfeld, from the fairy tale by Hans Christian Andersen

The Little Mermaid ★★★★★ [U]

Animated musical adventure
1989 · US · Colour · 85mins

What a splash this adventure made on its release, marking as it did the beginning of a new "golden age" of Disney animated features. The story of the plucky Ariel (who set the tone for a new generation of Disney heroines) features impressive animation and a catchy, show-stopping score by Academy Award-nominated Alan Menken – including the instant hit *Under the Sea*, sung with Caribbean verve by Sebastian, composer to the court of King Triton and Ariel's reluctant minder. While some of the scenes could frighten very young children, especially those featuring the loathesome Ursula, this remains an enduring delight. KFS DVD

Jodi Benson *Ariel* • Samuel E Wright *Sebastian* • Jason Marin *Flounder* • Christopher Daniel Barnes *Eric* • Pat Carroll *Ursula* • Edie McClurg *Carlotta* • Buddy Hackett *Scuttle* • Kenneth Mars *Triton* • Ben Wright (1) *Grimsby* • René Auberjonois *Louis* ■ *Dir* John Musker, Ron Clements • *Scr* John Musker, Ron Clements, from the fairy tale by Hans Christian Andersen

The Little Mermaid II: Return to the Sea ★★★ [U]

Animated musical adventure
2000 · US · Colour · 72mins

By the generally poor standards of straight-to-video Disney sequels, this second aquatic outing provides reasonable entertainment. The film's new heroine is Ariel's 12-year-old daughter Melody, whose underwater ancestry has been kept hidden to protect her from the evil influence of Ursula's bitter sister Morgana. The animation is unexceptional and the tunes aren't in the same Oscar winning league as the buoyant originals. On the positive side, the same voice cast return, joined by some new characters. JC DVD

Jodi Benson *Ariel* • Samuel E Wright *Sebastian* • Tara Charendoff *Melody* • Pat Carroll *Morgana* • Buddy Hackett *Scuttle* • Kenneth Mars *King Triton* • Max Casella *Tip* • Stephen Furst *Dash* ■ *Dir* Jim Kammerud, Brian Smith (3) • *Scr* Elizabeth Anderson, Temple Mathews

The Little Minister ★★★

Drama 1934 · US · BW · 104mins

Adapted from a novel and play by JM Barrie, this screen incarnation of the tale (several silent versions were made) stars Katharine Hepburn as a gypsy girl, an exotic outsider in a strictly religious Scottish community. Her romantic relationship with new, handsome young minister John Beal causes a furore among the village congregation. Beal gives a competent portrayal of a rigid cleric gradually melting under the influence of love, while Hepburn offers one of her livelier performances. RK

Katharine Hepburn *Babbie* • John Beal *Gavin* • Alan Hale *Rob Dow* • Donald Crisp *Dr McQueen* • Lumsden Hare *Thammas* • Andy Clyde *Wearyworld* • Beryl Mercer *Margaret* ■ *Dir* Richard Wallace • *Scr* Jane Murfin, Sarah Y Mason, Victor Heerman, Mortimer Offner, Jack Wagner, from the play by JM Barrie

Little Miss Broadway ★★★ [U]

Musical 1938 · US · BW · 71mins

A characteristic vehicle for the world's most famous child star phenomenon, Shirley Temple, now a veteran at ten years old and looking a mite plump. The idiotic plot is a variation on a number of other Temple vehicles in which the little moppet brings sunshine into a dozen lives and melts the stoniest of hearts – in this case mean Edna May Oliver who wants to close the hotel for stage troupers where Temple, rescued from an orphanage, lives with the family that has adopted her. The precocious child is both ghastly and irresistible. RK

Shirley Temple *Betsy Brown* • George Murphy *Roger Wendling* • Jimmy Durante *Jimmy Clayton* • Phyllis Brooks *Barbara Shea* • Edna May Oliver *Sarah Wendling* • George Barbier *Fiske* • Edward Ellis *Pop Shea* • Jane Darwell *Miss Hutchins* ■ *Dir* Irving Cummings • *Scr* Harry Tugend, Jack Yellen

Little Miss Marker ★★★

Comedy 1934 · US · BW · 78mins

This was the film that clinched Shirley Temple's claim to stardom. The diminutive phenomenon, six years old at the time, is utterly disarming and captivating as the moppet who is left with a bookie (Adolphe Menjou) as an IOU, and proceeds to reform the gambling fraternity with her charm. Based on a Damon Runyon story, the cast is peopled with the author's typically amusing guys and dolls. This is a warm and witty tale with the inestimable advantage of Temple's performance. TV

Adolphe Menjou *Sorrowful Jones* • Dorothy Dell *Bangles Carson* • Charles Bickford *Big Steve* • Shirley Temple *Miss Marker* • Lynne Overman *Regret* ■ *Dir* Alexander Hall • *Scr* William R Lipman, Sam Hellman, Gladys Lehman, from the story by Damon Runyon

Little Miss Marker ★ [U]

Comedy 1980 · US · Colour · 97mins

This remake of the 1934 Shirley Temple vehicle is so sickly sweet it's guaranteed to give you toothache. Sara Stimson has the unenviable role of following Temple as the titular Little Miss, who is handed over by her father to Walter Matthau's bookie as the guarantee for a racing debt. Matthau soon becomes putty in her childish hands in an unconvincing tale of a cute kid softening a grumpy old man. Throw a simpering Julie Andrews and a mincing Tony Curtis into the melting pot and you'll have Damon Runyon turning in his grave. LH

Walter Matthau *Sorrowful Jones* • Julie Andrews *Amanda* • Tony Curtis *Blackie* • Bob Newhart *Regret* • Lee Grant *The Judge* • Brian Dennehy *Herbie* • Kenneth McMillan *Brannigan* • Sara Stimson *The Kid* ■ *Dir* Walter Bernstein • *Scr* Walter Bernstein, from the story by Damon Runyon

Little Monsters ★ [PG]

Fantasy adventure
1989 · US · Colour · 97mins

Funnyman Howie Mandel is the wart hog-like creature who lives under Fred Savage's bed, in this adolescent *Beetle Juice* copy. Together they venture into a land of monsters and get up to all manner of childish pranks. Some of that mischief is actually quite vicious and dark so parents of young children should take note. Everyone tries hard to mine the fantasy for all the quirky comedy value they can, but the clumsy script defeats them. A dismal disaster. AJ

Fred Savage *Brian* • Howie Mandel *Maurice* • Ben Savage *Eric* • Daniel Stern *Glen Stevenson* • Margaret Whitton *Holly Stevenson* ■ *Dir* Richard Alan Greenberg • *Scr* Terry Rossio, Ted Elliott

Little Moon & Jud McGraw ★

Western 1978 · US · Colour · 92mins

This comedy western was previously known by the even less appealing title *Bronco Busters*. James Caan finds himself in one of the many troughs that have characterised his rollercoaster career. He's the falsely accused Jud McGraw, trying to clear his name and track down the real villain. Unoriginal. DA

James Caan *Jud McGraw* • Aldo Ray *Nemo* • Stefanie Powers • Sammy Davis Jr ■ *Dir* Bernard Girard • *Scr* J AS McCombie, Douglas Stewart, Monroe Manning, Marcus Devian

Little Murders ★★★★

Black comedy 1971 · US · Colour · 108mins

Satiric cartoonist Jules Feiffer adapted his play for the screen under the direction of actor Alan Arkin. Elliott Gould (who also co-produced) plays a young photographer who specialises in taking pictures of excrement. As a hardened New Yorker he's blithely unconcerned about crime and violence – even when he's the victim. Into this life of apathy comes optimist Marcia Rodd who thinks he will make ideal husband material. This black comedy of Manhattan manners hasn't dated – if anything its chilling view of alienation and arbitrary violence is more relevant than when it was made. A wonderful cast makes this little-known, thought-provoking film worth seeking out. TH

Elliott Gould *Alfred Chamberlain* • Marcia Rodd *Patsy Newquist* • Vincent Gardenia *Mr Newquist* • Elizabeth Wilson *Mrs Newquist* • Jon Korkes *Kenny* • John Randolph *Mr Chamberlain* • Doris Roberts *Mrs Chamberlain* • Donald Sutherland *Minister* • Alan Arkin *Detective* ■ *Dir* Alan Arkin • *Scr* Jules Feiffer, from his play

Little Nellie Kelly ★★★ [U]

Musical drama 1940 · US · BW · 98mins

Judy Garland was solo billed for the first time in this awkward slice of blarney, playing not only the young title character but also her dying mother! Today, some may well find this MGM adaptation rather mawkish, but Garland, as ever, delivers a wonderfully sincere performance, her talent shining through. George Murphy has the right surname but too bland a manner as Judy's husband/father, and Charles Winninger blusters along as usual. TS

Judy Garland *Nellie Kelly/Little Nellie Kelly* • George Murphy *Jerry Kelly* • Charles Winninger *Michael Noonan* • Douglas McPhail *Dennis Fogarty* • Arthur Shields *Timothy Fogarty* • Rita Page *Mary Fogarty* • Forrester Harvey *Moriarty* • James Burke *Sergeant McGowan* ■ *Dir* Norman Taurog • *Scr* Jack McGowan, from the musical comedy by George M Cohan

Little Nemo: Adventures in Slumberland ★★★

Animated adventure
1992 · Jpn/US · Colour · 85mins

This animated adaptation of Winsor McCay's pioneering comic-strip will delight young and old alike, thanks to its songs by legendary Disney stalwarts the Sherman brothers and the involvement of sci-fi maestro Ray Bradbury and French illustrator Moebius in the story. Nothing quite matches the eye-popping opening, but the twin worlds of Slumberland and Nightmareland are beautifully drawn, blending 19th-century imagination with modern graphic techniques. Plus there's a wonderfully mischievous voiceover from Mickey Rooney as the likeable con artist, Flip. DP

Gabriel Damon *Nemo* • Mickey Rooney *Flip* • René Auberjonois *Professor Genius* • Danny Mann *Icarus* • Laura Mooney *Princess Camille* • Bernard Erhard *King Morpheus* • William E Martin *Nightmare King* • Alan Oppenheimer *Oomp* ■ *Dir* William T Hurtz, Masami Hata • *Scr* Chris Columbus, Richard Outten, from a story by Jean Moebius Giraud, Yutaka Fujioka, from the comic strip by Winsor McCay

Little Nicky ★★★ [12]

Comedy 2000 · US · Colour · 86mins

This might be stupid, crass and vulgar, but it is also – in places – gloriously funny. For the first time, comedian Adam Sandler gets to perform his trademark moronic schtick against a backdrop of visually imaginative production values and devilishly good special effects. Sandler plays the son of Satan (Harvey Keitel), dispatched to Earth to bring his brothers (Rhys Ifans and Tom "Tiny" Lister Jr) back to the underworld before they can gather up enough evil souls to stage a coup in Hades. AJ DVD

Adam Sandler *Nicky* • Patricia Arquette *Valerie* • Harvey Keitel *Dad* • Rhys Ifans *Adrian* • Allen Covert *Todd* • Tommy "Tiny" Lister Jr [Tom "Tiny" Lister Jr] *Cassius* • Quentin Tarantino *Deacon* • Rodney Dangerfield *Lucifer* ■ *Dir* Steven Brill • *Scr* Steven Brill, Tim Herlihy, Adam Sandler

A Little Night Music ★★★ [12]

Musical
1977 · Austria/US/W Ger · Colour · 119mins

Stephen Sondheim's Broadway musical *A Little Night Music*. It's brought to the screen here with glamorous Elizabeth Taylor and Diana Rigg as two of the guests at a country estate. Appropriately, Taylor is cast as an actress with a colourful past but now looking for some stability in her life. Other visitors include her current lover and his wife (Rigg) and a past beau with his new bride. Stage director Hal Prince can't replicate the pace of the Broadway show but fans of Stephen Sondheim will enjoy the music, and the costume design received an Oscar nomination. TH

Elizabeth Taylor *Desiree Armfeldt* • Diana Rigg *Charlotte Mittelheim* • Len Cariou *Frederick Egerman* • Lesley-Anne Down *Anne Egerman* • Hermione Gingold *Mme Armfeldt* • Laurence Guittard *Carl-Magnus Mittelheim* • Christopher Guard *Erich Egerman* • Chloe Franks *Fredericka Armfeldt* ■ *Dir* Harold Prince • *Scr* Hugh Wheeler, from the musical by Hugh Wheeler, Stephen Sondheim, from the film *Smiles of a Summer Night* by Ingmar Bergman • *Costume Designer* Florence Klotz

Little Nikita ★★★ [15]

Spy thriller 1988 · US · Colour · 92mins

Teenager River Phoenix has parents who are "sleepers" – spies planted in key locations with orders to live unremarkable lives until "activated". But when Phoenix applies to join the US Air Force, the suspicions of FBI agent Sidney Poitier are aroused. Director Richard Benjamin wastes the intriguing premise, and settles for a game of cat and mouse as Poitier and Phoenix join forces to catch the real Soviet snakes. DP

Sidney Poitier *Roy Parmenter* • River Phoenix *Jeff Grant* • Richard Jenkins *Richard Grant* • Caroline Kava *Elizabeth Grant* • Richard Bradford *Konstantin Karpov* • Richard Lynch *Scuba* ■ *Dir* Richard Benjamin • *Scr* John Hill, Bo Goldman, from a story by Tom Musca, Terry Schwartz

Little Noises ★★★ 15

Drama 1992 · US · Colour · 87mins

A muddled, offbeat fable about greed, guilt and wanting more than you truly deserve. Struggling would-be writer Crispin Glover steals poems written by his friend Matthew Hutton who, though gifted with words, is actually mute. This unscrupulous behaviour brings Glover fame, fortune and success in the publishing world in director Jane Spencer's deliberately small-scale, character-driven opus. Fine work by Glover (who doesn't come across quite as strange as he usually does) and the eclectic cast make this ambitious chamber piece worth a look. AJ

Crispin Glover *Joey Kremple* • Tatum O'Neal *Stella Winslow* • John C McGinley *Stu Slovack* • Rik Mayall *Mathias Lichtenstein* • Steven Schub *Timmy Smith* • Tate Donovan *Elliott* • Nina Siemaszko *Dolores* • Matthew Hutton *Marty Slovack* • Carole Shelley *Aunt Shirley* ■ *Dir* Jane Spencer • *Scr* Jane Spencer, Jon Zeiderman, from the story by Anthony Brito, Jane Spencer

L

Little Odessa ★★★ 15

Crime thriller 1994 · US · Colour · 94mins

In this intimate character study, chilly both in setting and in atmosphere, a hitman (Tim Roth) is forced to return to his old Russian-Jewish Brooklyn neighbourhood to carry out an execution. But contact with his family only serves to re-ignite old feuds. Writer/director James Gray, here making a promising debut, elicits meaty performances from Roth, Edward Furlong and Maximilian Schell. However, his tendency to swamp key moments with excessive visual stylistics does sometimes blunt this movie's dramatic edge. JC. Contains violence, swearing and nudity.

Tim Roth *Joshua Shapira* • Edward Furlong *Reuben Shapira* • Moira Kelly *Alla Shustervich* • Vanessa Redgrave *Irina Shapira* • Maximilian Schell *Arkady Shapira* • Paul Guilfoyle (2) *Boris Volkoff* • Natasha Andreichenko *Natasha* • David Vadim *Sasha* ■ *Dir/Scr* James Gray

A Little of What You Fancy ★★★ U

Music documentary 1968 · UK · Colour · 79mins

A treat for anyone who laments the passing of *The Good Old Days*. Using a variety of photographs, posters, theatre bills and other memorabilia, this slickly produced documentary traces the history of British music hall from 1854 to 1968. Although much of this nostalgic wallow is occupied by a glorified *son et lumière* show, director Robert Webb tacks on an interesting finale in which he explores how the music hall tradition survived in the pubs, clubs and cabarets of the late 1960s, thanks to such performers as Helen Shapiro and Barry Cryer. DP

Dir Robert Webb [Robert D Webb] • *Scr* Ray Mackender

Little Old New York ★★★ U

Comedy drama 1940 · US · BW · 100mins

The story of Robert Fulton, who, back in 1807, managed to achieve his dream of building the first ever steamboat, is turned here by 20th Century-Fox into a vehicle for Alice Faye. She plays a breezy Irish saloon-keeper torn between sturdy Fred MacMurray and callow but bright Richard Greene as Fulton. Director Henry King wisely concentrates on the boat-building sequences, which are actually rather good. But the eternal triangle plot is silly and this style of movie has dated rather badly. TS

Alice Faye *Pat O'Day* • Fred MacMurray *Charles Browne* • Richard Greene *Robert Fulton* • Brenda Joyce *Harriet Livingstone* • Andy Devine *Commodore* • Henry Stephenson *Chancellor Livingstone* ■ *Dir* Henry King • *Scr* Harry Tugend, from a story by John Balderson, from the play by Rita Johnson Young

Little Otik ★★★★ 15

Part-animated black comedy fantasy 2000 · Cz Rep/UK/Jpn · Colour · 126mins

Veteran Czech surrealist Jan Svankmajer makes another foray into the world of dissatisfaction and decay in this deliriously macabre comedy. Unable to have children of their own, Prague couple Veronica Zilkova and Jan Hartl fashion a baby out of a tree stump, only for it to evolve into a flesh-eating monster. In giving a traditional fable a bitingly modern makeover, Svankmajer not only succeeds in satirising contemporary Czech society, but also in conveying an ecology-conscious subtext about the dangers of tinkering with the natural order. Uncompromising and provocative, this is an urban horror film of chilling simplicity and intelligence. DP. In Czech with English subtitles. DVD

Veronika Zilkova *Bozena Horakova* • Jan Hartl *Karel Horak* • Jaroslava Kretschmerova *Mrs Stadlerova* • Pavel Novy *Frantisek Stadler* • Kristina Adamcova *Alzbetka* ■ *Dir* Jan Svankmajer • *Scr* Jan Svankmajer, from his story

The Little Polar Bear ★★★ U

Animated adventure 2001 · Ger/Swi/US · Colour · 73mins

This enchanting tale has the titular fur-covered cutie, Lars, taking a trip to the tropics courtesy of a drifting ice floe, while an eco-aware subplot has him tackling a sinister automated super-trawler that's decimating the local fish stocks. The animation has a nicely retro feel, the storyline is clear and simple, and Lars is a love – although a passle of terminally depressed lemmings manage to steal the show. Short and most definitely sweet, this animated adventure is ideal for younger kids. DA. German dialogue dubbed into English. DVD

Wesley Singerman *Lars* • Brianne Siddall *Robby* • Michael McConnohie *Mika* • Daran Norris *Brutus* • Neil Kaplan *Bert* • Tom Fahn *Boris* • Steve Kramer *Screenplay* ■ *Dir* Thilo Graf Rothkirch, Piet de Rycker • *Scr* Piet de Rycker, Thilo Rothkirch, Bert Schrickel, Thomas Wittenburg, from the books by Hans de Beer

The Little Prince ★★ U

Musical 1974 · UK · Colour · 84mins

Antoine de Saint-Exupéry's much-loved allegory on the importance of childhood becomes a ponderous musical fable with few sparkling moments under Stanley Donen's stodgy direction. Pilot Richard Kiley crashes in the Sahara desert and is discovered by the Little Prince (Steven Warner), an emissary from another planet, who proceeds to teach him the true meaning of life through surreal intergalactic flashbacks. Lumbered with pointless songs by Alan Jay Lerner and Frederick Loewe, Donen's inability to meld the achingly real with the strangely fantastic turns the material to heavy-handed whimsy. AJ DVD

Richard Kiley *Pilot* • Steven Warner *Little Prince* • Bob Fosse *Snake* • Gene Wilder *Fox* • Joss Ackland *King* • Clive Revill *Businessman* • Victor Spinetti *Historian* • Graham Crowden *General* • Donna McKechnie *Rose* ■ *Dir* Stanley Donen • *Scr* Alan Jay Lerner, from the book *Le Petit Prince* by Antoine De Saint-Exupéry

The Little Princess ★★★★ U

Musical drama 1939 · US · Colour · 93mins

Made when the career of dimpled darling Shirley Temple was waning, this is now considered her best film. A lovingly produced version of Frances Hodgson Burnett's classic story of a little rich girl moved to the cold attic of her boarding school when her father is reported dead. Beautifully crafted and filmed in gorgeous Technicolor, this is a little gem. Arthur Treacher accompanies the star in a delightful song and dance number. TV DVD

Shirley Temple *Sara Crewe* • Richard Greene *Geoffrey Hamilton* • Anita Louise *Rose* • Ian Hunter *Capt Crewe* • Cesar Romero *Ram Dass* • Arthur Treacher *Bertie Minchin* • Mary Nash *Amanda Minchin* • Sybil Jason *Becky* ■ *Dir* Walter Lang • *Scr* Ethel Hill, Walter Ferris, from the novel by Frances Hodgson Burnett • *Producer* Darryl F Zanuck

A Little Princess ★★★★★ U

Period fantasy drama 1995 · US · Colour · 93mins

Simple for children to understand, yet sophisticated enough for adults to enjoy too, this wonderful adaptation of the novel by Frances Hodgson Burnett (who also wrote *The Secret Garden*) is an instant classic. The importance of magic and imagination in all our lives is engagingly conveyed through the entrancing tale of a schoolgirl escaping into exotic flights of fancy after news of her father's death. Mexican director Alfonso Cuarón gives his spellbinding fable a dazzling look and an astonishing atmosphere that prove hard to resist. You'll be enthralled by this little marvel from colourful start to heart-rending finish. AJ DVD

Eleanor Bron *Miss Minchin* • Liam Cunningham *Captain Crewe/Prince Rama* • Liesel Matthews *Sara Crewe* • Rusty Schwimmer *Amelia Minchin* • Arthur Malet *Charles Randolph* • Vanessa Lee Chester *Becky* • Errol Sitahal *Ram Dass* • Heather DeLoach *Ermengarde* ■ *Dir* Alfonso Cuarón • *Scr* Richard LaGravenese, Elizabeth Chandler, from the novel *Sara Crewe* and the play *The Little Princess* by Frances Hodgson Burnett

The Little Rascals ★ U

Comedy 1994 · US · Colour · 78mins

Launched by Hal Roach in 1922, the *Our Gang* series ran until 1944, ending its days at MGM. A decade later, around 100 of these comic shorts resurfaced on TV under the title *The Little Rascals*. Having failed the previous year to capture the magic of *The Beverly Hillbillies* on film, director Penelope Spheeris thought she'd take a crack at bringing Alfalfa, Darla and Spanky to a new audience, only to miss the target again and by a much wider margin. DP

Travis Tedford *Spanky* • Bug Hall *Alfalfa* • Brittany Ashton Holmes *Darla* • Kevin Jamal Woods *Stymie* • Zachary Mabry *Porky* • Ross Elliot Bagley *Buckwheat* • Sam Saletta *Butch* • Blake McIver Ewing *Waldo* • Mel Brooks *Mr Welling* • Whoopi Goldberg *Buckwheat's Mom* • Daryl Hannah *Miss Crabtree* • Donald Trump *Waldo's Dad* • George Wendt *Lumberyard Clerk* ■ *Dir* Penelope Spheeris • *Scr* Paul Guay, Stephen Mazur, Penelope Spheeris, from a story by Penelope Spheeris, Robert Wolterstorff, Mike Scott, Paul Guay, Stephen Mazur

Little Red Monkey ★★★

Spy drama 1955 · UK · BW · 77mins

Ken Hughes honed his skills as a director of thrillers working on the Scotland Yard B-movie series. Consequently, this quota quickie has a great deal more substance and style than many of its contemporaries. A top Russian boffin defects and American agent Richard Conte must escort him across the Atlantic. Hughes keeps the action on the boil, while Russell Napier and Rona Anderson are fine as a Scotland Yard detective and his niece, but Conte just looks old and bored. DP

Richard Conte *Bill Locklin* • Rona Anderson *Julia* • Russell Napier *Superintendent Harrington* • Colin Gordon *Martin* • Arnold Marlé *Dushenko* • Sylvia Langova *Hilde* • Donald Bisset *Editor* ■ *Dir* Ken Hughes • *Scr* Ken Hughes, James Eastwood, from the TV serial *Case of the Red Monkey* by Eric Maschwitz

Little Richard ★★★

Biographical drama 2000 · US · Colour · 97mins

Robert Townsend goes for a rose-tinted approach in this tribute to one of rock's most outrageous characters. The fact that this TV movie was made with the star's blessing gives Townsend little latitude where matters of sexual orientation are concerned, but Richard Penniman's progress from backstreet nobody to pop icon and born-again Christian is never dull and his legend is well served by an energetic performance from Leon. DP

Leon *Little Richard* • Jenifer Lewis *Muh Penniman* • Carl Lumbly *Bud Penniman* • Tamala Jones *Lucille* • Mel Jackson *Bump Blackwell* • Garrett Morris *Preacher Rainey* ■ *Dir* Robert Townsend • *Scr* Bill Kerby, Daniel Taplitz

A Little Romance ★★★ PG

Romantic comedy 1979 · US/Fr · Colour · 105mins

That Laurence Olivier could ham it up with the best, or worst, of them is proved unquestionably as he takes on the role of a Maurice Chevalier-like boulevardier helping lovelorn youngsters to a happy ending. The adults (Sally Kellerman, Arthur Hill, David Dukes) are so overdrawn there's inevitable sympathy for Diane Lane, the American girl in Paris falling for Thelonious Bernard despite family pressure. Charming and entertaining fluff; watch for Broderick Crawford's abrasive cameo appearance. TH

Laurence Olivier *Julius Edmond Santorin* • Diane Lane *Lauren King* • Thelonious Bernard *Daniel Michon* • Arthur Hill *Richard King* • Sally Kellerman *Kay King* • Broderick Crawford • David Dukes *George de Marco* • Andrew Duncan *Bob Duryea* • Claudette Sutherland *Janet Duryea* ■ *Dir* George Roy Hill • *Scr* Allan Burns, from the novel *E=MC Mon Amour* by Patrick Cauvin

A Little Sex ★★ 15

Comedy 1981 · US · Colour · 90mins

Mary Tyler Moore became a major player behind the screen when she set up MTM Enterprises, which produced such hit series as *Hill Street Blues*, *St Elsewhere* and *Lou Grant*. Their first theatrical production stayed loyal to its small screen roots, featuring Tim Matheson as a successful director of TV commercials who is also a hit with the ladies. Matheson tries to commit to his girlfriend Kate Capshaw but finds temptation at every turn. DF

Tim Matheson *Michael* • Kate Capshaw *Katherine* • Edward Herrmann *Brother* • John Glover *Walter* • Joan Copeland *Mrs Harrison* • Susanna Dalton *Nancy* ■ *Dir* Bruce Paltrow • *Scr* Robert DeLaurentiis

The Little Shop of Horrors ★★★ PG

Horror comedy 1960 · US · BW · 71mins

According to Hollywood legend, this riotous no-budget comedy horror from cult director Roger Corman was shot in three days on a leftover set. Jonathan Haze plays the browbeaten florist's apprentice who breeds a carnivorous plant that starts terrorising the neighbourhood. Look out for Jack Nicholson, who's hilarious as Wilbur Force, the masochistic dental patient reading *Pain* magazine in the waiting room. AJ [video] DVD

Jonathan Haze *Seymour Krelboined* • Jackie Joseph *Audrey Fulguard* • Mel Welles *Gravis Mushnik* • Myrtle Vail *Winifred Krelboined* • Leola Wendorff *Mrs Shiva* • Jack Nicholson *Wilbur Force* ■ *Dir* Roger Corman • *Scr* Charles B Griffith

Little Shop of Horrors ★★★★ PG

Musical black comedy horror
1986 · US · Colour · 89mins

Frank Oz here brings Howard Ashman's off-Broadway musical to the big screen in a way that Roger Corman (who directed a 1960 version) could only have dreamed of. It's packed with great doo-wop songs, a killer line-up of stars (Steve Martin shines brightest as the sadistic dentist) and clever horticultural special effects that underline, but never swamp, the charming theatricality of the stylised whole. The Four Tops' Levi Stubbs voices the alien Venus People-Trap that causes deliciously nerdy Rick Moranis to hack up victims for plant food and impress his Monroe-inspired lover, Ellen Greene, who reprises her award-winning stage role. This memorably weird musical is in the grand old Hollywood tradition. AJ. Contains violence, swearing. [video] DVD

Rick Moranis *Seymour Krelborn* • Ellen Greene *Audrey* • Vincent Gardenia *Mushnik* • Steve Martin *Orin Scrivello, DDS* • Tichina Arnold *Crystal* • Tisha Campbell *Chiffon* • Michelle Weeks *Ronette* • James Belushi *Patrick Martin* • John Candy *Wink Wilkinson* • Christopher Guest *First customer* • Bill Murray *Arthur Denton* • Levi Stubbs *Audrey II* ■ *Dir* Frank Oz • *Scr* Howard Ashman, from his play, from the film by Charles B Griffith

The Little Theatre of Jean Renoir ★★★ U

Portmanteau drama
1969 · Fr/It/W Ger · Colour · 107mins

Made for television, Jean Renoir's final feature is a delightful compendium, revisiting the humanist concerns that had preoccupied him for over forty years. In *Le Dernier Reveillon*, a homeless old couple find peace in companionship and dreams; *Le Cireuse Electrique* is a recitative denunciation of the evils of urban progress; *Quand l'Amour Se Meurt* is a musical interlude, sung by Jeanne Moreau in Belle Epoque costume; while *Le Roi d'Yvetot* centres on a cuckold forgiving both his wife and his best friend in a paean to the consoling joys of the countryside. A mixed bag, but a master's folly. DP. In French with English subtitles.

Nino Fornicola *Tramp* • Minny Monti *Tramp* • Marguerite Cassan *Isabelle* • Pierre Olaf *Gustave, her husband* • Jeanne Moreau *Singer* • Fernand Sardou *Duvallier* • Françoise Arnoul *Isabelle Duvallier* • Jean Carmet *Féraud* • Jean Renoir *Jean Renoir, master of ceremonies* ■ *Dir/Scr* Jean Renoir

Little Treasure ★★★ 15

Comedy adventure
1985 · US · Colour · 94mins

Margot Kidder is a loudmouthed topless dancer, summoned to Mexico for a reunion with her father, Burt Lancaster. She spends most of her time hanging out with Ted Danson and pursuing some elusive stolen cash. These are characters at the end of the line, and in some way the movie resembles a softened-up, distaff version of *Bring Me the Head of Alfredo Garcia*. AT [video]

Margot Kidder *Margo* • Ted Danson *Eugene* • Burt Lancaster *Teschemacher* • Joseph Hacker *Norman Kane* • Malena Doria *Evangelina* • John Pearce *Joseph* • Gladys Holland *Sadie* ■ *Dir/Scr* Alan Sharp

The Little Unicorn ★★ U

Fantasy adventure
1998 · UK · Colour · 90mins

Like *Black Beauty* before it, this story occasionally touches on darker issues, such as the death of the orphaned Brittney Bomann's beloved mare and the cruelty meted out to its unicorn foal by the dastardly Joe Penny. But this is primarily an uplifting fable, with shysters such as failed magician George Hamilton getting their just desserts and Bomann leading a rescue mission to save her stolen pet from the circus. DP [video] DVD

Brittney Bomann *Polly Regan* • David Warner *Grandfather* • George Hamilton *The Great Allonso* • Joe Penny *Tiny* • Christopher Atkins *Aunt Lucy's fiancé* • Emma Samms *Aunt Lucy* ■ *Dir/Scr* Paul Matthews

The Little Vampire ★★★ U

Horror fantasy adventure
2000 · Ger/Neth/UK/US · Colour · 91mins

A human boy helps a young vampire and his blood-sucking family escape the attentions of a vampire slayer in this entertaining adventure. Jonathan Lipnicki as the human and bright British newcomer Rollo Weeks as his undead friend turn in good performances, while Richard E Grant and Alice Krige camp it up as the vampire parents and Jim Carter is in slightly unhinged mode as the slayer. Witty and well written, this is that rarity – a children's film that doesn't patronise its audience. DA [video] DVD

Jonathan Lipnicki *Tony Thompson* • Richard E Grant *Frederick Sackville-Bagg* • Jim Carter *Rookery* • Alice Krige *Freda* • Pamela Gidley *Dottie Thompson* • Tommy Hinkley *Bob Thompson* • Anna Popplewell *Anna* • Dean Cook *Gregory* • Rollo Weeks *Rudolph* • John Wood *Lord McAshton* ■ *Dir* Uli Edel • *Scr* Karey Kirkpatrick, Larry Wilson, from the novels by Angela Sommer-Bodenburg

Little Vegas ★★★★ 15

Comedy 1990 · US · Colour · 87mins

This small-scale comedy/drama compensates for a lack of stars with lovely ensemble playing from Anthony John Denison, Catherine O'Hara and Jerry Stiller. They're part of the community of oddballs and eccentrics who live in in a Nevada trailer park. Bruce McGill dreams of turning the town into a mini gambling mecca, but he's opposed Stiller who has seen it all before with the pioneering mobsters of the real Vegas. Directed by Perry Lang, this intriguing story has director John Sayles in a small role. TH [video]

Anthony John Denison *Carmine* • Catherine O'Hara *Lexie* • Anne Francis *Martha* • Michael Nouri *Frank* • Perry Lang *Steve* • Bruce McGill *Harvey* • Jerry Stiller *Sam* • John Sayles ■ *Dir/Scr* Perry Lang

Little Vera ★★ 15

Drama 1988 · USSR · Colour · 133mins

For all its cultural significance as one of the first *glasnost* movies to present a reasonably accurate picture of everyday Soviet life, this is a cinematically pedestrian picture. Director Vasili Pichul never stints in his depiction of the peeling walls, the sozzled citizens and the limited opportunities, but a few astute compositions shot with a grainy film stock and some apposite vignettes do not make a classic in themselves. DP. In Russian with English Subtitles. Contains sex scenes and nudity.

Natalya Negoda *Vera* • Andrei Sokolov *Sergei* ■ *Dir* Vasili Pichul • *Scr* Mariya Khmelik

Little Voice ★★★★ 15

Comedy drama 1998 · UK · Colour · 92mins

Jane Horrocks reprises her stage performance as the reclusive girl whose virtuoso impersonations of the great singers – among them Shirley Bassey and Judy Garland – contrast with her almost total shyness. Her talents are belatedly recognised by sleazy agent Michael Caine, who's prepared to endure the attentions of her sexually predatory mother (Brenda Blethyn) as long as he can make some money out of that voice. The brilliance of Horrocks is slightly undermined by director Mark Herman's crude depiction of working-class life in a northern seaside town. Blethyn's strident squawking almost threatens to drown out the more subtle, *Cinderella*-like undertones of the story but there's good support from nightclub boss Jim Broadbent and Ewan McGregor. TH. Contains swearing, nudity. [video] DVD

Brenda Blethyn *Mari Hoff* • Jane Horrocks *"LV"* • Ewan McGregor *Billy* • Philip Jackson *George* • Annette Badland *Sadie* • Michael Caine *Ray Say* • Jim Broadbent *Mr Boo* ■ *Dir* Mark Herman • *Scr* Mark Herman, from the play *The Rise and Fall of Little Voice* by Jim Cartwright

Little Women ★★★★ U

Period drama 1933 · US · BW · 110mins

The first of three talkie versions of Louisa May Alcott's classic novel, starring Katharine Hepburn, Joan Bennett, Frances Dee and Jean Parker as the four sisters growing up in New England during the Civil War period. Director George Cukor had an early opportunity to show his affinity with the great female stars of the era. The film struck a chord with audiences at the time but lost out on the Oscars for best film and best director. This remains an entrancing film, with Hepburn perfectly cast. AT [video]

Katharine Hepburn *Jo* • Joan Bennett *Amy* • Paul Lukas *Prof Fritz Bhaer* • Edna May Oliver *Aunt March* • Jean Parker *Beth* • Frances Dee *Meg* • Henry Stephenson *Mr Laurence* • Douglass Montgomery *Laurie* • John Davis Lodge [John Lodge] *Brooke* • Spring Byington *Marmee* ■ *Dir* George Cukor • *Scr* Sarah Y Mason, Victor Heerman, from the novel by Louisa May Alcott

Little Women ★★★ U

Period drama 1949 · US · Colour · 121mins

This lush adaptation of Louisa May Alcott's novel has the benefit of a good cast, but the studio settings and the MGM production requirements really get in the way of the storytelling. Elizabeth Taylor and Janet Leigh are far too knowing for their roles, and top-billed June Allyson is too coy (and too old) for Jo. There's charm, certainly, whenever Margaret O'Brien and Peter Lawford are around, and the whole is very pretty to look at, but the classic original demanded sterner stuff than this cotton-candy confection. TS

June Allyson *Jo March* • Peter Lawford *Laurie Laurence* • Margaret O'Brien *Beth March* • Elizabeth Taylor *Amy March* • Janet Leigh *Meg March* • Rossano Brazzi *Professor Bhaer* • Mary Astor *Marmee March* • Lucile Watson *Aunt March* • C Aubrey Smith *Mr Laurence* • Elizabeth Patterson *Hannah* • Leon Ames *Mr March* ■ *Dir* Mervyn LeRoy • *Scr* Andrew Solt, Sarah Y Mason, Victor Heerman, from the novel by Louisa May Alcott

Little Women ★★★ U

Period drama 1994 · US · Colour · 113mins

Mother hen Susan Sarandon dominates this adaptation of Louisa May Alcott's much-loved novel about four impoverished sisters growing up during the American Civil War. Australian director Gillian Armstrong jettisons some of the schmaltz that adorned the earlier film versions, allowing Winona Ryder, who's superbly cast as the spirited Jo, to emote like mad. As a result, this 1990s take on the tale is less cosy and, therefore, less memorable, despite its wonderful pedigree. TH [video] DVD

Winona Ryder *Jo March* • Susan Sarandon *Marmee March* • Gabriel Byrne *Professor Friedrich Baer* • Eric Stoltz *John Brooke* • Samantha Mathis *Amy, aged 16* • Trini Alvarado *Meg* • Kirsten Dunst *Amy, aged 12* • Claire Danes *Beth* • Christian Bale *Laurie* • Mary Wickes *Aunt March* • Matthew Walker *Mr March* ■ *Dir* Gillian Armstrong • *Scr* Robin Swicord, from the novel by Louisa May Alcott

The Little World of Don Camillo ★★★★ U

Comedy 1951 · Fr/It · BW · 102mins

This was the first of Fernandel's five outings as the Po valley priest with a surfeit of sense and a hotline to God. With his equine features beaming bonhomie, he's perfectly cast in a role demanding comic charm and unforced humility. Yet, this is anything but a one-man show, as Gino Cervi more than holds his own as the communist mayor who not only delights in pitting his principles against his rival's religious beliefs, political but also rallies round at times of crises. This time he helps with a tangled romance and Don Camillo's possible transfer. Filmed in French, Italian and English language versions. DP

Fernandel *Don Camillo* • Gino Cervi *Peppone* • Sylvie *Christina* • Vera Talchi *Gina* • Franco Interlenghi *Mariolino* • Orson Welles *Narrator (American version)* ■ *Dir* Julien Duvivier • *Scr* René Barjavel, Julien Duvivier, from stories by Giovanni Guareschi

The Littlest Horse Thieves ★★★ U

Period drama 1976 · UK · Colour · 99mins

This Disney period piece (also known as *Escape from the Dark*) provided Alastair Sim with his last screen role, and there are echoes of the unreformed Scrooge in his performance as an Edwardian mine owner. Director Charles Jarrott makes the most of the Yorkshire scenery, but the most exciting scenes take place underground as the three scamps who rescue the ponies use them to save some trapped miners. DP [video]

Alastair Sim *Lord Harrogate* • Peter Barkworth *Richard Sandman* • Maurice Colbourne *Luke Armstrong* • Susan Tebbs *Violet Armstrong* • Geraldine McEwan *Miss Coutts* • Prunella Scales *Mrs Sandman* ■ *Dir* Charles Jarrott • *Scr* Rosemary Anne Sisson, from a story by Rosemary Anne Sisson, Burt Kennedy

The Littlest Rebel ★★★ PG

Musical war drama 1935 · US · BW · 73mins

This was a quintessential vehicle for Shirley Temple, made when the incredibly talented moppet was the top box-office attraction around the world. In this Civil War tale, Temple displays all the facets that made her so unique. The scene in which she pleads with President Lincoln to set her father free from a prisoner-of-war camp displays both humour and pathos, and she chirpily performs two dance duets with Bill Robinson. Only those violently allergic to Temple could fail to warm to this. TV [video]

Shirley Temple *Virginia "Virgie" Houston Cary* • John Boles *Confederate Capt Herbert Cary* • Jack Holt *Union Colonel Morrison* • Karen Morley *Mrs Cary* • Bill Robinson *Uncle Billy* • Guinn Williams [Guinn "Big Boy" Williams] *Sgt Dudley* • Willie Best *James Henry* • Frank McGlynn Sr *President Abraham Lincoln* • Bessie Lyle *Mammy* ■ *Dir* David Butler • *Scr* Edwin Burke, Harry Tugend, from the play by Edward Peple

L

Live a Little, Love a Little ★★ PG

Musical 1968 · US · Colour · 85mins

An enjoyable romp, at least by Presley standards, with several tuneful songs. Elvis plays a photographer who digs himself into a hole when he tries to shuttle between two jobs for publishers with very different editorial policies – both in the same office building. Watch out for Rudy Vallee, a singing star from an earlier era, as a publisher. Reasonably frothy. JG

Elvis Presley *Greg* • Michele Carey *Bernice* • Don Porter *Mike Landsdown* • Rudy Vallee *Penlow* • Dick Sargent *Harry* • Sterling Holloway *Milkman* ■ *Dir* Norman Taurog • *Scr* Michael A Hoey, Dan Greenburg, from the novel *Kiss My Firm But Pliant Lips* by Dan Greenburg

Live a Little, Steal a Lot ★★ 15

Crime comedy 1974 · US · Colour · 101mins

Robert Conrad and Don Stroud play real-life heist-meisters Allan Kuhn and Jack Murphy who, when the film was made, were locked up in a Florida prison. Jumped-up beach boys in flash clothes, they specialised in fleecing Miami and Bahamian hotels and beach houses; they then went big time by removing a priceless sapphire called the Star of India from the Natural History Museum in New York. It's filled with the requisite number of chases, close shaves and "characterful" performances designed to glamourise the criminals. AT

Robert Conrad *Allan Kuhn* • Don Stroud *Jack Murphy* • Donna Mills *Ginny Eaton* • Robyn Millan *Sharon Kagel* • Luther Adler *Max "The Eye"* • Paul Stewart *Avery* • Burt Young *Sergeant Bernasconi* ■ *Dir* Marvin J Chomsky • *Scr* E Arthur Kean, from a story by Allan Dale Kuhn

Live and Let Die ★★★★ PG

Spy adventure 1973 · UK · Colour · 116mins

Roger Moore's first tour of duty as James Bond, in the eighth of the licensed-to-kill series, has him up against the dark powers of voodoo in the bulky shape of Yaphet Kotto, while embracing the more curvaceous figure of tarot-reader Jane Seymour. Boasting as many cliff-hanging moments as a Saturday-matinée serial, this tale of a plan to turn everyone into drug addicts allows Bond's adversaries to be as mechanical as Moore himself. There are some splendid spasms of action, however, notably a speedboat leap that set a world record, as well as the usual hi-tech gadgetry. TH DVD

Roger Moore *James Bond* • Yaphet Kotto *Dr Kananga/Mr Big* • Jane Seymour (2) *Solitaire* • Clifton James *Sheriff Pepper* • Julius W Harris [Julius Harris] *Tee Hee* • Geoffrey Holder *Baron Samedi* • David Hedison *Felix Leiter* • Gloria Hendry *Rosie* • Bernard Lee *"M"* • Lois Maxwell *Miss Moneypenny* • Ruth Kempf *Mrs Bell* • Joie Chitwood *Charlie* ■ *Dir* Guy Hamilton • *Scr* Tom Mankiewicz, from the novel by Ian Fleming

Live Bait ★★★

Comedy 1995 · Can · BW · 84mins

Considering he was debuting as writer, director, editor and producer, Bruce Sweeney made a decent fist of this Generation X comedy. Overshadowed by his brother, pampered by his mother and taunted by his ambitious father, Tom Scholte has little going for him until he meets sculptress Micki Maunsell, who not only awakens his sense of self, but also becomes his sexual muse. Smart dialogue, exceptional performances and a fond nostalgia for the passing of mis-spent youth raise this above the average slacker or rites-of-passage picture. DP

Tom Scholte *Trevor MacIntosh* • Kevin McNulty *John MacIntosh* • Babs Chula *Helen MacIntosh* • David Lovgren *Brian MacIntosh* • Micki Maunsell *Charlotte Peacock* ■ *Dir/Scr* Bruce Sweeney

Live Fast, Die Young ★★

Crime 1958 · US · BW · 82mins

A genuine European "Ladies' Man" (the title of his autobiography), actor Paul Henreid directed several movies including this effort aimed squarely at the teen audience. It's about a young woman who gets involved in crime, and makes a bundle until her more law-abiding older sister spoils the party. Deeply moral, it stars Mary Murphy from *The Wild One* and teen heart-throb Troy Donahue. AT

Mary Murphy *Kim Winters* • Norma Eberhardt *Jill Winters* • Sheridan Comerate *Jerry Beckitt* • Michael Connors [Mike Connors] *Rick* • Carol Varga *Violet* • Jay Jostyn *Knox* • Peggy Maley *Sue Hawkins* • Troy Donahue *Artie* ■ *Dir* Paul Henreid • *Scr* Allen Rivkin, Ib Melchior, from a story by Edwin B Watson, Ib Melchior

Live Flesh ★★★★ 18

Black comedy thriller
1997 · Sp/Fr · Colour · 96mins

Excruciatingly funny, fearlessly frank and gloriously ironic, Spanish director Pedro Almodóvar's engaging take on the Ruth Rendell thriller is a deliciously twisted tale of destiny, desire and death. Using the central concept of how a single bullet fired during a botched police investigation causes a ricochet effect through the lives of five different characters, the camp iconoclast serves up a pulse-quickening cocktail of subversion and sexual tension where truth and humanity are used as clever red herrings. Featuring amazing performances from Javier Bardem and Angela Molina, this crime of passion is a must-see. AJ. In Spanish with English subtitles. Contains violence, swearing, sex scenes and nudity. DVD

Francesca Neri *Elena* • Javier Bardem *David* • Liberto Rabal *Victor Plaza* • José Sancho *Sancho* • Angela Molina *Clara* • Penélope Cruz *Isabelle* • Pilar Bardem *Dona Centro* ■ *Dir* Pedro Almodóvar • *Scr* Pedro Almodóvar, Ray Loriga, Jorge Guerricaechevarría, from the novel by Ruth Rendell

Live Forever ★★ 15

Music documentary
2002 · UK · Colour · 82mins

Britpop was a social phenomenon that heralded the dawn of New Labour. At least that's the contention of this lively, but narrowly focused, insight into the 1990s music scene. Ignoring the Spice Girls and the entire dance-music sector, first-time director John Dower concentrates on guitar bands with vague political agendas in a specious bid to celebrate a single cultural constituency that several of the interviewees actively deny. The issue of laddism is also airbrushed, yet the class fissures remain clearly evident. Damon Albarn, Jarvis Cocker and Noel Gallagher offer valuable analysis, but other contributions range from the peripheral to the downright embarrassing. DP DVD

Dir John Dower • *Cinematographer* Frédéric Fabre • *Editor* Jake Martin

Live from Baghdad ★★★ 15

Historical war drama
2002 · US · Colour · 108mins

This award-winning TV movie tells the story of a group of CNN reporters who stayed to cover the unfolding Gulf War crisis in 1991 after all the other networks had pulled out of the Iraqi capital, Baghdad. Co-written by one of the key players, veteran CNN producer Robert Wiener (played by Michael Keaton), it seamlessly mixes genuine news footage with taut, well-shot and impressively acted drama. Though the film's gung-ho attitude and occasionally too convenient scenarios smack of low-level propaganda, there's no denying the power of the tale, which makes even the dullest mechanics of journalism exciting. SF. Contains swearing. DVD

Michael Keaton *Robert Wiener* • Helena Bonham Carter *Ingrid Formanek* • Lili Taylor *Judy Parker* • Bruce McGill *Peter Arnett* • David Suchet *Naji Al-Hadithi* • Robert Wisdom *Bernard Shaw* • Paul Guilfoyle (2) *Ed Turner* ■ *Dir* Mick Jackson • *Scr* Robert Wiener, Richard Chapman, John Patrick Shanley, Timothy J Sexton, from the non-fiction book *Live from Baghdad: Making Journalism History behind the Lines* by Robert Wiener

Live It Up ★★ U

Musical comedy 1963 · UK · BW · 71mins

You'd hardly know that the Beatles were in the process of transforming the British pop scene from some of the sounds presented in this determinedly traditional musical. Lance Comfort was a decent director, but he was hardly cutting edge and he handles the drama as unimaginatively as he stages the songs. Icon-in-waiting David Hemmings looks distinctly uncomfortable as the Post Office messenger who defies trad dad Ed Devereux to bid for the top, prompting a hackneyed subplot about an audition and a big American producer. DP

David Hemmings *Dave Martin* • Jennifer Moss *Jill* • John Pike *Phil* • Heinz Burt *Ron* • Steven Marriott *Ricky* • Joan Newell *Margaret Martin* • Ed Devereaux *Herbert Martin* ■ *Dir* Lance Comfort • *Scr* Lyn Fairhurst, from his story, from an idea by Harold Shampan

Live, Love and Learn ★★★

Comedy 1937 · US · BW · 78mins

Rich girl Rosalind Russell marries impoverished artist Robert Montgomery and the two enjoy bohemian bliss in Greenwich Village until success for the artist rears its corrupting head. The two stars are delightful in the early portions of this mixture of screwball comedy and melodrama, but get little help from the script when things get tougher. The stars, the MGM polish and a sterling supporting cast give the fluffy concoction enough substance to keep it watchable. TV

Robert Montgomery *Bob Graham* • Rosalind Russell *Julie Stoddard Graham* • Robert Benchley *Oscar* • Helen Vinson *Lily Chalmers* • Monty Woolley *Mr Charles C Bawltitude* • EE Clive *Mr Palmiston* • Mickey Rooney *Jerry Crump* ■ *Dir* George Fitzmaurice • *Scr* Charles Brackett, Cyril Hume, Richard Maibaum, from a story by Marion Parsonnet, Helen Grace Carlisle

Live Now – Pay Later ★★★★

Comedy 1962 · UK · BW · 103mins

A remarkably cynical and revealing portrait of Britain shifting from postwar austerity into rampant consumerism and the swinging sixties. Ian Hendry plays a seedy, on-the-make, door-to-door salesman who pressurises his customers – usually housewives – into bed and into hock. Hendry's character is appalling, yet he is also sympathetic since he's the only person who ever does anything in a society built on inertia and the sense of defeat that only wartime victory can bring. AT

Ian Hendry *Albert Argyle* • June Ritchie *Treasure* • John Gregson *Callendar* • Liz Fraser *Joyce Corby* • Geoffrey Keen *Reggie Corby* • Jeannette Sterke *Grace* • Peter Butterworth *Fred* • Nyree Dawn Porter *Marjorie Mason* • Ronald Howard *Cedric Mason* • Harold Berens *Solly Cowell* ■ *Dir* Jay Lewis • *Scr* Jack Trevor Story, from the novel *All on the Never-Never* by Jack Lindsay

Live Nude Girls ★★ 18

Comedy drama 1995 · US · Colour · 91mins

Kim Cattrall and Dana Delaney star in this stream of consciousness comedy drama from writer/director Julianna Levin. They're just two of the 30-something women at a reunion party, sitting around talking frankly about sex, relationships, family and friends, as people tend to do on such soul-baring occasions. You'll either get bored really fast by the group's petty, self-indulgent ramblings, or be riveted by the caring and sharing. AJ. Contains nudity and sexual references.

Dana Delany *Jill* • Kim Cattrall *Jamie* • Cynthia Stevenson *Marcy* • Laila Robins *Rachel* • Lora Zane *Georgina* • Olivia D'Abo *Chris* ■ *Dir/Scr* Julianna Lavin

Live Virgin ★★ 15

Comedy 2000 · US/Fr · Colour · 83mins

Mena Suvari finds herself at the centre of a tug-of-war between rival porn barons in this decidedly dubious comedy. Jean-Pierre Marois purposes a scathing satire on everything from pay-per-view to the internet and consenting smut., but his film rapidly descends into a bawdy farce. Robert Loggia and Bob Hoskins toss restraint to the winds, while Gabriel Mann's geeky boyfriend and Sally Kellerman's talk show hostess are lazy clichés. As for Suvari, readying to lose her virginity for the cameras, better things were just around the corner. DP DVD

Bob Hoskins *Joey* • Mena Suvari *Katrina* • Robert Loggia *Ronny* • Gabriel Mann *Brian* • Sally Kellerman *Quaint* • Lamont Johnson *Nick* ■ *Dir* Jean-Pierre Marois • *Scr* Ira Israel, Jean-Pierre Marois

Live Wire ★★★ 15

Thriller 1992 · US · Colour · 81mins

Pierce Brosnan stars in this better-than-average TV movie with a strong cast and an ingenious storyline. The future 007 plays an FBI agent trying to stop the villainous Ben Cross blowing up Washington politicians. The twist here is that Cross has developed a liquid explosive that gives new meaning to the phrase "don't drink the water": if you do, you effectively become a human bomb. That's the cue for some truly stunning explosive effects. His dodgy American accent aside, Brosnan is as charismatic as ever. JF. Contains swearing, violence and a sex scene.

Pierce Brosnan *Danny O'Neill* • Ron Silver *Frank Traveres* • Ben Cross *Mikhail Rashid* • Lisa Eilbacher *Terry O'Neill* • Tony Plana *Al-Red* • Al Waxman *James Garvey* • Philip Baker Hall *Senator Thyme* ■ *Dir* Christian Duguay • *Scr* Bart Baker

The Lives of a Bengal Lancer ★★★★ U

Action adventure 1935 · US · BW · 104mins

A fabulous chunk of "Hollywood colonial", this wonderful, rip-roaring tale was a smash hit in its day and still manages to stir the hearts of adventure lovers. Gary Cooper, in a career-defining performance, and the urbane Franchot Tone are terrific as buddies on the North-West Frontier, fighting an array of evil, turbaned character actors, and looking after new recruit Richard Cromwell, who just happens to be the son of their commanding officer, Guy Standing. Multi-Oscar nominated, this has been highly influential. TS

Gary Cooper *Lieutenant Alan McGregor* • Franchot Tone *Lieutenant "Fort" Forsythe* • C Aubrey Smith *Major Hamilton* • Richard Cromwell *Lieutenant Donald Stone* • Guy Standing *Colonel Stone* • Kathleen Burke *Tania Volkanskaya* • Douglass Dumbrille *Mohammed Khan* • Monte Blue *Hamzulla Khan* • Akim Tamiroff *Emir of Gopal* • J Carrol

Naish *Grand Vizier* ■ *Dir* Henry Hathaway • *Scr* Waldemar Young, John L Balderston, Achmed Abdullah, from the novel by Major Francis Yeats-Brown, adapted by Grover Jones, Wiliam Slavens McNutt

The Living Daylights ★★ PG

Spy adventure 1987 · UK · Colour · 125mins

This was Timothy Dalton's debut as 007 and it was already pretty clear that he lacked the necessary ironic touch that made the credibility-straining action seem fun rather than ridiculous. Although adapted from an Ian Fleming story, the plot is merely an excuse for a little globe-trotting, as Bond tries to help Soviet general Jeroen Krabbé to defect. Maryam D'Abo's Czech cellist and Joe Don Baker's arms dealer don't help much, either. DP. Contains violence and nudity. VIDEO DVD

Timothy Dalton *James Bond* • Maryam D'Abo *Kara Milovy* • Jeroen Krabbé *General Georgi Koskov* • Joe Don Baker *Brad Whitaker* • John Rhys-Davies *General Leonid Pushkin* • Art Malik *Kamran Shah* • Andreas Wisniewski *Necros* • Thomas Wheatley *Saunders* • Desmond Llewelyn *"Q"* • Robert Brown *"M"* • Caroline Bliss *Miss Moneypenny* ■ *Dir* John Glen • *Scr* Richard Maibaum, Michael G Wilson, from a story by Ian Fleming

The Living Dead ★★★★

Horror fantasy 1932 · Ger · BW · 98mins

Paul Wegener, the great German actor and director, notably of *The Golem* (1914 and 1920), made his talkie debut in one of the last films of the Expressionist movement. Set in a shadowy England, it was based on two Edgar Allan Poe stories and one from Robert Louis Stevenson's *The Suicide Club*. Wegener plays a crazed inventor who kills his wife accidentally and conceals her body in a wall. The film, which seems to herald incipient Nazism, contains effective scenes in a waxworks museum and in an asylum where the lunatics have taken over. RB. In German with English subtitles.

Paul Wegener *The murderer* • Harald Paulsen *Frank Briggs* • Mary Parker *Briggs's fiancée* • Paul Henckels *Doctor* ■ *Dir* Richard Ornstein [Richard Oswald] • *Scr* Heinz Goldberg, Eugen Szatmari, from stories by Edgar Allan Poe and from a short story by Robert Louis Stevenson

The Living Dead at the Manchester Morgue ★★★ 18

Horror 1974 · Sp/It · Colour · 95mins

Night of the Living Dead gets an extreme gore makeover in this high-level Spanish shocker from splatter-maestro Jorge Grau. An experimental pesticide developed by the government not only succeeds in killing bugs but also raising the corpses in a nearby Manchester hospital. Wooden Ray Lovelock is the hippy hero who tries to stop the flesh-eating hordes. There's a bleak twist involving fascist cop Arthur Kennedy, and although nauseatingly graphic, Grau's cannibal holocaust is stylishly presented and effectively orchestrated by Giuliano Sorgini's chilling score. AJ VIDEO DVD

Raymond Lovelock *George* • Christina Galbo *Edna* • Arthur Kennedy *Inspector McCormick* • Jeanine Mestre *Katie* • Jose Lifante *Martin* ■ *Dir* Jorge Grau • *Scr* Sandro Continenza, Marcello Coscia

The Living Desert ★★★★ U

Documentary 1953 · US · Colour · 71mins

Keen to exploit the success of the "True-Life Adventures" series, Walt Disney moved into feature documentaries with this Oscar-winning study of the wildlife that endures the climatic extremes of Death Valley, the Yuma sand dunes and the Salton Sea mud pots. Disney's regular distributor, RKO, was convinced the film would fail at the box-office and so Walt founded his own company, Buena Vista, to launch the phenomenally profitable picture. Critics denounced the fact that the bobcat's escape from some wild pigs was staged rather than "discovered", but with a lively commentary by Winston Hibler, it remains a classic of its kind. DP

Dir James Algar • *Scr* James Algar, Winston Hibler, Ted Sears, Jack Moffitt

The Living End ★★★ 18

Road movie 1992 · US · Colour · 81mins

Shot on a shoestring by Gregg Araki, the *enfant terrible* of American independent cinema, this film gleefully advertised itself as an "irresponsible" black comedy about society's attitude towards HIV-positive gay men. While Araki sometimes tries a little too hard to shock and the acting is always the wrong side of raw, this is a film that is not ashamed to make a fool of itself in order to convey its audacious mix of comedy and anger. DP. Contains violence, swearing and nudity. VIDEO

Mike Dytri *Luke* • Craig Gilmore *Jon* • Mark Finch *Doctor* • Mary Woronov *Daisy* ■ *Dir/Scr* Gregg Araki

Living Free ★★ U

Wildlife adventure
1972 · UK · Colour · 88mins

This sequel to the ever-popular *Born Free* follows the fate of Elsa the lioness's three cubs after she is killed. The Adamsons are determined to keep them out of the zoo, but, unfortunately, their 700-mile journey across the wilds of Kenya to the Serengeti National Park has too few moments of high drama. However, the scenery is stunning, and, of course, the cubs are as cute and cuddly as ever. Richard Harris starred as George Adamson in an excellent follow-up film, 1999's *To Walk with Lions*. DP VIDEO DVD

Nigel Davenport *George Adamson* • Susan Hampshire *Joy Adamson* • Geoffrey Keen *John Kendall* • Edward Judd *Game Warden Weaver* ■ *Dir* Jack Couffer • *Scr* Millard Kaufman, from the books by Joy Adamson

The Living Idol ★

Adventure 1955 · US · Colour · 100mins

Director Albert Lewin's sixth and final movie was this preposterous Mexican-set fantasy. An archaeological expedition discovers a strange temple dedicated to the Mayan jaguar god; before long possession and reincarnation decimate the mission. Matinée idol Steve Forrest, bumbling British stalwart James Robertson-Justice and Broadway legend Liliane Montevecchi enliven the proceedings – but not by much. AJ

Steve Forrest *Terry Matthews* • Liliane Montevecchi *Juanita* • James Robertson-Justice *Dr Alfred Stones* • Sara Garcia *Elena* • Eduardo Noriega (1) *Manuel* ■ *Dir/Scr* Albert Lewin

Living in a Big Way ★★

Comedy drama 1947 · US · BW · 103mins

Marrying in haste before being drafted overseas, a GI returns to repent at leisure when his wife turns out to be wealthy, pampered, intent on a good time and a totally unsuitable mate. A box-office disaster in its day and hardly seen since, this confused mix of comedy, drama, social message, and sentimentality is not without some entertainment value. Gene Kelly stars as the idealistic hero, Marie "The Body" McDonald is the wife, and the experienced Gregory La Cava directs with some style. RK

Gene Kelly *Leo Gogarty* • Marie McDonald *Margaud Morgan* • Charles Winninger *D Rutherford Morgan* • Phyllis Thaxter *Peggy Randall* • Spring Byington *Mrs Morgan* ■ *Dir* Gregory La Cava • *Scr* Gregory La Cava, Irving Ravetch, from a story by Gregory La Cava

Living in Fear ★

Thriller 2001 · US · Colour · 86mins

This hackneyed thriller is supposed to be a mystery, but, even though just about everyone bears a grudge against a late, unlamented clergyman, it won't take you long to figure out who's behind the murders that are committed when one-time asylum inmate William R Moses returns to his home town for the reading of his father's will. Then again, it doesn't help that the cast is stuffed with soap-opera cast-offs and slipping celebs. DP

William R Moses *Chuck Hausman* • Marcia Cross *Rebecca Hausman* • Daniel Quinn *Art* • Katherine Helmond *Mrs Ford* • John Saxon *Rev Leo Hausman* ■ *Dir/Scr* Martin Kitrosser

Living in Hope ★ 15

Comedy drama 2001 · UK · Colour · 83mins

Another embarrassing British attempt to emulate the US campus movie, this is guaranteed to draw howls of derision. Guy de Beaujeu's screenplay is rigid with clichés and caricatures, while John Miller's direction wouldn't pass basic drama society muster. Consequently, the cast hasn't an earthly of luring us into the Bristol University world of babes, booze and bungee jumping. DP DVD

Tom Harper *"Posh"/Alistair* • Paul Foster *Footsie* • Liam McMahon *Liam* • Bennet Thorpe *Animal* • Robin Edwards *Harry* • Naomie Harris *Ginny* • Jade Ball *Michaela* ■ *Dir* John Miller • *Scr* Guy de Beaujeu

Living in Oblivion ★★★★ 15

Comedy 1995 · US · Colour and BW · 86mins

The tribulations of low-budget independent film-making are sent up with glorious wit in this low-budget independent film from director Tom DiCillo. Steve Buscemi is hilarious as the harassed director contending with egomaniacal leading man James LeGros, inept stagehands, back-stabbing assistants, off-screen love affairs and a temperamental dwarf, all in one day of production. Packed with movie-buff in-jokes, DiCillo's sparkling satire recalls François Truffaut's similarly themed 1973 movie *Day for Night*. AJ. Contains swearing, sex scenes and nudity. VIDEO

Steve Buscemi *Nick Reve* • Catherine Keener *Nicole* • Dermot Mulroney *Wolf* • Danielle Von Zerneck *Wanda* • James LeGros *Chad Palomino* ■ *Dir/Scr* Tom DiCillo

Living It Up ★★★ U

Musical comedy 1954 · US · Colour · 93mins

This good-natured Dean Martin and Jerry Lewis comedy is actually a remake of the 1937 black comedy movie *Nothing Sacred*. Lewis takes the Carole Lombard role as the victim of radiation poisoning, with smoothie Martin as Jerry's medic, and sexy Janet Leigh in the Fredric March part of the ambitious reporter. Highlights include Sheree North's sizzling performance of what was arguably the first rock 'n' roll number on celluloid. Very funny indeed. TS

Dean Martin *Steve* • Jerry Lewis *Homer* • Janet Leigh *Wally Cook* • Edward Arnold *The Mayor* • Fred Clark *Oliver Stone* • Sheree North *Jitterbug Dancer* ■ *Dir* Norman Taurog • *Scr* Jack Rose, Melville Shavelson, from the musical *Hazel Flagg* by Ben Hecht, Jule Styne, Bob Hilliard, from a story by James Street

Living It Up ★★ 15

Screwball comedy
2000 · Sp · Colour · 108mins

Bereft of ideas outside its basic premise, this is nothing more than a droll vignette. Yet Antonio Cuadri persists in dragging it out long after the laughs have stopped. Salma Hayek stars as a waitress, but the focus falls on bus driver Carmelo Gomez, who borrows money from the Mob to finance one last fling before his suicide, only to fall in love and realise he has a reason to live. DP. In Spanish with English subtitles. VIDEO DVD

Salma Hayek *Lola* • Carmelo Gomez *Martin* • Tito Valverde *Salva* • Alicia Agut *Rosa* • Miguel Ayones *Montero* ■ *Dir* Antonio Cuadri • *Scr* Carlos Asorey, Fernando León de Aranoa, from an idea by Antonio Cuadri

Living Out Loud ★★★ 15

Comedy drama 1998 · US · Colour · 95mins

Screenwriter Richard LaGravenese's directorial debut is a bittersweet comedy with Holly Hunter terrific as the chic Manhattan 40-something trying to make it on her own after her husband of 15 years leaves her. Ensconced in her deluxe high-rise apartment, she passes the time of day with lift operator Danny DeVito and has imaginary conversations with singer Queen Latifah at a jazz bar. An interesting look at 1990s' relationships and one woman's journey in particular, the film unfortunately loses its power towards the end. JB. Contains swearing. VIDEO DVD

Holly Hunter *Judith* • Danny DeVito *Pat* • Queen Latifah *Liz Bailey* • Martin Donovan (2) *Bob Nelson* • Richard Schiff *Philly* • Elias Koteas *The Kisser* • Suzanne Shepherd *Mary* • Mariangela Pino *Donna* ■ *Dir* Richard LaGravenese • *Scr* Richard LaGravenese, from stories by Anton Chekhov

Lizzie ★★★

Psychological drama 1957 · US · BW · 81mins

Eleanor Parker is very fine as the woman with three personalities: one quiet and shy, another raunchy and boisterous and the third together and caring. Psychiatric treatment from a stolidly able Richard Boone swiftly ensues. Hugo Haas's rather humdrum and plodding movie has all the hallmarks of 1950s psychiatric knowledge and practice. SR

Eleanor Parker *Elizabeth Richmond* • Richard Boone *Dr Neal Wright* • Joan Blondell *Aunt Morgan* • Hugo Haas *Walter Brenner* • Ric Roman *Johnny Valenzo* • Dorothy Arnold *Elizabeth's Mother* • John Reach *Robin* • Marion Ross *Ruth Seaton* • Johnny Mathis *Nightclub Singer* ■ *Dir* Hugo Haas • *Scr* Mel Dinelli, from the novel *The Bird's Nest* by Shirley Jackson

The Lizzie McGuire Movie ★★ U

Part-animated comedy drama
2003 · US · Colour · 89mins

Only ardent fans of the Disney Channel's sitcom princess will like director Jim Fall's retake on *Gidget Goes to Rome*. Everyone else should give this synthetic soap opera a wide berth. Fluffy to the point of nearly blowing off the screen, the clumsy TV eighth-grader (Hilary Duff) goes on a graduation school trip to the Eternal City where she's mistaken for the female half of a sensational Italian pop duo. This inane confection is sugar-coated blandness personified and not remotely funny. AJ VIDEO DVD

Hilary Duff *Lizzie McGuire/Isabella* • Adam Lamberg *David "Gordo" Gordon* • Robert Carradine *Sam* • Hallie Todd *Jo* • Jake Thomas *Matt* • Yani Gellman *Paolo* • Ashlie Brillault *Kate* • Clayton Snyder *Ethan* ■ *Dir* Jim Fall • *Scr* Susan Estelle Jansen, Ed Decter, John J Strauss, from the TV series by Terri Minsky

The Llano Kid ★★

Western 1939 · US · BW · 69mins

A mild little Paramount western featuring imported Latin-American crooner Tito Guizar as writer O Henry's legendary "kissing bandit", previously played by the great Gary Cooper in *The*

L

Texan. This was made to cash in on the then-popular Cisco Kid (also an O Henry hero) style of exotic cowboy lead. Guizar has an interesting co-star in Jan Clayton, but since the other woman is evil Gale Sondergaard, her co-stars barely get a look-in. TS

Tito Guizar *The Llano Kid* • Alan Mowbray *John Travers* • Gale Sondergaard *Lora Travers* • Jan Clayton *Lupita* • Emma Dunn *Donna Teresa* • Minor Watson *Sheriff McLane* ■ *Dir* Edward Venturini • *Scr* Wanda Tuchock, from the short story *The Double-Dyed Deceiver* by O Henry

Lloyd's of London ★★★★

Historical epic 1936 · US · BW · 115mins

No facet of history was safe from 20th Century-Fox, who managed to turn both Rothschild and Lloyd's into household names in America. The presence of the young Tyrone Power undeniably helped in the latter instance, and this is the movie that launched the matinée idol's stardom. Power's character begins, though, as an apprentice (played by Freddie Bartholomew) in the famous brokerage house. He grows up to vie with suave George Sanders for the beauteous Madeleine Carroll. It's extremely handsomely mounted and director Henry King treats it all as though it's a solid piece of Americana. TS

Freddie Bartholomew *Young Jonathan Blake* • Tyrone Power *Jonathan Blake* • Madeleine Carroll *Lady Elizabeth Stacy* • Sir Guy Standing [Guy Standing] *John Julius Angerstein* • George Sanders *Lord Everett Stacy* • C Aubrey Smith *Old "Q"* • Virginia Field *Polly* • Montagu Love *Hawkins* • Una O'Connor *Widow Blake* • JM Kerrigan *Brook Watson* ■ *Dir* Henry King • *Scr* Ernest Pascal, Walter Ferris, from a story by Curtis Kenyon

Loaded ★★ 18

Psychological thriller
1994 · UK/NZ · Colour · 91mins

Anna Campion, sister of the Oscar-winning Jane, makes her directing debut with this modest, yet intriguing thriller. The story focuses on a vaguely pretentious group of Generation X school-leavers who travel to the country to make a horror film. Things go pear-shaped when they collectively drop some tabs of acid one night. Campion summons up an air of quiet psychological menace, although it's hard to work up much sympathy for the self-centred characters. JF DVD

Oliver Milburn *Neil* • Nick Patrick *Giles* • Catherine McCormack *Rose* • Thandie Newton *Zita* • Matthew Eggleton *Lionel* • Danny Cunningham *Lance* • Biddy Hodson *Charlotte* ■ *Dir/Scr* Anna Campion

Lobster Man from Mars ★★ PG

Science-fiction comedy
1989 · US · Colour · 78mins

Borrowing liberally from Mel Brooks's classic *The Producers*, this good-natured spoof of all those drive-in monster movies of the 1950s is just about tacky and smart enough to be intermittently enjoyable. Tony Curtis stars as movie mogul JP Shelldrake who, upon being told he needs a flop for tax purposes, sets out to make the biggest howler in Hollywood history. The performances are enthusiastic and suitably ripe, but director Stanley Sheff fails to maintain the high level of inspirational parody that made *Airplane!* and *The Naked Gun* such comedy classics. RS

Tony Curtis *JP Shelldrake* • Deborah Foreman *Mary* • Anthony Hickox *John* • Tommy Sledge • Dean Jacobson *Stevie Horowitz* • Fred Holliday *Colonel Ankrum* • Bobby Pickett *King of Mars, the Astrologer* • SD Nemeth *Dreaded Lobster Man* ■ *Dir* Stanley Sheff • *Scr* Bob Greenberg

Local Hero ★★★★ PG

Comedy 1983 · UK · Colour · 107mins

This comedy drama firmly established Bill Forsyth as a major British film-maker. It's a lyrical, almost mystical, tale that follows the attempts of Texas oilman Burt Lancaster and his minion Peter Riegert to buy up an isolated Scottish village in order to build an oil refinery, without bargaining on the village's integral strength of community. This avoids the relentless whimsy of Forsyth's previous outing, *Gregory's Girl*, while the scenery is gorgeous, and the performances funny, ironic and moving. SR. Contains swearing. DVD

Peter Riegert *MacIntyre* • Burt Lancaster *Happer'* • Denis Lawson *Urquhart* • Peter Capaldi *Oldsen* • Fulton Mackay *Ben* • Jenny Seagrove *Marina* • Jennifer Black *Stella* • Christopher Asante *Reverend MacPherson* • Rikki Fulton *Geddes* ■ *Dir/Scr* Bill Forsyth • *Cinematographer* Chris Menges

Loch Ness ★★★ PG

Fantasy drama 1994 · UK · Colour · 96mins

There's more than a hint of *Local Hero* in this feel-good fantasy drama from director John Henderson. The script had been around for a decade before Ted Danson signed up as the scientist sent to the Highlands to disprove the existence of Nessie. Naturally, his investigation is sidetracked by romance and the self-interested schemes of the locals before he, too, becomes convinced by the legend. Although Danson is a touch bland, Joely Richardson turns in a doughty performance as the single mum whose daughter knows a thing or two about "water kelpies". DP DVD

Ted Danson *Dempsey* • Joely Richardson *Laura* • Ian Holm *Water Bailiff* • Harris Yulin *Doctor Mercer* • James Frain *Adrian Foote* • Keith Allen *Gordon Shoals* • Nick Brimble *Andy Maclean* • Kirsty Graham *Isabel* • Harry Jones *Wee Wullie* • Philip O'Brien *Doctor Abernathy* ■ *Dir* John Henderson • *Scr* John Fusco

Lock, Stock and Two Smoking Barrels ★★★★ 18

Crime comedy 1998 · UK · Colour · 102mins

Widely regarded as the best British crime movie since *The Long Good Friday*, the youthful exuberance of Guy Ritchie's debut feature is truly infectious. The superb cast is spiced up with the presence of celebrities such as Sting, and especially Vinnie Jones in a well-received henchman-with-a-heart role. The action revolves around young cardsharp Nick Moran, who loses £500,000 he doesn't have to a crime king. With a week to come up with the shortfall, he and mates Dexter Fletcher, Jason Flemyng and Jason Statham plan to hijack the proceeds of a robbery hatched by their gangster neighbours, but things go horribly wrong very quickly. Cheerfully amoral and featuring some canny carnage, it's fun from start to finish. JF. Contains violence, swearing, nudity and drug abuse. DVD

Jason Flemyng *Tom* • Dexter Fletcher *Soap* • Nick Moran *Eddy* • Jason Statham *Bacon* • Steven Mackintosh *Winston* • Nicholas Rowe *J* • Nick Marcq *Charles* • Charlie Forbes *Willie* • Vinnie Jones *Big Chris* • Lenny McLean *Barry the Baptist* • Peter McNicholl *Little Chris* • PH Moriarty *Hatchet Harry* • Stephen Marcus *Nick the Greek* • Vas Blackwood *Rory Breaker* • Sting *JD* ■ *Dir/Scr* Guy Ritchie

Lock Up ★★ 18

Prison drama 1989 · US · Colour · 104mins

Sylvester Stallone opts for some grittier material after the cartoon heroics of his Rambo and Rocky characters, but this proves to be almost as disastrous as his forays into comedy. He plays a nice criminal on the verge of being released who is whisked away to a Gothic prison hell presided over by a wildly over-the-top Donald Sutherland. Director John Flynn loses his way in a flood of testosterone and prison clichés. JF. Contains swearing, violence. DVD

Sylvester Stallone *Frank Leone* • Donald Sutherland *Warden Drumgoole* • John Amos *Meissner* • Tom Sizemore *Dallas* • Frank McRae *Eclipse* • Sonny Landham *Chink* • Larry Romano *First Base* • Darlanne Fluegel *Melissa* ■ *Dir* John Flynn • *Scr* Richard Smith, Jeb Stuart, Henry Rosenbaum

Lock Up Your Daughters! ★★ 15

Period comedy 1969 · UK · Colour · 97mins

The story of three sex-starved sailors on leave and at large isn't just confined to *On the Town*, as this adaptation of an 18th-century comedy demonstrates. This version of the London stage musical comes to the screen minus the songs. Despite its distinguished origins – and a cast that includes Christopher Plummer, Susannah York and Glynis Johns – it comes across as non-musical slapstick that's as loud and vulgar as a cheapjack panto. TH. Contains violence, swearing, sex scenes.

Christopher Plummer *Lord Foppington* • Susannah York *Hilaret* • Glynis Johns *Mrs Squeezum* • Ian Bannen *Ramble* • Tom Bell *Shaftoe* • Elaine Taylor *Cloris* • Jim Dale *Lusty* • Kathleen Harrison *Lady Clumsey* • Roy Kinnear *Sir Tunbelly Clumsey* • Georgia Brown *Nell* • Roy Dotrice *Gossip* • Fenella Fielding *Lady Eager* ■ *Dir* Peter Coe • *Scr* Keith Waterhouse, Willis Hall, from the musical *Lock Up Your Daughters!* by Bernard Miles, Laurie Johnson, Lionel Bart, from the play *Rape upon Rape* by Henry Fielding and the play *The Relapse* by John Vanbrugh

The Locket ★★★

Film noir 1946 · US · BW · 85mins

A minor league *film noir*, tightly directed by John Brahm and starring Laraine Day, about a little girl who allegedly stole a locket and whose kleptomania as a woman leads to murder, suicide and nervous breakdowns for everyone around her. Every flashbacked scene is a crisis, every performance over the top. Day is convincingly neurotic, while Robert Mitchum gives her solid support as the first of her men to crack. AT

Laraine Day *Nancy* • Brian Aherne *Dr Blair* • Robert Mitchum *Norman Clyde* • Gene Raymond *John Willis* • Sharyn Moffett *Nancy, aged 10* • Ricardo Cortez *Mr Bonner* • Henry Stephenson *Lord Wyndham* ■ *Dir* John Brahm • *Scr* Sheridan Gibney

Los Locos ★★★ 15

Western 1997 · US/UK · Colour · 95mins

After the overtly political *Posse*, writer/star/producer Mario Van Peebles loosens up considerably for this engaging western. This time around ace gunslinger Peebles finds himself the unwitting saviour of a group of patients at a very primitive mental asylum, after the inmates save him from death. The star is as charismatic as before and his script nods slyly towards Clint Eastwood's classic *The Outlaw Josey Wales*. Western purists may wince at some of the modern liberties that are taken, but it's always watchable. JF

Mario Van Peebles *Chance* • René Auberjonois *Presidente* • Tom Dorfmeister *Baby Brother* • Paul Lazar *Buck* • Rusty Schwimmer *Sister Drexel* • Danny Trejo *Manuel Batista* • Melora Walters *Allison* • Eric Winzenried *Spackman* • Jean Speegle Howard *Mother Superior* ■ *Dir* Jean-Marc Vallée • *Scr* Mario Van Peebles

The Lodger ★★★★ PG

Classic silent thriller 1926 · UK · BW · 92mins

Alfred Hitchcock once called this the "first true Hitchcock movie". In addition to being the first in which he explored his favourite theme of the innocent in danger, it also marked his debut before the camera in one of those celebrated fleeting cameos. Clearly reflecting the influence of German expressionism, this was dismissed as a disaster by the distributors, but the critics proclaimed it the best British film made to date. The action is based on a novel about Jack the Ripper and played with extravagance by matinée idol Ivor Novello and a truly creepy cast. DP DVD

Ivor Novello *The Lodger/Jonathan Drew* • June *Daisy Bunting* • Marie Ault *Mrs Bunting* • Arthur Chesney *Mr Bunting* • Malcolm Keen *Joe Betts* ■ *Dir* Alfred Hitchcock • *Scr* Alfred Hitchcock, Eliot Stannard, Ivor Montagu, from the novel by Marie Belloc-Lowndes

The Lodger ★★★★

Thriller 1944 · US · BW · 80mins

In his first big starring role, the massive young character actor Laird Cregar makes an excellent job of portraying the lodger in Victorian London who is really the notorious killer, Jack the Ripper. Merle Oberon is the singer living in the same house, and George Sanders is the Scotland Yard inspector. A fine script is enhanced by the striking visual sense of director John Brahm and cameraman Lucien Ballard, who later married Oberon. Sadly, Cregar's promising career ended when he died from crash-dieting. AE

Merle Oberon *Kitty* • George Sanders *John Garrick* • Laird Cregar *The Lodger* • Sir Cedric Hardwicke [Cedric Hardwicke] *Robert Burton* • Sara Allgood *Ellen* • Aubrey Mather *Supt Sutherland* • Queenie Leonard *Daisy* • David Clyde *Sgt Bates* ■ *Dir* John Brahm • *Scr* Barré Lyndon, from the novel by Marie Belloc-Lowndes

Logan's Run ★★★ PG

Science-fiction thriller
1976 · US · Colour · 113mins

Michael York and Jenny Agutter star in this tale that earnestly depicts a society that dooms those over the age of 30 to the myth of "renewal". Director Michael Anderson takes a while to make his point here, but puts on a real spurt when the runners head for the outside. Dale Hennesy and Robert De Vestel's Oscar-nominated, imaginative designs compensate for the rather cumbersome plot. TH. Contains violence, nudity.

Michael York *Logan* • Jenny Agutter *Jessica* • Richard Jordan *Francis* • Roscoe Lee Browne *Box* • Farrah Fawcett-Majors [Farrah Fawcett] *Holly* • Peter Ustinov *Old man* • Michael Anderson Jr *Doc* • Gary Morgan *Billy* ■ *Dir* Michael Anderson • *Scr* David Zelag Goodman, from the novel by William F Nolan, George Clayton Johnson • *Costume Designer* Bill Thomas

Logan's War: Bound by Honor ★★ 15

Action drama 1998 · US · Colour · 87mins

Chuck Norris sticks to pretty much to his usual formula here in a story co-written by his brother, Aaron. It's a no-nonsense drama with plenty of bruising fight sequences and even more corny dialogue. Accepting his advancing years, Norris passes the buck to Eddie Cibrian, who stars as an army ranger out to avenge the family murdered when he was a child. Primordial, but professional. DP DVD

Chuck Norris *Jake Fallon* • Eddie Cibrian *Logan Fallon* • Joe Spano *Agent Downing* • Jeff Kober *Sal Mercado* • RD Call *Al Talgorno*

■ *Dir* Michael Preece • *Scr* Walter Klenhard, from a story by Chuck Norris, Aaron Norris, Walter Klenhard

Lola ★★★★★ PG

Romantic comedy drama
1960 · Fr/It · BW · 83mins

Dedicated to Max Ophüls but bearing the hallmarks of a Gene Kelly musical, Jacques Demy's debut feature is a charming paean to his home town of Nantes, here given a monochrome gloss by cinematographer Raoul Coutard that evokes both the poetic realism of the 1930s and the vibrancy of the *Nouvelle Vague*. Demy sweeps his camera around the port as cabaret dancer Anouk Aimée has a few affairs while awaiting the return of her daughter's absentee father. Gleefully playing games with chance and coincidence, this fond satire on movie romance remains as fresh, enchanting and deliciously superficial as it seemed on its original release. Demy remade this in 1969 as *Model Shop* for his Hollywood debut. DP. In French with English subtitles.

Anouk Aimée *Lola* • Marc Michel *Roland* • Elina Labourdette *Mme Desnoyers* • Alan Scott *Frankie* • Annie Duperoux *Cecile* ■ *Dir/Scr* Jacques Demy

Lola ★★★★ 15

Black comedy
1982 · W Ger · Colour · 109mins

Coming between *The Marriage of Maria Braun* and *Veronika Voss*, the second in Rainer Werner Fassbinder's trilogy is unusual in that it has a happy ending. Or, at least as happy as possible considering that brothel chanteuse Barbara Sukowa is bedding corrupt construction boss Mario Adorf within minutes of marrying idealistic town planner Armin Mueller-Stahl. Arguing that fascism did not die with Hitler, Fassbinder mischievously makes a hero of Adorf's petty dictator by having every citizen acquiesce so compliantly in his imposed conformity. A daringly dark, yet gaudily colourful comedy. DP. In German with English subtitles.

Barbara Sukowa *Lola* • Armin Mueller-Stahl *Von Bohm* • Mario Adorf *Schuckert* • Matthias Fuchs *Esslin* • Helga Feddersen *Frau Hettich* • Karin Baal *Lola's mother* • Ivan Desny *Wittich* ■ *Dir* Rainer Werner Fassbinder • *Scr* Peter Marthesheimer, Pea Frohlich

Lola ★★★

Thriller
1986 · Sp · Colour · 106mins

As the factory worker who escapes an abusive relationship to find all-too-brief contentment with her daughter, Angela Molina is both passionate and vulnerable, particularly in the early scenes with Feodor Atkine, the true love who reappears on the scene to investigate her seemingly respectable French husband, Patrick Bauchau. Packed with moments of graphic physicality, psychological intensity and sadistic violence, Bigas Luna's three-act melodrama is sordid and compelling in equal measure. DP. Spanish dialogue dubbed into English.

Angela Molina *Lola* • Patrick Bauchau *Robert* • Feodor Atkine *Mario* • Assumpta Serna *Silvia* ■ *Dir* Bigas Luna • *Scr* Bigas Luna, Luis Herce, Enrique Viciano

Lola and Bilidikid ★★★ 18

Drama
1999 · Tur/Ger · Colour · 91mins

This provocative drama, set on the fringes of Berlin's gay and Turkish communities, has a raw and busy style, in keeping with writer/director Kutlug Ataman's preoccupation with the messiness of life rather than neat fictional contrivance. The performances are honest, with Gandi Mukli outstanding as the drag queen ostracised from his family and pressurised by his macho lover (Erdal Yildiz) to have a sex-change operation. With moments of revelation and tenderness shattered by explosive violence, this study of racism and homophobia burns deep. DP. In German and Turkish with English subtitles. DVD

Baki Davrak *Murat* • Gandi Mukli *Lola* • Erdal Yildiz *Bili* ■ *Dir/Scr* Kutlug Ataman

Lola Montès ★★★★★

Historical romantic drama
1955 · Fr/W Ger · Colour · 140mins

Max Ophüls was inspired to film this story of the rise and fall of the famous mistress of King Ludwig I and Franz Liszt by Judy Garland's nervous breakdown and Zsa Zsa Gabor's romances. Ophüls's final film, his only work in colour, transcends the trappings of a conventional historical romance by his brilliant use of the CinemaScope screen and the virtuoso camerawork. Sadly, on its initial release, the producers reduced the 140-minute film to 90 minutes. It was not until 1969, when it was shown in a restored form, that the film was recognised as the masterpiece it is. RB. In French with English subtitles.

Martine Carol *Lola Montès* • Peter Ustinov *Circus Master* • Anton Walbrook *Ludwig I, King of Bavaria* • Ivan Desny *James* • Will Quadflieg *Liszt* • Oskar Werner *The Student* • Lise Delamare *Mrs Craigie* • Henri Guisol *Maurice* • Paulette Dubost *Joséphine* ■ *Dir* Max Ophüls • *Scr* Max Ophuls, Annette Wademant, Franz Geiger, from the novel *La Vie Extraordinaire de Lola Montès* by Cécil St Laurent, Jacques Natanson • *Cinematographer* Christian Matras

Lolita ★★★★★ 15

Black comedy drama
1961 · UK · BW · 147mins

"How did they ever make a film of *Lolita*?" asked the posters for this brilliant Stanley Kubrick film. Well, in Vladimir Nabokov's adaptation of his own famous novel about the professor and the 12-year-old girl, there are added layers of black comedy and only slight compromise: James Mason seems to love Sue Lyon rather than lust after her, and Lolita's age is increased to 15. Shelley Winters's hilarious and sad portrayal of Lolita's mother is American momism incarnate, while Peter Sellers as Clare Quilty is like a creepy chameleon. For economic and censorship reasons the picture was made in England, so the nightmare vision of urban America and its seedy motels is reduced to obvious back projection and even more obvious Elstree locations. This apart, a perfect movie. AT DVD

James Mason *Humbert Humbert* • Sue Lyon *Lolita Haze* • Shelley Winters *Charlotte Haze* • Peter Sellers *Clare Quilty* • Diana Decker *Jean Farlow* • Jerry Stovin *John Farlow* • Gary Cockrell *Dick* • Marianne Stone *Vivian Darkbloom* ■ *Dir* Stanley Kubrick • *Scr* Vladimir Nabokov, from his novel

Lolita ★★★ 18

Black comedy drama
1997 · Fr/US · Colour · 131mins

To be fair, this 1997 version of Vladimir Nabokov's notorious 1955 novel isn't as sacrilegious as it might have been, with the flashy, superficial Adrian Lyne (*Fatal Attraction*, *Indecent Proposal*) at the helm. However, it is Lyne's bid for artistic "respectability" (the artful shots, the fidelity to the book) that is also the film's undoing. It looks good, but lacks danger. Despite a compelling, tortured turn from Jeremy Irons as Humbert – and a seductive one from Dominique Swain as Lolita – it's all a little too cosmetic and soft-focused. AC DVD

Jeremy Irons *Humbert Humbert* • Melanie Griffith *Charlotte Haze* • Frank Langella *Clare Quilty* • Dominique Swain *Lolita Haze* • Suzanne Shepherd *Miss Pratt* • Keith Reddin *Reverend Rigger* • Erin J Dean *Mona* • Joan Glover *Miss LeBone* ■ *Dir* Adrian Lyne • *Scr* Stephen Schiff, from the novel by Vladimir Nabokov

The Lolly-Madonna War ★★★

Drama
1973 · US · Colour · 105mins

Let backwoods battle commence! Rod Steiger and Robert Ryan are the heads of the feuding families in this variable drama. The two sides have been brought to the brink of violence by a land dispute and matters come to a head with a bizarre case of mistaken identity involving Season Hubley as the presumed "Lolly-Madonna". Director Richard C Sarafian piles a lot of enthusiasm into the mayhem, and the cast is strong. Unfortunately, the film's mood-swings make it only a superior example of Peckinpah-lite. TH

Rod Steiger *Laban Feather* • Robert Ryan *Pap Gutshall* • Jeff Bridges *Zack Feather* • Scott Wilson *Thrush Feather* • Katherine Squire *Mrs Feather* • Tresa Hughes *Mrs Gutshall* • Season Hubley *Roonie Gill* • Randy Quaid *Finch Feather* • Gary Busey *Seb Gutshall* ■ *Dir* Richard C Sarafian • *Scr* Rodney Carr-Smith, Sue Grafton, from the novel by Sue Grafton

Londinium ★★

Comedy
1999 · US · Colour · 90mins

Writer/director Mike Binder also stars in this misfiring comedy of marital manners. It all begins brightly enough, with Binder arriving in London to pen fading US star Mariel Hemingway's new TV series, and falling for French make-up artist Irène Jacob. But once Binder and Hemingway embark on an affair and seek to assuage their guilt by pairing off Jacob with Hemingway's producer husband (Colin Firth), the story begins to stutter and the dialogue becomes self-conscious. DP

Mike Binder *Ben Greene* • Colin Firth *Allen Portland* • Mariel Hemingway *Carly Matthews Portland* • Irène Jacob *Fiona Delgrazia* • Stephen Fry *Nigel* • Jack Dee *Glen* • Stephen Marcus *Davey* ■ *Dir/Scr* Mike Binder

London ★★★★ U

Documentary drama
1994 · UK · Colour · 81mins

After a series of shorts, documentarist Patrick Keiller made his feature debut with this unique portrait of the English capital. With its highly literate commentary from Paul Scofield, this is essentially the story of three expeditions as the narrator and his friend Robinson go in search of London's literary past as well as exploring the reasons why the city sold its soul to suburbia. However, distractions abound as contemporary events such as the 1992 General Election and IRA bomb attacks intrude upon their musings. The juxtaposition of text and image is intriguing as Keiller lilts between travelogue, love letter and lament. Keiller's follow-up to this, a journey around England called *Robinson in Space*, is equally as fascinating. DP DVD

Paul Scofield *Narrator* ■ *Dir/Scr* Patrick Keiller

London after Midnight

Silent mystery
1927 · US · BW

Now sadly lost, this is on the American Film Institute's "most wanted" list. One of the first American films to deal with vampirism, this silent classic was a memorable collaboration between Lon Chaney and that other horror genius, producer/director Tod Browning. Chaney plays multiple roles in a complex plot about a pair of actors terrorising the inhabitants of a cursed Gothic mansion into believing a vampire stalks the premises. This seminal shocker was remade as *Mark of the Vampire* in 1935. AJ

Lon Chaney *Burke* • Marceline Day *Lucille Balfour* • Henry B Walthall *Sir James Hamlin* • Percy Williams *Butler* • Conrad Nagel *Arthur Hibbs* ■ *Dir* Tod Browning • *Scr* Tod Browning, Waldemar Young, from a story by Tod Browning

London Belongs to Me ★★★

Drama
1948 · UK · BW · 112mins

Richard Attenborough as the mechanic charged with murder might be the central character in this Frank Launder and Sidney Gilliat production, but the film belongs fairly and squarely to Alastair Sim. As the fake medium desperately trying to dupe Joyce Carey into marriage, he is hilariously sinister, and the scenes can't pass quickly enough before he's back on the screen. For once, the US title, *Dulcimer Street*, is probably more apposite, as this is one of those sentimentalised "strength in the community" pictures that postwar British cinema was so fond of. DP

Richard Attenborough *Percy Boon* • Alastair Sim *Mr Squales* • Fay Compton *Mrs Josser* • Stephen Murray *Uncle Henry* • Wylie Watson *Mr Josser* • Susan Shaw *Doris Josser* • Ivy St Helier *Connie* ■ *Dir* Sidney Gilliat • *Scr* Sidney Gilliat, JB Williams, from the novel by Norman Collins

London by Night ★★★

Crime
1937 · US · BW · 70mins

Actor/dancer and future US senator George Murphy is the star of this snappy and suspenseful thriller from MGM. A well-crafted script, with punchy dialogue, has Murphy and sassy Rita Johnson (in her film debut) on the trail of a blackmailer who fakes two murders to build his reputation. Genuine English accents were provided by London-born Virginia Field and, as a Scotland Yard detective, Manchester-born George Zucco. RB

George Murphy *Michael Denis* • Rita Johnson *Patricia Herrick* • Virginia Field *Bessie* • Leo G Carroll *Correy* • George Zucco *Inspector Jefferson* • Montagu Love *Sir Arthur Herrick* ■ *Dir* William Thiele • *Scr* George Oppenheimer, from the play *The Umbrella Man* by Will Scott

London Kills Me ★ 18

Comedy drama
1991 · UK · Colour · 102mins

A disappointing directorial debut from Hanif Kureishi, the provocative writer of *My Beautiful Laundrette* and *Sammy and Rosie Get Laid*. Justin Chadwick is a Notting Hill drug-dealer of no fixed abode, who wants to get his life together, but needs a nice pair of shoes in order to land a waiter's job at a restaurant. Whatever Kureishi was trying to say about London criminal culture is lost among boring characters and meaningless story. JC

Justin Chadwick *Clint* • Steven Mackintosh *Muffdiver* • Emer McCourt *Sylvie* • Roshan Seth *Dr Bubba* • Fiona Shaw *Headley* • Brad Dourif *Hemingway* • Tony Haygarth *Burns* • Stevan Rimkus *Tom Tom* • Eleanor David *Lily* • Alun Armstrong *Stone* • Nick Dunning *Faulkner* ■ *Dir/Scr* Hanif Kureishi

London Melody ★★

Musical romance
1937 · UK · BW · 75mins

Slight musical romance from the Anna Neagle/Herbert Wilcox partnership. Neagle, a street singer and dancer, attracts the attention of Tullio Carminati's wealthy, sophisticated diplomat who secretly pays for dancing lessons, enabling her to become a cabaret star. He even takes the blame for a mistake made by the cad (Robert Douglas) to whom she was engaged. Although started at Elstree, its one claim to fame is that it was the very first production to shoot on the sound stages of the new Pinewood Studios in September 1936. AE

Anna Neagle *Jacqueline* • Tullio Carminati *Marius Andreani* • Robert Douglas *Nigel Taplow* • Horace Hodges *Father Donnelly* ■ *Dir* Herbert Wilcox • *Scr* Florence Tranter, Monckton Hoffe, from a story by Ray Lewis

London Town ★ U

Musical comedy 1946 · UK · Colour · 127mins

A comedian from the provinces arrives in London for his big break, only to find he has been hired as the understudy. Thanks to the devious machinations of his daughter, he goes on as the main comic attraction. A huge budget was lavished on this film, with American director Wesley Ruggles imported for the occasion. Unfortunately, it turned out a major disaster.The plot is unappealing, the script weak, the pace laboured and the film too long. RK

Sid Field *Jerry* • Greta Gynt *Mrs Barry* • Petula Clark *Peggy* • Sonnie Hale *Charlie* • Kay Kendall *Patsy* • Jerry Desmonde *George* ■ *Dir* Wesley Ruggles • *Scr* Elliot Paul, Val Guest, Siegfried Herzig, from a story by Wesley Ruggles

The Lone Hand ★★ U

Western 1953 · US · Colour · 79mins

A routine western from Universal, with Joel McCrea posing as an outlaw to bring a criminal gang to justice. McCrea's stolid sturdiness nearly sinks the film; you keep wanting him to show more emotion, but, after all, he is in disguise, even from his own son. George Sherman's direction is undistinguished, but two subsequent TV stars make a creditable showing Barbara Hale from *Perry Mason* and *Gunsmoke*'s James Arness. TS

Joel McCrea *Zachary Hallock* • Barbara Hale *Sarah Jane Skaggs* • Alex Nicol *Jonah Varden* • Charles Drake *George Hadley* • Jimmy Hunt *Joshua Hallock* • Jim Arness [James Arness] *Gus Varden* • Roy Roberts *Mr Skaggs* ■ *Dir* George Sherman • *Scr* Joseph Hoffman, from a story by Irving Ravetch

The Lone Ranger ★★ U

Western 1956 · US · Colour · 85mins

Clayton Moore and Jay Silverheels filled a break from their long-running black-and-white TV series by starring in this deluxe Warner Bros western, still playing their usual characters of the masked avenger and his Indian sidekick, Tonto. The hills of Utah echo to the cry of "Hi-ho, Silver!" as the duo carry out more brave exploits, exposing rancher Lyle Bettger as the man stirring up the Indians to break their treaty so that he can mine the silver in their sacred mountain. AE

Clayton Moore *Lone Ranger* • Jay Silverheels *Tonto* • Lyle Bettger *Reece Kilgore* • Bonita Granville *Welcome* • Perry Lopez *Ramirez* • Robert J Wilke *Cassidy* • John Pickard *Sheriff Kimberly* • Beverly Washburn *Lila* • Michael Ansara *Angry Horse* ■ *Dir* Stuart Heisler • *Scr* Herb Meadow, from characters created by Fran Striker, George W Trendle

The Lone Ranger and the Lost City of Gold ★★ U

Western 1958 · US · Colour · 81mins

The Lone Ranger (Clayton Moore) and his sidekick Tonto (Jay Silverheels) made a comeback after their TV series had ended to celebrate the 25th anniversary of the masked avenger's debut as a radio serial. The childish plot has hooded riders murdering Indians for medallions that, pieced together, show the location of a lost city of gold. The writers and former B-western director Lesley Selander keep the action coming, though, and kids everywhere should still enjoy it. AE

Clayton Moore *Lone Ranger* • Jay Silverheels *Tonto* • Douglas Kennedy *Ross Brady* • Charles Watts *Oscar Matthison* • Noreen Nash *Frances Henderson* • Lisa Montell *Paviva* • Ralph Moody *Padre Vincente Esteban* ■ *Dir* Lesley Selander • *Scr* Robert Schaefer, Eric Freiwald, from characters created by Fran Striker, George W Trendle

The Lone Rider in Ghost Town ★★ U

Western 1941 · US · BW · 55mins

Deemed the best of the 1941 *Lone Riders*, this was released first to whet the public appetite for a new cowboy hero. In 1944, however, star George Houston died of a heart attack in his mid-40s. The majority of the nine-strong series was directed by the prolific Sam Newfield, and produced by his brother Sigmund Neufeld, chief of production at PRC. The series waned rapidly in popularity, and the last few were released without the words "Lone Rider" in the actual titles. TS

George Houston *Tom Cameron* • Al St John *Fuzzy* • Alaine Brandes *Helen* • Budd Buster *Moosehide* • Frank Hagney *O'Shead* • Alden Chase *Sinclair* • Reed Howes *Gordon* • Charles King (2) *Roberts* • George Chesebro *Jed* • Edward Peil Sr *Clark* ■ *Dir* Sam Newfield • *Scr* Joe O'Donnell

Lone Star ★★ U

Western 1952 · US · BW · 94mins

Heavy-going saga of Texas in 1845 when the big question was whether it should become part of the United States or remain a republic. Clark Gable is the rancher favouring statehood, dispatched by Andrew Jackson (Lionel Barrymore) to scupper any possible deal with the Mexicans. His main adversary is Broderick Crawford, a staunch republican senator, while Ava Gardner is the newspaperwoman caught in the middle. Some brief but well handled action sequences aren't enough to compensate for the verbose script. AE

Clark Gable *Devereaux Burke* • Ava Gardner *Martha Ronda* • Broderick Crawford *Thomas Craden* • Lionel Barrymore *Andrew Jackson* • Beulah Bondi *Minniver Bryan* • Ed Begley *Sen Anthony Demmett* • William Farnum *Sen Tom Crockett* • Lowell Gilmore *Capt Elliott* ■ *Dir* Vincent Sherman • *Scr* Borden Chase, from a stories by Howard Estabrook, Borden Chase

Lone Star ★★★★★ 15

Murder mystery drama
1995 · US · Colour · 129mins

An engrossing storyline and a superb ensemble cast make this deeply textured account of the burden of history people carry with them a graceful slow-burner. Sheriff Chris Cooper discovers a skeleton buried in the desert outskirts of his Mexican border town and launches a murder investigation. So begins a multi-generation mosaic of family ties, local legend, interracial romance and political tinkering as he discovers the murky past of his own late father (Matthew McConaughey), also a cop. Confident direction combines with intelligent drama to craft a bittersweet delicacy. AJ

Kris Kristofferson *Charlie Wade* • Chris Cooper *Sam* • Matthew McConaughey *Buddy Deeds* • Elizabeth Peña *Pilar* • Frances McDormand *Bunny* • Stephen Mendillo *Cliff* • Stephen Lang *Mickey* • Oni Faida Lampley *Celie* • Eleese Lester *Molly* • Joe Stevens *Deputy Travis* ■ *Dir/Scr* John Sayles

Lone Wolf ★★ 18

Horror science-fiction
1988 · US · Colour · 94mins

Standard horror fare about high school computer hackers and a struggling rock band tracking down a killer that's terrorising Denver, Colorado, which the police think is a wild dog. The teenagers however are convinced that the killings are due to a werewolf, while the police force bumble around getting nowhere. A quite gory, but minor, entry in *The Howling*-inspired sweepstakes. AJ

Kevin Hart *Joel* • Jamie Newcomb *Eddie* • Ann Douglas *Deirdre* • Tom Henry *The Wolf* ■ *Dir* John Callas • *Scr* Michael Krueger, John Callas, Nancy M Gallanis

Lone Wolf McQuade ★★★ 18

Action adventure
1983 · US · Colour · 102mins

Probably the best movie action-man hero Chuck Norris has ever made. He's a Texas Ranger battling evil gunrunner David Carradine in this modern western, which is styled after the work of Italian maestro Sergio Leone. Barbara Carrera provides the love interest in a sticky subplot, but the thrust of director Steve Carver (another Roger Corman protégé) always remains geared towards the super-macho elements – strong, silent heroes and villains, loads of weaponry and self-styled enigmatic warriors playing rough. AJ. Contains swearing, violence and brief nudity.

Chuck Norris *JJ McQuade* • David Carradine *Rawley Wilkes* • Barbara Carrera *Lola Richardson* • Leon Isaac Kennedy *Jackson* • Robert Beltran *Kayo* • LQ Jones *Dakota* ■ *Dir* Steve Carver • *Scr* BJ Nelson, from the story by H Kaye Dyal, BJ Nelson

The Lone Wolf Meets a Lady ★★★

Mystery adventure 1940 · US · BW · 70mins

The third of nine films starring Warren William as the former jewel thief-turned-sleuth who can never resist helping a damsel in distress, in this case a lady involved in murder and the theft of a valuable necklace. Neatly plotted and briskly paced, this is an entertaining adventure, with former Warner star Jean Muir a captivating heroine in her penultimate film – she was later nearly ruined by the McCarthy hearings. TV

Warren William *Michael Lanyard, "The Lone Wolf"* • Jean Muir *Joan Bradley* • Eric Blore *Jamison* • Victor Jory *Clay Beaudine* • Roger Pryor *Pete Rennick* • Warren Hull *Bob Penyon* • Thurston Hall *Inspector Crane* ■ *Dir* Sidney Salkow • *Scr* John Larkin, Sidney Salkow, from a story by John Larkin, Wolfe Kaufman, from the character created by Louis Joseph Vance

The Lone Wolf Returns ★★★

Mystery adventure 1936 · US · BW · 64mins

Although Warren William is most closely associated with Michael Lanyard, it was Melvyn Douglas who took the title role in Columbia's first adventure featuring Louis Joseph Vance's troubleshooting sleuth. Directed by Roy William Neill (who would later handle Universal's Sherlock Holmes series), this is a rattling comedy thriller, in which Douglas's jewel thief is lured out of retirement by Gail Patrick's necklace. However, he resists temptation and merely steals her photograph, only to be blackmailed and then framed for robbery by Douglass Dumbrille. Somewhat undervalued these days, Douglas is splendidly dapper as he keeps both cops and crooks at bay DP

Melvyn Douglas *Michael Lanyard/"The Lone Wolf"/Col Thompson* • Gail Patrick *Marcia Stewart* • Tala Birell *Liane Mallison* • Henry Mollison *Mallison* • Thurston Hall *Crane* • Raymond Walburn *Jenkins* • Douglass Dumbrille *Morphew* ■ *Dir* Roy William Neill • *Scr* Joseph Krumgold, Bruce Manning, Lionel Houser, from the novel by Louis Joseph Vance

The Lone Wolf Spy Hunt ★★★

Mystery adventure 1939 · US · BW · 67mins

Smoothly accomplished Warren William, out of the same mould as William Powell and Melvyn Douglas, plays Michael Lanyard, alias the Lone Wolf, a gentleman jewel thief turned sleuth, in this agreeably old-fashioned comedy-thriller which finds Lanyard tangling with a ruthless international spy ring. Columbia's modestly entertaining 19-picture Lone Wolf series, based on thriller-writer Louis Joseph Vance's creation, survived from 1926 to 1949, with a five-year gap. Bert Lytell played Lanyard from 1926 to 1930; Melvyn Douglas starred in *The Lone Wolf Returns* in 1936, followed by Francis Lederer in 1938 before William took over for nine in a row. After his departure, the formula ran out of steam and after three with the lacklustre Gerald Mohr the films ended with Ron Randell in *The Lone Wolf and His Lady*. RK

Warren William *Michael Lanyard, "The Lone Wolf"* • Ida Lupino *Val Carson* • Rita Hayworth *Karen* • Virginia Weidler *Patricia Lanyard* • Ralph Morgan *Spiro Gregory* • Tom Dugan *Sgt Devan* ■ *Dir* Peter Godfrey • *Scr* Jonathan Latimer, from the novel *The Lone Wolf's Daughter* by Louis Joseph Vance

The Loneliness of the Long Distance Runner ★★★★★ 12

Drama 1962 · UK · BW · 99mins

Having already scored successes with *Look Back in Anger* and *A Taste of Honey*, director Tony Richardson completed his outstanding "kitchen sink" collection with this stirring tale of the borstal boy who dares to buck the system just as it offers him a lifeline. Tom Courtenay delivers a remarkable debut performance as the embittered delinquent whose talent for running gives governor Michael Redgrave the means to raise the profile of his institution. Masterfully adapted by Alan Sillitoe and unobtrusively shot by Walter Lassally, this is as powerful and relevant today as it ever was. DP DVD

Tom Courtenay *Colin Smith* • Michael Redgrave *Governor* • Avis Bunnage *Mrs Smith* • Peter Madden *Mr Smith* • James Bolam *Mike* • Julia Foster *Gladys* • Topsy Jane *Audrey* ■ *Dir* Tony Richardson • *Scr* Alan Sillitoe, from his novel

Lonely Are the Brave ★★★★

Western 1962 · US · BW · 105mins

This moving story about a contemporary cowboy is Kirk Douglas's own favourite among his films. It highlights the dignity of the individual as Douglas's law-breaking loner is pursued across the mountains by sheriff Walter Matthau. Matthau's posse uses helicopters and mountain jeeps, making the power and speed of Douglas on his horse tragically irrelevant. The symbolism in former blacklisted writer Dalton Trumbo's script becomes a little too obvious, especially at the end, but the location photography (by Philip Lathrop) is stunning and the cast is superb. TS

Kirk Douglas *Jack Burns* • Gena Rowlands *Jerri Bondi* • Walter Matthau *Sheriff Johnson* • Michael Kane *Paul Bondi* • Carroll O'Connor *Hinton* • William Schallert *Harry* • Karl Swenson *Reverend Hoskins* • George Kennedy *Guitierrez* ■ *Dir* David Miller • *Scr* Dalton Trumbo, from the novel *Brave Cowboy* by Edward Abbey

The Lonely Guy ★★ 15

Comedy 1984 · US · Colour · 86mins

After he finds his girlfriend in bed with another man, Steve Martin is escorted through the rather sad world of the "lonely guy" by a sympathetic Charles Grodin. It's slickly directed by Arthur Hiller and there are some genuinely funny passages. However, Martin is strangely subdued and the film is stolen from under his nose by the ever-excellent Grodin. JF. Contains some swearing and brief nudity. [video]

Steve Martin *Larry Hubbard* • Charles Grodin *Warren Evans* • Judith Ivey *Iris* • Steve Lawrence *Jack Fenwick* • Robyn Douglass *Danielle* • Merv Griffin • Dr Joyce Brothers ■ *Dir* Arthur Hiller • *Scr* Ed Weinberger, Stan Daniels, from the novel *The Lonely Guy's Book of Life* by Bruce Jay Friedman, adapted by Neil Simon

Lonely Hearts ★★★★ 15

Romantic comedy
1981 · Aus · Colour · 91mins

Paul Cox delivers another of his idiosyncratic insights into the soul of the misfit in this charming tale of late-life love. Norman Kaye, harbouring fantasies that are both innocent and desperate, expertly assumes the mantle of the timid everyman, as he begins to live after years of tending to his mother. His impersonation of a blind piano teacher and his encounter with a smarmy toupee salesman are just dotty enough to come off. But it's his hesitant relationship with Wendy Hughes, who has waited until her 30s to rebel against her parents, that gives the film its heart. DP [video]

Wendy Hughes *Patricia Curnov* • Norman Kaye *Peter Thompson* • Jon Finlayson *George* • Julia Blake *Pamela* • Jonathan Hardy *Bruce* ■ *Dir/Scr* Paul Cox

Lonely in America ★★★

Romantic comedy
1990 · US · Colour · 96mins

We may be more used to films about the experience of the Asian community in Britain, but American examples are comparatively rare. While Mira Nair's *Mississippi Masala* played it straight, Barry Alexander Brown employs a light touch as he charts Ranjit Chowdhry's introduction to the Big Apple. The story turns on the clash between tradition and progress, as Chowdhry has to decide how much of his heritage he can jettison without alienating his family. An engaging ensemble cast, some unusual views of New York and several neat cultural asides make this an unexpected pleasure. DP. Contains swearing and sex scenes.

Ranjit Chowdhry *Arun* • Tirlok Malik *Max* • Adelaide Miller *Faye* • Robert Kessler *Jim* • David Toney *Duncan* • Melissa Christopher *Becky* • Frankie Hughes *Carlos* ■ *Dir* Barry Alexander Brown • *Scr* Satyajit Joy Palit, Barry Alexander Brown, from a story by Tirlok Malik

The Lonely Lady ★ 18

Drama 1983 · US · Colour · 87mins

The fact that it's based on a novel by Harold Robbins should offer a big clue as to the quality of the material. The link between career success and sexual promiscuity is explored in the antics of aspiring screenwriter Pia Zadora, who's rescued from rapist Ray Liotta by successful writer Lloyd Bochner. Badly scripted, shot and acted, with turgid and offensive sex scenes, this is possibly one of the worst films of all time. LH [video]

Pia Zadora *Jerilee Randall* • Lloyd Bochner *Walter Thornton* • Bibi Besch *Veronica Randall* • Joseph Cali *Vincent Dacosta* • Anthony Holland *Guy Jackson* • Jared Martin *George Ballantine* • Ray Liotta *Joe Heron* ■ *Dir* Peter Sasdy • *Scr* John Kershaw, Shawn Randall, from the novel by Harold Robbins, adapted by Ellen Shepard

The Lonely Man ★★★

Western 1957 · US · BW · 87mins

Jack Palance and Anthony Perkins, as estranged father and son, tried to out-smoulder each other in this taut, offbeat, psychological western. Perkins, who blames his long-absent father for the death of his mother, reluctantly links up with ex-bandit Palance. It turns out that Perkins isn't the only one who has a few old scores to settle with him. RB

Jack Palance *Jacob Wade* • Anthony Perkins *Riley Wade* • Neville Brand *King Fisher* • Robert Middleton *Ben Ryerson* • Elaine Aiken *Ada Marshall* • Elisha Cook Jr *Willie* • Claude Akins *Blackburn* • Lee Van Cleef *Faro* • Denver Pyle *Sheriff* ■ *Dir* Henry Levin • *Scr* Harry Essex, Robert Smith

The Lonely Passion of Judith Hearne ★★★ 15

Drama 1987 · UK · Colour · 111mins

Nobody does it better than Maggie Smith when it comes to forlorn, middle-aged Irish spinsters trying to look on the bright side, but finding the silver gleam tarnished by experience. Director Jack Clayton counterbalances booze and religion as the most powerful passions in Judith Hearne's life, so that Bob Hoskins's flirtatious entrepreneur never really stands a chance. Too sombre for what little it has to say, but the performances manage to redeem it. TH. Contains swearing and nudity. [video]

Maggie Smith *Judith Hearne* • Bob Hoskins *James Madden* • Wendy Hiller *Aunt D'Arcy* • Marie Kean *Mrs Rice* • Ian McNeice *Bernard* • Alan Devlin *Father Quigley* • Rudi Davies *Mary* • Prunella Scales *Moira O'Neill* ■ *Dir* Jack Clayton • *Scr* Peter Nelson, from the novel by Brian Moore

Lonely Woman Seeks Lifetime Companion ★★★

Romantic drama
1987 · USSR · Colour · 91mins

This touching Moscow-set drama would have been unthinkable in the pre-*glasnost* era, but such *bytove* or "everyday" pictures became something of a staple of Soviet cinema in the late 1980s. Desperate to escape from her midlife cul-de-sac, Irina Kupchenko sticks lonely hearts advertisements to lampposts in the hope of finding Mr Right. Homeless, alcoholic ex-acrobat Aleksandr Zbruyev is hardly what she has in mind, but love comes in all guises. Shooting in a fly-on-the-wall style, director Vyacheslav Krishtofovich is rewarded with touching and believable performances. DP. In Russian with English subtitles.

Irina Kupchenko *Kladvia* • Aleksandr Zbruev *Valentin* ■ *Dir* Vyacheslav Krishtofovich • *Scr* Viktor Merezhko

Lonelyhearts ★★

Drama 1958 · US · BW · 103mins

Fans of Nathanael West's famous 1933 novella *Miss Lonelyhearts*, which deals in the despair of a male agony aunt columnist, will despair at this attempt to broaden and contemporise the story with earnest moral and political platitudes. That said, there are convincing performances from Montgomery Clift, sensitive in the title role, Robert Ryan as his hard-bitten editor, and Broadway actress Maureen Stapleton, making her screen debut (and earning an Oscar nomination) as the sexually frustrated wife of a crippled husband. RK

Montgomery Clift *Adam White* • Robert Ryan *William Shrike* • Myrna Loy *Florence Shrike* • Dolores Hart *Justy Sargent* • Maureen Stapleton *Fay Doyle* • Frank Maxwell *Pat Doyle* • Jackie Coogan *Gates* ■ *Dir* Vincent J Donehue • *Scr* Dore Schary, from the novella *Miss Lonelyhearts* by Nathanael West

The Loners ★★

Crime drama 1971 · US · Colour · 79mins

This modern-day western has angst-ridden biker Dean Stockwell as a mixed-race Indian, who accidentally kills a highway patrolman and goes on the run with his best buddy Todd Susman. They pick up Pat Stich on the way and romance, murder and mayhem ensue. Here's a film that wants to cash in on everything from biker movies like *Easy Rider* to the social banditry of *Bonnie and Clyde*, Peckinpah-style shoot-outs, and the whole counterculture thing as an expression of antiwar sentiment. AT

Dean Stockwell *Stein* • Pat Stich [Patricia Stich] *Julio* • Todd Susman *Allan* • Scott Brady *Hearn* • Gloria Grahame *Annabelle* • Alex Dreier *Police Chief Peters* • Tim Rooney *Howie* • Ward Wood *Sheriff* ■ *Dir* Sutton Roley • *Scr* John Lawrence, Barry Sandler, from a story by John Lawrence

Lonesome Cowboys ★★★ 18

Experimental western
1968 · US · Colour · 104mins

One of the last films to feature artist Andy Warhol as director, this gay cowboy fantasy does raise the fundamental question conventional westerns have failed to address. If cowboys live, ride and die together, surely they must have sex with each other, too? The plot is a thin excuse to indulge in camp and erotic posing as Viva and Taylor Mead, both desperate for male company, pounce on Louis Waldon's homosexual gang when they ride into their desert town. By turn boring, bizarre and hilarious, this amateur Factory film captures the decadence and ennui of 1960s counterculture. AJ [video]

Viva *Ramona Alvarez* • Tom Hompertz *Drifter* • Louis Waldon *Mickey, the eldest brother* • Eric Emerson *Eric* • Taylor Mead *Nurse* • Joe Dallesandro *Little Joe* • Francis Francine *Sheriff* • Julian Burroughs *Julian, the brother* ■ *Dir/Scr* Andy Warhol

The Long Absence ★★★★ U

Drama 1961 · Fr/It · BW · 96mins

The fact that it shared the Palme d'Or at Cannes with Luis Buñuel's *Viridiana*, at the height of New Wave euphoria, itself suggests the quality of this study of isolation and enduring love. Retaining the subtle melancholy of Marguerite Duras's orginal story, director Henri Colpi refuses to hurry the relationship between Alida Valli and Georges Wilson as the Parisian café owner and the amnesiac vagabond she believes to be the husband she lost in Germany during the war. Consequently, her hope and his confusion are conveyed with a delicacy that's almost too painful to endure. DP. In French with English subtitles.

Alida Valli *Thérèse Langlois* • Georges Wilson *Tramp* • Jacques Harden *Truckdriver* • Diana Lepvrier *Martine* • Catherine Fontenay *Alice* ■ *Dir* Henri Colpi • *Scr* Marguerite Duras, Gérard Jarlot, from a story by Marguerite Duras

The Long and the Short and the Tall ★★★ PG

Second World War drama
1960 · UK · BW · 101mins

Time hasn't been kind to this studio-bound version of a Royal Court Second World War play that originally starred Frank Finlay. The film was shatteringly powerful in its day but seems rather weak now with its lack of realistic dialogue, its palpably phoney Elstree jungle sets and the uncomfortable star performance from Richard Todd, whose well-spoken tones are overlaid with a laboured regional accent. TS [video]

Richard Todd *Sergeant Mitchem* • Laurence Harvey *Private Bamforth* • Richard Harris *Corporal Johnstone* • Ronald Fraser *Lance-Corporal MacLeish* • John Meillon *Private Smith* • David McCallum *Private Whitaker* • John Rees *Private Evans* • Kenji Takaki *Tojo* ■ *Dir* Leslie Norman • *Scr* Wolf Mankowitz, Willis Hall, from the play by Willis Hall

The Long Arm ★★★ U

Police drama 1956 · UK · BW · 92mins

This rather glum insight into the policeman's lot was the final film made at Ealing Studios. Jack Hawkins wears a suitably hangdog expression as the detective faced with a series of robberies and a rocky marriage to neglected Dorothy Alison. Far from adding to the realism of the tale, the domestic crisis is a crashing bore and it's with evident relief that director Charles Frend abandons Bromley to head back to the side streets of Covent Garden and, finally, to the Festival Hall to provide an exciting conclusion to the case. DP [video]

Jack Hawkins *Detective Superintendent Tom Halliday* • Dorothy Alison *Mary Halliday* • Michael Brooke Jr *Tony Halliday* • John Stratton *Sergeant Ward* • Geoffrey Keen *Superintendent Malcolm* • Newton Blick *Commander Harris* • Ralph Truman *Colonel Blenkinsop* • Joss Ambler *Cashier* • Ian Bannen *Workman* • Nicholas Parsons *Police Constable Bates* • Alec McCowen *Surgeon* ■ *Dir* Charles Frend • *Scr* Janet Green, Robert Barr, Dorothy Christie, Campbell Christie, from a story by Robert Barr

The Long Dark Hall ★

Crime thriller 1951 · UK · BW · 86mins

Off-screen spouses (at the time) Rex Harrison and Lilli Palmer star in this risible courtroom drama in which Harrison stands trial for murder, while the real killer canoodles with his wilting wife. Co-director Anthony Bushell also plays Harrison's defence lawyer, but there are no sparks in his clashes with prosecutor Denis O'Dea. About as tense as snapped elastic. DP

Rex Harrison *Arthur Groome* • Lilli Palmer *Mary Groome* • Raymond Huntley *Chief Inspector Sullivan* • Anthony Dawson *The Man* • Denis O'Dea *Sir Charles Morton* • Anthony Bushell *Clive Bedford* ■ *Dir* Anthony Bushell, Reginald Beck • *Scr* Nunnally Johnson, William EC Fairchild, from the novel *A Case to Answer* by Edgar Lustgarten

The Long Day Closes ★★★★★ PG

Biographical drama
1992 · UK · Colour · 81mins

Anyone who has ever been lost in wonder at the magic of the movies will find that this enchanting feature strikes repeated chords. In the second of his films set in the Liverpool of his childhood, Terence Davies fondly recalls those marvellous moments at the local fleapit when the drabness of everyday life receded the instant the opening credits appeared on screen. Leigh McCormack is absolutely superb as the 11-year-old whose life revolves around film and family, and his performance lends dramatic unity to this kaleidoscopic autobiography. Unmissable. DP [video]

Marjorie Yates *Mother* • Leigh McCormack *Bud* • Anthony Watson *Kevin* • Nicholas Lamont *John* • Ayse Owens *Helen* • Tina Malone *Edna* • Jimmy Wilde *Curly* ■ *Dir/Scr* Terence Davies

The Long Day's Dying ★★

Second World War drama
1968 · UK · Colour · 93mins

Heavily allegorical war drama about three British soldiers who parachute behind enemy lines and take a German prisoner. All three are expert killers but the drawing of straws allows their German prisoner to live and be escorted to the British HQ. Along the way there are skirmishes, debates about the morality of war, and differing degrees of psychopathy. The ending is irony writ large since everything is laid on with a trowel. AT

David Hemmings *John* • Tom Bell *Tom* • Tony Beckley *Cliff* • Alan Dobie *Helmut* ■ *Dir* Peter Collinson • *Scr* Charles Wood, from the novel by Alan White

Long Day's Journey into Night ★★★ PG

Drama 1962 · US · BW · 170mins

Set in 1912, Eugene O'Neill's epic play about a self-destructive Connecticut family is a challenge for any actor and, indeed, audience. Katharine Hepburn picked up an inevitable Oscar nomination as the morphine-addicted mother of alcoholic Jason Robards and tubercular Dean Stockwell, but the star turn here is Ralph Richardson as the miserly head of the ill-fated Tyrone clan. AT

Katharine Hepburn *Mary Tyrone* • Ralph Richardson *James Tyrone Sr* • Jason Robards Jr [Jason Robards] *James Tyrone Jr* • Dean Stockwell *Edmund Tyrone* • Jeanne Barr *Cathleen* ■ *Dir* Sidney Lumet • *Scr* from the play by Eugene O'Neill

Long Day's Journey into Night ★★

Drama 1996 · Can · Colour · 174mins

Eugene O'Neill's family saga about the Tyrones, an Irish-American family raddled with alcoholism and a lifetime's worth of emnities is a challenge to any actor. This version is a filmed record of a stage production which received rave notices when first performed during the Stratford Festival in Canada. William Hutt plays James senior, the head of the household so miserable he refuses to pay for medical treatment for his sick wife (Martha Henry) and son (Tom McCamus), while Peter Donaldson is the alcholic elder son. AT

William Hutt *James Tyrone* • Martha Henry *Mary Tyrone* • Tom McCamus *Edward Tyrone* • Peter Donaldson *Jamie Tyrone* • Martha Burns *Cathleen* ■ *Dir* David Wellington • *Scr* from the play by Eugene O'Neill

The Long Duel ★★ U

Adventure 1966 · UK · Colour · 115mins

It's big, it's British and it's trying very hard to be spectacular. Director Ken Annakin makes the 1920s Indian setting look authentic and keeps the conflict bubbling, but Yul Brynner's rebel tribal leader is prone to ranting and speechifying, police officer Trevor Howard conveys the feeling that he'd rather be in Tunbridge Wells, and the true-life story of obsessed antagonism rings false thanks to stilted dialogue and clichéd situations. TS

Yul Brynner *Sultan* • Trevor Howard *Freddy Young* • Harry Andrews *Stafford* • Andrew Keir *Gungaram* • Charlotte Rampling *Jane Stafford* • Virginia North *Champa* • Laurence Naismith *McDougal* • Maurice Denham *Governor* • Imogen Hassall *Tara* ■ *Dir* Ken Annakin • *Scr* Ernest Bornemann, Geoffrey Orme, Peter Yeldham, from a story by Ranveer Singh

The Long Good Friday ★★★★ 18

Crime drama 1979 · UK · Colour · 109mins

Bob Hoskins got his big break playing the East End gangster who realises his gang is being ruthlessly picked off by the IRA. Owing something to American thrillers of the 1940s, and rather more to *Get Carter* and TV crime shows, John Mackenzie's film remains both an explosively violent thriller and a sharp evocation of the enterprise culture of the time (Hoskins's dream is to build a new city in London's docklands with Mafia money). Helen Mirren offers seductive support, while Pierce Brosnan appears as an anonymous IRA hitman. AT. Contains violence, swearing and nudity. DVD

Bob Hoskins *Harold* • Helen Mirren *Victoria* • Eddie Constantine *Charlie* • Dave King *Parky* • Bryan Marshall *Harris* • George Coulouris *Gus* • Derek Thompson *Jeff* • Bruce Alexander *Mac* • Pierce Brosnan *First Irishman* ■ *Dir* John Mackenzie • *Scr* Barrie Keefe

The Long Goodbye ★★★★★ 18

Detective drama 1973 · US · Colour · 111mins

This semi-spoof update of Raymond Chandler's novel from director Robert Altman ranks as one of the most intelligent adaptations of the celebrated thriller writer's work since *The Big Sleep* in 1946. Elliott Gould may seem an odd choice to play the world-weary Philip Marlowe, but his laid-back take on the legendary gumshoe is a masterstroke. By brilliantly deconstructing the standard private eye thriller with irony and affection, Altman comments on the changes in American society and the American Dream to starkly satirical effect. One of the finest films of the 1970s. AJ. Contains violence, swearing and nudity. DVD

Elliott Gould *Philip Marlowe* • Nina Van Pallandt *Eileen Wade* • Sterling Hayden *Roger Wade* • Mark Rydell *Marty Augustine* • Henry Gibson *Dr Verringer* • David Arkin *Harry* • Jim Bouton *Terry Lennox* • Jack Knight *Mabel* ■ *Dir* Robert Altman • *Scr* Leigh Brackett, from the novel by Raymond Chandler

The Long Gray Line ★★★ U

Drama 1955 · US · Colour · 131mins

One of director John Ford's most sentimental movies, this will only excite those who believe West Point Military Academy is an institution to be valued for its righteous place in the American way of life. A uniformed *Goodbye, Mr Chips*, it stars Tyrone Power, who arrives at the academy as a menial worker, becomes a cadet-instructor, marries Maureen O'Hara, and stays on teaching boys to be men, until time immemorial and a Ford-blessed sunset. Beautifully crafted, but appallingly banal. TH

Tyrone Power *Marty Maher* • Maureen O'Hara *Mary O'Donnell* • Robert Francis *James Sundstrom Jr* • Donald Crisp *Old Martin* • Ward Bond *Capt Herman J Koehler* • Betsy Palmer *Kitty Carter* • Phil Carey [Philip Carey] *Charles Dotson* • William Leslie *Red Sundstrom* • Harry Carey Jr *Dwight Eisenhower* • Patrick Wayne *Cherub Overton* ■ *Dir* John Ford • *Scr* Edward Hope, from the novel *Bringing up the Brass* by Marty Maher, Nardi Reeder Campion

The Long Hair of Death ★★★

Gothic horror 1964 · It · BW · 97mins

Director Antonio Margheriti isn't quite up to Mario Bava standards, but serves up enough plague-riddled peasants and cobweb festooned secret passageways to keep genre fans happy. Horror queen Barbara Steele plays an unfortunate 15th-century wench accused of murder and burnt as a witch who, years later, returns to torment and engineer the death of the real culprit. The script wanders and the dubbing is clumsy, but Steele's resurrection scene is worth staying up for on its own. RS. Italian dialogue dubbed into English.

Giorgio Ardisson [George Ardisson] *Kurt* • Halina Zalewska *Lizabeth* • Robert Rains *Von Klage* ■ *Dir* Anthony Dawson [Antonio Margheriti] • *Scr* Robert Bohr, Julian Berry [Ernesto Gastaldi], Renato Caldonazzo (English translation)

The Long Hot Summer ★★★★ PG

Drama 1958 · US · Colour · 111mins

Two short stories and a novel by William Faulkner were glued together to form the script of this torrid Deep South melodrama with a simply marvellous cast. Paul Newman is the drifter and redneck who catches the eye of Lee Remick and wins the favour of her father-in-law, local tyrant Orson Welles, who tries to pair him off with daughter Joanne Woodward. Ludicrously overheated but magnificent with it, this was the first of several pictures Newman made with Woodward; the couple married shortly after filming was completed. AT

Paul Newman *Ben Quick* • Joanne Woodward *Clara Varner* • Orson Welles *Will Varner* • Anthony Franciosa *Jody Varner* • Lee Remick *Eula* • Richard Anderson *Alan Stewart* ■ *Dir* Martin Ritt • *Scr* Irving Ravetch, Harriet Frank Jr, from the stories *Barn Burning*, *The Spotted Horse*, and the novel *The Hamlet* by William Faulkner

Long John Silver ★★ U

Swashbuckling adventure 1954 · Aus · Colour · 105mins

Fresh from hijacking Disney's *Treasure Island*, Robert Newton reprised the role of the infamous peg-legged pirate in this mediocre adventure that owes little to the genius of Robert Louis Stevenson. Martin Rackin's screenplay is a patchwork of episodes discarded from the original adaptation, making the action seem both confused and incidental. But the real problem is Newton, whose affinity for the bottle clearly clouded his judgement of tone, as he overplays every scene. DP

Robert Newton *Long John Silver* • Kit Taylor *Jim Hawkins* • Connie Gilchrist *Purity Pinker* • Lloyd Berrell *Captain Mendoza, "El Toro"* • Eric Reiman *Trip Fenner* • Syd Chambers *Ned Shill* ■ *Dir* Byron Haskin • *Scr* Martin Rackin, from characters created by Robert Louis Stevenson

The Long Journey ★★★★

Drama 1949 · Cz · BW · 78mins

The last picture completed in Czechoslovakia before the Stalinist takeover, Alfred Radok's extraordinary account of the Nazi Occupation chronicles the strain placed upon the Jewish-Gentile marriage of Viktor Ocasek and doctor Blanka Waleska. Had it simply been a human melodrama, this would still have been a highly courageous achievement. But the fact that Radok inserted much controversial newsreel footage meant that he re-created the role played by the Czechs in the Final Solution with such accuracy that the film was banned until the Velvet Revolution. DP. In Czech with English subtitles.

Blanka Waleska *Dr Hannah Kaufman* • Otomar Krejca *Dr Tony Bures* • Viktor Ocasek *Mr Kaufman* • Zdenka Baldova *Mrs Kaufman* • Jiri Spirit *Johnny* ■ *Dir* Alfred Radok • *Scr* Mojmir Drvota, Erik Kolar, Alfred Radok

The Long Kiss Goodnight ★★★★ 18

Action thriller 1996 · US · Colour · 115mins

This vehicle for Geena Davis is one of the loudest, sassiest and most entertaining action blockbusters in recent years. Directed by her then-husband Renny Harlin, it's wonderfully over the top in virtually every respect, from *Lethal Weapon* scriptwriter Shane Black's barmy story and even crazier characters to the nonstop, reality defying action set pieces. Davis stars as a small-town housewife suffering from amnesia who discovers that she was once a ruthless assassin working for a shadowy government agency. JF. Contains swearing, violence. DVD

Geena Davis *Samantha Caine/Charly Baltimore* • Samuel L Jackson *Mitch Hennessey* • Yvonne Zima *Caitlin* • Craig Bierko *Timothy* • Tom Amandes *Hal* • Brian Cox *Nathan* • Patrick Malahide *Perkins* • David Morse *Luke/Daedalus* ■ *Dir* Renny Harlin • *Scr* Shane Black

Long Live Life ★★

Science-fiction thriller
1984 · Fr · Colour · 110mins

According to Claude Lelouch, the idea for this film came to him in a dream on the day that *Edith and Marcel* opened to disastrous reviews. The nub of the story concerns the claims of businessman Michel Piccoli and actress Evelyne Bouix that they were kidnapped by aliens and sent back to Earth to preach anti-nuclear pacifism. Over-elaborate hokum. DP. In French with English subtitles.

Charlotte Rampling *Catherine Perrin* • Michel Piccoli *Michel Perrin* • Jean-Louis Trintignant *François Gaucher* • Evelyne Bouix *Sarah Gaucher* • Anouk Aimée *Anouk* • Charles Aznavour *Edouard Takvorian* ■ *Dir* Claude Lelouch • *Scr* Claude Lelouch

Long Live the Lady! ★★★★ 15

Comedy 1987 · It · Colour · 106mins

Six young graduates of a catering school are engaged to wait at table at a grand banquet being given in a medieval castle by a mysterious old lady. Like the bespectacled pimpled youth, through whose eyes we see the feast, the director Ermanno Olmi minutely observes, by turns fascinated and repulsed, the rituals of a strictly hierarchical, decaying society whose dominant symbol is the huge, ugly fish which the guests consume with relish. By the use of eloquent gestures, faces and looks, rather than dialogue, Olmi has created a witty and sharp satire on the haute bourgeoisie. RB. In Italian with English subtitles.

Marco Esposito *Libenzio* • Simona Brandalise *Corinna* • Stefania Busarello *Anna* • Simone Dalla Rosa *Mao* • Lorenzo Paolini *Ciccio* • Tarcisio Tosi *Pigi* ■ *Dir/Scr* Ermanno Olmi

The Long, Long Trailer ★★ U

Comedy 1954 · US · Colour · 96mins

After mediocre cinema careers, Lucille Ball and Desi Arnaz became household names on TV in *I Love Lucy*. They returned in triumph to MGM for this episodic comedy feature which essentially preserves their small screen images of madcap wife and long-suffering husband. Playing newlyweds, Lucille persuades Desi that they should invest in a mobile home and use it for their honeymoon trip, leading to scrapes and disasters. AE

Lucille Ball *Tacy Collini* • Desi Arnaz *Nicholas Carlos Collini* • Marjorie Main *Mrs Hittaway* • Keenan Wynn *Policeman* • Gladys Hurlbut *Mrs Bolton* • Moroni Olsen *Mr Tewitt* ■ *Dir* Vincente Minnelli • *Scr* Albert Hackett, Frances Goodrich, from the novel by Clinton Twiss

Long Lost Father ★★

Drama 1934 · US · BW · 64mins

John Barrymore was never too choosy with his later screen roles, and this was one of his lesser efforts. Barrymore, in his world-weary manner, plays a man who deserted his family many years before but finds his grown-up daughter (Helen Chandler) working in the same nightclub as he is. Naturally, he wins back her love. The director Ernest B Schoedsack shows no feeling for the material. RB

John Barrymore *Carl Bellairs* • Helen Chandler *Lindsey Lane* • Donald Cook *Dr Bill Strong* • Alan Mowbray *Sir Anthony Gelding* • Claude King *Inspector* • EE Clive *Spot Hawkins* • Reginald Sharland *Lord Vivyan* ■ *Dir* Ernest B Schoedsack • *Scr* Dwight Taylor, from the novel by GB Stern

The Long Memory ★★

Thriller 1952 · UK · BW · 96mins

Robert Hamer will always be remembered as the director of the classic Ealing comedy *Kind Hearts and*

Coronets, but he also had an excellent eye for local detail. Here he cleverly captures the murky side of life in London's marshlands, but he is beaten from the start by the utterly predictable wrong man story. John Mills is badly miscast as an old lag desperate to discover who framed him for murder, while detective John McCallum is clueless in every sense. DP

John Mills *Davidson* • John McCallum *Detective Inspector Lowther* • Elizabeth Sellars *Fay Lowther* • Eva Bergh *Elsa* • Geoffrey Keen *Craig* • Michael Martin-Harvey *Jackson* • John Chandos *Boyd* • John Slater *Pewsey* • Thora Hird *Mrs Pewsey* ■ *Dir* Robert Hamer • *Scr* Robert Hamer, Frank Harvey, from a novel by Howard Clewes

The Long Night ★★★

Drama 1947 · US · BW · 96mins

Few movies have ever aroused as much critical fury as *The Long Night* when it was (mistakenly) believed that the producers of this remake of *Le Jour Se Lève* had destroyed every copy of the original. Marcel Carné's great film has survived, while this effective, more socially orientated version is rarely revived. Henry Fonda performs sensitively as the ex-serviceman turned killer who keeps the police at bay during a long night in which he looks back on the disastrous sequence of events that have left him trapped. AE

Henry Fonda *Joe Adams* • Barbara Bel Geddes *Jo Ann* • Vincent Price *Maximilian* • Ann Dvorak *Charlene* • Howard Freeman *Sheriff* • Moroni Olsen *Chief of Police* • Elisha Cook Jr *Frank* • Queenie Smith *Janitor's wife* ■ *Dir* Anatole Litvak • *Scr* John Wexley, from the film *Le Jour Se Lève* by Jacques Viot

Long Pants ★★★★

Silent comedy 1927 · US · BW · 60mins

This bizarre black comedy is the last of three silent features which display the full genius of baby-faced Harry Langdon, following *Tramp, Tramp, Tramp* and *The Strong Man*. Here he plays the boy who has just graduated to long pants and dreams of being a great lover. The attractions of long-time sweetheart Priscilla Bonner pale in comparison with Alma Bennett's more exciting big city vamp and our "hero" decides that drastic measures are required. Langdon's effectiveness stems from the astute direction of the young Frank Capra. When Langdon fired Capra and tried to go it alone, he wrecked his career. AE

Harry Langdon *The boy* • Gladys Brockwell *His mother* • Alan Roscoe *His father* • Alma Bennett *The vamp* • Priscilla Bonner *Priscilla* ■ *Dir* Frank Capra • *Scr* Robert Eddy, from a story by Arthur Ripley

The Long Ride ★★ 15

Second World War adventure
1984 · US/Hun · Colour · 88mins

In this Second World War drama, American airman John Savage is shot down over Hungary, where he joins the horsemen and resistance fighters who roam the Hortobagy plain. In civilian life, Savage is a cowboy from Wyoming, so he has no trouble fitting in, but the vast, treeless landscape is the real star here. AT [VIDEO]

John Savage *Brady* • Kelly Reno *Miki* • Ildiko Bansagi *Klara* • Laszlo Mensaros *Dr Dussek* • Ferenc Bacs *Wortmann* • Dzsoko Roszics *Csorba* • Laszlo Horvath *Moro* • Matyas Usztics *Swede* ■ *Dir* Pal Gabor • *Scr* William W Lewis, from a story by Pal Gabor

The Long Riders ★★★★ 18

Western 1980 · US · Colour · 95mins

Powerful novelty casting and a superb score by guitar maestro Ry Cooder are major draws in this authentic-looking western that concerns the events surrounding the notorious Northfield, Minnesota, bank raid. Directed by Walter Hill, it's very reminiscent of *The Wild Bunch* in its use of slow-motion violence and flashbacks. Three Carradines (David, Keith and Robert) play the Younger brothers, with Stacy and James Keach as Frank and Jesse James; Randy and Dennis Quaid portray the less familiar Miller boys, while the Fords (Bob and Charlie) are brought to life by Nicholas and Christopher Guest. Not to be outdone by the siblings, Pamela Reed gives a heartfelt performance. TS. Contains violence, swearing, nudity. [VIDEO] DVD

Stacy Keach *Frank James* • David Carradine *Cole Younger* • Keith Carradine *Jim Younger* • Robert Carradine *Bob Younger* • James Keach *Jesse James* • Dennis Quaid *Ed Miller* • Randy Quaid *Clell Miller* • Kevin Brophy *John Younger* • Harry Carey Jr *George Arthur* • Christopher Guest *Charlie Ford* • Nicholas Guest *Bob Ford* ■ *Dir* Walter Hill • *Scr* Bill Bryden, Steven Phillip Smith, Stacy Keach, James Keach, Ry Cooder

The Long Run ★★ 15

Sports drama 2000 · S Afr · Colour · 107mins

This is another story about a disciplinarian coach who drives his prodigy to the edge in a bid to fulfil her athletic potential. But what sets Jean Stewart's drama apart is that it's set in democratic South Africa and that the budding champion in Armin Mueller-Stahl's care is Namibian refugee Nthati Moshesh. Stewart fully exploits the forbidding scenery, but she fails to generate any sense of sporting scale or excitement. DP [VIDEO] DVD

Armin Mueller-Stahl *Bertold "Berry" Bohmer* • Nthati Moshesh *Christine* • Paterson Joseph *Gasa* • Desmond Dube *Miso* ■ *Dir* Jean Stewart (2) • *Scr* Johann Potgieter

The Long Shadow ★★

Drama 1992 · US/Isr/Hun · Colour · 89mins

After 35 years in America, establishing himself as one of Hollywood's finest cinematographers, Vilmos Zsigmond returned to his native Hungary to make his directorial debut. Unfortunately, even the visual aspects of this pretentious film are substandard, with the glossy style trivialising what is supposed to be an intense study of delicate feelings. As the actor son of an archaeologist, Michael York fails to convince either as a master thespian or as a lover caught in the throes of passion for his stepmother, Liv Ullmann. DP

Liv Ullmann *Katherine* • Michael York *Raphael Romondy/Gabor* • Teomi Oded *Johann Grabier* • Ava Haddad *Rachel* ■ *Dir* Vilmos Zsigmond • *Scr* Paul Salamon, Janos Edelenyi

The Long Ships ★★ PG

Period adventure
1963 · UK/Yug · Colour · 120mins

This eager co-production has almost everything you would expect of a lavish screen epic. There's plenty of action and more than a hint of sin, the costumes and sets are opulent, and Christopher Challis's colour photography shimmers with richness. But, while Richard Widmark plays his Viking role with pantomimic brio, Sidney Poitier chooses to play the Moorish prince as a sort of medieval civil rights activist. In other words, like many epics before and since, it's too self-indulgent for its own good. DP. [VIDEO]

Richard Widmark *Rolfe* • Sidney Poitier *El Mansuh* • Rosanna Schiaffino *Aminah* • Russ Tamblyn *Orm* • Oscar Homolka *Krok* • Lionel Jeffries *Aziz* • Edward Judd *Sven* • Beba Loncar *Gerda* • Clifford Evans *King Harald* • Colin Blakely *Rhykka* • Gordon Jackson *Vahlin* • David Lodge *Olla* ■ *Dir* Jack Cardiff • *Scr* Berkely Mather, Beverley Cross, from the novel by Frans T Bengtsson

Long Shot ★★

Drama 1978 · UK · Colour · 85mins

This unusual docu-comedy set in and around the Edinburgh Festival should be required viewing for any aspiring film-makers. Film producer and proud Scot Charles Gormley is attempting to find backers for his movie entitled *Gulf and Western*. Naturally this proves to be problematic but some farcical comedy ensues and movie buffs will enjoy spotting luminaries like Wim Wenders, Stephen Frears, John Boorman and Susannah York in the supporting cast. LH

Charles Gormley *Charlie* • Neville Smith *Neville* • Ann Zelda *Annie* • David Stone *Distributor* • Suzanne Danielle *Sue* • Ron Taylor (1) *American director* • Wim Wenders *Another director* • Stephen Frears *Biscuit Man* • Maurice Bulbulian *French-Canadian director* • William Forsythe [Bill Forsyth] *Billie* • Alan Bennett *Neville's doctor* • Susannah York *Actress* • John Boorman *The Director* ■ *Dir* Maurice Hatton • *Scr* Eoin McCann, Maurice Hatton

The Long Summer of George Adams ★★★★

Drama 1982 · US · Colour · 100mins

Director Stuart Margolin excels himself here with an ambitious TV movie that stars his longtime pal James Garner as a married man suffering a midlife crisis. Joan Hackett, in one of her last roles, matches the masterful Garner and their beautifully modulated performances are the heart of this small-town drama. Unsentimental, humorous and intelligently scripted, this is a low-key work about an all too human relationship. BB

James Garner *George Adams* • Joan Hackett *Norma Adams* • Alex Harvey *Ernie Lankford* • Juanin Clay *Ann Sharp* • David Graf *Olin Summers* • Anjanette Comer *Venida Pierce* ■ *Dir* Stuart Margolin • *Scr* John Gay, from the novel by Weldon Hill

Long Time Dead ★ 15

Horror 2001 · UK/US · Colour · 90mins

Everything about this south London-set *Scream* – featuring college students summoning up an ancient fire demon during a Ouija board session – is obvious, third-hand and bogus. Former *EastEnders* pin-up Joe Absolom and obligatory American "name" Lukas Haas add little to this supernatural tosh, which is further marred by a vague denouement and some sloppy editing. AJ [VIDEO] DVD

Lukas Haas *Webster* • Joe Absolom *Rob* • Lara Belmont *Stella* • Melanie Gutteridge *Annie* • James Hillier *Spence* • Alec Newman *Liam* • Tom Bell *Becker* ■ *Dir* Marcus Adams • *Scr* Eitan Arrusi, Daniel Bronzite, Chris Baker, Andy Day, from a story by Marcus Adams, Daniel Bronzite, James Gay-Rees

The Long Voyage Home ★★★★ PG

Second World War drama
1940 · US · BW · 100mins

This near masterpiece from director John Ford was scripted from four one-act seafaring plays by Eugene O'Neill, and it bears that satisfying streak of grim melancholy that typifies the finest work of one of America's greatest writers. Although relentlessly studio bound, the magnificent photography captures the dangerous atmosphere as a freighter transports a cargo of dynamite across the Atlantic during the Second World War. John Wayne plays a Swedish merchant seaman, and he's backed up by an extremely effective supporting cast. TS [VIDEO]

John Wayne *Ole Olsen* • Thomas Mitchell *Aloysius Driscoll* • Ian Hunter *Smitty* • Barry Fitzgerald *Cocky* • Wilfrid Lawson *Captain* • Mildred Natwick *Freda* • John Qualen *Axel Swanson* • Ward Bond *Yank* ■ *Dir* John Ford • *Scr* Dudley Nichols, from four one-act plays by Eugene O'Neill • *Cinematographer* Gregg Toland

The Long Wait ★★

Crime drama 1954 · US · BW · 94mins

What was a tasteful British film-maker like Victor Saville doing forming Parklane Productions to film the lurid crime novels of Mickey Spillane? He tried his hand at directing this one, but lacked the edgy style that Robert Aldrich brought to *Kiss Me Deadly*. Still, it has a certain seamy atmosphere as Anthony Quinn's amnesiac tries to figure out which of four sexy dames might be the one who can clear him of murder. AE

Anthony Quinn *Johnny McBride* • Charles Coburn *Gardiner* • Gene Evans *Servo* • Peggie Castle *Venus* • Mary Ellen Kay *Wendy* • Shawn Smith *Carol* • Dolores Donlon *Troy* ■ *Dir* Victor Saville • *Scr* Alan Green, Lesser Samuels, from the novel by Mickey Spillane

The Long Walk Home ★★★ PG

Period drama 1990 · US · Colour · 91mins

Whoopi Goldberg plays Sissy Spacek's housemaid in this convincing drama set during the early years of the civil rights movement. Tensions rise in Spacek's Alabama household as blacks and whites grow further apart when the blacks boycott the segregated buses and the whites up the ante with an arson attack on Martin Luther King's house. Solid acting, a no-nonsense script, a convincing 1950s look and marvellous gospel music all distinguish this. AT [VIDEO]

Whoopi Goldberg *Odessa Cotter* • Sissy Spacek *Miriam Thompson* • Dwight Schultz *Norman Thompson* • Ving Rhames *Herbert Cotter* • Dylan Baker *Tunker Thompson* • Erika Alexander *Selma Cotter* • Lexi Faith Randall [Lexi Randall] *Mary Catherine* • Richard Habersham *Theodore Cotter* • Jason Weaver *Franklin Cotter* ■ *Dir* Richard Pearce • *Scr* John Cork

L

The Long Way Home ★★★★

Documentary
1996 · US · BW and Colour · 110mins

The winner of the Oscar for best feature documentary, this is a devastating exposé of the events that followed the liberation of the European concentration camps at the end of the Second World War. Narrated by Morgan Freeman and combining archive footage, stills, interviews and personal testimonies, the shameful catalogue of oversights, errors and wilful acts of neglect can only astonish those unaware that the suffering of the Holocaust survivors did not end with the defeat of the Nazis. Conducting his exhaustive research in conjunction with Rabbi Marvin Hier, Mark Jonathan Harris has produced a fitting tribute to these forgotten victims. DP

Morgan Freeman *Narrator* ■ *Dir/Scr* Mark Jonathan Harris

The Long Way Home ★★★

Drama 1998 · US · Colour · 96mins

Jack Lemmon provides the extra bit of class that lifts this sudsy TV melodrama out of the ordinary. The veteran star plays a lonely widower, staying with his son and daughter-in-law, who gets a new lease of life when his friendship with feisty young Sarah Paulson leads to a chance encounter. Lemmon relishes this juicy role, while director Glenn Jordan does his best to sidestep the more sugary moments. JF

Jack Lemmon *Tom Gerrin* • Betty Garrett *Veronica* • Sarah Paulson *Leanne Bossert* • Kristin Griffith *Bonnie Gerrin* • Garwin Sanford

Ken Gerrin ■ *Dir* Glenn Jordan • *Scr* William Hanley, from the TV film *Thomas Guerin, Retraite* by Louise Vincent, Patrick Jamain

Long Weekend ★★ 15

Thriller 1977 · Aus · Colour · 92mins

The eco-thriller is one of the coming genres of western cinema, but this is a pretty resistible early effort. The sequences of events that befall bickering marrieds John Hargreaves and Briony Behets are not mysterious or shocking enough and their lack of curiosity soon rubs off on the viewer. By following each new occurrence with a renewed outburst of squabbling, this reinforces the view that whatever is going to happen to this ghastly pair is more than due. DP

John Hargreaves *Peter* • Briony Behets *Marcia* ■ *Dir* Colin Eggleston • *Scr* Everett De Roche

The Longest Day ★★★★ PG

Second World War drama
1962 · US · BW · 168mins

This war film has a lot going for it: a huge budget and masses of military co-operation; the clever idea of providing a composite picture of the Allied invasion of Occupied France on D-Day 6 June 1944 from the British, American, French Resistance and German viewpoints; well-known actors from each nationality to help audiences cope with the large number of characters; and black-and-white photography to convey a sense of newsreel authenticity. The picture holds its three-hour length well and is far from gung ho in highlighting the errors and miscalculations on both sides. The battle scenes are memorably staged and the major Hollywood stars fit in particularly well – but it's let down by over-acting from many of the European players, some crude characterisation and pretentious vignettes. AE. In English and German with subtitles. DVD

John Wayne *Col Benjamin Vandervoort* • Robert Mitchum *Brig Gen Norman Cota* • Henry Fonda *Brig Gen Theodore Roosevelt* • Robert Ryan *Brig Gen James Gavin* • Rod Steiger *Destroyer commander* • Robert Wagner *US ranger* • Richard Beymer *Schultz* • Mel Ferrer *Maj Gen Robert Haines* • Jeffrey Hunter *Sgt Fuller* • Paul Anka *US ranger* • Sal Mineo *Pte Martini* • Roddy McDowall *Pte Morris* • Stuart Whitman *Lt Sheen* • Eddie Albert *Col Newton* • Edmond O'Brien *Gen Raymond O Barton* • Fabian *Ranger* • Red Buttons *Pte Steel* • Tom Tryon *Lt Wilson* • Alexander Knox *Maj Gen Walter Bedell Smith* • Richard Burton *RAF pilot* • Kenneth More *Capt Maud* • Peter Lawford *Lord Lovat* • Richard Todd *Maj Howard* • Sean Connery *Pte Flanagan* • Christopher Lee *Bit* ■ *Dir* Andrew Marton, Ken Annakin, Bernhard Wicki • *Scr* Cornelius Ryan, Romain Gary, James Jones, David Pursall, Jack Seddon, from the novel by Cornelius Ryan

The Longest Yard ★★★ 12A

Prison sports comedy
2005 · US · Colour · 113mins

In this remake of the Burt Reynolds 1974 comedy, *The Mean Machine*, Adam Sandler plays a washed-up football star who lands in prison. Warden James Cromwell asks him to train a group of convicts to play against the guards' team for a warm-up match but, encouraged by Chris Rock, the failed player sets his sights on winning the game. Lazy, deeply predictable but warmly humorous, this eschews complex characterisation in favour of well-worn prison genre clichés, but is still entertaining. GM

Adam Sandler *Paul "Wrecking" Crewe* • Chris Rock *Caretaker* • Burt Reynolds *Coach Nate Scarborough* • Nelly *Earl Megget* • James Cromwell *Warden Hazen* • William Fichtner *Captain Knauer* • Michael Irvin *Deacon Moss* ■ *Dir* Peter Segal • *Scr* Sheldon Turner, from the 1974 film by Tracy Keenan Wynn, from a story by Albert S Ruddy

The Longshot ★★ PG

Comedy 1986 · US · Colour · 85mins

Paul Bartel's eccentric style and off-kilter view of the world has resulted in some unusual and interesting films, but this substandard comedy isn't one of his best. Four luckless friends are conned into borrowing a fortune to bet on a "sure thing" race. Predictably it all goes horribly wrong and they find themselves pursued by the thugs who loaned them the money. DF

Tim Conway *Dooley* • Harvey Korman *Lou* • Jack Weston *Elton* • Ted Wass *Stump* • Anne Meara *Madge* • Jorge Cervera [Jorge Cervera Jr] *Santiago* • Jonathan Winters *Tyler* ■ *Dir* Paul Bartel • *Scr* Tim Conway

Longtime Companion ★★★★ 15

Drama 1990 · US · Colour · 95mins

The riveting, gut-wrenching account of eight friends' experiences from the day a newspaper reports "a rare cancer affecting the homosexual community" to the mounting impact Aids has on their lives and loves. Charting the way affluent gays were shocked out of their Calvin Klein lifestyles into dealing with bigotry and misunderstanding as they coped with bewildering loss, this quasi-documentary is a most accessible Aids history lesson. Oscar-nominee Bruce Davison gives the standout performance in a powerful, courageous testament. AJ. Contains swearing.

Bruce Davison *David* • Campbell Scott *Willy* • Stephen Caffrey *Fuzzy* • Mark Lamos *Sean* • Patrick Cassidy *Howard* • Mary-Louise Parker *Lisa* • John Dossett *Paul* ■ *Dir* Norman René • *Scr* Craig Lucas

Look at Me ★★★★ 12

Comedy drama 2004 · Fr/It · Colour · 106mins

Young music student Marilou Berry, a voluptuous beauty who is obsessed with her weight, pines for the affection of her self-absorbed novelist father Jean-Pierre Bacri. Director Agnès Jaoui plays Lolita's singing teacher, who is brought into the family's orbit when her own novelist husband befriends Bacri. Another half dozen characters, each lovelorn or damaged in some way, populate the seemingly casual but deftly constructed plot, which climaxes with a huge row in a country house. This is a wise and elegant comedy in which the dialogue fizzes. LF. In French with English subtitles. DVD

Marilou Berry *Lolita Cassard* • Agnès Jaoui *Sylvia Miller* • Jean-Pierre Bacri *Etienne Cassard* • Laurent Grévill *Pierre Miller* • Virginie Desarnauts *Karine* • Keine Bouhiza *Sébastien* • Grégoire Oestermann *Vincent* • Serge Riaboukine *Felix* • Michèle Moretti *Edith* ■ *Dir* Agnès Jaoui • *Scr* Jean-Pierre Bacri, Agnès Jaoui

Look Back in Anger ★★★★ PG

Drama 1959 · UK · BW · 95mins

Richard Burton is on a whingeing streak as the ever-complaining Jimmy Porter in Tony Richardson's version of the John Osborne play, the epitome of the kitchen-sink drama that heralded the liberated Swinging Sixties. As the downtrodden, middle-class wife taking the brunt of his tirades, Mary Ure poignantly deserves better from life than a husband who believes the world owes him a living, because Burton makes the man totally unsympathetic. As an emblem of its time, though, not to be missed. TH

Richard Burton *Jimmy Porter* • Claire Bloom *Helena Charles* • Mary Ure *Alison Porter* • Edith Evans *Mrs Tanner* • Gary Raymond *Cliff Lewis* • Glen Byam Shaw *Corporal Redfern* • Phyllis Nielson-Terry *Mrs Redfern* • Donald Pleasence *Hurst* • Jane Eccles *Miss Drury* ■ *Dir* Tony Richardson • *Scr* Nigel Kneale, John Osborne, from the play by John Osborne

Look for the Silver Lining ★★★ U

Musical biography
1949 · US · Colour · 106mins

An under-rated Warner Bros biopic of Broadway legend Marilyn Miller (after whom Marilyn Monroe was named), vivaciously played here by June Haver. Large chunks of Miller's New York hits *Sunny* and *Sally* are re-created, with highstepping Ray Bolger as her partner Jack Donahue, the man who taught Eleanor Powell to dance. In reality, Miller married three times, the second of her husbands being Mary Pickford's brother Jack, but here she's been given a fictional husband played by Gordon MacRae. David Butler directs it all with style. TS

June Haver *Marilyn Miller* • Ray Bolger *Jack Donahue* • Gordon MacRae *Frank Carter* • Charlie Ruggles [Charles Ruggles] *Pop Miller* • Rosemary DeCamp *Mom Miller* • Lee Wilde *Claire Miller* • Lynn Wilde *Ruth Miller* • Will Rogers Jr *Will Rogers* ■ *Dir* David Butler • *Scr* Henry Ephron, Phoebe Ephron, Marian Spitzer, from the story *Life of Marilyn Miller* by Bert Kalmar, Harry Ruby

Look in Any Window ★★

Drama 1961 · US · BW · 86mins

Pop star and composer Paul Anka had just missed a starring role in *West Side Story* when he took a risk with his image by playing a deeply disturbed teenager who gets his kicks by donning a mask and spying on the neighbours. Coming from a unhappy home, Anka is halfway to being committed to an asylum, but then so are the majority of the characters in this indie psychodrama. AT

Paul Anka *Craig Fowler* • Ruth Roman *Jackie Fowler* • Alex Nicol *Jay Fowler* • Gigi Perreau *Eileen Lowell* • Carole Mathews *Betty Lowell* • George Dolenz *Carlo* • Jack Cassidy *Gareth Lowell* • Robert Sampson *Lindstrom* ■ *Dir* William Alland • *Scr* Laurence E Mascott

Look Up and Laugh ★★ U

Comedy 1935 · UK · BW · 74mins

Celebrated author JB Priestley supplied the story for this Gracie Fields vehicle. Gracie and her fellow market traders discover an ancient Royal Charter that enables them to declare independence from Britain and so confound the takeover plans of a department-store chain. Look out for an uncredited Kenneth More making his screen debut and Vivien Leigh in only her third film. DP

Gracie Fields *Grace Pearson* • Alfred Drayton *Belfer* • Douglas Wakefield *Joe Chirk* • Billy Nelson *Alf Chirk* • Harry Tate *Turnpenny* • Huntley Wright *Old Ketley* • Vivien Leigh *Marjorie Belfer* • Kenneth More ■ *Dir* Basil Dean • *Scr* Gordon Wellesley, from a story by JB Priestley

Look Who's Laughing ★★ U

Comedy 1941 · US · BW · 78mins

Not many people manage to become national celebrities through a radio ventriloquism act. But that's what happened to Edgar Bergen, who teams once more with his cheeky dummy Charlie McCarthy for this slight, but tolerable flag-waver. He's joined by radio regulars Fibber McGee and Molly (Jim and Marian Jordan) and Harold Peary in one of his five film ventures as the Great Gildersleeve. DP

Edgar Bergen • Jim Jordan *Fibber McGee* • Marian Jordan *Molly McGee* • Lucille Ball *Julie Patterson* • Lee Bonnell *Jerry* • Dorothy Lovett *Marge* • Harold Peary *The Great Gildersleeve* ■ *Dir* Allan Dwan • *Scr* James V Kern, Don Quinn, Leonard L Levinson, Zeno Klinker, Dorothy Kingsley

Look Who's Talking ★★★ 12

Comedy 1989 · US · Colour · 95mins

This is the smash hit that brought John Travolta back from the wilderness into the public eye and spawned two increasingly silly sequels. Kirstie Alley is the single mother on the lookout for the perfect husband, even though we know lowly taxi driver Travolta is the safe bet from the outset. Bruce Willis, the wisecracking voice of baby Mikey, has the best lines, although Travolta and Alley are an amiable pairing, and there's nice support from Olympia Dukakis and George Segal. JF. Contains swearing, sexual references. DVD

John Travolta *James* • Kirstie Alley *Mollie* • Olympia Dukakis *Rosie* • George Segal *Albert* • Abe Vigoda *Grandpa* • Bruce Willis *Mikey* • Twink Caplan *Rona* ■ *Dir/Scr* Amy Heckerling

Look Who's Talking Too ★★ 15

Comedy 1990 · US · Colour · 76mins

Although this sequel succeeded in reuniting the stars of the first movie, it is a pallid retread. The twist this time around is that precocious Mikey (voiced again by Bruce Willis) gets a baby sister (vocals courtesy of Roseanne Barr), but, just to be doubly sure, director Amy Heckerling throws in a couple of other big name "cameos" – the voice talent of Damon Wayans and Mel Brooks. A worrying strain of sentimentality starts to seep through. JF. Contains swearing. DVD

John Travolta *James* • Kirstie Alley *Mollie* • Olympia Dukakis *Rosie* • Elias Koteas *Stuart* • Twink Kaplan *Rona* • Neal Israel *Mr Ross* • Bruce Willis *Mikey* • Roseanne Barr *Julie* • Damon Wayans *Eddie* • Mel Brooks *Mr Toilet Man* ■ *Dir* Amy Heckerling • *Scr* Amy Heckerling, Neal Israel, from characters created by Amy Heckerling

Look Who's Talking Now! ★★ 12

Comedy 1993 · US · Colour · 95mins

The talking baby concept had been exhausted by the first two *Look Who's* films, so the makers moved on to animals for this second sequel. However, even the presence of Danny DeVito and Diane Keaton couldn't breathe life into a tired formula. John Travolta and Kirstie Alley go through the motions again as the bickering couple, while DeVito and Keaton, providing the voices for two dogs from different sides of the tracks, snap away in similar fashion. Good gags are thin on the ground. JF DVD

John Travolta *James Ubriacco* • Kirstie Alley *Mollie Ubriacco* • David Gallagher *Mikey Ubriacco* • Tabitha Lupien *Julie Ubriacco* • Lysette Anthony *Samantha* • Olympia Dukakis *Rosie* • Danny DeVito *Rocks* • Diane Keaton *Daphne* • George Segal *Albert* ■ *Dir* Tom Ropelewski • *Scr* Tom Ropelewski, Leslie Dixon, from characters created by Amy Heckerling

Looker ★★★★ 15

Science-fiction thriller
1981 · US · Colour · 89mins

This under-rated blend of techno horror and suspense is a slick outing about subliminal advertising, in which plastic surgeon Albert Finney joins pin-up Susan Dey to investigate the deaths of his supermodel clients and their association with advertising agency chief James Coburn. Although it's confusing at times, the design is fabulous, and the time-continuum blaster gizmo is a brilliant device allowing Michael Crichton to indulge in some great visual effects. The acting, from Finney especially, is outstanding. AJ. Contains nudity.

Albert Finney *Dr Larry Roberts* • James Coburn *John Reston* • Susan Dey *Cindy* • Leigh Taylor-

Young *Jennifer Long* • Dorian Harewood *Lieutenant Masters* • Tim Rossovich *Moustache Man* ■ *Dir/Scr* Michael Crichton

Lookin' Italian ★★ 18

Crime drama 1994 · US · Colour · 97mins

This is a rather embarrassing skeleton from *Friends* star Matt LeBlanc's closet. He is actually a supporting player here, appearing as the hot-headed nephew of the Mafia-connected Jay Acovone, who is attempting to begin a new peaceful life in Los Angeles. The performances are wildly over the top and Guy Magar's script is stacked with every gangster cliché in the book. JF DVD

Jay Acovone *Vinny Pallazzo* • Matt LeBlanc *Anthony Manetti* • Stephanie Richards *Danielle* • John LaMotta *Don Dinardo* • Ralph Manza *Manza* • Lou Rawls *Willy* ■ *Dir/Scr* Guy Magar

Lookin' to Get Out ★★ 15

Comedy 1982 · US · Colour · 100mins

The title probably sums up director Hal Ashby's feelings about this dud comedy that marked the beginning of his career decline in the 1980s. Stars Jon Voight and Burt Young are the two losers who arrive in Las Vegas hoping to win back the fortune they have just managed to lose. To this end they con their way into a luxury hotel suite and – with a little help from Ann-Margret – hit the tables. There's solid character back-up from the likes of Bert Remsen but it needed more flair upfront to make it work. TH

Jon Voight *Alex Kovac* • Ann-Margret *Patti Warner* • Burt Young *Jerry Feldman* • Bert Remsen *Smitty* • Jude Farese *Harry* • Allen Keller *Joey* ■ *Dir* Hal Ashby • *Scr* Al Schwartz, Jon Voight

Looking for Mr Goodbar ★★★★ 18

Drama 1977 · US · Colour · 130mins

Although not the most obvious choice to play the man-hungry heroine in this adaptation of Judith Rossner's bestseller, Diane Keaton manages a wonderfully fraught performance in writer/director Richard Brooks's overcharged sexual melodrama. Keaton plays a teacher of deaf children who haunts singles bars at night, taking the sadistic rough (Richard Gere) with the decent smooth (William Atherton) until she meets a bisexual killer (Tom Berenger). Although reminiscent of the German classic *Pandora's Box*, this has a glib puritanism pervading the sleaze and, even if some aspects of the novel are glossed over, it's still very raw. TH. Contains violence, sex scenes, swearing, drug abuse.

Diane Keaton *Theresa Dunn* • Tuesday Weld *Katherine Dunn* • Richard Gere *Tony Lopanto* • William Atherton *James Morrissey* • Richard Kiley *Mr Dunn* • Alan Feinstein *Professor Engle* • Tom Berenger *Gary Cooper White* ■ *Dir* Richard Brooks • *Scr* Richard Brooks, from the novel by Judith Rossner

Looking for Richard ★★★★ 12

Documentary drama 1996 · US · Colour · 107mins

Al Pacino's unusual and very personal tribute to Shakespeare follows his attempts to adapt *Richard III* for the screen. It's partly a documentary (containing interviews with the likes of Kenneth Branagh and John Gielgud), partly a filmed adaptation of the play, as Pacino plays out scenes with fellow Americans Kevin Spacey, Winona Ryder, Aidan Quinn and Alec Baldwin. Demonstrating genuine love and understanding of the Bard as well as great skill as a Shakespearean actor, Pacino explores the classic text in a compelling and original way. LH. Contains violence, swearing. DVD

Al Pacino *Richard III* • Alec Baldwin *Clarence* • Kevin Spacey *Buckingham* • Winona Ryder *Lady Anne* • Aidan Quinn *Richmond* • Estelle Parsons *Margaret* ■ *Dir* Al Pacino

Looking for Trouble ★★

Crime drama 1934 · US · BW · 77mins

Spencer Tracy and Jack Oakie play two telephone line repairmen in this action-packed and sometimes confusing drama from director William Wellman. These macho stalwarts get involved in every kind of crisis from fire and earthquake, to robbery, romance and murder. Constance Cummings co-stars, and there are enough dramatics to keep the action moving and hold – if not exactly grip – one's attention. RK

Spencer Tracy *Joe Graham* • Jack Oakie *Casey* • Constance Cummings *Ethel Greenwood* • Morgan Conway *Dan Sutter* • Arline Judge *Maizie* ■ *Dir* William A Wellman • *Scr* Leonard Praskins, Elmer Harris, from a story by JR Bren

Looking for Trouble ★★

Comedy 1996 · US · Colour · 73mins

This old-fashioned creature feature is co-directed by Peter Tors, whose father produced the classic 1960s animal TV shows *Flipper* and *Daktari*. However, the story of Holly Butler's bid to rescue an elephant calf from a travelling circus is more likely to appeal to nostalgic parents than youngsters. DP

Holly Butler *Jamie Miller* • Susan Gallagher *Susan Miller* • Gerry Russell *Ben* • Shawn McAllister *Harry* ■ *Dir* Jay Aubrey, Peter Tors • *Scr* Jay Aubrey, Jeffrey Dowdy, Peter Tors, Christopher Wooden

The Looking Glass War ★★★ 15

Spy drama 1969 · UK · Colour · 102mins

The spymasters come out best, but that's because they're played by Ralph Richardson and Paul Rogers in this John le Carré adaptation in which a Polish refugee (Christopher Jones) is persuaded to enter East Germany to verify Russian missile sites. The foot soldiers of espionage (including a young Anthony Hopkins) have a tough time of it, and its Cold War climate now seems long ago and far away. TH. Contains violence and swearing.

Christopher Jones *Leiser* • Pia Degermark *The Girl* • Ralph Richardson *Leclerc* • Anthony Hopkins *John Avery* • Paul Rogers *Haldane* • Susan George *Susan* • Ray McAnally *Starr* • Robert Urquhart *Johnson* ■ *Dir* Frank R Pierson [Frank Pierson] • *Scr* Frank R Pierson, from the novel by John le Carré

Looking on the Bright Side ★★★ U

Musical comedy 1931 · UK · BW · 78mins

Gracie Fields hit the movie big time with this sprightly musical comedy, which was co-directed by theatre impresario Basil Dean and silent specialist Graham Cutts. As ever, she plays a spirited working lass, who keeps her wits around her, even when things are at their bleakest. Quitting her job as a manicurist, when the hairdresser she adores gets the chance to write songs for a superstar, she joins the police and not only rediscovers her self-esteem, but also arrives on stage to save her beau's flagging career. DP

Gracie Fields *Gracie* • Richard Dolman *Laurie* • Julian Rose *Oscar Schultz* • Wyn Richmond *Miss Joy* ■ *Dir* Basil Dean, Graham Cutts • *Scr* Basil Dean, Archie Pitt, Brock Williams

Looks and Smiles ★★★★

Drama 1981 · UK · Colour · 103mins

The rising damp of despair permeates this Ken Loach docudrama about the effect of redundancies on teenagers living in Sheffield, South Yorkshire. One boy opts for enlistment and ends up in Belfast; another stays at home, condemning himself to the futility of the job search and a relationship with shopgirl Carolyn Nicholson. Loach elicits marvellous performances from his three leads, all amateur actors behaving like true professionals. TH

Graham Green *Mick Walsh* • Carolyn Nicholson *Karen Lodge* • Tony Pitts *Alan Wright* • Roy Haywood *Phil Adams* • Phil Askham *Mr Walsh* • Pam Darrell *Mrs Walsh* • Tracey Goodlad *Julie* ■ *Dir* Kenneth Loach [Ken Loach] • *Scr* Barry Hines

Looney Looney Looney Bugs Bunny Movie ★★★ U

Animation 1981 · US · Colour · 69mins

Forty-one years after *A Wild Hare*, the most famous character in the Warner Bros cartoon stable returns in another greatest hits compilation. Bugs Bunny is always good value and the selection made here by Friz Freleng, one of the animators who first brought him to life (based on sketches by a story man named Bugs Hardaway, hence the name) is often very funny indeed. The highlight is *Knighty Knight Bugs*, which won the Oscar for best animated short subject in 1958. DP

Mel Blanc *Bugs Bunny/Daffy Duck/Sylvester/Tweety Pie/Porky Pig* ■ *Dir* Friz Freleng, Gerry Chiniquy • *Scr* David Detiege, John W Dunn

Looney Tunes: Back in Action ★★ PG

Part-animated fantasy adventure 2004 · US · Colour · 87mins

The live actors interact awkwardly with the animation in a dumb story that has studio security guard DJ Drake (Brendan Fraser), Daffy Duck and Bugs Bunny attempting to foil the world domination plans of Mr Chairman (Steve Martin). Director Joe Dante packs every frame with his brand of referential humour, but the most inspired moments of this uneven adventure come during a classic *Looney Tunes* chase through the Louvre. AJ DVD

Brendan Fraser *DJ Drake/Brendan Fraser* • Jenna Elfman *Kate Houghton* • Timothy Dalton *Damien Drake* • Joan Cusack *Mother* • Bill Goldberg *Mr Smith* • Heather Locklear *Dusty Tails* • Steve Martin *Mr Chairman* ■ *Dir* Joe Dante • *Scr* Larry Doyle

Loophole ★★ PG

Crime drama 1980 · UK · Colour · 99mins

Albert Finney and Susannah York star in this lacklustre heist caper. Martin Sheen is the obligatory American import, whose in-depth knowledge of bank security systems and hefty overdraft make him the ideal partner for Finney's mastermind. The blag itself is pretty routine, although the action picks up slightly when the gang's escape through the London sewers is hindered by a torrential downpour. Drably directed, not even Lalo Schifrin's score can enliven the proceedings. DP

Albert Finney *Mike Daniels* • Martin Sheen *Stephen Booker* • Susannah York *Dinah Booker* • Colin Blakely *Gardner* • Jonathan Pryce *Taylor* • Robert Morley *Godfrey* • Alfred Lynch *Harry* • Tony Doyle *Nolan* ■ *Dir* John Quested • *Scr* Jonathan Hales, from a novel by Robert Pollock

Loose Cannons ★ 15

Comedy 1990 · US · Colour · 90mins

This dire buddy comedy marked a new low for the excellent Gene Hackman. He is the tough cop who finds himself reluctantly paired on a case with oddball detective Dan Aykroyd, who happens to suffer from a form of multiple personality disorder brought on by imminent danger. An unwatchable mess. JF. Contains swearing, violence and nudity. DVD

Gene Hackman *Mac Stern* • Dan Aykroyd *Ellis Fielding* • Dom DeLuise *Harry "The Hippo" Gutterman* • Ronny Cox *Bob Smiley* • Nancy Travis *Riva* • Robert Prosky *Curt Von Metz* ■ *Dir* Bob Clark • *Scr* Richard Christian Matheson, Richard Matheson, Bob Clark

Loose Connections ★★★ PG

Comedy 1983 · UK · Colour · 95mins

This attempt by theatre director Richard Eyre to resurrect the screwball comedies of the 1930s has unlikely duo Lindsay Duncan and Stephen Rea as the protagonists. Duncan plays an uptight Germaine Greer type, driving through Germany with co-"pilot" Rea as her unfortunate companion. Their inability to see eye to eye fits well with the film's general depiction of the Brits abroad. Turns from Robbie Coltrane and Gary Olsen add to the fun and the two leads carry the film with style. Eyre nearly obtains his objective with the genre – but not quite. LH

Stephen Rea *Harry* • Lindsay Duncan *Sally* • Carol Harrison *Kay* • Frances Low *Laurie* • Andrew De La Tour *Journalist* • David Purcell *Photographer* • Keith Allen *Keith* • Robbie Coltrane *Drunk* • Ruth Bruck *Wirtin* ■ *Dir* Richard Eyre • *Scr* Maggie Brooks

Loot ★★★★ 15

Comedy 1970 · UK · Colour · 97mins

Joe Orton's mordant play is about a bundle of stolen money hidden in a coffin that gets buried in the churchyard. It's a ruthless satire on authoritarianism as well as a send-up of the Agatha Christie-style whodunnit which had kept the British theatre ticking over for decades. The play had gone from disaster to prize-winning success but the film version flopped badly. Reworked by TV writers Ray Galton and Alan Simpson, it's wholly faithful to Orton's surreal sense of humour and the extreme tackiness of the characters, especially Richard Attenborough who clearly delights in playing the creepiest, kinkiest detective you'll ever see. AT

Richard Attenborough *Inspector Truscott* • Lee Remick *Fay* • Hywel Bennett *Dennis* • Roy Holder *Hal* • Milo O'Shea *Mr McLeavy* • Dick Emery *Mr Bateman* • Joe Lynch *Father O'Shaughnessy* • John Cater *Meadows* • Aubrey Woods *Undertaker* ■ *Dir* Silvio Narizzano • *Scr* Ray Galton, Alan Simpson, from the play by Joe Orton

The Looters ★★

Action adventure 1955 · US · BW · 87mins

Rory Calhoun and Ray Danton are two buddies who reach four survivors of a plane crash in the Rockies, only to fall out over money found on board. Calhoun is forced at gunpoint to lead the group to safety, biding his time to turn the tables. Calhoun and Danton are not particularly interesting as actors, and the plot might have worked better as a western. AE

Rory Calhoun *Jesse Hill* • Julie Adams *Sheryl Gregory* • Ray Danton *Pete Corder* • Thomas Gomez *George Parkinson* • Frank Faylen *Stan Leppich* • Rod Williams *Co-pilot* • Russ Conway *Major Knowles* ■ *Dir* Abner Biberman • *Scr* Richard Alan Simmons, from a story by Paul Schneider

The Looters ★★

Crime drama 1966 · Fr/It · Colour · 102mins

Ex-criminal Frederick Stafford falls for Jean Seberg, but finds that her gangster father has other plans for him. He's recruited to crack a safe and steal some gold owned by a would-be dictator who is planning a coup. Despite these political undertones, the film is a straightforward crime caper which could have been livelier. JG. French and Italian dialogue dubbed into English.

L

Frederick Stafford *Sam Morgan* • Jean Seberg *Colleen O'Hara* • Mario Pisu *Patrick O'Hara* • Maria-Rosa Rodriguez *Estella* • Serge Gainsbourg *Clyde* ■ *Dir* Jacques Besnard • *Scr* Pierre Foucaud, Michel Lebrun

Lorca and the Outlaws

★★ PG

Science fiction 1985 · UK · Colour · 86mins

Another dreary *Star Wars* clone with a bit of *Mad Max* thrown in. About a miner's strike on a remote desert world put down by militaristic police, the irony of this British-financed production (shot in the Australian outback) being made in the year of Arthur Scargill was seemingly lost on the film-makers. Despite killer robots and numerous fights and chases the whole affair is a chaotic bore. RS

John Tarrant *Lorca* • Donogh Rees *Abbie* • Deep Roy *Kid* • Cassandra Webb *Suzi* • Ralph Cotterill *Jowitt* • Hugh Keays-Byrne *Danny* ■ *Dir* Roger Christian • *Scr* Roger Christian, Matthew Jacobs • *Music* Tony Banks

Lord Edgware Dies

★

Murder mystery 1934 · US · BW · 81mins

Agatha Christie's 13th whodunnit was filmed the year after its publication. It was intended to be the start of a series of Hercule Poirot movie adventures, with Austin Trevor as the fastidious Belgian sleuth. But such was the wave of apathy that greeted this lacklustre adaptation that the plans were shelved. Trevor is wincingly bad, completely missing the trademark mannerisms of Poirot that later actors would bring to the character. DP

Austin Trevor *Hercule Poirot* • Jane Carr (1) *Lady Edgware* • Richard Cooper *Captain Hastings* • John Turnbull *Inspector Japp* • Michael Shepley *Captain Ronald Marsh* • Leslie Perrins *Bryan Martin* • CV France *Lord Edgware* • Esme Percy *Duke of Merton* ■ *Dir* Henry Edwards • *Scr* H Fowler Mear, from the novel by Agatha Christie

Lord Jim

★★★★ PG

Period adventure

1965 · UK · Colour · 154mins

Peter O'Toole gives one of his finest performances in this adaptation of Joseph Conrad's story about a merchant seaman branded a coward after jumping ship during a storm. His search for salvation in South East Asia results in action against a fanatical tyrant lording it over oppressed natives. Writer/director Richard Brooks allows the plot to meander out of control, but Freddie Young's photography of the mist-shrouded rivers and jungles emphasises the weird spirituality of Lord Jim's quest for redemption. TH DVD

Peter O'Toole *Lord Jim* • James Mason *Gentleman Brown* • Curt Jurgens *Cornelius* • Eli Wallach *The General* • Jack Hawkins *Marlow* • Paul Lukas *Stein* • Akim Tamiroff *Schomberg* • Daliah Lavi *The Girl* ■ *Dir* Richard Brooks • *Scr* Richard Brooks, from the novel by Joseph Conrad

Lord Love a Duck

★★★

Black comedy 1966 · US · BW · 105mins

George Axelrod made a notable directorial debut with this wickedly funny and beautifully acted satire on 1960s California lifestyles. It is centred on a bizarre high school, where clairvoyant Roddy McDowall grants wishes for the students, notably those of teen vamp Tuesday Weld. This is a real one-off: a wacky black comedy unfettered by taste, written and performed with great élan, with an interesting supporting cast including eccentric Ruth Gordon and Lola Albright as Weld's suicidal mom. TS

Roddy McDowall *Alan "Mollymauk" Musgrave* • Tuesday Weld *Barbara Ann Greene* • Lola Albright *Marie Greene* • Martin West *Bob Barnard* • Ruth Gordon *Stella Barnard* • Harvey Korman *Weldon Emmett* • Sarah Marshall *Miss Schwartz* ■ *Dir* George Axelrod • *Scr* Larry H Johnson, George Axelrod, from the novel by Al Hine

Lord of Illusions

★★ 18

Horror 1995 · US · Colour · 116mins

An unfocused and meandering dark fairy tale directed by *Hellraiser* horror novelist Clive Barker featuring his literary creation, the world-weary private eye Harry D'Amour (Scott Bakula). The troubled detective is on the trail of an evil cult spiritualist and his murder investigation takes him into the illusory world of professional theatre magicians. Barker's keen visual flair is evident throughout this gory intrigue, but there's far too much style and not enough content to fully engage the fear senses. AJ DVD

Scott Bakula *Harry D'Amour* • Famke Janssen *Dorothea Swann* • Trevor Edmond *Young Butterfield* • Daniel Von Bargen *Nix* • Kevin J O'Connor *Philip Swann* • Joseph Latimore *Caspar Quaid* ■ *Dir/Scr* Clive Barker

Lord of the Flies

★★★★ PG

Drama 1963 · UK · BW · 86mins

Novelist William Golding's fierce morality tale about schoolboys marooned on a desert island and reverting to religious savagery is given the larger-than-life treatment by theatrical director Peter Brook, who can't quite cope with cinematic character, but who keeps the tension tight as a crossbow. The wider implications of the idea, as a comment on mankind's original sin don't come across, but, taken as a parable limited to a bleak blueprint, it's vividly memorable. TH DVD

James Aubrey *Ralph* • Tom Chapin *Jack* • Hugh Edwards *Piggy* • Roger Elwin *Roger* • Tom Gaman *Simon* ■ *Dir* Peter Brook • *Scr* Peter Brook, from the novel by William Golding

Lord of the Flies

★★★ 15

Drama 1990 · US · Colour · 87mins

This is a worthy but misfired attempt to feed William Golding's classic tale to the masses. The switch from British public schoolboys to American military cadets works better than it sounds and, at one level, makes the boys' savage transformation even more believable. Director Harry Hook coaxes wonderful performances out of a young, largely unknown cast led by Balthazar Getty. However, he doesn't quite succeed in recapturing the dark, disturbing undercurrents of the novel. JF. Contains swearing and violence. DVD

Balthazar Getty *Ralph* • Chris Furrh *Jack* • Danuel Pipoly *Piggy* • Gary Rule *Roger* • Terry Wells *Andy* • Braden MacDonald *Larry* ■ *Dir* Harry Hook • *Scr* Sara Schiff, from the novel by William Golding

The Lord of the Rings

★★ PG

Animated fantasy adventure

1978 · US · Colour · 127mins

Unlikely to satisfy fans of JRR Tolkien's novels, this animated version is also small beer compared to recent animated spectaculars. It seems less concerned with Tolkien than the West Coast druggie culture of the mid-1970s and as a herald of New Ageism. It's also rather slow and virtually impossible to follow unless you know the books. AT DVD

Christopher Guard *Frodo* • Michael Scholes *Samwise* • John Hurt *Aragorn "Strider"* • William Squire *Gandalf* • Simon Chandler *Merry* • Dominic Guard *Pippin* • Norman Bird *Bilbo* • Anthony Daniels *Legolas* ■ *Dir* Ralph Bakshi • *Scr* Chris Conkling, Peter S Beagle, from the novels by JRR Tolkien

The Lord of the Rings: The Fellowship of the Ring

★★★★★ PG

Fantasy adventure

2001 · NZ/US · Colour · 171mins

In the first chapter of director Peter Jackson's $300-million adaptation of JRR Tolkien's classic trilogy, Middle-earth is the fictional setting, but it's no backdrop; it's a living, breathing universe, in which mild-mannered hobbit Frodo Baggins (Elijah Wood) is forced to turn hero when he inherits the ring of absolute power. Assisted by powerful wizard Gandalf (a perfectly cast Ian McKellen) and a ragtag group of warriors and friends, he must journey across mountain, forest and plain to return the talisman to its source. The computer-generated images transform the New Zealand locations into views that will take your breath away and only someone with a pathological aversion to fantasy could fail to be absorbed and transported by this stunning, sincere and frequently terrifying adaptation. AC DVD

Elijah Wood *Frodo Baggins* • Ian McKellen *Gandalf the Grey* • Liv Tyler *Arwen Undómiel* • Viggo Mortensen *Aragorn/Strider* • Sean Astin *Samwise "Sam" Gamgee* • Cate Blanchett *Galadriel* • Hugo Weaving *Elrond* • Sean Bean *Boromir* • Ian Holm *Bilbo Baggins* • Christopher Lee *Saruman the White* • John Rhys-Davies *Gimli* • Billy Boyd *Peregrin "Pippin" Took* • Dominic Monaghan *Meriadoc "Merry" Brandybuck* • Orlando Bloom *Legolas Greenleaf* • Andy Serkis *Sméagol/Gollum* ■ *Dir* Peter Jackson • *Scr* Peter Jackson, Philippa Boyens, Fran Walsh, from the novel *The Fellowship of the Ring* by JRR Tolkien • *Cinematographer* Andrew Lesnie • *Music* Howard Shore

The Lord of the Rings: The Two Towers

★★★★★ 12

Fantasy adventure

2002 · NZ/US/Ger · Colour · 171mins

Under the assumption that everyone has seen *The Fellowship of the Ring*, director Peter Jackson jumps straight back into the action. With the fellowship fractured, the story diverges into three separate strands: Frodo and Sam's trek to Mordor, on which they are joined by the deranged Gollum; Gimli, Legolas and Aragorn's new allegiance with the imperilled kingdom of Rohan; and Merry and Pippin's affiliation with the sentient trees of Fangorn Forest. Darker and more urgent than the first film, Jackson again displays an unparalleled grasp of storytelling on a grand scale – the siege of Helm's Deep in the final hour is as heroic and spectacular as any battle scene ever committed to film. The performances are uniformly excellent, but the most impressive contribution comes from Andy Serkis, who provides the creepy tones and fluid physical movements of Gollum, the most convincing CGI character created to date. JC DVD

Elijah Wood *Frodo Baggins* • Ian McKellen *Gandalf the White* • Liv Tyler *Arwen Undómiel* • Viggo Mortensen *Aragorn/Strider* • Sean Astin *Samwise "Sam" Gamgee* • Cate Blanchett *Galadriel* • John Rhys-Davies *Gimli/Treebeard* • Billy Boyd *Peregrin "Pippin" Took* • Dominic Monaghan *Meriadoc "Merry" Brandybuck* • Orlando Bloom *Legolas Greenleaf* • Christopher Lee *Saruman the White* • Hugo Weaving *Elrond* • Miranda Otto *Eowyn of Rohan* • Bernard Hill *King Théoden* • Andy Serkis *Sméagol/Gollum* ■ *Dir* Peter Jackson • *Scr* Peter Jackson, Philippa Boyens, Fran Walsh, Stephen Sinclair, from the novel *The Two Towers* by JRR Tolkien

The Lord of the Rings: The Return of the King

★★★★★ 12

Fantasy adventure

2003 · NZ /US/Ger · Colour · 192mins

Peter Jackson deservedly won the best director Oscar for this powerful and enchanting concluding episode to his massively ambitious adaptation of JRR Tolkien's trilogy. It also became the first fantasy film to receive the best picture Oscar and won awards in all the categories for which it was nominated, equalling the record haul of 11 set by *Ben-Hur* and *Titanic*. One staggeringly beautiful sight follows another as the brilliant ensemble cast mix man, myth and magic together with astonishing scope and intoxicating invention. The action picks up from *The Two Towers* with Frodo crawling to Mount Doom to destroy the ring, while Aragorn enlists an army of the dead to help Gandalf defend the besieged city of Minas Tirith from the Witch-king and his armies. The ending does drag on with its series of teary farewells, but this is a minor gripe considering his towering achievement in creating a literate masterpiece. AJ DVD

Elijah Wood *Frodo Baggins* • Ian McKellen *Gandalf the White* • Liv Tyler *Arwen Undómiel* • Viggo Mortensen *Aragorn/Strider* • Sean Astin *Samwise "Sam" Gamgee* • Cate Blanchett *Galadriel* • John Rhys-Davies *Gimli* • Bernard Hill *King Théoden* • Billy Boyd *Peregrin "Pippin" Took* • Dominic Monaghan *Meriadoc "Merry" Brandybuck* • Orlando Bloom *Legolas Greenleaf* • Hugo Weaving *Elrond* • Miranda Otto *Eowyn of Rohan* • David Wenham *Faramir* • John Noble *Denethor, Steward of Gondor* • Andy Serkis *Sméagol/Gollum* ■ *Dir* Peter Jackson • *Scr* Peter Jackson, Fran Walsh, Philippa Boyens, from the novel *The Return of the King* by JRR Tolkien

The Lords of Discipline

★★★ 15

Drama 1983 · US · Colour · 98mins

Having hanged himself in *An Officer and a Gentleman*, David Keith goes back to military school for this sinister thriller in which he combats the racist bigotry of a secret society known as "The Ten". Director Franc Roddam is comfortable with the sights and sounds of 1960s Carolina, but once the scene has been set he rather loses the plot, spending a disturbing amount of time on the acts of cruelty perpetrated upon the academy's first black cadet and not enough time sleuthing the culprits. DP. Contains swearing and violence.

David Keith *Will McClean* • Robert Prosky *Colonel "Bear" Berrineau* • GD Spradlin *General Durrell* • Barbara Babcock *Abigail* • Michael Biehn *Alexander* • Rick Rossovich *Pig* • John Lavachielli *Mark* • Judge Reinhold *Macabbee* • Bill Paxton *Gilbreath* • Jason Connery *MacKinnon* ■ *Dir* Franc Roddam • *Scr* Thomas Pope, Lloyd Fonvielle, from the novel by Pat Conroy

Lords of Dogtown

★★★ 12A

Action sports drama

2005 · US · Colour · 106mins

Stacy Peralta, who directed the documentary *Dogtown and Z-Boys* (2001) that charted the rise of three young skateboarders in California in the early 1970s, provides the script for this dramatisation of the same events. It's a fast, good-looking movie, thanks to director Catherine Hardwicke, who gives the film an intense immediacy. The weaknesses are all down to the script, with the young heroes walking a well-trodden path. However, the leads are charismatic and the soundtrack outstanding. GM

Emile Hirsch *Jay Adams* • Victor Rasuk *Tony Alva* • John Robinson (3) *Stacy Peralta* • Michael Angarano *Sid* • Nikki Reed *Kathy Alva* • Heath Ledger *Skip Engblom* • Rebecca De

Mornay *Philaine* • Johnny Knoxville *Topper Banks* ■ *Dir* Catherine Hardwicke • *Scr* Stacy Peralta

The Lords of Flatbush ★★★★ 15

Drama 1974 · US · Colour · 80mins

Sylvester Stallone (in his first top-billed role), *Happy Days* star Henry Winkler, B-movie heart-throb Perry King and Paul Mace are members of a Brooklyn gang in this brilliant coming-of-age saga set in the late 1950s. Stallone sets the seal on his future success as a tough-talker pushed into marriage by his pregnant girlfriend when all he really wants to do is hang out with the guys and tend his pigeons. This evokes a strong sense of time and place, with a great nostalgic soundtrack. AJ [video]

Perry King *Chico Tyrell* • Sylvester Stallone *Stanley Rosiello* • Henry Winkler *Butchey Weinstein* • Paul Mace *Wimpy Murgalo* • Susan Blakely *Jane Bradshaw* • Maria Smith *Frannie Malincanico* • Renee Paris *Annie Yuckamanelli* • Ray Sharkey *Student* • Paul Jabara *Crazy Cohen* ■ *Dir* Stephen Verona, Martin Davidson • *Scr* Stephen Verona, Martin Davidson, Gayle Gleckler, Sylvester Stallone

Lorenzo's Oil ★★★ 15

Biographical drama
1992 · US · Colour · 129mins

This glossy, at times harrowing, heart-tugger is dominated by the towering performance of Susan Sarandon as the determined Michaela Odone, who takes on the medical establishment when her young son is diagnosed with a rare and normally fatal wasting disease. But Nick Nolte is less successful as the boy's father, Augusto, sporting a bizarre Italian accent. You'll either love or loathe this intelligent, well-made wallow that's ably directed by *Mad Max* veteran George Miller. SH [video] DVD

Nick Nolte *Augusto Odone* • Susan Sarandon *Michaela Odone* • Peter Ustinov *Professor Nikolais* • Kathleen Wilhoite *Deirdre Murphy* • Gerry Bamman *Doctor Judalon* • Margo Martindale *Wendy Gimble* • Zack O'Malley Greenburg *Lorenzo* • Laura Linney *Young teacher* ■ *Dir* George Miller (2) • *Scr* George Miller, Nick Enright

Lorna ★★ 18

Satirical melodrama 1964 · US · BW · 79mins

Part gothic melodrama, part sex morality play, this was the notorious Russ Meyer's first serious effort at "legitimate" film-making. Certainly it's his first plot-driven movie and casts buxom Lorna Maitland as the eponymous heroine, a backwoods wife who strays from her dull husband and begins an affair with an escaped con. Meyer, with his typically flamboyant editing and direction, does a pretty good job of things considering the mediocre acting talent and script at his disposal. RS. Contains sex scenes, swearing and violence. [video] DVD

Lorna Maitland *Lorna* • Mark Bradley *Fugitive* • James Rucker *James* • Hal Hopper *Luther* • Doc Scortt *Jonah* • James Griffith *Prophet/Narrator* ■ *Dir* Russ Meyer • *Scr* James Griffith, from a story by R Albion Meyer

Lorna Doone ★★★ U

Period drama 1934 · UK · BW · 82mins

RD Blackmore's novel is a full-blooded melodrama set in 17th century Exmoor where two feuding families – the Doones and the Ridds – are at each other's throats. As in *Romeo and Juliet*, there is a cross-feudal romance between strappingly handsome John Ridd and pretty Lorna who, it transpires, isn't a Doone at all but a kidnapped aristocrat. Victoria Hopper, the wife of the producer/director Basil Dean, stars as Lorna. John Loder, as the hero Ridd, was always a rather wooden actor, though Margaret Lockwood, in her screen debut, is a ravishing beauty. AT [video]

Victoria Hopper *Lorna Doone* • John Loder *John Ridd* • Margaret Lockwood *Annie Ridd* • Roy Emerton *Carver Doone* • Mary Clare *Mistress Ridd* • Edward Rigby *Reuben Huckaback* • Roger Livesey *Tom Faggus* • George Curzon *King James II* ■ *Dir* Basil Dean • *Scr* Dorothy Farnum, Miles Malleson, Gordon Wellesley, from the novel by RD Blackmore

Lorna Doone ★★ U

Period drama 1951 · US · Colour · 83mins

Hollywood has a go at the classic yarn of a rustic feud, a hulking hero and a smart heroine who turns out to be a kidnapped heiress. It's made on a slimmed down budget and shot in the Yosemite National Park, California, rather than on Exmoor, but the studio did put up the money for Technicolor. B-movie director Phil Karlson treats it just like a western. AT

Barbara Hale *Lorna Doone* • Richard Greene *John Ridd* • Carl Benton Reid *Sir Ensor Doone* • William Bishop *Carver Doone* • Ron Randell *Tom Faggus* • Sean McClory *Charleworth Doone* • Onslow Stevens *Counsellor Doone* • Lester Matthews *King Charles II* ■ *Dir* Phil Karlson • *Scr* Jesse L Lasky Jr [Jesse Lasky Jr], Richard Schayer, from the novel by RD Blackmore

The Loser ★★★

Comedy thriller 1971 · Fr · Colour · 96mins

An amusing "worm turns" story that provides an admirable showcase for Claude Brasseur. As the petty crook whose stint in the cells lands him an introduction to the big time, Brasseur milks every gag as he not only begins blackmailing the town's crooked dignitaries, but also moves in on a murdered mobster's moll (Marthe Keller). The prolific Gilles Grangier directs with a glib charm owing much to the fact that his speciality was the sort of crime drama he so gleefully spoofs here. DP. French dialogue dubbed into English.

Claude Brasseur *Granier* • André Weber *Laigneau* • Marthe Keller *Catherine* • Pierre Tornade *Fernier* ■ *Dir* Gilles Grangier • *Scr* Albert Simonin, from a novel by Jean Stuart

Loser ★ 12

Comedy romance 2000 · US · Colour · 91mins

Teen films often plumb the depths of good taste, but rarely do they hit rock bottom like this one. Outrage and amorality have long been staples of the genre – especially since the success of *American Pie* – but it's a fine line between chucklesome grossness and unfunny crassness. Date-rape drugs and under-age sex are just two of the areas mined for so-called mirth as callow country kid Jason Biggs bids to be accepted by his sex-obsessed, boorish and room-mates at a big-city college. DA [video] DVD

Jason Biggs *Paul Tannek* • Mena Suvari *Dora Diamond* • Zak Orth *Adam* • Tom Sadoski *Chris* • Jimmi Simpson *Noah* • Greg Kinnear *Professor Edward Alcott* • Dan Aykroyd *Dad* ■ *Dir/Scr* Amy Heckerling

Loser Takes All ★

Comedy drama 1956 · UK · Colour · 88mins

Given that this screenplay was written by Graham Greene from his own book, its awfulness defies explanation. The casting of Glynis Johns and Rossano Brazzi as a newlywed couple honeymooning in Monte Carlo at the invitation of a vaguely characterised and only intermittently seen Robert Morley is a pairing so unlikely as to sink the enterprise on its own. However, the screenplay, about the husband developing a gambling obsession, is not much better. RK

Rossano Brazzi *Bertrand* • Glynis Johns *Cary* • Robert Morley *Dreuther* • Felix Aylmer *The Other* ■ *Dir* Ken Annakin • *Scr* Graham Greene, from his novella

Loser Takes All ★ PG

Comedy 1990 · UK/US · Colour · 81mins

Robert Lindsay and Molly Ringwald take over from Rossano Brazzi and Glynis Johns as the British couple who are gifted a honeymoon in Monte Carlo, only for staid hubbie to become seduced by the casino. Lindsay does his best with the ploddingly predictable material but Ringwald is grievously miscast as his wife and even the presence of a distinguished supporting cast can't save it. JF [video]

Robert Lindsay *Ian Bertram* • Molly Ringwald *Cary Porter* • John Gielgud *Herbert Dreuther* • Simon de la Brosse *Philippe* • Max Wall *Bowles* • Margi Clarke *Bowles's nurse* • Frances de la Tour *Mrs De Vere* ■ *Dir* James Scott • *Scr* James Scott, from the novella by Graham Greene

Losin' It ★★ 18

Comedy drama 1983 · US · Colour · 95mins

Tom Cruise, in one of his earliest roles, adds curiosity value to an unexceptional coming-of-age-tale about three teenagers heading for Tijuana to gain a broader perspective on life and lose their virginity. Strictly routine in every area, with Shelley Long coming along for the ride as a woman hoping to get a quick divorce. AJ [video]

Tom Cruise *Woody* • Jackie Earle Haley *Dave* • John Stockwell *Spider* • Shelley Long *Kathy* • John P Navin Jr *Wendell the Wimp* • Henry Darrow *El Jefe, Sheriff* • Hector Elias *Chuey* ■ *Dir* Curtis Hanson • *Scr* BWL Norton, from his story

Losing Isaiah ★★★ 15

Drama 1995 · US · Colour · 102mins

This emotionally-charged drama examines the custody battle between a young black mother (Halle Berry), who three years earlier had abandoned her baby while high on drugs, and the loving white couple (Jessica Lange and David Strathairn) who have adopted him. The strong cast adds dramatic weight to a "TV movie of the week" plot. A tad contrived, but still believable. JC. Contains violence, swearing and drug abuse. [video] DVD

Jessica Lange *Margaret Lewin* • Halle Berry *Khaila Richards* • David Strathairn *Charles Lewin* • Cuba Gooding Jr *Eddie Hughes* • Daisy Eagan *Hannah Lewin* • Marc John Jeffries *Isaiah* • Samuel L Jackson *Kadar Lewis* ■ *Dir* Stephen Gyllenhaal • *Scr* Naomi Foner, from the novel by Seth J Margolis

The Loss of Sexual Innocence ★★ 18

Drama 1999 · US/UK · Colour · 105mins

Specked with fascinating moments, this is an otherwise over-indulgent hobby horse from writer/director Mike Figgis. A fragmentary memoir of a movie producer called Nic (played variously by Jonathan Rhys Meyers and Julian Sands), it traces his development from school bullying and love on the Tyne to marital discord and tragedy in the Sahara. Alas, the decision to intercut the action with a mixed race re-telling of the Adam and Eve story proves calamitously self-conscious. DP. Contains sex scenes and nudity. [video]

Julian Sands *Nic (as an adult)* • Saffron Burrows *English twin/Italian twin* • Stefano Dionisi *Lucca* • Kelly Macdonald *Susan* • Gina McKee *Susan's mother* • Jonathan Rhys Meyers *Nic (age 16)* • Bernard Hill *Susan's father* ■ *Dir/Scr* Mike Figgis

Lost ★★★

Crime drama 1955 · UK · Colour · 89mins

A film that succeeds because it confronts every parent's nightmare: what happens when you suddenly look away and find your child is missing when you look back? Of course, this being a class-riddled Rank picture, it's the nanny who loses the baby, but it's pretty harrowing nonetheless, despite the casting of insipid David Knight and Julia Arnall as the parents. Granite-faced cop David Farrar is on hand to bring grit to this earnest chase movie and Harry Waxman's colour location photography is superb. TS

David Farrar *Inspector Craig* • David Knight *Lee Cochrane* • Julia Arnall *Sue Cochrane* • Anthony Oliver *Sergeant Lyel* • Thora Hird *Landlady* • Eleanor Summerfield *Sergeant Cook* • Ann Paige *Nanny* • Anna Turner *Mrs Robey* ■ *Dir* Guy Green • *Scr* Janet Green

Lost and Found ★ 15

Romantic comedy
1979 · UK/US · Colour · 100mins

Re-uniting George Segal and Glenda Jackson, the delightful duo of *A Touch of Class*, might have seemed like a good plan, but this story of a widowed American professor meeting a British divorcee on a skiing holiday, marrying, and living unhappily ever after makes us regret the very idea. The couple's incompatability degenerates into shouted slanging matches to the extent that, like a ski-run, the film heads downhill all the way. TH. Contains swearing. [video]

George Segal *Adam Watson* • Glenda Jackson *Patricia Brittenham* • Maureen Stapleton *Jemmy* • Hollis McLaren *Eden* • John Cunningham (1) *Lenny* • Paul Sorvino *Reilly* • John Candy *Carpentier* • Martin Short *Engel* ■ *Dir* Melvin Frank • *Scr* Melvin Frank, Jack Rose

Lost & Found ★★ 12

Romantic comedy
1999 · US · Colour · 96mins

Dependable comic actor David Spade finally cracked the big time with his role in the US sitcom *Just Shoot Me*. His success led to a starring role in this romantic comedy in which Spade plays a restaurateur who falls in lust with his attractive French neighbour Sophie Marceau. Spade's smarmy persona can be an acquired taste, so add a star if you're a fan, take one off if you find his bitchy asides and pointed sarcasm hard to take. DF [video]

David Spade *Dylan Ramsey* • Sophie Marceau *Lila Dubois* • Patrick Bruel *Rene* • Artie Lange *Wally* • Mitchell Whitfield *Mark Glidewell* • Martin Sheen *Millstone* • Jon Lovitz *Uncle Harry* ■ *Dir* Jeff Pollack • *Scr* David Spade, Marc Meeks, JB Cook

Lost Angel ★★★ U

Drama 1943 · US · BW · 90mins

Foundling child Margaret O'Brien, made the subject of a scientific experiment, reveals herself as a genius by the age of six, but at the cost of the normal joys of childhood. The situation is remedied when police reporter James Craig takes her under his wing. The film demonstrates O'Brien's talent and appeal and, although an implausible exercise in sentimentality designed to tug at the heartstrings, its saccharine content is nicely modulated. RK

Margaret O'Brien *Alpha* • James Craig *Mike Regan* • Marsha Hunt *Katie Mallory* • Philip Merivale *Professor Peter Vincent* • Keenan Wynn *Packy* • Alan Napier *Dr Woodring* ■ *Dir* Roy Rowland • *Scr* Isobel Lennart, from an idea by Angna Enters

The Lost Boys ★★ 15

Horror comedy 1987 · US · Colour · 93mins

There's a nasty surprise in store for divorcee Dianne Wiest when she

L

moves her family to the Californian coast. The local teenage gang is a pack of punk vampires with designs on her kids. A slick, noisily empty, and ultimately desperate attempt to update the undead genre for the MTV generation, director Joel Schumacher's neon-drenched violent nightmare is an anaemic blend of Hollywood glitz and endless pop culture references. AJ. Contains swearing. DVD

Jason Patric *Michael Emerson* • Kiefer Sutherland *David* • Corey Feldman *Edgar Frog* • Corey Haim *Sam Emerson* • Dianne Wiest *Lucy Emerson* • Barnard Hughes *Grandpa* • Edward Herrmann *Max* • Jami Gertz *Star* ■ *Dir* Joel Schumacher • *Scr* Janice Fischer, James Jeremias, Jeffrey Boam, from a story by Janice Fischer, James Jeremias

Lost Command ★★ 15

War drama 1966 · US · Colour · 129mins

French soldier Anthony Quinn gathers his old unit from the Indo-China war and heads for Algeria, ready to crush the independence movement. But his hopes to recruit old buddy George Segal are dashed when he discovers that Segal heads up the rebel army. In between all this is Claudia Cardinale, looking gorgeous and changing sides according to which man she shares a scene with. Alain Delon and Maurice Ronet guaranteed the movie a huge audience in France. AT DVD

Anthony Quinn *Lt Col Raspeguy* • Alain Delon *Capt Esclavier* • George Segal *Mahidi* • Michèle Morgan *Countess de Clairefons* • Maurice Ronet *Boisfeuras* • Claudia Cardinale *Aicha* • Grégoire Aslan *Ben Saad* • Jean Servais *General Meliès* ■ *Dir* Mark Robson • *Scr* Nelson Gidding, from the novel *Les Centurions* by Jean Lartéguy

The Lost Continent ★★

Science-fiction adventure
1968 · US · Colour · 103mins

Director Leslie Norman probably heaved a huge sigh of relief when he parted company with this Hammer stinker just a few days into production. Michael Carreras took over and immediately ran the project on to the cinematic rocks. The script is wonderfully bizarre, with Eric Porter and his crew setting foot on an island ruled by the Spanish Inquisition. But it's the monsters that will have you shrieking with laughter, though, not terror. Crass or classic? You choose. DP

Eric Porter *Captain Lansen* • Hildegarde Neff *Eva* • Suzanna Leigh *Unity* • Tony Beckley *Harry Tyler* • Nigel Stock *Dr Webster* • Neil McCallum *First Officer Hemmings* ■ *Dir* Michael Carreras • *Scr* Michael Nash [Michael Carreras], from the novel *Uncharted Seas* by Dennis Wheatley

Lost Embrace ★★★

Drama 2004 · Arg/Sp/Fr/It · Colour · 97mins

Set in a working-class, predominantly Jewish corner of Buenos Aires, Daniel Burman's affirming drama suggests that there's more to multiculturalism than racial tension and political correctness. Frustrated by his dead-end existence, college dropout Daniel Hendler is keen to acquire a Polish passport and start afresh, but most people around him are too busy making the most of every day to collude in his plans. Celebrating the neighbourhood's cultural diversity, Burman creates a palpable sense of community that is reinforced by the splendid ensemble. DP. In Spanish with English subtitles.

Daniel Hendler *Ariel* • Sergio Boris *Joseph* • Adriana Aizenberg *Sonia* • Jorge D'Elia *Elias* • Rosita Londner *Ariel's grandmother* • Diego Korol *Mitelman* • Silvina Bosco *Rita* • Melina Petriella *Estela* ■ *Dir* Daniel Burman • *Scr* Daniel Burman, Marcelo Birmajer

Lost Highway ★★★★ 18

Psychological thriller
1996 · US · Colour · 128mins

David Lynch's narrative-defying psychological thriller is about a jazz saxophonist (an exemplary Bill Pullman) in a disturbed domestic limbo who suddenly and inexplicably transforms into a younger man (Balthazar Getty). Though never together in a scene, the men share what appears to be the same elusive, deceptive woman (Patricia Arquette). It's not the most accessible scenario, but the delivery is hypnotising. And while other modern films about bad people, paranoia and deceptive women get labelled *film noir*, Lynch reinvents the form of that genre rather than just relying on its storyline formula. Painterly, impenetrable and creepy. DO. Contains violence, swearing, sex scenes and nudity. DVD

Bill Pullman *Fred Madison* • Patricia Arquette *Renee Madison/Alice Wakefield* • Balthazar Getty *Pete Dayton* • Robert Blake *Mystery man* • Natasha Gregson Wagner *Sheila* • Robert Loggia *Mr Eddy/Dick Laurent* • Gary Busey *Bill Dayton* • Richard Pryor *Arnie* • Michael Massee *Andy* • Henry Rollins *Guard Henry* • Jack Nance *Phil* • Mink Stole *Forewoman* • Giovanni Ribisi *Steve "V"* ■ *Dir* David Lynch • *Scr* David Lynch, Barry Gifford • *Cinematographer* Peter Deming

The Lost Honour of Katharina Blum ★★★★ 15

Political thriller
1975 · W Ger · Colour · 101mins

Slightly shifting the emphasis of Heinrich Böll's novel to inculcate the police, as well as the media, in the downfall of an innocent victim, Volker Schlöndorff and Margarethe von Trotta have created a chilling tale of state paranoia and tabloid sensationalism that remains a depressingly familiar tale for our times. Displaying enviable dignity in the face of provocation, Angela Winkler is harrowingly credible as the apolitical woman whose unwitting one night stand with a suspected terrorist results in the ruination of her life. Filmed with a realism that adds to its menace, this is a key example of New German Cinema. DP

Angela Winkler *Katharina Blum* • Mario Adorf *Beizmenne* • Dieter Laser *Werner Toetgess* • Heinz Bennent *Dr Blorna* • Hannelore Hoger *Trude Blorna* • Harald Kuhlmann *Moeding* • Karl Heinz Vosgerau *Alois Straubleder* • Jürgen Prochnow *Ludwig Götten* ■ *Dir* Volker Schlöndorff, Margarethe von Trotta • *Scr* Volker Schlöndorff, Margarethe von Trotta, from the novel by Heinrich Böll

Lost Horizon ★★★★★ U

Fantasy adventure 1937 · US · BW · 131mins

Here's one of the great dream fulfilment movies, showing there is a better place, a heaven on Earth with lasting peace and happiness, tucked away in the Himalayas. In his enthusiasm to film James Hilton's novel, Columbia's ace director Frank Capra persuaded the studio to spend a record $2.5 million. The money was well utilised to create a Shangri-la of Art Deco cleanliness and simplicity populated with unfamiliar faces – most memorably Sam Jaffe as the 250-year-old High Lama – to contrast with the typecasting of Ronald Colman, Thomas Mitchell, Edward Everett Horton and others as the outsiders. Colman ensures the film's success – his sincerity and passion make believers of us all. AE DVD

Ronald Colman *Robert Conway* • Jane Wyatt *Sondra* • Edward Everett Horton *Alexander P Lovett* • John Howard (1) *George Conway* • Thomas Mitchell *Henry Barnard* • Margo *Maria* • Isabel Jewell *Gloria Stone* • HB Warner *Chang* • Sam Jaffe *High Lama* ■ *Dir* Frank Capra • *Scr* Robert Riskin, from the novel by James Hilton • *Music* Dimitri Tiomkin [Dmitri Tiomkin] • *Cinematographer* Joseph Walker • *Art Director* Stephen Goosson

Lost Horizon ★ U

Musical 1973 · US · Colour · 132mins

In his 1937 adaptation, Frank Capra managed to make sense of the fanciful ideas raised in James Hilton's novel, but they are rendered risible in this ill-conceived musical remake. Aiming for the glossy sophistication he brought to his earlier projects, producer Ross Hunter presents Shangri-La as a Himalayan country club instead of a utopian sanctuary. Peter Finch, meanwhile, looks as though he's in purgatory as he exchanges trite truisms with High Lama Charles Boyer, though he's not alone in struggling with the dire ditties penned by Burt Bacharach and Hal David. DP

Peter Finch *Richard Conway* • Michael York *George Conway* • Liv Ullmann *Catherine* • Sally Kellerman *Sally Hughes* • George Kennedy *Sam Cornelius* • Olivia Hussey *Maria* • Bobby Van *Harry Lovett* • James Shigeta *Brother To-Lenn* • Charles Boyer *High Lama* • John Gielgud *Chang* ■ *Dir* Charles Jarrott • *Scr* Larry Kramer, from the novel by James Hilton

The Lost Hours ★★ U

Murder mystery 1952 · UK · BW · 70mins

This is one of Director David MacDonald's least distinguished ventures, being another of the dreaded quota quickies in which a third-rate Hollywood star gets to play the lead in a threadbare crime story, notable for the cheapness of the sets, the dismal dialogue and the eagerness of the supporting cast. Mark Stevens is the luckless Yank in this ham-fisted tale about amnesia, smuggling and jealousy, which is lifted only by Jean Kent's elegance and Garry Marsh as the dogged flatfoot. DP

Mark Stevens *Paul Smith* • Jean Kent *Louise Parker* • Garry Marsh *Foster* • John Bentley *Clark Sutton* • Dianne Foster *Dianne Wrigley* • Jack Lambert *John Parker* • Thora Hird *Maid* ■ *Dir* David MacDonald • *Scr* Steve Fisher, John Gilling

Lost in a Harem ★★★

Comedy 1944 · US · BW · 88mins

Abbott and Costello are way out east as two prop men with a travelling show touring a desert kingdom. Thrown in jail along with the show's star Marilyn Maxwell, they are freed by dispossessed prince John Conte to help him recapture his lost kingdom. This is well up to standard for the boys and there's good value from Douglass Dumbrille as the villainous Sultan Nimativ – the funnier routines involve his hypnotic rings. DF

Bud Abbott *Peter Johnson* • Lou Costello *Harvey Garvey* • Marilyn Maxwell *Hazel Moon* • John Conte *Prince Ramo* • Douglass Dumbrille *Nimativ* ■ *Dir* Charles Reisner • *Scr* John Grant, Harry Crane, Harry Ruskin

Lost in Alaska ★ PG

Comedy 1952 · US · BW · 76mins

This feels like a two-reeler that's been teased out (not to say tormented) to reach feature length. Abbott and Costello play a couple of San Franciscan firemen who head for the Yukon determined to track down the $2 million in gold that's been stolen from suicidal prospector Tom Ewell. The tunes intoned by saloon singer Mitzi Green were part-scored by Henry Mancini, who was making his movie debut. DP

Bud Abbott *Tom Watson* • Lou Costello *George Bell* • Mitzi Green *Rosette* • Tom Ewell *Nugget Joe McDermott* • Bruce Cabot *Jake Stillman* • Emory Parnell *Sherman* • Jack Ingram *Henchman* ■ *Dir* Jean Yarbrough • *Scr* Martin A Ragaway [Martin Ragaway], Leonard Stern, from a story by Elwood Ullman

Lost in America ★★★ 15

Comedy 1985 · US · Colour · 87mins

Albert Brooks is one of Hollywood's most engaging, oddball talents, a sort of West Coast Woody Allen who writes, directs and stars in his own projects. In this satire, he's a nervously successful advertising executive in LA who, with wife Julie Hagerty, drops out and sets off to discover America "just like *Easy Rider*", he says. The story takes as many byways as highways and is always unpredictable and engaging, with weird characters seen through Brooks's askew lens. Maybe it lacks that extra bite – an easy ride, but always an enjoyable one. AT

Albert Brooks *David Howard* • Julie Hagerty *Linda Howard* • Maggie Roswell *Patty* • Michael Greene *Paul Dunn* • Tom Tarpey *Brad Tooley* • Raynold Gideon *Ray* ■ *Dir* Albert Brooks • *Scr* Albert Brooks, Monica Johnson

Lost in La Mancha ★★★★ 15

Documentary 2002 · UK · Colour · 89mins

Keith Fulton and Louis Pepe's compelling documentary charts the derailment of Terry Gilliam's film *The Man Who Killed Don Quixote*. The film opens with clips from Orson Welles's ill-fated attempt to bring the Cervantes classic to the screen, and from there draws upon over 80 hours of video footage, widescreen rushes and animated storyboards to tell the whole "un-making" of Gilliam's project. With Jean Rochefort as the eccentric knight and Johnny Depp as a time-traveller mistaken for Sancho Panza, everything looks set. But an air of *Munchausen* madness pervades both pre-production and the brief shoot, leaving one to lament the loss of a potential masterpiece and marvel at the terrifying unpredictability of the movie business. DP DVD

Jeff Bridges *Narrator* ■ *Dir/Scr* Keith Fulton, Louis Pepe

Lost in Siberia ★★★ 15

Period drama
1991 · UK/USSR · Colour · 103mins

Among the first Russian films to consider the notorious gulags, this forceful drama may be set in the early days of the Cold War, but the implication is that matters scarcely improved in the intervening years. In a radical departure from his *Brideshead* image, Anthony Andrews gives one his strongest performances as the Russo-British geologist, who is wrongly arrested for spying on the Persian border and consigned to a Siberian labour camp. Alexander Mitta focuses on the empowerment the inmates derive from their unshakeable friendships. Made in both Russian and English versions. DP

Anthony Andrews *Andrei Miller* • Yelena Mayorova *Doctor Anna* • Vladimir Ilyin *Captain Malakhov* • Ira Mikhalyova *Lilka* • Yevgeni F Mironov [Yevgeni Mironov] *Volodya* ■ *Dir* Alexander Mitta • *Scr* Alexander Mitta, Valery Fried, Yuri Korotkov, James Brabazon (English version)

Lost in Space ★★ PG

Science-fiction adventure
1998 · US · Colour · 124mins

This big-budget screen version of Irwin Allen's cult 1960s TV series is a charmless if flashy affair under the too-straightforward direction of Stephen Hopkins. The Robinson family's Earth migration experiment is sabotaged by evil Doctor Smith (Gary Oldman) and they are forced to land on a mysterious planet where time becomes distorted and where they encounter mutated monster spiders. The special effects, the nostalgia, the varying tone and the acting never jell in what is basically a cynical marketing exercise. AJ. Contains violence. VIDEO DVD

Gary Oldman *Dr Smith* • William Hurt *John Robinson* • Matt LeBlanc *Don West* • Mimi Rogers *Maureen Robinson* • Heather Graham *Judy Robinson* • Lacey Chabert *Penny Robinson* • Jack Johnson *Will Robinson* • Jared Harris *Older Will* ■ *Dir* Stephen Hopkins • *Scr* Akiva Goldsman, from the TV series

Lost in the Stars ★★★ PG

Musical drama 1974 · US · Colour · 93mins

This was the last musical score by *The Threepenny Opera's* Kurt Weill, an operetta that translates Alan Paton's poignant anti-apartheid novel *Cry, the Beloved Country* into ironic harmonies. Brock Peters gives a fine performance as the black clergyman in search of his son in Johannesburg, who finds instead cruel racism and repression. While the music is memorable and the production sincere, this "stage record" also somewhat predictable and ponderous. TH DVD

Brock Peters *Stephen Kumalo* • Melba Moore *Irina* • Raymond St Jacques *John Kumalo* • Clifton Davis *Absalom* • Paul Rogers *James Jarvis* • Paulene Myers *Grace* ■ *Dir* Daniel Mann • *Scr* Alfred Hayes, from the play by Maxwell Anderson, Kurt Weill, from the novel *Cry, the Beloved Country* by Alan Paton

Lost in Translation ★★★★★ 15

Romantic comedy drama
2003 · US · Colour · 97mins

Bill Murray gives a delicately restrained and masterful performance in Sofia Coppola's marvellous follow-up to her debut movie *The Virgin Suicides*. He stars as a world-weary film actor who's in Japan to make a whisky commercial. There he meets an unhappily married younger woman, played by Scarlett Johansson. She is equally as good as the woman trapped in a loveless marriage, and Coppola wisely underlies the bittersweet soul-searching with a healthy dose of humour. By expertly using the neon-drenched backdrop of night-time Tokyo as an alien landscape against which the couple delicately explore each other's ambiguous feelings, this talented young director has produced a sad, funny, magical and almost irresistibly moving experience. AS VIDEO DVD

Bill Murray *Bob Harris* • Scarlett Johansson *Charlotte* • Giovanni Ribisi *John* • Anna Faris *Kelly* • Fumihiro Hayashi *Charlie* • Catherine Lambert *Jazz singer* • Akiko Takeshita *Ms Kawasaki* ■ *Dir/Scr* Sofia Coppola

Lost in Yonkers ★★★ PG

Comedy drama 1993 · US · Colour · 109mins

Richard Dreyfuss stars as a small-time gangster who returns to his childhood home in Yonkers to lie low, regaling his young nephews Brad Stoll and Mike Damus with tall tales of his life of crime. Grandma Irene Worth rules the household with a rod of iron that has broken the spirit of Dreyfuss's sister Mercedes Ruehl. This is another of playwright Neil Simon's semi-autobiographical dramas along the lines of his *Brighton Beach Memoirs*, but, despite some wonderful acting turns, this can be humdrum. TH VIDEO DVD

Richard Dreyfuss *Louie* • Mercedes Ruehl *Bella* • Irene Worth *Grandma* • Brad Stoll *Jay* • Mike Damus *Arty* • David Strathairn *Johnny* ■ *Dir* Martha Coolidge • *Scr* Neil Simon, from his play

The Lost Lover ★★ PG

Drama 1999 · It/UK · Colour · 93mins

For all its liberalism and committed playing, this is a morose and, ultimately, inconsequential melodrama from Italian director Roberto Faenza. Living in Israel after the death of his son, garage owner Ciaran Hinds goes in search of mysterious stranger Stuart Bunce in the hope of preventing his withdrawn wife, Juliet Aubrey, from drifting into another bout of depression. Neither enlightening nor engaging. DP VIDEO

Ciaran Hinds *Adam* • Juliet Aubrey *Asya* • Stuart Bunce *Gabriel* • Clara Bryant *Dafi* • Erick Vazquez *Naim* • Phyllida Law *Grandmother* ■ *Dir* Roberto Faenza • *Scr* Sandro Petraglia, Roberto Faenza

The Lost Man ★★

Drama 1969 · US · Colour · 122mins

Sidney Poitier plays a black radical who plans a robbery on a factory that only employs whites. The heist backfires and Poitier, with white love interest Joanna Shimkus, finds himself on the run. As the highly equivocal hero, partially modelled on Malcolm X, Poitier probably thought this was a brave movie to make, but it's hardly a radical movie, just another caper-gone-wrong action film. There's also a twist at the end that signals a rapid descent into treacle. AT

Sidney Poitier *Jason Higgs* • Joanna Shimkus *Cathy Ellis* • Al Freeman Jr *Dennis Laurence* • Michael Tolan *Hamilton* • Leon Bibb *Eddie Moxy* • Richard Dysart *Barnes* ■ *Dir* Robert Alan Aurthur • *Scr* Robert Alan Aurthur, from the novel *Odd Man Out* by FL Green

The Lost Moment ★★★

Period drama 1947 · US · BW · 88mins

Henry James's novel *The Aspern Papers*, is a highly theatrical, as well as an intimate and intriguing work. The simple story concerns the quest of a publisher for the letters of a famous poet, which are now in the possession of a very old woman who lives with her spinster niece. Set in a convincing and studio-built Venice, this film version stars Robert Cummings, a superb Agnes Moorehead as the old lady and, in an unexpected piece of casting, Susan Hayward as her niece. A compelling, stylised period drama, elegantly directed by Martin Gabel, and with a surprise denouement. RK

Robert Cummings *Lewis Venable* • Susan Hayward *Tina* • Agnes Moorehead *Juliana* • Joan Lorring *Amelia* • John Archer *Charles* • Eduardo Ciannelli *Father Rinaldo* ■ *Dir* Martin Gabel • *Scr* Leonardo Bercovici, from the novel *The Aspern Papers* by Henry James

The Lost One ★★★

Drama 1951 · W Ger · BW · 97mins

The wonderful character actor Peter Lorre only directed this one film and it has a melancholic sense of self-reference that probably would have been difficult to follow. He returned to Germany (from which he exiled himself in 1933) in the doldrums days of the postwar national cinema and starred in this harrowing work about a scientist who has been trapped into working for the Nazis. The consequences of the relationship bring death and betrayal to his existence and eventually lead him to seek salvation in a refugee camp. Lorre directs fluently in a somewhat dated expressionist style that is reminiscent of the great German master, Fritz Lang. BB. In German with English subtitles.

Peter Lorre *Dr Karl Rothe* • Karl John *Hoesch* • Helmut Rudolf *Colonel Winkler* • Renate Mannhardt *Inge Hermann* • Johanna Hofer *Frau Hermann* • Eva-Ingeborg Scholz *Ursula Weber* ■ *Dir* Peter Lorre • *Scr* Peter Lorre, Benno Vigny, Axel Eggebrecht

Lost Paradise ★★★

Drama 1997 · Jpn · Colour · 119mins

Koji Yakusho is engagingly adept at conveying the ennui of the middle-aged "salaryman". He turns here to an adulterous affair to deflect his disappointment at being passed over for promotion at the magazine to which he's given years of faithful service. Equally impressive is Hitomi Kuroki, as the married printer who shares his reluctance to go public with their passion. Director Yoshimitsu Morita dissects Japanese social mores with a steady hand. DP. In Japanese with English subtitles.

Koji Yakusho *Kuki* • Hitomi Kuroki ■ *Dir* Yoshimitsu Morita • *Scr* Tomomi Tsutsui

The Lost Patrol ★★

First World War adventure
1934 · US · BW · 74mins

In the Mesopotamian desert during the First World War, a small group of lost British cavalrymen search for their comrades while being gradually decimated by Arab snipers, the scorching sun and lack of water. As directed by John Ford, it's more of a western than a war movie and the climactic skirmish looks like Custer's Last Stand. AT

Victor McLaglen *Sergeant* • Boris Karloff *Sanders* • Wallace Ford *Morelli* • Reginald Denny *Brown* • JM Kerrigan *Quincannon* • Billy Bevan *Hale* • Alan Hale *Cook* ■ *Dir* John Ford • *Scr* Dudley Nichols, Garrett Fort, from the story *Patrol* by Philip MacDonald

The Lost People ★

Drama 1949 · UK · BW · 89mins

Bridget Boland's play, *Cockpit*, which tackled the problem of Europeans left stateless and homeless after the Second World War, meant well and was excitingly experimental. This film version, still confined to one set, doesn't work. It's all talk and no action, and additional love scenes, written by Muriel Box, stick out like sore thumbs. Worse, the efforts of British officer Dennis Price to get people of many nationalities to co-operate with each other now come across as xenophobic. DM

Dennis Price *Captain Ridley* • Mai Zetterling *Lili* • Richard Attenborough *Jan* • Siobhan McKenna *Marie* • Maxwell Reed *Peter* • William Hartnell *Sgt Barnes* • Gerard Heinz *Professor* • Zena Marshall *Anna* ■ *Dir* Bernard Knowles, Muriel Box • *Scr* Bridget Boland, Muriel Box, from the play *Cockpit* by Bridget Boland

The Lost Son ★★ 18

Crime drama 1998 · UK/Fr · Colour · 102mins

This is Daniel Auteuil's first English language film, but that's not the only problem here. This deeply ambitious movie, following Auteuil as an ex-cop turned private investigator who unearths a paedophile ring while on the trail of a missing son, is sadly flawed. Aside from the interestingly bleak nature of the story and Auteuil's watchability, the casting is bizarre. Billie Whitelaw, Ciaran Hinds – whose accent is so atrocious one is left wondering where he's supposed to be from – and Nastassja Kinski all fail to convince. LH VIDEO DVD

Daniel Auteuil *Xavier Lombard* • Nastassja Kinski *Deborah* • Katrin Cartlidge *Emily* • Ciaran Hinds *Carlos* • Marianne Denicourt *Nathalie* • Bruce Greenwood *Friedman* • Billie Whitelaw *Mrs Spitz* • Cyril Shaps *Mr Spitz* ■ *Dir* Chris Menges • *Scr* Eric Leclere, Margaret Leclere, Mark Mills

Lost Souls ★★ 15

Supernatural horror thriller
2000 · US · Colour · 93mins

This stars Winona Ryder as a traumatised victim of demonic possession, who learns that author Ben Chaplin is destined to be "reborn" as Christianity's arch-enemy. Ryder is a credible witness to events, but Chaplin faces impending reincarnation with all the foreboding of a man whose bus is late, while John Hurt (as a priest) seems to think that merely looking soulful will pass for acting. The directorial debut of Oscar-winning cinematographer Janusz Kaminski, this is visually striking but disappointingly short on dramatic tension. TH VIDEO DVD

Winona Ryder *Maya Larkin* • Ben Chaplin *Peter Kelson* • Philip Baker Hall *Father James* • Elias Koteas *John Townsend* • Sarah Wynter *Claire Van Owen* • John Beasley *Mike Smythe* • John Hurt *Father Lareaux* ■ *Dir* Janusz Kaminski • *Scr* Pierce Gardner, from a story by Pierce Gardner, Betsy Stahl

The Lost Squadron ★★★★

Adventure drama 1932 · US · BW · 72mins

A fascinating movie that is a genuine cinematic equivalent of the great "lost generation" postwar writings of Ernest Hemingway and F Scott Fitzgerald. A group of First World War fighter pilots find themselves reduced to postwar stunt flying in the movies under the direction of demented Erich von Stroheim. The atmosphere of disillusionment is quite palpable, thanks to a knowing original story by Dick Grace, himself a stunt flyer. The acting and the plot structure may seem creaky now, but the tone is brilliantly sustained and Von Stroheim's performance – lampooning himself – is a tour de force. TS

Richard Dix *Captain Gibson* • Mary Astor *Follette Marsh* • Erich von Stroheim *Von Furst* • Joel McCrea *Red* • Robert Armstrong *Woody* • Dorothy Jordan *The Pest* ■ *Dir* George Archainbaud • *Scr* Wallace Smith, Herman J Mankiewicz, Robert Presnell, from a story by Dick Grace

The Lost Weekend ★★★★ PG

Drama 1945 · US · BW · 96mins

Billy Wilder's ground-breaking drama about an alcoholic writer trying to kick the bottle, won Oscars for best film, direction, screenplay and and actor. Ray Milland is the booze-afflicted antihero, suffering from writer's block and a frighteningly convincing case of the DTs. Despite the grim subject matter, there are glimpses of Wilder's characteristic mordant wit and the director's location work in New York's Third Avenue district is exemplary. Casting the hitherto bland Milland was a stroke of genius, but the scenes involving his brother (Phillip Terry) and girlfriend (Jane Wyman) are soft-centred and don't really work. AT DVD

Ray Milland *Don Birnam* • Jane Wyman *Helen St James* • Phillip Terry *Nick Birnam* • Howard Da Silva *Nat the bartender* • Doris Dowling *Gloria* ■ *Dir* Billy Wilder • *Scr* Charles Brackett, Billy Wilder, from the novel by Charles R Jackson • *Cinematographer* John F Seitz • *Music* Miklos Rozsa • *Special Effects* Farciot Edouart, Gordon Jennings

The Lost World ★★★ U

Silent fantasy adventure
1925 · US · BW · 92mins

Of great historical interest, this film of Arthur Conan Doyle's novel was a smash hit in 1925 because of its sensational representation of prehistoric creatures by the special effects team headed by Willis O'Brien, who later perfected his skills on *King Kong*. Wallace Beery stars as Professor Challenger, leading an expedition to a South American plateau where an abundance of wild life previously thought extinct still lives. O'Brien combined live action and stop-action animation to convincing effect for the first time. AE DVD

Bessie Love *Paula White* • Lloyd Hughes *Edward J Malone* • Lewis Stone *Sir John Roxton* • Wallace Beery *Prof Challenger* • Arthur Hoyt *Prof Summerlee* • Margaret McWade *Mrs Challenger* ■ *Dir* Harry O Hoyt •

L

Scr Marion Fairfax, from the novel by Sir Arthur Conan Doyle • *Cinematographer* Arthur Edeson • *Special Effects* Willis H O'Brien

The Lost World ★★★

Fantasy adventure
1960 · US · Colour · 94mins

Long before Steven Spielberg and Michael Crichton got there, the "master of disaster" Irwin Allen had already transported audiences to a lost world – author Sir Arthur Conan Doyle's South American plateau forgotten by time. In one of his later roles, Claude Rains leads the cast of lesser stars on an Amazon expedition where they confront a host of magnified pet-shop lizards with plastic fins in a glossy, if conventionally plotted, adventure with intermittent thrills. Clips from this would be a mainstay of Allen's TV fantasy series for years to come. AJ

Michael Rennie *Lord Roxton* • Jill St John *Jennifer Holmes* • David Hedison *Ed Malone* • Claude Rains *Professor Challenger* • Fernando Lamas *Gomez* • Richard Haydn *Professor Summerlee* • Ray Stricklyn *David* ■ *Dir* Irwin Allen • *Scr* Irwin Allen, Charles Bennett, from the novel by Sir Arthur Conan Doyle

The Lost World: Jurassic Park ★★★ PG

Science-fiction adventure
1997 · US · Colour · 123mins

There's another island full of genetically created dinosaurs in director Steven Spielberg's exuberantly calculated sequel to his own *Jurassic Park*. But while the cloned prehistoric package does elicit a sense of *déjà vu*, such feelings never get in the way of the excitement or special effects spectacle served up in deliciously scary dollops. With Richard Attenborough and Jeff Goldblum on hand once more to test the balance of nature off the coast of Costa Rica, Spielberg ensures his thrill-ride runs smoothly along well-oiled tracks. AJ. Contains violence, swearing. DVD

Jeff Goldblum *Dr Ian Malcolm* • Julianne Moore *Dr Sarah Harding* • Pete Postlethwaite *Roland Tembo* • Arliss Howard *Peter Ludlow* • Richard Attenborough *John Hammond* • Vince Vaughn *Nick Van Owen* ■ *Dir* Steven Spielberg • *Scr* David Koepp, from the novel by Michael Crichton

A Lot like Love ★★★ 12A

Romantic comedy
2005 · US · Colour · 106mins

Ashton Kutcher and Amanda Peet are the strangers who meet by joining the mile-high club, only to cross paths again (and again...) in a rollercoaster journey spanning seven years. Even when they're rubbing each other the wrong way, Kutcher and Peet create dazzling sparks. Direct Nigel Cole teases out human insecurities with humour and sensitivity, which, together with inspired casting, makes this a fling worth embarking on. SP. Contains sexual references.

Ashton Kutcher *Oliver Martin* • Amanda Peet *Emily Friehl* • Kathryn Hahn *Michelle* • Kal Penn *Jeeter* • Ali Larter *Gina* • Taryn Manning *Ellen Geary* • Gabriel Mann *Peter* • Jeremy Sisto *Ben Miller* • Ty Giordano *Graham Martin* ■ *Dir* Nigel Cole • *Scr* Colin Patrick Lynch

Louisiana Purchase ★★★ U

Musical comedy 1941 · US · Colour · 97mins

Hard, perhaps, to whip up much enthusiasm for a musical satire on the notoriously corrupt politicians of Louisiana, but this is worth a look. For most of the way, it is unusually faithful to the Broadway hit, with veteran comedian Victor Moore reprising his role as Senator Loganberry and featuring dancer Vera Zorina and others from the original cast. The major change is bringing in Bob Hope as the fall guy for the scheming politicians, but he filibusters his way out of trouble in style. AE

Bob Hope *Jim Taylor* • Vera Zorina *Marina Von Minden* • Victor Moore *Sen Oliver P Loganberry* • Irene Bordoni *Madame Bordelaise* • Dona Drake *Beatrice* • Raymond Walburn *Colonel Davis Sr* • Maxie Rosenbloom *The Shadow* • Frank Albertson *Davis Jr* ■ *Dir* Irving Cummings • *Scr* Jerome Chodorov, Joseph Fields, from the musical by Morrie Ryskind, BG "Buddy" DeSylva • *Cinematographer* Ray Rennahan, Harry Hallenberger • *Music/lyrics* Irving Berlin

Louisiana Story ★★★ U

Documentary drama 1948 · US · BW · 77mins

Documentary director Robert Flaherty (*Nanook of the North*) went to the bayou country of Louisiana and recruited non-professionals to tell a simple but affecting story of a small boy, whose father ekes out a living by hunting and fishing while oil prospectors set up a floating derrick and sink a well. With sparse dialogue and a notable score by Virgil Thomson, the film has little action other than the boy's fight with an alligator. Flaherty was backed by a major oil company, which must have been delighted by the entirely favourable impression the film gives of the oil drillers. AE

Dir Robert J Flaherty [Robert Flaherty] • *Scr* Robert J Flaherty, Frances Flaherty • *Cinematographer* Richard Leacock • *Music* Virgil Thomson

Loulou ★★★★ 18

Drama 1980 · Fr · Colour · 100mins

This is an unforgettable exercise in street naturalism from director Maurice Pialat. Rarely has Paris looked less inviting as it provides the backdrop for the picaresque adventures of Depardieu's blue-collar boor and the bourgeois Huppert, who abandons husband Guy Marchand out of boredom and unadulterated lust. While acknowledging the courage of the performances, however, this is much more than just an "odd couple" romance, as Pialat's accumulation of telling details exposes the soulless social and sexual state of contemporary France. DP. In French with English subtitles.

Isabelle Huppert *Nelly* • Gérard Depardieu *Loulou* • Guy Marchand *André* • Humbert Balsan *Michel* ■ *Dir* Maurice Pialat • *Scr* Arlette Langmann, Maurice Pialat, from a story by Arlette Langmann

The Lovable Cheat ★★ U

Comedy drama 1949 · US · BW · 78mins

Charles Ruggles is the bankrupt Parisian who'll stop at nothing to keep his creditors at bay in this stagey comedy drama. Ruggles hopes that marrying off his daughter Peggy Ann Garner to a suitable suitor might be the answer to his problems. A strong cast (including Buster Keaton) do their best with the material but this has nothing new going for it apart from a fascination with money and the way it makes both love, and the world, go round – and wrong. TH

Charles Ruggles *Claude Mercadet* • Peggy Ann Garner *Julie Mercadet* • Richard Ney *Jacques Minard* • Alan Mowbray *Justin* • John Wengraf *Pierquin* • Curt Bois *Count de la Brive* • Buster Keaton *Goulard* ■ *Dir* Richard Oswald • *Scr* Richard Oswald, Edward Lewis, from the play *Mercadet le Falseur* by Honoré de Balzac

Love ★★

Silent drama 1927 · US · BW · 97mins

This silent version of Tolstoy's *Anna Karenina* from MGM was a box-office hit in its day, thanks to the starring of Greta Garbo as Anna and John Gilbert as Vronsky, the lover who ruins her. Directed by Edmund Goulding, it's not uninteresting, especially for Garbo fans, but has been long superseded by the studio's much superior sound remake *Anna Karenina* (1935) in which Garbo repeats the role under Clarence Brown's direction. RK

Greta Garbo *Anna Karenina* • John Gilbert (1) *Vronsky* • George Fawcett *Grand Duke* • Emily Fitzroy *Grand Duchess* • Brandon Hurst *Karenin* ■ *Dir* Edmund Goulding • *Scr* Frances Marion, Lorna Moon, from the novel *Anna Karenina* by Leo Nikolayevich Tolstoy

Love ★★★★

Drama 1971 · Hun · BW · 88mins

Set in the twilight of the Stalinist era, and passing sly asides on the cult of personality, this adroit study of the dissemination and reception of propaganda is cleverly couched in terms of a delicate chamber drama. Handled with great finesse by Karoly Makk, there's genuine affection in the relationship between a wife who tries to assuage her bedridden mother-in-law's fears about her son by fabricating letters about his Hollywood success, while hiding her own pain at the knowledge he's in a labour camp. DP. In Hungarian with English subtitles.

Lili Darvas *Mother* • Mari Torocsik *Luca, the wife* • Ivan Darvas *Janos, the son* ■ *Dir* Karoly Makk • *Scr* Tibor Dery, from his novella

Love Actually ★★★ 15

Romantic comedy
2003 · UK/US/Fr · Colour · 129mins

A film so drenched in upbeat sentiment that it makes Frank Capra seem emotionally reserved, this ensemble romantic comedy from writer Richard Curtis is an unashamedly saccharine proposition. In his debut behind the camera, Curtis unfurls eight ongoing stories, headed by Hugh Grant's new Prime Minister falling for junior staff member Martine McCutcheon, and writer Colin Firth enchanted by his Portuguese housekeeper (Lucia Moniz). Boasting an attractive cast, this deliberately commercial Christmas package may be guilty of spreading its acting talent a bit thin, but even the most cynical of hearts couldn't fail to be lifted by its charm. JC DVD

Alan Rickman *Harry* • Bill Nighy *Billy Mack* • Colin Firth *Jamie* • Emma Thompson *Karen* • Hugh Grant *David, the Prime Minister* • Laura Linney *Sarah* • Liam Neeson *Daniel* • Martine McCutcheon *Natalie* • Keira Knightley *Juliet* • Rowan Atkinson *Rufus* • Billy Bob Thornton *The US President* • Lucia Moniz *Aurelia Barros* ■ *Dir/Scr* Richard Curtis

Love Affair ★★

Romantic drama 1932 · US · BW · 68mins

The main reason to watch this antique romantic drama is for an early performance from Humphrey Bogart. He's a handsome but impoverished aviator who attracts the attentions of an heiress who invests in the plane and then in Bogart himself. Further characters complicate the romantic situation which is resolved – naturally enough – aloft. AT

Dorothy Mackaill *Carol Owen* • Humphrey Bogart *Jim Leonard* • Jack Kennedy *Gilligan* • Barbara Leonard *Felice* • Astrid Allwyn *Linda Lee* • Bradley Page *Georgie* ■ *Dir* Thornton Freeland • *Scr* Jo Swerling, Dorothy Howell, from a story by Ursula Parrott

Love Affair ★★★★★ U

Romantic comedy drama
1939 · US · BW · 86mins

Charles Boyer and Irene Dunne meet on an ocean liner bound for New York and, despite their determination to avoid involvement, fall hopelessly in love. They agree to meet six months later at an appointed time at the top of the Empire State Building if they still feel the same, but when the day comes, she is not there... One word suffices for Leo McCarey's film, which garnered six Academy Award nominations – perfect. Witty, sophisticated, romantic and poignant, it is extremely well-written, immaculately directed, and beautifully played by the stars. It remains one of the best love stories ever to emerge from Hollywood, and McCarey remade it faithfully as *An Affair to Remember* (1957), with Cary Grant and Deborah Kerr, while Nora Ephron paid it tribute with *Sleepless in Seattle*. RK

Irene Dunne *Terry McKay* • Charles Boyer *Michel Marnet* • Maria Ouspenskaya *Grandmother Janou* • Lee Bowman *Kenneth Bradley* • Astrid Allwyn *Lois Clarke* • Maurice Moscovich *Maurice Cobert* ■ *Dir* Leo McCarey • *Scr* Delmer Daves, Donald Ogden Stewart, from a story by Leo McCarey, Delmer Daves, Mildred Cram

Love Affair ★★★ 12

Romantic drama
1994 · US · Colour · 103mins

This remake of *Love Affair* and *An Affair to Remember* failed to impress the critics and never even got to cinemas in the UK. But it is an undeniably polished production and if Glenn Gordon Caron's direction is occasionally sluggish and Ennio Morricone's score is stiflingly lush, the story of the lovers who are torn apart by the cruellest twist of fate can still get the tears flowing. However, the most heartbreaking moment is the all-too-brief appearance of Katharine Hepburn, gamely fighting against the effects of Parkinson's Disease. DP

Warren Beatty *Mike Gambril* • Annette Bening *Terry McKay* • Katharine Hepburn *Aunt Ginny* • Garry Shandling *Kip DeMay* • Chloe Webb *Tina Wilson* • Pierce Brosnan *Ken Allen* • Kate Capshaw *Lynn Weaver* • Brenda Vaccaro *Nora Stillman* • Paul Mazursky *Herb Stillman* ■ *Dir* Glenn Gordon Caron • *Scr* Robert Towne, Warren Beatty, from the 1939 film

Love among the Ruins ★★★★

Romantic comedy
1975 · US · Colour · 72mins

An extremely classy made-for-television film from veteran director George Cukor which stars Katharine Hepburn as a dowager in the early 20th century being sued by a young upstart. Sadly her defence barrister Laurence Olivier also has it in for her as she has failed to recollect their affair from years before. Olivier thus decides to portray the poor woman as short of her marbles throughout the court case. Comic, painful and insightful, Cukor extracts excellent performances from Hepburn and Olivier and it makes for a rare televisual treat. LH

Katharine Hepburn *Jessica Medlicott* • Laurence Olivier *Sir Arthur Granville-Jones* • Colin Blakely *JF Devine* • Richard Pierson *Druce* • Joan Sims *Fanny Pratt* • Leigh Lawson *Alfred Pratt* ■ *Dir* George Cukor • *Scr* James Costigan

Love and a .45 ★★★★ 18

Thriller 1994 · US · Colour · 97mins

Although the Tarantino influences are clear to see, this matt-black trailer trash thriller is an impressively nasty treat. Gil Bellows is the nice-ish convenience store robber who is forced to go on the run with his devoted girlfriend (an electric early showing from Renee Zellweger) after a raid goes horribly wrong. The body count continues to multiply as they are pursued by Bellows's old partner in crime (Rory Cochrane) and two psycho debt collectors, along with massed ranks of law enforcement. CM Talkington's direction is hip and amoral and the performances uniformly good. JF DVD

Gil Bellows *Watty Watts* • Renee Zellweger *Starlene Cheatham* • Rory Cochrane *Billy Mack Black* • Jeffrey Combs *Dino Bob* • Jace

Alexander *Creepy Cody* • Ann Wedgeworth *Thaylene* • Peter Fonda *Vergil* ■ *Dir/Scr* CM Talkington

Love & Basketball ★★★ 12

Romantic sports drama
2000 · US · Colour · 119mins

Sanaa Lathan and Omar Epps are young athletes with a lifelong love of basketball and each other. The movie follows them from childhood games to professional careers, all the while contrasting the different challenges men and women face while playing the same sport. Gina Prince-Bythewood's feature debut captures the characters' passion for the game, though she struggles with scenes that take place off the court. While Lathan delivers a passionate, star-making performance, her fellow actors are hobbled by underdeveloped roles. ST [video] DVD

Sanaa Lathan *Monica Wright* • Omar Epps *Quincy McCall* • Alfre Woodard *Camille Wright* • Dennis Haysbert *Zeke McCall* • Debbi Morgan *Mona McCall* • Harry Lennix *Nathan Wright* ■ *Dir/Scr* Gina Prince-Bythewood

Love and Bullets ★★ 15

Thriller 1978 · UK · Colour · 97mins

Charles Bronson stars as an American policeman on a mission to break a crime syndicate in Switzerland, in director Stuart Rosenberg's dull and predictable thriller. Rather surprisingly, Bronson struggles to portray the toughness required of his role, while Rod Steiger goes way over the top as a Mafia boss. Only Jill Ireland impresses as the gangster's moll. Unintentional laughs can be had from watching Steiger in Mussolini-mode, and the Swiss locations are breathtaking. AT [video] DVD

Charles Bronson *Charlie Congers* • Jill Ireland *Jackie Pruitt* • Rod Steiger *Joe Bomposa* • Henry Silva *Vittorio Faroni* • Strother Martin *Louis Monk* • Bradford Dillman *Brickman* ■ *Dir* Stuart Rosenberg • *Scr* Wendell Mayes, John Melson, from a story by Wendell Mayes

Love and Death ★★★★ PG

Satirical comedy 1975 · US · Colour · 81mins

You never know where Woody Allen is coming from. With homages to Sergei Eisenstein and Bob Hope – among others – this satire is located in the fatalistic Russian territory of *War and Peace* and is one of Woody Allen's early greats. In 1812 a condemned Allen looks back in bemusement at the historical events, and a hysterical Diane Keaton, that have brought him to his execution. The Grim Reaper scythes through from *The Seventh Seal*, but the jokes are strictly New York Jewish. The plotting is too desultory, but the fun comes at you from all directions, but mainly from off the wall. TH [video] DVD

Woody Allen *Boris* • Diane Keaton *Sonja* • Georges Adet *Old Nehamkin* • Frank Adu *Drill sergeant* • Edmond Ardisson *Priest* • Feodor Atkine *Mikhail* ■ *Dir/Scr* Woody Allen

Love and Death on Long Island ★★★ 15

Comedy drama
1998 · UK/Can · Colour · 93mins

This touching comedy provides John Hurt with one of his best roles of the 1990s, and he doesn't miss a beat. He plays a naive, unworldly writer/scholar who becomes besotted by the American star (Jason Priestley) of *Hotpants College 2*, a low-budget teen movie he mistakenly wanders into. Hurt then travels to Long Island to meet what he thinks will be his true love. There is a sense of impending tragedy throughout but Hurt's wonderful performance ensures that it never slips into melodramatic gloom. Priestley has fun sending up his teen idol image, while Richard Kwietniowksi directs with affection. JF. Contains swearing. [video] DVD

John Hurt *Giles De'Ath* • Jason Priestley *Ronnie Bostock* • Fiona Loewi *Audrey* • Sheila Hancock *Mrs Barker* • Harvey Atkin *Lou* • Gawn Grainger *Henry, Giles's agent* • Elizabeth Quinn *Mrs Reed* • Maury Chaykin *Irving Buckmuller* ■ *Dir* Richard Kwietniowski • *Scr* Richard Kwietniowski, from the novel by Gilbert Adair

Love and Human Remains ★★ 18

Drama 1993 · Can · Colour · 99mins

The activities of a serial killer cast a shadow over this drama of modern relationships, as does the spectre of Aids. This was the first English language film from Québecois film-maker Denys Arcand, director of the 1989 art house hit *Jesus of Montreal*. Though Arcand is widely regarded as being more comfortable working in his native French, this remains a watchable drama focusing on the sexual pursuits, fears and fetishes of a bunch of adult cityfolk. DA [video]

Thomas Gibson *David* • Ruth Marshall *Candy* • Cameron Bancroft *Bernie* • Mia Kirshner *Benita* • Rick Roberts *Robert* • Joanne Vannicola *Jerri* • Matthew Ferguson *Kane* ■ *Dir* Denys Arcand • *Scr* Brad Fraser, from his play *Unidentified Human Remains and the True Nature of Love*

Love and Money ★★

Thriller 1982 · US · Colour · 90mins

Director James Toback, presented with natural drama, doesn't know how to commit himself to his material and so turns what should be high octane into an afternoon stroll. Financier Ray Sharkey decides to inject some excitement into his life by getting mixed up with Klaus Kinski's Latin-American business schemes. Sharkey, Ornella Muti (as his love interest) and Klaus Kinski perform adequately, but they are upstaged by an appearance from celebrated director King Vidor. JM. Contains swearing.

Ray Sharkey *Byron Levin* • Ornella Muti *Catherine Stockheinz* • Klaus Kinski *Frederick Stockheinz* • Armand Assante *Lorenzo Prado* • King Vidor *Walter Klein* • Susan Heldfond *Vicky* ■ *Dir/Scr* James Toback • *Music* Aaron Copland

Love and Other Catastrophes ★★★ 15

Comedy drama 1996 · Aus · Colour · 75mins

This spirited Australian comedy recounts an incident-packed day in the life of five college students. All human experience seems condensed into the 24-hour period as the protagonists cope with unrequited love, romantic entanglements and life-changing decisions. Reputedly shot in just 17 days, the speed of the production translates to the screen and the film whizzes by delightfully. A strong ensemble cast ensures that all the characters are well rounded and believable. DF. Contains swearing and sex scenes. [video]

Alice Garner *Alice* • Frances O'Connor *Mia* • Matthew Dyktynski *Ari* • Matt Day *Michael* • Radha Mitchell *Danni* • Suzi Dougherty *Savita* • Kim Gyngell *Professor Leach* ■ *Dir* Emma-Kate Croghan • *Scr* Emma-Kate Croghan, Yael Bergman, Helen Bandis, from a story by Stavros Andonis Efthymiou [Stavros Kazantzidis]

Love and Pain and the Whole Damn Thing ★★★★

Drama 1973 · US · Colour · 113mins

Alan J Pakula's political thrillers *Klute* (1971), *The Parallax View* (1974) and *All the President's Men* (1976), make him seem a social warrior, but this is an out-of-character delight with unexpected and refreshing romanticism. Maggie Smith plays a terminally ill spinster in Spain whose heartbeats click like castanets when she meets youngster Timothy Bottoms. Despite the fatal-illness undercurrent, sentimentality is kept at bay in this rare gem. TH

Maggie Smith *Lila Fisher* • Timothy Bottoms *Walter Elbertson* • Emiliano Redondo *Spanish gentleman* • Charles Baxter *Dr Elbertson* • Margaret Modlin *Mrs Elbertson* • May Heatherly *Melanie Elbertson* ■ *Dir* Alan J Pakula • *Scr* Alvin Sargent

Love & Sex ★★★ 15

Romantic comedy
2000 · US · Colour · 82mins

Famke Janssen plays a magazine journalist who, while re-writing a feature about love and relationships, muses on her own experiences in this romantic comedy from writer/director Valerie Breiman. Though she can recall a whole candelabra of old flames, Janssen's thoughts keep returning to a key romance with artist Jon Favreau. While Breiman doesn't cover any new ground, the combined energies of her snappy script and the two lead performances will have you nodding as you watch the pair. JB [video] DVD

Famke Janssen *Kate Welles* • Jon Favreau *Adam* • Noah Emmerich *Eric* • Ann Magnuson *Ms Steinbacher* • Cheri Oteri *Mary* • Josh Hopkins *Joey Santino* • Robert Knepper *Gerard* ■ *Dir/Scr* Valerie Breiman

Love and the Midnight Auto Supply ★★

Comedy 1977 · US · Colour · 93mins

This is a breezy, comic cheapo about a gang of car thieves whose nocturnal activities are given an altruistic slant when they're asked to help out some impoverished farm workers. Part youth movie, part political comment on America's economic problems, it has a weird cast led by Michael Parks. AT

Michael Parks *Duke* • Linda Cristal *Annie* • Scott Jacoby *Justin* • Bill Adler *Ramon* • Colleen Camp *Billie Jean* • Monica Gayle *Kathy* • Sedena Spivey *Violet* • George McCallister *Peter Santore* • John Ireland *Tony Santore* • Rory Calhoun *Len Thompson* ■ *Dir/Scr* James Polakof

Love at First Bite ★★★★ 15

Horror spoof 1979 · US · Colour · 91mins

This very funny spoof of the Dracula legend has George Hamilton as the uprooted, undead count, who's trying to adjust to life in the modern Big Apple. Former MGM heart-throb Hamilton camps it up delightfully as he clumsily romances fashion model Susan Saint James, much to the chagrin of her psychiatrist lover Richard Benjamin, who gets his vampire lore amusingly scrambled when he tries to intervene. It's fast and furious fun, superbly scripted by Robert Kaufman, and wonderfully pulled together by director Stan Dragoti. AJ. Contains swearing. [video]

George Hamilton *Count Dracula* • Susan Saint James *Cindy Sondheim* • Richard Benjamin *Dr Jeff Rosenberg* • Dick Shawn *Lieutenant Ferguson* • Arte Johnson *Renfield* • Sherman Hemsley *Reverend Mike* • Isabel Sanford *Judge* ■ *Dir* Stan Dragoti • *Scr* Robert Kaufman, from a story by Robert Kaufman, Mark Gindes

Love at Large ★★ 15

Crime drama 1990 · US · Colour · 93mins

Tom Berenger's career took a downward turn with this daft, if imaginative, attempt at a light-hearted *film noir* by writer/director Alan Rudolph. A private detective, hired by a beautiful woman, ends up following the wrong man and is himself followed by a female detective. Still with us? Well, you won't be after an hour and a half of mistaken identities, tortuous plot twists and below-par acting. JB. Contains violence and swearing. [video]

Tom Berenger *Harry Dobbs* • Elizabeth Perkins *Stella Wynkowski* • Anne Archer *Miss Dolan* • Kate Capshaw *Ellen McGraw* • Annette O'Toole *Mrs King* ■ *Dir/Scr* Alan Rudolph

Love at Stake ★★★ 15

Comedy drama 1987 · US · Colour · 83mins

Kelly Preston plays the town baker (Sara Lee!) in this farcical comedy set amid a colony of Puritans in 17th-century Salem. The local judge and mayor have devised a fiendish plan to steal villagers' land by accusing them of witchcraft. Very much *The Crucible* meets *The Naked Gun*, this is awash with toilet humour and screamingly bad gags. Barbara Carrera does a great turn as the only actual witch, and this will keep lovers of the genre heartily amused. LH [video]

Patrick Cassidy *Miles* • Kelly Preston *Sara Lee* • Bud Cort *Parson Babcock* • David Graf *Nathaniel* • Stuart Pankin *Judge Samuel John* • Dave Thomas *Mayor Upton* • Barbara Carrera *Faith* ■ *Dir* John Moffitt • *Scr* Terrence Sweeney, Lanier Laney

Love at Twenty ★★★

Portmanteau drama
1962 · Fr/It/Jpn/W Ger/Pol · BW · 115mins

The most significant entry in this portmanteau picture is *Antoine et Colette*, which furthered the Antoine Doinel cycle launched by François Truffaut in *The 400 Blows*. However, there's much to enjoy elsewhere. In Renzo Rossellini's *Rome* a rich woman fights to keep her lover from a beautiful innocent, while Marcel Ophüls's *Munich* sees a photographer develop a passion for the mother of his child. A factory worker murders the student who refuses his advances in Shintaro Ishihara's *Tokyo*, while in Andrzej Wajda's intriguing *Warsaw* a man's life changes after he rescues a child from the bear pit at the zoo. DP. In French with English subtitles.

Jean-Pierre Léaud *Antoine Doinel "Paris–Antoine et Colette"* • Marie-France Pisier *Colette* • Eleonora Rossi-Drago *Valentina* • Koji Furuhata *Hiroshi* • Nami Tamura *Fukimo* • Christian Doermer *Tonio* • Barbara Frey *Ursula* • Barbara Lass *Basia* ■ *Dir* François Truffaut, Renzo Rossellini, Shintaro Ishihara, Marcel Ophüls, Andrzej Wajda • *Scr* François Truffaut, Yvon Samuel, Renzo Rossellini, Shintaro Ishihara, Marcel Ophüls, Jerzy Stefan Stawinski

Love before Breakfast ★★

Comedy 1936 · US · BW · 65mins

A middle-of-the-road lightweight romantic comedy given A-grade treatment in casting and production values. The title is meaningless and the flimsy plot concerns Cesar Romero and Preston Foster as suitors vying for the affections of New York socialite Carole Lombard. Foster schemes to get his rival out of the way – even out of the country – but Lombard smells a rat. Walter Lang directs what, in most circumstances, would be a waste of time, but anything starring the lovely Lombard is worth a look. RK

Carole Lombard *Kay Colby* • Preston Foster *Scott Miller* • Cesar Romero *Bill Wadsworth* • Janet Beecher *Mrs Colby* • Betty Lawford *Contessa Janie Campanella* ■ *Dir* Walter Lang • *Scr* Herbert Fields, from the novel *Spinster Dinner* by Faith Baldwin

The Love Bug ★★★★ U

Comedy 1969 · US · Colour · 107mins

In this classic Disney comedy, plain good fun is at the wheel, with its foot down to the floor. Herbie, the Volkswagen with as much bottle as throttle, is a brilliant invention, and Dean Jones, as his racing driver

L

owner, and David Tomlinson, as Jones's ruthless rival, work wonders to stop the little Beetle running away with the film. Having shown a flair for fantasy with *Mary Poppins*, director Robert Stevenson here demonstrates a sure slapstick touch. *Herbie Rides Again*, the first of three of sequels, followed in 1974. DP DVD

Dean Jones *Jim Douglas* • Michele Lee *Carole Bennett* • David Tomlinson *Peter Thorndyke* • Buddy Hackett *Tennessee Steinmetz* • Joe Flynn *Havershaw* • Benson Fong *Mr Wu* ■ *Dir* Robert Stevenson • *Scr* Don DaGradi, Bill Walsh, from a story by Gordon Buford

The Love Cage ★★

Crime romance 1964 · Fr · BW · 96mins

Jane Fonda in her sex-kitten phase – that's before the leftie radical phase, the great actress phase and the mogul's wife phase. It was her first French movie, originally titled *Les Félins*. France's biggest star, Alain Delon, plays a gangster who is given refuge in a vast chateau by Fonda and her aunt, Lola Albright, whose lover, another gangster, has murdered her husband. It's a game of sexual charades – clothes come off and then a gun goes off, spoiling all the fun. AT. French dialogue dubbed into English.

Alain Delon *Marc* • Jane Fonda *Melinda* • Lola Albright *Barbara* • Carl Studer *Loftus* • Sorrell Booke *Harry* • André Oumansky *Vincent* • Arthur Howard (2) *Rev Nielson* ■ *Dir* René Clément • *Scr* René Clément, Charles Williams, Pascal Jardin, from the novel *Joy House* by Day Keene

Love, Cheat & Steal ★★ 18

Thriller 1994 · US · Colour · 91mins

An unpleasant modern *film noir* featuring Eric Roberts as a vengeful escaped convict who shows-up at ex-wife Mädchen Amick's house posing as her estranged brother. John Lithgow is Amick's new, rich banker husband, whose vaults full of Colombian drug money are targeted by Roberts. The attractively elf-like, but fatally wooden, Amick goes through more skimpy costume changes than a fashion show. Things do perk up, however, in the satisfying, twist-laden robbery climax. JC. Contains violence, swearing and sex scenes.

John Lithgow *Paul Harrington* • Eric Roberts *Reno Adams* • Mädchen Amick *Lauren Harrington* • Richard Edson *Billy Quayle* • Donald Moffat *Paul's father* • David Ackroyd *Tom Kerry* • Dan O'Herlihy *Hamilton Fisk* ■ *Dir/Scr* William Curran

Love Child ★★★ 18

Drama based on a true story
1982 · US · Colour · 92mins

Amy Madigan made her big screen debut here as Terry Jean Moore, a condemned criminal who is initially sentenced to 15 years for robbery, increased to 20 years for starting a fire in jail. Moore campaigns for her right to keep her baby which is fathered by one of the prison guards, played by Beau Bridges. The real-life case attracted a lot of press coverage in America, turning the volatile Moore into a celebrity and feminist icon. The approach is level-headed and semi-documentary in style. AT

Amy Madigan *Terry Jean Moore* • Beau Bridges *Jack Hansen* • Mackenzie Phillips *JJ* • Albert Salmi *Captain Ellis* • Joanna Merlin *Superintendent Sturgis* • Margaret Whitton *Jacki Steinberg* • Lewis Smith *Jesse Chaney* • Dennis Lipscomb *Arthur Brady* ■ *Dir* Larry Peerce • *Scr* Anne Gerard, Katherine Specktor, from a story by Anne Gerard

Love Crazy ★★★

Screwball comedy 1941 · US · BW · 98mins

The favourite box-office team of William Powell and Myrna Loy (Nick and Nora Charles of the *Thin Man* series) are the beleaguered couple in this madcap farce. Instead of celebrating a wedding anniversary it looks as though they're heading for the rocks when her mother comes to stay and he meets up with an old flame. Directed at a rollicking pace by Jack Conway, this is complete nonsense and lots of fun. RK

William Powell *Steven Ireland* • Myrna Loy *Susan Ireland* • Gail Patrick *Isobel Grayson* • Jack Carson *Ward Willoughby* • Florence Bates *Mrs Cooper* • Sidney Blackmer *George Hennie* • Vladimir Sokoloff *Dr Klugle* • Kathleen Lockhart *Mrs Bristol* ■ *Dir* Jack Conway • *Scr* William Ludwig, Charles Lederer, David Hertz, from a story by David Hertz, William Ludwig

Love Crimes ★ 18

Erotic thriller 1991 · US · Colour · 86mins

Director Lizzie Borden's unbelievable thriller has lawyer Sean Young going undercover to trap con artist Patrick Bergin, a man who preys on unsuspecting women by posing as a fashion photographer and offering them the chance of a modelling career. The ridiculous story makes little sense and wooden performances by both leads don't help much. AJ. Contains violence, swearing and nudity.

Sean Young *Dana Greenway* • Patrick Bergin *David Hanover* • Arnetia Walker *Maria Johnson* • James Read *Stanton Gray* • Ron Orbach *Detective Eugene Tully* • Fern Dorsey *Colleen Dells* • Tina Hightower *Anne Winslow* ■ *Dir* Lizzie Borden • *Scr* Allan Moyle, Laurie Frank, from a story by Allan Moyle

Love Don't Cost a Thing ★★ 15

Romantic comedy
2003 · US · Colour · 97mins

Having bought the remake rights to *Can't Buy Me Love*, director Troy Beyer clearly didn't have enough left over to pay for either a decent screenplay or a capable cast. There's virtually no spark between high-school nobody Nick Cannon and Christina Milian, as the girl who helps secure him an entrée to the in-crowd in return for repairing her mom's car. Beyer's choice of camera angles often beggars belief in this mixed-message movie. DP. Contains sexual references. DVD

Nick Cannon *Alvin Johnson* • Christina Milian *Paris Morgan* • Steve Harvey *Alvin's dad* • Al Thompson *Big Ted* • Kal Penn *Kenneth* • Kenan Thompson *Walter* • Vanessa Bell Calloway *Mrs Johnson* • Melissa Schuman *Zoe* ■ *Dir* Troy Beyer • *Scr* Troy Beyer, Michael Swerdlick, from the film *Can't Buy Me Love* by Michael Swerdlick

Love etc ★★★ 15

Romantic drama 1997 · Fr · Colour · 99mins

It's not just the title and setting that director Marion Vernoux jettisons in her Gallicisation of Julian Barnes's novel *Talking It Over*. The confessional narrative style is also reined in to permit a more traditionally structured account of the romantic triangle that forms between timid executive Yvan Attal, art restorer Charlotte Gainsbourg and the indolent Charles Berling. While fitfully amusing, this is essentially a rather sad story. However, uncertain pacing mars both the opening exposition and the resolution of what is an overly familiar and frequently flatly played scenario. DP. In French with English subtitles. Contains swearing and sex scenes. DVD

Charlotte Gainsbourg *Marie* • Yvan Attal *Benoît* • Charles Berling *Pierre* • Thibault de Montalembert *Bernard* • Elodie Navarre *Eléonore* ■ *Dir* Marion Vernoux • *Scr* Marion Vernoux, Dodine Henry, from the novel *Talking It Over* by Julian Barnes

Love Field ★★★★ 15

Romantic drama
1992 · US · Colour · 100mins

Michelle Pfeiffer may have been nominated for an Oscar for her role in this neglected drama, but that still didn't guarantee it a cinema release in this country, where it slipped quietly straight to video. Pfeiffer is superb as the bleach-blonde Jackie Kennedy-obsessed housewife who walks out on her husband to travel to President Kennedy's funeral, and Dennis Haysbert (replacing Denzel Washington, who turned down the role) is equally watchable as the secretive black man travelling with his daughter, with whom she makes friends on the journey. Political intrigue aside, this is a fascinating tale of innocent enthusiasm in a bigoted world. JB. Contains violence, swearing. DVD

Michelle Pfeiffer *Lurene Hallett* • Dennis Haysbert *Paul Cater* • Stephanie McFadden *Jonell Cater* • Brian Kerwin *Ray Hallett* • Louise Latham *Mrs Enright* • Peggy Rea *Mrs Heisenbuttal* • Beth Grant *Hazel* • Rhoda Griffis *Jacqueline Kennedy* ■ *Dir* Jonathan Kaplan • *Scr* Don Roos

Love Finds Andy Hardy ★★★

Comedy drama 1938 · US · BW · 90mins

The fourth and one of the freshest films in the Andy Hardy series, with Mickey Rooney muddling dance dates and getting in a dreadful mess. Judy Garland makes the first of three appearances in the series – she sings three songs – and seems relatively natural when compared to the precocious talent of Rooney. Another star-in-waiting, Lana Turner, plays one of Rooney's girlfriends. AT

Mickey Rooney *Andy Hardy* • Lewis Stone *Judge James K Hardy* • Judy Garland *Betsy Booth* • Ann Rutherford *Polly Benedict* • Lana Turner *Cynthia Potter* • Cecilia Parker *Marian Hardy* • Fay Holden *Mrs Emily Hardy* • Betty Ross Clark [Betty Ross Clarke] *Aunt Milly* ■ *Dir* George B Seitz • *Scr* William Ludwig, from stories by Vivian R Bretherton, from characters created by Aurania Rouverol

Love from a Stranger ★★★

Crime drama 1936 · UK · BW · 86mins

Having come into a fortune but quarrelled with her fiancé, Ann Harding is swept off her feet into marriage by Basil Rathbone, whom she barely knows. They settle in luxury in Europe, only for her to be warned that he murders wealthy women. Directed by Rowland V Lee, this is a neat, smooth suspense drama, in which the stars give polished performances. RK

Basil Rathbone *Gerald Lovell* • Ann Harding *Carol Howard* • Binnie Hale *Kate Meadows* • Bruce Seton *Ronald Bruce* • Jean Cadell *Aunt Lou* • Bryan Powley *Dr Gribble* • Joan Hickson *Emmy* ■ *Dir* Rowland V Lee • *Scr* Frances Marion, from the play by Frank Vosper, from the short story *Philomel Cottage* by Agatha Christie in the collection *The Listerdale Mystery and Other Stories*

Love from a Stranger ★★

Period mystery 1947 · US · BW · 81mins

Based on an Agatha Christie story *Philomel Cottage*, in which a wealthy young woman has a whirlwind courtship and marries a habitual wife murderer, this is a pointless and markedly inferior remake of the splendid 1936 version. Sylvia Sidney, her once great career by then in shreds but her talent intact, stars as the intended victim, with John Hodiak as the Bluebeard-style villain, here turned into an absurd South American adventurer. RK

John Hodiak *Manuel Cortez/Pedro Ferrara* • Sylvia Sidney *Cecily Harrington* • Ann Richards *Mavis Wilson* • John Howard (1) *Nigel Lawrence* • Isobel Elsom *Auntie Loo-Loo* • Ernest Cossart *Billings* ■ *Dir* Richard Whorf • *Scr* Philip MacDonald, from the play *Love from a Stranger* by Frank Vosper, from the short story *Philomel Cottage* by Agatha Christie in the collection *The Listerdale Mystery and Other Stories*

The Love God? ★★

Comedy 1969 · US · Colour · 103mins

Girlie magazine publisher Edmond O'Brien faces bankruptcy when a change in status means he can no longer claim cheap mailing privileges. He sees salvation in the ailing ornithological magazine edited by Don Knotts. O'Brien convinces Knott he can save the magazine, then sends him away to photograph exotic birds, while he turns the publication into another nudie rag. Low-octane comedy. DF

Don Knotts *Abner Peacock* • Anne Francis *Lisa* • Edmond O'Brien *Osborn Tremain* • James Gregory *Hughes* • Maureen Arthur *Eleanor Tremain* ■ *Dir/Scr* Nat Hiken

The Love Goddesses ★★★★

Compilation
1965 · US · BW and Colour · 78mins

This is a marvellous compilation of clips featuring Hollywood's finest sex symbols. Trouble is, the producers were obviously constrained by availability and copyright, so where you would perhaps expect more you might get less, and vice versa. Paramount stars are favoured, but, nevertheless, many of the great ladies of the silver screen are present and correct, and the makers refreshingly cast their nets wider than the US, including Hedy Lamarr (as Hedwig Keisler), famously nude in *Ecstasy*, and that wanton Lulu, Louise Brooks, abroad in Europe. There's even a sizeable chunk of *Expresso Bongo*, one of the most daring (and under-rated) flicks of its day. Sylvia Syms a love goddess? You bet! TS. Contains nudity.

Dir Saul J Turrell, Graeme Ferguson • *Scr* Saul J Turrell, Graeme Ferguson • *Editor* Howard Kuperman • *Music* Percy Faith

Love Happy ★★ U

Comedy 1949 · US · BW · 84mins

The Marx Brothers' penultimate film together is hardly worth the effort – unless you hanker for a glimpse of Marilyn Monroe. Harpo wrote the story and gets most of the spotlight as the shoplifting member of a penniless group of actors who unwittingly picks up a sardine can filled with diamonds. Raymond Burr is one of the villains trying to get the jewels back and Vera-Ellen plays Harpo's love interest. Groucho fans should note that his appearance is a brief one. TH

Harpo Marx *Harpo* • Chico Marx *Faustino the Great* • Ilona Massey *Madame Egilichi* • Vera-Ellen *Maggie Phillips* • Marion Hutton *Bunny Dolan* • Raymond Burr *Alphonse Zoto* • Melville Cooper *Lefty Throckmorton* • Paul Valentine *Mike Johnson* • Leon Belasco *Mr Lyons* • Eric Blore *Mackinaw* • Bruce Gordon (1) *Hannibal Zoto* • Marilyn Monroe *Grunion's client* • Groucho Marx *Detective Sam Grunion, narrator* ■ *Dir* David Miller • *Scr* Frank Tashlin, Mac Benoff, from a story by Harpo Marx

Love Has Many Faces ★

Romantic drama
1965 · US · Colour · 105mins

The title of this witless farrago is as unintentionally hilarious as its content. The many faces include Lana Turner as a millionairess in Acapulco and Cliff Robertson as her husband, a former beach lothario who married her for her money and is now lusting after Stefanie Powers. Turner has her hands full with bullfighter Jaime Bravo, and Hugh O'Brian – a gigolo on the make with both Lana and the equally wealthy Ruth Roman. RK

Lana Turner *Kit Jordan* • Cliff Robertson *Pete Jordan* • Hugh O'Brian *Hank Walker* • Ruth Roman *Margot Eliot* • Stefanie Powers *Carol Lambert* • Virginia Grey *Irene Talbot* ■ *Dir* Alexander Singer • *Scr* Marguerite Roberts

Love, Honour and Obey ★★ 18

Comedy drama 2000 · UK · Colour · 94mins

This is the second film from the self-styled Fugitives, a loose artists' collective centred around actors Ray Winstone, Jude Law and Sadie Frost. Jonny Lee Miller, Rhys Ifans and Denise Van Outen join the trio in this tale of a courier who wheedles his way into a London crime family, only to embroil them in a deadly feud with a rival gang. The humour is laddish, lowbrow and not especially funny, while some improvised scenes should never have made the final cut. DA [video] DVD

Ray Winstone *Ray* • Jonny Lee Miller *Jonny* • Jude Law *Jude* • Kathy Burke *Kathy* • Sadie Frost *Sadie* • Sean Pertwee *Sean* • Denise Van Outen *Denise* • Rhys Ifans *Mathew* ■ *Dir/Scr* Dominic Anciano, Ray Burdis

Love Hurts ★★ 15

Comedy drama 1990 · US · Colour · 102mins

Jeff Daniels's reluctant divorcee is the only believable character in this well-meaning comedy drama from veteran director Bud Yorkin. But Cloris Leachman is way over the top as our hero's zany mum, as this plodding effort attempts to look at the idea of civilised parting, what to do with the extended relatives and how to comfort the children. It's a good try, but it comes unstuck after the first reel and the inappropriately crass comedy all too often fails to hit the button. SR. Contains violence and swearing. [video]

Jeff Daniels *Paul Weaver* • Cynthia Sikes *Nancy Weaver* • Judith Ivey *Susan Volcheck* • John Mahoney *Boomer* • Cloris Leachman *Ruth Weaver* • Amy Wright *Karen Weaver* • Mary Griffin *Sarah Weaver* ■ *Dir* Bud Yorkin • *Scr* Ron Nyswaner

Love in a Goldfish Bowl ★★

Romantic comedy
1961 · US · Colour · 88mins

Teen idols Tommy Sands and Fabian star in this unassuming romantic comedy about youthful love. Teenager Sands and his friend, fellow student Toby Michaels, decide to take an (innocent) vacation together at Sands's mother's beach house. During the holiday Michaels falls for the charms of local sailor Fabian. Average, but not without charm, and the leads are attractive enough. DF

Tommy Sands *Gordon Slide* • Fabian *Giuseppe La Barba* • Jan Sterling *Sandra Slide* • Toby Michaels *Blythe Holloway* • Edward Andrews *Senator Clyde Holloway* • John McGiver *Dr Frowley* • Majel Barrett *Alice* ■ *Dir* Jack Sher • *Scr* Jack Sher, from a story by Irene Kamp, Jack Sher

Love in Ambush ★★

Drama 1997 · Aus/Fr · Colour

This glossy if somewhat contrived melodrama is set in Cambodia in 1972, prior to Pol Pot's disastrous takeover. Sigrid Thornton is the woman who returns to South East Asia to find her brother (Grant Piro), a soldier who disappeared during the conflict. Old wounds are reopened when she is forced to call on her ex-husband and plantation owner Jacques Perrin, now a Khmer Rouge sympathiser. It looks great, but both the performances and the plotting are sudsy. JF. Contains swearing, violence.

Sigrid Thornton *Shelley Kincaird* • Jacques Perrin *Pascal Lasalle* • Gary Sweet *Eddie Norton* • James Tolkan *Price* • Grant Piro *Lt Jon Kincaird* ■ *Dir* Carl Schultz • *Scr* Loupe Durand, David Ambrose, Christine Miller, John Howlett, Tom Hegarty

Love in Pawn ★ U

Comedy 1953 · UK · BW · 70mins

Britain's popular radio (and later TV) imports from Canada, Bernard Braden and his wife Barbara Kelly, star in this indescribably puerile and unfunny comedy directed by Charles Saunders. It concerns a penniless artist who must prove his respectability in order to inherit a fortune from his wealthy uncle. Best forgotten, which it was. RK

Bernard Braden *Roger Fox* • Barbara Kelly *Jean Fox* • Jean Carson *Amber Trusslove* • Reg Dixon *Albert Trusslove* ■ *Dir* Charles Saunders • *Scr* Guy Morgan, Frank Muir, Denis Norden, from a story by Humphrey Knight

Love in the Afternoon ★★★★★

Romantic comedy 1957 · US · BW · 129mins

Filmed and set in Paris, Billy Wilder's romantic comedy will delight fans of his earlier *Sabrina*. Audrey Hepburn again stars, this time as the daughter of French private eye Maurice Chevalier who becomes obsessed by one of his targets: American businessman and serial adulterer Gary Cooper who lives at the Ritz and has a gypsy band serenade his love-making sessions. Critics at the time found the crinkly Cooper much too old to romance the gorgeous Hepburn, but that's precisely the point: she humanises and energises him with her European vivacity. This first collaboration between Wilder and co-writer IAL Diamond features some lovely scenes and colourful secondary characters. AT

Gary Cooper *Frank Flannagan* • Audrey Hepburn *Ariane Chavasse* • Maurice Chevalier *Claude Chavasse* • John McGiver *Monsieur X* • Van Doude *Michel* • Lise Bourdin *Madame X* ■ *Dir* Billy Wilder • *Scr* Billy Wilder, IAL Diamond, from the novel *Ariane* by Claude Anet

Love in the Afternoon ★★★★ 15

Comedy drama 1972 · Fr · Colour · 93mins

Eric Rohmer winds up his "Six Moral Tales" series with this delightful comedy drama, also known by its American title *Chloë in the Afternoon*. Rather than exploring the doubts that beset those contemplating marriage, Rohmer here considers the temptations that take the sheen off wedded bliss. Real-life husband and wife Bernard and Françoise Verley play a couple whose contentment is jeopardised by his secret meetings with old friend Zouzou. The acting is impeccable, and Rohmer's skilful use of location adds to the atmosphere and charm. DP. In French with English subtitles. [video] DVD

Zouzou *Chloë* • Bernard Verley *Frédéric* • Françoise Verley *Hélène* • Daniel Ceccaldi *Gérard* • Malvina Penne *Fabienne* • Babette Ferrier *Martine* • Frederique Hender *Madame M* ■ *Dir/Scr* Eric Rohmer

Love in the City ★★

Portmanteau comedy drama
1953 · It · BW · 110mins

In the early 1950s, Italian cinema was arguably the liveliest and most innovative in Europe, and this brought together many of its major writers and directors. But, like most of these compilation films, it's a mixed blessing. The idea was to film real-life stories and real people, but Federico Fellini copped out (well, of course he would) and made a fantasy about a werewolf who uses a marriage agency because he thinks getting hitched will cure him. Michelangelo Antonioni offers some interviews with girls who attempted suicides. Other stories scour the gutter. AT. In Italian with English subtitles.

Dir Michelangelo Antonioni, Federico Fellini, Alberto Lattuada, Carlo Lizzani, Francesco Maselli, Dino Risi, Cesare Zavattini • *Scr* Aldo Buzzi, Luigi Chiarini, Luigi Malerba, Tullio Pinelli, Vittorio Veltroni

Love in the Strangest Way ★★ 15

Thriller 1994 · Fr · Colour · 102mins

Seeking to break with his amiable screen image, Thierry Lhermitte plays a ruthless debt collector whose dangerous liaison with a mystery woman can only lead to one thing. Devoid of passion, suspense or social grit, this mildly salacious suspense film isn't worth waiting up for. DP. In French with English subtitles. Contains violence, mild swearing and nudity. [video]

Thierry Lhermitte *Julien Bernier* • Maruschka Detmers *Anne Bernier* • Nadia Farès *Angela Galli* • Johann Martel *Charles* • Umberto Orsini *Vienne* ■ *Dir* Christopher Frank • *Scr* Christopher Frank, Jean Nachbaur, from an idea by Jean-Marc Roberts

Love Is a Ball ★★

Romantic comedy
1963 · US · Colour · 112mins

The early 1960s was plagued with this kind of French Riviera tosh. Acres of bikini-clad bottoms, tinkling champagne glasses on clifftop terraces, Ferraris taking hairpin bends at ridiculous speeds and a plethora of Equity no-hopers who make the entire "We're having a jolly privileged time" premise appear more wooden than a barn door. A prime example of the style. SH

Charles Boyer *Monsieur Etienne Pimm* • Glenn Ford *John Davis* • Hope Lange *Millie Mehaffey* • Ricardo Montalban *Gaspard* • Telly Savalas *Dr Gump* • Ruth McDevitt *Mathilda* ■ *Dir* David Swift • *Scr* David Swift, Tom Waldman, Frank Waldman, from the novel *The Grand Duke and Mr Pimm* by Lindsay Hardy

Love Is a Gun ★★★ 18

Erotic thriller 1994 · US · Colour · 102mins

Eric Roberts, that actor who just can't seem to say no to any script, shows better judgment with this nifty little thriller. The territory is familiar enough – police snapper Roberts becomes a murder suspect when he falls for a *femme fatale* – but director David Hartwell's jump-start direction and quirky eye distinguish it from other straight-to-video fodder. Roberts is well supported by Kelly Preston and R Lee Ermey. JF [video]

Eric Roberts *Jack Hart* • Kelly Preston *Jean* • Eliza Garrett *Isabel* • Joe Sirola [Joseph Sirola] *Al Kinder* • John Toles-Bey *Jay Leibowitz* • R Lee Ermey *Frank Deacon* ■ *Dir/Scr* David Hartwell

Love Is a Many-Splendored Thing ★★ U

Romantic drama 1955 · US · Colour · 97mins

Despite having one of the most famous romantic titles of all time, this soap opera's distinction rests largely with its hit title ballad and director Henry King's imaginative use of early CinemaScope, which captures stars Jennifer Jones and William Holden horizontal at every possible opportunity. Trouble is, both Jones and Holden fail to convince in this occasionally trite tale of forbidden love, which is a shame, because the source book by Han Suyin is actually very moving. Alfred Newman's Oscar-winning score will convince you that this tosh, a huge success at the time, is better than it is. TS [video] DVD

William Holden (2) *Mark Elliot* • Jennifer Jones *Han Suyin* • Torin Thatcher *Mr Palmer-Jones* • Isobel Elsom *Adeline Palmer-Jones* • Murray Matheson *Dr Tam* • Virginia Gregg *Ann Richards* • Richard Loo *Robert Hung* • Soo Young *Nora Hung* • Philip Ahn *Third Uncle* ■ *Dir* Henry King • *Scr* John Patrick, from the book *A Many Splendored Thing* by Han Suyin

Love Is a Racket ★★★

Crime comedy drama
1932 · US · BW · 72mins

Douglas Fairbanks Jr is the Broadway gossip columnist who falls for an ambitious but financially irresponsible young actress (Frances Dee). She becomes indebted to a ruthless gangster, who then meets with an untimely death. Fairbanks is terrific as the cynical reporter with sudden stardust in his eyes, and he is well supported by a cast that includes Lee Tracy, Lyle Talbot and Ann Dvorak. A pacy comedy/drama, smartly scripted and, under William Wellman's immaculate direction, offering lots of New York nightlife atmosphere. RK

Douglas Fairbanks Jr *Jimmy Russell* • Ann Dvorak *Sally* • Frances Dee *Mary Wodehouse* • Lee Tracy *Stanley Fiske* • Lyle Talbot *Eddie Shaw* • George Raft *Stinky* ■ *Dir* William A Wellman • *Scr* Courtenay Terrett [Courtney Terrett], from the novel *Love Is a Racket* by Rian James

Love Is All There Is ★ 12

Comedy drama 1996 · US · Colour · 101mins

An oafish update of *Romeo and Juliet*, with competing catering companies as the families linked by star-crossed love. Crass, loud and a lot less funny than it thinks it is, the main interest here is an early performance from Oscar-winner Angelina Jolie as the "Juliet" character. Joseph Bologna (who also co-directed), Barbara Carrera and Paul Sorvino fill out the mid-quality cast. If food be the music of love, *don't* play on! DA [video] DVD

Lainie Kazan *Sadie* • Paul Sorvino *Piero* • Barbara Carrera *Maria* • Joseph Bologna *Mike* • Angelina Jolie *Gina* • Nathaniel Marston *Rosario* • Renee Taylor *Mona* • William Hickey *Monsignor* • Dick Van Patten *Dr Rondino* • Abe Vigoda *Rudy* • Connie Stevens *Miss DeLuca* • Blessed Roscoe ■ *Dir/Scr* Renee Taylor, Joseph Bologna

Love Is Better Than Ever ★★ U

Romantic comedy 1951 · US · BW · 80mins

A naive dance teacher comes to New York for a dance convention and meets a slick theatrical agent. He shows her around but she misinterprets his attentiveness as honorable intentions and falls in love with him. Directed by Stanley Donen, this wisp of a forgotten romantic comedy is definitely lower-half-of-the-bill stuff, even though the girl is a young Elizabeth Taylor. Her love interest is Larry Parks, starring in his last film before the McCarthy hearings destroyed his career. RK

Larry Parks *Jud Parker* • Elizabeth Taylor *Anastacia Macaboy* • Josephine Hutchinson *Mrs Macaboy* • Tom Tully *Mr Macaboy* • Ann Doran *Mrs Levoy* • Elinor Donahue *Pattie Marie Levoy* • Kathleen Freeman *Mrs Kahmey* • Doreen McCann *Albertina Kahmey* • Gene Kelly *Guest star* ■ *Dir* Stanley Donen • *Scr* Ruth Brooks Flippen

Love Is Colder Than Death ★★★★

Romantic crime comedy
1969 · W Ger · BW · 88mins

Clearly taking up where Jean-Luc Godard had left off in his assault on traditional cinema, Rainer Werner Fassbinder made his remarkable debut with this micro-budget deconstruction of the crime thriller. Much of the action is staged as tableaux before a doggedly static camera. The minimalist plot is presented in fragmentary form, while lowlifes Ulli Lommel and Fassbinder (and Hannah Schygulla as the girl caught between them) scarcely exchange a word. It's almost wilfully obscure, but compelling nonetheless. DP. In German with English subtitles.

Ulli Lommel *Bruno* • Hanna Schygulla *Johanna* • Rainer Werner Fassbinder *Franz* • Katrin Schaake *Lady in train* • Hans Hirschmüller *Peter* ■ *Dir/Scr* Rainer Werner Fassbinder

Love Is News ★★★

Screwball comedy 1937 · US · BW · 78mins

This screwball battle-of-the-sexes romantic comedy pits heart-throb newshound Tyrone Power against beautiful heiress Loretta Young. Fed up with being chased by journalists, she takes her revenge on Power by announcing that she's leaving fiancé George Sanders for him, whereupon he's sacked by boss Don Ameche, and on goes a plot of escalating lunacy and pace. This is often hilarious fare, well cast and delightfully played. Remade as a beguiling Fox musical, *Sweet Rosie O'Grady*, in 1943, and again in 1948 as *That Wonderful Urge* (also starring Power). RK

Tyrone Power *Steve Leyton* • Loretta Young *Tony Gateson* • Don Ameche *Martin J Canavan* • Slim Summerville *Judge Hart* • Dudley Digges *Cyrus Jeffrey* • Walter Catlett *Eddie Johnson* • Pauline Moore *Lois Westcott* • Jane Darwell *Mrs Flaherty* • Stepin Fetchit *Penrod* • George Sanders *Count André de Guyon* • Elisha Cook Jr *Egbert Eggleston* ■ *Dir* Tay Garnett • *Scr* Harry Tugend, Jack Yellen, from a story by William R Lipman, Frederick Stephani

Love Is the Devil: Study for a Portrait of Francis Bacon ★★★ 18

Biographical drama
1998 · UK · Colour · 86mins

John Maybury's film is a highly stylised account of the painter's abrasive affair with reformed thief George Dyer. As lovers divided by culture and class, Derek Jacobi gives a remarkable physical impersonation of Bacon, while Daniel Craig is a model of repressed anger and bemused despair. The director's use of distorting lenses, reflective surfaces, angular close-ups and split-screen devices conveys both the couple's dislocated world and the style of Bacon's paintings. However, the film needs momentum, while the dialogue is pretentiously epigrammatic. DP. Contains nudity, sex scenes and some swearing. [video] DVD

Derek Jacobi *Francis Bacon* • Daniel Craig *George Dyer* • Anne Lambton *Isabel Rawsthorne* • Karl Johnson *John Deakin* • Annabel Brooks *Henrietta Moraes* • Adrian Scarborough *Daniel Farson* • Tilda Swinton *Muriel Belcher* • Richard Newbold *Blonde Billy* ■ *Dir* John Maybury • *Scr* John Maybury, James Cohen, Don Jordan

Love Jones ★★★ 15

Romantic comedy
1997 · US · Colour · 104mins

Writer Theodore Witcher made his directorial debut with this funny, funky tale of love among a group of Chicago middle-class African Americans. Nia Long and Larenz Tate are the star-crossed lovers who meet, make love and then part, leading to the usual romantic complications. Portraying blacks as successful urbanites rather than the usual clichéd, downbeat characters, this features superb performances from the leads. Stylishly shot and with a snappy script, this is a knowing look at the pitfalls of love and romance in the 1990s. JB. Contains swearing, sexual references. [video]

Larenz Tate *Darius Lovehall* • Nia Long *Nina Mosley* • Isaiah Washington *Savon Garrison* • Lisa Nicole Carson *Josie Nichols* • Bill Bellamy *Hollywood* ■ *Dir/Scr* Theodore Witcher

Love Kills ★★★ 18

Comedy 1998 · US · Colour · 90mins

Mario Van Peebles stars a masseur and con artist who specialises in scamming recently widowed women in ingenious ways dreamed up by his insanely jealous girlfriend Loretta Devine. His new target is Lesley Ann Warren who is actually broke, but whose flakey stepson (Donovan Leitch) is about to inherit jewels worth millions. Into this stew comes Daniel Baldwin as a *Columbo*-style cop who might not be what he seems. Glossily produced for indie fodder, this is worth checking out if only for Van Peebles's extraordinary dreadlocks. JF [video] DVD

Mario Van Peebles *Poe Finklestein* • Lesley Ann Warren *Evelyn Heiss* • Daniel Baldwin *Danny Tucker* • Donovan Leitch *Dominique* • Alexis Arquette *James* • Louise Fletcher *Alena Heiss* • Loretta Devine *Sylvia Finklestein* • Melvin Van Peebles *Abel* ■ *Dir/Scr* Mario Van Peebles

Love Laughs at Andy Hardy ★★ U

Comedy drama 1946 · US · BW · 92mins

This was the fifteenth and last genuine Andy Hardy movie (though there was a nostalgic straggler in 1958). Andy and his dad (Lewis Stone) had entertained America through the war years and kept alive small-town values, but Mickey Rooney couldn't conceal the fact that he was now 26 years old. In any case, these were the days of *film noir*, romantic fatalism and venetian blinds, all of which meant curtains for the boyish Hardy. This instalment sees Rooney back from the war and crushed when his fiancée (Bonita Granville) runs off with someone else. AT DVD

Mickey Rooney *Andy Hardy* • Lewis Stone *Judge James K Hardy* • Fay Holden *Mrs Emily Hardy* • Sara Haden *Aunt Milly* • Bonita Granville *Kay Wilson* ■ *Dir* Willis Goldbeck • *Scr* Harry Ruskin, William Ludwig, from a story by Howard Dimsdale, from characters created by Aurania Rouverol

The Love Letter ★★ 15

Romantic comedy
1999 · US · Colour · 83mins

This film about a divorced single mother is very much a family affair. Actress Kate Capshaw bought the rights to Cathleen Schine's novel in order to produce it for husband Steven Spielberg's DreamWorks company, while one of the Spielberg children, Sasha, has a walk-on role. Capshaw finds an anonymous letter written in amorously endearing terms and thinks it's for her. The film's romantic focus is unsteady and soapily blurred. TH. Contains swearing, a sex scene and nudity. [video]

Kate Capshaw *Helen* • Blythe Danner *Lillian* • Ellen DeGeneres *Janet* • Geraldine McEwan *Miss Scattergoods* • Julianne Nicholson *Jennifer* • Tom Everett Scott *Johnny* • Tom Selleck *George* • Gloria Stuart *Eleanor* • Jessica Capshaw *Kelly* • Sasha Spielberg *Girl with sparkler* ■ *Dir* Peter Ho-Sun Chan • *Scr* Maria Maggenti, from the novel by Cathleen Schine

Love Letters ★★★

Melodrama 1945 · US · BW · 101mins

Mogul David O Selznick loaned his protégée and future wife, Jennifer Jones, to producer Hal B Wallis and Paramount for this glitzy romantic soap opera. In Ayn Rand's screenplay, Jones suffers a number of shocks, including amnesia and the traumatic discovery that her treasured collection of love letters was written not by her husband (Robert Sully) but by co-star Joseph Cotten. This stylish and enjoyable nonsense was directed by William Dieterle and received several Oscar nominations including one for Jones (as best actress). RK

Jennifer Jones *Singleton* • Joseph Cotten *Alan Quinton* • Ann Richards *Dilly Carson* • Anita Louise *Helen Wentworth* • Cecil Kellaway *Mack* • Gladys Cooper *Beatrice Remington* • Byron Barr *Derek Quinton* • Robert Sully *Roger Morland* ■ *Dir* William Dieterle • *Scr* Ayn Rand, from the novel *Pity My Simplicity* by Chris Massie

Love Letters ★★★★ 18

Drama 1983 · US · Colour · 84mins

This hugely impressive emotional drama is beautifully played and sensitively directed by Amy Jones. The story centres on a single woman who discovers evidence of an affair among her dead mother's letters, then takes up herself with a married man. The film intelligently probes the emotions of infidelity, and its frequent justification on the grounds that it's sometimes right to do the wrong thing. The starry cast includes Jamie Lee Curtis, Amy Madigan, Bud Cort and James Keach. DA [video]

Jamie Lee Curtis *Anna* • James Keach *Oliver* • Amy Madigan *Wendy* • Bud Cort *Danny* • Matt Clark *Winter* • Bonnie Bartlett *Mrs Winter* ■ *Dir/Scr* Amy Jones [Amy Holden Jones]

Love, Life and Laughter ★★ U

Musical comedy drama
1934 · UK · BW · 81mins

This self-conscious musical romance – a variation on *The Prince and the Showgirl* scenario – is not one of Gracie Fields's finest hours, as it sacrifices her trademark realism for neverland fantasy. Fields seems slightly inhibited as the actress who lures the heir to the throne away from his Ruritanian kingdom, and fiancée Norah Howard, but John Loder, as the prince, rises to the challenge admirably. The idea that movies have become the new fairy tales is a good one, however, even if director Maurice Elvey occasionally confuses the fake glamour of celebrity with the pomp and pageantry that mask the heavy burden of official duty. DP [video]

Gracie Fields *Nellie Gwyn* • John Loder *Prince Charles* • Norah Howard *Princess Grapfel* • Alan Aynesworth *King* • Esme Percy *Goebschen* • Veronica Brady *Mrs Gwyn* • Horace Kenney *Mr Gwyn* ■ *Dir* Maurice Elvey • *Scr* Robert Edmunds, from a story by Maurice Braddell

Love Liza ★★★ 15

Drama 2001 · US/Fr/Ger · Colour · 86mins

Director Todd Louiso's feature debut is something of a family affair, with actor Philip Seymour Hoffman excelling in a story that won his brother Gordy the prestigious Waldo Salt Screenwriting Award at the 2002 Sundance Festival. As a widower coming to terms with his loss, Hoffman courageously conveys the slow erosion of surface calm by inner turmoil, as he succumbs to sniffing petrol fumes to obliterate the guilt and rejection inspired by his wife's unexplained suicide. Some of his misadventures may seem overly eccentric, but the raw emotion of Hoffman's performance is authentic. DP DVD

Philip Seymour Hoffman *Wilson Joel* • Kathy Bates *Mary Ann Bankhead* • Jack Kehler *Denny* • Sarah Koskoff *Maura* • Stephen Tobolowsky *Tom Bailey* • Erika Alexander *Brenda* ■ *Dir* Todd Louiso • *Scr* Gordy Hoffman

The Love Lottery ★★★ U

Comedy 1953 · UK · Colour · 83mins

David Niven is his usual smooth self and the part of a 1950s celluloid heart-throb was made for him. Charles Crichton directs with his tongue well placed in his cheek. The plot is about as daft as you can possibly get – Niven agrees to be first prize in a love lottery for fans – but nobody really cares as there's just enough satire to keep this fizzy, old-fashioned romp afloat. SR

David Niven *Rex Allerton* • Peggy Cummins *Sally* • Anne Vernon *Jane* • Herbert Lom *Amico* • Charles Victor *Jennings* • Gordon Jackson *Ralph* • Humphrey Bogart ■ *Dir* Charles Crichton • *Scr* Harry Kurnitz, from the story by Charles Neilson-Terry, Zelma Bramley-Moore

The Love Machine ★ 18

Drama 1971 · US · Colour · 103mins

Jacqueline Susann hit paydirt with this tacky adaptation of her bestselling novel. The setting is the power-crazed, sexually torrid world of television news and if you can believe John Philip Law as the head honcho you will believe anything. Dyan Cannon pouts, Robert Ryan looks bored as a company chairman and David Hemmings plays a hyped-up photographer – a not very subtle in-joke about his role in *Blowup*. This lacks the really bad taste and send-up performances to make it even vaguely enjoyable. AT [video]

John Phillip Law *Robin Stone* • Dyan Cannon *Judith Austin* • Robert Ryan *Gregory Austin* • Jackie Cooper *Danton Miller* • David Hemmings *Jerry Nelson* ■ *Dir* Jack Haley Jr • *Scr* Samuel Taylor, from the novel by Jacqueline Susann

The Love Match ★★★ U

Comedy 1955 · UK · BW · 86mins

Although this is an admirable enough comedy, it is also one of those unforgivably patronising pictures that bourgeois British film-makers believed presented an authentic picture of working-class life. Arthur Askey stars as a football crazy railway employee whose passion for a team of no-hopers lands him in all sorts of trouble. Struggling against a shortage of genuinely funny situations, the cast does well to keep the action alive. The highlight is Askey's heckling of the referee, a wonderful moment of football hooliganism. DP

Arthur Askey *Bill Brown* • Thora Hird *Sal Brown* • Glenn Melvyn *Wally Binns* • Robb Wilton *Mr Muddlecombe* • James Kenney *Percy Brown* • Shirley Eaton *Rose Brown* ■ *Dir* David Paltenghi • *Scr* Geoffrey Orme, Glenn Melvyn, from the play by Glenn Melvyn

Love Me If You Dare ★★★ 15

Romantic comedy drama
2003 · Fr/Bel · Colour · 89mins

Taking a childhood game to adult extremes, Yann Samuell's anti-romance asks us to root for a couple destined to be together, but wilfully determined to remain apart. The dares that young Thibault Verhaeghe and Josephine Lebas Joly make to get them through the pain of growing up are mischievous and sweet. But the fact that Guillaume Canet and Marion Cotillard continue to disrupt each others' lives periodically over the next 15 years seems capricious, contrived and occasionally cruel. Technically accomplished, this is entertaining, but never wholly engaging. DP. In French with English subtitles. Contains swearing and sex scenes. DVD

Guillaume Canet *Julien* • Marion Cotillard *Sophie* • Thibault Verhaeghe *Julien, aged 8* • Josephine Lebas Joly *Sophie, aged 8* • Emmanuelle Grönvold *Julien's mother* • Gérard Watkins *Julien's father* • Gilles Lellouche *Sergueï* • Julia Faure *Sophie's sister* • Laetizia Venezia *Christelle* • Elodie Navarre *Aurélie* ■ *Dir/Scr* Yann Samuell

Love Me or Leave Me ★★★★

Musical drama 1955 · US · Colour · 121mins

This cracking biopic of 1920s chanteuse Ruth Etting was originally intended as a vehicle for Ava Gardner, but MGM wisely brought in Doris Day, giving her a sexy new image and pairing her with tough guy James Cagney, and, boy, how those sparks fly! Though censorship has diluted this tawdry saga of a kept woman and her obsessive and sexually inadequate gangster sponsor, the truth is not glossed over, despite the top-notch production values that make the tale less squalid than it was. Day is a knockout, performing the title number and *Ten Cents a Dance* with great understanding, but it's Cagney who walks away with the movie. TS

Doris Day *Ruth Etting* • James Cagney *Martin "the Gimp" Snyder* • Cameron Mitchell *Johnny Alderman* • Robert Keith (1) *Bernard V Loomis* • Tom Tully *Frobisher* • Harry Bellaver *Georgie* • Richard Gaines *Paul Hunter* ■ *Dir* Charles Vidor • *Scr* Daniel Fuchs, Isobel Lennart, from a story by Daniel Fuchs

Love Me Tender ★★★ PG

Western 1956 · US · BW · 85mins

When 20th Century-Fox made a cheap black-and-white CinemaScope western called *The Reno Brothers*, they couldn't possibly have foreseen how one lucky stroke of casting would bring their production costs back within the first three days of opening. For, as younger brother Clint Reno, rock 'n' roll sensation Elvis Presley made his screen debut, and the title of the movie was changed to that of its ballad, *Love Me Tender*. Elvis proved to be a natural screen presence and, although third-billed to stars Richard Egan and Debra Paget, effortlessly dominates the film. TS [VIDEO] DVD

Richard Egan *Vance* • Debra Paget *Cathy* • Elvis Presley *Clint* • Robert Middleton *Siringo* • William Campbell *Brett Reno* • Neville Brand *Mike Gavin* • Mildred Dunnock *Mother* ■ *Dir* Robert D Webb • *Scr* Robert Buckner, from a story by Maurice Geraghty

Love Me Tonight ★★★★★

Musical comedy 1932 · US · BW · 104mins

This is one of Hollywood's most clever and influential film musicals, with a sublime Rodgers and Hart score illuminating director Rouben Mamoulian's successful attempt at freeing the production from its staid, stage-bound forerunner. The irrepressible Maurice Chevalier is "the son-of-a-gun who's nothing but a tailor" who falls for princess Jeanette MacDonald, long before MGM put her in a straitjacket opposite the sexless Nelson Eddy. And those songs – *Mimi*, *Lover*, *Isn't It Romantic?* – and, ooh, that risqué dialogue: make a note of Myrna Loy's pre-censorship response to "Could you go for a doctor?". TS

Maurice Chevalier *Maurice Courtelin* • Jeanette MacDonald *Princess Jeanette* • Myrna Loy *Countess Valentine* • Charlie Ruggles [Charles Ruggles] *Vicomte de Vareze* • C Aubrey Smith *Duke* • Charles Butterworth *Count de Savignac* • Joseph Cawthorn *Dr Armand de Fontinac* • Robert Greig *Flamond* ■ *Dir* Rouben Mamoulian • *Scr* Samuel Hoffenstein, Waldemar Young, George Marion Jr, from the play *Tailor in the Chateau* by Léopold Marchand, by Paul Armont

Love, Mother ★★ 15

Drama 1987 · Hun · Colour · 105mins

Occasionally guilty of being too mischievous for his own good, Hungarian director Janos Rozsa still produces a witty morality story about the dangers of lust and greed. Spied on by the young son by means of a network of periscopes dotted around the house, the family at the centre of this satire is so preoccupied by upward mobility and sexual gratification that its members communicate only through chalked messages on a blackboard in the kitchen. DP. In Hungarian with English subtitles.

Dorottya Udvaros *Juli Kalmar* • Robert Koltai *Geza Kalmar* • Kati Lajtai *Mari Kalmar* • Simon G Gevai *Peti Kalmar* • Sandor Gáspár *Doctor* ■ *Dir* Janos Rozsa • *Scr* Miklos Vamos, from his story

Love Nest ★★ U

Comedy 1951 · US · BW · 81mins

This piece of harmless fluff stars sweet and pretty June Haver in one of her rare non-musical roles. She and bland William Lundigan are a married couple who have invested their life savings in an apartment building, but a number of problems arise. One of them comes in the comely shape of Marilyn Monroe – on the eve of stardom – tossed in to create jealousy. It's difficult to believe that this ineptly contrived screenplay was written by IAL Diamond, who was to co-write some of Billy Wilder's best movies. RB DVD

June Haver *Connie Scott* • William Lundigan *Jim Scott* • Frank Fay *Charley Patterson* • Marilyn Monroe *Roberta Stevens* • Jack Paar *Ed Forbes* • Leatrice Joy *Eadie Gaynor* ■ *Dir* Joseph M Newman • *Scr* IAL Diamond, from the novel by Scott Corbett

The Love of Jeanne Ney ★★★★

Silent romance 1927 · Ger · BW · 144mins

Made in the heyday of UFA, the famed German production company, just prior to GW Pabst's best works, *Pandora's Box* and *Diary of a Lost Girl*, this epic love story deserves to be better known. A mixture of social realism and Hollywood-style romance, the rather complicated plot moves from the Crimea (studio sets) during the Russian Revolution to Paris, where sequences were shot in the streets. The lovers, portrayed by Edith Jehanne and Uno Henning, are outplayed by Fritz Rasp, a wonderfully sleazy villain, and Brigitte Helm, uncharacteristically cast as a lonely blind girl. RB

Edith Jehanne *Jeanne Ney* • Brigitte Helm *Gabrielle Ney* • Hertha von Walther *Margot* • Uno Henning *Andreas Labov* • Fritz Rasp *Khalibiev* • Adolph Edgar Licho *Raymond Ney* • Eugen Jensen *Alfred Ney* • Hans Jaray *Emile Poitras* • Wladimir Sokoloff [Vladimir Sokoloff] *Zacharkiewitsch* ■ *Dir* GW Pabst • *Scr* Ladislao Vajda, Rudolph Leonhardt, Ilya Ehrenburg, from the novel *Die Liebe der Jeanne Ney* by Ilya Ehrenburg

The Love of Sumako the Actress ★★★

Biographical drama 1947 · Jpn · BW · 93mins

Although he had inate sympathy for geishas and others who suffered from patriarchal injustice, Kenji Mizoguchi was perhaps less astute in his handling of successful females. Consequently, although he stages this biopic of Sumako Matsui with a genuine feel for the Japanese theatre at a time when actresses and western techniques were virtually unknown, he is less certain in his presentation of the melodramatic events surrounding her affair with married director, Hogetsu Shimamura. DP. In Japanese with English subtitles.

Kinuyo Tanaka *Sumako Matsui* • So Yamamura *Hogetsu Shimamura* • Eijiro Tono *Shoyo Tsubouchi* • Kikue Mori *Ichiko Shimamura* ■ *Dir* Kenji Mizoguchi • *Scr* Yoshikata Yoda, from the play *Karumen Yukinu* by Hideo Nagata

Love on the Dole ★★★★ PG

Drama 1941 · UK · BW · 94mins

This dramatisation of Walter Greenwood's influential novel about working-class life stars Deborah Kerr as a mill girl caught on the horns of a classic 1930s dilemma: become a kept woman and escape poverty, or keep faith with the morality of her class. Director John Baxter has summoned all the usual slum-dwelling stereotypes – local sharp-suited bookie and cruel paterfamilias – yet the movie resonates with strong feeling for the harshness and brutal truths of life in Depression-era Salford, and Kerr is subtly affecting. SH [VIDEO] DVD

Deborah Kerr *Sally Hardcastle* • Clifford Evans *Larry Meath* • Joyce Howard *Helen Hawkins* • George Carney *Mr Hardcastle* • Mary Merrall *Mrs Hardcastle* • Geoffrey Hibbert *Harry Hardcastle* • Frank Cellier *Sam Grundy* • Martin Walker *Ned Narkey* ■ *Dir* John Baxter • *Scr* Walter Greenwood, Barbara K Emery, Rollo Gamble, from the play by Ronald Gow, from the novel by Walter Greenwood

Love on the Run ★★★

Comedy 1936 · US · BW · 80mins

This is class. It may not seem very clever or original today, but it never really had to be. The stars are Joan Crawford and Clark Gable, and for many movie fans of the era that's all that matters. One of those globetrotting romances that never get off the backlot, this is whipped along ever-so-lightly by director WS Van Dyke ("One-take Woody"), an expert craftsman who knew exactly how to handle material like this. TS

Joan Crawford *Sally Parker* • Clark Gable *Michael Anthony* • Franchot Tone *Barnabas Pells* • Reginald Owen *Baron Spandermann* • Mona Barrie *Baroness* • Ivan Lebedeff *Prince Igor* ■ *Dir* WS Van Dyke • *Scr* John Lee Mahin, Manuel Seff, Gladys Hurlbut, from the story *Beauty and the Beast* by Alan Green, Julian Brodie

Love on the Run ★★★ 12

Comedy drama 1979 · Fr · Colour · 91mins

The fifth, last and least of François Truffaut's films about his alter ego Antoine Doinel, first seen in the director's debut feature, *The 400 Blows*, made 20 years earlier. This is also a nostalgic movie, with many of Antoine's former female conquests making guest appearances, some in sequences from earlier films, as he prepares to write a novel of his romantic career. It's more than a shade indulgent, and some may find Jean-Pierre Léaud a real pain as the lead. Yet it's still a funny and humane movie. AT. In French with English subtitles. [VIDEO] DVD

Jean-Pierre Léaud *Antoine Doinel* • Marie-France Pisier *Colette* • Claude Jade *Christine* • Dani *Liliane* • Dorothée *Sabine* ■ *Dir* François Truffaut • *Scr* François Truffaut, Suzanne Schiffman, Marie-France Pisier, Jean Aurel

Love or Money ★★ 15

Comedy 1990 · US · Colour · 86mins

This routine comedy, about a pushy home-seller who finds himself in a real (e)state when he faces the eternal dilemma – success in business or a shot at romantic happiness. The film stars personable Timothy Daly, plus veterans Kevin McCarthy and former beach movie and Elvis co-star Shelley Fabares. DA [VIDEO]

Kevin McCarthy *William Reed* • Timothy Daly *Chris Murdoch* • Haviland Morris *Jennifer Reed* • Shelley Fabares *Lu Ann Reed* • David Doyle *Arthur Reed* ■ *Dir* Todd Hallowell • *Scr* Bart Davis, Elyse England, Michael Zausner

The Love Parade ★★★★

Musical comedy 1929 · US · BW · 107mins

Soprano Jeanette MacDonald, the queen of screen operetta, made her film debut as Queen Louise, being wooed by Maurice Chevalier's Count Alfred Renard in Ernst Lubitsch's first talkie. His Gallic charm and her Anglo-Saxon reserve and self-mockery produced a seductive, piquant combination in this saucy fairy tale set in Paris and the fictional land of Sylvania. With its lavish settings, songs integrated into the scenario and sexual innuendo, it set the pattern for future Hollywood musicals. RB

Maurice Chevalier *Count Alfred Renard* • Jeanette MacDonald *Queen Louise* • Lupino Lane *Jacques* • Lillian Roth *Lulu* • Edgar Norton *Major-Domo* • Jean Harlow ■ *Dir* Ernst Lubitsch • *Scr* Ernst Vajda, Guy Bolton, from the play *The Prince Consort* by Leon Xanrof, Jules Chancel

The Love Pill ★ 18

Erotic comedy 1971 · UK · Colour · 79mins

In the early 1970s, the pill was still held responsible in many quarters for the onset of the permissive society and so this crass picture takes the argument to its illogical conclusion by having dozens of women take a tablet that transforms them into nymphomaniacs. Instantly forgettable soft-core comedy. DP [VIDEO]

Henry Woolf *Libido* • Toni Sinclair *Sylvia, Libido's secretary* • David Pugh *Arnold* • Melinda Churcher *Linda* • Kenneth Waller *Professor Edwards* ■ *Dir* Kenneth Turner • *Scr* from a story by John Lindsay

Love Potion No 9 ★★ PG

Romantic fantasy comedy 1992 · US · Colour · 92mins

Taking its plot cues from the lyrics of the famous pop hit, this is silly, cute and randomly amusing. Tate Donovan and Sandra Bullock are the nerdy lab assistants who discover a spray formula that makes them irresistible to the opposite sex. The expected complications ensue. Writer/director Dale Launer knows his limitations and deftly creates an unassuming feel-good factor around them. Worth seeing for Anne Bancroft's uncredited mystic gypsy cameo, Madame Ruth. AJ [VIDEO] DVD

Tate Donovan *Paul Matthews* • Sandra Bullock *Diane Farrow* • Mary Mara *Marisa* • Dale Midkiff *Gary Logan* • Hillary Bailey Smith *Sally* • Dylan Baker *Prince Geoffrey* • Anne Bancroft *Madame Ruth (uncredited)* ■ *Dir* Dale Launer • *Scr* Dale Launer, from a song by Jerry Leiber, Mike Stoller

Love Serenade ★★

Comedy 1996 · Aus · Colour · 101mins

Typically quirky Australian comedy, about a top DJ who relocates to a remote outback town. But it isn't his discs that he puts in a spin, it's the lives of the two love-hungry sisters who live next door. The storyline teeters on the edge of tastelessness, but the engagingly oddball handling and strong performances keep it just the right side of sleazy. DA

Miranda Otto *Dimity Hurley* • Rebecca Frith *Vicki-Ann Hurley* • George Shevtsov *Ken Sherry* • John Alansu *Albert Lee* • Jessica Napier *Deborah* • Jill McWilliam *Curler victim* ■ *Dir/Scr* Shirley Barrett

A Love Song for Bobby Long ★★★

Drama 2004 · US · Colour · 119mins

John Travolta tackles the inevitable fact of ageing in this tale of a young woman (Scarlett Johansson), who returns to her home after her mother's death only to find it occupied by a group of alcoholic literary types who have every intention of staying put. Despite Travolta's best efforts (and impressively silvered hair), he never quite convinces as an ageing, drunk writer, but what director Shainee Gabel's debut movie lacks slightly in dramatic credibility it more than makes up for in New Orleans atmosphere. AS

John Travolta *Bobby Long* • Scarlett Johansson *Pursy* • Gabriel Macht *Lawson* • Deborah Kara Unger *Georgianna* • Dane Rhodes *Cecil* • David Jensen (2) *Junior* • Clayne Crawford *Lee* ■ *Dir* Shainee Gabel • *Scr* Shainee Gabel, from the novel *Off Magazine Street* by Ronald Everett Capps

Love Songs ★★

Drama 1984 · Fr · Colour · 109mins

The prospect of watching Christopher Lambert and Richard Anconina camp it up as wannabe rock stars will probably dissuade many from sticking with this showbiz melodrama, particularly as the ditties are hardly the finest. But the romance that develops between Lambert and record mogul Catherine Deneuve is not without interest. The leads' contrasting acting styles also add to this otherwise pedestrian picture. DP. French dialogue dubbed into English.

Catherine Deneuve *Margaux* • Christopher Lambert *Jeremy* • Richard Anconina *Michel* • Jacques Perrin *Yves* • Dayle Haddon *Corinne* • Nick Mancuso *Peter* • Charlotte Gainsbourg *Charlotte* • Dominique Lavanant *Florence* • Lionel Rocheman *Gruber* ■ *Dir/Scr* Elie Chouraqui

Love Stinks ★

Comedy 1999 · US · Colour · 93mins

Unpleasant characters populate this story about two lovers, French Stewart and Bridgette Wilson, who torture each other with malicious pranks once their romance goes south. The film presents women as greedy, manipulative ice queens while men are seen as sex-obsessed, commitment-phobic pigs. Flat jokes and non-existent chemistry between the leads also contribute to a truly excruciating experience. ST

French Stewart *Seth Winnick* • Bridgette Wilson *Chelsea Turner* • Bill Bellamy *Larry Garnett* • Tyra Banks *Holly Garnett* • Steve Hytner *Marty Mark* • Jason Bateman *Jesse Travis* • Tiffani-Amber Thiessen *Rebecca Melini* ■ *Dir/Scr* Jeff Franklin

Love Story ★★ U

Romantic melodrama
1944 · UK · BW · 108mins

This is one of those tragic romances in which all concerned would have been spared a lot of tears if just one of the lovers had bothered to give the other an inkling of the truth. But with former pilot Stewart Granger keeping mum about his incipient blindness and pianist Margaret Lockwood equally reticent about her terminal illness, we are guaranteed angst aplenty. Stiff-upper-lipped hokum. DP

Margaret Lockwood *Lissa Campbell* • Stewart Granger *Kit Firth* • Patricia Roc *Judy Martin* • Tom Walls *Tom Tanner* • Reginald Purdell *Albert* • Moira Lister *Carol* • Dorothy Bramhall *Susie* • Vincent Holman *Prospero* • Joan Rees *Ariel* ■ *Dir* Leslie Arliss • *Scr* Leslie Arliss, Doreen Montgomery, Rodney Ackland, from the story by JW Drawbell

Love Story ★★★ PG

Romantic drama 1970 · US · Colour · 95mins

This heady mixture of love and life-threatening illness was roundly condemned by critics in its day, but became a massive box-office hit nevertheless. Drown in the excess of it all as the ill-starred romance between tragic Ali MacGraw and Ryan O'Neal takes its course and you'll require two boxes of Kleenex. On the other hand, bring even the remotest hint of cynicism to bear and it will grate like fingernails on a blackboard. A sequel, *Oliver's Story*, followed belatedly in 1978. SH. Contains swearing and sex scenes. DVD

Ali MacGraw *Jenny Cavilleri* • Ryan O'Neal *Oliver Barrett IV* • John Marley *Phil Cavilleri* • Ray Milland *Oliver Barrett III* • Russell Nype *Dean Thompson* • Katherine Balfour *Mrs Oliver Barrett III* • Sydney Walker *Dr Shapeley* • Robert Modica *Dr Addison* • Tom Lee Jones [Tommy Lee Jones] *Hank* ■ *Dir* Arthur Hiller • *Scr* Erich Segal, from his novel • *Music* Francis Lai

Love Streams ★★ 15

Drama 1984 · US · Colour · 134mins

Not one of John Cassavetes's better efforts, this casts the director's wife, Gena Rowlands, as a woman going through marital breakdown who finds solace with her alcoholic brother, played by Cassavetes. Much of the dialogue sounds like typical American psycho-babble, making the movie less of a drama and more of a confessional therapy session. The result is intense, well-acted and more than a little tedious. AT

Gena Rowlands *Sarah Lawson* • John Cassavetes *Robert Harmon* • Diahnne Abbott *Susan* • Seymour Cassel *Jack Lawson* • Margaret Abbott *Margarita* ■ *Dir* John Cassavetes • *Scr* John Cassavetes, Ted Allan, from a play by Ted Allan

The Love Test ★★★

Comedy 1935 · UK · BW · 63mins

This early romantic comedy from director Michael Powell features one of Bernard Miles's first appearances, as well as an early outing for Googie Withers, whom Powell claimed "brings sunshine into dull lives, makes bald hair grow". Judy Gunn stars as a laboratory overseer up against her male employees. Initially successful, Gunn has to work to outwit her adversaries, who plot to oust her by making her fall in love. Only rediscovered in the late 1980s, this demonstrates Powell's fascination with strong women. LH

Judy Gunn *Mary* • Louis Hayward *John* • David Hutcheson *Thompson* • Morris Harvey *President* • Googie Withers *Minnie* • Aubrey Dexter *Vice-President* • Bernard Miles *Allan* ■ *Dir* Michael Powell • *Scr* Selwyn Jepson, from a story by Jack Celestin

Love That Brute ★★★

Crime comedy 1950 · US · BW · 85mins

Good-natured fun in a Runyonesque tale of a soft-hearted gangster (Paul Douglas) who falls for a naive innocent (Jean Peters). He pretends to have children in order to hire her as a governess. The prohibition-era story is a remake of *Tall, Dark and Handsome* (1941), which starred Cesar Romero, who takes the villain's role this time round. If the earlier version was a little livelier, this one has the advantage of a fine portrayal of blustering surface toughness from Douglas. TV

Paul Douglas *Big Ed Hanley* • Jean Peters *Ruth Manning* • Cesar Romero *Pretty Willie* • Keenan Wynn *Bugs* • Joan Davis *Mamie* • Arthur Treacher *Quentin* • Jay C Flippen *Biff* ■ *Dir* Alexander Hall • *Scr* Karl Tunberg, Darrell Ware, John Lee Mahin

Love Thy Neighbour ★

Comedy 1973 · UK · Colour · 84mins

The attitudes on display in this film based on the 1970s TV comedy series are so dated that they are more laughable than offensive. Time hasn't dimmed its spectacular unfunniness. Watch it only to boggle at a career low point for a number of well known British faces. JF

Jack Smethurst *Eddie Booth* • Rudolph Walker *Bill Reynolds* • Nina Baden-Semper *Barbie* • Kate Williams *Joan Booth* ■ *Dir* John Robins • *Scr* Vince Powell, Harry Driver

Love to Kill ★★ 15

Comedy thriller 1997 · US · Colour · 102mins

Modestly offbeat gangster thriller, with a video-friendly cast of familiar faces. Tony Danza is a gunrunner looking to go to straight who gets dragged back into his old world when he and his partner (co-writer Rustam Branaman) go on a double date with girlfriend Elizabeth Barondes and her sister (Amy Locane). The latter ends up dead and the duo must then get rid of her body while avoiding rival crook Michael Madsen. Nicely played, but it tries a little too hard to be quirky. JF

Tony Danza *Moe* • Elizabeth Barondes *Monica* • James Russo *Brannigan* • Louise Fletcher *Gloria* • Rustam Branaman *Franco* • Amy Locane *Beth* • Michael Madsen *Donnelly* • Brian Brophy *Harry* ■ *Dir* James Bruce • *Scr* Rustam Branaman, Monica Clemens

Love! Valour! Compassion! ★★★ 15

Comedy drama 1997 · US · Colour · 109mins

Joe Mantello's poignant adaptation of Terrence McNally's award-winning play explores the differing emotions and attitudes (sexual and otherwise) of eight gay men staying at a glorious country retreat. Set over three American holiday weekends, this is an involving if overly sentimental study of human relationships, with a talented ensemble cast. Despite the absence of any straight characters, the film's honesty and insight into human nature makes it accessible to all audiences. JC. Contains swearing and nudity.

Jason Alexander *Buzz Hauser* • Randy Becker *Ramon Fornos* • Stephen Bogardus *Gregory Mitchell* • John Glover *John Jeckyll/James Jeckyll* • John Benjamin Hickey *Arthur Pape* • Justin Kirk *Bobby Brahms* • Stephen Spinella *Perry Sellars* ■ *Dir* Joe Mantello • *Scr* Terrence McNally, from his play

Love Walked In ★★ 15

Crime thriller 1997 · US/Arg · Colour · 87mins

Having won an Emmy for *Life Stories*, director Juan José Campanella attempted a latterday *noir* here, as struggling pianist Denis Leary and singer wife Aitana Sanchez-Gijon conspire with sleazy private eye Michael Badalucco to sting wealthy Terence Stamp with a divorce scam. But, while the thriller elements are established efficiently, Campanella spends too much time on staging episodes from Leary's horror scribblings, which distract from the action. DP. Contains swearing and violence.

Denis Leary *Jack Morrisey* • Aitana Sanchez-Gijon *Vicky* • Terence Stamp *Fred Moore* • Michael Badalucco *Eddie* • Gene Canfield *Joey* • Marj Dusay *Mrs Moore* • Moira Kelly *Vera* • Neal Huff *Howard* ■ *Dir* Juan José Campanella • *Scr* Lynn Geller, Larry Golin, Juan José Campanella, from the novel *Ni el Tiro del Final* by Jose Pablo Feinmann

The Love Waltz ★★★

Comedy 1930 · Ger · BW · 70mins

The operettas produced by UFA, the famed German production company, in the early sound era were so universally popular, they were often remade in foreign language versions. John Batten steps in for Willy Fritsch in this English re-working of the romance between a commoner and a princess destined for marriage to an ageing archduke. With her beautiful voice and deliciously light comic touch, London-born Lilian Harvey shows why she was one of Germany's biggest stars, but Batten lacks the charisma to justify her jilting Georg Alexander. Producer Erich Pommer provides the plushest of sets, but the going gets a little heavy. DP

Julia Serda *Duchess of Lauenburg* • Lilian Harvey *Princess Eva* • Karl Ludwig Diehl *Count Marshal* • Lotte Spira *Archduchess Melany* • Georg Alexander *Archduke Peter Ferdinand* • Hans Junkermann *Fould* • John Batten *Bobby* • Viktor Schwannecke *Dr Lemke* ■ *Dir* Wilhelm Thiele [William Thiele], Carl Winston • *Scr* Hans Müller, Robert Liebmann

Love Will Tear Us Apart ★★

Drama 1999 · HK · Colour · 114mins

Cinematographer Nelson Lik-Wai Yu's directorial debut resembles the work of Wong Kar-Wai. With four mainland exiles trying to acclimatise to the frantic pace of Hong Kong, the picture gets off to a busy start. But there's less here than meets the eye, in spite of a touching performance from Lu Liping as the lame ex-dancing teacher now reduced to operating an elevator. Less effective is Tony Leung Kar-Fai as the manager of a porn video shop. DP. In Cantonese with English subtitles.

Tony Kar-Fai Leung [Tony Leung (1)] *Jian* • Lu Liping *Yan* • Wong Ning *Ying* • Rolf Chow *Chun* ■ *Dir/Scr* Nelson Lik-Wai Yu

Love with the Proper Stranger ★★★★

Comedy drama 1963 · US · BW · 100mins

After a one-night stand, demure Natalie Wood gets pregnant and jazz musician Steve McQueen does one of those wonderful, trademark double-takes when she tells him the news. This is a fresh and very touching drama, set against the religious and staunch family traditions of New York's Italian community. Even when the script begins to run out of ideas – you can only have so many "will she have an abortion?" scenes – the gorgeous Wood and McQueen have more than enough charisma to fill the screen without saying a single word. AT

Natalie Wood *Angie Rossini* • Steve McQueen *Rocky Papasano* • Edie Adams *Barbie, Barbara of Seville* • Herschel Bernardi *Dominick Rossini* • Tom Bosley *Anthony Colombo* • Harvey Lembeck *Julio Rossini* ■ *Dir* Robert Mulligan • *Scr* Arnold Schulman

Loved ★ 15

Drama 1996 · US · Colour · 99mins

This fumbles the sensitive subject of domestic violence. Writer/director Erin Dignam manages to turn in an almost insulting and poorly paced drama which does its well-meaning cast a disservice. Robin Wright Penn is the woman still in love with her ex-partner despite his abuse, who is asked to testify against him by DA William Hurt, after another of the man's lovers throws herself in front of a car. Wright Penn walks around barefoot to convey her distress, while Hurt sleepwalks through his part. JB. Contains some swearing and nudity.

William Hurt *KD Dietrickson* • Robin Wright [Robin Wright Penn] *Hedda* • Amy Madigan *Brett* • Joanna Cassidy *Elenore* • Paul Dooley *Leo* • Anthony Lucero *Defendent* • Jennifer Rubin *Debra* • Sean Penn *Michael* ■ *Dir/Scr* Erin Dignam

The Loved One ★★★

Black comedy farce
1965 · US · BW · 122mins

Although he ranks among the most admired British novelists of the century, the cinema has not been kind to Evelyn Waugh. Given that this novel, set in a California pet cemetery, is overladen with scathing swipes at Hollywood and American notions of the afterlife, screenwriters Terry Southern and Christopher Isherwood (themselves acclaimed novelists) might have produced a darker, more bitingly satirical script. However, director Tony Richardson and his all-star cast make the most of their opportunities before events descend into broad farce. TH

Robert Morse *Dennis Barlow* • Rod Steiger *Mr Joyboy* • Jonathan Winters *Harry Glenworthy/Wilbur Glenworthy* • Anjanette Comer *Aimee Thanatogenos* • Dana Andrews *General Brinkman* • Milton Berle *Mr Kenton* • John Gielgud *Sir Francis Hinsley* • James Coburn *Immigration Officer* • Tab Hunter *Guide* • Liberace *Mr Starker* • Lionel Stander *Guru*

Brahmin ■ *Dir* Tony Richardson • *Scr* Terry Southern, Christopher Isherwood, from the novel by Evelyn Waugh

The Loveless ★★ 18

Drama 1981 · US · Colour · 79mins

Willem Dafoe's first major screen role was in this comatose existential biker movie co-directed by Kathryn Bigelow. Dafoe and neo-rockabilly singer Robert Gordon are members of a rough-and-tumble biker gang who, on en route to Daytona, get stranded in a small southern town where they swagger and sneer a lot and put the narrow-minded locals' backs up. Worth a look for Dafoe alone. AJ [video]

Willem Dafoe *Vance* • Robert Gordon *Davis* • Marin Kanter *Telena* • J Don Ferguson *Tarver* • Tina L'Hotsky *Sportster Debbie* • Lawrence Matarese *LaVille* ■ *Dir* Monty Montgomery, Kathryn Bigelow • *Scr* Kathryn Bigelow

Lovely & Amazing ★★★ 15

Comedy 2001 · US · Colour · 87mins

Writer/director Nicole Holofcener explores the emotional fallout that accrues when self-absorption meets low self-esteem in this caustic, expertly played and restrained comedy drama. Although widowed mother Brenda Blethyn is undergoing liposuction and younger sister Emily Mortimer is seized by doubts about her beauty despite a burgeoning acting career, it's the underachieving Catherine Keener who experiences the gravest identity crisis, as she veers from a loveless marriage into a romance with her teenage boss at a one-hour photo shop. DP. Contains swearing, sex scenes and nudity. [video] DVD

Catherine Keener *Michelle Marks* • Brenda Blethyn *Jane Marks* • Emily Mortimer *Elizabeth Marks* • Raven Goodwin *Annie Marks* • Aunjanue Ellis *Lorraine* • Clark Gregg *Bill* • Jake Gyllenhaal *Jordan* • James LeGros *Paul* • Michael Nouri *Dr Crane* • Dermot Mulroney *Kevin McCabe* ■ *Dir/Scr* Nicole Holofcener

Lovely Rita ★★★ 15

Drama 2000 · Austria/Ger · Colour · 79mins

Director Jessica Hausner uses the misdaventures of a sullen adolescent girl to cast a disparaging eye over the current state of Austria in an impressive debut feature. Barbara Osika plays the titular teen misfit who sustains a front of self-indulgent petulance that only drops when she's fooling around with sickly schoolfriend Christoph Bauer or flirting with bus driver Peter Fiala. However, despite fine naturalistic performances from an entirely non-professional cast, the impact of the drama is lessened by the urgent digital camerawork and the improbable melodramatic climax. DP. In German with English subtitles.

Barbara Osika *Rita* • Christoph Bauer *Fexi* • Peter Fiala *Bus driver* • Wolfgang Kostal *Norbert, Rita's father* • Karina Brandlmayer *Inge, Rita's mother* ■ *Dir/Scr* Jessica Hausner • *Cinematographer* Martin Gschlacht

Lovely to Look At ★★★ U

Musical comedy 1952 · US · Colour · 101mins

This is the sumptuous MGM remake of the old RKO musical hit *Roberta*, an early vehicle for Fred Astaire and Ginger Rogers. The superb Jerome Kern score has been retained, and the songs, notably *Smoke Gets in Your Eyes* and *I Won't Dance*, still scintillate, especially when they're handled by such marvellous musical movie artists as Howard Keel, Ann Miller, and Marge and Gower Champion. Although the whole film is nominally directed by Mervyn LeRoy, the wonderfully Technicolored fashion show sequence was actually directed by one of the great stylists of the screen, Vincente Minnelli. TS

Kathryn Grayson *Stephanie* • Red Skelton *Al Marsh* • Howard Keel *Tony Naylor* • Marge Champion *Clarisse* • Gower Champion *Jerry Ralby* • Ann Miller *Bubbles Cassidy* • Zsa Zsa Gabor *Zsa Zsa* ■ *Dir* Mervyn LeRoy • *Scr* George Wells, Harry Ruby, Andrew Solt, from the musical *Roberta* by Jerome Kern, Dorothy Fields, Otto Harbach, from the novel *Roberta* by Alice Duer Miller

A Lovely Way to Go ★

Thriller 1968 · US · Colour · 103mins

This is a lifeless, excessively complicated detective story that fails to deliver suspense, wit or romance. Kirk Douglas is wasted as the ex-cop hired by Eli Wallach's wily lawyer to protect Sylva Koscina, young unfaithful wife, on trial for murdering her husband. Douglas brings his usual vitality to bear but Koscina is bland and there is no energy between them. Look out for Ali McGraw making her screen debut. AE

Kirk Douglas *Jim Schuyler* • Sylva Koscina *Rena Westabrook* • Eli Wallach *Tennessee Fredericks* • Kenneth Haigh *Jonathan Fleming* • Sharon Farrell *Carol* • Gordon Peters *Eric* • Martyn Green *Finchley* • Doris Roberts *Feeney* • Carey Nairnes *Harris* • Ralph Waite *Sean Magruder* • Ali MacGraw *Melody* ■ *Dir* David Lowell Rich • *Scr* AJ Russell

The Lover ★★ 18

Erotic drama 1992 · Fr/UK · Colour · 110mins

Jean-Jacques Annaud raised a few eyebrows with this steamy tale of a girl's sexual awakening in 1920s Indo-China. It did feature young star Jane March in various states of undress, but there was really nothing much to get steamed up about. March plays a 15-year-old schoolgirl who ends up losing more than her inhibitions with older man Tony Leung – cue a voiceover by Jeanne Moreau, and a few deep and meaningful moments which March is too out of her (acting) depth to convey. JB [video]

Jane March *Young Marguerite Duras* • Tony Kar-Fai Leung [Tony Leung (1)] *Chinese man* • Frédérique Meininger *Mother* • Arnaud Giovaninetti *Elder brother* • Melvil Poupaud *Younger brother* • Lisa Faulkner *Hélène Lagonelle* ■ *Dir* Jean-Jacques Annaud • *Scr* Jean-Jacques Annaud, Gérard Brach, from the novel by Marguerite Duras

A Lover and His Lass ★★★

Comedy 1975 · Swe · Colour · 94mins

This is the debut feature of Lasse Hallström, the Swedish director who went on to achieve international fame in Hollywood. Brasse Brännström (who also provided the story for the film) stars as a shiftless young man who is charm personified, but whose vocabulary does not include the words "fidelity" or "employment". Also known as *A Guy and His Gal*, this is a ribald, well-observed comedy, with winning performances. DP. In Swedish with English subtitles.

Brasse Brännström *Lasse* • Mariann Rudberg *Lena* • Christer Jonsson *Bosse* • Börje Ahlstedt *Lasse's Brother* • Chatarina Larsson *Ulla* ■ *Dir* Lasse Hallström • *Scr* Lasse Hallström, from a story by Brasse Brännström

Lover Come Back ★★

Romantic comedy 1946 · US · BW · 91mins

This romantic comedy has war correspondent George Brent returning from a couple of years away on assignment. Wife Lucille Ball's warm welcome is soon frozen by the discovery that her hubby hasn't lacked for female company and she takes off for a Vegas divorce. Naturally, he follows. Some zany shenanigans along the way pep up a mildly entertaining movie, disadvantaged by its dull leading man and dancer Vera Zorina, whose acting leaves a lot to be desired, in the role of the glamorous "other woman". RK

George Brent *Bill Williams* • Lucille Ball *Kay Williams* • Vera Zorina *Madeline Laslo* • Charles Winninger *Pa Williams* • Carl Esmond *Paul* • Raymond Walburn *JP Winthrop* • Elisabeth Risdon *Ma Williams* • Louise Beavers *Martha* ■ *Dir* William A Seiter • *Scr* Michael Fessier, Ernest Pagano

Lover Come Back ★★★ PG

Romantic comedy
1961 · US · Colour · 102mins

Another dig at the world of advertising featuring Doris Day, this time reuniting her with her *Pillow Talk* co-star Rock Hudson. This ultra-glossy romantic comedy is very much of its period, but the idea of Madison Avenue executives marketing a nonexistent product (called VIP) remains a good one, and the anti-advertising jokes are still funny. Stanley Shapiro and Paul Henning's script was Oscar-nominated, though the finale is astoundingly tasteless. TS [video] DVD

Rock Hudson *Jerry Webster* • Doris Day *Carol Templeton* • Tony Randall *Peter Ramsey* • Edie Adams *Rebel Davis* • Jack Oakie *J Paxton Miller* ■ *Dir* Delbert Mann • *Scr* Stanley Shapiro, Paul Henning • *Costume Designer* Irene

Lover's Knot ★

Romantic comedy
1995 · US · Colour · 88mins

This dire romantic comedy stars Tim Curry as a cosmic matchmaker in the service of Cupid, instructed to splice Jennifer Grey and Bill Campbell together forever. The pair, it turns out, have been karmically entwined for several lifetimes but have failed to clinch a happy ending. With a peculiar mishmash of documentary-style interviews, past life flashbacks and comments from the likes of William Shakespeare this is a mess. LH

William Campbell [Bill Campbell] *Steve Hunter* • Jennifer Grey *Megan Forrester* • Tim Curry *Cupid Caseworker* • Adam Baldwin *John Reed* • Mark Sheppard *Nigel Bowles* • Tom McTigue *Doug Meyers* • Holly Fulger *Gwen Meyers* • Adam Ant *Marvell* ■ *Dir/Scr* Pete Shaner

Loverboy ★★★ 15

Comedy 1989 · US · Colour · 94mins

Patrick Dempsey is the pizza delivery boy bringing more than just a deep pan with extra cheese to a somewhat silly comedy from director Joan Micklin Silver. Carrie Fisher, Kirstie Alley and Barbara Carrera are just three of the women falling for his charms, and Dempsey is an engaging lead. Light-hearted and well played nonsense. JB. Contains some swearing. [video]

Patrick Dempsey *Randy Bodek* • Kate Jackson *Diane Bodek* • Kirstie Alley *Joyce Palmer* • Carrie Fisher *Monica Delancy* • Robert Ginty *Joe Bodek* • Nancy Valen *Jenny Gordon* • Charles Hunter Walsh *Jory Talbot* • Barbara Carrera *Alex Barnett* ■ *Dir* Joan Micklin Silver • *Scr* Robin Schiff, Tom Ropelewski, Leslie Dixon, from a story by Robin Schiff

The Lovers! ★★★

Comedy 1972 · UK · Colour · 88mins

Lasting just 13 episodes on ITV in the early 1970s, this popular sitcom was another stepping stone in the careers of creator Jack Rosenthal and director Michael Apted. It didn't exactly harm the prospects of Richard Beckinsale or Paula Wilcox, either, as the couple who tiptoe towards commitment in spite of his passion for Manchester United and her refusal to entertain encounters with "Percy Filth". Hardly hilarious, but rather sweet. DP

Paula Wilcox *Beryl* • Richard Beckinsale *Geoffrey* • Joan Scott (1) *Beryl's mum* • Stella Moray *Geoffrey's mum* • Nikolas Simmonds *Roland* • Susan Littler *Sandra* • Anthony Naylor *Neville* • Bruce Watt *Jeremy* • John Comer *Geoffrey's dad* ■ *Dir* Herbert Wise • *Scr* Jack Rosenthal

Lovers ★★★ 18

Erotic thriller 1991 · Sp · Colour · 104mins

Victoria Abril won the Best Actress award at Berlin for her performance in this re-enactment of a true-life *crime passionnel*. Set in mid-1950s Madrid, the film concentrates on the romantic entanglements of soldier Jorge Sanz, who honours fiancée Maribel Verdú's virginity by satiating his lust with landlady Abril. The action is beautifully shot but it lacks the sense of smouldering passion that might precipitate murder. While Abril and Verdú are excellent, Sanz is unconvincing. DP. In Spanish with English subtitles. Contains violence, swearing and nudity. [video]

Victoria Abril *Luisa* • Jorge Sanz *Paco* • Maribel Verdú *Trini* • Enrique Cerro *Commandant* • Mabel Escano *Commandant's wife* ■ *Dir* Vicente Aranda • *Scr* Carlos Perez Merinero, Alvaro Del Amo, Vicente Aranda • *Cinematographer* José Luis Alcaine

Lovers ★★★

Romantic drama 1999 · Fr · Colour · 100mins

The fifth film made under the auspices of Dogme 95, and the first to be directed by a non-Dane, Jean-Marc Barr's movie owes as much to the stylistic devices of the French New Wave as it does to Lars von Trier's much vaunted Vow of Chastity. However, such is Barr's preoccupation with achieving spontaneous video visuals that he neglects the dramatic aspects of his disjointed, episodic tale. Deciding to live outside the law in order to love freely, bookseller Elodie Bouchez and painter Sergej Trifunovic (an illegal exile from the former Yugoslavia) are credibly desperate. But the jarringly edited hand-held footage undermines their efforts. DP. In French with English subtitles.

Sergej Trifunovic *Dragan* • Elodie Bouchez *Jeanne* • Genevieve Page • Dragan Nikolic • Thibault de Montalembert ■ *Dir* Jean-Marc Barr • *Scr* Jean-Marc Barr, Pascal Arnold

Lovers and Other Strangers ★★★★ 15

Comedy 1970 · US · Colour · 104mins

This caustic and very funny wedding comedy shows what happens to a couple's extended family when they decide to get married. The cast contains so many exquisite performances that it seems invidious to single out anyone in particular. Gig Young, however, is simply terrific as the father of the bride (Bonnie Bedelia.) Director Cy Howard knows when to step back and let the excellent script speak for itself. Look out for Diane Keaton in her screen debut. TS [video]

Bonnie Bedelia *Susan Henderson* • Gig Young *Hal Henderson* • Michael Brandon *Mike Vecchio* • Beatrice Arthur *Bea Vecchio* • Richard Castellano *Frank Vecchio* • Robert Dishy [Bob Dishy] *Jerry* • Harry Guardino *Johnny* • Diane Keaton *Joan* ■ *Dir* Cy Howard • *Scr* Renee Taylor, Joseph Bologna, David Zelag Goodman, from a play by Renee Taylor, Joseph Bologna

The Lovers of the Arctic Circle ★★★★ 15

Romantic drama
1998 · Sp/Fr · Colour · 104mins

Basque director Julio Medem's metaphysical romance is one of his most inventive and accessible works to date. From the age of eight, Otto (Fele Martínez) and Ana (Najwa Nimri) know they are destined to be together. However, fate keeps intervening well into adulthood, forcing their on again/

off again relationship to weather their being apart for long stretches. Employing an unusual narrative technique that blurs both lovers' perspectives together, and a dazzling style that confuses time periods and repeats certain key scenes, this dreamy rumination on unrequited love, chance and coincidence is a wonderfully rich and potent fable for our times. AJ. In Spanish with English subtitles. DVD

Fele Martínez *Otto* • Najwa Nimri *Ana* • Nancho Novo *Alvaro* • Maru Valdivielso *Olga* ■ *Dir/Scr* Julio Medem

The Loves and Times of Scaramouche ★★

Swashbuckling comedy 1976 · It · Colour · 95mins

Italian director Enzo Girolami Castellari was one of the most under-rated makers of spaghetti westerns and he handles the battle sequences in this costume adventure with vigorous assurance. But he was not at his best with comedy and neither the slapstick swashbuckling nor the cod history merit more than the occasional wry smile. As the womanising scoundrel caught up in an assassination attempt on Napoleon, Michael Sarrazin hams it up shamelessly. DP. An Italian film dubbed into English.

Michael Sarrazin *Scaramouche* • Ursula Andress *Josephine* • Aldo Maccione *Napoleon* • Giancarlo Prete • Michael Forest • Nico Il Grande • Romano Puppo • Massimo Vanni • Alex Togni • Damir Mejovsek • Lucia De Oliveira ■ *Dir* Enzo G Castellari • *Scr* Enzo G Castellari, Tito Carpi

L

Love's Labour's Lost ★★★ U

Romantic musical comedy 1999 · US/Fr/UK · Colour · 89mins

Kenneth Branagh gives his Shakespearean adaptation a lift by combining this story of four sets of lovers with a host of 1930s and 40s song-and-dance numbers. Adrian Lester shines in a sublime musical set piece, and Natascha McElhone again demonstrates her depth and beauty. The film is flawed, though. The environment never transcends the feel of a studio, American stars Alicia Silverstone and Matthew Lillard are clumsy and miscast, and Branagh has lost some of the play's complexity by oversimplifying the text. LH DVD

Kenneth Branagh *Berowne* • Nathan Lane *Costard, the clown* • Adrian Lester *Dumaine* • Matthew Lillard *Longaville* • Natascha McElhone *Rosaline* • Alessandro Nivola *King* • Alicia Silverstone *Princess* • Timothy Spall *Don Armado* • Richard Briers *Nathaniel* • Richard Clifford *Boyet* • Carmen Ejogo *Maria* • Daniel Hill *Mercade* • Geraldine McEwan *Holofernia* • Emily Mortimer *Katherine* ■ *Dir* Kenneth Branagh • *Scr* Kenneth Branagh, from the play by William Shakespeare

The Loves of Carmen ★★★

Drama 1948 · US · Colour · 96mins

There's no Bizet here, and hardly much of author Prosper Mérimée's great original either, as the director and stars of the immortal drama *Gilda* reunite to tell another tale of *amour fou* beneath blazing skies. Sadly, it doesn't quite gel. Not only is there no darker underside, but the 1940s Technicolor casts a bizarre and garish glow over the proceedings. Glenn Ford is arguably the most unlikely Don Jose ever, but Hayworth looks ravishing. TS

Rita Hayworth *Carmen Garcia* • Glenn Ford *Don Jose* • Ron Randell *Andres* • Victor Jory *Garcia* • Luther Adler *Dancaire* • Arnold Moss *Colonel* • Joseph Buloff *Remendado* ■ *Dir* Charles Vidor • *Scr* Helen Deutsch, from the story *Carmen* by Prosper Mérimée

The Loves of Count Iorga, Vampire ★★★

Horror 1970 · US · Colour · 89mins

Robert Quarry entered the "Horror Hall of Fame" thanks to his convincing turn here as an amoral Californian bloodsucker in this low-budget gross-out, blending crude horror with macabre wit. Originally planning to make a sex film (hence the inclusion of numerous soft-core starlets as vampire brides in the cast), director Bob Kelljan saw the light when *Night of the Living Dead* mopped up at the box office. So in came the ashen-faced undead feasting on cat's intestines, plus other moments of shock sleaze. An even better sequel, *The Return of Count Iorga*, followed. DP

Robert Quarry *Count Iorga* • Roger Perry *Dr Hayes* • Michael Murphy *Paul* • Michael Macready *Michael* • Donna Anders *Donna* • Judy Lang [Judith Lang] *Erica* ■ *Dir/Scr* Bob Kelljan

The Loves of Joanna Godden ★★★

Drama 1947 · UK · BW · 89mins

A classic example of how the documentary-style story (so popular with postwar British film-makers) could result in pictures as crashingly dull as they were worthy. The story centres on Edwardian farmer Googie Withers, whose determination to make good as a sheep breeder and protect her spoiled sister (Jean Kent) forces her to discard a trio of eager beaus (John McCallum, Chips Rafferty and Derek Bond). There is plenty of incident, but the realism beloved of director Charles Frend is scarcely appropriate for such ripe melodrama. DP

Googie Withers *Joanna Godden* • Jean Kent *Ellen Godden* • John McCallum *Arthur Alce* • Derek Bond *Martin Trevor* • Henry Mollison *Harry Trevor* • Chips Rafferty *Collard* ■ *Dir* Charles Frend • *Scr* He Bates, Angus MacPhail, from the novel *Joanna Godden* by Sheila Kaye-Smith

The Loves of Three Queens ★★

Drama 1954 · It/Fr · Colour · 90mins

Having been frustrated by the cancellation of her comeback picture, *Queen Esther and the King of Egypt*, Hedy Lamarr signed up for this project for Marc Allégret. Originally intended to be a three-hour investigation into the mysteries of womanhood, the oft-altered screenplay had Lamarr question three male friends about which historical figure she should impersonate at a masquerade ball and then appear in vignettes prompted by their answers. Edgar G Ulmer shot some uncredited linking sequences and this was released to little acclaim. DP

Hedy Lamarr *Hedy Windsor/Helen of Troy/Empress Josephine/Geneviève de Brabant* • Gérard Oury *Napoleon Bonaparte* • Massimo Serato *Paris* • Robert Beatty *Menelaus* • Cathy O'Donnell *Oenone* • Guido Celano *Jupiter* • Rico Glori *Priamus* • Seren Michelotti *Cassandra* • Alba Arnova *Venus* ■ *Dir* Marc Allégret • *Scr* Nino Novarese, Marc Allégret, Salka Viertel, from a story by Aeneas MacKenzie, Vadim Plenianikov, Marc Allégret, Hugh Gray

Lovesick ★★★ 15

Romantic comedy 1983 · US · Colour · 91mins

Long-time Woody Allen collaborator Marshall Brickman made his second outing as writer/director with this droll comedy in which psychiatrist Dudley Moore falls helplessly in love with patient Elizabeth McGovern. The unlikely pairing works a treat thanks to the coy performances and several nifty one-liners. There are also some knowing cameos from Ron Silver, Wallace Shawn and legendary director John Huston. DP

Dudley Moore *Saul Benjamin* • Elizabeth McGovern *Chloe Allan* • Alec Guinness *Sigmund Freud* • Renee Taylor *Mrs Mondragon* • Ron Silver *Ted Caruso* • Gene Saks *Frantic patient* • Christine Baranski *Nymphomaniac* • David Strathairn *Zuckerman* ■ *Dir/Scr* Marshall Brickman

Lovespell ★

Drama 1979 · US · Colour · 91mins

Even die-hard Wagner fans will detest this incompetent retelling of the amorous tragedy of Tristan and Isolde. Richard Burton makes a splendid king, but Kate Mulgrew is rather too mature to play his Juliet-like bride. Filmed on lush Irish locations, the language is as parched as a desert, while Tom Donovan's direction is woefully lacking for a story that needs tender, loving care if audiences are to be convinced of its contemporary relevance. TH

Richard Burton *King Mark of Cornwall* • Kate Mulgrew *Iseult* • Nicholas Clay *Tristan* • Cyril Cusack • Geraldine Fitzgerald ■ *Dir* Tom Donovan • *Scr* Claire Labine

Lovin' Molly ★★

Drama 1974 · US · Colour · 97mins

A misfire from director Sidney Lumet who misjudges himself after his success with *Serpico*, as if he wanted to be known for more artier things than just New York crime movies. This sprawling yarn covers 40 years – from 1925 onwards – in the lives, loves and deaths of a Texan family. Based on Larry McMurtry's novel, it needed a far more melodramatic approach than Lumet's more cerebral style, and the running time is inadequate to cope with the soapy story. AT

Anthony Perkins *Gid* • Beau Bridges *Johnny* • Blythe Danner *Molly* • Edward Binns *Mr Fry* • Susan Sarandon *Sarah* • Conrad Fowkes *Eddie* ■ *Dir* Sidney Lumet • *Scr* Stephen J Friedman, from the novel *Leaving Cheyenne* by Larry McMurtry

Loving ★★★

Comedy drama 1970 · US · Colour · 89mins

It takes all George Segal's under-used skill to touch our sympathy here, playing a character who is well out of charm's way – an ageing commercial artist heading for mental and marital breakdown. As his emotionally devoted but drained wife, Eva Marie Saint is outstandingly forbearing, enough to make us wonder why she married him in the first place. But then again, there is a glimmer in Segal that explains it. TH. Contains swearing.

George Segal *Brooks Wilson* • Eva Marie Saint *Selma Wilson* • Sterling Hayden *Lepridon* • Keenan Wynn *Edward* • Nancie Phillips *Nelly* • Janis Young *Grace* • David Doyle *Will* • Paul Sparer *Marve* • Andrew Duncan *Willy* • Sherry Lansing *Susan* ■ *Dir* Irvin Kershner • *Scr* Don Devlin, from the novel *Brooks Wilson, Ltd* by JM Ryan

Loving Couples ★★

Romantic comedy 1980 · US · Colour · 97mins

Shirley MacLaine and James Coburn are the middle-aged married couple who spice up their relationship with a spot of partner-swapping with younger (and more glamorous) Susan Sarandon and Stephen Collins. While MacLaine enjoys the charms of her toyboy, Coburn looks extremely uncomfortable with a woman almost young enough to be his daughter on his arm. All the embarrassing May-September clichés are dredged up, and this never gets beyond the predictable. JB

Shirley MacLaine *Evelyn* • James Coburn *Walter* • Susan Sarandon *Stephanie* • Stephen Collins *Gregg* • Sally Kellerman *Mrs Liggett* • Nan Martin *Walter's nurse* ■ *Dir* Jack Smight • *Scr* Martin Donovan

Loving in the Rain ★★

Romantic drama 1974 · Fr · Colour · 90mins

Considering he had emerged as an actor during the auteur era and that this was the fourth of his six outings as a director, Jean-Claude Brialy invests surprisingly little personality in this understated melodrama. Experienced scenarist Jean-Claude Carrière co-wrote the script that makes only a cursory exploration of the emotions experienced by Romy Schneider and Bénédicte Boucher, as the mother and teenage daughter indulging in a holiday romance. It's a proficient job, but pretty pictures and steady performances don't make for enthralling cinema. DP. In French with English subtitles.

Romy Schneider *Elisabeth* • Nino Castelnuovo *Giovanni* • Suzanne Flon *Edith* • Bénédicte Boucher *Cecile* ■ *Dir* Jean-Claude Brialy • *Scr* Jean-Claude Brialy, Jean-Claude Carrière, from a story by Yves Simon

Loving You ★★★ U

Musical drama 1957 · US · Colour · 101mins

Elvis Presley's second movie (the first under famous producer Hal B Wallis) gives us a precious look at the King in his rock 'n' roll prime. The plot allows Presley to re-enact his rise to stardom, under the guidance here of director Hal Kanter, who studied Presley on stage beforehand for authenticity. Musical highlights include *Teddy Bear* and *Lonesome Cowboy* (the film's original title). Scorned in its day (but not by fans), this looks better by the decade, and Presley's natural screen presence reminds us of his considerable early raw talent. TS DVD

Elvis Presley *Deke Rivers* • Lizabeth Scott *Glenda Markle* • Wendell Corey *Tex Warner* • Dolores Hart *Susan Jessup* • James Gleason *Carl Meade* ■ *Dir* Hal Kanter • *Scr* Herbert Baker, Hal Kanter, from the story *A Call from Mitch Miller* by Mary Agnes Thompson

The Low Down ★★★ 18

Drama 2000 · UK · Colour · 95mins

This feature debut from writer/director Jamie Thraves has film-school experimentation written all over it, some of which works, some of which doesn't. Focusing on the excellent Aidan Gillen, one of a group of lost 20-something bohemian Londoners, the movie follows his burgeoning romance with Kate Ashfield, which parallels his journey out of a Peter Pan complex into adulthood. Honest, true and cinematographically original, this suffers from an all-too-familiar rites-of-passage plot with an overkill feel that's reminiscent of a Nick Hornby or Helen Fielding novel. LH DVD

Aidan Gillen *Frank* • Kate Ashfield *Ruby* • Dean Lennox Kelly *Mike* • Tobias Menzies *John* • Rupert Proctor *Terry* ■ *Dir/Scr* Jamie Thraves

A Low Down Dirty Shame ★★ 18

Action spoof 1994 · US · Colour · 100mins

After scoring several direct hits with his blaxploitation spoof, *I'm Gonna Git You Sucka*, Keenen Ivory Wayans shoots high and wide with this scattergun parody of *film noir* crime pictures. Clearly spreading himself too thin, Wayans seems to be the only performer with real faith in his script, which is woefully predictable and too often settles for the easy (and occasionally offensive) gag. His direction is equally sloppy. DP

Keenen Ivory Wayans *Andre Shame* • Charles S Dutton *Sonny Rothmiller* • Jada Pinkett [Jada Pinkett Smith] *Peaches Jordan* • Salli

Richardson *Angela Flowers* • Andrew Divoff *Ernesto Mendoza* • Corwin Hawkins *Wayman* • Gary Cervantes *Luis* • Gregory Sierra *Captain Nunez* • Kim Wayans *Diane* ■ *Dir/Scr* Keenen Ivory Wayans

The Low Life ★★

Comedy drama 1995 · US · Colour · 98mins

Excellent central performances from a first-rate young cast can't save this depressing character study. There's no life in this tale of wannabe writer Rory Cochrane coming to LA only to find himself stuck in low-paying temp jobs and lumbered with a girlfriend (Kyra Sedgwick) uninterested in serious commitment. Occasionally funny and touching, ultimately this takes too long in getting nowhere in particular. RS

Rory Cochrane *John* • Kyra Sedgwick *Bevin* • Ron Livingston *Chad* • Christian Meoli *Leonard* • Sara Melson *Suzie* • James LeGros *Mike Jr* • Sean Astin *Andrew* • JT Walsh *Mike Sr* • Renee Zellweger *Poet* ■ *Dir* George Hickenlooper • *Scr* George Hickenlooper, from the story by John Enbom

The Lower Depths ★★★

Drama 1936 · Fr · BW · 95mins

Having secured the dying Maxim Gorky's permission to rework parts of his celebrated socialist play, cinema's leading humanist, Jean Renoir, proceeded to produce his darkest film of the Popular Front period. Although there's a rapport between impoverished baron Louis Jouvet and petty thief Jean Gabin, the sense of community that existed in *Le Crime de Monsieur Lange* has been replaced by a survivalist individualism, as they seek to out-manoeuvre landlord Vladimir Sokoloff. As ever, Renoir's compositional flair is to the fore, with a strolling, deep-focus camera endlessly picking up significant expressions, gestures and details. DP. In French with English subtitles.

Jean Gabin *Pépel* • Louis Jouvet *The baron* • Suzy Prim *Vassilissa* • Jany Holt *Nastia* • Vladimir Sokoloff *Kostyley* • André Gabriello *Commisaire Toptun* ■ *Dir* Jean Renoir • *Scr* Eugène Zamiatine, Jacques Companeez, Jean Renoir, Charles Spaak, from the play *Na Dne* by Maxim Gorky

The Lower Depths ★★★★ PG

Period drama 1956 · Jpn · BW · 119mins

The longest and most intense version of Maxim Gorky's claustrophobic play about slum dwellers is here transposed by Akira Kurosawa from Moscow to Edo, towards the end of the Tokugawa period. The action is confined to just two sets and the magnificent ensemble playing (he rehearsed for six weeks before the quick shoot) creates an unsentimental portrait of transitory lives, without hope. The ending is abrupt, when during a boisterous drinking session an announcement is made about the suicide of one of the group. A close-up, characteristic of the film's style, and another man says, "A pity just when the party was getting started". BB. In Japanese with English subtitles. [VIDEO]

Toshiro Mifune *Sutekichi, the thief* • Isuzu Yamada *Osugi, the landlady* • Ganjiro Nakamura *Rokubei, her husband* • Kyoko Kagawa *Okayo, her sister* • Bokuzen Hidari *Kahei, the priest* ■ *Dir* Akira Kurosawa • *Scr* Shinobu Hashimoto, Akira Kurosawa, Hideo Oguni, from the play *Na Dne* by Maxim Gorky

The Loyal 47 Ronin ★★★★

Historical epic 1941 · Jpn · BW · 222mins

Threatened with closure by the government for its failure to produce enough National Policy pictures, the Shochiku studio was reprieved by Kenji Mizoguchi's offer to shoot the second part of this historical epic under its auspices. Set in the early 18th century, the action follows the revenge of Oishi and his fellow samurai on Kira, the evil warlord who had tricked their master into committing hara-kiri. Large scale historicals were not the director's forte, but he opened out this fact-based Kabuki standard to spectacular effect. DP. In Japanese with English subtitles.

Chojuro Kawarazaki *Kuranosuke Oishi* • Yoshisaburo Arashi *Takuminokami, Lord Asano* • Mantoyo Mimasu *Kozunosuke, Lord Kira* • Kanemon Nakamura *Sukeemon Tomimori* • Utaemon Ichikawa *Tsunatoyo Tokugawa* • Mitsuko Miura *Yosenin, Lady Asano* ■ *Dir* Kenji Mizoguchi • *Scr* Kenichiro Hara, Yoshikata Yoda, from the play by Seika Mayama, from a well-known story that took place in 1703

Lucas ★★★★ 15

Comedy drama 1986 · US · Colour · 95mins

Corey Haim gives an excellent performance in this sweet, simple and cliché-free study of first love. As the serious kid whom half the school wouldn't notice unless they tripped over him, he is witty and wise beyond his years, and his earnest conversations with heart's desire Kerri Green are small masterpieces of observation. But true love can never run smoothly, especially when there are sporty bozos like school football star Charlie Sheen bestriding the primrose path. Winona Ryder made her debut in this delightful comedy. DP. Contains swearing. [VIDEO] DVD

Corey Haim *Lucas Blye* • Kerri Green *Maggie* • Charlie Sheen *Cappie* • Courtney Thorne-Smith *Alise* • Winona Ryder *Rina* • Thomas E Hodges [Tom Hodges] *Bruno* • Ciro Poppiti *Ben* ■ *Dir/Scr* David Seltzer

Lucia ★★ 15

Opera drama 1998 · UK · Colour · 102mins

Drawing on the old "life imitating art" formula, Don Boyd uses scenes from the opera *Lucia di Lammermoor* to comment on the doomed romance between soprano Amanda Boyd and tenor Richard Coxon. The pair are to co-star in *Lucia* just as she enters into a loveless marriage (sanctioned by her impoverished brother) to a dissolute millionaire. Essentially this is a feature-length opera video, with stylised visuals that often distract from the determinedly contemporary arrangements. Stiffly acted and archly staged, yet filmed with imagination and passion, this has its rewards. DP

Amanda Boyd *Kate Ashton, "Lucia"* • Richard Coxon *Sam Ravenswood, "Edgardo"* • Ann Taylor *Alice, "Alisa"* • John Daszak *Norman, "Normanno"* • Andrew Greenan *Raymond, "Raimondo"* • John Osborn *Oliver Hickox, "Arturo"* • Mark Holland *Hamish Ashton, "Enrico"* • Mark Shanahan *Conductor, London Studio* ■ *Dir* Don Boyd • *Scr* Don Boyd, from the opera *Lucia Di Lammermoor* by Gaetano Donizetti, from the novel *The Bride of Lammermoor* by Sir Walter Scott

Lucie Aubrac ★★ 12

Wartime drama based on a true story
1997 · Fr · Colour · 111mins

Daniel Auteuil stars as a French resistance worker taken prisoner by the Gestapo, and Carole Bouquet is the devoted wife who risks all to save him. Surprisingly, considering cast calibre and intrinsic drama of storyline, the film is a dull and plodding affair, with director Claude Berri more concerned with sticking faithfully to facts rather than exploiting the story's full cinematic potential. DA. In French with English subtitles. [VIDEO] DVD

Carole Bouquet *Lucie Bernard* • Daniel Auteuil *Raymond Samuel* • Patrice Chéreau *Max* • Eric Boucher *Serge* • Jean-Roger Milo *Maurice* • Heino Ferch *Klaus Barbie* • Jean Martin *Paul Lardanchet* • Andrzej Seweryn *Lieutenant Schlöndorff* • Pascal Greggory *Hardy* ■ *Dir* Claude Berri • *Scr* Claude Berri, Arlette Langmann, from the novel *Outwitting the Gestapo (Ils Partiront dans l'Ivresse)* by Lucie Aubrac, Claude Berri

Lucifer Rising ★★★

Experimental movie
1981 · US · Colour · 29mins

Using rather startling free-association imagery, such as flying saucers hovering over the Temple of Luxor, this is one of the better Kenneth Anger "visual music" avant-garde movies (ie no plot or acting to speak of). Anger himself plays a Magus who invokes Lucifer, celebrating his rebirth with a birthday cake with Lucifer Mark VI written in pink icing. The eclectic cast includes Marianne Faithfull, director Donald Cammell, and Leslie Huggins, a hunky young Middlesbrough steel worker. An earlier version of the film, shot in 1966, was stolen and buried in the Mojave desert by the musician Bobby Beausoleil, currently serving a life sentence for murder. RB

Miriam Gibril *Isis* • Donald Cammell *Osiris* • Haydn Couts *The Adept* • Kenneth Anger *The Magus* • Sir Francis Rose *Chaos* • Marianne Faithfull *Lilith* • Leslie Huggins *Lucifer* ■ *Dir* Kenneth Anger • *Scr* Kenneth Anger, from the poem *Hymn to Lucifer* by Aleister Crowley

The Luck of Ginger Coffey ★★★

Drama 1964 · US/Can · BW · 99mins

Robert Shaw and Mary Ure star as Irish immigrants in freezing Montreal, coping with his unemployment, their separation and their daughter's decision to live with her father. A slight story but an affecting one, due to the wealth of everyday detail created by writer Brian Moore and director Irvin Kershner. Shaw and Ure, a tempestuous married couple off-screen, give a satisfying portrayal of a love that somehow endures. AT

Robert Shaw *Ginger Coffey* • Mary Ure *Vera* • Liam Redmond *MacGregor* • Tom Harvey *Joe McGlade* • Libby McClintock *Paulie* • Leo Leyden *Brott* ■ *Dir* Irvin Kershner • *Scr* Brian Moore, from his novel

Luck of the Draw ★★

Action crime drama
2000 · US · Colour · 108mins

This crime thriller opens promisingly, with a rattling gunfight involving rival French and American mobsters and a gang of corrupt cops. But, as James Marshall's ex-con witness makes off with the counterfeit $100 plates that the gangs are squabbling over, director Luca Bercovici fails to spot the obvious fact that his hero is incapable of holding the viewer's attention against the scene-chewing abilities of Dennis Hopper, Eric Roberts and Michael Madsen. Add to that the lack of novelty in plot and style, and the tale soon becomes humdrum. DP

Dennis Hopper *Gianni Ponti* • William Forsythe *Max Fenton* • James Marshall *Jack Sweeney* • Michael Madsen *Zippo* • Ice-T *Macneilly* • Eric Roberts *Carlo* • Frank Gorshin *Sterling Johnson* ■ *Dir* Luca Bercovici • *Scr* Namon Ami, Rick Joe Bloggs [Rick Bloggs], Kandice King

Luck, Trust & Ketchup: Robert Altman in Carver ★★★ 15

Documentary 1994 · US · Colour · 89mins

Try to excuse the lousy title, for this is a highly entertaining and informative documentary about director Robert Altman, his films and his methods. Recorded during the making of *Short Cuts*, it has a day-in-the-life feel that makes it an ideal companion piece to that film, but there are also dozens of little insights that have a bearing on Altman's entire output. Co-directed by longtime colleague Mike Kaplan, this little-seen feature also contains interviews with the principal members of the *Short Cuts* cast, not all of whom present themselves in the most favourable light. DP. Contains some swearing. [VIDEO]

Dir Mike Kaplan, John Dorr

The Luckiest Man in the World ★★

Comedy 1989 · US · Colour · 82mins

Unassuming but nicely played drama about a businessman discovering a conscience after a near death experience. Philip Bosco delivers a believable performance as the middle-aged man out to make up for past mistakes and he is ably supported by a largely unknown cast. JF

Philip Bosco *Sam Posner* • Doris Belack *Mrs Posner* • Joanne Camp *Laura* • Matthew Gottlieb *Sheldon* • Arthur French *Cleveland* • Stan Lachow *Schwartz* • Moses Gunn *The Voice* ■ *Dir/Scr* Frank D Gilroy

Lucky and Zorba ★★★★

Animation 1998 · It · Colour · 75mins

This charming animation is not only uplifting in its simple message of acceptance and co-operation, but also refreshingly free of the lazy sentimentality that characterises so much commercial cartooning. The most expensive animated film ever made in Italy, Enzo D'Alo's feature chronicles the friendship between an orphan seagull named Lucky and Zorba, the cat who teaches her to fly. Beautifully drawn and touchingly entertaining, this is a delight. DP. Italian dialogue dubbed into English.

Dir Enzo D'Alo • *Scr* Enzo D'Alo, Umberto Marino, from the story *Story of a Seagull and the Cat Who Taught Her to Fly* by Luis Sepulveda

L

Lucky Break ★★★★ 12

Crime comedy
2001 · UK/Ger/US · Colour · 103mins

It took director Peter Cattaneo four years to follow up *The Full Monty*, and he has chosen his next project wisely. On the surface, this brilliantly cast prison comedy has much in common with the Sheffield strippers – a group of men bonding through showbiz (here, they stage a prison musical as cover for an escape) – but this is more of a character study than a social satire. Although the idea of the climactic amateur show acts as a magnet for great farce moments, it's the more subtle relationships between the cons that give the film its depth. AC. Contains swearing. [VIDEO] DVD

James Nesbitt *Jimmy Hands* • Olivia Williams *Annabel Sweep* • Timothy Spall *Cliff Gumbell* • Bill Nighy *Roger Chamberlain* • Lennie James *Rudy Guscott* • Ron Cook *Perry* • Christopher Plummer *Governor Graham Mortimer* ■ *Dir* Peter Cattaneo • *Scr* Ronan Bennett

Lucky Devils ★★★

Action adventure 1933 · US · BW · 64mins

Based on a story by stuntman Bob Rose, who also appears in the film, this is just an excuse for stuntmen William Boyd (later Hopalong Cassidy) and William Gargan to go through their paces. Boyd also gets the girl in the person of Dorothy Wilson. Among the cast is Lon Chaney Jr, credited under his real name of Creighton Chaney. The highlights of the movie are the spectacular stunts, including a climactic ride over a waterfall. RB

Bill Boyd [William Boyd (1)] *Skipper* • William Gargan *Bob* • Bruce Cabot *Happy* • William Bakewell *Slugger* • Creighton Chaney [Lon Chaney Jr] *Frankie* • Bob Rose *Rusty* • Dorothy Wilson *Fran* • Sylvia Picker *Toots* ■ *Dir* Ralph Ince • *Scr* Ben Markson, Agnes Christine Johnston, from a story by Casey Robinson, Bob Rose

Lucky Jim ★★★★ U

Comedy 1957 · UK · BW · 91mins

Kingsley Amis's comic masterpiece was one of the most influential English novels of the 1950s. The Boulting brothers' film adaptation misses some of the subtle nuances, barbed satire and deliciously sly characterisation of the book, but you will find that this still makes for very agreeable entertainment. Ian Carmichael gives a good account of himself as Jim Dixon, the disaster-prone lecturer whose career in the red-bricked halls of academe gets off to the worst possible start, while those masters of comic support Hugh Griffith and Terry-Thomas are bang on form. DP DVD

Ian Carmichael *Jim Dixon* • Terry-Thomas *Bertrand Welch* • Hugh Griffith *Professor Welch* • Sharon Acker *Christine Callaghan* • Jean Anderson *Mrs Welch* • Maureen Connell *Margaret Peel* • Clive Morton *Sir Hector Gore-Urquhart* ■ *Dir* John Boulting • *Scr* Jeffrey Dell, Patrick Campbell, from the novel by Kingsley Amis

The Lucky Lady ★★

Silent romantic comedy
1926 · US · BW · 62mins

A silent movie, directed by the admirable Raoul Walsh early in his career, in which young princess Greta Nissen sneaks out of her convent school to see a travelling theatre show. There she meets youthful American William Collier Jr and falls in love with him. This doesn't go down well at the palace where they have lined up lecherous Lionel Barrymore as her future husband. Set in the fictional principality of San Guido, this romantic comedy has a certain charm, but it's well past its sell-by date for all but silent movie devotees. RK

Greta Nissen *Antoinette* • Lionel Barrymore *Count Ferranzo* • William Collier Jr *Clarke* • Marc MacDermott *Franz Garletz* ■ *Dir* Raoul Walsh • *Scr* James T O'Donohoe, Robert Emmet Sherwood [Robert E Sherwood], from a story by Bertram Bloch • *Cinematographer* Victor Milner

Lucky Lady ★

Comedy 1975 · US · Colour · 118mins

Gene Hackman and Liza Minnelli were both recent Oscar-winners, and Burt Reynolds was at the peak of his stardom. Yet audiences somehow sensed *Lucky Lady* was a stinker and stayed away in droves. The romantic rivalry between the two leading men is negligible, while Minnelli never seems comfortable in her role as the nightclub singer they fall for. The plot, meanwhile – which has Hackman and Reynolds trying to smuggle bootleg liquor across the Mexican border – sinks like a stone. AT

Gene Hackman *Kibby* • Liza Minnelli *Claire* • Burt Reynolds *Walker* • Geoffrey Lewis *Captain Aaron Mosley* • John Hillerman *Christy McTeague* • Robby Benson *Billy Webber* • Michael Hordern *Captain Rockwell* • Anthony Holland *Mr Tully* ■ *Dir* Stanley Donen • *Scr* Willard Huyck, Gloria Katz

Lucky Luciano ★★★★ 18

Biographical crime drama
1973 · Fr/It · Colour · 105mins

Francesco Rosi's sociological melodrama, set in America and Italy, reveals the criminal network – both legal and illegal – for which Lucky Luciano was the crime kingpin. While Rod Steiger was the leading gangster in *Al Capone* (1959), here it's Gian Maria Volonté. This is more complex than a simple dirty-rat-tat-tat view of the world, and Volonte is excellent, but Steiger's hard-man performance upstages all the political nuances by sheer power. TH DVD

Gian Maria Volonté *Lucky Luciano* • Rod Steiger *Gene Giannini* • Charles Siragusa • Vincent Gardenia *American colonel* ■ *Dir* Francesco Rosi • *Scr* Francesco Rosi, Tonino Guerra

Lucky Me ★★ U

Comedy musical 1954 · US · Colour · 96mins

Doris Day sings as delightfully as ever and acts with gusto, but this musical about showbusiness hopefuls – her penultimate film under her contract at Warner Bros – is substandard. Talents such as Phil Silvers, Nancy Walker and Eddie Foy are wasted, and Day is saddled with an inappropriate leading man in Robert Cummings. The songs, by the *Calamity Jane* team of Sammy Fain and Paul Francis Webster, also disappoint. Angie Dickinson can be spotted making her screen debut as a guest in a party scene near the film's end. TV DVD

Doris Day *Candy Williams* • Robert Cummings *Dick Carson* • Phil Silvers *Hap Snyder* • Eddie Foy Jr *Duke McGee* • Nancy Walker *Flo Neely* • Martha Hyer *Lorraine Thayer* • Bill Goodwin *Otis Thayer* • Marcel Dalio *Anton* • Hayden Rorke *Tommy Arthur* • Angie Dickinson *Party guest* ■ *Dir* Jack Donohue • *Scr* James O'Hanlon, Robert O'Brien, Irving Elinson, from a story by James O'Hanlon

Lucky Partners ★★★ U

Comedy 1940 · US · BW · 99mins

This frothy comedy is somewhat let down by the uncomfortable pairing of its two leads. Perky Ginger Rogers, then under contract to RKO and at her professional peak, and urbane Ronald Colman fail to spark in an American remake of Sacha Guitry's 1935 French film *Bonne Chance*. The romance seems too lightweight for Colman, under Lewis Milestone's experienced, if slightly heavy-handed, direction. Still, fans of the two great stars won't want to miss this. TS

Ginger Rogers *Jean Newton* • Ronald Colman *David Grant* • Jack Carson *Freddie* • Spring Byington *Aunt* • Cecilia Loftus *Mrs Sylvester* • Harry Davenport *Judge* • Billy Gilbert *Charles* ■ *Dir* Lewis Milestone • *Scr* Allan Scott, John Van Druten, from the film *Bonne Chance* by Sacha Guitry

The Lucky Star ★★★

Second World War drama
1980 · Can · Colour · 110mins

A Texan twist on the idea of Nazi occupation makes this Canadian family adventure original, to say the least. A young Dutch Jew (Brett Marx), fascinated by westerns, sees his parents taken away by the Germans. So he sets about kidnapping the colonel (Rod Steiger) he holds responsible. Directed by Max Fischer from a script he co-wrote with TV playwright Jack Rosenthal, it manages to say something imaginative about this emotive period of history. TH

Rod Steiger *Col Gluck* • Louise Fletcher *Loes Bakker* • Lou Jacobi *Elia Goldberg* • Brett Marx *David Goldberg* • Helen Hughes *Rose Goldberg* ■ *Dir* Max Fischer • *Scr* Max Fischer, Jack Rosenthal, from an idea by Roland Topor

The Lucky Stiff ★★

Comedy drama 1949 · US · BW · 99mins

Jack Benny produced this undistinguished comedy/whodunnit, but decided against appearing in it, just as top director Leo McCarey thought about taking it on and then didn't. Leading lady Dorothy Lamour, on loan from Paramount, ended up co-starring with character actor Brian Donlevy under the direction of writer Lewis R Foster. Lamour is too pallid for her part of a shady nightclub singer. Donlevy pursues a gang of protection racketeers, while Claire Trevor does all the scene stealing as his long-suffering secretary. Jack Benny never produced another picture. AE

Dorothy Lamour *Anna St Claire* • Brian Donlevy *John J Malone* • Claire Trevor *Marguerite Seaton* • Irene Hervey *Mrs Childers* • Marjorie Rambeau *Hattie Hatfield* • Robert Armstrong *Von Flanagan* • Billy Vine *Joe Di Angelo* • Warner Anderson *Eddie Britt* ■ *Dir* Lewis R Foster • *Scr* Lewis R Foster, from the novel by Craig Rice

The Lucky Texan ★★ U

Western 1934 · US · BW · 54mins

One of those irritating programme fillers that mixes contemporary icons – in this case a model "T" Ford in a chase sequence – with traditional western elements. The clean-cut John Wayne provides the heroism, and Lloyd Whitlock and stuntman Yakima Canutt the villainy. But really, unless these minor movies are your cup of tea, it's not very good. TS DVD

John Wayne *Jerry Mason* • Barbara Sheldon *Betty* • George Hayes [George "Gabby" Hayes] *Jake Benson* • Yakima Canutt *Cole* • Gordon DeMaine *Sheriff* ■ *Dir/Scr* Robert N Bradbury

Lucky to Be a Woman ★★★

Comedy drama 1955 · It · BW · 95mins

Marcello Mastroianni and Sophia Loren team up for what is, in many ways, a dry run for *La Dolce Vita*. Oozing languid charm, Mastroianni revels in the anti-heroic antics of the scurrilous paparazzo whose cheeky snap of Loren's legs persuades lecherous aristocrat Charles Boyer to transform her into a movie star. Strewn with in-jokes and satirical pot-shots at the supposedly sophisticated worlds of film and high fashion, this polished comedy is as artificial as its target. But the smooth direction and the accomplished performances give it an easy charm. DP. An Italian language film.

Sophia Loren *Antoinette* • Charles Boyer *Count Gregorio* • Marcello Mastroianni *Corrado* • Nino Besozzi *Film producer* ■ *Dir* Alessandro Blasetti • *Scr* Suso Cecchi D'Amico, Ennio Flaiano, Alessandro Continenza, Alessandro Blasetti

Lucy Gallant ★★★ U

Drama 1955 · US · Colour · 104mins

Dressmaker Jane Wyman devotes herself to work and becomes a successful female fashion-house mogul, but the price of her independence is a rocky ride in her love life. Charlton Heston is the man involved in this particular battle of the sexes. The supporting cast includes Thelma Ritter and Claire Trevor (both irresistible) and a rare on-screen appearance from Edith Head, winner of eight Oscars, who also designed the costumes. Haute couture, VistaVision and deft direction by Robert Parrish contribute to the enjoyment of this typical 1950s "woman's picture". RK

Jane Wyman *Lucy Gallant* • Charlton Heston *Casey Cole* • Claire Trevor *Lady MacBeth* • Thelma Ritter *Molly Basserman* • William Demarest *Charles Madden* • Wallace Ford *Gus Basserman* • Tom Helmore *Jim Wardman* • Gloria Talbott *Laura Wilson* • Edith Head ■ *Dir* Robert Parrish • *Scr* John Lee Mahin, Winston Miller, from the novel *The Life of Lucy Gallant* by Margaret Cousins

Ludwig ★★

Historical drama
1973 · It/W Ger/Fr · Colour · 136mins

This is director Luchino Visconti's study of mad King Ludwig of Bavaria, whose obsession with Wagner's music inspired him to build a series of fairy-tale castles and lose what was already a tenuous hold on sanity before his operatic death by drowning. In the title role, Helmut Berger looks the part – pouting, wild and very pretty – and the castles themselves are stunning backdrops. Trevor Howard makes an honourable stab at Wagner and Romy Schneider is simply gorgeous as Ludwig's unhappy bride Empress Elizabeth. But Visconti's approach is rather too solemn, and the movie drags. AT. An Italian language film.

Helmut Berger *Ludwig* • Romy Schneider *Empress Elisabetta* • Trevor Howard *Richard Wagner* • Silvana Mangano *Cosima Von Bulow* • Gert Fröbe *Father Hoffman* • Helmut Griem *Captain Durckeim* • Isabella Telezynska *Queen Mother* • Umberto Orsini *Count Von Holstein* ■ *Dir* Luchino Visconti • *Scr* Luchino Visconti, Enrico Medioli, Suso Cecchi D'Amico

Ludwig – Requiem for a Virgin King ★★★

Historical drama
1972 · W Ger · Colour · 139mins

The inner and outer life, real and imagined, of the mad castle-building King of Bavaria is told in 28 chapters, or tableaux vivants. Cheaply made, and using a blend of theatrical techniques such as backdrops and back projections, Hans Jürgen Syberberg's collage of German history, culture and psychology – at different moments puerile, fatuous, stimulating, amusing and over-extended – says far more about Ludwig than Luchino Visconti's glossy film on the same subject. RB. In German with English subtitles.

Harry Baer *Ludwig II of Bavaria* • Balthasar Thomas *Small Ludwig* • Peter Kern *Lackey Mayr/Hairdresser Hoppe/Röhm* • Oscar von Schab *Ludwig I/Karl May* ■ *Dir/Scr* Hans Jürgen Syberberg

Lullaby of Broadway ★★ U

Musical comedy 1951 · US · Colour · 88mins

Despite its promising title and the presence of Doris Day, this tailor-made vehicle is one of Warner Bros's least effective movies. Still, there are points in its favour: the songs though seriously underperformed and staged, are nevertheless memorable, and the amiable and talented Gene Nelson is an effective leading man. Warners veteran Gladys George brings all her experience to bear playing Day's wayward mum, and presumably taught Doris a trick or two about acting in the process, but, if ever a movie looked undirected, it's this one. TS

Doris Day *Melinda Howard* • Gene Nelson *Tom Farnham* • SZ Sakall *Adolph Hubbell* • Billy De Wolfe *"Lefty" Mack* • Gladys George *Jessica Howard* • Florence Bates *Mrs Hubbell* ■ *Dir* David Butler • *Scr* Earl Baldwin, from his story *My Irish Molly O*

Lulu Belle ★★★

Drama 1948 · US · BW · 86mins

This tougher than usual melodrama marked an attempt to change Dorothy Lamour's screen image. The amoral chanteuse she plays here is as far removed from the saronged lovelies of the *Road* series as it's possible to be. Unfortunately, such a character is hard to like, though today's more cynical audiences might be better disposed to Lulu's manner of dealing with anyone who gets in her way. Lamour's early career as a singer provides her with real insights into the role and she proves how good an actress she could be, but she's not helped by the bland performance of leading man George Montgomery and Leslie Fenton's routine direction. TS

Dorothy Lamour *Lulu Belle* • George Montgomery *George Davis* • Albert Dekker *Mark Brady* • Otto Kruger *Harry Randolph* • Glenda Farrell *Molly Benson* • Greg McClure *Butch Cooper* • Charlotte Wynters *Mrs Randolph* ■ *Dir* Leslie Fenton • *Scr* Everett Freeman, Karl Kamb, from the play by Charles MacArthur, Edward Sheldon

U = SUITABLE FOR ALL Uc = SUITABLE FOR ALL, ESPECIALLY FOR YOUNG CHILDREN (VIDEO ONLY) PG = PARENTAL GUIDANCE

Lulu on the Bridge ★

Romantic mystery drama
1998 · US · Colour · 103mins

What begins promisingly – Harvey Keitel is a musician starting over after a shooting ends his career – quickly takes a turn for the bizarre. He finds a mysterious glowing stone, which not only leads him to aspiring actress Mira Sorvino but also causes them to fall in love. A first-rate cast is wasted in this esoteric and monotonous film. A twist ending doesn't help clear up any of the confusion, it just makes you happy that the movie is over. ST

Harvey Keitel *Izzy Maurer* • Mira Sorvino *Celia Bums* • Willem Dafoe *Dr Van Horn* • Gina Gershon *Hannah* • Mandy Patinkin *Philip Kleinman* • Vanessa Redgrave *Catherine Moore* ■ *Dir/Scr* Paul Auster

Lumière Noire ★★★

Crime thriller 1994 · Fr · Colour · 107mins

Best known for *Sarraounia*, his portrait of the 19th-century African warrior queen, the Mauritanian director Med Hondo is one of the most politically contentious and courageous of black African film-makers. This conspiracy thriller is something of a disappointment, therefore, with its theme of asylum-seeking and deportation shunted into a subplot. However, Hondo sustains the tension admirably, as French hologram engineer Patrick Poivey seeks the illegal immigrant from Mali whose eyewitness testimony alone can prove that the state has blood on its hands. DP. In French with English subtitles.

Patrick Poivey *Yves Guyot* • Ines Demedeiros *Ghislaine Guyot* • Charlie Bauer *Detective Londrin* • Gilles Ségal *Inspector Cadin* • Roland Bertin *Judge Berthier* ■ *Dir* Med Hondo • *Scr* Med Hondo, Didier Daeninckx, from the novel by Didier Daeninckx

La Luna ★★★

Drama 1979 · It · Colour · 141mins

This deliberately artificial tale of an opera diva, her heroin-addicted son, their almost incestuous relationship and his search for a father figure caused quite a stir on its release. In the role of the diva, Jill Clayburgh seems to be mimicking Kiri Te Kanawa as she sings her way through the Verdi back catalogue. Sadly, the other performances are wooden. The real star of Bernardo Bertolucci's film is Vittorio Storaro's exquisite photography. AT

Jill Clayburgh *Caterina Silveri* • Matthew Barry *Joe* • Laura Betti *Ludovica* • Fred Gwynne *Douglas Winter* • Veronica Lazar *Marina* • Renato Salvatori *Communist* • Tomas Milian *Giuseppe* • Alida Valli *Giuseppe's mother* • Roberto Benigni *Upholsterer* ■ *Dir* Bernardo Bertolucci • *Scr* Bernardo Bertolucci, Giuseppe Bertolucci, Clare Peploe, George Malko, from a story by Franco Arcalli, Bernardo Bertolucci, Giuseppe Bertolucci • *Music* Ennio Morricone

The Lunatic ★★ 15

Comedy 1992 · US · Colour · 94mins

Lol Creme, founder member of the pop group 10CC and renowned rock video director, makes his feature debut with this genial oddity which boasts a low-key quirky charm. Paul Campbell is the resident idiot of a Jamaican village who has a fling with insatiable German tourist Julie T Wallace. But it's when she also starts having an affair with Rastafarian butcher Carl Bradshaw that the romantic complications begin, especially once he sucks them both into burgling a white landowner. A film of minor appeal, but reasonably beguiling all the same. AJ [video]

Julie T Wallace *Inga* • Paul Campbell *Aloysius* • Reggie Carter *Busha/Voice of Strongheart Tree* • Carl Bradshaw *Service* • Winston Stona *Linstrom* • Linda Gambrill *Sarah* • Rosemary Murray *Widow Dawkins* • Lloyd Reckord *Judge* ■ *Dir* Lol Creme • *Scr* Anthony C Winkler, from his novel

Lunatics: a Love Story ★★★ 15

Black comedy romance
1991 · US · Colour · 83mins

In this bizarre comedy about the relationship between a mismatched pair of kooks, Ted Raimi (Sam's brother) plays Hank, whose psychological problems include hallucinations about doctors trying to "treat" him with outsize needles, and an inability to leave his tin-foil lined apartment. The object of his affections is Deborah Foreman, who is convinced that she causes mayhem for anyone who comes into contact with her. Eccentric and surprisingly charming, the film puts a comedic rather than horrific spin on Raimi's visions. DA [video]

Ted Raimi *Hank* • Deborah Foreman *Nancy* • Bruce Campbell *Ray* • George Aguilar *Comet* • Brian McCree *Presto* ■ *Dir/Scr* Josh Becker

Lunch Hour ★★

Comedy 1962 · UK · BW · 73mins

A well constructed but predictable bedroom farce adapted from his own play by John Mortimer. Tired of being interrupted during their midday trysts, wallpaper executive Robert Stephens and designer Shirley Anne Field book a hotel room, but then their problems really start. Directed at a fair lick by James Hill, this lively romp is admirably played, with Kay Walsh and Nigel Davenport's supporting turns particularly worthy of note, but there's often an excess of chat between the excruciating moments. DP

Shirley Anne Field *Girl* • Robert Stephens *Man* • Kay Walsh *Manageress* • Hazel Hughes *Aunty* • Michael Robbins *Harris* • Nigel Davenport *Manager* ■ *Dir* James Hill • *Scr* John Mortimer, from his play

Lunch on the Grass ★★★

Romantic drama 1959 · Fr · Colour · 92mins

Jean Renoir, then 65, took 21 days to shoot this late work at Les Collettes, the house of his father Auguste, in the south of France. This hymn to nature is the great film director's only direct homage to his great Impressionist painter parent. Paul Meurisse is amusing as a supercilious biology professor experimenting with artificial insemination until he gets a beautiful peasant pregnant by conventional means. The rather reactionary satire also takes a dig at nuclear weapons, space travel and a united Europe, but delivers its message simplistically. RB. In French with English subtitles.

Paul Meurisse *Etienne* • Catherine Rouvel *Nenette* • Fernand Sardou *Nino* • Jacqueline Morane *Titine* • Jean-Pierre Granval *Ritou* ■ *Dir/Scr* Jean Renoir

Lured ★★

Crime drama 1947 · US · BW · 102mins

A preposterous and bizarrely cast would-be thriller that, alas, is over-plotted beyond redemption. It's not helped by director Douglas Sirk's ham-fisted direction of his players, particularly Cedric Hardwicke. The incredible story involves showgirl Lucille Ball being used by Scotland Yard to trap a killer in a London seemingly made up of left-over Hollywood sets. Along the way Ball falls for suspect George Sanders. Neither camp nor self-knowingly funny, it gets by as a genuine oddity. TS

George Sanders *Robert Fleming* • Lucille Ball *Sandra Carpenter* • Charles Coburn *Inspector Temple* • Boris Karloff *Artist* • Alan Mowbray *Maxwell* • Cedric Hardwicke *Julian Wilde* • George Zucco *Officer Barrett* ■ *Dir* Douglas Sirk • *Scr* Leo Rosten, from the 1939 film *Pièges* by Jacques Companeez, Ernest Neuville, Simon Gantillon

Lured Innocence ★★

Thriller 1999 · US · Colour · 99mins

Marley Shelton valiantly attempts to smoulder as the southern small-town temptress who seeks to exploit both the ailing Talia Shire (delicately distressed) and her frustrated husband Dennis Hopper (gleefully *Grand Guignol*) in their mutual murder plans. But the weakest link is Devon Gummersall who plays the reporter returning to his home town to try to save his erstwhile sweetheart in some of the most tension-free courtroom scenes you'll ever see. DP

Dennis Hopper *Rick Chambers* • Marley Shelton *Elsie Townsend* • Devon Gummersall *Elden Tolbert* • Talia Shire *Marsha Chambers* • Cheri Oteri *Molly* • John M Sullivan II *Bill Beckman* ■ *Dir/Scr* Kikuo Kawasaki

Lush Life ★★★ 15

Drama 1993 · US · Colour · 105mins

Forest Whitaker stars in this well-above-average TV movie. Jeff Goldblum co-stars as his sax-playing partner, living life to the full around the smoky clubs of New York, until Whitaker is diagnosed as having a brain tumour. But if you've gotta go, then what better way than with the mother of all jazz gigs. A little melancholic in places, but the stars make a fine team and Lennie Niehaus's music will keep your toes tapping. DP. Contains swearing, sex scenes and drug abuse. [video] DVD

Jeff Goldblum *Al Gorky* • Forest Whitaker *Buddy Chester* • Kathy Baker *Janice Gorky* • Tracey Needham *Sarah* • Lois Chiles *Lucy* • Don Cheadle *Jack* ■ *Dir/Scr* Michael Elias

Lust for a Vampire ★★ 18

Gothic horror 1970 · UK · Colour · 91mins

Hammer veteran Jimmy Sangster called it "an embarrassment" in his autobiography, and Ralph Bates regretted ever starring in something so "tasteless". This is the second of Hammer's Karnstein trilogy (which began with *The Vampire Lovers*) inspired by Sheridan Le Fanu's story *Carmilla*, with gratuitous lesbianism thrown in. A shallow performance by Yutte Stensgaard and some pretty ragged sets fix the lurid tone even lower as terror stalks the corridors of an exclusive girls' finishing school. *Twins of Evil* completed the trilogy in 1971. AJ. Contains nudity. [video] DVD

Ralph Bates *Giles Barton* • Yutte Stensgaard *Mircalla/Carmilla* • Barbara Jefford *Countess Herritzen* • Suzanna Leigh *Janet Playfair* • Michael Johnson *Richard Lestrange* ■ *Dir* Jimmy Sangster • *Scr* Tudor Gates, from the story *Carmilla* by J Sheridan Le Fanu

Lust for Life ★★★★ PG

Biographical drama
1956 · US · Colour · 117mins

This tortuous tale of Vincent van Gogh is a superior example of the Hollywood biopic. The painter is uncannily well played by Kirk Douglas, who seems to capture the very essence of the tormented artist, though it was actually Anthony Quinn's Gauguin that won the Oscar. It's lovingly crafted by brilliant director Vincente Minnelli, the superb colour and CinemaScope cinematography is by the great Freddie Young, while the authentic Arles location and a fine Miklos Rozsa score are also major plus points. This intelligent, beautifully made film was never a commercial success, but it acquired a cult following. TS [video]

Kirk Douglas *Vincent van Gogh* • Anthony Quinn *Paul Gauguin* • James Donald *Theo van Gogh* • Pamela Brown *Christine* • Everett Sloane *Dr Gachet* • Niall MacGinnis *Roulin* • Noel Purcell *Anton Mauve* • Henry Daniell *Theodorus van Gogh* • Madge Kennedy *Anna Cornelia van Gogh* • Jill Bennett *Willemien* ■ *Dir* Vincente Minnelli • *Scr* Norman Corwin, from the novel by Irving Stone

Lust in the Dust ★★ 15

Comedy western 1984 · US · Colour · 80mins

Considering this lame parody of vintage American and spaghetti westerns was directed by *Eating Raoul* director Paul Bartel and features a fabulous cult cast, the end result should have been much wilder and funnier than it actually is. Greedy gunslinger Tab Hunter, fiery cantina owner Lainie Kazan, saloon singer Divine and desperado Geoffrey Lewis team up to search for gold. A lifeless and lewd lampoon. AJ [video]

Tab Hunter *Abel Wood* • Divine *Rosie Velez* • Lainie Kazan *Marguerita Ventura* • Geoffrey Lewis *Hard Case Williams* • Henry Silva *Bernardo* • Cesar Romero *Father Garcia* • Woody Strode *Blackman* ■ *Dir* Paul Bartel • *Scr* Philip John Taylor

Lust of the Vampire ★★★★

Horror 1956 · It · BW · 65mins

Director Riccardo Freda fought with the producers of this seminal vampire chiller, walked out, and left ace cinematographer Mario Bava to complete the undead saga in two days. The stunning result set the seal on the future of Italian horror and prompted Hammer to mine the same Gothic vein in Britain. Beautiful "vampire" Gianna Maria Canale is kept artificially young by transfusions of blood from kidnapped girls in this haunting *Grand Guignol* tale of immortal obsession given the monstrously atmospheric spark of emotion by incredible black-and-white photography and amazing in-camera special effects. One of the most influential horror movies of all time. AJ. An Italian language film.

Gianna Maria Canale *Duchess Mararethe Du Grand* • Antoine Balpêtré *Professor Julien Du Grand* • Paul Muller *Joseph Signoret* ■ *Dir* Riccardo Freda • *Scr* Piero Regnoli, Rik Sjostrom • *Cinematographer* Mario Bava

The Lusty Men ★★★ U

Western 1952 · US · BW · 95mins

This touching, realistic drama stars Robert Mitchum as the former rodeo champ forced to retire through injury, and Arthur Kennedy as the young man whom Mitchum coaches. Of course, there's also a woman – Susan Hayward, who's married to Kennedy and takes Bob's fancy. Mitchum extended his range considerably with this role, and Lee Garmes's sombre black-and-white photography mirrors the characters' drab existence. A critical and box-office failure at the time, it is now regarded as one of director Nicholas Ray's finest films. AT

Susan Hayward *Louise Merritt* • Robert Mitchum *Jeff McCloud* • Arthur Kennedy *Wes Merritt* • Arthur Hunnicutt *Booker Davis* • Frank Faylen *Al Dawson* • Walter Coy *Buster Burgess* • Carol Nugent *Rusty Davis* • Maria Hart *Rosemary Maddox* ■ *Dir* Nicholas Ray • *Scr* Horace McCoy, David Dortort, from a story by Claude Stanush

Luther ★★★

Biographical drama
1974 · US/UK · Colour · 111mins

Playwright John Osborne's vivid portrayal of the religious revolutionary who famously broke with the Roman Catholic Church gets a rather lacklustre treatment here from director Guy Green, though Stacy Keach sweats a bundle as the cleric whose heavenly aspirations were always of the earthy variety. Osborne's deliberately matey dialogue is reduced to the level of tonsured chatter by a largely underused cast that includes Patrick

L

Magee and Hugh Griffith, although Judi Dench is a rose among all those thorny tenets of faith. TH

Stacy Keach *Martin Luther* • Patrick Magee *Hans* • Hugh Griffith *Tetzel* • Robert Stephens *Von Eck* • Alan Badel *Cajetan* • Judi Dench *Katherine* • Leonard Rossiter *Weinand* • Maurice Denham *Staupitz* • Julian Glover *The Knight* ■ *Dir* Guy Green • *Scr* Edward Anhalt, from the play by John Osborne

Luv ★

Sex comedy 1967 · US · Colour · 95mins

In this tasteless sex comedy, Jack Lemmon is saved from suicide by former schoolmate Peter Falk; he repays the favour by wooing and then wedding Falk's unwanted wife (Elaine May). After that, things get embarrassing for all concerned. This is an unmitigated disaster, not helped by the fact that Lemmon and Falk switched parts just days before shooting started. AT

Jack Lemmon *Harry Berlin* • Peter Falk *Milt Manville* • Elaine May *Ellen Manville* • Nina Wayne *Linda* • Eddie Mayehoff *Attorney Goodhart* ■ *Dir* Clive Donner • *Scr* Elliott Baker, from a play by Murray Schisgal

The Luzhin Defence ★★★ 12

Period romantic drama
2000 · UK/Fr/It/Hun/US · Colour · 104mins

Adapted from a story by Vladimir Nabokov, this is both an emotional drama and a psychological thriller. Can unworldly chess master John Turturro suppress the doubts caused by his parents' failed marriage and find love with socialite Emily Watson, while also breaking the ruinous hold exerted over him by former mentor Stuart Wilson? Director Marleen Gorris was drawn to the project by the prospect of analysing a man torn between two passions. But she has also succeeded in exploiting the romantic beauty of Lake Como in the 1920s to fashion a moving love story, well played by an impressive cast. DP DVD

John Turturro *Alexander Luzhin* • Emily Watson *Natalia* • Geraldine James *Vera* • Stuart Wilson (1) *Valentinov* • Christopher Thompson *Stassard* • Fabio Sartor *Turati* • Peter Blythe *Ilya* ■ *Dir* Marleen Gorris • *Scr* Peter Berry, from the novel by Vladimir Nabakov

M

Lydia ★★★ U

Romantic drama 1941 · US · BW · 94mins

Sumptuously mounted but leisurely paced, this is an unofficial Hollywood retread of the French classic *Un Carnet de Bal*, made by the same director, Julien Duvivier. Here he reworks and actively improves upon the original, working for the émigré Hungarian producer/director Alexander Korda, who provides Duvivier with a fine cast, headed by Merle Oberon (Mrs Korda), in the title role. Extravagantly romantic, and some would say overly sentimental, it nevertheless sustains a fine bittersweet tone. The marvellous score by the great Miklos Rozsa received an nomination. TS

Merle Oberon *Lydia MacMillan* • Edna May Oliver *Granny* • Alan Marshal *Richard Mason* • Joseph Cotten *Michael Fitzpatrick* • Hans Jaray *Frank Audry* • George Reeves *Bob Willard* • John Halliday *Fitzpatrick the Butler* ■ *Dir* Julien Duvivier • *Scr* Ben Hecht, Samuel Hoffenstein, from a story by Julien Duvivier, Laslo Bush-Fekete

Lydia Bailey ★★ U

Adventure 1952 · US · Colour · 87mins

Kenneth Roberts's epic novel, set during Haiti's war with Napoleonic forces in the 1880s, was so simplified for this screen version that the result seems like an empty, cut-price *Gone with the Wind*. The scenic splendours and Harry Jackson's gorgeous colour camerawork are the film's prime attractions. Veteran director Jean Negulesco handles the drama professionally enough, but this suffers from the underpowered casting and a shallow script. TV

Dale Robertson *Albion Hamlin* • Anne Francis *Lydia Bailey* • Charles Korvin *d'Autremont* • William Marshall (2) *King Dick* • Luis Van Rooten *General LeClerc* • Adeline De Walt Reynolds *Madame d'Autremont* • Angos Perez *Paul* • Bob Evans [Robert Evans] *Soldier* ■ *Dir* Jean Negulesco • *Scr* Michael Blankfort, Philip Dunne, from the novel by Kenneth Roberts

The Lyons in Paris ★★★ U

Comedy 1955 · UK · BW · 81mins

The popular radio series, *Life with the Lyons*, starring Ben Lyon, Bebe Daniels and their troublesome children, Barbara and Richard, produced two film spin-offs. This, the second, looks suspiciously like three radio episodes joined together. Bebe mistakenly thinks Ben has forgotten their wedding anniversary, but he's secretly been planning a trip to Paris (there are some genuine location shots); Ben and Richard are wooed by a naughty mademoiselle; Barbara falls in love with an existentialist (a bit of satire here). Director Val Guest maintains a brisk pace, and the Lyons are really rather endearing. DM DVD

Bebe Daniels *Bebe* • Ben Lyon *Ben* • Barbara Lyon *Barbara* • Richard Lyon *Richard* • Reginald Beckwith *Capt le Grand* • Martine Alexis *Fifi le Fleur* ■ *Dir* Val Guest • *Scr* Val Guest, from the radio series *Life with the Lyons* by Bebe Daniels, Bob Block, Bill Harding

M ★★★★★ PG

Classic crime drama
1931 · Ger · BW · 110mins

Peter Lorre is the most under-rated actor in the history of Hollywood. In his later years, he was content to parody the sinister snivelling that made him so compelling to watch. Here, the familiar persona has a real edge of menace, as he plays the self-loathing child murderer whose crimes are always preceded by a chilling whistle. Making his talkie debut, Fritz Lang continues to fill the screen with the atmospheric expressionist images that made him Europe's pre-eminent silent director, but his use of sound is also inspired, whether in crowd scenes or details like the clicking-open of Lorre's knife. A masterpiece. DP. In German with English subtitles. DVD

Peter Lorre *Franz Becker* • Otto Wernicke *Inspector Lohmann* • Gustaf Gründgens *Safebreaker* • Theo Lingen *Con man* • Inge Landgut *Child* • Ellen Widmann *Mother* • Fritz Odemar *Cheat* • Theodore Loos [Theodor Loos] *Groeber* ■ *Dir* Fritz Lang • *Scr* Thea von Harbou, Paul Falkenberg, Karl Vash, Adolf Jansen, from an article by Egon Jacobson

M ★★★

Crime drama 1951 · US · BW · 88mins

Independent producer Seymour Nebenzal was behind this Hollywood remake of his acclaimed 1931 German production. The idea of the underworld helping to catch a murderer of children doesn't ring true in a Los Angeles setting. Yet director Joseph Losey creates a visually powerful picture with some brilliantly chosen locations and effective use of music, while David Wayne comes close to matching Peter Lorre as the pathetic murderer. AE

David Wayne *Martin Harrow* • Howard Da Silva *Carney* • Luther Adler *Langley* • Martin Gabel *Marshall* • Steve Brodie *Lt Becker* • Raymond Burr *Pottsy* • Glenn Anders *Riggert* • Karen Morley *Mrs Coster* • Jim Backus *Mayor* ■ *Dir* Joseph Losey • *Scr* Norman Reilly Raine, Leo Katcher, Waldo Salt, from the 1931 film, from an article by Egon Jacobson

M Butterfly ★★ 15

Drama 1993 · US · Colour · 96mins

Director David Cronenberg came horribly unstuck with this insipid adaptation of David Henry Hwang's successful Broadway play about sexual deception and espionage. Jeremy Irons is a minor French diplomat in Beijing who falls under the spell of beautiful Chinese diva Song Liling. But not only is Song a spy, she's also a man! While it's obvious why Cronenberg would be attracted to such an operatic story of blurred identity, this should be filed under "interesting failure". AJ. Contains violence, swearing, sex scenes.

Jeremy Irons *René Gallimard* • John Lone *Song Liling* • Barbara Sukowa *Jeanne Gallimard* • Ian Richardson *Ambassador Toulon* • Annabel Leventon *Frau Baden* • Shizuko Hoshi *Comrade Chin* • Richard McMillan *Embassy colleague* • Vernon Dobtcheff *Agent Etancelin* ■ *Dir* David Cronenberg • *Scr* David Henry Hwan, from his play

MGM's Big Parade of Comedy ★★★ U

Comedy compilation 1964 · US · BW · 89mins

This patchy celebration of MGM's comic past is another of the compilation films assembled by producer Robert Youngson. There are a couple of funny episodes featuring Laurel and Hardy and Buster Keaton, but neither did their best work for the studio and we are forced to spend too long in the company of performers such as Wallace Beery and Marie Dressler, whose brand of humour is now very dated. The high points are provided by William Powell, Myrna Loy, Jean Harlow and Marion Davies, who was a much better actress than critics at the time gave her credit for. DP

Dir Robert Youngson

Ma and Pa Kettle ★★

Comedy 1949 · US · BW · 76mins

As the hillbilly couple of the 1947 hit comedy *The Egg and I*, Marjorie Main and Percy Kilbride scored so many laughs they were given a film of their own, which developed into a hugely successful annual series that ran until 1957. Here the Kettles, facing eviction from their ramshackle abode, win a futuristic new home in which to live with their 15 offspring. Their efforts to cope with its gadgets provide much of the slapstick humour. AE

Marjorie Main *Ma Kettle* • Percy Kilbride *Pa Kettle* • Richard Long *Tom Kettle* • Meg Randall *Kim Parker* • Patricia Alphin *Secretary* • Esther Dale *Mrs Birdie Hicks* • Barry Kelley *Mr Tomkins* • Harry Antrim *Mayor Swiggins* ■ *Dir* Charles Lamont • *Scr* Herbert Margolis, Louis Morheim, Al Lewis, from the characters created by Betty MacDonald

Ma Femme Est une Actrice ★★★ 15

Comedy 2001 · Fr · Colour · 91mins

Actor Yvan Attal makes his feature debut as director with this attractive French comedy that he also wrote and co-stars in. Attal's off-screen wife Charlotte Gainsbourg appears as the superstar actress whose success begins to make her sportswriter husband feel uneasy. This knowing satire lacks a certain sparkle, but with Terence Stamp preening himself as the suave English thespian Attal suspects as a romantic rival and the screenplay supplying some sly asides on both the male and artistic ego, it is enjoyable. DP. In French with English subtitles. DVD

Charlotte Gainsbourg *Charlotte* • Yvan Attal *Yvan* • Terence Stamp *John* • Noémie Lvovsky *Nathalie* • Laurent Bateau *Vincent* • Ludivine Sagnier *Géraldine* • Lionel Abelanski *Georges* • Keith Allen *David* ■ *Dir/Scr* Yvan Attal

Ma Mère ★★ 18

Drama
2004 · Fr/Sp/Austria · Colour · 107mins

Isabelle Huppert here explores the dark heart of human sexuality, playing a licentious mother who falls for the physical charms of her 17-year-old son (Louis Garrel). Director Christophe Honoré goes all out to challenge contemporary taboos, depicting incest as just another form of decadent tension-relief in a holiday resort where everyone's bed-hopping. In trying so hard to shock, however, Honoré creates a voyeuristic movie that sadly never delves into the minds of its unrestrained protagonists. SF. In French with English subtitles. Contains sex scenes. DVD

Isabelle Huppert *Hélène* • Louis Garrel *Pierre* • Emma de Caunes *Hansi* • Joana Preiss *Réa* • Jean-Baptiste Montagut *Loulou* • Dominique Reymond *Marthe* • Olivier Rabourdin *Robert* •

Philippe Duclos *Father* ■ *Dir* Christophe Honoré • *Scr* Christophe Honoré, from the novel by Georges Battaille

Ma Saison Préferée ★★ 15

Drama 1993 · Fr · Colour · 121mins

Daniel Auteuil and Catherine Deneuve are brother and sister brought together after many years to attend the imminent demise of their mother. The familial strife around a death-bed recalls those hothouse dramas by Tennessee Williams and Eugene O'Neill, and this effort offers few surprises. The main point of interest is the fact that Deneuve's daughter is played by her real-life daughter, Chiara, whose father was famed actor Marcello Mastroianni. AT. In French with English subtitles.

Catherine Deneuve *Emilie* • Daniel Auteuil *Antoine* • Marthe Villalonga *Berthe* • Jean-Pierre Bouvier *Bruno* • Chiara Mastroianni *Anne* ■ *Dir* André Téchiné • *Scr* André Téchiné, Pascal Bonitzer

Ma Vie en Rose ★★★ 12

Drama
1997 · Fr/Bel/UK/Swi · Colour · 85mins

Both director Alain Berliner and his young star, Georges Du Fresne, make auspicious debuts with this bittersweet tale of sexual confusion and bourgeois prudery. Berliner's clever shifts in colour, as reality intrudes upon the boy's Barbie-doll daydreams, are inspired, while as the pre-teen convinced he'll eventually turn into a girl, Du Fresne is so disingenuously trusting that he almost atones for the film's muddled blend of social satire and whimsical fantasy. Mother Michèle Laroque is so delightfully sympathetic that the trite ending has just the right ring of optimism. DP. In French with English subtitles. DVD

Michèle Laroque *Hanna* • Jean-Philippe Ecoffey *Pierre* • Hélène Vincent *Elisabeth* • Georges Du Fresne *Ludovic* • Daniel Hanssens *Albert* • Laurence Bibot *Lisette* ■ *Dir* Alain Berliner • *Scr* Alain Berliner, from a story by Chris Vander Stappen

Ma Vie Sexuelle ★★★ 15

Drama 1996 · Fr · Colour · 172mins

Directed with a genuine curiosity about his characters that is too rare in 1990s cinema, Arnaud Desplechin's leisurely study of Parisian 20-something angst has its moments, but too few to justify the running time. As the wannabe intellectual trapped in a dead-end teaching post, Mathieu Amalric deserves credit for creating such a introspective loser. But his relationships with neglected girlfriend Emmanuelle Devos, unhinged student Marianne Denicourt and his cousin's lover, Chiara Mastroianni, only occasionally flicker into life. DP. In French with English subtitles. DVD

Mathieu Amalric *Paul* • Emmanuelle Devos *Esther* • Emmanuel Salinger *Nathan* • Marianne Denicourt *Sylvia* • Chiara Mastroianni *Patricia* ■ *Dir* Arnaud Desplechin • *Scr* Arnaud Desplechin, Emmanuel Bourdieu

Ma Vraie Vie à Rouen ★★★ 15

Comedy drama 2002 · Fr · Colour · 100mins

Olivier Ducastel and Jacques Martineau take a technical risk in presenting the whole of this teasingly self-reflexive picture from the camcorded perspective of an unprepossessing Rouen teenager. But what emerges is a touchingly honest portrait of a wannabe figure skater coming to terms with his sexuality and the fact that most of his dreams won't come true. Jimmy Tavares impresses in his limited screen time, but Ariane Ascaride excels as the doting, widowed mother both amused and irritated by his fixation with turning family and friends into characters in his personal soap. DP. In French with English subtitles. DVD

Ariane Ascaride *Caroline* • Jonathan Zaccaï *Laurent* • Hélène Surgère *Grandmother* • Jimmy Tavares *Etienne* • Lucas Bonnifait *Ludovic* ■ *Dir/Scr* Olivier Ducastel, Jacques Martineau

Maachis ★★ 12

Drama 1996 · Ind · Colour · 159mins

The winner of numerous domestic awards, yet denounced because of its allegedly pro-terrorist stance, this is designed to appeal more to the emotions than to the intellect. In following a couple of lovers on their road from romance to political violence, director Gulzar is guilty of frequently ignoring plot and character logic if they are at odds with his explosive set pieces. Yet the performance of Om Puri, as the leader of a band of mountain rebels, does much to redeem the shortcomings. DP. In Punjabi with English subtitles.

Chandrachur Singh *Kripal* • Raj Zutshi *Jassi* • Tabu *Veeran* • Om Puri *Santan* • Ravi Gosain • Kulbushan Karband ■ *Dir/Scr* Gulzar

Maborosi 

Drama 1995 · Jpn · Colour · 109mins

Made three years before his celestial masterpiece, *After Life*, one-time documentarist Hirokazu Koreeda's fictional debut also tackles the subject of death, but the focus here is how it affects those left behind. Traumatised by childhood memories of her beloved grandmother's departure and then her husband's apparent suicide, Makiko Esumi becomes convinced she curses everyone she loves and resists the chance of a fresh start with her new husband in a sleepy fishing village. This is a deeply felt film that eschews cheap sentiment and leaves one genuinely moved and uplifted. DP. In Japanese with English subtitles. Contains brief nudity.

Makiko Esumi *Yumiko* • Takashi Naito *Tamio (Yumiko's husband)* • Tadanobu Asano *Ikuo (Yumiko's ex-husband)* • Gohki Kashiyama *Yuichi (Yumiko's son)* • Naomi Watanabe *Tomoko (Tamio's daughter)* ■ *Dir* Hirokazu Koreeda • *Scr* Yoshihisa Ogita, from a story by Teru Miyamoto

Mac ★★★ 18

Period drama 1992 · US · Colour · 113mins

Three brothers from Queens try to set themselves up as business contractors in actor John Turturro's accomplished directing debut. But fraternal rivalry rears its ugly head in an absorbing, 1950s-set ensemble piece that is brutal and warmly humorous by turns. Turturro plays Mac, the bullying perfectionist who wants to make his father proud, with a painful honesty that's both touching and believable. This is an intimate drama of great depth and keen observation. AJ

John Turturro *Niccolo "Mac" Vitelli* • Michael Badalucco *Vico Vitelli* • Carl Capotorto *Bruno Vitelli* • Katherine Borowitz *Alice Vitelli* • John Amos *Nat* • Olek Krupa *Polowski* • Ellen Barkin *Oona* ■ *Dir* John Turturro • *Scr* John Turturro, Brandon Cole

Mac and Me ★★ U

Adventure 1988 · US · Colour · 94mins

After ET's jaunt to our planet captured the hearts of Earthlings of all ages, it was only to be expected that he would be followed by a positive star fleet of cute critters from outer space. Mac was not one of the more endearing, although there are moments when his relationship with Jade Calegory (who doesn't allow spina bifida to detract from her courageous performance) is quite touching. Director Stewart Raffill's film is otherwise an unashamed rip-off and only remembered as the picture that gave product placement a bad name. DP

Christine Ebersole *Janet Cruise* • Jonathan Ward *Michael Cruise* • Katrina Caspary [Tina Caspary] *Courtney* • Lauren Stanley *Debbie* • Jade Calegory *Eric Cruise* • Vinnie Torrente *Mitford* • Martin West *Wickett* • Ivan Jorge Rado *Zimmerman* ■ *Dir* Stewart Raffill • *Scr* Stewart Raffill, Steve Feke

Macabre ★★

Horror 1958 · US · BW · 71mins

The first gimmick horror movie from showman producer/director William Castle is more a mystery whodunnit than a ghoulish chiller, filled with fog-shrouded cardboard graveyards and numerous surprises. Doctor William Prince has just five hours to find his daughter, who has been buried alive as part of an elaborate charade. Castle arranged a $1,000 life insurance policy with Lloyd's of London to cover audience members from "death by fright" – a successful ploy that found him mounting ever more outlandish stunts. AJ

William Prince *Dr Rodney Barrett* • Jim Backus *Jim Tyloe* • Jacqueline Scott *Polly Baron* • Philip Tonge *Jode Wetherby* • Ellen Corby *Miss Kushins* • Susan Morrow *Sylvia Stevenson* • Christine White *Nancy Wetherby* ■ *Dir* William Castle • *Scr* Robb White, from the novel by Theo Durrant

Macao ★★★ PG

Crime drama 1952 · US · BW · 77mins

This piece of low-budget exotica was directed by Josef von Sternberg, who was at odds with some of his cast as well as the project as a whole. When Nicholas Ray, who also directed some sequences of Robert Mitchum's *The Racket*, was given credit for shooting some of the final scenes, von Sternberg denounced the film. It's a diversion, with Mitchum and Jane Russell beautifully matched as a fugitive from justice and a nightclub singer who become involved in a bid to ensnare a local crime boss. If only the story and script were on a par with them as well. AT

Robert Mitchum *Nick Cochran* • Jane Russell *Julie Benson* • William Bendix *Lawrence Trumble* • Thomas Gomez *Lt Sebastian* • Gloria Grahame *Margie* • Brad Dexter *Halloran* • Edward Ashley *Martin Stewart* ■ *Dir* Josef von Sternberg, Nicholas Ray • *Scr* Bernard C Schoenfeld, Stanley Rubin, from a story by Bob Williams

Macario ★★★★

Period fantasy 1960 · Mex · BW · 89mins

Like the film that beat it to the Oscar for best foreign film, Ingmar Bergman's *The Virgin Spring*, this Mexican drama focuses on faith, superstition and death. But there's little optimism in Roberto Gavaldon's period fantasy, evocatively shot by master cinematographer Gabriel Figueroa and drawing heavily on the magic realist tradition. The story turns on the fate of starving woodsman, Ignacio Lopez Tarso, who, having refused to share a turkey with either God or the Devil, is tricked into a pact with Death. DP. A Spanish language film.

Ignacio Lopez Tarso *Macario* • Pina Pellicer *Macario's wife* • Enrique Lucero *Death* ■ *Dir* Roberto Gavaldon • *Scr* Roberto Galvadon, Emilio Carballido, from the story *The Third Guest* by Bruno Traven

Macaroni ★★★ PG

Comedy drama 1985 · It · Colour · 101mins

It sounds so improbable it could never work. Yet, in the hands of Jack Lemmon and Marcello Mastroianni, Ettore Scola's tale of the surly businessman who rediscovers the simple joys of life from an eccentric Neapolitan exercises an irresistible charm right through to its closing note of quiet optimism. Discovering that Marcello has continued writing love letters to the heartbroken sister GI Jack jilted at the end of the war, Lemmon gratefully succumbs to the companionship absent from his troubled life. DP. In English and Italian with subtitles.

Jack Lemmon *Robert Traven* • Marcello Mastroianni *Antonio* • Daria Nicolodi *Laura* • Isa Danieli *Carmelina* • Patrizia Sacchi *Virginia* • Bruno Esposito *Giulio* • Giovanna Sanfilippo *Maria* ■ *Dir* Ettore Scola • *Scr* Ruggero Maccari, Furio Scarpelli, Ettore Scola

MacArthur ★★★ PG

Biographical drama
1977 · US · Colour · 123mins

Though not in the same league as *Patton*, this solid, old-fashioned war epic deals with a similarly controversial and complex military commander. Gregory Peck is well cast as the martinet/genius, who famously said, "I will return" after being forced to evacuate Corregidor, the last American stronghold in the Philippines. He did go back, defeating the Japanese and later leading the US forces in the Korean War. He didn't become the US President, but Peck's tremendous performance is presidential in every respect. AT DVD

Gregory Peck *General Douglas MacArthur* • Ivan Bonar *General Sutherland* • Dan O'Herlihy *President Roosevelt* • Ward Costello *General Marshall* • Nicolas Coster *Colonel Huff* • Marj Dusay *Mrs MacArthur* • Ed Flanders *President Harry S Truman* ■ *Dir* Joseph Sargent • *Scr* Hal Barwood, Matthew Robbins

MacArthur's Children ★★★

Second World War drama
1985 · Jpn · Colour · 120mins

On the remote island of Awaji Shima at the end of the Second World War, a large cast of characters reacts in different ways to defeat. There's the aggressive pupil who decides to become a gangster as a way of exorcising the military surrender; there is also an admiral who expects to be arrested and tried for war crimes. Weaving together several strands of narrative, Masahiro Shinoda's film broke new ground for Japanese cinema in confronting defeat and America's cultural and economic colonisation. AT. In Japanese with English subtitles.

Takaya Yamauchi *Ryuta Ashigara* • Yoshiyuki Omori *Saburo Masaki* • Shiori Sakura *Mume Hatano* • Masako Natsume *Komako Nakai* ■ *Dir* Masahiro Shinoda • *Scr* Takeshi Tamura, from a novel by Yu Aku

McBain ★★ 15

Action adventure 1991 · US · Colour · 99mins

Rescued from prison on the day the Vietnam War ended, Christopher Walken vows to return the favour to his liberator. But it's the sister (Maria Conchita Alonso) who calls in the debt, so Walken and other Viet vets wash up in Colombia, fighting on the side of the peasants against the drug cartel-backed forces of El Presidente. Despite its violence, the movie is pitched as an updated send-up of *The Magnificent Seven*, while in other respects it resembles an episode of TV's *The A-Team*. AT

Christopher Walken *McBain* • Maria Conchita Alonso *Christina* • Michael Ironside *Frank Bruce* • Steve James (1) *Eastland* • Jay Patterson *Doctor Dalton* • Victor Argo *El Presidente* ■ *Dir/Scr* James Glickenhaus

Macbeth ★★★★ PG

Tragedy 1948 · US · BW · 102mins

Orson Welles's rendition of *Macbeth* may be the least of his Shakespeare

M

adaptations but, bearing in mind the brilliance of *Chimes at Midnight* and *Othello*, this can hardly be taken as a denunciation. Admittedly, the Scottish accents are often impenetrable thanks to the indifferent sound quality, and Jeanette Nolan may not be the incarnation of merciless ambition that is most people's idea of Lady Macbeth. But Welles gives a towering performance, vacillating between ambition, indecision and conscience with supreme skill. The film's design conveys an atmosphere of evil and unease far more effectively than the plush trappings of Roman Polanski's 1971 version. DP DVD

Orson Welles *Macbeth* • Jeanette Nolan *Lady Macbeth* • Dan O'Herlihy *Macduff* • Roddy McDowall *Malcolm* • Edgar Barrier *Banquo* • Erskine Sanford *Duncan* • John Dierkes *Ross* • Keene Curtis *Lennox* • Peggy Webber *Lady Macduff* • Alan Napier *A Holy Father* ■ *Dir* Orson Welles • *Scr* Orson Welles, from the play by William Shakespeare

Macbeth ★★★★ 15

Tragedy 1971 · UK · Colour · 134mins

A controversial adaptation by Roman Polanski (with Kenneth Tynan advising), this sacrifices some of Shakespeare's bleak poetry in favour of great barbaric imagery. A bloody account of Macbeth (Jon Finch) and his intimidating wife (Francesca Annis) making their way to the top of the medieval heap via murder and treachery, it was Polanski's first film after the murder of his wife, Sharon Tate, and has a savagery that seems tinged with paranoia. Lady Macbeth's nude sleepwalking scene resulted in critical flak and was seen as evidence of the malign influence of production company Playboy. It deserves better than that jibe. TH DVD

Jon Finch *Macbeth* • Francesca Annis *Lady Macbeth* • Martin Shaw *Banquo* • Nicholas Selby *Duncan* • John Stride *Ross* • Stephan Chase *Malcolm* • Paul Shelley *Donalbain* • Terence Baylor *Macduff* ■ *Dir* Roman Polanski • *Scr* Roman Polanski, from the play by William Shakespeare • *Cinematographer* Gilbert Taylor

Macbeth ★★ 12

Tragedy 1997 · UK · Colour · 142mins

This doggedly low-budget affair lacks the power or cinematic imagination of earlier efforts by Orson Welles, Akira Kurosawa (*Throne of Blood*) and Roman Polanski. As Macbeth, a role long coveted by his father, Jason Connery is suitably hesitant in his ambition, but there's a suspicion this owes more to his discomfort with the difficult dialogue than character insight. Helen Baxendale is similarly troubled as his scheming wife. Director Jeremy Freeston has some splendid locations to work with; a pity, then, he shoots much of the dialogue in suffocating close-up. DP DVD

Jason Connery *Macbeth* • Helen Baxendale *Lady Macbeth* • Graham McTavish *Banquo* • Kenny Bryans *Macduff* • Kern Falconer *Seyton* • Hildegard Neil *1st witch* • Brian Blessed *Edward the Confessor* ■ *Dir* Jeremy Freeston • *Scr* Bob Carruthers, Jeremy Freeston, from the play by William Shakespeare

McCabe and Mrs Miller ★★★★ 15

Western 1971 · US · Colour · 115mins

Warren Beatty stars as McCabe, a gambler who sets up his girlfriend Julie Christie as a whorehouse madam, in a bleak western set against the backdrop of a developing town in the American North West. It's an interesting tale with all the classic elements of the genre, and the affair is given added weight by the solid performances of Beatty and Christie. A reminder of just how good *Short Cuts* director Robert Altman can be when he's on form. JB DVD

Warren Beatty *John McCabe* • Julie Christie *Constance Miller* • René Auberjonois *Sheehan* • John Schuck *Smalley* • Bert Remsen *Bart Coyle* • Keith Carradine *Cowboy* • William Devane *Lawyer* • Corey Fischer *Mr Elliott* • Shelley Duvall *Ida Coyle* ■ *Dir* Robert Altman • *Scr* Robert Altman, Brian McKay, from the novel *McCabe* by Edmund Naughton

The McConnell Story ★★ U

Biographical drama
1955 · US · Colour · 102mins

Alan Ladd was terrified of flying, but he had no qualms about playing Captain Joseph C McConnell Jr, a real-life pilot ace of the Korean War. It's standard stuff, with Ladd putting duty first and his patient wife (June Allyson) second, though the script had to be revised when McConnell was killed testing a new type of plane shortly before production started. The jingoistic embellishments are somewhat sickening, however. AE

Alan Ladd *Captain Joseph C "Mac" McConnell Jr* • June Allyson *"Butch"* • James Whitmore *Ty Whitman* • Frank Faylen *Sykes* • Robert Ellis *Bob* • Willis Bouchey *Newton Bass* ■ *Dir* Gordon Douglas • *Scr* Ted Sherdeman, Sam Rolfe, from a story by Ted Sherdeman

McHale's Navy ★★★ U

War comedy 1964 · US · Colour · 92mins

McHale's Navy first aired on US TV in 1962 and was an immediate hit, showing the antics of the crew of a PT boat. This film version preserves the main cast and production team, giving Ernest Borgnine the plum role as Lt Comdr Quinton McHale, the least likely officer in the Pacific. Very much a product of its times, it includes some genuinely funny, even surreal moments such as a Japanese peering through his periscope and seeing a racehorse on the bows of the PT boat. AT

Ernest Borgnine *Lt Cmdr Quinton McHale* • Joe Flynn *Capt Wallace Burton Binghamton* • Tim Conway *Ensign Charles Parker* • Carl Ballantine *Torpedoman Lester Gruber* • Gary Vinson *QM George "Christy" Christopher* ■ *Dir* Edward J Montagne • *Scr* Frank Gill Jr, G Carleton Brown, from a story by Si Rose

McHale's Navy ★★ PG

Comedy 1997 · US · Colour · 104mins

Tom Arnold stars in this update of the 1960s TV series. Lt Cmdr Quinton McHale is lured out of retirement in the Caribbean to fight dangerous international terrorist Tim Curry, who is trying to build his own nuclear silo and fire a missile at the Pentagon. So much attention was paid to getting an impressive cast of B-movie actors that somebody forgot to write any jokes. ST. Contains some swearing.

Tom Arnold *Lt Cmdr Quinton McHale* • Dean Stockwell *Capt Wallace B Binghampton* • Debra Messing *Lt Penelope Carpenter* • David Alan Grier *Ensign Charles T Parker* • Tim Curry *Major Vladikov* • Ernest Borgnine *Cobra* ■ *Dir* Bryan Spicer • *Scr* Peter Crabbe, from a story by Andy Rose, Peter Crabbe

La Machine ★★★ 18

Science-fiction horror thriller
1994 · Fr/Ger · Colour · 91mins

Gérard Depardieu is a psychologist with a particular fascination for the criminal mind. He develops a machine that enables him to swap brains with Didier Bourdon, a man convicted of stabbing three women to death. Unfortunately, the experiment becomes permanent. But does his wife, Nathalie Baye, still recognise him? This exercise in schlock provides some effective jolts as Depardieu surfs someone else's brainwaves. AT. A French language film.

Gérard Depardieu *Marc* • Nathalie Baye *Marie* • Didier Bourdon *Zyto* • Natalia Woerner *Marianne* • Erwan Baynaud *Leonard* ■ *Dir* François Dupeyron • *Scr* François Dupeyron, from a novel by René Belletto

Machine Gun Kelly ★★★ 12

Biographical crime drama
1958 · US · BW · 83mins

One of the first films to gain cult director Roger Corman international recognition and critical acclaim, this is a vivid and fast-moving biopic about the infamous 1930s bank robber. Charles Bronson (in his first starring role) brings an edgy intensity to Kelly, the audacious gangster who finally surrendered to the FBI rather than be killed in a shoot-out. Rapid-fire dialogue and effective characterisations make this a winner. AJ DVD

Charles Bronson *Machine Gun Kelly* • Susan Cabot *Flo* • Morey Amsterdam *Fandango* • Jack Lambert *Howard* • Wally Campo *Maize* ■ *Dir* Roger Corman • *Scr* R Wright Campbell

The Machinist ★★★ 15

Psychological mystery thriller
2003 · Sp · Colour · 97mins

The most astonishing thing about this bleak, underplayed psychological thriller is Christian Bale's incredible physical transformation. Bale deliberately withered to the point where his appearance is shockingly reminiscent of undernourished PoWs. Reportedly losing over 60 pounds to get into the role, Bale plays a factory worker whose emaciated condition and chronic insomnia may be linked to a mysterious stranger and a secret from his past. Director Brad Anderson cultivates a studied, effectively creepy atmosphere but his determination to move everything at a pace that would disgrace a slothful snail finally undermines some of the tension. AS. Contains swearing, violence. DVD

Christian Bale *Trevor Reznik* • Jennifer Jason Leigh *Stevie* • Aitana Sanchez-Gijon *Marie* • John Sharian *Ivan* • Michael Ironside *Miller* • Larry Gilliard *Jackson* • Reg E Cathey *Jones* • Anna Massey *Mrs Shrike* ■ *Dir* Brad Anderson • *Scr* Scott Kosar

Macho Callahan ★★ 15

Period war drama
1970 · US/Sp · Colour · 94mins

Union soldier David Janssen busts out of jail and sets out to kill Lee J Cobb, murdering Jean Seberg's one-armed husband in the process. The fact that Seberg falls in love with Janssen *after* she's hired some bounty hunters to bump him off makes life complicated for all concerned. Seldom has a western shown such relish for pain and cruelty, while Seberg has to strip off for the obligatory rape scene. The bleached look of the film gives it a certain realism, but no one's heart seems to be in it. AT

David Janssen *Diego "Macho" Callahan* • Jean Seberg *Alexandra Mountford* • Lee J Cobb *Duffy* • James Booth *"King Harry" Wheeler* • Pedro Armendáriz Jr *Juan Fernandez* • Anne Revere *Crystal* • David Carradine *Colonel David Mountford* • Diane Ladd *Girl* ■ *Dir* Bernard L Kowalski • *Scr* Clifford Newton Gould, from a story by Richard Carr

Machuca ★★★ 15

Period drama
2004 · Chil/Sp/UK/Fr · Colour · 121mins

Andrés Wood's emotive drama was a huge success in the director's native Chile and is set against the fall of the Allende government in 1973. It shrewdly views events from a child's perspective, charting the growing friendship between pampered Matías Quer and shantytown kid Ariel Mateluna, after the latter is awarded a place at Quer's prestigious school. Quer develops a crush on Mateluna's cousin Manuela Martelli, who divides her time between menial jobs and social protest. Wood captures the period mood well, even though he laces the occasionally fraught melodrama with some bombastic political rhetoric. DP. In Spanish with English subtitles. Contains swearing.

Matías Quer *Gonzalo Infante* • Ariel Mateluna *Pedro Machuca* • Manuela Martelli *Silvana* • Aline Küppenheim *María Luisa Infante* • Federico Luppi *Roberto Ochagavía* • Ernesto Malbrán *Father McEnroe* • Tamara Acosta *Juana* • Francisco Reyes *Patricio Infante* ■ *Dir* Andrés Wood • *Scr* Andrés Wood, Roberto Brodsky, Mamoun Hassan

The Mack ★★ 18

Blaxploitation 1973 · US · Colour · 87mins

One of the most popular of all the blaxploitation movies, this followed in the bloody wake of *Shaft* (1971) and, if anything, is even more violent. Max Julien is a black pimp who comes up against white cops and an evil drugs lord. The morals are as sleazy as the hero, while Michael Campus directs at a pace as urgent as the slashing knives Julien uses. TH

Max Julien *Goldie* • Don Gordon *Hank* • Richard Pryor *Slim* • Carol Speed *Lulu* • Roger E Mosley *Olinga* • Dick Williams [Dick Anthony Williams] *Pretty Tony* ■ *Dir* Michael Campus • *Scr* Robert J Poole

Mack the Knife ★ 15

Musical drama 1989 · US · Colour · 98mins

An all-star British cast gives support to Raul Julia's MacHeath in this version of Bertolt Brecht and Kurt Weill's *Threepenny Opera*. However, the impressive line-up conceals an appalling travesty of a theatrical classic that's totally alien to the spirit of the original. Set in deprived Victorian London, this is a forced affair, full of turgid scenes and dialogue. It's no surprise to learn that Anthony Hopkins walked off set complaining of "creative differences"; the real mystery is why everybody else didn't follow suit. LH

Raul Julia *MacHeath* • Julia Migenes-Johnson *Jenny* • Richard Harris *Mr Peachum* • Julie Walters *Mrs Peachum* • Roger Daltrey *Street singer* • Rachel Robertson *Polly Peachum* • Clive Revill *Money Matthew* • Miranda Garrison *Esmerelda* ■ *Dir* Menahem Golan • *Scr* Menahem Golan, from the musical *The Threepenny Opera* by Bertolt Brecht, Kurt Weill

Mackenna's Gold ★★★ 15

Western 1969 · US · Colour · 122mins

How could this possibly fail – a western about hidden Apache gold with more stars in the cast than there are twists, swindles and red herrings in the plot? Yet fail it did, and there was nothing that such powerhouse performers as Gregory Peck, Omar Sharif and Edward G Robinson could do about it. Carl Foreman's script may be cliché ridden, but J Lee Thompson's direction is vigorous. DP DVD

Gregory Peck *Mackenna* • Omar Sharif *Colorado* • Telly Savalas *Sergeant Tibbs* • Camilla Sparv *Inga* • Keenan Wynn *Sanchez* • Julie Newmar *Heshke* • Ted Cassidy *Hachita* • Lee J Cobb *Editor* • Raymond Massey *Preacher* • Burgess Meredith *Storekeeper* • Anthony Quayle *Older Englishman* • Edward G Robinson *Old Adams* • Eli Wallach *Ben Baker* ■ *Dir* J Lee Thompson • *Scr* Carl Foreman, from the novel by Will Henry

The McKenzie Break ★★★★ 12

Second World War drama
1970 · UK · Colour · 105mins

An unusual slant on the prisoner-of-war escape movie – here, members of a German U-boat crew in a Scottish internment camp plan to make their getaway. Brian Keith's intelligence officer finds himself opposing Helmut Griem's fanatical Nazi, who is willing to sacrifice others for the glory of the Fatherland. Directed by Lamont Johnson, this rare and interesting movie acknowledges that guards can only run such lock-ups efficiently with the tacit permission of the prisoners. Keith and Griem turn in admirable performances, and the tense script ensures a nail-biting finish. TH. Contains violence, swearing. [video] DVD

Brian Keith *Captain Jack Connor* • Helmut Griem *Kapitan Schluetter* • Ian Hendry *Major Perry* • Jack Watson *General Kerr* • Patrick O'Connell *Sergeant Major Cox* • Horst Janson *Neuchl* • Alexander Allerson *Von Sperrle* • John Abineri *Kranz* ■ *Dir* Lamont Johnson • *Scr* William Norton, from the novel *The Bowmanville Break* by Sidney Shelley

The Mackintosh Man ★★ 15

Spy thriller 1973 · UK · Colour · 95mins

A movie with everything you would expect of a Cold War thriller – and therein lies its problem. Walter Hill has made a smooth enough job of adapting Desmond Bagley's novel, but John Huston handles the cleverly crafted frame-up, the ingenious escapes and the finale in Malta with little conviction. Paul Newman and James Mason seem equally distracted as, respectively, the undercover agent and the high-ranking MP who is not what he seems. DP [video]

Paul Newman *Joseph Rearden* • James Mason *Sir George Wheeler* • Dominique Sanda *Mrs Smith* • Harry Andrews *Angus Mackintosh* • Nigel Patrick *Soames-Trevelyan* • Ian Bannen *Slade* • Peter Vaughan *Brunskill* ■ *Dir* John Huston • *Scr* Walter Hill, from the novel *The Freedom Trap* by Desmond Bagley

McLintock! ★★★ U

Comedy western
1963 · US · Colour · 126mins

Rollicking John Wayne vehicle that's a real Wayne family affair – it co-stars one son, Patrick, and another, Michael, produced the movie. He also issued it in varying forms, shortened, and with different music, but the best version, is the full two hours-plus Panavisioned opus. It's basically a rewrite of *The Taming of the Shrew*, with all the pre-feminist attitudes endemic to that Shakespeare comedy; attitudes, one suspects, held by the Duke himself. Be warned: it's rowdy, rude and rather dated. TS [video] DVD

John Wayne *George Washington McLintock* • Maureen O'Hara *Katherine McLintock* • Yvonne De Carlo *Louise Warren* • Patrick Wayne *Devlin Warren* • Stefanie Powers *Becky McLintock* • Jack Kruschen *Birnbaum* • Chill Wills *Drago* ■ *Dir* Andrew V McLaglen • *Scr* James Edward Grant

The McMasters ★★

Western 1970 · US · Colour · 97mins

This weird western was directed by a disciple of Ingmar Bergman, Alf Kjellin, who predictably makes the atmosphere as bleak as possible. The central theme is racial prejudice, as white rancher Burl Ives and native American Indians, led by David Carradine, come to the aid of black soldier-turned-rancher Brock Peters, who faces hostility from local white farmers. Really a critique of the Vietnam War, this is always interesting, rarely exciting. AT. Contains violence.

Brock Peters *Benjie* • Burl Ives *Neal McMasters* • David Carradine *White Feather* • Nancy Kwan *Robin* • Jack Palance *Kolby* • Dane Clark *Spencer* • John Carradine *Preacher* • LQ Jones *Russell* ■ *Dir* Alf Kjellin • *Scr* Harold Jacob Smith

The Macomber Affair ★★★

Romantic drama 1947 · US · BW · 89mins

Based on a brilliant story by Ernest Hemingway, this is a serious – perhaps too serious – film attempt at translating the author's prose to the silver screen. Gregory Peck is wooden in the lead, but Robert Preston and Joan Bennett both have a rare intelligence as a sparky married couple who are on safari under Peck's wing. A hard film to like, but an easy one to admire, and a must for collectors of filmed Hemingway. TS

Gregory Peck *Robert Wilson* • Robert Preston *Francis Macomber* • Joan Bennett *Margaret Macomber* • Reginald Denny *Captain Smollet* • Carl Harbord *Coroner* ■ *Dir* Zoltan Korda • *Scr* Casey Robinson, Seymour Bennett, Frank Arnold, from the story *The Short Happy Life of Francis Macomber* by Ernest Hemingway

Macon County Line ★★★

Crime drama 1973 · US · Colour · 88mins

Max Baer Jr (*The Beverly Hillbillies*) wrote, produced and co-starred in this minor drive-in classic. Two footloose brothers, one of whom is about to go into the army, pick up a girl and go on one last hellraising spree in 1950s Georgia, only to run foul of a redneck sheriff who hunts them down for a murder they didn't commit. Supposedly based on a true story, this isn't your average "good ol' boy" flick. Although director Richard Compton has much to say about gun use and small town mores, the melodrama of the piece swamps any message. Compton directed a disappointing sequel, *Return to Macon County* (1975). RS

Alan Vint *Chris Dixon* • Cheryl Waters *Jenny* • Geoffrey Lewis *Hamp* • Joan Blackman *Carol Morgan* • Jesse Vint *Wayne Dixon* • Max Baer Jr *Deputy Morgan* • Sam Gilman *Deputy Bill* ■ *Dir* Richard Compton • *Scr* Max Baer Jr, Richard Compton, from a story by Max Baer Jr

McQ ★★ 15

Thriller 1974 · US · Colour · 106mins

Star John Wayne and director John Sturges were both past their action prime when they collaborated on this ill-conceived excursion into *Dirty Harry* territory. Cop Wayne hands in his badge as he pursues the truth about his murdered pal. The car-chase finale on the beach is particularly poorly staged, but this will come as no surprise. Shot in Seattle, this is watchable mainly for the scenery and the solid supporting performances. TS. Contains violence, swearing. [video]

John Wayne *Detective Lt Lon McQ* • Eddie Albert *Capt Ed Kosterman* • Diana Muldaur *Lois Boyle* • Colleen Dewhurst *Myra* • Clu Gulager *Franklin Toms* • David Huddleston *Edward M "Pinky" Farrow* ■ *Dir* John Sturges • *Scr* Lawrence Roman

Macu, the Policeman's Wife ★★★

Drama based on a true story
1987 · Ven · Colour · 91mins

Solveig Hoogesteijn had already explored the themes of culture and identity in a couple of pictures before adding feminist and political concerns in this disturbing melodrama. The story of a policeman who murders his teenage wife's lover is told through flashbacks which also reveal the shocking part played by young Maria Luisa Mosquera's mother in her troubled life. This complex analysis of the role of women in Venezuelan society isn't an easy watch. DP. In Spanish with English subtitles.

Daniel Alvarado *Ismael* • Maria Luisa Mosquera *Macu* • Frank Hernandez *Simon* • Tito Aponte *Willy* ■ *Dir/Scr* Solveig Hoogesteijn

McVicar ★★ 18

Prison drama 1980 · UK · Colour · 107mins

This is an ill-conceived account, based on his autobiography, of folk hero John McVicar's escape from Durham prison. The Who's Roger Daltrey was one of the producers and the band had a hand in the noisy, inappropriate rock score. Daltrey also attempts the role of McVicar, while another pop singer, Adam Faith, plays his mate Walter. Tom Clegg directs it all in slam-bang *Sweeney* style. DM [video] DVD

Roger Daltrey *John McVicar* • Adam Faith *Walter Probyn* • Cheryl Campbell *Sheila* • Billy Murray *Joey Davis* • Georgina Hale *Kate* • Ian Hendry *Hitchens* • Steven Berkoff *Ronnie Harrison* ■ *Dir* Tom Clegg • *Scr* Tom Clegg, John McVicar, from the autobiography *McVicar by Himself* by John McVicar

Mad about Mambo ★★★ 12

Romantic comedy
1999 · UK/US · Colour · 88mins

Actor Gabriel Byrne executive produced this agreeable fairy-tale romance, set in Belfast, about a talented schoolboy footballer (William Ash). Inspired by the words of a Brazilian player, who says "we don't run with the ball, we dance", he starts taking samba lessons in order to find some rhythm. Soon he is catching the eye of pretty dance champion Keri Russell, but their class differences, his football commitments and her obnoxious ex-boyfriend threaten to ruin the happy ending. Engagingly played by the two young stars, this is a sweet feel-good confection. JC [video] DVD

William Ash *Danny Mitchell* • Keri Russell *Lucy McLoughlin* • Brian Cox *Sidney McLoughlin* • Theo Fraser Steele *Oliver* • Julian Littman *Rudi Morelli* • Maclean Stewart *Mickey* ■ *Dir/Scr* John Forte

Mad about Men ★★ U

Fantasy 1954 · UK · Colour · 85mins

Director Ralph Thomas, so effective with the *Doctor* series, is out of his depth with this slice of outdated hokum, a cliché-ridden story that's a sequel to the first mermaid movie *Miranda*. Glynis Johns still looks good as the aquatic star, swapping roles with a sports mistress who's going on holiday, but this is certainly not the equal of the charming original. TH

Glynis Johns *Miranda/Caroline* • Anne Crawford *Barbara* • Donald Sinden *Jeff Saunders* • Margaret Rutherford *Nurse Cary* • Dora Bryan *Berengaria* • Nicholas Phipps *Barclay Sutton* • Peter Martyn *Ronald* • Noel Purcell *Old Salt* • Joan Hickson *Mrs Forster* • Irene Handl *Madame Blanche* ■ *Dir* Ralph Thomas • *Scr* Peter Blackmore

Mad about Music ★★★ U

Drama 1938 · US · BW · 91mins

In her third starring role, Deanna Durbin plays the daughter of a vain actress (Gail Patrick) who keeps her hidden away at a Swiss school. There the parentless girl invents a romantic explorer father and regales her fellow pupils with his exploits. When her deception looks about to be revealed, she dragoons a bemused but co-operative Herbert Marshall into impersonating her fantasy. Like all of Durbin's vehicles, this is charming, delightful nonsense. RK [video] DVD

Deanna Durbin *Gloria Harkinson* • Herbert Marshall *Richard Todd* • Arthur Treacher *Tripps* • Gail Patrick *Gwen Taylor* • William Frawley *Dusty Rhodes* • Jackie Moran *Tommy* • Helen Parrish *Felice* ■ *Dir* Norman Taurog • *Scr* Bruce Manning, Felix Jackson, from a story by Marcella Burke, Frederick Kohner

Mad at the Moon ★★

Horror western 1992 · US · Colour · 97mins

Fur-out blend of *The Wolf Man* and *Little House on the Prairie*, with Mary Stuart Masterson as a rancher's wife who wonders why hubby Hart Bochner keeps nipping out at night and baying at the moon. Yes, you've guessed it: he's a lycanthrope. But can beauty tame the beast before he wolfs her down for his next meal? Low on gore and long on talk and atmosphere, Martin Donovan's horror western failed to find an audience. DA

Mary Stuart Masterson *Jenny* • Hart Bochner *Miller Brown* • Fionnula Flanagan *Jenny's mom* • Stephen Blake *James Miller* • Daphne Zuniga *Jenny's mom as a young woman* • Cec Verrell *Sally* ■ *Dir* Martin Donovan (1) • *Scr* Martin Donovan, Richard Pelusi

Mad City ★★★★ 12

Crime drama 1997 · US · Colour · 110mins

John Travolta is the museum security guard who resorts to the desperate measure of holding a group of schoolkids hostage after he loses his job. In this 1990s version of *Ace in the Hole*, Dustin Hoffman is the ageing newsman in need of a career break, who decides to manipulate the unsuspecting Travolta for his own ends. Surprisingly dark for a Hollywood movie, this works exceptionally well thanks to a well thought-out script, subtle direction and superb performances from Travolta, Hoffman and Alan Alda as his news rival. JB. Contains swearing, violence. [video] DVD

Dustin Hoffman *Max Brackett* • John Travolta *Sam Baily* • Alan Alda *Kevin Hollander* • Mia Kirshner *Laurie Callahan* • Ted Levine *Alvin Lemke* • Robert Prosky *Lou Potts* • Blythe Danner *Mrs Banks* • William Atherton *Dohlen* ■ *Dir* Costa-Gavras • *Scr* Tom Matthews, Eric Williams, from a story by Tom Matthews

Mad Cows ★ 15

Comedy 1999 · UK · Colour · 86mins

Kathy Lette's bestselling comic novel transfers to the screen with tiresomely over-the-top characters, amateurish direction and a witless script. Anna Friel nails the accent as Australian single mum Maddy, but her gamine looks and limited skills render her character unconvincing. If the poor performances and stupid story don't drive you mad, the heavy-handed, "wacky" camerawork should finish the job. JC. Contains drug abuse and nudity. [video] DVD

Anna Friel *Maddy* • Joanna Lumley *Gillian* • Anna Massey *Dwina Phelps* • Phyllida Law *Lady Drake* • Greg Wise *Alex* • John Standing *Johnny Vaguelawn* • Prunella Scales *Dr Minny Stinkler* • Mohamed Al-Fayed *Harrods doorman* • Meg Mathews *Harrods shopper* ■ *Dir* Sara Sugarman • *Scr* Sasha Hails, Sara Sugarman, from the novel by Kathy Lette

The Mad Doctor of Market Street ★★★

Drama 1942 · US · BW · 60mins

Slyly derivative of HG Wells's *The Island of Dr Moreau*, this schlocky drama stars Lionel Atwill as a deranged doctor forced to quit his plush New York surgery for indulging in strange practices. Fleeing by boat, he is shipwrecked on a desert island with a bunch of survivors whom he decides to turn into zombies. Cult director Joseph H Lewis keeps his tongue firmly in cheek, but his film has quite a narrative pull and the title is terrific. TH

Una Merkel *Aunt Margaret* • Lionel Atwill *Dr Benson* • Nat Pendleton *"Red"* • Claire Dodd *Patricia Wentworth* ■ *Dir* Joseph H Lewis • *Scr* Al Martin

Mad Dog ★★★★ 18

Biographical action drama
1976 · Aus · Colour · 93mins

Australia, 1854, and young Dennis Hopper, partaking of opium in Chinatown, survives a massacre and is sentenced to a dozen years after stealing some clothing. Raped in jail, he gets out after six years and becomes a legendary outlaw, Mad Dog Morgan. With his boomerang-throwing, didgeridoo-playing partner, played by David Gulpilil from *Walkabout*, Hopper is every inch the social bandit, and

M

writer/director Philippe Mora surely skews a few facts to make us regard him as a hero. Superbly shot and pacily directed. AT DVD

Dennis Hopper *Daniel Morgan* • Jack Thompson *Detective Manwaring* • David Gulpilil *Billy* • Frank Thring *Superintendent Cobham* • Michael Pate *Superintendent Winch* • Wallas Eaton *Macpherson* • Bill Hunter *Sgt Smith* ■ *Dir* Philippe Mora • *Scr* Philippe Mora, from the book *Morgan the Bold Bushranger* by Margaret Carnegie

Mad Dog and Glory ★★★ [15]

Romantic drama
1992 · US · Colour and BW · 97mins

In this intriguing oddity, Robert De Niro stars as the "Mad Dog" of the title, a shy, quiet police forensics photographer who saves the life of mobster and aspiring stand-up comedian Bill Murray. In return, he gets a "present" – Uma Thurman – but the arrangement becomes complicated when the mismatched duo fall in love. The direction from John McNaughton is subtle, even though he has difficulty keeping the diverse elements of the story together, but he's helped by an understated performance from De Niro, and a rather strange one from Murray. JF. Contains violence, swearing and nudity. DVD

Robert De Niro *Wayne Dobie* • Uma Thurman *Glory* • Bill Murray *Frank Milo* • David Caruso *Mike* • Mike Starr *Harold* • Tom Towles *Andrew* • Kathy Baker *Lee* ■ *Dir* John McNaughton • *Scr* Richard Price

Mad Dog Coll ★★

Biographical crime drama
1961 · US · BW · 87mins

Initially rejected by the British censor, this violent biopic of the eponymous gangster marked the film debut of Gene Hackman, in a small role as a policeman. The eagle-eyed will also spot early screen appearances by a hirsute Telly Savalas and a youthful Vincent Gardenia. The movie was one of a handful directed by Burt Balaban, an ex-marine and combat cameraman, who died in 1965. BB

John Davis Chandler *Vincent Coll* • Kay Doubleday *Clio* • Brooke Hayward *Elizabeth* • Neil Nephew *Rocco* • Jerry Orbach *Joe* • Telly Savalas *Lieutenant Darrell* • Vincent Gardenia *Dutch Schultz* • Gene Hackman *Cop* ■ *Dir* Burt Balaban • *Scr* Edward Schreiber, from material by Leo Lieberman

Mad Dog Murderer ★★★

Action crime drama
1977 · It · Colour · 96mins

Vicious psychopath Helmut Berger breaks out of jail with three colleagues and goes on a score-settling killing spree in one of the most shocking crime thrillers ever made in Italy. Berger is on top form with his pitiless depiction of a homicidal maniac who kidnaps and brutalises an informer's girlfriend, played by sex siren Marisa Mell. Director Sergio Grieco highlights the violence and sexual sadism with a prurience that the squeamish will find sickening. AJ. In Italian and Spanish with English subtitles.

Helmut Berger *Nanni Vitali* • Marisa Mell *Giulianna* • Richard Harrison *Comm Giulio Santini* • Marina Giordana *Santini's sister* • Vittorio Duse *Santini's father* ■ *Dir/Scr* Sergio Grieco

Mad Dogs and Englishmen ★★

Music documentary
1971 · US · Colour · 111mins

An uneven record of Joe Cocker's 1970 American tour, with split-screen clips from concerts held in New York, Dallas, Minneapolis and San Francisco. The gravel-throated bluesman flails his arms through 14 of his best-loved songs, including *Delta Lady, With a Little Help from My Friends* and *She Came in through the Bathroom Window*. Cocker's classics make a powerful impact, but it's event organiser Leon Russell who grabs the backstage attention. AJ

Dir Pierre Adidge • *Scr* Pierre Adidge, Harry Marks, Robert Abel

Mad Dogs and Englishmen ★ [18]

Thriller 1994 · UK · Colour · 93mins

The links between drug addiction and the privileged classes form the basis of this completely misguided thriller. In an awful performance, Elizabeth Hurley plays an upper-class heroin addict who floats through stately homes surrounded by pompous twits and listless "Hooray Henriettas". Joss Ackland puts in an even worse turn as the investigating cockney policeman, while everyone else gamely tries to make sense of the dreadful dialogue. AJ. Contains swearing, violence, drug abuse and sex scenes.

Elizabeth Hurley *Antonia Dyer* • C Thomas Howell *Mike Stone* • Joss Ackland *Inspector Sam Stringer* • Claire Bloom *Liz Stringer* • Jeremy Brett *Tony Vernon-Smith* • Frederick Treves *Sir Harry Dyer* • Andrew Connolly *Clive Nathan* ■ *Dir* Henry Cole • *Scr* Tim Sewell, from a story by Henry Cole

The Mad Game ★★★

Crime drama 1933 · US · BW · 73mins

When the former partners-in-crime of imprisoned bootlegger Spencer Tracy kidnap the children of the judge (Ralph Morgan) who put him away, Tracy is let loose to help track down the guilty men. Directed by Irving Cummings and co-starring Claire Trevor as a reporter who takes a shine to Tracy, this routine crime movie is kept very watchable by the star. RK

Spencer Tracy *Edward Carson* • Claire Trevor *Jane Lee* • Ralph Morgan *Judge Penfield* • J Carrol Naish *Chopper Allen* • John Miljan *William Bennett* ■ *Dir* Irving Cummings • *Scr* William Conselman, Henry Johnson

The Mad Genius ★★★

Drama 1931 · US · BW · 81mins

Matinée idol John Barrymore had tremendous success with the movie version of *Svengali*, and Warner Bros ordered an immediate follow-up. This virtual sequel was released later the same year, and, helped by a better director in Michael Curtiz, Barrymore is sensational. This movie does seem freer than *Svengali* in dealing with similar themes, though its plot is based on the bizarre relationship between ballet impresario Diaghilev and his star dancer Nijinsky. TS

John Barrymore *Ivan Tzarakov* • Marian Marsh *Nana* • Donald Cook *Fedor* • Charles Butterworth *Karinsky* • Luis Alberni *Serge Bankieff* • Carmel Myers *Preskoya* • André Luguet *Bartag* • Frankie Darro *Fedor as a boy* • Boris Karloff *Fedor's father* ■ *Dir* Michael Curtiz • *Scr* J Grubb Alexander, Harvey Thew, from the play *The Idol* by Martin Brown

Mad Love ★★★★

Horror 1935 · US · BW · 67mins

Peter Lorre made his American debut in this, one of the all-time classic horror stories, the first sound remake of the 1925 silent shocker *The Hands of Orlac*. Colin Clive is the concert pianist given the hands of an executed killer when his own are lost in an accident. Lorre brilliantly conveys twisted compassion and obsessive madness as the surgeon who performs the operation because he loves the pianist's actress wife. A real chiller about psychological fear, made even more effective by Karl Freund's hard-edged poetic direction, way ahead of its time for atmosphere, eerie visuals and imaginative camera technique. AJ

Peter Lorre *Doctor Gogol* • Frances Drake *Yvonne Orlac* • Colin Clive *Stephen Orlac* • Ted Healy *Reagan* • Sara Haden *Marie* • Edward Brophy *Rollo* • Henry Kolker *Prefect Rosset* • May Beatty *Françoise* ■ *Dir* Karl Freund • *Scr* Guy Endore, PJ Wolfson, John L Balderston, from the novel *Les Mains d'Orlac* by Maurice Renard • *Cinematographer* Gregg Toland, Chester Lyons

Mad Love ★★ [15]

Romantic drama 1995 · US · Colour · 92mins

British director Antonia Bird made her Hollywood debut with this uninspired reworking of the tired teens-on-the-run theme. She puts her foot on the emotional pedal just as the action needs to be approached with care, with the consequence that Drew Barrymore's increasingly unpredictable behaviour becomes irritating rather than harrowing. Without depth, Paula Milne's script is a hotchpotch of half-digested clichés. DP. Contains violence, swearing, nudity. DVD

Chris O'Donnell *Matt* • Drew Barrymore *Casey* • Matthew Lillard *Eric* • Richard Chaim *Duncan* • Robert Nadir *Coach* • Joan Allen *Margaret* • Jude Ciccolella *Richard* • Amy Sakasitz *Joanna* ■ *Dir* Antonia Bird • *Scr* Paula Milne

The Mad Magician ★★★

Horror 1954 · US · BW · 72mins

When *House of Wax* became a huge hit, Vincent Price was thrown into a quickie imitation with a similar turn-of-the-century setting, fantastic plot and lurid murders. He hams it up endearingly as a deranged illusionist who kills the rival who stole his outrageous tricks, and then assumes his identity. Wonderfully over-the-top nonsense, with Price badly dubbed each time he's in disguise. It was originally shot in 3-D, which explains some of the weirder effects. AJ

Vincent Price *Gallico* • Mary Murphy *Karen Lee* • Eva Gabor *Claire* • John Emery *Rinaldi* • Donald Randolph *Ross Ormond* • Lenita Lane *Alice Prentiss* • Patrick O'Neal *Bruce Allen* ■ *Dir* John Brahm • *Scr* Crane Wilbur

Mad Max ★★★★★ [18]

Futuristic action adventure
1979 · Aus · Colour · 88mins

Despite its low budget, this highly inventive, violent action picture became an international hit, made a star of Mel Gibson and spawned two sequels. Gibson is at his mean and moody best as a heroic cop, one of the few who are left trying to hold together a disintegrating society in a bleak and desolate future. What the film lacks in repartee, it makes up for in rip-roaring spectacle, marvellous chase sequences, terrific stunts and natty leather costumes, setting an early example of grunge chic. In his debut feature, director George Miller exhibits a striking visual style, particularly with his use of fender-level cameras that help crank up the excitement. A landmark classic. AJ. Contains violence, swearing and nudity. DVD

Mel Gibson *Max Rockatansky* • Joanne Samuel *Jessie* • Hugh Keays-Byrne *Toecutter* • Steve Bisley *Jim Goose* • Tim Burns (1) *Johnny the Boy* • Roger Ward *Fifi Macaffee* • Vince Gil *Nightrider* • Geoff Parry *Bubba Zanetti* ■ *Dir* George Miller (2) • *Scr* George Miller (2), James McCausland, from a story by George Miller (2), Byron Kennedy

Mad Max 2 ★★★★ [18]

Futuristic action adventure
1981 · Aus · Colour · 91mins

After the low-budget nihilism of the original movie, director George Miller moved up a gear and the result was this violent, slick and exhilarating action thriller that further helped launch Mel Gibson into superstardom. His police days now well behind him, Mel the road warrior comes to the aid of a peace-loving group that owns a valuable source of fuel and is being threatened by the voracious gangs that patrol the highways of the future. Gibson is charismatic as the hero, and Miller doesn't take his foot off the accelerator for a second. The ingeniously designed and staged road action is stunning. JF. Contains violence, swearing and nudity. DVD

Mel Gibson *Max Rockatansky* • Bruce Spence *Gyro captain* • Vernon Wells *Wez* • Emil Minty *Feral Kid* • Mike Preston [Michael Preston] *Pappagallo* • Kjell Nilsson *Humungus* • Virginia Hey *Warrior woman* • Syd Heylen *Curmudgeon* ■ *Dir* George Miller (2) • *Scr* Terry Hayes, George Miller (2), Brian Hannant

Mad Max beyond Thunderdome ★★★ [15]

Futuristic action adventure
1985 · Aus · Colour · 102mins

The third in Mel Gibson's sci-fi series is the weakest, but it remains a hugely entertaining futuristic spectacular. This time around Gibson finds himself a reluctant surrogate father to a lost tribe of youngsters, as well as getting mixed up with gladiatorial battles in the thunderdome of the wild city of Bartertown, ruled over by the extraordinary Tina Turner. Directors George Miller and George Ogilvie stage some exhilarating set pieces and keep the action bustling along nicely, even if there are also some daft dollops of new ageism. JF. Contains violence and swearing. DVD

Mel Gibson *Mad Max* • Tina Turner *Aunty Entity* • Bruce Spence *Jedediah* • Adam Cockburn *Jedediah Jr* • Frank Thring *The collector* • Angelo Rossitto *The master* • Paul Larsson *The blaster* • Angry Anderson *Ironbar* ■ *Dir* George Miller (2), George Ogilvie • *Scr* Terry Hayes, George Miller (2)

The Mad Miss Manton ★★★

Screwball comedy 1938 · US · BW · 65mins

Barbara Stanwyck is a delight as the Manhattan debutante and amateur detective, and so is Henry Fonda as the obsessive but romantically rather awkward newspaper editor who finds they are both chasing the same murder story. There are borrowings from *The Thin Man* and any number of screwball comedies here, and the result is slight and completely artificial. Thanks to the appeal of its stars, it's also thoroughly enjoyable. AT

Barbara Stanwyck *Melsa Manton* • Henry Fonda *Peter Ames* • Sam Levene *Lieutenant Brent* • Frances Mercer *Helen Frayne* • Stanley Ridges *Edward Norris* • Whitney Bourne *Pat James* • Vicki Lester *Kit Beverly* • Hattie McDaniel *Hilda* ■ *Dir* Leigh Jason • *Scr* Phillip J Epstein, Hal Yates, from a story by Wilson Collison

Mad Monster Party ★★★ [U]

Animated comedy horror
1966 · US · Colour · 90mins

Baron Boris von Frankenstein (voiced by Boris Karloff) throws a retirement party and invites all his celebrity monster friends in this fun animated feature, filmed in the "Animagic" process using stop-motion puppets. Co-written by Harvey Kurtzman, the creator of *Mad* magazine, the film also includes contributions by Forrest J Ackerman, editor of *Famous Monsters of Filmland*. Dracula, the Creature from the Black Lagoon, Dr Jekyll and Mr Hyde, the Mummy, the Invisible Man and the Hunchback of Notre Dame all make the guest list in an enchanting blend of horror and comedy. AJ

Boris Karloff *Baron Boris von Frankenstein* • Ethel Ennis • Gale Garnett • Phyllis Diller *Frankenstein's wife* • Allen Swift • Jack Davis *Puppet Designer* ■ *Dir* Jules Bass • *Scr* Len

Korobkin, Harvey Kurtzman, Forrest J Ackerman (uncredited), from a story by Arthur Rankin Jr

The Mad Room ★★

Drama 1969 · US · Colour · 92mins

In this remake of the Ida Lupino movie *Ladies in Retirement* (1941), Shelley Winters plays a rich widow whose companion and housekeeper (Stella Stevens) gets her younger brother and sister to move in with them. The problem is that the siblings are recently released mental patients who may have murdered their parents. Pitched as a whodunnit, with a shock ending that's easy to predict, the film needs spookier styling, but Stevens does well in a rare dramatic role. AT

Stella Stevens *Ellen Hardy* • Shelley Winters *Mrs Gladys Armstrong* • Skip Ward *Sam Aller* • Carol Cole *Chris* • Severn Darden *Nate* • Beverly Garland *Mrs Racine* ■ *Dir* Bernard Girard • *Scr* Bernard Girard, AZ Martin, from the film *Ladies in Retirement* by Garrett Ford, Reginald Denham, from the play *Ladies in Retirement* by Reginald Denham, Edward Percy

Mad Wednesday ★★★ U

Comedy 1950 · US · BW · 76mins

Originally released in 1947 as *The Sin of Harold Diddlebock*, Preston Sturges's film was re-edited and re-released in 1950 as this. The brilliant premise has elegant silent movie clown Harold Lloyd (in his final role) in a story showing what has happened to one of his earlier creations, the football hero star of *The Freshman* (1925). Thus two comic giants were united on one project and, although this is not a masterpiece, it still features some wonderful comic moments. The longer (89-minute) original merits another star. DF

Harold Lloyd *Harold Diddlebock* • Frances Ramsden *Miss Otis* • Jimmy Conlin *Wormy* • Raymond Walburn *EJ Waggleberry* • Edgar Kennedy *Jake, the bartender* • Arline Judge *Manicurist* • Franklin Pangborn *Formfit Franklin* • Lionel Stander *Max* • Margaret Hamilton *Flora* ■ *Dir/Scr* Preston Sturges

Madagascar ★★★ U

Animated comedy adventure
2005 · US · Colour · 86mins

In this entertaining family film from Dreamworks, Chris Rock and Ben Stiller provide the voices for Marty the zebra and Alex, a preening lion, who enjoy a comfortable existence in Manhattan's Central Park Zoo until Marty expresses a desire to return the wild. What follows is a predictable but engaging series of mishaps that land the pair, along with a neurotic giraffe (David Schwimmer) and a no-nonsense hippo (Jada Pinkett Smith), in Africa. The pace drags in the last third of the movie, but the film is always marvellous to look at and the sight gags come thick and fast. GM

Ben Stiller *Alex the Lion* • Chris Rock *Marty the Zebra* • David Schwimmer *Melman the Giraffe* • Jada Pinkett Smith *Gloria the Hippo* • Sacha Baron Cohen *King Julien* • Cedric the Entertainer *Maurice* • Andy Richter *Mort* ■ *Dir* Eric Darnell, Tom McGrath • *Scr* Mark Burton, Billy Frolick, Eric Darnell, Tom McGrath

Madagascar Skin ★★★ 15

Drama 1995 · UK · Colour · 91mins

Slow-moving and often wordless, director Chris Newby's follow-up to the enigmatic *Anchoress* is a weird boy-meets-boy fable. Bored with the big city, John Hannah (his face covered with a birthmark in the shape of Madagascar) heads for the coast where he discovers cheeky Bernard Hill buried up to his neck in sand. When the two outcasts set up home together in a semi-derelict cottage, this strangely endearing chamber piece becomes an inventive and brave drama. AJ. Contains swearing. [VIDEO]

Bernard Hill *Flint* • John Hannah *Harry* • Mark Anthony *Adonis* • Mark Petit *Lover* • Danny Earl *Lover* • Robin Neath *Thug* • Simon Bennett *Thug* ■ *Dir/Scr* Chris Newby

Madam Satan ★

Comedy musical 1930 · US · BW · 80mins

Directed by Cecil B DeMille, this must be one of the most bizarre films ever made. It begins as a supposed comedy of manners, with socialite Kay Johnson catching on to the fact that her frivolous husband, Reginald Denny, is having an affair with good-time girl Lillian Roth. Played as a mind-numbingly unfunny and badly acted farce for the first half, it becomes a characteristic DeMille extravaganza in the second, when Roland Young throws a costume party aboard a dirigible hovering over Manhattan. For collectors of curiosities only. RK

Kay Johnson *Angela Brooks* • Reginald Denny *Bob Brooks* • Roland Young *Jimmy Wade* • Lillian Roth *Trixie* • Elsa Peterson *Martha* ■ *Dir* Cecil B DeMille • *Scr* Jeanie Macpherson, Gladys Unger, Elsie Janis

Madame ★★

Period comedy
1961 · Fr/It/Sp · Colour · 100mins

Sophia Loren plays the woman who does Napoleon's laundry, though this is before he started to own most of Europe. This adaptation, directed by swashbuckler specialist Christian-Jaque, is a pleasantly frothy affair, with Loren falling for Robert Hossein's nobleman, marrying him and generally leading from the front in the manner of her Italian comedies. AT. Italian dialogue dubbed into English.

Sophia Loren *Madame Catherine Hubscher* • Robert Hossein *Lefebvre* • Julien Bertheau *Napoleon Bonaparte* • Marina Berti *Elisa* • Carlo Giuffrè *Jerome* ■ *Dir* Christian-Jaque • *Scr* Henri Jeanson, Ennio De Concini, Christian-Jaque, Franco Solinas, Jean Ferry, from the play *Madame Sans-Gêne* by Emile Moreau, Victorien Sardou

Madame Bovary ★★★★

Period romance 1933 · Fr · BW · 101mins

What a tragedy that the producers of this fascinating adaptation of Flaubert's classic novel should have felt the need to cut over an hour from the three-hour original in the interests of commercial viability. Director Jean Renoir had attempted to translate the novel's subtle symbolism into cinematic terms and, through his pioneering use of deep-focus photography, he succeeded in visibly locating his heroine in the stifling provincial surroundings that so repressed her spirit. You'll either love or loathe Valentine Tessier's Emma Bovary, but there's no doubting the quality of Renoir's elder brother Pierre's performance as the insensitive doctor. A remarkable film. DP. In French with English subtitles.

Valentine Tessier *Emma Bovary* • Pierre Renoir *Charles Bovary* • Fernand Fabre *Rodolphe Boulanger* • Daniel Lecourtois *Leon* • Pierre Larquey *Hippolyte* • Christiane Dor *Madame Le François* • Monette Dinay *Félicité* • Alice Tissot *Madame Bovary, Charles's mother* ■ *Dir* Jean Renoir • *Scr* Jean Renoir, from the novel by Gustave Flaubert

Madame Bovary ★★★

Period romance 1949 · US · BW · 114mins

James Mason, as author Gustave Flaubert, defends his renowned tale in flashback from a Paris court in which he finds himself accused of violating contemporary morality. The story he recounts is dressed in MGM's finest 1940s production values, and directed by master of style Vincente Minnelli, whose wonderful ball sequence is one of the cinema's great unrecognised set pieces. Unfortunately, Jennifer Jones lacks the range for Emma Bovary, but she tries gamely, while Van Heflin and Louis Jourdan as her husband and lover respectively are both perfectly cast. This film was critically abused in its day, but now stands up well against other screen versions. TS

Jennifer Jones *Emma Bovary* • James Mason *Gustave Flaubert* • Van Heflin *Charles Bovary* • Louis Jourdan *Rodolphe Boulanger* • Christopher Kent [Alf Kjellin] *Leon Dupuis* • Gene Lockhart *J Homais* • Frank Allenby *L'hereux* • Gladys Cooper *Madame Dupuis* ■ *Dir* Vincente Minnelli • *Scr* Robert Ardrey, from the novel by Gustave Flaubert

Madame Bovary ★★★ PG

Period romance 1991 · Fr · Colour · 136mins

Isabelle Huppert's third movie collaboration with Claude Chabrol promised much. But their fidelity to Flaubert's novel makes this a less effective film than previous adaptations by Jean Renoir and Vincente Minnelli. As the doctor's wife tempted into adultery by the tedium of rural life, Huppert brilliantly conveys the stifled passions that bring about her ruin, while Chabrol uses all his skill at psychological dissection to expose the social and moral rigidity of the mid-19th century. Yet this internality and literariness prevent us from engaging with the action. DP. In French with English subtitles. [VIDEO] DVD

Isabelle Huppert *Emma Bovary* • Jean-François Balmer *Charles Bovary* • Jean Yanne *Monsieur Homais, Pharmacist* • Christophe Malavoy *Rodolphe Boulanger* • Lucas Belvaux *Leon Dupuis* • Jean-Louis Maury *L'heureux* ■ *Dir* Claude Chabrol • *Scr* Claude Chabrol, from the novel by Gustave Flaubert

Madame Butterfly ★

Drama 1932 · US · BW · 86mins

Paramount came a cropper with this film version of the classic tragedy, an updated presentation told as straight melodrama. Directed at a snail's pace by Marion Gering, with Cary Grant not at his best as Lieutenant Pinkerton, it's a turgid bore. Sylvia Sidney has the perfect face and sad soulful eyes for Butterfly, the Japanese girl whose heart is broken by Pinkerton's desertion. In the end, though, it's just not enough. RK

Sylvia Sidney *Cho-cho San* • Cary Grant *Lt BF Pinkerton* • Charlie Ruggles [Charles Ruggles] *Lt Barton* • Irving Pichel *Yamadori* • Helen Jerome Eddy *Cho-cho San's mother* • Edmund Breese *Cho-cho San's grandfather* • Louise Carter *Suzuki* ■ *Dir* Marion Gering • *Scr* Josephine Lovett, Joseph Moncure March, from the play by David Belasco, from the novel by John Luther Long

Madame Butterfly ★★ PG

Opera
1995 · Fr/Jpn/Ger/UK · Colour · 128mins

Directed by Frédéric Mitterrand, this adaptation of Puccini's opera has the advantage of an admirable cast and some magnificent locations. But, like so many filmed operas before it, it fails to reproduce the thrill that comes from hearing the live operatic voice. Mitterrand wastes his settings either by clumping his cast together in huddled groups or by filming the important arias in tight close-up. Ying Huang gives a superb rendition of *One Fine Day* and Richard Troxell is solid as the American sailor who breaks a geisha's heart. Disappointingly unimaginative. DP. In Italian with English subtitles. [VIDEO] DVD

Huang Ying *Madame Butterfly* • Richard Troxell *Pinkerton* • Liang Ning *Suzuki* • Richard Cowan *Sharpless* • Ma Fan Jing *Goro* • Christopheren Nomura *Prince Yamadori* • Constance Hauman *Kate Pinkerton* • Yo Kusakabe *Uncle Bonze* ■ *Dir* Frédéric Mitterrand • *Scr* Frédéric Mitterrand, from the opera by Giacomo Puccini

Madame Curie ★★★ U

Biographical drama 1943 · US · BW · 124mins

Two hours of MGM gloss canonising the discoverer of radium might be a bit much for modern palates, but this thoughtful and finely acted biopic was the epitome of taste in its day. Greer Garson and Walter Pidgeon – as Marie and Pierre Curie – X-ray themselves into dramatic bliss, with hardly a thought for the side effects (like audiences falling into a coma, for instance). It still represents the studio at its worthy, educational and sincere best, receiving seven Academy Award nominations. TS

Greer Garson *Madame Marie Curie* • Walter Pidgeon *Pierre Curie* • Robert Walker *David LeGros* • Dame May Whitty *Madame Eugene Curie* • Henry Travers *Eugene Curie* • C Aubrey Smith *Lord Kelvin* • Albert Basserman *Professor Jean Perot* ■ *Dir* Mervyn LeRoy • *Scr* Paul Osborn, Paul H Rameau, from a biography by Eve Curie

Madame de... ★★★★ U

Drama 1953 · Fr/It · BW · 95mins

Although Max Ophüls's penultimate film was Oscar-nominated for its costumes, it really should have brought him a direction award, as he sends his camera on a series of gliding shots around the luxurious haunts of the idle rich, revealing their every secret and laying bare their empty souls. Danielle Darrieux is the unnamed noblewoman of the title, whose precious earrings, which she has already sold, return to her via husband Charles Boyer's mistress and her own lover, Vittorio De Sica. The script is witty, the performances beyond sophistication. This is just about as polished as European cinema gets. DP. In French with English subtitles. [VIDEO]

Danielle Darrieux *Countess Louise De...* • Charles Boyer *General André De...* • Vittorio De Sica *Baron Fabrizio Donati* • Mireille Perrey *Madame De...'s nurse* • Jean Debucourt *Monsieur Rémy, the jeweller* • Serge Lecointe *Jérome, his son* • Lia Di Léo *Lola, the general's mistress* • Jean Galland *Monsieur De Bernac* ■ *Dir* Max Ophüls • *Scr* Marcel Achard, Max Ophüls, Annette Wademant, from the novel by Louise de Vilmorin

Madame Du Barry ★★

Historical drama 1934 · US · BW · 79mins

The life and times of Louis XV's court at Versailles, seen through the eyes of his famed mistress from the time the king takes her up to her banishment when Louis XVI succeeds to the throne. Dolores Del Rio is ravishingly beautiful, as befits the legendary Du Barry. Sadly, though, she lacks the personality required to carry this lavishly mounted but disappointingly dull historical romance. Reginald Owen is the king, while the large cast impersonating the usual figures of the period includes Osgood Perkins, father of Anthony, as Cardinal Richelieu. RK

Dolores Del Rio *Mme Du Barry* • Reginald Owen *King Louis XV* • Victor Jory *Duke D'Aiguillon* • Osgood Perkins *Richelieu* • Verree Teasdale *Duchess De Granmont* • Henry O'Neill *Duc De Choiseul* • Anita Louise *Marie Antoinette* ■ *Dir* William Dieterle • *Scr* Edward Chodorov

Madame du Barry ★★★

Historical drama
1954 · Fr/It · Colour · 110mins

Martine Carol was France's leading sex symbol and top box-office attraction in the years preceding the rise of Brigitte Bardot, and many of her greatest hits were directed by her husband Christian-Jaque. Though the director was not a favourite with the critics, the

M

public loved his work. This example has a typical mix of gorgeous settings, exuberant performances and an emphasis on entertainment rather than historical accuracy. TV. A French language film.

Martine Carol *Madame Du Barry* • André Luguet *Louis XV* • Daniel Ivernel *Count Du Barry* • Gianna-Maria Canale *Madame Gramont* ■ *Dir* Christian-Jaque • *Scr* Christian-Jaque, Albert Valentin, Henri Jeanson

Madame Rosa ★

Drama 1977 · Fr · Colour · 105mins

Sentimental and manipulative rubbish about an Auschwitz survivor and ex-prostitute who lives out her final days in Paris cared for by an Arab youth (Samy Ben Youb). The movie is full of Arab-Israeli pieties, flashbacks to the Holocaust and a performance from Simone Signoret that was calculated to win prizes and publicity. The movie's badness didn't stop it winning an Oscar for best foreign film. AT. In French with English subtitles.

Simone Signoret *Madame Rosa* • Samy Ben Youb *Mohammed, "Momo"* • Claude Dauphin *Dr Katz* • Gabriel Jabbour *Monsieur Hamil* • Michal Bat-Adam *Madame Nadine* • Costa-Gavras *Ramon* ■ *Dir* Moshe Mizrahi • *Scr* Moshe Mizrahi, from the novel *Momo* by Emile Ajar [Romain Gary]

Madame Sata ★★★

Drama 2002 · Bra/Fr · Colour · 105mins

Karim Ainouz's disjointed biopic of Joao Francisco dos Santos only tells a fraction of the remarkable story of the uneducated black Brazilian who found fame as a drag artist and infamy as a ruthless street hood. Lazaro Ramos's electrifying displays of fierce anger and flamboyant pride fail to provide much insight into the psyche of an enduring icon, but with Walter Carvalho's cinematography capturing the decadence and deprivation of 1930s Rio, this remains an engaging portrait of a character and a society riven with contradictions. DP. In Portuguese with English subtitles.

Lazaro Ramos *Madame Sata/Joao Francisco* • Marcelia Cartaxo *Laurita* • Flavio Bauraqui *Taboo* • Felipe Marques *Renatinho* • Emiliano Queiroz *Amador* • Renata Sorrah *Vitoria dos Anjos* ■ *Dir/Scr* Karim Ainouz

M

Madame Sin ★★ PG

Spy thriller 1972 · US · Colour · 86mins

Made for television originally, but released theatrically over here, this cramped-looking melodrama offers a splendid character part to Bette Davis, who loses no opportunity to chew all the scenery in sight. Co-star Robert Wagner has little to do but observe this awesome spectacle, while director David Greene has the good sense to stand well back and let Davis queen it over a batch of English worthies. The plot, by the way, is some tortuous spy stuff about flogging off a Polaris submarine. TS

Bette Davis *Madame Sin* • Robert Wagner *Tony Lawrence* • Denholm Elliott *Malcolm* • Gordon Jackson *Commander Teddy Cavandish* • Dudley Sutton *Monk* • Catherine Schell *Barbara* • Paul Maxwell *Connors* • Roy Kinnear *Holidaymaker* ■ *Dir* David Greene • *Scr* David Greene, Barry Oringer

Madame Sousatzka ★★★ 15

Drama 1988 · UK · Colour · 115mins

Rather lost in the crowd on its release, this an engaging picture that slowly draws you into the quietly tragic lives of the inhabitants of Peggy Ashcroft's rundown London house. As the imperious piano teacher of the title, Shirley MacLaine beautifully combines the wistful regret for her own disappointments with a commitment to the future of her students. Navin Chowdhry is an excellent foil as her teenage prodigy, while Twiggy and Geoffrey Bayldon do well as fellow tenants worn down by their everyday lives. DP. Contains swearing.

Shirley MacLaine *Madame Sousatzka* • Peggy Ashcroft *Lady Emily* • Twiggy *Jenny* • Navin Chowdhry *Manek Sen* • Shabana Azmi *Sushila Sen* • Leigh Lawson *Ronnie Blum* • Geoffrey Bayldon *Mr Cordle* • Lee Montague *Vincent Pick* ■ *Dir* John Schlesinger • *Scr* Ruth Prawer Jhabvala, John Schlesinger, from the novel by Bernice Rubens

Madame X ★★

Melodrama 1929 · US · BW · 95mins

After a romantic indiscretion, a Parisian wife is thrown out by her eminent but unbending lawyer husband. Forbidden to see her beloved son, she sinks into a life of alcoholic degradation. This classic melodrama fascinated film-makers and audiences for decades. The title role is here played by the splendid Broadway actress Ruth Chatterton, with Lewis Stone as the husband. Both Chatterton and director Lionel Barrymore were Oscar-nominated, but the film now seems slow, mannered and stagey. RK

Ruth Chatterton *Jacqueline* • Lewis Stone *Floriot* • Raymond Hackett *Raymond* • Holmes Herbert *Noel* • Eugenie Besserer *Rose* ■ *Dir* Lionel Barrymore • *Scr* Willard Mack, from the play *La Femme X* by Alexandre Bisson

Madame X ★★★★

Melodrama 1937 · US · BW · 75mins

Gladys George takes the title role in the second, and best, talkie version of the melodrama to end them all. She meets the challenge head on in a powerful performance that pulls no punches, and the film as a whole is played with a seriousness that undercuts the soap opera, at least until the sentimental histrionics of the courtroom finale. Warren William is perfectly cast as George's husband, while Henry Daniell is suitably slimy as the conman who undoes her. This treatment is much fuller than Lionel Barrymore's 1929 film, charting the various steps in the heroine's tragic descent. RK

Gladys George *Jacqueline Fleuriot* • John Beal *Raymond Fleuriot* • Warren William *Bernard Fleuriot* • Reginald Owen *Maurice Dourel* • Henry Daniell *Lerocle* • Jonathan Hale *Hugh Fariman Sr* • William Henry *Hugh Fariman Jr* ■ *Dir* Sam Wood • *Scr* John Meehan, from the play *La Femme X* by Alexandre Bisson

Madame X ★★

Melodrama 1966 · US · Colour · 100mins

This is the last – to date – cinema version (there was a TV-movie remake in 1981 starring Tuesday Weld) of Alexandre Bisson's play about a woman on trial for murder unknowingly defended by her son. Here producer Ross Hunter casts Lana Turner in the leading role; trouble is, Turner seems to have aged suddenly, and the lame direction also does her no favours. Still, there's a super support cast, including Constance Bennett in her last screen appearance. TS

Lana Turner *Holly Parker* • John Forsythe *Clay Anderson* • Ricardo Montalban *Phil Benton* • Burgess Meredith *Dan Sullivan* • Constance Bennett *Estelle* • Teddy Quinn *Clay Jr as a child* • Keir Dullea *Clay Jr as an adult* ■ *Dir* David Lowell Rich • *Scr* Jean Holloway, from the play *La Femme X* by Alexandre Bisson

The Maddening ★★ 18

Horror thriller 1995 · US · Colour · 92mins

Mia Sara's trip to see her sister turns nasty when she takes a short cut proposed to her by shifty gas station owner Burt Reynolds. That's because Reynolds is a nutcase who kidnaps Mia Sara and her daughter to keep his own deranged wife (Angie Dickinson) and child company. This slickly produced thriller is fairly well-acted, but it's too exploitative and sordid to provide much entertainment. ST

Burt Reynolds *Roy Scudder* • Angie Dickinson *Georgina Scudder* • Mia Sara *Cassie Osborne* • Brian Wimmer *David Osborne* • Josh Mostel *Chicky Ross* • William Hickey *Daddy* ■ *Dir* Danny Huston • *Scr* Henry Slesar, Leslie Greif

Made ★★ 15

Crime comedy drama
2001 · US · Colour · 90mins

Containing an uncharacteristically showy performance by Vince Vaughn, this irritates and annoys as it explores the dual themes of male friendship and loyalty. Vaughn and Jon Favreau play boxing buddies who moonlight as muscle for the local Mob. When they're sent on simple courier duty to New York, it's a recipe for trouble. Favreau just wants to get the job done, and then get back to keeping other people's paws off his stripper girlfriend Famke Janssen. Vaughn, by contrast, sees the job as his chance to take a step up the Mob hierarchy. Contrasting ambitions lead to Laurel and Hardy-style humour. DA DVD

Jon Favreau *Bobby* • Vince Vaughn *Ricky* • Sean Combs *Ruiz* • Famke Janssen *Jessica* • Peter Falk *Max* ■ *Dir/Scr* Jon Favreau

Made for Each Other ★★★ U

Comedy drama 1939 · US · BW · 90mins

A besotted young couple who marry in indecent haste face a mounting series of travails in the form of her difficult mother-in-law (Lucile Watson), his failure to gain promotion in his law firm and, climactically, the potentially fatal illness of their baby son. James Stewart and Carole Lombard star, while Charles Coburn is terrific as the crusty law boss; the director is John Cromwell, a master of soap opera. Although certainly not one of the best of its kind (Stewart's self-deprecating persona is almost irritating here), the formula is gold-plated. RK DVD

Carole Lombard *Jane Mason* • James Stewart *Johnny Mason* • Charles Coburn *Judge Joseph Doolittle* • Lucile Watson *Mrs Mason* • Harry Davenport *Dr Healy* • Ruth Weston *Eunice Doolittle* ■ *Dir* John Cromwell • *Scr* Jo Swerling, Frank Ryan

Made in America ★★ 12

Romantic comedy
1993 · US · Colour · 106mins

The central idea of this comedy has potential – a young black teenager discovers that her biological father is white because of a mix-up at the sperm bank – and the cast just about makes it watchable. Whoopi Goldberg and Ted Danson turn in engaging performances as the unsuspecting parents, and Nia Long is entirely believable as their confused offspring, while Will Smith provides confident support. Sadly, the finished product is low on laughs and thin on content, with merely workmanlike direction. JF. Contains swearing.

Whoopi Goldberg *Sarah Mathews* • Ted Danson *Hal Jackson* • Nia Long *Zora Mathews* • Will Smith *Tea Cake Walters* • Paul Rodriguez *Jose* • Jennifer Tilly *Stacy* • Peggy Rea *Alberta* • Clyde Kusatsu *Bob Takashima* ■ *Dir* Richard Benjamin • *Scr* Holly Goldberg Sloan, from a story by Marcia Brandwynne, Nadine Schiff, Holly Goldberg Sloan

Made in Heaven ★★ U

Comedy 1952 · UK · Colour · 81mins

This sprightly comedy was inspired by the ancient English custom of the "Dunmow Flitch", in which married couples sought to win a sizeable side of bacon by swearing on Whit Monday to an uninterrupted year of wedded bliss. However, the chances of the ideally suited Petula Clark and David Tomlinson take a dip when they employ pouting Hungarian maid Sonja Ziemann. Vicar Richard Wattis and his stern sister Athene Seyler add to the fun, which is glossily photographed by Geoffrey Unsworth. DP

Petula Clark *Julie Topham* • David Tomlinson *Basil Topham* • Sonja Ziemann *Marta* • AE Matthews *Grandpa* • Charles Victor *Mr Topham* • Sophie Stewart *Mrs Topham* • Richard Wattis *Vicar* • Athene Seyler *Miss Honeycroft* ■ *Dir* John Paddy Carstairs • *Scr* William Douglas Home, George H Brown

Made in Heaven ★★ PG

Romantic fantasy
1987 · US · Colour and BW · 98mins

This quirky fantasy was cult director Alan Rudolph's bid for a box-office hit, but he too often strains for effect. Timothy Hutton stars as a dead man who meets his future love (Kelly McGillis) in heaven when she's not yet been born. It looks good, like most Rudolph movies, and Hutton handles the comedy with aplomb. Hutton's then wife Debra Winger gives an uncredited performance as the male administrative head of heaven. DP

Timothy Hutton *Mike Shea/Elmo Barnett* • Kelly McGillis *Annie Packert/Ally Chandler* • Maureen Stapleton *Aunt Lisa* • Ann Wedgeworth *Annette Shea* • James Gammon *Steve Shea* • Mare Winningham *Brenda Carlucci* • Don Murray *Ben Chandler* • Timothy Daly *Tom Donnelly* ■ *Dir* Alan Rudolph • *Scr* Bruce A Evans, Raynold Gideon

Made in Hong Kong ★★★★ 15

Crime drama 1997 · HK · Colour · 104mins

Fruit Chan's searching study of a community in transition was shot on discarded scraps of film stock and makes powerful use of its authentic locations and unfamiliar performers. Prone to technical gimmickry and overdoing the political symbolism, Chan nevertheless brings an abrasive energy to this story of a Triad wannabe imprisoned by both his social circumstances and fate. Sam Lee captures the disillusion shared by many Hong Kong youths as he tries to protect both his slow-witted mate and his dying girlfriend, while haunted by the memory of a suicide victim he never knew. DP. In Cantonese with English subtitles. Contains swearing, violence and sexual references.

Sam Lee Chan-Sam [Sam Lee] *To Chung-Chau, "Moon"* • Neiky Hui-Chi Yim *Lam Yuk-Ping, "Ping"* • Wenbers Tung-Chuen Li *Ah-Lung, "Sylvester"* • Amy Ka-Chuen Tam *Hui Bo-San, "Susan"* ■ *Dir/Scr* Fruit Kuo Chan [Fruit Chan]

Made in Paris ★★

Romantic comedy
1966 · US · Colour · 103mins

Desperately dated comedy with Ann-Margret as an American fashion buyer in Paris discovering that, like her predecessor, she is expected to wind up in bed with seductive couturier Louis Jourdan. There's a story about lopsided morals at the heart of this, but this MGM offering devotes itself to glad rags, Ann-Margret's dancing abilities and the tourist attractions of Gay Paree. AT

Ann-Margret *Maggie Scott* • Louis Jourdan *Marc Fontaine* • Richard Crenna *Herb Stone* • Edie Adams *Irene Chase* • Chad Everett *Ted Barclay* • John McGiver *Roger Barclay* ■ *Dir* Boris Sagal • *Scr* Stanley Roberts • *Music/lyrics* Burt Bacharach, Hal David

Made in USA ★★★ 18

Crime drama 1966 · Fr · Colour · 78mins

There is a story of sorts – Anna Karina on the trail of her lover's killer – but this Jean-Luc Godard movie shows the

U = SUITABLE FOR ALL Uc = SUITABLE FOR ALL, ESPECIALLY FOR YOUNG CHILDREN (VIDEO ONLY) PG = PARENTAL GUIDANCE

director moving inexorably and often excitingly away from conventional narrative. As a piece of 1960s Pop Art, this movie takes some beating but today's viewers, largely unaware of the impact Godard made on world cinema, will soon tire of his playing with the medium, his political slogans and passing thoughts on JFK and the Algerian war. By the time the film was made, Karina and Godard were divorced; this was their final film together. AT. In French with English subtitles. [VIDEO] DVD

Anna Karina *Paula Nelson* • Laszlo Szabo *Richard Widmark* • Jean-Pierre Léaud *Donald Siegel* • Yves Alfonso *David Goodis* • Ernest Menzer *Edgar Typhus* ■ *Dir* Jean-Luc Godard • *Scr* Jean-Luc Godard, from the novel *The Juggler* by Richard Stark [Donald E Westlake]

Made Men ★★★ 15

Action thriller 1999 · US · Colour · 86mins

In this derivative though solidly made action thriller, James Belushi is forced to flee from the gangster he not only shopped to the cops, but from whom he also pilfered the tidy sum of $12 million. Director Louis Morneau's previous picture, *Bats*, was disappointing, but this time round there are dramatic fireworks to match the explosions, as Belushi finds that the head of a backwoods drugs racket and corrupt sheriff Timothy Dalton are also on his tail. DP [VIDEO] DVD

James Belushi *Bill Manucci* • Timothy Dalton *Sheriff Dex Drier* • Michael Beach *Miles* • Steve Railsback *Kyle* • Carlton Wilborn *Felix* • Vanessa Angel *Debra* ■ *Dir* Louis Morneau • *Scr* Robert Franke, Miles Millar, Alfred Gough

Madeleine ★★ U

Drama 1949 · UK · BW · 109mins

Only two films blot David Lean's otherwise immaculate copybook (*The Passionate Friends* is the other), and both feature Ann Todd, whom he married in 1949. Todd was never the most expressive of actresses, but here her face a blank and her delivery as modulated as the speaking clock. Uncomfortable with the courtroom format and confounded by the deadliness of dialogue drawn from original trial transcripts, Lean allows love to cloud his judgement, at the expense of what might otherwise have been an intriguing tale of murder in Victorian Glasgow. DP [VIDEO]

Ann Todd *Madeleine Smith* • Norman Wooland *William Minnoch* • Ivan Desny *Emile l'Angelier* • Leslie Banks *James Smith* • Edward Chapman *Dr Thompson* • Barbara Everest *Mrs Smith* • André Morell *Dean* • Barry Jones *Lord Advocate* ■ *Dir* David Lean • *Scr* Stanley Haynes, Nicholas Phipps

Madeline ★★★ U

Comedy 1998 · US/Ger · Colour · 85mins

This sweet, but not entirely successful, children's film is based on Ludwig Bemelmans's books. Hatty Jones is cute as the young orphan, but adults are more likely to be charmed by a warm turn from Frances McDormand as the engaging Miss Clavel, who runs the orphanage and dispenses wisdom to her charges. This well-meaning entertainment for young girls may get overlooked in favour of big-budget productions full of special effects, but it will certainly hold its target audience's attention on a rainy afternoon. JB [VIDEO] DVD

Frances McDormand *Miss Clavel* • Nigel Hawthorne *Lord Covington* • Hatty Jones *Madeline* • Ben Daniels *Leopold, the tutor* • Stéphane Audran *Lady Covington* ■ *Dir* Daisy von Scherler Mayer • *Scr* Mark Levin, Jennifer Flackett, from a story by Malia Scotch Marmo, Mark Levin, Jennifer Flackett, from the books by Ludwig Bemelmans

Madeline: Lost in Paris ★★

Animated adventure
1999 · US · Colour · 76mins

Following a mixed reception for Columbia's live-action adaptation of Ludwig Bemelmans's popular books, Disney returned to the original graphic style for this dark, but always engaging adventure. Madeline, the smallest of the 12 girls residing at Miss Clavel's Parisian orphanage thinks she's finally found a family when a long-lost Viennese uncle comes to claim her. This should keep younger viewers entertained, but the grown-ups might wince at the songs. DP

Lauren Bacall *Madame Lacroque* • Jason Alexander *Uncle Horst/Henri* • Christopher Plummer *Narrator* • Andrea Libman *Madeline* • Stephanie Louise Vallance *Miss Clavel* ■ *Dir* Stan Phillips • *Scr* from the character created by Ludwig Bemelmans

Mademoiselle ★★★

Psychological drama
1966 · Fr/UK · BW · 102mins

Scripted by Jean Genet, the controversial French playwright, this has Jeanne Moreau in the title role as a sexually frustrated schoolmarm in a French farming community. Her secret acts of terrorism – arson, the poisoning of a well, flooding fields – lead the hatred of the village to be directed at the object of her desires, an Italian woodcutter (Ettore Manni). It has a weird compulsion, but director Tony Richardson's over-decorative style is too ponderous for the subject. TH. A French/English language film.

Jeanne Moreau *Mademoiselle* • Ettore Manni *Manou* • Keith Skinner *Bruno* • Umberto Orsini *Antonio* • Jane Beretta *Annette* • Mony Reh *Vievotte* ■ *Dir* Tony Richardson • *Scr* Jean Genet, Bernard Frechtman

Mademoiselle Docteur ★★★★

First World War spy drama
1936 · Fr · BW · 86mins

This melodramatic account of Germany's most famous spy, Anne-Marie Lesser, is given distinction by a fine cast and the evocative direction of GW Pabst. The plotting and assignations during the First World War are vividly re-created in salons, cabarets and railway stations, while delicately beautiful Dita Parlo makes an ethereal heroine. An English language version was made similtaneously by Edmond T Gréville with Erich von Stroheim in the role played by here Louis Jouvet. The same story had been filmed by MGM in 1934 as *Stamboul Quest* with Myrna Loy, but this is by far the better version. TV. In French with English subtitles.

Dita Parlo *Anne-Marie Lesser/Mademoiselle Docteur* • Pierre Blanchar *Gregor Courdane/Condoyan* • Pierre Fresnay *Capt Georges Carrère* • Louis Jouvet *Simonis* • Charles Dullin *Col Matthesius* • Viviane Romance *Gaby* ■ *Dir* GW Pabst • *Scr* Irma von Cube, Georges Neveux, Leo Birinski, Herman J Mankiewicz, Jacques Natanson

Madhouse ★★★ 18

Horror spoof 1974 · UK · Colour · 87mins

In the early 1970s, Vincent Price came to the UK for a string of delightfully black horror comedies, among them *Theatre of Blood* and the *Dr Phibes* movies. *Madhouse* is not in the same class, but it's an entertaining enough romp all the same. The horror legend plays a distinguished actor whose return to the small screen coincides with a series of brutish murders. There is a sterling support cast, and director Jim Clark delivers enough gory chuckles to keep Price fans more than happy. JF. Contains swearing. [VIDEO]

Vincent Price *Paul Toombes* • Peter Cushing *Herbert Flay* • Robert Quarry *Oliver Quayle* • Adrienne Corri *Faye Flay* • Natasha Pyne *Julia* • Michael Parkinson *Television interviewer* • Linda Hayden *Elizabeth Peters* ■ *Dir* Jim Clark • *Scr* Greg Morrison, Ken Levison, from the novel *Devilday* by Angus Hall

Madhouse ★★★ 15

Comedy 1990 · US · Colour · 86mins

The unwanted guest has long been a staple of cinematic comedy. The situation is taken to its extreme in this uneven farce, in which Kirstie Alley and John Larroquette find their new love nest overrun by the kind of relatives you hope you only see at weddings and funerals. The contrast between down-on-their-luck John Diehl and Jessica Lundy and wealthy wife Alison LaPlaca makes for contrived satire, but writer/director Tom Ropelewski comes up with a couple of cracking moments, the best involving a spaced-out moggie. DP. Contains swearing. [VIDEO]

John Larroquette *Mark Bannister* • Kirstie Alley *Jessie Bannister* • Alison LaPlaca *Claudia* • John Diehl *Fred* • Jessica Lundy *Bernice* • Bradley Gregg *Jonathan* • Dennis Miller *Wes* • Robert Ginty *Dale* ■ *Dir/Scr* Tom Ropelewski

Madigan ★★★★ 12

Crime drama 1968 · US · Colour · 96mins

Gifted director Don Siegel amassed a critical and cult following with such hard-boiled movies as this terrific New York-based crime drama. The superb Richard Widmark gives one of his finest performances in the title role, but the laconic Henry Fonda is more than a match for him as the troubled police commissioner. There's a marvellously gritty supporting cast, and the film contains its fair share of sex and violence. Only the cheapness of Universal's Techniscope process disappoints, though the inherent grain oddly suits the night scenes. TS [VIDEO]

Richard Widmark *Det Dan Madigan* • Henry Fonda *Commissioner Anthony Russell* • Inger Stevens *Julia Madigan* • Harry Guardino *Det Rocco Bonaro* • James Whitmore *Chief Inspector Charles Kane* • Sheree North *Jonesy* ■ *Dir* Don Siegel • *Scr* Henri Simoun, Harry Kleiner, Abraham Polonsky, from the novel *The Commissioner* by Richard Dougherty

Madigan's Millions ★

Crime caper 1967 · Sp/It · Colour · 78mins

This Dustin Hoffman film was made in Italy in 1966, before he made *The Graduate* and shot to stardom. It's a caper comedy, with Dustin playing a US tax inspector sent to Europe to look into a murdered mobster's murky accounts. Cesar Romero is seen briefly as the gangster (he replaced George Raft in the role), while Elsa Martinelli plays his daughter. AT. An English/Spanish/Italian language film.

Dustin Hoffman *Jason Fister* • Elsa Martinelli *Vicky Shaw* • Cesar Romero *Mike Madigan* ■ *Dir* Stanley Prager, Dan Ash, Giorgio Gentili • *Scr* James Henaghan, Jose Luis Bayonas

Madison Avenue ★★★ U

Drama 1962 · US · BW · 93mins

The final feature from prolific 20th Century-Fox director H Bruce Humberstone, this is a late round-up of once major Fox stars, in a turgid but nevertheless entertaining melodrama set in the world of advertising. "Lucky" Humberstone uses the black-and-white photography very effectively, especially on those desk-bound interiors, while stars Dana Andrews, Jeanne Crain and the wonderful Eleanor Parker shine as though they knew this was going to be one of the last gasps of the once beloved Fox studio system. TS

Dana Andrews *Clint Lorimer* • Eleanor Parker *Anne Tremaine* • Jeanne Crain *Peggy Shannon* • Eddie Albert *Harvey Ames* • Howard St John *JD Jocelyn* • Henry Daniell *Stipe* • Kathleen Freeman *Miss Haley* • David White *Stevenson Brock* ■ *Dir* H Bruce Humberstone • *Scr* Norman Corwin, from the novel *The Build-Up Boys* by Jeremy Kirk

Madman ★ 18

Horror 1981 · US · Colour · 88mins

Supposedly based on the legend of Madman Marz, who took an axe to his family and then escaped the local lynch mob to disappear without a trace, this is a derivative bore. The disfigured maniac returns and soon the leafy glades are splattered with blood as headless corpses, strangulation victims and mutilated bodies are dragged back to the Marz shack to be meat-hooked. AJ [VIDEO] DVD

Alexis Dubin *Betsy* • Tony Fish *TP* • Harriet Bass *Stacey* • Seth Jones *Dave* • Jan Claire *Ellie* ■ *Dir/Scr* Joe Giannone

The Madness of King George ★★★★★ PG

Biographical historical drama
1995 · UK · Colour · 105mins

Nigel Hawthorne gives an inspired, funny and deeply moving performance in the title role of this celebrated, Oscar-winning film of Alan Bennett's play. The king is married to Charlotte (Helen Mirren), dallying with Lady Pembroke (Amanda Donohoe), and is not only father of 15 children but also of a nation and an empire. Problem is, Farmer George – a nickname the king delights in – is showing signs of madness, or at least that's the official diagnosis. Surgeon Ian Holm is brought in to put the king into a straitjacket (providing some of the film's most disturbing scenes). Behind the sardonic jokes and colloquialisms that are Bennett's trademark is a serious study of 18th-century politics and the monarchy. Immaculately directed by Nicholas Hytner, this is an unmissable treat. AT. Contains some swearing. [VIDEO] DVD

Nigel Hawthorne *George III* • Helen Mirren *Queen Charlotte* • Ian Holm *Willis* • Rupert Graves *Greville* • Amanda Donohoe *Lady Pembroke* • Rupert Everett *Prince of Wales* • Julian Rhind-Tutt *Duke of York* • Julian Wadham *Pitt* • Jim Carter *Fox* • Geoffrey Palmer *Warren* ■ *Dir* Nicholas Hytner • *Scr* Alan Bennett, from his play • *Production Designer* Ken Adam

Madness of the Heart ★★ PG

Drama 1949 · UK · BW · 85mins

Margaret Lockwood's career was already in terminal decline by the time she made this unpersuasive melodrama. As the London lass convinced she's been blinded by lust, she does what she can with a preposterous plot that has her marrying her French lover, Paul Dupuis, only to become the target of a mysterious assassin. Kudos to the supporting cast for keeping straight faces throughout. DP [VIDEO]

Margaret Lockwood *Lydia Garth* • Paul Dupuis *Paul De Vandiere* • Maxwell Reed *Joseph Rondolet* • Thora Hird *Rosa* • Kathleen Byron *Verite Faimont* • Raymond Lovell *Comte De Vandiere* • Maurice Denham *Dr Simon Blake* ■ *Dir* Charles Bennett • *Scr* Charles Bennett, from the novel by Flora Sandstrom

Mado ★★★★

Crime drama 1976 · Fr · Colour · 135mins

This scathing snapshot of France under President Giscard d'Estaing is a typically perceptive study of the country's disconcerted, middle-aged middle classes from director Claude Sautet. Shaken by the suicide of his partner, Michel Piccoli gets lured into Julien Guiomar's attempt to swindle Charles Denner. More important than the real estate MacGuffin, however, are Piccoli's relationships with Ottavia Piccolo, a prostitute at the centre of the scam, and Romy Schneider, whose desperate loyalty to this confused yet undeserving man is heartbreaking. Riveting and revealing. DP. In French with English subtitles.

Michel Piccoli *Simon* • Ottavia Piccolo *Mado* • Jacques Dutronc *Pierre* • Romy Schneider *Helene* • Charles Denner *Manecca* • Julien Guiomar *Boss* ■ *Dir* Claude Sautet • *Scr* Claude Sautet, Claude Néron • *Cinematographer* Jean Boffety

Madonna of the Seven Moons ★★★ U

Romantic drama 1944 · UK · BW · 104mins

A huge box-office success in its day, this Gainsborough costume drama divided the critics, with many denouncing it as a piece of overblown twaddle. Director Arthur Crabtree was a first-class cinematographer, and he brings a lurid glamour to the proceedings. However, he is all at sea where plotting and pacing are concerned. Only the experience of his cast prevents the more melodramatic passages becoming even more over-the-top. DP

Phyllis Calvert *Maddalena Lambardi/Rosanna* • Stewart Granger *Nino Barucci* • Patricia Roc *Angela Lambardi* • Peter Glenville *Sandro Barucci* • John Stuart *Giuseppi* • Jean Kent *Vittoria* • Nancy Price *Madame Barucci* • Peter Murray Hill *Logan* ■ *Dir* Arthur Crabtree • *Scr* Roland Pertwee, Brock Williams, from the novel by Margery Lawrence

La Madre Muerta ★★★★ 18

Thriller 1993 · Sp · Colour · 106mins

Exploring dark and dangerous themes, Juanma Bajo Ulloa's intense film treads a fine line between the disturbing and the distasteful with an agility remarkable for a director making only his second feature. Set in the Basque region, the film considers the controversial topic of sex and the emotionally arrested through the eyes of both a killer (who kidnaps, years later, the mute daughter of his victim to prevent her from identifying him) and his lover (whose jealousy of the girl becomes more threatening than his fear). The acting is excellent, but it's Bajo Ulloa's relentless direction that makes this so troubling. DP. In Spanish with English subtitles.

Karra Elejalde *Ismael Lopez De Matauko* • Ana Alvarez *Leire* • Lio *Maite* • Silvia Marso *Blanca* • Elena Irureta *Female director* • Ramón Barea *Nightclub owner* • Gregoria Mangas *Mrs Millas* • Marisol Sez *Mother* ■ *Dir* Juanma Bajo Ulloa • *Scr* Juanma Bajo Ulloa, Eduardo Bajo Ulloa

Madron ★★

Western 1970 · US · Colour · 93mins

Richard Boone gives one of the craggiest of his many craggy performances in this western about a glowering gunslinger with a soft spot for the kindly nun (Leslie Caron) he's escorting through hostile Apache territory. Shot on location in Israel's Negev desert, there are shades of *The Wild Bunch* in the way the action unfolds; the occasional brutality is another thing it shares with Sam Peckinpah's film. PF

Richard Boone *Madron* • Leslie Caron *Sister Mary* • Paul Smith *Gabe Price* • Gabi Amrani *Angel* • Chaim Banai *Sam Red* ■ *Dir* Jerry Hopper • *Scr* Edward Chappell, Leo McMahon, from a story by Leo McMahon

The Madwoman of Chaillot ★ U

Comedy 1969 · US · Colour · 142mins

An eccentric Parisian countess (Katharine Hepburn) and her batty companions (Margaret Leighton, Edith Evans and Giulietta Masina) foil a fiendish plan to turn the city into a giant oilfield in this wordy, repetitive and boring tale. It's not helped either by the overloading of the cast with star names in even the smallest of the many roles. The opulent sets and costumes, reminiscent of Versailles rather than modern Paris, fail to rescue a misconceived enterprise. RK

Katharine Hepburn *Countess Aurelia* • Charles Boyer *The Broker* • Claude Dauphin *Dr Jadin* • Edith Evans *Josephine* • John Gavin *Reverend* • Paul Henreid *The General* • Oscar Homolka *Commissar* • Margaret Leighton *Constance* • Giulietta Masina *Gabrielle* • Nanette Newman *Irma* • Richard Chamberlain *Roderick* • Yul Brynner *Chairman* • Donald Pleasence *Prospector* • Danny Kaye *Ragpicker* ■ *Dir* Bryan Forbes • *Scr* Edward Anhalt, from the play *La Folle de Chaillot* by Jean Giraudoux

Maelström ★★★

Psychological drama
2000 · Can · Colour · 95mins

The curious caprices of life inform this handsomely atmospheric, but self-consciously surreal melodrama. Boutique owner Marie-Josée Croze's brushes with death and her fortuitous discovery of a reason to live are chronicled with an unnervingly bleak optimism. But it's difficult to see how they gain any additional intensity or macabre irony by being narrated by a soon-to-be-slaughtered fish. DP. In French, Norwegian and English with subtitles.

Marie-Josée Croze *Bibianne Champagne* • Jean-Nicolas Verreault *Evian Karlsen* • Stephanie Morgenstern *Claire Gunderson* • Pierre Lebeau *Fish* • Klimbo *Head-Annstein Karlsen* ■ *Dir/Scr* Denis Villeneuve

Il Maestro ★

Drama 1989 · Fr/Bel · Colour · 90mins

British Malcolm McDowell and French Charles Aznavour co-star as Italians. It's a convoluted story about an orchestra conductor (McDowell) who gets a touch of the vapours when rehearsing *Madame Butterfly*. This leads to a flashback to an era when both McDowell and Aznavour were on the run from the Nazis. The result is a dramatic mess. AT

Malcolm McDowell *Goldberg* • Charles Aznavour *Romualdi* • Andréa Ferréol *Dolores* • Francis Lemaire *Administrator* • Carmela Locantore *Paola* • Pietro Pizzuti *Father Superior* • Serge-Henri Valcke *Major Wyatt* • Chen Qilian *Margerita* ■ *Dir* Marion Hänsel • *Scr* Marion Hänsel, from the story *La Giacca Verde* by Mario Soldati

The Magdalene Sisters ★★★★ 15

Period drama
2002 · UK/Ire · Colour · 114mins

Religious repression and moral hypocrisy are targeted by writer/director Peter Mullan in this bitter indictment of the Magdalene Asylums – convent laundries that were run like workhouses – into which "fallen women" were forced in order to cleanse their "sins". Following three wayward teenagers sent to one such asylum in the 1960s, Mullan's fictionalised version of actual events keeps soapy sentimentality at bay, thanks mainly to the compelling performances of a young cast of unknowns – Eileen Walsh is especially outstanding as the tragic Crispina – while Geraldine McEwan is frighteningly good as the bullying Mother Superior. AJ DVD

Geraldine McEwan *Sister Bridget* • Anne-Marie Duff *Margaret* • Nora-Jane Noone *Bernadette* • Dorothy Duffy *Rose/Patricia* • Eileen Walsh *Crispina* • Mary Murray *Una* • Britta Smith *Katy* • Frances Healy *Sister Jude* ■ *Dir/Scr* Peter Mullan

The Maggie ★★★★ U

Comedy 1953 · UK · BW · 87mins

Ostensibly, this most underestimated of Ealing comedies is a whimsical story about a crew of canny Clydebankers giving a brash American a torrid time after being assigned to carry his property aboard their clapped-out steamer. Don't be fooled, however, by the leisurely pace, the gentle humour and the relatively good-natured conclusion. This is a wicked little satire on the mutual contempt that underlies Euro-American relations, and few could have handled it with such incisive insight as American-born Scot Alexander Mackendrick. Cruel rather than quaint. DP DVD

Paul Douglas *Marshall* • Alex Mackenzie *Skipper* • James Copeland *Mate* • Abe Barker *Engineer* • Tommy Kearins *Wee boy* • Hubert Gregg *Pusey* • Geoffrey Keen *Campbell* • Dorothy Alison *Miss Peters* ■ *Dir* Alexander Mackendrick • *Scr* William Rose, from a story by Alexander Mackendrick

Magic ★★ 15

Thriller 1978 · US · Colour · 106mins

A low-key update of the old "ventriloquist taken over by his evil dummy" theme, scripted by William Goldman. Richard Attenborough overstretches an already thin premise and deliberately minimises the horror elements by placing the emphasis on warped entertainer Anthony Hopkins's unbalanced psychological condition. The result is a sadly sentimental effort, lacking both suspense and atmosphere. AJ. Contains swearing and some violence.

Anthony Hopkins *Corky/"Fats"* • Ann-Margret *Peggy Ann Snow* • Burgess Meredith *Ben Greene* • Ed Lauter *Duke* • EJ André *Merlin* • Jerry Houser *Cab driver* • David Ogden Stiers *George Hudson Todson* • Lillian Randolph *Sadie* ■ *Dir* Richard Attenborough • *Scr* William Goldman, from his novel

The Magic Bow ★★ U

Biographical drama 1946 · UK · BW · 105mins

The few facts that have been retained in this biopic of the violin virtuoso Niccolo Paganini have been submerged in melodramatic scenes that are notable only for a certain pomposity of dialogue, while such invented details as the duel and the pawning of his Stradivarius betray the penny-dreadful imagination of the scriptwriters. Yet somehow this film still manages to get under the skin, thanks to the vigorous vulgarity of Stewart Granger's performance and Yehudi Menuhin's vibrant playing on the soundtrack. DP

Stewart Granger *Paganini* • Phyllis Calvert *Jeanne* • Jean Kent *Blanchi* • Dennis Price *Paul De La Roche* • Cecil Parker *Germi* • Felix Aylmer *Pasini* ■ *Dir* Bernard Knowles • *Scr* Roland Pertwee, Norman Ginsbury, from the novel by Manuel Komroff

The Magic Box ★★★★ U

Biographical drama
1951 · UK · Colour · 103mins

Produced for the Festival of Britain, this biopic of William Friese-Greene is more a piece of wishful thinking than an accurate portrait of Britain's pre-eminent cinema pioneer. So what if Friese-Greene failed in his attempt to project moving images, and who cares if he "borrowed" many of his ideas from forgotten collaborators like John Rudge and Mortimer Evans? This is charming and thoroughly entertaining myth-making, made all the more palatable by the engaging performance of Robert Donat. DP

Robert Donat *William Friese-Greene* • Maria Schell *Helena* • Margaret Johnston *Edith Friese-Greene* • Robert Beatty *Lord Beaverbrook* • Renée Asherson *Miss Tagg* • Michael Redgrave *Mr Lege* • Richard Attenborough *Jack Carter* • Laurence Olivier *Second Holborn policeman* • Eric Portman *Arthur Collings* • Glynis Johns *May Jones* • Margaret Rutherford *Lady Pond* • Peter Ustinov *Industry man* • Stanley Holloway *Broker's man* ■ *Dir* John Boulting • *Scr* Eric Ambler, from the book *Friese-Greene, Close-up of an Inventor* by Ray Allister

The Magic Bubble ★★★ 12

Fantasy comedy 1992 · US · Colour · 90mins

In a thought-provoking film, a downtrodden mum who's just turned 40 is finally able to stick two fingers up to her bullying hubby after a magic bubble grants her deepest desire, and she finds she can no longer remember her age. Renewed "youthfulness" leads to changes in appearance, personality and permissiveness. Diane Salinger and John Calvin star, but the main cast interest resides in an early role for George Clooney. DA DVD

Diane Salinger *Julia Cole* • John Calvin *Charles Cole* • Priscilla Pointer *Grandma* • George Clooney *Mac* • Colleen Camp *Deborah* • Wallace Shawn *Dr Block* • Shera Danese *Letty* ■ *Dir* Deborah Ringel, Alfredo Ringel • *Scr* Meridith Baer, Geoff Prysirr

The Magic Christian ★★ 15

Comedy 1969 · UK · Colour · 88mins

Admiring Terry Southern's satirical novel of 1959, Peter Sellers sent it to Stanley Kubrick who liked its humour so much he hired Southern to work on *Dr Strangelove*. Then Sellers reunited with Southern for this comedy about the richest man in the world who adopts a drop-out son, Ringo Starr, to prove his and the rest of humanity's worthlessness. A dreadful mess, very much part of the Swinging Sixties culture, this film is also unmissable for an eye-popping cast. AT

Peter Sellers *Sir Guy Grand* • Ringo Starr *Youngman Grand* • Richard Attenborough *Oxford coach* • Leonard Frey *Psychiatrist on ship* • Laurence Harvey *Hamlet* • Christopher Lee *Dracula* • Spike Milligan *Traffic warden* • Yul Brynner *Lady singer* • Roman Polanski *Man listening to lady singer* • Raquel Welch *Slave-driver* • Wilfrid Hyde White *Ship's captain* • Graham Chapman *Oxford stroke* • John Cleese *Director in Sotheby's* • Clive Dunn *Sommelier* • Hattie Jacques *Ginger Horton* ■ *Dir* Joseph McGrath • *Scr* Terry Southern, Joseph McGrath, Peter Sellers, Graham Chapman, John Cleese from the novel *The Magic Christian* by Terry Southern,

The Magic Donkey ★★★ U

Fantasy 1970 · Fr · Colour · 89mins

Following their exemplary collaboration on *The Umbrellas of Cherbourg*, director Jacques Demy and composer Michel Legrand reunited for this adaptation of Charles Perrault's distinctly dubious fairy tale. The film achieves its neverland atmosphere through the enchanting decor and some glorious colour photography from Ghislain Cloquet. However, it's hard to identify with the story of a king (Jean Marais) whose promise to his dying queen that he will only marry someone of comparable beauty sets him after his daughter (Catherine Deneuve). DP. French dialogue dubbed in English.

Catherine Deneuve *Peau d'Ane/Queen* • Jacques Perrin *Prince* • Jean Marais *King* • Delphine Seyrig *Fairy* • Fernand Ledoux *Red King* • Micheline Presle *Red Queen* ■ *Dir* Jacques Demy • *Scr* Jacques Demy, from the fairy tales *Les Contes de Ma Mère l'Oye* by Charles Perrault

Magic Fire ★★

Biographical drama
1956 · US · Colour · 112mins

Long-delayed in reaching the screen, then barely released, this biography of composer Richard Wagner proved to be too ambitious for Republic Studios. Despite a finely upholstered look and a flamboyant performance from Alan Badel, the film is scuppered by his

M

wooden Argentinian co-star Carlos Thompson and leaden direction from veteran William Dieterle. TS

Alan Badel *Richard Wagner* • Yvonne De Carlo *Minna* • Carlos Thompson *Franz Liszt* • Rita Gam *Cosima* • Valentina Cortese *Mathilde* • Peter Cushing *Otto Wesendonk* • Frederick Valk *Minister von Moll* • Gerhard Riedmann *King Ludwig II* ■ *Dir* William Dieterle • *Scr* Bertita Harding, EA Dupont, David Chantler, from the novel by Bertita Harding • *Music* Erich Wolfgang Korngold • *Cinematographer* Ernest Haller

The Magic Flute ★★★ U

Opera 1974 · Swe · Colour · 134mins

Aiming both to re-create the contemporary experience of watching Mozart's final operatic masterpiece and make opera accessible to viewers of all races and ages, Ingmar Bergman's stylised staging only fitfully succeeds. A surfeit of audience reaction shots and some rather twee backstage docu-snaps interfere with the flow of the story. However, the studio re-creation of the handsome Drottningholm Theatre and its 18th-century paraphernalia is delightful, while the cast is admirable. DP. In Swedish with English subtitles.

Josef Köstlinger *Tamino* • Irma Urrila *Pamina* • Hakan Hagegard *Papageno* • Elisabeth Eriksson *Papagena* • Ulrik Cold *Sarastro* ■ *Dir* Ingmar Bergman • *Scr* Ingmar Bergman

The Magic Garden of Stanley Sweetheart ★★

Drama 1970 · US · Colour · 111mins

For a time in the 1960s, Hollywood studios thought that all they had to do to tempt kids from the TV was to pack movies with "shocking" sex, drugs and rock 'n' roll. Here, Don Johnson plays a disaffected college student who experiments with casual sex, drugs and alternative lifestyles. The hippy philosophy, the music and the fashions are now pleasantly nostalgic, but Johnson's aimless odyssey does seem to go on forever. DM

Don Johnson *Stanley Sweetheart* • Linda Gillin *Shayne/Barbara* • Michael Greer *Danny* • Dianne Hull *Cathy* • Holly Near *Fran* • Victoria Racimo *Andrea* ■ *Dir* Leonard Horn • *Scr* Robert T Westbrook, from his novel

Magic Hunter ★★★

Fantasy
1994 · Hun/Swi/Fr/Can · Colour · 106mins

Executive produced by David Bowie and starring Gary Kemp and Sadie Frost, this is a surreal though beautiful treatise from director Ildiko Enyedi. Set in medieval Hungary and contemporary Budapest, the film interweaves two tales. One tells the story of a policeman (Kemp) who loses his ability to shoot on target just when he is assigned to protect a chess master from assassination. The other involves a painting of the Virgin Mary (Natalie Conde) coming to life to save a rabbit! LH. In Hungarian with English subtitles.

Gary Kemp *Max* • Sadie Frost *Eva* • Alexander Kaidanovsky *Maxim* • Peter Vallai *Kaspar* • Mathias Gnadinger *Police chief* • Alexandra Wasscher *Lili* • Ildiko Toth *Lina* • Natalie Conde *Virgin Mary* ■ *Dir* Ildiko Enyedi • *Scr* Ildiko Enyedi, Laszlo Revesz, from the opera *Der Freischutz* by Carl Maria von Weber

Magic in the Water ★★★ PG

Fantasy adventure
1995 · Can/US · Colour · 96mins

A charming family film about a mythical water creature that helps a psychiatrist realise he's so wrapped up in his work that he's making a mess of both his life and his relationship with his kids. Rick Stevenson's film wisely goes easy on the special effects, emphasising instead the magic inherent in its basic scenario. Mark Harmon and Harley Jane Kozak star in a slice of delightful escapism that will enchant children and their parents. DA [video]

Mark Harmon *Jack Black* • Joshua Jackson *Joshua Black* • Harley Jane Kozak *Dr Wanda Bell* • Sarah Wayne *Ashley Black* • Willie Nark-Orn *Hiro* • Frank Sotonoma Salsedo [Frank Salsedo] *Uncle Kipper* ■ *Dir* Rick Stevenson • *Scr* Rick Stevenson, Icel Dobell Massey, from a story by Ninian Dunnett, Rick Stevenson, Icel Dobell Massey

The Magic of Lassie ★★

Drama 1978 · US · Colour · 99mins

Not even the presence of James Stewart, Mickey Rooney and Alice Faye can save this otherwise unremarkable attempt to resurrect the world's most famous collie. Director Don Chaffey sticks closely to the story of the original *Lassie Come Home*, as nasty Pernell Roberts takes Lassie away from a debt-ridden family. The 1943 classic was genuinely uplifting – this is just cloyingly sentimental. JF

James Stewart *Clovis Mitchell* • Mickey Rooney *Gus* • Alice Faye *Alice* • Pernell Roberts *Jamison* • Stephanie Zimbalist *Kelly Mitchell* • Michael Sharrett *Chris Mitchell* ■ *Dir* Don Chaffey • *Scr* Jean Holloway, Robert B Sherman, Richard M Sherman

The Magic Pudding ★★★ U

Animated fantasy adventure
2000 · Aus · Colour · 75mins

Norman Lindsay was the controversial Australian artist whose story was retold in *Sirens*. Surprisingly, he was also the author of the children's favourite on which this animated feature is based. Some of the continent's finest performers contribute voices to the story of Bunyip Bluegum (Geoffrey Rush), a koala who is joined in the search for his missing parents by Bill Barnacle the sailor (Hugo Weaving) and the penguin, Sam Sawnoff (Sam Neill). With Jack Thompson as the wicked wombat Buncle, who tries to steal Albert (John Cleese), the pudding that never runs out, this should keep the whole family amused. DP [video]

John Cleese *Albert the Magic Pudding* • Geoffrey Rush *Bunyip Bluegum* • Sam Neill *Sam Sawnoff* • Hugo Weaving *Bill Barnacle* • Toni Collette *Meg Bluegum* • Jack Thompson *Buncle* ■ *Dir* Karl Zwicky • *Scr* Harry Cripps

The Magic Roundabout ★★★ U

Animated fantasy adventure
2005 · UK/Fr · Colour · 81mins

The much-loved children's TV classic is re-imagined for 21st-century youngsters in this attractive computer-animated adventure. Using the original characters as a springboard, the film broadens and updates their escapades to satisfy contemporary tastes. The result is a colourful tribute to the eccentric 1960s show, in which Dougal the dog inadvertently releases imprisoned sorcerer Zeebad (voiced by Tom Baker). The dialogue and comic scenarios still have their knowing undertones, while the slightly beefed-up characters retain their simple charm. SF

Tom Baker *Zeebad* • Jim Broadbent *Brian* • Joanna Lumley *Ermintrude* • Kylie Minogue *Florence* • Robbie Williams *Dougal* • Ian McKellen *Zebedee* • Bill Nighy *Dylan* • Ray Winstone *Soldier Sam* • Lee Evans *Train* ■ *Dir* Dave Borthwick, Jean Duval, Frank Passingham • *Scr* Paul Bassett, Raolf Sanoussi, Stephane Sanoussi, from characters created by Serge Danot, Martine Danot

The Magic Sword ★★★

Fantasy 1962 · US · Colour · 80mins

This medieval fantasy never really takes off, coming across as a blunt version of *Excalibur*. Gary Lockwood plays a young knight who sets out to rescue princess Anne Helm from wicked sorcerer Basil Rathbone. The latter is magnificent, as usual, while Estelle Winwood's witch is a wonderful piece of dithery expertise. Otherwise, though, this not really cutting-edge material, despite some neat special effects by Milt Rice. TH

Basil Rathbone *Lodac* • Estelle Winwood *Sybil* • Gary Lockwood *St George* • Anne Helm *Princess Helene* • Liam Sullivan *Sir Branton* • John Mauldin *Sir Patrick* • Jacques Gallo *Sir Dennis* • Leroy Johnson *Sir Ulrich* ■ *Dir* Bert I Gordon • *Scr* Bernard Schoenfeld, from a story by Bert I Gordon

The Magic Sword: Quest for Camelot ★★★ U

Animated period adventure
1997 · US · Colour · 82mins

The daughter of a murdered knight searches for King Arthur's magic sword, Excalibur, which has been stolen and is lost in a mythic wood. Adapted from the novel *The King's Damosel* by British writer Vera Chapman, it's hot on character but rather devoid of action. There's an interesting cast of voices, from Gary Oldman's evil Sir Ruber to John Gielgud's magical Merlin, and Pierce Brosnan is a very smooth-talking King Arthur. TH [video] DVD

Cary Elwes *Garrett* • Bryan White *Garrett* • Jessalyn Gilsig *Kayley* • Andrea Corr *Kayley* • Gary Oldman *Sir Ruber* • Eric Idle *Devon* • Don Rickles *Cornwall* • Pierce Brosnan *King Arthur* • John Gielgud *Merlin* ■ *Dir* Frederik Du Chau • *Scr* Kirk De Micco, William Schiffrin, Jacqueline Feather, David Seidler, from the novel *The King's Damosel* by Vera Chapman

Magic Town ★★★ U

Comedy drama 1947 · US · BW · 98mins

This intriguing comedy drama, deftly directed by William A Wellman, provides a fascinating insight into small-town America. James Stewart is convinced that the white-picket-fence haven of Grandview can be used as a statistical yardstick for the country as a whole, while Jane Wyman's strong newspaper editor seeks positive social change. The old and new vie for supremacy in postwar society, and Wellman uses his film as a metaphor for the debate while staying in touch with the human story. SH DVD

James Stewart *Lawrence Rip Smith* • Jane Wyman *Mary Peterman* • Kent Smith *Hoopendecker* • Ned Sparks *Ike Sloan* • Wallace Ford *Lou Dicketts* • Regis Toomey *Ed Weaver* • Ann Doran *Mrs Weaver* • Donald Meek *Mr Twiddle* ■ *Dir* William A Wellman • *Scr* Robert Riskin, from a story by Robert Riskin, Joseph Krumgold

The Magic Voyage ★★

Animated musical adventure
1992 · Ger · Colour · 80mins

The handful of films made to commemorate the 500th anniversary of Columbus's discovery of America were a pretty lacklustre lot, with the serious dramas *1492: Conquest of Paradise* and *Christopher Columbus: the Discovery* too overblown for some tastes. At least this feature-length cartoon musical achieves what it sets out to do to – inform and entertain its young audience with the charming story of how a woodworm helped Columbus reach the New World and how a glow-worm guided him home. DP

Dom DeLuise *Columbus* • Corey Feldman *Pico* • Irene Cara *Marilyn* • Samantha Eggar *Queen Isabella* • Dan Haggerty *King Ferdinand* • Mickey Rooney *Narrator* ■ *Dir* Michael Schoemann • *Scr* Scott Santoro

The Magician ★★★ PG

Fantasy drama 1958 · Swe · BW · 107mins

Winner of the special jury prize at Venice, Ingmar Bergman's Gothic drama has been described as a comedy without jokes and a horror film without chills. Focusing on the artist's value to society and exploring such themes as illusion, faith, science and truth, this has the feel of a man trying too hard to repeat the success of the previous year's masterpieces. Max von Sydow gives a bravura performance as the 19th-century mesmerist Vogler and Gunnar Fischer's photography creates the right mood of uncertainty, but, for all the director's sleights of hand, there's no magic. DP. In Swedish with English subtitles. [video] DVD

Max von Sydow *Vogler* • Ingrid Thulin *Manda* • Gunnar Björnstrand *Dr Vergerus* • Naima Wifstrand *Grandmother* • Bengt Ekerot *Spegel* • Bibi Andersson *Sara* • Gertrud Fridh *Ottilia* • Lars Ekborg *Simson* • Erland Josephson *Egerman* ■ *Dir/Scr* Ingmar Bergman • *Cinematographer* Gunnar Fischer

The Magician of Lublin ★★★ 15

Drama 1979 · Is/W Ger · Colour · 108mins

Isaac Bashevis Singer's novel gets a halfway decent adaptation from, of all people, ex-Cannon boss and trash director Menahem Golan. Alan Arkin stars as a Jewish entertainer, who becomes the toast of late 19th and early 20th-century Warsaw society thanks to his talent as an ace illusionist and escape artist. But greed, lust and his giant ego soon cause his rapid fall from grace. A good cast invest this rarefied period piece with a high-tone atmosphere and its unusual fantasy elements provide a surprising conclusion. AJ [video]

Alan Arkin *Yasha Mazur* • Louise Fletcher *Emilia* • Valerie Perrine *Zeftel* • Shelley Winters *Elizabeta* • Maia Danziger *Magda* • Linda Bernstein *Esther* • Lou Jacobi *Wolsky* ■ *Dir* Menahem Golan • *Scr* Irving S White, Menahem Golan, from the novel by Isaac Bashevis Singer

M

The Magnet ★★ U

Comedy 1950 · UK · BW · 74mins

This was one of Ealing superscribe TEB Clarke's least distinguished efforts. The story of a young boy who steals a magnet and becomes the toast of his community after his accidental heroics is contrived, but it's the totally false characters that let it down. Moreover, director Charles Frend fails to exploit the run-down urban locations. Young William Fox would later change his first name to James and become a front-rank star. DP [video] DVD

Stephen Murray *Dr Brent* • Kay Walsh *Mrs Brent* • William Fox [James Fox] *Johnny Brent* • Meredith Edwards *Harper* • Gladys Henson *Nannie* • Thora Hird *Nannie's friend* • Michael Brooke Jr *Kit* • Wylie Watson *Pickering* ■ *Dir* Charles Frend • *Scr* TEB Clarke

The Magnetic Monster ★★★

Science fiction 1953 · US · Colour · 75mins

An excellent, low-budget slice of science-fiction about a new radioactive element, created by scientists' unauthorised experiments, that doubles its size every 12 hours by converting surrounding energy into matter. Confidently directed by Curt Siodmak with an accent on approximate authenticity, and incorporating stock footage to good effect, this cosmic *Frankenstein* makes full use of its interesting cast. AJ

Richard Carlson *Dr Jeffrey Stewart* • King Donovan *Dr Dan Forbes* • Jean Byron *Connie Stewart* • Harry Ellerbe *Dr Allard* • Leo Britt *Dr Benton* • Leonard Mudie *Dr Denker* • Byron Foulger *Simon* • Michael Fox *Dr Serny* ■ *Dir* Curt Siodmak • *Scr* Curt Siodmak, Ivan Tors

The Magnetist's Fifth Winter ★★★

Period drama
1999 · Nor/Swe/Den/Fr · Colour · 119mins

A stylish tale of charlatanism, superstition and the inexplicable. The action turns on the seemingly miraculous ministrations of Ole Lemmeke, an itinerant magnetist whose cure of doctor Rolf Lassgård's blind daughter, Johanna Sällström, prompts jilted physician Gard B Eidsvold to delve into the stranger's scandalous past. Possessing both an eerie spirituality and a susceptibility to temptation, Lemmeke is truly mesmerising as he seeks to exploit attitudes which, despite the 1820 setting, are positively medieval. DP. In Swedish with English subtitles.

Rolf Lassgård *Doctor Selander* • Ole Lemmeke *Friedrich Meisner* • Johanna Sällström *Maria* • Gard B Eidsvold *Doctor Stenius* ■ *Dir* Morten Henriksen • *Scr* Morten Henriksen, Jonas Cornell, from a novel by Per Olov Enquist

The Magnificent Ambersons ★★★★★ U

Classic period drama
1942 · US · BW · 84mins

Orson Welles's follow-up to *Citizen Kane* is one of cinema's flawed masterpieces. Adapted from Booth Tarkington's novel, it tells the compelling story of the decline of a once-proud family in the face of sprawling industrialisation. We shall never see the director's version, as executives at RKO felt the film was too long and depressing, and so ordered over 40 minutes of cuts, destroyed the footage and tacked on a happy ending directed by production manager Freddie Fleck. Out of the country on location, Welles was powerless to do anything about it. It says much for his genius that this is still a brilliant exercise in nostalgia and film technique. DP [video]

Joseph Cotten *Eugene Morgan* • Agnes Moorehead *Fanny Minafer* • Dolores Costello *Isabel Amberson Minafer* • Anne Baxter *Lucy Morgan* • Tim Holt *George Amberson Minafer* • Don Dillaway [Donald Dillaway] *Wilbur Minafer* • Ray Collins *Jack Amberson* • Richard Bennett *Major Amberson* • Erskine Sanford *Roger Bronson* • Charles Phipps *Uncle John* • Orson Welles *Narrator* ■ *Dir* Orson Welles • *Scr* Orson Welles, from the novel by Booth Tarkington • *Cinematographer* Stanley Cortez • *Editor* Robert Wise • *Music* Bernard Herrmann • *Costume Designer* Edward Stevenson • *Production Designer* Mark-Lee Kirk

Magnificent Doll ★

Historical drama 1946 · US · BW · 90mins

One of the great romantic dramas of American history is rendered flatter than a pancake by grotesque miscasting and direction that completely fails the subject matter. Ginger Rogers is spectacularly wrong as Dolly Payne Madison, one of the White House's great ladies, in a screenplay by Irving Stone that plays fast and loose with the facts. David Niven, as Aaron Burr, gives a truly awful performance. TS

Ginger Rogers *Dorthea "Dolly" Payne Madison* • David Niven *Aaron Burr* • Burgess Meredith *James Madison* • Horace McNally [Stephen McNally] *John Todd* • Peggy Wood *Mrs Payne* • Frances Williams *Amy, the maid* • Grandon Rhodes *Thomas Jefferson* ■ *Dir* Frank Borzage • *Scr* Irving Stone, from his story

The Magnificent Dope ★★ U

Comedy drama 1942 · US · BW · 83mins

A minor vehicle for Henry Fonda as a lazy country hick who arrives in New York and teaches everyone how to chill out, relax and take things easy. This amazes city slicker Don Ameche and charms secretary Lynn Bari, a starlet whom 20th Century-Fox promoted as the "girl with the million dollar figure" as well as "the woo woo girl": American GIs apparently rated her second only to Betty Grable in pin-up power. As corny as Kansas in August, but entertaining enough. AT

Henry Fonda *Tad Page* • Lynn Bari *Claire* • Don Ameche *Dawson* • Edward Everett Horton *Horace Hunter* • George Barbier *Barker* • Frank Orth *Messenger* • Roseanne Murray *Dawson's secretary* • Marietta Canty *Jennie* ■ *Dir* Walter Lang • *Scr* George Seaton, from a story by Joseph Schrank

The Magnificent Matador ★★

Romantic drama 1955 · US · Colour · 94mins

Anthony Quinn plays a bullfighter who falls for rich American tourist Maureen O'Hara and worries about his illegitimate son entering the arena. The director of this effort, Budd Boetticher, was a matador himself who quit the arena for a career in Hollywood. Typically, there is a lot of macho posturing, snorting and hooves scratching at the sand – and that's just Anthony Quinn! AT

Maureen O'Hara *Karen Harrison* • Anthony Quinn *Luis Santos* • Manuel Rojas *Rafael Reyes* • Thomas Gomez *Don David* • Richard Denning *Mark Russell* • Lola Albright *Mona Wilton* • William Ching *Jody Wilton* • Eduardo Noriega (1) *Miguel* ■ *Dir* Budd Boetticher • *Scr* Charles Lang, from a story by Budd Boetticher

Magnificent Obsession ★★★★

Melodrama 1935 · US · BW · 112mins

Directed by a master of the soap opera, Universal's John M Stahl, this romantic melodrama has Robert Taylor as a wealthy, irresponsible playboy who is partly responsible for the death of a revered doctor and, subsequently, for an accident that blinds the doctor's widow Irene Dunne, with whom he falls in love. Filled with remorse, Merrick becomes a Nobel Prize-winning brain surgeon and, years later, finds her again, hoping to redeem himself. Beautifully made and well-acted, it's a more restrained and credible version than the Douglas Sirk remake, but not half as much fun! RK

Irene Dunne *Helen Hudson* • Robert Taylor (1) *Bobby Merrick* • Charles Butterworth *Tommy Masterson* • Betty Furness *Joyce Hudson* • Sara Haden *Nancy Ashford* • Ralph Morgan *Randolph* • Henry Armetta *Tony* • Gilbert Emery *Dr Ramsay* ■ *Dir* John M Stahl • *Scr* George O'Neil, Sarah Y Mason, Victor Heerman, Finley Peter Dunne, from the novel by Lloyd C Douglas

Magnificent Obsession ★★★★ U

Classic melodrama
1954 · US · Colour · 107mins

Luscious, glorious Technicolor entry from Universal's memorable Ross Hunter/Douglas Sirk cycle of no-holds-barred melodramas, and the one that turned beefcake Rock Hudson into a romantic superstar. Adapted from the syrupy novel by Lloyd C Douglas, it was a box-office hit the first time around (in 1935). This time an Oscar-nominated Jane Wyman plays the woman who loses her husband and then goes blind, partly through Hudson's irresponsibility. While she is cared for by Agnes Moorehead, he mends his ways and becomes a brilliant surgeon before seeking her out years later. RK

Jane Wyman *Helen Phillips* • Rock Hudson *Bob Merrick* • Barbara Rush *Joyce Phillips* • Agnes Moorehead *Nancy Ashford* • Otto Kruger *Randolph* • Gregg Palmer *Tom Masterson* ■ *Dir* Douglas Sirk • *Scr* Robert Blees, Wells Root, from the 1935 film, from the novel by Lloyd C Douglas

The Magnificent Rebel ★★ U

Biographical drama
1961 · US/W Ger · Colour · 94mins

Karlheinz Böhm plays a brooding and intense Ludwig van Beethoven in this Disney biography, shot in Germany. It was originally shown in two parts on American television, but released as a film elsewhere. Böhm does well, but the screenplay is poor, the direction turgid and the dubbing distracting. However, the photography and, of course, the music make this watchable. TS. German dialogue dubbed into English.

Karlheinz Böhm *Ludwig van Beethoven* • Giulia Rubini *Giulietta* • Ivan Desny *Lichnowsky* • Peter Arens *Amenda* • Oliver Grimm *Stefan* ■ *Dir* Georg Tressler • *Scr* Joanne Court [Joan Scott] • *Cinematographer* Göran Strindberg

The Magnificent Seven ★★★★★ PG

Classic western 1960 · US · Colour · 127mins

Director John Sturges was extremely fortunate in securing a near-perfect cast for this enduringly popular western reworking of the Japanese classic *Seven Samurai*. Not content with forging a new iconic image for Yul Brynner as a black-clad gunslinger, he also created key star-making roles for 1960s sensations Steve McQueen, James Coburn and Charles Bronson. The use of Panavision landscape is glorious to behold, Eli Wallach is a suitably slimy villain and the action sequences are tremendously exciting. There's also one of the greatest musical themes ever written for a movie, in an altogether fine brass-led score by composer Elmer Bernstein. Three sequels followed, beginning with *Return of the Seven* in 1966 and *Guns of the Magnificent Seven* (1969). TS. Contains violence. [video] DVD

Yul Brynner *Chris* • Steve McQueen *Vin* • Eli Wallach *Calvera* • Horst Buchholz *Chico* • Charles Bronson *O'Reilly* • Robert Vaughn *Lee* • Brad Dexter *Harry Luck* • James Coburn *Britt* • Vladimir Sokoloff *Old man* • Rosenda Monteros *Petra* ■ *Dir* John Sturges • *Scr* William Roberts, Walter Bernstein, Walter Newman (uncredited) • *Cinematographer* Charles Lang Jr [Charles Lang]

The Magnificent Seven Deadly Sins ★★ PG

Comedy 1971 · UK · Colour · 103mins

Having packed his short film *Simon, Simon* with cameos by his famous friends, comic actor Graham Stark enticed even more comedians and comic writers to contribute to this, his only feature. It comprises seven sketches, each one a mildly amusing illustration of a deadly sin. The film is very much a product of its time, with familiar TV faces performing glorified sitcom (two of the segments are adaptations of TV episodes), while busty starlets remove their clothes. DM [video] DVD

Bruce Forsyth • Joan Sims • Roy Hudd • Harry Secombe • Leslie Phillips • Julie Ege • Harry H Corbett • Ian Carmichael • Alfie Bass • Spike Milligan • Ronald Fraser ■ *Dir* Graham Stark • *Scr* Marty Feldman, Graham Stark, Ray Galton, Alan Simpson, Barry Cryer, John Esmonde, Graham Chapman, Dave Freeman, Bob Larbey, Spike Milligan

The Magnificent Seven Ride! ★★★ PG

Western 1972 · US · Colour · 96mins

Not really, they don't. This is the fourth and last outing for the famous title and, as in the previous sequel, no members of the original cast are to be found. Still, Lee Van Cleef makes a perfectly acceptable substitute for Yul Brynner, and the theme remains true to the original's concept. Here the bandits kidnap Van Cleef's wife and the seven are rounded up to seek vengeance, but the real star is Elmer Bernstein's score. TS [video] DVD

Lee Van Cleef *Chris* • Stefanie Powers *Laurie Gunn* • Mariette Hartley *Arilla* • Michael Callan *Noah Forbes* • Luke Askew *Skinner* • Pedro Armendáriz Jr *Pepe Carral* • Ralph Waite *Jim Mackay* • William Lucking *Walt Drummond* ■ *Dir* George McCowan • *Scr* Arthur Rowe • *Music* Elmer Bernstein

The Magnificent Showman ★★★ U

Action adventure
1964 · US · Colour · 131mins

This entertaining big-top saga features John Wayne as a circus owner whose business faces a variety of crises. Begun as *Circus World* by director Frank Capra, the film was then entrusted to the much more suitable Henry Hathaway, who makes the lengthy tale race by in a jiffy. The climactic fire and the capsize of the circus ship (special effects by Alex Weldon) were amazingly effective. And what other movie features Rita Hayworth and Claudia Cardinale as mother and daughter, each trying to upstage the other? TS [video]

John Wayne *Matt Masters* • Rita Hayworth *Lili Alfredo* • Claudia Cardinale *Toni Alfredo* • Lloyd Nolan *Cap Carson* • Richard Conte *Aldo Alfredo* • John Smith *Steve McCabe* • Henri Dantes *Emile Schuman* • Wanda Rotha *Mrs Schuman* ■ *Dir* Henry Hathaway • *Scr* Ben Hecht, Julian Halevy [Julian Zimet], James Edward Grant, from the story by Philip Yordan, Nicholas Ray

The Magnificent Two ★★ PG

Comedy 1967 · UK · Colour · 91mins

Like most British comedians of the 1960s and 1970s, Morecambe and Wise failed to make it in movies because the situations that made their TV series so successful simply could not be sustained beyond an hour or the confines of a studio setting. Here Eric and Ernie do their utmost to kick-start this poor comedy of errors about travelling salesmen caught up in a South American revolution. But the plot is paper thin, the jokes aren't funny and the use of a bikini-clad army to install Margit Saad as president is unworthy of the duo. DP [video] DVD

Eric Morecambe *Eric* • Ernie Wise *Ernie* • Margit Saad *Carla* • Cecil Parker *British ambassador* • Virgilio Teixeira *Carillo* • Isobel Black *Juanita* • Martin Benson *President Diaz* ■ *Dir* Cliff Owen • *Scr* SC Green, RM Hills, Michael Pertwee, Peter Blackmore

The Magnificent Yankee ★★★ U

Biographical drama 1950 · US · BW · 88mins

A biopic of Oliver Wendell Holmes (1841-1935), the Supreme Court judge famous for his witticisms and his espousal of liberal causes, which earned him the nickname "The Great Dissenter". The story charts Holmes's career between the presidencies of two Roosevelts, taking in such key historical events as the Great War and the Depression. As Holmes, Louis Calhern has to age considerably, dispense justice *and* have a private life with his wife (Ann Harding). No wonder his performance earned him an Oscar nomination. A stagey, talky movie that oozes prestige. AT

Louis Calhern *Oliver Wendell Holmes* • Ann Harding *Fanny Bowditch Holmes* • Eduard Franz *Judge Louis Brandeis* • Philip Ober *Mr Owen Wister* • Ian Wolfe *Mr Adams* • Edith Evanson *Annie Gough* • Richard Anderson *Reynolds* ■ *Dir* John Sturges • *Scr* Emmet Lavery, from the play by Emmet Lavery, from the novel *Mr Justice Holmes* by Francis Biddle

M

Magnolia ★★★★★ 18

Drama 1999 · US · Colour · 180mins

Paul Thomas Anderson seals his growing reputation as one of Hollywood's most ambitious and audacious film-makers with this dark, daring and dazzling take on Robert Altman's *Short Cuts*. Boldly tossing aside storytelling conventions, Anderson's offbeat epic charts 24 hours in the weird lives of a dozen San Fernando Valley inhabitants. The cast is just superb, with Tom Cruise's supremely arrogant sex guru standing out. But Jason Robards, Julianne Moore, Melora Walters, John C Reilly and William H Macy are also brilliant in their one-of-a-kind roles. Although the running time is a little indulgent, the film's increasingly frantic pace, manic camerawork and unpredictable scenarios command the attention. JC. Contains violence, swearing, sex scenes, drug abuse, nudity. [video] DVD

Tom Cruise *Frank TJ Mackey* • Julianne Moore *Linda Partridge* • William H Macy *Quiz Kid Donnie Smith* • Philip Seymour Hoffman *Phil Parma* • Melora Walters *Claudia Wilson Gator* • John C Reilly *Jim Kurring* • Jason Robards *Earl Partridge* • Philip Baker Hall *Jimmy Gator* • Melinda Dillon *Rose Gator* • Luis Guzman *Luis* • Orlando Jones *Worm* • Alfred Molina *Solomon Solomon* • Henry Gibson *Thurston Howell* ■ *Dir/Scr* Paul Thomas Anderson • *Cinematographer* Robert Elswit

Magnum: Don't Eat the Snow in Hawaii ★★★ PG

Crime drama 1980 · US · Colour · 89mins

Tom Selleck must have an ambivalent attitude towards Thomas Sullivan Magnum, as his commitment to the Hawaii-based series prevented him from being cast as Indiana Jones. Using his position as head of security on the estate of absent crime writer Robin Masters as a cover for his activities as a private detective, Selleck would continue to solve cases over the next eight years. Here he's suitably imposing as he pursues the killer of a Vietnam veteran. DP [video]

Tom Selleck *Thomas Sullivan Magnum* • John Hillerman *Jonathan Quayle Higgins* • Roger E Mosley *Theodore "T C" Calvin* • Larry Manetti *Orville "Rick" Wright* • Pamela Susan Shoop [Pamela Shoop] *Alice Cook* • Fritz Weaver *Captain Cooly* ■ *Dir* Roger Young • *Scr* Donald P Bellisario, Glen A Larson

Magnum Force ★★★ 18

Crime thriller 1973 · US · Colour · 117mins

An all-guns-blazing follow-up to *Dirty Harry*, with a storyline different enough from the original to grip the attention. Clint Eastwood is on fine form as no-nonsense cop "Dirty" Harry Callahan, yet again relying on his own instincts as he investigates the ruthless killings of prominent criminals in San Francisco. There's excellent support, and the chase scene involving motorbikes during the climax is superbly staged, but this lacks much of the original's moral complexity, with more action favoured. *The Enforcer* (1976) continued the series. NF. Contains violence, swearing. [video] DVD

Clint Eastwood *Harry Callahan* • Hal Holbrook *Lieutenant Briggs* • Felton Perry *Early Smith* • Mitchell Ryan *Charlie McCoy* • David Soul *Davis* • Tim Matheson *Sweet* • Robert Urich *Grimes* • Kip Niven *Astrachan* ■ *Dir* Ted Post • *Scr* John Milius, Michael Cimino, from a story by John Milius, from original material by Harry Julian Fink, RM Fink

The Magus ★

Fantasy drama 1968 · UK · Colour · 116mins

Asked whether he would do everything the same if he had to live his life all over again, Peter Sellers thought for a moment and said: "Yes. But I would not see *The Magus*." Here's a movie so pretentious, it's worth sampling a reel or two just to confirm that, yes, they *can* make them as bad as this. The producers committed a double whammy by choosing an unfilmable novel and then getting its author – John Fowles – to adapt it himself. It's about a British schoolteacher (played by Michael Caine) cast sexually and metaphysically adrift on a Greek island. Anthony Quinn is in it, with Candice Bergen and Anna Karina. AT

Anthony Quinn *Maurice Conchis* • Michael Caine *Nicholas Urfe* • Candice Bergen *Lily* • Anna Karina *Anne* • Julian Glover *Anton* • Takis Emmanuel *Kapetan* ■ *Dir* Guy Green • *Scr* John Fowles, from his novel

Mahler ★★★ 15

Biographical drama 1974 · UK · Colour · 110mins

This was one of the more successful and less outré outings from Ken Russell, in which he returned to familiar turf, having directed a series of television dramatisations of famous composers' lives during the 1960s. Gustav Mahler is played with some depth and subtlety by Robert Powell and there's excellent support from Georgina Hale as his self-sacrificing wife. The director here considerably tones down the cinematic excesses for which he has become notorious, and this is a brief, interesting, finely scripted film. SH [video] DVD

Robert Powell *Gustav Mahler* • Georgina Hale *Alma Mahler* • Richard Morant *Max* • Lee Montague *Bernhard Mahler* • Rosalie Crutchley *Marie Mahler* • Benny Lee *Uncle Arnold* • Miriam Karlin *Aunt Rosa* • Angela Down *Justine* ■ *Dir/Scr* Ken Russell

Mahogany ★

Melodrama 1975 · US · Colour · 108mins

The only good thing to come out of this mess is the theme song, the Diana Ross classic *Do You Know Where You're Going To*. Ross stars as a humble Chicago secretary who becomes a fashion model called Mahogany, then a fashion designer with the help of fruitcake photographer Anthony Perkins. Pitched as a full-blooded melodrama, it's banality has to be seen to be believed. AT

Diana Ross *Tracy/Mahogany* • Billy Dee Williams *Brian* • Anthony Perkins *Sean* • Jean-Pierre Aumont *Christian Rosetti* • Beah Richards *Florence* • Nina Foch *Miss Evans* • Marisa Mell *Carlotta Gavina* ■ *Dir* Berry Gordy • *Scr* John Byrum, from a story by Toni Amber

The Maid ★★ PG

Romantic comedy 1991 · US/Fr · Colour · 86mins

A soft-centred romantic comedy that wastes the talents of its stars, Martin Sheen and Jacqueline Bisset. The former is a besotted businessman who poses as a servant to be with his newly discovered true love Bisset. There are some nice role-reversal moments, but the script lacks bite and there is little to work with. Supporting players Jean-Pierre Cassel and James Faulkner fare the best, but it's slim pickings all round. JF [video]

Martin Sheen *Anthony Wayne* • Jacqueline Bisset *Nicole Chantrelle* • Victoria Shalet *Marie* • Jean-Pierre Cassel *CP Oliver* • James Faulkner *Laurent Leclair* • Dominique Varda *Nicole's secretary* ■ *Dir* Ian Toynton • *Scr* Timothy Prager

Maid in Manhattan ★★ PG

Romantic comedy 2002 · US · Colour · 100mins

Director Wayne Wang swaps originality and sophistication for feel-good froth in this predictable Cinderella story. Ralph Fiennes piles on the charm as a would-be senatorial candidate who falls for Manhattan hotel maid and single parent Jennifer Lopez in the mistaken belief she's a socialite. Comic mishaps and schmaltzy soul-searching ensue, but the two leads are unconvincing. SF [video] DVD

Jennifer Lopez *Marisa Ventura* • Ralph Fiennes *Christopher Marshall* • Natasha Richardson *Caroline Lane* • Stanley Tucci *Jerry Siegel* • Bob Hoskins *Lionel Bloch* • Tyler Garcia Posey *Ty Ventura* • Frances Conroy *Paula Burns* • Chris Eigeman *John Bextrum* ■ *Dir* Wayne Wang • *Scr* Kevin Wade, from a story by Edmond Dantes [John Hughes]

Maid to Order ★★★ 15

Comedy 1987 · US · Colour · 89mins

This is a story of wish fulfilment, but if the majority of the cast were given the chance they would probably have wished for a sharper script than this one, in which poor little rich girl Ally Sheedy learns about life the hard way after she is erased from her father's memory. Sheedy is too nice to convince as a spoilt brat, but Valerie Perrine and Dick Shawn are good value as the vulgar wannabes who hire her as their maid. DP [video]

Ally Sheedy *Jessie Montgomery* • Beverly D'Angelo *Stella* • Michael Ontkean *Nick McGuire* • Valerie Perrine *Georgette Starkey* • Dick Shawn *Stan Starkey* • Tom Skerritt *Charles Montgomery* • Merry Clayton *Audrey James* • Begona Plaza *Maria* ■ *Dir* Amy Jones [Amy Holden Jones] • *Scr* Amy Jones [Amy Holden Jones], Perry Howze, Randy Howze

The Maids ★★ 12

Drama 1974 · UK/Can · Colour · 90mins

This is a dull screen version of the dreary Jean Genet play about two Parisian maids who concoct a sado-masochistic plan to murder their hated mistress, but then never actually go through with it. It's that sort of play, and film. The main interest resides in the quality acting from a top-notch British cast. DA DVD

Glenda Jackson *Solange* • Susannah York *Claire* • Vivien Merchant *Madame* • Mark Burns *Monsieur* ■ *Dir* Christopher Miles • *Scr* Robert Enders, Christopher Miles, from the play *Les Bonnes* by Jean Genet

Maid's Night Out ★★★

Comedy 1938 · US · BW · 64mins

To win a bet with his self-made father, millionaire Allan Lane becomes a milkman for a month and falls for rich girl Joan Fontaine whom he thinks is the maid. RKO dropped their budding star Fontaine the same year she made this jolly little film, played and directed (by Ben Holmes) with evident enjoyment; she would shortly bounce back by making *Rebecca* for Hitchcock. Gossip columnist Hedda Hopper, who began her career as an actress, is in the supporting cast. RK

Joan Fontaine *Sheila Harrison* • Allan Lane *Bill Norman* • Hedda Hopper *Mrs Harrison* • George Irving *Rufus Norman* • William Brisbane *Wally Martin* • Billy Gilbert *Papalapoulas* • Cecil Kellaway *Geoffrey* ■ *Dir* Ben Holmes • *Scr* Bert Granet, from a story by Willoughby Speyers

Maigret Sets a Trap ★★★

Detective drama 1957 · Fr · BW · 110mins

The work of Georges Simenon – especially that featuring Inspector Maigret – has reputedly been more often adapted to the screen than those of any other 20th-century writer. This entertaining whodunnit benefits from the presence of the incomparable Jean Gabin, who brings grace and gravitas to the role of the detective in pursuit of a night stalker and killer. Annie Girardot and Lino Ventura lend support in this atmospheric film. BB. A French language film.

Jean Gabin *Inspector Jules Maigret* • Annie Girardot *Yvonne Maurin* • Jean Desailly *Marcel Maurin* • Olivier Hussenot *Inspector Lagrume* • Jeanne Boitel *Mme Maigret* • Lucienne Bogaert *Mme Maurin* ■ *Dir* Jean Delannoy • *Scr* RM Arlaud, Michel Audiard, Jean Delannoy, from a novel by Georges Simenon

Mail Order Bride ★★★

Western 1963 · US · Colour · 83mins

In this slight but rather charming western, Buddy Ebsen tries to tame Keir Dullea, the hotheaded son of a dead friend, by making him marry Lois Nettleton, a widow with a young son. Writer/director Burt Kennedy's dialogue is splendid, and he extracts fine performances from his cast; his use of the camera could have been more dynamic, though. Warren Oates contributes some colourful work as the villain, while Marie Windsor figures nicely as the saloon keeper. AE

Buddy Ebsen *Will Lane* • Keir Dullea *Lee Carey* • Lois Nettleton *Annie Boley* • Warren Oates *Jace* • Barbara Luna *Marietta* • Paul Fix *Jess Linley* • Marie Windsor *Hanna* • Denver Pyle *Preacher Pope* ■ *Dir* Burt Kennedy • *Scr* Burt Kennedy, from the story *Mail-Order Bride* by Van Cort in *The Saturday Evening Post*

The Main Attraction ★★

Romantic drama 1962 · UK · Colour · 89mins

Keen to kick against his clean-cut image, American crooner Pat Boone hightailed it to Europe for this ludicrous circus melodrama, in which he trifles with the affections of ventriloquist Mai Zetterling, while holding a candle for bareback rider Nancy Kwan. Yet Boone isn't the most miscast member of this sorry ensemble. That honour goes to Lionel Blair as the clown who becomes pathologically jealous of Boone's relationship with Zetterling. DP

Pat Boone *Eddie* • Nancy Kwan *Tessa* • Mai Zetterling *Gina* • Yvonne Mitchell *Elenora* • Kieron Moore *Ricco* • John Le Mesurier *Bozo* • Warren Mitchell *Proprietor* • Lionel Blair *Clown* ■ *Dir* Daniel Petrie • *Scr* John Patrick

The Main Event ★★ 15

Romantic comedy 1979 · US · Colour · 104mins

This is one of those self-centred films that Barbra Streisand produces, in which she takes her favourite role of sexual predator. Her target is Ryan O'Neal but the stars fail to re-create the comic success they had in *What's Up, Doc?*. Streisand plays the bankrupt owner of a perfume company whose only asset is washed-up boxer O'Neal. Sadly, director Howard Zieff's comedy falls a long way short of going the distance. TH [video] DVD

Barbra Streisand *Hillary Kramer* • Ryan O'Neal *Eddie "Kid Natural" Scanlon* • Paul Sand *David* • Whitman Sand *Percy* • Patti D'Arbanville *Donna* • Chu Chu Malave *Luis* • Richard Lawson *Hector Mantilla* ■ *Dir* Howard Zieff • *Scr* Gail Parent, Andrew Smith

Main Hoon Na ★★ 12

Romantic comedy drama 2004 · Ind · Colour · 174mins

Major Shah Rukh Khan's dying father, played by Naseeruddin Shah, always hoped that his scheme "Mission Milaap" would end the tension between India and Pakistan. However, physics master Sunil Shetty is out to sabotage his plans and so Shah Rukh has to go undercover and return to school. This is a proficient star vehicle, but the shifts from international espionage to romantic triangle aren't always smooth. DP. In Hindi with English subtitles. [video] DVD

Shah Rukh Khan *Major Ram Prasad Sharma* • Zayed Khan *Lucky Laxman* • Amrita Rao *Sanjana* • Sushmita Sen *Chandni* • Naseeruddin Shah *Brigadier Shekhar Sharma* • Sunil Shetty *Raghavan* ■ *Dir* Farah Khan • *Scr* Abbas Tyrewala, Farah Khan, from a story by Farah Khan

Main Prem Ki Diwani Hoon ★★ PG

Musical romantic drama
2003 · Ind · Colour · 175mins

Everything in this disappointing film is played at fever pitch, whether it's spoilt Kareena Kapoor's frequent tantrums or Johny Lever's foolish antics with the family pets. Even Hrithik Roshan overdoes the charm as the gregarious employee of bashful American-based tycoon Abhishek Bachchan, who is mistaken for Kapoor's prospective husband until her grasping mother, Himani Shivpuri, intervenes. It's a simple comedy of errors, but the action is unnecessarily strung out. DP. In Hindi with English subtitles. DVD

Hrithik Roshan *Prem* • Kareena Kapoor *Sanjana* • Abhishek Bachchan *Prem* • Johny Lever [Johnny Lever] • Pankaj Kapur *Sanjana's father* • Himani Shivpuri *Sanjana's mother* ■ *Dir* Sooraj R Barjatya [Sooraj Barjatya] • *Scr* Sooraj R Barjatya [Sooraj Barjatya], from a story by Subodh Ghosh

Main Street to Broadway ★★

Romantic comedy 1953 · US · BW · 101mins

The professional struggles of aspiring young playwright Tom Morton and his involvement with actress Mary Murphy offer a flimsy excuse for fleeting appearances by just about every star on MGM's books. The result is a dull and uninteresting look at Broadway's backstage life, marginally enlivened by Tallulah Bankhead's guest turn. RK

Tom Morton *Tony Monaco* • Mary Murphy *Mary Craig* • Agnes Moorehead *Mildred Waterbury* • Herb Shriner *Frank Johnson* • Rosemary DeCamp *Mrs Craig* • Clinton Sundberg *Mr Craig* • Tallulah Bankhead • Ethel Barrymore ■ *Dir* Tay Garnett, Joel Newton • *Scr* Samson Raphaelson, from a story by Robert E Sherwood

Les Mains Sales ★★

Drama 1951 · Fr · BW · 106mins

Jean-Paul Sartre co-adapted his once controversial play to the screen, ensuring – given the date – that the inherent conflict between disillusioned politico Pierre Brasseur and dedicated young communist and potential assassin Daniel Gélin was retained. Sadly, Fernand Rivers displays little filmic invention so we're left with a talkative battle between the revolutionaries, past and present, when the younger man, accompanied by his wife (Monique Artur) agrees to murder his colleague, who might compromise their cause. Plenty of discussion and no resolution. BB. In French with English subtitles.

Pierre Brasseur *Hoederer* • Daniel Gélin *Hugo* • Claude Nollier *Olga* • Monique Artur *Jessica* • Jacques Castelot *Prince* • Marcel André *Karski* ■ *Dir* Fernand Rivers • *Scr* Jacques-Laurent Bost, Fernand Rivers, Jean-Paul Sartre, from the play by Jean-Paul Sartre

Maisie ★★★

Comedy 1939 · US · BW · 74mins

MGM cast Ann Sothern in this programmer about a curly-headed showgirl stranded without a dime in a one-horse rodeo town. After a chapter of accidents and misunderstandings involving taciturn ranch manager Robert Young, she cons her way into a job as maid to the owner (Ian Hunter) and his faithless wife (Ruth Hussey). Directed by Edwin L Marin, the success of this fresh, breezy and inconsequential film spawned a ten-picture series, making Maisie/Sothern a 1940s institution. Seen in our jaded age, the picture is both sociologically fascinating and enormous good fun. RK

Robert Young (1) *"Slim" Martin* • Ann Sothern *Maisie Ravier* • Ruth Hussey *Sybil Ames* • Ian Hunter *Clifford Ames* • Cliff Edwards *Shorty* • Anthony Allan [John Hubbard] *Richard Raymond* • Art Mix *"Red"* • George Tobias *Rico* ■ *Dir* Edwin L Marin • *Scr* Mary C McCall Jr, from the novel *Dark Dame* by Wilson Collison

Le Maître d'Ecole ★★★

Comedy 1981 · Fr · Colour · 95mins

At this point in his career, Claude Berri was known for blending autobiographical incident with social satire. Yet he resorted to slapstick and sitcom for this fish-out-of-water tale of the novice supply teacher forced to deal with an uncooperative class and eccentric colleagues. Reliant on borrowed notes and his own wits, Michel Coluche rises to the challenge, without falling back on the kind of cornball feel-good that characterises similar Hollywood romps. DP. In French with English subtitles.

Michel Coluche *Gérard Barbier* • Josiane Balasko *Miss Joyful* • Jacques Debary *Headmaster* • Charlotte De Turckheim *Charlotte* ■ *Dir/Scr* Claude Berri

Maîtresse ★★★ 18

Erotic black comedy
1976 · Fr · Colour · 108mins

Walking the tightrope between titillation and tact, this study of sadomasochism stars Bulle Ogier as a "mistress" or dominatrix, who inflicts pain and various sorts of humiliation upon her clients. Coming into this secret world is petty crook Gérard Depardieu, who becomes not only Ogier's lover but also her willing assistant. At once explicit and discreet, Barbet Schroeder's film certainly looks weird enough; through the perversion, the purity of Ogier and Depardieu's affair emerges and enters a surreal zone of its own. AT. In French with English subtitles. DVD

Gérard Depardieu *Olivier* • Bulle Ogier *Ariane* • André Rouyer *Mario* • Nathalie Keryan *Lucienne* ■ *Dir* Barbet Schroeder • *Scr* Barbet Schroeder, Paul Voujargol

The Majestic ★★★ PG

Romantic comedy drama
2001 · US/Aus · Colour · 146mins

This unashamedly Capra-esque film endorses the values of small-town America and their redemptive effects. Jim Carrey stars as a blacklisted screenwriter in 1950s Hollywood who – in a state of drunken despair – accidentally drives his car off a bridge and is later found washed up on the shores of a proverbial small town, suffering from amnesia. He closely resembles the missing soldier son of Martin Landau, who owns the town's Majestic cinema. With his part in the renovation of the crumbling movie-house, Carrey is able to find his true worth and the town's spirit is revived. Overlong, but caring. TH DVD

Jim Carrey *Peter Appleton/Luke Trimble* • Martin Landau *Harry Trimble* • Laurie Holden *Adele Stanton* • David Ogden Stiers *Doc Stanton* • James Whitmore *Stan Keller* • Jeffrey DeMunn *Ernie Cole* • Hal Holbrook *Congressman Doyle* • Bob Balaban *Majority Counsel Elvin Clyde* • Allen Garfield *Leo Kubelsky* ■ *Dir* Frank Darabont • *Scr* Michael Sloane

The Major and the Minor ★★★ U

Romantic comedy 1942 · US · BW · 101mins

A 12-year-old girl on a train awakens the concern of army officer Ray Milland. She also awakens his sexual interest and that of the boys at the military academy where he's stationed. This romantic comedy marked Billy Wilder's Hollywood directing debut. The girl, of course, is not underage at all, but Ginger Rogers masquerading to avoid paying full fare. Famous wit and sometime character actor Robert Benchley offers support, and Ginger's real-life mother Lela plays her mom. Daft, sparkling entertainment. RK

Ginger Rogers *Susan Applegate* • Ray Milland *Maj Kirby* • Rita Johnson *Pamela Hill* • Robert Benchley *Mr Osborne* • Diana Lynn *Lucy Hill* • Edward Fielding *Col Hill* • Frankie Thomas *Cadet Osborne* • Raymond Roe *Cadet Wigton* • Lela Rogers *Mrs Applegate* ■ *Dir* Billy Wilder • *Scr* Billy Wilder, Charles Brackett, from the play *Connie Goes Home* by Edward Childs Carpenter, from the story *Sunny Goes Home* by Fannie Kilbourne

Major Barbara ★★★★

Satirical comedy 1941 · UK · BW · 125mins

This is a superbly cast adaptation of George Bernard Shaw's morality study of the Salvation Army and armaments manufacture. Wendy Hiller in the title role, Rex Harrison as her admirer and a marvellous array of British stage and screen names acquit themselves with distinction. The only flawed performance comes from Robert Morley, who plays Hiller's capitalist father as a fool. Although direction is originally credited to the Hungarian producer Gabriel Pascal, who had acquired the sole rights to film Shaw, this was in fact an early directorial effort by the young David Lean and Harold French. Deborah Kerr looks radiant in an early appearance, and the sophistication of the comedy is perfectly balanced by Ronald Neame's photography and Vincent Korda's splendid interior sets. TS

Wendy Hiller *Major Barbara Undershaft* • Rex Harrison *Adolphus Cusins* • Robert Morley *Andrew Undershaft* • Emlyn Williams *Snobby Price* • Robert Newton *Bill Walker* • Sybil Thorndike *The General* • Deborah Kerr *Jenny Hill* • David Tree *Charles Lomax* ■ *Dir* Gabriel Pascal, Harold French, David Lean • *Scr* Anatole de Grunwald, George Bernard Shaw, from the play by George Bernard Shaw

Major Dundee ★★★ PG

Western 1965 · US · Colour · 117mins

Sam Peckinpah's third feature stars Charlton Heston as a Union officer leading a wild bunch of Confederate prisoners, including Richard Harris, to capture an even wilder bunch of marauding Apaches. While Peckinpah had in mind a dark, violent epic about the Civil War, Columbia wanted a breezy cavalry and Indians adventure. When Columbia threatened to fire Peckinpah in mid-schedule, Heston backed him up and offered to return his $200,000 fee. The studio, of course, accepted this rash offer and let Peckinpah continue, though it still cut 40 minutes of footage. AT

Charlton Heston *Major Amos Dundee* • Richard Harris *Captain Benjamin Tyreen* • Senta Berger *Teresa Santiago* • Jim Hutton *Lieutenant Graham* • James Coburn *Samuel Potts* • Michael Anderson Jr *Tim Ryan* • Mario Adorf *Sergeant Gomez* • Brock Peters *Aesop* ■ *Dir* Sam Peckinpah • *Scr* Harry Julian Fink, Oscar Saul, Sam Peckinpah, from a story by Harry Julian Fink

Major League ★★★ 15

Sports comedy 1989 · US · Colour · 101mins

In this amiable, if predictable sporting comedy, the players of a deadbeat baseball team, led by Tom Berenger, decide to fight back when they discover that their new boss (Margaret Whitton) is determined to see them finish bottom of the league. The misfits include the short-sighted pitcher Charlie Sheen and the hopelessly vain Corbin Bernsen. Director David S Ward, who wrote *The Sting*, allows it to get by on star power alone, while the sharp-eyed will spot the pre-stardom Rene Russo and Wesley Snipes. JF

Tom Berenger *Jake Taylor* • Charlie Sheen *Rickie Vaughn* • Corbin Bernsen *Roger Dorn* • Margaret Whitton *Rachel Phelps* • James Gammon *Lou Brown* • Rene Russo *Lynn Wells* • Wesley Snipes *Willie Mays Hayes* ■ *Dir/Scr* David S Ward

Major League II ★★ PG

Sports comedy 1994 · US · Colour · 100mins

Five years after the Cleveland Indians baseball team stepped out in *Major League*, the same sorry crew (minus Wesley Snipes and Rene Russo) reassembles for another season, with the team's original nemesis, owner Margaret Whitton, once again determined to dismantle the club. The acting is minor league, while the bawdy locker-room banter and the endless on-the-field foul-ups become tiresome. DP. Contains swearing.

Charlie Sheen *Rick "Wild Thing" Vaughn* • Tom Berenger *Jake Taylor* • Corbin Bernsen *Roger Dorn* • Dennis Haysbert *Pedro Cerrano* • James Gammon *Lou Brown* • Omar Epps *Willie Mays Hayes* • Margaret Whitton *Rachel Phelps* ■ *Dir* David S Ward • *Scr* RJ Stewart, from a story by Tom S Parker, Jim Jennewein, RJ Stewart

Major League: Back to the Minors ★★ 12

Sports comedy 1998 · US · Colour · 95mins

It's strike three for this baseball comedy franchise, and it's out – of ideas. Scott Bakula should have been suspicious when even the non-selective Charlie Sheen declined to return for this second sequel. Slimy Corbin Bernsen is back, though, offering ex-player Bakula the job of managing the worst team in the league. There's the usual array of eccentric players and reversals of fortune, but don't expect too many surprises. JC. Contains swearing.

Scott Bakula *Gus Cantrell* • Corbin Bernsen *Roger Dorn* • Takaaki Ishibashi *Taka Tanaka* • Ted McGinley *Leonard Huff* • Bob Uecker *Harry Doyle* • Dennis Haysbert *Pedro Cerrano* ■ *Dir/Scr* John Warren (2)

A Majority of One ★ U

Comedy drama 1961 · US · Colour · 153mins

The unlikely love affair between a middle-aged Jewish widow and a Japanese diplomat is the subject of this movie, adapted by Leonard Spigelgass from his hit Broadway play. The film, however, directed by Mervyn LeRoy at interminable length, falls flat on its face, due in no small part to disastrous miscasting. The blue-blooded Rosalind Russell never quite convinces as a Brooklyn mother, while Alec Guinness substitutes inscrutability for character. RK

Rosalind Russell *Mrs Jacoby* • Alec Guinness *Koichi Asano* • Ray Danton *Jerome Black* • Madlyn Rhue *Alice Black* • Mae Questel *Mrs Rubin* ■ *Dir* Mervyn LeRoy • *Scr* Leonard Spigelgass, from his play

Make Haste to Live ★★

Thriller 1954 · US · BW · 90mins

Dorothy McGuire fans need no persuading to watch this splendidly titled melodrama, in which McGuire is confronted by a neurotic criminal husband (a glowering Stephen McNally) who's come back to seek vengeance. This is a very average programme filler, from that period in McGuire's career when she was past her 1940s peak and before she superbly re-invented her screen image as an older, wiser woman. Director William A Seiter is hamstrung by a tight budget and a short shooting schedule. TS

Dorothy McGuire *Crystal Benson* • Stephen McNally *Steve* • Mary Murphy *Randy Benson* • Edgar Buchanan *Sheriff* • John Howard (1)

Josh ■ *Dir* William A Seiter • *Scr* Warren Duff, from a novel by Mildred Gordon, Gordon Gordon

Make Me a Star ★★★

Comedy drama 1932 · US · BW · 86mins

Stuart Erwin stars as the screen-struck hick who goes to Hollywood and becomes a movie star when cast in a comedy western that he thinks is a serious film. Great fun, with Joan Blondell the sympathetic co-star, ZaSu Pitts and Ben Turpin in support, and a host of the famous (Claudette Colbert, Tallulah Bankhead, Gary Cooper, Charlie Ruggles, Fredric March et al) flitting through Paramount studios as themselves. RK

Joan Blondell *"Flips" Montague* • Stuart Erwin *Merton Gill* • ZaSu Pitts *Mrs Scudder* • Ben Turpin *Ben* • Charles Sellon *Mr Gashwiler* • Florence Roberts *Mrs Gashwiler* ■ *Dir* William Beaudine • *Scr* Sam Mintz, Walter DeLeon, Arthur Kober, from the play *Merton of the Movies* by George S Kaufman, Marc Connelly, from the novel *Merton of the Movies* by Harry Leon Wilson

Make Mine a Million ★★★ U

Comedy 1959 · UK · BW · 77mins

Diminutive funster Arthur Askey had often spoofed the BBC on radio and in films and, when he made the transition from the BBC to ITV (in 1956), he likewise took the rise out of his new employers. In this satire on TV advertising, Arthur Askey is a make-up man who falls under the influence of dodgy promoter Sidney James and becomes the star of soap powder commercials. A pacey romp. DF

Arthur Askey *Arthur Ashton* • Sidney James *Sid Gibson* • Dermot Walsh *Martin Russell* • Sally Barnes *Sally* • Olga Lindo *Mrs Burgess* • Bernard Cribbins *Jack* • Kenneth Connor *Anxious husband* ■ *Dir* Lance Comfort • *Scr* Peter Blackmore, Talbot Rothwell, Arthur Askey, from a story by Jack Francis

Make Mine Mink ★★ U

Comedy 1960 · UK · BW · 96mins

This is so awash with whimsy that the comedy only occasionally manages to bob to the surface. But, while it's not an uproarious laughfest, there's still plenty to enjoy as the dependable Terry-Thomas masterminds a series of robberies for his gang of old dears in order to raise money for a children's home. Athene Seyler, Elspeth Duxbury and Hattie Jacques are good value as the respectable rogues, and Kenneth Williams is fun as their fence. But Billie Whitelaw is less convincing as the reformed delinquent. DP DVD

Terry-Thomas *Major Albert Rayne* • Hattie Jacques *Nanette Parry* • Athene Seyler *Dame Beatrice Appleby* • Billie Whitelaw *Lily* • Elspeth Duxbury *Elizabeth Pinkerton* • Irene Handl *Madame Spolinski* • Jack Hedley *Jim Benham* • Kenneth Williams *Freddy Warrington* ■ *Dir* Robert Asher • *Scr* Michael Pertwee, Peter Blackmore, from the play *Breath of Spring* by Peter Coke

Make Mine Music ★★★★ U

Musical animation
1946 · US · Colour · 71mins

This was Walt Disney's attempt to do for popular music what his studio's animation had achieved for classical music in *Fantasia*, but he failed to meet with similar box-office success. This beautifully crafted film is by no means as well known as it should be. As with *Fantasia*, the crass populism of this episodic treat divided critics and delighted children, and today there's even more to enjoy, not least the glorious period Technicolor and the display of major 1940s talent, including the Benny Goodman Orchestra, the Andrews Sisters, Dinah Shore and Nelson Eddy. TS

Nelson Eddy • Dinah Shore • Jerry Colonna • Andy Russell • Sterling Holloway ■ *Dir* Jack Kinney, Clyde Geronimi, Hamilton Luske, Robert Cormack, Joshua Meador • *Scr* Homer Brightman, Dick Huemer, Dick Kinney, John Walbridge, Tom Oreb, Dick Shaw, Eric Gurney, Sylvia Holland, T Hee, Dick Kelsey, Jesse Marsh, Roy Williams, Erdman Penner, James Bodrero, Cap Palmer, Erwin Graham

Make Way for Tomorrow ★★★★

Comedy drama 1937 · US · BW · 91mins

There aren't many films on the painful subject of growing old and becoming a burden to one's offspring: Yasujiro Ozu's *Tokyo Story*, *Kotch* with Walter Matthau and this heartrending Leo McCarey picture, a genuine tear-jerker thanks to its acute understanding of human nature. Victor Moore and Beulah Bondi play the retired couple who lose their home and are forced to separate when none of their children will take them in. The old pair are shown realistically, being quite difficult at times, but their continuing optimism makes their plight all the worse. AE

Victor Moore *Barkley Cooper* • Beulah Bondi *Lucy Cooper* • Fay Bainter *Anita Cooper* • Thomas Mitchell *George Cooper* • Porter Hall *Harvey Chase* • Barbara Read *Rhoda Cooper* • Maurice Moscovitch [Maurice Moscovich] *Max Rubens* • Elisabeth Risdon *Cora Payne* • Leo McCarey *Passerby/Man in overcoat/Carpet sweeper* ■ *Dir* Leo McCarey • *Scr* Viña Delmar [Vina Delmar], from the unpublished play *Years Are So Long* by Helen Leary, Nolan Leary, from the novel *Years Are So Long* by Josephine Lawrence

Make Your Own Bed ★ U

Comedy 1944 · US · BW · 82mins

Private detective Jack Carson and his girlfriend Jane Wyman accept an assignment from inventor Alan Hale to move into his house as servants in order to protect him from a gang of Nazis. Witless and desperately unfunny, directed by Peter Godfrey without a single idea to liven it up. RK

Jack Carson *Jerry Curtis* • Jane Wyman *Susan Courtney* • Alan Hale *Walter Whirtle* • Irene Manning *Vivian Whirtle* • George Tobias *Boris Murphy* ■ *Dir* Peter Godfrey • *Scr* Francis Swann, Edmund Joseph, Richard Weil, from a play by Harvey J O'Higgins, Harriet Ford

The Maker ★★★ 18

Crime drama 1997 · US · Colour · 94mins

Director Tim Hunter made his name with the startling *River's Edge*, a harrowing portrait of disaffected youth, and this sees him covering similar ground. Jonathan Rhys Meyers plays a teenage slacker who, along with his friends fills his days by hanging around malls and indulging in petty crime. Then his long-lost older brother Matthew Modine turns up out of the blue and initiates him into burglary. The thriller elements don't quite come off but Hunter still has a sharp eye for adolescent trauma. JF. Contains swearing and violence. DVD

Matthew Modine *Walter Schmeiss* • Mary-Louise Parker *Officer Emily Peck* • Jonathan Rhys Meyers *Josh Minnell* • Michael Madsen *Skarney* • Fairuza Balk *Bella Sotto* • Kate McGregor-Stewart *Mother Minnell* • Lawrence Pressman *Father Minnell* ■ *Dir* Tim Hunter • *Scr* Rand Ravich

Making Contact ★★★ 15

Supernatural adventure
1985 · W Ger · Colour · 75mins

An early film from director Roland Emmerich, made a decade before he went big and blockbustery with *Stargate*, *Independence Day* and *Godzilla*. Emmerich brings flair and imagination to this superior kids' film about a boy whose grief at his dad's death activates previously hidden telekinetic powers. DA

Joshua Morrell *Joey* • Eva Kryll *Laura, Joey's mother* • Jan Zierold *Martin, Joey's father* • Tammy Shields *Sally* • Barbara Klein *Dr Haiden* ■ *Dir* Roland Emmerich • *Scr* Hans J Haller, Thomas Lechner

Making Love ★★ 18

Drama 1982 · US · Colour · 106mins

Kate Jackson gets a shock when her doctor husband Michael Ontkean confesses he is in love with another. The other happens to be a man (Harry Hamlin). Arthur Hiller's restrained account of a repressed man coming out of the closet was something of a ground-breaking film for Hollywood at the time. But because such care has been taken not to offend anyone, this never rises above the uncomplicated, routine level of a soap opera. AME

Michael Ontkean *Zack* • Kate Jackson *Claire* • Harry Hamlin *Bart McGuire* • Wendy Hiller *Winnie Bates* • Arthur Hill *Henry* • Nancy Olson *Christine* • John Dukakis *Tim* ■ *Dir* Arthur Hiller • *Scr* Barry Sandler, from a story by A Scott Berg

Making Mr Right ★★★ 15

Science-fiction satire
1987 · US · Colour · 94mins

This quirky satire was Susan Seidelman's next movie after her big hit, *Desperately Seeking Susan*. John Malkovich plays both an inventor and the android he has created, while Ann Magnuson is a wacky PR whizz hired to promote the robot but soon falling in love with it. Zany stuff, combining shades of vintage B-movies with punk hairstyles and postmodern sensibilities. Less than the sum of its rather too diverse parts. PF DVD

John Malkovich *Dr Jeff Peters/Ulysses* • Ann Magnuson *Frankie Stone* • Glenne Headly *Trish* • Ben Masters *Congressman Steve Marcus* • Laurie Metcalf *Sandy* • Polly Bergen *Estelle Stone* • Harsh Nayyar *Dr Ravi Ramdas* • Susan Berman *Ivy Stone* ■ *Dir* Susan Seidelman • *Scr* Floyd Byars, Laurie Frank

The Making of Maps ★★ 15

Drama 1995 · UK · Colour · 102mins

In this film set at the height of the Cuban missile crisis, Welsh film-maker Endaf Emlyn contrasts adolescent trauma with the problems of a world in transition. However, this tale of a boy charting his course through the choppy waters of family life is much more personal than its predecessor, which explains the prevalence of mirror images throughout the film. It's earnestly acted, but a bit too solemn. DP. In Welsh with English subtitles.

Gavin Ashcroft *Griff* • Catherine Tregenna *Megan* • Maldwyn Pate *Robert* • Abigail Creel *Ruth* • Lara Ward *Alis* ■ *Dir/Scr* Endaf Emlyn

The Making of the Mahatma ★★

Biographical drama
1995 · Ind/S Afr · Colour · 147mins

While Richard Attenborough's Oscar winner dwelt on Mohandas Karamchand Gandhi's time in South Africa, Shyam Benegal's sprawling biopic focuses entirely on the young lawyer's diverse activities there between 1893 and 1914. There's less emphasis placed here on the Mahatma's destiny than on his humanitarianism, as he campaigns with equal vigour against racial prejudice and for East Indian rights. A ponderous portrait. DP

Rajit Kapur *Ghandi* • Pallavi Joshi *Kasturba* ■ *Dir* Shyam Benegal • *Scr* Fatima Meer, Shama Zaidi, Shyam Benegal

Making Up ★★★★ 15

Romantic comedy
1992 · Ger · Colour · 54mins

It only lasts 54 minutes, but this blind date comedy was a commercial and critical hit. Not bad for a graduation film. Man-mad nurse Nina Kronjäger and struggling cartoonist Katja Riemann have such a wonderfully knockabout relationship that it almost seems a shame to pair them off with a narcissistic hunk and his wiseacre mate. However, the star of the show is director Katja von Garnier, who gets extra mileage out of jokes in serious need of a retread. DP. In German with English subtitles.

Katja Riemann *Frenzy* • Nina Kronjäger *Maischa* • Gedeon Burkhard *René* • Max Tidof *Mark* • Daniela Lunkewitz *Susa* ■ *Dir* Katja von Garnier • *Scr* Katja von Garnier, Benjamin Taylor, Hannes Jaenicke

The Makioka Sisters ★★★★

Drama 1983 · Jpn · Colour and BW · 140mins

Adapted from Junichiro Tanizaki's novel, this is a sprawling study of Japanese society in the days preceding the Second World War. Bound by family wealth, but divided on everything else – from politics and progress to the role of women within an increasingly militaristic state – the four Makioka sisters take some time getting to know. But once Kon Ichikawa has established their attitudes and alliances, their ambitions, fears, romances and rivalries begin to engross. The result is impeccably played and beautifully designed and photographed. DP. In Japanese with English subtitles.

Keiko Kishi *Tsuruko, oldest sister* • Yoshiko Sakuma *Sachiko, second oldest sister* • Sayuri Yoshinaga *Yukiko, third oldest sister* • Yuko Kotegawa *Taeko, youngest sister* • Juzo Itami *Tsuruko's husband* ■ *Dir* Kon Ichikawa • *Scr* Kon Ichikawa, Shinya Hidaki, from the novel by Junichiro Tanizaki • *Production Designer* Shinobu Muraki • *Cinematographer* Kiyoshi Hasegawa

M

Mal ★★ 18

Drama 1999 · Por · Colour · 85mins

A gutsy performance by Pauline Cadell is the only thing to recommend this grindingly dull melodrama from Alberto Seixas Santos, who seems more interested in flouting traditional narrative conventions than in focusing on his characters. As the respectable wife who is distracted from her bid to wean a teenager off heroin by her HIV-positive husband's revelation of his serial adultery, Cadell keeps her head above the soap-operatic events. DP. In Portuguese with English subtitles.

Pauline Cadell *Cathy* • Rui Morrisson *Pedro* • Alexandre Pinto *Daniel* • Maria Santos *Marta* • Lia Gama *Emilia* • Zita Duarte *Assunçao* ■ *Dir/Scr* Alberto Seixas Santos

Malachi's Cove ★★ U

Period adventure 1973 · UK · Colour · 85mins

Based on a story by Anthony Trollope, this children's period adventure benefits from ripe, eye-rolling performances with a Cornish lilt from Donald Pleasence (as Malachi) and Peter Vaughan. But the direction and underwritten screenplay by Henry Herbert leave much to be desired, and this movie, perhaps because of its short running time, barely received a cinema release. Nevertheless, Dai Bradley and Veronica Quilligan are well-cast as youngsters Barty and Mally. Walter Lassally's location photography is attractive. TS

Donald Pleasence *Malachi* • David Bradley (2) *Barty* • Veronica Quilligan *Mally* • Peter Vaughan *Mr Gunliffe* • Lilias Walker *Mrs Gunliffe* • Arthur English *Jack Combes* ■ *Dir* Henry Herbert • *Scr* Henry Herbert, from a story by Anthony Trollope

Malaga ★ U

Action adventure 1954 · UK · Colour · 88mins

Tangier comes across vividly enough as the exotic setting for this British-produced thriller. Maureen O'Hara certainly looks gorgeous, but the queen of the redheads takes some swallowing as a modern Mata Hari working for the American government to expose a dope-smuggling ring. Macdonald Carey is flabby and uninspiring as her co-star. AE

Maureen O'Hara *Joanna Dane* • Macdonald Carey *Van Logan* • Binnie Barnes *Frisco* • Guy Middleton *Soames Howard* • Hugh McDermott *Richard Farrell* • James Lilburn *Danny Boy* ■ *Dir* Richard Sale • *Scr* Robert Westerby

Malarek ★★

Biographical action drama
1989 · Can · Colour · 95mins

Crusading dramas more intent on alerting than entertaining an audience are not the sole preserve of the TV-movie industry, as this true-life drama illustrates. The film reveals how inexperienced Montreal reporter Victor Malarek was driven to expose the abusive regime within the city's teenage detention centre after witnessing the murder of an inmate. Elias Koteas is solid enough in the title role, but this is uninvolving. DP

Elias Koteas *Victor Malarek* • Kerrie Keane *Claire* • Al Waxman *Stern* • Michael Sarrazin *Moorcraft* • Daniel Pilon *Max Middleton* ■ *Dir* Roger Cardinal • *Scr* Avrum Jacobson, from the novel *Hey Malarek* by Victor Malarek

Malaya ★★★

Second World War adventure
1949 · US · BW · 94mins

Enjoyable tosh from MGM with an amazing cast, though in the end it's not much more than a B-movie. Spencer Tracy and James Stewart play a convict and a reporter hired to smuggle rubber out of Japanese-occupied Malaya. (The fact that this was a British theatre of war doesn't seem to enter into the equation.) Greenstreet runs a bar in the jungle where Valentina Cortese sings while waiting to see which star she ends up with in the end. AT

Spencer Tracy *Carnahan* • James Stewart *John Royer* • Valentina Cortese *Luana* • Sydney Greenstreet *Dutchman* • John Hodiak *Keller* • Lionel Barrymore *John Manchester* • Gilbert Roland *Romano* • DeForest Kelley *Lt Glenson* ■ *Dir* Richard Thorpe • *Scr* Frank Fenton, from a story by Manchester Boddy

Malcolm ★★★ 15

Crime comedy 1986 · Aus · Colour · 82mins

This comedy tells the gently contrived story of Colin Friels, a simple, inarticulate man whose Heath Robinson-like constructions help his lodgers (John Hargreaves and Lindy Davies) pursue a career in remote-controlled crime. The directorial debut of Nadia Tass, whose husband, David Parker, wrote the script, it has a quaintness of observation that is never coy. It's a tribute to the actors that they are never upstaged by the scene-stealing inventions. TH

Colin Friels *Malcolm* • John Hargreaves *Frank* • Lindy Davies *Judith* • Chris Haywood *Willy* • Judith Stratford *Jenny* • Beverly Phillips *Mrs T* ■ *Dir* Nadia Tass • *Scr* David Parker

Malcolm X ★★★ 15

Biographical drama
1992 · US · Colour · 193mins

To describe a film as "worthy" is to damn it with faint praise. But, as much as one admires the ambition of Spike Lee's picture, it is surprisingly conventional and, at times, downright dull. There are speeches, reams and reams of them, and Denzel Washington as the black militant leader of the 1960s copes with them as best he can. Washington looks impressive and he has undoubted charisma, like Malcolm X himself, but he's stuck in a huge epic that lumbers on through the decades, continents and events. AT. Contains violence and swearing. DVD

Denzel Washington *Malcolm X* • Angela Bassett *Betty Shabazz* • Albert Hall *Baines* • Al Freeman Jr *Elijah Muhammad* • Delroy Lindo *West Indian Archie* • Spike Lee *Shorty* • Theresa Randle *Laura* • Kate Vernon *Sophia* • Lonette McKee *Louise Little* • Tommy Hollis *Earl Little* ■ *Dir* Spike Lee • *Scr* Arnold Perl, Spike Lee, from *The Autobiography of Malcolm X, as told to Alex Haley*

Male and Female ★★★★

Silent satire 1919 · US · BW · 115mins

Before Cecil B DeMille discovered the Bible, the flamboyant producer/director explored sex in a series of enjoyably risqué comedies, six of them with Gloria Swanson. In this free adaptation of JM Barrie's *The Admirable Crichton*, Swanson plays one of a group of shipwrecked aristocrats who find themselves dependent on their butler (Thomas Meighan). DeMille remade it in 1934 as *Four Frightened People*. RB

Thomas Meighan *Crichton* • Gloria Swanson *Lady Mary Lasenby* • Lila Lee *Tweeny* • Theodore Roberts *Lord Loam* • Raymond Hatton *Honorable Ernest Wolley* • Mildred Reardon *Agatha Lasenby* • Bebe Daniels *The King's favourite* ■ *Dir* Cecil B DeMille • *Scr* Jeanie Macpherson, from the play *The Admirable Crichton* by JM Barrie

The Male Animal ★★★★

Comedy 1942 · US · BW · 100mins

A punchy, apposite comedy, regarded as highly sophisticated in its day, which still stands the test of time. Henry Fonda is excellent as the college professor about to lose his wife Olivia de Havilland to old flame Jack Carson, and his job, if he reads a controversial letter written by anarchists to his students. All three leads are splendid, giving great light and shade to their characters and so immediately drawing us into the complex plot. SH

Henry Fonda *Tommy Turner* • Olivia de Havilland *Ellen Turner* • Joan Leslie *Patricia Stanley* • Jack Carson *Joe Ferguson* • Eugene Pallette *Ed Keller* • Herbert Anderson *Michael Barnes* • Hattie McDaniel *Cleota* • Ivan Simpson *Dr Damon* ■ *Dir* Elliott Nugent • *Scr* Julius J Epstein, Philip G Epstein, Stephen Morehouse Avery, from the play by James Thurber, Elliott Nugent

Male Hunt ★★

Comedy 1964 · Fr/It · BW · 92mins

A sex comedy about bachelors on the run from beautiful women, directed by Edouard Molinaro who later made *La Cages aux Folles*. A big hit in France, this is worth seeing only for its astonishing cast: the raffish charm of Jean-Claude Brialy is complemented by Jean-Paul Belmondo doing his trademark petty criminal act. The women are even more eye-catching and include Catherine Deneuve and her sister Françoise Dorléac, who died so tragically in a car crash in 1967. AT. In French with English subtitles.

Jean-Paul Belmondo *Fernand* • Jean-Claude Brialy *Tony* • Bernard Blier *Mons Heurtin* • Catherine Deneuve *Denise* • Françoise Dorléac *Sandra* • Micheline Presle *Isabelle* • Claude Rich *Julien* • Marie Laforêt *Gisèle* • Bernadette Lafont *Flora* ■ *Dir* Edouard Molinaro • *Scr* France Roche, Michel Audiard, from an idea by Yvon Guezel, from stories by Albert Simonin, Michel Duran

Malena ★★★ 15

Second World War romantic drama
2000 · It/US · Colour · 88mins

Set in a picturesque, fictional Sicilian town, Giuseppe Tornatore's two-toned rite-of-passage picture is set against the changing fortunes of the Second World War. Debuting Giuseppe Sulfaro manages a naivety that tempers his furtive imaginings, as the teenager besotted with local beauty Malena (Monica Bellucci). Tornatore revels in a gallery of Italianate caricatures, but the film belongs to Bellucci, who almost wordlessly conveys the allure, vulnerability and courage of a much-wronged outsider. DP. In Italian with English subtitles. Contains violence, swearing, sex scenes. DVD

Monica Bellucci *Malena Scordia* • Giuseppe Sulfaro *Renato Amoroso* • Luciano Federico *Renato's father* • Matilde Piana *Renato's mother* • Pietro Notarianni *Professor Bonsignore* • Gaetano Aronica *Nino Scordia* ■ *Dir* Giuseppe Tornatore • *Scr* Giuseppe Tornatore, from a story by Luciano Vincenzoni • *Music* Ennio Morricone • *Cinematographer* Lajos Koltai

Malibu's Most Wanted ★★ 15

Comedy 2003 · US · Colour · 82mins

As a skit on his TV comedy series, *The Jamie Kennedy Experiment*, Jamie Kennedy's portrayal of a white teen who acts like a black rap artist had plenty of comic scope. But stretched out for a full feature, the joke soon wears thin. Though B-Rad's gangsta posturing is amusing in his over-privileged Malibu environment, once transposed to the LA "ghetto" the film becomes a Caucasian pastiche of black urban life. It gets tedious watching the same old ethnic clichés, while the repetitive gags are as transparent as the plotline. SF. Contains swearing, violence. DVD

Jamie Kennedy *B-Rad* • Taye Diggs *Sean* • Anthony Anderson *P J* • Blair Underwood *Tom Gibbons* • Regina Hall *Shondra* • Damien Dante Wayans [Damien Wayans] *Tec* • Ryan O'Neal *Bill Gluckman* • Snoop Dogg *Ronnie Rizzat* • Bo Derek *Bess Gluckman* • Jeffrey Tambor *Dr Feldman* ■ *Dir* John Whitesell • *Scr* Fax Bahr, Adam Small, Jamie Kennedy, Nick Swardson, from the character created by Jamie Kennedy

Malice ★★★ 15

Psychological thriller
1993 · US · Colour · 102mins

Nicole Kidman has surprised the cynics by forging a very individual career of her own. Here she plays the seemingly innocent young newlywed who ensnares nice-but-dim husband Bill Pullman and charismatic surgeon Alec Baldwin in a deadly scam. Kidman is smart and sexy as the *femme fatale* figure, while Baldwin, always better at being bad, excels as the arrogant doc. The screenplay is a mite too tortuous, but director Harold Becker has fun piling on the red herrings. JF. Contains violence, swearing, sex scenes and nudity. DVD

Alec Baldwin *Jed Hill* • Nicole Kidman *Tracy Safian* • Bill Pullman *Andy Safian* • Bebe Neuwirth *Dana* • George C Scott *Dr Kessler* • Anne Bancroft *Claire Kennsinger* • Peter Gallagher *Dennis Riley* • Gwyneth Paltrow *Paula Bell* ■ *Dir* Harold Becker • *Scr* Aaron Sorkin, Scott Frank, from a story by Aaron Sorkin, Jonas McCord

Mallrats ★★★ 18

Comedy 1995 · US · Colour · 91mins

Director Kevin Smith's follow-up to his no-budget independent hit *Clerks* was this under-rated comic look at pop Americana, junk culture and adolescent angst that gained enormously from the use of a professional cast (Shannen Doherty, Claire Forlani, Ben Affleck). Focusing on a pair of slackers mooching around the local shopping mall after being dumped by their girlfriends, Smith's vulgar and amusing diversion is equally irreverent and desperately spot-on as its eye-opening predecessor. AJ DVD

Shannen Doherty *Rene* • Jeremy London *TS Quint* • Jason Lee *Brodie Bruce* • Claire Forlani *Brandi Svenning* • Ben Affleck *Shannon Hamilton* • Joey Lauren Adams *Gwen Turner* • Renee Humphrey *Tricia Jones* • Jason Mewes *Jay* • Stan Lee • Kevin Smith (2) *Silent Bob* ■ *Dir/Scr* Kevin Smith (2)

Malone ★★ 18

Action drama 1987 · US · Colour · 87mins

Burt Reynolds is in standard macho form as a former CIA agent on the trail of a baddie who's busy building his personal paramilitary empire. Apart from the fact that Reynolds and co-star Cliff Robertson know their way around the all-action scenario like maps of their home town, there's nothing much of merit here. SH. Contains swearing and violence.

Burt Reynolds *Malone* • Cliff Robertson *Delaney* • Cynthia Gibb *Jo Barlow* • Scott Wilson *Paul Barlow* • Kenneth McMillan *Hawkins* • Lauren Hutton *Jamie* ■ *Dir* Harley Cokliss • *Scr* Christopher Frank, from the novel *Shotgun* by William Wingate

Malpertuis ★★★★ 18

Horror fantasy
1971 · Fr/W Ger/Bel · Colour · 91mins

A triumph of conception and design that's slightly betrayed by its execution, this is, nevertheless, a dazzlingly audacious attempt to realise Jean Ray's fantasy novel, in which the deities of Mount Olympus eke out a woeful bourgeois existence inside a labyrinthine mansion. Director Harry Kümel cleverly uses the fabulous Gothic sets to generate a real sense of earthbound ethereality, which is reinforced by cinematographer Gerry Fisher's confident use of texture and colour. But, while Orson Welles and Charles Janssens invest their roles with knowing humour, Mathieu Carrière's sailor and Susan Hampshire's Gorgon are markedly less successful. A glorious curio. DP. In Flemish and French with English subtitles.

Orson Welles *Cassavius* • Susan Hampshire *Nancy/Euryale/Alice/Nurse* • Michel Bouquet *Dideloo* • Mathieu Carrière *Jan* • Jean-Pierre Cassel *Lampernisse* • Charles Janssens *Philarette* • Daniel Pilon *Mathias Crook* ■ *Dir* Harry Kümel • *Scr* Jean Ferry, from the novel by Jean Ray

Malpractice ★★★

Documentary drama
1989 · Aus · Colour · 94mins

Bill Bennett is one of Australia's most accomplished documentary directors and this is a laudable experiment in having a fictional courtroom drama heard by real-life jurors. The story, about a junior doctor who mishandles a difficult birth, suffers from too many clichéd characterisations, particularly within the family who sue the hospital. But the conflicts between the exhausted junior and the arrogant consultant, and the desire of the doughty nurse to see justice done are credible enough. DP

Caz Lederman *Coral Davis* • Bob Baines *Doug Davis* • Ian Gilmour *Dr Frank Harrison* • Pat Thomson *Sister Margaret Beattie* • Charles Little *Dr Tom Cotterslow* • Janet Stanley *Sister Diane Shaw* • Dorothy Alison *Maureen Davis* ■ *Dir* Bill Bennett • *Scr* Jenny Ainge

Malta Story ★★★ U

Second World War drama
1953 · UK · BW · 98mins

Intended as a cinematic tribute to the island that was awarded the George Cross for its courage during the Second World War, this is a remarkably restrained drama in comparison to other British-made accounts of wartime heroics. Blending romance and intrigue with convincing combat sequences, director Brian Desmond Hurst presents a moving human story without slipping into melodrama. Alec Guinness is perhaps overly subdued as the aerial photographer, but Flora Robson is superb as the mother whose children experience the sharply contrasting fortunes of war. DP

Alec Guinness *Peter Ross* • Jack Hawkins *Air Commanding Officer* • Anthony Steel *Bartlett* • Muriel Pavlow *Maria* • Flora Robson *Melita* • Renée Asherson *Joan* • Ralph Truman *Banks* • Reginald Tate *Payne* ■ *Dir* Brian Desmond Hurst • *Scr* William Fairchild, Nigel Balchin, Thorold Dickinson, Peter de Sarigny

The Maltese Bippy ★

Comedy 1969 · US · Colour · 92mins

At the height of their TV fame with *Laugh In*, comedians Dan Rowan and Dick Martin parlayed one of their catch phrases – "You bet your sweet bippy" – into a brainless, feature-length horror send-up. Rowan plays a nudie movie producer who takes his lead star, Martin, to a Long Island haunted house. Cue lots of alternative endings, none of which are remotely funny. AJ

Dan Rowan *Sam Smith* • Dick Martin *Ernest Grey* • Carol Lynley *Robin Sherwood* • Julie Newmar *Carlotta Ravenswood* • Mildred Natwick *Molly Fletcher* • Fritz Weaver *Mr Ravenswood* • Robert Reed *Lt Tim Crane* ■ *Dir* Norman Panama • *Scr* Everett Freeman, Ray Singer, from a story by Everett Freeman

The Maltese Falcon ★★★★★ PG

Classic film noir 1941 · US · BW · 96mins

Superb cinematic entertainment, this third version of Dashiell Hammett's hard-boiled crime drama completely obliterated memories of the two perfectly fine earlier versions (*Dangerous Lady* and *Satan Met a Lady*) and created a brand new movie icon in Humphrey Bogart's cynical private detective Sam Spade. This was the beginning of a beautiful friendship between Bogie and John Huston, who was then a screenwriter making his feature debut as director, and whose tart screenplay retains most of the sharp dialogue and sleazy amorality of Hammett's original. Among the supporting cast, stage actor Sydney Greenstreet made his screen debut as Gutman, lusting after the Black Bird; Peter Lorre is the whiny, effeminate Joel Cairo; Mary Astor is cast against type as the *femme fatale* supreme: an extraordinary combination that couldn't be bettered. TS DVD

Humphrey Bogart *Samuel Spade* • Mary Astor *Brigid O'Shaughnessy/Miss Wonderly* • Gladys George *Iva Archer* • Peter Lorre *Joel Cairo* • Barton MacLane *Lt of Detectives Dundy* • Lee Patrick *Effie Perine* • Sydney Greenstreet *Kasper Gutman* • Ward Bond *Det Tom Polhaus* • Jerome Cowan *Miles Archer* • Elisha Cook Jr *Wilmer Cook* ■ *Dir* John Huston • *Scr* John Huston, from the novel by Dashiell Hammett • *Cinematographer* Arthur Edeson • *Music* Adolph Deutsch

Mamá Cumple 100 Años ★★★

Black comedy 1979 · Sp · Colour · 100mins

In *Anna and the Wolves*, Carlos Saura used Rafaela Aparicio's three sons to symbolise what he considered to be the primary evils of Franco's Spain: religion, sexual repression and authoritarian fascism. This Oscar-nominated follow-up shows the two surviving siblings joining with the rest of Aparicio's grasping family to celebrate her centenary, though they soon abandon their false bonhomie to scrap for a chunk of her fortune. The satire is ferocious, the caricatures grotesque, yet Saura is more intent on amusing than denouncing. DP. In Spanish with English subtitles.

Geraldine Chaplin *Anna* • Amparo Muñoz *Natalia* • Rafaela Aparicio *Mother* • Fernando Fernán Gómez *Fernando* • Norman Briski *Antonio* • Charo Soriano *Luchi* ■ *Dir/Scr* Carlos Saura

La Maman et la Putain ★★★★★ 18

Drama 1973 · Fr · BW · 208mins

A sprawling study of sexual politics and smug 1960s intellectualism, Jean Eustache's masterpiece was the last hurrah of the French New Wave. Based on actual conversations, the screenplay was delivered verbatim by a superb cast that deserves considerable credit for making every line seem so spontaneous – particularly Françoise Lebrun, a first-time non-professional whose epic speech about the futility of sex without love is remarkable for its power and intensity. But Jean-Pierre Léaud's indolent student and his sensible girlfriend, Bernadette Lafont, are equally impressive in a brilliantly observed portrait that remains as compelling as it is controversial. DP. In French with English subtitles. Contains swearing and sex scenes.

Bernadette Lafont *Marie* • Jean-Pierre Léaud *Alexandre* • Françoise Lebrun *Veronika* • Isabelle Weingarten *Gilberte* ■ *Dir/Scr* Jean Eustache

Mama's Dirty Girls ★

Black comedy 1974 · US · Colour · 80mins

A witless melange of attempted murders and inane seduction, this supposed black comedy was another nail in the coffin of one-time Hollywood *femme fatale* Gloria Grahame's illustrious career. She plays a black widow who, after dispatching one idiot husband, lures another allegedly rich man into marrying her. Moribund. AJ

Gloria Grahame *Mama Love* • Paul Lambert *Harold* • Sondra Currie *Addie* • Candice Rialson *Becky* • Christopher Wines *Sheriff* ■ *Dir* John Hayes • *Scr* Gil Lasky

Mama's Guest ★★★ PG

Comedy 2004 · Iran · Colour · 107mins

Dariush Mehrjui, Iranian film's great survivor, raises copious smiles with this gentle, if slightly protracted satire on tradition, hospitality and snobbery on the margins of Islamic society. The gradual manner in which various impoverished neighbours rally to help highly strung Golab Adineh feed her soldier nephew and his new bride allows Mehrjui to touch on topics as diverse as women's education, union activism, cinema and the disenfranchised's blind faith in authority. The ensemble lurches between minor crises with such a sense of communal calamity that it's impossible not to be both amused and touched. DP. A Farsi language film.

Golab Adineh *Mrs Effat* • Amin Hayaee *Doctor* • Parsa Piroozfar *Yousef* ■ *Dir* Dariush Mehrjui • *Scr* Dariush Mehrjui, Hooshang M Kermani, Vahideh Mohammadifar

Mambo ★★

Romantic drama 1954 · US/It · BW · 93mins

This clumsy American-Italian co-production stars Silvana Mangano as a lowly shopgirl who becomes an internationally known dancer while juggling the affections of a small-time crook and a dying count. Piling agony upon agony, Robert Rossen's movie staggers from one risible scene to the next, while Michael Rennie and Shelley Winters heighten the absurdity by adopting lasagne accents. AT

Silvana Mangano *Giovanna Masetti* • Vittorio Gassman *Mario Rossi* • Michael Rennie *Count Enrico* • Shelley Winters *Tony Burns* • Katherine Dunham • Mary Clare *Contessa Marisoni* • Eduardo Cianelli [Eduardo Ciannelli] *Padre di Giovanna* ■ *Dir* Robert Rossen • *Scr* Guido Piovene, Ivo Perilli, Ennio De Concini, Robert Rossen

Mambo Italiano ★★ 15

Comedy 2003 · Can · Colour · 88mins

The dramatic impetus of this adaptation is provided by wannabe TV writer Luke Kirby's gradual acceptance of his homosexuality. However, the thematic emphasis is firmly on the socio-cultural mores of Kirby's traditionalist Italian family. It's a pity, therefore, that both Paul Sorvino (as Kirby's father) and Mary Walsh (as the mother of Kirby's Italian-Canadian policeman lover) overdo the ethnic caricatures as they strive to come to terms with the relationship of their sons. Both the social commentary and the sitcom-style humour lack bite. DP. Contains swearing.

Ginette Reno *Maria Barberini* • Sophie Lorain *Pina Lunetti* • Paul Sorvino *Gino Barberini* • Luke Kirby *Angelo Barberini* • Peter Miller (3) *Nino Paventi* • Mary Walsh *Lina Paventi* • Claudia Ferri *Anna Barberini* • Pierrette Robitaille *Rosetta* • Dino Tavarone *Giorgio* ■ *Dir* Emile Gaudreault • *Scr* Emile Gaudreault, Steve Galluccio, from the play by Steve Galluccio

The Mambo Kings ★★★★ 15

Musical drama
1992 · US/Fr · Colour · 99mins

Antonio Banderas made the jump from Spanish star to international hunk with this, his first big English-language movie, a musical drama based on the Pulitzer Prize-winning novel by Oscar Hijuelos. Banderas and Armand Assante star as two Cuban musicians who arrive in postwar America seeking love, fame and fortune. The film positively sizzles when the music gets going, and the mambo itself is as much a character in the movie as the actors. Debut director Arne Glimcher went on to make the Sean Connery thriller *Just Cause*. JB

Armand Assante *Cesar Castillo* • Antonio Banderas *Nestor Castillo* • Cathy Moriarty *Lanna Lake* • Maruschka Detmers *Delores Fuentes* • Pablo Calogero *Ramon* • Scott Cohen *Bernardito* • Mario Grillo *Mario* ■ *Dir* Arne Glimcher • *Scr* Cynthia Cidre, from the novel *The Mambo Kings Play Songs of Love* by Oscar Hijuelos

Mame ★ PG

Musical comedy 1974 · US · Colour · 125mins

You need a better voice than Lucille Ball's to carry this dreary, predictable and almost embarrassing paean to American matriarchy at its most egocentric. Lumbered with a weak plotline and sketchy characterisation, the original show relied on one great, thumping performance to win the day, and Gene Saks's film is no different. There are plenty of stars who could have pulled it off, but this sitcom queen is not one of them. SH

Lucille Ball *Mame* • Robert Preston *Beauregard* • Beatrice Arthur *Vera* • Bruce Davison *Older Patrick* • Joyce Van Patten *Sally Cato* • Don Porter *Mr Upson* • Audrey Christie *Mrs Upson* ■ *Dir* Gene Saks • *Scr* Paul Zindel, from the musical Jerome Lawrence, Jerry Herman, Robert E Lee, from the play *Auntie Mame* by Jerome Lawrence, Robert E Lee, from the novel *Auntie Mame* by Patrick Dennis

Mamma Roma ★★★★ 15

Drama 1962 · It · BW · 101mins

Following the acclaim for *Accatone*, Pier Paolo Pasolini refined his unique blend of Marxism, Catholicism, kitchen-sink naturalism, classicism and street poetry in this unforgettable portrait of a Rome that never makes the guide books. As the only professional in an outstanding cast, Anna Magnani gives a typically extrovert performance as the prostitute whose bid to prevent her beloved teenage son from being sucked into the perilous underworld of vice and crime is hamstrung by her grasping pimp. This has none of the sentimentality that so clouded the neorealist vision. DP. In Italian with English subtitles.

Anna Magnani *Mamma Roma* • Ettore Garofolo *Ettore* • Franco Citti *Carmine* • Silvana Corsini *Bruna* • Luisa Loiano *Biancofiore* • Paolo Volponi *Priest* • Luciano Gonini *Zacaria* ■ *Dir/Scr* Pier Paolo Pasolini • *Cinematographer* Tonino Delli Colli

Mammy ★★

Musical comedy
1930 · US · BW and Colour · 83mins

This is a star vehicle for Al Jolson, here playing the leading light of a touring minstrel act. Unjustly accused of shooting the troupe's MC (Lowell Sherman), the two-timing fiancé of Lois Moran, Jolson briefly goes on the run and visits the mother he adores (Louise Dresser) before returning for the happy ending. This was a smash hit in its day, and boasts a score by Irving Berlin, but it has dated badly. RK

Al Jolson *Al Fuller* • Lois Moran *Nora Meadows* • Louise Dresser *Mrs Fuller* • Lowell Sherman *Westy* • Hobart Bosworth *Meadows* • Tully Marshall *Slats* ■ *Dir* Michael Curtiz • *Scr* Joseph Jackson, Gordon Rigby, from the play *Mr Bones* by Irving Berlin, James Gleason

The Man ★★★

Drama 1972 · US · Colour · 93mins

When the US president and Speaker of the House are killed in a freak accident and the Vice-President is rendered insensible by a stroke, senate leader James Earl Jones becomes the first black man to live in the White House. Based on the bestselling novel by Irving Wallace, the drama skips rather nervously over several key issues, including apartheid in South Africa. Jones, though, is impressive as the unelected president fighting for acceptance. AT

James Earl Jones *Douglas Dilman* • Martin Balsam *Jim Talley* • Burgess Meredith *Senator Watson* • Lew Ayres *Noah Calvin* • William Windom *Arthur Eaton* • Barbara Rush *Kay Eaton* • Georg Stanford Brown *Robert Wheeler* • Janet MacLachlan *Wanda* • Jack Benny ■ *Dir* Joseph Sargent • *Scr* Rod Serling, from a novel by Irving Wallace

A Man, a Woman and a Bank ★★ 15

Comedy thriller 1979 · Can · Colour · 101mins

A loopy heist movie with Donald Sutherland and Paul Mazursky plugging in their computer to a new electronic bank, hoping to transfer $4 million to their hideaway in Macao. Despite some very funny scenes and the engaging performances, including Brooke Adams as Sutherland's romantic interest, the movie is rather too ramshackle for its own good, though its predictions about computerised banking procedures seem right on the money. AT

Donald Sutherland *Reese Halperin* • Brooke Adams *Stacey Bishop* • Paul Mazursky *Norman Barrie* • Allan Migicovsky *Peter* • Leigh Hamilton *Marie* • Nick Rice *Gino* • Peter Erlich *Jerry* ■ *Dir* Noel Black • *Scr* Ronald Gideon, Bruce A Evans, Stuart Margolin

A Man about the House ★★ PG

Period thriller 1947 · UK · BW · 89mins

Two English spinster sisters (Margaret Johnston, Dulcie Gray) take up residence in a Neapolitan villa they have inherited and are charmed by the handsome young Italian (Kieron Moore) who is caring for the place. He marries

M

Johnston, but slowly poisons her in order to get back the property, which once belonged to his family. A suitably brooding British-made melodrama, directed by Leslie Arliss, this seems rather drearily predictable now. RK

Margaret Johnston *Agnes Isit* • Dulcie Gray *Ellen Isit* • Kieron Moore *Salvatore* • Guy Middleton *Sir Benjamin Dench* • Felix Aylmer *Richard Sanctuary* • Lilian Braithwaite *Mrs Armitage* ■ *Dir* Leslie Arliss • *Scr* Leslie Arliss, JB Williams, from the play by John Perry, from the novel by Francis Brett Young

Man about the House ★★ PG

Comedy 1974 · UK · Colour · 85mins

Not the product you would normally associate with Hammer, this spin-off from the popular TV series was the kind of project the House of Horror was forced to resort to as the fright business took a down turn in the mid-1970s. The material is thinner than a bedsit wall as housemates Richard O'Sullivan, Sally Thomsett and Paula Wilcox team up with their inimitable landlords Brian Murphy and Yootha Joyce to see off unscrupulous property developers. DP DVD

Richard O'Sullivan *Robin Tripp* • Paula Wilcox *Chrissy* • Sally Thomsett *Jo* • Brian Murphy *Mr Roper* • Yootha Joyce *Mrs Roper* • Doug Fisher *Larry Simmonds* • Peter Cellier *Morris Pluthero* • Patrick Newell *Sir Edmund Weir* • Spike Milligan • Arthur Lowe *Spiros* ■ *Dir* John Robins • *Scr* Johnnie Mortimer, Brian Cooke

Man about Town ★★★★

Period romantic comedy
1947 · Fr/US · BW · 89mins

René Clair's first French film for over a decade is a bittersweet, regretful look at the silent cinema in which he began his career. Maurice Chevalier plays an ageing ex-actor, now a director, who teaches his assistant (François Périer) the arts of seduction, unaware that they are both in love with the same young girl (an insipid Marcelle Derrien). The re-creation of the era is rather more convincing than the plot, but Chevalier shows a rare depth. RB. French dialogue dubbed into English.

Maurice Chevalier *Emile Clément* • François Périer *Jacques* • Marcelle Derrien *Madeleine Célestin* • Mme Dany Robin [Dany Robin] *Lucette* ■ *Dir* René Clair • *Scr* René Clair, Robert Pirosh, from a story by René Clair

A Man Alone ★★★ U

Western 1955 · US · Colour · 95mins

Ray Milland joined up with Republic as a producer, director and star, and acquitted himself well on all three counts in making this offbeat western. Milland doesn't say a word for the first third of the film, which casts him as a mysterious loner who arrives in town, only to be accused of committing a stagecoach robbery. The house he takes refuge in belongs to sheriff Ward Bond, who's quarantined with yellow fever. Although it becomes more routine towards the end, this is still a jump ahead of most westerns of the time, especially Republic's. AE

Ray Milland *Wes Steele* • Mary Murphy *Nadine Corrigan* • Ward Bond *Gil Corrigan* • Raymond Burr *Stanley* • Arthur Space *Dr Mason* • Lee Van Cleef *Clantin* • Alan Hale [Alan Hale Jr] *Anderson* ■ *Dir* Ray Milland • *Scr* John Tucker Battle, from a story by Mort Briskin

A Man and a Woman: 20 Years Later ★★ 15

Romantic drama 1986 · Fr · Colour · 107mins

Two decades after racing driver Jean-Louis Trintignant and script girl Anouk Aimée parted in *Un Homme et une Femme*, Claude Lelouch reunited them for this self-reflexive look at how film shapes life for its own ends. Trintignant is now scouting for younger talent and big-shot producer Aimée is so desperate for a hit that she resorts to a musical version of her own *amour fou*. This glossily empty confection is overwhelmed by a stupid subplot, gratuitous structural gimmickry and a gloating sense of cinematic significance. DP. In French with English subtitles.

Anouk Aimée *Anne Gauthier* • Jean-Louis Trintignant *Jean-Louis Duroc* • Evelyne Bouix *Françoise* • Marie-Sophie L Pochat *Marie-Sophie* ■ *Dir* Claude Lelouch • *Scr* Claude Lelouch, Pierre Uytterhoeven, Monique Lange, Jérôme Tonnerre • *Music* Francis Lai

Man and Boy ★★ U

Western 1971 · US · Colour · 77mins

Comedian Bill Cosby launched his big-screen career as star and executive producer of this mild, old-fashioned western drama about blacks out West after the Civil War. Cosby is good as the homesteader who takes his young son in pursuit of a stolen horse, but director EW Swackhamer lets too many actors chew the scenery and stages some unconvincing shoot-outs. Yaphet Kotto plays a powerful bully, Douglas Turner Ward is a cantankerous outlaw, while Leif Erickson has the only substantial white role as a lawman. AE

Bill Cosby *Caleb Revers* • George Spell *Billy Revers* • Gloria Foster *Ivy Revers* • Douglas Turner Ward *Lee Christmas* • Yaphet Kotto *Nate Hodges* • Shelley Morrison *Rosita* • Leif Erickson *Sheriff Mossman* ■ *Dir* EW Swackhamer • *Scr* Harry Essex, Oscar Saul

A Man Apart ★★ 18

Crime action thriller
2003 · US/Ger · Colour · 105mins

Vin Diesel doesn't display any acting muscle in this by-the-numbers action thriller. Diesel's DEA agent reluctantly enlists the help of an imprisoned drugs lord in order to track down the mysterious new cartel boss who may be responsible for the murder of his wife. As bland as its title, this isn't helped by unbelievable characters and action scenes of perfunctory viciousness. AJ. In English and Spanish with subtitles. Contains violence, swearing and drug abuse. DVD

Vin Diesel *Sean Vetter* • Larenz Tate *Demetrius Hicks* • Timothy Olyphant *"Hollywood" Jack Slayton* • Jacqueline Obradors *Stacy Vetter* • Geno Silva *Memo Lucero* • Juan Fernandez *Mateo Santos* • Steve Eastin *Ty Frost* ■ *Dir* F Gary Gray • *Scr* Christian Gudegast, Paul T Scheuring

Man Beast ★★

Adventure 1956 · US · BW · 60mins

Virginia Maynor and Lloyd Nelson mount an expedition to the Himalayas to search for her missing brother, only to uncover a dastardly plot by Abominable Snowmen to lure women into their domain. Cobbled together by cheapskate producer/director Jerry Warren from Mexican-shot location footage, with a cast full of game has-beens and men in Yeti suits, this is dumb fun in a non-scary sort of way. AJ

Rock Madison *Lon Raynon* • Virginia Maynor *Connie Hayward* • Tom Maruzzi *Steve Cameron* • Lloyd Nelson *Trevor Hudson* • George Wells Lewis *Dr Erickson* ■ *Dir* Jerry Warren • *Scr* B Arthur Cassidy

A Man Betrayed ★★ U

Drama 1941 · US · BW · 81mins

John Wayne became Republic's biggest asset thanks to the good films he made elsewhere. But his home studio repeatedly let him down with feeble pictures such as this, also known as *Citadel of Crime* and *Wheel of Fortune*, which tries to combine an exposé of crooked politics with doses of screwball comedy and fails on both counts. On the plus side, Wayne is appealing as a crusading lawyer, while Frances Dee is vivacious as the daughter of a corrupt politician. AE

John Wayne *Lynn Hollister* • Frances Dee *Sabra Cameron* • Edward Ellis *Tom Cameron* • Wallace Ford *Casey* • Ward Bond *Floyd* ■ *Dir* John H Auer • *Scr* Isabel Dawn, Tom Kilpatrick, from a story by Jack Moffitt

The Man Between ★★ U

Spy drama 1953 · UK · BW · 94mins

Set in partitioned Berlin at the height of the Cold War, this is a less than convincing return to *Third Man* territory by Carol Reed. Using some of the most outrageously oblique camera angles of his career to suggest a city out of kilter and its citizens beset by fear and doubt, Reed strains for a visual edginess that might atone for the flatness of this melodramatic and suspenseless tale. Recognising that their characters have no depth, the members of the cast fail to rouse themselves, although James Mason is as watchable as ever. DP

James Mason *Ivo Kern* • Claire Bloom *Susanne Mallison* • Hildegarde Neff *Bettina* • Geoffrey Toone *Martin Mallison* • Aribert Wäscher *Halendar* • Ernst Schroeder [Ernst Schröder] *Kastner* ■ *Dir* Carol Reed • *Scr* Harry Kurnitz, Eric Linklater, from the novel *Susanne in Berlin* by Walter Ebert

Man Bites Dog ★★★★ 18

Satirical black comedy
1992 · Bel · Colour · 92mins

A prize winner at Cannes, this searing satire caused a storm of protest on its original release. Were its co-directors exposing our lust for media sensationalism? Or were they merely getting away with explicit scenes of rape and slaughter in the name of social commentary? Many will bridle at the graphic imagery, while others will resent the cockiness of the approach as documentarists André Bonzel and Rémy Belvaux play an increasingly active role in the crimes of serial killer Benoît Poelvoorde. Yet this is an undeniably bold contribution to the debate on screen violence and the responsibilities of both film-makers and audiences. DP. In French with English subtitles. DVD

Benoît Poelvoorde *Ben* • Rémy Belvaux *Reporter* • André Bonzel *Cameraman* • Jacqueline Poelvoorde-Pappaert *Ben's mother* ■ *Dir* Rémy Belvaux, André Bonzel, Benoît Poelvoorde • *Scr* Rémy Belvaux, André Bonzel, Benoît Poelvoorde, Vincent Tavier, from an idea by Rémy Belvaux

A Man Called Adam ★★

Drama 1966 · US · Colour · 103mins

Trying to yoke an allegory about race to this story of a black trumpeter (Ossie Davis) battling discrimination and feelings of inadequacy makes for a rather queasy mix. The guest stars make it enjoyable, though – Sammy Davis Jr, Louis Armstrong and Mel Tormé – while Cicely Tyson shines in a supporting role. The director is Leo Penn, father of Chris and Sean. TH

Sammy Davis Jr *Adam Johnson* • Ossie Davis *Nelson Davis* • Cicely Tyson *Claudia Ferguson* • Louis Armstrong *Willie "Sweet Daddy" Ferguson* • Frank Sinatra Jr *Vincent* • Peter Lawford *Manny* • Mel Tormé ■ *Dir* Leo Penn • *Scr* Tina Rome, Les Pine

The Man Called Flintstone ★★ U

Animated comedy
1966 · US · Colour · 86mins

Directed by creators William Hanna and Joseph Barbera, this feature-length spin-off from the hit TV series is a spoof of all the films and TV shows about spies that emerged during the 1960s. Fred takes over from a lookalike secret agent to pursue the Green Goose and his evil henchmen, the men from SMIRK. The strength of the basic *Flintstones* concept just about carries this film. DA

Alan Reed *Fred Flintstone* • Mel Blanc *Barney Rubble* • Jean Vander Pyl *Wilma Flintstone* • Gerry Johnson *Betty Rubble* ■ *Dir* Joseph Barbera, William Hanna • *Scr* Harvey Bullock, RS Allen, from a story by Harvey Bullock, RS Allen, from material by Joseph Barbera, William Hanna, Warren Foster, Alex Lovy

A Man Called Gannon ★★

Western 1969 · US · Colour · 105mins

Quite pointless Universal remake of its own minor classic *Man without a Star*, a torrid western that benefited greatly from King Vidor's direction and the intensely masochistic presence of Kirk Douglas in the lead. Here, talented director James Goldstone does what he can, but the hyper-erotic elements of the original are missing and the cast, headed by Tony Franciosa, has little to get its teeth into. TS

Tony Franciosa [Anthony Franciosa] *Gannon* • Michael Sarrazin *Jess Washburn* • Judi West *Beth* • Susan Oliver *Matty* • John Anderson *Capper* • David Sheiner *Sheriff Polaski* • James Westerfield *Amos* • Gavin Macleod *Lou* ■ *Dir* James Goldstone • *Scr* Gene Kearney, Borden Chase, DD Beauchamp, from the novel by Dee Linford

A Man Called Hero ★★ 15

Period martial arts fantasy
1999 · HK/Chi · Colour · 102mins

In this period actioner, Andrew Lau succeeds in evoking a time of fear and despair, when arrivals at New York's Ellis Island were as likely to find themselves entering a nightmare as embarking on the American Dream. The fight sequences are staged with typical ebullience, but the flashback structure complicates an already tortuous plot, in which Ekin Cheng is eventually joined by his son, Nicholas Tse, in his bid to find the Japanese ninjas responsible for the murder of his wife. DP. In Cantonese with English subtitles. DVD

Ekin Cheng *Hero Hua* • Qi Shu *Mu* • Kristy Yang *Jade* • Nicholas Tse *Sword Hua* • Yuen Biao *Yuen Mo* ■ *Dir* Andrew Lau • *Scr* Manfred Wong, from a comic book by Ma Wing Shing

A Man Called Horse ★★★ 15

Western 1970 · US · Colour · 109mins

This key film in the trend towards a more realistic depiction of life in the Old West provides a thorough study of the Sioux tribe's mores as experienced by an English aristocrat who is unfortunate enough to become its prisoner. Richard Harris gives a compelling performance as the man who is tortured, ridiculed and turned into a beast of burden before finding ways to improve his lot. You'll need a strong stomach to watch Harris undergoing the elaborate (and accurately depicted) Sun Vow ceremony in which he is impaled by hooks. Followed in 1976 by *Return of a Man Called Horse*, the first of two sequels. AE DVD

Richard Harris *Lord John Morgan* • Judith Anderson *Buffalo Cow Head* • Manu Tupou *Yellow Hand* • Jean Gascon *Batise* • Corinna Tsopei *Running Deer* • Dub Taylor *Joe* • William Jordan *Bent* ■ *Dir* Elliot Silverstein • *Scr* Jack DeWitt, from the story by Dorothy M Johnson

A Man Called Peter ★★★ U

Biographical drama
1955 · US · Colour · 119mins

An earnest and solidly mounted biopic about Peter Marshall, the Scottish cleric who began as an assistant at the Church of the Presidents and rose to become chaplain to the US Senate.

Richard Todd brings dignity and zeal to the part of the Presbyterian whose uncompromising sermons did not always endear him to listeners at opposite ends of the political spectrum, while Jean Peters is quiet and loyal as his wife Catherine. DP

Richard Todd *Peter Marshall* • Jean Peters *Catherine Marshall* • Marjorie Rambeau *Miss Fowler* • Jill Esmond *Mrs Findlay* • Les Tremayne *Senator Harvey* • Robert Burton *Mr Peyton* • Gladys Hurlbut *Mrs Peyton* • Gloria Gordon *Barbara* ■ *Dir* Henry Koster • *Scr* Eleanore Griffin, from the memoirs by Catherine Marshall

A Man Could Get Killed ★★★ U

Spy spoof 1966 · US · Colour · 98mins

James Garner's air of suave bafflement comes in handy for this spoof thriller, in which he plays a businessman in Portugal suspected of being a secret agent. The cast is a curious mix of nationalities – Greek spitfire Melina Mercouri fizzes exotically, while Cecil Parker and Dulcie Gray keep the British end up – though a better-balanced plot would have been more to the point. TH

James Garner *William Beddoes* • Melina Mercouri *Aurora-Celeste da Costa* • Sandra Dee *Amy Franklin* • Tony Franciosa [Anthony Franciosa] *Steve-Antonio* • Robert Coote *Hatton-Jones* • Roland Culver *Dr Mathieson* • Grégoire Aslan *Florian* • Cecil Parker *Sir Huntley Frazier* • Dulcie Gray *Mrs Mathieson* • Jenny Agutter *Linda Frazier* ■ *Dir* Ronald Neame, Cliff Owen • *Scr* Richard Breen [Richard L Breen], TEB Clarke, from the novel *Diamonds for Danger* by David Esdaile Walker

Man Dancin' ★★ 15

Crime drama 2003 · UK · Colour · 109mins

Norman Stone directs this ambitious, but leadenly symbolic gangland parable. Ex-con Alex Ferns, bristling with compassion and righteous anger, accepts the lead in priest Tom Georgeson's Passion play – his participation being a condition of his parole. But Ferns's former boss James Cosmo and bent copper Kenneth Cranham suspect his motives, and a modern-day tragedy that mirrors the trials of Christ unfolds. An improvement on many recent British crime flicks, this drama doesn't always avoid the genre's clichés. DP. Contains violence and drug abuse. DVD

Alex Ferns *Jimmy Kerrigan* • Tom Georgeson *Father Gabriel Flynn* • Kenneth Cranham *Detective Inspector "Pancho" Villers* • James Cosmo *Donnie McGlone* • Jenny Foulds *Maria Gallagher* • Cas Harkins *Terry Kerrigan* • Tam White *Johnny Bus-Stop* ■ *Dir* Norman Stone • *Scr* Sergio Casci

A Man Escaped ★★★★★ U

Prison drama 1956 · Fr · BW · 95mins

Robert Bresson's story of an imprisoned and condemned French Resistance fighter who plans an escape with his teenage cellmate is one of the great classics of European art cinema. As usual, Bresson uses non-professional actors and a technique that is utterly hypnotic despite being almost totally devoid of stylistic flourish. Many subsequent prison movies are deeply indebted to it – most notably *Birdman of Alcatraz*, *Escape from Alcatraz* and *The Shawshank Redemption*, all of which attempted to evoke the director's peculiar mood of quietitude and contemplation as the two men conduct their meticulous plan of escape. AT. In French with English subtitles. [video]

François Leterrier *Fontaine* • Charles Le Clainche *Jost* • Roland Monod *Priest* • Jacques Ertaud *Orsini* • Maurice Beerblock *Blanchet* ■ *Dir* Robert Bresson • *Scr* Robert Bresson, from the articles by André Devigny

A Man for All Seasons ★★★★ U

Historical drama
1966 · UK · Colour · 115mins

Fred Zinnemann's Oscar-laden version of Robert Bolt's 1960 play, with Paul Scofield as Sir Thomas More who wins the moral argument but loses the more vital one, concerning custody of his head, to Henry VIII. Robert Shaw's Henry is a man of formidable intelligence and political skill, while Orson Welles's Cardinal Wolsey is a beached, purple whale and John Hurt (in his first major role) is eloquent in Parliament. But it's Scofield's picture – an inspired performance of virtue with a dash of vanity. AT [video] DVD

Paul Scofield *Sir Thomas More* • Wendy Hiller *Alice More* • Leo McKern *Thomas Cromwell* • Robert Shaw *King Henry VIII* • Orson Welles *Cardinal Wolsey* • Susannah York *Margaret More* • Nigel Davenport *Duke of Norfolk* • John Hurt *Richard Rich* • Corin Redgrave *William Roper* • Colin Blakely *Matthew* • Vanessa Redgrave *Anne Boleyn* ■ *Dir* Fred Zinnemann • *Scr* Robert Bolt, Constance Willis, from the play by Robert Bolt

Man Friday ★★ PG

Drama 1975 · UK · Colour · 109mins

In revising Daniel Defoe's 1719 novel, *Robinson Crusoe*, screenwriter Adrian Mitchell clearly intended both to denounce the idea of the white man's burden and to preach a code of racial equality. Unfortunately, he has succeeded only in destroying the narrative tension of the original. Jack Gold's hesitant direction doesn't help, while Peter O'Toole and Richard Roundtree have nothing to do but mouth platitudes. DP [video]

Peter O'Toole *Robinson Crusoe* • Richard Roundtree *Friday* • Peter Cellier *Carey* • Christopher Cabot *McBain* • Sam Seabrook *Young girl* ■ *Dir* Jack Gold • *Scr* Adrian Mitchell, from his play by Adrian Mitchell, from the novel *The Adventures of Robinson Crusoe* by Daniel Defoe

The Man from Bitter Ridge ★★

Western 1955 · US · Colour · 80mins

Despite the presence of distinguished cameraman Russell Metty, this Universal western is nothing special. It stars former Tarzan Lex Barker as a lawman investigating stagecoach robberies. His chief suspects are Stephen McNally and John Dehner, while Mara Corday provides the glamour. Directing his first western, Jack Arnold keeps the pace up and the bullets flying. TS

Lex Barker *Jeff Carr* • Mara Corday *Holly Kenton* • Stephen McNally *Alec Black* • John Dehner *Ranse Jackman* • Trevor Bardette *Walter Dunham* ■ *Dir* Jack Arnold • *Scr* Lawrence Roman, Teddi Sherman, from the novel by William MacLeod Raine

The Man from Button Willow ★★ U

Animated western
1965 · US · Colour · 77mins

Set in the 1860s, this is a so-so children's animated tale about a rancher who leads a double life as a secret agent. Young children may be entertained, but it's unlikely that anyone brought up on the new generation of Disney animation will be too impressed. Dale Robertson and Howard Keel are among the actors lending their voices. JB [video]

Dale Robertson *Justin Eagle* • Edgar Buchanan *Sorry* • Barbara Jean Wong *Stormy* • Howard Keel ■ *Dir/Scr* David Detiege

The Man from Cairo ★ U

Crime drama 1953 · US/It · BW · 81mins

The man in question is George Raft, and he's in Algiers, not Cairo, turning the Casbah upside down in a search for Nazi gold. Along the way he meets all the usual suspects: black marketeers, shady café owners, torch singers, Arab pickpockets and shifty spies. Raft's career was then in terminal decline due to his underworld connections, failing casinos and a flop TV series that he financed himself. AT

George Raft *Mike Canelli* • Gianna Maria Canale *Lorraine* • Massimo Serato *Basil Constantine* • Irene Papas *Yvonne* • Guido Celano *Emile Touchard* ■ *Dir* Ray Enright • *Scr* Eugene Ling, Janet Stevenson, Philip Stevenson, from a story by Ladislas Fodor

The Man from Colorado ★★★

Psychological western
1948 · US · Colour · 98mins

Before he adopted a crew cut for *The Blackboard Jungle* and went Method, Glenn Ford was seldom more than mildly interesting. Here, unusually, he portrays a sadistic military tyrant, appointed as judge to govern the territory. The story by Borden Chase can be read as an allegory of the brutalising effect the Second World War had on its returning veterans, and the insinuations are clearly there if you look for them. Ford is confronted by hero William Holden, in the type of colourless role he found himself trapped in before *Sunset Boulevard*. TS

Glenn Ford *Colonel Owen Devereaux* • William Holden (2) *Captain Del Stewart* • Ellen Drew *Caroline Emmett* • Ray Collins *Big Ed Carter* • Edgar Buchanan *Doc Merriam* • Jerome Courtland *Johnny Howard* • James Millican *Sergeant Jericho Howard* • Jim Bannon *Nagel* ■ *Dir* Henry Levin • *Scr* Robert D Andrews, Ben Maddow, from a story by Borden Chase

The Man from Dakota ★★★

Western 1940 · US · BW · 75mins

In this American Civil War tale a couple of Yankee soldiers escape from imprisonment in the South, become spies and hook up with a glamorous Russian refugee while they're on the run. This unlikely, not to mention fanciful, idea sounds like a Bob Hope spoof, but it's actually an action-packed period adventure. The men are Wallace Beery and John Howard; the lady is Dolores Del Rio. RK

Wallace Beery *Sgt Barstow* • John Howard (1) *Oliver Clark* • Dolores Del Rio *Eugenia, "Jenny"* • Donald Meek *Mr Vestry* • Robert Barrat *Parson Summers* • Addison Richards *Provost Marshal* • Frederick Burton *Leader* ■ *Dir* Leslie Fenton • *Scr* Laurence Stallings, from the novel *Arouse and Beware* by MacKinlay Kantor

The Man from Down Under ★★

Drama 1943 · US · BW · 103mins

Charles Laughton stars as an Australian army sergeant who adopts two orphaned Belgian children after the Great War and takes them back with him to Oz, raising one of them to become a boxing champion. The film was produced by a certain Orville O Dull and lives up to his name. That said, Laughton's Australian accent is good for a laugh. AT

Charles Laughton *Jocko Wilson* • Binnie Barnes *Aggie Dawlins* • Richard Carlson *"Nipper" Wilson* • Donna Reed *Mary Wilson* • Christopher Severn *Young "Nipper"* • Clyde Cook *Ginger Gaffney* • Horace McNally [Stephen McNally] *"Dusty" Rhodes* • Arthur Shields *Father Polycarp* ■ *Dir* Robert Z Leonard • *Scr* Wells Root, Thomas Seller, from a story by Bogart Rogers, Mark Kelly

The Man from Hong Kong ★

Martial arts action
1975 · Aus/HK · Colour · 103mins

Jimmy Wang Yu – a sort of low-rent Bruce Lee – stars in this action mess with erstwhile 007 George Lazenby, cast more for gimmick value than anything else. The tiresome Wang is a Hong Kong cop who travels to Sydney to apprehend a drugs baron (Lazenby) who also happens to run a kung fu academy. To describe Lazenby as wooden is an understatement – he's an entire forestry commission. AT

Jimmy Wang Yu *Inspector Fang Sing-Ling* • George Lazenby *Jack Wilton* • Frank Thring *Willard* • Hugh Keays-Byrne *Morrie Grosse* ■ *Dir/Scr* Brian Trenchard-Smith

The Man from Laramie ★★★★ U

Western 1955 · US · Colour · 98mins

In partnership with director Anthony Mann, James Stewart helped change the very nature of the western. Considerably tougher than Mann's other psychological entries in the genre, this is a tale of vengeance, as Stewart seeks the man responsible for supplying the Apaches with the guns that killed his brother. The infighting between rancher Donald Crisp and sons Alex Nicol and Arthur Kennedy (one natural, one adopted) dominates the action, but the scenes in which Stewart is shot in the hand and the final shoot-out on the cliffs are the ones you'll remember. DP [video] DVD

James Stewart *Will Lockhart* • Arthur Kennedy *Vic Hansbro* • Donald Crisp *Alec Waggoman* • Cathy O'Donnell *Barbara Waggoman* • Alex Nicol *Dave Waggoman* • Aline MacMahon *Kate Canaday* • Wallace Ford *Charley O'Leary* • Jack Elam *Chris Boldt* ■ *Dir* Anthony Mann • *Scr* Philip Yordan, Frank Burt, from a story by Thomas T Flynt

M

The Man from Morocco ★★

Second World War adventure
1944 · UK · BW · 117mins

What should have been an intriguing drama of espionage is rendered tedious thanks to the moribund direction. Even the usually watchable Anton Walbrook, playing a Czech refugee who is interned by the Vichy regime and sent as slave labour to help build the Saharan railroad for the Germans, is defeated by the film's lack of pace. TS

Anton Walbrook *Karel Langer* • Margaretta Scott *Manuela* • Mary Morris *Sarah Duboste* • Reginald Tate *Ricardi* • Peter Sinclair *Jock Sinclair* • David Horne *Dr Duboste* • Hartley Power *Colonel Bagley* ■ *Dir* Max Greene • *Scr* Edward Dryhurst, Marguerite Steen, Warwick Ward, from a story by Rudolph Cartier

The Man from Planet X ★★★

Science fiction 1951 · US · BW · 70mins

Shot in six days by B-movie maven Edgar G Ulmer, this mini-classic was one of the first science-fiction movies to accent sombre and serious issues above gung-ho fantasy. A lonely alien seeking assistance for his freezing planet finds a similar coldness in humanity when he lands his spaceship on the Scottish moors. Ulmer's odd camera angles create a real sense of unease in this decent cosmic fable, while the extraterrestrial – a bubble-headed midget with an immobile white face and chest-plate speaker – is one of sci-fi's most haunting creations. AJ [video]

Robert Clarke *Lawrence* • Margaret Field *Enid Elliot* • Raymond Bond *Prof Elliot* • William Schallert *Mears* • Roy Engel *Constable* • Charles Davis *Geordie* ■ *Dir* Edgar G Ulmer • *Scr* Aubrey Wisberg, Jack Pollexfen

The Man from Snowy River ★★★ PG

Adventure 1982 · Aus · Colour · 103mins

Based on AB "Banjo" Paterson's poem (known to every Australian from an early age), this epic from Down Under offers a surprising dual role to Kirk Douglas, who plays both the grizzled mountain man and his autocratic landowner brother. Jack Thompson has little to do in support and youthful co-star Tom Burlinson can't quite carry the picture. Behind the camera is the "other" George Miller, not the *Mad Max/Lorenzo's Oil* director of the same name, and he makes the most of the impressive locations. TS

Kirk Douglas *Harrison/Spur* • Tom Burlinson *Jim Craig* • Sigrid Thornton *Jessica* • Jack Thompson *Clancy* • Lorraine Bayly *Rosemary* • Chris Haywood *Curly* • Tony Bonner *Kane* • Gus Mercurio *Frew* • David Bradshaw *AB "Banjo" Paterson* ■ *Dir* George Miller (1) • *Scr* John Dixon, Fred Cullen, from the poem by AB "Banjo" Paterson

Man from Tangier ★★ U

Crime drama 1957 · UK · BW · 66mins

This barely acceptable B-thriller was made at a time when British cinemas habitually ran supporting features to give you time to buy your soft drinks and popcorn. Directed by the indefatigable Lance Comfort, it's a forgery caper involving shifty foreigners, an international criminal mastermind, a lady without a passport and a film stuntman, played by Robert Hutton (an American actor whose Hollywood career never took off). AT

Robert Hutton *Chuck Collins* • Lisa Gastoni *Michele* • Martin Benson *Voss* • Leonard Sachs *Heinrich* • Robert Raglan *Inspector Meredith* • Derek Sydney *Darracq* • Jack Allen *Rex* • Richard Shaw *Johnny* ■ *Dir* Lance Comfort • *Scr* P Manning O'Brine

The Man from the Alamo ★★★ U

Western 1953 · US · Colour · 76mins

Glenn Ford is branded a coward after surviving the massacre at the Alamo, but proves himself a hero, fighting Victor Jory's band of rampaging renegades. This vigorous western has a rather perfunctory script, but director Budd Boetticher and cameraman Russell Metty stage the exciting action scenes with some real imagination, while Julie Adams is a forceful leading lady. AE DVD

Glenn Ford *John Stoud* • Julia Adams [Julie Adams] *Beth Anders* • Chill Wills *John Gage* • Victor Jory *Jess Wade* • Hugh O'Brian *Lieutenant Lamar* • Jeanne Cooper *Kate Lamar* ■ *Dir* Budd Boetticher • *Scr* Steve Fisher, DD Beauchamp, from a story by Niven Busch, Oliver Crawford

The Man from the Diner's Club ★★

Comedy 1963 · US · BW · 96mins

Telly Savalas is a mobster, while Danny Kaye plays the eponymous man from the Diner's Club. Both men share a physical peculiarity – one foot bigger than the other – which gives Savalas the idea of faking his own death with the help of Kaye's corpse. There's a gentle (read toothless) satire here about American capitalism, life on credit and the growing importance of computerisation. AT

Danny Kaye *Ernie Klenk* • Cara Williams *Sugar Pye* • Martha Hyer *Lucy* • Telly Savalas *Foots Pulardos* • Everett Sloane *Martindale* • Kay Stevens *Bea Frampton* • Howard Caine *Bassanio* • George Kennedy *George* • Harry Dean Stanton *First beatnik* ■ *Dir* Frank Tashlin • *Scr* Bill Blatty [William Peter Blatty], from a story by John Fenton Murray, Bill Blatty [William Peter Blatty]

The Man from Utah ★★ U

Western 1934 · US · BW · 51mins

A very routine example of John Wayne's B-western output, from his period at Monogram Studios. Despite the estimable Yakima Canutt as villain, the rodeo setting holds no surprises, and nor does a plot which features the Duke turning down the offer of sheriff in order to enter a horse race. Very average, but the fist-fight at the beginning is a corker. TS DVD

John Wayne *John Weston* • Polly Ann Young *Marjorie Carter* • George "Gabby" Hayes *George Higgins* • Yakima Canutt *Cheyenne Kent* • Edward Peil Sr *Barton* • Anita Campillo *Aurora* • Lafe McKee *Judge Carter* • George Cleveland *Sheriff* ■ *Dir* Robert N Bradbury • *Scr* Lindsley Parsons, from his story

The Man from Yesterday ★★

First World War romance
1932 · US · BW · 68mins

The "yesterday" of the title is more a matter of "yesteryear", when British officer Clive Brook married American Claudette Colbert and went off to fight in the First World War, but does not return. Years later he reappears, but when it becomes apparent that his wife loves army surgeon Charles Boyer, he bravely vanishes again. This lachrymose melodrama strains credibility and lacks interest, despite the top-notch trio of leads. RK

Claudette Colbert *Sylvia Suffolk* • Clive Brook *Tony Clyde* • Charles Boyer *Rene Goudin* • Andy Devine *Steve Hand* • Alan Mowbray *Dr Waite* • Greta Meyer *Proprietress of Swiss inn* ■ *Dir* Berthold Viertel • *Scr* Oliver HP Garrett, from the play *The Wound Stripe* by Nell Blackwell, Rowland G Edwards

Man Hunt ★★★

Second World War spy drama
1941 · US · BW · 105mins

From its riveting opening, as Walter Pidgeon, perched on a ridge above Hitler's "Eagle's Nest" at Berchtesgaden, fixes the Führer in his rifle sight and prepares to pull the trigger, this fine adaptation of Geoffrey Household's *Rogue Male* substantially changes the tenor of the original. Under the direction of Fritz Lang, the Germans, including svelte George Sanders and gaunt John Carradine, are genuinely chilling, but heroine Joan Bennett's English accent leaves a lot to be desired. Pidgeon was seldom better. An inferior 1976 TV-movie remake starred Peter O'Toole. TS

Walter Pidgeon *Captain Thorndike* • Joan Bennett *Jerry* • George Sanders *Quive-Smith* • John Carradine *Mr Jones* • Roddy McDowall *Vaner* • Ludwig Stossel *Doctor* • Heather Thatcher *Lady Risborough* • Frederic Worlock [Frederick Worlock] *Lord Risborough* ■ *Dir* Fritz Lang • *Scr* Dudley Nichols, from the novel *Rogue Male* by Geoffrey Household

The Man I Killed ★★★

Drama 1932 · US · BW · 77mins

Phillips Holmes is a young Frenchman who seeks out the family of a German soldier he killed during the war. Pretending he was a friend of their son's, he falls in love with the dead man's fiancée (Nancy Carroll). Though sombre and oversentimental at times, this sensitively wrought and perfectly crafted drama is, surprisingly, the work of Ernst Lubitsch, straying far from his usual territory. Critics acclaimed it, but audiences stayed away, and the great director of romantic comedy never made another serious film. RK

Lionel Barrymore *Dr Holderlin* • Nancy Carroll *Elsa* • Phillips Holmes *Paul* • Tom Douglas *Walter Holderin* • ZaSu Pitts *Anna* ■ *Dir* Ernst Lubitsch • *Scr* Ernest Vajda, Samson Raphaelson, Reginald Berkeley, from the play *L'Homme Que J'ai Tué* by Maurice Rostand

The Man I Love ★★★★

Musical drama 1946 · US · BW · 96mins

This Ida Lupino/Robert Alda vehicle is a glittering, highly professional potboiler that grabs its audience by the scruff of the neck and refuses to let go. Lupino is suitably sassy as the charismatic nightclub singer relentlessly chased by Alda's feckless hood. There are more holes in the plot than in Nora Batty's tights, but who cares? Sit back and enjoy. SH

Ida Lupino *Petey Brown* • Robert Alda *Nicky Toresca* • Andrea King *Sally Otis* • Martha Vickers *Virginia Brown* • Bruce Bennett *Sam Thomas* • Alan Hale *Riley* • Dolores Moran *Gloria O'Connor* ■ *Dir* Raoul Walsh • *Scr* Catherine Turney, Jo Pagano, from the novel *Night Shift* by Maritta Wolff

The Man I Married ★★★★

Second World War drama
1940 · US · BW · 77mins

A riveting topical drama featuring Joan Bennett as the American wife of handsome Francis Lederer, who returns to Germany on holiday only to be swept up on a tide of Nazi propaganda. Oliver HP Garrett's clever screenplay is unsparing in its depiction of Hitler's prewar regime, and the plot, in which Lederer discovers that his own grandmother is Jewish, is brilliantly constructed. Twentieth Century-Fox's stark black-and-white studio look suits this film very well. TS

Joan Bennett *Carol* • Francis Lederer *Eric Hoffman* • Lloyd Nolan *Kenneth Delane* • Anna Sten *Freda Heinkel* • Otto Kruger *Heinrich Hoffman* • Maria Ouspenskaya *Frau Gerhardt* • Ludwig Stossel *Dr Hugo Gerhardt* • Johnny Russell *Ricky* ■ *Dir* Irving Pichel • *Scr* Oliver HP Garrett, from the articles *I Married a Nazi* by Oscar Schisgall

The Man in Grey ★★★ PG

Period drama 1943 · UK · BW · 88mins

This rip-roaring costume drama thrilled war-weary audiences with its shameless depiction of the lawlessness and lasciviousness of Regency England. No longer likely to set pulses racing, this remains an excellent example of the kind of bodice-ripping escapism churned out by Gainsborough Studios. Directed with gusto by Leslie Arliss, the picture sags when the virtuous Phyllis Calvert and Stewart Granger are on screen, but from the moment Margaret Lockwood and James Mason take centre stage, the action begins to smoulder. DP

James Mason *Rohan* • Phyllis Calvert *Clarissa* • Margaret Lockwood *Hesther Shaw* • Stewart Granger *Rokeby* • Nora Swinburne *Mrs Fitzherbert* • Martita Hunt *Miss Patchett* • Raymond Lovell *Prince Regent* ■ *Dir* Leslie Arliss • *Scr* Margaret Kennedy, Doreen Montgomery, Leslie Arliss, from the novel by Lady Eleanor Smith

A Man in Love ★★ 18

Romantic drama 1987 · Fr · Colour · 105mins

This French production filmed in Italy was the first mainly English-language film from Diane Kurys, the award-winning French writer/director, but it is not, unfortunately, among her finest efforts. Greta Scacchi brings her usual sensuality to some passionate scenes with Peter Coyote but, despite moments of intelligence and insight, the tale about love and adultery on a movie set in Rome ultimately outstays its welcome. PF. In English, French and Italian with subtitles.

Greta Scacchi *Jane Steiner* • Peter Coyote *Steve Elliott* • Peter Riegert *Michael Pozner* • Claudia Cardinale *Julia Steiner* • John Berry *Harry Steiner* • Vincent Lindon *Bruno Schlosser* • Jamie Lee Curtis *Susan Elliott* ■ *Dir/Scr* Diane Kurys

Man in the Attic ★★★

Horror mystery 1953 · US · BW · 79mins

Marie Belloc-Lowndes's novel *The Lodger*, about a man suspected of being Jack the Ripper, was filmed twice in Britain with Ivor Novello, then again in Hollywood with Laird Cregar. Fox dug out its old script, had a new writer make some unhelpful alterations and turned out this modestly budgeted thriller to exploit Jack Palance's sudden rise to villainous stardom. He's too obviously sinister and the other players are weak, but the story is virtually fool-proof and director Hugo Fregonese whips up some chills and a good Victorian atmosphere. AE

Jack Palance *Slade* • Constance Smith *Lily Bonner* • Byron Palmer *Paul Warwick* • Frances Bavier *Helen Harley* • Rhys Williams *William Harley* ■ *Dir* Hugo Fregonese • *Scr* Robert Presnell Jr, Barre Lyndon, from the novel *The Lodger* by Marie Belloc-Lowndes

The Man in the Back Seat ★★★

Thriller 1961 · UK · BW · 57mins

The phrase "quota quickie" was synonymous with cheaply made, under-plotted films notable only for the ineptitude of the acting. It's a rare treat, therefore, to stumble across a British B with an intriguing idea that's been ingeniously executed. Director Vernon Sewell outdoes himself with this haunting story that obviously has its roots in the Banquo's ghost segment of *Macbeth*. Derren Nesbitt and Keith Faulkner turn in creditable performances, but you can't help wondering what it would have been like with Peter Lorre and Elisha Cook Jr. DP

Derren Nesbitt *Tony* • Keith Faulkner *Frank* • Carol White *Jean* • Harry Locke *Joe Carter* ■ *Dir* Vernon Sewell • *Scr* Malcolm Hulke, Eric Paice, from the novel by Edgar Wallace

Man in the Dark ★★

Crime drama 1953 · US · BW · 67mins

It's nothing more than a B-feature, but this crime melodrama was dressed up with two lesser stars (Edmond O'Brien and Audrey Totter) and rush-released as one of the first features in the 3-D boom of 1953. Director Lew Landers is out of his depth and overloads the picture with 3-D gimmicks, but at least the climactic shoot-out on a rollercoaster track has some life. AE

Edmond O'Brien *Steve Rawley/James Blake* • Audrey Totter *Peg Benedict* • Ted De Corsia *Lefty* • Horace McMahon *Arnie* • Nick Dennis *Cookie* • Dayton Lummis *Dr Marston* ■ *Dir* Lew Landers • *Scr* George Bricker, Jack Leonard, William Sackheim, from a story by Tom Van Dycke, Henry Altimus

The Man in the Glass Booth ★★ 12

Courtroom drama
1975 · US · Colour · 111mins

Maximilian Schell stars as a charming New Yorker who is suddenly bundled off to Israel, put in a glass cage in a courtroom and accused of murdering millions of Jews in a Nazi death camp. Actor Robert Shaw's play was inspired by the trial of Adolph Eichmann. Shaw, however, was unhappy with this adaptation by playwright Edward Anhalt and had his name removed from the credits. It's a rather stilted effort that makes great demands on its cast and the stamina of its audience. AT DVD

Maximilian Schell *Arthur Goldman* • Lois Nettleton *Miriam Rosen* • Luther Adler *Presiding Judge* • Lawrence Pressman *Charlie Cohn* • Henry Brown *Jack Arnold* • Richard Rasof *Moshe* ■ *Dir* Arthur Hiller • *Scr* Edward Anhalt, from the play by Robert Shaw

M

The Man in the Gray Flannel Suit ★★★

Drama 1956 · US · Colour · 152mins

An overlong, self-important yet compelling melodrama, with Gregory Peck as the appealingly flawed hero choosing between his family and a high-powered but time-consuming job. To add to his woes, his marriage to Jennifer Jones is undermined by the revelation that he fathered a child in Italy during the war. The excellent Peck and Jones are joined by the ever-reliable Fredric March and Lee J Cobb, as well as Marisa Pavan, twin sister of Pier Angeli. AT

Gregory Peck *Tom Rath* • Jennifer Jones *Betsy Rath* • Fredric March *Ralph Hopkins* • Marisa Pavan *Maria* • Ann Harding *Mrs Hopkins* • Lee J Cobb *Judge Bernstein* • Keenan Wynn *Caesar Gardella* • Gene Lockhart *Hawthorne* ■ *Dir* Nunnally Johnson • *Scr* Nunnally Johnson, from the novel by Sloan Wilson

The Man in the Iron Mask ★★★ U

Period adventure 1939 · US · BW · 111mins

Louis Hayward gives a riveting performance in this adaptation of Alexandre Dumas's splendid swashbuckling tale about the twin heirs to the throne of France. Under the sympathetic direction of the great James Whale, Hayward exhibits just the right amount of baroque arrogance as Louis XIV plus a genuine feeling of romantic helplessness as the imprisoned Philippe. Warren William is fine as D'Artagnan, Philippe's guardian, but the other musketeers are blithely cast, as is Joan Bennett as Maria Theresa. Watch closely for Peter Cushing in his movie debut. TS

Louis Hayward *Louis XIV/Philippe* • Joan Bennett *Maria Theresa* • Warren William *D'Artagnan* • Joseph Schildkraut *Fouquet* • Alan Hale *Porthos* • Miles Mander *Aramis* • Bert Roach *Athos* • Walter Kingsford *Colbert* • Peter Cushing *King's messenger* ■ *Dir* James Whale • *Scr* George Bruce, from the novel by Alexandre Dumas

The Man in the Iron Mask ★★★ PG

Period adventure
1977 · US/UK · Colour · 100mins

This sprightly TV adaptation of the classic Alexandre Dumas adventure has Richard Chamberlain as the unfortunate twin of Louis XIV who's trapped in an iron mask. Money was obviously thrown at the production and it stuck: it looks good and has a certain bravura. There's a strong supporting cast, plus zippy direction by Mike Newell. AT [video] DVD

Richard Chamberlain *Philippe/Louis XIV* • Patrick McGoohan *Fouquet* • Louis Jourdan *D'Artagnan* • Jenny Agutter *Louise de la Valliere* • Ian Holm *Duval* • Ralph Richardson *Colbert de Voliere* • Vivien Merchant *Queen Maria Theresa* • Brenda Bruce *Anne of Austria* ■ *Dir* Mike Newell • *Scr* William Bast, from the novel by Alexandre Dumas

The Man in the Iron Mask ★★★ 12

Period adventure
1997 · US · Colour · 126mins

Leonardo DiCaprio has a dual role as both the wicked King Louis XIV and his mistreated twin Phillippe. The three musketeers (Jeremy Irons, John Malkovich, Gérard Depardieu) ride to the rescue, while the fourth musketeer (Gabriel Byrne) decides to support Louis, despite riots in the street and rats in the court. The performances are uniformly good in this rousing version, and the French locations are beautifully shot by cinematographer Peter Suschitzky. TH [video] DVD

Leonardo DiCaprio *King Louis/Phillippe* • Jeremy Irons *Father Aramis* • John Malkovich *Athos* • Gérard Depardieu *Porthos* • Gabriel Byrne *D'Artagnan* • Anne Parillaud *Queen Anne* • Judith Godrèche *Christine Balfour* • Hugh Laurie *King's advisor* ■ *Dir* Randall Wallace • *Scr* Randall Wallace, from the novel by Alexandre Dumas

The Man in the Iron Mask ★★ PG

Period adventure 1997 · US · Colour · 85mins

This probably would never have seen the light of day had a smart video label not spotted it and rushed it out just as Leonardo DiCaprio's version hit the big screen. It's faithful, cheerfully cheap stuff, with a strictly second-division cast , and another frustratingly erratic effort from actor/director William Richert. JF. [video]

Nick Richert *Philippe/King Louis XIV* • William Richert *Count Aramis* • Dennis Hayden *D'Artagnan* • Edward Albert *Athos* • Rex Ryon *Porthos* • Dan Coplan *Molière* • Dana Barron *Vallière* • Timothy Bottoms *Fouquet* ■ *Dir* William Richert • *Scr* William Richert, from the novel by Alexandre Dumas

The Man in the Middle ★★ U

Drama 1964 · US/UK · BW · 78mins

In India after the war, tensions rise between the US and Britain when an American lieutenant murders a British staff sergeant. Evidence that the American is insane and a racist is covered up, since the big brass on both sides want him executed. This is a tightly compressed drama that deals with the hangover of the war and associated moral issues. However, it's rather stodgy. AT

Robert Mitchum *Lt Col Barney Adams* • France Nuyen *Kate Davray* • Barry Sullivan *General Kempton* • Trevor Howard *Major Kensington* • Keenan Wynn *Lt Winston* • Sam Wanamaker *Major Kaufman* • Alexander Knox *Colonel Burton* ■ *Dir* Guy Hamilton • *Scr* Keith Waterhouse, Willis Hall, from the novel *The Winston Affair* by Howard Fast

The Man in the Mirror ★★

Fantasy comedy 1936 · UK · BW · 83mins

Lugubrious Edward Everett Horton, American master of the double-take, stars in this low-rent British fantasy as a dithering businessman whose looking-glass alter ego takes over his battles in life. Interesting more for the social assumptions of its time than for any cinematic adroitness, it was directed by Maurice Elvey, who made more than 300 unmemorable features in his career. TH

Edward Everett Horton *Jeremy Dike* • Genevieve Tobin *Helen* • Garry Marsh *Tarkington* • Ursula Jeans *Veronica* • Alastair Sim *Interpreter* • Aubrey Mather *Bogus of Bokhara* • Renée Gadd [Renee Gadd] *Miss Blake* ■ *Dir* Maurice Elvey • *Scr* McGrew Willis, Hugh Mills, from the novel by William Garrett

Man in the Moon ★★ U

Comedy 1960 · UK · BW · 98mins

Apart from an amiable performance by Kenneth More as the test pilot whose A1 fitness makes him the ideal candidate to become Britain's first astronaut, this British spoof on the Nasa space programme never leaves the launch pad. Seemingly stuck for ideas, writers Michael Relph and Bryan Forbes fall back on that old plot stand-by, the rival with his nose out of joint, to enliven the scenes of More's training with a few acts of unfunny sabotage. Mildly amusing. DP

Kenneth More *William Blood* • Shirley Anne Field *Polly* • Norman Bird *Herbert* • Michael Hordern *Dr Davidson* • John Glyn-Jones *Dr Wilmot* • John Phillips (1) *Professor Stephens* • Charles Gray *Leo* ■ *Dir* Basil Dearden • *Scr* Michael Relph, Bryan Forbes

The Man in the Moon ★★★ PG

Period drama 1991 · US · Colour · 95mins

To Kill a Mockingbird director Robert Mulligan is an old hand in dealing with coming-of-age stories. Here he lovingly re-creates the rural Americana of the 1950s in this tasteful, if somewhat anachronistic drama. Reese Witherspoon, making her feature film debut, is the troubled adolescent who has a crush on an older teen equally smitten by her older sister. There are memorable performances from the youngsters, and nicely underplayed supporting turns. JF [video] DVD

Sam Waterston *Matthew Trant* • Tess Harper *Abigail Trant* • Gail Strickland *Marie Foster* • Reese Witherspoon *Dani Trant* • Jason London *Court Foster* • Emily Warfield *Maureen Trant* • Bentley Mitchum *Billy Sanders* ■ *Dir* Robert Mulligan • *Scr* Jenny Wingfield

The Man in the Net ★★

Crime mystery 1959 · US · BW · 97mins

Artist Alan Ladd is suspected of murdering his wife, an alcoholic two-timer. Hiding out in the woods, he is given sanctuary by a group of children who help him solve the mystery. Directed by Michael Curtiz, this story has a potential that is never fully realised. Ladd has a rather haunted look as he and the children check out his dead wife's lovers, but the film remains bogged down in plot. AT

Alan Ladd *John Hamilton* • Carolyn Jones *Linda Hamilton* • Diane Brewster *Vickie Carey* • John Lupton *Brad Carey* • Charles McGraw *Steve Ritter* ■ *Dir* Michael Curtiz • *Scr* Reginald Rose, from the novel *Man in a Net* by Patrick Quentin

The Man in the Road ★★ U

Spy mystery 1957 · UK · BW · 86mins

A surprisingly fine cast was assembled for this unremarkable quickie adapted from the espionage thriller by Anthony Armstrong. Derek Farr stars as a scientist whose loss of memory alone prevents a vital secret from falling into the hands of the communists who have abducted him. Donald Wolfit was knighted the same year, but surely not on the strength of his performance here as a blustering professor. DP

Derek Farr *Ivan Mason* • Ella Raines *Rhona Ellison* • Donald Wolfit *Professor Cattrell* • Lisa Daniely *Mitzi* • Karel Stepanek *Dmitri Palenkov* • Cyril Cusack *Dr Kelly* • Olive Sloane *Mrs Lemming* • Bruce Beeby *Dr Manning* ■ *Dir* Lance Comfort • *Scr* Guy Morgan, from the novel *He Was Found in the Road* by Anthony Armstrong

Man in the Saddle ★★★ U

Western 1951 · US · Colour · 87mins

An excellent Randolph Scott western, with the star somewhat unusually cast in a love triangle involving Joan Leslie and Alexander Knox. Directed by the under-rated Andre De Toth, the film contains some marvellous Technicolor night scenes. John Russell is a terrific tight-lipped villain and has a great punch-up with Scott, while Ellen Drew's schoolmarm makes a very sexy other woman. Great stuff. TS

Randolph Scott *Owen Merritt* • Joan Leslie *Laure Bidwell* • Ellen Drew *Nan Melotte* • Alexander Knox *Will Isham* • Richard Rober *Fay Dutcher* • John Russell *Hugh Clagg* ■ *Dir* Andre De Toth • *Scr* Kenneth Gamet, from the novel by Ernest Haycox

Man in the Shadow ★★★ U

Western 1957 · US · BW · 99mins

This modern western pits new sheriff Jeff Chandler against Orson Welles as the rancher who owns everything as far as the eye can see. Chandler insists on investigating the death of a Mexican labourer and eventually topples Welles's empire. Producer Albert Zugsmith and director Jack Arnold use Gene L Coon's script as a springboard for some action that was considered rather violent for its time, while Welles's posturing performance overwhelms both the picture and Colleen Miller, who plays his appalled daughter. The film was retitled *Pay the Devil* for its original UK release. AE

Jeff Chandler *Ben Sadler* • Orson Welles *Virgil Renchler* • Colleen Miller *Skippy Renchler* • Barbara Lawrence *Helen Sadler* • Ben Alexander *Ab Begley* • John Larch *Ed Yates* • Royal Dano *Aiken Clay* • James Gleason *Hank James* ■ *Dir* Jack Arnold • *Scr* Gene L Coon

The Man in the Sky ★★ U

Drama 1956 · UK · BW · 85mins

Although he excelled at playing principled everymen, Jack Hawkins was never at his most convincing when called upon to express emotion. Thus, he contributes a rather uneven performance to this mediocre Ealing outing about the trials and tribulations of a test pilot. While at the controls of a prototype aeroplane, he's every inch the action hero – particularly during the final test flight. But once Hawkins gets home to demanding wife Elizabeth Sellars, Charles Crichton's melodrama loses all sense of direction. DP

Jack Hawkins *John Mitchell* • Elizabeth Sellars *Mary Mitchell* • Walter Fitzgerald *Conway* • Eddie Byrne *Ashmore* • John Stratton *Peter Hook* • Victor Maddern *Joe Biggs* • Lionel Jeffries *Keith* • Donald Pleasence *Crabtree* ■ *Dir* Charles Crichton • *Scr* John Eldridge, William Rose, from a story by William Rose

The Man in the Trunk ★

Comedy mystery drama
1942 · US · BW · 71mins

The title character is a murder victim who has been in a trunk for ten years. When the trunk is opened, his ghost appears and assists a young lawyer in capturing the murderer. This mediocre B-movie has one saving grace, the performance of reliable Raymond Walburn as the restless spirit. But the script is poor, the romantic leads colourless and Mal St Clair's direction doggedly uninspired. TV

Lynne Roberts *Peggy* • George Holmes *Dick Burke* • Raymond Walburn *Jim Cheevers* • J Carrol Naish *Reginald DeWinters* • Dorothy Peterson *Lola DeWinters* • Eily Malyon *Abbie Addison* • Arthur Loft *Sam Kohler* ■ *Dir* Malcolm St Clair • *Scr* John Larkin

M

Man in the Trunk ★★★

Comedy drama 1973 · Fr · Colour · 100mins

Georges Lautner pulls off the tricky task of finding the lighter side of the Arab-Israeli conflict, without offending anyone's political sensibilities, in this lively spy spoof. Mireille Darc gives a customarily lively performance as the music-hall chanteuse who joins with embassy official Michel Constantin to help Israeli agent Jean-Pierre Marielle flee Tunisia during an airport strike. Lautner does well to raise a few unexpected smiles. DP. French dialogue dubbed into English.

Mireille Darc *Françoise* • Michel Constantin *Augier* • Jean-Pierre Marielle *Bloch* • Jean Lefebvre *Baggage controller* • Amidou *Abdul* • Raoul Saint-Yves *Ambassador* ■ *Dir* Georges Lautner • *Scr* Francis Veber

The Man in the White Suit ★★★★★ U

Classic satire 1951 · UK · BW · 81mins

Telling the story of a scientist who is undone by the seeming perfection of his own invention, Alexander Mackendrick's astute film is the only Ealing comedy to truly bare its teeth. Capitalist greed, professional jealousy, the spectre of unemployment and a fear of progress are just some of the provocative themes explored in this razor-sharp satire that spurns the studio's customary whimsy. Alec Guinness is wonderfully unworldly as the boffin whose indestructible cloth unites the textile industry against him, while Joan Greenwood is also impressive as the spirited daughter of mill owner Cecil Parker. DP

Alec Guinness *Sidney Stratton* • Joan Greenwood *Daphne Birnley* • Cecil Parker *Alan Birnley* • Michael Gough *Michael Corland* • Ernest Thesiger *Sir John Kierlaw* • Vida Hope *Bertha* • Howard Marion-Crawford *Cranford* • Miles Malleson *Tailor* • Henry Mollison *Hoskins* ■ *Dir* Alexander Mackendrick • *Scr* Roger MacDougall, John Dighton, Alexander Mackendrick, from the play by Roger MacDougall • *Cinematographer* Douglas Slocombe

Man in the Wilderness ★★ PG

Adventure 1971 · US/Sp · Colour · 100mins

Richard Harris here exhibits the same sort of macho masochism he affected in *A Man Called Horse*, enduring the rigours of both nature and native American tribal rituals as a 19th-century fur trapper left to die after being mauled by a bear and vowing revenge. The resemblance is not surprising as this movie was made by the same team that saddled up *Horse*. Allegedly based on a true story, it's too much like the earlier film to be anything other than predictable. TH

Richard Harris *Zachary Bass* • John Huston *Captain Filmore Henry* • Henry Wilcoxon *Indian chief* • Percy Herbert *Fogarty* • Dennis Waterman *Lowrie* • Prunella Ransome *Grace* • Norman Rossington *Ferris* ■ *Dir* Richard C Sarafian • *Scr* Jack DeWitt

The Man Inside ★★★

Crime drama 1958 · UK · Colour · 96mins

This old-fashioned yarn has Nigel Patrick on the lam with a priceless diamond and Hollywood hunk Jack Palance as the private eye in hot pursuit. This dashes from one eye-catching European capital to the next, picking up the statuesque Anita Ekberg en route. With Anthony Newley as a Spanish cabbie, Donald Pleasence as an organ grinder and Sid James as a wideboy, the cast alone makes this worth watching, even if the plot is as old as the hills. AT

Jack Palance *Milo March* • Anita Ekberg *Trudie Hall* • Nigel Patrick *Sam Carter* • Anthony Newley *Ernesto* • Bonar Colleano *Martin Lomer* • Sean Kelly *Rizzio* • Sidney James *Franklin* • Donald Pleasence *Organ grinder* ■ *Dir* John Gilling • *Scr* David Shaw, John Gilling, Richard Maibaum, from a novel by ME Chaber

The Man Inside ★★ 15

Thriller based on a true story
1990 · Fr/US · Colour · 94mins

This real-life tale of a German investigative journalist going undercover at a right-wing newspaper doesn't ring true. The film's main failing is that the characters seem like a work of fiction. Jürgen Prochnow's crusading Gunter Wallraff is so singleminded in his pursuit of justice, he's almost ridiculous; while Peter Coyote's alcoholic hack and Dieter Laser's aggressive editor resemble bad caricatures of people in other "paper" movies. Pretty tame. JC

Jürgen Prochnow *Gunter Wallraff* • Peter Coyote *Henry Tobel* • Nathalie Baye *Christine* • Dieter Laser *Leonard Schroeter* • Monique van de Ven *Tina Wallraff* • Philip Anglim *Rolf Gruel* ■ *Dir* Bobby Roth • *Scr* Bobby Roth, from articles by Gunter Wallraff

Man Is a Woman ★ 15

Comedy 1998 · Fr · Colour · 99mins

This trite French reworking of Ang Lee's excellent comedy, *The Wedding Banquet*, is clearly unsafe in the hands of director Jean-Jacques Zilbermann. *Eurotrash's* Antoine de Caunes stars as a gay clarinettist offered money to marry Jewish virgin Elsa Zylberstein. On their wedding night she can tell all is not well, despite her fetish for Antoine's clarinet. Zylberstein's convincing performance almost rescues the film from its poor plot, bad script and an inadequate de Caunes. LH. In French with English subtitles.

Antoine de Caunes *Simon* • Elsa Zylberstein *Rosalie* • Gad Elmaleh *David* • Michel Aumont *Uncle Salomon* ■ *Dir* Jean-Jacques Zilbermann • *Scr* Gilles Taurand, Jean-Jacques Zilbermann, from an idea by Jean-Jacques Zilbermann, Joele Van Effenterre

Man Made Monster ★★★

Science-fiction horror
1941 · US · BW · 56mins

Lon Chaney Jr made his horror acting debut in this above-average Universal B-movie, which lacks the verve and gusto of the studio's earlier genre hits. Chaney is circus sideshow performer "Dynamo Dan, the Electric Man", and ever-reliable Lionel Atwill the mad doctor who wants to turn up his voltage and convert him into a zombie killer with a lethal touch. Make-up genius Jack Pierce provided Chaney's fiendish look as the natty rubber-suited "atomic monster" (the film's re-release title). AJ

Lionel Atwill *Dr Paul Rigas* • Lon Chaney Jr *Dan McCormick* • Anne Nagel *June Lawrence* • Frank Albertson *Mark Adams* • Samuel S Hinds *Dr Lawrence* • William B Davidson *District Attorney* • Ben Taggart *Detective Sergeant* • Connie Bergen *Nurse* ■ *Dir* George Waggner • *Scr* Joseph West [George Waggner], from the short story *The Electric Man* by HJ Essex, Sid Schwartz, Len Golos

The Man Next Door ★★ 15

Drama 1996 · US · Colour · 93mins

Lamont Johnson, probably best known for the controversial rape drama *Lipstick*, tackles the same subject, albeit in a less sensational manner, for this made-for-TV drama. Michael Ontkean plays a released rapist who decides to build a new life for himself in a small town, only to discover his past catching up with him. It takes an age to get going, but it's reasonably watchable. JF

Michael Ontkean *Eli Cooley* • Pamela Reed *Wanda Gilmore* • Annette O'Toole *Annie Hodges* • Sam Anderson *Dwight Cooley* • Richard Gilliland *Moe Hurley* • Vonetta McGee *Pamela* • Tracy O'Neil Heffernan *Sally Cooley* ■ *Dir* Lamont Johnson • *Scr* Susan Baskin

The Man Next Door ★★ 15

Horror 1998 · US · Colour · 94mins

Movie legend Virginia Mayo adds a little undeserved value to this otherwise undistinguished straight-to-video horror flick, which revolves around a troubled young woman who develops a worrying fixation on a beau from her youth; the problem is that he's no longer the sweet young boy from next door. Mayo and veteran character actor David Huddleston stand out among the otherwise unknown cast. JF

Laura Lael Ellis *Vivian* • John Hardison *Clayton* • Virginia Mayo *Lucia* • John Furlong *George* • Karen Carlson *Grace* • Ricky Simpson *Carey* • David Huddleston *Sheriff Dawkins* ■ *Dir/Scr* Rod C Spence

Man of a Thousand Faces ★★

Biographical drama 1957 · US · BW · 121mins

The life and work of silent actor and special make-up genius Lon Chaney is brought into less than sharp focus in a heavily fictionalised biopic starring the impressive James Cagney. It's a typical rags-to-riches saga of the humble boy raised by deaf-mute parents whose talent for playing grotesquely deformed screen villains made him a Hollywood legend. Cagney gets to appear in re-creations of Chaney's two most famous roles – the Phantom of the Opera and the Hunchback of Notre Dame – in a hokey but reasonably entertaining tribute. AJ

James Cagney *Lon Chaney* • Dorothy Malone *Cleva Creighton Chaney* • Jane Greer *Hazel Bennet* • Marjorie Rambeau *Gert* • Jim Backus *Clarence Logan* • Robert Evans *Irving Thalberg* • Celia Lovsky *Mrs Chaney* • Jeanne Cagney *Carrie Chaney* ■ *Dir* Joseph Pevney • *Scr* R Wright Campbell, Ivan Goff, Ben Roberts, from a story by Ralph Wheelwright

Man of Africa ★★★ U

Documentary drama
1954 · UK · Colour · 84mins

Although this tale of the Ugandan bush was made 20 years after Robert Flaherty's seminal *Man of Aran*, it's a shade disappointing to see how little producer John Grierson had moved away from that style of drama documentary. Still, his influence is considerably more evident than that of his acolyte, Cyril Frankel. Following the migration of the Bakija and Batwa tribes, the action centres on farming couple Frederick Bijuerenda and Violet Mukabuerza as they endure everything from malaria and internecine strife to marauding elephants and pygmies. DP

Dir Cyril Frankel • *Scr* Montagu Slater

Man of Aran ★★★ U

Documentary 1934 · UK · BW · 73mins

Film-maker Robert Flaherty made a huge impact in the silent era with his film about Inuit life, *Nanook of the North* (1922). This account of life's daily grind on the Aran Islands (just west of Ireland) follows a similar "against the elements" theme, as the local farmers struggle to eke a living from their barren surroundings. Flaherty's films are best described as dramatised documentaries – the intention is to show life as it really is, but the method involves staging and re-staging events as necessary to fit the loose "script", and the natives are not always strictly native. Issues of authenticity aside, there's no doubt that this is a heartfelt piece of cinema, and the imagery of craggy cliffs and pounding waves is frequently breathtaking. RT

Dir Robert Flaherty • *Scr* John Goldman, Robert Flaherty, Frances Flaherty • *Cinematographer* John Goldman, Harces Flaherty

Man of Conquest ★★ U

Biographical western
1939 · US · BW · 98mins

Republic Pictures ventured into the bigger budget league for the first time with this popular contribution to the western cycle. The studio had so little top talent of its own that it had to borrow most of the talent from RKO. Richard Dix plays Sam Houston, the man who brought Texas into the Union, and the biopic includes the defeat at the Alamo and victory at San Jacinto. Stunt directors B Reeves Eason and Yakima Canutt bring some life into a static and talkative picture. AE

Richard Dix *Sam Houston* • Gail Patrick *Margaret Lea* • Edward Ellis *Andrew Jackson* • Joan Fontaine *Eliza Allen* • Victor Jory *William B Travis* • Robert Barrat *Davy Crockett* ■ *Dir* George Nichols Jr • *Scr* Wells Root, EE Paramore Jr [Edward E Paramore Jr], from the story *Wagons Westward* by Wells Root, Harold Shumate

Man of Flowers ★★★ 18

Drama 1984 · Aus · Colour · 86mins

After making his name as one of Australia's most respected photographers and documentarists, Dutch-born film-maker Paul Cox brought his distinctive, compassionate take on alienation and eccentricity to his adopted country's cinema resurgence. Here Norman Kaye is a lonely, mother-fixated bachelor who finds quiet delight in gardening and the artist's model (Alyson Best) he employs to undress for him once a week. Renowned German director Werner Herzog plays Kaye's fearsome father in the flashbacks. AME

Norman Kaye *Charles Bremer* • Alyson Best *Lisa* • Chris Haywood *David* • Sarah Walker *Jane* • Julia Blake *Art teacher* • Bob Ellis *Psychiatrist* • Werner Herzog *Father* ■ *Dir* Paul Cox • *Scr* Paul Cox, Bob Ellis

Man of Iron ★★★★

Drama 1981 · Pol · Colour · 152mins

The winner of the Palme d'Or at Cannes, this semi-sequel sees Krystyna Janda return to the documentary fray, this time to chart the career of her husband, a Solidarity leader and the son of her subject in *Man of Marble*. But the main focus falls on Marian Opania, a broken-down reporter whose mission to spy on the rebellious Gdansk shipworkers is undermined by his growing politicisation. Capturing history in the making and neatly weaving it into his fictional tale, Andrzej Wajda expertly manages to convey the optimism of Lech Walesa's working class heroes without losing a sense of perspective. DP. In Polish with English subtitles.

Jerzy Radziwilowicz *Tomczyk* • Krystyna Janda *Agnieszka* • Marian Opania *Winkiel* • Irene Byrska *Anna Hulewicz's mother* ■ *Dir* Andrzej Wajda • *Scr* Aleksandar Scibor-Rylski

Man of La Mancha ★ PG

Musical 1972 · US · Colour · 123mins

The Broadway show was a massive hit, but this movie adaptation bungles everything, including the big number – *The Impossible Dream* – and the moment when Don Quixote tilts at the windmills. Peter O'Toole fights a losing battle as both Miguel de Cervantes and the hopelessly idealistic knight. Arthur Hiller's direction is heavy-going, tricksy and self-consciously arty, while Sophia Loren unwisely singing her own songs. A costly box-office dud. AT

Peter O'Toole *Miguel de Cervantes/Don Quixote/Quijana* • Sophia Loren *Aldonza/Alonso Dulcinea* • James Coco *Manservant/Sancho Panza* • Harry Andrews *Governor/Innkeeper* • John Castle *Duke/Dr Carrasco/Black Knight/Knight of the Mirrors* • Brian Blessed *Pedro* ■ *Dir* Arthur Hiller • *Scr* Dale Wasserman, from his play *Man of La Mancha*, from the novel *El Ingenioso Hidalgo Don Quijote de la Mancha* by Miguel de Cervantes Saavedra

Man of Marble ★★★★ U

Drama 1977 · Pol · Colour · 153mins

Employing a "talking heads" style redolent of both *Citizen Kane* and the polemics of Jean-Luc Godard, this is a superbly controlled treatise on the power of the Party, the transience of reputation and the veracity of visual evidence. Expertly manufacturing "contemporary" newsreel footage, Andrzej Wajda turns a pseudo-documentary into a disturbing thriller as film student Krystyna Janda relentlessly investigates the part played by the Communist authorities in the tragedy of Mateusz Birkut, a Stakhanovite hero of the 1950s who was destroyed when his influence became too great. DP. In Polish with English subtitles.

U = SUITABLE FOR ALL Uc = SUITABLE FOR ALL, ESPECIALLY FOR YOUNG CHILDREN (VIDEO ONLY) PG = PARENTAL GUIDANCE

Jerzy Radziwilowicz *Mateusz Birkut* • Krystyna Janda *Agnieszka* • Tadeusz Lomnicki *Jerzy Burski* • Jacek Lomnicki *Younger Burski* • Michal Tarkowski *Witek* ■ *Dir* Andrzej Wajda • *Scr* Aleksandar Sciber-Rylski

A Man of No Importance

★★★★ 15

Drama 1994 · UK/Ire · Colour · 94mins

Albert Finney gives a great performance as the eccentric Alfie, the poetry-loving Dublin bus conductor with a tenacious dream to stage Oscar Wilde's play *Salome* in the local village hall, an ambition that sets off a train of unfortunate events. One of the film's splendidly handled central themes is the painful comparison between Finney's ebullient public face and his sexually repressed, private hell. Dublin in 1963 is realistically brought to life in this major treat. SH. Contains a sex scene, violence. [video]

Albert Finney *Alfie Byrne* • Rufus Sewell *Robbie Fay* • Brenda Fricker *Lily Byrne* • Tara FitzGerald *Adele Rice* • Michael Gambon *Carney* • Patrick Malahide *Carson* • Anna Manahan *Mrs Grace* ■ *Dir* Suri Krishnamma • *Scr* Barry Devlin

Man of the House

★★ U

Comedy 1994 · US · Colour · 92mins

A vehicle more for Jonathan Taylor Thomas (from TV's *Home Improvement*), than the nominal star Chevy Chase, reprising his now familiar nice-but-dim persona. In this one, well-meaning Chase moves in with girlfriend Farrah Fawcett and attempts to bond with her son (Thomas) with disastrous consequences. There's a syrupy undertone to much of the juvenile slapstick and not even *Cheers* star George Wendt can wring many laughs out of the dull script. JF [video] DVD

Chevy Chase *Jack Sturges* • Farrah Fawcett *Sandra Archer* • Jonathan Taylor Thomas *Ben Archer* • George Wendt *Chet Bronski* • David Shiner *Lloyd Small* • Art LaFleur *Red Sweeney* ■ *Dir* James Orr • *Scr* James Orr, Jim Cruickshank, from a story by David Peckinpah, Richard Jefferies

Man of the House

★★ 12A

Action comedy 2005 · US · Colour · 99mins

Tommy Lee Jones plays a lawman again, this time baby-sitting a bunch of college cheerleaders who are the only eyewitnesses to a Mob hit. Predictably, when crusty cop meets exuberant airheads, it's a learning experience for all. As lowbrow comedy, this is breezy enough, but there's something rather sad about seeing an actor of Jones's calibre slumming it in such mediocrity. DA. Contains violence and sexual references.

Tommy Lee Jones *Roland Sharp* • Anne Archer *Professor Molly McCarthy* • Brian Van Holt *Eddie Zane* • Christina Milian *Anne* • Paula Garcés *Teresa* • Monica Keena *Evie* • R Lee Ermey *Captain Nichols* • Cedric the Entertainer *Percy Stevens* • Vanessa Ferlito *Heather* ■ *Dir* Stephen Herek • *Scr* Robert Ramsey, Matthew Stone, John J McLaughlin, from a story by John J McLaughlin, Scott Lobdell

Man of the Moment

★★★ U

Comedy 1955 · UK · BW · 85mins

Norman Wisdom is almost at the peak of his powers in this typically silly comedy, in which slapstick and sentiment jostle for centre stage. Norman is a Whitehall nobody who suddenly finds himself a target for foreign agents after he stalls the entire United Nations with his support for the island of Tarawaki. Although we usually think of Norman as a bashful bungler, he also did a nice line in cockiness, and it's surprisingly amusing to watch Whitehall and Geneva dance to his tune. Jerry Desmonde again proves to be the supreme stooge. DP [video] DVD

Norman Wisdom *Norman* • Lana Morris *Penny* • Belinda Lee *Sonia* • Jerry Desmonde *Jackson* • Karel Stepanek *Lom* • Garry Marsh *British delegate* • Inia Te Wiata *Toki* • Evelyn Roberts *Sir Horace* ■ *Dir* John Paddy Carstairs • *Scr* Vernon Sylvaine, John Paddy Carstairs, from a story by Maurice Cowan

Man of the West

★★★★

Western 1958 · US · Colour · 100mins

This fine, relentlessly grim western was accorded scant critical approval on its original release. A study of choice and injustice, it stars Gary Cooper, whose haggard, ageing features lend the tale an almost biblical intensity. Director Anthony Mann's use of CinemaScope is exemplary, although the sometimes savage story suffered cuts – the rape of saloon singer Julie London, for example. The screenplay, by *12 Angry Men* writer Reginald Rose, is particularly literate, and Lee J Cobb's ferocious study in villainy is wonderful to watch. TS

Gary Cooper *Link Jones* • Julie London *Billie Ellis* • Lee J Cobb *Dock Tobin* • Arthur O'Connell *Sam Beasley* • Jack Lord *Coaley* • John Dehner *Claude* • Royal Dano *Trout* • Robert Wilke [Robert J Wilke] *Ponch* ■ *Dir* Anthony Mann • *Scr* Reginald Rose, from the novel *The Border Jumpers* by Will C Brown

Man of the World

★★★

Drama 1931 · US · BW · 71mins

Smooth, sophisticated gigolo-turned-blackmailer William Powell chooses fellow Americans in Paris as his victims. But he comes unstuck when he falls in love with one of them (Carole Lombard) and is threatened with exposure by his hard-boiled mistress Wynne Gibson. Scripted by Herman J Mankiewicz, this high society drama, characteristic of the period, more than gets by thanks to its star casting. Powell is impeccable, while Lombard – his off-screen wife from 1931 to 1933 – is clearly on her way to major stardom. RK

William Powell *Michael Trevor* • Carole Lombard *Mary Kendall* • Wynne Gibson *Irene Hoffa* • Guy Kibbee *Harold Taylor* • Lawrence Gray *Frank Thompson* • Andre Cheron *Victor* ■ *Dir* Richard Wallace, Edward Goodman • *Scr* Herman J Mankiewicz, from his story

Man of the Year

★★★ 15

Drama documentary
1995 · US · Colour · 85mins

Playgirl's 1992 Man of the Year, actor/model-turned-film-maker Dick Shafer, blends fact and fiction to good effect in this tale of his year as every woman's fantasy, while hiding the fact that he was gay. Because Shafer is so involved in the movie, it sometimes becomes a bit of a vanity project. But there are also a lot of interesting comments about sexual stereotypes and prejudices, as well as plenty of self-deprecating humour on the part of Shafer that makes this an interesting and unusual documentary. JB [video]

Dirk Shafer *Dirk Schafer* • Vivian Paxton • Claudette Sutherland *Tammy Shafer* • Michael Ornstein *Mike Miller* • Calvin Bartlett [Cal Bartlett] *Ken Shafer* • Beth Broderick *Kelly Bound* ■ *Dir/Scr* Dirk Shafer

The Man of the Year

★★★ 15

Crime action comedy
2002 · Bra · Colour · 104mins

Working with a screenplay by his father Rubem, debutant director Jose Enrique Fonseca delves into the murky layer of corruption, decadence and violence that insulates Brazilians aspiring to bourgeois respectability from those existing in backstreet squalor. The tone vacillates between bleak comedy and urban parable. But the story of an accidental hero who is duped into becoming the people's vigilante tries to cover too much ground, particularly after Murilo Benicio's teenage mistress, Natalia Lage, gets religion following the murder of his wife, Claudia Abreu. It's intriguing, but never wholly convincing. DP. In Portuguese with English subtitles. Contains drug abuse, swearing, violence. DVD

Murilo Benicio *Maiquel Jorge* • Claudia Abreu *Cledir* • Natalia Lage *Erica* • Jorge Doria *Dr Carvalho* • José Wilker *Silvio* • Agildo Ribeiro *Zilmar* ■ *Dir* José Henrique Fonseca • *Scr* Rubem Fonseca, from the novel *O Matador [The Killer]* by Patricia Melo

Man on a Tightrope

★★★

Drama based on a true story
1953 · US · BW · 103mins

A professionally made and absorbing drama, based on real-life events, about a circus troupe escaping across the border from communist Czechoslovakia to Austria. This is well acted, particularly by Fredric March and Robert Beatty, and effectively directed by Elia Kazan, but the fact that this was the movie Kazan was working on when he shamefully "named names" to the House Un-American Activities Committee makes the story ironic. TS

Fredric March *Karel Cernik* • Terry Moore *Tereza Cernik* • Gloria Grahame *Zama Cernik* • Cameron Mitchell *Joe Vosdek* • Adolphe Menjou *Fesker* • Robert Beatty *Barovic* • Alex D'Arcy *Rudolph* ■ *Dir* Elia Kazan • *Scr* Robert E Sherwood, from the story *International Incident* by Neil Peterson

Man on Fire

★★ 18

Thriller 1987 · It/Fr · Colour · 87mins

In an often unintentionally funny mix of big-blast set pieces and patently ludicrous plot shenanigans, Scott Glenn plays a former CIA agent-turned-pacifist who becomes a Rambo-style avenger when the 12-year-old girl in his charge is kidnapped. Alongside Glenn, Jonathan Pryce, Danny Aiello and Joe Pesci are confounded by the mediocrity of the project. JM. Contains swearing and violence. [video]

Scott Glenn *Chris Creasy* • Jade Malle *Samantha "Sam" Balletto* • Joe Pesci *David* • Brooke Adams *Jane Balletto* • Jonathan Pryce *Michael* • Paul Shenar *Ettore Balletto* • Danny Aiello *Conti* • Laura Morante *Julia* ■ *Dir* Elie Chouraqui • *Scr* Elie Chouraqui, Sergio Donati, from the novel by AJ Quinnell

Man on Fire

★★★ 18

Action thriller
2004 · US/UK · Colour · 140mins

Denzel Washington excels here as a burned-out former US government agent, who reluctantly takes a job in Mexico City as bodyguard to Dakota Fanning, the child of wealthy parents who needs protection during a wave of kidnappings. Director Tony Scott hits the right notes early on when the girl's charm begins to win over her emotionally closed-off protector. But once Fanning is kidnapped, this becomes a drawn-out revenge thriller, as the second half of the film degenerates into a showcase of imaginative ultra-violence with Washington hunting down the perpetrators. GM. In English and Spanish with subtitles. Contains violence. [video] DVD

Denzel Washington *John Creasy* • Dakota Fanning *Lupita "Pita" Martin Ramos* • Marc Anthony *Samuel Ramos* • Radha Mitchell *Lisa Martin Ramos* • Christopher Walken *Rayburn* • Giancarlo Giannini *Manzano* • Rachel Ticotin *Mariana* • Mickey Rourke *Jordan Kalfus* ■ *Dir* Tony Scott • *Scr* Brian Helgeland, from the novel by AJ Quinnell

A Man on the Beach

★ U

Crime drama 1955 · UK · Colour · 28mins

This obscure half-hour featurette, derived from a story by Victor Canning, has promising credentials: stars Donald Wolfit and Michael Medwin, a script by Jimmy Sangster and direction by Joseph Losey. Its somewhat bizarre plot requires Medwin to rob a French casino in drag, become wounded killing his accomplice and take refuge in the bungalow of Wolfit's retired, blind doctor. But it is notable only as the first occasion since arriving in Britain that the blacklisted Losey could put his own name on a film. AE

Donald Wolfit *Carter* • Michael Medwin *Max* • Michael Ripper *Chauffeur* • Edward Forsyth *Inspector Clement* ■ *Dir* Joseph Losey • *Scr* Jimmy Sangster, from a story by Victor Canning

The Man on the Eiffel Tower

★★

Detective thriller 1949 · US · Colour · 83mins

Charles Laughton stars as Georges Simenon's Inspector Maigret, with Franchot Tone as his fiendish and arrogant adversary. Burgess Meredith plays an impoverished knife-grinder and directed most of the picture, filmed in Paris using the untried Ansco Color process. Laughton directed some scenes, including the one in which Meredith turns burglar and comes upon two women stabbed to death in the bedroom. There are some striking touches but never any real suspense. AE

Charles Laughton *Inspector Maigret* • Franchot Tone *Johann Radek* • Burgess Meredith *Joseph Huertin* • Robert Hutton *Bill Kirby* • Jean Wallace *Edna Wallace* • Patricia Roc *Helen Kirby* • Belita *Gisella* • George Thorpe *Comelieu* • Wilfrid Hyde White *Prof Grollet* ■ *Dir* Burgess Meredith • *Scr* Harry Brown, from the novelette *La Tête d'un Homme (A Battle of Nerves)* by Georges Simenon

The Man on the Flying Trapeze

★★

Comedy 1935 · US · BW · 65mins

WC Fields, who dreamed up the storyline with Sam Hardy, is the characteristically curmudgeonly star of this misleadingly titled comedy, released more accurately in Britain as *The Memory Expert*. Fields plays a man who capitalises on his astonishing feats of memory to reduce all those around him, including his nagging wife, to gibbering submission. The sole exception is his daughter, played by Mary Brian. Clyde Bruckman directs what is essentially a showcase for a series of Fields gags. RK

WC Fields *Ambrose Wolfinger* • Mary Brian *Hope Wolfinger* • Kathleen Howard *Leona Wolfinger* • Grady Sutton *Claude Neselrode* • Vera Lewis *Mrs Cordelia Neselrode* • Lucien Littlefield *Mr Peabody* • Walter Brennan *"Legs" Garnett* ■ *Dir* Clyde Bruckman • *Scr* Ray Harris, Sam Hardy, Jack Cunningham, Bobby Vernon, from a story by Sam Hardy, Charles Bogle [WC Fields]

Man on the Moon

★★★★ 15

Biographical comedy drama
1999 · US · Colour · 113mins

The strange, self-destructive career of comedian Andy Kaufman is re-created by Jim Carrey and director Milos Forman in this challenging, off-the-wall biography. Carrey gives everything he's got to portray the man who found fame as the squeaky-voiced Latka in 1980s sitcom *Taxi*. In an audacious piece of casting, Kaufman's *Taxi* co-star Danny DeVito portrays his manager, and he too is first-rate. From the bizarre credits scene onwards, Forman keeps the audience unsure of how to perceive Kaufman, a decision that prompted some critics to complain he does not allow enough insight into the off-stage man. JC [video] DVD

Jim Carrey *Andy Kaufman* • Danny DeVito *George Shapiro* • Courtney Love *Lynne Margulies* • Paul Giamatti *Bob Zmuda* • Vincent Schiavelli *Maynard Smith* • Jerry

M

Lawler • Gerry Becker *Stanley Kaufman* • Leslie Lyles *Janice Kaufman* ■ *Dir* Milos Forman • *Scr* Scott Alexander, Larry Karaszewski

Man-Proof ★★★

Comedy drama 1937 · US · BW · 74mins

Shenanigans among the sophisticated set as an uncharacteristically predatory Myrna Loy sets her sights on Walter Pidgeon and keeps them there, even when he marries her rival (Rosalind Russell). Rescue, however, is at hand in the shape of Franchot Tone. A mildly diverting romantic comedy drama, directed by Richard Thorpe, that holds the attention thanks to the easy expertise of the classy cast. RK

Myrna Loy *Mimi Swift* • Franchot Tone *Jimmy Kilmartin* • Rosalind Russell *Elizabeth Kent* • Walter Pidgeon *Alan Wythe* • Rita Johnson *Florence* • Nana Bryant *Meg Swift* • Ruth Hussey *Jane* • Leonard Penn *Bob* ■ *Dir* Richard Thorpe • *Scr* George Oppenheimer, Vincent Lawrence, Waldemar Young, from the novel *The Four Marys* by Fanny Heaslip Lea

The Man They Could Not Hang ★★★

Horror 1939 · US · BW · 64mins

While not exactly the "holocaust of horror" promised at the time, this incredibly prophetic sci-fi thriller is laced with enough sinister menace to get by. British bogeyman Boris Karloff plays a crazed scientist dabbling in heart transplant surgery who is sentenced to death by the medical authorities. After his execution, his own technology is used to turn him into a vengeful maniac with a mechanical ticker. As usual, kindly Karloff elevates standard fear fare with wit, grace and presence. AJ

Boris Karloff *Dr Henryk Savaard* • Lorna Gray *Janet Saavard* • Robert Wilcox *Scoop Foley* • Roger Pryor *District Attorney Drake* • Don Beddoe *Lt Shane* ■ *Dir* Nick Grinde • *Scr* Karl Brown, from a story by Leslie T White, George W Sayre

A Man to Respect ★★

Heist thriller
1972 · It/W Ger · Colour · 110mins

Kirk Douglas came to Europe for this middling entry in the series of "impossible" heist movies inspired by *Rififi*. In addition to tackling a state-of-the-art computerised safe, Douglas has to teach his blagging skills to circus acrobat Giuliano Gemma, so he can get past the devilish security system. It starts slowly, with Florinda Bolkan trying to talk her newly liberated hubby out of the job. Not exactly nail-biting, but still proficiently tense. DP. Italian dialogue dubbed into English.

Kirk Douglas *Wallace* • Florinda Bolkan *Anna* • Giuliano Gemma *Marco* • Rene Kolldehoff [Reinhard Kolldehoff] *Police detective* • Wolfgang Preiss *Miller* ■ *Dir* Michele Lupo • *Scr* Franco Bucceri, Roberto Leoni, Michele Lupo, Mino Roli

Man-Trap ★★

Crime drama 1961 · US · BW · 93mins

Jeffrey Hunter stars in this grubby exploitation movie, in which he plays the husband of drunken slut Stella Stevens, lured into a heist by war buddy David Janssen. Actor Edmond O'Brien directed this quickie after recovering from the heart attack which forced him to abandon his role as the journalist in *Lawrence of Arabia*. AT

Jeffrey Hunter *Matt Jameson* • David Janssen *Vince Biskay* • Stella Stevens *Nina Jameson* • Elaine Devry *Liz Adams* ■ *Dir* Edmond O'Brien • *Scr* Ed Waters, from the novella *Taint of the Tiger* by John D MacDonald

Man Trouble ★★ 15

Romantic comedy
1992 · US · Colour · 95mins

Proof that even the most talented actors – in this case, Jack Nicholson and Ellen Barkin – can make bad choices and turn in mediocre performances in a below-par film. When opera singer Barkin thinks she's being stalked, she enlists the help of oddball dog trainer Nicholson to find her an attack dog. Naturally, the pair are soon sparring along the path to true love. Ridiculous and insignificant complications ensue. JB [video] DVD

Jack Nicholson *Harry Bliss* • Ellen Barkin *Joan Spruance* • Harry Dean Stanton *Redmond Layls* • Beverly D'Angelo *Andy Ellerman* • Michael McKean *Eddy Revere* • Saul Rubinek *Laurence Moncrief* ■ *Dir* Bob Rafelson • *Scr* Carole Eastman

The Man Upstairs ★★★ PG

Drama 1958 · UK · Colour · 84mins

Le Jour Se Lève (1939) starred Jean Gabin as a killer who barricades himself in his attic flat. It was remade in 1947 as *The Long Night* with Henry Fonda, and this too is a remake, with Richard Attenborough going bonkers upstairs while the police downstairs try to calm him down. The motivation has changed (he blames himself for his fiancée's brother's death), but the dramatic set-up is identical and makes for some agreeable tension. AT [video]

Richard Attenborough *Peter Watson, the man* • Bernard Lee *Inspector Thompson* • Donald Houston *Sanderson* • Dorothy Alison *Mrs Barnes* • Patricia Jessel *Mrs Lawrence* • Virginia Maskell *Helen Grey* ■ *Dir* Don Chaffey • *Scr* Alun Falconer, Robert Dunbar, Don Chaffey, from a story by Alun Falconer

The Man Who Broke the Bank at Monte Carlo ★★

Comedy 1935 · US · BW · 70mins

The popular song is played over the titles, but this movie is initially set in Paris where Russian émigré Ronald Colman works as a cab driver. He decides to try his luck in Monte Carlo and lands a multi-million franc windfall at the tables. Joan Bennett is the casino employee sent to woo him and his winnings back. This would-be sophisticated comedy fall flats under the heavy-handed direction of former stuntman Stephen Roberts. AT

Ronald Colman *Paul Gallard* • Joan Bennett *Helen Berkeley* • Colin Clive *Bertrand Berkeley* • Nigel Bruce *Ivan* • Montagu Love *Director* • Ferdinand Gottschalk *Office man* ■ *Dir* Stephen Roberts • *Scr* Howard Ellis Smith, Nunnally Johnson, from the play *Monsieur Alexandre, Igra, Lepy and the Gamble* by Illia Surgutchoff, Frederick Albert Swann

The Man Who Came to Dinner ★★★★ U

Comedy 1941 · US · BW · 116mins

New York character actor Monty Woolley transferred his stage role to the screen, playing irascible lecturer Sheridan Whiteside in this sparkling Warner Bros comedy based on the Broadway hit. Incapacitated after slipping on ice outside the home of Grant Mitchell, Woolley becomes an unwelcome guest who takes control of the house, leaving a respectable family totally bewildered. Despite Woolley's screen-hogging, the presence of the dynamic Bette Davis and Ann Sheridan lends Woolley the star power he personally lacks. Splendid entertainment. TS

Bette Davis *Maggie Cutler* • Monty Woolley *Sheridan Whiteside* • Ann Sheridan *Lorraine Sheldon* • Richard "Dick" Travis [Richard Travis] *Bert Jefferson* • Jimmy Durante *Banjo* • Reginald Gardiner *Beverly Carlton* • Billie Burke *Mrs Stanley* • Mary Wickes *Miss Preen* ■ *Dir* William Keighley • *Scr* Julius J Epstein, Philip G Epstein, from the play by George S Kaufman, Moss Hart

The Man Who Captured Eichmann ★★★★ PG

Historical drama 1996 · US · Colour · 92mins

A great actor was needed to find a shred of humanity in Nazi Adolf Eichmann and this made-for-cable movie has that actor in Robert Duvall. He portrays the bureaucrat who sent millions of people to the gas chambers as an aged, infirm exile, kidnapped in Argentina by masterspy Peter Malkin (Arliss Howard) and taken to Israel to face trial. Concentrating on the excitement of the chase, the film nevertheless carries the horror of the Holocaust across the years. TH [video]

Robert Duvall *Adolf Eichmann* • Arliss Howard *Peter Malkin* • Jeffrey Tambor *Isser Harel* • Jack Laufer *Uzi* • Nicolas Surovy *Hans* ■ *Dir* William A Graham • *Scr* Lionel Chetwynd, from the memoirs *Eichmann in My Hands* by Peter Malkin, Harry Stein

The Man Who Changed His Mind ★★★

Science fiction 1936 · UK · BW · 61mins

Boris Karloff is up to his brain transference tricks again in this seldom-seen British chiller. As Dr Laurience, he's in love with lab assistant Anna Lee. Unfortunately, she's planning to marry John Loder. So Karloff plans to switch brains with him using the usual strange scientific apparatus so popular in 1930s borderline sci-fi melodrama. Karloff gives one of his best performances in the amusing leading role. AJ

Boris Karloff *Dr Laurience* • Anna Lee *Dr Clare Wyatt* • John Loder *Dick Haslewood* • Frank Cellier *Lord Haslewood* • Donald Calthrop *Clayton* • Cecil Parker *Dr Gratton* • Lyn Harding *Professor Holloway* ■ *Dir* Robert Stevenson • *Scr* L DuGarde Peach, Sidney Gilliat, John L Balderston

The Man Who Changed His Name ★★

Crime drama 1934 · UK · BW · 71mins

A millionaire causes his wife and her unscrupulous lover to think he is a notorious murderer in this above-average B-feature, based on a typically ingenious work by Edgar Wallace. Its stage origins are evident in the static, talkative development, but it's carried by Lyn Harding's characteristically powerful performance as the husband. Betty Stockfield is adequate as the foolish wife, though Leslie Perrins is miscast as the philanderer. AE

Lyn Harding *Selby Clive* • Betty Stockfeld *Nita Clive* • Leslie Perrins *Frank Ryan* • Ben Welden *Jerry Muller* • Aubrey Mather *Sir Ralph Whitcomb* • Richard Dolman *John Boscombe* ■ *Dir* Henry Edwards • *Scr* H Fowler Mear, Edgar Wallace, from the play by Edgar Wallace

The Man Who Could Cheat Death ★★

Horror 1959 · UK · Colour · 82mins

A strange Hammer horror about a 104-year-old doctor who is able to look like a 30-year-old thanks to annual glandular transplants taken from living donors. When he murders his own doctor, however, things starts to unravel. This has its moments, but not very many. That said, it does provide a rare starring role to Anton Diffring, who usually played sadistic SS officers. AT

Anton Diffring *Dr Georges Bonnet* • Hazel Court *Janine* • Delphi Lawrence *Margo* • Christopher Lee *Dr Pierre Gerard* • Francis De Wolff *Inspector Legris* ■ *Dir* Terence Fisher • *Scr* Jimmy Sangster, from the play *The Man in Half Moon Street* by Barré Lyndon

The Man Who Could Work Miracles ★★ U

Fantasy comedy 1936 · UK · BW · 78mins

Having produced HG Wells's *Things to Come*, British movie mogul Alexander Korda went straight on to another Wells story, a rather corny fantasy about a bashful draper's assistant (Roland Young) who acquires miraculous powers when the gods look kindly upon him. The comedy soon gives way to pomposity, as Young gathers world leaders and tells them to be nice to each other. While Ralph Richardson is delightfully eccentric throughout, it's embarrassingly dated and simplistic. AT [video]

Roland Young *George McWhirter Fotheringay* • Ralph Richardson *Colonel Winstanley* • Edward Chapman *Major Grigsby* • Ernest Thesiger *Mr Maydig* • Joan Gardner *Ada Price* • Sophie Stewart *Maggie Hooper* • Robert Cochran *Bill Stoker* • Lawrence Hanray *Mr Bamfylde* ■ *Dir* Lothar Mendes • *Scr* HG Wells, Lajos Biró, from the short story by HG Wells

The Man Who Cried ★★ 12

Period romantic drama
2000 · UK/Fr/US · Colour · 95mins

Set mostly in France just prior to Nazi occupation, this theatrically staged romance follows Christina Ricci's Jewish émigré as she moves from her native Russia to London then Paris, dependent on the kindness of others, notably showgirl Cate Blanchett. Ricci falls in love with Johnny Depp's unintentionally comic gypsy horseman, although their onscreen chemistry is nil. The charcters in Sally Potter's colourful film are little more than chocolate-box cut-outs. AC. Contains violence and sex scenes. [video] DVD

Christina Ricci *Suzie* • Cate Blanchett *Lola* • John Turturro *Dante Domino* • Johnny Depp *Cesar* • Oleg Yankovskiy *Father* • Harry Dean Stanton *Felix Perlman* • Miriam Karlin *Madame Goldstein* ■ *Dir/Scr* Sally Potter

The Man Who Cried Wolf ★★

Crime drama 1937 · US · BW · 66mins

An actor keeps making false confessions of murder to the police to avoid suspicion when he kills his wife's lover. But then, in a clever twist, he needs to persuade the police that he did commit the crime to prevent his son carrying the can. Lewis Stone does his best in the lead, while Tom Brown plays his son, but the film is content to remain an ordinary B-feature. AE

Lewis Stone *Lawrence Fontaine* • Tom Brown *Tommy Bradley* • Barbara Read *Nan* • Marjorie Main *Amelia Bradley* ■ *Dir* Lewis R Foster • *Scr* Charles Grayson, Sy Bartlett, from the story *Too Clever to Live* by Arthur Rohlsfel

The Man Who Fell to Earth ★★★★ 18

Cult science-fiction drama
1976 · UK · Colour · 133mins

This typically eccentric and multidimensional movie from director Nicolas Roeg transforms Walter Tevis's novel into an enigmatic and chilling mosaic of corporate satire and effective science fiction. In his feature debut, David Bowie is exactly right as the Swiftian starman who becomes fabulously wealthy from his intergalactic inventions, but soon gets corrupted by such earthbound vices as alcohol, television and sex. Already an established sci-fi classic, this is a fascinating new-age fairy tale, with Bowie's "fall" open to numerous allegorical interpretations. AJ. Contains violence, swearing, sex scenes and nudity. [video] DVD

David Bowie *Thomas Jerome Newton* • Rip Torn *Nathan Bryce* • Candy Clark *Mary-Lou* • Buck Henry *Oliver Farnsworth* • Bernie Casey *Peters* • Jackson D Kane *Professor Canutti* •

Rick Riccardo *Trevor* • Tony Mascia *Arthur* ■ *Dir* Nicolas Roeg • *Scr* Paul Mayersburg, from the novel by Walter Tevis

The Man Who Finally Died ★

Drama 1962 · UK · BW · 100mins

Stanley Baker goes to Bavaria to find out about his long-lost German father; while there, he gets involved in espionage. A routine spy thriller based on a TV series which plods more than it surprises, though the actors deserve some credit for delivering the deathless lines with a conviction that's way beyond the call of duty. AJ

Stanley Baker *Joe Newman* • Peter Cushing *Dr von Brecht* • Eric Portman *Hofmeister* • Mai Zetterling *Lisa* • Niall MacGinnis *Brenner* • Nigel Green *Hirsch* • Barbara Everest *Martha* ■ *Dir* Quentin Lawrence • *Scr* Lewis Greifer, Louis Marks, from a story by Lewis Greifer

The Man Who Had Power over Women ★

Comedy 1970 · UK · Colour · 89mins

This awful, cringe-inducing story about a public relations executive and his obnoxious pop star client was filmed at the fag end of the Swinging Sixties, and it has dated very badly. Although the film toys around with the moral issue of abortion, it never achieves more than a glossy vacuity. AT

Rod Taylor *Peter Reaney* • Carol White *Jody Pringle* • James Booth *Val Pringle* • Penelope Horner *Angela Reaney* • Charles Korvin *Alfred Felix* • Alexandra Stewart *Frances* ■ *Dir* John Krish • *Scr* Allan Scott, Chris Bryant, Andrew Meredith, from the novel by Gordon M Williams

The Man Who Haunted Himself ★★★ PG

Thriller 1970 · UK · Colour · 89mins

This wonderfully improbable chiller affords the rare opportunity to see Roger Moore being acted off the screen – by Roger Moore! The respectable business executive whose life is transformed by a car crash is a drip of the first order, but the sinister alter ego who escapes while he is unconscious is a rip-roaring cad. Veteran director Basil Dearden just manages to sustain the eerie atmosphere and, even though the mistaken identity card is overplayed, it's very watchable. DP [video] DVD

Roger Moore *Harold Pelham* • Hildegard Neil *Eve Pelham* • Alastair Mackenzie (1) *Michael* • Hugh Mackenzie *James* • Kevork Malikyan *Luigi* • Thorley Walters *Bellamy* • Anton Rodgers *Tony Alexander* • Olga Georges-Picot *Julie* ■ *Dir* Basil Dearden • *Scr* Basil Dearden, Michael Relph, from the short story *The Case of Mr Pelham* by Anthony Armstrong

The Man Who Knew Too Little ★★★ 12

Spy comedy 1997 · US/Ger · Colour · 89mins

As the parodic Hitchcock title suggests, this sweet-natured Bill Murray comedy is an entertaining throwback to the espionage thrillers of yesteryear. The naive Murray is visiting brother Peter Gallagher in London and unwittingly becomes entangled in an assassination plot, the inspired twist being that Murray thinks it's all part of a participatory drama group. Enjoyable, but the one-joke premise does eventually lose its lustre. JC. Contains violence, sex scenes. [video]

Bill Murray *Wallace Ritchie* • Peter Gallagher *James Ritchie* • Joanne Whalley-Kilmer [Joanne Whalley] *Lori* • Alfred Molina *Boris, the Butcher* • Richard Wilson *Sir Roger Daggenhurst* • Geraldine James *Dr Ludmilla Kropotkin* • John Standing *Gilbert Embleton* • Anna Chancellor *Barbara Ritchie* ■ *Dir* Jon Amiel • *Scr* Robert Farrar, Howard Franklin, from the novel *Watch That Man* by Robert Farrar

The Man Who Knew Too Much ★★★★ U

Thriller 1934 · UK · BW · 75mins

With a finale inspired by the 1911 Sidney Street siege, this early Hitchcock – the only film he remade – was originally devised as a case for Bulldog Drummond. A taut, twisting thriller, the film sweeps from Switzerland to London's Albert Hall as Leslie Banks and Edna Best seek to rescue kidnapped daughter Nova Pilbeam and prevent a political assassination. Laced with gallows humour, this expertly structured tale marked the English-language debut of Peter Lorre, whose delight in his own villainy is tempered with an unexpected touch of humanity. DP [video] DVD

Leslie Banks *Bob Lawrence* • Edna Best *Jill Lawrence* • Peter Lorre *Abbott* • Frank Vosper *Ramon Levine* • Hugh Wakefield *Clive* • Nova Pilbeam *Betty Lawrence* • Pierre Fresnay *Louis Bernard* • Cicely Oates *Nurse Agnes* ■ *Dir* Alfred Hitchcock • *Scr* Edwin Greenwood, AR Rawlinson, Emlyn Williams, Charles Bennett, DB Wyndham-Lewis, from a story by DB Wyndham-Lewis

The Man Who Knew Too Much ★★★ PG

Thriller 1956 · US · Colour · 114mins

Alfred Hitchcock once told François Truffaut that his 1934 version of this exciting thriller was "the work of a talented amateur and the second was made by a professional". There's no doubt that this colour remake is technically more accomplished, while the deft tinkering with the finale adds considerably to the suspense. Not all of the additional minutes are as well spent. *Que Sera, Sera* might have won the Oscar, but its inclusion was solely to mollify Doris Day fans and the storytelling is occasionally over-deliberate, but James Stewart is superb. DP [video] DVD

James Stewart *Dr Ben McKenna* • Doris Day *Jo McKenna* • Bernard Miles *Mr Drayton* • Brenda de Banzie *Mrs Drayton* • Ralph Truman *Buchanan* • Daniel Gélin *Louis Bernard* • Reggie Nalder *Rien, the assassin* • Mogens Wieth *Ambassador* • Alan Mowbray *Val Parnell* • Hillary Brooke *Jan Peterson* ■ *Dir* Alfred Hitchcock • *Scr* John Michael Hayes, Angus MacPhail, from a story by DB Wyndham-Lewis, Charles Bennett

The Man Who Laughs ★★★★

Silent period drama 1928 · US · BW · 110mins

The third of four moody and mysterious films German-born director Paul Leni made in Hollywood was released a year after it was made in order to add music and sound effects. Based on Victor Hugo's tale, it tells of a man whose face is distorted into a hideous grin. Becoming a circus clown, he falls in love with a blind girl. Conrad Veidt plays the protagonist, while Mary Philbin is touching as his beloved. RB

Conrad Veidt *Gwynplaine* • Mary Philbin *Dea* ■ *Dir* Paul Leni • *Scr* J Grubb Alexander, Charles E Whittaker, Marion Ward, May McLean, Walter Anthony (titles), from the novel *L'Homme Qui Rit* by Victor Hugo

The Man Who Laughs ★

Period horror 1966 · It/Fr · Colour · 97mins

Under Sergio Corbucci's surprisingly confused and unfocused eye Victor Hugo's macabre romance is shifted to 16th-century Italy. Jean Sorel is the man whose face has been tortured into a hideous fixed grin who becomes court assassin for effete Edmund Purdom's Cesare Borgia. This travesty is a typically overblown product of its era: chintzy costumes, third-rate acting, over-operatic score and badly dubbed. AJ. Italian dialogue dubbed into English.

Jean Sorel *Angelo/Astorre Manfredi* • Lisa Gastoni *Lucrezia Borgia* • Edmund Purdom *Cesare Borgia* • Ilaria Occhini *Dea* • Linda Sini ■ *Dir* Sergio Corbucci • *Scr* E Sanjust, L Ronconi, Sergio Corbucci, F Rossetti [Franco Rossetti], A Bertolotto, from the novel by Victor Hugo

The Man Who Liked Funerals ★★ U

Comedy 1959 · UK · BW · 59mins

Leslie Phillips landed his first starring role in this brisk B-picture. Reining in the trademark charm, he plays a printer who attempts to fill the coffers of a struggling boys' club by blackmailing the relatives of recently departed bigwigs, whose scandalous (albeit forged) memoirs he threatens to publish. However, it all goes horribly wrong when he picks on the family of a notorious gangster. The film is nothing to get excited about, but it does raise the odd smile. DP

Leslie Phillips *Simon Hurd* • Brian Tyler (1) *Nutter* • Anthony Green *Tommy* • Shaun O'Riordan *Reverend Pitt* • Susan Beaumont *Stella* • Bill Fraser *Jeremy Bentham* ■ *Dir* David Eady • *Scr* Margot Bennett, from a story by C Finn, Joan O'Connor

The Man Who Lived Twice ★★★

Crime drama 1936 · US · BW · 73mins

Before Ralph Bellamy became cast as the typical "other man" – notably in 1937's *The Awful Truth* – he was known as a useful and recognisable tough lead. Here, he's excellent as a murderer who has brain and facial surgery which turns him into quite literally another person. Never a big hit, this average feature has an interesting period sheen. TS

Ralph Bellamy *James Blake/Slick Rawley* • Marian Marsh *Janet Haydon* • Thurston Hall *Dr Schuyler* • Isabel Jewell *Peggy Russell* • Nana Bryant *Mrs Margaret Schuyler* • Ward Bond *Gloves Baker* ■ *Dir* Harry Lachman • *Scr* Tom Van Dycke, Fred Niblo Jr, Arthur Strawn, from the story by Tom Van Dycke, Henry Altimus

The Man Who Loved Cat Dancing ★ 18

Western 1973 · US · Colour · 118mins

Rumour has it that Robert Bolt did a bit of script doctoring to improve this western, which starred his wife Sarah Miles and Burt Reynolds. Imagine how awful it must have been before he got hold of it. Directed with no sense of narrative, let alone the old West, what starts out as a revenge story soon turns into a soppy romance. Lee J Cobb and Jack Warden are left cooling their heels while Reynolds and Miles make little effort to hide their obvious antipathy towards one another. DP [video]

Burt Reynolds *Jay Grobart* • Sarah Miles *Catherine Crocker* • Lee J Cobb *Lapchance* • Jack Warden *Dawes* • George Hamilton *Crocker* • Bo Hopkins *Billy* • Robert Donner *Dub* • Jay Silverheels *The Chief* ■ *Dir* Richard C Sarafian • *Scr* Eleanor Perry, from the novel by Marilyn Durham

The Man Who Loved Redheads ★★★

Comedy 1954 · UK · Colour · 100mins

An elegant and witty screenplay by Terence Rattigan, based on his play, helps make this extremely civilised and sophisticated entertainment. It also benefits immensely from an early Eastmancolor process and photography by the great Georges Perinal, a combination that proved ideal for showing off the titian tresses of Moira Shearer. The idea is nicely bittersweet, as Shearer plays all the "other" women in the recollections of John Justin, married to Gladys Cooper in the film. The denouement is genuinely moving, and a marvellous line-up of supporting players speeds the slight tale pleasurably on its way. TS

Moira Shearer *Sylvia/Daphne/Olga/Colette* • John Justin *Mark St Neots* • Roland Culver *Oscar* • Gladys Cooper *Caroline* • Denholm Elliott *Denis* • Harry Andrews *Williams* • Patricia Cutts *Bubbles* • John Hart *Sergei* ■ *Dir* Harold French • *Scr* Terrence Rattigan, from his play *Who Is Sylvia?*

The Man Who Loved Women ★★★ 15

Comedy 1977 · Fr · Colour · 114mins

Attacked for its chauvinism, François Truffaut's wry comedy is actually a shrugging admission that men are little boys who don't deserve the women who love them. As he recalls each pair of legs that has enticed him, Charles Denner emerges less as a manipulative cad and more a sad man who has missed so many opportunities to live a fuller life. Unfortunately, Truffaut turns his memoirs into a long series of flashbacks, which prevents him from exploring Denner's motives and emotions. A touch more gravitas might have made his tale more poignant. DP. In French with English subtitles. DVD

Charles Denner *Bertrand Morane* • Brigitte Fossey *Genevieve Bigey* • Nelly Borgeaud *Delphine Grezel* • Genevieve Fontanel *Helene* • Nathalie Baye *Martine Desdoits* • Sabine Glaser *Bernadette* • Leslie Caron *Vera* ■ *Dir* François Truffaut • *Scr* François Truffaut, Michel Fermaud, Suzanne Schiffman

The Man Who Loved Women ★★ 15

Comedy 1983 · US · Colour · 105mins

This is an early example of the American trend of adapting (and usually ruining) a French success for the US market. Director Blake Edwards takes François Truffaut's minor film and balloons it into something grander, yet emptier. Burt Reynolds works well as a women-obsessed sculptor whose story is played out via flashbacks at his funeral. Julie Andrews is the psychiatrist to whom Reynolds confesses all. The cast is pleasing, but this fails to hit the mark. DF [video]

Burt Reynolds *David* • Julie Andrews *Marianna* • Kim Basinger *Louise* • Marilu Henner *Agnes* • Cynthia Sikes *Courtney* • Sela Ward *Janet* ■ *Dir* Blake Edwards • *Scr* Blake Edwards, Milton Wexler, Geoffrey Edwards, from the 1977 film by François Truffaut

The Man Who Never Was ★★ U

Second World War spy drama
1955 · UK · Colour · 102mins

A lacklustre Second World War espionage caper about a plan to fool the Nazis into believing that the Allies had no interest in invading Sicily from North Africa. Scripted by Nigel Balchin, the plan hinges on a corpse, a British one, washed ashore with secret papers marking Greece as the invasion site. But the Germans aren't so easily convinced and send Irish agent Stephen Boyd to London to investigate. Stodgily directed by Ronald Neame, this is less a thriller than a game of wartime charades. AT

Clifton Webb *Lt Cmdr Ewen Montagu* • Gloria Grahame *Lucy* • Stephen Boyd *O'Reilly* • Robert Flemyng *George Acres* • Josephine Griffin *Pam* • André Morell *Sir Bernard Spilsbury* • Laurence Naismith *Admiral Cross* • Michael Hordern *General Coburn* ■ *Dir* Ronald Neame • *Scr* Nigel Balchin, from the book by Ewen Montagu

M

The Man Who Played God ★★★★

Drama 1932 · US · BW · 81mins

The great George Arliss, with his death's-head face, effete elegance and mannered theatrical style, might at first strike modern audiences as faintly comical. However, in this intriguing fable about love, faith and redemption, he is mesmerising as a wealthy international concert pianist who becomes an embittered recluse after going deaf from a bomb explosion. Eventually, he learns to lip-read the conversations of passers-by and uses his wealth to play God. Bette Davis made her striking Warner Bros debut as his youthful and passionate disciple, and John Adolfi directed this compelling drama with imagination and sensitivity. It was embarrassingly updated in 1955 as *Sincerely Yours*, a starring vehicle for Liberace. RK

George Arliss *Montgomery Royale* • Violet Heming *Mildred Miller* • Ivan Simpson *Battle* • Louise Closser Hale *Florence Royale* • Bette Davis *Grace Blair* • André Luguet *The King* • Donald Cook *Harold Van Adam* • Charles E Evans *The Doctor* ■ *Dir* John G Adolfi • *Scr* Julien Josephson, Maude Howell, from the play by Jules Eckert Goodman, from the short story *The Silent Voice* by Gouverneur Morris

The Man Who Shot Liberty Valance ★★★★★ U

Western 1962 · US · BW · 118mins

This key late John Ford western has James Stewart top-billed over John Wayne, and a superb Lee Marvin in support as the ironically titled Valance. The film's most famous epigram "Print the legend" effectively sums up the plot, which, told in flashback, depends on a twist that only a spoilsport would reveal. On its release, the movie was taken for granted, but with hindsight it can be reassessed as a major work. In Tom Doniphon and "Pilgrim" Ransom Stoddard, Wayne and Stewart created indelible western icons, and the film clearly shows the impact of the arrival of literacy upon an innocent, more primitive West. TS DVD

James Stewart *Ransom Stoddard* • John Wayne *Tom Doniphon* • Vera Miles *Hallie Stoddard* • Lee Marvin *Liberty Valance* • Edmond O'Brien *Dutton Peabody* • Andy Devine *Link Appleyard* • Woody Strode *Pompey* • Ken Murray *Doc Willoughby* • John Carradine *Major Cassius Starbuckle* ■ *Dir* John Ford • *Scr* Willis Goldbeck, James Warner Bellah, from a story by Dorothy M Johnson • *Cinematographer* William H Clothier [William Clothier]

The Man Who Sued God ★★★ 15

Comedy drama 2001 · Aus · Colour · 96mins

Unashamedly Capra-esque in its championing of the little feller against the system, Mark Joffe's comedy provides a charming, but acute indictment of the self-serving attitudes of established religion and the insurance industry. Angered at the decision that the destruction of his boat by lightning was an act of God, fisherman Billy Connolly teams up with journalist Judy Davis to challenge establishment truisms. The romantic subplot sugars the pill, but this is still entertaining. DP. Contains swearing. DVD

Billy Connolly *Steve Myers* • Judy Davis *Anna Redmond* • Colin Friels *David Myers* • Bille Brown *Gerry Ryan* • Wendy Hughes *Jules Myers* • Blair Venn *Les* • Emily Browning *Rebecca Myers* ■ *Dir* Mark Joffe • *Scr* Don Watson, from a screenplay (unproduced) by John Clarke, from an idea by Patrick McCarville

The Man Who Understood Women ★★

Satirical drama 1959 · US · Colour · 135mins

Leslie Caron and Henry Fonda make up a May-December partnership in this overlong mix of comedy, romance and drama. Fonda is a film-maker who finds popular success by turning his new love, Caron, into a star. When she becomes involved with pilot Cesare Danova, however, Fonda gets jealous, and what could have been a hilarious satire on Hollywood turns into an unconvincing melodrama. The stars are good, but Nunnally Johnson, who writes, produces *and* directs, seems to lose his focus and his grip. RK

Leslie Caron *Ann Garantier* • Henry Fonda *Willie Bauche* • Cesare Danova *Marco Ranieri* • Myron McCormick *Preacher* • Marcel Dalio *Le Marne* • Conrad Nagel *GK* ■ *Dir* Nunnally Johnson • *Scr* Nunnally Johnson, from the novel *The Colors of Day* by Romain Gary

The Man Who Wasn't There ★★★★ 15

Period crime drama
2001 · US/UK · BW · 106mins

It would be simplistic to call the Coen brothers' latest movie a pastiche of *film noir*. Certainly it is set in small-town California in 1949 and involves an ordinary Joe embroiled in a murder plot – and it's shot in period black and white – but the veneer of homage masks something far more complex and clever. The story, in which Billy Bob Thornton's inscrutable barber attempts to escape from his humdrum life through blackmail, is typical of the Coens. With its dash of flying-saucer paranoia, it's tempting to interpret the film as a broader examination of western existential dread. There is sublime acting from Thornton and Coen regular Frances McDormand, aided by the stunning photography of Roger Deakins. AC. Contains violence and swearing. DVD

Billy Bob Thornton *Ed Crane* • Frances McDormand *Doris Crane* • Michael Badalucco *Frank* • James Gandolfini *Big Dave* • Katherine Borowitz *Ann Nirdlinger* • Jon Polito *Creighton Tolliver* • Scarlett Johansson *Birdy Abundas* • Richard Jenkins *Walter Abundas* • Tony Shalhoub *Freddy Riedenschneider* ■ *Dir* Joel Coen • *Scr* Joel Coen, Ethan Coen

The Man Who Watched Trains Go By ★★★

Mystery 1952 · UK · Colour · 78mins

Adapted from the novel by the prolific Georges Simenon, this was one of Claude Rains's rare assignments in his homeland. Notwithstanding the dreadful colour, the tale of a clerk who takes advantage of the accidental death of crooked boss Herbert Lom quickly involves, with director Harold French capturing the atmosphere of provincial France and Rains essaying the decent little man with ease. DP

Claude Rains *Kees Popinga* • Michael Nightingale *Clerk* • Felix Aylmer *Merkemans* • Herbert Lom *Julius de Koster Jr* • Gibb McLaughlin *Julius de Koster Sr* • Marius Goring *Lucas* • Marta Toren *Michele* ■ *Dir* Harold French • *Scr* Harold French, from the novel by Georges Simenon

The Man Who Would Be King ★★★★★ PG

Period adventure
1975 · US · Colour · 123mins

This colourful movie version of Rudyard Kipling's right royal 19th-century adventure stars Sean Connery and Michael Caine as the veteran army squaddies who bamboozle a remote mountain tribe in Afghanistan into accepting Connery's regal credentials. Greed and circumstances topple the comic elements of the tale into a serious fable about the vanity of human endeavour and the folly of imperialism. Director John Huston matches character to action in masterly fashion, aided by the brief bonus of an aloof commentary on the situation by Christopher Plummer, as Kipling himself. Packed with sly dialogue and memorable scenes, plus a stirring score from Maurice Jarre. TH. Contains violence, swearing. DVD

Sean Connery *Daniel Dravot* • Michael Caine *Peachy Carnehan* • Christopher Plummer *Rudyard Kipling* • Saeed Jaffrey *Billy Fish* • Karroum Ben Bouih *Kafu-Selim* • Jack May *District commissioner* • Doghmi Larbi *Ootah* • Shakira Caine *Roxanne* ■ *Dir* John Huston • *Scr* John Huston, Gladys Hill, from the story by Rudyard Kipling • *Cinematographer* Oswald Morris • *Music* Maurice Jarre

The Man Who Would Not Die ★★

Mystery thriller 1975 · US · Colour · 83mins

There's a fascinating plot struggling to get out of this muddled affair, in which Alex Sheafe investigates a series of mysterious deaths only to discover that they are tied to an elaborate robbery scam. Screen veterans Keenan Wynn, Dorothy Malone and Aldo Ray are unable to muster much enthusiasm, and director Robert Arkless seems to have less idea about what is going on than the audience. JF

Dorothy Malone *Paula Stafford* • Keenan Wynn *Victor Slidell* • Aldo Ray *Frank Keefer* • Alex Sheafe *Marc Rogers* • Joyce Ingalls *Pat Reagan* • Fred Scollay *Lieutenant Willetts* • James Monks *Mr Reagan* ■ *Dir* Robert Arkless • *Scr* Robert Arkless, George Chesbro, Stephen Taylor, from the novel *The Sailcloth Shroud* by Charles Williams

The Man Who Wouldn't Talk ★★★

Crime drama 1940 · US · BW · 72mins

Lloyd Nolan has one of his strongest roles playing the mysterious figure who confesses to killing a businessman, yet steadfastly refuses to reveal his true identity or motive. This entertaining Fox B-feature was the second screen version of a 1920s play, having previously served as the basis of Paul Muni's film, *The Valiant* (1929), but the previously tragic ending is discarded. AE

Lloyd Nolan *Joe Monday* • Jean Rogers *Alice Stetson* • Richard Clarke (1) *Steve Phillips* • Onslow Stevens *Frederick Keller* • Eric Blore *Horace Parker* ■ *Dir* David Burton • *Scr* Robert Ellis, Helen Logan, Lester Ziffren, Edward Ettinger, from the play *The Valiant* by Holworthy Hall, Robert M Middlemass

The Man Who Wouldn't Talk ★★ U

Courtroom drama 1957 · UK · BW · 108mins

Producer/director Herbert Wilcox makes a moderately entertaining film out of this courtroom drama in which Anthony Quayle's American scientist, accused of murder, refuses to testify in his own defence. Wilcox's wife, Anna Neagle, gives another of her great lady portraits as Britain's leading Queen's Counsel, demonstrating her deductive brilliance in spotting a bullet hole in a witness's window pane and her oratorical skills in a dramatic five-minute courtroom address. AE

Anthony Quayle *Dr Frank Smith* • Anna Neagle *Mary Randall QC* • Zsa Zsa Gabor *Eve Trent* • Katherine Kath *Yvonne Delbeau* • Dora Bryan *Telephonist* • Patrick Allen *Kennedy* • Hugh McDermott *Bernie* ■ *Dir* Herbert Wilcox • *Scr* Edgar Lustgarten, from the book by Stanley Jackson

The Man with a Cloak ★★ U

Period drama 1951 · US · BW · 80mins

In 19th-century New York, villainous housekeeper Barbara Stanwyck schemes to murder Louis Calhern and cheat innocent young Leslie Caron out of her inheritance. Mysterious stranger Joseph Cotten arrives on the scene to save the day, turning out, quite inexplicably, to be Edgar Allan Poe. A bemusing period farrago, directed by Fletcher Markle, that would deserve to sink without trace were it not for Stanwyck's characteristically uncompromising performance. RK

Joseph Cotten *Dupin* • Barbara Stanwyck *Lorna Bounty* • Louis Calhern *Thevenet* • Leslie Caron *Madeline Minot* • Joe De Santis *Martin* • Jim Backus *Flaherty* • Margaret Wycherly *Mrs Flynn* • Richard Hale *Durand* ■ *Dir* Fletcher Markle • *Scr* Frank Fenton, from a story by John Dickson Carr

Man with a Movie Camera ★★★★★

Silent experimental documentary
1929 · USSR · BW · 67mins

Dziga Vertov claimed that his purpose in making this remarkable panorama of Moscow life – the workers, shoppers, holidaymakers and machines that keep the city moving – was to film "life as it is". To achieve this, Vertov displayed all the techniques of cinema at his disposal: split-screen, dissolves, slow-motion and freeze frames. Indeed, it's the camera that is the hero of this influential documentary. Born Denis Kaufman, Vertov took his name from the Ukrainian words meaning spinning, turning or, appropriately, revolution. RB

Dir/Scr Dziga Vertov • *Cinematographer* Mikhail Kaufman

The Man with Bogart's Face ★★★

Detective comedy mystery
1980 · US · Colour · 111mins

An enjoyable, unassuming movie buff in-joke about a second-rate private eye called Sam Marlow who has plastic surgery to make him look like his role model, Humphrey Bogart. It's a neat idea, and Bogart clone Robert Sacchi could certainly be mistaken for Bogie on a darkly lit mean street. The *Maltese Falcon*-style plot involves Alexander the Great's sapphires, with Victor Buono and Herbert Lom in the Greenstreet and Lorre roles. AT

Robert Sacchi *Sam Marlow* • Michelle Phillips *Gena* • Franco Nero *Hakim* • Olivia Hussey *Elsa* • Victor Buono *Commodore Anastas* • Herbert Lom *Mr Zebra* • George Raft *Petey Cane* ■ *Dir* Robert Day • *Scr* Andrew J Fenady, from his novel

The Man with One Red Shoe ★★ PG

Comedy 1985 · US · Colour · 88mins

Hollywood has no qualms about trawling foreign climes for inspirational ideas and turning them into blandly inoffensive pap. This time around, however, the source is the French farce *The Tall Blond Man with One Black Shoe*, which itself limps along unfunnily in the slow lane. Unsurprisingly, so does the remake, making little use of Tom Hanks's comic talents. Marooned by inanity and mistiming, he plays a violinist who is mistaken for a spy. JM

Tom Hanks *Richard* • Dabney Coleman *Cooper* • Lori Singer *Maddy* • Charles Durning *Ross* • Carrie Fisher *Paula* • Edward Herrmann *Brown* • Jim Belushi [James Belushi] *Morris* ■ *Dir* Stan Dragoti • *Scr* Robert Klane, from the film *The Tall Blond Man with One Black Shoe* by Francis Veber, Yves Robert

The Man with the Deadly Lens ★★★ 15

Satirical thriller 1982 · US · Colour · 113mins

This thriller finds roving TV journalist Sean Connery uncovering a hornet's nest of conspiracies and terrorist links at the heart of the US Government.

The tone is often satirical but there are so many plots, subplots and red herrings that it's hard to figure out if it's a mess or immensely sophisticated. However, Connery is an anchorman in every respect, giving the film a firm foundation and a moral centre. AT [video] DVD

Sean Connery *Patrick Hale* • George Grizzard *President Lockwood* • Robert Conrad *General Wombat* • Katharine Ross *Sally Blake* • GD Spradlin *Philindros* • John Saxon *Homer Hubbard* • Henry Silva *Rafeeq* • Leslie Nielsen *Mallory* ■ *Dir* Richard Brooks • *Scr* Richard Brooks, from the novel *The Better Angels* by Charles McCarry

The Man with the Golden Arm ★★★★ 15

Drama 1955 · US · BW · 119mins

This is to drug addiction what *The Lost Weekend* was to alcoholism – a trailblazer. From Saul Bass's opening credits to Elmer Bernstein's jazzy score, Otto Preminger's movie boasts its modernity in its unflinching approach to the story of an aspiring musician and heroin addict. In the clean-cut Eisenhower era, this movie shocked audiences deeply. Frank Sinatra's Oscar-nominated performance still impresses, as do those of Eleanor Parker as his wife and Kim Novak as Sinatra's object of desire. AT [video] DVD

Frank Sinatra *Frankie Machine* • Kim Novak *Molly* • Eleanor Parker *Zosch Machine* • Arnold Stang *Sparrow* • Darren McGavin *Louie* • Robert Strauss *Schwiefka* • George Mathews *Williams* • John Conte *Drunky* ■ *Dir* Otto Preminger • *Scr* Walter Newman, Lewis Meltzer, from the novel by Nelson Algren

The Man with the Golden Gun ★★★ PG

Spy adventure 1974 · UK · Colour · 119mins

This is an improvement on Ian Fleming's novel, with Christopher Lee making a fine villain, sporting a golden gun, a third nipple and a tiny henchman called Nick Nack, wittily played by Herve Villechaize. Britt Ekland is funny, too, sending herself up as Bond's clueless assistant and surviving the most sexist scene in the entire 007 series. There are major faults as well – notably the repeat of the pre-credit scene for the climax (borrowing from Orson Welles's *The Lady from Shanghai*). Thailand's Phang-Nga Bay was a stunning choice of location, though it was soon to become a tourist trap. AT [video] DVD

Roger Moore *James Bond* • Christopher Lee *Scaramanga* • Britt Ekland *Mary Goodnight* • Maud Adams *Andrea* • Herve Villechaize *Nick Nack* • Clifton James *Sheriff JW Pepper* • Soon Taik Oh [Soon-Teck Oh] *Hip* • Richard Loo *Hai Fat* • Bernard Lee *"M"* • Lois Maxwell *Miss Moneypenny* • Marc Lawrence (1) *Rodney* • Desmond Llewelyn *"Q"* ■ *Dir* Guy Hamilton • *Scr* Richard Maibaum, Tom Mankiewicz, from the novel by Ian Fleming

Man with the Gun ★★★

Western 1955 · US · BW · 83mins

One of Robert Mitchum's strengths was his ability to grab a western like this by its throat and turn it into a personal statement. Mitchum plays a brooding gunman who cleans up a town to try to win back his estranged wife, played by the excellent Jan Sterling. There's a fair amount of sadism on show, and the mood and tone are satisfyingly grim. It's an impressive directorial debut from former Orson Welles associate Richard Wilson, featuring fine photography from the great veteran Lee Garmes. TS

Robert Mitchum *Clint Tollinger* • Jan Sterling *Nelly Bain* • Karen Sharpe *Stella Atkins* • Henry Hull *Marshal Sims* • Emile Meyer *Saul Atkins* • John Lupton *Jeff Castle* • Angie Dickinson *Kitty* ■ *Dir* Richard Wilson • *Scr* NB Stone Jr, Richard Wilson

The Man with the X-Ray Eyes ★★★★ PG

Science-fiction thriller
1963 · US · Colour · 75mins

Ray Milland plays one of his best remembered roles in Roger Corman's pocket-sized, yet highly potent, sci-fi shocker. He is scientist Dr Xavier, who experiments on himself and gains the power to see through solid materials. But as his sight gets stronger, so do the side-effects – Corman's cue to move from playful sideshow terror to mystical allegory, with plenty of engaging surreal imagery along the way. The Bible provided the inspiration for this cult classic, something clearly evident in the unforgettable revival-meeting climax. AJ [video]

Ray Milland *Dr James Xavier* • Diana Van Der Vlis *Dr Diane Fairfax* • Harold J Stone *Dr Sam Brant* • John Hoyt *Dr Willard Benson* • Don Rickles *Crane* • Lorie Summers *Carnival owner/party dancer* • Vicki Lee *Young girl patient* • Kathryn Hart *Mrs Mart* ■ *Dir* Roger Corman • *Scr* Robert Dillon, Ray Russell, from the story by Ray Russell

The Man with Two Brains ★★★★★ 15

Comedy 1983 · US · Colour · 85mins

There have been more accomplished Steve Martin films – *Roxanne*, *LA Story* – but this dazzlingly inventive comedy remains his finest hour. Martin is Doctor Hfuhruhurr, the brilliant brain surgeon who marries black widow Kathleen Turner but falls for a disembodied brain, voiced by Sissy Spacek. Turner hilariously sends up the *femme fatale* persona she established in *Body Heat*, David Warner co-stars as a fellow mad scientist, and there is also a surprise cameo in the form of the Elevator Killer. Sublime. JF [video]

Steve Martin *Dr Michael Hfuhruhurr* • Kathleen Turner *Dolores Benedict* • David Warner *Dr Necessiter* • Paul Benedict *Butler* • Richard Brestoff *Dr Pasteur* • James Cromwell *Realtor* • George Furth *Timon* • Peter Hobbs *Dr Brandon* • Earl Boen *Dr Conrad* • Sissy Spacek *Anne Uumellmahaye* ■ *Dir* Carl Reiner • *Scr* Steve Martin, Carl Reiner, George Gipe

The Man Within ★★★

Period adventure 1947 · UK · BW · 87mins

Set in 19th-century Sussex, Graham Greene's first published novel tells the story of an orphaned teenager, played by Richard Attenborough, who shops his guardian (Michael Redgrave), a smuggler. Greene thought this tale of guilt, identity and moral redemption was "embarrassingly sentimental", and he dismissed Bernard Knowles's film version as a treachery. AT

Michael Redgrave *Richard Carlyon* • Jean Kent *Lucy* • Joan Greenwood *Elizabeth* • Richard Attenborough *Francis Andrews* • Francis L Sullivan *Mr Braddock* • Felix Aylmer *Priest* • Ronald Shiner *Cockney Harry* • Basil Sydney *Sir Henry Merriman* • Ernest Thesiger *Farne* ■ *Dir* Bernard Knowles • *Scr* Muriel Box, Bernard Box, from the novel by Graham Greene

The Man without a Body ★

Horror 1957 · UK · BW · 80mins

Rock-bottom British shocker with an almost wilfully stupid story about a surgeon who revives Nostradamus's head and later grafts it on to someone else's body. (Don't ask why.) The only interesting thing is that both directors had more famous siblings: W Lee Wilder was Billy's brother, while Charles Saunders is the brother of *Mousetrap* producer Peter. Some of the same team went on to produce the similarly maniacal *Woman Eater*. DM

Robert Hutton *Dr Phil Merritt* • George Coulouris *Karl Brussard* • Julia Arnall *Jean Kramer* • Nadja Regin *Odette Vernet* • Sheldon Lawrence *Dr Lew Waldenhaus* • Michael Golden *Nostradamus* ■ *Dir* W Lee Wilder, Charles Saunders • *Scr* William Grote

The Man without a Face ★★★ 12

Drama 1993 · US · Colour · 114mins

Mel Gibson marked his directorial debut with this low-key, coming-of-age drama set in the late 1960s. Gibson plays the horribly scarred former teacher, who lives a reclusive life away from the gossip of his small-town neighbours. He is gradually drawn out of his shell by an unhappy young boy (Nick Stahl), but their close relationship eventually comes back to haunt him. Gibson takes a back seat to his young lead, and Stahl doesn't disappoint, delivering a moving, intense performance. Although the direction sometimes errs on the side of sentimentality, it remains an assured debut. JF [video] DVD

Mel Gibson *Justin McLeod* • Margaret Whitton *Catherine* • Fay Masterson *Gloria* • Gaby Hoffman [Gaby Hoffmann] *Megan* • Geoffrey Lewis *Chief Stark* • Richard Masur *Carl* • Nick Stahl *Chuck Norstadt* • Michael DeLuise *Douglas Hall* ■ *Dir* Mel Gibson • *Scr* Malcolm MacRury, from the novel by Isabelle Holland

The Man without a Past ★★★★ 12

Romantic comedy drama
2002 · Fin/Ger/Fr · Colour · 93mins

Although Timo Salminen's lustrous photography and Aki Kaurismäki's ripe dialogue evoke the Hollywood melodramas of yesteryear, this has a distinctively Finnish feel. Deadpan delivery, quirky humour and compassion for ordinary people quietly striving to get by are established Kaurismäki trademarks, but there's nothing predictable about the way in which Markku Peltola recovers his sense of identity, notably through his chaste relationship with Salvation Army member, Kati Outinen. The community on the outskirts of Helsinki belongs to a rock 'n' roll fairy tale, but Kaurismäki's detached style is too rooted in reality to proffer unfettered escapism. DP. In Finnish with English subtitles. Contains violence. [video] DVD

Markku Peltola *M* • Kati Outinen *Irma* • Juhani Niemela *Nieminen* • Sakari Kuosmanen *Anttila* ■ *Dir/Scr* Aki Kaurismäki

Man without a Star ★★★★

Western 1955 · US · Colour · 89mins

This fine Technicolor western was made by King Vidor and features the wonderful Kirk Douglas in an all-grinning, all-snarling portrayal, the kind of role he was born to play. There's tremendous sexual tension generated between Douglas and manipulative ranch owner Jeanne Crain, and the psychological slant is also cleverly integrated, as juvenile William Campbell idolises the no-good Douglas. Remade, poorly, in 1969 as *A Man Called Gannon*. TS

Kirk Douglas *Dempsey Rae* • Jeanne Crain *Reed Bowman* • Claire Trevor *Idonee* • Richard Boone *Steve Miles* • William Campbell *Jeff Jimson* • Jay C Flippen *Strap Davis* • Myrna Hansen *Tess Cassidy* • Mara Corday *Moccasin Mary* • Eddy C Waller [Eddy Waller] *Bill Cassidy* ■ *Dir* King Vidor • *Scr* Borden Chase, DD Beauchamp, from the novel by Dee Linford

Man, Woman and Child ★★★ PG

Drama 1983 · US · Colour · 96mins

Adapting his own novel, Erich Segal teamed with David Zelag Goodman for this unashamed weepie. It provides an unusually soft-centred role for Martin Sheen, as the happily married man who discovers that the French dalliance of a decade ago resulted in a son. But it's Blythe Danner who will have you reaching for the tissues as the wife trying to come to terms with the new member of her family. DP [video]

Martin Sheen *Robert Beckwith* • Blythe Danner *Sheila Beckwith* • Craig T Nelson *Bernie Ackerman* • David Hemmings *Gavin Wilson* • Nathalie Nell *Nicole Guerin* • Maureen Anderman *Margo* ■ *Dir* Dick Richards • *Scr* Erich Segal, David Zelag Goodman, from the novel by Erich Segal

Manchester United: beyond the Promised Land ★ PG

Documentary 2000 · UK/US · Colour · 80mins

Even the diehards are going to find this self-congratulatory tribute to MUFC plc hard to swallow. Less a documentary than a corporate video designed to attract potential investors, it's more about selling a brand than chronicling a season. Strenuous attempts are made to demonstrate the club's sensitivity to its sponsors, the internationalism of its fans and how much fun Sir Alex Ferguson really is. But fan-friendly issues such as player crises and United's farcical involvement in Fifa's World Club Championship are glossed over. Crude cinematic spin-doctoring. DP [video] DVD

Dir Bob Potter • *Cinematographer* Ferdia de Buitléar • *Editor* Paul Doyle Jr

The Manchurian Candidate ★★★★★ 15

Psychological thriller
1962 · US · BW · 130mins

Laurence Harvey is wonderfully creepy as the war hero brainwashed and programmed by Korean communists to eliminate a presidential candidate in this fearfully prophetic thriller. Frank Sinatra plays Harvey's old war buddy who tries to establish the truth and Angela Lansbury is Harvey's doting and utterly terrifying mother. Co-written by George Axelrod and director John Frankenheimer from the novel by Richard Condon, this blackly comic and suspenseful film ranks with Stanley Kubrick's *Dr Strangelove* as one of the toughest and most original movies of the 1960s. Following President Kennedy's assassination in 1963, Sinatra had the film withdrawn for many years. AT [video] DVD

Frank Sinatra *Bennett Marco* • Laurence Harvey *Raymond Shaw* • Janet Leigh *Rosie* • Angela Lansbury *Raymond's mother* • Henry Silva *Chunjim* • James Gregory *Senator John Iselin* • Leslie Parrish *Jocie Jordon* • John McGiver *Senator Thomas Jordon* ■ *Dir* John Frankenheimer • *Scr* George Axelrod, John Frankenheimer, from the novel by Richard Condon • *Cinematographer* Lionel Lindon • *Art Director* Richard Sylbert

The Manchurian Candidate ★★★★ 15

Psychological thriller
2004 · US · Colour · 124mins

An intelligent and chillingly believable tale of brainwashing, exploitation and political corruption, this update of John Frankenheimer's classic 1962 film relocates the military conflict at the heart of the story from Communist Korea to the first Gulf War in Kuwait. Denzel Washington steps into Frank Sinatra's shoes, playing a tormented US Army major who unwittingly becomes the key to a complex political conspiracy. Jonathan Demme's controlled direction is exhilarating, and he elicits brilliant performances from a fine cast. Liev Schreiber finally gets a part to sink his teeth into, as Washington's former sergeant who becomes a vice presidential candidate, but it's Meryl Streep, as Schreiber's

M

unscrupulous senator mother, who leaves the deepest impression. SF. Contains violence, swearing. DVD

Denzel Washington *Bennett "Ben" Marco* • Meryl Streep *Senator Eleanor Prentiss Shaw* • Liev Schreiber *Raymond Shaw* • Jon Voight *Senator Thomas Jordan* • Kimberly Elise *Rosie* • Jeffrey Wright *Al Melvin* • Ted Levine *Colonel Howard* • Bruno Ganz *Richard Delp* • Miguel Ferrer *Colonel Garret* • Dean Stockwell *Mark Whiting* ■ *Dir* Jonathan Demme • *Scr* Daniel Pyne, Dean Georgaris, from the film by George Axelrod, from the novel by Richard Condon

Mandalay ★★

Melodrama 1934 · US · BW · 65mins

Good-time girl Kay Francis, doctor Lyle Talbot and gunrunner Ricardo Cortez are all up the Irrawaddy without a paddle in this Warner Bros melodrama. Set in a Burma that exists only on the studio backlot, Michael Curtiz's film seems to draw most of its inspiration from MGM's *Red Dust*, in which Clark Gable got all steamed up over Jean Harlow. Unfortunately, the creaky plot and arthritic performances mean that *Mandalay* is really showing its age. AT

Kay Francis *Tanya Borisoff/Spot White* • Ricardo Cortez *Tony Evans* • Warner Oland *Nick* • Lyle Talbot *Dr Gregory Burton* • Ruth Donnelly *Mrs Peters* • Reginald Owen *Police commissioner* • Shirley Temple *Betty Shaw* ■ *Dir* Michael Curtiz • *Scr* Austin Parker, Charles Kenyon, from a story by Paul Hervey Fox

Mandela ★★★★ PG

Biographical documentary
1995 · US · Colour · 117mins

This Oscar-nominated documentary about the father of the new South Africa benefits immeasurably from having much of it fronted by Mandela himself. Afforded apparently unlimited access to the man and his mind, the film-makers trace Mandela's life from his humble village origins, through his early ANC involvement and subsequent lengthy incarceration by the country's white minority government, right up to his very public distancing from second wife Winnie. Particularly moving are Mandela's returns to the village of his birth and the cell where he was imprisoned for almost three decades. DA

Dir Jo Menell, Angus Gibson

Mandela and de Klerk ★★★ PG

Political drama 1997 · US · Colour · 109mins

One of the problems of making a film about recent events is that the screenwriter has to tiptoe around the sensibilities of extant characters. Consequently, this worthy TV movie can only tell part of the story of how Nelson Mandela and FW de Klerk jointly earned the Nobel Peace Prize for their efforts in bringing about democracy in South Africa. As the ANC leader who is thrust back into the limelight after 27 years' imprisonment, Sidney Poitier has the requisite dignity and determination. But Michael Caine's Afrikaaner president is the more grounded performance. DP

Sidney Poitier *Nelson Mandela* • Michael Caine *FW de Klerk* • Tina Lifford *Winnie Mandela* • Gerry Maritz *PW Botha* • Terry Norton *Marike de Klerk* ■ *Dir* Joseph Sargent • *Scr* Richard Wesley

Mandi ★★★ 15

Black comedy 1983 · Ind · Colour · 155mins

Respected film-maker Shyam Benegal made a rare foray into comedy with this tale centred around a brothel. The resulting class satire brings out the hypocrisy and lechery of the bourgeois males who frequent Shabana Azmi's Hyderabad kotha (a brothel with traditional cabaret on the side), and portrays the brothel as just another local business. Benegal highlights the corruption, amorality and greed that are awoken when local bigwig Saeed Jaffrey discovers that his son has fallen for his illegitimate daughter (Smita Patil). DP. In Hindi with English subtitles.

Shabana Azmi *Rukmini Bai* • Smita Patil *Zeenat* • Naseeruddin Shah *Dungdoo* • Saeed Jaffrey *Major Agarwal* • Kulbhushan Kharbanda *Mr Gupta* ■ *Dir* Shyam Benegal • *Scr* Shama Zaidi

Mandingo ★★★★ 18

Period drama 1975 · US · Colour · 120mins

Hollywood always had a romantic and sanitised view of what really went on in the Old South. This full-blooded excursion into American Gothic puts the lie to all that. Plantation owner James Mason festers away in a rotten old mansion, his feet resting on a black boy so that his disease will feed from him to the child. Mason's son (Perry King) keeps a harem of women slaves, while his wife, a sweaty Susan George, has sex with one of the slaves Mason trains to be a fighter. Vilified by most critics at the time, this is a head-on examination of the period; it's also one of the bravest American movies of the 1970s. Don't bother with the dire 1976 sequel, *Drum*. AT

James Mason *Warren Maxwell* • Susan George *Blanche* • Perry King *Hammond Maxwell* • Richard Ward *Agamemnon* • Brenda Sykes *Ellen* • Ken Norton *Mede* • Lillian Hayman *Lucrezia Borgia* ■ *Dir* Richard Fleischer • *Scr* Norman Wexler, from the play by Jack Kirkland, from the novel by Kyle Onstott

Mandragora ★★★ 18

Crime drama
1997 · Cz Rep/UK · Colour · 129mins

According to legend, the mandragora is a plant that grows under the gallows from the sperm of dead men. It's a powerful symbol for this harrowing, fact-based study of Prague's gay sex market, as each youth is condemned as soon as he steps on to the streets. Miroslav Caslavka heads a largely non-professional cast (many of whom are rent boys) that pumps itself with drink and drugs to withstand the exploitation of tourists and the brutality of their pimps. Directed with an unerring sense of pity by Wiktor Grodecki. DP. In Czech with English subtitles. DVD

Miroslav Caslavka *Marek Nedela* • David Svec *David* • Pavel Skripal *Honza* • Kostas Zedraloglu *Krysa* • Miroslav Breu *Libor* • Jiri Kodet *Otec* ■ *Dir* Wiktor Grodecki • *Scr* Wiktor Grodecki, David Svec

Mandy ★★★★ PG

Drama 1952 · UK · BW · 89mins

Whisky Galore! director Alexander Mackendrick's only non-comedy during his stay at Ealing is a highly intelligent film with much to say about the generation gap. Mandy Miller gives a performance of remarkable charm and insight as the deaf-mute child whose silent world is opened up by committed headmaster Jack Hawkins. An unusually unsympathetic Phyllis Calvert and Terence Morgan do well as Mandy's feuding parents and there is a standout turn from Godfrey Tearle as her embittered grandfather. DP

Phyllis Calvert *Christine* • Jack Hawkins *Searle* • Terence Morgan *Harry* • Godfrey Tearle *Mr Garland* • Mandy Miller *Mandy* • Marjorie Fielding *Mrs Garland* • Nancy Price *Jane Ellis* • Edward Chapman *Ackland* ■ *Dir* Alexander Mackendrick • *Scr* Nigel Balchin, Jack Whittingham, from the novel *The Day is Ours* by Hilda Lewis

The Mangler ★★ 18

Horror 1994 · US · Colour · 101mins

This Stephen King-based nonsense is about a possessed speed-ironing machine at a rural laundry that demands a virgin sacrifice every so often if the town's bigwigs want to remain prosperous. Horror icon Robert Englund chews the scenery in this shock-less wonder as the crotchety laundry owner, covered in old-age make-up and wearing leg braces, who made a pact with the Devil years before. The direction is also on crutches. AJ DVD

Robert Englund *Bill Gartley* • Ted Levine *John Hunton* • Daniel Matmor *Mark Jackson* • Jeremy Crutchley *Pictureman Mortician* • Vanessa Pike *Sherry Ouelette* ■ *Dir* Tobe Hooper • *Scr* Tobe Hooper, Stephen Brooks, Peter Welbeck [Harry Alan Towers], from a story by Stephen King

Manhatta ★★★

Silent experimental documentary
1921 · US · BW · 9mins

Although Hollywood dominated the mainstream, experimental cinema was largely the preserve of European artists during the silent era. However, that changed with the release of this portrait of New York, which anticipated the "city symphony" style that would reach its apogee in Walter Ruttman's *Berlin, Symphony of a Great City* (1927). Accompanied by extracts from a poem by Walt Whitman, the photographic vistas assembled by Charles Sheeler and Paul Strand are meticulously composed. But there's little action within the frame and less sense of urban rhythm. Shown as a trailer in the States and exhibited at a French Dadaist happening, it was subsequently hailed as the keystone of the American avant-garde. DP

Dir Paul Strand, Charles Sheeler

Manhattan ★★★★★ 15

Romantic comedy 1979 · US · BW · 92mins

This early masterpiece from Woody Allen celebrates his beloved New York. Allen stars as a neurotic TV writer who's taken up with 17-year-old Mariel Hemingway, but who's being diverted by fast-talking Diane Keaton and – more dangerously – by the book written about him by his lesbian ex-wife Meryl Streep. Allen and his fellow New Yorkers swan in and out of the cultural byways of the Big Apple, indulging in psychiatric therapy that's never quite the cure-all they crave. The characters could have become over-articulate bores, but Allen invests them with the saving grace of humanity. A wonderful film, with a George Gershwin score that adds poignancy. TH. Contains swearing. DVD

Woody Allen *Isaac Davis* • Diane Keaton *Mary Wilke* • Michael Murphy *Yale* • Mariel Hemingway *Tracy* • Meryl Streep *Jill* • Anne Byrne *Emily* • Karen Ludwig *Connie* • Michael O'Donoghue *Dennis* • Wallace Shawn *Jeremiah* ■ *Dir* Woody Allen • *Scr* Woody Allen, Marshall Brickman • *Cinematographer* Gordon Willis

Manhattan Melodrama ★★

Crime drama 1934 · US · BW · 93mins

On 22 July 1934, John Dillinger went to see *Manhattan Melodrama* at the Biograph in Chicago. He was shot dead by government men on leaving the cinema. The film he saw is a heavily moralistic drama featuring Mickey Rooney in a childhood flashback that explains why Blackie Gallagher (Clark Gable) became a racketeer and killer. While *Manhattan Melodrama* has its wisecracking, stylish moments, it's mostly cringe-inducing – though it does mark the first teaming of William Powell and Myrna Loy, who went on to make the successful *Thin Man* films. AT

Clark Gable *Blackie Gallagher* • William Powell *Jim Wade* • Myrna Loy *Eleanor* • Leo Carrillo *Father Joe* • Nat Pendleton *Spud* • George Sidney (1) *Poppa Rosen* • Mickey Rooney *Blackie as a boy* ■ *Dir* WS Van Dyke II [WS Van Dyke] • *Scr* Oliver HP Garrett, Joseph L Mankiewicz, from the story *Three Men* by Arthur Caesar

Manhattan Murder Mystery ★★★★ PG

Comedy thriller 1993 · US · Colour · 103mins

This lightweight comedy clearly bears the hallmark of being an uncontentious romp that would keep Woody Allen occupied while he awaited his day in court with ex-partner Mia Farrow. Another couple of hours pounding away at the typewriter clearly wouldn't have gone amiss, but this is a hugely enjoyable little film that slyly mocks the pretensions of Manhattan's well-heeled intelligentsia. The role originally intended for Farrow is taken by Diane Keaton, and the ease with which she and Allen combine leaves you longing for just one more reunion. DP. Contains violence, swearing. DVD

Alan Alda *Ted* • Woody Allen *Larry Lipton* • Diane Keaton *Carol Lipton* • Anjelica Huston *Marcia Fox* • Jerry Adler *Paul House* • Joy Behar *Marilyn* • Ron Rifkin *Sy* • Lynn Cohen *Lillian House* ■ *Dir* Woody Allen • *Scr* Woody Allen, Marshall Brickman

Manhunter ★★★★ 18

Thriller 1986 · US · Colour · 114mins

Whether or not, as some contend, this is a better movie than *The Silence of the Lambs*, the second and more celebrated film adaptation of novelist Thomas Harris's source material, it is undoubtedly a gripping psycho-chiller. William Petersen plays the former FBI whizz, hauled from retirement to help hunt a sophisticated serial murderer. Strong performances, especially from Brian Cox as Hannibal Lecktor, combine with a clever plot and top-notch direction by Michael Mann to produce an atmospheric and arresting thriller. PF. Contains violence and swearing. DVD

William Petersen [William L Petersen] *Will Graham* • Brian Cox *Dr Hannibal Lecktor* • Dennis Farina *Jack Crawford* • Kim Greist *Molly Graham* • Stephen Lang *Freddie Lounds* • Tom Noonan *Francis Dollarhyde* • Joan Allen *Reba* • Benjamin Hendrickson *Dr Chilton* ■ *Dir* Michael Mann • *Scr* Michael Mann, from the novel *Red Dragon* by Thomas Harris

Maniac ★★★

Psychological thriller
1962 · UK · BW · 88mins

This psychological horror film is a typical Hammer programme-filler of the 1960s. The convoluted mystery takes ages to set up, but some of the shocks (most memorably an attempted murder by blowtorch) have stood the test of time, and the twist ending is brilliant. Kerwin Mathews plays an American artist who becomes involved with a young woman (Liliane Brousse) and her stepmother (Nadia Gray) and agrees to help them spring Brousse's father (Donald Houston) from the loony bin. Not a good idea. DM

Kerwin Mathews *Geoff Farrell* • Nadia Gray *Eve Beynat* • Donald Houston *Georges Beynat* • Liliane Brousse *Annette Beynat* • George Pastell *Inspector Etienne* ■ *Dir* Michael Carreras • *Scr* Jimmy Sangster

Maniac ★★★

Crime drama 1977 · US · Colour · 84mins

A solid crime drama, in which a psychotic killer starts to bump off a small town's populace before demanding a million-dollar ransom to stop. The town's richest man isn't having any of it, though, and hires a mercenary to kill the killer. Oddball but interesting casting sees the likes of Stuart Whitman and Deborah Raffin acting opposite Oliver Reed. The film has its dull spots, but it remains watchable. DA. Contains violence.

Oliver Reed *Nick McCormick* • Deborah Raffin *Cindy Simmons* • Stuart Whitman *William Whitaker* • Jim Mitchum [James Mitchum] *Tracker* • John Ireland *Chief Haliburton* ■ *Dir* Richard Compton • *Scr* John C Broderick, Ron Silkosky

Maniac Cop ★★ 18

Action horror 1988 · US · Colour · 81mins

True to its title, this features a maniac in a policeman's uniform loose on the streets of New York City, killing any innocent people who stray into his path and giving the NYPD a bad reputation they don't deserve. (Stop laughing!) Bruce Campbell is the cop who takes the fall for the true killer and eventually hunts him down. Fairly well written (by Larry Cohen of *It's Alive* fame), but the acting can't keep up and *Evil Dead* star Campbell is given too little to do. ST [VIDEO] DVD

Tom Atkins *Lieutenant Frank McCrae* • Bruce Campbell *Jack Forrest* • Laurene Landon *Theresa Mallory* • Richard Roundtree *Commissioner Pike* • William Smith *Captain Ripley* • Robert Z'Dar *Matt Cordell* ■ *Dir* William Lustig • *Scr* Larry Cohen

Maniac Cop 2 ★★ 18

Action horror 1990 · US · Colour · 83mins

An undead ex-cop goes on another gruesome killing rampage in this sequel, this time in concert with a serial killer who targets strippers – presumably to get the maximum amount of skin on screen. Screenwriter Larry Cohen decides to clean up the killer's image this time: now we're told he was an honest cop who was willing to prosecute powerful people, as opposed to the first movie, in which he was known for violating suspects' civil rights. ST [VIDEO] DVD

Robert Davi *Detective Sean McKinney* • Claudia Christian *Susan Riley* • Michael Lerner *Edward Doyle* • Bruce Campbell *Jack Forrest* • Laurene Landon *Teresa Mallory* • Robert Z'Dar *Matt Cordell* • Clarence Williams III *Blum* ■ *Dir* William Lustig • *Scr* Larry Cohen

Manic ★★ 15

Drama 2001 · US · Colour · 96mins

First-time director Jordan Melamed tips his hat to the Dogme school of film-making with this gruelling exploration of teen psychosis. Shot on hand-held digital video, this unfolds in the adolescent wing of a psychiatric institution, where teenager Joseph Gordon-Levitt has been sent after viciously attacking a classmate. Under the watchful eye of a recovering drug addict doctor (an impressive Don Cheadle), the patients confront their personal demons during group therapy. Although the performances are accomplished, the film remains sterile and tediously banal. SF DVD

Joseph Gordon-Levitt *Lyle* • Michael Bacall *Chad* • Zooey Deschanel *Tracey* • Cody Lightning *Kenny* • Elden Henson *Michael* • Sara Rivas *Sara* • Don Cheadle *Dr David Monroe* ■ *Dir* Jordan Melamed • *Scr* Michael Bacall, Blayne Weaver

The Manitou ★★ 15

Horror 1978 · US · Colour · 98mins

Something very nasty is growing on Susan Strasberg's neck in this preposterous *Exorcist* clone. This time around, the demon is a 400-year-old Indian witch doctor seeking reincarnation in modern-day San Francisco. Tony Curtis, as a fake medium suddenly flung into the real world of the supernatural, is always worth watching, while the monster's first appearance has a certain visceral impact. The title derives from the native Indian word for a human's spirit inhabiting all things. According to this film, that includes typewriters. RS [VIDEO]

Tony Curtis *Harry Erskine* • Michael Ansara *Singing Rock* • Susan Strasberg *Karen Tandy* • Stella Stevens *Amelia Crusoe* • Jon Cedar *Dr Jack Hughes* • Ann Sothern *Mrs Karmann* ■ *Dir* William Girdler • *Scr* William Girdler, Jon Cedar, Tom Pope, from the novel by Graham Masterson

Mannequin ★★★

Drama 1937 · US · BW · 92mins

The fabulous Joan Crawford works her way out of the Lower East Side slums and into the arms of Spencer Tracy. Crawford, whose exquisite gowns come complete with influential Adrian shoulder pads, is totally miscast as the lower-class working girl. But this is an MGM star vehicle, with all that that implies: you've never seen such glossy tenements! Director Frank Borzage seems at home with this corny melodrama, which audiences loved. DP

Joan Crawford *Jessie Cassidy* • Spencer Tracy *John L Hennessey* • Alan Curtis *Eddie Miller* • Ralph Morgan *Briggs* • Mary Phillips [Mary Philips] *Beryl* • Oscar O'Shea *"Pa" Cassidy* • Elisabeth Risdon *Mrs Cassidy* • Leo Gorcey *Clifford* ■ *Dir* Frank Borzage • *Scr* Lawrence Hazard, from the story *Marry For Money* by Katherine Brush • *Costume Designer* Adrian

Mannequin ★★ PG

Comedy 1987 · US · Colour · 85mins

A bewilderingly successful comedy about sculptor Andrew McCarthy who falls for a shop window dummy (Kim Cattrall). To everybody else, however, Cattrall is just an ordinary mannequin, which makes for a rather tricky romance. It requires a light, frothy touch, but director Michael Gottlieb instead takes it as a cue for some helpless mugging and crude slapstick. McCarthy is even more plastic than Cattrall, Meshach Taylor is a gruesome caricature as his sympathetic co-worker, while James Spader simply looks embarrassed. JF [VIDEO] DVD

Andrew McCarthy *Jonathan Switcher* • Kim Cattrall *Emmy* • Estelle Getty *Claire Timkin* • James Spader *Richards* • GW Bailey *Felix* • Carole Davis *Roxie* • Stephen Vinovich [Steve Vinovich] *BJ Wert* • Meshach Taylor *Hollywood* ■ *Dir* Michael Gottlieb • *Scr* Edward Rugoff, Michael Gottlieb

Mannequin on the Move ★ PG

Comedy 1991 · US · Colour · 91mins

If ever a movie didn't need a sequel, it was *Mannequin*. In another story of a lovesick woman returning from the past as a shop dummy, statuesque beauty Kristy Swanson asks us to spot when she's acting and when she's deliberately being inanimate. It's not all her fault: the script is so full of old gags it must have been chiselled on stone tablets. DP [VIDEO]

Kristy Swanson *Jessie* • William Ragsdale *Jason Williamson/Prince William* • Meshach Taylor *Hollywood Montrose/Doorman* • Terry Kiser *Count Spretzle/Sorcerer* • Stuart Pankin *Mr James* ■ *Dir* Stewart Raffill • *Scr* Edward Rugoff, David Isaacs, Ken Levine, Betsy Israel, from characters created by Edward Rugoff, Michael Gottlieb

Manon des Sources ★★★ U

Drama 1952 · Fr · BW · 144mins

Even though Marcel Pagnol was working from his own screenplay (later expanded into a novel, *L'Eau des Collines*), this poetic, over-ambitious adaptation is never as captivating as Claude Berri's 1986 remake. Originally running nearly five hours, the action meanders as Pagnol places a lyrical emphasis on the beauty of the landscape at the expense of taut storytelling. His wife, Jacqueline, struggles to convince in the title role, as she seeks revenge on the Soubeyrans for the death of her hunchbacked father. DP. A French language film.

Jacqueline Pagnol *Manon Cadoret* • Raymond Pellegrin *Maurice, the schoolmaster* • Rellys *Ugolin* • Robert Vattier *Monsieur Belloiseau* • Henri Poupon *Le Papet, the uncle* • Henri Vilbert *The Priest* ■ *Dir/Scr* Marcel Pagnol

Manon des Sources ★★★★ PG

Period drama 1986 · Fr/It/Swi · Colour · 108mins

The conclusion to Claude Berri's adaptation of Marcel Pagnol's *L'Eau des Collines* takes place ten years after the death of Jean de Florette. Once more the photography borders on the sublime and the direction is paced to suit life under the scorching sun. The script is less convincing, however, with melodrama seeping into too many scenes and an uncomfortable number of loose ends being neatly tied up in the closing moments. Yves Montand and Daniel Auteuil maintain the quality of their performances, with the latter impressive as he tries to atone for the wrong done to Manon (Emmanuelle Béart) and her family. DP. In French with English subtitles. [VIDEO] DVD

Yves Montand *César Soubeyran, le Papet* • Daniel Auteuil *Ugolin Soubeyran* • Emmanuelle Béart *Manon Cadoret* • Elisabeth Depardieu *Aimée Cadoret* • Hippolyte Girardot *Bernard Olivier* • Margarita Lozano *Baptistine* • Gabriel Bacquier *Victor* • Ernestine Mazurowna *Young Manon* ■ *Dir* Claude Berri • *Scr* Gérard Brach, Claude Berri, from the novel *L'Eau des Collines* by Marcel Pagnol • *Cinematographer* Bruno Nuytten

Manpower ★★★

Drama 1941 · US · BW · 102mins

Two power linesmen, Edward G Robinson and George Raft, compete for the favours of seductive café hostess Marlene Dietrich, with fatal results. While not an unfamiliar tale, it's given heavyweight treatment thanks to the three-way star chemistry and tough direction by Raoul Walsh. It plays like a gangster movie, slightly marred by some misfiring attempts at comic relief. The sassy Eve Arden is featured in support. RK

Edward G Robinson *Hank McHenry* • Marlene Dietrich *Fay Duval* • George Raft *Johnny Marshall* • Alan Hale *Jumbo Wells* • Frank McHugh *Omaha* • Eve Arden *Dolly* • Barton MacLane *Smiley Quinn* • Ward Bond *Eddie Adams* ■ *Dir* Raoul Walsh • *Scr* Richard Macaulay, Jerry Wald

Man's Best Friend ★★ 15

Science-fiction thriller 1993 · US · Colour · 83mins

You'd have thought Stephen King's *Cujo* was the last word on mad dogs. Not according to this sci-fi thriller, in which reporter Ally Sheedy rescues a big pooch from a laboratory, only to discover there's a reason why scientist Lance Henriksen keeps it in a cage. It's because the initially lovable canine has been genetically mutated and is now a furry killer! Daftly enjoyable for genre fans. JB [VIDEO]

Ally Sheedy *Lori Tanner* • Lance Henriksen *Dr Jarret* • Robert Costanzo *Detective Kovacs* • Fredric Lehne *Perry* ■ *Dir/Scr* John Lafia

Man's Castle ★★★

Romantic drama 1933 · US · BW · 66mins

A marvellously romantic view of love during the Depression, fashioned by one of Hollywood's most sensitive directors, the double Academy Award-winner Frank Borzage. His acute romanticising is sometimes hard to stomach, and Spencer Tracy's aggressively macho leading character ultimately becomes grating. But Loretta Young is genuinely charming and gives a lovely, winsome performance. On the downside, the shantytown setting looks relentlessly studio-bound, and the use of miniatures still looks phoney. TS

Spencer Tracy *Bill* • Loretta Young *Trina* • Glenda Farrell *Fay Larue* • Walter Connolly *Ira* • Arthur Hohl *Bragg* • Marjorie Rambeau *Flossie* • Dickie Moore *Joie* • Harvey Clark *Café manager* ■ *Dir* Frank Borzage • *Scr* Jo Swerling, from a play by Lawrence Hazard

Man's Favorite Sport? ★★★★ U

Screwball comedy 1964 · US · Colour · 119mins

This is one of the great under-rated American comedies, with a simple plot and layer upon layer of delicious sexual innuendo. Director Howard Hawks has fashioned a film that's the true successor to his comic masterpiece *Bringing Up Baby*. Filmed in glossy Technicolor, it features Rock Hudson as a fishing expert who can't fish: work out the sexual subtext yourself. Paula Prentiss, an unfairly overlooked actress, is simply fabulous as Hudson's nemesis, and the supporting cast is genuinely funny. TS

Rock Hudson *Roger Willoughby* • Paula Prentiss *Abigail Page* • Maria Perschy *Isolde "Easy" Mueller* • Charlene Holt *Tex Connors* • John McGiver *William Cadwalader* • Roscoe Karns *Major Phipps* • Forrest Lewis *Skaggs* • Norman Alden *John Screaming Eagle* ■ *Dir* Howard Hawks • *Scr* John Fenton Murray, Steve McNeil, from the story *The Girl Who Almost Got Away* by Pat Frank

Man's Hope ★★★★

War drama 1945 · Sp/Fr · BW · 72mins

Based on his novel *L'Espoir*, the only feature directed by André Malraux began shooting in Barcelona in 1938, but was interrupted when General Franco took the city. Completed in a studio in Paris, it was not shown until after the Second World War, with different editing. Malraux, who was still at the front, was not consulted; indeed, when he saw the film for the first time, he did not recognise the cutting. Nevertheless, despite the professional actors and the studio work, this semi-documentary about a small group of Republican fighters in the Spanish Civil War attempting to blow up a bridge gives the impression that the actual war is being filmed. RB. In Spanish with English subtitles.

Andres Mejuto *Capt Munoz* • Nicolas Rodriguez *Pilot Marquez* • Jose Lado *The peasant* ■ *Dir* André Malraux • *Scr* André Malraux, from his novel *L'Espoir*

Mansfield Park ★★★★ 15

Period drama 1999 · UK/US · Colour · 107mins

Writer/director Patricia Rozema looks beyond Jane Austen's third novel for inspiration and uses the author's own letters and journals to beef up this cleverly constructed and lively update. Frances O'Connor dazzles as Fanny Price, plucked from poverty and sent to live with her wealthy relatives on the Mansfield Park estate. There she must choose between true love and social duty. Austen purists may be offended by the liberties taken, but Rozema's bracing rumination on class hypocrisy and social hierarchy is a compelling revision of traditional costume drama. AJ. Contains violence, a sex scene and nudity. [VIDEO] DVD

Frances O'Connor *Fanny Price* • Embeth Davidtz *Mary Crawford* • Jonny Lee Miller *Edmund Bertram* • Alessandro Nivola *Henry Crawford* • Harold Pinter *Sir Thomas Bertram* • Lindsay Duncan *Lady Bertram/Frances Price* • Sheila Gish *Mrs Norris* • James Purefoy *Tom Bertram* ■ *Dir* Patricia Rozema • *Scr* Patricia Rozema, from the novel by Jane Austen

M

Mansion of the Doomed ★

Horror 1975 · US · Colour · 86mins

An utterly repugnant horror film that at least has the courage of its gruesome convictions. An eminent surgeon abducts victims and removes their eyes in the hope of restoring the sight of his daughter, blinded in a car wreck. Director Michael Pataki piles on the banality and reduces Richard Basehart and Gloria Grahame to embarrassed shells of their former selves. Squeamish viewers beware! RS

Richard Basehart *Dr Leonard Chaney* • Trish Stewart *Nancy Chaney* • Gloria Grahame *Katherine* • Lance Henriksen *Dr Dan Bryan* ■ *Dir* Michael Pataki • *Scr* Frank Ray Perilli

Manslaughter ★★

Drama 1930 · US · BW · 85mins

The lives of a district attorney (Fredric March) and the rich and idle society girl (Claudette Colbert) with whom he is in love are complicated when she runs over a traffic cop and kills him, forcing March to send her to jail. Written and directed by George Abbott, this updated version of a more flamboyant silent made by Cecil B DeMille in 1922 is notable mainly for Colbert's fine dramatic performance. RK

Claudette Colbert *Lydia Thorne* • Fredric March *Dan O'Bannon* • Emma Dunn *Miss Bennett* • Natalie Moorhead *Eleanor* • Richard Tucker *Albee* • Hilda Vaughn *Evans* • G Pat Collins *Drummond* ■ *Dir* George Abbott • *Scr* George Abbott, from the story by Alice Duer Miller

The Manson Family ★★ 18

Horror based on a true story
2003 · US/UK · Colour · 91mins

Fifteen years in the making, maverick director Jim VanBebber's legendary micro-budget horror (originally titled *Charlie's Family*) is an ultra-graphic and often powerful examination of the 1969 Tate–La Bianca slayings. This manic meditation draws on court transcriptions from the murder trial and restages interviews from the 1972 documentary *Manson* to reconstruct the Manson Family's infamous attack on director Roman Polanski's house, which left his pregnant wife (the actress Sharon Tate) and four others dead. The amateur acting and deliberate evocation of the 1970s exploitation Z-movie style severely hampers the director's choppy, celluloid orgy. Be warned, many will find the gore-drenched detail of the replicated homicidal attack beyond the pale. AJ. Contains violence, sex scenes and drug abuse. DVD

Marcelo Games *Charlie* • Marc Pitman *Tex* • Leslie Orr *Patty* • Maureen Allisse *Sadie* • Amy Yates *Leslie* • Jim VanBebber *Bobbi* ■ *Dir/Scr* Jim VanBebber

Mantrap ★★★

Silent comedy drama
1926 · US · BW · 66mins

Bored to tears with her marriage to small-town businessman Ernest Torrence, sexy flapper Clara Bow falls into the arms of visiting lawyer Percy Marmont and plans to run off with him to the big city. One of Bow's more substantial vehicles, adapted for the silent screen from a novel by Sinclair Lewis and directed by her then-lover, Victor Fleming. A good example of the screen persona that made the "It Girl" box-office dynamite in the 1920s. RK

Ernest Torrence *Joe Easter* • Clara Bow *Alverna* • Percy Marmont *Ralph Prescott* • Eugene Pallette *E Wesson Woodbury* • Tom Kennedy *Curly Evans* • Josephine Crowell *Mrs McGavity* • William Orlamond *Mr McGavity* • Charles Stevens *Lawrence Jackfish* ■ *Dir* Victor Fleming • *Scr* Adelaide Heilbron, Ethel Doherty, George Marion Jr (titles), from a novel by Sinclair Lewis

Mantrap ★★

Thriller 1952 · UK · BW · 78mins

Paul Henreid, that oily smoothie from *Casablanca* and *Now, Voyager*, here washes up in the torrid, tawdry, cheapskate world of the British quota quickie. Lois Maxwell plays a wife who changes her name and begins a new life after her husband is convicted of murder. When he escapes, she goes to private detective Henreid for help. Maxwell later found fame as Miss Moneypenny in the Bond films. AT

Paul Henreid *Hugo Bishop* • Lois Maxwell *Thelma Tasman* • Kieron Moore *Mervyn Speight* • Hugh Sinclair *Maurice Jerrard* ■ *Dir* Terence Fisher • *Scr* Paul Tabori, Terence Fisher, from the novel *Queen in Danger* by Elleston Trevor

Manuela ★★

Romantic drama 1957 · UK · BW · 105mins

This unlikely shipboard romance was later gently lampooned in *Carry On Jack*. Director Guy Hamilton does a fair job of reining in Trevor Howard's natural bullishness, coming as close as anyone ever did to discovering vulnerability in his gruff make-up. Elsa Martinelli never really convinces in her boyish disguise, but it's clear to see why tipsy Captain Howard would fall for her. This frippery is beneath the cast, but it still has an easy charm. DP

Trevor Howard *James Prothero* • Elsa Martinelli *Manuela* • Leslie Weston *Bleloch* • Donald Pleasence *Evans* • Jack MacGowran *Tommy* • Warren Mitchell *Moss* • Pedro Armendáriz *Mario Constanza* ■ *Dir* Guy Hamilton • *Scr* William Woods, Guy Hamilton, Ivan Foxwell, from the novel by William Woods

The Manxman ★★ U

Silent drama 1929 · UK · BW · 79mins

Alfred Hitchcock's last silent film is a brooding melodrama concerning a love triangle that ends in tragedy. Anny Ondra is loved by two men who are best friends – fisherman Carl Brisson and lawyer Malcolm Keen. She loves Brisson but when her father forbids marriage, he leaves the island and Keen steps in. Unfamiliar territory for present-day Hitchcock fans, this is competently done and atmospheric, but too old-fashioned to be of more than limited interest. RK

Carl Brisson *Pete Quilliam* • Malcolm Keen *Philip Christian* • Anny Ondra *Kate Cregeen* ■ *Dir* Alfred Hitchcock • *Scr* Eliot Stannard, from the novel by Sir Hall Caine

Many Rivers to Cross ★★★ U

Comedy western 1955 · US · Colour · 94mins

A good-natured buckskin-clad MGM pre-western frontier comedy, sold on the back of the similarly themed *Seven Brides for Seven Brothers*. Robert Taylor and Eleanor Parker make an attractively spunky pair, but the script lets them down, being neither as hilarious nor as perceptive about the female condition as it thinks it is. Under-rated director Roy Rowland does what he can, but the constant need to roister defeats him and exhausts the audience's patience. Quite funny, though, and lovely to look at. TS

Robert Taylor (1) *Bushrod Gentry* • Eleanor Parker *Mary Stuart Cherne* • Victor McLaglen *Cadmus Cherne* • Jeff Richards *Fremont* • Russ Tamblyn *Shields* • James Arness *Esau Hamilton* • Alan Hale Jr *Luke Radford* ■ *Dir* Roy Rowland • *Scr* Harry Brown, Guy Trosper, from a story by Steve Frazee

Map of the Human Heart ★★★★ 15

Drama
1992 · UK/Aus/Can/Fr · Colour · 104mins

Spanning several decades and told as an elongated flashback to cartographer John Cusack, this is a rare blend of imagination and insight. Memorable moments abound, from a plane landing on the Arctic ice to Inuit Jason Scott Lee and mixed-race Anne Parillaud finally consummating their on-off affair atop a deflating barrage balloon. It would be too easy to say that it is only the stunning visuals that prevent this romantic triangle drama from lapsing into sentimental platitude, but it has the intelligence and humanity to make its tale seem like life, not fictional contrivance. DP

Jason Scott Lee *Avik* • Robert Joamie *Young Avik* • Anne Parillaud *Albertine* • Annie Galipeau *Young Albertine* • Patrick Bergin *Walter Russell* • Clotilde Courau *Rainee* • John Cusack *Mapmaker* • Jeanne Moreau *Sister Banville* ■ *Dir* Vincent Ward • *Scr* Louis Nowra, from a story by Vincent Ward

A Map of the World ★★★★ 15

Drama 1999 · US · Colour · 120mins

Sigourney Weaver gives what is perhaps the finest performance of her career – as a rural housewife not just on the verge of a nervous breakdown, but engulfed by it. She's the lone bright woman in a Wisconsin farming community, but her mundane life is disturbed when a neighbour's two-year-old daughter drowns while in her care and young local Marc Donato accuses her of sexual abuse. Director Scott Elliott loses his grip in the second half, but Weaver's performance transcends the flaws. TH DVD

Sigourney Weaver *Alice Goodwin* • Julianne Moore *Theresa Collins* • David Strathairn *Howard Goodwin* • Arliss Howard *Paul Reverdy* • Chloë Sevigny *Carole Mackessy* • Louise Fletcher *Nellie* • Marc Donato *Robbie* ■ *Dir* Scott Elliott • *Scr* Peter Hedges, Polly Platt, from the novel by by Jane Hamilton

Mapantsula ★★★★ 15

Crime drama 1988 · S Afr · Colour · 99mins

With its title coming from the Soweto slang for "spiv", this was one of the few South African films of the apartheid era to background the political situation and eschew fashionable caucasian liberalism. Thomas Mogotlane excels as the thief who reveals levels of determination and dignity as he endures the same sadistic brutality as the militant activists with whom he shares a cell. The township sequences teem with life, drawing additional authenticity from the fact that Mogotlane doesn't care which side of the racial divide he operates. DP. In Sotho, Zulu and Afrikaans with English subtitles.

Thomas Mogotlane *Panic* • Marcel Van Heerden *Stander* • Thembi Mtshali *Pat* • Dolly Rathebe *Ma Mobise* • Peter Sephuma *Buma* • Darlington Michaels *Dingaan* • Eugene Majola *Sam* ■ *Dir* Oliver Schmitz • *Scr* Oliver Schmitz, Thomas Mogotlane

El Mar ★★ 18

Melodrama
1999 · Fr/Sp/Ger · Colour · 107mins

Set either side of the Spanish Civil War, Augustin Villaronga's simmering study of unrequited passion and unremitting guilt sadly develops into an overheated melodrama. The inexperienced cast certainly contributes to the atmosphere of excess, as racketeering opportunist Roger Casamajor, religious zealot Bruno Bergonzini and nursing nun Antonia Torrens reunite in a TB sanitorium for the first time since they lost their childhood buddy at the height of the conflict. DP. In Spanish with English subtitles. DVD

Roger Casamajor *Andreu Ramallo* • Bruno Bergonzini *Manuel Tur* • Antonia Torrens *Francisca* • Hernan Gonzalez *Galindo* • Juli Mira *Don Eugeni Morell* • Simon Andreu *Alcantara* • Angela Molina *Carmen* ■ *Dir* Augustin Villaronga • *Scr* Antonio Aloy, Biel Mesquida, Agustin Villaronga, from the novel by Blai Bonet

Mara Maru ★★

Adventure 1952 · US · BW · 97mins

Approaching the end of his romantic swashbuckler career, but still making a handsome fist of it, Errol Flynn stars as a deep-sea diver who knows the whereabouts of a bejewelled cross, sunk on a PT boat in the China Seas during the Second World War. Flynn is hired by wealthy villain Raymond Burr to retrieve the treasure, and sets out on a voyage rife with deception and chicanery. Mildly entertaining. RK

Errol Flynn *Gregory Mason* • Ruth Roman *Stella Callahan* • Raymond Burr *Brock Benedict* • Paul Picerni *Steven Ranier* • Richard Webb *Andy Callahan* ■ *Dir* Gordon Douglas • *Scr* N Richard Nash, from a story by Philip Yordan, Sidney Harmon, Hollister Noble

Maracaibo ★

Adventure drama 1958 · US · Colour · 88mins

In this disjointed mess, Cornel Wilde struggles manfully to douse a fire in an undersea oil well in Venezuela. Then Wilde has to give his real-life wife, Jean Wallace, something to do. So a second plot is trumped up about an American woman novelist who learns about the personal tragedy of the owner of the blazing well. The two halves quickly come unglued in a welter of travelogue footage of watersports and flamenco dancing. AT

Cornel Wilde *Vic Scott* • Jean Wallace *Laura Kingsley* • Abbe Lane *Elena Holbrook* • Francis Lederer *Senor Miguel Orlando* • Michael Landon *Lago* • Joe E Ross *Milt Karger* ■ *Dir* Cornel Wilde • *Scr* Ted Sherdeman, from a novel by Stirling Silliphant

Marat/Sade ★★

Historical drama
1966 · UK · BW and Colour · 115mins

The Marquis de Sade (Patrick Magee) directs his insane asylum inmates in a morality play-within-a-play about the assassination of French Revolutionary leader Jean-Paul Marat (Ian Richardson). The bedlam governor (Clifford Rose) continually stops the performance to demand cuts in the polemic. Arty and worthy, with de Sade and Marat mainly shouting political rhetoric at each other, Peter Brook's hard-going film adaptation adds extra Brechtian close-up nuance to his controversial stage hit. AJ

Ian Richardson *Jean-Paul Marat* • Patrick Magee *Marquis de Sade* • Glenda Jackson *Charlotte Corday* • Clifford Rose *M Coulmier* • Brenda Kempner *Mme Coulmier* • Ruth Baker *Mlle Coulmier* • Michael Williams *Herald* • Freddie Jones *Cucurucu* ■ *Dir* Peter Brook • *Scr* Adrian Mitchell, from the play *The Persecution and Assassination of Jean-Paul Marat as Performed by the Inmates of the Asylum of Charenton under the Direction of the Marquis de Sade* by Peter Weiss, as translated by Geoffrey Skelton, Adrian Mitchell of the play *Die Verfolgung und Ermordung Jean Paul Marats, Dargestellt durch die Schauspielgruppe des Hospizes zu Charenton unter Anleintung des Herrn de Sade*

Marathon Man ★★★★ 18

Thriller 1976 · US · Colour · 119mins

Dustin Hoffman stars as the bewildered New York student training to run a marathon who inadvertently becomes mixed up in a hunt for a haul of Nazi diamonds in director John Schlesinger's gripping thriller. Laurence Olivier is the essence of evil as the former concentration camp sadist who leaves South America to claim his legacy – the priceless gems taken from Jewish victims during the war. Also making an impact is Roy Scheider as Hoffman's secret agent older brother.

Schlesinger's film is not without its flaws – it takes rather too long to get started and is too dislocated – but it's a very classy package. TH. Contains violence, swearing, a sex scene and nudity. [VIDEO] DVD

Dustin Hoffman *Babe Levy* • Laurence Olivier *Szell* • Roy Scheider *Doc Levy* • William Devane *Janeway* • Marthe Keller *Elsa* • Fritz Weaver *Professor Biesenthal* • Richard Bright *Karl* • Marc Lawrence (1) *Erhard* • Allen Joseph *Babe's father* ■ *Dir* John Schlesinger • *Scr* William Goldman, from his novel

The Marauders ★★

Western 1947 · US · BW · 63mins

William Boyd, who played Hopalong Cassidy throughout the 1930s and 1940s, here once again saddles up as the Wild West's B-movie good guy. In this tale, he tracks a gang of outlaws intent on plundering the oil under land occupied by a small town. Routine heroics are given a comedy twist by Boyd's sidekick, rasp-voiced Andy Clyde – a downmarket best-buddy. TH

William Boyd (1) *Hopalong Cassidy* • Andy Clyde *California Carlson* • Rand Brooks *Lucky Jenkins* • Ian Wolfe *Black* • Dorinda Clifton *Susan* • Mary Newton *Mrs Crowell* ■ *Dir* George Archainbaud • *Scr* Charles Belden, from characters created by Clarence E Mulford

The Marauders ★★

Western 1955 · US · Colour · 81mins

A western staple, this – the powerful ranchers who hire muscle to force squatters, lowlifes and emigrants off their land. At the first skirmish the squatters win, killing the rancher and his son. But then Dan Duryea, a book-keeper who fancies himself as a military strategist and calls himself "The General", gets control of the ranch and initiates all-out range war. This MGM effort never rises above its B-movie station. AT

Dan Duryea *Mr Avery* • Jeff Richards *Corey Everett* • Keenan Wynn *Hook* • Jarma Lewis *Hannah Ferber* • John Hudson (1) *Roy Rutherford* • Harry Shannon *John Rutherford* ■ *Dir* Gerald Mayer • *Scr* Jack Leonard, Earl Felton, from a novel by Alan Marcus

Marcello Mastroianni: I Remember ★★★★★

Documentary
1997 · It · Colour and BW · 198mins

Although directed by his partner, Anna Maria Tato, this is essentially a cinematic self-portrait from Marcello Mastroianni, who amassed over 170 credits in his glittering, yet ceaselessly questing career. He emerges from these glorious clips and monologues as a charming, erudite, cosmopolitan gentleman, with a love of literature, a pride in his career and a passion for life. Lamenting the artistic decline of mainstream cinema, he fondly recalls his collaborations with Vittoria De Sica, Federico Fellini and Marco Ferreri, while deriding his international reputation as a Latin lover. However, these mercurial memoirs also provide many personal insights that make them as invaluable as Mastroianni is irreplaceable. DP. In Italian with English subtitles.

Dir Anna Maria Tato

March Comes in like a Lion ★★★

Drama 1991 · Jpn · Colour · 118mins

Hitoshi Yazaki tackles the controversial subject of incest in this laconic yet tantalisingly lyrical drama. There's also a tense undercurrent to the action, as it's only a matter of time before Cho Bang-Ho recovers his memory and realises that Yoshiko Yura, who rescued him from a Tokyo hospital, isn't just his lover, but also his sister. Imbuing the lengthy, taciturn takes with simmering eroticism and a mischievous visual sense, Yazaki avoids judging his passionate protagonists, while keeping in mind the storm gathering around their dread secret. DP. A Japanese language film.

Yoshiko Yura *Ice* • Cho Bang-Ho *Haruo* ■ *Dir* Hitoshi Yazaki • *Scr* Hitoshi Yazaki, Hiroshi Miyazaki, Sachio Ono

The March Hare ★★★ U

Drama 1956 · UK · Colour · 84mins

This British Lion horse-racing romp gains from the fact that it was photographed in colour and CinemaScope by the great Jack Hildyard. It also has good-looking leads in handsome Terence Morgan and sultry Peggy Cummins who, together with a sly performance from Cyril Cusack, keep the whole thing a good deal more watchable than it deserves to be. TS

Peggy Cummins *Pat McGuire* • Terence Morgan *Sir Charles Hare* • Martita Hunt *Lady Anne* • Cyril Cusack *Lazy Mangan* • Wilfrid Hyde White *Colonel Keene* • Charles Hawtrey *Fisher* ■ *Dir* George More O'Ferrall • *Scr* Gordon Wellesley, Paul Vincent Carroll, Allan Mckinnon, from the novel *Gamblers Sometimes Win* by TH Bird

March or Die ★★ PG

Adventure 1977 · UK · Colour · 102mins

Producer Lew Grade's good intentions often led to disappointing results. So it proved in this *Beau Geste*-style tale about the French Foreign Legion. Much of the blame must lie with Terence Hill, who got by (just!) in comic westerns where his accent and lack of ability weren't too apparent. Alongside such seasoned talents as Gene Hackman and Max von Sydow, however, he is totally lost, slowing the pace down to a snail's crawl. Catherine Deneuve looks radiant, though, while John Alcott's photography is a treat. TS [VIDEO] DVD

Gene Hackman *Major William Sherman Foster* • Terence Hill *Marco Segrain* • Catherine Deneuve *Simone Picard* • Max von Sydow *François Marneau* • Ian Holm *El Krim* • Jack O'Halloran *Ivan* ■ *Dir* Dick Richards • *Scr* David Zelag Goodman, from a story by David Zelag Goodman, Dick Richards

Marci X ★★ 15

Comedy 2003 · US · Colour · 80mins

Lisa Kudrow plays a Jewish New York socialite who enters into the world of hardcore rap artist Damon Wayans to save her ailing father's company. In a role far removed from her small screen character in *Friends*, Kudrow is endearing and sassy, but, like Wayans, she's wasted in an imprudent film that tries too hard to be hip and trendy. The picture is often patronising and stereotypical; consequently, most of the laughs come from the questionable taste of Richard Benjamin's subject matter. SF. Contains swearing and drug abuse. [VIDEO] DVD

Lisa Kudrow *Marci Feld* • Damon Wayans *Dr S* • Richard Benjamin *Ben Feld* • Christine Baranski *Sen Mary Ellen Spinkle* • Paula Garcés *Yolanda Quinones* • Billy Griffith *Tubby Fenders* • Jane Krakowski *Lauren* ■ *Dir* Richard Benjamin • *Scr* Paul Rudnick

Marco ★★★

Period musical 1973 · US · Colour · 109mins

The exploits of the medieval explorer Marco Polo have proved unlucky for film-makers. This little-known musical version of Marco Polo's travels is in fact the best of the lot, with the benefit of actual Oriental locations, serviceable songs and a pleasing cast. Desi Arnaz Jr has youthful exuberance as the explorer and Zero Mostel is a scene-stealing Kublai Khan. TV

Desi Arnaz Jr *Marco Polo* • Zero Mostel *Kublai Khan* • Jack Weston *Maffio Polo* • Win Cie Cie *Aigiarm* • Aimee Eccles *Kuklatoi* • Fred Sadoff *Niccolo Polo* ■ *Dir* Seymour Robbie • *Scr* Romeo Muller • *Music* Maury Laws

Mardi Gras ★★ U

Musical 1958 · US · Colour · 107mins

It must have seemed a good idea to team pop idols Pat Boone and Tommy Sands with Gary Crosby (son of Bing) as military cadets on a spree in New Orleans. Frankly, however, 20th Century-Fox could have come up with a better plot. This one's some hokum about winning a date on a raffle, which wouldn't matter too much if the songs were any good, but they're not. This empty piece of entertainment marked the downward spiral of Boone's movie career as his amiable, ingratiating smile was becoming tiresome. TS

Pat Boone *Pat Newell* • Christine Carère *Michelle Marton* • Tommy Sands *Barry Denton* • Sheree North *Eadie West* • Gary Crosby *Tony Runkle* • Fred Clark *Hal Curtis* • Richard Sargent [Dick Sargent] *Dick Saglon* ■ *Dir* Edmund Goulding • *Scr* Winston Miller, Hal Kanter, from a story by Curtis Harrington

Mare Nostrum ★★★

Silent First World War drama 1926 · US · BW

Directed by Rex Ingram, a master at epic romances, this tragic First World War love story touched nerves as well as hearts with its story of a German spy (Alice Terry, Ingram's wife) who falls in love with a Spanish captain (Antonio Moreno). Nowadays, of course, it feels dreadfully dated, but the film still has a narrative charge. TH

Alice Terry *Freya Talberg* • Antonio Moreno *Ulysses Ferragut* • Uni Apollon *The Triton* ■ *Dir* Rex Ingram (1) • *Scr* Willis Goldbeck, from the novel by Vicente Blasco-Ibañez

Marebito ★★

Horror 2004 · Jpn · Colour · 91mins

Shot on grainy digital video in eight days, *The Grudge* director Takashi Shimizu's haphazard horror is an empty exercise in unease that never builds into anything coherently creepy. Shinya Tsukamoto plays a news cameraman obsessed with understanding the true nature of fear. He follows the ghost of a suicide into the Tokyo netherworld and returns with a vampire girl whom he is compelled to feed with the blood of murdered victims. AJ. In Japanese with English subtitles.

Shinya Tsukamoto *Masuoka* • Tomomi Miyashita • Kazuhiro Nakahara • Shun Sugata ■ *Dir* Takashi Shimizu • *Scr* Chiaka Konaka

Margaret's Museum ★★★ 15

Period drama
1995 · Can/UK · Colour · 95mins

A powerful period piece, set in a Canadian coal-mining community during the 1940s. Helena Bonham Carter is Margaret, whose father and brother have already perished down the mines, and who is determined that the new love in her life, a bagpipe-playing, Gaelic-speaking dishwasher, won't follow suit. But times are hard, jobs are scarce and history looks bound to repeat itself. Clive Russell and Kate Nelligan offer strong support, but it's Bonham Carter's film. DA. Contains sex scenes. [VIDEO]

Helena Bonham Carter *Margaret MacNeil* • Clive Russell *Neil Currie* • Craig Olejnik *Jimmy MacNeil* • Kate Nelligan *Catherine MacNeil* • Kenneth Welsh *Angus MacNeil* • Andrea Morris *Marilyn Campbell* ■ *Dir* Mort Ransen • *Scr* Mort Ransen, Gerald Wexler, from the short story *The Glace Bay Miner's Museum* by Sheldon Currie

Margie ★★★★ U

Musical comedy 1946 · US · Colour · 93mins

In the wake of MGM's *Meet Me in St Louis*, the other studios dusted off their songbooks and petticoats, and 20th Century-Fox produced this little Technicolored charmer, which set a style and standard that endured at the studio for well over a decade. Set in the 1920s, the era of the raccoon coat and the charleston, this is a captivating work, lovingly directed, and starring Jeanne Crain in the role of her career. Completely evading the schmaltz and vulgarity that hampered later entries in the same vein, this remains a model of wit, taste and good musical sense. TS

Jeanne Crain *Margie McDuff* • Glenn Langan *Professor Ralph Fontayne* • Lynn Bari *Miss Isabelle Palmer* • Alan Young *Roy Hornsdale* • Barbara Lawrence *Marybelle Tenor* • Conrad Janis *Johnny Green* • Esther Dale *Grandma McSweeney* • Hattie McDaniel *Cynthia* ■ *Dir* Henry King • *Scr* F Hugh Herbert, from a story by Ruth McKinney, Richard Bransten

Margin for Error ★★★

Black comedy 1943 · US · BW · 74mins

After an unhappy start in Hollywood as a producer turned director, Otto Preminger returned to Broadway. Among the most successful plays he directed was this black comedy by Clare Boothe about the Nazi consul in Brooklyn and the Jewish policeman ordered to protect him. Preminger played the role of the arrogant Nazi himself and repeats it on screen, typecasting himself forever in the process, while future TV comedian Milton Berle plays the cop. To improve the script Preminger hired Samuel Fuller, who worked without credit while he was on leave from the army. AT

Joan Bennett *Sophie Baumer* • Milton Berle *Moe Finkelstein* • Otto Preminger *Karl Baumer* • Carl Esmond *Baron Max von Alvenstor* • Howard Freeman *Otto Horst* • Poldy Dur *Frieda Schmidt* ■ *Dir* Otto Preminger • *Scr* Lillie Hayward, Samuel Fuller, from the play by Clare Boothe [Clare Boothe Luce]

M

Marguerite de la Nuit ★★★

Drama 1955 · Fr · Colour · 130mins

Complete with Art Deco backdrops from Max Douy and plenty of photographic tricks from Jacques Natteau, this is a stylish, if dramatically unsatisfactory updating of the Faust myth to the mid-1920s. Shifting the emphasis of Goethe's story away from the ageing doctor who signs away his soul to regain his youth, director Claude Autant-Lara concentrates instead on the relationship between the satanic Pigalle drug-dealer and Marguerite, the long-suffering object of Faust's affections. Jean-François Calvé is out of his depth, but Yves Montand and Michèle Morgan generate plenty of spark. DP. A French language film.

Michèle Morgan *Marguerite* • Yves Montand *M Léon* • Jean-François Calvé *Georges Faust* • Massimo Girotti *Valentin* • Fernand Sardou *Le patron du café* • Pierre Palau *Dr Faust* ■ *Dir* Claude Autant-Lara • *Scr* Ghislaine Autant-Lara, Gabriel Arout, from the novel *Marguerite de la Nuit* by Pierre Mac Orlan [Pierre Dumarchais], from the writings *Faust* by Johann Wolfgang von Goethe

Maria Chapdelaine ★★★

Romantic drama
1982 · Can/Fr · Colour · 108mins

Clearly intent on commenting on Quebec's nationalist aspirations throughout the 20th century, Gilles Carle gives Carole Laure's romantic quandary an allegorical edge that intensifies an already engrossing drama. Torn between timid farmer Pierre Curzi, swarthy trapper Nick Mancuso and dapper sophisticate

Donald Lautrec, Laure spiritedly personifies Québecois fervour. Pierre Mignot's images of the forbidding far north also impress. DP. In French with English subtitles.

Carole Laure *Maria Chapdelaine* • Nick Mancuso *François Paradis* • Claude Rich *Father Cordelier* • Amulette Garneau *Laura Chapdelaine* • Yoland Guérard *Samuel Chapdelaine* • Pierre Curzi *Eutrope Gagnon* • Donald Lautrec *Lorenzo Suprenant* ■ *Dir* Gilles Carle • *Scr* Gilles Carle, Guy Fournier, from the novel by Louis Hémon

Maria do Mar ★★★★

Silent drama 1930 · Por · BW · 104mins

The reputation of Manoel de Oliveira casts such a long shadow over Portuguese cinema that it's easy to forget that there were not only accomplished film-makers who predated him, but also those whose work inspired his own. Two things are significant about José Leitao de Barros's silent melodrama. Firstly, it marries the Soviet visual style with the authenticity that would characterise both the British documentary movement and Italian neorealism. But, secondly, this tale of feuding fisherfolk is impassioned to the point of provocation, with the non-professionals of Nazaré revelling in their roles, while also providing an invaluable record of everyday life. DP

Rosa Maria *Maria do Mar* • Oliveira Martins *Manuel* • Adelina Abranches *Aunt Aurélia* • Alves da Cunha *Falacha* • Perpetua dos Santos *Falacha's wife* ■ *Dir* José Leitão de Barros • *Scr* José Leitão de Barros, Norberto Lopes (titles)

Maria Full of Grace ★★★ 15

Crime drama
2003 · US/Col/Ecu · Colour · 100mins

Writer/director Joshua Marston's first feature – the story of drug mule Maria (Catalina Sandino Moreno) – is told with a forensic eye for detail and a sure sense of suspense. Frustrated by the lack of opportunities in her rural Colombian community, the pregnant 17-year-old elects to ingest a consignment of heroin for trafficker Jaime Osorio Gomez. Her journey from Bogota to New York is both riveting and revealing. The subtlety of Moreno's Oscar-nominated performance conveys the pressures that drive the dispossessed to take such potentially fatal risks. DP. In Spanish and English with subtitles. Contains swearing.

Catalina Sandino Moreno *Maria* • Yenny Paola Vega *Blanca* • Giulied Lopez *Lucy* • Jhon Alex Toro *Franklin* • Patricia Rae *Carla* • Orlando Tobon *Don Fernando* ■ *Dir/Scr* Joshua Marston

Maria Marten, or the Murder in the Red Barn ★★

Melodrama 1935 · UK · BW · 67mins

Based on a true story, this creaky melodrama tells of a rotten squire who gets a young innocent girl pregnant, then murders her. Director Milton Rosmer strives unsuccessfully for a suitably gothic air, but the cast (Eric Portman and Tod Slaughter in their movie debuts, and Sophie Stewart) has a fine time hamming things up. JF

Tod Slaughter *Squire William Corder* • Sophie Stewart *Maria Marten* • DJ Williams *Farmer Marten* • Clare Greet *Mrs Marten* • Eric Portman *Carlos* • Gerrard Tyrell *Tim* • Ann Trevor *Nan* • Antonia Brough *Maud Sennett* ■ *Dir* Milton Rosmer • *Scr* Randall Faye

El Mariachi ★★★ 15

Action adventure 1992 · US · Colour · 81mins

Carlos Gallardo, the *mariachi* of the title, is an innocent musician mistaken for a lethal killer who's gunning for Mob boss Peter Marquardt. Robert Rodriguez's debut feature is a no-budget, no-frills effort but the director carries off the action set pieces with confidence and style. *Desperado*, the Hollywood remake, may have had more money and Antonio Banderas as the hero, but this is still the more endearing film. AJ. In Spanish with English subtitles. Contains violence. DVD

Carlos Gallardo *El Mariachi* • Consuelo Gomez *Domino* • Jaime De Hoyos *Bigoton* • Peter Marquardt *Mauricio (Moco)* • Reinol Martinez *Azul* • Ramiro Gomez *Cantinero* • Jesus Lopez *Viejo clerk* ■ *Dir/Scr* Robert Rodriguez

Marianna Ucria ★★

Period drama
1997 · It/Fr/Port · Colour · 108mins

A stoic performance from Emmanuelle Laborit is the main asset of Roberto Faenza's otherwise pedestrian drama. As the deaf-mute teenager enduring the indignity of marriage to her lascivious uncle, she conveys a range of complex emotions without resorting to silent-style gesticulation. Tonino Delli Colli's lustrous photography adds to the 18th-century grandeur, but Faenza's direction is airless. DP. In Italian with English subtitles.

Emmanuelle Laborit *Marianna Ucria* • Eva Grieco *Marianna as a child* • Roberto Herlitzka *Duke Pietro* • Philippe Noiret *Duke Signoretto* • Laura Morante *Maria* • Lorenzo Crespi *Saro* • Laura Betti *Giuseppa* ■ *Dir* Roberto Faenza • *Scr* Roberto Faenza, Sandro Petraglia, from a novel by Dacia Maraini

Marianne de Ma Jeunesse ★★★

Fantasy romantic drama
1955 · Fr · BW · 105mins

This was a huge hit with adolescent French audiences in the mid-1950s, though critics were more restrained in their enthusiasm. However, Marianne Hold is delightfully coquettish as the mysterious young girl who persuades student Pierre Vaneck (who's been locked in an eerie Bavarian castle as an initiation prank by his classmates) that she is being held captive by a pitiless ogre. Equally, there's no denying the visual fascination of Julien Duvivier's fantasy, while special effects wizard Eugen Schüfftan's trickery enhances Léonce-Henry Burel's already atmospheric photography. DP. A French language film.

Marianne Hold *Marianne* • Pierre Vaneck *Vincent* • Isabella Pia *Lise* • Gil Vidal *Manfred* ■ *Dir* Julien Duvivier • *Scr* Julien Duvivier, from the novel *Douloureuse Arcadie* by P De Mendelssohn

Maria's Lovers ★★★ 15

Romantic drama
1984 · US · Colour · 104mins

Traumatised Second World War veteran John Savage cannot consummate his marriage to childhood sweetheart Nastassja Kinski, so she runs off with various men, including Keith Carradine. The plot sounds a little like Tennessee Williams, but it's actually far less melodramatic than that. Indeed, the mining community setting, the Russian émigré community and the presence of Savage makes Soviet director Andrei Konchalovsky's American debut tender, touching and well acted. AT

Nastassja Kinski *Maria Bosic* • John Savage *Ivan Bibic* • Robert Mitchum *Ivan's father* • Keith Carradine *Clarence Butts* • Anita Morris *Mrs Wynic* • Bud Cort *Harvey* • Karen Young *Rosie* • John Goodman *Frank* ■ *Dir* Andrei Konchalovsky • *Scr* Andrei Konchalovsky, Gérard Brach, Paul Zindel, Marjorie David

Marie: a True Story ★★★ 15

Biographical drama
1985 · US · Colour · 106mins

Sissy Spacek gives an impressive performance as Marie Ragghianti, a single mother with three kids who attempts to rid Tennessee's parole board of corruption. This utter paragon actually existed, and Roger Donaldson's well paced biography zings with some great performances and truthful set pieces which grip from the word go. There are a few dull patches, however, largely due to the fact that Donaldson can't bear to speak ill of the put-upon. SH DVD

Sissy Spacek *Marie Ragghianti* • Jeff Daniels *Eddie Sisk* • Keith Szarabajka *Kevin McCormack* • Don Hood *Governor Ray Blanton* • Morgan Freeman *Charles Traughber* • Lisa Banes *Toni Greer* ■ *Dir* Roger Donaldson • *Scr* John Briley, from the book by Peter Maas

Marie Antoinette ★★★★

Biographical romantic epic
1938 · US · Sepia · 160mins

This highly romanticised version of the life of France's most famous queen is, in a word, sumptuous. An Oscar-nominated Norma Shearer takes the title role, dazzlingly dressed by Adrian and lovingly photographed by William Daniels under the direction of WS Van Dyke II. Robert Morley (also Oscar-nominated) plays her husband, Tyrone Power is her self-sacrificing lover, Joseph Schildkraut makes a devious Duke of Orleans and Gladys George is the infamous Madame DuBarry. This is MGM at its most extravagant. RK

Norma Shearer *Marie Antoinette* • Tyrone Power *Count Axel de Fersen* • John Barrymore *King Louis XV* • Gladys George *Mme DuBarry* • Robert Morley *King Louis XVI* • Anita Louise *Princess DeLamballe* • Joseph Schildkraut *Duke of Orleans* • Henry Stephenson *Count Mercey* ■ *Dir* WS Van Dyke II [WS Van Dyke], Julien Duvivier • *Scr* Claudine West, Donald Ogden Stewart, Ernest Vajda, F Scott Fitzgerald, from the book by Stefan Zweig

Marie Antoinette ★★★

Biographical drama
1956 · Fr · Colour · 120mins

Tracing Marie Antoinette's life from her leave of Austria, through her affair with a dashing ambassador, to her dignified appearance before the Revolutionary Tribunal, this is a markedly less melodramatic take on the life of France's last queen than the Norma Shearer vehicle. Filmed simultaneously in French and English, Jean Delannoy's lavish biopic is strong on period detail and makes a laudable attempt to reclaim the tragic consort from the maelstrom of historical events. But, just as Michèle Morgan's regality errs towards coldness, so the screenplay tends dryly towards the academic. DP

Michèle Morgan *Marie Antoinette* • Richard Todd *Count Axel De Fresen* • Jacques Morel *Louis XVI* • Aimé Clariond *Louis XV* • Jeanne Boitel *Madame Campan* • Guy Tréjan *Lafayette* • Marina Berti *Comtesse de Polignac* • Madeleine Rousset *Madame de Tourzel* ■ *Dir* Jean Delannoy • *Scr* Jean Delannoy, Bernard Zimmer, Philippe Erlanger

Marie Galante ★★ PG

Spy adventure 1934 · US · BW · 84mins

Cinematographer John F Seitz's mastery of moody atmosphere gives this pulp novel adaptation some unmerited class. The project was intended to showcase the talents of French import Ketti Gallian, as a kidnap victim who becomes embroiled in a plot to sabotage the Panama Canal. However, she's upstaged at every turn by Spencer Tracy as the pugnacious secret agent who falls for her charms. The supporting cast is unfussily proficient, but wisecracking adventure clearly isn't director Henry King's forte. DP DVD

Spencer Tracy *Crawbett* • Ketti Gallian *Marie Galante* • Ned Sparks *Plosser* • Helen Morgan (1) *Tapia* • Sig Rumann [Sig Ruman] *Brogard* • Leslie Fenton *Tenoki* • AS Byron [Arthur Byron] *General Phillips* ■ *Dir* Henry King • *Scr* Reginald Berkeley, from a novel by Jacques Deval

Marie in the City ★★★

Drama 1987 · Can · Colour · 72mins

Pursuing a feminist agenda with some subtlety, Marquise LePage's drama drags us through Montreal's sleazy streets with abused runaway Marie (Geneviève Lenoir). Her friendship with world-weary hooker Sarah (Fredérique Collin) becomes a predictable mother-daughter set-up, but the fearsome intensity of the acting cuts through a naive situation with the serrated edge of credibility. TH. In French with English subtitles.

Geneviève Lenoir *Marie* • Fredérique Collin *Sarah* • Denis Levasseur • Robert H Boivin ■ *Dir/Scr* Marquise LePage

Marine Raiders ★★

Second World War drama
1944 · US · BW · 90mins

This Second World War adventure salutes the marines who trained and then fought for the island of Guadalcanal in the South Pacific. Filmed in pseudo-documentary style, it takes a handful of marines, led by blokeish Pat O'Brien, and plonks them down in California for basic training before showing how they fare in battle. Australia serves as a halfway house, where there's time for romance for Robert Ryan and Ruth Hussey. AT

Robert Ryan *Capt Dan Craig* • Pat O'Brien *Major Steve Lockhard* • Ruth Hussey *Ellen Foster* • Frank McHugh *Sgt Louis Leary* • Barton MacLane *Sgt Maguire* • Richard Martin (1) *Jimmy* • Edmund Glover *Miller* ■ *Dir* Harold Schuster • *Scr* Warren Duff, from a story by Warren Duff, Martin Rackin

Marius ★★★★

Drama 1931 · Fr · BW · 125mins

Hungarian-born Alexander Korda directed *Marius* in France, written and produced by Marcel Pagnol. Rich in depth of characterisation and exquisitely played, it launched the famous Marseille trilogy that continued with *Fanny* (1932), and *César* (1936). Throughout, the same actors play the principal roles: blunt but lovable café owner César (Raimu); his son Marius (Pierre Fresnay); Fanny, Marius' sweetheart (Orane Demazis); and elderly widower Panisse (Fernand Charpin). Establishing the relationships for what is to come, Marius here pursues his dream of going to sea and joins the merchant navy, unknowingly leaving Fanny pregnant with their child. RK. In French with English subtitles.

Pierre Fresnay *Marius* • Orane Demazis *Fanny* • Raimu *César* • Alida Rouffe *Honorine* • Fernand Charpin *Panisse* • Paul Dullac *Escartefigue* ■ *Dir* Alexander Korda • *Scr* Marcel Pagnol, from his play

Marius et Jeannette ★★★★ 15

Romantic comedy drama
1997 · Fr · Colour · 97mins

Set in a Marseille backwater, this kitchen sink romance resembles both Marcel Pagnol's famous *Marius* trilogy and the poetic realist films of Vigo, Renoir and René Clair. Soft-centred spitfire Ariane Ascaride is superb as the single mum struggling to provide for her kids and make sense of her relationship with taciturn nightwatchman Gérard Meylan. Touching on everything from the failure of Communism to the overlapping doctrines of Christianity and Islam, this bristling pageant is observed with a keen eye by under-rated director Robert Guédiguian. DP. In French with English subtitles. Contains swearing, sexual references and nudity.

M

Ariane Ascaride *Jeannette* • Gérard Meylan *Marius* • Pascale Roberts *Caroline* • Jacques Boudet *Justin* • Frédérique Bonnal *Monique* • Pierre Banderet *M Ebrard* ■ *Dir* Robert Guédiguian • *Scr* Robert Guédiguian, Jean-Louis Milesi

Marjorie Morningstar ★★★ U

Drama 1958 · US · Colour · 122mins

Natalie Wood stars as a New York Jewish princess with unconventional ambitions who falls for the supposed glamour of showbusiness, as represented by the producer of a summer stock theatrical company, played by Gene Kelly. Irving Rapper's film underplays the sex and Jewish angles and ends up as a rather bland "woman's picture", though Wood is very good and Kelly is fine in a non-musical role. RK [video]

Natalie Wood *Marjorie* • Gene Kelly *Noel Airman* • Claire Trevor *Rose* • Carolyn Jones *Marsha* • Ed Wynn *Uncle Samson* • Everett Sloane *Arnold* • Martin Milner *Wally* • Martin Balsam *Dr David Harris* ■ *Dir* Irving Rapper • *Scr* Everett Freeman, from the novel by Herman Wouk

The Mark ★★★

Crime drama 1961 · UK · BW · 125mins

An apparently reformed paedophile starts a relationship with a young widow who has a little daughter. Things begin to unravel, however, when the press start taking an interest in his new life. Pitched as a rather sentimentalised melodrama, this is still an unusually frank and adult treatment of a serious topic, set in Britain but performed by two major Hollywood stars: an Oscar-nominated Stuart Whitman and Rod Steiger, who plays the hero's psychiatrist. AT

Maria Schell *Mrs Ruth Leighton* • Stuart Whitman *Jim Fuller* • Rod Steiger *Dr Edmund McNally* • Brenda de Banzie *Mrs Cartwright* • Donald Houston *Austin, reporter* • Donald Wolfit *Mr Clive* ■ *Dir* Guy Green • *Scr* Sidney Buchman, Stanley Mann, from the novel by Charles Israel

The Mark of Cain ★★ PG

Period crime drama 1947 · UK · BW · 84mins

This morose melodrama never wrestles free of its penny-dreadful origins. One reason for this is the heavy-handed direction of Brian Desmond Hurst. But, primarily, there's simply no spark between the leads. Distraught that her French manners don't appeal to bluff Northern industrialist Patrick Holt, Sally Gray seeks advice from brother-in-law, Eric Portman. However, he's got plans for her himself, although they don't involve being charged with her husband's murder. DP [video]

Sally Gray *Sarah Bonheur* • Eric Portman *Richrad Howard* • Patrick Holt *John Howard* • Dermot Walsh *Jerome Thorn* • Denis O'Dea *Sir William Godfrey* • Edward Lexy *Lord Rochford* ■ *Dir* Brian Desmond Hurst • *Scr* Christianna Brand, Francis Crowdy, WP Lipscomb, from the novel *Airing in a Closed Carriage* by Joseph Shearing

Mark of the Devil ★★ 18

Horror 1970 · W Ger/UK · Colour · 87mins

The plot of this notorious "sex and sadism" shocker revolves around witchfinder Herbert Lom and assistant Udo Kier, who falls in love with a suspected witch. But it's essentially a succession of graphically violent scenes "justified" by spurious historical references. When the film was released in the US, cinema patrons were issued with sick bags and the result was a huge box office success (and a sequel in 1972). DM. German dialogue dubbed into English. [video] DVD

Herbert Lom *Count Cumberland* • Olivera Vuco *Vanessa* • Udo Kier *Christian* • Reggie Nalder *Albino* • Herbert Fux *Chief executioner* ■ *Dir* Michael Armstrong • *Scr* Sergio Casstner [Michael Armstrong], Percy Parker [Adrian Hoven]

The Mark of the Hawk ★★ U

Drama 1957 · US · Colour · 82mins

This is Sidney Poitier's most obscure film: a dramatisation of black Africa's desire for self-determination. Poitier plays the ambitious, well-educated African workers' representative facing a choice between pursuing racial equality through terrorism, as advocated by his younger brother, or via the peaceful means urged by Juano Hernandez's pastor and John McIntire's American missionary. After Southern Rhodesia banned the film's makers, location shooting was done in eastern Nigeria. Eartha Kitt, miscast as Poitier's wife, sings one wildly inappropriate song. AE

Sidney Poitier *Obam* • Juano Hernandez *Amugu* • John McIntire *Craig* • Eartha Kitt *Renee* • Helen Horton *Barbara* • Marne Maitland *Sander Lal* ■ *Dir* Michael Audley, Gilbert Gunn • *Scr* H Kenn Carmichael, from a story by Lloyd Young

Mark of the Phoenix ★ U

Thriller 1957 · UK · BW · 77mins

This dismal low-budget thriller has a corkscrew plot involving rare metals, jewel thieves, international blackmail, the Cold War and much else. Made in 1957, it was shelved for two years until a suitably worthy main feature was found to accompany it. The mediocre cast is typical of British B-movies of the period, with the sole exception of Anton Diffring. AT

Julia Arnall *Petra* • Sheldon Lawrence *Chuck Martin* • Anton Diffring *Inspector Schell* • Eric Pohlmann *Duser* • George Margo *Emilson* • Michael Peake *Koos* • Martin Miller *Brunet* ■ *Dir* Maclean Rogers • *Scr* Norman Hudis, from a story by Desmond Cory

Mark of the Vampire ★★★

Horror 1935 · US · BW · 60mins

Bela Lugosi is on chilling form in this stylish horror from Tod Browning. It's a remake of Browning's own silent classic *London after Midnight*. Lionel Barrymore is the vampire hunter, and his over-the-top performance prompted critics to acclaim the film as an astute parody. Carol Borland looks bemused as Lugosi's accomplice, which is hardly surprising since her part had been slashed after the censors detected references to incest. DP

Bela Lugosi *Count Mora* • Lionel Barrymore *Professor Zelen* • Lionel Atwill *Inspector Neumann* • Elizabeth Allan *Irena Borotyn* • Holmes Herbert *Sir Karell Borotyn* • Jean Hersholt *Baron Otto Von Zinden* • Carol Borland *Luna Mora* • Donald Meek *Dr Doskil* ■ *Dir* Tod Browning • *Scr* Guy Endore, Bernard Schubert

The Mark of Zorro ★★★

Silent swashbuckling adventure
1920 · US · BW · 89mins

Don Diego Vega is a sort of American-Mexican Scarlet Pimpernel who leads a double life as Zorro, a masked avenger and expert swordsman, waging war on tyranny. Combining adventure with a dash of romance and comedy, the film gave Douglas Fairbanks the first of the swashbuckling roles that earned him immortality. Directed by Fred Niblo, it co-stars Marguerite De La Motte as the woman who has no time for Don Diego, but is in love with Zorro. Fairbanks returned as Zorro in 1925's *Don Q, Son of Zorro*. RK

Douglas Fairbanks *Don Diego Vega/Señor Zorro* • Noah Beery *Sergeant Pedro* • Charles Hill Mailes *Don Carlos Pulido* • Claire McDowell *Don Catalina, his wife* • Marguerite De La Motte *Lolita* • Robert McKim *Captain Juan Ramon* ■ *Dir* Fred Niblo • *Scr* Eugene Miller, from the short story *The Curse of Capistrano* by Johnston McCulley

The Mark of Zorro ★★★★ U

Swashbuckling adventure
1940 · US · BW · 89mins

This wonderful, definitive adaptation of the great romantic legend stars matinée idol Tyrone Power as the swashbuckling Don Diego Vega, alias the masked avenger known as Zorro. Amazingly, Power is the equal (well, almost) of predecessor Douglas Fairbanks Sr in this lavish black-and-white 20th Century-Fox spectacular. Basil Rathbone makes a superb villain, and the swordfights are terrific. For schoolboys of all ages. TS [video] DVD

Tyrone Power *Don Diego Vega* • Linda Darnell *Lolita Quintero* • Basil Rathbone *Captain Esteban Pasquale* • Gale Sondergaard *Inez Quintero* • Eugene Pallette *Fra Felipe* • J Edward Bromberg *Don Luis Quintero* • Montagu Love *Don Alejandro Vega* • Janet Beecher *Senora Isabella Vega* ■ *Dir* Rouben Mamoulian • *Scr* John Tainton Foote, Garrett Fort, Bess Meredyth, from the novel *The Curse of Capistrano* by Johnston McCulley

Marked for Death ★★★ 18

Action thriller 1990 · US · Colour · 89mins

Steven Seagal plays a former Drug Enforcement Agency operative who gets involved in a war between local drug dealers and Jamaican Yardies when he "retires" to his home town of Chicago. Basil Wallace is wildly over the top as the bizarrely named Yardie leader Screwface, and female leads Joanna Pacula and Elizabeth Gracen are given little to do. The action sequences are superbly choreographed and it's efficiently directed by Dwight H Little. JF. Contains violence, swearing, sex scenes and drug abuse. [video] DVD

Steven Seagal *John Hatcher* • Basil Wallace *Screwface* • Keith David *Max* • Tom Wright *Charles* • Joanna Pacula *Leslie* • Elizabeth Gracen *Melissa* • Bette Ford *Kate Hatcher* • Danielle Harris *Tracey* ■ *Dir* Dwight H Little • *Scr* Michael Grias, Mark Victor

The Marked One ★

Crime drama 1963 · UK · BW · 65mins

This British B-movie, barely an hour long, casts William Lucas as a truck driver and ex-con who uses his criminal contacts to help the police locate a kidnapped child. Lucas was a familiar face in threadbare capers like this one, while his co-star Zena Marshall is best remembered for her performance as the comely Miss Taro, one of James Bond's conquests in *Dr No*. AT

William Lucas *Don Mason* • Zena Marshall *Kay Mason* • Patrick Jordan *Inspector Mayne* • Laurie Leigh *Maisie* • David Gregory *Ed Jones* ■ *Dir* Francis Searle • *Scr* Paul Erickson

Marked Woman ★★★★ PG

Crime drama 1937 · US · BW · 91mins

This terrific Warner Bros crime exposé melodrama is based on the real-life case of a group of prostitutes testifying against their gangland boss. No punches are pulled in this taut dramatisation, which stars Bette Davis as a battered victim of the hoodlum, and Humphrey Bogart on the right side of the law as a crusading attorney. Neither star had yet found their respective trademark style, but both display a compulsively watchable dynamic presence. Eduardo Ciannelli is particularly persuasive as the slimy hood, and the screenplay is surprisingly explicit. TS [video]

Bette Davis *Mary Dwight* • Humphrey Bogart *David Graham* • Jane Bryan *Betty Strauber* • Eduardo Ciannelli *Johnny Vanning* • Isabel Jewell *Emmy Lou Egan* • Allen Jenkins *Louie* • Mayo Methot *Estelle Porter* • Lola Lane *Gabby Marvin* ■ *Dir* Lloyd Bacon • *Scr* Robert Rossen, Abem Finkel, Seton I Miller

Marlene ★★★ PG

Biographical documentary
1984 · W Ger · Colour and BW · 92mins

A mesmerising documentary from distinguished actor/director Maximilian Schell about the legendary Marlene Dietrich, based on a series of tape-recorded interviews. (She wouldn't let him point the camera at her, but had no objection to the sound rolling.) Although the image is necessarily blunted, Dietrich's comments are utterly revelatory, and Schell utilises film clips and archive material to flesh out his unseen subject. The style palls after a while, but this is still essential viewing for film students and quite unmissable for fans. TS. An English and German language film. [video]

Marlene Dietrich • Maximilian Schell ■ *Dir* Maximilian Schell • *Scr* Maximilian Schell, Meir Dohnal

Marlowe ★★★

Mystery thriller 1969 · US · Colour · 95mins

Raymond Chandler always preferred Dick Powell to Humphrey Bogart as his great private eye, but had he been alive he may well have liked James Garner's quizzical, slightly bemused charm. Taking on a missing person case, chivalrous Marlowe tries to track down Sharon Farrell's brother. Bruce Lee, in his first American movie, makes a big impression as the heavy. TH. Contains drug abuse.

James Garner *Philip Marlowe* • Gayle Hunnicutt *Mavis Wald* • Carroll O'Connor *Lt Christy French* • Rita Moreno *Dolores Gonzales* • Sharon Farrell *Orfamay Quest* • William Daniels *Mr Crowell* • HM Wynant *Sonny Steelgrave* • Jackie Coogan *Grant W Hicks* • Bruce Lee *Winslow Wong* ■ *Dir* Paul Bogart • *Scr* Sterling Silliphant, from the novel *The Little Sister* by Raymond Chandler

Marnie ★★★★ 15

Psychological drama
1964 · US · Colour · 124mins

Rumours abounded that Grace Kelly would be making a comeback before this adaptation of Winston Graham's novel went into production. Her icy aloofness would have been perfect for this tale of kleptomania, frigidity, fetishism and suppressed anxiety, and Tippi Hedren was considered no substitute by contemporary critics. Hindsight has established this as one of Hitchcock's more interesting misfires. Some of the conspicuously artificial set design and back projection may not suit all tastes, but watch for Robert Burks's suave colour photography and the mental duel between a man (Sean Connery) turned on by crime and a woman who steals to forget. DP [video] DVD

"Tippi" Hedren [Tippi Hedren] *Marnie Edgar* • Sean Connery *Mark Rutland* • Diane Baker *Lil Mainwaring* • Martin Gabel *Sidney Strutt* • Louise Latham *Bernice Edgar* • Bob Sweeney *Cousin Bob* • Milton Selzer *Man at the track* • Alan Napier *Mr Rutland* • Mariette Hartley *Susan Clabon* • Bruce Dern *Sailor* • S John Launer *Sam Ward* ■ *Dir* Alfred Hitchcock • *Scr* Jay Presson Allen, from the novel by Winston Graham.

Maroc 7 ★★

Crime drama 1966 · UK · Colour · 91mins

The heavily insured, flashing pins of Cyd Charisse are on display in this lacklustre crime caper about an international jewel thief and a priceless medallion, with a support cast that includes such acting luminaries as Elsa Martinelli and Leslie Phillips. It makes you wonder why someone in the production line didn't cry out "Stop, abandon ship". SH

Gene Barry *Simon Grant* • Elsa Martinelli *Claudia* • Cyd Charisse *Louise Henderson* • Leslie Phillips *Raymond Lowe* • Denholm

Elliott *Inspector Barrada* • Alexandra Stewart *Michele Craig* ■ *Dir* Gerry O'Hara • *Scr* David Osborn, from his story

Marooned ★★★ U

Science-fiction adventure
1969 · US · Colour · 123mins

Winner of the Oscar for best special visual effects, this astute blend of science fact and fiction eerily anticipated the kind of lost-in-space crisis that would actually occur during the *Apollo 13* mission. Gene Hackman, Richard Crenna and James Franciscus successfully combine public confidence with private misgivings as the stranded crew, while Gregory Peck heads the Nasa operation with typical reserve. Director John Sturges makes the most of his space hardware but never gets the domestic drama off the ground, with Lee Grant and the other wives being reduced to mere cardboard cut-outs. DP [video] DVD

Gregory Peck *Charles Keith* • Richard Crenna *Jim Pruett* • David Janssen *Ted Dougherty* • James Franciscus *Clayton Stone* • Gene Hackman *Buzz Lloyd* • Lee Grant *Celia Pruett* • Nancy Kovack *Teresa Stone* • Mariette Hartley *Betty Lloyd* ■ *Dir* John Sturges • *Scr* Mayo Simon, from the novel by Martin Caidin • *Special Effects* Lawrence Butler, Donald C Glouner, Robie Robinson

Marquis ★★★ 18

Historical fantasy satire
1989 · Bel/Fr · Colour · 79mins

It's hard to know whether to applaud this for its sheer audacity or to decry its many misfiring ideas. Certainly, director Henri Xhonneux and his designer Roland Topor can't be accused of taking a traditional approach to the Marquis de Sade's last days in the Bastille, as scenes from his books are presented as claymation diversions, while their much-maligned author spends most of the time in earnest conversation with his penis, an extended, human-faced member named Colin. All the cast wear symbolic animal heads, while the dialogue could have come from a bawdy pantomime. DP. In French with English subtitles. [video]

François Marthouret *Marquis/Dog* • Valérie Kling *Colin/Colin's Sex* • Michel Robin *Ambert/Rat* • Isabelle Canet-Wolfe *Justine/Cow* ■ *Dir* Henri Xhonneux • *Scr* Roland Topor, Henry Xhonneux, from the novel *Justine* by the Marquis de Sade

Marquise ★★ 15

Historical romance
1997 · Fr/It/Swi/Sp · Colour · 110mins

Meticulously re-creating the 17th-century theatrical milieu, this handsome film still has all the vigour of a waxwork tableau. Véra Belmont's directorial inexperience counts against her, as the action veers between melodrama and classicism. As the dancer thrust into the rivalry between Molière (Bernard Giraudeau) and Racine (Lambert Wilson), Sophie Marceau pouts persuasively, but her rendition of *Andromaque* is anything but the work of a great tragedienne. DP. In French with English subtitles. Contains sex scenes and nudity. [video]

Sophie Marceau *Marquise* • Bernard Giraudeau *Molière* • Lambert Wilson *Jean Racine* • Patrick Timsit *Gros-René* • Thierry Lhermitte *Louis XIV* ■ *Dir* Véra Belmont • *Scr* Jean-François Josselin, Véra Belmont, Marcel Beaulieu

The Marquise of O ★★★★ PG

Period drama
1976 · W Ger/Fr · Colour · 98mins

One of Eric Rohmer's extremely rare departures from France and the present, this elegant version of Heinrich von Kleist's classic novella is set during the Franco-Prussian War. A virtuous widow is drugged, then raped by an officer in the invading Russian army. When she finds herself pregnant, she marries the man, not realising it was he who raped her. Rohmer seems perfectly at ease with the ironic nuances of the delicate story; he and his cinematographer Nestor Almendros were inspired by German Romantic painters and bathe the interiors in an unearthly light. RB. In German with English subtitles. [video] DVD

Edith Clever *Marquise* • Bruno Ganz *Count* • Peter Lühr *Marquise's father* • Edda Seippel *Marquise's mother* • Otto Sander *Marquise's brother* • Ruth Drexel *Midwife* ■ *Dir* Eric Rohmer • *Scr* Eric Rohmer, from a novella by Heinrich von Kleist

The Marriage Circle ★★★★★

Silent comedy 1924 · US · BW · 90mins

The first, and perhaps best, of the six silent films Ernst Lubitsch made at Warner Bros in his first years in Hollywood is a daring and sophisticated comedy of manners. Set in Vienna, the scenario (by Paul Bern, later married to Jean Harlow) tells of the intricate intrigues between two married couples and their suspicions of infidelity, both justified and unjustified. What distinguishes the "Lubitsch touch" is the way he works by suggestion rather than direct statement, coupled with casually significant close-ups of objects. The playing, notably by Florence Vidor (recently separated from director King Vidor), Marie Prevost and Adolphe Menjou, is particularly subtle. RB

Florence Vidor *Charlotte Braun* • Monte Blue *Dr Franz Braun* • Marie Prevost *Mizzie Stock* • Creighton Hale *Dr Gustav Mueller* • Adolphe Menjou *Prof Josef Stock* ■ *Dir* Ernst Lubitsch • *Scr* Paul Bern, from the play *Nur ein Traum, Lustspiel in 3 Akten (Only a Dream)* by Lothar Schmidt [Lothar Goldschmidt]

The Marriage Fool ★★★

Comedy drama 1998 · US · Colour · 86mins

The chemistry between Walter Matthau and Carol Burnett is irresistible in this TV movie. A recently widowed man is ready to enter into a new romantic relationship, only to have his conservative son John Stamos get in the way. Matthau's director son Charles displays a fine hand at comedy in this poignant ode to love. Also known as *Love after Death*. MC

Walter Matthau *Frank Walsh* • Carol Burnett *Florence* • John Stamos *Robert Walsh* • Teri Polo *Susan Prescot* ■ *Dir* Charles Matthau • *Scr* Richard Vetere, from the play by Richard Vetere

The Marriage-Go-Round ★★

Romantic comedy
1960 · US · Colour · 98mins

The marriage of James Mason and Susan Hayward is upset when Swedish beauty Julie Newmar comes to stay. Newmar decides that the brains of brilliant anthropology professor Mason, combined with her physical attributes, would make for the perfect child. In adapting his play for the screen, Leslie Stevens mislays the laugh quotient, resulting in a faintly embarrassing comedy that falls flat on its face. Hayward is terrific, however. RK

Susan Hayward *Content Delville* • James Mason *Paul Delville* • Julie Newmar *Katrin Sveg* • Robert Paige *Dr Ross Barnett* • June Clayworth *Flo Granger* • Joe Kirkwood Jr *Henry* • Mary Patton *Mamie* ■ *Dir* Walter Lang • *Scr* Leslie Stevens, from his play

Marriage Is a Private Affair ★★★

Romantic comedy 1944 · US · BW · 116mins

A spoilt but insecure New York beauty (Lana Turner), fearful of following in the footsteps of her shallow, much-married mother, makes a hasty wartime marriage to a stuffed-shirt air force officer (John Hodiak) and has a baby. Tempted to commit infidelity with an old flame (James Craig), she finally grows up and finds herself. Under Robert Z Leonard's direction, the inexperienced Turner does well in this intelligent drama, slightly marred by extraneous and silly excesses. RK

Lana Turner *Theo Scofield West* • James Craig *Captain Miles Lancing* • John Hodiak *Lieutenant Tom West* • Frances Gifford *Sissy Mortimer* • Hugh Marlowe *Joseph I Murdock* • Keenan Wynn *Major Bob Wilton* ■ *Dir* Robert Z Leonard • *Scr* David Hertz, Lenore Coffee, from the novel by Judith Kelly

Marriage – Italian Style ★★ 12

Comedy drama 1964 · Fr/It · Colour · 95mins

Businessman Marcello Mastroianni hires a prostitute to double as his live-in lover and his aged mother's nursemaid. Years later, she traps him into marriage by pretending she's terminally ill; in fact, she's hiding three children, one of whom may be Mastroianni's. Male chauvinist pigs may admire Mastroianni's behaviour, while feminists will revel in Loren's sly scheming. Few will laugh, though. AT. An Italian language film. [video]

Sophia Loren *Filomena Marturano* • Marcello Mastroianni *Domenico Soriano* • Aldo Puglisi *Alfredo* • Tecla Scarano *Rosalie* • Marilu Tolo *Diane* ■ *Dir* Vittorio De Sica • *Scr* Eduardo De Filippo, Renato Castellani, Tonino Guerra, Leo Benvenuti, Piero De Bernardi, from the play *Filumena Marturano* by Eduardo De Filippo

The Marriage of a Young Stockbroker ★★

Comedy drama 1971 · US · Colour · 94mins

Lawrence Turman, producer of *The Graduate*, here directs another Charles Webb novel. Richard Benjamin and Joanna Shimkus are trapped in an unhappy marriage: he just likes to eye young girls, so she moves in with her sister and plans to divorce. What follows is certainly in the satirical vein of a dozen other comedies aimed at mildly shocking the middle-aged, middle-class audience. AT

Richard Benjamin *William Alren* • Joanna Shimkus *Lisa Alren* • Elizabeth Ashley *Nan* • Adam West *Chester* • Patricia Barry *Psychiatrist* • Tiffany Bolling *Girl in the rain* ■ *Dir* Lawrence Turman • *Scr* Lorenzo Semple Jr, from the novel by Charles Webb

The Marriage of Maria Braun ★★★★ 15

Romantic drama
1978 · W Ger · Colour · 114mins

Hanna Schygulla won the best actress prize at Berlin for her work in Rainer Werner Fassbinder's most avowedly commercial film. This owes much to the glossy 1950s melodramas of Douglas Sirk and works just as well as soap opera as socio-political treatise. The choices Maria makes for survival during her husband's prolonged absences clearly reflect those made by Germany in the post-Hitler era, and Fassbinder evidently disapproves of Maria's (and the nation's) notion of paradise postponed. Accessible, yet also complex and ambiguous. DP. In German with English subtitles. [video]

Hanna Schygulla *Maria Braun* • Klaus Löwitsch *Hermann Braun* • Ivan Desny *Karl Oswald* • Gottfried John *Willi Klenze* ■ *Dir* Rainer Werner Fassbinder • *Scr* Peter Marthesheimer, Pea Fröhlich, Rainer Werner Fassbinder, from a story by Rainer Werner Fassbinder

Marriage on the Rocks ★★

Comedy 1965 · US · Colour · 109mins

An unfunny and tasteless farrago that looks like an attempt by Frank Sinatra and Dean Martin to have a holiday on location in Mexico away from fellow clan members, while dragging along an awkwardly cast Deborah Kerr. There's a moderately entertaining turn from Cesar Romero, plus a motley collection of supporting players including Sinatra's daughter Nancy. Beautifully photographed by Garbo's cameraman William H Daniels, it's not entirely without interest either, but it's surprisingly underdirected by one-time dance supremo Jack Donohue. TS

Frank Sinatra *Dan Edwards* • Deborah Kerr *Valerie Edwards* • Dean Martin *Ernie Brewer* • Cesar Romero *Miguel Santos* • Hermione Baddeley *Jeannie MacPherson* • Tony Bill *Jim Blake* • John McGiver *Shad Nathan* • Nancy Sinatra *Tracy Edwards* • Trini Lopez ■ *Dir* Jack Donohue • *Scr* Cy Howard

The Marriage Playground ★★★

Drama 1929 · US · BW · 70mins

This was the fourth of five films made in 1929 by the undeservedly neglected German director, Lothar Mendes. Elegantly adapted from an Edith Wharton novel, it also confirmed Broadway actor Fredric March as a Hollywood fixture. As the wealthy American touring Italy, he comes to the rescue of young Mary Brian, who has been left by her pleasure-loving parents (Huntley Gordon and Lilyan Tashman) to care for her siblings. Ben Kingsley starred in the 1990 remake, *The Children*. DP

Fredric March *Martin Boyne* • Mary Brian *Judith Wheater* • Lilyan Tashman *Joyce Wheater* • Huntley Gordon *Cliffe Wheater* • Kay Francis *Zinnia La Crosse* ■ *Dir* Lothar Mendes • *Scr* J Walter Ruben, Doris Anderson, from the novel *The Children* by Edith Wharton

Married to It ★★ 15

Romantic comedy drama
1991 · US · Colour · 107mins

Shot in 1991 but unreleased until 1993, this marital comedy from Arthur Hiller tries hard to raise a laugh but instead suffocates us in sugar. Harking back to the golden days of the 1960s and sexual liberation, it's about the tribulations of three married New York couples and looks like out-takes from various sitcoms glued together. The members of the cast are good, though, and they do their best with the substandard material. AT. Contains swearing. [video]

Beau Bridges *John Morden* • Stockard Channing *Iris Morden* • Robert Sean Leonard *Chuck Bishop* • Mary Stuart Masterson *Nina Bishop* • Cybill Shepherd *Claire Laurent* • Ron Silver *Leo Rothenberg* ■ *Dir* Arthur Hiller • *Scr* Janet Kovalcik

Married to the Mob ★★★★ 15

Comedy thriller 1988 · US · Colour · 99mins

Michelle Pfeiffer proves she's a deft hand at light-hearted fare in Jonathan Demme's gangster comedy thriller. She plays the widow of mobster Alec Baldwin, who decides to make a new life for herself and her child, but doesn't allow for the attentions of crime boss Dean Stockwell and the FBI's Matthew Modine. The cast is superb – especially Mercedes Ruehl in over-the-top mode as Stockwell's brassy, jealous wife – and Demme keeps both the action and the laughs perfectly tuned. JB. Contains swearing, violence and nudity. [video] DVD

Michelle Pfeiffer *Angela De Marco* • Matthew Modine *Mike Downey* • Dean Stockwell *Tony "The Tiger" Russo* • Alec Baldwin *Frank "The Cucumber" De Marco* • Mercedes Ruehl *Connie Russo* • Joan Cusack *Rose Boyle* ■ *Dir* Jonathan Demme • *Scr* Barry Strugatz, Mark R Burns

Married/Unmarried ★★ 18

Drama 2001 · UK/US/Aus · Colour · 98mins

Already an established playwright, Noli demonstrates an edgy flair for cinema in his directorial debut. His use of colour and close-up are admirable, but he fails to create the intimacy that the frank sexual actions and revelations of two bed-hopping couples require. Ben Daniels's brutal humiliation of lover Kristen McMenamy always feels self-consciously shocking, while his mistress Gina Bellman's crisis-riven marriage to Paolo Seganti seems blissfully dull by comparison. DP. Contains swearing and sex scenes. DVD

Paolo Seganti *Paul* • Ben Daniels *Danny* • Gina Bellman *Amanda* • Kristen McMenamy *Kim* • Denis Lavant *Love* • Lidija Zovkic *Tania* ■ *Dir* Noli • *Scr* Noli, from his play

The Married Woman ★★★★

Drama 1964 · Fr · BW · 98mins

Jean-Luc Godard's movie gained immediate notoriety for its sex scenes, and no less a personage than General De Gaulle objected to the morality of its heroine. Macha Méril is married to a pilot, has an affair with an actor and seems to fill her head with glamorous images from magazines. As with all Godard movies, this is like a scrapbook of bits and pieces that, glued together, reveal the impact of the consumer society. AT. In French with English subtitles.

Macha Méril *Charlotte Giraud* • Bernard Noël *Robert, the lover* • Philippe Leroy *Pierre, the husband* • Roger Leenhardt • Rita Maiden *Madame Celine* ■ *Dir/Scr* Jean-Luc Godard

Marry Me! ★★

Romantic comedy 1949 · UK · BW · 97mins

The story of four couples introduced by a matrimonial agency run by two spinster sisters, this Gainsborough Picture languishes in obscurity through its lack of major stars and poor reputation. Inevitably, it's a hit-and-miss affair with Susan Shaw and Patrick Holt faring best in the most serious relationship as an ill-matched dance hall hostess and country parson. But Guy Middleton brings a deft lighter touch as the aristocrat who fancies the schoolteacher introduced to his manservant. AE

Derek Bond *Andrew* • Susan Shaw *Pat* • Patrick Holt *Martin* • Carol Marsh *Doris* • David Tomlinson *David Haig* • Zena Marshall *Marcelle* • Guy Middleton *Sir Gordon Blake* ■ *Dir* Terence Fisher • *Scr* Denis Waldock, Lewis Gilbert

Marry Me Again ★★★

Comedy 1953 · US · BW · 73mins

Writer/director Frank Tashlin's cartooning experience intermittently livens up this tame satire in which garage hand Robert Cummings leaves blonde scatterbrain Marie Wilson at the altar to become a Korean War hero, then won't marry her because she's inherited a fortune. Tashlin, who married supporting player Mary Costa at the end of shooting, has mild fun with nutty psychiatrists, empty shoes and the vogue for 3-D movies, but it's a far cry from his best work. AE

Robert Cummings *Bill* • Marie Wilson *Doris* • Ray Walker *Mac* • Mary Costa *Joan* • Jess Barker *Jenkins* • Lloyd Corrigan *Mr Taylor* • June Vincent *Miss Craig* • Richard Gaines *Dr Pepperdine* ■ *Dir* Frank Tashlin • *Scr* Frank Tashlin, from a story by Alex Gottlieb

Marry Me! Marry Me! ★★★

Comedy drama 1968 · Fr · Colour · 89mins

Years before his tragic rural masterpieces, *Jean de Florette* and *Manon des Sources* (both 1986), writer/producer/director Claude Berri allowed himself a little levity with this inconsequential trifle about Parisienne love and marriage. Berri stars as an encyclopedia salesman wavering between two women. Airy, but nicely ventilated. TH. A French language film.

Claude Berri *Claude* • Elisabeth Wiener *Isabelle Schmoll* • Luisa Colpeyn [Louisa Colpeyn] *Madame Schmoll* • Grégoire Aslan *Monsieur Schmoll* • Régine *Marthe Schmoll* ■ *Dir/Scr* Claude Berri

The Marrying Kind ★★★★

Comedy drama 1952 · US · BW · 92mins

A post office worker (Aldo Ray) and his ex-secretary wife (Judy Holliday) are on the brink of divorce. As they tell their story to an understanding judge (one-time silent screen star Madge Kennedy), we watch their relationship in flashback, from first meeting through marriage and children. Well directed by George Cukor, this is a perfect vehicle for the quirky, brilliant Holliday. Overlaid with incisive wit and beautifully played by both stars, this combination of domestic drama and comedy is a winner. RK

Judy Holliday *Florence Keefer* • Aldo Ray *Chet Keefer* • Madge Kennedy *Judge Carroll* • Sheila Bond *Joan Shipley* • John Alexander *Howard Shipley* • Rex Williams *George Bastian* • Phyllis Povah *Mrs Derringer* • Peggy Cass *Emily Bundy* ■ *Dir* George Cukor • *Scr* Ruth Gordon, Garson Kanin

Mars Attacks! ★★★★ 12

Satirical science-fiction 1996 · US · Colour · 101mins

In Tim Burton's acutely delectable satire, when the Martian Ambassador announces that he'd like to pay a visit, the welcoming Earthlings convene in the desert only to receive the kind of zap they'd not been expecting. World domination follows, seamlessly choreographed using digital wizardry and stop-motion puppets (inspired by animation master Ray Harryhausen). Both spoof and homage, this features an amazing roster of stars, including Pierce Brosnan, hilarious as a presidential adviser, and Lisa Marie, weirdly creepy as a disguised alien temptress. AJ [video] DVD

Jack Nicholson *President James Dale/Art Land* • Glenn Close *Marsha Dale* • Annette Bening *Barbara Land* • Pierce Brosnan *Donald Kessler* • Danny DeVito *Rude gambler* • Martin Short *Jerry Ross* • Sarah Jessica Parker *Nathalie Lake* • Michael J Fox *Jason Stone* • Rod Steiger *General Decker* • Tom Jones • Lisa Marie *Martian girl* ■ *Dir* Tim Burton • *Scr* Jonathan Gems, from his story, from the illustrated card series by the Topps Company

La Marseillaise ★★★ U

Historical drama 1938 · Fr · BW · 116mins

Sponsored by the trades union movement, this is the "official" film of the French Revolution. It's not one of Renoir's greatest films: he seems torn between the need to make a big populist epic and his own instinct to produce a humane document, in which both the doomed aristocracy and the revolting peasantry are accorded a sympathetic hearing. Thus the king has toothache and worries about his wig; the approaching army has foot sores; and, when the national anthem is first heard, someone says how awful it is. AT. In French with English subtitles.

Pierre Renoir *Louis XVI* • Lise Delamare *Marie Antoinette* • Léon Larive *Picard* • William Aguet *La Rochefoucald-Liancourt* • Louis Jouvet *Roederer* ■ *Dir* Jean Renoir • *Scr* Jean Renoir, Carl Koch, N Martel Dreyfus, Mme Jean-Paul Dreyfus

The Marseille Contract ★★ 15

Thriller 1974 · UK/Fr · Colour · 87mins

Despite an endearing performance from Michael Caine as a hitman, this carefree slice of mayhem involving drug smuggling, an assassination attempt and executive double-crosses never quite gets into top gear. Only the presence of Anthony Quinn and James Mason, along with some eye-catching Paris and Marseille locations, adds any interest to the stereotypical characters and overly familiar plot. TH [video]

Michael Caine *Deray* • Anthony Quinn *Steve Ventura* • James Mason *Brizard* • Maureen Kerwin *Lucianne* • Marcel Bozzuffi *Calmet* • Catherine Rouvel *Brizard's mistress* • Maurice Ronet *Inspector Briac* • André Oumansky *Marsac* • Alexandra Stewart *Rita* ■ *Dir* Robert Parrish • *Scr* Judd Bernard, from his story *What Are Friends For?*

Marshal Law ★★ 18

Action thriller 1996 · US · Colour · 92mins

When is a disaster movie just a disaster? Jimmy Smits is a lovable construction worker who's just about to go home after overseeing the building of a posh apartment complex when an earthquake hits. If that weren't bad enough, an escaped convict and his band of punk desperadoes arrive on the scene, looking to take advantage of the chaos. Kristy Swanson co-stars, while Smits kids are tossed in for pathos. ST. Contains swearing, violence. [video]

Jimmy Smits *Jack Coleman* • Ethan Peck *Josh Coleman* • Kristy Swanson *Betty* • Camilla Belle *Boot Coleman* • Vonte Sweet *Weathers* • James LeGros *Cougar* ■ *Dir* Stephen Cornwell • *Scr* Stephen Cornwall, Nick Gregory

Martha ★★★ 15

Thriller 1973 · W Ger · Colour · 111mins

Rainer Werner Fassbinder laid waste the "woman's picture" with this highly stylised study of the dark desires that lurk behind even the most respectable façades. Sunny, naturalistic compositions take on unexpectedly sinister aspects, as Karlheinz Böhm dominates and then destroys Margit Carstensen, the 30-something virgin whose yearning for romance contributes to her own downfall. Littering the Hollywood-style melodrama with Freudian dream symbols and allusions to Germany's fascist past, Fassbinder also encourages a florid performance from Carstensen. DP. In German with English subtitles. [video]

Margit Carstensen *Martha* • Karlheinz Böhm *Helmut Salomon* • Barbara Valentin *Marianne* • Peter Chatel *Kaiser* • Gisela Fackeldey *Mother* ■ *Dir/Scr* Rainer Werner Fassbinder

Martha & Ethel ★★★★ U

Documentary 1993 · US · Colour · 80mins

There is an uncomfortable tension underlying nearly all the relationships in this riveting documentary about the impact of two nannies on the lives of their charges. Although they are both genuinely fond of their nannies, both director Jyll Johnstone and co-producer Barbara Ettinger rather resent the way in which their parents parcelled them off while they got on with their own lives. Johnstone's respect for Martha, for example, is tempered by mixed memories of the German immigrant's strict approach, while Ettinger's mother still seems to see the African-American Ethel as some sort of servant. Full of knowing asides, this is a real curio. DP

Ruth Fuglistaller *Martha's voiceover* ■ *Dir* Jyll Johnstone • *Scr* Alysha Cohen, Barbara Ettinger, Christina Houlihan, Jyll Johnstone, Frank Ortega, Sharon Woods

Martha and I ★★★★

Period drama
1990 · W Ger/It/Fr · Colour · 107mins

Set on the eve of the Second World War, this is a moving and unforced plea for tolerance. Defying conventional wisdom about class, race and physical appearance, Michel Piccoli marries the family's portly maid (Marianne Sägebrecht) and finds a contentment that young Ondrej Vetchy immediately appreciates when he is sent to stay with his uncle by his haughty parents in the hope that he will be cured of a similar obsession. DP. In German with English subtitles.

Marianne Sägebrecht *Martha* • Michel Piccoli *Dr Ernst Fuchs* • Vaclav Chalupa *Emil as a teenager* • Ondrej Vetchy *Emil as an adult* ■ *Dir/Scr* Jiri Weiss

Martha – Meet Frank, Daniel and Laurence ★★★ 15

Romantic comedy drama
1997 · UK · Colour · 83mins

Three hapless British chaps (Rufus Sewell, Joseph Fiennes and Tom Hollander) fall for gorgeous American Monica Potter when she arrives in London hoping to start a new life. There's the odd rough patch, but the witty script uses coincidence as a springboard for plot, and shows that a British movie can be both romantic and funny. Potter is an adept comedian, and, despite its dreadful title, this deserves attention. SR. Contains swearing, sexual references. [video] DVD

Monica Potter *Martha* • Rufus Sewell *Frank* • Tom Hollander *Daniel* • Joseph Fiennes *Laurence* • Ray Winstone *Pedersen* ■ *Dir* Nick Hamm • *Scr* Peter Morgan

Martians Go Home ★★ 15

Science-fiction comedy
1990 · US · Colour · 82mins

Alien invasion is played strictly for laughs in this sporadically entertaining sci-fi comedy. Randy Quaid is the musician whose sci-fi movie theme unwittingly encourages hordes of Martian wiseguys to make a complete nuisances of themselves on Earth. Quaid is as good as ever and there is solid support from the likes of Ronny Cox and Anita Morris. Although much of the humour is hit-and-miss, this is still a refreshingly bonkers take on a familiar sci-fi theme. JF [video] DVD

Randy Quaid *Mark Devereaux* • Margaret Colin *Sara Brody* • Anita Morris *Dr Jane Buchanan* • Vic Dunlop *Martian* • Barry Sobel *Martian* ■ *Dir* David Odell • *Scr* Charles S Haas, from a novel by Fredrick Brown

Martin ★★★★ 18

Horror 1978 · US · Colour and BW · 93mins

A neglected minor masterpiece from cult horror director George A Romero. Is teenager John Amplas a sexually repressed oddball with a Dracula fixation, or an octogenarian kept youthful by blood? Romero doesn't give the game away easily, instead telling his highly intelligent story with overdoses of atmosphere, gore and jet-black humour. The film also features a splendid central performance from Amplas, who stalks suburbia killing frenziedly with razor blades instead of the traditional fangs. Not everyone's cup of tea (or blood), this is well worth a look for horror addicts with a craving for the offbeat. RS [video] DVD

John Amplas *Martin* • Lincoln Maazel *Tati Cuda* • Christine Forrest *Christina* • Elayne Nadeau *Mrs Santini* • Tom Savini *Arthur* • George A Romero *Father Howard* ■ *Dir/Scr* George A Romero

M

Martin Roumagnac ★★

Crime drama 1946 · Fr · BW · 88mins

Directed by Georges Lacombe, this French drama concerns an affair between Jean Gabin, a provincial builder, and Marlene Dietrich, a sophisticated new arrival from the city for whom he is building a house. On discovering that she is a high-class whore, Gabin murders her. The potentially erotic pairing of Dietrich and Gabin promises much. Sadly, it delivers little more than a run-of-the-mill courtroom drama, with the story of the affair told in flashback. RK

Marlene Dietrich *Blanche Ferrand* • Jean Gabin *Martin Roumagnac* • Margo Lion *Martin's sister* • Marcel Herrand *Consul* • Jean d'Yd *Blanche's uncle* ■ *Dir* Georges Lacombe • *Scr* Pierre Véry, from a novel by Pierre-René Wolf

Martin Scorsese Presents the Blues: Feel like Going Home ★★★★★ U

Documentary
2003 · US · Colour and BW · 81mins

This is the first in the seven-film documentary series, and the only instalment to be directed by the man himself. Tracing the progress and evolution of the music from Mali to the Mississippi, Scorsese never loses sight of the historical legacy of slavery, poverty and repression that underpins its pain and pathos. But he also succeeds in recapturing the mood, method and message of such Delta legends as Robert Johnson and Charley Patton. Guitarist Corey Harris proves an amiable travelling companion – his conversations with the likes of Ali Farka Toure, Taj Mahal and Keb' Mo' are as captivating as the music, which retains all its affecting power. DP DVD

Dir Martin Scorsese • *Scr* Peter Guralnick

Martin Scorsese Presents the Blues: Godfathers and Sons ★★★★ 15

Documentary
2003 · US · Colour and BW · 95mins

In 1968, Muddy Waters released *Electric Mud* on the Chess label and was slammed by the critics for betraying the spirit of the Blues. Director Marc Levin attempts to reassess the reputation of this much-maligned album in this stylish, but always gutsy entry in the documentary series. Levin follows Chicago producer Marshall Chess (whose father, Leonard, co-founded the label) and rapper Chuck D as they bid to reunite Waters's band and rethink the music for a new generation. In so doing, he succeeds in establishing the links between Muddy and Howlin' Wolf and the hip-hop stars of today. DP DVD

Dir Marc Levin • *Cinematographer* Mark Benjamin

Martin Scorsese Presents the Blues: Piano Blues ★★★ 15

Documentary
2003 · US · Colour and BW · 88mins

Clint Eastwood's penchant for jazz blurs the lines in this highly personal contribution to the series. Starting off with 1930s ragtime and boogie-woogie, Eastwood detours around Art Tatum and Oscar Peterson, trades tales with Dave Brubeck before meandering back – via some Kansas City big band and pseudo-classical interludes – to West Coast Blues in the company of Ray Charles. Purists are going to protest at every turn, but newcomers will be intrigued by the intermingling of styles, and no one can object to the archive footage of such greats as Professor Longhair and Fats Domino. DP DVD

Dir Clint Eastwood

Martin Scorsese Presents the Blues: Red, White & Blues ★★★ 15

Documentary
2003 · US · Colour and BW · 92mins

British director Mike Figgis has always lavished care on his film soundtracks and this passion for music comes across in his contribution the series. Taking 1940s British jazz as his starting point, Figgis shows how this evolved into 1950s skiffle and the 1960s electric Blues perfected by the likes of The Rolling Stones, The Animals and The Spencer Davis Group. The musical highlights are provided by Van Morrison and the unlikely duo of Jeff Beck and Lulu. More reliant on talking heads than other entries, this is still fascinating. DP DVD

Dir Mike Figgis

Martin Scorsese Presents the Blues: The Road to Memphis ★★★★ PG

Documentary 2003 · US · Colour · 88mins

The sense of a parade passing along Beale Street and into history drives director Richard Pearce's melancholic entry in the series. A veteran film-maker who got his start on DA Pennebaker's Bob Dylan documentary *Don't Look Back*, Pearce is torn between celebrating Memphis's almost forgotten black musical roots and emphasising the struggle experienced by the city's remaining blues practitioners. Consequently, the reminiscences are more telling and the sound produced by the quartet of BB King, Rosco Gordon, Ike Turner and Bobby Rush is all the more poignant. As much about the artists as their music, this is a nostalgic and authentic portrait of what the Blues is all about. DP DVD

Dir Richard Pearce • *Scr* Robert Gordon

Martin Scorsese Presents the Blues: The Soul of a Man ★★★★ 12

Documentary
2003 · US/Ger · Colour and BW · mins

One of the highlights of the series, this technically audacious and musically sincere tribute to Blind Willie Johnson, Skip James and JB Lenoir from director Wim Wenders reveals the enduring legacy of three bluesmen whose songs have previously been the preserve of aficionados. The performances of Lou Reed, Bonnie Raitt and John Mayall and the Bluesbreakers are memorable in themselves. What makes this documentary so enticing, however, are the archive pastiches by cinematographer Lisa Rinzler, which not only bring these elusive figures back to life, but also re-create the Depression-era realities in which they lived and worked. DP DVD

Dir/Scr Wim Wenders • *Narrator* Laurence Fishburne

Martin Scorsese Presents The Blues: Warming by the Devil's Fire ★★ 12

Drama documentary
2003 · US · Colour and BW · 88mins

We don't learn as much as we should about such 78rpm recording stars as Ma Rainey, Rosetta Tharpe, Charley Patton and T-Bone Walker in this lacklustre episode of the series. Director Charles Burnett rather capriciously elects to explore their careers through the encyclopedic anecdotes told by a streetwise 1950s New Orleans uncle to his barely enthralled 11-year-old nephew. The fact that so much superb music is short-changed makes the selection of this contrived road movie format all the more disappointing. DP DVD

Dir/Scr Charles Burnett

The Martins ★★★ 15

Black comedy drama
2001 · UK · Colour · 83mins

Crassly sold as a knockabout comedy, this fares better if approached as a tragic drama about social exclusion. The eponymous family are Hatfield's "neighbours from hell": unemployable dad, pregnant 14-year-old daughter, et al. It is to the credit of writer/first-time-director Tony Grounds that these apparent undesirables elicit such sympathy. A nicely understated Lee Evans loves Kathy Burke and both would do anything for their family. This stretches to armed robbery, and thus we have the film's essentially comedic plot. Sad rather than hilarious, and richer for that. AC DVD

Lee Evans *Robert Martin* • Kathy Burke *Angie Martin* • Linda Bassett *Anthea* • Frank Finlay *Mr Heath* • Ray Winstone *Mr Marvel* • Lorraine Ashbourne *Lil* • Barbara Leigh-Hunt *Mrs Heath* ■ *Dir/Scr* Tony Grounds

Martin's Day ★★ 15

Drama 1984 · Can · Colour · 94mins

This Canadian drama managed to attract a notable cast (Richard Harris, Linday Wagner, James Coburn, Karen Black) but little attention. Director Alan Gibson struggles with the emotionally driven material, which revolves around an escaped convict and his adventures with his young hostage, and he doesn't manage to get even half the performance out of Justin Henry that Robert Benton did in *Kramer vs Kramer* five years earlier. NF

Richard Harris *Martin Steckert* • Lindsay Wagner *Dr Mennen* • James Coburn *Lieutenant Lardner* • Justin Henry *Martin* • Karen Black *Karen* • John Ireland *Brewer* ■ *Dir* Alan Gibson • *Scr* Allan Scott, Chris Bryant

Marty ★★★★★ U

Drama 1955 · US · BW · 88mins

Beginning life as a TV drama, Paddy Chayefsky's slice-of-life tale became part of the fabric of the 1950s, and won Oscars for best picture, Delbert Mann's direction, Chayefsky's marvellous screenplay and Ernest Borgnine's performance. Audiences used to seeing Borgnine in more menacing roles in films warmed to his sympathetic portrayal of the Bronx butcher with low self-esteem. Equally good is Betsy Blair as the vulnerable schoolteacher Marty falls in love with. This moving film was a major triumph for its uncredited co-producer Burt Lancaster, who, allegedly, made it as a tax loss. TS DVD

Ernest Borgnine *Marty* • Betsy Blair *Clara* • Esther Minciotti *Mrs Pilletti* • Joe Mantell *Angie* • Augusta Ciolli *Catherine* • Karen Steele *Virginia* • Jerry Paris *Thomas* • Frank Sutton *Ralph* ■ *Dir* Delbert Mann • *Scr* Paddy Chayefsky, from his TV play

Marvin and Tige ★

Drama 1983 · US · Colour · 104mins

John Cassavetes stars as a middle-aged dropout reduced to earning a little cash by collecting the deposits on discarded bottles. For company he ties up with 11-year-old Gibran Brown, a street urchin whom he saves from committing suicide. Working like one of the corniest, most manipulative products of the Depression era, this eminently missable tear-jerker has a banality that is hard to credit. AT

John Cassavetes *Marvin Stewart* • Billy Dee Williams *Richard Davis* • Denise Nicholas-Hill [Denise Nicholas] *Vanessa Jackson* • Gibran Brown *Tige Jackson* • Fay Hauser *Brenda Davis* ■ *Dir* Eric Weston • *Scr* Wanda Dell, Eric Weston, from a novel by Frankcina Glass

Marvin's Room ★★★★ 12

Drama 1996 · US · Colour · 94mins

Based on the play by Scott McPherson, who adapted his work for the screen before dying of an Aids-related illness, this character-driven tale benefits from restrained and impressive performances. Diane Keaton plays a carer who has been looking after her bedridden father for years, but who is forced to ask her estranged sister Meryl Streep for help after she is told she has leukaemia. To complicate family relations further, Streep arrives with her two sons, Hal Scardino and Leonardo DiCaprio. Keaton was nominated for an Oscar for her portrayal of the proud spinster battling a debilitating disease, but kudos should go to the entire cast. JB DVD

Meryl Streep *Lee* • Leonardo DiCaprio *Hank* • Diane Keaton *Bessie* • Robert De Niro *Dr Wally* • Hume Cronyn *Marvin* • Gwen Verdon *Ruth* • Hal Scardino *Charlie* • Dan Hedaya *Bob* ■ *Dir* Jerry Zaks • *Scr* Scott McPherson, from his play

Mary Higgins Clark's Let Me Call You Sweetheart ★★★ 12

Murder mystery 1997 · US · Colour · 88mins

A sinister plastic surgeon and a long-closed murder case lie at the heart of this convoluted but surprisingly effective TV thriller from the pen of Mary Higgins Clark. Attorney Meredith Baxter's pursuit of the "Sweetheart Killer" isn't without its clichés, however, as she falls headlong for her sidekick, Victor Garber, and risks her boss's political future by delving into the trial on which his reputation is based. But the doppelgänger aspect of the plot is decidedly creepy, as are Baxter's nightmares. DP DVD

Meredith Baxter *DA Kerry McGrath* • Sophie Lang *Robin McGrath* • Tony LoBianco *Dr Charles Smith* • Victor Garber *Geoff Dorso* • Nick Mancuso *Bob Kinellen* ■ *Dir* Bill Corcoran • *Scr* Christopher Lofton, from the novel by Mary Higgins Clark

Mary, Mary ★★

Comedy 1963 · US · Colour · 126mins

This rather dour comedy is based on the play by Jean Kerr (whose own life was filmed as *Please Don't Eat the Daisies*) about a divorced couple bent on destroying each other's future happiness. Brash Debbie Reynolds is miscast, and the men in her life – amiable Barry Nelson and gaunt Michael Rennie – are colourless. Director Mervyn LeRoy, meanwhile, fails to disguise the obvious theatrical origins. TS

Debbie Reynolds *Mary McKellaway* • Barry Nelson *Bob McKellaway* • Michael Rennie *Dirk Winston* • Diane McBain *Tiffany Richards* • Hiram Sherman *Oscar Nelson* ■ *Dir* Mervyn LeRoy • *Scr* Richard Breen [Richard L Breen], from the play *Mary, Mary* by Jean Kerr

Mary of Scotland ★★★ U

Historical drama 1936 · US · BW · 122mins

Despite sterling work by Katharine Hepburn in the title role, and moody, shadowy photography by the great Joseph H August, director John Ford fails to make this screen version of the Maxwell Anderson play very cinematic. Fredric March (as the Earl of Bothwell) and Mrs Fredric March, Florence Eldridge (as Queen Elizabeth I), are too contemporary and therefore feel miscast, though John Carradine and

M

Donald Crisp – the only member of the cast with a genuine Scottish accent – seem quite at home at court. TS

Katharine Hepburn *Mary Stuart* • Fredric March *Bothwell* • Florence Eldridge *Elizabeth Tudor* • Douglas Walton *Darnley* • John Carradine *Rizzio* • Robert Barrat *Morton* • Gavin Muir *Leicester* • Donald Crisp *Huntley* ■ *Dir* John Ford • *Scr* Dudley Nichols, from the play by Maxwell Anderson

Mary Poppins ★★★★★ U

Classic musical fantasy
1964 · US · Colour · 133mins

Easily the best of Disney's experiments in combining animation and live action, this is one of the studio's best-loved films. The last feature compiled by Walt Disney before his death, it was nominated for 13 Oscars and scooped five, including best actress for Julie Andrews on her screen debut. She is splendid as the prim nanny who transforms the lives of her young charges through their visits to her charming fantasy world. Quite why Dick Van Dyke was not even nominated for his performance as Bert the chimney sweep remains a mystery, as his energy is one of the picture's main assets (though his cockney accent does leave something to be desired). Packed with unforgettable sequences, adorable cartoon characters and timeless songs, it's simply supercalifragilisticexpialidocious. DP DVD

Julie Andrews *Mary Poppins* • Dick Van Dyke *Bert/Mr Dawes Sr* • David Tomlinson *Mr Banks* • Glynis Johns *Mrs Banks* • Hermione Baddeley *Ellen* • Karen Dotrice *Jane Banks* • Matthew Garber *Michael Banks* • Reta Shaw *Mrs Brill* • Elsa Lanchester *Katie Nanna* • Arthur Treacher *Constable Jones* • Reginald Owen *Admiral Boom* • Ed Wynn *Uncle Albert* • Jane Darwell *Bird woman* ■ *Dir* Robert Stevenson • *Scr* Bill Walsh, Don DaGradi, from the *Mary Poppins*,books by PL Travers • *Costume Designer* Tony Walton • *Music/lyrics* Richard M Sherman, Robert B Sherman

Mary, Queen of Scots ★★★★

Historical drama
1971 · UK · Colour · 126mins

Here the great Tudor power play is laid out like a richly embroidered carpet with, in the blue corner, Glenda Jackson as Elizabeth I and, in the red corner, Vanessa Redgrave as her deeply principled cousin Mary Stuart. In short, two of Britain's finest actresses shine in tailor-made roles. There are a few liberties taken with historical fact, but who cares? This is a splendid costume drama with the stars ably assisted by the likes of Ian Holm, Nigel Davenport and Trevor Howard. Wonderful stuff. SH

Vanessa Redgrave *Mary, Queen of Scots* • Glenda Jackson *Queen Elizabeth I* • Patrick McGoohan *James Stuart* • Timothy Dalton *Henry, Lord Darnley* • Nigel Davenport *Lord Bothwell* • Trevor Howard *William Cecil* • Ian Holm *David Riccio* • Daniel Massey *Robert Dudley, Earl of Leicester* ■ *Dir* Charles Jarrott • *Scr* John Hale

Mary Reilly ★★★ 15

Psychological horror
1995 · US · Colour · 103mins

This is a clever twist on *Dr Jekyll and Mr Hyde*, as seen through the eyes of his housemaid, played by a totally miscast but oddly touching Julia Roberts. As the famous split personality, John Malkovich gives a typically complex and powerful performance. Director Stephen Frears's lavish, black-bricked and gaslit production is satisfying both as a meditation on a literary classic and as an old-fashioned Victorian horror story. But this was a jinxed production, virtually disowned by the studio that financed it. AT DVD

Julia Roberts *Mary Reilly* • John Malkovich *Dr Jekyll/Mr Hyde* • George Cole *Mr Poole* • Michael Gambon *Mary's father* • Kathy Staff *Mrs Kent* • Glenn Close *Mrs Farraday* • Michael Sheen *Bradshaw* • Bronagh Gallagher *Annie* ■ *Dir* Stephen Frears • *Scr* Christopher Hampton, from the novel by Valerie Martin, from the story *The Strange Case of Dr Jekyll and Mr Hyde* by Robert Louis Stevenson

Mary Shelley's Frankenstein ★★ 15

Horror 1994 · US · Colour · 118mins

Kenneth Branagh's version of the much-filmed story is as pompous as it is perverse in the way it wastes not only his own talents (as Victor Frankenstein), but also those of Robert De Niro (who boasts a few moving moments as the man-made monster) and Helena Bonham Carter. The creation of the creature is undoubtedly spectacular, but the rest of the movie is not a fraction as frightening or funny as the 1931 classic with Boris Karloff. In attempting to keep faith with the original novel, Branagh concentrates too much on design and content, and loses the heart and soul of the story in the process. TH. Contains violence, sex scenes and nudity. DVD

Robert De Niro *Creature/Sharp-featured man* • Kenneth Branagh *Victor Frankenstein* • Tom Hulce *Henry* • Helena Bonham Carter *Elizabeth* • Aidan Quinn *Captain Walton* • Ian Holm *Victor's father* • Richard Briers *Grandfather* • John Cleese *Prof Waldman* • Robert Hardy *Prof Krempe* ■ *Dir* Kenneth Branagh • *Scr* Steph Lady, Frank Darabont, from the novel by Mary Shelley

Maryland ★★★ U

Drama 1940 · US · Colour · 91mins

One of a seemingly unending series of 20th Century-Fox horse-racing sagas, superbly photographed in breathtaking Technicolor. Veteran director Henry King extracts the maximum drama from an awkward plot about a mother who won't let her son ride because that's how his father died. As vapid John Payne plays the son, however, who really cares? Fay Bainter and Walter Brennan, Oscar winners both, ride out the grimmer moments and prove to be more than a match for the scenery. TS

Walter Brennan *William Stewart* • Fay Bainter *Charlotte Danfield* • Brenda Joyce *Linda* • John Payne *Lee Danfield* • Charles Ruggles *Dick Piper* • Hattie McDaniel *Hattie* • Marjorie Weaver *Georgie Tomlin* • Sidney Blackmer *Spencer Danfield* ■ *Dir* Henry King • *Scr* Ethel Hill, Jack Andrews • *Cinematographer* George Barnes, Ray Rennahan

Masala ★★★ 18

Comedy drama 1991 · Can · Colour · 105mins

Srinivas Krishna makes an impressive debut with this deceptively serious study of the problems facing Asians settling in the New World. Besides the black comedy and the pastiches of Bollywood's trademark musical sequences, what gives the film its appeal is the superb characterisation, whether it's Krishna himself as the outsider who scandalises his adoptive family with his attitude to sex and drugs; Zohra Segal, who uses her VCR to communicate with the gods; or Saeed Jaffrey as both Krishna's grasping uncle and the impoverished father of the girl he loves. Quirky, inventive and socially astute. DP

Saeed Jaffrey *Lallu Bhai Solanki/Mr Tikkoo/Lord Krishna* • Zohra Segal *Grandma Tikkoo* • Srinivas Krishna *Krishna* • Sakina Jaffrey *Rita Tikkoo* ■ *Dir/Scr* Srinivas Krishna

Mascara ★★ 18

Psychological thriller
1987 · Bel/Neth/Fr/US · Colour · 94mins

An unabashed exploitation movie, with oodles of sex and swearing, about a kinky relationship between a brother and his sister. Charlotte Rampling and Michael Sarrazin star in a film that one suspects doesn't exactly hold pride of place on their respective CVs. Lurid and rather nasty. DA

Charlotte Rampling *Gaby Hart* • Michael Sarrazin *Bert Sanders* • Derek De Lint *Chris Brine* • Jappe Claes *Colonel March* • Herbert Flack *David Hyde* ■ • *Scr* Hugo Claus, Pierre Drouot, Patrick Conrad, from an idea by Patrick Conrad

La Maschera ★★

Period romance 1988 · It · Colour · 90mins

With landscapes as picturesque as a Claude Lorrain painting, Fiorella Infascelli's feature debut is a visual delight. Striking masks and costumes add to the lustre of this 18th-century romance between a dissolute Italian aristocrat and a fiery actress. What undermines the production is that too little takes place beneath the surface, with Michael Maloney and Helena Bonham Carter unable to overcome the two-dimensionality of their characters. DP. In Italian with English subtitles.

Helena Bonham Carter *Iris* • Michael Maloney *Leonardo* • Roberto Herlitzka *Elia* • Alberto Cracco *Viola* • Valentina Lainati *Maria* ■ *Dir* Fiorella Infascelli • *Scr* Fiorella Infascelli, Adriano Apra

Masculine Feminine ★★★ 15

Romantic comedy drama
1966 · Fr/Swe · Colour · 100mins

Jean-Pierre Léaud is best known for playing Antoine Doinel, the shambolic but incurable romantic in a series of Truffaut films. In this, his first of many films for Jean-Luc Godard, Léaud plays a more politicised Doinel: demobbed from the army, dallying with several girls and dabbling with radical politics. Fans at the time hailed this as a vital Godard masterpiece about 1960s youth; others saw it as a self-indulgent mess. AT. In French with English subtitles. DVD

Jean-Pierre Léaud *Paul* • Chantal Goya *Madeleine* • Marlène Jobert *Elisabeth* • Michel Debord *Robert* • Catherine-Isabelle Duport [Catherine Duport] *Catherine* • Brigitte Bardot ■ *Dir* Jean-Luc Godard • *Scr* Jean-Luc Godard, from the short stories *La Femme de Paul* and *Le Signe* by Guy de Maupassant

The Masculine Mystique ★★★

Documentary drama
1984 · Can · Colour · 87mins

This intriguing example of docudrama, by Canadian film-makers John N Smith and Giles Walker, has a style and structure that has rarely been pursued since. Four men discuss the impact of women's lib on their attitudes, re-enacting situations to echo those reactions. These days TV does this sort of thing better, and it's easy to dismiss it all as glib. But the intention is sincere, the technique is skilful, and the witty quartet manage to save the picture from pretentiousness. TH

Stefan Wodoslawsky *Blue* • Char Davies *Amurie* • Sam Grana *Alex* • Eleanor MacKinnon *Shelley* • Mort Ransen *Mort* • Annebet Zwartsenberg *Bet* • Ashley Murray *Ashley* ■ *Dir* John N Smith, Giles Walker • *Scr* John N Smith, Giles Walker, David Wilson

MASH ★★★★★ 15

Wartime black comedy
1969 · US · Colour · 110mins

The quality of Robert Altman's acerbic study of life in a Korean War field hospital has been too often overlooked because of the popularity of the TV series it spawned. It takes a while to get used to Donald Sutherland in the role of Hawkeye that Alan Alda later made his own; similarly, you keep expecting Loretta Swit and not Sally Kellerman to appear whenever "Hot Lips" is mentioned. But the glorious wit of Ring Lardner Jr's Oscar-winning script soon has you under its spell. Altman and Kellerman were both rewarded with Oscar nominations, only to lose out to Franklin J Schaffner and Helen Hayes, while the film lost to *Patton*. DP. Contains swearing and brief nudity. DVD

Donald Sutherland *Hawkeye Pierce* • Elliott Gould *Trapper John McIntyre* • Tom Skerritt *Duke Forrest* • Sally Kellerman *Major "Hot Lips" Houlihan* • Robert Duvall *Major Frank Burns* • Jo Ann Pflug *Lieutenant Dish* • René Auberjonois *Dago Red* • Roger Bowen *Colonel Henry Blake* • Gary Burghoff *Radar O'Reilly* ■ *Dir* Robert Altman • *Scr* Ring Lardner Jr, from the novel by Richard Hooker

The Mask ★

Horror 1961 · Can · BW and Colour · 79mins

Donning a cursed sacrificial mask causes the wearer to commit atrocities under the spell of hallucinatory visions. Audiences at the time donned 3-D glasses so they could witness colour segments of hooded satanists, a ghoul rowing a coffin through a sea of mist and mouldering corpses jumping into view in "thrilling depth dimension". Without that extra incentive, this cult revival flick is a weakly-acted bore. AJ

Paul Stevens *Dr Allan Barnes* • Claudette Nevins *Pamela Albright* • Bill Walker *Lt Martin* • Anne Collings *Jill Goodrich* • Martin Lavut *Michael Randin* ■ *Dir* Julian Roffman, Slavko Vorkapich • *Scr* Frank Taubes, Sandy Haber, Slavko Vorkapich

Mask ★★★★ 15

Biographical drama
1985 · US · Colour · 114mins

This film features what is perhaps Cher's finest role as the mother of Eric Stoltz, a teenager trying to cope with disfigurement caused by a rare bone disease and the prospect of imminent death. Peter Bogdanovich's direction shrewdly reveals the strengths and weaknesses of both mother and son as she tries to give him the confidence he lacks and encourage him to follow her example and live life to the full. The end result is a moving and life-affirming experience. TH DVD

Cher *Rusty Dennis* • Eric Stoltz *Rocky Dennis* • Sam Elliott *Gar* • Estelle Getty *Evelyn* • Richard Dysart *Abe* • Laura Dern *Diana* • Micole Mercurio *Babe* • Harry Carey Jr *Red* • Dennis Burkley *Dozer* ■ *Dir* Peter Bogdanovich • *Scr* Anna Hamilton Phelan

The Mask ★★★★★ PG

Fantasy comedy 1994 · US · Colour · 97mins

Jim Carrey consolidated his "Ace Ventura" position as America's most successful comedian with this stunning tribute to the zany style of Tex Avery and other Warner Bros animators from the golden age of cartoons. Amazing computer-generated special effects drive this slick showcase for Carrey's explosively unpredictable talents, as he plays a mild-mannered banker who turns into a wild and crazy superhero when he finds a magical ancient mask. Highlights include the Bugs Bunny-style *Cuban Pete* routine, Carrey's pet dog donning the mask and gorgeous Cameron Diaz as the star's love interest. But mainly it's an excuse for Carrey to move with whirlwind speed, pop his eyeballs and swap parts of his anatomy for the cartoon equivalents in hysterically funny and tremendously imaginative ways. AJ DVD

Jim Carrey *Stanley Ipkiss/The Mask* • Cameron Diaz *Tina Carlyle* • Peter Riegert *Lieutenant Mitch Kellaway* • Peter Greene *Dorian* • Amy Yasbeck *Peggy Brandt* • Richard Jeni *Charlie Schumaker* • Orestes Matacena *Niko* • Timothy Bagley *Irv* ■ *Dir* Charles Russell [Chuck Russell] • *Scr* Mike Werb, from a story by Michael Fallon, Mark Verheiden

The Mask of Dimitrios
★★★★

Spy drama 1944 · US · BW · 95mins

Peter Lorre and Sidney Greenstreet, those beloved character actors best known for *Casablanca* and *The Maltese Falcon*, co-star in this marvellous *film noir*. Terrifically directed by *Johnny Belinda's* Jean Negulesco, it's a scorching adaptation of Eric Ambler's novel that provides a fine example of Warner Bros literacy at work. Dimitrios himself is played by Zachary Scott in his screen debut – his acting ability would later earn him the nickname "The Eyebrow". TS

Sydney Greenstreet *Mr Peters* • Zachary Scott *Dimitrios* • Faye Emerson *Irana Preveza* • Peter Lorre *Cornelius Latimer Leyden* • George Tobias *Fedor Muishkin* ■ *Dir* Jean Negulesco • *Scr* Frank Gruber, from the novel *A Coffin for Dimitrios* by Eric Ambler

Mask of Dust
★ U

Sports drama 1954 · UK · BW · 74mins

In this cheap action drama from Hammer's pre-horror days, its American partner imposed a Hollywood scriptwriter and sent over not one, but two minor US stars. British racing drivers such as Stirling Moss appear as themselves and double for lead Richard Conte and other players in this cliché-ridden tale. The intercut footage of real races shows up the artificiality of the studio work. AE DVD

Richard Conte *Peter Wells* • Mari Aldon *Pat Wells* • George Coulouris *Dallapiccola* • Peter Illing *Bellario* • Alec Mango *Guido Rizetti* • Meredith Edwards *Lawrence* • Jimmy Copeland [James Copeland] *Johnny* • Jeremy Hawk *Martin* ■ *Dir* Terence Fisher • *Scr* Richard Landau, Paul Tabori, from the novel *The Last Race* by Jon Manchip White

The Mask of Fu Manchu
★★★

Horror adventure 1932 · US · BW · 72mins

Boris Karloff only played Sax Rohmer's ruthless Asian madman once, but the result is a wonderfully outrageous exercise in campy exotica. Forget the story – something about stealing Genghis Khan's ceremonial mask and sword to take over the world. Just marvel at the fabulous sets and costumes artfully and stylishly employed to disguise the thin content. A death ray, crocodile pits, dungeons and assorted torture devices provide this classic "Yellow Peril" adventure with enough colourful incident to pack an entire 1930s serial. AJ

Boris Karloff *Dr Fu Manchu* • Lewis Stone *Nayland Smith* • Karen Morley *Sheila Barton* • Charles Starrett *Terence Granville* • Myrna Loy *Fah Lo See* • Jean Hersholt *Professor Von Berg* • Lawrence Grant *Sir Lionel Barton* ■ *Dir* King Vidor, Charles Brabin • *Scr* Irene Kuhn, Edgar Allen Woolf, John Willard, from the novel by Sax Rohmer

The Mask of Satan
★★★★ 15

Horror 1960 · It · BW · 83mins

For his directing debut, Italian cinematographer Mario Bava cast British starlet Barbara Steele as the soul-snatching witch Asa and shot the whole grisly tale of vengeance from beyond the grave in stunning black and white. He created an instant horror classic that established his cutting-edge reputation, confirmed over the next two decades. A masterpiece of the macabre, it had censors worldwide up in arms over its still powerful opening torture sequence, in which a mask of nails is hammered onto Steele's screaming face. Steele launched an entire career playing vamps, vampires and victims on the strength of her impact in this atmospheric stunner. AJ. Italian dialogue dubbed in English. DVD

Barbara Steele *Katia/Asa* • John Richardson *Dr Andrej Gorobek* • Ivo Garrani *Prince Vajda* • Andrea Checchi *Dr Kruvajan* • Arturo Dominici *Javutich* • Clara Bindi *Innkeeper* • Enrico Olivieri *Constantine* • Mario Passante *Nikita* ■ *Dir* Mario Bava • *Scr* Mario Bava, Marcello Coscia, Ennio De Concini, Mario Serandrei, from the story *The Vij* by Nikolay Vasilyevich Gogol [Nikolai Gogol]

The Mask of Zorro
★★★★ PG

Swashbuckling action adventure
1998 · US · Colour · 131mins

Zorro may wear a mask, but there's no disguising the fact that this is a splendid swashbuckler. Anthony Hopkins plays the original righter of wrongs who hands over his rapier, and his mission, to a younger man, Antonio Banderas, while Catherine Zeta-Jones, as the fiery heroine, proves she a match for the men in the action sequences. Director Martin Campbell makes the most of the dramatic swordplay and paces the film perfectly to its explosive conclusion. TH. Contains violence. DVD

Antonio Banderas *Alejandro Murrieta/Zorro* • Anthony Hopkins *Zorro/Don Diego de la Vega* • Stuart Wilson (1) *Don Rafael Montero* • Catherine Zeta-Jones *Elena* • Matt Letscher *Captain Harrison Love* • Maury Chaykin *Prison warden* • LQ Jones *Three-Fingered Jack* ■ *Dir* Martin Campbell • *Scr* John Eskow, Ted Elliott, Terry Rossio, from a story by Randall Johnson, from characters created by Johnston McCulley

Masked and Anonymous
★ 12

Drama 2003 · US/UK · Colour · 101mins

Written by Bob Dylan with director Larry Charles under pseudonyms (hence the title), this a vacuous, self-indulgent mess, set in a futuristic, post-revolutionary America. John Goodman and Jessica Lange play dodgy promoters who spring Dylan's aging rocker from prison to give a charity benefit concert. What follows is the most pretentious ego trip, in which a host of cameoing stars spout his hideously pompous dialogue, while wandering apathetically through the unstructured scenes. A criminal waste of a fantastic cast. SF DVD

Jeff Bridges *Tom Friend* • Penélope Cruz *Pagan Lace* • Bob Dylan *Jack Fate* • John Goodman *Uncle Sweetheart* • Jessica Lange *Nina Veronica* • Luke Wilson *Bobby Cupid* ■ *Dir* Larry Charles • *Scr* Sergei Petrov [Bob Dylan], Rene Fontaine [Larry Charles]

Maslin Beach
★★

Romantic comedy
1997 · Aus · Colour · 80mins

Set on the eponymous Fleurieu Peninsula nudist paradise south of Adelaide, this episodic comedy is never going to shock or titillate, despite the naturist setting. But it's not likely to provide much entertainment, either. Michael Allen Khan and Eliza Lovell play a couple who arrive for a day at the beach with different ideas about their relationship. Pure tosh. DP. Contains swearing, sex scenes and nudity.

Michael Allen Khan [Michael Allen (2)] *Simon* • Bonnie-Jaye Lawrence *Gail* • Eliza Lovell *Marcie* • Gary Waddell *Ben* ■ *Dir/Scr* Wayne Groom

Le Masque de Fer
★★★

Historical swashbuckling adventure
1962 · Fr/It · Colour · 127mins

In his efforts to install Louis XIV's identical brother on the throne, D'Artagnan proves invincible with a sword but perilously susceptible to feminine wiles in this rousing adventure. The period trappings and historical characters are just an exotic backdrop against which Jean Marais can demonstrate his dashing athleticism and irresistibility to Claudine Auger and Sylva Koscina. DP. A French language film.

Jean Marais *D'Artagnan* • Jean-François Poron *Louis XIV/Henri* • Germaine Montero *Anne d'Autriche* • Claudine Auger *Isabelle de Saint-Mars* • Jean Rochefort *Lastreaumont* • Jean Davy *Marchal de Turenne* • Sylva Koscina *Marion* ■ *Dir* Henri Decoin • *Scr* Cécil Saint-Laurent, Gerard Devries, from the novel *The Man in the Iron Mask* by Alexandre Dumas

The Masque of the Red Death
★★★★ 15

Horror 1964 · UK/US · Colour · 84mins

This is easily the finest of director Roger Corman's Edgar Allan Poe adaptations, with Vincent Price the very essence of evil as the sadistic devil-worshipper trying to keep the plague at bay in 12th-century Italy by indulging in degenerate revels. While there are touches of deliciously wicked humour, the aura of terror comes from the doom-laden tone Corman creates by reaching as much into sombre Ingmar Bergman territory (the poignant tableaux showing crimson-cloaked Death stalking through fog-shrouded woods) as atmospheric Hammer shock. AJ. Contains violence. DVD

Vincent Price *Prince Prospero* • Hazel Court *Juliana* • Jane Asher *Francesca* • David Weston *Gino* • Patrick Magee *Alfredo* • Nigel Green *Ludovico* ■ *Dir* Roger Corman • *Scr* Charles Beaumont, R Wright Campbell, from the short stories by Edgar Allan Poe • *Cinematographer* Nicolas Roeg

Masquerade
★★ U

Comedy adventure
1965 · UK · Colour · 99mins

This slack send-up of British imperialism and James Bondism has Jack Hawkins and Cliff Robertson as British and American agents involved in the kidnapping of an Arab oil sheik. The plot is sometimes impossible to follow, so one is left half-smiling at the familiar turns from the likes of Bill Fraser, John Le Mesurier and Charles Gray. Robertson, who was brought in at the last minute to replace Rex Harrison, enlisted screenwriter William Goldman to rewrite his scenes. AT

Cliff Robertson *David Frazer* • Jack Hawkins *Col Drexel* • Marisa Mell *Sophie* • Michel Piccoli *Sarrasin* • Bill Fraser *Dunwoody* • Charles Gray *Benson* • John Le Mesurier *Sir Robert* ■ *Dir* Basil Dearden • *Scr* Michael Relph, William Goldman, from the novel *Castle Minerva* by Victor Canning

Masquerade
★★ 18

Thriller 1988 · US · Colour · 87mins

Director Bob Swaim's misfiring attempt at a Hitchcock-style thriller set among the Long Island yachting fraternity has the advantage of good performances by Rob Lowe and Meg Tilly. Otherwise, it's a rather dumb and violent affair as timid heiress Tilly is married to gigolo Lowe as part of a long-term plot to kill her and get her millions. Sleek boats and beautiful beaches give it the glossy look of a holiday commerical, but out-of-the-blue character changes make it implausible. TH DVD

Rob Lowe *Tim Whalan* • Meg Tilly *Olivia Lawrence* • Kim Cattrall *Brooke Morrison* • Doug Savant *Mike McGill* • John Glover *Tony Gateworth* • Dana Delany *Anne Briscoe* • Erik Holland *Chief of police* • Brian Davies *Granger Morrison* ■ *Dir* Bob Swaim • *Scr* Dick Wolf

The Masquerader
★★★ PG

Drama 1933 · US · BW · 73mins

Suave Ronald Colman essays a dual role in a virtual rehearsal for *The Prisoner of Zenda* four years later. He plays a drug-addicted MP who hires his cousin to impersonate him and make a major speech in parliament. Of course, this has a knock-on effect on his love life (can the lovely Elissa Landi tell them apart?) and his conniving butler (brilliant Halliwell Hobbes). Intelligent stuff, though a little creaky. TS

Ronald Colman *Sir John Chilcote/John Loder* • Elissa Landi *Eve Chilcote* • Juliette Compton *Lady Joyce* • Halliwell Hobbes *Brock* • David Torrence *Fraser* • Creighton Hale *Lakely* ■ *Dir* Richard Wallace • *Scr* Howard Estabrook, from the play by John Hunter Booth, from the novel by Katherine Cecil Thurston

Masques
★★★★ 15

Thriller 1987 · Fr · Colour · 100mins

The name of Alfred Hitchcock is often bandied around during the discussion of suspense thrillers, but French director Claude Chabrol has consistently demonstrated a near-understanding of the master's style and preoccupations. This isn't Chabrol at his best, but the tale of writer Robin Renucci trying to uncover the guilty secret of game show host Philippe Noiret's country chateau is endlessly entertaining. Flashy, but littered with delicious moments. DP. In French with English subtitles.

Philippe Noiret *Christian Legagneur* • Robin Renucci *Roland Wolf* • Bernadette Lafont *Patricia Marquet* • Monique Chaumette *Colette* • Anne Brochet *Catherine* • Roger Dumas *Manuel Marquet* ■ *Dir* Claude Chabrol • *Scr* Odile Barski, Claude Chabrol

Mass Appeal
★★★ 15

Comedy drama 1984 · US · Colour · 95mins

Not quite as funny as *The Apartment*, this is another film comedy with a theatrical feel and Jack Lemmon in the lead. Directed by Glenn Jordan, it's an enjoyable screen adaptation of Bill C Davis's hit Broadway play, in which a live wire theology student (Zeljko Ivanek) challenges an easy-going, affable priest (played by the ever-excellent Lemmon). The picture has appeal, though not necessarily of the mass variety. PF

Jack Lemmon *Father Farley* • Zeljko Ivanek *Mark Dolson* • Charles Durning *Monsignor Burke* • Louise Latham *Margaret* • Alice Hirson *Mrs Hart* • Helene Heigh *Mrs Hart's mother* • Sharee Gregory *Marion Hart* ■ *Dir* Glenn Jordan • *Scr* Bill C Davis, from his play

Massacre in Rome
★ 15

Wartime drama based on a true story
1973 · It/Fr · Colour · 95mins

Richard Burton, as the German commandant in Rome, and Marcello Mastroianni, as a priest trying to prevent mass executions, have to gargle with some awful dialogue here. The pace would make a snail itch with impatience, and this was a resounding flop everywhere except Italy. AT

Richard Burton *Col Kappler* • Marcello Mastroianni *Father Pietro Antonelli* • Leo McKern *General Kurt Maelzer* • John Steiner *Colonel Dollmann* • Delia Boccardo *Elena* ■ *Dir* George Pan Cosmatos • *Scr* George Pan Cosmatos, Robert Katz, from the novel *Death in Rome* by Robert Katz

The Master
★★ 18

Martial arts action
1989 · HK · Colour · 88mins

Jet Li enjoyed moderate Hong Kong success via a series of period martial arts movies that highlighted his balletic prowess. In this modern action thriller Li plays a martial arts student in America who contacts his old teacher and gets caught up in a local gang war. A flop at first, it was re-released in 1992 to cash in on the success of *Once upon a Time in China*. Lovers of kung fu set pieces will enjoy the stunning final fight. DF. In Cantonese with English subtitles. Contains violence and some swearing. DVD

U = SUITABLE FOR ALL Uc = SUITABLE FOR ALL, ESPECIALLY FOR YOUNG CHILDREN (VIDEO ONLY) PG = PARENTAL GUIDANCE

Jet Li *Jet* • Yuen Wah *Uncle Tak* • Crystal Hwoh *May* • Jerry Trimble *Jonny* ■ *Dir* Tsui Hark • *Scr* Lam Hee To, Lau Tai Mo, from a story by Tsui Hark

Master and Commander: the Far Side of the World

★★★★ 12

Period adventure drama
2003 · US · Colour · 132mins

Like the much-loved series of novels by Patrick O'Brian, Peter Weir's film immerses the audience in the day-to-day life on board a 19th-century British warship as it pursues a "phantom" French vessel. Purists will endlessly discuss the casting of Russell Crowe as Captain Aubrey (here deploying his self-described "RSC two pints after lunch" English accent) and Paul Bettany as his ship's doctor and best friend, Maturin, but both give full-blooded performances. It might be a little repetitive but thankfully the likeable characters, Weir's meticulous attention to period detail and the stunningly realised action more than compensate. AS. Contains violence and swearing. VIDEO DVD

Russell Crowe *Captain Jack Aubrey* • Paul Bettany *Dr Stephen Maturin* • Billy Boyd *Barrett Bonden* • James D'Arcy *First Lt Thomas Pullings* • Lee Ingleby *Hollom* • George Innes *Joe Plaice* • Mark Lewis Jones *Mr Hogg* • Chris Larkin *Captain Howard* ■ *Dir* Peter Weir • *Scr* Peter Weir, John Collee, from the novels *Master and Commander* and *The Far Side of the World* by Patrick O'Brian

The Master Gunfighter ★

Western 1975 · US · Colour · 110mins

This sloppy western is credited to Frank Laughlin, the nine-year-old son of real director and star Tom Laughlin. That family in-joke sets the tone for a painfully self-indulgent mess. Laughlin is a gun expert pitted against a Mexican warlord. There are obvious nods to Vietnam, the peace movement and native American consciousness amid the clumsily shot bloodletting. AT. Contains violence.

Tom Laughlin *Finley McCloud* • Ron O'Neal *Paulo* • Lincoln Kilpatrick *Jacques St Charles* • Geo Anne Sosa *Chorika* • Barbara Carrera *Eula* • Victor Campos *Maltese* • Hector Elias *Juan* ■ *Dir* Frank Laughlin [Tom Laughlin] • *Scr* Harold Lapland, from the film *Goyokin* by Kei Tasaka, Hideo Gosha

The Master of Ballantrae

★★★ U

Period swashbuckling adventure
1953 · US/UK · Colour · 88mins

Errol Flynn was beginning to look old and tired when he made this colourful adaptation of the Robert Louis Stevenson story (changed almost beyond recognition) in Europe. Nevertheless, with the help of Warner Bros veteran director William Keighley, the ailing star revived enough to make his mark in a movie that's not entirely without charm. There's a fine British cast and a lovely leading lady in Beatrice Campbell. TS

Errol Flynn *James Durrisdeer* • Roger Livesey *Colonel Francis Burke* • Anthony Steel *Henry Durrisdeer* • Beatrice Campbell *Lady Alison* • Yvonne Furneaux *Jessie Brown* • Jacques Berthier *Arnaud* • Felix Aylmer *Lord Durrisdeer* • Mervyn Johns *MacKellar* • Gillian Lynne *Marianne* ■ *Dir* William Keighley • *Scr* Herb Meadow, Harold Medford, from the novel by Robert Louis Stevenson

The Master of Bankdam

★★★

Period drama 1947 · UK · BW · 105mins

This is a thunderingly good melodrama spanning virtually the entire Victorian era. Tom Walls is all accent and folly as the head of a mill-owning northern family who entrusts the business to the wrong son. But the feud between swaggering Stephen Murray and his gritty brother Dennis Price is nothing compared to the rivalry between the foppish David Tomlinson and the down-to-earth Jimmy Hanley. DP

Anne Crawford *Annie Pickersgill* • Dennis Price *Joshua Crowther* • Tom Walls *Simeon Crowther Sr* • Stephen Murray *Zebediah Crowther* • Linden Travers *Clara Baker* • Jimmy Hanley *Simeon Crowther Jr* • Nancy Price *Lydia Crowther* • David Tomlinson *Lancelot Handel Crowther* ■ *Dir* Walter Forde • *Scr* Edward Dryhurst, Moie Charles, from the novel *The Crowthers of Bankdam* by Thomas Armstrong

The Master of Disguise ★ PG

Fantasy comedy 2002 · US · Colour · 76mins

This lamentably limp comedy cruelly demonstrates why Dana Carvey does not enjoy the superstar status of his *Wayne's World* co-star Mike Myers. Carvey plays a sheltered Italian youth who discovers that he has amazing powers of disguise and uses them to rescue his parents from the clutches of evil mastermind Brent Spiner. The nearest thing to a genuine joke is the bad guy's propensity for breaking wind whenever he laughs. AS VIDEO DVD

Dana Carvey *Pistachio Disguisey* • Jennifer Esposito *Jennifer* • Harold Gould *Grandfather* • James Brolin *Fabbrizio* • Brent Spiner *Devlin Bowman* • Edie McClurg *Mother* • Maria Canals *Sophia* • Bo Derek ■ *Dir* Perry Andelin Blake • *Scr* Dana Carvey, Harris Goldberg

Master of the House

★★★★★ U

Silent romantic drama
1925 · Den · BW · 91mins

This domestic tragicomedy with a feminist slant was Danish director Carl Th Dreyer's seventh feature and anticipates his greatest films. The deceptively simple story tells of a husband whose disregard for his wife's feelings causes her to become ill. When she is sent away to recuperate, his old nanny moves in and teaches him to mend his ways. Dreyer filmed in an exact replica of a real two-roomed flat built in a studio, using its limitations to his advantage. A film of close-ups and gestures, it contains a wonderful performance from Mathilde Nielsen as the nanny. RB VIDEO

Johannes Meyer *Victor Frandsen* • Astrid Holm *Ida, his wife* • Karin Nellemose *Karen Frandsen* • Clara Schonfeld *Alvilda Kryger* • Mathilde Nielsen *Mads* ■ *Dir* Carl Th Dreyer • *Scr* Carl Th Dreyer, Svend Rindom, from the play *Tyraennens Fald (The Fall of a Tyrant)* by Svend Rindom

Master of the World ★★ U

Fantasy adventure
1961 · US · Colour · 98mins

An uneven mixture of two Jules Verne novels to make one highly moralistic antiwar fable. Vincent Price plays a 19th-century inventor planning to destroy all of mankind's weapons from a flying airship with his usual suave and sinister panache. Spiced up with stock battle footage taken from other costume epics (the reason why the Globe theatre suddenly appears in Victorian London), it's a cheap and cheerful fantasy. AJ

Vincent Price *Robur* • Charles Bronson *Strock* • Henry Hull *Prudent* • Mary Webster *Dorothy* • David Frankham *Philip* • Richard Harrison *Alistair* • Vito Scotti *Topage* ■ *Dir* William Witney • *Scr* Richard Matheson, from the novels *Master of the World* and *Robur, the Conqueror* by Jules Verne

The Master Plan ★★★ U

Spy drama 1954 · UK · BW · 77mins

Blacklisted in Hollywood during the communist witch-hunt, South African-born Cy Endfield worked uncredited on three British thrillers with Charles De Lautour. This was his first solo venture in exile, made under the pseudonym Hugh Raker. It is an above-average quota quickie, with war hero and B-movie stalwart Wayne Morris as a government troubleshooter fighting against the double agent who is leaking secrets to the enemy. DP

Wayne Morris *Major Brent* • Tilda Thamar *Helen* • Norman Wooland *Colonel Cleaver* • Mary Mackenzie *Miss Gray* • Arnold Bell *General Goulding* • Marjorie Stewart *Yvonne* • Laurie Main *Johnny Orwell* • Frederick Schrecker *Dr Morgan Stern* ■ *Dir* Hugh Raker [Cy Endfield] • *Scr* Hugh Raker [Cy Endfield], Donald Bull, from the TV play *Operation North Star* by Harold Bratt

The Master Race ★★

Second World War drama
1944 · US · BW · 101mins

A bizarre wartime curio about a Nazi officer who hides out in Belgium and tries to keep the fascist fires burning by causing dissent among the newly liberated countries. Made promptly after the D-Day landings, it's a heavy slice of peace propaganda, with George Coulouris deeply sinister as the villain. Director Herbert J Biberman, blacklisted in 1948 as a result of his communist sympathies, was one of the original Hollywood Ten. AT

George Coulouris *Von Beck* • Stanley Ridges *Phil Carson* • Osa Massen *Helena* • Carl Esmond *Andrei* • Nancy Gates *Nina* • Morris Carnovsky *Old Man Bartoc* • Lloyd Bridges *Frank* ■ *Dir* Herbert J Biberman • *Scr* Herbert J Biberman, Anne Froelick, Rowland Leigh, from a story by Herbert J Biberman

Master Spy ★ U

Spy drama 1964 · UK · BW · 70mins

There isn't an atom of suspense in Montgomery Tully's tepid thriller about spying scientists. Indeed, the most exciting moments are the games of chess during which defector Stephen Murray passes vital secrets to communist squire, Alan Wheatley. There's a valiant attempt to put a sting in the tail, but only lab assistant June Thorburn fails to see through the slenderest web of deception. DP

Stephen Murray *Boris Turganev* • June Thorburn *Leila* • Alan Wheatley *Paul Skelton* • John Carson *Richard Colman* • John Brown *John Baxter* • Jack Watson *Captain Foster* ■ *Dir* Montgomery Tully • *Scr* Maurice J Wilson, from the story *They Also Serve* by Gerald Anstruther, Paul White

Mastermind ★★★

Spoof detective drama
1976 · US · Colour · 131mins

Shot in 1969 and left on the shelf for seven years, this curiosity is worth seeking out. It's a Charlie Chan parody, with the great blacklisted clown Zero Mostel as a bumbling oriental detective, and a sterling supporting cast including a last appearance from *On the Town's* Jules Munshin. Plus there's a knockout car chase and some voluble slapstick, too. TS

Zero Mostel *Inspector Hoku* • Bradford Dillman *Jabez Link* • Keiko Kishi *Nikki Kono* • Gawn Grainger *Nigel Crouchback* • Jules Munshin *Israeli agent* ■ *Dir* Alex March • *Scr* Terence Klein, Ian McLellan Hunter, from a story by Terence Klein

Masterminds ★ 12

Action adventure
1997 · US · Colour · 100mins

It's hard to understand why accomplished actor Patrick Stewart agreed to appear in this odious adventure movie. Stewart poses as a security expert, installing surveillance systems at a posh private school in order to hold a small number of the wealthiest kids in the world hostage. But he doesn't count on the school's biggest troublemaker, who has the school rigged for his own mischievous ends. ST. Contains violence. VIDEO

Patrick Stewart *Rafe Bentley* • Vincent Kartheiser *Ozzie* • Brenda Fricker *Principal Claire Maloney* • Brad Whitford [Bradley Whitford] *Miles Lawrence* • Matt Craven *Jake Paxton* ■ *Dir* Roger Christian • *Scr* Floyd Byars, from a story by Alex Siskin, Chris Black, Floyd Byars

The Masters ★★★

Mystery drama 1975 · It · Colour · 113mins

A naive schoolmistress (Jennifer O'Neill), newly arrived in a tiny Sicilian town, is insulted by a local peasant who is then murdered by the local Mafia. It's all to do with the corrupt police, but the teacher takes a long time to figure out exactly what's going on. Director Luigi Zampa gives the mystery more credibility than it deserves, while James Mason supplies a menacing turn. TH. Italian dialogue dubbed into English.

James Mason *Antonio Bellocampo* • Franco Nero *Prof Belcore* • Jennifer O'Neill *Elena Bardi* • Orazio Orlando • Claudio Gora ■ *Dir* Luigi Zampa • *Scr* Piero Bernardi, from the novel by Giuseppe Fava

Masters of Menace ★ 15

Comedy 1990 · US · Colour · 93mins

David Rasche is a Hell's Angel-style gang leader and Catherine Bach is his pregnant wife in this juvenile comedy from director Daniel Raskov, who seems to think the dumber the gag, the funnier it is. Adding embarrassing support to a farcical fiasco with very questionable undertones are slumming jokers Dan Aykroyd, John Candy and James Belushi. AJ. Contains violence, swearing and drug abuse. VIDEO

David Rasche *Buddy* • Catherine Bach *Kitty* • Lance Kinsey *Wallace* • Teri Copley *Sunny* • Ray Baker *Hoover* • Malcolm Smith *Schouweiller* • George "Buck" Flower *Sheriff Julip* ■ *Dir* Daniel Raskov • *Scr* Tino Insana

M

Masters of the Universe

★★ PG

Fantasy adventure
1987 · US · Colour · 101mins

It is difficult to make convincing live-action versions of cult cartoon strips, and this big-screen version of the momentarily popular TV series is one of the least successful attempts. Dolph Lundgren has the necessary physique for He-Man, and Frank Langella has been splendidly made-up for the role of Skeletor. But the story – about a cosmic key that will enable its holder to become master of the universe – is uninspired, while the effects look painfully cheap. DP VIDEO

Dolph Lundgren *He-Man* • Frank Langella *Skeletor* • Meg Foster *Evil-Lyn* • Billy Barty *Gwildor* • Courteney Cox *Julie Winston* • Robert Duncan McNeill *Kevin* ■ *Dir* Gary Goddard • *Scr* David Odell

Masti ★★★ 12

Comedy 2004 · Ind · Colour · 165mins

This is a men-behaving-badly scenario, with newlyweds Ritesh Deshmukh, Aftab Shivdasani and Vivek Oberoi pining for their bachelor days. However, the decision to spice up their social lives backfires when they cross swords with cop Ajay Devgan. So now, not only do they have to extricate themselves from their predicament, but they also have to prevent their wives finding out how they landed there in the first place. This is cheekier than most Bollywood movies, and, consequently, more fun. DP. In Hindi with English subtitles.

Vivek Oberoi *Meet* • Amrita Rao *Aanchal* • Aftab Shivdasani *Prem* • Tara Sharma *Geetha* • Ritesh Deshmukh *Amar* • Genelia D'Souza

Bindiya • Ajay Devgan *Inspector Sikander* ■ *Dir* Indra Kumar • *Scr* Tushar Hiranandani, Milap Zaveri

Mata Hari ★★★★

Spy melodrama 1931 · US · BW · 91mins

Greta Garbo's transcendent persona found an ideal outlet as the First World War spy who operates above all laws yet is brought down by a fatally romantic detour. The film is sensual and atmospheric and ranks as one of the few vehicles actually worthy of the celluloid goddess. Director George Fitzmaurice and cameraman William Daniels capture the story in stylishly visual terms, while there is a poignant chemistry between Garbo and the intense Ramon Novarro. And revealing a contradiction that is at once fascinating and modern, Garbo applies her customary sense of elsewhere to situations that call for desire, drive and purpose in a mercenary role. DO

Greta Garbo *Mata Hari* • Ramon Novarro *Lt Alexis Rosanoff* • Lionel Barrymore *General Serge Shubin* • Lewis Stone *Andriani* • C Henry Gordon *Dubois* • Karen Morley *Carlotta* • Alec B Francis *Caron* • Blanche Frederici *Sister Angelica* ■ *Dir* George Fitzmaurice • *Scr* Benjamin Glazer, Leo Birinski, Doris Anderson, Gilbert Emery

Mata Hari ★ 18

Spy drama 1985 · US · Colour · 103mins

This soft-core sex version of the old World War One yarn has Sylvia Kristel (*Emmanuelle*) as the French spy, taking off her clothes at the drop of a proverbial hat. Handsome Christopher Cazenove is her opposite number in Germany – the spy who loved her. Director Curtis Harrington may have intended a satire but the producers wanted a bit of hot stuff. AT

Sylvia Kristel *Mata Hari* • Christopher Cazenove *Karl Von Byerling* • Oliver Tobias *Captain Ladoux* • Gaye Brown *Fraulein Doktor* • William Fox *Maître Clunet* ■ *Dir* Curtis Harrington • *Scr* Joel Ziskin

Matador ★★★ 18

Black comedy drama
1986 · Sp · Colour · 101mins

Flashy, trashy and vibrantly colourful, Pedro Almodóvar's film explores the links between eroticism and violence. Antonio Banderas gives a courageous performance as the trainee bullfighter whose overpowering fantasies and his own sexual misdemeanours prompt him to confess to a series of kinky killings. Some of the dialogue is laughably pretentious, while Almodóvar's emphasis on voyeuristic titillation and cheap black comedy comes at the expense of developing some interesting themes. DP. In Spanish with English subtitles. Contains violence, nudity. DVD

Assumpta Serna *Maria Cardenal* • Antonio Banderas *Angel Giminez* • Nacho Martinez *Diego Montes* • Eva Cobo *Eva* • Julieta Serrano *Berta* • Chus Lampreave *Pilar* • Carmen Maura *Julia* ■ *Dir* Pedro Almodóvar • *Scr* Pedro Almodóvar, Jesus Ferrero, from a story by Pedro Almodóvar

Matango ★★ 15

Science-fiction horror
1963 · Jpn · BW · 72mins

Japanese tourists on a luxury get-away-from-it-all yachting holiday are shipwrecked on a mysterious Pacific island where they eat narcotic mushrooms and turn into walking, phallic-shaped fungi. Told in flashback by a padded-cell survivor, director Inoshiro Honda's drug allegory-cum-monster movie is an insanely illogical romp suffused with dream logic and startling sexual imagery. AJ. A Japanese language film.

Akira Kubo *Kenji Murai* • Kenji Sahara *Senzo Koyama* • Yoshio Tsuchiya *Fumio Kasai* • Hiroshi Koizumi *Naoyuki Sakeda* ■ *Dir* Inoshiro Honda • *Scr* Takeshi Kimura

The Match ★★★ 15

Comedy drama
1999 · UK/US/Ire · Colour · 96mins

Apparently an attempt at reviving the spirit of the Ealing comedy, this tells the story of young Scottish milkman Max Beesley, looking forward to the return of girlfriend Laura Fraser from university. Despite Beesley's physical disadvantages, he finds himself involved in a soccer match-cum-feud between two local watering holes. An amiable movie with no pretensions, this presents a host of familiar British faces and plenty of cosy characters. TH. Contains swearing. DVD

Max Beesley *Wullie Smith* • Isla Blair *Sheila Bailey* • James Cosmo *Billy Bailey* • Laura Fraser *Rosemary Bailey* • Richard E Grant *Gorgeous Gus* • Ian Holm *Big Tam* • Tom Sizemore *Buffalo* • Pierce Brosnan *John McGee* ■ *Dir/Scr* Mick Davis

The Match Factory Girl ★★★ 15

Drama 1990 · Fin/Swe · Colour · 65mins

Finnish film-maker Aki Kaurismäki claimed that this picture was intended to make Robert Bresson seem like the director of epic action movies. While it certainly shares the French master's minimalist style, the story of a plain Jane who defies the harshest of odds, finally to take control of her life, lacks the compassion that characterised even the bleakest Bresson scenario. But Kati Outinen is superb in the title role, overcoming the odd improbable plot twist to convince you that she is one of the countless Eleanor Rigbys totally dependent on dreams to sweeten their bitter reality. DP. In Finnish with English subtitles.

Kati Outinen *Iris* • Elina Salo *Mother* • Esko Nikkari *Stepfather* • Vesa Vierikko *Aarne* • Reijo Taipale *Singer* • Silu Seppala *Brother* • Outi Maenpaa *Workmate* • Marja Packalen *Doctor* ■ *Dir/Scr* Aki Kaurismäki

The Matchmaker ★★★ U

Period comedy 1958 · US · BW · 102mins

This is *Hello, Dolly!* without the tunes or, indeed, Barbra Streisand. Shirley Booth is Dolly Levi, the widowed, interfering busybody who arranges marriages like flowers in a vase. In her own sights is Paul Ford's merchant; getting tangled up in her plans are Shirley MacLaine and Anthony Perkins. The performances are perfectly attuned to the 1880s ambience, which is nicely enhanced when the actors address the camera directly. AT

Shirley Booth *Dolly Levi* • Anthony Perkins *Cornelius Hackl* • Shirley MacLaine *Irene Molloy* • Paul Ford *Horace Vandergelder* • Robert Morse *Barnaby Tucker* • Wallace Ford *Malachi Stack* • Perry Wilson *Minnie Fay* ■ *Dir* Joseph Anthony • *Scr* John Michael Hayes, from the play by Thornton Wilder

The Matchmaker ★★★ 15

Romantic comedy
1997 · Ire/UK/US · Colour · 97mins

The under-rated Janeane Garofalo gets to flex her acting muscles as Marcy, dispatched to the Emerald Isle to round up a US senator's ancestors. Inadvertently she finds herself at a matchmaking festival, where sparks are soon flying between her and gauche barman David O'Hara. Matchmaker Milo O'Shea bets he can get them together and sends them on a wild goose chase to the Aran islands. It's unfortunate that the movie begins and ends in America, but what's in between has all the charm that Ireland can offer. LH

Janeane Garofalo *Marcy Tizard* • David O'Hara *Sean Kelly* • Milo O'Shea *Dermot O'Brien* • Jay O Sanders *Senator John McGlory* • Denis Leary *Nick* ■ *Dir* Mark Joffe • *Scr* Karen Janszen, Louis Nowra, Graham Linehan, from a screenplay (unproduced) by Greg Dinner

Matchstick Men ★★★ 12

Crime comedy drama
2003 · US · Colour · 111mins

Director Ridley Scott's low-key movie stars Nicolas Cage as a conman who is also afflicted by an obsessive-compulsive disorder that makes him nervous and a cleanliness freak. That this is at odds with his lifestyle choice does stretch credibility, but it also allows Scott to indulge in all sorts of appropriately edgy cuts and compositions. Cage and partner Sam Rockwell embark on a high-stakes scam, just as the former discovers he has a bright teenage daughter (Alison Lohman). The bonding scenes are played beautifully, yet the script cheapens this sharp setup with a predictable con of its own. JC. Contains swearing, violence. DVD

Nicolas Cage *Roy Waller* • Sam Rockwell *Frank Mercer* • Alison Lohman *Angela* • Bruce McGill *Chuck Frechette* • Bruce Altman *Dr Harris Klein* • Sheila Kelley *Kathy* • Beth Grant *Laundry lady* ■ *Dir* Ridley Scott • *Scr* Ted Griffin, Nicholas Griffin, from the novel by Eric Garcia

Matewan ★★★★ 15

Historical drama
1987 · US · Colour · 127mins

When the local coal company cuts the pay of its mainly white workforce and begins using blacks and Italian immigrants at cheaper rates, tensions run high in the West Virginian mining town of Matewan. Union organiser Joe Kenehan (Chris Cooper) arrives to sort out the increasingly violent confrontation. Set in the 1920s, this resembles a western: the good, the bad and the ugly characters are clearly delineated, even if writer/director John Sayles often gives them speeches instead of dialogue. Films about the American labour movement are rare, so this uncompromising, fact-based drama is to be savoured. The glowing cinematography is by Haskell Wexler. AT. Contains swearing. DVD

Chris Cooper *Joe Kenehan* • James Earl Jones *"Few Clothes" Johnson* • Will Oldham *Danny Radnor* • Jace Alexander *Hillard* • Ken Jenkins *Sephus Purcell* • Bob Gunton *CE Lively* • Gary McCleery *Ludie* • Kevin Tighe *Hickey* ■ *Dir/Scr* John Sayles

Matilda ★★ U

Sports comedy 1978 · US · Colour · 87mins

Screen version of the Paul Gallico book, about a boxing kangaroo and the small-time theatrical agent who becomes the marsupial's manager. The budget obviously didn't stretch to special effects, so the kangaroo is played by a man in a costume. This cute comedy looks a little dated these days, but kids might want to hop along to see it. Elliott Gould and Robert Mitchum head the humans, while Gary Morgan is the guy in the suit. DA

Elliott Gould *Bernie Bonnelli* • Robert Mitchum *Duke Parkhurst* • Harry Guardino *Uncle Nono* • Clive Revill *Billy Baker/Narration* • Lionel Stander *Pinky Schwab* • Karen Carlson *Kathleen Smith* • Gary Morgan ■ *Dir* Daniel Mann • *Scr* Albert S Ruddy, Timothy Galfas, from the novel by Paul Gallico

Matilda ★★★★ PG

Comedy fantasy 1996 · US · Colour · 94mins

Director Danny DeVito revels in the black comedy of this typically dark Roald Dahl story, in which monstrous adults consider children as inconvenient accessories. DeVito – who also stars as Matilda's boorish dad – cleverly emphasises the point by shooting much of the film from a child's-eye view, making people and buildings alike look forbidding and cold. Mara Wilson is excellent in the lead, while Embeth Davidtz prevents beloved teacher Miss Honey from being too sweet, but stealing the acting honours is Pam Ferris, who brings vicious headmistress Miss Trunchbull to terrifying life. DP DVD

Mara Wilson *Matilda* • Danny DeVito *Harry Wormwood* • Rhea Perlman *Zinnia Wormwood* • Embeth Davidtz *Miss Honey* • Pam Ferris *Agatha Trunchbull* • Paul Reubens *FBI agent* ■ *Dir* Danny DeVito • *Scr* Nicholas Kazan, Robin Swicord, from the novel by Roald Dahl

Matinee ★★★★ PG

Comedy drama 1993 · US · Colour · 94mins

This glorious coming-of-age saga from Joe Dante is a paean to growing up in the early 1960s, using the twin backdrops of nuclear bomb paranoia and "Atom Age" monster flicks. It's also a loving tribute to legendary producer/director William Castle, the schlock showman responsible for gimmick B-movies such as *The Tingler* and *House on Haunted Hill.* Charming John Goodman is the Castle clone launching his new giant insect horror film in Key West during the Cuban missile crisis, and it's the contrast between fake movie scares and real-life ones that makes Dante's nostalgic film so engaging. AJ DVD

John Goodman *Lawrence Woolsey* • Cathy Moriarty *Ruth Corday/Carole* • Simon Fenton *Gene Loomis* • Omri Katz *Stan* • Kellie Martin *Sherry* • Lisa Jakub *Sandra* • Lucinda Jenney *Anne Loomis* • Jesse Lee *Dennis Loomis* ■ *Dir* Joe Dante • *Scr* Charlie Haas, from a story by Jerico, Charlie Haas

The Matinee Idol ★★

Silent comedy 1928 · US · BW · 60mins

A Broadway star catches a Civil War drama performed by a theatrical troupe out in the boondocks. It's so badly done that he takes it to the city as a comedy and has a hit. Bessie Love is the appealing star of this silent, the second to be directed for Columbia by Frank Capra. (Romance blossoms between Love and the actor who plays a black soldier and only declares his affection when rain washes off his make-up.) Although Capra could have given more weight to the fact that the actors have been made fools of, the film is frequently very funny. RK

Bessie Love *Ginger Bolivar* • Johnnie Walker *Don Wilson/Harry Mann* • Lionel Belmore *Col Jasper Bolivar* ■ *Dir* Frank Capra • *Scr* Peter Milne, Elmer Harris, from the story *Come Back to Aaron* by Robert Lord

The Mating Game ★★★★ U

Comedy 1959 · US · Colour · 96mins

The Darling Buds of May is better known here as the popular TV series which introduced us to Catherine Zeta-Jones. But this MGM version of HE Bates's novel is actually much funnier and more faithful to the spirit of the original. The cast is also much classier: Paul Douglas is a truly estimable father to Debbie Reynolds, the farm girl who falls for taxman Tony Randall, while director George Marshall keeps it all zipping along. TS

Debbie Reynolds *Mariette Larkin* • Tony Randall *Lorenzo Charlton* • Paul Douglas *Pop Larkin* • Fred Clark *Oliver Kelsey* • Una Merkel *Ma Larkin* ■ *Dir* George Marshall • *Scr* William Roberts, from the novel *The Darling Buds of May* by HE Bates

The Mating Habits of the Earthbound Human ★ 15

Romantic comedy
1999 · US · Colour · 86mins

David Hyde Pierce is the narrator (an anthropologist from an alien world) in this awful comedy, helping us to understand how humans relate and mate. Badly written, woodenly performed and, overall, an ill-advised and badly executed disaster. JB

David Hyde Pierce *Narrator* • MacKenzie Astin *Billy Masterson* • Carmen Electra *Jenny Smith* • Lucy Liu *Jenny's friend* • Marcus Redmond *Billy's friend* • Lisa Rotondi *Jenny's friend* • Marc Blucas *Jenny's ex-boyfriend* ■ *Dir/Scr* Jeff Abugov

The Mating Season ★★ U

Comedy 1951 · US · BW · 101mins

Working man John Lund ascends the social ladder through marriage to Gene Tierney, daughter of an ambassador, whose family is unaware of his humble origins. His mother Thelma Ritter pretends to be a servant and comes to work for the newlyweds. Given his somewhat lifeless co-stars and a workmanlike script, director Mitchell Leisen wisely lets Thelma Ritter walk away with this comedy. Her performance earned her the second of her record six Oscar nominations for best supporting actress. RK

Gene Tierney *Maggie Carleton* • John Lund *Van McNulty* • Miriam Hopkins *Fran Carleton* • Thelma Ritter *Ellen McNulty* • Jan Sterling *Betsy* • Larry Keating *Mr Kallinger Sr* ■ *Dir* Mitchell Leisen • *Scr* Charles Brackett, Walter Reisch, Richard Breen [Richard L Breen]

The Matrix ★★★★★ 15

Science-fiction action thriller
1999 · US · Colour · 136mins

Keanu Reeves reclaims his action hero crown in the Wachowski Brothers' super-smart science-fiction action adventure set across two dimensions. Thematically complex, yet intelligently integrating eastern philosophy, Lewis Carroll and ancient mysticism, the film has Reeves as Neo, a reclusive computer hacker who may just be the one to save the world from the evils of cyberspace slavery. Taking a quantum leap beyond anything the fantasy sensation seeker has seen before in the special effects department, this mixes ultra-cool visuals, vertigo-inducing kung fu and a deliciously paranoid scenario for an adrenalin-pumping rollercoaster ride of extraordinary vision and power. AJ. Contains violence, swearing. DVD

Keanu Reeves *Thomas A Anderson/Neo* • Carrie-Anne Moss *Trinity* • Laurence Fishburne *Morpheus* • Hugo Weaving *Agent Smith* • Joe Pantoliano *Cypher* • Marcus Chong *Tank* • Gloria Foster *Oracle* ■ *Dir/Scr* Larry Wachowski, Andy Wachowski

The Matrix Reloaded ★★★ 15

Science-fiction action thriller
2002 · US/Aus · Colour · 132mins

Creating a sequel to the superlative sci-fi action blockbuster *The Matrix* was always going to be a Herculean task. The Wachowski brothers set themselves such a high standard that the second chapter in their epic man-versus-machines trilogy was never likely to match the impact of the first. The duo add a handful of fantastic – though underused – new villains and deliver an array of astonishing set pieces, as Neo (Keanu Reeves) and his associates fight to save Zion, Earth's last human enclave. Disappointingly, however, such elements fail to lift a film that suffers from stilted dialogue, cheesy scripting and a plodding pace. SF. Contains violence. DVD

Keanu Reeves *Thomas A Anderson/Neo* • Laurence Fishburne *Morpheus* • Carrie-Anne Moss *Trinity* • Hugo Weaving *Agent Smith* • Jada Pinkett Smith *Niobe* • Gloria Foster *Oracle* • Monica Bellucci *Persephone* • Collin Chou *Seraph* • Nona Gaye *Zee* • Randall Duk Kim *Keymaker* ■ *Dir/Scr* Larry Wachowski, Andy Wachowski

The Matrix Revolutions ★★★ 15

Science-fiction action thriller
2003 · US · Colour · 123mins

Continuing straight on from the events of *Reloaded*, the first hour of this more substantial second sequel plays like an extended version of the previous film: annoyingly cryptic conversations, overfamiliar acrobatic shoot-outs and inert pacing. But, in a great second half, the Wachowski Brothers get the trilogy back on track, as humans in huge combat armour battle valiantly to protect their Zion stronghold against a million robotic Sentinels. Both technically and artistically, this extended siege is perhaps the most impressive set piece of the series. JC. Contains violence. DVD

Keanu Reeves *Thomas A Anderson/Neo* • Carrie-Anne Moss *Trinity* • Laurence Fishburne *Morpheus* • Hugo Weaving *Agent Smith* • Jada Pinkett Smith *Niobe* • Mary Alice *The Oracle* • Tanveer Atwal *Sati* • Monica Bellucci *Persephone* ■ *Dir/Scr* Larry Wachowski, Andy Wachowski

The Mattei Affair ★★★★ U

Historical crime drama
1972 · It · Colour · 115mins

Dubbed by *Time* magazine "the most powerful Italian since Augustus Caesar", Enrico Mattei was a wartime hero who rose through the ranks of the AGIP utility to head ENI, a state-sponsored body that he moulded into an operation capable of transforming the nation's petro-chemical industry. However, his ambitions died with him in a plane crash in 1962. Delving into the murky worlds of international capitalism and postwar Italian politics, Francesco Rosi's compelling, Palme d'Or-winning reconstruction seeks to prove that this deeply flawed man (impeccably played by Gian Maria Volonté) was the victim of a conspiracy inspired by corruption and greed. DP. In Italian with English subtitles.

Gian Maria Volonté *Enrico Mattei* • Luigi Squarzina *Journalist* • Gianfranco Ombuen *Ferrari* • Edda Ferronao *Mrs Mattei* ■ *Dir* Francesco Rosi • *Scr* Francesco Rosi, Tonino Guerra, Nerio Minuzzo, Tito Di Stefano

A Matter of Dignity ★★★

Drama 1957 · Gr · BW · 102mins

Michael Cacoyannis's fourth feature is an exacting domestic melodrama centring on the morality of three very different women. Ellie Lambetti drew the most plaudits as the daughter of an impoverished household who contemplates marrying a man she detests for his money. However, there's much to admire in the supporting performances of both Athena Michaelidou, as her grasping, snobbish mother, and Eleni Zafiriou, as the maid who has endured exploitation and incurred ruinous debts in order to care for her ailing son. DP. In Greek with English subtitles.

Ellie Lambetti *Chloé* • Georges Pappas *Cléon Pellas* • Athena Michaelidou *Roxane* • Eleni Zafiriou *Katerina* ■ *Dir/Scr* Michael Cacoyannis

A Matter of Life and Death ★★★★★ U

Romantic fantasy
1946 · UK · BW and Colour · 99mins

The theatrical stylisation of Michael Powell and Emeric Pressburger sometimes deflected their thematic purpose, but in this dazzling fantasy they succeed in marrying the two to perfection. Although the film was intended to celebrate the Anglo-American alliance that had prevailed in the Second World War, the Archers production company instead delivered a barbed allegory that called into question not only the strength of the ties between the Allies, but also Britain's continued status as a world power. Its political outspokenness, visual audacity and mannered playing now make it one of the most fondly recalled British movies. DP DVD

David Niven *Squadron Leader Peter Carter* • Kim Hunter *June* • Roger Livesey *Dr Reeves* • Robert Coote *Bob Trubshawe* • Marius Goring *Conductor 71* • Raymond Massey *Abraham Farlan* • Kathleen Byron *Angel* • Richard Attenborough *English pilot* • Bonar Colleano *American pilot* • Joan Maude *Chief recorder* ■ *Dir/Scr* Michael Powell, Emeric Pressburger • *Cinematographer* Jack Cardiff • *Production Designer* Alfred Junge

A Matter of Time ★ PG

Drama 1976 · It/US · Colour · 99mins

Movie star Liza Minnelli recalls her encounters with aged contessa Ingrid Bergman whose rambling tales of her life inspired the young girl. Made up of a series of utterly confusing flashbacks-within-flashbacks, this maudlin rubbish is not helped by Minnelli's undisciplined, edgy performance – or that of Bergman, done up as a dessicated crone. Isabella Rossellini has a cameo as the old contessa's nurse. RK

Liza Minnelli *Nina* • Ingrid Bergman *Contessa Sanziani* • Charles Boyer *Count* • Spiros Andros *Mario* • Tina Aumont *Valentina* • Gabriele Ferzetti *Antonio Vicari* • Isabella Rossellini *Sister Pia* ■ *Dir* Vincente Minnelli • *Scr* John Gay, from the novel *The Film of Memory* by Maurice Druon

A Matter of WHO ★★

Detective comedy thriller
1961 · UK · BW · 98mins

Wanting to stretch himself after his comedy successes in the 1950s, Terry-Thomas accepted what was intended to be a straight role in a thriller designed to highlight the work of the World Health Organisation. He plays an investigator who, while trying to locate the source of an outbreak of smallpox, uncovers a typically British B-movie criminal plot. Everything becomes very intricate yet unexciting and the gap-toothed one mistakenly tries to liven things up by slipping into comic mode, which does not work at all well. DM

Terry-Thomas *Archibald Bannister* • Alex Nicol *Edward Kennedy* • Sonja Ziemann *Michèle Cooper* • Richard Briers *Jamieson* • Clive Morton *Hatfield* • Vincent Ball *Doctor Blake* • Honor Blackman *Sister Bryan* ■ *Dir* Don Chaffey • *Scr* Milton Holmes, Patricia Lee, from a story by Patricia Lee, Paul Dickson

Maurice ★★★ 15

Period drama 1987 · UK · Colour · 134mins

EM Forster's autobiographical novel about homosexuals at Cambridge was written in 1914, but withheld from publication until after his death in 1970. From its opening scenes, in which Simon Callow camply tells the young Maurice what great things he can expect from his body, James Ivory's film skips rather gingerly around the subject matter. The older Maurice, now played by James Wilby, goes up to Cambridge where Hugh Grant awaits; eventually, though, he ends up with a bit of rough trade, played by Rupert Graves. As with all Merchant Ivory films, it's impeccably mounted, prim and a tad dull. AT DVD

James Wilby *Maurice Hall* • Hugh Grant *Clive Durham* • Denholm Elliott *Dr Barry* • Simon Callow *Mr Ducie* • Billie Whitelaw *Mrs Hall* • Ben Kingsley *Lasker-Jones* • Judy Parfitt *Mrs Durham* • Rupert Graves *Alec Scudder* ■ *Dir* James Ivory • *Scr* Kit Hesketh-Harvey, James Ivory, from the novel by EM Forster

Mausoleum ★ 18

Horror 1983 · US · Colour · 92mins

Self-styled sleaze starlet Bobbie Bresee plays a housewife who, due to a family curse, becomes possessed by a demon that turns her into a ritually homicidal nymphomaniac. Bresee dances around topless a lot and, in the film's only fun moment, reveals her breasts have teeth. Otherwise the special effects are cheesy (Bresee sports glowing green eyes when feeling lustful), the acting amateurish and the dialogue dreadful. AJ

Marjoe Gortner *Oliver Farrell* • Bobbie Bresee *Susan Farrell* • Norman Burton *Dr Simon Andrews* • Maurice Sherbanee *Ben, the gardener* • LaWanda Page *Elsie* ■ *Dir* Michael Dugan • *Scr* Robert Madero, Robert Barich, from a story by Katherine Rosenwink

Maverick ★★★ PG

Comedy western
1994 · US · Colour · 121mins

This comedy western written by script doctor supreme William Goldman was clearly in need of a little attention itself. Goldman has produced a gentle tribute to the hit TV series, but misses a golden opportunity for a razor-sharp spoof. Mel Gibson and Jodie Foster sparking nicely as the eponymous gambler and the con artist who is more than his match. But it's left to James Garner (the original Bret Maverick) to demonstrate what comic acting is really all about. DP. Contains violence. DVD

Mel Gibson *Bret Maverick* • Jodie Foster *Annabelle Bransford* • James Garner *Zane Cooper* • Graham Greene (2) *Joseph* • Alfred Molina *Angel* • James Coburn *Commodore Duval* • Dub Taylor *Room clerk* • Geoffrey Lewis *Matthew Wicker* ■ *Dir* Richard Donner • *Scr* William Goldman, from the TV series by Roy Huggins

The Maverick Queen ★★ U

Western 1955 · US · Colour · 90mins

Barbara Stanwyck stars in a cheaply-made, lurid western that vaguely resembles Republic's far more successful *Johnny Guitar*. Stanwyck plays a saloon owner who gives young studs the runaround before falling in love with Barry Sullivan, a Pinkerton agent on the trail of the Sundance Kid. This was directed by workhorse Joseph Kane and shot in the studio's widescreen process, Naturama. AT

Barbara Stanwyck *Kit Banion* • Barry Sullivan *Jeff* • Scott Brady *Sundance* • Mary Murphy *Lucy Lee* • Wallace Ford *Jamie* • Howard Petrie *Butch Cassidy* ■ *Dir* Joseph Kane • *Scr* Kenneth Gamet, DeVallon Scott, from the novel by Zane Grey, Romer Grey

Max ★★★

Drama 1994 · Can · Colour · 94mins

This intelligent and involving drama takes an occasionally bitter look at how the ideals of the 1960s have been sold out by the 1990s. The film follows a family's bid to escape the tensions and dangers of the city by settling in the desert, only to discover that their new environment brings new problems. RH Thomson and Denise Crosby head a credible cast. JF

RH Thomson *Andy Blake* • Denise Crosby *Jayne Blake* • Walter Dalton *Jayne's Dad* • Garwin Sanford *Doctor Kaye* • Don Davis [Don S Davis] *Earl* ■ *Dir/Scr* Charles Wilkinson

Max ★★ 15

Period drama
2002 · Hun/Can/UK · Colour · 104mins

Menno Meyjes's feature debut is a brave and, at least thematically, fascinating work. Controversially

M

focusing on Adolf Hitler the man, Meyjes offers a fictional account of the early events that set a demobbed soldier and frustrated artist on the road to genocide. Fellow First World War veteran and Jewish art dealer John Cusack befriends the obnoxious young Adolf (Noah Taylor) and tries to persuade him to put as much passion into his painting as he does into his embryonic hate politics. While the drama is well shot and Taylor gives a striking performance, the film is too contrived and simplistic. SF DVD

John Cusack *Max Rothman* • Noah Taylor *Adolf Hitler* • Leelee Sobieski *Liselore* • Molly Parker *Nina Rothman* • Ulrich Thomsen *Captain Mayr* • David Horovitch *Max's father* • Janet Suzman *Max's mother* • Peter Capaldi *David Cohn* ■ *Dir/Scr* Menno Meyjes

Max Dugan Returns ★★★ PG

Comedy 1983 · US · Colour · 93mins

A Neil Simon comedy starring his then wife, Marsha Mason, as a widow struggling against the foibles of modern life to bring up her 15-year-old son (Matthew Broderick). Just as we get to know them and their world – a world in which every domestic appliance is against them – Jason Robards shows up as Mason's father. He abandoned her when she was nine; now he's terminally ill and stinking rich. Easy on the eye and the mind, with a very attractive cast. AT

Marsha Mason *Nora* • Jason Robards *Max Dugan* • Donald Sutherland *Brian* • Matthew Broderick *Michael* • Dody Goodman *Mrs Litke* • Sal Viscuso *Coach* • Panchito Gomez *Luis* • Kiefer Sutherland *Bill* ■ *Dir* Herbert Ross • *Scr* Neil Simon

Max Keeble's Big Move ★★ PG

Comedy 2001 · US · Colour · 82mins

Alex D Linz plays the boy trying to get by at school without being bullied, or caught out by the mean-minded principal. But when dad Robert Carradine announces the family is decamping to Chicago, Linz has just a week to wreak revenge on bullying Noel Fisher, unprincipled principal Larry Miller and grumpy ice-cream man Jamie Kennedy, while also trying to impress dream-girl Zena Grey. Frantic, dumbed-down fun with neither charm nor credibility. DP

Alex D Linz *Max Keeble* • Larry Miller *Principal Jindraike* • Jamie Kennedy *Evil Ice Cream Man* • Zena Grey *Megan* • Josh Peck *Robe* • Nora Dunn *Lily Keeble* • Robert Carradine *Don Keeble* ■ *Dir* Tim Hill • *Scr* Jonathan Bernstein, Mark Blackwell, James Greer, from a story by David Watts, Jonathan Bernstein, Mark Blackwell, James Greer

Max Mon Amour ★★ 18

Black comedy 1986 · Fr/US · Colour · 97mins

A clever idea from director Nagisa Oshima who obviously tries to follow in Luis Buñuel's surreal footsteps by taking apart the hypocrisies of the French bourgeoisie. Charlotte Rampling is the diplomat's deeply bored wife in Paris who takes a chimpanzee as a lover, and Anthony Higgins is her non-plussed husband who is determined to take it on the stiff upper lip and chin. The satire fails to bite, however, owing to a pair of stultifying performances from the main stars, though Max the chimp is actually rather good. SH. In French and English with subtitles.

Charlotte Rampling *Margaret Jones* • Anthony Higgins *Peter Jones* • Bernard-Pierre Donnadieu *Archibald* • Victoria Abril *Maria* • Anne-Marie Besse *Suzanne* • Nicole Calfan *Hélène* ■ *Dir* Nagisa Oshima • *Scr* Nagisa Oshima, Jean-Claude Carrière, from an idea by Jean-Claude Carrière

Max Q: Emergency Landing ★★★ PG

Space thriller 1998 · US · Colour · 83mins

Hot on the tail of his own blockbusting disaster-in-space adventure, *Armageddon*, producer Jerry Bruckheimer set his production company on a mission to produce this efficient TV-movie sci-fi thriller. Director Michael Shapiro has turned out an admirably absorbing adventure, in which the crew of a shuttle mission braces itself for a perilous re-entry after an accident leaves the craft crippled. DP DVD

William Campbell [Bill Campbell] *Commander Clay Jarvis* • Paget Brewster *Rena Wynter* • Ned Vaughn *Scott Hines* • Tasha Smith *Karen Daniels* • Geoffrey Blake *Jonah Randall* ■ *Dir* Michael Shapiro • *Scr* Marty Kaplan, Robert J Avrech

Maxie ★★★ PG

Comedy fantasy 1985 · US · Colour · 93mins

An old-fashioned fantasy, with Glenn Close as the bishop's secretary whose body is taken over by a free spirit from the 1920s called Maxie Malone. Close has fun with the dual role of the conservative working wife and the jazz-age flapper, but it is *Chicago Hope's* Mandy Patinkin who, as Close's husband, comes across as most at home with the light romantic comedy. Slight but enjoyable. JB

Glenn Close *Jan/Maxie* • Mandy Patinkin *Nick* • Ruth Gordon *Mrs Lavin* • Barnard Hughes *Bishop Campbell* • Valerie Curtin *Miss Sheffer* • Googy Gress *Father Jerome* ■ *Dir* Paul Aaron • *Scr* Patricia Resnick, from the novel *Marion's Wall* by Jack Finney

Maximum Overdrive ★★ 18

Horror 1986 · US · Colour · 93mins

Horror writer Stephen King decided his neon-lit prose needed his neon-lit direction. It's a courageous debut, with the machinery in a North Carolina small town coming to lethal life and besieging a group headed by Emilio Estevez and Pat Hingle. The trouble is that writer King should have explained to director King that you must not outpace your audience's interest, however well-managed the action. TH. Contains violence, swearing. DVD

Emilio Estevez *Bill Robinson* • Pat Hingle *Hendershot* • Laura Harrington *Brett* • Yeardley Smith *Connie* • John Short *Curt* • Ellen McElduff *Wanda June* ■ *Dir* Stephen King • *Scr* Stephen King, from his story.

Maximum Risk ★★ 18

Action thriller 1996 · US · Colour · 96mins

In *Double Impact*, we suffered the agony of two Jean-Claude Van Dammes for the entire movie. Here, thankfully, his twin gets bumped off in the opening few minutes. It's still hard work, but at least in the hands of Hong Kong director Ringo Lam (*City on Fire*) there are plenty of tremendous action set pieces to relish as Van Damme takes on the might of the Russian Mafia with the help of his late sibling's girlfriend (Natasha Henstridge from *Species*). JF DVD

Jean-Claude Van Damme *Alain/Mikhail* • Natasha Henstridge *Alex* • Jean-Hugues Anglade *Sebastien* • Zach Grenier *Ivan* • Stéphane Audran *Chantal Moreau* ■ *Dir* Ringo Lam • *Scr* Larry Ferguson

May Wine ★★★ 15

Romantic comedy
1990 · Fr/US · Colour · 80mins

Lara Flynn Boyle is on good form here as a troublesome daughter whose refusal to dump an unsuitable boyfriend prompts mother Joanna Cassidy to sweep her off to Paris. No sooner have they arrived than they both fall for the same doctor, Guy Marchand. Cassidy is one of Hollywood's more under-rated actresses, while Marchand is among French cinema's most accomplished supporting players. Consequently, the cast brings out the best in director Carol Wiseman's frothy script. DP. Contains swearing and nudity.

Joanna Cassidy *Lorraine* • Lara Flynn Boyle *Camille* • Guy Marchand *Dr Paul Charmant* • Paul Freeman *Tom* • Andre Penvern *Concierge* • Emmanuel Fouquet *Porter* ■ *Dir* Carol Wiseman • *Scr* Carol Wiseman, from a screenplay (unproduced) by Peter Lefcourt

Maya ★★★ 15

Drama 1992 · Ind/UK · Colour · 121mins

Ketan Mehta emerged as one of India's foremost directors with *Mirch Masala* and he further enhanced his reputation with this imaginative adaptation of Flaubert's *Madame Bovary*. Set in the days following independence from Britain, Mehta manages to be faithful to the spirit of the novel while also developing his own themes, using Deepa Sahi's passionate fantasies and unrewarding affairs to highlight the mood of the Indian people in 1949, torn between the notion of nationhood and nostalgia for the Raj. DP. In Hindi with English subtitles.

Deepa Sahi *Maya* • Farooque Sheikh *Charudatta Das* • Raj Babbar *Rudrapratap Singh* • Shah Rukh Khan *Lalit Kumar* • Satyadev Dubey *Old interrogator* • Shrivallabh Vyas *Young interrogator* • Dr Shree Ram Lagoo *Maya's father* ■ *Dir* Ketan Mehta • *Scr* Sitanshu Yashashchandra, Ketan Mehta

Maybe Baby ★ 15

Romantic comedy
1999 · UK · Colour · 100mins

Debut writer/director Ben Elton tries and fails to step into the winning comedy shoes of erstwhile *Blackadder* partner Richard Curtis. Revolving around Hugh Laurie and Joely Richardson's attempts to have a child, this is a clichéd, caricatured and dreadfully acted tale, while Elton's direction is colourless. JC DVD

Hugh Laurie *Sam Bell* • Joely Richardson *Lucy Bell* • Adrian Lester *George* • James Purefoy *Carl Phipps* • Tom Hollander *Ewan Proclaimer* • Joanna Lumley *Sheila* • Emma Thompson *Druscilla* • Rowan Atkinson *Mr James* • Dawn French *Charlene* ■ *Dir/Scr* Ben Elton

Mayerling ★★★★

Historical romance 1936 · Fr · BW · 96mins

An exquisite French account of one of history's most famous and poignant love affairs: that of Crown Prince Rudolph, heir to the Austro-Hungarian throne, and the youthful Marie Vetsera, a well-born commoner. Denied a release from his loveless marriage, Rudolph and Marie escape for a 24-hour idyll to Mayerling, his hunting lodge, at the end of which he shoots her and then himself in a suicide pact. Charles Boyer and Danielle Darrieux are faultlessly cast as the ill-fated lovers under Anatole Litvak's stylish and sensitive direction. The film led to a Hollywood contract for Litvak and made an international heart-throb of Boyer. RK. A French language film.

Charles Boyer *Archduke Rudolph of Austria* • Danielle Darrieux *Marie Vetsera* • Suzy Prim *Countess Larisch* • Jean Dax *Emperor Franz Joseph* • Gabrielle Dorziat *Empress Elizabeth* • Jean Debucourt *Count Taafe* • Marthe Régnier *Baroness Vetsera/Helene* ■ *Dir* Anatole Litvak • *Scr* Joseph Kessel, Irma Von Cube, from the novel by Claude Anet

Mayerling ★★ PG

Historical romance
1968 · Fr/UK · Colour · 132mins

Omar Sharif is Crown Prince Rudolf of Austria, helplessly in love with young Marie Vetsera (Catherine Deneuve). Unable to free himself from his marriage, he enters a suicide pact with his lover. After spending 24 idyllic hours together at Mayerling, his country retreat, he shoots her and then himself. This love story was definitively filmed in France in 1936 by Anatole Litvak. Terence Young's version is overblown, unmoving and overlong, with the presence of James Mason, Ava Gardner and Genevieve Page adding only surface gloss. RK

Omar Sharif *Crown Prince Rudolf* • Catherine Deneuve *Baroness Maria Vetsera* • James Mason *Emperor Franz Josef* • Ava Gardner *Empress Elizabeth* • James Robertson-Justice *Edward, Prince of Wales* • Genevieve Page *Countess Larisch* ■ *Dir* Terence Young • *Scr* Terence Young, Denis Cannan, Joseph Kessel, from the novel by Claude Anet and the novel *The Archduke* by Michael Arnold

The Mayor of Hell ★★

Crime drama 1933 · US · BW · 85mins

A typical Warner Bros social melodrama, with James Cagney as a racketeer who suddenly takes an interest in a reform school and the conditions of the youngsters inside. Will he corrupt them or does he become a do-gooder? Despite Cagney's energy, the picture is hopelessly dated, full of mawkish moments, dire knockabout humour and bouts of violence as Cagney carries on with his profession. AT

James Cagney *Patsy Gargan* • Madge Evans *Dorothy Griffith* • Arthur Byron *Judge Gilbert* • Allen Jenkins *Mike* • Dudley Digges *Thompson* • Frankie Darro *Jimmy Smith* • Sheila Terry *The girl* ■ *Dir* Archie Mayo • *Scr* Edward Chodorov, from a story by Islin Auster

Mayor of the Sunset Strip ★★★ 15

Biographical musical documentary
2003 · US · Colour and BW · 93mins

An unlikely hybrid of John Peel and Andy Warhol, Rodney Bingenheimer moved from the fringes of the 1960s music scene to become a hugely influential Los Angeles radio DJ, bringing glam rock and punk across the Atlantic, and went on to champion more recent bands such as Coldplay. This intriguing music documentary, which is packed with contributions from the likes of David Bowie, Cher, Deborah Harry and Oasis, also offers us an insight into the private disillusionment of a wannabe who never really received the credit he deserved. As a shrewdly observed indictment of celebrity and disposable culture. DP. Contains swearing.

Dir/Scr George Hickenlooper

Maytime ★★★★ U

Romantic musical
1937 · US · Sepia · 131mins

Singing duo Jeanette MacDonald and Nelson Eddy were in their prime in this splendid version of Rida Johnson Young and Sigmund Romberg's melancholy operetta, and the theme song *Will You Remember?* became for ever identified with them. The classy MGM production is particularly lavish, and director Robert Z Leonard manages a marvellous tragic tone, unusual for this type of mainstream light entertainment. The film is further enhanced by the presence of the great John Barrymore, in one of his last worthwhile roles. TS

Jeanette MacDonald *Miss Morrison/Marcia Morney* • Nelson Eddy *Paul Allison* • John Barrymore *Nicolai Nazaroff* • Herman Bing *August Archipenco* • Tom Brown *Kip Stuart* • Lynn Carver [Lynne Carver] *Barbara Roberts* • Rafaela Ottiano *Ellen* ■ *Dir* Robert Z Leonard • *Scr* Noel Langley, from the operetta by Rida Johnson Young, Sigmund Romberg

Maytime in Mayfair ★★★ U

Romantic musical
1949 · UK · Colour · 98mins

This is virtually a remake of the previous year's Anna Neagle/Michael Wilding smash hit *Spring in Park Lane*. The plot resembles an earlier Neagle movie, *Irene*, with its dress-shop rivalry, once so fashionable and today so dated. Neagle looks rather too old and staid to partner the charming Wilding, but a hard-working supporting cast keeps the fun bubbling. TS

Anna Neagle *Eileen Grahame* • Michael Wilding *Michael Gore-Brown* • Peter Graves (1) *D'Arcy Davenport* • Nicholas Phipps *Sir Henry Hazelrigg* • Thora Hird *Janet* • Michael Shepley *Shepherd* • Tom Walls *Inspector* ■ *Dir* Herbert Wilcox • *Scr* Nicholas Phipps

The Maze ★★★

Horror 1953 · US · BW · 80mins

Filmed in monochrome 3-D (but since made available in a duo-colour print), this adaptation was an early venture into stereoscopy. As you'd expect of someone with William Cameron Menzies's genius for art design, this atmospheric shocker, set in an isolated Scottish castle, looks superb (in spite of some of the more gimmicky shots). However, there's little tension in Veronica Hurst's pursuit of runaway fiancé Richard Carlson, who is now a prematurely aged recluse. Moreover, the supposedly Kafkaesque resolution is more than slightly preposterous. DP

Richard Carlson *Gerald McTeam* • Veronica Hurst *Kitty Murray* • Katherine Emery *Mrs Murray* • Michael Pate *William* • John Dodsworth *Dr Bert Dilling* ■ *Dir* William Cameron Menzies • *Scr* Dan Ullman [Daniel B Ullman], from a novel by Maurice Sandoz

Me & Isaac Newton ★★★

Documentary 2000 · US · Colour · 105mins

Although he's had his share of blockbusters, Michael Apted has never forgotten his roots in documentary. Following his study of artistic endeavour in Inspirations, he turns his attention to scientific genius in this lively and accessible survey. It's a talking heads affair, but this is anything but dry and academic. There are genuinely touching moments, like Nobel laureate Gertrude Elion's recollection of the fiancé whose death sparked her interest in chemistry. But everyone has something interesting to say, whether it's Steven Pinker ascribing his love of language to his argumentative parents or string-theorist Michio Kaku considering the therapeutic benefits of ice skating. DP

Dir Michael Apted

Me and My Gal ★★★

Comedy drama 1932 · US · BW · 78mins

This charming but creaky 20th Century-Fox comedy drama is given a lift by its tart dialogue and the naturalistic playing of stars Spencer Tracy and Joan Bennett. The bulk of the plot turns out to be some nonsense about Bennett's sister falling for a gangster, with Tracy playing a cop who's keen on Bennett. Director Raoul Walsh tries to keep sentimentality at bay, but the whole turns out to be rather ramshackle, if short and sweet. TS

Spencer Tracy *Danny Dolan* • Joan Bennett *Helen Riley* • Marion Burns *Kate Riley* • George Walsh *Duke Castenega* • J Farrell MacDonald *Pat "Pop" Riley* • Noel Madison *Baby Face* • Henry B Walthall *Sarge* • Bert Hanlon *Jake* ■ *Dir* Raoul Walsh • *Scr* Arthur Kober, Frank J Dolan (uncredited), Philip Dunne (uncredited), Charles Vidor (uncredited), Al Cohn (uncredited), from a story by Barry Connors, from a story by Phillip Klein

Me and the Colonel ★★★ U

Second World War comedy
1958 · US · BW · 105mins

Danny Kaye gained new admirers with his subdued performance and altered appearance in this serious comedy, playing one half of an odd couple: a self-effacing, resourceful Jew fleeing the German occupation of Paris in 1940. Joining the journey of escape is an arrogant, aristocratic Polish colonel, played by Curt Jurgens, who ultimately overcomes his anti-Semitism. Director Peter Glenville draws finely judged performances from his leads, and there are some expert supporting performances, particularly from Martita Hunt as a mother superior. AE [video]

Danny Kaye *SL Jacobowsky* • Curt Jurgens *Colonel Tadeusz Boleslav Prokoszny* • Nicole Maurey *Suzanne Roualet* • Françoise Rosay *Madame Bouffier* • Akim Tamiroff *Szabuniewicz* • Martita Hunt *Mother Superior* • Alexander Scourby *Major Von Bergen* ■ *Dir* Peter Glenville • *Scr* George Froeschel, SN Behrman, from the play *Jacobowsky and the Colonel* by Franz Werfel

Me and the Kid ★★

Crime comedy drama
1993 · US · Colour · 97mins

In this plodding semi-comedy, bungling burglars break into a rich man's home, find the safe empty and decide to kidnap the rich guy's neglected kid instead. The thieves fall out when one decides to return the boy, only to find that he prefers his new life and doesn't want to go back. Poor pacing makes the film heavy going. DA. Contains some swearing.

Danny Aiello *Harry* • Alex Zuckerman *Gary Feldman* • Joe Pantoliano *Roy* • Cathy Moriarty *Rose* • David Dukes *Victor Feldman* • Anita Morris *Mrs Feldman* ■ *Dir* Dan Curtis • *Scr* Richard Tannenbaum, from the novel *Taking Gary Feldman* by Stanley Cohen

Me and the Mob ★★ 15

Crime comedy 1992 · US · Colour · 83mins

Corny crime caper with James Lorinz as an author suffering from writer's block who joins the Mob to get some background information for his next book. An insignificant release at the time, this energetic but inane comedy has more resonance now due to the presence of Sandra Bullock in a small role. Steve Buscemi also makes a fleeting appearance. DF [video] DVD

James Lorinz *Jimmy Corona* • Stephen Lee *Bobby Blitzer* • Sandra Bullock *Lori* • Tony Darrow *Tony Bando* • Vinny Pastore [Vincent Pastore] *"Birdman" Badamo* • Frank Gio *"Fixer" Giachetti* • John Costelloe *"Bink-Bink" Borelli* • Steve Buscemi *Conspiracy nut* ■ *Dir* Frank Rainone • *Scr* Rocco Simonelli, James Lorinz, Frank Rainone

Me, Myself & Irene ★★★ 15

Comedy 2000 · US · Colour · 116mins

As a Rhode Island state trooper, Jim Carrey's a sweet-hearted loser falls in love with Renée Zellweger, even though he's lumbered with three delightful grown-up black sons from his wife's adulterous liaison. Unfortunately, his vicious alter-ego has also fallen for her, and comic mayhem ensues as when Jekyll wrestles with Hyde for Zellweger's affections. The jokes are outrageously tasteless, but the movie delivers its vulgarity with almost surreal panache. TH. Contains violence, swearing, nudity. [video] DVD

Jim Carrey *Charlie Baileygates/Hank* • Renée Zellweger [Renee Zellweger] *Irene P White* • Chris Cooper *Lieutenant Gerke* • Robert Forster *Colonel Partington* ■ *Dir* Bobby Farrelly, Peter Farrelly • *Scr* Peter Farrelly, Mike Cerrone, Bobby Farrelly

Me Myself I ★★★★ 15

Romantic comedy fantasy
1999 · Fr/Aus · Colour · 100mins

Rachel Griffiths delivers an engaging performance as a single 30-something journalist who wonders what would have happened if she had married her former sweetheart David Roberts and settled down to the life of a housewife and mother. After a freak (and never explained) occurrence, she wakes up to discover that her old life has disappeared and she is *that* woman, complete with annoying children and a sexless marriage. Brilliantly written and directed by Pip Karmel, this realistically presents the pros and cons of both of lives, while Griffiths proves she has a deft comic touch. JB [video]

Rachel Griffiths *Pamela* • David Roberts *Robert* • Sandy Winton *Ben* • Yael Stone *Stacey* • Shaun Loseby *Douglas* • Trent Sullivan *Rupert* • Rebecca Frith *Terri* • Felix Williamson *Geoff* ■ *Dir/Scr* Pip Karmel

Me without You ★★★★ 15

Comedy drama
2001 · UK/Ger · Colour · 103mins

This film about female friendship was a deserved hit for director Sandra Goldbacher at the Venice film festival. Detailing the relationship between childhood friends Anna Friel and Michelle Williams, the film follows the girls from 1970s spacehoppers through teenage sex, drugs and rock 'n' roll, to university and into the present day. The fabulous attention to period detail is matched by equally strong emotional observation, as the difference between Friel's brittle bitch and Williams's bright but delicate innocent gets more exaggerated and the friendship disintegrates from undying loyalty to an almost claustrophobic curse. LH [video] DVD

Anna Friel *Marina* • Michelle Williams *Holly* • Kyle MacLachlan *Daniel* • Oliver Milburn *Nat* • Trudie Styler *Linda* • Marianne Denicourt *Isabel* • Nicky Henson *Ray* ■ *Dir* Sandra Goldbacher • *Scr* Sandra Goldbacher, Laurence Coriat

Me, You, Them ★★★ PG

Comedy drama
2000 · Bra/US/Por · Colour · 102mins

This is an amiable, if unambitious, attempt to explore socio-sexual mores in a tightly knit Brazilian community. Regina Case romps through the fact-based proceedings as the jilted bride amassing a motley collection of beaus and babies. But much of the humour is centred on cuckolded chauvinist Lima Duarte and Stenio Garcia, the poacher who turns gamekeeper when Case begins spending her lunch hours cavorting in the fields with handsome drifter Luiz Carlos Vasconcelos. Andrucha Waddington employs camera and character intelligently, but this is largely undemanding fare. DP. In Portuguese with English subtitles. [video]

Regina Case *Darlene* • Lima Duarte *Osias Linhares* • Stenio Garcia *Zezinho* • Luiz Carlos Vasconcelos *Ciro* • Nilda Spencer *Raquel* ■ *Dir* Andrucha Waddington • *Scr* Elena Soarez

Mean Creek ★★★★ 15

Thriller 2004 · US · Colour · 89mins

Rory Culkin gives a more-than-competent performance in this compelling tale of teenage revenge, playing an unremarkable schoolkid who is harassed by bully Josh Peck. When his older brother (Trevor Morgan) finds out about it, he cooks up a plan for some payback with town bad-boy Scott Mechlowicz. This is a gripping, original thriller that boasts an unusual level of moral engagement and is studded with outstanding performances. Jacob Aaron Estes, in his debut feature, takes what could have been hackneyed material and transforms it into something surprising and serious. AS. Contains swearing and sexual references.

Rory Culkin *Sam* • Ryan Kelley *Clyde* • Scott Mechlowicz *Marty* • Trevor Morgan *Rocky* • Josh Peck *George* • Carly Schroeder *Millie* • James W Crawford *Tom* ■ *Dir/Scr* Jacob Aaron Estes

Mean Dog Blues ★★ 18

Prison drama 1978 · US · Colour · 104mins

After a hit-and-run incident, musician Gregg Henry ends up in prison and comes up against nasty guard George Kennedy. Prison is predictably hell – especially in a chain gang. Director Mel Stuart has had a varied career that includes *Willy Wonka and the Chocolate Factory*, but despite his efforts, this is basically a B-movie with slim production values. TH [video]

Gregg Henry *Paul Ramsey* • Kay Lenz *Linda Ramsey* • Scatman Crothers *Mudcat* • Tina Louise *Donna Lacey* • Felton Perry *Jake Turner* • Gregory Sierra *Jesus Gonzales* • James Wainwright *Sergeant Hubbell Wacker* • George Kennedy *Captain Omar Kinsman* ■ *Dir* Mel Stuart • *Scr* George Lefferts

Mean Girls ★★★ 12

Comedy 2004 · US · Colour · 92mins

Inspired by a real life high-school survival manual for teenage girls and their mothers, this is a bracingly dark comedy. Lindsay Lohan stars as a bright, pretty kid who has been home-schooled in Africa by her anthropologist parents, and is thrown in at the deep end when she attends high school in the US for the first time. Befriended by the geek clique, she also infiltrates the "plastics" – a troika of Barbie-like popular girls. Despite descending into slightly saccharine moralising towards the end, this is a snappily written, acerbic account of the American high-school experience. AS. Contains swearing and sexual references. [video] DVD

Lindsay Lohan *Cady Heron* • Rachel McAdams *Regina George* • Tina Fey *Ms Norbury* • Tim Meadows *Mr Duvall* • Amy Poehler *Mrs George* • Ana Gasteyer *Betsy Heron* • Lacey Chabert *Gretchen Wieners* • Lizzy Caplan *Janis Ian* • Daniel Franzese *Damian* • Neil Flynn *Chip Heron* ■ *Dir* Mark S Waters [Mark Waters] • *Scr* Tina Fey, from the non-fiction book *Queen Bees and Wannabes: Helping Your Daughter Survive Cliques, Gossip, Boyfriends and Other Realities of Adolescence* by Rosalind Wiseman

Mean Guns ★★★ 18

Action thriller 1996 · US · Colour · 93mins

Highlander star Christopher Lambert and rapper Ice-T strut their lethal stuff in this blood-soaked and slightly surreal action thriller. Ice-T is a sinister gangster who invites scores of criminal honchos, including troubled hitman Lambert, to an empty prison to atone for their sins against the syndicate. There they must fight each other to the death, with the last three survivors emerging with $10 million so they can retire from crime forever. Set-bound but stylish, it is one of the better films from director Albert Pyun. JF [video]

Christopher Lambert *Lou* • Ice-T *Vincent Moon* • Michael Halsey *Marcus* • Deborah Van Valkenburgh *Cam* • Tina Cote *Barbie* • Yuji Okumoto *Hoss* ■ *Dir* Albert Pyun • *Scr* Andrew Witham, Nat Whitcomb

The Mean Machine ★★★★ 15

Prison sports comedy
1974 · US · Colour · 121mins

This is the film that fixed Burt Reynolds's "good old boy" image in the minds of audiences everywhere and helped propel him to superstardom. Reynolds exudes star quality as an imprisoned football pro who's forced to organise a team of

M

convicts for a match against their guards. Full of references to *The Dirty Dozen* and the corrupt regime of President Nixon, Robert Aldrich's feature is a little heavy-handed as a political satire. But as a boisterous comedy, with a few choice asides on dignity, loyalty and liberty, it's pretty hard to beat. Released in the US as *The Longest Yard*, the UK DVD release is also under this title. DP [video] DVD

Burt Reynolds *Paul Crewe* • Eddie Albert *Warden Hazen* • Ed Lauter *Captain Knauer* • Michael Conrad *Nate Scarboro* • Jim Hampton [James Hampton] *Caretaker* • Harry Caesar *Granville* • John Steadman *Pop* • Charles Tyner *Unger* ■ *Dir* Robert Aldrich • *Scr* Tracy Keenan Wynn, from a story by Albert S Ruddy

Mean Machine ★★★ 15

Prison sports comedy
2001 · US/UK · Colour · 95mins

Vinnie Jones doesn't stray too far from home for his first leading part, starring in this remake of Robert Aldrich's 1974 movie. If you can overlook the rather thin characters and simplistic plot, the film's final third – an ill-tempered soccer match between warders and inmates – is very well filmed and entertaining. Jones isn't bad in a made-to-measure role, though the movie's best shots on goal come from Jason Statham's maverick keeper and Jason Flemyng's unconventional commentator. JC [video] DVD

Vinnie Jones *Danny Meehan* • David Kelly *Doc* • David Hemmings *Governor* • Ralph Brown *Burton* • Vas Blackwood *Massive* • Robbie Gee *Trojan* • Jason Flemyng *Bob Likely* • Jason Statham *Monk* ■ *Dir* Barry Skolnick • *Scr* Barry Fletcher, Chris Baker, Andrew Day, from the 1974 film by Tracy Keenan Wynn, from a story by Albert S Ruddy

M

The Mean Season ★★★ 15

Thriller 1985 · US · Colour · 103mins

This is a cracker of a thriller, marred only by some seriously duff moments, most notably supplied by poor Mariel Hemingway, who is saddled with the weak "girlfriend under threat from a psychopath" role. Her boyfriend is cynical journalist Kurt Russell, who gives a mesmerising performance as a man who finds himself dragged further into his latest crime story than is comfortable. A taut, atmospheric and potentially distressing movie, with the odd dull spell. SH. Contains violence, swearing and nudity. [video] DVD

Kurt Russell *Malcolm Anderson* • Mariel Hemingway *Christine Connelly* • Richard Jordan *Alan Delour* • Richard Masur *Bill Nolan* • Joe Pantoliano *Andy Porter* • Richard Bradford *Phil Wilson* • Andy Garcia *Ray Martinez* ■ *Dir* Phillip Borsos • *Scr* Leon Piedmont, from the novel *In the Heat of the Summer* by John Katzenbach

Mean Streets ★★★★ 18

Drama 1973 · US · Colour · 107mins

In his breakthrough film, director Martin Scorsese drew on his upbringing in New York's Little Italy for this semi-autobiographical story about two friends. Harvey Keitel is the older of the two and a debt-collector for the Mob, while tearaway hoodlum Robert De Niro is in hock to loan sharks. This explicitly European-influenced film establishes Scorsese's masterful use of music, mixing a 1960s pop soundtrack with grubby pool-hall violence. This keystone of 1970s American cinema hinges on the power of its lead performances; Keitel exhibits simmering anguish as he struggles to reconcile his religion and lifestyle while dating the epileptic Amy Robinson against his boss's wishes, while the freewheeling De Niro is full of edgy humour, life and barely concealed danger. AC. Contains violence and swearing. [video] DVD

Harvey Keitel *Charlie* • Robert De Niro *Johnny Boy* • David Proval *Tony* • Amy Robinson *Teresa* • Richard Romanus *Michael* • Cesare Danova *Giovanni* • Vic Argo [Victor Argo] *Mario* • Robert Carradine *Assassin* ■ *Dir* Martin Scorsese • *Scr* Martin Scorsese, Mardik Martin, from a story by Martin Scorsese

The Meanest Man in the World ★★★ U

Comedy 1943 · US · BW · 57mins

This is a cracking vehicle for the inimitable partnership of Jack Benny and Eddie "Rochester" Anderson. Few comics could milk a gag as well as Benny, whose expression, as he steals a lollipop from a child in an effort to prove to both his prospective father-in-law and millionaire Edmund Gwenn that he is a lawyer to be reckoned with, is priceless. Priscilla Lane is under-used as Benny's fiancée, but Anne Revere is splendid as his wavering secretary. DP

Jack Benny *Richard Clark* • Priscilla Lane *Janie Brown* • Eddie "Rochester" Anderson *Shufro* • Edmund Gwenn *Frederick P Leggitt* • Matt Briggs *Mr Brown* • Anne Revere *Kitty Crockett* • Margaret Seddon *Mrs Leggitt* • Harry Hayden *Mr Chambers* ■ *Dir* Sidney Lanfield • *Scr* George Seaton, Allan House, from a play by Augustin MacHugh, George M Cohan

Meatballs ★★ 15

Comedy 1979 · Can · Colour · 89mins

This early collaboration for *Ghostbusters* director Ivan Reitman and Bill Murray is solely dependent on its star for laughs, and there aren't that many. Murray plays a goofy counsellor at a Canadian summer camp who takes a young loner under his wing. No better or worse than dozens of other similarly-plotted comedies, but Reitman has the good sense to get Murray on screen as often as possible. JC [video]

Bill Murray *Tripper* • Harvey Atkin *Morty* • Kate Lynch *Roxanne* • Russ Banham *Crockett* • Kristine DeBell *AL* • Sarah Torgov *Candace* • Jack Blum *Spaz* • Keith Knight *Fink* ■ *Dir* Ivan Reitman • *Scr* Len Blum, Dan Goldberg, Janis Allen, Harold Ramis

Meatballs 2 ★ 15

Comedy 1984 · US · Colour · 83mins

Quite why it took five years to come up with this sequel is a mystery, since they seem to be making it up as they go along. This time, the plot revolves around a big boxing match, but Richard Mulligan is no Bill Murray. The only bright spots come from the weirdness of Paul Reubens, aka Pee-wee Herman. JC [video]

Archie Hahn *Jamie* • John Mengatti *Flash* • Tammy Taylor *Nancy* • Kim Richards *Cheryl* • Ralph Seymour *Eddie* • Richard Mulligan *Giddy* • Hamilton Camp *Hershey* • John Larroquette *Foxglove* • Paul Reubens *Albert* ■ *Dir* Ken Wiederhorn • *Scr* Bruce Singer, from a story by Martin Kitrosser, Carol Watson

Meatballs III: Summer Job ★★ 18

Comedy 1987 · US · Colour · 89mins

The original *Meatballs* was notable only for the fact that it gave an early starring role to Bill Murray. Two sequels on, this mix of smut and slapstick looks very dated indeed. Patrick Dempsey plays a randy young teen at summer camp desperate to lose his virginity and receiving unexpected help from a ghostly porn queen (Sally Kellerman). JF. Contains swearing and sex scenes. [video]

Sally Kellerman *Roxy Du Jour* • Patrick Dempsey *Rudy Gerner* • Al Waxman *Saint Peter* • Isabelle Mejias *Wendy* • Shannon Tweed *The Love Goddess* • Jan Taylor *Rita* • George Buza *Mean Gene* ■ *Dir* George Mendeluk • *Scr* Michael Paseornek, Bradley Kesden, from a story by Chuck Workman

The Mechanic ★★★ 15

Action thriller 1972 · US · Colour · 95mins

No-frills direction from Michael Winner creates the right tone of seething disquiet for star Charles Bronson in this forerunner to *Death Wish*. No one is better at suggesting silent menace than Bronson, who here plays a hitman capable of making his messy work look accidental and training a young pretender to the throne. Winner, though sometimes disrupting the action with unnecessary gloss, keeps his film suspenseful. JM Contains violence and swearing. [video] DVD

Charles Bronson *Arthur Bishop* • Jan-Michael Vincent *Steve McKenna* • Keenan Wynn *Harry McKenna* • Jill Ireland *Prostitute* • Linda Ridgeway *Louise* • Frank De Kova *Syndicate head* • Lindsay H Crosby *Policeman* ■ *Dir* Michael Winner • *Scr* Lewis John Carlino

A Medal for Benny ★★★ U

Satirical drama 1945 · US · BW · 80mins

Though Benny himself is never seen, his trouble-making has got him evicted from the small town on the California coast, home to Mexican immigrants. Then his shamed family and the townspeople learn he's a war hero, having killed 100 Japanese single-handed before being killed himself. Interesting, untypical casting and a semi-satirical script that manages (just) to veer off easy sentimentality make this little-known picture well worth a look. The story, partly by John Steinbeck, was Oscar-nominated. AT

Dorothy Lamour *Lolita Sierra* • Arturo de Cordova *Joe Morales* • J Carrol Naish *Charley Martin* • Mikhail Rasumny *Raphael Catalina* • Fernando Alvarado *Chito Sierra* • Charles Dingle *Zach Mibbs* • Frank McHugh *Edgar Lovekin* • Douglass Dumbrille *General* ■ *Dir* Irving Pichel • *Scr* Frank Butler, Jack Wagner, from a story by Jack Wagner, John Steinbeck

The Medallion ★ PG

Action fantasy
2003 · HK/US · Colour · 84mins

In a Jackie Chan film only two elements really matter: the chemistry between the two inevitable buddies/partners and the quality of the action. Sadly both are well below par in this Dublin-set farrago. Chan stars as a cop whose search for evil crime lord Julian Sands leads to the discovery of an ancient medallion and a kidnapped boy. Looking like it was edited on a bacon slicer, this mess couldn't possibly get any worse until Lee Evans applies the tin lid with an excruciating performance. AS [video] DVD

Jackie Chan *Eddie Yang* • Lee Evans *Arthur Watson* • Claire Forlani *Nicole James* • Julian Sands *Snakehead* • John Rhys-Davies *Commander Hammerstock-Smythe* • Anthony Wong (1) *Lester Wong* ■ *Dir* Gordon Chan • *Scr* Bey Logan, Gordon Chan, Alfred Cheung, Bennett Joshua Davlin, Paul Wheeler, from a story by Alfred Cheung, from characters created by Alfred Cheung

Medea ★★ PG

Tragedy
1970 · It/Fr/W Ger · Colour · 105mins

Following his 1967 adaptation of Sophocles's *Oedipus Rex*, this was Pier Paolo Pasolini's second venture into Greek mythology. But this version of Euripides's play suffers as much from miscasting as it does from lacklustre direction. Opera legend Maria Callas is stripped of much of her power by the fact that her voice is dubbed, while Giuseppe Gentile brings little but physique to the part of Jason. The locations have been exploited to the full, but Pasolini's overambitious mix of myth, Marxism and psychology makes for heavy going. DP. In Italian with English subtitles. [video]

Maria Callas *Medea* • Giuseppe Gentile *Jason* • Massimo Girotti *Creon* • Laurent Terzieff *Centaur* • Margareth Clementi *Glauce* ■ *Dir* Pier Paolo Pasolini • *Scr* Pier Paolo Pasolini, from the play by Euripides

Medea ★★★

Tragedy 1988 · Den · Colour · 76mins

Danish director Lars von Trier's version of Euripedes's classical tragedy has an icy calm and muted colours that give its locations an unworldly feel. Working from an unproduced 1960s screenplay by influential Danish director Carl Theodor Dreyer and poet Preben Thomsen, von Trier artfully uses his video camera to approximate Dreyer's atmospheric austerity. But the bravura technique and liberal interpretation are pure von Trier. DP. In Danish with English subtitles.

Kirsten Olesen *Medea* • Udo Kier *Jason* ■ *Dir* Lars von Trier • *Scr* Lars von Trier, from a screenplay (unproduced) by Preben Thomsen, Carl Theodor Dreyer [Carl Th Dreyer], from the play by Euripides

Medicine Man ★★ PG

Drama 1992 · US · Colour · 100mins

Giving an effortlessly charismatic performance, Sean Connery overcomes an unfocused script and an even worse ponytail. He plays a grumpy scientist who has discovered a cure for cancer deep in the heart of the South American rainforest, but is now unable to reproduce it. He also has to cope with the twin threats of destructive developers and Lorraine Bracco (badly miscast), who has been sent to supervise him. JF [video]

Sean Connery *Dr Robert Campbell* • Lorraine Bracco *Dr Rae Crane* • José Wilker *Dr Miguel Ornega* • Rodolfo De Alexandre *Tanaki* • Francisco Tsirene Tsere Rereme *Jahausa* • Elias Monteiro Da Silva *Palala* • Edinei Maria Serrio Dos Santos *Kalana* ■ *Dir* John McTiernan • *Scr* Tom Schulman, Sally Robinson

Mediterraneo ★★★★ 15

Comedy drama 1991 · It · Colour · 86mins

As with so many recent winners of the Oscar for best foreign language film, this is an undemanding picture closer to the Hollywood brand of light entertainment than to art house *gravitas*. Set in a largely forgotten theatre of the Second World War, the action centres on eight Italian soldiers sent to guard the strategically negligible Greek island of Kastellorizo. The interaction between the mismatched squad and its increasingly amicable relationship with the islanders throws up few novel situations, but everything is done with such sleepy good humour that it makes for easy watching. DP. In Italian with English subtitles. [video] DVD

Claudio Bigagli *Lieutenant Montini* • Giuseppe Cederna *Farina* • Claudio Bisio *Noventa* • Gigio Alberti *Strazzabosco* • Ugo Conti *Colosanti* • Memo Dini *Felice Munaron* • Vasco Mirondola *Libero Munaron* ■ *Dir* Gabriele Salvatores • *Scr* Vincenzo Monteleone

The Medium ★★

Opera 1951 · US · BW · 80mins

A fake medium is driven to murder by her paranoiac fear of a resentful spirit world in Gian-Carlo Menotti's adaptation of his own one-act opera. It might have made for an atmospheric night at the theatre, but it falls prey to staginess and bombast when subjected to the unforgiving gaze of the camera. Both opera lovers and film fans will find this a frustrating experience, despite a spirited performance from Marie Powers. DP

Marie Powers *Mme Flora* • Anna Maria Alberghetti *Monica* • Leo Coleman *Toby* • Belva Kibler *Mrs Nolan* • Beverly Dame *Mrs*

Gobineau • Donald Morgan *Mr Gobineau* ■ *Dir* Gian-Carlo Menotti • *Scr* Gian-Carlo Menotti, from his opera

Medium Cool ★★★★★

Drama 1969 · US · Colour · 110mins

The Oscar-winning cameraman Haskell Wexler turned director with this semi-documentary study of America's political temperature in the turbulent late-1960s. Robert Forster plays a TV news cameraman who covers various major events, notably the riots at the Democratic Convention in Chicago, while trying to prevent his personal life from falling apart. Much of the movie's thrust derives from media pundit Marshall McLuhan's dictum that "the medium is the message". The film's flaws are obvious, but never mind: this is a provocative and hugely influential movie that ends on a note of deep pessimism with the famous chant, "The whole world is watching". AT

Robert Forster *John Cassellis* • Verna Bloom *Eileen Horton* • Peter Bonerz *Gus* • Marianna Hill *Ruth* • Harold Blankenship *Harold Horton* • Sid McCoy *Frank Baker* ■ *Dir* Haskell Wexler • *Scr* Haskell Wexler, from the novel *The Concrete Wilderness* by Jack Couffer • *Cinematographer* Haskell Wexler

The Medusa Touch ★★★ PG

Supernatural thriller
1978 · UK/Fr · Colour · 104mins

This is a quietly effective thriller that combines the kinetic thrills of a disaster movie with *Omen*-style shocks. Richard Burton is a novelist driven to the brink of insanity by his murderous mental powers, while Lee Remick is the psychiatrist attempting to piece together the puzzle. Director Jack Gold keeps this amiable tosh ticking along, aided by some spectacular disaster footage and an impressive roster of British support players. RS [video] DVD

Richard Burton *John Morlar* • Lee Remick *Dr Zonfeld* • Lino Ventura *Detective Inspector Brunel* • Harry Andrews *Assistant Commissioner* • Marie-Christine Barrault *Patricia Morlar* • Michael Hordern *Atropos* • Gordon Jackson *Dr Johnson* • Derek Jacobi *Townley* ■ *Dir* Jack Gold • *Scr* John Briley, Jack Gold, from a novel by Peter Van Greenaway

Meet Boston Blackie ★★★

Detective drama 1941 · US · BW · 60mins

Pulp novelist Jack Boyle's thief-turned-troubleshooter debuted on screen in 1918. But this film, directed with aplomb by Robert Florey, launched Columbia's 14-strong B series, which boasted Chester Morris as the wisecracking maverick with an eye for the girls and a nose for trouble. Richard Lane was ever present as the perpetually suspicious Inspector Farraday (here as Faraday), as was Morris's sidekick, The Runt (played here by Charles Wagenhaim and later by George E Stone and then Sid Tomack, for the franchise finale). Lloyd Corrigan had an occasional role in the series as thrill-seeking playboy Arthur Manleder. Diamonds, jailbreaks and murder feature strongly, as does Morris's penchant for magic. DP

Chester Morris *Boston Blackie/Horatio Black* • Rochelle Hudson *Cecelia Bradley* • Richard Lane *Inspector Faraday* • Charles Wagenheim *The Runt* • Constance Worth *Marilyn Howard* • Nestor Paiva *Martin Vestrick* ■ *Dir* Robert Florey • *Scr* Jay Dratler, from a story by Jay Dratler, from the character created by by Jack Boyle

Meet Danny Wilson ★★★

Musical drama 1952 · US · BW · 87mins

Frank Sinatra stars a crooner who rises to the top through his ultimately disastrous association with a racketeering thug (Raymond Burr). Playing a role that, in the context of the star's own life, is pretty close to the bone, Ol' Blue Eyes does justice to his twin talents as actor and singer in a tight drama, directed by Joseph Pevney and laced with some of Frank's best-loved standards. Shelley Winters is the girl caught between Sinatra and his best friend, Alex Nicol. RK

Frank Sinatra *Danny Wilson* • Shelley Winters *Joy Carroll* • Alex Nicol *Mike Ryan* • Raymond Burr *Nick Driscoll* • Tommy Farrell *Tommy Wells* • Vaughn Taylor *TW Hatcher* • Donald MacBride *Sergeant* • Barbara Knudson *Marie* • Tony Curtis *Man in nightclub* ■ *Dir* Joseph Pevney • *Scr* Don McGuire, from his story

Meet Dr Christian ★★★ U

Medical drama 1939 · US · BW · 63mins

This is the first in a six-film series spun-off from a long-running radio show inspired by the exploits of Allan Dafoe, the Canadian medic who famously delivered the Dionne Quintuplets. Having played the good doctor in three previous films, Jean Hersholt (the Danish star after whom the Oscar people named their Humanitarian Award) was the natural choice to headline these sentimental B-movies, in which his folksy wisdom was as crucial to the citizens of River's End, Minnesota, as his surgical skill. Nurse Dorothy Lovett's complicated love life, housekeeper Maude Eburne's kvetching and storekeeper Edgar Kennedy's irritability leavened Hersholt's saintliness with some much-needed human foibles. DP

Jean Hersholt *Dr Christian* • Dorothy Lovett *Judy Price* • Robert Baldwin *Roy Davis* • Enid Bennett *Anne Hewitt* • Paul Harvey *John Hewitt* • Marcia Mae Jones *Marilee* ■ *Dir* Bernard Vorhaus • *Scr* Ian McLellan Hunter, Ring Lardner Jr, Harvey Gates, from a story by Harvey Gates

Meet Joe Black ★★ 12

Romantic fantasy drama
1998 · US · Colour · 172mins

Brad Pitt stars as the Grim Reaper in this remake of the 1930s classic *Death Takes a Holiday*, giving ailing media magnate Anthony Hopkins an offer he can't refuse – extra life, provided Death can spend a few days living among mortals. However, no one is more startled by Pitt's arrival than Hopkins's daughter Claire Forlani, because Death has taken over the body of the stranger she met earlier in a coffee shop. Nicely played but ridiculously overlong. JF. Contains a sex scene, swearing. [video] DVD

Brad Pitt *Joe Black/Young man in coffee shop* • Anthony Hopkins *William Parrish* • Claire Forlani *Susan Parrish* • Jake Weber *Drew* • Marcia Gay Harden *Allison* • Jeffrey Tambor *Quince* ■ *Dir* Martin Brest • *Scr* Ron Osborn, Jeff Reno, Kevin Wade, Bo Goldman, from the film *Death Takes a Holiday* by Maxwell Anderson, Gladys Lehman, Walter Ferris, from the play *Death Takes a Holiday* by Alberto Casella

Meet John Doe ★★ U

Drama 1941 · US · BW · 122mins

This sombre fantasy from Frank Capra starts off interesting, but by the end it's almost unwatchable. Capra failed to solve the film's structural problems and allegedly shot five different endings. Gary Cooper and Barbara Stanwyck head a fine cast, but Capra provides no colour and far too much worthy dialogue. "John Doe" is here the signature on a powerful letter from a mystery man promising to commit suicide by Christmas and atone for the sins of the world. TS [video] DVD

Gary Cooper *John Doe/Long John Willoughby* • Barbara Stanwyck *Ann Mitchell* • Edward Arnold *DB Norton* • Walter Brennan *The "Colonel"* • Spring Byington *Mrs Mitchell* • James Gleason *Henry Connell* • Gene Lockhart *Mayor Lovett* ■ *Dir* Frank Capra • *Scr* Robert Riskin, Myles Connolly (uncredited), from the short story *A Reputation* by Richard Connell in *Century Magazine*

Meet Me after the Show ★★ U

Musical comedy 1951 · US · Colour · 86mins

A feeble Betty Grable vehicle with precious little to recommend it. A perfunctory plot and appallingly static direction from Richard Sale battle in vain to hold the attention, though Grable's co-stars Macdonald Carey and Rory Calhoun are likeable. More of the healthy vulgarity that characterised Grable's other Fox features would have helped, and the faked amnesia plot is strictly for the birds. TS

Betty Grable *Delilah* • Macdonald Carey *Jeff* • Rory Calhoun *David Hemingway* • Eddie Albert *Christopher Leeds* • Fred Clark *Tim* • Lois Andrews *Gloria Carstairs* ■ *Dir* Richard Sale • *Scr* Mary Loos, Richard Sale, from a story by Erna Lazarus, W Scott Darling

Meet Me at Dawn ★★

Romantic comedy 1946 · UK · BW · 98mins

After making his name with *Flying down to Rio*, this was something of a crash-landing for American director Thornton Freeland. His understanding of the peculiarities of British humour seems to have deserted him after his wartime sojourn in Hollywood, for he misses every laughter cue (and goodness knows there are precious few) in this feeble comedy. His fellow Yank in exile, William Eythe, looks increasingly uncomfortable as this tale of duelling and duplicity develops. DP

William Eythe *Charles Morton* • Stanley Holloway *Emile* • Hazel Court *Gabrielle Vermorel* • George Thorpe *Senator Philipe Renault* • Irene Browne *Madame Renault* • Beatrice Campbell *Margot* • Basil Sydney *Georges Vermorel* • Margaret Rutherford *Madame Vermorel* ■ *Dir* Thornton Freeland, Peter Cresswell • *Scr* Lesley Storm, James Seymour, from the play *La Tueur* by Marcel Achard, Anatole Litvak

Meet Me at the Fair ★★★ U

Musical romantic drama
1952 · US · Colour · 87mins

When a travelling show's medicine man (Dan Dailey) takes in an orphan boy (Chet Allen) who has run away from a cruel institution, he is accused of kidnapping and must battle with a politician's social worker fiancée (Diana Lynn). No prizes for guessing how things are resolved in this amiable, folksy musical, which combines a dose of drama with romance and features some pleasing numbers. RK

Dan Dailey *"Doc" Tilbee* • Diana Lynn *Zerelda Wing* • Chet Allen *"Tad" Bayliss* • Scatman Crothers *Enoch Jones* • Hugh O'Brian *Chilton Corr* • Carole Mathews *Clara Brink* • Rhys Williams *Pete McCoy* ■ *Dir* Douglas Sirk • *Scr* Irving Wallace, Martin Berkeley, from the novel *The Great Companions* by Gene Markey

Meet Me in Las Vegas ★★★ U

Musical 1956 · US · Colour · 112mins

This late MGM musical is a delight. A showcase for Vegas itself, the negligible plot (every time Dan Dailey holds Cyd Charisse's hand he comes up trumps) serves as a framing device for a whole slew of talent: here are on-screen numbers from Lena Horne and Frankie Laine, and uncredited guest slots from some of the biggest stars of the day. Charisse dances up a storm, but the sizzle is stolen by Cara Williams, who lights up the screen. Better known here by its British title *Viva Las Vegas!* TS

Dan Dailey *Chuck Rodwell* • Cyd Charisse *Maria Corvier* • Agnes Moorehead *Miss Hattie* • Lili Darvas *Sari Hatvani* • Jim Backus *Tom Culdane* • Oscar Karlweis *Loisi* • Liliane Montevecchi *Lilli* • George Kerris [George Chakiris] *Young groom* • Betty Lynn *Young bride* ■ *Dir* Roy Rowland • *Scr* Isobel Lennart

Meet Me in St Louis ★★★★★ U

Classic musical 1944 · US · Colour · 108mins

This portrayal of a perfect American family was too sugary for some critical tastes at the time, but it can be viewed today as a vintage MGM musical. Whatever the film's minor flaws, they are more than made up for by some dazzling musical numbers – such as *Have Yourself a Merry Little Christmas*, *The Trolley Song* and *Skip to My Lou* – enhanced by the masterly direction of Vincente Minnelli at the top of his form. Providing a romanticised but still uplifting depiction of life in St Louis at the beginning of the 20th century, with Mary Astor as mom and Judy Garland as one of four daughters, this is a tale that only works against the backdrop of a more innocent age. PF [video] DVD

Judy Garland *Esther Smith* • Margaret O'Brien *"Tootie" Smith* • Mary Astor *Mrs Anna Smith* • Lucille Bremer *Rose Smith* • Leon Ames *Mr Alonzo "Lon" Smith* • Tom Drake *John Truett* • Marjorie Main *Katie, the maid* • Harry Davenport *Grandpa Prophater* • June Lockhart *Lucille Ballard* • Henry H Daniels Jr *Lon Smith Jr* • Joan Carroll *Agnes Smith* ■ *Dir* Vincente Minnelli • *Scr* Irving Brecher, Fred F Finklehoffe, from the novel by Sally Benson • *Cinematographer* George Folsey • *Costume Designer* Irene

Meet Me Tonight ★★ PG

Portmanteau comedy
1952 · UK · Colour · 80mins

This below par portmanteau picture comprises three one-act plays written by Noël Coward. There are too few examples of the urbane Coward wit to atone for the banality of the stories, while the observations on the types produced by the British class system are shallow to the point of platitude. However, the performances stand up rather well. DP [video]

Kay Walsh *Lily Pepper* • Ted Ray *George Pepper* • Stanley Holloway *Henry Gow* • Betty Ann Davies *Doris Gow* • Valerie Hobson *Stella Cartwright* • Nigel Patrick *Toby Cartwright* • Jack Warner *Murdoch* ■ *Dir* Anthony Pelissier • *Scr* Noël Coward, from his play *Tonight at 8:30*

Meet Mr Lucifer ★★ U

Fantasy comedy 1953 · UK · BW · 82mins

For every Ealing comedy gem there is at least one poor imitation, packed with cosy caricatures and devoid of the usual satirical bite. This tepid assault on television has Stanley Holloway as a pantomime demon who is sent as an emissary from hell to ensure that TV sets throughout the nation bring nothing but misery. DP

Stanley Holloway *Sam Hollingsworth/Mr Lucifer* • Peggy Cummins *Kitty Norton* • Jack Watling *Jim Norton* • Barbara Murray *Patricia Pedelty* • Joseph Tomelty *Mr Pedelty* • Kay Kendall *Lonely hearts singer* • Gordon Jackson *Hector McPhee* ■ *Dir* Anthony Pelissier • *Scr* Monja Danischewsky, Peter Myers, Alec Graham, from the play *Beggar My Neighbour* by Arnold Ridley

Meet Nero Wolfe ★★★ U

Detective murder mystery
1936 · US · BW · 71mins

Edward Arnold plays the corpulent gourmet and orchid cultivator Nero Wolfe, who solves most of his cases from the comfort of his own home. Directed by Herbert Biberman with Lionel Stander, Victor Jory and Rita Cansino (later Hayworth) in the cast, this neat little thriller finds the sleuth connecting and solving the murders of a college president and a mechanic.

M

Columbia intended to build a series around Rex Stout's popular detective, but there was just one more picture, *League of Frightened Men* (1937). RK

Edward Arnold *Nero Wolfe* • Lionel Stander *Archie Goodwin* • Joan Perry *Ellen Barstow* • Victor Jory *Claude Roberts* • Nana Bryant *Sarah Barstow* • Rita Cansino [Rita Hayworth] *Maria Maringola* ■ *Dir* Herbert Biberman [Herbert J Biberman] • *Scr* Howard J Green, Bruce Manning, Joseph Anthony, from a story by Rex Stout, from his novel *Fer-de-Lance*

Meet Simon Cherry ★

Detective drama 1949 · UK · BW · 66mins

This early Hammer B-feature is based on *Meet the Rev*, a popular radio series about a parson turned detective. Its star, Hugh Moxey, made his screen debut in this feeble story in which the Reverend Simon Cherry tries to take a much-needed holiday. Of course, his car breaks down and an overnight stay at the nearest manor produces a corpse by morning. AE

Zena Marshall *Lisa Colville* • John Bailey *Henry Dantry* • Hugh Moxey *Rev Simon Cherry* • Anthony Forwood *Alan Colville* ■ *Dir* Godfrey Grayson • *Scr* Gale Pedrick, Godfrey Grayson, AR Rawlinson, from the radio series *Meet the Rev* by Gale Pedrick

Meet the Applegates ★★★★ 15

Satirical fantasy 1991 · US · Colour · 86mins

Giant insects take on human form and move to Ohio from the Amazon rainforest to take revenge on humanity for destroying their home in director Michael Lehmann's surreal send-up of 1950s monster insect flicks, environmental issues and life in semi-detached suburbia. But while their creepy-crawly spirits are willing, their flesh-and-blood disguises are weak and soon they succumb to human nature: sex, drugs and drink ("grasshopper cocktail, anyone?"). It's a stinging satire on brainless pop culture and trashy Americana, and great fun, too. AJ. Contains swearing.

Ed Begley Jr *Dick Applegate* • Stockard Channing *Jane Applegate* • Dabney Coleman *Aunt Bea* • Bobby Jacoby *Johnny Applegate* • Cami Cooper [Camille Cooper] *Sally Applegate* • Glenn Shadix *Greg Samson* • Susan Barnes *Opal Withers* • Adam Biesk *Vince Samson* ■ *Dir* Michael Lehmann • *Scr* Redbeard Simmons, Michael Lehmann

Meet the Baron ★★

Comedy 1933 · US · BW · 65mins

Complete with his catch phrase "Vas you dere, Sharlie?", Jack Pearl was a big star on American radio in the 1930s. So Louis B Mayer surrounded him with impressive backstage talents to ensure his feature debut was a roaring success. Yet, the story of an opportunist who masquerades as the celebrated fabulist Baron Munchausen fails to gel, despite the presence of the ever-willing Jimmy Durante, plus ZaSu Pitts and Ted Healy and His Stooges. DP

Jack Pearl *Julius/Baron Munchausen* • Jimmy Durante *Joe McGoo* • ZaSu Pitts *ZaSu* • Ted Healy *Ted* • Edna May Oliver *Dean Primrose* • Henry Kolker *Baron Munchausen* • Moe Howard • Jerry Howard • Larry Fine ■ *Dir* Walter Lang • *Scr* Allen Rivkin, PJ Wolfson, from a story by Herman J Mankiewicz, from a story by Norman Krasna

Meet the Deedles ★ PG

Comedy 1998 · US · Colour · 90mins

This downmarket cousin to *Bill & Ted's Excellent Adventure* has two surf bum twins (Paul Walker and Steve Van Wormer) accidentally becoming rangers in Yellowstone National Park. There they are given the task of thwarting former employee Dennis Hopper, who plans to sabotage the landscape with help from a pack of prairie dogs. Only for teenagers who have absolutely nothing better to do. LH

Steve Van Wormer *Stew Deedle* • Paul Walker *Phil Deedle* • AJ Langer *Jesse Ryan* • John Ashton *Captain Douglas Pine* • Dennis Hopper *Frank Slater* • Eric Braeden *Elton Deedle* • Robert Englund *Nemo* ■ *Dir* Steve Boyum • *Scr* Jim Herzfeld, Dale Pollock

Meet the Feebles ★★★ 18

Puppet comedy 1989 · NZ · Colour · 96mins

In the sickest and most offensive puppet movie ever made, Peter Jackson presents his muppets as violent, perverted and just plain unpleasant. Taking the form of an animal backstage musical, the unhinged creatures and debauched behaviour are often amusing, mainly because you can't believe someone made a fluffy animal movie this twisted. JC DVD

Dir Peter Jackson • *Scr* Peter Jackson, Frances Walsh, Stephen Sinclair, Daniel Mulheron

Meet the Fockers ★★★ 12

Comedy 2004 · US · Colour · 110mins

In this sequel to *Meet the Parents*, Robert De Niro's anal ex-CIA man returns to spar with accident-prone, soon-to-be son-in-law Ben Stiller and travels to Florida to meet Stiller's mother and father. It is testament to the cracking performances of Dustin Hoffman and Barbra Streisand as Stiller's parents that they steal the film from De Niro. In their roles as earth mother sex therapist and hippy househusband, Streisand and Hoffman are utterly credible, while playing everything for the broadest of laughs. The least successful parts of the film are those that depend on knowledge of the original or that simply reuse the same jokes. AC. Contains sexual references. DVD

Robert De Niro *Jack Byrnes* • Ben Stiller *Greg Focker* • Dustin Hoffman *Bernie Focker* • Barbra Streisand *Roz Focker* • Blythe Danner *Dina Byrnes* • Teri Polo *Pam Byrnes* • Tim Blake Nelson *Officer Le Flore* • Owen Wilson *Kevin Rawley* ■ *Dir* Jay Roach • *Scr* Jim Herzfeld, John Hamburg, from a story by Jim Herzfeld, Marc Hyman, from characters created by by Greg Glienna, Mary Ruth Clarke

Meet the Parents ★★★★ 12

Comedy 2000 · US · Colour · 103mins

Teri Polo takes her potential groom Ben Stiller home to meet her parents. In the course of the weekend, he loses the cat, floods the garden and has his various weaknesses painfully exposed by her father, a former CIA operative. Given the set-up, this comedy could have been predictable and cliché-ridden, but the sheer class of the cast elevates this into something really special. Ben Stiller gives the unfortunate beau humanity and realism; Robert De Niro's gravitas makes "dad" an intimidating presence and Blythe Danner is a quirky prospect as the mother-in-law. Ridiculously funny and somehow rather endearing. LH. Contains swearing. DVD

Robert De Niro *Jack Byrnes* • Ben Stiller *Greg Focker* • Teri Polo *Pam Byrnes* • Blythe Danner *Dina Byrnes* • Nicole DeHuff *Debbie Byrnes* • Jon Abrahams *Denny Byrnes* • James Rebhorn *Larry Banks* • Owen Wilson *Kevin Rawley* ■ *Dir* Jay Roach • *Scr* John Hamburg, from a story by Greg Glienna, Mary Ruth Clarke • *Music* Randy Newman

Meet the People ★★★ U

Musical comedy 1944 · US · BW · 100mins

Masquerading as a minor MGM musical, this is a delight, featuring such period entertainers as frozen-faced Virginia O'Brien, crooner Vaughn Monroe and vaudevillian (and Cowardly Lion) Bert Lahr. The plot is extraordinarily liberal, with committed activist Dick Powell causing Broadway star Lucille Ball to abandon showbusiness and work as a riveter in the shipyards. Well, it was wartime, but even so, this is pre-McCarthy era political dynamite. TS

Lucille Ball *Julie Hampton* • Dick Powell *William "Swanee" Swanson* • Virginia O'Brien *"Woodpecker" Peg* • Bert Lahr *Commander* • Rags Ragland *Mr Smith* • June Allyson *Annie* ■ *Dir* Charles Reisner • *Scr* SM Herzig, Fred Saidy, from a story by Sol Barzman, Ben Barzman, Louis Lantz

Meeting at Midnight ★★ PG

Mystery 1944 · US · BW · 62mins

Originally released as *Black Magic*, this is the third in Monogram's Charlie Chan series. When his daughter, Frances Chan, is caught up in the murder of a medium, Chinese sleuth Sidney Toler sets out to expose the victim's fraudulent operation and discover the significance of events that happened almost a decade before in London. Too much time is devoted to the slapstick antics of Mantan Moreland, although the sequence in which Toler teeters on a rooftop under the influence of a mind-controlling drug is effective. DP DVD

Sidney Toler *Charlie Chan* • Mantan Moreland *Birmingham Brown* • Frances Chan • Joseph Crehan *Matthew* • Jacqueline de Wit *Justine Bonner* • Ralph Peters *Rafferty* • Helen Beverly *Norma Duncan* • Richard Gordon [Dick Gordon] *Bonner* ■ *Dir* Phil Rosen • *Scr* George Callahan, from characters created by Earl Derr Biggers

Meeting Venus ★★★ 15

Satirical romantic drama
1990 · UK · Colour · 114mins

Kiri Te Kanawa provides the arias for Glenn Close's Swedish high diva in director István Szabó's up-market romantic comedy drama. Close has fun as the man-eating prima donna whose infamous temperament threatens the career-enhancing project of young conductor Niels Arestrup. Wagner's music ponderously matches the melodrama, as hardline politics are exposed along with naked ambition. Szabó keeps a tight rein on his cast as the backstage passions flare, and if you can't stand the tantrums, the soundtrack is marvellous. TH

Glenn Close *Karin Anderson* • Niels Arestrup *Zoltan Szanto* • Marian Labuda *Von Schneider* • Maite Nahyr *Maria Krawiecki* • Victor Poletti *Stefano Del Sarto* • Jay O Sanders *Stephen Taylor* ■ *Dir* István Szabó • *Scr* István Szabó, Michael Hirst

Meetings with Remarkable Men ★★ U

Biographical drama
1979 · UK · Colour · 102mins

With Gilbert Taylor's camera rejoicing in the beauty of the Afghan mountainscapes, this is an uncomfortable combination of the gloriously cinematic and the doggedly theatrical. In electing to employ his famous technique of "forced improvisation" to adapt the memoirs of GI Gurdjieff, Peter Brook conveys something of the assiduity of the mystic's lifelong search for enlightenment. But neither his ideas nor his unique methods of meditation make for riveting viewing. DP

Dragan Maksimovic *Gurdjieff* • Terence Stamp *Prince Lubovedsky* • Athol Fugard *Professor Skridlov* • Warren Mitchell *Gurdjieff's father* • Natasha Parry *Vitvitskaia* ■ *Dir* Peter Brook • *Scr* Peter Brook, Jeanne DeSalzmann, from the book by GI Gurdjieff

Melancholia ★★★★ 15

Political thriller
1989 · UK/W Ger · Colour · 83mins

It may look distinctly unpromising and yet this political thriller is extremely well made and becomes increasingly exciting. Jeroen Krabbé plays a German art critic whose old anarchist fervour is reignited by the opportunity to assassinate a member of the Chilean military, but with escalating consequences. Surprisingly, this suspenseful movie is the only feature directed by Andi Engel, a larger-than-life film distributor with a wealth of cinematic knowledge. Camera shots are full of sleek, clean lines, while well-chosen London locations make the city look great. DM

Jeroen Krabbé *David Keller* • Ulrich Wildgruber *Manfred* • Susannah York *Catherine* • Kate Hardie *Rachel* • Jane Gurnett *Sarah Yelin* • Saul Reichlin *Dr Vargas* ■ *Dir* Andi Engel • *Scr* Andi Engel, Lewis Rodia

Melinda and Melinda ★★★ 12A

Comedy drama 2004 · US · Colour · 99mins

Cleverly structured, Woody Allen's comedy drama runs along parallel plotlines – one tragic, one comic – that are both initiated by a troubled woman named Melinda (Radha Mitchell), who subtly disrupts the lives of those around her. In one tale, Melinda falls for a suave pianist (Chiwetel Ejiofor), but finds herself betrayed by a close friend. In the other, Melinda's upstairs neighbour – a married, out-of-work actor played by Will Ferrell – falls for her. Trying to keep the separate stories straight can be a little confusing, but that's the point: that sadness and joy are inextricably entwined. LF. Contains sexual references.

Chiwetel Ejiofor *Ellis Moonsong* • Will Ferrell *Hobie* • Jonny Lee Miller *Lee* • Radha Mitchell *Melinda* • Amanda Peet *Susan* • Chloë Sevigny *Laurel* • Wallace Shawn *Sy* • David Aaron Baker *Steve* ■ *Dir/Scr* Woody Allen

Mélo ★★★★ PG

Romantic drama 1986 · Fr · Colour · 109mins

Surprisingly opting for a traditionally linear (and rather theatrical) approach, Alain Resnais explores his perennial theme of memory by peeling away the sophisticated veneer to reveal the genuine pain felt by Sabine Azéma, the adulterous wife of violinist Pierre Arditi, who is driven to suicide by the loyalty of his more celebrated virtuoso friend, André Dussolier. Impeccably played and outwardly old-fashioned, this is a powerful study of ruthless decency and emotional anguish. DP. In French with English subtitles.

Sabine Azéma *Romaine Belcroix* • Pierre Arditi *Pierre Belcroix* • André Dussollier *Marcel Blanc* • Fanny Ardant *Christiane Levesque* • Jacques Dacqmine *Dr Remy* • Catherine Arditi *Yvonne* ■ *Dir* Alain Resnais • *Scr* Alain Resnais, from the play by Henri Bernstein

Melody ★★ PG

Drama 1971 · UK · Colour · 106mins

David Puttnam's first production – from Alan Parker's first script – was retitled *SWALK*, as in *Sealed with a Loving Kiss*. Puttnam had bought the rights to a handful of songs by the Bee Gees which had to be incorporated into a story. So Parker came up with this tale of two kids (played by Jack Wild and Mark Lester) at a south London comprehensive whose friendship is tested when a pretty girl comes into their social orbit. AT

Jack Wild *Ornshaw* • Mark Lester (2) *Daniel* • Tracy Hyde *Melody* • Colin Barrie *Chambers* • Billy Franks *Burgess* • Ashley Knight *Stacey* • Craig Marriott *Dadds* ■ *Dir* Waris Hussein • *Scr* Alan Parker, Andrew Birkin

Melody Cruise ★★

Musical comedy 1933 · US · BW · 76mins

Phil Harris – the voice of Disney favourites Baloo the bear and O'Malley the alley cat – stars as a millionaire pursued by a shipful of gold diggers in this likeable musical comedy. Stealing the show, however, is flustered *farceur* Charles Ruggles as the minder hired to keep Harris on the straight and narrow. Mark Sandrich overdoes the camera trickery, but he handles the song and dance routines with some flair. DP

Charles Ruggles *Pete Wells* • Phil Harris *Alan Chandler* • Greta Nissen *Ann* • Helen Mack *Laurie Marlowe* • Chick Chandler *Steward* • Betty Grable *Stewardess* ■ *Dir* Mark Sandrich • *Scr* Mark Sandrich, Ben Holmes, Allen Rivkin, RG Wolfson, from a story by Mark Sandrich, Ben Holmes

Melody Time ★★ U

Animation 1948 · US · Colour · 75mins

A hit-and-miss Disney short story collection with each tale inspired by a popular tune. Whereas *Fantasia* was founded on established pieces from the classical repertoire, this relies on numbers that have not stood the test of time, and younger viewers may struggle to identify with the songs. Best of the bunch is *Little Toot* about a mischievous tugboat, and *Bumble Boogie*, a jazz variation on *The Flight of the Bumble Bee*. DP [video] DVD

Dir Clyde Geronimi, Hamilton Luske, Jack Kinney, Wilfred Jackson

Melvin and Howard ★★★★

Comedy drama 1980 · US · Colour · 94mins

In 1976, hard-up, much-married Melvin Dummar learned he had been left $156 million in the will of a man he barely knew. And all, according to this delightful film from Jonathan Demme, because Melvin treated the reclusive tycoon Howard Hughes to a slice of real life just when he needed it most. Jason Robards is typically bluff as the bedraggled eccentric, while Paul Le Mat is so good as the amiable everyman it's hard to fathom why his career has never really taken off. Mary Steenburgen won the Oscar for best supporting actress. DP

Paul Le Mat *Melvin Dummar* • Jason Robards *Howard Hughes* • Mary Steenburgen *Lynda Dummar* • Elizabeth Cheshire *Darcy Dummar* • Chip Taylor *Clark Taylor* • Michael J Pollard *Little Red* • Denise Galik *Lucy* • Gloria Grahame *Mrs Sisk* ■ *Dir* Jonathan Demme • *Scr* Bo Goldman

The Member of the Wedding ★★★

Drama 1952 · US · BW · 89mins

This interesting drama would have been wonderful if it had shifted up a gear. Carson McCullers's highly intelligent novel and stage play are transferred delicately to the screen and directed with some flair by Fred Zinnemann. Julie Harris is sublime as the unworldly child forced to face reality as the arrangements for her brother's wedding gather steam; it was her film debut, and she was nominated for an Oscar. Well worth catching for the beautifully rendered, claustrophobic atmosphere. SH

Ethel Waters *Berenice Sadie Brown* • Julie Harris *Frankie Addams* • Brandon de Wilde *John Henry* • Arthur Franz *Jarvis* • Nancy Gates *Janice* • William Hansen *Mr Addams* • James Edwards *Honey Camden Brown* ■ *Dir* Fred Zinnemann • *Scr* Edna Anhalt, Edward Anhalt, from the novel and play by Carson McCullers

Memento ★★★★★ 15

Thriller 2000 · US · Colour and BW · 108mins

This dazzling, highly original "anti-thriller" has a complex narrative that moves backwards in time. Thus we begin with the climactic murder, then regress through the events that led up to it. Matters are complicated by the fact that the killer (Guy Pearce) suffers from a rare form of amnesia, leaving him with no short-term memory. The mystery requires a lot of concentration, but the stunning final scene is ample reward. The ingenious structure makes the point that memory, although unreliable, is what we depend upon for our sense of reality. Writer/director Christopher Nolan's first film, the similar *Following*, signalled his brilliantly individual talent. DM. Contains violence, swearing. [video] DVD

Guy Pearce *Leonard Shelby* • Carrie-Anne Moss *Natalie* • Joe Pantoliano *Teddy* • Mark Boone Junior *Burt* • Stephen Tobolowsky *Sammy Jankis* • Harriet Sansom Harris *Mrs Jankis* • Callum Keith Rennie *Dodd* ■ *Dir* Christopher Nolan • *Scr* Christopher Nolan, from a short story by Jonathan Nolan

Memoirs of an Invisible Man ★★★ PG

Comedy thriller 1992 · US · Colour · 94mins

Director John Carpenter returned to the Hollywood mainstream with this flawed thriller. While Carpenter ensures that the action whips along at a cracking pace and the effects are stunning, the main problem is the uncertainty of tone. Chevy Chase, the innocent man who inadvertently becomes invisible, looks at home with the comic elements but is less convincing as a straightforward action hero, and it's left to Sam Neill, as the scheming spy who wants Chase's invisibility kept secret, and Stephen Tobolowsky to take the acting honours. JF [video]

Chevy Chase *Nick Halloway* • Daryl Hannah *Alice Monroe* • Sam Neill *David Jenkins* • Michael McKean *George Talbot* • Stephen Tobolowsky *Warren Singleton* • Jim Norton *Dr Bernard Wachs* • Pat Skipper *Morrissey* • Paul Perri *Gomez* ■ *Dir* John Carpenter • *Scr* Robert Collector, Dana Olsen, William Goldman, from the novel by HF Saint

Memories of Me ★ 15

Comedy drama 1988 · US · Colour · 98mins

When funny man Billy Crystal is good, he's very good, but when he's bad, he's terrible. This mawkish comedy drama falls in the latter category, as Crystal tries to put his life in order after a mind-altering heart attack. This means searching out his estranged father – the cue for even more sickly sentiment and some hopelessly artificial, angst-ridden emotion. The laughs are certainly there, but they're mostly unintentional. AJ [video] DVD

Billy Crystal *Dr Abbie Polin* • Alan King *Abe Polin* • JoBeth Williams *Lisa McConnell* • Sean Connery • Janet Carroll *Dorothy Davis* • David Ackroyd *First assistant director* ■ *Dir* Henry Winkler • *Scr* Eric Roth, Billy Crystal

Memories of Murder ★★★ 15

Murder mystery based on a true story
2003 · S Kor · Colour · 130mins

Inspired by the unsolved crimes of South Korea's first serial killer, Bong Joon-ho's simmering police procedural focuses as much on the relationship between incompetent small-town cop Song Kang-ho and his city superior, Kim Sang-kyung, as it does on the search for the brutal rapist who has claimed ten victims on a sadistic spree. Initially, there's a comic edge to the town-and-country posturing, but the tone grows darker once female officer Koh Seo-hee establishes a link with a radio request show. DP. In Korean with English subtitles. Contains swearing and violence. DVD

Song Kang-ho *Detective Park Doo-man* • Kim Sang-kyung *Detective Seo Tae-yoon* • Kim Rwe-ha *Detective Cho Yong-koo* • Song Jae-ho *Sergeant Shin Dong-chul* • Byun Hee-bong *Sergeant Koo Hee-bong* • Koh Seo-hee *Officer Kweon Kwi-ok* ■ *Dir* Bong Joon-ho • *Scr* Bong Joon-ho, Shim Sung-bo, from a story by Kim Gwang-rim

Memories of Underdevelopment ★★★★

Political drama 1968 · Cub · BW · 97mins

Already acclaimed for *Death of a Bureaucrat*, Cuban director Tomás Gutiérrez Alea came of age with this scathing satire, in which bourgeois intellectual Sergio Corrieri refuses the chance to flee to Miami. Instead he finds himself caught between his socialist ideals, European aspirations and the comfortable trappings of his lifestyle as he tries to sustain a new love affair and assimilate to the new regime. Slotting newsreel footage into the exhilarating visuals, this is a shrewd insight into a society struggling to come to terms with its post-colonial identity and the Cold War. DP. In Spanish with English subtitles.

Sergio Corrieri *Sergio* • Daisy Granados *Elena* ■ *Dir* Tomás Gutiérrez Alea • *Scr* Tomás Gutiérrez Alea, Edmundo Desnoes, from a novel by Edmundo Desnoes

Memory Run ★★ 18

Science-fiction action thriller
1995 · US · Colour · 89mins

An unnecessarily complicated slice of sci-fi which sees Karen Duffy going on the run from an evil corporate empire after she discovers that its executives have been literally playing with her mind. Saul Rubinek and Matt McCoy add respectability, but this one is really for genre fans only. JF [video] DVD

Karen Duffy *Celeste/Josette* • Saul Rubinek *Dr Munger* • Matt McCoy *Gabriel* • Chris Makepeace *Andre Fuller* ■ *Dir* Allan A Goldstein • *Scr* David Gottlieb, Dale Hildebrand, from the novel *Season of the Witch* by Hank Stine

Memphis Belle ★★★★ U

Second World War documentary
1943 · US/UK · Colour · 39mins

This is one of the finest combat documentaries of the Second World War. The Flying Fortress *Memphis Belle* had flown 24 successful missions and this daylight bombing raid was to be its last. Director William Wyler's pulsating short film uses diagrams to explain the mission and then takes us on board as the crew encounters flak and enemy fighters before hitting its targets. Footage from the film was used in the 1990 feature of the same name, which was co-produced by Wyler's daughter, Catherine. DP

Eugene Kern *Narrator* • Corp John Beal *Narrator* ■ *Dir* Lt Col William Wyler [William Wyler] • *Scr* Capt Edwin Gilbert, Tech Sgt Lester Koenig • *Cinematographer* Major William Clothier [William Clothier], Lt Col William Wyler [William Wyler], Lt Harold Tannenbaum [Harold Tannenbaum]

Memphis Belle ★★★ PG

Historical Second World War drama
1990 · UK · Colour · 102mins

Co-producer David Puttnam was the force behind this moving and nostalgic trip back to the Second World War. The focus is upon the crew of a B-17 bomber bidding to complete its final mission. It's a bit too predictable – the usual "will they make it back or not" heroics – but the characters, all slickly played by a strong cast including Matthew Modine and Eric Stoltz, are endearing and the crew's final flight is grippingly filmed. Most of the plaudits, though, must go to the stunning aerial effects and photography. NF. Contains some violence and swearing. [video] DVD

Matthew Modine *Dennis Dearborn* • John Lithgow *Colonel Bruce Derringer* • Eric Stoltz *Danny Daly* • Sean Astin *Richard "Rascal" Moore* • Harry Connick Jr *Clay Busby* • Reed Edward Diamond [Reed Diamond] *Virgil* • Tate Donovan *Luke Sinclair* • DB Sweeney *Phil Rosenthal* • Billy Zane *Val Kozlowski* • Jane Horrocks *Faith* ■ *Dir* Michael Caton-Jones • *Scr* Monte Merrick • *Cinematographer* David Watkin

The Men ★★★★ PG

Drama 1950 · US · BW · 86mins

This film is now remembered for the remarkable screen debut of Marlon Brando, who changed the very nature of screen acting with his mesmerising, naturalistic, self-pitying performance as a paraplegic war veteran. Brando first appears after the notable opening address by doctor Everett Sloane, a clever ploy used by director Fred Zinnemann to set the tone and prepare the audience for what follows. The sexual aspect of the tale is superbly circumvented (made necessary by the censors) in Carl Foreman's sensitive screenplay and it may all seem dated and overly melodramatic today. At the time, however, it was ground-breaking stuff. TS [video] DVD

Marlon Brando *Ken "Bud" Wilozek* • Teresa Wright *Ellen* • Everett Sloane *Dr Brock* • Jack Webb *Norm Butler* • Richard Erdman *Leo* • Arthur Jurado *Angel* • Virginia Farmer *Nurse Robbins* ■ *Dir* Fred Zinnemann • *Scr* Carl Foreman, from his story

Men... ★★★ 15

Comedy 1985 · W Ger · Colour · 99mins

Originally made for German television, this is an astute satire on the emotional immaturity of the average male. As the womanising businessman who moves in with his wife's bohemian lover in a bid to turn him into an equally unregenerate cad, Heiner Lauterbach gives a wonderfully sleazy display of bitter insecurity. Yet Doris Dörrie shrewdly presents this behaviour as only marginally more heinous than the lazy charm of artist Uwe Ochsenknecht and the disillusioned self-absorption of Ulrike Kreiner. Although straining credibility in places, this is still an amusing skirmish in cinema's ongoing battle of the sexes. DP. In German with English subtitles.

Heiner Lauterbach *Julius Armbrust* • Uwe Ochsenknecht *Stefan Lachner* • Ulrike Kriener *Paula Armbrust* • Janna Marangosoff *Angelika* ■ *Dir/Scr* Doris Dörrie

Men Are Not Gods ★★ U

Drama 1936 · UK · BW · 90mins

A chance to see a youthful Rex Harrison in a supporting role in this languid luvvie yarn about an actor (Sebastian Shaw) playing Othello, who takes his work too seriously and attempts to strangle his wife Gertrude Lawrence (who's playing Desdemona) because he's fallen for Miriam Hopkins. Essentially an excuse to look at the incestuous antics within a theatre company, this is daft from the portentous title onwards. SH [video]

Miriam Hopkins *Ann Williams* • Gertrude Lawrence *Barbara Halford* • Sebastian Shaw *Edmund Davey* • Rex Harrison *Tommy Stapleton* • AE Matthews *Skeates* • Val Gielgud *Producer* • Laura Smithson *Katherine* ■ *Dir* Walter Reisch • *Scr* GB Stern, Iris Wright, Walter Reisch

Men at Work ★★ 15

Comedy thriller 1990 · US · Colour · 94mins

Emilio Estevez wrote and directed this comedy action tale about two dustbin men (played by Estevez and his brother Charlie Sheen) who uncover a corpse on their daily route. Together with a nutty Vietnam vet (Keith David), they attempt to solve the crime and keep their community clean. Unsurprisingly, Sheen and Estevez have a chemistry which charms, though the subject

M

matter and genre require you to watch *sans* brain. LH DVD

Charlie Sheen *Carl Taylor* • Emilio Estevez *James St James* • Leslie Hope *Susan Wilkins* • Keith David *Louis Fedders* • Dean Cameron *Pizza man* • John Getz *Maxwell Potterdam III* ■ *Dir/Scr* Emilio Estevez

Men Don't Leave ★★★★ 15

Drama 1990 · US · Colour · 109mins

Jessica Lange gives another powerful performance as a mother coping with starting life anew after the death of her husband. Trying to pay off mounting debts and reduced to living in a small apartment with her sons (Charlie Korsmo and Chris O'Donnell, in one of his first roles), she also tries to begin a new relationship while battling against depression. Honest and absorbing, this confirms Lange as one of the best actresses of her generation. Watch out, too, for strong supporting turns from the excellent Joan Cusack and Kathy Bates. JB. Contains violence and swearing.

Jessica Lange *Beth Macauley* • Chris O'Donnell *Chris Macauley* • Charlie Korsmo *Matt Macauley* • Arliss Howard *Charles Simon* • Tom Mason *John Macauley* • Joan Cusack *Jody* • Kathy Bates *Lisa Coleman* ■ *Dir* Paul Brickman • *Scr* Barbara Benedek, Paul Brickman, from a story by Barbara Benedek, suggested by the film *La Vie Continue*

Men in Black ★★★★ PG

Science-fiction comedy
1997 · US · Colour · 93mins

This smash-hit science-fiction comedy, based on a short-lived 1980s comic strip, has secret agent Tommy Lee Jones and new recruit Will Smith as part of a top-secret agency responsible for regulating all alien activity on Earth. While investigating an alien sighting the pair become involved in the search for a missing galaxy to appease an interstellar force and avert the Earth's destruction. Great special effects, inventive alien designs and Smith and Jones's hip, hilarious double act make director Barry Sonnenfeld's bug-eyed *Lethal Weapon*-style buddy picture a fast-paced pleasure. AJ DVD

Tommy Lee Jones *K* • Will Smith *J* • Linda Fiorentino *Laurel* • Vincent D'Onofrio *Edgar* • Rip Torn *Zed* • Tony Shalhoub *Jeebs* ■ *Dir* Barry Sonnenfeld • *Scr* Ed Solomon, from the comic book by Lowell Cunningham

Men in Black 2 ★★ PG

Science-fiction comedy
2002 · US · Colour · 84mins

The smart-suited alien immigration agents Jay (Will Smith) and Kay (Tommy Lee Jones) return to save the planet, along with other familiar supporting players (including the hilarious talking pug Frank). This time, however, it's a super sexy Lara Flynn Boyle who's causing the cosmic chaos as evil alien queen Serleena. Her restrained performance lacks depth and menace, and adds no meat to an already emaciated plot. But there are enough flashy special effects and sharp humour to keep fans happy. SF. Contains some violence. DVD

Tommy Lee Jones *Agent Kay* • Will Smith *Agent Jay* • Lara Flynn Boyle *Serleena* • Johnny Knoxville *Scrad/Charlie* • Rosario Dawson *Laura* • Tony Shalhoub *Jeebs* • Rip Torn *Zed* • Patrick Warburton *Agent Tee* ■ *Dir* Barry Sonnenfeld • *Scr* Robert Gordon, Barry Fanola, from a story by Robert Gordon, from characters created by Lowell Cunningham

The Men in Her Life ★★

Drama 1941 · US · BW · 89mins

An ambitious former circus performer rises to become a famous ballerina and has several romances, at the cost of her relationship with her daughter. A trite and unconvincing melodrama, with the lovely but totally miscast Loretta Young at the centre. The under-characterised men in her life are Dean Jagger, John Shepperd (a pseudonym for Shepperd Strudwick) and Conrad Veidt as the strict ballet master who helps her to the top. Gregory Ratoff directs more stylishly than one might expect in the circumstances. RK

Loretta Young *Lina Varasvina/Polly Varley* • Conrad Veidt *Stanislas Rosing* • Dean Jagger *David Gibson* • Eugenie Leontovich *Marie* • John Shepperd [Shepperd Strudwick] *Sir Roger Chevis* • Otto Kruger *Victor* • Ann Todd [Ann E Todd] *Rose* ■ *Dir* Gregory Ratoff • *Scr* Frederick Kohner, Michael Wilson, Paul Trivers, from the novel *Ballerina* by Lady Eleanor Smith

Men in War ★★★

War drama 1957 · US · BW · 102mins

One of those minor war movies that were thick on the ground in the 1950s. But this account of a US infantry platoon in Korea is given distinction by the intelligent script and Anthony Mann's in-your-face direction, while the music by Elmer Bernstein is also a bonus. Robert Ryan's battle-exhausted lieutenant is a character whose attitude says more about war's futility than many a major epic. TH

Robert Ryan *Lieutenant Benson* • Aldo Ray *Montana* • Robert Keith (1) *Colonel* • Phillip Pine *Riordan* • Vic Morrow *Zwickley* • Nehemiah Persoff *Lewis* • LQ Jones *Editor* ■ *Dir* Anthony Mann • *Scr* Philip Yordan (front for Ben Maddow), from the novel *Combat* by Van Van Praag

Men in White ★★★

Drama 1934 · US · BW · 80mins

Clark Gable is a brilliant and dedicated young intern who is chosen to work with veteran physician Jean Hersholt – Hollywood's resident kindly doctor – to the distress of his socialite fiancée Myrna Loy. This modest, decently-made drama is a flag-waver for the medical profession. Gable's tragic involvement with a student nurse (marvellously played by Elizabeth Allan) strays into unconvincing melodrama, but the rest is believable and absorbing. RK

Clark Gable *Dr Ferguson* • Myrna Loy *Laura* • Jean Hersholt *Dr Hochberg* • Elizabeth Allan *Barbara* • Otto Kruger *Dr Levine* ■ *Dir* Richard Boleslawski • *Scr* Waldemar Young, from the play by Sidney Kingsley

Men o' War ★★★★ U

Comedy 1929 · US · BW · 19mins

One of 100-plus movie appearances for beloved comedy double act Laurel and Hardy, this 20-minute short is one of the team's best talkies. It's especially important for being the film that demonstrated that the duo could succeed with sound. The boys play sailors on leave enjoying a series of comic encounters – in a park, at an ice cream parlour and on a lake in a rowing boat. DF DVD

Stan Laurel *Stan* • Oliver Hardy *Ollie* • James Finlayson *Soda jerk* ■ *Dir* Lewis R Foster • *Scr* HM Walker

Men of Boys Town ★

Drama 1941 · US · BW · 106mins

Unspeakably yucky farrago, with Spencer Tracy reprising his Oscar-winning role as Father Edward J Flanagan, first seen in *Boys Town*, who seems to think there's a saint in every delinquent. At one point, Tracy even employs a pet pooch to help win over the kids. Tracy's rehabilitation of cute little Mickey Rooney from an unforgiving reform school will probably leave today's audiences nauseous. AT

Spencer Tracy *Father Flanagan* • Mickey Rooney *Whitey Marsh* • Bobs Watson *Pee Wee* • Larry Nunn *Ted Martley* • Darryl Hickman *Flip* • Henry O'Neill *Mr Maitland* • Lee J Cobb *Dave Morris* ■ *Dir* Norman Taurog • *Scr* James Kevin McGuinness

Men of Honor ★★★ 15

Action drama based on a true story
2000 · US · Colour · 123mins

This earnest but enjoyable film is based on the experiences of Carl Brashear, who joined the US Navy in the late 1940s, just as segregation was abolished. In George Tillman Jr's film, Brashear (played by Cuba Gooding Jr) sets his sights on becoming the first African-American deep-sea navy diver. Sent to boot camp, he finds himself under the strict regime of hostile diving master Billy Sunday (Robert De Niro), and so begins a long struggle to win respect and achieve his goal. There are some spectacular underwater sequences, but they tend to overshadow the performances of both leads. LH DVD

Robert De Niro *Billy Sunday* • Cuba Gooding Jr *Carl Brashear* • Charlize Theron *Gwen* • Aunjanue Ellis *Jo* • Hal Holbrook *Mr Pappy* • David Keith *Capt Hartigan* • Michael Rapaport *Snowhill* • Powers Boothe *Capt Pullman* ■ *Dir* George Tillman Jr • *Scr* Scott Marshall Smith

Men of Means ★★★

Crime drama 1997 · Can · Colour · 80mins

Michael Paré here goes part way to justifying the claims of those who rate him above the pack of direct-to-video action stars, turning in a measured performance as the hoodlum who decides to quit the racket before he falls victim to gang boss Raymond Serra's increasingly psychotic paranoia. However, the plaudits go to Austin Pendleton's scene-stealing cameo as the melancholic gambler whose loose talk sets Paré on the road to redemption. Avoiding the more obvious Mob clichés and including some briskly handled gunplay, this is slick but undemanding fare. DP

Michael Paré *Rico "Bullet" Burke* • Raymond Serra *Tommy Costa* • Kaela Dobkin *Cleo* • Mark Hutchinson *Joey* • Austin Pendleton *Jerry Trask* ■ *Dir* George Mendeluk • *Scr* Shane Perez, Todd Baker (uncredited)

Men of Respect ★★ 18

Crime drama 1990 · US · Colour · 108mins

The idea of translating William Shakespeare's "Scottish play" to the Mafia underworld is a good one but this film, like 1956's *Joe Macbeth*, fails to capitalise on the high concept. Writer/director William Reilly's dialogue teeters between the clever and the unintentionally hysterical. As the hood who becomes head of the Mob by bumping off his rivals, John Turturro is occasionally very sinister, and Katherine Borowitz (as his wife) eggs him on with sadistic glee. But there are just too many sniggers for a tough crime drama. DP. Contains violence and swearing.

John Turturro *Mike Battaglia* • Katherine Borowitz *Ruthie Battaglia* • Rod Steiger *Charlie D'Amico* • Peter Boyle *Duffy* • Dennis Farina *Bankie Como* • Stanley Tucci *Mal* ■ *Dir* William Reilly • *Scr* William Reilly, from the play *Macbeth* by William Shakespeare

Men of Sherwood Forest ★★ U

Adventure 1954 · UK · Colour · 77mins

A cheap and cheerful Hammer outing to Sherwood. American nobody Don Taylor lacks both the dash and the devilment to convince as he leads his Merrie Men on a mission to aid Richard the Lionheart. Leonard Sachs similarly makes a lightweight Sheriff of Nottingham, while Eileen Moore provides some rather soppy love interest. Val Guest directs with little feel for the boisterous action. DP

Don Taylor *Robin Hood* • Reginald Beckwith *Friar Tuck* • Eileen Moore *Lady Alys* • David King-Wood *Sir Guy Belton* • Patrick Holt *King Richard* • John Van Eyssen *Will Scarlett* • Leonard Sachs *Sheriff of Nottingham* ■ *Dir* Val Guest • *Scr* Allan MacKinnon

Men of Texas ★★★ U

Western 1942 · US · BW · 82mins

Chicago reporter Robert Stack is sent to investigate the aftermath of the Civil War in Texas and confronts Broderick Crawford, who refuses to admit defeat. The interesting interplay between the characters suggests that the pen is mightier than the sword, a strange concept to be advocating in the dark days of the Second World War. This is a good-looking western, pacily directed by Ray Enright. Anne Gwynne makes a very attractive leading lady, while Leo Carrillo supplies the humour as Stack's photographer sidekick. TS

Robert Stack *Barry Conovan* • Broderick Crawford *Henry Clay Jackson* • Jackie Cooper *Robert Houston Scott* • Anne Gwynne *Jane Baxter Scott* • Ralph Bellamy *Major Lamphere* • Leo Carrillo *Sam Sawyer* ■ *Dir* Ray Enright • *Scr* Harold Shumate, Richard Brooks, from the story *Frontier* by Harold Shumate • *Cinematographer* Milton Krasner

Men of the Fighting Lady ★

War drama 1954 · US · Colour · 79mins

A commie-bashing Korean war yarn about a US aircraft carrier, *The Fighting Lady*, and the brave men who fly her bombers, aim their rockets at the enemy's railway network, then return to base to exchange some of the corniest dialogue ever to emerge from the MGM studio. Louis Calhern plays author James A Michener, whose reports in *The Saturday Evening Post* formed the basis for the script. AT

Van Johnson *Lieutenant Howard Thayer* • Walter Pidgeon *Commander Kent Dowling* • Louis Calhern *James A Michener* • Dewey Martin *Ensign Kenneth Schechter* • Keenan Wynn *Lieutenant Commander Ted Dodson* • Frank Lovejoy *Lieutenant Commander Paul Grayson* • Robert Horton *Ensign Neil Conovan* • Bert Freed *Lieutenant Andrew Szymanski* ■ *Dir* Andrew Marton • *Scr* Art Cohn, from the stories *The Forgotten Heroes of Korea* by James A Michener and *The Case of the Blind Pilot* by Commander Harry A Burns

Men of Two Worlds ★

Drama 1946 · UK · Colour · 107mins

A well-intentioned but terribly tedious attempt to portray the beneficial side of British colonialism in helping the indigenous population achieve social and economic progress. Robert Adams is the educated black musician who overcomes the superstitious powers of Orlando Martins's witch doctor to persuade a tribe to move away from an area infected with tsetse fly. Almost all the extensive Technicolor footage filmed in Tanganyika had to be re-shot at Denham, ruining the semi-documentary approach taken by director Thorold Dickinson. AE

Eric Portman *District Commissioner Randall* • Phyllis Calvert *Dr Caroline Munro* • Robert Adams *Kisenga* • Orlando Martins *Magole* • Arnold Marlé *Professor Gollner* • Cathleen Nesbitt *Mrs Upjohn* • Sam Blake *Chief Raki* ■ *Dir* Thorold Dickinson • *Scr* Thorold Dickinson, Herbert W Victor, from a story by E Arnot Robertson, Joyce Cary

Men of War ★★★ 18

Action drama 1995 · US · Colour · 98mins

Although the testosterone-laden action is plentiful in this jungle-island war drama, the script (partially written by John Sayles) is startlingly good. A group of mercenaries sent to the island is charged with convincing the natives to sign over the mineral rights, but some of the group find themselves siding with the islanders. This unusually intelligent commando movie is probably the best film of Lundgren's career, with a standout perfomance from BD Wong as a wisecracking local. ST

Dolph Lundgren *Nick* • Charlotte Lewis *Loki* • BD Wong *Po* • Anthony John Denison *Jimmy* • Don Harvey *Nolan* • Tom "Tiny" Lister Jr *Blades* • Kevin Tighe *Merrick* ■ *Dir* Perry Lang • *Scr* John Sayles, Ethan Reiff, Cyrus Voris, from a story by Stan Rogow

Men with Guns ★★★★★ 15

Drama 1997 · US · Colour · 127mins

John Sayles, one of America's most impressive and enterprising independent film-makers, makes this Spanish-language film a socially significant fable about tyranny. An elderly doctor (Federico Luppi) goes to visit former students working in poor Latin American villages, only to find they've been killed by the dictatorial regime. Made with a feeling and sincerity that is never undermined by sentimentality, it's a poignant reminder of how we all turn a blind eye to that which would inconvenience us. TH. In Spanish with English subtitles.

Federico Luppi *Doctor Humberto Fuentes* • Damián Alcázar *Padre Portillo, the priest* • Tania Cruz *Graciela, the mute girl* • Damian Delgado *Domingo, the soldier* • Dan Rivera González *Conejo, the boy* • Iguandili Lopez *Mother* • Mandy Patinkin *Andrew* ■ *Dir* John Sayles • *Scr* John Sayles, inspired by a character in *The Long Night of White Chickens* by Francisco Goldman

Men with Wings ★★

Drama 1938 · US · Colour · 105mins

Starting with a re-enactment of the Wright Brothers' first manned flight in 1903, this flying epic from *Wings* director William "Wild Bill" Wellman isn't nearly exciting enough. Childhood buddies Fred MacMurray and Ray Milland grow up to become aerial obsessives, building and inventing planes, fighting in the wars and having a protracted and rather dull dogfight over Louise Campbell. The end result was an expensive flop. AT

Fred MacMurray *Patrick Falconer* • Ray Milland *Scott Barnes* • Louise Campbell *Peggy Ranson* • Andy Devine *Joe Gibbs* • Lynne Overman *Hank Rinebow* • Porter Hall *Hiram F Jenkins* • Walter Abel *Nick Ranson* • Virginia Weidler *Peggy Ranson, as a child* • Donald O'Connor *Pat Falconer, as a child* ■ *Dir* William A Wellman • *Scr* Robert Carson

Men without Women ★★★

Drama 1930 · US · BW · 77mins

Filmed as an early talkie but apparently surviving only in the alternative silent version, director John Ford's first collaboration with writer Dudley Nichols is the compelling drama of the attempts to rescue the crew of a crippled American submarine from the floor of the China Sea. John Wayne has a bit part as a sailor relaying messages with earphones and mouthpiece. Kenneth MacKenna and Frank Albertson are the stars, but it's Ford masterly direction that is the film's main attraction now. AE

Kenneth MacKenna *Chief Torpedoman Burke* • Frank Albertson *Ens Price* • Paul Page *Handsome* • Walter McGrail *Cobb* • Warren Hymer *Kaufman* • John Wayne ■ *Dir* John Ford • *Scr* Dudley Nichols, from a story by John Ford, James Kevin McGuiness

Men, Women: a User's Manual ★★★ 12

Satire 1996 · Fr · Colour · 122mins

Disregard the title. Look instead to the subtitle, *An Inhuman Comedy*, to find a clue to this wry tale about a cruel practical joke. The perpetrator is doctor Alessandra Martines, whose long-harboured lover's grudge prompts her to inform oversexed tycoon Bernard Tapie that he is terminally ill, while telling dying cop Fabrice Luchini the opposite. In spite of the plot's preposterous contrivance, you are still drawn to director Claude Lelouch's rather resistible characters, although the subplots are less successful. DP. In French with English subtitles.

Bernard Tapie *Benoît Blanc* • Fabrice Luchini *Fabio Lini* • Alessandra Martines *Doctor Nitez* • Pierre Arditi *Dr Pierre Lerner* • Caroline Céllier *Madame Blanc* • Ophélie Winter *Pretty blonde of Crillon* • Anouk Aimée *The widow* ■ *Dir* Claude Lelouch • *Scr* Claude Lelouch, René Bonnell, Jean-Phillipe Chatrier

Menace II Society ★★★ 18

Drama 1993 · US · Colour · 97mins

A searing, if bleak portrait of life in the 'hood from Allen and Albert Hughes, twins who were just 20 at the time it was made. Tyrin Turner is the surly adolescent, the son of a junkie mother and a drug-pushing dad, who's torn between nice single mom Jada Pinkett or a life of drive-by shootings and petty crime. There's no denying the visceral power of the Hughes brothers' vision, but – with the exception of Pinkett – it's hard to have sympathy for any of the characters. JF DVD

Jada Pinkett [Jada Pinkett Smith] *Ronnie* • Tyrin Turner *Caine* • Larenz Tate *O-Dog* • Charles S Dutton *Mr Butler* • Bill Duke *Detective* • Samuel L Jackson *Tat Lawson* ■ *Dir* Allen Hughes, Albert Hughes • *Scr* Tyger Williams, Allen Hughes, Albert Hughes, from their story

The Men's Club ★ 18

Drama 1986 · US · Colour · 96mins

A static and stagey bore about seven men who meet up to swap sexual stories, throw knives at a wall and howl like wolves before heading off to the weirdest brothel in the US. One-dimensional, misogynistic garbage, with flat direction from Peter Medak and unengaging performances. The second half is plain embarrassing, though Jennifer Jason Leigh shines as an enthusiastic prostitute. JC

David Dukes *Phillip* • Richard Jordan *Kramer* • Harvey Keitel *Solly Berliner* • Frank Langella *Harold Canterbury* • Roy Scheider *Cavanaugh* • Craig Wasson *Paul* • Treat Williams *Terry* • Stockard Channing *Nancy* • Jennifer Jason Leigh *Teensy* ■ *Dir* Peter Medak • *Scr* Leonard Michaels, from his novel

La Mentale ★★ 15

Crime thriller 2002 · Fr · Colour · 102mins

Once again it seems there's no honour among thieves. But director Manuel Boursinhac is clearly more interested in referencing crime classics than he is in the domestic, ethnic and emotional pressures ex-jailbird Samuel Le Bihan faces as cousin Samy Naceri tries to coax him into one last blag before he settles down with loyal wife, Marie Guillard. Michel Duchaussoy snarls effectively as a ruthless Mob boss and Clotilde Courau pulls off a bizarre scene involving some diamonds, but the rest is abrasive, formulaic and forgettable. DP. In French with English subtitles. Contains swearing, violence and sex scenes DVD

Samuel Le Bihan *Dris* • Samy Naceri *Yanis* • Clotilde Courau *Nina* • Marie Guillard *Lise* • Michel Duchaussoy *Fêche* • Philippe Nahon *Simon* • Francis Renaud *Niglo* • Lucien Jean-Baptiste *Foued* • Bibi Naceri *Rouquin* ■ *Dir* Manuel Boursinhac • *Scr* Bibi Naceri, Manuel Boursinhac

Mephisto ★★★★★ 15

Drama 1981 · Hun · Colour · 138mins

Winner of the Oscar for best foreign film, this was the first of István Szabó's loose trilogy on the theme of treachery and ambition. As in the subsequent *Colonel Redl* and *Hanussen*, Klaus Maria Brandauer plays a character who sells his soul for power, here as an actor who ignores the implications of Nazi patronage to achieve stardom. Klaus Mann's source novel is a revision of the Faust legend, but Szabó never loses a sense of historical perspective and delineates the seductive allure of fascism with chilling detachment to make its evil tenets all the more hideous. Brandauer is majestic and this is a masterpiece. DP. In German with English subtitles.

Klaus Maria Brandauer *Hendrik Höfgen* • Ildiko Bansagi *Nicoletta von Niebuhr* • Rolf Hoppe *General* • Gyorgy Cserhalmi *Hans Miklas* • Peter Andorai *Otto Ulrichs* • Karin Boyd *Juliette Martens* • Christine Harbort *Lotte Lindenthal* ■ *Dir* István Szabó • *Scr* Peter Dobai, István Szabó, Klaus Mann

The Mephisto Waltz ★★★

Horror drama 1971 · US · Colour · 108mins

An under-rated occult thriller blending urban Gothic trappings with psychological insights. Dying concert pianist Curt Jurgens uses black magic to possess journalist Alan Alda's body in this unnerving shocker. It's when Alda's wife, Jacqueline Bisset, finds out what's going on that things start getting really scary. Director Paul Wendkos uses soap-opera clichés and dazzling psychedelic colours to distort the boundary between reality and fantasy in this diabolical tale of enigmatic paranoia. AJ

Alan Alda *Myles Clarkson* • Jacqueline Bisset *Paula Clarkson* • Barbara Parkins *Roxanne* • Curt Jurgens *Duncan Ely* • Brad Dillman [Bradford Dillman] *Bill* • William Windom *Dr West* • Kathleen Widdoes *Maggie West* • Pamelyn Ferdin *Abby Clarkson* ■ *Dir* Paul Wendkos • *Scr* Ben Maddow, from the novel by Fred Mustard Stewart

Le Mépris ★★★ 15

Satire 1963 · Fr/It · Colour · 98mins

Jean-Luc Godard's weird satire on Hollywood's invasion of Europe stars Jack Palance as the American producer who says: "When I hear the word culture I reach for my cheque book." Fritz Lang plays the director of an intended version of Homer's *Odyssey*, while the sex interest is provided by – who else? – Brigitte Bardot. It sounds relatively straightforward, and probably would be if Godard didn't veer off at tangents in a desperate attempt not to be swamped by his biggest budget and cast to date. AT. In English and French with subtitles. DVD

Brigitte Bardot *Camille Javal* • Michel Piccoli *Paul Javal* • Jack Palance *Jeremy Prokosh* • Fritz Lang • Giorgia Moll *Francesca Vanini* ■ *Dir/Scr* Jean-Luc Godard

The Merchant of Four Seasons ★★★★ 15

Drama 1971 · W Ger · Colour · 84mins

Recalling the fate of his own uncle, Rainer Werner Fassbinder explores the emotional tyranny of women in this archly realist melodrama. Having failed in the Foreign Legion and the police, been neglected by his mother, jilted by his romantic ideal and humiliated by his jealous wife, greengrocer Hans Hirschmüller is trapped in an irrelevant, drink-sodden existence. Fassbinder employs a series of perfectly judged flashbacks to piece together this life just as it's falling apart. What results is both a sympathetic portrait of a far from blameless nobody and a pessimistic vision of everyday life. DP. In German with English subtitles.

Hans Hirschmüller *Hans Epp* • Irm Hermann *Irmgard Epp* • Hanna Schygulla *Anna* • Andrea Schober *Renate Epp* ■ *Dir/Scr* Rainer Werner Fassbinder

Merci Docteur Rey ★ 15

Comedy drama
2002 · UK/Fr · Colour · 98mins

Andrew Litvack's debut feature is a gross miscalculation that is woefully over-written and shamefully overplayed. Dianne Wiest is primarily culpable as the operatic diva whose return to the Parisian stage is blighted by the murder of her ex-husband (Simon Callow). Pretentious, preposterous and embarrassing. DP. In English and French with subtitles. Contains swearing, drug abuse, sexual references. DVD

Dianne Wiest *Elisabeth Beaumont* • Jane Birkin *Penelope* • Stanislas Merhar *Thomas Beaumont* • Bulle Ogier *Claude Sabrie* • Karim Saleh *Murderer* • Didier Flamand *Detective* • Jerry Hall *Sybil* • Simon Callow *Bob* • Vanessa Redgrave ■ *Dir/Scr* Andrew Litvack

Merci la Vie ★★★ 18

Surreal fantasy drama
1991 · Fr · Colour and BW · 113mins

At times dazzling, Bertrand Blier's film teems with ideas, but it too often finds itself at a loss with what to do with them. Charlotte Gainsbourg and Anouk Grinberg give spellbinding performances as the social misfits confronted with a melange of maladjusted males, including doctor Gérard Depardieu and Nazi officer Jean-Louis Trintignant. It's a challenging, violent and often outrageously funny movie. DP. In French with English subtitles. Contains violence, swearing and sex scenes. DVD

Charlotte Gainsbourg *Camille* • Anouk Grinberg *Joëlle* • Gérard Depardieu *Marc Antoine* • Michel Blanc *Young father* • Jean Carmet *Old father* • Catherine Jacob *Young mother* • Thierry Frémont *François* • François Perrot *Director* • Jean-Louis Trintignant *Officer* ■ *Dir/Scr* Bertrand Blier

Merci pour le Chocolat ★★★ PG

Crime thriller 2000 · Fr/Swi · Colour · 96mins

Alfred Hitchcock always wanted to set a film in a Swiss chocolate factory and he would doubtless have been amused by this realisation of his dream by his most fervent disciple, Claude Chabrol. A typically rich mixture of malice and mockery, his ultra-cool approach perhaps removes some of the spice from the tale, making the central pursuit (by an undetected murderess, Isabelle Huppert, of her pianist husband's new protégée) somewhat lacking in suspense. Yet Chabrol's talent for social satire remains undimmed and the clinical way in which he exposes the murderess's bourgeois foibles is deliciously excruciating to watch. DP. In French with English subtitles. DVD

Isabelle Huppert *Marie-Claire "Mika" Muller* • Jacques Dutronc *André Polonski* • Anna Mouglalis *Jeanne Pollet* • Rodolphe Pauly *Guillaume Polonski* • Michel Robin *Patou Dufreigne* • Mathieu Simonet *Axel* ■ *Dir* Claude Chabrol • *Scr* Claude Chabrol, Caroline Eliacheff, from the novel *The Chocolate Cobweb* by Charlotte Armstrong

Mercury Rising ★★★ 15

Action thriller 1998 · US · Colour · 106mins

Bruce Willis stars as a renegade government operative who becomes protector of an autistic child (Miko Hughes) who has cracked the supposedly impenetrable Mercury security code; Alec Baldwin is the crooked national security man hunting them down. Director Harold Becker manages to impart a little depth to the relationship between Willis and Hughes – in between the chases and shoot-outs – but the psychological backdrop is too contrived. JF. Contains swearing and violence. DVD

Bruce Willis *Art Jeffries* • Alec Baldwin *Nicholas Kudrow* • Miko Hughes *Simon Lynch* • Chi McBride *Tommy B Jordan* • Kim Dickens *Stacey* • Robert Stanton *Dean Crandell* ■ *Dir* Harold Becker • *Scr* Lawrence Konner, Mark Rosenthal, from the novel *Simple Simon* by Ryne Douglas Pearson

Mercy ★★ 18

Erotic detective thriller
2000 · US · Colour · 112mins

Ellen Barkin is the cop investigating the murders of a series of women who have been tortured to death, while socialite Peta Wilson and therapist Julian Sands (giving his usual wooden performance) are two of her chief suspects. The cast is more interesting than the plot, which goes from "erotic" to "moralistic" just when it was looking intriguing – but there are nice performances here even if the script isn't up to much. JB

Ellen Barkin *Catherine Palmer* • Wendy Crewson *Bernadine Mello* • Peta Wilson *Vickie Kittrie* • Karen Young *Mary* • Julian Sands *Dominick Broussard* • Stephen Baldwin *Mechanic* • Marshall Bell *Gil Reynolds* • Beau Starr *Lt Frisch* ■ *Dir* Damian Harris • *Scr* Damian Harris, from the novel by David L Lindsey

Merlin the Return ★★ PG

Action fantasy 2000 · UK · Colour · 87mins

As dumbed-down derring do for the kids, this has its entertaining moments. The plot has King Arthur's evil half-brother, Mordred, concocting an escape from the Netherworld, while Merlin tries to awaken the slumbering King Arthur and his knights so that they can face their old foe. Craig Sheffer makes a nicely hissable Mordred, but Rik Mayall plays Merlin as if he were auditioning to be the next Doctor Who. The film has one genuinely scary sequence, and there's enough action hokum to please the under-tens. DA DVD

Rik Mayall *Merlin* • Tia Carrere *Joan Maxwell, a scientist* • Patrick Bergin *King Arthur* • Adrian Paul *Lancelot* • Craig Sheffer *Mordred* • Julie Hartley *Guinevere* ■ *Dir/Scr* Paul Matthews

Mermaids ★★★★ 15

Romantic comedy
1990 · US · Colour · 105mins

In this gentle romantic comedy, director Richard Benjamin coaxes a deft performance from Winona Ryder as a confused 1960s teen, caught between her lust for a local handyman (Michael Schoeffling) and her desire to be a nun. She's surrounded by an eccentric mother (Cher) who's romantically involved with a local shopkeeper (Bob Hoskins), and a younger sister (Christina Ricci) who practises being a swimmer by holding her breath in the bath. This is a curious, light-hearted tale, with Ryder the greatest surprise. DP. Contains some swearing. DVD

Cher *Mrs Flax* • Bob Hoskins *Lou Landsky* • Winona Ryder *Charlotte Flax* • Michael Schoeffling *Joe Peretti* • Christina Ricci *Kate Flax* • Caroline McWilliams *Carrie* • Jan Miner *Mother Superior* • Betsey Townsend *Mary O'Brien* ■ *Dir* Richard Benjamin • *Scr* June Roberts, from the novel by Patty Dann

Merrill's Marauders ★★★★ U

Second World War drama
1962 · US · Colour · 94mins

Grey-haired Jeff Chandler never made it to the top rung of Hollywood stardom, and this, his last and finest movie, makes us wonder why. As Brigadier General Frank Merrill, he's a vivid and boisterous leader of a top US Army unit in 1942 Burma. What marks it out from other battle movies is William Clothier's dramatic photography and director Samuel Fuller's understanding of soldiers in action. He knows that war is hell but that the heat of action can strengthen character. TH

Jeff Chandler *Brig Gen Frank Merrill* • Ty Hardin *Lieutenant Lee Stockton* • Peter Brown *Bullseye* • Andrew Duggan *Major "Doc" Nemeny* • Will Hutchins *Chowhound* • Claude Akins *Sergeant Kolowicz* • Luz Valdez *Burmese girl* • John Hoyt *General Stilwell* • Charles Briggs *Muley* ■ *Dir* Samuel Fuller • *Scr* Samuel Fuller, Milton Sperling, from the novel by Charlton Ogburn Jr

Merrily We Go to Hell ★★★

Comedy 1932 · US · BW · 78mins

Sylvia Sidney once commented that she had been "paid by the tear", and her on-screen suffering was indeed relentless. At least this melodrama allowed her to leave the milieu of poverty and crime in which she was so often placed. Here she plays an heiress whose marriage to attractive writer Fredric March disintegrates as a result of his alcoholism and womanising. Deft direction and the strong presence of the stars rescue a plot that is short on substance. Look out for Cary Grant in a bit part. RK

Sylvia Sidney *Joan Prentice* • Fredric March *Jerry Corbett* • Adrianne Allen *Claire Hempstead* • Richard "Skeets" Gallagher *Buck* • Cary Grant *Charlie Baxter* ■ *Dir* Dorothy Arzner • *Scr* Edwin Justus Mayer, from the story *I, Jerry, Take Thee, Joan* by Cleo Lucas

Merrily We Live ★★★

Screwball comedy 1938 · US · BW · 90mins

This delightful screwball comedy might be better known if the plot were not so similar to *My Man Godfrey*, made only two years earlier. The earlier film had a crazy rich family employing as a butler an educated bum who tames the spoilt daughter, while this has a crazy family (headed by Billie Burke) employing as a chauffeur an educated bum (Brian Aherne) who tames the spoilt daughter (Constance Bennett). The pacing is a little off, but the timing of the cast cannot be faulted. RB

Constance Bennett *Jerry Kilbourne* • Brian Aherne *Wade Rawlins* • Billie Burke *Mrs Emily Kilbourne* • Alan Mowbray *Grosvenor* • Patsy Kelly *Cook* • Ann Dvorak *Minerva Harlan* • Tom Brown *Kane Kilbourne* • Bonita Granville *Marion Kilbourne* ■ *Dir* Norman Z McLeod • *Scr* Eddie Moran, Jack Jevne

Merry Andrew ★★★ U

Musical romantic comedy
1958 · US · Colour · 102mins

This is by no means the funniest Danny Kaye vehicle, but it is energetic and good-humoured. Kaye is a teacher at a stuffy boys' school in England who sets out on an archaeological dig but ends up joining a circus, where he falls in love with Pier Angeli. Saul Chaplin and Johnny Mercer's score includes *The Square on the Hypotenuse* and *Salud*, the latter given a spirited production number with some dazzling dancing by Tommy Rall. TV

Danny Kaye *Andrew Larabee* • Pier Angeli *Selena* • Salvatore Baccaloni *Antonio Gallini* • Robert Coote *Dudley Larabee* • Noel Purcell *Matthew Larabee* • Patricia Cutts *Letitia Fairchild* • Rex Evans *Gregory Larabee* • Tommy Rall ■ *Dir* Michael Kidd • *Scr* Isobel Lennart, IAL Diamond, from the story *The Romance of Henry Menafee* by Paul Gallico

Merry Christmas Mr Lawrence ★★★★ 15

Second World War drama
1982 · UK/Jpn · Colour · 118mins

Nagisa Oshima, the most controversial director of the Japanese New Wave, made his English-language debut with this affecting story set in a PoW camp during the Second World War. Tom Conti stars as a bilingual prisoner who is forced to act as intermediary between commandant Ryuichi Sakamoto and his sadistic number two Takeshi "Beat" Kitano, and the blustering British CO Jack Thompson. Treading carefully in matters of duty and culpability, Oshima creates credible and complex characters, played with distinction by his international cast. DP. Contains some swearing. DVD

David Bowie *Major Jack "Straffer" Celliers* • Tom Conti *Colonel John Lawrence* • Ryuichi Sakamoto *Captain Yonoi* • Takeshi [Takeshi Kitano] *Sergeant Gengo Hara* • Jack Thompson *Group Captain Hicksley* • Johnny Okura *Kanemoto* • Alistair Browning *De Jong* ■ *Dir* Nagisa Oshima • *Scr* Nagisa Oshima, Paul Mayersberg, from the novel *The Seed and the Sower* and the stories *A Bar of Shadow* and *The Sword and the Doll* by Laurens van der Post

Merry-Go-Round ★★★

Romance 1956 · Hun · BW · 100mins

Zoltan Fabri emerged as a leading figure in Hungarian "New Course" cinema with this rural *Romeo and Juliet* fable. Although the film's main purpose was to extol the virtues of collective farming, the romance between Bela Barsi and the debuting Mari Torocsik is full of touching moments, particularly during their whirlwind fairground courtship. Yet, in spite of the vivacious performances, Fabri's direction is stickily sentimental. DP. In Hungarian with English subtitles.

Mari Torocsik *Pataki Mari* • Imre Soos *Mate* • Bela Barsi *Pataki Istvan* ■ *Dir* Zoltan Fabri • *Scr* Zoltan Fabri, from a novel by Imre Sarkadi

The Merry Monahans ★★★

Musical comedy 1944 · US · BW · 90mins

This seen-it-all-before but delightfully nostalgic musical details the ups and downs, onstage and backstage, of the Monahans, a family of vaudeville entertainers. Jam-packed with musical favourites, the movie stars pint-sized dancing powerhouse Donald O'Connor, Jack Oakie and Peggy Ryan as the family in question. Ann Blyth, soon to play Joan Crawford's monster daughter in *Mildred Pierce*, turns up in more winsome mode. RK

Donald O'Connor *Jimmy Monahan* • Peggy Ryan *Patsy Monahan* • Jack Oakie *Pete Monahan* • Ann Blyth *Sheila DeRoyce* • Rosemary DeCamp *Lillian Rice DeRoyce* • John Miljan *Arnold Pembroke* • Gavin Muir *Weldon Laydon* • Isabel Jewell *Rose Monahan* ■ *Dir* Charles Lamont • *Scr* Michael Fessier, Ernest Pagano

The Merry Widow ★★★★

Silent romantic drama
1925 · US · BW · 110mins

Erich von Stroheim transformed the Ruritanian romance of Franz Lehar's operetta into an erotic black comedy that carries with it a whiff of decay. Von Stroheim dwells on the lechery of Prince Danilo (John Gilbert) before he is sent to Paris to woo a wealthy American widow (Mae Murray) and thereby save his bankrupt country. Despite the fact that von Stroheim and Murray fought throughout the shooting, she gave one of her best performances, and the lavish pre-sound musical was a great success with both the public and the critics. RB

Mae Murray *Sally O'Hara* • John Gilbert (1) *Prince Danilo* • Roy D'Arcy *Crown Prince Mirko* • Tully Marshall *Baron Sadoja* ■ *Dir* Erich von Stroheim • *Scr* Erich von Stroheim, Benjamin Glazer, from the operetta *Die Lustique Witwe* by Victor Leon, Leo Stein, Franz Lehar

The Merry Widow ★★★★

Musical comedy 1934 · US · BW · 99mins

A scintillating version of Franz Lehar's operetta, with all the favourite tunes included and a fabulous pairing of the great Maurice Chevalier (as Danilo) and Jeanette MacDonald (as the widow). If you only know MacDonald for the films she made with Nelson Eddy, you'll find she's a revelation here – a very merry widow indeed! The film's wit, style and polish is down to the talents of brilliant director Ernst Lubitsch, whose risqué "touch" is apparent in every scene. This is a real pleasure, dated only in its fashions and its view of a long-gone Europe. TS

Maurice Chevalier *Prince Danilo* • Jeanette MacDonald *Sonia* • Edward Everett Horton *Ambassador Popoff* • Una Merkel *Queen Dolores* • George Barbier *King Achmed* • Minna Gombell *Marcelle* • Ruth Channing *Lulu* • Sterling Holloway *Mischka* ■ *Dir* Ernst Lubitsch • *Scr* Samson Raphaelson, Ernest Vajda, from the operetta *Die Lustique Witwe* by Victor Leon, Leo Stein, Franz Lehar

The Merry Widow ★★ U

Musical 1952 · US · Colour · 104mins

Oodles of MGM money and all-stops-out Technicolor were lavished on this version of Franz Lehar's much-loved operetta, set in the fantasy principality of Marshovia, but to little avail. A new and pedestrian screenplay, heavy-handed direction and the casting of an unsubtle Lana Turner (dubbed by Trudy Erwin) and a stereotypical Fernando Lamas as Count Danilo drains the material of its romantic charm. RK

Lana Turner *Crystal Radek* • Fernando Lamas *Count Danilo* • Una Merkel *Kitty Riley* • Richard Haydn *Baron Popoff* • Thomas Gomez *King of Marshovia* ■ *Dir* Curtis Bernhardt • *Scr* Sonya Levien, William Ludwig, from the operetta *Die Lustique Witwe* by Victor Leon, Leo Stein, Franz Lehar

Merton of the Movies ★★ U

Comedy 1947 · US · BW · 81mins

The George S Kaufman–Marc Connelly play about a small-town youth, who crashes Hollywood on a mission to be a movie star, would seem to be a splendid vehicle for comedian Red Skelton, but it just fails to ignite. Gloria Grahame, Virginia O'Brien and Alan Mowbray are among the fine talents on parade here, but they are all at sea in a generally lifeless affair. TV

Red Skelton *Merton Gill/Clifford Armitage* • Virginia O'Brien *Phyllis Montague* • Gloria Grahame *Beulah Baxter* • Leon Ames *Lawrence Rupert* • Alan Mowbray *Frank Mulvaney* ■ *Dir* Robert Alton • *Scr* George Wells, Lou Breslow, from the play by George S Kaufman, Marc Connelly, from the novel by Harry Leon Wilson

Meshes of the Afternoon ★★★★ PG

Silent experimental drama
1943 · US · BW · 18mins

The visual signature of such French film Impressionists as Germaine Dulac is evident throughout this feminist dream play, which was primarily responsible for reinvigorating the postwar American avant-garde. Shot on a shoestring in their own home by Maya Deren and her Czech husband, Alexander Hammid, this audaciously abstract visual poem concerns a slumbering woman's attempts to catch the hooded figure who keeps intruding upon her subconscious. Employing unexpected juxtapositions, abrupt camera angles and variegated speeds to disorientate the woman into a fear of familiar objects and spaces, this ultimately tragic tale is also a disturbing study of psychological and physical reality. DP

Alexander Hammid *Man* • Maya Deren *Woman* ■ *Dir* Maya Deren • *Scr* Maya Deren, Alexander Hackenschmied

Mesmer ★★

Biographical drama
1994 · UK/Ger · Colour · 107mins

This biography of Franz Anton Mesmer, the 18th-century psychiatrist and father of mesmerism, is a classic Europudding. Alan Rickman stars in a film which chronicles both Mesmer's unorthodox healing practices, based on a theory of "animal magnetism", and his affair with a blind pianist, which so scandalised Viennese society that he was booted out of the city. Roger Spottiswoode directs from a screenplay by Dennis Potter. DA

Alan Rickman *Franz Anton Mesmer* • Amanda Ooms *Maria Teresa Paradies* • Gillian Barge *Mrs Mesmer* • David Hemblen *Dr Inginhousz* • Jan Rubes *Professor Stoerk* • Anna Thalbach *Francisca* • Simon McBurney *Franz* • Beatie Edney *Marie Antoinette* ■ *Dir* Roger Spottiswoode • *Scr* Dennis Potter

Mesmerized ★★ 15

Period drama
1984 · Aus/NZ/UK · Colour · 94mins

In this sluggish and visually uninspired film, young innocent Jodie Foster is forced into marrying an older man (John Lithgow) in 19th-century New Zealand. Unable to tolerate his sexual peccadilloes, Foster kills him in self-defence and has to stand trial as a result. Foster delivers a strong performance, but this is not one of her better efforts. LH [video] DVD

Jodie Foster *Victoria* • John Lithgow *Oliver Thompson* • Michael Murphy *Reverend Wilson* • Harry Andrews *Old Thompson* • Dan Shor *George Thompson* • Philip Holder *Dr Finch* • Reg Evans *Mr Simmons* • Beryl Te Wiata *Mrs Simmons* ■ *Dir* Michael Laughlin • *Scr* Michael Laughlin, from a treatment by Jerzy Skolimowski

The Message ★★ PG

Religious epic
1976 · Lebanon/UK · Colour · 170m

Also known as *Mohammed, Messenger of God*, this three-hour epic re-creates the feudal life and times of the seventh-century leader of the religious movement that became known as Islam. Whatever sense of drama director Moustapha Akkad might have intended to create is undercut by the decision – as with early films of Christ – not to show the prophet himself, but instead have Anthony Quinn, as his uncle Hamza, an honoured warrior, take centre stage. Nonetheless the film caused an uproar among the faithful for daring to tell the tale at all. Non-believers may well find it sprawling and reverentially tedious. TH [video] DVD

Anthony Quinn *Hamza* • Irene Papas *Hind* • Michael Ansara *Abu-Sofyan* • Johnny Sekka *Bilal* • Michael Forest *Khalid* • Damien Thomas *Zaid* • Garrick Hagon *Ammar* ■ *Dir* Moustapha Akkad • *Scr* HAL Craig, AB Jawdat Al-Sahhar, Tawfik Al-Hakim, AB Rahman Al-Sharkawi, Mohammad Ali Maher

Message in a Bottle ★★★ 12

Romantic drama
1998 · US · Colour · 125mins

Kevin Costner stars as a strong, silent and sensitive boat builder living in North Carolina, who's tracked down by newspaper researcher Robin Wright Penn after she finds a heart-rending love letter to his late wife in a bottle on the seashore. Her hard-nosed reporter's edge soon softens as she decides to learn more about the man. Although the inevitable happens – with a twist! – the beauty of director Luis Mandoki's intelligent tear-jerker is how all the emotions ring true. This is warm-hearted stuff, with a scene-stealing performance from Paul Newman as Costner's grizzled father. AJ. Contains a sex scene. [video] DVD

Kevin Costner *Garret Blake* • Robin Wright Penn *Theresa Osborne* • Paul Newman *Dodge Blake* • John Savage *Johnny Land* • Illeana Douglas *Lina Paul* • Robbie Coltrane *Charlie Toschi* • Jesse James *Jason Osborne* ■ *Dir* Luis Mandoki • *Scr* Gerald DiPego, from the novel by Nicholas Sparks

A Message to Garcia ★★

Historical war adventure
1936 · US · BW · 77mins

It's the Hollywood version of the Spanish-American war, as army envoy John Boles goes in search of the titular general, surrounded by a cast of fine character actors, all of whom, alas, look quite out of place in the phoney Cuban setting. Unfortunately, George Marshall's direction lacks the vitality this type of film really needs, but it's entertaining enough. Rogue Wallace Beery and Barbara Stanwyck are the leads helping bland Boles deliver that message. TS

Wallace Beery *Sergeant Dory* • Barbara Stanwyck *Raphaelita Maderos* • John Boles *Lieutenant Andrew Rowan* • Herbert Mundin *Henry Piper* • Martin Garralaga *Rodriquez* • Juan Torena *Luis Maderos* • Alan Hale *Dr Krug* • Enrique Acosta *General Garcia* ■ *Dir* George Marshall • *Scr* WP Lipscomb, Gene Fowler, Sam Hellman, Gladys Lehman, from the non-fiction book by Lieutenant Andrew S Rowan and an essay by Elbert Hubbard

Message to Love ★★★ 18

Concert documentary
1995 · US/UK · Colour · 138mins

Proof that the dying embers of the 1960s were still flickering into the next decade is provided in this account of the 1970 Isle of Wight rock festival. Britain's answer to Woodstock (in organisational, as well as musical terms), the five-day jamboree drew a crowd of some 600,000, of whom only 50,000 actually paid. Twenty-five years later, film-maker Murray Lerner finally secured the funds to complete his film, albeit without the Bob Dylan footage. However, there's still a chance to see the flipside of flower power and keynote performances by Jimi Hendrix, the Who, Joan Baez, Donovan, Kris Kristofferson and the Doors. DP [video] DVD

Dir Murray Lerner

Messenger of Death ★★★ 18

Crime thriller 1988 · US · Colour · 92mins

The title promises the usual Charles Bronson bloodfest, but the script is by Paul Jarrico, a mild-mannered intellectual who was blacklisted and then produced the provocative, Union-financed *Salt of the Earth*. Bronson plays a Denver crime reporter whose snooping into a multiple killing leads him into Mormon society and a family who seem to be ritualistically following the examples of Cain and Abel. Director J Lee Thompson juggles the various elements – mystery, biblical allegory, bloody thriller – with great assurance. AT [video]

Charles Bronson *Garret Smith* • Trish Van Devere *Jastra Watson* • Laurence Luckinbill *Homer Foxx* • Daniel Benzali *Chief Barney Doyle* • Marilyn Hassett *Josephine Fabrizio* • Charles Dierkop *Orville Beecham* ■ *Dir* J Lee Thompson • *Scr* Paul Jarrico, from the novel *The Avenging Angel* by Rex Burns

Messidor ★★★

Crime drama 1978 · Swi/Fr · Colour · 122mins

Alain Tanner's road movie caused a stir not just because of the amorality of its hitch-hiking heroines, but also because of its unflattering portrait of his native Switzerland. From the moment student Clémentine Amouroux and shop assistant Catherine Rétoré decide to embark on a robbery spree, Tanner is less concerned with the nature of their crimes or their impact upon the women themselves than with the response of this unrepentantly capitalist country. DP. In French with English subtitles.

Clémentine Amouroux *Jeanne* • Catherine Rétoré *Marie* • Franziskus Abgottspon • Gérald Battiaz ■ *Dir/Scr* Alain Tanner

Metallica: Some Kind of Monster ★★★ 15

Music documentary
2004 · US · Colour · 140mins

Audience members expecting insights into the creative process behind global rock brand Metallica and those looking for a few *Spinal Tap*-style laughs at the expense of stadium-sized egos will walk away happy from this curiously affecting rock 'n' roll chronicle. Film-makers Joe Berlinger and Bruce Sinofsky first met the band while filming a documentary, *Paradise Lost: the Child Murders at Robin Hood Hills*, about three Metallica fans accused of "ritual" murders. But this is no fanboy tribute. The band's ridiculous behaviour is at times hilariously exposed as they struggle to record the album *St Anger* – unfortunately not one of their best – amid walkouts, stints in rehab, ego clashes, belly-aching and group therapy sessions. TH DVD

Dir Joe Berlinger, Bruce Sinofsky

Meteor ★ PG

Disaster movie 1979 · US · Colour · 102mins

Director Ronald Neame here places the planet on star-studded collision course with a gigantic asteroid. Spectacle has never looked cheaper or more pathetic than the tidal waves, avalanches and mud-slides on view in this celluloid catastrophe that reaches an apex of absurdity when America (in the person of Sean Connery) and Russia (Natalie Wood) bury the hatchet to nuke the big rock. AJ [video]

Sean Connery *Dr Paul Bradley* • Natalie Wood *Tatiana Donskaya* • Karl Malden *Harry Sherwood* • Brian Keith *Dr Dubov* • Martin Landau *General Adlon* • Trevor Howard *Sir Michael Hughes* • Richard Dysart *Secretary of Defense* • Henry Fonda *President* ■ *Dir* Ronald Neame • *Scr* Stanley Mann, Edmund H North, from a story by Edmund H North

The Meteor Man ★★ PG

Science-fiction comedy
1993 · US · Colour · 95mins

After *Hollywood Shuffle* and *The Five Heartbeats*, this was third time unlucky for young, gifted and black actor/writer/director Robert Townsend. It's certainly about time we had more non-Caucasian superheroes, but there's something a little too fallible about this emerald-clad warrior whose powers have a nasty habit of waning at crucial moments. Similarly, although tackling the neighbourhood drug barons is a worthy mission, the heavy-handed social commentary provides surprisingly few laughs or thrills. DP [video]

Robert Townsend *Jefferson Reed* • Marla Gibbs *Mrs Reed* • Eddie Griffin *Michael* • Robert Guillaume *Mr Reed* • James Earl Jones *Mr Moses* • Roy Fegan *Simon* • Bill Cosby *Marvin* ■ *Dir/Scr* Robert Townsend

Metro ★★ 18

Action thriller 1997 · US · Colour · 112mins

Eddie Murphy returns to the genre that made him a star with this misfiring action vehicle. It has a harder centre than usual as negotiator Murphy uses his motormouth talents to haggle with hostage takers. However, his persuasive charms are tested when he comes up against psychotic jewel thief Michael Wincott. The highlight set piece is a car chase involving a runaway tram, but otherwise director Thomas Carter displays little flair in the action department. JF. Contains violence, swearing, nudity. [video] DVD

Eddie Murphy *Scott Roper* • Michael Rapaport *Kevin McCall* • Kim Miyori *Detective Kimura* • James Carpenter *Officer Forbes* • Art Evans *Lieutenant Sam Baffert* • Michael Wincott *Michael Korda* ■ *Dir* Thomas Carter • *Scr* Randy Feldman

Metroland ★★ 18

Drama 1997 · UK/Fr/Sp · Colour · 96mins

Philip Saville directs this disappointing adaptation of Julian Barnes's knowing novel. Every choice is so safe, whether it's a tell-tale period detail or an identikit character trait. As a result, there's no urgency in bored suburbanite Christian Bale's dilemma after his hippy friend Lee Ross reappears and tries to persuade him to leave his wife (Emily Watson) and return to the hedonistic lifestyle they shared ten years before. DP. Contains sex scenes and swearing. [video] DVD

Christian Bale *Chris Lloyd* • Emily Watson *Marion Lloyd* • Lee Ross *Toni* • Elsa Zylberstein *Annick* • Rufus *Henri* ■ *Dir* Philip Saville • *Scr* Adrian Hodges, from the novel by Julian Barnes

Metropolis ★★★★★ PG

Silent science-fiction fantasy
1926 · Ger/US · BW · 119mins

No sooner had it been premiered – at approximately 153 minutes in length – than Fritz Lang's sci-fi masterpiece was subjected to commercially inspired abridgement. But now, thanks to the efforts of a team of unsung archivists, a new 119-minute version has been compiled from the various extant prints. A quarter of the picture appears irretrievably lost. Nevertheless, what remains still stands as a monument to both the ingenuity of the UFA art department and Lang's vision as a film-maker. The muddled political message of the film – in which the master of a futuristic city attempts to quell the simmering discontent among his workforce – has been the subject of much conjecture, but few can deny the majesty of the cityscapes and the inhumanity of the subterranean caverns. Among the most famous and influential silents ever made, this has lost none of its ability to inspire awe and provoke debate. DP [video] DVD

Alfred Abel *John Fredersen* • Gustav Fröhlich *Freder* • Rudolf Klein-Rogge *Rotwang* • Brigitte Helm *Maria/Robot* • Fritz Rasp *Slim* • Theodor Loos *Josaphat/Joseph* ■ *Dir* Fritz Lang • *Scr* Fritz Lang, Thea von Harbou, from the novel by Thea von Harbou • *Cinematographer* Karl Freund, Günther Rittau

Metropolis ★★★ PG

Animated futuristic drama
2001 · Jpn · Colour · 103mins

Re-imagining the core of Fritz Lang's 1926 silent masterpiece as an *animé* feature was always going to be a considerable challenge. Like its illustrious namesake, Metropolis is a grand city of the future; however the Japanese model comprises a strictly divided society of humans and robots, not thinkers and workers as in the German original. Into this chaotic mix are pitched a pair of detectives who are on the trail of a renegade robot scientist and his latest creation. Despite a script by *Akira* auteur Katsuhiro Otomo, this fails to live up to the reputation of its creators. DP. Japanese dialogue dubbed into English. [video] DVD

Dave Mallow *Pero* • Scott Weinger *Atlas* • Rebecca Olkewski *Tima* • Dave Whittenberg *Rock* • Tony Pope *Shunsaku Ban* ■ *Dir* Tarô Rin [Rintaro] • *Scr* Katsuhiro Otomo, from the comic strip by Osamu Tezuka

Metropolitan ★★★ 15

Comedy 1990 · US · Colour · 94mins

Director Whit Stillman sold his Manhattan apartment to raise the

M

budget for his debut movie. Using a cast of unknowns, it tells the story of a group of young, privileged New Yorkers who call themselves the SFRP (Sally Fowler Rat Pack, named after a party hostess) and do little other than spend the Christmas season attending balls, having party postmortems, swapping *bons mots* and courting each other. It's the world of F Scott Fitzgerald caught in a time warp, complete with social interloper. Stillman's witty, sophisticated screenplay was Oscar-nominated. AT

Edward Clements *Tom Townsend* • Carolyn Farina *Audrey Rouget* • Christopher Eigeman [Chris Eigeman] *Nick Smith* • Taylor Nichols *Charlie Black* • Allison Rutledge-Parisi *Jane Clarke* • Dylan Hundley *Sally Fowler* ■ *Dir/Scr* Whit Stillman

The Mexican ★★★ 15

Comedy drama 2001 · US · Colour · 118mins

Audiences wishing to see Julia Roberts and Brad Pitt sizzle for more than two hours will be disappointed to find they only spend 15 minutes together on screen. However, this offbeat comedy thriller does have its merits: an ace script and quirkily appealing performances from the two leads. Pitt is a useless Mafia appendage, trying to extricate himself from the Mob by doing one last job: retrieving an antique pistol (the "Mexican" of the title). Meanwhile, his girlfriend, Roberts, is kidnapped by James Gandolfini to ensure Pitt will return, gun in hand. LH. Contains violence and swearing. DVD

Brad Pitt *Jerry Welbach* • Julia Roberts *Samantha* • James Gandolfini *Leroy* • Bob Balaban *Bernie Nayman* • Gene Hackman *Arnold Margolese* ■ *Dir* Gore Verbinski • *Scr* JH Wyman

Mexican Bus Ride ★★★★

Comedy drama 1951 · Mex · BW · 85mins

Esteban Marquez plays a young man dragged away on his wedding night by his avaricious elder brothers, who need his endorsement of their dying mother's will. A perilous and incident-packed mountain bus trip ensues, during which a woman gives birth and Marquez has to fend off the attentions of the local floozy. From Spain's great Luis Buñuel, who based this deftly-made film on a real journey made by his poet friend Altolaguirre, it's one of the director's lightest works. RB. In Spanish with English subtitles.

Lilia Prado *Raquel* • Carmelita Gonzalez *Oliviero's wife* • Esteban Marquez *Oliviero* • Manuel Donde *Eladio Gonzales* • Roberto Cobo *Juan* • Luis Aceves Castañeda *Silvestre* ■ *Dir* Luis Buñuel • *Scr* Manuel Altolaguirre, Luis Buñuel, Juan De La Cabada

Mexican Spitfire ★★ U

Comedy 1940 · US · BW · 67mins

The spitfire of the title is Lupe Velez, married to Donald Woods's advertising executive and fighting off efforts by his disapproving aunt (Elisabeth Risdon) and jealous ex-fiancée (Linda Hayes) to break them up. Based on characters introduced in *The Girl from Mexico*, this cleverly orchestrated, lowbrow farce has Leon Errol as both a benevolent uncle and a visiting English whisky baron. The pie-throwing finale recalls Mack Sennett in his prime. Six sequels followed. AE

Lupe Velez *Carmelita Lindsay* • Leon Errol *Uncle Matt Lindsay/Lord Basil Epping* • Donald Woods *Dennis Lindsay* • Linda Hayes *Elizabeth* • Cecil Kellaway *Chumley* • Elisabeth Risdon *Aunt Della Lindsay* ■ *Dir* Leslie Goodwins • *Scr* Joseph Fields, Charles E Roberts, from a story by Joseph Fields

Mi Vida Loca ★★★ 15

Drama 1993 · US · Colour · 91mins

Allison Anders's third feature is a much tougher picture than her poignantly moving *Gas, Food, Lodging*, being closer to the uncompromising portrait of inner city life presented in the films of the African-American new wave. Although some of the dialogue recalls the work of longtime friend Quentin Tarantino, their concerns could not be more diverse, with Anders showing how religion and pulp romance sustain Hispanic teenage girls in a world where violence and loss are commonplace. The use of real street gangsters adds to the urgency and authenticity, although the dramatic quality suffers. DP. Contains swearing and substance abuse.

Angel Aviles *Sad girl* • Seidy Lopez *Mousie* • Jacob Vargas *Ernesto* • Marlo Marron *Giggles* • Jesse Borrego *El Duran* • Magali Alvarado *La Blue Eyes* ■ *Dir/Scr* Allison Anders

Miami Blues ★★★★ 18

Crime thriller 1990 · US · Colour · 92mins

Alec Baldwin has never been better than as a vicious ex-con who takes up with naive hooker Jennifer Jason Leigh in Miami. Things get complicated when he steals investigating cop Fred Ward's gun, badge and false teeth and sets about robbing and shooting just about everyone in his path, while masquerading as a police officer. An absorbing, gripping (and often very violent) battle of wits, this has some wonderfully dark comic moments and superb performances. JB DVD

Fred Ward *Sergeant Hoke Moseley* • Alec Baldwin *Frederick J Frenger Jr* • Jennifer Jason Leigh *Susie Waggoner* • Nora Dunn *Ellita Sanchez* • Charles Napier *Sergeant Bill Henderson* • Obba Babatunde *Blink Willie* ■ *Dir* George Armitage • *Scr* George Armitage, from the novel by Charles Willeford

Miami Rhapsody ★★★ 15

Romantic comedy
1995 · US · Colour · 91mins

You could be forgiven here for thinking that you are watching a Woody Allen comedy. The setting may be Miami, not Manhattan, but there is the central character (Sarah Jessica Parker) bemoaning her lot, a dysfunctional family and Mia Farrow in a co-starring role as Parker's mother. But as the action develops, it's clear that writer/director David Frankel is more of a Woody wannabe than a genuine pretender to the throne. If this lacks the deft touches that make Allen's work so uniquely enjoyable, it's still a clever and satisfying counterfeit. DP. Contains swearing.

Sarah Jessica Parker *Gwyn Marcus* • Gil Bellows *Matt* • Antonio Banderas *Antonio* • Mia Farrow *Nina Marcus* • Paul Mazursky *Vic Marcus* • Kevin Pollak *Jordan Marcus* • Barbara Garrick *Terri* • Naomi Campbell *Kaia* ■ *Dir/Scr* David Frankel

Micha ★★★

Drama 1992 · Ire/Rus · Colour · 97mins

Having worked in St Petersburg for several years, Irish director Gerard Michael MacCarthy was almost on home soil for this debut feature. His rite-of-passage drama is a heady cocktail of visual styles which echoes the many different facets of the city. It also captures the conflicting emotions of 11-year-old Genya Korhin as he wanders between his strict school, the spartan flat he shares with his mum and the TV location where he hangs out with the star of a cop show (Igor Kostolevsky). Ambitiously stylised yet movingly authentic. DP. In Russian with English subtitles.

Genya Korhin *Micha* • Victoria Korhina *Julia, Micha's mother* • Igor Kostolevsky ■ *Dir/Scr* Gerard Michael MacCarthy

Michael ★★★ PG

Fantasy comedy 1996 · US · Colour · 100mins

John Travolta stars as an angel living in backwoods Iowa. Even though he comes with feathers on his back, he's close to being white trash, but when some journalists arrive to write a story about him Travolta turns their hardboiled hearts into slush. William Hurt is dependably strange and often very funny as one of the hacks, but Bob Hoskins is embarrassing as Hurt's editor and Andie MacDowell fails to make her mark as the female lead. AT. Contains some swearing.

John Travolta *Michael* • Andie MacDowell *Dorothy Winters* • William Hurt *Frank Quinlan* • Bob Hoskins *Vartan Malt* • Robert Pastorelli *Huey Driscoll* • Jean Stapleton *Pansy Milbank* • Teri Garr *Judge Esther Newberg* ■ *Dir* Nora Ephron • *Scr* Nora Ephron, Delia Ephron, Pete Dexter, Jim Quinlan, from a story by Pete Dexter, Jim Quinlan

Michael Collins ★★★★ 15

Biographical drama
1996 · US/UK · Colour · 126mins

Neil Jordan's screen biography of the founder of the IRA, an intellectual who virtually invented urban terrorism and bombed his way to talks in Downing Street before being assassinated by his own side in 1922. The movie begins with an impressively filmed Easter uprising, in which Jordan appears to demolish Dublin, yet there's also an even-handedness when it comes to depicting and simplifying the political struggle for Irish independence. As Collins, Liam Neeson is both charming and menacing, while Alan Rickman is superbly cast as Eamon De Valera. Julia Roberts, however, looks hopelessly lost. AT. Contains swearing and violence. DVD

Liam Neeson *Michael Collins* • Julia Roberts *Kitty Kiernan* • Aidan Quinn *Harry Boland* • Ian Hart *Joe O'Reilly* • Stephen Rea *Ned Broy* • John Kenny *Patrick Pearse* • Alan Rickman *Eamon De Valera* • Charles Dance *Soames* ■ *Dir/Scr* Neil Jordan

Michael Shayne, Private Detective ★★

Crime mystery 1940 · US · BW · 76mins

The first in an interesting series of programme fillers from 20th Century-Fox, important today because it featured a tough, resilient and self-reliant private eye before the popularity of those moody Humphrey Bogart movies later on in the decade. Shayne was incarnated on screen by the excellent Lloyd Nolan, an actor whose very persona suggested he brooked no nonsense. This pilot movie is abrasive, sexy and eminently watchable within its B-budget confines. Nolan reprised the role in two further films. TS

Lloyd Nolan *Michael Shayne* • Marjorie Weaver *Phyllis Brighton* • Joan Valerie *Marsha Gordon* • Walter Abel *Elliott Thomas* • Elizabeth Patterson *Aunt Olivia* • Donald MacBride *Chief Painter* • Douglass Dumbrille *Gordon* ■ *Dir* Eugene Forde • *Scr* Stanley Rauh, Manning O'Connor, from a novel by Brett Halliday

Mickey Blue Eyes ★★★ 15

Comedy 1999 · US/UK · Colour · 98mins

Hugh Grant is sublimely ridiculous as an English auctioneer in New York, who learns that marrying sweetheart Jeanne Tripplehorn means getting spliced to the Mob. Tripplehorn's father, James Caan, is the local don and Grant quickly finds himself up to his neck in linguine as he fakes the identity of out-of-town mobster "Mickey Blue Eyes". Gently entertaining. LH. Contains swearing, violence. DVD

Hugh Grant *Michael Felgate* • James Caan *Frank Vitale* • Jeanne Tripplehorn *Gina Vitale* • Burt Young *Vito Graziosi* • James Fox *Philip Cromwell* • Joe Viterelli *Vinnie* • Gerry Becker *Agent Connell* • Maddie Corman *Carol* ■ *Dir* Kelly Makin • *Scr* Mark Lawrence, Adam Scheinmann, Robert Kuhn

Mickey One ★★★

Crime drama 1965 · US · BW · 92mins

Warren Beatty made *Mickey One* right after *Lilith* and the result was another flop. It's easy to see why. Essentially a thriller about a nightclub comic, the plot fragments into a psychological drama about the Mob. The style, though, is something else. This is an American art movie, incredibly flash and tricksy, with a melodramatic Hurd Hatfield as a homosexual club owner and oblique references to the Kennedy assassination and Jack Ruby. A fascinating mess. AT

Warren Beatty *Mickey One* • Alexandra Stewart *Jenny* • Hurd Hatfield *Castle* • Franchot Tone *Ruby Lopp* • Teddy Hart *Berson* • Jeff Corey *Fryer* • Kamatari Fujiwara *Artist* ■ *Dir* Arthur Penn • *Scr* Alan M Surgal

Micki & Maude ★ PG

Comedy 1984 · US · Colour · 112mins

Dudley Moore's cinematic career reached its height with the movies *10* and *Arthur*, but by the time this weak Blake Edwards comedy was made in 1984 it was in a trough as deep as the Grand Canyon. This farcical tale of a man who wants to marry his pregnant mistress while still remaining married to his equally expectant wife didn't help matters, and the blame has to be laid at the feet of the similarly out-of-luck Edwards. JB

Dudley Moore *Rob Salinger* • Amy Irving *Maude Guillory* • Ann Reinking *Micki Salinger* • Richard Mulligan *Leo Brody* • George Gaynes *Dr Eugene Glztski* • Wallace Shawn *Dr Elliot Fibel* • John Pleshette *Hap Ludlow* • HB Haggerty *Barkhas Guillory* ■ *Dir* Blake Edwards • *Scr* Jonathan Reynolds

Microcosmos ★★★★ U

Documentary
1996 · Fr/Swi/It · Colour · 72mins

Directors Claude Nuridsany and Marie Pérennou redefine the boundaries of the nature documentary with this astounding look at the insect life in a French meadow. Filmed over three years using revolutionary camera and sound equipment, it presents a bug's-eye view of the world in a series of visually amazing close-ups highlighting a stag beetle battle, an ant colony hatching and the deliberate movement of a caterpillar. The soundtrack contains the startling noises of the insects themselves and an eclectic array of music, and the result is an overpowering experience. AJ DVD

Kristin Scott Thomas *Narrator* ■ *Dir* Claude Nuridsany, Marie Pérennou

Midaq Alley ★★ 15

Melodrama 1995 · Mex · Colour · 138mins

Apparently, this film has won 45 international film awards, yet it would undoubtedly have remained buried if it wasn't for the presence of one Salma Hayek. Unreleased on video until 1999, it was made when she was largely unknown outside her native Mexico. Hayek is the young innocent who is plunged into the world of prostitution in one of three loosely linked stories, which take place over the same time period but are viewed from different perspectives. JF. In Spanish with English subtitles.

Ernesto Gómez Cruz *Don Rutilio* • Maria Rojo *Doña Cata* • Salma Hayek *Alma* • Bruno Bichir *Abel* ■ *Dir* Jorge Fons • *Scr* Vicente Leñero, from the novel by Naguib Mahfouz

Midas Run ★★

Crime mystery 1969 · US · Colour · 106mins

Swedish actor/director Alf Kjellin – so memorable in *Torment* (1944), a tale of troubled adolescence – comes a cropper with this Hollywood hokum about an elderly spymaster determined to steal a load of gold bullion. (Hence the alternative title, *A Run On Gold.*) It has a splendid job-lot of class actors: Fred Astaire, Richard Crenna, Ralph Richardson, Cesar Romero. They don't help much, though. TH

Richard Crenna *Mike Warden* • Anne Heywood *Sylvia Giroux* • Fred Astaire *John Pedley* • Roddy McDowall *Wister* • Ralph Richardson *Henshaw* • Cesar Romero *Dodero* • Adolfo Celi *Aldo Ferranti* • Maurice Denham *Crittenden* • John Le Mesurier *Wells* ■ *Dir* Alf Kjellin • *Scr* James Buchanan, Ronald Austin, Berne Giler, from a story by Berne Giler

Middle Age Crazy ★★★

Comedy drama 1980 · Can · Colour · 91mins

Bruce Dern has a midlife crisis, though his gangling frame, thinning hair, buck teeth and country hick voice make him look a little unhinged to begin with. He's a Texan architect – nothing fancy, just fast food stands – who has just clocked 40. So when his dad dies, he buys a Porsche, dresses like JR Ewing, leaves his wife (played by the wittily voluptuous Ann-Margret) and runs off with sexy Deborah Wakeham. All the clichés of a movie marriage on the rocks fall into place, but it's none the worse for that. AT

Bruce Dern *Bobby Lee* • Ann-Margret *Sue Ann* • Graham Jarvis *JD* • Eric Christmas *Tommy* • Helen Hughes *Ruth* • Geoffrey Bowes *Greg* • Deborah Wakeham *Nancy* ■ *Dir* John Trent • *Scr* Carl Kleinschmitt, from the song by Jerry Lee Lewis

Middle of the Night ★★

Drama 1959 · US · BW · 117mins

A typically overwrought drama from Paddy Chayefsky about life and love in the garment industry. The factory is run by unhappily married Albert Dekker and lonely widower Fredric March, who suddenly falls for pretty secretary Kim Novak. As usual with these wordy, liberal dramas, characters make speeches and there's a dollop of psychobabble to make us understand them better. A strong cast, though. AT

Kim Novak *Betty Preisser* • Fredric March *Jerry Kingsley* • Lee Philips *George* • Glenda Farrell *Mrs Mueller* • Albert Dekker *Lockman* • Martin Balsam *Jack* • Lee Grant *Marilyn* • Edith Meiser *Evelyn Kingsley* ■ *Dir* Delbert Mann • *Scr* Paddy Chayefsky, from his play

The Middleman ★★★★

Satirical drama 1975 · Ind · BW · 122mins

This knowing satire from Satyajit Ray on the corruption that grips all aspects of Indian commerce completes the Calcutta trilogy that began with *The Adversary* and *Company Limited*. Providing an unflattering picture of both the middle classes and inner-city life, the film focuses on the shady dealings of a university graduate as he searches for an escort for a client. Deftly switching between comedy and social comment, Ray draws a fine performance from Pradip Mukherjee as the ambitious 20-something who has been reduced to behaving like the Arthur Daley of Calcutta. DP. In Bengali with English subtitles.

Pradip Mukherjee *Somnath Bannerji* • Satya Bannerji [Satya Bannerjee] *Somnath's father* • Dipankar Dey *Bhombol* • Lily Chakravarty *Kamala* • Aparna Sen *Somnath's girlfriend* • Goutam Chakravarti *Sukumar, Somnath's friend* ■ *Dir* Satyajit Ray • *Scr* Satyajit Ray, from the novel by Shankar

Middleton's Changeling ★ 18

Tragedy 1997 · UK · Colour · 85mins

Based on the classic Jacobean tragedy about doomed love, betrayal and madness, director Marcus Thompson's film is a total bore. His interpretation involves much poetic license with the text and period (heroine Amanda Ray-King wears sneakers under her petticoats). Although such gimmickry is shrouded in visually arresting images, the film remains an infuriating curiosity. AJ. Contains swearing, sex scenes and violence. DVD

Ian Dury *De Flores* • Amanda Ray-King *Beatrice Joanna* • Colm O Maonlai *Alsemero* • Billy Connolly *Alibius* • Campbell Morrison *Lollio* • Moya Brady *Isabella* • Richard Mayes *Vermandero* ■ *Dir* Marcus Thompson • *Scr* Marcus Thompson, from the play by Thomas Middleton, William Rowley

Midnight ★★

Drama 1934 · US · BW · 68mins

A crime of passion repeats itself: just as a jury foreman announces the guilty verdict that sends a woman to the electric chair, his daughter shoots her lover to stop him going away. The daughter is Sidney Fox, and the lover is a racketeer played by the young Humphrey Bogart. The film is rather pretentious, and Bogart is quite unremarkable in his small role – though that didn't stop an American distributor reissuing it in 1947 as *Call It Murder*, billing Bogie as the star. AE

Humphrey Bogart *Gar Boni* • Henry Hull *Bob Nolan* • Sidney Fox *Stella Weldon* • OP Heggie *Edward Weldon* • Richard Whorf *Arthur Weldon* • Lynne Overman *Joe "Leroy" Biggers* • Granville Bates *Henry McGrath* • Margaret Wycherly *Mrs Weldon* ■ *Dir* Chester Erskine • *Scr* Chester Erskine, from a play by Paul Sifton, Claire Sifton

Midnight ★★★★★

Classic comedy 1939 · US · BW · 94mins

Written by the incomparable team of Charles Brackett and Billy Wilder, starring Claudette Colbert, Don Ameche and John Barrymore (in one of his best late roles), this is right up there with *Ninotchka*, another Wilder and Brackett classic. Add Mary Astor and Francis Lederer in support and expert direction from Mitchell Leisen, and the result is one of the most stylish and enduring comedies of the era. The story involves an American girl (Colbert) who arrives penniless in Paris at midnight. After catching the eye of a Hungarian taxi driver (Ameche), she finds herself masquerading as a wealthy baroness, hired by a wealthy man (Barrymore) to lure away his wife's lover. Sophisticated and hilarious, it sparkles and sizzles. RK

Claudette Colbert *Eve Peabody/"Baroness Czerny"* • Don Ameche *Tibor Czerny* • John Barrymore *Georges Flammarion* • Francis Lederer *Jacques Picot* • Mary Astor *Helene Flammarion* • Elaine Barrie *Simone* • Hedda Hopper *Stephanie* • Rex O'Malley *Marcel* • Monty Woolley *Judge* ■ *Dir* Mitchell Leisen • *Scr* Charles Brackett, Billy Wilder, from a story by Edwin Justus Mayer, Franz Shulz

Midnight ★★ 18

Horror thriller 1980 · US · Colour · 90mins

Occasionally scary, but too often pedestrian, this cheap horror movie marked the directorial debut of John A Russo. Melanie Verlin flees from her wicked stepfather (1940s star Lawrence Tierney) only to be captured by satanists in need of a human sacrifice. It's all weighed down by reams of dialogue and too many scenes of driving and walking. DM [video]

Lawrence Tierney *Bert Johnson* • Melanie Verliin *Nancy Johnson* • John Hall *Tom* • Charles Jackson *Hank* • Doris Hackney *Harriet Johnson* • John Amplas *Abraham* ■ *Dir* John A Russo • *Scr* John A Russo, from his novel

Midnight ★

Horror satire 1989 · US · Colour · 84mins

Low-grade horror rubbish, this is a lame lampoon on showbiz. Lynn Redgrave plays an Elvira-style TV horror hostess, complete with frizzy wig and gothic costume, whose entourage is being killed off. There's good support from Tony Curtis as her greedy network boss and Frank Gorshin as a double-crossing agent, but director Norman Thaddeus Vane generates no suspense whatsoever. RS

Lynn Redgrave *Midnight (Vera)* • Tony Curtis *Mr B* • Steve Parrish *Mickey Modine* • Rita Gam *Heidi* • Gustav Vintas *Siegfried* • Karen Witter *Mitty* • Frank Gorshin *Ron* ■ *Dir/Scr* Norman Thaddeus Vane

Midnight ★★★

Drama 1998 · Bra/Fr · Colour · 76mins

Walter Salles's follow-up to *Central Station* may be set on Millennium Eve, but by the time an escaped prisoner and an abandoned teacher meet on a Rio rooftop, it's clear this is no nostalgic paean to the passing century or expression of hope for the future. Instead it's a grim reminder that, for all the high-minded resolutions of the establishment, life grinds on for those ordinary people caught in time's relentless mechanism. DP. In Portuguese with English subtitles.

Fernanda Torres *Maria* • Luiz Carlos Vasconcelos *Joao* • Carlos Vereza *Pedro* ■ *Dir* Walter Salles, Daniela Thomas • *Scr* Daniela Thomas, José de Carvalho, Walter Salles, Joao Emanuel Carneiro

Midnight at Madame Tussaud's ★★

Thriller 1936 · UK · BW · 66mins

Made at Highbury studios, this creaky old chiller benefits from some superb sets, but the story, about a famous explorer who hopes to reduce his debts by betting he can spend the night in the famous Chamber of Horrors, is pretty limp. Not even a subplot involving his daughter's shady love life can pep it up. Bernard Miles is good value as the ghoulish sculptor, but James Carew as the explorer is less animated than the exhibits. DP

James Carew *Sir Clive Cheyne* • Lucille Lisle *Carol Cheyne* • Charles Oliver *Harry Newton* • Kim Peacock *Nick Frome* • Patrick Barr *Gerry Melville* • William Hartnell *Stubbs* • Lydia Sherwood *Brenda* • Bernard Miles *Modeller* ■ *Dir* George Pearson • *Scr* Kim Peacock, Roger MacDougall, from a story by James S Edwards, Roger MacDougall

A Midnight Clear ★★★★ 15

Second World War drama
1991 · US · Colour · 103mins

The shifting group dynamics of a Second World War infantry squad are put under the psychological microscope in director Keith Gordon's gripping morality play about the personal price exacted by battle. It's when the GIs meet some German soldiers, just back from the disastrous campaign on the Russian front, that the main thrust of this insightful drama snaps into focus. Former actor Gordon gives his ensemble cast a chance to shine in a powerful tragedy full of surprises and visual style. AJ [video]

Peter Berg *Bud Miller* • Kevin Dillon *Mel Avakian* • Arye Gross *Stan Shutzer* • Ethan Hawke *Will Knott* • Gary Sinise *"Mother" Wilkins* • Frank Whaley *"Father" Mundy* • John C McGinley *Major Griffin* • Larry Joshua *Lieutenant Ware* ■ *Dir* Keith Gordon • *Scr* Keith Gordon, from the novel by William Wharton

Midnight Cop ★★★ 18

Thriller 1988 · W Ger · Colour · 92mins

This passable police thriller benefits enormously from Armin Mueller-Stahl's strong central performance as an eccentric, ageing Berlin cop hunting down a vicious serial killer. Director Peter Patzak works wonders with a meandering storyline and deserves a medal for the sheer temerity of casting TV soap bimbette Morgan Fairchild as a call girl who acts as a decoy to trap the killer. RS [video]

Armin Mueller-Stahl *Inspector Alex Glas* • Morgan Fairchild *Lisa* • Michael York *Karstens* • Frank Stallone *Jack Miskowski* • Julia Kent *Shirley* ■ *Dir* Peter Patzak • *Scr* Julia Kent, Paul Nicholas, Peter Patzak

Midnight Cowboy ★★★★★ 18

Drama 1969 · US · Colour · 108mins

This tawdry, strident yet deeply affecting tale of a naive Texas stud striking up a relationship with a tubercular conman deservedly won several Oscars. British film-maker John Schlesinger was the perfect director to cast an alien eye on Manhattan's sexual permissiveness and Warhol weirdness, and exposes the jaundiced stratum beneath the hip surface with scalpel-sharp precision. Jon Voight and Dustin Hoffman are a perfectly matched odd couple adrift on the sea of amorality in a warped buddy picture that cleverly walks a fine line between warmth and cruelty. AJ. Contains violence, swearing, sex scenes, drug abuse and nudity. [video] DVD

Dustin Hoffman *Ratso Rizzo* • Jon Voight *Joe Buck* • Sylvia Miles *Cass* • Brenda Vaccaro *Shirley* • John McGiver *Mr O'Daniel* • Barnard Hughes *Towny* • Ruth White *Sally Buck* • Jennifer Salt *Annie* ■ *Dir* John Schlesinger • *Scr* Waldo Salt, from the novel by James Leo Herlihy • *Music* John Barry (1)

Midnight Crossing ★★ 18

Thriller 1988 · US · Colour · 92mins

Faye Dunaway demonstrates here that even the most illustrious career can suffer a nose dive. Daniel J Travanti takes blind wife Dunaway on a Caribbean holiday; unbeknown to her, though, he's actually there to recover some stolen money. The plot gets seriously twisted as everyone starts crossing and double-crossing each other, but the script and the performances don't generate much interest. JB [video] DVD

Faye Dunaway *Helen Barton* • Daniel J Travanti *Morely Barton* • Kim Cattrall *Alexa Schubb* • Ned Beatty *Ellis* • John Laughlin *Jeffrey Schubb* • Pedro De Pool *Capt Mendoza* • Doug Weiser *Miller* ■ *Dir* Roger Holzberg • *Scr* Roger Holzberg, Doug Weiser, from a story by Roger Holzberg

Midnight Dancers ★★★ 18

Drama 1994 · Phil · Colour · 122mins

Directed in almost documentary style by Mel Chionglo, this is an uncompromising insight into the risks and realities faced by the "macho dancers" of Manila. Ricky Lee's script focuses on three brothers forced on to the street in order to survive. Although the emphasis is firmly on the youngest and his transvestite lover as they cruise the city's clubs and bars, the attention regularly switches to the eldest, as he juggles his wife and gay lover, and to the middle boy, who lives for the danger of street hustling. Revealing, provocative and often deeply disturbing. DP. In English and Tagalog with subtitles. [video]

Axel Del Rosario • Grandong Cervantes • Lawrence David • Luis Cortez ■ *Dir* Mel Chionglo • *Scr* Ricky Lee

M

Midnight Express ★★★★★ 18

Biographical drama
1978 · UK/US · Colour · 115mins

It's hard to counter some of the criticisms about the sympathetic depiction of drug traffickers, the pitiless violence, the stereotypical representation of the Turkish jailers and the over-simplistic approach to the key issues raised that greeted this film on its release. Yet it is still a superbly staged drama, which exploits its excesses to force the viewer into considering the broader moral and humanitarian themes, as well as the harrowing events on the screen. Scripted by Oliver Stone from the memoirs of Billy Hayes, it is directed with power and intelligence by Alan Parker, while Brad Davis is outstanding in the lead. DP. Contains violence, swearing, sex scenes, drug abuse and nudity. DVD

Brad Davis *Billy Hayes* • Randy Quaid *Jimmy Booth* • John Hurt *Max* • Irene Miracle *Susan* • Bo Hopkins *Tex* • Paolo Bonacelli *Rifki* • Paul Smith *Hamidou* • Norbert Weisser *Erich* ■ *Dir* Alan Parker • *Scr* Oliver Stone, from the non-fiction book by Billy Hayes, William Hoffer

Midnight in St Petersburg ★★ 15

Thriller 1995 · UK/Can/Rus · Colour · 85mins

Harry Palmer really should have stayed in retirement, but Michael Caine was persuaded to resurrect the bespectacled spy character that made his name back in the 1960s for two new adventures, shot back-to-back on location in Russia. However, his heart doesn't really seem in it and the result is the worst sort of Europudding. This is the second of the two films (following *Bullet to Beijing*), with Harry running a security firm in Moscow. JF. Contains violence and swearing.

Michael Caine *Harry Palmer* • Jason Connery *Nick* • Michael Sarrazin *Craig* • Michael Gambon *Alex Alexovich* • Michelle Rene Thomas [Michelle Burke] *Brandy* • Tanya Jackson *Tatiana* • Yuri Limonty *Circus clown* • Michael Scherer *Mafioso* ■ *Dir* Doug Jackson [Douglas Jackson] • *Scr* Peter Welbeck [Harry Alan Towers], from the novel by Len Deighton

Midnight in the Garden of Good and Evil ★★★★ 15

Crime drama 1997 · US · Colour · 148mins

John Berendt's bestseller was an audacious blend of travel journalism and true-life crime that gave a tremendous boost to the tourist industry of Savannah, Georgia. Clint Eastwood's long and leisurely adaptation is so seduced by the town's sultry, seedy atmosphere that the plot sometimes seems incidental. John Cusack is the naive New York journalist who stumbles into Savannah's sinister underbelly, meeting Kevin Spacey's wealthy antiques dealer and getting lost in a demimonde of soirées, rent boys and murder. Under-rated by most critics, this grows in stature and lingers long in the memory. AT. Contains swearing and violence. DVD

Kevin Spacey *Jim Williams* • John Cusack *John Kelso* • Jack Thompson *Sonny Seiler* • Irma P Hall *Minerva* • Jude Law *Billy Hanson* • Alison Eastwood *Mandy Nichols* • Paul Hipp *Joe Odom* • The Lady Chablis [Lady Chablis] *Chablis Deveau* ■ *Dir* Clint Eastwood • *Scr* John Lee Hancock, from the novel by John Berendt

Midnight Lace ★★ PG

Psychological thriller
1960 · US · Colour · 103mins

With Doris Day and Rex Harrison, one expects a comedy. But this is a thriller in which Day, married to businessman Harrison, is stalked, receives abusive phone calls and is nearly pushed under a bus. The police think she's fibbing; Harrison claims she losing her marbles. What on earth is going on? Well, it's not too hard to figure out. Set in London and filmed entirely in Hollywood, the supporting cast of such veterans as Myrna Loy and Herbert Marshall, plus the inimitable John Williams as the man from Scotland Yard, are distinct bonuses. AT

Doris Day *Kit Preston* • Rex Harrison *Tony Preston* • John Gavin *Brian Younger* • Myrna Loy *Aunt Bea* • Roddy McDowall *Malcolm* • Herbert Marshall *Charles Manning* • Natasha Parry *Peggy Thompson* • John Williams *Inspector Byrnes* • Hermione Baddeley *Dora* ■ *Dir* David Miller • *Scr* Ivan Goff, Ben Roberts, from the play *Matilda Shouted Fire* by Janet Green • *Costume Designer* Irene

Midnight Madness ★★ PG

Comedy 1980 · US · Colour · 107mins

This juvenile campus comedy is notable for the fact it was only the second movie from the Disney stable to carry a PG certificate (the first was *The Black Hole*). It's a juvenile take on *It's a Mad Mad Mad Mad World*, with five teams of student stereotypes – nerds, jocks, sorority girls, slobs – cavorting around Los Angeles in a 24-hour scavenger hunt for the clues deposited by the uncharismatic Alan Solomon. Michael J. Fox fans will wince at the sight of their 18-year-old hero debuting as a pre-teen. DP

David Naughton *Adam* • Debra Clinger *Laura* • Eddie Deezen *Wesley* • Brad Wilkin *Lavitas* • Maggie Roswell *Donna* • Stephen Furst *Harold* • Michael J Fox *Scott* • Alan Solomon *Leon* ■ *Dir* Michael Nankin, David Wechter • *Scr* David Wechter, Michael Nankin

The Midnight Man ★★

Mystery 1974 · US · Colour · 118mins

Burt Lancaster stars as a former cop, jailed for the murder of his wife's lover, who investigates another murder on the university campus where he now works as a janitor. Set in South Carolina, this is never more than routine; Lancaster later admitted he made it as a favour to his longtime buddy and partner, Roland Kibbee, who needed the money and got a co-writer and co-director credit. AT

Burt Lancaster *Jim Slade* • Susan Clark *Linda* • Cameron Mitchell *Quartz* • Morgan Woodward *Clayborn* • Harris Yulin *Sheriff Casey* • Joan Lorring *Judy* ■ *Dir* Roland Kibbee, Burt Lancaster • *Scr* Roland Kibbee, Burt Lancaster, from the novel *The Midnight Lady and the Mourning Man* by David Anthony

Midnight Movie Massacre ★

Science-fiction comedy horror
1987 · US · Colour · 86mins

An alien monster closes in on a movie theatre packed with 1950s teens watching a sci-fi double bill, in this cobbled-together mess of lame nostalgia, nerd humour, real trailers and bad re-creations of black-and-white serials that uses unreleased footage from shelved projects. The idea of hack producer Wade Williams, who shoehorns his uncompleted production of *Space Patrol* into director Mark Stock's *Animal House*-style antics, the result is a gory but completely nonsensical farrago. AJ

Ann Robinson *Dr Van Buren* • Robert Clarke *Colonel Carlyle* ■ *Dir/Scr* Mark Stock

Midnight Run ★★★★ 18

Comedy thriller 1988 · US · Colour · 121mins

Robert De Niro played this action picture for laughs and, as a result, had his first hit in years. It's a variant on the odd-couple theme, as De Niro's bounty hunter goes on the run with an accountant who has embezzled $15 million from the Mob. The accountant is Charles Grodin, whose underplaying is an absolute joy: he looks like a puppy that's lost its poop tray. As with all the best road movies – and this is one of the best – the picture really moves, as a simple air trip from New York to LA turns into a saga of trains and automobiles, car crashes and skirmishes with the FBI and a dozen other interested parties. AT. Contains swearing, violence. DVD

Robert De Niro *Jack Walsh* • Charles Grodin *Jonathan Mardukas* • Yaphet Kotto *Alonzo Mosely* • John Ashton *Marvin Dorfler* • Dennis Farina *Jimmy Serrano* • Joe Pantoliano *Eddie Moscone* • Richard Foronjy *Tony Darvo* ■ *Dir* Martin Brest • *Scr* George Gallo

Midnight Sting ★★★ 15

Sports drama 1992 · US · Colour · 93mins

This sparky comedy drama packs such a punch, that it's hard to believe it sank without trace on its British cinema release. This boxing variation on *The Sting* bristles with sassy dialogue, dynamic fight sequences and truly dastardly villainy (provided by the ever-hissable Bruce Dern). As the cons who hope to clean up with a boxing scam in a small rural backwater, James Woods, Louis Gossett Jr and Oliver Platt are bang on form, but director Michael Ritchie lets the side down by wasting time on a tiresome romantic interlude and a sentimental subplot. DP DVD

James Woods *Gabriel Caine* • Louis Gossett Jr *"Honey" Roy Palmer* • Bruce Dern *John Gillon* • Oliver Platt *Fitz* • Heather Graham *Emily Forrester* • Randall "Tex" Cobb *Wolf Forrester* • Thomas Wilson Brown *Robby Gillon* • Duane Davis *Hambone Busby* ■ *Dir* Michael Ritchie • *Scr* Steven McKay, from the novel *The Diggstown Ringers* by Leonard Wise

The Midnight Story ★★★

Crime mystery 1957 · US · BW · 90mins

Traffic cop Tony Curtis is refused a transfer to homicide, so he resigns from the force in order to investigate the murder of his best friend, the Catholic priest who raised him as an orphan. Curtis's main quarry is restaurateur Gilbert Roland, who invites him to lodge at his house. Set in the Italian community of San Francisco, it's as much about Curtis's need for a family, a faith and a sense of belonging as it is a whodunnit. Unpretentious, compelling and with a neat twist at the end. AT

Tony Curtis *Joe Martini* • Marisa Pavan *Anna Malatesta* • Gilbert Roland *Sylvio Malatesta* • Jay C Flippen *Sergeant Jack Gillen* • Argentina Brunetti *Mama Malatesta* ■ *Dir* Joseph Pevney • *Scr* John Robinson, Edwin Blum, from a story by Edwin Blum

A Midsummer Night's Dream ★★★★ U

Romantic comedy fantasy
1935 · US · BW · 111mins

One of the pottiest movies ever made in Hollywood – a loose rendition of Shakespeare's play, set amid lavish and fantastical woodland sets and with some extraordinary performances from James Cagney as Bottom, Olivia de Havilland as Hermia, Dick Powell as Lysander and Mickey Rooney as Puck. Rooney broke his leg during production and was moved around the set on a bicycle. Warner Bros gave theatre maestro Max Reinhardt carte blanche to create a masterwork and, when he set too slow a pace and got into a muddle, decided to give him a co-director, studio hack William Dieterle. From the mess came two Oscars, the debut of a movie composer Erich Wolfgang Korngold, and a breathtaking, if kitsch classic. AT

James Cagney *Bottom, the weaver* • Dick Powell *Lysander* • Mickey Rooney *Puck, or Robin Goodfellow* • Joe E Brown *Flute, the bellows-mender* • Victor Jory *Oberon* • Ian Hunter *Theseus, Duke of Athens* • Verree Teasdale *Hippolyta* • Hobart Cavanaugh *Philostrate* • Ross Alexander (1) *Demetrius* • Olivia de Haviland [Olivia de Havilland] *Hermia* • Jean Muir *Helena* • Grant Mitchell *Egeus* • Frank McHugh *Quince* • Anita Louise *Titania* • Kenneth Anger *Changeling prince* ■ *Dir* Max Reinhardt, William Dieterle • *Scr* Charles Kenyon, Mary C McCall Jr, from the play by William Shakespeare • *Cinematographer* Hal Mohr, Ernest Haller • *Art Director* Anton Grot

A Midsummer Night's Dream ★★★★

Animated romantic fantasy
1961 · Cz · Colour · 76mins

Three years in the making, Jiri Trnka's masterpiece seeks to dispense with the Shakespearean text and tell the still-enchanting story by means of pantomimic puppetry and dance. Trnka and his co-animator, Bretislav Pojar, lavished considerable care on both the costumes and the forest settings. For all the richness of the visual detail, though, there was still room for the simple exhilaration created by Puck and the mechanicals. The balletic quality of the action left international audiences confused, however, and a voiceover quoting from and commenting on the Bard's play was added against Trnka's wishes. DP

Richard Burton *Narrator* • Tom Criddle *Lysander* • Ann Bell *Hermia* • Michael Meacham *Demetrius* • John Warner *Egeus* • Barbara Leigh-Hunt *Helena* • Hugh Manning *Theseus* • Joss Ackland *Quince* • Alec McCowen *Bottom* • Stephen Moore *Flute* • Barbara Jefford *Titania* • Jack Gwillim *Oberon* ■ *Dir* Jiri Trnka, Howard Sackler • *Scr* Jiri Trnka, Jiri Brdecka, Howard Sackler, from the play by William Shakespeare

A Midsummer Night's Dream ★★ U

Romantic comedy fantasy
1969 · UK · Colour · 119mins

Sir Peter Hall's early attempt at translating this Shakespearean classic from stage to screen is too close to the original RSC production to achieve a new lease of life on film. Diana Rigg, Helen Mirren, Judi Dench and Ian Richardson star in this tale of four lovers and a "rude mechanical", lost in the forest and at the mercy of mischievous fairies. Hall, an opera and theatre veteran, betrays his lack of film experience by making some very strange editing and sound choices. LH

Derek Godfrey *Theseus* • Barbara Jefford *Hippolyta* • Hugh Sullivan *Philostrate* • Nicholas Selby *Egeus* • David Warner *Lysander* • Michael Jayston *Demetrius* • Diana Rigg *Helena* • Helen Mirren *Hermia* • Ian Richardson *Oberon* • Judi Dench *Titania* • Ian Holm *Puck* ■ *Dir* Peter Hall • *Scr* from the play by William Shakespeare

A Midsummer Night's Dream ★★ PG

Romantic comedy fantasy
1996 · UK · Colour · 99mins

The great tragedy of this screen version of director Adrian Noble's Royal Shakespeare Company production is that, on stage, it would be absolutely electrifying. The hanging lightbulbs that comprise the Athenian forest, the stylised costumes and the glittery make-up help convey some of the play's magic. But the fairies in glowing wigs and the tacky conceit of having the whole thing dreamed by a young boy are ghastly misjudgements. The leaden camera movements are matched only by the clumsiness of the editing. DP DVD

Lindsay Duncan *Hippolyta/Titania* • Alex Jennings *Theseus/Oberon* • Desmond Barrit *Nick Bottom* • Barry Lynch *Puck/Philostrate* • Monica Dolan *Hermia* • Kevin Doyle *Demetrius* • Daniel Evans *Lysander* • Emily Raymond *Helena* ■ *Dir* Adrian Noble • *Scr* Adrian Noble, from the play by William Shakespeare

A Midsummer Night's Dream ★★★ PG

Romantic comedy fantasy
1999 · US · Colour · 120mins

Kevin Kline steals the show as Bottom in this stilted version of Shakespeare's ode to blighted love. As played by Kline, not only is Bottom a garrulous bumbler, but he's also – when transformed into a donkey by Oberon (Rupert Everett) to fool Titania (Michelle Pfeiffer) – an object of abject poignancy. Updated to 19th-century Italy, Michael Hoffman's film looks most elegant – Calista Flockhart makes a beautiful Helena, and Stanley Tucci's Puck should get a prize for the best-dressed fairy – but without an animating core of real magic the result is simply a pretty enchantment. TH. Contains brief semi-nudity. VIDEO DVD

Kevin Kline *Nick Bottom* • Michelle Pfeiffer *Titania* • Rupert Everett *Oberon* • Stanley Tucci *Puck* • Calista Flockhart *Helena* • Anna Friel *Hermia* • Christian Bale *Demetrius* • Dominic West *Lysander* • Sophie Marceau *Hippolyta* • Bernard Hill *Egeus* • John Sessions *Philostrate* ■ *Dir* Michael Hoffman • *Scr* Michael Hoffman, from the play by William Shakespeare

A Midsummer Night's Sex Comedy ★★★★ 15

Comedy 1982 · US · Colour · 84mins

Woody Allen pays homage to Ingmar Bergman in this re-vamp of *Smiles of a Summer Night*, in which six characters gather at a turn-of-the-century farmhouse in search of sexual satisfaction. José Ferrer is the pedantic scholar engaged to Mia Farrow; Allen is the stockbroker trying to bed his frigid wife, Mary Steenburgen. The jokes come thin and slow for a Woody movie, with the result that Allen's oddball inventions (which include a flying bicycle) are at least as interesting as the oddball people. Gordon Willis's photography is exquisite, however. TH VIDEO DVD

Woody Allen *Andrew* • Mia Farrow *Ariel Weymouth* • José Ferrer *Leopold* • Julie Hagerty *Dulcy Ford* • Tony Roberts *Maxwell* • Mary Steenburgen *Adrian* • Michael Higgins *Reynolds* • Adam Redfield *Student Foxx* ■ *Dir/Scr* Woody Allen

Mifune ★★★ 15

Romantic comedy drama
1999 · Swe/Den · Colour · 101mins

Less abrasive than earlier Dogme outings, this surprisingly traditional comedy is similar in storyline and tone to the 1998 Dutch film *The Polish Bride*. Spurning the shock tactics and hand-held camera style of *Festen* and *The Idiots*, director Søren Kragh-Jacobsen uses the beautiful Lolland light to bring a pleasing rustic ambience to the piece. The tale centres on the romance between prostitute Iben Hjejle and Anders W Berthelsen, a newly married yuppie who hides his country origins. A predictable but rather pleasing little film. DP. In Danish with English subtitles. Contains swearing and sexual references.

Anders W Berthelsen *Kresten* • Jesper Asholt *Rud* • Iben Hjejle *Liva Psilander* • Sofie Grabol *Claire* • Emil Tarding *Bjarke Psilander* ■ *Dir* Søren Kragh-Jacobsen • *Scr* Søren Kragh-Jacobsen, Anders Thomas Jensen

The Mighty ★★★★ PG

Fantasy drama 1998 · US · Colour · 96mins

Lumbering outcast Elden Henson doesn't fit in with the other kids in school, but he finally finds a friend when Kieran Culkin is instructed to tutor him. Culkin is a disabled hunchback, but he is also a lover of stories who introduces Henson to an imaginary life outside their own depressing existence. Both boys are superb, and they are ably supported by a cast which includes Sharon Stone, Gena Rowlands, Gillian Anderson and Harry Dean Stanton. A moving, wonderfully-played tale. JB VIDEO DVD

Sharon Stone *Gwen Dillon* • Harry Dean Stanton *Grim* • Gena Rowlands *Gram* • Kieran Culkin *Kevin Dillon* • Gillian Anderson *Loretta Lee* • Elden Henson *Maxwell Kane* • Meat Loaf Aday [Meat Loaf] *Iggy* ■ *Dir* Peter Chelsom • *Scr* Charles Leavitt, from the novel *Freak the Mighty* by Rodman Philbrick

Mighty Aphrodite ★★★ 15

Comedy 1995 · US · Colour · 90mins

It's all Greek (myth) to Woody Allen in this story of a sportswriter (Allen) who, with his gallery-owner wife (Helena Bonham Carter), adopts a baby boy. When Allen decides to seek out the boy's birth mother, he finds she's a hooker (the Oscar-winning Mira Sorvino) and becomes entangled in a web of convoluted plot twists that not even an occasional and rather boring Greek chorus can explain. Too self-conscious, the never-ending radio-play dialogue needs gagging rather than more gags. TH VIDEO DVD

Woody Allen *Lenny* • Helena Bonham Carter *Amanda* • Mira Sorvino *Linda* • F Murray Abraham *Chorus leader* • Claire Bloom *Amanda's mother* • Olympia Dukakis *Jocasta* • Michael Rapaport *Kevin* • David Ogden Stiers *Laius* ■ *Dir/Scr* Woody Allen

The Mighty Barnum ★★★

Biographical drama 1934 · US · BW · 87mins

Wallace Beery made Phineas T Barnum his own in this breezy 20th Century-Fox biography of the self-styled greatest showman of them all. Beery seemed born to espouse Barnum's phrases and philosophy, such as "There's one born every minute", and if the plot errs a little on the fanciful side, that would have been just dandy for old Phineas. Adolphe Menjou makes an unlikely reluctant partner. Virginia Bruce, as the "Swedish Nightingale" Jenny Lind, is lovely. TS

Wallace Beery *Phineas T Barnum* • Adolphe Menjou *Mr Bailey Walsh* • Virginia Bruce *Jenny Lind* • Rochelle Hudson *Ellen* • Janet Beecher *Nancy Barnum* • Tammany Young *Todd* • Lucille La Verne *Joyce Heth* • Herman Bing *Farmer Schultz* • George Brasno *General Tom Thumb* ■ *Dir* Walter Lang • *Scr* Gene Fowler, Bess Merdeyth, from their story

The Mighty Ducks ★★ PG

Sports comedy 1992 · US · Colour · 99mins

As a disgraced lawyer coaching the world's worst ice-hockey team as part of his community service, former Brat Packer Emilio Estevez makes the best of what, the ice apart, could hardly be called a cool assignment. This is *The Bad News Bears* with skates on, and you know from the first face-off how it's going to end. But director Stephen Herek pitches every gag and moment of melodrama at just the right level. Two sequels (*D2: the Mighty Ducks* and *D3: the Mighty Ducks*) followed. This was released in the UK as *Champions*. DP VIDEO DVD

Emilio Estevez *Gordon Bombay* • Joss Ackland *Hans* • Lane Smith *Coach Reilly* • Heidi Kling *Casey* • Josef Sommer *Gerald Ducksworth* • Joshua Jackson *Charlie Conroy* • Elden Ratliff *Fulton Reed* • Shaun Weiss *Goldberg* ■ *Dir* Stephen Herek • *Scr* Steven Brill

Mighty Joe Young ★★★ U

Fantasy adventure 1949 · US · BW · 93mins

As an emasculated *King Kong*, this variation on the monster theme is, nevertheless, entertaining enough. Terry Moore is persuaded to bring her enormous pet gorilla from Africa to America to become part of a nightclub act which includes, in superlatively kitsch style, her playing *Beautiful Dreamer* while being held aloft by the gorilla. Directed by Ernest B Schoedsack, who co-directed *King Kong*, with special effects by *King Kong* originator Willis O'Brien and, among others, Ray Harryhausen, it's excruciatingly schmaltzy but keeps its innocence intact. TH

Terry Moore *Jill Young* • Robert Armstrong *Max O'Hara* • Ben Johnson *Gregg Ford* • Frank McHugh *Press agent* • Douglas Fowley *Jones* ■ *Dir* Ernest B Schoedsack • *Scr* Ruth Rose, from a story by Merian C Cooper

Mighty Joe Young ★★★ PG

Fantasy adventure
1998 · US · Colour · 109mins

This entertaining remake of the 1949 family drama has beautiful Charlize Theron as the woman who befriends a colossal, but cute, gorilla hidden in the deepest jungle. Of course, Joe doesn't remain concealed for long after explorer Bill Paxton discovers him, and he's soon pursued by nasty hunters who want to capture him for some rich collector's amusement. It's a fun romp with some impressive ape effects and luscious scenery. JB VIDEO DVD

Charlize Theron *Jill Young* • Bill Paxton *Gregg O'Hara* • Rade Serbedzija *Strasser* • Peter Firth *Garth* • David Paymer *Harry Ruben* • Regina King *Cecily Banks* • Robert Wisdom *Kweli* • Naveen Andrews *Pindi* ■ *Dir* Ron Underwood • *Scr* Mark Rosenthal, Lawrence Konner, from the 1949 film

Mighty Morphin Power Rangers: the Movie ★★★ PG

Science-fiction adventure
1995 · US · Colour · 91mins

A few years ago, these superheroes in vinyl tights were the hottest thing around. Now the tie-in toys are about as fashionable as Cabbage Patch dolls. Here the Power Rangers battle their old enemy Rita Repulsa, fight off slime creatures and squash the world domination plans of evil Ivan Ooze. If your children are feeling nostalgic, then this colourful junk will while away a couple of very mindless hours. A second film, *Power Rangers 2*, followed. AJ VIDEO DVD

Karan Ashley *Aisha/Yellow Ranger* • Johnny Yong Bosch *Adam/Black Ranger* • Stephen Antonio Cardenas *Rocky/Red Ranger* • Jason David Frank *Tommy/White Ranger* • Amy Jo Johnson *Kimberly/Pink Ranger* • David Harold Yost *Billy/Blue Ranger* • Paul Schrier *Bulk* • Paul Freeman *Ivan Ooze* • Julia Cortez *Rita Repulsa* ■ *Dir* Bryan Spicer • *Scr* Arne Olsen, from a story by John Kamps, Arne Olsen

The Mighty Quinn ★★★ 15

Detective drama 1989 · US · Colour · 94mins

Denzel Washington hasn't made many wrong moves in his movie career, but he nearly came a cropper with this lightweight Caribbean thriller. He is his usual charismatic self as the determined police chief on a small former colony who gets mixed up in murder and political corruption, and there is a solid enough supporting cast. But director Carl Schenkel seems to have been seduced by the beautiful locations and laid-back lifestyle, as there is little in the way of suspense. JF. Contains swearing. VIDEO DVD

Denzel Washington *Xavier Quinn* • James Fox *Elgin* • Mimi Rogers *Hadley* • Robert Townsend *Maubee* • M Emmet Walsh *Miller* • Sheryl Lee Ralph *Lola* • Art Evans *Jump* • Esther Rolle *Ubu Pearl* ■ *Dir* Carl Schenkel • *Scr* Hampton Fancher, from the novel *Finding Maubee* by AHZ Carr

A Mighty Wind ★★★★ 12

Satirical comedy 2003 · US · Colour · 88mins

This Is Spinal Tap's Christopher Guest takes the mickey out of the folk music scene in this musical satire. Director and co-writer Guest is called upon to reform acoustic trio The Folksmen for a memorial concert for the late promoter Irving Steinbloom. Headlining the event above the ridiculously upbeat New Main Street Singers are Mitch & Mickey (played by Eugene Levy and Catherine O'Hara), once the sweethearts of the folk world, who haven't spoken to each other for nearly three decades following a messy divorce. This mockumentary can't match the satirical bite of the classic *Spinal Tap*, but there are still many laugh-out-loud moments. TH VIDEO DVD

Bob Balaban *Jonathan Steinbloom* • Ed Begley Jr *Lars Olfen* • Jennifer Coolidge *Amber Cole* • Christopher Guest *Alan Barrows* • John Michael Higgins *Terry Bohner* • Eugene Levy *Mitch Cohen* • Jane Lynch *Laurie Bohner* • Michael McKean *Jerry Palter* • Catherine O'Hara *Mickey Crabbe* • Parker Posey *Sissy Knox* • Harry Shearer *Mark Shubb* • Fred Willard *Mike LaFontaine* ■ *Dir* Christopher Guest • *Scr* Christopher Guest, Eugene Levy

Mignon Has Left ★★★ 12

Drama 1988 · It/Fr · Colour · 98mins

Italian director Francesca Archibugi made a considerable impact with this, her debut feature. Ostensibly a tale of two cities, the story focuses on Céline Beauvallet, a chic Parisian teen who is sent to stay with working-class relatives in Rome when her father is jailed. Beauvallet's abrupt awakening and her bashful cousin's achingly true-to-life crush are delicately handled, but it's the upward struggle of her put-upon aunt (the excellent Stefania Sandrelli) that gives this drama its poignancy and credibility. DP. In Italian with English subtitles.

Stefania Sandrelli *Mama* • Jean-Pierre Duriez *Federico* • Leonardo Ruta *Giorgio* • Céline Beauvallet *Mignon* • Francesca Antonelli *Chiara* • Lorenzo De Pasqua *Cacio* • Eleonora Sambiagio *Antonella* ■ *Dir* Francesca Archibugi • *Scr* Francesca Archibugi, Gloria Malatesta, Claudia Sbarigia

The Mikado ★★★

Operetta 1939 · UK · Colour · 93mins

A lavish, British production of the famed Gilbert and Sullivan Savoy operetta, faithfully directed by imported American Victor Schertzinger, a composer himself. Also imported from the States was radio crooner Kenny Baker to star as Nanki-Poo, and he seems ill-at-ease among the D'Oyly Carte players, notably Martyn Green as Ko-Ko and Sydney Granville as Pooh-Bah, playing as if born to their roles. The marvellous use of early Technicolor makes this rather dull adaptation very watchable today, and the score is remarkably complete, and superbly played by the now-defunct Royal Symphony Orchestra. TS

Kenny Baker (1) *Nanki-Poo* • Martyn Green *Ko-Ko* • Sydney Granville *Pooh-Bah* • John Barclay *The Mikado* • Gregory Stroud *Pish-Tush* • Jean Collin *Yum-Yum* • Constance Willis *Katisha* • Elizabeth Paynter *Pitti-Sing* ■ *Dir* Victor Schertzinger • *Scr* Geoffrey Toye, from the operetta by WS Gilbert, Arthur Sullivan • *Cinematographer* William Skall [William V Skall], Bernard Knowles

Mike Bassett: England Manager ★★★ 15

Sports satire 2001 · UK · Colour · 85mins

Thanks to the minimal use of on-field action football sequences, we are spared the embarrassment of watching players who can't act and actors who can't play in this funny sports satire. Instead, the film focuses on the boardroom, back-room and dressing-room shenanigans that ensue after a lower-league soccer boss is made England manager. Ricky Tomlinson plays Bassett with a nice mix of humour and pathos. When the team flukes its way into the World Cup in Brazil, Bassett is faced with the task of turning his individual allsorts into a winning side. DA. Contains violence, swearing and brief nudity. DVD

Ricky Tomlinson *Mike Bassett* • Amanda Redman *Karine Bassett* • Philip Jackson *Lonnie Urquart* • Bradley Walsh *Dave Dodds* • Phill Jupitus *Tommo Thompson* • Pelé • Gabby Logan ■ *Dir* Steve Barron • *Scr* Rob Sprackling, JRN Smith

Mike's Murder ★★ 18

Psychological thriller
1984 · US · Colour · 104mins

Long-delayed and barely released, this murky thriller reunites Debra Winger with her *Urban Cowboy* director, James Bridges. Here she's sleuthing over a drug deal that went wrong – though not half as wrong as the movie itself, which spent a couple of years being edited, restructured, cut again and then finally dubbed in England. TS. Contains swearing.

Debra Winger *Betty Parrish* • Mark Keyloun *Mike* • Paul Winfield *Phillip* • Darrell Larson *Pete* • Brooke Alderson *Patty* • Robert Crosson *Sam* ■ *Dir/Scr* James Bridges • *Music* Joe Jackson, John Barry (1)

Mikey and Nicky ★★ 15

Drama 1976 · US · Colour · 101mins

Elaine May is perhaps most infamous for huge money-loser *Ishtar*, but she is also the director of a handful of odd comedies that are virtually two-handers. This one is a gangland tale of cross and double-cross. Nicky (John Cassavetes) is a holed-up and scared gangster, Mikey (Peter Falk) is his supposed friend who may or may not be setting him up for a hit. An uncomfortable, often painfully funny film. DF DVD

Peter Falk *Mikey* • John Cassavetes *Nicky* • Ned Beatty *Kinney* • Rose Arrick *Annie* • Carol Grace *Nell* • William Hickey *Sid Fine* • Sanford Meisner *Dave Resnick* • M Emmet Walsh *Bus driver* ■ *Dir/Scr* Elaine May

M

The Milagro Beanfield War ★★★★ 15

Drama 1988 · US · Colour · 112mins

With *Quiz Show* and *Ordinary People*, former heart-throb Robert Redford revealed himself to be one of America's finest directors of actors. Here he proves adept at handling a large ensemble cast in this adaptation of John Nichols's whimsical novel about a New Mexican farmer (Chick Vennera), who deflects water from a housing development to start his own beanfield. Watch out for Melanie Griffith, John Heard and Christopher Walken, enjoy Dave Grusin's Oscar-winning score, and don't be put off by that title. TS. Contains swearing.

Rubén Blades *Sheriff Bernabe Montoya* • Richard Bradford *Ladd Devine* • Sonia Braga *Ruby Archuleta* • Julie Carmen *Nancy Mondragon* • James Gammon *Horsethief Shorty* • Melanie Griffith *Flossie Devine* • John Heard *Charlie Bloom* • Christopher Walken *Kyril Montana* ■ *Dir* Robert Redford • *Scr* David Ward, John Nichols, from the novel by John Nichols

Mildred Pierce ★★★★★ PG

Classic film noir melodrama
1945 · US · BW · 106mins

Although it will forever be known as the movie that relaunched Joan Crawford's flagging career, there is much more to this classic "woman's picture" than an Oscar-winning performance. Crawford is fabulous as the woman who, after the breakdown of her marriage, goes to work to pay for her daughters' education and builds up a successful business. Tragedy, naturally, awaits. While it reworks the original plot, Ranald MacDougall's script retains the sharp edge of James M Cain's novel, while Michael Curtiz's cool direction keeps the action moving and Crawford, Ann Blyth and Zachary Scott away from caricature. Ernest Haller's moody photography and Anton Grot's sets (which, at a glance, convey Mildred's changing social status) are also outstanding. Screen suffering was never so sophisticated. DP

Joan Crawford *Mildred Pierce* • Jack Carson *Wally Fay* • Zachary Scott *Monte Beragon* • Eve Arden *Ida Corwin* • Ann Blyth *Veda Pierce* • Bruce Bennett *Bert Pierce* • Lee Patrick *Mrs Maggie Biederhof* • Moroni Olsen *Inspector Peterson* • Jo Ann Marlowe *Kay Pierce* • Butterfly McQueen *Lottie* ■ *Dir* Michael Curtiz • *Scr* Ranald MacDougall, from the novel by James M Cain • *Music* Max Steiner

Milena ★★★

Biographical drama
1990 · Can/Fr/W Ger · Colour · 139mins

Those familiar with Valérie Kaprisky solely as Richard Gere's co-star in *Breathless* will be overwhelmed by the way she comports herself in this biography of Milena Jesenka, the communist confidante of Franz Kafka whose outspoken journalism resulted in her incarceration by the Nazis in Ravensbruck concentration camp. For all its evident admiration for its subject, however, Véra Belmont's film spends too much time gazing on the gorgeous costumes and conducting intellectual debates that neither engross nor provoke. The sequences in Vienna, where Milena lived with music critic Ernst Pollack, are particularly decorative, but the later politicised scenes have more passion. DP

Valérie Kaprisky *Milena Jesenka* • Philip Anglim *Franz Kafka* • Peter Gallagher *Polak* • Gudrun Landgrebe *Olga* • Stacy Keach *Jesenski* • Nick Mancuso *Jaromir* ■ *Dir/Scr* Véra Belmont

Miles from Home ★★★ 15

Drama 1988 · US · Colour · 103mins

Richard Gere, whose career was somewhat in the doldrums at the time, made a stab for credibility with this worthy, if uneven, rural drama. Gere is the farmer whose property is in danger of being seized by the banks, forcing him into increasingly drastic action. Actor Gary Sinise here directs ably, but it is the playing that really makes the picture; if Gere is not entirely convincing in the leading role, Kevin Anderson, as his younger brother, is terrific, while the supporting turns more than compensate for the weaknesses in the script. JF. Contains violence, swearing and drug abuse.

Richard Gere *Frank Roberts Jr* • Kevin Anderson *Terry Roberts* • Brian Dennehy *Frank Roberts Sr* • Jason Campbell *Young Frank* • Austin Bamgarner *Young Terry* • Larry Poling *Nikita Khrushchev* • Laurie Metcalf *Ellen* • John Malkovich *Barry Maxwell* ■ *Dir* Gary Sinise • *Scr* Chris Gerolmo

Military Policeman ★★ U

Comedy 1953 · US · BW · 90mins

The Bob Hope style of wise-cracking comedy was showing some strain by the time of this effort, and 1953 was the last year in which he figured in the top ten box-office stars. His teaming with the exuberant Mickey Rooney does not always gel, either, but there are sufficient laughs to make this a pleasant enough time-passer. Eddie Mayehoff shines as a military policeman who despairs at the ineptitude of Hope, playing a boxer's manager unwittingly stuck with a term in the army. TV

Bob Hope *Wally Hogan* • Mickey Rooney *Herbert Tuttle* • Marilyn Maxwell *Connie Curtis* • Eddie Mayehoff *Karl Danzig* • Stanley Clements *Bullet Bradley* • Jack Dempsey ■ *Dir* George Marshall • *Scr* Hal Kanter, Jack Sher, from a story by Hal Kanter

Militia ★★ 15

Action thriller 2000 · US · Colour · 85mins

TV's Superman Dean Cain has not made much on an impact on the movie scene and, despite a better than average cast, the main problem here is the typically sloppy direction of Jim Wynorski. Cain is the Government agent who is paired with former right-wing extremist Frederic Forrest to infiltrate a shadowy new militia headed by crazy Stacy Keach. JF DVD

Dean Cain *Ethan Carter* • Jennifer Beals *Julie Sanders* • Frederic Forrest *William Fain* • Stacy Keach *Mr Montgomery* • Brett Butler *Bobbie* ■ *Dir* Jay Andrews [Jim Wynorski] • *Scr* Steve Latshaw, William Carson

Milk ★★ 15

Black comedy
1999 · UK/Aus · Colour · 92mins

An enviable British ensemble is under-employed in William Brookfield's directorial debut. James Fleet is rather swept away by the grasping relatives who descend on his Wiltshire dairy farm following the death of his martinet mother. Consequently, we're much more interested in the antics of such scene-stealers as Peter Jones and Dawn French than in Fleet's machinations and his tentative relationship with back-packer, Clotilde Courau. This is never macabre nor comic enough. DP DVD

James Fleet *Adrian* • Phyllida Law *Veronica* • Joss Ackland *Vicar* • Clotilde Courau *Ilaria* • Peter Jones *Harry* • Francesca Annis *Harriet* • Dawn French *Virginia* • Lesley Manville *Fiona* • Richard Johnson *John* ■ *Dir/Scr* William Brookfield

Milk Money ★★★ 12

Romantic comedy
1994 · US · Colour · 104mins

Four years after *Pretty Woman* came another implausible "prostitute finds love with a nice man" romantic comedy. This is more warm-hearted than the successful Julia Roberts film, with Melanie Griffith sexy and down-to-earth as the hooker brought home by a young boy as a prospective wife for his lonely dad (Ed Harris). Both Harris and Griffith give nice, unshowy performances, while Malcolm McDowell is convincingly nasty as the pimp who's after Griffith. Utterly preposterous, but thoroughly enjoyable entertainment. JB DVD

Melanie Griffith *V* • Ed Harris *Tom Wheeler* • Michael Patrick Carter *Frank Wheeler* • Malcolm McDowell *Waltzer* • Anne Heche *Betty* • Casey Siemaszko *Cash* • Philip Bosco *Jerry the Pope* • Brian Christopher *Kevin Clean* ■ *Dir* Richard Benjamin • *Scr* John Mattson

The Milky Way ★★★★

Sports comedy 1936 · US · BW · 89mins

Perhaps the last great Harold Lloyd comedy classic (this was later remade as *The Kid from Brooklyn* with Danny Kaye, becoming blandly pasteurised in the process). Lloyd plays a mild-mannered milkman who, mistaken for a potential world boxing champion, gets caught up with a gang of crooked fixers. Adolphe Menjou, Helen Mack and Lionel Stander provide wonderful back-up for his endeavours. TH

Harold Lloyd *Burleigh "Tiger" Sullivan* • Adolphe Menjou *Gabby Sloan* • Verree Teasdale *Ann Westley* • Helen Mack *Mae Sullivan* • William Gargan *Elwood "Speed" MacFarland* • George Barbier *Wilbur Austin* • Dorothy Wilson *Polly Pringle* • Lionel Stander *Spider Schultz* ■ *Dir* Leo McCarey • *Scr* Grover Jones, Frank Butler, Richard Connell, from a play by Lynn Root, Harry Clork

The Milky Way ★★★★★ 15

Drama 1968 · Fr/It · Colour · 97mins

A pilgrim's regress by the great surrealist master Luis Buñuel, which, while being among his most anti-clerical and enigmatic movies, is still marvellously accessible even for those not in tune with Catholic concerns. His two tramps, progressing from Paris to a shrine in Spain, slip through time to encounter the Devil, the Virgin Mary and many zealots. They conclude, on their road to religious ruin, that intolerance is next to godliness. Buñuel, who was always on the side of the heretics, makes his points with sarcastic compassion. TH. In French with English subtitles. DVD

Laurent Terzieff *Jean* • Paul Frankeur *Pierre* • Delphine Seyrig *Prostitute* • Edith Scob *Virgin Mary* • Bernard Verley *Jesus* • Georges Marchal *Jesuit* • Jean Piat *Jansenist* • Pierre Clémenti *The Devil* ■ *Dir* Luis Buñuel • *Scr* Luis Buñuel, Jean-Claude Carrière

The Mill on the Floss ★★

Period drama 1937 · UK · BW · 82mins

Director, Tim Whelan was also one of four writers attempting to adapt George Eliot's famous novel about the tragic feud between the Tullivers and the Wakems, and the resulting Victorian period piece is to be recommended for its polished British cast. RK

Geraldine Fitzgerald *Maggie Tulliver* • James Mason *Tom Tulliver* • Felix Aylmer *Mr Wakem* • Frank Lawton *Philip Wakem* • Fay Compton *Mrs Tulliver* • Griffith Jones *Stephen Guest* • Mary Clare *Mrs Moss* • Victoria Hopper *Lucy Deane* ■ *Dir* Tim Whelan • *Scr* Tim Whelan, John Drinkwater, Garnett Weston, Austin Melford, from the novel by George Eliot

Millennium ★★ PG

Science-fiction drama
1989 · US · Colour · 101mins

Based on an interesting short story, this doesn't have enough meat on it for a feature and it's a struggle to stay watching to the end. Kris Kristofferson is the investigator trying to work out what happened after an air disaster, who discovers that the passengers were whisked off by time traveller Cheryl Ladd before the crash. Unfortunately, a promising premise gets lost among the clichés and B-movie performances. JB

Kris Kristofferson *Bill Smith* • Cheryl Ladd *Louise Baltimore* • Daniel J Travanti *Arnold Mayer* • Robert Joy *Sherman* • Lloyd Bochner *Walters* • Brent Carver *Coventry* • Maury Chaykin *Roger Keane* ■ *Dir* Michael Anderson • *Scr* John Varley, from the short story *Air Raid* by John Varley

Miller's Crossing ★★★★★ 18

Crime drama 1990 · US · Colour · 110mins

The Coen brothers' sublime Prohibition-era gangster saga is a magnificent display of compelling acting, spellbinding storytelling and fine film-making. A dark-hued, richly operatic mood piece, with machine gun-fire dialogue and twisted meaty substance to spare, it focuses on the friendship between politician Albert Finney and Gabriel Byrne, the power behind his throne, and the bloody mob war that erupts when they fall in love with the same woman, Marcia Gay Harden. The title refers to a lonely, leafy glade where somebody's murder will take place. Byrne is simply outstanding as the cool, calculating catalyst around whom the whole vivid spectacle revolves. AJ. Contains violence, sex scenes, swearing, nudity. DVD

Gabriel Byrne *Tom Reagan* • Marcia Gay Harden *Verna* • John Turturro *Bernie Bernbaum* • Jon Polito *Johnny Caspar* • JE Freeman *Eddie Dane* • Albert Finney *Leo* • Mike Starr *Frankie* • Al Mancini *Tic-Tac* • Steve Buscemi *Mink* ■ *Dir* Joel Coen • *Scr* Joel Coen, Ethan Coen • *Cinematographer* Barry Sonnenfeld

The Miller's Wife ★

Period comedy 1955 · It · Colour · 95mins

The governor of Naples (Vittorio De Sica), lusting after the sexy wife (Sophia Loren) of the local miller (Marcello Mastroianni), has the man arrested on a trumped-up charge, then offers the wife her husband's release in return for her favours. A melodramatic plot is the basis for a vulgar and unfunny Neapolitan farce, directed without a trace of inspiration. RK. An Italian language film.

Vittorio De Sica *The Governor* • Marcello Mastroianni *Luca, the miller* • Sophia Loren *Carmela* • Paolo Stoppa *Gardunia* ■ *Dir* Mario Camerini • *Scr* Mario Camerini, Ennio De Concini, Augusto Camerini, Alessandro Continenza, Ivo Perilli, from the play by Pedro DeAlacon

Le Million ★★★★

Comedy 1931 · Fr · BW · 85mins

René Lefèvre stars as a poor painter who wins a fortune on the lottery, only to discover that the ticket is in the pocket of an old jacket that's been stolen. His chase across Paris to recover it, which lands him on the stage of the opera house, forms the delightfully funny substance of this famously charming, innovative and influential early sound film from French director René Clair. The lovely Annabella and the fluent camera of future cinematographic ace Georges Périnal contribute to the stylishness. RK. A French language film.

Annabella *Beatrice* • René Lefèvre *Michel* • Paul Olivier *"Father Tulipe" Crochard, a gangster* • Louis Allibert *Prosper* ■ *Dir* René Clair • *Scr* René Clair, from the musical by Georges Berr, M Guillemaud

Million Dollar Baby ★★

Romantic comedy 1941 · US · BW · 100mins

This modest little comedy was one of eight movies in which Warner Bros paired sparky and wholesome Priscilla Lane with handsome Jeffrey Lynn. The plot has Lane inheriting a million dollars from crotchety May Robson, only to arrive at the unrealistic conclusion that money doesn't bring happiness. Along the way she dallies with Ronald Reagan, improbably cast as a concert pianist. RB

Priscilla Lane *Pamela McAllister* • Jeffrey Lynn *James Amory* • Ronald Reagan *Peter Rowan* • May Robson *Cornelia Wheelwright* • Lee Patrick *Josie LaRue* • Helen Westley *Mrs Galloway* ■ *Dir* Curtis Bernhardt • *Scr* Casey Robinson, Richard Macaulay, Jerry Wald, from the story *Miss Wheelwright Discovers America* by Leonard Spigelgass

Million Dollar Baby ★★★★★ 12

Sports drama 2004 · US · Colour · 127mins

For those who thought *Unforgiven* was the masterpiece of Clint Eastwood's autumn years, this sharp, moving and brutally bleak drama proves that he can bring the same grizzled genius to the sports arena. Eastwood stars as a washed-up coach whose fighters abandon him as soon as they hit the big time. Dumped by his latest slugger, he reluctantly turns his attentions to Hilary Swank, a 31-year-old waitress who turns up at his gym begging for lessons. Eastwood tutors Swank to success, but then this otherwise standard underdog story takes a shocking turn in its final third that gives the movie an unexpected depth and immense power. Morgan Freeman is impressive as the trainer's crumpled sidekick, and Oscar winner Swank is terrific, too, but this is Clint's film, both as its tortured hero and as a great American director. DW. Contains violence and swearing. [VIDEO] DVD

Clint Eastwood *Frankie Dunn* • Hilary Swank *Maggie Fitzgerald* • Morgan Freeman *Eddie "Scrap-Iron" Dupris* • Anthony Mackie *Shawrelle Berry* • Jay Baruchel *Danger Barch* • Mike Colter *Big Willie Little* • Lucia Rijker *Billie "The Blue Bear"* • Brian O'Byrne *Father Horvak* ■ *Dir* Clint Eastwood • *Scr* Paul Haggis, from the short stories *Rope Burns: Stories from the Corner* by FX Toole

The Million Dollar Duck ★★★ U

Comedy 1971 · US · Colour · 92mins

Disney's unofficial remake of the Douglas Fairbanks Jr vehicle, *Mr Drake's Duck*, provides yet another twist on the nutty professor story. Dean Jones is a scientist whose experiments on the behaviour of ducks go haywire when his prize specimen, Charley, dips his beak into some radioactive apple sauce and begins laying golden eggs. From then on, it's the familiar tale of bungling baddies and government agents seeking to snatch the remarkable bird from the prof and his young friends. DP [VIDEO]

Dean Jones *Professor Albert Dooley* • Sandy Duncan *Katie Dooley* • Joe Flynn *Finley Hooper* • Tony Roberts *Fred Hines* • James Gregory *Rutledge* • Lee Harcourt Montgomery [Lee Montgomery] *Jimmy Dooley* • Jack Kruschen *Dr Gottlieb* ■ *Dir* Vincent McEveety • *Scr* Roswell Rogers, from a story by Ted Key

The Million Dollar Hotel ★ 15

Comedy drama
1999 · Ger/US · Colour · 116mins

Director Wim Wenders applies his art house touch to this Hollywood tale of an FBI agent investigating a suspicious death at a bizarre, bohemian hotel. Kept simple, it could have worked; unfortunately, Wenders cloaks everything in needless complexity and wilful obscurity. Mel Gibson, whose Icon company produced the film, plays the agent and winds up looking considerably less than a million dollars. DA [VIDEO] DVD

Jeremy Davies *Tom Tom* • Milla Jovovich *Eloise* • Mel Gibson *Skinner* • Jimmy Smits *Geronimo* • Peter Stormare *Dixie* • Amanda Plummer *Vivien* • Bud Cort *Shorty* • Julian Sands *Terence Scopey* • Tim Roth *Izzy Goldkiss* ■ *Dir* Wim Wenders • *Scr* Nicholas Klein, from a story by Bono, Nicholas Klein

Million Dollar Legs ★★ U

Comedy 1932 · US · BW · 64mins

As the President of Klopstokia, a mythical principality that's bankrupt, WC Fields plays very much second fiddle to Jack Oakie in this nonsensical slapstick farce. Oakie is a visiting American brush salesman, who falls in love with the President's daughter and comes up with the money-making scheme of entering Klopstokia in the Los Angeles Olympics. Directed by Edward Cline, it plays like an inferior version of a Marx Brothers excursion into silliness, with pratfalls, non-sequiturs and really terrible gags. RK

Jack Oakie *Migg Tweeny* • WC Fields *The President of Klopstokia* • Andy Clyde *The Major-domo* • Lyda Roberti *Mata Machree* • Susan Fleming *Angela* ■ *Dir* Edward Cline • *Scr* Henry Myers, Nick Barrows, from a story by Joseph L Mankiewicz

Million Dollar Legs ★★ U

Comedy 1939 · US · BW · 64mins

A college student takes up a collection and bets the money on a horse named Million Dollar Legs, thus raising the cash to buy badly needed equipment for the college rowing team. This is most interesting for a cast that includes future stars Betty Grable, 14-year-old Donald O'Connor and William Holden, in a two-word bit part. Also cast was Jackie Coogan, the real-life husband of Grable, whose stardom ended with his coming of age. RK

Betty Grable *Carol Parker* • John Hartley *Greg Melton* • Donald O'Connor *Sticky Boone* • Jackie Coogan *Russ Simpson* • Larry Crabbe [Larry "Buster" Crabbe] *Coach Baxter* ■ *Dir* Nick Grinde • *Scr* Lewis R Foster, Richard English, from a story by Lewis R Foster

Million Dollar Mermaid ★★★ U

Biographical drama
1952 · US · Colour · 115mins

Who else but the divine water-goddess of MGM, Esther Williams, this time afloat in a highly-fictionalised biopic of her predecessor, silent screen sensation Annette Kellerman? Of course, this being MGM, the plot is just an excuse for some wonderfully ornate Busby Berkeley routines, which today seem hilarious or camp. Williams is as radiant as ever, but the period sense is nonexistent. TS

Esther Williams *Annette Kellerman* • Victor Mature *James Sullivan* • Walter Pidgeon *Frederick Kellerman* • David Brian *Alfred Harper* • Donna Corcoran *Annette, aged ten* • Jesse White *Doc Cronnel* • Maria Tallchief *Pavlova* • Howard Freeman *Aldrich* ■ *Dir* Mervyn LeRoy • *Scr* Everett Freeman

The Million Pound Note ★★★★ U

Classic satirical comedy
1953 · UK · Colour · 84mins

In this lovely comedy, Gregory Peck plays a bankrupt American abroad, who is given the title bank note and told to keep it intact for a month. As the butt of a joke between two rich gamblers, Peck has problems at first, but then finds the note means he never has to spend a penny because his credit rating is so good. Set in Edwardian London, the picture has a lot of charm and humour, owing to Peck's delight in the role and to Ronald Neame's unobtrusive direction. The witty script was based on the story by Mark Twain. AT [VIDEO]

Gregory Peck *Henry Adams* • Jane Griffiths *Portia Lansdowne* • Ronald Squire *Oliver Montpelier* • Wilfrid Hyde White *Roderick Montpelier* • Joyce Grenfell *Duchess of Cromarty* • Reginald Beckwith *Rock* • Hartley Power *Hastings* • Brian Oulton *Lloyd* ■ *Dir* Ronald Neame • *Scr* Jill Craigie, from the story by Mark Twain

A Million to Juan ★★★

Comedy 1994 · US · Colour · 97mins

This is a Hispanic reworking of that old Gregory Peck favourite, *The Million Pound Note*. Loosely based on the story by Mark Twain, the film marked the directorial debut of comedian Paul Rodriguez, who also stars as the hard-working father who is given a cheque for a million dollars by a stranger. A reward is promised, providing he does good with the money without actually spending it. If Rodriguez occasionally gets a little tacky, he still does enough to raise a smile. DP

Paul Rodriguez *Juan Lopez* • Polly Draper *Olivia Smith* • Gerardo *Flaco* • Jonathan Hernandez *Alejandro Lopez* • Edward James Olmos *Mr Angel* • Victor Rivers *Hector Delgado* • Bert Rosario *Alvaro* • Pepe Serna *Jorge/Mr Ortiz* ■ *Dir* Paul Rodriguez • *Scr* Robert Grasmere, Francisca Matos, Paul Rodriguez, from the story *The Million Pound Note* by Mark Twain

A Million to One ★★★

Drama 1937 · US · BW · 59mins

One of the main functions of film is as a recording medium, and this artless, fictionalised true story is of real value as a social record, featuring 1932 Olympic shot-putter Herman Brix as an athlete preparing for an Olympic decathlon. If Brix looks vaguely familiar, it's because he did actually become a film star, initially as Tarzan, and latterly changing his name to Bruce Bennett. A young Joan Fontaine rather sweetly plays a society lass who falls for Brix, and the film has a overall charm, despite static direction and a pace which may well deter all but the hardiest of Olympic fans. TS

Herman Brix [Bruce Bennett] *Johnny Kent* • Joan Fontaine *Joan Stevens* • Reed Howes *Duke Hale* • Monte Blue *John Kent Sr* • Kenneth Harlan *William Stevens* • Suzanne Kaaren *Pat Stanley* • Ed Piel *Mac* • Ben Hall *Joe* ■ *Dir* Lynn Shores • *Scr* John T Neville

Millionaire Dogs ★★ U

Animation 1999 · Ger · Colour · 80mins

Few German cartoons have made it to this country and if this crude canine comedy is anything to go by, it's easy to see why. The storyline clearly owes a debt to *The Aristocats*, even though this time it's a pair of malevolent (and very odd looking) twins who attempt to prevent a pet from inheriting a fortune. The graphic style is way below Disney standard, but what will alienate younger viewers is the resistibility of the stars. DP. German dialogue dubbed into English. [VIDEO] DVD

Dir Michael Schoemann • *Scr* Karin Howard, Joe Steuben, from an idea by Ute Schoemann-Koll

A Millionaire for Christy ★★★★ U

Romantic comedy 1951 · US · BW · 91mins

A good old-fashioned madcap comedy has always been a pleasing way to pass the time and this latter-day screwball provides more than its fair share of laughs. Fred MacMurray gives a droll performance as a folksy radio celebrity who becomes the target of legal secretary Eleanor Parker after he unexpectedly becomes a millionaire. Adding to the fun is MacMurray's on/off wedding with Kay Buckley and his chaotic pursuit of absconded best man Richard Carlson. Ken Englund's script brings plenty of verbal wit to the breezy situations, while director George Marshall outdoes himself with the hilarious beach scene. DP

Fred MacMurray *Peter Ulysses Lockwood* • Eleanor Parker *Christy Sloane* • Richard Carlson *Dr Roland Cook* • Kay Buckley *June Chandler* • Una Merkel *Patsy* • Douglass Dumbrille *AK Thompson* • Raymond Greenleaf *Benjamin Chandler* • Nestor Paiva *Mr Rapello* ■ *Dir* George Marshall • *Scr* Ken Englund, from a story by Robert Harari

The Millionairess ★★★ U

Comedy 1960 · UK · Colour · 86mins

An important film for British comedy actor Peter Sellers, this would give him his first real international audience. Sophia Loren was already a Sellers fan and was happy to have him play the Indian doctor opposite her spoiled heiress in this adaptation of the George Bernard Shaw play. Sellers brings a gentle charm to his character and avoids taking the easy route to laughter by racial caricature. Loren is stunning and excels at the light comedy. Romance blossomed on set between the two and perhaps helped to make plausible the unlikely on-screen romance. DF [VIDEO] DVD

Sophia Loren *Epifania Parerga* • Peter Sellers *Dr Ahmed el Kabir* • Vittorio De Sica *Joe* • Alastair Sim *Sagamore* • Dennis Price *Dr Adrian Bond* • Gary Raymond *Alastair* • Alfie Bass *Fish Curer* • Miriam Karlin *Mrs Joe* ■ *Dir* Anthony Asquith • *Scr* Wolf Mankowitz, Riccardo Aragno, from the play by George Bernard Shaw

Millions ★★★★ 12A

Comedy drama 2004 · UK · Colour · 98mins

Two schoolboy brothers have a week to spend a load of stolen sterling before the UK switches to the euro in this charming comedy drama from

M

director Danny Boyle. Alex Etel is wonderful as the angel-faced seven-year-old whose hilarious visitations from saints lead him to believe that the mislaid robbery loot that lands in his lap is actually a gift from God. But while he wants to use the money for worthy causes, his nine-year-old brother Lewis McGibbon favours entirely personal consumption, leading to a clash of wills that attracts the wrong kind of attention. Boyle handles the material deftly, delivering a morality tale that's sweet but never nauseating. SF

James Nesbitt *Ronnie Cunningham* • Daisy Donovan *Dorothy* • Alex Etel *Damian Cunningham* • Lewis McGibbon *Anthony Cunningham* • Christopher Fulford *The Man* • Pearce Quigley *Community policeman* • Jane Hogarth *Mum* • Alun Armstrong *St Peter* ■ *Dir* Danny Boyle • *Scr* Frank Cottrell Boyce

Millions like Us ★★★★ U

Second World War drama
1943 · UK · BW · 103mins

Frank Launder and Sidney Gilliat are better known for their comedies, but here they have produced one of the finest home-front dramas of the Second World War. Adopting the docudramatic approach that characterised many British flag-wavers, the co-directors present a nation pulling together in spite of class differences. The sequences in the factory and at the workers' dormitory are fascinating for the way in which they depict the emergence of both a new kind of woman and a new social order. Patricia Roc and Eric Portman stand out in the excellent cast. DP

Eric Portman *Charlie Forbes* • Patricia Roc *Celia Crowson* • Gordon Jackson *Fred Blake* • Anne Crawford *Jennifer Knowles* • Joy Shelton *Phyllis Crowson* • Megs Jenkins *Gwen Price* • Terry Randall *Annie Earnshaw* • Basil Radford *Charters* • Naunton Wayne *Caldicott* ■ *Dir/Scr* Frank Launder, Sidney Gilliat

Milou en Mai ★★★ 15

Black comedy 1989 · Fr · Colour · 102mins

Louis Malle's final French film may not stand comparison with his earlier classics, but it is still a polished piece from a director whose willingness to tackle the more controversial aspects of France's recent past established him as one of the most fascinating artists to emerge from the New Wave era of the early 1960s. He handles the family flirting and bickering with assurance, but fumbles the serious and satirical political themes. DP. In French with English subtitles.

Michel Piccoli *Milou* • Miou-Miou *Camille* • Michel Duchaussoy *Georges* • Dominique Blanc *Claire* • Harriet Walter *Lily* • Bruno Carette *Grimaldi* • François Berléand *Daniel* • Martine Gautier *Adèle* ■ *Dir* Louis Malle • *Scr* Louis Malle, Jean-Claude Carrière • *Music* Stéphane Grappelli

Milwaukee, Minnesota ★★★ 15

Comedy drama 2002 · US · Colour · 91mins

With Bernd Heinl's camera evocatively capturing the frozen desolation of small-town Wisconsin, this is a quirky film in the true indie tradition. Yet, Allan Mindel is occasionally over-conscious of the need to operate in left field; consequently, the scramble for the affections of unworldly ice fisherman Troy Garity' by various exploitative predators feels like an assemblage of set pieces rather than a cogent narrative. However, Bruce Dern and Randy Quaid seize the opportunity to act to the hilt, while Alison Folland impresses as the damaged survivor. DP. Contains swearing and violence. DVD

Troy Garity *Albert Burroughs* • Alison Folland *Tuey Stites* • Bruce Dern *Sean McNally* • Hank Harris *Stan Stites* • Debra Monk *Edna Burroughs* • Josh Brolin *Gary* • Holly Woodlawn *Transvestite* • Randy Quaid *Jerry James* ■ *Dir* Allan Mindel • *Scr* RD Murphy [Richard Murphy (2)]

Mimic ★★★ 15

Science-fiction horror
1997 · US · Colour · 101mins

Mira Sorvino stars as an entomologist determined to find out what has invaded the New York subway system. It's preposterous stuff, but the tale of oversized insects (a genetically enhanced species developed to eradicate an epidemic-spreading breed of cockroaches) is suitably gruesome and atmospheric thanks to director Guillermo del Toro's dark direction. Sorvino is believably tough, too, and smartly supported by Jeremy Northam, Charles S Dutton and Josh Brolin as potential monster munchies. Two made-for-video sequels followed. JB. Contains violence, swearing. DVD

Mira Sorvino *Dr Susan Tyler* • Jeremy Northam *Dr Peter Mann* • Josh Brolin *Josh Maslow* • Giancarlo Giannini *Manny* • Alexander Goodwin *Chuy* • Alix Koromzay *Remy* • F Murray Abraham *Doctor Gates* • Charles S Dutton *Leo* ■ *Dir* Guillermo del Toro • *Scr* Matthew Robbins, Guillermo del Toro, from a story by Matthew Robbins, Guillermo del Toro, Donald A Wollheim

Min and Bill ★★★

Comedy drama 1930 · US · BW · 66mins

Dated but of considerable historical interest, this comedy drama was MGM's biggest hit of 1930 and won Marie Dressler an Academy Award for best actress. Dressler portrays the hard-boiled owner of a ramshackle waterfront hotel who kills to protect the waif she has raised (Dorothy Jordan). Cast as her fisherman sweetheart, Wallace Beery registered so well opposite her that they were teamed in another smash hit, *Tugboat Annie*. AE

Marie Dressler *Min Divot* • Wallace Beery *Bill* • Dorothy Jordan *Nancy Smith* • Marjorie Rambeau *Bella Pringle* • Donald Dillaway *Dick Cameron* • DeWitt Jennings *Groot* ■ *Dir* George Hill • *Scr* Frances Marion, Marion Jackson, from the novel *Dark Star* by Lorna Moon

Mina Tannenbaum ★★★★ 12

Drama 1993 · Fr/Bel/Neth · Colour · 123mins

Martine Dugowson made her directorial debut with this tragicomic rites-of-passage story. Tackling such diverse topics as heredity, conformity, compatibility, Jewishness and the nature of friendship in a competitive world, the film employs an impressive range of cinematic devices, including jump cuts, speeches direct to camera, Truffaut-like movie references and trick photography. Romane Bohringer and Elsa Zylberstein are superb as the lifelong friends, while Jean-Philippe Ecoffey stands out among the dreadful men they encounter over the years. DP. In French with English subtitles. Contains swearing.

Romane Bohringer *Mina Tannenbaum* • Elsa Zylberstein *Ethel Bénégui* • Nils Tavernier *François* • Stéphane Slima *Didier* • Florence Thomassin *The cousin* • Chantal Krief *Daisy* • Jany Gastaldi *Gisèle* • Jean-Philippe Ecoffey *Jacques Dana* ■ *Dir/Scr* Martine Dugowson

Minbo – or the Gentle Art of Japanese Extortion ★★★

Comedy 1992 · US/Jpn · Colour · 123mins

In this darkly humorous thriller, director Juzo Itami turns his attention to the underworld and the grip it exerts on all aspects of life. Nobuko Miyamoto plays a crusading lawyer who helps the management of a hotel resist a gang of extortionists. Smartly spoofing the stylised violence and downbeat toughness of the cult *yakuza eiga* or gangster pictures, the film earned notoriety when Itami was slashed across the face by three hoods as punishment for mocking gangland. DP. In Japanese with English subtitles.

Nobuko Miyamoto *Mahiru Inoue* • Akira Takarada *Kobayashi* • Masahiro Murata *Takehiro Murata* • Yasuo Daichi *Yuki Suzuki* • Hideji Otaki *Hotel owner* • Noboru Mitani *Gang boss* • Shiro Ito *Iriuchijima* • Akira Nakao *Ibagi* ■ *Dir/Scr* Juzo Itami

The Mind Benders ★★

Science-fiction drama
1963 · UK · BW · 113mins

Ahead of its time in 1963 and now hopelessly dated, this melodrama about spying, brainwashing and Oxford dons was ill-fated from the start. Dirk Bogarde is just one of the scientists who spends a few hours in an isolation tank and ends up even more unpleasant than he was before. The film boasts some fine performances – not to mention the screen debut of Edward Fox – but Basil Dearden's direction is far too straightforward for such a bizarre story. AT

Dirk Bogarde *Dr Henry Longman* • Mary Ure *Oonagh Longman* • John Clements *Major Hall* • Michael Bryant *Dr Tate* • Wendy Craig *Annabelle* • Harold Goldblatt *Professor Sharpey* • Geoffrey Keen *Calder* • Terry Palmer *Norman* • Edward Fox *Stewart* ■ *Dir* Basil Dearden • *Scr* James Kennaway

The Mind of Mr Soames ★★★★

Science-fiction thriller
1970 · UK · Colour · 97mins

A thought-provoking psychological study of human behaviour, director Alan Cooke's sensitive work signalled an exciting new direction for Amicus, Hammer's nearest British rival, as they entered the horror-swamped 1970s. Terence Stamp is brought out of a 30-year coma by neurosurgeon Robert Vaughn and, following a crash course in the ways of society, is sent into the terrifying outside world. In one of his finest roles, Stamp is outstanding; his subtle character shadings ooze a captivating truth. An overlooked, intelligent thriller. AJ

Terence Stamp *John Soames* • Robert Vaughn *Dr Michael Bergen* • Nigel Davenport *Dr Maitland* • Donal Donnelly *Dr Joe Allen* • Christian Roberts *Thomas Fleming* • Vickery Turner *Naomi* • Scott Forbes *Richard Bannerman* • Judy Parfitt *Jenny Bannerman* ■ *Dir* Alan Cooke (1) • *Scr* John Hale, Edward Simpson, from the novel by Charles Eric Maine

The Mind Reader ★★★

Drama 1933 · US · BW · 68mins

Warren William stars as a failed carnival grifter who turns fake clairvoyant, gets into trouble, and then tries to go straight for the sake of the wife who believes in him. This is a rather curious but watchable mix of satirical humour, sentimentality and near melodrama, distinguished by a first-rate performance from William and an excellent supporting cast, including the classy Constance Cummings as the loyal wife. RK

Warren William *Chandra Chandler/Dr Munro* • Constance Cummings *Sylvia* • Allen Jenkins *Frank* • Natalie Moorhead *Mrs Austin* • Mayo Methot *Jenny* • Clarence Muse *Sam* ■ *Dir* Roy Del Ruth • *Scr* Robert Lord, Wilson Mizner, from a story by Vivian Crosby

The Mind Snatchers ★★ 15

Drama 1972 · US · Colour · 92mins

In this slow-moving drama, army scientists use controversial shock therapy on overly aggressive soldiers who find it difficult to conform to army life. Ronny Cox and a pre-stardom Christopher Walken play two victims who respond to the pleasure-centre brain treatment in differing ways. Despite powerful moments, the movie never fully conquers its stage play origins, although it does manage to put across the trauma inherent in the experimental euphoria. AJ DVD

Christopher Walken *Private James Reese* • Joss Ackland *Dr Frederick* • Ralph Meeker *Major* • Ronny Cox *Miles* • Marco St John *Orderly* ■ *Dir* Bernard Girard • *Scr* Ron Whyte, from the play by Dennis Reardon

Mindhunters ★★ 15

Crime thriller
2003 · US/Neth/UK/Fin · Colour · 105mins

A group of FBI trainees is sent to a remote island for an elaborate exercise by their predictably unorthodox mentor, Val Kilmer. They are joined at the last minute by police officer LL Cool J and new recruit Christian Slater. When Slater is murdered, the group begins to suspect that there may be a serial killer on the loose. However, the characters are so bland and Renny Harlin's direction so full of meaningless slow-motion gloss that it's difficult to care. GM. Contains violence and swearing.

James Todd Smith [LL Cool J] *Gabe Jensen* • Jonny Lee Miller *Lucas Harper* • Kathryn Morris *Sara Moore* • Patricia Velasquez *Nicole Willis* • Clifton Collins Jr *Vince Sherman* • Eion Bailey *Bobby Whitman* • Will Kemp *Rafe Perry* • Val Kilmer *Jake Harris* • Christian Slater *JD Reston* ■ *Dir* Renny Harlin • *Scr* Wayne Kramer, Kevin Brodbin, from a story by Wayne Kramer

Mindwalk ★

Drama 1990 · US · Colour · 112mins

A group of ecologists talk at length about environmental philosophy in the medieval French town of St Michel, in director Bernt Capra's tortuous adaptation of his brother Fritjof's New Age bestseller. With virtually no action, drama or narrative, this deathly dull variation on *My Dinner with Andre* is a vanity production of epic proportions. Despite the presence of Liv Ullman and Sam Waterston, it's a film that gives conversation a bad name. AJ

Liv Ullmann *Sonia Hoffman* • Sam Waterston *Jack Edwards* • John Heard *Thomas Harriman* • Ione Skye *Kit Hoffman* • Emmanuel Montes *Romain* ■ *Dir* Bernt Capra • *Scr* Fritjof Capra, Floyd Byars, from a story by Bernt Capra, from the non-fiction book *The Turning Point* by Fritjof Capra

Mine Own Executioner ★★★

Psychological drama
1947 · UK · BW · 110mins

A nerve-shattered former prisoner of war, who has tried to kill the wife he loves, is treated by a lay psychiatrist with problems of his own. This is a brave and intelligent piece of film-making, which allowed Nigel Balchin to adapt his novel with almost no box-office concessions. The psychiatrist becomes Canadian to suit American actor Burgess Meredith, but he plays the part brilliantly. Under the direction of Anthony Kimmins, Kieron Moore is also excellent as the disturbed man. The climax on the ledge of a high building will make your feet tingle. AE

Burgess Meredith *Felix Milne* • Dulcie Gray *Patricia Milne* • Kieron Moore *Adam Lucian* • Barbara White *Molly Lucian* • Christine Norden *Barbara Edge* • John Laurie *Dr James Garsten* • Michael Shepley *Peter Edge* • Lawrence Hanray *Dr Lefage* ■ *Dir* Anthony Kimmins • *Scr* Nigel Balchin, from his novel

The Minion ★ 15

Supernatural thriller
1998 · US/Can · Colour · 91mins

Fallen star Dolph Lundgren reaches rock bottom in this absurdly expensive straight-to-video movie. The muddled storyline has something to do with a spirit that travels from body to body, searching for a holy door that will release evil on earth if opened. Lundgren plays a preacher intent on stopping it; this he does by punching possessed people in the back of their heads with a spiked glove. KB

Dolph Lundgren *Lukas* • Françoise Robertson *Karen Goodleaf* • Roc Lafortune *David Schulman* ■ *Dir* Jean-Marc Piche • *Scr* Matt Roe

Ministry of Fear ★★★

Spy drama 1945 · US · BW · 86mins

Paramount snapped up the rights to Graham Greene's novel because they liked the title. The plot that came with it was largely disposable, and the book was turned into a pursuit thriller starring Ray Milland as a mental patient who has spent two years in an insane asylum for murdering his wife. Fritz Lang turns this into a creepily effective work, full of bravura set pieces and subtle suggestions and somehow creating, in Hollywood, an impression of the London Blitz. AT

Ray Milland *Stephen Neale* • Marjorie Reynolds *Carla Hilfe* • Carl Esmond *Willi Hilfe* • Hillary Brooke *Mrs Bellane* • Percy Waram *Inspector Prentice* • Dan Duryea *Cost/Travers* • Alan Napier *Dr Forrester* • Erskine Sanford *Mr Rennit* ■ *Dir* Fritz Lang • *Scr* Seton I Miller, from the novel by Graham Greene

The Miniver Story ★ U

Drama 1950 · UK/US · BW · 104mins

MGM's *Mrs Miniver* (1942) won six Oscars and remains a famous beacon of patriotic light in the darkest days of the Second World War. This disastrously ill-judged sequel brings back the stars, with a new cast playing the now grown-up Miniver children. Directed by HC Potter, this irrelevant follow-up is a second-rate soap opera, bleak and depressing. RK

Greer Garson *Kay Miniver* • Walter Pidgeon *Clem Miniver* • John Hodiak *Spike Romway* • Leo Genn *Steve Brunswick* • Cathy O'Donnell *Judy Miniver* • Reginald Owen *Mr Foley* • Anthony Bushell *Dr Kanesley* • Peter Finch *Polish officer* ■ *Dir* HC Potter • *Scr* Ronald Millar, George Froeschel, from characters created by Jan Struther

Minnie and Moskowitz ★★★

Comedy drama 1971 · US · Colour · 114mins

Two sad and lonely people meet and fall in love against the hectic, heedless backdrop of the big city. Minnie (Gena Rowlands) works in a museum; Moskowitz (Seymour Cassel) is a car park attendant. The setting, Los Angeles, is important, since the movie is about the ribbon of dreams that people tie up their lives with. As always with Cassavetes, the film goes out of its way to show how different it is from conventional Hollywood fare. AT

Gena Rowlands *Minnie Moore* • Seymour Cassel *Seymour Moskowitz* • Val Avery *Zelmo* • Timothy Carey *Morgan* • Katherine Cassavetes *Sheba Moskowitz* • Elizabeth Deering *Girl* • Elsie Ames *Florence* • Lady Rowlands *Georgia Moore* ■ *Dir/Scr* John Cassavetes

Minor Mishaps ★★★★ 15

Drama 2002 · Den · Colour · 104mins

With its improvised approach to dysfunction, there's more than a hint of Mike Leigh about Annette K Olesen's directorial debut. Yet, this Danish domestic drama also contains elements of those Dogme favourites, *Festen* and *Italian for Beginners*, as the various everyday and extraordinary crises facing a working-class Copenhagen family combine both the pugnacity of a soap and the geniality of a sitcom. Focusing on the frustrations of middle age, it also succeeds in presenting widower Jorgen Kiil's unprepossessing offspring – reclusive chef Maria Würgler Rich, overworked contractor Henrik Prip and eccentric artist, Jannie Faurschou – without ever demonising or patronising them. A minor triumph. DP. In Danish with English subtitles. DVD

Jorgen Kiil *John Olsen, father* • Maria Würgler Rich *Marianne Olsen, younger daughter* • Jannie Faurschou *Eva Olsen, older daughter* • Henrik Prip *Tom Olsen, John's son* • Jesper Christensen *Soren Olsen, John's brother* • Karen-Lise Mynster *Hanne, Soren's wife* • Tina Gylling Mortensen *Ellen* • Julie Wieth *Lisbeth, Tom's wife* • Vigga Bro *Ulla Olsen, mother* ■ *Dir* Annette K Olesen • *Scr* Kim Fupz Aakeson

Minority Report ★★★★ 12

Futuristic action thriller
2002 · US · Colour · 139mins

Steven Spielberg's masterfully sleek vision of the future is an awesome mix of sensationally skewed science fiction, twisty Hitchcock-style thrills, stunning blue-grey tinged photography and outstanding design. Set in 2054, when police can use precognitive mutants to detect homicides before they're even committed, the plot sees top "Pre-cop" Tom Cruise identified as a future killer and forced to go on the run to discover why he's been set up and by whom. Adroitly realised by Spielberg, this is what sci-fi cinema should always be about but rarely is – mind-boggling images and a literate, witty script skilfully working together in perfect harmony. AJ DVD

Tom Cruise *Chief John Anderton* • Colin Farrell (2) *Danny Witwer* • Samantha Morton *Agatha* • Max von Sydow *Director Lamar Burgess* • Lois Smith *Dr Iris Hineman* • Peter Stormare *Dr Solomon Eddie* • Tim Blake Nelson *Gideon* ■ *Dir* Steven Spielberg • *Scr* Scott Frank, Jon Cohen, from the story by Philip K Dick

The Minus Man ★★★★

Psychological thriller
1999 · US · Colour · 115mins

This is a low-key tension-builder of the unbearable kind. The pleasant boy-next-door manner of drifter Owen Wilson hides the fact that he's a serial killer. It's when he lodges with troubled marrieds Brian Cox and Mercedes Ruehl that fate selects his next mark, and his precarious union with postal worker Janeane Garofalo suggests his poisoning days might be numbered. A very creepy, jet-black psychological thriller, this is made more unsettling by having Wilson meditate on his actions in comically-toned voiceover. A true original steeped in macabre chills and tightly-coiled emotions. AJ. Contains swearing and drug abuse.

Owen Wilson *Vann Siegert* • Janeane Garofalo *Ferrin* • Brian Cox *Doug* • Mercedes Ruehl *Jane* • Dwight Yoakam *Blair* • Dennis Haysbert *Graves* • Sheryl Crow *Caspar* • Eric Mabius *Gene* ■ *Dir* Hampton Fancher • *Scr* Hampton Fancher, from the novel by Lew McCreary

Mio in the Land of Faraway ★★ U

Fantasy adventure
1987 · Swe/USSR/Nor · Colour · 94mins

This is the kind of tosh that gives sword and sorcery a bad name. Young Nicholas Pickard's bid to defeat evil knight Christopher Lee has all the necessary quest ingredients. But director Vladimir Grammatikov assembles them too slowly and Lee arrives too late to revive flagging interest. Lacking in charm, but suffused with shoestring mediocrity, it's Tolkein for *Tweenie* tots. DP

Nicholas Pickard *Mio* • Christian Bale *Yum-Yum* • Christopher Lee *Wicked knight* • Timothy Bottoms *King* • Susannah York *Weaver woman* ■ *Dir* Vladimir Grammatikov • *Scr* William Aldridge, from the novel *Mio, My Son* by Astrid Lindgren

The Miracle ★★ U

Period drama 1959 · US · Colour · 121mins

Carroll Baker plays a Spanish novice who falls for British dragoon Roger Moore as he drifts across Spain towards the battle of Waterloo. Lavish, wooden and ridiculous, with bullfights, duels, droughts, plagues and an astonishing rainstorm at the end, this is hilariously awful. AT

Carroll Baker *Teresa* • Roger Moore *Captain Michael Stuart* • Walter Slezak *Flaco* • Vittorio Gassman *Guido* • Katina Paxinou *La Roca* • Gustavo Rojo *Cordoba* ■ *Dir* Irving Rapper • *Scr* Frank Butler, Jean Rouverol (uncredited), from the play by Karl Vollmoeller

The Miracle ★★★★ 15

Drama 1990 · UK · Colour · 92mins

Set in a small Irish seaside town, Neil Jordan's wonderful drama is often overlooked. Teenagers Lorraine Pilkington and Niall Byrne spend most of their time imagining the secret lives of their neighbours. Then glamorous actress Beverly D'Angelo turns up and pulls them into a real world of romance and mystery. Deliciously affecting, this was a small-scale comeback for Jordan after a couple of disasters. JB

Beverly D'Angelo *Renee* • Donal McCann *Sam* • Niall Byrne *Jimmy* • Lorraine Pilkington *Rose* • JG Devlin *Mr Beausang* • Cathleen Delaney *Miss Strange* ■ *Dir/Scr* Neil Jordan

Miracle ★★★ PG

Sports drama based on a true story
2004 · US · Colour · 130mins

You don't need to be a sports fan to enjoy this real-life hockey drama. A rousing strength-through-adversity tale, it shows how a team of American underdogs managed to defeat the seemingly invincible Soviet Union side in the 1980 Winter Olympics. The gruelling training and accompanying emotional fall-out are compelling, giving the movie a very human core. Kurt Russell is particularly good as unorthodox coach Herb Brooks, but as strong as his performance is, it's the well-shot action sequences that steal the show. SF DVD

Kurt Russell *Herb Brooks* • Patricia Clarkson *Patty Brooks* • Noah Emmerich *Craig Patrick* • Sean McCann *Walter Bush* • Kenneth Welsh *Doc Nagobads* • Eddie Cahill *Jim Craig* • Patrick O'Brien Demsey *Mike Eruzione* • Michael Mantenuto *Jack O'Callahan* • Nathan West *Rob McClanahan* ■ *Dir* Gavin O'Connor • *Scr* Eric Guggenheim

Miracle in Milan ★★★ U

Fantasy drama 1950 · It · BW · 91mins

Vittorio De Sica's follow-up to the internationally acclaimed *Bicycle Thieves* is a modern biblical parable that begins with the words, "Once upon a time". Abandoned in a cabbage patch, the hero, Toto, is brought up by a kindly old lady. The boy grows up to become one of life's saints, and the poverty that surrounds him in the shanty town outside Milan only sharpens his faith in human nature. Like a piece of 16th-century Renaissance art seen through a neorealist lens, this will probably seem very corny and simplistic to modern audiences. AT. In Italian with English subtitles.

Branduani Gianni *Little Toto, aged 11* • Francesco Golisano *Good Toto* • Paolo Stoppa *Bad Rappi* • Emma Gramatica *Old Lolatta* • Guglielmo Barnabo *Mobbi the rich man* ■ *Dir* Vittorio De Sica • *Scr* Cesare Zavattini, Vittorio De Sica, Suso Cecchi D'Amico, Mario Chiari, Adolfo Franci, from the story *Toto Il Buono* by Cesare Zavattini

Miracle in Soho ★★ U

Drama 1957 · UK · Colour · 97mins

Emeric Pressburger's screenwriting outings in Britain, without Michael Powell, were few and far between and this dour little drama might go some way to explaining why. Pressburger's script aims for the sort of semi-documentary tone that had become fashionable at the time, but this romance between a roadsweeper and an Italian girl needed a little local colour to buck it up, not grey sociological pronouncements. The grim images of Soho do have a certain historical value. DP

John Gregson *Michael Morgan* • Belinda Lee *Julia Gozzi* • Cyril Cusack *Sam Bishop* • Rosalie Crutchley *Mafalda Gozzi* • Peter Illing *Papa Gozzi* • Marie Burke *Mama Gozzi* • Ian Bannen *Filippo Gozzi* • Brian Bedford *Johnny* ■ *Dir* Julian Amyes • *Scr* Emeric Pressburger

Miracle in the Rain ★★ U

Romantic drama 1956 · US · BW · 107mins

Fine performances from stars Jane Wyman (as a timid office girl) and the ever-dependable Van Johnson (as an extrovert soldier) keep this soapy melodrama watchable, but its ending takes an awful lot of swallowing. Director Rudolph Maté sketches a credible working class New York, unusual for a period in American cinema when gloss ruled. The film is well made, but it comes across as either very moving or rather tacky. TS

Jane Wyman *Ruth Wood* • Van Johnson *Arthur Hugenon* • Peggie Castle *Millie Kranz* • Fred Clark *Stephen Jalonkik* • Eileen Heckart *Grace Ullman* • Josephine Hutchinson *Agnes Wood* • Alan King *Sgt Gil Parker* • Barbara Nichols *Arleene* ■ *Dir* Rudolph Maté • *Scr* Ben Hecht, from a novel by Ben Hecht

The Miracle Maker ★★★ U

Biblical animation
1999 · UK/Rus · Colour · 86mins

This co-production uses clay puppets and Wallace and Gromit-style techniques to tell the tale of Christ's life, his eventual crucifixion, resurrection and ascension. The puppets are beautifully carved, if a tad creepy, while the stop-motion animation is state-of-the-art, especially during crowd scenes that feature dozens of little figures pootling about. Somewhat dull and reverential side. DA DVD

Ralph Fiennes *Jesus* • Michael Bryant *God/The Doctor* • Julie Christie *Rachel* • Richard E Grant *John the Baptist* • Ian Holm *Pilate* • William Hurt *Jairus* • Bob Peck *Joseph of Arimathea* • Miranda Richardson *Mary Magdalene* • Antony Sher *Ben Azra* • David Thewlis *Judas* ■ *Dir* Derek Hayes, Stanislav Sokolov • *Scr* Murray Watts

Miracle Mile ★★★ 15

Science-fiction drama
1989 · US · Colour · 83mins

Anthony Edwards plays a musician who accidentally intercepts a phone call in which a man reveals that a nuclear Armageddon is on its way, with an hour to go before the world's destruction. Writer/director Steve De Jarnatt specifically zeroes in on Edwards to capture the impact of the bad news. The man is caught between his moral responsibilities and his desire to see his new love (Mare Winningham) one last time. But will it be that? De Jarnatt keeps you guessing right up to the end. JF

Anthony Edwards *Harry Washello* • Mare Winningham *Julie Peters* • John Agar *Ivan Peters* • Lou Hancock *Lucy Peters* • Mykelti Williamson *Wilson* • Kelly Minter [Kelly Jo Minter] *Charlotta* • Kurt Fuller *Gerstead* • Denise Crosby *Landa* ■ *Dir/Scr* Steve De Jarnatt

M

The Miracle of Bern
★★★★ PG

Sports drama based on a true story
2003 · Ger · Colour · 113mins

In 1954, the West German team staged one of the most remarkable comebacks in World Cup football history. Having been battered 8-3 by Hungary in the group stages, they exacted their revenge by beating them 3-2 in the final held in Bern, Switzerland. Director Sönke Wortmann satisfyingly relates the story of the unexpected triumph, but this is not just a feel-good sports movie. It is also a moving domestic drama, as young footie fan Louis Klamroth tries to get to know his father who has just returned from a Soviet labour camp, 11 years after being taken prisoner in the war. The performances are splendid, but even more impressive are the soccer sequences. DP. In German with English subtitles. DVD

Peter Lohmeyer *Richard Lubanski* • Louis Klamroth *Matthias Lubanski* • Lucas Gregorowicz *Paul Ackermann* • Katharina Wackernagel *Annette Ackermann* • Johanna Gastdorf *Christa Lubanski* • Mirko Lang *Bruno Lubanski* • Birthe Wolter *Ingrid Lubanski* • Sascha Göpel *Helmut Rahn* ■ *Dir* Sönke Wortmann • *Scr* Sönke Wortmann, Rochus Hahn

The Miracle of Morgan's Creek
★★★★★

Classic comedy 1944 · US · BW · 98mins

With its controversial (at the time) subject matter, the real miracle was that this film was allowed to be made in the first place. Writer/director Preston Sturges thumbed his nose at the Hays Office (administrators of the film censorship code) delivering a fast-paced story of a girl (Betty Hutton) who finds herself pregnant after attending a GI party and has no idea of the identity of the father from the men present. Sturges was the great Hollywood satirist of the 1940s and he made a slew of trailblazing films that remain some of the period's finest. This is a blistering comedy with marvellous moments all the way through and terrific interplay between the leads. DF

Eddie Bracken *Norval Jones* • Betty Hutton *Trudy Kockenlocker* • Diana Lynn *Emmy Kockenlocker* • Brian Donlevy *Governor McGinty* • Akim Tamiroff *Boss* • William Demarest *Officer Kockenlocker* • Porter Hall *Justice of the Peace* ■ *Dir/Scr* Preston Sturges • *Cinematographer* John F Seitz

M

The Miracle of Our Lady of Fatima
★★★ U

Religious drama 1952 · US · Colour · 102mins

Never approaching the Oscar-winning standard of *The Song of Bernadette*, this is, nevertheless, a sincere account of the 1917 apparition of the Virgin Mary to the Cova of Iria outside the Portuguese village of Fatima. The trio claim to have heard prophecies from a "lady in the sky" on the 13th of six consecutive months. But even though director John Brahm makes such moments as the cure of the lame and blind truly inspirational, the reverential approach will be harder to take for many than the episode's religious implications. DP

Gilbert Roland *Hugo Da Silva* • Susan Whitney *Lucia Dos Santos* • Sherry Jackson *Jacinta Marto* • Sammy Ogg *Francisco Marto* • Angela Clark *Maria Rosa* • Frank Silvera *Arturo Dos Santos* • Jay Novello *Antonio* • Richard Hale *Father Ferreira* ■ *Dir* John Brahm • *Scr* Cran Wilbur, James O'Hanlon

The Miracle of the Bells
★★★

Drama 1948 · US · BW · 119mins

Definitely one for those who like religious themes tied up in a neat parcel and featuring bearded men on fluffy clouds. Frank Sinatra, Fred MacMurray and Alida Valli star in an undemanding slice of whimsy, in which movie star Valli is laid to rest in her mining home town to rather dramatic effect. It's all a shade too sugary and daft, with stereotypes firmly in place, but still charming. SH

Fred MacMurray *Bill Dunnigan* • Valli [Alida Valli] *Olga Treskovna* • Frank Sinatra *Father Paul* • Lee J Cobb *Marcus Harris* • Jim Nolan *Ted Jones* • Veronika Pataky *Anna Klovna* • Philip Ahn *Ming Gow* ■ *Dir* Irving Pichel • *Scr* Ben Hecht, Quentin Reynolds, DeWitt Bodeen, from the novel by Russell Janney

Miracle of the White Stallions
★★★ U

Wartime adventure based on a true story
1963 · US · Colour · 89mins

In this real-life adventure, the famous white Lippizaner stallions of the Spanish Riding School in Vienna are evacuated to the countryside during the final days of the war. The head of the School leads the horses to safety and puts on a show for General Patton, thus securing American protection from the advancing Russians. The Disney brand might induce a certain cynicism, but this is a fairly sugar-free yarn. AT [video]

Robert Taylor (1) *Colonel Podhajsky* • Lilli Palmer *Verena Podhajsky* • Curt Jurgens *General Tellheim* • Eddie Albert *Rider Otto* • James Franciscus *Major Hoffman* • John Larch *General Patton* ■ *Dir* Arthur Hiller • *Scr* AJ Carothers, from the non-fiction book *The Dancing White Stallions of Vienna* by Colonel Alois Podhajsky

Miracle on Main Street
★★★

Seasonal drama 1940 · US · BW · 76mins

A tight little Columbia programme filler, this derives great strength from the performance of Margo, who stars as a dance-hall girl who finds an abandoned baby on Christmas Eve in a Los Angeles alley. Director Steve Sekely keeps sentiment at bay, and Jane Darwell and Veda Ann Borg provide potent cameos. TS

Margo *Maria Porter* • Walter Abel *Jim Foreman* • William Collier Sr *Doctor Miles* • Jane Darwell *Mrs Herman* • Lyle Talbot *Dick Porter* • Wynne Gibson *Sade "Coochie" Blake* • Veda Ann Borg *Flo* • Pat Flaherty *Detective* ■ *Dir* Steve Sekely • *Scr* Frederick Jackson, from a story by Samuel Ornitz, Boris Ingster

Miracle on 34th Street
★★★★★ U

Christmas fantasy 1947 · US · BW · 92mins

Natalie Wood is a jaded youngster who knows there's no such thing as Father Christmas because her mother, Maureen O'Hara, organises a New York department store's yearly parade, and Wood has always seen Santa played by drunken old men. The great plot was rightly awarded Oscars for best screenplay and original story, while Edmund Gwenn also won as best supporting actor. Indeed, Gwenn became so identified with the role of Kris Kringle that every holiday he found himself hired to hand out presents at the houses of such Hollywood notables as Louis B Mayer. TS [video] DVD

Maureen O'Hara *Doris Walker* • John Payne *Fred Gailey* • Edmund Gwenn *Kris Kringle* • Gene Lockhart *Judge Henry X Harper* • Natalie Wood *Susan Walker* • Porter Hall *Mr Sawyer* • William Frawley *Charles Halloran* • Jerome Cowan *Thomas Mara* • Philip Tonge *Mr Shellhammer* • James Seay *Dr Pierce* ■ *Dir* George Seaton • *Scr* George Seaton, from a story by Valentine Davies

Miracle on 34th Street
★★★ U

Christmas fantasy
1994 · US · Colour · 109mins

Richard Attenborough plays Kriss Kringle in this remake of the classic 1947 fantasy. He positively twinkles in the role in an attempt to convince moppet Mara Wilson, and the audience, that he is a living legend. Yet, although the film as a whole is a much more glamorous affair, and Wilson and Elizabeth Perkins as her mother are undoubtedly charming, it does lack some of the magic of the original. TH [video] DVD

Richard Attenborough *Kriss Kringle* • Elizabeth Perkins *Dorey Walker* • Dylan McDermott *Bryan Bedford* • JT Walsh *Ed Collins* • Mara Wilson *Susan Walker* • James Remar *Jack Duff* • Jane Leeves *Alberta Leonard* • Simon Jones *Shellhammer* ■ *Dir* Les Mayfield • *Scr* John Hughes, from the 1947 film, from a story by Valentine Davies

The Miracle Woman
★★★

Drama 1931 · US · BW · 90mins

A rarely-seen, extraordinary early work from director Frank Capra. Its theme of fake evangelism made it a controversial film in its day, based as it was on a play featuring a thinly disguised portrait of popular evangelist Aimée Semple McPherson. Barbara Stanwyck gives a remarkable performance, combining rare delicacy with great strength of purpose. Interestingly, this movie was produced in the days before the Hays Code censored such dialogue and sequences dealing with religious issues. Only a few years later such content would not be deemed fit material for US audiences. TS

Barbara Stanwyck *Florence "Faith" Fallon* • David Manners *John Carson* • Sam Hardy *Bob Hornsby* • Beryl Mercer *Mrs Higgins* • Russell Hopton *Bill Welford* • Charles Middleton *Simpson* • Eddie Boland *Collins* • Thelma Hill *Gussie* ■ *Dir* Frank R Capra [Frank Capra] • *Scr* Dorothy Howell, Jo Swerling, from the play *Bless You Sister* by John Meehan

The Miracle Worker
★★★★★ PG

Biographical drama 1962 · US · BW · 102mins

This is a marvellously moving biopic about the youth of deaf, dumb and blind Helen Keller, and her remarkable teacher Annie Sullivan. There are outstanding Oscar-winning performances from Anne Bancroft as Sullivan and Patty Duke as Keller, while Arthur Penn's direction is superb, remaining solidly unsentimental throughout. Unsettling and thought-provoking, this is a fine American humanitarian work, brilliantly photographed in harsh black and white by Ernesto Caparros. Duke later played the Sullivan role in a 1979 TV movie remake. TS [video] DVD

Anne Bancroft *Annie Sullivan* • Patty Duke *Helen Keller* • Victor Jory *Captain Keller* • Inga Swenson *Kate Keller* • Andrew Prine *James Keller* • Kathleen Comegys *Aunt Ev* • Beah Richards *Viney* ■ *Dir* Arthur Penn • *Scr* William Gibson, from his play, from the non-fiction book *The Story of My Life* by Helen Keller

Miracles
★★ PG

Comedy 1985 · US · Colour · 83mins

In this predictable, frantic caper, Teri Garr and her ex-husband Tom Conti suffer various indignities in the South American desert. Conti gives us his floppy-haired, shyly charming act, while Garr, a passably talented actress on occasion, is once again handed a script requiring little more than constant hysterics. If you're in a tolerant mood, this piece of visual chewing gum may amuse. SH [video]

Tom Conti *Roger* • Teri Garr *Jean* • Christopher Lloyd *Harry* • Paul Rodriguez *Juan* • Adalberto Martinez *Kayum, witch doctor* • Jorge Russek *Judge* • Paco Morayta *Sgt Gomez* ■ *Dir/Scr* Jim Kouf

Miracles for Sale
★★

Murder mystery 1939 · US · BW · 71mins

A change of pace for director Tod Browning, best known for controversial cult favourite *Freaks*, with a story about a magician (Robert Young) who gets involved in some supernatural murders. Browning plays it fairly straight in his final film but builds the tension nicely, aided by the capable performances of his cast. JF

Robert Young (1) *Michael Morgan* • Florence Rice *Judy Barclay* • Frank Craven *Dad Morgan* • Henry Hull *Dave Duvallo* • Lee Bowman *La Clair* • Cliff Clark *Inspector Gavigan* • Astrid Allwyn *Zelma La Clair* • Walter Kingsford *Colonel Watrous* ■ *Dir* Tod Browning • *Scr* Harry Ruskin, Marion Parsonnet, James Edward Grant, from the novel *Death from a Top Hat* by Clayton Rawston

Mirage
★★★★

Mystery thriller 1965 · US · Colour · 108mins

Corkscrew plots come no screwier than in this corker. The plot is unfathomable, and it's not certain whether that's deliberate or simply a symptom of poor film-making. Gregory Peck stars as an amnesiac who finds himself in a variety of tense situations, aided, abetted and threatened by a fine supporting cast of spooks that includes George Kennedy and Walter Matthau. One could regard this paranoid nightmare as a reflection of director Edward Dmytryk's experience of the Hollywood blacklist. This was remade three years later as *Jigsaw*. AT

Gregory Peck *David Stillwell* • Diane Baker *Sheila* • Walter Matthau *Ted Caselle* • Kevin McCarthy *Josephson* • Jack Weston *Lester* • Leif Erickson *Major Crawford* • Walter Abel *Charles Calvin* • George Kennedy *Willard* ■ *Dir* Edward Dmytryk • *Scr* Peter Stone, from the novel *Fallen Angel* by Walter Ericson [Howard Fast]

Miranda
★★★

Comedy fantasy 1947 · UK · BW · 79mins

Glynis Johns gives one of the best performances of her career as Miranda the mermaid, in this fishy tale that had more than a passing influence on the Ron Howard hit *Splash*. Griffith Jones is something of a stuffed shirt as the doctor who pulls her out of the sea and gives her the run of his bathroom, but Googie Withers is good value as his suspicious wife, yet no one can compare with the marvellous Margaret Rutherford as the local nurse. Never exactly funny, but enjoyable all the same. A sequel, *Mad about Men*, followed in 1954. DP

Glynis Johns *Miranda* • Googie Withers *Clare Marten* • Griffith Jones *Dr Paul Marten* • John McCallum *Nigel Hood* • Margaret Rutherford *Nurse Cary* • David Tomlinson *Charles* • Yvonne Owen *Betty* • Sonia Holm *Isobel* ■ *Dir* Ken Annakin • *Scr* Peter Blackmore, Denis Waldock, from the play by Peter Blackmore

Miranda
★ 15

Romantic thriller 2001 · UK · Colour · 88mins

Grubby, artificial and showcasing one of Christina Ricci's worst performances to date, this dull embarrassment is supposedly a comedy romance, but features little of either. John Simm is a librarian who falls in love with the enigmatic Ricci, only to learn she's a conwoman. When director Marc Munden shifts this listless mediocrity into tepid thriller territory the whole farrago becomes more indigestible by the second. AJ [video] DVD

Christina Ricci *Miranda* • John Simm *Frank* • Kyle MacLachlan *Nailor* • John Hurt *Christian* •

Julian Rhind-Tutt *Rod* • Cavan Clerkin *Gerry* • Matthew Marsh *Charles* ■ *Dir* Marc Munden • *Scr* Rob Young

Mirch Masala ★★★ 15

Drama 1987 · Ind · Colour · 119mins

Although it loses track of its intellectual purpose and ends up being a rather bland melodrama, this political allegory made the international reputation of Indian director Ketan Mehta. Naseeruddin Shah plays the Raj-obsessed tax collector, or subedar, whose passion for Smita Patil is drawn with considerable ferocity. Om Puri is also impressive as the sage watchman who protects the frightened Patil in an otherwise all-female spice factory. It's beautifully photographed, but much of the symbolism will lack significance for western audiences. DP. In Hindi with English subtitles.

Naseeruddin Shah *Subedar* • Smita Patil *Sonbai* • Suresh Oberoi *Mukhi* • Om Puri ■ *Dir* Ketan Mehta

Mirror ★★★★ U

Experimental biographical drama
1974 · USSR · Colour and BW · 101mins

Cinema doesn't get much more personal than this. Casting his mother as the old woman and using his famous father, Arseni Tarkovsky's poetry on the soundtrack, director Andrei Tarkovsky draws on childhood memories, artistic fantasies and actual events to explore the ways in which the history of his country impinged on the lives of three generations of his family. It's a bewildering blend of documentary footage and stylised imagery, that can only be described as cinematic poetry. Some of the references are decidedly obscure and demand concentration to keep in step, but it is an awesome achievement, nevertheless. DP. In Russian with English subtitles. DVD

Margarita Terekhova *Alexei's mother/Natalia* • Ignat Daniltsev *Ignat/Alexei, aged 12* • Maria Tarkovskaya *Alexei's mother, as an old woman* • Alla Demidova *Lisa* • Fillip Yankovsky *Alexei, aged five* • Oleg Yankovsky *Father* ■ *Dir* Andrei Tarkovsky • *Scr* Andrei Tarkovsky, Aleksandr Misharin

The Mirror Crack'd ★★ PG

Mystery 1980 · UK · Colour · 101mins

This mediocre mystery gave Angela Lansbury the chance to rehearse her role as a crime-solving novelist in *Murder She Wrote*. Here, she takes on the mantle of Agatha Christie's Miss Marple. Frankly, with the clash of the titans going on between Elizabeth Taylor and Kim Novak, nobody else really gets a look in, not even Tony Curtis and Rock Hudson (in his penultimate picture). DP DVD

Angela Lansbury *Miss Marple* • Elizabeth Taylor *Marina Rudd* • Tony Curtis *Marty N Fenn* • Edward Fox *Inspector Craddock* • Rock Hudson *Jason Rudd* • Geraldine Chaplin *Ella Zielinsky* • Kim Novak *Lola Brewster* ■ *Dir* Guy Hamilton • *Scr* Jonathan Hales, Barry Sandler, from the novel by Agatha Christie

The Mirror Has Two Faces ★★★ 15

Romantic comedy
1996 · US · Colour · 121mins

Barbra Streisand directs and stars in this so-so romantic comedy. She plays a dowdy professor who agrees to have a purely platonic relationship with Jeff Bridges, which is his solution to years of empty sexual romances. Of course, Babs secretly fancies the pants off him, so she decides to turn herself into a sensual swan and seduce him. While Streisand and Bridges fumble with their roles, the movie is stolen out from under them by supporting cast members Mimi Rogers, as Barbra's glamour-puss sister, and Lauren Bacall as her critical mother. JB DVD

Barbra Streisand *Rose Morgan* • Jeff Bridges *Gregory Larkin* • Lauren Bacall *Hannah Morgan* • George Segal *Henry Fine* • Mimi Rogers *Claire* • Pierce Brosnan *Alex* • Brenda Vaccaro *Doris* • Austin Pendleton *Barry* • Elle Macpherson *Candy* ■ *Dir* Barbra Streisand • *Scr* Richard LaGravenese, from his story, from the film *Le Miroir A Deux Faces* by André Cayatte, Gérard Oury • *Music* Marvin Hamlisch • *Cinematographer* Dante Spinotti, Andrzej Bartkowiak

The Misadventures of Margaret ★★ 15

Romantic comedy
1998 · Fr/UK/US · Colour · 88mins

The art of screwball comedy was dead long before writer/director Brian Skeet banged this nail into its coffin. As she attempts valiantly to impersonate Katharine Hepburn, star Parker Posey succeeds only in being irritatingly overeager in the role of the novelist whose marriage, to genial academic Jeremy Northam, begins to unravel as she researches her latest book. Despite a few clever touches and its strong cast, this is a misadventure from start to finish. DP. Contains swearing and sex scenes.

Parker Posey *Margaret Nathan* • Jeremy Northam *Edward Nathan* • Craig Chester *Richard Lane* • Elizabeth McGovern *Till Turner* • Brooke Shields *Lily* • Corbin Bernsen *Art Turner* • Justine Waddell *Young girl* ■ *Dir* Brian Skeet • *Scr* Brian Skeet, from the novel *Rameau's Niece* by Cathleen Schine

The Misadventures of Merlin Jones ★★ U

Comedy 1964 · US · Colour · 90mins

A pleasant, undemanding Disney comedy from the director of *The Absent-Minded Professor*. A college genius accidentally develops a means of reading minds. Turning this new ability to good use – in contrast to the way some of us might be tempted to exploit it – he tries to solve crimes, but winds up in court himself. The characters returned in a 1965 sequel, *The Monkey's Uncle*. JG

Tommy Kirk *Merlin Jones* • Annette Funicello *Jennifer* • Leon Ames *Judge Holmby* • Stuart Erwin *Police Capt Loomis* • Alan Hewitt *Prof Shattuck* • Connie Gilchrist *Mrs Gossett* ■ *Dir* Robert Stevenson • *Scr* Tom August [Alfred Lewis Levitt], Helen August [Helen Levitt], from a story by Bill Walsh

Mischief ★★

Crime thriller 1983 · W Ger · Colour · 98mins

We hear so much about the decline of the British film industry, but that is nothing in comparison to the collapse of the German cinema. The situation is unlikely to improve if directors of the calibre of Peter Fleischmann can find nothing better than this quirky murder mystery. Fleischmann also stars as a workaholic cop who postpones a holiday to investigate the death of a child. The friction between the policeman and Angelika Stute, the child's mother and chief murder suspect, generates the odd spark, but there are few surprises. DP. German dialogue dubbed into English.

Peter Fleischmann *Detective Inspector Lohmann* • Angelika Stute *Annette* • Isolde Barth *Gilla* • Balduin Baas *Dürkheimer* • Horst Kummeth *Vesselitz* ■ *Dir* Peter Fleischmann • *Scr* Peter Fleischmann, Jacques Rozier, Werner Sommer

Mischief ★★ 15

Comedy 1985 · US · Colour · 92mins

The predictable teen comedy, set in the 1950s, tries to be a cross between *Porky's* and *American Graffiti* – a daft combination if ever there was one. Doug McKeon and Catherine Mary Stewart are two of the youngsters trying to find love and a decent plot in a cast that includes Jami Gertz and Kelly Preston. JB. Contains swearing, violence and nudity.

Doug McKeon *Jonathan* • Catherine Mary Stewart *Bunny* • Kelly Preston *Marilyn* • Chris Nash *Gene* • DW Brown *Kenny* • Jami Gertz *Rosalie* • Maggie Blye *Claire Miller* ■ *Dir* Mel Damski • *Scr* Noel Black

Les Misérables ★★★★★

Period epic 1934 · Fr · BW · 305mins

Since 1909, there have been nearly two dozen film versions of Victor Hugo's vast novel. The story is trifling yet monumental. After serving a massive prison sentence for petty theft, Jean Valjean's spiritual transformation into a pillar of society is undermined by Javert, the policeman who obsessively pursues him. Add to this an epic panorama of French Revolutionary history and a doomed love affair, and you have a humanist masterpiece that works on a multitude of levels. Raymond Bernard's epic version of 1934 might be compared to Abel Gance's *Napoleon* (it shares the same cameraman, Jules Krüger): it's slow, unfailingly faithful to the source, and contains towering performances by Harry Bauer and Charles Vanel. AT. In French with English subtitles.

Harry Baur *Jean Valjean* • Charles Vanel *Javert* • Henry Krauss *Monseignor Myriel* • Odette Florelle [Florelle] *Fantine* ■ *Dir* Raymond Bernard • *Scr* Raymond Bernard, Andre Lang, from the novel by Victor Hugo • *Music* Arthur Honneger

Les Misérables ★★★★

Period epic 1935 · US · BW · 111mins

Victor Hugo's classic novel had been filmed several times in the silent era, and there was an impressive French version in 1934. Despite cuts to the text, however, this lavish 20th Century-Fox production (which imported MGM talent for the occasion) is generally considered to be the best. Fredric March, as condemned criminal Jean Valjean, gives a solid and noble performance, but the film is dominated by Charles Laughton as the policeman Javert, a magnificent portrayal of dark obsession. The film's emotional and ironic climax was regarded by Laughton as "the finest thing I have ever been able to accomplish on the screen". AT

Fredric March *Jean Valjean* • Charles Laughton *Javert* • Cedric Hardwicke *Bishop Bienvenu* • Rochelle Hudson *Big Cosette* • Marilyn Knowlden *Little Cosette* • Frances Drake *Eponine* • John Beal *Marius* • Jessie Ralph *Madame Magloire* ■ *Dir* Richard Boleslawski • *Scr* WP Lipscomb, from the novel by Victor Hugo • *Cinematographer* Gregg Toland

Les Misérables ★★

Period epic 1946 · It · BW · 120mins

This Italian version of the Victor Hugo story puts the emphasis not on Jean Valjean (Gino Cervi) and Inspector Javert (Hans Hinrich), but on Valentina Cortese, who plays both Fantine and her daughter Cosette. Original versions played in two parts – *Manhunt* and *Storm Over Paris* – of 90 minutes each. A foreign version, with lamentable English dubbing, was released in 1952 at 140 minutes; it was later cut to two hours. AT. Italian dialogue dubbed into English.

Valentina Cortese *Fantine/Cosette* • Gino Cervi *Jean Valjean* • Hans Hinrich *Inspector Javert* • Aldo Nicodemi *Marius* ■ *Dir* Riccardo Freda • *Scr* Riccardo Freda, Mario Monicelli, Stefano Vanzina, from the novel by Victor Hugo • *Cinematographer* Rodolfo Lombardi

Les Misérables ★★★ U

Period epic 1952 · US · BW · 105mins

Lewis Milestone's film is a faithful but undeniably pedestrian version of Victor Hugo's masterpiece. Michael Rennie makes a decent Valjean, but he comes in some way behind Harry Baur, Fredric March and Jean Gabin, all of whom invested the part with considerably more truth and emotion. Robert Newton plays Javert as an eye-rolling villain whose fanaticism is at odds with Milestone's contention that personality has no part to play in the enforcement of the law. Edmund Gwenn alone captures the novel's humanity as a benevolent bishop. DP

Michael Rennie *Jean Valjean* • Robert Newton *Javert* • Debra Paget *Cosette* • Edmund Gwenn *Bishop* • Sylvia Sidney *Fantine* • Cameron Mitchell *Marius* • Elsa Lanchester *Madame Magloire* • James Robertson-Justice *Robert* ■ *Dir* Lewis Milestone • *Scr* Richard Murphy, from the novel by Victor Hugo

Les Misérables ★★

Period epic
1957 · E Ger/It/Fr · Colour · 210mins

Despite the presence of France's greatest screen actor, Jean Gabin, this version of Victor Hugo's classic is likely to lose many viewers during the course of its three-and-a-half hours. Gabin's performance as the petty criminal turned saintly hero Jean Valjean is perfectly adequate, and Bernard Blier is also good as Javert, the cop who obsessively haunts him. The problem lies in the stolid direction by former Resistance fighter Jean-Paul Le Chanois, while filming in the state-run studios of communist East Germany benefited only the budget. AT. In French with English subtitles.

Jean Gabin *Jean Valjean* • Bernard Blier *Javert* • Bourvil *Thenardier* • Danièle Delorme *Fantine* • Fernand Ledoux *Myriel* • Béatrice Altariba *Cosette* • Gianni Esposito *Marius* • Silvia Montfort *Eponine* ■ *Dir* Jean-Paul Le Chanois • *Scr* Jean-Paul Le Chanois, Michel Audiard, René Barjavel, from the novel by Victor Hugo,

M

Les Misérables ★★★ PG

Period epic 1978 · US · Colour · 137mins

Richard Jordan and Anthony Perkins take on the challenging roles of Valjean (the hunted) and Javert (the hunter) in Victor Hugo's classic tale, investing this impressive TV movie with intelligence and depth. Director Glenn Jordan, a TV movie specialist whose early career was in the theatre, gives a luxurious (and thus ironic) feel to the claustrophobic world of Hugo's characters, providing plenty of room for his stars to shine. JM DVD

Richard Jordan *Jean Valjean* • Anthony Perkins *Inspector Javert* • Cyril Cusack *Fauchelevent* • Claude Dauphin *Bishop Myriel* • John Gielgud *Gillenormand* • Ian Holm *Thenardier* • Celia Johnson *Sister Simplice* • Flora Robson *Prioress* ■ *Dir* Glenn Jordan • *Scr* John Gay, from the novel by Victor Hugo

Les Misérables ★★★

Period epic 1982 · Fr · Colour · 180mins

A middling *Misérables*, better than the 1957 version with Jean Gabin, but not in the same league as the 1934 and 1935 versions or Claude Lelouch's radical update of 1995. Made for French TV and shown in six 50-minute episodes (a cinema version of three hours was shown first), Hossein's exhaustive and exhausting effort boasts an excellent Valjean and Javert in the charismatic, Bogart-like Lino Ventura and the creepy Michel Bouquet. It's a bit like a primer for French lit students, but some of it is spectacular to look at, with marvellous use of the medieval town of Sarlat. AT. In French with English subtitles.

Lino Ventura *Jean Valjean* • Michel Bouquet *Inspector Javert* • Jean Carmet *Thenardier* •

Françoise Seigner *La Thenardier* • Evelyne Bouix *Fantine* • Christine Jean *Cosette* • Frank David *Marius* • Candice Patou *Eponine* ■ *Dir* Robert Hossein • *Scr* Robert Hossein, Alain Decaux, from the novel by Victor Hugo

Les Misérables ★★★★ 12

Period epic 1995 · Fr · Colour · 167mins

Director Claude Lelouch makes an ambitious attempt to update Victor Hugo's tale to the 20th century. Although he provides a provocative portrait of France under the Nazi occupation, this sprawling epic is very much a picaresque adventure, with Jean-Paul Belmondo outstanding as the former boxer for whom the task of keeping a Jewish family out of the clutches of the Nazis is no less daunting than completing Hugo's mammoth tome. Brimming with incident and with excellent support from Annie Girardot, this is both exhilarating and moving. DP. In French with English subtitles.

Jean-Paul Belmondo *Henri Fortin/Jean Valjean* • Michel Boujenah *André Ziman* • Alessandra Martines *Elise Ziman* • Salomé [Salomé Lelouch] *Salomé Ziman* • Annie Giradot *Théardière farmer woman* • Philippe Léotard *Thénardier* ■ *Dir* Claude Lelouch • *Scr* Claude Lelouch, from the novel by Victor Hugo

Les Misérables ★★ 12

Period epic 1997 · US · Colour · 127mins

Liam Neeson stars as the reformed criminal, Jean Valjean; Geoffrey Rush is the obsessive detective, Javert; Uma Thurman and Claire Danes play the women Valjean cares for. On paper, this is an impressive cast; on screen, though, the performances are distinctly underwhelming. Bille August's production, mostly shot in Prague, looks like a TV mini-series that's been hacked down for cinema release and the rhythm is all wrong. AT. Contains some swearing and violence. DVD

Liam Neeson *Jean Valjean* • Geoffrey Rush *Javert* • Uma Thurman *Fantine* • Claire Danes *Cosette* • Hans Matheson *Marius* • Reine Brynolfsson *Captain Beauvais* • Peter Vaughan *Bishop* ■ *Dir* Bille August • *Scr* Rafael Yglesias, from the novel by Victor Hugo

Misery ★★★★ 18

Psychological thriller
1990 · US · Colour · 102mins

Director Rob Reiner's superb adaptation of Stephen King's bestseller deals with the trappings of celebrity, fanatical devotion, artistic dilemmas and the worthiness of commercial fiction within a psychological suspense context. Kathy Bates deservedly won an Oscar for her monstrously scary performance as novelist James Caan's "Number One Fan", turning from caring nurse to insane torturer after learning he's killed off her favourite character. Reiner's adept exercise in chilling claustrophobia contains numerous jolts, with the "hobbling" scene certain to evoke screams of revulsion. AJ. Contains violence, swearing. DVD

James Caan *Paul Sheldon* • Kathy Bates *Annie Wilkes* • Richard Farnsworth *Buster, Sheriff* • Frances Sternhagen *Virginia* • Lauren Bacall *Marcia Sindell* • Graham Jarvis *Libby* • Jerry Potter *Pete* ■ *Dir* Rob Reiner • *Scr* William Goldman, from the novel by Stephen King • *Cinematographer* Barry Sonnenfeld

The Misfits ★★★★ PG

Drama 1961 · US · BW · 119mins

The last film of both Marilyn Monroe and Clark Gable, and some might say containing the last real performance by Montgomery Clift, it went from box-office flop to cult status within the space of a year. Written by Monroe's then husband, Arthur Miller, it's a grey, solemn and at times pretentious piece about three drifters who hunt horses destined to become pet food. Somehow the flat, arid Nevada landscape mirrors the characters' bleak existence and sets the overall mood of despair and depression. Dogged by various production problems (Monroe's emotional upheavals, Clift's substance abuse, United Artists freezing the budget), John Huston's film is easy to admire but hard to enjoy fully. AT DVD

Clark Gable *Gay Langland* • Marilyn Monroe *Roslyn Taber* • Montgomery Clift *Perce Howland* • Eli Wallach *Guido* • Thelma Ritter *Isabelle Steers* • James Barton *Old man in bar* • Estelle Winwood *Church lady* • Kevin McCarthy *Raymond Taber* ■ *Dir* John Huston • *Scr* Arthur Miller

Mishima: a Life in Four Chapters ★★★★ 15

Biographical drama
1985 · US/Jpn · Colour and BW · 115mins

This is an astonishing account by Paul Schrader of the life and works of Yukio Mishima, the Japanese literary icon who committed *seppuku* (ritual suicide) on 25 November 1970. Audaciously cutting between the events of that day, monochrome flashbacks and stylised excerpts from Mishima's writings, Schrader produces a film of exemplary control and penetrating insight – a feat made all the more impressive by the fact that Mishima's widow forbade any explicit reference to her late husband's sexuality and controversial politics. Exquisitely designed by Eiko Ishioka, the scenes from Mishima's works are mesmerisingly beautiful and enlightening. DP. In English and Japanese with subtitles.

Ken Ogata *Yukio Mishima* • Masayuki Shionoya *Morita* • Junkichi Orimoto *General Mashita* • Naoko Otani *Mother* • Go Riju *Mishima, aged 18-19* • Masato Aizawa *Mishima, aged 9-14* • Yuki Nagahara *Mishima, aged 5* • Haruko Kato *Grandmother* ■ *Dir* Paul Schrader • *Scr* Leonard Schrader, Paul Schrader, Chieko Schrader, from various literary works by Yukio Mishima

Misplaced ★★★

Drama 1989 · US · Colour · 98mins

The feature debut of Polish-born Louis Yansen was barely seen outside the film festival circuit, but this intelligent exploration of coming to terms with an entirely new way of life deserves a wider audience. The melting-pot theme has long been a Hollywood standby, but this is one of the few films to focus on the struggles of an exile whose life has been ruined. DP. An English and Polish language film.

John Cameron Mitchell *Jacek Nowak* • Viveca Lindfors *Zofia* • Elzbieta Czyzewska *Halina Nowak* • Drew Snyder *Bill* • Deirdre O'Connell *Ela* • Debralee Scott *Mrs Padway* • John Christopher Jones *David* • Tico Wells *Clayton* ■ *Dir* Louis Yansen • *Scr* Louis Yansen, Lonnie Carter, Thomas De Wolfe, from a story by Louis Yansen

Miss Amerigua ★★★

Political satire
1994 · Chil/Swe · Colour · 97mins

Chilean director Luis R Vera is currently based in Sweden, but he returns to his homeland for this stylish tale of love and revenge. The story follows a young revolutionary as he returns to avenge his father's murder just as the town is gripped by a beauty contest, in which the three favourites are his sister, his beloved and the daughter of his father's killer. Forget the complex political allegory, this is a sizzling melodrama. DP. In Spanish with English subtitles.

Hector Silva *Evaristo* • Sonia Marchewka *Maria Desamparo* • Jesus Perez *Colonel Banderas* • Jorge Baez *Inocencio Periodista* • Carlos Cristaldo *Reencarnacion* ■ *Dir* Luis R Vera • *Scr* Andras Colman, Luis R Vera

Miss Annie Rooney ★★

Drama 1942 · US · BW · 86mins

At the age of 14, former childhood sweetheart Shirley Temple was having trouble sustaining her popularity, and this is one of the mild vehicles she found herself in after leaving Fox. The star sings and jitterbugs, but its chief selling point was the fact that Temple received her first screen kiss (though it's little more than a peck on the cheek). It was given by another former child star Dickie Moore, who would state that the kiss was a first for him, too. Moore couldn't dance, so those scenes were performed by Roland Dupree, wearing a rubber face-mask in the image of his co-star. TV

Shirley Temple *Annie Rooney* • William Gargan *Tim Rooney* • Guy Kibbee *Grandpop Rooney* • Dickie Moore *Marty White* • Peggy Ryan *Myrtle* • Roland DuPree *Joey* • Jonathan Hale *Mr White* • Gloria Holden *Mrs White* ■ *Dir* Edwin L Marin • *Scr* George Bruce

Miss Congeniality ★★★★ 12

Action comedy 2000 · US · Colour · 105mins

Sandra Bullock returns to form in director Donald Petrie's energetic comedy that focuses on the world of beauty pageants. When a terrorist threatens the Miss United States competition, Bullock's determinedly unfeminine FBI agent is drafted in as a contestant. Pampered and preened by contest expert Michael Caine, Bullock uncovers her own feminine side and has some of her preconceptions shattered. Her relationship with FBI colleague Benjamin Bratt sparkles with sexual chemistry and the gags come thick and fast. The antics of the competition's hosts, Candice Bergen and William Shatner, are slightly overplayed, but on the whole this is great fun. LH. Contains swearing and some violence. DVD

Sandra Bullock *Gracie Hart* • Michael Caine *Victor Melling* • Benjamin Bratt *Eric Matthews* • Candice Bergen *Kathy Morningside* • William Shatner *Stan Fields* • Ernie Hudson *McDonald* • Heather Burns *Cheryl "Rhode Island"* ■ *Dir* Donald Petrie • *Scr* Marc Lawrence (2), from a story by Katie Ford, Caryn Lucas, Marc Lawrence (2)

Miss Congeniality 2: Armed & Fabulous ★★ 12

Action comedy
2005 · US/Aus · Colour · 110mins

Sandra Bullock returns as clumsy FBI agent Gracie Hart in this lazy sequel. Picking up where the original movie left off, the story involves Hart reluctantly accepting a PR role after her newfound fame makes it impossible for her to operate undercover. Groomed to perfection, the Bureau's poster girl soon begins to relish her position, much to the distaste of her tough new bodyguard (Regina King). Were it not for Bullock's natural comic timing, this would fall apart. SF. Contains violence. DVD

Sandra Bullock *Gracie Hart* • William Shatner *Stan Fields* • Heather Burns *Cheryl* • Regina King *Sam Fuller* • Ernie Hudson *McDonald* • Treat Williams *Collins* ■ *Dir* John Pasquin • *Scr* Marc Lawrence (2)

Miss Evers' Boys ★★★★

Period drama based on a true story
1997 · US · Colour · 118mins

This Emmy Award-winning true story brilliantly dramatises a dark and shameful chapter in America's recent past. Alfre Woodard stars as a caring nurse who tries to alleviate her patients' suffering while working on a federal health project in 1930s Alabama. The study, intended to monitor and treat syphilis among poor African-American men, instead lapses into a heartless experiment on patients deteriorating into madness from the untreated disease. Writer Walter Bernstein's sensitive adaptation, Joseph Sargent's direction and a distinguished cast make this TV movie a drama of rare power and eloquence. MC. Contains swearing.

Alfre Woodard *Eunice Evers* • Laurence Fishburne *Caleb Humphries* • Craig Sheffer *Dr Douglas* • Joe Morton *Dr Brodus* • Ossie Davis *Mr Evers* • EG Marshall *Senate chairman* ■ *Dir* Joseph Sargent • *Scr* Walter Bernstein, from the play by David Feldshuh

Miss Firecracker ★★★ PG

Comedy drama 1989 · US · Colour · 98mins

Dazzling Holly Hunter is full of energetic snap, crackle and pop as she re-creates the part she made her own on stage. It's Hunter's dream to win the Yazoo City beauty contest, and the tale of how she makes it to the finals against all the odds is beautifully told by director Thomas Schlamme. A gentle comedy, filled with Southern eccentrics deliciously brought to scene-stealing life by the likes of Mary Steenburgen, Alfre Woodard and Tim Robbins. AJ DVD

Holly Hunter *Carnelle Scott* • Mary Steenburgen *Elain Rutledge* • Tim Robbins *Delmount Williams* • Alfre Woodard *Popeye Jackson* • Scott Glenn *Mac Sam* • Veanne Cox *Tessy Mahoney* • Ann Wedgeworth *Miss Blue* ■ *Dir* Thomas Schlamme • *Scr* Beth Henley, from her play

Miss Grant Takes Richmond ★★★ U

Crime comedy 1949 · US · BW · 88mins

An archetypal dumb blonde takes a job as a secretary in a real-estate office, unaware that it's a fake outfit fronting a crooked betting syndicate. When she concerns herself with the problems of the homeless, her boss finds himself organising a low-cost housing scheme as a way of paying off his bad gambling debts. A lightweight comedy, directed with a suitably light touch by Lloyd Bacon, the movie's main attraction is Lucille Ball in a role tailor-made for her kooky talents. She's ably supported by a personable William Holden as her bemused boss. RK

Lucille Ball *Ellen Grant* • William Holden (2) *Dick Richmond* • Janis Carter *Peggy Donato* • James Gleason *J Hobart Gleason* • Gloria Henry *Helen White* • Frank McHugh *Kilcoyne* ■ *Dir* Lloyd Bacon • *Scr* Nat Perrin, Devery Freeman, Frank Tashlin, from the story by Everett Freeman

Miss Julie ★★★★

Period drama 1951 · Swe · BW · 90mins

Considered shocking in its day for the eroticism of its exchanges, Alf Sjöberg's adaptation of August Stringberg's one-act play shared the Grand Prix at Cannes with Vittorio De Sica's *Miracle in Milan*. Defying her inexperience, Anita Björk gives a wickedly wilful performance as the spoilt daughter who takes out the resentment she feels towards her ex-fiancé (and men in general) by goading the family's misanthropic valet, Ulf Palme, into seducing her. The flashback/flash forward structure dissipates the intensity, but enables Sjöberg to explore the attitudes Björk inherited from her mother, and the price she pays for her cruelty. DP. A Swedish language film.

Anita Björk *Miss Julie* • Ulf Palme *Jean* • Inger Norberg *Miss Julie as a child* • Jan Hagerman *Jean as a child* ■ *Dir* Alf Sjöberg • *Scr* Alf Sjöberg, from the play by August Strindberg

Miss Julie ★★★ 15

Period drama 1999 · UK/US · Colour · 96mins

Mike Figgis directs this screen adaptation of August Strindberg's play as a vehicle for the statuesque Saffron Burrows. She plays the eponymous

M

Julie, the spoilt daughter of a wealthy family, whose nocturnal dalliance with footman Peter Mullan threatens to bring destruction down on both their heads. Claustrophobically filmed on a single set, this virtual two-hander (the third main character, played by Maria Doyle Kennedy, sleeps through most of the action) suffers from a marked height imbalance between the leads, which renders much of their interaction faintly ludicrous. Mullan, however, brings an intensity and rage to the upstart Jean. NS. Contains swearing and a sex scene. DVD

Saffron Burrows *Miss Julie* • Peter Mullan *Jean* • Maria Doyle Kennedy *Christine* ■ *Dir* Mike Figgis • *Scr* Helen Cooper, from the play by August Strindberg

Miss London Ltd ★★★

Musical comedy 1943 · UK · BW · 99mins

This was the first feature film directed by Val Guest, who had written several scripts for comics Will Hay and Arthur Askey. For this lively musical, Guest also co-wrote the script and provided the lyrics for the eight Manning Sherwin melodies. The story – perky blonde Evelyn Dall inherits half of a rundown escort agency and sets out to make it a success with partner Askey – is an excuse for songs and lots of comic business. TV

Arthur Askey *Arthur Bowman* • Evelyn Dall *Terry Arden* • Anne Shelton *Gail Martin* • Richard Hearne *Commodore* • Max Bacon *Romeo* • Jack Train *Joe Nelson* • Peter Graves (1) *Capt Rory O'More* ■ *Dir* Val Guest • *Scr* Val Guest, Marriott Edgar

Miss Mary ★★★ 15

Drama 1986 · Arg/US · Colour · 95mins

One of those strange but all too vacuous roles that the highly politicised Julie Christie took on during the 1980s. She plays a sexually repressed but simmering governess, employed by an aristocratic Argentinian family in the late 1930s. The pot never boils over sufficiently to make it interesting. Christie looks great in high-cut, flouncy collars and the scenery is spectacular. SH. Some dialogue in Spanish with English subtitles. Contains some swearing.

Julie Christie *Mary Mulligan* • Nacha Guevara *Mecha* • Luisina Brando *Perla* • Eduardo Pavlovsky *Alfredo* • Gerardo Romano *Ernesto* • Iris Marga *Grandmother* • Guillermo Battaglia *Grandfather* • Sofia Viruboff *Carolina* ■ *Dir* Maria Luisa Bemberg • *Scr* Maria Luisa Bemberg, Jorge Goldenberg

Miss Nobody ★★★

Drama 1997 · Pol · Colour · 103mins

Few of Andrzej Wajda's films have focused solely on female protagonists, and an uncertainty of tone undermines the account of rural teenager Anna Wielgucka's tempestuous relationships with the girls at her Warsaw school. These include New Age devotee Anna Mucha and Anna Powierza, whose brusque cynicism arouses rebellious emotions. Overstressing the allegorical undertones and uncomfortable with both the philosophical and sexual aspects of the story, this is one of Wajda's lesser achievements. DP. A Polish language film.

Anna Wielgucka *Marysia Kawaczak* • Anna Mucha *Kasia* • Anna Powierza *Ewa* • Stanislawa Celinska *Marysia's mother* ■ *Dir* Andrzej Wajda • *Scr* Radoslaw Piwowarski, from a novel by Tomek Tryzna

Miss Oyu ★★★

Drama 1951 · Jpn · Colour · 95mins

Kenji Mizoguchi's first collaboration with cinematographer Kazuo Miyagawa disappointed the critics and the director alike. However, this had little to do with the long, fluid takes, nor the intensity of the performances. The problem lies with Junichiro Tanizaki's source novel, which offered Mizoguchi little chance to explore his usual social and gynocentric themes. The film stars Kinuyo Tanaka as the respectable widow who persuades her younger sister, Nobuko Otowa, to marry the wealthy Yuji Hori so that she can continue their affair while protecting her son's inheritance. DP. A Japanese language film.

Kinuyo Tanaka *Oyu Kayukawa* • Nobuko Otowa *Shizu* • Yuji Hori *Shinnosuke Seribashi* • Kiyoko Hirai *Osumi* ■ *Dir* Kenji Mizoguchi • *Scr* Yoshikata Yoda, from the novel *Ashikari* by Junichiro Tanizaki • *Cinematographer* Kazuo Miyagawa

Miss Robin Hood ★★ U

Comedy 1952 · UK · BW · 76mins

This disappointing comedy gave the much-loved Margaret Rutherford a rare chance to star. Considering the infectious enthusiasm of her performance as the mischievous Miss Honey, she deserved better material than this slight skirmish with a gang of crooks over a valuable whisky recipe. There are solid turns from such stalwarts as Sid James and James Robertson-Justice, but writers Val Valentine and Patrick Campbell have over-diluted the mixture for most tastes. DP

Margaret Rutherford *Miss Honey* • Richard Hearne *Henry Wrigley* • Michael Medwin *Ernest* • Peter Jones *Lidstone* • James Robertson-Justice *McAllister* • Sidney James *Sidney* • Dora Bryan *Pearl* ■ *Dir* John Guillermin • *Scr* Val Valentine, Patrick Campbell, from a story by Reed de Rouen

Miss Rose White ★★★★

Drama 1992 · US · Colour · 95mins

Kyra Sedgwick stars as a Polish Jew in a moving story of two sisters exiled in New York – one who escaped the Holocaust and one who survived it. Describing her terrifying experiences with heartrending conviction, Amanda Plummer will surprise those used to seeing her in more manic roles, while Maximilian Schell and Maureen Stapleton provide solid support. This won three Emmys, for outstanding made-for-TV movie, Plummer (supporting actress) and director Joseph Sargent. DP

Kyra Sedgwick *Rayzell Weiss/Rose White* • Amanda Plummer *Lusia* • Penny Fuller *Miss Ryan* • Maureen Stapleton *Tanta Perla* • Maximilian Schell *Mordechai* • DB Sweeney *Dan* • Milton Selzer *Shimon* • Gina Gershon *Angie* ■ *Dir* Joseph Sargent • *Scr* Anna Sandor, from the play *A Shayna Maidel* by Barbara Lebow

Miss Sadie Thompson ★★★

Drama 1953 · US · Colour · 90mins

It's Somerset Maugham's *Rain* again, this time with sexy Rita Hayworth in the title role as the hooker who floors a religious fanatic. Originally this movie was made in 3-D and composed for widescreen, so if watching on TV you see too many floors and ceilings and a lot of room above the actors' heads in close-up. Try to ignore all that, and enjoy instead an over-the-top performance from the smitten José Ferrer. TS

Rita Hayworth *Sadie Thompson* • José Ferrer *Alfred Davidson* • Aldo Ray *Sergeant Phil O'Hara* • Russell Collins *Dr Robert MacPhail* • Diosa Costello *Ameena Horn* • Harry Bellaver *Joe Horn* • Wilton Graff *Governor* • Charles Bronson *Edwards* ■ *Dir* Curtis Bernhardt • *Scr* Harry Kleiner, from the short story *Rain* by W Somerset Maugham

Miss Susie Slagle's ★★★

Period drama 1945 · US · BW · 87mins

Lillian Gish runs a boarding house in Baltimore for medical students training at the famed John Hopkins institution and keeps a motherly eye on their concerns and love affairs. John Berry, a newcomer to film but an alumnus of Orson Welles and John Houseman's Mercury Theatre company, directs. A charming and gentle period piece set in 1910, this is illuminated, as always, by the presence of Gish. She'd been in film for three decades, and had another four to go. RK

Veronica Lake *Nan Rogers* • Sonny Tufts *Pug Prentiss* • Joan Caulfield *Margaretta Howe* • Ray Collins *Dr Elijah Howe* • Billy De Wolfe *Ben Mead* • Lillian Gish *Miss Susie Slagle* • Lloyd Bridges *Silas Holmes* ■ *Dir* John Berry • *Scr* Anne Froelick, Hugo Butler, Theodore Strauss, Adrian Scott, from the novel by Augusta Tucker

Miss Tatlock's Millions ★★★★ U

Comedy 1948 · US · BW · 100mins

One of the brighter comedies of the late 1940s, this verges perilously close to bad taste, with lead John Lund pretending to be an idiot for most of the picture. Hired to attend the reading of a will, Lund continues the deception after the lunatic he is portraying unexpectedly becomes co-heir to a fortune. Character actor Richard Haydn proves an astute choice of director, milking the situations for all their worth as the family endures Lund's outrageous behaviour to remain in favour. AE

John Lund *Burke* • Wanda Hendrix *Nan Tatlock* • Barry Fitzgerald *Denno Noonan* • Monty Woolley *Miles Tatlock* • Ilka Chase *Cassie Van Alen* • Robert Stack *Nickey Van Alen* • Ray Milland • Richard Rancyd [Richard Haydn] *Fergel* ■ *Dir* Richard Haydn • *Scr* Charles Brackett, Richard Breen [Richard L Breen], from the play *Oh – Brother* by Jacques Deval

Missing ★★★★ 15

Drama based on a true story 1981 · US · Colour · 117mins

The US State Department denounced Costa-Gavras's uncompromising human drama when it was first released because of possible political repercussions. But then the director of *Z* and *State of Siege* was used to causing controversy, and this riveting true saga proved to be his most accessible Kafkaesque nightmare. What happened to American writer Charles Horman, who disappeared during the military coup that overthrew the Allende government of Chile in 1973? That's what his liberal wife Sissy Spacek and staunchly conservative father Jack Lemmon try to find out in a compelling moral tale. AJ. Contains swearing and nudity.

Jack Lemmon *Ed Horman* • Sissy Spacek *Beth Horman* • Melanie Mayron *Terry Simon* • John Shea *Charles Horman* • Charles Cioffi *Captain Ray Tower* • David Clennon *Consul Phil Putnam* • Richard Venture *US Ambassador* • Jerry Hardin *Colonel Sean Patrick* ■ *Dir* Costa-Gavras • *Scr* Costa-Gavras, Donald Stewart, from a non-fiction book by Thomas Hauser • *Music* Vangelis

The Missing ★★ 15

Western 2003 · US · Colour · 131mins

After a moderately promising start, director Ron Howard's stab at creating an epic western soon degenerates into a bloated chase movie. Cate Blanchett stars as an unmarried frontier woman whose hard life gets a whole lot harder when her estranged father (Tommy Lee Jones) turns up on her doorstep, and her eldest daughter is kidnapped by slave traders. Blanchett gives an agreeable performance, while Jones makes the most of his ludicrous role as a mystical wanderer. AS. Contains violence. DVD

Tommy Lee Jones *Samuel Jones* • Cate Blanchett *Maggie Gilkeson* • Eric Schweig *Chidin* • Evan Rachel Wood *Lilly Gilkeson* • Jenna Boyd *Dot Gilkeson* • Steve Reevis *Two Stone* • Ray McKinnon *Russell J Wintick* • Val Kilmer *Lt Jim Ducharme* ■ *Dir* Ron Howard • *Scr* Ken Kaufman, from the novel *The Last Ride* by Thomas Eidson

The Missing Gun ★★★ 12

Comedy thriller 2002 · Chi · Colour · 86mins

Lu Chuan makes confident, if occasionally careless use of film speeds, camera angles and intriguing inserts in this directorial debut. But it's the performance of Jiang Wen, as a rural Chinese policeman searching for the service revolver he lost at a drunken wedding, that melds the plot's gently satirical social critique and murder mystery sub-plot into a satisfying whole. Indeed, the arrest of Ning Jing's killer remains a secondary consideration, as Jiang contemplates the shame of exposure. With Wu Yujuan, as his teacher wife, heading an impeccable ensemble, this is a captivating study of character and community. DP. In Mandarin with English subtitles. Contains swearing and violence. DVD

Jiang Wen *Ma Shan* • Ning Jing • Shi Liang ■ *Dir* Lu Chuan • *Scr* Lu Chuan, from the story *The Search for a Missing Gun* by Fan Yiping

Missing in Action ★★ 15

Action thriller 1984 · US · Colour · 97mins

Chuck Norris is an American soldier who was held illegally in a Vietnamese PoW camp for seven years after the war ended. Now he returns to Vietnam to prove that other Americans are still being held. When diplomatic means fail, Norris arms himself and goes on a one-man commando mission to liberate the GIs. Stupid and simplistic, but with lots of action and posturing by Norris. ST. Contains violence, swearing. DVD

Chuck Norris *Colonel Braddock* • M Emmet Walsh *Tuck* • David Tress *Senator Porter* • Lenore Kasdorf *Ann* • James Hong *General Tran* ■ *Dir* Joseph Zito • *Scr* James Bruner, from a story by John Crowther, Lance Hool, from characters created by Arthur Silver, Larry Levinson, Steve Bing

Missing in Action 2: the Beginning ★ 18

Action adventure 1985 · US · Colour · 91mins

This prequel, which shows us the origins of Colonel Braddock, Norris's self-righteous, gun-toting patriot, is even more blockheaded than the first film. Norris may be the one being tortured by scheming commanders and brutal guards, but you'll beg for mercy long before he does. A second sequel, *Braddock: Missing in Action III* followed in 1988. ST

Chuck Norris *Colonel Braddock* • Soon-Teck Oh *Colonel Yin* • Cosie Costa *Mazilli* • Steven Williams *Captain David Nester* • David Chung *Dou Chou* • Joe Michael Terry *Opelka* ■ *Dir* Lance Hool • *Scr* Arthur Silver, Larry Levinson, Steve Bing

Missing Link ★★ PG

Prehistoric documentary drama 1989 · US · Colour · 87mins

The travails of the last apeman, doomed to extinction by Man's invention of the axe circa one million years BC, provide the basis for this odd, non-dialogue "mockumentary". Gifted mime artist Peter Elliott, who choreographed the primates in *Greystoke*, brings a savage wistfulness to a prehistory lesson resembling the "Dawn of Man" prologue from *2001* in both look and tone. Shot on stunning Namibian locations, it contains unsubtle ecological messages and dire warnings, but fans of nature shows will love the wildlife footage. AJ

M

Peter Elliott *Apeman* • Michael Gambon *Narrator* ■ *Dir/Scr* David Hughes (3), Carol Hughes • *Cinematographer* David Hughes (3), Carol Hughes

Missing Pieces ★★ PG

Comedy thriller 1991 · US · Colour · 88mins

Unlike Messrs Cleese and Palin, ex-Monty Python member Eric Idle hasn't had much success in movies. In this mongrel of a comedy, he plays a man who, fired by a greetings card company, teams up with unemployed cellist Robert Wuhl. What follows is a mystery about an inheritance that leads our heroes to Los Angeles and up several blind alleys. This falls flat in most departments, though there is a decent *femme fatale* in Lauren Hutton. AT. Contains swearing.

Eric Idle *Wendel Dickens* • Robert Wuhl *Lou Wimpole* • Lauren Hutton *Jennifer* • Bob Gunton *Mr Gabor* • Richard Belzer *Baldesari* • Bernie Kopell *Dr Gutman* • Kim Lankford *Sally* ■ *Dir/Scr* Leonard Stern [Leonard B Stern]

The Mission ★★★ PG

Historical drama
1986 · UK · Colour · 119mins

Winner of the Palme d'Or at Cannes, but accorded a mixed critical reception, this is a studied, elegant and very moving drama set in 18th-century South America. There's no denying the existence of longueurs in Robert Bolt's script, a certain flabbiness in Roland Joffé's direction and a detached contribution from a curiously cast Robert De Niro. However, Jeremy Irons gives a performance of great sincerity as the head of a Jesuit mission under threat from the greed of Iberian slavers and the whim of Ray McAnally's cardinal. Chris Menges's Oscar-winning photography is glorious, while Ennio Morricone's score sends shivers down the spine. DP. Contains violence and some nudity. DVD

Robert De Niro *Mendoza* • Jeremy Irons *Father Gabriel* • Ray McAnally *Altamirano* • Aidan Quinn *Felipe* • Cherie Lunghi *Carlotta* • Ronald Pickup *Hontar* • Liam Neeson *Fielding* • Chuck Low *Cabeza* ■ *Dir* Roland Joffé • *Scr* Robert Bolt, from his story

Mission: Impossible ★★★★ PG

Action spy thriller
1996 · US · Colour · 105mins

Superstar Tom Cruise and director Brian De Palma join forces for this thrilling extravaganza of jaw-dropping special effects and amazing stunts. Based on the cult 1960s TV series about a covert strike force designing situations villains believe to be real, it's best to forget the complicated plot – something about Cruise clearing his name and proving to the CIA he's not a treacherous mole – and simply enjoy the epic roller-coaster ride that De Palma brings to life with his customary brilliance. The burglary of a guarded vault and the Channel Tunnel helicopter pursuit alone put other thrillers in intensive care. AJ DVD

Tom Cruise *Ethan Hunt* • Jon Voight *Jim Phelps* • Emmanuelle Béart *Claire* • Henry Czerny *Kittridge* • Jean Reno *Krieger* • Ving Rhames *Luther* • Kristin Scott Thomas *Sarah Davies* • Vanessa Redgrave *Max* • Dale Dye *Frank Barnes* • Marcel Iures *Golitsyn* ■ *Dir* Brian De Palma • *Scr* David Koepp, Robert Towne, from a story by David Koepp, Steven Zaillian, from the TV series by Bruce Geller

Mission: Impossible 2 ★★★★ 15

Action spy thriller
1999 · US · Colour · 118mins

By junking the tired spy shenanigans of the original TV series and replacing them with the slick, slow-motion mayhem that has become his trademark, John Woo creates a sequel very different from the first *Mission: Impossible*. Admittedly, there's a distinct shortage of pulse-quickening, slam-bang action in the first hour, which finds Tom Cruise wooing lithe lady thief Thandie Newton before heading Down Under to stop bad guy Dougray Scott holding the world to ransom. Around the halfway mark, though, Woo cranks the pace up a gear. If it's adrenalin you're after, look no further. NS DVD

Tom Cruise *Ethan Hunt* • Dougray Scott *Sean Ambrose* • Thandie Newton *Nyah Hall* • Ving Rhames *Luther Stickell* • Richard Roxburgh *Hugh Stamp* • John Polson *Billy Baird* • Anthony Hopkins *Misson Commander Swanbeck* ■ *Dir* John Woo • *Scr* Robert Towne, Ronald D Moore, from a story by Brannon Braga, from the TV series by Bruce Geller • *Cinematographer* Jeffrey L Kimball

Mission of Justice ★★ 18

Martial arts action
1992 · US · Colour · 94mins

Brigitte Nielsen's presence is the first sign that the proceedings here are unlikely to be taken too seriously. As a mayoral candidate, she runs the titular mission, a training centre for ersatz Guardian Angels, though she is already secretly executing her sinister plans. Jeff Wincott, stiff as ever, is the cop who goes undercover to expose her. Cheerfully mindless. KB

Jeff Wincott *Kurt Harris* • Brigitte Nielsen *Rachel K Larkin* • Tony Burton *Cedric Williams* • Luca Bercovici *Roger Stockwell* • Matthias Hues *Titus Larkin* • Karen Sheperd *Lynn Steele* • Cyndi Pass *Erin Miller* ■ *Dir* Steve Barnett • *Scr* George Saunders, John Bryant Hedberg, from a story by Pierre David

Mission to Mars ★★★ PG

Science-fiction drama
1999 · US · Colour · 108mins

Brian De Palma slums it with his first science-fiction melodrama, which comes loaded with sentiment, camp moments and risible dialogue. However, while there's nothing new in this red planet space opera, the *Carrie* director covers its drawbacks with pristine craftsmanship, trademark suspense sequences and a full quota of sharp computer visuals. Nasa astronauts Gary Sinise and Tim Robbins embark on a rescue mission to the planet and make an extraordinary discovery. AJ DVD

Gary Sinise *Jim McConnell* • Don Cheadle *Mission Commander Luke Graham* • Connie Nielsen *Mars Rescue Mission specialist Dr Terri Fisher* • Tim Robbins *Commander Woody Blake* • Jerry O'Connell *Mission Specialist Phil Ohlmyer* • Armin Mueller-Stahl *Ray Beck* ■ *Dir* Brian De Palma • *Scr* John Thomas, Jim Thomas, Graham Yost, from a story by John Thomas, Jim Thomas, Lowell Cannon

Mission to Moscow ★★★★ U

Drama 1943 · US · BW · 121mins

This prestigious Warner Bros epic is based on US ambassador Joseph E Davies's bestseller about his pre-Second World War years in the Soviet Union, and is introduced by Davies himself. What lends it particular piquancy today is its documentary-style depiction of a pre-Cold War, pre-Red Scare Russia, filmed at an impressive pace by director Michael Curtiz. Walter Huston is ideally cast as the avuncular Davies, and it's sobering to realise that in subsequent years the film was denounced as pro-Communist propaganda because of its view of Stalin as a benevolent ruler. TS

Walter Huston *Ambassador Joseph E Davies* • Ann Harding *Mrs Davies* • Oscar Homolka *Maxim Litvinov* • George Tobias *Freddie* • Gene Lockhart *Vyacheslav Molotov* • Frieda Inescort *Madame Molotov* • Eleanor Parker *Emlen Davies* • Richard Travis *Paul Grosjean* ■ *Dir* Michael Curtiz • *Scr* Howard Koch, from the non-fiction book by Joseph E Davies

The Missionary ★★★ 15

Period comedy 1982 · UK · Colour · 77mins

In his first solo film venture away from the Pythons, Michael Palin came up with this saucy comedy. Palin is pleasing enough as an innocent abroad in the crinoline jungle of Edwardian prostitution, but the supporting cast has all the fun, with Maggie Smith in fine fettle as a frustrated aristocrat. Palin struggles to sustain the comedy, but Richard Loncraine lashes on the period style to good effect. DP. Contains swearing. DVD

Michael Palin *Reverend Charles Fortescue* • Maggie Smith *Lady Ames* • Trevor Howard *Lord Ames* • Denholm Elliott *The Bishop* • Michael Hordern *Slatterthwaite* • Graham Crowden *Reverend Fitzbanks* • Phoebe Nicholls *Deborah* • Tricia George *Ada* ■ *Dir* Richard Loncraine • *Scr* Michael Palin

Mississippi ★★

Musical comedy 1935 · US · BW · 80mins

To escape accusations of cowardice, a creamy-voiced Southerner joins a showboat on the Mississippi, finds true love and rescues his reputation. Directed by A Edward Sutherland as a vehicle for Bing Crosby, this rambling period musical is partly redeemed by several Rodgers and Hart numbers, while WC Fields is splendid as the boat's captain. RK

Bing Crosby *Tom Grayson/Col Steele* • WC Fields *Commodore Orlando Jackson* • Joan Bennett *Lucy Rumford* • Queenie Smith *Alabam'* • Gail Patrick *Elvira Rumford* ■ *Dir* A Edward Sutherland • *Scr* Francis Martin, Jack Cunningham, Claude Binyon, Herbert Fields, from the play *Magnolia* by Booth Tarkington

Mississippi Burning ★★★★ 18

Drama based on a true story
1988 · US · Colour · 121mins

In this powerful drama from director Alan Parker, Gene Hackman gives a mesmerising performance as a Southern States FBI agent fighting racism with local knowledge and canny psychology. Willem Dafoe is equally impressive, if more restrained, as his rule-obsessed Ivy League partner. Parker's wonderful creation crackles with dramatic tension and simmering violence that often reaches boiling point. Loosely based on a true story and shot with great visual flair (Peter Biziou won the Oscar for best cinematography), this is a gripping evocation of the early days of the civil rights movement. SH. Contains violence and swearing. DVD

Gene Hackman *Rupert Anderson* • Willem Dafoe *Alan Ward* • Frances McDormand *Mrs Pell* • Brad Dourif *Deputy Pell* • R Lee Ermey *Mayor Tilman* • Gailard Sartain *Sheriff Stuckey* • Stephen Tobolowsky *Townley* • Michael Rooker *Frank Bailey* • Pruitt Taylor Vince *Lester Cowens* ■ *Dir* Alan Parker • *Scr* Chris Gerolmo

The Mississippi Gambler ★★★ U

Adventure 1953 · US · Colour · 98mins

Matinée idol Tyrone Power stars as a handsome and honest riverboat gambler, forced to jump ship with partner John McIntire to chase comely Piper Laurie in New Orleans. The studio sets and location photography look superb, but the leads are dull and the plot unnecessarily complicated. TS

Tyrone Power *Mark Fallon* • Piper Laurie *Angelique Duroux* • Julia Adams [Julie Adams] *Ann Conant* • John McIntire *Kansas John Polly* • William Reynolds *Pierre* • Paul Cavanagh *Edmund Duroux* • John Baer *Laurent Duroux* ■ *Dir* Rudolph Maté • *Scr* Seton I Miller

Mississippi Masala ★★★★ 15

Romantic drama
1991 · US · Colour · 112mins

A "masala" is a culinary collection of hot and colourful spices used in curry dishes. Here, though, it's a good word to describe the Mississippi community where black American Denzel Washington falls in love with Asian woman Sarita Choudhury, causing tension between their families. As a mix of romance and racism, Mira Nair's follow-up to *Salaam Bombay!* (1988) ends on an ingenuously optimistic note. Roshan Seth is powerfully credible as Choudhury's bigoted father, however. TH

Denzel Washington *Demetrius* • Sarita Choudhury *Mina* • Roshan Seth *Jay* • Sharmila Tagore *Kinnu* • Charles S Dutton *Tyrone* • Joe Seneca *Williben* • Ranjit Chowdhry *Anil* ■ *Dir* Mira Nair • *Scr* Sooni Taraporevala

Mississippi Mermaid ★★ 12

Romantic mystery
1969 · Fr/It · Colour · 117mins

Catherine Deneuve arrives on the island of Réunion to marry plantation owner Jean-Paul Belmondo in this adaptation of a Cornell Woolrich novel, transformed by Truffaut into a lavish study of obsessive love. Things turn decidedly darker when the tropics give way to winter in the French Alps and romance turns to murder. This was the director's first major flop, only released abroad in a slightly cut and badly dubbed version that rendered the dialogue utterly risible. AT. The UK DVD release version is subtitled. DVD

Jean-Paul Belmondo *Louis Mahé* • Catherine Deneuve *Marion/Julie Roussel* • Michel Bouquet *Comolli* • Nelly Borgeaud *Berthe Roussel* • Marcel Berbert *Jardine* ■ *Dir* François Truffaut • *Scr* François Truffaut, from the novel *Waltz into Darkness* by William Irish [Cornell Woolrich]

The Missouri Breaks ★★★★ 15

Western 1976 · US · Colour · 121mins

As a clash of titans, this film – despite a shambles of a plot – is exciting stuff because of the ego battle between Marlon Brando and Jack Nicholson. Brando's a hired bounty hunter, pitting his wits against horse-thief Nicholson amid the conflict between Montana ranchers and rustlers, and both actors twitch their way through an upstaging duel that is mesmerising in its brazen arrogance. Director Arthur Penn seems to stand back from the proceedings, though his view of pioneer days is still so fascinatingly uncluttered and fresh that you can almost smell the raw wood of log cabins. TH. Contains some violence. DVD

Marlon Brando *Robert E Lee Clayton* • Jack Nicholson *Tom Logan* • Randy Quaid *Little Tod* • Kathleen Lloyd *Jane Braxton* • Frederic Forrest *Cary* • Harry Dean Stanton *Calvin* • John McLiam *David Braxton* ■ *Dir* Arthur Penn • *Scr* Thomas McGuane • *Music* John Williams

The Missouri Traveler ★★ U

Drama 1958 · US · Colour · 100mins

This pleasant but overlong slice of Americana has something of John Ford about it. Ford's son, Patrick, is the producer; the superb Technicolor photography is by one of the director's favourite cameramen, Winton Hoch; while the epic fight at the end recalls *The Quiet Man*. However, Jerry Hopper's direction is hardly in the Ford class. Brandon de Wilde stars as the friendly 15-year-old runaway who stops in a small Missouri town and falls foul of Lee Marvin's surly farmer. AE

Brandon de Wilde *Brian Turner* • Lee Marvin *Tobias Brown* • Gary Merrill *Doyle Magee* • Paul Ford *Finas Daugherty* • Mary Hosford *Anna Love Price* • Ken Curtis *Fred Mueller* ■ *Dir* Jerry Hopper • *Scr* Norman S Hall, from the novel by John Burress

Mistaken Identity ★★ PG

Drama 1999 · US · Colour · 84mins

This melodrama packs in all the TV-movie clichés for its journey from a hospital ward to the inevitable courtroom. Inspired by a real-life mix-up that saw two mothers swap babies, the events depicted here wouldn't pass muster as fiction. Only the committed performances of Melissa Gilbert and Rosanna Arquette will keep you from switching off. DP DVD

Melissa Gilbert *Sarah* • Rosanna Arquette *Linda* • David Andrews *James Barlow* • James McCaffrey *Darryl* • Mary Mara *Judy* • Susan Barnes *Marie* • Ron Silver *Bert* • Lester B Hanson *Dr Lee* ■ *Dir* Douglas Barr • *Scr* Arlene Sarner, Jerry Leichtling

Mr and Mrs Bridge ★★★ PG

Period drama 1990 · UK · Colour · 125mins

The winning Merchant Ivory partnership is off target in this pretty but ultimately disappointing vehicle for Paul Newman and his wife Joanne Woodward. It's another of director James Ivory's polite studies of emotional repression, but the rambling, episodic tale of American family life in the 1930s and 1940s lacks cohesion. However, the two stars are superb as the eponymous married couple: Newman all starched conservatism as the stiff-necked lawyer, stubbornly resisting the changes around him; and Woodward the devoted wife attempting in her own quiet way to open his eyes. JF [video]

Paul Newman *Walter Bridge* • Joanne Woodward *India Bridge* • Robert Sean Leonard *Douglas Bridge* • Margaret Welsh *Carolyn Bridge* • Kyra Sedgwick *Ruth Bridge* • Blythe Danner *Grace Barron* • Simon Callow *Dr Alex Sauer* ■ *Dir* James Ivory • *Scr* Ruth Prawer Jhabvala, from the novels *Mr Bridge* and *Mrs Bridge* by Evan S Connell

Mr and Mrs '55 ★★★★ U

Romantic comedy drama
1955 · Ind · BW · 129mins

Even Busby Berkeley would have been proud of the musical numbers in this classic Bollywood masala from Guru Dutt. Ostensibly a satire at the expense of the urban upper echelons, this is also a delightfully romantic comedy, in which Dutt is hired as a groom by heiress Madhubala for the wedding of convenience that will fulfil the terms of her father's will. Don't look for any plot sophistication, just revel in the joyous performances of the leads and the wholly cinematic, endlessly inventive song-and-dance routines. DP. In Hindi with English subtitles. [video] DVD

Madhubala *Anita* • Lalita Pawar *Seeta Devi* • Guru Dutt *Preetam Kumar* • Johnny Walker *Johnny* • Tuntun *Lily D'Silva* ■ *Dir* Guru Dutt • *Scr* Abrar Alvi, Majrooh Sultanpuri

Mr and Mrs North ★★

Comedy mystery 1941 · US · BW · 66mins

Gracie Allen (minus George Burns on this occasion) is Mrs North, the wife of William Post Jr, in this comedy suspense drama from MGM's programmer department. The couple return home from a weekend trip to find a dead body in a cupboard in their apartment. Instead of leaving it to the cops, they decide to play detective and line up their friends as suspects. A moderately amusing, even occasionally tense spoof, this is competently directed by Robert B Sinclair. RK

Gracie Allen *Pamela North* • William Post Jr *Gerald P North* • Paul Kelly (1) *Lt Weigand* • Rose Hobart *Carol Brent* • Virginia Grey *Jane Wilson* • Tom Conway *Louis Berex* ■ *Dir* Robert B Sinclair • *Scr* SK Lauren, from a story by Richard Lockridge, Frances Lockridge, from the play by Owen Davis

Mr and Mrs Smith ★★★ U

Screwball comedy 1941 · US · BW · 90mins

Carole Lombard had always wanted to star in an Alfred Hitchcock film and, although situation comedy was far from Hitchcock's forte, he agreed to take the assignment as a favour for a friend. The result is a patchy farce in which Lombard and Robert Montgomery discover that their marriage is invalid and set about trying to outdo each other in their pleasure at being single. Even a screwball maestro like Howard Hawks would have been pushed to do much with the clunky script, and Hitch's lack of interest is apparent. Lombard took over the director's chair for Hitch's obligatory cameo in which he plays a drunk asking for money. DP [video] DVD

Carole Lombard *Ann Smith* • Robert Montgomery *David Smith* • Gene Raymond *Jeff* • Jack Carson *Chuck* • Philip Merivale *Mr Custer* • Lucile Watson *Mrs Custer* • William Tracy *Sammy* • Charles Halton *Mr Deever* ■ *Dir* Alfred Hitchcock • *Scr* Norman Krasna

Mr & Mrs Smith ★★★ 15

Romantic action thriller
2005 · US · Colour · 119mins

In this enjoyably daft action comedy, Brad Pitt and Angelina Jolie play a married couple who are bored with each other (to many, the movie's most preposterous conceit) and also professional killers (unknown to one another) hired to rub each other out. Director Doug Liman combines wit with stylish mayhem to great effect here, though some will feel that he lurches into overkill in the last half hour. Although it's supremely silly, Pitt and Jolie look outrageously good in their roles and it's fun while it lasts. AS. Contains violence, swearing, sex scenes.

Brad Pitt *John Smith* • Angelina Jolie *Jane Smith* • Vince Vaughn *Eddie* • Adam Brody *Benjamin Danz* • Kerry Washington *Jasmine* • Keith David *Father* • Chris Weitz *Martin Coleman* • Rachael Huntley *Suzy Coleman* • Michelle Monaghan *Gwen* ■ *Dir* Doug Liman • *Scr* Simon Kingberg

Mr Baseball ★★ 15

Comedy 1992 · US · Colour · 103mins

Tom Selleck was never much of an actor for detail and here paints his has-been hero with too broad a brush. Even though his character, a faded baseball player transferred to Japan, is meant to be annoying the locals because of his tendency for arrogance, Selleck just can't resist letting his natural charm wash over the screen. Director Fred Schepisi reduces the pace to a tepid canter. JM. Contains swearing. [video]

Tom Selleck *Jack Elliot* • Ken Takakura *Uchiyama* • Aya Takanashi *Hiroko Uchiyama* • Dennis Haysbert *Max "Hammer" Dubois* • Toshi Shioya *Yoji Nishimura* • Kosuke Toyohara *Toshi Yamashita* • Toshizo Fujiwara *Ryoh Mukai* ■ *Dir* Fred Schepisi • *Scr* Gary Ross, Kevin Wade, Monte Merrick, Theo Pelletier, John Junkerman

Mr Belvedere Goes to College ★★ U

Comedy 1949 · US · BW · 82mins

Clifton Webb had made a spectacular success playing the egocentric genius Lynn Belvedere in the previous year's *Sitting Pretty*, and this was the first of two sequels in which he played the same character. Proposing to earn a four-year degree in one year, he enters college; alas, his escapades are too predictable to generate the amusement intended. Shirley Temple, nearing the end of her film career, and Tom Drake provide romance. TV

Clifton Webb *Lynn Belvedere* • Shirley Temple *Ellen Baker* • Tom Drake *Bill Chase* • Alan Young *Avery Brubaker* • Jessie Royce Landis *Mrs Chase* • Kathleen Hughes *Kay Nelson* ■ *Dir* Elliott Nugent • *Scr* Richard Sale, Mary Loos, Mary McCall Jr, from the character created by Gwen Davenport

Mr Belvedere Rings the Bell ★★★ U

Comedy 1951 · US · BW · 87mins

Former Broadway musical star Clifton Webb (and his infamous mother, who went with him everywhere) had been around since the silent days, but it took his portrayal of the sour-tongued misanthrope Belvedere in 1948's *Sitting Pretty* to actually endear him to movie audiences. In this light-hearted nonsense, the second sequel to *Sitting Pretty*, Belvedere takes up residence in an old people's home to prove age is no barrier to living a full life. TS

Clifton Webb *Lynn Belvedere/Oliver Erwenter* • Joanne Dru *Miss Tripp* • Hugh Marlowe *Reverend Watson* • Zero Mostel *Emmett* • William Lynn *Mr Beebe* • Doro Merande *Mrs Hammer* • Frances Brandt *Miss Hoadley* ■ *Dir* Henry Koster • *Scr* Ranald MacDougall, from the play *The Silver Whistle* by Robert C McEnroe and the character created by Gwen Davenport

Mr Billion ★★ PG

Drama 1977 · US · Colour · 88mins

As Terence Hill, the Italian actor Mario Girotti starred in several spaghetti westerns and seemed unhealthily fixated on Clint Eastwood. *Mr Billion* was Hill's Hollywood debut, a chase thriller clearly modelled on Hitchcock but with a little bit of social moralising thrown in. Hill plays an Italian who inherits a fortune and must travel to San Francisco to claim it; Valerie Perrine is the double agent who gets in his way. AT [video]

Terence Hill *Guido Falcone* • Valerie Perrine *Rosi Jones* • Jackie Gleason *John Cutler* • Slim Pickens *Duane Hawkins* • William Redfield *Leopold Lacy* • Chill Wills *Colonel Clayton T Winkle* • Dick Miller *Bernie* • RG Armstrong *Sheriff TC Bishop* ■ *Dir* Jonathan Kaplan • *Scr* Ken Friedman, Jonathan Kaplan

Mr Blandings Builds His Dream House ★★★★ U

Comedy 1948 · US · BW · 94mins

Many viewers will identify with the plight of Cary Grant and Myrna Loy in this sublime comedy. As the married couple who move to the countryside and do, quite literally, what the title states, Grant and Loy get conned by every cowboy builder along the way. The film was remade in 1985 as *The Money Pit*, but it wasn't as funny or stylish as this original, as neither Tom Hanks nor Shelley Long could compete with Grant and Loy at their best – just watch Loy recite her proposed colour scheme! TS [video]

Cary Grant *Jim Blandings* • Myrna Loy *Muriel Blandings* • Melvyn Douglas *Bill Cole* • Sharyn Moffett *Joan Blandings* • Connie Marshall *Betsy Blandings* • Louise Beavers *Gussie* • Harry Shannon *Mr Tesander* ■ *Dir* HC Potter • *Scr* Norman Panama, Melvin Frank, from the novel by Eric Hodgins

Mister Buddwing ★★

Drama 1965 · US · BW · 96mins

This is what can happen when a Hollywood director sees the work of French New Wave folk like Godard and Resnais and thinks: "Hey, I can do that!" *Mister Buddwing* is *Last Year at Marienbad* relocated to New York, with James Garner waking up in Central Park not knowing who he is or where he's from. Three beautiful women – Jean Simmons, Suzanne Pleshette and Katharine Ross – are seen in the multiple flashbacks. With its first-person camera, jump cuts and other "look at me" devices, it's rather tedious, despite Garner's efforts. AT

James Garner *Mister Buddwing* • Jean Simmons *The blonde* • Suzanne Pleshette *Fiddle* • Katharine Ross *Janet* • Angela Lansbury *Gloria* • Jack Gilford *Mr Schwartz* ■ *Dir* Delbert Mann • *Scr* Dale Wasserman, from the novel *Buddwing* by Evan Hunter

Mister Cinders ★★★

Musical romance 1934 · UK · BW · 72mins

The popular British stage musical, with music by Vivian Ellis, is basically *Cinderella* with a sex change. (Poor relation Jim, wrongly suspected of being a thief, has two Ugly Brothers). Although only one tune, *Spread a Little Happiness*, has stood the test of time, the whole score is charming. This film version, although still stagey, has been efficiently opened out by a talented German director, who stayed in Britain to make more musicals. The location work is very pretty and the whole cast, including many well-known stage names of the day, is sound. DM

Clifford Mollison *Jim Lancaster* • Zelma O'Neal *Jill Kemp* • Esme Church *Lady Agatha Lancaster* • Edmund Breon *Sir George Lancaster* • Kenneth Western *Lumley Lancaster* • George Western *Guy Lancaster* • Finlay Currie *Henry Kemp* ■ *Dir* Friedrich Zelnik [Fred Zelnik] • *Scr* Clifford Grey, Frank Miller, Jack Davies, George Western, Kenneth Western, from the play by Greatrex Newman

Mister Cory ★★★

Drama 1957 · US · Colour · 92mins

Tony Curtis emerges from the slums of Chicago, becomes a dishwasher at a swish country club, teams up with gambler Charles Bickford and ends up owning a casino. It's a rags-to-riches tale close to Curtis's heart and which helped move him out of the matinée idol, sword-and-sandal ghetto. As written by Blake Edwards – this was also his third directing stint – the story is shot through with a certain cynicism as Curtis is clearly on the make. The use of CinemaScope and colour, though, tends to blunt the film's sharp edge. AT

Tony Curtis *Cory* • Martha Hyer *Abby Vollard* • Charles Bickford *Biloxi* • Kathryn Grant *Jen Vollard* • William Reynolds *Alex Wyncott* • Henry Daniell *Earnshaw* • Russ Morgan *Ruby Matrobe* ■ *Dir* Blake Edwards • *Scr* Blake Edwards, from a story by Leo Rosten

Mr Death: the Rise and Fall of Fred A Leuchter Jr ★★★★

Documentary 1999 · US · Colour · 90mins

Errol Morris has always fed on obsessional outsiders, but none has been so dangerously deluded as Fred A Leuchter, the American executioner whose vanity led to his becoming a reviled apologist for Holocaust denial. This is certainly an ironic portrait of a man who takes pride in his work and pleasure at his expertise. But Morris avoids mockery, as he demonstrates Leuchter's commitment to bringing humanity and efficiency to the various death penalty procedures, before following him to Auschwitz, where he spent his honeymoon illicitly and inexpertly collecting evidence to support Ernst Zündel's theories denying the existence of the gas chambers. Chilling and compelling. DP

Dir Errol Morris • *Cinematographer* Peter Donohue, Robert Richardson

M

Mr Deeds ★ 12

Comedy 2002 · US · Colour · 92mins

In this remake of *Mr Deeds Goes to Town*, comedian Adam Sandler takes on the Gary Cooper role of the country bumpkin who inherits a business empire. Whereas Cooper was an Everyman, Sandler is just the man in the street, and director Steven Brill is no Frank Capra; he has replaced wit with smut and sentiment with saccharin. StH. Contains swearing, violence. DVD

Adam Sandler *Longfellow Deeds* • Winona Ryder *Babe Bennett/Pam Dawson* • Peter Gallagher *Chuck Cedar* • Jared Harris *Mac McGrath* • John Turturro *Emilio Lopez* • Conchata Ferrell *Jan* • Steve Buscemi *Crazy Eyes* ■ *Dir* Steven Brill • *Scr* Tim Herlihy, from the film *Mr Deeds Goes to Town* by Robert Riskin, from the story *Opera Hat* by Clarence Budington Kelland

Mr Deeds Goes to Town ★★★★ U

Comedy 1936 · US · BW · 110mins

A popular and critical success in its day, this slight morality tale won an Oscar for director Frank Capra, but today's more cynical audience might find it too full of Capra-corn. Lanky Gary Cooper is wonderful as Longfellow Deeds, the tuba-playing "Cinderella Man" who inherits a small fortune. But the character of the investigative reporter played by Jean Arthur rings false, as do the myriad minor roles, although many are well cast. TS

Gary Cooper *Longfellow Deeds* • Jean Arthur *Babe Bennett* • George Bancroft *MacWade* • Lionel Stander *Cornelius Cobb* • Douglass Dumbrille *John Cedar* • Raymond Walburn *Walter* • Margaret Matzenauer *Madame Pomponi* • HB Warner *Judge Walker* • Warren Hymer *Bodyguard* ■ *Dir* Frank Capra • *Scr* Robert Riskin, from the story *Opera Hat* by Clarence Budington Kelland

M

Mr Denning Drives North ★★★

Comedy thriller 1951 · UK · BW · 93mins

John Mills looked brooding in the startling red-and-black poster for this film, and audiences might have found themselves somewhat disappointed by this genteel drama. Mills is excellent as the father who accidentally bumps off his daughter's devious lover, but acting honours are stolen by Sam Wanamaker as the truth-seeking boyfriend, and there's one of those excellent supporting casts of stalwarts that makes films of this era so watchable. TS

John Mills *Tom Denning* • Phyllis Calvert *Kay Denning* • Eileen Moore *Liz Denning* • Sam Wanamaker *Chick Eddowes* • Herbert Lom *Mados* • Raymond Huntley *Wright* • Russell Waters *Harry Stopes* • Wilfrid Hyde White *Woods* • Bernard Lee *Inspector Dodds* ■ *Dir* Anthony Kimmins • *Scr* Alec Coppel, from his novel

Mr Destiny ★★ PG

Comedy drama 1990 · US · Colour · 105mins

You might expect this fantasy to live up to its wistful plotline, as Michael Caine's bartender dispenses what-if potions to a baseball fan (James Belushi) who regrets the day all those years ago when he missed a home run. Yet as Belushi lives his life again, more successful but wishing he was still married to Linda Hamilton rather than his new wife (Rene Russo), it's hard not to see him as a tedious slob who can't make up his mind. TH

James Belushi *Larry Burrows* • Linda Hamilton *Ellen Burrows* • Michael Caine *Mike* • Jon Lovitz *Clip Metzler* • Hart Bochner *Niles Pender* • Bill McCutcheon *Leo Hansen* • Rene Russo *Cindy Jo* • Jay O Sanders *Jackie Earle* • Maury Chaykin *Guzelman* ■ *Dir* James Orr • *Scr* James Orr, Jim Cruickshank

Mr Drake's Duck ★★★ U

Comedy 1950 · UK · BW · 85mins

A bright, breezy comedy from British writer/director Val Guest about a duck that lays uranium eggs, filmed in an innocent postwar era when the long-term effects of radiation poisoning were still unknown. Mrs Guest, the blonde and perky Yolande Donlan, plays Mrs Drake, who's married to suave Douglas Fairbanks Jr and who, together with her husband, breeds ducks on their Sussex farm, one of which turns out to be a source of possible riches. Very enjoyable, and deservedly popular in its day. TS

Douglas Fairbanks Jr *Don Drake* • Yolande Donlan *Penny Drake* • Howard Marion-Crawford *Major Travers* • Reginald Beckwith *Mr Boothby* • Wilfrid Hyde White *Mr May* • John Boxer *Sergeant* • Jon Pertwee *Reuben* • Peter Butterworth *Higgins* ■ *Dir* Val Guest • *Scr* Val Guest, from the play by Ian Messiter

Mister 880 ★★★ U

Comedy drama 1950 · US · BW · 89mins

Amazingly based on a true story, this is a delightful light comedy about an old codger who has forged dollar bills for years and bewilderingly left the authorities in his wake. Lovable Edmund Gwenn, everybody's favourite Santa, is the junk collector with his own printing press, and Burt Lancaster, on the cusp of stardom, is all teeth and shoulders as the federal agent chasing him. TS

Burt Lancaster *Steve Buchanan* • Dorothy McGuire *Ann Winslow* • Edmund Gwenn *Skipper Miller* • Millard Mitchell *Mac* • Minor Watson *Judge O'Neil* • Howard St John *Chief* • Hugh Sanders *Thad Mitchell* • James Millican *Olie Johnson* ■ *Dir* Edmund Goulding • *Scr* Robert Riskin, from the *New Yorker* article *Old Eight Eighty* by St Clair McKelway

Mister Frost ★★ 15

Horror 1990 · Fr/UK · Colour · 99mins

Jeff Goldblum makes an unlikely Satan in this tale about a mass murderer whose countryside estate is littered with mutilated victims. Arrested and sent to a mental institution, he confides to psychiatrist Kathy Baker that he is in fact the Devil. His mission is simple: to get her to kill him. Policeman Alan Bates is also involved, making for an overly earnest and rather ridiculous film. LH

Jeff Goldblum *Mister Frost* • Alan Bates *Felix Detweiler* • Kathy Baker *Dr Sarah Day* • Roland Giraud *Raymond Reynhardt* • François Négret *Christophe Kovac* • Jean-Pierre Cassel *Inspector Correlli* ■ *Dir* Philippe Setbon • *Scr* Philippe Setbon, Brad Lynch

Mr Hobbs Takes a Vacation ★★★ U

Comedy 1962 · US · Colour · 114mins

James Stewart made some amiable movies during the 1960s, lightweight fluff that warmed the heart without stretching the brain. Here he's married to the lovely Maureen O'Hara, and the slight plot is encapsulated in the title. Contemporary heart-throbs Fabian and John Saxon add to the period charm, and the ingénue is Cliff Richard's flame from *Summer Holiday*, Lauri Peters. It's all rather endearing in a ramshackle kind of way. TS

James Stewart *Mr Hobbs* • Maureen O'Hara *Peggy Hobbs* • Fabian *Joe* • Lauri Peters *Katey* • Lili Gentle *Janie* • John Saxon *Byron* • John McGiver *Martin Turner* • Marie Wilson *Emily Turner* ■ *Dir* Henry Koster • *Scr* Nunnally Johnson, from the novel *Hobb's Vacation* by Edward Streeter

Mr Holland's Opus ★★★★ PG

Drama 1995 · US · Colour · 136mins

Richard Dreyfuss strikes just the right note of sentiment and truth as music teacher Glenn Holland, who wonders if 30 years at the high school chalkface have been worthwhile, especially as he sacrificed his ambitions to be a composer. A shrewd mix of *Goodbye Mr Chips* and *It's a Wonderful Life*, it adds harsher ingredients including Mr Holland's neglect of his wife and hearing-impaired son to further the education of his students. The way Richard Dreyfuss lightens up his character makes the film satisfyingly accessible to young and old. TH. Contains some swearing. DVD

Richard Dreyfuss *Glenn Holland* • Glenne Headly *Iris Holland* • Jay Thomas *Bill Meister* • Olympia Dukakis *Principal Jacobs* • William H Macy *Vice Principal Wolters* • Alicia Witt *Gertrude Lang* • Terrence Howard *Louis Russ* • Damon Whitaker *Bobby Tidd* ■ *Dir* Stephen Herek • *Scr* Patrick Sheane Duncan

Mr Imperium ★ U

Drama 1951 · US · Colour · 86mins

Lana Turner stars as a glamorous vocalist with a cowboy quartet who falls in love with European prince Ezio Pinza. When he inherits the throne, though, he can't consort with a commoner. Marking the screen debut of Metropolitan Opera star Pinza, this cardboard drivel was a disastrous bomb. Directed by Don Hartman, it boasts good-looking locations and sumptuous clothes for Lana; Pinza is in good voice on the rare occasions he's permitted to sing. RK

Lana Turner *Fredda Barlo* • Ezio Pinza *Mr Imperium* • Marjorie Main *Mrs Cabot* • Barry Sullivan *Paul Hunter* • Cedric Hardwicke *Prime Minister Bernand* • Keenan Wynn *Motor cop* • Debbie Reynolds *Gwen* ■ *Dir* Don Hartman • *Scr* Don Hartman, Edwin H Knopf, from a play by Edwin H Knopf

Mr In-Between ★ 15

Romantic thriller 2001 · UK · Colour · 94mins

Atom Egoyan's regular cinematographer Paul Sarossy makes his directorial debut with this disappointing adaptation. Much of the problem lies in Peter Waddington's plodding script and the lifeless performance of Andrew Howard as the dispassionate hitman whose ruthless streak is softened by a chance re-acquaintance with the object of his teenage affection, Geraldine O'Rawe. But the pitilessly sadistic sequences involving gentleman bad guys David Calder, Saeed Jaffrey and Clive Russell also undermine Sarossy's attempts to imbue proceedings with a sense of pessimistic realism. DP DVD

Andrew Howard *Jon* • Geraldine O'Rawe *Cathy* • David Calder *The Tattooed Man* • Andrew Tiernan *Andy* • Mark Benton *Phil* • Clive Russell *Mr Michaelmas* • Clint Dyer *Rickets* • Peter Waddington *Priest* • Saeed Jaffrey *Mr Basmati* ■ *Dir* Paul Sarossy • *Scr* Peter Waddington, from the novel by Neil Cross

Mr India ★★★ U

Drama 1986 · Ind · Colour · 133mins

An entertaining Hindi fantasy about the clash between good and evil which was hugely successful on its release in India. There's a rousing portrait of villainy from Amrish Puri, while Anil Kapoor plays his nemesis, a scientist's son who has discovered the secret of invisibility. It's stylishly directed by Shekhar Kapur, who went on to direct *Bandit Queen*. RT. In Hindi with English subtitles. DVD

Amrish Puri *Mugambo* • Anil Kapoor *Arun* ■ *Dir* Shekhar Kapur

Mr Jealousy ★★★

Romantic comedy drama
1997 · US · Colour · 105mins

Eric Stolz plays the mister of the title, a guy permanently obsessed about his dates' fidelity. His latest flame is Annabella Sciorra, but his relentless stalking and green-eyed psychology work against him. Director Noah Baumbach is sadly too concerned with "clever" pastiches of Truffaut and Woody Allen to create a focused film. His script is good, as is his depiction of a generation of 30-year-olds refusing to grow old gracefully, but the end result is mixed. LH

Eric Stoltz *Lester Grimm* • Annabella Sciorra *Ramona Ray* • Chris Eigeman *Dashiell Frank* • Carlos Jacott *Vince* • Marianne Jean-Baptiste *Lucretia* • Brian Kerwin *Stephen* • Peter Bogdanovich *Dr Poke* • Bridget Fonda *Irene* ■ *Dir/Scr* Noah Baumbach

Mister Jerico ★★ U

Comedy adventure
1969 · US · Colour · 85mins

A run-of-the-mill comedy adventure, chiefly of interest today for fans of Patrick Macnee, better known even then as John Steed in *The Avengers*. The usual ingredients of diamonds, crooks and blonde sirens can't make up for the lack of plot, although Herbert Lom is on hand to remind viewers of the *Pink Panther* capers. RT

Patrick Macnee *Dudley Jerico* • Connie Stevens *Susan* • Herbert Lom *Victor Russo* • Marty Allen *Wally* • Leonardo Pieroni *Angelo* ■ *Dir* Sidney Hayers • *Scr* Philip Levene, from an idea by David T Chantler

Mister Johnson ★★★ PG

Period drama 1991 · US · Colour · 96mins

Following on from *Driving Miss Daisy*, Bruce Beresford returned to the idea of a white master and a black servant, possibly hoping to garner the best director Oscar he didn't get the year before. It's colonial West Africa in the 1920s, and Mr Johnson (Maynard Eziashi) is the clerk of English administrator Harry Rudbeck. Unfortunately, this slight film has none of the depth of the Joyce Cary novel upon which it is based, and much of the blame can be laid at the director's door. Although Beresford peppers the movie with beautiful landscapes, there is not enough characterisation to really engage the viewer. JB

Pierce Brosnan *Harry Rudbeck* • Maynard Eziashi *Mister Johnson* • Edward Woodward *Sargy Gollup* • Beatie Edney *Celia Rudbeck* • Denis Quilley *Bulteen* • Nick Reding *Tring* ■ *Dir* Bruce Beresford • *Scr* William Boyd, Bruce Beresford, from the novel by Joyce Cary

Mr Jones ★★ 15

Romantic drama
1993 · US · Colour · 109mins

Here's one Jones that audiences won't want to keep up with, as manic-depressive Richard Gere suffers a Freudian slip-up by having an affair with his psychiatrist, Lena Olin. Gere's mood-swinging hero displays surprising energy and verve, which was probably not the original intention: studio executives ordered extensive recutting in order to lighten up what was by all accounts a sombre movie, and the result makes uncomfortable viewing. TH. Contains swearing. DVD

Richard Gere *Mr Jones* • Lena Olin *Dr Libbie Bowen* • Anne Bancroft *Dr Catherine Holland* • Tom Irwin *Patrick* • Delroy Lindo *Howard* • Bill Pullman *Construction site foreman* ■ *Dir* Mike Figgis • *Scr* Eric Roth, Michael Cristofer, from a story by Eric Roth

Mr Kingstreet's War ★★★

Adventure drama 1970 · US · Colour · 92mins

Former Alfred Hitchcock leading lady Tippi Hedren became a lady with a cause after marrying African safari ecologist Noel Marshall, and made a worthy series of movies espousing wildlife campaigns. This film, not thought good enough for a cinema release in the UK, is an unusual and fascinating study of pre-Second World

U = SUITABLE FOR ALL Uc = SUITABLE FOR ALL, ESPECIALLY FOR YOUNG CHILDREN (VIDEO ONLY) PG = PARENTAL GUIDANCE

War Africa, where, despite the encroachment of the opposing Italian and British forces, the wildlife sanctuaries are preserved by a determined couple. In spite of its amateur origins, the casting of former heart-throbs John Saxon and Rossano Brazzi keeps the movie watchable. TS

John Saxon *Jim Kingstreet* • Tippi Hedren *Mary Kingstreet* • Rossano Brazzi *Count Ugo Bernadelli* • Brian O'Shaughnessy *Morgan* ■ *Dir* Percival Rubens

Mr Klein ★★★★ 12

Second World War thriller
1976 · Fr · Colour · 118mins

Set in Paris during the Nazi occupation, this thriller by director Joseph Losey is one of his most poignant and Kafkaesque. Alain Delon is the Roman Catholic antiques dealer who fleeces Jews desperate to flee France. His world starts to unravel when he is mistaken for another Robert Klein, a Jew who is using his identity as a cover for subversive activities. Delon gives one of his greatest performances in this undervalued drama. TH. French dialogue dubbed into English. [VIDEO]

Alain Delon *Mr Klein* • Jeanne Moreau *Florence* • Suzanne Flon *Concierge* • [Michel Lonsdale] *Pierre* • Juliet Berto *Janine* ■ *Dir* Joseph Losey • *Scr* Franco Solinas

Mr Love ★★★ 15

Comedy 1985 · UK · Colour · 87mins

A very satisfying British gem, originally intended for Channel 4's *First Love* series, but made as a feature and awarded a short-lived theatrical outing. With a better-known cast, this might have been a real winner. As it stands, though, it's a cleverly made minor item, with the virtually unknown but excellent Barry Jackson as a sort of British version of François Truffaut's "Man Who Loved Women". Rewarding, with a knock-out send-up of *Casablanca*. TS [VIDEO]

Barry Jackson *Donald Lovelace* • Maurice Denham *Theo* • Margaret Tyzack *"Pink Lady"* • Linda Marlowe *Barbara* • Christina Collier *Esther* • Helen Cotterill *Lucy Nuttall* • Julia Deakin *Melanie* ■ *Dir* Roy Battersby • *Scr* Kenneth Eastaugh

Mr Lucky ★★★ U

Comedy 1943 · US · BW · 95mins

Cary Grant stars as a cynical professional gambler who romances heiress Laraine Day. Having cheated the American War Relief Society, he redeems himself by turning his gambling ship into a vessel laden with medical supplies. It sounds tacky, and it is a bit, but the movie was a big hit in 1943 and Grant always rated it as one of his favourites "because the character I played was more like the real Cary Grant than any before". First-time screenwriter Milton Holmes was in fact a pro at the Beverly Hills Tennis Club who pitched the idea to Grant in the parking lot. AT [VIDEO]

Cary Grant *Joe Adams* • Laraine Day *Dorothy Bryant* • Charles Bickford *Hard Swede* • Gladys Cooper *Capt Steadman* • Alan Carney *Crunk* • Henry Stephenson *Mr Bryant* • Paul Stewart *Zepp* ■ *Dir* HC Potter • *Scr* Milton Holmes, Adrian Scott, from the story *Bundles for Freedom* by Milton Holmes

Mr Magoo ★ PG

Comedy 1997 · US · Colour · 83mins

The main joke of the original cartoon was the myopia of its hero, the lugubrious Magoo. In a squirm-inducing sop to political correctness, a title at the end of this live-action feature points out that short-sighted people are not being ridiculed – which, of course, they are. As Magoo, Leslie Nielsen shows his limitations as a comedian: he barely raises a smile, let alone a laugh. The plot, about the chase for a stolen jewel, is pathetic. AT. Contains some violence. [VIDEO] DVD

Leslie Nielsen *Mr Magoo* • Kelly Lynch *Luanne* • Matt Keeslar *Waldo* • Nick Chinlund *Bob Morgan* • Stephen Tobolowsky *Agent Chuck Stupak* • Ernie Hudson *Agent Gus Anders* • Jennifer Garner *Stacey* • Malcolm McDowell *Austin Cloquet* ■ *Dir* Stanley Tong • *Scr* Pat Proft, Tom Sherohman

Mr Majestyk ★★ 18

Action thriller 1974 · US · Colour · 99mins

Charles Bronson is cast here in the unlikely role of a melon farmer. But when the Mafia starts interfering with his peaceful rural life, the star soon resorts to his violent ways to protect his workers and his harvest. Director Richard Fleischer has come up with a sort of *Death Wish* in Colorado – a combination that doesn't really work despite decent performances. Notably, the screenplay is written by Elmore Leonard. TS. Contains violence and swearing. [VIDEO] DVD

Charles Bronson *Vince Majestyk* • Al Lettieri *Frank Renda* • Linda Cristal *Nancy Chavez* • Lee Purcell *Wiley* • Paul Koslo *Bobby Kopas* • Taylor Lacher *Gene Lundy* • Frank Maxwell *Det Lt McAllen* • Alejandro Rey *Larry Mendoza* ■ *Dir* Richard Fleischer • *Scr* Elmore Leonard

Mr Mom ★★ PG

Comedy drama 1983 · US · Colour · 87mins

A role-reversal comedy about a dad who gets fired from his high-powered job and winds up as a househusband while his wife goes out to work. Probably something of a novelty back in 1983, nowadays the tendency would be to tell "Mr Mom" to stop flapping and start coping. Michael Keaton and Teri Garr star, with support from Christopher Lloyd and Martin Mull, and they're all likeable enough, but the film takes the easy options, plumping for farce and slapstick. DA [VIDEO] DVD

Michael Keaton *Jack Butler* • Teri Garr *Caroline Butler* • Frederick Koehler *Alex Butler* • Taliesin Jaffe *Kenny Butler* • Courtney White *Megan Butler* • Brittany White *Megan Butler* • Martin Mull *Ron Richardson* • Christopher Lloyd *Larry* ■ *Dir* Stan Dragoti • *Scr* John Hughes

Mister Moses ★★ U

Adventure 1965 · US · Colour · 126mins

Robert Mitchum plays a diamond smuggler who gets the name of Moses when he leads the population of an African village out of harm's way, parting the waters of a vast dam which will drown the village. Irritants on the journey include a mobile menagerie, magic spells cast by the witch doctor, a dull missionary and his daughter (Carroll Baker). The film never allows us to forget its biblical parallels, though the stars share some witty repartee. AT

Robert Mitchum *Joe Moses* • Carroll Baker *Julie Anderson* • Ian Bannen *Robert* • Alexander Knox *Reverend Anderson* • Raymond St Jacques *Ubi* • Orlando Martins *Chief* ■ *Dir* Ronald Neame • *Scr* Charles Beaumont, Monja Danischewsky, from the novel by Max Catto

Mr Moto in Danger Island ★★★

Detective drama 1939 · US · BW · 63mins

The last filmed of the *Mr Moto* series (that began in 1937 with *Think Fast, Mr Moto*), although it was released before *Mr Moto Takes a Vacation*. Beginning to look bored with the part of the wily Japanese troubleshooter, Peter Lorre finds himself in Puerto Rico, where he loads the evidence against himself in order to lure a gang of murderous diamond smugglers into the open. There was a belated attempt to revive the detective in 1965 with *The Return of Mr Moto*. DP

Peter Lorre *Mr Moto* • Jean Hersholt *Sutter* • Amanda Duff *Joan Castle* • Warren Hymer *Twister McGurk* • Richard Lane *Commissioner Gordon* • Leon Ames *Commissioner Madero* • Douglass Dumbrille *Commander La Costa* ■ *Dir* Herbert I Leeds • *Scr* Peter Milne, from ideas by John Reinhardt, George Bricker, from the novel *Murder in Trinidad* by John W Vandercook, from the character created by JP Marquand

Mr Moto Takes a Chance ★★

Detective drama 1938 · US · BW · 63mins

Inspired by JP Marquand's stories, the *Mr Moto* movies are hardly known for the clarity of their storylines. This one, though, is impenetrable. On his fourth outing as the Japanese detective, Peter Lorre finds himself in Cambodia in order to discover the secret of the caverns beneath a ruined temple. J Edward Bromberg has a ball as the chieftain. DP

Peter Lorre *Mr Moto* • Rochelle Hudson *Victoria Mason* • Robert Kent *Marty Weston* • J Edward Bromberg *Rajah Ali* • Chick Chandler *Chick Davis* • George Regas *Boker, High Priest* ■ *Dir* Norman Foster • *Scr* Lou Breslow, John Patrick, from a story by Willis Cooper, Norman Foster, from the character created by JP Marquand

Mr Moto Takes a Vacation ★★★

Detective drama 1939 · US · BW · 65mins

One of the last entries in the *Mr Moto* series; by the end of 1939, with Japan flexing its military muscles in South East Asia, the character was considered unsuitably heroic. This time, JP Marquand's master meddler is asked to protect an ancient African crown before it falls into the hands of a collector who has already nabbed some of the crown jewels. DP

Peter Lorre *Mr Moto* • Joseph Schildkraut *Hendrik Manderson* • Lionel Atwill *Professor Hildebrand* • Virginia Field *Eleanor Kirke* • John King *Howard Stevens* • Iva Stewart *Susan French* ■ *Dir* Norman Foster • *Scr* Norman Foster, Philip MacDonald, from the character created by JP Marquand

Mr Moto's Gamble ★★★

Detective drama 1938 · US · BW · 71mins

Returning for the third time to the role of the wily Japanese detective, Peter Lorre cruises through this undemanding boxing mystery, originally intended as a case for Charlie Chan. However, Keye Luke, who played Chan's "Number One Son", puts in a welcome appearance alongside Maxie Rosenbloom as a trainee sleuth. The latter helps Moto discover how poison got on the gloves of contender Dick Baldwin during a bout on which gangster Douglas Fowley had placed a sizeable bet. DP

Peter Lorre *Mr Moto* • Keye Luke *Lee Chan* • Dick Baldwin *Bill Steele* • Lynn Bari *Penny Kendall* • Douglas Fowley *Nick Crowder* • Jayne Regan *Linda Benton* ■ *Dir* James Tinling • *Scr* Charles Belden, Jerry Cady [Jerome Cady], from the character created by JP Marquand

Mr Moto's Last Warning ★★★

Detective drama 1939 · US · BW · 71mins

The sixth in the series featuring Peter Lorre as JP Marquand's Japanese sleuth sees Mr Moto in the Middle East, doing battle with spies intent on sabotaging French ships in the Suez canal and blaming it on the British. The formula is B-movie basic, with lots of rat-a-tat chat, plenty of plot twists and a scarcity of clues. The supporting cast is premier league, though. DP

Peter Lorre *Mr Moto* • Ricardo Cortez *Fabian* • Virginia Field *Connie Porter* • John Carradine *Danforth* • George Sanders *Eric Norvel* • Joan Carol *Mary Delacour* • Robert Coote *Rollo Venables* ■ *Dir* Norman Foster • *Scr* Philip MacDonald, Norman Foster, from the character created by JP Marquand

Mr Muggs Rides Again ★★ U

Comedy 1945 · US · BW · 63mins

Not even the presence of Leo Gorcey as Muggs could endear this weak entry in the East Side Kids series to its fans, and the following year the kids were disbanded, to resurface as the Bowery Boys. Gorcey is typecast as a jockey who gets suspended from racing owing to some alleged dirty doings. Unfortunately, it's neither very funny nor remotely fast-moving. TS

Leo Gorcey *Ethelbert Aloysius "Muggs" McGinnis* • Huntz Hall *Glimpy* • Billy Benedict *Skinny* • Johnny Duncan *Squeegie Robinson* • Bud Gorman *Danny* • Mende Koenig *Sam* • Minerva Urecal *Nora "Ma" Brown* • Bernard B Brown *Gaby O'Neill* • George Meeker *Dollar Davis* ■ *Dir* Wallace Fox • *Scr* Harvey H Gates

Mr Murder ★★ 15

Thriller
1998 · US/Ger/Neth · Colour · 126mins

Though based on a book by horror maestro Dean R Koontz, this TV thriller places the emphasis on action rather than chills. Stephen Baldwin plays a writer of bizarre murder mysteries who becomes embroiled in a deadly real-life game, when a mix-up involving blood samples during a shady genetics experiment results in the creation of Baldwin's evil clone. The end result is enjoyable, if a tad unbelievable. JF. Contains violence, swearing and nudity. [VIDEO] DVD

Stephen Baldwin *Marty Stillwater/Alfie* • Julie Warner *Paige Stillwater* • Bill Smitrovich *Lieutenant Lowbock* • James Coburn *Drew Oslett Sr* • Thomas Haden Church *Drew Oslett Jr* ■ *Dir* Dick Lowry • *Scr* Stephen Tolkin, from a novel by Dean R Koontz

M

Mr Music ★★★ U

Musical 1950 · US · BW · 114mins

This agreeable musical remake of 1935's *Accent on Youth*, itself based on a play, was tailor-made for the easy-going talents of Bing Crosby. Bing, who plays a middle-aged songwriter who would rather play golf than write songs, gets to sing several lively Burke/Van Heusen numbers. However, the film – under the direction of prissy comic actor Richard Haydn is even more laid-back than its star. It's also far too long for its flimsy subject matter. The guest stars, including Peggy Lee and Groucho Marx, perk things up considerably. RB

Bing Crosby *Paul Merrick* • Nancy Olson *Katherine Holbrook* • Charles Coburn *Alex Conway* • Ruth Hussey *Lorna* • Robert Stack *Jefferson* • Ida Moore *Aunt Amy* • Tom Ewell *Haggerty* ■ *Dir* Richard Haydn • *Scr* Arthur Sheekman, from the play *Accent on Youth* by Samson Raphaelson

Mr Nanny ★★ PG

Comedy 1992 · US · Colour · 80mins

This is the one where "Hulk" Hogan gets to dress up like a ballerina and aims to entertain what one assumes is his main fan base: young children. In a variation on the concept of youngsters inflicting humiliation on grown-ups, Hogan plays a former wrestler who winds up as bodyguard-cum-nanny to two troublesome brats, whose father is under threat because he has invented a super microchip. Hogan draws on his wrestling training to make the most of his many pratfalls. JF. Contains some swearing and violence. [VIDEO]

Terry "Hulk" Hogan [Hulk Hogan] *Sean Armstrong* • Sherman Hemsley *Bert Wilson* • Austin Pendleton *Alex Mason Sr* • Robert

Gorman [Robert Hy Gorman] *Alex Mason Jr* • Madeline Zima *Kate Mason* • Raymond O'Connor *Frank Olsen* • Mother Love *Corinne* ■ *Dir* Michael Gottlieb • *Scr* Edward Rugoff, Michael Gottlieb

Mr Nice Guy ★★ 15

Martial arts action comedy
1996 · HK · Colour · 84mins

This Melbourne-set vehicle for Hong Kong action star Jackie Chan may have been shot in English, but something definitely got lost in the translation. Chan plays a TV chef who gets mixed up with journalist Gabrielle Fitzpatrick's investigation into a drugs ring led by Richard Norton. The fight sequences are as inventive and imaginative as ever, but all the performances border on the hysterical. JF DVD

Jackie Chan *Jackie* • Richard Norton *Giancarlo "The Saint" Lucchetti* • Miki Lee *Miki* • Karen McLymont *Lakeisha* • Gabrielle Fitzpatrick *Diana* • Vince Poletto *Romeo Baggio* ■ *Dir* Sammo Hung • *Scr* Edward Tang, Fibe Ma

Mr North ★★★ PG

Comedy drama 1988 · US · Colour · 88mins

An exceptional amalgam of American greats – Robert Mitchum, Lauren Bacall, a script co-written by John Huston – adds much to this gently amusing tale. Anthony Edwards performs healing miracles among the Newport elite in the 1920s and finds himself going head to head with the local doctor. Very much a family affair – executive produced by Huston, the film stars his daughter Anjelica and is directed by his son Danny – this is a quality period fare and well worth watching. LH

Anthony Edwards *Theophilus North* • Robert Mitchum *James McHenry Bosworth* • Lauren Bacall *Mrs Amelia Cranston* • Harry Dean Stanton *Henry Simmons* • Anjelica Huston *Persis Bosworth-Tennyson* • Mary Stuart Masterson *Elspeth Skeel* • Virginia Madsen *Sally Boffin* • David Warner *Dr McPherson* ■ *Dir* Danny Huston • *Scr* Janet Roach, John Huston, James Costigan, from the novel *Theophilus North* by Thornton Wilder

Mr Peabody and the Mermaid ★★★ U

Comedy fantasy 1948 · US · BW · 89mins

This gentle and now-forgotten romantic comedy was the first mermaid movie to make postwar movie censors tremble. Not that there is much to worry about, since lovely Ann Blyth is a most provocative, but totally covered-up, former denizen of the deep. William Powell catches her while fishing, and his urbanity makes this Nunnally Johnson-scripted tosh acceptable, though it would have benefited from a stronger director than Irving Pichel. TS

William Powell *Mr Peabody* • Ann Blyth *Mermaid* • Irene Hervey *Polly Peabody* • Andrea King *Cathy Livingston* • Clinton Sundberg *Mike Fitzgerald* • Art Smith *Dr Harvey* ■ *Dir* Irving Pichel • *Scr* Nunnally Johnson, from the novel *Peabody's Mermaid* by Guy Jones, Constance Jones

Mr Perrin and Mr Traill ★★★

Drama 1948 · UK · BW · 91mins

Hugh Walpole's novel becomes a well-performed but obvious drama of life in a boys' public school. Marius Goring plays the stuffy, frustrated, ageing house master, while David Farrar is the virile and popular new games teacher. The problems start when they clash disastrously over Greta Gynt's glamorous school nurse. Lacking the subtlety of the later, rather similar *The Browning Version*, this swaps any sense of tragedy for melodrama, with a climax that makes use of the school's location on a Cornish clifftop. AE

Marius Goring *Vincent Perrin* • David Farrar *David Traill* • Greta Gynt *Isobel Lester* • Raymond Huntley *Moy-Thompson* • Edward Chapman *Birkland* • Mary Jerrold *Mrs Perrin* • Ralph Truman *Comber* • Finlay Currie *Sir Joshua Varley* ■ *Dir* Lawrence Huntington • *Scr* LAG Strong, TJ Morrison, from the novel by Hugh Walpole

Mister Quilp ★★ U

Musical 1975 · UK · Colour · 122mins

Anthony Newley plays the mean-spirited, hunchbacked money-lender Quilp in this film version of Charles Dickens's *The Old Curiosity Shop*. The star also composed the songs in the manner of Lionel Bart's *Oliver!*. This is principally a sanitised, Americanised, family-orientated affair that nevertheless preserves some of the darker elements of the original. The performances, particularly Newley's, put the emphasis on grotesquerie. AT

Anthony Newley *Daniel Quilp* • David Hemmings *Richard Swiveller* • David Warner *Sampson Brass* • Michael Hordern *Grandfather/Edward Trent* • Paul Rogers *Single gent/Henry Trent* • Jill Bennett *Sally Brass* • Mona Washbourne *Mrs Jarley* ■ *Dir* Michael Tuchner • *Scr* Louis Kamp, Irene Kamp, from the novel *The Old Curiosity Shop* by Charles Dickens

Mr Reliable ★★★★ 15

Comedy drama based on a true story
1996 · Aus · Colour · 108mins

Down Under in the late 1960s, dim-witted crook Colin Friels and his new girlfriend, single mum Jacqueline McKenzie, scare off an irritating policeman with a shotgun, sparking a full-scale hostage crisis. However, much to the embarrassment of the local Establishment, the fair dinkum general public are firmly on the lovestruck couple's side. Friels and McKenzie are terrific as the dopey heroes, and all the characters are fleshed out with great affection. A beaut. JF. Contains swearing, violence and some sex scenes.

Colin Friels *Wally Mellish* • Jacqueline McKenzie *Beryl Muddle* • Paul Sonkkila *Norman Allan* • Fred Gallacher *Don Fergusson* • Lisa Hensley *Penny Wilberforce* ■ *Dir* Nadia Tass • *Scr* Don Catchlove, Terry Hayes

Mr Ricco ★★ 15

Crime drama 1975 · US · Colour · 93mins

This humdrum crime drama gave Dean Martin his last leading role before his career lapsed into the occasional wry cameo appearance. As a liberal lawyer in San Francisco, he successfully defends a black militant accused of murder who then appears to be responsible for a vicious killing spree. No Matt Helm dramatics here, this film's tired Dino is a lonely widower who keeps a shaggy dog to retrieve his golf balls, drinks milk, and has a lady friend of a suitable age – neatly portrayed by Geraldine Brooks. AE

Dean Martin *Joe Ricco* • Eugene Roche *George Cronyn* • Thalmus Rasulala *Frankie Steele* • Denise Nicholas *Irene Mapes* • Cindy Williams *Jamison* • Geraldine Brooks *Katherine Fremont* • Philip Thomas [Philip Michael Thomas] *Purvis Mapes* ■ *Dir* Paul Bogart • *Scr* Robert Hoban, from a story by Ed Harvey, Francis Kiernan

Mister Roberts ★★★★★ U

Comedy drama 1955 · US · Colour · 115mins

This magnificent adaptation of the hit Broadway comedy sees Henry Fonda returning to the screen after a long absence to re-create his stage role as a supply-ship officer who longs to be part of the action during the Second World War. Fonda clashed with original director John Ford over how to play the part, which led to director Mervyn LeRoy taking over, but the transfer was seamless and the qualities of the play were retained. The film has a cast to die for: James Cagney as the captain, William Powell (his last movie) as the wise old doc, and young Jack Lemmon, winning his first Oscar as the brash, irresistible and irrepressible Ensign Pulver. Perhaps if Lemmon had reprised the role in 1964's disappointing spin-off *Ensign Pulver* that might have been a better movie. This, however, is a great one. TS

Henry Fonda *Lieutenant Doug Roberts* • James Cagney *Captain* • Jack Lemmon *Ensign Frank Thurlowe Pulver* • William Powell *Doc* • Betsy Palmer *Lieutenant Ann Girard* • Ward Bond *Chief Petty Officer Dowdy* ■ *Dir* John Ford, Mervyn LeRoy • *Scr* Joshua Logan, Frank S Nugent, from the play by Joshua Logan, Thomas Heggen, from the novel by Thomas Heggen

Mr Sardonicus ★★★ 12

Horror 1961 · US · BW · 86mins

Director William Castle worked overtime on this unofficial reworking of the 1928 chiller *The Man Who Laughs*. Having personally introduced the picture, Castle concluded proceedings with a Punishment Poll, in which the audience decided the fate of Guy Rolfe as Sardonicus, the 19th-century aristocrat who kidnaps Audrey Dalton to compel her surgeon sweetheart, Ronald Lewis, to operate on his face, which was frozen in childhood into a hideous grin. Eerily shot by Burnett Guffey with a surprisingly literate script from Ray Russell, all is primed for Oscar Homolka to steal the show as Rolfe's embittered servant. DP

Ronald Lewis *Sir Robert Cargrave* • Audrey Dalton *Maude Sardonicus* • Guy Rolfe *Sardonicus* • Oscar Homolka *Krull* • Vladimir Sokoloff *Father* ■ *Dir* William Castle • *Scr* Ray Russell, from a short story by Ray Russell

Mr Saturday Night ★★★ 15

Comedy drama 1992 · US · Colour · 114mins

Billy Crystal builds on a character he developed during his early stand-up days for this affectionate, fictional biopic. Crystal's Buddy Young Jr is a stand-up comedian whose career spans more than 50 years; however, he is less successful with personal relationships, notably with his brother and manager David Paymer. The best bits are the scenes of his initial bids for success on stage; the dramatic elements are less successfully incorporated into the picture. Watch for a cameo from Jerry Lewis. JF. Contains swearing. DVD

Billy Crystal *Buddy Young Jr* • David Paymer *Stan Yankelman* • Julie Warner *Elaine* • Helen Hunt *Annie* • Mary Mara *Susan* • Jerry Orbach *Phil Gussman* • Ron Silver *Larry Meyerson* • Jerry Lewis ■ *Dir* Billy Crystal • *Scr* Billy Crystal, Lowell Ganz, Babaloo Mandel

Mr Skeffington ★★★★

Melodrama 1944 · US · BW · 116mins

A narcissistic, selfish, faithless and rich society woman marries a loyal, dignified and adoring businessman to protect her feckless brother's reputation, and treats him like dirt. Retribution arrives when diphtheria ravages her looks, redemption when he returns blind from a Nazi concentration camp. It's well directed by Vincent Sherman on opulent sets and contains fabulous performances from the Oscar-nominated Bette Davis and Claude Rains, who are both at the height of their powers. Against a Franz Waxman score that emphasises the drama, Davis delivers a synthesis of the vain bitch roles she made uniquely her own; Rains is the perfect foil. Absolutely irresistible. RK

Bette Davis *Fanny Trellis* • Claude Rains *Job Skeffington* • Walter Abel *George Trellis* • Richard Waring *Trippy Trellis* • George Coulouris *Dr Byles* • Marjorie Riordan *Young Fanny* • Robert Shayne *MacMahon* ■ *Dir* Vincent Sherman • *Scr* Philip G Epstein, Julius J Epstein, James Leicester, from the novel by "Elizabeth" [Mary Annette Beauchamp Russell] • *Art Director* Robert Haas

Mr Smith Goes to Washington ★★★★★ U

Political comedy drama
1939 · US · BW · 124mins

This superb discourse on corruption in American politics is one of Hollywood's finest achievements. Director Frank Capra remarkably (for him) keeps sentimentality at bay in his film of Lewis R Foster's Oscar-winning original story (adapted by Sidney Buchman) about an idealistic young senator who finally realises that he is not his own man. Washington hated this movie, but the public flocked to see James Stewart in, arguably, his finest hour. Few movies are as well cast: the bell-voiced Jean Arthur is wonderful as a super-cynical secretary, but veteran western star Harry Carey is quite magnificent as the vice president, one of the greatest supporting roles in all cinema, and alone a reason for viewing. TS DVD

Jean Arthur *Clarissa Saunders* • James Stewart *Jefferson Smith* • Claude Rains *Senator Joseph Paine* • Edward Arnold *Jim Taylor* • Guy Kibbee *Governor Hubert Hopper* • Thomas Mitchell *Diz Moore* • Eugene Pallette *Chick McGann* • Beulah Bondi *Ma Smith* • HB Warner *Senate majority leader* • Harry Carey *President of the Senate* ■ *Dir* Frank Capra • *Scr* Sidney Buchman, Myles Connolly, from the story *The Gentleman from Montana* by Lewis R Foster

Mr Sycamore ★ PG

Comedy drama 1974 · US · Colour · 84mins

They don't make them like this any more, with good reason. A fine cast is ill-used in this whimsical comedy about one man's attempt to escape the rat race. A mild-mannered postman (Jason Robards), under the heel of his overbearing wife, decides to become a tree. Luckily for Robards, his cinema career perked up shortly afterwards with an Oscar-winning role in *All the President's Men*. JG

Jerome Thor *Higgins* • Jason Robards *John Gwilt* • Sandy Dennis *Jane Gwilt* • Jean Simmons *Estelle Benbow* • Robert Easton *Fred Staines* • Brenda Smith *Daisy* ■ *Dir* Pancho Kohner • *Scr* Pancho Kohner, Ketti Frings, from a story by Robert Ayre, from a play by Ketti Frings

Mister Ten Per Cent ★★ U

Comedy 1967 · UK · Colour · 85mins

For all his success on TV, Charlie Drake has failed to make an impact on the big screen, with only four movies in 13 years before this flop. Co-scripted by Drake and Norman Hudis, it's a comedy about the deliberate staging of a box-office bomb to claim the insurance, which predated Mel Brooks's similarly themed *The Producers* by a year. In spite of an accomplished cast, it is killed stone dead by Drake himself, who was so hurt by its failure that he went into temporary retirement. DP

Charlie Drake *Percy Pointer* • Derek Nimmo *Tony* • Wanda Ventham *Kathy* • John Le Mesurier *Jocelyn Macauley* • Anthony Nicholls *Casey* • Noel Dyson *Mrs Gorman* • John Hewer *Townsend* ■ *Dir* Peter Graham Scott • *Scr* Norman Hudis, Charlie Drake

Mr Topaze ★★ U

Comedy 1961 · UK · Colour · 96mins

Peter Sellers directed himself in this adaptation of a Marcel Pagnol play, so he has only himself to blame. He plays an ex-schoolmaster in a small French town who falls among thieves and comes up wealthy. Beset by the likes of Herbert Lom, Leo McKern and Nadia Gray, Sellers makes an endearing innocent at large. Alas, his direction lacks the edge the idea needed. TH

Peter Sellers *Mr Topaze* • Nadia Gray *Suzy* • Herbert Lom *Castel Benac* • Leo McKern *Muche* • Martita Hunt *Baroness* • John Neville *Roger* • Billie Whitelaw *Ernestine* • Michael Gough *Tamise* • Joan Sims *Colette* ■ *Dir* Peter Sellers • *Scr* Pierre Rouve, from the play *Topaze* by Marcel Pagnol

Mr Vampire ★★★★ 15

Comedy horror 1986 · HK · Colour · 93mins

Slapstick comedy, mystic martial arts and astonishing gore appear in the first of a long line of popular, and much copied, period Chinese horror films. Lam Ching Ying is the voodoo priest hired by a prominent merchant to exorcise his bouncing bloodsucker father. Complications arise thanks to Lam's two over-enthusiastic apprentices, lured by lonely ghosts into exhausting nights of spectral passion, and the eight zombies left in his undertaking care. This is oriental knockabout horror at its most entertaining. AJ. In Cantonese with English subtitles. [video] DVD

Ricky Hui *Man Chor* • Moon Lee *Ting Ting* • Lam Ching Ying *Master* • Pauline Wong *Jade Ah Wai* • Anthony Chan *Brother* ■ *Dir* Ricky Lau • *Scr* Wong Ching, Szeto Cheuk Hon

Mr Winkle Goes to War ★

Second World War drama
1944 · US · BW · 79mins

One of the crassest wartime propaganda movies ever made, with Edward G Robinson as a meek little bank clerk who's bullied by his wife (Ruth Warrick) – until he's drafted, that is. This same little man becomes a hero when he fetches up on a Pacific island and drives a bulldozer straight through the Japanese defences. Give that man a medal and watch his wife dissolve with pride. The manipulative calculation of this movie has to be seen to be believed. Released as *Arms and the Woman* in the UK. AT

Edward G Robinson *Wilbert George Winkle* • Ruth Warrick *Amy Winkle* • Ted Donaldson *Barry* • Bob Haymes *Jack Pettigrew* • Richard Lane *Sgt "Alphabet"* • Robert Mitchum *Corporal* ■ *Dir* Alfred E Green • *Scr* Waldo Salt, George Corey, Louis Solomon, from a novel by Theodore Pratt

Mr Wonderful ★★★★ 15

Romantic drama 1992 · US · Colour · 95mins

Director Anthony Minghella made his American debut with this quaint comedy that scores so heavily on the performance level that you can forgive it its contrived plot and odd lapses in logic. Matt Dillon's plans to open a bowling alley depend entirely on cutting the alimony paid to ex-wife Annabella Sciorra, but she's dating married academic William Hurt and has no plans to tie the knot. It's obvious Dillon's schemes to find her a new husband will rekindle his own passion – romantics will not be disappointed. DP [video]

Matt Dillon *Gus* • Annabella Sciorra *Lee* • Mary-Louise Parker *Rita* • William Hurt *Tom* • Vincent D'Onofrio *Dominic* • David Barry Gray *Pope* • Dan Hedaya *Harvey* ■ *Dir* Anthony Minghella • *Scr* Anthony Minghella, from a screenplay (unproduced) by Amy Schor, Vicki Polon

Mr Wrong ★★★ 15

Thriller 1985 · NZ · Colour · 88mins

This psycho-thriller concerns a woman who buys a Jaguar car that turns out to be haunted. Alfred Hitchcock himself once showed interest in filming Elizabeth Jane Howard's story and, while this is certainly not in the master's class, it is still a skilful and enjoyable feature debut by former documentary-maker Gaylene Preston. PF

Heather Bolton *Meg* • David Letch *Mr Wrong* • Margaret Umbers *Samantha* • Suzanne Lee *Val* • Gary Stalker *Bruce* • Danny Mulheron *Wayne* ■ *Dir* Gaylene Preston • *Scr* Gaylene Preston, Geoff Murphy, Graeme Tetley, from a story by Elizabeth Jane Howard

Mr Wrong ★ 12

Romantic comedy
1996 · US · Colour · 92mins

You will discover how truly unfunny a comedy can be if you subject yourself to this unfortunate fare, made as a big-screen vehicle for TV star Ellen DeGeneres. She's the lonely single woman who meets hunky Bill Pullman and discovers, too late, what a loser he really is – by which point she can't seem to get rid of him. Unfortunately, director Nick Castle lets this tedious tale amble along, and DeGeneres, Pullman and Joan Cusack can't save it. JB. Contains some swearing and sexual references. [video]

Ellen DeGeneres *Martha Alston* • Bill Pullman *Whitman Crawford* • Joan Cusack *Inga* • Dean Stockwell *Jack Tramonte* • Joan Plowright *Mrs Crawford* • John Livingston *Walter* • Robert Goulet *Dick Braxton* • Ellen Cleghorne *Jane* • Hope Davis *Annie* ■ *Dir* Nick Castle • *Scr* Chris Matheson, Kerry Ehrin, Craig Munson

Mistress ★★ 15

Satirical comedy
1992 · US · Colour · 105mins

This Tinseltown comedy keeps threatening to blow the lid off the whole movie-making business. Yet, while the script wickedly captures the nitty-gritty of wheeler-dealing, the story lacks originality and direction. As the trio willing to back Robert Wuhl's film (providing there are starring roles for their mistresses), Eli Wallach, Danny Aiello and Robert De Niro are hugely disappointing, although Martin Landau shines as a grubbing producer. DP [video]

Robert Wuhl *Marvin Landisman* • Martin Landau *Jack Roth* • Jace Alexander *Stuart Stratland Jr* • Robert De Niro *Evan M Wright* • Laurie Metcalf *Rachel Landisman* • Eli Wallach *George Lieberhoff* • Danny Aiello *Carmine Rasso* • Christopher Walken *Warren Zell* ■ *Dir* Barry Primus • *Scr* Barry Primus, JF Lawton, from a story by Barry Primus

Misunderstood ★★ PG

Drama 1984 · US · Colour · 90mins

Gene Hackman is an industrialist living in some splendour in Tunisia. Recently widowed and consumed by grief, he has to raise two young boys, the older of whom is played by Henry Thomas, then basking in worldwide fame as the young hero of *ET*. Hackman and young Thomas are complete strangers who slowly start to understand each other, a process heightened when the latter is seriously hurt in an accident. This is a serious, sometimes sombre study of human relationships, though director Jerry Schatzberg disowned the cop-out, freeze-frame ending added by the producers. AT [video]

Gene Hackman *Ned* • Henry Thomas *Andrew* • Rip Torn *Will* • Huckleberry Fox *Miles* • Maureen Kerwin *Kate* • Susan Anspach *Lilly* • June Brown *Mrs Paley* • Nadim Sawalha *Ahmed* ■ *Dir* Jerry Schatzberg • *Scr* Barra Grant, from a novel by Florence Montgomery

Mitchell ★★

Action crime drama
1975 · US · Colour · 96mins

Joe Don Baker stars as the bull-headed cop on the trail of two big-time drug dealers, played by Martin Balsam and John Saxon. Trawling through the sewer of life, Baker finds a tart-with-heart (Linda Evans) and a whole range of pimps, bent cops, Bel Air socialites and mob members. Baker certainly has a physical presence but here he lacks the material that made his sheriff hero of *Walking Tall*, or his hitman in *Charley Varrick*, such memorable screen characters. AT

Joe Don Baker *Mitchell* • Martin Balsam *James Arthur Cummins* • John Saxon *Walter Deaney* • Linda Evans *Greta* • Merlin Olsen *Benton* ■ *Dir* Andrew V McLaglen • *Scr* Ian Kennedy Martin

Mitsou ★★★

Romantic drama 1957 · Fr · Colour · 98mins

Delighting in toying with the scruples of the hypocritical, this adaptation of Colette's short novel was, in its day, considered risqué both in its frank imagery and its bold approach to love. Viewed from afar, it seems a perfect specimen of the "tradition of quality" so despised by the young bucks of the *Nouvelle Vague*. For all the occasional starchiness of the dialogue, though, this is a charmingly coquettish picture, with Danièle Delorme radiantly naive as the music-hall singer who turns to ageing roué Fernand Gravey for a crash course in the refinements that will turn the head of priggish soldier François Guérin. DP. A French language film.

Danièle Delorme *Mitsou* • Fernand Gravey [Fernand Gravet] *Pierre Duroy-Lelong* • François Guérin *Lieutenant Bleu* • Claude Rich *Lieutenant Kaki* • Odette Laure *Petite Chose* ■ *Dir* Jacqueline Audry • *Scr* Pierre Laroche, from the novel by Colette

Mix Me a Person ★★

Crime drama 1962 · UK · BW · 112mins

Like most early British pop stars, Adam Faith appeared in a few movies. Unlike the majority, though, he didn't shy away from meatier roles more usually reserved for "proper" actors. In this routine courtroom drama, he rather woodenly plays a teenage garage mechanic convicted of killing a policeman. Anne Baxter is the psychiatrist wife of his barrister Donald Sinden who sets out to prove his innocence. A pedestrian thriller, and, yes, Faith does sing the title song. AJ

Anne Baxter *Dr Anne Dyson* • Donald Sinden *Philip Bellamy QC* • Adam Faith *Harry Jukes* • David Kernan *Socko* ■ *Dir* Leslie Norman • *Scr* Ian Dalrymple, Roy Kerridge, from the novel by Jack Trevor Story

Mixed Blood ★★★

Black comedy drama
1984 · US/Fr · Colour · 99mins

There's shades of *Bloody Mama* in this violent tale of gang warfare in New York's Alphabet City. The focus is on the Brazilian immigrant "Maceteros", a group of teenage hoodlums dominated by matriarch Marilia Pêra, who become involved in an escalating conflict with their Puerto Rican opposite numbers. Written and directed by Warhol acolyte Paul Morrissey, this meanders in tone, but it deserves some marks for at least attempting to challenge, and Pêra is barnstorming. RT

Marilia Pêra *Rita La Punta* • Richard Ulacia *Thiago* • Linda Kerridge *Carol* • Geraldine Smith *Toni* • Angel David *Juan the Bullet* • Ulrich Berr *The German* • Marcelino Rivera *Hector* ■ *Dir* Paul Morrissey • *Scr* Paul Morrissey, Alan Browne

Mixed Company ★★

Comedy drama 1974 · US · Colour · 108mins

A mildly entertaining but overly simplistic look at what happens when a couple adopt a string of ethnic children and naively introduce them into their secretly bigoted neighbourhood. It's an honourable attempt by director Melville Shavelson and stars Barbara Harris and Joseph Bologna to treat an important subject with some lightness of touch, and not the worst film on racial prejudice ever made by any means, but its overall effect is sadly one of sporadically relieved tedium. SH. Contains some swearing and nudity.

Barbara Harris *Kathy* • Joseph Bologna *Pete* • Lisa Gerritsen *Liz* • Ariane Heller *Mary* • Stephen Honanie *Joe* • Haywood Nelson *Freddie* • Eric Olson *Rob* • Jina Tan *Quan* • Tom Bosley *Al* ■ *Dir* Melville Shavelson • *Scr* Melville Shavelson, Mort Lachman

Mixed Nuts ★★ 12

Comedy 1994 · US · Colour · 93mins

An off-form Steve Martin stars as the manager of a struggling telephone help-line that's about to be disconnected in this California-set adaptation of French comedy *Le Père Noël Est une Ordure*. It's so tasteless you'd scarcely believe it's by Nora Ephron, director of that eminently inoffensive romantic comedy *Sleepless in Seattle*. There's also little to warm the heart in the bleak Christmas context. TH. Contains swearing. [video]

Steve Martin *Philip* • Rita Wilson *Catherine* • Madeline Kahn *Mrs Munchnik* • Robert Klein *Mr Lobel* • Anthony LaPaglia *Felix* • Juliette Lewis *Gracie* • Rob Reiner *Dr Kinsky* • Garry Shandling *Stanley* • Adam Sandler *Louie* • Liev Schreiber *Chris* ■ *Dir* Nora Ephron • *Scr* Nora Ephron, Delia Ephron, from the 1982 film *Le Père Noël est une Ordure*

Mixing Nia ★★★

Romantic comedy drama
1998 · US · Colour · 92mins

Bermuda-born documentarist Alison Swan made her feature debut as the writer/director of this perky romantic comedy drama, a reworking of 1949's *Pinky* in which Jeanne Crain starred as an African-American whose skin colour was pale enough to pass as white. Here Karyn Parsons gives a truly vibrant performance as the yuppie daughter of a mixed-race marriage who quits her copywriting job and embarks on a voyage of self-discovery. Swan gets a little carried away with the recurrent fantasy sequences, but she handles her themes with care. DP

Karyn Parsons *Nia* • Eric Thal *Matt* • Isaiah Washington *Lewis* • Diego Serrano *Joe* • Rosalyn Coleman *Renee* • Heidi Schanz *Jen* ■ *Dir/Scr* Alison Swan

Mo' Better Blues ★★★ 15

Drama 1990 · US · Colour · 123mins

Spike Lee suffers under the weight of his own ambition here, trying to cram his film with so many ideas (the nature of obsession, the avoidance of reality, the conflict between art and life) that it comes unglued at an early stage, especially as there's not enough plot to shore it up. Yet Denzel Washington, as a single-minded trumpeter, gingerly steps over the cracks to provide plenty of powerful scenes. He is helped by Wesley Snipes and Lee himself, and the lack of coherence is offset by vigorous, stylish camerawork and a killer jazz score. JM. Contains violence, swearing, sex scenes and nudity. [video]

Denzel Washington *Bleek Gilliam* • Spike Lee *Giant* • Wesley Snipes *Shadow Henderson* • Joie Lee *Indigo Downes* • Cynda Williams *Clarke Bentancourt* • Dick Anthony Williams *Big Stop Gilliam* • Giancarlo Esposito *Left Hand Lacey* ■ *Dir/Scr* Spike Lee

Mo' Money ★ 15

Action comedy 1992 · US · Colour · 89mins

Written and executive produced by its star, Damon Wayans, this is a ridiculous and gratuitously violent action movie which also professes to be a comedy. Wayans tries to impress his girlfriend (Stacey Dash) by getting a lowly job at the credit card company where she works. In no time at all, he's up to his neck in blackmail and fraud. Poorly scripted, this does Wayans few favours. LH [video] DVD

M

Damon Wayans *Johnny Stewart* • Stacey Dash *Amber Evans* • Joe Santos *Lt Raymond Walsh* • John Diehl *Keith Heading* • Harry J Lennix [Harry Lennix] *Tom Dilton* • Marlon Wayans *Seymour Stewart* ■ *Dir* Peter MacDonald • *Scr* Damon Wayans

Moana ★★★★

Silent documentary 1926 · US · BW · 77mins

Because of the success of Robert Flaherty's first feature, *Nanook of the North* (1922), Paramount asked the ethnological director to make a "Nanook of the South Seas". So, with an unlimited budget, Flaherty spent two years in the Samoan islands making *Moana*. He returned with a lyrical, beautifully photographed, idealised picture of an island paradise where noble savages hunt, fish and cook. Although it did not as successful as the earlier film, it inspired British film producer John Grierson to coin the word "documentary". RB

Dir Robert Flaherty • *Scr* Robert Flaherty, Julian Johnson (titles) • *Cinematographer* Robert Flaherty

The Mob ★★★

Crime drama 1951 · US · BW · 86mins

When talented, under-rated director Robert Parrish worked as an editor, he managed to help pull together the shambles that was *All the King's Men*, not only winning himself an Oscar nomination (with Al Clark), but securing the best picture award and the best actor statuette for star Broderick Crawford. Crawford paid back the debt by lending his considerable (and bulky) presence to this, Parrish's second film as a director. Crawford brings great credibility to the role of a cop passing for a thug, and is especially good at the sexy repartee with forgotten actress Lynne Baggett. TS

Broderick Crawford *Johnny Damico* • Betty Buehler *Mary Kiernan* • Richard Kiley *Thomas Clancy* • Otto Hulett *Lieutenant Banks* • Matt Crowley *Smoothie* • Neville Brand *Gunner* • Ernest Borgnine *Joe Castro* • Charles Buchinski [Charles Bronson] *Jack* ■ *Dir* Robert Parrish • *Scr* William Bowers, from the novel *Waterfront* by Ferguson Findley

The Mobster ★★

Crime drama 1958 · US · BW · 79mins

After gaining critical attention with *Machine Gun Kelly*, director Roger Corman quickly followed up that historical gangster thriller with one set in the modern era. Told in flashback to a Senate investigating committee, it charts the rise and fall of gangland leader Steve Cochran, from his lowly slum beginnings working a numbers racket and dealing drugs to becoming head of the syndicate. While the script is nowhere near as strong as *Kelly*, Corman captures the grimy criminal atmosphere in broad strokes and with swift action pacing. AJ

Steve Cochran *Joe Sante* • Lita Milan *Teresa Porter* • Robert Strauss *Black Frankie* • Celia Lovsky *Mrs Sante* • Lili St Cyr • John Brinkley *Ernie Porter* • Yvette Vickers *Blonde* • Grant Withers *Joe Moran* ■ *Dir* Roger Corman • *Scr* Steve Fisher, from the novel *I, Mobster* by Joseph Hilton Smyth

Mobsters ★★ 18

Crime thriller 1991 · US · Colour · 115mins

It is extraordinary that, with gangster-era America providing such a natural source of drama, director Michael Karbelnikoff should turn gritty reality into such an empty tale. Hampered by inanity and a tortuous plot, Christian Slater (as "Lucky" Luciano), Patrick Dempsey (Meyer Lansky) and Richard Grieco ("Bugsy" Siegel) still look credible in period suits, while Anthony Quinn and Michael Gambon, as two hard mobsters, supply the flair and fire. JM. Contains sex scenes, swearing, violence, nudity. [video] DVD

Christian Slater *Charlie "Lucky" Luciano* • Patrick Dempsey *Meyer Lansky* • Richard Grieco *Benjamin "Bugsy" Siegel* • Costas Mandylor *Frank Costello* • Anthony Quinn *Don Masseria* • F Murray Abraham *Arnold Rothstein* • Michael Gambon *Don Faranzano* • Lara Flynn Boyle *Mara Motes* ■ *Dir* Michael Karbelnikoff • *Scr* Michael Mahern, Nicholas Kazan, from a story by Michael Mahern

Moby Dick ★★

Adventure drama 1930 · US · BW · 75mins

A bowdlerised version of Herman Melville's classic novel, this has Captain Ahab (John Barrymore) losing his leg to a whale as a result of being pushed overboard by an evil stepbrother who is after the preacher's daughter (Joan Bennett) Ahab loves. Directed by Lloyd Bacon, the sequences where Ahab hunts the whale are let down by the clumsily obvious model of the predator. Barrymore almost holds the nonsensically melodramatic plot together with a fine performance. RK

John Barrymore *Captain Ahab* • Joan Bennett *Faith* • Lloyd Hughes *Derek* • May Boley *Whale Oil Rosie* • Walter Long *Stubbs* • Tom O'Brien *Starbuck* • Nigel de Brulier *Elijah* ■ *Dir* Lloyd Bacon • *Scr* J Grubb Alexander, from the novel by Herman Melville

Moby Dick ★★★ PG

Adventure drama
1956 · UK/US · Colour · 110mins

John Huston's long-cherished adaptation of Herman Melville's novel has some wonderful scenes but must be counted as a noble failure. The great white whale always looks phoney; it performed badly in high seas off the coasts of Ireland and the Canaries, pushing the budget through the roof. Gregory Peck as Captain Ahab is miscast, lacking the required demonic presence. Wags at the time joked that Orson Welles, who plays Father Mapple, should have played the whale, while Peck himself thought that Huston should have played Ahab. AT [video] DVD

Gregory Peck *Captain Ahab* • Richard Basehart *Ishmael* • Leo Genn *Starbuck* • Orson Welles *Father Mapple* • Friedrich Ledebur *Queequeg* • Harry Andrews *Stubb* • Bernard Miles *Manxman* • James Robertson-Justice *Captain Boomer* ■ *Dir* John Huston • *Scr* John Huston, Ray Bradbury, from the novel by Herman Melville • *Cinematographer* Oswald Morris, Freddie Francis

The Mod Squad ★ 15

Crime action drama
1999 · US · Colour · 90mins

This remake of the popular 1960s TV series about three former criminals who become undercover cops is a good example of how not to make a movie. It spends 40 minutes establishing the hipness of its trio of main characters before getting to the plot, and then buries the rest in a mishmash of strangeness and 20-something angst. ST. Contains swearing and violence. [video] DVD

Claire Danes *Julie Barnes* • Giovanni Ribisi *Pete Cochrane* • Omar Epps *Linc Hayes* • Josh Brolin *Billy Waites* • Dennis Farina *Captain Adam Greer* • Steve Harris *Detective Briggs* ■ *Dir* Scott Silver • *Scr* Scott Silver, Stephen Kay, Kate Lanier, from characters created by Buddy Ruskin

The Model and the Marriage Broker ★★★

Comedy drama 1951 · US · BW · 103mins

A minor but charming movie from "women's director" George Cukor, here slightly overdependent on the undoubted talents and weather-beaten features of character actress and notorious scene-stealer Thelma Ritter. Ritter is marvellous, trying to pair friend Jeanne Crain with handsome radiographer Scott Brady, while trying not to let Crain know matchmaking is her real profession. Others in the marriage market include a pre-blacklist Zero Mostel. TS

Jeanne Crain *Kitty Bennett* • Scott Brady *Matt Hornbeck* • Thelma Ritter *Mae Swazey* • Zero Mostel *Wixted* • Michael O'Shea *Doberman* • Helen Ford *Emmy Swazey* • Frank Fontaine *Johannson* ■ *Dir* George Cukor • *Scr* Charles Brackett, Walter Reisch, Richard Breen [Richard L Breen]

Model Shop ★

Romantic comedy drama
1969 · US/Fr · Colour · 95mins

Jacques Demy made some fine films in France, but his Hollywood debut was a mistake from start to finish. Made in LA during the time of anti-Vietnam demos, the counterculture and the sexual revolution, it's a frivolous thing about fashion design and photography. Gary Lockwood has all the personality of a paper cup, while Anouk Aimée, who revives her 1960 character from Demy's *Lola*, does little but stare vacantly into the middle distance. AT

Anouk Aimée *Lola* • Gary Lockwood *George Matthews* • Alexandra Hay *Gloria* • Carol Cole *Barbara* • Severn Darden *Portly man* • Tom Fielding *Gerry* ■ *Dir* Jacques Demy • *Scr* Jacques Demy, Adrien Joyce

A Modern Affair ★★ 15

Romantic comedy drama
1996 · US · Colour · 90mins

This film harps on about the plight of the single career girl whose biological clock is thumping while her life is a man-free zone. Lisa Eichhorn is the workaholic Manhattan-ite dragging herself to the sperm bank. Once up the proverbial duff, she inevitably decides she must meet the sperm donor herself and tracks down photographer Stanley Tucci. Entirely two dimensional, this has little to recommend it bar the standard of performance from Tucci. LH [video]

Lisa Eichhorn *Grace Rhodes* • Stanley Tucci *Peter Kessler* • Caroline Aaron *Elaine* • Mary Jo Salerno *Lindsey* • Tammy Grimes *Dr Gresham* • Wesley Addy *Ed Rhodes* ■ *Dir* Vern Oakley • *Scr* Paul Zimmerman, from a story by Vern Oakley, Paul Zimmerman

Modern Love ★★ 15

Romantic comedy
1990 · US · Colour · 104mins

This lame, hackneyed look at the problems of modern relationships and the family adds nothing new to the great American middle income debate. Robby Benson co-opted his real-life wife, Karla DeVito, and their own daughter to play his family, which gives the whole plodding affair a smug, incestuous air. Benson cobbled this one together as part of a university film course; he should have listened to the old maxim "those who can, do; those who can't, teach". SH [video]

Robby Benson *Greg* • Karla DeVito *Dr Billie Parker* • Burt Reynolds *Colonel Frank Parker* • Debra Port *Annabell* • Cliff Bemis *Dirk Martin* • Rue McClanahan *Evelyn* • Frankie Valli *Mr Hoskins* ■ *Dir/Scr* Robby Benson

Modern Problems ★

Comedy 1981 · US · Colour · 90mins

Stressed-out air traffic controller Chevy Chase is driving along the freeway when a truck carrying nuclear waste springs a leak, drenching our hero in radioactive slime. Instead of making him grow an extra head or simply killing him, the incident causes Chase to develop telekinetic powers. These help him sort out the problems in his life and enable him to take sweet revenge on his enemies. An idea that might have occupied a five-minute sketch on a TV show is overstretched to feature-film length. AT

Chevy Chase *Max* • Patti D'Arbanville *Darcy* • Mary Kay Place *Lorraine* • Nell Carter *Dorita* • Brian Doyle-Murray *Brian* • Dabney Coleman *Mark* • Mitch Kreindel *Barry* ■ *Dir* Ken Shapiro • *Scr* Ken Shapiro, Tom Sherohman, Arthur Sellers

Modern Romance ★★★ 15

Romantic comedy
1981 · US · Colour · 89mins

A neglected and totally original comedy from co-writer/director/star Albert Brooks. He plays a film editor, and the sequences involving the cutting process are insightful and truthful, as he and the excellent Bruno Kirby go to work on a sci-fi flick with the mercilessly hamming George Kennedy as space leader Zeron. The man behind the camera for the schlock movie is played by real-life director James L Brooks, who would later offer Albert (no relation) the role of his career in *Broadcast News*. The plot's slight, but the film is enjoyable and interesting, especially for movie buffs. TS. Contains swearing. [video]

Albert Brooks *Robert Cole* • Kathryn Harrold *Mary Harvard* • Tyann Means *Waitress* • Bruno Kirby *Jay* • Jane Hallaren *Ellen* • Karen Chandler *Neighbour* • James L Brooks *David* • George Kennedy *Zeron* ■ *Dir* Albert Brooks • *Scr* Albert Brooks, Monica Johnson

Modern Times ★★★★★ U

Comedy 1936 · US · Colour · 86mins

Charles Chaplin's ridiculing of an increasingly mechanised and mechanical society is an inspired assembly line of gags, similar to *A Nous la Liberté* by the French director René Clair, who declared he had always been inspired by Chaplin so was honoured if "the master" had been inspired by him. As machines chew up our hero and spit him out, Charlie finds solace in the love of Paulette Goddard and a sunset stroll into a happy-ever-after. Naive this may be, but what else could Chaplin do? He was in the business of redemption and this was the only way out he could find in darkening days. TH [video] DVD

Charlie Chaplin [Charles Chaplin] *Factory worker* • Paulette Goddard *Gamine* • Henry Bergman *Café owner* • Stanley Sanford [Tiny Sanford] *Big Bill/Worker* • Chester Conklin *Mechanic* ■ *Dir/Scr* Charlie Chaplin [Charles Chaplin] • *Cinematographer* Rollie Totheroh, Ira Morgan

The Moderns ★★★ 15

Drama 1988 · US · Colour and BW · 121mins

Alan Rudolph's wry study of the cabal that gathered itself around Ernest Hemingway in 1920s Paris is short on drama, but stuffed with arch academic allusions. As convincingly fake as the pictures Keith Carradine is commissioned to paint, the neverland of bons mots and chic cafés is superbly sustained by the brilliance of the screenplay and Rudolph's lightness of touch, which enables his cast to shine without dazzling. With Wallace Shawn impressive as the journalist feeding off the "lost generation" and Linda Fiorentino as Carradine's ex-wife, this is both ambitious and accessible. DP. Contains nudity. [video]

Keith Carradine *Nick Hart* • Linda Fiorentino *Rachel Stone* • Geneviève Bujold *Libby Valentin* • Geraldine Chaplin *Nathalie de Ville* • Wallace Shawn *Oiseau* • John Lone *Bertram Stone* • Kevin J O'Connor *Ernest Hemingway* • Elsa Raven *Gertrude Stein* • Ali Giron *Alice B Toklas* ■ *Dir* Alan Rudolph • *Scr* Alan Rudolph, John Bradshaw

Modesty Blaise ★★ PG

Spy spoof 1966 · UK · Colour · 114mins

With its dizzy set designs and flamboyant costumes, Joseph Losey's misguided screen adaptation of Peter O'Donnell's seminal cartoon strip is a paean to the excesses of the mid-1960s. The years have not been kind, however, and the film now exists in a pop art time-bubble of its own making. In a plot that makes virtually no sense, Monica Vitti is miscast as the sexy female spy, a sort of earthbound Barberella out to thwart effete arch fiend Dirk Bogarde (in a silver wig and sunglasses). Camper than a lift full of Graham Nortons. RS

Monica Vitti *Modesty Blaise* • Dirk Bogarde *Gabriel* • Terence Stamp *Willie Garvin* • Michael Craig *Paul Hagan* • Harry Andrews *Sir Gerald Tarrant* • Rossella Falk *Mrs Fothergill* • Scilla Gabel *Melina* • Clive Revill *McWhirter/Sheik Abu Tahir* • Joe Melia *Crevier* ■ *Dir* Joseph Losey • *Scr* Evan Jones, from a story by Peter O'Donnell, Stanley Dubens, from the comic strip by Peter O'Donnell, Jim Holdaway

Mogambo ★★★ U

Romantic adventure
1953 · US · Colour · 111mins

In 1932, Clark Gable made a picture for MGM called *Red Dust*, and very steamy it was too. A story of lust set in the jungles of south-east Asia, it featured Gable as a rubber planter choosing between temptress Jean Harlow and demure Mary Astor. *Mogambo*, directed by John Ford, is the remake, transposed to Africa with Gable again, plus Ava Gardner and Grace Kelly. Gone is the steaminess of the original: this is a Technicolor adventure romp fit for the postwar era of healthy living. AT DVD

Clark Gable *Victor Marswell* • Ava Gardner *Eloise Y Kelly* • Grace Kelly *Linda Nordley* • Donald Sinden *Donald Nordley* • Philip Stainton *John Brown Pryce* • Eric Pohlmann *Leon Boltchak* • Laurence Naismith *Skipper* ■ *Dir* John Ford • *Scr* John Lee Mahin, from the play *Red Dust* by Wilson Collison

Mohabbatein ★★★ PG

Romantic musical drama
2000 · Ind · Colour · 215mins

Aditya Chopra's second feature is a titanic battle of generational wills. Veteran superstar Amitabh Bachchan confirms he's made the transition from action hero with a glaring display as the unbending head of a prestigious college who vents his wrath on music teacher Shah Rukh Khan, after he dares not only to encourage six of his amorous students to pair off, but also to make eyes at Bachchan's daughter, Aishwarya Rai. DP. In Hindi with English subtitles. DVD

Amitabh Bachchan *Narayan Shankar* • Shah Rukh Khan *Raj Aryan* • Uday Chopra *Vicky* • Shamita Shetty *Ishika* • Jugal Hansraj *Sameer* • Kim Sharma *Sanjana* • Jimmy Shergill *Karan* • Preeti Jhangiani *Kiran* • Aishwarya Rai *Megha, Narayan Shanker's daughter* ■ *Dir/Scr* Aditya Chopra

Mohawk ★★ U

Western 1956 · US · Colour · 79mins

Splendidly camp stuff, as a quintessential bevy of 1950s movie icons throw themselves at devil-may-care artist Scott Brady. Director Kurt Neumann's baroque style was way ahead of contemporary audiences' tastes – this film is really for collectors only. Despite the presence of Neville Brand in the cast, true western devotees should steer clear. TS

Scott Brady *Jonathan Adams* • Rita Gam *Onida* • Neville Brand *Rokhawah* • Lori Nelson *Cynthia Stanhope* • Allison Hayes *Greta* • John Hoyt *Butler* • Vera Vague [Barbara Jo Allen] *Aunt Agatha* ■ *Dir* Kurt Neumann • *Scr* Maurice Geraghty, Milton Krims

Mojave Moon ★★

Romantic comedy
1996 · US · Colour · 85mins

This determinedly "difficult" indie movie has a decent cast trying desperately to make sense of a wilfully wacky script and coping manfully with indifferent direction. Danny Aiello plays a lovelorn LA car salesman who drives a young woman back to her Mojave desert home. There, he's drawn into the weird world of the girl's mom and her paranoid boyfriend. The super cast also includes Angelina Jolie, in an early screen appearance. DA. Contains violence, nudity, swearing, drug abuse and sexual situations.

Danny Aiello *Al* • Angelina Jolie *Ellie* • Anne Archer *Julie* • Jack Noseworthy *Kaiser* • Alfred Molina *Sal* • Michael Biehn *Boyd* ■ *Dir* Kevin Dowling • *Scr* Leonard Glasser

Mojo ★★ 15

Period drama 1998 · UK · Colour · 92mins

Revealing the dark underside of London in the late 1950s, this brutal Soho-set drama by Jez Butterworth was a big hit at London's Royal Court theatre. But, in spite of a nervously energetic camera and diverse directorial flourishes, this adaptation remains a stubbornly theatrical experience. There's a laudable eagerness about the performances, as ambitious henchman Ian Hart gets embroiled in Harold Pinter's scheme to move in on a singing sensation at Ricky Tomlinson's seedy club. DP. Contains swearing and violence.

Ian Hart *Mickey* • Ewen Bremner *Skinny Luke* • Aidan Gillen *Baby* • Martin Gwynn Jones *Sweets* • Hans Matheson *Silver Johnny* • Andy Serkis *Sid Potts* • Ricky Tomlinson *Ezra* • Harold Pinter *Sam Ross* ■ *Dir* Jez Butterworth • *Scr* Jez Butterworth, Tom Butterworth, from the play by Jez Butterworth

The Mole People ★★

Science fiction 1956 · US · BW · 77mins

Anthropologists John Agar and Hugh Beaumont fall into a deep cave in Asia, discover a lost Sumerian city, and get captured by albino natives who have Mole Men as slaves. Armed with only flashlights to keep the sunlight-hating race at bay, they make their escape when the Mole Men stage a revolt. This nonsensical pulp is made more fun thanks to the weird rubber Mole suits, Agar and Beaumont making a hilarious hero team and a few fanciful directorial glimmers by Virgil Vogel. A minor cult classic. AJ

John Agar *Dr Roger Bentley* • Cynthia Patrick *Adad Gizelle* • Hugh Beaumont *Dr Jud Bellamin* • Alan Napier *Elinu High Priest* • Nestor Paiva *Prof Etienne Lafarge* ■ *Dir* Virgil Vogel [Virgil W Vogel] • *Scr* Laszlo Gorog

Moll Flanders ★★★ 12

Period drama 1995 · US · Colour · 117mins

Daniel Defoe's story of the hard-edged young woman with dubious virtues gets the Hollywood treatment in a classy, if sometimes yawn-inducing reworking of the 18th-century romp. Robin Wright is well cast as Moll, whose sad, eventful life is recounted to her abandoned daughter Aisling Corcoran by manservant Morgan Freeman. Far grittier than you would expect from a Tinseltown interpretation, director Pen Densham's convincing period evocation is bolstered by Wright's terrific work as the abused heroine. JC. Contains swearing, sexual situations.

Robin Wright [Robin Wright Penn] *Moll Flanders* • Morgan Freeman *Hibble* • Stockard Channing *Mrs Allworthy* • John Lynch *Fielding* • Brenda Fricker *Mrs Mazzawatti* • Geraldine James *Edna* • Aisling Corcoran *Flora* ■ *Dir* Pen Densham • *Scr* Pen Densham, from the novel by Daniel Defoe

Molly ★ 15

Drama 1999 · US · Colour · 98mins

Elisabeth Shue plays a 28-year-old autistic woman who undergoes an operation that brings her out of her shell. Unfortunately, the changed persona does little to improve the star's performance, which is so over-the-top it's embarrassing. Worse still are their attempts to punctuate the drama with various kinds of offensive humour. KB

Elisabeth Shue *Molly McKay* • Aaron Eckhart *Buck McKay* • Thomas Jane *Sam* • Jill Hennessy *Susan Brookes* • DW Moffett *Mark Cottrell* • Elizabeth Mitchell *Beverly Trehare* ■ *Dir* John Duigan • *Scr* Dick Christie

Molly and Lawless John ★★★

Western 1972 · US · Colour · 97mins

There's a ingenious storyline and a distinct feminist slant to this undiscovered western, directed by TV-movie expert Gary Nelson. Vera Miles plays the unhappy, 40-something wife of staid local sheriff John Anderson who has blond and dashing young outlaw Sam Elliott in his jail. Elliott persuades Miles to organise his escape and they elope together, though it's not long before Miles begins to despise her new man. AT

Vera Miles *Molly Parker* • Sam Elliott *Johnny Lawler* • Clu Gulager *Deputy* • John Anderson *Sheriff Parker* • Cynthia Myers *Dolly* ■ *Dir* Gary Nelson • *Scr* Terry Kingsley-Smith

Molly and Me ★★★

Musical comedy 1945 · US · BW · 76mins

Gracie Fields and Monty Woolley co-star in this engaging variation on the *Pollyanna* story, in which Our Gracie and a bunch of "resting" entertainers transform Woolley's staid existence while working as his servants. Brightly directed by Lewis Seiler, the film is as interesting for its supporting cast as it is for its leads. DP

Gracie Fields *Molly* • Monty Woolley *Graham* • Roddy McDowall *Jimmy Graham* • Reginald Gardiner *Peabody* • Natalie Schafer *Kitty* • Edith Barrett *Julia* • Clifford Brooke *Pops* • Aminta Dyne *Musette* • Queenie Leonard *Lily* • Doris Lloyd *Mrs Graham* ■ *Dir* Lewis Seiler • *Scr* Leonard Praskins, Roger Burford, from the novel by Frances Marion

The Molly Maguires ★★ PG

Period drama 1970 · US · Colour · 119mins

With a cast that features Sean Connery as a rebellious coalminer, Richard Harris as a mining company *agent provocateur* and Samantha Eggar as Harris's above-the-ground love interest, it's sad that the end result proves so disappointing. All the effort here has gone into the depiction of mining conditions in 19th-century Pennsylvania, but the script seems to have been written by a mechanical digger. Every scene rams home some kind of message, and Martin Ritt directs from a soapbox. AT. Contains violence and swearing. DVD

Richard Harris *James McParlan/McKenna* • Sean Connery *Jack Kehoe* • Samantha Eggar *Mary Raines* • Frank Finlay *Captain Davies* • Anthony Zerbe *Dougherty* • Bethel Leslie *Mrs Kehoe* • Art Lund *Frazier* ■ *Dir* Martin Ritt • *Scr* Walter Bernstein, from the novel *Lament for the Molly Maguires* by H Arthur Lewis

Moloch ★★★

Historical drama
1999 · Rus/Ger/Fr · Colour · 108mins

Owing the same visual debt to the German Romantic artist, Caspar David Friedrich, as his previous outing, *Mother and Son*, Aleksandr Sokurov's Berchtesgaden dissertation on the nature of power also nods, occasionally, in the direction of the Reich's official film-maker, Leni Riefenstahl. However, instead of presenting a revealing portrait of the Führer through the eyes of his long-suffering mistress, Eva Braun, Sokurov succeeds only in presenting an illustrated digest of the table talk of Adolf Hitler. DP. In German with English subtitles.

Leonid Mosgovoi *Adolf Hitler* • Elena Rufanova *Eva Braun* • Leonid Sokol *Josef Goebbels* • Elena Spiridonova *Magda Goebbels* • Vladimir Bogdanov *Martin Bormann* ■ *Dir* Aleksandr Sokurov • *Scr* Yuri Arabov, Marina Koreneva

Mom and Dad Save the World ★ PG

Science-fiction comedy
1992 · US · Colour · 86mins

When middle-class parents Teri Garr and the wonderful Jeffrey Jones are spirited away to a far distant planet whose ruler intends making Garr his bride, Jones is forced into warrior mode to oust the tyrant and put rightful heir Eric Idle onto the throne. With its tasteless sets and rubber-suited monsters, the film's modest budget is flaunted as if it were a selling point. Yet director Greg Beeman can't disguise the lamentable script which, despite the best efforts of a likeable cast, falls flat. RS DVD

Teri Garr *Marge Nelson* • Jeffrey Jones *Dick Nelson* • Jon Lovitz *Tod Spengo* • Dwier Brown *Sirk* • Kathy Ireland *Semage* • Thalmus Rasulala *General Afir* • Wallace Shawn *Sibor* • Eric Idle *Raff* ■ *Dir* Greg Beeman • *Scr* Ed Solomon, Chris Matheson

Moment by Moment ★

Romantic comedy
1978 · US · Colour · 93mins

Jane Wagner writes and directs this embarrassing romance, a vehicle for her longtime companion and collaborator, Lily Tomlin. The latter stars as a bored Malibu housewife whose juices are stirred by John Travolta, playing a drifter with the hilarious name of Strip. Alas, audiences showed little interest in their May-December relationship. FL

Lily Tomlin *Trisha Rawlings* • John Travolta *Strip* • Andra Akers *Naomi* • Bert Kramer *Stu Rawlings* • Shelley R Bonus *Peg* • Debra Feuer *Stacie* ■ *Dir/Scr* Jane Wagner

M

Un Moment d'Egarement ★★

Comedy 1977 · Fr · Colour · 85mins

It's hard to forgive this comedy since it spawned one of the most charmless movies ever made, *Blame It on Rio*. The story hinges on two friends, Jean-Pierre Marielle – newly divorced – and Victor Lanoux, holidaying together in the South of France, each with their 17-year-old daughters in tow. When Marielle has a brief affair with Agnes Soral, the premise turns farcical, as her outraged father mistakes another man as the seducer. Glamorous locations and French panache stop the film lapsing into the crass vulgarity of the British revamp. BB. In French with English subtitles.

Jean-Pierre Marielle *Pierre* • Victor Lanoux *Jacques* • Christine Dejoux *Martine* • Agnes Soral *Françoise* ■ *Dir/Scr* Claude Berri

Moment of Danger ★★

Crime drama 1960 · UK · BW · 97mins

Meek locksmith and cuckolded husband Trevor Howard is recruited by debonair Edmund Purdom to rob a Mayfair jewellers'. After the robbery, Purdom vanishes with all the swag so Howard pursues him to Spain with Purdom's jilted girlfriend, Dorothy Dandridge. Part thriller, part romantic tangle, this is produced by Douglas Fairbanks Jr and directed by Laslo Benedek. AT

Trevor Howard *John Bain* • Dorothy Dandridge *Gianna* • Edmund Purdom *Peter Carran* • Michael Hordern *Inspector Farrell* • Paul Stassino *Juan Montoya* ■ *Dir* Laslo Benedek • *Scr* David Osborn, Donald Ogden Stewart, from the novel *The Scent of Danger* by Donald MacKenzie

A Moment of Innocence ★★★

Comedy drama
1996 · Iran/Fr/Swi · Colour · 77mins

Iranian cinema's preoccupation with the mechanics of movie-making once again comes to the fore in this teasing treatise on idealism, love, coincidence and the selectivity of memory. Recalling an incident from the days of the Shah when he stabbed a policeman, Mohsen Makhmalbaf cross-cuts between this moment of revolutionary zeal and the production of a film re-creating the event. With the actual cop, Mirhadi Tayebi, playing himself and coaching his young alter ego, the action challenges the viewer to question the motives of the participants and the relevance of distinguishing between fact and fiction. Genuinely intriguing. DP. In Farsi with English subtitles.

Mirhadi Tayebi *The policeman* • Mohsen Makhmalbaf *The director* • Ali Bakhshi *The young director* • Ammar Tafti *The young policman* ■ *Dir/Scr* Mohsen Makhmalbaf

The Moment of Truth ★★★★

Drama 1964 · It/Sp · Colour · 105mins

The infamous "sport" of bullfighting is depicted here, although it could equally be boxing or professional football that entices the poor with nothing but nerves and strength to offer in return for wealth and fame. In Francesco Rosi's superb docudrama, a poor Andalusian boy (played by then famous matador "Miguelin"), living in arid poverty, determines to confront beasts rather than live like one. Making his name in the *corrida*, he becomes a minnow among sharks as entrepreneurs and the wealthy, who respect his skill not his life, encircle him. Rosi depicts society in a harsh glare and finds it wanting, while the cameramen led by Gianni Di Venanzo, help capture the perverse glamour and cruelty. BB. An Italian language film.

"Miguelin" [Miguel "Miguelin" Mateo] *Miguel* • Pedro Basauri *Maestro Pedrucho* • Jose Gomez Sevillano *Impresario* • Linda Christian *American woman* ■ *Dir* Francesco Rosi • *Scr* Francesco Rosi, Pedro Portabella, Ricardo Muñoz Suay, Pedro Beltran, Raffaele La Capria, from a story by Francesco Rosi

Moment to Moment ★★

Romantic thriller
1966 · US · Colour · 107mins

A psychiatrist's wife, left alone on the French Riviera during her husband's frequent absences, becomes involved with a young officer who is later shot and left for dead. The result is a ludicrous brew of adultery and attempted murder, directed by Mervyn LeRoy, dressed by Yves Saint-Laurent and photographed by Harry Stradling. Alas, the overlay of gloss and glamour fails to disguise the dreadful script or the inert performances. RK

Jean Seberg *Kay Stanton* • Honor Blackman *Daphne Fields* • Sean Garrison *Mark Dominic* • Arthur Hill *Neil Stanton* • Peter Robbins *Timmy Stanton* • Grégoire Aslan *Edward DeFargo* • Donald Woods *Mr Singer* • Walter Reed *Hendricks* ■ *Dir* Mervyn LeRoy • *Scr* John Lee Mahin, Alec Coppel, from the short story *Laughs With a Stranger* by Alec Coppel

Mommie Dearest ★★★★ 15

Biographical drama
1981 · US · Colour · 122mins

This riveting melodrama about Joan Crawford is based on her daughter Christina's vengeful memoir. Faye Dunaway is astonishing as Crawford, risen from rags to bitches, who still scrubs the floors, runs rings around studio bosses and creates a living hell for her daughter (brilliantly played by young Mara Hobel and, later, by Diana Scarwid). This is lavish and pretty accurate as far as Hollywood lore is concerned, but Dunaway makes Norma Desmond look like Doris Day. AT. Contains violence, swearing. DVD

Faye Dunaway *Joan Crawford* • Diana Scarwid *Christina Crawford* • Steve Forrest *Greg Savitt* • Howard Da Silva *Louis B Mayer* • Mara Hobel *Christina as a child* • Rutanya Alda *Carol Ann* • Harry Goz *Al Steele* ■ *Dir* Frank Perry • *Scr* Frank Yablans, Frank Perry, Tracy Hotchner, Robert Getchell, from the memoirs by Christina Crawford

The Mommy Market ★★ PG

Fantasy comedy 1994 · US · Colour · 79mins

Sissy Spacek's virtuosity isn't enough to save this lame satire on children's expectations of their parents, adapted by Tia Brelis from her mother Nancy's 1966 novel. Anna Chlumsky plays one of a trio of siblings whose dissatisfaction with their mother prompts them to trade her in at a magical market. But each alternative (played with mischievous insight by Spacek) falls short of their exacting standards. It should have been fun, but it will barely raise a smile. DP

Sissy Spacek *Mrs Martin/Maman/Mom/Natasha* • Anna Chlumsky *Elizabeth* • Aaron Michael Metchik *Jeremy* • Asher Metchik *Harry* • Maureen Stapleton *Mrs Cavour* ■ *Dir* Tia Brelis • *Scr* Tia Brelis, from the novel *The Mommy Market* by Nancy Brelis

Mon Homme ★★★ 18

Drama 1996 · Fr · Colour · 95mins

A typically outrageous and undisciplined effort from Bertrand Blier, with Anouk Grinberg as the proverbial tart with a heart who decides to rescue the homeless man (Gérard Lanvin) living in the garbage dump of her apartment block. After she cooks for him and sleeps with him, he becomes her pimp. Buried beneath the sexual frolics, however, there lies a chaste tale of redemption. AT. In French with English subtitles.

Anouk Grinberg *Marie* • Gérard Lanvin *Jeannot* • Valéria Bruni-Tedeschi *Sanguine* • Olivier Martinez *Jean-François* • Sabine Azéma *Bérangère* • Mathieu Kassovitz *Client* • Jean-Pierre Léaud *Claude* ■ *Dir/Scr* Bertrand Blier

Mon Oncle ★★★★★ U

Satirical comedy 1958 · Fr · Colour · 103mins

Jacques Tati revived Monsieur Hulot for this typically gentle yet incisive satire on the mechanised madness of the modern world. Although shot in widescreen for the maximum democracy of viewing and patterned with plenty of symbolic colour, Hulot's baffled encounter with his sister's soulless, state-of-the-art residence depends as much on the meticulously constructed soundtrack as the visual humour for its comic impact. Belying hours of puntilious preparation, each gag seems positively spontaneous as Tati puts progress in its place by extolling the virtues of human contact. Two versions were actually shot simultaneously, although the English one is some ten minutes shorter than the French. DP. In French with English subtitles. DVD

Jacques Tati *Monsieur Hulot* • Jean-Pierre Zola *Monsieur Arpel* • Adrienne Servantie *Madame Arpel* • Alain Bécourt *Gérard* • Lucien Frégis *Monsieur Pichard* • Betty Schneider *Betty* • Yvonne Arnaud *Georgette, the maid* • Dominique Marie *Neighbour* ■ *Dir* Jacques Tati • *Scr* Jacques Tati, Jacques Lagrange, Jean L'Hote

Mon Oncle d'Amérique ★

Drama 1980 · Fr · Colour · 123mins

We all know that life is a rat race. To underline the point, though, Alain Resnais uses the staggeringly original device of filming rats scurrying about! He also indulges animal behaviourist Dr Henri Laborit as he laboriously passes comment on the three main characters: a suicidal middle manager (Gérard Depardieu), an actress (Nicole Garcia) and a TV executive (Roger Pierre). A complete waste of time. AT. A French language film.

Gérard Depardieu *Rene Ragueneau* • Nicole Garcia *Janine Garnier* • Roger Pierre *Jean Le Gall* • Marie Dubois *Therese Ragueneau* • Nelly Borgeaud *Arlette Le Gall* • Henri Laborit ■ *Dir* Alain Resnais • *Scr* Jean Gruault, from the works of Henri Laborit

Mon Père Ce Héros ★★★★ PG

Romantic comedy 1991 · Fr · Colour · 99mins

There are moments in this boisterous French comedy that will cause many politically correct brows to knit in disapproval. However, without ever atoning for its lapses, Gérard Lauzier's one-joke comedy rather creeps up on you, almost solely on account of the performance of Gérard Depardieu as the indulgent father who becomes the talk of a holiday hotel when his 14-year-old daughter tells all and sundry he is her lover. Marie Gillain bristles with coquettish charm, but the pace dips when Depardieu is off screen. Consequently, he was the obvious choice for the 1994 Hollywood remake, *My Father the Hero*. DP. In French with English subtitles.

Gérard Depardieu *André* • Marie Gillain *Véronique* • Patrick Mille *Benjamin* • Catherine Jacob *Christelle* • Charlotte De Turckheim *Irina* • Jean-François Rangasamy *Pablo* • Koomaren Chetty *Karim* ■ *Dir/Scr* Gérard Lauzier

Mona Lisa ★★★★ 18

Crime drama 1986 · UK · Colour · 99mins

A haunting, if often disturbing, London-set thriller, in which Bob Hoskins manages to convey some deeper emotion than his more usual thuggery. As the gangster's chauffeur madly in love with Cathy Tyson's detached, emotionally bruised prostitute, Hoskins brings rich pathos to a plot not overloaded with such feelings. Neil Jordan directs with great flair and insight, and the photography lingers long in the mind. Summing up a certain 1980s soullessness, this is still a thought-provoking gem. SH. Contains violence, swearing, sex scenes and nudity. DVD

Bob Hoskins *George* • Cathy Tyson *Simone* • Michael Caine *Mortwell* • Robbie Coltrane *Thomas* • Clarke Peters *Anderson* • Kate Hardie *Cathy* • Zoe Nathenson *Jeannie* • Sammi Davis *May* • Joe Brown (2) *Dudley* ■ *Dir* Neil Jordan • *Scr* Neil Jordan, David Leland • *Cinematographer* Roger Pratt

Mona Lisa Smile ★★★ 12

Period drama 2003 · US · Colour · 114mins

Julia Roberts stars as an unconventional teacher in an emotionally manipulative chick flick with a quasi-intellectual veneer. Kirsten Dunst, Julia Stiles and a vampy Maggie Gyllenhaal are among the students at a New England girls' college in 1953 whose lives are changed by the arrival of art history lecturer Roberts and her scandalous free-spirited ways. Though the characters are all recognisable stereotypes, they're solidly performed, while Roberts makes a sympathetic lead, despite her often anachronistic behaviour and appearance. SF DVD

Julia Roberts *Katherine Ann Watson* • Kirsten Dunst *Betty Warren* • Julia Stiles *Joan Brandwyn* • Maggie Gyllenhaal *Giselle Levy* • Dominic West *Bill Dunbar* • Juliet Stevenson *Amanda Armstrong* • Marcia Gay Harden *Nancy Abbey* • Ginnifer Goodwin *Connie Baker* • John Slattery *Paul Moore* ■ *Dir* Mike Newell • *Scr* Lawrence Konner, Mark Rosenthal

Monday Morning ★★★★ PG

Comedy drama 2002 · Fr/It · Colour · 122mins

Otar Iosseliani won the Best Director prize at Berlin for this midlife satire, which suggests that the grass is rarely greener regardless of the location of the fence. Irked by the petty restrictions and domestic vexations that blight his existence, factory worker and frustrated artist Jacques Bidou heads to Venice to look up an old pal. But Arrigo Mozzo's life is no better, despite the beauty of the city and the eccentric presence of a bogus aristocrat (played with delicious pomposity by Iosseliani himself). Comprised of small moments and wry smiles, this is observational comedy at its most congenial. DP. In French, Italian and Romanian with English subtitles. DVD

Jacques Bidou *Vincent* • Arrigo Mozzo *Carlo* • Anne Kravz-Tarnavsky *Josephine* • Narda Blanchet *Vincent's mother* • Otar Iosseliani *Enzo di Martini* ■ *Dir/Scr* Otar Iosseliani

Mondays in the Sun ★★★ 15

Drama 2002 · Sp/Fr/It · Colour · 113mins

Fernando Léon de Aranoa relies on a solid ensemble cast and some downbeat realism to explore the social and psychological pressures borne by a group of working-class men who've been deprived of the dignity of labour. The story centres on Javier Bardem's rebellious shipbuilder, who's been reduced to baby-sitting for pocket money. But Luis Tosar's gnawing envy at wife Nieve de Medina's soul-destroying job at a tuna-canning factory and José Angel Egido's pathetic attempts to cut it in a younger man's world are equally affecting. DP. In Spanish with English subtitles. Contains swearing.

Javier Bardem *Santa* • Luis Tosar *José* • José Angel Egido *Lino* • Nieve de Medina *Ana* • Enrique Villén *Reina* • Celso Bugallo *Amador* • Joaquín Climent *Rico* • Aida Folch *Nata* ■ *Dir* Fernando León de Aranoa • *Scr* Fernando León de Aranoa, Ignacio del Moral

Le Monde du Silence ★★★★

Documentary 1956 · Fr · Colour · 82mins

The first feature of Jacques-Yves Cousteau, the famous French oceanographer, diver and documentary film-maker, is an exploration of the fascinating fauna and flora of the ocean's depths. Cousteau, and his underwater cameramen, went beyond the bounds of a scientific documentary by capturing the poetry of the "silent world". Cousteau's co-director was 24-year-old Louis Malle, getting his first director's credit. His work on the film caused him ear problems for the rest of his life. RB. A French language film.

Dir Jacques-Yves Cousteau, Louis Malle • *Scr* James Dugan (commentary)

Mondo Cane ★

Documentary 1962 · It · Colour · 91mins

The British censor initially banned this "shockumentary", which looks at the weirdest, freakiest and least pleasant aspects of life in a way that defines prurience. Examples include irradiated creatures on Bikini Atoll; religious self-flagellation; restaurants which serve dogs, insects or crocodile; street kids

M

polishing the skulls of their Roman ancestors; islanders taking hideous revenge on sharks; and "stone age" Papuans making an air strip, then waiting for the plane that never comes. An unedifying experience for all. AT. An Italian language film.

Stefano Sibaldi *Narrator* ■ *Dir* Gualtiero Jacopetti, Franco Prosperi • *Scr* Gualtiero Jacopetti, Paolo Cavara, Franco Prosperi,

Mondo Trasho ★★

Satirical melodrama 1970 · US · BW · 94mins

The first widely-seen feature from John Waters, the "Pope of Trash", was made on a shoestring budget of $2,000 with no synchronised sound. An engagingly overwrought porn parody, it details a single day in the lives of hit-and-run driver Divine and her tormented victim, Mary Vivian Pearce. Foot fetishism, 1950s rock 'n' roll, visions of the Virgin Mary and a tacky homage to Tod Browning's controversial horror film *Freaks* are thrown around with typical gay abandon in this Fellini-esque lampoon. AJ

Mary Vivian Pearce *Girl* • John Leisenring *Shrimper* • Sharon Sandrock *Stepsister* • Berenica Cipcus *Stepsister/Nurse* • Divine *Hit-and-run driver* • Margie Skidmore *Madonna* • Mink Stole *Tapdancer* • David Lochary *Dr Coathanger* ■ *Dir/Scr* John Waters (2)

Mondovino ★★★★ PG

Documentary 2004 · US/Fr · Colour · 131mins

It's clear where director Jonathan Nossiter's sympathies lie in this fascinating study of how globalisation has impinged upon something as traditionally localised as wine making. He may mistrust the motives and methods of the California-based Mondavi corporation, but he allows them to reveal their own agenda (along with those of the critics who have sought to engineer a "democritisation" – pro-US monopoly – of the industry). The French producers who are holding out against what they consider cultural imperialism are essentially depicted as maverick heroes. But Nossiter's film is also even-handed enough to recognise why impoverished farmers in Latin America could succumb to the Napa Valley invaders. DP. In English, French, Italian, Portuguese and Spanish with subtitles. DVD

Dir/Scr Jonathan Nossiter

Money for Nothing ★★ 15

Black comedy based on a true story 1993 · US · Colour · 96mins

The problem with this black comedy is that it's based on actual events that are anything but amusing. Joey Coyle's decision to keep the $1.2 million he found after it fell out of a casino security van was the worst he ever made. Not only did he have to plea temporary insanity to escape jail, but he committed suicide shortly before this film was released. John Cusack has the unenviable task of playing the docker, but not even his geniality can save this frantic misfire. DP. Contains swearing. [video] DVD

John Cusack *Joey Coyle* • Debi Mazar *Monica Russo* • Michael Madsen *Detective Pat Laurenzi* • Benicio Del Toro *Dino Palladino* • Michael Rapaport *Kenny Kozlowski* • Maury Chaykin *Vincente Goldoni* • James Gandolfini *Billy Coyle* • Fionnula Flanagan *Mrs Coyle* ■ *Dir* Ramon Menendez • *Scr* Ramon Menendez, Tom Musca, Carol Sobieski

Money from Home ★★ U

Comedy 1953 · US · Colour · 100mins

Dean Martin and Jerry Lewis meet Damon Runyon in this rather weak entry in the Paramount canon, its combination of racetrack high-jinks and comic Arabs defeating even Martin and Lewis. It certainly seemed funnier and more convincing in its original 3-D format, but it was shown "flat" on release in the UK. This largely uninspired and rather juvenile romp is really just fan fodder. TS

Dean Martin *"Honey Talk" Nelson* • Jerry Lewis *Virgil Yokum* • Marjie Millar *Phyllis Leigh* • Pat Crowley *Autumn Claypool* • Richard Haydn *Bertie Searles* • Robert Strauss *Seldom Seen Kid* ■ *Dir* George Marshall • *Scr* Hal Kanter, James Allardice, from a story by Damon Runyon

Money Mania ★ U

Comedy 1987 · US · Colour · 90mins

This truly abysmal picture tried to cash in on the get-rich-quick ethos by offering its audience a prize of one million dollars if anyone could find the money while the characters rushed around losing it. A sort of board game turned into a movie, it was titled *Million Dollar Mystery* on its brief American release. AT [video]

Royce D Applegate *Tugger* • Pam Matteson *Dotty* • Rich Hall *Slaughter* • Eddie Deezen *Rollie* • Wendy Sherman *Lollie* • Rick Overton *Stuart Briggs* • Mona Lyden *Barbara Briggs* • Tom Bosley *Sidney Preston* ■ *Dir* Richard Fleischer • *Scr* Tim Metcalfe, Miguel Tejada-Flores, Rudy DeLuca

Money Movers ★★★

Thriller 1978 · Aus · Colour · 94mins

A fast, furious and tough Australian heist movie, which writer/director Bruce Beresford has paced with all the agility of a kangaroo stampede. Apart from Bryan Brown, the cast is largely unknown, but the theme of corruption among police and crooks is one that keeps the cynicism as well as the adrenalin on the boil. TH

Terence Donovan *Eric Jackson* • Ed Devereaux *Dick Martin* • Bryan Brown *Brian Jackson* • Tony Bonner *Leo Bassett* • Lucky Grills *Robert Conway* ■ *Dir* Bruce Beresford • *Scr* Bruce Beresford, from the novel by Devon Minchin

The Money Pit ★★★ 15

Comedy 1985 · US · Colour · 87mins

There are belly laughs aplenty in this unofficial remake of *Mr Blandings Builds His Dream House*, but director Richard Benjamin eventually runs out of inspiration. In this home renovation comedy, Tom Hanks does enough to remind us of what we've been missing since he made his mark in serious drama, while Shelley Long's perfect timing leaves you wondering why she has never quite made the transition from sitcom to cinema. DP. Contains swearing. [video] DVD

Tom Hanks *Walter Fielding* • Shelley Long *Anna Crowley* • Alexander Godunov *Max Beissart* • Maureen Stapleton *Estelle* • Joe Mantegna *Art Shirk* • Philip Bosco *Curly* • Josh Mostel *Jack Schnittman* ■ *Dir* Richard Benjamin • *Scr* David Giler

Money Talks ★★ 18

Action comedy 1997 · US · Colour · 91mins

This mediocre action comedy sees complete opposites Chris Tucker and Charlie Sheen forced to rely on each other when the former, a small-time crook, crosses a gang of jewel thieves. Sheen is a TV reporter who sees the unfolding story as a way to save his ailing career. Endless explosions, tedious car chases and brainless shoot-outs punctuate a drearily crass plot whose appeal wholly depends on one's reaction to helium-voiced comedian Tucker. AJ. Contains swearing and violence. [video] DVD

Chris Tucker *Franklin Hatchett* • Charlie Sheen *James Russell* • Heather Locklear *Grace Cipriani* • Paul Sorvino *Guy Cipriani* • Veronica Cartwright *Connie Cipriani* • David Warner *Barclay* • Paul Gleason *Detective Bobby Pickett* ■ *Dir* Brett Ratner • *Scr* Joel Cohen, Alec Sokolow

Money Train ★★ 18

Comedy thriller 1995 · US · Colour · 105mins

Die Hard meets *Speed*, but with the brakes on, as transport cop Wesley Snipes tries to stop his flaky foster brother Woody Harrelson robbing the New York subway transit system. Lightning doesn't strike twice for the *White Men Can't Jump* dynamic duo, and director Joseph Ruben's recycling of exhausted gags is lacklustre in the extreme. On the plus side, Jennifer Lopez is dynamite as the Hispanic rookie cop. AJ. Contains swearing, violence and sex scenes. [video] DVD

Wesley Snipes *John* • Woody Harrelson *Charlie* • Robert Blake *Patterson* • Jennifer Lopez *Grace Santiago* • Chris Cooper *Torch* ■ *Dir* Joseph Ruben • *Scr* Doug Richardson, David Loughery, from a story by Doug Richardson

The Money Trap ★★

Crime drama 1966 · US · BW · 92mins

Glenn Ford plays a cop, married to pretty rich girl Elke Sommer and stretched financially as a result. When the opportunity arises, Ford crosses over to the wrong side of the law, with predictable results. What wouldn't pass muster as a 10-minute subplot on *Kojak* is here turned into a dusty showcase for a distinctly secondhand Ford. Adding to the aura of faded glamour is Rita Hayworth, playing a drug dealer's widow and a former flame of Ford's. AT

Glenn Ford *Joe Baron* • Elke Sommer *Lisa Baron* • Rita Hayworth *Rosalie Kenny* • Joseph Cotten *Dr Horace Van Tilden* • Ricardo Montalban *Pete Delanos* • Tom Reese *Matthews* • James Mitchum *Detective Wolski* ■ *Dir* Burt Kennedy • *Scr* Walter Bernstein, from the novel by Lionel White

Money, Women and Guns ★★ U

Western 1958 · US · Colour · 80mins

A negligible western programme filler from Universal, given distinction by the casting of Kim Hunter, who'd won a best supporting actress Oscar for *A Streetcar Named Desire*, opposite former stuntman Jock Mahoney. The script concerning the investigation into the murder of an old prospector is clever but feebly executed, although the photography is impressive. TS

Jock Mahoney *Hogan* • Kim Hunter *Mary Kingman* • Tim Hovey *Davey Kingman* • Gene Evans *Sheriff Crowley* • Tom Drake *Jess Ryerson* • Lon Chaney Jr *Art Birdwell* ■ *Dir* Richard Bartlett • *Scr* Montgomery Pittman • *Cinematographer* Philip Lathrop

The Mongols ★★

Historical drama 1961 · Fr/It · Colour · 105mins

Jack Palance stars as Ogotai, son of Genghis Khan, who invades Europe in AD 1240 and gets as far as Cracow, Poland, where the local bigwig, Franco Silva, tries to negotiate peace. Also in the invasion party is the absurdly statuesque Anita Ekberg. Palance goes from one outlandish act of cruelty to the next, grinning madly. Such sadism, though, doesn't quite prepare us for the masochism of the climax. Made in Italy by three directors, it has the usual hilarious dubbing. AT. Italian dialogue dubbed into English.

Jack Palance *Ogotai* • Anita Ekberg *Huluna* • Antonella Lualdi *Amina* • Franco Silva *Stephen* • Gianni Garko *Henry* • Roldano Lupi *Genghis Khan* ■ *Dir* Andre De Toth, Leopoldo Savona • *Scr* Ugo Guerra, Luciano Martino, Ottavio Alessi, Alessandro Ferrau

The Monk ★★★

Drama 1972 · Fr/W Ger/It · Colour · 92mins

Luis Buñuel and Jean-Claude Carrière attempted to film Matthew Lewis's famous gothic novel in the mid-1960s, but the project was shelved for lack of funds. Their screenplay was used in this multinational production, with Buñuel's friend, Greek surrealist Ado Kyrou, in the director's chair. Franco Nero stars as the intellectual cleric whose attempts to resist the allure of novice Nathalie Delon draw him into the world of magic and an alliance with Satan. All Buñuel's preoccupations with religious hypocrisy and repressed sexuality are present and correct, but Kyrou's direction lacks the master's touch. DP. A French language film.

Franco Nero *Ambrosio* • Nathalie Delon *Mathilde* • Nicol Williamson *Duke of Talamur* • Nadja Tiller *Elvira* • Elisabeth Wiener *Nun* • Eliana De Santis *Antonia* ■ *Dir* Ado Kyrou • *Scr* Luis Buñuel, Jean-Claude Carrière, from the novel by Matthew Lewis

The Monk ★★★ 15

Gothic drama 1990 · UK/Sp · Colour · 101mins

Paul McGann stars as the brother in brown whose quiet life begins to unravel spectacularly when a young woman with designs on him disguises herself and slips into his monastery. The source novel by Matthew Lewis caused a sensation on its publication at the end of the 18th century, but here Paco Lara eschews the gothic delights of the book in favour of a more ironic approach, shooting on stylised sets that seem to parody their Hammer counterparts from the 1960s. Later released on video in the UK as *Seduction of a Priest*. RT [video]

Paul McGann *Father Lorenzo* • Sophie Ward *Juan/Matilda* • Isla Blair *Mother Agueda* • Freda Dowie *Sister Ursula* • Aitana Sanchez-Gijon *Sister Ines* ■ *Dir* Paco Lara • *Scr* Paco Lara, from the novel by Matthew Lewis

M

Monk Dawson ★★ 18

Religious drama 1997 · UK · Colour · 107mins

This is a mildly entertaining tale of a monk who rapidly falls into bad habits when he quits cloistered monastery life and re-enters the real world. John Michie makes an engaging hero, and there's strong support from Martin Kemp. The film's "real" world never convinces, however, and the tone is wildly inconsistent. It's as if debut director Tom Waller wasn't really sure what sort of movie he wanted to make. DA. Contains some swearing and sex scenes. [video] DVD

John Michie *Eddie Dawson* • Ben Taylor *Bobby Winterman* • Paula Hamilton *Jenny Stanten* • Martin Kemp *David Allenby* • Rupert Vansittart *Father Timothy* • Frances Tomelty *Mrs Carter* ■ *Dir* Tom Waller • *Scr* James Magrane, from a novel by Piers Paul Read

Monkey Business ★★★★ U

Comedy 1931 · US · BW · 74mins

This is the one in which Groucho Marx dances the tango (with Thelma Todd) and the little-seen Zeppo gets tough with a gangster. One of the funniest early Marx Brothers comedies, it was the first to be written for the screen (by SJ Perelman among others) instead of being adapted from their stage routines. As stowaways on an ocean liner, the brothers have to keep on the move from cabin to cabin to avoid being clapped in irons. Harpo works in a Punch and Judy show, while Chico tickles the ivories – gentle competition for Groucho's acerbic one-liners. TH [video] DVD

Groucho Marx *Groucho* • Harpo Marx *Harpo* • Chico Marx *Chicago* • Zeppo Marx *Zeppo* • Thelma Todd *Lucille* • Tom Kennedy *Gibson* • Ruth Hall *Mary Helton* • Rockliffe Fellowes *Joe Helton* ■ *Dir* Norman Z McLeod • *Scr* Arthur Sheekman, from a story by SJ Perelman, WB Johnstone, Roland Pertwee

Monkey Business ★★★★★ U

Screwball comedy 1952 · US · BW · 92mins

One of the funniest, smartest and most under-rated Hollywood comedies, this has never secured the reputation it deserves, considering its pedigree. It was made by Howard Hawks, arguably Hollywood's greatest studio director, who was also responsible for the scatty *Bringing Up Baby* and dynamic *His Girl Friday*. Hawks is reunited here with his star from those films, Cary Grant, who gives a sublime performance as a man reduced to juvenility for arcane plot reasons too complex to divulge. Ginger Rogers is a great foil, but it's Marilyn Monroe who steals the movie. Hawks jazzes up the story with witty optical effects, and, all in all, this one is a humdinger. TS DVD

Cary Grant *Professor Barnaby Fulton* • Ginger Rogers *Edwina Fulton* • Charles Coburn *Mr Oliver Oxley* • Marilyn Monroe *Lois Laurel* • Hugh Marlowe *Harvey Entwhistle* • Henri Letondal *Dr Siegfried Kitzel* ■ *Dir* Howard Hawks • *Scr* Ben Hecht, Charles Lederer, IAL Diamond, from a story by Harry Segall

Monkey Grip ★★ 18

Drama 1983 · Aus · Colour · 101mins

Based on a prize-winning novel and highly praised by local critics, *Monkey Grip* takes a look at life on the margins in Melbourne. Noni Hazlehurst stars as a divorcee with a ten-year-old daughter who leaves her regular boyfriend for a struggling actor, initially unaware that's he's a junkie. The drug and rock scene has a certain authenticity, but the project seems dated and contrived. AT

Noni Hazlehurst *Nora* • Colin Friels *Javo* • Alice Garner *Gracie* • Harold Hopkins *Willie* • Candy Raymond *Lillian* • Michael Caton *Clive* ■ *Dir* Ken Cameron • *Scr* Ken Cameron, Helen Garner, from the novel by Helen Garner

A Monkey in Winter ★★★

Comedy drama 1962 · Fr · BW · 104mins

Having vowed to remain teetotal if he survives the war, Jean Gabin's innkeeper is tempted off the straight and narrow by Jean-Paul Belmondo, a stranger who needs a drop of courage before visiting his daughter at the local school. Henri Verneuil's attention is fixed on these cinematic icons, but he also recognises the importance of character to establishing the rural Norman atmosphere and so Gabin's wife, Suzanne Flon, the eccentric Noël Roquevert and the chauffeur Charles Bouillaud are all excellent. DP. In French with English subtitles.

Jean Gabin *Albert Quentin* • Jean-Paul Belmondo *Gabriel Fouquet* • Suzanne Flon *Suzanne Quentin* • Noël Roquevert *Landru* • Paul Frankeur *Esnault* • Gabrielle Dorziat *Victoria* • Charles Bouillaud *Chauffeur* ■ *Dir* Henri Verneuil • *Scr* François Boyer, Michel Audiard, from the novel *Un Singe en Hiver* by Antoine Blondin

Monkey Shines ★★★★ 18

Horror 1988 · US · Colour · 108mins

This provocative shocker from *Night of the Living Dead* director George A Romero contains some of his finest and most disturbing visions. Jason Beghe is the wheelchair-bound student who gradually realises the genetically brain-altered monkey trained to assist him is acting out his darkest desires and revenge impulses. Intense yet surprisingly tender, Romero's confident chiller is an intelligent nail-biter that takes a highly unusual look at the warped laws of the jungle one man must combat to survive. AJ DVD

Jason Beghe *Allan Mann* • John Pankow *Geoffrey Fisher* • Kate McNeil *Melanie Parker* • Joyce Van Patten *Dorothy Mann* • Christine Forrest *Maryanne Hodges* • Stephen Root *Dean Burbage* • Stanley Tucci *Dr John Wiseman* • Janine Turner *Linda Aikman* ■ *Dir* George A Romero • *Scr* George A Romero, from the novel by Michael Stewart

Monkey Trouble ★★★ U

Action comedy 1994 · US · Colour · 92mins

A cute family film from director Franco Amurri, this stars accomplished child actress Thora Birch *AmericanBeauty*) as the young girl who finds and adopts a capuchin monkey, unaware the creature is actually a trained jewel thief belonging to petty criminal Harvey Keitel. Quite what the hard-as-nails star of *Reservoir Dogs* and *Bad Lieutenant* is doing in this comedy adventure is anyone's guess, but his performance will delight adults as much as the monkey business will enchant young children. JB DVD

Harvey Keitel *Azro* • Mimi Rogers *Amy* • Thora Birch *Eva* • Christopher McDonald *Tom* • Adrian Johnson *Jack* ■ *Dir* Franco Amurri • *Scr* Franco Amurri, Stu Krieger

Monkeybone ★★★ 12

Part-animated fantasy comedy
2000 · US · Colour · 88mins

Quirky comedy and gallows humour mix uncomfortably in this strange little film from director Henry Selick. Brendan Fraser stars as a cartoonist who, following a freak accident, ends up comatose and trapped in a nightmare populated by weird creatures – including his cuddly but slightly racy creation, Monkeybone. Some of the humour is very juvenile and even Fraser's comic talents can't stop the film from sliding into complete silliness. However, the mix of animation and live action is strikingly done. JB. Contains violence. DVD

Brendan Fraser *Stu Miley* • Bridget Fonda *Julie McElroy* • Chris Kattan *Stu, organ donor* • Dave Foley *Herb* • Giancarlo Esposito *Hypnos* • Lisa Zane *Medusa* • John Turturro *Monkeybone* • Whoopi Goldberg *Death* ■ *Dir* Henry Selick • *Scr* Sam Hamm, from the graphic novel *Dark Town* by Kaja Blackley

Monkeys, Go Home! ★★ U

Comedy 1966 · US · Colour · 86mins

Maurice Chevalier bade movies farewell with this Disney offering that will have animal activists reaching for their placards. The sight of four chimps being trained to harvest olives might have delighted youngsters in the mid-1960s, but it's doubtful whether it will have quite the same quaint impact today. The studio spared no expense to re-create Provence in its backyard, even planting its own olive grove. But the story of Dean Jones's contretemps with his disgruntled French neighbours is less than gripping. DP

Maurice Chevalier *Father Sylvain* • Dean Jones *Hank Dussard* • Yvette Mimieux *Maria Riserau* • Bernard Woringer *Marcel Cartucci* • Clément Harari *Emile Paraulis* ■ *Dir* Andrew V McLaglen • *Scr* Maurice Tombragel, from the short story *The Monkeys* by GK Wilkinson

The Monkey's Mask ★★★ 18

Erotic thriller
2000 · Aus/Fr/Jpn/It · Colour · 89mins

This Australian thriller has a plot that suggests yet another steamy entry in the late-night TV schedules – yet fortunately Samantha Lang's film is a lot more interesting than that. In classic *noir* style, a private investigator is hired by a Sydney family to find their student daughter and is soon drawn into a liaison with the prime suspect in the girl's murder. The twist here is that the detective (played by Susie Porter) is a gay woman, instantly attracted to Kelly McGillis, a married poetry lecturer with a penchant for cigarettes and illicit sex. This is a stylish movie that relies more on atmosphere than narrative coherence. JF DVD

Susie Porter *Jill Fitzpatrick* • Kelly McGillis *Diana* • Marton Csokas *Nick* • Abbie Cornish *Mickey* • Jean-Pierre Mignon *Tony Brach* • Caroline Gillmer *Barbara Brach* ■ *Dir* Samantha Lang • *Scr* Anne Kennedy, from the verse novel by Dorother Porter

A Monkey's Tale ★ U

Animated adventure
1999 · Fr/UK/Ger/Hun · Colour · 75mins

This European attempt to board the Disney bandwagon boasts a hackneyed plot, a clutch of dreadful songs and some ghastly animation. A tree-dwelling ape takes up residence with his clothes-wearing, "civilised" brethren, though it's not long before he becomes embroiled in a plot to usurp the monkey throne. NS DVD

Matt Hill *Kom* • John Hurt *Chancellor Sebastian* • Michael York *The King* • Sally Ann Marsh *Gina* • Rik Mayall *Gerard* • Michael Gambon *Master Martin* • Shirley Anne Field *Governess* • French Tickner *Korkonak* ■ *Dir* Jean-François Laguionie • *Scr* Norman Hudis, Jean-François Laguionie

The Monkey's Uncle ★★ U

Comedy 1965 · US · Colour · 86mins

A chimpanzee called Stanley is the real star of this droopy Disney sequel to *The Misadventures of Merlin Jones*, in which young inventor Tommy Kirk helps two kids pass a test and constructs a bike-powered flying machine. The chimp gets the best of it, spending most of the movie in the arms Annette Funicello. The latter dropped her surname on the billing, but it didn't help her acting much. TH

Tommy Kirk *Merlin Jones* • Annette [Annette Funicello] *Jennifer* • Leon Ames *Judge Holmsby* • Frank Faylen *Mr Dearborne* • Arthur O'Connell *Darius Green III* • Leon Tyler *Leon* • Norman Grabowski *Norman* ■ *Dir* Robert Stevenson • *Scr* Tom August [Alfred Lewis Levitt], Helen August [Helen Levitt]

The Monolith Monsters ★★★

Science fiction 1957 · US · Colour · 77mins

Meteor fragments land on Earth, absorb moisture and grow to epic proportions. After a rainstorm, they start covering the world like living skyscrapers. An effective minor entry from sci-fi's golden era, based on a story by 1950s icon Jack Arnold (*The Incredible Shrinking Man, Creature from the Black Lagoon*) and set in his favourite small-town desert locale. AJ

Grant Williams *Dave Miller* • Lola Albright *Cathy Barrett* • Les Tremayne *Martin Cochrane* • Trevor Bardette *Arthur Flanders* • Phil Harvey *Ben Gilbert* • William Flaherty *Police Chief Dan Corey* ■ *Dir* John Sherwood • *Scr* Norman Jolley, Robert M Fresco, from a story by Jack Arnold, Robert M Fresco

Monrak Transistor ★★★★ 15

Musical comedy drama
2001 · Thai · Colour · 120mins

This adaptation of Wat Wanlayangkoon's bestseller is a charming blend of misadventure and star-crossed love that delights in its kitsch without lapsing into the high camp that undermined *Tears of the Black Tiger*. As the wannabe singer with a genius for ruinous accidents, Suppakorn Kitsuwan is akin to a Thai Norman Wisdom, as he combines pathos and pugnacity in the face of a club owner's unwanted advances and a plantation foreman's brutality. However, director Pen-ek Ratanaruang might have placed more emphasis on Kitsuwan's abandoned, but unswervingly loyal wife, played by Siriyakorn Pukkavesa. DP. In Thai with English subtitles.

Suppakorn Kitsuwan *Pan* • Siriyakorn Pukkavesa *Sadaw* • Black Pomtong *Yod* • Somlek Sakdikul *Suwat* ■ *Dir* Pen-ek Ratanaruang • *Scr* Pen-ek Ratanaruang, from the novel by Wat Wanlayangkoon

Monsieur Beaucaire ★★★

Comedy 1946 · US · BW · 93mins

Made at the peak of Bob Hope's popularity, this remake of a Rudolph Valentino silent (based on a novel by Booth Tarkington) is played strictly for laughs as Hope, a barber at the court of Louis XV, is forced to masquerade as a great lover and swordsman. Joan Caulfield makes a colourless leading lady, but those scene-stealing stalwarts Joseph Schildkraut and Constance Collier add to the fun. TV

Bob Hope *Mons Beaucaire* • Joan Caulfield *Mimi* • Patric Knowles *Duc de Chandre* • Marjorie Reynolds *Princess Maria of Spain* • Cecil Kellaway *Count D'Armand* • Joseph Schildkraut *Don Francisco* • Reginald Owen *King Louis XV of France* • Constance Collier *The Queen* ■ *Dir* George Marshall • *Scr* Melvin Frank, Norman Panama, from the novel by Booth Tarkington

Monsieur Hire ★★★★★ 15

Thriller 1989 · Fr · Colour · 75mins

Previously filmed by Julien Duvivier as *Panique*, Georges Simenon's chilling tale of murder and obsession is turned into a tender and compelling love story by Patrice Leconte. The director's insight, restraint and humanity is reinforced by Michael Nyman's achingly beautiful score and echoed in the superb performances. Never has the pain of loneliness been more truthfully depicted on screen than by Michel Blanc as the timid little man who willingly sacrifices all to assist his stunning neighbour, Sandrine Bonnaire. DP. In French with English subtitles.

Michel Blanc *Monsieur Hire* • Sandrine Bonnaire *Alice* • Luc Thuillier *Emile* • André Wilms *Inspector* ■ *Dir* Patrice Leconte • *Scr* Patrice Leconte, Patrick Dewolf, from the novel *Les Fiançailles de M Hire* by Georges Simenon

Monsieur Hulot's Holiday ★★★★★ U

Satirical comedy 1953 · Fr · BW · 83mins

Inspired by the sophisticated silent clowning of Max Linder and Buster Keaton, Jacques Tati's masterpiece is a sublime blend of satire, slapstick and character comedy that was itself a key influence on the *nouvelle vague*. With the genial Hulot invariably at its centre, much of the hilarious seaside action was filmed in long shot – not only to allow the gags to develop in their own time and space, but also to enable audiences to discover for themselves Tati's intuitive use of the film frame, his acute understanding of human behaviour, and his gently mocking appreciation of the absurdities of life. DP. In French with English subtitles. DVD

Jacques Tati *Monsieur Hulot* • Nathalie Pascaud *Martine* • Michèle Rolla *Aunt* • Raymond Carl *Waiter* • Lucien Frégis *Hotel proprietor* • Valentine Camax *Englishwoman* ■ *Dir* Jacques Tati • *Scr* Jacques Tati, Henri Marquet, Pierre Aubert, Jacques Lagrange

Monsieur Ibrahim and the Flowers of the Koran ★★★

Drama 2003 · Fr · Colour · 94mins

As a Turkish shopkeeper with a wise word for every occasion, Omar Sharif gives his most accomplished performance in years in this genial, if ultimately fanciful meeting of clashing cultures. Director François Dupeyron unshowily captures the sights and sounds of Paris's Rue Bleue in the 1960s and ably establishes the strained relationship between teenager Pierre Boulanger and his inconsolable single father, Gilbert Melki. But the closer the Jewish boy and the kindly Muslim grow. DP. In French and Turkish with English subtitles.

Omar Sharif *Monsieur Ibrahim* • Pierre Boulanger *Momo* • Gilbert Melki *Momo's father* • Isabelle Renauld *Momo's mother* • Lola Naynmark *Myriam* • Anne Suarez *Sylvie* • Mata Gavin *Fatou* • Céline Samie *Eva* • Isabelle Adjani *"La Star"* ■ *Dir* François Dupeyron • *Scr* François Dupeyron, Eric-Emmanuel Schmitt, from the play *Monsieur Ibrahim et les Fleurs du Coran* by Eric-Emmanuel Schmitt

Monsieur N ★★★★ [12]

Historical mystery thriller
2003 · Fr/UK/S Afr · Colour · 123mins

Concentrating on the latter days of Napoleon – but far less fancifully than in Alan Taylor's *The Emperor's New Clothes* – Antoine de Caunes's historical conspiracy thriller may not be entirely credible, but remains utterly intriguing. Philippe Torreton captures Bonaparte's complexities with a finesse that is slightly lacking in Richard E Grant's British governor. But the aristocratic ensemble trapped on the island of St Helena, from motives of selflessness and self-interest, also excels and the period look and feel is impeccable. DP. In English and French with subtitles. Contains nudity.

Philippe Torreton *Napoleon* • Richard E Grant *Sir Hudson Lowe* • Jay Rodan *Basil Heathcote* • Elsa Zylberstein *Albine de Montholon* • Roschdy Zem *Marshal Bertrand* • Bruno Putzulu *Cipriani* • Stéphane Freiss *General Montholon* • Frédéric Pierrot *General Gourgaud* ■ *Dir* Antoine de Caunes • *Scr* René Manzor, from an idea by Pierre Kubel

Monsieur Verdoux ★★★★ [PG]

Black comedy 1947 · US · BW · 123mins

One of the best of the latter-day sound movies by Charles Chaplin, this is a chilling black comedy in which a bank clerk (watch him riffling through those bank-notes!) turns to killing wealthy women. Sentiment sneaks in with the appearance of the waifish Marilyn Nash, but it's soon dispelled by the vulgarity of Martha Raye as an intended victim. There's a fastidious cruelty about it all, reflecting Chaplin's deep-seated contempt for the middle-class, and the final speech allies the bank clerk's Bluebeard tendencies with the activities of the major political powers. Adapted from an idea by Orson Welles, this is an astringent treat. TH [video] DVD

Charles Chaplin *Henri Verdoux/Varney/Bonheur/Floray/Narrator* • Mady Correll *Mona Verdoux* • Allison Roddan *Peter Verdoux* • Robert Lewis (1) *Maurice Bottello* • Martha Raye *Annabella* ■ *Dir* Charles Chaplin • *Scr* Charles Chaplin, from an idea by Orson Welles • *Cinematographer* Rollie Rotheroh

Monsieur Vincent ★★★★

Biographical religious drama
1947 · Fr · BW · 118mins

The winner of only the second Oscar awarded to the best foreign film, this inspirational biopic also enabled Pierre Fresnay to land the best actor prize at the Venice Film Festival for his self-abasing performance as Vincent de Paul, the saintly priest who used his influence with the aristocracy to help relieve poverty in 17th-century France. Considering it was made with the backing of the Catholic Church, it's anything but a hagiography. Indeed, director Maurice Cloche is as keen to expose the disinterest of Cardinal Richelieu's regime as to extol the cleric's compassion for the poor. DP. In French with English subtitles.

Pierre Fresnay *Saint Vincent de Paul* • Lise Delamare *Countess de Gondi* • Aimé Clariond *Cardinal de Richelieu* • Gabrielle Dorziat *Mme Groussault* • Jean Debucourt *Count de Philippe de Gondi* • Germaine Dermoz *Queen Anne of Austria* • Pierre Dux *Chancellor Seguier* ■ *Dir* Maurice Cloche • *Scr* Jean Anouilh, Maurice Cloche, Jean Bernard Luc

Monsignor ★★★ [15]

Drama 1982 · US · Colour · 116mins

Christopher Reeve stars as an ambitious young priest who greases his way up the Vatican's slippery pole and faces various temptations along the way, including lusty nuns and Mafia gangsters. The film rests on a knife edge between schlock and solemnity – when *The Exorcist*'s Jason Miller pops up, you start wondering when the green vomit will start flying. AT [video]

Christopher Reeve *Flaherty* • Geneviève Bujold *Clara* • Fernando Rey *Santoni* • Jason Miller *Appolini* • Joe Cortese *Varese* • Adolfo Celi *Vinci* • Leonardo Cimino *Pope* ■ *Dir* Frank Perry • *Scr* Abraham Polonsky, Wendell Mayes, from the novel by Jack Alain Leger

Monsoon Wedding ★★★★ [15]

Comedy drama
2001 · US/It/Ger/Fr · Colour · 109mins

This was a surprise winner of the Golden Lion at Venice, but, while the emphasis here is on fun – as Punjabi Vasundhara Das prepares for her nuptials with US-based engineer Parvin Dabas – there's still social comment to add backbone to the comedy. The various vignettes skirt over the family saga, pausing only to chart wedding planner Vijay Raaz's growing infatuation with maid Tilotama Shome. Celebrating the wisps of tradition that hold Indian society together while also exposing its less salubrious facets, Mira Nair draws vigorous performances from an impeccable ensemble cast and bathes the action in an irresistible Holly/Bollywood glow. DP. English, Hindi and Punjabi with English subtitles. Contains swearing. [video] DVD

Naseeruddin Shah *Lalit Verma* • Lillete Dubey *Pimma Verma* • Shefali Shetty *Ria Verma* • Vijay Raaz *PK Dubey* • Tilotama Shome *Alice* • Vasundhara Das *Aditi Verma* • Kulbhushan Kharbanda *CL Chadha* • Parvin Dabas *Hemant Rai* ■ *Dir* Mira Nair • *Scr* Sabrina Dhawan

The Monster ★★★

Silent horror comedy
1925 · US · BW · 71mins

One of Lon Chaney's more tongue-in-cheek horror films, this is a delight, if less memorable than *The Unholy Three* and *The Phantom of the Opera*, released in the same year. Here he's without elaborate make-up as the dapper Dr Ziska, a mad surgeon who arranges car accidents on a lonely road, thereby obtaining subjects for his experiments to discover the secret of life. Director Roland West handles the story with considerable humour. AE

Lon Chaney *Dr Ziska* • Johnny Arthur *Under clerk* • Gertrude Olmsted *Betty Watson* • Hallam Cooley *Watson's head clerk* • Charles A Sellon [Charles Sellon] *Constable* ■ *Dir* Roland West • *Scr* Willard Mack, Albert Kenyon, from a play by Crane Wilbur • *Cinematographer* Hal Mohr

Monster ★★★ [18]

Horror comedy 1980 · US · Colour · 80mins

Pollution-spawned creatures go on a carnal rampage in a lively update of the concepts Roger Corman adeptly used for his own cult films of the 1950s. Director Barbara Peeters complained producer Corman spliced in the sensationalised rape scenes after she had finished with the project, but they only add to the lurid, lip-smacking sleaze of the whole enjoyably tacky enterprise. AJ [video]

Doug McClure *Jim Hill* • Ann Turkel *Dr Susan Drake* • Vic Morrow *Hank Slattery* • Cindy Weintraub *Carol Hill* • Anthony Penya *Johnny Eagle* • Denise Galik *Linda Beale* ■ *Dir* Barbara Peeters • *Scr* Frederick James, from a story by Frank Arnold, Martin B Cohen

Monster ★★★★ [18]

Crime drama based on a true story
2003 · US/Ger · Colour · 104mins

More an intense portrait of doomed romance than a serial-killer thriller, writer/director Patty Jenkins's brutal biopic of prostitute turned-multiple-murderer Aileen Wuornos burrows deep into the woman's psyche with the help of an Oscar-winning turn from Charlize Theron. Theron's performance goes beyond the weight-gain and dental prosthetics, finding both compassion and coldness in Wuornos's descent into homicidal mania, as she fights both to survive and to protect her burgeoning relationship with the naive outcast lesbian Selby (a superbly understated Christina Ricci). Tender, chilling and heartbreaking. IF [video] DVD

Charlize Theron *Aileen Wuornos* • Christina Ricci *Selby Wall* • Bruce Dern *Thomas* • Lee Tergesen *Vincent Corey* • Annie Corley *Donna Tentler* • Marco St John *Evan/"undercover john"* • Pruitt Taylor Vince *Gene/"stuttering john"* • Scott Wilson *Horton/"last john"* ■ *Dir/Scr* Patty Jenkins

The Monster Club ★★★ [15]

Horror 1980 · UK · Colour · 93mins

John Carradine (as famed horror writer R Chetwynd-Hayes) travels to a Transylvanian disco where bloodsucker Vincent Price (playing a vampire for the first and only time) relates three macabre stories of varying quality in a shaky anthology based on Chetwynd-Hayes's tales of terror and complicated ghoul genealogy. Included in the pseudo-hip monster mash is a Shadmock whose silent whistle is fatal to mortals, a band of Mafia-type undead chasers with stakes in their violin cases, and the Humgoos who wreak havoc on a film director looking for a creepy location. Worth watching for the all-star cast alone. AJ. Contains brief nudity. [video]

Vincent Price *Erasmus* • John Carradine *R Chetwynd-Hayes* • James Laurenson *Raven* • Barbara Kellerman *Angela* • Simon Ward *George* • Geoffrey Bayldon *Psychiatrist* • Donald Pleasence *Pickering* • Britt Ekland *Lintom's mother* • Richard Johnson *Lintom's father* ■ *Dir* Roy Ward Baker • *Scr* Edward Abraham, Valerie Abraham, from the short story collection by R Chetwynd-Hayes

Monster from Green Hell ★★ [PG]

Science fiction 1958 · US · BW · 67mins

Jim Davis leads an expedition of scientists through the African jungle, courtesy of stock footage from *Stanley and Livingstone* (1939) and some cheap backlot trimmings. He's looking for a crashed space probe and its cargo of radioactively enlarged wasps, but he needn't have bothered: after going on a weakly rendered trail of destruction, the inept wasps eventually stumble into an erupting volcano. An enjoyable, thick-witted trek through 1950s clichés. AJ [video]

Jim Davis *Quent Brady* • Robert E Griffin [Robert Griffin] *Dan Morgan* • Barbara Turner *Lorna Lorentz* • Eduardo Ciannelli *Mahri* • Vladimir Sokoloff *Dr Lorentz* • Joel Fluellen *Arobi* ■ *Dir* Kenneth Crane • *Scr* Louis Vittes, Endre Boehm

Monster in a Box ★★★

Biographical documentary
1991 · US · Colour · 90mins

Following the success of *Swimming to Cambodia*, writer/actor Spalding Gray embarked upon a second one-man show. The film tells of the interruptions Gray experienced while writing his autobiographical novel, *Impossible Vacation*, including an account of a trip to the Soviet Union along with several Hollywood stars for a Soviet film festival. Shot in London by Nick Broomfield, this country's master documentarist, the film suffers from audience laughter intruding into the soundtrack. DP. Contains swearing.

Dir Nick Broomfield • *Scr* Spalding Gray

Monster-in-Law ★★★ [12A]

Romantic comedy
2005 · US · Colour · 101mins

It's Gucci handbags at dawn for Jane Fonda and Jennifer Lopez in this comedy with bite from director Robert Luketic. While it stumbles a little with a corny courtship between J-Lo's bohemian babe and well-heeled doctor Michael Vartan, once Fonda turns up, the battle – and laughter – lines are very quickly drawn. After a 15-year sabbatical from movies, Fonda relishes the part of maniacal mommy, displaying a surprising gift for physical humour. The ending is sappy, but Lopez manages to hold her own. SP

Jennifer Lopez *Charlie Cantilini* • Jane Fonda *Viola Fields* • Michael Vartan *Kevin Fields* • Wanda Sykes *Ruby* • Adam Scott *Remy* • Monet Mazur *Fiona* • Annie Parisse *Morgan* • Elaine Stritch *Gertrude* ■ *Dir* Robert Luketic • *Scr* Anya Kochoff

Monster in the Closet ★★ [15]

Horror comedy 1983 · US · Colour · 85mins

Released by Troma (though produced independently), this amusing update of 1950s horror movies works because its earnest cast deliver their absurd dialogue in a relatively straight fashion. Across the land, people are being killed by a monster (Kevin Peter Hall) who pops out of their closets. Rookie reporter Donald Grant pounds the streets for an answer and helps save the day when the monster comes out into the open. Lots of cameos add to the nostalgic feel. KB [video]

Donald Grant *Richard Clark* • Denise DuBarry *Diane Bennett* • Claude Akins *Sheriff Ketchum* • Howard Duff *Father Finnegan* • Henry Gibson *Dr Pennyworth* • Donald Moffat *General Turnbull* • Paul Dooley *Roy Crane* • Stella Stevens *Margo Crane* • John Carradine *Old Joe* • Kevin Peter Hall *Monster* ■ *Dir* Bob Dahlin • *Scr* Bob Dahlin, from a story by Peter Bergquist, Bob Dahlin

The Monster Maker ★

Horror 1944 · US · BW · 62mins

This repellent horror movie – more closely allied to surgical fiction than imaginative fantasy – casts J Carrol Naish (later to play Charlie Chan on TV) as a mad scientist who infects his enemies with distorting bacteria. Directed by Sam Newfield and co-starring Ralph Morgan and Wanda McKay, it has little to recommend it apart from its freak-show novelty and an audience-pulling title. TH

J Carrol Naish *Dr Igor Markoff* • Ralph Morgan *Lawrence* • Tala Birell *Maxine* • Wanda McKay *Patricia Lawrence* • Terry Frost *Blake* • Glenn Strange *Giant* ■ *Dir* Sam Newfield • *Scr* Pierre Gendron, Martin Mooney, from a story by Lawrence Williams

Monster Man ★★ [18]

Comedy horror 2003 · US · Colour · 91mins

Redneck clichés flow as freely as the gore in this derivative comedy horror. Wimpy Eric Jungmann and his obnoxious buddy Justin Urich find a cross-country road trip turning to terror when they become the target of a disfigured fiend driving a monster truck. Throw in a scantily clad hitch-hiker (Aimee Brooks), the occult and puerile female genitalia jokes, and you've got a daft genre hybrid best suited to teenagers and fans of trashy B-movies. Yet the film still has a few effective moments. SF DVD

Eric Jungmann *Adam* • Justin Urich *Harley* • Aimee Brooks *Sarah* • Joe Goodrich *Brother*

Fred • Michael Bailey Smith *Brother Bob/ Monster Man* • Robert R Shafer *Deputy Dang* ■ *Dir/Scr* Michael Davis (3)

The Monster of Highgate Ponds ★★ U

Fantasy adventure 1961 · UK · BW · 58mins

Although Michael Balcon usually gets all the credit for the creative stature of Ealing Studios, the director Alberto Cavalcanti was the major force, pouring oil on troubled waters and encouraging brilliance from the film-makers. This is a lacklustre example of his work in decline, a children's film set in north London and featuring Roy Vincente and Ronald Howard. Although it includes some neat touches, which show the talent that Cavalcanti was, it's too obviously aimed at its target audience of youngsters. TH

Roy Vincente *The monster* • Ronald Howard *Uncle Dick* • Rachel Clay *Sophie* • Michael Wade *David* • Terry Raven *Chris* • Frederick Piper *Sam* • Michael Balfour *Bert* ■ *Dir* Alberto Cavalcanti • *Scr* Mary Cathcart Borer, from a story by Joy Batchelor

Monster on the Campus ★★

Science fiction 1958 · US · BW · 76mins

This typically wacky 1950s monster movie might have scared the pants off teen audiences back in the days of drive-ins, but will probably send today's youngsters straight to sleep. Still, there's much to enjoy in this corny tale of a fossilised fish whose blood transforms everything it touches into snarling monsters. The effects are quaint, but the stilted script makes this perhaps the least interesting of Jack Arnold's genre efforts. RS

Arthur Franz *Donald Blake* • Joanna Moore *Madeline Howard* • Judson Pratt *Mike Stevens* • Nancy Walters *Sylvia Lockwood* • Troy Donahue *Jimmy Flanders* • Phil Harvey *Sergeant Powell* • Helen Westcott *Molly Riordan* ■ *Dir* Jack Arnold • *Scr* David Duncan

M

The Monster Squad ★★★ 15

Comedy horror 1987 · US · Colour · 78mins

This horror movie scares just enough and amuses quite a lot. A well-cast Duncan Regehr is Count Dracula, journeying to suburban America to search for a mysterious amulet with the help of Frankenstein's monster and the Wolf Man, among others. But he reckons without a group of excitable children who are soon rustling up a few stakes in woodwork class. Enormous fun. SH

André Gower *Sean Crenshaw* • Robby Kiger *Patrick* • Stephen Macht *Del Crenshaw* • Duncan Regehr *Count Dracula* • Tom Noonan *Frankenstein's monster* • Brent Chalem *Horace* • Ryan Lambert *Rudy* ■ *Dir* Fred Dekker • *Scr* Shane Black, Fred Dekker

The Monster That Challenged the World ★★★

Science fiction 1957 · US · BW · 84mins

A fun, low-budget sci-fi horror movie, in which the eggs of an extinct sea monster are released during an earthquake and hatch as giant snail-like creatures that kill humans for their blood and water. Tim Holt came out of retirement to play the naval officer teaming up with Hans Conried's boffin to prevent the monsters breeding and spreading. An effective piece of film-making results from the good script by Pat Fielder, suspenseful direction by Arnold Laven and convincing monsters by Augie Lohman. AE

Tim Holt *Lieutenant Commander John Twillinger* • Audrey Dalton *Gail MacKenzie* • Hans Conried *Dr Jess Rogers* • Harlan Warde *Lieutenant Bob Clemens* • Casey Adams [Max Showalter] *Tad Johns* ■ *Dir* Arnold Laven • *Scr* Pat Fielder, from a story by David Duncan

Monster's Ball ★★★★ 15

Romantic crime drama
2001 · US · Colour · 108mins

The complexities of the heart are examined against a background of bigotry, despair and redemption in German-born director Marc Forster's blistering Deep South drama. Anchored by compelling and provocative performances of Billy Bob Thornton and Oscar-winner Halle Berry, the story focuses on the relationship between a grieving black widow and the white prison guard who presided over her convict husband's execution. A film of rare emotional depth and power, this is so centred on the irrationalities of human sentiment that many of the plot's implausibilities can be forgiven. SF. Contains violence, swearing, a sex scene and nudity. DVD

Billy Bob Thornton *Hank Grotowski* • Halle Berry *Leticia Musgrove* • Heath Ledger *Sonny Grotowski* • Peter Boyle *Buck Grotowski* • Sean Combs *Lawrence Musgrove* • Mos Def *Ryrus Cooper* ■ *Dir* Marc Forster • *Scr* Milo Addica, Will Rokos

Monsters, Inc ★★★★★ U

Animated comedy
2001 · US · Colour · 88mins

In this frantic, funny and very furry animated feature from computer animation pioneers Pixar, the focus is on the creatures that lurk inside the bedroom closets of children and who terrify their human prey when the lights are off. The creatures are employees of Monsters Inc, a power provider for the city of Monstropolis which is fuelled by the screams of human children. Then Sulley (voiced by John Goodman) accidentally lets a little girl into a realm where kids are believed to be highly toxic. Packed with the sort of artistry and storytelling panache we've come to expect from Pixar, the film creates a believable monsters' universe full of colour, energy and amusing creatures – especially the two horned, one-eyed joker known as Mike (voiced by Billy Crystal at his wisecracking best). JC DVD

John Goodman *James P "Sulley" Sullivan* • Billy Crystal *Michael "Mike" Wazowski* • Mary Gibbs *Boo* • Steve Buscemi *Randall Boggs* • James Coburn *Henry J Waternoose* • Jennifer Tilly *Celia* • Bob Peterson *Roz* • John Ratzenberger *Yeti* • Frank Oz *Fungus* ■ *Dir* Peter Docter • *Scr* Andrew Stanton, Daniel Gerson, from a story by Peter Docter, Jill Culton, Jeff Pidgeon, Ralph Eggleston

Montana ★★ PG

Western 1950 · US · Colour · 73mins

A routine western in glorious Technicolor, this stars an amiable Errol Flynn as the sheep farmer daring to seek grazing land in cattle country. The film lacks any real bite, suffering in particular from the absence of an authoritative villain. Douglas Kennedy does his best, but it is the redheaded cattle queen played by Alexis Smith who wants to shoot it out with him at the end. AE

Errol Flynn *Morgan Lane* • Alexis Smith *Maria Singleton* • SZ "Cuddles" Sakall [SZ Sakall] *Poppa Schultz* • Douglas Kennedy *Rodney Ackroyd* • James Brown (1) *Tex Coyne* • Ian MacDonald *Slim Reeves* • Paul E Burns *Tecumseh Burke* ■ *Dir* Ray Enright • *Scr* James R Webb, Borden Chase, Charles O'Neal, from a story by Ernest Haycox

Montana ★★ 18

Crime drama 1997 · US · Colour · 92mins

Though directed by a woman (Jennifer Leitzes) and centering around a female assassin (Kyra Sedgwick) framed and pursued by gun-wielding mobsters, this crime drama doesn't have any ambitions to offer a feminist perspective. The focus is definitely more on dialogue and characters than violence, though, which makes the bloody shoot-outs seem slightly out of place. The best and most original parts of the movie are its bizarre flashes of humour, while the cast is certainly worth a look. KB DVD

Kyra Sedgwick *Claire* • Stanley Tucci *Nick* • Robin Tunney *Kitty* • John Ritter *Dr Wexler* • Robbie Coltrane *The Boss* • Philip Seymour Hoffman *Duncan* ■ *Dir* Jennifer Leitzes • *Scr* John Hoeber, Erich Hoeber

Montana Trap ★★

Western 1976 · W Ger · Colour · 96mins

Originally released in a cut version called *Potato Fritz*, this German-made western stars Hardy Krüger as the potato farmer who settles in Indian territory, shows his good intentions by hanging his gun on a flag-pole and dreams of eating bratwurst and mash. Filmed in Yugoslavia, with bought-in footage of Montana buffalos. AT. A German language film.

Hardy Kruger *Potato Fritz* • Stephen Boyd *Bill Addison* • Anton Diffring *Lieutenant Slade* • Paul Breitner *Sergeant Black* • Christiane Gött *Jane Antrim* • Arthur Brauss *James Wesley* • Peter Schamoni *Reverend Cavenham* ■ *Dir* Peter Schamoni • *Scr* Paul Hengge

Monte Carlo ★★★ PG

Musical comedy 1930 · US · BW · 184mins

On the French Riviera, a count (Jack Buchanan) poses as a hairdresser and woos a countess (Jeanette MacDonald) in this feather-light musical romance from Ernst Lubitsch. What follows is enjoyable and characteristically stylish, though not as good as those to come which paired MacDonald with Maurice Chevalier. English stage star Buchanan is witty and appealing but lacks Chevalier's Gallic charm. RK

Jack Buchanan *Count Rudolph Falliere* • Jeanette MacDonald *Countess Vera von Conti* • ZaSu Pitts *Maria, Vera's maid* • Claude Allister [Claud Allister] *Prince Otto von Seibenheim* • Lionel Belmore *Duke Gustave von Seibenheim, his father* • Tyler Brooke *Armand, Rudolph's friend* ■ *Dir* Ernst Lubitsch • *Scr* Ernest Vajda, Vincent Lawrence, from the play *The Blue Coast* by Hans Muller and the novel *Monsieur Beaucaire* by Booth Tarkington

Monte Carlo or Bust ★★★ PG

Comedy 1969 · Fr/UK/It · Colour · 119mins

This is a well-intentioned sequel to the massively popular *Those Magnificent Men in Their Flying Machines* from the same director, Ken Annakin, and with many of the same cast, only this time it's about a 1,500-mile car race. It's a long haul, but star Tony Curtis makes the most of the journey and there's a rare opportunity to see Peter Cook and Dudley Moore in the same movie, plus accomplished turns from the likes of Terry-Thomas, Eric Sykes and the splendid Bourvil. TS

Tony Curtis *Chester Schofield* • Susan Hampshire *Betty* • Terry-Thomas *Sir Cuthbert* • Peter Cook *Major Dawlish* • Dudley Moore *Lt Barrington* • Eric Sykes *Perkins* • Gert Frobe [Gert Fröbe] *Willi Schickel/Horst Muller* • Hattie Jacques *Lady journalist* • Mireille Darc *Marie-Claude* • Jack Hawkins *Count Levinovitch* • Bourvil *Monsieur Dupont* ■ *Dir* Ken Annakin, Sam Itzkovitch • *Scr* Ken Annakin, Jack Davis

The Monte Carlo Story ★★ U

Comedy drama
1957 · It/US · Colour · 101mins

Italian count Vittorio De Sica, bankrupted by gambling, looks for a rich woman to finance his "system" at the tables. He falls in love with Marlene Dietrich, but they part when he discovers she is also penniless. Writer/director Samuel Taylor trespasses into Lubitsch territory with this well-worn tale, but he lacks the latter's gift for transforming this kind of story and setting into witty and romantic magic. The result is a desperately overplotted affair. RK

Marlene Dietrich *Marquise Maria de Crevecoeur* • Vittorio De Sica *Count Dino della Fiaba* • Arthur O'Connell *Mr Hinkley* • Jane Rose *Mrs Freeman* • Clelia Matania *Sophia* • Alberto Rabagliati *Albert* • Mischa Auer *Hector* ■ *Dir* Sam Taylor • *Scr* Samuel Taylor, from a story by Marcello Girosi, Dino Risi

Monte Walsh ★★★ PG

Western 1970 · US · Colour · 94mins

This evocative, painterly and melancholy western marks the directing debut of William A Fraker, the cameraman on *Bullitt* and *Paint Your Wagon*. It was the star of the latter, Lee Marvin, who enabled Fraker to make this movie about two cowboy friends, Marvin and Jack Palance, who see their way of life ending yet find their attempts to forge domesticated lives also doomed. It's a pity that Fraker's directing career all but fizzled out after this striking, beautifully cast first feature. AT. Contains some violence.

Lee Marvin *Monte Walsh* • Jack Palance *Chet Rollins* • Jeanne Moreau *Martine Bernard* • Mitch Ryan [Mitchell Ryan] *Shorty Austin* • Jim Davis *Cal Brennan* • John Hudkins *Sonny Jacobs* • Raymond Guth *Sunfish Perkins* • John McKee *Petey Williams* ■ *Dir* William A Fraker • *Scr* David Z Goodman, Lukas Heller, from the novel by Jack Warner Schaefer

Montenegro ★★ 18

Surreal comedy
1981 · Swe/UK · Colour · 92mins

It's not often that a scene involving a toy tank and a stripper provides the most arresting moment in a film, but that's the case with this comedy. Serbian director Dusan Makavejev coaxes a vibrant performance out of Susan Anspach as the bored housewife who gets to sample the wild side of life after missing a flight. But chauvinistic husband Erland Josephson is less impressive, and the symbolism is heavy-handed. DP. Contains swearing, sex scenes and nudity.

Susan Anspach *Marilyn Jordan* • Erland Josephson *Martin Jordan* • Jamie Marsh *Jimmy* • Per Oscarsson *Dr Pazardjian* • Bora Todorovic *Alex* • Marianne Jacobi *Cookie* ■ *Dir/Scr* Dusan Makavejev

Monterey Pop ★★★★

Music documentary
1968 · US · Colour · 79mins

This breakthrough concert movie, which paved the way for *Woodstock* with its ground-breaking, *cinéma vérité* style, was directed by DA Pennebaker, who made the Bob Dylan documentary *Don't Look Back* one year earlier. Over 45 hours of 16mm film was shot at the 1967 Monterey International Pop Festival and edited into the first major rock festival documentary, capturing some of the greatest music legends of the hippy era. In between shots of sexy chicks, arrays of sleeping bags and queues for the toilets, Janis Joplin wails her way through *Ball and Chain*, The Who trash sound equipment to *My Generation*, Otis Redding warbles *I've Been Loving You Too Long* and Jimi Hendrix sets his guitar aflame to *Wild Thing* – the highlight. AJ

Dir/Scr DA Pennebaker

A Month by the Lake ★★★ PG

Period romantic drama
1994 · UK/US · Colour · 87mins

John Irvin's period drama is a *ménage à quatre* set on the shores of Italy's Lake Como on the eve of the Second

World War. Vanessa Redgrave's flirtation with English major Edward Fox becomes more serious thanks to the intervention of American nanny Uma Thurman and the attentions of Italian youth Alessandro Gassman, who has a taste for older women. There's little emotional depth, but the acting is impeccable. TH [video] DVD

Vanessa Redgrave *Miss Bentley* • Edward Fox *Major Wilshaw* • Uma Thurman *Miss Beaumont* • Alida Valli *Signora Fascioli* • Alessandro Gassman *Vittorio Balsari* • Carlo Cartier *Mr Bonizzoni* • Paolo Lombardi *Enrico* • Riccardo Rossi *Guido* • Sonia Martinelli *Maria* ■ *Dir* John Irvin • *Scr* Trevor Bentham, from the novella by HE Bates

A Month in the Country ★★★★ PG

Drama 1987 · UK · Colour · 87mins

This moving and sensitive meditation on the aftereffects of the First World War shows shell-shocked survivors Colin Firth and Kenneth Branagh learning to live with each other's idiosyncracies and quirks of sexual nature while preserving and restoring relics from a bygone age. Working from Simon Gray's adaptation of JL Carr's book, director Pat O'Connor fashions a poignant gem, with a finale that brings one close to tears. TH [video] DVD

Colin Firth *Tom Birkin* • Kenneth Branagh *Charles Moon* • Natasha Richardson *Alice Keach* • Patrick Malahide *Reverend Keach* • Jim Carter *Ellerbeck* • Richard Vernon *Colonel Hebron* ■ *Dir* Pat O'Connor • *Scr* Simon Gray, from the novel by JL Carr

Montparnasse 19 ★★★

Biographical drama
1958 · Fr/It · BW · 110mins

What an ill-fated film! Having developed the project, Max Ophüls died before shooting, while both his replacement, Jacques Becker, and star, Gérard Philipe, would be dead within three years. Philipe was only 36 when he died, one year older than Amedeo Modigliani, the reckless artist he portrays here. The film revels in both his various addictions and the cut-throat nature of bohemian Paris in the early 20th century, but Becker leaves too little room for drama by refusing to stray from the facts. DP. In French with English subtitles.

Gérard Philipe *Amedeo Modigliani* • Lilli Palmer *Béatrice Hastings* • Anouk Aimée *Jeanne Hébuterne* • Gérard Séty *Sborowski* • Lila Kedrova *Mme Sborowski* • Lea Padovani *Rosalie* • Jean Lanier *Monsieur Hébuterne* ■ *Dir* Jacques Becker • *Scr* Henri Jeanson, Max Ophüls, Jean Cocteau, from the novel *Les Montparnos* by Georges-Michel Michel

Monty Python and the Holy Grail ★★★★ 15

Comedy 1975 · UK · Colour · 85mins

Complete with some inspired digressions and shorn of some of the weaker sketches, the soundtrack album of the Pythons' first story-based feature is even funnier than the film itself. Yet this remains a wonderfully inventive comedy that brilliantly debunks the Dark Ages and the legends of chivalry through King Arthur's encounters with an anarcho-syndicalist commune, the Black Knight, God (courtesy of Terry Gilliam) and the "knights who say ni". The *Camelot* and *Sir Robin* songs also get beneath the visor, but the highlights are the trial of Connie Booth's witch and the Holy Hand Grenade of Antioch sequence. DP. Contains swearing, some violence and nudity. [video] DVD

Graham Chapman *King Arthur* • John Cleese *Black Knight/Sir Lancelot* • Terry Gilliam *Patsy/Green Knight* • Eric Idle *Sir Robin/Brother Maynard* • Terry Jones *Dennis' mother/Sir Bedevere* • Michael Palin *Dennis/Sir Galahad* • Connie Booth *Witch* ■ *Dir* Terry Gilliam, Terry Jones • *Scr* Graham Chapman, John Cleese, Terry Gilliam, Eric Idle, Terry Jones, Michael Palin • *Music/lyrics* Neil Innes

Monty Python Live at the Hollywood Bowl ★★★ 15

Comedy 1982 · UK · Colour · 77mins

Suffering from writer's block during the scripting on *Monty Python's The Meaning of Life*, the Pythons decided to play the famous open-air Hollywood Bowl to revive their creative spirits. Under-rehearsed and prone to fits of giggles, the team still ran through such favourites as *The Ministry of Silly Walks*, the *Bruces*, the *Four Yorkshiremen* and the *Lumberjack Song* with consummate skill. It's a mixed bag but, because HandMade decided to cut parts of the show for the film version, it's all over far too soon. DP. Contains swearing. [video]

Graham Chapman • John Cleese • Terry Gilliam • Eric Idle • Terry Jones • Michael Palin • Neil Innes • Carol Cleveland ■ *Dir* Terry Hughes, Ian MacNaughton • *Scr* Graham Chapman, John Cleese, Terry Gilliam, Eric Idle, Terry Jones, Michael Palin

Monty Python's Life of Brian ★★★★ 15

Comedy 1979 · UK · Colour · 89mins

The controversy that surrounded this inspired send-up of religious epics overshadows the fact that this is the Monty Python team's most assured work. Graham Chapman ("he's not the Messiah, he's just a naughty boy") is the Judaean whose life bears some resemblance to a certain carpenter's around the same time, although the shambling story serves mainly as an excuse to take pot shots at some of their favourite targets and serve up some joyfully juvenile gags. Michael Palin gets some memorable roles, notably the Roman governor with a speech impediment ("Welease Wodewick"); Spike Milligan makes a very funny and quite irrelevant cameo. JF. Contains violence, swearing and nudity. [video] DVD

Terry Jones *The Virgin Mandy/The mother of Brian, a ratbag/Colin/Simon the holy man/Saintly passer-by* • Graham Chapman *First Wise Man/Brian called Brian/Biggus Dickus* • Michael Palin *Second Wise Man/Mr Big Nose/Francis a Revolutionary/Mrs A who casts the second stone/Ex-leper/Ben, an ancient prisoner/Pontius Pilate, Roman governor/A boring prophet/Eddie/Nisus Wettus* • John Cleese *Third Wise Man/Reg, leader of the Judean People's Front/Jewish official at the stoning/Centurion of the Yard/Deadly Dirk/Arthur* • Eric Idle *Mr Cheeky/Stan called Loretta, a confused revolutionary/Harry the Haggler, beard and stone salesman/Culprit Woman, who casts the first stone/Intensely dull youth/Otto, the Nazarene jailer's assistant/Mr Frisbee III* • Terry Gilliam *Another person further forward/Revolutionaries and masked commandos/A blood and thunder prophet/Geoffrey/Jailer* ■ *Dir* Terry Jones • *Scr* Graham Chapman, John Cleese, Terry Gilliam, Eric Idle, Terry Jones, Michael Palin

Monty Python's The Meaning of Life ★★★ 18

Comedy 1983 · UK · Colour · 86mins

A pick 'n' mix selection of comedy sketches by the anarchic, surrealistic team of John Cleese, Terry Gilliam, Eric Idle, Terry Jones, Michael Palin and Graham Chapman. Exploring the stages of human existence, ranging from conception to death, this is British humour at its most tasteless and occasionally brilliant – the sequence in which a financial institution is boarded by swashbuckling pirates is superb, while the one in which a glutton explosively overeats is wholly nasty. TH. Contains violence, swearing and brief nudity. [video] DVD

Graham Chapman • John Cleese • Terry Gilliam • Eric Idle • Terry Jones • Michael Palin ■ *Dir* Terry Jones • *Scr* Terry Jones (HYF), Graham Chapman, John Cleese, Terry Gilliam, Eric Idle, Michael Palin

Moolaadé ★★★★ 15

Drama
2004 · Sen/Fr/Burkina Faso · Col · 124m

The subject of female genital mutilation, which is still practised in many African countries, has been tackled before, but no film has managed to emphasise the human aspect of this bitter dispute with such compassion and poetry as the continent's finest film-maker, Ousmane Sembene. A violent showdown ensues between the elders of a Burkina Faso village and the courageous Collé (Fatoumata Coulibaly) when she refuses to hand over four young girls for ritual "purification". Sembene captures the tensions between the Islamic patriarchs and progressive womenfolk with an irresistible satirical power. Crusading cinema at its best. DP. In Wolof, various African languages and French with English subtitles.

Fatoumata Coulibaly *Collé Ardo Gallo Sy* • Hélène Diarra *Hadjatou Maïmouna* • Salimata Traoré *Amasatou* • Dominique T Zeïda *Mercenary* • Mah Campaoré *Leader of the purifiers* • Aminata Dao *Alima Ba* ■ *Dir/Scr* Ousmane Sembene

The Moon and Sixpence ★★★

Melodrama
1942 · US · BW and Colour · 88mins

George Sanders stars as a London stockbroker who becomes a painter in Paris, goes all Bohemian and then drops out in the South Seas. Somerset Maugham's novel was partly inspired by Gauguin and his sojourn in the Marquesas Islands, but Sanders's performance is more Oscar Wilde than Maugham. (It's certainly far removed from Anthony Quinn's piratical Gauguin in *Lust for Life*.) Don't look for luscious location photography either; this is an effete, studio-bound exploration of artistic temperament. AT

George Sanders *Charles Strickland* • Herbert Marshall *Geoffrey Wolfe* • Steve Geray [Steven Geray] *Dirk Stroeve* • Doris Dudley *Blanche Stroeve* • Eric Blore *Captain Nichols* • Albert Basserman *Doctor Coutras* ■ *Dir* Albert Lewin • *Scr* Albert Lewin, from the novel by W Somerset Maugham

Moon 44 ★ 15

Science-fiction action drama
1990 · W Ger/US · Colour · 95mins

Before his Hollywood successes, Roland Emmerich directed this German-financed sci-fi thriller about cop Michael Paré going undercover as a convict on an industrial planet to investigate ongoing sabotage. Over-plotted, cliché-ridden and highly derivative. JC [video]

Michael Paré *Felix Stone* • Lisa Eichhorn *Terry Morgan* • Dean Devlin *Tyler* • Malcolm McDowell *Major Lee* • Brian Thompson *Jake O'Neal* • Stephen Geoffreys *Cookie* ■ *Dir* Roland Emmerich • *Scr* Dean Heyde, Oliver Eberle, from a story by Dean Heyde, Eberle, Roland Emmerich, PJ Mitchell

The Moon in the Gutter ★★★ 18

Mystery romance
1983 · Fr/It · Colour · 132mins

Critically panned and reviled by even its star, Gérard Depardieu, director Jean-Jacques Beneix's follow-up to *Diva* is another glittering visual delight that suffers from a cumbersome and pretentious plot. Depardieu is a poor stevedore searching for the man who raped his sister. While on his traumatic odyssey, he ends up pursuing rich Nastassja Kinski who is, literally, the girl of his dreams. Deliriously obscure and dazzlingly superficial by turns, this curiosity contains the most erotic images of Kinski, Depardieu and Victoria Abril ever captured on film. AJ. In French with English subtitles. [video]

Gérard Depardieu *Gerard* • Nastassja Kinski *Loretta* • Victoria Abril *Bella* • Vittorio Mezzogiorno *Newton Channing* • Dominique Pinon *Frank* • Bertice Reading *Lola* ■ *Dir* Jean-Jacques Beineix • *Scr* Jean-Jacques Beineix, Olivier Mergault, from the novel by David Goodis

The Moon Is Blue ★★★ PG

Comedy 1953 · US · BW · 95mins

William Holden meets actress Maggie McNamara on top of the Empire State Building, only for McNamara to be pursued by older man David Niven. This mildly amusing comedy of romantic errors was a huge box-office success when director Otto Preminger defied the censor and released the film with dialogue that was considered extreme for its day. Preminger also gave a boost to Niven's career simply by casting him. Niven had broken with a vindictive Sam Goldwyn and was described by this film's production company, United Artists, as "all washed up". Given the chance to prove himself once again, Niven rose to the challenge brilliantly. TH [video]

William Holden (2) *Donald Gresham* • David Niven *David Slater* • Maggie McNamara *Patty O'Neill* • Tom Tully *Michael O'Neill* • Dawn Addams *Cynthia Slater* ■ *Dir* Otto Preminger • *Scr* F Hugh Herbert, from his play

The Moon Is Down ★★

Second World War drama
1943 · US · BW · 90mins

This clumsy piece of wartime propaganda sees some plucky Norwegians overcome the might of the Nazis. Doubtless such acts of selfless heroism occurred throughout the Second World War, but Hollywood (particularly its European exiles) could never resist setting them in fairy-tale towns populated by quaint characters. Cedric Hardwicke credits his Nazi commander with having some intelligence, but he's no match for Henry Travers, who's armed to the teeth with decency. DP

Cedric Hardwicke *Colonel Lanser* • Henry Travers *Mayor Orden* • Lee J Cobb *Dr Winter* • Dorris Bowdon *Molly Morden* • Margaret Wycherly *Madame Orden* • Peter Van Eyck *Lieutenant Tonder* • Irving Pichel *Innkeeper* ■ *Dir* Irving Pichel • *Scr* Nunnally Johnson, from the novel by John Steinbeck

Moon over Miami ★★★ U

Musical 1941 · US · Colour · 87mins

One of the very best of the 20th Century-Fox Technicolor Betty Grable vehicles: a pleasingly bright, garish and utterly unsophisticated version of Fox's great stand-by plot about money-hungry gals on a spree (*Three Blind Mice*, *Three Little Girls in Blue*, *How to Marry a Millionaire*). There's some fun dancing here from Jack Cole and the Condos Brothers, and some nice songs, such as *You Started Something* and the title tune. Easy on the eye and ear, this is prime viewing for nostalgists. TS [video]

Don Ameche *Phil O'Neil* • Betty Grable *Kay Latimer* • Robert Cummings *Jeff Bolton* • Charlotte Greenwood *Aunt Susie Latimer* • Jack Haley *Jack O'Hara* • Carole Landis *Barbara Latimer* • Cobina Wright Jr *Connie Fentress* ■ *Dir* Walter Lang • *Scr* Vincent Lawrence, Brown Holmes, George Seaton, Lynn Starling, from the play *Three Blind Mice* by Stephen Powys

Moon over Parador ★★ 15

Comedy 1988 · US · Colour · 99mins

Director Paul Mazursky, whose instinct for comic mores is usually razor-sharp, resorts to a lazy trawl through a decent

M

comedy idea, blunting the edges of any comic potential in the process. However, Richard Dreyfuss puts plenty of energy into his scenes as a frustrated actor turned South American despot, using his nervy tics and schoolboy charm to advantage, and there are a handful of pointed barbs at the expense of dictatorship. JM. Contains swearing.

Richard Dreyfuss *Jack Noah* • Raul Julia *Roberto Strausmann* • Sonia Braga *Madonna* • Jonathan Winters *Ralph* • Fernando Rey *Alejandro* • Sammy Davis Jr • Michael Greene *Clint* • Charo *Madame Loop* ■ *Dir* Paul Mazursky • *Scr* Leon Capetanos, Paul Mazursky, from a story by Charles G Booth

Moon Pilot ★★★ U

Science-fiction comedy
1962 · US · Colour · 98mins

In one of the better Disney live-action pictures of this period, Tom Tryon is selected to become the first man in space by a test-flight chimpanzee. The unwilling Tryon's resolve to remain on Earth is reinforced when he falls for Dany Saval, but when he discovers that she is a visitor from another planet, his feelings about outer space quickly change. The leads are engaging, and there are plenty of smart jokes at the expense of Nasa. DP

Tom Tryon *Captain Richmond Talbot* • Brian Keith *Maj Gen John Vanneman* • Edmond O'Brien *McClosky* • Dany Saval *Lyrae* • Bob Sweeney *Senator McGuire* ■ *Dir* James Neilson • *Scr* Maurice Tombragel, from a story by Robert Buckner

The Moon-Spinners ★★★ U

Mystery 1964 · US/UK · Colour · 113mins

Walt Disney fashioned numerous star vehicles for young Hayley Mills, and here she's involved, along with Joan Greenwood, in some likeable nonsense about jewel thieves in Crete. But it's the supporting cast that makes this worth watching: silent screen vamp Pola Negri came out of retirement to play the mysterious Madame Habib, only to be upstaged by the evil Eli Wallach and Greek star Irene Papas as his sister. Unfortunately, it doesn't come off as a Hitchcock-style mystery, and Mary Stewart's original novel should have been reworked. TS

Hayley Mills *Nikky Ferris* • Eli Wallach *Stratos* • Pola Negri *Madame Habib* • Peter McEnery *Mark Camford* • Joan Greenwood *Aunt Frances* • Irene Papas *Sophia* • Sheila Hancock *Cynthia Gamble* • Michael Davis (2) *Alexis* • John Le Mesurier *Anthony Chelmscott Gamble* ■ *Dir* James Neilson • *Scr* Michael Dyne, from the novel by Mary Stewart

Moon Zero Two ★★ U

Science-fiction adventure
1969 · UK · Colour · 100mins

In an effort to diversify, Hammer attempted this "U" certificate space western, in which James Olson and Ori Levy do battle with the bad guys for prospecting rights on a somewhat bleak-looking moon. It's exactly what you might expect from a western set on the moon, complete with shoot-outs, ambushes and dancing girls. The plot and dialogue are terrible, though there are a few thrills for the kids. DM

James Olson *Bill Kemp* • Catherina von Schell [Catherine Schell] *Clementine Taplin* • Warren Mitchell *JJ Hubbard* • Adrienne Corri *Liz Murphy* • Ori Levy *Karminski* • Dudley Foster *Whitsun* • Bernard Bresslaw *Harry* ■ *Dir* Roy Ward Baker • *Scr* Michael Carreras, from a story by Gavin Lyall, Frank Hardman, Martin Davison

Moondance ★★

Romantic drama
1995 · Ger/Ire/UK · Colour · 92mins

Two eccentric young brothers are torn apart when a beautiful woman enters their lives. The Irish scenery is gorgeous, as is German actress Julia Brendler, but the two brothers (Ian Shaw and Ruaidhri Conroy) are so eccentric they're hardly believable. The characters' motivations are obscure, and the movie often leaves the viewer behind. Since this story has been told better many times before, it's tough to recommend this version. ST. An English/German language film.

Ruaidhri Conroy *Dominic* • Ian Shaw *Patrick* • Julia Brendler *Anya* • Marianne Faithfull *Mother* ■ *Dir* Dagmar Hirtz • *Scr* Mark Watters, Bert Weinshanker, from the novel *The White Hare* by Francis Stuart

Moonfleet ★★★

Period adventure 1955 · US · Colour · 86mins

While a long way from being the best film on director Fritz Lang's illustrious CV, this adaptation of J Meade Falkner's swashbuckling classic still makes for rousing entertainment. Set in Dorset in the 1770s, this fast-moving tale of smuggling and secret identities provides Stewart Granger with the chance to add a touch of devilment to the expected romantic dash and derring-do. George Sanders gives his usual performance of silky smooth malevolence in this solid piece of old-fashioned escapism. DP

Stewart Granger *Jeremy Fox* • Joan Greenwood *Lady Ashwood* • George Sanders *Lord Ashwood* • Viveca Lindfors *Mrs Minton* • Liliane Montevecchi *Gypsy* ■ *Dir* Fritz Lang • *Scr* Jan Lustig, Margaret Fitts, from the novel by J Meade Falkner

Moonlight and Valentino ★★★ 15

Drama 1995 · US · Colour · 99mins

A talky but well-acted adaptation of Ellen Simon's stage play about the struggles of a young widow to cope with life without her husband. Elizabeth Perkins's moving performance as the widow is the centrepiece of this beautifully shot, intimately detailed drama, but the supporting cast is equally praiseworthy, with special mention for star-in-the-making Gwyneth Paltrow as Perkins's eccentric sister. The sluggish, grief-drenched first half is pretty heavy going, though the tone is lightened by the introduction of charismatic rock star turned actor Jon Bon Jovi, who helps to re-awaken Perkins. JC. Contains some sex scenes and swearing.

Elizabeth Perkins *Rebecca Trager Lott* • Whoopi Goldberg *Sylvie Morrow* • Gwyneth Paltrow *Lucy Trager* • Kathleen Turner *Alberta Russell* • Jon Bon Jovi *The painter* • Peter Coyote *Paul* ■ *Dir* David Anspaugh • *Scr* Ellen Simon, from her play

Moonlight Mile ★★★ 15

Period drama 2002 · US · Colour · 112mins

Writer/director Brad Silberling's polished drama blends a simple premise (grieving parents take in their murdered daughter's fiancé) with more complex emotional undercurrents. While the veteran actors – Dustin Hoffman and Susan Sarandon, in roles written especially for them – credibly convey the emotional highs and lows, it's the youthful Jake Gyllenhaal's awkwardness and vulnerability that connects most satisfyingly. Silberling's final-act catharsis for every character and conflict is laid on too thickly, but there's no doubting the film-maker's sincerity. JC. Contains swearing. DVD

Jake Gyllenhaal *Joe Nast* • Dustin Hoffman *Ben Floss* • Susan Sarandon *JoJo Floss* • Holly Hunter *Mona Camp* • Ellen Pompeo *Bertie Knox* • Richard T Jones *Ty* • Allan Corduner *Stan Michaels* • Dabney Coleman *Mike Mulcahey* ■ *Dir/Scr* Brad Silberling

Moonlight Sonata ★★

Romantic drama 1937 · UK · BW · 86mins

A plane makes a forced landing in the grounds of a Swedish country house owned by the music-loving Baroness Lindenborg (Marie Tempest). The passengers needing refuge include a fortune-hunting cad (Eric Portman), who temporarily sweeps the baroness's granddaughter off her feet. This British film exists only as an excuse for the great pianist Ignace Jan Paderewski to make his screen debut at the age of 77 as one of the passengers. RK

Ignace Jan Paderewski • Charles Farrell *Eric Molander* • Marie Tempest *Baroness Lindenborg* • Barbara Greene *Ingrid* • Eric Portman *Mario de la Costa* • Graham Browne *Dr Broman* • Queenie Leonard *Margit, his niece* • Lawrence Hanray *Bishop* ■ *Dir* Lothar Mendes • *Scr* Edward Knoblock, EM Delafield, from a story by Hans Rameau

The Moonlighter ★★

Western 1953 · US · BW · 77mins

Barbara Stanwyck and Fred MacMurray, the doomed lovers from the classic *Double Indemnity*, are reunited in a western that was originally released in 3-D. The weird plot is about a cattle rustler (MacMurray) who escapes a lynch mob and robs a bank. He is then pursued by his girlfriend (Stanwyck), who also happens to be the sheriff. The title derives from western lore that says rustlers work only in moonlight. AT

Barbara Stanwyck *Rela* • Fred MacMurray *Wes Anderson* • Ward Bond *Cole* • William Ching *Tom Anderson* • John Dierkes *Sheriff Daws* • Morris Ankrum *Prince* • Jack Elam *Strawboss* ■ *Dir* Roy Rowland • *Scr* Niven Busch

Moonlighting ★★★★ 15

Political drama 1982 · UK · Colour · 93mins

Directed with vigour and assurance by the exiled Polish director Jerzy Skolimowski, this razor-sharp satire brilliantly equates the experiences of a crew of moonlighting Polish builders in Thatcherite London with the plight of the workers in the Gdansk shipyard at the height of the Solidarity uprising. As the leader of the gang, Jeremy Irons gives one of the finest performances of his career as he imposes curfews and news blackouts to prevent his colleagues learning of the momentous events back home before the job is done. The shoplifting sequence is the highlight of an enthralling and intelligent picture. DP

Jeremy Irons *Nowak* • Eugene Lipinski *Banaszak* • Jiri Stanislaw *Wolski* • Eugeniusz Haczkiewicz *Kudaj* ■ *Dir/Scr* Jerzy Skolimowski

The Moonraker ★★★ U

Period adventure 1957 · UK · Colour · 78mins

Although it lacks a decent budget and big stars, this is still an enjoyable romp. George Baker is the Cavalier who keeps the future Charles II out of the clutches of Oliver Cromwell (portrayed with visible relish by John Le Mesurier). Sylvia Syms provides the glamour and *Doctor Who* fans will recognise Patrick Troughton, who played the time-traveller in his second incarnation. DP

George Baker *Earl Anthony of Dawlish, "the Moonraker"* • Sylvia Syms *Anne Wyndham* • Peter Arne *Edmund Tyler* • Marius Goring *Colonel Beaumont* • Clive Morton *Lord Harcourt* • Gary Raymond *Prince Charles Stuart* • John Le Mesurier *Oliver Cromwell* • Patrick Troughton *Captain Wilcox* ■ *Dir* David MacDonald • *Scr* Robert Hall, Wilfrid Eades, Alistair Bell, from the play by Arthur Watkyn

Moonraker ★★ PG

Spy adventure 1979 · UK · Colour · 121mins

The 11th Bond movie jettisons Ian Fleming's marvellous novel and sends 007 into space. Weighed down by its often clunky special effects and non-existent plotting, the movie seems to be merely an attempt to update Bond in the wake of *Star Wars*. Roger Moore is at his least convincing as Bond, Michael Lonsdale makes a lacklustre master criminal and Jaws, the towering sub-villain from *The Spy Who Loved Me*, makes a return appearance. Too much of the budget was wasted on overblown spectacle, without enough attention being given to the basics. AT. Contains violence. DVD

Roger Moore *James Bond* • Lois Chiles *Holly Goodhead* • Michael Lonsdale [Michel Lonsdale] *Hugo Drax* • Richard Kiel *Jaws* • Corinne Cléry *Corinne Dufour* • Bernard Lee *"M"* • Desmond Llewelyn *"Q"* • Lois Maxwell *Miss Moneypenny* ■ *Dir* Lewis Gilbert • *Scr* Christopher Wood, from the novel by Ian Fleming • *Music* John Barry (1)

Moonrise ★★★★ PG

Film noir 1948 · US · BW · 86mins

This sombre but compelling rural drama is a tribute to the skill of director Frank Borzage, a fine example of his tender feelings for young lovers in adversity. Dane Clark gives his best performance as the murderer's son who kills one of his tormentors, while Gail Russell brings her fragile beauty to the part of the girl who believes in him. Though tracked by the sheriff and his posse, his biggest enemy is himself. The film is a visual treat, and a true mood piece. AE

Dane Clark *Danny Hawkins* • Gail Russell *Gilly Johnson* • Ethel Barrymore *Grandma* • Allyn Joslyn *Clem Otis* • Henry Morgan [Harry Morgan] *Billy Scripture* • Rex Ingram (2) *Mose* ■ *Dir* Frank Borzage • *Scr* Charles Haas, from the novel by Theodore Strauss

The Moon's Our Home ★★★

Romantic comedy 1936 · US · BW · 80mins

The major attraction of this romantic comedy is the pairing of Margaret Sullavan and Henry Fonda, two of Hollywood's most attractive and gifted stars of the 1930s, who were married in real life for a stormy couple of years from 1931 to 1933. She plays a movie star, he's a writer and explorer; they fly in the face of temperamental incompatibility and marry. The rest of the film, directed by William Seiter from a witty script that includes contributions from Dorothy Parker, is concerned with how they sort out their differences. Warm and charming. RK

Margaret Sullavan *Sarah Brown/Cherry Chester* • Henry Fonda *John Smith/Anthony Amberton* • Charles Butterworth *Horace Van Steedan* • Beulah Bondi *Mrs Boyce Medford* • Margaret Hamilton *Mitty Simpson* • Henrietta Crosman *Lucy Van Steedan* ■ *Dir* William A Seiter • *Scr* Isabel Dawn, Boyce DeGaw, Dorothy Parker, Alan Campbell, from the story by Faith Baldwin

Moonshine County Express ★★

Action crime drama
1977 · US · Colour · 95mins

A hillbilly is murdered and his three daughters decide to sell his ocean of illicit whiskey, thereby incurring the wrath of local moonshine big shot William Conrad. This sort of slipshod, sour mash jape features Susan Howard, Claudia Jennings and Maureen McCormick as the three hoochettes. John Saxon works for Conrad but fancies Howard, which adds a dash of romance to the original recipe of car chases and banjo music. AT

John Saxon *JB Johnson* • Susan Howard *Dot Hammer* • William Conrad *Jack Starkey* • Morgan Woodward *Sweetwater* • Claudia Jennings *Betty Hammer* • Jeff Corey *Preacher Hagen* • Dub Taylor *Uncle Bill* • Maureen McCormick *Sissy Hammer* ■ *Dir* Gus Trikonis • *Scr* Hubert Smith, Daniel Ansley

The Moonstone ★★

Mystery 1934 · US · BW · 62mins

Wilkie Collins's novel has always been a hard nut for film-makers to crack, so it comes as no surprise to learn that there have been no film versions since this one (although there have been some made-for-TV efforts). David Manners makes a stiff and unappealing hero, though the result does have some historical interest. Collins fared much better with Warner Bros's 1948 version of *The Woman in White*, which came complete with all the requisite Gothic trimmings. TS

David Manners *Franklin Blake* • Phyllis Barry *Anne Verinder* • Jameson Thomas *Godfrey Ablewhite, rare book dealer* • Gustav von Seyffertitz *Septimus Lucker, money-lender* • Herbert Bunston *Sir John Verinder* ■ *Dir* Reginald Barker • *Scr* Adele Buffington, from the novel by Wilkie Collins

Moonstruck ★★★★ PG

Romantic comedy
1987 · US · Colour · 97mins

An unashamedly romantic comedy that established once and for all that Cher could act. She gives an Oscar-winning performance as a widow who looks set for a safe marriage to Danny Aiello, but falls instead for his moody younger brother Nicolas Cage. John Patrick Shanley, who won an Oscar for best original screenplay, paints a warm and affectionate picture of Italian-American life, and there are enough quirky touches to prevent it from toppling into treacle. Norman Jewison directs subtly and unobtrusively, allowing the splendid cast to make the most of Shanley's fine writing. JF [video] DVD

Cher *Loretta Castorini* • Nicolas Cage *Ronny Cammareri* • Olympia Dukakis *Rose Castorini* • Vincent Gardenia *Cosmo Castorini* • Danny Aiello *Mr Johnny Cammareri* • Julie Bovasso *Rita Cappomaggi* • John Mahoney *Perry* ■ *Dir* Norman Jewison • *Scr* John Patrick Shanley

Moontide ★★★

Drama 1942 · US · BW · 94mins

Jean Gabin is a heavy-drinking, rootless Frenchman who wanders from job to job in dockside towns supporting "buddy" Thomas Mitchell, who has a hold over him and clings like a leech. Gabin saves Ida Lupino from suicide, setting in motion a chain of dramatic events. A modest, grittily effective and absorbing drama, with French idol Gabin impressive and Lupino appealing. Mitchell is excellent as the weak and scummy villain, while Claude Rains is unlikely but sympathetic as an educated night watchman. Archie Mayo's direction is uneven, but there are some fine sequences of brooding tension – doubtless explained by the fact that an uncredited Fritz Lang directed some of the film. RK

Jean Gabin *Bobo* • Ida Lupino *Anna* • Thomas Mitchell *Tiny* • Claude Rains *Nutsy* • Jerome Cowan *Dr Frank Brothers* • Helene Reynolds *Woman on boat* • Ralph Byrd *Rev Wilson* ■ *Dir* Archie Mayo • *Scr* John O'Hara, from the novel by Willard Robertson

Moonwalker ★★★ PG

Musical fantasy 1988 · US · Colour · 89mins

Made when Michael Jackson was still the biggest pop star in the world, this is, unfortunately, a bit of a mess. However, fans will still love the music and the innovative pop promo interludes, while some older viewers might enjoy the discomfort of Joe Pesci as the evil Mr Big. Look out for Sean Lennon as one of Jackson's chums. JF. Contains violent scenes. [video] DVD

Michael Jackson (3) *Michael* • Joe Pesci *Mr Big* • Sean Lennon *Sean* • Kellie Parker *Katie* • Brandon Adams *Zeke/"Baby Bad" Michael* ■ *Dir* Colin Chilvers, Jerry Kramer • *Scr* David Newman, from a story by Michael Jackson

More ★ 18

Drama 1969 · Lux /Fr · Colour · 110mins

The fag end of the Swinging Sixties, as seen by debutant director Barbet Schroeder. More soft-core porn than social comment, it's about a German lad who hitch-hikes across Europe, gets into drugs and ends up in Ibiza with Mimsy Farmer. This is the full druggie nightmare, complete with acid trips, skinny-dipping, hippy speak and a music score by Pink Floyd. AT DVD

Mimsy Farmer *Estelle* • Klaus Grunberg *Stefan* • Heinz Engelmann *Wolf* • Michel Chanderli *Charlie* • Louise Wink *Cathy* • Henry Wolf *Henry* ■ *Dir* Barbet Schroeder • *Scr* Paul Gegauff, Barbet Schroeder, from a story by Barbet Schroeder

More American Graffiti ★★ 12

Comedy drama 1979 · US · Colour · 106mins

How do you follow a modern masterpiece like *American Graffiti*? Not with this plodding, inferior sequel, which catches up with the Class of 1962 as they live through the Vietnam-dominated, hippy sixties. The only saving grace is yet another brilliant soundtrack, featuring golden oldies from the Supremes, Mary Wells, the Byrds, Bob Dylan and Cream. Wolfman Jack and Country Joe and the Fish also make appearances in this aimlessly directed failure. AJ [video]

Candy Clark *Debbie Dunham* • Bo Hopkins *Little Joe* • Ron Howard *Steve Bolander* • Paul Le Mat *John Milner* • Mackenzie Phillips *Carol Rainbow* • Charles Martin Smith *Terry the Toad* • Cindy Williams *Laurie Bolander* • Harrison Ford *Motorcycle cop* ■ *Dir* BWL Norton [Bill L Norton] • *Scr* BWL Norton, from characters created by George Lucas, Gloria Katz, Willard Huyck

More Dead than Alive ★★

Western 1969 · US · Colour · 100mins

A potentially interesting western, obviously influenced by Sergio Leone's *Dollars* trilogy and starring TV hunk Clint Walker as a hired gun readjusting to life after 18 years in jail. Unemployable and harassed by former enemies, Walker gets a job in a Wild West show owned by kindly impresario Vincent Price. It's only now that the real plot emerges – Price has hired Walker to replace another crack shot who proceeds to turn psychotic. There're bags of potential here for an off-kilter drama, but Walker has all the charisma of a sack of concrete. AT

Clint Walker *"Killer" Cain* • Vincent Price *Dan Ruffalo* • Anne Francis *Monica Alton* • Paul Hampton *Billy Eager* • Mike Henry *Luke Santee* • Craig Littler *Rafe Karma* ■ *Dir* Robert Sparr • *Scr* George Schenck

More than a Miracle ★★★ U

Fantasy romantic drama
1967 · It/Fr · Colour · 103mins

Sophia Loren and Omar Sharif are paired in this Italian film, directed by Francesco Rosi, about a Spanish aristocrat who falls in love with a peasant girl. The path of true love, however, runs anything but smoothly. Despite being weakened by a running time that's a little too long to support the tale, this is a charming mix of romance, social comment and whimsy, directed and played with a suitably light touch and photographed in the style of an illustrated fairy tale. RK. Italian dialogue dubbed into English.

Sophia Loren *Isabella* • Omar Sharif *Prince Ramon* • Dolores Del Rio *Queen Mother* • Georges Wilson *Monzu* • Leslie French *Brother Joseph of Copertino* • Carlo Pisacane *Witch* • Marina Malfatti *Devout princess* ■ *Dir* Francesco Rosi • *Scr* Francesco Rosi, Tonino Guerra, Raffaele La Capria, Giuseppe Patroni Griffi • *Cinematographer* Pasquale De Santis [Pasqualino De Santis]

The More the Merrier ★★★★ U

Comedy 1943 · US · BW · 99mins

The wartime housing shortage in Washington DC forces government employee Jean Arthur and Joel McCrea to share an apartment with kindly businessman Charles Coburn. Part screwball comedy, part message movie about the need to pull together, it's a piece of fluff effortlessly carried by the charm of its stars and by George Stevens's elegant direction. A scene on the steps of the apartment, when McCrea makes a pass at Arthur, aroused a good deal of comment at the time for being shockingly sexy. There was a 1966 remake, *Walk, Don't Run*, set in Tokyo with Cary Grant in the Coburn role. AT [video]

Jean Arthur *Connie Milligan* • Joel McCrea *Joe Carter* • Charles Coburn *Benjamin Dingle* • Richard Gaines *Charles J Pendergast* • Bruce Bennett *Evans* • Frank Sully *Pike* • Clyde Fillmore *Senator Noonan* ■ *Dir* George Stevens • *Scr* Robert Russell, Frank Ross, Richard Flournoy, Lewis R Foster, from a story by Robert Russell, Frank Ross, Garson Kanin

The More Things Change ★★★ PG

Comedy drama 1985 · Aus · Colour · 90mins

Robyn Nevin was already one of Australia's most respected theatrical directors when she embarked on this, her debut as a film director. She is evidently more at home with coaching her cast than she is with moving a camera and creating dramatic tension through editing, but the strength of the story carries the day. Judy Morris and Barry Otto impress as the Melbourne couple whose relationship becomes strained when he drops out of city life to renovate a run-down farm. Deftly handled, but the melodramatic subplot involving their pregnant teenage nanny gets in the way. DP [video]

Judy Morris *Connie* • Barry Otto *Lex* • Victoria Longley *Geraldine* • Lewis Fitz-Gerald *Barry* • Peter Carroll *Roley* • Louise Le Nay *Lydia* • Owen Johnson *Nicholas* • Brenda Addie *Angela* ■ *Dir* Robyn Nevin • *Scr* Moya Wood

Morgan – a Suitable Case for Treatment ★★★ PG

Comedy drama 1966 · UK · Colour · 92mins

Angry young men were abundant in the British cinema of the 1960s, but they were never so irate as working-class artist David Warner, who tries to sabotage the second marriage of his middle-class ex-wife Vanessa Redgrave to art dealer Robert Stephens by rewiring their house and dressing in a gorilla suit. Adapted from David Mercer's television play, it's really a fable about the class society. Yet its dream sequences and surreal touches make it more odd than meaningful, and it now feels dated. TH [video]

Vanessa Redgrave *Leonie Delt* • David Warner *Morgan Delt* • Robert Stephens *Charles Napier* • Irene Handl *Mrs Delt* • Newton Blick *Mr Henderson* • Nan Munro *Mrs Henderson* • Bernard Bresslaw *Policeman* ■ *Dir* Karel Reisz • *Scr* David Mercer, from his TV play *A Suitable Case for Treatment*

Morgan the Pirate ★★ U

Swashbuckling adventure
1960 · It/Fr · Colour · 95mins

Bodybuilder Steve Reeves shakes off the loincloth of his usual Greek heroes and dons the costume of legendary pirate Henry Morgan. Reeves sticks in the craw of the Spanish, launches a raid on Panama and sweeps the governor's daughter off her feet. His performance is fairly gormless but he's got a bigger chest than his leading ladies and a jawline that would make a crocodile shed tears. AT

Steve Reeves *Sir Henry Morgan* • Valérie Lagrange *Dona Inez* • Lidia Alfonsi *Dona Maria* • Chelo Alonso *Concepcion* • Armand Mestral *L'Olannais* • Ivo Garrani *Governor* ■ *Dir* Andre De Toth, Primo Zeglio • *Scr* Andre De Toth, Primo Zeglio, Filippo Sanjust

The Morning After ★★★ 15

Thriller 1986 · US · Colour · 102mins

Sidney Lumet is best known for his New York stories of civic crime and corruption. This, though, was the first film Lumet directed that was set in LA and he gives it an abstract gloss and uses some bizarre locations, including a Gaudi-esque house that hides away behind Rodeo Drive. The plot is rather more ordinary: Jane Fonda wakes up next to a man with a knife through his chest. An alcoholic actress, she hasn't a clue what happened, so ex-cop Jeff Bridges helps her out. There are false trails, red herrings and Raul Julia as Fonda's hairdresser husband, but, for Lumet, it's a rare exercise in style and mood. AT. Contains swearing and violence. [video]

Jane Fonda *Alex Sternbergen* • Jeff Bridges *Turner Kendall* • Raul Julia *Joaquin "Jacky" Manero* • Diane Salinger *Isabel Harding* • Richard Foronjy *Sergeant Greenbaum* • Geoffrey Scott *Bobby Korshack* ■ *Dir* Sidney Lumet • *Scr* James Hicks

Morning Departure ★★★

Drama 1950 · UK · BW · 102mins

An atmospheric "confined space" drama, with John Mills in one of his best roles as the commander of a submarine, holed by a mine and plunging to the sea bed. Twelve crew members survive the initial impact, but only eight will be able to use the escape equipment. A spot of bother, in other words, but everyone makes you proud to be British, apart from Richard Attenborough, playing a weak-willed stoker with his trademark intensity. PF

John Mills *Lieutenant Commander Armstrong* • Helen Cherry *Helen* • Richard Attenborough *Stoker Snipe* • Lana Morris *Rose Snipe* • Nigel Patrick *Lieutenant Harry Manson* • Andrew Crawford *Warrant Officer McFee* • Michael Brennan *Chief Petty Officer Barlow* ■ *Dir* Roy Baker [Roy Ward Baker] • *Scr* WEC Fairchild, from the play by Kenneth Woollard

Morning Glory ★★★

Drama 1933 · US · BW · 74mins

"The calla lillies are in bloom again" in Katharine Hepburn's stunningly mannered performance, which won her the first of her unequalled (and likely to remain so) four best actress Oscars. Cast as young Broadway hopeful Eva Lovelace, she's all angles and angst in this adaptation of Zoe Akins's play about a starry-eyed Cinderella. Despite Hepburn's worthy co-stars, who include Adolphe Menjou as a lecherous producer and Douglas Fairbanks Jr as an earnest playwright, the movie belongs totally to Kate. Remade in 1958 as *Stage Struck*. TS

Katharine Hepburn *Eva Lovelace* • Douglas Fairbanks Jr *Joseph Sheridan* • Adolphe Menjou *Louis Easton* • Mary Duncan *Rita Vernon* • C Aubrey Smith *Robert Harley Hedges* ■ *Dir* Lowell Sherman • *Scr* Howard J Green, from the play by Zoe Akins

Morocco ★★★★★

Romance 1930 · US · BW · 90mins

This is screen goddess Marlene Dietrich's first American-made movie, sumptuously directed by her *Blue Angel* mentor Josef von Sternberg and ravishingly photographed by the great Lee Garmes and Lucien Ballard. Dietrich's romantic partner is handsome foreign legionnaire Gary Cooper, and the audience is left wondering whether she'll choose between him or dapper, worldly Adolphe Menjou. Dietrich makes her

M

displaced cabaret chanteuse very real and touching, and her first appearance in the Moroccan nightclub is an ultra-sophisticated piece of staging that is as ornate as it is outrageous. This movie set the seal on Dietrich's image for ever. TS

Marlene Dietrich *Amy Jolly* • Gary Cooper *Tom Brown* • Adolphe Menjou *Le Bessier* • Ullrich Haupt *Adjutant Caesar* • Juliette Compton *Anna Dolores* • Francis McDonald *Cpl Tatoche* ■ *Dir* Josef von Sternberg • *Scr* Jules Furthman, from the novel *Amy Jolly* by Benno Vigny • *Art Director* Hans Dreier

Morons from Outer Space ★ PG

Science-fiction spoof
1985 · UK · Colour · 86mins

Mel Smith and Griff Rhys Jones's lamentable lampoon is a shambling spoof with little wit. Directed by Mike Hodges, who really should have known better, the pathetic story concerns aliens from the planet Blob crash-landing on Earth and forming a glam-rock band. But the end result wouldn't have made the grade during the Oxbridge duo's student rag week. AJ. Contains swearing. DVD

Mel Smith *Bernard* • Griff Rhys Jones *Graham Sweetley* • James B Sikking *Col Laribee* • Dinsdale Landen *Cdr Matteson* • Jimmy Nail *Desmond* • Joanne Pearce *Sandra* • Paul Bown *Julian* ■ *Dir* Mike Hodges • *Scr* Mel Smith, Griff Rhys Jones, Bob Mercer

Mortal Fear ★★ 12

Medical thriller 1994 · US · Colour · 86mins

This TV thriller based on the novel by Robin Cook bears a remarkable similarity to his earlier bestseller, *Coma*. Joanna Kerns is the high-flying medic who suspects something is not quite right when her hospital begins to lose patients at a rate even an overworked junior doctor might notice. You've seen it all before. DP DVD

Joanna Kerns *Dr Jennifer Kessler* • Gregory Harrison *Philip Montgomery* • Robert Englund *Dr Ralph Wanamaker* • Max Gail *Det Michael Curran* • Rebecca Schull *Dr Danforth* ■ *Dir* Larry Shaw • *Scr* Rob Gilmer, Roger Young, from the novel by Robin Cook

Mortal Kombat ★★★ 15

Martial arts action adventure
1995 · US · Colour · 97mins

At the time this film was made, *Mortal Kombat* was the world's biggest-selling game franchise, so it was a natural choice for a Hollywood makeover. And unlike other games-inspired turkeys (*Super Mario Bros*, *Street Fighter*), this one actually works, thanks mainly to director Paul Anderson's single-minded dedication to nonstop, expertly choreographed martial arts action. Christopher Lambert is the nominal star, but the best work comes from Cary-Hiroyuki Tagawa, who steals the show with a typically charismatic performance. JF. Contains violence and some swearing. DVD

Christopher Lambert *Lord Rayden* • Bridgette Wilson *Sonya Blade* • Linden Ashby *Johnny Cage* • Talisa Soto *Princess Kitana* • Cary-Hiroyuki Tagawa *Shang Tsung* ■ *Dir* Paul Anderson • *Scr* Kevin Droney, from the computer game by Ed Boon, John Tobias

Mortal Kombat: Annihilation ★★ 15

Martial arts action adventure
1997 · US · Colour · 90mins

The martial arts arcade game spawns a second movie incarnation that offers even bigger helpings of action and special effects than the original. Robin Shou is back from the first outing, though Christopher Lambert's role is now taken by James Remar. Evil warlords from the sinister Outworld are bent on dominating Earth again, and only a handful of fearless heroes can save the day. Undemanding fun. JF. Contains violence. DVD

Robin Shou *Liu Kang* • Talisa Soto *Princess Kitana* • James Remar *Lord Rayden* • Sandra Hess *Sonya Blade* ■ *Dir* John R Leonetti • *Scr* Brent V Friedman, Bryce Zabel, from a story by John Tobias, Lawrence Kasanoff, Joshua Wexler, from the computer game by Ed Boon, John Tobias

Mortal Passions ★★ 18

Black comedy thriller
1989 · US · Colour · 91mins

David Warner adds a little bit of class to this otherwise routine erotic thriller, which went straight to video over here. Krista Errickson is the *femme fatale* who leads innocent husband Zach Galligan into a web of sexual and murderous intrigue. Warner plays the psychiatrist who is Galligan's only confidante. Director Andrew Lane throws in plenty of sex and nudity, but is less sure when it comes to the unnecessarily complicated plotting. JF. Contains violence and swearing.

Zach Galligan *Todd* • David Warner *Dr Powers* • Krista Errickson *Emily* • Sheila Kelley *Adele* • Michael Bowen *Berke* • Luca Bercovici *Darcy* ■ *Dir* Andrew Lane • *Scr* Alan Moskowitz

Mortal Sins ★★

Detective drama 1989 · US · Colour · 90mins

Private investigator Brian Benben is hired by a local TV evangelist to investigate the death of an associate, and he is approached shortly afterwards by the reverend's daughter on another matter. Signs point to a competing televangelist as the culprit, but Benben discovers that little is as it seems and the stern righteousness displayed by the fundamentalist church leaders may be no more than a veneer. Benben has some funny moments, but there's a lot of melodrama slowing things down. ST

Brian Benben *Nathan* • Debrah Farentino *Laura Rollins* • Anthony LaPaglia *Vito* • James Harper *Malcolm Rollins* • Brick Hartney *Billy Beau Backus* • James Saito *Park Sung* ■ *Dir* Yuri Sivo • *Scr* Allen Blumberg

The Mortal Storm ★★★

Drama 1940 · US · BW · 100mins

This version was daring in its time for alerting American audiences to the dangers of Nazism, though the horror is softened by the casting of resolutely all-American types as Germans and by a very Culver City Reich. Director Frank Borzage does not keep sentimentality at bay, but his drama is nevertheless moving and tragic by turns. It also features the marvellous Margaret Sullavan and the lanky but lovable James Stewart. Frank Morgan is genuinely touching as the father who watches his family disintegrate, and there's a chilling early cameo from later dance master Dan Dailey. TS

Margaret Sullavan *Freya Roth* • James Stewart *Martin Brietner* • Robert Young (1) *Fritz Marlberg* • Frank Morgan *Professor Roth* • Robert Stack *Otto Von Rohn* • Bonita Granville *Elsa* • Irene Rich *Mrs Roth* • William T Orr *Erich Von Rohn* ■ *Dir* Frank Borzage • *Scr* Claudine West, Anderson Ellis, George Froeschel, from the novel by Phyllis Bottome

Mortal Thoughts ★★★ 18

Thriller 1991 · US · Colour · 98mins

Told in flashback, this drama (co-produced by star Demi Moore) follows two women friends (Moore and Glenne Headly) who are both unhappy in their marriages, and who end up being linked with the murder of Headly's husband (Bruce Willis). The acting from the three protagonists, and Harvey Keitel as the investigating detective, is superb, lifting what could have been a depressing tale into an intriguing mystery. JB. Contains swearing and violence. DVD

Demi Moore *Cynthia Kellogg* • Glenne Headly *Joyce Urbanski* • Bruce Willis *James Urbanski* • John Pankow *Arthur Kellogg* • Harvey Keitel *Detective John Woods* • Billie Neal *Linda Nealon* • Frank Vincent *Dominic Marino* • Karen Shallo *Gloria Urbanski* • Crystal Field *Jeanette Marino* ■ *Dir* Alan Rudolph • *Scr* William Reilly, Claude Kerven

Mortgage ★★★

Documentary drama
1989 · Aus · Colour · 92mins

Former documentary director Bill Bennett was the pioneer of the docudrama in which real-life professionals played themselves in situations built around a couple of fictional characters. This often engrossing film recalls the Cary Grant-Myrna Loy comedy *Mr Blandings Builds His Dream House*, only without the laughs, as the string of setbacks that beset this couple are staged to arouse the anger of any viewer who has ever applied for a mortgage, sought planning permission or been ripped off by cowboy builders. DP

Brian Vriends *Dave Dodd* • Doris Younane *Tina Dodd* • Bruce Venables *George Shooks* • Andrew Gilbert [Andrew S Gilbert] *Kevin Grant* • Paul Coolahan *Jack Napper* ■ *Dir/Scr* Bill Bennett

Morvern Callar ★★★★ 15

Drama 2001 · UK/Can · Colour · 93mins

Based on Alan Warner's cult novel, this is director Lynne Ramsay's follow-up to her acclaimed debut *Ratcatcher*. Preserving the novel's quirky and oblique originality, Ramsay relates the tale of the eponymous Oban shopgirl (an intelligent and compelling performance from Samantha Morton) who wakes on Christmas morning to find that her boyfriend has committed suicide. Morvern casually dismembers and buries his body, and then deletes her boyfriend's name from the novel he has bequeathed her, keys in her own and sends it to a publisher. Using money from his bank account, she departs for a hedonistic holiday in Spain, where the film shifts gear. With its assured directorial style, this confirms Ramsay's reputation as a true cinematic artist. AC DVD

Samantha Morton *Morvern Callar* • Kathleen McDermott *Lanna* • Raife Patrick Burchell *Boy in room 1022* • Dan Cadan *Dazzer* • Carolyn Calder *Tequila Sheila* • Jim Wilson (3) *Tom Boddington* • Dolly Wells *Susan* • Ruby Milton *Couris Jean* ■ *Dir* Lynne Ramsay • *Scr* Lynne Ramsay, Liana Dognini, from the novel by Alan Warner

Moscow Distrusts Tears ★★★

Romantic comedy drama
1979 · USSR · Colour · 147mins

A surprise winner of the Oscar for best foreign film, Vladimir Menshov's "that was then, this is now" melodrama harks back to the ensemble "women's pictures" made in Hollywood in the 1950s. Beginning in a Moscow factory hostel in the Khrushchev era, the action jumps forward 20 years to see how socially ambitious Irina Muravyova, conservative Raisa Ryazanova and ditzy Vera Alentova made out. Despite the broken marriages, illegitimate births, compromises and disappointments, the trio remain inseparable. For all the energetic performances and politicised setting, however, there's nothing particularly remarkable here. DP. In Russian with English subtitles.

Vera Alentova *Katya* • Alexei Batalov *Goscha* • Irina Muravyova *Ludmilla* • Raisa Ryazanova *Antonia* • Yuri Vasilyev *Rudolf* ■ *Dir* Vladimir Menshov • *Scr* Valentin Chernykh

Moscow Nights ★★

Drama 1935 · UK · BW · 100mins

The daughter of impoverished Russian aristocrats (a colourless Penelope Dudley Ward), forced into marriage with a boorish but wealthy tradesman (Harry Baur), really loves a handsome army officer (Laurence Olivier). In debt to her husband after losing a card game, the officer's efforts to pay up lead him into the spy game and a charge of treason. Directed by Anthony Asquith, this tangled and creaky brouhaha offers good performances from Olivier and the splendid French actor Baur, but is curiously uninteresting. RK

Harry Baur *Brioukow* • Laurence Olivier *Capt Ignatoff* • Penelope Dudley Ward *Natasha* • Robert Cochran *Polonsky* • Morton Selten *Kovrin* • Athene Seyler *Mme Sabline* ■ *Dir* Anthony Asquith • *Scr* Anthony Asquith, Erich Seipmann, from the novel *Les Nuits de Moscou* by Pierre Benoit

Moscow on the Hudson ★★★ 15

Comedy drama 1984 · US · Colour · 112mins

There's a gentle, sweet-natured core to Robin Williams's screen personality that is too often camouflaged by the hysteria that forms the basis of his performances. This rather melancholy comedy lets that attractive side surface to good effect, with Williams playing a Soviet circus musician who defects while shopping in New York. He then finds, once he's part of the immigrant experience, that life is as racist and rancid as back home, with freedom as a meagre bonus. Director Paul Mazursky gallops off in too many directions, but Williams's performance is a real treat. TH. Contains swearing, violence and nudity. DVD

Robin Williams *Vladimir Ivanoff* • Maria Conchita Alonso *Lucia Lombardo* • Cleavant Derricks *Lionel Witherspoon* • Alejandro Rey *Orlando Ramirez* • Savely Kramarov *Boris* • Oleg Rudnik *Yury* ■ *Dir* Paul Mazursky • *Scr* Paul Mazursky, Leon Capetanos

Moses ★★ 15

Biblical epic 1975 · UK/It · Colour · 135mins

Burt Lancaster does everything you'd expect as Moses: he orders up plagues, leads his people out of Egypt, parts the Red Sea, climbs Mount Sinai and comes back down with the Ten Commandments. This Lew Grade production was originally a six-hour mini-series, partly written by Anthony Burgess; the latter also composed his own music score, but it was rejected in favour of one from Ennio Morricone. However, where Cecil DeMille's 1956 version was a ponderous but occasionally juicy religious epic, this is more of a dreary historical drama that breaks the 11th commandment: "Thou Shalt Not Bore." AT

Burt Lancaster *Moses* • Anthony Quayle *Aaron* • Ingrid Thulin *Miriam* • Irene Papas *Zipporah* • Mariangela Melato *Princess Bithia* • William Lancaster *Young Moses* ■ *Dir* Gianfranco de Bosio • *Scr* Anthony Burgess, Victorio Bonicelli, Gianfranco de Bosio

The Mosquito Coast ★★★★ PG

Drama 1986 · US · Colour · 113mins

This absorbing journey into the heart of darkness provides Harrison Ford with one of the most unsympathetic characters of his film career. He plays an idealistic, obsessive inventor who begins a slow slide into madness when he moves his family to Central America in a doomed attempt to bring ice to the jungle. Paul Schrader intelligently adapts Paul Theroux's source novel and, if director Peter Weir loses his way a little, the performances are uniformly superb. Ford is surprisingly convincing as the outwardly charming control freak, while River Phoenix gives a portrayal beyond his years as his troubled son. JF. Contains some mild violence.

Harrison Ford *Allie Fox* • Helen Mirren *Mother* • River Phoenix *Charlie* • Jadrien Steele *Jerry* • Hilary Gordon *April* • Rebecca Gordon *Clover* • Jason Alexander *Clerk* • Martha Plimpton *Emily Spellgood* ■ *Dir* Peter Weir • *Scr* Paul Schrader, from the novel by Paul Theroux

Mosquito Squadron ★★ PG

Second World War adventure
1968 · UK · Colour · 89mins

A host of familiar faces that you can't quite put a name to keep their upper lips stiff as our boys try to destroy a French chateau containing the Nazis' super-duper doodlebug, the V3, in this derivative war drama. David McCallum plays an RAF pilot who must comfort his missing friend's wife and lead the mission. Only some nice flying sequences and the support of Charles Gray pass muster. DP DVD

David McCallum *Quint Munroe* • Suzanne Neve *Beth Scott* • David Buck *Squadron Leader David Scott* • David Dundas *Flight Lieutenant Douglas Shelton* • Dinsdale Landen *Wing Commander Penrose* • Charles Gray *Air Commodore Hufford* • Michael Anthony *Father Bellague* ■ *Dir* Boris Sagal • *Scr* Donald S Sanford, Joyce Perry

Moss Rose ★★

Period detective drama
1947 · US · BW · 81mins

Who is murdering Victor Mature's lovers and leaving behind the clue of a bible marked with a dried moss rose? Vincent Price plays the sly detective in charge of the cryptic case, proving he could be just as convincing on the right side of the law as he would soon be on the wrong. Mature isn't interesting or enigmatic enough in this muddled whodunnit, but solid trouping by a good supporting cast gives it a much needed lift. AJ

Peggy Cummins *Belle Adair* • Victor Mature *Sir Alexander Sterling* • Ethel Barrymore *Lady Sterling* • Vincent Price *Inspector Clinner* • Margo Woode *Daisy Arrow* • George Zucco *Craxton* • Patricia Medina *Audrey Ashton* • Felippa Rock *Liza* ■ *Dir* Gregory Ratoff • *Scr* Jules Furthman, Tom Reed, Niven Busch, from the novel by Joseph Shearing

The Most Dangerous Game ★★★★ 12

Classic horror 1932 · US · BW · 62mins

Originally released in the UK as *The Hounds of Zaroff*, this teaming of star Fay Wray and co-director Ernest Schoedsack predates their classic *King Kong*, and traverses similar action territory, with the genius of composer Max Steiner vividly illuminating both movies. Richard Connell's story was a natural for filming, but none of the subsequent versions live up to the sheer exuberance of this cracker. Leslie Banks's mad Count Zaroff remains hard to replicate and the theme of hunting human game was never quite so chilling as here. No question, this is the best movie version of the tale. TS DVD

Joel McCrea *Bob Rainsford* • Fay Wray *Eve Trowbridge* • Leslie Banks *Count Zaroff* • Robert Armstrong *Martin Trowbridge* • Steve Clemento *Tartar servant* • Noble Johnson *Tartar servant* ■ *Dir* Ernest B Schoedsack, Irving Pichel • *Scr* James A Creelman, from the story *The Most Dangerous Game* by Richard Connell

The Most Dangerous Man Alive ★

Science fiction 1961 · US · Colour · 80mins

Escaped convict Ron Randell is accidentally exposed to radiation by a cobalt bomb explosion and becomes an unstoppable superman, hell-bent on revenge against the gangsters who framed him. The last film directed by silent pioneer Allan Dwan is an over-familiar, poverty-row mix of science-fiction thriller and mob melodrama. AJ

Ron Randell *Eddie Candell* • Debra Paget *Linda Marlow* • Elaine Stewart *Carla Angelo* • Anthony Caruso *Andy Damon* • Gregg Palmer *Lt Fisher* ■ *Dir* Allan Dwan • *Scr* James Leicester, Phillip Rock, from the story *The Steel Monster* by Michael Pate, Phillip Rock

The Most Desired Man ★★★ 18

Romantic comedy
1994 · Ger · Colour · 90mins

Highly rated by those who know their German movies, *The Most Desired Man* is proof that the phrase "German comedy" isn't always an oxymoron. The film concerns a heterosexual man and incorrigible womaniser who, having been booted out of his girlfriend's flat, moves in with a gay friend. When the girlfriend discovers she's pregnant, she sets out to get him back, ignorant of the circle he now moves in. DA. In German with English subtitles.

Til Schweiger *Axel Feldheim* • Katja Riemann *Doro Feldheim* • Joachim Król *Norbert Brommer* • Antonia Lang *Elke Schmitt* ■ *Dir* Sönke Wortmann • *Scr* Sönke Wortmann, from the comic books *Der Bewegte Mann* and *Pretty Baby* by Ralf König

The Most Fertile Man in Ireland ★★ 15

Romantic comedy
1999 · UK/Ire · Colour · 92mins

Debutant director Dudi Appleton opts for a broad and bawdy approach to the discovery that dating agent Kris Marshall has the potency to impregnate even the most infertile female. Consequently, the round of comic couplings soon loses its novelty, while subplots involving Marshall's crush on undertaker's assistant Kathy Keira Clarke and his brush with angry Orangeman James Nesbitt prompt a shift in tone that deflates the fun without adding much insight. DP DVD

Kris Marshall *Eamon Manley* • Kathy Keira Clarke *Rosie* • Bronagh Gallagher *Millicent* • James Nesbitt *"Mad Dog" Billy Wilson* • Kenneth Cranham *Da* • Olivia Nash *Ma* • Pauline McLynn *Maeve* • Toyah Willcox *Dr Johnson* ■ *Dir* Dudi Appleton • *Scr* Jim Keeble

The Most Terrible Time in My Life ★★

Detective drama 1993 · Jpn · BW · 92mins

This Japanese crime comedy, a yakuza spoof, is simply too knowing for its own good. Director Kaizo Hayashi is too intent on pace and pastiche to make the plot intelligible, while the flashy camerawork is dizzying rather than dazzling. Indeed, the director is so pleased with his efforts that he even tacks on a cod trailer for star Masatoshi Nagase's return as private eye Maiku Hama (get it?). DP. In Japanese with English subtitles.

Masatoshi Nagase *Maiku Hama* • Shiro Sano *Kanno* • Kiyotaka Nanbara *Hoshino* • Yang Haitin *Yang Hai Tin* • Hou De Jian *De Jian* • Akaji Maro *Lt Nakayama* • Shinya Tsukamoto *Yamaguchi* ■ *Dir* Kaizo Hayashi • *Scr* Daisuke Tengan, Kaizo Hayashi

Most Wanted ★★★ 15

Action adventure 1997 · US · Colour · 94mins

In the conspiracy thriller stakes, this is minor league stuff, but very entertaining nonetheless. In a more serious role than usual, writer/star Keenen Ivory Wayans plays a former army sniper recruited into a shadowy government organisation, only to find himself framed for the murder of the First Lady. The political machinations don't bear close scrutiny, but director David Glenn Hogan stages some immaculate action set pieces and the cast is top quality, with Jon Voight staging a dress rehearsal for his role in *Enemy of the State*. JF. Contains some swearing and violence. DVD

Keenen Ivory Wayans *James Dunn* • Jon Voight *Casey/General Woodward* • Jill Hennessy *Dr Victoria Constantini* • Paul Sorvino *CIA Deputy Director Kenny Rackmill* • Robert Culp *Donald Bickhart* ■ *Dir* David Glenn Hogan [David Hogan] • *Scr* Keenen Ivory Wayans

Mostly Martha ★★★ PG

Romantic comedy
2001 · Ger/Austria/Swi/It · Colour · 102mins

Director Sandra Nettelbeck – here making her feature debut – opts for the tart rather than the saccharine approach in this food-themed romantic comedy. The ordered existence of Hamburg chef Martina Gedeck is disrupted by the arrival at home of her orphaned eight-year-old niece (Maxime Foerste) and at work of a handsome Italian rival (Sergio Castellitto). Nettelbeck questions the place of cuisine in the pantheon of sophistication while making sly observations about gender and cultural stereotypes. DP. In German with English subtitles. DVD

Martina Gedeck *Martha Klein* • Sergio Castellitto *Mario* • Maxime Foerste *Lina* • Sibylle Canonica *Frida* • Katja Studt *Lea* • Oliver Broumis *Jan* • August Zirner *Therapist* • Ulrich Thomsen *Sam Thalberg* ■ *Dir/Scr* Sandra Nettelbeck

Motel ★★

Murder mystery
1983 · Mex/US · Colour · 99mins

Having partly trained in London and drawn acclaim for a series of assured shorts, Mexican-born Luis Mandoki made his feature debut with this slow-burning thriller, which is less a whodunnit than an intriguing clash of personalities. Hired to investigate the death of a wealthy socialite, detective José Alonso seems to be confronted by the perfect crime. But his sole clue takes him to an isolated motel, where the peculiar behaviour of the couple in charge arouses his suspicions. DP. In Spanish with English subtiltes.

Blanca Guerra *Marta Holtz* • José Alonso *Andres Camargo* • Salvador Sanchez *Julian Vargas* • Carmelita Gonzalez *Carolina Lopez* ■ *Dir* Luis Mandoki • *Scr* Abraham Cherem, Jordi Arenas

Motel Blue ★★ 18

Erotic thriller 1997 · US · Colour · 90mins

Sean Young was briefly on the cusp of great things, but now she camps it up in soft-focus romps that tend to raise titters rather than titillate. Here she plays a top-level scientist, whose request for additional security clearance sparks a government inquiry that reveals much more than trade secrets. Soleil Moon Frye is out of her depth alongside such inveterate scene-stealers as Robert Vaughn and Seymour Cassel. DP

Sean Young *Lana Hawking* • Soleil Moon Frye *Agent Kyle Rivers* • Seymour Cassel *Old priest* • Robert Vaughn *Chief MacIntyre* ■ *Dir* Sam Firstenberg • *Scr* Cormac Wibberley, Marianne Wibberley

Motel Hell ★★★ 18

Cult black comedy horror
1980 · US · Colour · 97mins

A gory horror spoof that successfully walks the fine line between bad taste and nutty wit, Amicus alumnus Kevin Connor's remarkable slice of backwoods American Gothic is a classy shocker that stands out from the usual stalk-and-slash pack. Farmer Rory Calhoun ambushes passers-by at his roadside motel, buries them alive up to their necks, fattens them up and then uses their flesh for his famous spicy smoked meats. Explicit, gruesome, harrowing (the human harvesting is very nasty) and outrageously funny (mainly because of Calhoun's endearingly nonchalant performance). AJ DVD

Rory Calhoun *Vincent Smith* • Paul Linke *Bruce Smith* • Nancy Parsons *Ida Smith* • Nina Axelrod *Terry* • Wolfman Jack *Reverend Billy* • Elaine Joyce *Edith Olson* ■ *Dir* Kevin Connor • *Scr* Robert Jaffe, Steven-Charles Jaffe

Mother ★★★★★

Silent drama 1926 · USSR · BW · 106mins

Vsevolod Pudovkin's first feature is one of the classics of the golden age of Russian cinema. The tightly constructed narrative, adapted from Maxim Gorky's rambling novel, concerns a mother (the extraordinary Vera Baranovskaya) who, at the time of the abortive revolution of 1905, accidentally gives up her communist son to the police. The superb cast is made up of members of the Moscow Arts Theatre, with Pudovkin himself playing the interrogating officer. By an ingenious juxtaposition of images, the director creates an illusion of sound, and the emotional impact has not diminished with time. RB

Vera Baranovskaya *Pelageya Vlasova, the mother* • A Tchistyakova *Vlasov, her husband* • Nikolai Batalov *Pavel, her son* • Vsevolod I Pudovkin *Police officer* ■ *Dir* Vsevolod I Pudovkin • *Scr* Nathan Zarkhi, Vsevolod Pudovkin, from the novel *Mat* by Maxim Gorky

Mother ★★★ 12

Comedy 1996 · US · Colour · 99mins

Albert Brooks writes, directs and stars in this uneven but intermittently hilarious ode to mothers. He plays a writer who returns to his childhood home when his relationship and career go down the pan, only to be driven over the edge by his mom (hilariously played by Debbie Reynolds) and her sly, sarcastic comments. Brooks gives a nice performance, but this is Reynolds's film, and she steals every scene she's in. JB

Albert Brooks *John Henderson* • Debbie Reynolds *Beatrice Henderson* • Rob Morrow *Jeff Henderson* • Lisa Kudrow *Linda* • John C McGinley *Carl* • Paul Collins *Lawyer* • Laura Weekes *Karen Henderson* ■ *Dir* Albert Brooks • *Scr* Albert Brooks, Monica Johnson

M/Other ★★★

Drama 1999 · Jpn · Colour · 147mins

Through his resolute adherence to improvisation, Nobuhiro Suwa has become a distinctive voice in Japanese cinema. Not everyone will appreciate his patient objectivity, as graphic designer Makiko Watanabe attempts to impress restaurateur boyfriend Tomokazu Miura by playing the perfect surrogate to his young son, while his real mother recovers from a broken leg. But Suwa achieves a rare naturalism that becomes almost too painful to watch, as an already shaky relationship starts to come apart at the seams. Heroically honest. DP. In Japanese with English subtitles.

Tomokazu Miura *Tetsuro* • Makiko Watanabe *Aki* • Ryudai Takahashi *Shun* ■ *Dir* Nobuhiro Suwa • *Scr* Nobuhiro Suwa, Tomokazu Miura, Makiko Watanabe

The Mother ★★★★ 15

Romantic drama
2003 · UK · Colour · 107mins

Not since *Harold And Maude* has a film so affectionately addressed the controversial theme of autumn–spring romance. While visiting her children in West London, recently widowed grandmother Anne Reid gradually finds herself in lust with Daniel Craig, the

M

much younger handyman renovating her son's house. Craig happens to be having an affair with Reid's daughter (Cathryn Bradshaw), but it's not long before Reid and Craig begin a sexual relationship of their own. Roger Michell's film thankfully avoids the pitfalls of its toy-boy premise, and it challenges taboos insightfully, with great emotional maturity. TH. Contains swearing and drug abuse. DVD

Anne Reid *May* • Cathryn Bradshaw *Paula* • Daniel Craig *Darren* • Steven Mackintosh *Bobby* • Oliver Ford Davies *Bruce* • Anna Wilson-Jones *Helen* • Peter Vaughan *Toots* • Harry Michell *Harry* • Rosie Michell *Rosie* ■ *Dir* Roger Michell • *Scr* Hanif Kureishi

Mother and Son ★★★★ U

Drama 1997 · Ger/Rus · Colour · 70mins

The agony of seeing a loved one draw close to death is presented in such intimate detail in this meticulous Russian drama, that watching it feels like an intrusion on the grief of the ailing mother and her devoted son. Considering neither Gudrun Geyer nor Alexei Ananishnov are professionals, they give performances of remarkable power and simplicity as they explore their mutual dependence. Rarely has silence been so poignant as director Aleksandr Sokurov fashions images that draw as heavily on the romantic art of Caspar David Friedrich as they do on the cinema of Vsevolod Pudovkin and Andrei Tarkovsky. Intense, moving and memorable. DP. In Russian with English subtitles.

Gudrun Geyer *Mother* • Alexei Ananishnov *Son* ■ *Dir* Aleksandr Sokurov • *Scr* Yuri Arabov

Mother India ★★★★ U

Drama 1957 · Ind · Colour · 159mins

Regarded by some as Bollywood's *Gone with the Wind*, Mehboob Khan's film shows a heartbroken mother winning the support of her neighbours, thus becoming a symbol of national pain and perseverance. The action is told as an extended flashback, as Nargis remembers the hardships that ultimately drove her to kill her own rebellious son, Sunil Dutt (Nargis's future husband). Sacrificing realism for epic spectacle, the film was nominated for the best foreign film Oscar. DP. In Hindi with English subtitles. DVD

Nargis *Radha* • Sunil Dutt *Birju* • Rajendra Kumar *Ramu* • Raaj Kumar *Shamoo* ■ *Dir* Mehboob Khan • *Scr* S Ali Raza, Vajahat Mirza, Mehboob Khan

Mother Is a Freshman ★★★ U

Comedy 1949 · US · Colour · 80mins

This utterly charming Loretta Young vehicle has a very silly plot but is so ravishingly filmed in that rich and garish 1940s Technicolor that it hardly matters if mother Loretta or daughter Betty Lynn ends up with charmer Van Johnson. Veteran director Lloyd Bacon, responsible for *42nd Street*, just lets the laughs fall where they may, and there's a nice supporting turn from the one-time king of the megaphone, former heart-throb Rudy Vallee. TS

Loretta Young *Abigail "Abby" Fortitude Abbott* • Van Johnson *Professor Richard Michaels* • Rudy Vallee *John Heaslip* • Barbara Lawrence *Louise Sharpe* • Robert Arthur *Beaumont Jackson* • Betty Lynn *Susan Abbott* ■ *Dir* Lloyd Bacon • *Scr* Mary Loos, Richard Sale, from a story by Raphael Blau

Mother, Jugs & Speed ★★★ 15

Black comedy 1976 · US · Colour · 98mins

Guess who's who in the title roles as Bill Cosby, Harvey Keitel and Raquel Welch charge around as private ambulance drivers in this dark comedy with slapstick moments from *Bullitt* director Peter Yates. The cast acquits itself well, and there's an especially funny pre-JR Larry Hagman playing a randy driver, but the whole enterprise really comes to a halt thanks to the lack of narrative. TS. Contains some violence, swearing, drug abuse.

Bill Cosby *Mother* • Raquel Welch *Jugs* • Harvey Keitel *Speed* • Allen Garfield *Harry Fishbine* • LQ Jones *Davey* • Bruce Davison *Leroy* • Dick Butkus *Rodeo* • Larry Hagman *Murdoch* ■ *Dir* Peter Yates • *Scr* Tom Mankiewicz, from a story by Stephen Manes, Tom Mankiewicz

Mother Küsters Goes to Heaven ★★★★

Drama 1975 · W Ger · Colour · 108mins

Banned from the Berlin Film Festival for its scathing exposé of the self-seeking agendas of both political activists and the press, Rainer Werner Fassbinder's bitterly ironic fable was filmed in a remarkable 20 days. Widowed after her working-class husband kills both his boss and himself, Brigitte Mira is cast into isolation before being besieged by new exploitative "friends". That she emerges having discovered both herself and her fate owes much to Mira's astute performance and to Fassbinder's world-weary cynicism. DP. In German with English subtitles.

Brigitte Mira *Mother Küsters* • Ingrid Caven *Corinna Corinne* • Armin Meier *Ernst* • Irm Hermann *Helene* • Gottfried John *Journalist* • Karlheinz Böhm *Thalmann* • Margit Carstensen *Mrs Thalmann* ■ *Dir* Rainer Werner Fassbinder • *Scr* Rainer Werner Fassbinder, Kurt Raab, from a story by Heinrich Zille

Mother Lode ★★ PG

Adventure 1982 · US · Colour · 98mins

Kim Basinger and Nick Mancuso fly into the Canadian wilderness in the hope of finding gold. But all they find is Charlton Heston, a wild man of the forest with a weird Scottish accent and a twin brother. Written and produced by Chuck's son, Fraser, and financed outside the studio system, this is almost a Heston home movie; what drew them to make it, however, remains buried underground. The usual things happen – Basinger and Mancuso's plane crashes on landing, leaving them stranded – but there's little to enjoy here except some spectacular scenery. AT

Charlton Heston *Silas McGee/Ian McGee* • Nick Mancuso *Jean Dupre* • Kim Basinger *Andrea Spalding* • John Marley *Elijah* • Dale Wilson *Gerard Elliot* • Ricky Zantolas *George Patterson* ■ *Dir* Charlton Heston • *Scr* Fraser Clarke Heston

Mother Night ★★★ 15

Drama 1996 · US · Colour and BW · 109mins

Kurt Vonnegut's source novel about a Nazi war criminal – a sort of Lord Haw-Haw figure – standing trial in Israel, whose memoirs claim he was in fact an American spy, proves a hard nut to crack. It's a diffuse story told in flashback that stretches over five decades and also deals with racism in Harlem in the 1950s. Director Keith Gordon's film is brave and ambitious but not completely successful, though Nick Nolte is excellent in an especially demanding central role, and there is strong support from John Goodman and Alan Arkin. AT DVD

Nick Nolte *Howard Campbell* • Sheryl Lee *Helga Noth/Resi Noth* • Alan Arkin *George Kraft* • John Goodman *Major Frank Wirtanen* • Kirsten Dunst *Young Resi Noth* • Arye Gross *Abraham Epstein* ■ *Dir* Keith Gordon • *Scr* Robert B Weide, from the novel by Kurt Vonnegut Jr

Mother Wore Tights ★★★ U

Musical 1947 · US · Colour · 106mins

An immensely popular Betty Grable musical, in which she's teamed with the likeable and talented Dan Dailey as 20th Century-Fox tells the story of the early days of vaudeville in garish Technicolor. Neither clever nor sophisticated, this effortlessly whiles away the time. It also has the benefit of a superb Oscar-winning Alfred Newman/Charles Henderson score, and contains a rare opportunity to see the great ventriloquist Senor Wences on celluloid. The story itself, however, which is held together by off-screen narration from Anne Baxter, rambles rather and lacks any real climax. TS

Betty Grable *Myrtle McKinley Burt* • Dan Dailey *Frank Burt* • Mona Freeman *Iris Burt* • Connie Marshall *Mikie Burt* • Vanessa Brown *Bessie* • Robert Arthur *Bob Clarkman* • Sara Allgood *Grandmother McKinley* • William Frawley *Mr Schneider* • Ruth Nelson *Miss Ridgeway* • Anne Baxter *Narrator* ■ *Dir* Walter Lang • *Scr* Lamar Trotti, from the novel by Miriam Young

Motherhood ★★★ 15

Black comedy 1993 · US · Colour · 86mins

There are equal parts gore and guffaw in this spirited horror romp, notable for a cast that includes the cream of America's wackier character actors. Tombstone-toothed Steve Buscemi plays a mummy's boy who'll do anything to bring his dearly departed back from the dead. Trouble is, anything works and back mum comes. But now she's dead different, her new appetite for insects being a particular bugbear. DA DVD

Steve Buscemi *Ed Chilton* • Miriam Margolyes *Mother* • Ned Beatty *Uncle Benny* • John Glover *AJ Pattie* • Sam Jenkins *Storm Reynolds* ■ *Dir* Jonathan Wacks • *Scr* Chuck Hughes

Mother's Boys ★★ 15

Thriller 1993 · US · Colour · 91mins

Psycho-mum Jamie Lee Curtis is the disturbed ex-wife of Peter Gallagher, and she doesn't like the way his new partner, Joanne Whalley-Kilmer, has taken over her former role. Yves Simoneau's direction is competent, but it's not really nasty enough to please ardent chiller fans and the ending is just plain daft. JF. Contains swearing, violence and brief nudity.

Jamie Lee Curtis *Jude* • Peter Gallagher *Robert* • Joanne Whalley-Kilmer [Joanne Whalley] *Callie* • Vanessa Redgrave *Lydia* • Luke Edwards *Kes* • Colin Ward *Michael* • Joey Zimmerman *Ben* • Joss Ackland *Lansing* • Paul Guilfoyle (2) *Mark Kaplan* ■ *Dir* Yves Simoneau • *Scr* Barry Schneider, Richard Hawley, from the novel by Bernard Taylor

The Mothman Prophecies ★★★ 12

Supernatural thriller
2001 · US · Colour · 113mins

The presence of Richard Gere in this paranormal thriller (based on "true" events) may suggest a rather mainstream approach to the material. Yet this eerie and engrossing movie is far from conventional, combining off-kilter camera work and spooky sound mixing with enough narrative ambiguity to fill several David Lynch movies. Gere plays a political reporter who one night inexplicably drives hundreds of miles out of his way to a small West Virginia town. He discovers that the confused inhabitants are plagued by strange visitations from a large winged creature that seem to foreshadow disaster. Although many questions are left unanswered, this is a well-crafted and grown-up chiller. JC DVD

Richard Gere *John Klein* • Laura Linney *Connie Parker* • Will Patton *Gordon Smallwood* • Lucinda Jenney *Denise Smallwood* • Debra Messing *Mary Klein* • Alan Bates *Dr Alexander Leek* ■ *Dir* Mark Pellington • *Scr* Richard Hatem, from the non-fiction book by John A Keel

Mothra ★★★

Monster horror 1962 · Jpn · Colour · 90mins

This introduction to one of Japan's most famous radioactive monsters was one of Toho Studios' best efforts, boasting colourful photography, a more ambitious story and good special effects. Surprisingly, Mothra here stays in egg or caterpillar form for most of the movie before finally growing wings, leaving less time than usual for monster mayhem. Much of the movie instead concerns Mothra's guardians – two tiny twin girls – and the greedy businessman who covets them. This is cute, though a sober reminder of the campiness that would later give the genre a bad name. KB. Japanese dialogue dubbed into English.

Frankie Sakai *"Bulldog" Tsinchan/Junichiro Fukada* • Hiroshi Koizumi *Dr Shinichi Chujo* • Kyoko Kagawa *Photographer Michi Hanamura* • Emi Ito *Mothra's priestess* • Yumi Ito *Mothra's priestess* ■ *Dir* Ishiro Honda [Inoshiro Honda] • *Scr* Shinichi Sekizawa, Robert Myerson (English dialogue), from a story by Shinichiro Nakamura, Takehiko Fukunaga, Yoshie Hotta as published in *Asahi Shimbun*

Motor Psycho ★★ 18

Crime drama 1965 · US · BW · 72mins

In this slightly more tasteful companion to sexploitation director Russ Meyer's legendary *Faster, Pussycat! Kill! Kill!*, a three-man gang of bikers led by deranged Vietnam veteran Stephen Oliver bring terror, rape and mayhem to a small town. Country vet Alex Rocco teams up with Meyer regular Haji to take revenge on the hoodlums. Not as wild or as sordid as your typical Meyer melodrama, this homage to *The Wild One* is one of the mammary maestro's less memorable offerings. AJ. Contains violence, sexual situations, swearing. DVD

Haji *Ruby Bonner* • Alex Rocco *Cory Maddox* • Stephen Oliver *Brahmin* • Holle K Winters *Gail Maddox* • Joseph Cellini *Dante* ■ *Dir* Russ Meyer • *Scr* William E Sprague, Russ Meyer, from a story by Russ Meyer, James Griffith, Hal Hopper • *Cinematographer* Russ Meyer

Motorama ★★★★ 15

Fantasy road movie comedy
1991 · US · Colour · 85mins

Director Barry Shils's weird and wonderful road movie is an undervalued gem. Starring a Who's Who of B-movie cult-dom, this highly engaging oddity follows the bizarre exploits of ten-year-old Gus (Jordan Christopher Michael) who drives across a mythical kingdom in a car customised with wooden leg extenders (so he can reach the pedals) in search of cards given free at Chimera gas stations. If he collects the eight cards that spell the word "motorama" he'll win $1 million. He traverses the strange terrain populated by eccentric adults, aging all the time as his innocence is destroyed by the darkly comic encounters. AJ

Jordan Christopher Michael *Gus* • Martha Quinn *Bank teller* • Susan Tyrrell *Bartender* • John Diehl *Phil* • Robert Picardo *Jerry the policeman* • Michael J Pollard *Lou* • Sandy Baron *Kidnapping husband* • Mary Woronov *Kidnapping wife* • Drew Barrymore *Fantasy girl* • Meat Loaf *Vern* • Jack Nance *Motel clerk* ■ *Dir* Barry Shils • *Scr* Joseph Minion

The Motorcycle Diaries ★★★★★ 15

Biographical road movie drama
2004 · US/UK/Fra · Colour · 120mins

It started as a fun road trip across Latin America for two Argentinian friends in 1952, but the social struggles and injustices witnessed en route awakened their political consciousness – and in the case of Ernesto "Che" Guevara de la Serna sealed his future as a revolutionary icon. Director Walter Salles's remarkably involving biography humanises Che, portraying the man rather than a propagandist myth. By turns funny (witness the duo's pick-up lines), lyrical (the gorgeously photographed locations in Argentina, Chile and Peru) and moving (their ultimate destination, the leper colony), Salles's film is astonishing in its emotional and physical scope. AJ. In Spanish with English subtitles. Contains swearing. DVD

Gael García Bernal *Ernesto Guevara de la Serna* • Rodrigo de la Serna *Alberto Granado* • Mia Maestro *Chichina Ferreyra* • Gustavo Bueno *Dr Hugo Pesce* • Jorge Chiarella *Dr Bresciani* • Mercedes Morán *Celia de la Serna* ■ *Dir* Walter Salles • *Scr* José Rivera, from the memoirs by Ernesto Che Guevara, from the memoirs *With Che through Latin America* by Alberto Granado

Motorcycle Gang ★ PG

Drama 1957 · US · BW · 77mins

Four years after Marlon Brando terrorised a town in *The Wild One*, this film breezed into drive-in cinemas, double-billed with Roger Corman's *Sorority Girl*. Compared to the Brando picture, this is a pink Lambretta with a puncture – a daft, woodenly-acted and underwritten saga about teenagers and a police-organised bikers' club. AT. Contains violence and swearing. DVD

Anne Neyland *Terry* • Steven Terrell *Randy* • John Ashley *Nick* • Carl Switzer [Carl "Alfalfa" Switzer] *Speed* • Raymond Hatton *Uncle Ed* • Russ Bender *Joe* • Jean Moorhead *Marilyn* ■ *Dir* Edward L Cahn • *Scr* Lou Rusoff

Mouchette ★★★★★ 15

Tragedy 1966 · Fr · BW · 77mins

A documentary fidelity underpins Robert Bresson's rigorous, though accessible, adaptation of Georges Bernanos's novel. Mouchette (Nadine Nortier) inhabits a world of spiritual and physical brutality. School and family offer nothing, and the comfort of strangers leads to rejected charity and rape, providing solace through cruelty. With sparse dialogue, this elliptical film never sentimentalises and contains Bresson's most lyrical sequence when, from a single act of generosity, Nortier relishes a dodgem ride, rebelling against her pious, alcoholic father and God. The climax is devastating, compassionate and powerful. BB. In French with English subtitles. Contains swearing, violence and a sex scene. DVD

Nadine Nortier *Mouchette* • Marie Cardinal *Mother* • Paul Hébert *Father* • Jean Vimenet *Mathieu* • Jean-Claude Guilbert *Arsène* ■ *Dir* Robert Bresson • *Scr* Robert Bresson, from the novel *Nouvelle Histoire de Mouchette* by Georges Bernanos

Moulin Rouge ★★

Silent melodrama 1928 · UK · BW · 90mins

Using German production facilities and creative personnel and opening with a long portrait of Paris by night, this silent drama – one of the costliest ever made in Britain – turns into a melodrama about a stripper whose aristocratic boyfriend plans to marry her own daughter, then decides to kill himself in his racing car. The film was was heavily cut between its European and American premieres; when the original version was restored, it was given a jazz soundtrack specially composed by Mike Westbrook and performed by the Matrix Ensemble. AT

Olga Tschechowa *Parysia* • Eve Gray *Margaret, her daughter* • Jean Bradin *Andre* • Georges Treville *Father* ■ *Dir/Scr* EA Dupont

Moulin Rouge ★★★★ PG

Biographical drama
1952 · US/UK · Colour · 114mins

The first 20 minutes of this movie are truly exhilarating, with cancan dancers, amazing lookalike re-creations of period characters and a magnificent sense of the vibrancy of 1880s Paris. This segment is one of director John Huston's finest achievements, and rightly helped the film win its Oscars for best art direction and best costume design. The film then goes on to tell the morbid tale of artist Henri de Toulouse-Lautrec, memorably played by José Ferrer. The women in his life are well cast, notably an unusually credible Zsa Zsa Gabor, but the real co-star is Georges Auric's lovely main theme, recorded by both Percy Faith and Mantovani. TS DVD

José Ferrer *Henri de Toulouse-Lautrec/Comte de Toulouse-Lautrec* • Colette Marchand *Marie Charlet* • Suzanne Flon *Myriamme Hayem* • Zsa Zsa Gabor *Jane Avril* • Katherine Kath *La Goulue* • Claude Nollier *Countess de Toulouse-Lautrec* ■ *Dir* John Huston • *Scr* Anthony Veiller, John Huston, from the novel by Pierre La Mure • *Cinematographer* Oswald Morris • *Art Director* Paul Sheriff, Marcel Vertes • *Costume Designer* Marcel Vertes

Moulin Rouge! ★★★★ 12

Musical romantic drama
2001 · US/Aus · Colour · 122mins

This opulent, no-holds-barred and multi-layered musical revolves around a simple story: struggling writer Ewan McGregor falls in love with beautiful courtesan Nicole Kidman at the famous Parisian nightclub of the title, but their love is threatened by her tuberculosis, as well as the fact she is betrothed to unscrupulous duke Richard Roxburgh. This is wrapped up in an audacious mix of traditional and contemporary song – including David Bowie, Elton John, Madonna and Nirvana – and staged with a near-insane visual ambition by Baz Luhrmann. You will either fall in love with every camp flourish, or find yourself soon exhausted. A singular achievement either way. AC DVD

Nicole Kidman *Satine* • Ewan McGregor *Christian* • John Leguizamo *Toulouse-Lautrec* • Jim Broadbent *Zidler* • Richard Roxburgh *Duke of Worcester* • Kylie Minogue *Green Fairy* ■ *Dir* Baz Luhrmann • *Scr* Baz Luhrmann, Craig Pearce • *Music* Craig Armstrong • *Production Designer* Catherine Martin • *Costume Designer* Catherine Martin, Angus Strathie

The Mountain ★★★ U

Drama 1956 · US · Colour · 104mins

When a plane crashes on top of a mountain, vile wastrel Robert Wagner plans to loot it with the help of his older brother, Spencer Tracy. What follows is a well-made, heavily symbolic drama about greed and the nature of heroism, further complicated by the fact that one person survives the plane crash. The survivor, an Indian girl, is played by Anna Kashfi, who was chosen for the part because she was skinny, and therefore less of a burden for Tracy to carry down the mountain. Shortly afterwards Kashfi became Mrs Marlon Brando, though the marriage was short-lived. AT

Spencer Tracy *Zachary Teller* • Robert Wagner *Chris Teller* • Claire Trevor *Marie* • William Demarest *Father Belacchi* • Barbara Darrow *Simone* • Richard Arlen *Rivial* • EG Marshall *Solange* • Anna Kashfi *Hindu girl* ■ *Dir* Edward Dmytryk • *Scr* Ranald MacDougall, from the novel by Henri Troyat

Mountain Family Robinson ★★ Uc

Adventure 1979 · US · Colour · 95mins

Updated spin on the *Swiss Family Robinson* story, about a couple with kids who've swapped big-city crime and grime for a back-to-nature life in the spectacular Rocky Mountains. Predictably, they discover mountain life also has its ups and downs, just different ones. Corny but fun family film, the third in a series. DA

Robert Logan *Skip* • Susan Damante Shaw [Susan Shaw] *Pat* • Heather Rattray *Jenny* • Ham Larsen *Toby* ■ *Dir* John Cotter • *Scr* Arthur R Dubs

The Mountain Men ★★ 15

Period adventure 1980 · US · Colour · 95mins

Charlton Heston and Brian Keith play fur trappers hounded by Indians in the 1830s in this Disney-style wilderness adventure, albeit with considerably more violence. The script is by Heston's son, Fraser, who apparently lived with Alaskan Indians as a "part-time 20th-century mountain man". Yet the story also chimes with Heston's public political posturings on the freedom of the individual and the right to bear arms (and chest). AT

Charlton Heston *Bill Tyler* • Brian Keith *Henry Frapp* • Victoria Racimo *Running Moon* • Stephen Macht *Heavy Eagle* • John Glover *Nathan Wyeth* • Seymour Cassel *La Bont* • David Ackroyd *Medicine Wolf* ■ *Dir* Richard Lang • *Scr* Fraser Clarke Heston

The Mountain Road ★★ U

Second World War drama
1960 · US · BW · 102mins

The great James Stewart is always worth watching, but even he could be defeated by weak material and feeble direction. He does what he can here, but this overlong war drama set in a very Hollywood-backlot China as the Second World War nears its end remains one of his least successful vehicles. Director Daniel Mann has problems with the tone, and Stewart looks uncomfortable. TS

James Stewart *Major Baldwin* • Lisa Lu *Madame Sue-Mei Hung* • Glenn Corbett *Collins* • Harry Morgan *Michaelson* • Frank Silvera *General Kwan* • James Best *Niergaard* ■ *Dir* Daniel Mann • *Scr* Alfred Hayes, from the novel by Theodore White

Mountains of the Moon ★★★ 15

Historical adventure
1989 · US · Colour · 129mins

Five Easy Pieces director Bob Rafelson is not perhaps the first film-maker you would associate with a tale of Victorian explorers bonding manfully in the search for the source of the Nile. Yet he turned this long-cherished project into a stirring, offbeat and often compelling adventure. Patrick Bergin (as the adventurer Richard Burton) and Iain Glen (as the aristocratic John Hanning Speke) are both excellent, and there are neat turns from Richard E Grant and Bernard Hill as Dr Livingstone. DP. Contains violence and nudity. DVD

Patrick Bergin *Richard Burton* • Iain Glen *John Hanning Speke* • Richard E Grant *Laurence Oliphant* • Fiona Shaw *Isabel Arundell* • John Savident *Lord Murchison* • James Villiers *Lord Oliphant* • Adrian Rawlins *Edward* • Peter Vaughan *Lord Houghton* • Delroy Lindo *Mabruki* • Bernard Hill *Dr Livingstone* ■ *Dir* Bob Rafelson • *Scr* William Harrison, Bob Rafelson, from the novel by William Harrison and the journals by Richard Burton, John Hanning Speke

Mourning Becomes Electra ★★★

Melodrama 1947 · US · BW · 159mins

A heavy-duty adaptation of Eugene O'Neill's Civil War play based on Aeschylus's *Oresteia*. It's an impressive but over-ambitious and terribly stagey attempt from director Dudley Nichols. Rosalind Russell is miscast in the lead, having neither the range nor the intensity for Lavinia, and the mix 'n' match gathering of distinguished US and European thespians doesn't gel, but there's no denying that, for Hollywood, getting this made at all ranked as a major achievement. TS

Rosalind Russell *Lavinia Mannon* • Michael Redgrave *Orin Mannon* • Raymond Massey *Ezra Mannon* • Katina Paxinou *Christine Mannon* • Leo Genn *Adam Brent* • Kirk Douglas *Peter Niles* • Nancy Coleman *Hazel Niles* • Henry Hull *Seth Beckwith* ■ *Dir* Dudley Nichols • *Scr* Dudley Nichols, from the play by Eugene O'Neill

The Mouse and His Child ★★ U

Animation 1977 · US · Colour · 80mins

Animation is at its best when propelled by imaginative action. But American animators Charles Swenson and Fred Wolf, perhaps worshipping at the shrine of British costume drama, overdo the chit-chat in this feature-length cartoon about two toy mice and their attempts to become self-winding. There are some sequences which border on the lively, though, and the distinctive vocal intelligence of Peter Ustinov also freshens up the character of Manny the rat. JM

Peter Ustinov *Manny* • Cloris Leachman *Euterpe* • Sally Kellerman *Seal* • Andy Devine *Frog* • Alan Barzman *Mouse* • Marcy Swenson *Mouse child* ■ *Dir* Fred Wolf, Chuck Swenson [Charles Swenson] • *Scr* Carol Mon Pere, from the novel by Russell Hoban

The Mouse on the Moon ★★ U

Comedy 1963 · UK · Colour · 86mins

The combination of a witty Michael Pertwee script, the exuberant direction of Richard Lester and the unique talents of Margaret Rutherford would normally have been enough to guarantee comic gold. But, perhaps because Peter Sellers in a triple role was a hard act to follow, this sequel to *The Mouse That Roared* never gets off the ground. Fitfully amusing, it wastes a splendid cast. DP

Margaret Rutherford *The Grand Duchess Gloriana* • Ron Moody *Mountjoy* • Bernard Cribbins *Vincent* • David Kossoff *Kokintz* • Terry-Thomas *Spender* • June Ritchie *Cynthia* • John Le Mesurier *British delegate* ■ *Dir* Richard Lester • *Scr* Michael Pertwee, from the novel by Leonard Wibberley

The Mouse That Roared ★★★ U

Comedy 1959 · UK · Colour · 79mins

This wry little comedy opens brightly, but quickly loses direction as its one joke is stretched to breaking point. The idea of a tiny country declaring war on America to benefit from aid in defeat is a lovely one, but not even Peter Sellers in three widely differing roles can compensate for the longueurs that occupy the film's final hour. Jean Seberg is wasted in decorous support, along with David Kossoff and William Hartnell. DP DVD

Peter Sellers *Tully Bascombe/Grand Duchess Gloriana XII/PM Count Mountjoy* • Jean Seberg *Helen* • David Kossoff *Professor Kokintz* • William Hartnell *Will* • Leo McKern *Benter* • MacDonald Parke *Snippet* • Timothy Bateson *Roger* ■ *Dir* Jack Arnold • *Scr* Roger MacDougall, Stanley Mann, from the novel *The Wrath of Grapes* by Leonard Wibberley

Mouse Trouble ★★★★ U

Animated comedy 1944 · US · Colour · 7mins

This archetypal *Tom and Jerry* cartoon finds the series fully realised only four years after its inception. The simple plot revolves around Tom the cat's use of a guide book to help him catch Jerry the mouse. For his pains he is caught in his own mouse trap, tied to a tree,

M

punched in the face, yelled at through a stethoscope, shot, hit with a mallet, pierced with needles, sawn in half and blown up with explosives. For some reason, modern audiences find this sort of thing violent. In the 1940s, they gave it an Academy Award – and quite right, too, for it's very funny and, for all its sadism, subtly done. CLP

Dir William Hanna, Joseph Barbera

Mousehunt ★★★★ PG

Comedy 1997 · US · Colour · 93mins

In this energetic and highly inventive comedy, hapless brothers Nathan Lane and Lee Evans inherit a valuable old house but find it is already occupied by a pesky rodent. There's stacks of Laurel and Hardy-style visual comedy as the pair wreak havoc in their bid to rid themselves of the furry fiend, though adults may prefer Christopher Walken's hilarious turn as an exterminator. The darker touches might upset younger children, and the film is definitely not for viewers with a phobia of rodents. But for sheer verve, this family entertainment is hard to beat. JB. Contains swearing. DVD

Nathan Lane *Ernie Smuntz* • Lee Evans *Lars Smuntz* • Christopher Walken *Caesar* • Maury Chaykin *Alexander Falko* • Vicki Lewis *April Smuntz* • Eric Christmas *The lawyer* • William Hickey *Rudolf Smuntz* ■ *Dir* Gore Verbinski • *Scr* Adam Rifkin

The Mouth Agape ★★★★

Drama 1974 · Fr · Colour · 82mins

Shot in a series of intense long takes, this movingly natural drama explores the effect the news that she has terminal cancer has on 50-year-old Monique Mélinand's philandering husband and impotent son. Exploring the connection between sex and death and the inextricable bonds that somehow keep unhappy couples together, Maurice Pialat's analysis of physical and emotional pain is never moralistic or sentimental. DP. In French with English subtitles.

Monique Melinand *Mother* • Hubert Deschamps *Father* • Philippe Léotard *Philippe* • Nathalie Baye *Nathalie* ■ *Dir/Scr* Maurice Pialat

Mouth to Mouth ★★★

Black comedy thriller
1995 · Sp · Colour · 97mins

A screwball Spanish comedy about actor Javier Bardem who, after a spell of unemployment, devotes his talent to a phone sex company. Unfortunately, his most regular callers are all male! When Aitana Sanchez-Gijon suggests a rendezvous, he jumps at the opportunity – and walks straight into a ploy to enrage her unfaithful husband. Director Manuel Gomez Pereira gives his Spanish peer Almodóvar a real run for his money with a compelling, cheeky and genuinely funny film. LH. In Spanish with English subtitles.

Javier Bardem *Victor Ventura* • Jose Maria Flotats *Ricardo/Bill* • Aitana Sanchez-Gijon *Amanda* • Maria Barranco *Angela* • Myriam Mézières *Sheila* • Fernando Guillen-Cuervo *Raul* ■ *Dir* Manuel Gomez Pereira • *Scr* Manuel Gomez Pereira, Joaquin Oristrell, Juan Luis Iborra, Naomi Wise

Move Over, Darling ★★★★ U

Comedy 1963 · US · Colour · 99mins

This Doris Day classic – a remake of 1940's *My Favorite Wife* – features the star as a woman who returns from a desert island to find that her husband James Garner has remarried. Providing perfect support for Day and Garner are Polly Bergen as the "other woman" and Chuck Connors as the hunk who was marooned with Day. Stealing the show, however, is the wonderful Thelma Ritter as Day's outspoken mother-in-law. Day's popularity suffered from the onset of the sexual revolution in the mid-1960s when her wholesome image seemed out of step with the time, but this film shows how her great talent has endured. SH

Doris Day *Ellen Wagstaff Arden* • James Garner *Nicholas Arden* • Polly Bergen *Bianca Steele Arden* • Thelma Ritter *Grace Arden* • Elliott Reid *Dr Herman Schlick* • Don Knotts *Shoe salesman* • Chuck Connors *Stephen "Adam" Burkett* • Fred Clark *Codd* ■ *Dir* Michael Gordon • *Scr* Hal Kanter, Jack Sher, from the film *My Favorite Wife* by Bella Spewack, Samuel Spewack, from a story by Leo McCarey, Samuel Spewack, Bella Spewack

Movers and Shakers ★ 15

Comedy 1985 · US · Colour · 76mins

Charles Grodin is undoubtedly a superb comic actor who never really gets the material worthy of his talents. With this woeful comedy, however, he really only has himself to blame, as he wrote and co-produced it. A wonderful cast (Walter Matthau, Steve Martin, Gilda Radner, Vincent Gardenia) is reduced to mugging furiously in a supposedly satirical look at the movie business. JF. Contains swearing.

Walter Matthau *Joe Mulholland* • Charles Grodin *Herb Derman* • Vincent Gardenia *Saul Gritz* • Tyne Daly *Nancy Derman* • Steve Martin *Fabio Longio* • Bill Macy *Sid Spokane* • Gilda Radner *Livia Machado* • Michael Lerner *Arnie* • Penny Marshall *Reva* ■ *Dir* William Asher • *Scr* Charles Grodin

Movie Crazy ★★★ U

Comedy 1932 · US · BW · 79mins

One of the great silent film clowns, Harold Lloyd was a master of physical comedy whose exploits delighted and thrilled early audiences. Made later in his career, this is undoubtably his best talkie. Lloyd plays Harold Hall, an unassuming type who yearns to be in the movies and gets his break when he meets starlet Constance Cummings. The brilliant set pieces include the famous sequence in which Lloyd wears a magician's suit to a swanky ball, only to find it contains more than he bargained for. DF

Harold Lloyd *Harold Hall* • Constance Cummings *Mary Sears* • Kenneth Thomson *Vance, a gentleman heavy* ■ *Dir* Clyde Bruckman • *Scr* Agnes Christine Johnston, John Grey, Felix Adler, Vincent Lawrence

Movie Movie ★★★ PG

Comedy 1978 · US · BW and Colour · 101mins

Stanley Donen's attempt to recapture the spirit of 1930s double-bills is in the form of two B-movies – a boxing melodrama, *Dynamite Hands*, and a backstage musical, *Baxter's Beauties of 1933*. Donen even offers a trailer in the middle. It's a smart idea which all film buffs will warm to, even if the execution doesn't quite do justice to the concept. It was one of several movies at the time – such as *Nickelodeon* and *Silent Movie* – that cashed in on the perceived nostalgia for old movies, but all that this inspired was some bad jokes from critics – "Lousy, Lousy", for instance. It's actually better than that and the musical sequence has some delectable moments. AT

George C Scott *Gloves Malloy/Spats Baxter* • Trish Van Devere *Betsy McGuire/Isobel Stewart* • Barbara Harris *Trixie Lane* ■ *Dir* Stanley Donen • *Scr* Larry Gelbart, Sheldon Keller

Moving ★ 15

Comedy 1988 · US · Colour · 85mins

Director Alan Metter appears perfectly content to replace bona fide comedy with Richard Pryor's exaggerated racket in this lame suburban farce. Showing off is no substitute for acting, and letting Pryor roam free is a big mistake. Desperation sinks its jaws into this mediocrity at an early stage, as director and star latch on to anything in the vain hope of laughter. Children, removal men and Randy Quaid (playing a lawn-trimming slob) are all pushed into service, to meagre effect. JM. Contains swearing.

Richard Pryor *Arlo Pear* • Beverly Todd *Monica Pear* • Dave Thomas *Gary Marcus* • Dana Carvey *Brad Williams* • Randy Quaid *Frank/Cornell Crawford* • Stacey Dash *Casey Pear* • Raphael Harris *Marshall Pear* • Ishmael Harris *Randy Pear* ■ *Dir* Alan Metter • *Scr* Andy Breckman

Moving Violations ★ 15

Comedy 1985 · US · Colour · 85mins

It takes some skill to aim even more downmarket than *Police Academy*, but this dire cash-in certainly succeeds in that respect. The story revolves around the usual lovable collection of anarchic misfits who run rings around the establishment when they are sentenced to traffic school. James Keach, Sally Kellerman and Jennifer Tilly have doubtless erased this from their CVs. JF. Contains swearing.

John Murray *Dana Cannon* • Jennifer Tilly *Amy Hopkins* • James Keach *Deputy Halik* • Sally Kellerman *Judge Nedra Henderson* • Brian Backer *Scott Greeber* • Ned Eisenberg *Wink Barnes* • Clara Peller *Emma Jean* ■ *Dir* Neal Israel • *Scr* Neal Israel, Pat Proft, from a story by Paul Boorstin, Sharon Boorstin

Mrs 'arris Goes to Paris ★★★

Comedy 1992 · US · Colour · 97mins

This is one of those projects that spent decades doing the Hollywood rounds before finally being made as a TV movie. Angela Lansbury is the housekeeper who saves and saves so she can fulfil her lifelong dream of going to Paris and buying a Christian Dior dress. Lightweight stuff indeed, but Lansbury and co-stars Diana Rigg and Omar Sharif all seem to be having so much fun you can't help but laugh along with them. JB

Angela Lansbury *Mrs Harris* • Omar Sharif *Marquis DeChassange* • Diana Rigg *Madame Colbert* • Lothaire Bluteau *André* • John Savident *Armand* • Lila Kaye *Mrs Butterfield* • Tamara Gorski *Natasha* ■ *Dir* Anthony Shaw [Anthony Pullen Shaw] • *Scr* John Hawkesworth, from the novella *Mrs 'arris Goes to Paris* by Paul Gallico

Mrs Brown ★★★★★ PG

Historical drama
1997 · UK/US/Ire · Colour · 100mins

Judi Dench and Billy Connolly are a wonderfully regal double-act in this perceptive blend of fact and fiction. The story examines the relationship between Queen Victoria and her Scottish gillie John Brown, who audaciously dispelled her gloom after the death of Prince Albert and with whom she became so close that gossips gave her his name. The Oscar-nominated Dench provides a wonderfully dignified counter-balance to comedian Connolly, whose forthright bluntness causes consternation among her tradition-bound household staff. Director John Madden and scriptwriter Jeremy Brock have created an engrossing account of an attachment that might have fulfilled itself romantically had it not been for the conventions of the time. TH DVD

Judi Dench *Queen Victoria* • Billy Connolly *John Brown* • Antony Sher *Benjamin Disraeli* • Geoffrey Palmer *Henry Ponsonby* • Richard Pasco *Doctor Jenner* • David Westhead *Bertie, Prince of Wales* • Gerard Butler *Archie Brown* • Bridget McConnel *Lady Ely* • Georgie Glen *Lady Churchill* ■ *Dir* John Madden • *Scr* Jeremy Brock, from an idea by George Rosie

Mrs Caldicot's Cabbage War ★★ 12

Comedy drama 2000 · UK · Colour · 106mins

This adaptation of Vernon Coleman's novel has the feel of an overgrown, over-familiar sitcom. Yet initially the story shows promise, with the formerly browbeaten Pauline Collins embracing widowhood with vengeful gusto. However, once avaricious son Peter Capaldi consigns her to John Alderton's rest home, the gallows humour is replaced by a glutinous plea for a revision of society's dismissive attitude towards the elderly. The veteran supporting cast is game enough, but not even it can enliven the sluggish proceedings. DP DVD

Pauline Collins *Thelma Caldicot* • Peter Capaldi *Derek Caldicot, her son* • Anna Wilson-Jones *Veronica Caldicot* • Gwenllian Davies *Audrey* • Sheila Reid *Joyce* • Frank Mills *Leslie* • Frank Middlemass *Bernard* • John Alderton *Hawksmoor* ■ *Dir* Ian Sharp • *Scr* Malcolm Stone, from the novel by Vernon Coleman

Mrs Dalloway ★★★ PG

Period drama
1997 · US/UK/Neth · Colour · 93mins

A day in the life of Vanessa Redgrave, the emotionally troubled wife of an MP, and Rupert Graves, a shell-shocked war veteran. They never meet, but fate still brings them together at the end of a series of flashbacks that sketch in Redgrave's early life and feature Natascha McElhone as her younger self. Adapting Virginia Woolf's intricate novel, Eileen Atkins juggles time and emotional choices with skill, while the performances are uniformly excellent. Yet it's also rather smug, trapped in an ivory tower of its own making. AT. Contains brief nudity. DVD

Vanessa Redgrave *Mrs Clarissa Dalloway* • Natascha McElhone *Young Clarissa Dalloway* • Rupert Graves *Septimus Warren Smith* • Michael Kitchen *Peter Walsh* • Alan Cox *Young Peter Walsh* • Sarah Badel *Lady Rosseter* • Lena Headey *Young Sally* • John Standing *Richard Dalloway* ■ *Dir* Marleen Gorris • *Scr* Eileen Atkins, from the novel by Virginia Woolf

Mrs Delafield Wants to Marry ★★★★

Romantic comedy
1986 · US · Colour · 94mins

This delightful romantic TV comedy features the incomparable Katharine Hepburn as a rich, high society widow who scandalises her friends and family when she decides to marry her divorced, Jewish doctor (Harold Gould). As usual, Hepburn is watchable in a role created for her by Broadway playwright James Prideaux. The premise is hardly original, but the execution is deft and the underlying issues of race and class bigotry are dealt with in an entertaining way. MC

Katharine Hepburn *Mrs Delafield* • Harold Gould *Dr Marvin Elias* • Denholm Elliott *George Parker* • Brenda Forbes *Gladys Parker* • David Ogden Stiers *Horton* ■ *Dir* George Schaefer • *Scr* James Prideaux

Mrs Doubtfire ★★★★ PG

Comedy drama 1993 · US · Colour · 120mins

This knowing blend of comedy and common sense is family entertainment *par excellence*. Aided by Oscar-winning make-up, Robin Williams gives one of the performances of his career as an actor who disguises himself as a Scottish nanny to be close to his children after he splits with wife Sally Field. Director Chris Columbus reins in the Williams exuberance, while retaining enough of his quick-fire personality to ensure that just about every gag hits its target. Pierce Brosnan also does well as the bachelor looking for a ready-made family, but Sally Field overdoes the

M

exasperation at times. DP. Contains swearing. [video] DVD

Robin Williams *Daniel Hillard/Mrs Doubtfire* • Sally Field *Miranda Hillard* • Pierce Brosnan *Stu* • Harvey Fierstein *Frank* • Polly Holliday *Gloria* • Lisa Jakub *Lydia Hillard* • Matthew Lawrence *Chris Hillard* • Mara Wilson *Natalie Hillard* ■ *Dir* Chris Columbus • *Scr* Randi Mayem Singer, Leslie Dixon, from the novel *Alias Mrs Doubtfire* by Anne Fine • *Make-up* Ve Neill, Greg Cannom, Yolanda Toussieng

Mrs Mike ★★

Romantic drama 1949 · US · BW · 98mins

At the end of the 19th century, Boston girl Evelyn Keyes ventures to the rugged north-west of Canada, where she meets and falls in love with Mountie Dick Powell. They marry, and our heroine sets about adjusting to an unfamiliar way of life. Louis King directs this sentimental drama that's neither memorable nor absorbing, but does have believable performances. RK

Dick Powell *Sergeant Mike Flannigan* • Evelyn Keyes *Kathy O'Fallon* • JM Kerrigan *Uncle John* • Angela Clarke *Sarah Carpentier* • John Miljan *Mr Howard* • Nan Boardman *Georgette Beauclaire* • Will Wright *Dr McIntosh* ■ *Dir* Louis King • *Scr* Alfred Lewis Levitt, DeWitt Bodeen, from the novel by Benedict Freedman, Nancy Freedman

Mrs Miniver ★★★★★ U

Classic wartime drama
1942 · US · BW · 128mins

This superb wartime melodrama was "more valuable than the combined efforts of six army divisions", according to Winston Churchill. Greer Garson and Walter Pidgeon play the British couple suffering in the Second World War, bringing this country's plight to the American public, and today this MGM production is best viewed in that propagandist light. The film won six Oscars, including best picture, best actress and best direction for William Wyler, and it's easy to understand why. Trivia buffs might like to note that Garson's real-life lover at the time, Richard Ney, plays her son in this movie – the couple married the following year. The sequel *The Miniver Story*, filmed eight years later, is nowhere near as good. TS [video] DVD

Greer Garson *Mrs Miniver* • Walter Pidgeon *Clem Miniver* • Teresa Wright *Carol Beldon* • Dame May Whitty *Lady Beldon* • Reginald Owen *Foley* • Henry Travers *Mr Ballard* • Richard Ney *Vin Miniver* • Henry Wilcoxon *Vicar* • Christopher Severn *Toby Miniver* ■ *Dir* William Wyler • *Scr* Arthur Wimperis, George Froeschel, James Hilton, Claudine West, from the novel by Jan Struther • *Cinematographer* Joseph Ruttenberg

Mrs O'Malley and Mr Malone ★★★

Comedy mystery 1950 · US · BW · 69mins

Outspoken Montana widow Marjorie Main, en route to collect a prize from a radio show, and small-time lawyer James Whitmore, chasing a client for money, meet on the train to New York, where they turn amateur sleuths when his errant client turns up as a corpse. A snappy, enjoyable comedy thriller with an excellent supporting cast, and a memorably eccentric rendition by Main (best known as Ma Kettle) of *Possum up a Gum Stump*. RK

Marjorie Main *Hattie O'Malley* • James Whitmore *John J Malone* • Ann Dvorak *Connie Kepplar* • Phyllis Kirk *Kay* • Fred Clark *Tim Marino* • Dorothy Malone *Lola Gillway* • Douglas Fowley *Steve Kepplar* ■ *Dir* Norman Taurog • *Scr* William Bowers, from a story by Craig Rice, Stuart Palmer

Mrs Parker and the Vicious Circle ★★★★ 15

Biographical drama
1994 · US · Colour and BW · 119mins

You'll either love or loathe Jennifer Jason Leigh's mannered performance here as Dorothy Parker (the brilliant wit of the 1920s and 30s). But her portrayal is still a constant delight of looks and language in director Alan Rudolph's biographical drama about the Algonquin hotel's Round Table (which consisted of writers and celebrities who gathered around Parker). Her affair with Charles MacArthur (played here by Matthew Broderick) and her subsequent affairs and fractured marriage chime a note of doom and despair that counters the show-off cleverness of the rest. TH. Contains swearing and nudity. [video]

Jennifer Jason Leigh *Dorothy Parker* • Campbell Scott *Robert Benchley* • Matthew Broderick *Charles MacArthur* • Andrew McCarthy *Eddie Parker* • Tom McGowan *Alexander Woollcott* • Nick Cassavetes *Robert Sherwood* ■ *Dir* Alan Rudolph • *Scr* Alan Rudolph, Randy Sue Coburn

Mrs Parkington ★★

Drama 1944 · US · BW · 123mins

This drama gained Greer Garson an Oscar nomination more deserved by the make-up department. She starts the picture as an octagenarian widow and matriarch who suffers from flashback disease, thereby revealing her early life as the brash mining-town girl who married Pidgeon's millionaire and became a society figure. Garson learned card tricks for the film, but the lumbering script deprives director Tay Garnett of a winning hand. In the original American version, Edward, Prince of Wales (played by Cecil Kellaway) is entranced by Garson, but British audiences were given Hugo Haas as a Balkan monarch to avoid offending Buckingham Palace. AE

Greer Garson *Susie Parkington* • Walter Pidgeon *Maj Augustus Parkington* • Edward Arnold *Amory Stilham* • Frances Rafferty *Jane Stilham* • Agnes Moorehead *Aspasia Conti* • Selena Royle *Mattie Trounsen* • Gladys Cooper *Alice, Duchess de Brancourt* • Lee Patrick *Madeleine* • Dan Duryea *Jack Stilham* ■ *Dir* Tay Garnett • *Scr* Robert Thoeren, Polly James, from the novel by Louis Bromfield • *Costume Designer* Irene

Mrs Pollifax – Spy ★

Spy parody 1970 · US · Colour · 110mins

This unfunny comedy adventure brought Rosalind Russell's big screen career to an end. She had only herself and husband Frederick Brisson to blame, though, since she wrote it pseudonymously and he produced it and employed the undistinguished Leslie Martinson to direct. Russell plays a middle-aged woman who joins the CIA and embarks on a series of unlikely and over-energetic adventures. (As she was over 60 at the time, stunt doubles are much in evidence.) BB

Rosalind Russell *Emily Pollifax* • Darren McGavin *Johnny Farrell* • Nehemiah Persoff *General Berisha* • Harold Gould *Colonel Nexdhet* • Albert Paulsen *General Perdido* • John Beck *Sgt Lulash* ■ *Dir* Leslie Martinson [Leslie H Martinson] • *Scr* CA McKnight [Rosalind Russell], from the novel *The Unexpected Mrs Pollifax* by Dorothy Gilman

Mrs Soffel ★★★ PG

Biographical drama
1984 · US · Colour · 106mins

Based on the true story of a prison warden's wife who fell in love with an inmate and plotted his escape, this turn-of-the-century costume romance is too dour for its own good. Australia's Gillian Armstrong directs the potentially passionate content with a cool detachment that mirrors the wintry landscapes across which the lovers flee, while Diane Keaton's contemporary style is also at odds with the piece. But there's plenty of appeal in the young Mel Gibson, appropriately seductive as the convicted murderer, and Matthew Modine is nicely cast as his dimwit brother. AME [video]

Diane Keaton *Kate Soffel* • Mel Gibson *Ed Biddle* • Matthew Modine *Jack Biddle* • Edward Herrmann *Peter Soffel* • Trini Alvarado *Irene Soffel* • Jennie Dundas *Margaret Soffel* • Danny Corkill *Eddie Soffel* ■ *Dir* Gillian Armstrong • *Scr* Ron Nyswaner

Mrs Wiggs of the Cabbage Patch ★★

Melodrama 1934 · US · BW · 80mins

Director Norman Taurog's film recounts the poverty-stricken but incident-packed existence of Pauline Lord and her five children, whose father has disappeared without trace. Always cheerful in the face of struggle, the family is helped by a local rich girl (Evelyn Venable). At times Dickensian in flavour, at others Chaplinesque, it's at its best in the second half when WC Fields arrives on the scene and courts family friend ZaSu Pitts. RK

Pauline Lord *Mrs Elvira Wiggs* • WC Fields *Mr C Ensworth Stubbins* • ZaSu Pitts *Miss Tabitha Hazy* • Evelyn Venable *Lucy Olcott* • Kent Taylor *Bob Redding* • Charles Middleton *Mr Bagby* • Donald Meek *Mr Hiram Wiggs* • Clara Lou Sheridan [Ann Sheridan] *Girl* ■ *Dir* Norman Taurog • *Scr* William Slavens McNutt, Jane Storm, from the play by Anne Crawford Flexner, from the novel by Alice Hegan Rice

Mrs Winterbourne ★★★ 12

Romantic comedy
1996 · US · Colour · 101mins

This comic remake of the far more serious *No Man of Her Own* stars US talk-show queen Ricki Lake as a young girl with a baby on the way who, following a train crash, adopts the identity of the late Patricia Winterbourne. She is promptly whisked off to meet the rich Winterbourne family, who had never met their dead son's bride. Shirley MacLaine steals the show as the *grande dame* of the family, but Lake holds her own and there is nice support from Brendan Fraser as the brother-in-law with whom she falls in love. JB. Contains swearing, sexual references. [video] DVD

Shirley MacLaine *Grace Winterbourne* • Ricki Lake *Connie Doyle* • Brendan Fraser *Bill Winterbourne/Hugh Winterbourne* • Miguel Sandoval *Paco* • Loren Dean *Steve DeCunzo* • Peter Gerety *Father Brian* • Jane Krakowski *Christine* ■ *Dir* Richard Benjamin • *Scr* Phoef Sutton, Lisa-Marie Radano, from the novel *I Married a Dead Man* by Cornell Woolrich

Ms 45 ★★★ 18

Crime drama 1981 · US · Colour · 75mins

Abel Ferrara was once Public Enemy No 1 as far as the UK censors were concerned: his first two movies ended up on the banned list. The notorious *Driller Killer* was the first; *Ms 45* was the second, and it's a far more accomplished affair. Zoe Tamerlis plays a mute woman who, after being raped twice in one day, decides to get her own back on mankind. It was billed as a feminist *Death Wish*, but it's a lot more disturbing than that, even if Ferrara and his regular scriptwriter Nicholas St John once again go overboard on the religious guilt. It was eventually approved for release, with a few minor cuts. JF [video]

Zoe Tamerlis *Thana* • Bogey *Phil* • Albert Sinkys *Albert* • Darlene Stuto *Laurie* • Jimmy Laine [Abel Ferrara] *First rapist* • Peter Yellen *Second rapist* ■ *Dir* Abel Ferrara • *Scr* Nicholas St John

Much Ado about Nothing ★★★★ PG

Comedy drama 1993 · UK · Colour · 106mins

A real luvvies outing, as the then married Kenneth Branagh and Emma Thompson decamp to Tuscany with pals to film an exciting, joyful and rollicking version of William Shakespeare's tale of frenetic wooing. Branagh, who stars and directs, gives the story an enormous *joie de vivre* and is aided by a star-studded supporting cast that includes Thompson's mother Phyllida Law, Imelda Staunton, Ben Elton, Keanu Reeves and Denzel Washington. SH. Contains brief nudity. [video] DVD

Kenneth Branagh *Benedick* • Richard Briers *Leonato* • Michael Keaton *Dogberry* • Denzel Washington *Don Pedro* • Robert Sean Leonard *Claudio* • Keanu Reeves *Don John* • Emma Thompson *Beatrice* • Kate Beckinsale *Hero* • Imelda Staunton *Margaret* • Phyllida Law *Ursula* • Ben Elton *Verges* ■ *Dir* Kenneth Branagh • *Scr* Kenneth Branagh, from the play by William Shakespeare

Much Too Shy ★★ U

Comedy 1942 · UK · BW · 95mins

Although he was still Britain's biggest box-office attraction, George Formby was already showing signs of the novelty fatigue that would result in the collapse of his screen career four years later. Too bashful to paint anything below the neck, he gets into hot water when his portraits of three village matrons end up in a soap advertisement attached to nude torsos. The cheeky wit that informed so many of Formby's songs is to the fore in this contrived comedy. DP

George Formby *George Andy* • Kathleen Harrison *Amelia Peabody* • Hilda Bayley *Lady Driscoll* • Eileen Bennett *Jackie Somers* • Joss Ambler *Sir George Driscoll* ■ *Dir* Marcel Varnel • *Scr* Ronald Frankau

Muddy River ★★★★ PG

Drama 1981 · Jpn · BW · 103mins

Clearly inspired by Yasujiro Ozu's delightful studies of childhood friendship, Kohei Oguri's Oscar-nominated debut makes striking use of its black-and-white imagery to evoke a sense of both nostalgic innocence and the grinding poverty that so many Japanese experienced, even at the height of the 1950s boom. As the nine-year-old son of comfortable restaurateurs, Nobutaka Asahara is touchingly awestruck as he learns some harsh lessons about class and sex from the widow who works as a prostitute on the houseboat she shares with her kids. Dramatically satisfying, visually authentic and beautifully played. DP. In Japanese with English subtitles.

Nobutaka Asahara *Nobuo* • Takahiro Tamura *Shinpei* • Yumiko Fujita *Nobuo's mother* • Minoru Sakurai *Kiichi* ■ *Dir* Kohei Oguri • *Scr* Takako Shigemuri, from the novel by Teru Miyamoto

Mudhoney ★★★★ 18

Melodrama 1965 · US · BW · 92mins

This early film by soft porn maestro Russ Meyer has been hailed as an undiscovered masterpiece, and it's easy to see why. Apart from some brief glimpses of nudity, this Southern melodrama, set in the Prohibition era, could easily have been made by any of Hollywood's all-time greats. The plot (desperate men feuding over sex and power on a farm) is straight out of a dime novel, but the action builds to a rivetingly horrible denouement, while the high standard of photography and performances has rarely been equalled in low-budget exploitation. Among the best of its kind. DM [video] DVD

Hal Hopper *Sidney Brenshaw* • Lorna Maitland *Clara Belle* • Antoinette Cristiani *Hannah Brenshaw* • John Furlong *Calif McKinney* • Stuart Lancaster *Lute Wade* ■ *Dir* Russ Meyer • *Scr* Raymond Friday Locke, William E Sprague • *Cinematographer* Walter Schenk

The Mudlark ★★★ U

Period drama 1950 · UK · BW · 99mins

This achieved minor notoriety for its relatively daring casting, with noted Hollywood *grande dame* Irene Dunne playing Queen Victoria to Alec Guinness's elegant Disraeli. Dunne acquits herself well enough, and Guinness is superb, particularly in a long speech that seems to be uninterrupted by cutting: bravura screen acting indeed. The story is about one of those Oliver Twist-like foundlings, played here by Andrew Ray, and the sentimental plot is hard to take seriously. TS

Irene Dunne *Queen Victoria* • Alec Guinness *Benjamin Disraeli* • Andrew Ray *Wheeler, the mudlark* • Beatrice Campbell *Lady Emily Prior* • Finlay Currie *John Brown* • Anthony Steel *Lieutenant Charles McHatten* • Raymond Lovell *Sergeant Footman Naseby* ■ *Dir* Jean Negulesco • *Scr* Nunnally Johnson, from the novel by Theodore Bonnet

Mughal-e-Azam ★★★★ PG

Historical epic
1960 · Ind · Colour and BW · 197mins

Re-creating the feud between the Emperor Akbar and his son Salim over his passion for the low-born dancer, Anarkali, this is one of the undisputed classics of Bollywood cinema. It's also one of the most sensual, with the lavish period trappings providing a fabulous setting for the intense love scenes between Dilip Kumar and Madhubala. Indeed, it's this unforced juxtaposition between scale and intimacy that characterises K Asif's direction, although he's not slow to recognise the emotional value of a grandiose, full-colour set piece. DP. In Hindi with English subtitles. DVD

Dilip Kumar *Prince Salim* • Madhubala *Anarkali* • Prithviraj [Prithviraj Kapoor] *Emperor Akbar* • Durga Khote *Empress Jodha Bai* ■ *Dir* K Asif • *Scr* Aman, K Asif, Kamal Amrohi, Wajahat Mirza, Ehsan Rizvi

Muhammad Ali: King of the World ★ PG

Biographical sports drama
2000 · US · Colour · 89mins

This TV movie is the weakest of the plethora of Ali biopics. The sporting focus here is on the Cassius Clay era, as the former Olympic champion gears up for his tilt at the title against world heavyweight legend, Sonny Liston. Melodramatic, with neither Terrence Dashon Howard nor Gary Dourdan credible as the boxer and his mentor. DP DVD

Terrence Dashon Howard [Terrence Howard] *Cassius Clay* • Gary Dourdan *Malcolm X* • Saint Adeogba *Betty X* • Rodger Boyce *Bill McDonald* • Darryl Cox *Howard Cosell* • Blue Deckert *Gorgeous George* ■ *Dir* John Sacret Young • *Scr* John Sacret Young, from the non-fiction book *King of the World: Muhammad Ali and the Rise of an American Hero* by David Remnick

Muhammad Ali, the Greatest ★★★★ PG

Documentary
1974 · Fr · Colour and BW · 110mins

The first segment of William Klein's seminal portrait of a sporting legend begins in the monochrome days of 1964 and chronicles the furore that surrounded the then Cassius Clay at the time of his notorious bouts with Sonny Liston. Accompanying him on the road and into the changing rooms, director Klein produces Direct Cinema at its most immediate and provides an intimate insight into the fighter's lifestyle, emerging showmanship and growing potency as a black superstar in the Civil Rights era. The second half of this superb biography was filmed a decade after Clay's triumphs over Liston, by which time "The Louisville Lip" was known as Muhammad Ali and on his way to his greatest victory at the "Rumble in the Jungle" in Zaire. DP DVD

Dir William Klein • *Cinematographer* [William Klein]

Mujhse Dosti Karoge! ★★ U

Musical romantic drama
2002 · Ind · Colour · 148mins

Returning to Shimla after 15 years in London, Hrithik Roshan has convinced that Kareena Kapoor has been sending him the doting e-mails that have really been written by their mutual childhood friend, Rani Mukherji. However, the route to the truth in this contrived romantic comedy of errors offers few surprises. Debuting director Kunal Kohli borrows too liberally from recent box-office hits, while only the demure Mukherji manages a performance approximating psychological depth. DP. In Hindi with English subtitles. DVD

Hrithik Roshan *Raj* • Rani Mukherji *Pooja* • Satish Shah *Mr Sahani* • Kareena Kapoor *Tina* • Uday Chopra *Rohan* • Kiran Kumar *Mr Khanna* ■ *Dir/Scr* Kunal Kohli

Mujhse Shaadi Karogi ★★★ PG

Romantic comedy
2004 · Ind · Colour · 156mins

David Dhawan, known as Bollywood's king of comedy, directs this sparky romantic comedy set in the coastal town of Goa. Salman Khan and Akshay Kumar are the hunky lifeguard and his free-spirited flatmate who find themselves competing for the affections of aspiring designer Priyanka Chopra. The leads bounce off each other to good effect, but Rajpal Yadav steals the show in the dual role of an astrologer and his troublemaking biker twin. DP. In Hindi with English subtitles. DVD

Salman Khan *Samir* • Priyanka Chopra *Rani* • Amrish Puri *Colonel Dugraj Singh* • Akshay Kumar *Sunny* • Satish Shah *Surya Prakash* • Rajpal Yadav *Raj/Paul* ■ *Dir* David Dhawan • *Scr* Anees Bazmee, Rumi Jaffrey

Mulan ★★★★ U

Animated musical adventure
1998 · US · Colour · 87mins

Set in ancient China, this recounts the adventures of the eponymous heroine who dons man's clothing and goes to war to save her family honour. Some splendid set pieces, the inevitable love between Mulan and her brave captain, and the often uproarious presence of a snappy little dragon (voiced by Eddie Murphy) are the highlights. Aspects of the story go a bit over young children's heads, but it's an enthralling narrative for everyone else and there's plenty of slapstick fun to keep youngsters happy. A startling addition to the Disney studio's catalogue. A belated straight-to-video sequel followed in 2004. TH DVD

Ming-Na *Mulan* • Eddie Murphy *Mushu* • Lea Salonga *Mulan* • BD Wong *Shang* • Donny Osmond *Shang* • Miguel Ferrer *Shan-Yu* • Harvey Fierstein *Yao* • Miriam Margolyes *Matchmaker* • Pat Morita *Emperor* • George Takei *First ancestor* ■ *Dir* Barry Cook, Tony Bancroft • *Scr* Rita Hsiao, Christopher Sanders, Philip Lazebnik, Raymond Singer, Eugenia Bostwick-Singer, from a story by Robert D San Souci

Mule Train ★★ U

Western 1950 · US · Sepia · 70mins

The song of the title was a million-selling pop hit for Frankie Laine, and this Gene Autry programme filler was made quickly to capitalise on the song's success. But threading a plot around the lyrics wasn't easy and resulted in this loose thriller about the construction of a dam and, bizarrely, cement claim jumping. The popular Autry is his usual likeable self, but Robert Livingston's evil freight shipper is actually far more interesting than the bland hero. The movie was originally filmed in the now forgotten screen process of Sepiatone. TS

Gene Autry • Pat Buttram *Smokey Argyle* • Sheila Ryan *Carol Bannister* • Robert Livingston *Sam Brady* • Frank Jacquet *Clayton Hodges* • Vince Barnett *Barber Mulkey* • Syd Saylor *Skeeter* • Sandy Sanders *Bud* ■ *Dir* John English • *Scr* Gerald Geraghty, from a story by Alan James

Mulholland Drive ★★★★★ 15

Psychological thriller
2001 · US/Fr · Colour · 140mins

As twisted as the Los Angeles road it takes its name from, David Lynch's film is a typically weird and wonderful rumination on the American Dream, the Hollywood nightmare and the mysterious grey area in between. Lynch's dazzling thriller reaches new heights of mesmeric fascination thanks to scintillating visuals and an offbeat emotional intensity. Although many plot strands are thrown into the suspenseful mix, the main focus is on the bizarre relationship between amnesiac movie star Laura Elena Harring and wannabe actress Naomi Watts, who slowly helps the accident victim recover her memory and identity. With a sensational performance by Watts, it's a triple-strength masterpiece that will more than satisfy die-hard Lynch fans and may even gain a receptive new audience for the Sultan of Strange. AJ DVD

Justin Theroux *Adam Kesher* • Naomi Watts *Betty Elms/Diane Selwyn* • Laura Elena Harring [Laura Harring] *Rita/Camilla Rhodes* • Ann Miller *Coco Lenoix* • Dan Hedaya *Vincenzo Castigliane* • Mark Pellegrino *Joe* • Brent Briscoe *Detective Domgaard* • Robert Forster *Det Harry McKnight* • Lee Grant *Louise Bonner* • Michael J Anderson *Mr Rocque* • Billy Ray Cyrus *Gene* • Chad Everett *Jimmy Katz* • Angelo Badalamenti *Luigi Castigliane* ■ *Dir/Scr* David Lynch

Mulholland Falls ★★★ 18

Thriller 1996 · US · Colour · 102mins

Nick Nolte heads a very starry cast as the hard-nosed head of the Hat Squad – a group of detectives prepared to take the law into their own hands to deal with mobsters. Nolte becomes entangled in a political conspiracy when investigating the death of a beautiful woman (Jennifer Connelly) who had been his lover. Director Lee Tamahori stylishly evokes the sleazy glamour of postwar Los Angeles and elicits excellent performances from the cast, but all are let down by a muddled script. JF. Contains violence, swearing, nudity and sex scenes. DVD

Nick Nolte *Hoover* • Melanie Griffith *Katherine* • Chazz Palminteri *Coolidge* • Michael Madsen *Eddie Hall* • Chris Penn *Arthur* • Treat Williams *Fitzgerald* • Jennifer Connelly *Allison Pond* • John Malkovich *Timms* ■ *Dir* Lee Tamahori • *Scr* Pete Dexter, from a story by Floyd Mutrux, Pete Dexter

Mullet ★★★

Comedy drama 2001 · Aus · Colour · 90mins

Prodigal Ben Mendelsohn returns from exile in Sydney to the fishing port of Coollawarra to discover that everything's different but nothing has really changed. However, by the end of this straight-talking comedy, there's room for optimism as he finds his niche in a community that had branded him worthless. Presenting dysfunction as a fact of life rather than using it as a convenient dramatic device, writer/director David Caesar delivers a splendid ensemble effort. DP

Ben Mendelsohn *Eddie "Mullet" Maloney* • Susie Porter *Tully* • Andrew S Gilbert *Peter Maloney* • Belinda McClory *Kay* ■ *Dir/Scr* David Caesar

Multiple Maniacs ★★ 18

Satirical melodrama 1970 · US · BW · 90mins

John Waters, the self-styled "Sovereign of Sleaze", dubbed this early work a "celluloid atrocity", while its title is a homage to the 1964 gorefest *Two Thousand Maniacs!*. Waters's most overtly Catholic tale to date centres on "Lady Divine's Cavalcade of Perversions", a travelling freak show that pitches its tent in Baltimore. The moral is that the world at large contains far worse horrors than those featured in Divine's ghoulish gallery. An eye-opening gutter parable that comes complete with the Infant of Prague (Michael Renner Jr). AJ

Divine *Lady Divine* • David Lochary *Mr David* • Mary Vivian Pearce *Bonnie* • Mink Stole • Cookie Mueller *Cookie* • Paul Swift *Steve* • Rick Morrow *Ricky* • Michael Renner Jr *Infant of Prague* ■ *Dir/Scr* John Waters (2)

Multiplicity ★★★ 12

Fantasy comedy 1996 · US · Colour · 112mins

Michael Keaton finds his time stretched to the limit between his wife, career and family, until he meets a scientist who offers to clone him, in director Harold Ramis's inventive comedy. Of course, one clone ends up not being enough and soon he has an attic full of them – all played by Keaton and each with a different personality – while his unsuspecting wife (Andie MacDowell) wonders what is going on. A sprightly romp that benefits from very funny multiple performances by Keaton. JB DVD

Michael Keaton *Doug Kinney* • Andie MacDowell *Laura Kinney* • Zack Duhame *Zack Kinney* • Katie Schlossberg *Jennifer Kinney* • Harris Yulin *Dr Leeds* • Richard Masur *Del King* • Eugene Levy *Vic* • Ann Cusack *Noreen* ■ *Dir* Harold Ramis • *Scr* Chris Miller, Mary Hale, Lowell Ganz, Babaloo Mandel, from a short story by Chris Miller

Mumbai Matinee ★★★ 12

Comedy 2003 · Ind · Colour · 125mins

This enjoyable comedy from Anant Balani takes something of a Bollywood risk by focusing on the subject of virginity. Star Rahul Bose is suitably despairing as the 32-year-old innocent who accidentally becomes a porn star through the underhand dealings of immoral fixer Vijay Raaz and down-at-heel director Saurabh Shukla, while Perizaad Zorabian co-stars as the unflappable journalist who rescues Bose's flagging reputation. DP. In Hindi and English with subtitles. DVD

Rahul Bose *Debashish Chatterjee* • Perizaad Zorabian *Sonali Verma* • Vijay Raaz *Baba Hindustani* • Saurabh Shukla *Nitin Kapoor* ■ *Dir/Scr* Anant Balani

Mumford ★★ 15

Comedy drama
1999 · US · Colour and BW · 107mins

Though advertised as a riotous comedy, this story of a small town psychiatrist with a deep secret and his wondrous effect on the locals is really more of a light-hearted drama. While never boring, and filled with moments both touching and humorous, it moves at a snail's pace. Relieved of its multiple subplots, the film might have felt less congested. Even then, some unexplained changes in the characters – particularly Martin Short's – would remain. KB. Contains drug abuse, sex scenes, nudity, swearing. [VIDEO] DVD

Loren Dean *Mumford* • Hope Davis *Sofie Crisp* • Jason Lee *Skip Skipperton* • Alfre Woodard *Lily* • Mary McDonnell *Althea Brockett* • Pruitt Taylor Vince *Henry Follett* • Zooey Deschanel *Nessa Watkins* • Martin Short *Lionel Dillard* • Ted Danson *Jeremy Brockett* • Robert Stack ■ *Dir/Scr* Lawrence Kasdan

The Mummy ★★★★ 15

Classic horror 1932 · US · BW · 72mins

Boris Karloff's next film after *Frankenstein* shows what an intensely subtle actor he was compared with the walking-dead performances of the supporting cast. He plays the ancient Egyptian Im-Ho-Tep who has been buried alive for trying to restore life to his beloved princess. Brought back to life in the present day, he pursues his lost love, believing her to be reincarnated as the fiancée of a member of an archaeological expedition. Master photographer Karl Freund directs without shock tactics, apart from the burying alive scene, but with images of death and decay worthy of Edgar Allan Poe. TH [VIDEO] DVD

Boris Karloff *Imhotep/Ardeth Bey* • Zita Johann *Helen Grosvenor/Princess Ankh-es-en-Amon* • David Manners *Frank Whemple* • Arthur Byron *Sir Joseph Whemple* • Edward Van Sloan *Doctor Muller* • Bramwell Fletcher *Ralph Norton* • Eddie Kane *Doctor* ■ *Dir* Karl Freund • *Scr* John L Balderston, from the story *Cagliostro* by Nina Wilcox Putnam, Richard Schayer

The Mummy ★★★ PG

Horror 1959 · UK · Colour · 84mins

After its huge success with Dracula and Frankenstein, Hammer turned to another vintage Universal monster for its scream dream team of Peter Cushing, Christopher Lee and director Terence Fisher. Although rather talky and undemanding plot-wise, Cushing is marvellously crisp as the tomb-desecrating archaeologist, fending off the malevolent attentions of gauze-wrapped Lee. And, unlike your usual shambling mummy, Lee captures the murderously powerful ferocity of the bandaged reincarnation as he stomps through foggy London. AJ [VIDEO] DVD

Peter Cushing *John Banning* • Christopher Lee *Kharis, the Mummy* • Yvonne Furneaux *Isobel Banning/Princess Ananka* • Eddie Byrne *Inspector Mulrooney* • Felix Aylmer *Stephen Banning* • Raymond Huntley *Joseph Whemple* ■ *Dir* Terence Fisher • *Scr* Jimmy Sangster, from the 1932 film

The Mummy ★★★ 12

Period horror adventure
1999 · US · Colour · 119mins

In the good old days, the Mummy merely met Abbott and Costello. Now, thanks to the wizards of the special effects industry, this digitally manipulated villain can meet his adversaries in a world of vibrant action adventure. Stephen Sommers has embroidered the original story to excess at times, with flesh-eating beetles and battling zombie slaves just two of the gruesome modern additions. Yet Brendan Fraser does his goofy macho best and Arnold Vosloo has the perfect bone structure for the brooding menace returned from the dead. AJ [VIDEO] DVD

Brendan Fraser *Rick O'Connell* • Rachel Weisz *Evelyn* • John Hannah *Jonathan* • Kevin J O'Connor *Beni* • Arnold Vosloo *Imhotep* • Jonathan Hyde *Egyptologist* ■ *Dir* Stephen Sommers • *Scr* Stephen Sommers, from a story by Lloyd Fonvielle, Kevin Jarre, Stephen Sommers

The Mummy Returns ★★★ 12

Period horror adventure
2001 · US · Colour · 124mins

You have to admire them for getting a sequel into the cinemas just two years after the first *Mummy* became a surprise hit. This sense of continuity pulls the franchise in line with the *Indiana Jones* films, to which this owes so much with its tomb-raiding themes, period colour and deft mix of comedy and action. To praise it faintly as more of the same does a disservice to the slick bravado of writer/director Stephen Sommers and the technical wizardry of Industrial Light and Magic, who created the screen-dominating CGI effects. AC [VIDEO] DVD

Brendan Fraser *Rick O'Connell* • Rachel Weisz *Evelyn* • John Hannah *Jonathan* • Arnold Vosloo *Imhotep* • Oded Fehr *Ardeth Bay* • Patricia Velasquez *Meela/Anck-Su-Namun* • The Rock *The Scorpion King* ■ *Dir/Scr* Stephen Sommers

The Mummy's Curse ★ PG

Horror 1944 · US · BW · 57mins

This carbon copy chiller finds Kharis the Mummy (Lon Chaney Jr in his third and last bandaged big-screen outing) once more terrorising swamp dwellers and archaeologists in the monotonous search for the reincarnation of his Princess Ananka (Virginia Christine). The striking opening – the only sequence given any visual flair by director Leslie Goodwins – has Ananka dug out of the quicksand she sank into during the finale of *The Mummy's Ghost*. Otherwise, this is a slow-moving, predictable potboiler. AJ [VIDEO]

Lon Chaney [Lon Chaney Jr] *Kharis, the Mummy* • Peter Coe *Dr Ilzor Zandaab* • Virginia Christine *Princess Ananka* • Kay Harding *Betty Walsh* • Dennis Moore *Dr James Halsey* • Martin Kosleck *Ragheb* ■ *Dir* Leslie Goodwins • *Scr* Bernard Schubert, Leon Abrams, Dwight V Babcock, from a story by Leon Abrams, Dwight V Babcock

The Mummy's Ghost ★ PG

Horror 1944 · US · BW · 57mins

A creaky programme-filler carelessly directed by Z-movie maven Reginald Le Borg with little originality on show. Priest George Zucco sends disciple John Carradine to New England to help Kharis the Mummy (Lon Chaney Jr, in his second bandaged appearance) find the Princess Ananka. Her soul has been reincarnated in student Ramsay Ames. As musty as the soiled wrappings swathing Kharis's body and as murky as the swamp mud he and his ancient lover sink into during the film's climax. AJ [VIDEO]

John Carradine *Yousef Bey* • Lon Chaney [Lon Chaney Jr] *Kharis, the Mummy* • Robert Lowery *Tom Hervey* • Ramsay Ames *Amina Mansouri* • Barton MacLane *Inspector Walgreen* • George Zucco *High priest* • Frank Reicher *Professor Matthew Norman* ■ *Dir* Reginald LeBorg [Reginald Le Borg] • *Scr* Griffin Jay, Henry Sucher, Brenda Weisberg, from a story by Griffin Jay, Henry Sucher

The Mummy's Hand ★★

Horror 1940 · US · BW · 67mins

This first sequel to Boris Karloff's *The Mummy* plagiarises its predecessor and is a cheap and cheerful precursor to a series of cumbersome follow-ups. The head of the Cairo Museum (George Zucco) balefully revives the 3,000-year-old Kharis (Tom Tyler) as a prelude to Mummy mayhem. Predictably, Universal spent little money, making use of sets from earlier movies, and there's minimal shock-horror as the bandaged threat lurches into view with only a dodgy left leg and memories of things long past to propel his murderous ambitions. BB

Dick Foran *Steve Banning* • Peggy Moran *Marta Solvani* • Wallace Ford *Babe Jenson* • Eduardo Cianelli [Eduardo Ciannelli] *High priest* • George Zucco *Andoheb* • Cecil Kelloway [Cecil Kellaway] *Mr Solvani* • Tom Tyler *Kharis, the Mummy* ■ *Dir* Christy Cabanne • *Scr* Griffin Jay, Maxwell Shane, from a story by Griffin Jay

The Mummy's Shroud ★★ PG

Horror 1966 · UK · Colour · 86mins

Hammer could never resist dabbling with the dark forces of ancient Egypt, but this third descent into the mummy's tomb was one of the studio's least accomplished horrors. After dwelling a bit too long in the land of the pharaohs, the action shifts to 1920 as André Morell's expedition ventures into the vault. We know it's doomed because a) it's sponsored by treasure-seeking rogue John Phillips and b) local malcontent Roger Delgado knows the spell to revive the avenging mummy. There are some particularly grisly murders and a terrific finale, but it's mostly dry as dust. DP DVD

André Morell *Sir Basil Walden* • John Phillips (1) *Stanley Preston* • David Buck *Paul Preston* • Elizabeth Sellars *Barbara Preston* • Maggie Kimberley *Claire de Sangre* • Michael Ripper *Longbarrow* • Roger Delgado *Hasmid Ali* ■ *Dir* John Gilling • *Scr* John Gilling, from a story by John Elder [Anthony Hinds]

The Mummy's Tomb ★★ PG

Horror 1942 · US · BW · 58mins

The tedious cost-cutting sequel to *The Mummy's Hand* features flashbacks to that 1940 pot-boiler, angry villager scenes borrowed from *Frankenstein* and, despite being promoted on Lon Chaney Jr's rising horror appeal, stuntman Eddie Parker doubled for the overweight star as the bandaged Kharis in numerous shots. Ageing high priest George Zucco sends disciple Turhan Bey to America with Kharis to wreak vengeance on the expedition members who defiled his Egyptian resting place. An uninspired addition to the musty formula that should have stayed under wraps. AJ [VIDEO]

Lon Chaney [Lon Chaney Jr] *Kharis, the Mummy* • Dick Foran *Stephen A Banning* • John Hubbard *John Banning* • Elyse Knox *Isobel Evans Banning* • George Zucco *Andoheb* • Wallace Ford *Babe Hanson* • Turhan Bey *Mehemet Bey* ■ *Dir* Harold Young • *Scr* Griffin Jay, Henry Sucher, from a story by Neil P Varnick

Mumsy, Nanny, Sonny & Girly ★

Horror thriller 1970 · UK · Colour · 101mins

The title promises rubbish, and the film obliges. Michael Bryant falls prey to a weird gang – a mother, two children and a maid – who kidnap men, play with them and then kill them. Neither comedy or horror, this is merely a mess. The director is Freddie Francis, a former house cameraman for Hammer Films who would later collaborate with David Lynch on *Dune* and *The Elephant Man*. AT

Michael Bryant *"New Friend"* • Ursula Howells *Mumsy* • Pat Heywood *Nanny* • Howard Trevor *Sonny* • Vanessa Howard *Girly* • Robert Swann *Soldier* • Imogen Hassall *Girlfriend* • Michael Ripper *Zoo attendant* ■ *Dir* Freddie Francis • *Scr* Brian Comport, from the play *The Happy Family* by Maisie Mosco

Munchie ★★ PG

Fantasy comedy 1992 · US · Colour · 77mins

A magical furry creature (voiced by Dom DeLuise) befriends a precocious young boy struggling to adjust at his new school. Munchie's appearance may actually frighten kids, especially since the puppetry is so poor that his lip movements rarely match DeLuise's voice. Loni Anderson plays the kid's mom, but it rather looks as if she's doing a favour for pal DeLuise. Watch for a young Jennifer Love Hewitt as the obligatory "cute girl". ST. Contains drug abuse. [VIDEO]

Loni Anderson *Cathy* • Dom DeLuise *Munchie* • Andrew Stevens *Elliott* • Jaime McEnnan *Gage Dobson* • Arte Johnson *Professor Cruikshank* • Mike Simmrin *Leon* • Scott Ferguson *Ashton* • Love Hewitt [Jennifer Love Hewitt] *Andrea* ■ *Dir* Jim Wynorski • *Scr* Jim Wynorski, RJ Robertson

Munchie Strikes Back ★★ PG

Fantasy comedy 1994 · US · Colour · 85mins

In this second sequel to the poor man's *Gremlins*, the troublesome space creature gets one final chance to do some good on Earth when he is assigned to the household of Lesley-Anne Down. Andrew Stevens, Loni Anderson and Dom DeLouise return from the first sequel, with *WKRP Cincinnati* alumnus Howard Hesseman providing the voice of Munchie. Director Jim Wynorksi keeps the action racing along and undemanding children will probably like it. JF [VIDEO]

Lesley-Anne Down *Linda McClelland* • Howard Hesseman *Munchie* • Angus Scrimm *Kronus* • Trenton Knight *Chris* • Corey Mendelsohn *Brett Carlisle* • Andrew Stevens *Shelby* • Loni Anderson • Dom DeLuise ■ *Dir* Jim Wynorski • *Scr* Jim Wynorski, RJ Robertson

Munchies ★ PG

Comedy horror 1987 · US · Colour · 78mins

What's worse than a rip-off of *Gremlins*? A rip-off of *Gremlins* with Harvey Korman in multiple roles, of course. Alien-hunter Korman thinks he's found definitive proof in the form of a cute little creature who eats junk food. His evil brother (Korman again) gets hold of the little guy and, before you know it, there are scads of them, causing trouble for everyone. ST [VIDEO]

Harvey Korman *Cecil/Simon Waterman* • Charles Stratton *Paul* • Nadine Van Der Velde *Cindy* • Alix Elias *Melvis* • Charlie Phillips *Eddie* • Hardy Rawls *Big Ed* • Jon Stafford *Dude* • Robert Picardo *Bob Marvelle* ■ *Dir* Bettina Hirsch • *Scr* Lance Smith

M

Munimji ★★★ U

Drama 1955 · Ind · BW · 149mins

Subodh Mukherjee made his directorial debut with this typically tangled Hindi tale. At the centre of events are Pran and Dev Anand as half-brothers who were switched at birth and now find themselves on opposite sides of the law, yet in love with the same girl. However, the film's main interest lies in the fact that it provided the prolific Nirupa Roy, who would go on to become the most famous mother figure in Indian cinema, with her first maternal role. Indeed, fans used to seeing her play goddesses might be a little shocked to see the way she schemes here. DP. In Hindi with English subtitles. [VIDEO]

Dev Anand *Amar* • Pran *Ratan* • Nirupa Roy *Malati* • Nalini Jaywant *Roopa* ■ *Dir* Subodh Mukherjee • *Scr* Subodh Mukherjee, Ranjan, from a story by Ranjan

Munster, Go Home! ★★★ U

Comedy 1966 · US · Colour · 96mins

Popular sitcoms rarely make the grade when they are extended to feature-film length. Here's one of the few exceptions, originally made for television but deemed good enough for theatrical release. The family inherits an English estate that is being used by their nefarious relatives as the centre of a counterfeiting ring. When they turn up to inspect Munster Hall, their aristocratic next-of-kin (under the deliciously plummy command of Hermione Gingold) try and scare them away with fake apparitions and musty scares. Terry-Thomas and genre veteran John Carradine enter into the spirit of a charming, colourful and funny affair. AJ

Fred Gwynne *Herman* • Yvonne De Carlo *Lily* • Al Lewis *Grandpa* • Butch Patrick *Eddie* • Debbie Watson *Marilyn* • Terry-Thomas *Freddie* • Hermione Gingold *Lady Effigie* • Robert Pine *Roger* • John Carradine *Cruikshank* • Richard Dawson *Joey* ■ *Dir* Earl Bellamy • *Scr* George Tibbles, Joe Connelly, Bob Mosher, from the TV series *The Munsters*

The Muppet Christmas Carol ★★★★ U

Comedy drama 1992 · US · Colour · 85mins

With Michael Caine as Scrooge, Kermit and Miss Piggy as the Cratchits, and Gonzo as Dickens, this is quite simply corking Christmas entertainment. Although the story has been Muppetised (with Fozzie Bear as Fozziwig, the owner of a rubber chicken factory), no attempt has been made to water down the story, and the poignance of the moral tale is as affecting as ever. Caine hasn't been this good in years, and his scenes with those hecklers supreme Statler and Waldorf, as the Marley brothers, are the highlight of the film. DP DVD

Michael Caine *Scrooge* • Steve Whitmire *Screenplay* • Frank Oz *Source Writer* • Dave Goelz *Source Writer* • David Rudman *Source Writer* • Jerry Nelson *Statler/Floyd/Ma Bear/Tiny Tim/The Ghost of Christmas Present* ■ *Dir* Brian Henson • *Scr* Jerry Juhl, from the story by Charles Dickens

The Muppet Movie ★★★★ U

Comedy adventure
1979 · US · Colour · 94mins

Jim Henson's beloved, zany puppets made their feature film debut in this entertaining adventure relating Kermit the Frog's inspirational journey from Georgia swamp tadpole to Hollywood star. Comedy director James Frawley imposes pleasing order on the charming proceedings while Henson and his long-time associate Frank Oz delightfully dominate as the manipulators and voices of Kermit and Miss Piggy. An indication of how big the Muppets were at the time is the more than a dozen silly star cameos. The only letdown is Paul Williams and Kenny Ascher's disappointingly forgettable song score. AME

Jim Henson *Kermit the Frog/Rowlf/Dr Teeth/Waldorf* • Frank Oz *Miss Piggy/Fozzie Bear/Animal/Sam the Eagle* • Jerry Nelson *Floyd Pepper/Crazy Harry/Robin the Frog/Lew Zealand* • Richard Hunt *Scooter/Statler/Janice/Sweetums/Beaker* • Dave Goelz *Gonzo/Zoot/Dr Bunsen Honeydew* ■ *Dir* James Frawley • *Scr* Jerry Juhl, Jack Burns

Muppet Treasure Island ★★★★ U

Comedy adventure
1996 · US · Colour · 95mins

The Muppets take on Robert Louis Stevenson in their inimitable way in this rollicking musical version of the pirate saga. Using the bare bones of the classic story as a framework, director Brian Henson press-gangs the likes of Billy Connolly, Jennifer Saunders and Tim Curry into service for a series of hilarious cameos, accompanied by some rousing songs and the now customary "romance" between Miss Piggy and Kermit. Adults may find the voyage a long haul, but children will love it. AJ DVD

Steve Whitmire *Captain Abraham Smollet (Kermit the Frog)/Rizzo the Rat* • Frank Oz *Benjamina Gunn (Miss Piggy)* • Tim Curry *Long John Silver* • Kevin Bishop *Jim Hawkins* • Billy Connolly *Billy Bones* • Jennifer Saunders *Mrs Bluveridge* • Dave Goelz *The Great Gonzo* ■ *Dir* Brian Henson • *Scr* Jerry Juhl, Kirk R Thatcher, James V Hart

Muppets from Space ★★★★ U

Science-fiction comedy adventure
1999 · UK/US · Colour · 85mins

Although more earthbound than the title suggests, this achieves a high chuckle factor. Nasally challenged Gonzo believes his long-lost family are aliens and that they're coming to take him home. Aspiring TV reporter Miss Piggy and assorted government agents, led by Jeffrey Tambor, want to abduct him for their own ends. Movies from *Close Encounters* to *The Shawshank Redemption* are wickedly parodied, while F Murray Abraham, Ray Liotta and Andie MacDowell seem to be having a great time. SR DVD

Frank Oz *Miss Piggy/Fozzie Bear/Animal/Sam Eagle* • Dave Goelz *Gonzo/Bunsen Honeydew/Waldorf/The Birdman* • Steve Whitmire *Kermit the Frog/Rizzo the Rat/Beaker/Cosmic Fish No 1* • Bill Barretta *Pepe the Prawn/Bobo as Rentro/Bubba the Rat/Johnny Fiama/Cosmic Fish No 2* • F Murray Abraham *Noah* • Ray Liotta *Gate guard* • Andie MacDowell *Shelley Snipes* ■ *Dir* Tim Hill • *Scr* Jerry Juhl, Joseph Mazzarino, Ken Kaufman

The Muppets Take Manhattan ★★★ U

Comedy 1984 · US · Colour · 93mins

The third big-screen outing for Jim Henson's puppets has playwright Kermit frog-marching his pals to New York to stage his college show on Broadway. Alas, he finds that biting the Big Apple can leave a sour taste in the mouth. It's not quite up to the standards of the two earlier outings, but the bouncy songs and clever use of Manhattan locations are bonuses. Muppet movies always feature a vast array of guest stars: watch out here for cameos from Liza Minnelli, Brooke Shields, Joan Rivers and Gregory Hines, among others. RT DVD

Jim Henson *Kermit the Frog/Rowlf/Dr Teeth/Ernie/Muppet newsman/Swedish chef/Waldorf* • Frank Oz *Miss Piggy/Fozzie Bear/Animal/Sam the Eagle/Bert/Cookie Monster* • Dave Goelz *Gonzo/Chester Rat/Bill the Frog/Dr Bunsen Honeydew/Zoot* • Steve Whitmire *Rizzo the Rat/Gil the Frog* ■ *Dir* Frank Oz • *Scr* Frank Oz, Tom Patchett, Jay Tarses, from a story by Tom Patchett, Jay Tarses

Murder ★★★ PG

Mystery 1930 · UK · BW · 99mins

Alfred Hitchcock's third talkie is a creaky murder mystery, co-adapted by Hitch's wife Alma Reville. Herbert Marshall does well in only his second sound film as a juror who conducts his own inquiries after he suspects an actress isn't a killer. Without giving too much away, the denouement was considered rather daring in its day, as was the use of a stream-of-consciousness voiceover, which established Hitchcock as one of the most inventive of sound directors. The acting now seems rather stagey and the whodunnit isn't particularly taxing, but it's still fascinating. DP

Herbert Marshall *Sir John Menier* • Norah Baring *Diana Baring* • Phyllis Konstam *Dulcie Markham* • Edward Chapman *Ted Markham* • Miles Mander *Gordon Druce* • Esme Percy *Handel Fane* ■ *Dir* Alfred Hitchcock • *Scr* Alma Reville, Walter C Mycroft, Alfred Hitchcock, from the novel and play *Enter Sir John* by Clemence Dane, Helen Simpson

Murder à la Mod ★★★

Mystery comedy drama
1968 · US · BW · 80mins

After several acclaimed shorts, Brian De Palma moved into features with *The Wedding Party*, which he co-directed with Cynthia Munroe and Wilford Leach in 1966. However, by the time it was released, three years later, he had completed his solo feature bow with this enigmatic comedy thriller, which he also wrote and edited. Centred on the murder of a pornographer's lover, this is a Rashomonesque exercise, with each segment reflecting the lifestyle of the protagonist – soap opera for the victim, Hitchcockian thriller for the blackmailed husband and silent slapstick for the deaf-mute horror actor. The result is intriguing, but inconsistent. DP

Margo Norton *Karen* • Andra Akers *Tracy* • Jared Martin *Christopher* • William Finley *Otto* • Ken Burrows *Wiley* ■ *Dir/Scr* Brian De Palma

Murder Ahoy ★★★ U

Murder mystery comedy
1964 · UK · BW · 88mins

The final entry in Margaret Rutherford's Miss Marple casebook is the only one not reworked from a story by Agatha Christie. While David Pursall and Jack Seddon's original screenplay has all the characteristics of a Christie whodunnit, closer scrutiny reveals too many offbeat characters, a glut of inconsequential chat and more comedy than you'd ever find in a well-stocked shelf of the great Dame's mysteries. Having said that, it's neatly staged and the solution is neither blatantly obvious nor buried under a mass of barely perceptible clues. DP

Margaret Rutherford *Miss Marple* • Lionel Jeffries *Captain de Courcy Rhumstone* • Charles Tingwell *Detective Inspector Craddock* • William Mervyn *Commander Breeze-Connington* • Joan Benham *Matron Alice Fanbraid* • Stringer Davis *Mr Stringer* • Nicholas Parsons *Dr Crump* • Miles Malleson *Bishop Faulkner* • Henry Oscar *Lord Rudkin* • Derek Nimmo *Sub-Lt Humbert* ■ *Dir* George Pollock • *Scr* David Pursall, Jack Seddon, from the character created by Agatha Christie

Murder at Devil's Glen ★★★ 15

Thriller 1999 · US · Colour · 88mins

A nifty made-for-TV variation on *I Know What You Did Last Summer*, which makes up for what it lacks in thrills with some cunning plotting. The film opens with four students burying a body in the deserted Devil's Glen. Fast forward eight years and one of the number (Rick Schroder) emerges from prison with some bad news for his now respectable buddies: their burial ground is about to be redeveloped and they need to move the body. JF. Contains violence, swearing. DVD

Rick Schroder *Henry* • Jack Noseworthy *Oliver* • Jayce Bartok *Doc* • Michael Easton *Charlie* • Tara Reid *Girl* ■ *Dir* Paul Shapiro • *Scr* Eric Harlacher

Murder at My Door ★★ 15

Thriller 1996 · US · Colour · 90mins

In this grimmer-than-usual TV-movie chiller, Judith Light plays a mother still grieving following the death of her son and worrying about his surviving twin (Johnny Galecki), who is developing some rather morbid pastimes. Meanwhile, a serial killer is stalking the town's students. There are few surprises in the script, but director Eric Till generates some suspense. JF. Contains violence.

Judith Light *Irene McNair* • RH Thomson *Ed McNair* • Johnny Galecki *Teddy McNair* ■ *Dir* Eric Till • *Scr* Patti Sullivan, Chris Canaan [Christopher Canaan]

Murder at 1600 ★★ 15

Political thriller 1997 · US · Colour · 102mins

Wesley Snipes delivers another of his one-note tough guys in an uninspired, cliché-ridden action thriller about a Washington DC cop called in to investigate a murder at the White House. As he delves deeper into the crime with the help of Secret Service agent Diane Lane, he uncovers a conspiracy which may reach all the way to the President himself. Director Dwight Little's routine mystery generates little suspense and even less interest. AJ. Contains violence, swearing, a sex scene. DVD

Wesley Snipes *Detective Harlan Regis* • Diane Lane *Nina Chance* • Alan Alda *Alvin Jordan* • Daniel Benzali *Nick Spikings* • Dennis Miller *Detective Stengel* • Ronny Cox *President Jack Neil* • Diane Baker *Kitty Neil* ■ *Dir* Dwight H Little • *Scr* Wayne Beach, David Hodgin

Murder at the Gallop ★★★ U

Murder mystery comedy
1963 · UK · BW · 77mins

Robert Morley and Flora Robson add a touch of class to the list of suspects as Miss Marple investigates the murder of a rich recluse. While detective Charles Tingwell scratches his head in bewilderment, the divine Margaret Rutherford lures the killer into a trap using herself as bait. Director George Pollock effortlessly blends clues and comedy in Rutherford's second outing as the doyenne of St Mary Mead (after 1961's *Murder She Said*), but the most striking thing about this lively whodunnit is that it was inspired by the novel *After the Funeral*, in which the case was actually solved by Hercule Poirot! DP

Margaret Rutherford *Miss Marple* • Stringer Davis *Mr Stringer* • Robert Morley *Hector Enderby* • Flora Robson *Miss Gilchrist* • Charles Tingwell *Det Insp Craddock* • Gordon Harris *Sgt Bacon* • Robert Urquhart *George Crossfield* • Katya Douglas *Rosamund Shane* • James Villiers *Michael Shane* • Noel Howlett *Mr Trundell* • Finlay Currie *Old Enderby* ■ *Dir* George Pollock • *Scr* James P Cavanagh, David Pursall, Jack Seddon, from the novel *After the Funeral* by Agatha Christie

Murder at the Vanities ★★★

Thriller 1934 · US · BW · 95mins

A rare breed, this – a musical thriller set inside the famous Vanities vaudeville theatre and opening with a dance routine that features nude ladies inside huge models of powder compacts. There's also a near-Hitchcock moment when one of the girls finds blood dripping from the catwalk on to her shoulder. Director Mitchell Leisen's biographer, David Chierichetti, claimed the film "pushed the limits of bawdiness and nudity farther than they would go in any American film until the sixties". AT

Victor McLaglen *Bill Murdock* • Carl Brisson *Eric Lander* • Jack Oakie *Jack Ellery* • Kitty Carlisle *Ann Ware* • Gertrude Michael *Rita Ross* • Jessie Ralph *Mrs Smith* • Gail Patrick *Sadie Evans* • Charles B Middleton [Charles Middleton] *Homer* • Clara Lou Sheridan [Ann Sheridan] *Lou* ■ *Dir* Mitchell Leisen • *Scr* Carey Wilson, Joseph Gollomb, Sam Hellman, from the play by Earl Carroll, Rufus King

Murder at the Windmill ★★

Musical 1949 · UK · BW · 70mins

Comic policemen Garry Marsh and Jon Pertwee investigate a murder at London's Windmill theatre, famous for its nude tableaux and the fact that it remained open throughout the Second World War. Partly filmed *in situ*, with performers and staff playing themselves, this creaky whodunnit is a valuable record, within the bounds of the strict censorship of the day, of the lowbrow songs and sketches that made the theatre famous. Jimmy Edwards's spot, dreadful now, was thought hilarious at the time, and won the whiskery comic his part in radio's celebrated *Take It from Here*. DM

Garry Marsh *Detective Inspector* • Jon Pertwee *Sergeant* • Jack Livesey *Vivian Van Damm* •

Eliot Makeham *Gimpy* • Jimmy Edwards *Jimmy* • Diana Decker *Frankie* • Donald Clive *Donald* • Jill Anstey *Patsy* ■ *Dir/Scr* Val Guest

Murder between Friends ★★★ 15

Crime drama based on a true story
1993 · US · Colour · 91mins

This TV movie tells the story of a perplexing murder in Louisiana. Stephen Lang and Martin Kemp play friends who are spotted leaving the house where Lang's wife has been beaten to death; both then insist the other is guilty of the murder, and it's left to assistant DA Timothy Busfield to unravel the mystery. It borders on the melodramatic, but Lang and Kemp deliver chilling performances. JF DVD

Timothy Busfield *Assistant DA John Thorn* • Stephen Lang *Kerry Meyers* • Martin Kemp *Bill Fontanille* • Lisa Blount *Janet Myers* • O'Neal Compton *Detective Easby* • Alex Courtney *Rene LeGallais* ■ *Dir* Waris Hussein • *Scr* Philip Rosenberg

Murder by Contract ★★★

Thriller 1958 · US · BW · 80mins

Here's a real gem and total justification for the existence of the B-movie. X-certificated in the UK on release, this darkly sinister plot masks a deeply original screenplay proffering philosophical insights into what makes hitman Vince Edwards tick. Ostensibly he wants more cash on discovering that his victim is female, but really he begins to ruminate on himself and his ambitions. Stunningly directed by Irving Lerner and cleverly produced on a shoestring, this is original, clever and absorbing. TS

Vince Edwards *Claude* • Phillip Pine *Marc* • Herschel Bernardi *George* • Michael Granger *Moon* • Caprice Toriel *Billie Williams* ■ *Dir* Irving Lerner • *Scr* Ben Simcoe

Murder by Death ★★ PG

Detective spoof 1976 · US · Colour · 90mins

A bizarre hotch-potch of greats, also-rans and has-beens combine to pay the mortgage in one of those whodunnits in a big house. Truman Capote has gathered together the world's top sleuths to present them with a slaying due to take place at midnight, and only Maggie Smith is worth watching as the hands creep round. This one belongs firmly in the genre that maintains that as long as you can get enough famous names on the poster the public will accept anything. Not true. SH DVD

Peter Sellers *Sidney Wang* • Peter Falk *Sam Diamond* • David Niven *Dick Charleston* • Maggie Smith *Dora Charleston* • Alec Guinness *Butler Bensonumum* • Truman Capote *Lionel Twain* • Eileen Brennan *Tess Skeffington* • James Coco *Milo Perrier* • Elsa Lanchester *Jessica Marbles* ■ *Dir* Robert Moore • *Scr* Neil Simon

Murder by Decree ★★ 15

Detective drama
1978 · Can/UK · Colour · 118mins

Rather than having Holmes and Watson plod wearily around London, director Bob Clark gives them a surprisingly imaginative lift. The film proposes politicians, freemasons and royalty as links to the Jack the Ripper murders. Such speculation is made with a fair degree of gothic credibility, even though the flabby plot wanders off up too many byways. Also, Donald Sutherland is not the best choice as a fruitcake visionary. Still, even during moments of slack, Christopher Plummer and James Mason interpret their roles as Holmes and Watson with plenty of heart. JM DVD

Christopher Plummer *Sherlock Holmes* • James Mason *Dr Watson* • David Hemmings *Inspector Foxborough* • Anthony Quayle *Sir Charles Warren* • Geneviève Bujold *Annie Crook* • Frank Finlay *Inspector Lestrade* • John Gielgud *Prime Minister* • Donald Sutherland *Robert Lees* ■ *Dir* Bob Clark • *Scr* John Hopkins, from a story by Bob Clark, from characters created by Sir Arthur Conan Doyle

Murder by Numbers ★★ 15

Detective thriller
2002 · US · Colour · 115mins

Michael Pitt and Ryan Gosling play bored teenagers who kill a defenceless woman simply to get away with it. Of course, their mistake is to underestimate unconventional homicide detective Sandra Bullock who smells a rat and confronts a few skeletons in her own cupboard to come after them. Bullock plays the maverick detective rather well, but there's little else to get excited about in this dull and predictable thriller. LH. Contains violence, swearing, sex scenes and drug abuse. DVD

Sandra Bullock *Cassie Mayweather* • Ben Chaplin *Sam Kennedy* • Ryan Gosling *Richard Haywood* • Michael Pitt *Justin Pendleton* • Agnes Bruckner *Lisa Mills* • Chris Penn *Ray* • RD Call *Captain Rod Cody* ■ *Dir* Barbet Schroeder • *Scr* Tony Gayton

Murder by Phone ★★ 15

Mystery thriller 1982 · Can · Colour · 89mins

If you answer the phone in this picture you end up dead. The killer has devised a system that sends an electric pulse down the line, which sends the brain into immediate meltdown. The room you are in also gets a makeover. Richard Chamberlain is the science lecturer investigating the death of a student, John Houseman is a glorified telephone engineer and Sara Botsford an artist who taps into phone company files to trap the killer. AT

Richard Chamberlain *Nat Bridger* • John Houseman *Dr Stanley Markowitz* • Sara Botsford *Ridley Taylor* • Robin Gammell *Noah Clayton* • Gary Reineke *Detective Meara* • Barry Morse *Fred Waits* ■ *Dir* Michael Anderson • *Scr* Michael Butler, Dennis Shryack, John Kent Harrison

Murder by Rope ★★

Thriller 1936 · UK · BW · 64mins

A man who laughed in the dock at his death sentence appears to return from the gallows to take revenge on the people involved in his trial and execution. This dramatic set-up is frittered away in a cheap British B-feature which helped fulfil Paramount's quota obligations as a distributor. After a judge dies at a country house gathering, DA Clarke-Smith's handwriting expert interrogates the usual suspects. The explanation is delightfully preposterous. AE

Constance Godridge *Daphne Farrow* • DA Clarke-Smith *Hanson* • Sunday Wilshin *Lucille Davine* • Wilfrid Hyde White *Alastair Dane* • Donald Read *Peter Paxton* • Daphne Courtney *Flora* ■ *Dir* George Pearson • *Scr* Ralph Neale

Murder, He Says ★★★

Comedy 1945 · US · BW · 94mins

This slapstick comedy is one of the most bizarre pictures made in Hollywood, a kind of *Arsenic and Old Lace* in hillbilly country that's either very funny or totally unendurable, depending on your point of view. Fred MacMurray stars as the insurance investigator who runs into Marjorie Main's mad brood in a house where poisoned food glows in the dark (along with anyone foolish enough to eat it) and secret passages lead to hidden treasure. Veteran director George Marshall claimed to have made it up as he went along with the help of writer Lou Breslow and suggestions from the cast. AE

Fred MacMurray *Pete Marshall* • Helen Walker *Claire Mathews* • Marjorie Main *Mamie Johnson* • Jean Heather *Elany Fleagle* • Porter Hall *Mr Johnson* • Peter Whitney *Mert Fleagle/Bert Fleagle* ■ *Dir* George Marshall • *Scr* Lou Breslow, from a story by Jack Moffitt

Murder in a Small Town ★★★

Period murder mystery
1999 · US · Colour · 100mins

In addition to headlining, Gene Wilder also co-wrote this pleasing TV whodunnit, which is given additional charm by its 1930s setting. Self-exiled from Broadway following the murder of his wife, Wilder's impresario takes to managing a small theatre in Connecticut. However, when an anti-Semitic industrialist is found murdered, Wilder uses his understanding of character motivation to help detective Mike Starr solve the case. Wilder's energy somewhat swamps his lesser-known co-stars, but this was successful enough for Wilder to reprise the role in *The Lady in Question*. DP

Gene Wilder *Larry "Cash" Carter* • Mike Starr *Tony* • Cherry Jones *Mimi* • Frances Conroy *Martha Lassiter* ■ *Dir* Joyce Chopra • *Scr* Gene Wilder, Gilbert Pearlman

Murder in Mind ★★★ 18

Psychological thriller
1996 · US/UK · Colour · 84mins

Nigel Hawthorne leads an impressive cast as a respected psychiatrist who uses hypnosis to question a disturbed Mary-Louise Parker, the prime suspect in the murder of her husband. As the mind games are played out, the lines between victim, suspect and investigator become blurred. It's a claustrophobic, sometimes erratic affair, but there are striking supporting turns from Jimmy Smits and Jason Scott Lee. JF. Contains violence, swearing and nudity. DVD

Nigel Hawthorne *Dr Ellis* • Mary Louise Parker [Mary-Louise Parker] *Caroline* • Jimmy Smits *Peter* • Jason Scott Lee *Holloway* • Gailard Sartain *Charlie* • Jon Cedar *Superior officer* ■ *Dir* Andrew Morahan • *Scr* Michael Cooney, from his play

Murder in Mississippi ★★★★ 15

Drama based on a true story
1990 · US · Colour · 92mins

This US TV movie was made just two years after Alan Parker's Oscar-nominated *Mississippi Burning*. However, while Parker's movie was only loosely based on truth, this small-screen film sticks more closely to the known facts about the murder of three civil rights activists by the Ku Klux Klan in the Deep South. Parker's movie was a hard act to follow yet, thanks to a strong narrative, superior acting and a mournful score, this powerful and violent stab at the story makes almost equally compelling viewing. PF

Tom Hulce *Mickey Schwerner* • Blair Underwood *James Chaney* • Josh Charles *Andrew Goodman* • Jennifer Grey *Rita Schwerner* • Eugene Byrd *Ben Chaney Jr* • Donzaleigh Abernathy *Sue Brown* • CCH Pounder *Fannie Lee Chaney* ■ *Dir* Roger Young • *Scr* Stanley Weiser, from an article by Ben Stein • *Music* Mason Daring

Murder in New Hampshire ★★ 15

Crime drama based on a true story
1991 · US · Colour · 89mins

A TV movie based on an infamous real-life case in which a small-town schoolteacher plans to murder her husband with the help of her student lover. Not the most obvious role for Oscar-winner Helen Hunt, but she attacks it with gusto and, even though the whole farrago has a rather "filming by numbers" feel, it still packs a generous punch. SH DVD

Helen Hunt *Pamela Smart* • Chad Allen *Billy Flynn* • Michael Learned *Judy Smart* • Ken Howard *Bill Smart* • Howard Hesseman *DA Paul Maggiotto* • Larry Drake *Mark Sisti* ■ *Dir* Joyce Chopra • *Scr* William Wood, Joe Cacaci

Murder in the Cathedral ★★ U

Religious drama 1952 · UK · BW · 145mins

TS Eliot's play about Thomas à Becket and the political and theosophical complexities surrounding his murder by Henry II's henchmen was first performed in 1935. Negligible as a piece of cinema, this film version preserves Eliot's text and allows us to see National Theatre actors much as theatre audiences would have seen them. We hear Eliot himself, as the "Fourth tempter", goading Henry into killing his Archbishop. AT

John Groser *Thomas à Becket* • Alexander Gauge *King Henry II* • David Ward *First tempter* • George Woodbridge *Second tempter* • Basil Burton *Third tempter* • TS Eliot *Fourth tempter* • Donald Bisset *First priest* • Clement McCallin *Second priest* • Leo McKern *Third knight* ■ *Dir* George Hoellering • *Scr* George Hoellering, from the play by TS Eliot

Murder in the First ★★★★ 15

Drama based on a true story
1994 · US · Colour · 122mins

Kevin Bacon gives the performance of his career in this sensational assault on the prison system. Based on the actual experiences of Henri Young, Marc Rocco's uncompromising picture alternates between Alcatraz and a forbidding courtroom, as lawyer Christian Slater tries to pin Bacon's murder of a fellow inmate on the regime that maltreated him to the verge of madness. A little over-intense at times, this is essentially a showcase for its two leads, although Gary Oldman is terrifyingly sinister as the nasty Warden Glenn. Exhausting but enthralling. DP. Contains swearing, violence and a sex scene. DVD

Christian Slater *James Stamphill* • Kevin Bacon *Henri Young* • Gary Oldman *Associate Warden Glenn* • Embeth Davidtz *Mary McCasslin* • Bill Macy [William H Macy] *William McNeil* • Stephen Tobolowsky *Mr Henkin* • Brad Dourif *Byron Stamphill* • R Lee Ermey *Judge Clawson* ■ *Dir* Marc Rocco • *Scr* Dan Gordon

Murder in the Music Hall ★★

Mystery 1946 · US · BW · 87mins

Former Olympic skater Vera Hruba Ralston donned her blades for this hammy hogwash from the biggest studio on Hollywood's "poverty row", Republic. The skating sequences rather slow down the action in a fair-to-middlin' whodunnit which, in typical B-movie style, is taken at such a lick that it's next to impossible to follow what's going on. Ann Rutherford, Julie Bishop and Helen Walker are on cop William Gargan's list of suspects, but where is the blind man who is the key to the mystery? DP

Vera Hruba Ralston [Vera Ralston] *Lila* • William Marshall (1) *Don* • Helen Walker *Millicent* • Nancy Kelly *Mrs Morgan* • William Gargan *Inspector Wilson* • Ann Rutherford *Gracie* • Julie Bishop *Diane* ■ *Dir* John English • *Scr* Frances Hyland, Laszlo Gorog, from a story by Arnold Phillips, Maria Matray

Murder, Inc ★★

Crime drama 1960 · US · BW · 103mins

A Mob movie about the Depression-era gang headed by Albert Anastasia and Louis "Lepke" Buchalter, whose hitmen later went freelance and rubbed out to order. Set in 1930s New York, it

M

stars Stuart Whitman and May Britt as nightclub performers caught up in a spiral of blackmail and extortion. What should have been an 80-minute firecracker is extended in a futile stab at social significance and gets hopelessly bogged down in plot and subplot. Peter Falk overacts hilariously as a hissable, cartoon-strip killer, though jazz fans will welcome the appearance by Sarah Vaughn. AT

Stuart Whitman *Joey* • May Britt *Eadie* • Henry Morgan *Turkus* • Peter Falk *Reles* • David J Stewart *Lepke* • Simon Oakland *Tobin* • Warren Fennerty *Bug* • Sarah Vaughn • Howard I Smith [Howard Smith] *Albert Anastasia* ■ *Dir* Burt Balaban, Stuart Rosenberg • *Scr* Irv Tunick, Mel Barr, Sid Feder, from the non-fiction book by Burton Turkus

Murder Man ★★★

Crime drama 1935 · US · BW · 70mins

From a time when newspapermen were the folk heroes that psychiatrists and counter-agents became in later years, comes this low-budget but gutsy crime drama. Spencer Tracy is the boozy reporter who plots the perfect revenge for the crooks who ruined his father and caused the suicide of his estranged wife, while Virginia Bruce is the girl who loves him. The great Lionel Atwill articulates authority with every word, while a briefly-glimpsed James Stewart is starting to drawl his way to stardom. TH

Spencer Tracy *Steve Gray* • Virginia Bruce *Mary Shannon* • Lionel Atwill *Capt Cole* • Harvey Stephens *Henry Mander* • Robert Barrat *Robbins* • James Stewart *Shorty* • William Collier Sr *Pop Gray* • William Demarest *Rod McGuire* ■ *Dir* Tim Whelan • *Scr* Tim Whelan, John C Higgins, from a story by Tim Whelan, Guy Bolton

M

The Murder Men ★★

Crime drama 1961 · US · BW · 74mins

Dorothy Dandridge's fortunes dwindled rapidly after starring in lover Otto Preminger's disappointing version of *Porgy and Bess*. Bankrupt and limited in her options by cinema's strict rules on mixed-race romance, she ended up giving her farewell (and pathetically poignant) performance in this melancholic melodrama about a washed-up jazz singer that was originally made for television. DP

Mark Richman [Peter Mark Richman] *Nick Cain* • Dorothy Dandridge *Norma Sherman* • James Coburn *Arthur Troy* • Joe Mantell *Maury Troy* • Ivan Dixon *Joe Sherman* • Edward Asner *Dave Keller* ■ *Dir* John Peyser • *Scr* Mel Goldberg

Murder Most Foul ★★★ U

Murder mystery 1964 · UK · BW · 86mins

Margaret Rutherford dons the tweed twinset of Miss Marple for the third time after *Murder She Said* and *Murder at the Gallop* in this rather contrived adaptation of *Mrs McGinty's Dead*, the second Hercule Poirot case to be reworked as a vehicle for Agatha Christie's spinster sleuth. Having hung a jury during a murder trial, Miss M treads the boards with a shambolic theatre company to find the real culprit. Ron Moody is over the top as a temperamental thesp, but director George Pollock sustains the suspense and there is solid support from Rutherford's real-life husband, Stringer Davis. DP [video]

Margaret Rutherford *Miss Marple* • Ron Moody *Driffold Cosgood* • Charles Tingwell *Detective Inspector Craddock* • Andrew Cruickshank *Justice Crosby* • Megs Jenkins *Mrs Thomas* • Ralph Michael *Ralph Summers* • James Bolam *Bill Hanson* • Stringer Davis *Mr Stringer* • Francesca Annis *Sheila Upward* ■ *Dir* George Pollock • *Scr* David Pursall, Jack Seddon, from the novel *Mrs McGinty's Dead* by Agatha Christie

A Murder of Crows ★★★ 15

Murder mystery thriller
1998 · US · Colour · 96mins

This slick if barely credible suspense yarn has Cuba Gooding Jr as a disbarred lawyer-turned-writer who appropriates a dead man's unpublished novel and passes it off as his own. The novel's a huge hit, but Gooding Jr is hauled up on homicide charges when killings in the book are found to mirror real-life murders and include details that only the killer himself could have known. Some of the dialogue tries too hard to sound hardboiled, but this TV movie is stylishly made and well acted by a quality cast. DA DVD

Cuba Gooding Jr *Lawson Russell* • Eric Stoltz *Thurman Parks III* • Tom Berenger *Clifford Dubose* • Marianne Jean-Baptiste *Elizabeth Pope* • Ashley Lauren [Ashley Laurence] *Janine DeVrie* • Doug Wert *Billy Ray* ■ *Dir/Scr* Rowdy Herrington

Murder of Innocence ★★ 18

Crime drama based on a true story
1993 · US · Colour · 94mins

Judging by the glut of American TV movies on the subject, there must be a neighbourhood eccentric around every corner in the USA. This tells the tale of a seemingly normal housewife whose increasingly oddball behaviour begins to deeply concern her husband. It soon becomes clear that his worries are tragically justified. Stars Valerie Bertinelli and Stephen Caffrey are competent enough, but there are few surprises in either the script or the direction. JF [video] DVD

Valerie Bertinelli *Laurie Wade* • Stephen Caffrey *Matthew Wade* • Graham Beckel *Frank Kendall* • Jerry Hardin *Mort Webber* • Millie Perkins *Edna Webber* ■ *Dir* Tom McLoughlin • *Scr* Philip Rosenberg, from the book by Joel Kaplan, George Papajohn, Eric Zorn

Murder on a Bridle Path ★★

Comedy mystery 1936 · US · BW · 63mins

It took two directors and four writers to fashion this fourth entry in the Hildegarde Withers RKO series, which began in 1932 with *The Penguin Pool*. This time Helen Broderick takes over as the sleuthing schoolmarm from the redoubtable Edna May Oliver, but to lesser effect. James Gleason is still aboard as cigar-chomping cop Oscar Piper, but unfortunately is lumbered here with some very silly dialogue. That and the slowish pace make this a weaker entry in the generally excellent series. TS

James Gleason *Inspector Oscar Piper* • Helen Broderick *Hildegarde Withers* • Louise Latimer *Barbara Foley* • Owen Davis Jr *Eddie Fry* • John Arledge *Joey* ■ *Dir* William Hamilton, Edward Killy • *Scr* Dorothy Yost, Thomas Lennon, Edmund H North, James Gow, from the novel by Stuart Palmer

Murder on a Honeymoon ★★★

Mystery 1935 · US · BW · 94mins

The third film in RKO's splendid series featuring schoolteacher sleuth Hildegarde Withers (played by Edna May Oliver in her last appearance in the role) and detective partner Oscar Piper (James Gleason). Wittily co-scripted by famed humourist Robert Benchley, it has the distinction of actually being filmed on location on Catalina Island off the coast of California. Very enjoyable indeed. Helen Broderick took over the role in 1936's *Murder on a Bridle Path*. TS

Edna May Oliver *Hildegarde Withers* • James Gleason *Inspector Oscar Piper* • Lola Lane *Phyllis La Font* • Chick Chandler *Pilot French* • George Meeker *Kelsey* • Dorothy Libaire *Kay Deving* • Harry Ellerbe *Marvin Deving* ■ *Dir* Lloyd Corrigan • *Scr* Seton I Miller, Robert Benchley, from the novel *Puzzle of the Pepper Tree* by Stuart Palmer

Murder on a Sunday Morning ★★★ 12

Documentary 2001 · US/Fr · Colour · 111mins

French director Jean-Xavier de Lestrade won an Oscar for this account of black teenager Brenton Butler's ordeal after being charged with the murder of a 65-year-old woman in a Florida motel. Outrage is the initial response, but indignant jubilation takes over as public defender Pat McGuinness exposes both the institutional racism within the Jacksonville police department and the flaws in a legal system that could allow such a prosecution to reach trial. Lestrade clearly takes sides, but his concern for the boy and his pious parents is evident and his presentation of the courtroom revelations is highly suspenseful. DP DVD

Dir Jean-Xavier de Lestrade

Murder on the Blackboard ★★

Mystery 1934 · US · BW · 71mins

In the second, after *The Penguin Pool*, of RKO's series based on Stuart Palmer's stories, Edna May Oliver and James Gleason as Hildegarde Withers and Oscar Piper investigate the death of a schoolteacher. Also returning from the first film is delightful character actor Edgar Kennedy, as one of Gleason's colleagues. Not as good as the original, but still fun. TS

Edna May Oliver *Hildegarde Withers* • James Gleason *Inspector Oscar Piper* • Bruce Cabot *Asst principal Addison Stevens* • Gertrude Michael *Janey Davis* • Regis Toomey *Smiley* • Edgar Kennedy *Detective Donahue* • Tully Marshall *MacFarland* • Jackie Searle *Leland Jones* ■ *Dir* George Archainbaud • *Scr* Willis Goldbeck, from the story by Stuart Palmer

Murder on the Orient Express ★★★★ PG

Murder mystery 1974 · UK · Colour · 122mins

Easily the best screen adaptation of an Agatha Christie whodunnit and, for those unfamiliar with either book or film, the solution will take your breath away. Albert Finney makes fussy Belgian detective Hercule Poirot seem every bit as preposterous as Christie intended and he earned an Oscar nomination for his wonderful performance. The supporting cast does everything that is expected of it, with Ingrid Bergman's Oscar-winning turn just about the pick of a stellar selection. Praise should also go to director Sidney Lumet for keeping you guessing right to the end. DP. Contains violence and swearing. [video] DVD

Albert Finney *Hercule Poirot* • Lauren Bacall *Mrs Hubbard* • Martin Balsam *Bianchi* • Ingrid Bergman *Greta Ohlsson* • Jacqueline Bisset *Countess Andrenyi* • Jean-Pierre Cassel *Pierre Paul Michel* • Sean Connery *Colonel Arbuthnot* • John Gielgud *Beddoes* • Wendy Hiller *Princess Dragomiroff* • Anthony Perkins *Hector McQueen* • Vanessa Redgrave *Mary Debenham* • Rachel Roberts (1) *Hildegarde Schmidt* • Richard Widmark *Ratchett* • Michael York *Count Andrenyi* • Colin Blakely *Hardman* ■ *Dir* Sidney Lumet • *Scr* Paul Dehn, from the novel by Agatha Christie

Murder on the Orient Express ★★

Murder mystery 2001 · US · Colour · 100mins

Agatha Christie's classic whodunnit had already been brought to the screen with aplomb by Sidney Lumet, so it was hard to fathom the need for this TV-movie remake. With the exception of Leslie Caron, the cast list is nowhere near as star-studded and the characters are much less subtly drawn, with the result that Alfred Molina's Poirot seems all the more eccentric. Just as damaging, however, is the decision to update the action to the present day. DP

Alfred Molina *Hercule Poirot* • Meredith Baxter *Mrs Caroline Hubbard* • Leslie Caron *Senora Alvarado* • Amira Casar *Helena von Strauss* • Peter Strauss *Mr Samuel Ratchett* • David Hunt *Bob Arbuthnot* ■ *Dir* Carl Schenkel

Murder on the Waterfront ★

Second World War mystery
1943 · US · BW · 49mins

Using minor contract players, Warner Bros kept this B-mystery brief, making it ideal to accompany its lengthier main features of the time. But this dim-witted tale of wartime espionage in a Pacific Coast navy yard turns into an endurance test before the traitor responsible for murdering the inventor of a vital new thermostat is exposed. AE

Warren Douglas *Joe Davis* • Joan Winfield *Gloria Davis* • John Loder *Lt Com Holbrook* • Ruth Ford *Lana Shane* ■ *Dir* B Reeves Eason • *Scr* Robert E Kent, from the play *Without Warning* by Ralph Spencer Zink • *Cinematographer* Harry Neumann

Murder She Said ★★ PG

Murder mystery 1961 · UK · BW · 83mins

Through the window of a passing train, Miss Marple (Margaret Rutherford) spots a woman being murdered. When no corpse can be found, however, her suspicions are dismissed as the ravings of an eccentric elderly spinster. Determined to solve the mystery, she takes a job as a maid at the estate of James Robertson-Justice. The first screen adaptation to star Rutherford as Agatha Christie's amateur sleuth only holds the interest now because of its star's unique persona and comic timing. RK [video]

Margaret Rutherford *Miss Marple* • Arthur Kennedy *Dr Quimper* • Muriel Pavlow *Emma Ackenthorpe* • James Robertson-Justice *Mr Ackenthorpe* • Charles Tingwell *Inspector Craddock* • Thorley Walters *Cedric Ackenthorpe* • Joan Hickson *Mrs Kidder* ■ *Dir* George Pollock • *Scr* David Pursall, Jack Seddon, David Osborn, from the novel *4.50 from Paddington* by Agatha Christie

Murder without Crime ★★

Crime thriller 1950 · UK · BW · 78mins

Director J Lee Thompson was also a playwright, and this is his own adaptation of his play, *Double Error*. It's basically a four-hander about a marriage, a murder and a third party who sees an opportunity for blackmail. The result is a film of modest budget and ambition with a nice performance by Dennis Price, as suave and duplicitous as ever. AT

Derek Farr *Stephen* • Dennis Price *Matthew* • Patricia Plunkett *Jan* • Joan Dowling *Grena* ■ *Dir* J Lee Thompson • *Scr* J Lee Thompson, from his play *Double Error*

The Murderers Are amongst Us ★★★

Drama 1946 · W Ger · BW · 87mins

This was one of the earliest German films to examine the notion of collective guilt in the Nazi era. A sombre, well-intentioned film shot in a style reminiscent of the expressionist films of the 1920s, it concerns a doctor tormented by the terrible things he witnessed in a concentration camp. His anguish is accentuated by the presence of a man, responsible for mass executions, living a comfortable, untroubled life nearby. There is also an important early role for Hildegarde Neff who subsequently became a Hollywood leading lady. BB. In German with English subtitles.

Hildegarde Knef [Hildegarde Neff] *Susanna Wallner* • Ernst Borchert *Dr Hans Mertens* • Arno Paulsen *Capt Bruckner* • Erna Sellner *Frau Bruckner* ■ *Dir/Scr* Wolfgang Staudte

Murderers' Row ★★

Spy spoof 1966 · US · Colour · 108mins

In this sequel to *The Silencers*, Dean Martin returns as secret agent Matt Helm to save Washington from dastardly Karl Malden and his "Helio Beam". Martin's "morning after the night before" performance has a certain louche appeal, but, like any self-respecting Bond rip-off, Harry Levin's film has problems spoofing a spoof. (Indeed, the plot is remarkably similar to *Thunderball*.) The decor is hard on the eye, while Ann-Margret's disco gyrations are cringeworthy. Martin played Helm in two further films: *The Ambushers* (1967) and *The Wrecking Crew* (1969). AT

Dean Martin *Matt Helm* • Ann-Margret *Suzie Solaris* • Karl Malden *Julian Wall* • Camilla Sparv *Coco Duquette* • James Gregory *MacDonald* • Beverly Adams *Lovey Kravezit* • Richard Eastman *Dr Norman Solaris* ■ *Dir* Henry Levin • *Scr* Herbert Baker, from the novel by Donald Hamilton

A Murderous Affair ★★ 15

Drama based on a true story 1992 · US · Colour · 89mins

In this TV movie Virginia Madsen plays another in a long line of *femmes fatales*. The Carolyn Warmus case made headline news in the States, as a seemingly respectable teacher not only had an affair with a married man, but also murdered his wife. The frankly sensational events have been toned down from their tabloid origins for TV consumption. William H Macy also appears. DP [video] DVD

Virginia Madsen *Carolyn Warmus* • Chris Sarandon *Paul Solomon* • Ned Eisenberg *Richard Freeman* • Tom Mason *Mike McCormick* • Robert Picardo *David Lewis* • William H Macy *Sean Hammel* • Olivia Burnette *Kristan Solomon* ■ *Dir* Martin Davidson • *Scr* Earl Wallace, Pamela Wallace, Martin Davidson

Murders in the Rue Morgue ★★★ 12

Horror 1932 · US · BW · 57mins

Director Robert Florey plunders German expressionism and atmospheric shocks while allowing plenty of room for Bela Lugosi to enjoy his Dr Caligari-esque mad scientist role. Lugosi runs an offbeat carnival attraction featuring a giant gorilla by day. By night, however, he's engaged in diabolical blood transfusion experiments involving apes and beautiful virgins. Although far removed from its Edgar Allan Poe inspiration, the lurid overtones of the pulp plot are handled with surprising candour. AJ [video]

Bela Lugosi *Dr Mirakle* • Sidney Fox *Camille* • Leon Waycoff [Leon Ames] *Pierre Dupin* • Bert Roach *Paul* • Brandon Hurst *Prefect of Police* • Noble Johnson *Janos* ■ *Dir* Robert Florey • *Scr* Tom Reed, Dale Van Every, John Huston, from the story by Edgar Allan Poe

Murders in the Rue Morgue ★★★

Horror 1971 · US · Colour · 87mins

Director Gordon Hessler's fourth collaboration with Hammer scriptwriter Christopher Wicking is one of the most undervalued horror movies of the 1970s. A superb Eurotrash cast populate this clever revenge story, in which a series of grisly murders strike members of Jason Robards's *Grand Guignol* theatre company while they are presenting a stage version of the Edgar Allan Poe classic. Hessler's suspense shocker is packed with sophisticated insight, surrealistic poetry and a nightmarish delirium. AJ

Jason Robards *Cesar Charron* • Herbert Lom *Marot* • Christine Kaufmann *Madeleine* • Adolfo Celi *Vidocq* • Lilli Palmer *Madeleine's mother* • Maria Perschy *Genevre* ■ *Dir* Gordon Hessler • *Scr* Christopher Wicking, Henry Slesar, from the story by Edgar Allan Poe

Murders in the Zoo ★★

Horror 1933 · US · BW · 66mins

Lionel Atwill overacts a storm as a sadistic zookeeper using the animals in his care to kill anyone who so much as looks at his gorgeous wife, Kathleen Burke. Lions, snakes and alligators are called on to do their worst by the insanely jealous warden, but it's the moment where he sews up the mouth of one paramour which provides the most chills. Randolph Scott is the hero and Charles Ruggles provides the comic relief in a menacing melodrama considered highly shocking and tasteless in its day. AJ

Charles Ruggles *Peter Yates* • Lionel Atwill *Eric Gorman* • Gail Patrick *Jerry Evans* • Randolph Scott *Dr Woodford* • John Lodge *Roger Hewitt* • Kathleen Burke *Evelyn Gorman* • Harry Beresford *Professor Evans* ■ *Dir* Edward Sutherland [A Edward Sutherland] • *Scr* Phillip Wylie, Seton I Miller

Muriel ★★★★

Drama 1963 · Fr/It · Colour · 115mins

With her stepson Jean-Baptiste Thierrée home from army service in Algeria, Delphine Seyrig invites her erstwhile lover Jean-Pierre Kérien, together with his niece Nita Klein, to visit her in Boulogne. The son is haunted by memories of a dead girl called Muriel, while the ex-lovers are similarly caught in memories of their past. From the unique poetic and metaphysical imagination of French director Alain Resnais, this is an opaque mix of memory and imagination, past and present. Faultlessly assembled, acted and photographed, it's certainly intriguing and generally regarded as one of Resnais's masterworks. RK. A French language film.

Delphine Seyrig *Helene Aughain* • Jean-Pierre Kérien *Alphonse Noyard* • Nita Klein *Françoise* • Jean-Baptiste Thierrée *Bernard* • Laurence Badie *Claudie* • Martine Vatel *Marie-Dominique* ■ *Dir* Alain Resnais • *Scr* Jean Cayrol, from his story

Muriel's Wedding ★★★★ 15

Comedy drama 1994 · Aus · Colour · 101mins

The Ugly Duckling is given a delightful Down Under spin in this congenial comedy. Flabby Muriel (Toni Collette) lives in a frothy fantasy world of Abba songs, husband-shopping and wedding-dress dreams. It's when she leaves her small-minded home town under a cloud to flat-share with an old acquaintance from school (snappily played by Rachel Griffiths), that the initially hilarious humour begins to turn a shade more poignant. Collette is tremendously affecting as the mousey no-mark who spends her life flicking through bridal catalogues, while PJ Hogan (*My Best Friend's Wedding*) directs with a breezy touch. AJ. Contains swearing, nudity. [video] DVD

Toni Collette *Muriel Heslop* • Bill Hunter *Bill Heslop* • Rachel Griffiths *Rhonda* • Jeanie Drynan *Betty Heslop* • Gennie Nevinson *Deidre* • Matt Day *Brice* ■ *Dir* PJ Hogan • *Scr* PJ Hogan, from a story by PJ Hogan, Jocelyn Moorhouse

Murphy's Law ★★ 18

Action thriller 1986 · US · Colour · 96mins

The Defiant Ones meets *Death Wish* in a formula Charles Bronson crime thriller, which casts him as an alcoholic cop framed for murdering his estranged wife by a psychopathic criminal with a grudge. There's lots of shouting and shooting, as Bronson escapes arrest handcuffed to a female offender, but not much in the way of gripping suspense. AJ [video]

Charles Bronson *Jack Murphy* • Kathleen Wilhoite *Arabella McGee* • Carrie Snodgress *Joan Freeman* • Robert F Lyons *Art Penney* • Richard Romanus *Frank Vincenzo* • Bill Henderson *Ben Wilcove* ■ *Dir* J Lee Thompson • *Scr* Gail Morgan Hickman

Murphy's Romance ★★★ 15

Drama 1985 · US · Colour · 103mins

Six years after she won the best actress Oscar for *Norma Rae*, Sally Field teamed up with director Martin Ritt again for this easy-going comedy about a *May to December*-style romance between an ambitious horse trainer and a widowed pharmacist. The result? Her rugged love interest, twinkle-eyed James Garner, gained a first-time nomination instead. Quite why is the question; while eager to please, this is flimsy stuff that lacks the director's usual hard edge. AJ [video]

James Garner *Murphy Jones* • Sally Field *Emma Moriarty* • Brian Kerwin *Bobby Jack Moriarty* • Corey Haim *Jake Moriarty* • Dennis Burkley *Freeman Coverly* • Georgann Johnson *Margaret* • Carole King *Tillie* ■ *Dir* Martin Ritt • *Scr* Harriet Frank Jr, Irving Ravetch, from the novella by Max Schott

Murphy's War ★★★

Second World War action adventure 1971 · UK · Colour · 106mins

This trifle has hints of *The African Queen*, with Peter O'Toole as a manic Irish seaman teaming up with a Quaker missionary (O'Toole's then wife, Sian Phillips) and a French oil engineer, convincingly played by Philippe Noiret. O'Toole's scheme is to repair an old plane and use it to sink a German U-boat down on the Orinoco delta. Shot in the jungles of Venezuela, the film is a blend of whimsy and battle, skilfully handled by director Peter Yates, who was riding high on the success of *Bullitt*. AT. Contains some swearing.

Peter O'Toole *Murphy* • Sian Phillips *Dr Hayden* • Philippe Noiret *Louis Brezan* • Horst Janson *Kapitan Lauchs* • John Hallam *Lieutenant Ellis* • Ingo Mogendorf *Lieutenant Voght* ■ *Dir* Peter Yates • *Scr* Stirling Silliphant, from the novel by Max Catto

Musashi Miyamoto ★★★ PG

Drama 1944 · Jpn · BW · 93mins

This was the first film made by Kenji Mizoguchi after his wife, Chieko, was declared insane and committed to the asylum where she was to spend the rest of her life. Yet his lack of interest in the project owes as much to the fact that he had little empathy for either the samurai genre or the nationalist sentiments that lay behind it. Mizoguchi was incapable of making an unwatchable film, however, and so it proves here. The story shows how Kinuyo Tanaka and Kigoro Ikushima's determination to avenge the murder of their father leads to a showdown between two legendary swordsmen. DP. A Japanese language film. [video]

Chojuro Kawarazaki *Musashi Miyamoto* • Kinuyo Tanaka *Shinobu Nonomiya* • Kanemon Nakamura *Kojiro Sasaki* • Kigoro Ikushima *Genichiro Nonomiya* ■ *Dir* Kenji Mizoguchi • *Scr* Matsutaro Kawaguchi, from a serialised story by Kan Kikuchi in the newspaper *Mainichi Shinbun*

Muscle Beach Party ★★

Musical 1964 · US · Colour · 94mins

This one is so dated that it practically has cobwebs hanging off it. The quiffed crooner Frankie Avalon starred in a plethora of these jivin' beach party movies, in which everyone hops around in shorts shaking their heads wildly to truly terrible music. The original *Beach Party* was a big teen success, so the producers came up with this lacklustre sequel. Avalon warbles horribly, Annette Funicello dances as if she has a live octopus attached to her derrière, while the plot involves clashing teenage rivals. SH

Frankie Avalon *Frankie* • Annette Funicello *Dee Dee* • Luciana Paluzzi *Julie* • John Ashley *Johnny* • Don Rickles *Jack Fanny* • Peter Turgeon *Theodore* • Jody McCrea *Deadhead* • Little Stevie Wonder [Stevie Wonder] • Peter Lorre *Mr Strangdour* ■ *Dir* William Asher • *Scr* Robert Dillon, from a story by Robert Dillon, William Asher

The Muse ★★★ PG

Satirical comedy 1999 · US · Colour · 92mins

American satirist Albert Brooks casts his waspish eye over the film business, writing, directing and starring in this tale of a screenwriter who has lost his touch. Though he is sceptical when successful writer chum Jeff Bridges claims to be inspired by a real-life muse, Brooks nonetheless woos the temperamental Sharon Stone, only to find her turning his life with wife Andie MacDowell upside down. Despite Brooks's ever-present cynicism about life, his film is full of lovely, gentle humour, while film fans will love the cameos from Stone's other "clients", among them James Cameron and Martin Scorsese. SR [video] DVD

Albert Brooks *Steven Phillips* • Sharon Stone *Sarah Liddle/Christine* • Andie MacDowell *Laura Phillips* • Jeff Bridges *Jack Warrick* • Mark Feuerstein *Josh Martin* • Steven Wright *Stan Spielberg* ■ *Dir* Albert Brooks • *Scr* Albert Brooks, Monica Johnson

Mushrooms ★★

Comedy 1995 · Aus · Colour · 93mins

Writer/director Alan Madden clearly intended this curio to be a quaintly black comedy, but what he ended up with is a fine showcase for his elderly co-stars and a ragbag of decidedly dubious gags. Julia Blake and Lynette Curran are most engaging as the 60-somethings who decide to take in lodgers, only to find themselves needing to dispose of a new tenant's body. One of Australia's finest character actresses, Blake has a ball as she twitters around the shop that's below the widows' home, but you never feel Madden is totally in control. DP. Contains violence and swearing.

Julia Blake *Flo* • Lynette Curran *Minnie* • Simon Chilvers *Instep* • Brandon Burke *Lynch* • Boris Brkic *Grubb* ■ *Dir/Scr* Alan Madden

The Music Box ★★★★★ U

Classic comedy 1932 · US · BW · 28mins

Perhaps the best-loved of all the Laurel and Hardy shorts (albeit a longish one, at just under 30 minutes), it won the pair an Oscar and rightly so. In this classic outing they must deliver a piano to an address at the top of a vast flight of steps, and the duo certainly deliver the comedy, with assorted variations on the theme of the instrument jangling down the stairs in its box, and some fine slapstick involving an ornamental pond. Even when they finally get it inside Professor von Schwarzenhoffen's (Billy Gilbert) house, the trouble isn't over. The result is a definitive (and partly improvised) display. AC [video] DVD

Stan Laurel *Stan* • Oliver Hardy *Ollie* • Billy Gilbert *Professor Theodore von Schwarzenhoffen* • William Gillespie *Piano salesman* • Charlie Hall *Postman* ■ *Dir* James Parrott • *Scr* HM Walker

Music Box ★★★★ 15

Drama 1989 · US · Colour · 120mins

In Costa-Gavras's political melodrama, Jessica Lange stars as a lawyer who defends her blue-collar Hungarian father (Armin Mueller-Stahl) from a charge of being the leader of an SS-run death squad during the Second World War. Courtroom battles generally make riveting viewing and this is no exception. We are kept on a knife-edge of suspense as we wonder if the now kindly veteran could have been a hideous monster in his past. The film raises more questions than it answers and Costa-Gavras's direction is perhaps a little too detached, but the intensity of Lange and Mueller-Stahl more than makes amends. TH. Contains swearing.

Jessica Lange *Ann Talbot* • Armin Mueller-Stahl *Mike Laszlo* • Frederic Forrest *Jack Burke* • Donald Moffat *Harry Talbot* • Lukas Haas *Mikey Talbot* • Cheryl Lynn Bruce *Georgine Wheeler* ■ *Dir* Costa-Gavras • *Scr* Joe Eszterhas

Music for Millions ★★★

Musical drama 1944 · US · BW · 117mins

Child prodigy Margaret O'Brien co-stars with June Allyson in this family entertainment from MGM that mixes wartime sentiments and tear-jerking sentimentality with comedy, songs and classical music. O'Brien is the younger sister dispensing comfort to pregnant older sibling Allyson, a cellist with José Iturbi's orchestra whose husband is away fighting in the Pacific. Pianist Iturbi supplies outpourings of Debussy, Tchaikovsky, Dvorak and Grieg, while Jimmy Durante (as the maestro's manager) leavens the mix with a couple of characteristic numbers. RK

Margaret O'Brien *"Mike"* • José Iturbi *Jose Iturbi* • June Allyson *Barbara "Babs" Ainsworth* • Jimmy Durante *Andy Andrews* • Marsha Hunt *Rosalind* • Hugh Herbert *Uncle Ferdinand, "Bish"* ■ *Dir* Henry Koster • *Scr* Myles Connolly • *Costume Designer* Irene

The Music Freelancers ★★★

Drama 1998 · Fr · Colour · 90mins

Exploring the perils of liberty, the temperament of the artiste and the sheer pleasure that music can bring, this is a delightful ensemble comedy from writer/director Denis Dercourt. Amid all the instrumental rivalries and personality clashes that occur as a freelance chamber orchestra rehearses for a one-off concert, a baby is born, a mournful maestro dies and a petty thief reforms. (Well, almost.) Despite this, these disparate *cachetonneurs* still manage to make beautiful music. Taken at a pleasingly relaxed tempo, the humour flows from the situations without a hint of contrivance. DP. In French with English subtitles.

Pierre Lacan *Roberto* • Marc Citti *Lionel* • Philippe Clay *The aristocrat* • Henri Garcin *Svarowski* • Marie-Christine Laurent *Therese* ■ *Dir/Scr* Denis Dercourt

Music from Another Room ★★★ 12

Romantic comedy drama
1998 · US · Colour · 99mins

Jude Law stars in this whimsical, watchable romance with a high-calibre cast. As a small boy, Law's character helps his doctor father deliver Brenda Blethyn's latest baby, a girl. Years later, Law sets out to woo the girl (Gretchen Mol), who's engaged to be married to Jon Tenney. Various distractions include a dying Blethyn, a blind sister (Jennifer Tilly) and assorted other dysfunctional siblings. This is either engagingly offbeat or irritatingly quirky, depending on your point of view, but the cast merits attention, even if the material is lightweight and contrived. DA DVD

Jude Law *Danny* • Jennifer Tilly *Nina Swan* • Gretchen Mol *Anna Swan* • Martha Plimpton *Karen Swan* • Brenda Blethyn *Grace Swan* • Jon Tenney *Eric* • Jeremy Piven *Billy* ■ *Dir/Scr* Charlie Peters

Music Hath Charms ★

Musical 1935 · UK · BW · 70mins

Henry Hall merits his place in musical legend for that children's classic *The Teddy Bears' Picnic*. However, he goes down in cinematic infamy for this dismal collection of sketches in which people around the world have their cares soothed away by the soporific melodies of Henry and his orchestra. Strictly for nostalgia nuts. DP

Henry Hall (2) • WH Berry *Basil Turner* • Carol Goodner *Mrs Norbray* • Arthur Margetson *Alan Sterling* • Lorna Hubbard *Marjorie Turner* • Antoinette Cellier *Joan* • Billy Milton *Jack Lawton* • Aubrey Mallalieu *Judge* ■ *Dir* Thomas Bentley, Alexander Esway, Walter Summers, Arthur Woods [Arthur B Woods] • *Scr* Jack Davies, Courtney Terrett, from a story by L DuGarde Peach

Music in Manhattan ★★

Musical comedy 1944 · US · BW · 80mins

Song-and-dance hopeful Anne Shirley is mistaken for war hero Phillip Terry's bride when she visits Washington to promote her act with Dennis Day in this professionally produced, albeit lacklustre musical comedy. There are lots of songs, but few are any good, though it's a pleasant enough period piece that includes a rare appearance by Charlie Barnet and his band. TS

Anne Shirley *Frankie* • Dennis Day *Stanley* • Phillip Terry *Johnny* • Raymond Walburn *Professor* • Jane Darwell *Mrs Pearson* • Patti Brill *Gladys* ■ *Dir* John H Auer • *Scr* Lawrence Kimble, from a story by Maurice Tombragel, Hal Smith, Jack Scholl

Music in My Heart ★★

Musical 1940 · US · BW · 69mins

Someone once described Tony Martin as a "singing tuxedo". Although he was rather a stiff actor, he was handsome and charming, with a winning, dimpled smile and, most importantly, a mellifluous tenor voice. In the silly paper-thin plot of this low-budget musical, Martin plays a foreign singer fighting deportation from the US. He's given a few pleasant songs and a lovely partner in Rita Hayworth, in her first musical for Columbia. RB

Tony Martin *Robert Gregory* • Rita Hayworth *Patricia O'Malley* • Edith Fellows *Mary O'Malley* • Alan Mowbray *Charles Gardner* • Eric Blore *Griggs* • George Tobias *Sascha* ■ *Dir* Joseph Santley • *Scr* James Edward Grant, from his story *Passport to Happiness*

The Music Lovers ★★ 18

Historical drama
1970 · UK · Colour · 118mins

Overwrought to the point of muddled confusion, Ken Russell's "biography" of Tchaikovsky is a crescendo of images which portray the Russian composer as a homosexual whose wife (Glenda Jackson) is so appalled by his lack of loving that she goes mad. Russell keeps up a shrill note of hysteria throughout, though Richard Chamberlain does at least attempt to understand the workings of a tortured soul. Outrageous in its time, it is now almost charmingly quaint, while its account of the *1812 Overture* is so over the top as to be risible. TH

Richard Chamberlain *Tchaikovsky* • Glenda Jackson *Nina Milyukova* • Max Adrian *Nicholas Rubenstein* • Christopher Gable *Chiluvsky* • Isabella Telezynska *Madame Von Meck* • Kenneth Colley *Modeste Tchaikovsky* ■ *Dir* Ken Russell • *Scr* Melvyn Bragg, from the novel *Beloved Friend* by Catherine Drinker Bowen, Barbara von Meck

Music Man ★★ U

Musical comedy 1948 · US · BW · 66mins

The sheer expense of staging the song 'n' dance routines meant that few Poverty Row studios dabbled with musicals, but Monogram hardly broke the bank on Will Jason's tale of feuding brothers who terminate their songwriting partnership, only for their secretary to dupe them into a collaboration by persuading each they're working with a mysterious new talent. Freddie Stewart and Phil Brito singularly lack charm, but June Preisser provides sparky support. DP

Phil Brito *Phil Russo* • Freddie Stewart *Freddie Russo* • Jimmy Dorsey • Alan Hale Jr *Joe* • June Preisser *June Larkin* • Noel Neill *Kitty* • Grazia Narciso *Mrs Russo* ■ *Dir* Will Jason • *Scr* Sam Mintz

The Music Man ★★★★ U

Musical comedy 1962 · US · Colour · 144mins

Morton DaCosta, who directed Meredith Willson's hit musical on Broadway, was given carte blanche by Jack Warner to re-create it on the screen. He did so with the aid of his Broadway leading man, the dynamic Robert Preston, and came up with an Oscar-winning blockbuster. Preston plays the energetic, charming and silver-tongued conman who charms the elders of River City, Iowa, to finance a band. Also involved is Shirley Jones, the romantic interest and subject of the song *Marian the Librarian*. Onna White's electric choreography and a score that includes *Till There Was You* and *76 Trombones* contribute to an invigorating experience. Matthew Broderick starred in a made-for-TV remake in 2003. RK

Robert Preston *Harold Hill* • Shirley Jones *Marian Paroo* • Buddy Hackett *Marcellus Washburn* • Hermione Gingold *Eulalie Mackechnie Shinn* • Paul Ford *Mayor Shinn* • Pert Kelton *Mrs Paroo* • Timmy Everett *Tommy Djilas* • Susan Luckey *Zaneeta Shinn* • Ronny Howard [Ron Howard] *Winthrop Paroo* ■ *Dir* Morton Da Costa • *Scr* Marion Hargrove, from the musical by Meredith Willson, Franklin Lacey

The Music of Chance ★★★ 15

Drama 1993 · US · Colour · 94mins

This is a beguiling adaptation of Paul Auster's disquieting novel from ex-documentary director Philip Haas, who extracts every ounce of intelligence, wit and insight from a slight tale without ever straining for effect. He is well served by some exceptional performances, notably from James Spader and Mandy Patinkin as the gamblers forced to build a medieval stone wall to pay off a debt. The conclusion is disappointing, but this neglected curio is worth watching. DP. Contains swearing. DVD

James Spader *Jack Pozzi* • Mandy Patinkin *James Nashe* • Charles Durning *Bill Flower* • Joel Grey *Willie Stone* • M Emmet Walsh *Calvin Murks* • Samantha Mathis *Tiffany* • Chris Penn *Floyd* • Pearl Jones *Louise* ■ *Dir* Philip Haas • *Scr* Philip Haas, Belinda Haas, from the novel by Paul Auster

Music of the Heart ★★ PG

Biographical drama
1999 · US · Colour · 118mins

Horror maestro Wes Craven's first non-fantasy is a bland bust. The true story of violin teacher Roberta Guaspari (Meryl Streep), who brought music and hope to the school kids of East Harlem, gets nothing more than a vacuous TV-movie treatment under Craven's restrained direction. Streep merely plays a parody of herself in this mix of *Fame* and *Dangerous Minds*, while salsa superstar Gloria Estefan couldn't have made a more ineffectual feature debut. AJ DVD

Meryl Streep *Roberta* • Angela Bassett *Janet* • Aidan Quinn *Brian* • Cloris Leachman *Assunta* • Gloria Estefan *Isabel* • Jane Leeves *Dorothea* • Itzhak Perlman • Isaac Stern ■ *Dir* Wes Craven • *Scr* Pamela Gray

The Music Room ★★★ U

Drama 1958 · Ind · BW · 100mins

In addition to scripting the majority of his pictures, Bengali director Satyajit Ray also regularly composed the soundtracks. Few films better showcased his command of Indian music than this poignant tale of an aristocrat who spends everything he has on a concert to serenade a passing age. There is much to admire in Chhabi Biswas's mournful performance and the way in which Ray maintains the delicate balance between progress and decay. But you really need an ear for Indian classical music to fully appreciate this. DP. In Hindi with English subtitles.

Chhabi Biswas *Bishwambar Roy* • Padmadevi *Roy's wife* • Pinaki Sengupta *Khoka* • Tulsi Lahiri *Manager of Roy's estate* ■ *Dir* Satyajit Ray • *Scr* Satyajit Ray, from a short story by Tarashankar Bannerjee

The Music Teacher ★★ U

Drama 1988 · Bel · Colour · 93mins

The director Gérard Corbiau has received an Oscar nomination each time he has ventured into the world of opera. Snippets from Verdi, Mozart, Schubert and Bellini pop up like selections from a classical jukebox, as retiring tenor José Van Dam pits his pickpocketing protégé against bisexual prince Patrick Bauchau's toyboy baritone. The action is often pretentious, but the art direction and cinematography look good enough to eat. DP. In French with English subtitles. DVD

José Van Dam *Joachim Dallayrac* • Anne Roussel *Sophie* • Philippe Volter *Jean* • Sylvie Fennec *Estelle* • Patrick Bauchau *Prince Scotti* • Johan Leysen *François* ■ *Dir* Gérard Corbiau • *Scr* Gérard Corbiau, André Corbiau, from a story by Luc Jabon, Gérard Corbiau • *Cinematographer* Walther van den Ende

The Musketeer ★ PG

Swashbuckling action adventure
2001 · Ger/US/UK/Lux · Colour · 100mins

Falling flat from the clumsy opening titles, this fails entirely in its aim to update Alexandre Dumas's classic by adding *Matrix*-style fight choreography. The confrontation sequences between Justin Chambers's vengeful musketeer and Cardinal Richelieu's henchman Tim Roth are tension free, while the ludicrous collection of mullet haircuts, beards and inconsistent accents adds an extra air of farce to a movie crammed with hammy dialogue and wooden performances. SF DVD

Catherine Deneuve *The Queen* • Mena Suvari *Francesca* • Stephen Rea *Cardinal Richelieu* • Tim Roth *Febre* • Justin Chambers *D'Artagnan* • Nick Moran *Aramis* • Bill Treacher *Bonacieux* ■ *Dir* Peter Hyams • *Scr* Gene Quintano, Fabrice Ziolkowski, from the novel *Les Trois Mousquetaires* by Alexandre Dumas

The Musketeers of Pig Alley ★★★★

Silent drama 1912 · US · BW · 17mins

Advertised as "a depiction of the gangster evil", the finest of DW Griffith's short films is also one of the first gangster pictures. Lillian Gish, whom Griffith was to make into one of the silent screen's greatest stars, in only her third film, shines as a young wife who becomes the object of a hoodlum's attentions. This realistic drama, which reflected the director's increased interest in social concerns, was shot in authentic locations and is of lasting historical interest as a

M

picture of New York's slums in 1912. RB

Lillian Gish *Little Lady* • Elmer Booth *Snapper Kid, "Chief of the Musketeers"* • Walter Miller *A musician* • Harry Carey ■ *Dir* DW Griffith • *Scr* DW Griffiths, Anita Loos

Mustang Country ★★ U

Western 1976 · US · Colour · 79mins

There's more than a little biographical irony in this solidly crafted western. The action is set in 1925, around the time that a young hopeful named Joel McCrea was working as a movie stuntman and horse wrangler. Here, 51 years on, McCrea is making his final appearance in a distinguished screen career, playing a retired rodeo star and rancher who helps a native American lad track down and tame a wild horse in time for a big meet. DP

Joel McCrea *Dan Treego* • Nika Mina *Nika* • Robert Fuller *Griff* • Patrick Wayne *Tee Jay* ■ *Dir/Scr* John C Champion

Mutant ★★ 18

Science-fiction horror
1984 · US · Colour · 95mins

A small midwestern town is menaced by zombie mutants who have been contaminated by a toxic waste spill. As usual, the local corporation is trying to cover up the scandal that has endangered the whole community. Although the zombies do little more than lunge at people with outstretched arms, the movie is well paced, but it lacks the tension and relentless suspense of the *Living Dead* landmarks that it's so clearly trying to copy. AJ [video] DVD

Wings Hauser *Josh Cameron* • Bo Hopkins *Sheriff Will Stewart* • Jody Medford *Holly Pierce* • Lee Montgomery *Mike Cameron* • Marc Clement *Albert* • Cary Guffey *Billy* • Jennifer Warren *Dr Myra Tate* ■ *Dir* John "Bud" Cardos • *Scr* Peter Orton, Michael Jones, from a story by John Kruize

The Mutations ★★ 18

Horror 1973 · UK · Colour · 88mins

Veteran cinematographer-turned-director Jack Cardiff's mind-boggling mad scientist extravaganza triumphantly embraces bad taste to provide queasy *frissons* rarely witnessed in British horror. Demented biologist Donald Pleasence crosses humans with plants and sends his gruesome failures to Michael Dunn, a dwarf who runs a circus sideshow. His most successful hybrid is a man-sized Venus fly trap (Scott Antony) who ingests a tramp before traumatising Jill Haworth and Julie Ege. Mixing genuinely deformed performers with made-up actors, the discomfiting template may be that of *Freaks*, but its prurient atmosphere is rooted in 1970s British sleaze. AJ [video]

Donald Pleasence *Dr Nolter* • Tom Baker *Lynch* • Brad Harris *Brian* • Julie Ege *Hedi* • Michael Dunn *Burns* • Scott Antony *Tony* • Jill Haworth *Lauren* ■ *Dir* Jack Cardiff • *Scr* Robert D Weinbach, Edward Mann

Mute Witness ★★★★ 18

Thriller 1995 · UK/Ger · Colour · 92mins

A mute special-effects make-up artist accidentally sees a "snuff" movie being filmed in a Moscow studio, then spends the rest of this super-cool thriller running for her life. Reminiscent of early Brian De Palma shockers, Anthony Waller's witty fright stuff revitalises the "woman in peril" genre with jet-black humour, tons of superbly controlled style, grisly corkscrew twists and the sinister appearance of Alec Guinness as "the Reaper". The Russian locations only add to the edge-of-your-seat atmosphere. AJ. Contains violence, swearing, sex scenes and nudity. [video] DVD

Marina Sudina *Billie Hughes* • Fay Ripley *Karen Hughes* • Evan Richards *Andy Clarke* • Oleg Jankowskij [Oleg Jankowski] *Larsen* • Igor Volkov *Arkadi* • Sergej Karlenkov *Lyosha* • Alexander Buriev *Strohbecker* • Alec Guinness *"The Reaper"* ■ *Dir/Scr* Anthony Waller

Mutiny ★★ U

Period adventure 1952 · US · Colour · 77mins

A rousing action adventure aboard a war ship on the high seas during the War of 1812. An event-filled plot involves a heroic sea captain (Mark Stevens), a mutinous English sailor (Patric Knowles), and a duplicitous firebrand (Angela Lansbury) who is the object of both their affections. Mutiny, gold bullion, the sinking of British ships, and a horde of colourful peg-leg and one-eyed pirates are all on hand to add to the excitement. RK

Mark Stevens *James Marshall* • Angela Lansbury *Leslie* • Patric Knowles *Ben Waldridge* • Gene Evans *Hook* • Rhys Williams *Redlegs* ■ *Dir* Edward Dmytryk • *Scr* Sidney Harmon, Philip Yordan, from a story by Hollister Noble

Mutiny ★★★ U

Historical drama 1999 · US · Colour

Actor Morgan Freeman produced this made-for-TV true historical drama illuminating a dark episode in American history. In 1944, a segregated unit of black seamen, who are poorly trained and ill-equipped, are forced by belittling, racist officers to load dangerous munitions at a navy base in California. After an explosion kills more than 300 men, 50 black sailors take a stand and refuse to work. Although conventionally told, the film is powerful and full of convincing period detail. MC

Michael Jai White *Ben Cooper* • Duane Martin *BJ Teach* • David Ramsey *Vernon Nettles* • Adrian Pasdar *Lieutenant Maravich* • Joe Morton *Thurgood Marshall* • Matthew Glave *Lieutenant Kirby* • James B Sikking *Lieutenant Commander Tynan* ■ *Dir* Kevin Hooks • *Scr* James Henerson [James S Henerson]

Mutiny on the Bounty ★★★★ PG

Classic adventure 1935 · US · BW · 132mins

Clark Gable squirmed at the idea of wearing a pigtail, knickerbockers and shoes with silver buckles to play the part of Fletcher Christian, in what was to be his first costume movie. But he and Charles Laughton (as Captain Bligh) teamed to bracing effect in this lavish and stirring adventure on the high seas, based, of course, on the famous real-life mutiny. Director Frank Lloyd won best director Oscars for *The Divine Lady* and *Cavalcade*, but this may be his best movie of all. The Academy certainly thought so: they voted it best picture. PF [video] DVD

Charles Laughton *Captain William Bligh* • Clark Gable *Fletcher Christian* • Franchot Tone *Roger Byam* • Herbert Mundin *Smith* • Eddie Quillan *Ellison* • Dudley Digges *Bacchus* • Donald Crisp *Burkitt* • Henry Stephenson *Sir Joseph Banks* • James Cagney • David Niven ■ *Dir* Frank Lloyd • *Scr* Talbot Jennings, Jules Furthman, Carey Wilson, from the novels *Mutiny on the Bounty* and *Men against the Sea* by Charles Nordhoff, James Norman Hall

Mutiny on the Bounty ★★★★ 15

Historical adventure
1962 · US · Colour · 177mins

This version of the famous nautical adventure from Lewis Milestone is a memorable successor to the Oscar-winning 1935 movie. Milestone deserves credit for surviving laborious re-shoots and difficulties caused by Marlon Brando's temperament. Though controversial, Brando's performance as Fletcher Christian is impressive as he moves from arrogant fop to gallant hero, despite his somewhat strangulated English accent. Trevor Howard is fine as the sadistic Captain Bligh, but the Tahiti interlude is a sequence to be missed. TH [video]

Marlon Brando *Fletcher Christian* • Trevor Howard *Captain William Bligh* • Richard Harris *John Mills* • Hugh Griffith *Alexander Smith* • Richard Haydn *William Brown* • Tarita *Maimiti* • Tim Seely *Edward Young* • Percy Herbert *Matthew Quintal* • Gordon Jackson *Edward Birkett* ■ *Dir* Lewis Milestone • *Scr* Charles Lederer, Eric Ambler, William L Driscoll, Borden Chase, John Gay, Ben Hecht, from the novel by Charles Nordhoff, James Norman Hall

Mutiny on the Buses ★ PG

Comedy 1972 · UK · Colour · 84mins

Things must have been bad at Hammer for the once-famous horror studio to resort to big screen TV spin-offs such as this woefully unfunny comedy based on the popular ITV series. You'd have thought there was simply no more mileage left in the jokes about Blakey's schedules, Olive and Arthur's marriage and Stan and Jack's allergy to work, but they managed to squeeze out a third movie – *Holiday on the Buses* – the following year. DP [video] DVD

Reg Varney *Stan Butler* • Doris Hare *Mrs Butler* • Anna Karen *Olive* • Michael Robbins *Arthur* • Bob Grant *Jack* • Stephen Lewis *Inspector Blake* ■ *Dir* Harry Booth • *Scr* Ronald Wolfe, Ronald Chesney

My Ain Folk ★★★★ PG

Biographical drama 1973 · UK · BW · 52mins

The second part of Bill Douglas's autobiographical trilogy (that began the previous year with *My Childhood*) owes more to the style of the Soviet cinema of the 1920s and 1930s than the others in the series. Extreme close-ups leave us nowhere to hide from the misery Stephen Archibald experiences as he goes to stay with his father's parents after his maternal grandma dies and his half-brother is packed off to a home. Such is the loveless nature of the relationship between his grandparents and the bitterness they feel towards the boy's mother that you are left with that uncomfortable feeling you get when you hear the neighbours having a blazing row. The concluding segment is *My Way Home*. DP [video]

Stephen Archibald *Jamie* • Hughie Restorick *Tommy* • Jean Taylor-Smith *Grandmother* • Bernard McKenna *Tommy's father* • Mr Munro *Jamie's grandfather* • Paul Kermack *Jamie's father* ■ *Dir/Scr* Bill Douglas

My American Cousin ★★★ PG

Comedy drama 1985 · Can · Colour · 85mins

A delightful coming-of-age tale made and set in Canada. It's the summer of 1959, and all there is to do is some cherry picking until a pre-teen girl's Californian cousin rides into town in his red Cadillac and sets everyone's hearts a-flutter. The film won six Genies (the Canadian equivalent of the Oscar), and it's easy to see why, thanks to the charming script and enjoyable performances by a relatively unknown cast. An equally charming sequel, *American Boyfriends*, followed in 1989. JB [video]

Margaret Langrick *Sandy* • John Wildman *Butch Walker* • Richard Donat *Major Wilcox* • Jane Mortifee *Kitty Wilcox* • TJ Scott *Lenny McPhee* • Camille Henderson *Shirley Darling* ■ *Dir/Scr* Sandy Wilson

My Architect ★★★★ PG

Documentary 2003 · US · Colour · 116mins

In this meditative and poetic documentary, Nathaniel Kahn – one of two illegitimate children that the architect Louis Kahn had with two different women – seeks to find out who his late father really was. In interviews with architectural greats such as IM Pei and Frank Gehry, we learn of Kahn's brilliance and the respect accorded to him by his peers. Unfortunately, the film-maker shies away from asking tough questions of the women who could perhaps give more insight into Kahn's private life. Like Nathaniel (who was only 11 when his father died), we are left to discover what we can of the man through his influential work, which includes the impressive Capital building in Bangladesh. Almost as fascinating is how Louis Kahn's own journey took him from greatness to bankruptcy and a lonely death from a heart attack in the men's room at New York's Penn Station in 1974. GM

Nathaniel Kahn *Narrator* ■ *Dir/Scr* Nathaniel Kahn • *Cinematographer* Bob Richman

My Beautiful Laundrette ★★★★★ 15

Drama 1985 · UK · Colour · 93mins

A seminal 1980s movie which launched a plethora of now distinguished careers, including those of director Stephen Frears and Daniel Day-Lewis. The latter shines here in his first major role as the scabrous punk and friend to Gordon Warnecke's entrepreneurial Asian, who dreams of creating the most glittering laundrette in London. The movie's undoubted importance lies in the way it takes many of the decade's Thatcherite characteristics – grafting in the free market, the desire for material acquisitions, the establishment of stability – and turns everything on its head with a merciful lack of polemic. A marvellously played film. SH. Contains violence and sex scenes. [video] DVD

Daniel Day-Lewis *Johnny* • Gordon Warnecke *Omar* • Saeed Jaffrey *Nasser* • Roshan Seth *Papa* • Derrick Branche *Salim* • Shirley Anne Field *Rachel* • Rita Wolf *Tania* ■ *Dir* Stephen Frears • *Scr* Hanif Kureishi

M

My Best Fiend ★★★ 15

Documentary
1999 · Ger/UK/US · Colour and BW · 98mins

Even though the tensions that existed between them bordered on genuine hatred, director Werner Herzog and actor Klaus Kinski made five quite remarkable films together. Yet, as Herzog recalls in this bittersweet documentary memoir, he only prevented the native Indians from killing his star on the Amazonian set of *Fitzcarraldo* because he needed him for a few more scenes. Almost fondly philosophical about the tantrums and abuse, Herzog recalls them at length, and he virtually regards the infrequent ceasefires as wasted opportunities. This is clearly only one side of the story, but it's still a fascinating one. DP. In German with English subtitles. Contains swearing. DVD

Werner Herzog *Narrator* ■ *Dir* Werner Herzog

My Best Friend's Wedding ★★★★ 12

Romantic comedy
1997 · US · Colour · 104mins

This sparkling comedy proved to be a career-resurrecting movie for Julia Roberts, and for once she plays someone who may not get the guy. When she hears her best friend and former lover (Dermot Mulroney) is getting married to Cameron Diaz, Roberts realises she wants to be more than just friends after all. What makes this film work so well is that it's not just "The Julia Roberts Show". While she does the bumbling, adorable stuff she's best at, the stunning Diaz and superb Rupert Everett (as Roberts's gay friend and accomplice) battle it out for best supporting performance. (They both win.) Terrific stuff. JB [video] DVD

Julia Roberts *Julianne Potter* • Dermot Mulroney *Michael O'Neal* • Cameron Diaz *Kimmy Wallace* • Rupert Everett *George Downes* • Philip Bosco *Walter Wallace* • M Emmet Walsh *Joe O'Neal* • Rachel Griffiths *Samantha Newhouse* • Carrie Preston *Mandy Newhouse* ■ *Dir* PJ Hogan • *Scr* Ronald Bass

My Best Girl ★★★ U

Silent romantic comedy
1927 · US · BW · 66mins

Made for her own production company under the auspices of United Artists, which she co-founded with Douglas Fairbanks, Charlie Chaplin and DW Griffith, this was one of Mary Pickford's last silent films. As the only normal member of a hopelessly irresponsible family, Pickford works in a Five-and-Dime and becomes romantically involved with the new clerk (Charles "Buddy" Rogers), who is really the boss's son. Other than asking us to believe that the 34-year-old "Little Mary" is 18, this is sweetly pleasing, if inconsequential. RK

Mary Pickford *Maggie Johnson* • Charles "Buddy" Rogers *Joe Grant* • Sunshine Hart *Ma Johnson* • Lucien Littlefield *Pa Johnson* • Carmelita Geraghty *Liz Johnson* ■ *Dir* Sam Taylor • *Scr* Hope Loring, Allen McNeil, Tim Whelan, from a story by Kathleen Norris

My Big Fat Greek Wedding ★★★★ PG

Romantic comedy
2002 · US/Can · Colour · 91mins

This perky, low-budget romantic comedy – adapted by star Nia Vardalos from her autobiographical one-woman stage show – was the unexpected success story of 2002. Vardalos shines as a frumpy waitress at her Greek family's restaurant who goes against her father's traditionalist views when she finds a new job, gets a confidence-boosting makeover and hooks handsome American teacher John Corbett. While the happy couple-to-be – who share charming screen chemistry – are played relatively straight, Vardalos's in-your-face relatives are a source of buoyant comic vitality, played to the hilt by a delightful cast. JC. In English and Greek with subtitles. DVD

Nia Vardalos *Toula Portokalos* • John Corbett *Ian Miller* • Michael Constantine *Gus Portokalos* • Lainie Kazan *Maria Portokalos* • Andrea Martin *Aunt Voula* • Joey Fatone *Angelo* • Gia Carides *Nikki* • Louis Mandylor *Nick* • Ian Gomez *Mike* ■ *Dir* Joel Zwick • *Scr* Nia Vardalos, from her one-woman show

My Blood Runs Cold ★★

Thriller
1965 · US · BW · 103mins

This chiller has an intriguing enough premise, with Troy Donahue attempting to worm his way into heiress Joey Heatherton's bank account by claiming they were lovers in a previous life. However, with both directorial and actorly restraint at a premium, the reincarnation angle is soon forgotten and the psychopathic Donahue embarks on the inevitable stalk-and-slash mission. DP

Troy Donahue *Ben Gunther* • Joey Heatherton *Julie Merriday* • Barry Sullivan *Julian Merriday* • Nicolas Coster *Harry Lindsay* • Jeanette Nolan *Aunt Sarah* ■ *Dir* William Conrad • *Scr* John Mantley, from the story *The Girl Who Was Two* by John Meredyth Lucas

My Blue Heaven ★★★ U

Musical comedy
1950 · US · Colour · 95mins

Another teaming of Betty Grable and Dan Dailey from 20th Century-Fox following the surprise success of 1947's *Mother Wore Tights*. This isn't bad, but its plot about vaudevillians wanting to adopt a child may seem a little tasteless, and, frankly, it's hard to accept Grable drooling over a baby and admitting that she wants to wash nappies! The songs are nice, the Technicolor is ravishing and the result is fairly typical of a Fox musical. TS

Betty Grable *Molly Moran* • Dan Dailey *Jack Moran* • David Wayne *Walter Pringle* • Jane Wyatt *Janet Pringle* • Mitzi Gaynor *Gloria Adams* • Una Merkel *Miss Gilbert* • Louise Beavers *Selma* ■ *Dir* Henry Koster • *Scr* Lamar Trotti, Claude Binyon, from the story *Storks Don't Bring Babies* by SK Lauren

My Blue Heaven ★★ PG

Comedy
1990 · US · Colour · 91mins

With Steve Martin and Rick Moranis in the leads and a script by Nora Ephron, this satire on suburban America promises much. Sadly, it delivers very little, largely because the supply of gags runs out too quickly and Martin rather overdoes it as a hood hidden away near San Diego prior to testifying in a mob murder trial. Moranis's FBI agent won't be the only one not to see the funny side as Martin commits a few crimes for old time's sake. DP. Contains swearing and violence.

Steve Martin *Vinnie Antonelli* • Rick Moranis *Barney Coopersmith* • Joan Cusack *Hannah Stubbs* • Melanie Mayron *Crystal Rybak* • William Irwin [Bill Irwin] *Kirby* • Carol Kane *Shaldeen* • William Hickey *Billy Sparrow* • Deborah Rush *Linda* • Daniel Stern *Will Stubbs* ■ *Dir* Herbert Ross • *Scr* Nora Ephron

My Bodyguard ★★★ PG

Drama
1980 · US · Colour · 92mins

School bully Matt Dillon persecutes rich kid Chris Makepeace, who retaliates by attempting to hire the morose and overgrown Adam Baldwin as his personal bodyguard. First-time director Tony Bill creates a believable atmosphere at this Chicago school while gradually shifting attention away from Makepeace's plight to Baldwin's troubled past. Cameos from Ruth Gordon and John Houseman, plus the debut of Joan Cusack, are bonuses. AT

Chris Makepeace *Clifford* • Adam Baldwin *Linderman* • Matt Dillon *Moody* • Paul Quandt *Carson* • Joan Cusack *Shelley* • Dean R Miller *Hightower* • Richard Bradley *Dubrow* • Ruth Gordon *Gramma* • John Houseman *Dobbs* ■ *Dir* Tony Bill • *Scr* Alan Ormsby

My Boss's Daughter ★ 12

Romantic comedy
2003 · US · Colour · 86mins

David Zucker's clunker of a comedy is utterly devoid of wit. Following a misunderstanding with Tara Reid, his heart's desire who also happens to be his boss's daugher, publishing researcher Ashton Kutcher finds himself housesitting for her scrupulous dad (Terence Stamp). But none of the misfortunes that befall Stamp's prized home are the remotest bit amusing and it's hard to see how a cast this stellar could be attracted to a project this dire. DP DVD

Ashton Kutcher *Tom Stansfield* • Tara Reid *Lisa Taylor* • Jeffrey Tambor *Ken* • Andy Richter *Red Taylor* • Michael Madsen *T J* • Jon Abrahams *Paul* • David Koechner *Speed* • Carmen Electra *Tina* • Terence Stamp *Jack Taylor* ■ *Dir* David Zucker • *Scr* David Dorfman

My Boyfriend's Back ★★★★

Comedy drama
1989 · US · Colour · 96mins

Sandy Duncan, Judith Light and Jill Eikenberry star as the members of a 1960s trio who reunite 25 years on for a television music concert in a TV movie that does more than just skate across the surface. The three leads give carefully layered performances, personal and social insights abound, real emotion is built into every frame and drama is fused seamlessly with wit. Actual pop stars of the 1960s appear, including Mary Wells, Gary Puckett and the Penguins. JM

Sandy Duncan *Chris Henry* • Jill Eikenberry *Deborah McGuire* • Judith Light *Vicki Vine* • John Sanderford *Harry Simons* • Stephen Macht *Joseph, Deborah's boyfriend* ■ *Dir* Paul Schneider • *Scr* Lindsay Harrison, from a story by April Campbell, Bruce Jones

My Boyfriend's Back ★ 15

Comedy
1993 · US · Colour · 81mins

As naff and dreadful as the title suggests, this gross comedy regurgitates that old chestnut about the high school geek who woos the prettiest girl in school. Andrew Lowery is the bespectacled teen who gets shot just before his dream prom date with Traci Lind. In absolute absurdist style, he returns from the dead and goes to the ball regardless. Things go from bad to worse when his body parts start dropping off. LH DVD

Andrew Lowery *Johnny Dingle* • Traci Lind *Missy McCloud* • Danny Zorn *Eddie* • Edward Herrmann *Mr Dingle* • Mary Beth Hurt *Mrs Dingle* • Jay O Sanders *Sheriff McCloud* • Libby Villari *Camille McCloud* • Matthew Fox *Buck* ■ *Dir* Bob Balaban • *Scr* Dean Lorey

My Brilliant Career ★★★★ U

Period drama
1979 · Aus · Colour · 95mins

A key film in the Australian film renaissance of the 1970s, this sensitive story of a fiercely independent young woman with aspirations to be a writer in male-dominated turn-of-the-century Australia made international reputations for director Gillian Armstrong and her remarkably assured 23-year-old star, Judy Davis. With Sam Neill and Wendy Hughes providing attractive support, the one drawback is being expected to believe any woman in her right mind would turn down Neill's charming, wealthy suitor. AME DVD

Judy Davis *Sybylla Melvyn* • Sam Neill *Harry Beecham* • Wendy Hughes *Aunt Helen* • Robert Grubb *Frank Hawdon* • Max Cullen *Mr McSwat* • Patricia Kennedy *Aunt Gussie* ■ *Dir* Gillian Armstrong • *Scr* Eleanor Witcombe, from the novel by Miles Franklin

My Brother Jonathan ★★ U

Drama
1947 · UK · BW · 103mins

Time has not been kind to the films featuring husband and wife Michael Denison and Dulcie Gray. Yet Denison's clipped tones and stiff acting style and Gray's mousey loyalty turned this into a respectable hit. It follows the fortunes of Black Country doctor Denison, whose ambitions to become a surgeon are thwarted by family ties. Harold French directs steadily, but without a feel for small-town life. DP

Michael Denison *Jonathan Dakers* • Dulcie Gray *Rachel Hammond* • Stephen Murray *Doctor Craig* • Ronald Howard *Harold Dakers* • Mary Clare *Mrs Dakers* • Finlay Currie *Doctor Hammond* • James Robertson-Justice *Eugene Dakers* ■ *Dir* Harold French • *Scr* Leslie Landau, Adrian Alington, from the novel by Francis Brett Young

My Brother Talks to Horses ★★★ U

Comedy
1946 · US · BW · 92mins

This MGM co-feature served to show off the burgeoning talent of director Fred Zinnemann, who would later make such Oscar-winning classics as *High Noon* and *From Here to Eternity*. There's not much sign of the promise to come in this silly but charming picture, however, which is succinctly summed up by its title. Young Jackie "Butch" Jenkins plays the original horse whisperer, and there's interesting period support, but the central gimmick becomes tiresome and the plot has nowhere to go. TS

"Butch" Jenkins [Jackie "Butch" Jenkins] *Lewis Penrose* • Peter Lawford *John S Penrose* • Spring Byington *Mrs Penrose* • Beverly Tyler *Martha* • Edward Arnold *Mr Bledsoe* • Charlie Ruggles [Charles Ruggles] *Richard Pennington Roeder* ■ *Dir* Fred Zinnemann • *Scr* Morton Thompson

My Brother the Pig ★★ PG

Comedy fantasy
1999 · US · Colour · 91mins

Scarlett Johansson has found fame since she starred in this comedy fantasy about a boy's accidental transformation into a pig. Though Johansson has the starring role, much of the focus falls on Eva Mendes, as the nanny whose magical powers bring misfortune upon the curious Nick Fuoco. It's a predictable race-against-time romp, but the Mexican setting is interesting. DP DVD

Nick Fuoco *George Caldwell* • Scarlett Johansson *Kathy Caldwell* • Judge Reinhold *Richard Caldwell* • Romy Walthall [Romy Windsor] *Dee Dee Caldwell* • Eva Mendes *Matilda* • Alex D Linz *Freud* ■ *Dir* Erik Fleming • *Scr* Matthew Flynn

My Brother Tom ★★★ 18

Romantic drama
2001 · UK/Ger · Colour · 104mins

Dom Rotheroe's debut feature is an interesting psychodrama that takes a walk on the wilder side of teenage love. Jenna Harrison is a Home Counties schoolgirl who falls for loner Ben Whishaw, and the two adolescents seek refuge in their own private world. Photographed on digital video by *Breaking the Waves* cameraman Robby Müller, the film has an aura of sullen inevitability that hangs over the couple like a cloud, though their love-in-a-mist attitude is redeemed by some wonderful acting. The later lurch into murder and melodrama is a step too far. TH. Contains violence.

Jenna Harrison *Jessica* • Ben Whishaw *Tom* • Adrian Rawlins *Jack* • Judith Scott *Jessica's mum* • Richard Hope *Jessica's dad* ■ *Dir* Dom Rotheroe • *Scr* Dom Rotheroe, Alison Beeton-Hilder

My Brother's Keeper ★★

Drama
1948 · UK · BW · 86mins

A decade before Tony Curtis and Sidney Poitier played *The Defiant Ones*, Jack Warner and George Cole star as a couple of convicts whose escape is hindered by the fact that they are handcuffed together. Replacing the racial theme is the neat twist that only one of the runaways is guilty. Under the direction of Alfred Roome and Roy Rich, however, their perils are often predictable. DP

Jack Warner *George Martin* • George Cole *Willie Stannard* • Jane Hylton *Nora Lawrence* • David Tomlinson *Ronnie Waring* • Bill Owen *Syd Evans* • Yvonne Owen *Margaret "Meg" Waring* • Raymond Lovell *Bill Wainwright* ■ *Dir* Alfred Roome, Roy Rich • *Scr* Frank Harvey, from a story by Maurice Wiltshire

My Chauffeur ★★ 15

Comedy
1986 · US · Colour · 97mins

Feisty Deborah Foreman stars as a girl who makes it in the predominantly male profession of limousine driving. Picking up a depressed and drunk millionaire's son, she is dismissed when he wakes up the next day on her couch. But the pair are thrown together yet again. An inconsequential attempt at screwball comedy and farce, with a truly terrible combination of bad jokes thrown in for good measure. LH

Deborah Foreman *Casey Meadows* • Sam J Jones [Sam Jones] *Battle Witherspoon* • Sean McClory *O'Brien* • Howard Hesseman *McBride* • EG Marshall *Witherspoon* • Penn Jillette *Bone* • Teller *Abdul* ■ *Dir/Scr* David Beaird

My Childhood ★★★ PG

Biographical drama 1972 · UK · BW · 44mins

Costing some £4,000 to make and lasting less than an hour, this is the first part of director Bill Douglas's autobiographical trilogy, one of the most painful evocations of childhood ever brought to the screen. Set in a run-down Scottish mining village, the film explores the strained relationships between an eight-year-old boy, his half-brother, his uncompromising grandmother and a kindly German prisoner of war. Stephen Archibald gives a remarkable performance, while Jean Taylor-Smith sends shivers as the very antithesis of a loving granny. *My Ain Folk* (1973) continues his story. DP

Stephen Archibald *Jamie* • Hughie Restorick *Tommy* • Jean Taylor-Smith *Grandmother* • Karl Fieseler *Helmuth* • Bernard McKenna *Tommy's father* • Paul Kermack *Jamie's father* ■ *Dir/Scr* Bill Douglas

My Cousin Rachel ★★★ PG

Romantic mystery 1952 · US · BW · 176mins

Based on Daphne du Maurier's novel, this overwrought melodrama has Richard Burton first detesting, then obsessively loving Olivia de Havilland, who married and may have murdered his beloved cousin. Set on the clifftops of 19th-century Cornwall, it puts the story of *Rebecca* into reverse gear and delivers great dollops of emotion. The dashingly handsome, brooding Burton picked up the first of his seven unsuccessful Oscar nominations for his first Hollywood role. AT

Olivia de Havilland *Rachel Ashley* • Richard Burton *Philip Ashley* • Audrey Dalton *Louise* • Ronald Squire *Nick Kendall* • George Dolenz *Rainaldi, Rachel's lawyer* • John Sutton *Ambrose Ashley* • Tudor Owen *Seecombe* ■ *Dir* Henry Koster • *Scr* Nunnally Johnson, from the novel by Daphne du Maurier

My Cousin Vinny ★★★★ 15

Comedy 1992 · US · Colour · 114mins

Joe Pesci plays the Vinny of the title, an extremely inept lawyer (who has never tried a case in court), who comes to the rescue of his young cousin (Ralph Macchio) when the lad runs into a bit of trouble with the law in the Deep South. Pesci has great fun with his role but the biggest surprise is Marisa Tomei, who plays his coarse Brooklyn girlfriend. Although she's great in what was her first major role, there was widespread surprise when she walked off with the best supporting actress Oscar. JB. Contains swearing. DVD

Joe Pesci *Vinny Gambini* • Marisa Tomei *Mona Lisa Vito* • Ralph Macchio *Bill Gambini* • Mitchell Whitfield *Stan Rothenstein* • Fred Gwynne *Judge Chamberlain Haller* • Lane Smith *Jim Trotter III* • Austin Pendleton *John Gibbons* • Bruce McGill *Sheriff Farley* ■ *Dir* Jonathan Lynn • *Scr* Dale Launer

My Darling Clementine ★★★★★ U

Classic western 1946 · US · BW · 92mins

In this classic western, Henry Fonda's Wyatt Earp and Victor Mature's Doc Holliday are heading for that close shave at the OK Corral. Owing rather less to historical accuracy than more recent movies, this John Ford picture boasts some fine sequences. The best is a dance in an unfinished church, a fine symbol of the "garden being fashioned from the wilderness" by the strong-arm methods of Fonda's self-righteous lawman. Filmed in expressive black-and-white against Monument Valley backdrops, the picture combines both the grandeur and the folksiness so typical of its director. AT

Henry Fonda *Wyatt Earp* • Victor Mature *Doc Holliday* • Linda Darnell *Chihuahua* • Walter Brennan *Old Man Clanton* • Cathy Downs *Clementine* • Tim Holt *Virgil Earp* • Ward Bond *Morgan Earp* • John Ireland *Billy Clanton* ■ *Dir* John Ford • *Scr* Samuel G Engel, Winston Miller, from a story by Sam Hellman, from the novel *Wyatt Earp, Frontier Marshal* by Stuart N Lake • *Cinematographer* Joe MacDonald

My Dear Secretary ★★ U

Romantic comedy 1948 · US · BW · 94mins

Bestselling novelist Kirk Douglas, who suffers from an irresistible drive to make passes at his secretaries, gets more than he bargained for when he hires Laraine Day. He ends up marrying her – whereupon she becomes jealous of her replacement. This mindless variant on the familiar wife-versus-secretary idea, directed by Charles Martin from his own thin script, is made thinner still by Douglas's lack of comic flair. What laughs there are come from Keenan Wynn and Rudy Vallee. RK DVD

Laraine Day *Stephanie Gaylord* • Kirk Douglas *Owen Waterbury* • Keenan Wynn *Ronnie Hastings* • Helen Walker *Elsie* • Rudy Vallee *Charles Harris* • Florence Bates *Mrs Reeves* ■ *Dir/Scr* Charles Martin

My Demon Lover ★★ 15

Horror comedy 1987 · US · Colour · 83mins

A typical 1980s horror comedy, enlivened by an enthusiastic cast and some good make-up effects. Brat Pack wannabe Scott Valentine is subject to an ancient curse that turns him into a whole menagerie of monsters whenever he is sexually aroused. Shot on location in New York, one wonders if director Charles Loventhal has ever been there, especially when he places a huge gothic castle straight out of a Bela Lugosi movie slap-bang in the middle of Central Park. RS

Scott Valentine *Kaz* • Michelle Little *Denny* • Arnold Johnson *Fixer* • Robert Trebor *Charles* • Alan Fudge *Captain Phil Janus* ■ *Dir* Charles Loventhal • *Scr* Leslie Ray

My Dinner with Andre ★★★

Drama 1981 · US · Colour · 111mins

Few films polarise critical opinion more than this love it or loathe it chat-fest from director Louis Malle. Your response to the film depends entirely on whether you consider avant-garde theatre director Andre Gregory to be a man of charm, imagination and questing intellect, or a pompous narcissist in love with the sound of his own voice. Wallace Shawn is altogether easier to take as Gregory's straight man with a nice line in barbed quippery. Drawn from the pair's actual conversations, the adventures and ideas Gregory relates range from the fascinating to the preposterous. DP

Wallace Shawn *Wally* • Andre Gregory *Andre* • Jean Lenauer *Waiter* ■ *Dir* Louis Malle • *Scr* Wallace Shawn, Andre Gregory

My Dog Skip ★★★ U

Biographical drama 1999 · US · Colour · 95mins

Though corny at times, this is less sentimental than most boy-and-dog movies. Against the backdrops of the Second World War and Deep South segregation, this heartwarming family film traces the bonding between an eight-year-old Mississippi youngster and a Jack Russell terrier. It's old-fashioned entertainment for adults and older children, though the under-tens may find it a touch talky. DA DVD

Frankie Muniz *Willie Morris* • Diane Lane *Ellen Morris* • Luke Wilson *Dink Jenkins* • Kevin Bacon *Jack Morris* • Mark Beech *Army buddy* ■ *Dir* Jay Russell • *Scr* Gail Gilchriest, from the memoir by Willie Morris

My Dream Is Yours ★★★

Musical 1949 · US · Colour · 99mins

Doris Day stars in this extremely pleasant Warner Bros film, a very gentle satire on radio, with a swipe at the movies. Day and co-star Jack Carson clown and croon sweetly under Michael Curtiz's competent direction. Scene-stealing honours go to Bugs Bunny, who appears in a super dream sequence. TS

Jack Carson *Doug Blake* • Doris Day *Martha Gibson* • Lee Bowman *Gary Mitchell* • Adolphe Menjou *Thomas Hutchins* • Eve Arden *Vivian Martin* • SZ Sakall *Felix Hofer* • Selena Royle *Freda Hofer* • Edgar Kennedy *Uncle Charlie* ■ *Dir* Michael Curtiz • *Scr* Harry Kurnitz, Dane Lussier, Allen Rivkin, Laura Kerr, from the story *Hot Air* by Jerry Wald, Paul Moss

My English Grandfather ★★★

Comedy 1986 · USSR · BW and Colour · 76mins

This is an engagingly offbeat story about a British communications engineer who seeks refuge from the events of the Russian Revolution and its aftermath by camping out on the three metres he claims for England at the foot of a recently erected telegraph pole. Slyly exploring the adverse effects of communism on a previously contented community, Nana Dzhordzhadze's film has all the energy and inventiveness of *glasnost* cinema. If the conversations and confrontations of the revolutionary era are not entertaining enough, the latter-day search for the man's murderer by his Georgian lover is quite compelling. DP. In Georgian with English subtitles.

Zhanri Lolashvili *Hughes* • Nineli Chankvetadze • Guram Pirtskhalava ■ *Dir* Nana Dzhordzhadze • *Scr* Irakly Kvirikadze

My Fair Lady ★★★★★ U

Classic musical 1964 · US · Colour · 171mins

This sumptuous record of Lerner and Loewe's smash Broadway version of George Bernard Shaw's play *Pygmalion* won eight well-deserved Oscars. It boasts superb performances from Rex Harrison repeating his stage success as Henry Higgins and Stanley Holloway as Alfred P Doolittle. At the time, there was criticism that Julie Andrews didn't re-create her original Broadway role, but Audrey Hepburn is still quite wonderful as Eliza. If not coarse enough for the Covent Garden flower girl, nobody, but nobody, could ever blossom as beautifully as Hepburn does in the Cecil Beaton costumes later on, and, despite being dubbed in the songs by Marni Nixon, her portrayal is funny and heart-warming in equal doses. A more visually inspired director might have brought a little more élan to the work, but George Cukor rightly preserves the theatricality of the enterprise and provides a film to savour again and again. TS DVD

Audrey Hepburn *Eliza Doolittle* • Rex Harrison *Professor Henry Higgins* • Stanley Holloway *Alfred P Doolittle* • Wilfrid Hyde White *Colonel Hugh Pickering* • Gladys Cooper *Mrs Higgins* • Jeremy Brett *Freddy Eynsford-Hill* • Theodore Bikel *Zoltan Karpathy* • Isobel Elsom *Mrs Eynsford-Hill* • Mona Washbourne *Mrs Pearce* ■ *Dir* George Cukor • *Scr* Alan Jay Lerner, from the musical by Alan Jay Lerner, Frederick Loewe, from the play *Pygmalion* by George Bernard Shaw • *Cinematographer* Harry Stradling • *Art Director* Cecil Beaton, Gene Allen • *Music Director* Andre Previn

My Family ★★★★ 15

Drama 1994 · US · Colour · 121mins

Writer/director Gregory Nava's drama charts the trials, triumphs and tribulations of a family of Mexican immigrants in Los Angeles over three generations. What sets this picture apart from other such films are the striking performances from the cast, which includes Jimmy Smits, Esai Morales and Edward James Olmos, plus an admirable lack of sentimentality from Nava. Both moving and funny, this is a treat. JB

Jimmy Smits *Jimmy Sanchez* • Esai Morales *Chucho* • Edward James Olmos *Paco* • Eduardo Lopez Rojas *Jose Sanchez* • Jenny Gago *Maria Sanchez* • Elpidia Carrillo *Isabel Magana* ■ *Dir* Gregory Nava • *Scr* Gregory Nava, Anna Thomas

My Father Is Coming ★★★ 18

Comedy drama 1991 · US/Ger · Colour · 80mins

This is a surprisingly restrained mainstream comedy from Monika Treut. Caught in the oh-so-familiar fib of telling the folks back home that all is going swimmingly, waitress Shelley Kästner is torn between a lesbian affair and a mysterious male when her strait-laced German father (Alfred Edel) arrives in New York to see his "stage star" daughter in action. Enlivening the usual round of farcical deceptions is real-life porn star Annie Sprinkle, who keeps Edel mind-bogglingly occupied while Käster ponders her future. DP

Shelley Kästner *Vicky* • Alfred Edel *Hans* • Mary-Lou Graulau *Lisa* • Dominique Gaspar *Christa* • Flora Gaspar *Dora* • David Bronstein *Ben* • Annie Sprinkle *Annie* ■ *Dir* Monika Treut • *Scr* Bruce Benderson, Monika Treut

My Father the Hero ★★★ PG

Comedy drama 1994 · US · Colour · 86mins

If you enjoyed the French original, *Mon Père Ce Héros*, then steer well clear of this Hollywood remake. However, if you are coming to the film with an open mind, there's every chance you will glean some enjoyment from this frivolous comedy in which Katherine Heigl tries to impress the admiring Dalton James by pretending that her father, Gérard Depardieu, is really her sugar daddy. The film has the distinction of being the only American remake of a Gallic hit to retain the original star, but Depardieu is obviously aware of the gulf between the two pictures. DP DVD

Gérard Depardieu *André* • Katherine Heigl *Nicole* • Dalton James *Ben* • Lauren Hutton *Megan* • Faith Prince *Diana* • Stephen Tobolowsky *Mike* • Ann Hearn *Stella* ■ *Dir* Steve Miner • *Scr* Francis Veber, Charlie Peters, from the film *Mon Père Ce Héros* by Gérard Lauzier

My Favorite Blonde ★★★★

Comedy 1942 · US · BW · 78mins

Vaudeville entertainer Bob Hope meets gorgeous blonde Madeleine Carroll who, it turns out, is a British spy being pursued by Nazi villains, notably the sinister duo of George Zucco and glamorous Gale Sondergaard. It's Bob to the rescue in one of his best vehicles. Directed at a laugh a minute and a thrilling pace by Sidney Lanfield, this is a glorious spoof on the espionage-chase films so beloved of Alfred Hitchcock. RK

Bob Hope *Larry Haines* • Madeleine Carroll *Karen Bentley* • Gale Sondergaard *Mme Stephanie Runick* • George Zucco *Dr Hugo Streger* • Lionel Royce *Karl* • Walter Kingsford *Dr Faber* • Bing Crosby *Man giving directions* ■ *Dir* Sidney Lanfield • *Scr* Don Hartman, Frank Butler, from a story by Melvin Frank, Norman Panama

My Favorite Brunette ★★★ PG

Comedy mystery 1947 · US · BW · 86mins

Bob Hope (starring in the first film for his own production company, which made him richer than ever) plays a guy who, mistaken for a Philip Marlowe-type private eye, decides to live out

M

the role in order to help mysterious Dorothy Lamour, who's in a spot of bother involving gangsters. Only moderately successful as a spoof of Raymond Chandler's thrillers, it's amusing enough. RK DVD

Bob Hope *Ronnie Jackson* • Dorothy Lamour *Carlotta Montay* • Peter Lorre *Kismet* • Lon Chaney Jr *Willy* • Charles Dingle *Major Simon Montague* • John Hoyt *Dr Lundau* • Reginald Denny *James Collins* • Jack LaRue *Tony* • Bing Crosby *Executioner* • Alan Ladd *Sam McCloud* ■ *Dir* Elliott Nugent • *Scr* Edmund Beloin, Jack Rose

My Favorite Martian ★ PG

Science-fiction comedy 1999 · US · Colour · 93mins

This farce is a pointless farrago that's nowhere near as fun as the 1960s TV series that inspired it, despite an in-joke appearance by original Martian Ray Walston. Here, unemployed TV-news producer Jeff Daniels hides crash-landed alien Christopher Lloyd in his car as the manic shape-shifter searches for spaceship spare parts. A highly talented cast drowns in a mass of bad quips, slapstick pratfalls and shameless mugging. AJ DVD

Jeff Daniels *Tim O'Hara* • Christopher Lloyd *Uncle Martin* • Elizabeth Hurley *Brace Channing* • Daryl Hannah *Lizzie* • Christine Ebersole *Mrs Lorelei Brown* • Wallace Shawn *Coleye* • Michael Lerner *Mr Channing* • Jeremy Hotz *Billy* • Ray Walston *Armitan* ■ *Dir* Donald Petrie • *Scr* Deanna Oliver, Sherri Stoner, from the TV series by John L Greene

My Favorite Spy ★ U

Musical comedy 1942 · US · BW · 85mins

Bandleader/comedian Kay Kyser is an aquired taste, and though some of his films prove ingenuous fun, this is the weakest of the five films he made for RKO in the early 1940s. Produced by former silent star Harold Lloyd with too much reliance on Kyser's minimal flare for comedy, it has surprisingly lifeless direction by Tay Garnett. Pleasant songs by Jimmy Van Heusen and Johnny Burke provide some respite from the antics of Kyser as a bandleader chosen by Army Intelligence to infiltrate a spy ring. TV

Kay Kyser • Jane Wyman *Connie* • Ellen Drew *Terry Kyser* • Robert Armstrong *Harry Robinson* • Helen Westley *Aunt Jessie* • Una O'Connor *Cora* ■ *Dir* Tay Garnett • *Scr* William Bowers, Sig Herzig, from a story by M Coates Webster

My Favorite Spy ★★★

Comedy 1951 · US · BW · 93mins

This is Bob Hope's third *My Favorite* outing, directed this time by Norman Z McLeod, and with the stunningly beautiful Hedy Lamarr following in the footsteps of Madeleine Carroll and Dorothy Lamour as the comedian's co-star. The nonsensical plot has Hope as a minor-league vaudeville comic being persuaded to take the place of an agent in Tangier and foil a conspiracy. Less funny than its predecessors but offering some adroit slapstick, fans will enjoy it. RK

Bob Hope *Peanuts White/Eric Augustine* • Hedy Lamarr *Lily Dalbray* • Francis L Sullivan *Karl Brubaker* • Arnold Moss *Tasso* • John Archer *Henderson* • Luis Van Rooten *Hoenig* • Stephen Chase (1) *Donald Bailey* ■ *Dir* Norman Z McLeod • *Scr* Edmund Hartmann [Edmund L Hartmann], Jack Sher, Edmund Beloin, Lou Breslow, Hal Kanter, from a story by Edmund Beloin, Lou Breslow

My Favorite Wife ★★★★ U

Romantic comedy 1940 · US · BW · 84mins

Irene Dunne, having disappeared seven years earlier in a shipwreck, shows up alive and well just after her husband, Cary Grant, has remarried (to Gail Patrick). With a screenplay that burns brightly for most of the way and a cast that scintillates to the last, this hit romantic comedy remains a delight. Producer Leo McCarey had directed the 1937 Dunne-Grant smash *The Awful Truth* and was due to direct this one, but had to let Garson Kanin take over after being involved in a serious car crash. It was remade in 1963 as *Move Over, Darling*, with Doris Day and James Garner. RK DVD

Cary Grant *Nick Arden* • Irene Dunne *Ellen Arden* • Randolph Scott *Stephen Burkett* • Gail Patrick *Bianca* • Ann Shoemaker *Ma* • Scotty Beckett *Tim Arden* • Mary Lou Harrington *Chinch Arden* • Donald MacBride *Hotel clerk* ■ *Dir* Garson Kanin • *Scr* Sam Spewack, Bella Spewack, from a story by Sam Spewack, Bella Spewack, Leo McCarey

My Favorite Year ★★★★ PG

Comedy 1982 · US · Colour · 88mins

Peter O'Toole's deliciously unbalanced portrayal of a legendary Hollywood star falling off the wagon is one of the joys of this farcical excursion to the relatively early days (1954) of American TV. Lots of echoes here, as naive writer Mark Linn-Baker tries to keep the Errol Flynn-like hero sober for a television interview in the way Budd Schulberg was minder for F Scott Fitzgerald. The show's despotic boss, Joseph Bologna, has more than a touch or two of comedian Sid Caesar. TH. Contains swearing.

Peter O'Toole *Alan Swann* • Mark Linn-Baker *Benjy Stone* • Jessica Harper *KC Downing* • Joseph Bologna *King Kaiser* • Bill Macy *Sy Benson* • Lainie Kazan *Belle Carroca* • Anne De Salvo *Alice Miller* • Basil Hoffman *Herb Lee* • Lou Jacobi *Uncle Morty* ■ *Dir* Richard Benjamin • *Scr* Norman Steinberg, Dennis Palumbo, from a story by Dennis Palumbo

My Fellow Americans ★★★ 12

Satirical comedy 1996 · US · Colour · 96mins

In this clever twist on *The Odd Couple* format, two grouchy ex-Presidents – one Democrat, the other Republican – hit the road pursued by the secret service. Old-timers Jack Lemmon and James Garner squabble for the best lines in this gentle satire on American politics and middle America. The notable supporting cast includes Dan Aykroyd and John Heard, while Lauren Bacall makes a memorable ex-First Lady. AT. Contains sexual references and swearing.

Jack Lemmon *Russell P Kramer* • James Garner *Matt Douglas* • John Heard *Ted Matthews* • Dan Aykroyd *William Haney* • Sela Ward *Kaye Griffin* • Wilford Brimley *Joe Hollis* • Lauren Bacall *Margaret Kramer* ■ *Dir* Peter Segal • *Scr* E Jack Kaplan, Richard Chapman, Peter Tolan, from a story by E Jack Kaplan, Richard Chapman

My First Mister ★★★ 15

Drama 2001 · US/Ger · Colour · 104mins

A sweet film about the relationship between two lonely people, this benefits from superb performances from leads Albert Brooks and Leelee Sobieski. She plays the alienated teenager who spends her days wandering around the mall until she sees a middle-aged man rearranging the window of a men's clothing shop. She asks for a job, and once she's agreed to tone down her appearance to work there, the two become friends. Unfortunately, writer Jill Franklyn loses courage about the relationship before the film ends, and we are left with a contrived plot twist. JB. Contains swearing and drug abuse. DVD

Albert Brooks *Randall, "R"* • Leelee Sobieski *Jennifer, "J"* • Desmond Harrington *Randy* • Carol Kane *Mrs Benson* • Mary Kay Place *Patty, nurse* • John Goodman *Benjamin* ■ *Dir* Christine Lahti • *Scr* Jill Franklyn

My First Wife ★★★★ 15

Drama 1984 · Aus · Colour · 97mins

This frankly autobiographical tale from writer/director Paul Cox is a harrowing and highly personal account of marital break-up. Memories and emotions tumble over each other as DJ/composer John Hargreaves learns that not only is his father dying, but his wife is also having an affair. As Hargreaves resorts to increasingly desperate measures to keep his family together, it would have been easy for Cox to turn Wendy Hughes's character into a callous bitch. However, such is the honesty and intensity of this curiously poetic treatise on desire we are too shattered to take sides. DP

John Hargreaves *John* • Wendy Hughes *Helen* • Lucy Angwin *Lucy* • David Cameron *Tom* ■ *Dir* Paul Cox • *Scr* Paul Cox, Bob Ellis

My Foolish Heart ★★★ U

Romantic drama 1949 · US · BW · 94mins

Susan Hayward gives one of her least mechanical performances here as the wife and mother unhappily married to Kent Smith and remembering past moments with pilot Dana Andrews. Written by Julius J and Philip G Epstein from a JD Salinger short story, this weepie has the customary gloss associated with its producer, Samuel Goldwyn, but the direction never really achieves the emotional depth required. Sadly, Salinger was so unhappy with this adaptation that he decided against agreeing to any further films of his work. TH

Dana Andrews *Walt Dreiser* • Susan Hayward *Eloise Winters* • Kent Smith *Lew Wengler* • Lois Wheeler *Mary Jane* • Jessie Royce Landis *Martha Winters* • Robert Keith (1) *Henry Winters* ■ *Dir* Mark Robson • *Scr* Julius J Epstein, Philip G Epstein, from the short story *Uncle Wiggily in Connecticut* by JD Salinger

My Forbidden Past ★

Drama 1951 · US · BW · 80mins

With the starry line-up of beautiful Ava Gardner, cool Robert Mitchum and debonair Melvyn Douglas, you'd assume this RKO feature would be well nigh unmissable. Actually it's a Deep South potboiler of staggering banality, not even raised above its own low level by the stars. Director Robert Stevenson has to be held partly responsible for the slow pace and lack of action. The casual attitude accorded this New Orleans-set melodrama is indicated by the fact that nobody even attempts a southern accent. TS

Robert Mitchum *Dr Mark Lucas* • Ava Gardner *Barbara Beaurevel* • Melvyn Douglas *Paul Beaurevel* • Lucile Watson *Aunt Eula* • Janis Carter *Corinne* • Gordon Oliver *Clay Duchesne* ■ *Dir* Robert Stevenson • *Scr* Marion Parsonnet, Leopold Atlas, from the novel *Carriage Entrance* by Polan Banks

My Friend Flicka ★★★★ U

Drama 1943 · US · Colour · 85mins

This is one of those films for all the family carelessly referred to by hardened hacks as heartwarming. But it really is. Roddy McDowall is the lonely son of Rocky Mountain rancher Preston Foster, whose dearest wish comes true when he is entrusted with raising his own horse. The story is simply irresistible, the photography glows and the scenes in which McDowall trains the animal and nurses it through sickness put the film up among the best of its kind. McDowell returned for a sequel, *Thunderhead – Son of Flicka* two years later. DP DVD

Roddy McDowall *Ken McLaughlin* • Preston Foster *Rob McLaughlin* • Rita Johnson *Nell* • James Bell *Gus* • Jeff Corey *Tim Murphy* • Diana Hale *Hildy* • Arthur Loft *Charley Sargent* ■ *Dir* Harold Schuster • *Scr* Lillie Hayward, Frances Edwards Faragoh

My Friend Irma ★★

Comedy 1949 · US · BW · 102mins

Based on a hit radio show starring Marie Wilson as the ultimate dumb blonde (a characterisation exceedingly sexist by today's standards), this mild comedy is notable only for marking the screen debut of Dean Martin and Jerry Lewis. They raise more laughs than Wilson, whose predictably daffy reactions as she tries to help her larcenous boyfriend (John Lund) in his money-making schemes lack the sublimely convoluted logic of the more endearingly eccentric Gracie Allen. TV

John Lund *Al* • Diana Lynn *Jane Stacey* • Don DeFore *Richard Rhinelander* • Marie Wilson *Irma Peterson* • Dean Martin *Steve Baird* • Jerry Lewis *Seymour* • Hans Conried *Prof Kropotkin* • Kathryn Givney *Mrs Rhinelander* ■ *Dir* George Marshall • *Scr* Cy Howard, Parke Levy, from a radio series by Cy Howard

My Friend Irma Goes West ★★

Comedy 1950 · US · BW · 90mins

This sequel to *My Friend Irma* (1949) has dumb blonde Marie Wilson heading for California with her friends to try their luck in movies. It is marginally superior to its predecessor, due mainly to the extra time given to the comedy team of Dean Martin and Jerry Lewis, who had received an enthusiastic response from audiences with their debut in the earlier film. Martin is given French actress Corinne Calvet as love interest, while Lewis has some classic comic moments, including some inventive business with a plate of spaghetti. TV

John Lund *Al* • Marie Wilson *Irma Peterson* • Diana Lynn *Jane Stacey* • Dean Martin *Steve Baird* • Jerry Lewis *Seymour* • Corinne Calvet *Yvonne Yvonne* • Lloyd Corrigan *Sharpie* ■ *Dir* Hal Walker • *Scr* Cy Howard, Parke Levy, from a radio series by Cy Howard

My Friend Ivan Lapshin ★★★★ 15

Period drama 1982 · USSR · Colour and BW · 98mins

Adapted from his father Yuri's stories, Alexei Gherman's third feature is a compelling, understated portrait of Soviet provincial life in the days before the Stalinist purges. Opening in colour, the action flashes back into atmospheric monochrome to follow police chief Andrei Boltnev as he divides his time between tracking down an unscrupulous gang and pursuing actress Nina Ruslanova. Even the subplots, focusing on his relationships with a recently widowed friend and a neighbour and his nine-year-old son, are packed with acute observations that not only evoke the everyday, but also suggest the carnage to come. DP. In Russian with English subtitles.

Andrei Boltnev *Ivan Lapshin* • Nina Ruslanova *Natasha Adashova* • Andrei Mironov *Khanin* • Z Adamovich *Patrikeyevna* ■ *Dir* Alexei German • *Scr* Eduard Volodarsky, from stories by Yuri Gherman

My Friend Joe ★★

Drama 1996 · UK/Ger/Ire · Colour · 100mins

In this self-consciously provocative drama, Pauline McLynn spends much of her time carving voluptuous statues. But she's a voice of reason beside the chauvinistic rantings of Stephen McHattie, a soured ex-acrobat who insists on raising his orphaned niece, Schuyler Fisk, as a nephew. The friendship between the young American and John Cleere's timid Irish outcast is pleasingly developed. But once Fisk's secret emerges, the mood shifts and Chris Bould settles for a sentimental solution. DP. Contains swearing.

Schuyler Fisk *Joe* • John Cleere *Chris Doyle* • Stephen McHattie *Curt* • Stanley Townsend *Mr Doyle* • Pauline McLynn *Ms Doyle* ■ *Dir* Chris Bould • *Scr* David Howard

My Gal Sal ★★★ U

Biographical musical drama
1942 · US · Colour · 103mins

They really don't make 'em like this any more: a musical, set in the 1890s, that bounces along on enough high-octane energy to run the National Grid for a week. Rita Hayworth is at her most luscious and appealing as the chanteuse love object of Victor Mature, playing popular songwriter Paul Dresser, whose wonderful old songs give this warm, engaging movie its fuel. What unites the movie's feel-good ingredients is the sublime choreography of Hermes Pan, the man partly responsible for Fred Astaire's legendary routines, and Val Raset. SH

Rita Hayworth *Sally Elliott* • Victor Mature *Paul Dresser* • John Sutton *Fred Haviland* • Carole Landis *Mae Collins* • James Gleason *Pat Hawley* • Phil Silvers *Wiley* ■ *Dir* Irving Cummings • *Scr* Seton I Miller, Darrell Ware, Karl Tunberg, from the biography *My Brother Paul* by Theodore Dreiser

My Geisha ★★

Romantic comedy
1962 · US · Colour · 119mins

When a movie director (Yves Montand) refuses to cast his wife (Shirley MacLaine) in his film of *Madame Butterfly*, she disguises herself as a geisha girl in order to change his mind. Produced in Japan by Steve Parker as a vehicle for his powerhouse wife MacLaine, and directed by Oscar-winning cinematographer Jack Cardiff, the film looks gorgeous. The mildly amusing idea fails to take fire, however, and what should have been a sprightly comedy becomes a yawn. RK

Shirley MacLaine *Lucy Dell/Yoko Mori* • Yves Montand *Paul Robaix* • Edward G Robinson *Sam Lewis* • Bob Cummings [Robert Cummings] *Bob Moore* ■ *Dir* Jack Cardiff • *Scr* Norman Krasna

My Giant ★★ PG

Comedy 1998 · US · Colour · 99mins

Billy Crystal plays a second-rate talent agent who, while in Romania to visit his latest signing, has a close encounter with a seven-foot-seven giant (basketball player Gheorghe Muresan). Crystal sees potential in this soft-hearted titan and promptly whisks him off to America, promising to reunite him with his childhood sweetheart. What follows is a less than scintillating mawkish family flick. NS. Contains some swearing. [VIDEO]

Billy Crystal *Sammy* • Kathleen Quinlan *Serena* • Gheorghe Muresan *Max* • Joanna Pacula *Lillianna* • Zane Carney *Nick* • Jere Burns *Weller* • Harold Gould *Milt* • Dan Castellaneta *Partlow* ■ *Dir* Michael Lehmann • *Scr* David Seltzer, from a story by Billy Crystal, David Seltzer

My Girl ★★ PG

Romantic drama 1991 · US · Colour · 98mins

Macaulay Culkin doesn't have much screen time in this occasionally charming tale. Anna Chlumsky plays a young tomboy who is trying to come to terms with life and the fact that her mortician father (Dan Aykroyd) is starting a relationship with the woman (Jamie Lee Curtis) who makes up the bodies at his funeral parlour. It's one for the less cynical members of the family, although younger viewers may find some of the unhappier moments distressing. JB. Contains swearing. [VIDEO] DVD

Dan Aykroyd *Harry Sultenfuss* • Jamie Lee Curtis *Shelly DeVoto* • Macaulay Culkin *Thomas J Sennett* • Anna Chlumsky *Vada Sultenfuss* • Richard Masur *Phil Sultenfuss* • Griffin Dunne *Mr Bixler* ■ *Dir* Howard Zieff • *Scr* Laurice Elehwany

My Girl 2 ★★ PG

Drama 1994 · US · Colour · 94mins

This unthreatening, absolutely redundant sequel has the now adolescent Anna Chlumsky trekking off to Los Angeles to find out what her real mother (who died during childbirth) was like. The nominal adult leads (Dan Aykroyd and Jamie Lee Curtis) are left stuck at home with little to do but wring their hands with concern. JF [VIDEO] DVD

Dan Aykroyd *Harry Sultenfuss* • Jamie Lee Curtis *Shelly Sultenfuss* • Anna Chlumsky *Vada Sultenfuss* • Austin O'Brien *Nick Zsigmond* • Richard Masur *Phil Sultenfuss* • Christine Ebersole *Rose Zsigmond* • John David Souther [JD Souther] *Jeffrey Pommeroy* ■ *Dir* Howard Zieff • *Scr* Janet Kovalcik

My Girl Tisa ★★★ U

Drama 1948 · US · BW · 95mins

A starring vehicle for Lilli Palmer, an actress who successfully combined beauty, intelligence and acting ability. She plays a young immigrant trying to bring her father to America, a role which must have had many resonances for Palmer, who herself grew up in Germany, the daughter of a Jewish surgeon, and fled with her sister Irene to Paris to avoid the persecution of the Jews by the Nazis. Here she co-stars with other noted refugees Sam Wanamaker, Akim Tamiroff and Hugo Haas in a deeply committed movie that doesn't quite reach the heights of social realism to which it aspires. TS

Lilli Palmer *Tisa Kepes* • Sam Wanamaker *Mark Denek* • Akim Tamiroff *Mr Grumbach* • Alan Hale *Dugan* • Hugo Haas *Tescu* • Gale Robbins *Jenny Kepes* • Stella Adler *Mrs Faludi* ■ *Dir* Elliott Nugent • *Scr* Allen Boretz, from the play *Ever the Beginning* by Lucille S Prumbs, Sara B Smith

My Girlfriend's Boyfriend ★★★★ PG

Comedy drama 1987 · Fr · Colour · 99mins

Eric Rohmer effortlessly blends the old and the new in this typically deft study of the inconsequential love lives of his youthful, self-obsessed protagonists. Inspired by the social wit of the 18th-century playwright, Marivaux, yet set against the futuristic landscape of the antiseptic Parisian suburb of Cergy-Pontoise, the focus falls on Emmanuelle Chaulet, who finds herself irresistibly drawn to her best friend's swain, Eric Viellard. While the characters endlessly analyse emotions which seem as artificial as their surroundings, Rohmer experiments with colour and language as he explores the nature of fidelity and friendship. A delight. DP. In French with English subtitles. [VIDEO] DVD

Emmanuelle Chaulet *Blanche* • Sophie Renoir *Léa* • Anne-Laure Meury *Adrienne* • Eric Viellard *Fabien* • François-Eric Gendron *Alexandre* ■ *Dir/Scr* Eric Rohmer

My Heroes Have Always Been Cowboys ★★★

Western 1991 · US · Colour · 106mins

It would be all too easy to write off Stuart Rosenberg's film as a pale imitation of Sam Peckinpah's rodeo classic, *Junior Bonner*. But that would be unfair to a fine ensemble cast that rises above a formulaic screenplay to create some highly credible characters. There's a real air of disappointment about Scott Glenn's battle-scarred rider, while Kate Capshaw makes light of the clichés as a woman torn between the thrill of love and the pain of bitter experience. But stealing the show is Ben Johnson as Glenn's contrarily cantankerous father. DP. Contains violence and swearing.

Scott Glenn *HD Dalton* • Kate Capshaw *Jolie Meadows* • Ben Johnson *Jesse Dalton* • Tess Harper *Cheryl Hornby* • Paul Balthazar Getty [Balthazar Getty] *Jud Meadows* • Gary Busey *Clint Hornby* • Mickey Rooney *Junior* • Clarence Williams III *Virgil* • Dub Taylor *Gimme Cap* ■ *Dir* Stuart Rosenberg • *Scr* Joel Don Humphreys

My House in Umbria ★★★ 12

Drama 2002 · US/UK/It · Colour · 98mins

Maggie Smith won an Emmy Award for her typically mannered performance as an English romance novelist in this adaptation of William Trevor's 1991 novella. On a trip to Milan, Smith's train compartment is wrecked by an explosion and she is one of the few survivors. She invites the others to recover at her palatial country house in Umbria. Director Richard Loncraine's HBO cable movie features glorious vistas but is weak-kneed and overly sentimental. Best to forget the artificiality of the lazy plot and focus on the high standard of acting. AJ. Contains sexual references. DVD

Maggie Smith *Mrs Emily Delahunty* • Chris Cooper *Thomas "Tom" Riversmith* • Timothy Spall *Quinty* • Benno Fürmann *Werner* • Ronnie Barker *The General* • Giancarlo Giannini *Inspector Girotti* • Libero De Rienzo *Dr Innocenti* ■ *Dir* Richard Loncraine • *Scr* Hugh Whitemore, from the novella by William Trevor

My Hustler ★★

Drama 1965 · US · BW · 79mins

One of 18 films Andy Warhol made in 1965, this has, unusually for Warhol, some sort of plot. It concerns a young hustler, hired for the weekend through "Dial-a-Hustler", who bronzes himself on Fire Island beach while a trio of admirers bitch and banter about who will seduce him first. Be advised that the sexually explicit film also contains lengthy shots of men shaving. Mainly for Warhol fans. PF

Paul America *Young hustler* • Ed Hood *The "John"* • Joseph Campbell *Sugar Plum Fairy* • John MacDermott *Houseboy* ■ *Dir* Andy Warhol • *Scr* Chuck Wein

My Kingdom ★★★ 18

Crime drama 2001 · It/UK · Colour · 111mins

King Lear meets *Get Carter* in this entertaining tribute to the British gangster movie from director Don Boyd. As the Liverpool hood realising his day is done in the wake of his wife's murder, Richard Harris produces a display of rage and despair that's all the more powerful for its restraint. Every aspect of this pitiless family feud drips with corrosive criminality, whether it's scheming sisters Louise Lombard and Lorraine Pilkington fighting over bent cop Aiden Gillen, or their husbands, Paul McGann and Jimi Mistry, vying for supremacy. DP. Contains violence, swearing. [VIDEO] DVD

Richard Harris *Sandeman* • Lynn Redgrave *Mandy* • Louise Lombard *Kath* • Lorraine Pilkington *Tracy* • Emma Catherwood *Jo* • Paul McGann *Dean* • Jimi Mistry *Jughinder "Jug" Singh* • Aidan Gillen *Detective Sergeant Barry Puttnam* • Tom Bell *Richard Quick* ■ *Dir* Don Boyd • *Scr* Nick Davies, Don Boyd

My Learned Friend ★★★★ PG

Comedy 1943 · UK · BW · 70mins

Will Hay's last film is a devilishly black comedy in which he not only stars, but also co-directs with Basil Dearden. Reduced to writing begging letters after he's disbarred, shyster lawyer Hay joins forces with bungling barrister Claude Hulbert to end the reign of terror being waged by Mervyn Johns, an ex-jailbird bent on taking murderous revenge on all who convicted him for forgery. Hay is on tip-top form and Johns indulges himself as the eye-rolling maniac. There are laughs aplenty and the Big Ben finale skilfully marries Hitchcock and Harold Lloyd. DP [VIDEO]

Will Hay *William Fitch* • Claude Hulbert *Claude Babbington* • Mervyn Johns *Grimshaw* • Laurence Hanray [Lawrence Hanray] *Sir Norman* • Aubrey Mallalieu *Magistrate* • Charles Victor *"Safety" Wilson* ■ *Dir* Will Hay, Basil Dearden • *Scr* John Dighton, Angus MacPhail

My Left Foot ★★★★★ 15

Biographical drama
1989 · UK/Ire · Colour · 98mins

A superb movie chronicling the life of writer and artist Christy Brown, who was born with cerebral palsy, portrayed with astonishing passion and sensitivity by Daniel Day-Lewis. All concerned were rightly showered with praise and plaudits at the time, including Oscars for Day-Lewis and Brenda Fricker as Christy's stoical mum. There were some low rumblings that Day-Lewis's role should have been given to a disabled actor, a view which won some sympathy, but nothing can be taken away from this all-round great movie. It's also notable for the penultimate screen appearance of the marvellous Ray McAnally. SH. Contains swearing. [VIDEO] DVD

Daniel Day-Lewis *Christy Brown* • Ray McAnally *Mr Brown* • Brenda Fricker *Mrs Brown* • Ruth McCabe *Mary Carr* • Fiona Shaw *Dr Eileen Cole* • Eanna MacLiam *Benny* • Alison Whelan *Sheila* • Hugh O'Conor *Younger Christy* ■ *Dir* Jim Sheridan • *Scr* Shane Connaughton, Jim Sheridan, from the autobiography by Christy Brown • *Music* Elmer Bernstein

M

My Life ★★★ 15

Drama 1993 · US · Colour · 112mins

The directorial debut of screenwriter Bruce Joel Rubin, who won an Oscar for his screenplay for *Ghost*, and a passable effort it is, too. Michael Keaton is very effective as the hotshot public relations executive given only months to live, and Nicole Kidman is nicely sparky as his newly pregnant wife. Rubin keeps everything just the right side of pathos until the final reel, when he jettisons all semblance of reality. The film is at its most endearing and revealing, however, when Keaton videotapes messages to leave to his unborn child. SH. Contains swearing. [VIDEO] DVD

Michael Keaton *Bob Jones* • Nicole Kidman *Gail Jones* • Bradley Whitford *Paul* • Queen Latifah *Theresa* • Michael Constantine *Bill* • Rebecca Schull *Rose* • Mark Lowenthal *Doctor Mills* • Lee Garlington *Carol Sandman* • Haing S Ngor *Mr Ho* ■ *Dir/Scr* Bruce Joel Rubin

My Life as a Dog ★★★★ PG

Period comedy drama
1985 · Swe · Colour · 101mins

Oscar-nominated Lasse Hallström invests this delightful rites-of-passage picture with as many autobiographical references as he does incidents from Reidar Jonsson's popular novel to produce a film of great warmth and wit. He shows a keen appreciation of the workings of a young mind, as he chronicles the misadventures of an imaginative 12-year-old packed off by his tubercular mother to stay with his uncle in the southern Swedish countryside of the 1950s. Hallström elicits a performance of innocence and spirit from Anton Glanzelius, who is wonderfully natural. DP. In Swedish with English subtitles. Contains swearing. [VIDEO] DVD

Anton Glanzelius *Ingemar Johansson* • Anki Liden *Ingemar's mother* • Tomas von Brömssen *Uncle Gunnar* • Manfred Serner *Erik Johansson* ■ *Dir* Lasse Hallström • *Scr* Lasse

Hallström, Brasse Brännström, Pelle Berglund, Reidar Jonsson, from the novel *Mitt Liv som Hund* by Reidar Jonsson

My Life So Far ★★★ 12

Period drama 1999 · UK/US · Colour · 98mins

This is a small, intimate portrait of one eccentric family in the Scottish highlands of the 1920s. Seen from the perspective of the family's ten-year-old son, the movie follows the traumatic events of one tumultuous year as the boy's madcap inventor dad (Colin Firth) has a fling with a visiting uncle's French fiancée (Irène Jacob). Crammed with quirkily memorable characters, the film's subject matter may be too twee for some tastes, though others will enjoy its fine evocation of an era long gone. DA

Colin Firth *Edward Pettigrew* • Rosemary Harris *Gamma Macintosh* • Irène Jacob *Heloise* • Tcheky Karyo *Gabriel Chenoux* • Mary Elizabeth Mastrantonio *Moira Pettigrew* • Malcolm McDowell *Uncle Morris Macintosh* • Kelly Macdonald *Elspeth Pettigrew* • Robert Norman *Fraser Pettigrew* ■ *Dir* Hugh Hudson • *Scr* Simon Donald, from the memoir *Son of Adam* by Sir Denis Forman

My Life with Caroline ★★

Romantic comedy 1941 · US · BW · 80mins

When his wife (British actress Anna Lee in her Hollywood debut) decides that she might be better off married to either Reginald Gardiner or Gilbert Roland, Ronald Colman must constantly woo her to retain her affections. Considering the talents involved – playwright John Van Druten wrote it, Lewis Milestone directs – this misfiring romantic comedy is remarkably devoid of amusement. It's always a pleasure, though, to watch the elegant Colman. RK

Ronald Colman *Anthony Mason* • Anna Lee *Caroline Mason* • Charles Winninger *Bliss* • Reginald Gardiner *Paul Martindale* • Gilbert Roland *Paco Del Valle* • Katherine Leslie *Helen* ■ *Dir* Lewis Milestone • *Scr* John Van Druten, Arnold Belgard, from the play *Train to Venice* by Louis Verneuil, Georges Berr

My Life without Me ★★★★ 15

Drama 2002 · Sp/Can · Colour · 101mins

The small details we take for granted in everyday life are celebrated with passion in this warm and bittersweet drama. It follows a 23-year-old working-class mother of two (Sarah Polley) who learns to appreciate the value of existence when she's diagnosed as terminally ill. This beautifully shot tale is a wonderfully perceptive, wryly amusing and occasionally surreal experience. Spanish writer/director Isabel Coixet's soulful heroine is as much an eternal optimist as she is a realist, despite her convict father, work-shy husband and resentful mother (singer Deborah Harry). Heart-rending and joyfully uplifting. SF DVD

Sarah Polley *Ann* • Amanda Plummer *Laurie* • Scott Speedman *Don* • Leonor Watling *Neighbour Ann* • Deborah Harry *Ann's mother* • Maria de Medeiros *Hairdresser* • Mark Ruffalo *Lee* • Julian Richings *Dr Thompson* • Alfred Molina *Ann's father* ■ *Dir* Isabel Coixet • *Scr* Isabel Coixet, from the short story *Pretending the Bed Is a Raft* by Nanci Kincaid

My Little Chickadee ★★★

Comedy western 1940 · US · BW · 83mins

The teaming of WC Fields and Mae West should have resulted in one of the funniest wisecracking movies of all time, but this spoof western never came close to hilarity and ended up as merely rollicking fun. Returning to the screen after two years, West (aided by Fields) penned a script that suited her style of precisely timed innuendo, but which also reined in Fields's unique brand of off-the-cuff rambling. There are some memorable moments, such as their wedding night, the crooked poker game and the scene in which they trade catch phrases, but the linking narrative is ponderous. DP

Mae West *Flower Belle Lee* • WC Fields *Cuthbert J Twillie* • Joseph Calleia *Jeff Badger* • Dick Foran *Wayne Carter* • Ruth Donnelly *Aunt Lou* • Margaret Hamilton *Mrs Gideon* • Donald Meek *Amos Budge* • Fuzzy Knight *Cousin Zeb* ■ *Dir* Edward Cline • *Scr* Mae West, WC Fields

My Little Eye ★★★ 18

Horror
2002 · UK/US/Fr/Can · Colour · 91mins

Five "lucky" strangers are put under constant 24-hour surveillance for an internet reality show. The group will all win $1 million if they live together in a remote, snowbound Nova Scotia house for six months with their every move being watched. As the deadline approaches, a mysterious stranger arrives, causing sexual havoc and pushing this bleak chiller into an unrelenting frenzy of intense, bloody carnage. Too many genre clichés early on test the patience but the grainy fly-on-the-wall style builds up a disturbingly authentic atmosphere. AJ DVD

Jennifer Sky *Charlie* • Stephen O'Reilly *Danny* • Laura Regan *Emma* • Sean CW Johnson *Matt* • Kris Lemche *Rex* • Bradley Cooper *Travis Patterson* ■ *Dir* Marc Evans • *Scr* David Hilton, James Watkins, from a story by David Hilton

My Little Girl ★★★ 15

Drama 1986 · US · Colour · 112mins

A little contrived and a tad sentimental, this well-meaning melodrama marked Connie Kaiserman's directorial debut. As the poor little rich girl spending her summer in a hostel for underprivileged kids, Mary Stuart Masterson conveys something of a teenager's confusion at coming face to face with the real world. She's well supported by James Earl Jones, who adds some down-to-earth dignity to the proceedings as the hostel's director. DP. Contains violence and swearing.

James Earl Jones *Ike Bailey* • Geraldine Page *Molly* • Mary Stuart Masterson *Franny Bettinger* • Anne Meara *Mrs Shopper* • Pamela Payton-Wright *Cordelia "Delly" Bettinger* • Peter Michael Goetz *Norman Bettinger* ■ *Dir* Connie Kaiserman • *Scr* Connie Kaiserman, Nan Mason

My Little Pony ★★ U

Animated adventure
1986 · US · Colour · 83mins

This children's favourite is from those bygone days when Pokémons and Power Rangers were still mere twinkles in their merchandisers' eyes, and when collectibles were altogether softer, more cuddly things. A feature-length spin-off from the TV series and toy range, this was indifferently animated in Japan and voiced rather better than it deserved to be by Danny DeVito, Cloris Leachman and Rhea Perlman. The plot has the rainbow-maned ponies fighting hoof and nail against a wicked witch with a living lava weapon. DA DVD

Danny DeVito *Grundle King* • Madeline Kahn *Draggle* • Cloris Leachman *Hydia* • Rhea Perlman *Reeka* ■ *Dir* Michael Joens • *Scr* George Arthur Bloom, from characters created by Hasbro

My Love Has Been Burning ★★★★

Political drama 1949 · Jpn · BW · 96mins

Made quickly and cheaply, yet anticipating director Kenji Mizoguchi's mature style, this *film à clef* was based on the autobiography of the 19th-century women's rights campaigner, Hideko Kageyama. As played by Kinuyo Tanaka, Eiko is a typical Mizoguchi heroine: she sees her school closed down on account of her political views, suffers imprisonment and then marries a prominent liberal who refuses to support her demand for female suffrage. The action, inspired by the postwar art of Picasso, is unexpectedly violent. DP. In Japanese with English subtitles.

Kinuyo Tanaka *Eiko Hirayama* • Mitsuko Mito *Chiyo* • Eitaro Ozawa *Hayase* • Ichiro Sugai *Kentaro Omoi* • Kuniko Miyake *Toshiko Kishida* ■ *Dir* Kenji Mizoguchi • *Scr* Yoshikata Yoda, Kaneto Shindo, from the autobiography *Warawa no Hanshogai (My Half Life)* by Hideko Kageyama

My Lucky Star ★★★

Musical comedy
1938 · US · BW and Tinted · 63mins

This minor Sonja Henie vehicle has a nice Mack Gordon-Harry Revel score and a daft plot that gives the dimpled skater plenty of opportunity to strut her stuff. Henie plays a department store clerk who catches the eye of the boss's son, Cesar Romero; the latter's wife is played by Louise Hovick, better known as Gypsy Rose Lee. The rest of the supporting cast is way above par, though leading man Richard Greene is a bit bland. The *Alice in Wonderland* ice ballet was originally tinted pink. TS

Sonja Henie *Kristina Nielson* • Richard Greene *Larry Taylor* • Joan Davis *Mary Dwight* • Cesar Romero *George Cabot Jr* • Buddy Ebsen *Buddy* • Arthur Treacher *Whipple* • George Barbier *George Cabot Sr* • Louise Hovick [Gypsy Rose Lee] *Marcelle La Verne* • Billy Gilbert *Nick* • Elisha Cook Jr *Waldo* ■ *Dir* Roy Del Ruth • *Scr* Harry Tugend, Jack Yellen, from the story *They Met in Chicago* by Karl Tunberg, Don Ettlinger

My Man Adam ★★ 15

Comedy 1985 · US · Colour · 83mins

Page Hannah (sister of Daryl) is the object of Raphael Sbarge's fantasies in this weak comedy about a high school student who finds his daydreams aren't nearly as exciting as real life when he inadvertently becomes involved in a murderous crime. A very slight comedy which goes some way to explain why Page's career didn't take off like her sister's. JB

Raphael Sbarge *Adam Swit* • Page Hannah *Sabrina McKay* • Veronica Cartwright *Elaine Swit* • Dave Thomas *Jerry Swit* • Charlie Bennett *Leroy* • Larry B Scott *Donald* • John Kapelos *Mr Rangle* ■ *Dir* Roger L Simon • *Scr* Roger L Simon, Renee Missel

My Man Godfrey ★★★★ U

Screwball comedy 1936 · US · BW · 89mins

A derelict (William Powell) finds himself rescued by a wealthy Park Avenue family's irrepressible younger daughter (Carole Lombard) and installed as the latest in a succession of butlers. Who he really is, and how he withstands the pressure of the family's insane antics, is the stuff of this classic comedy. It would be faultless if the family's farcical behaviour didn't strain credibility. Yet it's no surprise that both stars, director Gregory La Cava and the screenplay he co-wrote were all nominated for Oscars, as were Alice Brady for her portrayal of the featherbrained mother of the clan and Mischa Auer for his performance as her posturing protégé. RK DVD

William Powell *Godfrey Parke* • Carole Lombard *Irene Bullock* • Alice Brady *Angelica Bullock* • Gail Patrick *Cornelia Bullock* • Jean Dixon *Molly* • Eugene Pallette *Alexander Bullock* • Alan Mowbray *Tommy Gray* • Mischa Auer *Carlo* • Franklin Pangborn *Master of ceremonies* ■ *Dir* Gregory La Cava • *Scr* Morrie Ryskind, Eric Hatch, Robert Presnell, Zoë Akins [Zoe Akins], from the novel by Eric Hatch

My Man Godfrey ★★ U

Comedy 1957 · US · Colour · 91mins

Perhaps it was a mistake to try to recapture the atmosphere of the well-loved classic 1930s screwball comedy, but Universal did try gamely here, casting David Niven and June Allyson and throwing in the dubious benefits of colour and CinemaScope. This may pass the time, especially if you're a fan of either star, but Niven is too often reduced to eyebrow-raising double takes, while Allyson seems outclassed by her leading man. TS

David Niven *Godfrey* • June Allyson *Irene* • Jessie Royce Landis *Angelica* • Robert Keith (1) *Mr Bullock* • Eva Gabor *Francesca* • Jay Robinson *Vincent* • Martha Hyer *Cordelia* • Herbert Anderson *Hubert* ■ *Dir* Henry Koster • *Scr* Everett Freeman, Peter Berneis, William Bowers, from the 1936 film, from the novel *1101 Park Avenue* by Eric Hatch

My Mother Frank ★★★

Comedy drama 2000 · Aus · Colour · 95mins

This is an astute Australian comedy about an overbearing Catholic mother who undergoes a transformation on enrolling at her son's university. Sinead Cusack's conversion is made all the more enjoyable by the fact that it's partly brought about by her dismissively arrogant tutor, who is played with typically self-effacing nonchalance by Sam Neill. Admittedly, there are distinct echoes of *Educating Rita*, but writer/director Mark Lamprell is smart enough to muffle them with a subplot involving Cusack's son Matthew Newton. DP

Sinead Cusack *Frances "Frank" Kennedy* • Matthew Newton *David Kennedy* • Sam Neill *Professor Mortlock* • Celia Ireland *Maggie* • Rose Byrne *Jenny* ■ *Dir/Scr* Mark Lamprell

My Mother's Courage ★★★★ 12

Wartime biographical drama
1995 · Ger/UK/Austria · Colour · 90mins

This is a powerful, moving and decidedly different telling of a true Holocaust tale about the deportation of 4,000 Hungarian Jews from Budapest to Auschwitz in 1944. Told in flashback, the film focuses on the narrator's mother (Pauline Collins), who survived due to a mix of coincidence, courage and help from a most unexpected quarter. Director Michael Verhoeven also made *The Nasty Girl* (1990), and there are similar touches of surrealism here. DA

Pauline Collins *Elsa Tabori* • Ulrich Tukur *SS officer* • Heribert Sasse *Kelemen* • Natalie Morse *Maria* • Robert Giggenbach *Cornelius Tabori* • Günter Bothur *"Moustache"* • Simon Verhoeven *Young SS man* ■ *Dir* Michael Verhoeven • *Scr* Michael Verhoeven, from the novel by George Tabori

My Name Is Bill W ★★★★

Drama based on a true story
1989 · US · Colour · 100mins

This is a generally impressive TV drama about the founding of Alcoholics Anonymous. Few of the familiar Hollywood clichés about drunks are present in the script, and Daniel Petrie's direction is sensitive and well tuned to the remarkable actors. James Woods is compelling as Bill Wilson, living and drinking himself to an early grave until he meets Dr Bob Smith, another alcoholic, played by the excellent James Garner. Together they put the cork in the bottle and start the famous meetings. AT

James Woods *Bill Wilson* • JoBeth Williams *Lois Wilson* • James Garner *Dr Bob Smith* •

Gary Sinise *Ebby Thatcher* • George Coe *Frank Shaw* • Fritz Weaver *Dr Burnham* ■ *Dir* Daniel Petrie • *Scr* William G Borchert

My Name Is Joe ★★★★★ 15

Drama
1998 · UK/Ger/Fr/It/Sp · Colour · 100mins

This trawl through the Glaswegian underworld by director Ken Loach tells the story of Joe (Peter Mullan), a recovering alcoholic who falls in love with a social worker (Louise Goodall). However, his past comes back to haunt him when he vainly tries to help a young friend and his junkie wife who are being threatened by local gangsters. Downbeat and buoyant by turns, Loach's poignant drama boasts laugh-out-loud moments and a host of splendid performances. Mullan won the best actor prize at Cannes. TH. Contains violence, swearing, a sex scene and drug abuse. VIDEO DVD

Peter Mullan *Joe* • Louise Goodall *Sarah* • Gary Lewis *Shanks* • Lorraine McIntosh *Maggie* • David McKay *Liam* • Annemarie Kennedy *Sabine* • Scott Hannah *Scott* ■ *Dir* Ken Loach • *Scr* Paul Laverty

My Name Is Julia Ross ★★★

Film noir 1945 · US · BW · 64mins

With unusual acumen, the bosses of Columbia realised they had a rather good little thriller on their hands and gave this a major launch, earning some rave reviews despite the lack of box-office names. Nina Foch takes the principal role of the secretary who is given a new identity against her will and imprisoned in a remote mansion. Dame May Whitty plays against type as the villainess, supported by the ever-sinister George Macready as her murderous son. The setting is Hollywood's idea of England, but it's still an entertaining, commendably brief picture. AE

Nina Foch *Julia Ross* • May Whitty [Dame May Whitty] *Mrs Williamson Hughes* • George Macready *Ralph Hughes* • Roland Varno *Dennis Bruce* • Anita Bolster *Sparkes* • Doris Lloyd *Mrs Mackie* ■ *Dir* Joseph H Lewis • *Scr* Muriel Roy Bolton, from the novel *The Woman in Red* by Anthony Gilbert

My Name Is Nobody ★★★ 12

Spaghetti western
1973 · It/Fr/W Ger · Colour · 111mins

Sergio Leone produced this spaghetti western and again cast Henry Fonda, the star of *Once upon a Time in the West*, as a notorious gunfighter who plans to take an ocean liner from New Orleans and retire in Europe. Terence Hill plays "Nobody", who idolises Fonda and seduces him into one last, ultimate showdown. The story has epic pretensions, but the knockabout mood is poorly judged, while Hill is no substitute for Clint Eastwood. Leone's involvement is clear from the gunfights, huge close-ups and Ennio Morricone score. AT. Some dialogue dubbed into English. VIDEO DVD

Henry Fonda *Jack Beauregard* • Terence Hill *Nobody* • Jean Martin *Sullivan* • Piero Lulli *Sheriff* • Leo Gordon *Red* • RG Armstrong *Honest John* ■ *Dir* Tonino Valerii • *Scr* Ernesto Gastaldi, from a story by Fulvio Morsella, Ernesto Gastaldi, from an idea by Sergio Leone

My New Gun ★★★ 15

Black comedy 1992 · US · Colour · 94mins

A charming, eccentric slice of Americana that provides Diane Lane with probably her best role to date, playing an ordinary suburban housewife who strikes up a curious relationship with wild neighbour James LeGros. When LeGros steals the gun Lane's husband Stephen Collins bought her for protection, a series of events unfolds that changes her life for ever. Writer/director Stacy Cochran, in her first feature, pokes some wry fun at the American obsession with weaponry, and there are winning performances from Lane, LeGros, Tess Harper and the cast-against-type Collins. JF. Contains swearing. VIDEO

Diane Lane *Debbie Bender* • James LeGros *Skippy* • Stephen Collins *Gerald Bender* • Tess Harper *Kimmy Hayes* • Bill Raymond *Andrew* • Bruce Altman *Irwin* • Maddie Corman *Myra* ■ *Dir/Scr* Stacy Cochran

My Night with Maud ★★★★ U

Drama 1969 · Fr · BW · 105mins

Oscar-nominated for best foreign language film, this is one of Eric Rohmer's few films to boast a star-studded cast. It is an engrossing study of temptation and moral rectitude, with a delicious twist in which Rohmer questions the validity of religious and philosophical conviction in the face of human caprice. As the staunchly Catholic engineer, Jean-Louis Trintignant gives one of his finest performances as he resists the seduction of sophisticated divorcee Françoise Fabian out of fidelity to Marie-Christine Barrault, a woman he adores silently from afar. DP. In French with English subtitles. VIDEO

Jean-Louis Trintignant *Jean-Louis/Narrator* • Françoise Fabian *Maud* • Marie-Christine Barrault *Françoise* • Antoine Vitez *Vidal* • Leonide Kogan *Concert violinist* ■ *Dir/Scr* Eric Rohmer • *Cinematographer* Nestor Almendros

My Own Private Idaho ★★★★ 18

Drama 1991 · US · Colour · 99mins

A narcoleptic rent boy's doomed quest to find his mother is all the story director Gus Van Sant needs to explore the meaning of home and family in this unsettling tone poem. Using hallucinatory dream sequences, *cinéma vérité* confessions with male hustlers, artful sexual posing and impressionistic effects to hammer home the disturbed state of River Phoenix's mind, Van Sant also manages to extract a mould-breaking performance from Keanu Reeves (playing the object of Phoenix's affections). Audacious, controversial, directional, important and unique. AJ. Contains swearing, sex scenes, drug abuse, nudity. VIDEO DVD

River Phoenix *Mike Waters* • Keanu Reeves *Scott Favor* • James Russo *Richard Waters* • William Richert *Bob Pigeon* • Rodney Harvey *Gary* • Chiara Caselli *Carmella* • Michael Parker *Digger* • Jessie Thomas *Denise* • Grace Zabriskie *Alena* ■ *Dir* Gus Van Sant • *Scr* Gus Van Sant, with additional dialogue by William Shakespeare

My Pal Gus ★★

Comedy drama 1952 · US · BW · 83mins

Somewhat glib and predictable, this features Richard Widmark as a divorced businessman and George Winslow as his neglected, misbehaving son. Joanne Dru is the schoolteacher who takes the youngster in hand and Audrey Totter as the ex-wife who comes back to cause trouble. Winslow, the boy with the foghorn voice from *Gentlemen Prefer Blondes*, has a meatier role here, but the film could have done with a lighter touch. AE

Richard Widmark *Dave Jennings* • Joanne Dru *Lydia Marble* • Audrey Totter *Joyce* • George Winslow *Gus Jennings* • Joan Banks *Ivy Tolliver* • Regis Toomey *Farley Norris* ■ *Dir* Robert Parrish • *Scr* Fay Kanin, Michael Kanin

My Pal Trigger ★★ U

Western 1946 · US · BW · 79mins

Roy Rogers declared this a favourite among his westerns, though it's hard to see why – except for the fact that it gives Trigger more prominence than usual. Horse breeding is central to the dramatic storyline, which sees one champion steed shot dead, Rogers accused of the crime, and a mare being injured by a mountain lion while protecting her offstring. Former star Jack Holt plays the lead heavy. AE

Roy Rogers • George "Gabby" Hayes *Gabby Kendrick* • Dale Evans *Susan* • Jack Holt *Brett Scoville* • LeRoy Mason *Carson* • Roy Barcroft *Hunter* • Kenne Duncan *Croupier* ■ *Dir* Frank McDonald • *Scr* Jack Townley, John K Butler, from a story by Paul Gangelin

My Reputation ★★

Melodrama 1946 · US · BW · 92mins

This typical Barbara Stanwyck vehicle has her playing a widow who creates a scandal by dating too soon after her husband's death (hence the title). She's got two suitors, one of whom is George Brent, playing against type as a womaniser, and there are no real surprises, except for the fact that Stanwyck fairly drips with furs and jewellery when rolling bandages for the local Red Cross. Eve Arden as Stanwyck's best friend steals the movie, but it's petty larceny. TS

Barbara Stanwyck *Jessica Drummond* • George Brent *Major Scott Landis* • Warner Anderson *Frank Everett* • Lucile Watson *Mrs Kimball* • John Ridgely *Cary Abbott* • Eve Arden *Ginna Abbott* • Jerome Cowan *George Van Orman* ■ *Dir* Curtis Bernhardt • *Scr* Catherine Turney, from the novel *Instruct My Sorrows* by Clare Jaynes

My Science Project ★★ 15

Science-fiction adventure
1985 · US · Colour · 90mins

This laugh-free comedy typifies the problems that the Disney studios have always had in producing films for kids who've outgrown their cartoons. The plot is OK: high school students get their hands on an extraterrestrial gizmo that lets them summon up objects from the past and future. But its development, especially the emphasis on clumsily portrayed and badly integrated adolescent sex, leaves a nasty taste in the mouth.Dennis Hopper is truly funny as an ageing hippy science teacher. DA VIDEO DVD

John Stockwell *Michael Harlan* • Danielle Von Zerneck *Ellie Sawyer* • Fisher Stevens *Vince Latello* • Raphael Sbarge *Sherman* • Dennis Hopper *Bob Roberts* • Barry Corbin *Lew Harlan* • Richard Masur *Detective Isadore Nulty* ■ *Dir/Scr* Jonathan Betuel

My Side of the Mountain ★★★ U

Adventure 1969 · Can/US · Colour · 100mins

A touching celebration of nature, this children's film is about a highly intelligent 13-year-old who, after a family trip to the country is called off, runs away from home and manages to survive in the Montana wilds. It's attractively photographed, well-acted (particularly by Teddy Eccles in the lead) and thankfully unsentimental. JG

Teddy Eccles [Ted Eccles] *Sam Gribley* • Theodore Bikel *Bando* • Tudi Wiggins *Miss Turner* • Frank Perry *Mr Gribley* • Peggi Loder *Mrs Gribley* ■ *Dir* James B Clark • *Scr* Ted Sherdeman, Jane Klove, Joanna Crawford, from the novel by Jean Craighead George

My Sin ★★★

Drama 1931 · US · BW · 77mins

About to marry into wealthy New York society, former nightclub singer Tallulah Bankhead, who shot and killed a man in Panama, is confronted by her murky hidden past when the lawyer (Fredric March) who defended her appears on the scene. This was Paramount's second attempt in a year (the first was *Tarnished Lady*) to turn stage, society and gossip-column legend Tallulah into a big-time movie star. However, the wild girl's charismatic sex appeal once again failed to transfer itself to celluloid in this rather creaky melodrama. RK

Tallulah Bankhead *Carlotta/Ann Trevor* • Fredric March *Dick Grady* • Harry Davenport *Roger Metcalf* • Scott Kolk *Larry Gordon* • Anne Sutherland *Mrs Gordon* • Margaret Adams *Paula Marsden* • Lily Cahill *Helen Grace* ■ *Dir* George Abbott • *Scr* Owen Davis, Adelaide Heilbron, George Abbott, from the play *Her Past* by Frederick Jackson

My Sister Eileen ★★★ U

Comedy 1942 · US · BW · 96mins

This film version of the hit play was a great success in its day, though it seems somewhat forced and strident now. Yet Rosalind Russell's expert comic timing is a joy to behold in her role as an aspiring writer, trying her luck in Manhattan and finding opportunity comes more easily to her beautiful sister (Janet Blair). Russell won an Oscar nomination for her performance, which she re-created to enormous acclaim in the stage musical *Wonderful Town*. Columbia, however, who owned the rights to the original play, made a completely different musical of the property in 1955. TV

Rosalind Russell *Ruth Sherwood* • Brian Aherne *Robert Baker* • Janet Blair *Eileen Sherwood* • George Tobias *Landlord Appopolous* • Allyn Joslyn *Chick Clark* • Richard Quine *Frank Lippincott* ■ *Dir* Alexander Hall • *Scr* Joseph Fields, Jerome Chodorov, from their play, from the stories by Ruth McKenney

My Sister Eileen ★★★ U

Musical comedy 1955 · US · Colour · 96mins

This charming musical remake of the 1942 comedy details the adventures of two girls from the Ohio backwoods getting to grips with the fleshpots of New York. Starring a whole host of early 1950s faces, the whole enterprise zings with an amiable kookiness. Betty Garrett in particular shines as the plain older sister with a heart of fractured gold. SH

Janet Leigh *Eileen Sherwood* • Betty Garrett *Ruth Sherwood* • Jack Lemmon *Bob Baker* • Robert Fosse [Bob Fosse] *Frank Lippencott* • Kurt Kasznar *Appopolous* • Richard York [Dick York] *"Wreck"* • Lucy Marlow *Helen* • Tommy Rall *Chick Clark* ■ *Dir* Richard Quine • *Scr* Blake Edwards, Richard Quine, from the play by Joseph Fields, Jerome Chodorov, from the stories by Ruth McKenney

My Sister, My Love ★★

Period romantic drama
1966 · Swe · BW · 97mins

The story of Bibi Andersson's incestuous relationship with long-absent brother Per Oscarsson labours under the misapprehension that it's a serious and shocking work of art, when it's actually a shoddy bodice-ripper that fritters away its hard-working cast and forbidding setting. Undeterred, Vilgot Sjöman went on to confirm his reputation as the bad boy of Swedish cinema with *I Am Curious – Yellow*. DP

Per Oscarsson *Jacob* • Bibi Andersson *Charlotte* • Jarl Kulle *Alsmeden* • Gunnar Björnstrand *Count Schwartz* • Tina Hedström *Ebba Livin* • Berta Hall *Mrs Kuller* ■ *Dir* Vilgot Sjöman • *Scr* Vilgot Sjöman, inspired by the play *'Tis Pity She's a Whore* by John Ford

My Six Convicts ★★

Prison drama 1952 · US · BW · 104mins

John Beal plays a psychologist who enters Harbour State Prison to interview a variety of prisoners, including a safecracker, an embezzler and a killer. Based on Donald Powell Wilson's bestselling novel, this quasi-documentary was produced by message movie maestro Stanley Kramer and was intended to give convicts a human face, even a sense of humour. Some scenes were shot inside the actual San Quentin prison, using real convicts as extras. AT

Millard Mitchell *James Connie* • Gilbert Roland *Punch Pinero* • John Beal *Doc* • Marshall Thompson *Blivens Scott* • Alf Kjellin *Clem Randall* • Henry Morgan [Harry Morgan] *Dawson* • Jay Adler *Steve Kopac* • Regis Toomey *Doctor Gordon* • Charles Buchinski [Charles Bronson] *Jocko* ■ *Dir* Hugo Fregonese • *Scr* Michael Blankfort, from a novel by Donald Powell Wilson

My Six Loves ★★★ U

Romantic comedy
1962 · US · Colour · 100mins

As a film director, ace choreographer Gower Champion never achieved the heights he reached on Broadway. Nor did he equal his popularity as half of the dance team of Marge and Gower Champion who appeared in a series of superbly entertaining MGM features. Here he reunites with another MGM alumnus, Debbie Reynolds, in a likeable tale of theatrical folk. This is either mawkish or genuinely sentimental, according to taste, but certainly professional. TS

Debbie Reynolds *Janice Courtney* • Cliff Robertson *Rev Jim Larkin* • David Janssen *Martin Bliss* • Eileen Heckart *Ethel Swenson* • Jim Backus *The Sheriff* • Pippa Scott *Diane Soper* • John McGiver *Judge Harris* • Hans Conried *Kingsley Cross* ■ *Dir* Gower Champion • *Scr* John Fante, Joseph Calvelli, William Wood, from the novel by Peter VK Funk

My Son John ★ U

Drama 1952 · US · BW · 121mins

A patriotic American family goes into shock when they learn their beloved son is a communist. All is forgiven when he recants and dies. For this abysmal anti-Red movie, Helen Hayes returned to the screen after a long absence to play the mother, while Robert Walker died before the film's completion, forcing the production to fill in the gaps with footage from *Strangers on a Train*. To the astonishment of many, Leo McCarey was Oscar-nominated for his original story. RK

Helen Hayes *Lucille Jefferson* • Van Heflin *Stedman of the FBI* • Robert Walker *John Jefferson* • Dean Jagger *Dan Jefferson* • Minor Watson *Dr Carver* • Frank McHugh *Father O'Dowd* • Richard Jaeckel *Chuck Jefferson* • James Young *Ben Jefferson* ■ *Dir* Leo McCarey • *Scr* Myles Connolly, Leo McCarey, John Lee Mahin, from a story by Leo McCarey

My Son, My Son! ★★★★

First World War drama
1940 · US · BW · 116mins

A stellar cast, under Charles Vidor's sober and well-judged direction, brings Howard Spring's powerful bestseller to life. The always attractive Brian Aherne plays William Essex who, born into a poverty-stricken background, has become a successful novelist. He dotes on his son (Louis Hayward), but the latter grows into cruel manhood, mocking his father, destroying his own childhood sweetheart (Laraine Day) and attempting to seduce the woman his father loves (Madeleine Carroll). An absorbing drama of the highest order. RK

Madeleine Carroll *Livia Vaynol* • Brian Aherne *William Essex* • Louis Hayward *Oliver Essex* • Laraine Day *Maeve O'Riordan* • Henry Hull *Dermot O'Riordan* • Josephine Hutchinson *Nellie Moscrop Essex* • Sophie Stewart *Sheila O'Riordan* • Bruce Lester *Rory O'Riordan* ■ *Dir* Charles Vidor • *Scr* Leonore Coffee, from the novel by Howard Spring

My Son the Fanatic ★★★ 15

Drama 1997 · UK · Colour · 83mins

Caricature and cliché come close to scuppering this Yorkshire-based drama from screenwriter Hanif Kureishi. But such is the excellence of leads Om Puri and Rachel Griffiths that this study of religious intolerance, class snobbery and the seeming impossibility of social integration is never less than absorbing. As the immigrant cab driver whose hopes for acceptance are dashed by his son's involvement with a strict Islamic sect, Puri strikes up a rapport with Griffiths's harassed prostitute and thus deepens his crisis. DP. Contains swearing, sex scenes and drug abuse. [video]

Om Puri *Parvez* • Rachel Griffiths *Bettina* • Stellan Skarsgård *Schitz* • Akbar Kurtha *Farid* • Gopi Desai *Minoo* • Harish Patel *Fizzy* • Bhasker Patel [Bhasker] *The Maulvi* • Sarah Jane Potts *Madelaine* ■ *Dir* Udayan Prasad • *Scr* Hanif Kureishi, from his short story

My Stepmother Is an Alien ★★★ 15

Science-fiction comedy
1988 · US · Colour · 103mins

"Barbarella Goes Shopping" is the premise of this clunky cosmic satire, saved by Kim Basinger's untapped flair for light comedy. She plays a gorgeous ET who shacks up with scientist slob Dan Aykroyd to save her planet from destruction. Forget the plot, just settle down and watch a series of goofy culture-clash sketches revolving around Basinger coping with suburban life on Earth armed only with her talking alien handbag. Fine moments of inspired lunacy jostle with predictably slight comic relief, but Basinger's eager-to-please freshness and verve make this muddle impossible to dislike. AJ. Contains swearing. [video] DVD

Dan Aykroyd *Dr Steven Mills* • Kim Basinger *Celeste Martin* • Jon Lovitz *Ron Mills* • Alyson Hannigan *Jessie Mills* • Joseph Maher *Dr Lucas Budlong* • Seth Green *Fred Glass* • Wesley Mann *Grady* • Adrian Sparks *Dr Morosini* ■ *Dir* Richard Benjamin • *Scr* Jerico, Herschel Weingrod, Timothy Harris, Jonathan Reynolds

My Summer of Love ★★★ 15

Drama 2004 · UK · Colour · 82mins

This loose adaptation of Helen Cross's Yorkshire-set novel makes several astute contrasts between surface illusion and bitter reality. Ryszard Lenczewski's cinematography perfectly captures a balmy atmosphere of rural contentment, as working-class teenager Natalie Press falls for well-heeled Emily Blunt. The intensity of their relationship soon threatens to overwhelm them, and seems as fragile as Paddy Considine's fervent, prison-inspired dalliance with born-again Christianity. The naive optimism of the central characters is sensitively conveyed, but the assault on religion is heavy-handed and the dialogue occasionally ponderous. DP. Contains swearing and sex scenes. DVD

Natalie Press *Mona* • Emily Blunt *Tamsin* • Paddy Considine *Phil* • Dean Andrews *Ricky* • Michelle Byrne *Ricky's wife* • Paul Antony-Barber *Tamsin's father* • Lynette Edwards *Tamsin's mother* • Kathryn Summer *Sadie* ■ *Dir* Pawel Pawlikowski • *Scr* Pawel Pawlikowski, Michael Wynne, from the novel by Helen Cross

My Sweet Little Village ★★★ PG

Comedy 1986 · Cz · Colour · 99mins

Touching obliquely on bureaucratic corruption, the underdevelopment of the countryside and the shortage of decent housing, this is one of Jirí Menzel's mildest political allegories. It's a benign gaze that falls upon the villagers of a muddle-along collective, where the doctor is accident-prone, a bashful student becomes besotted with his teacher, a young wife strays from nuptial bliss and a truck driver and his doltish assistant fall out over repeated bungling. It all makes for amiable entertainment. DP. A Czech language film.

Janos Ban *Otik Rakosnik* • Marian Labuda *Pavek* • Rudolf Hrusinsky *Dr Skruzny* • Petr Cepek *Turek* ■ *Dir* Jirí Menzel • *Scr* Zdenek Sverak

My Teenage Daughter ★

Drama 1956 · UK · BW · 102mins

Anna Neagle stars in this ludicrous and staggeringly awful melodrama about the problems of motherhood in the fiifties. Neagle plays a magazine editor whose teenage daughter (Sylvia Syms) gets a new boyfriend and ends up in jail for manslaughter. The villain of the piece is jive dancing, while everyone speaks with Mayfair accents and seems to think they're making a statement about the youth of today. AT

Anna Neagle *Valerie Carr* • Sylvia Syms *Janet Carr* • Wilfrid Hyde White *Sir Joseph* • Norman Wooland *Hugh Manning* • Kenneth Haigh *Tony Ward Black* • Julia Lockwood *Poppet Carr* • Helen Haye *Aunt Louisa* ■ *Dir* Herbert Wilcox • *Scr* Felicity Douglas

My Tutor ★★ 18

Comedy drama 1983 · US · Colour · 92mins

A desperately dated and awful teen comedy drama, this is only saved by a wacky supporting performance from Crispin Glover. Matt Lattanzi stars as the teenager whose father hires him a tutor so he can get into Yale and luckily for him, Caren Kaye is blonde and beautiful. Director George Bowers tries to handle their relationship sympathetically rather than gratuitously, but it is overshadowed by a silly subplot. JB [video]

Caren Kaye *Terry* • Matt Lattanzi *Bobby Chrystal* • Kevin McCarthy *Mr Chrystal* • Clark Brandon *Billy* • Bruce Bauer *Don* • Arlene Golonka *Mrs Chrystal* • Crispin Glover *Jack* • Kitten Natividad *Ana Maria* ■ *Dir* George Bowers • *Scr* Joe Roberts, from the story by Mark Tenser

My 20th Century ★★

Surreal comedy drama
1988 · Hun/Can · BW · 104mins

Winner of the Caméra d'Or at Cannes for best first feature, Ildiko Enyedi's period comedy is illuminated by the triple performance of Dorotha Segda as a mother and her twins. The latter come together 20 years after they were orphaned as passengers on the Orient Express. One is now the mistress of a powerful man; the other is a radical activist. This might have made for an amusing comedy of errors; instead, Enyedi intersperses the sisters' adventures with surreal diversions and references to the dehumanising advance of progress. DP. A Hungarian language film.

Dorotha Segda *Dora/Lili/Mother* • Oleg Jankowski *Z* • Peter Andorai *Thomas Alva Edison* • Gabor Mathe *X* • Paulus Manker *Weininger* ■ *Dir/Scr* Ildiko Enyedi

My Uncle Antoine ★★★

Drama 1971 · Can · Colour · 110mins

This small-scale, 1940s-set rural drama is sometimes regarded as one of the best Canadian films ever made. Dealing with life and death in a Québec village, it gently juggles a gallery of characters, focusing on teenage Jacques Gagnon and his uncle, the local undertaker. Director Claude Jutra has a small role as the town clerk, but his career was tragically cut short by Alzheimer's disease. In 1986, he vanished; a year later, his decomposed body was found in the frozen St Lawrence river with a note to identify himself. AT. In French with English subtitles.

Jacques Gagnon *Benoît* • Lyne Champagne *Carmen* • Jean Duceppe *Antoine* • Monique Mercure *Alexandrine* • Lionel Villeneuve *Joseph Poulin* • Olivette Thibault *Cecile* • Claude Jutra *Fernand* ■ *Dir* Claude Jutra • *Scr* Clement Perron, Claude Jutra, from a story by Clement Perron

My Voyage to Italy ★★★★

Documentary 1999 · It/US · Colour · 246mins

This insightful documentary provides as much of a window into the thematic and stylistic preoccupations of Martin Scorsese as a history of Italian cinema prior to 1963. Some might find the choice of the films that illuminated Scorsese's Little Italy boyhood a touch conservative. But the director's decision to stick to the critical classics enables him to show in admirable detail (and with lengthy clips) how the neorealism of Roberto Rossellini, Luchino Visconti and Vittorio De Sica shaped the increasingly personal work of Federico Fellini and Michelangelo Antonioni. Moreover, the lengthy clips also allow the audience to catch Scorsese's infectious enthusiasm for a time when social commitment, intellectual rigour and artistic vision weren't things for film-makers to be ashamed of. DP

Dir Martin Scorsese

My Way Home ★★★★ 15

Biographical drama 1978 · UK · BW · 68mins

Having endured endless poverty and rejection, Stephen Archibald emerges from the dark tunnel of his childhood in the concluding part of Bill Douglas's magnificent film autobiography, that began with *My Childhood* (1972). After all the pain of family life, it is, unsurprisingly, a stranger whom Archibald meets on National Service in Egypt who transforms the boy's life. Taken together, Douglas's trilogy is one of the finest achievements in British cinema history. DP [video]

Stephen Archibald *Jamie* • Paul Kermack *Jamie's father* • Jessie Combe *Father's wife* • William Carrol *Archie* • Morag McNee *Father's girlfriend* • Lennox Milne *Grandmother* ■ *Dir/Scr* Bill Douglas

My Wild Irish Rose ★★ U

Biographical musical
1947 · US · Colour · 100mins

The subject of this rather feeble biopic is Chauncey Olcott, an Irish-American tenor who co-wrote the title song, *Mother Machree* and *When Irish Eyes Are Smiling*. The songs are well sung by charming Dennis Morgan, who plays the composer with a wobbly Irish brogue. If the film is to be believed (and it isn't), Olcott was enamoured with glamorous singer Lillian Russell (Andrea King) before settling down with his wife. The latter is portrayed by beautiful redhead Arlene Dahl. RB

Dennis Morgan *Chauncey Olcott/Jack Chancellor* • Arlene Dahl *Rose Donovan* • Andrea King *Lillian Russell* • Alan Hale *John Donovan* • George Tobias *Nick Popolis* • George O'Brien *William "Duke" Muldoon* • Sara Allgood *Mrs Brennan* ■ *Dir* David Butler • *Scr* Peter Milne, Edwin Gilbert, Sidney Fields, from the story *Song in His Heart* by Rita Olcott

Myra Breckinridge ★★★ 18

Comedy 1970 · US · Colour · 89mins

Time has tempered the scandalised revulsion that initially greeted director Michael Sarne's ultra-melodramatic adaptation of Gore Vidal's transsexual satire. Clouded by the controversy, contemporary critics failed to see it as a rather sly essay on gender, all-American movie-star stereotypes and vintage Hollywood nostalgia. Despite Mae West's barnstorming comeback after a 27-year absence from the big screen to play a triple-entendre "talent agent", the movie belongs to Raquel Welch in her most under-rated role. AJ. Contains swearing, nudity. [video] DVD

Mae West *Leticia* • John Huston *Buck Loner* • Raquel Welch *Myra Breckinridge* • Rex Reed *Young man* • Farrah Fawcett *Mary Ann* • Roger C Carmel *Dr Montag* • Jim Backus *Doctor* • John Carradine *Surgeon* • Andy Devine *Coyote Bill* • Tom Selleck *Stud* ■ *Dir* Michael Sarne • *Scr* Michael Sarne, David Giler, from the novel by Gore Vidal

Le Mystère Picasso ★★★★ U

Documentary
1956 · Fr · BW and Colour · 77mins

Pablo Picasso creates 15 original artworks in this majestic study of a genius at work. However, as they were all destroyed after the documentary was finished, they exist only as moving sketches that are captured with graceful simplicity through a transparent canvas by cinematographer Claude Renoir (whose grandfather was the Impressionist, Auguste Renoir). Director Henri-Georges Clouzot occasionally tinkers with time-lapse and at one point splendidly shifts into widescreen when the Spaniard complains that he needs more space. But, essentially, he keeps his distance to allow Picasso's personality and inspiration to mesmerise and delight, even when he produces a muddled misfire. DP. A French language film.

Dir Henri-Georges Clouzot • *Cinematographer* Claude Renoir • *Music* Georges Auric

The Mysteries of Paris ★★★ U

Period adventure 1962 · Fr · Colour · 95mins

This lavish production was adapted from Eugène Sue's story of kidnap and murder, set during the reign of Louis Philippe. The novel's socio-political themes have been excised to leave a lively adventure in which master of disguise Jean Marais sweeps through the Paris underworld avenging evil and rewarding good. Packed with reformed crooks, vile urchins, mischievous artists and gullible do-gooders, André Hunebelle's film blends thrills and laughs to good effect, while Marais is suitably mysterious amid the splendid period trappings. DP. French dialogue dubbed into English.

Jean Marais *Rodolphe De Sambreuil* • Dany Robin *Irene* • Raymond Pellegrin *Baron De Lansignac* • Jill Haworth *Marie* • Pierre Mondy *Le Chourineur* • Renée Gardes *"The Witch"* ■ *Dir* André Hunebelle • *Scr* Jean Halain, Pierre Foucaud, Diego Fabbri, from a novel by Eugène Sue

The Mysterious Island ★★★

Science-fiction adventure
1929 · US · Colour and BW · 95mins

Three years in the making, shot mostly in brilliant two-strip Technicolour and featuring wonderfully elaborate sets, miniature work and special effects, this is the first of a number of adaptations of Jules Verne's sequel to *20,000 Leagues under the Sea*. Using only basic plot elements from the novel and minimal dialogue, Lionel Barrymore (in one of his best roles) plays the scientist ruler of a mythical kingdom who invents a submarine to search the oceans for sea monsters. Director Lucien Ballard took over the troubled production from Maurice Tourneur and Benjamin Chistensen when storms wrecked the sets, and he finds exactly the right melodramatic tenor for the fantastical elements that keep both tension and interest at an unusually high level for transitional silent films of this period. AJ

Lionel Barrymore *Count Dakkar* • Lloyd Hughes *Nicolai* • Montagu Love *Falon* • Harry Gribbon *Mikhail* • Snitz Edwards *Anton* • Gibson Gowland *Dmitry* • Dolores Brinkman *Teresa* ■ *Dir* Lucien Hubbard • *Scr* Lucien Hubbard, from the novel by Jules Verne

Mysterious Island ★★★ U

Science-fiction adventure
1961 · UK/US · Colour · 96mins

Based on Jules Verne's sequel to *20,000 Leagues under the Sea*, this enjoyable British production blends Sinbad-style giant monster thrills, pirates, volcanic eruptions and, of course, Captain Nemo (Herbert Lom). As ever, stop-frame animation maestro Ray Harryhausen's monstrous menagerie provides most of the film's highlights, as oversized bees and colossal crabs threaten Michael Craig, Joan Greenwood and their companions. Although the rather colourless cast doesn't do much to raise excitement levels, Harryhausen's fine work and Bernard Herrman's atmospheric score make this fantasy island worth an excursion. SG [video] DVD

Michael Craig *Captain Cyrus Harding* • Joan Greenwood *Lady Mary Fairchild* • Michael Callan *Herbert Brown* • Gary Merrill *Gideon Spilett* • Herbert Lom *Captain Nemo* • Beth Rogan *Elena* ■ *Dir* Cy Endfield • *Scr* John Prebble, Daniel Ullman, Crane Wilbur, from the novel *L'Ile Mysterieuse* by Jules Verne

The Mysterious Lady ★★

Silent romantic drama
1928 · US · BW · 99mins

In her sixth Hollywood film, Greta Garbo stars as a Russian spy who has an affair with Austrian officer Conrad Nagel in order to steal some secret documents. But she falls in love with him for real, eventually betraying her masters. Competently directed by Fred Niblo to capitalise on the camera's love affair with Garbo, it's actually the most risible nonsense, only good for a giggle and an opportunity for her fans to gaze upon her beauty and savour her mysterious persona. RK

Greta Garbo *Tania* • Conrad Nagel *Karl von Heinersdorff* • Gustav von Seyffertitz *General Alexandroff* • Albert Pollet *Max* ■ *Dir* Fred Niblo • *Scr* Bess Meredyth, Marian Ainslee (titles), Ruth Cummings (titles), from the novel *Der Krieg im Dunkel* by Ludwig Wolff

Mysterious Mr Moto ★★★

Detective drama 1938 · US · BW · 62mins

Master of disguise and intrepid meddler in other people's business, Mr Moto sweeps from Scotland Yard to Devil's Island in pursuit of an international crime ring in one of the weaker entries in 20th Century-Fox's amiable B-movie series. The production has an all-expenses-spared feel about it and the plot is hardly out of the top drawer. Such is the pace of Norman Foster's direction, though, that you barely have time to notice. Apart from Leon Ames and Erik Rhodes, the supporting line-up is third-rate, but Peter Lorre more than atones. DP

Peter Lorre *Mr Moto* • Mary Maguire *Ann Richman* • Henry Wilcoxon *Anton Darvak* • Erik Rhodes *David Scott-Frensham* • Harold Huber *Ernst Litmar* • Leon Ames *Paul Brissac* ■ *Dir* Norman Foster • *Scr* Norman Foster, Philip MacDonald, from the character created by JP Marquand

Mysterious Skin ★★★ 18

Drama 2004 · US/Neth · Colour · 105mins

A poignant and disturbing exploration of paedophilia and its emotional fallout, this poetic and elegantly constructed drama is Gregg Araki's most accessible work to date, and also his most perceptive. In powerful performances, Joseph Gordon-Levitt and Brady Corbet play polar-opposite teens, linked together by an unsettling experience that they shared aged eight. The painful journey that each young man undertakes is difficult to watch, addressing extreme facets of abuse in an impartial manner that some viewers will find offensive. SF. Contains violence.

Brady Corbet *Brian Lackey* • Joseph Gordon-Levitt *Neil McCormick* • Michelle Trachtenberg *Wendy Peterson* • Jeff Licon *Eric Preston* • Bill Sage *Coach Heider* • Mary Lynn Rajskub *Avalyn Friesen* • Elisabeth Shue *Mrs McCormick* • Billy Drago *Zeke* ■ *Dir* Gregg Araki • *Scr* Gregg Araki, from the novel by Scott Heim

Mystery, Alaska ★★★ 15

Sports comedy drama
1999 · US · Colour · 113mins

Ice hockey forms the backbone of this likeable comedy. The remote town of Mystery makes the headlines thanks to its passion for the game, prompting a sports network to arrange a challenge between the locals and a major league New York team. The tale loses its way under a welter of characters and subplots, but compensation comes courtesy of the excellent cast and plenty of laughs. There's even a cameo from Mike Myers as a TV commentator. RT [video] DVD

Russell Crowe *John Biebe* • Hank Azaria *Charles Danner* • Mary McCormack *Donna Biebe* • Burt Reynolds *Judge Walter Burns* • Colm Meaney *Mayor Scott Pitcher* • Lolita Davidovich *Mary Jane Pitcher* • Maury Chaykin *Bailey Pruitt* • Mike Myers *Donnie Shulzhoffer* • Little Richard ■ *Dir* Jay Roach • *Scr* David E Kelley, Sean O'Byrne

Mystery Date ★★ 15

Comedy thriller 1991 · US · Colour · 93mins

What's the real reason behind Ethan Hawke's shady older brother organising a blind date for him with the sexy next door neighbour? Could it have something to do with the corpse in his car? A wildly uneven, but nonetheless fun black comedy with many surprising touches, not least how endearing Hawke proves to be in a thankless role. For optimum enjoyment, Jonathan Wacks's film should be viewed as a teenage *After Hours*. AJ. Contains some swearing and violence. [video]

Ethan Hawke *Tom McHugh* • Teri Polo *Geena Matthews* • Brian McNamara *Craig McHugh* • Fisher Stevens *Dwight* • BD Wong *James Lew* • Tony Rosato *Sharpie* ■ *Dir* Jonathan Wacks • *Scr* Terry Runte, Parker Bennett

Mystery in Mexico ★

Crime drama 1948 · US · Colour · 65mins

RKO made this B-feature as a cost-cutting experiment at the Churubusco Studios in Mexico City which it half-owned. Little money was saved and even with a talented director, Robert Wise, it was no spicier than the average B because of weak stars and a by-the-numbers script that has insurance investigator William Lundigan flying to Mexico City to find a missing colleague with the help of the man's sister, Jacqueline White. AE

William Lundigan *Steve Hastings* • Jacqueline White *Victoria Ames* • Ricardo Cortez *Norcross* • Tony Barrett *Carlos* • Jacqueline Dalya *Dolores* • Walter Reed *Glenn Ames* ■ *Dir* Robert Wise • *Scr* Lawrence Kimble, from a story by Muriel Roy Bolton

Mystery Men ★★★ PG

Comedy action adventure
1999 · US · Colour · 116mins

An eclectic cast adds a quality sheen to this mildly diverting superhero spoof, based on the Dark Horse comic. The gimmick is that these saviours of Champion City possess abilities that are of no use whatsoever – fork-throwing expertise, shovel-wielding skills, noxious bodily odours and so on. At a shade over two hours, Kinka Usher's film is much too long to sustain the script's slender humour quotient. However, with actors of the calibre of William H Macy, Greg Kinnear, Ben Stiller, Wes Studi and Geoffrey Rush, it's never short of quirky appeal. JC [video] DVD

Hank Azaria *The Blue Raja* • Janeane Garofalo *The Bowler* • William H Macy *The Shoveler* • Kel Mitchell *Invisible Boy* • Paul Reubens *The Spleen* • Ben Stiller *Mr Furious* • Wes Studi *The Sphinx* • Greg Kinnear *Captain Amazing/ Lance* ■ *Dir* Kinka Usher • *Scr* Neil Cuthbert, from the comic book by Bob Burden

The Mystery of Edwin Drood ★★★

Mystery 1935 · US · BW · 87mins

Faced with the unenviable prospect of concocting a credible finale to the tale Charles Dickens left unfinished at his death, John L Balderston and his fellow screenwriters wisely place the emphasis on character in this atmospheric adaptation of the novelist's most sinister opus. The exceptional cast thrives under Stuart Walker's generous direction, with Claude Rains responding particularly well as the opium-addled chorister whose love for Heather Angel spells disaster for her fiancé, David Manners. The stylised Gothic sets add to the overall sense of unease, but the wildly melodramatic ending undermines an otherwise effective production. DP

Claude Rains *John Jasper* • Douglass Montgomery *Neville Landless* • Heather Angel *Rosa Bud* • David Manners *Edwin Drood* • Valerie Hobson *Helena Landless* • Francis L Sullivan *Mr Crisparkle* • Walter Kingsford *Hiram Grewigious* • EE Clive *Thomas Sapsea* ■ *Dir* Stuart Walker • *Scr* John L Balderston, Gladys Unger, Leopold Atlas, Bradley King, from the novel by Charles Dickens

The Mystery of Edwin Drood ★ 15

Mystery 1993 · UK · Colour · 97mins

Filming Charles Dickens's unfinished novel presents two distinct, but equally difficult challenges: to capture the style of what is a decidedly atypical tome, and to devise a feasible finale. Timothy Forder fails to come close on either count, shooting the opening section with stuffy reverence with a static camera before launching into a hand-held Hammer pastiche that lacks both imagination and credibility. DP [video]

Robert Powell *John Jasper* • Nanette Newman *Mrs Crisparkle* • Gemma Craven *Miss Twinkleton* • Rosemary Leach *Mrs Tope* • Finty Williams *Rosa* • Glyn Houston *Grewgious* • Ronald Fraser *Dean* ■ *Dir* Timothy Forder • *Scr* Timothy Forder, from the novel by Charles Dickens

Mystery of the Wax Museum ★★★★ PG

Horror 1933 · US · Colour · 74mins

Lionel Atwill stars in this golden-era fright classic as a mad sculptor repopulating his burnt-down museum with wax-covered murder victims. Fay Wray supplies the screams (as she did so memorably in *King Kong* in the same year), plus the magic moment where she cracks Atwill's false face to reveal the scars beneath. Glenda Farrell also shines, as a wise-cracking reporter. The inspiration for the later *House of Wax*, this *Grand Guignol* outing boasts fabulous sets, zippy pacing, surprising frankness and marvellously evocative early two-strip Technicolor. AJ [video] DVD

Lionel Atwill *Ivan Igor* • Fay Wray *Charlotte Duncan* • Glenda Farrell *Florence Dempsey* • Frank McHugh *Jim* • Gavin Gordon *Harold Winton* • Edwin Maxwell *Joe Worth* ■ *Dir* Michael Curtiz • *Scr* Don Mullally, Carl

M

Erickson, from a play by Charles S Belden [Charles Belden] • *Art Director* Anton F Grot [Anton Grot]

Mystery Science Theater 3000: the Movie ★★★ PG

Science-fiction comedy
1996 · US · Colour · 70mins

In this big-screen version of the long-running American cable TV series, we eavesdrop on Michael J Nelson and his two robot friends (voiced by Trace Beaulieu and Kevin Murphy) as they watch the 1950s sci-fi movie *This Island Earth*. Nelson and the droids are adept at poking fun at the bad movies they're forced to watch by evil scientist Dr Forrester (Beaulieu again), though *This Island Earth* is cut above the vast majority of films featured on the original TV show. ST

Trace Beaulieu *Dr Clayton Forrester/Crow T Robot* • Michael J Nelson *Mike Nelson* • Jim Mallon *Gypsy* • Kevin Murphy *Tom Servo* • John Brady *Benkitnorf* ■ *Dir* Jim Mallon • *Scr* Michael J Nelson, Trace Beaulieu, Jim Mallon, Kevin Wagner Murphy [Kevin Murphy], Mary Jo Pehl, Paul Chaplin, Bridget Jones, from the TV series by Joel Hodgson

Mystery Street ★★★

Crime thriller 1950 · US · Colour · 92mins

MGM's B-movies were quite unlike any other studio's: they had a professional, glossy look to them and often featured players who would be quite at home in costlier fare. This is a rattlingly good example: a tight little caper tale expertly directed by John Sturges, who over the next decade-and-a-half would be producing such heavyweight movies as *Gunfight at the OK Corral*, *The Magnificent Seven* and *The Great Escape*. Sturges does well by the Boston setting, and he's helped by an expert cast headed by the versatile Ricardo Montalban. TS

Ricardo Montalban *Lieutenant Peter Moralas* • Sally Forrest *Grace Shanway* • Bruce Bennett *Dr McAdoo* • Elsa Lanchester *Mrs Smerrling* • Marshall Thompson *Henry Shanway* • Jan Sterling *Vivian Heldon* ■ *Dir* John Sturges • *Scr* Sydney Boehm, Richard Brooks, from a story by Leonard Spiegelgass

N

Mystery Submarine ★ U

Spy drama 1950 · US · BW · 78mins

Of interest only to close observers of the career of its director, Douglas Sirk, this minor work was his first as a contract director at Universal. The extravagant plot has Robert Douglas's U-boat captain, who has survived the Second World War in South America along with his vessel, kidnapping a German atomic scientist and offering him for sale to a foreign power. Fortunately, Macdonald Carey's US agent has infiltrated the crew. AE

Macdonald Carey *Dr Brett Young* • Marta Toren *Madeline Brenner* • Robert Douglas *Comdr Eric Von Molter* • Carl Esmond *Lt Heldman* • Ludwig Donath *Dr Adolph Guernitz* ■ *Dir* Douglas Sirk • *Scr* George W George, George F Slavin, from a story by George W George, George F Slavin, Ralph Dietrich

Mystery Train ★★★★ 15

Comedy drama
1989 · US/Jpn · Colour · 105mins

Demonstrating his customary, quirky genius for character, director Jim Jarmusch effortlessly weaves together three stories set in a moth-eaten Memphis hotel, which is little more than a seedy shrine to Elvis Presley, whose spirit pervades the entire picture. The scenes involving Japanese rock pilgrims Masatoshi Nagase and Youki Kudoh are a delight, while the postmortem into Joe Strummer and Steve Buscemi's bungled robbery is tantamount to a Tarantino prototype. Capping the lot are the exchanges between night clerk Screamin' Jay Hawkins and bellboy Cinque Lee. DP. In English and Japanese with subtitles. Contains violence, swearing, nudity and drug abuse. DVD

Masatoshi Nagase *Jun* • Youki Kudoh *Mitzuko* • Screamin' Jay Hawkins *Night clerk* • Cinqué Lee *Bellboy* • Nicoletta Braschi *Luisa* • Elizabeth Bracco *Dee Dee* • Joe Strummer *Johnny* • Steve Buscemi *Charlie* • Tom Waits *Voice of radio DJ* ■ *Dir/Scr* Jim Jarmusch

The Mystic Masseur ★★★ PG

Period satirical drama
2001 · UK/Ind · Colour · 113mins

Ismail Merchant's previous directorial offerings have been tainted by a tendency to gild the lily. But while this adaptation of VS Naipaul's novel is admirably restrained in its depiction of Asian society in Trinidad, it misses the nuances of the original prose and instead opts for broad satire. Aasif Mandvi's rise from poet to politician seems more like a pantomime than a parable, with Om Puri reduced to caricature as the village grocer seduced by his son-in-law's celebrity. Entertaining enough. DP DVD

Om Puri *Ramlogan* • James Fox *Mr Stewart* • Aasif Mandvi *Ganesh* • Sanjeev Bhaskar *Beharry* • Ayesha Dharkar *Leela* ■ *Dir* Ismail Merchant • *Scr* Caryl Phillips, from the novel by VS Naipaul

Mystic Pizza ★★★★ 15

Romantic comedy
1988 · US · Colour · 103mins

This features one of Julia Roberts's first major roles, and it's still one of her best. It follows the ups and downs of Roberts, pal Lili Taylor and sister Annabeth Gish, who get into trouble with love while working at a pizza parlour in their home town of Mystic, Connecticut. Donald Petrie serves up a fine coming-of-age tale, interlacing the story of the girls' problems of the heart with some delightfully comic moments and astute observations about romance. JB. Contains sex scenes, swearing. DVD

Julia Roberts *Daisy Araujo* • Annabeth Gish *Kat Araujo* • Lili Taylor *Jojo Barboza* • Vincent Phillip D'Onofrio [Vincent D'Onofrio] *Bill Montijo* • William R Moses *Tim Travers* • Adam Storke *Charles Gordon Winsor* • Conchata Ferrell *Leona Valsouano* • Joanna Merlin *Margaret* ■ *Dir* Donald Petrie • *Scr* Amy Jones [Amy Holden Jones], Perry Howze, Randy Howze, Alfred Uhry, from a story by Amy Jones [Amy Holden Jones]

Mystic River ★★★★ 15

Murder mystery drama
2003 · US/Aus · Colour · 132mins

This ambitious, well-crafted adult drama is a welcome return to form for Clint Eastwood the director. It features sterling performances from an excellent cast and only just misses greatness by a whisker. Sean Penn, Tim Robbins and Kevin Bacon play childhood friends whose lives are shattered when Penn's daughter is brutally murdered, an event that forces them to confront a horrific episode from their own shared past. Eastwood directs with crisp efficiency but Brian Helgeland's screenplay somehow fails to convince, emerging as a sequence of well-written individual scenes rather than an integrated whole, while the plot relies too much on coincidence. Judged to the highest standards then, this is a flawed piece of work, but it still ranks as must-see, grown-up cinema. AS. Contains swearing and violence. DVD

Sean Penn *Jimmy Markum* • Tim Robbins *Dave Boyle* • Kevin Bacon *Sean Devine* • Laurence Fishburne *Whitey Powers* • Marcia Gay Harden *Celeste Boyle* • Laura Linney *Annabeth Markum* • Kevin Chapman *Val Savage* • Emmy Rossum *Katie Markum* • Spencer Treat Clark *Silent Ray Harris* • Tom Guiry *Brendan Harris* ■ *Dir* Clint Eastwood • *Scr* Brian Helgeland, from the novel by Dennis Lehane

The Myth of Fingerprints ★★★★ 15

Drama 1996 · US · Colour · 86mins

Julianne Moore and *ER's* Noah Wyle are two of four grown-up siblings who return to their New England home for the traditional Thanksgiving dinner. Cue the airing of family grudges, secrets and emotions in this sly and subdued drama from writer/director Bart Freundlich. Blythe Danner and Roy Scheider stand out as the overwrought parents, but what is most attractive about the film is that it offers no jaw-dropping revelations or happily-ever-after resolutions. Instead it allows us to draw our own conclusions. JB. Contains swearing, sex scenes.

Roy Scheider *Hal* • Julianne Moore *Mia* • Blythe Danner *Lena* • Noah Wyle *Warren* • Hope Davis *Margaret* • James LeGros *Cezanne* • Brian Kerwin *Elliot* • Laurel Holloman *Leigh* ■ *Dir/Scr* Bart Freundlich

Na Tum Jaano Na Hum ★★★ PG

Romantic drama
2002 · Ind · Colour · 158mins

Actor Arjun Sablok makes his feature directorial debut with this old-fashioned tale of a romantic triangle. It's certainly a stellar affair, with all three leads being the offspring of established stars. Playing an introvert with a heart of gold, Hrithik Roshan makes the perfect foil for Saif Ali Khan, the brash go-getter with a callous approach to women – that is, until he falls for Esha Deol, a dreamer who is convinced that love is a matter of divine intervention. This is pure corn, but its heart is in the right place. DP. In Hindi with English subtitles. DVD

Saif Ali Khan *Akshay* • Hrithik Roshan *Rahul* • Esha Deol *Esha* ■ *Dir/Scr* Arjun Sablok

Naach ★★ PG

Musical romantic drama
2004 · Ind · Colour · 140mins

Simply shot but technically sound, this charts the growing relationship between struggling actor Abhishek Bachchan and aspiring choreographer Antara Mali, as they both try to further their careers in the competitive world of the Hindi film industry. Talented cinematographer (and co-director) Kiran Reddy paints every scene with cloying emotion, but the absence of chemistry between the two leads and a dreary screenplay scupper the film. OA. A Hindi language film.

Abhishek Bachchan *Abhi* • Antara Mali *Rewa* ■ *Dir* Ram Gopal Varma, Kiran Reddy

Nada ★★★★ 18

Political crime drama
1974 · Fr/It · Colour · 106mins

Claude Chabrol here adopts the style of the exciting political thrillers of Costa-Gavras, though he adds his special brand of cynicism and black humour and refuses to take sides. Nada, the Spanish for "nothing", is the name of a group of anarchists who decide to kidnap the American ambassador in Paris during his weekly visit to a high-class bordello. Conflicts grow within the group and among the police, who are viewed as the flip side of the same coin. This rather overlong film came as a surprise after Chabrol's series of murder stories featuring his wife, Stéphane Audran. RB. In French with English subtitles.

Fabio Testi *Buenaventura Diaz* • Michel Duchaussoy *Marcel Treufais* • Maurice Garrel *André Epaulard* • Michel Aumont *Goémond* • Lou Castel *D'Arey* ■ *Dir* Claude Chabrol • *Scr* Claude Chabrol, Jean-Patrick Manchette, from a novel by Jean-Patrick Manchette

Nadine ★★ PG

Comedy thriller 1987 · US · Colour · 79mins

Director Robert Benton scores something of a misfire with this well-intentioned but uneven comedy. The story of a manicurist who witnesses a murder and teams up with her soon-to-be ex-husband to solve the crime has its moments. But the problems lie mainly with Kim Basinger and Jeff Bridges, neither of whom makes this broad comedy work. JB. Contains violence and swearing. [video]

Jeff Bridges *Vernon Hightower* • Kim Basinger *Nadine Hightower* • Rip Torn *Buford Pope* • Gwen Verdon *Vera* • Glenne Headly *Renee* • Jerry Stiller *Raymond Escobar* • Jay Patterson *Dwight Estes* ■ *Dir/Scr* Robert Benton

Nadja ★★★★ 15

Horror 1995 · US · BW · 88mins

David Lynch (who pops up in a cameo as a mortuary attendant) executive-produced this erotic vampire thriller, stylishly shot in black and white. Elina Lowensohn is the Nadja of the title, an enthusiastic creature of the night who just happens to be the daughter of Dracula. She prowls the clubs of New York for her prey, but vampire-hunter Van Helsing (Peter Fonda) is on her trail. It's a bizarre update of the vampire legend by independent film-maker Michael Almereyda, a deft hand at powerful visual images. JB [video]

Elina Lowensohn *Nadja* • Suzy Amis *Cassandra* • Peter Fonda *Dracula/Dr Van Helsing* • Martin Donovan (2) *Jim* • Galaxy Craze *Lucy* • Karl Geary *Renfield* • Jared Harris *Edgar* ■ *Dir/Scr* Michael Almereyda

Naked ★★★★ 18

Drama 1993 · UK · Colour · 125mins

Mike Leigh prowls new working class territory with this grim tale about a Mancunian misfit who turns up at his ex-girlfriend's London flat and proceeds to tell the naked truth regarding the city's uncaring society by lashing out unmercifully at everyone he meets. David Thewlis is outstanding as a deeply nasty 1990s version of Alfie, and Leigh's bravura mix of comedy, tragedy, violence and warmth marks this uncompromising exposé as British film-making at its finest. AJ. Contains swearing, drug abuse and nudity. [video]

David Thewlis *Johnny* • Lesley Sharp *Louise* • Katrin Cartlidge *Sophie* • Greg Cruttwell *Jeremy* • Claire Skinner *Sandra* • Peter Wight *Brian* • Ewen Bremner *Archie* • Susan Vidler *Maggie* ■ *Dir/Scr* Mike Leigh

Naked Alibi ★★

Crime drama 1954 · US · BW · 85mins

After he is dismissed for harassing suburban baker Gene Barry whom he's convinced is a violent killer, senior cop Sterling Hayden continues to hunt his quarry. When he finds himself in trouble in a Mexican bordertown, he is helped by Barry's girlfriend Gloria Grahame. Directed by Jerry Hopper, this mix of detective thriller, gangster movie and *film noir* starts promisingly enough but degenerates about a third of the way through as a result of a derivative screenplay and some unconvincing characterisation. RK

Sterling Hayden *Joseph Conroy* • Gloria Grahame *Marianna* • Gene Barry *Al Willis* • Marcia Henderson *Helen Willis* • Casey Adams [Max Showalter] *Lieutenant Parks* • Billy Chapin *Petey* • Chuck Connors *Captain Owen Kincaide* ■ *Dir* Jerry Hopper • *Scr* Lawrence Roman, from the story *Cry Copper* by J Robert Breen, Gladys Atwater

The Naked and the Dead ★★★ PG

Second World War drama
1958 · US · Colour · 130mins

Since it was clearly impossible to film the vigorous intensity, not to mention the language, of Norman Mailer's superb antiwar first novel, director Raoul Walsh opted for a virtual remake of his 1955 hit *Battle Cry*, but this time the characters are not realistic enough. Aldo Ray is the sadistic sergeant, handling most of the diatribes and virtually holding the long movie together by himself. The battle scenes are fine and shot through a green night filter. TS [video]

Aldo Ray *Croft* • Cliff Robertson *Hearn* • Raymond Massey *General Cummings* • Lili St Cyr *Lily* • Barbara Nichols *Mildred* • William Campbell *Brown* • Richard Jaeckel *Gallagher* • James Best *Ridges* • Joey Bishop *Roth* ■ *Dir* Raoul Walsh • *Scr* Denis Sanders, Terry Sanders, from the novel by Norman Mailer • *Cinematographer* Joseph LaShelle

Naked as Nature Intended ★★ 15

Documentary drama
1961 · UK · Colour · 64mins

Not the first British nudie, but easily the most celebrated, its title still common parlance even if everything else about it is forgotten. In its day, this first feature film by glamour photographer George Harrison Marks was a sensation. It comes as a surprise to find that it consists almost entirely of a prettily photographed travelogue. A group of attractive young women, one of whom is Marks's mistress and muse Pamela Green, travels to Cornwall. There are dire comic interludes along the way, and only in the last 20 minutes do the girls romp in the nude. DM [video]

Pamela Green • Jackie Salt • Petrina Forsyth • Bridget Leonard • Angela Jones • Stuart Samuels • Guy Kingsley-Poynter *Narrator* ■ *Dir* George Harrison Marks

The Naked City ★★★★

Crime drama 1948 · US · BW · 95mins

Hugely influential, thanks to its innovative documentary-style and character-driven treatment of an otherwise conventional cop drama (murdered blonde in bathtub, homicide squad gets moving). The movie is hard-hitting, gripping and a hymn to the excitement of New York City, where it was shot entirely on location. Narrated by its producer, former crime reporter Mark Hellinger, it stars Barry Fitzgerald as the police lieutenant heading the investigation. There were Oscars for cinematography and editing, and the voiceover proclaiming "there are eight million stories in the naked city" passed into popular culture, thanks to the long-running TV series. RK

Barry Fitzgerald *Lt Dan Muldoon* • Howard Duff *Frank Niles* • Dorothy Hart *Ruth Morrison* • Don Taylor *Jimmy Halloran* • Ted De Corsia *Garzah* • House Jameson *Dr Stoneman* • Mark Hellinger *Narrator* ■ *Dir* Jules Dassin • *Scr* Albert Maltz, Malvin Wald, from a story by Malvin Wald • *Music* Miklos Rozsa, Frank Skinner • *Cinematographer* William H Daniels • *Editor* Paul Weatherwax

The Naked Country ★★★ 18

Thriller 1985 · Aus · Colour · 87mins

Set in the Australian outback, this is a gripping outdoors thriller from Tim Burstall, one of the key directors of the 1970s "new wave". Based on the novel by Morris West, it's about a ranch owner who gets caught up in a bitter struggle with an unruly tribe of Aborigines. Burstall conjures up a taut, well paced drama that builds up nicely to a tense chase climax. NF [video]

John Stanton *Lance Dillon* • Rebecca Gilling *Mary Dillon* • Ivar Kants *Sergeant Neil Adams* • Tommy Lewis *Mundaru* • Simon Chilvers *Inspector Poole* • John Jarratt *Mick Conrad* ■ *Dir* Tim Burstall • *Scr* Ross Dimsey, Tim Burstall, from the novel by Morris West

The Naked Dawn ★★★

Crime drama 1955 · US · Colour · 82mins

Arthur Kennedy plays the likeable Mexican bandit whose booty tempts the impoverished farmer he befriends, and whose way of life appeals to the farmer's dissatisfied young wife. This character study was made on a shoestring in Mexico by the low-budget maestro Edgar G Ulmer, who shapes the material into a moving study of salvation. It could have been an intense, brooding piece, but it's shot in colour and displays a generosity of spirit that is ultimately moving. AE

Arthur Kennedy *Santiago* • Betta St John *Maria* • Eugene Iglesias *Manuel* • Charlita *Tita* • Roy Engel *Guntz* ■ *Dir* Edgar G Ulmer • *Scr* Nina Schneider, Herman Schneider (fronts for Julian Zimet)

The Naked Earth ★★

Adventure 1958 · UK · BW · 96mins

The husky-voiced French singer Juliette Greco, protégée of studio boss Darryl F Zanuck, livens up this slow-paced saga with her volatile personality and offbeat looks. She plays the former whore who teams up with Richard Todd's penniless Irishman and helps him grow tobacco in Uganda in 1895. When they fail to harvest the crop, he takes up shooting crocodiles for their skins. Milton Holmes's intelligent script deserved a more interesting lead and a less plodding director. AE

Richard Todd *Danny* • Juliette Greco *Maria* • John Kitzmiller *David* • Finlay Currie *Father Verity* • Laurence Naismith *Skin trader* ■ *Dir* Vincent Sherman • *Scr* Milton Holmes, Harold Buchman (uncredited)

The Naked Edge ★★

Mystery thriller 1961 · UK · BW · 103mins

This bleak and undistinguished thriller, about an American businessman based in London whose wife (Deborah Kerr) comes to suspect him of murder, marked a most unfitting end to Gary Cooper's illustrious career. The actor died shortly after giving one last wooden performance and floundering among the plot's red herrings. RK

Gary Cooper *George Radcliffe* • Deborah Kerr *Martha Radcliffe* • Eric Portman *Jeremy Clay* • Diane Cilento *Mrs Heath* • Hermione Gingold *Lilly Harris* • Peter Cushing *Mr Wrack* • Michael Wilding *Morris Brooke* • Ray McAnally *Donald Heath* ■ *Dir* Michael Anderson • *Scr* Joseph Stefano, from the novel *First Train to Babylon* by Max Ehrlich

The Naked Face ★★ 18

Crime thriller 1984 · US · Colour · 100mins

Psychiatrist Roger Moore is the prime suspect when one of his patients is murdered in director Bryan Forbes's tepid adaptation of an early Sidney Sheldon bestseller. When it becomes clear he's the next target, he takes the law into his own hands to unmask the killer, despite the suspicions of cops Rod Steiger and Elliott Gould. Reasonably well-acted, the complex plot has too many red herrings to be completely satisfying. AJ. Contains swearing, violence and brief nudity. [video]

Roger Moore *Dr Judd Stevens* • Rod Steiger *Lieutenant McGreavy* • Elliott Gould *Angeli* • Art Carney *Morgens* • Anne Archer *Ann Blake* • David Hedison *Dr Hadley* • Deanna Dunagan *Mrs Hadley* ■ *Dir* Bryan Forbes • *Scr* Bryan Forbes, from the novel by Sidney Sheldon

Naked Fury ★ U

Crime drama 1959 · UK · BW · 64mins

As with many other crime capers of the late 1950s, this gives the impression of being a routine TV episode that has had a bit of money thrown at it. This is a sordid little tale about a gang of safe-crackers who are forced to kill a night watchman and kidnap his daughter to make good their escape. Journeyman director Charles Saunders and his willing cast are left high and dry by the desperate script. DP

Leigh Madison *Carol* • Reed De Rouen *Eddy* • Kenneth Cope *Johnny* • Arthur Lovegrove *Syd* • Thomas Eytle *Steve* • Alexander Field *Vic* ■ *Dir* Charles Saunders • *Scr* Brock Williams, from a story by Guido Coen

The Naked Gun ★★★★★ 15

Comedy 1988 · US · Colour · 81mins

The team behind *Airplane!* first turned their wicked talents on to the police force with the short-lived cult TV series *Police Squad!*, but it took this feature-length version to make Leslie Nielsen's inspired Frank Drebin a worldwide star. He remains wonderfully stone-faced as he proceeds to wreak havoc in Los Angeles while investigating the shooting of a colleague. The supporting players – George Kennedy as his captain and Priscilla Presley as the equally clumsy love interest – are delightfully deadpan, and the determinedly juvenile gags never stop flowing. JF. Contains swearing. [video] DVD

Leslie Nielsen *Lieutenant Frank Drebin* • Priscilla Presley *Jane Spencer* • Ricardo Montalban *Vincent Ludwig* • George Kennedy *Captain Ed Hocken* • OJ Simpson *Nordberg* • Nancy Marchand *Mayor* ■ *Dir* David Zucker • *Scr* Jerry Zucker, Jim Abrahams, David Zucker, Pat Proft, from the TV series *Police Squad!* by David Zucker, Jerry Zucker, Jim Abrahams

The Naked Gun 2½: the Smell of Fear ★★★★ 15

Comedy 1991 · US · Colour · 81mins

This second instalment from the files of *Police Squad* is deliriously funny. Leslie Nielsen, as the steadfastly stupid Frank Drebin, starts off by wrecking a White House reception, then proceeds to blunder his way through an investigation into a group of corrupt businessmen plotting to stave off radical new changes to the energy industry. Many of the original cast return for this sequel, and while it's not quite up to the standard set by the first film, it's still a treat. AJ. Contains swearing. [video] DVD

Leslie Nielsen *Lieutenant Frank Drebin* • Priscilla Presley *Jane Spencer* • George Kennedy *Ed Hocken* • Robert Goulet *Quentin Hapsburg* • Richard Griffiths *Dr Meinheimer/Earl Hacker* • OJ Simpson *Nordberg* • Anthony James *Hector Savage* • Lloyd Bochner *Baggett* • Tim O'Connor *Fenzwick* ■ *Dir* David Zucker • *Scr* David Zucker, Pat Proft, from the TV series *Police Squad!* by David Zucker, Jerry Zucker, Jim Abrahams

N

Naked Gun 33⅓: the Final Insult ★★★★ 12

Comedy 1994 · US · Colour · 79mins

The first two *Naked Guns* were comedy classics, but this is only very, very funny. Leslie Nielsen and the team return for another endearingly silly, gag-filled spoof in which house-husband Frank Drebin comes out of retirement to pursue a lethal bomber. Although it trades a little too casually on the jokes and slapstick of the first two, Nielsen delivers another wonderfully deadpan performance, and there are a host of neat cameos. JF. Contains swearing. [video] DVD

Leslie Nielsen *Lieutenant Frank Drebin* • Priscilla Presley *Jane Spencer* • George Kennedy *Ed Hocken* • OJ Simpson *Nordberg* • Fred Ward *Rocco* • Kathleen Freeman *Muriel* • Anna Nicole Smith *Tanya* • Ellen Greene *Louise* ■ *Dir* Peter Segal • *Scr* David Zucker, Pat Proft, Robert LoCash, from the TV series *Police Squad!* by David Zucker, Jerry Zucker, Jim Abrahams

Naked in New York ★★★ 15

Romantic comedy
1994 · US · Colour · 87mins

Daniel Algrant got Martin Scorsese to executive produce his autobiographical first feature – in other words, help raise the money and encourage some big names to guest star. The story is slight enough: Eric Stoltz grows up without a dad, decides to be a playwright and becomes a magnet to women. But it's the guest appearances that make the most impact – Tony

Curtis, Timothy Dalton and Kathleen Turner, camping it up as a Broadway star. AT [video]

Eric Stoltz *Jake Briggs* • Mary-Louise Parker *Joanne White* • Ralph Macchio *Chris* • Jill Clayburgh *Shirley Briggs* • Tony Curtis *Carl Fisher* • Timothy Dalton *Elliot Price* • Kathleen Turner *Dana Coles* • Whoopi Goldberg *Tragedy Mask* • Quentin Crisp ■ *Dir* Dan Algrant [Daniel Algrant] • *Scr* Dan Algrant [Daniel Algrant], John Warren

The Naked Jungle ★★★★

Adventure drama 1953 · US · Colour · 93mins

Charlton Heston is the South American plantation owner battling both his red-haired wife (Eleanor Parker) and a plague of red ants, which provides a spectacular climax to this riveting tale directed by Byron Haskin (*The War of the Worlds*). Both an adventure and a thought-provoking drama, the movie is beautifully photographed by Ernest Laszlo and remains one of Heston's most interesting early films. JB

Eleanor Parker *Joanna Leiningen* • Charlton Heston *Christopher Leiningen* • William Conrad *Commissioner* • Romo Vincent *Boat captain* • Douglas Fowley *Medicine man* • John Dierkes *Gruber* • Leonard Strong *Kutina* ■ *Dir* Byron Haskin • *Scr* Philip Yordan (front for Ben Maddow), Ranald MacDougall, from the story *Leiningen versus the Ants* by Carl Stephenson

The Naked Kiss ★★★★ 18

Cult drama 1964 · US · BW · 86mins

This is a typically bleak and brutal tale from maverick American independent director Samuel Fuller, who this time turns his cynical eye to the corrupt values lurking beneath small-town life. Constance Towers gives a dignified performance as a former prostitute who attempts to build a new life in a new town, but finds her past coming back to haunt her when she tries to establish a relationship with the local leading citizen. The storyline is pure melodrama, but the harsh photography and startling images make this a cult classic. JF [video] DVD

Constance Towers *Kelly* • Anthony Eisley *Griff* • Michael Dante *Grant* • Virginia Grey *Candy* • Patsy Kelly *Mac* • Betty Bronson *Miss Josephine* • Marie Devereux *Buff* • Karen Conrad *Dusty* ■ *Dir/Scr* Samuel Fuller • *Cinematographer* Stanley Cortez

Naked Lies ★★ 18

Thriller 1997 · US · Colour · 89mins

Formulaic, straight-to-video fare, spiced up with bit of sex and nudity. Shannon Tweed plays a tough FBI agent who is suspended from duty when she accidentally kills a child during a drugs bust. With her career at a crossroads, she finds herself falling for an international counterfeiter. JF. Contains violence, swearing, sex scenes and nudity. [video] DVD

Shannon Tweed *Cara Landry* • Fernando Allende *Damian Medina* • Steven Bauer *Kevin Dowd* • Hugo Stiglitz *Santiago* ■ *Dir* Ralph Portillo • *Scr* D Alvelo

Naked Lunch ★★★ 18

Fantasy drama
1991 · UK/Can · Colour · 110mins

This is one to admire more than enjoy – only horror maestro David Cronenberg could have filmed William S Burroughs's notorious cult novel as an intellectual paranoid acid trip through the creative writing process. Cronenberg underlines Burroughs's autobiographical concerns over abuses of power (metaphorically disguised as fantasy drug addiction and surreal sexual acts), crafting a uniquely slanted mind-blower with more than a hint of highbrow inaccessibility. AJ. Contains violence, swearing, sex scenes, drug abuse, nudity. [video] DVD

Peter Weller *William Lee* • Judy Davis *Joan Frost/Joan Lee* • Ian Holm *Tom Frost* • Julian Sands *Yves Cloquet* • Roy Scheider *Dr Benway* • Monique Mercure *Fadela* • Nicholas Campbell *Hank* • Michael Zelniker *Martin* ■ *Dir* David Cronenberg • *Scr* David Cronenberg, from the novel by William S Burroughs

The Naked Maja ★★

Biographical drama
1959 · US/It · Colour · 111mins

Despite the title, there's nothing particularly revelatory in this account of the life of the Spanish painter Goya (Anthony Franciosa), who grew from peasant stock to become a painter of royalty. The script revolves around Goya's scandalous nude portrait of a duchess (Ava Gardner), but director Henry Koster gives no more than a surface gloss to the proceedings. Movies about artists were all the rage at the time, but this one is a still life in more ways than one. TH

Ava Gardner *Duchess of Alba* • Anthony Franciosa *Francisco Goya* • Amedeo Nazzari *Manuel Godoy* • Gino Cervi *King Carlos IV* • Lea Padovani *Queen Maria Luisa* ■ *Dir* Henry Koster, Mario Russo • *Scr* Norman Corwin, Giorgio Prosperi, from a story by Oscar Saul, Talbot Jennings

The Naked Man ★★ 15

Comedy drama 1998 · US · Colour · 93mins

Shades of *Barton Fink*'s film-within-a-film colour this misfiring comedy, which is hardly surprising since it was co-scripted by Ethan Coen and debutant director J Todd Anderson, who has been the Coens' storyboard artist since *Raising Arizona*. Some credit is due to Michael Rapaport for attempting such a cockeyed performance as the small-town chiropractor who masquerades as a wrestler in his spare time. But his potentially amusing feud with spine-gnarled pharmaceutical tycoon Michael Jeter stubbornly refuses to spark into life. DP [video]

Michael Rapaport *Dr Edward Bliss Jr* • Michael Jeter *Sticks Varona* • Arija Bareikis *Kim Bliss* • Joe Grifasi *Lt Albert Karski* • John Slattery *Ferris* • Rachael Leigh Cook *Delores* ■ *Dir* J Todd Anderson • *Scr* J Todd Anderson, Ethan Coen

The Naked Prey ★★★ PG

Period adventure 1966 · US · Colour · 91mins

Filmed entirely in South Africa, this offbeat adventure was directed by ex-matinée idol Cornel Wilde, who also stars as a 19th-century white hunter whose safari expedition is captured and tortured by tribesmen. Set free in a skimpy loincloth that would make even Johnny Weissmuller blush, Wilde is then relentlessly hunted down like prey. Bolstered by a documentary-style realism, if dated in its stereotypes, this remains a riveting tale of survival against the odds. Wilde gives a fine performance, despite being ill for much of the filming. RS [video]

Cornel Wilde *Man* • Gert Van Den Bergh *Second man* • Ken Gampu *Warrior leader* • Patrick Mynhardt *Safari overseer* ■ *Dir* Cornel Wilde • *Scr* Clint Johnston, Don Peters

The Naked Runner ★★ PG

Spy drama 1967 · UK · Colour · 99mins

This Stanley Mann-scripted slice of Cold War shenanigans is bland, thanks to unappealing characters and a far-fetched narrative. Frank Sinatra stars as a wartime crack shot reluctantly reactivated for an assassination plot in East Germany; Edward Fox and Peter Vaughan represent British intelligence. Sidney J Furie's gimmicky direction is jarring, while Sinatra can do nothing with a monotonous role that merely requires him to be shunted around like a pawn on a chessboard. RS [video]

Frank Sinatra *Sam Laker* • Peter Vaughan *Martin Slattery* • Derren Nesbitt *Colonel Hartmann* • Nadia Gray *Karen Gisevius* • Toby Robins *Ruth* • Inger Stratton *Anna* • Cyril Luckham *Cabinet minister* • Edward Fox *Ritchie Jackson* ■ *Dir* Sidney J Furie • *Scr* Stanley Mann, from the novel by Francis Clifford

Naked Souls ★ 18

Erotic science-fiction thriller
1995 · US · Colour · 81mins

Pamela Anderson's main assets unsurprisingly play a prominent role in this daft erotic science-fiction thriller. The pneumatic former *Baywatch* babe portrays an artist – don't laugh – whose geeky scientist boyfriend Brian Krause gets into trouble when he starts playing around with the memories of dead serial killers and messing with sinister rival David Warner. JF. Contains violence, sex scenes, swearing, nudity. [video] DVD

Pamela Anderson Lee [Pamela Anderson] *Britanny "Brit" Clark* • Brian Krause *Edward Adams* • David Warner *Everett Longstreet* • Dean Stockwell *Duncan Ellis* ■ *Dir* Lyndon Chubbuck • *Scr* Frank Dietz

The Naked Spur ★★★

Western 1953 · US · Colour · 91mins

In the third of the great collaborations between James Stewart and director Anthony Mann, Stewart stars as a neurotic bounty hunter on the trail of Robert Ryan, hoping to make enough money to buy a ranch in California, but threatened by madness. This melodramatic western aspires to Greek or Shakespearean tragedy and, set in the truly Olympian Rocky Mountains of Colorado, the characters look suitably puny and pitiful. Janet Leigh, however, looks gorgeous. AT

James Stewart *Howard Kemp* • Robert Ryan *Ben Vandergroat* • Janet Leigh *Lina Patch* • Ralph Meeker *Roy Anderson* • Millard Mitchell *Jesse Tate* ■ *Dir* Anthony Mann • *Scr* Sam Rolfe, Harold Jack Bloom

The Naked Street ★★

Crime drama 1955 · US · BW · 84mins

In this lurid melodrama, Anthony Quinn is the racketeer who, not unlike Paul Muni in *Scarface*, has an almost unhealthy fixation with his sister, played by Anne Bancroft. When she becomes pregnant by Farley Granger's two-bit hood, Quinn gets him off a murder rap and tries to make him go straight. Writer/director Maxwell Shane draws effective performances from his three lead players but the contrived plot deprives this of tragic force. AE

Farley Granger *Nicky Bradna* • Anthony Quinn *Phil Regal* • Anne Bancroft *Rosalie Regalzyk* • Peter Graves (2) *Joe McFarland* • Else Neft *Mrs Regalzyk* • Jerry Paris *Latzi Franks* • Frank Sully *Nutsy* • John Dennis *Big Eddie* ■ *Dir* Maxwell Shane • *Scr* Maxwell Shane, from a story by Leo Katcher

Naked Tango ★★ 18

Erotic thriller 1990 · US/Arg · Colour · 88mins

An overheated and rather silly melodrama set in Argentina in the days when Rudolph Valentino was "tango-ing" a swooning female audience. Mathilda May is the young wife en route to South America who takes on a new identity and ends up being fought over by gangster Esai Morales and "dirty dancer" Vincent D'Onofrio. It's beautifully designed, and the much put-upon May delivers a sensual performance. Unfortunately, D'Onofrio lacks charisma and writer/director Leonard Schrader's script is dripping with pretension. JF. Contains swearing, violence, sex scenes and nudity. [video]

Vincent D'Onofrio *Cholo* • Mathilda May *Stephanie/Alba* • Esai Morales *Zico Borenstein* • Fernando Rey *Judge Torres* • Josh Mostel *Bertoni the jeweller* ■ *Dir* Leonard Schrader • *Scr* Leonard Schrader, from the works of Manuel Puig

The Naked Truth ★★★★ U

Black comedy 1957 · UK · BW · 88mins

An early Peter Sellers comedy that supplied him with some of his funniest and finest material. He plays a crowd-pleasing TV host who's being blackmailed by smarmy Dennis Price, editor of a muck-raking magazine. Terry-Thomas and Peggy Mount are among the victims who gang up against their persecutor. Based on class and sex, as the best British humour often is, it's satisfyingly scripted by Michael Pertwee and directed with superb timing by Mario Zampi. TH [video] DVD

Peter Sellers *Sonny MacGregor* • Terry-Thomas *Lord Mayley* • Peggy Mount *Flora Ransom* • Dennis Price *Michael Dennis* • Shirley Eaton *Belinda Wright* • Georgina Cookson *Lady Mayley* • Joan Sims *Ethel Ransom* ■ *Dir* Mario Zampi • *Scr* Michael Pertwee

Naked Werewolf Woman ★★ 18

Erotic horror 1976 · It · Colour · 89mins

Annik Borel believes she's the reincarnation of a wolf creature from two centuries ago in this delightfully silly sex, sleaze and horror outing. But it's only her sexual drive that's causing fur to grow all over her body as she runs around foaming at the mouth and killing people in nasty ways. Graphic blood-letting, obligatory lesbian and rape scenes, virtually nonexistent direction from Rino Di Silvestro and hilariously hairy special effects make this loser a schlock treat. AJ. Italian dialogue dubbed into English. [video]

Annik Borel *Daniela Messeri* • Frederick Stafford *Police inspector* • Tino Carraro *Count Messeri* ■ *Dir* Rino Di Silvestro • *Scr* Rino Di Silvestro, Howard Ross

The Name of the Rose ★★★★ 18

Period mystery
1986 · It/W Ger/Fr · Colour · 123mins

Sean Connery is in majestic form as the Franciscan friar who, with novice Christian Slater, investigates a series of murders in a remote 14th-century abbey, incurring the wrath of vicious inquisitor F Murray Abraham in the process. Director Jean-Jacques Annaud has decoded Umberto Eco's cryptic bestseller with an eye-blinkingly ornate visual style. While the inhabitants of the abbey are mostly as grotesque as gargoyles, the Holmesian figure of Connery dominates and elucidates with the kind of deductive brilliance that Conan Doyle's sleuth was to display centuries later. TH. Contains violence, nudity and a sex scene. [video] DVD

Sean Connery *William of Baskerville* • F Murray Abraham *Bernardo Gui* • Christian Slater *Adso of Melk* • Elya Baskin *Severinus* • Feodor Chaliapin Jr *Jorge de Burgos* • William Hickey *Ubertino de Casale* • Michael Lonsdale [Michel Lonsdale] *Abbot* • Ron Perlman *Salvatore* ■ *Dir* Jean-Jacques Annaud • *Scr* Andrew Birkin, Gerard Brach, Howard Franklin, Alain Godard, from the novel *Il Nome Della Rosa* by Umberto Eco

Namu, the Killer Whale ★★★ U

Adventure based on a true story
1966 · US · Colour · 88mins

Laslo Benedek directs this factually-based drama, superbly photographed on location in Puget Sound off the Washington State coast. The film follows the struggle of marine biologist Robert Lansing to prevent local fishermen from killing the trapped whale which is threatening their livelihood. The story can't fail to stir the emotions, but Benedek deserves credit for presenting the case for both sides with admirable fairness. DP

Robert Lansing *Hank Donner* • John Anderson *Joe Clausen* • Robin Mattson *Lisa Rand* • Richard Erdman *Deke* • Lee Meriwether *Kate Rand* ■ *Dir* Laslo Benedek • *Scr* Arthur Weiss • *Cinematographer* Lamar Boren

Nana ★★★

Silent period drama 1926 · Fr · BW · 161mins

JeanRenoir distils Zola's novel via just three characters, Nana, Vandeuvres and Muffat, while sumptuously re-creating the end of the Second Empire. The story follows Nana's brief success as an "actress", her period as a courtesan and grim death. Catherine Hessling, the director's wife, gives a somewhat laboured performance but there are many pleasures in this apprentice work. Although well received critically, *Nana* was badly distributed and cost Renoir a million francs of an inheritance from his father, whose influence is apparent in the film. BB

Catherine Hessling *Nana* • Werner Krauss *Comte Muffat* • Jean Angelo *Comte de Vandeuvres* • Raymond Guérin-Catelain *Georges Hugon* • Pierre Philippe [Pierre Lestringuez] *Bordenave* • Pierre Champagne *La Faloise* ■ *Dir* Jean Renoir • *Scr* Pierre Lestringuez, Jean Renoir, from the novel by Emile Zola

Nana ★★★ PG

Period romantic melodrama
1934 · US · BW · 83mins

Dorothy Arzner was one of the few women directors working in Hollywood during its Golden Age. Her films have recently been given a feminist slant, but it is hard to see this loose adaptation of Emile Zola's novel as anything other than pure melodrama. In place of Zola's gritty naturalism is producer Samuel Goldwyn's glossy sensationalism, as waif Anna Sten plunges into the seedy world of the French music hall and finds herself torn between amorous brothers Lionel Atwill and Phillips Holmes. DP [video]

Anna Sten *Nana* • Phillips Holmes *Lieutenant George Muffat* • Lionel Atwill *Colonel André Muffat* • Richard Bennett *Gaston Greiner* • Mae Clarke *Satin* • Muriel Kirkland *Mimi* ■ *Dir* Dorothy Arzner • *Scr* Willard Mack, Harry Wagstaff Gribble, from the novel by Emile Zola

Nana ★★

Period drama 1955 · Fr · Colour · 122mins

Emile Zola's gritty realism is virtually dispensed with altogether in favour of Second Empire opulence in this glossy adaptation. Never the most cerebral of directors, Christian-Jaque has produced an undemanding melodrama that spends a disproportionate amount of time eavesdropping on romantic trysts, at the expense of exploring the motives and emotions of Zola's complex characters. The director's passion for his then-wife, Martine Carol, is clearly evident. But the excellent Charles Boyer outshines her as the rich man she betrays. DP. French dialogue dubbed into English.

Charles Boyer *Count Muffat* • Martine Carol *Nana* • Walter Chiari *Fontan* • Jacques Castelot *Count de Vandeuvres* • Noël Roquevert *Steiner* • Paul Frankeur *Bordenave* ■ *Dir* Christian-Jaque • *Scr* Christian-Jaque, Henri Jeanson, Albert Valentin, Jean Ferry, from the novel by Emile Zola

Nancy Drew – Detective ★★★ U

Mystery adventure 1938 · US · BW · 66mins

Warners launched its four-film series based on Carolyn Keene's popular teenage mysteries, with the gymslip sleuth being played by Bonita Granville. Partnered by devoted sidekick Frankie Thomas, the gutsy Granville cracks cases with an energy and ingenuity that was typical of the studio's no-nonsense ethos. Here she tries to stop a house owned by two elderly ladies from falling into the hands of some ruthless gangsters. The films are bracingly enjoyable, but fjourneyman director William Clemens's attitude to the crude realities of crime was surprisingly uncompromising. DP

Bonita Granville *Nancy Drew* • John Litel *Carson Drew* • James Stephenson *Challon* • Frankie Thomas *Ted Nickerson* • Frank Orth *Inspector Milligan* • Charles Trowbridge *Hollister* ■ *Dir* William Clemens • *Scr* Kenneth Gamet, from the novel *The Password to Larkspur Lane* by Carolyn Keene

Nancy Goes to Rio ★★★ U

Musical 1950 · US · Colour · 99mins

MGM's resident soubrette, pert and pretty Jane Powell, was the true successor to Deanna Durbin, as underlined by this remake of Durbin's *It's a Date* (1940). This time around, instead of a trip to Hawaii and black and white, Powell and her actress mother (Ann Sothern) are on a luxury liner on their way to Rio in glorious Technicolor. There are some good numbers, especially *Shine on Harvest Moon*, sung by Powell, Sothern and (unexpectedly) Louis Calhern. RB

Jane Powell *Nancy Barklay* • Ann Sothern *Frances Elliott* • Barry Sullivan *Paul Berten* • Carmen Miranda *Marina Rodriguez* • Louis Calhern *Gregory Elliott* ■ *Dir* Robert Z Leonard • *Scr* Sidney Sheldon, from a story by Jane Hall, Frederick Kohner, Ralph Block

Nancy Steele Is Missing ★★★

Drama 1937 · US · BW · 84mins

Lindbergh baby kidnapper Bruno Hauptmann had been sent to the electric chair the year before this film opened, so the timing could not have been entirely coincidental. This rambling production confronts the Hays Office head on by using lovable Victor McLaglen as a sympathetic abductor who eventually ends up as a gardener after reuniting his victim with her real father. George Marshall's direction is on the slow side, but McLaglen keeps it watchable. TS

Victor McLaglen *Dannie O'Neill* • Walter Connolly *Michael Steele* • Peter Lorre *Professor Sturm* • June Lang *Sheila O'Neill/ Nancy Steele* • Robert Kent *Jimmie Wilson* • Shirley Deane *Nancy* • John Carradine *Harry Wilkins* ■ *Dir* George Marshall • *Scr* Hal Long, Gene Fowler, from the story *Ransom* by Charles Francis Coe

Nang Nak ★★★

Supernatural period drama
1999 · Thai · Colour · 99mins

A huge box-office hit in its native Thailand, this mixture of folklore, gore fest and love story will either affect with its intensity or alienate with its minimalist approach and stylised acting. Set in the 1860s, the story centres on Winai Kraibutr, a young bride who lingers in ghostly form beside the Prakanong canal after dying in childbirth while her husband, Intira Jaroenpura, is away at war. The tenderness of their romance contrasts sharply with her violent assaults on those who challenge her ethereal idyll, including a Buddhist ghostbuster hired by the terrified villagers. DP. In Thai with English subtitles.

Intira Jaroenpura *Mak* • Winai Kraibutr *Nak* ■ *Dir* Nonzee Nimibutr • *Scr* Wisit Sasanatieng

The Nanny ★★★ 15

Thriller 1965 · UK · BW · 89mins

The first of two movies Bette Davis made for Britain's Hammer films is a genuinely chilling horror tale, with a clever plot written by Hammer regular Jimmy Sangster. However, movie purists may well object to the fact that the flashbacks reveal incidents that never actually happened, manipulating the expectations of the audience. Despite valiant work from Davis and director Seth Holt, the narrative weaknesses and the general unpleasantness of the piece spoil what could have been an interesting addition to the genre. TS [video] DVD

Bette Davis *Nanny* • Wendy Craig *Virgie Fane* • Jill Bennett *Pen* • James Villiers *Bill Fane* • William Dix *Joey* • Pamela Franklin *Bobby* • Jack Watling *Dr Medman* • Alfred Burke *Dr Wills* • Maurice Denham *Dr Beamaster* ■ *Dir* Seth Holt • *Scr* Jimmy Sangster from a novel by Evelyn Piper

Nanook of the North ★★★ U

Classic silent documentary
1922 · US · BW · 49mins

Sponsored by furriers Revillon Frères, shot in the frozen wastes of Hudson Bay and re-edited in 1948 with commentary and music added, this remains a historic, ground-breaking work by the great pioneering documentarist Robert Flaherty. According his subject matter the dignity it deserves, Flaherty recorded, with insight and touches of humour, the life of Inuit Nanook, his wife Nyla and their family and their harsh daily struggle for survival. A truthful, unembellished account of Inuit life – building an igloo, capturing a seal, fishing in ice for food – the film looks undeniably primitive by today's standards, but present-day documentarists owe it a debt. RK

Dir Robert Flaherty • *Scr* Robert Flaherty, Carl Stearns Clancy (titles), Robert Flaherty (titles) • *Cinematographer* Robert Flaherty

Nanou ★★ 15

Drama 1986 · UK/Fr · Colour · 110mins

Writer/director Conny Templeman's only feature to date displays the characteristic urge of 1980s British cinema to fuse the personal with the political. In this instance English teenager Imogen Stubbs's pre-college trip to Europe results in a liaison with French activist Jean-Philippe Ecoffey, who is intent on making his feelings about local unemployment heard. The opening act is well played, with a light, surprisingly humorous touch, and Stubbs shows considerable talent, but as the demands of Ecoffey and his cronies become increasingly extreme, so credibility is stretched. RT. In English and French with subtitles.

Imogen Stubbs *Nanou* • Jean-Philippe Ecoffey *Luc* • Christophe Lidon *Charles* • Valentine Pelka *Jacques* • Roger Ibanez *Michel* • Nathalie Becue *Chantal* • Daniel Day-Lewis *Max* ■ *Dir* Conny Templeman • *Scr* Conny Templeman, Antione Lacomblez

Napoléon ★★★★★

Silent historical drama
1927 · Fr · BW · 234mins

Intended as the first instalment of a six-part biography, Abel Gance's factitious account of Bonaparte's life from military school to the Italian campaign originally ran for over five hours. Achieving his audacious movements by variously attaching the camera to a galloping horse's back, a pendulum and a flying football, Gance pushed the technology of silent cinema to its limits, even shooting several scenes in a triptych process called Polyvision. His energetic metaphorical editing was also innovative, at one point filling the screen with 16 superimposed images. Albert Dieudonné gives a spirited performance in the title role, but the accolades all belong to the director. DP

Albert Dieudonné *Napoleon Bonaparte* • Gina Manès *Josephine de Beauharnais* • Vladimir Roudenko *Young Napoleon* • Alexandre Koubitzky *Georges Jacques Danton* • Antonin Artaud *Jean-Paul Marat* • Abel Gance *Louis Saint-Just* ■ *Dir/Scr* Abel Gance

Napoléon ★★★★

Biographical drama
1955 · Fr · Colour · 190mins

One of the most entertaining of Sacha Guitry's witty all-star extravaganzas, it featured the 70-year-old actor/writer/ director as Talleyrand, recounting a series of anecdotes about the life and loves of Napoléon Bonaparte (played first by Daniel Gélin and then Raymond Pellegrin). The film, which cost $1.8 million, then a record for a French film, was shot at the Parc des Expositions because no studio was large enough to accommodate the sets. Yet the three-hour film has an intimate feel as Guitry holds court, introducing a mouth-watering cast. RB. In French with English subtitles.

Jean-Pierre Aumont *Renault de Saint-Jean d'Angely* • Pierre Brasseur *Barras* • Danielle Darrieux *Eleonore Denuelle* • Jean Gabin *Marshal Lannes* • Daniel Gélin *Bonaparte* • Sacha Guitry *Talleyrand* • Jean Marais *Count de Montholon* • Yves Montand *Marshal Lefebvre* • Michèle Morgan *Joséphine de Beauharnais* • Raymond Pellegrin *Napoléon* • Serge Reggiani *Lucien Bonaparte* • Maria Schell *Marie-Louis d'Autriche* • Erich von Stroheim *Beethoven* • Orson Welles *Hudson Lowe* ■ *Dir/Scr* Sacha Guitry

Napoleon ★★★ U

Adventure
1995 · Aus/Jpn/US · Colour · 77mins

This Australian adventure will delight those who prefer their animal magic with a touch of authenticity. The encounters of a golden-retriever puppy who runs away to join the outback's wild dogs are often gleefully eccentric – whether they're with a psycho cat, a Dame Edna Everage-voiced kangaroo or with Joan Rivers's mother kangaroo. Cannily directed by Mario Andreacchio, it's cute, but never tacky. DP [video]

Adam Wylie *Muffin/Napoleon* • Bronson Pinchot *Birdo Lucci* • Dame Edna Everage [Barry Humphries] *Kangaroo* • Carol Kane *Spider* • Joan Rivers *Mother Penguin* • David Ogden Stiers *Koala/Owl* • Blythe Danner *Mother Dingo* ■ *Dir* Mario Andreacchio • *Scr* Mario Andreacchio, Michael Bourchier, Mark Saltzman

Napoleon and Samantha ★★★ U

Adventure 1972 · US · Colour · 91mins

Just think how much it would cost to team Michael Douglas and Jodie Foster today. Back in 1972, Disney had to shell out next to nothing to land the relatively unknown Douglas and the debuting Foster for this amiable adventure about a couple of runaway kids and their pet lion. No one will be able to resist Major, the retired circus lion who was also a veteran of several movies and TV episodes opposite Ron Ely's Tarzan. DP

Michael Douglas *Danny* • Will Geer *Grandpa* • Arch Johnson *Chief of Police* • Johnny Whitaker *Napoleon Wilson* • Jodie Foster *Samantha* • Henry Jones *Mr Gutteridge* ■ *Dir* Bernard McEveety • *Scr* Stewart Raffill

Napoleon Dynamite ★★★ PG

Comedy 2004 · US · Colour · 89mins

Like the central character's bizarre name, there's something self-consciously quirky about this whimsical tale of a super-nerd's small-town life. The eponymous Napoleon (Jon Heder), a blank-faced teen with carrot-coloured hair and seriously underdeveloped interpersonal skills, tries to help his equally nerdish best friend (Efren Ramirez) win the school elections. Heder's performance is entertainingly eccentric, while the supporting

N

characters are amusing though a tad one-dimensional. AS DVD

Jon Heder *Napoleon Dynamite* • Jon Gries [Jonathan Gries] *Uncle Rico* • Aaron Ruell *Kip* • Efren Ramirez *Pedro* • Tina Majorino *Deb* • Diedrich Bader *Rex* • Haylie Duff *Summer Wheatley* ■ *Dir* Jared Hess • *Scr* Jared Hess, Jerusha Hess

Naqoyqatsi ★★★ PG

Documentary 2002 · US · Colour · 85mins

Godfrey Reggio completes the trilogy begun with *Koyaanisqatsi* and *Powaqqatsi* in this visually striking, if self-consciously provocative montage documentary. Translating as "war as a way of life" in the the Hopi language, the title allows Reggio to explore a range of socio-political issues in loose segments centring on the pros and cons of technology, modern society's obsession with success and celebrity, and humanity's irresistible urge to self-destruct. Philip Glass's score is again sublime, but some may object to Reggio's manipulation of archival footage as a means of persuading us to look again at a planet in crisis. DP. Contains nudity. DVD

Dir/Scr Godfrey Reggio

Narc ★★★ 18

Police thriller 2001 · US · Colour · 100mins

Joe Carnahan deftly manipulates all the clichés of the hard-boiled cop thriller in this intriguing example of the genre. Jason Patric is suspended after a drugs surveillance operation ends with him accidentally shooting a pregnant woman. Almost two years later, he returns to the force to investigate the homicide of a colleague. The dead man's partner, played with hair-raising energy by Ray Liotta, seems to be quite willing to break all the rules to get the killer, but Patric begins to suspect his motives. While the over-familiar plot often fails to convince, strong performances from the well-matched leads hold the attention. AS DVD

Ray Liotta *Lt Henry Oak* • Jason Patric *Nick Tellis* • Chi McBride *Capt Cheevers* • Busta Rhymes *Darnell "Big D Love" Beery* • Anne Openshaw *Katherine Calvess* • John Ortiz *Octavio Ruiz* ■ *Dir/Scr* Joe Carnahan

The Narrow Margin ★★★★ PG

Crime drama 1952 · US · BW · 71mins

This rattlingly good train thriller epitomises the very best of the style now known and recognised as *film noir*, directed with a wonderful sense of the claustrophobic by Richard Fleischer and terrifically performed by tough guy Charles McGraw. He's the cop taking floozy Marie Windsor to testify to the grand jury, with evidence that will send a mobster gang to the chair. Naturally enough, they don't want her to squeal. The suspense is acute, nobody is quite who they seem to be, and the action is riveting. A classic B-movie. TS

Charles McGraw *Walter Brown* • Marie Windsor *Mrs Neil* • Jacqueline White *Ann Sinclair* • Gordon Gebert *Tommy Sinclair* • Queenie Leonard *Mrs Troll* • David Clarke *Kemp* • Peter Virgo *Densel* ■ *Dir* Richard Fleischer • *Scr* Earl Fenton, from a story by Martin Goldsmith, Jack Leonard

Narrow Margin ★★★ 15

Thriller 1990 · US · Colour · 92mins

Gene Hackman stars as the assistant district attorney who faces a nightmarish train journey when he escorts a key witness (Anne Archer) to a Mob trial in this efficient remake of Richard Fleischer's cracking 1950s B-movie. Director Peter Hyams doesn't bring anything particularly new or innovative to his update, but the cat-and-mouse games between Hackman and chief assassin James B Sikking are a delight, and the action sequences on the roof of the speeding train are exhilaratingly shot. JF. Contains violence, swearing. DVD

Gene Hackman *Robert Caulfield* • Anne Archer *Carol Hunnicut* • James B Sikking *Nelson* • JT Walsh *Michael Tarlow* • M Emmet Walsh *Sergeant Dominick Benti* • Susan Hogan *Kathryn Weller* ■ *Dir* Peter Hyams • *Scr* Peter Hyams, from the 1952 film

Nashville ★★★★★

Comedy drama 1975 · US · Colour · 160mins

Produced in time for the American bicentennial, this is Robert Altman's magnum opus, breathtaking in its scope and ambition. Set in Nashville, it is less a story than a mosaic with two dozen characters who connect, disconnect and reflect aspects of America, notably its music and politics. Ronee Blakley is one of the principal characters, supported by, among others, Geraldine Chaplin, Shelley Duvall and Ned Beatty, with cameos from Elliott Gould and Julie Christie. Its blend of country and western music, comedy and tragedy is never less than dazzling, and represents a major technical achievement for its visual and sound editors. AT. Contains violence, swearing and nudity.

David Arkin *Norman* • Barbara Baxley *Lady Pearl* • Ned Beatty *Delbert Reese* • Karen Black *Connie White* • Ronee Blakley *Barbara Jean* • Timothy Brown *Tommy Brown* • Keith Carradine *Tom Frank* • Geraldine Chaplin *Opal* • Robert DoQui *Wade* • Shelley Duvall *LA Joan* • Allen Garfield *Barnett* • Henry Gibson *Haven Hamilton* • Lily Tomlin *Linnea Reese* • Jeff Goldblum *Tricycle man* ■ *Dir* Robert Altman • *Scr* Joan Tewkesbury

The Nasty Girl ★★★★ PG

Political satire based on a true story 1990 · W Ger · Colour and BW · 92mins

Barely seen in this country on its original release, this bitingly brilliant film is a searing study of the way in which modern Germany has assuaged its conscience following the Nazi era. Writer/director Michael Verhoeven based his script on the experiences of Anja Rosmus, whose rummaging into the history of her own town led to her becoming a social outcast. The dazzling use of back projection and the unexpected transitions between scenes give the film a vibrancy that both invigorates and disturbs. DP. In German with English subtitles. Contains some violence. DVD

Lena Stolze *Sonja* • Monika Baumgartner *Maria* • Michael Garr *Paul Rosenberger* • Fred Stillkrauth *Uncle* • Elisabeth Bertram *Grandmother* ■ *Dir/Scr* Michael Verhoeven • *Cinematographer* Axel de Roche

Nasty Habits ★★ PG

Comedy 1976 · US/UK · Colour · 87mins

An appropriate title for a mildly sacrilegious comedy, based on the novel *The Abbess of Crewe* by Muriel Spark, about nuns who smoke, drink, swear and cheat. As the nuns attempt to rig the election of a new abbess, it gradually becomes apparent that the events are those of the Watergate scandal transferred to a Philadelphia convent. Today, though, few people will appreciate the political references. Glenda Jackson seems to have little interest in the proceedings, but Sandy Dennis is very funny. DM

Glenda Jackson *Sister Alexandra* • Melina Mercouri *Sister Gertrude* • Geraldine Page *Sister Walburga* • Sandy Dennis *Sister Winifred* • Anne Jackson *Sister Mildred* • Anne Meara *Sister Geraldine* • Susan Penhaligon *Sister Felicity* ■ *Dir* Michael Lindsay-Hogg • *Scr* Robert Enders, from the novel *The Abbess of Crewe* by Muriel Spark

Nasty Neighbours ★★ 15

Black comedy 2000 · UK · Colour · 85mins

Ricky Tomlinson plays a pompous Middle Englander whose quiet life in semi-detached suburbia conceals the turmoil of job problems and mounting debts. When moneyed wide boy Phil Daniels and his wife Rachel Fielding move next door, it's hate at first sight, with mutual loathing escalating into a war of words, and worse. Director Debbie Isitt's black comedy was adapted from her own stage play and features some good performances, but it's a one-note film. DA

Ricky Tomlinson *Harold Peach* • Phil Daniels *Robert Chapman* • Rachel Fielding *Ellen Chapman* • Hywel Bennett *The boss* • Debbie Isitt *Pauline Peach* ■ *Dir* Debbie Isitt • *Scr* Debbie Isitt, from her play

Nathalie... ★★★ 15

Drama 2003 · Fr/Sp · Colour · 101mins

In this intense psychological drama, middle-aged gynaecologist Fanny Ardant pays sex-club hostess Emmanuelle Béart to lure her errant husband (Gérard Depardieu) into an affair. Ardant is motivated by revenge for a casual fling and meets Béart after each of the encounters with her husband for an explicit recounting of events. However, there is no palpable friction between Ardant and Béart, so their meetings lack sexual tension, while the conceit depends on a surprise ending that might have worked in a novel, but which is glaringly apparent on screen. DP. In French with English subtitles. Contains swearing. DVD

Fanny Ardant *Catherine* • Emmanuelle Béart *Nathalie/Marlène* • Gérard Depardieu *Bernard* • Wladimir Yordanoff *François* • Judith Magre *Catherine's mother* • Rodolphe Pauly *Thierry* ■ *Dir* Anne Fontaine • *Scr* Jacques Fieschi, Anne Fontaine, François-Olivier Rousseau, from an idea by Philippe Blasband

The National Health ★★★

Satire 1973 · UK · Colour · 97mins

This adaptation of Peter Nichols's play shows the United Kingdom in intensive care. The setting is a rundown, ramshackle hospital, where the grisly reality of life on a men's ward contrasts with the slippery fiction of a TV soap opera entitled *Nurse Norton's Affair*. Director Jack Gold assembles some sprightly set pieces and fine actors (Donald Sinden, Lynn Redgave, Jim Dale) who give real clout to the sometimes contrived satire. TH

Lynn Redgrave *Nurse Sweet/Betty* • Donald Sinden *Mr Carr/Dr Boyd* • Jim Dale *Barnet/Neil* • Eleanor Bron *Nurse McFee/Sister Mary* • Colin Blakely *Loach* • Clive Swift *Ash* • Bob Hoskins *Foster* ■ *Dir* Jack Gold • *Scr* Peter Nichols, from his play

National Lampoon's Animal House ★★★★ 15

Comedy 1978 · US · Colour · 108mins

It spawned a number of puerile spin-offs, but this cheerfully vulgar offering deserves the status of comedy classic. As well as providing John Belushi with his best ever role, it also helped launch the career of a number of rising young actors (Kevin Bacon, Tom Hulce, Peter Riegert), not to mention director John Landis and co-writer Harold Ramis. There's not much of a plot to speak of: at a US college in the early 1960s, dean John Vernon plots to remove the depraved Delta House fraternity from the campus; Belushi and his fellow students decide to fight back. The film is crammed with smart sight gags and one-liners. JF. Contains swearing, nudity. DVD

John Belushi *John "Bluto" Blutarsky* • Tim Matheson *Eric "Otter" Stratton* • John Vernon *Dean Vernon Wormer* • Verna Bloom *Marion Wormer* • Thomas Hulce [Tom Hulce] *Larry "Pinto" Kroger* • Peter Riegert *Donald "Boon" Schoenstein* • Stephen Furst *Kent "Flounder" Dorfman* • Kevin Bacon *Chip Diller* ■ *Dir* John Landis • *Scr* Harold Ramis, Douglas Kenney, Chris Miller • *Music* Elmer Bernstein

National Lampoon's Christmas Vacation ★★ PG

Comedy 1989 · US · Colour · 92mins

Following on from the funnier *National Lampoon's Vacation* and *European Vacation*, the plot here again revolves around the Griswold family, led by Chevy Chase and Beverly D'Angelo. This time the family stays at home, and, of course, is beset by a series of disasters during the Christmas holiday. Silly in the extreme, it is only saved by Randy Quaid's performance as an obnoxious relative. A TV-movie sequel followed in 2003. JB. Contains swearing. DVD

Chevy Chase *Clark W Griswold Jr* • Beverly D'Angelo *Ellen Griswold* • Randy Quaid *Cousin Eddie* • Miriam Flynn *Catherine, Eddie's wife* • Johnny Galecki *Rusty Griswold* • Juliette Lewis *Audrey Griswold* • John Randolph *Clark W Griswold Sr* • Diane Ladd *Nora Griswold* • EG Marshall *Art, Ellen's father* • Doris Roberts *Frances, Ellen's mother* ■ *Dir* Jeremiah S Chechik [Jeremiah Chechik] • *Scr* John Hughes

National Lampoon's Class Reunion ★ 18

Comedy horror 1982 · US · Colour · 85mins

An appalling comedy horror, this has a bunch of obnoxious ex-students locked in at their class reunion and stalked by a psychotic killer. The script is so inept, repulsive and agonisingly humour-free that it's hard to believe it was written by the usually dependable John Hughes. JC DVD

Gerrit Graham *Bob Spinnaker* • Michael Lerner *Dr Robert Young* • Fred McCarren *Gary Nash* • Miriam Flynn *Bunny Packard* • Stephen Furst *Hubert Downs* • Marya Small *Iris Augen* ■ *Dir* Michael Miller (2) • *Scr* John Hughes

National Lampoon's European Vacation ★★★ 15

Comedy 1985 · US · Colour · 90mins

Amy Heckerling's politically incorrect comedy should be dismissed without hesitation. But there is something endearing about the Griswold family, and Chevy Chase and Beverly D'Angelo's infectious enthusiasm manages to sweep you along on this cliché-ridden package tour. Every conceivable national stereotype is pressed into service, as polite British cyclists, rude French waiters, aggressive Germans in lederhosen and Mafia hitmen are trotted out with soothing predictability. DP. Contains swearing and nudity.

Chevy Chase *Clark W Griswold* • Beverly D'Angelo *Ellen Griswold* • Dana Hill *Audrey Griswold* • Jason Lively *Rusty Griswold* • John Astin *Quiz host* • Eric Idle *Bike rider* • Mel Smith *Hotel manager* • Robbie Coltrane *Man in bathroom* • Maureen Lipman *Lady in bed* ■ *Dir* Amy Heckerling • *Scr* John Hughes, Robert Klane, from a story by John Hughes

National Lampoon's Loaded Weapon 1 ★★★ PG

Comedy 1993 · US · Colour · 79mins

This bid by the *National Lampoon* team to cash in with some *Naked Gun*-style spoofery lacks the brainless invention of those films but still manages to score quite a few laughs. The *Lethal Weapon* series is its main target, with Emilio Estevez taking over the Mel Gibson role and Samuel L Jackson standing in for Danny Glover. Often the targets and gags are far too obvious, but much of the fun is in watching out for the cameos. JF. Contains violence and swearing. DVD

Emilio Estevez *Jack Colt* • Samuel L Jackson *Wes Luger* • Tim Curry *Jigsaw* • Jon Lovitz *Becker* • Kathy Ireland *Destiny Demeanor* • William Shatner *General Mortars* • Frank McRae *Captain Doyle* • F Murray Abraham *Harold Leacher* ■ *Dir* Gene Quintano • *Scr* Don Holley, Gene Quintano, from a story by Don Holley, Tori Tellem

National Lampoon's Movie Madness ★ 15

Comedy 1981 · US · Colour · 85mins

This is one of the worst films in the series: a bloated, desperately unfunny trilogy of mini-spoofs which unforgivably wastes the talents of an exceptional cast. Personal growth films, cop movies and soaps are the predictable targets; a fourth segment on disaster movies never saw the light of day. JF. Contains swearing. [video]

Christopher Lloyd *Samuel Starkman* • Robby Benson *Brent Falcone* • Richard Widmark *Stan Nagurski* • Barry Diamond *Junkie* • Elisha Cook Jr *Mousy* • Julie Kavner *Mrs Falcone* • Henny Youngman *Lawyer* • Robert Culp *Paul Everest* • Olympia Dukakis *Helena Naxos* • Peter Riegert *Jason Cooper* • Diane Lane *Liza* ■ *Dir* Henry Jaglom, Bob Giraldi • *Scr* Tod Carroll, Shary Slenniken

National Lampoon's Scuba School ★★ 12

Comedy 1994 · US · Colour · 88mins

Although energetic and with the usual hedonistic shenanigans, this is a far cry from *Animal House* and not as much fun as vacationing with the Griswolds. The simplistic plot has Corey Feldman and Corey Haim rushing to the aid of Feldman's uncle Geoffrey Lewis on a Caribbean resort. The two pose as CIA agents-cum-scuba instructors and thwart the villain Robert Mandan. DF [video]

Corey Haim *Dave* • Corey Feldman *Sam* • Geoffrey Lewis *Uncle Rex* • Robert Mandan *Hemlock* • Demetra Hampton *Alex* • Maureen Flannigan *Sonja* ■ *Dir* Rafal Zielinski • *Scr* Damian Lee, Patrick Labyorteaux

National Lampoon's Senior Trip ★ 15

Comedy 1995 · US · Colour · 87mins

Each successive entry in this once hilariously irreverent series is denounced as its nadir, but this risible comedy has stronger claims than most. Every character is a walking cliché, while every gag is designed to be cheap, and often offensive, rather than funny. Satire is at a premium as a gang of high school students write to the President lamenting the state of the nation and receive an invitation to the White House. Inept twaddle. DP. Contains some swearing and sexual references. [video]

Matt Frewer *Principal Moss* • Valerie Mahaffey *Miss Tracy Milford* • Lawrence Dane *Senator John Lerman* • Tommy Chong *Red* • Jeremy Renner *Mark "Dags" D'Agostino* • Rob Moore *Reggie* ■ *Dir* Kelly Makin • *Scr* Roger Kumble, I Marlene King

National Lampoon's Vacation ★★★ 15

Comedy 1983 · US · Colour · 94mins

National Lampoon's first outing (1978's *Animal House*) is still the funniest by far, but this is a decent effort. Chevy Chase is the put-upon dad who sets off to take his family across America to an amusement park, encountering numerous mishaps and disasters along the way. Director Harold Ramis, who went on to make the comedy *Groundhog Day*, keeps the silliness coming fast and furious, and he is ably abetted by a supporting cast that includes Beverly D'Angelo, Randy Quaid and John Candy. JB. Contains swearing and nudity. [video] DVD

Chevy Chase *Clark Griswold* • Beverly D'Angelo *Ellen Griswold* • Imogene Coca *Aunt Edna* • Randy Quaid *Cousin Eddie* • Anthony Michael Hall *Rusty Griswold* • Dana Barron *Audrey Griswold* • Eddie Bracken *Roy Walley* • James Keach *Motorcycle cop* • John Candy *Lasky* • Christie Brinkley *Girl in red Ferrari* ■ *Dir* Harold Ramis • *Scr* John Hughes

National Security ★★ 12

Action comedy
2002 · US/UK · Colour · 84mins

This poorly executed buddy movie is a vehicle for Martin Lawrence and Steve Zahn. Lawrence plays a wannabe cop who's booted out of the academy and becomes a security guard; Zahn is an ex-policeman who was sent down for six months after being falsely accused, by Lawrence, of a racist assault and is also forced to find work as a guard. They are thrown together and end up on the trail of the ruthless crooks who were responsible for the death of Zahn's partner. Dumb, tasteless and short on laughs. JC [video] DVD

Martin Lawrence *Earl Montgomery* • Steve Zahn *Hank Rafferty* • Colm Feore *Det Frank McDuff* • Bill Duke *Lt Washington* • Eric Roberts *Nash* • Timothy Busfield *Charlie Reed* • Robinne Lee *Denise* • Matt McCoy *Robert Barton* ■ *Dir* Dennis Dugan • *Scr* Jay Scherick, David Ronn

National Treasure ★★ PG

Action adventure
2004 · US · Colour · 125mins

This is part historical detective story, part conspiracy thriller and part *Boys' Own* adventure, but director Jon Turteltaub never quite finds a successful way to marry all these elements together. Nicolas Cage sleepwalks his way through the role of Benjamin Franklin Gates, who embarks on a cross-country treasure hunt to discover the whereabouts of booty hidden by the Founding Fathers of the United States. En route, there are some limp action moments, colourless characters and sluggish storytelling, but this Jerry Bruckheimer production still has enough to keep the undemanding interested. IF [video] DVD

Nicolas Cage *Benjamin Franklin Gates* • Hunter Gomez *Young Ben Gates* • Jon Voight *Patrick Gates* • Harvey Keitel *Agent Sadusky* • Diane Kruger *Dr Abigail Chase* • Sean Bean *Ian Howe* • Justin Bartha *Riley Poole* • Christopher Plummer *John Adams Gates* ■ *Dir* Jon Turteltaub • *Scr* Jim Kouf, Cormac Wibberley, Marianne Wibberley, from a story by Jim Kouf, Oren Aviv, Charles Segars

National Velvet ★★★★ U

Classic drama 1944 · US · Colour · 118mins

In this adaptation of Enid Bagnold's novel, 12-year-old Elizabeth Taylor gives a star-making performance as the girl who dreams of racing her horse in the Grand National. Director Clarence Brown knows how to tug at the heartstrings and this film has become a classic, even though the story has to be taken with a large pinch of salt. Thanks to a strong performance from Mickey Rooney, an Oscar-winning one from Anne Revere, and the appeal of Taylor, this is a richly satisfying movie. A misguided British sequel, *International Velvet*, followed in 1978. TS [video]

Mickey Rooney *Mi Taylor* • Donald Crisp *Mr Herbert Brown* • Elizabeth Taylor *Velvet Brown* • Anne Revere *Mrs Brown* • Angela Lansbury *Edwina Brown* • Jackie "Butch" Jenkins *Donald Brown* • Juanita Quigley *Malvolia Brown* • Arthur Treacher *Race patron* • Reginald Owen *Farmer Ede* • Norma Varden *Miss Simms* ■ *Dir* Clarence Brown • *Scr* Theodore Reeves, Helen Deutsch, from the novel by Enid Bagnold

Nationale 7 ★★★★ 15

Comedy drama 1999 · Fr · Colour · 95mins

Director/co-writer Jean-Pierre Sinapi avoids any patronising pitfalls in this droll drama, which was inspired by the experiences of his nursing sister and a dying friend with a lust for life. Indeed, Olivier Gourmet's wheelchair-bound socialist is so human he's unbearable, at least until nurse Nadia Kaci agrees to chaperone his visits to a prostitute in a Nationale 7 lay-by. The theme may be physical, racial, sexual and religious acceptance, but Sinapi never preaches and succeeds in affirming life however it's lived. DP. In French with English subtitles. Contains swearing and sexual references.

Nadia Kaci *Julie* • Olivier Gourmet *René* • Lionel Abelanski *Roland* • Chantal Neuwirth *Sandrine* ■ *Dir* Jean-Pierre Sinapi • *Scr* Jean-Pierre Sinapi, Anne-Marie Catois

Native Land ★★★ PG

Documentary drama 1942 · US · BW · 88mins

Based on testimony given to the US Senate Civil Liberties Committee, this docudrama focuses on the cruel irony entailed in the American boast to be the Land of the Free. With narration by Paul Robeson, episodes set in a Midwest farm, a bustling metropolis, a Southern village and a factory town proffer a potent amalgam of rhetoric, image and score. But in depicting those who demean the Bill of Rights as the "enemy within" and those striving for labour representation as the "new pioneers", the Frontier Film pairing of Leo Hurwitz and Paul Strand betrays the naivety of their political stance. DP [video]

Paul Robeson *Narrator/Singer* • Fred Johnson *Fred Hill, the farmer* • Mary George *Farmer's wife* • John Rennick *Farmer's son* ■ *Dir* Leo Hurwitz, Paul Strand • *Scr* David Wolff [Ben Maddow], Leo Hurwitz, Paul Strand

Native Son ★★

Crime drama 1951 · US/Arg · BW · 91mins

The work of American author Richard Wright probably offers the harshest portrait of the South ever published. Shortly after he exiled himself to Paris in 1950, Wright was persuaded by director Pierre Chenal to star in his own adaptation of his most famous novel, about a boy from the slums who gets a job as a chauffeur to a white family. When the daughter of the family gets drunk, the youngster tries to keep her quiet and accidentally kills her. Sadly, Wright was no actor and he was twice the age of his protagonist so this tame version of his work failed. BB

Richard Wright *Bigger Thomas* • Jean Wallace *Mary Dalton* • Nicholas Joy *Mr Dalton* • Gloria Madison *Bessie Mears* ■ *Dir* Pierre Chenal • *Scr* Pierre Chenal, Richard Wright, from the novel by Richard Wright

Native Son ★★★ 15

Drama 1986 · US · Colour · 106mins

Native Son has an impressive pedigree. It began as a 1940 novel by Richard Wright about a maladjusted, malcontented black youth who is taken for a night out by his employer's pretty daughter and her boyfriend. Both are active communists who make a show of equality. Later he accidentally murders the girl, incinerates the body and gets sentenced to death. This 1986 adaptation is pitched as a full-blooded melodrama and is worth seeing for its splendid cast: Carroll Baker as the blind mother, Elizabeth McGovern and Matt Dillon as the young communists, Victor Love as the central character and Oprah Winfrey in a cringe-making final scene. AT [video]

Carroll Baker *Mrs Dalton* • Akosua Busia *Bessie* • Matt Dillon *Jan* • Art Evans *Doc* • John Karlen *Max* • Victor Love *Bigger Thomas* • Elizabeth McGovern *Mary Dalton* • John McMartin *Mr Dalton* • Geraldine Page *Peggy* • Oprah Winfrey *Mrs Thomas* ■ *Dir* Jerrold Freedman • *Scr* Richard Wesley, from the novel by Richard Wright

The Natural ★★★★ PG

Sports drama 1984 · US · Colour · 116mins

Based on Bernard Malamud's 1952 novel, this is a wistful and often memorable look at the world of baseball by director Barry Levinson. Robert Redford is at his beautiful best as the player who experiences the highs and lows of the game in a film that's more *Field of Dreams* than *Bull Durham*. Baseball here is seen as something magical – Redford has a mystical bat named "Wonderboy", which he fashioned from a tree struck by lightning – rather than merely a sport. If you can suspend disbelief, you'll be rewarded with an emotional and heart-warming experience. JB. Contains swearing. [video] DVD

Robert Redford *Roy Hobbs* • Robert Duvall *Max Mercy* • Glenn Close *Iris* • Kim Basinger *Memo Paris* • Wilford Brimley *Pop Fisher* • Barbara Hershey *Harriet Bird* • Robert Prosky *The Judge* • Richard Farnsworth *Red Blow* • Joe Don Baker *The Whammer* ■ *Dir* Barry Levinson • *Scr* Roger Towne, Phil Dusenberry, from the novel by Bernard Malamud

Natural Born Killers ★★★★ 18

Crime drama
1994 · US · Colour and BW · 114mins

Woody Harrelson and Juliette Lewis are serial killers turned into folk heroes by media excesses in this striking movie, criticised by original story author Quentin Tarantino after being largely rewritten by director Oliver Stone and others. Ambitious, unrelenting and inventive, Stone's controversial landmark movie excites the intellect while bludgeoning the senses, blending naturalistic violence with stylised visuals, and commandeering every available cinematic trick to put across its searing message. A dazzling display of technique underscoring the media's obsession with violent crime, this is the most provocative addition to the debate since *A Clockwork Orange*. AJ. Contains violence, swearing, sex scenes and nudity. [video] DVD

Woody Harrelson *Mickey Knox* • Juliette Lewis *Mallory Knox* • Robert Downey Jr *Wayne Gale* • Tommy Lee Jones *Dwight McClusky* • Tom Sizemore *Jack Scagnetti* • Rodney Dangerfield *Mallory's dad* ■ *Dir* Oliver Stone • *Scr* David Veloz, Richard Rutowski, Oliver Stone, from a story by Quentin Tarantino

Naughty but Nice ★★★ U

Musical 1939 · US · BW · 89mins

Crooner Dick Powell's last movie under his Warner Bros contract is an amiable lightweight tale, in which Powell – courtesy of some demon rum – plays a Jekyll-and-Hyde music professor. This loose satire on Tin Pan Alley is really a vehicle for top-billed Ann Sheridan, the lovely and talented Texas sophisticate who Warners tagged the "Oomph Girl". But even she can't salvage this silly movie, in which the only satirical content is a look at how popular songs always steal from the classics. Look out for an early appearance from a callow Ronald Reagan. TS

Ann Sheridan *Zelda Manion* • Dick Powell *Professor Hardwick* • Gale Page *Linda McKay* • Helen Broderick *Aunt Martha* • Allen Jenkins *Joe Dirk* • ZaSu Pitts *Aunt Penelope* • Ronald Reagan *Ed Clark* ■ *Dir* Ray Enright • *Scr* Richard Macaulay, Jerry Wald, from their story *Always Leave Them Laughing*

Naughty Marietta ★★★

Musical 1935 · US · BW · 103mins

This was the first movie to team "America's Sweethearts", Jeanette

MacDonald and Nelson Eddy. The somewhat sickly mixture of Nelson as a lecherous rake and Jeanette as a maligned loose woman might seem old hat today, but there's no denying the sheer panache of the production, and the undoubted pleasure (if you like that sort of thing) of a Victor Herbert score that includes *Tramp, Tramp, Tramp* and *Ah, Sweet Mystery of Life*. Louis B Mayer liked it so much that he willed MacDonald to sing *Sweet Mystery* at his funeral. She did. TS

Jeanette MacDonald *Princess Marie de Namours de la Bonfain/"Marietta Franini"* • Nelson Eddy *Captain Richard Warrington* • Frank Morgan *Governor Gaspard d'Annard* • Elsa Lanchester *Madame d'Annard* • Douglass Dumbrille *Prince de Namours de la Bonfain* ■ *Dir* WS Van Dyke II [WS Van Dyke] • *Scr* John Lee Mahin, Frances Goodrich, Albert Hackett, from the operetta by Victor Herbert, Rida Johnson Young

The Naughty Nineties ★★

Period comedy 1945 · US · BW · 76mins

Bud and Lou: names that terrorise hardened moviegoers or evoke rapture at the prospect of their comic antics. While they lack the genius of Stan and Ollie – it's slapstick and music hall, not sublime comedies of errors – Abbott and Costello were once the highest paid comics in Hollywood. Often they are best remembered for incident rather than narrative, which here involves the duo helping out an elderly steamboat owner. The highlight for many will be the six-minute "Who's on First" dualogue, about the playing order of the St Louis baseball team. It's a routine that defies description and eschews a question mark. BB

Bud Abbott *Dexter Broadhurst* • Lou Costello *Sebastian Dinwiddie* • Alan Curtis *Crawford* • Rita Johnson *Bonita Farrow* • Henry Travers *Captain Sam Jackson* • Lois Collier *Caroline Jackson* ■ *Dir* Jean Yarbrough • *Scr* Edmund L Hartmann, John Grant, Edmund Joseph, Hal Fimberg, Felix Adler

N

Navajo Joe ★★

Spaghetti western
1966 · It/Sp · Colour · 90mins

Burt Reynolds made this spaghetti western shortly after he saw his friend Clint Eastwood in *A Fistful of Dollars*. "They'll love you in Italy," Eastwood told Reynolds. "You're quarter Indian, you can ride a horse like no one I know and you like to hug people." Reynolds plays a Navajo Indian who sees his entire tribe murdered, including his wife, and in revenge kills a lot of people. AT. Italian dialogue dubbed into English.

Burt Reynolds *Joe* • Aldo Sambrell *Marvin "Vee" Duncan* • Nicoletta Machiavelli *Estella* • Tanya Lopert *Maria* • Fernando Rey *Rattigan* • Franca Polesello *Barbara* ■ *Dir* Sergio Corbucci • *Scr* Dean Craig [Mario Pierotti], Fernando Di Leo, from a story by Ugo Pirro

The Navigator ★★★★ U

Classic silent comedy
1924 · US · BW · 57mins

A gorgeous Buster Keaton comedy set aboard a real ocean liner – the SS *Buford*, which was destined for the scrapyard before Keaton turned it into a marvellous prop. The story has Keaton playing Rollo Treadway – "heir to the Treadway fortune and and living proof that every family tree must have its sap" – who becomes adrift on the ship with his girlfriend. There are encounters with cannibals, an impromptu duel between swordfish, and an extraordinary underwater sequence with Keaton in full frogman's gear, filmed in 20 feet of water in Lake Tahoe, Nevada. AT

Buster Keaton *Rollo Treadway* • Kathryn McGuire *Betsy O'Brien* • Frederick Vroom *John O'Brien* • Clarence Burton *Spy* • HM Clugston *Spy* • Noble Johnson *Cannibal chief* ■ *Dir* Donald Crisp, Buster Keaton • *Scr* Clyde Bruckman, Joseph Mitchell, Jean Havez

The Navigator – a Medieval Odyssey ★★★★ PG

Fantasy adventure
1988 · Aus/NZ · Colour and BW · 87mins

An outstanding fable from New Zealand director Vincent Ward, which switches in time between Cumbria in the Middle Ages and the Antipodes of today. A medieval village threatened by the plague sends a group on a journey to find a miraculous church located on the other side of the world. The intrepid miners, however, burrow through the earth and end up in 20th-century New Zealand. The story could have been the basis for a knockabout time-travel comedy; indeed, there are some nice gags. Yet Ward is more interested in creating a mythical tale that subtly alludes to the Aids crisis and the nuclear apocalypse. JF

Bruce Lyons *Connor* • Hamish McFarlane *Griffin* • Noel Appleby *Ulf* • Marshall Napier *Searle* • Chris Haywood *Arno* • Paul Livingston *Martin* ■ *Dir/Scr* Vincent Ward

The Navigators ★★★ 15

Political drama
2001 · UK/Ger/Sp/It/Fr · Colour · 92mins

New Labour may be in the ascendancy, but little has changed for the average worker according to Ken Loach in this stinging swipe at post-socialist Britain. Joe Duttine and Tom Craig demonstrate Yorkshire grit as the rail gangers whose livelihoods and self-esteem are jeopardised by privatisation. The humanity that gave Loach's earlier socio-dramas an integrity to match their commitment has been replaced by a more strident politicking. Yet, this still rings all too true. DP DVD

Joe Duttine *Paul* • Tom Craig *Mick* • Dean Andrews *John* • Steve Huison *Jim* • Venn Tracey *Gerry* • Andy Swallow *Len* ■ *Dir* Ken Loach • *Scr* Rob Dawber

Navy Blue and Gold ★★ U

Drama 1937 · US · BW · 93mins

One of dozens of movies set in the naval training academy of Annapolis. There's an important football game coming up against the army, and a question mark hangs over James Stewart's vital participation. It seems he slipped into Annapolis under an assumed name, because his navy father had a major blemish on his career. Can Stewart redeem his family name and get to the game on time? AT

Robert Young (1) *Roger Ash* • James Stewart *John "Truck" Cross* • Lionel Barrymore *Capt "Skinny" Dawes* • Florence Rice *Patricia Gates* • Billie Burke *Mrs Alyce Gates* • Tom Brown *Richard Arnold Gates Jr* • Samuel S Hinds *Richard A Gates Sr* ■ *Dir* Sam Wood • *Scr* George Bruce, from his novel

The Navy Comes Through ★★ U

Second World War drama
1942 · US · BW · 81mins

There's a convoy heading across the ocean, and it's Pat O'Brien's job to sink the enemy subs, shoot the fighters out of the sky and keep George Murphy guessing about his promotion prospects. That's because Murphy has been having an affair with O'Brien's sister (Jane Wyatt), who also happens to be aboard. The action scenes mainly comprise stock footage from a dozen other RKO efforts. AT

Pat O'Brien *Mallory* • George Murphy *Sands* • Jane Wyatt *Myra* • Jackie Cooper *Babe* • Carl Esmond *Kroner* • Max Baer *Berringer* • Desi Arnaz *Tarriba* ■ *Dir* A Edward Sutherland • *Scr* Earl Baldwin, Roy Chanslor, John Twist, Aeneas MacKenzie, from the story *Pay to Learn* by Borden Chase

The Navy Lark ★★ U

Comedy 1959 · UK · BW · 82mins

The Navy Lark was a BBC Home Service comedy show that tickled people pink throughout the 1950s. Filmed in CinemaScope and running three times its normal length, it's a nostalgia trip for those who remember and a completely baffling experience for those who don't. The idea was to show naval life as a jolly jape, so the plot deals with life aboard a mine sweeper whose skipper invents an outbreak of yellow fever. It's wrapped up in *Carry On*-style puns and saucy seaside postcard situations. AT

Cecil Parker *Commander Stanton* • Ronald Shiner *CPO Banyard* • Leslie Phillips *Lieutenant Pouter* • Elvi Hale *Leading Wren Heather* • Nicholas Phipps *Captain Povey* • Cardew Robinson *Lieutenant Binns* • Gordon Jackson *Leading Seaman Johnson* • Hattie Jacques *Fortune teller* ■ *Dir* Gordon Parry • *Scr* Sid Colin, Laurie Wyman, from the radio series by Laurie Wyman

Navy SEALS ★★ 15

Action thriller 1990 · US · Colour · 108mins

Charlie Sheen has proved to be more convincing sending up action heroes (namely in the *Hot Shots!* films) than playing it straight, and this uninspired adventure yarn is a perfect case in point. Sheen is the slightly crazy crack commando who, with colleagues such as Michael Biehn and Rick Rossovich, sets out to rid the world of baddies. Director Lewis Teague lets off the requisite amount of explosions, but the script is riddled with clichés and Sheen is hardly a charismatic lead. JF. Contains swearing and violence.

Charlie Sheen *Lieutenant Dale Hawkins* • Michael Biehn *Lieutenant Commander James Curran* • Joanne Whalley-Kilmer [Joanne Whalley] *Claire Verens* • Rick Rossovich *Leary* • Bill Paxton *Dane* ■ *Dir* Lewis Teague • *Scr* Chuck Pfarrer, Gary Goldman

The Navy Steps Out ★★★ U

Comedy 1941 · US · BW · 90mins

Produced by the great silent comedian Harold Lloyd, this lightweight farce starts merrily enough as stenographer Lucille Ball and her wacky family and friends show stuffed-shirt tycoon Edmond O'Brien how to get some fun out of life. The rapid pace and slapstick situations keep the fun bubbling until the last reel. Worth a look, if only to see Ball displaying the assurance and talent that Hollywood took so long to acknowledge. TV

Lucille Ball *Dot Duncan* • George Murphy *Coffee Cup* • Edmond O'Brien *Stephen Herrick* • George Cleveland *Pokey* • Henry Travers *Abel Martin* • Franklin Pangborn *Pet shop owner* • Kathleen Howard *Jawme* ■ *Dir* Richard Wallace • *Scr* Bert Granet, Frank Ryan, from a story by Grover Jones

The Navy vs the Night Monsters ★★ 12

Science-fiction drama
1966 · US · Colour · 85mins

Antarctic vegetable samples replanted on an island naval base grow into acid-bleeding, walking trees and terrorise the inhabitants of a South Seas navy base. But most of the cast are too busy ogling 1950s blonde bombshell Mamie Van Doren to even notice. A terrible script, awful direction and ham acting from an eclectic bunch of Z-movie celebrities make this a camp, mind-boggling must-see. AJ

Mamie Van Doren *Lt Nora Hall* • Anthony Eisley *Lt Charles Brown* • Pamela Mason [Pamela Kellino] *Maria, a scientist* • Billy Gray *Petty Officer Fred Twining* • Bobby Van Ens *Rutherford Chandler* ■ *Dir* Michael A Hoey • *Scr* Michael A Hoey, from the novel *Monster from Earth's End* by Murray Leinster

Naya Daur ★★★ U

Drama 1957 · Ind · BW · 172mins

Directed by BR Chopra, this is a solid example of the politically conscious movie known as the "masala social". Just about every problem besetting the inhabitants of India's outlying rural communities comes under the microscope in this relentless melodrama, in which the arrival of new technology blows the lid off a long-simmering class and caste crisis. As if this wasn't enough to be getting on with, there is also a romantic triangle, a villain and a handful of those extravagant song-and-dance routines that make Indian cinema so unique. DP. In Hindi with English subtitles.

Jeevan *Kundan* • Dilip Kumar *Shankar* • Ajit (1) *Krishna* • Nasir Hussain *Seth Maganlal* ■ *Dir* BR Chopra • *Scr* Akhtar Mirza

Nazarín ★★★★

Religious drama 1958 · Mex · BW · 94mins

Rejecting the chance to adapt *The House of Bernarda Alba*, Luis Buñuel instead chose to direct this distressing odyssey through rural Mexico, which is sufficiently ambiguous to be claimed as both a scathing attack on the Catholic Church and a humanist lament at the impossibility of evangelising a determinedly secular world. Francisco Rabal wears an increasingly haunted look as his journey (which frequently echoes events from the Gospels) reveals the virtual irrelevance of religion, even to people beset by plague and poverty. DP. A Spanish language film.

Francisco Rabal *Nazarín* • Marga Lopez *Beatriz* • Rita Macedo *Andara* • Ignacio Lopez Tarso *Sacrilegist* • Ofelia Guilmain *Chanfa* ■ *Dir* Luis Buñuel • *Scr* Luis Buñuel, Julio Alejandro, from a novel by Benito Perez Galdos

Nazi Hunter: the Beate Klarsfeld Story ★★★★

Drama based on a true story
1986 · US · Colour · 100mins

Every now and then a star pulls out a performance that leaves you dumbfounded because you simply didn't think they had it in them. Farrah Fawcett is the performer working wonders here, in the title role of this genuinely affecting TV movie about the capture of the Butcher of Lyons, Klaus Barbie, who, at the end of the war, had fled into exile in Bolivia. Director Michael Lindsay-Hogg also draws expert performances from Tom Conti as Fawcett's devoted husband, and Geraldine Page as a camp survivor whose testimony helps nail the fugitive. It's just a shame it dips too frequently into melodrama. DP

Farrah Fawcett *Beate Klarsfeld* • Tom Conti *Serge Klarsfeld* • Geraldine Page *Itta Halaunbrenner* • Catherine Allégret *Madame Simone Lagrange* • Feodor Atkine *Luc Pleyel* • Helene Vallier *Raissa Klarsfeld* • Vincent Gauthier *Barbie in 1944* ■ *Dir* Michael Lindsay-Hogg • *Scr* Frederic Hunter

Near Dark ★★★★ 18

Horror 1987 · US · Colour · 90mins

An undead revamp of *Bonnie and Clyde*, director Kathryn Bigelow's tense road movie combines the western and horror genres in one visually stunning and frightening package. Adrian Pasdar is the farm boy inducted by Jenny Wright into her itinerant family of gangster bloodsuckers as they manage to keep one step ahead of the law and daylight. Bigelow spins a genuinely scary tale, slickly examining the violent lifestyle of the outlaw gang, with Lance Henriksen and Bill Paxton giving standout performances. AJ. Contains violence and swearing. [video] DVD

Adrian Pasdar *Caleb Colton* • Jenny Wright *Mae* • Lance Henriksen *Jesse* • Bill Paxton *Severen* • Jenette Goldstein *Diamondback* • Joshua Miller *Homer* • Marcie Leeds *Sarah Colton* • Tim Thomerson *Loy Colton* • Kenny Call *Deputy Sheriff* ■ *Dir* Kathryn Bigelow • *Scr* Eric Red, Kathryn Bigelow

Near Mrs ★★ 15

Romantic comedy
1990 · Fr/US · Colour · 89mins

Judge Reinhold strains to amuse as the executive whose bigamous double life is exposed when he persuades doltish Casey Siemaszko to stand in for him on the annual Army Reserve fortnight while he romances his latest mistress. The farce that follows Siemaszko's kidnap by the Soviets is laboured, in spite of the frantic pace. DP. Contains swearing. [video]

Judge Reinhold *Claude Jobert* • Casey Siemaszko *Colin Phipps* • Cécile Paoli *Molly* • Rebecca Pauly *Maggie* • Muriel Combeau *Toni* • Katarzyna Figura *Sasha* ■ *Dir* Baz Taylor • *Scr* Peter I Baloff [Peter Baloff], David W Wollert

The Near Room ★★ 18

Thriller 1995 · UK · Colour · 85mins

The third feature from actor/director David Hayman (*Silent Scream*, *The Hawk*) is a rather grim thriller about a gutter-press journalist (Adrian Dunbar) on the trail of his long-lost teenage daughter. The search takes him through child sex rackets, pornography rings and other underworld horrors. Some viewers may find the relentless squalor, thick accents and foul language hard to take. AT [video]

Adrian Dunbar *Charlie Colquhoun* • David O'Hara *Harris Hill* • David Hayman *Dougie Patterson* • Julie Graham *Elise Grey* ■ *Dir* David Hayman • *Scr* Robert Murphy

Nearest and Dearest ★★

Comedy 1972 · UK · Colour · 84mins

Responsible for some of Hammer's most grisly horrors, Michael Carreras was perhaps a surprise choice to produce this spin-off from the long-running ITV comedy series. Released the year before this fondly remembered sitcom departed our screens, it provides a worthy record of the word-mangling sniping between Hylda Baker and Jimmy Jewel as they try to suppress their sibling rivalry and make a go of their father's pickle factory. Bawdy, music hall entertainment. DP

Hylda Baker *Nellie Pledge* • Jimmy Jewel *Eli Pledge* • Eddie Malin *Walter* • Madge Hindle *Lily* • Joe Gladwin *Stan* • Norman Mitchell *Vernon Smallpiece* • Pat Ashton *Freda* • Yootha Joyce *Mrs Rowbottom* ■ *Dir* John Robins • *Scr* Tom Brennand, Roy Bottomley, from the TV series

Nearly a Nasty Accident ★★★ U

Comedy 1961 · UK · BW · 89mins

Jimmy Edwards teams with Kenneth Connor for this old-fashioned blend of slapstick and bluster. Although Edwards, his handlebar moustache bristling with indignation, is the nominal star as the RAF officer whose cushy lifestyle is shattered by the arrival of an accident-prone mechanic, it's Connor's talent for timidity and catastrophe that makes this catalogue of disasters so amusing. Don Chaffey directs with undue fuss, and there's practised support from Richard Wattis and Shirley Eaton. DP

Jimmy Edwards *Group Captain Kingsley* • Kenneth Connor *AC2 Alexander Wood* • Shirley Eaton *Jean Briggs* • Ronnie Stevens *Fl Lt Pocock* • Richard Wattis *Wagstaffe* • Jon Pertwee *General Birkenshaw* • Eric Barker *Minister* • Peter Jones *Fl Lt Winters* ■ *Dir* Don Chaffey • *Scr* Jack Davies, Hugh Woodhouse, from the play *Touch Wood* by David Stringer

'Neath the Arizona Skies ★★ U

Western 1934 · US · BW · 51mins

There's little to get excited about here in a very routine John Wayne Monogram programme filler, except for a spectacular, waterlogged fistfight between the Duke and stuntman Yakima Canutt at the climax. The rest of the tale is flimsily plotted around a far-fetched case of mistaken identity. This is for Wayne fans only, and even they might blanch at such a minor opus. TS [video] DVD

John Wayne *Chris Morrell* • Sheila Terry *Clara Moore* • Jay Wilsey [Buffalo Bill Jr] *Jim Moore* • Shirley Ricketts [Shirley Jane Ricketts] *Nina* • George "Gabby" Hayes *Matt Downing* • Yakima Canutt *Sam Black* ■ *Dir* Harry Fraser • *Scr* Burl Tuttle, from his story

Necessary Roughness ★★ 15

Comedy 1991 · US · Colour · 103mins

This American football comedy replays all the situations and clichés from the baseball saga *Major League*, but with a minor-league cast and clumsy direction. Scott Bakula is the hero, a mature college student and member of the team that must clear itself of a reputation for foul play. Marginal amusement can be had from the team's coach (Hector Elizondo), but this is eminently missable. AT. Contains swearing. [video] DVD

Scott Bakula *Paul Blake* • Robert Loggia *Wally Riggendorf* • Hector Elizondo *Ed Gennero* • Harley Jane Kozak *Suzanne Carter* • Sinbad *Andre Krimm* • Larry Miller *Dean Elias* ■ *Dir* Stan Dragoti • *Scr* Rick Natkin, David Fuller

Necronomicon ★★ 18

Horror 1993 · US · Colour · 92mins

Pacts with sea devils, mad scientists searching for eternal life and alien sacrifices are the themes of this trilogy of terror based on the works of HP Lovecraft. Nothing too remarkable is on offer here, although the gothic lyricism of Christophe Gans's episode *The Drowned* is noteworthy and the gruesome Edgar Allan Poe poetry of Shu Kaneko's *The Cold* gets a lift from the manic performance of David Warner. Brian Yuzna's *Whispers* is the goriest and daftest of the three horrors. AJ [video]

Jeffrey Combs *HP Lovecraft* • Tony Azito *Librarian* • Brian Yuzna *Cabbie* • Bruce Payne *Edward de la Poer* • Richard Lynch *Jethro de la Poer* • David Warner *Dr Madden* ■ *Dir* Christophe Gans, Shu Kaneko [Shusuke Kaneko], Brian Yuzna • *Scr* Brent V Friedman, Christophe Gans, Kazunori Ito, Brian Yuzna, from stories by HP Lovecraft

Ned Kelly ★★ 15

Biographical drama
1970 · UK · Colour · 99mins

One of the unfortunate temptations of hiring a rock star to carry a film is for the director to rely rather lazily on that star's charisma instead of trying to mould him into a character. Witness Mick Jagger, here cast as Australia's most memorable outlaw, who is so similar to his stage image that you half expect him to start shrieking, "Thank you, Sydney, you've been a great audience!". Director Tony Richardson's handling sometimes obscures the message and buries the drama. JM. Contains swearing. [video]

Mick Jagger *Ned Kelly* • Allen Bickford *Dan Kelly* • Geoff Gilmour *Steve Hart* • Mark McManus *Joe Byrne* • Serge Lazareff *Wild Wright* • Peter Sumner *Tom Lloyd* • Ken Shorter *Aaron Sherritt* • James Elliott *Pat O'Donnell* ■ *Dir* Tony Richardson • *Scr* Tony Richardson, Ian Jones

Ned Kelly ★★★ 15

Biographical drama
2003 · Aus/UK/US/Fr · Colour · 105mins

Gregor Jordan's film about Australia's famous outlaw casts as rosy a light as possible on the outback legend. Heath Ledger gives a growling performance as Ned, while the oppressive nature of the world in which he lived is evocatively presented. Misjudged and set up by the police, especially Superintendent Hare (Geoffrey Rush), he is forced to go on the run and form a gang. The outback is filmed in tones as sumptuous as any tourist brochure, but the idolisation of Kelly rings only as true as the stature accorded to Billy the Kid. TH [video] DVD

Heath Ledger *Ned Kelly* • Orlando Bloom *Joe Byrne* • Geoffrey Rush *Superintendent Francis Hare* • Naomi Watts *Julia Cook* • Laurence Kinlan *Dan Kelly* • Philip Barantini *Steve Hart* • Joel Edgerton *Aaron Sherritt* • Kiri Paramore *Alex Fitzpatrick* ■ *Dir* Gregor Jordan • *Scr* John McDonagh, from the novel *Our Sunshine* by Robert Drewe

Needful Things ★★ 15

Horror 1993 · US · Colour · 115mins

The Devil arrives in the sleepy coastal town of Castle Rock to open a curiosity shop selling bric-a-brac with nasty surprises attached. Director Fraser C Heston's adaptation of the Stephen King novel is overlong, if mechanically efficient, and the script can't make up its mind whether to mine the humour or the horror. Despite capable performances, this "Antiques Creepshow" fails to generate any sympathy for its characters, and the episodic format is annoying. AJ. Contains swearing and violence. [video]

Max von Sydow *Leland Gaunt* • Ed Harris *Sheriff Alan Pangborn* • Bonnie Bedelia *Polly Chalmers* • Amanda Plummer *Nettie Cobb* • JT Walsh *Danforth Keeton III* • Ray McKinnon *Deputy Norris Ridgewick* • Duncan Fraser *Hugh Priest* ■ *Dir* Fraser C Heston • *Scr* WD Richter, from the novel by Stephen King

Nefertite, Queen of the Nile ★★★

Historical epic 1961 · It · Colour · 97mins

Part of a deal made by 20th Century-Fox with Italian studios, this is a negligible trip to Ancient Egypt. Contract player Edmund Purdom is the sculptor who falls for the high priest's daughter (Jeanne Crain) and is sentenced to death. She's meant to be a bride of the new pharaoh so it's a case of "less majesty" if she loses her virginity. There are some cherishable lines, but otherwise it's a very dull excursion to the past. TH. Italian dialogue dubbed into English.

Jeanne Crain *Tanit/Nefertite* • Vincent Price *Benakon* • Edmund Purdom *Tumos* • Amedeo Nazzari *Amenophis IV* • Liana Orfei *Merith* ■ *Dir* Fernando Cerchio • *Scr* John Byrne, Ottavio Poggi, Fernando Cerchio

The Negotiator ★★★★ 15

Action drama
1998 · US/Ger · Colour · 133mins

Cluttered with clichés from other thrillers, this is still efficiently exciting cinema because of the electrifying chemistry between Samuel L Jackson and Kevin Spacey as Chicago police negotiators – cops skilled at talking hostage-takers out of the dead ends into which they put themselves. Jackson, fresh from persuading a madman not to kill his daughter, is accused of stealing from police funds. So he takes captives until his name is cleared, and Spacey has the job of "talking him down". It's that stand-off that director F Gary Gray makes such a cunningly dramatic centrepiece. TH. Contains swearing, violence. [video] DVD

Samuel L Jackson *Danny Roman* • Kevin Spacey *Chris Sabian* • David Morse *Commander Adam Beck* • Ron Rifkin *Commander Grant Frost* • John Spencer *Chief Al Travis* • JT Walsh *Terence Niebaum* • Siobhan Fallon *Maggie* • Paul Giamatti *Rudy Timmons* ■ *Dir* F Gary Gray • *Scr* James DeMonaco, Kevin Fox

Neighbors ★★★★ U

Silent comedy 1920 · US · BW · 17mins

Set amid rundown city tenements, this tale of thwarted lovers provides the impetus for some of Buster Keaton's most inspired sight gags. The sequence in which he uses a washing-line to escape from Virginia Fox's third-storey apartment is a masterclass in gymnastic slapstick, which culminates in him careering back into his beloved's room and straight into the arms of her seething pop, Joe Roberts. The clothes-line shenanigans with his own father, Joe Keaton, were a glorious throwback to their vaudeville days. DP [video]

Buster Keaton *Boy* • Joe Keaton *His father* • Virginia Fox *Girl* • Joe Roberts *Her father* • Eddie Cline [Edward Cline] *Cop* ■ *Dir/Scr* Buster Keaton, Eddie Cline [Edward Cline]

Neighbors ★★★ 15

Comedy 1981 · US · Colour · 91mins

This swan song of the John Belushi/Dan Aykroyd partnership is a flawed but fascinating stab by the comedians at breaking away from their traditional knockabout slapstick. The two stars even swap their usual comic personae, with Belushi playing a geeky, mild-mannered suburbanite who is slowly being driven mad by his crazy neighbours (Aykroyd and Cathy Moriarty). Director John G Avildsen shows little affinity for the material, but Aykroyd and especially Belushi are excellent and make it worth a look. JF. Contains swearing. [video]

John Belushi *Earl Keese* • Dan Aykroyd *Vic* • Kathryn Walker *Enid Keese* • Cathy Moriarty *Ramona* • Igors Gavon *Chic* ■ *Dir* John G Avildsen • *Scr* Larry Gelbart, from the novel by Thomas Berger

Neither the Sea nor the Sand ★★

Fantasy drama 1972 · UK · Colour · 95mins

Based on the novel by one-time newsreader Gordon Honeycombe, this romantic ghost story is a genuine oddity that was sadly overlooked at the time. Susan Hampshire retreats to Jersey where she meets and falls in love with lighthouse keeper Michael Petrovitch. When he dies, her friends and family (including Anthony Booth, Cherie's dad) are dismayed to find that death is no barrier to their love. FL

Susan Hampshire *Anna Robinson* • Michael Petrovitch *Hugh Dabernon* • Frank Finlay *George Dabernon* • Michael Craze *Collie* • Jack Lambert *Dr Irving* • David Garth *Mr Mackay* • Betty Duncan *Mrs Mackay* • Anthony Booth *Delamare* ■ *Dir* Fred Burnley • *Scr* Gordon Honeycombe, Rosemary Davies, from the novel by Gordon Honeycombe

Nell ★★★ 12

Drama 1994 · US · Colour · 108mins

Jodie Foster plays a young woman living in the North Carolina woods who has never seen the outside world and speaks a strange indecipherable language. Psychologist Natasha Richardson wants to take her into psychiatric care for research; sympathetic local doctor Liam Neeson believes she should be left alone. Although Foster is perhaps a little too showy in the title role (and was again Oscar-nominated for her pains), she still delivers a marvellous performance,

N

and director Michael Apted, making the most of the stunning locations, keeps the syrup at bay. JF. Contains some swearing and brief nudity.

Jodie Foster *Nell* • Liam Neeson *Jerome Lovell* • Natasha Richardson *Paula Olsen* • Richard Libertini *Alexander Paley* • Nick Searcy *Todd Peterson* • Robin Mullins *Mary Peterson* • Jeremy Davies *Billy Fisher* ■ *Dir* Michael Apted • *Scr* William Nicholson, Mark Handley, from the play *Idioglossia* by Mark Handley

Nell Gwyn ★★★ U

Historical drama 1934 · UK · BW · 71mins

The American censors were appalled when Herbert Wilcox's bawdy historical drama about Charles II's mistress was presented to them. In addition to 35 cuts, they suggested that a much more suitable ending would be to have Nell marry the king! A box-office smash in this country, the film benefits from a script by Miles Malleson that took much of its dialogue from Samuel Pepys's famous diary. Cedric Hardwicke has a rare old time as Charles, but Anna Neagle is just a touch too refined as Nell and comes off second best in her court intrigues with Jeanne de Casalis. DP DVD

Anna Neagle *Nell Gwyn* • Cedric Hardwicke *King Charles II* • Miles Malleson *Chiffinch* • Esme Percy *Samuel Pepys* • Jeanne de Casalis *Duchess of Portsmouth* • Lawrence Anderson *Duke of York* • Helena Pickard *Mrs Pepys* ■ *Dir* Herbert Wilcox • *Scr* Miles Malleson, from the diaries of Samuel Pepys

Nelly & Monsieur Arnaud ★★★★ PG

Drama 1995 · Fr/It /Ger · Colour · 106mins

Director Claude Sautet's distinctively cool style is wonderfully suited to this melancholy study of a young woman (Emmanuelle Béart) who becomes involved in a fragile, unfulfilled relationship with the elderly businessman (Michel Serrault) for whom she works as a secretary. There are more emotional insights than you find in many a so-called romantic movie – looks that are loaded with meaning, touches that bruise with the suggestion of passion – while the tale of obsession is told so discreetly it makes the film all the more haunting. TH. In French with English subtitles.

Emmanuelle Béart *Nelly* • Michel Serrault *Monsieur Arnaud* • Jean-Hugues Anglade *Vincent* • Claire Nadeau *Jacqueline* • Françoise Brion *Lucie* ■ *Dir* Claude Sautet • *Scr* Claude Sautet, Jacques Fieschi

Nemesis ★ 18

Science-fiction action
1993 · US · Colour · 91mins

Cyborg ex-cop Olivier Gruner is forced by police chief Tim Thomerson into stopping a band of techno-terrorists planning to disrupt a summit meeting. If he refuses, he'll die from a bomb implanted in his body. Schlockmeister Albert Pyun has had a long fascination with futuristic stories involving cyborgs, but this effort is just as threadbare and unconvincing as all his other attempts. Sue Price took over as the lead for three sequels. KB DVD

Olivier Gruner *Alex Rain* • Tim Thomerson *Farnsworth* • Deborah Shelton *Julian* • Marjorie Monaghan *Jared* • Merle Kennedy *Max Impact* • Cary-Hiroyuki Tagawa *Angie Liv* ■ *Dir* Albert Pyun • *Scr* Rebecca Charles

The Neon Bible ★★★ 15

Drama 1995 · UK/US · Colour · 87mins

This measured, beautifully photographed but harrowing study of family angst in Georgia around the time of the Second World War marked the American debut of director Terence Davies. He breathes some new life into the familiar small-town formula, thanks to his keen eye for detail and a supremely assured performance from Gena Rowlands as the nightclub singer aunt who shakes up the lives of ten-year-old Drake Bell and his parents Diana Scarwid and Denis Leary. DP. Contains violence and swearing.

Gena Rowlands *Aunt Mae* • Diana Scarwid *Sarah* • Denis Leary *Frank* • Jacob Tierney *David aged 15* • Leo Burmester *Bobbie Lee Taylor* • Frances Conroy *Miss Scover* • Peter McRobbie *Reverend Watkins* • Joan Glover *Flora* • Drake Bell *David aged ten* ■ *Dir* Terence Davies • *Scr* Terence Davies, from the novel by John Kennedy Toole • *Cinematographer* Mick Coulter

The Nephew ★★ 12

Drama 1997 · Ire · Colour · 104mins

In yet another Irish rural saga, a young American man returns to the village from which his deceased mother came, sending the residents into a turmoil. Sounds familiar? The only twist in the tale is that the man is black, but that's not enough to keep you entertained throughout this well-meaning but cliché-ridden tale. Taking a break from the Bond films, Pierce Brosnan is one of the film's producers, and he also stars as the local publican. JB. Contains swearing and violence. DVD

Pierce Brosnan *Joe Brady* • Donal McCann *Tony Egan* • Sinead Cusack *Brenda O'Boyce* • Hill Harper *Chad Egan-Washington* • Aislin McGuckin *Aislin Brady* • Niall Toibin *Sean Post* ■ *Dir* Eugene Brady • *Scr* Jacqueline O'Neill, Sean P Steele, from a story by Eugene Brady, Douglas Mayfield, Jacqueline O'Neill

The Neptune Factor ★ U

Science-fiction adventure
1973 · Can · Colour · 98mins

"The most fantastic undersea odyssey ever filmed," bragged the poster. Hardly – the producers should have been done under the trades description act for this feeble slice of aquatic sci-fi. Ben Gazzara and Ernest Borgnine are in charge of a mini-submarine, which offers the only chance of rescuing the crew of a sea-lab trapped by an earthquake on the ocean floor. A huge letdown. RS

Ben Gazzara *Commander Adrian Blake* • Yvette Mimieux *Leah Jansen* • Walter Pidgeon *Dr Samuel Andrews* • Ernest Borgnine *"Mack" MacKay* • Chris Wiggins *Captain Williams* ■ *Dir* Daniel Petrie • *Scr* Jack DeWitt

Neptune's Daughter ★★★ U

Musical comedy 1949 · US · Colour · 92mins

A super-fun all-star MGM Technicolor musical, this is as good-natured as they come. Metro's aqua-queen Esther Williams stars along with Red Skelton, Ricardo Montalban and the ever-wonderful Betty Garrett, and she gets to sing one of the nicest numbers ever to win the Academy Award for best song, Frank Loesser's catchy *Baby, It's Cold Outside*. The mistaken-identity plot is purely functional, but keep a beady eye out for a rare appearance on screen of the great Mel Blanc, the voice of all the Warner Bros cartoon characters. TS

Esther Williams *Eve Barrett* • Red Skelton *Jack Spratt* • Ricardo Montalban *Jose O'Rourke* • Betty Garrett *Betty Barrett* • Keenan Wynn *Joe Backett* • Xavier Cugat • Mike Mazurki *Mac Mozolla* • Mel Blanc *Julio* ■ *Dir* Edward Buzzell • *Scr* Dorothy Kingsley, Ray Singer, Dick Chevillat

The Nesting ★ 18

Horror 1981 · US · Colour · 99mins

Tame ghost story about an author (Robin Groves) who moves to an old, dark house, unaware that it is full of vengeful ghosts (two of whom are played by veterans John Carradine and Gloria Grahame). It all looks terribly cheap, while the attempts at special effects appear desperate. Another example of a porno director failing to cross to the mainstream. DM

Robin Groves *Lauren Cochran* • Christopher Loomis *Mark Felton* • Michael David Lally *Daniel Griffith* • John Carradine *Colonel LeBrun* • Gloria Grahame *Florinda Costello* • Bill Rowley *Frank Beasley* ■ *Dir* Armand Weston • *Scr* Daria Price, Armand Weston

The Net ★★ U

Spy drama 1953 · UK · BW · 82mins

This tepid thriller might have enjoyed more box-office success under its American title, *Project M7*. Although best known for his literary adaptations, director Anthony Asquith was no stranger to suspense movies but he plods through this story about aviation espionage with little enthusiasm. The surprisingly strong cast probably deserved better, and only Herbert Lom manages to give a good account of himself. DP

Phyllis Calvert *Lydia Heathley* • James Donald *Michael Heathley* • Robert Beatty *Sam Seagram* • Herbert Lom *Alex Leon* • Muriel Pavlow *Caroline Cartier* • Noel Willman *Dr Dennis Bord* • Walter Fitzgerald *Sir Charles Cruddock* • Patric Doonan *Brian Jackson* • Maurice Denham *Carrington* • Marjorie Fielding *Mama* ■ *Dir* Anthony Asquith • *Scr* William Fairchild, from the novel by John Pudney

The Net ★★ 12

Thriller 1995 · US · Colour · 109mins

Sandra Bullock's star charisma raises this mediocre computer-age paranoia fantasy to the level of watchable entertainment. The *Speed* heroine plays a lonely hacker who uncovers a criminal conspiracy. How she copes with the threat of cyberspace annihilation from an unknown assassin turns an already slow-moving thriller into a predictable game of hide-and-seek. AJ. Contains violence and swearing. DVD

Sandra Bullock *Angela Bennett* • Jeremy Northam *Jack Devlin* • Dennis Miller *Dr Alan Champion* • Diane Baker *Mrs Bennett* • Wendy Gazelle *Imposter* • Ken Howard *Bergstrom* • Ray McKinnon *Dale* ■ *Dir* Irwin Winkler • *Scr* John Brancato, Michael Ferris

Network ★★★★ 15

Drama 1976 · US · Colour · 116mins

This was a thunderous, strangely eerie swan song for Peter Finch, who plays a bilious and increasingly demented TV anchorman, ranting on air against his powerlessness. It's is a bravura performance from Finch – who was awarded a posthumous Oscar – given full flight by Paddy Chayefsky's daring, sumptuously satirical script, which throws a continuous hail of barbs at the electronic eye. Sidney Lumet directs with wild aplomb, allowing Finch free rein and keeping up a furious pace. Criticised by some at the time for a certain naivety and lack of subtlety, this remains one of the most devastating condemnations of the media's urge to exploit. SH. Contains swearing. DVD

Peter Finch *Howard Beale* • Faye Dunaway *Diana Christensen* • William Holden (2) *Max Schumacher* • Robert Duvall *Frank Hackett* • Wesley Addy *Nelson Chaney* • Ned Beatty *Arthur Jensen* • Beatrice Straight *Louise Schumacher* ■ *Dir* Sidney Lumet • *Scr* Paddy Chayefsky

Neutral Port ★★

Second World War drama
1940 · UK · BW · 92mins

Will Fyffe stars in this wartime romp as the irrepressible skipper who decides to replace his torpedoed cargo vessel with a brand new German ship. He plans to steal one from a neutral port, much to the horror of the British consul (Leslie Banks). As directed by Marcel Varnel, it has the mood of a French movie. AT

Will Fyffe *Capt Ferguson* • Leslie Banks *George Carter* • Yvonne Arnaud *Rosa Pirenti* • Phyllis Calvert *Helen Carter* • Hugh McDermott *Jim Grey* • Hugh Griffith ■ *Dir* Marcel Varnel • *Scr* JB Williams, TJ Morrison

Nevada ★★ U

Western 1944 · US · BW · 61mins

After RKO signed up Robert Mitchum in 1946, it tested his starring potential in a couple of B westerns as a replacement for Tim Holt who was away in the Armed Services. Mitchum is drearily deadpan and uncharismatic as a cowboy who is almost lynched after stumbling across the body of a murdered miner. Between chatting up not one, but two, leading ladies, Anne Jeffreys and Nancy Gates, he exposes the villain out to collar some hidden silver deposits. AE

Bob Mitchum [Robert Mitchum] *Jim "Nevada" Lacy* • Anne Jeffreys *Julie Dexter* • Nancy Gates *Hattie Ide* • Craig Reynolds *Crash Burridge* • Guinn "Big Boy" Williams *Dusty* • Richard Martin (1) *Chito Rafferty* ■ *Dir* Edward Killy • *Scr* Norman Houston, from the novel *Nevada* by Zane Grey

Nevada Smith ★★★ 15

Western 1966 · US · Colour · 125mins

An epic western with a fascinating premise – a young man tracks down the outlaws who killed his white father and Indian mother – is suffocated by lethargic direction from veteran Henry Hathaway, though the film is redeemed by Lucien Ballard's lush photography and an outstanding supporting cast. A miscast Steve McQueen brings star presence to a film that was backed by his own production company, Solar, and was a hit in its day. RS DVD

Steve McQueen *Nevada Smith/Max Sand* • Karl Malden *Tom Fitch* • Brian Keith *Jonas Cord* • Arthur Kennedy *Bill Bowdre* • Suzanne Pleshette *Pilar* • Raf Vallone *Father Zaccardi* • Janet Margolin *Neesa* • Pat Hingle *Big Foot* • Howard Da Silva *Warden* • Martin Landau *Jesse Coe* ■ *Dir* Henry Hathaway • *Scr* John Michael Hayes, from characters created by Harold Robbins

Never a Dull Moment ★★★ U

Comedy 1950 · US · BW · 89mins

A Manhattan lady songwriter and a widowed farmer meet at a charity show and fall in love. Transplanted to his rustic ranch, she has to cope with her precocious stepdaughters as well as the living conditions, the horses and the local characters. Irene Dunne and Fred MacMurray co-star in this good-natured, sometimes near-farcical romantic comedy. It's a lot of fun and didn't deserve the scathing critical reception it received upon release. RK

Irene Dunne *Kay* • Fred MacMurray *Chris* • William Demarest *Mears* • Andy Devine *Orvie* • Gigi Perreau *Tina* • Natalie Wood *Nan* • Philip Ober *Jed* • Jack Kirkwood *Papa Dude* ■ *Dir* George Marshall • *Scr* Lou Breslow, Doris Anderson, from the novel *Who Could Ask for Anything More* by Kay Swift

Never a Dull Moment ★★ U

Crime comedy 1968 · US · Colour · 84mins

In fact, there are too many dull moments in this formula comedy. Starring Dick Van Dyke and directed by Jerry Paris (who cut his directorial teeth on Van Dyke's TV show), it's a caper story, with our hero as a TV actor who is mistaken for a professional hitman and tries to prevent art fancier and mobster Edward G Robinson from stealing a priceless masterpiece. AT

Dick Van Dyke *Jack Albany* • Edward G Robinson *Leo Joseph Smooth* • Dorothy Provine *Sally Inwood* • Henry Silva *Frank Boley*

• Joanna Moore *Melanie Smooth* • Tony Bill *Florian* • Slim Pickens *Cowboy Schaeffer* • Jack Elam *Ace Williams* ■ *Dir* Jerry Paris • *Scr* AJ Carothers, from the novel *A Thrill a Minute with Jack Albany* by John Godey

Never Been Kissed ★★★ 12

Romantic comedy
1999 · US · Colour · 107mins

Drew Barrymore does what she does best – cute, funny romance – in this simple teen comedy about a bumbling young copy editor who gets a chance to prove herself as a reporter when she is sent undercover to a high school to find out just what sort of nefarious things students get up to nowadays. It also gives her the chance to rewrite her own painful school memories – she was the class nerd. Thanks to Barrymore's infectious performance and a fun turn from David Arquette as her older brother, this is enjoyably sweet fare. JB DVD

Drew Barrymore *Josie Geller* • David Arquette *Rob Geller* • Michael Vartan *Sam Coulson* • Molly Shannon *Anita* • John C Reilly *Gus* • Garry Marshall *Rigfort* • Leelee Sobieski *Aldys* ■ *Dir* Raja Gosnell • *Scr* Abby Kohn, Marc Silverstein, Jenny Bicks

Never Cry Wolf ★★★ PG

Adventure based on a true story
1983 · US · Colour · 100mins

After his directorial debut with the superb *Black Stallion*, Carroll Ballard spent two years on location in British Columbia making this captivating adaptation of Farley Mowat's autobiographical account of his time spent with a pack of wolves. With the help of the Inuit who saved his life, he not only learns all about the frozen wilderness and the people who live there, but also discovers who is responsible for ravaging the local caribou herds. As you'd expect of Ballard, a cameraman on *Star Wars*, the photography is awesome. DP. Contains brief nudity.

Charles Martin Smith *Tyler* • Brian Dennehy *Rosie* • Zachary Ittimangnaq *Ootek* • Samson Jorah *Mike* • Hugh Webster *Drunk* ■ *Dir* Carroll Ballard • *Scr* Curtis Hanson, Sam Hamm, Richard Kletter, Charles Martin Smith, Eugene Corr, Christina Luescher, from the non-fiction book by Farley Mowat

Never Die Alone ★★★ 18

Crime drama 2004 · US · Colour · 84mins

Director Ernest Dickerson gives a hackneyed topic an interesting spin in this gritty gangster thriller based on the novel by career criminal Donald Goines. Centred around a strong performance from rapper DMX, it tells the posthumous story of a drug dealer and all-round brute. Thematically there's nothing new in the cocktail of guns, addiction and crime, but it's the film's stylish execution that makes its mark. The urban *noir* atmosphere as aspiring reporter David Arquette unravels events has a pulpy appeal, while the unusually inventive visuals help offset the plot's predictability. SF. Contains violence, swearing and drug abuse. DVD

DM X *King David* • David Arquette *Paul* • Michael Ealy *Mike* • Clifton Powell *Moon* • Reagan Gomez-Preston *Juanita* • Jennifer Sky *Janet* • Antwon Tanner *Blue* ■ *Dir* Ernest Dickerson [Ernest R Dickerson] • *Scr* James Gibson, from the novel *Holloway House* by Donald Goines

Never Give a Sucker an Even Break ★★★★ U

Comedy 1941 · US · BW · 70mins

Although only credited (as Otis Criblecoblis) with devising the story, WC Fields actually scripted his final feature because director Edward Cline felt the rewrite imposed by the Universal front office was abysmal. In addition to being a dart directed at the empty heart of Hollywood, this is also a joyously anarchic assault on the sort of film narrative that Tinseltown held dear. By linking a series of bizarre, unrelated incidents and by blurring the line between reality and fantasy, Fields was way ahead of his time. A blistering parting gesture to an industry that failed to appreciate his genius. DP

WC Fields *The Great Man, WC "Uncle Bill" Fields* • Gloria Jean *His niece, Gloria Jean* • Leon Errol *His rival, Leon Errol* • Butch [Billy Lenhart] *Heckler* • Buddy [Kenneth Brown] *Heckler* • Margaret Dumont *Mrs Hemogloben* • Susan Miller *Ouliotta Hemogloben* • Franklin Pangborn *Producer, Franklin Pangborn* • Mona Barrie *Producer's wife* • Anne Nagel *Madame Gorgeous* ■ *Dir* Edward Cline • *Scr* John T Neville, Prescott Chaplin, from a story by Otis Criblecoblis [WC Fields]

Never Let Go ★ PG

Crime drama 1960 · UK · BW · 87mins

What was intended to be a gritty insight into the brutality of the underworld ends up being a tatty melodrama in this misfire from director John Guillermin. Peter Sellers is cast against type as the leader of a stolen car racket, whose ruthless methods prompt victim Richard Todd and street punk Adam Faith to forge an unlikely alliance against him. Alun Falconer's script does nobody any favours, with Sellers reduced to embarrassing histrionics in the bid to shed his comic image. DP DVD

Richard Todd *John Cummings* • Peter Sellers *Lionel Meadows* • Elizabeth Sellars *Anne Cummings* • Adam Faith *Tommy Towers* • Carol White *Jackie* • Mervyn Johns *Alfie Barnes* • Peter Jones *Alec Berger* • John Le Mesurier *Pennington* ■ *Dir* John Guillermin • *Scr* Alun Falconer, from a story by John Guillermin, Peter De Sarigny

Never Let Me Go ★★★ U

Romantic adventure
1953 · US/UK · BW · 93mins

An American news reporter in Russia falls in love with a ballerina and marries her, only for him to be deported by the authorities. A middle-aged Clark Gable and the glamorous Gene Tierney are the stars in this love story, which turns into a rescue drama halfway through. Directed by Delmer Daves, it was made by MGM's British arm, which explains the presence of Kenneth More, Bernard Miles and Frederick Valk in the cast. No surprises, but respectably escapist. RK

Clark Gable *Philip Sutherland* • Gene Tierney *Marya Lamarkina* • Richard Haydn *Christopher Wellington St John Denny* • Bernard Miles *Joe Brooks* • Belita *Valentina Alexandrovna* • Kenneth More *Steve Quillan* • Karel Stepanek *Commissar* • Theodore Bikel *Lieutenant* • Frederick Valk *Kuragin* ■ *Dir* Delmer Daves • *Scr* Ronald Millar, George Froeschel, from the novel *Came the Dawn* by Roger Bax

Never Love a Stranger ★★ PG

Crime drama 1958 · US · BW · 87mins

John Drew Barrymore stars as a Jewish orphan who becomes a New York crime kingpin in this tacky mixture of *Dead End Kids*-style schmaltz and Mob warfare, covering the early years of the 20th century to the Depression. Produced and co-written by Harold Robbins from his own potboiling novel, the only reason to watch today is for Steve McQueen in his first significant screen role as Barrymore's teenage buddy who grows up to become assistant DA. AT

John Drew Barrymore *Frank Kane* • Lita Milan *Julie* • Robert Bray *"Silk" Fennelli* • Steven McQueen [Steve McQueen] *Martin Cabell* • Salem Ludwig *Moishe Moscowitz* • Douglas Rodgers *Brother Bernard* ■ *Dir* Robert Stevens • *Scr* Harold Robbins, Richard Day, from the novel by Harold Robbins

Never on Sunday ★★★ PG

Comedy drama 1960 · Gr · BW · 98mins

Melina Mercouri won the best actress prize at Cannes for her boisterous performance in this rarified romp that owes more than a little to the Pygmalion myth. As the waterfront prostitute who receives a cultural crash course from a besotted American professor, she gleefully casts restraint to the winds, much to the approval of her director, co-star and future husband, Jules Dassin. Although Dassin successfully soaks up the local atmosphere, his script too often errs on the side of laboured bons mots and intellectual snobbery. Manos Hadjidakis's bouzouki music is also an acquired taste, although his theme song landed him an Oscar. DP

Melina Mercouri *Ilya* • Jules Dassin *Homer* • George Foundas *Tonio* • Titos Vandis *Jorgo* ■ *Dir/Scr* Jules Dassin

Never on Tuesday ★★ 15

Comedy 1988 · US · Colour · 86mins

Writer/director Adam Rifkin was barely in his 20s when he made this slight but amiable "stranded on the road" movie. Andrew Lauer and a very youthful Peter Berg are the jocks stranded in the desert after a car collision with Claudia Christian, fantasising about getting lucky while an assortment of characters – including some celebrity cameos – fail to get them up and running again. RT

Andrew Lauer *Matt* • Peter Berg *Eddie* • Claudia Christian *Tuesday* • Charlie Sheen *Thief* • Judd Nelson *Motorcycle cop* • Emilio Estevez *Tow-truck driver* • Gilbert Gottfried *Lucky Larry Lupin* • Nicolas Cage *Man in red sports car* • Cary Elwes *Tow-truck driver* ■ *Dir/Scr* Adam Rifkin

Never Say Die ★★

Comedy 1939 · US · BW · 80mins

This is one of Bob Hope's lesser efforts, in which he plays an eccentric millionaire who, believing he has only weeks to live, marries Martha Raye so that she can inherit his money. Though the script (co-written by Preston Sturges) has its fair share of gags, too much of the film is silly rather than funny and Raye tries to compensate with a surfeit of mugging. Alan Mowbray provides some of the best moments with his droll underplaying of a disagreeable prince. TV

Martha Raye *Mickey Hawkins* • Bob Hope *John Kidley* • Andy Devine *Henry Munch* • Alan Mowbray *Prince Smirnov* • Gale Sondergaard *Juno* • Sig Rumann [Sig Ruman] *Poppa Ingleborg* • Ernest Cossart *Jeepers* • Paul Harvey *Jasper Hawkins* ■ *Dir* Elliott Nugent • *Scr* Don Hartman, Frank Butler, Preston Sturges, from a play by William H Post

Never Say Goodbye ★★

Romantic comedy 1946 · US · BW · 97mins

The small daughter (Patti Brady) of a devil-may-care commercial artist (Errol Flynn) and a Park Avenue mother (Eleanor Parker) must live alternately with each of her recently divorced parents who, of course, still really love each other. Directed by James V Kern, this romantic comedy, while admittedly a collection of recycled clichés devoid of substance and populated by stereotypes, is nonetheless an entertainingly breezy affair. RK

Errol Flynn *Phil Gayley* • Eleanor Parker *Ellen Gayley* • Lucile Watson *Mrs Hamilton* • SZ "Cuddles" Sakall [SZ Sakall] *Luigi* • Forrest Tucker *Fenwick Lonkowski* • Donald Woods *Rex DeVallon* • Hattie McDaniel *Cozy* • Patti Brady *Phillippa "Flip" Gayley* ■ *Dir* James V Kern • *Scr* James V Kern, IAL Diamond, Lewis R Foster, from the story *Don't Ever Leave Me* by Ben Barzman, Norma Barzman

Never Say Goodbye ★★ U

Romantic drama 1955 · US · Colour · 95mins

American doctor Rock Hudson marries Cornell Borchers in Europe, but later walks out on her, taking their small daughter with him. Reconciliation is prevented by her incarceration in a Russian labour camp, but he runs into her ten years later in America... A shameless attempt by Universal to recycle the hit formula of their five-handkerchief weepie *Magnificent Obsession*, right down to Hudson operating on Borchers after she is hit by a truck in Chicago! The result is a cornucopia of wilted clichés. RK

Rock Hudson *Dr Michael Parker* • Cornell Borchers *Lisa Gosting/Dorian Kent* • George Sanders *Victor* • Ray Collins *Dr Bailey* • David Janssen *Dave* • Shelley Fabares *Suzy Parker* ■ *Dir* Jerry Hopper, Douglas Sirk • *Scr* Charles Hoffman, from the film *This Love of Ours* by Bruce Manning, John Klorer, Leonard Lee, from the play *Come Prima Meglio de Prima* by Luigi Pirandello

Never Say Never Again ★★★ PG

Spy adventure 1983 · UK · Colour · 128mins

Even though the Bond genre had long been steeped in self-parody, aided hugely by the smirking frivolity of Roger Moore, it was down to Sean Connery, returning to the role after 12 years, to balance the comic hysteria with action-man authenticity. Connery, ever-aware that he's at the centre of a big, expensive joke, still makes you believe that he's heroic to the core. His well-groomed presence holds the screen with ease and he's flanked here by three charismatic ne'er-do-wells, Klaus Maria Brandauer, Max von Sydow and Barbara Carrera. The plot, which owes much to *Thunderball*, lurches badly at times, but the wild action set pieces are to be cherished. JM DVD

Sean Connery *James Bond* • Klaus Maria Brandauer *Largo* • Max von Sydow *Blofeld* • Barbara Carrera *Fatima Blush* • Kim Basinger *Domino* • Bernie Casey *Felix Leiter* • Alec McCowen *"Q"/Algy* • Edward Fox *"M"* • Pamela Salem *Miss Moneypenny* ■ *Dir* Irvin Kershner • *Scr* Lorenzo Semple Jr, from a story by Kevin McClory, Jack Whittingham, Ian Fleming

Never So Few ★★

Second World War drama
1959 · US · Colour · 124mins

This MGM drama about wartime activity in Burma is notable mainly for its use of Ceylon locations. But the discussion of key moral issues is quickly discarded for the sake of a hot romance between Frank Sinatra and the immaculate Gina Lollobrigida. Today, this film is a fascinating relic of a studio in decline. The story is undimmed by the star casting of Sinatra, who had yet to acquire the image that would undermine his credibility in such roles forever. TS

Frank Sinatra *Captain Tom C Reynolds* • Gina Lollobrigida *Carla Vesari* • Peter Lawford *Captain Grey Travis* • Steve McQueen *Bill Ringa* • Richard Johnson *Captain Danny de Mortimer* • Paul Henreid *Nikko Regas* • Brian Donlevy *General Sloane* • Dean Jones *Sergeant Jim Norby* • Charles Bronson *Sergeant John Danforth* ■ *Dir* John Sturges • *Scr* Millard Kaufman, from the novel by Tom T Chamales

Never Steal Anything Small ★★★★

Musical crime drama
1959 · US · Colour · 94mins

Terrific if little-known semi-musical starring James Cagney, based on a play about trade unionism that never made it to Broadway. This is colourful and funny stuff, classily shot in CinemaScope and with some knockout production numbers, especially from

N

moll Cara Williams. Cagney shines throughout, though, in truth, he's a mite old for the role. Shirley Jones is just a little too sweet to be Cagney's other half, but there's super character work from the likes of Nehemiah Persoff and Royal Dano. TS

James Cagney *Jake MacIllaney* • Shirley Jones *Linda Cabot* • Roger Smith *Dan Cabot* • Cara Williams *Winnipeg* • Nehemiah Persoff *Pinelli* • Royal Dano *Words Cannon* • Anthony Caruso *Lieutenant Tevis* • Horace McMahon *OK Merritt* ■ *Dir* Charles Lederer • *Scr* Charles Lederer, from the play *The Devil's Hornpipe* by Maxwell Anderson, Rouben Mamoulian

Never Take No for an Answer ★★★ U

Drama 1951 · UK/It · BW · 83mins

Awash with sentimentality, yet rejoicing in the innocence and faith of its young hero, Paul Gallico's novel, *The Small Miracle*, is given a light coating of neorealism by its joint directors Maurice Clocheand Ralph Smart. As Peppino, the seven-year-old war orphan convinced that his ailing donkey will be cured if they visit the tomb of St Francis, the patron saint of animals, Vittorio Manunta is miraculously natural. DP

Vittorio Manunta *Peppino* • Denis O'Dea *Father Damico* • Guido Celano *Strotti* • Nerio Bernardi *Father Superior* ■ *Dir* Maurice Cloche, Ralph Smart • *Scr* Paul Gallico, Pauline Gallico, Maurice Cloche, Ralph Smart, from the novella *The Small Miracle* by Paul Gallico

Never Take Sweets from a Stranger ★★★

Drama 1960 · UK · BW · 91mins

An extremely audacious film for its time, dealing with the problem of paedophilia and building towards a surprisingly grim and disturbing climax. The story concerns an English family who emigrate to a small town in Canada. The father, Patrick Allen, takes up the post of headmaster at a school, but then his nine-year-old daughter is sexually abused by a local bigwig, played by Felix Aylmer. It's made by Hammer Films, so the movie walks a tightrope between seriousness and sensation. AT

Gwen Watford *Sally Carter* • Patrick Allen *Peter Carter* • Felix Aylmer *Clarence Olderberry Sr* • Niall MacGinnis *Defense counsel* • Alison Leggatt *Martha* • Bill Nagy *Clarence Olderberry Jr* ■ *Dir* Cyril Frankel • *Scr* John Hunter, from the play *The Pony Cart* by Roger Garis

Never Talk to Strangers ★★ 18

Erotic thriller
1995 · US/Can · Colour · 82mins

One of theatre director Peter Hall's occasional, unsuccessful forays into the cinema, this stars Rebecca De Mornay as an ice-cool criminal psychologist whose self-possession leaves her when she meets Antonio Banderas. They embark upon a torrid affair, but strange things start happening to De Mornay, and her new beau is soon under suspicion. AT. Contains violence, swearing, sex scenes and nudity. DVD

Rebecca De Mornay *Dr Sarah Taylor* • Antonio Banderas *Tony Ramirez* • Dennis Miller *Cliff Raddison* • Len Cariou *Henry Taylor* • Harry Dean Stanton *Max Cheski* • Eugene Lipinski *Dudakoff* • Martha Burns *Maura* ■ *Dir* Peter Hall • *Scr* Jordan Rush, Lewis Green

Never Too Late ★★★

Comedy 1965 · US · Colour · 103mins

Adapting his own Broadway hit, Sumner Arthur Long succeeds better than most in opening out a play for the big screen. He's helped in no small measure by Paul Ford and Maureen O'Sullivan, who expertly reprise their stage roles as the not exactly youthful couple whose ordered existence is thrown into turmoil by an unexpected pregnancy. Less effective, however, are Connie Stevens and Jim Hutton as their self-obsessed daughter and incompetent son-in-law, who milk the gags their elders time to perfection. DP

Paul Ford *Harry Lambert* • Maureen O'Sullivan *Edith Lambert* • Connie Stevens *Kate Clinton* • Jim Hutton *Charlie Clinton* • Jane Wyatt *Grace Kimbrough* • Henry Jones *Doctor Kimbrough* ■ *Dir* Bud Yorkin • *Scr* Sumner Arthur Long, from his play

Never Too Late ★ PG

Comedy drama 1996 · Can · Colour · 92mins

This takes the talents of Olympia Dukakis, Cloris Leachman and Jan Rubes, then buries their performances under a pile of bizarre plot twists and uneven farce. All you need to know is that the old folks include a manic depressive and a paraplegic lesbian, Corey Haim brings S&M to the proceedings and Matt Craven overacts to the point of absurdity as the retirement home's suspicious manager. Terrible stuff. JB

Olympia Dukakis *Rose* • Cloris Leachman *Olive* • Jan Rubes *Joseph* • Jean Lapointe *Woody* • Corey Haim *Max* • Matt Craven *Carl O'Neal* ■ *Dir* Giles Walker • *Scr* Donald Martin

Never Too Young to Rock ★★ U

Musical 1975 · UK · Colour · 101mins

Fans of *TOTP2* won't want to miss this crucial guide to mid-1970s glam rock, featuring the tinsel tonsils of the Rubettes, Mud and the Glitter Band. 1960s heart-throb Peter Noone (of Herman's Hermits) bridges the generation gap in the daftest plot imaginable. But the whole point to this sequined extravaganza is hearing such jukebox jives as *Angel Face*, *Tiger Feet* and *Sugar Baby Love* again. AJ

Peter Denyer *Hero* • Freddie Jones *Mr Rockbottom* • Sheila Steafel *Café proprietress* • Joe Lynch *Russian soldier* • John Clive *Bandsman* • Peter Noone *Army captain* ■ *Dir* Dennis Abey • *Scr* Ron Inkpen, Dennis Abey

Never Wave at a WAC ★★★

Comedy 1952 · US · BW · 87mins

Delightful, light-hearted farce in which a divorced Washington hostess joins the Women's Army Corps in order to get to Paris and meet her boyfriend. Rosalind Russell has fun playing the unworldly heroine – when she goes to sign up, she takes her secretary with her to fill in the forms – and when not in uniform she wears a succession of eye-catching James Galanos gowns. When the script flags, the top-flight cast keeps things bubbling. TV

Rosalind Russell *Jo McBain* • Paul Douglas *Andrew McBain* • Marie Wilson *Clara Schneiderman* • William Ching *Lt Col Schuyler Fairchild* • Leif Erickson *Sgt Noisy Jackson* • Arleen Whelan *Sgt Toni Wayne* • Charles Dingle *Senator Tom Reynolds* • Lurene Tuttle *Capt Murchison* ■ *Dir* Norman Z McLeod • *Scr* Ken Englund, from the story *The Private Wore Skirts* by Frederick Kohner, Fred Brady

The NeverEnding Story ★★★★ U

Fantasy adventure
1984 · W Ger · Colour · 89mins

German director Wolfgang Petersen is now perhaps best known for action-packed blockbusters, but in his first English-language movie he proves to be equally at home in the world of fantasy. Barret Oliver plays the young boy drawn by a magical book into a wondrous alternative world that is threatened by evil forces. The story is a touch simplistic, but Petersen's direction is assured and children will be dazzled by the imaginative effects and stunning sets. JF

Noah Hathaway *Atreyu* • Barret Oliver *Bastian* • Tami Stronach *Childlike empress* • Moses Gunn *Cairon* • Patricia Hayes *Urgl* • Gerald McRaney *Bastian's father* • Thomas Hill *Koreander* ■ *Dir* Wolfgang Petersen • *Scr* Wolfgang Petersen, Herman Weigel, from the novel by Michael Ende

The NeverEnding Story II: the Next Chapter ★★ U

Fantasy adventure
1991 · Ger/US · Colour · 85mins

Bastian returns (albeit in a different guise) for another adventure in the imaginary land of Fantasia in this frankly disappointing sequel. Australian director George Miller (not the *Mad Max* one) assumes the storyteller's chair only to find that, for all its empresses, towers and enchanted creatures, he's been given a dull tale to relate. He does what he can with some engaging special effects, but Jonathan Brandis is too feeble a hero to get excited about. DP

Jonathan Brandis *Bastian* • Kenny Morrison *Atreyu* • Clarissa Burt *Xayide* • Alexandra Johnes *Childlike empress* • Martin Umbach *Nimbly* • John Wesley Shipp *Barney Bux* ■ *Dir* George Miller (1) • *Scr* Karin Howard, from the novel *The NeverEnding Story* by Michael Ende

The NeverEnding Story III ★★ U

Fantasy 1994 · Ger · Colour · 91mins

By now the *NeverEnding Story* franchise was, well, heading towards an end. This one is more firmly anchored in real life, possibly to its detriment, with young Bastian being badly bullied at school by a bunch of no-gooders called the "Nasties". His only sanctuary is the library where he can escape to the world of Fantasia via the *NeverEnding Story* book. JF

Jason James Richter *Bastian Bux* • Melody Kay *Nicole* • Freddie Jones *Mr Coreander/Old Man of Wandering Mountain* • Jack Black *Slip* • Ryan Bollman *Dog* • Carole Finn *Mookie* ■ *Dir* Peter MacDonald • *Scr* Jeff Lieberman, from a story by Karin Howard, from characters created by Michael Ende

The New Adventures of Pinocchio ★★ PG

Fantasy adventure
1999 · US/Lux · Colour · 84mins

Veteran director Michael Anderson may seem an odd choice to handle this special effects-laden fairy-tale. But he invests the "sequel" to Carlo Collodi's classic story with a certain old-fashioned charm. Now a real 12-year-old boy, Gabriel Thompson is transformed back into a puppet after drinking a potion given to him by a carnival crone, who turns out to be sinister puppeteer Udo Kier. Technically, it's quietly impressive. If only the same could be said for the song-and-dance routines. DP DVD

Martin Landau *Geppetto* • Udo Kier *Mme Flambeau/Lorenzini* • Gabriel Thomson *Pinocchio* • Gemma Gregory *Blue Fairy* • Warwick Davis *Dwarf* ■ *Dir* Michael Anderson • *Scr* Sherry Mills, Tom Sheppard, from characters created by Carlo Collodi

The New Adventures of Pippi Longstocking ★ U

Adventure 1988 · US · Colour · 96mins

There was absolutely no point whatsoever in Americanising the popular creation of Swedish children's novelist Astrid Lindgren, whose character had already featured in several home-grown film versions. Despite a much publicised quest to find a new Pippi, this new movie barely saw the light of day. Leaden and unwatchable. TS

Tami Erin *Pippi Longstocking* • David Seaman Jr *Tommy* • Cory Crow *Annika* • Eileen Brennan *Miss Bannister* • Dennis Dugan *Mr Settigren* • Dianne Hull *Mrs Settigren* ■ *Dir* Ken Annakin • *Scr* Ken Annakin, from the books by Astrid Lindgren

The New Adventures of Tarzan ★★★ U

Adventure 1935 · US · BW · 74mins

The jungle swinger from Edgar Rice Burroughs's famous yarns goes to Guatemala to rescue an old friend and encounters a dangerous cult religion. Also known as *Tarzan and the Lost Goddess*, this B-picture was originally a Saturday matinée serial, but was later released as a feature. It lacks any kind of sophistication, but is still mildly compelling. Tarzan is played by Herman Brix, who later changed his name to Bruce Bennett. TH

Herman Brix [Bruce Bennett] *Tarzan* • Frank Baker *Major Martling, archaeologist* • Dale Walsh *Alice Martling* • Harry Ernest *Gordon Hamilton* • Lewis Sargent *George* • Ula Holt *Ula Vale* • Don Castello *Raglan* ■ *Dir* Edward Kull, WF McGaugh • *Scr* Edwin Blum, Charles Francis Royal, from the novels by Edgar Rice Burroughs

The New Age ★★ 18

Satire 1994 · US · Colour · 107mins

Since arriving in Hollywood from Australia in the early 1990s, Judy Davis has all too rarely been given the chance to show what she can do. Given that it was written and directed by *The Player* screenwriter Michael Tolkin, this should have been the perfect vehicle – an LA couple's yuppie lifestyle takes a turn for the worse, ushering the pair in to running their own upmarket fashion boutique. Yet, Tolkin infuriatingly misses the target. Davis and *RoboCop* star Peter Weller are splendid as the downwardly spiralling husband and wife, but what should have been a savage satire emerges merely as a collection of clever ideas gone sadly awry. DP

Peter Weller *Peter Witner* • Judy Davis *Katherine Witner* • Patrick Bauchau *Jean Levy* • Rachel Rosenthal *Sarah Friedberg* • Adam West *Jeff Winter* • Paula Marshall *Alison Gale* ■ *Dir/Scr* Michael Tolkin

The New Babylon ★★★ U

Silent political drama
1929 · USSR · BW · 76mins

Babylon is a fashionable Paris department store where salesgirl Elena Kuzmina works for the capitalist bourgeoisie. A significant silent film from the influential Soviet partnership of Grigori Kozintsev and Leonid Trauberg, this utilises the montage techniques that characterised the films of Eisenstein. Satirical, cynical and inventive, the film is also episodic and emblematic – capitalists are cowardly and greedy, the workers patriotic and brave – as it observes the devastating effects of the Franco-Prussian war through a Marxist/Stalinist eye. RK

Elena Kuzmina *Louise Poirier* • Pyotr Sobolevsky *Jean, a soldier* • David Gutman *Grasselin* • Sophie Magarill *An actress* • Sergei Gerasimov *Lutro, journalist* ■ *Dir/Scr* Grigori Kozintsev, Leonid Trauberg

The New Centurions ★★★★ 15

Police drama 1972 · US · Colour · 98mins

Virtually dismissed on release, this cracking crime drama is violent and humorous by turns and superbly directed by the estimable Richard Fleischer from a top-notch screenplay by Stirling Silliphant. The real star of the movie, despite competition from a high-calibre cast, is cop-turned-author Joseph Wambaugh, whose own police experiences form the basis of the movie. Many of the cast went on to play similar roles in TV series; this one, though, is the real thing, with star George C Scott particularly outstanding. TS

George C Scott *Sergeant Kilvinsky* • Stacy Keach *Roy Fehler* • Jane Alexander *Dorothy Fehler* • Scott Wilson *Gus* • Rosalind Cash *Lorrie* • Erik Estrada *Sergio* • Clifton James *Whitey* • Richard Kalk *Milton* • James Sikking [James B Sikking] *Sergeant Anders* ■ *Dir* Richard Fleischer • *Scr* Stirling Silliphant, from the novel by Joseph Wambaugh

New Face in Hell ★★

Crime thriller 1968 · US · Colour · 108mins

Wealthy tycoon Raymond Burr suspects that his wife is trying to murder his mistress, so he hires shabby private eye George Peppard to be her bodyguard. Making his first Hollywood movie, British director John Guillermin pays passing nods to all the old Bogart movies. However, this is essentially an essay in late 1960s graphic violence and James Bond-style glamour. AT

George Peppard *PJ Detweiler* • Raymond Burr *William Orbison* • Gayle Hunnicutt *Maureen Preble* • Coleen Gray *Betty Orbison* • Susan Saint James *Linette Orbison* • Wilfrid Hyde White *Billings-Browne* • Brock Peters *Police Chief Waterpark* ■ *Dir* John Guillermin • *Scr* Philip Reisman Jr, from a story by Philip Reisman Jr, Edward Montagne Jr [Edward J Montagne]

New Faces ★★★

Musical comedy revue
1954 · US · Colour · 98mins

No attempt was made to open out this hit-and-miss filmed record of the popular Broadway revue, and CinemaScope only enhanced the feeling of a proscenium arch. Yet it's interesting to see a cast of talented newcomers headed by Eartha Kitt, who sings (or rather purrs) five wittily sexy songs. Comedienne Alice Ghostley has an ironic number called *Boston Beguine*, while Carol Lawrence sings and dances. RB

Ronny Graham • Eartha Kitt • Robert Clary • Carol Lawrence • Alice Ghostley • June Carroll • Paul Lynde ■ *Dir* Harry Horner • *Scr* Melvin Brooks [Mel Brooks], Ronny Graham, Paul Lynde, Luther Davis, John Cleveland, from the revue *New Faces of 1952* by Leonard Sillman

New Faces of 1937 ★★ U

Musical 1937 · US · BW · 98mins

A theatrical producer sells 85 per cent of a show to four backers, then tries to make sure it's a flop so he can pocket the surplus. Yes, it's the plot of *The Producers* some 30 years earlier, though this version lacks both the wit and the flair of the Mel Brooks classic, with even the great Milton Berle straining to compensate for poor material. An undistinguished score is no help, but musical fans will find it watchable for the variety acts. TV

Joe Penner *Seymore Semor* • Milton Berle *Wellington Wedge* • Parkyakarkus *Parky* • Harriet Hilliard [Harriet Nelson] *Patricia* • William Brady *Jimmy* • Jerome Cowan *Robert Hunt* • Thelma Leeds *Elaine* • Lorraine Krueger *Suzy* • Ann Miller ■ *Dir* Leigh Jason • *Scr* Nat Perrin, Philip G Epstein, Irving S Brecher, Harold Kusell, Harry Clork, Howard J Green, David Freedman, from the story *Shoestring* by George Bradshaw

The New Gulliver ★★★★

Puppet fantasy 1935 · USSR · BW · 85mins

Russian special effects expert Alexander Ptushko chose Jonathan Swift's satire *Gulliver's Travels* as the basis for the world's first feature-length puppet film. The laborious process – it took Ptushko almost three years to complete – also made it one of the last of the genre. Effective use is made of tiny, grotesque wax puppets, created in conjunction with an actor playing Gulliver, while the tale itself was adapted to fit the Soviet ideology of the time. RB. In Russian with English subtitles.

Vladimir Konstantinov *Gulliver* ■ *Dir* Alexander Ptushko • *Scr* Alexander Ptushko, Grigori Roshal, from the novel *Gulliver's Travels* by Jonathan Swift • *Puppet Maker* Sarra Mokil

The New Guy ★ 12

Comedy 2002 · US · Colour · 84mins

Directed by *There's Something about Mary* co-writer Ed Decter, this excruciating teen comedy is a formulaic jumble of crass visual gags, limp dialogue and social stereotyping. DJ Qualls plays drippy senior Dizzy, who reinvents himself as the epitome of high-school cool and, of course, gets the hottest girl (Eliza Dushku) with the assistance of a black convict with attitude. It's blatantly unfunny and infuriatingly repetitious, underscoring its faults with a saccharine ending that patronisingly proclaims "it's OK to be an outcast". SF DVD

DJ Qualls *Dizzy Gillespie Harrison/Gil Harris* • Eliza Dushku *Danielle* • Zooey Deschanel *Nora* • Lyle Lovett *Bear* • Jerod Mixon *Kirk* • Illeana Douglas *Kiki Pierce* ■ *Dir* Ed Decter • *Scr* David Kendall

The New Interns ★★

Medical melodrama
1964 · US · BW · 122mins

The sequel to the 1962 hit *The Interns* again turns the medical profession into racy melodrama. Original cast members Michael Callan, Telly Savalas and Stefanie Powers remain in post while George Segal and Dean Jones are the new surgeons on the block, along with a bevy of young Hollywood hopefuls. Several separate stories are interwoven, notably Jones's low sperm count and Segal's background as a juvenile delinquent. AT

Michael Callan *Dr Alec Considine* • Dean Jones *Dr Lew Worship* • Telly Savalas *Dr Riccio* • Stefanie Powers *Gloria Worship* • Barbara Eden *Laura Rogers* • Kay Stevens *Didi Loomis* • Inger Stevens *Nancy Terman* • George Segal *Dr Tony Parelli* ■ *Dir* John Rich • *Scr* Wilton Schiller, from characters created by Richard Frede

New Jack City ★★★★ 18

Action drama 1991 · US · Colour · 96mins

Mario Van Peebles made his directorial debut with this hard-hitting mix of crime thriller and social drama, which is as indebted to the urban realism of Spike Lee as it is to gangster movies such as Brian De Palma's *Scarface*. Based on actual events, the film suggests that the problems facing black inner-city kids are often as much caused by exploitative drugs barons as they are by racial discrimination. Wesley Snipes achieves a chilling mix of arrogance and malevolence as a ruthless drugs lord, while Van Peebles and fellow cops Ice-T and Judd Nelson successfully convey a sense of crusade rather than mere law enforcement. DP. Contains swearing, violence and sex scenes. DVD

Wesley Snipes *Nino Brown* • Ice-T *Scotty Appleton* • Allen Payne *Gee Money* • Chris Rock *Pookie* • Mario Van Peebles *Detective Stone* • Michael Michele *Selina* • Bill Nunn *Duh Duh Duh Man* • Judd Nelson *Officer Nick Peretti* ■ *Dir* Mario Van Peebles • *Scr* Barry Michael Cooper, Thomas Lee Wright, from a story by Thomas Lee Wright

New Jersey Drive ★★★ 18

Drama 1995 · US · Colour · 93mins

Director Nick Gomez here explores the world of disillusioned urban youth in Newark, "the car theft capital of the world". It has grit, attitude and pseudo-documentary realism to spare as it adds new insightful twists to the time-honoured tale of youths up to no good. Sharron Corley and Gabriel Casseus are excellent as the petty criminal joyriders hounded by sadistic cop Saul Stein. AJ. Contains violence, swearing, drug abuse.

Sharron Corley *Jason Petty* • Gabriel Casseus *Midget* • Saul Stein *Roscoe* • Gwen McGee *Renee Petty* • Andre Moore *Ritchie* • Donald Adeosun Faison *Tiny Dime* • Michele Morgan *Coreen* • Samantha Brown *Jackie Petty* ■ *Dir* Nick Gomez • *Scr* Nick Gomez, from a story by Michel Marriott, Nick Gomez

A New Kind of Love ★★

Comedy 1963 · US · Colour · 110mins

Paul Newman has had his moments as a screen comedian, but this is not one of them. In this undistinguished battle of the sexes, he plays a struggling writer who makes his name penning a newspaper column based on the romantic exploits of a smart Parisienne, unaware that she is the tomboy fashion designer he met on the plane. While not in the screwball class of a Katharine Hepburn, Joanne Woodward is nevertheless highly engaging as both the dippy career girl and the fibbing socialite. DP

Paul Newman *Steve Sherman* • Joanne Woodward *Samantha Blake* • Thelma Ritter *Lena O'Connor* • Eva Gabor *Felicianne Courbeau* • George Tobias *Joseph Bergner* ■ *Dir/Scr* Melville Shavelson

The New Land ★★★★

Adventure drama
1972 · Swe · Colour · 160mins

Having survived the perilous passage depicted in *The Emigrants*, Swedish farmer Max von Sydow and his wife, Liv Ullmann, endeavour to make their mark upon the unrelenting plains of Minnesota in this concluding part of Jan Troell's epic adaptation of Vilhelm Moberg's literary saga. As before, Troell's refusal to romanticise either the landscape or the daily grind heightens the authenticity of the struggle, as well as its dramatic intensity. Proud but vulnerable, von Sydow is superb as he tries to comprehend his kinsmen's lust for gold and the politics that will plunge his adopted nation into civil war. DP. In Swedish with English subtitles.

Max von Sydow *Karl Oskar* • Liv Ullmann *Kristina* • Eddie Axberg *Robert* • Hans Alfredson *Jonas Petter* • Halvar Bjork *Anders Mansson* • Allan Edwall *Danjel* ■ *Dir* Jan Troell • *Scr* Bengt Forslund, Jan Troell, from the novel *The Emigrants* by Vilhelm Moberg

A New Leaf ★★★★ U

Black comedy 1971 · US · Colour · 101mins

A sophisticated, cynical black comedy from writer/director/star Elaine May about middle-aged playboy Walter Matthau who, lacking the resources to sustain his extravagant lifestyle, decides to marry wealthy wallflower Elaine May to keep himself in the luxury to which he's accustomed. Matthau intends to bump his new bride off, only to find himself afflicted by a guilty conscience. This is a wonderfully mordant Manhattan fairy tale. TH

Walter Matthau *Henry Graham* • Elaine May *Henrietta Lowell* • Jack Weston *Andrew McPherson* • George Rose *Harold* • James Coco *Uncle Harry* • Doris Roberts *Mrs Traggert* • Renee Taylor *Sharon Hart* • William Redfield *Beckett* ■ *Dir* Elaine May • *Scr* Elaine May, from the short story *The Green Heart* by Jack Ritchie

A New Life ★★★ 15

Comedy drama 1988 · US · Colour · 99mins

Alan Alda, still trying to break free from his *MASH* TV image, here takes control of his career by writing and directing, as well as starring in, this comedy drama. He and his screen wife Ann-Margret divorce after more than 20 years, leaving Alda to drink and wisecrack his way through a series of one-night stands before both he and Ann-Margret start up relationships with younger people (Veronica Hamel and John Shea). It's all sub-Woody Allen stuff, but the performances are amiable. JB. Contains swearing.

Alan Alda *Steve Giardino* • Ann-Margret *Jackie Giardino* • Hal Linden *Mel Arons* • Veronica Hamel *Dr Kay Hutton* • John Shea *Doc* • Mary Kay Place *Donna* ■ *Dir/Scr* Alan Alda

New Moon ★★★ U

Musical 1940 · US · BW · 104mins

A splendid and popular Jeanette MacDonald/Nelson Eddy version of Sigmund Romberg's operetta, which was filmed a decade earlier with Metropolitan Opera stars Grace Moore and Lawrence Tibbett. MGM changed the setting from pre-revolutionary Russia to a very anti-British New Orleans, but it makes no difference. The terrific score includes *Softly as in a Morning Sunrise*, *Lover Come Back* and *One Kiss*, all with marvellous Oscar Hammerstein lyrics. TS

Jeanette MacDonald *Marianne de Beaumanoir* • Nelson Eddy *Charles Mission/Duc de Villiers* • Mary Boland *Valerie de Rossac* • George Zucco *Vicomte de Ribaud* • HB Warner *Father Michel* • Richard Purcell [Dick Purcell] *Alexander* • Stanley Fields *Tambour* • Bunty Cutler *Julie the maid* ■ *Dir* Robert Z Leonard • *Scr* Jacques Deval, Robert Arthur, from the operetta by Sigmund Romberg, Oscar Hammerstein II, Frank Mandel, Lawrence Schwab

New Port South ★★★ 12

Drama 2001 · US · Colour · 89mins

This John Hughes-produced exploration of the cause and effect of youthful idealism is a sophisticated affair. Stylishly shot and featuring strong performances, it's a well-executed, non-patronising movie with a powerful message. Events unfold in a suburban Chicago high school, where a former pupil's escape from a mental institute prompts student Blake Shields to investigate his mysterious case. Believing that the school's restrictive rules were to blame for the boy's incarceration, Shields persuades his friends to initiate a campaign against their teachers. SF DVD

Blake Shields *Maddox* • Todd Field *Mr Walsh* • Will Estes *Chris* • Melissa George *Amanda* • Raymond J Barry *Preston Foster* ■ *Dir* Kyle Cooper • *Scr* James Hughes

New Rose Hotel ★

Science-fiction drama
1998 · US · Colour · 92mins

Based on a William Gibson short story, cult director Abel Ferrara's cyberpunk *Pygmalion* is an incomprehensible mess. It's an arrogantly arty sci-fi reverie about Willem Dafoe's life unravelling as the dirty deals he's involved in finally catch up with him and he anguishes over the true meaning of love. AJ

Christopher Walken *Fox* • Willem Dafoe *X* • Asia Argento *Sandii* • Yoshitaka Amano *Hiroshi* • Annabella Sciorra *Madame Rosa* ■ *Dir* Abel Ferrara • *Scr* Christi Zois, Abel Ferrara, from a short story by William Gibson

New Town Original ★★ 15

Drama 2004 · UK · Colour · 86mins

The banality of estate life in Blair's Britain is exposed in this ambitious but undistinguished independent feature. Set in the concrete jungle that is Basildon, writer/director Jason Ford's first movie is a low-budget tale about everyman Elliott Jordan, who becomes convinced that he's in danger after sleeping with the ex-girlfriend (Katharine Peachey) of local hard man Paul McNeilly. Sadly, it's impossible to ignore the inexperience of the young cast, whose overplaying tips the tone from gritty realism into amateurish melodrama. DP. Contains swearing, sex scenes, violence.

Elliott Jordan *Mick* • Nathan Thomas *Johnno* • Katharine Peachey *Nicki* • Richard Gooch *Ozzy* • Kal Aise *Bal* • Paul McNeilly *Si Naylor* • Steve Gibbs *Dave Milner* • Terry Bird *Darren Tutt* ■ *Dir/Scr* Jason Ford

New World Disorder ★★ 18

Action thriller 1999 · US · Colour · 89mins

If this computer thriller is anything to go by, villainy is clearly not Andrew McCarthy's forte. Rutger Hauer plays the veteran detective forced to learn new tricks from his tech-savvy partner Tara FitzGerald as they track down evil hacker McCarthy. Director Richard Spence hurls his actors through a series of barely competent set pieces while forcing them to spout risible dialogue. DP

Rutger Hauer *David Marx* • Andrew McCarthy *Kurt Bishop* • Tara FitzGerald *Kris Paddock* • Hari Dhillon *Mark Ohai* ■ *Dir* Richard Spence • *Scr* Jeffrey Smith, Ehren Kruger

New Year's Day ★★ 18

Drama 1999 · UK/Fr · Colour · 97mins

In this low-budget British attempt to explore the adolescent response to loss, Andrew Lee-Potts and Bobby Barry play the sole survivors of a tragic accident that killed all their schoolfriends and put their teacher in a coma. The two friends embark on a series of therapeutic, but increasingly preposterous pranks with the intention of committing cliff-top suicide in a year's time. Unfortunately the courageous performances of the two lead actors are compromised throughout by a calculating blend of social realism, macabre comedy and overt sentimentality. DP DVD

Marianne Jean-Baptiste *Veronica* • Anastasia Hille *Shelley* • Andrew Lee-Potts *Jake* • Bobby Barry *Steven* • Michael Kitchen *Robin* • Sue Johnston *Mrs Fisher* • Jacqueline Bisset *Geraldine* ■ *Dir* Suri Krishnamma • *Scr* Ralph Brown

N

New York Confidential ★★★

Crime drama 1955 · US · BW · 87mins

This gangster thriller, a precursor to *The Godfather*, was among the first to show the Mafia as a business linked as much by blood as bloodiness. Written by Clarence Greene and Russell Rouse, who also directs, it marked the end of an era for Warner Bros, home of Cagney, Bogart and Robinson, and the beginning of a new one. Broderick Crawford is the godfather, Anne Bancroft is his daughter, while Richard Conte is the assassin he takes under his wing. TH

Broderick Crawford *Charlie Lupo* • Richard Conte *Nick Magellan* • Marilyn Maxwell *Iris Palmer* • Anne Bancroft *Kathy Lupo* • J Carrol Naish *Ben Dagajanian* ■ *Dir* Russell Rouse • *Scr* Clarence Greene, Russell Rouse, from a book by Jack Lait, Lee Mortimer

New York Cop ★ 18

Police drama 1995 · US/Jpn · Colour · 84mins

This is as bland and generic as its title, despite being supposedly based on a true story. An attempt to emulate US cop movies, complete with sporadic action sequences, it lacks their energy and even a basic understanding of their conventions, while its treatment of African-Americans will be considered by many to be offensive. Toru Nakamura brings nothing to his character except an accent that makes much of his dialogue hard to understand. KB

Toru Nakamura *Toshi* • Chad McQueen *Hawk* • Andreas Katsulas *Ferrara* • Conan Lee *Konen Li* • Mira Sorvino *Maria* • Tony Sirico *Mr C* ■ *Dir* Toru Murakawa • *Scr* Hiroshi Kashiwabara, from the non-fiction book *New York Undercover Cop* by Jiro Ueno

New York Minute ★★ PG

Comedy adventure
2004 · US · Colour · 87mins

This action comedy is the project that twins Mary-Kate and Ashley Olsen selected as their first "grown-up" movie, building on their successful careers as child actors. Aiming to demonstrate the teens' very individual personalities, the film sees Mary-Kate's school-skipping rebel heading to New York to try to slip her rock band's demo to music executives, accompanied by her overachieving sibling who's there to compete for a university scholarship. Too predictable and cutesy to appeal much beyond its adolescent audience. SF DVD

Ashley Olsen *Jane Ryan* • Mary-Kate Olsen *Roxy Ryan* • Eugene Levy *Max Lomax* • Andy Richter *Bennie Bang* • Riley Smith *Jim, the bike messenger* • Jared Padalecki *Trey Lipton* • Dr Drew Pinsky *Dr Ryan* • Darrell Hammond *Hudson McGill* • Andrea Martin *Sen Anne Baxter-Lipton* ■ *Dir* Dennie Gordon • *Scr* Emily Fox, Adam Cooper, Bill Collage, from a story by Emily Fox

New York, New York ★★★★ PG

Musical drama 1977 · US · Colour · 156mins

This neglected gem from Martin Scorsese, traces the love-hate relationship of saxophonist Robert De Niro and singer Liza Minnelli. The action fairly swings along from the couple's first meeting on VJ Day, through De Niro's rise to bandleader and the birth of their baby, to Minnelli's big break in the movies. Although the tempo drops occasionally, Scorsese's re-creation of the postwar era is faultless, and he handles the musical numbers with aplomb. De Niro packs plenty of swaggering sax appeal, but the effervescent Minnelli steals the spotlight with a series of show stoppers. DP. Contains swearing. DVD

Robert De Niro *Jimmy Doyle* • Liza Minnelli *Francine Evans* • Lionel Stander *Tony Harwell* • Mary Kay Place *Bernice* • George Memmoli *Nicky* • Murray Moston *Horace Morris* • Barry Primus *Paul Wilson* • Georgie Auld *Frankie Harte* ■ *Dir* Martin Scorsese • *Scr* Earl MacRauch, Mardik Martin, from a story by Earl MacRauch

New York Stories ★★★ 15

Portmanteau movie
1989 · US · Colour · 119mins

A word to the wise. As soon as Martin Scorsese's *Life Lessons* episode ends, you have 33 minutes to yourself – unless, of course, you feel you really have to sit through Francis Coppola's atrocious aberration *Life without Zoe*. Scorsese's contribution, on the other hand, is a superbly controlled drama focusing on artist Nick Nolte's relationship with his muse, Rosanna Arquette. But the real showstopper comes from Woody Allen, whose *Oedipus Wrecks* is one of the funniest things he's ever done, thanks largely to a monstrous performance by mother-from-hell Mae Questel. DP. Contains swearing. DVD

Nick Nolte *Lionel Dobie* • Rosanna Arquette *Paulette* • Steve Buscemi *Gregory Stark* • Peter Gabriel • Heather McComb *Zoe* • Talia Shire *Charlotte* • Giancarlo Giannini *Claudio* • Woody Allen *Sheldon Mills* • Mia Farrow *Lisa* • Julie Kavner *Treva* • Mae Questel *Sadie Millstein* ■ *Dir* Martin Scorsese, Francis Coppola [Francis Ford Coppola], Woody Allen • *Scr* Richard Price, Francis Coppola [Francis Ford Coppola], Sophia Coppola, Woody Allen

Newman's Law ★★

Police drama 1974 · US · Colour · 98mins

George Peppard stars in this suitably dour and predictable cop movie. Squaring up against big city politics and corrupt police colleagues, he's framed and then suspended for getting too close to a drug kingpin. Director Richard T Heffron deals efficiently with the requisite physical action and bolsters the routine good cop/bad cop plot with diverting insights into bureaucratic police methods. RS

George Peppard *Vince Newman* • Roger Robinson *Garry* • Eugene Roche *Reardon* • Gordon Pinsent *Eastman* • Abe Vigoda *Dellanzia* • Louis Zorich *Falcone* • Michael Lerner *Frank Acker* • Victor Campos *Jimenez* ■ *Dir* Richard T Heffron • *Scr* Anthony Wilson

The News Boys ★★ PG

Musical 1992 · US · Colour · 116mins

This is a Disney concoction about the Manhattan newsboys' strike of 1899, which *Variety* shrewdly described as "a strange cross between *Oliver!* and Samuel Fuller's *Park Row*". Yes, it's a musical, directed by choreographer Kenny Ortega in traditional – rather than MTV – style. Christian Bale leads the strike against Robert Duvall as miserly publisher Joseph Pulitzer, who gave his name to the prize. AT

Christian Bale *Jack Kelly/Frances Sullivan* • Bill Pullman *Bryan Denton* • Ann-Margret *Medda Larkson* • Robert Duvall *Joseph Pulitzer* ■ *Dir* Kenny Ortega • *Scr* Bob Tzudiker, Noni White

News from the Good Lord ★★★

Black comedy
1996 · Fr/Swi/Por · Colour · 100mins

Didier Le Pêcheur's debut rewards patient attention with a surfeit of audaciously original thinking and some bravura performances. Convinced they are characters in a badly written celestial novel, Christian Charmetant and his passionate sister, Marie Trintignant, set off in search of God to query his literary prowess. However, the idea that moral responsibility lies with one's creator is somewhat sidetracked by the designer violence of a road movie crime spree. DP. In French with English subtitles.

Marie Trintignant *Evangila* • Maria de Medeiros *Karenina* • Christian Charmetant *North* • Isabelle Candelier *Edwarda* • Michel Vuillermoz *Zhivago* • Jean Yanne *God* • Mathieu Kassovitz ■ *Dir* Didier Le Pêcheur • *Scr* Didier Le Pêcheur, from his novel

Newsfront ★★★★

Drama 1978 · Aus · Colour and BW · 110mins

Set during the 1940s and 1950s, this is a humane, witty and affectionate tribute to Australia's cinema newsreel cameramen. It beautifully conveys the mood of a nation, still tied emotionally and politically to Britain, and details both domestic crises and national disasters such as the Maitland floods. Clever use of black-and-white archive footage and a strong central performance from the burly, no-nonsense Bill Hunter distinguishes this fine movie from other first features. It's the movie directing debut of Phillip Noyce, who has since rather squandered his talent on Hollywood action blockbusters. AT

John Dease *Ken* • Wendy Hughes *Amy McKenzie* • Gerard Kennedy *Frank Maguire* • John Ewart *Charlie* • Angela Punch McGregor *Fay Maguire* • Bryan Brown *Geoff* • Bill Hunter *Len Maguire* ■ *Dir* Phillip Noyce • *Scr* Phillip Noyce, Bob Ellis, from an idea by David Elfick, Philippe Mora

The Newton Boys ★★★ 15

Western crime drama
1998 · US · Colour · 117mins

In the early 1920s, the four Texan-born Newton brothers were the most successful bank robbers in history. *Slacker* director Richard Linklater gives this little-known piece of Americana a pumped-up modern spin and crafts a well constructed, highly entertaining romantic adventure. Matthew McConaughey, Skeet Ulrich, Ethan Hawke and Vincent D'Onofrio make the boys a personable bunch with their differing traits, and Dwight Yoakam's portrayal of a nervous explosives expert is a blast. AJ DVD

Matthew McConaughey *Willis Newton* • Skeet Ulrich *Joe Newton* • Ethan Hawke *Jess Newton* • Gail Cronauer *Ma Newton* • Vincent D'Onofrio *Dock Newton* • Julianna Margulies *Louise Brown* • Dwight Yoakam *Brentwood Glasscock* • Bo Hopkins *KP Aldrich* ■ *Dir* Richard Linklater • *Scr* Richard Linklater, Claude Stanush, Clark Lee Walker, from a story by Willis Newton, Joe Newton, from the book *The Newton Boys: Portrait of an Outlaw Gang* by Claude Stanush, David Middleton

The Next Best Thing ★★ 12

Comedy drama 2000 · US · Colour · 103mins

Madonna stars in this humdrum comedy drama, as an LA yoga instructor whose life takes a dramatic turn when she sleeps with her gay best friend (Rupert Everett) and ends up pregnant. The couple set up house together for the good of their son, but problems arise when she falls for hunky Benjamin Bratt and Everett sues for custody. Veteran British director John Schlesinger handles his stars with kid gloves, and both deliver self-conscious performances. NS DVD

Madonna *Abbie* • Rupert Everett *Robert* • Illeana Douglas *Elizabeth Ryder* • Michael Vartan *Kevin* • Josef Sommer *Richard Whittaker* • Malcolm Stumpf *Sam* • Lynn Redgrave *Helen Whittaker* • Benjamin Bratt *Ben Cooper* • Neil Patrick Harris *David* ■ *Dir* John Schlesinger • *Scr* Thomas Ropelewski, Leslie Dixon, Rupert Everett, Mel Bordeaux

Next Friday ★★ 15

Comedy 1999 · US · Colour · 94mins

Rapper turned actor Ice Cube grabs writing, producing and performing credits for this follow-up to his hit US comedy *Friday*. Just as lowbrow in its laughs, but sadly lacking the original's darkish hue, this has Cube's street-savvy character hiding out in an affluent LA suburb where, thanks to a lottery win, his uncle is the richest man on the block. Add gangsters, a curvy señorita and a doped-up dog, and you have the recipe for some undemanding hokum. DA DVD

Ice Cube *Craig Jones* • Mike Epps *Day-Day* • Justin Pierce *Roach* • John Witherspoon *Mr Jones* • Don "D C" Curry *Uncle Elroy* ■ *Dir* Steve Carr • *Scr* Ice Cube, from characters created by Ice Cube, DJ Pooh

The Next Karate Kid ★★ PG

Martial arts adventure
1994 · US · Colour · 102mins

Ralph Macchio may have departed, but at least the fourth instalment in this series could still call on the services of Pat Morita. Essentially, this is a case of "same stunts, different sex", as future Oscar-winner Hilary Swank becomes Morita's prize pupil. A few pre-prom dance lessons are the only significant departure from the chop-socky formula, although Michael Ironside is good value as Swank's sinister gym teacher. DP

Noriyuki "Pat" Morita [Pat Morita] *Mr Miyagi* • Hilary Swank *Julie Pierce* • Michael Ironside *Colonel Dugan* • Constance Towers *Louisa* • Chris Conrad *Eric* • Arsenio "Sonny" Trinidad

Abbot Monk • Michael Cavalieri *Ned* ■ *Dir* Christopher Cain • *Scr* Mark Lee, from characters created by Robert Mark Kamen

The Next Man ★★ 15

Thriller 1976 · US · Colour · 99mins

This confused thriller is a long way from Sean Connery's best, while the plot certainly takes a lot of swallowing. A hired killer (Cornelia Sharpe) is sent to murder a high-flying Arab diplomat (Connery), but finds herself falling for his charms. However, Connery is charismatic even when sleepwalking through a role and the locations are certainly exotic. JF

Sean Connery *Khalil Abdul Muhsen* • Cornelia Sharpe *Nicole Scott* • Albert Paulsen *Hamid* • Adolfo Celi *Al Sharif* • Marco St John *Justin* • Ted Beniades *Dedario* ■ *Dir* Richard C Sarafian • *Scr* Mort Fine, Alan Trustman, David M Wolf, Richard C Sarafian, from a story by Martin Bregman, Alan Trustman

Next of Kin ★★★★ PG

Second World War propaganda drama
1942 · UK · BW · 95mins

Thorold Dickinson's eerily credible account of Fifth Column activity started life as a propaganda short, only to be expanded (at the MOI's behest) into a feature on the dangers of careless talk. Mervyn Johns gives a chillingly unassuming performance as the Nazi agent whose dual ability to invite confidences and blend into the background enables him to learn key secrets about an impending commando raid on a continental stronghold. Dickinson planned to use the failure of the attack to ram home his message. But Churchill intervened, fearing the film's effect on morale, and insisted the assault succeded, but with heavy casualties. DP

Mervyn Johns *Mr Davis, No 23* • Basil Sidney *Naval captain* • Frederick Leister *Colonel* • John Chandos *Davis's contact, No 16* • Sqn/ Ldr Reginald Tate [Reginald Tate] *Major Richards* • 2nd Lt Jack Hawkins [Jack Hawkins] *Brigade Major Harcourt* • Torin Thatcher *German general* • Thora Hird *ATS girl* ■ *Dir* Thorold Dickinson • *Scr* Thorold Dickinson, Basil Bartlett, Angus MacPhail, John Dighton

Next of Kin ★★ 15

Crime drama 1989 · US · Colour · 103mins

From the days when Liam Neeson was serving his Hollywood apprenticeship, this sleazy muddle of a movie at least gives him a chance to flex his acting muscles as the hillbilly brother of Chicago cop Patrick Swayze. They unite in vengeance when another brother is killed by the Mob. British director John Irvin seems to have little idea of movie momentum or the way characters are developed, but these weaknesses are also the fault of the banal script. TH. Contains swearing, violence.

Patrick Swayze *Truman Gates* • Liam Neeson *Briar Gates* • Adam Baldwin *Joey Rossellini* • Helen Hunt *Jessie Gates* • Andreas Katsulas *John Isabella* • Bill Paxton *Gerald Gates* • Ben Stiller *Lawrence Isabella* ■ *Dir* John Irvin • *Scr* Michael Jenning, Jeb Stuart

Next One ★

Science-fiction fantasy drama
1984 · US · Colour · 105mins

This is a tedious fantasy with quasi-religious overtones has Adrienne Barbeau and her son Jeremy Licht are living on the island of Mykonos when stranger Keir Dullea washes ashore. It turns out he's a Jesus Christ figure from the future. As well as being totally ludicrous, this is slow-paced from the start. If the Greeks don't have a word for it, they should – pathetic, dull... AJ

Keir Dullea *Glenn/The Next One* • Adrienne Barbeau *Andrea Johnson* • Jeremy Licht *Timmy* ■ *Dir/Scr* Nico Mastorakis

Next Stop, Greenwich Village ★★★

Comedy 1976 · US · Colour · 111mins

Set in New York in 1953, aspiring actor Lenny Baker has finally escaped his momma, Shelley Winters. Or so he thinks, for Winters shows up to steal a scene and to give her son some maternal advice and clean underwear. That makes the movie funny, but the evocation of bohemian New York is also splendidly realised. Of course, it's autobiographical since writer/director Paul Mazursky lived this life himself, brushed up against Brando, Strasberg and Actors' Studio types and finally went to Hollywood to play in Stanley Kubrick's first film, *Fear and Desire*. AT

Lenny Baker *Larry Lapinsky* • Shelley Winters *Mrs Lapinsky* • Ellen Greene *Sarah* • Lois Smith *Anita* • Christopher Walken *Robert* • Dori Brenner *Connie* • Antonio Fargas *Bernstein* ■ *Dir/Scr* Paul Mazursky

Next Stop Wonderland ★★★★

Romantic comedy
1998 · US · Colour · 111mins

Terrific romantic comedy, all the more laudable for being the first feature from up-and-coming indie director Brad Anderson. Hope Davis plays Erin, a Boston night-shift nurse who swears off men after she's dumped by her boyfriend. Her mother, though, has other ideas and places a personal ad on her daughter's behalf. The film then chronicles Erin's reluctant return to the meet market. Philip Seymour Hoffman (*Happiness*) is the best-known face among the supporting cast. DA

Hope Davis *Erin Castleton* • Alan Gelfant *Alan Monteiro* • Victor Argo *Frank* • Jon Benjamin *Eric* • Cara Buono *Julie* • Larry Gilliard Jr *Brett* • Philip Seymour Hoffman *Sean* ■ *Dir* Brad Anderson • *Scr* Brad Anderson, Lyn Vaus

Next Time We Love ★★★

Romantic melodrama
1936 · US · BW · 86mins

The marriage between a Broadway actress and a news correspondent suffers from a conflict in career interests. A top-billed Margaret Sullavan co-stars with James Stewart in his first important role, while Ray Milland plays a stalwart friend of the couple who nurses an unrequited love for the wife. Beautifully mounted and superbly cast, this has all the makings of a first-class movie. Under Edward H Griffith's direction, though, it just plods along, just about held together by the polish and personality of the stars. RK

Margaret Sullavan *Cicely Tyler* • James Stewart *Christopher Tyler* • Ray Milland *Tommy Abbott* • Grant Mitchell *Michael Jennings* • Robert McWade *Frank Carteret* ■ *Dir* Edward H Griffith • *Scr* Melville Baker, Preston Sturges, from the novel *Say Goodbye Again* by Ursula Parrott

Next to No Time ★★★ U

Comedy 1958 · UK · Colour · 92mins

This whimsical comedy was something of a disappointment considering it marked the reunion of director Henry Cornelius with his *Genevieve* star Kenneth More. Sadly, it proved to be Cornelius's last picture before his tragically early death the same year during the production of *Law and Disorder*. More is curiously out of sorts as an engineer who uses a voyage on the *Queen Elizabeth* to persuade wealthy Roland Culver to back his latest project. His romantic interest is provided by Betsy Drake, who was then married to Cary Grant. DP

Kenneth More *David Webb* • Betsy Drake *Georgie Brant* • Harry Green *Saul* • Patrick Barr *Jerry* • Maureen Connell *Mary* • Bessie Love *Becky* • Reginald Beckwith *Warren* • Roland Culver *Sir Godfrey Cowan* ■ *Dir* Henry Cornelius • *Scr* Henry Cornelius, from the story *The Enchanted Hour* by Paul Gallico

The Next Voice You Hear ★★★

Drama 1950 · US · BW · 82mins

MGM's new studio head Dore Schary had made some interesting, relevant, and mildly liberal (by MGM standards) programme fillers during his tenure at RKO, and attempted to raise the thought and quality content at Metro, with varying degrees of success. This oddity, produced by Schary himself, concerns the effects on an allegorical US town when no less than the voice of God is heard over the radio. It's a fascinating idea, but action director William A Wellman handles it like a tub of molasses. TS

James Whitmore *Joe Smith* • Nancy Davis *Mary Smith* • Gary Gray *Johnny Smith* • Lillian Bronson *Aunt Ethel* • Art Smith *Mr Brannan* • Tom D'Andrea *Hap Magee* • Jeff Corey *Freddie* ■ *Dir* William A Wellman • *Scr* Charles Schnee, from a story by George Sumner Albee

Ngati ★★★

Drama 1987 · NZ · Colour · 88mins

Made by a predominantly Maori cast and crew, this was the first feature produced anywhere by an indigenous community resident within a primarily white country. Set in 1948 and tackling the age-old theme of tradition versus progress, Barry Barclay's drama demonstrates the importance of ethnic unity by linking three distinct plot strands, concerning a dying child, an obsolete meat-freezing depot and an Australian doctor making a pilgrimage to the place of his birth. This may be rough around the edges, but the political points are soundly made. DP

Michael Tibble *Tione* • Oliver Jones *Ropata* • Judy McIntosh *Jenny Bennett* • Ross Girven *Greg Shaw* • Wi Kuki Kaa *Iwi, Ropata's father* ■ *Dir* Barry Barclay • *Scr* Tama Poata

Niagara ★★★★ PG

Thriller 1953 · US · Colour · 85mins

If ever a film poster could be said to have created a star's image, it was the one for this movie – Marilyn Monroe draped across said falls with a certain look in her eye and a come-on caption to match her décolletage: "A raging torrent of emotion that even nature can't control!" Monroe, top-billed for the first time in her career, is a sensation, but the film itself is a sordid melodrama, daft and clever by turns. There's a fine performance from Joseph Cotten and some interesting location shots of the falls, but this is Monroe's star-making movie and, boy, does she know it. TS DVD

Marilyn Monroe *Rose Loomis* • Joseph Cotten *George Loomis* • Jean Peters *Polly Cutler* • Casey Adams [Max Showalter] *Ray Cutler* • Denis O'Dea *Inspector Sharkey* • Richard Allen *Patrick* • Don Wilson *Mr Kettering* • Lurene Tuttle *Mrs Kettering* ■ *Dir* Henry Hathaway • *Scr* Charles Brackett, Walter Reisch, Richard Breen [Richard L Breen]

Niagara Niagara ★★ 15

Romantic drama 1997 · US · Colour · 90mins

Playing a victim of Tourette syndrome, Robin Tunney won the best actress prize at Venice for her convincing outbursts and involuntary acts of violence. But there are too many echoes of other road movies to elevate Bob Gosse's film above the crowd. Travelling with the taciturn Henry Thomas, it's only a matter of time before Tunney's lack of medication renders her unpredictable and the pair turn to crime. DP DVD

Robin Tunney *Marcy* • Henry Thomas *Seth* • Stephen Lang *Pharmacist* • John MacKay *Seth's father* • Michael Parks *Walter* ■ *Dir* Bob Gosse • *Scr* Matthew Weiss

The Nibelungen ★★★★

Silent fantasy epic 1924 · Ger · BW · 249mins

Fritz Lang's adaptation of the 13th-century German saga is a superb example of the craftsmanship at the UFA studios. Paul Richter is Siegfried, married to Margarete Schön; together the two journey from Iceland to Burgundy with Hanna Ralph, who is to be the bride of Theodor Loos. Adventures, magical and otherwise, death and revenge all ensue. The stylised sets create a mysterious beauty, especially the misty forest (constructed in a Zeppelin hangar) and the romantic castles. There is also a wonderful dragon that the hero slays early in Part I (*Siegfried*) and a massively staged battle to end Part II (*Kriemhild's Revenge*). The characters are deliberately one-dimensional as befits the epic mode. RB

Paul Richter *Siegfried* • Margarete Schön *Kriemhild* • Theodor Loos *King Gunther* • Hanna Ralph *Brunhild* ■ *Dir* Fritz Lang • *Scr* Fritz Lang, Thea von Harbou, from the anonymous 13th-century German poem *Das Nibelungenlied,and various Norse legends*

Nice Girl? ★★★ U

Musical comedy 1941 · US · BW · 97mins

Nice Deanna Durbin was at her most charming as a small-town girl who falls for a much older man (36-year-old Franchot Tone), a New York roué, because the boy next door (Robert Stack) is more interested in cars than in her. The situation, redolent with sexual possibilities, is rendered as innocently as possible, making the question mark in the title unnecessary. Among the pleasures here are the casting of humorist Robert Benchley as Deanna's father and Walter Brennan as a lovesick postman. RB

Deanna Durbin *Jane Dana* • Franchot Tone *Richard Calvert* • Walter Brennan *Hector Titus* • Robert Stack *Don Webb* • Robert Benchley *Oliver Dana* • Helen Broderick *Cora Foster* • Ann Gillis *Nancy Dana* ■ *Dir* William A Seiter • *Scr* Richard Connell, Gladys Lehman, from the play by Phyllis Duganne

A Nice Girl like Me ★

Comedy 1969 · UK · Colour · 90mins

This abysmal comedy has Barbara Ferris going to France and Italy and coming back pregnant both times. If you want to see it as an allegory about Britain's thwarted desire to join the Common Market, the film has significance and irony; but seen as a comedy its ability to send its audience into a deep sleep is unrivalled. AT

Barbara Ferris *Candida* • Harry Andrews *Savage, caretaker* • Gladys Cooper *Aunt Mary* • Bill Hinnant *Ed* • James Villiers *Freddie* • Joyce Carey *Aunt Celia* • Christopher Guinee *Pierre* ■ *Dir* Desmond Davis • *Scr* Anne Piper, Desmond Davis, from the novel *Marry at Leisure* by Anne Piper

Nice Girls Don't Explode ★★ PG

Horror spoof 1987 · US · Colour · 78mins

Michelle Meyrink is a girl who can make things explode, usually whenever she gets amorous – a curse she's inherited from her mother (Barbara Harris). With its unabashed lifts from *Carrie*, this peculiar hybrid is rarely amusing and only distinguished by the presence of Harris, a delightfully quirky actress. AJ

Barbara Harris *Mom* • Michelle Meyrink *April* • William O'Leary *Andy* • Wallace Shawn *Ellen* ■ *Dir* Chuck Martinez • *Scr* Paul Harris

A Nice Little Bank That Should Be Robbed ★★ U

Crime comedy 1958 · US · BW · 87mins

Despite its whimsical title, a script by one of Fox's star writers (Sydney Boehm) and the presence of Mickey Rooney and Tom Ewell, this is a rather pathetic attempt at heist comedy. Two incompetent crooks rob a small-town bank, then buy a racehorse that is just as much of a loser as they are. Henry Levin directs with little of the flair such a subject needs, while the stars seem to know they're in a stinker. TH

Tom Ewell *Max Rutgers* • Mickey Rooney *Gus Harris* • Mickey Shaughnessy *Harold "Rocky" Baker* • Dina Merrill *Margie Solitaire* • Madge Kennedy *Grace Havens* • Frances Bavier *Mrs Solitaire* ■ *Dir* Henry Levin • *Scr* Sydney Boehm, from an article by Evan Wylie

Nicholas and Alexandra ★★★ PG

Historical drama
1971 · UK · Colour · 164mins

This sumptuous, if overlong epic about the last days of the Russian Romanov dynasty, before the Bolsheviks executed Tsar Nicholas II and his family, shows the stretchmarks of too much padding, though Michael Jayston and Janet Suzman, as the Tsar and Tsarina, are a poignant reminder that a royal marriage can be both faithful and true. It overwhelms us with its detail, though Tom Baker is a lot of fun as the leering mystic Rasputin, and there are cameo appearances from Timothy West, Laurence Olivier and Michael Redgrave among others. TH DVD

Michael Jayston *Tsar Nicholas II* • Janet Suzman *Empress Alexandra* • Fiona Fullerton *Princess Anastasia* • Tom Baker *Rasputin* • Candace Glendenning *Princess Marie* • Lynne Frederick *Princess Tatiana* • Ania Marson *Princess Olga* • Roderic Noble *Prince Alexis* • John McEnery *Kerensky* ■ *Dir* Franklin Schaffner [Franklin J Schaffner] • *Scr* James Goldman, Edward Bond, from a non-fiction book by Robert K Massie

Nicholas' Gift ★★ PG

Drama based on a true story
1998 · It/US · Colour · 86mins

As true weepies go, this TV movie is definitely in the premier league, if only for the top quality cast. Jamie Lee Curtis and Alan Bates play tourists on holiday in Italy whose young son is seriously wounded when they are attacked by jewel thieves. With the child given no chance of surviving, the grieving couple agree to donate his organs. Unbeknown to them, though, Italy has an appalling record in this area of medicine, and they come up against a brick wall of bureaucracy. Sentimentality runs riot. JF DVD

Jamie Lee Curtis *Maggie Green* • Alan Bates *Reginald Green* • Gene Wexler *Nicholas Green* • Hallie Kate Eisenberg *Eleanor Green* ■ *Dir* Robert Markowitz • *Scr* Christine Berardo

Nicholas Nickleby ★★★★ U

Period drama 1947 · UK · BW · 102mins

Alberto Cavalcanti was the Brazilian-born film-maker who joined Michael Balcon's famous team of Ealing directors after helping to develop the documentary movement at the GPO Film Unit. One of his infrequent outings as a director, this was to be overshadowed by David Lean's *Oliver Twist* and *Great Expectations*, but it still deserves attention as a screen version of a Dickens fable that has relevance today. Derek Bond is hopelessly wooden as Nicholas, but Alfred Drayton is suitably loathsome as the head of Dotheboys Hall and Cedric Hardwicke is an Uncle Ralph of diabolical villainy. TH DVD

Derek Bond *Nicholas Nickleby* • Cedric Hardwicke *Ralph Nickleby* • Stanley Holloway *Vincent Crummles* • Alfred Drayton *Wackford Squeers* • Cyril Fletcher *Alfred Mantalini* • Bernard Miles *Newman Noggs* • Sally Ann Howes *Kate Nickleby* • Mary Merrall *Mrs Nickleby* • Sybil Thorndike *Mrs Squeers* ■ *Dir* Alberto Cavalcanti • *Scr* John Dighton, from the novel by Charles Dickens

Nicholas Nickleby ★★★ U

Animation 1985 · Aus · Colour · 72mins

Live-action adaptations of the world's literary classics are hard enough to do well, but producing successful animated versions is almost impossible, especially on the kind of budget allocated to this project. However, this is a laudable attempt to bring Dickens to a younger audience. Naturally, the narrative has been simplified and some of the characters have been omitted. But the story of Nicholas and the unfortunate Smike remains as tragic as ever. DP

Dir Warwick Gilbert • *Scr* Rob Mowbray, from the novel by Charles Dickens

Nicholas Nickleby ★★★★ PG

Period drama
2002 · US/UK · Colour · 127mins

The actors in any film of a novel by Charles Dickens have to guard against caricature – so extreme in vice or virtue are his characters. Not a chance of parody, though, with this bustling, personality-packed account. Young Nicholas (Charlie Hunnam) is the innocent at large in a world controlled by Uncle Ralph (Christopher Plummer), one of the most evil men in English literature. First there is the tour to the lower depths of educational hell at Dotheboys Hall, run by Wackford Squeers (Jim Broadbent) and his wife (Juliet Stevenson). Then there is light at the end of the tunnel with the Cheeryble brothers (Timothy Spall and Gerard Horan) and the hope of love with Madeline (Anne Hathaway). Written and directed by Douglas McGrath, the original tale has been slightly truncated, but this is still a treat. TH DVD

Charlie Hunnam *Nicholas Nickleby* • Christopher Plummer *Ralph Nickleby* • Jamie Bell *Smike* • Jim Broadbent *Wackford Squeers* • Tom Courtenay *Newman Noggs* • Edward Fox *Sir Mulberry Hawk* • Juliet Stevenson *Mrs Squeers* • Nathan Lane *Vincent Crummles* • Dame Edna Everage [Barry Humphries] *Mrs Crummles* • Timothy Spall *Charles Cheeryble* • Alan Cumming *Mr Folair* • Anne Hathaway *Madeline Bray* • Gerard Horan *Ned Cheeryble* • Stella Gonet *Mrs Nickleby* ■ *Dir* Douglas McGrath • *Scr* Douglas McGrath, from the novel by Charles Dickens

Nick and Jane ★★★ 15

Romantic comedy
1996 · US · Colour · 88mins

This is a watchable enough romantic comedy that includes all the staple elements of the genre. Dana Wheeler-Nicholson is businesswoman Jane who, after catching her unfaithful boyfriend *in flagrante*, dives into a getaway cab driven by James McCaffrey. Chalk and cheese, the two are attracted to each other and, at the same time, repelled. Inevitably, they spend the rest of the movie getting together. LH

Dana Wheeler-Nicholson *Jane* • James McCaffrey *Nick* • Gedde Watanabe *Enzo* • David Johansen *Carter* • George Coe *Mr Morgan* ■ *Dir* Richard Mauro • *Scr* Richard Mauro, Neil Alumkal, Peter Quigley, from a story by Richard Mauro

Nick Carter, Master Detective ★★

Detective spy drama 1939 · US · BW · 60mins

This polished MGM B-feature was the first of three films in which Walter Pidgeon played the screen incarnation of a popular dime-novel sleuth. The topical story has Carter preventing blueprints of a new high-speed plane falling into the hands of spies. The film gives director Jacques Tourneur little chance to display the skill he would later bring to *Cat People* and *I Walked with a Zombie*, but it moves briskly and painlessly through its brief duration. *Phantom Raiders* and *Sky Murder*, both 1940, followed. AE

Walter Pidgeon *Nick Carter/Robert Chalmers* • Rita Johnson *Lou Farnsby* • Henry Hull *John A Keller* • Stanley C Ridges [Stanley Ridges] *Dr Frankton* • Donald Meek *Bartholomew* ■ *Dir* Jacques Tourneur • *Scr* Bertram Millhauser, from a story by Bertram Millhauser, Harold Buckley

Nick of Time ★★ 15

Action thriller 1995 · US · Colour · 85mins

In director John Badham's weak suspense thriller, accountant Johnny Depp is told he has 90 minutes, and six bullets, to murder the governor of California or his daughter will be killed. Supposedly playing out his shock predicament in real-time, with lots of close-ups of clocks, Badham fluffs the tension by accenting the preposterous plot contrivances rather than creating any real emotional empathy with the plight of the characters. AJ DVD

Johnny Depp *Gene Watson* • Christopher Walken *Mr Smith* • Courtney Chase *Lynn Watson* • Charles S Dutton *Huey* • Roma Maffia *Ms Jones* • Marsha Mason *Governor Eleanor Grant* • Peter Strauss *Brendan Grant* • Gloria Reuben *Krista Brooks* ■ *Dir* John Badham • *Scr* Patrick Sheane Duncan

Nickel & Dime ★★ PG

Action comedy 1991 · US · Colour · 91mins

Small-time heir hunter C Thomas Howell is down on his luck, but he thinks if he can just make that one big case, everything will turn around. Too bad he's been saddled with a by-the-book certified public accountant Wallace Shawn. The middle portion of the film drags terribly, but if you're a fan of Shawn's unique acting style, you may want to check it out. ST

C Thomas Howell *Jack Stone* • Wallace Shawn *Everett Willis* • Lise Cutter *Cathleen Markson* • Roy Brocksmith *Sammy Thornton* • Lynn Danielson *Destiny Charm* • Kathleen Freeman *Judge Lechter* ■ *Dir* Ben Moses • *Scr* Eddy Pollon, Seth Front

Nickelodeon ★★★ U

Comedy 1976 · US · Colour · 116mins

Critic-turned-director Peter Bogdanovich intended this tribute to the early days of film-making to be his masterwork, but it turned out to be one of his biggest flops. Ryan O'Neal plays the director, Burt Reynolds the handsome star, Stella Stevens a vamp and Brian Keith a fledgeling movie mogul. It was a critical and commercial disaster, but it's still a charmer, with nice performances and impeccable period atmosphere. AT DVD

Ryan O'Neal *Leo Harrigan* • Burt Reynolds *Buck Greenway* • Tatum O'Neal *Alice Forsyte* • Brian Keith *HH Cobb* • Stella Stevens *Marty Reeves* • John Ritter *Franklin Frank* • Jane Hitchcock *Kathleen Cooke* • Harry Carey Jr *Dobie* ■ *Dir* Peter Bogdanovich • *Scr* Peter Bogdanovich, WD Richter

Nico ★★ 18

Martial arts action
1988 · US · Colour · 94mins

Released in the US as *Above the Law*, this was Steven Seagal's action debut. Despite his obvious limitations as an actor, Seagal's rock-fisted martial arts style made this a massive video hit and paved the way for his lengthy career in similar biff-em-ups. He's a cop whose massive drug bust is suddenly stolen from under his nose by pushy FBI men for complex, and possibly criminal, reasons. Providing the actual acting talent are Pam Grier, Sharon Stone and villainous Henry Silva. JF. Contains swearing, violence and drug abuse. DVD

Steven Seagal *Nico Toscani* • Pam Grier *Delores Jackson* • Sharon Stone *Sara Toscani* • Daniel Faraldo *Salvano* • Henry Silva *Zagon* ■ *Dir* Andrew Davis • *Scr* Steven Pressfield, Ronald Shusett, Andrew Davis, from a story by Steven Seagal, Andrew Davis

Nico the Unicorn ★★★

Fantasy drama 1998 · Can · Colour · 90mins

A Canadian gem based on the Frank Sacks novel that allows both children and adults to share something magical. Anne Archer moves house after her husband is killed and her son Kevin Zegers is crippled in the same accident. Feeling alone and somewhat bitter, the son visits a nearby circus and cajoles his mother into buying a neglected pony. When it gives birth to a unicorn, both their lives take a turn for the better. AJ

Anne Archer *Julie Hastings* • Kevin Zegers *Billy Hastings* • Michael Ontkean *Tom Gentry* ■ *Dir* Graeme Campbell • *Scr* Frank Sacks, from his novel

Night after Night ★★

Comedy drama 1932 · US · BW · 70mins

Ex-prizefighter George Raft, looking to make something of his life, buys a ritzy nightclub, mingles with the smart set and falls in love with a socialite. Constance Cummings and Alison Skipworth co-star in this small-scale drama, which is long on Prohibition-era atmosphere but short on interesting content. The film is remembered, however, for promoting Raft to leading man status, and is unforgettable for marking the screen debut of Mae West. "Goodness, what diamonds!" remarks a hat-check girl as she makes her entrance. "Goodness had nothing to do with it, dearie," Mae replies. RK

George Raft *Joe Anton* • Constance Cummings *Jerry Healy* • Wynne Gibson *Iris Dawn* • Mae West *Maudie Triplett* • Alison Skipworth *Mrs Mabel Jellyman* ■ *Dir* Archie Mayo • *Scr* Vincent Lawrence, Kathryn Scola, Mae West, from the novel *Single Night* by Louis Bromfield

Night and Day ★★★ U

Musical biography
1946 · US · Colour · 122mins

This is a mawkish yet mesmerising biopic, whose casting of Cary Grant as Cole Porter completely eliminated any suggestion of Porter's homosexuality and reduced his tragic riding accident (Porter eventually lost a leg) to Grant using a walking stick to get around. But the truth doesn't matter much in this kind of movie, and director Michael Curtiz does a smashing job, helped by ravishing Technicolor and a marvellous cast. TS DVD

Cary Grant *Cole Porter* • Alexis Smith *Linda Lee Porter* • Monty Woolley • Ginny Simms *Carole Hill* • Jane Wyman *Gracie Harris* • Eve Arden *Gabrielle* • Victor Francen *Anatole Giron* • Alan Hale *Leon Dowling* • Dorothy Malone *Nancy* ■ *Dir* Michael Curtiz • *Scr* Charles Hoffman, Leo Townsend, William Bowers, from a biography by Jack Moffit

Night and Day ★★★★ 15

Romantic drama
1991 · Bel/Fr/Swi · Colour · 95mins

Bearing the influence of François Truffaut (to whom the film is dedicated), Chantal Akerman's delicately-played morality tale continues her fascination with the way emotion reveals itself through the banalities of everyday life. Radiant in the atmospheric nocturnal photography, Guilaine Londez gives a disarmingly truthful performance as the provincial girl whose love for cabbie Thomas Langmann is supplanted by a passion for François Négret, who

N

drives the same taxi on the day shift. Thanks to Akerman's genuine interest in her characters, the dialogue is as authentic as the resolution. DP. In French with English subtitles.

Guilaine Londez *Julie* • Thomas Langmann *Jack* • François Négret *Joseph* • Nicole Colchat *Jack's mother* • Pierre Laroche *Jack's father* ■ *Dir* Chantal Akerman • *Scr* Chantal Akerman, Pascal Bonitzer

Night and the City ★★★★ PG

Crime drama 1950 · UK/US · BW · 91mins

Here's a really interesting crime drama, a genuine 20th Century-Fox *film noir* set and filmed entirely in London, with imported American stars and a British supporting cast. Surprisingly, it works, largely because of star Richard Widmark's brilliant, desperate portrayal of a hustler on the edge, and skilled director Jules Dassin's cleverly atmospheric use of London locations, plus expertly controlled pacing. The plot hangs on a wrestling fix, and is both adult and original. TS

Richard Widmark *Harry Fabian* • Gene Tierney *Mary Bristol* • Googie Withers *Helen Nosseross* • Hugh Marlowe *Adam Dunn* • Francis L Sullivan *Phil Nosseross* • Herbert Lom *Kristo* • Stanley Zbyszko [Stanislaus Zbyszko] *Gregorius* • Mike Mazurki *Strangler* ■ *Dir* Jules Dassin • *Scr* Jo Eisinger, from the novel by Gerald Kersh

Night and the City ★★★ 15

Crime drama 1992 · US · Colour · 103mins

A respectful update of Jules Dassin's 1950 classic, with the setting switched from London to New York. Robert De Niro takes the Richard Widmark role of the small-time promoter desperately trying to hustle his way to the big time, while Jessica Lange is the woman who gets too close to his dreams. Irwin Winkler's direction is functional, but he is smart enough to surround himself with an impressive array of talent. The two stars are joined by a wonderful supporting cast (comedian Alan King in particular), while the deft script comes from Richard Price (*Sea of Love*). JF. Contains violence, swearing. [VIDEO] DVD

Robert De Niro *Harry Fabian* • Jessica Lange *Helen* • Cliff Gorman *Phil* • Alan King *"Boom Boom" Grossman* • Jack Warden *Al Grossman* • Eli Wallach *Peck* • Barry Primus *Tommy Tessler* • Gene Kirkwood *Resnick* • Pedro Sanchez [Ignazio Spalla] *Cuda Sanchez* ■ *Dir* Irwin Winkler • *Scr* Richard Price, from the 1950 film

A Night at the Opera ★★★★★ U

Comedy 1935 · US · BW · 87mins

At Paramount, the Marx Brothers had specialised in zany, freewheeling comedies that owed much to the anarchic antics of their vaudeville shows. This first outing for MGM was also honed on the stage, but producer Irving Thalberg used the three-week pre-production tour to chip away at the rough edges that made their humour so unique. But the Brothers' anarchic spirit triumphs, and the plot involving Groucho's bid to dupe wealthy socialite Margaret Dumont into investing in his opera company is almost an irrelevance. Certainly the romantic interludes with songbirds Allan Jones and Kitty Carlisle are. The madcap lunacy is unforgettable – whether it's Groucho's inimitable line in patter or the slapstick ruination of *Il Trovatore*. DP [VIDEO] DVD

Groucho Marx *Otis B Driftwood* • Chico Marx *Fiorello* • Harpo Marx *Tomasso* • Margaret Dumont *Mrs Claypool* • Allan Jones *Riccardo Baroni* • Kitty Carlisle *Rosa Castaldi* • Siegfried "Sig" Rumann [Sig Ruman] *Herman Gottlieb* ■ *Dir* Sam Wood • *Scr* George S Kaufman, Morrie Ryskind, Al Boasberg, Bert Kalmar, Harry Ruby, from a story by James Kevin McGuinness

A Night at the Roxbury ★ 15

Comedy 1998 · US · Colour · 81mins

Beware movies based on comedy sketches as, with very few exceptions (*Wayne's World* being one), they are rarely very good. This tale, based on a *Saturday Night Live* skit about two dumber-than-dumb, sexist brothers trying to get into the coolest clubs in LA, is utterly devoid of any redeeming features. The actors are irritating, the script is humourless, and at under an hour-and-a-half it is still 80 minutes too long. JB. Contains sexual references and some swearing. [VIDEO]

Will Ferrell *Steve Butabi* • Chris Kattan *Doug Butabi* • Richard Grieco • Loni Anderson *Barbara Butabi* • Dan Hedaya *Kamehl Butabi* ■ *Dir* John Fortenberry • *Scr* Steven Koren, Will Ferrell, Chris Kattan

Night Beat ★★

Crime drama 1948 · UK · BW · 102mins

A relishably bad British crime drama set in an unreal Soho underworld of spivs and nightclubs. It's a compendium of clichés as two army friends end up on opposite sides of the law – one a policeman, the other a black-market racketeer who marries a good girl but dallies with a glamorous cabaret singer. Particularly enjoyable are Maxwell Reed as the swaggering villain, Christine Norden as the vicious blonde vamp, and Michael Medwin in a spot of light relief as an indignant pickpocket. Benjamin Frankel's score is better than the film deserves. AE

Maxwell Reed *Felix Fenton* • Ronald Howard *Andy Kendall* • Anne Crawford *Julie Kendall* • Christine Norden *Jackie* • Michael Medwin *Spider* ■ *Dir* Harold Huth • *Scr* Guy Morgan, TJ Morrison, Robert Westerby, Roland Pertwee, from a story by Guy Morgan

The Night Before ★ 15

Comedy 1988 · US · Colour · 86mins

Keanu Reeves's first starring vehicle was understandably shelved for two years before its minuscule release. The future star of *The Matrix* shows no charisma as he stumbles through this *After Hours* for the adolescent crowd, playing a prom-bound teenager who retraces his steps after he wakes up in an alley with no car, no date and no memory of how he got there. The surreal touches are self-conscious and distracting and do not blend well with the movie's comic tone. KB [VIDEO]

Keanu Reeves *Winston Connelly* • Lori Loughlin *Tara Mitchell* • Theresa Saldana *Rhonda* • Trinidad Silva *Tito* • Suzanne Snyder *Lisa* • Morgan Lofting *Mom* • Gwil Richards *Dad* ■ *Dir* Thom Eberhardt • *Scr* Gregory Scherick, Thom Eberhardt, from a story by Gregory Scherick

Night Boat to Dublin ★★

Second World War spy drama
1946 · UK · BW · 91mins

This B-thriller is worth seeing for its treatment of a topical theme – atomic weapons – and the performance of Robert Newton, then on the cusp of stardom. Newton plays a British secret service agent who travels to Dublin, where a Swedish scientist is giving atomic secrets to the Nazis. AT

Robert Newton *Captain David Grant* • Raymond Lovell *Paul Faber* • Guy Middleton *Captain Tony Hunter* • Muriel Pavlow *Marion Decker* • Herbert Lom *Keitel* • John Ruddock *Bowman* • Martin Miller *Professor Hansen* • Marius Goring *Frederick Jannings* ■ *Dir* Lawrence Huntington • *Scr* Robert Hall, Lawrence Huntington

The Night Caller ★★

Science-fiction thriller
1965 · UK · BW · 83mins

You are an alien sent to Earth to find women to help repopulate your planet. How would you go about recruiting them? A wanted advert in *Bikini Girl* magazine, of course. This cheerful piece of nonsense has John Saxon as the scientist who is called in to investigate the arrival of a mysterious pod, and Alfred Burke as the copper unable to explain a spate of disappearances of young women. DP

John Saxon *Jack Costain* • Maurice Denham *Professor Morley* • Patricia Haines *Ann Barlow* • Alfred Burke *Superintendent Hartley* • Jack Carson *Major* • Jack Watson *Sergeant Hawkins* • Warren Mitchell *Lilburn* ■ *Dir* John Gilling • *Scr* Jim O'Connolly, from the novel *The Night Callers* by Frank Crisp

The Night Caller ★★ 18

Thriller 1998 · US · Colour · 89mins

Tracy Nelson is a loser who has delusions that radio psychologist, Shanna Reed is talking directly to her. Nelson subsequently acquires a new job as Reed's babysitter and keeps it by killing anyone who threatens her happiness. While the premise is derivative and the treatment surprisingly violent, Nelson does an effective job at keeping her demented character sympathetic. ST [VIDEO] DVD

Shanna Reed *Dr Lindsay Roland* • Tracy Nelson *Beth Needham* • Mary Crosby *Nikki Rogers* • Cyndi Pass *Marge Hampton* • Eve Sigall *Mama* • Howard Miller *Lee Dixon* ■ *Dir* Robert Malenfant • *Scr* Mark Bomback, Frank Rehwaldt, from a story by George Saunders

Night Comes Too Soon ★★

Supernatural drama 1949 · UK · BW · 57mins

While Valentine Dyall became famous for radio shows such as *The Man in Black* and *Appointment with Fear*, he never quite made his mark on the big screen. However, his mellifluous tones add considerably to this tricksy chiller, in which he plays a "paranormalist" called in by newlyweds to remove the curse from their dream home. With only meagre resources to play with, most of the eerie effects are achieved by lighting changes and good old-fashioned dissolves. That said, the ghostly visions are effective. DP

Valentine Dyall *Dr Clinton* • Anne Howard *Phyllis* • Alec Faversham *John* • Beatrice Marsden *Mrs Paxton* • Howard Douglas • Anthony Baird *Lionel Waddell* • Arthur Brander • Frank Dunlop ■ *Dir* Denis Kavanagh • *Scr* Pat Dixon, from the play *The Haunted and the Haunters* by Lord Lytton [Edward George Bulwer-Lytton]

Night Crossing ★★ PG

Adventure based on a true story
1981 · UK/US · Colour · 102mins

Disney attempts to impose cuteness on a true Cold War story about two East German families who float perilously over the border to western life, liberty and the pursuit of capitalism in a home-made balloon. Director Delbert Mann conveys little of the truth of what must have been a terrifying business. John Hurt, Jane Alexander and Beau Bridges give their all, but it's just hot air. TH [VIDEO] DVD

John Hurt *Peter Strelzyk* • Jane Alexander *Doris Strelzyk* • Doug McKeon *Frank Strelzyk* • Keith McKeon *Fitscher Strelzyk* • Beau Bridges *Gunter Wetzel* • Glynnis O'Connor *Petra Wetzel* ■ *Dir* Delbert Mann • *Scr* John McGreevey

Night Eyes ★★ 18

Erotic thriller 1990 · US · Colour · 94mins

This is the first in what has turned out to be a very profitable franchise, already spawning three very similar sequels. Called in to protect Tanya Roberts, Andrew Stevens plays a security guard whose voyeuristic tendencies get the better of him. The sex and thrills are strictly soft-core, the performances little more than adequate. JF. Contains violence, swearing and nudity. [VIDEO]

Andrew Stevens *Will* • Tanya Roberts *Nikki* • Cooper Huckabee *Ernie* • Veronica Henson-Phillips *Lauretta* • Stephen Meadows *Michael Vincent* • Karen Elise Baldwin *Ellen* • Warwick Sims *Brian Walker* ■ *Dir* Jag Mundhra • *Scr* Tom Citrano, Andrew Stevens

Night Falls on Manhattan ★★ 15

Crime drama 1997 · US · Colour · 108mins

Assistant DA Andy Garcia finds himself promoted following his successful, high-profile prosecution of a big-time drug dealer and cop killer. Then a skeleton is hauled out of the river, opening a hornet's nest of corruption. Despite some good performances this is really just another drive around the block for Sidney Lumet: he not only lets the pace slacken, but also sanctions a corny romance between Garcia and legal rival Lena Olin that turns the gritty realism into soapy melodrama. AT. Contains violence and swearing. [VIDEO] DVD

Andy Garcia *Sean Casey* • Richard Dreyfuss *Sam Vigoda* • Lena Olin *Peggy Lindstrom* • Ian Holm *Liam Casey* • James Gandolfini *Joey Allegretto* • Colm Feore *Elihu Harrison* ■ *Dir* Sidney Lumet • *Scr* Sidney Lumet, from the novel *Tainted Evidence* by Robert Daley

Night Flight ★★

Adventure 1933 · US · BW · 84mins

MGM wheeled out a lot of stars for this flying yarn: two Barrymores, Clark Gable, Robert Montgomery and two fine leading ladies, Myrna Loy and Helen Hayes. The story is about the setting up of a company that delivers mail across the high Andes. In the air, it's all turbulence, fog and mountain peaks; on the ground, it's all macho posturing and romantic clinches. Its box-office success spawned a whole series of imitators. AT

John Barrymore *Riviere* • Helen Hayes *Mme Fabian* • Clark Gable *Jules* • Lionel Barrymore *Robineau* • Robert Montgomery *Auguste Pellerin* • Myrna Loy *Brazilian pilot's wife* ■ *Dir* Clarence Brown • *Scr* Oliver HP Garrett, from the story by Antoine de Saint-Exupéry

Night Game ★★ 18

Thriller 1989 · US · Colour · 91mins

Over-familiar story of a Texas police chief trying to track down a serial lady-killer before he can claim his next victim. The reliable Roy Scheider and Karen Young deliver good performances, but their efforts are wasted on mediocre material. DA [VIDEO]

Roy Scheider *Seaver* • Karen Young *Roxy* • Richard Bradford *Nelson* • Paul Gleason *Broussard* • Carlin Glynn *Alma* ■ *Dir* Peter Masterson • *Scr* Spencer Eastman, Anthony Palmer, from a story by Spencer Eastman

Night Games ★ 18

Erotic thriller 1979 · US · Colour · 101mins

Risible soft-core erotica from Roger Vadim, the man who "discovered", then married Brigitte Bardot and Jane Fonda (though not at the same time). Vadim's protégée Cindy Pickett isn't bad in her feature debut, playing a Beverly Hills housewife terrified of sexual contact due to a traumatic childhood incident. When she's reduced to having sex with a man dressed as a bird, though, it's fatally unclear whether Vadim is being mocking or serious. RS [VIDEO]

Cindy Pickett *Valerie St John* • Joanna Cassidy *Julie Miller* • Barry Primus *Jason St John* • Paul Jenkins *Sean Daniels* • Gene Davis *Timothy* • Juliet Fabriga *Alicia* • Clem Parsons *Jun* • Mark Hanks *"The Phantom"* ■ *Dir* Roger Vadim • *Scr* Anton Diether, Clarke Reynolds, from a story by Barth Jules Sussman, Anton Diether

N

Night Has a Thousand Eyes ★★

Mystery 1948 · US · BW · 81mins

The assumption that a vaudeville show clairvoyant (Edward G Robinson) is a fake turns out to be unfounded when he proves he really can foretell the future. John Farrow directs this efficiently made but bland entertainment, it co-stars Gail Russell, John Lund, Virginia Bruce and William Demarest. RK

Edward G Robinson *John Triton* • Gail Russell *Jean Courtland* • John Lund *Elliott Carson* • Virginia Bruce *Jenny* • William Demarest *Lt Shawn* • Richard Webb *Peter Vinson* ■ *Dir* John Farrow • *Scr* Barre Lyndon, Jonathan Latimer, from a novel by Cornell Woolrich

The Night Has Eyes ★★★

Thriller 1942 · UK · BW · 79mins

The saturnine side of James Mason's screen persona was exploited to the full in this studio-bound melodrama, set on the Yorkshire moors. Mason plays a reclusive composer and wounded veteran of the Spanish Civil War who is subject to fits. He could well be a threat to Joyce Howard, one of two female teachers taking refuge from a storm. On the other hand, there's something not quite right about Wilfrid Lawson and Mary Clare, the couple who run the house. Director Leslie Arliss develops the sinister atmosphere with some skill. AE

James Mason *Stephen Deremid* • Joyce Howard *Marian Ives* • Wilfrid Lawson *Sturrock* • Mary Clare *Mrs Ranger* • Tucker McGuire *Doris* • John Fernald *Dr Barry Randall* ■ *Dir* Leslie Arliss • *Scr* John Argyle, Leslie Arliss, Alan Kennington, from a story by Alan Kennington

The Night Holds Terror ★★

Crime drama 1955 · US · BW · 85mins

Watch this and you'll spend the night checking all locks and doors three times over. One of those post-*film noir* movies where everything is shadow and promised substance, but you get little more than a lot of characters with their mouths hanging open and jauntily angled fedoras. Here, a family is held to ransom by crooks John Cassavetes (in only his second major role), Vince Edwards and David Cross. Quite exciting for the first 20 minutes, and immensely tedious thereafter. SH

Jack Kelly *Gene Courtier* • Hildy Parks *Doris Courtier* • Vince Edwards *Victor Gosset* • John Cassavetes *Robert Batsford* • David Gross *Luther Logan* • Edward Marr [Eddie Marr] *Captain Cole* ■ *Dir* Andrew Stone [Andrew L Stone] • *Scr* Andrew Stone

A Night in Casablanca ★★★ U

Comedy 1946 · US · BW · 84mins

While it has none of the sustained genius of their earlier outings, this Marx Brothers' picture has enough moments of inspired lunacy to merit a place on most viewers' "must see" lists. Although freed from the constraints placed upon them by MGM, the trio (ending a five-year screen exile) are forced to play second fiddle to a contrived plot about spies and buried treasure, which was supposed to invite cheeky comparisons with the classic Bogart/Bergman drama. Groucho goes into one-liner overdrive to compensate for the absence of Margaret Dumont, but Harpo has the best gag in the opening minutes. DP DVD

Groucho Marx *Ronald Kornblow* • Harpo Marx *Rusty* • Chico Marx *Corbaccio* • Lisette Verea *Beatrice Reiner* • Charles Drake *Pierre* • Lois Collier *Annette* • Dan Seymour *Captain Brizzard* • Sig Rumann [Sig Ruman] *Count Pfefferman* ■ *Dir* Archie Mayo • *Scr* Joseph Fields, Roland Kibbee

A Night in Havana: Dizzy Gillespie in Cuba ★★★

Music documentary 1988 · US · Colour · 84mins

An intriguing account of the great jazz trumpeter's 1985 tour of Cuba, a country which had particular relevence to him since for 40 years he had been pioneering the use of Afro-Cuban rhythms within American music. Educational as well as entertaining, the affable bebopper is shown performing full-length versions of *A Night in Tunisia* and *Manteca*, cracking jokes, relating anecdotes and offering illuminating historical and musical analyses of Cuban rhythms. TH

Allen Honigberg *Interviewer* ■ *Dir* John Holland

A Night in Heaven ★★ 18

Romantic drama 1983 · US · Colour · 79mins

College professor Lesley Ann Warren goes to a male strip club and finds that the featured dancer is Christopher Atkins, who happens to be one of her students. A contrived May-December romantic drama, this coasts along thanks mainly to Warren's captivating turn and "Heaven", the Chippendales-style locale. Watch out for Andy Garcia in his first screen role. AJ

Christopher Atkins *Rick* • Lesley Ann Warren *Faye* • Robert Logan *Whitney* • Deborah Rush *Patsy* • Deney Terrio *Tony* • Sandra Beall *Slick* • Alix Elias *Shirley* • Carrie Snodgress *Mrs Johnson* • Amy Levine *Eve* • Andy Garcia *TJ* ■ *Dir* John G Avildsen • *Scr* Joan Tewkesbury

A Night in the Life of Jimmy Reardon ★★★ 15

Drama 1988 · US · Colour · 88mins

River Phoenix strayed from his usual thoughtful pubescent role to play a romeo teenager with a gravity-defying hairdo in this hit-and-miss comedy. Although Phoenix is as engaging as ever, he seems ill at ease playing such an extrovert character. Nonetheless, the movie has its moments, notably Phoenix's assignations with older woman Ann Magnuson. JB. Contains swearing.

River Phoenix *Jimmy Reardon* • Meredith Salenger *Lisa* • Matthew L Perry [Matthew Perry] *Fred* • Ione Skye *Denise* • Ann Magnuson *Joyce* • Louanne *Suzie* • Paul Koslo *Mr Reardon* • Jane Hallaren *Mrs Reardon* ■ *Dir* William Richert • *Scr* William Richert, from his novel *Aren't You Even Gonna Kiss Me Goodbye?*

Night Is My Future ★★★

Drama 1948 · Swe · BW · 87mins

Ingmar Bergman's fourth feature was the first to turn a profit. His mentor, producer Lorens Marmstedt, insisted he adhered closely to the storyline, even though it was awash with sentimentality: from the fact that Birger Malmsten is blinded while trying to rescue a puppy from a firing range, to the final reunion with a waifish Mai Zetterling. However, there's a persuasive poetic realism about the picture, with the hallucinatory dream sequence allowing Bergman to break out of the film's melodramatic straitjacket. DP. A Swedish language film.

Mai Zetterling *Ingrid Olofsdotter* • Birger Malmsten *Bengt* • Bengt Eklund *Ebbe* ■ *Dir* Ingmar Bergman • *Scr* Dagmar Edqvist, from her novel

The Night Is Young ★★★ 15

Romantic thriller 1986 · Fr · Colour · 114mins

For all his visual flair, director Léos Carax's storytelling skills leave a lot to be desired. There's a carelessly pulpy quality about this futuristic thriller, in which Denis Lavant's commitment to the theft of a serum that cures a fatal disease afflicting only the romantically insincere is diminished by his growing obsession with Juliette Binoche, the mistress of fellow gang member Michel Piccoli. The compositions irresistibly recall the pictorial genius of film-makers as different as Fritz Lang and Jean-Luc Godard. Fascinating, but frustrating. DP. In French with English subtitles.

Denis Lavant *Alex* • Juliette Binoche *Anna* • Michel Piccoli *Marc* • Hans Meyer *Hans* • Julie Delpy *Lise* • Carroll Brooks *The American* • Hugo Pratt *Boris* • Serge Reggiani *Charlie* ■ *Dir/Scr* Léos Carax

Night Mail ★★★★★ U

Documentary 1936 · UK · BW · 23mins

The jewel of British cinema in the 1930s was the documentary movement presided over by John Grierson (the man who coined the term "documentary" for factual films). Grierson and Stuart Legg provide the commentary for this evocative short, directed by Harry Watt and Basil Wright for the GPO Film Unit. Never have the dry statistics about the operation of the London-Glasgow mail train been presented with such flair. The beautiful shots of steaming engines, Benjamin Britten's pulsing score and WH Auden's adroit verses combine to form a film poem that delights both the ear and the eye. DP DVD

Dir Harry Watt, Basil Wright • *Scr* WH Auden, Basil Wright, Harry Watt

'Night, Mother ★★★★ 15

Drama 1986 · US · Colour · 92mins

Sissy Spacek, who won an Oscar six years earlier for her performance in *Coal Miner's Daughter*, tells her mother she's going to commit suicide in this drama based on Marsha Norman's Pulitzer Prize-winning play. Both Spacek and Anne Bancroft (an Academy Award-winner herself for *The Miracle Worker*) are excellent, and though this character-driven piece sometimes feels a bit stagey, the performances are mesmerising enough to keep you riveted. JB

Sissy Spacek *Jessie Cates* • Anne Bancroft *Thelma Cates* • Ed Berke *Dawson Cates* • Carol Robbins *Loretta Cates* • Jennifer Roosendahl *Melodie Cates* • Michael Kenworthy *Kenny Cates* ■ *Dir* Tom Moore • *Scr* Marsha Norman, from her play

Night Moves ★★★★ 18

Mystery thriller 1975 · US · Colour · 95mins

Despite its title, this brilliantly self-conscious gumshoe movie by director Arthur Penn from Alan Sharp's sparkling script lights up a time of post-Watergate confusion, when bloodshot private eye Gene Hackman seeks a client's lost daughter and his own lost honour. It's a bleak, pointless quest, encapsulated by the final shot of a boat going round in meaningless circles, but there's a sour wit that can mock other directors. An enigmatic masterpiece whose pleasures are allusive and cinematic. TH. Contains some violence and swearing.

Gene Hackman *Harry Moseby* • Jennifer Warren *Paula* • Edward Binns *Joey Ziegler* • Harris Yulin *Marty Heller* • Kenneth Mars *Nick* • Janet Ward *Arlene Iverson* • James Woods *Quentin* • Anthony Costello *Marv Ellman* • John Crawford *Tom Iverson* • Melanie Griffith *Delly Grastner* • Susan Clark *Ellen Moseby* ■ *Dir* Arthur Penn • *Scr* Alan Sharp

Night Must Fall ★★★★

Thriller 1937 · US · BW · 116mins

Emlyn Williams's famous shocker has had many incarnations, but this MGM version is very good indeed, largely due to the casting against type of the totally plausible Robert Montgomery as the suspected killer, and a marvellous performance from Rosalind Russell as the woman who slowly but surely discovers the killer's identity for herself. Several of the cast MGM employed had played their parts on stage in both London and New York, and the film is especially notable for the appearance of May Whitty, in one of her first talking roles, as a foolish, isolated old woman. TS

Robert Montgomery *Danny* • Rosalind Russell *Olivia* • May Whitty [Dame May Whitty] *Mrs Bransom* • Alan Marshal *Justin* • Merle Tottenham *Dora* • Kathleen Harrison *Mrs Terence* ■ *Dir* Richard Thorpe • *Scr* John van Druten, from the play by Emlyn Williams

Night Must Fall ★★★

Thriller 1964 · UK · BW · 104mins

Emlyn Williams's popular, if shakily plotted, stage thriller was originally filmed in 1937. In this flashy remake, Susan Hampshire steps into the shoes of the woman who gradually comes to realise who is responsible for a series of countryside killings. Director Karel Reisz's attempts to explore the murderer's mental instability through camera movements and cross-cuts are undone by the staginess of the dialogue. Yet Freddie Francis's photography is highly atmospheric and Albert Finney's performance is occasionally electrifying. DP

Albert Finney *Danny* • Susan Hampshire *Olivia* • Mona Washbourne *Mrs Bramson* • Sheila Hancock *Dora* • Michael Medwin *Derek* • Joe Gladwin *Dodge* ■ *Dir* Karel Reisz • *Scr* Clive Exton, from the play by Emlyn Williams

The Night My Number Came Up ★★★

Drama 1955 · UK · BW · 94mins

This intriguing film bears more than a passing resemblance to the James Stewart airplane melodrama *No Highway*. Similarly held together by a first-rate central performance, the film features Michael Redgrave intent on grounding his flight to Tokyo as events alarmingly begin to resemble those in a nightmare. Exploring with a keen intelligence the coincidences and implausibilities generated by fear, RC Sherriff's tense screenplay is full of unsympathetic, self-obsessed characters, played to a nicety by a model supporting cast. DP

Michael Redgrave *Air Marshal John Hardie* • Sheila Sim *Mary Campbell* • Alexander Knox *Owen Robertson* • Denholm Elliott *Flight Lieutenant McKenzie* • Ursula Jeans *Mrs Robertson* • Michael Hordern *Commander Lindsay* • Ralph Truman *Lord Wainwright* ■ *Dir* Leslie Norman • *Scr* RC Sherriff, from an article by Air Marshal Sir Victor Goddard

Night Nurse ★★★

Crime drama 1931 · US · BW · 72mins

A fast-moving melodrama with a great cast headed by Barbara Stanwyck and Joan Blondell, who were accused by contemporary critics of boosting the film's audiences by spending an inordinate amount of screen time dressing and undressing. Ben Lyon is the co-star, but the screen is well and truly stolen by a young actor in the supporting role of sadistic chauffeur: a clean-shaven Clark Gable on the road to stardom. This kind of tough, sexy drama vanished with the coming of the restrictive Hays Code, and it's always interesting to see what Hollywood could get away with before. TS

Barbara Stanwyck *Lora Hart* • Ben Lyon *Mortie* • Joan Blondell *Maloney* • Charles Winninger *Dr Arthur Bell* • Charlotte Merriam *Mrs Ritchey* • Edward Nugent *Eagan* • Blanche Frederici *Mrs Maxwell* ■ *Dir* William A Wellman • *Scr* Oliver HP Garrett, Charles Kenyon, from the novel by Dora Macy [Grace Perkins Oursler]

The Night of Counting the Years ★★★★

Historical drama
1969 · Egy · Colour · 102mins

Recalling the actual theft by members of the Horrabat tribe of artefacts from a tomb in Thebes in 1881, this stunningly photographed picture considers whether an impoverished people should sell its antiquities to survive or resist the export of its heritage. Shadi Abdelsalam's background in art direction is evident in his hypnotic selection of deep-focus shots and his control of light and contrasting colours. Yet he also manages to keep this slow-moving story absorbing throughout. DP. In Arabic with English subtitles.

Ahmed Marei *Wanniss* • Zouzou El Hakim *Mother* • Ahmad Hegazi *Brother* • Nadia Loutfy *Zeena* • Gaby Karraz *Maspero* ■ *Dir/Scr* Shadi Abdelsalam

Night of Dark Shadows ★★

Horror 1971 · US · Colour · 93mins

The presence of Jonathan Frid as Barnabas the vampire is greatly missed in this second film sequel (after *House of Dark Shadows*) to the cult TV daytime serial *Dark Shadows*. The tale of the haunting of a newlywed couple who have recently moved in to their ancestral home unfolds in haphazard fashion. Barking more than terrifying, this will be best enjoyed by fans of the soap opera and its misbegotten 1990s update. AJ

David Selby *Quentin Collins/Charles Collins* • Grayson Hall *Carlotta Drake* • John Karlen *Alex Jenkins* • Nancy Barrett *Claire Jenkins* • Lara Parker *Angélique* • Kate Jackson *Tracy Collins* • James Storm *Gerard Styles* • Diana Millay *Laura Collins* • Christopher Pennock *Gabriel Collins* • Thayer David *Reverend Strack* ■ *Dir* Dan Curtis • *Scr* Sam Hall, from a story by Sam Hall, Dan Curtis, from the TV series created by Dan Curtis, Art Wallace

The Night of San Lorenzo ★★★★ [12]

Second World War drama
1981 · It · Colour · 102mins

Told as an extended flashback by a woman who was just six when Tuscany was liberated by the Allies, this pacifist drama draws on both the Taviani brothers' own memories of the summer of 1944 and their cinematic influences to create an unforgettable, neorealist fairy tale. Against the visual poetry, small instances of surrealist fantasy and warm moments of simple humanity, however, is set the horror of war, as the Nazis and their Italian collaborators deal peremptorily with the partisans undermining their defence of San Martino. Thus the film's glowing romanticism lies less in the hard-won victory than in the people's unity and indomitability. DP. In Italian with English subtitles.

Paolo Hendel *Dilvo* • Omero Antonutti *Galvano* • Margarita Lozano *Concetta* • Claudio Bigagli *Corrado* • Massimo Bonetti *Nicola* • Norma Martelli *Ivana* ■ *Dir* Vittorio Taviani, Paolo Taviani • *Scr* Paolo Taviani, Vittorio Taviani, Giuliani G De Negri, Tonino Guerra

Night of the Big Heat ★★ [15]

Science-fiction horror
1967 · UK · Colour · 90mins

The ever-reliable team of Peter Cushing and Christopher Lee put a crisp British cast through its paces as mystified islanders are plagued by a winter heatwave caused by energy-starved aliens. Most of the action takes place at a local inn, where the helpless survivors get on each other's nerves. However, the final arrival of the monsters signals a few tepid thrills, even if they do resemble badly fried eggs with tinned spaghetti innards. AJ. Contains some violence. DVD

Christopher Lee *Hanson* • Peter Cushing *Dr Stone* • Patrick Allen *Jeff Callum* • Sarah Lawson *Frankie Callum* • Jane Merrow *Angela Roberts* • William Lucas *Ken Stanley* • Kenneth Cope *Tinker Mason* ■ *Dir* Terence Fisher • *Scr* Ronald Liles, Pip Baker, Jane Baker, from the novel by John Lymington

Night of the Comet ★★★ [15]

Science fiction 1984 · US · Colour · 94mins

Full of fun scares, gleeful unease and touching warmth, director Thom Eberhardt's tongue-in-cheek cult item pastes together numerous ideas from other science-fiction flicks and takes them the full distance. The same comet that wiped out the dinosaurs reappears to make most of mankind extinct this time. Catherine Mary Stewart and Kelli Maroney are two tough talking Valley girls who survive to take on the remaining flesh-eating zombies, marauding punks and sinister scientists in this upbeat and funky metaphor for maturity. AJ

Catherine Mary Stewart *Regina* • Robert Beltran *Hector* • Kelli Maroney *Samantha* • Geoffrey Lewis *Carter* • Mary Woronov *Audrey* ■ *Dir/Scr* Thom Eberhardt

Night of the Demon ★★★★ [15]

Horror 1957 · UK · BW · 90mins

A remarkably well-constructed essay on the realm of the supernatural, *Cat People* director Jacques Tourneur's classic devil-cult chiller is a superb adaptation of the MR James short story *Casting the Runes*. Pitting rational scientist Dana Andrews against sinister mystic Niall MacGinnis, this top-notch suspense drama works marvellously well, despite studio interference insisting that the scary demon Tourneur wanted to avoid showing be included at the last minute. Edge-of-the-seat stuff, with a truly memorable climax. Released on video as *Curse of the Demon*. AJ

Dana Andrews *John Holden* • Peggy Cummins *Joanna Harrington* • Niall MacGinnis *Dr Karswell* • Maurice Denham *Professor Harrington* • Athene Seyler *Mrs Karswell* • Liam Redmond *Mark O'Brien* • Reginald Beckwith *Mr Meek* • Ewan Roberts *Lloyd Williamson* ■ *Dir* Jacques Tourneur • *Scr* Charles Bennett, Hal E Chester, from the story *Casting the Runes* by MR James

Night of the Demons ★★ [18]

Horror 1988 · US · Colour · 85mins

A high schoolers' Halloween party at the local spook house goes predictably wrong in this goofy 1980s horror film. Think *The Breakfast Club* crossed with *The Evil Dead* and you'll get the basic idea. Sadly, it's nowhere near as funny as the first, or as scary as the second. Scream queen Linnea Quigley provides most of the requisite nudity, while Steve Johnson (Quigley's future husband) supplies the gore. There are a few bright moments, but mostly it's the same old schtick. ST DVD

Lance Fenton *Jay* • Cathy Podewell *Judy* • Alvin Alexis *Roger* • Hal Havins *Stooge* • Amelia Kinkade *Angela* • Linnea Quigley *Suzanne* ■ *Dir* Kevin S Tenney • *Scr* Joe Augustyn • *Special Effects* Steve Johnson

Night of the Demons 2 ★★★

Horror 1994 · US · Colour · 96mins

This belated follow-up to the 1988 film is actually a more imaginative and outrageous ride, despite the clichéd plot about a group of brattish students holding a Halloween bash in a creepy old house. Director Brian Trenchard-Smith plays it for laughs at every opportunity and throws a smidgen of gratuitous nudity and gore into the teen-slasher brew. There are some truly inspired moments, such as when a nun saves the day using holy water in a squirt gun Uzi. A third instalment, *Demon House*, followed in 1997. RS

Cristi Harris *Bibi* • Bobby Jacoby *Perry* • Merle Kennedy *Mouse* • Amelia Kinkade *Angela* • Rod McCary *Father Bob* • Johnny Moran *Johnny* • Rick Peters *Rick* ■ *Dir* Brian Trenchard-Smith • *Scr* Joe Augustyn, from a story by James Penzi, Joe Augustyn

Night of the Eagle ★★★ [15]

Horror 1961 · UK · BW · 83mins

A woman uses witchcraft to further her husband's career in this nifty adaptation of Fritz Leiber Jr's classic tale. Despite being over-melodramatic at times, Sidney Hayers's solid direction creates a great deal of terror out of the unseen to make it above average in the spine-tingling department. You'll still be unnerved even though you can glimpse the wires on the stone eagle as it comes to life in the eerie coda. AJ DVD

Peter Wyngarde *Norman Taylor* • Janet Blair *Tansy Taylor* • Margaret Johnston *Flora Carr* • Anthony Nicholls *Harvey Sawtelle* • Colin Gordon *Professor Lindsay Carr* • Kathleen Byron *Evelyn Sawtelle* • Reginald Beckwith *Harold Gunnison* • Jessica Dunning *Hilda Gunnison* ■ *Dir* Sidney Hayers • *Scr* Charles Beaumont, Richard Matheson, George Baxt, from the novel *Conjure Wife* by Fritz Leiber Jr

The Night of the Following Day ★★ [18]

Crime thriller 1968 · UK/US · Colour · 89mins

Marlon Brando wears a blonde wig and a black T-shirt to show off his lithe figure in this deservedly obscure thriller, shot in Normandy under conditions of considerable chaos and tension, not least due to Brando's on-off relationship with co-star Rita Moreno. British actress Pamela Franklin is kidnapped by drug addict Moreno, tough cookie Richard Boone and chauffeur Brando. It's around this point that the movie becomes extremely arty in a way that suggests the director had been watching too much Godard. AT

Marlon Brando *Bud the chauffeur* • Richard Boone *Leer* • Rita Moreno *Vi* • Pamela Franklin *Girl* • Jess Hahn *Wally* ■ *Dir* Hubert Cornfield • *Scr* Hubert Cornfield, Robert Phippeny, from the novel *The Snatchers* by Lionel White

The Night of the Generals ★★★ [15]

Second World War drama
1966 · UK/Fr · Colour · 137mins

Three Nazi generals are the prime suspects following a series of Jack the Ripper-style murders in this lurid Second World War drama. Omar Sharif heads the inquiry while Peter O'Toole is top-billed as one of the officers under investigation. Director Anatole Litvak gives up on the whodunnit element early on and the plot just about muddles through, with Tom Courtenay representing the powerless ordinary soldier. TH

Peter O'Toole *General Tanz* • Omar Sharif *Major Grau* • Tom Courtenay *Corporal Hartmann* • Donald Pleasence *General Kahlenberge* • Joanna Pettet *Ulrike von Seidlitz-Gabler* • Philippe Noiret *Inspector Morand* • Charles Gray *General von Seidlitz-Gabler* • Coral Browne *Eleanore von Seidlitz-Gabler* ■ *Dir* Anatole Litvak • *Scr* Joseph Kessel, Paul Dehn, from the novels *Die Nacht der Generale* by Hans Helmut Kirst and *The Wary Transgressor* by James Hadley Chase

Night of the Ghouls ★ [PG]

Horror 1959 · US · BW · 66mins

Even by the standards of Edward D Wood Jr, generally acknowledged as the worst director ever, this is woeful stuff. In this sequel of sorts to *Bride of the Monster*, Kenne Duncan, in a role originally written for Bela Lugosi, plays a fake medium who unwittingly resurrects the dead. The opening shot of Criswell arising from his coffin to warn the audience of things that go bump in the night is funnier than every Abbott and Costello film put together. This was one of Wood's last movies, though it was never released in his lifetime. RS

Criswell • Kenne Duncan *Dr Acula* • Maila Nurmi [Vampira] *Black ghost* • Tor Johnson *Lobo* • Valda Hansen *Fake ghost* • Lon Chaney Jr ■ *Dir/Scr* Edward D Wood Jr

The Night of the Grizzly ★★ [PG]

Western 1966 · US · Colour · 97mins

TV star Clint Walker is a homesteader who arrives on his slice of Wyoming with his wife and family. Almost at once he runs into opposition from the locals, but there is also a greedy grizzly bear that seems to single Walker out for special treatment, slaughtering Walker's valuable herd and bringing about the mortgaging of the property. Part *Jaws*, part *Shane*, it's really a children's film that relies on its bear and some attractive mountain photography. AT

Clint Walker *Jim Cole* • Martha Hyer *Angela Cole* • Keenan Wynn *Jed Curry* • Nancy Kulp *Wilhelmina Peterson* • Kevin Brodie *Charlie Cole* • Ellen Corby *Hazel Squires* • Jack Elam *Hank* • Ron Ely *Tad Curry* ■ *Dir* Joseph Pevney • *Scr* Warren Douglas

The Night of the Hunter ★★★★★ [12]

Classic thriller 1955 · US · BW · 88mins

Charles Laughton's only film as a director is one of the great masterpieces of American cinema, a movie so strangely repellent, so poetic and so utterly hypnotic that it sadly never found an audience. It features Robert Mitchum's finest screen performance as a bogus priest and psychopath who has "love" and "hate" tattooed on his knuckles. Mitchum's always imposing, menacing presence is heightened by Laughton to an extraordinary degree, and this stunning collaboration is enhanced by Lillian Gish's portrayal of a gun-toting spinster. Set during the Depression in a rural backwater, this is a fairy tale turned into a dark night of the soul. Remade, unnecessarily, in 1991 as a TV movie. AT DVD

Robert Mitchum *Preacher Harry Powell* • Shelley Winters *Willa Harper* • Lillian Gish *Rachel* • Evelyn Varden *Icey Spoon* • Peter Graves (2) *Ben Harper* • Billy Chapin *John* • Sally Jane Bruce *Pearl* • James Gleason *Birdie* ■ *Dir* Charles Laughton • *Scr* James Agee, from the novel by Davis Grubb • *Cinematographer* Stanley Cortez

The Night of the Iguana ★★★ [12]

Drama 1964 · US · Colour · 112mins

It says much for the quality of the performances here that, from a cast that includes Richard Burton, Ava Gardner and Deborah Kerr, it was the little-known Grayson Hall who was nominated for an Oscar. As you would expect of a Tennessee Williams play, every performer has something to sink their teeth into. Yet Burton's defrocked cleric, Gardner's hotelier and Kerr's artist owe more to polished technique than flesh and blood. This may have something to do with director John Huston viewing this steamy story from his own laconic perspective. DP

Richard Burton *Rev T Lawrence Shannon* • Ava Gardner *Maxine Faulk* • Deborah Kerr *Hannah Jelkes* • Sue Lyon *Charlotte Goodall* • James Ward *Hank Prosner* • Grayson Hall *Judith Fellowes* • Cyril Delevanti *Nonno* ■ *Dir* John Huston • *Scr* Anthony Veiller, John Huston, from the play by Tennessee Williams

Night of the Juggler ★★ 18

Action thriller 1980 · US · Colour · 96mins

This overblown urban thriller achieves the rare feat of making New York look even uglier than it is in real life. When his daughter is mistakenly kidnapped by a candidate for "psycho of the month", ex-cop James Brolin trashes the city looking for her. Director Robert Butler brings technical craft to the numerous scenes of car crashes, but he seems rather less interested in the human beings in the cast. RS

James Brolin *Sean Boyd* • Cliff Gorman *Gus Soltic* • Richard Castellano *Lieutenant Tonelli* • Abby Bluestone *Kathy Boyd* • Dan Hedaya *Sergeant Otis Barnes* • Julie Carmen *Marie* • Mandy Patinkin *Cabbie* ■ *Dir* Robert Butler • *Scr* William Norton Sr, Rick Natkin, from the novel by William P McGivern

Night of the Lepus ★

Science fiction 1972 · US · Colour · 88mins

When a laboratory rabbit, injected with an experimental pest control serum, escapes into the Arizona desert and starts breeding with the local wild bunny population you either have the potential for an eco-thriller of the stature of *Them!* or you have the ingredients of a Monty Python sketch. Alas, this giant killer bunny flick is as unintentionally hilarious as anything Cleese and company could have dreamt up. RS

Stuart Whitman *Roy Bennett* • Janet Leigh *Gerry Bennett* • Rory Calhoun *Cole Hillman* • DeForest Kelley *Dr Elgin Clark* • Paul Fix *Sheriff Cody* ■ *Dir* William F Claxton • *Scr* Don Holliday, Gene Kearney, from the novel *The Year of the Angry Rabbit* by Russell Braddon

Night of the Living Dead ★★★★★ 18

Classic horror 1968 · US · BW · 95mins

Director George Romero's seminal classic redefined the meaning of horror for fear-sated audiences in the 1960s. It starts suddenly with a jolting attack in a cemetery and relentlessly continues on a downward spiral of frantic despair as terrified people take fragile shelter in a secluded house to fight off an army of cannibalistic zombies. Conveying visceral terror through an unrelieved black-and-white documentary atmosphere, Romero's graphic cult chiller no longer scares the daylights out of viewers because of its countless imitations. But his radical style and lethal wit still impress. Two sequels, *Dawn of the Dead* (1978) and *Day of the Dead* (1985) complete his masterful trilogy. AJ DVD

Judith O'Dea *Barbara* • Russell Streiner *Johnny* • Duane Jones *Ben* • Karl Hardman *Harry Cooper* • Keith Wayne *Tom* ■ *Dir* George A Romero • *Scr* John A Russo, from a story by George A Romero

Night of the Living Dead ★★★★ 18

Horror 1990 · US · Colour · 84mins

This highly acceptable remake of George A Romero's 1968 horror classic sticks close to the events of the original, as a group of people becomes trapped inside a farmhouse by a gang of flesh-eating zombies. However, the masterstroke here is to keep the viewer off-guard by introducing some fresh slants, courtesy of Romero (who updated his own script). Well acted and shot in atmospheric muted colours, this succeeds thanks to director Tom Savini's sure hand, bringing flair, intelligence and imagination to the task. AJ. Contains violence and swearing. DVD

Tony Todd *Ben* • Patricia Tallman *Barbara* • Tom Towles *Harry* • McKee Anderson *Helen* • William Butler *Tom* • Katie Finneran *Judy Rose* • Bill Mosley [Bill Moseley] *Johnnie* • Heather Mazur *Sarah* ■ *Dir* Tom Savini • *Scr* George A Romero, from the 1968 film

Night of the Party ★★

Detective drama 1934 · UK · BW · 60mins

In this typical 1930s murder mystery, a press magnate with many enemies seems to have invited them all to the same party. He is shot during a murder game with the lights out and anyone could have done it. The film's surviving interest is as one of the earliest extant works of Michael Powell, still in his 20s at the time. The project offered little artistic challenge, but he directs fluently enough and seems to have cut short the lengthy courtroom denouement in favour of a lively, if implausible, interruption by the culprit. AE

Leslie Banks *Sir John Holland* • Ian Hunter *Guy Kennington* • Jane Baxter *Peggy Studholme* • Ernest Thesiger *Chiddiatt* ■ *Dir* Michael Powell • *Scr* Ralph Smart, from a play by Roland Pertwee, John Hastings Turner

Night of the Prowler ★ U

Crime drama 1962 · UK · BW · 61mins

British director Francis Searle had the distinction of making only one bill-topping feature in his entire 27-film career, the daft comedy *A Girl in a Million*. The remainder of his output consisted of B-movies, including this offering. Devotees of laughably bad low-budget crime movies should enjoy this tawdry tale of ambition, murder and deceit, set in the cut-throat world of the motor trade! DP

Patrick Holt *Robert Langton* • Colette Wilde *Marie Langton* • Bill Nagy *Paul Conrad* • Mitzi Rogers *Jacky Reed* • John Horsley *Inspector Cameron* • Marianne Stone *Mrs Cross* ■ *Dir* Francis Searle • *Scr* Paul Erickson

Night of the Strangler ★

Thriller 1975 · US · Colour · 88mins

The sight of ex-Monkee Micky Dolenz investigating the mysterious deaths of a white woman and her black lover is the only noteworthy aspect of this violent thriller. Lots of nudity and a racism subplot do little to perk the interest in an awkwardly acted programme filler, set in New Orleans and directed by Joy N Houck Jr. AJ

Mickey Dolenz [Micky Dolenz] *Vance* • Chuck Patterson *Priest* • James Ralston *Dan* ■ *Dir* Joy N Houck Jr

Night on Earth ★★★ 15

Comedy drama 1992 · US · Colour · 123mins

Five taxi rides take place on the same night in Los Angeles, New York, Paris, Rome and Helsinki. In each cab, a moving story about life's little ironies unfolds. While the two American-based tales in Jim Jarmusch's highly accessible compendium fall flat, the European segments – Roberto Benigni confessing all to his priest-passenger, blind Béatrice Dalle teaching her cabbie a thing or two – hit the right note of quirkiness that has become the art house director's trademark. Well worth watching. AJ. In English, French, Finnish and Italian with subtitles. DVD

Winona Ryder *Corky* • Gena Rowlands *Victoria Snelling* • Giancarlo Esposito *Yoyo* • Armin Mueller-Stahl *Helmut Grokenberger* • Rosie Perez *Angela* • Isaach de Bankole *Driver* • Béatrice Dalle *Blind woman* • Roberto Benigni *Gino* ■ *Dir/Scr* Jim Jarmusch

A Night on the Town ★★★ 15

Comedy 1987 · US · Colour · 102mins

Also known as *Adventures in Babysitting*, this is one of the lightweight comedies Chris Columbus made before he directed the blockbusting hit *Home Alone*. It's a daft but fun teen movie with Elisabeth Shue as a girl who has a series of ridiculous adventures on the streets of Chicago one night with the children she's supposed to be baby-sitting. JB. Contains violence, swearing. DVD

Elisabeth Shue *Chris Parker* • Maia Brewton *Sara Anderson* • Keith Coogan *Brad Anderson* • Anthony Rapp *Daryl Coopersmith* • Calvin Levels *Joe Gipp* • Vincent Phillip D'Onofrio [Vincent D'Onofrio] *Dawson* • Penelope Ann Miller *Brenda* ■ *Dir* Chris Columbus • *Scr* David Simkins

Night Passage ★★ U

Western 1957 · US · Colour · 86mins

James Stewart, director Anthony Mann and writer Borden Chase already had a whole string of hit westerns under their belt when they started work on this below-par effort. Mann quit after a few days, sensing that the script wasn't quite ready, and made way for TV director James Neilson. Stewart plays a former railroad man who comes up against his own brother, train robber Audie Murphy, when he is hired to deliver a payroll. AT DVD

James Stewart *Grant McLaine* • Audie Murphy *Utica Kid* • Dan Duryea *Whitey Harbin* • Dianne Foster *Charlotte Drew* • Elaine Stewart *Verna Kimball* • Brandon de Wilde *Joey Adams* ■ *Dir* James Neilson • *Scr* Borden Chase, from a story by Norman A Fox

Night Patrol ★ 18

Comedy 1984 · US · Colour · 81mins

With a cast that would make any B-movie fan drool, this *Police Academy*-inspired comedy seems to have been constructed to become an instant cult film. It actually gets halfway there, thanks to an eager-to-please cast and vigorous direction. The other half, however, is made unbearable by an idiotic script that recycles old jokes, groan-inducing puns and tasteless attempts at humour involving nudity and bodily functions. KB DVD

Linda Blair *Sue* • Pat Paulsen *Kent* • Jaye P Morgan *Kate* • Jack Riley *Dr Ziegler* • Billy Barty *Captain Lewis* • Murray Langston *Melvin* • Noriyuki "Pat" Morita [Pat Morita] *Rape victim* ■ *Dir* Jackie Kong • *Scr* Jackie Kong, Murray Langston, William A Levey, Bill Osco

Night People ★★

Spy drama 1954 · US · Colour · 92mins

Gregory Peck plays an American intelligence officer who flies to Berlin to secure the release of a US soldier kidnapped by the communists. There he runs into a giant conspiracy involving the young man's father, an influential magnate (Broderick Crawford), and the failed assassination plot against Hitler. This blend of Cold War jitters and Nazi hangover makes for a moderately gripping thriller that uses the real bombed-out city as its location, though gritty black and white might have served the story better than touristy Technicolor. AT

Gregory Peck *Colonel Van Dyke* • Broderick Crawford *Leatherby* • Anita Björk *Hoffy* • Rita Gam *Miss Cates* • Buddy Ebsen *Sergeant McColloch* • Walter Abel *Foster* ■ *Dir* Nunnally Johnson • *Scr* Nunnally Johnson, from a story by Jed Harris, Thomas Reed

The Night Porter ★★★ 18

Drama 1973 · It · Colour · 112mins

What happens when former SS officer Dirk Bogarde and concentration camp inmate Charlotte Rampling meet years later and pick up their sadomasochistic sexual relationship more or less where they left off? Not quite the examination of the Nazi legacy in political and allegorical terms that director Liliana Cavani probably hoped for; hence the reason why her celebration of self-disgust and degradation so preoccupied the censors. Mere sexploitation or a serious analysis of guilty repression? The debate still rages. AJ. Contains violence and nudity.

Dirk Bogarde *Max* • Charlotte Rampling *Lucia* • Philippe Leroy *Klaus* • Gabriele Ferzetti *Hans* • Giuseppe Addobbati *Stumm* • Isa Miranda *Countess Stein* ■ *Dir* Liliana Cavani • *Scr* Liliana Cavani, Italo Moscati, from a story by Liliana Cavani, Barbara Alberti, Amedeo Pagani

Night Ride Home ★★★

Drama 1999 · US · Colour · 94mins

Rebecca De Mornay and Keith Carradine star in this TV movie as a couple whose life is ripped apart when their 17-year-old son is killed in a riding accident. Plagued by grief and guilt, the family struggle to heal their wounds. Thora Birch as angst-ridden daughter Clea and Ellen Burstyn as the caring grandmother round out this powerful drama, subtly directed by Glenn Jordan. MC

Rebecca De Mornay *Nora Mahler* • Keith Carradine *Neal Mahler* • Ellen Burstyn *Maggie* • Jordan Brower *Simon Mahler* • Thora Birch *Clea Mahler* • Lynne Thigpen *Fran* • Ryan Merriman *Justin* ■ *Dir* Glenn Jordan • *Scr* Ronald Parker, Darrah Cloud, from the novel by Barbara Esstman

The Night Runner ★★★

Film noir 1957 · US · BW · 78mins

Ray Danton, who went on to play the title role in *The Rise and Fall of Legs Diamond* (1960), is well-cast in this sharp shocker about a schizophrenic mental patient who takes up with Colleen Miller, much to the displeasure of her father. Abner Biberman directs with occasional flashes of insight, but the film never lets Danton show off his acting skills. TH

Ray Danton *Roy Turner* • Colleen Miller *Susan Mayes* • Merry Anders *Amy Hansen* • Willis Bouchey *Loren Mayes* • Harry Jackson *Hank Hansen* • Robert Anderson (2) *Ed Wallace* ■ *Dir* Abner Biberman • *Scr* Gene Levitt, from a story by Owen Cameron

Night Shapes ★★★★

Drama 1999 · Ger · Colour · 103mins

Imbuing the realist style of Ken Loach with the urban nightmare atmosphere of Martin Scorsese's *After Hours*, this is a deceptively perceptive comic exploration of the difficulties of integration faced by the citizens of the former East Germany. Marshalling a splendid ensemble cast, director Andreas Dresen neatly links together the experiences of three disparate couples during the Pope's visit to Berlin. Exposing just how little impact religion has on everyday lives, the film does, however, show that even in a world overrun by prostitution, drug abuse, racial prejudice and urban alienation, there's still a shred of human decency if you dig deep enough. DP. A German language film.

Meriam Abbas *Hanna* • Dominique Horwitz *Victor* • Oliver Bassler *Jochen* • Susanne Bormann *Patty* • Michael Gwisdek *Henrik Peschke* • Ricardo Valentim *Feliz* ■ *Dir/Scr* Andreas Dresen • *Cinematographer* Andreas Hofer

Night Shift ★★★★ 15

Comedy 1982 · US · Colour · 101mins

It was intended as a vehicle for director Ron Howard's old *Happy Days* chum Henry "the Fonz" Winkler, but future Batman Michael Keaton steals the show. Winkler is the shy mortuary attendant who gets involved in a call-girl operation run from the morgue by sharp-talking Keaton. The broad script doesn't attempt to milk the black opportunities in the scenario, but it is still very funny. This also gave early exposure to a number of other future stars, including Kevin Costner and Shannen Doherty. JF. Contains violence, swearing and nudity.

Henry Winkler *Chuck Lumley* • Michael Keaton *Bill Blazejowski* • Shelley Long *Belinda Keaton* • Gina Hecht *Charlotte Koogle* • Pat Corley *Edward Koogle* • Bobby DiCicco *Leonard* • Clint Howard *Jefferey* • Kevin Costner *Frat boy* • Shannen Doherty *Bluebird* ■ *Dir* Ron Howard • *Scr* Lowell Ganz, Babaloo Mandel

Night Song ★★★ U

Romantic drama 1947 · US · BW · 102mins

Merle Oberon gets to weep buckets in this sudsy melodrama in which she poses as a blind young woman to help her sightless protégé Dana Andrews fulfil his potential as a composer. Director John Cromwell could churn out this kind of sentimental nonsense in his sleep, and he knows just when to play on the heartstrings or lighten the atmosphere through the knowing performances of Ethel Barrymore and Hoagy Carmichael. The best part is watching Artur Rubinstein and the New York Philharmonic treating Andrews's lousy tune as a masterpiece. DP

Dana Andrews *Dan* • Merle Oberon *Cathy* • Ethel Barrymore *Miss Willey* • Hoagy Carmichael *Chick* • Artur Rubinstein • Jacqueline White *Connie* ■ *Dir* John Cromwell • *Scr* DeWitt Bodeen, Frank Fenton, Dick Irving Hyland, from a story by Dick Irving Hyland

The Night Stalker ★★★ 18

Thriller 1985 · US · Colour · 89mins

In this neatly compact B-thriller, Charles Napier – usually cast in supporting roles in such films as *The Blues Brothers* and *The Grifters* – is outstanding as a cop on skid row in pursuit of a serial killer who targets prostitutes. Directed by Max Kleven, it has some gripping moments, but the pace slackens. TH

Charles Napier *Sergeant JJ Striker* • Michelle Reese *Rene* • Katherine Kelly Lang *Denise* • Robert Viharo *Charlie Garrett* • Joseph Gian *Buddy Brown* • Robert Z'Dar *Sommers* ■ *Dir* Max Kleven • *Scr* John Goff, Don Edmonds

Night Sun ★★★ 15

Historical drama
1990 · It/Fr/W Ger · Colour · 107mins

Tolstoy's story, *Father Sergius*, is translated to 18th-century Italy in this handsome yet minimalist study of asceticism, idealism and the perils of pride and fame. Quitting the Neapolitan court on discovering that his bride-to-be, Nastassja Kinski, was once the king's mistress, ennobled trooper Julian Sands embraces desert monasticism, only to be beset by worldly temptation (in the form of the minxish Charlotte Gainsbourg) after he's hailed as a miracle worker by pilgrims to Mount Petra. DP. In Italian with English subtitles.

Julian Sands *Sergio Giuramondo* • Charlotte Gainsbourg *Matilda* • Nastassja Kinski *Cristina* • Massimo Bonetti *Prince Santobuono* • Margarita Lozano *Sergio's mother* • Patricia Millardet *Aurelia* ■ *Dir* Paolo Taviani, Vittorio Taviani • *Scr* Paolo Taviani, Vittorio Taviani, Tonino Guerra, from the story *Father Sergius* by Leo Tolstoy

The Night the Lights Went Out in Georgia ★ 15

Drama 1981 · US · Colour · 107mins

Appealing performances by Dennis Quaid and Kristy McNichol can't save this road movie. They play sibling country and western singers. McNichol is trying to invest her rowdy brother with some of her Nashville ambition, but he's more interested in the women he gets to meet backstage. Stereotypical situations, barely functional dialogue and directional incompetence doesn't give the fine cast any chance at all. AJ

Kristy McNichol *Amanda Child* • Dennis Quaid *Travis Child* • Mark Hamill *Conrad* • Don Stroud *Seth* • Arlen Dean Snyder *Andy* ■ *Dir* Ronald F Maxwell • *Scr* Bob Bonney, from the song by Bobby Russell

The Night They Raided Minsky's ★★★

Comedy 1968 · US · Colour · 98mins

An amiably eccentric story of America's burlesque theatre with Norman Wisdom (yes, our Norm!) upstaging everyone, including Jason Robards. It's an atmospheric comedy with Britt Ekland as the Amish girl who eventually rebels against her father and takes off her clothes on a commercial basis. The scattershot narrative never quite gets its act together, but director William Friedkin, injects enough enthusiasm to make it enjoyable, if boisterous viewing. TH. Contains brief nudity.

Jason Robards *Raymond Paine* • Britt Ekland *Rachel Schpitendavel* • Norman Wisdom *Chick Williams* • Forrest Tucker *Trim Houlihan* • Harry Andrews *Jacob Schpitendavel* • Joseph Wiseman *Louis Minsky* • Denholm Elliott *Vance Fowler* • Elliott Gould *Billy Minsky* • Jack Burns *Candy Butcher* ■ *Dir* William Friedkin • *Scr* Arnold Schulman, Sidney Michaels, Norman Lear, from the novel by Rowland Barber

Night Tide ★★ PG

Thriller drama 1961 · US · BW · 86mins

Avant-garde film-maker Curtis Harrington made his feature debut with this strange story of a sailor who meets a mysterious woman who may or may not be a mermaid. The principal setting is the Californian amusement pier where the woman works under the care of her guardian, who claims she was found on a Greek island. The sailor, played by Dennis Hopper, is thoroughly smitten despite being warned that she brought death to two previous admirers. One for Hopper completists only. AT

Dennis Hopper *Johnny Drake* • Linda Lawson *Mora* • Gavin Muir *Capt Murdock* • Luana Anders *Ellen Sands* • Marjorie Eaton *Madame Romanovitch* ■ *Dir/Scr* Curtis Harrington

A Night to Remember ★★★ PG

Comedy thriller 1942 · US · BW · 88mins

This witty and clever mystery tale has Brian Aherne and Loretta Young well cast as a husband and wife trying to solve a murder. He is an author of whodunnits who knows he has a romantic novel in him; she is simply radiant and for some will be the whole reason for watching. Editor turned director Richard Wallace lacks the requisite style to bring anything special to the mix, but he lets the stars shine and marshals a fine supporting cast of suspects. TS

Loretta Young *Nancy Troy* • Brian Aherne *Jeff Troy* • Jeff Donnell *Ann Carstairs* • William Wright *Scott Carstairs* • Sidney Toler *William Wright* • Gale Sondergaard *Mrs Devoe* • Lee Patrick *Polly Franklin* ■ *Dir* Richard Wallace • *Scr* Richard Flournoy, Jack Henley, from the story by Kelly Roos

A Night to Remember ★★★★ PG

Historical drama 1958 · UK · BW · 117mins

While this drama about the sinking of the *Titanic* can't compete in terms of spectacle with James Cameron's blockbuster, it still presents the facts of the disaster in a deeply moving and compelling manner. Director Roy Baker opts for a documentary style that focuses on the human interest angle without recourse to melodramatics. The result is a gripping account of the tragedy, impeccably acted by a sterling British cast, with Kenneth More excelling as the heroic second officer, from whose perspective we see events unfolding. DP DVD

Kenneth More *Herbert Lightoller* • Ronald Allen *Clarke* • Honor Blackman *Mrs Lucas* • Anthony Bushell *Captain Rostron* • John Cairney *Murphy* • David McCallum *Bride* • Robert Ayres *Peuchen* • Jill Dixon *Mrs Clarke* • Sean Connery ■ *Dir* Roy Baker [Roy Ward Baker] • *Scr* Eric Ambler, from the book by Walter Lord

Night Train ★★ 15

Romantic drama 1998 · Ire · Colour · 89mins

Brenda Blethyn plays a timid spinster who strikes up a friendship with ex-con John Hurt when he rents a room in her house. Hurt, who's on the run from some gangsters, has a passion for model trains and uses them to worm his way into Blethyn's heart. The two stars are fine, but this uneasy mix of crime thriller and romance takes some swallowing. NS DVD

John Hurt *Michael Poole* • Brenda Blethyn *Alice Mooney* • Pauline Flanagan *Mrs Mooney* • Lorcan Cranitch *Billy* ■ *Dir* John Lynch • *Scr* Aodhan Madden

Night Train to Munich ★★★★

Spy thriller 1940 · UK · BW · 90mins

Witty and suspenseful, Frank Launder and Sidney Gilliat's screenplay about a missing Czech scientist bears an uncanny resemblance to the earlier classic they had a hand in, Alfred Hitchcock's *The Lady Vanishes*. Reinforcing the link is the reappearance of Basil Radford and Naunton Wayne as the cricket-mad eccentrics Charters and Caldicott. The dashing Rex Harrison evidently enjoys himself as the bemused British spy and Margaret Lockwood as the scientist's daughter does well to keep up with him. It's fast, furious and funny but, even with that master of atmosphere Carol Reed as director, it could have done with a couple of fresh tricks to keep us guessing. DP

Margaret Lockwood *Anna Bomasch* • Rex Harrison *Gus Bennett* • Paul Henreid *Karl Marsen* • Basil Radford *Charters* • Naunton Wayne *Caldicott* • James Harcourt *Axel Bomasch* ■ *Dir* Carol Reed • *Scr* Sidney Gilliat, Frank Launder, from a story by Gordon Wellesley

Night Train to Venice ★ 18

Thriller 1993 · Ger · Colour · 94mins

Journalist and neo-Nazi expert Hugh Grant is victimised by skinheads during his train trip from Munich to Venice and spends the rest of the film agonising over his plight. Malcolm McDowell is "the stranger" who looks on with smug delight. Of course, the skinheads aren't finished with him just yet. Erratically edited and incoherently directed, this is as repulsive as it sounds. ST

Hugh Grant *Martin Gamil* • Tahnee Welch *Vera Cortese* • Malcolm McDowell *Stranger* • Samy Langs *Pedro* ■ *Dir* Carlo U Quinterio • *Scr* Leo Tichat, Toni Hirtreiter

Night unto Night ★★

Romantic drama 1949 · US · BW · 92mins

Directed by Don Siegel, this obviously well-intended movie emerges as verbose, portentous claptrap that criminally wastes the gifts of the beautiful and talented Swedish-born actress Viveca Lindfors (Siegel's wife from 1949–53). She stars as a woman grieving over her husband's death, whose suffering is temporarily relieved by a lot of introspective talk with a troubled epileptic scientist, played by Ronald Reagan. RK

Ronald Reagan *John* • Viveca Lindfors *Ann* • Broderick Crawford *Shawn* • Rosemary DeCamp *Thalia* • Osa Massen *Lisa* • Craig Stevens *Tony* ■ *Dir* Don Siegel • *Scr* Kathryn Scola, from the novel by Philip Wylie

The Night Visitor ★★★

Thriller 1970 · Swe/US · Colour · 101mins

Very odd and rarely shown, this intriguing, arty horror movie was shot in Sweden by Hungarian director Laslo Benedek and stars a handful of Ingmar Bergman's repertory company of actors. Max von Sydow is a farmer accused of murder he didn't commit, who ingeniously escapes from his insane asylum prison nightly to kill the people who put him there. This spooky gothic thriller has a compelling atmosphere that's most unusual. AJ

Max von Sydow *Salem* • Trevor Howard *Inspector* • Liv Ullmann *Esther Jenks* • Per Oscarsson *Dr Anton Jenks* • Rupert Davies *Clemens, the attorney* • Andrew Keir *Dr Kemp* ■ *Dir* Laslo Benedek • *Scr* Guy Elmes, from the short story *Salem Came to Supper* by Samuel Roecca

Night Visitor ★★

Horror 1989 · US · Colour · 93mins

Strange that a film boasting satanists, hookers, ritual butchery and voyeurism should prove such a dull watch. Yet this proves to be the case with Rupert Hitzig's uninspired slant on the boy-who-cried-wolf story. Derek Rydall stars as a school kid given to outrageous lies who witnesses the murder of a neighbourhood prostitute. Police captain Richard Roundtree doesn't believe him, so Rydall turns to retired cop Elliott Gould for help. An awkward blend of thrills and cheap laughs. RS

Elliott Gould *Ron Devereaux* • Richard Roundtree *Captain Crane* • Allen Garfield *Zachary Willard* • Michael J Pollard *Stanley Willard* • Derek Rydall *Billy Colton* • Teresa Van Der Woude *Kelly Fremont* • Shannon Tweed *Lisa Grace* ■ *Dir* Rupert Hitzig • *Scr* Randal Viscovich

N

The Night Walker ★★

Horror thriller 1964 · US · BW · 85mins

Barbara Stanwyck's last theatrical feature is a lame *Psycho* imitation from producer/director William Castle, who lit up the 1950s with such ingenious gimmick flicks as *Homicidal* and *The Tingler*. Starring with her real-life ex-husband Robert Taylor, Stanwyck is a widow suffering from recurring dreams about her dead spouse (Hayden Rorke). This is a tepid chiller with laughable special effects; Stanwyck is great value, though. AJ

Barbara Stanwyck *Irene Trent* • Robert Taylor (1) *Barry Morland* • Hayden Rorke *Howard Trent* • Lloyd Bochner *The man in the dream* • Judith Meredith [Judi Meredith] *Joyce* • Rochelle Hudson *Hilda* • Ted Durant *Narrator* ■ *Dir* William Castle • *Scr* Robert Bloch, from the story *Witches' Friday* by Elizabeth Kata

Night Warning ★

Horror 1981 · US · Colour · 96mins

Bo Svenson's sour and homophobic cop character gets in the way of making this horror mystery funnier than it already is. Investigating the death of a gay TV repairman, Svenson sees Jimmy McNichol as the chief suspect. Actually, it was McNichol's aunt (Susan Tyrrell) who did it in a rage of fury when the guy wouldn't have sex with her. Tyrrell's acting makes this film a must for bad movie fans. Not content to chew the scenery, she tears it up, digests it and asks for seconds. KB

Jimmy McNichol *Billy* • Susan Tyrrell *Aunt Cheryl* • Bo Svenson *Detective Carlson* ■ *Dir* William Asher • *Scr* Stephen Breimer, Boon Collins, Alan Jay Glueckman

Night Was Our Friend ★★

Psychological drama 1951 · UK · BW · 61mins

Michael Gough is best known now for playing butler Alfred in the *Batman* movies. But this dowdy little drama from his dim and distant past is one picture he'd probably prefer to forget. Long believed to have perished in the Brazilian jungle, he returns to haunt wife Elizabeth Sellars and her new beau Ronald Howard. DP

Michael Gough *Martin Raynor* • Elizabeth Sellars *Sally Raynor* • Ronald Howard *Dr John Harper* • Marie Ney *Emily Raynor* • Edward Lexy *Arthur Glanville* • Nora Gordon *Kate* • Felix Felton *Jury foreman* ■ *Dir* Michael Anderson • *Scr* Michael Pertwee, from his play

Night Watch ★★★ 15

Mystery thriller 1973 · UK · Colour · 98mins

Reminiscent of *Gaslight*, this thriller stars Elizabeth Taylor as a woman recovering from a nervous breakdown who thinks she sees a corpse outside her window. Could it be the work of her husband (Laurence Harvey in his final film), who may or may not be having an affair with her best friend (Billie Whitelaw)? The actors give the tired plot all they've got, but director Brian G Hutton is more concerned with action than atmosphere, abbreviating tension where it should be given time to accumulate. TH

Elizabeth Taylor *Ellen Wheeler* • Laurence Harvey *John Wheeler* • Billie Whitelaw *Sarah Cooke* • Robert Lang *Appleby* • Tony Britton *Tony* • Bill Dean *Inspector Walker* ■ *Dir* Brian G Hutton • *Scr* Tony Williamson, Evan Jones, from a play by Lucille Fletcher

Night Watch ★★ 15

Crime thriller 1995 · UK/US · Colour · 94mins

Inspired by the work of Alistair MacLean, this leaden caper is forced by budgetary constraint to serve up an uninvolving combination of hi-tech gadgetry and bruising stuntwork. This sub-007 adventure was Pierce Brosnan's last assignment before his debut as James Bond. Reprising the role of Mike Graham that he had previously played in *Death Train*, Brosnan turns art detective in a bid to recover a Rembrandt painting before it falls into the hands of a Hong Kong crime lord. DP. Contains violence and swearing. DVD

Pierce Brosnan *Mike Graham* • Alexandra Paul *Sabrina Carver* • William Devane *Nick Caldwell* • Michael J Shannon *Martin Schrader* • Lim Kay Siu *Mao Yixin* • Irene Ng *Myra Tang* ■ *Dir* David S Jackson [David Jackson] • *Scr* David S Jackson, from the novel by Alistair MacLean

N

Night Watch ★★★

Fantasy horror thriller
2004 · Rus · Colour · 115mins

The highest-grossing Russian movie of all time is a horror fantasy about an ancient truce being broken between the forces of Light and Darkness, and the prophetic coming of the "Great Other" who will tip the outcome of the human v vampires final battle. Director Timur Bekmambetov flings special effects around, but his lightning pace rarely bothers to explain the plot, probably a good thing because it's essentially very silly. Although this epic production is something new for Russia budget-wise and technically, it's the same old blockbuster in Hollywood terms. However, stylised subtitling adds to the experience, often becoming its own artistic statement. AJ. In Russian with English subtitles.

Konstantin Khabensky *Anton Gorodetsky* • Vladimir Menshov *Boris Geser* • Valery Zolotukhin *Kostya's father* • Maria Poroshina *Svetlana* • Galina Tyunina *Olga* • Viktor Verzhbitsky *Zavulon* • Gosha Kutsenko *Ignat* • Alexei Chadov *Kostya* • Zhanna Friske *Alisa* ■ *Dir* Timur Bekmambetov • *Scr* Sergei Lukyanenko, Timur Bekmambetov, from the novel by Sergei Lukyanenko

The Night We Called It a Day ★★★

Drama based on a true story
2003 · Aus/US · Colour · 96mins

Dennis Hopper delivers a credible turn as the legendary crooner Frank Sinatra in this engaging romp, based on real-life events. The year is 1974 and a small-time Australian rock promoter (Joel Edgerton) lands the coup of the decade when he convinces Ol' Blue Eyes to come to Australia for some live shows. However, Sinatra quickly falls foul of the local media and the war of words escalates into a full blown crisis involving the local trade unions, led by future prime minister Bob Hawke (David Field). But although there are some lovely moments, Paul Goldman's direction lacks fizz and the pace flags towards the end. JF

Dennis Hopper *Frank Sinatra* • Melanie Griffith *Barbara Marx* • Portia de Rossi *Hilary Hunter* • Joel Edgerton *Rod Blue* • Rose Byrne *Audrey Rose Appleby* • David Hemmings *Mickey Rudin* • David Field *Bob Hawke* • Victoria Thaine *Penny* ■ *Dir* Paul Goldman • *Scr* Michael Thomas, Peter Clifton

The Night We Dropped a Clanger ★★ U

Second World War comedy
1959 · UK · BW · 84mins

This identity switch picture set during the Second World War stretches its comic notions to breaking point. More disciplined comic timing would have provided an effective cure. However, farce king Brian Rix is a sensible choice for this wartime foolishness and he switches convincingly from military rigour (in one guise) to gormlessness (in the other). JM

Brian Rix *Arthur Atwood/Wing Commander Blenkinsop* • Cecil Parker *Sir Bertram* • William Hartnell *Sergeant Bright* • Leslie Phillips *Squadron Leader Thomas* • Leo Franklyn *Sergeant Belling* • John Welsh *Squadron Leader Grant* • Toby Perkins *Flight Lieutenant Spendal* • Liz Fraser *Lulu* ■ *Dir* Darcy Conyers • *Scr* John Chapman

The Night We Got the Bird ★

Comedy 1960 · UK · BW · 88mins

Your heart will go out to the splendid cast that found itself lumbered with this turkey. Ronald Shiner has the most luck, as he at least gets to spend much of the picture as a reincarnated parrot, thus leaving doltish egghead Brian Rix to carry the can for his misdemeanours as an antiques forger. There are bedroom mix-ups, courtroom chaos and a break-in at a top secret space lab, but it's all dismally unfunny. DP

Brian Rix *Bertie Skidmore* • Dora Bryan *Julie Skidmore* • Leo Franklyn *Victor* • Irene Handl *Ma* • Liz Fraser *Fay* • John Slater *Wolfie Green* • Reginald Beckwith *Chippendale Charlie* • Robertson Hare *Dr Vincent* • John Le Mesurier *Court clerk* • Ronald Shiner *Cecil Gibson* • Terry Scott *PC Lovejoy* ■ *Dir* Darcy Conyers • *Scr* Ray Cooney, Tony Hilton, Darcy Conyers, from the play *The Love Birds* by Basil Thomas

The Night We Never Met ★★★★ 15

Romantic comedy
1993 · US · Colour · 94mins

This is a sharp and cute study of young New Yorkers sharing a studio apartment on an alternate-days rota. Writer/director Warren Leight tinges the light comedy with a touch of Woody Allen-style angst, but whenever the story gets down-hearted his three leads (Kevin Anderson, yuppie slob; Annabella Sciorra, bored housewife; Matthew Broderick, dumped nice guy) perk it up with ensemble acting that dovetails perfectly. Love among the skyscrapers has rarely been such a delight. TH. Contains swearing and nudity. DVD

Matthew Broderick *Sam Lester* • Annabella Sciorra *Ellen Holder* • Kevin Anderson *Brian McVeigh* • Justine Bateman *Janet Beehan* • Jeanne Tripplehorn *Pastel* • Michael Mantell *Aaron Holder* • Christine Baranski *Lucy* ■ *Dir/Scr* Warren Leight

Night without Stars ★★★ U

Crime drama 1951 · UK · BW · 82mins

David Farrar is virtually blind and retires to the Riviera where he falls in love with Nadia Gray. Then he tangles with murderers, blackmailers and forgers when he discovers she is the widow of a resistance fighter. He's pushed off a cliff which forces him to get his sight restored and – very smart this – return to the Riviera still claiming to be blind so that he can trap the dirty rotters. Winston Graham adapted his own novel for this enjoyable little thriller. AT

David Farrar *Giles Gordon* • Nadia Gray *Alix Delaisse* • Maurice Teynac *Louis Malinay* • Gilles Quéant *Deffand* • Gérard Landry *Pierre Chaval* • June Clyde *Claire* • Robert Ayres *Walter* ■ *Dir* Anthony Pelissier • *Scr* Winston Graham, from his novel

Night Zoo ★★★ 18

Crime drama
1987 · Can/Fr · Colour · 116mins

Time hasn't been particularly kind to Jean-Claude Lauzon's award-winning, uncompromising study of the Montreal underworld. The 1980s look has dated very badly and Gilles Maheu's attempts to look mean and moody leave him occasionally looking like a third-rate Fonz impersonator. However, the story of a jailbird's bid to build bridges with both forgiving father Roger Le Bel and girlfriend-turned-hooker Lynne Adams – in the face of hostility from a couple of corrupt cops after their share of a drugs stash – still simmers with sexual and criminal menace. DP. In French with English subtitles. Contains violence, nudity and sex scenes.

Roger Le Bel *Albert* • Gilles Maheu *Marcel* • Lorne Brass *Georges* • Germaine Houde *Charlie* • Lynne Adams *Julie* ■ *Dir/Scr* Jean-Claude Lauzon

Nightbreaker ★★★ 15

Historical drama 1989 · US · Colour · 94mins

After such hits as *Stakeout* and *Young Guns*, Emilio Estevez opted for a change of pace and appeared alongside his father Martin Sheen in this modest, worthy drama. The subject matter concerns the postwar nuclear tests in the Nevada desert and the tragic consequences for the unwitting soldiers forced to witness them. Estevez plays the naive young doctor who gets involved in the test programme, with Sheen playing the same character in the 1980s. It's a tad overwrought at times, but the two leads are excellent. JF

Martin Sheen *Dr Alexander Brown (present)* • Emilio Estevez *Dr Alexander Brown (past)* • Lea Thompson *Sally Matthews* • Melinda Dillon *Paula Brown* • Joe Pantoliano *Jack Russell* • Nicholas Pryor *Colonel William Devereau* ■ *Dir* Peter Markle • *Scr* TS Cook, from the novel *Atomic Soldiers* by Howard Rosenberg

Nightbreed ★★★ 18

Horror 1990 · US · Colour · 97mins

Hellraiser established Clive Barker as a major force in modern horror, but nothing he's done since has ever quite matched its unique visceral power. The trump up Barker's sleeve this time is the casting of cult horror director David Cronenberg as a malevolent shrink. He dupes a patient into believing that he's a serial killer and then tracks him down to the netherworld of Midian, a secret sanctuary for mutants and freaks. While this is certainly self-indulgent – Barker directs and adapted the screenplay from his own novel *Cabal* – the imagination on view certainly impresses. RS

Craig Sheffer *Boone* • Charles Haid *Captain Eigerman* • David Cronenberg *Dr Decker* • Anne Bobby *Lori* • Hugh Quarshie *Detective Joyce* ■ *Dir* Clive Barker • *Scr* Clive Barker, from his novel *Cabal*

The Nightcomers ★★ 18

Thriller 1972 · UK · Colour · 92mins

Marlon Brando is at his most loutishly sexual, tearing the clothes off Stephanie Beacham in this prequel to Henry James's *The Turn of the Screw*. It's a cod-Freudian exercise in sadomasochism, with Brando playing the groundsman and Beacham the governess to the two children destined to see ghosts later. Filmed with a distinct lack of subtlety and stretching early 1970s permissiveness to the limit, it was the last picture Brando made before he revived his flagging fortunes with *The Godfather* and *Last Tango in Paris*. It's trashily enjoyable, though. AT. Contains sex scenes, some swearing and violence. DVD

Marlon Brando *Quint* • Stephanie Beacham *Miss Jessel* • Thora Hird *Mrs Grose* • Verna Harvey *Flora* • Christopher Ellis *Miles* • Harry Andrews *Master of the house* ■ *Dir* Michael Winner • *Scr* Michael Hastings, from characters created by Henry James

Nightfall ★★★

Crime drama 1956 · US · BW · 78mins

Aldo Ray was a briefly glimpsed star who burned himself out all too quickly, but he was a formidable presence even as the "wronged man" in this pacey thriller by *noir*-meister Jacques Tourneur. It's an early outing for scriptwriter Stirling Silliphant from a cult-pulp by David Goodis, and he's fashioned a bleak morality tale about a man who thinks he can't win after being framed for murder and robbery, but then discovers gleams of hope. Anne Bancroft is particularly good as the ambiguous figure of salvation. TH

Aldo Ray *James Vanning* • Brian Keith *John* • Anne Bancroft *Marie Gardner* • Jocelyn Brando *Laura Fraser* • James Gregory *Ben Fraser* • Frank Albertson *Dr Edward Gurston* ■ *Dir* Jacques Tourneur • *Scr* Stirling Silliphant, from a novel by David Goodis

Nightflyers ★ 18

Science fiction 1987 · US · Colour · 85mins

This futuristic tale had potential, but lacked the budget and the expertise to capitalise on it. (The production had a troubled history, while a major re-edit by the producers made director Robert Collector opt for the pseudonym TC Blake.) The fog machine works overtime to hide the substandard sets as the motley crew of a decrepit spaceship goes in search of an alien race. KB

Catherine Mary Stewart *Miranda* • John Standing *D'Branin* • Michael Praed *Royd* • Lisa Blount *Audrey* • Michael Des Barres *Jon Winderman* ■ *Dir* TC Blake [Robert Collector] • *Scr* Robert Jaffe, from a novella by George RR Martin

Nighthawks ★★★ 18

Action thriller 1981 · US · Colour · 95mins

At this stage in his career Sylvester Stallone was not known as an action star, and in some ways this is his first real stab at the genre with which he is now most closely associated. Stallone and Billy Dee Williams play two New

York cops who are sent scampering all over the Big Apple on the trail of a vicious international terrorist (Rutger Hauer, making an electrifying Hollywood debut). Director Bruce Malmuth keeps the action zipping along at a pleasing pace. JF. Contains swearing and violence. [video] DVD

Sylvester Stallone *Deke DaSilva* • Billy Dee Williams *Matthew Fox* • Lindsay Wagner *Irene* • Persis Khambatta *Shakka* • Nigel Davenport *Peter Hartman* • Rutger Hauer *Wulfgar* • Hilarie Thompson *Pam* ■ *Dir* Bruce Malmuth • *Scr* David Shaber, from a story by David Shaber, Paul Sylbert

A Nightingale Sang in Berkeley Square ★★★ PG

Comedy thriller 1979 · UK · Colour · 105mins

This pleasing, if predictable, heist caper boasts an extraordinary cast. Giving one of the better performances of his twilight years, David Niven plays a criminal mastermind who blackmails old lag Richard Jordan into joining his assault on a swanky bank. Making his first film in five years, veteran director Ralph Thomas fails to impose himself on the familiar sequence of events, but coaxes a splendid performance from Gloria Grahame. DP [video] DVD

Richard Jordan *Pinky Green* • David Niven *Ivan the Terrible* • Oliver Tobias *Foxy* • Gloria Grahame *Ma* • Elke Sommer *Miss Pelham* • Richard Johnson *Inspector Watford* • Joss Ackland *Governor* • Michael Angelis *Pealer Bell* ■ *Dir* Ralph Thomas • *Scr* Guy Elmes

Nightmare ★★★★

Crime drama 1956 · US · BW · 89mins

Director Maxwell Shane here remakes his 1947 film *Fear in the Night*. Kevin McCarthy gives a good performance as the musician who becomes convinced he's a murderer, but Edward G Robinson is better as the detective who sees the flaw in what appears to be an open-and-shut case. Cameraman Joseph Biroc's moody photography adds real menace to the disturbing idea, and there's a jazz score by Herschel Burke Gilbert that's as jumpy as a neurotic's bad dream. TH

Edward G Robinson *Rene Bressard* • Kevin McCarthy *Stan Grayson* • Connie Russell *Gina* • Virginia Christine *Sue* • Rhys Williams *Torrence* • Gage Clarke *Belknap* ■ *Dir* Maxwell Shane • *Scr* Maxwell Shane, from the short story by William Irish [Cornell Woolrich]

Nightmare ★★★

Horror 1963 · UK · BW · 82mins

Ace cameraman Freddie Francis directs this Hammer-financed production, with English rose Jennie Linden having terrible nightmares about being tossed into a loony bin. The poor dear is taken to one of those dark, foreboding country houses where things go bump in the night. It isn't too long before the knives come out and everyone starts screaming. Brimming with sexual imagery and the odd reference to Henry James's *The Turn of the Screw*, this is let down by a pallid hero (David Knight) but pulls off quite a few decent shocks. AT

David Knight *Henry Baxter* • Moira Redmond *Grace* • Brenda Bruce *Mary* • Jennie Linden *Janet* • George A Cooper *John* ■ *Dir* Freddie Francis • *Scr* Jimmy Sangster

Nightmare Alley ★★★

Horror 1947 · US · BW · 111mins

Tyrone Power, 20th Century-Fox's most bankable and romantic leading man at the time, gave his image a jolt with this bizarre study of mental breakdown, in which he was reunited with his *Razor's Edge* director, Edmund Goulding. Power is a bogus mind-reader in a small-time carnival who revives Joan Blondell and Ian Keith's long forgotten act as a means to get rich, with tragic results. The script, by Jules Furthman, is based on a novel by William Lindsay Gresham, a writer obsessed by the emotional nakedness of circus performance who eventually committed suicide. AT

Tyrone Power *Stanton Carlisle* • Joan Blondell *Zeena* • Coleen Gray *Molly* • Helen Walker *Dr Lilith Ritter* • Taylor Holmes *Ezra Grindle* • Mike Mazurki *Bruno* • Ian Keith *Pete* • Julia Dean *Mrs Peabody* ■ *Dir* Edmund Goulding • *Scr* Jules Furthman, from the novel by William Lindsay Gresham

The Nightmare before Christmas ★★★★★ PG

Animated musical fantasy
1993 · US · Colour · 76mins

Producing here, Tim Burton called on the services of innovative animation director Henry Selick and composer Danny Elfman (a regular Burton collaborator, who wrote the ten surreal songs and lends his singing voice to the lead character) for this wonderfully weird fable that's packed with scary spooks, gags and dazzling decor. It enchants with every busy frame as spindly Jack Skellington, the mastermind behind Halloween, hijacks Christmas out of boredom, becoming a frightening Santa delivering nasty surprises instead of presents to terrified children. Its affectionate trashing of Christmas traditions is conceptually cunning and clever enough to please every generation. An unmissable treat. AJ [video] DVD

Danny Elfman *Jack Skellington* • Chris Sarandon *Jack Skellington* • Catherine O'Hara *Sally/Shock* • William Hickey *Evil scientist* • Glenn Shadix *Mayor* • Paul Reubens *Lock* • Ken Page *Oogie Boogie* • Ed Ivory *Santa* ■ *Dir* Henry Selick • *Scr* Caroline Thompson, from a story and characters created by Tim Burton

Nightmare in Chicago ★★★★

Crime drama 1968 · US · Colour · 80mins

Robert Altman was working in television when he directed this tale of a psychotic murderer known to the police and press as the Georgie Porgie killer. Featuring Philip Abbott, Ted Knight and Charles McGraw, it was shot entirely on location in Chicago and has the creepy atmosphere of an authentic bad dream. TV movies don't come much better than this. TH

Charles McGraw *Georgie Porgie* • Robert Ridgely • Ted Knight • Philip Abbott ■ *Dir* Robert Altman • *Scr* David Moessinger, from the novel *Killer on the Turnpike* by William P McGivern

Nightmare in the Sun ★★

Crime drama 1964 · US · Colour · 81mins

This innocent-on-the-run thriller finds the sexy wife (Ursula Andress) of a rich ranch owner picking up a hitch-hiker (John Derek, her then real-life husband) and bringing him home. The hitch-hiker decides to leave, but in a fit of rage the ranch boss kills Andress, leaving the drifter blamed for the murder by a corrupt, blackmailing sheriff. Less suspenseful than it sounds, but there are some early walk-ons from the likes of Robert Duvall and Richard Jaeckel. JG

Ursula Andress *Marsha* • John Derek *Hitch-hiker* • Aldo Ray *Sheriff* • Arthur O'Connell *Sam Wilson* • Sammy Davis Jr *Truck driver* • Allyn Joslyn *Junk dealer* • Keenan Wynn *Song-and-dance misfit* • Chick Chandler *Tavern owner* • Richard Jaeckel *Motorcyclist* • Robert Duvall *Motorcyclist* ■ *Dir* Marc Lawrence (1) • *Scr* Ted Thomas, Fanya Lawrence, from a story by Marc Lawrence, Fanya Lawrence, George Fass

A Nightmare on Elm Street ★★★★ 18

Horror 1984 · US · Colour · 87mins

Four teenagers experience identical nightmares and are haunted by the shockingly popular supernatural fiend Freddy Krueger (known here as Fred), in this pioneering fright flick from director Wes Craven. Craven's ingenious merging of dreams with reality gives a markedly different horror jolt as Heather Langenkamp realises she can only save her friends from violent death by staying awake and keeping the razor-fingered maniac at bay. Bloody special effects and suspenseful murders disguise the weakish script, but the performances (look for Johnny Depp in his screen debut) and Craven's command of the chilling concept make it a classic that spawned six sequels and a TV series. AJ [video] DVD

Robert Englund *Fred Krueger* • John Saxon *Lt Thompson* • Ronee Blakley *Marge Thompson* • Heather Langenkamp *Nancy Thompson* • Amanda Wyss *Tina Gray* • Johnny Depp *Glen Lantz* ■ *Dir/Scr* Wes Craven

A Nightmare on Elm Street 2: Freddy's Revenge ★ 18

Horror 1985 · US · Colour · 81mins

Mark Patton moves into the sinister Elm Street house, and Freddy Krueger just as quickly moves into his dreams in this damp squib of a sequel. Surprisingly homoerotic in content, Jack Sholder's sub-standard shocker replaces clever dream imagery with the more conventional theme of possession, while Patton contributes a one-expression performance. AJ [video] DVD

Mark Patton *Jesse Walsh* • Robert Englund *Freddy Krueger* • Kim Myers *Lisa Webber* • Robert Rusler *Ron Grady* • Clu Gulager *Mr Walsh* • Hope Lange *Mrs Walsh* ■ *Dir* Jack Sholder • *Scr* David Chaskin, from a character created by Wes Craven

A Nightmare on Elm Street 3: Dream Warriors ★★★ 18

Horror 1987 · US · Colour · 92mins

Anything can happen, and does, in this imaginative sequel that stretches the boundaries of 1980s horror to new limits with wildly inventive mayhem. Thanks to the psychic ability of Patricia Arquette, a group of youngsters terrorised by Freddy Krueger take part in a controlled experiment where they enter each other's nightmares on a time-share basis to exorcise his malevolent spirit. Full of great special effects, this is a roller-coaster ride from the opening Edgar Allan Poe quotation to the final Ray Harryhausen homage. AJ [video] DVD

Heather Langenkamp *Nancy Thompson* • Patricia Arquette *Kristen Parker* • Larry Fishburne [Laurence Fishburne] *Max* • Priscilla Pointer *Dr Elizabeth Simms* • Craig Wasson *Dr Neil Goldman* • Robert Englund *Freddy Krueger* ■ *Dir* Chuck Russell • *Scr* Wes Craven, Bruce Wagner, Chuck Russell, Frank Darabont, from a story by Wes Craven, Bruce Wagner, from characters created by Wes Craven

A Nightmare on Elm Street 4: The Dream Master ★★★ 18

Horror 1988 · US · Colour · 88mins

Lisa Wilcox goes through the blood-stained looking glass in this strong Freddy Krueger episode, given a wonderfully different European art-horror feel by future blockbuster director Renny Harlin, who puts a fresh spin on the recurring nightmare cliché. Wilcox takes on the talents of her deceased friends to become the Dream Master, the ancient guardian of positive scenarios, poised to counterattack Freddy's negative nightmares in this beautifully photographed redefinition of the pop-culture formula. AJ [video] DVD

Robert Englund *Freddy Krueger* • Lisa Wilcox *Alice* • Rodney Eastman *Joey* • Danny Hassel *Danny* • Andras Jones *Rick* • Tuesday Knight *Kristen Parker* ■ *Dir* Renny Harlin • *Scr* Brian Helgeland, Scott Pierce, from a story by William Kotzwinkle, Brian Helgeland, from a character created by Wes Craven

A Nightmare on Elm Street 5: The Dream Child ★★ 18

Horror 1989 · US · Colour · 86mins

Lisa Wilcox thinks she's banished Freddy Krueger from her life until she's made pregnant by college jock Danny Hassel. According to the jumbled script, a foetus can dream a few days after conception, and Freddy seizes this chance to enter her subconscious once more and finger-blade her unbelieving friends to death. Director Stephen Hopkins valiantly tries to paper over the huge cracks in the derivative low-energy thrills by replacing vapid gore with furious pacing, sudden shock cuts and rock video-style cartoonish imagery. The series continued with two further sequels – *Freddy's Dead: the Final Nightmare* (1991) and *Wes Craven's New Nightmare* (1994). AJ [video] DVD

Robert Englund *Freddy Krueger* • Lisa Wilcox *Alice Johnson* • Danny Hassel *Dan* • Kelly Jo Minter *Yvonne* • Erika Anderson *Greta* • Joe Seely *Mark* ■ *Dir* Stephen Hopkins • *Scr* Leslie Bohem, from a story by John Skip, Craig Spector, Leslie Bohem, from a character created by Wes Craven

Nightmares ★★ 15

Science-fiction horror
1983 · US · Colour · 94mins

This uneven four-part anthology is more miss than hit. A housewife under murderous threat, a deadly video game obsessing Emilio Estevez, a priest losing faith on the eve of battling a possessed truck, and a giant rat terrorising a suburban family jostle for attention in a workmanlike collection accenting substandard eerieness and few scares. While the first two tales are OK, the other two are dire. AJ [video]

Emilio Estevez *JJ Cooney* • Cristina Raines *Lisa* • Joe Lambie *Phil* • Anthony James *Clerk* • Clare Nono *Newswoman* • Raleigh Bond *Neighbour* • Robert Phelps *Newsman* • Dixie Lynn Royce *Little girl* ■ *Dir* Joseph Sargent • *Scr* Christopher Crowe, Jeffrey Bloom

Nightmares in a Damaged Brain ★★★ 18

Horror 1981 · US · Colour · 95mins

From its beginning, this is a cut above the average slasher movie. Italian director Romano Scavolini keeps tight control of his dark, disturbing story of a man thought cured of schizophrenia, who embarks on an apparently random killing spree. Though this gorefest contains dated elements such as girls in showers and cod-Freudian psychology, it now looks like a precursor to John McNaughton's *Henry: Portrait of a Serial Killer*. In Britain, Scavolini's incredibly graphic tale became one of the best known "video nasties". DM [video] DVD

Baird Stafford *George Tatum* • Sharon Smith *Susan Temper* • CJ Cooke *CJ Temper* • Mik Cribben *Bob Rosen* • Kathleen Ferguson *Barbara* ■ *Dir/Scr* Romano Scavolini

Nightmaster ★ 15

Martial arts action thriller
1987 · Aus/Can · Colour · 87mins

You need a masochistic taste for awful movies to watch this shoddily made, vaguely futuristic action thriller (also known as *Watch the Shadows Dance*). A tedious plodder, it focuses on teen

N

students whose late night ninja-style war games take on a deadly dimension when two of them discover sinister secrets about their martial arts tutor. Only notable for an early screen role for Nicole Kidman. SF [subtitles] DVD

Tom Jennings *Robby Mason* • Nicole Kidman *Amy Gabriel* • Joanne Samuel *Sonia Spane* • Vince Martin *Steve Beck* • Craig Pearce *Guy Duncan* • Doug Parkinson *Pete "Pearly" Gates* • Jeremy Shadlow *Simon* ■ *Dir* Mark Joffe • *Scr* Michael McGennan

Nights of Cabiria ★★★★★ 15

Drama 1957 · It · BW · 106mins

Often dismissed as grating and sentimental, this is one of Federico Fellini's most accessible films, which harks back to his days as a screenwriter during Italy's neorealist phase. The winner of the 1957 Oscar for best foreign film, it boasts a bravura performance from the director's wife, Giulietta Masina, as the childlike prostitute who is misused by everyone she encounters, yet still has the sense of self-worth to come bouncing back. Every bit as vulnerable as Shirley MacLaine in the Hollywood musical remake, *Sweet Charity*, Masina eschews sentiment to meet fate with enviable grace. DP. An Italian language film. [subtitles]

Giulietta Masina *Cabiria* • François Périer *Oscar D'Onofrio, accountant* • Amedeo Nazzari *Alberto Lazzari, movie star* • Aldo Silvani *Hypnotist* ■ *Dir* Federico Fellini • *Scr* Federico Fellini, Ennio Flaiano, Tullio Pinelli, Pier Paolo Pasolini (additional dialogue) • *Music* Nino Rota • *Art Director* Piero Gherardi

Nightshift ★★★ 15

Psychological drama
2000 · Fr · Colour · 92mins

Director Philippe Le Guay's unusually low-key blue-collar psychodrama is deliberately gloss-free and was shot using naturalistic lighting – elements that add enormous realism to its central story of a power struggle between co-workers. When Gérald Laroche switches to the lucrative nightshift in a glass factory, he becomes the target of a sadistic colleague's motiveless and increasingly brutal practical jokes. Striking a menacing and disorientating chord, Le Guay brilliantly explores the oddly compelling – even homoerotic – relationship between the two men, superbly portrayed by Laroche and Marc Barbé. AJ. In French with English subtitles. [subtitles] DVD

Gérald Laroche *Pierre* • Marc Barbé *Fred* • Bernard Ballet *Franck* • Michel Cassagne *Alain* • Alexandre Carrière *Danny* • Jean-François Lapalus *Mickey* ■ *Dir/Scr* Philippe Le Guay

Nightwatch ★★★★ 18

Thriller 1994 · Den · Colour · 102mins

A young student becomes night watchman at a mortuary where sinister things are happening and, before long, he's suspected of being a serial killer. Danish director Ole Bornedal's tense chiller is a quality genre item full of slow-burning suspense and high shock value. Everything good about this nerve-racking original was dumbed down for the US remake. AJ. In Danish with English subtitles. [subtitles] DVD

Nikolaj Coster-Waldau *Martin Bork* • Sofie Grabol *Kalinka Martens* • Kim Bodnia *Jens Arnkiel* ■ *Dir/Scr* Ole Bornedal

Nightwatch ★★ 18

Horror thriller 1997 · US · Colour · 96mins

Director Ole Bornedal takes his original 1994 Danish terror masterpiece – about a rookie morgue night watchman suspected of being a serial killer – and replaces the scary tension with formula gruesome shocks. The artful blend of hairy humour and creepy horror that graced the original doesn't quite survive in this good-looking poor relation. Ewan McGregor is fine, but Nick Nolte and Patricia Arquette sleepwalk through their roles. AJ. Contains violence, swearing, sex scenes. [subtitles] DVD

Ewan McGregor *Martin* • Nick Nolte *Inspector Thomas Cray* • Patricia Arquette *Katherine* • Josh Brolin *James* • Lauren Graham *Marie* • Brad Dourif *Duty doctor* ■ *Dir* Ole Bornedal • *Scr* Steven Soderbergh, Ole Bornedal, from the 1994 film

Nightwing ★★ 15

Horror 1979 · US · Colour · 100mins

The native Americans of New Mexico are in an uproar thanks to nightly raids by swarms of vampire bats that leave their cattle dead and their people horribly mutilated. Time to call in bat biologist David Warner, who's had it in for the beasts ever since they ate his father. Arthur Hiller's uninspired direction and the absurd fake bats (built by Carlo Rambaldi of *ET* fame) doom this laughable version of Martin Cruz Smith's bestseller. AJ [subtitles]

Nick Mancuso *Youngman Duran* • David Warner *Phillip Payne* • Kathryn Harrold *Anne Dillon* • Stephen Macht *Walker Chee* • Strother Martin *Selwyn* ■ *Dir* Arthur Hiller • *Scr* Steve Shagan, Bud Shrake, Martin Cruz Smith, from the novel by Martin Cruz Smith

Nijinsky ★★★★ 15

Biographical drama
1980 · UK · Colour · 119mins

Originally a Ken Russell project, this biopic of the tormented Russian ballet dancer has enough sex, angst and controversy to keep it boiling. Based on Nijinsky's diaries and Mrs Nijinsky's memoirs, it stars George De La Pena as the dancer and Alan Bates as his jilted inamorata, the impresario Diaghilev. As a study of life, art and ego, it's often close to Powell and Pressburger's *The Red Shoes* – powerfully acted and convincingly staged, with wonderful music. AT [subtitles]

Alan Bates *Sergei Diaghilev* • George De La Pena *Vaslav Nijinsky* • Leslie Browne *Romola DePulsky* • Alan Badel *Baron De Gunzberg* • Carla Fracci *Tamara Karsavina* • Colin Blakely *Vassili* • Ronald Pickup *Igor Stravinsky* ■ *Dir* Herbert Ross • *Scr* Hugh Wheeler, from the memoirs by Romola Nijinsky and the diary by Vaslav Nijinsky

Nikita ★★★★ 18

Thriller 1990 · Fr/It · Colour · 112mins

After being involved in a robbery, vicious junkie Anne Parillaud is reprogrammed as an assassin for a secret government agency in French director Luc Besson's extremely exciting thriller with a feminist slant. In paying homage to American action movies, Besson goes one better than his clear inspirations, to craft a beautifully stylised, enthralling and very violent comic strip. Parillaud (married to Besson at the time) is tremendous as the unscrupulous hit woman and Jeanne Moreau's Charm Teacher cameo is a gem. Besson's boldly modern approach to traditional *film noir* material makes this elemental mind-blower striking. A Hollywood remake (*Point of No Return*) followed in 1993, starring Bridget Fonda. AJ. In French with English subtitles. Contains violence and swearing. [subtitles] DVD

Anne Parillaud *Nikita* • Jean-Hugues Anglade *Marco* • Tcheky Karyo *Bob* • Jeanne Moreau *Amande* • Jean Reno *Victor the cleaner* • Marc Duret *Rico* • Philippe Leroy-Beaulieu *Grossman* ■ *Dir/Scr* Luc Besson

Nil by Mouth ★★★★★ 18

Drama 1997 · UK/US · Colour · 128mins

A harrowing directorial debut by actor Gary Oldman, this centres on violence and alcoholism within a working-class south London family. Although the film is not specifically autobiographical, Oldman has drawn from his own background to create a portrait of dysfunctional domestic life that is both convincing and compelling. Ray Winstone hulks brilliantly in the central role as the alienated husband and father trapped in a descending spiral of drunken rage. Kathy Burke matches Winstone's intensity – and won the best actress award at Cannes – for her performance as the brutalised wife. *Nil by Mouth* tempers its bleakness with tender understanding and wounding insight. TH. Contains swearing, sexual references and violence. [subtitles] DVD

Ray Winstone *Raymond* • Kathy Burke *Valerie* • Charlie Creed-Miles *Billy* • Laila Morse *Janet* • Edna Doré *Kath* • Chrissie Cotterill *Paula* ■ *Dir/Scr* Gary Oldman

La Niña Santa ★★★ 15

Drama
2004 · Arg/Sp/It/Neth/Swi · Colour · 103mins

Lucrecia Martel quickly establishes a simmering, claustrophobic atmosphere before turning up the sexual temperature by imbuing each principal with a sense of dissatisfaction that tempts them towards indiscretion. Mercedes Morán plays a divorcee who seeks solace among the misbehaving medics assembled for a conference in her run-down hotel. Meanwhile, her teenage daughter María Alché devotes herself to redeeming a timid ear, nose and throat specialist (Carlos Belloso) after he lasciviously brushes against her in a crowded street. This is a teasing study of lust, repression, naivety and guilt that relieves its aching sadness with moments of understated tenderness and wit. DP. In Spanish with English subtitles.

Mercedes Morán *Helena* • Carlos Belloso *Dr Jano* • Alejandro Urdapilleta *Freddy* • María Alché *Amalia* • Julieta Zylberberg *Josefina* • Monica Villa *Josefina's mother* • Marta Lubos *Mirta* ■ *Dir/Scr* Lucrecia Martel

Nina Takes a Lover ★★ 18

Romantic comedy
1993 · US · Colour · 93mins

This initially intriguing romantic comedy has Laura San Giacomo as a young married woman who decides to have an affair with a photographer (played by Welsh actor Paul Rhys) while her husband is away. The story is related in flashbacks with San Giacomo relating the tale of her now-over fling to a journalist, and it soon becomes clear that things are not quite as they seem. But the main weakness of this run-of-the-mill movie is the fact that all the characters come across as so self-absorbed. JB [subtitles]

Laura San Giacomo *Nina* • Paul Rhys *Photographer* • Michael O'Keefe *Journalist* • Fisher Stevens *Paulie* ■ *Dir/Scr* Alan Jacobs

9 Ages of Nakedness ★

Farce 1969 · UK · Colour · 97mins

George Harrison Marks began as a music-hall performer and later drifted into pornography, but always saw himself as a versatile comedian. In this film, he severely overstretches himself, producing, directing and writing a series of sketches in which he plays himself and eight of his ancestors. The bludgeoningly puerile humour, features great names of the music hall (Max Wall, Max Bacon) and a reputed 112 topless lovelies. The last sequence, set in the future, has to be seen to be believed. DM

George Harrison Marks *George Harrison Marks/Ancestors* • Charles Gray *Narrator* ■ *Dir/Scr* George Harrison Marks

Nine ½ Weeks ★★ 18

Erotic drama 1985 · US · Colour · 94mins

Despite the high production values and a starry cast, this remains mild, soft-core entertainment. Kim Basinger is the career woman who falls under the spell of the mysterious Mickey Rourke and finds herself being led into dangerous sexual waters. It's complete tosh, of course, and the storyline is so slim that it just becomes a series of beautifully composed nude encounters. JF. Contains sex scenes, violence, swearing. [subtitles] DVD

Mickey Rourke *John* • Kim Basinger *Elizabeth* • Margaret Whitton *Molly* • David Margulies *Harvey* • Christine Baranski *Thea* • Karen Young *Sue* • William De Acutis *Ted* ■ *Dir* Adrian Lyne • *Scr* Patricia Knop, Zalman King, Sarah Kernochan, from the novel by Elizabeth McNeill

9 Dead Gay Guys ★★ 18

Crime comedy 2001 · UK · Colour · 79mins

Lab Ky Mo's debut seeks to shock with its politically incorrect caricatures and self-conscious bad taste. But, in fact, it's nowhere near outrageous enough, either to work as a black comedy or as an in-joke on the London gay scene. Most successful is the running gag about Irish rent boys Brendan Mackey and Glenn Mulhern's insistence that they're straight while seeking an enormous pile of money following the deaths of wealthy queen Michael Praed and kinky widower Steven Berkoff. Crude and lacking wit. DP. Contains swearing. [subtitles] DVD

Glenn Mulhern *Kenny* • Brendan Mackey *Byron* • Steven Berkoff *Jeff* • Michael Praed *The Queen* • Vas Blackwood *Donkey-Dick Dark* ■ *Dir/Scr* Lab Ky Mo

Nine Hours to Rama ★★

Historical drama
1963 · UK/US · Colour · 125mins

While David Lean tried but gave up and Richard Attenborough battled for 20 years to make biopics of Gandhi, this melodrama about the assassination simply cut through all the red tape. German actor Horst Buchholz is rather good as the Hindu extremist, Naturam Godse, who believed that Gandhi should die, though Robert Morley in Indian make-up lacks credibility, and some of the lesser characters fail to come to life. AT

Horst Buchholz *Naturam Godse* • José Ferrer *Superintendent Gopal Das* • Valerie Gearon *Rani Mehta* • Don Borisenko *Naryan Apte* • Robert Morley *PK Mussadi* • Diane Baker *Sheila* • Harry Andrews *General Singh* ■ *Dir* Mark Robson • *Scr* Nelson Gidding, from the novel by Stanley Wolpert

The Nine Lives of Fritz the Cat ★ 18

Animated erotic comedy
1974 · US · Colour · 73mins

This uninspired sequel to *Fritz the Cat* finds the stoned feline imagining his other lives in the past and future. The astute social comment of both Robert Crumb's original strips and the first film directed by Ralph Bakshi is mostly gone, and instead the animators seem more intent on creating psychedelic effects. DM [subtitles] DVD

Skip Hinnant *Fritz* • Reva Rose *Fritz's old lady* ■ *Dir* Robert Taylor (3) • *Scr* Fred Halliday, Eric Monte, Robert Taylor

The Nine Lives of Tomas Katz ★ 15

Fantasy 1999 · UK/Ger · BW · 88mins

Set in a monochrome London on the eve of a possible apocalypse, this ambitious but wholly unsatisfactory fantasy is hamstrung by the juvenile humour and self-serving flamboyance of its director. Such is Ben Hopkins's eagerness to show off his familiarity with everything from expressionism to MTV, that the misadventures of alien Tomas Katz (Thomas Fisher) almost become an irrelevance. This is a muddle of obscure symbols and half-baked ideas. DP

Thomas Fisher *No/Tomas Katz* • Ian McNeice *The inspector* • Tim Barlow *Mr Browne* • Janet Henfrey *Janice Waily* • Tony Maudsley *Taxi driver* ■ *Dir* Ben Hopkins • *Scr* Ben Hopkins, Thomas Browne, from a story by Ben Hopkins, Robert Cheek

Nine Months ★★★

Comedy 1994 · Fr · Colour · 107mins

This French comedy is infinitely superior to its Hollywood remake., primarily because it is less coy in its depiction of the sexual and gynaecological aspects of pregnancy than Chris Columbus's film. It is therefore able to develop its relationships and shifting attitudes on more than a superficially comic level. Similarly, Patrick Braoudé is less mannered than Hugh Grant and genuinely appears to be perturbed by the prospect of fatherhood, despite the assurances of his long-suffering wife, Philippine Leroy-Beaulieu. DP

Philippine Leroy-Beaulieu *Mathilde* • Catherine Jacob *Dominique* • Patrick Braoudé *Samuel* • Daniel Russo *Georges* • Patrick Bouchitey *Marc* ■ *Dir/Scr* Patrick Braoudé

Nine Months ★★ 12

Comedy 1995 · US · Colour · 98mins

This attempt to cement Hugh Grant's reputation as the Cary Grant of the 1990s following the massive international success of *Four Weddings and a Funeral* collapses under sentimental crudity, as child psychologist Grant tries to come to terms with his fear of impending fatherhood when girlfriend Julianne Moore announces she is pregnant. TH. Contains swearing. [video] DVD

Hugh Grant *Samuel Faulkner* • Julianne Moore *Rebecca Taylor* • Tom Arnold *Marty Dwyer* • Joan Cusack *Gail Dwyer* • Jeff Goldblum *Sean Fletcher* • Robin Williams *Dr Kosevich* ■ *Dir* Chris Columbus • *Scr* Chris Columbus, from the 1994 film by Patrick Braoudé

Nine Queens ★★★★ 15

Crime drama 2000 · Arg · Colour · 109mins

Initially an entry in a screenwriting contest, Fabian Bielinsky's debut feature is dextrously assured. The story is set in Argentina and hinges on the meeting of incompetent con Gaston Pauls and experienced swindler Ricardo Darin. Their dubious deal involves a tycoon who's about to be deported and a forged set of priceless stamps. The endlessly inventive twists and turns are baffling, but the performances will keep you watching, with Darin outstanding as the small-time operator dripping with seedy charisma. Brisk without being brash, slick but never smug, this deftly handled tale is destined for cult status. DP. In Spanish with English subtitles. [video] DVD

Gaston Pauls *Juan* • Ricardo Darin *Marcos* • Leticia Bredice *Valeria* • Tomas Fonzi *Federico* ■ *Dir/Scr* Fabian Bielinsky

976-EVIL ★ 18

Horror 1988 · US · Colour · 94mins

Nerdy Stephen Geoffreys calls a "horrorscope" hot line and obtains supernatural powers that enable him to take revenge on his tormentors. A confusing mess directed by horror icon Robert Englund who falls back on Freddy Krueger wisecracks and other lifts from *A Nightmare on Elm Street* to beef up his demonic disaster. Sandy Dennis as Geoffreys's kooky religious aunt makes this stale tale almost worthwhile. AJ [video]

Patrick O'Bryan *Spike* • Sandy Dennis *Aunt Lucy* • Stephen Geoffreys *Hoax* • Jim Metzler *Marty Palmer* • Maria Rubell *Angella Martinez* • Lezlie Deane *Suzie* ■ *Dir* Robert Englund • *Scr* Rhet Topham, Brian Helgeland

976-EVIL 2 ★ 18

Horror 1992 · US · Colour · 86mins

In this awful sequel to the 1988 original, a serial killer is revealed to be a rotting zombie who murders via astral projection. Completely devoid of imagination, apart from one sequence where a victim is trapped in a black-and-white mix of *Night of the Living Dead* and *It's a Wonderful Life*, this horror cheapie is royally fouled up by director Jim Wynorski. AJ [video]

Patrick O'Bryan *Spike* • René Assa *Professor Grubeck* • Debbie James *Robin* • Brigitte Nielsen ■ *Dir* Jim Wynorski • *Scr* Erik Anjou

9 Songs ★★ 18

Erotic drama 2004 · UK · Colour · 66mins

Heralded as the first British film featuring "frequent strong real sex" to receive an 18 rating, *9 Songs* is director Michael Winterbottom's ode to physical love. Unfolding against the backdrop of a series of concerts, this explores the sexual relationship between lanky American student Margo Stiller and British research scientist Keiran O'Brien. Instead of a lesson in how hedonistic two people can be, their romp-fuelled four months together demonstrates how a generation deals with loneliness. This is very much an exercise in style over content and, as such, some will find it a rewarding art house experiment with much to recommend it. Others watching simply for the explicit and unsimulated lovemaking may well find it boring and pretentious. KK DVD

Margo Stilley *Lisa* • Keiran O'Brien *Matt* ■ *Dir* Michael Winterbottom • *Cinematographer* Marcel Zyskind

Nine to Five ★★★ 15

Comedy 1980 · US · Colour · 109mins

Dolly Parton makes her movie debut and belts the Oscar-nominated title song in this cheery comedy, which went on to spawn a sitcom series of the same name. Parton, Lily Tomlin and Jane Fonda play three office colleagues who scheme revenge on their chauvinist boss. It was Fonda who came up with the idea of making a Hollywood version of a feminist comedy, but it is Tomlin, as the junior manager overlooked for promotion, and Parton, as a personal secretary, whose performances impress the most. PF. Contains drug abuse and some swearing. [video]

Jane Fonda *Judy Bernly* • Lily Tomlin *Violet Newstead* • Dolly Parton *Doralee Rhodes* • Dabney Coleman *Franklin Hart Jr* • Sterling Hayden *Russell Tinsworthy* • Elizabeth Wilson *Roz Keith* • Henry Jones *Hinkle* ■ *Dir* Colin Higgins • *Scr* Colin Higgins, Patricia Resnick, from a story by Patricia Resnick

1918 ★★★

Period drama 1985 · US · Colour · 91mins

A fact-based period drama, set in rural Texas, this chronicles the death and despair brought to one small town by the killer flu epidemic that swept much of the US in the year of the title. Adapted from a Horton Foote play, the film seems understandably stagey at times. Nonetheless, the innate strength of story and some powerful performances carry it through. Look out for an early screen appearance by a young Matthew Broderick. Followed by a number of sequels. DA

William Converse-Roberts *Horace Robedaux* • Hallie Foote *Elizabeth Robedaux* • Rochelle Oliver *Mrs Vaughn* • Matthew Broderick *Brother* • Jeannie McCarthy [Jeanne McCarthy] *Bessie* • Bill McGhee *Sam* • Horton Foote Jr *Jessie* ■ *Dir* Ken Harrison • *Scr* Horton Foote, from his play

1984 ★★★

Futuristic drama 1955 · UK · BW · 89mins

Michael Anderson's adaptation of George Orwell's dystopian novel is reasonably faithful to its source, concentrating on the possibility of love and humanity in a totalitarian state ruled by a powerful bureaucratic elite, a world of "Big Brother", "Thought Police" and "Doublethink". It's not quite the equal of Michael Radford's 1984 version, but both pale beside the chilling, authentically Orwellian vision of Terry Gilliam's *Brazil*. AT

Edmond O'Brien *Winston Smith* • Michael Redgrave *O'Connor* • Jan Sterling *Julia* • David Kossoff *Charrington* • Mervyn Johns *Jones* • Donald Pleasence *Parsons* ■ *Dir* Michael Anderson • *Scr* William P Templeton, Ralph Bettinson, from the novel by George Orwell

Nineteen Eighty-Four ★★★★ 15

Futuristic drama
1984 · UK · Colour · 110mins

Inspired less by Soviet tyranny than the paranoia induced by British wartime censorship and propaganda, George Orwell's study of a dystopian future has lost none of its pessimism and dread. Much bleaker than the 1955 version, Michael Radford's superbly designed return to Oceania holds out little hope that the human spirit will be able to withstand the onset of totalitarianism. John Hurt is perfectly cast as the government cog who enters into a relationship with co-worker Suzanna Hamilton as an act of rebellion. But it's his encounter with Richard Burton, as the personification of "Big Brother's" omnipresence, that provides the dramatic highlight. DP. Contains violence, nudity. [video] DVD

John Hurt *Winston Smith* • Richard Burton *O'Brien* • Suzanna Hamilton *Julia* • Cyril Cusack *Charrington* • Gregor Fisher *Parsons* • James Walker *Syme* • Andrew Wilde *Tillotson* • Phyllis Logan *Telescreen announcer* • Roger Lloyd Pack *Waiter* ■ *Dir* Michael Radford • *Scr* Michael Radford, Jonathan Gems, from the novel by George Orwell

1941 ★★★ PG

Comedy 1979 · US · Colour · 113mins

Widely regarded as the one Steven Spielberg disaster, this sprawling comedy never deserved all the flak. True, it's a messy, hysterical affair and many of the gags are strictly puerile. However, the sentimentality that mars many of Spielberg's more acclaimed works is nowhere to be seen, and there is a mischievous, anarchic edge to the story of how LA collapsed into chaos over fear of Japanese invasion following Pearl Harbor. JF. Contains swearing. [video]

Dan Aykroyd *Sergeant Tree* • Ned Beatty *Ward Douglas* • John Belushi *Wild Bill Kelso* • Lorraine Gary *Joan Douglas* • Murray Hamilton *Claude* • Christopher Lee *Von Kleinschmidt* • Tim Matheson *Birkhead* • Toshiro Mifune *Commander Mitamura* • Warren Oates *Maddox* • Robert Stack *General Stilwell* • Treat Williams *Sitarski* • Nancy Allen *Donna* • John Candy *Foley* • Elisha Cook [Elisha Cook Jr] *Patron* • Slim Pickens *Hollis Wood* • Sam Fuller [Samuel Fuller] *Interceptor commander* • John Landis *Mizerany* • Mickey Rourke *Reese* ■ *Dir* Steven Spielberg • *Scr* Robert Zemeckis, Bob Gale, from a story by Robert Zemeckis, Bob Gale, John Milius

1942: a Love Story ★★★ 12

Drama 1994 · Ind · Colour · 151mins

As the Quit India movement gathered momentum at the height of the Second World War, the British response to the growing unrest (much of which came in the form of the passive resistance advocated by Gandhi) was often swift and brutal. Packed with songs that topped the Indian charts, this Romeo and Juliet story stars Anil Kapoor and Manisha Koirala as a Himalayan couple whose fathers are on opposite sides in the conflict. Director Vidhu Vinod Chopra admirably combines the human and the historical elements of the story. DP. In Hindi with English subtitles. [video] DVD

Anil Kapoor *Nandu* • Manisha Koirala *Rajjo* • Brian Glover *General Douglas* ■ *Dir* Vidhu Vinod Chopra • *Scr* Kamna, Chandra, Shiv Subrahmanyam, Vidhu Vinod Chopra

1900 ★★★★ 18

Epic period drama
1976 · It · Colour · 303mins

This stunning but demanding Marxist epic spans 45 years of Italian political history. Tracing the rise and fall of Fascism, Bernardo Bertolucci uses characters to symbolise entire social groups. Gérard Depardieu and Robert De Niro are born on the same day in the year 1901, in the same rural region, one to poor sharecroppers, the other to landowners. As they grow from childhood friends to antagonistic men, Depardieu becomes an inspirational Communist leader. His nemesis, Donald Sutherland, is the local blackshirt and De Niro's foreman. Operatically staged and swollen with symbolism, this is Bertolucci's flawed masterpiece, best viewed as polemic as much as history. AC. In Italian with English subtitles. [video]

Burt Lancaster *Alfredo Sr* • Robert De Niro *Alfredo Jr* • Gérard Depardieu *Olmo* • Donald Sutherland *Attila* • Dominique Sanda *Ada* • Sterling Hayden *Leo Dalco* • Stefania Sandrelli *Anita* • Alida Valli *Signora Pioppi* • Laura Betti *Regina* ■ *Dir* Bernardo Bertolucci • *Scr* Bernardo Bertolucci, Franco Arcalli, Giuseppe Bertolucci • *Music* Ennio Morricone

N

1919 ★★★

Period drama 1983 · Sp · Colour · 85mins

Despite its visual lustre, this is a less nostalgic picture than its predecessor, *Valentina*. Again recounted by a Republican PoW at the end of the Spanish Civil War, the story has now moved on to 1919, with Miguel Molina assuming the role of the young poet, Pepe. The hero is still devoted to his childhood sweetheart, Emma Suarez, but his passion is compromised by an encounter with Cristina Marsillach, the domestic he meets while studying in Zaragoza. DP. In Spanish with English subtitles.

Anthony Quinn *Mosen Joaquin* • Miguel Molina *Pepe* • Cristina Marsillach *Isabelita* • Saturno Cerra *Don Jose* • Conchita Leza *Doña Luisa* • Walter Vidarte *Checa* • Emma Suarez *Valentina* ■ *Dir* Antonio Jose Betancor • *Scr* Lautaro Murúa, Antonio José Betancor, Carlos Escobedo, Javier Moro, from the novel *Crónica del Alba (Days Of Dawn)* by Ramón J Sender

Nineteen Nineteen ★★ 15

Drama 1984 · UK · Colour · 98mins

Paul Scofield and Maria Schell co-star in this very solemn movie about Freudian analysis. The leads meet up in Vienna and recall their separate consultations with Dr Freud, given voice (but not a physical presence) by Frank Finlay. Scofield remembers the war, his marriage and his impossible love objects; Schell relives her lesbian relationship, marriage and divorce. AT

Maria Schell *Sophie Ruben* • Paul Scofield *Alexander Scherbatov* • Frank Finlay *Dr Freud* • Diana Quick *Anna* • Clare Higgins *Young Sophie* • Colin Firth *Young Alexander* ■ *Dir* Hugh Brody • *Scr* Hugh Brody, Michael Ignatieff

1991: The Year Punk Broke ★★

Music documentary
1992 · US · Colour · 99mins

This documentary records Sonic Youth's 1991 European tour as they moved from small club venues to the much bigger outdoor festival circuit. Nicely shot and edited, but rather dull overall; other bands featured include Nirvana, Dinosaur Jr and the Ramones. Gumball and Babes in Toyland also appear, but neither group shows the talent or class of Sonic Youth, despite frontman Thurston Moore failing to live up to his legendary image as a vicious wit. AJ

Dir Dave Markey

1969 ★★★ 15

Drama 1988 · US · Colour · 91mins

This is an effective and often moving portrayal of life in America at the end of the 1960s, with Kiefer Sutherland and Robert Downey Jr as two friends who find themselves on opposite sides of US involvement in Vietnam. Downey takes a moral stance; Sutherland loses himself in drink and drugs while waiting for his number to come up on Nixon's Vietnam draft lottery. Although clichéd in places and definitely slow towards the middle, it's an interesting look at the war that never should have been. JB. Contains violence, swearing, nudity. DVD

Robert Downey Jr *Ralph Carr* • Kiefer Sutherland *Scott Denny* • Bruce Dern *Cliff Denny* • Mariette Hartley *Jessie Denny* • Winona Ryder *Beth Carr* • Joanna Cassidy *Ev Carr* ■ *Dir/Scr* Ernest Thompson

90 Days ★★★ 15

Romantic comedy
1986 · Can · Colour · 99mins

This cute little comedy, shot in mock documentary style, isabout a Canadian who invites his Korean penpal to come and be his wife. The film amusingly explores the consequent clash of cultures as east and west not only meet but mate – or, at least, try to. Director Giles Walker would explore broadly similar culture clashes seven years later in *Ordinary Magic*, about an Indian orphan sent to live with his Canadian aunt. DF

Stefan Wodoslawsky *Blue* • Christine Pak *Hyang-Sook* • Sam Grana *Alex* • Fernanda Tavares *Laura* ■ *Dir* Giles Walker • *Scr* David Wilson, Giles Walker

99 and 44/100% Dead ★★ 15

Crime comedy 1974 · US · Colour · 97mins

Arguably cinema's first pop-art gangster movie, this offbeat black comedy matches up to the strangeness of its title. In a role meant for Robert Mitchum, the always superb Richard Harris plays a hitman who is hired by a gang leader struggling for supremacy over a criminal colleague. A below-par John Frankenheimer brings a comic-book feel to the various bloody shoot-outs and keeps the action moving at a fair clip, but he seems to get lost amid the nonsense. RS

Richard Harris *Harry Crown* • Edmond O'Brien *Uncle Frank* • Bradford Dillman *Big Eddie* • Ann Turkel *Buffy* • Constance Ford *Dolly* • David Hall *Tony* • Katherine Baumann *Baby* • Chuck Connors *Marvin "Claw" Zuckerman* ■ *Dir* John Frankenheimer • *Scr* Robert Dillon

99 River Street ★★★

Film noir 1953 · US · BW · 83mins

Peggie Castle, the wife of boxer-turned-cab driver John Payne deserts him for jewel thief Brad Dexter. When Dexter grows bored with the blonde, he kills her and leaves the corpse in Payne's cab. Payne, with help from Evelyn Keyes, has to run the gauntlet of the seedy underworld and its gun-happy dangers in an effort to prove his innocence. A modest but taut, tough and atmospheric crime movie. RK

John Payne *Ernie Driscoll* • Evelyn Keyes *Linda James* • Brad Dexter *Victor Rawlins* • Frank Faylen *Stan Hogan* • Peggie Castle *Pauline Driscoll* ■ *Dir* Phil Karlson • *Scr* Robert Smith, from a story by George Zuckerman

92 in the Shade ★★★

Comedy drama
1975 · US/UK · Colour · 83mins

Peter Fonda stars in this amiable coast-along playing a fishing guide in the Florida Keys at odds with the captain of another boat. He's in the company of such specialists in eccentricity as Warren Oates, Margot Kidder, Burgess Meredith and Harry Dean Stanton, and this makes up for directorial inexperience with atmosphere and quirkiness. TH

Peter Fonda *Tom Skelton* • Warren Oates *Nichol Dance* • Margot Kidder *Miranda* • Burgess Meredith *Goldsboro* • Harry Dean Stanton *Carter* • Sylvia Miles *Bella* • Elizabeth Ashley *Jeannie Carter* • William Hickey *Mr Skelton* ■ *Dir* Thomas McGuane • *Scr* Thomas McGuane, from his novel

Ninotchka ★★★★★ U

Comedy 1939 · US · BW · 105mins

This is without doubt one of the funniest, most original screen comedies ever made, and from the greatest year in Hollywood's history. Director Ernst Lubitsch brings his magic touch to bear on this inspired tale of a Russian emissary (the great Greta Garbo in a startling change of image) sent to Paris to retrieve three errant communists who have fallen in love with the ways of the west. Of course, it's just a matter of time before Garbo melts and falls in love, in her case with debonair count Melvyn Douglas. Witty, sophisticated, immaculately cast and superbly performed, this film was advertised in its day simply as "Garbo laughs!". That she does, and so will you, long and loud, especially at the utterly charming café scene. TS

Greta Garbo *Ninotchka, Nina Ivanova Yakushova* • Melvyn Douglas *Count Leon d'Algout* • Ina Claire *Grand Duchess Swana* • Bela Lugosi *Commissar Razinin* • Sig Rumann [Sig Ruman] *Iranoff* • Felix Bressart *Buljanoff* • Alexander Granach *Kopalski* • Gregory Gaye *Count Alexis Rakonin* ■ *Dir* Ernst Lubitsch • *Scr* Charles Brackett, Billy Wilder, Walter Reisch, from a story by Melchior Lengyel • *Cinematographer* William H Daniels • *Costume Designer* Adrian

The Ninth Configuration ★★★ 15

Psychological thriller
1979 · US · Colour · 113mins

Produced, directed and scripted by *The Exorcist* creator William Peter Blatty, this surreal exercise in Freudian vaudeville stars Stacy Keach as a psychiatrist who provides radical therapy to possibly insane military veterans in a remote Gothic mansion. Of course, Keach has a gruesome secret and is going through his own apocalyptic catharsis. At times absolutely bewildering, at others completely gripping and harrowing, this overly literate and obtuse thriller has become the thinking man's cult classic. AJ. Contains swearing and violence. DVD

Stacy Keach *Colonel Hudson Kane* • Scott Wilson *Captain Billy Cutshaw* • Jason Miller *Lieutenant Reno* • Ed Flanders *Colonel Fell* • Neville Brand *Major Groper* • Moses Gunn *Major Nammack* • Robert Loggia *Lieutenant Bennish* ■ *Dir* William Peter Blatty • *Scr* William Peter Blatty, from the novel *Twinkle, Twinkle, Killer Kane* by William Peter Blatty

The Ninth Gate ★★★ 15

Supernatural thriller
1999 · Fr/Sp/US · Colour · 127mins

This is a largely successful return to the horror genre by Roman Polanski, and features sardonic wit, subtle suspense tricks and razor-sharp irony. Johnny Depp stars as a rare books expert hired by billionaire Frank Langella to authenticate his copy of an ancient tome that was supposedly written in conjunction with the Devil. This Gothic chiller has moody atmosphere and a stunning score (from Wojciech Kilar), but the hallucinatory climax is a disappointment. AJ DVD

Johnny Depp *Dean Corso* • Frank Langella *Boris Balkan* • Lena Olin *Liana Telfer* • Emmanuelle Seigner *The girl* • Barbara Jefford *Baroness Kessler* • Jack Taylor *Victor Fargas* • James Russo *Bernie* ■ *Dir* Roman Polanski • *Scr* Enrique Urbizu, John Brownjohn, Roman Polanski, from the novel *El Club Dumas* by Arturo Pérez-Reverte

Nirvana ★★★★

Science-fiction thriller
1996 · It/Fr · Colour · 112mins

A stunning cyber-fantasy, rich in design and innovative ideas, that intellectually engages the mind while always remaining enjoyable on the purest pulp levels. Superstar video game inventor Christopher Lambert creates a new game called *Nirvana*, then realises his virtual reality hero (Italian matinée idol Diego Abatantuono) has a human consciousness. How he tries to erase the game before its mass-market Christmas release, which would condemn Abantantuono to a never-ending existence, pits Lambert against a ruthless multi-national corporation and takes him through the seedy underworlds of a future metropolis known as the Northern Agglomerate. AJ. An Italian language film.

Christopher Lambert *Jimi* • Diego Abatantuono *Solo* • Sergio Rubini *Joystick* • Emmanuelle Seigner *Lisa* • Stefania Rocca *Naima* ■ *Dir* Gabriele Salvatores • *Scr* Gabriele Salvatores, Gloria Corica, Pino Cacucci

Nirvana Street Murder ★★★

Black comedy 1990 · Aus · Colour · 75mins

Mark Little proves himself a more than capable actor in this uncompromising black comedy that anticipates the mix of violence and dark humour now so common in American independent cinema. Any film in which someone attempts murder by drowning the victim in a waterbed has got to be worth seeing. DP

Mark Little *Boady* • Ben Mendelsohn *Luke* • Mary Coustas *Helen* • Tamara Saulwick *Penny* • Sheila Florance *Molly* • Roberto Micale *Hector* ■ *Dir/Scr* Aleksi Vellis

Nishant ★★★ 15

Crime drama 1975 · Ind · Colour · 136mins

Shabana Azmi stars in Shyam Benegal's examination of the hypocrisy and corruption of rural society. The story centres on teacher Girish Karnad's determination to avenge the abduction and rape of his wife by Naseeruddin Shah, the youngest son of a feared landowner. Despite Benegal owing more to Satyajit Ray's style of cinema than the mainstream, this powerful, realist tale nevertheless turned the debuting Shah into a Bollywood legend, while Azmi confirmed her status as one of India's finest actresses. But it's Amrish Puri who dominates proceedings as Shah's vicious brother. DP. In Hindi with English subtitles.

Girish Karnad *Schoolmaster* • Shabana Azmi *Sushila* • Anant Nag *Anjaiya* • Amrish Puri *Eldest Zamindar* • Satyadev Dubey *Priest* • Smita [Smita Patil] *Rukmani* • Mohan Agashe *Prasad* • Kulbhushan Kharbanda *Policeman Patel* • Naseeruddin Shah *Vishwam* ■ *Dir* Shyam Benegal • *Scr* Vijay Tendulkar

Nixon ★★★★ 15

Biographical drama
1995 · US · Colour and BW · 182mins

Near the end of this biographical drama, the disgraced President gazes at a painting of John Kennedy and says, "When people look at you, they see what they want to be. When they look at me, they see what they are." That's a great line, the key to Oliver Stone's movie, which, like his earlier *JFK*, is three hours of brilliance, provocation and information overload. The movie makes great demands on the viewer and on Anthony Hopkins, whose brave performance is more an impression than an impersonation. At one point Paul Sorvino's sinister Henry Kissinger says, "He had greatness within his grasp but he had the defects of his qualities." Much the same can be said of this mesmerising movie. AT. Contains swearing. DVD

Anthony Hopkins *Richard Milhous Nixon* • Joan Allen *Pat Nixon* • Powers Boothe *Alexander Haig* • Ed Harris *E Howard Hunt* • Bob Hoskins *J Edgar Hoover* • EG Marshall *John Mitchell* • David Paymer *Ron Ziegler* • David Hyde Pierce *John Dean* • Paul Sorvino *Henry Kissinger* • Mary Steenburgen *Hannah Nixon* • JT Walsh *John Ehrlichman* • James Woods *HR Haldeman* • Brian Bedford *Clyde Tolson* ■ *Dir* Oliver Stone • *Scr* Stephen J Rivele, Christopher Wilkinson, Oliver Stone

Nô ★★ 15

Comedy drama
1998 · Can · Colour and BW · 84mins

This ambitous study in cultural and national dualism unsuccessfully seeks to combine high politics and low farce as it alternates between a monochrome Montreal and a vividly hued Osaka. Director Robert Lepage raises the occasional smile and makes some pertinent political points, but he fails to rein in an over-exuberant cast, with Anne-Marie Cadieux voluble as the pregnant actress fretting over the activities of her terrorist lover (Alexis Martin). DP. In French with English subtitles. Contains swearing, nudity and drug abuse.

Anne-Marie Cadieux *Sophie* • Alexis Martin *Michel* • Marie Brassard *Hanako* • Richard Fréchette *Walter* • Marie Gignac *Patricia* ■ *Dir* Robert Lepage • *Scr* Robert Lepage, André Morency, from the play *The Seven Streams of the River Ota* by Robert Lepage

No Big Deal ★ PG

Drama 1983 · US · Colour · 86mins

This teen movie strains to be hip and hammers home its social message, and even the least discerning couch potato will reach for the remote. A lifeless tale of a troubled misfit at a strictly-run school, it needs charismatic rebels, but all Kevin Dillon can do is sulk. DP

Kevin Dillon *Arnold Borberry* • Christopher Gartin *Michael Parker* • Mary Joan Negro *Jennifer Kirkpatrick* • Sylvia Miles *Principal* ■ *Dir* Robert Charlton • *Scr* Jeff Kindley, from the novel *Would You Settle for Improbable* by PJ Petersen

No Blade of Grass ★★★ 15

Science-fiction drama
1970 · UK · Colour · 91mins

This bleak but affecting eco-message drama from director Cornel Wilde casts Nigel Davenport and, in her last film, Jean Wallace (Wilde's real-life wife) as parents leading their family across a British countryside devastated by environmental pollution and blighted by anarchy. Wilde's rough-edged handling of the material oddly gives it a semi-documentary feel that's intermittently effective. It's a sober, well-meaning

U = SUITABLE FOR ALL Uc = SUITABLE FOR ALL, ESPECIALLY FOR YOUNG CHILDREN (VIDEO ONLY) PG = PARENTAL GUIDANCE

film that, despite not quite coming off, is well worth catching. RS

Nigel Davenport *John Custance* • Jean Wallace *Ann Custance* • John Hamill *Roger Burnham* • Lynne Frederick *Mary Custance* • Patrick Holt *David Custance* • Anthony May *Andrew Pirrie* • Wendy Richard *Clara* ■ *Dir* Cornel Wilde • *Scr* Sean Forestal, Jefferson Pascal, from the novel *The Death of Grass* by John Christopher

No Code of Conduct ★★ 18

Crime action drama 1998 · US · Colour · 85mins

Martin and Charlie Sheen are together again in this distinctly average crime drama. This time around, Charlie plays a maverick cop who's prepared to use any means necessary to bust a gigantic heroin ring, while Martin is a police executive waging his own war against high-level corruption. Expect the body count to mount rapidly. JF. Contains swearing and violence. DVD

Martin Sheen *Bill Peterson* • Charles Sheen [Charlie Sheen] *Jake Peterson* • Bret Michaels *Shane* • Mark Dacascos *Paul DeLucca* • Joe Lando *Willdog* • Meredith Salenger *Rebecca Peterson* ■ *Dir* Bret Michaels • *Scr* Bill Gucwa, Ed Masterson, Bret Michaels, Charlie Sheen, Shane Stanley

No Deposit No Return ★★ U

Comedy 1976 · US · Colour · 106mins

This Disney live-action picture is basically fine, with a couple of kids co-operating in their own kidnap in an attempt to avoid spending the summer with their uncaring grandfather. But it takes much more than a car chase, a pet skunk and David Niven hanging upside down by his heels to please kids. Darren McGavin and Don Knotts do their best as the dim-witted kidnappers, but the result isn't up to much. DP

David Niven *JW Osborne* • Darren McGavin *Duke* • Don Knotts *Bert* • Herschel Bernardi *Sergeant Turner* • Barbara Feldon *Carolyn* • Kim Richards *Tracy* • Brad Savage *Jay* ■ *Dir* Norman Tokar • *Scr* Arthur Alsberg, Don Nelson, from a story by Joe L McEveety

No Dessert Dad, Till You Mow the Lawn ★

Comedy 1994 · US · Colour · 89mins

This rare foray by producer Roger Corman into PG territory is a surprisingly reprehensible family film. When a brother/sister duo accidentally discover they can manipulate the self-hypnosis tapes of their parents (Robert Hays and Joanna Kerns), they use this knowledge to get everything they want. The movie is never able to justify this pseudo-range of the mind, even when the siblings' tape manipulation becomes unselfish (at least as far as they're concerned). KB

Robert Hays *Ken Cochran* • Joanna Kerns *Carol Cochran* • Richard Moll • Lyman Ward • Larry Linville *JJ* ■ *Dir* Howard McCain • *Scr* Cathy Moran, Martha Moran

No Down Payment ★★★

Drama 1957 · US · BW · 105mins

Four couples who seek upward mobility by buying homes in a suburban housing estate must face the reality of paying the mortgage and must cope with the dramas that arise as their lives intersect. Some commentators consider the movie sociologically significant as an accurate picture of 1950s suburban America; as entertainment, it's a reasonable compendium of soap opera clichés. RK

Joanne Woodward *Leola Boone* • Sheree North *Isabelle Flagg* • Tony Randall *Jerry Flagg* • Jeffrey Hunter *David Martin* • Cameron Mitchell *Troy Boone* • Patricia Owens *Jean Martin* • Barbara Rush *Betty Kreitzer* • Pat Hingle *Herman Kreitzer* ■ *Dir* Martin Ritt • *Scr* Philip Yordan (front for Ben Maddow), from the novel by John McPartland

No Drums, No Bugles ★★★

Drama 1971 · US · Colour · 86mins

A fascinating, low-budget movie in which Martin Sheen plays a Civil War soldier who, sickened by the killing, deserts and goes to live in the depths of the West Virginian forests. Vowing never to kill a living thing, Sheen turns into a mountain man with flowers in his hair and eco-awareness in his veins. This Vietnam allegory is artfully made – Sheen is the only real character, although others are briefly glimpsed or heard – and probably influenced by the Oscar-winning 1963 short, *Incident at Owl Creek*. AT

Martin Sheen *Ashby Gatrell* • Davey Davison *Callie Gatrell* • Rod McCary *Lieutenant* • Denine Terry *Sarah* ■ *Dir/Scr* Clyde Ware

No End ★★★ 15

Drama 1984 · Pol · Colour · 103mins

Watched by the ghost of lawyer Jerzy Radziwilowicz, both his widow, Grazyna Szapolowska, and his trade unionist client, Artur Barcis, face impossible moral dilemmas. She agonises over dishonouring his memory through physical need, while he debates whether to compromise his principles for freedom or become a martyr for the cause of liberty. Made in 1984, director Krzysztof Kieslowski's first collaboration with screenwriter Krzysztof Piesiewicz was withheld for two years from international release because of its pro-Solidarity sentiments. DP. In Polish with English subtitles. DVD

Grazyna Szapolowska *Ula Zyro* • Maria Pakulnis *Joanna* • Aleksander Bardini *Labrador* • Jerzy Radziwilowicz *Antoni "Antek" Zyro* • Artur Barcis *Darius* ■ *Dir* Krzysztof Kieslowski • *Scr* Krzysztof Kieslowski, Krzysztof Piesiewicz

No Escape ★★★ 15

Futuristic action thriller 1994 · US · Colour · 118mins

Ray Liotta gives it his best shot in this cheerfully trashy futuristic thriller from British director Martin Campbell. In the 21st century, Liotta finds himself imprisoned on an isolated island where the convicts have split into caring hippies and warmongering tribesmen. Lance Henriksen and Stuart Wilson ham it up for all they're worth as the leaders of the rival factions and, although his direction is a little erratic, Campbell delivers some satisfying set pieces. JF. Contains swearing and violence. DVD

Ray Liotta *Robbins* • Lance Henriksen *The Father* • Stuart Wilson (1) *Marek* • Kevin Dillon *Casey* • Kevin J O'Connor *Stephano* • Don Henderson *Killian* • Ian McNeice *King* • Jack Shepherd *Dysart* ■ *Dir* Martin Campbell • *Scr* Michael Gaylin, Joel Gross, from the novel *The Penal Colony* by Richard Herley

No Exit ★★

Drama 1954 · Fr · BW · 95mins

Quite why screenwriter Pierre Laroche felt it necessary to emasculate Jean-Paul Sartre's existential masterpiece remains a mystery. Yet it's plain to see what a disservice his decision to add extra characters and incorporate other-worldly flashbacks does to the relentless intensity of the original drama, in which a recently deceased trio discover the bitter truth that "hell is other people". DP. A French language film.

Arletty *Inès* • Frank Villard *M Garcin* • Gaby Sylvia *Estelle* • Nicole Courcel *Olga* ■ *Dir* Jacqueline Audry • *Scr* Pierre Laroche, from the play *Huis Clos* by Jean-Paul Sartre

No Good Deed ★★ 15

Crime thriller 2002 · Can/US/Ger · Colour · 93mins

Based on Dashiell Hammett's short story *The House on Turk Street* (the film's original title), this mediocre crime thriller has Samuel L Jackson's cello-playing detective kidnapped by bank robbers after he stumbles on their lair while hunting for a friend's missing daughter. The talents of the attractive cast are undermined by an increasingly preposterous script and this disappointment belies director Bob Rafelson's illustrious past. SF. Contains swearing, violence and nudity. DVD

Samuel L Jackson *Jack Friar* • Milla Jovovich *Erin* • Stellan Skarsgård *Tyrone* • Doug Hutchison *Hoop* • Joss Ackland *Mr Quarre* • Grace Zabriskie *Mrs Quarre* • Jonathan Higgins *David Brewster* ■ *Dir* Bob Rafelson • *Scr* Christopher Canaan, Steve Barancik, from the short story *The House on Turk Street* by Dashiell Hammett

No Greater Glory ★★★ U

Thriller 1934 · US · BW · 73mins

Frail young George Breakston gains courage, confidence and happiness when he is allowed into a gang, but his life is cut tragically short. No, this is not a juvenile crime movie, but a poignant, sensitive portrait of courage and love. Based on an autobiographical novel by Hungarian-born playwright Ferenc Molnar, Frank Borzage's film is acutely scripted by Jo Swerling and makes for a compelling, if sentimental, little drama. RK

George Breakston *Nemecsek* • Jimmy Butler *Boka* • Jackie Searl [Jackie Searle] *Gereb* • Frankie Darro *Feri Ats* • Donald Haines *Csonakos* • Rolf Ernest *Ferdie Pasztor* ■ *Dir* Frank Borzage • *Scr* Jo Swerling, from the novel *The Paul Street Boys* by Ferenc Molnar

No Higher Love ★★ PG

Drama 1999 · US · Colour · 86mins

In this sentimental TV-movie, Katey Sagal plays a happily married woman with a career in real estate who is diagnosed with terminal cancer shortly after giving birth to a daughter. Annabeth Gish plays the divorced nurse who comes into their lives and gives the family hope for the future. Even though it's based on a true story, it's a very contrived scenario, full of brave smiles and lachrymose lapses calculated to leave the viewer misty eyed. DP DVD

Katey Sagal *Ellen Young* • Annabeth Gish *Claire Hutton* • Tom Irwin *Brian Young* • Alison Pill *Samantha Hutton* • Katie Boland *Lindsay Hutton* • Brenda Bazinet *Sandy Russo* • Roger Dunn *Bill Young* ■ *Dir* Michael Switzer • *Scr* Richard Leder

No Highway ★★★ U

Thriller 1951 · UK · BW · 98mins

James Stewart is in his best absent-minded professor mode as a scientist whose obstinacy prevents a series of flying disasters in this watchable thriller, based on Nevil Shute's novel. It's about a boffin (Stewart) who can't find his own front door, but who confidently predicts metal fatigue in a new type of British aircraft. Naturally, he's branded a loony. Marlene Dietrich has an inflated part as a film star who believes in him, along with Glynis Johns as a friendly stewardess and Janette Scott as his daughter. Directed by Henry Koster, this is much better than the family comedies he later made with Stewart in Hollywood. AE

James Stewart *Theodore Honey* • Marlene Dietrich *Monica Teasdale* • Glynis Johns *Marjorie Corder* • Jack Hawkins *Dennis Scott* • Ronald Squire *Sir John* • Janette Scott *Elspeth Honey* ■ *Dir* Henry Koster • *Scr* RC Sherriff, Oscar Millard, Alec Coppel, from the novel by Nevil Shute

No Holds Barred ★ 15

Action comedy 1989 · US · Colour · 88mins

Rip (Hulk Hogan) is the world's most beloved wrestler. He's also a man of his word. His morals won't let him take on a lucrative contract for an upstart network mogul, and this sets him up for a fight with the mogul's anointed hero Zeus (Tom "Tiny" Lister). If you think that pro wrestlers are actors, Hogan's performance will probably convince you otherwise, and the script is so simplistic that you'll yearn for the relative sophistication of cable grappling shows. ST

Hulk Hogan *Rip* • Kurt Fuller *Brell* • Joan Severance *Samantha Moore* • Tom "Tiny" Lister [Tom "Tiny" Lister Jr] *Zeus* • Mark Pellegrino *Randy* • David Palmer *Unger* ■ *Dir* Thomas J Wright • *Scr* Dennis Hackin

No Kidding ★★ PG

Comedy drama 1960 · UK · BW · 82mins

The *Carry On* team of producer Peter Rogers and director Gerald Thomas are responsible for this wallow in whimsy in which a couple inherit a large house and convert it into a holiday home for rich kids. As the house fills up with the offspring of oil sheikhs, royals and sundry millionaires, the locals speak up for the underprivileged kids in the area. Leslie Phillips and Geraldine McEwan play the couple who kick off the plot, Joan Hickson is their conspiratorial cook, while Irene Handl is the local busybody. AT

Leslie Phillips *David Robinson* • Geraldine McEwan *Catherine Robinson* • Julia Lockwood *Vanilla* • Noel Purcell *Tandy* • Irene Handl *Mrs Spicer* • Joan Hickson *Cook* • Francesca Annis *Priscilla* • Christopher Witty *Richard Robinson* ■ *Dir* Gerald Thomas • *Scr* Norman Hudis, Robin Estridge, from the novel *Beware of Children* by Verily Anderson

No Limit ★★ PG

Comedy 1935 · UK · BW · 77mins

This was George Formby's debut for Associated Talking Pictures, but the star struggles to impose his inimitable personality on a plot that resembles an episode of the *Wacky Races* cartoon series. Sabotaged throughout the Isle of Man's famous TT Races, George eventually wins the day, thanks to the love of Florence Desmond and the assistance of a donkey. DP

George Formby *George Shuttleworth* • Florence Desmond *Florrie Dibney* • Howard Douglas *Turner* • Beatrix Fielden-Kaye *Mrs Horrocks* • Peter Gawthorne *Mr Higgins* • Alf Goddard *Norton* • Florence Gregson *Mrs Shuttleworth* • Jack Hobbs *Bert Tyldesley* ■ *Dir* Monty Banks • *Scr* Tom Geraghty, Fred Thompson, from a story by Walter Greenwood

No Looking Back ★★ 15

Romantic comedy drama 1998 · US · Colour · 92mins

Waitress Lauren Holly must decide between safe and dependable mechanic boyfriend Jon Bon Jovi, or her ex-lover, an exciting but unreliable drifter (played by director Edward Burns). Although the stars have charm to spare, this is painfully bland and risk-free. The script and performances aren't bad – it's just difficult to distinguish it from hundreds of similar movies. JC. Contains swearing and sex scenes.

Lauren Holly *Claudia* • Edward Burns *Charlie* • Jon Bon Jovi *Michael* • Connie Britton *Kelly* • Nick Sandow *Goldie* • Kaili Vernoff *Alice* • Shari Albert *Shari* • Blythe Danner *Claudia's mother* ■ *Dir/Scr* Edward Burns

No Love for Johnnie ★★★★

Political drama 1960 · UK · BW · 110mins

Labour win the general election but Peter Finch MP is overlooked for the cabinet post he was expecting. Instead, his communist wife leaves

N

him, he falls in with shifty communist-leaning MP Donald Pleasence and has a passionate affair with Mary Peach, a fashion model. Based on a novel by a Labour MP, this prefigures the Profumo affair with its then outspoken blend of sex and politics and remains eminently watchable and wholly plausible, due mainly to Finch's totally believable, award-winning portrayal. AT

Peter Finch *Johnnie Byrne* • Stanley Holloway *Fred Andrews* • Mary Peach *Pauline West* • Donald Pleasence *Roger Renfrew* • Billie Whitelaw *Mary* • Dennis Price *Flagg* • Hugh Burden *Tim Maxwell* • Rosalie Crutchley *Alice Byrne* ■ *Dir* Ralph Thomas • *Scr* Nicholas Phipps, Mordecai Richler, from the novel by Wilfred Fienburgh

No Man of Her Own ★★

Comedy drama 1932 · US · BW · 80mins

Clark Gable, on loan to Paramount from MGM, co-stars with Carole Lombard in this tale of romance between a shady New York gambler and a librarian in the small town where he hides out. Wesley Ruggles directs an essentially routine script, elevated by the personalities of the attractive stars and their evident chemistry. (They would marry a few years later.) Dorothy Mackaill is the jealous woman whose threats to destroy Gable have a beneficial outcome. RK

Clark Gable *Jerry "Babe" Stewart* • Carole Lombard *Connie Randall* • Dorothy Mackaill *Kay Everly* • Grant Mitchell *Charlie Vane* • George Barbier *Mr Randall* • Elizabeth Patterson *Mrs Randall* ■ *Dir* Wesley Ruggles • *Scr* Maurine Watkins, Milton Gropper, from a story by Edmund Goulding, Benjamin Glazer

No Man of Her Own ★★★

Melodrama 1950 · US · BW · 97mins

Barbara Stanwyck fires on all cylinders as the unmarried mother-to-be who adopts the identity of an also pregnant but much wealthier woman after the latter dies in a train crash. Just as she's enjoying her new life of deception, her baby's father shows up and starts blackmailing her. Given that the story is complete and utter tosh, and that John Lund is a lummox as Stanwyck's new beau, this *film noir* is gripping stuff. Remade 46 years later as *Mrs Winterbourne*, with the unlikely Ricki Lake taking the Stanwyck role. AT

Barbara Stanwyck *Helen Ferguson* • John Lund *Bill Harkness* • Jane Cowl *Mrs Harkness* • Phyllis Thaxter *Patrice Harkness* • Lyle Bettger *Stephen Morley* • Henry O'Neill *Mr Harkness* • Richard Denning *Hugh Harkness* ■ *Dir* Mitchell Leisen • *Scr* Sally Benson, Catherine Turney, from the novel *I Married a Dead Man* by William Irish [Cornell Woodrich]

No Man's Land ★★★ 15

Thriller 1987 · US · Colour · 100mins

Welcome to the "chop shop", a scrap yard where stolen cars are broken up and reassembled as new. This stylish use of the locale has rookie cop DB Sweeney going undercover in a Porsche garage. He becomes a close friend of crooked proprietor Charlie Sheen, a fast-lane traveller who dazzles our hero not only with his lifestyle, but also with his sister (Lara Harris). A low-budget thriller that nevertheless makes a big impact. TH. Contains swearing and violence. [video]

Charlie Sheen *Ted Varrick* • DB Sweeney *Benjy Taylor* • Randy Quaid *Lieutenant Vincent Bracey* • Lara Harris *Ann Varrick* • Bill Duke *Malcolm* • M Emmet Walsh *Captain Haun* ■ *Dir* Peter Werner • *Scr* Dick Wolf

No Man's Land ★★★ 15

Satirical black comedy
2001 · Bosnia/Fr/It/UK/Bel · Colour · 93mins

Winner of the Oscar for best foreign film, this is a bleak Balkan satire in which the intransigence of the combatants is both maddening and devastatingly funny. Trapped in a bunker with a booby-trapped corpse, Bosnian Branko Djuric and Serb Rene Bitorajac engage in pointless bouts of brinkmanship, while the media and the United Nation's peace-keeping forces look on with a dispiriting mix of self-aggrandisement and indifference. Debutant writer/director Danis Tanovic's observations on the nature of warfare in general and this conflict in particular are fairly orthodox, but his chronicling of the escalating chaos and its cynical resolution is astute. DP. In Bosnian, Croatian, English, French, Serbian and Serbo-Croat with English subtitles. [video] DVD

Branko Djuric *Chiki* • Rene Bitorajac *Nino* • Filip Sovagovic *Cera* • Georges Siatidis *Sergeant Marchand* • Serge-Henri Valcke *Captain Dubois* • Sacha Kremer *Michel* ■ *Dir/Scr* Danis Tanovic

No Mercy ★★★ 18

Thriller 1986 · US · Colour · 103mins

Richard Gere here stars to real effect in the film that prompted critics to note how much greyer, older and better he was. He plays a Chicago cop seeking vengeance in New Orleans following the death of his partner. Crime lord Jeroen Krabbé is his target and Kim Basinger is the gangster's reluctant moll, with whom Gere takes off into the Louisiana bayous for the rousing action finale. It's predictable hokum, but director Richard Pearce spins an artful story, helped by Gere's slick performance. TH. Contains swearing, violence, sex scenes and drug abuse. [video] DVD

Richard Gere *Eddie Jillette* • Kim Basinger *Michel Duval* • Jeroen Krabbé *Losado* • George Dzundza *Capt Stemkowski* • Gary Basaraba *Joe Collins* • Ray Sharkey *Angles Ryan* • William Atherton *Allan Deveneux* • Terry Kinney *Paul Deveneux* ■ *Dir* Richard Pearce • *Scr* Jim Carabatsos

No Mercy ★★

Drama 1994 · Peru/Mex/Fr · Colour · 117mins

In transferring the action of Dostoyevsky's *Crime and Punishment* to modern-day Lima, Francisco José Lombardi clearly seeks to link the central character's torment with the problems facing Peruvian society. However, such is the narrowness of his approach to both murderous student Diego Bertie's soul-crushing guilt and devout prostitute Adriana Davila's guileless promise of redemption that there's little room left to explore the squalor and exploitation that drove Bertie to kill his landlady and steal her cash. DP. In Spanish with English subtitles.

Diego Bertie *Ramon Romano* • Adriana Davila *Sonia Martinez* • Jorge Chiarella *Mayor Portillo* • Hernan Romero *Alejandro Velaochaga* • Marcello Rivera *Julian Razuri* • Mariella Trejos *Senora Aliaga* ■ *Dir* Francisco José Lombardi • *Scr* Augusto Cabada, from the novel *Crime and Punishment* by Fyodor Dostoyevsky

No Minor Vices ★★

Comedy 1948 · US · BW · 95mins

This is a slight piece about an eccentric artist who attempts to separate a stuffy paediatrician from his wife. The doctor is Dana Andrews, the artist is dashing foreigner Louis Jourdan, and the lady in question is the charming Lilli Palmer. Oh, and Jane Wyatt's in there, too, as Andrews's devoted assistant. This type of time-wasting tosh needs a far lighter touch than that of Lewis Milestone. TS

Dana Andrews *Dr Perry Aswell* • Lilli Palmer *April Aswell* • Louis Jourdan *Otavio Quaglini* • Jane Wyatt *Miss Darlington* • Norman Lloyd *Dr Sturdivant* • Bernard Gorcey *Mr Zitzfleisch* ■ *Dir* Lewis Milestone • *Scr* Arnold Manoff

No My Darling Daughter ★★ U

Romantic comedy 1961 · UK · BW · 96mins

The quality cast deserves something far better than this tepid British comedy. Juliet Mills does a feisty turn as the tomboy daughter of Michael Redgrave, whose romance with an American student leads to scandal. Both Redgrave and Roger Livesey are totally wasted as director Ralph Thomas squeezes all the fun out of a screwball plot that would have been meat and drink to even the most plodding Hollywood hack. DP

Michael Redgrave *Sir Matthew Carr* • Michael Craig *Thomas Barclay* • Juliet Mills *Tansy Carr* • Roger Livesey *General Henry Barclay* • Rad Fulton *Cornelius Allingham* • Renee Houston *Miss Yardley* • Joan Sims *Second typist* • Peter Barkworth *Charles* ■ *Dir* Ralph Thomas • *Scr* Frank Harvey, from the play *Handful of Tansy* by Harold Brooke, Kay Bannerman

No Name on the Bullet ★★★★ U

Western 1959 · US · Colour · 76mins

A mean and moody Audie Murphy is brilliantly cast in this study in paranoia as a gunman on the prowl, threatening a whole town, whose inhabitants each seem to have a guilty reason to be the assassin's potential victim. Director Jack Arnold keeps the action tense and the supporting cast, particularly Whit Bissell, is excellent. This Universal western contains plenty to watch even if you don't care for baby-faced Second World War hero Murphy. TS

Audie Murphy *John Gant* • Joan Evans *Anne Benson* • Charles Drake *Dr Luke Canfield* • RG Armstrong *Asa Canfield* • Virginia Grey *Mrs Fraden* • Warren Stevens *Lou Fraden* • Whit Bissell *Thad Pierce* • Karl Swenson *Earl Stricker* ■ *Dir* Jack Arnold • *Scr* Gene L Coon, from a story by Howard Amacker

No, No, Nanette ★★ U

Musical 1940 · US · BW · 96mins

In the early 1940s, British producer/director Herbert Wilcox and Anna Neagle (who married in 1943) landed a contract with RKO, but their combined career in Hollywood was short-lived. Not surprising given this filming of the 1925 Broadway musical, in which the best things were songs such as *Tea for Two* and *I Want to Be Happy*. Unwisely, Wilcox relegated the score to the background at the expense of the silly plot about a young woman who helps her uncle out of his financial and amorous difficulties. RB

Anna Neagle *Nanette* • Richard Carlson *Tom* • Victor Mature *William* • Roland Young *Mr Smith* • Helen Broderick *Mrs Smith* • ZaSu Pitts *Pauline* • Eve Arden *Winnie* • Tamara *Sonya* • Billy Gilbert *Styles* ■ *Dir* Herbert Wilcox • *Scr* Ken Englund, from the musical by Frank Mandel, Otto Harbach, Emil Nyitray, Vincent Youmans

No, Not Yet ★★

Drama 1993 · Jpn · Colour · 134mins

A meditation on death, and the final film directed by famed Japanese director Akira Kurosawa, then aged 83. The film's hero is a university professor who decides to give up teaching for writing. The setting, though, is the Second World War and its aftermath, during which the professor and his wife lose their home in a bombing raid, though most drama comes from the heartache caused by a missing cat. It's a long, philosophical and very talkative movie that may entrance the director's admirers but will test the patience of more casual viewers. AT. A Japanese language film.

Hisashi Igawa *Takayama* • Kyoko Kagawa *Professor's wife* • Tatsuo Matsumura *Professor Hyakken Uehida* • George Tokoro *Amaki* ■ *Dir/Scr* Akira Kurosawa

No Nukes ★★

Concert documentary
1980 · US · Colour · 103mins

Over five nights at Madison Square Garden in September 1979, and at an outdoor rally in Battery Park, a socially conscious group of rockers got together for pro-solar energy, anti-nuclear benefit concerts. Despite an impressive list of artists – including Bruce Springsteen, Carly Simon, Bonnie Raitt, Jackson Browne – this well-intentioned rockumentary is a thinly stretched effort, with only Bruce Springsteen shaking any life into the "right on" blandness. AJ

Dir Julian Schlossberg, Danny Goldberg [Dan Goldberg], Anthony Potenza

No One Could Protect Her ★★★ 18

Thriller 1996 · US · Colour · 87mins

A superior slice of TV-movie suspense, which almost inevitably is based on true events. Joanna Kerns plays a victim recruited by the police to draw out a rapist/killer who has been stalking a quiet, respectable neighbourhood. The performances are uniformly strong and director Larry Shaw orchestrates the action with confidence. JF. Contains some violence and swearing. [video] DVD

Joanna Kerns *Jessica Rayner* • Anthony John Denison *Dan Rayner* • Dan Lauria *Detective Greg Corning* • Christina Cox *Detective Elizabeth Jordan* • Dan Lett *Nick Foster* ■ *Dir* Larry Shaw • *Scr* Bruce Miller

No One Man ★

Drama 1932 · US · BW · 71mins

Wealthy Florida divorcee Carole Lombard, eager to snare a new husband, is torn between two contenders: Ricardo Cortez, handsome and oozing charm but a feckless creature of questionable character, and the less dazzling but decent and dependable Paul Lukas, an Austrian physician. How Lombard, her natural charms dulled under the weight of a trivial, unconvincing and boring script, makes her choice takes up the thankfully short running time of Lloyd Corrigan's pointless film. RK

Carole Lombard *Penelope Newbold* • Ricardo Cortez *Bill Hanaway* • Paul Lukas *Dr Karl Bemis* • Juliette Compton *Sue Folsom* • George Barbier *Alfred Newbold* • Virginia Hammond *Mrs Newbold* ■ *Dir* Lloyd Corrigan • *Scr* Sidney Buchman, Agnes Brand Leahy, Percy Heath, from the novel by Rupert Hughes

No One Writes to the Colonel ★★★

Period drama
1999 · Mex/Sp/Fr · Colour · 118mins

While this compassionate study of love in a time of adversity is restrained by his usual baroque standards, Mexican director Arturo Ripstein still overcooks this adaptation of Gabriel Garcia Marquez's novel. Driven to the brink of despair by the murder of his son, Fernando Lujan's melancholic optimist invests heavily in his cock-fighting dreams and the overdue military pension that his asthmatic wife, Marisa Paredes, knows will never come. The acting is impeccable, while Ripstein expertly captures the ambience of their 1940s coastal town. Yet the director allows inconsequential subplots and slack pacing to dissipate the story's dramatic intensity. DP. A Spanish language film.

Fernando Lujan *The Colonel* • Salma Hayek *Julia* • Marisa Paredes *Lola* • Ernesto Yanez

Don Sabas • Rafael Inclan *Father Angel* ■ *Dir* Arturo Ripstein • *Scr* Paz Alicia Garciadiego, from the novel by Gabriel Garcia Marquez

No Orchids for Miss Blandish ★

Crime drama 1948 · UK · BW · 104mins

This British gangster film was once vilified for its violence and immorality – banned in many parts of Britain and naturally a huge hit everywhere else. George Melachrino's score is apt, but most of the dialogue and acting are phoney, the plot developments are ludicrous and the film never begins to explore the sexual attraction that Linden Travers's spoiled brat feels for her kidnapper, Jack LaRue. The same story forms the basis of Robert Aldrich's *The Grissom Gang*. AE

Jack LaRue *Slim Grisson* • Hugh McDermott *Fenner* • Linden Travers *Miss Blandish* • Walter Crisham *Eddie* • Leslie Bradley *Bailey* • Sidney James *Ted/Barman* • Lily Molnar *Ma Grissom* ■ *Dir* St John L Clowes • *Scr* St John L Clowes, from the novel by James Hadley Chase

No Ordinary Summer ★★ 15

Drama 1994 · US · Colour · 107mins

A decent coming-of-age story about a black New York teenager spending the summer of 1976 with wealthy relatives in snooty Martha's Vineyard. The characters are a shade underwritten, and less is made of the clash of cultures than might have been. But the 1970s fashions are fun to look at, and there are decent performances from the cast of rising black stars. DA. Contains nudity, sex scenes, drug abuse and swearing. DVD

Larenz Tate *Drew Tate* • Joe Morton *Kenny Tate* • Suzzanne Douglas *Brenda Tate* • Glynn Turman *Spencer Phillips* • Vanessa Bell Calloway *Frances Phillips* ■ *Dir* Matty Rich • *Scr* Trey Ellis, Paris Qualles

No Place for Jennifer ★★

Drama 1949 · UK · BW · 91mins

It's hard to believe that this tosh was one of the biggest box-office hits of 1949. Eleven-year-old Janette Scott (daughter of Thora Hird) plays the girl whose vanishing act brings about a change of heart in divorcing parents Leo Genn and Rosamund John. Scriptwriter and future director J Lee Thompson obviously had little enthusiasm for the task of adapting this penny-dreadful, while director Henry Cass fails to inject any sense of urgency into the search. DP

Leo Genn *William* • Rosamund John *Rachel Kershaw* • Beatrice Campbell *Paula* • Guy Middleton *Brian Stewart* • Janette Scott *Jennifer* • Anthony Nicholls *Baxter* ■ *Dir* Henry Cass • *Scr* J Lee Thompson, from the novel *No Difference to Me* by Phyllis Hambledon

No Place to Go ★★★★

Drama 2000 · Ger · BW · 100mins

Starkly shot in hope-sapping monochrome, this film *à clef* was inspired by the last days of director Oskar Röhler's mother, Gisela Elsner. But it's much more than just a moving portrait of a woman in crisis, as it also explores the fears and expectations of Germans on either side of the crumbling Berlin Wall in 1989. Driven to drink by her waning popularity as a novelist in the East, Hannelore Elsner is forced to reassess her implicit faith in Marxism as she encounters the frustrations of ordinary people during a dazed meander around Berlin's run-down suburbs. Personal, perceptive and superbly performed. DP. In German with English subtitles.

Hannelore Elsner *Hanna Flanders* • Vadim Glowna *Bruno* ■ *Dir/Scr* Oskar Röhler

No Place to Hide ★★★ 18

Thriller 1992 · US · Colour · 92mins

Some critics claim that Kris Kristofferson is so wooden, you can get splinters just watching him. But that's unfair. The country singer may not be the most dynamic of actors, but he boasts a certain screen presence which is evident in this fast-moving thriller, where his gruff manliness is in nice contrast to Drew Barrymore's precocious chirpiness. He's a rough, tough cop; she's a kid hunted by a murderer who's already slaughtered her sister. DA

Kris Kristofferson *Joe Garvey* • Drew Barrymore *Tinsel Hanley* • Martin Landau *Frank McCay* • OJ Simpson *Allie Wheeler* • Dey Young *Karen* • Bruce Weitz *Captain Nelson Silva* ■ *Dir/Scr* Richard Danus

No Problem! ★★★

Comedy 1975 · Fr · Colour · 105mins

This rousing romp tosses slapstick and farce into the road movie formula to produce an hilarious and surprisingly sophisticated chase comedy. Heading for a Swiss rendezvous, Jean Lefebvre's womanising innocent is blissfully unaware of the corpse his son (Bernard Menez) has stashed in the boot of his car. The son sets off in hot pursuit with the stranger (Miou-Miou) who had asked him to dispose of the body. Maintaining a cracking pace, director Georges Lautner keeps the gag count high without sacrificing too much character depth. DP. French dialogue dubbed into English.

Miou-Miou *Anita* • Jean Lefebvre *Michalon* • Bernard Menez *Jean-Pierre* • Henri Guybet *Daniel* • Anny Duperey *Janis* ■ *Dir* Georges Lautner • *Scr* Jean-Marie Poiré

No Regrets for Our Youth ★★★★

Political drama based on a true story 1946 · Jpn · BW · 110mins

Even though its critical reception was decidedly mixed, Akira Kurosawa's sixth feature marked his breakthrough as a major film-maker. Political subjects were never to be his strong point, but his conviction that postwar Japanese society needed to rediscover its self-respect drew him to the fact-based story of the young city sophisticate (played with a mix of romantic innocence and indomitable spirit by Setsuko Hara) who finds the will to survive while slaving as a peasant after her father is dismissed from his university post for his communist views and her lover is executed as a spy. DP. In Japanese with English subtitles.

Denjiro Okochi *Professor Yagihara* • Eiko Miyoshi *Madame Yagihara, his wife* • Setsuko Hara *Yukie Yagihara, his daughter* • Susumu Fujita *Ryukichi Noge* ■ *Dir* Akira Kurosawa • *Scr* Eijiro Hisaita, Akira Kurosawa

No Resting Place ★★

Drama 1950 · UK · BW · 85mins

Pioneer film historian and left-wing documentary maker Paul Rotha's film has as its strongest aspect the creation of a realistic background to the story, the fanciful tale of Irish tinker Michael Gough, who accidentally kills a gamekeeper. After a brawl with the police, he's heading for the gallows, but he escapes, briefly, to enjoy a reunion with his wife and child. Despite sympathetic observation and good performances, it is rather naive and cannot compare with Rotha's earlier documentary work. BB

Michael Gough *Alec Kyle* • Eithne Dunne *Meg Kyle* • Noel Purcell *Guard Mannigan* • Brian O'Higgins *Tom Kyle* • Jack MacGowran *Billy Kyle* • Diana Campbell *Bess Kyle* • Maureen O'Sullivan *Nan Kyle* ■ *Dir* Paul Rotha • *Scr* Gerard Healy, Colin Lesslie, Michael Orrom, Paul Rotha, from the novel by Ian Niall

No Retreat, No Surrender ★★ 15

Martial arts action drama 1985 · US/HK · Colour · 94mins

With a plot reminiscent of *The Karate Kid*, this has Kurt McKinney as a martial arts-enthusiast. He is victimised by his peers until he acquires an unexpected ally – the ghost of Bruce Lee. Almost charming in its silliness, the movie gets close to the so-bad-it's-good level but too often takes itself too seriously. This is most noteworthy as Jean-Claude Van Damme's first real role; two sequels followed. KB DVD

Kurt McKinney *Jason Stillwell* • Jean-Claude Van Damme *Karl Brezdin/Ivan the Russian* • JW Fails *RJ Madison* • Kathie Sileno *Kelly Reilly* • Kent Lipham *Scott* ■ *Dir* Corey Yuen • *Scr* Keith Strandberg, from a story by Ng See Yuen, Corey Yuen

No Road Back ★★

Crime melodrama 1957 · UK · BW · 62mins

Sean Connery had been a lifeguard and a coffin polisher before he began acting. He must have doubted the wisdom of giving up the day job after his first experience of film-making, as this is almost an identikit "quota quickie". The lead is a skid-row American star (Skip Homeier), the plot is a threadbare crime caper, the sets are cheap and much of the action takes place in dank inner city backstreets. Crooks Connery and Alfie Bass are convincing enough, with their botched robbery causing Homeier to question the honesty of his blind and deaf, club-owning ma. DP

Skip Homeier *John Railton* • Paul Carpenter *Clem Hayes* • Patricia Dainton *Beth* • Norman Wooland *Inspector Harris* • Margaret Rawlings *Mrs Railton* • Alfie Bass *Rudge Haven* • Sean Connery *Spike* ■ *Dir* Montgomery Tully • *Scr* Charles Leeds, Montgomery Tully, from the play *Madame Tictac* by Falkland D Cary, Philip Weathers

No Room at the Inn ★★★

Second World War drama 1948 · UK · BW · 82mins

A group of child evacuees in Second World War England find themselves in the care of the cruelly unsympathetic, alcoholic Freda Jackson, who keeps them in conditions of squalor, neglect and semi-starvation while she imbibes a steady diet of gin. Poet Dylan Thomas co-wrote the screenplay for this nasty but effective view of human nature at its worst, in which Jackson (repeating her successful West End performance) is compelling. RK

Freda Jackson *Mrs Voray* • Joy Shelton *Judith Drave* • Hermione Baddeley *Mrs Waters* • Joan Dowling *Norma Bates* • Ann Stephens *Mary O'Rane* • Harcourt Williams *Reverend Allworth* • Dora Bryan ■ *Dir* Daniel Birt • *Scr* Ivan Foxwell, Dylan Thomas, from the play by Joan Temple

No Room for the Groom ★★

Comedy 1952 · US · BW · 82mins

Piper Laurie is the young wife of a GI who moves in with her family while he is off on duty. When her husband (Tony Curtis) returns, he finds himself surrounded by her relatives, including Spring Byington as the mother trying to marry her off to someone else (Don DeFore). The breezy and attractive young leads help to keep this idiotic, frenzied and only mildly amusing comedy alive. RK

Tony Curtis *Alvah Morrell* • Piper Laurie *Lee Kingshead* • Don DeFore *Herman Strouple* • Spring Byington *Mamma Kingshead* • Jack Kelly *Will Stubbins* ■ *Dir* Douglas Sirk • *Scr* Joseph Hoffman, from the novel *My True Love* by Darwin L Teilhet

No Sad Songs for Me ★★★

Melodrama 1950 · US · BW · 88mins

The wistful Margaret Sullavan was a rare and special talent, and this was her last film, a Columbia melodrama about a dying woman preparing her family for her untimely but inevitable death. Sullavan makes this trite material unbearably moving, and there is real truth in her portrayal: tragic but uplifting, sad yet inspirational. Wendell Corey and Natalie Wood play the rest of the family, and Viveca Lindfors is admirable in support, but the film belongs totally to Sullavan. TS

Margaret Sullavan *Mary Scott* • Wendell Corey *Brad Scott* • Viveca Lindfors *Chris Radna* • Natalie Wood *Polly Scott* • John McIntire *Dr Ralph Frene* • Ann Doran *Louise Spears* • Richard Quine *Brownie* • Jeanette Nolan *Mona Frene* ■ *Dir* Rudolph Maté • *Scr* Howard Koch, from a story by Ruth Southard

No Sex Please – We're British ★★ PG

Comedy 1973 · UK · Colour · 93mins

One of the West End's longest running comic farces arrived on the screen virtually intact, but with a significantly different leading man. Whereas Michael Crawford had consolidated both career and image by instigating the gauche lead on stage, in the film the role went to the diminutive British comedian Ronnie Corbett. Corbett does well by the hackneyed plot, and under-rated director Cliff Owen keeps up the pace. TS

Ronnie Corbett *Brian Runnicles* • Beryl Reid *Bertha* • Arthur Lowe *Mr Bromley* • Ian Ogilvy *David Hunter* • Susan Penhaligon *Penny Hunter* • David Swift *Inspector Paul* • Cheryl Hall *Daphne* • Michael Bates *Needham* ■ *Dir* Cliff Owen • *Scr* Anthony Marriott, Johnnie Mortimer, Brian Cooke, from the play by Anthony Marriott, Alistair Foot

No Small Affair ★★ 15

Romantic comedy 1984 · US · Colour · 98mins

A teenage photographer develops an obsessive crush for an up-and-coming rock singer and goes to stalker-like lengths to get her to like him. This patchy tale has its clever and funny moments, but it also has its stupid ones, and the overall impression isn't improved by the basic unlikeability of the characters. The film could earn a third star for the calibre of its cast which, in addition to Jon Cryer and Demi Moore, also features early appearances by Tim Robbins and Jennifer Tilly. DA

Jon Cryer *Charles Cummings* • Demi Moore *Laura Victor* • George Wendt *Jake* • Peter Frechette *Leonard* • Elizabeth Daily *Susan* • Ann Wedgeworth *Joan Cummings* • Jeffrey Tambor *Ken* • Tim Robbins *Nelson* • Jennifer Tilly *Mona* ■ *Dir* Jerry Schatzberg • *Scr* Charles Bolt, Terrence Mulcahy, Craig Bolotin, from a story by Charles Bolt

No Smoking ★ U

Comedy 1954 · UK · BW · 72mins

A small-town boffin comes up with a swallowable version of the nicotine patch, and then wonders why the tobacco giants will stop at nothing to put a stop to his discovery. Notable only for its anti-smoking theme in a period where no one bothered about puffing away on a cigarette, this gentle comedy ends up a wasted opportunity, though the cast give their all. JF

Reg Dixon *Reg Bates* • Belinda Lee *Miss Tonkins* • Lionel Jeffries *George Pogson* • Myrtle Rowe *Milly* • Ruth Trouncer *Joyce* • Peter Martyn *Hal* ■ *Dir* Henry Cass • *Scr* Kenneth R Hayes, Phil Park, from a TV play by Rex Rientis, George Moresby-White

No Surrender ★ 15

Black comedy 1986 · UK · Colour · 99mins

This offensive little tale purports to be black comedy but verges on the tasteless. A Liverpool nightclub owner plays host to a party of Irish OAPs with entertainment provided by, among others, Elvis Costello (in a cameo role). Problem is, they're a warring bunch of Catholics and Protestants, and the evening threatens to be explosive. Alan Bleasdale's script isn't bad as much as misdirected – as are the talents of Joanne Whalley. LH

Michael Angelis *Mike Moriarty* • Avis Bunnage *Martha Gorman* • JG Devlin *George Corman* • James Ellis *Paddy Burke* • Tom Georgeson *Mr Ross* • Bernard Hill *Bernard* • Ray McAnally *Billy McRacken* • Joanne Whalley *Cheryl* • Elvis Costello *Rosco De Ville* ■ *Dir* Peter K Smith • *Scr* Alan Bleasdale

No Time for Comedy ★★★

Comedy drama 1940 · US · BW · 92mins

One of those romantic comedies set in the cosy world of Broadway theatreland, this stars James Stewart as a playwright who's down in the dumps because of a midlife crisis that has leaked into his work. Rosalind Russell co-stars as his acerbic but uncomplaining wife. It's directed by William Keighley with the same smooth-paced energy that he brought to many gangster movies. TH

James Stewart *Gaylord Esterbrook* • Rosalind Russell *Linda Esterbrook* • Charlie Ruggles [Charles Ruggles] *Philo Swift* • Genevieve Tobin *Amanda Swift* • Allyn Joslyn *Morgan Carrel, theatrical director* • Clarence Kolb *Richard Benson* ■ *Dir* William Keighley • *Scr* Julius J Epstein, Philip G Epstein, from the play by SN Behrman

No Time for Love ★★★ U

Romantic comedy 1943 · US · BW · 83mins

Claudette Colbert and Fred MacMurray star in yet another romantic comedy that revolves around hostility which is really true love. This time around, she's a professional photographer and he's the foreman of a tunnel-digging crew who becomes her assistant, inevitably leading to complications. The snappy screenplay, tailor-made for the two attractive stars, veers slightly more towards slapstick than sophistication, but is lent gloss by Paramount's first-rung production values and direction from the stylish Mitchell Leisen. RK

Claudette Colbert *Katherine Grant* • Fred MacMurray *Jim Ryan* • Ilka Chase *Hoppy Grant* • Richard Haydn *Roger, composer* • Paul McGrath *Henry Fulton, magazine publisher* • June Havoc *Darlene, chorus girl* ■ *Dir* Mitchell Leisen • *Scr* Claude Binyon, Warren Duff, from a story by Robert Lees

No Time for Sergeants ★★★ U

Comedy 1958 · US · BW · 114mins

Andy Griffith starred in the long-running Broadway play and in this screen adaptation, using his Carolina drawl to good effect as the simple-minded hillbilly drafted into the air force. He teams up with Nick Adams and they both manage to fall out of their plane and then attend their own military funeral. Directed by the veteran Mervyn LeRoy, there's more than a touch of Laurel and Hardy, as well as the Marx Brothers' brand of irreverence, about this comic caper. AT

Andy Griffith *Will Stockdale* • Myron McCormick *Sergeant King* • Nick Adams *Ben Whitledge* • Murray Hamilton *Irvin Blanchard* • Howard Smith *General Bush* • Will Hutchins *Lieutenant Bridges* • Don Knotts *Manual Dexterity Corporal* ■ *Dir* Mervyn LeRoy • *Scr* John Lee Mahin, from the play by Ira Levin, from the novel by Mac Hyman

No Time for Tears ★★ U

Medical drama 1957 · UK · Colour · 85mins

What else could you call a film whose sole intention is to have you blubbing your eyes out from the off? Anna Neagle stars in this mawkish account of life in a children's hospital. If the triumphs and tragedies of the kiddies don't have you reaching for tissues, then the torrid love life of nurse Sylvia Syms certainly will. The members of the cast work minor miracles despite the string of clichés. DP

Anna Neagle *Matron Eleanor Hammond* • George Baker *Nigel Barnes* • Sylvia Syms *Margaret* • Anthony Quayle *Dr Seagrave* • Flora Robson *Sister Birch* • Alan White *Dr Hugh Storey* • Joan Sims *Sister O'Malley* ■ *Dir* Cyril Frankel • *Scr* Anne Burnaby

No Time to Die ★★ U

Second World War drama 1958 · UK · Colour · 104mins

Set during the campaign in the Libyan desert, American hunk Victor Mature plays an American who serves as a sergeant in the British army. He organises an escape from an Italian PoW camp and is then captured and tortured by a shifty sheikh in league with the Nazis. Every racial stereotype in the book stands to attention as Mature lurches from one heroic deed to the next, culminating in a joust with a Panzer tank. AT

Victor Mature *Sgt David Thatcher* • Leo Genn *Sgt Kendall* • Anthony Newley *Tiger Noakes* • Bonar Colleano *Pole* • Luciana Paluzzi *Carola* • Anne Aubrey *Italian girl* ■ *Dir* Terence Young • *Scr* Richard Maibaum, Terence Young

No Trace ★★★

Crime thriller 1950 · UK · BW · 75mins

This is a better-than-average "quota quickie" from John Gilling, in which crime writer Hugh Sinclair tries to cover his tracks (and delude snooping cop John Laurie) after he kills a blackmailer from his gangland past. As we know from the outset that he won't get away with it, the fun lies in watching him make the slips that give him away to secretary Dinah Sheridan and her flatfoot admirer, Barry Morse. DP

Hugh Sinclair *Robert Southley* • Dinah Sheridan *Linda* • John Laurie *Inspector MacDougall* • Barry Morse *Harrison* • Dora Bryan *Maisie* ■ *Dir/Scr* John Gilling

No Trees in the Street ★★ PG

Drama 1958 · UK · BW · 92mins

Although a stalwart of stage and TV, screenwriter Ted Willis worked less in movies and it rather shows in this ludicrously sentimental adaptation of his own play. It was unlucky enough to be released in the same year that British cinema entered its great "kitchen sink" phase, but this thin-cut slice of street life could never feel anything but stale. Herbert Lom tries to inject a little menace as a small-time hoodlum, but, confronted with sickly sweet Sylvia Syms and teen tearaway Melvyn Hayes, he succumbs to the mediocrity all around him. DP

Sylvia Syms *Hetty* • Herbert Lom *Wilkie* • Ronald Howard *Frank* • Stanley Holloway *Kipper* • Joan Miller *Jess* • Melvyn Hayes *Tommy* ■ *Dir* J Lee Thompson • *Scr* Ted Willis, from his play

No Way Back ★ 18

Crime thriller 1996 · US/Jpn · Colour · 87mins

In this preposterous crime thriller, Russell Crowe plays an FBI agent who, after a sting operation goes wrong in the most unbelievable manner, tries to bring a yakuza boss (Etsushi Toyokawa) from New York to Los Angeles on a commercial flight. The boss gets loose and forces the plane down on a small field in the mountains. Somehow the agent, the crime boss and a stewardess (Helen Slater at her most annoying) end up pushing a broken car around the desert. ST DVD

Russell Crowe *Zack Grant* • Helen Slater *Mary* • Etsushi Toyokawa *Yuji* • Michael Lerner *Frank Serlano* • Kyusaku Shimada *Tetsuro* • Kristopher Logan *Mr Contingency* ■ *Dir/Scr* Frank Cappello

No Way Home ★★★ 18

Crime drama 1996 · US · Colour · 96mins

A grim yet uplifting story of rehabilitation and redemption, this is shot through with a dynamic tone and moody atmosphere by independent director Buddy Giovinazzo. Fresh out of prison, Tim Roth moves in with his older brother James Russo in an attempt to go straight. Alas, he's soon sucked back into the criminal life. Almost Pinteresque in the way silences convey as much heart-rending truth as the succinct dialogue, this touching moral tale is an uncompromising character study given a poignant level of honesty. Deborah Kara Unger steals the picture as Roth's suspicious sister-in-law. AJ DVD

Tim Roth *Joey* • James Russo *Tommy* • Deborah Kara Unger *Lorraine* • Bernadette Penotti *Ronnie* • Larry Romano *Carter* ■ *Dir/Scr* Buddy Giovinazzo

No Way Out ★★★

Drama 1950 · US · BW · 101mins

Joseph L Mankiewicz's drama about racial prejudice stars Sidney Poitier, launching his career as a persecuted doctor at a municipal hospital. The head of Fox, Darryl F Zanuck, said the picture would be as "real as sweat, dealing with the absolute blood and guts of negro hating." Mankiewicz said it was "the first time racial violence was shown on the screen except for *Birth of a Nation* in modern times." Both were rather overblown statements, and so is the picture, not least because of Richard Widmark's snarling, racist villain and the contrived, if ironic conclusion. AT

Richard Widmark *Ray Biddle* • Linda Darnell *Edie* • Stephen McNally *Dr Wharton* • Sidney Poitier *Dr Luther Brooks* • Mildred Joanne Smith *Cora* • Harry Bellaver *George Biddle* ■ *Dir* Joseph L Mankiewicz • *Scr* Joseph L Mankiewicz, Lesser Samuels

No Way Out ★★★★ 15

Thriller 1986 · US · Colour · 109mins

Famous for its limousine sex scene, this Kevin Costner spy thriller provides a gripping insight into the corridors of US power. This is a highly intelligent, intriguing movie containing some wonderful performances, most notably from Gene Hackman as an icily manipulative politician. For once, Costner's tendency to stay emotionally removed from his character pays dividends as we are left guessing about the man right up to the final reel. The "surprise" twist is a trifle daft, but overall this is a major treat. SH. Contains swearing, violence and nudity. DVD

Kevin Costner *Lieutenant Commander Tom Farrell* • Gene Hackman *David Brice* • Sean Young *Susan Atwell* • Will Patton *Scott Pritchard* • Howard Duff *Senator Willy Duvall* • George Dzundza *Dr Sam Hesselman* • Jason Bernard *Major Donovan* • Iman *Nina Beka* • Fred Dalton Thompson *Marshall* ■ *Dir* Roger Donaldson • *Scr* Robert Garland, from the novel *The Big Clock* by Kenneth Fearing

No Way to Treat a Lady ★★★★

Black comedy 1968 · US · Colour · 107mins

Romantic comedies don't come much blacker than this immensely enjoyable tale of a serial strangler, incarnated in several guises by Rod Steiger. George Segal plays a Jewish cop, hysterically henpecked by his mother Eileen Heckart, while co-star Lee Remick has never looked lovelier as the sophisticated Lincoln Center guide who graduates from witness to intended victim. New York's the star, too, thanks to Jack Priestley's glossy photography, which includes interiors in both Joe Allen's and Sardi's. TS

Rod Steiger *Christopher Gill* • Lee Remick *Kate Palmer* • George Segal *Morris Brummel* • Eileen Heckart *Mrs Brummel* • Murray Hamilton *Inspector Haines* • Michael Dunn *Mr Kupperman* ■ *Dir* Jack Smight • *Scr* John Gay, from the novel by William Goldman

Noah's Ark ★★ U

Biblical epic 1928 · US · BW · 135mins

This early Warner Bros epic parallels a First World War story with the flooding of the temple in the Old Testament; the cast, headed by George O'Brien and Dolores Costello, play roles in both periods. Some of the flood water was for real and reputedly cost the lives of three extras, though the miniatures of a crumbling city are rather obvious. Silent and sound versions were issued, the latter adding contrived banter in the trenches. AE

Dolores Costello *Mary/Miriam* • George O'Brien *Travis/Japheth* • Noah Beery *Nickoloff/King Nephilim* • Louise Fazenda *Hilda/Tavern maid* • Guinn "Big Boy" Williams *Al/Ham* • Paul McAllister *Minister/Noah* • Myrna Loy *Dancer/Slave girl* ■ *Dir* Michael Curtiz • *Scr* Anthony Coldeway, from a story by Darryl F Zanuck

Nob Hill ★★

Musical 1945 · US · Colour · 95mins

Nob Hill is where the nobs used to live in San Francisco, an area now the preserve of the city's swishest hotels. But this brash Fox musical is pretty downmarket, starring George Raft as the saloon owner who jilts torch singer Vivian Blaine for socialite Joan Bennett. The songs are strictly B-sides and Henry Hathaway's direction doesn't have the necessary light touch. Another drawback is Raft, never a convincing leading man, though he once laid claim to being the world's fastest Charleston dancer. AT

George Raft *Johnny Angelo* • Joan Bennett *Harriet Carruthers* • Vivian Blaine *Sally Templeton* • Peggy Ann Garner *Katie Flanagan* • Falstaff Openshaw [Alan Reed] *Dapper Jack Harrigan* • BS Pully *Joe the bartender* • Emil Coleman *Pianist* ■ *Dir* Henry Hathaway • *Scr* Wanda Tuchock, Norman Reilly Raine, from a story by Eleanore Griffin

Nobody Knows ★★★★ 12

Drama 2003 · Jpn · Colour · 140mins

In 1988, what was dubbed the "Affair of the Four Abandoned Children of Nishi-Sugamo" scandalised Japan and inspired Hirokazu Kore-eda's screenplay, which took 15 years to bring to the screen. The wait proved worthwhile, as this is a deeply moving study of juvenile endurance that earned Yuya Yagira the best actor prize at Cannes. As the oldest of the siblings left to fend for themselves by their mother, the 12-year-old displays both ingenuity and insecurity in trying to keep his secret from the outside world. Even more impressive, however, is Kore-eda's disjointed directorial style which mirrors the household's increasing pressures. DP. In Japanese with English subtitles. DVD

Yuya Yagira *Akira* • Ayu Kitaura *Kyoko* • Hiei Kimura *Shigeru* • Momoko Shimizu *Yuki* • Hanae Kan *Saki* ■ *Dir/Scr* Hirokazu Kore-eda [Hirokazu Koreeda]

Nobody Lives Forever ★★★

Romantic drama 1946 · US · BW · 99mins

Before method acting, John Garfield was doing it for real with a tough-talking style that seemed ad-libbed. It's that hard-bitten personality which saves this romance from sentimental stickiness. The star plays a conman who swindles rich widow Geraldine Fitzgerald, only to fall in love with his victim. Mills and Boon stuff, though Garfield transforms it into near-credible drama. Walter Brennan co-stars. TH

John Garfield *Nick Blake* • Geraldine Fitzgerald *Gladys Halvorsen* • Walter Brennan *Pop Gruber* • Faye Emerson *Toni* • George Coulouris *Doc Ganson* • George Tobias *Al Doyle* ■ *Dir* Jean Negulesco • *Scr* WR Burnett, from his story *I Wasn't Born Yesterday*

Nobody Runs Forever ★★ PG

Thriller 1968 · UK · Colour · 97mins

Rank threw together a motley array of B-list actors, plus Rod Taylor and Christopher Plummer, and let them fight it out among themselves with scant direction for this over-complicated yet weakly scripted thriller. The thrills are in distinctly short supply as an Australian cop is sent to London to arrest a dastardly diplomat for murder. SH [video]

Rod Taylor *Scobie Malone* • Christopher Plummer *Sir James Quentin* • Lilli Palmer *Sheila Quentin* • Camilla Sparv *Lisa Pretorius* • Daliah Lavi *Madame Cholon* • Franchot Tone *Ambassador Townsend* • Clive Revill *Joseph* • Lee Montague *Denzil* ■ *Dir* Ralph Thomas • *Scr* Wilfred Greatorex, from the novel *The High Commissioner* by Jon Cleary

Nobody Waved Goodbye ★★★

Drama 1964 · Can · BW · 84mins

This Canadian drama ventures into the mental jungle of the alienated teenager, dealing with youngster Peter Kastner and his problems with his parents and girlfriend (Julie Briggs). Keen insights and good acting make this a whole lot more pleasurable than others of the genre, while director Don Owen makes the adolescents comic and not merely self-absorbed. Owen revisited his characters, now grown up, in 1983's *Unfinished Business*. TH

Peter Kastner *Peter* • Julie Biggs *Julie* • Claude Rae *Father* • Toby Tarnow *Sister* • Charmion King *Mother* ■ *Dir/Scr* Don Owen

Nobody's Child ★★★★

Drama based on a true story
1986 · US · Colour · 100mins

The haunting isolation of mental illness is made vividly personal by the breathtaking performance of Marlo Thomas in this TV movie about Marie Balter, a woman who spent 20 harrowing years in a mental hospital until a compassionate doctor helped her regain her sanity. The first-rate script by Mary Gallagher and Ara Watson, sensitive direction by Lee Grant and Thomas's single-minded commitment to telling the story make this memorable and moving. MC

Marlo Thomas *Marie Balter* • Ray Baker *Joe Balter* • Caroline Kava *Dr Blackwell* • Kathy Baker *Lucy* • Blanche Baker *Shari* ■ *Dir* Lee Grant • *Scr* Mary Gallagher, Ara Watson

Nobody's Fool ★★★ 15

Romantic comedy
1986 · US · Colour · 102mins

A modest portrait of Arizona small-town life, with Rosanna Arquette as a waitress, aspiring actress and local "celebrity" learning to live with her chequered past. As she searches for love and redemption, Arquette's performance becomes a three-ring circus – funny here, touching there, veering off balance elsewhere. Sharply written by Beth Henley and co-starring Oscar-winner Louise Fletcher, it's a pleasing diversion, if lacking dramatic fireworks. AT. Contains swearing. [video]

Rosanna Arquette *Cassie* • Eric Roberts *Riley* • Mare Winningham *Pat* • Jim Youngs *Billy* • Louise Fletcher *Pearl* • Gwen Welles *Shirley* • Stephen Tobolowsky *Kirk* • Lewis Arquette *Mr Fry* ■ *Dir* Evelyn Purcell • *Scr* Beth Henley

Nobody's Fool ★★★★ 15

Drama 1994 · US · Colour · 105mins

Director Robert Benton's pleasingly low-key film stars Paul Newman as a grouchy town rogue who is forced to face up to his family responsibilities when his long-neglected son turns up for Thanksgiving. An old hand at this kind of heart-warming fare, Benton doesn't swamp it with sentimentality, allowing the crumpled charisma of Newman to carry the drama effortlessly. He is also well served by a starry cast in which the likes of Bruce Willis and Melanie Griffith line up with venerable character actors such as Jessica Tandy and Josef Sommer. JF. Contains swearing and brief nudity. [video]

Paul Newman *Donald Sullivan* • Jessica Tandy *Miss Beryl* • Bruce Willis *Carl Roebuck* • Melanie Griffith *Toby Roebuck* • Dylan Walsh *Peter* • Pruitt Taylor Vince *Rub Squeers* • Gene Saks *Wirf* • Josef Sommer *Clive Peoples Jr* ■ *Dir* Robert Benton • *Scr* Robert Benton, from the novel by Richard Russo

Nobody's Perfect ★★ U

Second World War comedy
1968 · US · Colour · 102mins

Blond action man Doug McClure teams with Nancy Kwan to star in this lame nautical comedy about exploits on board the USS *Bustard* stationed in the Pacific during the Second World War. Though amiable enough, the leads are seriously lightweight and struggle to bring this rather uninspired and unamusing movie to life. RT

Doug McClure *Doc Willoughby* • Nancy Kwan *Tomiko Momoyama* • James Whitmore *Capt Mike Riley* • James Shigeta *Toshi O'Hara* ■ *Dir* Alan Rafkin • *Scr* John DF Black, from the novel *The Crows of Edwina Hill* by Allan R Bosworth

Noce Blanche ★★ 15

Drama 1989 · Fr · Colour · 88mins

Films featuring pop stars can usually be labelled "For Fans Only", and this pouting piece of self-publicity thinly disguised as a tale of hopeless passion is a case in point. Aware that the camera loves her, French singing sensation Vanessa Paradis struts her stuff like a true pop video veteran, but doesn't display an ounce of emotion as a girl who suffers enough domestic strife to keep the social services busy for months. Bruno Cremer is slyly effective as the older man she stalks, but this is risible. DP. In French with English subtitles. Contains nudity. [video]

Bruno Cremer *François Hainaut* • Vanessa Paradis *Mathilde Tessier* • Ludmila Mikael *Catherine Hainaut* • François Négret *Carpentier* • Véronique Silver *Academic adviser* • Jean Dasté *Concierge* ■ *Dir/Scr* Jean-Claude Brisseau

Les Noces Rouges ★★★

Drama based on a true story
1973 · Fr/It · Colour · 90mins

Another variation on Claude Chabrol's pet theme of infidelity leading to murder, this was part of the cycle of films in which Stéphane Audran, Chabrol's then-wife, added spice by playing either the victim or cause of the crime. Chabrol based his own screenplay on a newspaper account of a *crime passionnel*, which got the film banned for a while as it concerned a real murder case. The film is elegant, cool and blackly humorous, and the playing of the unsympathetic characters is impeccable. RB. In French with English subtitles.

Michel Piccoli *Pierre Maury* • Stéphane Audran *Lucienne Delamare* • Claude Piéplu *Paul Delamare* • Eliana De Santis *Hélène* • Pipo Merisi *Berthier* ■ *Dir/Scr* Claude Chabrol

Nocturne ★★★

Crime drama 1946 · US · BW · 88mins

A wealthy, cold-blooded composer is shot, bringing a verdict of suicide. Detective George Raft sets out to investigate further and comes to suspect glamorous starlet Lynn Bari of killing him. This glossy *film noir*, slickly directed by Edwin L Marin, offers an appealing performance from Raft in cultivated good-guy mode; it also features a catch of well-played red herrings, led by Virginia Huston, Joseph Pevney and Diana Dors lookalike Myrna Dell. The nocturne of the title, composed by Leigh Harline, features heavily in the plot. RK

George Raft *Lt Joe Warne* • Lynn Bari *Frances Ransom* • Virginia Huston *Carol Page* • Joseph Pevney *Fingers* • Myrna Dell *Susan* ■ *Dir* Edwin L Marin • *Scr* Jonathan Latimer, from a story by Frank Fenton, Rowland Brown • *Music* Leigh Harline

Noi Albinoi ★★★ 15

Black comedy drama
2002 · Ice/Ger/UK/Den · Colour · 88mins

The striking visual contrast between the Arctic snowscapes and the confining interiors of an insular Icelandic backwater reinforces the sense of frustration experienced by non-conformist teenager Tomas Lemarquis in this offbeat comedy. Bored at school, yet fiercely bright, he's reduced to amusing himself with minor acts of rebellion until he hooks up with garage attendant Elin Hansdottir and decides to rob a bank and abscond to the city. However, things don't go according to plan and that sheer unpredictability is one of the delights of Dagur Kari's debut feature. DP. In Icelandic with English subtitles. [video] DVD

Tomas Lemarquis *Noi* • Throstur Leo Gunnarsson *Kiddi Beikon* • Elin Hansdottir *Iris* • Anna Fridriksdottir *Lina* • Hjalti Rognvaldsson *Oskar* • Petur Einarsson *priest* ■ *Dir/Scr* Dagur Kari

Noi Tre ★★★ PG

Biographical comedy drama
1984 · It · Colour · 85mins

In this interesting, but inconsistent, Italian feature, director Pupi Avati tries to create an adolescence for musical genius Mozart by following the course of a summer stay with a country aristocrat and his mischievous teenage kin. Although it impressively conveys a sense of the crushing level of expectation placed on Mozart's shoulders, the film falls down in its portrayal of the youthful brawls and pranks, and the romantic stirrings that could have made it more engaging. DP. An Italian language film. [video]

Christopher Davidson *Wolfgang Amadeus Mozart* • Lino Capolicchio *Leopoldo* • Gianni Cavina *Cousin* • Carlo Delle Piane *Count Pallovicini* • Ida DiBenedetto *Maria Caterino* • Dario Parisini *Giuseppe* • Barbara Rebeschini *Antonia-Leda* ■ *Dir* Pupi Avati • *Scr* Pupi Avati, Antonio Avati, Cesare Bornazzini

Noir et Blanc ★★★ 18

Drama 1986 · Fr · BW · 80mins

Claire Devers won the Caméra d'Or at Cannes for this debut feature. Shooting in monochrome, Devers explores the grey area between pain and pleasure as she chronicles the abrasive relationship between timid health centre accountant Francis Frappat and muscular masseur Jacques Martial. A study in sensuality without the sensationalism, this is an admirably controlled film, in which Devers dispassionately depicts both the unspoken emotion and the sadomasochistic desire that fuels the dangerous liaison. DP. A French language film. [video]

Francis Frappat *Antoine* • Jacques Martial *Dominique* • Josephine Fresson *Josy* • Marc Berman *Monsieur Roland* ■ *Dir* Claire Devers • *Scr* Claire Devers, Alain Bergala, from the story *Desire and the Black Masseur* by Tennessee Williams

Noises Off ★★★ 15

Comedy 1992 · US · Colour · 99mins

Robbed of its essentially theatrical device – the comic contrast between off-stage chaos and on-stage calculation – this American adaptation of Michael Frayn's West End play provides more than enough laughs to skim over the potholes of improbability. Peter Bogdanovich's quick-fire direction is matched and aided by some wondrously staccato performances, notably from Carol Burnett, Michael Caine and Christopher Reeve. Luvvies at play have never been so pompously vulnerable or so sympathetic. TH [video] DVD

Carol Burnett *Dotty Otley/Mrs Clackett* • Michael Caine *Lloyd Fellowes* • Denholm Elliott *Selsdon Mowbray/Burglar* • Julie Hagerty *Poppy Taylor* • Marilu Henner *Belinda Blair/Flavia Brent* • Mark Linn-Baker *Tim Allgood* • Christopher Reeve *Frederick Dallas/Philip Brent* • John Ritter *Garry Lejeune/Roger Tramplemain* ■ *Dir* Peter Bogdanovich • *Scr* Marty Kaplan, from the play by Michael Frayn

Nomads ★★★ 18

Supernatural thriller
1985 · US · Colour · 88mins

A fascinating and ambitious directorial debut from John McTiernan that bypasses the 1980s fad for excessive gore and sex and focuses instead on atmosphere and dramatic visual scares. Pierce Brosnan gives a restrained performance as a French anthropologist working in Los Angeles drawn to a disparate gang of street punks, led by one-time pop idol Adam Ant, who are in reality nomadic demons roaming the earth. McTiernan apparently based his tale on Inuit legends, though his intriguing supernatural chiller might perhaps have worked better as a shorter, made-for-TV movie. RS [video]

Pierce Brosnan *Pommier* • Lesley-Anne Down *Dr Flax* • Anna Maria Montecelli *Niki* • Adam Ant *Number One* • Hector Mercado *Ponytail* • Josie Cotton *Silver Ring* ■ *Dir/Scr* John McTiernan

None but the Brave ★★ PG

Second World War drama
1965 · US/Jpn · Colour · 101mins

You'd think Frank Sinatra might have chosen a better project for his only foray into direction than this wartime morality chestnut about enemy US and Japanese troops forced to co-exist on a remote Pacific island. As director, Sinatra succeeds moderately well, but the proceedings lose credibility during his moments on screen. TS [video]

Frank Sinatra *Chief Pharmacist's Mate Maloney* • Clint Walker *Captain Dennis Bourke* • Tommy Sands *Second Lieutenant Blair* • Brad Dexter *Sergeant Bleeker* • Tony Bill *Air Crewman Keller* • Tatsuya Mihashi *Lieutenant Kuroki* ■ *Dir* Frank Sinatra • *Scr* John Twist, Katsuya Susaki, from a story by Kikumaru Okuda • *Producer* Frank Sinatra

N

None but the Lonely Heart ★★ U

Drama 1944 · US · BW · 108mins

The great Cary Grant was surprisingly nominated for an Oscar for this pretentious drama, in which he's hopelessly miscast as the cockney drifter Ernie Mott, a punk philosopher who drifts easily into crime because of the poverty of his circumstances. The star found an affinity between Mott and his own upbringing and insisted the left-wing playwright Clifford Odets be hired as director. Unfortunately, the result is turgid and earnest. TS

Cary Grant *Ernie Mott* • Ethel Barrymore *Ma Mott* • Barry Fitzgerald *Twite* • June Duprez *Ada* • Jane Wyatt *Aggie Hunter* • George Coulouris *Jim Mordinoy* • Dan Duryea *Lew Tate* ■ *Dir* Clifford Odets • *Scr* Clifford Odets, from the novel by Richard Llewellyn

None Shall Escape ★★★

Drama 1944 · US · BW · 85mins

A very interesting and extremely clever movie, which examines in depth the career of a high-ranking German officer during his trial for war crimes. The film, though set after the First World War, was made and released before the end of the Second World War, and proved to be extraordinarily prescient. Director Andre De Toth keeps the story suspenseful and elicits excellent performances from Marsha Hunt and Henry Travers. TS

Marsha Hunt *Marja Pacierkowski* • Alexander Knox *Wilhelm Grimm* • Henry Travers *Father Warecki* • Erik Rolf *Karl Grimm* • Richard Crane *Willie Grimm as a man* • Dorothy Morris *Janina* • Richard Hale *Rabbi Levin* ■ *Dir* Andre De Toth • *Scr* Lester Cole, from a story by Alfred Neumann, Joseph Than

Noose ★★★

Crime thriller 1948 · UK · BW · 95mins

This is a sterling slice of British *film noir*, starring American sex symbol Carole Landis. As the fashion journalist who gets mixed up in the murky underworld of London's black market, Landis bravely goes up against spivs and wide-boy racketeers in this well-made little thriller. While blonde bombshell Landis provides the glamour, the best performance is by Nigel Patrick as the fast-talking, charismatic villain. On a sad note, Landis committed suicide shortly after completing the film. She was 29. DF

Carole Landis *Linda Medbury* • Joseph Calleia *Sugiani* • Derek Farr *Captain Jumbo Hoyle* • Stanley Holloway *Inspector Rendall* • Nigel Patrick *Bar Gorman* ■ *Dir* Edmond T Gréville • *Scr* Richard Llewellyn, Richard Dryhurst, from the play *The Silk Noose* by Richard Llewellyn

Noose ★★★ 18

Crime drama 1997 · US · Colour · 89mins

Mystifyingly straight-to-video here, this brutish tale of "boys from the O'Hood" is a cracking tale of bullets and blarney, carried along by a good cast. Set in Boston, it stars Denis Leary as the small-time car thief who is forced to examine his loyalty to local crime boss Colm Meaney when one of his relatives (Billy Crudup) falls foul of the gangster. With the supporting players including Famke Janssen, Ian Hart, Martin Sheen and Jeanne Tripplehorn, this is a classy affair directed with some sympathy by Ted Demme. JF. Contains swearing, some violence and sexual references. DVD

Denis Leary *Bobby O'Grady* • Jason Barry *Seamus* • Billy Crudup *Teddy* • Ian Hart *Moose Murphy* • Famke Janssen *Katy O'Connor* • Colm Meaney *Jackie O'Hara* • Martin Sheen *Hanolon* • Jeanne Tripplehorn *Annie* ■ *Dir* Ted Demme • *Scr* Mike Armstrong

The Noose Hangs High ★★ U

Comedy 1948 · US · BW · 76mins

Just when the fortunes of comedians Bud Abbott and Lou Costello seemed at their lowest, director Charles Barton brought in Leon Errol as guest star: a balding ditherer from countless B-pictures whose take on the double take was something to behold. Errol was the kind of trouper one could rely on, and he certainly raised the laughs in this predictable yarn about window cleaners mistaken for gamblers. TH

Bud Abbott *Ted Higgins* • Lou Costello *Homer Hinchcliffe* • Cathy Downs *Carol Scott* • Joseph Calleia *Mike Craig* • Leon Errol *Julius Caesar McBride* • Mike Mazurki *Chuck* ■ *Dir* Charles Barton • *Scr* John Grant, Howard Harris, from a story by Daniel Taradash, Julian Blaustein, Bernard Feins

Nor the Moon by Night ★★ U

Adventure 1958 · UK · Colour · 92mins

Guy Elmes was one of the busiest British screenwriters of the 1950s and 1960s. In addition to penning several "sword and sandal" adventures in Italy, he also adapted the Graham Greene short story *The Stranger's Hand* for producer John Stafford, with whom he reunited for this rather scrappy melodrama. There's little to be said in defence of either the acting or the story, in which the warden of an African game reserve finally meets his pen pal only to discover she's not the person he expected her to be. DP

Belinda Lee *Alice Lang* • Michael Craig *Rusty Miller* • Patrick McGoohan *Andrew Miller* • Anna Gaylor *Thea Boryslawski* • Eric Pohlmann *Anton Boryslawski* • Pamela Stirling *Mrs Boryslawski* ■ *Dir* Ken Annakin • *Scr* Guy Elmes, from the novel by Joy Packer

Nora ★★ 15

Biographical drama
1999 · UK/Ire/Ger/It · Colour · 102mins

Director Pat Murphy's exploration of James Joyce's relationship with his wife, Nora Barnacle, boasts a tour de force performance from Susan Lynch in the title role. She excels as a passionate woman rebelling against a repressive existence while struggling to understand her selfish, obsessive, literary genius of a husband. Telling Joyce's story from Nora's point of view is a clever stroke, but the movie is let down by Ewan McGregor's risible portrait of the artist. Slow and unbalanced, the result falls well short of the mark. LH DVD

Ewan McGregor *James Joyce* • Susan Lynch *Nora Barnacle* • Peter McDonald *Stanislas Joyce* • Roberto Citran *Roberto Prezioso* • Andrew Scott *Michael Bodkin* • Vincent McCabe [Vinnie McCabe] *Uncle Tommy* • Veronica Duffy *Annie Barnacle* ■ *Dir* Pat Murphy • *Scr* Pat Murphy, Gerard Stembridge, from the biography by Brenda Maddox

Nora Prentiss ★★★

Crime melodrama 1947 · US · BW · 111mins

This glossy "women's picture" romp can be enjoyed by all – if you leave your brains behind. Nightclub chanteuse Ann Sheridan ruins doctor Kent Smith when he falls for her and assumes the identity of a dead patient. Allegedly based on an actual insurance scandal, this is high-camp entertainment, with a technical crew of the very best to ensure that every ludicrous moment seems credible. It's a little overlong for its plot, but don't miss Sheridan's two solos. TS

Ann Sheridan *Nora Prentiss* • Kent Smith *Dr Richard Talbot* • Bruce Bennett *Dr Joel Merriam* • Robert Alda *Phil McDade* • Rosemary DeCamp *Lucy Talbot* • John Ridgely *Walter Bailey* • Robert Arthur *Gregory Talbot* ■ *Dir* Vincent Sherman • *Scr* N Richard Nash, Philip McDonald, from the story *The Man Who Died Twice* by Paul Webster, Jack Sobell

Norma Jean & Marilyn ★★ 15

Biographical drama
1996 · US · Colour · 108mins

The rise and fall of a 20th-century legend forms the basis of yet another TV-movie biography, which charts the life of Marilyn Monroe from her poor, rootless childhood as Norma Jean Baker, to her makeover as a blonde bombshell, to her final, tragic failure to resist her private demons. The unusual approach of having two actresses – Ashley Judd and Mira Sorvino – play the same character fails to overcome the fact that this a leering, pointless fantasy on the life of one of Hollywood's most discussed yet least understood icons. MC DVD

Ashley Judd *Norma Jean Baker* • Mira Sorvino *Marilyn Monroe* • David Dukes *Arthur Miller* • Josh Charles *Eddie Jordan* • Ron Rifkin *Johnny Hyde* • Peter Dobson *Joe DiMaggio* • Taylor Nichols *Fred Karger* • John Rubinstein *Darryl Zanuck* ■ *Dir* Tim Fywell • *Scr* Jill Isaacs

Norma Rae ★★★★ PG

Drama based on a true story
1979 · US · Colour · 109mins

Director Martin Ritt's last important film is typical of his best work. Based on the true story of a reluctant real-life heroine, this sincere drama with a social conscience makes its union cause authentic, heartfelt and grittily entertaining. Determinedly shedding her image as a perennially cute, bubbly comedian, Sally Field deservedly won her first Oscar for her committed performance as the widowed Southern textile worker who nervously allies herself with New York labour organiser Ron Leibman to fight appalling conditions and, with growing gumption, takes on the mill owners. There are fine performances all round, including Beau Bridges as her boorish man, but it's Field's triumph, for which she won an Oscar. AME DVD

Sally Field *Norma Rae* • Beau Bridges *Sonny Webster* • Ron Leibman *Reuben* • Pat Hingle *Vernon* • Barbara Baxley *Leona* • Gail Strickland *Bonnie Mae* • Morgan Paull *Wayne Billings* • Robert Broyles *Sam Bolen* ■ *Dir* Martin Ritt • *Scr* Irving Ravetch, Harriet Frank Jr

Normal ★★ 18

Comedy drama 2002 · US · Colour · 112mins

Jane Anderson directs this polished adaptation of her stage play in this TV movie about transsexuality. However, in striving to de-sensationalise Tom Wilkinson's decision to end his 25-year marriage to Jessica Lange and undergo gender realignment, Anderson overcompensates by suppressing his inner turmoil and highlighting, instead, the prejudice of his family and friends. DP. Contains swearing and sexual references. DVD

Jessica Lange *Irma* • Tom Wilkinson *Roy* • Hayden Panettiere *Patty Ann* • Clancy Brown *Frank* • Joe Sikora *Wayne* • Randall Arney *Reverend Muncie* ■ *Dir* Jane Anderson • *Scr* Jane Anderson, from her play *Looking for Normal*

Normal Life ★★ 18

Crime drama 1995 · US · Colour · 102mins

Director John McNaughton, of *Henry: Portrait of a Serial Killer* and *Wild Things* fame, here delivers a sub-*Badlands* drama whose ending is obvious even before the opening credits have finished. Strait-laced cop Luke Perry finds his world unravelling after he falls for wild child Ashley Judd and gets caught up in credit card fraud and bank robbery. JB

Ashley Judd *Pam Anderson* • Luke Perry *Chris Anderson* • Bruce Young [Bruce A Young] *Agent Parker* • Jim True *Mike Anderson* • Dawn Maxey *Eva* • Tom Towles *Frank Anderson* ■ *Dir* John McNaughton • *Scr* Peg Haller, Bob Schneider

Norman... Is That You? ★★

Comedy drama 1976 · US · Colour · 91mins

Veteran black comedian Redd Foxx become a huge TV star via the sitcom *Sandford and Son* (based on the UK's *Steptoe and Son*). Here he plays a man who, after discovering his wife's infidelity with his own brother, travels to LA to share his troubles with his son Michael Warren. Upon arrival, he discovers his son's live-in male lover and vows to straighten his boy out. Although pleasingly acerbic in places, the film, like many cutting-edge comedies of the time, now seems occasionally offensive. DF

Redd Foxx *Ben Chambers* • Pearl Bailey *Beatrice Chambers* • Dennis Dugan *Garson Hobart* • Michael Warren *Norman Chambers* • Tamara Dobson *Audrey* • Vernée Watson *Melody* ■ *Dir* George Schlatter • *Scr* Ron Clark, Sam Bobrick, George Schlatter, from the play by Ron Clark, Sam Bobrick

Norman Loves Rose ★★★

Comedy 1982 · Aus · Colour · 97mins

Typically offbeat Australian comedy about a lovestruck teenager (Tony Owen) who becomes enamoured of his sexy sister-in-law (Carol Kane). When the latter gets pregnant, it's less a case of how's-your-father than who's-the-father. The unsavoury-sounding plot actually raises more than its fair share of laughs – Aussies are good at handling this sort of quirky material – while Warren Mitchell, TV's Alf Garnett, shines in a supporting role. DA

Carol Kane *Rose* • Tony Owen *Norman* • Warren Mitchell *Morris* • Myra De Groot *Norman's mother* • David Downer *Michael* ■ *Dir/Scr* Henri Safran

The Norseman ★ PG

Period adventure 1978 · US · Colour · 86mins

A pathetic would-be historical adventure, with Lee Majors as a Viking named Thorvald who goes overseas looking for his lost father (played by Mel Ferrer). This is the sort of movie where men wear horns on their heads and say "Vrolop thar, gravad lax" to each other before hacking their enemies to pieces. The violence is of the slo-mo variety, the budget clearly nonexistent. Charles B Pierce writes, directs and produces at the sort of crass level that makes *Erik the Viking* look like a masterpiece. AT

Lee Majors *Thorvald Helge* • Cornel Wilde *Ragnar* • Mel Ferrer *King Eurich* • Jack Elam *Death Dreamer* • Chris Connelly [Christopher Connelly] *Rolf* • Deacon Jones *Thrall* ■ *Dir/Scr* Charles B Pierce

El Norte ★★★★ 15

Drama 1983 · US · Colour · 133mins

Hailed as the "first American independent epic", Gregory Nava's compassionate film eschews political sermonising to concentrate on the human aspect of the arduous trek undertaken by so many Latinos to that pitiless promised land to the north. Adeptly using a docudramatic style to ward off overt sentimentality, Nava draws wondrously naturalistic performances from David Villalpando and Zaide Silvia Gutierrez. They play a brother and sister who, following the murder of their peasant father, experience both the despair of the refugee and the optimism of the immigrant after quitting their remote Guatemalan village. An irresistibly involving drama. DP. In English and Spanish with subtitles.

Ernesto Gómez Cruz *Arturo Xuncax* • David Villalpando *Enrique Xuncax* • Zaide Silvia Gutierrez *Rosa Xuncax* • Alicia del Lago *Lupe Xuncax* ■ *Dir* Gregory Nava • *Scr* Gregory Nava, Anna Thomas

North ★★ PG

Fantasy comedy drama
1994 · US · Colour · 83mins

Tired of saving the world, Bruce Willis is out to save the soul of 11-year-old Elijah Wood. However, the casting of Willis as a guardian angel dressed as a pink bunny rabbit is laughably typical of the misjudgements in Rob Reiner's fantastical extravaganza. Wood "divorces" his selfish parents and sets out on a worldwide odyssey to audition possible alternatives. Meanwhile, the school swot has set up a youngsters-versus-adults political power base on the strength of Wood's revolution. TH [video]

Elijah Wood *North* • Bruce Willis *Narrator* • Jason Alexander *North's dad* • Julia Louis-Dreyfus *North's mom* • Mathew McCurley *Winchell* • Jon Lovitz *Arthur Belt* • Alan Arkin *Judge Buckle* • Dan Aykroyd *Pa Tex* ■ *Dir* Rob Reiner • *Scr* Alan Zweibel, Andrew Scheinman, from the novel by Alan Zweibel

North by Northwest ★★★★★ PG

Classic spy thriller
1959 · US · Colour · 130mins

This Hitchcock classic contains extra helpings of the ingredients that make his films so unmissable. Action, intrigue, romance and comedy are blended throughout with consummate skill; the attack by the crop-dusting plane and the finale on Mount Rushmore are simply the icing on the cake. Rarely did Hitchcock have as much fun with his favourite "innocent in peril" theme or make such inventive use of famous landmarks. In his fourth and final collaboration with the "Master of Suspense", Cary Grant is the personification of suaveness as he tackles a nest of enemy agents, led by James Mason. DP [video] DVD

Cary Grant *Roger Thornhill* • Eva Marie Saint *Eve Kendall* • James Mason *Phillip Vandamm* • Jessie Royce Landis *Clara Thornhill* • Leo G Carroll *Professor* • Philip Ober *Lester Townsend* • Martin Landau *Leonard* • Adam Williams *Valerian* ■ *Dir* Alfred Hitchcock • *Scr* Ernest Lehman • *Cinematographer* Robert Burks • *Music* Bernard Herrmann

North Dallas Forty ★★★ 18

Sports drama 1979 · US · Colour · 113mins

This all-American sports saga stars Nick Nolte, looking the part of the professional American football player, now almost over the hill, and wanting to escape the steroid culture and corruption surrounding the game. Since the National Football League declined to assist in the production, action footage is minimal until the climax, but this turns the spotlight on the characters involved and, it must be said, the clichés about heroism, role models and the girls on the sidelines. AT. Contains swearing and nudity. [video]

Nick Nolte *Phillip Elliott* • Mac Davis *Maxwell* • Charles Durning *Coach Johnson* • Dayle Haddon *Charlotte* • Bo Svenson *Jo Bob Priddy* • Steve Forrest *Conrad Hunter* • Dabney Coleman *Emmett* ■ *Dir* Ted Kotcheff • *Scr* Frank Yablans, Ted Kotcheff, Peter Gent, from the novel by Peter Gent

North of the Great Divide ★★

Western 1950 · US · Colour · 67mins

The Oseka tribe are starving after a new salmon cannery over-fishes a river but, with Roy Rogers as the friendly Indian agent, it's all sorted out before the natives take to the warpath. Roy Barcroft and a whip-cracking Jack Lambert dispense the villainy, while Penny Edwards is an attractive field nurse. With its conservation theme, colour photography and three songs, this is a tolerable late entry in a long-running series. AE

Roy Rogers • Penny Edwards *Ann Keith* • Gordon Jones *Splinters* • Roy Barcroft *Banning* • Jack Lambert *Stagg* ■ *Dir* William Witney • *Scr* Eric Taylor

North Sea Hijack ★★ 15

Action adventure 1979 · UK · Colour · 95mins

Presumably because it was assumed that American audiences might not know where the North Sea was, this action caper was retitled *Ffolkes* for the US market. In view of the age of the stars, they might have gone the whole hog and titled it *Old Ffolkes Home*. Roger Moore is the frogman hero, James Mason is an admiral and Anthony Perkins is planning to hijack a North Sea oil rig. It's sub-Bond, sub-Forsyth, even sub-Alistair MacLean. Ffeeble. AT. Contains swearing and violence. [video] DVD

Roger Moore *Rufus Excalibur Ffolkes* • James Mason *Admiral Sir Francis Brinsden* • Anthony Perkins *Lou Kramer* • Michael Parks *Shulman* • David Hedison *King* • Jack Watson *Olafsen* • Faith Brook *Prime Minister* ■ *Dir* Andrew V McLaglen • *Scr* Jack Davies, from his novel *Esther, Ruth and Jennifer*

North Shore ★★ PG

Action drama 1987 · US · Colour · 91mins

This is a daft attempt to construct a youth-oriented surfer movie while maintaining an Elvis Presley-style innocence. The result? Anodyne nonsense. Matt Adler is the top surfer in Arizona who hitches to Hawaii to do battle with the famous Oahu waves. Adler falls in love, but his inamorata's family is not too keen on the oval-eyed interloper. The script stinks, but the screen comes alive once surf's up. SH [video]

Matt Adler *Rick Kane* • Gregory Harrison *Chandler* • Nia Peeples *Kiani* • John Philbin *Turtle* • Gerry Lopez *Vince* ■ *Dir* William Phelps • *Scr* William Phelps, Tim McCanlies, from a story by William Phelps, Randall Kleiser

The North Star ★★★ PG

Second World War drama
1943 · US · BW · 99mins

This Second World War drama is lifted above the mundane by a fine Lillian Hellman script (from her own story) and some strong playing from Walter Huston as a Ukrainian village doctor and Erich von Stroheim as his urbane Nazi counterpart. When the action is concentrated on the battle of words, this is a multilayered, complex film that contains some insights on the struggle against oppression, but there are far too many lengthy and tedious scenes of combat. SH [video]

Anne Baxter *Marina* • Farley Granger *Damian* • Jane Withers *Claudia* • Eric Roberts *Grisha* • Dana Andrews *Kolya* • Walter Brennan *Karp* • Walter Huston *Dr Kurin* • Erich von Stroheim *Dr Otto Von Harden* ■ *Dir* Lewis Milestone • *Scr* Lillian Hellman, from her story • *Music* Aaron Copeland

North Star ★ 15

Period adventure
1996 · Fr/It/Nor/UK · Colour · 84mins

During the 1899 Alaskan Gold Rush, prospector James Caan battles Indian Christopher Lambert for land and the love of Catherine McCormack. Directed by the Norwegian Nils Gaup, this contrived action adventure is weak on both plot and logic, resulting in a freeze-dried potboiler with little to recommend it apart from some spectacular locations. AJ [video]

Christopher Lambert *Hudson Ipsehawk* • James Caan *Sean McLennon* • Catherine McCormack *Sarah* • Jacques François *Colonel Johnson* ■ *Dir* Nils Gaup • *Scr* Sergio Donati, Lorenzo Donati, Paul Ohl, from a story by Gilles Behat, Philippe Schwartz, from the novel by Heck Allen [Will Henry]

North to Alaska ★★★★ U

Comedy adventure
1960 · US · Colour · 116mins

This splendid comedy adventure boasts a sparkling cast. John Wayne stars as a gold prospector, with the always under-rated (especially by himself) Stewart Granger as his wily partner. The eclectic casting also includes teen idol Fabian as Granger's unlikely sibling, and the acerbic Ernie Kovacs as a confidence trickster. Director Henry Hathaway keeps up the pace and humour, and the movie contains one of the wackiest bar-room brawls in Hollywood history. TS [video] DVD

John Wayne *Sam McCord* • Stewart Granger *George Pratt* • Ernie Kovacs *Frankie Canon* • Fabian *Billy Pratt* • Capucine *Michelle, "Angel"* • Mickey Shaughnessy *Peter Boggs* ■ *Dir* Henry Hathaway • *Scr* John Lee Mahin, Martin Rackin, Claude Binyon, Wendell Mayes (uncredited), from an idea by John Kafka, from the play *Birthday Gift* by Laszlo Fodor

North West Frontier ★★★ U

Adventure 1959 · UK · Colour · 124mins

This adventure, directed with great pace and precision by J Lee Thompson, proves that an old-fashioned, all-action drama can still keep you on the edge of your seat without the benefit of flashy special effects. It could almost be called an "eastern", transplanting the old western plot of a railroad journey through hostile territory to turn-of-the-century India. Kenneth More gives an assured performance as the soldier entrusted with the safety of a Hindu prince. DP [video] DVD

Kenneth More *Captain Scott* • Lauren Bacall *Catherine Wyatt* • Herbert Lom *Van Leyden* • Wilfrid Hyde White *Bridie* • IS Johar *Gupta* • Ursula Jeans *Lady Windham* • Eugene Deckers *Peters* • Ian Hunter *Sir John Windham* • Jack Gwillim *Brigadier Ames* ■ *Dir* J Lee Thompson • *Scr* Robin Estridge, Frank S Nugent, from a story by Patrick Ford, Will Price

North West Mounted Police ★★ U

Period adventure
1940 · US · Colour · 125mins

Cecil B DeMille's flat-footed tribute to the Mounties has Gary Cooper as the Texas Ranger-turned-Mountie who, in the 1880s, helps suppress a 15-year revolt by settlers, many of whom are of mixed race. From these historical skirmishes came the Mounties' motto of always getting their man (or woman). A box-office blockbuster, this was shot on sound stages and in Oregon when DeMille's preferred location in the Canadian Rockies proved to be too expensive. AT

Gary Cooper *Dusty Rivers* • Madeleine Carroll *April Logan* • Paulette Goddard *Louvette Corbeau* • Preston Foster *Sgt Jim Brett* • Robert Preston *Constable Ronnie Logan* • George Bancroft *Jacques Corbeau* • Lynne Overman *Tod McDuff* • Akim Tamiroff *Dan Duroc* ■ *Dir* Cecil B DeMille • *Scr* Alan LeMay, Jesse Lasky Jr, C Gardner Sullivan, from the book *Royal Canadian Mounted Police* by RC Fetherston-Haugh

Northern Pursuit ★★

Second World War adventure
1943 · US · BW · 93mins

The idea of Nazi saboteurs secretly entering Canada had been cleverly explored in the British film *49th Parallel*, but here it gets a juvenile treatment by Warner Bros. Errol Flynn is the Mountie of German descent who goes undercover, foiling a German scheme to assemble a bomber and attack the Panama Canal. Made just after Flynn's acquittal on charges of rape, the film goes lightly on the romance with Julie Bishop. AE

Errol Flynn *Steve Wagner* • Julie Bishop *Laura McBain* • Helmut Dantine *Von Keller* • John Ridgely *Jim Austin* • Gene Lockhart *Ernst* • Tom Tully *Inspector Barnett* ■ *Dir* Raoul Walsh • *Scr* Frank Gruber, Alvah Bessie, from the story *Five Thousand Trojan Horses* by Leslie T White

The Northerners ★★★★ 15

Surreal comedy drama
1992 · Neth · Colour · 102mins

Director Alex Van Warmerdam first came to the attention of British audiences with his 1986 black comedy *Abel*. This is an equally offbeat offering, which presents a surreal and, ultimately, macabre portrait of life on an incomplete Dutch housing estate in 1960. Among the eccentric inhabitants are a sexually frustrated butcher and his saintly wife, a short-sighted forest ranger with delusions of grandeur, a couple of travelling missionaries and a postman (played by the director himself) who hides away in the forest to read people's mail. DP. In Dutch with English subtitles. [video]

Leonard Lucieer *Thomas* • Jack Wouterse *Jacob the butcher* • Rudolf Lucieer *Anton the ranger* • Alex Van Warmerdam *Simon the postman* • Annet Malherbe *Martha* ■ *Dir* Alex Van Warmerdam • *Scr* Alex Van Warmerdam, Aat Ceelen

Northfork ★★ PG

Period drama 2002 · US · Colour · 99mins

Writer/directors Mark and Michael Polish's film is a wonky study in magical realism that places absurdist tone and somnambulant pacing over cohesive plotting or interesting characterisation. It's 1955 and the small Montana town of Northfork will be flooded when a nearby dam is built. Six men in black attempt to evacuate the remaining stragglers, including a modern-day Noah who has turned his house into an ark and a dying orphan having visions of angels. A pretentious biblical allegory. AJ [video] DVD

Peter Coyote *Eddie* • Anthony Edwards *Happy* • Duel Farnes *Irwin* • Daryl Hannah *Flower Hercules* • Kyle MacLachlan *Mr Hope* • Nick Nolte *Father Harlan* • James Woods *Walter O'Brien* • Mark Polish *Willis O'Brien* • Graham Beckel *Marvin* • Jon Gries [Jonathan Gries] *Arnold* ■ *Dir* Michael Polish • *Scr* Michael Polish, Mark Polish

Northwest Outpost ★★

Western musical 1947 · US · BW · 91mins

After Nelson Eddy was reduced to working at Republic he had nowhere to go and this musical, with a weak score by Rudolf Friml, was his last. Eddy is the American captain at a Russian outpost in California in the 1830s who falls for Ilona Massey (in her third film with Eddy), who is the wife of Joseph Schildkraut's disgraced Count. The script is quite lively and Allan Dwan directs with a light touch, but it's never more than old-fashioned fluff. AE

Nelson Eddy *Capt James Laurence* • Ilona Massey *Natalia Alanova* • Joseph Schildkraut *Count Igor Savin* • Hugo Haas *Prince Nickolai Balinin* • Elsa Lanchester *Princess "Tanya" Tatiana* ■ *Dir* Allan Dwan • *Scr* Elizabeth Meehan, Laird Doyle, Richard Sale, from a story by Angela Stuart

Northwest Passage ★★★ PG

Epic adventure 1940 · US · Colour · 121mins

A richly textured, beautifully shot adventure tale from MGM, this is pretty sturdy stuff, featuring a rugged Spencer Tracy as Robert Rogers himself, setting out to find the passage of the title. Director King Vidor spares nothing, with the river sequences particularly well-filmed, and

N

there is a genuinely epic feel to the whole endeavour. The ending (shot by uncredited director Jack Conway) certainly leaves you wanting more, but all that followed was a feeble TV series in the late 1950s. TS

Spencer Tracy *Major Robert Rogers* • Robert Young (1) *Langdon Towne* • Walter Brennan *Hunk Marriner* • Ruth Hussey *Elizabeth Browne* • Nat Pendleton *Captain Huff* • Louis Hector *Reverend Browne* • Robert Barrat *Humphrey Towne* • Lumsden Hare *General Amherst* • Donald MacBride *Sergeant McNott* ■ *Dir* King Vidor • *Scr* Laurence Stallings, Talbot Jennings, from the novel by Kenneth Roberts

Northwest Stampede ★★ U

Western 1948 · US · Colour · 75mins

James Craig was an ineffective but handsome substitute for Clark Gable and Robert Taylor while those two estimable stars fought for their country in the Second World War. On their return, MGM downgraded Craig and loaned him out on films like this, co-starring former Warner Bros ingénue Joan Leslie. It's a romantic western with Leslie as a rancher who's trying to make rodeo-rider Craig settle down. TS

Joan Leslie *Chris Johnson* • James Craig *Dan Bennett* • Jack Oakie *Mike Kirby* • Chill Wills *Mileaway* • Victor Kilian *Mel Saunders* ■ *Dir* Albert S Rogell • *Scr* Art Arthur, Lillie Hayward, from *The Saturday Evening Post* story *Wild Horse Roundup* by Jean Muir

Nosferatu, a Symphony of Horrors ★★★★ PG

Classic silent horror
1922 · Ger · Tinted and BW · 79mins

Celebrated German director FW Murnau plundered Bram Stoker's *Dracula* without permission for this 1922 ground-breaker, and was successfully sued by Stoker's wife – all prints were ordered to be destroyed, but a few survived. The result is the most frightening incarnation of the vampire count in horror history. With his grasping claws, pointed fangs, bald pate and white cadaverous features, Count Orlock, played by the hideous Max Schreck, creeps through Murnau's archetypal silent imagery with a mesmerising authority that retains a surprising amount of tension. The chilling finale, highlighted by Schreck's terrifying shadow outside his victim's door, packs a powerful punch even by today's standards. AJ DVD

Max Schreck *Count Orlock, Nosferatu* • Alexander Granach *Knock, an estate agent* • Gustav von Wangenheim *Hutter, his employee* • Greta Schroeder *Ellen, his wife* • GH Schnell *Harding, ship owner* • Ruth Landshoff *Annie, his wife* ■ *Dir* Friedrich W Murnau [FW Murnau] • *Scr* Henrik Galeen, from the novel *Dracula* by Bram Stoker

Nosferatu, the Vampire ★★ 15

Horror 1979 · Fr/W Ger · Colour · 107mins

Director Werner Herzog's all-too literal remake of FW Murnau's 1922 silent horror classic is a beautiful-looking bore. It's such a plodding exercise in image re-creation – with exactly the same sets, lighting effects and Klaus Kinski's replication of Max Schreck's Count Orlock – that one wonders why Herzog even bothered. Leisurely paced, and coming close to parody, this redundant labour of love is a sometimes haunting yet mostly magnificent misfire. AJ. In German with English subtitles. DVD

Klaus Kinski *Count Dracula* • Isabelle Adjani *Lucy Harker* • Bruno Ganz *Jonathan Harker* • Roland Topor *Renfield* • Walter Ladengast *Dr Van Helsing* • Dan Van Husen *Warden* ■ *Dir* Werner Herzog • *Scr* Werner Herzog, from the 1922 film by Henrik Galeen, from the novel *Dracula* by Bram Stoker

Nostalgia ★★★★ 15

Drama
1983 · USSR/It · Colour and BW · 120mins

In rejecting a possible affair and his intellectual researches to undertake the eternal quest for enlightenment, Oleg Yankovsky finds redemption of sorts as he rises to the symbolic challenge of carrying a lighted candle across a sulphurous spa – a challenge posed by Erland Josephson, the apocalypse-obsessed resident of a Tuscan shrine town. Contrasting monochrome flashbacks with desaturated colour landscapes, Andrei Tarkovsky (in his first non-Soviet picture) poetically employs langorous takes which not only convey Yankovsky's fragile mental and spiritual condition, but also heighten the mesmerising mysticism of this metaphysical allegory. DP. In Italian with English subtitles. DVD

Oleg Yankovsky *Andrei Gorchakov* • Erland Josephson *Domenico* • Domiziana Giordano *Eugenia* • Patrizia Terreno *Gorchakov's wife* ■ *Dir* Andrei Tarkovsky • *Scr* Andrei Tarkovsky, Tonino Guerra

Nostradamus ★★★ 15

Biographical drama
1993 · UK/Ger · Colour · 114mins

Director Roger Christian paints the charismatic 16th-century rebel doctor as a person shaken by the relevance of his dreams, but whose reputation for accuracy eventually attracts the patronage of French queen Catherine de'Medici. Using bursts of newsreel footage depicting African famine, atomic bomb testing, re-creations of the Second World War and space travel to visualise Nostradamus's most important predictions, Christian's po-faced venture is a genuine oddity. AJ

Tcheky Karyo *Nostradamus* • F Murray Abraham *Scalinger* • Rutger Hauer *Mystic Monk* • Amanda Plummer *Catherine de'Medici* • Julia Ormond *Marie* • Assumpta Serna *Anne* • Anthony Higgins *King Henry II* • Diana Quick *Diane de Portier* ■ *Dir* Roger Christian • *Scr* Kurt Boeser, from a story by Piers Ashworth, Roger Christian

Not Another Teen Movie ★ 15

Parody 2001 · US · Colour · 85mins

A strong contender for the title of the year's most puerile and vulgar film. A popular teen makes a bet he can get the plainest girl to attend the prom with him, and this pathetic excuse for humour reinforces every possible negative social stereotype. Former MTV producer and first-time director Joel Gallen throws incest, aneurysms and an avalanche of human waste into the tasteless equation. SF DVD

Chyler Leigh *Janey Briggs (The Pretty Ugly Girl)* • Chris Evans *Jake Wyler (The Popular Jock)* • Jaime Pressly *Priscilla (The Bitchy Cheerleader)* • Eric Christian Olsen *Austin (The Cocky Blond Guy)* • Mia Kirshner *Catherine (The Cruelest Girl in School)* • Deon Richmond *Malik (The Token Black Guy)* • Mr T *Wise janitor* • Molly Ringwald *Flight attendant* • Randy Quaid *Mr Briggs* ■ *Dir* Joel Gallen • *Scr* Michael G Bender, Adam Jay Epstein, Andrew Jacobson, Phil Beauman, Buddy Johnson

Not as a Stranger ★★★

Medical drama 1955 · US · BW · 136mins

After producing many key films, Stanley Kramer turned director with this melodrama. It's about impoverished medical student Robert Mitchum, who marries Swedish nurse Olivia de Havilland because she can pay his tuition fees. Then Mitchum steps out with Gloria Grahame. Containing lots of lurid detail about surgical procedures, this is an occasionally lumpen effort, but the high-powered cast is always worth watching. AT

Olivia de Havilland *Kristina Hedvigson* • Robert Mitchum *Lucas Marsh* • Frank Sinatra *Alfred Boone* • Gloria Grahame *Harriet Lang* • Broderick Crawford *Dr Aarons* • Charles Bickford *Dr Runkleman* • Myron McCormick *Dr Snider* • Lon Chaney Jr *Job Marsh* • Lee Marvin *Brundage* ■ *Dir* Stanley Kramer • *Scr* Edna Anhalt, Edward Anhalt, from the novel by Morton Thompson

Not for Publication ★★★ 15

Comedy 1984 · US · Colour · 83mins

Nancy Allen works for *The Informer*, at one time a crusading newspaper run by her father, but now a sleazy scandal sheet. Sent to interview the mayor of New York (Laurence Luckinbill), Allen finds his campaign plans in a mess and agrees to help out – without revealing her links to the muckraking *Informer*. This 1980s attempt to capture the flavour and style of a 1940s screwball comedy never quite comes off, but delivers plenty of fun along the way. DF

Nancy Allen *Lois Thorndyke* • Laurence Luckinbill *Mayor Claude Franklyn* • David Naughton *Barry Denver* • Alice Ghostley *Doris* • Don Peoples *Cy Katz* • Richard Blackburn *Jim* • Cork Hubbert *Odo* ■ *Dir* Paul Bartel • *Scr* Paul Bartel, John Meyer

Not Now, Comrade ★

Comedy 1976 · UK · Colour · 89mins

It's hard to envisage anyone wanting to film any British stage farce. Yet what is so unforgivable about this woeful farrago is that it has been done in such a visually uninteresting way that it comes over as little more than illustrated radio. The fault lies squarely with Ray Cooney, who not only wrote and co-directed, but also co-stars in this horrid comedy of errors about a defecting Russian ballet dancer. DP

Leslie Phillips *Commander Rimmington* • Roy Kinnear *Hoskins* • Windsor Davies *Constable Pulford* • Don Estelle *Bobby Hargreaves* • Michele Dotrice *Nancy Rimmington* • Ray Cooney *Mr Laver* • June Whitfield *Janet Rimmington* ■ *Dir* Ray Cooney, Harold Snoad • *Scr* Ray Cooney

Not Now Darling ★★ PG

Comedy 1972 · UK · Colour · 89mins

What an appalling waste of a remarkable cast that provides a comic link between the golden age of music hall and the *Carry Ons*. Popular 1930s husband-and-wife team Jack Hulbert and Cicely Courtneidge were reunited on screen for the first time in 12 years for this clumsy version of Ray Cooney's long-running West End farce. Leslie Phillips holds this threadbare piece together, as the furrier up to his neck in girlfriends and cheap minks, but it's all rather tatty. DP

Leslie Phillips *Gilbert Bodley* • Ray Cooney *Arnold* • Moira Lister *Maude Bodley* • Julie Ege *Janie* • Joan Sims *Miss Tipdale* • Derren Nesbitt *Harry* • Barbara Windsor *Sue* • Jack Hulbert • Cicely Courtneidge ■ *Dir* Ray Cooney, David Croft • *Scr* John Chapman, from the play by Ray Cooney

Not of This Earth ★★★

Science-fiction horror
1956 · US · BW · 67mins

Cult director Roger Corman mixes science-fiction, horror and humour in his classic alien invasion quickie with vampiric overtones. Paul Birch is a visitor from the planet Davanna on the trail of human blood because his own race is facing extinction from nuclear anaemia. Death rays are generated whenever he removes his black sunglasses. Corman's elegantly styled, fast-paced gem was the first of his prolific output to successfully lace comedy with suspense, inspiring him to continue in the same vein. The head-crushing bat monster is a fine example of pure 1950s pulp sci-fi. AJ

Paul Birch *Paul Johnson* • Beverly Garland *Nadine Story* • Morgan Jones *Harry Sherbourne* • William Roerick *Dr Rochelle* • Jonathan Haze *Jeremy Perrin* • Richard Miller [Dick Miller] *Joe Piper* ■ *Dir* Roger Corman • *Scr* Charles Griffith, Mark Hanna

Not of This Earth ★ 18

Science-fiction horror
1988 · US · Colour · 77mins

Ex-porn queen Traci Lords tried to go respectable in this dire remake of Roger Corman's 1956 cult favourite. After opening, for no apparent reason, with numerous clips from the New World Pictures back catalogue, director Jim Wynorski's laughably cheap effort tells exactly the same story as the original (a vampire from outer space checks out Earthlings' blood types for possible invasion purposes). Trash with no flash, dash or cash. AJ

Traci Lords *Nadine Story* • Arthur Roberts *Mr Johnson* • Lenny Juliano *Jeremy* • Ace Mask *Dr Rochelle* • Roger Lodge *Harry* • Michael Delano *Vacuum cleaner salesman* • Rebecca Perle *Davanna Girl* ■ *Dir* Jim Wynorski • *Scr* Jim Wynorski, RJ Robertson, from the 1956 film

Not of This World ★★★

Drama 1998 · It · Colour · 100mins

Giuseppe Piccioni has become known as the "Italian Truffaut" for his humanity and eye for telling detail. He provides a clear-sighted analysis of the dehumanising effect of urban life in this moving drama, in which novice nun Margherita Buy's ordered world is thrown into turmoil on meeting miserly dry-cleaning boss Silvio Orlando, the presumed father of an abandoned baby thrust into her care by a passing jogger. As Buy struggles with her suppressed maternal instincts and a growing fondness for the misunderstood Orlando, Piccioni still has time for Carolina Freschi, the mother racked by a guilt intensified by her desperate domestic situation. DP. In Italian with English subtitles.

Margherita Buy *Caterina* • Silvio Orlando *Ernesto* • Carolina Freschi *Teresa* • Maria Cristina Minerva *Esmeralda* ■ *Dir* Giuseppe Piccioni • *Scr* Giuseppe Piccioni, Gualtiero Rosella, Lucia Zei

Not One Less ★★★★ U

Comedy drama 1999 · Chi · Colour · 102mins

This sentimental but engaging drama from Zhang Yimou is wryly humanist but politically outspoken, and won the Golden Lion at Venice. It starts out by castigating the shoddiness of the Chinese education system, especially in the poor rural regions. However, once 13-year-old stand-in teacher Wei Minzhi sets off to retrieve the runaway student who can deprive her of a bonus for keeping all 28 charges in class, the focus of protest switches to the exploitation of child labour on the urban black market. DP. In Mandarin with English subtitles. DVD

Wei Minzhi • Zhang Huike • Tian Zhenda *Village chief* • Gao Enman *Teacher Gao* ■ *Dir* Zhang Yimou • *Scr* Shi Xiangsheng

Not Quite Jerusalem ★★ 15

Comedy drama 1985 · UK · Colour · 109mins

Old-fashioned romance from Lewis Gilbert, director of *Alfie*, *Educating Rita* and *Shirley Valentine*. This film isn't quite up to those august standards, but it's a pleasant enough yarn about multinational volunteers working on an Israeli kibbutz and the budding relationship that develops between young American Sam Robards and local girl Joanna Pacula. The pacing is a little pedestrian, but it's still the sort of low-key love story that very easy to get lost in. DA

Joanna Pacula *Gila* • Sam Robards *Mike* • Kevin McNally *Pete* • Todd Graff *Rothwell T Schwartz* • Selina Cadell *Carrie* • Bernard Strother *Dave* ■ *Dir* Lewis Gilbert • *Scr* Paul Kember, from his play

Not Reconciled, or Only Violence Helps Where Violence Rules ★★★★

Classic experimental drama
1965 · W Ger · BW · 53mins

With this debut feature, a deconstruction of Heinrich Böll's novel, Jean-Marie Straub and his wife Danièle Huillet, who has a role in the film, immediately established themselves as among the most interesting film-makers in Germany at the time, helping herald the New German Cinema movement. In less than an hour, the film deals with three generations of a middle-class German family, against the background of the anti-communism of the early 20th century to the Nazism of the 1930s to the revolutionary politics of the 1960s. RB. In German with English subtitles.

Heinrich Hargesheimer *Heinrich Fähmel at 80* • Carlheinz Hargesheimer *Heinrich Fähmel at 35* • Martha Ständner *Johanna Fähmel at 70* • Danièle Straub [Danièle Huillet] *Johanna Fähmel as a young woman* • Henning Harmssen *Robert Fähmel at 40* • Ulrich Hopmann *Robert Fähmel at 18* ■ *Dir* Jean-Marie Straub • *Scr* Jean-Marie Straub, Danièle Huillet, from the novel *Billiard um Halbzehn* by Heinrich Böll

Not Wanted on Voyage ★ U

Comedy 1957 · UK · BW · 87mins

A story about a luxury liner and a stolen necklace – sounds familiar? The script of *Titanic* might not be poetry, but it's a darn sight better than the drivel that passes for dialogue in this dismal comedy. Co-screenwriter Michael Pertwee enjoyed considerable success both before and after making a contribution to this venture, which is so unfunny that even gallant troupers Ronald Shiner and Brian Rix cannot conceal their dismay. DP

Ronald Shiner *Steward Albert Higgins* • Brian Rix *Steward Cecil Hollebone* • Griffith Jones *Guy Harding* • Catherine Boyle *Julie Haines* • Fabia Drake *Mrs Brough* • Michael Brennan *Chief Steward* ■ *Dir* Maclean Rogers • *Scr* Michael Pertwee, Evadne Price, Roland Pertwee, Jack Marks, from a screenplay (unproduced) by Dudley Sturrock, from the play *Wanted On Voyage* by Evadne Price, Ken Attiwill

Not with My Wife, You Don't! ★★★

Romantic comedy
1966 · US · Colour · 118mins

George C Scott, usually associated with heavyweight drama rather than lightweight fluff, here proves his comic strength when he muscles in on the uneasy marriage of US Air Force aide Tony Curtis and Virna Lisi, intent on carrying off the woman for whom he and Curtis once vied when they were Korean War comrades. Comic director Norman Panama and co-writers Larry Gelbart and Peter Barnes make the non-stop contrivance of the situation appear seamless. TH

Tony Curtis *Tom Ferris* • Virna Lisi *Julie Ferris* • George C Scott *"Tank" Martin* • Carroll O'Connor *General Parker* • Richard Eastham *General Walters* • Eddie Ryder *Sgt Gilroy* • George Tyne *Sgt Dogerty* ■ *Dir* Norman Panama • *Scr* Norman Panama, Larry Gelbart, Peter Barnes, from a story by Norman Panama, Melvyn Frank

Not without My Daughter ★★ 15

Biographical drama
1990 · US · Colour · 111mins

A real-life nightmare is turned into an overwrought soap. Betty Mahmoody, played by Sally Field, went to Iran with her doctor husband and their daughter, only to find him becoming a violent tyrant and all rights being taken from her. It took an underground chain of helpers to aid her and her daughter's escape. Sympathy for Field's character is distanced by her hysterical performance, and not even the usually impressive Alfred Molina can believably convey the husband's personality switch. TH. Contains some violence and swearing. [video] DVD

Sally Field *Betty Mahmoody* • Alfred Molina *Moody* • Sheila Rosenthal *Mahtob* • Roshan Seth *Houssein* • Sarah Badel *Nicole* • Mony Rey *Ameh Bozorg* • Georges Corraface *Mohsen* ■ *Dir* Brian Gilbert • *Scr* David W Rintels, from the non-fiction book by Betty Mahmoody, William Hoffer

The Notebook ★★★ 12

Romantic drama
2003 · US · Colour · 118mins

A shameless tearjerker, this skilfully pushes all the right emotional buttons. The movie opens in the present day with elderly James Garner reading to nursing-home resident Gena Rowlands from an old notebook. We then flash back 60 years to an ill-starred teenage romance between poor country boy Ryan Gosling and Rachel McAdams, daughter of rich city folk. The film is slickly made by Rowlands's son, Nick Cassavetes, and the acting is uniformly excellent, but the director should have taken his foot slightly off the slush pedal. DA [video] DVD

Ryan Gosling *Noah Calhoun* • Rachel McAdams *Allie Hamilton* • James Garner *Duke* • Gena Rowlands *Allie Calhoun* • James Marsden *Lon* • Kevin Connolly *Fin* • David Thornton *John Hamilton* • Joan Allen *Anne Hamilton* • Sam Shepard *Frank Calhoun* ■ *Dir* Nick Cassavetes • *Scr* Jeremy Leven, Jan Sardi, from a novel by Nicholas Sparks

Notebook on Cities and Clothes ★★★ U

Documentary 1989 · W Ger · Colour · 81mins

Although this is not as engaging, amusing or as insightful as the somewhat similar *Unzipped*, this documentary by German director Wim Wenders nonetheless provides an astute look at the work and creative process of innovative Japanese fashion designer Yohji Yamamoto. We see him contemplating the relationship between cities, identity and the future of cinema in the digital age. The film culminates in a Paris spring catwalk show at the Louvre and the way in which Wenders draws comparisons between his own work and Yamamoto's high-chic designs is a fascinating exercise. An English language version was also released. AJ. A German language film.

Wim Wenders *Narrator* ■ *Dir* Wim Wenders • *Scr* Wim Wenders, from an idea by François Burkhardt

Nothing but a Man ★★★

Drama 1964 · US · BW · 91mins

This engrossing drama stars Ivan Dixon as the black railroad worker in a small Southern town who takes on racist bully-boys so that he can stand tall in front of his wife and family. By making the dilemma small and intimate instead of loud and declamatory, director Michael Roemer ensures the issues involved are relevant to all. TH

Ivan Dixon *Duff Anderson* • Abbey Lincoln *Josie Dawson* • Gloria Foster *Lee* • Julius Harris *Will Anderson* • Yaphet Kotto *Jocko* ■ *Dir* Michael Roemer • *Scr* Michael Roemer, Robert Young

Nothing but the Best ★★★★

Black comedy satire
1963 · UK · Colour · 97mins

Scripted by Frederic Raphael, photographed by Nicolas Roeg and directed by Clive Donner, this has all the credentials to be one of the best British big-screen satires. There's no denying it's a very funny film, a sort of *School for Scoundrels* in a *Room at the Top*, but the brushstrokes are so broad that there is no room for the finer detail that would have made it a classic. Alan Bates is splendid as a working-class wannabe, but Denholm Elliott steals every scene as an indolent aristocrat who tutors him in the delicate art of being a cad. DP

Alan Bates *Jimmy Brewster* • Denholm Elliott *Charlie Prince* • Harry Andrews *Mr Horton* • Millicent Martin *Ann Horton* • Pauline Delany *Mrs March* • Godfrey Quigley *Coates* • Alison Leggatt *Mrs Brewster* ■ *Dir* Clive Donner • *Scr* Frederic Raphael, from the short story *The Best of Everything* by Stanley Ellin

Nothing but the Night ★★

Supernatural murder mystery
1972 · UK · Colour · 90mins

The first and last production from Christopher Lee's own company, Charlemagne, is a silly, supernatural variant on *Village of the Damned*. The brooding atmosphere of John Blackburn's possession novel goes awry under horror stalwart Peter Sasdy's confusing direction, leading to a complete absence of menace or suspense. A patchy affair. AJ

Christopher Lee *Colonel Bingham* • Peter Cushing *Sir Mark Ashley* • Diana Dors *Anna Harb* • Georgia Brown *Joan Foster* • Keith Barron *Dr Haynes* • Gwyneth Strong *Mary Valley* • Fulton Mackay *Cameron* • John Robinson (1) *Lord Fawnlee* • Michael Gambon *Inspector Grant* ■ *Dir* Peter Sasdy • *Scr* Brian Hayles, from the novel by John Blackburn

Nothing but the Truth ★★★

Comedy 1941 · US · BW · 90mins

This has a sure-fire plot in its story of a young man who vows to tell the absolute truth for 24 hours. Though slow to start, it pays off in the second half during a party on a yacht at which the hero's dilemma becomes increasingly farcical. Bob Hope was a master at this sort of thing and the vivacious Paulette Goddard always teamed well with him – this was their third film together. TV

Bob Hope *Steve Bennett* • Paulette Goddard *Gwen Saunders* • Edward Arnold *TT Ralston* • Leif Erickson *Tom Van Deusen* • Helen Vinson *Linda Graham* • Willie Best *Samuel* • Clarence Kolb *Mr James P Van Deusen* ■ *Dir* Elliott Nugent • *Scr* Don Hartman, Ken Englund, from the play by James Montgomery, from the novel by Frederick S Isham

Nothing but Trouble ★★ U

Comedy 1944 · US · BW · 66mins

A mawkish late entry from Laurel and Hardy working for a studio (MGM) which didn't understand their needs, so straitjacketed them into an oddly unlikeable story. Stan and Ollie are descendants of a long line of butlers and chefs whose own culinary disasters make them pariahs. They befriend boy king David Leland, who is in peril from his uncle Philip Merivale. The attempted murder puts the glooms on Stan and Ollie's light-hearted spirits. TH [video] DVD

Stan Laurel *Stan* • Oliver Hardy *Oliver* • Mary Boland *Mrs Elvira Hawkley* • Philip Merivale *Prince Saul* • Henry O'Neill *Mr Basil Hawkley* • David Leland *King Christopher* • John Warburton *Ronetz* ■ *Dir* Sam Taylor • *Scr* Russell Rouse, Ray Golden, Bradford Ropes, Margaret Gruen, from an idea by Robert Halff

Nothing but Trouble ★ 15

Fantasy comedy 1991 · US · Colour · 89mins

"Wasn't Worth the Trouble" might have been a more suitable title for a lousy comedy that rips off the premise of Peter Weir's cult classic, *The Cars That Ate Paris*. Dan Aykroyd wrote and directed this calamity, in which he also stars as a sadistic judge who delights in tormenting unsuspecting motorists. Chevy Chase and Demi Moore deserve no sympathy: they read the script before they signed their contracts. DP [video]

Chevy Chase *Chris Thorne* • Dan Aykroyd *"JP"/Bobo* • John Candy *Dennis/Eldona* • Demi Moore *Diane Lightston* • Taylor Negron *Fausto* • Bertila Damas *Renalda* ■ *Dir* Dan Aykroyd • *Scr* Dan Aykroyd, from a story by Peter Aykroyd

Nothing in Common ★★ 15

Drama 1986 · US · Colour · 113mins

Once the king of American TV comedy, Jackie Gleason stars as the washed-up rag trader who foists himself on his yuppie son (Tom Hanks) after his wife of 36 years, Eva Marie Saint, walks out on him. Director Garry Marshall treats the veteran Gleason with far too much respect, allowing him to get away with a hugely self-indulgent performance. Even Hanks is below his usually sparkling best. DP. Contains swearing. [video] DVD

Tom Hanks *David Basner* • Jackie Gleason *Max Basner* • Eva Marie Saint *Lorraine Basner* • Hector Elizondo *Charlie Gargas* • Barry Corbin *Andrew Woolridge* • Bess Armstrong *Donna Mildred Martin* • Sela Ward *Cheryl Ann Wayne* ■ *Dir* Garry Marshall • *Scr* Rick Podell, Michael Preminger

Nothing Lasts Forever ★★★ 15

Comedy 1984 · US · Colour and BW · 155mins

This is a rather bizarre but entertaining comedy shot in colour and black and white, with Zach Galligan as an artist experiencing life in the New York of the future. Most notable for its quirky cast, this was produced by *Saturday Night Live*'s Lorne Michaels, but is far stranger than anything that appeared on that innovative show. Not to everyone's taste, but definitely worth a look. JB [video]

Zach Galligan *Adam Beckett* • Lauren Tom *Ely* • Apollonia Van Ravenstein *Mara Hofmeier* • Dan Aykroyd *Buck Heller* • Imogene Coca *Daisy Schackman* • Eddie Fisher • Mort Sahl *Uncle Mort* • Bill Murray ■ *Dir* Tom Schiller • *Scr* Tom Schiller

Nothing Personal ★★ 15

Comedy 1980 · US/Can · Colour · 96mins

Donald Sutherland is a college professor who teams up with hotshot Harvard law graduate Suzanne Somers to prevent the slaughter of baby seals on the Arctic Circle. This serious environmental issue sits rather uncomfortably in what is really a screwball comedy romance between Sutherland and Somers. AT [video]

Donald Sutherland *Roger Keller* • Suzanne Somers *Abigail Adams* • Lawrence Dane *Robert Ralston* • Roscoe Lee Browne *Mr Paxton* • Dabney Coleman *Tom Dickerson* • Saul Rubinek *Peter Braden* ■ *Dir* George Bloomfield • *Scr* Robert Kaufman

Nothing Personal ★★★ 15

Drama 1995 · UK/Ire · Colour · 81mins

In striving for balance, Thaddeus O'Sullivan's pre-Irish peace process drama fails to deliver its intended statement and ends up merely reinforcing the clichés and stereotypes that exist on either side of the divide, while its murderous conclusion is cheaply manipulative. John Lynch is too familiar as the father who finds

N

himself on the front line, while Ian Hart is wildly over-the-top as a trigger-happy bigot. Yet the solid work of Michael Gambon and James Frain, makes it worth watching. DP. Contains violence and swearing. DVD

Ian Hart *Ginger* • John Lynch *Liam* • James Frain *Kenny* • Michael Gambon *Leonard* • Gary Lydon *Eddie* • Ruaidhri Conroy *Tommy* ■ *Dir* Thaddeus O'Sullivan • *Scr* Daniel Mornin, from his novel *All Our Fault*

Nothing Sacred ★★★ U

Screwball comedy
1937 · US · Colour · 73mins

A cynical black comedy from the acid pen of former journalist Ben Hecht, this is terrifically acted by Fredric March as a tabloid reporter and Carole Lombard as a Vermont girl whose last wish before she dies of radium poisoning is to see New York. Of course, she isn't really dying, but that doesn't stop March from exploiting her case to the hilt, and allowing Hecht to take swipes at his former profession. Tasteless, certainly, and not quite as funny as it thinks it is. TS

Carole Lombard *Hazel Flagg* • Fredric March *Wally Cook* • Charles Winninger *Dr Downer* • Walter Connolly *Stone* • Sig Rumann [Sig Ruman] *Dr Eggelhoffer* • Frank Fay *Master of Ceremonies* • Maxie Rosenbloom *Max Levinsky* • Hattie McDaniel *Mrs Walker* • Hedda Hopper *Dowager* ■ *Dir* William Wellman [William A Wellman] • *Scr* Ben Hecht, Ring Lardner Jr, Budd Schulberg, from the story *Letter to the Editor* by James H Street [James Street]

Nothing to Lose ★★ 18

Action comedy 1997 · US · Colour · 92mins

Tim Robbins stars in this glossy but empty-headed buddy movie. He plays a stressed-out exec who thinks his wife (Kelly Preston) is having an affair with his boss (Michael McKean). Seeking revenge, he finds an unlikely ally in petty thief Martin Lawrence. The two stars do their best with the comic crumbs they are handed, but they are hampered by the fact that this is an action comedy where nothing really happens. JF. Contains swearing, violence and a sex scene. DVD

Martin Lawrence *T Paul* • Tim Robbins *Nick Beam* • John C McGinley *Davis "Rig" Lanlow* • Giancarlo Esposito *Charlie Dunt* • Kelly Preston *Ann* • Michael McKean *Phillip Barrow* ■ *Dir/Scr* Steve Oedekerk

Notorious ★★★★★ U

Classic romantic thriller
1946 · US · BW · 100mins

Scripted by hard-boiled veteran Ben Hecht and boasting a highly topical uranium MacGuffin, this isn't as thematically complex or technically audacious as some of Alfred Hitchcock's later classics. But it's still hard to beat for pure, polished entertainment. Cary Grant and Ingrid Bergman are perfectly paired as an American agent and the high-living daughter of a Nazi sympathiser whom he has under surveillance. Yet they're almost upstaged by Claude Rains, who invests his treacherous villain with a modicum of humanity. Hitch permits himself one moment of visual virtuosity (a stunning crane shot swooping towards a key in Bergman's hand), but mostly confines himself to spinning his yarn with customarily mischievous skill. DP DVD

Cary Grant *TR Devlin* • Ingrid Bergman *Alicia Huberman* • Claude Rains *Alexander Sebastian* • Louis Calhern *Paul Prescott* • Madame Konstantin [Leopoldine Konstantin] *Mme Anna Sebastian* • Reinhold Schünzel *Dr Anderson/Otto Rensler* ■ *Dir* Alfred Hitchcock • *Scr* Ben Hecht • *Cinematographer* Ted Tetzlaff

The Notorious Landlady ★★★

Comedy mystery 1962 · US · BW · 126mins

An eccentric comedy mystery set principally in London with a sparkling cast led by Jack Lemmon, Kim Novak and, briefly, Fred Astaire. Lemmon plays a newly arrived diplomat whose landlady, Miss Novak, is suspected of murdering her husband who has vanished. When the husband does appear, Novak promptly shoots him. After that twist the plot thickens. London was created entirely on studio sets, giving the film an arch theatricality. AT

Kim Novak *Carlye Hardwicke* • Jack Lemmon *William Gridley* • Fred Astaire *Franklyn Ambruster* • Lionel Jeffries *Inspector Oliphant* • Estelle Winwood *Mrs Dunhill* • Maxwell Reed *Miles Hardwicke* • Philippa Bevans *Mrs Brown* ■ *Dir* Richard Quine • *Scr* Larry Gelbart, Blake Edwards, from a story by Margery Sharp

Notre Musique ★★★ 12A

Political drama
2004 · Fr/Swi · Colour and BW · 79mins

The opening montage of harrowing war footage culled from both fictional and documentary sources is reason enough to tackle this typically provocative offering from director Jean-Luc Godard. But his modern variation on Dante's *Divine Comedy* also throws up all manner of contentious social and political issues, as Jewish journalist Sarah Adler seeks answers and inspiration at a literary conference in postwar Sarajevo. Godard consistently demonstrates a passion for cinema and imaginative use of imagery, and the result is eclectic and demanding. DP. In French, English, Spanish, Arabic and Serbo-Croat with subtitles.

Sarah Adler *Judith Lerner* • Nade Dieu *Olga Brodsky* • Jean-Luc Godard • Rony Kramer *Ramos Garcia* • Georges Aguilar *Indian* • Leticia Gutiérrez *Indian* • Simon Eine *Ambassador* ■ *Dir/Scr* Jean-Luc Godard

La Notte ★★★★★

Drama 1961 · Fr/It · BW · 121mins

Antonioni's famous study of a marriage on the rocks stars Marcello Mastroianni as a novelist who blames his wife, Jeanne Moreau, for his lack of inspiration. She, in turn, feels ignored and patronised. After visiting a friend in hospital, Mastroianni and Moreau have an argument and separate. She spends the night wandering through the ugly bits of Milan; he goes to a party and pursues a virtually catatonic Monica Vitti. Mastroianni and Moreau loathed their parts, their director and the favouritism that he showed to Vitti, who was then his mistress. Yet this is, first and foremost, a director's film: rigidly controlled, very slow and with dazzling shots of the modern city that seem to infect the characters' despair and alienation. Dated it may be, but *La Notte* remains a mesmeric movie that cracks open the shell of the human soul. AT. An Italian language film.

Marcello Mastroianni *Giovanni Pontano* • Jeanne Moreau *Lidia Pontano* • Monica Vitti *Valentina Gherardini* • Bernhard Wicki *Tommaso* ■ *Dir* Michelangelo Antonioni • *Scr* Michelangelo Antonioni, Ennio Flaiano, Tonino Guerra, from a story by Michelangelo Antonioni

Notting Hill ★★★★ 15

Romantic comedy
1999 · US/UK · Colour · 123mins

The *Four Weddings* team produced another smash with this charming tale of bumbling bookshop owner Hugh Grant falling for the "most famous actress in the world", Julia Roberts. Inevitably, the course of true love is a bumpy road, with friends, family and flatmates getting in the way, but that's the cue for a series of screamingly funny scenarios. Saturated with wit and well directed by Roger Michell, the film was bashed by sceptics for its fluffiness and lack of realism (for a racially mixed area of London, there's not a black face to be seen). But, if you can accept the context as 100 per cent white middle class, it's an intensely enjoyable experience. LH. Contains swearing. DVD

Julia Roberts *Anna Scott* • Hugh Grant *William Thacker* • Hugh Bonneville *Bernie* • Emma Chambers *Honey* • James Dreyfus *Martin* • Rhys Ifans *Spike* • Tim McInnerny *Max* • Gina McKee *Bella* • Richard McCabe *Tony* ■ *Dir* Roger Michell • *Scr* Richard Curtis

Nous Sommes Tous des Assassins ★★★

Drama 1952 · Fr · BW · 107mins

From the early 1950s, André Cayatte's popular films – more radical in content than form – tackled such topics as euthanasia, juvenile delinquency, police corruption and, until the film was suppressed, false arrest. This movie about French complacency towards the death penalty evoked heated debate in its depiction of the experiences of several men on death row. One of them – a war hero – is accused of killing a policeman, but we never learn his fate or whether or not he is guilty. The emphatic title leaves us in no doubt about Cayatte's attitude to "legalised murder". The film won the special jury prize at Cannes. BB. A French language film.

Marcel Mouloudji *René Le Guen* • Raymond Pellegrin *Gino* • Antoine Balpêtré *Dr Albert Dutoit* • Claude Laydu *Philippe Arnaud* • Paul Frankeur *Leon* ■ *Dir* André Cayatte • *Scr* André Cayatte, Charles Spaak

La Nouvelle Eve ★★★ 18

Romantic drama 1999 · Fr · Colour · 90mins

A lifeguard with a fierce sense of independence may sound like an unlikely *femme fatale*, but that's exactly what Karin Viard plays in this quirky romantic comedy, set in the new Eden of 1990s Paris. However, in ambitiously updating notions of the stock literary heroine, director Catherine Corsini tempers Viard's pursuit of a politically active family man (Pierre-Loup Rajot) by adopting the rosy view that everyone's soul mate is out there somewhere. DP. In French with English subtitles. Contains sex scenes.

Karin Viard *Camille* • Pierre-Loup Rajot *Alexis* • Catherine Frot *Isabelle* • Sergi Lopez *Ben* • Laurent Lucas *Emile* • Mireille Roussel *Louise* • Nozha Khouadra *Solveig* • Valentine Vidal *Sophie* ■ *Dir* Catherine Corsini • *Scr* Catherine Corsini, Marc Syrigas, Emmanuel Bourdieu, Denyse Rodriguez-Tome

Nouvelle Vague ★★★

Drama 1990 · Swi/Fr · Colour · 89mins

Seducing us with some lustrous visuals before disarming our expectations with a melodramatic storyline and dialogue taken from a range of literary, philosophical and cinematic sources, this is something of a curate's egg from Jean-Luc Godard. Despite his dual involvement, Alain Delon looks curiously detached from the proceedings as he returns to wreak his revenge on murderous aristocrat Domiziana Giordano. Everything from socio-political allegory to morality tale is there if you can be bothered to scour the stylised imagery, but few critics were. DP. A French language film.

Alain Delon *Roger Lennox/Richard Lennox* • Domiziana Giordano *Countess Elena Torlato-Favrini* • Roland Amstutz *Jules the gardener* ■ *Dir/Scr* Jean-Luc Godard

The November Conspiracy ★★

Political action thriller
1995 · US · Colour · 103mins

As ambitious journalist Paige Turco tries to interview Democratic presidential candidate George Segal, the latter twice becomes the target of attempts on his life. When Turner's boyfriend Dirk Benedict turns out to be a secret agent who seems responsible for the second bid, Turner becomes the hunted party with only her knowledge of self-defence to protect her. This agreeable junk thriller displays a canny appreciation of its limitations, resulting in a loose, spirited B-movie political suspenser. AJ

Paige Turco *Jennifer Barron* • Dirk Benedict *John Mackie* • Conrad Janis *Frank* • Bo Hopkins *Captain Brogan* • George Segal *Senator Ashton* • Elliott Gould *Kahn* ■ *Dir* Conrad Janis • *Scr* Maria Grimm

The November Men ★★ 15

Spoof political thriller
1993 · US · Colour · 95mins

An intriguing concept doesn't quite come off in this sluggishly paced drama about a politically obsessed film-maker who enlists a handful of actors for an improvised movie about the fake assassination of President Bush. There's a fair share of twists and turns, as almost everybody involved in the guerrilla film-making is suspected as being a real assassin using the film as a cover. However, all the characters – particularly the Secret Service agents – are phoney and implausible. JC

James Andronica *Duggo* • Leslie Bevis *Elizabeth* • Beau Starr *Chief Agent Granger* • Paul Williams *Arthur Gwenlyn* • Coralissa Gines *Lorina* • Rod Ellis *Special Agent Eric Clancy* • Shanda Cunningham *Waitress* ■ *Dir* Paul Williams • *Scr* James Andronica

Novo ★★

Comedy drama
2002 · Fr/Sp/Swi · Colour · 95mins

Arresting visuals and a kinky sense of the absurd set apart this acerbic take on the breakdown of communication in the modern world. But for all its narrative audacity and directorial dexterity, Jean-Pierre Limosin's comedy treats its characters like cyphers. Amnesiac Eduardo Noriega's romance with secretary Anna Mouglalis is essentially sweet, particularly in comparison with his exploitative relationship with boss Nathalie Richard. Slick and quirky, but also self-satisfied and superficial. DP. In French with English subtitles.

Eduardo Noriega (2) *Graham* • Anna Mouglalis *Irène* • Nathalie Richard *Sabine* • Eric Caravaca *Fred* • Paz Vega *Isabelle* ■ *Dir* Jean-Pierre Limosin • *Scr* Jean-Pierre Limosin, Christophe Honoré

Novocaine ★★ 15

Black comedy mystery
2001 · US · Colour · 90mins

Director David Atkins bites off more than he can chew with this numbingly mediocre comedy. Opening improbably and becoming increasingly implausible by the minute, the story turns on respectable dentist Steve Martin's dangerous liaison with tearaway Helena Bonham Carter and her drug-dealing brother, Scott Caan. Only Laura Dern, as Martin's prudish fiancée, makes an impression. DP DVD

Steve Martin *Dr Frank Sangster* • Helena Bonham Carter *Susan Ivey* • Laura Dern *Jean Noble* • Elias Koteas *Harlan Sangster* • Scott Caan *Duane* • Keith David *Detective Lunt* • Lynne Thigpen *Pat* • Kevin Bacon *Lance Phelps* ■ *Dir* David Atkins • *Scr* David Atkins, from a story by David Atkins, Paul Felopulos

Now and Forever ★★

Comedy drama 1934 · US · BW · 81mins

Gary Cooper steals some jewellery and hides it in the teddy bear belonging to his small daughter. When they're discovered, his mistress, Carole Lombard, takes the blame, and Cooper allows the owner of the gems to adopt his child. This is a run-of-the-mill affair, with neither star shining too brightly. Its main attraction is the appearance of six-year-old Shirley Temple as Coop's daughter. RK

Gary Cooper *Jerry Day* • Carole Lombard *Toni Carstairs* • Shirley Temple *Penelope Day* • Guy Standing *Felix Evans* • Charlotte Granville *Mrs JHP Crane* • Gilbert Emery *James Higginson* ■ *Dir* Henry Hathaway • *Scr* Vincent Lawrence, Sylvia Thalberg, from the story *Honor Bright* by Jack Kirkland, Melville Baker

Now and Forever ★★ 15

Melodrama 1983 · Aus · Colour · 88mins

Based on the Danielle Steel book, this routine "trauma of the week" movie stars Cheryl Ladd as a chic boutique owner who returns from a clothes-buying trip abroad to find her philandering hubby has been had up on rape charges. Not surprisingly, the accusation puts strain on their marriage. Decent performances make this ideal for fans of Mills and Boon-type melodramas. DA [VIDEO]

Cheryl Ladd *Jessie Clarke* • Robert Coleby *Ian Clarke* • Carmen Duncan *Astrid Bonner* • Christine Amor *Margaret Burton* ■ *Dir* Adrian Carr • *Scr* Richard Cassidy, from the novel by Danielle Steel

Now and Then ★★★ PG

Drama 1995 · US · Colour · 102mins

Demi Moore co-produced this female version of *Stand by Me*, which follows four young girls (Gaby Hoffmann, Christina Ricci, Thora Birch, Ashleigh Aston Moore) in 1970 as they attempt to solve the mystery of the death of a local boy. It's a simple, small-town story, bookended by the present-day revelations of the girls, now grown up into Moore, Melanie Griffith, Rita Wilson and Rosie O'Donnell. This sweet film should strike a chord with anyone who believes that life was better in the 1970s. JB. Contains swearing. [VIDEO] DVD

Demi Moore *Samantha Albertson* • Melanie Griffith *Tina "Teeny" Tercell* • Rosie O'Donnell *Roberta Martin* • Rita Wilson *Christina "Chrissy" Dewitt* • Christina Ricci *Young Roberta* • Thora Birch *Young Teeny* • Gaby Hoffmann *Young Samantha* • Ashleigh Aston Moore *Young Chrissy* ■ *Dir* Lesli Linka Glatter • *Scr* I Marlene King

Now Barabbas Was a Robber ★★★

Prison drama 1949 · UK · BW · 84mins

"Elsie's Dad is inside again" reads the chalk message on a prison wall, one of several humorous touches in an otherwise sombre story of prison life. The assorted inmates include a bigamist, an embezzler, an Irish terrorist (strikingly portrayed by Richard Burton in his second screen role) and a well-mannered murderer about to be executed (a likeable performance by Richard Greene). Ably directed by Gordon Parry, this film version of William Douglas Home's play argues against the death penalty, but had the development of a homosexual relationship cut by the censor. AE

Richard Greene *Tufnell* • Cedric Hardwicke *Governor* • Kathleen Harrison *Mrs Brown* • Ronald Howard *Roberts, bank cashier* • Stephen Murray *Chaplain* • William Hartnell *Warder Jackson* • Beatrice Campbell *Kitty* • Richard Burton *Paddy* • Kenneth More *Spencer* • Dora Bryan *Winnie* ■ *Dir* Gordon Parry • *Scr* Gordon Parry, from the play by William Douglas Home

Now or Never ★★

Drama 1986 · W Ger · Colour · 55mins

A less than inspired German melodrama that attempts to enliven its proceedings by falling back on that most trustworthy of novelettish devices, the dark secret. As a woman rekindling her passion for a long-discarded lover, Eva Mattes does a tolerable job of safeguarding said skeleton in the cupboard, but the looks of anguish and the pregnant pauses each time a raw nerve is touched soon become tiresome. DP. German dialogue dubbed into English.

Eva Mattes *Mo* • Werner Stocker *Tom* • Teo Gostischa *Benjamin* • Silke Wülfing *Sarah* • August Zirner *Paul* • Eva Zlonitzky *Mutter* ■ *Dir/Scr* Christel Buschmann

Now, Voyager ★★★★★ PG

Classic romantic melodrama
1942 · US · BW · 113mins

One of the all-time great weepies, with a consummate performance from Bette Davis as the lifelong spinster emerging from her confining chrysalis into the arms of Paul Henreid. A lush, beautifully acted movie, which has gone down in the annals of cinema history for Henreid's lighting of two cigarettes scene and a tear-jerking speech from Davis, at her best in front of a moonlit sky. Irving Rapper directs with suitably grand aplomb and cinematographer Sol Polito lights everything with an almost magical touch. A movie in which all the elements came together in perfect harmony to give a hackneyed theme the imprint of greatness. SH [VIDEO]

Bette Davis *Charlotte Vale* • Paul Henreid *Jerry Durrance* • Claude Rains *Dr Jaquith* • Gladys Cooper *Mrs Henry Windle Vale* • Bonita Granville *June Vale* • John Loder *Elliot Livingston* • Ilka Chase *Lisa Vale* • Mary Wickes *Dora Pickford* • Janis Wilson *Tina Durrance* ■ *Dir* Irving Rapper • *Scr* Casey Robinson, from the novel by Olive Higgins Prouty • *Music* Max Steiner

Now You See Him, Now You Don't ★★ U

Comedy adventure
1972 · US · Colour · 88mins

Kurt Russell returns in this follow-up to *The Computer Wore Tennis Shoes* (1969), this time using a revolutionary new invisibility serum to save his school from financial ruin. The Disney studio's trick is to cast squeaky-clean Russell against such old-time pros as Cesar Romero and Jim Backus, thus luring both teen and mature audiences to this undemanding mix of golf, bank robbery and car chases. Lightweight, but this does have some ingenious special effects. AT [VIDEO]

Kurt Russell *Dexter Riley* • Cesar Romero *AJ Arno* • Joe Flynn *Dean Higgins* • Jim Backus *Timothy Forsythe* • William Windom *Professor Lufkin* • Michael McGreevey *Richard Schuyler* ■ *Dir* Robert Butler • *Scr* Joseph McEveety, from a story by Robert L King

Nowhere ★★★ 18

Experimental comedy drama
1997 · US/Fr · Colour · 78mins

Gregg Araki is certainly a film-making original, expressing teenage disillusionment through an otherwordly Los Angeles populated by surreal characters, trippy production design (the pop-art decor echoes each teen's inner psyche) and pounding music. This charts a day in the lives of the young, the restless and the really disturbed. The attractive cast is a who's who of teen talent. JC. Contains violence, sex scenes, drug abuse. [VIDEO] DVD

James Duval *Dark* • Rachel True *Mel* • Nathan Bexton *Montgomery* • Chiara Mastroianni *Kriss* • Debi Mazar *Kozy* • Kathleen Robertson *Lucifer* • Heather Graham *Lilith* • Mena Suvari *Zoe* ■ *Dir/Scr* Gregg Araki

Nowhere in Africa ★★★★ 15

Period drama 2001 · Ger · Colour · 134mins

Writer/director Caroline Link has composed a love letter to Africa with this visually stunning and immaculately acted drama. Based on the autobiographical novel by Stefanie Zweig, it's the emotional tale of a family of German-Jewish refugees who settle on a remote farm in Kenya in 1938. Against a landscape that can be cruel as well as beautiful, Juliane Köhler and Merab Ninidze and their five-year-old daughter struggle to adjust and survive. Link's drama delivers fresh insight into the Jewish experience of that era for, despite the setting, it's very much a Holocaust story. However, its characters are not victims – they are rounded individuals who provide a striking, and often ironic, portrait of the tenacity of the human spirit. SF. In English, German and Swahili with subtitles. [VIDEO] DVD

Juliane Köhler *Jettel Redlich* • Merab Ninidze *Walter Redlich* • Sidede Onyulo *Owuor* • Matthias Habich *Süsskind* • Lea Kurka *Regina Redlich, younger* • Karoline Eckertz *Regina Redlich, older* • Gerd Heinz *Max* • Hildegard Schmahl *Ina* ■ *Dir* Caroline Link • *Scr* Caroline Link, from the novel *Nirgendwo in Afrika* by Stefanie Zweig

Nowhere in Sight ★★

Psychological thriller
2000 · US/Can · Colour · 93mins

This is a shameless rehash of *Wait until Dark* and although Helen Slater does her best, her impersonation of a blind woman left alone with some burglars is simply not in the same league as Audrey Hepburn's Oscar-nominated performance. Her co-star Andrew McCarthy plays against type, but doesn't impress. DP. Contains violence, swearing and nudity.

Helen Slater *Carly Bauers* • Christopher Heyerdahl *Lewis Gills* • Andrew McCarthy *Eric Shelton* • Richard Jutras *Darryl Higgins* ■ *Dir* Doug Jackson [Douglas Jackson] • *Scr* James Lemmo

Nowhere to Go ★★ U

Crime drama 1958 · UK · BW · 103mins

Don't be fooled by the label "Made at Ealing": this is nothing more than a low-budget programme filler. Co-written by director Seth Holt and critic Kenneth Tynan, it is a routine crime drama in which thief George Nader goes into partnership with unscrupulous Bernard Lee. Neither the central round of robberies and escapes nor the finale in the Brecon Beacons are presented with any imagination. Only Maggie Smith, making her film debut, rises above the material. DP

George Nader *Paul Gregory* • Maggie Smith *Bridget Howard* • Bernard Lee *Vic Sloane* • Bessie Love *Harriet Jefferson* • Geoffrey Keen *Inspector Scott* • Andrée Melly *Rosa* • Howard Marion-Crawford *Cameron* ■ *Dir* Seth Holt • *Scr* Seth Holt, Kenneth Tynan, from the novel by Donald MacKenzie

Nowhere to Hide ★★ 15

Action thriller 1987 · Can · Colour · 90mins

This Canadian action thriller boasts some surprisingly good performances, particularly from Amy Madigan as an ex-marine who flees into hiding with her son when crooked defence contractors kill her husband. Michael Ironside also does well as the survivalist who shelters her and helps her fight back. Though made for cinemas, the film has the dark look, tone and slow pacing of a typical, low-budget TV drama. KB [VIDEO]

Amy Madigan *Barbara Cutter* • Michael Ironside *Ben* • John Colicos *General Howard* • Daniel Hugh-Kelly *Rob Cutter* • Robin MacEachern *Johnny Cutter* ■ *Dir* Mario Azzopardi • *Scr* Alex Rebar, George Goldsmith, from a story by Alex Rebar

Nowhere to Hide ★★★ 15

Crime thriller 1999 · S Kor · Colour · 96mins

Although it looks riotously modern, Lee Myeong-Se's police tale owes as much to Georges Méliès as it does to John Woo. The rain-streaked, neon-tinted vistas lend the complex plot and sardonic voiceover the feel of a latterday *film noir*. But Lee's use of slapstick silhouettes, varied film speeds, caption cards, ironic inserts and the occasional digitised image only serves to emphasise the director's endearingly playful spirit. Park Jung-Hun gives a superbly hard-boiled performance as a world-weary cop enduring endless stakeouts with rookie partner Jang Dong-Keon in pursuit of a killer. DP. In Korean with English subtitles. [VIDEO] DVD

Park Joong-Hoon *Detective Woo* • Ang Seong-Ki *Chang Sungmin* • Jang Dong-Keon [Jang Dong-gun] *Detective Kim* ■ *Dir/Scr* Lee Myeong-Se

Nowhere to Run ★★ 15

Romantic action adventure
1992 · US · Colour · 90mins

Jean-Claude Van Damme comes unstuck when he attempts to show his more sensitive side in this soft-centred thriller. He plays a convict on the run who holes up with a pretty young widow (Rosanna Arquette) and her children. Bad guy Joss Ackland is trying to evict Arquette from her land, but Van Damme comes to her rescue. The fighting sequences are a letdown. JF. Contains swearing, violence and nudity. [VIDEO] DVD

Jean-Claude Van Damme *Sam* • Rosanna Arquette *Clydie* • Kieran Culkin *Mookie* • Ted Levine *Mr Dunston* • Tiffany Taubman *Bree* • Edward Blatchford *Lonnie* • Anthony Starke *Billy* • Joss Ackland *Franklin Hale* ■ *Dir* Robert Harmon • *Scr* Joe Eszterhas, Leslie Bohem, Randy Feldman

The Nude Bomb ★ PG

Spy spoof 1980 · US · Colour · 89mins

This feature-length adaptation of the 1960s TV spy spoof *Get Smart* has agent Maxwell Smart (Don Adams) called in to stop a madman who is threatening to destroy all the clothing in the world. One has to wonder why the film-makers bothered to get the rights to the show, considering Smart here bears little resemblance to the character in the TV series. This plays like a lame, expanded sitcom that's missing its laughter track. KB [VIDEO]

Don Adams *Maxwell Smart/Agent 86* • Sylvia Kristel *Agent 34* • Vittorio Gassman *Nino Salvatore Sebastiani/Norman Saint Sauvage* • Rhonda Fleming *Edith Von Secondberg* • Dana Elcar *Chief* ■ *Dir* Clive Donner • *Scr* Arne Sultan, Bill Dana, Leonard Stern, from characters created by Mel Brooks, Buck Henry

Nude on the Moon ★ 15

Cult science-fiction drama
1961 · US · Colour · 69mins

"You're acting like a schoolboy. Don't forget we're rocket scientists," says an ageing doctor to a multi-millionaire playboy as they lift off in this weird space oddity from bargain-basement cult director Doris Wishman. Their journey ends, as the title suggests, with the discovery of topless models on the Moon. This pitiful production contains Nasa stock footage and is decorated with toy spaceships, funny-coloured tights and star-covered astronaut boots. AJ DVD

Marietta *Cathy/Moon Goddess* ■ *Dir/Scr* Doris Wishman

N

The Nugget ★★★ 15

Comedy 2002 · Aus · Colour · 92mins

In this amiable comedy, Eric Bana, Stephen Curry and Dave O'Neil play a trio of likable losers who stumble across a massive gold nugget that has been unearthed by flooding. However, it's not long before their new-found fortune is threatening their friendship and attracting the unwanted attention of local crooks. While it never reaches the barmy delights of *The Castle*, this still possesses a ramshackle charm and writer/director Bill Bennett sketches the eccentricities of small-town life with affection. JF. Contains swearing. DVD

Eric Bana *Lotto* • Stephen Curry *Wookie* • Dave O'Neil *Sue* • Belinda Emmett *Cheryl* • Peter Moon *Ratner* • Vince Colosimo *Dimitri* • Max Cullen *Wally* ■ *Dir/Scr* Bill Bennett

La Nuit de Varennes ★★ 12

Historical drama 1983 · Fr · Colour · 144mins

A historical conceit in which various notables arrive by coach at Varennes where the fugitive king Louis XVI and Marie Antoinette were captured. Thus Casanova (Marcello Mastroianni), political theorist Tom Paine (Harvey Keitel) and an Austrian countess (Hanna Schygulla) gather to discuss politics, sex, art, history and everything that can be crammed into almost two and a half hours. An excellent supporting cast should delight followers of European cinema, but Ettore Scola's film is neither as witty nor clever as it thinks it is. AT. In French with English subtitles.

Marcello Mastroianni *Casanova* • Hanna Schygulla *Countess Sophie de la Borde* • Jean-Louis Barrault *Nicolas Edme Restif* • Harvey Keitel *Thomas Paine* • Michel Piccoli *King Louis XVI* • Eléonore Hirt *Queen Marie-Antoinette* • Jean-Louis Trintignant *M Sauce* • Jean-Claude Brialy *M Jacob* ■ *Dir* Ettore Scola • *Scr* Ettore Scola, Sergio Amidei

N

La Nuit du Carrefour ★★★★

Mystery 1932 · Fr · BW · 75mins

The first Georges Simenon story to reach the screen is a triumph of location film-making. Eschewing the studio artifice that characterises so many early Talkies, Jean Renoir shot this dense mystery in almost permanent shadow and with direct sound to enhance the atmosphere of Inspector Maigret's pursuit of a murderous jewel thief. Pierre Renoir holds centre stage, while Winna Winifried is the addled, but alluring *femme fatale*. Anticipating the look and feel of *film noir*, this is not just a compelling whodunnit, but also a superbly observed portrait of an isolated community. DP. In French with English subtitles.

Pierre Renoir *Inspector Maigret* • Georges Terof *Lucas* • Winna Winifried *Else Andersen* • Georges Koudria *Carl Andersen* • Dignimont *Oscar* • Lucie Vallat *Michelle* • GA Martin *Granjean* ■ *Dir* Jean Renoir • *Scr* Jean Renoir, from the novel by Georges Simenon

Nuit et Brouillard ★★★★★ 15

Documentary
1955 · Fr · Colour and BW · 30mins

Exploring his perennial themes of time and memory, Alain Resnais described this documentary as a "warning siren" to those who believed that the horrors of Auschwitz were now consigned to history. Transposing hideous monochrome images of the camp in wartime with prowling takes capturing the melancholic calm that descended in the ensuing decade, the footage is often as unbearable to watch as the crimes are impossible to comprehend. Former deportee Jean Cayrol contributes a commentary that, for all its poignancy, makes several incontrovertible points, which prompted François Truffaut to declare this the greatest film ever made. DP. In French with English subtitles. DVD

Michel Bouquet *Narrator* ■ *Dir* Alain Resnais • *Scr* Jean Cayrol

La Nuit Fantastique ★★★★

Wartime comedy fantasy
1942 · Fr · BW · 103mins

The most widely known of Marcel L'Herbier's sound films was one of the great successes of the French cinema during the occupation. Although this atmospheric comedy fantasy has a dark side, the film catered to a population that needed escapist entertainment. It tells of a student who continually dreams of a woman in white, whom he then meets. He and the woman have a series of fantastic adventures, so that he is still not sure whether he's dreaming or not. Fernand Gravey was soon to join the French Resistance movement, while co-star Micheline Presle continued to work under the Nazi occupation. RB. A French language film.

Fernand Gravey [Fernand Gravet] *Denis* • Micheline Presle *Irène* • Saturnin Fabre *Thalès* • Bernard Blier *Lucien* • Charles Granval *Adalbert* • Jean Parédès *Cadet* • Christiane Nèré *Nina* • Michel Vitold *Boris* ■ *Dir* Marcel L'Herbier • *Scr* Louis Chavance, Maurice Henry, Marcel L'Herbier, Henri Jeanson, from a story by Louis Chavance

Les Nuits Fauves ★★★★ 18

Biographical drama
1992 · Fr · Colour · 122mins

This brutally honest insight into the mind of an HIV-positive man was written and directed by its bisexual star, Cyril Collard, who succumbed to an Aids-related illness just three days before the film's triumph at the Césars. Also released under its English title *Savage Nights*, this uncompromising picture is made particularly compelling by the credibility of its characters. So what if Collard's actions are reckless, or if teenage waif Romane Bohringer's decision to have unprotected sex with him is incomprehensible? These are the failings and irrationalities of real people. DP. In French with English subtitles. Contains violence, swearing, sex scenes, drug abuse, nudity.

Cyril Collard *Jean* • Romane Bohringer *Laura* • Carlos Lopez (1) *Samy* • Corine Blue *Laura's mother* • Claude Winter *Jean's mother* • René-Marc Bini *Marc* • Maria Schneider *Noémie* ■ *Dir* Cyril Collard • *Scr* Cyril Collard, Jacques Fieschi, from the novel by Cyril Collard

Nukie ★ U

Science fiction 1992 · S Afr · Colour · 95mins

This has got to be the worst *ET* rip-off ever made, and that's against some stiff competition. Nukie, who looks like a char-broiled Tinky Winky, lands in Africa and befriends two twins from a rural village. He enlists their help to find his brother, who is the subject of cruel tests by the "Space Foundation" in Florida. Incoherent and frustrating, you have to wonder why anyone bothered. ST

Glynis Johns *Sister Anne* • Steve Railsback *Dr Eric Harvey* • Ronald France • Fats Dibeco • Michael McCabe • Kurtis Kent • Janice Honeyman ■ *Dir* Sias Odendal • *Scr* Benjamin Taylor, from a story by Sias Odendal

Number One ★★

Drama 1969 · US · Colour · 104mins

Seldom have actor and director shown such mutual understanding first time out as Charlton Heston and Tom Gries in the masterly western *Will Penny*. This contemporary version, about an ageing quarterback player with the New Orleans Saints, followed almost immediately, but turned out to be a complete failure. Heston is relatively convincing, albeit no football player, and the setting is interesting, but few scenes really work and the script and direction are slovenly. TS

Charlton Heston *Ron "Cat" Catlan* • Jessica Walter *Julie Catlan* • Bruce Dern *Richie Fowler* • John Randolph *Coach Jim Southerd* • Diana Muldaur *Ann Marley* • GD Spradlin *Dr Tristler* • Richard Elkins *Kelly Williams* ■ *Dir* Tom Gries • *Scr* David Moessinger

Number One ★★ 15

Drama 1984 · UK · Colour · 98mins

This British crime drama boasts the presence of two legendary pop stars – Bob Geldof in the lead role and Ian Dury. They put in admirable performances, Geldof as a snooker hustler and Dury as an ineffectual hold-up man. But they and the rest of the cast are let down by wayward direction and an unfocused script, which borrows too blatantly from films such as *The Cincinnati Kid*. AJ

Bob Geldof *Harry "Flash" Gordon* • Mel Smith *Billy Evans* • Alison Steadman *Doreen* • PH Moriarty *Mike the Throat* • Phil Daniels *Terry the Boxer* • Alfred Molina *Constable Rogers* • Ian Dury *Teddy Bryant* ■ *Dir* Les Blair • *Scr* GF Newman

Number One with a Bullet ★★ 15

Action thriller 1986 · US · Colour · 96mins

This is a standard action pic, which clearly apes the buddy cop formula of *Lethal Weapon*. Director Jack Smight can do little with the hackneyed cops-versus-drug lord plotline. He does at least manage to wring a few laughs out of the mismatched pairing of Billy Dee Williams, a smooth and urbane cop, and Robert Carradine. Known for his unorthodox police tactics, Carradine is obsessed with bringing down the Mr Big of the Los Angeles drug scene. RS

Robert Carradine *Berzak* • Billy Dee Williams *Hazeltine* • Valerie Bertinelli *Teresa Berzak* • Peter Graves (2) *Captain Ferris* • Doris Roberts *Mrs Berzak* ■ *Dir* Jack Smight • *Scr* Gail Morgan Hickman, Andrew Kurtzman, Rob Riley, James Belushi, from a story by Gail Morgan Hickman

Number Seventeen ★★★ U

Crime comedy 1932 · UK · BW · 65mins

Anne Grey is the member of a gang of criminals who falls for the gentlemanly detective (John Stuart) who is investigating their nefarious activities, and helps bring her former colleagues to justice. Little-seen and largely forgotten, this is an Alfred Hitchcock film of minor entertainment value but superb technical expertise. It's especially notable for a climactic chase sequence involving a train. RK

Leon M Lion *Ben* • Anne Grey *The girl* • John Stuart *Detective* • Garry Marsh *Sheldrake* • Ann Casson *Miss Ackroyd* • Henry Caine *Mr Ackroyd* ■ *Dir* Alfred Hitchcock • *Scr* Alma Reville, Alfred Hitchcock, Rodney Ackland, from a play by J Jefferson Farjeon

Number Two ★★

Experimental drama
1975 · Fr · Colour · 88mins

Absent from film-making for three years due to a motorcycle crash, influential French director Jean-Luc Godard returned with this dour tale of an ordinary family coping with the problems and pressures of modern life. However, Godard seems most preoccupied by the husband's impotence and the wife's constipation. But it's the style of the film that is most striking – Godard shot it all on video and uses a variety of split-screen effects. AT. A French language film.

Sandrine Battistella *Wife* • Pierre Oudrey *Husband* • Alexandre Rignault *Grandpa* • Rachel Stefanopoli *Grandma* • Jean-Luc Godard ■ *Dir* Jean-Luc Godard • *Scr* Anne-Marie Miéville, Jean-Luc Godard

The Nun and the Bandit ★★

Crime drama 1992 · Aus · Colour · 92mins

It's a truism that nuns don't fare too well on the screen (unless played by Deborah Kerr) since they are often the objects of menace. That's true here in Paul Cox's rather odd dramatic thriller. Sister Lucy is the frightened and none-too-worldly aunt of a kidnapped child who is being held for ransom in the Australian outback. The film is adapted from a novel set in the 1930s, but the story has been somewhat updated. BB

Gosia Dobrowolska *Sister Lucy* • Chris Haywood *Michael Shanley* • Victoria Eagger *Maureen* • Charlotte Hughes Haywood *Julie* • Norman Kaye *George Shanley* ■ *Dir* Paul Cox • *Scr* Paul Cox, from a novel by EL Grant Watson

Nuns on the Run ★★★ 15

Comedy 1990 · UK · Colour · 88mins

Writer/director Jonathan Lynn, one half of the team behind the scorching wit of *Yes, Minister*, has been swimming rather more lazily in the mainstream in recent years. Here, by trying to squeeze a whole film from the single joke of Robbie Coltrane and Eric Idle decked out as nuns, he was in danger of veering towards a comic dud. Yet there is a natural spark between the two performers that saves many a scene and, when the genial proceedings are not burdened by the full weight of cliché, they do catch fire. JM. Contains violence. DVD

Eric Idle *Brian Hope* • Robbie Coltrane *Charlie McManus* • Camille Coduri *Faith* • Janet Suzman *Sister Superior* • Doris Hare *Sister Mary of the Sacred Heart* • Lila Kaye *Sister Mary of the Annunciation* • Robert Patterson *"Case" Casey* ■ *Dir/Scr* Jonathan Lynn

The Nun's Story ★★★★★ PG

Drama 1959 · US · Colour · 145mins

Kathryn C Hulme's popular novel makes a magnificent vehicle for the luminous Audrey Hepburn, battling with her conscience and wondering if she is truly cut out for her calling. Hepburn is a marvel, whether flirting with passion in the Congo (in the guise of Peter Finch, terrific as an agnostic doctor) or discovering that some nuns (Dames Edith Evans and Peggy Ashcroft) are only human after all. This is arguably director Fred Zinnemann's finest movie; it won eight nominations, but no Oscars, in the year of *Ben-Hur*. Unjust, really, as you watch Franz Planer's superb photography, listen to Franz Waxman's haunting score and wonder to what greater heights popular cinema can aspire. TS

Audrey Hepburn *Sister Luke/Gabrielle Van Der Mal* • Peter Finch *Dr Fortunati* • Edith Evans *Mother Emmanuel* • Peggy Ashcroft *Mother Mathilde* • Dean Jagger *Dr Van Der Mal* • Mildred Dunnock *Sister Margharita/Mistress of Postulance* • Beatrice Straight *Mother Christophe* • Patricia Collinge *Sister William* • Rosalie Crutchley *Sister Eleanor* • Colleen Dewhurst *Archangel Gabriel* • Lionel Jeffries *Dr Goovaerts* ■ *Dir* Fred Zinnemann • *Scr* Robert Anderson, from the novel by Kathryn C Hulme

Nurse Betty ★★★ 18

Black comedy drama
2000 · US · Colour · 105mins

Renee Zellweger excels in director Neil LaBute's adroit blend of comic fantasy and social satire. Yet LaBute's trademark acerbity has been somewhat diluted by the fact that he didn't write the occasionally fanciful script. So, while it's possible to believe that witnessing her husband's brutal murder could send a TV-addicted waitress on an odyssey to romance her hospital soap hero, it takes a sizeable

U = SUITABLE FOR ALL Uc = SUITABLE FOR ALL, ESPECIALLY FOR YOUNG CHILDREN (VIDEO ONLY) PG = PARENTAL GUIDANCE

suspension of disbelief to accept that the actor playing that role (Greg Kinnear) would buy into her delusion. Her impact on chillingly professional hitman Morgan Freeman is similarly strained. Still, engagingly offbeat and enjoyable. DP. Contains violence, swearing, sex scenes. [VIDEO] DVD

Morgan Freeman *Charlie* • Renée Zellweger [Renee Zellweger] *Betty Sizemore* • Chris Rock *Wesley* • Greg Kinnear *Dr David Ravel/George McCord* • Aaron Eckhart *Del Sizemore* • Tia Texada *Rosa Herrera* • Crispin Glover *Roy Ostrey* • Pruitt Taylor Vince *Sheriff Eldon Ballard* ■ *Dir* Neil LaBute • *Scr* John C Richards, James Flamberg, from a story by John C Richards

Nurse Edith Cavell ★★ U

First World War drama
1939 · US · BW · 96mins

English producer/director Herbert Wilcox's first Hollywood film is an account of Nurse Edith Cavell, the brave and self-sacrificing heroine of the First World War who smuggled English soldiers out of German-occupied Belgium and was executed as a spy for her pains. Anna Neagle (Wilcox's wife), an actress not noted for her dramatic range, makes do with her natural regal dignity in a film that is sober, competent and dull, yet affecting. RK

Anna Neagle *Nurse Edith Cavell* • George Sanders *Captain Heinrichs* • Edna May Oliver *Countess de Mavon* • May Robson *Mme Rappard* • ZaSu Pitts *Mme Moulin* • Sophie Stewart *Sister Watkins* ■ *Dir* Herbert Wilcox • *Scr* Michael Hogan, from his novel

Nurse on Wheels ★★★ U

Comedy 1963 · UK · BW · 82mins

Peter Rogers and his wife Betty Box seem to have had an obsession with medical matters. She produced the popular *Doctor* series, while he was responsible for four hospital-based *Carry Ons* and this charming comedy that reunited him with Juliet Mills, who had played a nurse in the previous year's *Twice round the Daffodils*. It has its moments of broad humour, but old-fashioned family fun is to the fore as district nurse Mills encounters a range of eccentrics in a village. DP [VIDEO]

Juliet Mills *Joanna Jones* • Ronald Lewis *Henry Edwards* • Joan Sims *Deborah Walcott* • Athene Seyler *Miss Farthingale* • Norman Rossington *George Judd* • Barbara Everest *Nurse Merrick* • Ronald Howard *Dr Harold Golfrey* • Joan Hickson *Mrs Wood* ■ *Dir* Gerald Thomas • *Scr* Norman Hudis, from the novel *Nurse Is a Neighbour* by Joanna Jones

Nutcracker ★★ 18

Drama 1982 · UK · Colour · 96mins

When Russian ballerina Finola Hughes defects and joins an international ballet company, she soon realises she is being used by its owner (Joan Collins) as a high-class call girl to local politicians. Meanwhile, photojournalist Paul Nicholas goes to extraordinary lengths to snap a scoop picture of Collins's new star dancer in action. A thin plot full of soap-opera theatrics and soft-core erotica is played out against intensely cheap sets. AJ [VIDEO]

Joan Collins *Mme Carrere* • Carol White *Margaux Lasselle* • Paul Nicholas *Mike McCann* • Finola Hughes *Nadia* • William Franklyn *Sir Arthur Cartwright* ■ *Dir* Anwar Kawadri • *Scr* Raymond Christodoulou

Nutcracker ★ U

Ballet 1986 · US · Colour · 81mins

Another version of the Christmas classic, this time performed by the Pacific Northwest Ballet. Despite inspired design by Maurice Sendak and direction by Carroll Ballard, this never transcends its stage origins, regardless of Ballard's attempts to create a fourth wall. Similarly, his overly tricky, close-up shots of dancers' limbs in action give the film the feel of a pop promo. If you want to see how it should be done, watch *The Red Shoes*. LH [VIDEO]

Hugh Bigney *Herr Drosselmeier* • Vanessa Sharp *Young Clara* • Patricia Barker *Dream Clara/Ballerina Doll* • Wade Walthall *Nutcracker* • Maia Rosal *Frau Stahlbaum/Peacock* • Carey Homme *Dr Stahlbaum/Moor* ■ *Dir* Carroll Ballard • *Scr* Maurice Sendak, Kent Stowell, from the ballet by Peter Ilich Tchaikovsky, from the fairy tale *The Nutcracker and the Mouse King* by ETA Hoffman

The Nutcracker Prince ★★ U

Animated fantasy
1990 · Can · Colour · 70mins

Canada has a proud tradition of ground-breaking animation, but this lowbrow, low-budget offering is something of an embarrassment. The story sees a young girl shrink to the size of her toys to help her model soldiers overcome a tyrannical rodent. Kiefer Sutherland and Peter O'Toole provide effective voiceovers, and there's Tchaikovsky's music on the soundtrack. But the artwork looks shoddy and Paul Schibli's direction is anything but magical. DP [VIDEO]

Peter O'Toole *Pantaloon* • Kiefer Sutherland *Nutcracker/Hans* • Megan Follows *Clara* • Michael MacDonald *Mouse King* ■ *Dir* Paul Schibli • *Scr* Patricia Watson, from the fairy tale *The Nutcracker and the Mouse King* by ETA Hoffman

Nuts ★★★ 18

Drama 1987 · US · Colour · 110mins

You can imagine Tom Topor's play about a prostitute proving her sanity so that she can stand trial for manslaughter making for a cracking night at the theatre. That it is marginally less compelling as a film is down to director Martin Ritt's decision to reveal key facts via clumsily staged flashbacks rather than as courtroom testimony, as this considerably diminishes their impact. Even though the outcome is inevitable, this is still an involving drama thanks to the bullish performances of Barbra Streisand as the hooker and Richard Dreyfuss as her attorney. DP [VIDEO]

Barbra Streisand *Claudia Draper* • Richard Dreyfuss *Aaron Levinsky* • Maureen Stapleton *Rose Kirk* • Eli Wallach *Dr Herbert A Morrison* • Karl Malden *Arthur Kirk* • Robert Webber *Francis MacMillan* ■ *Dir* Martin Ritt • *Scr* Alvin Sargent, Darryl Ponicsan, Tom Topor, from the play by Tom Topor

The Nutty Professor ★★★★ PG

Comedy 1963 · US · Colour · 102mins

In spite of almost universal criticism, this immensely accomplished comedy remains Jerry Lewis's best and funniest screen work. It's really "Doctor Jerry and Mister Love" (the film's French title translated), as Lewis plays a nerdish chemistry professor who is hooked on lovely student Stella Stevens. Lewis makes and takes a potion that turns him into Buddy Love, singing lounge lizard *par excellence*. The witty design and the use of fabulously rich Technicolor are major bonuses, and this clever movie remains extremely funny. TS [VIDEO] DVD

Jerry Lewis *Professor Julius Kelp/Buddy Love* • Stella Stevens *Stella Purdy* • Del Moore *Dr Hamius R Warfield* • Kathleen Freeman *Millie Lemmon* ■ *Dir* Jerry Lewis • *Scr* Jerry Lewis, Bill Richmond, from a story by Jerry Lewis

The Nutty Professor ★★★★ 12

Comedy 1996 · US · Colour · 91mins

This reworking of the 1963 Jerry Lewis comedy finds Eddie Murphy back on form as Sherman Klump, a sweet-natured, obese science teacher who perfects a potion that turns him into a svelte, sexy love machine. Of course, the potion wears off at the most unfortunate times, making his attempts at romance with attractive teaching assistant Jada Pinkett a bit of a lottery. Murphy plays the professor to perfection; thanks to the genius of the Oscar-winning make-up and computer graphics departments, he also portrays three generations of his family. Snappily directed, this isn't quite as daft as the original, but it is a most enjoyable laughfest. JB [VIDEO] DVD

Eddie Murphy *Sherman Klump/Buddy Love* • Jada Pinkett [Jada Pinkett Smith] *Carla Purty* • James Coburn *Harlan Hartley* • Larry Miller *Dean Richmond* • Dave Chappelle *Reggie Warrington* • John Ales *Jason* • Patricia Wilson *Dean's secretary* ■ *Dir* Tom Shadyac • *Scr* David Sheffield, Barry W Blaustein, Tom Shadyac, Steve Oedederk, from the 1963 film

Nutty Professor 2: the Klumps ★★★ 12

Comedy 2000 · US · Colour · 102mins

In this sequel to Eddie Murphy's 1996 success, Murphy gets to play rotund scientist Sherman Klump and his corpulent family, including his father at two different ages. His performance is an amazing tour de force, which could be compared to the best work of Alec Guinness and Peter Sellers if it weren't for the fact that half the time he's unintelligible. Klump is desperate to rid himself of his slim, supercool alter ego, Buddy Love, but only manages to regenerate (and mutate) him. Janet Jackson is sweetly effective, playing it straight as Klump's long-suffering girlfriend. DM. Contains sexual references. [VIDEO] DVD

Eddie Murphy *Professor Sherman Klump/Cletus "Papa" Klump/Young Cletus Klump/Anna "Mama" Klump/Ernie Klump/Grandma Klump/Buddy Love/Lance Perkins* • Janet Jackson *Professor Denise Gaines* • Larry Miller *Dean Richmond* • John Ales *Jason* • Richard Gant *Denise's father* • Anna Maria Horsford *Denise's mother* • Melinda McGraw *Leanne Guilford* • Jamal Mixon *Ernie Klump Jr* • Freda Payne *Claudine* ■ *Dir* Peter Segal • *Scr* Barry W Blaustein, David Sheffield, Paul Weitz, Chris Weitz, from a story by Steve Oedekerk, Barry W Blaustein, David Sheffield, from characters created by Jerry Lewis, Bill Richmond

A Nymphoid Barbarian in Dinosaur Hell ★★ 18

Science-fiction fantasy
1991 · US · Colour · 81mins

Even the guys from Troma, who produced this sci-fi fantasy, would be the first to admit it isn't one of their finest hours. The plot outline is as scanty as Linda Corwin's costume, as she endures the nightmare of being the last female alive following a nuclear conflagration. Moreover, it's hard to dispute the claim that it cost a mere $5,000 to shoot somewhere in New England, though the hilarious stop-motion Tromasaurus and the one-eyed "D'ya-think-e-saurus" almost save the day. DP. Contains violence, nudity. [VIDEO] DVD

Linda Corwin *Lea* • Paul Guzzi *Marn* • Mark Deshaies *Man with No Face* ■ *Dir/Scr* Brett Piper

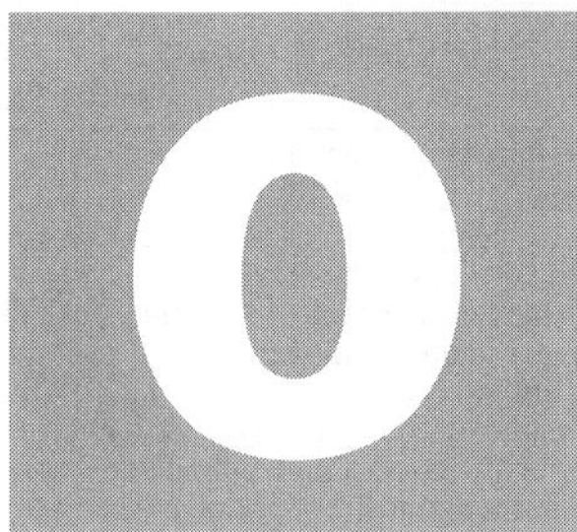

O ★★★★ 15

Drama 2001 · US · Colour · 90mins

Director Tim Blake Nelson's modern interpretation of Shakespeare's *Othello* is set in a high school in the American South, and the drama twists its themes of vengeance, jealousy and racism into a chilling and timely snapshot of contemporary teenage life. There's no glimmer of hope or salvation here, as black basketball hero Mekhi Phifer staggers like a sleepwalker into an inescapable hell. Set up by his embittered pal (a poisonously good Josh Hartnett), who envies him his sporting prowess and beautiful girlfriend Julia Stiles, Phifer's fall from grace is painfully bleak and downright nasty. SF. Contains violence, swearing, sex scenes, drug abuse and nudity. [VIDEO] DVD

Mekhi Phifer *Odin James* • Josh Hartnett *Hugo Goulding* • Julia Stiles *Desi Brable* • Martin Sheen *Coach Duke Goulding* • Andrew Keegan *Michael Casio* • Rain Phoenix *Emily* ■ *Dir* Tim Blake Nelson • *Scr* Brad Kaaya, from the play *Othello* by William Shakespeare • *Cinematographer* Russell Lee Fine

O Brother, Where Art Thou? ★★★★ 12

Comedy 2000 · US/UK/Fr · Colour · 102mins

The eighth collaborative effort produced and directed by brothers Ethan and Joel Coen concerns the attempts of escaped convict George Clooney (nicely self-mocking) to get back to his wife Holly Hunter (in a cameo appearance), and the picaresque adventures he has on the way. The title derives from Preston Sturges's 1941 movie *Sullivan's Travels*, whose humorous spirit hangs over this episodic tale. The movie also contrives to encapsulate every con-on-the-run picture one has ever seen, as well as southern period crime dramas. Yet again, the Coens' cinematic alchemy has worked a treat. RB [VIDEO] DVD

George Clooney *Ulysses Everett McGill* • John Turturro *Pete* • Tim Blake Nelson *Delmar* • Charles Durning *Pappy O'Daniel* • John Goodman *Big Dan Teague* • Michael Badalucco *George Nelson* • Holly Hunter *Penny* ■ *Dir* Joel Coen • *Scr* Ethan Coen, Joel Coen, from the poem *The Odyssey* by Homer • *Producer* Ethan Coen

OC and Stiggs ★★ 12

Comedy 1987 · US · Colour · 105mins

Before returning to fine, focused form with *The Player*, director Robert Altman barked up several wrong trees in the preceding years. This film was one of them: a meandering, stop-start sprawl, with a tone too blunt for satire. The eponymous characters are a couple of teen clowns who get up to all kinds of merry japes. There are, however, some semi-inspired moments of Altman strangeness. JM [VIDEO] DVD

Daniel H Jenkins [Daniel Jenkins] *OC Ogilvey* • Neill Barry *Mark Stiggs* • Jane Curtin *Elinore Schwab* • Paul Dooley *Randall Schwab* • Jon Cryer *Randall Schwab Jr* • Laura Urstein *Lenore Schwab* • Victor Ho *Frankie Tang* • Dennis Hopper *Sponson* ■ *Dir* Robert Altman • *Scr* Donald Cantrell, Ted Mann, from a story by Tod Carroll, Ted Mann, from a story in *National Lampoon* magazine

O

O Henry's Full House

★★★★ U

Portmanteau comedy drama
1952 · US · BW · 117mins

This compendium of five short stories by a genius of the form is beautifully adapted, well cast and directed. The most deeply moving tale is *The Last Leaf*, with Anne Baxter as a dying woman saved by self-sacrificing artist Gregory Ratoff. Charles Laughton stars as a tramp trying to get arrested in the cruelly ironic *The Cop and the Anthem*, in which Marilyn Monroe appears as a streetwalker; Dale Robertson is a cop who must arrest his good friend Richard Widmark in the tough-minded *The Clarion Call*; while *The Ransom of Red Chief* has kidnappers offering to pay the parents of the ghastly child they've nabbed to take him back. However, perhaps the most fondly remembered is the painfully tender *Gift of the Magi*, with Jeanne Crain and Farley Granger as the poverty-stricken young couple who each sacrifice a treasured possession to buy the other a Christmas gift. RK

Jeanne Crain *Della* • Farley Granger *Jim* • Sig Rumann [Sig Ruman] *Menkie* • Anne Baxter *Joanna* • Jean Peters *Susan* • Gregory Ratoff *Behrman* • Charles Laughton *Soapy* • Marilyn Monroe *Streetwalker* • Dale Robertson *Barney Woods* • Richard Widmark *Johnny Kernan* • Fred Allen *Sam* • Oscar Levant *Bill* • John Steinbeck *Narrator* ■ *Dir* Henry Hathaway, Henry Koster, Henry King, Howard Hawks, Jean Negulesco • *Scr* Lamar Trotti, Richard L Breen, Ben Roberts, Ivan Goff, Walter Bullock, Nunnally Johnson, from stories by O Henry

O-Kay for Sound

★★★

Comedy 1937 · UK · BW · 86mins

The much-loved Crazy Gang wreak their own particular brand of chaos in this breathless comedy in which they play extras who are mistaken for movie moguls and bring the production to a grinding halt. Unsurprisingly, it's Flanagan and Allen who catch the eye, but the Gang's other troublesome twosomes, Nervo and Knox and Naughton and Gold, chip in to good effect. Will Hay's regular backroom staff, writers Marriott Edgar and Val Guest, provide the ammunition, while director Marcel Varnel keeps the gags coming thick and fast. DP

Jimmy Nervo • Bud Flanagan • Chesney Allen • Teddy Knox • Charlie Naughton • Jimmy Gold ■ *Dir* Marcel Varnel • *Scr* Marriott Edgar, Val Guest

O Lucky Man!

★★★ 15

Satirical fantasy 1973 · UK · Colour · 169mins

This irreligious, updated *Pilgrim's Progress* through society remains a determined attempt to irritate, incite and entertain. The fine cast is led by director Lindsay Anderson's regular collaborator Malcolm McDowell, who plays an everyman adrift in a surreal landscape littered with British character actors such as Ralph Richardson, Rachel Roberts and Arthur Lowe, all playing multiple parts. The title is not so much ironic as downright sarcastic and, despite the jarring clash of symbols, it's a provocative fable not to be missed, even if it is now somewhat dated. Alan Price's energetic score is a bonus. TH. Contains sex scenes.

Malcolm McDowell *Mick Travis* • Ralph Richardson *Monty/Sir James Burgess* • Rachel Roberts (1) *Gloria/Mme Paillard/Mrs Richards* • Arthur Lowe *Mr Duff/Charlie Johnson/Dr Munda* • Helen Mirren *Patricia Burgess* • Dandy Nichols *Tea lady/Neighbour* ■ *Dir* Lindsay Anderson • *Scr* David Sherwin, from an idea by Malcolm McDowell • *Music/lyrics* Alan Price

OSS

★★★

Spy drama 1946 · US · BW · 105mins

Paramount's resident tough guy Alan Ladd finds himself spying in France during the Second World War in the dark days before D-Day. It's pretty routine action material for the studio, but it's given dignity by the strength of the star's performance. As the movie is so obviously a Ladd vehicle, there are no other stellar names in support; Geraldine Fitzgerald is an attractive though unexciting heroine, and Patric Knowles is as wooden as ever. TS. Contains violence.

Alan Ladd *John Martin* • Geraldine Fitzgerald *Ellen Rogers* • Patric Knowles *Commander Brady* • John Hoyt *Colonel Meister* • Gloria Saunders *Mary "Sparks" Kenny* • Richard Benedict *Bernay* ■ *Dir* Irving Pichel • *Scr* Richard Maibaum

The Oberwald Mystery

★★★

Drama 1980 · It/W Ger · Colour · 128mins

Sixteen years after *The Red Desert*, Michelangelo Antonioni and his muse, Monica Vitti, reunited for this flawed but fascinating reworking of Jean Cocteau's courtly melodrama. As the royal widow roused from a decade of mourning by anarchist poet Franco Branciaroli, Vitti is both vulnerable and tragic. However, Antonioni's attempt to fuse Cocteau's escapist flamboyance with his own coolly detached style was dramatically ill-conceived. Similarly, his scheme to shoot on video and then transfer the footage to 35mm proved visually unsatisfactory. DP. An Italian language film.

Monica Vitti *The Queen* • Luigi Diberti *Willenstein* • Paolo Bonacelli *Count of Foehn* • Franco Branciaroli *Sebastian* ■ *Dir* Michelangelo Antonioni • *Scr* Michelangelo Antonioni, Tonino Guerra, from the play *The Eagle Has Two Heads* by Jean Cocteau

The Object of Beauty

★★★ 15

Comedy drama
1991 · US/UK · Colour · 98mins

As the Americans who live on their wits and other people's money, Andie MacDowell and John Malkovich make an unexpectedly good team, with their on-screen limitations actually contributing to the credibility of their characters. Indeed, the insurance scam involving a Henry Moore sculpture rather gets in the way of their bantering, as it shifts the focus on to the deaf-mute maid who has purloined it. Smoothly directed by Michael Lindsay-Hogg, this is a pleasing comedy of crooked manners. DP DVD

John Malkovich *Jake* • Andie MacDowell *Tina* • Lolita Davidovich *Joan* • Rudi Davis *Jenny* • Joss Ackland *Mr Mercer* • Bill Paterson *Victor Swayle* • Ricci Harnett *Steve* • Peter Riegert *Larry* • Jack Shepherd *Mr Slaughter* • Rosemary Martin *Mrs Doughty* ■ *Dir/Scr* Michael Lindsay-Hogg

The Object of My Affection

★★★ 15

Romantic comedy
1998 · US · Colour · 106mins

Jennifer Aniston tries to escape her *Friends* persona in this uneven romantic comedy, directed by Nicholas Hytner. Aniston plays a girl who gets pregnant by her oafish ex-boyfriend, but decides to ask her gay friend Paul Rudd to help her bring up the child. She falls in love with him, of course, but the resulting mess it makes of both their lives is more sad than humorous, while the ending is contrived. Well-meaning, with some nice performances from co-stars Alan Alda and Nigel Hawthorne, but ultimately unsatisfying. JB. Contains swearing and a sex scene. DVD

Jennifer Aniston *Nina Borowski* • Paul Rudd *George Hanson* • John Pankow *Vince McBride* • Alan Alda *Sidney Miller* • Tim Daly [Timothy Daly] *Dr Robert Joley* • Nigel Hawthorne *Rodney Fraser* • Allison Janney *Constance Miller* • Amo Gulinello *Paul James* ■ *Dir* Nicholas Hytner • *Scr* Wendy Wasserstein, from the novel by Stephen McCauley

Objective, Burma!

★★★ PG

Second World War drama
1945 · US · BW · 135mins

A rousing Second World War drama, with Errol Flynn parachuting into the Burmese jungle with a company of paratroopers to destroy a Japanese radio station. It went unshown in Britain for seven years because it neglected the fact that the British played the major role in Burma. For some reason, action director Raoul Walsh stretches things out for over two hours, but, despite its frequent longueurs, it's exciting stuff, with Flynn bringing all his swashbuckling swagger to his role. AT DVD

Errol Flynn *Major Nelson* • James Brown (1) *Sergeant Treacy* • William Prince *Lieutenant Jacobs* • George Tobias *Gabby Gordon* • Henry Hull *Mark Williams* • Warner Anderson *Colonel Carter* • John Alvin *Hogan* ■ *Dir* Raoul Walsh • *Scr* Ranald MacDougall, Lester Cole, from a story by Alvah Bessie

Oblivion

★★

Science-fiction western
1993 · US · Colour · 94mins

Low-budget guru Charles Band tries setting a literal western on an alien planet. The cast of characters are amusingly eccentric, including reluctant sheriff Richard Joseph Paul (who, as an empathic psychic, feels the pain of anybody he kills), saloon owner Julie Newmar; and George Takei as Doc Valentine, who speaks in *Star Trek* puns. It probably looked a lot funnier on paper. ST

Richard Joseph Paul *Zack Stone* • Jackie Swanson *Mattie Chase* • Andrew Divoff *Redeye* • Meg Foster *Stell Barr* • Jimmie Skaggs [Jimmie F Skaggs] *Buteo* • George Takei *Doc Valentine* • Julie Newmar *Miss Kitty* • Isaac Hayes *Buster* ■ *Dir* Sam Irvin • *Scr* Peter David, from a story by Charles Band

Oblomov

★★★★ U

Satire 1980 · USSR · Colour · 140mins

Covering only half of Ivan Goncharov's sprawling novel, this two-part period piece dissects the dissolute charm of the aristocracy. Transfixed by ennui, corpulent 30-something Oleg Tabakov cannot be roused from his lethargy by a series of idyllic flashbacks prompted by his best friend, Yuri Bogatyrev. But the reformist zeal of Elena Solovei is another matter altogether. Criticised for a lack of incident and its stately pace, Nikita Mikhalkov's film is both intelligently faithful to the spirit of its source and meticulous in its blend of satire and sentimentality. Superbly photographed by Pavel Lebeshev, it's also slyly subversive in its stance on progress. DP. A Russian language film.

Oleg Tabakov *Oblomov* • Yuri Bogatyrev *Stoltz* • Elena Solovei *Olga* ■ *Dir* Nikita Mikhalkov • *Scr* Nikita Mikhalkov, Aleksander Adabashyan, from the novel by Ivan Goncharov

The Oblong Box

★★★ 15

Horror 1969 · UK · Colour · 87mins

Hitchcock protégé Gordon Hessler took over the direction of this obvious shocker when Michael Reeves committed suicide after planning it as his follow-up to *Witchfinder General*. A deranged and disfigured voodoo victim is buried alive by his brother, Vincent Price, only to return from the grave to wreak gory vengeance. A pervasive aura of evil is summoned up in a well-mounted period piece containing occasional flashes of Hessler's trademark visual flair. Yet, while Price is well used, adding weight to the clichéd dialogue, Christopher Lee in a wig is wasted. AJ

Vincent Price *Julian Markham* • Christopher Lee *Dr Neuhartt* • Alistair Williamson *Sir Edward Markham* • Hilary Dwyer *Elizabeth Markham* • Peter Arne *Samuel Trench* • Harry Baird *N Galo* • Carl Rigg *Mark Norton* • Maxwell Shaw *Tom Hackett* • Michael Balfour *Ruddock* ■ *Dir* Gordon Hessler • *Scr* Lawrence Huntingdon, Christopher Wicking, from the story by Edgar Allan Poe

Obsessed

★★★ 15

Thriller 1989 · Can · Colour · 99mins

An emotive and topical subject is sensitively handled by experienced Canadian documentary director Robin Spry. Kerrie Keane movingly portrays the mother whose grief increasingly turns to anger as the law fails to deal with the hit-and-run driver responsible for her young son's death. NF

Kerrie Keane *Dinah Middleton* • Saul Rubinek *Owen Hughs* • Daniel Pilon *Max Middleton* ■ *Dir* Robin Spry • *Scr* Douglas Bowie, from a story by Douglas Bowie, Robin Spry, from the novel *Hit and Run* by Tom Alderman

Obsession

★★★ PG

Thriller 1948 · UK · BW · 93mins

Blacklisted by the McCarthy witch-hunts for being a communist, director Edward Dmytryk came to Britain and made three films, including this suspenseful "perfect murder" thriller. Robert Newton over-acts as the doctor who plans the murder of his wife's American lover. Keeping the man alive and locked in a room, he plans to dissolve him in acid when the police call off the search. AT DVD

Robert Newton *Dr Clive Riordan* • Sally Gray *Storm Riordan* • Naunton Wayne *Superintendent Finsbury* • Phil Brown *Bill Kronin* • Olga Lindo *Mrs Humphreys* • Ronald Adam *Clubman* • James Harcourt *Aitkin* ■ *Dir* Edward Dmytryk • *Scr* Alec Coppel, from his novel *A Man about a Dog*

Obsession

★★

Crime drama 1954 · Fr/It · Colour · 105mins

Making her first film in colour, Michèle Morgan is the only reason to invest time in this hackneyed big-top melodrama. The sets are as woefully artificial as the performances, while the storyline feels like something from the silent era. Borrowing the central conceit from Alfred Hitchcock's *Suspicion* (a genial husband might be responsible for the death of his friend), Jean Delannoy never makes us care whether trapeze artist Raf Vallone or dog trainer Olivier Hussenot is a killer. DP. In French with English subtitles.

Michèle Morgan *Hélène Giovanni* • Raf Vallone *Aldo Giovanni* • Marthe Mercadier *Arlette Bernardin* • Jean Gaven *Alex* • Robert Dalbin *Inspector Chardin* ■ *Dir* Jean Delannoy • *Scr* Jean Delannoy, Roland Laudenbach, Antoine Blondin, from short stories by William Irish [Cornell Woolrich]

Obsession

★★★ 15

Thriller 1976 · US · Colour · 93mins

Director Brian De Palma makes a brave stab at a homage to his idol Alfred Hitchcock with this sexy thriller in which Paul Schrader's screenplay offers more than one nod to *Vertigo*. Further echoes of Hitch are supplied in the Oscar-nominated score by *Psycho* composer Bernard Herrmann. Geneviève Bujold is fetching as Cliff Robertson's dead wife and her double, but John Lithgow in his second movie steals the acting honours as Robertson's suspicious business partner. Nearly, but not quite, as clever as it thinks it is. TS DVD

Cliff Robertson *Michael Courtland* • Geneviève Bujold *Elizabeth Courtland/Sandra Portinari* •

John Lithgow *Robert LaSalle* • Sylvia "Kuumba" Williams *Judy* • Wanda Blackman *Amy Courtland* • J Patrick McNamara *Kidnapper* • Stanley J Reyes *Inspector Brie* ■ *Dir* Brian De Palma • *Scr* Paul Schrader, from a story by Brian De Palma, Paul Schrader

Ocean's Eleven ★★★★ PG

Crime caper 1960 · US · Colour · 127mins

One of the great (and one of the most critically under-rated) caper movies, this story was discovered by Peter Lawford and brought to fellow Rat Rack member Frank Sinatra, who effectively produced the movie. He cast himself as former sergeant Danny Ocean, who calls on his old wartime pals to help him in a raid on Las Vegas. Sleek, audacious and superbly cast, it's directed by veteran Lewis Milestone, who keeps a tight lid on the Rat Pack's antics. The ending, if rather derivative, is still brilliant. TS DVD

Frank Sinatra *Danny Ocean* • Dean Martin *Sam Harmon* • Sammy Davis Jr *Josh Howard* • Peter Lawford *Jimmy Foster* • Angie Dickinson *Beatrice Ocean* • Richard Conte *Anthony Bergdorf* • Cesar Romero *Duke Santos* • Patrice Wymore *Adele Ekstrom* • Joey Bishop *"Mushy" O'Conners* • Akim Tamiroff *Spyros Acebos* ■ *Dir* Lewis Milestone • *Scr* Harry Brown, Charles Lederer, from a story by George Clayton Johnson, Jack Golden Russell

Ocean's Eleven ★★★★ 12

Action crime caper
2001 · US/Aus · Colour · 111mins

George Clooney and his A-list pals have fun in the Las Vegas sun in this thoroughly enjoyable caper from director Steven Soderbergh. In a loose remake of the Rat Pack venture of the same name, Clooney comfortably steps into Frank Sinatra's shoes as Danny Ocean, who is fresh out of jail but still sets about putting together an audacious heist with the help of a ten-man crew. His star cronies include Brad Pitt, Matt Damon, Carl Reiner and Don Cheadle, who affects the worst cockney accent you've ever heard. The plan is to hit the vault containing the take from three of the biggest casinos in Vegas, all of which belong to Andy Garcia, the guy who just happens to be dating Ocean's ex-wife Julia Roberts. This is one of those films that's a joy from start to finish, but doesn't strain the brain for a second. JB DVD

George Clooney *Danny Ocean* • Brad Pitt *Rusty Ryan* • Julia Roberts *Tess Ocean* • Matt Damon *Linus Caldwell* • Andy Garcia *Terry Benedict* • Don Cheadle *Basher Tarr* • Bernie Mac *Frank Catton* • Elliott Gould *Reuben Tishkoff* • Carl Reiner *Saul Bloom* • Scott Caan *Turk Malloy* • Casey Affleck *Virgil Malloy* • Qin Shaobo *Yen* ■ *Dir* Steven Soderbergh • *Scr* Ted Griffin, from the 1960 film

Ocean's Twelve ★★ 12

Action crime caper
2004 · US/Aus · Colour · 120mins

Steven Soderbergh's *Ocean's Eleven* was a sharp, witty remake of a rather self-indulgent vehicle for Frank Sinatra's Rat Pack. With this sequel, George Clooney, Brad Pitt and company seem to have fallen into the same sort of trap. The lazy, convoluted plot has the smooth criminals hitting the robbery trail in Europe to raise the cash needed to pay back casino boss Andy Garcia. Soderbergh gives the movie a hip surface sheen and there's no denying the chemistry between the starry ensemble cast, but this is hopelessly contrived and a little too knowing for its own good. JF DVD

George Clooney *Danny Ocean* • Brad Pitt *Rusty Ryan* • Matt Damon *Linus Caldwell* • Catherine Zeta-Jones *Isabel Lahiri* • Andy Garcia *Terry Benedict* • Don Cheadle *Basher Tarr* • Bernie Mac *Frank Catton* • Julia Roberts *Tess Ocean* • Casey Affleck *Virgil Malloy* • Scott Caan *Turk Malloy* • Vincent Cassel *François Toulour* • Eddie Jemison *Livingston Dell* • Carl Reiner *Saul Bloom* • Elliott Gould *Reuben Tishkoff* • Qin Shaobo *Yen* • Eddie Izzard *Roman Nagel* • Robbie Coltrane *Matsui* • Jeroen Krabbé *van der Woude* ■ *Dir* Steven Soderbergh • *Scr* George Nolfi, from characters created by George Clayton Johnson, Jack Golden Russell

The Octagon ★★ 18

Martial arts action
1980 · US · Colour · 98mins

With his penchant for martial art butt-kicking and monosyllabic, mahogany-table acting, Chuck Norris was probably the precursor to the likes of Van Damme and Schwarzenegger. Here he plays a retired kung fu champ hired as a bodyguard for a wealthy woman against attack by sinister ninja types. As chop-socky movies go, this is better than most, but still devoid of a single brain cell. RS DVD

Chuck Norris *Scott James* • Karen Carlson *Justine* • Lee Van Cleef *McCarn* • Art Hindle *A J* • Carol Bagdasarian *Aura* ■ *Dir* Eric Karson • *Scr* Leigh Chapman, from a story by Paul Aaron, Leigh Chapman

Octane ★★★ 15

Horror 2003 · UK/Lux · Colour · 86mins

Embittered divorcee Madeleine Stowe searches for her teenage daughter, lost to a blood-drinking cult who scour motorway service stations for their victims. Laced with sex-and-splatter jolts, this unusual terror tale is a gripping collision of neon-lit car smashes, disorientating close-ups and well-oiled eeriness. Adams's haunting *danse macabre* exerts a lethal grip even when navigating a few climactic speed bumps. With a great soundtrack from Orbital, it's a canny package of surreal nightmare scenarios. AJ. Contains violence, swearing and drug abuse. DVD

Madeleine Stowe *Senga* • Norman Reedus *Recovery man* • Bijou Phillips *Backpacker* • Mischa Barton *Nat* • Jonathan Rhys Meyers *The Father* • Leo Gregory *Joyrider* • Gary Parker *Vacation man* • Amber Batty *Vacation woman* ■ *Dir* Marcus Adams • *Scr* Stephen Volk

October ★★★★ PG

Silent historical epic
1928 · USSR · Colour · 99mins

Despite being made to celebrate the tenth anniversary of the overthrow of Kerensky's provisional government, this impersonal tribute to the proletariat found little official or critical favour in the Soviet Union. Bitingly satirical and overtly political, it marked Sergei Eisenstein's most ambitious experiment in intellectual montage. However, despite such memorable set pieces as the assault on the Winter Palace, the raising of the bridge and the toppling of Alexander III's statue, the obscurity of some of its imagery and the uncomfortable blend of symbolism and realism renders it less dramatically unified, thematically consistent and emotionally overwhelming than its predecessor, *The Battleship Potemkin*. DP DVD

Nikandrof *Lenin* • N Popov *Kerensky* • Boris Livanov *Minister* ■ *Dir* Sergei Eisenstein, Grigori V Aleksandrov • *Scr* Sergei Eisenstein, Grigori Alexandrov • *Cinematographer* Edouard Tissé

The October Man ★★★★ PG

Murder mystery 1947 · UK · BW · 91mins

Sturdily scripted from his own novel by Eric Ambler, cannily directed by Roy Baker and atmospherically photographed by Erwin Hillier, this is one of British cinema's best stabs at *film noir*. John Mills gives a highly accomplished performance as the man who, having been responsible for an accidental death, now has to prove to himself and the authorities that he didn't kill fellow boarding-house tenant Kay Walsh. But what really makes this seedy thriller so compelling is the support playing of Joan Greenwood, Joyce Carey and Edward Chapman. Keep an eye out for a six-year-old Juliet Mills, making her third screen appearance. DP

John Mills *Jim Ackland* • Joan Greenwood *Jenny Carden* • Edward Chapman *Peachy* • Kay Walsh *Molly Newman* • Joyce Carey *Mrs Vinton* • Catherine Lacey *Miss Selby* • Adrianne Allen *Joyce Carden* • Felix Aylmer *Dr Martin* • Frederick Piper *Detective Inspector Godby* • Juliet Mills *Child* ■ *Dir* Roy Baker [Roy Ward Baker] • *Scr* Eric Ambler, from his novel

October Sky ★★★★ PG

Drama 1999 · US · Colour · 102mins

Joe Johnston, director of *Honey, I Shrunk the Kids*, reins himself in with this charming true story of pluck and determination in 1950s West Virginia. Although his dad (Chris Cooper) is superintendent of the town mine, schoolboy Jake Gyllenhaal is determined to avoid a life underground. With Sputnik launching the space age, he gathers a group of friends together to build their own rockets. Encouraged by teacher Laura Dern, the lads hope to enter the state science fair. Droll, touching and engrossing. SR DVD

Jake Gyllenhaal *Homer Hickam* • Chris Cooper *John Hickman* • Laura Dern *Miss Riley* • Chris Owen *Quentin* • William Lee Scott *Roy Lee* • Chad Lindberg *O'Dell* ■ *Dir* Joe Johnston • *Scr* Lewis Colick, from the autobiography *Rocket Boys* by Homer Hickam Jr

Octopussy ★★★ PG

Spy adventure 1983 · UK · Colour · 125mins

This was the 13th Bond movie and is possibly the most frivolous (and certainly the most careless) to date. The plot meanders as Roger Moore follows Maud Adams and renegade Soviet general Steven Berkoff across India and Central Europe. All the usual paraphernalia are on view (although the gadgets aren't quite up to Q's customary standard), but director John Glen never quite seems in control, either of the breathless action or the overly glib dialogue. DP. Contains violence. DVD

Roger Moore *James Bond* • Maud Adams *Octopussy* • Louis Jourdan *Kamal* • Kristina Wayborn *Magda* • Kabir Bedi *Gobinda* • Steven Berkoff *General Orlov* • David Meyer *One of twins* • Tony Meyer *One of twins* • Vijay Amritraj *Vijay* • Desmond Llewelyn *"Q"* • Robert Brown *"M"* • Walter Gotell *Gogol* • Geoffrey Keen *Minister of Defence* • Lois Maxwell *Miss Moneypenny* ■ *Dir* John Glen • *Scr* George MacDonald Fraser, Richard Maibaum, Michael G Wilson, from the stories *Octopussy* and *The Property of a Lady* by Ian Fleming

The Odd Angry Shot ★★★ 15

War comedy drama
1979 · Aus · Colour · 87mins

This Vietnam war movie fired off a barrage of controversy in its native Australia, with its story of a group of Aussie professional soldiers, bitterly complaining about a conflict they don't think is any of their business and feeling danger has been foisted on them by politicians. John Hargreaves and Bryan Brown are outstanding, despite having to play stereotypical boozing and brawling comrades, while director Tom Jeffrey catches the claustrophobia of the occasion as much as the violent action. TH

Graham Kennedy *Harry* • John Hargreaves *Bung* • John Jarratt *Bill* • Bryan Brown *Rogers* • Graeme Blundell *Dawson* • Richard Moir *Medic* • Brandon Burke *Isaacs* • Ian Gilmour *Scott* ■ *Dir* Tom Jeffrey • *Scr* Tom Jeffrey, from a novel by William Nagle

Odd Birds ★

Drama 1985 · US · Colour · 90mins

This tale of a Chinese immigrant girl in 1960s San Francisco is a no-hoper. Ming Lew gives a convincing performance as a teen who is told she can't be an actress by her mother, but, having sought advice and found solace in a friendship with priest Michael Moriarty she decides to have a go. Cue an audition and the ultimate "You could make it kid" scene. The film dumbs down any attempts by the performers to make it work and the ending is ridiculous. LH

Michael Moriarty *Brother TS Murphy* • Donna Lai Ming Lew *Joy Chan* • Nancy Yee *Mrs Chan* • Bruce Gray *Gower Champion* • Scott Crawford *Eric* ■ *Dir/Scr* Jeanne Collachia

The Odd Couple ★★★★ PG

Comedy 1968 · US · Colour · 101mins

Jack Lemmon, devastated by the break-up of his marriage, packs his sinuses and his nervous tics and moves in with happily divorced Walter Matthau. While Lemmon is the finicky housewife (crustless sandwiches, coasters for drinks, nifty hoover technique), Matthau is the arch slob (brimming ashtrays, unmade bed, linguini on the walls), and they inevitably drive each other nuts. Apart from a cringe-making scene with two English girls, Neil Simon's comedy has weathered well, bristling with one-liners timed to perfection. DP DVD

Jack Lemmon *Felix Ungar* • Walter Matthau *Oscar Madison* • John Fiedler *Vinnie* • Herb Edelman *Murray* • David Sheiner *Roy* • Larry Haines *Speed* • Monica Evans *Cecily* • Carole Shelley *Gwendolyn* ■ *Dir* Gene Saks • *Scr* Neil Simon, from his play

The Odd Couple II ★★★ 15

Comedy 1998 · US · Colour · 92mins

Although coming 30 years after the original, this belated sequel would have us believe it's really only 17 years since Jack Lemmon and Walter Matthau shared an apartment. The 78-year-old Matthau has retired to Florida to play poker with rich widows, but the impending marriage of his son to Jack's daughter brings the bickering pair together again. Scripted by original author Neil Simon, it's rarely more than a contrivance and a pension enhancement for all concerned, but Lemmon and Matthau are still eminently watchable. AT. Contains some swearing. DVD

Jack Lemmon *Felix Ungar* • Walter Matthau *Oscar Madison* • Richard Riehle *Detective* • Jonathan Silverman *Brucey Madison* • Lisa Waltz *Hannah Ungar* • Mary Beth Peil *Felice* • Christine Baranski *Thelma* • Jean Smart *Holly* • Barnard Hughes *Beaumont* ■ *Dir* Howard Deutch • *Scr* Neil Simon

The Odd Job ★★ 15

Comedy 1978 · UK · Colour · 84mins

A key member of the *Monty Python* team, Graham Chapman seemed lost without a little help from his friends in his solo ventures. The cast he gathers around him in this off-colour black comedy tries its hardest to tune into the cockeyed humour at which he excelled, but only David Jason, as the hitman hired by the heartbroken Chapman to kill him, and Bill Paterson, as a pompous flatfoot, come close. A one-joke movie. DP

Graham Chapman *Arthur Harris* • David Jason *Odd Job Man* • Diana Quick *Fiona Harris* • Simon Williams *Tony Sloane* • Edward Hardwicke *Inspector Black* • Bill Paterson *Sergeant Mull* • Michael Elphick *Raymonde* • Stewart Harwood *Bernard* ■ *Dir* Peter Medak • *Scr* Graham Chapman, Bernard McKenna, from a TV play by Bernard McKenna

Odd Jobs ★★ 15

Comedy 1986 · US · Colour · 84mins

Paul Reiser is takes top billing in this broad comedy, but in name only, for this is essentially an ensemble piece. Indeed, Robert Townsend has the best lines, as he and Reiser join a group of college friends spending their summer working as removal men with a little help from the Mob. Directed without a hint of subtlety by Mark Story, this is a crude compendium of obvious sight gags, and it's to the cast's credit that this is occasionally quite funny. DP. Contains swearing.

Paul Reiser *Max* • Robert Townsend *Dwight* • Scott McGinnis *Woody* • Rick Overton *Roy* • Paul Provenza *Bryon* • Leo Burmester *Wylie D Daiken* • Thomas Quinn *Frankie* • Savannah Smith Boucher *Loretta/Lynette* • Richard Dean Anderson *Spud* • Richard Foronjy *Manny* • Eleanor Mondale *Mandy* • Julianne Phillips *Sally* ■ *Dir* Mark Story • *Scr* Robert Conte, Peter Martin Wortmann

Odd Man Out ★★★★★ PG

Drama 1946 · UK · BW · 111mins

This is as agonising a piece of cinema as you are ever likely to see. James Mason gives the performance of a lifetime as an IRA man on the run in the backwaters of Belfast after he is fatally wounded during a robbery. Mason conveys his pain and isolation with consummate skill, but his desperate plight is made unbearable by the masterly direction of Carol Reed and the chillingly atmospheric photography of Robert Krasker – the unforgiving landscape is exploited with outrageous camera angles and photographic distortions to fashion a city that is at once forbiddingly cold and worth dying for. DP DVD

James Mason *Johnny* • Robert Newton *Lukey* • Kathleen Ryan *Kathleen* • Robert Beatty *Dennis* • FJ McCormick *Shell* • Kitty Kirwan *Granny* • Fay Compton *Rosie* • Cyril Cusack *Pat* ■ *Dir* Carol Reed • *Scr* FL Green, RC Sherriff, from the novel by FL Green

O

Oddball Hall ★ PG

Comedy 1990 · US · Colour · 83mins

This a smug joke at the expense of the developing world that no amount of spin could reposition as a satire on western civilisation. The mugging of Don Ameche and Burgess Meredith is as embarrassing as the plotline, which casts them as a couple of jewel thieves who are mistaken for members of a charitable fraternity with the powers to end a drought. DP

Don Ameche *G Paul Siebriese* • Burgess Meredith *Ingersol* • Bill Maynard *Copperthwaite* • Tullio Moneta *"Goose" Linguine* • Tiny Skefile *Meetoo-U* ■ *Dir/Scr* Jackson Hunsicker

Odds against Tomorrow ★★★★

Crime drama 1959 · US · BW · 96mins

A terrific heist movie, grimly told and well performed, this has a prescient and tough racist subtext that makes for compulsive viewing. Executive produced by Harry Belafonte and directed by master craftsman Robert Wise, it benefits from a high octane cast, headed by Belafonte himself, with Robert Ryan as the bigoted ex-con at his throat. There's also fine nervy back-up from Shelley Winters as Ryan's wife, Gloria Grahame as his mistress and Ed Begley, as the disgraced ex-cop who has the idea for the robbery. TS

Harry Belafonte *Johnny Ingram* • Robert Ryan *Earl Slater* • Shelley Winters *Lorry* • Ed Begley *Dave Burke* • Gloria Grahame *Helen* • Will Kuluva *Bacco* ■ *Dir* Robert Wise • *Scr* John O Killens [Abraham Polonsky], Nelson Gidding, from the novel by William P McGivern

Ode to Billy Joe ★★★★ 15

Drama 1976 · US · Colour · 101mins

The heartache of teenage love has rarely been so sensitively caught as in this romantic tragedy set in a Mississippi backwater, dramatising Bobby Gentry's 1967 hit-song lyric. Robby Benson is Billy Joe McAllister and Glynnis O'Connor the schoolgirl Bobbie Lee Hartley, while the Tallahatchie Bridge looms as the predestined doom. Although the ending is overly sentimental, the achievement of director Max Baer Jr and writer Herman Raucher is to mingle small-town behaviour with small-scale romance and to give a dramatic poignancy to both. TH

Robby Benson *Billy Joe McAllister* • Glynnis O'Connor *Bobbie Lee Hartley* • Joan Hotchkis *Mrs Hartley* • Sandy McPeak *Mr Hartley* • James Best *Dewey Barksdale* ■ *Dir* Max Baer Jr • *Scr* Herman Raucher, from the song by Bobbie Gentry

The Odessa File ★★★ PG

Thriller 1974 · UK · Colour · 123mins

A terrific Frederick Forsyth plot and impressive production values make this thriller eminently watchable, even if veteran director Ronald Neame lets the pace drag and the length feels excessive. However, the often undervalued Jon Voight is superb as the journalist tracking down a concentration camp commandant, his quest hindered at every turn by members of the sinister Odessa organisation. There are splendid moments along the way, but Derek Jacobi is wasted and female lead Mary Tamm is inadequate. TS. Contains violence and swearing. DVD

Jon Voight *Peter Miller* • Maximilian Schell *Eduard Roschmann* • Maria Schell *Frau Miller* • Mary Tamm *Sigi* • Derek Jacobi *Klaus Wenzer* • Peter Jeffrey *David Porath* • Klaus Lowitsch [Klaus Löwitsch] *Gustav Mackensen* • Kurt Meisel *Alfred Oster* ■ *Dir* Ronald Neame • *Scr* George Markstein, Kenneth Ross, from the novel by Frederick Forsyth

Odette ★★★ PG

Second World War drama 1950 · UK · BW · 112mins

There is an inescapable predictability about wartime exploits movies, even though there is no denying the magnitude of the achievements of people such as Odette Churchill who survived Nazi torture while working for the French Resistance. Director Herbert Wilcox has little new to offer in his depiction of underground activities and pulls his punches during Odette's interrogation by sadistic Gestapo types. Anna Neagle suggests a certain stiffness of the upper lip, but she is not at her best. DP

Anna Neagle *Odette* • Trevor Howard *Captain Peter Churchill* • Marius Goring *Henri* • Peter Ustinov *Arnaud* • Bernard Lee *Jack* • Marie Burke *Mme Glière* • Gilles Quéant *Jacques* • Alfred Shieske *Commandant* • Marianne Waller *Wardress* ■ *Dir* Herbert Wilcox • *Scr* Warren Chetham-Strode, from the book by Jerrard Tickell

The Odyssey ★★★ 12

Fantasy adventure 1997 · Ger/It/US · Colour · 172mins

Whittled down from a mini-series, this lavish dramatisation of Homer's epic poem has some breathtaking Mediterranean scenery, including the ruins of Troy that lend unrivalled authenticity to the famous Trojan Horse episode. Armand Assante is suitably heroic as the King of Ithaca, who encountered the Cyclops, the treacherous Eurymachus and the bewitching Circe and Calypso during his 20-year adventure. Andrei Konchalovsky directs with a judicious blend of mythical spectacle and philosophical insight, and expertly handles his stellar cast. DP

Armand Assante *Odysseus* • Greta Scacchi *Penelope* • Isabella Rossellini *Athene* • Bernadette Peters *Circe* • Eric Roberts *Eurymachus* • Irene Papas *Anticlea* • Jeroen Krabbé *King Alcinous* • Geraldine Chaplin *Eurycleia* ■ *Dir* Andrei Konchalovsky • *Scr* Andrei Konchalovsky, Christopher Solimine, from the poem by Homer

Oedipus Rex ★★★ 15

Tragedy 1967 · It · Colour · 100mins

Working from his own translation, Pier Paolo Pasolini seeks to emphasise the continued universality of Sophocles's tragedy by book-ending the action with episodes set in modern-day Bologna. He also imparts additional atmosphere by staging the play in the dramatic setting of a 15th-century adobe city deep in the Moroccan desert, and by employing a primordially powerful soundtrack. For all its impressive qualities, though, it's a strangely dispassionate picture. DP. In Italian with English subtitles. DVD

Franco Citti *Oedipus* • Silvana Mangano *Jocasta* • Carmelo Bene *Creon* • Julian Beck *Tiresias* • Ninetto Davoli *Messenger* • Pier Paolo Pasolini *High Priest* ■ *Dir* Pier Paolo Pasolini • *Scr* Pier Paolo Pasolini, from the play by Sophocles

Oedipus the King ★★

Tragedy 1967 · UK · Colour · 94mins

Neither a full-blooded epic nor an engrossing art house tale, *Oedipus the King* goes to show that even with a decent cast and with Sophocles as your source you can still come a cropper. As Oedipus, Christopher Plummer is far from compelling, despite the fact that he murders his father, marries his mother and then takes out his own eyes. This should be juicy stuff, but it just fails to ignite and even Orson Welles comes across as just the town bore. AT

Christopher Plummer *Oedipus* • Lilli Palmer *Jocasta* • Richard Johnson *Creon* • Orson Welles *Tiresias* • Cyril Cusack *Messenger* • Roger Livesey *Shepherd* • Donald Sutherland *Chorus leader* ■ *Dir* Philip Saville • *Scr* Philip Saville, Michael Luke, from the play by Paul Roche, from the play by Sophocles

Of a Thousand Delights ★★★

Psychological drama 1965 · It · BW · 100mins

Luchino Visconti's operatic tale of guilt, betrayal and incest, derived from the Electra myth, is pretty unconvincing. But it boasts fine black-and-white photography by Armando Nannuzzi, and powerful performances from Marie Bell and Claudia Cardinale as a mother and daughter in conflict while commemorating their husband and father respectively, a Jewish scientist killed by the Nazis. RB. An Italian language film.

Claudia Cardinale *Sandra* • Jean Sorel *Gianni* • Michael Craig *Andrew* • Renzo Ricci *Gilardini* ■ *Dir* Luchino Visconti • *Scr* Suso Cecchi D'Amico, Enrico Medioli, Luchino Visconti

Of Freaks and Men ★★★ 18

Drama 1998 · Rus · BW/Sepia · 88mins

Alexei Balabanov's sojourn in the sinful backwaters of early 20th century St Petersburg could not be any more different from his bruisingly realistic *Brother*. However, the swaggering disregard for political correctness is again to the fore as widows, virgins and Siamese twins are exploited by immigrant pornographer Sergei Makovetsky. Such shock tactics are not employed to titillate, but to expose the corruption inherent in Russian society throughout the last century. Littered with references to the nation's cinematic heritage, this is an eccentric and enthralling allegory. DP. In Russian with English subtitles.

Sergei Makovetsky *Johan* • Dinara Drukarova *Liza* • Lika Nevolina *Ekaterina Kirillovna* • Viktor Sukhorukov *Victor Ivanovich* ■ *Dir/Scr* Alexei Balabanov

Of Human Bondage ★★★★ PG

Drama 1934 · US · BW · 82mins

The first, and best, screen version of Somerset Maugham's famous novel. Leslie Howard is sensitive and polished as the gentlemanly artist turned medical student who almost ruins his life over his obsessive infatuation with a vindictive teashop waitress. Bette Davis proves her credentials in this latter role, offering a nuanced portrayal that rises above her cockney accent. There is excellent support, too, and plaudits must go to John Cromwell's tightly controlled and atmospheric direction. RK DVD

Leslie Howard *Philip Carey* • Bette Davis *Mildred Rogers* • Frances Dee *Sally Athelny* • Reginald Owen *Thorpe Athelny* • Reginald Denny *Harry Griffiths* • Kay Johnson *Norah* • Alan Hale *Emil Miller* • Reginald Sheffield *Dunsford* ■ *Dir* John Cromwell • *Scr* Lester Cohen, from the novel by W Somerset Maugham

Of Human Bondage ★★

Drama 1946 · US · BW · 105mins

This miscast effort stars Paul Henreid and Eleanor Parker: he too sophisticated and uncomfortably wooden, she doing her best to convince as a cockney. The film is solid and respectable, but ends up dull and unconvincing. For all its intrinsic deficiencies, however, one keeps watching, buoyed by a good supporting cast that includes Alexis Smith and Edmund Gwenn. RK

Eleanor Parker *Mildred Rogers* • Paul Henreid *Philip Carey* • Alexis Smith *Nora Nesbitt* • Edmund Gwenn *Athelny* • Janis Paige *Sally Athelny* • Patric Knowles *Griffiths* • Henry Stephenson *Dr Tyrell* • Marten Lamont *Dunsford* ■ *Dir* Edmund Goulding • *Scr* Catherine Turney, from the novel by W Somerset Maugham

Of Human Bondage ★★

Drama 1964 · UK · BW · 98mins

This unnecessary third version of W Somerset Maugham's tale of a doctor besotted with a floozy has both leads so miscast that it took three directors (Henry Hathaway, Bryan Forbes and the credited Ken Hughes) to get something credible on screen. Kim Novak is far too intelligent a person to cope with cockney Mildred's idiocies, and it's anyone's guess what Laurence Harvey thought he was up to. TS

Kim Novak *Mildred Rogers* • Laurence Harvey *Philip Carey* • Robert Morley *Dr Jacobs* • Siobhan McKenna *Norah Nesbitt* • Roger Livesey *Thorpe Athelny* • Jack Hedley *Griffiths* • Nanette Newman *Sally Athelny* ■ *Dir* Ken Hughes • *Scr* Bryan Forbes, from the novel by W Somerset Maugham

Of Human Hearts ★★★ U

Period drama 1938 · US · BW · 103mins

A period family drama, played out in rural surroundings and focusing on the conflict between heavily religious paterfamilias Walter Huston, his rebellious son James Stewart who wishes to break away and become a surgeon, and the lad's mother Beulah Bondi (Oscar-nominated), caught in the middle and making sacrifices to help him. Beautifully directed by Clarence Brown, with top-class production values and impeccable acting from a cast that includes stage actor Charles Coburn, virtually a newcomer to films at age 61, John Gilbert's daughter Leatrice

Joy Gilbert and John Carradine as Abraham Lincoln. RK

James Stewart *Jason Wilkins* • Walter Huston *Rev Ethan Wilkins* • Beulah Bondi *Mary Wilkins* • Guy Kibbee *Mr George Ames* • Charles Coburn *Dr Charles Shingle* • John Carradine *President Lincoln* • Ann Rutherford *Annie Hawks* • Charley Grapewin *Jim Meeker* • Leatrice Joy Gilbert *Annie Hawks at age 10* ■ *Dir* Clarence Brown • *Scr* Bradbury Foote, from the novel *Benefits Forgot* by Honoré Morrow

Of Love and Desire ★★

Drama 1963 · US · Colour · 96mins

Nobody comes off particularly well in this lurid melodrama set in Mexico about the lustful Merle Oberon who seduces an engineer and subsequently falls for him, to her great surprise. In her confused state, she is raped by one of her old flames, then tries to kill herself. Adult themes – loveless sex, nymphomania and incest – are in large supply and the general air of depravity undermines the positive ending. JG

Merle Oberon *Katherine Beckman* • Steve Cochran *Steve Corey* • Curt Jurgens *Paul Beckman* • John Agar *Gus Cole* • Steve Brodie *Bill Maxton* • Eduardo Noriega (1) *Mr Dominguez* • Elsa Cardenas *Mrs Dominguez* ■ *Dir* Richard Rush • *Scr* Laslo Gorog, Richard Rush, from a story by Victor Stoloff, Jacqueine Delessert

Of Love and Shadows ★ 18

Romantic political drama
1994 · Sp/Arg · Colour · 103mins

Antonio Banderas and Jennifer Connolly star as the lovers whose relationship is set against a backdrop of corruption in Chile. Connelly is unconvincing as a naive journalist, unfamiliar with Chile's criminal underbelly. Banderas is a photographer trying to expose her fiancé as a fascist involved in official torture and the corruption at the heart of government. Notable for appalling direction and dialogue, the film jolts from one dysfunctional scene to another. LH [VIDEO]

Antonio Banderas *Francisco* • Jennifer Connelly *Irene* • Stefania Sandrelli *Beatriz* • Diego Wallraff *Jose* • Camillo Gallardo *Gustavo* • Patricio Contreras *Mario* ■ *Dir* Betty Kaplan • *Scr* Donald Freed, from the novel by Isabel Allende

Of Mice and Men ★★★★

Drama 1939 · US · BW · 106mins

The aptly named Lewis Milestone created a little Hollywood history with this adaptation of John Steinbeck's best-loved novel, by commencing the action before the opening credits. However, its reputation really rests on the astute performances and Aaron Copland's superb score. Burgess Meredith and Lon Chaney Jr excel as the wiry drifter and genial giant wandering the west seeking refuge from the Depression. But every bit as effective is B-western star Bob Steele, who casts off his matinée idol persona to bring genuine menace to the part of the ranch owner's sadistic son, whose inability to control enticing wife Betty Field leads to tragedy. DP

Burgess Meredith *George* • Betty Field *Mae* • Lon Chaney Jr *Lennie* • Charles Bickford *Slim* • Roman Bohnen *Candy* • Bob Steele *Curley* • Noah Beery Jr *Whit* ■ *Dir* Lewis Milestone • *Scr* Eugene Solow, from the novel and by John Steinbeck • *Music* Aaron Copland

Of Mice and Men ★★★★ PG

Drama 1992 · US · Colour · 106mins

Twelve years after they first played George and Lennie on stage at Chicago's Steppenwolf Theater, Gary Sinise and John Malkovich reprised their roles in this sensitive screen adaptation of John Steinbeck's classic novel. Blending tenderness and confusion with temper and power, Malkovich is quite superb as the simple-minded hulk whose titanic strength brings the pair untold trouble. On the directorial side, Sinise acquits himself remarkably well, at times even managing to improve on the excellent Lewis Milestone version. DP. Contains violence and swearing. [VIDEO] DVD

John Malkovich *Lennie* • Gary Sinise *George* • Ray Walston *Candy* • Casey Siemaszko *Curley* • Sherilyn Fenn *Curley's wife* • John Terry *Slim* • Richard Riehle *Carlson* • Alexis Arquette *Whitt* • Joe Morton *Crooks* • Noble Willingham *The boss* ■ *Dir* Gary Sinise • *Scr* Horton Foote, from the novel and play by John Steinbeck

Of Unknown Origin ★★★★ 15

Horror 1983 · Can · Colour · 85mins

This minor gem insightfully outlines the psychological breakdown of a high-powered business executive which manifests itself in the form of a larger-than-life rat. Director George Pan Cosmatos wrings every ounce of terror and suspense from this simple premise, as Peter Weller believably fights for his sanity in a battle of wits with the vicious rodent when it moves into his Manhattan brownstone. Seat-edged tension is evoked by giving out horrendous facts concerning the very real threat rats are to our society and through nerve-racking dream sequences, which cleverly trade on universal phobias. AJ [VIDEO] DVD

Peter Weller *Bart Hughes* • Jennifer Dale *Lorrie Wells* • Lawrence Dane *Eliot Riverton* • Kenneth Welsh *James Hall* • Shannon Tweed *Meg Hughes* • Maury Chaykin *Dan* ■ *Dir* George Pan Cosmatos • *Scr* Brian Taggert, from the novel *The Visitor* by Chauncey G Parker III

Off and Running ★★ 15

Comedy 1991 · US · Colour · 86mins

It's obvious why this wannabe screwball comedy only premiered on cable five years after it was made. As the "resting" actress who is forced to work as a mermaid at a Miami hotel, Cyndi Lauper soon outstays her welcome. But, because she's now being pursued by the crooks who killed her boyfriend, we feel obliged to stick with her as she and failed golf pro David Keith encounter a kidnapped child and a nobbled racehorse. Too nasty to be romantic and too unfunny to be a comedy. DP. Contains violence, swearing, nudity and drug abuse [VIDEO]

Cyndi Lauper *Cyd* • David Keith *Jack* • Johnny Pinto *Pompey* • David Thornton *Reese* • Richard Belzer *Milt Zoloth* ■ *Dir* Edward Bianchi • *Scr* Mitch Glazer

Off Beat ★★ PG

Comedy 1986 · US · Colour · 88mins

Judge Reinhold – best known as the gormless LA detective in the *Beverly Hills Cop* trilogy – tries (and fails) to be a leading man in this below-average comedy about a librarian who poses as a police officer and ends up falling in love with unsuspecting policewoman Meg Tilly. Worth watching for John Turturro and Harvey Keitel in roles they'd now rather forget. JB [VIDEO] DVD

Judge Reinhold *Joe Gower* • Meg Tilly *Rachel Wareham* • Cleavant Derricks *Abe Washington* • Joe Mantegna *Pete Peterson* • Jacques d'Amboise *August* • Amy Wright *Mary Ellen Gruenwald* • John Turturro *Neil Pepper* • Fred Gwynne *Commissioner* • Harvey Keitel *Mickey* ■ *Dir* Michael Dinner • *Scr* Mark Medoff, from a story by Dezso Magyar

Off the Dole ★★

Detective comedy 1935 · UK · BW · 89mins

Shot on a shoestring in a primitive Manchester studio, George Formby's second feature for producer John E Blakeley offers an insight into 1930s music-hall humour. But as cinema it's something of a chore, with an often static camera, poor sound and negligible quality control. Thrown out of the queue at the labour exchange, Formby takes over his uncle's detective agency and blunders his way through cases. DP

George Formby *John Willie* • Beryl Formby *Grace, Charm and Ability* • Constance Shotter *Irene* • Dan Young *The Inimitable Dude* • James Plant *Crisp and Debonaire* • Stan Pell *A Most Inoffensive Parson* ■ *Dir* Arthur Mertz • *Scr* John E Blakeley, Arthur Mertz

Offbeat ★★

Crime drama 1960 · UK · BW · 72mins

Best known for his collaborations with Morecambe and Wise and 1970s sitcom spin-offs, Cliff Owen made his directorial debut with this rather forced thriller, which is also known as *The Devil Inside*. William Sylvester gives a good account of himself as the undercover cop who finds the life of crime to his liking, but Mai Zetterling is somewhat wasted as the gang widow for whom he falls. Given the budgetary restraints, it's not too bad, but, with the exception of the leads, the characters are a clichéd bunch. DP

William Sylvester *Steve Layton/Steve Ross* • Mai Zetterling *Ruth Lombard* • John Meillon *Johnny Remick* • Anthony Dawson *James Dawson* • Neil McCarthy *Leo Farrell* • Harry Baird *Gill Hall* • John Phillips (1) *Superintendent Gault* ■ *Dir* Cliff Owen • *Scr* Peter Barnes

The Offence ★★★ 18

Psychological drama
1972 · UK · Colour · 107mins

Gritty police programmes are now so much a part of the TV landscape that it is hard to realise that features like *The Offence* once packed quite a punch. Adapted by former *Z Cars* scriptwriter John Hopkins from his own play, this sordid study of evil and human weakness lacks the intensity of the stage production and suffers from director Sidney Lumet's uncharacteristically shaky handling of local colour and atmosphere. Yet, Sean Connery as the brutal, world-weary copper and Ian Bannen as the lowlife he suspects of child molesting still give compelling performances. DP. Contains violence, swearing. [VIDEO] DVD

Sean Connery *Detective Sergeant Johnson* • Trevor Howard *Lt Cartwright* • Vivien Merchant *Maureen Johnson* • Ian Bannen *Baxter* • Derek Newark *Jessard* • John Hallam *Panton* • Peter Bowles *Cameron* ■ *Dir* Sidney Lumet • *Scr* John Hopkins, from his play *This Story of Yours*

Offending Angels ★ 15

Romantic comedy fantasy
2000 · UK · Colour · 93mins

Conceived by writer/director Andrew Rajan as a vehicle for actors of ethnic origin (playing roles in which their ethnicity is irrelevant), the film at least has its heart in the right place, but has failed to locate any wit, style or invention. This tale of two greenhorn guardian angels (Susannah Harker and Shaun Parkes), who get a little too involved in the affairs of man, is dull, dreary and drawn out. DA

Susannah Harker *Paris* • Andrew Lincoln *Sam* • Shaun Parkes *Zeke* • Andrew Rajan *Baggy* • Paula O'Grady *Alison* ■ *Dir* Andrew Rajan • *Scr* Andrew Rajan, Tim Moyler

Office Space ★★★ 15

Satirical comedy 1999 · US · Colour · 89mins

This unconventional satire of work relationships and office politics comes courtesy of Mike Judge, one of the creators of the far from subtle *Beavis and Butt-head*. Jennifer Aniston (as a waitress) and Gary Cole (as a dreary boss) are the familiar faces, and the offbeat jokes range from droll references to singer Michael Bolton to swipes at restaurant etiquette and office technology. Not for all tastes. JC. Contains swearing, nudity and sex scenes. [VIDEO] DVD

Ron Livingston *Peter Gibbons* • Jennifer Aniston *Joanna* • David Herman *Michael Bolton* • Ajay Naidu *Samir* • Gary Cole *Bill Lumbergh* • Diedrich Bader *Lawrence* • John C McGinley *Bob Slydell* ■ *Dir/Scr* Mike Judge

An Officer and a Gentleman ★★★ 15

Romantic drama
1982 · US · Colour · 118mins

Hugely popular in its day, appealing to the incurable romantic in all of us, this is a highly manipulative mixture of boot camp is good for you and every girl loves a uniform. More sophisticated thoughts on human relationships form no part of Taylor Hackford's glossy hymn to overcoming a trailer-park background. Richard Gere looks a treat in his pristine white togs, and gives a performance more wooden than a wardrobe. Not even the combined talents of Debra Winger and Louis Gossett Jr can turn this one into a great movie, but if you're in the mood for a wallow, it's perfect. SH. Contains some violence, swearing, sex scenes and nudity. [VIDEO] DVD

Richard Gere *Zack Mayo* • Debra Winger *Paula Pokrifki* • David Keith *Sid Worley* • Robert Loggia *Byron Mayo* • Lisa Blount *Lynette Pomeroy* • Lisa Eilbacher *Casey Seeger* • Louis Gossett Jr *Sergeant Emil Foley* • David Caruso *Topper Daniels* • Grace Zabriskie *Esther Pokrifki* ■ *Dir* Taylor Hackford • *Scr* Douglas Day Stewart

The Officers' Ward ★★★★ 15

Wartime drama 2001 · Fr · Colour · 126mins

This is a sensitive yet unflinching examination of human indomitability. At the outset of the First World War, Eric Caravaca is hideously disfigured by a bomb blast to the face and spends the rest of the war in a Parisian hospital where he undergoes painful and primitive reconstructive surgery. The extent of Caravaca's injuries is not revealed for nearly an hour, so the reaction he elicits on the faces of the hospital staff is our only source for the severity of his plight. By refusing to capitalise on the visual horror of the officers' injuries, director François Dupeyron lends dignity to both their determination and despair. DP. In French with English subtitles. Contains violence and sex scenes. [VIDEO] DVD

Eric Caravaca *Adrien Fournier* • Denis Podalydès *Henri* • Grégori Derangère *Pierre* • Sabine Azéma *Anaïs* ■ *Dir* François Dupeyron • *Scr* François Dupeyron, from a novel by Marc Dugain

The Official Version ★★★★ 15

Drama 1985 · Arg · Colour · 109mins

The winner of the Oscar for best foreign film, this is the compelling story of a history teacher whose acquiescence in the military regime in Argentina is shaken when she begins to suspect she has adopted the child of a "disappeared" couple. It's an impressive effort from Luis Puenzo, who made his name directing commercials, that uses Norma Aleandro's credible conversion and the dignified determination of the ever-vigilant women of the Plaza del Mayo to make its political points. This subtly impassioned drama is both persuasive and uplifting. DP. In Spanish with English subtitles. [VIDEO] DVD

Héctor Alterio *Roberto* • Norma Aleandro *Alicia* • Chela Ruiz *Sara* • Chunchuna Villafane *Ana* ■ *Dir* Luis Puenzo • *Scr* Aida Bortnik, Luis Puenzo

Oh Dad, Poor Dad, Mama's Hung You in the Closet and I'm Feelin' So Sad ★

Comedy 1967 · US · Colour · 86mins

Rosalind Russell plays the horrendously awful, dominating mother of Robert Morse who is a worthless, emasculated creep. Morse's father, Jonathan Winters, is dead, murdered by Russell and stored in a coffin, but his ghost emerges on occasion to narrate the story. Barbara Harris is a sort of sex maniac who drives Morse so crazy with desire that he turns into Norman Bates. This black comedy about all-American "momism" is very much a product of its time. AT

Rosalind Russell *Madame Rosepettle* • Robert Morse *Jonathan* • Barbara Harris *Rosalie* • Hugh Griffith *Commodore Roseabove* • Jonathan Winters *Dad/Narrator* • Lionel Jeffries *Airport commander* ■ *Dir* Richard Quine, Alexander Mackendrick • *Scr* Ian Bernard, Pat McCormick, Herbert Baker, from the play by Arthur L Kopit

Oh, Daddy! ★★

Comedy drama 1935 · UK · BW · 77mins

Stage star Leslie Henson takes the title role in this cheeky farce, which typifies the kind of bawdy music-hall humour producer Michael Balcon brought to so many of his screen comedies. Henson is a puritanical toff whose conservative values are put to the test during a night in London, but the inimitable Robertson Hare (as his shockable sidekick) wins several scenes on points. DP

Leslie Henson *Lord Pye* • Frances Day *Benita de Lys* • Robertson Hare *Rupert Boddy* • Barry Mackay *Jimmy Ellison* • Marie Lohr *Lady Pye* • Alfred Drayton *Uncle Samson* ■ *Dir* Graham Cutts, Austin Melford • *Scr* Austin Melford, from his play

Oh, God! ★★★★ PG

Comedy 1977 · US · Colour · 93mins

This very, very funny original, together with *The Sunshine Boys*, revitalised the career of cigar-chomping veteran comedian George Burns. He plays the Almighty, visiting Earth to seek a messenger to convey to an indifferent world that He is still around, and choosing a supermarket assistant manager for the task (the perfectly cast country singer John Denver). Skilled director Carl Reiner works wonders with this material, which in other hands could have been extremely tasteless. Teri Garr and Ralph Bellamy provide wonderful support, and the whole has a marvellous feel-good quality to it. TS

George Burns *God* • John Denver *Jerry Landers* • Teri Garr *Bobbie Landers* • Donald Pleasence *Dr Harmon* • Ralph Bellamy *Sam Raven* • William Daniels *George Summers* ■ *Dir* Carl Reiner • *Scr* Larry Gelbart, from the novel by Avery Corman

Oh God! Book II ★ PG

Comedy 1980 · US · Colour · 89mins

Directed with cloying sentimentality, this follow-up should have spawned a new aphorism – never work with children or deities. The combination of George Burns growling out street-preacher wisdom and Louanne burbling kiddie banalities is enough to drive saints to sin. This story has God (Burns) ask a troubled schoolgirl to spearhead an advertising campaign to prove He's alive and well. DP

George Burns *God* • Suzanne Pleshette *Paula* • David Birney *Don* • Louanne *Tracy* • John Louie *Shingo* • Conrad Janis *Mr Benson* • Dr Joyce Brothers • Wilfrid Hyde White *Judge Miller* ■ *Dir* Gilbert Cates • *Scr* Josh Greenfeld, Hal Goldman, Fred S Fox, Seaman Jacobs, Melissa Miller, from a story by Josh Greenfeld

Oh, God! You Devil ★★ 15

Comedy 1984 · US · Colour · 91mins

A third heavenly outing for veteran vaudevillian George Burns, here playing both the Almighty and his Satanic counterpart, the Devil. The *Faust*-like plot reveals a lack of ideas and John Doolittle is not as affable a leading man as John Denver in the first of the series, but Burns is, nevertheless, watchable. TS. Contains swearing.

George Burns *God/the Devil* • Ted Wass *Bobby Shelton* • Ron Silver *Gary Frantz* • Roxanne Hart *Wendy Shelton* • Eugene Roche *Charlie Gray* • Robert Desiderio *Billy Wayne* ■ *Dir* Paul Bogart • *Scr* Andrew Bergman

Oh, Heavenly Dog! ★★ PG

Comedy 1980 · US · Colour · 98mins

Silly comedy, with Chevy Chase as a private investigator who's murdered, then comes back as a dog to sniff out his killer. If the plot gives you paws for thought, ponder this too: canine lead Benji was already a dog star in his own right, with two other films under his collar. Oddly, this film was shot in England, with a "local" support cast. Kids will like the cute stuff, whereas grown-ups will find it all rather tiresome. DA

Chevy Chase *Benjamin Browning* • Jane Seymour (2) *Jackie Howard* • Omar Sharif *Malcolm Bart* • Robert Morley *Bernie* • Alan Sues *Freddie* • Donnelly Rhodes *Montanero* • Barbara Leigh-Hunt *Margaret* ■ *Dir* Joe Camp • *Scr* Rob Browning, Joe Camp

Oh, Men! Oh, Women! ★★★ U

Comedy 1957 · US · Colour · 90mins

David Niven stars in this slightly farcical comedy but it's successful Broadway actor Tony Randall, making his screen debut, who runs away with the movie. Niven is a psychiatrist about to be married to screwball Barbara Rush, who's proud of how he manages to keep his personal and professional lives completely separate. Then he learns that Dan Dailey, the husband of his patient Ginger Rogers, is making a play for his fiancée, a situation topped by another patient (Randall), when he reveals his current amour as the same girl. The movie has its longueurs, but takes enough sideswipes at psychiatrists to provide some fun. RK

Ginger Rogers *Mildred Turner* • David Niven *Dr Alan Coles* • Dan Dailey *Arthur Turner* • Barbara Rush *Myra Hagerman* • Tony Randall *Cobbler* ■ *Dir* Nunnally Johnson • *Scr* Nunnally Johnson, from the play by Edward Chodorov (uncredited)

Oh, Mr Porter! ★★★★ U

Comedy 1937 · UK · BW · 80mins

This is easily the funniest film Will Hay made with his willing stooges Moore Marriott and Graham Moffatt. As the incompetent master of an Irish railway station, Hay is at his blustering best, whether trying to bring the facilities into the 20th century or curtailing the scrounging schemes of his staff. In addition to the endlessly inventive comic quips, there is also plenty of action, as the trio takes on a gang of gunrunners, with the confrontation in the windmill and the final chase (starring Gladstone the steam engine) particularly entertaining. DP DVD

Will Hay *William Porter* • Moore Marriott *Jeremiah Harbottle* • Graham Moffatt *Albert Brown* • Sebastian Smith *Charles Trimbletow* • Agnes Lauchlan *Mrs Trimbletow* ■ *Dir* Marcel Varnel • *Scr* JOC Orton, Val Guest, Marriott Edgar, from a story by Frank Launder

Oh, Rosalinda!! ★★★★ U

Musical 1955 · UK · Colour · 100mins

This splendidly original British musical is an update of the Strauss opera *Die Fledermaus*, set in postwar Vienna, though clearly based at Elstree Studios, with a marvellous international cast enjoying itself under co-directors Michael Powell and Emeric Pressburger. Time has been kind to this stylish exercise, which was derided on its first release. Michael Redgrave and Ludmilla Tcherina are the stars, with support from Anton Walbrook and Mel Ferrer. TS

Michael Redgrave *Colonel Eisenstein* • Ludmilla Tcherina *Rosalinda* • Anton Walbrook *Dr Falke* • Mel Ferrer *Captain Westerman* • Dennis Price *Major Frank* • Anthony Quayle *General Orlofsky* ■ *Dir* Michael Powell, Emeric Pressburger • *Scr* Michael Powell, Emeric Pressburger, from the opera *Die Fledermaus* by Johann Strauss

Oh! What a Lovely War ★★★★ PG

First World War musical satire
1969 · UK · Colour · 136mins

Based on Joan Littlewood's stage production, Richard Attenborough's first film as a director is a stylised, satirical and ultimately moving tribute to the soldiers who answered their country's call and fought in the Great War. An all-star cast performs the original's jingoistic music hall songs, which Attenborough cleverly stages in the Brighton Pavilion and on the old pier. While there was animosity behind the scenes – Len Deighton refused screen credit as the film's writer – this remains a distinctive piece of work and by far the most audacious film Attenborough has ever made. AT

Dirk Bogarde *Stephen* • Phyllis Calvert *Lady Haig* • Jean-Pierre Cassel *French Colonel* • John Clements *General Von Molke* • John Gielgud *Count Berchtold* • Jack Hawkins *Emperor Franz Joseph* • Kenneth More *Kaiser Wilhelm II* • Laurence Olivier *Field Marshal Sir John French* • Michael Redgrave *General Sir Henry Wilson* • Vanessa Redgrave *Sylvia Pankhurst* • Ralph Richardson *Sir Edward Grey* • Maggie Smith *Music hall star* • Susannah York *Eleanor* • John Mills *Sir Douglas Haig* • Ian Holm *President Poincaré* • Paul Daneman *Tsar Nicholas II* • Joe Melia *Photographer* • Mary Wimbush *Mary Smith* • Wendy Allnutt *Flo Smith* • Corin Redgrave *Bertie Smith* • Maurice Roëves *George Smith* • Angela Thorne *Betty Smith* ■ *Dir* Richard Attenborough • *Scr* Len Deighton (uncredited), from the stage musical, from the play *The Long, Long Trail* by Charles Chilton

Oh, What a Night ★★★ 15

Romantic comedy
1992 · Can · Colour · 87mins

This is a familiar enough rites-of-passage tale: at the end of the 1950s, Corey Haim is a troubled teenager who moves to the country with his father and stepmother and begins an affair with an older woman (Barbara Williams). Although director Eric Till overdoes the golden hue shots of the countryside, he brings a rare perception and wry sense of humour to the action. Robbie Coltrane pops up as Haim's confidant, and there's a great soundtrack. JF. Contains nudity.

Corey Haim *Eric* • Robbie Coltrane *Todd* • Barbara Williams (2) *Vera* • Keir Dullea *Thorvald* • Geneviève Bujold *Eva* ■ *Dir* Eric Till • *Scr* Richard Nielsen

Oh, You Beautiful Doll ★★★ U

Musical biography
1949 · US · Colour · 93mins

Broadway star, and later one of America's favourite raconteurs, George Jessel achieved some success later in his career as producer of a series of colourful vaudeville-based light musicals at 20th Century-Fox. This is a typical example of what were glossy star vehicles: a treasure trove of popular songs, in what is the alleged biography of little-known popular composer Fred Fisher. Fisher is portrayed by the wonderful character actor SZ "Cuddles" Sakall, whose delightful hamming is always watchable. TS

June Haver *Doris Breitenbach* • Mark Stevens *Larry Kelly* • SZ Sakall *Fred Fisher* • Charlotte Greenwood *Anna Breitenbach* • Gale Robbins *Marie Carle* • Jay C Flippen *Lippy Brannigan* • Andrew Tombes *Ted Held* ■ *Dir* John M Stahl • *Scr* Albert Lewis, Arthur Lewis

O'Hara's Wife ★★

Fantasy drama 1982 · US · Colour · 87mins

This comedy drama, one of a string of reassuring family movies Ed Asner made after TV's *Lou Grant* was axed, features a care-worn widower whose life, particularly his relationship with his children, improves after his dead wife comes back to haunt him. Undemanding, with a warm message and plenty of familiar faces in the cast, including Jodie Foster and Tom Bosley from *Happy Days*. DP

Edward Asner *Bob O'Hara* • Mariette Hartley *Harry O'Hara* • Jodie Foster *Barbara O'Hara* • Tom Bosley *Fred O'Hara* • Perry Lang *Rob O'Hara* ■ *Dir* William S Bartman • *Scr* James Nasella, William S Bartman, from a story by William S Bartman, Joseph Scott Kierland

Ohayo ★★★★ U

Comedy drama 1959 · Jpn · BW · 94mins

Director Yasujiro Ozu turns a feud between two small boys and their parents into a vibrant study of everyday life and a witty treatise on the importance of communication. Shooting in his typically unobtrusive style, Ozu demonstrates again how fully he understands the human condition, as two businessmen face up to their shortcomings, a woman is driven from her home by gossip and a couple hide their true feelings in platitudes. In the midst of this misunderstanding, the boys refuse to speak until their folks accept the westernising influence of television. DP. In Japanese with English subtitles.

Koji Shidara *Minoru Hayashi, older brother* • Masahiko Shimazu *Isamu Hayashi, younger brother* • Chishu Ryu *Keitaro Hayashi, father* • Kuniko Miyake *Tamiko Hayashi, mother* • Yoshiko Kuga *Setsuko Arita, aunt* • Keiji Sada *Heichiro Fukui, English teacher* • Haruo Tanaka *Tatsuko* • Haruko Sugimura *Kikue, Tatsuko's wife* ■ *Dir* Yasujiro Ozu • *Scr* Yasujiro Ozu, Kogo Noda

Oil for the Lamps of China ★★★

Drama 1935 · US · Colour · 104mins

A minor, but still very watchable, example of the sort of social message melodrama in which Warner Bros specialised in the early 1930s. Although he delivers his lines with the finesse and intonation of a cattle auctioneer, Pat O'Brien gives a fair impression of the little man who is prepared to sacrifice everything for a company that has given him nothing in return. Hampered by the patchiness of the script, director Mervyn LeRoy still maintains a cracking pace. DP

Pat O'Brien *Stephen Chase* • Josephine Hutchinson *Hester Chase* • Jean Muir *Alice Wellman* • John Eldredge *Don Wellman* • Lyle Talbot *Jim* • Arthur Byron *Ross* • Henry O'Neill *Hartford* • Donald Crisp *MacCargar* ■ *Dir* Mervyn LeRoy • *Scr* Laird Doyle, from the novel by Alice Tisdale Hobart

O

Okay ★★★ 15

Comedy drama
2002 · Den/Nor/Ger · Colour · 93mins

Following *Minor Mishaps* in proving that Danish realism doesn't have to abide by the Dogme manifesto, this unremitting tale of domestic dysfunction is held together by an impressive display of seething frustration from Paprika Steen. Unhappily married and estranged from her gay brother, she seeks to reassure herself she's not turning into her late unlamented mother by offering sanctuary to her terminally ill father. But Ole Ernst's turn for the better only adds to her woes. Jesper W Nielsen's wry direction owes much to Mike Leigh, but while his observations are as acute, he's much more forgiving of his characters' shortcomings. DP. In Danish with English subtitles. DVD

Paprika Steen *Nete* • Ole Ernst *Johannes Hermansen, Nete's father* • Troels Lyby *Kristian* • Nicolaj Kopernikus *Martin* • Molly Blixt Egelind *Kathrine* • Laura Drasbaek *Tanja* ■ *Dir* Jesper W Nielsen • *Scr* Kim Fupz Aakeson

Oklahoma! ★★★★ U

Musical 1955 · US · Colour · 145mins

The film version of the massively influential and, in its day, revolutionary Rodgers and Hammerstein Broadway musical preserves both the magnificent songs and the key Agnes DeMille choreography. Heading the notable cast is the under-rated Gordon MacRae as a finely shaded romantic Curly, while Shirley Jones, in her film debut, is superb as Laurey. If Rod Steiger is a shade morose and out of kilter, well, so is his character Jud Fry. Trouble is, director Fred Zinnemann can't quite manage the pizzazz the movie really needs, and messes up the stirring title number. Nevertheless, there's much to be thankful for. TS [video] DVD

Gordon MacRae *Curly* • Shirley Jones *Laurey* • Rod Steiger *Jud Fry* • Gloria Grahame *Ado Annie* • Gene Nelson *Will Parker* • Eddie Albert *Ali Hakim* • James Whitmore *Carnes* • Barbara Lawrence *Gertie* • Jay C Flippen *Skidmore* ■ *Dir* Fred Zinnemann • *Scr* Sonya Levien, William Ludwig, from the musical by Richard Rodgers, Oscar Hammerstein II, from the play *Green Grow the Lilacs* by Lynn Riggs

Oklahoma Crude ★★

Drama 1973 · US · Colour · 112mins

If ever a movie ran out of steam it's this one. Sumptuously produced and directed by Stanley Kramer on a high budget, it boasts terrific production values (though weak special effects work) and a fine cast led by Faye Dunaway and George C Scott at their respective ripsnorting bests. But once the oil gushers have gushed there's precious little plot or characterisation left, only the vicious Jack Palance, who wants Faye's oil well. TS

George C Scott *Noble "Mase" Mason* • Faye Dunaway *Lena Doyle* • John Mills *Cleon Doyle* • Jack Palance *Hellman* • William Lucking *Marion* • Harvey Jason *Wilcox* ■ *Dir* Stanley Kramer • *Scr* Marc Norman

The Oklahoma Kid ★★★ U

Western 1939 · US · BW · 77mins

Warner Bros achieved hit-and-miss results with its 1930s westerns, often making cowboy versions of its gangster movies. This film is no exception and no less effective for its unbelievable casting because the outlaw hero is played by none other than New York's own James Cagney, strapping on his six-guns and singing like the best of them. The villain is snarling Humphrey Bogart, and there's a lot of pleasure to be had from watching Bogie and Cagney out west. The plot is that old western stand-by about trying to find out who was responsible for the death of the hero's father. TS [video]

James Cagney *Jim Kincaid/"Oklahoma Kid"* • Humphrey Bogart *Whip McCord* • Rosemary Lane *Jane Hardwick* • Donald Crisp *Judge Hardwick* • Harvey Stephens *Ned Kincaid* • Hugh Sothern *John Kincaid* • Charles Middleton *Alec Martin* ■ *Dir* Lloyd Bacon • *Scr* Warren Duff, Robert Buckner, Edward E Paramore, from a story by Edward E Paramore, Wally Klein

The Oklahoma Woman ★★

Western 1956 · US · BW · 71mins

This was one of four low-budget westerns Roger Corman made for the drive-in market. Richard Denning is the reformed gunfighter who lines up against an old flame, the villainous Peggie Castle, when he falls for nice girl Cathy Downs. Corman assembles his usual eclectic cast but he shows little feel for the genre and the lack of production money doesn't help. JF

Richard Denning *Steve Ward* • Peggie Castle *Marie "Oklahoma" Saunders* • Cathy Downs *Susan Grant* • Tudor Owen *Ed Grant* ■ *Dir* Roger Corman • *Scr* Lou Rusoff

The Oklahoman ★★ U

Western 1957 · US · Colour · 79mins

This minor western features a too-old Joel McCrea in the lead and next to nothing spent on a wardrobe for leading lady Barbara Hale (Della Street from TV's *Perry Mason*). The screenplay's nothing either, as McCrea befriends an Indian (Michael Pate) and upsets some townies. Director Francis D Lyon was a superb editor (*Rembrandt, Things to Come, Body and Soul*) but turned into a truly mediocre director. TS

Joel McCrea *Dr John Brighton* • Barbara Hale *Anne Barnes* • Brad Dexter *Cass Dobie* • Gloria Talbott *Maria Smith* • Verna Felton *Mrs Waynebrook* • Douglas Dick *Mel Dobie* • Michael Pate *Charlie Smith* ■ *Dir* Francis D Lyon • *Scr* Daniel B Ullman

Okoge ★★★

Drama 1992 · Jpn · Colour · 120mins

With its title deriving from the Japanese for "fag hag" and the inclusion of a drag queen chorus, this refreshingly non-judgemental gay variation on *The Apartment* caused an uproar on its original release because of its frank discussion of a still-taboo topic and its provocatively graphic eroticism. Combining acerbic social commentary with camp comedy, director Takehiro Nakajima slickly establishes the unconventional menage constituted when Misha Shimizu offers the use of her bed to Takehiro Murata and his married salaryman lover. The resolution is messily unsatisfactory. DP. In Japanese with English subtitles.

Misa Shimizu *Sayoko* • Takehiro Murata *Goh* • Takeo Nakahara *Tochi* ■ *Dir/Scr* Takehiro Nakajima

Old Acquaintance ★★★

Drama 1943 · US · BW · 110mins

One of the great Bette Davis Warner Bros melodramas, this reteams her with Miriam Hopkins. The two stars battle it out as a pair of childhood friends who become lifelong literary rivals – art starts to imitate life and the resonances are plain to see, and enjoy, on screen. The unsympathetic Hopkins has a tough time holding the screen against Davis, but Vincent Sherman ensures that the scenery chewing is kept to a minimum. TS

Bette Davis *Kitty Marlowe* • Miriam Hopkins *Millie Drake* • Gig Young *Rudd Kendall* • John Loder *Preston Drake* • Dolores Moran *Deirdre* • Philip Reed *Lucian Grant* ■ *Dir* Vincent Sherman • *Scr* John Van Druten, Lenore Coffee, from the play by John Van Druten

Old Bill and Son ★★ U

Second World War comedy
1940 · UK · BW · 95mins

Envious of son John Mills enlisting in the army, First World War veteran Morland Graham blags his way into the Pioneer Corps and finds himself in France assisting in the capture of a Nazi platoon. With its cast of practised farceurs, this flagwaver is very much of its time. But its behind-the-scenes personnel is pretty remarkable, with Georges Périnal on camera, Vincent Korda responsible for the production design and Charles Crichton on duty in the cutting room. DP

Morland Graham *Old Bill Busby* • John Mills *Young Bill Busby* • Mary Clare *Maggie Busby* • Renee Houston *Stella Malloy* • René Ray *Sally* • Gus McNaughton *Alf* • Ronald Shiner *Bert* ■ *Dir* Ian Dalrymple • *Scr* Captain Bruce Bairnsfather [Bruce Bairnsfather], Ian Dalrymple, Arthur Wimperis, from the comic strip *Old Bill* by Bruce Bairnsfather

Old Bones of the River ★★ PG

Comedy 1938 · UK · BW · 86mins

This muddled lampoon at the expense of the colonial service completed a decidedly disappointing 1938 for Will Hay. A rather uninspired spoof of the old Edgar Wallace story *Sanders of the River*, this struggles to combine a worthwhile storyline with the endless stream of ancient music-hall gags. However, they are infinitely more preferable to the racist remarks, which are unacceptable today. DP [video] DVD

Will Hay *Prof Benjamin Tibbetts* • Moore Marriott *Jerry Harbottle* • Graham Moffatt *Albert* • Robert Adams *Bosambo* • Jack Livesey *Capt Hamilton* • Jack London *M'Bapi* • Wyndham Goldie *Commissioner Sanders* ■ *Dir* Marcel Varnel • *Scr* Marriott Edgar, Val Guest, JOC Orton, from the stories by Edgar Wallace

Old Boyfriends ★★

Comedy drama 1979 · US · Colour · 102mins

It should have worked, but somehow it doesn't. Talia Shire plays a clinical psychologist who, after a botched suicide attempt, goes on the trail of her past relationships. John Belushi and Keith Carradine are just two of the old beaus she meets up with in this lukewarm comedy drama. It marked the feature debut of Joan Tewkesbury, writer of *Nashville*, and was scripted by Paul and Leonard Schrader – which only goes to show that good pedigrees do not always a great movie make. FL

Talia Shire *Diane Cruise* • Richard Jordan *Jeff Turrin* • John Belushi *Eric Katz* • Keith Carradine *Wayne Van Til* • John Houseman *Dr Hoffman* • Buck Henry *Art Kopple* • Bethel Leslie *Mrs Van Til* • Joan Hotchkis *Pamela Shaw* ■ *Dir* Joan Tewkesbury • *Scr* Paul Schrader, Leonard Schrader

The Old Curiosity Shop ★★★ U

Drama 1934 · UK · BW · 91mins

A maligned adaptation of Dickens's tale of the destitute storekeeper and his granddaughter, Little Nell, who are forced to endure the hardship of the road after being terrorised by the monstrous money-lender, Quilp. Director Thomas Bentley was a former Dickens impersonator on the stage and had already filmed several silent versions of his novels. Here he does a commendable job of condensing the sprawling story, although his direction is occasionally lacklustre. Ben Webster and Elaine Benson make tolerably troubled Trents, but the film belongs to Hay Petrie, whose Quilp is the embodiment of evil. DP [video]

Ben Webster *Grandfather Trent* • Elaine Benson *Nell Trent* • Hay Petrie *Quilp* • Beatrix Thompson *Mrs Quilp* • Gibb McLaughlin *Sampson Brass* • Lily Long *Sally Brass* • Reginald Purdell *Dick Swiveller* • Polly Ward *Marchioness* • James Harcourt *Single gentleman* ■ *Dir* Thomas Bentley • *Scr* Margaret Kennedy, Ralph Neale, from the novel by Charles Dickens

The Old Dark House ★★★★ PG

Classic comedy horror
1932 · US · BW · 69mins

This is splendidly ghoulish nonsense, directed by that master of camp horror, James Whale. Charles Laughton and Boris Karloff are magnificent, and Melvyn Douglas is both suitably suave and puzzled, but, for fans of *Titanic*, it's the appearance of that movie's octogenarian Oscar nominee Gloria Stuart as the young female lead that will give most pleasure. The 1963 William Castle version isn't a patch on this marvellous original. TS [video]

Boris Karloff *Morgan* • Melvyn Douglas *Roger Penderel* • Charles Laughton *Sir William Porterhouse* • Gloria Stuart *Margaret Waverton* • Lillian Bond *Gladys DuCane* • Ernest Thesiger *Horace Femm* • Eva Moore *Rebecca Femm* • Raymond Massey *Philip Waverton* • Brember Wills *Saul Femm* • John Dudgeon [Elspeth Dudgeon] *Sir Roderick Femm* ■ *Dir* James Whale • *Scr* Benn W Levy, RC Sherriff, from the novel *Benighted* by JB Priestley

The Old Dark House ★★ PG

Comedy horror
1963 · US/UK · Colour · 82mins

William Castle forewent cinema audience-participation antics such as "Emergo" and "Coward's Corner" for this fumbling Hammer horror, in which the utterly inept Tom Poston comes to stay at Peter Bull's crumbling family pile. Instead, he concentrates on the macabre tics of such stalwarts as Joyce Grenfell (knitting manically), Robert Morley (perpetually tinkering with firearms) and Mervyn Johns (obsessively building an ark). Yet the transparency of the serial killer's identity and the overall sloppiness means this soon outstays its welcome. However, with credits drawn by the creator of *The Addams Family*, it has a certain so-bad-it's-fun value. DP [video]

Tom Poston *Tom Penderel* • Robert Morley *Roderick Femm* • Janette Scott *Cecily Femm* • Joyce Grenfell *Agatha Femm* • Peter Bull *Casper Femm/Jasper Femm* • Mervyn Johns *Potiphar* • Fenella Fielding *Morgana Femm* • Danny Green *Morgan Femm* ■ *Dir* William Castle • *Scr* Robert Dillon, from the novel *Benighted* by JB Priestley

O

Old Enough ★★ PG

Drama 1984 · US · Colour · 91mins

The sort of film that Jodie Foster would have been perfect in (before she grew up, that is), this stars Rainbow Harvest and Sarah Boyd as two young girls from the opposite ends of the social scale who strike up an unlikely friendship. Harvest is the girl from the wrong side of the tracks; Boyd is a rich, 12-year-old New Yorker. This has a certain charm. FL

Sarah Boyd *Lonnie Sloan* • Rainbow Harvest *Karen Bruckner* • Neill Barry *Johnny* • Danny Aiello *Bruckner* ■ *Dir/Scr* Marisa Silver

The Old-Fashioned Way ★★★★ U

Comedy 1934 · US · BW · 71mins

In one of WC Fields's greatest comedies, based on his own story, he appears as an impecunious impresario heading a travelling vaudeville troupe, outwitting landladies and writ-servers, putting on a full performance of the wheezy vintage melodrama *The Drunkard* and even finding time for his juggling routines. In addition, he conducts a running battle with Baby LeRoy – with the nipper inflicting the most damage. William Beaudine's direction gives it a polished look. AE

WC Fields *The Great McGonigle* • Judith Allen *Betty McGonigle* • Joe Morrison *Wally Livingston* • Jan Duggan *Cleopatra Pepperday* • Nora Cecil *Mrs Wendelschaffer* • Baby LeRoy *Albert Wendelschaffer* • Jack Mulhall *Dick Bronson* • Tammany Young *Marmaduke Gump* ■ *Dir* William Beaudine • *Scr* Garnett Weston, Jack Cunningham, from a story by Charles Bogle [WC Fields]

Old Gringo ★★★ 15

Period drama 1989 · US · Colour · 115mins

This adaptation of Carlos Fuentes's acclaimed novel is meticulously staged, played with great conviction and studiously faithful to the psychological and historical complexities of the original. The only problem is that it is just a tad dull. Set in Mexico at the time of Pancho Villa's uprising, it skirts around the political issues and takes the easy way out by concentrating on the romance that develops between Jane Fonda's wayward traveller and Jimmy Smits's revolutionary leader. Gregory Peck steals every scene he's in. DP. Contains swearing. DVD

Jane Fonda *Harriet Winslow* • Gregory Peck *Ambrose Bierce* • Jimmy Smits *Arroyo* • Patricio Contreras *Colonel Frutos Garcia* • Jenny Gago *La Garduna* • Jim Metzler *Ron* • Gabriela Roel *La Luna* • Pedro Armendáriz Jr *Pancho Villa* ■ *Dir* Luis Puenzo • *Scr* Aida Bortnik, Luis Puenzo, from the novel *Gringo Viejo* by Carlos Fuentes

The Old Lady Who Walked in the Sea ★★★ 18

Comedy 1991 · Fr · Colour · 90mins

As the haughty con artist seeking to pass on the tricks of her trade, Jeanne Moreau, gives a much better performance than this slight comedy really deserves. Although Michel Serrault stooges selflessly as her loyal partner, Moreau is badly let down by the feebleness of Luc Thuillier, as the beach baby she nominates as her protégé. Moreau thoroughly merited her César award. DP. In French with English subtitles. Contains swearing, sex scenes and nudity.

Jeanne Moreau *Lady M* • Michel Serrault *Pompilius* • Luc Thuillier *Lambert* • Géraldine Danon *Noémie* • Marie-Dominique Aumont *Muriel* ■ *Dir* Laurent Heynemann • *Scr* Dominique Roulet, from the novel *La Vieille Qui Marchait dans la Mer* by San Antonio

Old Louisiana ★

Period adventure drama
1938 · US · BW · 63mins

Former western hero Tom Keene starred in a series of period adventures made on a shoestring budget, of which this is a particularly poor specimen. Keene stars as an American living in Louisiana when it was still a Spanish colony. An actress called Rita Cansino plays the daughter of the Spanish governor; after she became famous as Rita Hayworth, the film was relaunched as *Louisiana Gal*, giving her top billing. AE

Tom Keene *John Colfax* • Rita Cansino [Rita Hayworth] *Dona Angela Gonzalez* • Will Morgan *Steve* • Robert Fiske *Luke E Gilmore* ■ *Dir* Irvin Willat • *Scr* Mary Ireland, from a story by John T Neville

The Old Maid ★★★★ U

Period drama 1939 · US · BW · 90mins

This wonderful slice of melodramatic soap opera froths and crackles with gloriously histrionic performances. This is Bette Davis at her best as an unmarried mother whose unsuspecting daughter prefers the company of Davis's deeply Machiavellian sister Miriam Hopkins. Davis and Hopkins spar like a pair of theatrical prizefighters. The period setting provides the perfect costumes to accompany all the flouncing. Never a dull moment. SH

Bette Davis *Charlotte Lovell* • Miriam Hopkins *Delia Lovell Ralston* • George Brent *Clem Spender* • Jane Bryan *Tina* • Donald Crisp *Dr Lanskell* ■ *Dir* Edmund Goulding • *Scr* Casey Robinson, from the play by Zoë Akins [Zoe Akins], from the novel by Edith Wharton

Old Man ★★★★

Period drama 1997 · US · Colour · 98mins

This outstanding adaptation of a William Faulkner story was written by Academy Award winning playwright/screenwriter Horton Foote. In 1928 rural Mississippi, after a disastrous flood, convict Arliss Howard is ordered to take a boat up river to save a pregnant single woman and becomes a reluctant hero while falling in love with the new mother. Howard eloquently captures the simple intelligence of his character; Jeanne Tripplehorn gives an elegant, understated performance, while director John Kent Harrison exhibits great finesse in capturing the natural essence of Faulkner's milieu. A rare TV-movie treat. MC

Jeanne Tripplehorn *Addie Rebecca Brice* • Arliss Howard *JJ Taylor* • Leo Burmester *Plump Convict* • Daro Latiolais *Cajun Man* • Ray McKinnon *Shanty Man with Gun* ■ *Dir* John Kent Harrison • *Scr* Horton Foote, from the short story by William Faulkner

The Old Man and the Sea ★★★ U

Drama 1958 · US · Colour · 86mins

Spencer Tracy is Ernest Hemingway's obsessed angler, riding the Caribbean with macho rubbish in his head and a giant marlin on the line. Inconsistent use of back projection and a certain monotony to the fishing sequences are drawbacks, but Tracy is tremendous, capturing the simple humanity and heroism of the central character and nearly capturing an Oscar as well. Director John Sturges, who took over the project after Fred Zinnemann had laboured for months on it. AT

Spencer Tracy *Old Man* • Felipe Pazos *Boy* • Harry Bellaver *Martin* ■ *Dir* John Sturges • *Scr* Peter Viertel, from the novella by Ernest Hemingway

Old Man Rhythm ★★★ U

Musical comedy 1935 · US · BW · 74mins

It's as lightweight as tissue paper but music buffs and film collectors still shouldn't miss this treat, which features a very young Betty Grable, and a rare appearance by the great songwriter Johnny Mercer as a college boy (he's the one on the train, with the southern accent). Watch out, too, for Lucille Ball. The plot, surprisingly, does have some relevance to its title, as George Barbier plays a businessman who goes back to college to keep a stern paternal eye on his playboy son, Charles "Buddy" Rogers, who is way too old for the part. TS

Charles "Buddy" Rogers *Johnny Roberts* • George Barbier *John Roberts Sr* • Barbara Kent *Edith* • Grace Bradley *Marion* • Betty Grable *Sylvia* • Eric Blore *Phillips* • Johnny Mercer *Colonel* • Lucille Ball *College girl* ■ *Dir* Edward Ludwig • *Scr* Sig Herzig, Ernest Pagano, HW Hanemann, from a story by Lewis Gensler, Sidg Herzig, Don Hartman • *Music/lyrics* Johnny Mercer, Lewis Gensler

The Old Man Who Read Love Stories ★★★

Drama
2000 · Fr/Aus/Sp/Neth · Colour · 111mins

Reluctantly rousing himself from his passion for penny dreadfuls to hunt a vengeful jaguar, Richard Dreyfuss grows into the role of the lonely widower who has eked out an existence in a small Amazonian village since setting out to colonise the region decades before. Exploring environmental, political and human themes with a deceptive insouciance, De Heer's primary concern lies with Dreyfuss's evolving relationships with tribal chief Victor Bottenbley, blustering mayor Timothy Spall and itinerant dentist Hugo Weaving and his sensuous mistress, Cathy Tyson. DP

Richard Dreyfuss *Antonio Bolivar* • Timothy Spall *Luis Agalla, mayor* • Hugo Weaving *Rubicondo, dentist* • Cathy Tyson *Josefina* • Victor Bottenbley *Nushino* ■ *Dir* Rolf De Heer • *Scr* Rolf de Heer, from the novel by Luis Sepulveda

The Old Mill ★★★★★ U

Animation 1937 · US · Colour · 9mins

This landmark Disney short marked the first use of the multiplane camera, a 14ft-tall construction that enabled several layers of artwork to be filmed simultaneously, giving a greater illusion of depth. Appropriately, the action mirrors the contraption that filmed it, as we are taken through the various stories of a ruined windmill and the wildlife living in it, from the ducks on the pond outside to the sleeping bats in the rafters. When a storm breaks out, the mill begins "working", jeopardising its inhabitants. Winner of the Oscar for best short cartoon of its year, the music-led, virtual plotlessness of the film looks forward to *Fantasia*, while the sophisticated animation of nature anticipates *Bambi*. With the animals' actions only slightly exaggerated for comic effect, it remains a lyrical mood piece. CLP

Dir Wilfred Jackson • *Music* Leigh Harlene

Old Mother Riley ★★ U

Comedy 1937 · UK · BW · 75mins

This is the first of 15 cross-dressing comedies starring Arthur Lucan (1937–52), although by the last he'd parted acrimoniously from singing sidekick, Kitty McShane. The husband-and-wife team had been playing the Irish washerwoman and her man-mad daughter since the 1920s, but their music-hall schtick always felt thinly spread on screen, despite efforts to vary the setting. Starting out at northern indie, Butchers, the duo were lured to Rank at the height of their fame, only to fade away at Renown. DP

Arthur Lucan *Old Mother Riley* • Kitty McShane *Kitty Riley* • Barbara Everest *Mrs Briggs* • Patrick Ludlow *Edwin Briggs* • J Hubert Leslie *Captain Lawson* • Edith Sharpe *Matilda Lawson* ■ *Dir* Oswald Mitchell • *Scr* Con West, from a story by John Argyle

Old School ★★★ 15

Comedy 2003 · US · Colour · 88mins

A well-scripted frat-boy flick with a twist, this tale's so irrepressible that it's hard not to warm to its infantile charms. Luke Wilson, Will Ferrell and Vince Vaughn let it all hang out as bored buddies who try to recapture the fun of their college years by establishing their own off-campus fraternity. While Wilson's dry comic style only really comes to life during the film's bolder set pieces, Vaughn and Ferrell are such natural clowns that they up the tempo whenever they're on screen. SF. Contains swearing, sex scenes, nudity. DVD

Luke Wilson *Mitch* • Will Ferrell *Frank* • Vince Vaughn *Beanie* • Jeremy Piven *Gordon Pritchard* • Ellen Pompeo *Nicole* • Juliette Lewis *Heidi* • Leah Remini *Lara* • Seann William Scott *Peppers* • Snoop Dogg ■ *Dir* Todd Phillips • *Scr* Todd Phillips, Scot Armstrong, from a story by Court Crandall, Todd Phillips, Scot Armstrong

Old Scores ★★★

Sports drama 1991 · UK/NZ · Colour · 93mins

This odd little rugby drama is a well played, if rather preachy, look at the re-match of a Wales–All Blacks game discovered to have been fixed 25 years previously. The players have long since scattered between God, drink and all points in between, but Windsor Davies and Glyn Houston round them up and add some gravitas. Lots of famous rugby faces are also featured. SH

Robert Pugh *Bleddyn Morgan* • Glyn Houston *Aneurin Morgan* • Alison Bruce *Ngaire Morgan* • Clayton Spence *Dai Morgan* • Dafydd Emyr *Owen Llewellyn* • John Francis *David Llewellyn* • Beth Morris *Bronwen Llewellyn* • Windsor Davies *Evan Price* ■ *Dir* Alan Clayton • *Scr* Dean Parker, Greg McGee

An Old Spanish Custom ★★

Comedy 1935 · UK · BW · 61mins

Working with British director Adrian Brunel, this comedy was an incongruous flop for Buster Keaton. The star plays a wealthy yachtsman who sails to Spain. While there, he falls under the spell of scheming siren Lupita Tovar. Pretty miserable stuff, especially when one remembers what the stone-faced genius was capable of when he really put his mind to it. TH

Buster Keaton *Leander Proudfoot* • Lupita Tovar *Lupita Malez* • Esme Percy *Jose* • Lyn Harding *Gonzalo Gonzalez* • Webster Booth *Serenader* ■ *Dir* Adrian Brunel • *Scr* Edwin Greenwood

Old Yeller ★★★★ U

Adventure drama 1957 · US · Colour · 80mins

This epic about man's best friend will not leave a dry eye in the house. This was Walt Disney's first boy-and-his-dog adventure and, despite all the *Savage Sams* and *Big Reds* that followed, remains resolutely the best, largely because of sensitive direction from British-born Robert Stevenson. Dorothy McGuire and Fess Parker make an upstanding and sympathetic Texas couple, and the frontier atmosphere is well re-created. TS

Dorothy McGuire *Katie Coates* • Fess Parker *Jim Coates* • Tommy Kirk *Travis Coates* • Kevin Corcoran *Arliss Coates* • Jeff York *Bud Searcy* • Beverly Washburn *Lisbeth Searcy* • Chuck Connors *Burn Sanderson* ■ *Dir* Robert Stevenson • *Scr* Fred Gipson, William Tunberg, from the novel by Fred Gipson

Oldboy ★★★★ 18

Action thriller 2003 · S Kor · Colour · 114mins

Director Park Chan-wook received the Grand Prix at 2004's Cannes film festival for this mind-bending action thriller. Choi Min-sik plays the happily married father, who is kidnapped and incarcerated for no apparent reason. He's then horrified to discover that his wife has been murdered with himself as the principal suspect. Fifteen years of unexplained Kafka-esque detention follow. Suddenly, he wakes up to find himself free, and gets down to the serious business of vengeance. Some viewers will be repulsed by scenes of self-mutilation; however, this has more to offer than action and violence – it's an imaginative tale of guilt and revenge, with a shocking twist in the tale. BP. In Korean with English subtitles. Contains violence. DVD

Choi Min-sik *Oh Dae-su* • Yu Ji-tae *Lee Woo-jin* • Gang Hye-jung *Mido* • Chi Dae-han *No Joo-hwan* • Oh Dal-su *Park Cheol-woong* • Kim Byoung-ok *Chief guard (Mr Han)* ■ *Dir* Park Chan-wook • *Scr* Hwang Jo-yun, Lim Joon-hyung, Park Chan-wook, from a story by Garon Tsuchiya, Nobuaki Minegishi

The Oldest Profession ★★

Comedy drama
1967 · Fr/It/W Ger · Colour · 97mins

Six vignettes exploring prostitution through the ages, yet only one has cinematic merit. Set in the then distant Y2K, Jean-Luc Godard's encounter between space traveller Jacques Charrier and Anna Karina was intended to be a bold experiment with colour, but the print undermined his efforts by daubing the pre-kiss sequences with a jaundiced yellow. Passing from prehistoric and Roman times to revolutionary and *fin de siècle* France, the other episodes are uninspiring, with Claude Autant-Lara loitering in an ambulance in the Bois de Boulogne, while Philippe de Broca and Michael Pfleghar succeed in making Jeanne Moreau and Raquel Welch seem dull. DP. A French language film.

Michèle Mercier *Brit* • Enrico Maria Salerno *Braque* • Elsa Martinelli *Empress* • Jeanne Moreau *Mimi* • Jean-Claude Brialy *Philibert* • Raquel Welch *Nini* • Martin Held *Banker* • Nadia Gray *Nadia* • Anna Karina *Miss Conversation* • Jean-Pierre Léaud *Bellboy* ■ *Dir* Franco Indovina, Mauro Bolognini, Philippe de Broca, Michael Pfleghar, Claude Autant-Lara, Jean-Luc Godard • *Scr* Ennio Flaiano, Daniel Boulanger, Georges Tabet, André Tabet, Jean Aurenche, Jean-Luc Godard

Oleanna ★★

Drama 1994 · US/UK · Colour · 89mins

Exploring the theme of inter-gender power-plays long before Michael Crichton dabbled with it in *Disclosure*, David Mamet's play enraged nearly all who saw it by forcing them to declare exactly where they stood on the subjects of sexual harassment and political correctness. Even though Mamet opts for a straight filmed record of the stage show, the screen version has markedly less impact, because the intensity of the theatrical experience cannot possibly be re-created, in spite of the spirited performances of William H Macy and Debra Eisenstadt. DP. Contains violence and swearing.

William H Macy *John* • Debra Eisenstadt *Carol* ■ *Dir* David Mamet • *Scr* David Mamet, from his play

Oliver! ★★★★ U

Musical 1968 · UK · Colour · 139mins

In this immensely popular film version of Lionel Bart's musical, Ron Moody – Oscar-nominated as Fagin – brings a certain magnificence to the role he had created on stage. The film collected six Oscars, including best picture and best director (Carol Reed, a last minute substitute for Lewis Gilbert, who probably would have brought the charm the fable sometimes lacks), and there's no denying that the Academy recognition for sound and art direction is justified. Today, the film works well as a child's introduction to Dickens, while adults can enjoy Shani Wallis's Nancy and Onna White's brisk Broadway choreography among other highlights. TS [video] DVD

Ron Moody *Fagin* • Oliver Reed *Bill Sikes* • Mark Lester (2) *Oliver* • Harry Secombe *Mr Bumble* • Shani Wallis *Nancy* • Jack Wild *Artful Dodger* • Hugh Griffith *Magistrate* • Sheila White *Bet* • Joseph O'Conor *Mr Brownlow* • Peggy Mount *Widow Corney* • Leonard Rossiter *Mr Sowerberry* • Hylda Baker *Mrs Sowerberry* ■ *Dir* Carol Reed • *Scr* Vernon Harris, from the musical play by Lionel Bart, from the novel *Oliver Twist* by Charles Dickens • *Cinematographer* Oswald Morris • *Production Designer* John Box

Oliver & Company ★★★ U

Animated drama 1988 · US · Colour · 73mins

Disney gives Oliver a new Twist with a Dickens of an animation job. A cute orphan kittycat is drafted into a doggy pack of streetwise New York pickpockets whose human master, Fagin, is up to his ears in debt to Sykes, the city's sinister kingpin of crime. It's a nicely told tale that, though a little lacking in Disney's customary charm, still provides fine family entertainment. DA [video] DVD

Joey Lawrence *Oliver* • Bette Midler *Georgette* • Billy Joel *Dodger* • Richard "Cheech" Marin *Tito* • Richard Mulligan *Einstein* • Roscoe Lee Browne *Francis* • Sheryl Lee Ralph *Rita* • Dom DeLuise *Fagin* • Robert Loggia *Sykes* ■ *Dir* George Scribner • *Scr* Jim Cox, Timothy J Disney, James Mangold, suggested by the novel *Oliver Twist* by Charles Dickens

Oliver the Eighth ★★★ U

Comedy 1934 · US · BW · 26mins

Typical Laurel and Hardy high-jinks in this short in which the great double act play a pair of barbers who both write to a rich widow who is advertising for a husband. However, Ollie neglects to post Stan's letter, planning to woo the widow by himself. She has, however, already seen off seven husbands and intends Ollie to be her eighth victim. In some territories the prefix "The Private Life of" was added to the title to mirror that of a hugely successful British film of the period, *The Private Life of Henry VIII* (1933). DF [video]

Stan Laurel *Stan* • Oliver Hardy *Ollie* • Mae Busch *Eccentric widow at Box 204J* • Jack Barty *Jitters, the butler* ■ *Dir* Lloyd French

Oliver Twist ★★

Silent drama 1922 · US · BW · 74mins

Wonderful lighting and production design, which beautifully evoke Dickensian London, are the saving grace of this otherwise disappointing silent version of the classic novel. Lon Chaney is ineffectual as Fagin, one of his few performances that fails to satisfy. Jackie Coogan, playing the title role, had become a phenomenal success the previous year starring with Chaplin in *The Kid* and this was one of the first films he made under a million-dollar contract with MGM. TV

Jackie Coogan *Oliver Twist* • Lon Chaney *Fagin* • Gladys Brockwell *Nancy Sikes* • George Siegmann *Bill Sikes* • Edouard Trebaol *Artful Dodger* • Lionel Belmore *Mr Brownlow* • Carl Stockdale *Monks* • Eddie Boland *Toby Crackit* ■ *Dir* Frank Lloyd • *Scr* Frank Lloyd, Harry Weil, Walter Anthony (titles), from the novel by Charles Dickens • *Art Director* Stephen Goosson • *Lighting* Lewis Johnson

Oliver Twist ★★★★★ U

Classic drama 1948 · UK · BW · 110mins

David Lean's masterly adaptation of the Dickens novel brims with unforgettable scenes and performances, notably Alec Guinness's Fagin and Robert Newton's genuinely frightening Bill Sikes. From the opening, with Oliver's mother struggling to the workhouse to give birth, to the climax on the roofs of Docklands, the picture brings the novel vividly to life. The movie caused riots in Germany and was initially banned and then heavily cut in America for its alleged anti-Semitism. AT [video] DVD

Alec Guinness *Fagin* • Robert Newton *Bill Sikes* • John Howard Davies *Oliver Twist* • Kay Walsh *Nancy* • Anthony Newley *Artful Dodger* • Ralph Truman *Monks* • Francis L Sullivan *Mr Bumble* • Henry Stephenson *Mr Brownlow* • Josephine Stuart *Oliver's mother* • Henry Edwards *Police official* • Diana Dors *Charlotte* • Maurice Denham *Chief of police* ■ *Dir* David Lean • *Scr* David Lean, Stanley Haynes, from the novel by Charles Dickens • *Cinematographer* Guy Green • *Art Director* John Bryan

Oliver Twist ★★★ PG

Drama 1982 · US · Colour · 98mins

Made for American television but released theatrically outside the States, this umpteenth version of Charles Dickens's famous tale poses no threat to David Lean's definitive British version. It does, however, boast a rumbunctious rasping Fagin played by George C Scott. He alone provides positive reason for viewing. However, director Clive Donner also gets value for money out of a slew of British thespians. The screenplay by James Goldman is adult and respectful. Literature the easy way. TS [video] DVD

George C Scott *Fagin* • Richard Charles *Oliver Twist* • Tim Curry *Bill Sikes* • Michael Hordern *George Brownlow* • Timothy West *Mr Bumble* • Eileen Atkins *Mrs Mann* • Cherie Lunghi *Nancy* • Oliver Cotton *Monks* • Martin Tempest *Artful Dodger* ■ *Dir* Clive Donner • *Scr* James Goldman, from the novel by Charles Dickens

Oliver's Story ★★

Romantic drama 1978 · US · Colour · 90mins

The less than successful sequel to schmaltzy *Love Story* has Ryan O'Neal trying to get his life together. The original was a complete one-off which should never have been revisited but even so director John Korty makes a game fist of dealing with the complexities of dating after your loved one's death. O'Neal looks a trifle jaded as well he might (his own personal life was going through several shades of hell at the time) but if you adored the blockbusting first picture you will be fascinated by this. SH

Ryan O'Neal *Oliver Barrett IV* • Candice Bergen *Marcie Bonwit* • Nicola Pagett *Joanna Stone* • Edward Binns *Phil Cavilleri* • Benson Fong *John Hsiang* • Charles Haid *Stephen Simpson* • Kenneth McMillan *James Francis* • Ray Milland *Mr Barrett* • Josef Sommer *Dr Dienhart* • Swoosie Kurtz *Gwen Simpson* ■ *Dir* John Korty • *Scr* Erich Segal, John Korty, from the novel by Erich Segal

Olivia ★★★★

Period psychological drama
1950 · Fr · BW · 91mins

The death, in a car accident, of Jacqueline Audrey, sister of Colette, robbed cinema of a respected talent. She directs this restrained adaptation of a pseudonymously published novel set in a girls' boarding school towards the end of the 19th century. In 1950, our censor cut ten minutes from it, although the lesbian undertones are just that. The story centres on two sisters, Edwige Feuillère and Simone Simon, who generate suppressed passions and affiliations among their charges. Dated in our permissive age, but still elegant, provocative and beautifully acted. BB. In French with English subtitles.

Edwige Feuillère *Mlle Julie* • Simone Simon *Mlle Cara* • Marie-Claire Olive *Olivia Realey* • Yvonne de Bray *Victoire* • Suzanne Dehelly *Mlle Dubois* ■ *Dir* Jacqueline Audry • *Scr* Colette Audry, Pierre Laroche, from the novel by Olivia

Olivier Olivier ★★★★ 15

Drama 1991 · Fr · Colour · 104mins

Anyone who enjoyed *The Return of Martin Guerre* and its Hollywood remake *Sommersby* will find themselves on familiar ground with this puzzling true-life tale of a runaway who returns. Is Grégoire Colin really the long-lost son of François Cluzet and the mollycoddling Brigitte Roüan, or is he, as his older sister Marina Golovine suspects, an impostor? Set in a rural idyll usually associated with innocence, this is both a mystery story and a disturbingly dark dissection of the modern family. Polish director Agnieszka Holland's persistent prying and the totally credible performances of the dysfunctional foursome make this compelling viewing. DP. In French with English subtitles. [video]

François Cluzet *Serge* • Brigitte Roüan *Elisabeth* • Jean-François Stévenin *Druot* • Grégoire Colin *Olivier* • Marina Golovine *Nadine* ■ *Dir/Scr* Agnieszka Holland

Los Olvidados ★★★★★

Drama 1950 · Mex · BW · 88mins

Luis Buñuel restored his critical reputation with this harsh, almost neorealist, study of street poverty that earned him the best director prize at Cannes in 1951. Shot in only 21 days and brimming with shrewd humanity, this keenly observed film is not without its surreal moments. But for all its political awareness, this is not a blindly liberal portrait of the pitiless crime, sexual corruption and cruel intimidation that is part and parcel of slum life. Society may be culpable for their plight, but Roberto Cobo and Alfonso Mejia, as the two leaders of a gang of boys who wreak havoc on their home town, are by no means saints. DP. In Spanish with English subtitles.

Estela Inda *Mother* • Alfonso Mejia *Pedro* • Roberto Cobo *Jaibo* ■ *Dir* Luis Buñuel • *Scr* Luis Buñuel, Luis Alcoriza • *Cinematographer* Gabriel Figueroa

Olympiad ★★★★

Documentary 1938 · Ger · BW · 225mins

After *Triumph of the Will* (1935), the documentary of the Nuremberg Rally, Leni Riefenstahl was commissioned by Hitler to film the 1936 Berlin Olympics "as a song of praise to the ideals of National Socialism". With over 30 cameramen as well as planes and airships at her disposal, Riefenstahl provided a two-part, near four-hour epic that links the Olympic ideal with that of the Third Reich. But even Riefenstahl couldn't avoid showing the victories of the black American Jesse Owens. Despite the bad taste it leaves in the mouth, one cannot be blind to the exceptional technique and beauty of the film, which many consider one of the greatest documentaries ever made. RB. A German language film. [video]

Dir/Scr Leni Riefenstahl

Omar Khayyam ★★ U

Period adventure
1957 · US · Colour · 100mins

There's only a slight inkling in this childish *Arabian Nights* adventure that Omar Khayyam was actually the medieval Persian poet of love and indolence and also a brilliant mathematician and astronomer. First and foremost he's a muscle-flexing, scimitar-swishing Cornel Wilde intent on saving Shah Raymond Massey from murderous foes while hazardously romancing his leader's beloved Debra Paget. Now so preposterously cute, this romp is watchably camp. TH

Cornel Wilde *Omar Khayyam* • Michael Rennie *Hasani* • Debra Paget *Sharain* • John Derek *Prince Malik* • Raymond Massey *Shah of Persia* • Sebastian Cabot *Nizam* • Yma Sumac *Karina* • Margaret Hayes *Zarada* ■ *Dir* William Dieterle • *Scr* Barré Lyndon

Omega Doom ★ 15

Science-fiction thriller
1996 · US · Colour · 80mins

Those familiar with director Albert Pyun's movies will not be surprised by the poor quality of this, or the fact it reworks the premise of a better-known film. This time, Pyun borrows from *A Fistful of Dollars*, updating the basic story to a post-apocalypse future. Rutger Hauer sleepwalks through his role as a mysterious robot who arrives in a ruined amusement park occupied by two robot groups. KB. Contains violence. [video]

Rutger Hauer *Omega Doom* • Shannon Whirry *Zed* • Tina Cote *Blackheart* • Anna Katarina *Bartender* • Norbert Weisser *The Head* • Jill

O

Pierce *Zinc* • Simon Pollard *Zed Too* • Cynthia Ireland *Ironface* ■ *Dir* Albert Pyun • *Scr* Albert Pyun, Ed Naha, from a story by Albert Pyun

The Omega Man ★★★★ PG

Science-fiction thriller
1971 · US · Colour · 93mins

If you're hooked on sci-fi, this is for you – a weirdly engrossing futuristic tale about the world after a viral apocalypse. The conflict between "normals" (led by Charlton Heston) and light-sensitive mutants (led by Anthony Zerbe) is one of science against superstition, and, while lacking the vampiristic teeth of Richard Matheson's novel, it still has an eerie topicality. TH. Contains violence and swearing. DVD

Charlton Heston *Robert Neville* • Anthony Zerbe *Matthias* • Rosalind Cash *Lisa* • Paul Koslo *Dutch* • Lincoln Kilpatrick *Zachary* • Eric Laneuville *Richie* ■ *Dir* Boris Sagal • *Scr* John William Corrington, Joyce H Corrington, from the novel *I Am Legend* by Richard Matheson

The Omen ★★★★ 18

Horror 1976 · US · Colour · 106mins

This big-budget horror blockbuster is given class by a distinguished cast and an unsettling atmosphere created by director Richard Donner. Cleverly borrowing a prophecy from the Book of Revelation about Armageddon, scriptwriter David Seltzer fashioned a supernatural terror tale of religious epic proportions. This carries its suspenseful premise with great uneasiness and David Warner's grisly beheading is only one of several remarkably imaginative ghastly deaths. Three sequels followed, beginning with *Damien – Omen II* (1978). AJ. Contains violence and swearing. DVD

Gregory Peck *Robert Thorn* • Lee Remick *Katherine Thorn* • David Warner *Jennings* • Billie Whitelaw *Mrs Baylock* • Harvey Stevens *Damien* • Leo McKern *Bugenhagen* • Patrick Troughton *Father Brennan* • Martin Benson *Father Spiletto* • Anthony Nichols *Dr Becker* • John Stride *Psychiatrist* ■ *Dir* Richard Donner • *Scr* David Seltzer

O

Omen III: the Final Conflict ★★ 18

Horror 1980 · US · Colour · 108mins

This second sequel to *The Omen* finds Devil-child Damien as US Ambassador to the Court of St James, thus following in father's footsteps. Intending to do a Herod by killing every male child born on a certain day, Damien unleashes a load of special effects, obliging the priests to dust off the seven daggers of Megiddo yet again. The climax is mind-bogglingly silly, but not final enough because there was yet another sequel, *Omen 4: The Awakening*, in 1991. AT DVD

Sam Neill *Damien Thorn* • Rossano Brazzi *Father DeCarlo* • Don Gordon *Harvey Dean* • Lisa Harrow *Kate Reynolds* • Barnaby Holm *Peter Reynolds* • Mason Adams *President* • Robert Arden *American Ambassador* ■ *Dir* Graham Baker • *Scr* Andrew Birkin, from characters created by Dave Seltzer

Omen IV: the Awakening ★ 15

Horror 1991 · US · Colour · 93mins

This is a desperate attempt to revive the successful horror series, with an adopted young girl this time attracting death and destruction. Faye Grant and Michael Lerner do their best with the tired material, but the absence of Damien means this late entry is doomed to failure from the start, and the fact that it was originally made for horror-shy American TV means there is also very little for gore fans. JF

Faye Grant *Karen York* • Michael Woods *Gene York* • Michael Lerner *Earl Knight* • Madison Mason *Dr Lou Hastings* • Ann Hearn *Jo Thueson* • Jim Byrnes *Noah* • Don S Davis *Jake Madison* • Asia Vieira *Delia York* ■ *Dir* Jorge Montesi, Dominique Othenin-Girard • *Scr* Brian Taggert, from a story by Harvey Bernhard, from a story by Brian Taggert, from characters created by David Seltzer

On a Clear Day ★★★ 12A

Drama 2005 · UK · Colour · 98mins

Peter Mullan plays a redundant, middle-aged shipyard worker who decides to swim the English Channel, aided and encouraged by a bunch of misfits that pass for friends. A man of steely determination but few words, he finds training to swim the Channel easier than communicating with his wife (Brenda Blethyn) and grown-up son (Jamie Sives), whose twin drowned in childhood. This just about survives its formulaic origins and some embarrassing characterisations from the supporting cast, and its qualified success is largely due to the convincing Mullan. BP

Peter Mullan *Frank* • Brenda Blethyn *Joan* • Sean McGinley *Eddie* • Jamie Sives *Rob* • Billy Boyd *Danny* • Ron Cook *Norman* • Jodhi May *Angela* • Benedict Wong *Chan* ■ *Dir* Gaby Dellal • *Scr* Alex Rose

On a Clear Day You Can See Forever ★★★ U

Musical 1970 · US · Colour · 124mins

A great libretto from Alan Jay Lerner is delivered with gusty force by Barbra Streisand as the Brooklyn "goil" who regresses to the 19th century while being hypnotised to stop smoking. Vincente Minnelli could direct these musical heart-twangers with his eyes closed, and it does, indeed, look like he has done just that in some wayward scenes. Yet it is hard to dislike a movie that combines so much talent at full throttle. It is a bit long-winded, but Minnelli's awesome gifts are deployed in full, especially in the glorious opening sequences. SH DVD

Barbra Streisand *Daisy Gamble* • Yves Montand *Dr Marc Chabot* • Bob Newhart *Dr Mason Hume* • Larry Blyden *Warren Pratt* • Simon Oakland *Dr Conrad Fuller* • Jack Nicholson *Tad Pringle* • John Richardson *Robert Tentrees* • Pamela Brown *Mrs Fitzherbert* • Irene Handl *Winnie Wainwhisle* • Roy Kinnear *Prince Regent* • John Le Mesurier *Pelham* ■ *Dir* Vincente Minnelli • *Scr* Alan Jay Lerner, from the musical play by Alan Jay Lerner, Burton Lane

On an Island with You ★★★ U

Musical 1948 · US · Colour · 103mins

Former Olympic swimmer Esther Williams proved that not only was she a superb athlete, but with her robust good humour and innate sexiness she was a major musical star. Trouble was, the inevitable swimming sequences placed ridiculous strictures on Esther's plots. Here she plays a movie star, on location in Hawaii, torn between dashing Ricardo Montalban and stalwart Peter Lawford. The production numbers are the thing, though, and the use of Technicolor is exquisite. TS

Esther Williams *Rosalind Reynolds* • Peter Lawford *Lt Larry Kingslee* • Ricardo Montalban *Ricardo Montez* • Jimmy Durante *Buckley* • Cyd Charisse *Yvonne* • Leon Ames *Commander Harrison* • Kathryn Beaumont *Penelope Peabody* • Dick Simmons *George Blaine* ■ *Dir* Richard Thorpe • *Scr* Dorothy Kingsley, Charles Martin, Hans Wilhelm, from a story by Charles Martin, Hans Wilhelm

On Any Sunday ★★★★ U

Documentary 1971 · US · Colour · 82mins

Steve McQueen's love of motorsport existed off screen as well as in films such as *The Great Escape*. So, it's appropriate there should be so much footage of him in this lyrical documentary that celebrates being on two wheels with no speed limit. There are crashes galore – though not for ace Mert Lawwill – and director Bruce Brown, who made the fine surfing movie *The Endless Summer*, exhibits his fascination for motorbiking, showing that road-surfing is just as much fun. And there are no Hell's Angels to bother the eye, even if the country-and-western soundtrack irritates the ear. TH DVD

Dir Bruce Brown

On Connaît la Chanson ★★★ PG

Musical comedy 1997 · Fr · Colour · 117mins

Alain Resnais's enjoyable comedy owes a debt to Dennis Potter, as its characters burst into lip-synched song at the least provocation. Polished, sophisticated, yet occasionally obvious, it will most intrigue those with a sound knowledge of French pop music, as the uninitiated not only miss out on the thrill of hearing familiar tunes, but they are also deprived of any socio-cultural significance they possess. The conceit is undermined by the slightness of the satire into which the tunes are inserted, as various self-obsessed bourgeois types fall prey to their passions. DP. In French with English subtitles.

Pierre Arditi *Claude* • Sabine Azéma *Odile Lalande* • Jean-Pierre Bacri *Nicolas* • André Dussollier *Simon* • Agnès Jaoui *Camille Lalande* • Lambert Wilson *Marc Duveyrier* • Jane Birkin *Jane* ■ *Dir* Alain Resnais • *Scr* Agnès Jaoui, Jean-Pierre Bacri

On Dangerous Ground ★★

Crime drama 1951 · US · BW · 82mins

Like many a major director, Nicholas Ray often did minor work, but even his lesser movies are of interest. This RKO crime drama has a terrific beginning, with tough cop Robert Ryan leading a manhunt and displaying a totally unsympathetic, even sadistic, temperament. Then he falls for blind Ida Lupino, his world is turned upside down and the movie loses its edge. Nevertheless, the mood is well maintained, boosted by a remarkable score, but it's not nearly grim enough for its subject matter. TS

Robert Ryan *Jim Wilson* • Ida Lupino *Mary Malden* • Ward Bond *Walter Brent* • Charles Kemper *Bill Daly* • Anthony Ross *Pete Santos* • Ed Begley *Captain Brawley* ■ *Dir* Nicholas Ray • *Scr* AI Bezzerides, Nicholas Ray, from the novel *Mad with Much Heart* by Gerald Butler • *Music* Bernard Herrmann

On Dangerous Ground ★★★ PG

Thriller 1986 · US · Colour · 91mins

If you catch this bizarrely plotted piece of hokum in the right mood, you might find much to enjoy in it. All-American Stephen Collins plays a physicist who takes on an evil industrialist illegally dumping nuclear waste. Filmed by former actor and stunt co-ordinator Chuck Bail, it's not surprising its limited dramatic appeal is significantly broadened by plentiful action and some dazzling aerial sequences. Only the sloppy editing disappoints. RS

Stephen Collins *David Lowell* • Janet Julian *Vanessa Pilgrim* • Lance Henriksen *Brook Alistair* • Bo Svenson *Captain* • Victoria Racimo *Rachel* • Nicholas Pryor *John Pilgrim* ■ *Dir* Chuck Bail • *Scr* Sheila Goldberg, Ovidio G Assonitis, Alfonso Brescia, Steve Luotto

On Deadly Ground ★★★ 15

Action adventure 1994 · US · Colour · 96mins

Action star Steven Seagal has always brought a vaguely liberal slant to his no-brain thrillers and his directorial debut is admirably politically correct. It's just a shame that the caring, sharing, eco-friendly message tends to overpower what Seagal does best – kicking the stuffing out of bad guys. Here he's a troubleshooter who goes into battle with oil tycoon Michael Caine who is about to pollute virtually all of Alaska. JF. Contains swearing, violence and nudity. DVD

Steven Seagal *Forrest Taft* • Michael Caine *Michael Jennings* • Joan Chen *Masu* • John C McGinley *MacGruder* • R Lee Ermey *Stone* • Shari Shattuck *Liles* • Billy Bob Thornton *Homer Carlton* • Richard Hamilton *Hugh Palmer* ■ *Dir* Steven Seagal • *Scr* Ed Horowitz, Robin U Russin

On Golden Pond ★★★★ PG

Drama 1981 · US · Colour · 104mins

Nominated for ten Oscars, this old-fashioned family melodrama won three – best adapted screenplay for Ernest Thompson and, more notably, Katharine Hepburn's fourth award for best actress and Henry Fonda's first as best actor. Considering neither was in the best of health, their performances are remarkable. The quiet authority of their acting is all the more apparent in their scenes with Jane Fonda, who overdoes the angst, particularly when opposite the father with whom she occasionally disagreed in real life. Complementing the subtle shades of performance are cinematographer Billy Williams's superb images, using to dramatic effect the changing light of the countryside in summer. DP DVD

Henry Fonda *Norman Thayer Jr* • Katharine Hepburn *Ethel Thayer* • Jane Fonda *Chelsea Thayer Wayne* • Doug McKeon *Billy Ray* • Dabney Coleman *Bill Ray* • William Lanteau *Charlie Martin* • Chris Rydell [Christopher Rydell] *Sumner Todd* ■ *Dir* Mark Rydell • *Scr* Ernest Thompson, from his play

On Her Majesty's Secret Service ★★★ PG

Spy adventure 1969 · UK · Colour · 127mins

This is the James Bond everyone forgets, mainly because it stars the Australian George Lazenby, who went from chocolate commercial to big-screen disaster. Wittily written (by Richard Maibaum and Simon Raven) and pacily directed (by Peter Hunt), it has excitement galore. Yet the chemistry between Diana Rigg and Lazenby is nonexistent – garlic-chewing did not endear the one to the other. Louis Armstrong is around to sing *We Have All the Time in the World*, which is some compensation. TH DVD

George Lazenby *James Bond* • Diana Rigg *Tracy* • Telly Savalas *Blofeld* • Ilse Steppat *Irma Bunt* • Gabriele Ferzetti *Draco* • Yuri Borienko *Gruenther* • Bernard Horsfall *Campbell* • George Baker *Sir Hilary Bray* • Bernard Lee *"M"* • Lois Maxwell *Miss Moneypenny* • Desmond Llewelyn *"Q"* ■ *Dir* Peter Hunt • *Scr* Richard Maibaum, Simon Raven, from the novel by Ian Fleming

On Moonlight Bay ★★★ U

Period musical comedy
1951 · US · Colour · 91mins

Doris Day shines as the tomboyish heroine in this elegantly designed but slight movie that beautifully evokes its early-20th-century setting. She's surrounded by warm-hearted character players such as Mary Wickes and Rosemary DeCamp. Based on stories by Booth Tarkington, this was so popular that the same cast was reunited two years later for an equally perky sequel, *By the Light of the Silvery Moon*. TS

Doris Day *Marjorie Winfield* • Gordon MacRae *William Sherman* • Jack Smith (1) *Hubert Wakeley* • Leon Ames *George Winfield* • Rosemary DeCamp *Mrs Winfield* • Mary Wickes *Stella* • Ellen Corby *Miss Stevens* • Billy Gray *Wesley Winfield* • Jeffrey Stevens *Jim Sherman* ■ *Dir* Roy Del Ruth • *Scr* Jack

Rose, Melville Shavelson, from the novel *Alice Adams* and the story *Penrod* by Booth Tarkington

On My Own ★★★

Drama 1992 · It/Can/Aus · Colour · 97mins

Australian actress Judy Davis proves once more that she is one of the most remarkable actresses around in this thoughtful drama from director Antonio Tibaldi. As a schizophrenic whose outbursts and shameless behaviour intrude upon the already troubled life of her adolescent son, she erupts on to the screen and lurches between reason and recklessness with a power that shocks with its intensity. Unfortunately, we get too little of her and the burden of carrying the action falls on Matthew Ferguson as her son. DP. Contains swearing and nudity.

Judy Davis *Mother* • Matthew Ferguson *Simon Henderson* • David McIlwraith *John Henderson* • Jan Rubes *The Colonel* • Michele Melega *Shammas* ■ *Dir* Antonio Tibaldi • *Scr* Antonio Tibaldi, Gill Dennis, John Frizzell

On My Way to the Crusades, I Met a Girl Who... ★

Farce 1967 · It/US · Colour · 110mins

Also known as *The Chastity Belt* and left waiting for two years on the shelf, this sex comedy stars Tony Curtis as a Middle Ages knight who keeps gamekeeper's daughter Monica Vitti securely locked up in order to preserve her "reputation". The bawdiness of the story owes something to the success of *Tom Jones*. Curtis remembered it mainly for Vitti's unwillingness to be photographed from any angle except head-on. He's quoted as saying, "She had a big nose and would never turn in profile." AT

Tony Curtis *Guerrando Da Montone* • Monica Vitti *Boccadoro* • Hugh Griffith *Ibn-el-Rascid* • John Richardson *Dragone* ■ *Dir* Pasquale Festa Campanile • *Scr* Luigi Magni, Larry Gelbart, from a story by Ugo Liberatore

On Our Merry Way ★★ U

Portmanteau comedy drama
1948 · US · BW · 107mins

A mediocre and unconvincing portmanteau movie, directed by (among others) the illustrious King Vidor on a bad day, this links its several episodic stories by means of a newspaper ad salesman (Burgess Meredith) who dreams of being an investigative journalist. He fibs to his new wife (Paulette Goddard, Meredith's then real-life wife) that he is the reporter responsible for a series of stories and then must make good the lie. The cast does include some notable names, with Henry Fonda and James Stewart teamed as jazz musicians in the best segment, which was actually directed – uncredited – by John Huston and George Stevens. RK

Burgess Meredith *Oliver Pease* • Paulette Goddard *Martha Pease* • Fred MacMurray *Al* • Hugh Herbert *Elisha Hobbs* • James Stewart *Slim* • Dorothy Lamour *Gloria Manners* • Victor Moore *Ashton Carrington* • Eilene Janssen *Peggy Thorndyke* • Henry Fonda *Lank* • William Demarest *Floyd* • Dorothy Ford *Lola* ■ *Dir* King Vidor, Leslie Fenton • *Scr* Laurence Stallings, Lou Breslow, from a story by John O'Hara, Arch Oboler

On Our Selection ★★★

Comedy drama 1932 · Aus · BW · 104mins

Steele Rudd's stories about a hard-pressed Australian farming family first appeared in 1895, while Raymond Longford brought the Rudds to the screen in 1920. However, ex-newsreel editor Ken G Hall's sound version is much broader in its comedy and transforms the older son, Dave (Fred MacDonald) from a genial everyman into a bungling buffoon. Yet, this folksy saga retains much of the humanity in Rudd's writings and Bert Bailey is splendidly resourceful as the head of the household. The ensemble would return for three more films. Remade in 1995 as *Dad and Dave: On Our Selection*. DP

Bert Bailey *Dad Rudd* • Alfreda Bevan *Mum* • Fred McDonald *Dave* • John McGowan *Maloney* • Molly Raynor *Kate* ■ *Dir* Ken G Hall • *Scr* Ken G Hall, Bert Bailey, from the play by Bert Bailey, from stories by Steele Rudd [Arthur Hoey]

On Purge Bébé ★★

Farce 1931 · Fr · BW · 62mins

Jean Renoir's silent films enjoyed scant success at the box office, so with this first move to sound he needed a commercial success. Adapted from a Georges Feydeau farce, it was shot quickly and was one of the first movies to contain the sound of a flushing toilet. The film, which betrays its stage origins by scarcely moving from its proscenium arch setting, tells the silly story of a porcelain manufacturer who attempts to sell thousands of chamber pots to the French army. It made enough profit for Renoir to move forward into his great period of film-making. BB. A French language film.

Marguerite Pierry *Julie Follavoine* • Jacques Louvigny *M Follavoine* • Sacha Tarride *Toto Follavoine* • Michel Simon *M Chouilloux* • Fernandel *Truchet* ■ *Dir* Jean Renoir • *Scr* Jean Renoir, Pierre Prévert, from the play by Georges Feydeau

On the Air Live with Captain Midnight ★★ PG

Drama 1979 · US · Colour · 79mins

This is very much a family project for the Sebastians with Ferd and Beverly sharing duties behind the camera and son Tracy taking the lead role. It's a shambolic affair about a young man who comes out of his shell with his anarchic pirate radio show. The budget constraints hardly help and the whole theme was better handled in the later *Pump Up the Volume*. JF [VIDEO]

Tracy Sebastian • John Ireland • Dena Dietrich • Ted Gehring • Mia Kovacs ■ *Dir/Scr* Beverly Sebastian, Ferd Sebastian

On the Avenue ★★★ U

Musical comedy 1937 · US · BW · 88mins

A host of classic Irving Berlin songs cut a swathe through this bright, cliché-free musical like gold in rock. Director Roy Del Ruth was well known for extracting thoughtful, multilayered performances from his stars, and Dick Powell as the showbiz charmer and Madeleine Carroll as the lovestruck uptown lady are both stunning. The movie has much to say on the nature of love and passion, serving it up with enormous verve and incisive wit. Upbeat. SH

Dick Powell *Gary Blake* • Madeleine Carroll *Mimi Caraway* • Alice Faye *Mona Merrick* • The Ritz Brothers [Al Ritz] • The Ritz Brothers [Jimmy Ritz] • The Ritz Brothers [Harry Ritz] • George Barbier *Commodore Caraway* • Alan Mowbray *Frederick Sims* • Cora Witherspoon *Aunt Fritz Peters* • Walter Catlett *Jake Dribble* • Douglas Fowley *Eddie Eads* • Joan Davis *Miss Katz* ■ *Dir* Roy Del Ruth • *Scr* Gene Markey, William Conselman

On the Beach ★★ PG

Drama 1959 · US · BW · 128mins

An atomic submarine boldly goes where no atomic sub has gone before: to survey a nuclear-wasted Earth. The few survivors suffer from contamination by cliché, a sickness of conversational banality. Stanley Kramer's film of Nevil Shute's bestseller means well, and Gregory Peck, Ava Gardner and Anthony Perkins certainly try their best, but it lacks any apocalyptic excitement to go with its appalling premise. Dreary and solemn. TH DVD

Gregory Peck *Dwight Towers* • Ava Gardner *Moira Davidson* • Fred Astaire *Julian Osborn* • Anthony Perkins *Peter Holmes* • Donna Anderson *Mary Holmes* • John Tate *Admiral Bridie* • Lola Brooks *Lieutenant Hosgood* ■ *Dir* Stanley Kramer • *Scr* John Paxton, James Lee Barrett, from the novel by Nevil Shute

On the Beat ★★ U

Comedy 1962 · UK · BW · 101mins

In this fitfully amusing comedy, Norman Wisdom plays a would-be policeman who is reduced to being a Scotland Yard car park attendant because he's not tall enough to be a bobby. Then it turns out that he's the spitting image of a criminal – you can probably guess the rest. Wisdom is funny enough, and a host of British character actors goes through the motions, but this is pretty simplistic stuff. TS [VIDEO] DVD

Norman Wisdom *Norman Pitkin/Giulio Napolitani* • Jennifer Jayne *Rosanna* • Raymond Huntley *Sir Ronald Ackroyd* • David Lodge *Superintendent Hobson* • Esma Cannon *Mrs Stammers* • Eric Barker *Doctor* ■ *Dir* Robert Asher • *Scr* Jack Davies, Norman Wisdom, Eddie Leslie

On the Black Hill ★★★ 15

Drama 1987 · UK · Colour · 110mins

Adapted from Bruce Chatwin's bestseller, this charming film balances its realism and whimsy with a light hand. Director Andrew Grieve's careful storytelling is rewarded with some lovely performances, notably from Bob Peck and Gemma Jones as a farming couple enduring the hardships and grasping the fleeting joys of life in the Welsh Marches. Mike and Robert Gwilym do well as the twins at the centre of the story, although their acting inexperience shows through during the weightier scenes. DP [VIDEO]

Mike Gwilym *Benjamin Jones* • Robert Gwilym *Lewis Jones* • Bob Peck *Amos Jones* • Gemma Jones *Mary Jones* • Jack Walters *Sam Jones* • Nesta Harris *Hannah Jones* ■ *Dir* Andrew Grieve • *Scr* Andrew Grieve, from the novel by Bruce Chatwin • *Cinematographer* Thaddeus O'Sullivan

On the Buses ★ PG

Comedy 1971 · UK · Colour · 84mins

This spin-off from a popular ITV comedy series was a box-office hit back in 1971. Nostalgia masochists should account for the bulk of those tuning in to this atrocious film, in which women drivers are taken on at Blakey's depot, much to the frustration of those "lovable" misogynists Reg Varney and Bob Grant. Two further films followed: *Mutiny on the Buses* (1972) and *Holiday on the Buses* (1973). DP [VIDEO] DVD

Reg Varney *Stan Butler* • Doris Hare *Mrs Butler* • Anna Karen *Olive* • Michael Robbins *Arthur* • Stephen Lewis *Inspector Blake* • Bob Grant *Jack* ■ *Dir* Harry Booth • *Scr* Ronald Chesney, Ronald Wolfe

On the Double ★★

Comedy 1961 · UK · Colour · 93mins

Danny Kaye plays a dual role as a soldier-mimic and the general he resembles. Most Kaye movies have their moments, and there are a few good laughs, notably a quick-change sequence in which Kaye does a breathtaking set of imitations (including Marlene Dietrich), and Diana Dors perks things up as a German spy, but the script and Melville Shavelson's direction are below par. TV

Danny Kaye *PFC Ernest Williams/Gen Sir Lawrence Mackenzie-Smith* • Dana Wynter *Lady Margaret Mackenzie-Smith* • Wilfrid Hyde White *Colonel Somerset* • Margaret Rutherford *Lady Vivian* • Diana Dors *Sergeant Bridget Stanhope* • Allan Cuthbertson *Captain Patterson* ■ *Dir* Melville Shavelson • *Scr* Jack Rose, Melville Shavelson

On the Edge ★★★ 15

Drama 1985 · US · Colour · 82mins

One of the most overlooked of American actors, Bruce Dern typically shines as a middle-aged runner on the fast track to redemption after previous sporting indiscretions. Along the way he teams up with his one-time coach John Marley and ex-lover Pam Grier. Exciting sports footage (Dern himself is a keen amateur runner) and solid camerawork is undermined by the all-too familiar formula and inaccessible characters. Ultimately Rob Nilsson's film falls short between art house pretension and mainstream acceptance. RS [VIDEO]

Bruce Dern *Wes Holman* • Pam Grier *Cora* • Bill Bailey (1) *Flash Holman* • Jim Haynie *Owen Riley* • John Marley *Elmo* ■ *Dir/Scr* Rob Nilsson

On the Fiddle ★★

Comedy 1961 · UK · BW · 96mins

Sean Connery was only a year away from becoming an international superstar in *Dr No* when he took the role of a dim-witted gypsy in this hit-and-miss comedy. He plays second fiddle to Alfred Lynch, who stars as a conman inducted into the army. Known in the States as *Operation Snafu*, this was presumably meant to be a minor variation on the Bilko theme. Sadly, it feels more like one of those wartime morale boosters featuring a couple of fading music-hall comics. DP

Alfred Lynch *Horace Pope* • Sean Connery *Pedlar Pascoe* • Cecil Parker *Group Captain Bascombe* • Stanley Holloway *Mr Cooksley* • Alan King *T/Sergeant Buzzer* • Eric Barker *Doctor* • Wilfrid Hyde White *Trowbridge* • Kathleen Harrison *Mrs Cooksley* • Eleanor Summerfield *Flora McNaughton* ■ *Dir* Cyril Frankel • *Scr* Harold Buchman, from the novel *Stop at a Winner* by RF Delderfield

On the Line ★★ PG

Romantic comedy
2001 · US · Colour · 82mins

It's hard to imagine even the most devoted fans of boy band NSync deriving much pleasure from this crass Chicago romantic comedy. Lance Bass and Joey Fatone star as roommates, but while party animal Fatone wallows in self-indulgence, Bass's bashful ad man covers the Windy City with handbills in a bid to trace Emmanuelle Chriqui, whom he met on the subway but was too tongue-tied to ask out. Neither band member has much screen presence. DP [VIDEO] DVD

Lance Bass *Kevin Gibbons* • Joey Fatone *Rod* • Emmanuelle Chriqui *Abbey* • G Q *Eric* • James Bulliard *Randy* • Al Green • Tamala Jones *Jackie* • Richie Sambora *Mick Silver* • Jerry Stiller *Nathan* ■ *Dir* Eric Bross • *Scr* Eric Aronson, Paul Stanton

On the Nickel ★★★

Drama 1979 · US · Colour · 96mins

This gloomy drama drowns in a splurge of sentimentality, but it has the power to move because of its autobiographical edge. Ralph Waite, a former alcoholic and the actor who played Daddy in the squeaky-clean TV series *The Waltons*, has retraced his own long night's journey into day, as a boozed down-and-out in Los Angeles. With Donald Moffat co-starring, Waite's film competently establishes the despair and the destitution of the characters' existences. TH

Donald Moffat *Sam* • Ralph Waite *CG* • Hal Williams *Paul* • Penelope Allen *Rose* • Jack Kehoe *Bad Mood* ■ *Dir/Scr* Ralph Waite

On the Right Track ★★ PG

Comedy 1981 · US · Colour · 93mins

Child star Gary Coleman was a hit with US TV audiences as one of a pair of black kids in *Diff'rent Strokes* (1978-86). Due to a congenital kidney complaint, Coleman looked much younger than his age and would play child roles for many years. This, his feature film debut, mined the same sentimental and gently humorous vein as the TV show, with Coleman playing a 10-year-old shoeshine boy who lives out of a locker at a train station and has an uncanny knack at picking winning horses. DF

Gary Coleman *Lester* • Michael Lembeck *Frank* • Lisa Eilbacher *Jill* • Maureen Stapleton *Mary* • Norman Fell *Mayor* • Herb Edelman *Sam* ■ *Dir* Lee Philips • *Scr* Tina Pine [Tina Rome], Avery Buddy, Richard Moses

On the Riviera ★★★

Musical comedy 1951 · US · Colour · 88mins

Here, Danny Kaye deserts his mentor Samuel Goldwyn for 20th Century-Fox, and a remake of one of the company's main plotlines – the dual identity stand-by used in *That Night in Rio* and *Folies Bergère*. As both musical star and military hero, Kaye makes the film very much his own, aided by glossy Technicolor and support from his two comely co-stars Gene Tierney and Corinne Calvet. TS

Danny Kaye *Henri Duran/Jack Martin* • Gene Tierney *Lilli* • Corinne Calvet *Colette* • Marcel Dalio *Philippe Lebrix* • Jean Murat *Periton* • Henri Letondal *Louis Forel* • Clinton Sundberg *Antoine* • Sig Rumann [Sig Ruman] *Gapeaux* • Gwyneth Verdon [Gwen Verdon] *Specialty dancer* ■ *Dir* Walter Lang • *Scr* Valentine Davies, Phoebe Ephron, Henry Ephron, from a play by Rudolph Lothar, Hans Adler

On the Run ★★

Action drama 1983 · Aus · Colour · 101mins

Rod Taylor returned to his native Australia for this routine thriller. Playing against type, he turns in a menacing performance as the respected, multi-lingual farmer who also masquerades as a calculating hitman, nicknamed "The Dingo". Director Mende Brown makes good use of the Sydney conurbation, but the action is derivative and predictable. DP

Paul Winfield *Harry* • Rod Taylor *Payette* • Beau Cox *Paul* ■ *Dir* Mende Brown • *Scr* Michael Fisher

On the Town ★★★★★ U

Musical 1949 · US · Colour · 93mins

This utterly exhilarating landmark movie musical gave Gene Kelly and choreographer Stanley Donen their directing break. The opening sequence is magnificent, as three sailors (Kelly, Frank Sinatra and Jules Munshin) hail the delights of *New York, New York* in Manhattan itself (it was unusual for MGM to leave its Hollywood lot). There are minor flaws: the substitution of dancers for Sinatra and Munshin in the ballet and a third act that's not as pithy as it should be. But these are quibbles, and the rest is a joy. TS

Gene Kelly *Gabey* • Frank Sinatra *Chip* • Vera-Ellen *Ivy Smith* • Jules Munshin *Ozzie* • Betty Garrett *Brunhilde Esterhazy* • Ann Miller *Claire Huddesen* • Florence Bates *Madame Dilyovska* • Alice Pearce *Lucy Shmeeler* • George Meader *Professor* ■ *Dir* Stanley Donen, Gene Kelly • *Scr* Adolph Green, Betty Comden, from the musical play by Adolph Green, Betty Comden, Leonard Bernstein, from the ballet *Fancy Free* by Jerome Robbins • *Cinematographer* Harold Rosson • *Music* Roger Edens, Adolph Green, Betty Comden, Leonard Bernstein

On the Waterfront ★★★★★ PG

Classic crime drama
1954 · US · BW · 103mins

In this seminal classic, Marlon Brando is unforgettable as Terry Malloy – a brooding misfit among the rampant corruption of the New York docks – and was rightly awarded an Oscar for best actor (the youngest ever at the time). The movie works on several levels. On the surface it's an extremely well-crafted and entertaining drama, but peel away some layers and you'll discover an apologia for informing. It's fascinating, then, to discover the superb direction is by Elia Kazan, who himself "named names" in McCarthyite America. Mix in Leonard Bernstein's Oscar-nominated score, memorable dialogue from screenwriter Budd Schulberg and truly great performances from screen newcomers Eva Marie Saint and Rod Steiger – if ever a movie deserved its eight Oscars, it was this one. Brando added the BFA award – the equivalent then of the Baftas – for best foreign actor to his Oscar. TS DVD

Marlon Brando *Terry Malloy* • Karl Malden *Father Barry* • Lee J Cobb *Johnny Friendly* • Rod Steiger *Charley Malloy* • Pat Henning *"Kayo" Dugan* • Eva Marie Saint *Edie Doyle* • Leif Erickson *Glover* • James Westerfield *Big Mac* • Marty Balsam [Martin Balsam] *Gillette* • Fred Gwynne *Slim* ■ *Dir* Elia Kazan • *Scr* Budd Schulberg, from a series of articles by Malcolm Johnson • *Cinematographer* Boris Kaufman • *Music* Leonard Bernstein • *Art Director* Richard Day

On the Yard ★★★ 15

Prison drama 1978 · US · Colour · 96mins

A rare return to the style of Warner Bros dramas of the 1930s, this prison-set tale is good at evoking the conflicts and conversation of convicts milling around the vast exercise yard into which they're released for daily recreation. While it's not so good at establishing a story and revealing the character of the four inmates who are at the centre of the narrative, director Raphael D Silver still efficiently summons up the atmosphere of a volatile community. TH

John Heard *Juleson* • Thomas Waites [Thomas G Waites] *Chilly* • Mike Kellin *Red* • Richard Bright *Nunn* • Joe Grifasi *Morris* • Lane Smith *Captain Blake* • Richard Hayes *Stick* ■ *Dir* Raphael D Silver • *Scr* Malcolm Braly, from his novel

On Top of Old Smoky ★★ U

Western 1953 · US · BW · 58mins

It's amazing that "Public Cowboy No 1" Gene Autry actually found time to churn out series movies like this one, since by the 1950s his many careers as radio station owner, publishing magnate, composer and recording artiste had turned him into one of the hardest working and richest men in America. His fans, though, expected films in which he practised his cowboy code: no hitting anyone smaller than him, no shooting men in the back, no gambling, drinking or smoking and, especially, no kissing. TS

Gene Autry • Smiley Burnette • Gail Davis *Jen Larrabee* • Grandon Rhodes *"Doc" Judson* • Sheila Ryan *Lila Maryland* • Kenne Duncan *McQuaid* ■ *Dir* George Archainbaud • *Scr* Gerald Geraghty, from his story

On Your Toes ★★ U

Musical comedy 1939 · US · BW · 94mins

The smash-hit Broadway musical came to the screen in a dispiritingly pale shadow of the original. The delightful tale of misunderstandings between an American composer and a visiting Russian ballet company, notably its ballerina, is worked over into a lacklustre screenplay and the gorgeous score denied its due. The high point of the movie is the *Slaughter on Tenth Avenue* ballet, choreographed by George Balanchine. RK

Eddie Albert *Phil Dolan Jr* • Zorina [Vera Zorina] *Vera Barnova* • Alan Hale *Sergei Alexandrovitch* • Frank McHugh *Paddy Reilly* • James Gleason *Phil Dolan Sr* • Donald O'Connor *Phil, as a boy* ■ *Dir* Ray Enright • *Scr* Jerry Wald, Richard Macaulay, Sig Herzig, Lawrence Riley, from the musical by Richard Rodgers, by Lorenz Hart, George Abbott

Once a Jolly Swagman ★★ U

Drama 1948 · UK · BW · 98mins

This is an improbably melodramatic tale of love, honour and speedway. Set in the 1930s, it scores with its realistic portrait of track life, but the wheels come off during the studio-bound sequences, in which ex-factory worker Dirk Bogarde is dazzled both by his new-found fame and the radiance of socialite Moira Lister. Bill Owen and Renée Asherson provide dependable support, but Bogarde never gets out of first gear. DP

Dirk Bogarde *Bill Fox* • Bonar Colleano *Tommy Possey* • Renée Asherson *Pat Gibbon* • Bill Owen *Lag Gibbon* • Cyril Cusack *Duggie Lewis* • Thora Hird *Ma Fox* • James Hayter *Pa Fox* ■ *Dir* Jack Lee • *Scr* Jack Lee, William Rose, Cliff Gordon, from a novel by Montagu Slater

Once a Thief ★★

Crime drama 1965 · US · BW · 106mins

This routine cops and robbers melodrama was French star Alain Delon's first American feature and he looks unusually awkward and out of place as an ex-con trying to go straight while being harassed by a vengeful cop and becoming a pawn in his brother's plans for a million-dollar heist. Director Ralph Nelson assembles an able support cast but the strength of his semi-documentary approach and the pre-*Bullitt* San Francisco locations are undercut by a cliché-ridden script. RS

Alain Delon *Eddie Pedak* • Ann-Margret *Kristine Pedak* • Van Heflin *Mike Vido* • Jack Palance *Walter Pedak* • John Davis Chandler *James Sargatanas* • Jeff Corey *Lt Kebner* ■ *Dir* Ralph Nelson • *Scr* Zekial Marko, from his novel *Scratch a Thief* • *Music* Lalo Schifrin

Once a Thief ★★★ 15

Romantic action comedy
1991 · HK · Colour · 103mins

John Woo remade this five years later for TV, yet wasn't able to touch this light-hearted caper movie, atypical for him. Beginning in France, three crooks (Chow Yun-Fat, Leslie Cheung, and Cherie Chung), who were raised as thieves after being orphaned in their childhood, plan one last caper to steal a valuable painting. Woo goes for comedy and less violent action in this effort, and the result is alternately charming and hilarious, frequently simultaneously. Those expecting the standard grandiose Woo shoot-outs will be disappointed – until the surprisingly violent climax. KB. In Cantonese with English subtitles. DVD

Chow Yun-Fat *Joe* • Leslie Cheung *Jim* • Cherie Chung *Cherie* ■ *Dir* John Woo • *Scr* John Woo, Clifton Ko, Janet Chung

Once Around ★★★ 15

Romantic comedy
1991 · US · Colour · 110mins

Some of the best talent Hollywood could muster graces this often affecting story of a repressed little rich girl, the excellent Holly Hunter, who falls madly in love with a garrulous salesman, a rather caricatured performance from Richard Dreyfuss, much to her family's chagrin. The tightly packed, occasionally lyrical script gives each character suitable depth and emotional history, but almost imperceptibly goes off the boil as the movie progresses. Oddly flat. SH. Contains swearing.

Holly Hunter *Renata Bella* • Richard Dreyfuss *Sam Sharpe* • Danny Aiello *Joe Bella* • Gena Rowlands *Marilyn Bella* • Laura San Giacomo *Jan Bella* • Roxanne Hart *Gail Bella* • Danton Stone *Tony Bella* • Tim Guinee *Peter Hedges* ■ *Dir* Lasse Hallström • *Scr* Malia Scotch Marmo, Lasse Hallström

Once Before I Die ★★

Second World War drama
1965 · US · Colour · 96mins

What on earth is Ursula Andress doing in the middle of the jungle and in the thick of the war in the Philippines? Well, appearing in then husband John Derek's movie is the answer. Viewers may find it difficult to fathom whether Derek wanted to deck a dull war movie out with glam shots of his wife, or vice versa. Either way, this is a blatant vanity project. AT

Ursula Andress *Alex* • John Derek *Major Bailey* • Rod Lauren *Captain* • Richard Jaeckel *Lt Custer* • Ron Ely *Soldier* ■ *Dir* John Derek • *Scr* Vance Skarstedt, from the story *Quit for the Next* by Anthony March

Once Bitten ★★ 15

Horror comedy 1985 · US · Colour · 88mins

This dumb teenage sex comedy with supernatural overtones has a very hit-and-miss gags quotient. Countess Lauren Hutton is a 400-year-old vampire looking for virgin blood in Los Angeles. Supplies are short until she picks up a student nerd (future superstar Jim Carrey) who hasn't managed to get his girlfriend Karen Kopins into bed. Cleavon Little as Hutton's gay manservant has some funny moments, but eventually the one-joke premise screeches to a halt under the lifeless direction. AJ

Lauren Hutton *Countess* • Jim Carrey *Mark Kendall* • Karen Kopins *Robin Pierce* • Cleavon Little *Sebastian* • Thomas Ballatore *Jamie* ■ *Dir* Howard Storm • *Scr* David Hines, Jeffrey Hause, Jonathan Roberts, from a story by Dimitri Villard

Once in Paris ★★★

Drama 1978 · US · Colour · 100mins

Frank D Gilroy drew on his own experiences of writing *The Only Game in Town* to piece together this warm, character-driven look at friendship and love. Wayne Rogers plays a screenwriter who is drafted to Paris to salvage a script. His chauffeur there is Jack Lenoir (Gilroy's real-life driver) against whom Rogers is warned, but despite finding out about his dodgy past, decides to keep him on and they become friends. A sympathetic and adult film. FL

Wayne Rogers *Michael Moore* • Gayle Hunnicutt *Susan Townsend* • Jack Lenoir *Jean-Paul Barbet* • Philippe March *Marcel Thery* • Clément Harari *Abe Wiley* • Tanya Lopert *Eve Carling* ■ *Dir/Scr* Frank D Gilroy

Once Is Not Enough ★★

Melodrama 1975 · US · Colour · 121mins

Adapted from Jacqueline Susann's potboiler novel, this is a forerunner of the *Dallas* and *Dynasty* soap operas, peppered with starry names and an appallingly camp plotline. Kirk Douglas plays a past-it producer and doting dad to Deborah Raffin. He is so keen to keep his darling daughter in the best that money can buy that he marries Alexis Smith – a rich, bisexual woman, who is still involved with her lesbian lover, Melina Mercouri. Brenda Vaccaro won a Golden Globe for her supporting role as a man-mad fashion editor. So bad it is almost good, but not quite. FL

Kirk Douglas *Mike Wayne* • Alexis Smith *Deidre Milford Granger* • David Janssen *Tom*

Colt • George Hamilton *David Milford* • Melina Mercouri *Karla* • Gary Conway *Hugh* • Brenda Vaccaro *Linda* • Deborah Raffin *January Wayne* ■ *Dir* Guy Green • *Scr* Julius J Epstein, from the novel by Jacqueline Susann

Once More, My Darling ★★

Romantic comedy 1949 · US · BW · 92mins

Robert Montgomery, past the peak of his stardom, directs himself in this romantic comedy about an actor turned lawyer who is hired by the army to romance lovely young heiress Ann Blyth and find out how she came by some stolen Nazi jewellery. The stars play well together, and Montgomery's direction is competent, but the end result is unconvincing. RK

Robert Montgomery *Collier Laing* • Ann Blyth *Marita Connell* • Lillian Randolph *Mamie the maid* • Jane Cowl *Mrs Laing* • Steven Geray *Kalzac* ■ *Dir* Robert Montgomery • *Scr* Robert Carson, Oscar Saul, from the story *Come Be My Love* by Robert Carson

Once More, with Feeling ★★

Comedy 1959 · UK · Colour · 92mins

Yul Brynner is a flamboyant and hot-headed conductor who enjoys a volatile relationship with his wife Kay Kendall, who is getting fed up with his egotistic excesses. This is a heavy-handed comedy with Brynner uncomfortable in the role and unable to milk laughs from the script. The piece is rescued from being totally worthless by the presence of Kendall, who turns in a performance way above the standard of the production. Kendall died from leukaemia in 1959, and this, her last film, was shelved for some months. DF

Yul Brynner *Victor Fabian* • Kay Kendall *Dolly Fabian* • Gregory Ratoff *Maxwell Archer* • Geoffrey Toone *Dr Hilliard* • Maxwell Shaw *Jascha Gendel/Grisha Gendel* • Mervyn Johns *Mr Wilbur Jr* ■ *Dir* Stanley Donen • *Scr* Harry Kurnitz, from his play

Once upon a Crime ★ PG

Comedy 1992 · US · Colour · 90mins

The comic genius of John Candy is there for all to see in this dismal crime caper. Only someone of his immense talent could raise a laugh out of material this bad. All around him flounder, particularly Richard Lewis and Sean Young as the couple who become embroiled in a trans-European murder mystery after finding a valuable dachshund. Inept and unwatchable. DP. Contains swearing. [VIDEO]

John Candy *Augie Morosco* • James Belushi *Neil Schwary* • Cybill Shepherd *Marilyn Schwary* • Sean Young *Phoebe* • Richard Lewis *Julian Peters* • Ornella Muti *Elena Morosco* • Giancarlo Giannini *Inspector Bonnard* • George Hamilton *Alfonso de la Pena* • Roberto Sbaratto *Detective Toussaint* • Joss Ackland *Hercules Popodopoulos* ■ *Dir* Eugene Levy • *Scr* Charles Shyer, Nancy Meyers, Steve Kluger, from a screenplay (unproduced) by Rodolfo Sonego, Giorgio Arlorio, Stefano Strucchi, Luciano Vincenzoni

Once upon a Dream ★★

Comedy 1948 · UK · BW · 87mins

Googie Withers is the attractive wife of army officer Guy Middleton. She conceives a fancy for her husband's former aide Griffith Jones, who comes to work as a servant in their household. When she wakes from a romantic dream about Jones, believing their love affair to be real, all kinds of complications ensue. The actors give their best, but the plot is paper-thin and the now-dated humour is only intermittently amusing. RK

Googie Withers *Mrs Carol Gilbert* • Griffith Jones *Jackson* • Guy Middleton *Major Gilbert* • Betty Lynne *Mlle Louise* • David Horne *Registrar* • Geoffrey Morris *Registrar's clerk* • Maurice Denham *Vicar* • Mona Washbourne *Vicar's wife* • Dora Bryan *Barmaid* ■ *Dir* Ralph Thomas • *Scr* Victor Katona, Patrick Kirwan

Once upon a Forest ★★ U

Musical animation
1992 · US · Colour · 67mins

The tone of this politically correct tale is often rather preachy, but the "furlings" who venture out into the big bad world to find the herbs needed to save one of their sickly playmates are cute and courageous, and their encounters with some unthinking humans and menacing machines should keep youngsters on the edge of their seats. Sadly, in common with so many non-Disney cartoons, the standard of the songs is poor and the animation lacks magic. DP [VIDEO] DVD

Michael Crawford *Cornelius, the Badger* • Ben Vereen *Phineas* • Ellen Blain *Abigail* • Ben Gregory [Benjamin Gregory] *Edgar* • Paige Gosney *Russell* • Elisabeth Moss *Michelle* ■ *Dir* Charles Grosvenor • *Scr* Mark Young, Kelly Ward, from the story by Rae Lambert

Once upon a Honeymoon ★★ PG

Wartime comedy drama
1942 · US · BW · 114mins

This lengthy and astoundingly tasteless comedy drama reveals how little America knew about the Nazis back in the early 1940s. The sequences involving Cary Grant and Ginger Rogers being mistaken for Jews and shipped off to a concentration camp leave a strange taste in the mouth. Director Leo McCarey later disowned the film, but it's well made and contemporary audiences simply accepted what was on screen; time has rendered that no longer possible. TS [VIDEO]

Cary Grant *Pat O'Toole* • Ginger Rogers *Katie O'Hara* • Walter Slezak *Baron Von Luber* • Albert Dekker *LeBlanc* • Albert Basserman *General Borelski* • Ferike Boros *Elsa* • Harry Shannon *Cumberland* ■ *Dir* Leo McCarey • *Scr* Sheridan Gibney, from a story by Sheridan Gibney, Leo McCarey

Once upon a Scoundrel ★★★

Comedy 1973 · US · Colour · 90mins

A morality tale directed by veteran US TV director George Schaefer and starring that bundle of explosive humour, Zero Mostel. He plays a duplicitous landowner who gets the fiancé of a girl he desires out of the way by having him thrown into prison. To teach Mostel a lesson, the girl and her aunt get together and contrive a ruse where they treat him as if he is dead. Mostel gradually comes round to believing he really has died and become a ghost. Clever idea, fairly well executed and with a smattering of amusing scenes. DF

Zero Mostel *Carlos del Refugio* • Katy Jurado *Aunt Delfina* • Titos Vandis *Dr Fernandez* • Priscilla Garcia *Alicia* • A Martinez *Luis* ■ *Dir* George Schaefer • *Scr* Rip Van Ronkel

Once upon a Texas Train ★★★ U

Western 1988 · US · Colour · 87mins

Texas Ranger Richard Widmark and ageing outlaw Willie Nelson discover that youngster Shaun Cassidy is about to disrupt their unlawful business by intercepting some ill-gotten loot in this entertaining TV movie. In addition to the stellar leads, there's a fine supporting cast of western stalwarts. The light-hearted tone might offend western purists, but others will probably enjoy this rollicking entertainment. TS [VIDEO] DVD

Willie Nelson *John Henry Lee* • Richard Widmark *Captain Oren Hayes* • Angie Dickinson *Maggie Hayes* • Shaun Cassidy *Cotton* • Chuck Connors *Nash Crawford* • Jack Elam *Jason Fitch* • Ken Curtis *Kelly Sutton* • Royal Dano *Nitro Jones* • Stuart Whitman *George Agnew* ■ *Dir/Scr* Burt Kennedy

Once upon a Time ★★★ U

Comedy 1944 · US · BW · 88mins

This amazing piece of whimsy is about impecunious theatre producer Cary Grant promoting a dancing caterpillar. Thanks to the deceptive skill of the ever-dependable Grant and the quiet cleverness of the screenplay, it works. Director Alexander Hall was skilled at this kind of fantasy and casts the quizzical James Gleason and Janet Blair, supporting the debonair Grant with some style. Slight and trivial in the extreme, but supremely watchable in its daffy, good-natured way. TS

Cary Grant *Jerry Flynn* • Janet Blair *Jeannie Thompson* • James Gleason *The Moke* • Ted Donaldson *Pinky Thompson* • Howard Freeman *McKenzie* • William Demarest *Brandt* ■ *Dir* Alexander Hall • *Scr* Lewis Meltzer, Oscar Saul, Irving Fineman, from the radio play *My Client Curly* by Norman Corwin, Lucille Fletcher Herrmann

Once upon a Time in America ★★★★★ 18

Epic crime drama
1984 · US · Colour · 217mins

Sergio Leone's final film is an extraordinary crime drama that runs for nearly four hours in its full length-version and chronicles the lives of two New York gangsters, played by Robert De Niro and James Woods. Four decades roll past in flashback, underpinned by a great Ennio Morricone score. The plotting is often arbitrary but, unlike *The Godfather*, Leone and his fine actors never try to win our sympathy: these are nasty people and there are two rape scenes, involving Tuesday Weld and Elizabeth McGovern, that may be among the most shocking ever filmed. But just gasp at the scale, at the immaculate period reconstruction and at that incredible opening with its endlessly ringing phone. A resounding flop on its US release, it fared better in Europe, where it was hailed as a masterpiece of 1980s cinema. AT. Contains violence, swearing, nudity. [VIDEO] DVD

Robert De Niro *Noodles* • James Woods *Max* • Elizabeth McGovern *Deborah* • Treat Williams *Jimmy O'Donnell* • Tuesday Weld *Carol* • Burt Young *Joe* • Joe Pesci *Frankie* • Danny Aiello *Police chief* • Bill Forsythe [William Forsythe] *Cockeye* ■ *Dir* Sergio Leone • *Scr* Leonardo Benvenuti [Leo Benvenuti], Piero De Bernardi, Enrico Medioli, Franco Arcalli, Franco Ferrini, Sergio Leone, Stuart Kaminsky, from the novel *The Hoods* by Harry Grey • *Cinematographer* Tonino Delli Colli

Once upon a Time in China ★★★★ 15

Martial arts action drama
1991 · HK · Colour · 128mins

Wong Fei-Hung (1847-1924) was one of the undisputed masters of such kung fu techniques as the no-shadow kick and drunken boxing. He was already a cult figure in pulp fiction before his exploits finally reached the screen in the late 1940s. Tsui Hark revitalised the legend with this box-office smash, which itself launched a whole new series of adventures that made a superstar of Jet Li. Notable for its stance against foreign influences, this is an explosive picture, with breakneck action sequences. DP. In Cantonese with English subtitles. Contains violence. [VIDEO] DVD

Jet Li *Wong Fei-Hung* • Yuen Biao *Leung Foon* • Jacky Cheung *Buck Teeth Sol* • Rosamund Kwan *Aunt Yee* ■ *Dir* Tsui Hark • *Scr* Tsui Hark, Yuen Kai-Chi, Leung Yiu-Ming

Once upon a Time in China II ★★★ 15

Martial arts action drama
1992 · HK · Colour · 107mins

The explosive combination of Tsui Hark and Jet Li as Wong Fei-Hung ensured a sequel to the smash hit *Once Upon a Time in China* and the result is another extravagant action pic. More sequels followed, culminating (so far) in *Once Upon a Time in China and America* (aka *Once Upon a Time in China VI*). Jet Li bowed out after episode three in the series but returned triumphantly for the most recent adventure. All of these films (even the non-Li ones) deliver some great cinematic action sequences. DF. In Cantonese with English subtitles. [VIDEO]

Jet Li *Wong Fei-Hung* • Rosamund Chi-Lam Kwan [Rosamund Kwan] *Aunt Yee* • Donnie Chi-Tan Yen [Donnie Yen] *Lan* • David Chiang *Luke* • Max Siu Chung Mok *Leung Fu* ■ *Dir* Tsui Hark • *Scr* Tsui Hark, Hanson Chan [Chan Tin Suen], Cheung Tan

Once upon a Time in Mexico ★★★ 15

Crime action adventure
2003 · US · Colour · 97mins

While you can see why director Robert Rodriguez might want to remake his 1992 ultra-low-budget debut *El Mariachi* as *Desperado* (1995) to take advantage of a studio-sized budget, remaking it yet again would seem to indicate that he's stuck in a groove. This third outing again stars Antonio Banderas as the wandering South American minstrel with an arsenal in his guitar case to take on evil drug lords. He's aided this time by an unorthodox CIA agent (Johnny Depp) who's the most entertaining thing in the film, although the action is certainly spectacular. AS. In English and Spanish with subtitles. Contains violence and swearing. [VIDEO] DVD

Antonio Banderas *El Mariachi* • Salma Hayek *Carolina* • Johnny Depp *Sands* • Mickey Rourke *Billy Chambers* • Eva Mendes *Ajedrez* • Danny Trejo *Cucuy* • Enrique Iglesias *Lorenzo* • Cheech Marin [Richard "Cheech" Marin] *Belini* • Rubén Blades *Jorge* • Willem Dafoe *Barillo* ■ *Dir* Robert Rodriguez • *Scr* Robert Rodriguez, from his characters

O

Once upon a Time in the Midlands ★★★ 15

Drama 2002 · UK · Colour · 100mins

Full of familiar Britpic faces and spaghetti western references, Shane Meadows's third feature opens with promise and panache. However, once petty crook Robert Carlyle arrives in Nottingham to prevent ex-wife Shirley Henderson from marrying garage boss Rhys Ifans, the Leone tone is replaced by a diluted brand of Ken Loach realism, in which quips and slapstick leaven the underlying atmosphere of aggression and despair. Consequently, the story loses momentum and minor characters are marginalised in favour of introspection. DP [VIDEO] DVD

Robert Carlyle *Jimmy* • Rhys Ifans *Dek* • Kathy Burke *Carol* • Shirley Henderson *Shirley* • Ricky Tomlinson *Charlie* • Finn Atkins *Marlene* • Vanessa Feltz *Vanessa* • Vic Reeves *Plonko the clown* • Bob Mortimer *Kung fu clown* • Shane Meadows *Bingo caller* ■ *Dir* Shane Meadows • *Scr* Paul Fraser, Shane Meadows

Once upon a Time in the West ★★★★★ 15

Spaghetti western
1968 · It/US · Colour · 158mins

In seeking to paint "a fresco on the birth of a great nation", Sergio Leone turned to the Hollywood western, rather than American history, for his inspiration. Set at the time when the dollar replaced the bullet as the currency of the frontier, this is a breathtaking tale of progress, greed and revenge. The story focuses on Henry Fonda, a gunfighter who dreams of becoming a tycoon, but who is still prepared to resort to trusted methods to drive widow Claudia Cardinale off the land coveted by a railroad company. Much of the action was improvised around the mood of the score, which Ennio Morricone had composed in advance. No wonder many critics described the film as an operatic masterpiece. DP DVD

Henry Fonda *Frank* • Claudia Cardinale *Jill McBain* • Jason Robards *Cheyenne* • Charles Bronson *Harmonica* • Frank Wolff *Brett McBain* • Gabriele Ferzetti *Morton* • Keenan Wynn *Sheriff* ■ *Dir* Sergio Leone • *Scr* Sergio Leone, Sergio Donati, from a story by Sergio Leone, Dario Argento, Bernardo Bertolucci • *Cinematographer* Tonino Delli Colli

Once Were Warriors

★★★★ 18

Drama 1994 · NZ · Colour · 98mins

Told in a bold, unflinching manner, director Lee Tamahori's drama grips and fascinates as it lifts the lid on ghetto Maori life. Rena Owen is drainingly moving as the put-upon housewife, pushed physically and mentally to the brink while trying to hold her family together, bearing the brunt of her unemployed husband's drink-fuelled frustrations. Tamahori's bleak film is raw, brutal cinema with a unique voice, showing a people adrift from their cultural roots and trapped in an urban nightmare of cheap housing and gangland controlled precincts. *What Becomes of the Broken Hearted?* was the belated 1999 sequel. AJ. Contains violence, swearing. DVD

Rena Owen *Beth Heke* • Temuera Morrison *Jake Heke* • Mamaengaroa Kerr-Bell *Grace Heke* • Julian Arahanga *Nig Heke* • Taungaroa Emile *Boogie Heke* • Rachael Morris Jr *Polly Heke* ■ *Dir* Lee Tamahori • *Scr* Riwia Brown, from the novel by Alan Duff

Once You Kiss a Stranger

★★

Drama 1969 · US · Colour · 105mins

This is a loose remake of Alfred Hitchcock's classic *Strangers on a Train* or, perhaps more accurately, it's another telling of the same source novel by Patricia Highsmith. Carol Lynley takes on the original, sinister Robert Walker role, meeting golf pro Paul Burke and offering to murder his rival if he, Burke, will murder Lynley's psychiatrist in return. When Burke's rival winds up dead, he finds himself blackmailed. Panned by most critics, it's only worth seeing to compare with the Hitchcock version. AT

Paul Burke *Jerry* • Carol Lynley *Diana* • Martha Hyer *Lee* • Peter Lind Hayes *Peter* • Philip Carey *Mike* • Stephen McNally *Lieutenant Gavin* ■ *Dir* Robert Sparr • *Scr* Frank Tarloff, Norman Katkov, from the novel *Strangers on a Train* by Patricia Highsmith

The One

★★★ 15

Science-fiction martial arts action
2001 · US · Colour · 83mins

Sci-fi action films don't come any more simplistic than this offering from James Wong, who goes all out to deliver an exhilarating, nonstop adrenalin rush. Jet Li gets to battle himself in his portrayal of two martial arts whirlwinds – one, a killer moving between parallel universes in order to murder his alter egos; the other, a Los Angeles police officer who's the last intergalactic double and next intended victim. Jaw-droppingly extreme set pieces punctuate this wildly over-the-top joy ride. SF DVD

Jet Li *Gabriel "Gabe" Yulaw/Lawless* • Delroy Lindo *Harry Roedecker/Attendant* • Carla Gugino *Traci "TK" Katherine/Massie Walsh* • Jason Statham *Ethan Funsch* • James Morrison *Aldrich/"A" World Inmate No 1* • Dylan Bruno *Yates* • Richard Steinmetz *D'Antoni* ■ *Dir* James Wong • *Scr* Glen Morgan, James Wong

One after the Other ★★

Spaghetti western
1968 · It/Sp · Colour · 105mins

Since his arrival in Italy in the late 1950s, American muscleman Richard Harrison had tried his hand at "sword and sandal" epics, spy spoofs and gangster movies. So it was only logical that he should also have a bash at Italian cinema's most celebrated export – the spaghetti western. However, he was unfortunate in his choice of this unremarkable effort, in which an unholy duo go in search of the thieves who have snatched the gold from a bank. DP. Italian dialogue dubbed into English.

Richard Harrison *Stan Ross* • Pamela Tudor *Sabine* • Paul Stevens [Paolo Stevens] *Glenn* • José Bodalo *Jefferson* ■ *Dir* Nick Howard [Nick Nostro] • *Scr* Nick Nostro, Carlos E Rodriquez, from a story by Simon O'Neill [Giovanni Simonelli]

One against the Wind

★★★★ PG

War drama based on a true story
1991 · US · Colour · 95mins

This excellent wartime drama is based on the real-life exploits of Mary Lindell, a British woman who used her Paris home as a halfway house for Allied soldiers trapped behind enemy lines. This TV movie is tense and emotive, mainly because of the array of talent on display: Judy Davis, one of the greatest and least "starry" actresses around, plays Lindell and brings the same sensivity that she brought to her roles in *A Passage to India* and Woody Allen's *Husbands and Wives*. There is also fine support from Sam Neill, Kate Beckinsale and the always dependable Denholm Elliott in one of his final screen appearances. AT

Judy Davis *Mary Lindell* • Sam Neill *Captain James Leggatt* • Denholm Elliott *Father LeBlanc* • Christien Anholt *Maurice* • Kate Beckinsale *Barbe* • Anthony Higgins *Herman Gruber* ■ *Dir* Larry Elikann • *Scr* Chris Bryant

A One and a Two ★★★★ 15

Drama 1999 · Tai/Jpn · Colour · 173mins

Notable for their complex structure, arresting visuals, measured pace and spare dialogue, Edward Yang's films have always provided a humanist insight into the modern urban experience. But rarely has he exhibited such poetry and precision as in this engrossing domestic epic. With his nerve-frazzled wife dabbling in religion and his kids experiencing growing pains, Wu Nianzhen hits a midlife crisis that not only proves the unpredictability of life, but also slyly mirrors Taiwan's political insecurity. The performances are superb. DP. In Mandarin and English with subtitles. Contains swearing. DVD

Wu Nianzhen *NJ Jian* • Issey Ogata *Ota* • Elaine Jin *Min-Min* • Kelly Lee *Ting Ting* • Jonathan Chang *Yang Yang* • Adrian Lin *Lili* ■ *Dir/Scr* Edward Yang

The One and Only ★★★

Comedy drama 1978 · US · Colour · 97mins

Henry Winkler plays a man whose huge ego is only matched by his determination to become an acting star. Convinced he knows better than anyone else, he alienates would-be employers by his insistence on changing lines and suggesting alterations in his roles. However he then does make a success as a wrestler, although his long-suffering wife and her parents are less enamoured with this new career. TV's Fonzie here finds a decent vehicle for his comedic talents and a sparkling script ensures plenty of laughs. DF

Henry Winkler *Andy Schmidt* • Kim Darby *Mary Crawford* • Gene Saks *Sidney Seltzer* • William Daniels *Mr Crawford* • Harold Gould *Hector Moses* • Polly Holliday *Mrs Crawford* • Herve Villechaize *Milton Miller* • Ed Begley Jr *Arnold the King* ■ *Dir* Carl Reiner • *Scr* Steve Gordon

The One and Only ★★ 15

Romantic comedy
2001 · UK/Fr · Colour · 87mins

Having triumphed on the small screen with *Our Friends in the North*, director Simon Cellan Jones and screenwriter Peter Flannery remain on Tyneside for this mirthless romantic comedy. Despite its meticulous contrivances, the storyline refuses to slot together as neatly as the fitted kitchen that the romantically attached Richard Roxburgh installs for pregnant footballer's wife, Justine Waddell. Consequently it's hard to summon up much enthusiasm, let alone sympathy, for their plight – both are trapped in loveless marriages and being pushed into parenthood by their respective spouses. DP DVD

Richard Roxburgh *Neil* • Justine Waddell *Stevie* • Jonathan Cake *Sonny* • Patsy Kensit *Stella* • Michael Hodgson *Stan* • Aisling O'Sullivan *Jenny* • Angel Thomas *Mgala* ■ *Dir* Simon Cellan Jones • *Scr* Peter Flannery, from the film *Den Eneste Ene* by Kim Fupz Aakeson

The One and Only, Genuine, Original Family Band ★★ U

Period musical drama
1968 · US · Colour · 105mins

This Disney family drama is notable only for the fact that it has a young Kurt Russell and Goldie Hawn appearing on screen together for the first time. Set during the 1888 presidential campaign, the film follows the efforts of Walter Brennan to win the right for his family band to perform in the face of both political opposition and domestic discord. The Sherman brothers' songs are of little interest. DP

Walter Brennan *Granpa Bower* • Buddy Ebsen *Calvin Bower* • John Davidson *Joe Carder* • Lesley Ann Warren *Alice Bower* • Janet Blair *Katie Bower* • Kurt Russell *Sidney Bower* • Steve Harmon *Ernie Stubbins* • Goldie Jeanne Hawn [Goldie Hawn] *Giggly girl* ■ *Dir* Michael O'Herlihy • *Scr* Lowell S Hawley, from the autobiography *Nebraska 1888* by Laura Bower Van Nuys

One Born Every Minute

★★★★

Comedy 1967 · US · Colour · 104mins

Also called *The Flim-Flam Man*, this is one of the choicest comedies in which George C Scott has starred. He's an elderly con-man of epic proportions, who takes on Michael Sarrazin as his apprentice, until the youngster falls in love and starts to reconsider his chosen path. Written by William Rose, it's directed by Irvin Kershner with panache, helped by his second unit director and stunt man, the legendary Yakima Canutt. TH

George C Scott *Mordecai Jones* • Sue Lyon *Bonnie Lee Packard* • Harry Morgan *Sheriff Slade* • Jack Albertson *Mr Packard* • Alice Ghostley *Mrs Packard* • Albert Salmi *Deputy Meshaw* • Slim Pickens *Jarvis Bates* • Michael Sarrazin *Curley Treadaway* ■ *Dir* Irvin Kershner • *Scr* William Rose, from the story *The Ballad of the Flim Flam Man* by Guy Owen

[One] Cavale ★★★★ 15

Thriller 2002 · Fr/Bel · Colour · 109mins

Writer/director Lucas Belvaux also headlines the first instalment in this laudably ambitious triptych, which succeeds in introducing the recurring characters, and is also a gripping thriller in its own right. As the one-time revolutionary who jumps jail in order to wreak revenge on the man he believes betrayed him, Belvaux becomes increasingly hamstrung by circumstance and the despair he feels at the self-seeking society that emerged as a result of the failure of 1960s radicalism. The work of the entire ensemble cast is impeccable, but Catherine Frot excels as the comrade-turned-teacher whose past loyalties jeopardise her future. Followed by *[Two] Un Couple Epatant*. DP. In French with English subtitles. Contains swearing, violence and drug abuse. DVD

Catherine Frot *Jeanne Rivet* • Lucas Belvaux *Bruno Le Roux* • Dominique Blanc *Agnès Manise* • Ornella Muti *Cécile Costes* • Gilbert Melki *Pascal Manise* • Alexis Tomassian *Banane* ■ *Dir/Scr* Lucas Belvaux

One Crazy Summer ★★ PG

Comedy 1986 · US · Colour · 89mins

There are youthful appearances by John Cusack and Demi Moore in this offbeat comedy about a college wannabe who has to learn about love on holiday in Nantucket before he goes off to the educational institution of his choice. It's filmed in a cartoon-style with some fun sight gags, witty dialogue and even a handful of well-integrated animation sequences, but there's little connective tissue. DA

John Cusack *Hoops McCann* • Demi Moore *Cassandra* • Curtis Armstrong *Ack Ack Raymond* • Joel Murray *George Calamari* • Joe Flaherty *General Raymond* • Bobcat Goldthwait *Egg Stork* • Mark Metcalf *Aguilla Beckersted* • William Hickey *Old Man Beckersted* ■ *Dir/Scr* Savage Steve Holland

One Dark Night ★★ 15

Supernatural horror
1982 · US · Colour · 88mins

Even by the early 1980s the teens-in-peril scenario was well past its sell-by-date. In her first leading role a young Meg Tilly, sister of Jennifer, is forced to spend the night in a creepy mausoleum as part of a gang initiation test unaware that its recently interned occupant is about to wake up! Director Tom McLoughlin manages to muster not one ounce of tension and the gore count is fatally low. At least the climax is adequately staged. RS

Meg Tilly *Julie* • Robin Evans *Carol* • Leslie Speights *Kitty* • Elizabeth Daily *Leslie* • Adam West *Allan* • Melissa Newman *Olivia* • Donald Hotton *Dockstader* • Kevin Peter Hall *Eddie* ■ *Dir* Tom McLoughlin • *Scr* Tom McLoughlin, Michael Hawes

One Day in September

★★★★ 12

Documentary 1999 · UK · Colour · 90mins

The protests of the victims' relatives have somewhat tarnished the sheen of Kevin Macdonald's Oscar-winning documentary. But it remains a revelatory account of the terrorist atrocity at the 1972 Munich Olympics. Narrated by Michael Douglas and linking news footage, interviews and graphics, this meticulously researched exposé of the hideously bungled German security operation simply beggars belief. Examples of poor communication, military inexpertise and governmental dithering almost overshadow the horror of the Black September action, which left 11 Israeli Olympians, five Palestinians and one policeman dead. A damning indictment of political violence and bureaucratic arrogance. DP

Michael Douglas *Narrator* ■ *Dir* Kevin Macdonald

O

One Day in the Life of Ivan Denisovich ★★★

Prison drama
1971 · UK/Nor · Colour · 108mins

Although meticulously adapted by Ronald Harwood from Alexander Solzhenitsyn's celebrated novel, this co-production only hints at the appalling conditions inside a Soviet labour camp in the late-Stalinist era, and the dignity and ingenuity with which Ivan survived them. Admittedly, it is a difficult novel to film, even when photographed by a genius like Sven Nykvist and interpreted with such intelligence by Tom Courtenay. But director Casper Wrede has turned it into the wrong sort of ordeal; overwhelmed by the political and literary significance of his material, he has missed both art and life. DP

Tom Courtenay *Ivan Denisovich* • Espen Skjonberg *Tiurin* • James Maxwell *Captain Buinovsky* • Alfred Burke *Alyosha* • Eric Thompson *Tsezar* • John Cording *Pavlo* • Mathew Guinness *Kilgas* ■ *Dir* Caspar Wrede [Casper Wrede] • *Scr* Ronald Harwood, from the novel by Alexander Solzhenitsyn

One Deadly Summer ★★★★ 18

Thriller 1983 · Fr · Colour · 127mins

Exploiting her beauty to disarming effect, Isabelle Adjani won a César for her smouldering performance in this deceptively complex thriller. Working from his own novel, Sébastien Japrisot fashions a script that consistently disconcerts the viewer as the narrative focus shifts between Adjani's vengeful temptress and her besotted husband, Alain Souchon. Similarly director Jean Becker refuses to mislead us simply with appearances, as what seems to be a study of provincial boorishness is overtaken by more sinister events. Atmospherically photographed with a roving camera by Etienne Becker, this meticulously paced picture is a tad overlong, but it's undeniably dark, daring and disturbing. DP. In French with English subtitles. [VIDEO] DVD

Isabelle Adjani *Eliane/Elle* • Alain Souchon *Florimond/Pin Pon* • Suzanne Flon *Cognata* • Jenny Clève *Pin Pon's mother* • Michel Galabru *Gabriel Devigne* • François Cluzet *Mickey* ■ *Dir* Jean Becker • *Scr* Sébastien Japrisot, from his novel

One Desire ★★

Period drama 1955 · US · Colour · 94mins

One of producer Ross Hunter's least interesting "women's pictures" of the 1950s, this stars Anne Baxter as the proprietor of an oil town's notorious gambling saloon whose big desire is to settle down and live a respectable life with Rock Hudson's handsome but carefree croupier. Baxter is too hard-as-nails to elicit much sympathy or tears while Hudson seems to be somewhere else. AE

Anne Baxter *Tacey Cromwell* • Rock Hudson *Clint Saunders* • Julie Adams *Judith Watrous* • Carl Benton Reid *Senator Watrous* • Natalie Wood *Seely* • William Hooper *MacBain* ■ *Dir* Jerry Hopper • *Scr* Lawrence Roman, Robert Blees, from the novel *Tacey Cromwell* by Conrad Richter

One Eight Seven ★★ 15

Drama 1997 · US · Colour · 114mins

Samuel L Jackson's typically intense work is the sole merit of this over-directed, uninvolving school drama. Jackson plays a New York teacher physically and psychologically scarred after a vicious knife assault by a student. He transfers to a new school in Los Angeles to rebuild his life, only to find equally violent conditions. Shot in a distracting MTV pop video style, Jackson's sincere performance is wasted on such clichéd fare. JC. Contains swearing, violence, nudity. [VIDEO]

Samuel L Jackson *Trevor Garfield* • John Heard *Dave Childress* • Kelly Rowan *Ellen Henry* • Clifton Gonzalez Gonzalez [Clifton Collins Jr] *Cesar* • Karina Arroyave *Rita* • Jonah Rooney *Stevie Middleton* • Lobo Sebastian *Benny* • Jack Kehler *Hyland* ■ *Dir* Kevin Reynolds • *Scr* Scott Yagemann

One-Eyed Jacks ★★★★ PG

Western 1961 · US · Colour · 135mins

This stunning and deeply satisfying western is the only film Marlon Brando directed, but Paramount had reason to regret indulging its star – not only does the movie contain levels of sadism and perversity that made it unique for a Hollywood studio film of the period, but it also failed to recoup its $6 million outlay in the States. In a story that is loosely based on the legend of Billy the Kid and Pat Garrett, Brando seeks revenge on his devious partner Karl Malden. It's a fine, adult work, with the Monterey seascapes (magnificently photographed by Charles Lang Jr) making an unusual setting. Incidentally, Brando took over from Stanley Kubrick, who left to direct *Spartacus*. TS [VIDEO] DVD

Marlon Brando *Rio* • Karl Malden *Dad Longworth* • Katy Jurado *Maria* • Pina Pellicer *Louisa* • Slim Pickens *Lon* • Ben Johnson *Bob Amory* ■ *Dir* Marlon Brando • *Scr* Guy Trosper, Calder Willingham, from the novel *The Authentic Death of Hendry Jones* by Charles Neider

One False Move ★★★★ 18

Crime drama 1992 · US · Colour · 101mins

For a mesmerising slice of modern *film noir*, director Carl Franklin skilfully steers past the usual clichés to deliver a thoughtful, ultimately tragic tale. A trio of criminals sets off on a murderous cross-country journey, fleeing Los Angeles with the takings from a brutal drugs heist. LA cops Jim Metzler and Earl Billings are convinced the criminals will head for the tiny southern town where one of their number (Cynda Williams) used to live, and lie in wait with the naive local cop (the ever excellent Bill Paxton). It's a gripping affair, punctuated with isolated splashes of shocking violence, and is superbly acted. JF. Contains swearing and drug abuse. [VIDEO] DVD

Cynda Williams *Fantasia/Lila* • Bill Paxton *Dale "Hurricane" Dixon* • Billy Bob Thornton *Ray Malcolm* • Jim Metzler *Dud Cole* • Michael Beach *Pluto* • Earl Billings *McFeely* • Natalie Canerday *Cheryl Ann* • Robert Ginnaven *Charlie* • Robert Anthony Bell *Byron* • Kevin Hunter *Ronnie* ■ *Dir* Carl Franklin • *Scr* Billy Bob Thornton, Tom Epperson

One Fine Day ★★★ PG

Romantic comedy
1996 · US · Colour · 104mins

In this warm-hearted but underwritten romantic comedy, George Clooney stars as a newspaper columnist saddled with parental responsibilities when he's forced to look after his five-year-old daughter while his ex-wife is on honeymoon. Into his life comes Michelle Pfeiffer, who's struggling to hold down a job and bring up a child, and the couple reluctantly agree to help each other out – only to find that what can go wrong does. The leads are suitably charming, but they are all let down by some uninspired direction from Michael Hoffman. JB [VIDEO] DVD

Michelle Pfeiffer *Melanie Parker* • George Clooney *Jack Taylor* • Mae Whitman *Maggie Taylor* • Alex D Linz *Sammy Parker* • Charles Durning *Lew* • Jon Robin Baitz *Yates Jr* • Ellen Greene *Elaine Lieberman* • Joe Grifasi *Manny Feldstein* ■ *Dir* Michael Hoffman • *Scr* Terrel Seltzer, Ellen Simon

One Flew over the Cuckoo's Nest ★★★★★ 18

Drama 1975 · US · Colour · 128mins

Adapted from Ken Kesey's novel, this film is one the classic movies of the 1970s, thanks in no small measure to the talents of director Milos Forman, who propelled the comic antics to a horrifyingly poignant finale and resounding critical and commercial success; it became one of the few to be awarded all the major Oscars, winning for best picture, director, screenplay, actor (Jack Nicholson) and actress (Louise Fletcher). Nicholson's performance as McMurphy, a free spirit at loose in a state mental home, is one of his greatest characterisations, as he stirs up rebellion against the oppressive regime of Fletcher's ward sister. And among the patients are such then almost unknowns as Danny DeVito, Brad Dourif and Christopher Lloyd. TH. Contains swearing and some violence. [VIDEO] DVD

Jack Nicholson *Randle P McMurphy* • Louise Fletcher *Nurse Mildred Ratched* • William Redfield *Harding* • Will Sampson *Chief Bromden* • Brad Dourif *Billy Bibbit* • Sydney Lassick *Charlie Cheswick* • Christopher Lloyd *Taber* • Danny DeVito *Martini* • Sherman "Scatman" Crothers [Scatman Crothers] *Turkle* ■ *Dir* Milos Forman • *Scr* Lawrence Hauben, Bo Goldman, from the play by Dale Wasserman, from the novel by Ken Kesey • *Cinematographer* Haskell Wexler

One Foot in Heaven ★★★ U

Biographical drama 1941 · US · BW · 107mins

The illustrious Fredric March is at the centre of this Oscar-nominated, pleasingly old-fashioned movie about William Spence, a Methodist minister who, at the turn of the 20th century, takes his message from parish to parish, and must grapple with the changes in society that conflict with his beliefs. This is a loving, if slighty mawkish, piece, peddling piety but not sanctimoniousness. March is well-supported, while Irving Rapper directs with a nice sense of period (and a generous supply of sentimentality). RK

Fredric March *William Spence* • Martha Scott *Hope Morris Spence* • Beulah Bondi *Mrs Lydia Sandow* • Gene Lockhart *Preston Thurston* • Grant Mitchell *Clayton Potter* • Moroni Olsen *Dr John Romer* • Harry Davenport *Elias Samson* • Elisabeth Fraser *Eileen Spence, aged 17* • Frankie Thomas *Hartzell Spence, aged 18* • Laura Hope Crews *Mrs Thurston* ■ *Dir* Irving Rapper • *Scr* Casey Robinson, from the biography by Hartzell Spence

One Foot in Hell ★★★

Western 1960 · US · Colour · 89mins

As an argument for America to introduce a National Health Service, this western takes some beating. Alan Ladd is the Civil War soldier whose wife dies in Arizona because he doesn't have the money to buy her medicine. Nevertheless, he becomes sheriff and plots revenge by robbing the bank and killing everyone he can. Giving a novel twist to the western formula, this has some fresh characters and doesn't readily cop out in the end. AT

Alan Ladd *Mitch Barrett* • Don Murray *Dan Keats* • Dan O'Herlihy *Harry Ivers* • Dolores Michaels *Julie Reynolds* • Barry Coe *Stu Christian* • Larry Gates *Doc Seltzer* • Karl Swenson *Sheriff Olson* ■ *Dir* James B Clark • *Scr* Aaron Spelling, Sydney Boehm, from the story by Aaron Spelling

One for the Road ★ 18

Black comedy 2003 · UK · Colour · 91mins

It's hard to think of a more inept outing than writer/director Chris Cooke's feature debut. Stripped of their licenses for drink driving, boy racer Greg Chisholm, cabbie Mark Devenport, salesman Rupert Procter and wealthy entrepreneur Hywel Bennett refuse to take their rehabilitation classes seriously. Few will care about these losers or their miserable lives. DP [VIDEO] DVD

Greg Chisholm [Gregory Chisholm] *Jimmy* • Hywel Bennett *Richard Stevens* • Rupert Procter [Rupert Proctor] *Paul* • Mark Devenport *Mark* • Julie Legrand *Liz* • Micaiah Dring *Eve* • Johnny Phillips [Jonathan Phillips] *Ian* ■ *Dir/Scr* Chris Cooke

One Froggy Evening ★★★★★

Animated comedy 1955 · US · Colour · 7mins

The best-known of Chuck Jones's Warner Bros one-shot cartoons (that is, those not featuring a recurring character) tells the story of a construction worker who dreams of riches when he finds a singing-and-dancing frog in the cornerstone of a building he is demolishing. His greed drives him to madness when it transpires the frog refuses to perform when others are present. Jones is probably alone among the great Hollywood cartoon directors in being able to tell a moral tale without drawing attention to the fact. The message that one should enjoy art for its own sake is subtly transmitted amid the exquisite, bitter-sweet humour. CLP

Bill Roberts *Frog, singing* ■ *Dir* Charles M Jones [Chuck Jones] • *Scr* Michael Maltese

One from the Heart ★★★ 15

Musical romance
1982 · US · Colour · 102mins

Francis Ford Coppola famously bankrupted his own studio Zoetrope making this $23 million-budget "musical Valentine" entirely on a sound stage, so its merits were subsumed by the commercial fiasco it turned into. It tells the simple tale of Frederic Forrest and Teri Garr, who split up and have affairs with a circus performer (Nastassja Kinski) and singing waiter (Raul Julia) while intoxicated by one neon-lit Las Vegas night. The songs, by Tom Waits and Crystal Gayle, are bittersweet gems, and the sets are magnificent. Unfortunately, the human element is dwarfed by the technical achievement. AC [VIDEO] DVD

Frederic Forrest *Hank* • Teri Garr *Frannie* • Nastassja Kinski *Leila* • Raul Julia *Ray* • Lainie Kazan *Maggie* • Harry Dean Stanton *Moe* • Allen Goorwitz [Allen Garfield] *Restaurant owner* ■ *Dir* Francis Ford Coppola • *Scr* Armyan Bernstein, Francis Ford Coppola, from a story by Armyan Bernstein • *Cinematographer* Vittorio Storaro

One Full Moon ★★★ 15

Drama 1991 · UK · Colour · 97mins

This poetic exercise in rural realism shifts between the 1950s and the 1920s, as Dyfan Roberts revisits the slate-mining community where he was raised by his mother. The relationship between Betsan Llwyd and young Tudor Roberts is both touching and unfeigned, as they put on a united front against the harshness of their existence and the censoriousness of the local preacher. But the nostalgic humour dissipates after Llwyd is assaulted by a travelling tinker and their grim idyll begins to unravel. DP. In Welsh with English subtitles.

Dyfan Roberts *Man* • Tudor Roberts *Boy* • Betsan Llwyd *Mother* • Delyth Einir *Jini* • Cian Ciaran *Huw* • Dilwyn Vaughn Thomas *Moi* ■ *Dir* Endaf Emlyn • *Scr* Gwenlyn Parry, Endaf Emlyn, from the novel by Caradog Prichard

One Good Cop ★★★ 15

Drama 1991 · US · Colour · 100mins

A smoothly orchestrated movie, veering unapologetically between shameless sentimentality and violent melodrama,

O

which is given a gritty reality by Michael Keaton's performance as a decent cop planning to adopt his murdered partner's three children. How he blots his record after robbing a local drug baron is a wrenching tale, skilfully told by writer/director Heywood Gould, whose true-life experiences were the basis of *Cocktail*. AJ. Contains violence, swearing. VHS DVD

Michael Keaton *Artie Lewis* • Rene Russo *Rita Lewis* • Anthony LaPaglia *Stevie Diroma* • Kevin Conway *Lieutenant Danny Quinn* • Rachel Ticotin *Grace* • Tony Plana *Beniamino* • Benjamin Bratt *Felix* ■ *Dir/Scr* Heywood Gould

One Good Turn ★★★ U

Comedy 1954 · UK · BW · 90mins

This is the cleverly constructed follow-up to Norman Wisdom's smash-hit debut *Trouble in Store*. Arguably the best of his vehicles, it features the bumbling star as a handyman trying to save the orphanage that employs him from collapse. His money-raising schemes are invariably hilarious, while his sequences with leading ladies Joan Rice and Australian zither girl Shirley Abicair are charming. Of course, the film is overly sentimental, but sentiment was part of Wisdom's stock-in-trade, and today we can recognise the rare quality of a true cinematic clown. TS VHS DVD

Norman Wisdom *Norman* • Joan Rice *Iris* • Shirley Abicair *Mary* • Thora Hird *Cook* • William Russell *Alec* • Richard Caldicot *Bigley* • Marjorie Fender *Tuppeny* ■ *Dir* John Paddy Carstairs • *Scr* Maurice Cowan, John Paddy Carstairs, Ted Willis, from a story by Dorothy Whipple, Sid Colin, Talbot Rothwell

One Good Turn ★★ 18

Thriller 1996 · US · Colour · 88mins

A whole lot of setup for very little pay-off. Lenny Von Dohlen is a successful software designer who spots James Remar living as a vagrant on the streets of LA. Since Remar had saved Von Dohlen's life years before when they were in the army together, he offers him a job, and then spends the next hour or so of screen time ignoring glaringly obvious clues that Remar has some insane agenda of his own. Little more than an average psycho-stalker movie. ST VHS

James Remar *Simon* • Suzy Amis *Laura* • Lenny Von Dohlen *Matt* • Richard Minchenberg *John* • Audie England *Kristen* • Rowena Guinness *Kim* • John Savage *Santapietro* ■ *Dir* Tony Randel • *Scr* Jim Piddock

One Heavenly Night ★★ U

Romantic musical
1931 · US · Colour · 76mins

Budapest flower-seller Evelyn Laye is persuaded by musical hall star Lilyan Tashman to take her place in her absence, in which guise Laye finds romance with handsome count John Boles. English star Laye was spirited away from the London stage by Samuel Goldwyn, who had this operetta especially written for her Hollywood debut. She is charming, pretty and graceful, but the film founders on an inadequate script and, when it lost money, Goldwyn dropped his protégée. RK VHS

Evelyn Laye *Lilli* • John Boles *Count Mirko Tibor* • Leon Errol *Otto* • Lilyan Tashman *Fritzi Vyez* • Hugh Cameron *Janos* • Marian Lord [Marion Lord] *Liska* • Lionel Belmore *Zagen* ■ *Dir* George Fitzmaurice • *Scr* Sidney Howard, from a story by Louis Bromfield

One Hour Photo ★★★★ 15

Psychological thriller
2001 · US · Colour · 91mins

Robin Williams is hauntingly moving as the supermarket photo processor, whose lonely existence feeds an escalating obsession with a glamorous local family. A simple yet effective reflection on modern society's fixation with so-called flawless lifestyles, it's meticulously composed and tautly executed. Each frame of this unnerving psychological chiller is a visually stunning snapshot of an innocent world distorted by human complexities. Director Mark Romanek draws on his music video background of storytelling through imagery, by applying varying degrees of colour and contrast to reflect the positive and negative emotions on display. SF. Contains swearing, violence, nudity. VHS DVD

Robin Williams *Seymour "Sy" Parrish* • Connie Nielsen *Nina Yorkin* • Michael Vartan *Will Yorkin* • Gary Cole *Bill Owens* • Eriq La Salle *Detective Van Der Zee* • Dylan Smith *Jakob "Jake" Yorkin* • Erin Daniels *Maya Burson* • Paul Hansen Kim *Yoshi Araki* ■ *Dir/Scr* Mark Romanek

One Hour with You ★★★

Musical romantic comedy
1932 · US · BW · 78mins

Parisian doctor Maurice Chevalier and his wife Jeanette MacDonald are still utterly devoted to each other after three years of marriage. But their harmony is disrupted when her devious, man-eating best friend Genevieve Tobin gets her clutches into Chevalier, and his best friend Charles Ruggles declares his passion for MacDonald. Paramount's master of sophistication, Ernst Lubitsch, remakes his 1924 silent hit, *The Marriage Circle*, beautifully orchestrating an experimental mix of verse, song and soliloquies delivered straight to camera. The result is frothy, sophisticated and risqué. RK

Maurice Chevalier *Dr André Bertier* • Jeanette MacDonald *Colette Bertier* • Genevieve Tobin *Mitzi Olivier* • Charlie Ruggles [Charles Ruggles] *Adolph* • Roland Young *Professor Olivier* • George Barbier *Police commissioner* ■ *Dir* Ernst Lubitsch • *Scr* Samson Raphaelson, from the play *Nur ein Traum, Lustspiel in 3 Akten (Only a Dream)* by Lothar Schmidt [Lothar Goldschmidt] • *Cinematographer* Victor Milner

One Hundred and One Dalmatians ★★★★★ U

Animated comedy adventure
1960 · US · Colour · 76mins

From the novel by Dodie Smith, this hardy perennial from Disney rivals the studio's *The Aristocats* for its deft mix of cute talking animals and largely foolish humans. While there's little faulting the draughtsmanship and personality of the Dalmatians, the two-legged foils are vital to the story's dynamic: monstrous, fur-loving villainess Cruella De Vil and her hapless Cockney henchmen Horace and Jasper. The "twilight bark" sequence, in which London's dogs communicate in woofs, brings poignancy to what is otherwise a thrilling caper created when the Disney artists where at the height of their powers. AC VHS DVD

Rod Taylor *Pongo* • Ben Wright (1) *Roger Radcliff* • J Pat O'Malley *Colonel/Jasper Badun* • Cate Bauer *Perdita* • Betty Lou Gerson *Cruella De Vil/Miss Birdwell* • Dave Frankham [David Frankham] *Sergeant Tibs* • Martha Wentworth *Nanny/Queenie/Lucy* • Frederick Worlock *Horace Badun/Inspector Craven* • Lisa Davis *Anita Radcliff* ■ *Dir* Wolfgang Reitherman, Hamilton S Luske [Hamilton Luske], Clyde Geronimi • *Scr* Bill Peet, from the novel by Dodie Smith

101 Dalmatians ★★★ U

Comedy adventure
1996 · US · Colour · 98mins

Disney updates its classic animated tale with this live-action version starring a deliciously over-the-top Glenn Close as infamous villain Cruella De Vil, who wants to turn loads of cuddly little dalmatian puppies into a fur coat. Jeff Daniels and Joely Richardson (as the couple trying to stop her) are slightly more subdued, but enjoyable to watch nonetheless. The only complaint for older viewers (and those sentimental about the original) is that live dogs lack the variety of expression – and the vocals – of their animated counterparts. That said, children will love it . JB VHS DVD

Glenn Close *Cruella De Vil* • Jeff Daniels *Roger* • Joely Richardson *Anita* • Joan Plowright *Nanny* • Hugh Laurie *Jasper* • Mark Williams *Horace* • John Shrapnel *Skinner* • Tim McInnerny *Alonzo* • Hugh Fraser *Frederick* ■ *Dir* Stephen Herek • *Scr* John Hughes, from the novel by Dodie Smith

101 Reykjavik ★★★ 18

Comedy 2000 · Ice/Den/Nor · Colour · 84mins

In this laconic comedy of sexual manners, wastrel Hilmir Snaer Gudnason impregnates both his on-off girlfriend Thrudur Vilhjalmsdottir, and Victoria Abril, the Spanish dance teacher who has just started a lesbian relationship with his newly liberated mother Hanna Maria Karlsdottir. The combination of Abril's hot-blooded sassiness and Gudnason's cool deadpan is highly effective, but what lingers longest are cinematographer Peter Steuger's snow-speckled backstreets. Made with additional funding from France and Germany. DP. In Icelandic and English with subtitles. Contains swearing and sex scenes. VHS DVD

Victoria Abril *Lola Milagros* • Hilmir Snaer Gudnason *Hlynur* • Hanna Maria Karlsdottir *Berglind* ■ *Dir* Baltasar Kormakur • *Scr* Baltasar Kormakur, from a novel by Hallgrímur Helgason

102 Dalmatians ★★★ U

Comedy adventure
2000 · US · Colour · 95mins

Glenn Close returns as the villainous Cruella De Vil in this follow-up to Disney's 1996 live-action hit *101 Dalmatians*. This is as much fun as the first film, with the supposedly reformed fur-lover Cruella released after a spell of incarceration and funding an animal rescue operation. Before you can say "cutesy wootsie puppies", she's got outrageous designer Gérard Depardieu preparing to make an overcoat out of you know who. JB VHS DVD

Glenn Close *Cruella De Vil* • Ioan Gruffudd *Kevin* • Alice Evans *Chloe* • Tim McInnerny *Alonso* • Ian Richardson *Mr Torte* • Gérard Depardieu *Le Pelt* • Eric Idle *Waddlesworth* ■ *Dir* Kevin Lima • *Scr* Kristen Buckley, Brian Regan, Brian Tzudiker, Noni White, from a story by Kristen Buckley, Brian Regan, from the novel *The One Hundred and One Dalmatians* by Dodie Smith • *Costume Designer* Anthony Powell

100 Days before the Command ★★★ 15

Drama 1990 · USSR · Colour · 66mins

Completed in 1990 but withheld for four years, Uzbek-born Hussein Erkenov's featurette is as compelling as it is complex. Shot secretly during the last days of Communism, this expressionist, elliptical and quietly subversive study of authority and obedience follows a unit of raw Red Army unit recruits as they are gradually dehumanised by the rigidity of their routine. Adhering to the prescribed socialist-realist style, this is a political, as well as a pacifist tract, which is given poetic power by cinematographer Vladimir Menshikov's astonishing use of light. DP. In Russian with English subtitles. VHS DVD

Oleg Vasilkov *Elin* • Vladimir Zamansky *The Unknown Man* • Oleg Khusainov *Angel* ■ *Dir* Hussein Erkenov • *Scr* Yuri Polyakov, Vladimir Kholodov, from a story by Yuri Polyakov

One Hundred Men and a Girl ★★★★ U

Musical 1937 · US · BW · 80mins

Deanna Durbin, the devoted daughter of a classical trombonist Adolphe Menjou, seeks the assistance of famous conductor Leopold Stokowski (playing himself) to form an Orchestra of the Unemployed. The result is a quintessential feel-good movie, played with precocious zest by Universal Studios' meal ticket and a splendid supporting cast that includes Mischa Auer and bombastic fat man Eugene Pallette. All one needs in order to enjoy this nonsense is the ability to surrender to its fairy-tale sweetness and enjoy the classical music under Stokowski's baton. RK VHS DVD

Deanna Durbin *Patricia "Patsy" Cardwell* • Adolphe Menjou *John Cardwell* • Leopold Stokowski • Alice Brady *Mrs Frost* • Eugene Pallette *John R Frost* • Mischa Auer *Michael Borodoff* • Billy Gilbert *Garage owner* • Alma Kruger *Mrs Tyler* ■ *Dir* Henry Koster • *Scr* Bruce Manning, Charles Kenyon, James Mulhauser

100 Rifles ★★ 15

Western 1969 · US · Colour · 104mins

A below-par western, filmed in Spain and directed by Tom Gries, who made the elegiac *Will Penny* with Charlton Heston. This is a breezier and more routine affair, with muscular black actor and former football star Jim Brown as a lawman in search of Burt Reynolds, a mixed race Mexican who has robbed a bank in order to build an arsenal for a revolution. Raquel Welch is the glamorous and scantily clad senorita of the piece who gets into bed with Brown, a startling scene for 1969. People sweat, say "Hey, gringo", and use up a lot of ammunition. AT VHS

Jim Brown *Lyedecker* • Raquel Welch *Sarita* • Burt Reynolds *Yaqui Joe* • Fernando Lamas *Verdugo* • Dan O'Herlihy *Grimes* • Hans Gudegast [Eric Braeden] *Von Klemme* • Michael Forest *Humara* ■ *Dir* Tom Gries • *Scr* Clair Huffaker, Tom Gries, from the novel *The Californio* by Robert MacLeod

One in a Million ★★★ U

Romantic musical comedy
1936 · US · BW · 94mins

Norwegian ice skating star Sonja Henie's first American film was a smash hit which resulted in a 20th Century-Fox contract and screen stardom. Viewed today it is probably her best vehicle; there's a winsome topicality attached to this film, dealing as it did with the pre-war Winter Olympics, where the blonde cutie wins the gold and is schlepped to Madison Square Garden by manager Adolphe Menjou. There she meets likeable Don Ameche. TS

Sonja Henie *Greta Muller* • Adolphe Menjou *Thadeus "Tad" Spencer* • Jean Hersholt *Heinrich Muller* • Ned Sparks *Danny Simpson* • Don Ameche *Bob Harris* • The Ritz Brothers [Al Ritz] *Ritz Brother* • The Ritz Brothers [Jimmy Ritz] *Ritz Brother* • The Ritz Brothers [Harry Ritz] *Ritz Brother* • Arline Judge *Billie Spencer* • Borrah Minevitch *Adolphe* • Dixie Dunbar *Goldie* • Montagu Love *Ratoffsky alias Sir Frederick Brooks* ■ *Dir* Sidney Lanfield • *Scr* Leonard Praskins, Mark Kelly, from a story by Leonard Praskins

One Is a Lonely Number ★★★ 15

Drama 1972 · US · Colour · 93mins

Trish Van Devere plays a wife who grapples with the aftermath of divorce, travelling the emotional rollercoaster with the help of Hollywood stalwarts Melvyn Douglas, who plays a lonely shopkeeper, and Janet Leigh, an acerbic president of a group for divorced women. Though a little lightweight at times, it has been treated perhaps more harshly than it deserves. FL

Trish Van Devere *Amy Brower* • Monte Markham *Howard Carpenter* • Janet Leigh *Gert Meredith* • Melvyn Douglas *Joseph Provo* • Jane Elliott *Madge Frazier* ■ *Dir* Mel Stuart • *Scr* David Seltzer, from the story *The Good Humor Man* by Rebecca Morris

One Kill ★★★

Courtroom drama 2000 · US · Colour · 96mins

Director Christopher Menaul's standard true-life court case TV drama, it doesn't matter that marine officer Anne Heche tried to break off her affair with married superior Sam Shepard or that she shot him in the genuine belief he intended to harm her. Only attorney Eric Stoltz stands between her and the prejudice of her brothers in arms. The star performances add lustre to what could have been run-of-the-mill. DP

Anne Heche *Mary Jane O'Malley* • Sam Shepard *Maj Nelson Gray* • Eric Stoltz *Captain Walker Randall* • Kate McNeil *Major Leslie Nesbitt* ■ *Dir* Christopher Menaul • *Scr* Shelley Evans

One Last Chance ★★ 15

Comedy drama
2003 · UK/Nor · Colour · 92mins

In this fitfully amusing caper set in the Scottish Highlands, Jamie Sives is desperate to leave the backwater of Tullybridge and steals a gold nugget that he hopes will finance his father's stay in an old people's home, enabling him to escape. However, his plan to sell the nugget to fence Dougray Scott goes awry, with Sives falling foul of gangster James Cosmo and a sinister curling club. Contrived, but well observed. DP. Contains swearing. DVD

Jamie Sives *Fitz* • Iain Robertson *Nellie* • Kevin McKidd *Seany* • Neve McIntosh *Barbara* • Jimmy Chisholm *Harry* • Ewan Stewart *Fitz's father* • James Cosmo *Big John* • Dougray Scott *Frankie the Fence* ■ *Dir/Scr* Stewart Svaasand

One Little Indian ★★ U

Western comedy drama
1973 · US · Colour · 86mins

In this sentimental Disney western, James Garner plays a cavalryman who tries to save the Indians during a massacre and is sentenced to hang. His neck and everyone else's conscience is saved by a white boy who has been brought up by Indians. Aimed firmly at the family audience, it boasts a Jerry Goldsmith score, the familiar backdrops of Utah's deserts and buttes, and an early appearance by a young Jodie Foster. AT

James Garner *Clint Keyes* • Vera Miles *Doris* • Pat Hingle *Capt Stewart* • Morgan Woodward *Sgt Raines* • John Doucette *Sgt Waller* • Clay O'Brien *Mark* • Robert Pine *Lt Cummins* • Bruce Glover *Schrader* • Jodie Foster *Martha* ■ *Dir* Bernard McEveety • *Scr* Harry Spalding • *Music* Jerry Goldsmith

One Magic Christmas ★★ U

Seasonal drama 1985 · US · Colour · 85mins

One suspects that the intention here was to put a modern slant on Dickens's tale *A Christmas Carol*. But quite how her husband's redundancy, impending homelessness and bankruptcy are supposed to rekindle the Christmas spirit in housewife Mary Steenburgen is anybody's guess. It takes a huge leap of faith for anyone to believe that an angel with an uncanny resemblance to Harry Dean Stanton can do much to rectify the situation, but then, this is Disney. Earnestly played, but far too downbeat for the festive season. DP

Mary Steenburgen *Ginnie Grainger* • Gary Basaraba *Jack Grainger* • Elisabeth Harnois *Abbie Grainger* • Arthur Hill *Caleb* • Wayne Robson *Harry Dickens* • Harry Dean Stanton *Gideon* • Jan Rubes *Santa Claus* • Elias Koteas *Eddie* ■ *Dir* Phillip Borsos • *Scr* Thomas Meehan, from a story by Thomas Meehan, Phillip Borsos, Barry Healey

One Man Force ★★ 18

Action thriller 1989 · US · Colour · 85mins

Former professional American football player John "the Tooz" Matuszak plays Jake Swan, who is a cop on the edge following the murder of his partner. He investigates the kidnapping of a singer, which then leads him on a tour of LA's nightclubs. This is somehow connected with a money-laundering scheme and naturally gives Jake the chance to get revenge for his partner. The Tooz isn't much of an actor, and this limp star vehicle doesn't even have very good action scenes. ST

John Matuszak *Jake Swan* • Ronny Cox *Lieutenant McCoy* • Charles Napier *Dante* • Sharon Farrell *Shirley* • Robert Tessier *Wilson* ■ *Dir/Scr* Dale Trevillion

One Man Jury ★

Action crime drama
1978 · US · Colour · 98mins

It seems like a B-movie dream: Jack Palance as a Dirty Harry-like cop who goes even further than Eastwood did, killing various street scum in cold blood. But despite the premise, the slow proceedings are actually rather tame. Palance's performance is half-hearted, and his character does more complaining than fighting. Cheesy. KB

Jack Palance *Wade* • Christopher Mitchum *Blake* • Pamela Shoop *Wendy* • Angel Tompkins *Kitty* • Joe Spinell *Mike* • Cara Williams *Nancy* • Alexandra Hay *Tessie* • Jeff McCracken *Billy Joe* ■ *Dir/Scr* Charles Martin

One Man's Way ★★ U

Biographical drama 1964 · US · BW · 104mins

This is a devout biopic about Norman Vincent Peale, a reporter who became one of those aspirational Dale Carnegie-types in American pop culture. Don Murray gives a sympathetically sanitised performance under Denis Sanders's direction. TH

Don Murray *Norman Vincent Peale* • Diana Hyland *Ruth Peale* • William Windom *Rev Clifford Peale* • Virginia Christine *Anna Peale* • Veronica Cartwright *Mary* ■ *Dir* Denis Sanders • *Scr* Eleanore Griffin, John W Bloch, from the biography *Norman Vincent Peale: Minister to Millions* by Arthur Gordon

One Million BC ★★ U

Science-fiction adventure
1940 · US · BW · 76mins

Hal Roach is best known as the producer who teamed Laurel and Hardy. Unfortunately, he got laughs in all the wrong places for this ambitious but ultimately preposterous prehistoric adventure. Yet the film does have a place in cinema history. This owes nothing to the story about the Rock and the Shell tribes, to the shoestring special effects, or to the grunting mime of Victor Mature, Carole Landis and Lon Chaney Jr in the principal roles. The claim to fame lies in the uncredited assistance of DW Griffith, the legendary silent director, working on his final picture after a decade in the wilderness. DP

Victor Mature *Tumak* • Carole Landis *Loana* • Lon Chaney Jr *Akhoba* • Conrad Nagel *Archaeologist/Narrator* • John Hubbard *Ohtao* • Robert Kent *Mountain guide* • Mamo Clark *Nupondi* ■ *Dir* Hal Roach, Hal Roach Jr • *Scr* Mickell Novak, George Baker, Joseph Frickert

One Million Years BC ★★★ PG

Adventure 1966 · US/UK · Colour · 96mins

Raquel Welch wears a furry bikini and roams the wilderness in this Jurassic lark. Welch has a stunning physique but no dialogue, merely some grunts and a furrowed brow, which is fine as she's not called upon to communicate much beyond fear or desire. Made by Hammer, it's an absolute hoot, as it follows the war between the Rock People and the Shell People, and throws in some wobbly prehistoric monsters, courtesy of effects maestro Ray Harryhausen. AT DVD

Raquel Welch *Loana* • John Richardson *Tumak* • Percy Herbert *Sakana* • Robert Brown *Akhoba* • Martine Beswick *Nupondi* • Jean Wladon *Ahot* • Lisa Thomas *Sura* ■ *Dir* Don Chaffey • *Scr* Michael Carreras, from the film *One Million BC* by Mickell Novak, George Baker, Joseph Frickert

One Minute to Zero ★★

War drama 1952 · US · BW · 105mins

Robert Mitchum goes into action during the Korean War, here teaming up with Ann Blyth who represents the United Nations and provides the love interest. Their romance comes under strain when Mitchum mows down some innocent refugees but, hey, they soon get together for a syrupy song called *Tell Me Golden Moon*. Despite the pains taken with the battle scenes, this is a pretty dismal job, designed to show how the UN was deep inside Uncle Sam's pocket. AT

Robert Mitchum *Colonel Steve Janowkski* • Ann Blyth *Linda Day* • William Talman *Colonel Parker* • Charles McGraw *Sgt Baker* • Margaret Sheridan *Mary Parker* • Richard Egan *Captain Ralston* ■ *Dir* Tay Garnett • *Scr* Milton Krims, William Wister Haines

One More Kiss ★★★★ 12

Romantic drama 1999 · UK · Colour · 97mins

Director Vadim Jean has taken a difficult subject – terminal illness – and created a beautiful movie that manages to be moving without being too sentimental. It tells the story of single-minded Valerie Edmond, who returns from New York to her home town of Berwick-upon-Tweed to patch things up with her father (James Cosmo) before she dies of cancer. She also meets up with now-married old flame Gerard Butler and becomes friends with fellow sufferer Danny Nussbaum. Thanks to some sterling performances, particularly from Cosmo, this is an uplifting, rewarding film that, while occasionally harrowing, is also full of gutsy humour. SR DVD

Gerard Butler *Sam* • James Cosmo *Frank* • Valerie Edmond *Sarah* • Valerie Gogan *Charlotte* • Carl Proctor *Barry* • Danny Nussbaum *Jude* • Dilys Miller *Mary* • Ron Guthrie *Robin* ■ *Dir* Vadim Jean • *Scr* Suzie Halewood

One More River ★★★

Drama 1934 · US · BW · 85mins

Looking fearfully dated today, this once prestigious Universal feature is based upon the last novel in John Galsworthy's *The Forsyte Saga*. Despite being directed by the talented expatriate Englishman James Whale, this Hollywood, England, study of a divorce remains relentlessly theatrical, although Diana Wynyard is sublime as the wife accused by Colin Clive of committing adultery with young Frank Lawton. Watch for the screen debut of Jane Wyatt. TS

Diana Wynyard *Clare Corven* • Frank Lawton *Tony Croom* • Mrs Patrick Campbell *Lady Mont* • Jane Wyatt *Dinny Cherrell* • Colin Clive *Sir Gerald Corven* • Reginald Denny *David Dornford* • C Aubrey Smith *General Charwell* • Henry Stephenson *Sir Lawrence Mont* • Lionel Atwill *Brough* • Alan Mowbray *Forsyte* ■ *Dir* James Whale • *Scr* RC Sherriff, from the novel by John Galsworthy

One More Time ★★

Comedy 1970 · UK · Colour · 95mins

Salt and Pepper, a lacklustre British-made comedy vehicle for Sinatra clan cronies Sammy Davis Jr and Peter Lawford, rather surprisingly spawned this even weaker sequel, in which the buddies are again Soho club-owners involved in crime. This time Lawford plays identical twin brothers; the death of one leads to attempts on the life of the other in a Scottish castle. Interesting (for a while) is the way director Jerry Lewis, who doesn't appear, transfers his zany persona to Davis and interpolates typical Lewis setups and sentimentality. DM

Sammy Davis Jr *Charlie Salt* • Peter Lawford *Chris Pepper/Lord Sydney Pepper* • Maggie Wright *Miss Tomkins* • Leslie Sands *Inspector Crook* • John Wood *Figg* • Sydney Arnold *Tombs* • Edward Evans *Gordon* • Christopher Lee • Peter Cushing ■ *Dir* Jerry Lewis • *Scr* Michael Pertwee

One More Train to Rob ★★

Western 1971 · US · Colour · 108mins

A breezy western with George Peppard as a train robber who tries to settle down with his girl and ends up in jail, only then realising that he has been set up by his partner in crime, John Vernon. Directed by Andrew V McLaglen, it's very much a post-*Butch Cassidy* picture, rarely more than a jolly jape, and Peppard makes for a pleasingly laconic hero. AT

George Peppard *Harker Fleet* • Diana Muldaur *Katy* • John Vernon *Timothy X Nolan* • France Nuyen *Ah Toy* • Steve Sandor *Jim Gant* • Soon-Teck Oh *Yung* ■ *Dir* Andrew V McLaglen • *Scr* Don Tait, Dick Nelson, from a story by William Roberts

One Night at McCool's ★★ 15

Black comedy 2001 · US · Colour · 88mins

Great cast, good start – shame, then, that this night out starts flagging by early evening. Set in McCool's bar, the film kicks off with the arrival of slinky, red-sheathed *femme fatale* Liv Tyler. She's the sort of woman that men don't so much live for as die for. And guess what? One does. Yet the killing further fuels the passions of besotted barman Matt Dillon, waterholing lawyer Paul Reiser and investigating homicide detective John Goodman. Starting out fine as a black comedy, the film loses its way with a desperate desire to be hip. Michael Douglas co-produced, and cameos as a hitman with an extremely weird wig. DA DVD

Liv Tyler *Jewel Valentine* • Matt Dillon *Randy* • John Goodman *Detective Dehling* • Paul Reiser *Carl Lumpke* • Michael Douglas *Mr Burmeister* • Reba McEntire *Dr Green* • Andrew Silverstein [Andrew Dice Clay] *Utah/Elmo* ■ *Dir* Harald Zwart • *Scr* Stan Seidel

One Night at the Music Hall ★★

Musical 1956 · Fr · Colour · 104mins

Eddie Constantine plays an American in Paris whose marriage seems to be heading for the final curtain after his wife, Zizi Jeanmaire, eclipses his singing celebrity. A kind of *A Star Is Born* without the tragedy, the film is most notable for Constantine's growling performance and a handful of ridiculous showstoppers. DP. French dialogue dubbed into English.

Eddie Constantine *Bob Hardie* • Zizi Jeanmaire *Claudie* • Yves Robert *Jeff* • Nadia Gray *Suzy Morgan* • Jacques Morel *Director* • Jacques Castelot *Philippe Loiselet* ■ *Dir* Henri Decoin • *Scr* Henri Decoin, Jacques Companeez, Georges Tabet, AndréTabet

O

One Night of Love ★★★★ U

Musical 1934 · US · BW · 83mins

This is the hit musical that made a movie star out of the diva Grace Moore, and brought opera to a wide film-going public. Somewhat mirroring her own career, it tells of an American soprano who studies in Italy and wins fame at the Met. After being turned down by MGM for *The Merry Widow* (1934), because she was considered too fat, Moore slimmed down and was signed with Columbia for this first (and best) of five deliriously silly, well-mounted and tuneful operettas she made for the studio. The director Victor Schertzinger, an accomplished musician, co-wrote the title song. RB

Grace Moore *Mary Barrett* • Tullio Carminati *Giulio Monteverdi* • Lyle Talbot *Bill Houston* • Mona Barrie *Lally* • Jessie Ralph *Angelina* • Luis Alberni *Giovanni* ■ *Dir* Victor Schertzinger • *Scr* SK Lauren, James Gow, Edmund North, from a play by Dorothy Speare, Charles Beahan

One Night Stand ★★ 15

Drama 1984 · Aus · Colour · 89mins

This Australian apocalypse movie concerns four disparate characters holed up in the Sydney Opera House on a New Year's Eve that may well be their last. A radio broadcast announces that nuclear bombs have been dropped in Europe, North America and Australia and advises people to stay where they are. Two terrified teenagers are joined in the Opera House by an AWOL soldier and a janitor. Good on the claustrophobia and characters but overall a little thin. FL

Tyler Coppin *Sam* • Cassandra Delaney *Sharon* • Jay Hackett *Brendan* • Saskia Post *Eva* ■ *Dir/Scr* John Duigan

One Night Stand ★★

Psychological thriller
1994 · US · Colour · 92mins

Francis Ford Coppola's actress sister Talia Shire takes a creditable stab at directing with this brooding stew of steamy psychodrama. Ally Sheedy is the lonely divorcee who becomes romantically involved with tall, dark and handsome A Martinez, only to discover that her new lover may well have murdered his first wife. Sheedy takes her acting duties seriously and delivers an engaging, if at times rather earnest performance. Frederic Forrest contributes a psychotic turn as Martinez's father-in-law, but otherwise this erotic thriller sticks to increasingly familiar territory as it progresses to its inevitable twist ending. RT

Ally Sheedy *Michelle Sanderson* • A Martinez *Jack Gillman* • Frederic Forrest *Michael Joslyn* • Diane Salinger *Barbara Joslyn* • Don Novello *Warren Miller* • Gina Hecht *Cy Watson* ■ *Dir* Talia Shire • *Scr* Marty Casella

One Night Stand ★★ 18

Romantic drama 1997 · US · Colour · 98mins

After the superb *Leaving Las Vegas*, director Mike Figgis took a misstep with this annoying drama about 1990s relationships and how one indiscretion can change the course of your life forever. The characters who swap beds and partners (Wesley Snipes, Nastassja Kinski, Kyle MacLachlan and Wen Ming-Na) are all unlikeable and annoying. Only Robert Downey Jr – as Snipes's dying friend – emerges unscathed, delivering a believable and meaningful performance. JB. Contains violence, swearing and sex scenes. DVD

Wesley Snipes *Max Carlyle* • Nastassja Kinski *Karen* • Kyle MacLachlan *Vernon* • Wen Ming-Na [Ming-Na] *Mimi Carlyle* • Robert Downey Jr *Charlie* ■ *Dir/Scr* Mike Figgis

One Night with You ★★ U

Musical comedy 1948 · UK · BW · 92mins

An Italian tenor and movie star, played by Italian tenor and movie star Nino Martini, and an English girl (Patricia Roc) meet on a station. While he rescues her dog from a fight, his bags are stolen, they miss their trains, and experience a night of adventures and mishaps before reaching their destination in Rome and a hearts-and-flowers denouement. This is occasionally diverting. RK

Nino Martini *Giulio Moris* • Patricia Roc *Mary Santell* • Bonar Colleano *Piero Santellini* • Hugh Wakefield *Santell* • Guy Middleton *Matty* • Stanley Holloway *Tramp* ■ *Dir* Terence Young • *Scr* Caryl Brahms, SJ Simon, from the film *Fuga a Due Voci* by Carlo Ludovico Bragaglia

One of Her Own ★★ 12

Drama based on a true story
1994 · US · Colour · 87mins

A made-for-TV police drama in which rookie officer Lori Loughlin is raped by colleague Greg Evigan, wrecking her career and turning her from victim into "villain" when she reports the incident. Martin Sheen adds some gravitas as the local Assistant DA and *Die Hard* fans will recognise Bruce Willis's ally Reginald VelJohnson. AT. Contains violence. DVD

Lori Loughlin *Toni Shroud* • Martin Sheen *Assistant DA Pete Maresca* • Greg Evigan *Charlie Lloyd* • Reginald VelJohnson *Detective Bob Hymes* • Valerie Landsburg *Stacy Schoep* ■ *Dir* Armand Mastroianni • *Scr* Valerie West

One of Our Aircraft Is Missing ★★★ U

Second World War drama
1942 · UK · BW · 102mins

This is an exciting enough Second World War adventure, as the crew of a crashed Wellington bomber attempts to evade Nazi patrols and reach home. Directors Michael Powell and Emeric Pressburger are more successful at re-creating the bomber raid and its spectacular crash than they are at capturing an authentic Dutch atmosphere. It's a classic example of the way in which fictional stories were given a documentary style in order to increase their propaganda impact, and the script received an Oscar nomination. However, the film looks rather dated now. DP

Godfrey Tearle *Sir George Corbett* • Eric Portman *Tom Earnshaw* • Hugh Williams *Frank Shelley* • Bernard Miles *Geoff Hickman* • Hugh Burden *John Glyn Haggard* • Emrys Jones *Bob Ashley* • Pamela Brown *Els Meertens* • Googie Withers *Jo de Vries* ■ *Dir/Scr* Michael Powell, Emeric Pressburger

One of Our Dinosaurs Is Missing ★★★ U

Comedy 1975 · US · Colour · 90mins

In this offering from Disney, a top secret formula is hidden by aristocrat Derek Nimmo inside the skeleton of a dinosaur at the Natural History Museum in London. There's not even a sniff of a velociraptor, but there is Peter Ustinov as a Chinese agent and Helen Hayes leading a gang of nannies that even Mary Poppins would be hard-pressed to join. A couple of kung fu fights, a very silly car chase and some wildly over-the-top acting help liven things up. DP DVD

Peter Ustinov *Hnup Wan* • Helen Hayes *Hettie* • Clive Revill *Quon* • Derek Nimmo *Lord Southmere* • Joan Sims *Emily* • Bernard Bresslaw *Fan Choy* • Natasha Pyne *Susan* • Roy Kinnear *Superintendent Grubbs* • Joss Ackland *BJ Spence* ■ *Dir* Robert Stevenson • *Scr* Bill Walsh, from the novel *The Great Dinosaur Robbery* by David Forrest

One of Our Spies Is Missing ★★★ U

Spy adventure 1966 · US · Colour · 91mins

The Man from UNCLE TV series began as a spoof of James Bond but took off with a life – albeit a mechanical one – of its own. This is one of the classier feature outings, with Robert Vaughn as indomitable Napoleon Solo and David McCallum as impassive Illya Kuryakin in an adventure that lives up to its title and to the series' hallmarks of well-groomed suspense and jingly music. Nostalgia buffs should have a ball with all those bouffant hairdos and the snappy stylised editing. TH

Robert Vaughn *Napoleon Solo* • David McCallum *Illya Kuryakin* • Leo G Carroll *Mr Waverly* • Vera Miles *Madame de Sala* • Maurice Evans *Sir Norman Swickert* • Ann Elder *Joanna Sweet* • Bernard Fox *Jordin* • Dolores Faith *Lorelei Lancer* • Anna Capri [Ahna Capri] *Do Do* • Harry Davis *Alexander Gritsky* • Yvonne Craig *Wanda* ■ *Dir* E Darrell Hallenbeck • *Scr* Howard Rodman, from a story by Henry Slesar

One of the Hollywood Ten ★★

Historical drama
2000 · UK/Sp · Colour · 110mins

Fear of the Red Menace prompted Senator Joseph McCarthy and his Hollywood acolytes to organise a blacklist in the early years of the Cold War. Among its victims was politically committed director Herbert Biberman, and his story is related in this impassioned, but somewhat strained drama. It doesn't help that neither Jeff Goldblum nor Greta Scacchi is comfortably cast as Biberman and his actress wife, Gale Sondergaard. DP

Jeff Goldblum *Herbert Biberman* • Greta Scacchi *Gale Sondergaard* • Angela Molina *Rosaura Revueltas* • Christopher Fulford *Riffkind* • John Sessions *Paul Jarrico* • Peter Bowles *Jack Warner* • Geraint Wyn Davies *Michael Wilson* • Sean Chapman *Edward Dmytryk* ■ *Dir/Scr* Karl Francis

One of Those Things ★★

Thriller 1970 · Den · Colour · 86mins

This bitter little film has little or nothing to say, and spends almost an hour and a half saying it. Ostensibly, it's a grim parable on how easily a cosy middle-class existence can be reduced to rubble by forces which it doesn't understand and can't control. Roy Dotrice gives a nice impression of the smug businessman whose vulnerability is cruelly exposed by scheming Judy Geeson after he covers up a hit-and-run accident. DP

Roy Dotrice *Henrik Vinther* • Judy Geeson *Susanne Strauss* • Zena Walker *Berit Vinther* • Frederick Jaeger *Melchior* • Ann Firbank *Sonja Melchior* • Geoffrey Chater *Falck* • Henry Okawa *Kawasaki* • Yvette Dotrice *Charlotte Vinther* ■ *Dir* Erik Balling • *Scr* Erik Balling, Anders Bodelsen, David Hohnen, Jesse Lasky Jr, from the novel *Hit and Run, Run, Run.* by Anders Bodelsen

One of Us ★★★★ U

Drama 1989 · Is · Colour · 110mins

This perceptive insight into the Middle East conflict brings home with some force the realisation that, for all the efforts of the politicians, peace depends on the actions of committed men whose convictions and loyalties do not always coincide with the greater good. Sharon Alexander gives an impressive performance as the army investigator who discovers that those suspected of the murder of an Arab are brothers in arms, his dilemma made all the more credible by the persuasive playing of Alon Aboutboul as the friend he must betray. DP. In Hebrew with English subtitles. Contains violence and some nudity.

Alon Aboutboul *Yotam* • Sharon Alexander *Rafa* • Dan Toren *Amir* • Dahlia Shimko *Tamar* • Arnon Tzadok *The Colonel* ■ *Dir* Uri Barbash • *Scr* Benny Barbash, from his play

One on One ★★ 15

Sports drama 1977 · US · Colour · 93mins

Having acted since the age of three, Robby Benson was twenty when he co-wrote and starred in this saga about college basketball, playing the blue-eyed nerd who becomes the champ. Two students fall head over heels in love with him – Annette O'Toole and Gail Strickland – and there's also Melanie Griffith in a minor supporting role. Drama is provided by GD Spradlin as the college coach who drives his athletes like a sadist. AT

Robby Benson *Henry Steele* • Annette O'Toole *Janet Hays* • GD Spradlin *Coach Moreland Smith* • Gail Strickland *BJ Rudolph* • Melanie Griffith *Hitchhiker* • James G Richardson *Malcolm* ■ *Dir* Lamont Johnson • *Scr* Robby Benson, Jerry Segal

One Plus One ★★ 15

Experimental documentary drama
1968 · UK · Colour · 96mins

Intended for large audiences because of the presence of the Rolling Stones, this turned out to be one of Jean-Luc Godard's most cryptic, fragmentary and irritating works. The Stones rehearsing their song *Sympathy for the Devil* in a recording studio is intercut with shots of a black man reading anticolonial texts, as well as a girl (Anne Wiazemsky, for whom Godard had left his wife Anna Karina) contemplating suicide when her boyfriend joins the Black Panther movement. After Iain Quarrier, one of the performers in the film, added a complete recording of the Stones' number at the end, he was attacked by the director at the 1968 London Film Festival. RB

Anne Wiazemsky *Eve Democracy* • Iain Quarrier *Bookman* • Frankie Dymon Jr *Black Power militant* • Sean Lynch *Narrator* ■ *Dir/Scr* Jean-Luc Godard

One Potato, Two Potato ★★★

Drama 1964 · US · BW · 89mins

This drama could have been quite a hot potato, made at a time of racial unrest in America and telling a story of a mixed romance that leads to marriage. The relationship is treated as utterly normal until the woman's former husband enters the frame, inciting a bitter dispute over the custody of their child. While a starry cast might have paid dividends at the box-office, the unknowns give this liberal film added authenticity, even though the Oscar-nominated script does lapse into sentimentality. AT

Barbara Barrie *Julie Cullen Richards* • Bernie Hamilton *Frank Richards* • Richard Mulligan *Joe Cullen* • Harry Bellaver *Judge Powell* • Marti Mericka *Ellen Mary* ■ *Dir* Larry Peerce • *Scr* Raphael Hayes, Orville H Hampton, from a story by Orville H Hampton

One Rainy Afternoon ★★★ U

Romantic comedy 1936 · US · BW · 80mins

This typical 1930s romance bears as much relevance to "real luv" as Ida Lupino to your average gal. But it works, with a deft combination of slick script, daft idea cleverly executed and wonderful light performances from all concerned. An innocuous kiss causes a major stir in Paris and sets the assembled company on a helter-skelter ride of rearranged lives. Lupino has a luminous screen presence. SH

Francis Lederer *Philippe Martin* • Ida Lupino *Monique Pelerin* • Hugh Herbert *Toto* • Roland Young *Maillot* • Erik Rhodes *Count Alfredo Donstelli* • Joseph Cawthorn *Mr Pelerin* •

Countess Liev de Maigret *Yvonne* • Donald Meek *Judge* ■ *Dir* Rowland V Lee • *Scr* Stephen Morehouse Avery, Maurice Hanline, from the film *Monsieur Sans-Gêne* by Emeric Pressburger, from the film by René Pujol

One Romantic Night ★

Romantic drama 1930 · US · BW · 73mins

Lillian Gish made her talking picture debut in this stumbling adaptation about a young aristocratic girl being groomed for marriage to a prince. The film, which co-stars a wooden Rod La Rocque, a ridiculously mannered Conrad Nagel and Marie Dressler doing battle with the script, went through three directors – George Fitzmaurice, Harry D'Abbadie D'Arrast and Paul L Stein (the only one credited) – only to emerge as a stilted bore. RK

Lillian Gish *Alexandra* • Rod La Rocque *Prince Albert* • Conrad Nagel *Dr Nicholas Haller* • Marie Dressler *Princess Beatrice* • OP Heggie *Father Benedict* • Albert Conti *Count Lutzen* • Edgar Norton *Col Wunderlich* ■ *Dir* Paul L Stein • *Scr* Melville Baker, from the play *The Swan* by Ferenc Molnar

One Single Night ★★★

Drama 1939 · Swe · BW · 90mins

Reunited with Gustaf Molander, the director who had done so much to make her a star in films such as *Intermezzo*, Ingrid Bergman gives a polished performance in this mildly shocking drama of illegitimacy and pre-marital sex. Bergman plays the ward of an aristocrat who has just discovered that he has an illegitimate son who has been raised by circus folk. The problem facing son Edvin Adolphson is whether to opt for romance with the well heeled Bergman or stay true to circus owner Aino Taube. The cross-class themes and the romantic interludes are handled with a sure touch by Molander. DP. In Swedish with English subtitles.

Ingrid Bergman *Eva Beckman* • Edvin Adolphson *Valdemar Moreaux* • Aino Taube *Helga Martenson* • Olof Sandborg *Colonel Magnus Von Brede* ■ *Dir* Gustaf Molander • *Scr* Gösta Stevens, from the story *En Eneste Natt* by Harald Tandrup

One Sings, the Other Doesn't ★★★

Drama 1976 · Fr/Bel/Cur · Colour · 120mins

Meeting in 1962, when student Valérie Mairesse helps single mother-of-two Thérèse Liotard terminate an unwanted pregnancy, the pair reunite a decade later to discover the former is fronting a radical all-girl band (awful songs!), while the latter works in a family planning clinic. As the shifting emotional and political attitudes suggest, this is an impartial film designed for the common woman, not critics and feminists, who detested it. DP. In French with English subtitles.

Valérie Mairesse *Pauline "Pomme"* • Thérèse Liotard *Suzanne* • Ali Raffi *Darius* • Jean-Pierre Pellegrin *Dr Pierre Aubanel* • Robert Dadies *Jérôme* ■ *Dir/Scr* Agnès Varda

One Special Night ★★★

Seasonal drama 1999 · US · Colour · 87mins

A simple premise – a man and a woman are stranded in a snowstorm on Thanksgiving, spend the night learning about each other and form an important friendship – becomes a moving TV movie thanks to the accomplished performances of James Garner and Julie Andrews. This is subtly directed by Roger Young and never descends into the mushiness you might expect from such a plot. The cast is uniformly good, but the real pleasure comes from watching the two leads go through their paces. JB

James Garner *Robert* • Julie Andrews *Catherine* • Patricia Charbonneau *Lori* • Stacy Grant *Jaclyn* • Stewart Bick *Jeff* ■ *Dir* Roger Young • *Scr* Nancey Silvers, from the play *A Winter Visitor* by Jan Hartman

One Spy Too Many ★★ PG

Spy adventure 1966 · US · Colour · 97mins

One of a number of features spun-off from the hit TV series *The Man from UNCLE* to be released in the 1960s, this lazy effort comprises situations from previously aired episodes and the result is most unsatisfactory. Robert Vaughn and David McCallum have the film stolen from under their noses by the excellent Rip Torn, who throws restraint to the winds. There are some hilarious dices with death along the way, but it's far too long for a cut-and-paste job. DP DVD

Robert Vaughn *Napoleon Solo* • David McCallum *Illya Kuryakin* • Rip Torn *Alexander* • Dorothy Provine *Tracey Alexander* • Leo G Carroll *Mr Waverly* • Yvonne Craig *Maude Waverly* ■ *Dir* Joseph Sargent • *Scr* Dean Hargrove

One Summer Love ★ 15

Romantic drama 1975 · US · Colour · 93mins

Also known as *Dragonfly*, this is a stinker under any name. Gilbert Cates directs this worn-out romantic tale about the relationship between a man recently released from a mental asylum and a young woman who works at a cinema. Despite Beau Bridges and Susan Sarandon giving it their all, this never engages, enthralls or amuses at any point in the proceedings. JB [video]

Beau Bridges *Jesse Arlington* • Susan Sarandon *Chloe* • Mildred Dunnock *Mrs Barrow* • Michael B Miller *Gabriel Arlington* • Linda Miller *Willa Arlington* • Martin Burke *Lonnie Arlington* • James Otis *Clifford* • James Noble *Dr Leo Cooper* ■ *Dir* Gilbert Cates • *Scr* N Richard Nash

The One That Got Away ★★★ U

Second World War drama
1957 · UK · BW · 106mins

A swaggering Hardy Kruger is excellent as Franz von Werra, the Luftwaffe pilot who not only escaped from several camps in this country, but who also absconded from Canada and crossed America in his bid to rejoin his outfit. Directed at a fair clip by Roy Baker, this true-life tale is more notable for its fair-minded approach than for its thrills, but still delivers the occasional exciting moment. DP [video] DVD

Hardy Kruger *Franz von Werra* • Colin Gordon *Army interrogator* • Michael Goodliffe *RAF interrogator* • Terence Alexander *RAF intelligence officer* • Jack Gwillim *Commandant at Grizedale* • Andrew Faulds *Lieutenant at Grizedale* • Alec McCowen *Duty Officer Hucknall* ■ *Dir* Roy Baker [Roy Ward Baker] • *Scr* Howard Clewes, from a book by Kendal Burt, James Leasor

One Third of a Nation ★★★

Drama 1939 · US · BW · 71mins

Wealthy New Yorker Leif Erikson helps a young boy who has escaped from a fire in a slum tenement fire and falls in love with the boy's sister. Sylvia Sidney, in her final film under her Paramount contract, stars as the girl; future director Sidney Lumet, in his only screen appearance, is the young boy. The screenplay was adapted from the controversial Broadway drama produced by the Works Progress Administration Federal Theater Project – part of President Franklin Roosevelt's New Deal – and places more emphasis on the love story than the horrors of slum conditions. It is nevertheless an affecting piece of social commentary. The title comes from Roosevelt's declaration that one third of Americans were inadequately housed. RK

Sylvia Sidney *Mary Rogers* • Leif Erikson *Peter Cortlant* • Myron McCormick *Sam Noon* • Hiram Sherman *Donald Hinchley* • Sidney Lumet *Joey Rogers* ■ *Dir* Dudley Murphy • *Scr* Oliver HP Garrett, Dudley Murphy, from the play by Arthur Arent

One Touch of Venus ★★★ U

Comedy fantasy 1948 · US · BW · 81mins

This is the movie where the love goddess herself, Ava Gardner, plays *the* love goddess, Venus, and comes to life for 24 hours on a window dresser's kiss. Gardner is fabulous: sexy, alluring, warm and womanly, and more than a match for feeble, miscast Robert Walker. The direction by William A Seiter isn't up to much, though, and neither are the production values. TS

Ava Gardner *Venus* • Robert Walker *Eddie Hatch* • Dick Haymes *Joe Grant* • Eve Arden *Molly* • Olga San Juan *Gloria* • Tom Conway *Whitfield Savory* ■ *Dir* William A Seiter • *Scr* Harry Kurnitz, Frank Tashlin, from the musical play by Kurt Weill, SJ Perelman, Ogden Nash, from the novel *The Tinted Venus* by F Anstey

One Tough Cop ★

Police drama 1998 · US · Colour · 90mins

A clunky crime drama "inspired" by the life of renegade NYPD cop Bo Dietl, as played with Neanderthal stoicism by Stephen Baldwin. Together with his heavy-gambling partner Duke Finnerty (Chris Penn), Dietl busts up an ethnic hostage crisis and uses his Mob connections to investigate the murder of a nun. (It was the latter brand of controversial policing that led to Bietl's enforced retirement at 35.) Cliché-ridden and generic to a fault. AJ

Stephen Baldwin *Bo Dietl* • Chris Penn *Duke Finnerty* • Mike McGlone *Rickie La Cassa* • Gina Gershon *Joey O'Hara* • Christopher Bregman *Gang Banger No 1* • Mike Santana *Gang Banger No 2* • Amy Irving *FBI Agent Jean Devlin* ■ *Dir* Bruno Barreto • *Scr* Jeremy Iacone, from the book *One Tough Cop: The Bo Dietl Story* by Bo Dietl, Ken Gross

One-Trick Pony ★★★ 15

Musical drama 1980 · US · Colour · 98mins

Paul Simon stars as a failing rock singer, facing up to an uncertain future after 14 years on the road, in this unusually harsh look at the realities of being a pop performer. Semi-autobiographical in the way it clearly reflects his post Simon and Garfunkel feelings, Simon fans will relish the ten new songs written for his vanity production even if they don't like his caustic screenplay. Vintage sets from Sam and Dave, the Lovin' Spoonful and the B52s, make this bitter pill easier to swallow. AJ. Contains swearing and nudity. [video]

Paul Simon *Jonah* • Blair Brown *Marion* • Rip Torn *Walter Fox* • Joan Hackett *Lonnie Fox* • [Allen Garfield] *Cal Van Damp* • Mare Winningham *Modeena Dandridge* • Michael Pearlman *Matty Levin* • Lou Reed *Steve Kunelian* ■ *Dir* Robert M Young • *Scr* Paul Simon

One True Love ★★

Romantic comedy drama
2000 · US · Colour · 96mins

You won't know whether to laugh or cry while watching this cornball TV romance. It's love at first sight when fireman David Hasselhoff rescues vet Terry Farrell from a blazing car. But how are they going to live happily ever after when they don't know each other's names? Moreover, they're both engaged to be married. Director Lorraine Senna lashes on the sentimental clichés with shameless assurance. DP

David Hasselhoff *Mike Grant* • Terry Farrell *Dana Boyer* • Paget Brewster *Tina* • Cameron Finley *Corey* • Karl Pruner *Phil Davis* • Doris Roberts *Lillian* ■ *Dir* Lorraine Senna [Lorraine Senna Ferrara] • *Scr* Richard Leder

One True Thing ★★★ 15

Drama 1998 · US · Colour · 122mins

Get those hankies out for this family weepie, which earned Meryl Streep an Oscar nomination. She's the cancer-stricken mum whom daughter Renee Zellweger comes home to look after, even though the pair have never got along. Rounding out the family are William Hurt, as Renee's revered father, and Tom Everett Scott as her brother, but it is Streep who steals every scene and wrings tears you didn't know you had out of you. Subtly handled by actor-turned-director Carl Franklin. JB [video] DVD

Meryl Streep *Kate Gulden* • Renee Zellweger *Ellen Gulden* • William Hurt *George Gulden* • Tom Everett Scott *Brian Gulden* • Lauren Graham *Jules* • Nicky Katt *Jordan Belzer* • James Eckhouse *District attorney* ■ *Dir* Carl Franklin • *Scr* Karen Croner, from the novel by Anna Quindlen

One, Two, Three ★★★★ U

Political comedy 1961 · US · BW · 103mins

If you count the punchlines per minute, this has to be one of the fastest, talkiest comedies ever made. Billy Wilder's satire never lets up and gives James Cagney his finest role for many years. Cagney plays a combustible Coca-Cola executive in West Berlin, desperate to improve sales at any cost, while his boss's visiting daughter falls for a communist named Piffl, played by Horst Buchholz. While some may find Wilder's scattershot approach a trifle obvious – capitalism and communism are both subjected to ridicule – it remains, like *Dr Strangelove*, a key product of the Cold War, when some things were just too serious to take seriously. AT [video] DVD

James Cagney *CR MacNamara* • Horst Buchholz *Otto Ludwig Piffl* • Pamela Tiffin *Scarlett Hazeltine* • Arlene Francis *Phyllis MacNamara* • Lilo Pulver [Liselotte Pulver] *Ingeborg* • Howard St John *Hazeltine* • Hanns Lothar *Schlemmer* • Lois Bolton *Mrs Hazeltine* • Leon Askin *Peripetchikoff* • Peter Capell *Mishkin* • Ralf Wolter *Borodenko* ■ *Dir* Billy Wilder • *Scr* Billy Wilder, IAL Diamond, from the play *Egy, Ketto, Harom* by Ferenc Molnar

O

One Way Out ★ U

Thriller 1955 · UK · BW · 61mins

John Chandos plays the ruthless jewel thief who blackmails Eddie Byrne's veteran police superintendent into dropping his investigations by implicating the cop's daughter, Jill Adams, in a robbery.The writing, acting and staging are weak in this B-thriller. AE

Jill Adams *Shirley Harcourt* • Eddie Byrne *Superintendent Harcourt* • Lyndon Brook *Leslie Parrish* • John Chandos *Danvers* • Arthur Lowe *Sam* ■ *Dir* Francis Searle • *Scr* Jonathan Roche, from story by John Temple-Smith, Jean Scott-Rogers

One Way Out ★★ 15

Crime drama 2002 · Can · Colour · 94mins

This TV-movie thriller's intriguing premise is frittered away by sloppy writing and injudicious casting. James Belushi is suitably self-absorbed as a cop whose addiction to gambling leaves him in thrall to a pair of club-owning mobsters. But things start to unravel when they suggest that Belushi pays off his debts by helping the hopelessly miscast Jason Bateman bump off his wife. DP. Contains sex scenes, swearing, violence. [video] DVD

James Belushi *Harry Woltz* • Angela Featherstone *Gwen Buckley* • Jason Bateman *John Farrow* • Guylaine St-Onge [Guylaine St Onge] *Evans Farrow* • Angelo Tsarouchas *Mickey Russell* ■ *Dir* Allan A Goldstein • *Scr* John Salvati

One Way Passage ★★★★

Romantic drama 1932 · US · BW · 68mins

Aboard an ocean liner homeward bound for the United States, William Powell (returning to face a murder charge) and Kay Francis (suffering from an incurable illness) enjoy a necessarily short-lived love affair. Very short, poignantly sweet, and discreetly directed by Tay Garnett, this is the kind of romantic drama redolent of 1930s Hollywood which, at its best, is involving and effective. Enhanced by Frank McHugh and Aline MacMahon as a pair of confidence tricksters (apparently an obligatory feature of Hollywood passenger lists), the movie won the Oscar for Robert Lord's original story. RK

William Powell *Dan Hardesty* • Kay Francis *Joan Ames* • Frank McHugh *Skippy* • Aline MacMahon *Betty the countess* • Warren Hymer *Steve Burke* • Frederick Burton *Doctor* ■ *Dir* Tay Garnett • *Scr* Wilson Mizner, Joseph Jackson, from a story by Robert Lord

One Way Pendulum ★★★ U

Comedy 1965 · UK · BW · 85mins

While Eric Sykes constructs a model of the Old Bailey in the living room, his son Jonathan Miller teaches his collection of I-Speak-Your-Weight machines to sing. The rest of the family are equally strange in this movie adaptation of NF Simpson's surreal stage play, which climaxes in a do-it-yourself murder trial organised by Sykes. The theatre production was a triumph of bizarre nonsense but the film never quite captures its spirit. DF

Eric Sykes *Mr Groomkirby* • George Cole *Defense Counsel/Friend* • Julia Foster *Sylvia* • Jonathan Miller *Kirby* • Peggy Mount *Mrs Gantry* • Alison Leggatt *Mrs Groomkirby* • Mona Washbourne *Aunt Mildred* ■ *Dir* Peter Yates • *Scr* NF Simpson, from his play

One Way Street ★★

Crime drama 1950 · US · BW · 79mins

A curious attempt to create a fatalistic crime drama is made all the more pretentious by the casting of the saturnine James Mason as the disillusioned doctor who double-crosses Dan Duryea's gang boss. He tries to make a new life in a primitive Mexican village but, of course, can't escape his past. Swedish actress Marta Toren plays the gangster's lover who deserts him for Mason. AE

James Mason *Doc Matson* • Marta Toren *Laura* • Dan Duryea *Wheeler* • William Conrad *Ollie* • King Donovan *Grieder* • Jack Elam *Arnie* • Tito Renaldo *Hank Torres* • Rock Hudson *Truck driver* ■ *Dir* Hugo Fregonese • *Scr* Lawrence Kimble, from his story *Death on a Side Street*

One Week ★★★★ U

Silent comedy 1920 · US · Colour · 17mins

Blissful mayhem for Buster Keaton fans as honeymooners Keaton and Sybil Sealey are given a home to assemble, only to watch it go cock-eyed because a rival to Buster has changed the numbers on the home components. The result is a lop-sided structure which gets swept away by an oncoming train. A tad mechanical, but it has some ground-breaking gags, most of which are still used by comedians today. TH

Buster Keaton *Newlywed husband* • Sybil Seeley *Newlywed wife* • Joe Roberts *Piano mover* ■ *Dir/Scr* Buster Keaton, Eddie Cline [Edward Cline]

One Woman's Courage ★★★ 15

Thriller 1994 · US · Colour · 86mins

The excellent Patty Duke stars in a laudable attempt to combine adultery, alcoholism, stalking and grievous bodily harm in one woman's rather hectic life. Margot Kidder appears in a cast which also includes the usually reliable James Farentino. If there is a soupçon too much going on, it is at least a TV movie which covers up any slack in the script. SH DVD

Patty Duke *Grace McKenna* • James Farentino *Lt Bill Lawson* • Keith Szarabajka *Wallace Bremer* • Margot Kidder *Stella Jenson* • Dennis Farina *Craig McKenna* ■ *Dir* Charles Robert Carner • *Scr* John Steven Owen

Onegin ★★★ 12

Period romantic drama
1999 · UK/US · Colour · 106mins

Ralph Fiennes is directed by his sister Martha in this ponderous adaptation of Pushkin's classic. Fiennes is well cast as Evgeny Onegin, a decadent, dissipated aristocrat who moves to his recently deceased uncle's estate in rural Russia. There he proceeds to devastate the lives of all around him, rejecting the advances of the luscious Liv Tyler and driving bumpkin Toby Stephens into a deadly duel. Though beautifully shot, this desperately needs pace, and the endless shots of Ralph's face show more sisterly devotion than emotion. LH. Contains a violent scene. DVD

Ralph Fiennes *Evgeny Onegin* • Liv Tyler *Tatyana Larin* • Toby Stephens *Vladimir Lensky* • Lena Headey *Olga Larin* • Martin Donovan (2) *Prince Nikitin* • Alun Armstrong *Zaretsky* • Harriet Walter *Madame Larina* • Irene Worth *Princess Alina* • Francesca Annis *Katiusha* ■ *Dir* Martha Fiennes • *Scr* Peter Ettedgui, Michael Ignatieff, from the novel *Eugene Onegin* by Alexander Pushkin

Ong-Bak ★★★★ 18

Martial arts action adventure
2003 · Thai · Colour · 108mins

Described as "the new Bruce Lee", Thai fighter Tony Jaa makes his movie debut in this back-to-basics martial arts outing that boasts the total absence of CGI and wirework. Jaa, who does all his own stunts, stars as a country bumpkin sent to Bangkok to retrieve his village's Buddha statue, which has been stolen and handed over to a big-city gangster. What sketchy plot there is matters little since it's the sheer spectacle of Jaa's astonishing muay thai skills that really takes the breath away. Despite the threadbare production values and questionable acting, this game of death is a gleeful throwback to the days when Bruce Lee was the only person wearing a yellow jump suit. JR. In Thai and English with subtitles. Contains violence and drug abuse.

Tony Jaa *Ting* • Petchthai Wongkamlao *George* • Pumwaree Yodkamol *Muay Lek* • Rungrawee Borrijindakul *Ngek* • Chetwut Wacharakun *Peng* • Wannakit Siriput *Don* • Sukhaaw Phongwilai *Khom Tuan* ■ *Dir* Prachya Pinkaew • *Scr* Suphachai Sittiaumponpan, from a story by Prachya Pinkaew, Panna Rittikrai

Onibaba ★★★ 15

Horror 1964 · Jpn · BW · 98mins

Set during the 16th-century Japanese civil wars, this cult favourite focuses on the tensions that arise when widow Jitsuko Yoshimura defies mother-in-law Nobuko Otowa by flirting with a neighbour and jeopardising their livelihood – the sale of armour stripped from murdered samurai. This is a frankly erotic and often hysterically acted tale, which director Kaneto Shindo clearly intended as an allegory on the modern world. However, it works best as a disturbing study of ruthless survivalism and supernatural punishment. DP. In Japanese with English subtitles.

Nobuko Otowa *Mother* • Jitsuko Yoshimura *Daughter-in-law* • Kei Sato *Hachi, farmer* • Jukichi Uno *Warrior* ■ *Dir/Scr* Kaneto Shindo

The Onion Field ★★★ 18

Police drama 1979 · US · Colour · 121mins

Cop-turned novelist-Joseph Wambaugh was so upset by the way *The Choirboys* was turned into a movie, he had complete control over this script based on a real-life case in 1963 when two small-time hoods kidnap two cops and murder one of them in an onion field. As a documentary-style record of police procedure and the fallibility of the legal system this is a gripping and disturbing movie, powerfully acted by John Savage as the surviving cop who quits the force to become a gardener and by Franklyn Seales and James Woods as the killers. AT

John Savage *Karl Hettinger* • James Woods *Gregory Powell* • Franklyn Seales *Jimmy Smith* • Ted Danson *Ian Campbell* • Priscilla Pointer *Chrissie Campbell* • Ronny Cox *Pierce Brooks* • David Huffman *DA Phil Halpin* • Christopher Lloyd *Jailhouse lawyer* ■ *Dir* Harold Becker • *Scr* Joseph Wambaugh, from his novel

Onionhead ★★

Comedy 1958 · US · BW · 96mins

Following the box-office success of *No Time for Sergeants*, Warner Bros pushed Andy Griffith into military service again, casting him as a cook, third class, aboard the USS *Periwinkle*, docked at Boston. On the run from one love affair, Griffith drops anchor with a decidedly promiscuous barfly, Felicia Farr, and jousts regularly with the ship's chief cook, a permanently sozzled Walter Matthau, who is the best thing in the movie. AT

Andy Griffith *Al Woods* • Felicia Farr *Stella* • Walter Matthau *"Red" Wildoe* • Erin O'Brien *Jo Hill* • Joe Mantell *"Doc" O'Neal* • Ray Danton *Ensign Dennis Higgins* • James Gregory *"The Skipper"* • Joey Bishop *Gutsell* ■ *Dir* Norman Taurog • *Scr* Nelson Gidding, from the novel by Weldon Hill

Only Angels Have Wings ★★★★★ U

Drama 1939 · US · BW · 115mins

One of the greatest films from the most memorable year in cinema history, overlooked at the time as a simple action adventure but now recognised as a superb study of grace under pressure. This Howard Hawks movie about a civil airline taking mail and freight over the treacherous Andes contains all of producer/director Hawks's key themes and some of his finest sequences, and boasts a splendid cast headed by hard-bitten Cary Grant and chirpy Jean Arthur. They are superbly backed by Rita Hayworth as a vamp and Richard Barthelmess as a disgraced flier. This is great cinema: supremely entertaining, mature storytelling. TS

Cary Grant *Geoff Carter* • Jean Arthur *Bonnie Lee* • Richard Barthelmess *Bat McPherson* • Rita Hayworth *Judith McPherson* • Thomas Mitchell *Kid Dabb* • Sig Rumann [Sig Ruman] *Dutchman* • Victor Killian [Victor Kilian] *Sparks* ■ *Dir* Howard Hawks • *Scr* Jules Furthman, from a story by Howard Hawks

The Only Game in Town ★★★

Drama 1970 · US · Colour · 113mins

And that game is love, if you can believe a word of this rather talky story of the love affair between chorus girl Elizabeth Taylor and gambling piano player Warren Beatty. The actors give it all they've got, and director George Stevens, making his last film, convincingly sets up the Las Vegas location as a place of glamour and sleaze, but it never quite involves. TH

Elizabeth Taylor *Fran Walker* • Warren Beatty *Joe Grady* • Charles Braswell *Thomas Lockwood* • Hank Henry *Tony* • Olga Valery *Woman with purple wig* ■ *Dir* George Stevens • *Scr* Frank D Gilroy, from his play

Only Human ★★★ 15

Romantic comedy
2004 · Sp/UK/Arg/Por · Colour · 89mins

This light and fast-paced comedy centres on a chaotic Jewish household in Madrid into which one of the family's daughters introduces her Palestinian partner. When a tub of frozen soup hurtles from the family's high-rise apartment and strikes a pedestrian, whether or not this is a "murder" that requires covering up elevates the near-slapstick farce. Sure-footed performances and immaculate comic timing make the most of a snappy script, but it gets a little predictable towards the end. KK. In Spanish with English subtitles. Contains swearing.

Norma Aleandro *Gloria Dalinsky* • Guillermo Toledo *Rafi* • María Botto *Tania Dalinsky* • Marián Aguilera *Leni Dalinsky* • Fernando Ramallo *David Dalinsky* • Max Berliner *Dudu Dalinsky* • Alba Molinero *Paula Dalinsky* • Mario Martín *Ernesto Dalinsky* ■ *Dir/Scr* Teresa de Pelegrí, Dominic Harari

The Only Son ★★★★

Drama 1936 · Jpn · BW · 103mins

Having demonstrated an intuitive mastery of silent technique, Yasujiro Ozu proved his sound credentials with this delicate, character-driven entry in the *shomin-geki* genre of lower middle-class dramas that would become his speciality. Chishu Ryu (an Ozu regular) is outstanding as the Tokyo teacher, who borrows a small fortune so he can prove to his doting small-town mother that the sacrifices she made for his education had all been worthwhile. DP. In Japanese with English subtitles.

Choko Iida *Otsune Nonomiya* • Shinichi Himori *Ryosuke, Otsune's son* • Masao Hayama *Ryosuke as a child* • Yoshiko Tsubouchi *Sugiko, Ryosuke's wife* ■ *Dir* Yasujiro Ozu • *Scr* Tadao Ikeda, Masao Arata, from a story by James Maki [Yasujiro Ozu]

Only the Brave ★★★ 15

Drama 1994 · Aus · Colour · 58mins

In keeping with many of the pictures produced in Australia during this period, Ana Kokkinos's coming-of-age drama deals with the frustrations experienced by an alienated urban youth. However, this featurette also has a lesbian agenda, as it traces the gradual disintegration of a close friendship after one of the girls realises the true nature of her feelings. Elena Mandalis cleverly conveys the confusions caused by the crushes on both her friend and her teacher, but the film is not always convincing in its portrayal either of Greek ethnicity or teenage disillusion. DP

Elena Mandalis *Alex* • Dora Kaskanis *Vicki* • Maude Davey *Kate Groves* • Helen Athanasiadis *Maria* • Tina Zerella *Sylvie* ■ *Dir* Ana Kokkinos • *Scr* Ana Kokkinos, Mira Robertson

Only the Lonely ★★★ 15

Romantic comedy
1991 · US · Colour · 100mins

Chris Columbus directs this understated little gem. It's a sweet, rather old-fashioned comedy about a shy policeman, John Candy, who falls for equally bashful mortician Ally Sheedy, much to the dismay of his overbearing mother, Maureen O'Hara. Although it occasionally lapses into sentimentality, it is sympathetically written and there are winning performances from the two leads. However, the film is all but stolen by O'Hara and that other veteran, Anthony Quinn. JF. Contains swearing.

John Candy *Danny Muldoon* • Maureen O'Hara *Rose Muldoon* • Ally Sheedy *Theresa Luna* • Kevin Dunn *Patrick Muldoon* • Milo O'Shea *Doyle Ryan* • Bert Remsen *Spats Shannon* •

Anthony Quinn *Nick Acropolis* • James Belushi *Sal Buonarte* • Macaulay Culkin *Billy* ■ *Dir/Scr* Chris Columbus

Only the Strong ★★ 15

Martial arts action drama
1993 · US · Colour · 92mins

An OK action thriller, this has martial-arts hero Mark Dacascos encouraged by his former teacher Geoffrey Lewis to instruct students in how to acquire self-discipline and battle the drug dealers infesting the high-school campus. The gimmick here is that Dacascos is a master of the Brazilian fighting skill *capoeira* – a sort of cross between kung fu and the lambada. Mild violence and samba music make this one an easy-listening no-brainer. AJ. Contains swearing.

Mark Dacascos *Louis Stevens* • Stacey Travis *Dianna* • Geoffrey Lewis *Kerrigan* • Paco Christian Prieto *Silverio* • Todd Susman *Cochran* ■ *Dir* Sheldon Lettich • *Scr* Sheldon Lettich, Luis Esteban

Only the Valiant ★★ PG

Western 1950 · US · BW · 104mins

Gregory Peck plays the cavalry commander whose harsh methods make him less than popular with his men, though everyone pulls together heroically when the Apaches gather at the mountain pass. This traditional, no-nonsense western gives Peck a decent role as the martinet, and the supporting cast includes many familiar faces. AT

Gregory Peck *Capt Richard Lance* • Barbara Payton *Cathy Eversham* • Ward Bond *Cpl Timothy Gilchrist* • Gig Young *Lt William Holloway* • Lon Chaney Jr *Trooper Kebussyan* • Neville Brand *Sgt Ben Murdock* • Jeff Corey *Joe Harmony* ■ *Dir* Gordon Douglas • *Scr* Edmund H North, Harry Brown, from the novel by Charles Marquis Warren

The Only Thrill ★★★ 15

Romantic drama
1997 · US · Colour · 103mins

In 1960s small-town America, Diane Keaton and Sam Shepard begin an illicit affair. Shepard, a second-hand shop owner with a comatose wife is attracted to widow Keaton and, ten years on, the two loners are still as linked to each other as Shepard's wife is to her life-support machine. Both leads are excellent, but director Peter Masterson misses opportunities to deal with illness and is loaded down with an unnecessary subplot involving the parallel relationship between Keaton and Shepard's kids. LH

Diane Keaton *Carol Fritzsimmons* • Sam Shepard *Reece McHenry* • Diane Lane *Katherine Fritzsimmons* • Robert Patrick *Tom McHenry* • Sharon Lawrence *Joleen Quillet* ■ *Dir* Peter Masterson • *Scr* Larry Ketron, from his play *The Trading Post*

Only Two Can Play ★★★★ PG

Comedy 1961 · UK · BW · 101mins

A misleading title because the players in this story of a would-be adulterous Welsh librarian (Peter Sellers) and his wannabe mistress (Mai Zetterling) also include Virginia Maskell as his dispirited wife and Richard Attenborough as the poet she flirts with. Adapted by Bryan Forbes from Kingsley Amis's *That Uncertain Feeling*, this small-town drama is played out as farce and makes its satirical points with comic deftness. That may be because Sellers is more than usually restrained and believable. TH

Peter Sellers *John Lewis* • Mai Zetterling *Elizabeth Gruffydd-Williams* • Virginia Maskell *Jean Lewis* • Richard Attenborough *Gareth Probert* • Kenneth Griffith *Iaeun Jenkins* • Maudie Edwards *Mrs Davies* • Frederick Piper *Davies* • Graham Stark *Hyman* • John Arnatt *Bill* • Sheila Manahan *Mrs Jenkins* • John Le Mesurier *Salter* ■ *Dir* Sidney Gilliat • *Scr* Bryan Forbes, from the novel *That Uncertain Feeling* by Kingsley Amis

Only When I Larf ★★★

Comedy 1968 · UK · Colour · 103mins

A jolly comedy about three confidence tricksters (Richard Attenborough, David Hemmings, Alexandra Stewart) who begin plotting against each other. The succession of scams, disguises and surprises is very entertaining and builds to a quadruple-cross (multiple double-crossing was very popular at the time). The production, in several glamorous locations, is amusingly trendy, in Swinging Sixties style, and Attenborough gives one of his most uninhibited comedy performances. DM

Richard Attenborough *Silas* • David Hemmings *Bob* • Alexandra Stewart *Liz* • Nicholas Pennell *Spencer* • Melissa Stribling *Diana* • Terence Alexander *Gee Gee Gray* • Edric Connor *Awana* • Clifton Jones *General Sakut* ■ *Dir* Basil Dearden • *Scr* John Salmon, from the novel by Len Deighton

Only When I Laugh ★★★ 15

Comedy drama 1981 · US · Colour · 114mins

This is a bittersweet Neil Simon comedy about a brilliant but boozy and self-destructive actress (Marsha Mason) striving to strike up a relationship with her teenage daughter (Kristy McNichol). Fine performances from the two leading ladies, and from support stars James Coco and Joan Hackett, as a failed gay actor and an ageing New York society beauty, respectively. DA

Marsha Mason *Georgia Hines* • Kristy McNichol *Polly* • James Coco *Jimmy Perino* • Joan Hackett *Toby Landau* • David Dukes *David Lowe* ■ *Dir* Glenn Jordan • *Scr* Neil Simon, from his play *The Gingerbread Lady*

Only Yesterday ★★★★

Romantic drama 1933 · US · BW · 106mins

During the First World War, innocent young Margaret Sullavan and a handsome lieutenant John Boles meet at a dance in Virginia and fall in love, but he is shipped to France before they can meet again. Pregnant with his child, she goes to live with her feminist aunt Billie Burke in New York, but when Boles returns he has forgotten her. Romantic soap opera to be sure but, as directed by genre specialist John M Stahl, of a superior kind. Sullavan, as ever, suffers with poignant dignity. RK

Margaret Sullavan *Mary Lane* • John Boles *James Stanton Emerson* • Edna May Oliver *Leona* • Billie Burke *Julia Warren* • Benita Hume *Phyllis Emerson* • Reginald Denny *Bob* • George Meeker *Dave Reynolds* • Marie Prevost *Amy* ■ *Dir* John M Stahl • *Scr* William Hurlbut, Arthur Richman, George O'Neill, from the novel *Briefe einer Unbekannten* by Stefan Zweig and the English-language translation *Letter from Unknown Woman* by Eden Paul, Cedar Paul, also inspired by the non-fiction book *Only Yesterday: an Informed History of the Nineteen-Twenties* by Frederick Lewis Allen

Only You ★★★ 15

Romantic comedy
1992 · US · Colour · 87mins

This romantic comedy features *St Elmo's Fire* brat-packer Andrew McCarthy as the shy bloke who finds himself lucking out when he falls for two different women – glamorous Kelly Preston and the more sensible, studious Helen Hunt. This is sweetly enjoyable, thanks to a witty script and nice performances from the cast. JB. Contains nudity,sexual situations.

Andrew McCarthy *Clifford Godfrey* • Kelly Preston *Amanda* • Helen Hunt *Claire* ■ *Dir* Betty Thomas • *Scr* Wayne Allan Rice

Only You ★★★★ PG

Romantic comedy
1994 · US · Colour · 103mins

Moonstruck director Norman Jewison successfully mines the same territory with this delicious "Cinderella Italian-style" romantic comedy. Following the prophecy of a childhood Ouija game, Pittsburgh schoolteacher Marisa Tomei runs out on her wedding and goes to Rome to find the man of her dreams. There she meets shoe salesman Robert Downey Jr, who may or may not fit the bill. The pairing of Tomei and Downey Jr works like a charm: both inject scintillating substance into an unashamedly lightweight affair through their winning chemistry. Billy Zane is also on hand to provide a neat twist in the tale, and the lush Italian scenery will have you changing your holiday plans. AJ DVD

Marisa Tomei *Faith Corvatch* • Robert Downey Jr *Peter Wright* • Bonnie Hunt *Kate* • Joaquim de Almeida *Giovanni* • Fisher Stevens *Larry* • Billy Zane *The false Damon Bradley* • Adam LeFevre *Damon Bradley* • John Benjamin Hickey *Dwayne* • Siobhan Fallon *Leslie* ■ *Dir* Norman Jewison • *Scr* Diane Drake

Ooh... You Are Awful ★★ PG

Comedy 1972 · UK · Colour · 92mins

No prizes will be handed out for guessing that this is a vehicle for the late Dick Emery. When Emery discovers his dead accountant has left the number of a safety deposit account tattooed to the derrière of several young models, he sets to with gusto. This is a McGill seaside postcard come to boozy, nudge-nudge, wink-wink life, and if that's to your taste then it belts along like a runaway Blackpool tram. SH DVD

Dick Emery *Charlie Tully* • Derren Nesbitt *Sid Sabbath* • Ronald Fraser *Reggie Campbell Peek* • Pat Coombs *Libby Niven* • William Franklyn *Arnold Van Cleef* • Cheryl Kennedy *Jo Mason* • Norman Bird *Warder Burke* • Liza Goddard *Liza Missenden Green* ■ *Dir* Cliff Owen • *Scr* John Warren, John Singer

Open All Night ★★

Drama 1934 · UK · BW · 61mins

An unusually ambitious little British "quota quickie", this gives Frank Vosper the kind of role associated with the German silent film tragedian Emil Jannings. As an elderly former Russian Grand Duke reduced to being night manager of a hotel, Vosper is given notice rather than the promotion he expected. Adding a dash of *Grand Hotel* melodrama, he sorts out some of the guests' problems on his final night. One of the better late works of pioneer director George Pearson. AE

Frank Vosper *Anton* • Margaret Vines *Elsie Warren* • Gillian Lind *Maysie* • Lewis Shaw *Bill Warren* • Leslie Perrins *Ranger* ■ *Dir* George Pearson • *Scr* Gerard Fairlie, from a play by John Chancellor

Open Doors ★★★★

Crime drama 1990 · It · Colour · 108mins

Adapted from Leonardo Sciascia's account of an actual court case that was heard in Sicily in the 1930s, Gianni Amelio's solemnly paced study of the quality of justice under the Fascist regime makes few dramatic concessions. However, impeccable performances and an oppressive sense of period ensure that it makes for compelling viewing. Realising that, far from being the "monster of Palermo", dedicated union official Ennio Fantastichini was driven to rape and multiple murder by his humiliating dismissal, liberal judge Gian Maria Volonté obdurately battles to save a victim of corruption and expediency from his self-willed fate. DP. In Italian with English subtitles.

Gian Maria Volonté *Vito Di Francesco* • Ennio Fantastichini *Tommaso Scalia* • Renzo Giovampietro *Judge Sanna* • Renato Carpentieri *Giovanni Consolo* • Tuccio Musumeci *Spadafora* ■ *Dir* Gianni Amelio • *Scr* Gianni Amelio, Vincenzo Cerami, from the novel by Leonardo Sciascia

Open Hearts ★★★★ 15

Romantic drama
2002 · Den · Colour · 108mins

The 28th feature to be shot in adherence to the Dogme aesthetic, this focuses wholly on the raw emotions of doctor Mads Mikkelsen and 20-something cook Sonja Richter. The pair are brought together when Mikkelsen's wife, Paprika Steen, is involved in a road accident that leaves Richter's fiancé, Nikolaj Lie Kaas, paralysed from the neck down. The most intriguing thing about this compelling story is the way director Susanne Bier explores the inevitability of the attraction, and all the performances are exceptional. DP. In Danish with English subtitles. DVD

Sonja Richter *Cecilie* • Nikolaj Lie Kaas *Joachim* • Mads Mikkelsen *Niels* • Paprika Steen *Marie* • Stine Bjerregaard *Stine* • Birthe Neumann *Hanne* • Niels Olsen *Finn* ■ *Dir* Susanne Bier • *Scr* Anders Thomas Jensen, from a story by Susanne Bier

Open Range ★★★★ 12

Western 2003 · US/UK · Colour · 133mins

Actor/director Kevin Costner's western is a beautifully crafted, well-acted example of the genre, that only occasionally lurches a little too close to cliché for comfort. It's set in a fascinating transitional period of frontier history – as the traditional free-ranging cattlemen and their herds were harassed and attacked by settled ranchers – but Costner finds most of the film's interest in the relationships between the main characters. He is impressive as the taciturn Charley, whose Civil War memories haunt him, but it is Robert Duvall's restrained performance as the de facto father to the "family" of travelling cow-pokes that is the movie's real powerhouse. AS. Contains violence. DVD

Robert Duvall *Boss Spearman* • Kevin Costner *Charley Waite* • Annette Bening *Sue Barlow* • Michael Gambon *Denton Baxter* • Michael Jeter *Percy* • Diego Luna *Button* • James Russo *Sheriff Poole* • Abraham Benrubi *Mose* • Dean McDermott *Doc Barlow* • Kim Coates *Butler* ■ *Dir* Kevin Costner • *Scr* Craig Storper, from the novel *The Open Range Men* by Lauran Paine

Open Season ★

Action 1974 · US/Sp · Colour · 106mins

Three Vietnam vets kidnap a man and a woman, force them to act as servants at the remote cabin, sexually abuse the woman, then hunt them down like game. Full of psychological baloney to justify its story, this exploitation effort makes some cheap shots about American democracy and justice before getting down to the nitty-gritty of gratuitous sex and violence. AT

Peter Fonda *Ken* • Cornelia Sharpe *Nancy* • John Phillip Law *Greg* • Richard Lynch *Art* • Albert Mendoza [Alberto de Mendoza] *Martin* • William Holden (2) *Wolkowski* ■ *Dir* Peter Collinson • *Scr* David Osborn, Liz Charles-Williams

Open Season ★★★

Comedy satire 1995 · US · Colour · 97mins

A sharp-edged satire on contemporary television in which a foul-up in the ratings mistakenly suggests that US viewers are giving dumb dross the thumbs down, and tuning in to shows of culture and intellect instead. Predictably, the very idea puts programmers in a tizz. Robert Wuhl stars, writes and directs, while Rod Taylor, Helen Shaver and Gailard Sartain co-star. A spot-on comedy, that retains its relevance. DA

Robert Wuhl *Stuart Sain* • Rod Taylor *Billy Patrick* • Gailard Sartain *George Plunkett* • Helen Shaver *Rachel Rowen* • Maggie Han *Cary Sain* • Dina Merrill *Doris Hays-Britton* • Saul Rubinek *Eric Schlockmeister* ■ *Dir/Scr* Robert Wuhl

Open Water ★★★ 15

Thriller based on a true story
2004 · US · Colour · 76mins

Blanchard Ryan and Daniel Travis play a couple who embark on a scuba diving excursion in the Caribbean, only to find themselves stranded in shark-infested waters with no sign of rescue. Shot on digital video, the film gains atmosphere from resembling an amateur undersea documentary; it's simple, short and effective because it leaves everything to the imagination. Anyone frightened of shark attacks can expect a full hands-in-front-of-eyes workout in this nail-biter with a surprising payoff. AJ. Contains swearing. DVD

Blanchard Ryan *Susan* • Daniel Travis *Daniel* • Saul Stein *Seth* • Estelle Lau *Estelle* • Michael E Williamson *Davis* • Cristina Zenarro *Linda* • John Charles *Junior* ■ *Dir/Scr* Chris Kentis

Open Your Eyes ★★★★ 15

Psychological thriller
1997 · Sp · Colour · 119mins

This is a dazzling second feature from young Spanish film-maker Alejandro Amenábar. As the pampered playboy whose life begins to unravel after a disfiguring car crash, Eduardo Noriega conveys both resentment and vulnerability as he strives to make sense of a relentless sequence of disconcerting events. This delirious treatise on appearance and reality requires total concentration, right through to its dissatisfyingly glib denouement. Penélope Cruz reprised her role in Cameron Crowe's remake, *Vanilla Sky*, with Tom Cruise in the César role . DP. In Spanish with English subtitles. DVD

Eduardo Noriega (2) *César* • Penélope Cruz *Sofia* • Chete Lera *Antonio* • Fele Martínez *Pelayo* • Najwa Nimri *Nuria* ■ *Dir* Alejandro Amenábar • *Scr* Alejandro Amenábar, Mateo Gil

Opening Night ★★★★ 15

Drama 1977 · US · Colour · 138mins

In addition to his own talent and daring as actor/writer/director, John Cassavetes was blessed in his wife and regular collaborator, Gena Rowlands, for whom this is a tour de force. Rowlands is spellbinding as the star experiencing an intense emotional and spiritual crisis before the first performance of her new play. A truthful testament to the self-absorption, fragility and art of actors, it's hard-going if you're not keen on Cassavetes's unconventional style. But the acting is suitably riveting: Cassavetes is compelling as Rowlands's leading man, and veteran Joan Blondell is on splendid form as her author friend. AME

Gena Rowlands *Myrtle Gordon* • John Cassavetes *Maurice Aarons* • Ben Gazzara *Manny Victor* • Joan Blondell *Sarah Goode* • Paul Stewart *David Samuels* • Zohra Lampert *Dorothy Victor* ■ *Dir/Scr* John Cassavetes

Opera ★★★ 18

Horror 1987 · It · Colour · 91mins

There's no phantom in Italian horror maestro Dario Argento's masterwork; just a mentally deranged maniac obsessed with ingénue singer Cristina Marsillach as she rehearses Verdi's *Macbeth*. But this aria of savage beauty contains Argento's single most potent and self-revelatory image: Marsillach, forced to watch orchestrated murders, is unable to close her eyes due to needles taped under the lids. Argento's relentless search for the outer limits of hardcore gore doesn't make much sense, but for those of a certain dispositon, it's bravura cinema. AJ. An Italian language film. DVD

Cristina Marsillach *Betty* • Urbano Barberini *Inspector Santini* • Daria Nicolodi *Mira* • Ian Charleson *Marco* ■ *Dir* Dario Argento • *Scr* Dario Argento, Franco Ferrini

Opera do Malandro ★★★★ 15

Musical fantasy
1986 · Bra · Colour · 107mins

This is less a stylised snapshot of Brazil on the eve of war than a tribute to the musical extravaganzas of MGM. Directing with visual and visceral panache, Ruy Guerra allows his camera to prowl around Rio's seedy bars and crumbling slums, as small-time racketeer Edson Celulari's plan to corrupt the daughter of his deadly, pro-Nazi rival calamitously backfires. It's sensual, surreal and subversive, and throbs with life. DP. In Portuguese with English subtitles.

Edson Celulari *Max* • Claudia Ohana *Ludmila* • Elba Ramalho *Margot* ■ *Dir* Ruy Guerra • *Scr* Chico Buarque, Orlando Senna, Ruy Guerra, from the play by Chico Buarque

Operation Amsterdam ★★★ U

Second World War drama
1958 · UK · BW · 104mins

It might seem like double Dutch these days, but director Michael McCarthy's final film (he died the following year) was convincing enough on its release – a British pseudo-documentary, set in 1940, about a bunch of spies sent into Holland to recover a hoard of industrial diamonds before the Nazis get to them. Diamond expert Alexander Knox looks grave and concerned, and Peter Finch is dashing and daring. TH

Peter Finch *Jan Smit* • Eva Bartok *Anna* • Tony Britton *Major Dillon* • Alexander Knox *Walter Keyser* • Malcolm Keen *Johann Smit* • Christopher Rhodes *Alex* ■ *Dir* Michael McCarthy • *Scr* Michael McCarthy, John Eldridge, from the book *Adventure in Diamonds* by David E Walker

Operation Bullshine ★★ U

Comedy 1959 · UK · Colour · 83mins

It's just feasible that this feeble comedy might have raised a smile in the darkest days of the Second World War, but more than a decade after the event there was simply no excuse for the tired collection of jokes that aren't worth a smutty snigger. This is a clear case of too much bull and not enough shine. Donald Sinden and Barbara Murray could do this sort of marital misunderstanding material in their sleep, and it's to their credit that they try to give it some pep, as does the splendid supporting cast. DP

Donald Sinden *Lt Gordon Brown* • Barbara Murray *Private Betty Brown* • Carole Lesley *Private Marge White* • Ronald Shiner *Gunner Slocum* • Naunton Wayne *Major Pym* • Dora Bryan *Private Cox* • John Cairney *Gunner Willie Ross* • Fabia Drake *Junior Commander Maddox, ATS* • Joan Rice *Private Finch* • Daniel Massey *Bombardier Palmer* ■ *Dir* Gilbert Gunn • *Scr* Anne Burnaby, Rupert Lang, Gilbert Gunn

Operation CIA ★★★

Spy action thriller 1965 · US · BW · 90mins

This nifty spy thriller sees agent Burt Reynolds (in one of his earliest roles) sent to Saigon during the Vietnam conflict to prevent an assassination. Not totally American propaganda, the film maintains a detached stance on the differing values of the goodies and the baddies, while director Christian Nyby keeps it all very lively. TH

Burt Reynolds *Mark Andrews* • Kieu Chinh *Kim-chinh* • Danielle Aubry *Denise, French agent* • John Hoyt *Wells* • Cyril Collick *Withers* • Vic Diaz *Prof Yen* • William Catching *Frank Decker* ■ *Dir* Christian Nyby • *Scr* Peer J Oppenheimer, Bill S Ballinger, from a story by Peer J Oppenheimer

Operation Condor: the Armour of God II ★★★★ 15

Martial arts adventure
1990 · HK · Colour · 102mins

Here, Hong Kong superstar Jackie Chan plays an Indiana Jones-style secret agent (codenamed Condor) searching for a stash of Nazi gold in the Sahara. Cue some wonderfully choreographed kung fu fights with militant desert rats, hugely entertaining action-hero parodies and silly slapstick for which Chan has the perfect timing. AJ. Cantonese dialogue dubbed into English. Contains violence.

Jackie Chan *Jackie* • Carol Cheng *Ada* • Eva Cobo de Garcia [Eva Cobo] *Elsa* • Shoko Ikeda *Momoko* • Alfredo Brel Sanchez *Adolf* ■ *Dir* Jackie Chan • *Scr* Jackie Chan, Edward Tang, Szeto Chuek-Hun, Ken Lowe, John Sheppard, from a story by Barry Wong

Operation Crossbow ★★★ PG

Second World War drama
1965 · It/US/UK · Colour · 111mins

The credits are impressive, the plot intriguing and the production values impeccable, but they only add up to an average wartime thriller. In common with many blockbuster writers, Emeric Pressburger and his colleagues were confounded by the dual task of telling a ripping yarn and finding enough to do for a big-name cast. As a result, the mission to replace German V-2 rocket scientists with Allied boffins is often of secondary interest to the stargazing. However, there is plenty of derring-do, although director Michael Anderson struggles to find a workable balance between action and chat. DP. In English and German with subtitles.

George Peppard *Lieutenant John Curtis* • Sophia Loren *Nora* • Trevor Howard *Professor Lindemann* • John Mills *General Boyd* • Richard Johnson *Duncan Sandys* • Tom Courtenay *Robert Henshaw* • Jeremy Kemp *Phil Bradley* • Anthony Quayle *Bamford* • Lilli Palmer *Frieda* • Paul Henreid *General Ziemann* ■ *Dir* Michael Anderson • *Scr* Richard Imrie [Emeric Pressburger], Derry Quinn, Ray Rigby, from a story by Duilio Coletti, Vittoriano Petrilli

Operation Daybreak ★★★ 15

Second World War thriller
1975 · US/UK/Cz · Colour · 114mins

A grimly exciting war drama about the Czech resistance's assassination of Reinhard Heydrich, deputy chief of the Gestapo and better known as "Hitler's Hangman". This is drily, if expertly, directed by veteran Lewis Gilbert, and features a motley cast including American Tim Bottoms and a particularly excellent Anthony Andrews as Czech patriots. Today, when the village of Lidice, which was razed by the Nazis in reprisal for the assassination, is hardly remembered, its telling is still timely. TS

Timothy Bottoms *Jan Kubis* • Martin Shaw *Karel Curda* • Joss Ackland *Janak* • Nicola Pagett *Anna* • Anthony Andrews *Joseph Gabcik* • Anton Diffring *Reinhard Heydrich* • Diana Coupland *Aunt Marie* • Cyril Shaps *Father Petrek* • Ray Smith *Hajek* • Timothy West *Vaclav* ■ *Dir* Lewis Gilbert • *Scr* Ronald Harwood, from the novel *Seven Men at Daybreak* by Alan Burgess

Operation Dead End ★★

Thriller 1986 · W Ger · Colour · 95mins

This passable thriller focuses on three strangers who volunteer for an experiment to monitor stress levels in the wake of a nuclear holocaust. However, 72 days in close confinement on a deserted island, and the discovery that the experiment is not all that it seems, cause tempers to fray. The claustrophobic shelter sequences are essentially chat-bound, but the pace picks up once the trio begins to investigate what the sinister scientists are really up to. DP. German dialogue dubbed into English.

Hannes Jaenicke *Leslie* • Uwe Oxenknecht *Boris* • Isabelle Willer *Kim* • Anton Diffring *Professor Lang* ■ *Dir* Nikolai Müllerschön • *Scr* Stanislav Barabas, Nikolai Müllerschön

Operation Delta Force ★★ 15

Action drama 1996 · US · Colour · 89mins

Jeff Fahey is the lead in this standard action cable-TV film, in which he plays the commander of a special military unit that is charged with retrieving a super-virus from Afrikaaner terrorists. The movie is fairly slickly made, but occasionally low-budget touches shine through the gloss: during a shoot-out in a train car, there are four or five people emptying machine guns at each other, yet the furnishing of the train never show the slightest damage! ST. Contains violence, swearing. DVD

Jeff Fahey *Lang* • Ernie Hudson *Tipton* • Rob Stewart *Sparks* • Frank Zagarino *McKinney* • Joe Lara *Nash* • Todd Jensen *Hutch* • Hal Holbrook *Henshaw* ■ *Dir* Sam Firstenberg • *Scr* David Sparling

Operation Delta Force II: Mayday ★★ 15

Action thriller 1998 · US · Colour · 103mins

This is not only numbingly predictable, but also robotically performed. Hurtling blindly between various unspecified locations, the plot turns around Edgar Allan Poe-quoting villain J Kenneth Campbell's plan to steal a Russian nuclear submarine by hijacking an American liner. But, unfortunately for him, the ship's skipper is Dale Dye, estranged father of Delta Force commander Michael McGrady. Director Yossi Wein stages the action sequences with the finesse of a bulldozer. Three further sequels (to date) followed. DP DVD

Michael McGrady *Captain Skip Long* • Simon Jones [John Simon Jones] *Vickers* • Robert Patteri *McKinney* • Todd Jensen *Lombardi* • Dale Dye *Captain Halsey Long* • Spencer Rochfort *Hutch* ■ *Dir* Yossi Wein • *Scr* David Sparling, from a story by Danny Lerner

Operation Dumbo Drop ★★★ PG

Comedy adventure
1995 · US · Colour · 103mins

This amiable family comedy has more than a fair share of surprisingly adult-orientated jokes. Director Simon Wincer's harmless allegory stars Danny Glover and Ray Liotta as the leaders of a group of Green Beret soldiers who promise to deliver an elephant to a Vietnamese village. The problems they face in order to carry out their pledge lead to lots of fun escapades and a winning climax. AJ DVD

Danny Glover *Captain Sam Cahill* • Ray Liotta *Captain Doyle* • Denis Leary *David Poole* • Doug E Doug *Harvey Ashford* • Corin Nemec *Lawrence Farley* • Tcheky Karyo *Goddard* ■ *Dir* Simon Wincer • *Scr* Gene Quintano, Jim Kouf, from a story by Jim Morris

Operation Kid Brother ★★

Spy comedy 1967 · It · Colour · 110mins

It must have seemed a good idea at the time: star Sean Connery's brother Neil as himself in a spy spoof and surround him with ex-James Bond girls, villains and associates. Unfortunately this Connery can't act and the story – something about his plastic surgeon character being blackmailed by Allied powers into smashing an international criminal conspiracy run by Adolfo Celi from an underground atomic city – just marks lethargic time between one lame lampoon and the next. AJ

Neil Connery • Daniela Bianchi *Maya* • Adolfo Celi *Thair Beta* • Agata Flori *Mildred* • Bernard Lee *Cmdr Cunningham* • Anthony Dawson [Antonio Margheriti] *Alpha* • Lois Maxwell *Max* ■ *Dir* Alberto De Martino • *Scr* Stefano Canzio, Paolo Levi, Frank Walker, Stanley Wright

Operation Mad Ball ★★★ U

Comedy 1957 · US · BW · 104mins

After his Oscar-winning turn in *Mister Roberts*, Jack Lemmon enlisted in the army for this breakneck comedy. It's set in Normandy in 1945 where the low-ranking soldiers in a military hospital stage a "mad ball" in order to fraternise with the otherwise off-limits nurses. Lemmon is in sparkling form as the "Mr Fixit" and Mickey Rooney's performance will either reduce you to hysterics or set your teeth on edge. Despite the setting, it's really a comedy about American sexual mores in the 1950s. AT

Jack Lemmon *Private Hogan* • Kathryn Grant *Lieutenant Betty Bixby* • Ernie Kovacs *Captain Paul Locke* • Arthur O'Connell *Colonel Rousch* • Mickey Rooney *Yancy Skibo* • Dick York *Corporal Bohun* • James Darren *Private Widowskas* ■ *Dir* Richard Quine • *Scr* Arthur Carter, Jed Harris, Blake Edwards, from the play by Arthur Carter

Operation Madonna ★★

Thriller 1987 · Neth/W Ger · Colour · 83mins

Dutch star Renée Soutendjik and versatile French character actor Michel Lonsdale add a touch of unmerited class to this humdrum thriller, in which a forged painting, a case of mistaken identity and a pair of identical twins singularly fail to raise the pulse rate. Director Hans-Christoph Blumenberg captures some of Hamburg's tawdry ambience, but he plods through the plot's predictable twists with little imagination. DP. In Dutch and German with English subtitles.

Marius Müller-Westernhagen *Martin Graves* • Renée Soutendijk *Juliane Mundt* • Michael Lonsdale [Michel Lonsdale] *Tanzmann* • Heinrich Schweiger *Arthur/Otto Wiegand* • Ingrid Van Bergen *Charly* • Nina Hoger *Monika* ■ *Dir* Hans-Christoph Blumenberg • *Scr* Jonathan Thornhill, Hans-Christoph Blumenberg

Operation Pacific ★★ U

Second World War drama
1951 · US · BW · 104mins

Like most of Wayne's war pictures, this is gung-ho, action-packed and grossly sentimental – the plot takes in homeless children, dewy-eyed nuns, a batch of dud torpedoes and marital difficulties. Wayne, of course, takes everything in his stride, scuppering the Japanese fleet, playing daddy to the youngsters and winning back the hand of Patricia Neal. The navy liked this one so much it held regular screenings at all its bases. AT DVD

John Wayne *"Duke" Gifford* • Patricia Neal *Mary Stuart* • Ward Bond *"Pop" Perry* • Scott Forbes *Larry* • Philip Carey *Bob Perry* • Paul Picerni *Jonesy* • William Campbell *Talker* • Kathryn Givney *Commander Steele* • Martin Milner *Caldwell* • Jack Pennick *Chief* ■ *Dir/Scr* George Waggner

Operation Petticoat ★★★★ U

Wartime comedy
1959 · US · Colour · 120mins

This wonderfully wacky comedy teams those two great *farceurs* Cary Grant and Tony Curtis in their only movie together. Here Grant is a submarine commander trying to keep his ropey old vessel in the water with the help of wheeler-dealer junior officer Curtis. Complications arise as the sub takes on board a number of unorthodox passengers. Grant is brilliant, with every reaction immaculately timed. Director Blake Edwards ensures no gag is missed, and the whole is a deliciously tasteless joy. TS DVD

Cary Grant *Admiral Matt Sherman* • Tony Curtis *Lt Nick Holden* • Joan O'Brien *Lt Dolores Crandall* • Dina Merrill *Lt Barbara Duran* • Gene Evans *Molumphrey* • Arthur O'Connell *Sam Tostin* • Richard Sargent [Dick Sargent] *Stovall* ■ *Dir* Blake Edwards • *Scr* Stanley Shapiro, Maurice Richlin, from a story by Paul King, Joseph Stone

Operation Snatch ★★★

Second World War comedy
1962 · UK · BW · 86mins

This enjoyably daft British comedy is inspired by the legend that if the Barbary apes leave Gibraltar, the Rock will leave the British Empire. During the Second World War, Lieutenant Terry-Thomas and his batman (Lionel Jeffries) are sent on a mission to find a breeding specimen to increase the dwindling colony. There are too many stock characters, but this does have several ridiculously funny scenes. DM

Terry-Thomas *Lt "Piggy" Wigg* • George Sanders *Maj Hobson* • Lionel Jeffries *Evans* • Jackie Lane [Jocelyn Lane] *Bianca Tabori* • Lee Montague *Miklos Tabori* • Michael Trubshawe *Colonel Marston* • James Villiers *Lt Keen* • Dinsdale Landen *Capt Whittington* ■ *Dir* Robert Day • *Scr* Alan Hackney, John Warren, Len Heath

Operator 13 ★★★ U

Period war drama 1934 · US · BW · 85mins

A vehicle for William Randolph Hearst's actress mistress, Marion Davies, who was much praised for her performance at the time, this is a tale of espionage and romance with a difference. Set during the American Civil War, this has an immensely complicated plot that revolves around actress Davies becoming a Yankee spy in Confederate territory and donning a series of disguises. In the course of the dramatic action, romance rears its head in the shape of enemy scout Gary Cooper. Engaging tosh, expensively filmed, this is strong on Southern atmosphere. RK

Marion Davies *Gail Loveless/Lucille/Operator 13/Anne Claybourne* • Gary Cooper *Capt Jack Gailliard* • Jean Parker *Eleanor Shackleford* • Katharine Alexander [Katherine Alexander] *Pauline Cushman/Mrs Vale/Operator 27* • Ted Healy *Capt/Doctor Hitchcock* • Russell Hardie *Littledale* ■ *Dir* Richard Boleslavsky [Richard Boleslawski] • *Scr* Harvey Thew, Zelda Sears, Eve Greene, from the novel *Secret Service Operator* by Robert W Chambers

Ophélia ★★

Drama 1962 · Fr · BW · 103mins

The textual influence may be Shakespeare, but the atmospheric sire of this dramatic curio from Claude Chabrol is clearly Franz Kafka. With Jean Rabier's camera prowling around the shabby grandeur of a murky mansion, the familiar story of the grieving son who becomes convinced that his mother and lecherous uncle were responsible for his father's death is laced with juvenile humour and melodramatic excess. DP. In French with English subtitles.

André Jocelyn *Yvan Lesurf* • Alida Valli *Claudia* • Juliette Mayniel *Lucie* • Claude Cerval *Adrien Lesurf* • Robert Burnier *André Lagrange* • Jean-Louis Maury *Sparkos* ■ *Dir* Claude Chabrol • *Scr* Claude Chabrol, Martial Matthieu [Paul Gégauff]

The Opportunists ★★★ 15

Heist drama 2000 · US/UK · Colour · 89mins

Hollywood's favourite psycho Christopher Walken is beautifully understated in this wryly melancholic crime caper about a bunch of small-time crooks. Walken is a former robber, an expert on cracking safes, who is dragged back into the life of crime by his Irish cousin (Peter McDonald) who offers him the opportunity to solve his financial woes. First time director Myles Connell stages some nifty robbery set pieces, but most of the enjoyment comes from the interplay between the disparate gang of losers. JF

Christopher Walken *Victor Kelly* • Peter McDonald *Michael* • Cyndi Lauper *Sally* • Donal Logue *Pat Duffy* • José Zuniga *Jesus Del Toro* • Vera Farmiga *Miriam* ■ *Dir/Scr* Myles Connell

Opportunity Knocks ★★ 15

Comedy 1990 · US · Colour · 96mins

Made two years before he struck paydirt as Garth in *Wayne's World*, Dana Carvey takes the lead in this fumbled comedy of errors. Trotting out the full repertoire of silly voices he made famous on *Saturday Night Live*, Carvey just about carries the story of a conman who wins the confidence of a wealthy family while on the run from a gangster. Robert Loggia contributes some assured support, but it's the script that lets the side down. DP

Dana Carvey *Eddie Farrell* • Robert Loggia *Milt Malkin* • Todd Graff *Lou Pasquino* • Julia Campbell *Annie Malkin* • Milo O'Shea *Max* • James Tolkan *Sal Nichols* ■ *Dir* Donald Petrie • *Scr* Mitchel Katlin, Nat Bernstein

The Opposite of Sex ★★★★ 18

Comedy 1998 · US · Colour · 96mins

Former screenwriter Don Roos cuts through the thicket of political correctness with rapier wit and rude humour in his eye-opening feature debut about contemporary sexual values and lifestyles. Christina Ricci is deadly funny as the white-trash teenager who steals her gay half-brother's boyfriend so she can have an instant father for the child she's carrying. With Lisa Kudrow from *Friends* also giving a spot-on turn as a self-righteous old maid, Roos's bitchy oddball comedy is hilarious. AJ. Contains violence, swearing. DVD

Christina Ricci *Dedee Truitt* • Martin Donovan (2) *Bill Truitt* • Lisa Kudrow *Lucia Dalury* • Lyle Lovett *Sheriff Carl Tippett* • Johnny Galecki *Jason Bock* • William Lee Scott *Randy* ■ *Dir/Scr* Don Roos

The Opposite Sex ★★★

Musical comedy 1956 · US · Colour · 116mins

The MGM classic *The Women* featured no men in its cast, but this musical remake makes the mistake of letting them in. Jeff Richards and a young Leslie Nielsen are pretty dreary, appearing opposite Joan Collins, Dolores Gray, Ann Sheridan, Ann Miller and Joan Blondell. Another fly in the ointment is top-billed June Allyson, who seems neither sophisticated nor brittle enough for the shenanigans in Clare Boothe Luce's play. There's good use of early CinemaScope, and the result is sexy, witty and glamorous. TS

June Allyson *Kay Hilliard* • Joan Collins *Crystal Allen* • Dolores Gray *Sylvia Fowler* • Ann Sheridan *Amanda Penrose* • Ann Miller *Gloria Dell* • Leslie Nielsen *Steve Hilliard* • Jeff Richards *Buck Winston* • Agnes Moorehead *Countess Lavaliere* ■ *Dir* David Miller • *Scr* Fay Kanin, Michael Kanin, from the play by Clare Boothe Luce

The Opposite Sex and How to Live with Them ★★ 15

Romantic comedy
1993 · US · Colour · 82mins

Courteney Cox plays the daughter of conservative parents who endures a mismatched, up-and-down relationship with Arye Gross. The two leads are fine, but the best performances and lines go to their respective best friends, Julie Brown and Kevin Pollak. Director Matthew Meshekoff attempts to spice up the formula with some raunchy scenes and characters talking directly to the camera. JF

Arye Gross *David* • Courteney Cox *Carrie* • Kevin Pollak *Eli* • Julie Brown *Zoe* • Jack Carter *Rabbi* • Kimber Sissons *Tracy* • Mitchell Ryan *Kenneth Davenport* ■ *Dir* Matthew Meshekoff • *Scr* Noah Stern

The Optimists of Nine Elms ★★★ PG

Drama 1973 · UK · Colour · 106mins

This was originally to have been a vehicle for Danny Kaye, but it's hard to see how his energetic style would have been suitable for the part of Sam the busker, who has little to sustain him apart from his music-hall memories and his faithful dog. Resisting the temptation for pathos, Peter Sellers gives a surprisingly sensitive and somewhat overlooked performance, made even more memorable by his generous encouragement of his young co-stars. Lionel Bart's songs aren't among his best, but these musings on poverty and community spirit are nicely expressed. DP

Peter Sellers *Sam* • Donna Mullane *Liz* • John Chaffey *Mark* • David Daker *Bob Ellis* • Marjorie Yates *Chrissie Ellis* ■ *Dir* Anthony Simmons • *Scr* Anthony Simmons, Tudor Gates, from the novel by Anthony Simmons

The Oracle ★★ U

Fantasy comedy 1952 · UK · BW · 85mins

Gilbert Harding voices the oracle at the bottom of a well in this piffling comedy in which whimsy is heaped on to make up for the absence of genuine humour. Ordinarily, Harding dispenses his wisdom to the inhabitants of a small Irish island. But then journalist Robert Beatty begins using him to predict horse races and other momentous events until the British mainland is reduced to chaos. Celebrated at the time as the rudest man on TV, Harding comes over today as an irascible prig and the threadbare story offers little to compensate for his blustering. DP

Robert Beatty *Bob Jefferson* • Joseph Tomelty *Terry Roche* • Michael Medwin *Timothy Blake* • Mervyn Johns *Tom Mitchum* • Virginia McKenna *Shelagh* • Gillian Lind *Jane Bond* • Ursula Howells *Peggy* • Gilbert Harding *Oracle's voice* ■ *Dir* CM Pennington-Richards • *Scr* Patrick Campbell, from the radio play *To Tell You the Truth* by Robert Barr

Orange County ★★★ 12

Comedy 2001 · US · Colour · 78mins

In addition to its offbeat observations, quirky sensibilities and marvelous performances, this is also noteworthy for showcasing the second generation Hollywood talents of Colin Hanks (Tom's son), Schuyler Fisk (Sissy Spacek's daughter) and Jake Kasdan (director Lawrence's son). Set in the "perfect" Californian region of the title, where Hanks finds his life changed when a clerical mistake means his brilliant grades are attributed to another student and he has 24 hours to fix the error before Stanford University closes its

O

application ranks. AJ. Contains swearing. [subtitles] DVD

Colin Hanks *Shaun Brumder* • Jack Black *Lance* • Catherine O'Hara *Cindy Beugler* • Schuyler Fisk *Ashley* • John Lithgow *Bud Brumder* • Brett Harrison [Bret Harrison] *Lonny Munsack* • Harold Ramis *Don Durkett* • Lily Tomlin *Charlotte Cobb* • Chevy Chase *Principal Harbert* • Kevin Kline *Marcus Skinner* • Ben Stiller *Fireman* ■ *Dir* Jake Kasdan • *Scr* Mike White

Orbit ★★ 15

Action adventure thriller
1996 · US · Colour · 79mins

An ambitious but unnecessarily complicated conspiracy thriller, which centres on an abortive attempt to sabotage a US shuttle mission via a virus in the computer system. Unfolded in flashback at a subsequent court case, the story stirs in right-wing American terrorists and even alien life forms into an already overheated brew and, for all the intriguing ideas on show, budgetary restraints means it's largely a static, earthbound affair. JF. Contains swearing. [subtitles]

Casper Van Dien • Bentley Mitchum • Kelly Ann Sweeney • Joe Estevez • Carrie Mitchum • Nick Wilder • Jan-Michael Vincent • Chris Mitchum [Christopher Mitchum] • Ulli Lommel *Max Braun* ■ *Dir* Mario Van Cleef [Ulli Lommel] • *Scr* Budd Garrison

Orca ... Killer Whale ★★ PG

Action adventure 1977 · US · Colour · 88mins

This man-versus-beast tale was an obvious attempt to jump on the *Jaws* bandwagon, but some of the scenes are just laughable. Richard Harris plays the macho hunter who incurs the wrath of a super-intelligent killer whale after he slaughters its pregnant mate. The female cast and some remarkable underwater photography fail to make up for the daft narrative. TH [subtitles] DVD

Richard Harris *Captain Nolan* • Charlotte Rampling *Rachel Bedford* • Will Sampson *Umilak* • Bo Derek *Annie* • Keenan Wynn *Novak* • Scott Walker *Swain* • Robert Carradine *Ken* • Peter Hooten *Paul* ■ *Dir* Michael Anderson • *Scr* Luciano Vincenzoni, Sergio Donati

Orchestra Rehearsal ★★★ PG

Drama 1978 · It/Fr/W Ger · Colour · 69mins

Prompted by the murder of ex-Prime Minister Aldo Moro, yet also clearly a swipe at the strikers who had disrupted the production of *Amarcord* and *Casanova*, Fellini's microcosmic burlesque on the shortcomings of both anarchy and authoritarianism was originally made for Italian television. Dismissed as a one-gag vignette, it's actually a revealing snapshot of late 1970s socio-political attitudes and an unconscious rebellion against the cult of auteurism. With Nino Rota's playfully banal score and production designer Dante Ferretti's symbolically crumbling edifice reinforcing the satire, this allegory may be Fellini in a minor key, but it's still wryly amusing. DP. In Italian with English subtitles. [subtitles]

Balduin Baas *Conductor* • Clara Colosimo *Harpist* • Elisabeth Labi *Pianist* ■ *Dir* Federico Fellini • *Scr* Federico Fellini, Brunello Rondi

Orchestra Wives ★★★ PG

Musical 1942 · US · BW · 93mins

Life on the road as lived by a touring swing orchestra and, more particularly the musicians' wives, with the new wife (Ann Rutherford) of trumpeter George Montgomery having to cope with the female rivalry and backbiting. The mediocre script and second-rung cast, however, are secondary to the delights of the Mack Gordon-Harry Warren score, the Glenn Miller Orchestra, vocalists Tex Beneke and Marion Hutton and the Modernaires, and dazzling tap-dancing team the Nicholas Brothers. RK [subtitles]

George Montgomery *Bill Abbott* • Ann Rutherford *Connie* • Glenn Miller *Gene Morrison* • Cesar Romero *Sinjin* • Lynn Bari *Jaynie* • Carole Landis *Natalie* • Virginia Gilmore *Elsie* • Jackie Gleason *Beck* • Nicholas Brothers *Specialty* • Tex Beneke • Marion Hutton ■ *Dir* Archie Mayo • *Scr* Karl Tunberg, Darrel Ware, from a story by James Prindle • *Music* Mack Gordon, Harry Warren

The Ordeal ★★★

Horror comedy
2004 · Bel/Fr/Lux · Colour · 94mins

Director Fabrice du Welz's spaced-out spooky feature debut has amateur cabaret singer Laurent Lucas taking a wrong turn to a Christmas gig and ending up in a remote inn run by demented Jackie Berroyer. Berroyer wants a perfect wife as a substitute for the one he never forgave for adultery, and soon Lucas is being debased in drag and facing mental torture and crucifixion in a woodland community of dangerous village idiots. This is disgusting, shocking and delightful in equal proportion. AJ. In French with English subtitles.

Laurent Lucas *Marc Stevens* • Jackie Berroyer *Paul Bartel* • Philippe Nahon *Robert Orton* • Jean-Luc Couchard *Boris* • Brigitte Lahaie *Mademoiselle Vicky* • Gigi Coursigni *Madame Langhoff* • Philippe Grand'Henry *Thomas Orton* • Jo Prestia *Mylène* ■ *Dir* Fabrice du Welz • *Scr* Fabrice du Welz, Romain Protat • *Cinematographer* Benoît Debie

Ordeal by Innocence ★★ 15

Detective drama
1984 · UK · Colour and BW · 86mins

A mediocre screen version of an Agatha Christie potboiler, about an explorer returning to England after two years in the Antarctic to find that a man he knows is on a murder rap from which he might have saved him. The bi-national cast all act on autopilot, especially Donald Sutherland, who looks as bemused as the audience about what an amateur American sleuth is doing in a Devon village. Equally out of place is Dave Brubeck's jazzy score. DA [subtitles]

Donald Sutherland *Dr Arthur Calgary* • Faye Dunaway *Rachel Argyle* • Ian McShane *Philip Durrant* • Sarah Miles *Mary Durrant* • Christopher Plummer *Leo Argyle* • Diana Quick *Gwenda Vaughan* • Annette Crosbie *Kirsten Lindstrom* • Michael Elphick *Inspector Huish* ■ *Dir* Desmond Davis • *Scr* Alexander Stuart, from the novel by Agatha Christie

The Order ★★ 15

Action thriller 2001 · US · Colour · 85mins

Jean-Claude Van Damme is always consistent. Whatever the storyline, he'll perform the same specific kick-boxing moves and at some stage bare his super-toned chest. So it's no surprise that this tired action thriller incorporates both these trademarks, along with all the requisite chase sequences and explosions. Here he plays an artefacts thief who gets embroiled with a religious cult in Israel after they kidnap his archaeologist father. It's tedious hokum, strewn with one-liners, but die-hard fans will no doubt lap it up. SF. Contains violence and swearing. [subtitles] DVD

Jean-Claude Van Damme *Rudy Cafmeyer* • Charlton Heston *Professor Finley* • Brian Thompson *Cyrus* • Ben Cross *Ben Ner* • Sofia Milos *Dalia* • Vernon Dobtcheff *Oscar Cafmeyer* ■ *Dir* Sheldon Lettich • *Scr* Les Weldon, Jean-Claude Van Damme

Order of Death ★★★ 18

Thriller 1983 · It · Colour · 96mins

Harvey Keitel has an early vicious role, with Sex Pistol John Lydon (aka Johnny Rotten) as his sociopathic confessor, in this genre-twisting spaghetti thriller. Lydon shows up at detective Keitel's secret Central Park apartment, paid for by drug dealers' backhanders, and admits he's the serial killer responsible for slaughtering numerous narcotics division cops. Is he telling the truth and what is Keitel going to do now the punk has seen his illicit apartment? A cleverly crafted, homoerotic minuet of strong wills. AJ [subtitles]

Harvey Keitel *Lt Fred O'Connor* • John Lydon *Leo Smith* • Nicole Garcia *Lenore Carvo* • Leonard Mann *Bob Carvo* • Sylvia Sidney *Margaret Smith* ■ *Dir* Roberto Faenza • *Scr* Ennio De Concini, Hugh Fleetwood, Roberto Faenza, from the novel by Hugh Fleetwood

Orders Are Orders ★★ U

Comedy 1954 · UK · BW · 74mins

A play from the 1930s was dug up to provide the basis for this army comedy, which pokes fun at American producers coming to Britain to make cheap science-fiction movies. The film is chiefly of interest today because of the amount of radio talent involved. Brian Reece, who had just finished a long run as PC49, stars, and up-and-coming Peter Sellers and Tony Hancock lend support, while even Eric Sykes was brought in to pep up the corny old script. DM [subtitles]

Peter Sellers *Private Goffin* • Sidney James *Ed Waggermeyer* • Brian Reece *Capt Harper* • Margot Grahame *Wanda Sinclair* • Raymond Huntley *Col Bellamy* • Tony Hancock *Lt Wilfrid Cartroad* • Clive Morton *Gen Grahame-Fox* • June Thorburn *Veronica Bellamy* • Bill Fraser *Private Slee* • Donald Pleasence *Lance Cpl Martin* • Eric Sykes *Private Waterhouse* ■ *Dir* David Paltenghi • *Scr* Donald Taylor, Eric Sykes, Geoffrey Orme, from the play by Ian Hay, Anthony Armstrong

Orders to Kill ★★★★

Second World War drama
1958 · UK · BW · 110mins

A forgotten gem of the British cinema, this wartime drama sends a French-speaking American bomber pilot, Paul Massie, to Paris to liquidate a double agent. However, when Massie meets his target and finds him to be friendly and mild-mannered, he questions the man's guilt. But orders are orders. After that comes a succession of major ironies and a complex moral argument, tightly directed by Anthony Asquith and co-written by Paul Dehn. AT

Eddie Albert *Major MacMahon* • Paul Massie *Gene Summers* • Lillian Gish *Mrs Summers* • James Robertson-Justice *Naval commander* • Irene Worth *Leonie* • Leslie French *Marcel Lafitte* • John Crawford *Kimball* • Lionel Jeffries *Interrogator* ■ *Dir* Anthony Asquith • *Scr* Paul Dehn, George St George, from a story by Donald C Downes

Ordet ★★★★★ 12

Religious drama 1955 · Den · BW · 119mins

Thirty-five years after he first saw Kaj Munk's play, Carl Th Dreyer finally brought this much-cherished project to the screen and won the Golden Lion at Venice. His only feature of the 1950s is filled with sharp contrasts – lively faith and dour dogma, optimism and fatalism, youth and age, cynical sanity and mystical madness – which are further highlighted by the authentic starkness of the Jutland setting and the deceptive simplicity of the long mobile takes. This establishes the atmosphere in which a family feud is resolved by a miraculous resurrection. It's simply a masterpiece. DP. In Danish with English subtitles. [subtitles]

Henrik Malberg *Morten Borgen* • Emil Hass Christensen *Mikkel Borgen* • Preben Lerdorff Rye *Johannes Borgen* • Cay Kristiansen *Anders Borgen* • Birgitte Federspiel *Inger, Mikkel's wife* ■ *Dir* Carl Th Dreyer • *Scr* Carl Th Dreyer, from the play by Kaj Munk • *Cinematographer* Henning Bendtsen

Ordinary Decent Criminal ★★★ 15

Crime caper
1999 · UK/Ger/Ire · Colour · 90mins

A thinly veiled attempt to retell the story of real-life Irish criminal Martin Cahill, the subject of John Boorman's critically acclaimed *The General*. This time Kevin Spacey plays Cahill (here renamed Michael Lynch), the cocky Dublin gangster who spent his days robbing the rich, annoying the police and falling foul of the IRA. Director Thaddeus O'Sullivan gives his star every possible moment of screen time. However, the man on whom Michael is based will bristle at his transformation into a lovable rogue who likes nothing better than flashing his naked bum at policemen. This is worth seeing thanks to another powerhouse performance from Spacey (dodgy accent notwithstanding). JB [subtitles] DVD

Kevin Spacey *Michael Lynch* • Linda Fiorentino *Christine Lynch* • Peter Mullan *Stevie* • Stephen Dillane *Noel Quigley* • Helen Baxendale *Lisa* • David Hayman *Tony Brady* • Patrick Malahide *Commissioner Daly* ■ *Dir* Thaddeus O'Sullivan • *Scr* Gerry Stembridge [Gerard Stembridge]

Ordinary Magic ★★

Drama 1993 · Can · Colour · 104mins

This is notable for the appearance of Paul Anka, pop star from the 1950s and early 1960s. Ryan Reynolds is a 15-year-old boy brought up in India by his social activist parents. He's shipped off to his aunt (Glenne Headly) in Canada after their death. When his aunt is unfairly evicted by a property developer (Anka), he puts into practice everything he has learned in India to right the wrong. An interesting if unsatisfying attempt to portray both alienation and Hindu ideals. FL

Glenne Headly *Charlotte* • Ryan Reynolds *Ganesh/Jeffrey* • David Fox *Father/Warren* • Heath Lamberts *Mayor* • Paul Anka *Joey Dean* ■ *Dir* Giles Walker • *Scr* Jefferson Lewis, from a novel by Malcolm Bosse

Ordinary People ★★★★ 15

Drama 1980 · US · Colour · 118mins

A critically acclaimed blockbuster in its time, *Ordinary People* won four Oscars, including best film and best director for Robert Redford, stepping behind the camera for the first time. There is one truly great performance from Mary Tyler Moore as the thin, elegant, golfing and social-mixing mother strung tighter than a piano wire, and she is ably assisted by Donald Sutherland and Timothy Hutton, who won a best supporting actor Oscar. There is something very pat about Redford's exposition of the seemingly cosy middle-class family simmering with unconscious angst after the death of a son, but it's still an auspicious directorial debut that stands as one of the first films to deal intelligently with the role of therapy. SH. Contains swearing. [subtitles] DVD

Donald Sutherland *Calvin* • Mary Tyler Moore *Beth* • Judd Hirsch *Berger* • Timothy Hutton *Conrad* • M Emmet Walsh *Swimming coach* • Elizabeth McGovern *Jeannine* • Dinah Manoff *Karen* • Fredric Lehne *Lazenby* • James B Sikking *Ray* ■ *Dir* Robert Redford • *Scr* Alvin Sargent, from the novel by Judith Guest

The Oregon Trail ★★ U

Western 1959 · US · Colour · 85mins

Fred MacMurray plays a New York reporter who gets kidnapped by Indians while investigating a story about the army's harsh treatment of the hostiles. Directed by Gene Fowler Jr, this atypical offering has a serious plot that gets positively controversial when MacMurray goes all dewy-eyed over a Indian maiden and marries her. There's even a song or two. AT

Fred MacMurray *Neal Harris* • William Bishop *Captain George Wayne* • Nina Shipman *Prudence Cooper* • Gloria Talbott *Shona Hastings* • Henry Hull *Seton* • John Carradine *Zachariah Garrison* ■ *Dir* Gene Fowler Jr • *Scr* Louis Vittes, Gene Fowler Jr, from a story by Louis Vittes

The Organization ★★★★ 15

Crime drama 1971 · US · Colour · 106mins

Sidney Poitier embarks on his third tour of duty as San Francisco homicide cop Virgil Tibbs – first seen in 1967's *In the Heat of the Night* – and there's still life left in his character. This story is neatly linked to the emerging youth culture of the time as Tibbs sets out to smash a drug syndicate with the help of young vigilantes out to get the organisation for what it's done to their family and friends. Director Don Medford keeps this moving in a convincingly tense manner and Poitier doesn't need to play the superhero to still come out on top. TH. Contains violence, swearing. DVD

Sidney Poitier *Lieutenant Virgil Tibbs* • Barbara McNair *Valerie Tibbs* • Gerald S O'Loughlin *Lieutenant Jack Pecora* • Sheree North *Gloria Morgan* • Fred Beir *Bob Alford* • Allen Garfield *Benjy* • Bernie Hamilton *Lieutenant Jessop* • Raul Julia *Juan Mendoza* • Ron O'Neal *Joe Peralez* • James A Watson Jr *Stacy Baker* ■ *Dir* Don Medford • *Scr* James R Webb, from characters created by John Ball

The Organizer ★★★★

Period drama
1963 · It/Fr/Yug · BW · 126mins

In Turin in the 1890s textile workers stage a massive and bitter strike and are organised by a radical intellectual played by Marcello Mastroianni. The government send in strikebreakers and then the army. Released when Italy was in the grip of industrial action, Monicelli's film, almost a black comedy, aroused considerable controversy. Mastroianni – hiding behind a beard and glasses – gives a superb performance, consolidating his position as Italy's pre-eminent actor. AT. In Italian with English subtitles.

Marcello Mastroianni *Professor Sinigaglia* • Renato Salvatori *Raoul* • Annie Girardot *Niobe* • Gabriella Giorgelli *Adele* • Bernard Blier *Martinetti* ■ *Dir* Mario Monicelli • *Scr* Mario Monicelli, Age, Scarpelli

Orgazmo ★★★ 18

Comedy 1997 · US · Colour · 88mins

The characters may be real-life actors rather than crudely drawn caricatures, but this second full-length feature from the co-creator of *South Park*, Trey Parker, admirably continues to flout all things tasteful, politically correct and sophisticated. Director Parker plays a naive Mormon actor doing the rounds of LA, who finds himself cast as the lead player in a porn movie. He intends to use the $20,000 salary for his impending marriage to his devoted fiancée back in Utah. Not quite as offensive as *South Park*, but sensitive souls will still be outraged by the relentless flow of lavatorial laughs and vulgarity. JF [video] DVD

Trey Parker *Joe Young* • Dian Bachar *Ben Chapleski* • Robyn Lynne Raab *Lisa, Joe's fiancée* • Michael Dean Jacobs *Maxxx Orbison* • Ron Jeremy *Clark* • Andrew W Kemler *Rodgers* • David Dunn *A-Cup* • Matt Stone *Dave the lighting guy* ■ *Dir/Scr* Trey Parker

Original Gangstas ★★★ 18

Crime drama 1996 · US · Colour · 98mins

Attention all blaxploitation fanatics! Five 1970s icons – Pam Grier, Fred Williamson, Jim Brown, Ron O'Neal and Richard Roundtree – team up to teach a Gary, Indiana, ghetto gang a tough-guy lesson in veteran B-movie director Larry Cohen's hip, black, badass action update. Exciting and thought-provoking (should fire be fought with fire?), it's both a contemporary morality tale and an affectionately nostalgic look back at the *Shaft* and *Foxy Brown* era. AJ [video]

Fred Williamson *John Bookman* • Jim Brown *Jake Trevor* • Pam Grier *Laurie Thompson* • Paul Winfield *Reverend Marshall Dorsey* • Ron O'Neal *Bubba* • Richard Roundtree *Slick* • Isabel Sanford *Gracie Bookman* ■ *Dir* Larry Cohen • *Scr* Aubrey Rattan

The Original Kings of Comedy ★★★★ 15

Documentary 2000 · US · Colour · 111mins

This is the least controversial of all director Spike Lee's movies: although the views on race in America are as hard-hitting as those in *Do the Right Thing* or *Bamboozled*, here they are embodied in the words and gestures of four black comedians. Lee's documentary, filmed in Charlotte, North Carolina, uses the quartet's blisteringly hilarious presence as a battering ram to jolt us into laughing at human bigotries. Steve Harvey, DL Hughley, Cedric the Entertainer and Bernie Mac are the wisecracking four, who draw on a vaudeville background that has all but disappeared. There are few British comics who can stand up to these stand-ups when it comes to outrageous comments on real life; with this film, Lee gives them a well-deserved global audience at last. TH. Contains swearing and sexual references. [video]

Dir Spike Lee • *Cinematographer* Malik Sayeed

Original Sin ★★ 18

Period melodrama
2001 · US/Fr · Colour · 111mins

Antonio Banderas and Angelina Jolie star in a corny, cliché-ridden bodice-ripper. Set in late 19th-century Cuba, Banderas plays a wealthy coffee merchant who orders a mail-order bride from the US to bear his children. What he gets is Ms Jolie so it's lust at first sight, but Jolie has a sinister secret agenda, and Banderas soon finds himself embroiled in a cat-and-mouse con game. DA. Contains violence, sex scenes and nudity. [video] DVD

Antonio Banderas *Luis Antonio Vargas* • Angelina Jolie *Julia Russell/Bonny Castle* • Thomas Jane *Walter Downs/Billy/Mephisto* • Jack Thompson *Alan Jordan* • Gregory Itzin *Colonel Worth* • Allison Mackie *Augusta Jordan* ■ *Dir* Michael Cristofer • *Scr* Michael Cristofer, from the novel *Waltz into Darkness* by Cornell Woolrich

Orion's Belt ★★★ PG

Thriller 1985 · Nor · Colour · 87mins

Starting out as an arresting, almost docudramatic insight into how a trio of opportunist North Sea boatmen supplement their meagre earnings by ferrying tourists, this big-budget Norwegian production slickly transforms itself into a sinister mystery, as the group seeks shelter on a remote Arctic outpost only to discover that it is actually the home of a Soviet spy station. But once he's past the spectacular helicopter sequence, director Ola Solum begins to run out of ideas and resorts to Cold War stereotypes. DP. In Norwegian with English subtitles. [video]

Helge Jordal *Tom Jansen* • Sverre Anker Ousdal *Larse* • Hans Ola Sorlie *Sverre* • Kjersti Holmen *Eva Jelseth* ■ *Dir* Ola Solum • *Scr* Richard Harris [Harald Paalgard, Ola Solum], from the novel by Jon Michelet

Orlando ★★★ PG

Historical fantasy
1992 · UK/Rus/Fr/It/Neth · Colour · 89mins

Director Sally Potter achieves the near-impossible task of bringing Virginia Woolf's complex tale to the screen in a series of burnished and glittering images. The film tells the story of young nobleman Orlando who lives for 400 years and mysteriously changes into a woman during the 18th century. As the hero/heroine, Tilda Swinton moves passively through the romantic, dramatic and intriguing events that befall Orlando, and there's an excellent supporting cast that includes Quentin Crisp as Elizabeth I. Sometimes puzzling, sometimes boring, but also sumptuous and atmospheric. RK [video] DVD

Tilda Swinton *Orlando* • Billy Zane *Shelmerdine* • John Wood *Archduke Harry* • Lothaire Bluteau *The Khan* • Charlotte Valandrey *Sasha* • Heathcote Williams *Nick Greene/Publisher* • Quentin Crisp *Queen Elizabeth I* • Dudley Sutton *King James I* • Thom Hoffman *King William of Orange* • Anna Healy *Euphrosyne* • Simon Russell Beale *Earl of Moray* • Ned Sherrin *Mr Addison* ■ *Dir* Sally Potter • *Scr* Sally Potter, from the novel by Virginia Woolf

Orphans ★★★ 15

Drama 1987 · US · Colour · 110mins

Albert Finney had played the drunken kidnap victim on stage in 1986 at the Hampstead Theatre Club, received rave reviews and filmed it a year later with Matthew Modine and Kevin Anderson as his kidnappers. Influenced by Harold Pinter, Lyle Kessler's play is a dark fable about domination, and director Alan J Pakula, respecting the source material, eschews the sort of visual flourishes that distinguish his other films. Stagey, but Finney is great. AT. Contains swearing. [video]

Albert Finney *Harold* • Matthew Modine *Treat* • Kevin Anderson *Phillip* • John Kellogg *Barney* • Anthony Heald *Man In Park* • Novella Nelson *Mattie* ■ *Dir* Alan J Pakula • *Scr* Lyle Kessler, from his play

Orphans ★★★★ 18

Black comedy drama
1998 · UK · Colour · 97mins

Actor Peter Mullan takes a turn behind the camera to write and direct this black comedy drama about four siblings and the long night they experience before burying their dearly departed mum. Star-in-the-making Douglas Henshall is the brother who ends up being stabbed following a bar brawl, while Rosemarie Stevenson – as the sister with cerebral palsy – gets stranded in an alley when her electric wheelchair breaks down. Unusual and quirky stuff indeed, yet Mullan deftly mixes humour with pathos. JB. Contains swearing, violence. [video] DVD

Douglas Henshall *Michael Flynn* • Gary Lewis *Thomas Flynn* • Stephen McCole *John Flynn* • Rosemarie Stevenson *Sheila Flynn* • Frank Gallagher *Tanga* • Alex Norton *Hanson* ■ *Dir/Scr* Peter Mullan

Orphans of the Storm ★★★★

Silent period melodrama
1921 · US · BW · 125mins

DW Griffith, writing under the name of Gaston de Tolignac, tackled the French Revolution, built a period Paris on 14 acres at his Mamaroneck studios, and had his luminous star, Lillian Gish, and her sister, Dorothy, play the orphaned sisters caught up in the bloody events. The plot, bursting with melodramatic incident, has Lillian, the carer of her blind sister, sent to the guillotine for harbouring her aristocrat lover (the splendid Joseph Schildkraut), only to be saved at the last minute by the intervention of Danton (Monte Blue). Not quite a silent masterpiece, it's still visually spectacular and largely absorbing. RK

Lillian Gish *Henriette Girard* • Dorothy Gish *Louise* • Joseph Schildkraut *Chevalier de Vaudrey* • Frank Losee *Count de Linières* • Katherine Emmett *Director* • Monte Blue *Danton* ■ *Dir* DW Griffith • *Scr* Marquis Gaston de Tolignac [DW Griffith], from the play *Les Deux Orphelines* by Adolphe Philippe Dennery, Eugène Cormon, adapted by N Hart Jackson, Albert Marshman Palmer

Orphée ★★★★★ PG

Fantasy 1950 · Fr · BW · 90mins

Jean Cocteau's updating of the Orpheus myth to post-Liberation Paris is one of the cinema's great artistic masterpieces, a piece of Méliès-like magic that is intensely powerful and moving even at its most bewildering. Jean Marais is the poet who falls in love with Death (Maria Casarès); her assistant, angel François Périer, snatches the poet's wife and forces him to enter the underworld to get her back. The use of images, especially the looking-glass that turns into water, is still daring and – it might be said – rich in gay iconography. In 1960, Cocteau made a sequel, *Le Testament d'Orphée*. AT. In French with English subtitles. [video] DVD

Jean Marais *Orphée* • François Périer *Heurtebise* • Maria Casarès *Princess* • Marie Déa *Eurydice* • Henri Cremieux *The editor* • Juliette Gréco [Juliette Greco] *Aglaonice* • Roger Blin *The writer* • Edouard Dermithe *Cégeste* • Pierre Bertin *The Inspector* • Jacques Varennes *First Judge* • Jean Cocteau *The voice* ■ *Dir/Scr* Jean Cocteau • *Cinematographer* Nicolas Hayer

Osaka Elegy ★★★★★

Drama 1936 · Jpn · BW · 71mins

Inspired by the sacrifices made by his own geisha sister, Kenji Mizoguchi's masterly drama marked the beginning of his longtime collaboration with screenwriter Yoshikata Yoda. Scrupulously avoiding sensationalism, it charts the descent into prostitution of a young telephonist, who becomes her boss's mistress in a bid to repay her embezzling father's debts and fund her brother's education. Mizoguchi regular Isuzu Yamada contributes a superb display of abused decency, but it's the director's astute visual sense that gives the picture its power, with the stylised realism of his claustrophobic compositions suggesting the exploitative repression of a corrupt patriarchal society. DP. A Japanese language film.

Isuzu Yamada *Ayako Murai* • Seiichi Takegawa *Junzo, Ayako's father* • Chiyoko Okura *Sachiko* • Shinpachiro Asaka *Hiroshi* • Benkei Shiganoya *Sonosuke Asai* • Yoko Umemura *Sumiko* • Kensaku Hara *Susumu Nishimura* • Shizuko Takizawa *Apartment maid* • Eitaro Shindo *Fujino* ■ *Dir* Kenji Mizoguchi • *Scr* Yoshikata Yoda, Kenjii Mizoguchi, from the serial *Mieko* by Saburo Okada in the magazine *Shincho*

Osama ★★★★ 12

Drama 2003 · Afg/Jpn/Ire · Colour · 79mins

The first feature produced in post-Taliban Afghanistan is a revealing political fairy tale, in which a plucky heroine attempts to challenge a chauvinist tyranny. Director Siddiq Barmak relies on trusted neorealist techniques to tell his tale and draws a moving performance from Marina Golbahari as the 12-year-old forced to disguise herself as a boy to find work after the closure of the hospital in which her war-widowed mother was a doctor. Indeed, the wholly untrained Golbahari exudes uncomprehending trust and innocent courage, until she is sent to a strict Koranic school where she lives in daily dread of her secret being exposed. DP. In Afghani with English subtitles. DVD

Marina Golbahari *Osama* • Arif Herati *Espandi* • Zubaida Sahar *Mother* • Khwaja Nader *Mullah* • Hamida Refah *Grandmother* ■ *Dir/Scr* Siddiq Barmak

O

The Oscar ★★★

Drama 1966 · US · Colour · 120mins

Stephen Boyd makes a fair fist of villainy here as actor Frank Fane who has been nominated for an Oscar and sits in the Shrine Auditorium waiting for the envelope to be opened. As he waits the flashback starts, showing how this slimeball walked over countless people and survived a slew of sex scandals to be a major movie star. It's hugely, trashily enjoyable and filled with a lot of in-jokes and bursting with cameos. AT

Stephen Boyd *Frank Fane* • Elke Sommer *Kay Bergdahl* • Milton Berle *Kappy Kapstetter* • Eleanor Parker *Sophie Cantaro* • Joseph Cotten *Kenneth H Regan* • Jill St John *Laurel Scott* • Tony Bennett *Hymie Kelly* • Edie Adams *Trina Yale* • Ernest Borgnine *Barney Yale* • Ed Begley *Grobard* • Walter Brennan *Orrin C Quentin* • Broderick Crawford *Sheriff* • Peter Lawford *Steve Marks* • Edith Head • Bob Hope • Merle Oberon • Frank Sinatra • Nancy Sinatra • Hedda Hopper ■ *Dir* Russell Rouse • *Scr* Harlan Ellison, Russell Rouse, Clarence Greene, from the novel by Richard Sale

Oscar ★★★ PG

Comedy 1991 · US · Colour · 105mins

The decline of John Landis is one of the cruellest blows to strike Hollywood comedy in recent years. However, he manages a semblance of form with this gangster farce based on a French play. Sylvester Stallone strives a touch too hard for laughs as the mobster whose plans to quit the rackets are confounded by a series of domestic crises and that old standby, the "mixed-up bags" routine. The main interest lies in the sly cameos, with Peter Riegert and Chazz Palminteri the standouts in the supporting cast. DP. Contains some swearing.

Sylvester Stallone *Angelo "Snaps" Provolone* • Ornella Muti *Sofia Provolone* • Peter Riegert *Aldo* • Vincent Spano *Anthony Rossano* • Marisa Tomei *Lisa Provolone* • Elizabeth Barondes *Theresa* • Kirk Douglas *Eduardo Provolone* • Art LaFleur *Officer Quinn* • Ken Howard *Kirkwood* • Don Ameche *Father Clemente* • Chazz Palminteri *Connie* • Tim Curry *Dr Thornton Poole* ■ *Dir* John Landis • *Scr* Michael Barrie, Jim Mulholland, from the play by Claude Magnier

Oscar and Lucinda ★★ 15

Romantic drama
1997 · US/Aus · Colour · 126mins

Adapted from Peter Carey's Booker Prize-winning novel, this story about two Victorian eccentrics with a passion for gambling was never going to be an easy choice to make into a film. Unfortunately, the end result is an irritating and generally incomprehensible art movie. Anglican minister Ralph Fiennes's wagers heiress Cate Blanchett that he can transport a glass chapel across the Australian outback. Pretentious twaddle. AT. Contains swearing, violence, sex scenes.

Ralph Fiennes *Oscar Hopkins/Oscar's great grandson* • Cate Blanchett *Lucinda Leplastrier* • Ciaran Hinds *Reverend Dennis Hasset* • Tom Wilkinson *Hugh Stratton* • Richard Roxburgh *Mr Jeffris* • Clive Russell *Theophilus* ■ *Dir* Gillian Armstrong • *Scr* Laura Jones, from the novel by Peter Carey

Oscar Wilde ★★★

Biographical drama 1959 · UK · BW · 96mins

Emboldened by the Government's Wolfenden Report, British film-makers at the turn of the 1960s began to deal frankly with homosexual themes. This modest production, directed by Russian actor Gregory Ratoff, who died months after the premiere, had its thunder stolen by the more ambitious *The Trials of Oscar Wilde*. Nevertheless it is well worth seeing, with Sir Ralph Richardson and Alexander Knox sparring in a grippingly staged courtroom scene, and Robert Morley, although too old, revealing hidden depths in the title role. DM

Robert Morley *Oscar Wilde* • Phyllis Calvert *Constance Wilde* • John Neville *Lord Alfred Douglas* • Ralph Richardson *Sir Edward Carson* • Dennis Price *Robert Ross* • Alexander Knox *Sir Edward Clarke* • Edward Chapman *Marquis of Queensbury* • Martin Benson *George Alexander* ■ *Dir* Gregory Ratoff • *Scr* Jo Eisinger, from a play by Leslie Stokes, Sewell Stokes

Osmosis Jones ★★★ PG

Part-animated comedy
2001 · US · Colour · 91mins

Bobby and Peter Farrelly have come up with an intriguing mix of live-action and inventive animation starring arch slob Bill Murray. He plays a sloppy zoo worker with bad eating habits who becomes infected with a killer cold virus (voiced by Laurence Fishburne) intent on murdering him within 48 hours. Here's where the audience gets to explore Murray's animated innards, "the city of Frank", and meet maverick police corpuscule Osmosis Jones (Chris Rock) and his cold-cure pal Drix (David Hyde Pierce). The puns on bodily functions and fluids are aimed at the young. TH DVD

Bill Murray *Frank Detorri* • Chris Rock *Osmosis Jones, "Ozzy"* • Laurence Fishburne *Thrax* • David Hyde Pierce *Drix* • Brandy Norwood [Brandy] *Leah* • William Shatner *Mayor Phlegmming* ■ *Dir* Bobby Farrelly, Peter Farrelly • *Scr* Marc Hyman

Ossessione ★★★★ PG

Drama 1942 · It · BW · 134mins

A drifter gets a job at a roadside café and has a torrid affair with the owner's wife who then asks her lover to murder her fat, loutish husband. Yes, this is the Italian version of *The Postman Always Rings Twice*, and it marked the directing debut of the Marxist aristocrat, Luchino Visconti. This transposition to the flat marshland of the Po Valley, with its working-class characters, drab settings and base morality, was banned by Mussolini's censors for its depiction of working-class life. The Fascists burned the negative, but Visconti managed to save a print. It was later credited with starting a new movement in Italian cinema called neorealism. AT. In Italian with English subtitles. DVD

Clara Calamai *Giovanna* • Massimo Girotti *Gino* • Juan de Landa *The husband* • Elia Marcuzzo *Giuseppe Tavolato, "The Spaniard"* • Dhia Cristani *Anita* • Vittorio Duse *The lorry driver* ■ *Dir* Luchino Visconti • *Scr* Mario Alicata, Antonio Pietrangeli, Gianni Puccini, Giuseppe De Santis, Luchino Visconti, from the novel *The Postman Always Rings Twice* by James M Cain

The Osterman Weekend ★★★ 18

Thriller 1983 · US · Colour · 97mins

In Sam Peckinpah's final film, Burt Lancaster is the CIA chief with presidential ambitions, who gets operative John Hurt to persuade TV journalist Rutger Hauer that there are Soviet agents among the guests assembled for a weekend get-together. Video gadgets push the atmosphere of post-Watergate paranoia to breaking point, but the confusion experienced by the characters is nothing compared to the audience's bafflement at the convoluted plot. TH. Contains violence, swearing and brief nudity. DVD

Rutger Hauer *John Tanner* • John Hurt *Lawrence Fassett* • Craig T Nelson *Bernard Osterman* • Dennis Hopper *Richard Tremayne* • Chris Sarandon *Joseph Cardone* • Burt Lancaster *Maxwell Danforth* • Meg Foster *Ali Tanner* • Helen Shaver *Virginia Tremayne* ■ *Dir* Sam Peckinpah • *Scr* Ian Sharp, Ian Masters, from the novel by Robert Ludlum

Otello ★★★★ U

Opera 1986 · It · Colour · 117mins

Franco Zeffirelli transposes Verdi's classic version of Shakespeare's tragedy into sweeping big-screen melodrama. Placido Domingo is magnificent as the jealous Moor, whose corruption by Iago crucifies his marriage to the gentle Desdemona. Domingo looks relaxed on screen, with Zeffirelli managing to remove the static tendencies of stage-bound singers to make a fluid and compelling film drama. Katia Ricciarelli is a delicate Desdemona, Justino Diaz a demonic Iago and Urbano Barberini a Cassio worthy of arousing crippling infidelity anxiety. One of the best films of opera ever made. LH. In Italian with English subtitles. DVD

Placido Domingo *Otello* • Katia Ricciarelli *Desdemona* • Justino Diaz *Iago* • Petra Malakova *Emilia* • Urbano Barberini *Cassio* ■ *Dir* Franco Zeffirelli • *Scr* Franco Zeffirelli, from the libretto by Arrigo Boito for the opera by Giuseppe Verdi

Othello ★★★★★ U

Tragedy
1952 · US/Fr/Mor/It · Colour · 89mins

Orson Welles found filming Shakespeare's tale about the Moor far from straightforward – most disruptively, he had to close production down three times so he could go away and earn the money to continue. But it's testimony to the master film-maker's tremendous talent that he continually turned the many setbacks to his advantage. When the costumes failed to arrive, he improvised one of the movie's finest scenes, the murder in the Turkish bath; and he compensates for the lack of purpose-built sets by making inspired use of the north African architecture to sculpt a world of shadows and treachery. Welles creates far more than a filmed version of the play – more like the most cinematic Shakespeare adaptation ever. NPF DVD

Orson Welles *Othello* • Michael MacLiammoir *Iago* • Suzanne Cloutier *Desdemona* • Robert Coote *Roderigo* • Hilton Edwards *Brabantio* • Michael Laurence (1) *Cassio* • Fay Compton *Emilia* ■ *Dir* Orson Welles • *Scr* Orson Welles, from the play by William Shakespeare

Othello ★★★★ U

Tragedy 1955 · USSR · Colour · 103mins

Having striven for 20 years to make this film, Sergei Yutkevitch got his just desserts by being named Best Director at Cannes. Working from a free translation by the novelist Boris Pasternak, and employing a symbolic palette to emphasise the play's physical and temperamental contrasts, Yutkevitch played down the Moor's rage to concentrate on the corruption of his nobility by the scheming Iago. Director-in-waiting Sergei Bondarchuk acquits himself admirably as Othello opposite his future wife, Irina Skobtseva, as the wrongfully accused Desdemona. DP. Russian dialogue dubbed into English.

Sergei Bondarchuk *Othello* • Irina Skobtseva *Desdemona* • Andrei Popov *Iago* • Vladimir Soshalsky *Cassio* • E Vesnik *Roderigo* • Antonina Maximova *Emilia* ■ *Dir* Sergei Yutkevitch • *Scr* Sergei Yutkevitch, from a translation by Boris Pasternak of the play by William Shakespeare

Othello ★★★★ U

Tragedy 1965 · UK · Colour · 158mins

Stagebound and elegantly lit by cinematographer Geoffrey Unsworth, this is a stunning transfer of Laurence Olivier's legendary National Theatre production to film. While it does not have the cinematic fireworks of Orson Welles's version, it is an indispensable record of Olivier's titanic, vigorously African performance as the Moor of Venice who "loved not wisely but too well". This also has the distinction of being the only Shakespearean film for which all four principals received Oscar nominations (Olivier, Maggie Smith, Frank Finlay and Joyce Redman) and features the screen debut of a young Derek Jacobi. AME DVD

Laurence Olivier *Othello* • Maggie Smith *Desdemona* • Frank Finlay *Iago* • Joyce Redman *Emilia* • Derek Jacobi *Cassio* • Robert Lang *Roderigo* • Kenneth Mackintosh *Lodovico* • Anthony Nicholls *Brabantio* • Sheila Reid *Bianca* ■ *Dir* Stuart Burge • *Scr* Margaret Unsworth, from the stage production by John Dexter of the play by William Shakespeare

Othello ★★★ 12

Tragedy 1995 · US/UK · Colour · 118mins

Laurence Fishburne follows in the footsteps of Orson Welles and Laurence Olivier. Young, gifted and appropriately black, he plays the title role as a sensual, bald and tattooed soldier, and is joined by Irène Jacob as Desdemona and Kenneth Branagh as a magnificently seething Iago. Shakespeare's tragedy has been hacked roughly in half by director Oliver Parker whose choice of locations is a plus but whose scaling down is generally a minus. AT

Laurence Fishburne *Othello* • Irène Jacob *Desdemona* • Kenneth Branagh *Iago* • Nathaniel Parker *Cassio* • Michael Maloney *Roderigo* • Anna Patrick *Emilia* • Nicholas Farrell *Montano* • Indra Ove *Bianca* • Michael Sheen *Lodovico* • André Oumansky *Gratiano* ■ *Dir* Oliver Parker • *Scr* Oliver Parker, from the play by William Shakespeare

The Other ★★★★

Horror 1972 · US · Colour · 99mins

A commercial flop, with no stars, too "arty" for popular taste, this highly atmospheric spook drama is much admired by aficionados. It is the only horror film from distinguished director Robert Mulligan, who adds beautiful visual touches to former actor Tom Tryon's screenplay, an adaptation of his own first novel. Set in 1935, the slow-moving but increasingly disturbing tale concerns a 10-year-old boy (a wonderful performance by Chris Udvarnoky) who claims that a series of murders are the work of his dead identical twin. The twins' grandmother is played by noted drama teacher Uta Hagen. Be prepared for a shocking climax. DM. Contains swearing.

Uta Hagen *Ada* • Chris Udvarnoky *Niles Perry* • Martin Udvarnoky *Holland Perry* • Diana Muldaur *Alexandra Perry* • Norma Connolly *Aunt Vee* • Victor French *Angelini* • Loretta Leversee *Winnie* • Lou Frizzell *Uncle George* • John Ritter *Rider* ■ *Dir* Robert Mulligan • *Scr* Thomas Tryon [Tom Tryon], from his novel

Other Halves ★★ 15

Drama 1984 · NZ · Colour · 104mins

Touching drama about the romance between two people who meet in a mental hospital. Lisa Harrow is a white woman who's recovering from a nervous breakdown; Mark Pilisi is a Maori teenager who's undergoing drug rehab. As soon as they're discharged, the pair move in together, but gradually find their relationship threatened by a clash of cultures and outlooks. There's a nice performance from Lisa Harrow but a slightly wooden one from Pilisi, who was found after a nationwide star-search across New Zealand. DA

Lisa Harrow *Liz* • Mark Pilisi *Tug* • Fraser Stephen-Smith *Michael* • Paul Gittins *Ken* • Emma Piper *Audrey* ■ *Dir* John Laing • *Scr* Sue McCanley, from her novel

The Other Love ★★ PG

Romantic drama 1947 · US · BW · 88mins

This larded, treacly plot comes firmly under the heading of Nonsense. Barbara Stanwyck is dying, as only a cinema diva can, but instead of taking the advice of devoted doctor David Niven, she hightails it with charismatic gambler Richard Conte. Niven pines, Conte leers and Stanwyck over-eggs the pudding alarmingly with every twinge. SH

Barbara Stanwyck *Karen Duncan* • David Niven *Dr Anthony Stanton* • Richard Conte *Paul Clermont* • Gilbert Roland *Croupier* • Joan Lorring *Celestine* • Richard Hale *Professor Linnaker* ■ *Dir* Andre De Toth • *Scr* Ladislas Fodor, Harry Brown, from the short story *Beyond* by Erich Maria Remarque

Other Men's Women ★★★★

Melodrama 1931 · US · BW · 69mins

Basically a conventional love-triangle story, this early talkie is given tremendous power and resonance by the vigorous direction of William A Wellman and the tight editing that was a trademark of the Warner Bros studio in the 1930s. Enacted in nocturnal, sometimes rainswept settings, it provides riveting viewing. In a typically audacious sequence, James Cagney, playing a minor role in his third film but clearly a star in the making, walks into a dance hall and breaks into an impromptu tap routine. A remarkable moment in an inventive movie. TV

Grant Withers *Bill* • Mary Astor *Lily* • Regis Toomey *Jack* • James Cagney *Ed* • Fred Kohler *Haley* • J Farrell MacDonald *Pegleg* • Joan Blondell *Marie* • Walter Long *Bixby* ■ *Dir* William A Wellman • *Scr* William K Wells, Maude Fulton, from a story by Maude Fulton

Other People's Money ★★★ 15

Comedy drama 1991 · US · Colour · 96mins

Danny DeVito plays Larry the Liquidator, whose asset-stripping gaze falls upon the old-fashioned New England company run by stubborn Gregory Peck. However, the battle becomes complicated when he falls for the company's lawyer, Penelope Ann Miller, who is leading the fight against him. DeVito is charmingly sleazy, while Peck embodies honourable liberal capitalism. Norman Jewison's direction is smooth and he is well served by cinematographer Haskell Wexler. JF. Contains swearing.

Danny DeVito *Lawrence Garfield* • Gregory Peck *Andrew Jorgenson* • Penelope Ann Miller *Kate Sullivan* • Piper Laurie *Bea Sullivan* • Dean Jones *Bill Coles* • RD Call *Arthur* • Mo Gaffney *Harriet* • Bette Henritze *Emma* • Tom Aldredge *Ozzie* ■ *Dir* Norman Jewison • *Scr* Alvin Sargent, from the play by Jerry Sterner

The Other Side of Midnight ★★★ 18

Melodrama 1977 · US · Colour · 158mins

Based on a blockbuster novel by Sidney Sheldon, this melodrama runs for nearly three hours, covers the whole of the Second World War and its aftermath, and flits between the continents without pausing for breath. It has the courage of its clichés, so sometimes we laugh as the characters bump into each other across the years, tears and oceans. AT

Marie-France Pisier *Noelle Page* • John Beck *Larry Douglas* • Susan Sarandon *Catherine Douglas* • Raf Vallone *Constantin Demeris* • Clu Gulager *Bill Fraser* • Christian Marquand *Armand Gautier* • Michael Lerner *Barbet* ■ *Dir* Charles Jarrott • *Scr* Herman Raucher, Daniel Taradash, from the novel by Sidney Sheldon

The Other Side of Sunday ★★★

Comedy drama 1996 · Nor · Colour · 103mins

Nominated for the best foreign film Oscar, this charming drama unassumingly captures the curiosity and contumacy of a strictly raised small-town teenager. But what sets it apart is a take on religion that unmistakably echoes that of the great Danish film-maker, Carl Theodor Dreyer. This tragicomic study of repression and rebellion adroitly avoids both melodrama and the clichés of the rites-of-passage picture. But, thanks to Maria Theisen's spirited performance, there is also subtle power in Berit Nesheim's attack on the patriarchal nature of both church and state. DP. In Norwegian with English subtitles.

Marie Theisen *Maria* • Bjorn Sundquist *Father* • Sylvia Salvesen *Mother* • Hildegunn Riise *Fru Tunheim* ■ *Dir* Berit Nesheim • *Scr* Berit Nesheim, Lasse Glomm, from the novel *Søndag (Sunday)* by Reidun Nortvedt

The Other Side of the Bed ★★★ 15

Romantic musical comedy
2002 · Sp · Colour · 104mins

With Ernesto Alterio cheating on Paz Vega with best pal Guillermo Toledo's girlfriend Natalia Verbeke, the plot of this romantic comedy couldn't be more formulaic. But such is the eloquence of the dialogue, the aptitude of the good-looking cast and the action's slick shifts in tone and pace that it's easy to forgive the familiarity. However, it's harder to comprehend the decision to interrupt the farce with a series of second-rate musical numbers. DP. In Spanish with English subtitles. Contains swearing and sex scenes. DVD

Ernesto Alterio *Javier* • Paz Vega *Sonia* • Guillermo Toledo *Pedro* • Natalia Verbeke *Paula* • Alberto San Juan *Rafa* • María Esteve *Pilar* • Ramón Barea *Sagaz* • Nathalie Poza *Lucía* ■ *Dir* Emilio Martínez-Lázaro • *Scr* David Serrano

The Other Side of the Mountain ★★★

Biographical drama
1975 · US · Colour · 99mins

Superior and heart-wrenching biopic about Jill Kinmont, an Olympic-standard skier whose career was cut short when a fall left her paralysed. Marilyn Hassett makes an impressive film debut as Kinmont, portraying her as a fighter whose gutsiness initially arouses expectations of recovery that were destined to be unfulfilled. The film's modest success prompted a sequel three years later. DA

Marilyn Hassett *Jill Kinmont* • Beau Bridges *Dick Buek* • Belinda J Montgomery *Audra-Jo* • Nan Martin *June Kinmont* • William Bryant *Bill Kinmont* • Dabney Coleman *Dave McCoy* ■ *Dir* Larry Peerce • *Scr* David Seltzer, from the biography *A Long Way Up* by EG Valens

The Other Side of the Mountain – Part 2 ★★

Biographical romantic drama
1978 · US · Colour · 105mins

Tear-jerking sequel to the 1975 movie based on the real-life story of Jill Kinmont. The film opens with Jill (again played by Marilyn Hassett) recovering from yet another emotional body blow with the death of the man who helped her after her accident, before continuing with her burgeoning romance with a truck driver played by Timothy Bottoms, whose real-life father James also appears in the film. FL

Marilyn Hassett *Jill Kinmont* • Timothy Bottoms *John Boothe* • Nan Martin *June Kinmont* • Belinda J Montgomery *Audra-Jo* • Gretchen Corbett *Linda* • William Bryant *Bill Kinmont* • James A Bottoms *Mr Boothe* • June Dayton *Mrs Boothe* ■ *Dir* Larry Peerce • *Scr* Douglas Day Stewart

The Other Sister ★★ 15

Romantic drama
1999 · US · Colour · 130mins

It needs a sure and delicate touch to use a mental disability as a dramatic device; otherwise, it's a tasteless gimmick to move the plot along. Sadly, despite a fine performance from Juliette Lewis, this is both clumsy and manipulative. Lewis is a rich San Francisco teenager fresh out of a mental institution. She wants to be a vet's assistant; despite the approval of father Tom Skerritt, but she has to fight mother Diane Keaton every step of the way. TH. Contains sexual references. DVD

Diane Keaton *Elizabeth* • Juliette Lewis *Carla Tate* • Tom Skerritt *Radley Tate* • Giovanni Ribisi *Danny* • Poppy Montgomery *Caroline* • Sarah Paulson *Heather* • Linda Thorson *Drew* • Joe Flanigan *Jeff* • Juliet Mills *Winnie* ■ *Dir* Garry Marshall • *Scr* Garry Marshall, Bob Brunner, from a story by Alexandra Rose, Blair Richwood

Other Voices, Other Rooms ★★ 12

Period drama 1995 · US/UK · Colour · 98mins

After producing a handful of enterprising documentaries, British director David Rocksavage made an inauspicious start to his feature career with this achingly dull adaptation of Truman Capote's debut novel. Trotting out all those tired Deep South Gothic clichés, Rocksavage seems uncertain whether to concentrate on atmosphere, plot or character, and ends up fudging all three. David Speck works hard as the teenager sent to live with his suspiciously infirm father. As his disturbed cousins, Anna Thomson is twitchily timid, while Lothaire Bluteau's effete aesthete is embarrassingly melodramatic. DP

Lothaire Bluteau *Randolph Skully* • Anna Thomson [Anna Levine] *Amy Skully* • David Speck *Joel Sansom* • April Turner *Zoo* • Frank Taylor *Edward "Ed" R Sansom* ■ *Dir* David Rocksavage • *Scr* Sara Flanigan, David Rocksavage, from the novel by Truman Capote

The Other Woman ★★ PG

Drama 1994 · US · Colour · 88mins

This is an unashamedly sentimental melodrama, in which bitter enmity turns to friendship in the face of terminal illness. As the finally reconciled women, Jill Eikenberry and Laura Leighton make the most of a glutinous script in a TV movie that really does have to be seen to be believed. DP DVD

Jill Eikenberry *Tessa* • Laura Leighton *Carolyn* • Lloyd Bridges *Jacob* • James Read *Michael Bryan* ■ *Dir* Gabrielle Beaumont • *Scr* Nancey Silvers

The Others ★★★ 12

Period horror thriller
2001 · US/Sp · Colour · 99mins

Nicole Kidman gives a powerful turn as a highly strung woman living alone in a postwar Jersey mansion with her two light-sensitive children. It's when she engages a trio of new servants that her shadowy home suddenly turns very creepy indeed, as her daughter starts to see "things" and they all experience seemingly supernatural events. Relying on deliberately old-fashioned bumps in the night for suspense, Alejandro Amenábar (in his English-language debut feature) creates a study in terror that relies on performance, atmosphere and mood. AJ DVD

Nicole Kidman *Grace* • Fionnula Flanagan *Mrs Mills* • Christopher Eccleston *Charles* • Alakina Mann *Anne* • James Bentley *Nicholas* • Eric Sykes *Mr Tuttle* • Elaine Cassidy *Lydia* • Renée Asherson *Old lady* ■ *Dir/Scr* Alejandro Amenábar

Otherworld ★★★ 12A

Part-animated adventure
2003 · UK · Colour · 108mins

This ambitious animation is based on a collection of Welsh myths, and director Derek Hayes concentrates on four "branches" to recount the tales of King Bendigeidfran's war with Ireland, Rhiannon's domestic woes and Lleu's adventures with his magician uncle, Gwydion. The live-action bookends involving three teenagers are an unfortunate miscalculation. However, once the trio's cartoon selves appear on a floating island, the complex plotlines begin to weave their spell. This occasionally gory fable may lack spectacle, but the folkloric aspects are fascinating. DP

Ioan Gruffud *King Bendigeidfran* • Matthew Rhys *Lleu* • Daniel Evans *Dan* • Jenny Livesy *Rhiannon* • Paul McGann *King Matholwch* • Philip Madoc *Gwydion* • Lisa Palfrey *Arianrhod* • Anton Lesser *Teyrnon* ■ *Dir* Derek Hayes • *Scr* Martin Lamb, Penelope Middleboe, inspired by the Celtic text *Y Mabinogi (The Mabinogion)/Tales of Young Men*

Otley ★★★ PG

Spy spoof 1968 · UK · Colour · 87mins

Even when it was released, this London-set Swinging Sixties spy spoof looked dreadfully old-fashioned. Indeed, without the comic genius of writers Dick Clement and Ian La Frenais it might have been a disaster. Forget about the labyrinthine plot that soon becomes impossible to follow and concentrate instead on the delightful performance of Tom Courtenay as the hapless petty criminal caught up in the slick world of spy Romy Schneider. DM

Tom Courtenay *Gerald Arthur Otley* • Romy Schneider *Imogen* • Alan Badel *Hadrian* • James Villiers *Hendrickson* • Leonard Rossiter *Johnston* • Freddie Jones *Proudfoot* • Fiona Lewis *Lin* • James Bolam *Albert* ■ *Dir* Dick Clement • *Scr* Ian La Frenais, Dick Clement, from the novel by Martin Waddell

O

Our Betters ★★★★

Comedy 1933 · US · BW · 79mins

RKO producer David O Selznick deployed the polished gifts of director George Cukor and actress Constance Bennett for this now dated screen version of W Somerset Maugham's equally dated but far from uninteresting play. An acid and brittle comedy of manners exposing the amorality of the English upper classes, it focuses on an American heiress (Bennett) who marries an English aristocrat (Alan Mowbray), only to realise that her money was what attracted him. Bennett gives a meticulous performance in this sophisticated film. RK

Constance Bennett *Lady Pearl Grayston* • Gilbert Roland *Pepi D'Costa* • Anita Louise *Bessie* • Hugh Sinclair *Lord Bleane* • Alan Mowbray *Lord George Grayston* • Grant Mitchell *Thornton Clay* • Charles Starrett *Fleming Harvey* • Phoebe Foster *Princess* ■ *Dir* George Cukor • *Scr* Jane Murfin, Harry Wagstaff Gribble, from the play by W Somerset Maugham

Our Children ★★★

Musical drama 1948 · Pol · BW · 75mins

Although the comedy duo of Shimon Dzigan and Yisroel Schumacher are nominally the stars of this affecting musical drama, the emphasis is firmly on the children they go to entertain at the Helenowek orphan colony near Lodz, whose recollections of life in the camps and ghettoes testify to the part played by kids in resisting the Nazi tyranny. However, the authorities resented the notion that striking Gentile miners would accept charity from Jewish children and banned the film as pro-Zionist propaganda. Believed lost for 30 years, its place in history is assured as the last Yiddish film ever made in Poland. DP. In Yiddish with English subtitles.

Shimon Dzigan *Dzigan* • Yisroel Schumacher *Schumacher* • Niusia Gold *Orphanage director* ■ *Dir* Natan Gross, Shaul Goskind, Shimon Dzigan, Yisroel Schumacher

Our Daily Bread ★★

Drama 1934 · US · BW · 75mins

A young couple (Karen Morley and Tom Keene), victims of the Depression, leave the city for a derelict farm they've inherited. Revisiting the socially conscious territory of *The Crowd*, his 1928 silent masterpiece about the Depression, master director King Vidor picks up the same protagonists (played by different actors), to make a film of admirable and serious intentions, though lacking in pace and clarity. However, the piece as a whole disappoints audience expectations. RK

Karen Morley *Mary Sims* • Tom Keene *John Sims* • John Qualen *Chris* • Barbara Pepper *Sally* • Addison Richards *Louie* • Harry Holman *Uncle Anthony* ■ *Dir* King Vidor • *Scr* King Vidor, Elizabeth Hill, Joseph L Mankiewicz

Our Dancing Daughters ★★★

Silent romantic drama 1928 · US · BW · 86mins

A melodrama reflecting the morals and mores of the jazz age, this is the movie that catapulted Joan Crawford to major stardom. She plays a wild-living, hard-drinking, man-eating socialite who pulls herself out of the fast lane in the nick of time, settling for true love with John Mack Brown. Some of her friends are less fortunate. It's directed with an accurate sense of its milieu by Harry Beaumont, who went on to make several more films with Crawford. RK

Joan Crawford *Diana Medford* • John Mack Brown [Johnny Mack Brown] *Ben Blaine* • Nils Asther *Norman* • Dorothy Sebastian *Beatrice* • Anita Page *Ann* • Kathlyn Williams *Ann's mother* • Edward Nugent *Freddie* • Dorothy Cumming *Diana's mother* ■ *Dir* Harry Beaumont • *Scr* Josephine Lovett, Marion Ainslee (titles), Ruth Cummings (titles), from a story by Josephine Lovett

O

Our Girl Friday ★★ U

Comedy 1953 · UK · Colour · 79mins

This is one of those films that you think you've seen before until you realise that all the oh-so-familiar scenes have come from many different pictures. The story of amorous castaways competing for a single woman makes for a one-joke movie, although George Cole and Robertson Hare are amusing as the no-hopers tilting their caps at Joan Collins's very sexy Sadie. DP

Joan Collins *Sadie* • Kenneth More *Pat* • George Cole *Jimmy Carroll* • Robertson Hare *Gibble* • Hermione Gingold *Spinster* • Walter Fitzgerald *Captain* • Hattie Jacques *Mrs Patch* ■ *Dir/Scr* Noel Langley

Our Guys: Outrage in Glen Ridge ★★★ 15

Crime drama 1999 · US · Colour · 90mins

This is an affecting fact-based TV drama with a solid cast, in which a group of affluent high-school jocks sexually assault a mildly retarded 17-year-old girl (Heather Matarazzo). Determined detective Ally Sheedy faces a conspiracy of silence from the community, the school board and the police who are intent on protecting the winning athletes. Matarazzo, although at times unsympathetic, gives a standout performance, while Eric Stoltz, as the prosecutor, invokes the moral outrage of his uphill battle for justice. MC [video] DVD

Ally Sheedy *Detective Kelly Brooks* • Heather Matarazzo *Leslie Faber* • Sara Botsford *Mrs Faber* • Eric Stoltz *Robert Laurino* • Scott Vickaryous *Paul Archer* ■ *Dir* Guy Ferland • *Scr* Paul Brown, from the book *Our Guys* by Bernard Lefkowitz

Our Hospitality ★★★★★ U

Silent comedy 1923 · US · BW · 65mins

A feudin' and fussin' masterpiece for Buster Keaton – which he co-directed with John Blystone – in which Buster is William, the last of the McKays, returning to Rockville to inherit his father's estate and falling foul of the vengeful Canfields, whose daughter (Natalie Talmadge) he's fallen in love with. Buster's beloved trains supply a hilarious track of running gags and there is some astonishing stuntwork, all of which Buster did himself. It's one of his few films in which he puts on drag – to escape the Canfields – and there's a sequence with a waterfall that is brilliant in its audacity. Three generations of Keatons are featured, from Joseph the elder to Buster's own son, while the period detail is at once comic and totally accurate. TH [video]

Buster Keaton *William McKay* • Kitty Bradbury *Aunt Mary* • Joseph Keaton [Joe Keaton] *Lem Doolittle, train engineer* • James Duffy *Sam Gardner, train guard* • Natalie Talmadge *Virginia Canfield* • Ralph Bushman *Clayton Canfield* • Buster Keaton Jr *William McKay as a baby* ■ *Dir* Buster Keaton, John Blystone [John G Blystone] • *Scr* Jean Havez, Clyde Bruckman, Joseph Mitchell

Our House ★★ 12

Black comedy 2003 · US · Colour · 85mins

This ham-fisted slapstick farce is as much a test of patience for the viewer as elderly Irish neighbour Eileen Essell is for Ben Stiller and Drew Barrymore, who find that their new Brooklyn residence comes with Essell's overbearing upstairs tenant . Soon the dotty pensioner is driving them crazy and Stiller and Barrymore hire hitman James Remar to solve their problem. Even Stiller's genius comic timing can't compensate for the tastelessness or clumsy tone of this wildly uneven film. AJ. Contains swearing. [video] DVD

Ben Stiller *Alex Rose* • Drew Barrymore *Nancy Kendricks* • Eileen Essell *Mrs Connelly* • Harvey Fierstein *Kenneth* • Justin Theroux *Coop* • Robert Wisdom *Officer Dan* • James Remar *Chick* • Swoosie Kurtz *Jean* • Wallace Shawn *Herman* ■ *Dir* Danny DeVito • *Scr* Larry Doyle

Our Lady of the Assassins ★★★

Drama 2000 · Col/Sp/Fr · Colour · 98mins

Shot on digital video in the Columbian town of Medellin, this is a visceral adaptation of Fernando Vallejo's novel about the rapidity with which corruption, brutality and greed can conquer a once proud community. Returning after 30 years in European exile, gay writer German Jaramillo is both appalled by the ruination of his home and determined to impart his memories to teenage hustler Anderson Ballesteros. However, by ensuring that the characters are as vibrant as the locale, Barbet Schroeder avoids designer violence, patronising miserableness and glib solutions. DP. In Spanish with English subtitles.

German Jaramillo *Fernando* • Anderson Ballesteros *Alexis* • Juan David Restrepo *Wilmar* • Manuel Busquets *Alfonso* ■ *Dir* Barbet Schroeder • *Scr* Fernando Vallejo, from his novel *La Virgen de los Sicarios*

Our Lips Are Sealed ★★ PG

Comedy 2000 · US · Colour · 89mins

Since striking out from the sitcom *Full House*, Mary-Kate and Ashley Olsen have built up quite a following in the United States. Unable to stay schtum after witnessing a crime, the twins are whisked off to Sydney under the FBI's Witness Protection Programme. But the mobsters soon catch up with them and a modicum of plot threatens to interrupt their shopping and sightseeing. With its patronising depiction of Australia as a land of endless beach parties, this is eminently resistible fluff. DP [video] DVD

Ashley Olsen *Ashley Parker/Abby Turtleby* • Mary-Kate Olsen *Mary Kate Parker/Maddy Turtleby* • Jim Meskimen *Rick Parker/Stanley Turtleby* • Tamara Clatterbuck *Teri Parker/Shirley Turtleby* ■ *Dir* Craig Shapiro • *Scr* Elizabeth Kruger, Craig Shapiro

Our Little Girl ★★ U

Drama 1935 · US · BW · 62mins

In this typical Shirley Temple vehicle, the star runs away to the circus while conspiring to reunite her estranged parents (Joel McCrea and Rosemary Ames) by driving the wolf (Lyle Talbot) from the door. Made at the peak of Temple's popularity, this was her weakest film of the period, an under-developed, slow-moving and predictable tale. The star is as charming as ever, particularly in her scenes with Poodles Hanneford as a clown, but this is only for her keenest admirers. TV DVD

Shirley Temple *Molly Middleton* • Rosemary Ames *Elsa Middleton* • Joel McCrea *Dr Donald Middleton* • Lyle Talbot *Rolfe Brent* • Erin O'Brien-Moore *Sarah Boynton* • Poodles Hanneford *Circus performer* ■ *Dir* John S Robertson • *Scr* Stephen Avery, Allen Rivkin, Jack Yellen, from the story *Heaven's Gate* by Florence Leighton Pfalzgraf

Our Man Flint ★★★ PG

Spy spoof 1966 · US · Colour · 102mins

As superspy Derek Flint, granite-faced James Coburn is equipped with the standard-issue suave mannerisms and harem of girls, plus one particular accessory that James Bond would have throttled Q for: a cigarette lighter with 83 uses (two-way radio, blowtorch and so on). No wonder ZOWIE (Zonal Organisation on World Intelligence Espionage) chooses Coburn to assassinate three villains who want to take over the world. Incredible action, credibly packaged – if only Coburn weren't so smug. A sequel, *In Like Flint* followed in 1967. TH [video] DVD

James Coburn *Derek Flint* • Lee J Cobb *Cramden* • Gila Golan *Gila* • Edward Mulhare *Malcolm Rodney* • Benson Fong *Dr Schneider* • Shelby Grant *Leslie* • Sigrid Valdis *Anna* • Gianna Serra *Gina* • Helen Funai *Sakito* ■ *Dir* Daniel Mann • *Scr* Hal Fimberg, Ben Starr, from a story by Hal Fimberg

Our Man in Havana ★★★

Comedy drama 1959 · UK · BW · 110mins

What a different film this would have been if Graham Greene had been able to overcome his antipathy towards Alfred Hitchcock. Instead, he offered the film rights to his amusing spy spoof to Carol Reed and Hitch went off to make *Psycho*. Reed drew deft performances from his superb cast, with Alec Guinness in fine fettle as the vacuum cleaner salesman-turned-agent. But he seemed uncertain how dark to make the action once the joke took its sinister turn. DP

Alec Guinness *Jim Wormold* • Burl Ives *Doctor Hasselbacher* • Maureen O'Hara *Beatrice Severn* • Ernie Kovacs *Captain Segura* • Noël Coward *Hawthorne* • Ralph Richardson *"C"* • Jo Morrow *Milly Wormold* ■ *Dir* Carol Reed • *Scr* Graham Greene, from his novel

Our Man in Marrakesh ★★ U

Spy spoof 1966 · UK · Colour · 93mins

The excellent Tony Randall stars as an American tourist caught up in spy antics in Morocco. The scenery is fabulous and the second-rung supporting cast fun to watch, but the script and production budget would defeat the hardiest director. Still, veteran professionals such as Herbert Lom, Wilfrid Hyde White and Terry-Thomas do what they can with the material, and Klaus Kinski and John Le Mesurier turn up, too. TS

Tony Randall *Andrew Jessel* • Senta Berger *Kyra Stanovy* • Terry-Thomas *El Caid* • Herbert Lom *Narim Casimir* • Wilfrid Hyde White *Arthur Fairbrother* • Grégoire Aslan *Achmed* • John Le Mesurier *George Lillywhite* • Klaus Kinski *Jonquil* ■ *Dir* Don Sharp • *Scr* Peter Yeldham, from a story by Peter Welbeck [Harry Alan Towers]

Our Miss Fred ★★ PG

Second World War comedy 1972 · UK · Colour · 91mins

Danny La Rue, Britain's most popular female impersonator during the 1970s, seems terribly constricted in his one major film, an old-fashioned wartime comedy written by distinguished playwright Hugh Leonard. Soldier La Rue is playing a woman on stage in France when the Germans invade. He escapes, wearing his costume, and, somewhat implausibly, remains in drag as he evades the enemy. The photography is quite pretty, which is more than can be said for La Rue, already somewhat matronly. DM [video]

Danny La Rue *Fred Wimbush* • Alfred Marks *General Brincker* • Lance Percival *Smallpiece* • Frances de la Tour *Miss Lockhart* ■ *Dir* Bob Kellett • *Scr* Hugh Leonard

Our Modern Maidens ★★

Silent drama 1929 · US · BW · 75mins

Capitalising on the success of *Our Dancing Daughters* (1928), MGM again starred Joan Crawford as a socialite in this follow-up romance, which was also released as a talkie. Anita Page returns as well for a second outing, and is joined by Rod La Rocque. But the main focus of the movie was the on-screen love affair between Crawford (dressed by Adrian, as she would be for many years) and Douglas Fairbanks Jr; they were the hot gossip item in Hollywood at the time and would soon be married in real life. RK

Joan Crawford *Billie* • Rod La Rocque *Abbott* • Douglas Fairbanks Jr *Gil* • Anita Page *Kentucky* • Edward Nugent *Reg* • Josephine Dunn *Ginger* ■ *Dir* Jack Conway • *Scr* Josephine Lovett, Marian Ainslee, Ruth Cummings, from a story by Josephine Lovett • *Costume Designer* Adrian

Our Mother's House ★★★

Drama 1967 · UK/US · Colour · 105mins

This weird and often chilling horror story is about some children (including a pre-*Oliver!* Mark Lester) who bury their mother's dead body in the garden and carry on as if she were still alive. Then shifty cockney Dirk Bogarde shows up, claiming to be their errant father. Bogarde and director Jack Clayton believed they had failed honourably, but Luchino Visconti thought it was a "beautiful" film and hired Bogarde for *The Damned* and *Death in Venice* on the strength of it. AT

Dirk Bogarde *Charlie Hook* • Margaret Brooks *Elsa Hook* • Pamela Franklin *Diana Hook* • Louis Sheldon Williams *Hubert Hook* • John Gugolka *Dunstan Hook* • Mark Lester (2) *Jiminee Hook* • Sarah Nicholls [Phoebe Nicholls] *Gerty Hook* • Gustav Henry *Willy Hook* ■ *Dir* Jack Clayton • *Scr* Jeremy Brooks, Haya Harareet, from the novel by Julian Gloag

Our Relations ★★★ U

Comedy 1936 · US · BW · 64mins

In this masterful double act, Laurel and Hardy turn in four great comic performances for the price of two. Comic mayhem is assured when family men Laurel and Hardy encounter their long lost identical twin brothers, a pair of jolly sailors who are enjoying shore leave. The inevitable mistaken identity occurs and our heroes find themselves up to their armpits in misunderstandings and sophisticated slapstick. Delightful, sometimes hilarious, shenanigans. DF [video]

Stan Laurel *Stan/Alfie Laurel* • Oliver Hardy *Ollie/Bert Hardy* • Sidney Toler *Captain of the SS Periwinkle* • Alan Hale *Joe Groagan, waiter* • Daphne Pollard *Mrs Daphne Hardy* • Betty Healy *Mrs Betty Laurel* ■ *Dir* Harry Lachman • *Scr* Richard Connell, Felix Adler, Charles Rogers, Jack Jevne, from the short story *The Money Box* by WW Jacobs

Our Town ★★

Period drama 1940 · US · BW · 89mins

An exercise in Hollywood bathos, based on Thornton Wilder's play about a small village in New Hampshire where a boy and girl's childhood friendship leads to adolescent romance, marriage and a tragic ending, which Hollywood tinkered with. An on-screen narrator – local pharmacist Frank Craven – guides us through the town and the 1901, 1904 and 1913 settings, but mostly we have William Holden and Martha Scott as the lovers. This is often like wading through an ocean of the stickiest maple syrup, but the Oscar-nominated music is by Aaron Copland. AT

Frank Craven *Mr Morgan, the narrator* • William Holden (2) *George Gibbs* • Martha Scott *Emily Webb* • Fay Bainter *Mrs Gibbs* • Beulah Bondi *Mrs Webb* • Thomas Mitchell *Dr Gibbs* • Guy Kibbee *Editor Webb* ■ *Dir* Sam Wood • *Scr* Thornton Wilder, Frank Craven, Harry Chandlee, from the play by Thornton Wilder • *Music* Aaron Copland

Our Very Own ★★ U

Drama 1950 · US · BW · 88mins

Whenever producer Samuel Goldwyn announced a serious drama about a socially significant subject, you could bet your bottom dollar that you were in for a cosy domestic melodrama with just the vaguest whiff of controversy about it. That's certainly what you get here in this underwritten and overplayed saga, in which spoiled teenager Ann Blyth snubs parents Jane Wyatt and Donald Cook on learning that she's been adopted. DP [video]

Ann Blyth *Gail* • Jane Wyatt *Lois Macaulay* • Donald Cook *Fred Macaulay* • Farley Granger *Chuck* • Joan Evans *Joan* • Ann Dvorak *Mrs Lynch* • Natalie Wood *Penny* • Gus Schilling *Frank* • Phyllis Kirk *Zaza* • Jessie Grayson *Violet* ■ *Dir* David Miller • *Scr* F Hugh Herbert • *Cinematographer* Lee Garmes

Our Vines Have Tender Grapes ★★★★ U

Drama 1945 · US · BW · 105mins

This warm-hearted MGM drama contains a simply superb performance from Edward G Robinson as the Norwegian dad of lovable little Margaret O'Brien, set against a Wisconsin (though largely studio) background. There's not a lot of plot as incident follows incident: the barn burns down, the floods come, there's a quarrel over some roller skates, the circus passes through town... There's a boring romance, too, but don't be put off: this is a movie of great charm, well directed by Roy Rowland. TS

Edward G Robinson *Martinius Jacobson* • Margaret O'Brien *Selma Jacobson* • James Craig *Nels Halverson* • Agnes Moorehead *Bruna Jacobson* • Jackie "Butch" Jenkins *Arnold Hanson* • Morris Carnovsky *Bjorn Bjornson* ■ *Dir* Roy Rowland • *Scr* Dalton Trumbo, from the novel by George Victor Martin

Our Wife ★★

Romantic comedy 1941 · US · BW · 92mins

Divorced classical trumpeter Melvyn Douglas, happily engaged to marry the supportive and inspirational young Ruth Hussey, finds himself caught in a no-holds barred battle for his affections when his ex-wife Ellen Drew decides she wants him back. A run-of-the-mill romantic triangle, with the polished Douglas reduced to a blank excuse for the women's rivalry. Neither actress has the high style necessary for the material, directed by John M Stahl in a manner more suited to heavy drama than light comedy. RK

Melvyn Douglas *Jerry Marvin* • Ruth Hussey *Susan Drake* • Ellen Drew *Babe Marvin* • Charles Coburn *Prof Drake* • John Hubbard *Tom Drake* • Harvey Stephens *Dr Cassell* • Theresa Harris *Hattie* ■ *Dir* John M Stahl • *Scr* PJ Wolfson, from the play by Lillian Day, Lyon Mearson • *Cinematographer* Franz F Planer [Franz Planer]

Out Cold ★★ 15

Black comedy 1989 · US · Colour · 87mins

Originally titled *Stiffs*, this lay on a marble slab for two years before it was released as *Out Cold*. It's a tale of two butchers, with the long-suffering John Lithgow thinking he has killed his loathsome partner, Bruce McGill, by locking him in the freezer. In fact, McGill's wife, Teri Garr, has done the deed after hiring private eye Randy Quaid. Macabre, and an acquired taste. AT [video]

Teri Garr *Sunny Cannald* • John Lithgow *Dave Geary* • Randy Quaid *Lester Atlas* • Bruce McGill *Ernie Cannald* • Lisa Blount *Phyllis* • Alan Blumenfeld *Lew* ■ *Dir* Malcolm Mowbray • *Scr* Leonard Glasser, George Malko, from a story by Leonard Glasser

Out for Justice ★★ 18

Action crime drama
1991 · US · Colour · 87mins

Steven Seagal gets more dialogue than in all his other movies put together, in this lukewarm attempt to give him a lot more heart and soul. He plays a Brooklyn cop who comes up against old neighbourhood foe William Forsythe, resulting in much retaliatory violence. Frankly, Seagal is no actor and his career has been founded upon his ability to look cool in combat situations, rather than convey the sort of softly spoken sadness he's aiming for here. JC. Contains swearing and violence. [video] DVD

Steven Seagal *Gino Felino* • William Forsythe *Richie Madano* • Jerry Orbach *Detective Ronnie Donziger* • Jo Champa *Vicky Felino* • Sal Richards *Frankie* • Gina Gershon *Patti Madano* ■ *Dir* John Flynn • *Scr* David Lee Henry, Steven Seagal

Out of Africa ★★★★ PG

Biographical drama
1985 · US · Colour · 154mins

Or "Afreeka" as Meryl Streep would have it, with a bizarre Danish accent that manages to overshadow her entire performance as awkward, free-spirited writer and farmer Karen Blixen. This is a beautifully filmed movie, with director Sydney Pollack propelling the camera across the lush, Kenyan country teeming with all manner of exotic beasts. The other exotic beasts – Streep, Klaus Maria Brandauer as her husband and Robert Redford as her adventurer lover – overact on a level to match the magnificence of the backdrop, but with this cast it is still eminently watchable stuff. What the movie loses in emotional realism it gains in epic audacity. SH [video] DVD

Meryl Streep *Karen* • Robert Redford *Denys Finch Hatton* • Klaus Maria Brandauer *Baron/Hans* • Michael Kitchen *Berkeley Cole* • Malick Bowens *Farah* • Joseph Thiaka *Kamante* • Stephen Kinyanjui *Kinanjui* • Michael Gough *Lord Delamere* • Suzanna Hamilton *Felicity* • Rachel Kempson *Lady Belfield* ■ *Dir* Sydney Pollack • *Scr* Kurt Luedtke, from the autobiographical books by Isak Dinesen [Karen Blixen], from *Isak Dinesen: the Life of a Storyteller* by Judith Thurman, from *Silence Will Speak* by Errol Trzebinski • *Cinematographer* David Watkin • *Music* John Barry (1)

Out of Darkness ★★★

Biographical drama
1990 · US · Colour · 89mins

This clumsy biopic rather dims the brightness of its subject, Albert Schweitzer, musician, intellectual, missionary and Nobel Peace Prize winner, who rejected European acclaim to minister to disease-ridden natives in the African jungle. It's not a whitewash – according to this he ran his deliberately run-down hospital like a tyrant – but its simplistic plot doesn't do the man justice. However, Malcolm McDowell is on top form. TH. Contains some violence and nudity.

Malcolm McDowell *Dr Albert Schweitzer* • Susan Strasberg *Helene Schweitzer* • Andrew Davis *Lionel Curtis* • Helen Jessop *Amanda Hampton* • John Carson *Horton Herschel* • Henry Cele *Onganga* ■ *Dir* Gray Hofmyer [Gray Hofmeyr] • *Scr* Michel Potts, Patrick Lee

Out of Depth ★★ 18

Crime drama 1998 · UK · Colour · 98mins

This chronicles the downward spiral of a young South London graphic designer (Sean Maguire) who makes the mistake of seeking retribution when his pub-worker mum (Rita Tushingham) is beaten up by a hardcase customer. Dissuaded by a mate from taking the law into his own hands, Maguire heads uptown, and enlists the fists of gangland enforcer Nicholas Ball. Sufficiently slick and well acted, this is basically just another of the numerous British gangster films that have been spawned by the success of *Lock, Stock and Two Smoking Barrels*. DA [video] DVD

Sean Maguire *Paul Nixon* • Danny Midwinter *Steve Wilshin* • Nicholas Ball *Lenny Walker* • Phil Cornwell *Ed Harris* • Josephine Butler *Sarah Callum* • Leigh Lawson *Richard Tate* • Clive Russell *Tinker* • Rita Tushingham *Maggie Nixon* ■ *Dir/Scr* Simon Marshall

Out of Order ★★★ 15

Thriller 1984 · W Ger · Colour · 83mins

German director Carl Schenkel mischievously takes Jean-Paul Sartre's contention that hell is other people and twists it by trapping his protagonists in a lift, with only some fraying cables keeping them from a 300-ft plunge. Naturally, there's not much to recommend about executive Götz George, mistress Renée Soutendijk, punk Hannes Jaenicke and embezzling accountant Wolfgang Kieling in the first place. But, as the tension mounts, their foibles and prejudices become voyeuristically irresistible. DP. In German with English subtitles. [video]

Götz George *Jörg* • Renée Soutendijk *Marion* • Wolfgang Kieling *Gössmann* • Hannes Jaenicke *Pit* ■ *Dir/Scr* Carl Schenkel

Out of Season ★★ 18

Drama 1975 · UK · Colour · 86mins

This stagey, moody, ambiguous love triangle, played in and around a holiday hotel in winter, will either intrigue or irritate, depending on one's predilection. The plot, such as it is, consists of the sex/power games played by three people: a middle-aged woman (Vanessa Redgrave), her teenage daughter (Susan George) and an American (Cliff Robertson) who enters their lives 20 years after his affair with the older woman. Director Alan Bridges cleverly teases suspense from the conflict, but the female roles are, by today's standards, sexual stereotypes. DM [video]

Vanessa Redgrave *Ann* • Cliff Robertson *Joe* • Susan George *Joanna* ■ *Dir* Alan Bridges • *Scr* Eric Bercovici, Reuben Bercovitch

Out of Sight ★★★★ 15

Romantic crime drama
1998 · US · Colour · 117mins

George Clooney and Jennifer Lopez sizzle in director Steven Soderbergh's sexy, sly and snappy crime caper, which neatly combines its 1970s heist-picture roots with sparkling romantic comedy. The Elmore Leonard plot gets a classy screen makeover as the stars on opposite sides of the law fight their instant attraction when robber Clooney escapes from prison and cop Lopez vows to bring him to justice. Using intricate flashbacks and a keen visual style, Soderbergh takes a sharp script and weaves it into an ambitious and accomplished work. AJ. Contains violence and swearing. [video] DVD

George Clooney *Jack Foley* • Jennifer Lopez *Karen Sisco* • Ving Rhames *Buddy Bragg* • Don Cheadle *Maurice (Snoopy) Miller* • Dennis Farina *Marshall Sisco* • Albert Brooks *Richard Ripley* • Michael Keaton *Ray Nicolette* • Samuel L Jackson *Hejira* ■ *Dir* Steven Soderbergh • *Scr* Scott Frank, from the novel by Elmore Leonard

Out of Sync ★

Action crime drama
1995 · US · Colour · 105mins

This is a confusing mix of typical action in the 'hood and 1940s *film noir*, with the hero led astray by a *femme fatale* who persuades him to assist in the robbery of his mobster boss. It's no wonder LL Cool J gets lost in the clash of styles and is unable to provoke any sympathy for his underground club DJ character. KB

LL Cool J *Jason "The Saint" St Julian* • Victoria Dillard *Monica Collins* • Ramy Zada *Danny Simon* • Howard Hesseman *Detective Caldwell* • Yaphet Kotto • Isaac Hayes • Aries Spears • Debbie Allen *Manicurist* ■ *Dir* Debbie Allen • *Scr* Robert Dorn

O

Out of the Blue ★★

Comedy 1947 · US · BW · 84mins

Displaying an unexpected flair for comedy, George Brent is a Greenwich Village resident, married to Carole Landis and feuding with his exotic artist neighbour (Turhan Bey). With Landis away, Brent invites interior designer Ann Dvorak in for a drink; already pretty loaded, she passes out. He thinks she's dead and dumps her body on Bey's porch. The plot might signal *film noir*, but what you actually get, under Leigh Jason's direction, is a chaotic mix of black farce, slapstick and screwball comedy. RK

George Brent *Arthur Earthleigh* • Virginia Mayo *Deborah Tyler* • Turhan Bey *David Gelleo* • Ann Dvorak *Olive Jensen* • Carole Landis *Mae Earthleigh* ■ *Dir* Leigh Jason • *Scr* Vera Caspary, Walter Bullock, Edward Eliscu, from a story by Vera Caspary

Out of the Blue ★★ 15

Drama 1980 · US/Can · Colour · 89mins

Dysfunctional family relationships are examined in a typically downbeat fashion by director Dennis Hopper. He also plays the ex-con whose return to his put-upon wife (Sharon Farrell) and rebellious teenage daughter (an exceptional Linda Manz) leads to intense conflict and inevitable tragedy. While not a pretty picture, it is one that occasionally resonates with honest emotion and truthful situations. AJ DVD

Linda Manz *Cindy "CeBe" Barnes* • Sharon Farrell *Kathy Barnes* • Dennis Hopper *Don Barnes* • Raymond Burr *Dr Brean* ■ *Dir* Dennis Hopper • *Scr* Leonard Yakir, Gary Jules Jouvenat, Brenda Nielson

Out of the Body ★ 18

Horror 1988 · Aus · Colour · 87mins

Journeyman Australian genre director Brian Trenchard-Smith comes unstuck in this reheated chiller inelegantly poised between slaughter and laughter. A supernatural monster is killing women in Sydney, Australia, and removing their eyes. Musician Mark Hembrow foresees the murders but the police think he's responsible for the crimes. Tedious terror. AJ

Mark Hembrow *David Gaze* • Tessa Humphries *Neva St Clair* • Carrie Zivetz *Dr Lydia Langton* • Linda Newton *Carla Dupré* • John Clayton *Detective Sergeant Whitaker* • John Ley *Sergeant Delgano* ■ *Dir* Brian Trenchard-Smith • *Scr* Kenneth Ross

Out of the Clouds ★★ U

Drama 1954 · UK · Colour · 87mins

This was the last and least in the series of compendium dramas made for Ealing Studios by director Basil Dearden and producer Michael Relph. This time, the newly expanded London Airport forms the backdrop for vignettes that put passengers and pilots alike through their clichéd paces. The documentary-style glimpses into the day-to-day running of the airport are fascinating, but the performances are no more than adequate. DP

Anthony Steel *Gus Randall* • Robert Beatty *Nick Milbourne* • David Knight *Bill Steiner* • Margo Lorenz *Leah Roche* • James Robertson-Justice *Captain Brent* • Eunice Gayson *Penny Henson* • Isabel Dean *Mrs Malcolm* • Michael Howard *Purvis* • Gordon Harker *Taxi driver* ■ *Dir* Basil Dearden • *Scr* John Eldridge, Michael Relph, Rex Rienits, from the novel *The Springboard* by John Fores

O

Out of the Dark ★★★ 18

Thriller 1988 · US · Colour · 83mins

An original take on the serial-killer genre in which a murderer in a clown mask kills staff members of a phone-sex service one by one. Director Michael Schroeder lays on the visual agony, while Cameron Dye and Lynn Danielson emote strenuously, but the real hysteria comes from actors such as Paul Bartel (a Roger Corman alumnus) and Divine, cast here a police detective! TH

Cameron Dye *Kevin/Bobo* • Karen Black *Ruth* • Lynn Danielson *Kristi* • Karen Witter *Jo Ann* • Starr Andreeff *Camille* • Karen Mayo-Chandler *Barbara* • Bud Cort *Stringer* • Divine *Detective Langella* • Paul Bartel *Motel clerk* • Tab Hunter *Driver* • Lainie Kazan *Hooker Nancy* ■ *Dir* Michael Schroeder • *Scr* Zane W Levitt, J Gregory DeFelice

Out of the Darkness ★★★★

Crime thriller based on a true story
1985 · US · Colour · 96mins

A strong central role in this TV movie attracted big name Martin Sheen, and he doesn't let anybody down. He is superb as detective Ed Zigo, who helped to solve the "Son of Sam" murders in the late 1970s, and he is almost matched by stage actor Robert Trebor as the killer. Sheen's son Charlie, later a major star in his own right, makes a brief appearance. NF

Martin Sheen *Ed Zigo* • Hector Elizondo *Father George* • Matt Clark *John Hubbard* • Jennifer Salt *Ann Zigo* • Eddie Egan *Tom Duncan* • Robert Trebor *David Berkowitz* • Charlie Sheen ■ *Dir* Jud Taylor • *Scr* TS Cook

Out of the Fog ★★★

Crime drama 1941 · US · BW · 84mins

A Brooklyn tailor and a short-order chef enjoy their little fishing trips around the bay, until a minor league gangster moves in, offering them protection and offering the tailor's daughter something else. More of a character study than a thriller, it spins on a surprising twist and then goes on to become a sentimental tale about exploitation. A good cast, though. AT

John Garfield *Harold Goff* • Ida Lupino *Stella Goodwin* • Thomas Mitchell *Jonah Goodwin* • Eddie Albert *George Watkins* • George Tobias *Gregor Propotkin* • John Qualen *Olaf Johnson* • Aline MacMahon *Florence Goodwin* ■ *Dir* Anatole Litvak • *Scr* Robert Rossen, Jerry Wald, Richard Macaulay, from the play *The Gentle People* by Irwin Shaw

Out of the Present ★★★★ U

Documentary
1995 · Ger/Fr/Bel/Rus · Colour · 99mins

After ten months in orbit, Sergei Krikalev returned to a homeland very different from the one he had left in May 1991. Yet, according to Andrei Ujica's documentary, the transition from Gorbachev's Soviet Union to Yeltsin's Russia was almost as painless as a change of crew on board the Mir space station. Combining grainy video footage with glossier imagery recorded with Krikalev's own camera, this account of the longest-ever space flight fascinates on a technical, political and human level. The immense silence, the awkward camaraderie and the fragility of the craft make a huge impression, but the spectacular views of Earth will live longest in the memory. DP. In Russian with English subtitles.

Dir/Scr Andrei Ujica

Out of the Rain ★★

Thriller 1991 · US · Colour · 91mins

Black sheep Michael O'Keefe attends the service of his brother, who apparently committed suicide. A bit of detective work reveals that it probably wasn't suicide after all, and a few talks with the locals (including dead brother's girlfriend Bridget Fonda) reveal that the culprit may be close to home. Vaguely intriguing but a bit too dialogue-heavy. ST

Bridget Fonda *Jolene* • Michael O'Keefe *Frank Reade* • John O'Keefe *Sheriff Norris* • Al Shannon *Drew* • John Seitz *Nat Reade* • Michael Mantell *Warren* ■ *Dir* Gary Winick • *Scr* Shem Bitterman, from his play

Out of This World ★★★

Musical 1945 · US · BW · 96mins

Bing Crosby is heard but not seen in this amusingly satirical look at fame and pop fans, 1940s-style. Eddie Bracken is the small-town telegram boy who sings like Crosby and is taken to New York by Diana Lynn, the leader of a girls' band. Crosby dubbed the songs, including the enduring title number by Harold Arlen and Johnny Mercer. Crosby's four sons can be seen as part of Bracken's adoring audience. TV

Eddie Bracken *Herbie Fenton* • Veronica Lake *Dorothy Dodge* • Diana Lynn *Betty Miller* • Cass Daley *Fanny the Drummer* • Parkyakarkus *Gus Palukas* • Donald MacBride *JC Crawford* • Bing Crosby ■ *Dir* Hal Walker • *Scr* Walter DeLeon, Arthur Phillips, from stories by Elizabeth Meehan, Sam Coslow

Out of Time ★★ 12

Crime thriller 2003 · US · Colour · 101mins

Carl Franklin reunites here with his *Devil in a Blue Dress* star Denzel Washington, but debutant screenwriter Dave Collard's laboured exposition saps any suspense from an already predictable premise. Washington's small-town cop is having an affair with married old flame Sanaa Lathan, for whose medical care he steals a vast sum of confiscated cash. Then he must stay one step ahead of his estranged wife (and fellow detective) Eva Mendes's investigation. Polished, but superficial. DP DVD

Denzel Washington *Matt Lee Whitlock* • Eva Mendes *Alex Diaz Whitlock* • Sanaa Lathan *Ann Merai Harrison* • Dean Cain *Chris Harrison* • John Billingsley *Chae* • Robert Baker (2) *Tony Dalton* • Alex Carter *Cabot* • Antoni Corone *Deputy Baste* • Terry Loughlin *Agent Stark* ■ *Dir* Carl Franklin • *Scr* Dave Collard • *Cinematographer* Theo van de Sande

The Out of Towners ★★★★ 12

Comedy 1970 · US · Colour · 97mins

Playwright Neil Simon blends comedy with pain in his first solo original screenplay, directed by Arthur Hiller. Jack Lemmon stars as the Ohio businessman who decides to combine a job interview in New York with a night on the town in the company of his wife Sandy Dennis. However, their excursion turns into a nightmare as they become increasingly bothered and bewildered by the Big Apple's ruthless manners. Lemmon takes it all with despairing aplomb, but Dennis seems less able to deal with the calamities; one wonders if comedy should be so serious. TH DVD

Jack Lemmon *George Kellerman* • Sandy Dennis *Gwen Kellerman* • Milt Kamen *Counterman* • Sandy Baron *TV man* • Anne Meara *Woman in police station* • Robert Nichols *Man in aeroplane* • Ann Prentiss *Airline stewardess* • Ron Carey *Boston cab driver* • Phil Bruns [Philip Bruns] *Officer Meyers* ■ *Dir* Arthur Hiller • *Scr* Neil Simon

The Out-of-Towners ★★ 15

Comedy 1999 · US · Colour · 86mins

This listless, pointless remake of Neil Simon's 1970 comedy stars Steve Martin and Goldie Hawn. They play a couple from the sticks who fly to New York for a job interview. No sooner have they left the ground than everything that could possibly go wrong (getting mugged, having their credit cards cancelled and so on), does. The two stars do their best, but they lack the desperation that Jack Lemmon and Sandy Dennis brought to the roles, while John Cleese's Basil Fawlty reprise is faintly embarrassing. JF. Contains swearing and some sexual references. DVD

Goldie Hawn *Nancy Clark* • Steve Martin *Henry Clark* • John Cleese *Mr Mersault* • Mark McKinney *Greg* • Oliver Hudson *Alan* • Valerie Perri *Stewardess* • Rudolph Giuliani *Mayor* ■ *Dir* Sam Weisman • *Scr* Marc Lawrence, from the 1970 film

Out on a Limb ★ PG

Comedy 1992 · US · Colour · 79mins

Turning his back on a $140 million business deal, yuppie Matthew Broderick heads for Buzzsaw, California, to save his sister from the clutches of a villain, played by Jeffrey Jones. The fact that Jones is a twin confuses things and makes this movie even less watchable than it already is. Indeed, this stinker was barely released. AT. Contains swearing.

Matthew Broderick *Bill Campbell* • Jeffrey Jones *Matt/Peter* • Heidi Kling *Sally* • John C Reilly *Jim Jr* • Marian Mercer *Ann* • Larry Hankin *Darren* • David Margulies *Buchenwald* ■ *Dir* Francis Veber • *Scr* Joshua Goldin, Daniel Goldin

Out 1: Spectre ★★★★

Experimental mystery
1973 · Fr · Colour · 260mins

Never one to worry about length, Jacques Rivette allowed this to run to over 12 hours. When it was reduced to this 4 hour 20 minute version, out of necessity, Rivette thought it was a mere ghost of the original, and changed the title. But, as the film doesn't seek to reach any conclusion, it could have gone on forever. A mystery story partly concerning a man and a woman who used to live together, separately rehearsing two plays by Aeschylus, this haunting film creates an unsettling atmosphere. The cast is brilliant, considering Rivette had virtually no shooting script. RB. A French language film.

Pierre Baillot *Quentin* • Juliet Berto *Frédérique* • Jacques Doniol-Valcroze *Etienne* • Françoise Fabian *Lucie* • Bernadette Lafont *Sarah* • Jean-Pierre Léaud *Colin* • Michel Lonsdale *Thomas* • Bulle Ogier *Pauline/Emilie* ■ *Dir* Jacques Rivette • *Scr* Jacques Rivette, Suzanne Schiffman, from the story *L'Histoire des Treize* by Honoré de Balzac

Out to Sea ★★ 12

Comedy 1997 · US · Colour · 102mins

Jack Lemmon and Walter Matthau are brothers-in-law working as dance partners for singles aboard a cruise ship. Lemmon and Matthau's schtick had a strange revival in the 1990s, as if adding wrinkles to the recipe might create a great new dish for moviegoers. This high-concept, low development movie has its moments, but the sub-standard screenplay means it's more embarrassing than it is funny. AT. Contains swearing, sexual references.

Jack Lemmon *Herb* • Walter Matthau *Charlie* • Dyan Cannon *Liz* • Gloria DeHaven *Vivian* • Brent Spiner *Gil Godwyn* • Elaine Stritch *Mavis* • Hal Linden *Mac* • Donald O'Connor *Jonathan* ■ *Dir* Martha Coolidge • *Scr* Robert Nelson Jacobs

Out West with the Hardys ★★ U

Comedy drama 1938 · US · BW · 83mins

Judge Hardy and family take a vacation on a dude ranch for this fifth in the series. While Lewis Stone gives his legal advice to the ranch owner, daughter Cecilia Parker runs off with the foreman and Mickey Rooney's ego is punctured by 11 year-old ranch temptress Virginia Weidler who steals the show something rotten. It's all quite witty and charming. AT

Lewis Stone *Judge James K Hardy* • Mickey Rooney *Andy Hardy* • Fay Holden *Mrs Emily Hardy* • Cecilia Parker *Marian Hardy* • Ann Rutherford *Polly Benedict* • Sara Haden *Aunt Milly* • Don Castle *Dennis Hunt* • Virginia Weidler *"Jake" Holt* ■ *Dir* George B Seitz • *Scr* Kay Van Riper, Agnes Christine Johnston, William Ludwig, from characters created by Aurania Rouverol

Outbreak ★★★★ 15

Thriller 1995 · US · Colour · 122mins

In this exciting eco-thriller, Dustin Hoffman plays an army medic who's trying to save the world from a lethal virus imported into America from Africa. You could read this as an Aids allegory, but it also works well as a regular against-the-clock jeopardy thriller with almost mandatory conspiracy cover-up overtones. Director Wolfgang Petersen marshals the effects superbly and there's terrific support from the likes of Morgan Freeman, Kevin Spacey and a nasty Donald Sutherland. TS. Contains violence and swearing. DVD

Dustin Hoffman *Col Sam Daniels* • Rene Russo *Dr Roberta "Robby" Keough* • Morgan Freeman *General Billy Ford* • Cuba Gooding Jr *Major Salt* • Kevin Spacey *Major Casey*

Schuler • Patrick Dempsey *Jimbo Scott* • Donald Sutherland *General Donald McClintock* ■ *Dir* Wolfgang Petersen • *Scr* Laurence Dworet, Robert Roy Pool

The Outcast ★★ U

Western 1954 · US · Colour · 90mins

John Derek stars in one of Republic's better-written westerns of the 1950s, playing a youngster who comes back to claim land stolen by his uncle, portrayed by Jim Davis. The film teeters on bedroom farce at one point when Davis insists on entering the hotel room of his fiancée, Catherine McLeod, while she's sheltering his wounded nephew, but director William Witney, a veteran of Republic serials and B-movies, stages the numerous outdoor action scenes with commendable vigour. AE

John Derek *Jet Cosgrave* • Joan Evans *Judy Polsen* • Jim Davis *Major Cosgrave* • Catherine McLeod *Alice Austin* • Ben Cooper *The Kid* • Taylor Holmes *Andrew Devlin* • Nana Bryant *Mrs Banner* • Slim Pickens *Boone Polsen* ■ *Dir* William Witney • *Scr* John K Butler, Richard Wormser, from a story by Todhunter Ballard

Outcast of the Islands ★★ PG

Drama 1951 · UK · BW · 95mins

Joseph Conrad's bustling, disquieting tale about a self-seeking wastrel's calamitous impact on a group of Far Eastern islands has, sadly, been turned into a loud, disjointed and rather disagreeable picture by Carol Reed. Such is the haphazard nature of the script that incidents come and go at an alarming rate, leaving the usually poised Reed powerless to tie them into a cohesive narrative. The exotic locations are exotic, and Ralph Richardson and Robert Morley controlled performances. DP [video]

Trevor Howard *Willems* • Ralph Richardson *Lingard* • Robert Morley *Almayer* • Kerima *Aissa* • Wendy Hiller *Mrs Almayer* • George Coulouris *Babalatchi* • Betty Ann Davies *Mrs Williams* • Peter Illing *Alagappan* • James Kenney *Ramsey* • Dharma Emmanuel *Ali* ■ *Dir* Carol Reed • *Scr* William Fairchild, from the novel by Joseph Conrad

The Outfit ★★★★ 15

Thriller 1973 · US · Colour · 98mins

In this brutish but compelling thriller, taken from the novel by Richard Stark (a pseudonym for Donald E Westlake), bank robber Robert Duvall leaves prison determined to find out who murdered his brother; the trail leads to ageing mobster Robert Ryan. Duvall is excellent, and there's a terrific supporting cast. The under-rated writer/director John Flynn lets the story unfold in an unflashy way, but stages some marvellous, if extremely violent, set pieces. JF. Contains swearing. [video]

Robert Duvall *Earl Macklin* • Joe Don Baker *Cody* • Robert Ryan *Mailer* • Karen Black *Bett* • Timothy Carey *Jake Menner* • Richard Jaeckel *Chemey* • Sheree North *Buck's wife* • Marie Windsor *Madge Coyle* • Jane Greer *Alma* • Henry Jones *Doctor* • Joanna Cassidy *Rita* • Elisha Cook [Elisha Cook Jr] *Carl* ■ *Dir* John Flynn • *Scr* John Flynn, from the novel by Richard Stark [Donald E Westlake]

The Outfit ★★ 18

Crime drama 1993 · US · Colour · 88mins

A charmless gangster flick that went straight-to-video in the States, this plays fast and loose with both historical setting and attention to period detail in its vain attempt to sustain interest. Director/co-writer J Christian Ingvordsen trots out the clichés of the genre to dress up a sub-standard action movie, as a maverick FBI agent (John Christian – Ingvordsen again) goes undercover to infiltrate the Mob. RT [video]

Lance Henriksen *Dutch Schultz* • Billy Drago *Lucky Luciano* • Martin Kove *Agent Baker* • Josh Mosby *Legs Diamond* • John Christian [J Christian Ingvordsen] *Bone Conn* • Rick Washburn *Red* • Jeffrey Howard *Max* • J Gregory Smith *Jimmy* ■ *Dir* J Christian Ingvordsen • *Scr* Steven Kaman, J Christian Ingvordsen, Whitney Ransick

Outland ★★ 15

Science-fiction action adventure
1981 · UK · Colour · 104mins

It's *High Noon* in outer space as mining colony marshal Sean Connery confronts the pushers peddling lethal drugs to Jupiter moon workers so they'll produce more ore. This bleak dramatisation of final frontier contamination comes complete with *Alien*-inspired decor and smooth direction by Peter Hyams. Hyams, however, sinks this far-flung fantasy with cheap scare tactics, illogical science and B-movie western-style laser gun battles that scupper credibility. AJ. Contains violence and swearing. [video] DVD

Sean Connery *O'Niel* • Peter Boyle *Sheppard* • Frances Sternhagen *Lazarus* • James B Sikking *Montone* • Kika Markham *Carol* • Clarke Peters *Ballard* • Steven Berkoff *Sagan* • John Ratzenberger *Tarlow* • Nicholas Barnes *Paul O'Niel* ■ *Dir/Scr* Peter Hyams

The Outlaw ★★★ U

Western 1943 · US · BW · 115mins

"Mean, moody, magnificent" was the advertising tag for this infamous movie, and it didn't refer to the outlaw of the title – Billy the Kid – but to Doc Holliday's delectable mistress, played so memorably here by Howard Hughes's exciting discovery, Jane Russell. Censorship and reshooting led to a three-year release delay for this languorous western, originally directed by the estimable Howard Hawks, which contrives strange fictional relationships between Billy (colourless newcomer Jack Buetel), Pat Garrett (Thomas Mitchell) and Holliday (the superb Walter Huston). Something of a kitsch curio. TS [video] DVD

Jack Buetel *Billy the Kid* • Jane Russell *Rio* • Thomas Mitchell *Pat Garrett* • Walter Huston *Doc Holliday* • Mimi Aguglia *Aunt Guadelupe* • Joseph Sawyer [Joe Sawyer] *Woodruff* • Gene Rizzi *Stranger* • Frank Darien *Shorty* ■ *Dir* Howard Hughes • *Scr* Jules Furthman

The Outlaw and His Wife ★★★

Silent drama 1917 · Swe · BW · 73mins

This fateful melodrama is set against the seasonal shifts of the Icelandic wilderness. Forced to flee after stealing a sheep to feed his family, 19th-century peasant Victor Sjöström falls for wealthy widow Edith Erastoff and they have a child during an idyllic summer in hiding from the authorities. However, as harsher conditions close in, psychological pressures impinge on the couple's relationship and tragedy ensues. Expertly locating his characters in the landscape that will destroy them, Sjöström brought a new visual and emotional maturity to Swedish cinema, thanks, in no small measure, to Julius Jaenzon's atmospheric photography. DP

Victor Sjöström *Berg-Ejvind* • Edith Erastoff *Halla* • John Ekman *Arnes* • Nils Arehn *Municipal official* ■ *Dir* Victor Sjöström • *Scr* Sam Ask, Victor Sjöström, from the play *Bjaerg-Ejvind og Hans Hustru* by Johan Sigurjónsson

Outlaw Blues ★★★ 15

Comedy drama 1977 · US · Colour · 96mins

If you can cope with Peter Fonda singing country and western ditties, then you might just find yourself having a good time with this scattershot mixture of comedy, musical and road movie. Fonda is clearly enjoying himself as a convict who breaks parole to get even with shyster singer James Callahan who has stolen his song. Director Richard T Heffron overdoes the motor mayhem, but does well to keep his cast at full throttle. DP [video]

Peter Fonda *Bobby Ogden* • Susan Saint James *Tina Waters* • John Crawford *Chief Cavenaugh* • James Callahan *Garland Dupree* • Michael Lerner *Hatch* ■ *Dir* Richard T Heffron • *Scr* BWL Norton

Outlaw Force ★ 18

Action adventure 1988 · US · Colour · 90mins

Surely one of the biggest vanity productions to date, with David Heavener not only starring, but taking the directing, writing, and producing reins, and also writing and singing seven of the eleven songs on the soundtrack. Only his singing gets a passing mark. Playing a dyed-in-the-wool modern-day cowboy, Heavener straps on his six guns and heads to the big city after the scum who raped and killed his wife, and kidnap his young daughter. Even if one disregards the blurred photography, dim lighting, and sound that makes some dialogue hard to make out, the movie is still ponderously slow. KB [video]

David Heavener *Billy Ray Dalton* • Paul L Smith [Paul Smith] *Inspector Wainwright* • Frank Stallone *Grady* • Robert Bjorklund *Washington* • Devin Dunsworth *Jesse* • Stephanie Cicero *Holly Dalton* • Warren Berlinger *Captain Morgan* ■ *Dir/Scr* David Heavener

The Outlaw Josey Wales ★★★★ 18

Western 1976 · US · Colour · 135mins

Clint Eastwood seized the directorial reins from Phil Kaufman and fashioned this tough, sprawling post-Civil War western epic into something approaching a personal testament. The tale of a wronged farmer bent on revenge consists more of a series of vignettes compared with the tightness of structure that so distinguishes the director's later *Unforgiven*. But there's much strength and power derived from the iconographic value of Eastwood the star, with Jerry Fielding's fine score and Chief Dan George's drily humorous Lone Watie also major pluses. TS. Contains violence, some swearing and brief nudity. [video] DVD

Clint Eastwood *Josey Wales* • Sondra Locke *Laura Lee* • Chief Dan George *Lone Watie* • Bill McKinney *Terrill* • John Vernon *Fletcher* • Paula Trueman *Grandma Sarah* • Sam Bottoms *Jamie* • Geraldine Keams *Little Moonlight* ■ *Dir* Clint Eastwood • *Scr* Phil Kaufman [Philip Kaufman], Sonia Chernus, from the novel *Gone to Texas* by Forrest Carter

The Outlaws Is Coming ★★★ U

Comedy western 1965 · US · BW · 88mins

Hardworking comedy team the Three Stooges appeared in nearly 200 shorts and over 20 feature films in their long career and this western spoof marks their last big-screen appearance together. Loved by millions, loathed by many, the Stooges never strayed far from their comic roots as violent exponents of lightning-paced slapstick. Here those skills are used to good effect in a story of the boys taking on gunslingers and other villains. DF

Moe Howard • Larry Fine • Joe De Rita • Adam West *Kenneth Cabot* • Nancy Kovack *Annie Oakley* • Mort Mills *Trigger Mortis* • Don Lamond *Rance Roden* ■ *Dir* Norman Maurer • *Scr* Elwood Ullman, from a story by Norman Maurer

Outpost in Morocco ★★ U

Romantic action adventure
1949 · US · BW · 92mins

Filmed in authentic locations with the full co-operation of the French Foreign Legion, this desert adventure is cited as one of the turning points in the career of George Raft. But, it also helped persuade that most under-rated of directors, Robert Florey, to consider his options in television, after a string of unworthy B-movie projects. There's nothing special about the plot, except for the fact that it rather daringly explores the idea of cross-racial romance, as Raft's beleagured legionnaire debates whether to slaughter emir Eduard Franz, the father of his beloved, Marie Windsor. DP

George Raft *Captain Paul Gerard* • Marie Windsor *Cara* • Akim Tamiroff *Lieutenant Glysko* • John Litel *Colonel Pascal* • Eduard Franz *Emir of Bel-Rashad* ■ *Dir* Robert Florey • *Scr* Charles Grayson, Paul de Sainte-Colombe, from a story by Joseph N Ermolieff

Outrage ★★

Drama 1950 · US · BW · 74mins

It took a female director, Ida Lupino, to make a film centred directly on the provocative subject of rape (although the word itself could not be used). Lupino's main concern is with the aftermath – the victim, well played by newcomer Mala Powers, feels so "dirty" that she runs away to start a new life. As the co-writer as well as director, Lupino avoids obvious sensationalism. AE

Mala Powers *Ann Walton* • Tod Andrews *Ferguson* • Robert Clarke *Jim Owens* • Raymond Bond *Mr Walton* • Lilian Hamilton *Mrs Walton* • Rita Lupino *Stella Carter* ■ *Dir* Ida Lupino • *Scr* Ida Lupino, Malvin Wald, Collier Young

The Outrage ★★★

Western 1964 · US · BW · 95mins

Having successfully remade Akira Kurosawa's *Seven Samurai* as *The Magnificent Seven*, Hollywood turned its sights on the Japanese maestro's earlier classic *Rashomon*, the story of a rape and a murder told by four people with differing perspectives. The story is transposed to the Wild West, with Paul Newman playing the killer, Claire Bloom and Laurence Harvey as the victims, and Edward G Robinson as a conman. It's a starry cast and worth watching for that reason alone, though Martin Ritt's direction labours every point and lacks the intensity of the original film. AT

Paul Newman *Juan Carrasco* • Laurence Harvey *Husband* • Claire Bloom *Wife* • Edward G Robinson *Con Man* • William Shatner *Preacher* • Howard Da Silva *Prospector* • Albert Salmi *Sheriff* • Thomas Chalmers *Judge* ■ *Dir* Martin Ritt • *Scr* Michael Kanin, from the stories by Ryunosuke Akutagawa, from the film *Rashomon* by Akira Kurosawa, Shinobu Hashimoto, and from the play *Rashomon* by Michael Kanin, Fay Kanin

Outrage ★★

Drama 1993 · Sp/It · Colour · 108mins

Francesca Neri's exotic circus artiste, an accomplished sharpshooter, hunts down the thugs who gang-raped her. Seasoned director Carlos Saura disappointingly undermines his powerful message with some gratuitous nudity and by romanticising her pitiless spree in having it viewed through the eyes of besotted journalist Antonio Banderas. The result, while staged with sophistication, is less shocking and provocative than Tony Garnett's similarly themed *Handgun*. DP. In Spanish with English subtitles. Contains violence and nudity.

Antonio Banderas *Marcos Vallez* • Francesca Neri *Ana* • Walter Vidarte *Manuel* • Eulalia Ramón *Mother* • Chema Manzo *Father* •

Archero Manas *Mario* ■ *Dir* Carlos Saura • *Scr* Carlos Saura, Enzo Monteleone, from the story *Spara Che Ti Pasa* by Giorgio Scerbanenco

Outrageous! ★★★

Drama 1977 · Can · Colour · 96mins

The hilarious and touching story of overweight Toronto hairdresser Craig Russell whose dream is to dazzle the world as a top-class female impersonator. His best friend, Hollis McLaren, is a certified schizophrenic who's pregnant. How director Richard Benner shows these misfits sticking two fingers up at society as they liberate their fantasies makes a sympathetic, uncompromising and well-acted feel-good gay movie. A well-rounded view of the way it was in the heady disco days, pre-Aids. A disappointing sequel, *Too Outrageous!*, followed in 1987. AJ

Craig Russell *Robin Turner* • Hollis McLaren *Liza Connors* • Richert Easley *Perry* • Allan Moyle *Martin* • David McIlwraith *Bob* • Gerry Salzberg *Jason* • Andrée Pelletier *Anne* • Helen Shaver *Jo* ■ *Dir* Richard Benner • *Scr* Richard Benner, from the story *Butterfly Ward* by Margaret Gibson

Outrageous Fortune ★★★ 15

Action comedy 1987 · US · Colour · 95mins

Bette Midler and Shelley Long team up for this buddy-buddy comedy to play two women from different sides of the tracks who find they have the same two-timing boyfriend (Peter Coyote, in a serious piece of miscasting). Director Arthur Hiller keeps the action and comedy rolling along at a fairly boisterous rate, and he is helped by the assured performances of Midler and Long, who refuse to let the humour lapse for a second. JB. Contains swearing. DVD

Bette Midler *Sandy Brozinsky* • Shelley Long *Lauren Ames* • Peter Coyote *Michael Sanchez* • Robert Prosky *Stanislav Korzenowski* • John Schuck *Atkins* • George Carlin *Frank* • Anthony Heald *Weldon* ■ *Dir* Arthur Hiller • *Scr* Leslie Dixon

The Outriders ★★ U

Western 1950 · US · Colour · 93mins

A very average Technicolor western from MGM with a seemingly uninterested Joel McCrea getting involved with Quantrill's Raiders and redhead Arlene Dahl. It's given some distinction by the studio's high production values and excellent location photography; the plot, though, is disappointingly routine. Director Roy Rowland manages an excellent and suspenseful river crossing, but the movie badly needs a grittier lead. TS

Joel McCrea *Will Owen* • Arlene Dahl *Jen Gort* • Barry Sullivan *Jesse Wallace* • Claude Jarman Jr *Roy Gort* • James Whitmore *Clint Priest* • Ramon Novarro *Don Antonio Chaves* • Jeff Corey *Keeley* ■ *Dir* Roy Rowland • *Scr* Irving Ravetch

The Outside Man ★★★

Crime thriller 1973 · Fr/US · Colour · 103mins

Director Jacques Deray adds Gallic cool to Californian chic in this meandering thriller, which relies more on character than mystery to sustain its suspense. Hired for a hit to pay his debts back in France, Jean-Louis Trintignant's mission seems to have gone without a hitch, until he becomes the target of rival assassin, Roy Scheider. The women's roles are somewhat stereotypical, with Ann-Margret as a tart with a heart and Angie Dickinson as the fatal femme. But it's Deray's assured shifts between amateur sleuthing and amoral slaughter that makes this so satisfyingly sordid. DP. In English and French with subtitles.

Jean-Louis Trintignant *Lucien* • Ann-Margret *Nancy Robson* • Roy Scheider *Lenny* • Angie Dickinson *Jackie* • Georgia Engel *Mrs Barnes* • Felice Orlandi *Anderson* • Talia Shire *Make-up girl* ■ *Dir* Jacques Deray • *Scr* Jean-Claude Carrière, Jacques Deray, Ian McLellan Hunter, from a story by Jacques Deray, Jean-Claude Carrière

Outside Providence ★★ 15

Comedy 1999 · US · Colour · 91mins

To say this demonstrates the sensitive side of the Farrelly brothers may be pushing it a little, but it's certainly a lot more tasteful than their usual fare. Set in the 1970s, it stars Shawn Hatosy as a working-class youth whose constant scrapes with the law lead his dad (Alec Baldwin) to pull a few strings to get him sent to an exclusive prep school. Although this doesn't break any new ground, the performances from the cast are appealing. JF

Alec Baldwin *Old Man Dunphy* • Shawn Hatosy *Tim Dunphy* • George Wendt *Joey* • Tommy Bone *Jackie Dunphy* • Samantha Lavigne *"Clops"* • Jonathan Brandis *Mousy* • Adam Lavorgna *Tommy the Wire* • Jesse Leach *Decenz* ■ *Dir* Michael Corrente • *Scr* Peter Farrelly, Michael Corrente, Bobby Farrelly, from a novel by Peter Farrelly

The Outsider ★★★

Biographical drama 1961 · US · BW · 108mins

One of the seminal images of the Second World War showed a group of US marines raising the flag at Iwo Jima; it was a photograph first, then a memorial in Washington. This ambitious biography tells the story of Ira Hamilton Hayes, a native American who volunteers for the navy and suffers from racial hostility, yet ends up a part of that famous photograph. After the war he becomes a celebrity, but alcoholism turns his life into a tragedy. A committed performance from Tony Curtis helps glide over the stickier parts of the script, resulting in a moving account of a tragic hero. AT

Tony Curtis *Ira Hamilton Hayes* • James Franciscus *Jim Sorenson* • Gregory Walcott *Sgt Kiley* • Bruce Bennett *General Bridges* • Vivian Nathan *Mrs Nancy Hayes* ■ *Dir* Delbert Mann • *Scr* Stewart Stern

The Outsider ★★★

Political thriller
1979 · US/Neth · Colour · 127mins

Irish-American Vietnam vet Craig Wasson is welcomed by the IRA who send him to Belfast, knowing that if he's killed he will become a martyr in America, aiding the organisation's fund-raising. Wasson's journey turns out to be through minefields of cross and double-cross and generations of hate. The whole film is somewhat partisan in its approach – the British security forces are depicted as the oppressors who are not above a little torture, something which got the film a lot of flak on its limited release. But as a thriller, it has tension and some superb location work. Blink and you'll miss Gabriel Byrne's screen debut. AT

Craig Wasson *Michael Flaherty* • Sterling Hayden *Seamus Flaherty* • Patricia Quinn *Siobhan* • Niall O'Brien *Emmet Donovan* • TP McKenna *John Russell* • Niall Tiobin *Farmer* • Frank Grimes *Tony Coyle* • Gabriel Byrne ■ *Dir* Tony Luraschi • *Scr* Tony Luraschi, from the novel *The Heritage of Michael Flaherty* by Cohn Leinster

The Outsider ★★

Crime drama 1983 · Fr · Colour · 100mins

How does Jean-Paul Belmondo keep getting away with it? This would go straight to video anywhere else in the world, but in France the man remains such a phenomenon that this umpteenth action adventure in the Belmondo canon broke all box-office records. Belmondo plays a maverick cop who invents a gang war to cover up his murderous pursuit of a Paris-Marseille drugs cartel. Director Jacques Deray keeps things brisk, but this is pretty unremarkable. DP. In French with English subtitles.

Henry Silva *Sauveur Meccaci* • Claude Brosset *Antonio Baldi* • Carlos Sotto Mayer *Livia Maria Dolores* • Pierre Vernier *Rojinsky* • Tcheky Karyo *Francis Pierron* ■ *Dir* Jacques Deray • *Scr* Jacques Deray, Jean Herman

The Outsiders ★★★ PG

Drama 1983 · US · Colour · 87mins

Francis Ford Coppola's re-creation of the sights and sounds of 1960s Tulsa is more than a little ham-fisted, a situation not helped by some stilted dialogue and a ludicrously over-the-top score by his father Carmine. If you think the rivalry between the gangs looks authentic, it was because Coppola pampered the Socs and persecuted the Greasers throughout the shoot so that a genuine resentment built up between them. DP. Contains violence and swearing.

Matt Dillon *Dallas Winston* • Ralph Macchio *Johnny Cade* • C Thomas Howell *Ponyboy Curtis* • Patrick Swayze *Darrel Curtis* • Rob Lowe *Sodapop Curtis* • Emilio Estevez *Two-bit Matthews* • Tom Cruise *Steve Randle* • Glenn Withrow *Tim Shepherd* • Diane Lane *Cherry Valance* • Leif Garrett *Bob Sheldon* • Tom Waits *Buck Merrill* ■ *Dir* Francis Ford Coppola • *Scr* Kathleen Knutsen Rowell, from the novel by SE Hinton

Outward Bound ★★

Fantasy drama 1930 · US · BW · 82mins

The first film version of Sutton Vane's once celebrated and controversial play concerns the passengers on an ocean liner who come to realise they are dead and drifting between heaven and hell. As an early talkie made by the director of the stage version, Robert Milton, with many members of the Broadway cast, it's extremely creaky with all the players overdoing their performances. Nevertheless, it's an intriguing historical curiosity that initiated Howard's Hollywood film career. Remade in 1944 as *Between Two Worlds*. AE

Leslie Howard *Tom Prior* • Douglas Fairbanks Jr *Henry* • Helen Chandler *Ann* • Beryl Mercer *Mrs Midget* • Alec B Francis *Scrubby* • Alison Skipworth *Mrs Cliveden-Banks* • Lyonel Watts *Rev William Duke* • Montagu Love *Mr Lingley* • Dudley Digges *Thompson, the Examiner* ■ *Dir* Robert Milton • *Scr* J Grubb Alexander, from the play by Sutton Vane

Over Her Dead Body ★★★ 15

Black comedy 1990 · US · Colour · 97mins

For some reason, at the tail end of the 1980s, there was a mini-vogue for body-disposal comedies. *Weekend at Bernie's* may be the most recognisable title, but this jet-black comedy is the funniest of the lot – that is, if you like your humour served as macabre as possible. Elizabeth Perkins shines as the woman who accidentally kills her much-hated sister after being caught in bed with the latter's cop husband. How she tries to elude discovery and bury the body gives rise to some very rewarding slapstick and laughter-inducing grossness. AJ. Contains violence and swearing.

Elizabeth Perkins *June* • Judge Reinhold *Harry* • Jeffrey Jones *Floyd* • Maureen Mueller *Enid Purley* • Rhea Perlman *Mavis* • Brion James *Trucker* • Charles Tyner *Man at Indian burial site* • Henry Jones *Old man* • Michael J Pollard *Hotel manager* ■ *Dir* Maurice Phillips • *Scr* AJ Tipping, James Whaley, Maurice Phillips

Over She Goes ★★★

Musical comedy 1937 · UK · BW · 77mins

One of the better films featuring British musical comedy star Stanley Lupino, father of actress/director Ida. This was a stage success for Stanley, and the film version manages to transfer all its unsubtleties intact. The hopelessly dated blackmail plot involves three girls quite literally falling for three men, one of whom is the likeable Lupino. TS

John Wood *Lord Drewsden* • Claire Luce *Pamela* • Laddie Cliff *Billy Bowler* • Sally Gray *Kitty* • Stanley Lupino *Tommy Teacher* • Gina Malo *Dolly Jordan* • Judy Kelly *Alice Mayhill* • Max Baer *Silas Morner* • Syd Walker *Inspector Giffnock* ■ *Dir* Graham Cutts • *Scr* Elizabeth Meehan, Hugh Brooke, from the play *Over She Goes* by Stanley Lupino

Over the Brooklyn Bridge ★★★ 15

Romantic comedy
1983 · US · Colour · 101mins

Elliott Gould is the owner of a Brooklyn nosherie who dreams of running a big-time Manhattan restaurant and is in love with a Catholic girl, played by Margaux Hemingway. This romance irks Gould's traditional Jewish relatives. Though it's set in the 1980s, this is the kind of film that could have been made 50 years earlier. Shelley Winters does her usual schtick as a Jewish momma, but it's Sid Caesar who steals the show – a great movie comeback for the TV legend. AT

Elliott Gould *Alby Sherman* • Margaux Hemingway *Elizabeth Anderson* • Sid Caesar *Uncle Benjamin* • Burt Young *Phil Romano* • Shelley Winters *Becky Sherman* • Carol Kane *Cheryl Goodman* ■ *Dir* Menahem Golan • *Scr* Arnold Somkin

Over the Edge ★★★★ 18

Drama 1979 · US · Colour · 90mins

Matt Dillon's first film – and a humdinger of a debut it is, too. Dillon plays a disaffected teenager in a sterile planned community that is more concerned with attracting big business than it is with providing amenities for its kids. Bored out of their skulls, and fuelled on drugs and drink, the kids start running riot and laying siege to the place. Jonathan Kaplan directs a genuinely powerful portrayal of alienated youth, with Dillon excellent in the causeless-rebel. Even the soundtrack is a stunner. DA

Michael Kramer *Carl* • Pamela Ludwig *Cory* • Matt Dillon *Richie* • Vincent Spano *Mark* • Tom Fergus *Claude* • Harry Northup *Doberman* • Andy Romano *Fred Willat* • Ellen Geer *Sandra Willat* ■ *Dir* Jonathan Kaplan • *Scr* Charles Haas, Tim Hunter

Over the Hill ★★★ PG

Drama 1992 · Aus · Colour · 97mins

A highly sentimental look at ageing, directed by the other Australian George Miller (not the one who directed *Mad Max*) in which Olympia Dukakis sets out on "a journey of personal odyssey" to prove to her selfish, chilly family that she is not, in fact, over the hill. Dukakis, an accomplished, always watchable actress, gives the rather hackneyed material a lift, and watch out for Bill Kerr and Derek Fowlds, who provide polished supporting performances. SH. Contains swearing, brief nudity.

Olympia Dukakis *Alma Harris* • Sigrid Thornton *Elizabeth* • Derek Fowlds *Dutch* • Bill Kerr *Maurio* • Steve Bisley *Benedict* • Martin Jacobs *Alan Forbes* ■ *Dir* George Miller (1) • *Scr* Robert Caswell, from the book *Alone in the Australian Wilderness* by Gladys Taylor

Over the Moon ★★ U

Romantic comedy
1937 · UK · Colour · 75mins

This was one of two early Technicolor movies set up by Alexander Korda for Merle Oberon – the other was *The Divorce of Lady X* – and her frozen-faced acting does little for the role of a sudden heiress who is helped in squandering her money by Ursula Jeans among others. Rex Harrison, as a village doctor, doesn't help much, either. There's usually a quaint charm about this sort of dated attempt at British sophistication, but it's not much in evidence here. TH

Merle Oberon *June Benson* • Rex Harrison *Dr Freddie Jarvis* • Ursula Jeans *Lady Millie Parsmill* • Robert Douglas *John Flight* • Louis Borell *Count Pietro d'Altamura* • Zena Dare *Julie Deethorpe* • Peter Haddon *Lord Petcliffe* • Elisabeth Welch *Cabaret singer* ■ *Dir* Thornton Freeland • *Scr* Anthony Pelissier, Alec Coppel, Arthur Wimperis, from a story by Robert E Sherwood, from a story by Lajos Biró • *Cinematographer* Harry Stradling, Robert Krasker

Over the Top ★★ PG

Drama 1987 · US · Colour · 89mins

This tacky action adventure has its roots in that old Wallace Beery classic, *The Champ*. Here, boxing is replaced by arm wrestling, as trucker Sly tries to re-establish a relationship with his military academy-trained son on a make-up or break trek across the States. The grapple scenes are so devoid of thrills that you long to return to the mushy melodramatics. DP. Contains violence, swearing. DVD

Sylvester Stallone *Lincoln Hawk* • Robert Loggia *Jason Cutler* • Susan Blakely *Christina Hawk* • Rick Zumwalt *Bob "Bull" Hurley* • David Mendenhall *Michael Cutler* • Chris McCarty *Tim Salanger* • Terry Funk *Ruker* ■ *Dir* Menahem Golan • *Scr* Stirling Silliphant, Sylvester Stallone, from a story by Gary Conway, David C Engelbach

Over 21 ★★

Second World War comedy
1945 · US · BW · 104mins

Successful writer Irene Dunne and her editor husband Alexander Knox move out of town, where the nearby army base attracts him to go for officer training. He leaves her to cope with wartime domestic difficulties, and his boss Charles Coburn to manage the newspaper without him. This adaptation of actress/writer Ruth Gordon's first play is kept afloat by Dunne's immaculate screen presence, Gordon's wit and Charles Vidor's sharp direction. Yet it remains essentially theatrical, Knox is dull, and the film hasn't much of interest to say. RK

Irene Dunne *Paula Wharton* • Alexander Knox *Max Wharton* • Charles Coburn *Robert Gow* • Jeff Donnell *Jan Lupton* • Loren Tindall *Roy Lupton* ■ *Dir* Charles Vidor • *Scr* Sidney Buchman, from the play by Ruth Gordon

Overboard ★★★★ PG

Romantic comedy
1987 · US · Colour · 107mins

A charming throwback to the screwball comedies of the 1930s and one of the better vehicles designed for Goldie Hawn. She plays the pampered heiress to a fortune, who loses her memory after falling off her luxury yacht. Carpenter Kurt Russell, who had clashed with her earlier, sees the chance for revenge, and convinces her that she is his wife. The chemistry between the two stars (a couple in real life) is complemented by the performances of an experienced support cast. The entire package is slickly directed by Garry Marshall, who juggles the sharp repartee and slapstick with ease. JF. Contains swearing. DVD

Goldie Hawn *Joanna Stayton/Annie* • Kurt Russell *Dean Proffitt* • Edward Herrmann *Grant Stayton III* • Katherine Helmond *Edith Mintz* • Michael Hagerty [Michael G Hagerty] *Billy Pratt* • Roddy McDowall *Andrew* • Jared Rushton *Charlie* • Jeffrey Wiseman *Joey* ■ *Dir* Garry Marshall • *Scr* Leslie Dixon

Overland Stage Raiders ★★ U

Western 1938 · US · BW · 54mins

This up-to-date Republic B-western features hold-ups not of stagecoaches but of motor coaches. The gang then rob a plane carrying gold in mid-flight, handing the passengers parachutes and booting them out. Its plot is of serial-like simplicity but it's directed by George Sherman with positive vigour. John Wayne is the upright leader of the "Three Mesquiteers" and the luminous silent star Louise Brooks (in her very last film role) displays a relaxed radiance and good humour. AE

John Wayne *Stony Brooke* • Ray "Crash" Corrigan *Tuscon Smith* • Max Terhune *Lullaby Joslin* • Louise Brooks *Beth Hoyt/Beth Vincent* • Anthony Marsh *Ned Hoyt/Ned Vincent* • Ralph Bowman *Bob Whitney* • Gordon Hart *Mullins* ■ *Dir* George Sherman • *Scr* Luci Ward, from a story by Bernard McConville, Edmond Kelso, from characters created by William Colt MacDonald

The Overlanders ★★★ U

War drama based on a true story
1946 · UK · BW · 91mins

This is a very impressive re-creation of a spectacular event that took place in Australia during the Second World War: the moving to safety of 500,000 head of cattle (reduced in the movie to a mere thousand), made necessary by the prospect of a Japanese invasion of the Northern Territory. This was one of Ealing's first Australian-made movies, and mightily effective it is under the direction of documentary film-maker Harry Watt. Trouble is, Watt also wrote the screenplay, and the clichés come thick and fast. Nevertheless, the action is very exciting. TS

Chips Rafferty *Dan McAlpine* • John Nugent Hayward *Bill Parsons* • Daphne Campbell *Mary Parsons* • Jean Blue *Mrs Parsons* • Helen Grieve *Helen Parsons* • John Fernside *Corky* ■ *Dir/Scr* Harry Watt

Overlord ★★

Second World War drama
1975 · UK · BW · 82mins

Made with the co-operation of the Imperial War Museum, this account of the D-Day landings attempts to convey the grim reality of the soldier's lot by combining newsreel footage with dramatic re-enactments. Unfortunately, too much time was spent rooting out clips and not enough on the script, which is a collection of clichéd ideas and utterances. A bold venture, but poorly executed. DP

Brian Stirner *Tom* • Davyd Harries *Jack* • Nicholas Ball *Arthur* • Julie Neesam *Girl* ■ *Dir* Stuart Cooper • *Scr* Stuart Cooper, Christopher Hudson

Overnight ★★ 15

Documentary 2003 · US · Colour · 82mins

Hubris is the name of the game in this slightly unsatisfactory documentary following heavy rock artiste and first-time director Troy Duffy as he tries to get his movie, *The Boondock Saints*, off the page and onto the big screen. Duffy reveals himself as an arrogant, foul-mouthed, temperamental egoist, and there's certainly some *schadenfreude* to be enjoyed as we watch him being screwed over by, among others, Miramax's Harvey Weinstein. However, half way through it's revealed that the film is actually being made by two disenchanted ex-band members and thus is anything but non-partisan. And for all their sniggering, Duffy did eventually get his movie made (though it was awful). AS. Contains swearing.

Dir Tony Montana, Brian Mark Smith

Overnight Delivery ★★ 15

Romantic comedy
1997 · US · Colour · 84mins

This could be regarded as one of Reese Witherspoon's misfires, though it's an entertaining enough teen romp. Paul Rudd plays a frustrated student who drowns his sorrows with a stripper (Witherspoon) when he discovers that his virginal girlfriend is apparently stepping out with a jock. Having sent compromising "evidence" of his sexual prowess through the post to his girlfriend, he is horrified to discover he was wrong and must intercept the mail. The two leads spark off each other quite nicely, but it's a slight affair. JF. Contains swearing.

Reese Witherspoon *Ivy Miller* • Paul Rudd *Wyatt Trips* • Larry Drake *Hal Ipswich* • Christine Taylor *Kimberly* • Tobin Bell *John Dwayne Beezly* ■ *Dir* Jason Bloom • *Scr* Marc Sedaka, Steven L Bloom

Overture to Glory ★★★ U

Musical melodrama 1940 · US · BW · 88mins

This was the first US feature made by exiled German director, Max Nosseck. It follows Vilna cantor Moishe Oysher, as he defies the synagogue authorities to find fame in the Warsaw opera, only to lose his voice on hearing of the death of his neglected son and find redemption on the Day of Atonement. With surprisingly lavish production values, this Yiddish film found little favour because of its downbeat ending, despite the superb singing of its star. DP. In Yiddish with English subtitles.

Moishe Oysher *Yoel David Strashunsky* • Florence Weiss *Chana Strashunsky* • Lazar Freed *Rabbi* • Helen Beverly *Countess Wanda Mirova* • Jack Mylong *Stanislaw Maniusko* ■ *Dir* Max Nosseck • *Scr* Max Nosseck, Ossip Dymow, Jacob Gladstone, from the legend *The Vilna Balabessel* by Ossip Dymow

Owd Bob ★★★ U

Drama 1938 · UK · BW · 75mins

Prepare to shed a tear at this shamelessly sentimental sheepdog drama set in the Lake District. The tale turns on the rift between ageing shepherd Will Fyffe and his new neighbour, John Loder, when the latter's dog – the Owd Bob of the title – upstages Fyffe's prized Black Wull at the local trials. With flavoursome support coming from the likes of Moore Marriott and Graham Moffatt, there's barely room for Margaret Lockwood to make an impression as Loder's love interest. DP

Will Fyffe *Adam McAdam* • John Loder *David Moore* • Margaret Lockwood *Jeannie* • Graham Moffatt *Tammas* • Moore Marriott *Samuel* • Wilfred Walter *Thwaites* ■ *Dir* Robert Stevenson • *Scr* Michael Hogan, JB Williams, from the novel *Bob, Son of Battle* by Alfred Ollivant

The Owl and the Pussycat ★★★ 15

Romantic comedy
1970 · US · Colour · 92mins

Barbra Streisand plays against type, as well as actually letting co-star George Segal get a word in edgeways, in this slick adaptation of Bill Manhoff's Broadway hit. She's an eccentric hooker who moves in with bookish neighbour Segal who had her evicted from her own flat in this Neil Simon-esque comedy. Director Herbert Ross and scriptwriter Buck Henry give the raucous original an extra glow of warmth and Streisand and Segal are so good together you wonder why they never did a sequel. TH DVD

Barbra Streisand *Doris* • George Segal *Felix* • Robert Klein *Barney* • Allen Garfield *Dress shop proprietor* • Roz Kelly *Eleanor* • Jacques Sandulescu *Rapzinsky* • Jack Manning *Mr Weyderhaus* ■ *Dir* Herbert Ross • *Scr* Buck Henry, from the play by Bill Manhoff

Owning Mahowny ★★ 15

Drama based on a true story
2002 · Can/UK · Colour · 100mins

As 1980s Canadian bank manager and gambling addict Dan Mahowny, Philip Seymour Hoffman works hard to convince, but his performance suffers under weak direction and a tedious script. The film is too bogged down with the mechanics of his multi-million dollar theft to offer any genuine insights into his motivations and emotions, while an almost unrecognisable Minnie Driver is underused as Mahowny's drippy girlfriend. But the real scandal is John Hurt's poor turn as an Atlantic City casino boss. SF DVD

Philip Seymour Hoffman *Dan Mahowny* • Minnie Driver *Belinda* • Maury Chaykin *Frank Perlin* • John Hurt *Victor Foss* • Sonja Smits *Dana Selkirk* • Ian Tracey *Detective Ben Lock* • Roger Dunn *Bill Gooden* • Jason Blicker *Dave Quinson* ■ *Dir* Richard Kwietniowski • *Scr* Maurice Chauvet, from the non-fiction book *Stung: the Incredible Obsession of Brian Molony* by Gary Stephen Ross

The Ox ★★★ 15

Period drama based on a true story
1991 · Swe · Colour · 88mins

Sven Nykvist, best known for his work as a cinematographer with Ingmar Bergman, here directs a heart-rending true-life drama set in 19th-century rural Sweden. Bergman regulars Liv Ullmann, Erland Josephson and Max von Sydow turn in polished support performances, but the action is carried by the excellent Stellan Skarsgård and Ewa Froling as the couple driven to desperate measures to survive a merciless famine. While Nykvist occasionally allows the pace to drop, he maintains an atmosphere worthy of his mentor. DP. In Swedish with English subtitles.

Stellan Skarsgård *Helge* • Ewa Fröling *Elfrida* • Lennart Hjulstrom *Svenning* • Max von Sydow *Pastor* • Liv Ullmann *Maria* • Erland Josephson *Silver* ■ *Dir* Sven Nykvist • *Scr* Sven Nykvist, Lasse Summanen

The Ox-Bow Incident ★★★★★

Western drama 1943 · US · BW · 75mins

This celebrated indictment of lynching remains a brave and unorthodox piece of film-making, based on the novel by Walter Van Tilburg Clark and pushed through the studio system by director William A Wellman as a personal project. It is a western only in setting (the exteriors are largely created on studio sound stages) and its grim tale lacks any heroes – Henry Fonda and Henry "Harry" Morgan are passing cattlemen who observe rather than intervene. The lynch mob mentality is tellingly explored, but the letter so beautifully read out by Fonda is far too literate and philosophical to be the last testament of a humble cowboy. AE

Henry Fonda *Gil Carter* • Dana Andrews *Donald Martin* • Mary Beth Hughes *Rose Mapen* • Anthony Quinn *The Mexican* • William Eythe *Gerald Tetley* • Henry Morgan [Harry Morgan] *Art Croft* • Jane Darwell *Ma Grier* • Matt Briggs *Judge Daniel Tyler* • Francis Ford *"Dad" Hardwick* ■ *Dir* William A Wellman • *Scr* Lamar Trotti, from the novel by Walter Van Tilburg Clark

Oxford Blues ★★ 15

Drama 1984 · US · Colour · 93mins

It's easy to see why this brat-pack version of *A Yank at Oxford* was delayed for two years before being released in the UK. It's familiar teen territory all the way as Rob Lowe finances an Oxford education via gambling, but fails to impress titled debutante Amanda Pays. With the bias towards bland travelogue footage, a major point of interest is noting how many actors in the student bit parts have now become stars. AJ. Contains swearing.

Rob Lowe *Nick Di Angelo* • Ally Sheedy *Rona* • Amanda Pays *Lady Victoria* • Julian Firth *Geordie* • Alan Howard *Simon* • Gail Strickland *Las Vegas Lady* • Michael Gough *Dr Ambrose* • Aubrey Morris *Dr Boggs* • Cary Elwes *Lionel* ■ *Dir/Scr* Robert Boris

Oxygen ★★★ 18

Psychological crime thriller
1999 · US · Colour · 88mins

This thriller doesn't score many points for originality, but it's well staged and has a decent twist. Adrien Brody stars as a psychopath who is obsessed with the feats of Harry Houdini. When he is caught, he plays a high-stakes game of cat and mouse with the police over the whereabouts of a woman he has buried alive. Maura Tierney gives a believable performance as the psychologically tortured cop on the case and Brody is everything you'd expect as the killer. ST DVD

Maura Tierney *Madeline* • Adrien Brody *Harry* • Terry Kinney *Tim* • Dylan Baker *Jackson* • Paul Calderon *Jessie* • James Naughton *Hannon* ■ *Dir/Scr* Richard Shepard

The Oyster Princess ★★★★

Silent romantic drama
1919 · Ger · BW · 65mins

Satirising Prussian militarism, American materialism and fadism, and snobbery in general, this was the first comedy that former slapstick clown Ernst Lubitsch felt demononstrated "the Lubitsch touch" of sly sophistication that would become his trademark. Combining visual opulence with narrative intricacy, the tale of the nouveau riche heiress and the impoverished prince, who are matchmade in the pursuit of dynastic and fiscal legitimacy, is packed with mistaken identities, unlikely developments and inspired resolutions. In short, it's a delight. DP

Ossi Oswalda *The Princess, daughter of the Oyster King* • Victor Janson *Quaker, the Oyster King* • Julius Falkenstein *Josef, servant of Nuki* • Harry Liedtke *Prince Nuki* ■ *Dir* Ernst Lubitsch • *Scr* Hans Kräly, Ernst Lubitsch • *Cinematographer* Theodor Sparkuhl

PCU ★★ 15

Comedy 1994 · US · Colour · 77mins

A flawed attempt to revive that 1980s staple, the fraternity house flick. This brings it bang up to date by making political correctness, rather than teachers, the main enemy, with the slobbish devotees of the old-style of campus education (drink, sex, pranks and parties) declaring war on the caring, liberal face of responsible studenthood. It's a nice idea, but the members of the largely unknown cast don't have the charisma to carry off the antics. JF. Contains swearing.

Jeremy Piven *Droz* • Chris Young *Tom Lawrence* • Megan Ward *Katy* • Jon Favreau *Gutter* • Sarah Trigger *Samantha* • David Spade *Rand McPherson* ■ *Dir* Hart Bochner • *Scr* Adam Leff, Zak Penn

PK and the Kid ★★★

Drama 1982 · US · Colour · 89mins

Molly Ringwald made her second screen appearance in this arm-wrestling melodrama, which languished on the shelf for five years before it was dusted down following the release of Sylvester Stallone's *Over the Top*. Paul Le Mat's decision to pick up a hitcher brings untold trouble, this time in the form of Alex Rocco, the abusive partner of runaway Ringwald's mom. It's tacky, teen wish-fulfilment, but director Lou Lombardo develops the unlikely friendship without prurient undertones. DP

Paul Le Mat *Kid Kane* • Molly Ringwald *PK Bayette* • Alex Rocco *Les* • Charles Hallahan *Bazooka* • John DiSanti *Benny* • Leigh Hamilton *Louise* • Esther Rolle *Mim* ■ *Dir* Lou Lombardo • *Scr* Neal Barbera

POW the Escape ★★ 15

War action adventure
1986 · US · Colour · 85mins

Yet another gung ho American Vietnam war movie that attempts to rewrite the history books while also apeing the *Rambo* movies. Shot in the Philippines, it stars David Carradine, who plays a high-ranking Vietcong prisoner determined to lead his comrades to freedom in the last days before the fall of Saigon. Oriental-for-hire Mako plays the camp commandant as if he's been cast as Ming the Merciless. Strictly second division. RS

David Carradine *Colonel Jim Cooper* • Charles R Floyd *Sparks* • Mako *Captain Vinh* • Steve James (1) *Jonston* • Phil Brock *Adams* ■ *Dir* Gideon Amir • *Scr* Jeremy Lipp, James Bruner, Malcolm Barbour, John Langley, from a story by Avi Kleinberger, Gideon Amir

PT 109 ★★★ U

Biographical Second World War drama
1963 · US · Colour · 134mins

During his war service, John F Kennedy's torpedo boat was blown in half by the Japanese. Towing a wounded shipmate for three miles by swimming with the wounded man's life belt clamped in his jaws, JFK landed on an uninhabited Pacific island and was rescued some days later. Cliff Robertson makes a fine pre-president, though the build-up to the incident is rather slow. But as a piece of hero worship and political propaganda, released just after the Cuban missile crisis, the movie is a fascinating relic from a less cynical age. AT

Cliff Robertson *Lieutenant John F Kennedy* • Ty Hardin *Ensign Leonard J Thom* • James Gregory *Commander CR Ritchie* • Robert Culp *Ensign "Barney" Ross* • Grant Williams *Lieutenant Alvin Cluster* • Lew Gallo *Yeoman Rogers* • Errol John *Benjamin Kevu* • Michael Pate *Lieutenant Reginald Evans* • Robert Blake *"Bucky" Harris* ■ *Dir* Leslie H Martinson • *Scr* Richard L Breen, Howard Sheehan, Vincent X Flaherty, from the non-fiction book *PT 109, John F Kennedy in World War II* by Robert J Donovan

Pacific Heights ★★★ 15

Thriller 1990 · US · Colour · 98mins

Michael Keaton enjoys himself immensely as the tenant from hell, turning the life of nice yuppie couple Matthew Modine and Melanie Griffith into a nightmare. It's a little hard to summon up much sympathy for a landlord, and it must be said that the story just gets sillier as the film progresses. However, director John Schlesinger is an old hand when it comes to this sort of thing and Keaton delivers a genuinely creepy performance. JF. Contains swearing, violence and nudity.

Melanie Griffith *Patty Palmer* • Matthew Modine *Drake Goodman* • Michael Keaton *Carter Hayes* • Mako *Toshio Watanabe* • Nobu McCarthy *Mira Watanabe* • Laurie Metcalf *Stephanie MacDonald* • Carl Lumbly *Lou Baker* • Dorian Harewood *Dennis Reed* • Tippi Hedren *Florence Peters* ■ *Dir* John Schlesinger • *Scr* Daniel Pyne

Pacific Inferno ★ 15

Second World War adventure
1979 · US/Phil · Colour · 85mins

This bottom-of-the-barrel Second World War action hokum was produced by and stars Jim Brown as the leader of a team of captured American Navy divers. They are forced by the Japanese to recover $16 million in silver pesos that General MacArthur dumped in Manila Bay to prevent them falling into enemy hands. RS

Jim Brown *Clyde Preston* • Richard Jaeckel *Dealer* • Tim Brown [Timothy Brown] *Zoe* • Tad Horino *Yamada* • Dindo Fernando *Totoy* • Wilma Reading *Tita* • Rik Van Nutter *Dennis* ■ *Dir/Scr* Rolf Bayer

The Pacifier ★★ PG

Action comedy 2005 · US · Colour · 95mins

Vin Diesel cheekily sends up his tough-guy persona in this uneven comedy. He plays a Navy SEAL who's assigned to protect the five unruly offspring of an assassinated scientist. Diesel camps it up wildly, but is let down by an underdeveloped script and an overall lack of vitality. Director Adam Shankman never achieves a boisterous sense of fun, and it's only in the final third that things pick up. SF

Vin Diesel *Shane Wolfe* • Lauren Graham *Principal Claire Fletcher* • Faith Ford *Julie Plummer* • Brittany Snow *Zoe Plummer* • Max Thieriot *Seth Plummer* • Chris Potter *Captain Bill Fawcett* • Morgan York *Lulu Plummer* • Scott Thompson *Director* • Carol Kane *Helga* ■ *Dir* Adam Shankman • *Scr* Thomas Lennon, Robert Ben Garant

The Pack ★★★ 15

Horror 1977 · US · Colour · 94mins

Snarlingly effective horror movie in which marine biologist Joe Don Baker is sent in to stop a bunch of ferocious dogs tearing and ravaging holidaymakers on a remote island. Although the idea is drawn from Alfred Hitchcock's *The Birds*, this film doesn't have the same terrifying sense of nature arbitrarily fighting back, but it comes across as an intriguing adventure nonetheless. TH

Joe Don Baker *Jerry* • Hope Alexander-Willis *Millie* • Richard B Shull *Hardiman* • RG Armstrong *Cobb* • Ned Wertimer *Walker* • Bibi Besch *Marge* • Delos V Smith Jr *McMinnimee* • Richard O'Brien *Dodge* ■ *Dir* Robert Clouse • *Scr* Robert Clouse, from a novel by Dave Fisher

Pack Up Your Troubles ★★★★★ U

Comedy 1932 · US · BW · 64mins

Seldom seen intact since it was made, this Laurel and Hardy delight has gone through the mincing machine of distributors' cuts but still remains one of their best movies for producer Hal Roach. After a disastrous wartime service, Stan and Ollie try to keep their promise to a dying buddy that they would look after his little girl (Jacquie Lyn). The usual ins-and-outs follow as they try to reunite her with her grandparents. It touches the nerves of comedy and pathos with just the right amount of pressure and also has a vivid portrayal of a revenge-crazed army cook by George Marshall, the film's co-director. TH DVD

Stan Laurel *Stan* • Oliver Hardy *Ollie* • Donald Dillaway *Eddie Smith* • Jacquie Lyn *Eddie's baby* • James Finlayson *General* • Mary Carr *Elderly woman* • Rychard Cramer [Richard Cramer] *Uncle Jack* • Grady Sutton *Eddie, the bridegroom* • Billy Gilbert *Mr Hathaway* • Paulette Goddard ■ *Dir* George Marshall, Raymond McCarey [Ray McCarey] • *Scr* HM Walker

Pack Up Your Troubles ★★★ U

Comedy 1939 · US · BW · 75mins

This is a very funny vehicle for the comedy team the Ritz Brothers, Jane Withers, the child star who memorably bullied Shirley Temple in *Bright Eyes*, here makes a successful transition to adolescent actress. The brothers play First World War soldiers mistaken for the enemy who escape in a balloon and find themselves actually in Germany. The team are an acquired taste but this is one of their best. TV

The Ritz Brothers [Al Ritz] • The Ritz Brothers [Jimmy Ritz] • The Ritz Brothers [Harry Ritz] • Jane Withers *Colette* • Lynn Bari *Yvonne* • Joseph Schildkraut *Hugo Ludwig* • Stanley Fields *Sergeant "Angel Face" Walker* • Fritz Leiber *Pierre Ferrand* ■ *Dir* H Bruce Humberstone • *Scr* Lou Breslow, Owen Francis, from their story

The Package ★★ 15

Political thriller 1989 · US · Colour · 103mins

This post-Cold War thriller comes apart like a package damaged in the post. In fact, "the package" is Tommy Lee Jones, whom sergeant Gene Hackman has to escort to America from Berlin, but the complications and coincidences are so formidable that not even the participants seem to know what's going on. Director Andrew Davis is used to working with action men such as Chuck Norris and Steven Seagal, so perhaps working with Hackman went to his head. TH. Contains swearing. DVD

Gene Hackman *Sgt Johnny Gallagher* • Tommy Lee Jones *Thomas Boyette* • Joanna Cassidy *Lt Col Eileen Gallagher* • John Heard *Col Glen Whitacre* • Kevin Crowley *Walter Henke* • Chelcie Ross *General Thomas Hopkins* • Joe Greco *General Robert Carlson* • Dennis Franz *Milan Delich* • Pam Grier *Ruth Butler* ■ *Dir* Andrew Davis • *Scr* John Bishop, from a story by Dennis Haggerty, John Bishop

Paco ★★

Comedy adventure
1975 · Col · Colour · 100mins

Puerto Rican-born José Ferrer is the star of this crime adventure in which eager kids lock horns with pantomimic villains. Combining Dickensian melodrama with a somewhat romanticised view of urban street poverty, Robert Vincent O'Neil's film

P

will seem old-fashioned to modern youngsters, in spite of a willing performance from Panchito Gómez, as the orphan who is forced to leave the family farm and head for the big city. DP

José Ferrer *Fermin Flores* • Allen Garfield *Padre* • Inès Elvira Cortès *Susana* • Panchito Gomez *Paco* ■ *Dir* Robert Vincent O'Neil • *Scr* Andrew Davis, Andre Marquis, Robert Vincent O'Neil

The Pad (and How to Use It) ★★

Comedy 1966 · US · Colour · 85mins

In this relic from the 1960s, based on a play by Peter Shaffer, shy, virginal Brian Bedford shares his bedsit with his hi-fi gear and really loves his music. Then he meet the smashing Julie Sommars and asks his lothario friend for advice on how to romance her. Now way beyond being merely dated and more in the realms of the historical comedy. The soundtrack features the Knickbockers. Groovy! AT

Brian Bedford *Bob Handman* • Julie Sommars *Doreen Marshall* • James Farentino *Ted* • Edy Williams *Lavinia* ■ *Dir* Brian G Hutton • *Scr* Thomas C Ryan, Ben Starr, from the play *The Private Ear* by Peter Shaffer

Padre Nuestro ★★

Comedy drama 1985 · Sp · Colour · 104mins

Francisco Regueiro aspired to Buñuelian heights with this seedy study of the shameless hypocrisy of those adhering to Catholicism and Marxism. But there's little of the master in this overblown melodrama, which its star, Fernando Rey (a four-time Buñuel collaborator), opted to omit from his official filmography. Ignoring a papal appeal, the dying Cardinal Rey leaves the Vatican for the first time in 30 years to settle the affairs of his family's vineyard. DP. A Spanish language film.

Fernando Rey *Cardinal* • Francisco Rabal *Abel* • Victoria Abril *Cardenala* • Emma Penella *Maria* • Amelia de la Torre *Valentina* • Rafaela Aparicio *Jerónima* • Lina Canalejas *Blanca* ■ *Dir* Francisco Regueiro • *Scr* Francisco Regueiro, Angel Fernandez Santos

Padre Padrone ★★★★ 15

Drama based on a true story
1977 · It · Colour · 108mins

Winner of the Palme d'Or at Cannes, brothers Paolo and Vittorio Taviani had their first international success with this portrayal of primitive patriarchal Sardinian life in the late 1940s. It tells of how a peasant father sends his small son to the mountains to look after the sheep all by himself for years. Deprived of company and language, the young man struggles to adapt when he re-enters society. Perhaps if the sibling directors had approached the tale in a more sober and detached manner, the film might have been even more moving. RB. In Italian with English subtitles.

Omero Antonutti *Efisio Ledda, Gavino's father* • Saverio Marconi *Gavino Ledda* • Marcella Michelangeli *Gavino's mother* ■ *Dir* Paolo Taviani, Vittorio Taviani • *Scr* Paolo Taviani, Vittorio Taviani, from the autobiographical novel *Padre Padrone: l'Educazione di un Pastore* by Gavino Ledda

Page Miss Glory ★★ U

Comedy 1935 · US · BW · 94mins

Promoter Pat O'Brien, something of a chancer, sends in a composite photograph of a girl for a beauty contest, wins, and then has to find a real girl to live up to the illustrated ideal. She comes along in the shape of Marion Davies, starring in the first of four pictures at Warner Bros under a deal made by her lover, William Randolph Hearst, for his Cosmopolitan Pictures. Mervyn LeRoy directed this pleasing lightweight comedy in which Davies, a better comedian than straight actress, is fine. RK

Marion Davies *Loretta Dalrymple/"Dawn Glory"* • Pat O'Brien *Dan "Click" Wiley* • Dick Powell *Bingo Nelson* • Mary Astor *Gladys Russell* • Frank McHugh *Ed Olsen* ■ *Dir* Mervyn LeRoy • *Scr* Delmer Daves, Robert Lord, from the play by Joseph Schrank, Philip Dunning

A Page of Madness ★★★★★

Silent melodrama 1926 · Jpn · BW · 60mins

Director Teinosuke Kinugasa, who made his name with a series of samurai movies, came across this lost silent masterpiece in his storeroom in the early 1970s, and released it with a music soundtrack. Relying on its eloquent images without the need for intertitles, the film tells of how an elderly man, working in a mental hospital where his wife is confined, hopes to set her free. Kinugasa, who would study with Sergei Eisenstein after this film, displays a remarkable range of cinematic techniques to give the impression of madness, in between the sane flashbacks to the wife's pre-asylum days. RB

Masao Inoue *Custodian* • Yoshie Nakagawa *Wife* • Ayako Iijima *Daughter* ■ *Dir* Teinosuke Kinugasa • *Scr* Yasunari Kawabata, Teinosuke Kinugasa • *Cinematographer* Kohei Sugiyama

The Pagemaster ★★ U

Adventure 1994 · US · Colour · 72mins

Macaulay Culkin takes refuge in a library during a thunderstorm, turns into a two-dimensional cartoon and is transported into an animated world where classic literature comes to life. Although the homilies "There's no place like home" and "Books are worth reading" are repeated continuously, the dull story and crude animation sabotage any well-intentioned message. None of the segments show any real imagination or artistry. AJ

Macaulay Culkin *Richard Tyler* • Ed Begley Jr *Alan Tyler* • Mel Harris *Claire Tyler* • Christopher Lloyd *Mr Dewey/Pagemaster* • Patrick Stewart *Adventure* • Whoopi Goldberg *Fantasy* • Frank Welker *Horror* • Leonard Nimoy *Dr Jekyll/Mr Hyde* ■ *Dir* Joe Johnston, Maurice Hunt • *Scr* David Casci, David Kirschner, Ernie Contreras, from a story by David Casci, David Kirschner

Pagliacci ★★

Musical 1936 · UK · BW and Colour · 92mins

While known for his glossy visuals, the Austrian director Karl Grune never really came to terms with sound (making him a rather odd choice for a musical) and this clumsy adaptation of Ruggiero Leoncavallo's masterpiece was to be his final film. His fellow countryman Richard Tauber gives a solid rendition of the insanely jealous Canio, while Steffi Duna makes a spirited Nedda. Grune is not the only film-maker to be confounded by opera, but he is the most pedestrian. DP

Richard Tauber *Canio Tonini* • Steffi Duna *Nedda Tonini* • Diana Napier *Trina* • Arthur Margetson *Tonio* • Esmond Knight *Silvio* ■ *Dir* Karl Grune • *Scr* Monckton Hoffe, John Drinkwater, Roger Burford, Ernest Betts, from the opera *I Pagliacci* by Ruggiero Leoncavallo

Pagliacci ★★★

Opera 1948 · It · BW · 80mins

Fresh from completing his version of *Don Giovanni*, Mario Costa embarked on this Calabrian-set adaptation of Ruggiero Leoncavallo's one-act opera about the lachrymose clown whose act of charity towards a homeless waif is repaid by treachery and heartache. Although the star of the show is, nominally, the celebrated baritone, Tito Gobbi, Costa was more interested in showcasing the talents of his "discovery", Gina Lollobrigida. Even though her singing voice was dubbed, "La Lollo" made sufficient impression to be prised away from her mentor by Lux Films, where stardom beckoned. DP. An Italian language film.

Tito Gobbi *Tonio/Silvio* • Gina Lollobrigida *Nedda* • Onelia Fineschi *Nedda (singing voice)* • Afro Poli *Canio* • Galliano Masini *Canio* ■ *Dir* Mario Costa • *Scr* from the opera by Ruggiero Leoncavallo

Paid in Full ★★

Drama 1950 · US · BW · 105mins

Feeling responsible for the death of her sister's child, a woman who knows pregnancy stands to endanger her own life, decides to get pregnant in order to give the sister a replacement baby. As if this isn't enough to contend with, the tormented heroine, played by Lizabeth Scott, is in love with her sister's husband. Oh dear. Efficient enough tearjerker, but so steeped in bleak and relentless suffering that even the presence of Eve Arden is unable to lift it from the depths. RK

Robert Cummings *Bill Prentice* • Lizabeth Scott *Jane Langley* • Diana Lynn *Nancy Langley* • Eve Arden *Tommy Thompson* • Ray Collins *Dr Fredericks* • Frank McHugh *Ben* ■ *Dir* William Dieterle • *Scr* Robert Blees, Charles Schnee, from a story by Frederic M Loomis

A Pain in the A...! ★★★★

Comedy crime drama
1973 · Fr/It · Colour · 84mins

A very funny ebony-hued comedy with Lino Ventura as the hitman trying to carry out a murder contract, who's constantly hindered by the suicidal Jacques Brel. The contrast between the implacable Ventura and Brel's walking nervous breakdown is a constant source of laughs. Edouard Molinaro directs this adaptation of Francis Veber's stage success, later remade by Billy Wilder as *Buddy Buddy*. This is the original and the best version. TH. A French language film.

Jacques Brel *Pignon* • Lino Ventura *Ralph* • Caroline Cellier *Louise* • Nino Castelnuovo *Bellhop* • Jean-Pierre Darras *Fuchs* ■ *Dir* Edouard Molinaro • *Scr* Edouard Molinaro, Francis Veber, from the play *Le Contrat* by Francis Veber • *Music* Jacques Brel • *Cinematographer* Raoul Coutard

Paint It Black ★★★ 18

Thriller 1989 · US · Colour · 96mins

A strange little psychodrama from Tim Hunter, the director who'd burst so promisingly on the independent movie scene two years earlier with quirky teen-murder tale *River's Edge*. This isn't quite in the same class, but it's impressive enough, with a strong performance from Rick Rossovich as an up-and-coming sculptor who's artistically and emotionally tied to unscrupulous art gallery owner Sally Kirkland. Things get a little weird when he also falls under the influence of an oddball art collector. DA

Sally Kirkland *Marion Easton* • Rick Rossovich *Jonathan Dunbar* • Doug Savant *Eric* • Julie Carmen *Gina Hayworth* • Martin Landau *Daniel Lambert* • Jason Bernard *Lt Wilder* ■ *Dir* Tim Hunter • *Scr* AH Zacharias [Timothy Harris], Michael Drexler [Herschel Weingrod]

Paint Your Wagon ★★★ PG

Musical comedy western
1969 · US · Colour · 153mins

Alan Jay Lerner invented a new "adult" plot, quite unnecessarily, for this screen version of his own Broadway show, in which Lee Marvin and Clint Eastwood share Jean Seberg in a *ménage à trois*. Joshua Logan directs with the heaviest of hands, and only Harve Presnell as Rotten Luck Willie emerges with credit, but then he does have all the best songs, even though Marvin topped the UK charts with *Wandrin' Star*. Clint uses his own singing voice charmingly, too, and there's some of the finest chorale work (directed by Roger Wagner) ever heard in a film musical. This overlong screen adaptation almost works. TS DVD

Lee Marvin *Ben Rumson* • Clint Eastwood *Pardner* • Jean Seberg *Elizabeth* • Harve Presnell *Rotten Luck Willie* • Ray Walston *Mad Jack Duncan* • Tom Ligon *Horton Fenty* • Alan Dexter *Parson* • William O'Connell *Horace Tabor* ■ *Dir* Joshua Logan • *Scr* Alan Jay Lerner, Paddy Chayefsky, from the musical play by Alan Jay Lerner, Frederick Loewe • *Cinematographer* William A Fraker

Painted Angels ★★ 15

Western drama
1997 · Can/UK · Colour · 105mins

Brenda Fricker and Kelly McGillis star in this tedious western about a prairie-town bordello in the 1870s, the whores who work there and the pragmatic madam who runs the place. The use of period lighting gives the film a murky, washed-out look, while director Jon Sanders taxes the patience with lengthy static takes where people just sit around, saying nothing and doing even less. DA. Contains swearing, a sex scene.

Brenda Fricker *Annie Ryan* • Kelly McGillis *Nettie* • Meret Becker *Katya* • Bronagh Gallagher *Eileen* • Lisa Jakub *Georgie* • Anna Mottram *Ada* ■ *Dir* Jon Sanders • *Scr* Anna Mottram, Jon Sanders

The Painted Desert ★★ U

Western 1931 · US · BW · 83mins

A western about two miners whose discovery of a six-month-old baby in the wilderness results in a long and bitter feud. Doubtless very creaky by modern standards, well worth seeing for its cast. The heroine is played by Helen Twelvetrees, a beautiful New York-born actress whose career collapsed in 1938. The hero is played by William Boyd, four years before he hit paydirt as Hopalong Cassidy. Plus Clark Gable has his first speaking role. AT

Bill Boyd [William Boyd (1)] *Bill Holbrook* • Helen Twelvetrees *Mary Ellen Cameron* • William Farnum *Cash Holbrook* • J Farrell MacDonald *Jeff Cameron* • Clark Gable *Rance Brett* ■ *Dir* Howard Higgin • *Scr* Howard Higgin, Tom Buckingham

Painted Desert ★

Western 1938 · US · BW · 58mins

George O'Brien was the star of two of the most famous silent movies ever made – John Ford's *The Iron Horse* and Murnau's *Sunrise* – but here he's slumming in a B-minus western. The plot is about a land deal and crams in the expected gunfights and chases, as well as three musical numbers performed by singing cowboy Ray Whitley, before the hour is up. AT

George O'Brien *Bob McVey* • Laraine Johnson [Laraine Day] *Carol Banning* • Ray Whitley *Steve* • Fred Kohler *Fawcett* • Maude Allen *Yukon Kate* ■ *Dir* David Howard • *Scr* John Rathmell, Oliver Drake, from a story by Jack Cunningham

Painted Heart ★★ 15

Thriller 1992 · US · Colour · 86mins

A complex thriller about a woman in love with two men. One's the painter next door, the other's her hubby, the painter's boss. Torn apart emotionally, she finds she could also wind up torn apart physically, because one of the men is a serial killer. The plot actually plays better than it reads, with the quality cast of Will Patton, Bebe Neuwirth and Robert Pastorelli creating credence out of confusion. DA

Will Patton *Wesley* • Bebe Neuwirth *Margaret* • Robert Pastorelli *Willie* • Casey Siemaszko *Cal* ■ *Dir/Scr* Michael Taav

The Painted Smile ★

Crime drama 1961 · UK · BW · 61mins

This dreadfully dull British B-movie makes its brief running time seem like an eternity. From the moment that Liz Fraser's partner-in-crime is murdered, fugitive Kenneth Griffith tries desperately to avoid the finger of suspicion pointing at him. The cast members do what they can with the script, but they clearly received little directorial encouragement. DP

Liz Fraser *Jo Lake* • Kenneth Griffith *Kleinie* • Peter Reynolds *Mark Davies* • Anthony Wickert *Tom* • Craig Douglas *Nightclub singer* • Nanette Newman *Mary* • Ray Smith *Glynn* • David Hemmings *Roy* ■ *Dir* Lance Comfort • *Scr* Pip Baker, Jane Baker, from an idea by Brock Williams

The Painted Veil ★★★

Drama 1934 · US · BW · 84mins

Greta Garbo, the newlywed wife of doctor Herbert Marshall, accompanies her husband to China, where his work leads to his frequent absence, and his absence to her affair with married diplomat George Brent. Several dramatic upheavals follow, including a cholera epidemic. This melodramatic hokum is glitzed up with Cedric Gibbons's oriental sets, Adrian's costumes and William H Daniels's photography, and given committed direction by Richard Boleslawski. Garbo is at her loveliest in her familiar "noble suffering" mode. RK

Greta Garbo *Katherine Koerber Fane* • Herbert Marshall *Dr Walter Fane* • George Brent *Jack Townsend* • Warner Oland *General Yu* • Jean Hersholt *Prof Koerber* • Beulah Bondi *Frau Koerber* • Katherine Alexander *Mrs Townsend* • Cecilia Parker *Olga* ■ *Dir* Richard Boleslawski • *Scr* John Meehan, Salka Viertel, Edith Fitzgerald, from the novel by W Somerset Maugham • *Cinematographer* William H Daniels

Painting the Clouds with Sunshine ★★★ U

Musical 1951 · US · Colour · 86mins

Here Warner Bros reworked its highly successful *Gold Diggers* format, updated to take in Las Vegas and dressed in glowing 1950s' Technicolor. Nothing to shout about, but this pleasant film does feature a cast of bright young performers (bland top-billed Dennis Morgan is the exception) entertaining us with recognisable songs and dances in glamorous settings. Worth watching for hoofer Gene Nelson alone, but keep an eye out for George Sanders's brother, the suave Tom Conway. TS

Dennis Morgan *Vince Nichols* • Virginia Mayo *Carol* • Gene Nelson *Ted Lansing* • Lucille Norman *Abby* • Tom Conway *Bennington* • Wallace Ford *Sam Parks* • Tom Dugan *Barney* ■ *Dir* David Butler • *Scr* Harry Clark, Roland Kibbee, Peter Milne, from the play *Gold Diggers of Broadway* by Avery Hopwood

A Pair of Briefs ★★

Comedy 1961 · UK · BW · 90mins

This tepid comedy falls flat for the simple reason that feuding barristers Michael Craig and Mary Peach just don't click. Not only is the romantic banter very poor, but there is also none of the knowing courtroom comedy that made the Boulting brothers' *Brothers in Law* so enjoyable. James Robertson-Justice contributes some bullish support, but this just isn't funny enough. DP

Michael Craig *Tony Stevens* • Mary Peach *Frances Pilbright* • Brenda de Banzie *Gladys Pudney* • James Robertson-Justice *Justice Hadden* • Roland Culver *Sir John Pilbright* • Liz Fraser *Pearly Girl* • Ron Moody *Sid Pudney* ■ *Dir* Ralph Thomas • *Scr* Nicholas Phipps, from the play *How Say You?* by Harold Brooke, Kay Bannerman

Paisà ★★★ PG

Second World War drama
1946 · It · BW · 120mins

Following *Rome, Open City*, Roberto Rossellini moved on from the dramas of resistance workers to the Allied invasion of Sicily to the declaration of victory. The film, using entirely unknown and largely non-professional actors, focuses on a series of individual encounters – one between a black American soldier and an Italian urchin, for example – as well as showing the arrest and execution of partisans. Not as good as its predecessor, but the documentary style and flavour make for a realistic, involving, and significant film. RK. In Italian with English subtitles.

Carmela Sazio *Carmela* • Robert Van Loon *Joe* • Alfonsino Pasca *Boy* • Harriet White [Harriet Medin] *Harriet* • Dots Johnson *MP* • William Tubbs *Capt Bill Martin* ■ *Dir* Roberto Rossellini • *Scr* Sergio Amidei, Federico Fellini, Roberto Rossellini, Annalena Limentani (English dialogue), from a story by Klaus Mann

The Pajama Game ★★★★ U

Musical 1957 · US · Colour · 96mins

Workers' demands for a seven-and-a-half per cent pay rise in a pajama factory is the unlikely subject for this bouncy, infectious musical. However, it provided an exuberant Doris Day with several terrific songs and one of her best roles as the head of the workers' grievance committee who falls in love with the foreman (John Raitt). Co-directors Stanley Donen and George Abbott demonstrated that it was possible to remain true to a stage original, in this case the Broadway hit, while using creative camerawork and editing. RB DVD

Doris Day *Katie "Babe" Williams* • John Raitt *Sid Sorokin* • Carol Haney *Gladys Hotchkiss* • Eddie Foy Jr *Vernon Hines* • Reta Shaw *Mabel* • Barbara Nichols *Poopsie* • Thelma Pelish *Mae* • Jack Straw *Prez* ■ *Dir* George Abbott, Stanley Donen • *Scr* George Abbott, Richard Bissell, from their musical, from the novel *Seven and a Half Cents* by Richard Bissell • *Music/lyrics* Richard Adler, Jerry Ross • *Choreographer* Bob Fosse

Pajama Party ★ U

Comedy 1964 · US · Colour · 84mins

One of those terribly kitsch movies so rooted in 1960s Californian beach parties that it erupts into hilarious entertainment. This is part of a teen culture series which began with *Beach Party* and was slowly strangled to death by awful scripts. In this one, "star" Tommy Kirk plays a Martian who drops in on the high jinks with suitably nonplussed results. It is meant to be gently amusing but is gut-wrenchingly unfunny. SH

Tommy Kirk *Go-Go* • Annette Funicello *Connie* • Elsa Lanchester *Aunt Wendy* • Harvey Lembeck *Eric Von Zipper* • Jesse White *J Sinister Hulk* • Buster Keaton *Chief Rotten Eagle* • Dorothy Lamour *Head saleslady* • Don Rickles • Frankie Avalon ■ *Dir* Don Weis • *Scr* Louis M Heyward

Pakeezah ★★★★ PG

Romantic drama
1971 · Ind · Colour · 145mins

Determined to showcase the talents of his alcoholic wife, Meena Kumari (who died shortly after the picture wrapped), director Kamal Amrohi finally realised this project some 13 years after he came up with its concept. Production started in 1964, but marital strife, money problems and Kumari's precarious health prevented the completion of this richly coloured, romantic period melodrama, which became an instant box-office hit. As both the abused courtesan rejected by her husband's snobbish Lucknow family and the daughter kept from her father and her beloved, the doe-eyed Kumari gives a career-best performance that makes her hopeless plight all the more distressing. DP. In Urdu with English subtitles.

Ashok Kumar *Shahab* • Meena Kumari *Sahebjaan* • Raaj Kumar *Salam Ahmed Khan* ■ *Dir/Scr* Kamal Amrohi

Pal Joey ★★★ PG

Musical comedy 1957 · US · Colour · 104mins

Frank Sinatra's Exocet delivery of some great Richard Rodgers/Lorenz Hart songs, which include *The Lady Is a Tramp* and *My Funny Valentine*, more than makes up for the whitewash here of the black-hearted hero from the stage version. Joey is now a crooner, not a hoofer as on stage, and his rapacious greed for bed (on the make for fading star Rita Hayworth, but really loving Kim Novak) and bright lights has been toned down to give it a happy ending. The heel proves to have a soul, which is rather a pity as novelist John O'Hara's original Broadway exposé deserves a more sarcastic treatment. TH DVD

Rita Hayworth *Vera Simpson* • Frank Sinatra *Joey Evans* • Kim Novak *Linda English* • Barbara Nichols *Gladys* • Bobby Sherwood *Ned Galvin* • Hank Henry *Mike Miggins* • Elizabeth Patterson *Mrs Casey* ■ *Dir* George Sidney (2) • *Scr* Dorothy Kingsley, from the musical play by John O'Hara, Richard Rodgers, Lorenz Hart, from stories in the *New Yorker* magazine by John O'Hara

Palais Royale ★★ 15

Crime comedy drama
1988 · Can · Colour · 87mins

The gangster movie gets a Canadian spin in this Toronto-shot *film noir*, set in the late 1950s, and starring Matt Craven as an adman whose unbridled ambition embroils him in a world of gunmen and goons. Dean Stockwell and Kim Cattrall provide sturdy support. But there's nothing really to distinguish this formulaic flick from a hundred other thrillers. DA

Kim Cattrall *Odessa* • Matt Craven *Gerald* • Kim Coates *Tony* • Dean Stockwell *Dattalico* • Brian George *Gus* • Michael Hogan (3) *Sergeant Leonard* ■ *Dir* Martin Lavut • *Scr* Hugh Graham, David Daniels, Lawrence Zack, Jo Ann McIntyre

Pale Rider ★★★ 15

Western 1985 · US · Colour · 110mins

This handsome mystical western is one of director/star Clint Eastwood's more sombre offerings. A small community of prospectors struggle to scrape a living in the shadow of a strip-mining company that is intent on driving them out, by any means necessary. A young girl (Sydney Penny) prays for deliverance from the violence – cue Eastwood's entrance as the enigmatic "Preacher". We are in classic "man with no name" territory here – with added religious symbolism – but despite a reliably good performance from Eastwood and excellent support from Penny and Carrie Snodgress, this takes itself a little too seriously. TS. Contains swearing. DVD

Clint Eastwood *Preacher* • Michael Moriarty *Hull Barret* • Carrie Snodgress *Sarah Wheeler* • Christopher Penn [Chris Penn] *Josh Lahood* • Richard Dysart *Coy Lahood* • Sydney Penny *Megan Wheeler* • Richard Kiel *Club* • Doug McGrath *Spider Conway* ■ *Dir* Clint Eastwood • *Scr* Michael Butler, Dennis Shryack

The Paleface ★★★★★ U

Silent comedy 1921 · US · Colour · 20mins

Although Buster Keaton's movie is in a comedy class of its own, containing gags that have survived through the years. In his quest to catch butterflies, a collector innocently wanders into an Indian encampment and becomes involved in a war between rival tribes with hilarious results. In one great sequence, Keaton is tied to a stake, then uproots it and walks away. In another, he is locked in an embrace with a pretty Indian; a title-card flashes up saying, "Two years later!" When it cuts back, they are still kissing. TH

Buster Keaton • Joe Roberts *Indian chief* • Virginia Fox *Indian maid* ■ *Dir* Buster Keaton, Eddie Cline [Edward Cline]

The Paleface ★★★ U

Comedy western 1948 · US · Colour · 91mins

One of Bob Hope's most popular films in which he plays a correspondence school-qualified dentist meeting up with sharpshooter Jane Russell (as Calamity Jane) out west. Russell proves here that she can handle droll comedy, and Hope provides a lively mix of wisecracks and slapstick. The film has fun spoofing the western genre and includes the Oscar-winning song by Jay Livingston and Ray Evans, *Buttons and Bows*. Hope's biggest box-office hit and very entertaining, though it is one of the rare cases where the sequel *Son of Paleface*, made in 1952, is even better. TV

Bob Hope *"Painless" Peter Potter* • Jane Russell *Calamity Jane* • Robert Armstrong *Terris* • Iris Adrian *Pepper* • Robert Watson [Bobby Watson] *Toby Preston* • Jack Searl [Jackie Searle] *Jasper Martin* • Joseph Vitale *Indian scout* • Charles Trowbridge *Governor Johnson* ■ *Dir* Norman Z McLeod • *Scr* Edmund Hartmann [Edmund L Hartmann], Frank Tashlin, Jack Rose

Palermo oder Wolfsburg ★★★

Drama 1980 · W Ger/Swi · Colour · 175mins

The rough cut of Werner Schroeter's operatic parable reportedly ran for some eight hours. He clearly trimmed it down drastically before it took the Golden Bear at the Berlin Film Festival. Yet time still hangs heavy after Nicola Zarbo leaves his impoverished family in Sicily to find work at the Volkswagen factory in Wolfsburg, only to be charged with murder after defending his honour in a knife fight. Considering he had never acted before, Zarbo admirably conveys the resentment of the exploited migrant. But once the trial sequence takes a messianic turn, the story's otherwise impressive realism succumbs to pompous polemic. DP. A German/Italian language film.

Nicola Zarbo *Nicola* • Ida Di Benedetto *Giovanna* • Brigitte Tilg *Brigitte Hahn* • Otto Sander *Staatsanwalt* • Magdalena Montezuma *Rechtsanwältin* • Johannes Wacker *Richter* • Antonio Orlando *Antonio* • Calogero Arancio *Nicola's father* ■ *Dir* Werner Schroeter • *Scr* Werner Schroeter, Giuseppe Fava, Klaus Dethloff

Palindromes ★★ 15

Black comedy drama
2004 · US/Fr · Colour · 99mins

No one but Todd Solondz's die-hard fans will find this film anything other than dull and distasteful. The episodic story follows Aviva, a 12-year-old girl – played for no discernible reason by eight actors of various ages, race and gender – who embarks on an odyssey intending to become pregnant. Along the way she encounters a paedophile truck driver, murderous pro-lifers and a brood of disabled evangelicals. Although there is the (very) occasional grim laugh along the way, this fulfils its promise and ends up where it begins – nowhere of any real interest. AS

Ellen Barkin *Joyce Victor* • Richard Masur *Steve Victor* • Stephen Adly Guirgis *Joe/Earl/*

Bob • Debra Monk *Mama Sunshine* • Jennifer Jason Leigh *Aviva* • Sharon Wilkins *Aviva* • Emani Sledge *Aviva* • Valerie Shusterov *Aviva* • Hannah Freiman *Aviva* • Rachel Corr *Aviva* • Will Denton *Aviva* • Shayna Levine *Aviva* ■ *Dir/Scr* Todd Solondz

The Pallbearer ★★ 12

Romantic comedy
1996 · US · Colour · 93mins

David Schwimmer gets himself into a pickle when he is asked to be a pallbearer at the funeral of a schoolfriend he doesn't remember by the deceased's mother (Barbara Hershey). You can see the young-man-older-woman seduction coming a mile off, and Schwimmer is so whiny it's hard to imagine that any woman would want him. Only worth enduring for the performances of Gwyneth Paltrow and the talented Michael Rapaport. JB. Contains swearing. [video] DVD

David Schwimmer *Tom Thompson* • Gwyneth Paltrow *Julie DeMarco* • Michael Rapaport *Brad Schorr* • Toni Collette *Cynthia* • Carol Kane *Tom's Mom* • Bitty Schram *Lauren* • Barbara Hershey *Ruth Abernathy* ■ *Dir* Matt Reeves • *Scr* Jason Katims, Matt Reeves

The Palm Beach Story ★★★★ U

Screwball comedy 1942 · US · BW · 82mins

Made by the brilliant writer/director of satirical comedy, Preston Sturges, this stars Claudette Colbert who, by the early 1940s, had become firmly established as Hollywood's queen of romantic comedy. Watching her antics and listening to her way with a witty line in the face of this film's absurdities, it's easy to see why. Teamed with Joel McCrea, Colbert is the young wife who decides that her poverty-stricken husband would be better off without her. So she leaves for Florida to seek a divorce and a rich man. RK

Claudette Colbert *Gerry Jeffers* • Joel McCrea *Tom Jeffers* • Mary Astor *Princess Centimillia* • Rudy Vallee *JD Hackensacker III* ■ *Dir/Scr* Preston Sturges • *Costume Designer* Irene

Palm Springs Weekend ★★

Comedy drama 1963 · US · Colour · 100mins

Various teens follow the spring exodus to Palm Springs, Florida, where grim police chief Andrew Duggan tries to keep order. One of them, Troy Donahue, is interested in Stefanie Powers, who unfortunately for him is the chief's daughter. Fans of TV''s *Lost in Space* will easily spot Will Robinson (Billy Mumy) as Boom Boom. Moderately entertaining. JG

Troy Donahue *Jim Munroe* • Connie Stevens *Gail Lewis* • Ty Hardin *Stretch Fortune* • Stefanie Powers *Bunny Dixon* • Robert Conrad *Eric Dean* • Andrew Duggan *Chief Dixon* • Jack Weston *Coach Campbell* • Billy Mumy [Bill Mumy] *Boom Boom* ■ *Dir* Norman Taurog • *Scr* Earl Hamner Jr

Palmer's Pick-Up ★★

Comedy 1999 · US · Colour · 106mins

Offered a lot of money to drive a crate to Florida in time for the millennium New Year, LA package delivery duo Robert Carradine and Richard Hillman hit the highway and rub hard shoulders with a gay ex-con, a nymphomaniac trucker (Rosanna Arquette) and an androgynous Mob boss. A quirky road movie that's the sum of its often camp and hilarious parts more than being an overall long-haul success. Disco diva Grace Jones adds a further level of kitsch to another entry from the multi-talented Coppola family. AJ

Robert Carradine *Bruce Palmer* • Richard Hillman *Pearl* • Patrick Kilpatrick *Bo* • Neil Giuntoli *Mac* • Rosanna Arquette *Dawn* • Alice Ghostley *Mrs Eleanor Palmer* • Grace Jones *Ms Remo* • Piper Laurie *Radio Evangelist* ■ *Dir* Christopher Coppola • *Scr* Christopher Coppola, Nick Johnson

Palmetto ★★ 15

Crime thriller
1998 · US/Ger · Colour · 109mins

This update of James Hadley Chase's 1961 novel *Just Another Sucker* to contemporary Florida is fudged and fuzzy. Ex-con Woody Harrelson returns home to the title town to get suckered into a fake kidnapping scam by a dying millionaire's trophy wife, Elisabeth Shue. Although at times an artful blend of atmosphere and sharp dialogue, Schlöndorff's low energy suspense film fails because Harrelson's pivotal role is so unremittingly unsympathetic it's hard to care what happens to him. AJ. Contains swearing, violence, sex scenes and nudity. [video]

Woody Harrelson *Harry Barber* • Elisabeth Shue *Rhea Malroux* • Gina Gershon *Nina* • Rolf Hoppe *Felix Malroux* • Michael Rapaport *Donnelly* • Chloë Sevigny *Odette Malroux* • Tom Wright *District Attorney John Renick* • Marc Macaulay *Miles Meadows* ■ *Dir* Volker Schlöndorff • *Scr* E Max Frye, from the novel *Just Another Sucker* by James Hadley Chase

Palmy Days ★★★ U

Musical comedy 1931 · US · BW · 73mins

An Eddie Cantor vehicle in which the banjo-eyed comedian frenetically gets involved with a gang of crooks masquerading as fortune tellers: one of them is a young George Raft. There's some funny stuff in a bakery involving high-kicking Charlotte Greenwood, but the credited ace choreographer Busby Berkeley was still a fair way from finding the unique style that made him a household name at Warner Bros. Despite the somewhat perfunctory direction, Cantor is genuinely amusing. TS [video]

Eddie Cantor *Eddie Simpson* • Charlotte Greenwood *Helen Martin* • Spencer Charters *Ab Clark* • Barbara Weeks *Joan Clark* • George Raft *Joe the Frog* • Paul Page *Steve Clayton* • Harry Woods *Plug Moynihan* ■ *Dir* A Edward Sutherland • *Scr* Morrie Ryskind, Eddie Cantor, from a story by Morrie Ryskind, Keene Thompson, David Freedman, David Freedman, Eddie Cantor

Palooka ★★★★

Comedy 1934 · US · BW · 87mins

Hey, youse guys this is the bee's knees! Promoter Knobby Walsh (the great Jimmy Durante) has plucked a comer (hick Stu Erwin) from the streets, and is grooming him for the big fight, only the Palooka doesn't know what's (about to) hit him. Fabulous stuff, with the Schnoz on top form. Heck of a support cast, too. A Joe Palooka series of B-movies followed, with Joe Kirkwood Jr as the chump champ. TS

Jimmy Durante *Knobby Walsh* • Lupe Velez *Nina Madero* • Stuart Erwin *Joe Palooka* • Marjorie Rambeau *Mayme Palooka* • Robert Armstrong *Pete Palooka* • Mary Carlisle *Anne* • William Cagney *Al McSwatt* • Thelma Todd *Trixie* • Franklyn Ardell *Doc Wise* ■ *Dir* Benjamin Stoloff [Ben Stoloff] • *Scr* Ben Ryan, Murray Roth, Gertrude Purcell, Jack Jevne, Arthur Kober, from the comic strip by Ham Fisher

Palookaville ★★★★ 15

Comedy crime drama
1995 · US · Colour · 88mins

Clever, richly atmospheric and perfectly pitched, Alan Taylor's directorial debut is a low-key delight that's strong on character and packed with sharp, witty dialogue. It's inspired by the works of Italian author Italo Calvino, but the story events are incidental to the superbly nuanced interplay between the uniformly excellent William Forsythe, Vincent Gallo and Adam Trese. They star as dead-end New Jersey buddies who turn to a life of petty crime to ease their boredom, with remarkably unspectacular results. Frances McDormand lends winning support as a hooker. AJ [video] DVD

Adam Trese *Jerry* • Vincent Gallo *Russ* • William Forsythe *Sid* • Gareth Williams *Ed* • Frances McDormand *June* ■ *Dir* Alan Taylor • *Scr* David Epstein

Pals ★★★ PG

Comedy 1986 · US · Colour · 86mins

This slight but amiable TV movie is distinguished by delightful performances from veterans George C Scott and Don Ameche. The duo play bored pensioners who discover a fortune in drugs money and decide to keep it. Scott and Ameche spark off each other superbly, there is a fine supporting performance from another old trouper, Sylvia Sidney, and director Lou Antonio keeps the action moving along briskly. JF [video]

George C Scott *Jack Stobbs* • Don Ameche *Art Riddle* • Sylvia Sidney *Fern* • James Greene *Leek* • Lenka Peterson *Betty* • Richard Hamilton *Herman* ■ *Dir* Lou Antonio • *Scr* Michael Norell

Le Paltoquet ★★★★ 15

Crime drama 1986 · Fr · Colour · 93mins

In this sophisticated surrealist whodunnit, director/writer Michel Deville allows his camera to rove around the bistro run by Jeanne Moreau and Michel Piccoli. The atmospheric visual symbolism complements the sparkling verbal exchanges between inspector Jean Yanne and the card-playing quartet he suspects of murder: journalist Daniel Auteuil, doctor Richard Bohringer, tradesman Philippe Léotard and teacher Claude Piéplu. Fanny Ardant adds support from a hammock in this cerebral delight, with Piccoli also excelling. DP. A French language film.

Fanny Ardant *Lotte* • Daniel Auteuil *Journalist* • Richard Bohringer *Doctor* • Philippe Léotard *Tradesman* • Jeanne Moreau *Proprietress* • Michel Piccoli *Paltoquet* • Claude Piéplu *Teacher* ■ *Dir* Michel Deville • *Scr* Michel Deville, from the novel *On A Tué Pendant l'Escale* by Franz-Rudolph Falk

Pan-Americana ★

Romantic comedy 1945 · US · BW · 84mins

The editor of a magazine (Eve Arden), her foreign editor (Robert Benchley), their girl reporter (Audrey Long) and a photographer (Philip Terry), make a whistle-stop tour of several South and Central American countries to research a feature on Latin America. Each venue is a cue to showcase an act. Unfurled in flashback and "narrated" by Benchley, this is a pathetic excuse for a musical exhibition. RK

Phillip Terry *Dan Jordan* • Audrey Long *Jo Anne Benson* • Robert Benchley *Charlie Corker* • Eve Arden *Helen "Hoppy" Hopkins* • Ernest Truex *Uncle Rudy* • Marc Cramer *Jerry Bruce* ■ *Dir* John H Auer • *Scr* Lawrence Kimble, from a story by Frederick Kohner, John H Auer

Pancho Villa ★★

Western 1971 · Sp · Colour · 91mins

Hammy *Kojak* star Telly Savalas might not be ideally cast as Mexico's saviour, yet this is still an interesting example of a Spanish western, set against a background of arid landscapes, with a watchable cast of Hollywood veterans. Director Eugenio Martin has a clever knack for handling train sequences. TS

Telly Savalas *Pancho Villa* • Clint Walker *Scotty* • Anne Francis *Flo* • Chuck Connors *Colonel Wilcox* • Angel Del Pozo *Lieutenant Eager* • José Maria Prada *Luis* ■ *Dir* Gene Martin [Eugenio Martin] • *Scr* Julian Halevy [Julian Zimet], from a story by Gene Martin [Eugenio Martin]

Pandaemonium ★★★ 12

Period drama
2000 · UK/US · Colour · 124mins

Julien Temple, film biographer of the Sex Pistols, conducts a fascinating, if superficial, study into the ramifications of intellectual curiosity in this archly anachronistic fantasy. Not content with conveying something of the excitement of both radical thought and the hallucinogenic effect of opium, Temple coaxes Linus Roach into playing Samuel Coleridge as an addled dreamer, while John Hannah's William Wordsworth becomes an envious dullard. The warnings about tinkering with nature are worth making, but a greater focus on poetry and personality might have reduced the need for directorial flamboyance. DP [video] DVD

John Hannah *William Wordsworth* • Linus Roache *Samuel Coleridge* • Samantha Morton *Sara Coleridge* • Emily Woof *Dorothy Wordsworth* • Emma Fielding *Mary Wordsworth* • Andy Serkis *John Thelwall* • Samuel West *Robert Southey* ■ *Dir* Julien Temple • *Scr* Frank Cottrell Boyce

Pandemonium ★ 15

Horror spoof 1982 · US · Colour · 77mins

Hard to believe that the numerous comic talents assembled for this shoddy *Friday the 13th* spoof in the *Airplane!* vein barely manage to raise a single smile between them. A Jason-type killer is spearing trainee cheerleaders and displaced Mountie Tom Smothers and his addled deputy Paul (Pee Wee) Reubens are sent to investigate. Nothing the able director Alfred Sole does with the weak script can generate a laugh. AJ [video]

Tom Smothers *Cooper* • Carol Kane *Candy* • Miles Chapin *Andy* • Debralee Scott *Sandy* • Marc McClure *Randy* • Judge Reinhold *Glenn* • Paul Reubens *Johnson* • O'Connor Donald *Glenn's dad* • Kaye Ballard *Glenn's mum* • Tab Hunter *Blue Grange* • Eve Arden *Warden June* ■ *Dir* Alfred Sole • *Scr* Jaime Klein, Richard Whitley

Pandora and the Flying Dutchman ★★★★

Romantic fantasy drama
1950 · UK · Colour · 123mins

Albert Lewin was in some ways Hollywood's answer to Michael Powell and Emeric Pressburger, as a maker of weird, exotic and often slightly barmy Technicolor fantasies. This bizarre British-made effort stars the ravishing Ava Gardner as a woman incapable of returning the love of her men, and James Mason as the sailor of legend, condemned to roam the seas for eternity until he meets a woman willing to give up her life for him. Set in Spain, its flights of romantic fantasy are heightened by the work of Powell and Pressburger's regular cinematographer, Jack Cardiff. An acquired taste, perhaps, but Lewin was a genuine maverick talent. AT

James Mason *Hendrick van der Zee* • Ava Gardner *Pandora Reynolds* • Nigel Patrick *Stephen Cameron* • Sheila Sim *Janet* • Harold Warrender *Geoffrey Fielding* • Mario Cabré *Juan Montalvo* • Marius Goring *Reggie Demarest* • John Laurie *Angus* ■ *Dir* Albert Lewin • *Scr* Albert Lewin, from a story by Albert Lewin, suggested by the legend of the Flying Dutchman

The Pandora Project ★ 15

Action thriller 1998 · US · Colour · 86mins

Daniel Baldwin specialises in straight-to-video stinkers like this dull thriller about a CIA agent on the trail of muscley madman Richard Tyson, who has acquired an unpleasant and very deadly new weapon. It's as flat and

P

formulaic as they come – hero and villain have sneering contests, Baldwin's girlfriend Erika Eleniak is kidnapped by Tyson and there's a climactic punch-up. JC

Daniel Baldwin *John Lacy* • Erika Eleniak *Wendy Lane* • Richard Tyson *Bill Stenwick* ■ *Dir* Jim Wynorski, John Terlesky • *Scr* John Terlesky

Pandora's Box ★★★★★ PG

Silent drama 1929 · Ger · BW · 104mins

American-born Louise Brooks is devastating as the *femme fatale* who murders her husband and tangos with a lesbian countess before falling victim herself to Jack the Ripper. Screenwriter Ladislaus Vajda makes a superb job of condensing Frank Wedekind's two Lulu plays, but it's the visual imagination of director GW Pabst that most fully conveys the story's brooding sexual tension and all-pervading atmosphere of latent violence. A masterly mix of expressionism and street realism, this ranks among the masterpieces of German silent cinema. DP DVD

Louise Brooks *Lulu* • Fritz Kortner *Dr Peter Schön* • Franz Lederer [Francis Lederer] *Alwa Schön* • Carl Götz *Schigolch* • Alice Roberts *Countess Anna Geschwitz* ■ *Dir* GW Pabst • *Scr* Ladislaus Vajda, from the plays *Erdgeist/Die Büchse der Pandora* by Frank Wedekind • *Cinematographer* Günther Krampf

Panhandle Calibre 38 ★★

Spaghetti western 1972 · It · Colour · 90mins

The plot twists may be signposted and the humour might have been laid on with a trowel, but this is a lively enough spaghetti western with a tough edge from director Toni Secchi. Keenan Wynn plays a has-been gunslinger hired to take a Confederate gold shipment across treacherous terrain in the company of his city slicker son, Scott Holden (son of William Holden and Brenda Marshall). Delia Boccardo (posing as a schoolteacher) leads the shiftless group hot on their trail. DP

Keenan Wynn *Billy Bronson* • Delia Boccardo *Connie* • Scott Holden *Bobo* ■ *Dir* Antonio Secchi [Toni Secchi] • *Scr* Mario Mendola, Massimo Franciosa, Louisa Montagnana

P

Panic ★★★

Crime drama 2000 · US · Colour · 88mins

Henry Bromwell emerges from his TV background to make an impressive feature debut with this assured blend of crime thriller, domestic drama and black comedy. There's a whisp of *Analyse This* about the way covert hitman William H Macy reveals to psychiatrist John Ritter the hold domineering father Donald Sutherland exerts over him. With Tracey Ullman and Neve Campbell competing for Macy's confused affections, this is adroit and discerningly downbeat. DP

William H Macy *Alex* • Donald Sutherland *Michael* • Neve Campbell *Sarah* • Tracey Ullman *Martha* • Barbara Bain *Deidre* • David Dorfman *Sammy* • John Ritter *Josh Parks* ■ *Dir/Scr* Henry Bromell

Panic Button ★★

Comedy 1964 · US · BW · 90mins

Michael Connors is the producer looking to make a flop as a tax write-off who hires forgotten movie star Maurice Chevalier – completely unsuited to the role – to play Romeo, and professional tart Jayne Mansfield as Juliet, for a TV pilot of Shakespeare's play. For good measure, he gets Akim Tamiroff as a director who is only too happy to give him the garbage he wants. Barely released, this is a minor but quite appealing comedy. RK

Maurice Chevalier *Philippe Fontaine* • Jayne Mansfield *Angela* • Michael Connors [Mike Connors] *Frank Pagano* • Eleanor Parker *Louise Harris* • Akim Tamiroff *Pandowski* ■ *Dir* George Sherman • *Scr* Hal Biller, from a story by Mort Friedman, Ron Gorton

The Panic in Needle Park ★★★★ 18

Drama 1971 · US · Colour · 103mins

Drug abuse movies can be hard to take, but this compelling drama has a superior screenplay (by Joan Didion and her husband John Gregory Dunne) and sensational performances from young Al Pacino and Kitty Winn. He's the cheeky bad boy and she the nice, sweet girl irresistibly drawn to him, and together their youthful dabbling in drugs drags them down into addiction and a harrowing spiral of squalor and loathing. Pacino's electrifying presence here convinced Francis Ford Coppola to fight enormous studio resistance to cast him as Michael Corleone in *The Godfather*. AME DVD

Al Pacino *Bobby* • Kitty Winn *Helen* • Alan Vint *Hotchner* • Richard Bright *Hank* • Angie Ortega *Irene* • Marcia Jean Kurtz *Marcie* • Raul Julia *Marco* • Kiel Martin *Chico* • Paul Sorvino *Samuels* ■ *Dir* Jerry Schatzberg • *Scr* Joan Didion, John Gregory Dunne, from a novel by James Mills

Panic in the City ★★ U

Thriller 1968 · US · Colour · 91mins

One of those all-too-possible thrillers, common in the 1960s, about the threat of Armageddon in which a revolutionary group try to start a Third World War ("The human race has been given its chance – and failed"). This particular group plan to explode an atomic bomb in Los Angeles in the hope that the US will blame the Soviet Union. Howard Duff tries to stop it all from happening but he cannot impede the banality of an idea which required more money and a better director. TH

Nehemiah Persoff *August Best* • Anne Jeffreys *Myra Pryor* • Howard Duff *Dave Pomeroy* • Linda Cristal *Dr Paula Stevens* • Stephen McNally *James Kincade* • Oscar Beregi *Dr Paul Cerbo* • Dennis Hopper *Goff* ■ *Dir* Eddie Davis • *Scr* Eddie Davis, Charles E Savage

Panic in the Streets ★★★★ PG

Drama 1950 · US · BW · 92mins

This tense drama might have seemed an unusual choice for director Elia Kazan. Yet, given the mood of xenophobia that prevailed in the United States at the time, the storyline – the killing of an illegal immigrant results in a potential plague outbreak – is very much in keeping with Kazan's preoccupation with racism. Richard Widmark gives one of his more restrained performances as the health inspector teaming up with cop Paul Douglas to apprehend the murderers, compellingly played by Jack Palance and Zero Mostel. DP DVD

Richard Widmark *Clinton Reed* • Paul Douglas *Police Captain Tom Warren* • Barbara Bel Geddes *Nancy Reed* • Walter (Jack) Palance [Jack Palance] *Blackie* • Zero Mostel *Raymond Fitch* • Dan Riss *Neff* ■ *Dir* Elia Kazan • *Scr* Richard Murphy, Daniel Fuchs, from the stories *Quarantine* and *Some Like 'Em Cold* by Edna Anhalt, Edward Anholt

Panic in Year Zero ★★★★

Science-fiction drama 1962 · US · BW · 91mins

Ray Milland directs and stars in this story about a nuclear war and the breakdown of society that follows. Milland's nondescript direction sometimes makes the film even more chilling, as survivors take the law into their own hands and head for the hills, through a traffic jam of surreal proportions. Milland plays the boring, everyday Joe who holds up a store, takes his wife and family to live in a cave and kills the thugs who threaten them. There's a lot going on in this movie, with much to think about. AT

Ray Milland *Harry Baldwin* • Jean Hagen *Ann Baldwin* • Frankie Avalon *Rick Baldwin* • Mary Mitchel *Karen Baldwin* • Joan Freeman *Marilyn Hayes* • Richard Garland *Mr Johnson* ■ *Dir* Ray Milland • *Scr* Jay Simms, John Morton, from a story by Jay Simms

Panic Room ★★★ 15

Thriller 2002 · US · Colour · 107mins

In this dark thriller, David Fincher exploits modern society's home-security paranoia, as a bunker-like safe room becomes a source of escalating horror for mother Jodie Foster and daughter Kristen Stewart, trapped by thieves in their New York brownstone. Though the plot is formulaic, it's ruthlessly executed, with the tension building to claustrophobic levels. However, Fincher seems obsessed with breakneck camera movement and unconventional angles, which means at times his extraordinary visual style gets in the way of the action. SF. Contains violence, swearing. DVD

Jodie Foster *Meg Altman* • Forest Whitaker *Burnham* • Dwight Yoakam *Raoul* • Jared Leto *Junior* • Kristen Stewart *Sarah Altman* • Ann Magnuson *Lydia Lynch* • Ian Buchanan *Evan Kurlander* • Patrick Bauchau *Stephen Altman* • Nicole Kidman *Stephen's girlfriend on the phone* ■ *Dir* David Fincher • *Scr* David Koepp

Panther ★★★ 15

Political drama 1995 · US · Colour · 124mins

The troubled rise of the Black Panther group, from their formation in Oakland, California, to their media hounding by J Edgar Hoover, is put under the spotlight by director Mario Van Peebles in a "factional" account of an important chapter in American race politics. Although densely plotted, the director's use of extreme close-ups and energetic flashy visuals keep the attention riveted. Highly controversial, this is a thought-provoking film that works on a number of levels. AJ. Contains violence, swearing and drug abuse.

Kadeem Hardison *Judge* • Bokeem Woodbine *Tyrone* • Joe Don Baker *Brimmer* • Courtney B Vance *Bobby Seale* • Tyrin Turner *Cy* • Marcus Chong *Huey Newton* • Anthony Griffith *Eldridge Cleaver* • Bobby Brown *Rose* ■ *Dir* Mario Van Peebles • *Scr* Melvin Van Peebles, from his novel

Paparazzi ★★ 15

Thriller 2004 · US · Colour · 84mins

Mel Gibson's ex-hair stylist Paul Abascal directs his debut feature (with Gibson co-producing), a rough-hewn revenge thriller that shows the effects of paparazzi persecution from the point of view of the celebrity. When up-and-coming movie action hero Cole Hauser antagonises unscrupulous snapper Tom Sizemore, he finds that his wife and child are targeted by the photographer and his three sleazy cronies. With the police unable to take action, Hauser decides to take matters into his own hands. Low on quality and virtually morality free, this crass film is all about making a point with a sledgehammer. KK. Contains violence.

Cole Hauser *Bo Laramie* • Robin Tunney *Abby Laramie* • Tom Sizemore *Rex Harper* • Dennis Farina *Detective Burton* • Daniel Baldwin *Wendell Stokes* • Tom Hollander *Leonard Clark* • Kevin Gage *Kevin Rosner* • Blake Bryan *Zach Laramie* • Mel Gibson *Man in waiting room* ■ *Dir* Paul Abascal • *Scr* Forrest Smith

Papa's Delicate Condition ★★★★ U

Period comedy 1963 · US · Colour · 97mins

Jackie Gleason has a touch of the staggers which, considering his size, is a risky lurch to be in the way of. It's a totter brought about by too many nips of liquor, an ailment his loving household in their turn-of-the-century Texas small town has to deal with or avoid. Based on memoirs by silent screen star Corinne Griffith and with an Oscar-winner of a song (*Call Me Irresponsible*) by James Van Heusen and Sammy Cahn, it's the kind of ode to old-time family values that has gone out of fashion, if not favour. TH

Jackie Gleason *Jack "Papa" Griffith* • Glynis Johns *Ambolyn Griffith* • Charles Ruggles *Grandpa Anthony Ghio* • Laurel Goodwin *Augusta Griffith* • Linda Bruhl *Corinne Griffith* ■ *Dir* George Marshall • *Scr* Jack Rose, from the non-fiction book by Corinne Griffith

The Paper ★★★★ 15

Comedy drama 1994 · US · Colour · 106mins

Michael Keaton heads a formidable cast as a city editor on the New York *Sun* in a highly engaging and absorbing look at 24 hours in the life of an ailing tabloid. As Keaton faces another day of decisions, deadlines and compromises both job-wise (he's being head-hunted by rival editor Spalding Gray) and personally (his pregnant wife, Marisa Tomei, is feeling neglected), director Ron Howard deftly ties the numerous story strands together with some vibrantly snappy dialogue. This is very much an ensemble film: Robert Duvall is superb as the editor who has sacrificed his life for the paper, while Glenn Close cleverly shows the difficulties of being a woman with power over men. DP. Contains swearing. DVD

Michael Keaton *Henry Hackett* • Glenn Close *Alicia Clark* • Robert Duvall *Bernie White* • Marisa Tomei *Martha Hackett* • Randy Quaid *McDougal* • Jason Robards *Graham Keighley* • Jason Alexander *Marion Sandusky* • Spalding Gray *Paul Bladden* • Catherine O'Hara *Susan* • Lynne Thigpen *Janet* ■ *Dir* Ron Howard • *Scr* David Koepp, Stephen Koepp

The Paper Chase ★★★★ PG

Comedy drama 1973 · US · Colour · 106mins

The 71-year-old John Houseman won a best supporting actor Oscar for his unforgettable portrayal of a Harvard law professor in this fine drama from James Bridges. While the central, intellectual duel between Houseman, an absolute stickler for excellence, and Timothy Bottoms as his rather obnoxious student makes for bracing entertainment, Bridges also tosses in some contrived subplots, including a rather gooey romance. Houseman repeated his role in the TV series that followed. AT

Timothy Bottoms *Hart* • Lindsay Wagner *Susan* • John Houseman *Kingsfield* • Graham Beckel *Ford* • Edward Herrmann *Anderson* • Bob Lydiard *O'Connor* • Craig Richard Nelson *Bell* ■ *Dir* James Bridges • *Scr* James Bridges, from the novel *The Paper Chase* by John Jay Osborn Jr

Paper Hearts ★★★

Drama 1993 · US · Colour · 90mins

Sally Kirkland is a good 'ole Southern gal, dutifully married to wandering lothario James Brolin with two grown-up daughters (Renée Estevez and Pamela Gidley) and a patient, biding-his-time cowboy boyfriend (Kris Kristofferson). It's an intelligent, grown-up movie that is both resonant and affecting, if a little pat. A reassuringly old-fashioned heart-tugger. FL

Sally Kirkland *Jenny* • James Brolin *Henry* • Kris Kristofferson *Tom* • Pamela Gidley

Samantha • Laura Johnson *Patsy* • Michael Moore (4) *Bill* • Renée Estevez *Kat* • Mickey Cottrell *Brady* ■ *Dir/Scr* Rod McCall

Paper Lion ★★★

Comedy drama based on a true story
1968 · US · Colour · 107mins

An engagingly good-tempered "mockumentary" from sports writer George Plimpton's bestseller about his time as quarterback for the Detroit Lions American football team. Technical knowledge of the game is unnecessary because Alan Alda, in his first starring role, interprets for us through his naive, amateurish actions, while Lauren Hutton is a pleasure to watch as Alda's secretary. There are also cameos from middleweight boxing champion Sugar Ray Robinson, and other American sporting heroes. TH. Contains swearing.

Alan Alda *George Plimpton* • Lauren Hutton *Kate* • David Doyle *Oscar* • Ann Turkel *Susan* ■ *Dir* Alex March • *Scr* Lawrence Roman, from the book by George Plimpton

Paper Marriage ★★ 15

Romantic comedy drama
1991 · UK/Pol · Colour · 84mins

A Polish woman arrives in Newcastle to marry a British man, but discovers he's decided against it. Reluctant to return to home, she blindly suggests marriage to the astonished Gary Kemp, hoping she can then get to stay in the country. As the down-on-his-luck artist desperately needs money, he goes along with her indecent proposal. Strong on characterisation and humour, low on plausibility, but shot through with engaging pathos. AJ [video]

Gary Kemp *Aiden Carey* • Joanna Trzepiecinska *Alicja Stralkowska* • Rita Tushingham *Lou* • Richard Hawley *Red* • William Ilkley *Jack* • Gary Whelan *Boss* • Ann Mitchell *Phyllida* • Fred Pearson *Officer Crane* ■ *Dir* Krzysztof Lang • *Scr* Krzysztof Lang, Marek Kreutz, Debbie Horsfield

Paper Mask ★★★ 15

Thriller 1990 · UK · Colour · 100mins

The stories you occasionally read in the papers about people who somehow manage to pass themselves off as medics are the inspiration for this dark tale. It stars Paul McGann as the hospital porter-turned-bogus doctor and Amanda Donohoe as the casualty department nurse who becomes involved in his deception. Director Christopher Morahan turns in a spookily plausible thriller. PF. Contains some violence and nudity. [video]

Paul McGann *Matthew Harris* • Amanda Donohoe *Christine Taylor* • Frederick Treves *Dr Mumford* • Tom Wilkinson *Dr Thorn* • Barbara Leigh-Hunt *Celia Mumford* • Jimmy Yuill *Alec Moran* • Mark Lewis Jones *Dr Lloyd* ■ *Dir* Christopher Morahan • *Scr* John Collee

Paper Moon ★★★★ PG

Period comedy drama
1973 · US · BW · 98mins

The wandering star of Peter Bogdanovich's directorial talent brilliantly lights up this cynical charmer of a story – set during the Depression – of a Bible-toting conman (Ryan O'Neal) forming a bizarre partnership with the brattish nine-year-old (real-life daughter Tatum O'Neal) who may or may not be his child. Laszlo Kovacs's outstanding monochromatic photography lends an affectionate sheen to a quest through the Kansas dustbowl in which the girl gradually becomes mother to the man. With this, *Targets*, and *The Last Picture Show*, Bogdanovich looked set to be one of Hollywood's finest but, sadly, he hasn't managed to repeat the excellence of these three movies. TH

Ryan O'Neal *Moses Pray* • Tatum O'Neal *Addie Loggins* • Madeline Kahn *Trixie Delight* • John Hillerman *Sheriff Hardin/Jess Hardin* • PJ Johnson *Imogene* • Randy Quaid *Leroy* ■ *Dir* Peter Bogdanovich • *Scr* Alvin Sargent, from the novel *Addie Pray* by Joe David Brown

Paper Tiger ★★★ PG

Comedy adventure
1974 · UK · Colour · 95mins

David Niven was a fine actor, at his best when playing life-cashiered failures, as in *Separate Tables* for which he won an Oscar, and in this otherwise tedious effort. He's the tutor to a Japanese child who finds he has to live up to the Walter Mitty-ish fantasies with which he's entertained the boy when both are kidnapped by terrorists. His performance as a man trying to make up for a loser's lifetime is at once noble and sad, but it lifts this rather leaden idea. TH [video]

David Niven *Walter Bradbury* • Toshiro Mifune *Ambassador Kagoyama* • Hardy Kruger *Muller* • Ando *Koichi Kagoyama* • Ivan Desny *Foreign minister* • Irene Tsu *Talah* • Ronald Fraser *Forster* ■ *Dir* Ken Annakin • *Scr* Jack Davies

A Paper Wedding ★★★

Drama 1989 · Can · Colour · 90mins

Released around the same time as *Green Card*, this Canadian drama also focuses on a marriage of convenience, only without the laughs. Although normally outspoken in his political views, director Michel Brault resists the temptation to soapbox about either the conditions in Chile at the time or the illogicalities of the Canadian immigration system. Consequently, what emerges is a film that argues its case without distracting from the human drama that unfolds when college professor Geneviève Bujold is given just three days to dispose of her married lover and get to know exiled Chilean dissident Manuel Aranguiz. DP. In French with English subtitles.

Geneviève Bujold *Claire* • Manuel Aranguiz *Pablo* • Dorothée Berryman *Annie* • Monique Lepage *Gaby* • Teo Spychalski *Milosh* ■ *Dir* Michel Brault • *Scr* Jefferson Lewis, Andrée Pelletier, with the collaboration of Sylvain Brault

Paperback Hero ★★★

Drama 1972 · Can · Colour · 93mins

Keir Dullea plays a small-town hockey hero and ladies' man who leads a double life as the town's gunfighter. In his daydreams, anyway. Nicely acted by a cast which also includes Elizabeth Ashley, the film holds interest but never quite scales the same heights of escapist excellence as *The Secret Life of Walter Mitty*. DA

Keir Dullea *Rick Dillon* • Elizabeth Ashley *Loretta* • John Beck *Pov* • Dayle Haddon *Joanna* • Franz Russell *Big Ed* ■ *Dir* Peter Pearson • *Scr* Les Rose, Barry Pearson

Paperback Hero ★★★ 15

Romantic comedy
1998 · Aus · Colour · 96mins

The karaoke love duet should be the nail in any film's coffin. Yet this outback-set romantic comedy survives reasonably intact thanks to the amiable performances of Hugh Jackman, as a handsome trucker who secretly pens period romances, and Claudia Karvan, as the feisty crop-dusting mate he persuades to front his popular novel on a PR campaign so that she can afford to marry the local vet. Writer/director Antony J Bowman clearly intended a 1990s variation on battle-of-the-sexes screwball, but ends up with a frothy concoction that might be dubbed a "Crocodile Mills and Boon". Pleasing but utterly predictable entertainment. DP [video]

Claudia Karvan *Ruby Vale* • Hugh Jackman *Jack Willis* • Angie Milliken *Ziggy Keane* • Andrew S Gilbert *Hamish* • Jeanie Drynan *Suzie* • Bruce Venables *Artie* • Barry Rugless *Mad Pete* • Barry Lea *Policeman* ■ *Dir/Scr* Antony J Bowman

Paperback Romance ★★

Romantic comedy
1994 · Aus · Colour · 93mins

Gia Carides is a writer of steamily erotic romances, living out in her imagination what she lacks in real life. Embarrassed by a paralysed leg (a result of childhood polio), she rejects the advances of Anthony LaPaglia. Then Carides breaks her leg and uses the cast to hide her disability. Carides and LaPaglia (a real-life couple) do their best to elevate this poor taste burlesque but they're not helped by unnecessary sex scenes. FL

Gia Carides *Sophie* • Anthony LaPaglia *Eddie* • Rebecca Gibney *Gloria* • Robyn Nevin *Anne-Marie LePine* • Marshall Napier *George LePine* ■ *Dir/Scr* Ben Lewin

Paperhouse ★★★ 15

Fantasy horror 1988 · UK · Colour · 88mins

This is a highly intelligent horror, in which the terror comes from the exploration of the subconscious rather than from banal schlock set pieces. Neglected by busy father Ben Cross and at loggerheads with (miscast) mother Glenne Headly, Charlotte Burke is the 11-year-old who enters a threatening world shaped by her dreams and the drawings in her notebook. DP. Contains some swearing. [video] DVD

Charlotte Burke *Anna Madden* • Elliott Spiers *Marc* • Glenne Headly *Kate* • Ben Cross *Dad* • Gemma Jones *Dr Sarah Nichols* • Sarah Newbold *Karen* • Samantha Cahill *Sharon* ■ *Dir* Bernard Rose • *Scr* Matthew Jacobs, from the novel *Marianne Dreams* by Catherine Storr

Papillon ★★★★ 15

Biographical prison drama
1973 · US · Colour · 144mins

On its original release, the critics had few good words to say about this adaptation of Henri Charrière's autobiographical account of his escape from Devil's Island. They sighed dejectedly at the stately pace and the careful development of the forbidding prison atmosphere. None could find any merit in Steve McQueen's performance as the convict bent on breaking free and even blamed him for bringing Dustin Hoffman down to his level. But this harrowing study of confinement and single-mindedness has been criminally hard done by. Occasionally McQueen is perhaps a little too enigmatic for his own good, but Hoffman's depiction of cunning corruption is splendid. DP. Contains violence, swearing, nudity. [video] DVD

Steve McQueen *Henri Charrière, Papillon* • Dustin Hoffman *Louis Dega* • Victor Jory *Indian Chief* • Don Gordon *Julot* • Anthony Zerbe *Toussaint, Leper Colony Chief* • Robert Deman *Maturette* • Woodrow Parfrey *Clusoit* • Bill Mumy *Lariot* • George Coulouris *Dr Chatal* ■ *Dir* Franklin J Schaffner • *Scr* Dalton Trumbo, Lorenzo Semple Jr, from the novel by Henri Charrière

Paracelsus ★★★

Historical drama 1943 · Ger · BW · 107mins

This is one of the most controversial films from the great impressionist director GW Pabst. Made for the Nazi regime, and starring the favourite actor of both Pabst and the Third Reich, Werner Krauss, the film transforms its hero, who rescues a city from the plague only to have its inhabitants turn on him, into a surrogate Führer, a poor-boy-made-good and a genius ahead of his time. Excessively talky, episodic and blatantly tendentious, it has been condemned by some as an example of a great talent reduced to studio hack, but at least one astounding sequence displays the director's celebrated pictorial imagination and flair. TV. In German with English subtitles.

Werner Krauss *Paracelsus* • Mathias Wieman *Ulrich von Hutten* • Harald Kreutzberg *Fliegenbein* • Martin Urtel *Johannes* • Harry Langewisch *Hans Pfefferkorn* • Annelies Reinhold *Renata Pfefferkorn, his daughter* ■ *Dir* GW Pabst • *Scr* Kurt Heuser • *Cinematographer* Herbert Stephan

Parade ★ U

Comedy documentary
1974 · Fr/Swe · Colour · 69mins

This Swedish TV co-production filmed in a circus tent in Sweden using video techniques was sadly Jacques Tati's last film. Basically, the film records a series of dismal repetitive provincial circus acts in between Tati's own appearances. As director, Tati attempts to demonstrate his whimsical philosophy that everyone's a clown by showing members of the audience. There are few more depressing experiences in the cinema than watching admired comedians in stuff far below their talent. RB

Jacques Tati *Circus performer* ■ *Dir/Scr* Jacques Tati • *Cinematographer* Jean Badal, Gunnar Fischer

The Parade ★★★★ PG

Drama 1984 · US · Colour · 91mins

Directed with considerable care by Peter Hunt, this compelling TV drama is set in a small Kansas town on the eve of the annual Fourth of July parade. The story focuses on the impact on three women of the return of a recently released prisoner. Frederic Forrest gives one of his best performances, inspiring solid work from his co-stars in the process. DP [video]

Michael Learned *Rachel Kirby* • Frederic Forrest *Matt Kirby* • Rosanna Arquette *Tilda Kirby* • Maxwell Caulfield *Jeff* • James Olson *Andy Janacek* • Geraldine Page *Sarah* ■ *Dir* Peter H Hunt • *Scr* N Richard Nash, Emily Tracy, from the story by N Richard Nash

The Paradine Case ★★★ U

Crime drama 1947 · US · BW · 114mins

This is one of those pictures that no amount of professional polish could save. Producer David O Selznick and director Alfred Hitchcock disagreed over the script, the shooting style and the leads (Hitchcock wanting Laurence Olivier and Greta Garbo for the roles filled by Peck and Alida Valli, in her US film debut), and the discord shows on screen. Peck looks uncomfortable as the lawyer who jeopardises his career and his marriage to help Valli, who's accused of murdering her wealthy husband. Hitchcock is always watchable, but this should have been so much better. DP [video] DVD

Gregory Peck *Anthony Keane* • Valli [Alida Valli] *Maddalena Paradine* • Ann Todd *Gay Keane* • Charles Laughton *Lord Horfield* • Charles Coburn *Sir Simon Flaquer* • Ethel Barrymore *Lady Sophie Horfield* • Louis Jourdan *Andre Latour* ■ *Dir* Alfred Hitchcock • *Scr* David O Selznick, Alma Reville, James Bridie, from the novel by Robert Hichens

Paradise ★★ 15

Period romantic adventure
1982 · US · Colour · 89mins

This daft period piece, sort of a *Blue Lagoon* without the water, has Phoebe Cates and Willie Aames as two 19th-century teenagers travelling by caravan from Baghdad to Damascus. It's harem-scarum time when Cates attracts the unwanted attentions of a desert rogue. There's plenty of flesh on display as the two abandoned teens find love in the sand. DA [video]

P

Willie Aames *David* • Phoebe Cates *Sarah* • Richard Curnock *Geoffrey* • Tuvia Tavi *The Jackal* • Neil Vipond *Reverend* ■ *Dir/Scr* Stuart Gillard

Paradise ★★★ PG

Drama 1991 · US · Colour · 106mins

Melanie Griffith and Don Johnson star in this remake of the French film *Le Grand Chemin*, playing a married couple at war over the loss of a child. Elijah Wood is the ten-year-old from Manhattan who comes to stay with them and makes friends with girl-next-door Thora Birch. It's less lurid and more convincing than its Gallic predecessor, and first-time director Mary Agnes Donoghue shows she can cope with people, not just special effects. Both Johnson and Griffith deliver honest and effective performances. TH. Contains swearing and nudity. DVD

Melanie Griffith *Lily Reed* • Don Johnson *Ben Reed* • Elijah Wood *Willard Young* • Thora Birch *Billie Pike* • Sheila McCarthy *Sally Pike* • Eve Gordon *Rosemary Young* • Louise Latham *Catherine Reston Lee* ■ *Dir* Mary Agnes Donoghue • *Scr* Mary Agnes Donoghue, from the film *Le Grand Chemin* by Jean-Loup Hubert

Paradise Alley ★★ 15

Comedy drama 1978 · US · Colour · 102mins

Having scripted *Rocky* and *FIST*, Sylvester Stallone made his debut as a writer/director with this sentimental story of three brothers trying to claw their way out of the poverty trap of Hell's Kitchen in the 1940s. When one brother, Lee Canalito, becomes a successful wrestler, the others climb aboard his bandwagon. Stallone's approach is strong on period atmosphere, but with a tendency to overcook the dialogue. AT DVD

Sylvester Stallone *Cosmo Carboni* • Lee Canalito *Victor "Kid Salami" Carboni* • Armand Assante *Lenny Carboni* • Frank McRae *Big Glory* • Anne Archer *Annie O'Sherlock* • Kevin Conway *"Stitch" Mahon* • Terry Funk *"Franky the Thumper"* • Joyce Ingalls *Bunchie* ■ *Dir/Scr* Sylvester Stallone

Paradise Canyon ★★ U

Western 1935 · US · BW · 52mins

Another of John Wayne's many films for poverty row studio Monogram, so like all the others that it's virtually impossible to tell them apart; plenty of scenes of horses galloping across the brush and a few fist fights. Once again stunt specialist Yakima Canutt plays the baddie and the Duke's undercover agent has to call on the help of suspicious locals to bring him to book. DP DVD

John Wayne *John Wyatt* • Marion Burns *Linda Carter* • Earle Hodgins *Dr Carter* • Yakima Canutt *Curly Joe Gale* • Reed Howes *Trigger* ■ *Dir* Carl Pierson • *Scr* Lindsley Parsons, Robert Tansey [Robert Emmett], from a story by Lindsley Parsons

Paradise for Three ★★★ U

Comedy 1938 · US · BW · 77mins

The delightful Mary Astor sues American millionaire soap-manufacturer Frank Morgan for breach of promise in this romantic comedy. Set in the German Alps on the eve of the Second World War, there are some thoughtful undertones, as Morgan's character tries to assimilate himself with the German people to understand their way of life. Eddie Buzzell directs with a light touch, and the supporting cast includes the indomitable Edna May Oliver as Morgan's housekeeper. TV

Frank Morgan *Rudolph Tobler/Edward Schultze* • Robert Young (1) *Fritz Hagedorn* • Mary Astor *Mrs Mallebre* • Edna May Oliver *Aunt Julia Kunkel* • Florence Rice *Hilde Tobler* • Reginald Owen *Johann Kesselhut* • Henry Hull *Sepp* ■ *Dir* Edward Buzzell • *Scr* George Oppenheimer, Harry Ruskin, from the novel *Three Men in the Snow* by Erich Kästner

Paradise Grove ★★ 15

Black comedy drama
2003 · UK · Colour · 93mins

Retirement-home carer Leyland O'Brien's existence among the Jewish OAPs of Paradise Grove is thrown into utter confusion by the arrival of waif-like beauty Lee Blakemore, who's on the run. Joining O'Brien as he attempts to help his ageing grandfather (Ron Moody) deal with the onset of senility, Blakemore offers proof that there is a life waiting beyond the four walls of "Death's departure lounge". This an uneven blend of Yiddish stereotypes and mawkish sentiment, with only Moody and Rula Lenska (as O'Brien's mother) hitting the right tone. JR. Contains swearing.

Ron Moody *Izzie Goldberg* • Rula Lenska *Dee Perry* • Lee Blakemore *Kim Wright* • Leyland O'Brien *Keith Perry* • John Cunningham (2) *Dr Norman* • Dorothea Alexander *Mrs Wallenstein* • Leelo Ross *Annie Libowitz* • Georgette Pallard *Carolina* • Andy Lucas *Garrison Moss* ■ *Dir/Scr* Charles Harris,

Paradise, Hawaiian Style ★★ U

Musical 1966 · US · Colour · 86mins

Elvis Presley struck box-office gold with the massive hit *Blue Hawaii* back in 1961, and the combination of sun, surf, girls and song was too good to let rest. Unfortunately, this time out, the formula looks decidedly shopworn, and this movie formed part of the downward spiral that would eventually destroy the on-screen credibility of the King of rock 'n' roll. Elvis himself reveals a charming persona, but the thin plot and unmemorable songs undermine his efforts. TS DVD

Elvis Presley *Rick Richards* • Suzanna Leigh *Judy Hudson* • James Shigeta *Danny Kohana* • Donna Butterworth *Jan Kohana* • Marianna Hill *Lani* • Irene Tsu *Pua* • Linda Wong *Lehua* ■ *Dir* Michael Moore (1) • *Scr* Allan Weiss, Anthony Lawrence, from a story by Allan Weiss

Paradise Is Somewhere Else ★★★ PG

Drama 2003 · Iran · Colour · 80mins

Abdolrasoul Golbon's documentary experience is evident in this provocative analysis of the old adage that the grass is always greener. His depiction of the impoverished community on the Iranian-Afghan border paints a telling picture by implication of post-Taliban conditions. Teenage refugee Jan-Mohammad Tajik is determined to bring his mother and sister to a backwater that shepherd Yar-Mohammed Damanipour can't wait to abandon for the Emirates. The conflict of loyalties that ensues when Damanipour takes revenge for his road-builder father's death only reinforces the drama's intensity and the desolation of its setting. DP. In Farsi with English subtitles.

Yar-Mohammad Damanipour *Eidok* • Jan-Mohammad Tajik *Gol-Mohammad* • Fereshteh Sarabandi *Mother* ■ *Dir/Scr* Abdolrasoul Golbon

Paradise Lost: the Child Murders at Robin Hood Hills ★★★★

Documentary 1996 · US · Colour · 150mins

Documentary film-makers Joe Berlinger and Bruce Sinofsky uncovered a sinister example of murder and miscarriage in the case of Damien Echols and his Metallica- worshipping buddies, who were accused of killing three boys found molested and mutilated in a woodland stream near West Memphis, Arkansas. This is as much an indictment of the media and the prejudices of small-town America as an assault on the justice system. But, even though the film-makers manipulate their material to melodramatic effect, there's still no doubt that the trio were condemned more for their looks and reputations than on hard evidence. Four years later, Berlinger and Sinofsky returned to West Memphis for *Paradise Lost 2: Revelations*, to focus on Mark Byers, the father of one of the victims, whose chequered career has led many to question the security of the original conviction. DP DVD

Dir/Scr Joe Berlinger, Bruce Sinofsky

Paradise Road ★★ 15

Second World War prison drama
1997 · Aus/US · Colour · 116mins

Director Bruce Beresford's drama about a Japanese PoW camp for women in hot and sticky Sumatra covers similar physical and emotional terrain as the 1980s BBC series *Tenko*. Unfortunately it has some glaring weaknesses – everyone is too well-nourished and too neatly made-up for one thing – and threatens to become syrupy. Still, it has an undeniable integrity and an outstandingly good cast. AT. Contains violence.

Glenn Close *Adrienne Pargiter* • Pauline Collins *Margaret Drummond* • Frances McDormand *Doctor Verstak* • Cate Blanchett *Susan Macarthy* • Jennifer Ehle *Rosemary Leighton-Jones* • Julianna Margulies *Topsy Merritt* • Wendy Hughes *Mrs Dickson* • Elizabeth Spriggs *Mrs Roberts* ■ *Dir* Bruce Beresford • *Scr* Bruce Beresford, from a story by David Giles, Martin Meader, from the non-fiction book *White Coolies* by Betty Jeffrey

Paradisio ★

Spy spoof 1962 · UK · BW and Tinted · 90mins

Even though Jacques Henrici does have a blink-and-you'll-miss-it screen credit, no one ever publicly owned up to directing this silly comedy and it's easy to see why. Arthur Howard (brother of the more famous Leslie) struggles as a dotty professor whose discovery of x-ray sunglasses makes him the target for spies and the bane of women everywhere. Downright odd, but nice European locations. DP. Contains nudity.

Arthur Howard (2) *Professor Sims* • Eva Waegner *Lisa Hinkle* ■ *Dir* Jacques Henrici • *Scr* Lawrence Zeitlin, Henri Haile, Jacques Henrici

Paragraph 175 ★★★★

Documentary
1999 · UK/Ger/US · BW and Colour · 76mins

This is another fine documentary from the makers of *The Celluloid Closet*, Rob Epstein and Jeffrey Friedman. By the fall of the Berlin Wall, only ten of the tens of thousands of gay men detained by the Nazis were left alive (lesbians were not subjected to such energetic oppression). Recalling the good old days of Weimar decadence and the living hell of the camps, these unassuming survivors piece together a genuinely moving "forgotten history" of the persecution that, like that of Romanies, has not received as much media or historical attention as the Jewish Holocaust . DP. In English, French and German with subtitles.

Rupert Everett *Narrator* ■ *Dir* Rob Epstein, Jeffrey Friedman • *Scr* Sharon Wood

The Parallax View ★★★★★ 15

Thriller 1974 · US · Colour · 97mins

Two years before *All the President's Men*, Alan J Pakula directed this potent and startling conspiracy thriller. Investigating a political assassination, reporter Warren Beatty uncovers evidence of a sinister agency called the Parallax Corporation, which recruits its marksmen from the dregs of disillusioned society. With an excellent script, stunning photography, and perfect acting, the story of Beatty's infiltration of the society and his attempt to foil yet another killing is riveting and fascinating. AJ. Contains violence and swearing. DVD

Warren Beatty *Joe Frady* • Paula Prentiss *Lee Carter* • William Daniels *Austin Tucker* • Walter McGinn *Jack Younger* • Hume Cronyn *Rintels* • Kelly Thordsen *LD* • Chuck Waters *Assassin* • Earl Hindman *Red* ■ *Dir* Alan J Pakula • *Scr* David Giler, Lorenzo Semple Jr, from the novel by Loren Singer • *Cinematographer* Gordon Willis

Paramount on Parade ★★

Musical revue
1930 · US · BW and Colour · 102mins

One of the earliest but not one of the best of a seemingly endless supply of studio revues designed to show off a roster of contract stars. In later years the formula occasionally had some flimsy excuse for a plot attached to it, but this overstuffed rag-bag, utilising the services of 11 directors offers no such distraction. Sometimes tedious, sometimes ill-judged in matching the players to the material, this is nonetheless a collector's piece. RK

Jean Arthur • Mischa Auer • Clara Bow • Clive Brook • Nancy Carroll • Ruth Chatterton • Maurice Chevalier • Gary Cooper • Mitzi Green • Helen Kane • Fredric March • Nino Martini • Jack Oakie • Eugene Pallette • William Powell • Lillian Roth • Fay Wray ■ *Dir* Dorothy Arzner, Otto Brower, Edmund Goulding, Victor Heerman, Edwin H Knopf, Rowland V Lee, Ernst Lubitsch, Lothar Mendes, Victor Schertzinger, Edward Sutherland [A Edward Sutherland], Frank Tuttle

Paranoiac ★★★

Horror 1963 · UK · BW · 80mins

This is one of the best of a cycle of psychological horror films Hammer made in the 1960s. Heiress Janette Scott and her crazy brother Oliver Reed are confronted by Alexander Davion, who claims to be their long-lost sibling. The plot and the devices (organ played in the middle of the night, car brakes tampered with) now seem very hackneyed. But this was very popular with rebellious teens, and the twist ending is still not easily guessable. DM

Janette Scott *Eleanor Ashby* • Oliver Reed *Simon Ashby* • Liliane Brousse *Françoise* • Alexander Davion *Tony Ashby* • Sheila Burrell *Aunt Harriet* • Maurice Denham *John Kossett* • John Bonney *Keith Kossett* ■ *Dir* Freddie Francis • *Scr* Jimmy Sangster

Parasite ★ 18

Science-fiction horror
1982 · US · Colour · 84mins

In a post-holocaust future, where paramilitary forces and mutant punks clash, scientist Robert Glaudini creates a parasitic monster that burrows into its victims and eats them from the inside. This is a crummy exploitation movie that wastes the talents of its cast. Its one feature of note is that it cashed in on the early 1980s 3-D revival frenzy, but it's junk. AJ

Robert Glaudini *Dr Paul Dean* • Demi Moore *Patricia Welles* • Luca Bercovici *Ricus* • James Davidson *Merchant* • Al Fann *Collins* • Tom Villard *Zeke* • Cherie Currie *Dana* ■ *Dir* Charles Band • *Scr* Michael Shoob, Frank Levering, Alan Adler [Alan J Adler]

Pardes ★★★ PG

Musical romantic drama
1997 · Ind · Colour · 189mins

This culture-clashing masala confirmed Subhash Ghai's status as a major Bollywood crowd pleaser. The common link is Shah Rukh Khan, who is detailed by US-based foster father

Amrish Puri to matchmake his decadent son, Apoorva Agnihotri, with his old friend Alok Nath's demure daughter, Mahima Chaudhary. However, in teaching the couple about each other's values, virtues and vices, he ends up forming the third side of an inevitable romantic triangle. Chaudhary impresses in a role originally intended for Madhuri Dixit. DP. In Hindi with English subtitles.

Shah Rukh Khan *Arjun* • Apoorva Agnihotri *Rajiv* • Mahima Chaudhary *Kusum Ganga* • Amrish Puri *Kishorilal* • Alok Nath *Suraj Dev* ■ *Dir* Subhash Ghai • *Scr* Subhash Ghai, Javed Siddiqi, from a story by Subhash Ghai

Pardners ★★

Musical western spoof
1956 · US · Colour · 90mins

Dean Martin and Jerry Lewis, making a last-ditch stand before splitting up their partnership, star as a ranch foreman and the well-intentioned but inept city greenhorn who helps him fend off a bunch of cattle raiders. Stomping about in buckskins and ten-gallon hats, the pair burlesques every cliché of the western tradition, but the one-dimensional screenplay yields insufficient hilarity. RK

Dean Martin *Slim Mosely Sr/Slim Mosely Jr* • Jerry Lewis *Wade Kingsley Sr/Wade Kingsley Jr* • Lori Nelson *Carol Kingsley* • Jeff Morrow *Rio* • Jackie Loughery *Dolly Riley* • John Baragrey *Dan Hollis* • Agnes Moorehead *Mrs Kingsley* • Lon Chaney Jr *Whitey* • Lee Van Cleef *Gus* ■ *Dir* Norman Taurog • *Scr* Sidney Sheldon, Jerry David, from the story *Rhythm on the Range* by Marvin J Houser

Pardon Mon Affaire ★★★

Comedy 1976 · Fr · Colour · 108mins

If you think Yves Robert's sex comedy looks familiar, that's probably because it borrows heavily from *The Seven Year Itch* and was remade as *The Woman in Red*. However, neither Tom Ewell nor Gene Wilder can hold a candle to the comic ingenuity of Jean Rochefort, whose deliciously restrained performance atones for the slightness of the story, in which he risks his happy marriage to Danièle Delorme to pursue poster girl Anny Duperey. DP. French dialogue dubbed into English.

Jean Rochefort *Etienne* • Claude Brasseur *Daniel* • Guy Bedos *Simon* • Victor Lanoux *Bouly* • Danièle Delorme *Marthe* • Anny Duperey *Charlotte* ■ *Dir* Yves Robert • *Scr* Jean-Loup Dabadie, Yves Robert

Pardon My Past ★★★

Comedy 1945 · US · BW · 88mins

While demobbed GI Fred MacMurray is on his way to start a mink farm with his pal William Demarest, he is hauled in by a gambler (Akim Tamiroff) who believes he is Francis Pemberton (also MacMurray), a playboy idler who owes Tamiroff money. MacMurray is appealing in his dual role, trying to deal with the complications that arise before this neat little comedy of mistaken identity resolves itself and he gets the girl (Marguerite Chapman). Director Leslie Fenton keeps an effective grip on the proceedings. RK

Fred MacMurray *Eddie York/Francis Pemberton* • Marguerite Chapman *Joan* • Akim Tamiroff *Jim Arnold* • William Demarest *Chuck Gibson* • Rita Johnson *Mary Pemberton* • Harry Davenport *Grandpa Pemberton* • Douglass Dumbrille *Uncle Wills* ■ *Dir* Leslie Fenton • *Scr* Earl Felton, Karl Kamb, from a story by Patterson McNutt, Harlan Ware

Pardon My Sarong ★★ U

Comedy 1942 · US · BW · 84mins

Director Erle C Kenton finds himself cast adrift with comedians Bud Abbott and Lou Costello. Made to cash in on the South Seas bubble of the time – Dorothy Lamour's sarong was much in vogue – the duo are bus drivers who find themselves all at sea with a jewel thief, the sinister Lionel Atwill from Universal's horror stable. TH

Bud Abbott *Algy Shaw* • Lou Costello *Wellington Phlug* • Virginia Bruce *Joan Marshall* • Robert Paige *Tommy Layton* • Lionel Atwill *Dr Varnoff* • Leif Erickson *Whaba* • William Demarest *Detective Kendall* ■ *Dir* Erle C Kenton • *Scr* True Boardman, Nat Perrin, John Grant

Pardon Us ★★★ U

Prison comedy 1931 · US · BW · 64mins

In this parody of the 1930 prison melodrama, *The Big House*, Laurel and Hardy play unintentional bootleggers who are imprisoned with two of their old faithfuls: spluttering James Finlayson and two-fisted hard man Walter Long. Some scenes are far from politically correct – the boys don blackface at one point – but Ollie warbles an attractive tenor, while Stan's loose tooth means it's raspberries all round. TH

Stan Laurel *Stan* • Oliver Hardy *Ollie* • June Marlowe *Warden's daughter* • Wilfred Lucas *Warden* • James Finlayson *Instructor* • Walter Long *Tiger* • Stanley J Sandford *Officer LeRoy Shields* ■ *Dir* James Parrott • *Scr* HM Walker • *Cinematographer* Jack Stevens

The Parent Trap ★★★ U

Comedy 1961 · US · Colour · 121mins

Hayley Mills stars in the dual role as twins trying to reunite their divorced parents, played by Maureen O'Hara and an undercast, and seemingly uncomfortable, Brian Keith. Like many Disney films of the period, it's overlong, drawn out by the interminable section at a summer camp. But David Swift's direction is adroit – he also guided Mills through her Oscar-winning performance in the previous year's *Pollyanna* – and Lucien Ballard's Technicolor photography is particularly fetching. Several sequels followed, and Disney remade the original in 1998. TS DVD

Hayley Mills *Sharon/Susan* • Maureen O'Hara *Maggie McKendrick* • Brian Keith *Mitch* • Charlie Ruggles [Charles Ruggles] *Charles McKendrick* • Una Merkel *Verbena* • Leo G Carroll *Rev Mosby* • Joanna Barnes *Vicky Robinson* • Cathleen Nesbitt *Louise McKendrick* ■ *Dir* David Swift • *Scr* David Swift, from the novel *Das Doppelte Lottchen* by Erich Kästner

The Parent Trap ★★★ PG

Comedy drama 1998 · US · Colour · 122mins

Freckle-faced Lindsay Lohan is the American youngster who steps into Hayley Mills's shoes for this update of the 1961 original. Lohan plays twins separated not long after birth, one growing up with British wedding-gown designer Natasha Richardson, the other with her ex-husband, American vineyard owner Dennis Quaid. Meeting by chance at an American summer camp, the twins plot to bring their parents back together. Thanks to seamless special effects, it's impossible to tell there aren't really two Lohans, and this sentimental comedy should delight its target audience of young girls. SR DVD

Lindsay Lohan *Hallie Parker/Annie James* • Dennis Quaid *Nick Parker* • Natasha Richardson *Elizabeth James* • Elaine Hendrix *Meredith Blake* • Lisa Ann Walter *Chessy* • Simon Kunz *Martin* ■ *Dir* Nancy Meyers • *Scr* Nancy Meyers, Charles Shyer, David Swift, from the novel *Das Doppelte Lottchen* by Erich Kästner

Parenthood ★★★★ 15

Comedy 1989 · US · Colour · 118mins

Director Ron Howard's feel-good family ensemble piece just manages to stay the right side of sentimentality, and the result is an affectionate, leisurely comedy about the joys (and otherwise) of bringing up children. Steve Martin grabs the comic honours as the elder son of a family headed by crotchety Jason Robards, although there are fine performances, too, from the rest of the star-studded cast. Howard handles the large number of different story strands adeptly and he makes the most of the sharp script and some neat set pieces, notably Martin's cowboy turn at his son's birthday party. JF. Contains swearing. DVD

Steve Martin *Gil Buckman* • Mary Steenburgen *Karen Buckman* • Dianne Wiest *Helen* • Jason Robards *Frank* • Rick Moranis *Nathan* • Tom Hulce *Larry* • Keanu Reeves *Tod* • Martha Plimpton *Julie* • Harley Kozak [Harley Jane Kozak] *Susan* • Leaf Phoenix [Joaquin Phoenix] *Garry* ■ *Dir* Ron Howard • *Scr* Lowell Ganz, Babaloo Mandel, from a story by Lowell Ganz, Babaloo Mandel, Ron Howard

Parents ★★★★ 18

Horror comedy 1988 · US · Colour · 78mins

If the BSE scare didn't put you off eating meat, then Bob Balaban's grim horror comedy certainly will. Could Bryan Madorsky's suburban parents really be the cannibals he thinks they are? Or is he just a disturbed child suffering from juvenile hallucinations brought on by the atom-age anxieties of the Eisenhower 1950s? Set firmly in *Blue Velvet* territory, with a spot-on big band Muzak soundtrack, this disquieting explosion of the nuclear family unit will have you screaming with both laughter and revulsion. AJ. Contains swearing.

Randy Quaid *Nick Laemle* • Mary Beth Hurt *Lily Laemle* • Sandy Dennis *Millie Dew* • Bryan Madorsky *Michael Laemle* • Juno Mills-Cockell *Sheila Zellner* • Kathryn Grody *Miss Baxter* • Deborah Rush *Mrs Zellner* • Graham Jarvis *Mr Zellner* ■ *Dir* Bob Balaban • *Scr* Christopher Hawthorne • *Music* Angelo Badalamenti

Les Parents Terribles ★★★★★

Drama 1948 · Fr · BW · 102mins

Making few alterations to his original text, Jean Cocteau proved with this tragicomic tale of dysfunction and sexual frustration that it was possible to adapt a play and be inventively cinematic at the same time. The credits may roll over a stage curtain, the acts may be divided by captions and the action may be confined to two stylised sets, but through judicious use of telephoto lenses, rigid framing and punctilious editing, Cocteau is able to register every twisted emotion and treacherous expression as the skeletons tumble out of the closet and domineering matriarch Yvonne de Bray's world slowly falls apart. This remains one of the finest examples of ensemble excellence in French screen history. DP. A French language film.

Jean Marais *Michel* • Yvonne de Bray *Yvonne* • Gabrielle Dorziat *Aunt Léo* • Marcel André *Georges* • Josette Day *Madeleine* • Jean Cocteau *Narrator* ■ *Dir* Jean Cocteau • *Scr* Jean Cocteau, from his play • *Cinematographer* Michel Kelber

Le Parfum d'Yvonne ★★★ 18

Drama 1994 · Fr · Colour · 85mins

Patrice Leconte always manages to create a world in which reality and fantasy happily co-exist. However, here he overdoes the unlikely to the extent that this charming but flimsy study of daydreaming and delusion has too little substance to support adequately its more serious undercurrents. Hippolyte Girardot, in Swiss exile to avoid Algerian War service, and Sandra Majani, as the girl dreaming of movie stardom, are as dull as Jean-Pierre Marielle is outrageously camp. DP. In French with English subtitles. Contains sex scenes and nudity. DVD

Jean-Pierre Marielle *René Meinthe* • Hippolyte Girardot *Victor Chmara* • Sandra Majani *Yvonne* • Richard Bohringer *Uncle Roland* • Paul Guers *Daniel Hendrickx* • Corinne Marchand *Tilleuls Patron* • Philippe Magnan *Pulli* ■ *Dir* Patrice Leconte • *Scr* Patrice Leconte, from the novel *Villa Triste* by Patrick Modiano

Parineeta ★★★★ 12A

Romantic drama
2005 · Ind · Colour · 130mins

This well crafted and spectacularly made love story exemplifies the stern determination Indian culture demands of the relationship between men and women. Saif Ali Khan plays the son of an affluent businessman whose deep friendship with neighbour Vidya Balan ignites with the arrival of outsider Sanjay Dutt. The literate script, rich colour schemes and wonderfully energetic song-and-dance set pieces evolve naturally in Pradeep Sarkar's splendid film. Khan brings his usual instinctive grace, but it's newcomer Balan who really catches the eye. OA. In Hindi with English subtitles.

Sanjay Dutt *Girish* • Vidya Balan *Lolita* • Raima Sen *Koel* • Saif Ali Khan *Shekhar* • Diya Mirza *Gayatri Tantia* • Sabyasachi Chakraborty *Navin* ■ *Dir* Pradeep Sarkar • *Scr* Vidhu Vinod Chopra, Pradeep Sarkar, from the novel by Sarat Chandra Chattopadhyay

Paris after Dark ★★

Second World War drama
1943 · US · BW · 84mins

Philip Dorn is a sick and defeated Frenchman, released from captivity by the Germans. He suspects his wife Brenda Marshall of having an affair with her employer, doctor George Sanders, but they turn out to be stalwarts of the Resistance who inspire him to stand up for freedom. Of all the Hollywood studios, 20th Century-Fox made the biggest effort to employ displaced European film-makers and here gave director Léonide Moguy and producer André Daven their first Hollywood picture. AE

George Sanders *Dr André Marbel* • Philip Dorn *Jean Blanchard* • Brenda Marshall *Yvonne Blanchard* • Madeleine Lebeau *Collette* • Marcel Dalio *Michel* • Peter Lawford ■ *Dir* Léonide Moguy • *Scr* Harold Buchman, from a story by George Kessel

Paris Blues ★★★★ 12

Romantic drama 1961 · US · BW · 94mins

Paul Newman and Sidney Poitier click as footloose, free-spirited American jazzmen on the razzle in Paris, where pretty tourists Joanne Woodward and Diahann Carroll are understandably captivated by the charismatic musicians. The sensational Duke Ellington score provides the film's highlight. This offbeat affair from one of Newman's favourite directors, Martin Ritt, is also one of the most delightful jazz movies ever made. AME. Contains some violence.

Paul Newman *Ram Bowen* • Joanne Woodward *Lillian Corning* • Sidney Poitier *Eddie Cook* • Louis Armstrong *Wild Man Moore* • Diahann Carroll *Connie Lampson* • Serge Reggiani *Michel Duvigne* ■ *Dir* Martin Ritt • *Scr* Jack Sher, Irene Kamp, Walter Bernstein, Lulla Adler, from the novel by Harold Flender

Paris by Night ★★★ 15

Drama 1988 · UK · Colour · 99mins

Film noir meets allegorical Thatcherite morality as the problems pile up for Conservative Euro MP Charlotte Rampling. Her marriage to alcoholic Michael Gambon is on the rocks and she's convinced she's being blackmailed. While in Paris for political talks, she is surprised by her suspected blackmailer and murders him. But can she avoid the

P

consequences of her deed with the same steely efficiency? Utilising brittle dialogue, wilful obscurity and nightmarish visuals, writer/director David Hare conjures up a symbolic and often devastating fable about warped values in the yuppie 1980s. AJ

Charlotte Rampling *Clara Paige* • Michael Gambon *Gerald Paige* • Robert Hardy *Adam Gillvray* • Iain Glen *Wallace Sharp* • Jane Asher *Pauline* • Andrew Ray *Michael Swanton* • Niamh Cusack *Jenny Swanton* ■ *Dir/Scr* David Hare

Paris Calling ★★

Second World War drama
1941 · US · BW · 95mins

Elisabeth Bergner's sole stab at a Hollywood career came with this routine wartime melodrama about underground resistance after the Germans capture Paris. She plays the wealthy Parisienne who joins the fight for freedom, with intrepid Randolph Scott as a downed RAF pilot and heinous Basil Rathbone as a French politician turned collaborator. Add Lee J Cobb as the top Nazi, and you have a cast that makes the proceedings just about watchable. AE

Elizabeth Bergner [Elisabeth Bergner] *Marianne* • Randolph Scott *Nick* • Basil Rathbone *Benoit* • Gale Sondergaard *Colette* • Lee J Cobb *Schwabe* ■ *Dir* Edwin L Marin • *Scr* Benjamin Glazer, Charles S Kaufman, from a story by John S Toldy

Paris France ★★ 18

Erotic drama
1993 · Can · Colour and BW · 112mins

Director Gérard Ciccoritti's intention here was obviously to make an erotic drama about the connection between the sexual and the creative urge. He certainly packs his picture with passionate encounters, but the pronouncements that he hoped would have the audience nodding sagely had them rolling in the aisles, such is their pompous absurdity. Leslie Hope plays a novelist married to publisher Victor Ertmanis, who is living life to the full after he believes that he has received an answerphone message from John Lennon telling him he's only got three days to live. DP. Contains swearing, sex scenes and nudity. DVD

Leslie Hope *Lucy Quick* • Peter Outerbridge *Randall Sloan* • Victor Ertmanis *Michael Quick* • Dan Lett *William* • Raoul Trujillo *Minter* ■ *Dir* Gerard Ciccoritti [Jerry Ciccoritti] • *Scr* Tom Walmsley, from his novel

Paris Holiday ★★ U

Comedy 1958 · US · Colour · 109mins

American comedian Bob Hope, while in Paris, buys a French script, unaware that it carries clues to a gang of counterfeiters. They send sexy blonde Anita Ekberg to lure Hope into their clutches, but she falls for him and shoves him into a lunatic asylum from where he is rescued by Fernandel. Wisecracker Hope and France's comic idol, Fernandel, prove an ill-matched pair, and this outing is strictly for committed fans of the two stars. RK

Bob Hope *Robert Leslie Hunter* • Fernandel *Fernydel* • Anita Ekberg *Zara* • Martha Hyer *Ann McCall* • Preston Sturges *Serge Vitry* • André Morell *American Ambassador* • Maurice Teynac *Dr Bernais* ■ *Dir* Gerd Oswald • *Scr* Edmund Beloin, Dean Riesner, from a story by Bob Hope

Paris Honeymoon ★★

Comedy 1939 · US · BW · 83mins

Texas millionaire Bing Crosby, complete with ten-gallon hat, falls for countess Shirley Ross, pursues her to Europe, and rents himself a castle. Once installed, he falls in love with a local peasant girl (Franciska Gaal). As insubstantial as gossamer, this nonsense, directed by Frank Tuttle with minimum style, includes a handful of forgotten songs and is definitely of interest only to Crosby fans. RK

Bing Crosby *"Lucky" Lawton* • Franciska Gaal *Manya* • Akim Tamiroff *Peter Karloca* • Shirley Ross *Barbara Wayne* • Edward Everett Horton *Ernest Figg* • Ben Blue *Sitska* • Albert Dekker *Drunken peasant* ■ *Dir* Frank Tuttle • *Scr* Frank Butler, Don Hartman, from a story by Angela Sherwood • *Cinematographer* Karl Struss

Paris Is Burning ★★★★

Documentary 1990 · US · Colour · 76mins

A brilliantly entertaining documentary peek into the New York subculture of drag queens and transsexuals centred around "The Ball", a regular event that's part competition, part performance art and part ritual. Director Jennie Livingston's acerbic look at gay society's fringe-dwellers is a rapturous mixture of high spirits (the vogueing dance craze started in its hallowed Harlem venue), camp (the legendary Pepper Labeija living out an outlandish parody of a Hollywood star's life) and pathos (long-time pro Dorian Corey ashamed that the upcoming she-males don't even know who Marlene Dietrich is). AJ

Dir Jennie Livingston

Paris Nous Appartient ★★★★

Mystery drama 1960 · Fr · BW · 158mins

Like many French New Wave film-makers, Jacques Rivette began his career as a critic. Indeed, he was still working for the famous journal *Cahiers du Cinéma* while making this intense conspiracy picture, for which he had to borrow film stock from François Truffaut and a camera from Claude Chabrol. The fact that the action was shot over a two-year period is clearly evident in the inconsistent quality of the performances, but Rivette still crafts a complex and intriguing story. Some critics labelled the film pretentious, but his fellow directors considered it one of the crowning achievements of the early New Wave. DP. In French with English subtitles.

Betty Schneider *Anne Goupil* • Gianni Esposito *Gérard Lenz* • Françoise Prévost *Terry Yordan* • Daniel Crohem *Philip Kaufman* • François Maistre *Pierre Goupil* • Jean-Claude Brialy *Jean-Marc* ■ *Dir* Jacques Rivette • *Scr* Jacques Rivette, Jean Gruault

Paris Qui Dort ★★

Silent fantasy 1923 · Fr · BW · 61mins

René Clair's first feature, completed in three weeks, reflected some of the anarchic preoccupations of the surrealist and Dadaist artists with whom Clair associated at the time. The story, which he wrote in one night, tells of a crazed inventor who creates a "sleep ray" that suspends animation throughout Paris. Although the film is full of comic invention and absurdity, it is sometimes too self-consciously in love with its own cleverness, and the cinematic tricks begin to pall. RB

Henri Rollan *Albert* • Madeleine Rodrigue *Woman passenger* • Marcel Vallée *Thief* • Albert Préjean *Pilot* ■ *Dir/Scr* René Clair

Paris, Texas ★★★★★ 15

Drama 1984 · W Ger/Fr · Colour · 138mins

Character actor Harry Dean Stanton enjoys a rare leading role in German director Wim Wenders's emotionally charged road movie. The odyssey begins as restless drifter Stanton walks out of the desert after a four-year absence and is reunited with his small son Hunter Carson, who's being cared for by his brother Dean Stockwell. Stanton then sets out to reclaim his family life by seeking out his estranged wife Nastassja Kinski, now a peep-show stripper. There's an urgency to the film, as Wenders brings an outsider's fresh eye to create this massive metaphor about rootless America. TH DVD

Harry Dean Stanton *Travis Anderson* • Nastassja Kinski *Jane* • Dean Stockwell *Walter R Anderson* • Aurore Clément *Anne Anderson* • Hunter Carson *Hunter Anderson* • Bernhard Wicki *Dr Ulmer* ■ *Dir* Wim Wenders • *Scr* Sam Shepard, from his story adapted by LM Kit Carson

Paris Trout ★★★★ 18

Drama 1991 · US · Colour · 95mins

Paris Trout is a person: played by Dennis Hopper, he's a bigoted Deep South storekeeper who murders the young sister of a black man who has reneged on a debt. Appalled wife Barbara Hershey finds herself becoming the target of Hopper's violence and eventually retreats to the arms of lawyer Ed Harris. This pressure cooker of a plot, set in 1949 and adapted by Pete Dexter from his own novel, is tensely directed by Stephen Gyllenhaal. Hopper – crewcut, wild-eyed and utterly horrific – delivers a mesmerising portrayal of a monster who believes he's behaving normally. AT. Contains violence.

Dennis Hopper *Paris Trout* • Barbara Hershey *Hanna Trout* • Ed Harris *Harry Seagraves* • Ray McKinnon *Carl Bonner* • Tina Lifford *Mary Sayers* • Darnita Henry *Rosie Sayers* • Eric Ware *Henry Ray Sayers* • Ronreaco Lee *Chester Sayers* ■ *Dir* Stephen Gyllenhaal • *Scr* Pete Dexter, from his novel

Paris Vu Par... ★★★ 15

Portmanteau drama
1965 · Fr · Colour · 91mins

Shot in 16mm and capturing the spontaneity of the *Nouvelle Vague*, this portmanteau picture is patchy but entertaining. Jean-Daniel Pollet chronicles a nervous man's encounter with a prostitute; an angry wife is too preoccupied to help a potential suicide in Jean Rouch's entry; an American in Paris swaps boyfriends for Jean Douchet; Eric Rohmer puts Jean-Michel Rouzière through the emotional wringer; Jean-Luc Godard has a woman mixing up her billets-doux; and in Claude Chabrol's contribution, a boy is frustrated by his parents' arguing. DP. A French language film.

Nadine Ballot *Odile* • Barbet Schroeder *Jean-Pierre* • Micheline Dax *Prostitute* • Claude Melki *Léon* • Jean-Michel Rouzière *Jean-Marc* • Marcel Gallon *Victim* • Joanna Shimkus *Monica* • Philippe Hiquilly *Roger* • Stéphane Audran *Wife* • Claude Chabrol *Husband* ■ *Dir* Jean Douchet, Jean Rouch, Jean-Daniel Pollet, Eric Rohmer, Jean-Luc Godard, Claude Chabrol • *Scr* Jean Douchet, Georges Keller, Jean Rouch, Jean-Daniel Pollet, Eric Rohmer, Jean-Luc Godard, Claude Chabrol

Paris Was a Woman ★★★

Documentary
1995 · UK/Ger/US · Colour and BW · 77mins

This is a compelling documentary about the creative community that haunted Left Bank Paris between the world wars. Using newsreel footage, stills and interviews, Greta Schiller marginalises the literary titans to discuss the likes of troubled novelist Djuna Barnes, photographer Gisele Freud, the tragic artist Romaine Brooks, Sapphic hostess Natalie Barney and essayist Janet Flanner. An inevitable air of nostalgia pervades the memoirs of Gertrude Stein and Alice B Toklas, Colette and Josephine Baker. But Schiller also celebrates the emergence of women as an intellectual force and the advent of their long-overdue social and sexual emancipation. DP DVD

Juliet Stevenson *Narrator* ■ *Dir* Greta Schiller • *Scr* from the non-fiction book by Andrea Weiss

Paris When It Sizzles ★★ U

Romantic comedy
1964 · US · Colour · 105mins

Gowned in her trademark Givenchy, the irresistible Audrey Hepburn does her best in director Richard Quine's leaden remake of a soufflé-light French comedy in which screenwriter William Holden, facing a deadline, is devoid of inspiration. He enlists the help of his secretary (Hepburn) in acting out possible scenarios, sending the film off into an unsuccessful hotch-potch of genres, periods and fantasy sequences. Hepburn is charming and keeps the nonsense and a dull Holden afloat. RK DVD

William Holden (2) *Richard Benson* • Audrey Hepburn *Gabrielle Simpson* • Grégoire Aslan *Police inspector* • Raymond Bussières *Gangster* • Christian Duvallex *Maître d'hôtel* • Noël Coward *Alexander Meyerheimer* • Tony Curtis *2nd policeman* • Marlene Dietrich *Guest star* • Mel Ferrer • Fred Astaire • Frank Sinatra ■ *Dir* Richard Quine • *Scr* George Axelrod, from the film *La Fête à Henriette* by Julien Duvivier, Henriette*by Henri Jeanson*

Une Parisienne ★★★ PG

Comedy 1957 · Fr/It · Colour · 81mins

This saucy comedy takes every opportunity to show Brigitte Bardot, France's favourite sex kitten, in a state of undress. Yet Michel Boisrond's romantic caper is nowhere near as naughty as it would like to suggest – hence the fact that "Bébé"'s politician's daughter succumbs to a cold rather than the charms of Charles Boyer's aristocratic roué after she decides to take revenge on her philandering husband, Henri Vidal. Bardot proves herself an adept comedienne, but Boisrand's direction lacks the sophistication his mentor, René Clair. DP. In French with English subtitles. DVD

Charles Boyer *Prince Charles* • Henri Vidal *Michel* • Brigitte Bardot *Brigitte Laurier* • Noël Roquevert *Herblay* • Madeleine Lebeau *Monique* • Fernand Sardou *Fernand* • André Luguet *Premier Laurier* • Nadia Gray *Queen Greta* ■ *Dir* Michel Boisrond • *Scr* Michel Boisrond, Jean Aurel, Jacques Emmanuel, Annette Wademant

Park Plaza 605 ★ U

Crime thriller 1953 · UK · BW · 79mins

Tom Conway's long experience of playing sleuths shows to advantage in this fair British B-feature which tees off with the accidental death of a carrier pigeon. Conway can't resist courting danger on his day off by keeping a mysterious appointment with Eva Bartok's blonde diamond smuggler. Joy Shelton has the thankless role of the detective's wary girlfriend while there's offbeat casting of Sid James as a police superintendent and Richard Wattis as a villain. AE

Tom Conway *Norman Conquest* • Eva Bartok *Nadina Rodin* • Joy Shelton *Pixie Everard* • Sidney James *Supt Williams* • Richard Wattis *Theodore Feather* • Carl Jaffe *Boris Roff* • Anton Diffring *Gregor* • Robert Adair *Baron Von Henschel* ■ *Dir* Bernard Knowles • *Scr* Bertram Ostrer, Albert Fennell, Bernard Knowles, Clifford Witting, from the novel *Daredevil Conquest* by Berkeley Gray

Park Row ★★★★ U

Period drama 1952 · US · BW · 82mins

Hard-boiled director Samuel Fuller returns to the profession that launched him – American big-city journalism – with this belter of a story about rivalry between two ruthless 19th-century newspaper owners. Gene Evans stars as the reporter who sets up his own paper, incurring the wrath of his former boss, played by Mary Welch, who resorts to underhand tactics to ensure he fails. In their dog-eat-dog world, they battle to feed sleaze-hungry readers with all the news that's fit to print or get away with. TH

Gene Evans *Phineas Mitchell* • Mary Welch *Charity Hackett* • Bela Kovacs *Ottmar Mergenthaler* • Herbert Heyes *Josiah Davenport* • Tina Rome *Jenny O'Rourke* • George O'Hanlon *Steve Brodie* ■ *Dir/Scr* Samuel Fuller

Parker ★★ 15

Thriller 1984 · UK · Colour · 93mins

A routine British suspense film, with Bryan Brown as a businessman who claims to have been kidnapped in Munich, but who finds police oddly reluctant to accept his allegation. The paranoia-fuelled plot has potential, but it's largely unrealised because of needless obscurity and ambivalence. A more simple tack might have paid better dividends. DA [video]

Bryan Brown *Parker* • Cherie Lunghi *Jenny* • Kurt Raab *Inspector Haag* • Hannelore Elsner *Jillian Schelm* • Bob Peck *Rohl* • Ingrid Pitt *Widow* • Tom Wilkinson *Tom* ■ *Dir* Jim Goddard • *Scr* Trevor Preston

Parlor, Bedroom and Bath ★★

Comedy 1931 · US · BW · 72mins

Suffocated by the studio system and uncomfortable with sound, Buster Keaton's spell at MGM became one of the unhappiest and least inspired of his career. Originally a Broadway hit and a popular 1920 silent, this frantic farce was bought specially for Keaton by production chief Irving G Thalberg to make amends after they fell out over the Great Stone Face's talkie debut, *Free and Easy*. A top-notch supporting cast was assembled and Keaton was given a measure of creative freedom, but farce just wasn't his forte. DP

Buster Keaton *Reginald Irving* • Charlotte Greenwood *Polly Hathaway* • Reginald Denny *Jeffery Haywood* • Cliff Edwards *Bellhop* • Dorothy Christy *Angelica Embrey* • Joan Peers *Nita Leslie* • Sally Eilers *Virginia Embrey* ■ *Dir* Edward Sedgwick • *Scr* Richard Schayer, Robert E Hopkins, from the play by Charles W Bell, Mark Swan

Parnell ★★

Biographical drama 1937 · US · BW · 117mins

This worthy, though deadly dull, Hollywood biopic suffers from the chronic miscasting of the then king and queen of Hollywood, Clark Gable and Myrna Loy, as top Irish statesman Charles Stewart Parnell and his mistress Kitty O'Shea. For years afterwards Gable would joke about *Parnell* ruefully and with good cause. The whole is unwatchable except for fans of serious miscasting. RT

Clark Gable *Charles Stewart Parnell* • Myrna Loy *Katie O'Shea* • Edna May Oliver *Aunt Ben* • Edmund Gwenn *Campbell* • Alan Marshal *Willie O'Shea* • Donald Crisp *Davitt* • Billie Burke *Clara* • Donald Meek *Murphy* • Montagu Love *Gladstone* • Randolph Churchill *MP* ■ *Dir* John M Stahl • *Scr* John Van Druten, SN Behrman, from the play *Parnell* by Elsie T Schauffler

The Parole Officer ★★★ 12

Crime comedy 2001 · UK · Colour · 90mins

This light, old-fashioned bank-job comedy in the Ealing vein is a departure for Australian director John Duigan, but a natural step for Steve Coogan, well established on TV as Alan Partridge, Paul and Pauline Calf and others. His parole officer character here is less frenetic and cutting edge than his previous creations, but that also makes him more immediately sympathetic. In a nice setup, Coogan must convince the only three ex-lags he has successfully put on the straight and narrow (Om Puri, Ben Miller, Steve Waddington) to return to crime and help him steal a videotape from a bank vault and thus clear his name, as he's been framed by bent cop Stephen Dillane. Well told, and peppered with smart lines. AC [video] DVD

Steve Coogan *Simon Garden* • Lena Headey *Emma* • Om Puri *George* • Steven Waddington *Jeff* • Ben Miller *Colin* • Jenny Agutter *Victor's wife* • Stephen Dillane *Inspector Burton* ■ *Dir* John Duigan • *Scr* Steve Coogan, Henry Normal

Parrish ★★

Drama 1961 · US · Colour · 137mins

One of several lurid Warner Bros melodramas from Delmer Daves showcasing young players and aimed principally at juvenile audiences. Blond hunk Troy Donahue plays the humble worker on a tobacco plantation who becomes involved with Connie Stevens, Diane McBain and Sharon Hugueny. It's sniggering fun for about half its running time, with Connie Stevens helpfully pointing out the location of her bedroom and her penchant for sleeping in the raw to the young stud. Claudette Colbert makes her final big screen appearance as Troy's mother. AE

Troy Donahue *Parrish McLean* • Claudette Colbert *Ellen McLean* • Karl Malden *Judd Raike* • Dean Jagger *Sala Post* • Connie Stevens *Lucy* • Diane McBain *Alison Post* • Sharon Hugueny *Paige Raike* ■ *Dir* Delmer Daves • *Scr* Delmer Daves, from the novel by Mildred Savage

The Parson and the Outlaw ★ U

Western 1957 · US · Colour · 70mins

In this B-western, Pat Garrett doesn't shoot Billy the Kid. He lets him go free when Billy promises to throw away his guns. But poor Billy can't escape his legend, nor those people who want to pick a fight with him. This nickel-and-dime effort may please devotees of sagebrush sagas because of its cast of has-beens. AT

Anthony Dexter *Billy the Kid* • Charles "Buddy" Rogers *Reverend Jericho Jones* • Jean Parker *Mrs Jones* • Sonny Tufts *Jack Slade* • Robert Lowery *Colonel Morgan* • Marie Windsor *Tonya* ■ *Dir* Oliver Drake • *Scr* Oliver Drake, John Mantley

Part 2, Sounder ★★★

Drama 1976 · US · Colour · 98mins

On the back of the low-budget success of the original *Sounder*, an American TV network (ABC) funded this sequel as a TV movie but was so impressed they gave it a theatrical release. It continues the story of the family of black sharecroppers in Depression-hit Louisiana in 1933, who are fighting poverty and prejudice with the help of activist teacher Annazette Chase. Her educational establishment is closed down by the white landowners but the black community get together to build their own school. FL

Harold Sylvester *Nathan Lee Morgan* • Ebony Wright *Rebecca Lee Morgan* • Taj Mahal *Ike Phillips* • Annazette Chase *Camille Johnson* • Darryl Young *David Lee Morgan* • Erica Young *Josie Mae Morgan* • Ronald Bolden *Earl Morgan* ■ *Dir* William A Graham • *Scr* Lonne Elder III, from a novel by William H Armstrong • *Music* Taj Mahal

Part 2 Walking Tall ★★ 15

Crime 1975 · US · Colour · 104mins

Here are the further adventures of real-life Tennessee sheriff Buford Pusser and his one-man crusade against organised crime, impersonated this time by the lightweight Bo Svenson, replacing original star Joe Don Baker. Pusser did agree to play himself but 24 hours after signing the contract he died in a car crash. Less violent than its predecessor, with a noticeable easing up on the glorification of vigilante cops. Svenson reprised the role in 1977 in *Final Chapter – Walking Tall*. RS [video]

Bo Svenson *Buford Pusser* • Luke Askew *Pinky Dobson* • Noah Beery Jr *Carl Pusser* • John Chandler [John Davis Chandler] *Ray Henry* • Robert DoQui *Obra Eaker* • Bruce Glover *Grady Coker* • Richard Jaeckel *Stud Pardee* • Leif Garrett *Mike Pusser* ■ *Dir* Earl Bellamy • *Scr* Howard B Kreitsek

Part-Time Wife ★★

Comedy 1961 · UK · BW · 69mins

Unsuccessful insurance salesman Anton Rodgers is a well-intentioned but gullible sort who's married to the vivacious Nyree Dawn Porter. Rodgers's ex-army friend, Kenneth J Warren, has a rich uncle visiting from Canada, and he is anxious to get in his good books. To this end, he persuades his friend to lend him his wife. Competent performances fail to add sparkle to the tired plot. DF

Anton Rodgers *Tom* • Nyree Dawn Porter *Jenny* • Kenneth J Warren *Drew* • Henry McCarthy *Whitworth* • Mark Singleton *Detective* ■ *Dir* Max Varnel • *Scr* MM McCormack

Une Partie de Campagne ★★★★★ PG

Romantic drama 1936 · Fr · BW · 38mins

Based on the Maupassant story, Jean Renoir's short feature is one of the most lyrical pieces of cinema ever produced. Set in 1880, it follows a Parisian family on a Sunday outing that results in a stolen moment of passion and a lifetime of regret. Slyly observing middle-class foibles, the film is exuberantly played and majestically photographed by Claude Renoir and Jean Bourgoin. Abandoned because of incessant rain (with only two scenes left to shoot), the picture was not released until 1946, and even then incomplete, with captions explaining the missing action. DP. In French with English subtitles. [video] DVD

Sylvia Bataille *Henriette* • Georges Saint Saens *Henri* • Jeanne Marken [Jane Marken] *Mme Dufour* • Gabriello [André Gabriello] *Monsieur Dufour* • Jacques Borel [Jacques Brunius] *Rudolph* • Paul Temps *Anatole* • Gabrielle Fontan *The Grandmother* • Jean Renoir *Papa Poulin* • Marguerite Renoir *Servant* ■ *Dir* Jean Renoir • *Scr* Jean Renoir, from the story by Guy de Maupassant

Une Partie de Plaisir ★★★ 18

Melodrama 1974 · Fr/It · Colour · 96mins

When Paul Gégauff, the screenwriter on many of Claude Chabrol's films, wrote this autobiographical account of the break-up of his marriage, Chabrol persuaded him, his real ex-wife and his daughter to play versions of themselves. Gégauff comes across as a chic poseur, who treats his wife abominably. Chabrol is fascinated and disgusted by his friend's behaviour, and the audience might feel the same, though the exhibitionism of the whole enterprise sometimes outweighs the interest. RB. In French with English subtitles. Contains violence, swearing and sex scenes. [video]

Paul Gégauff *Philippe* • Danièle Gégauff *Esther* • Paula Moore *Sylvia Murdoch* • Michel Valette *Katkof* ■ *Dir* Claude Chabrol • *Scr* Paul Gégauff

Parting Glances ★★★ 15

Drama 1985 · US · Colour · 86mins

Set during 24 hours in the Aids-ravaged confines of New York's swanky gay scene, director Bill Sherwood's earnestly tender drama is at heart about two men finishing their relationship because one gets a job transfer abroad. Basically a series of heartfelt farewells to friends and family, this character-driven ensemble piece tells its bittersweet tale with warmth, grace and droll humour. Sherwood himself died of an Aids-related illness in 1990. AJ. Contains swearing. [video] DVD

Richard Ganoung *Michael* • Steve Buscemi *Nick* • John Bolger *Robert* • Adam Nathan *Peter* • Kathy Kinney *Joan* • Patrick Tull *Cecil* ■ *Dir/Scr* Bill Sherwood

Parting Shots ★ 12

Black comedy 1998 · UK · Colour · 98mins

Michael Winner's serial killer comedy is excruciatingly awful, with every member of its august cast guilty of a gross error of judgement by agreeing to participate. As a dying man punishing those who've slighted him, singer Chris Rea's totally inadequate performance is made to look even more inept by a script of the smuggest sitcom variety. DP. Contains violence. [video]

Chris Rea *Harry Sterndale* • Felicity Kendal *Jill Saunders* • Bob Hoskins *Gerd Layton* • Ben Kingsley *Renzo Locatelli* • Joanna Lumley *Freda* • Oliver Reed *Jamie Campbell-Stewart* • Diana Rigg *Lisa* • John Cleese *Maurice Walpole* • Gareth Hunt *Inspector Bass* • Peter Davison *John* ■ *Dir* Michael Winner • *Scr* Michael Winner, Nick Mead, from a story by Michael Winner

Partner ★★★

Drama 1968 · It · Colour · 105mins

The fact that Pierre Clémenti speaks French while everyone else converses in Italian, rather betrays the fact that Bernardo Bertolucci was totally enthralled with Jean-Luc Godard at this stage of his career. The repressed, middle-class Clémenti adopts a cockily anarchic alter ego in a bid to impress Stefania Sandrelli. Brimming over with political and cinematic ideas, this has an exhuberance that compensates for its naiveté. DP. A French/Italian language film.

Pierre Clémenti *Jacob I/Jacob II* • Stefania Sandrelli *Clara* • Tina Aumont *Salesgirl* • Sergio Tofano *Petrushka* • Giulio Cesare Castello *Professor Mozzoni* ■ *Dir* Bernardo Bertolucci • *Scr* Bernardo Bertolucci, Gianni Amico, from the novel *The Double* by Fyodor Dostoyevsky

P

Partners ★★

Drama 1976 · Can · Colour · 96mins

Denholm Elliott was incapable of giving a bad performance, but he came very close to doing so in this lightweight film. He doesn't seem to care too much about his role as the owner of a large paper firm and the father of Hollis McLaren. When Dad's company is under threat from a rival corporation, both father and daughter discover their true capabilities. Mildly intriguing. FL

Denholm Elliott *John Grey* • Hollis McLaren *Heather Grey* • Michael Margotta *Paul Howard* • Lee Broker *Philip Rudd* • Judith Gault *Barbara* ■ *Dir* Don Owen • *Scr* Norman Snider, Don Owen

Partners ★★ 15

Comedy 1982 · US · Colour · 88mins

A twist is given to the stale conventions of the buddy-cop movie when two detectives, one straight (Ryan O'Neal) and one gay (John Hurt), step out on to the streets of Los Angeles. Hurt takes on the role of a gay cop with ease. O'Neal also pretends to be gay for the sake of the plot which involves a murder in the homosexual community. AT [video]

Ryan O'Neal *Benson* • John Hurt *Kerwin* • Kenneth McMillan *Wilkins* • Robyn Douglass *Jill* • Jay Robinson *Halderstam* ■ *Dir* James Burrows • *Scr* Francis Veber

Partners ★★

Action comedy 2000 · US · Colour · 87mins

Joey Travolta makes a tidy job of this odd couple caper, which trades effectively on the physical disparity of its stars. Having stolen a top secret programme, in order to flog it to some Japanese computer pirates, David Paymer finds himself in a shaky alliance with Casper Van Dien, an opportunist thief who ends up acting as his nerdy buddy's bodyguard. Brisk minor league fun. DP

Casper Van Dien *Drifter* • David Paymer *Bob* • Vanessa Angel *Angel* • Jenifer Lewis *Detective* ■ *Dir* Joey Travolta • *Scr* Jeff Ferrell, Timothy Puntillo [Tim Puntillo]

The Party ★★★ PG

Comedy 1968 · US · Colour · 94mins

Peter Sellers always had to be kept in check but director Blake Edwards was hardly the one to do it, especially in this straight-up farce which he'd promised Sellers as a diversion from Inspector Clouseau. The result is a one-joke idea in the two-reel style of a silent comedy. Sellers puts on the accent that enraptured Sophia Loren in *The Millionairess* to play a clumsy Indian actor who inadvertently wrecks a Hollywood production. There are some very funny moments, but Sellers, like the character he plays, overstays his welcome. TH DVD

Peter Sellers *Hrundi V Bakshi* • Claudine Longet *Michele Monet* • Marge Champion *Rosalind Dunphy* • Sharron Kimberly *Princess Helena* • Denny Miller *Wyoming Bill Kelso* • Gavin Macleod *CS Divot* • Buddy Lester *Davey Kane* • Corinne Cole *Janice Kane* ■ *Dir* Blake Edwards • *Scr* Blake Edwards, Tom Waldman, Frank Waldman, from a story by Blake Edwards

The Party and the Guests ★★★★ U

Political drama 1966 · Cz · BW · 70mins

A Kafkaesque portrait of modern Czechoslovakia, packed with resonating contemporary motifs, this sinister study of social conformity and political dissent was a collaboration between director Jan Nemec and his writer/designer wife, Ester Krumbachova. Set in Edenic woodlands, the film follows the pursuit, with savage dogs, of the sole self-determining individualist whose refusal to acquiesce in the system threatens the status quo. Nemec's film was withheld for two years because of government censure. DP. In Czech with English subtitles.

Ivan Vyskocil *The Host* • Jan Klusak *Rudolf* • Jiri Nemec *Josef* • Zdenka Skvorecka [Zdena Skvorecka] *Eva* • Pavel Bosek *Frantisek* • Helena Pejskova *Marta* • Karel Mares *Karel* • Jana Pracharova *Wife* • Evald Schorm *Husband* ■ *Dir* Jan Nemec • *Scr* Ester Krumbachova, Jan Nemec, from a short story by Ester Krumbachova

Party Girl ★★★

Drama 1930 · US · BW · 67mins

A society drama about escort services and respectable businessmen. Rich client Douglas Fairbanks Jr is blackmailed into marrying one of the girls (Marie Prevost). Even though this rather racy melodrama was made before the puritanical Hays Code came into being, it does try to suggest that the girls only ever dance and drink with their clients. Rather dated but enjoyable stuff, with lovely silent star Prevost, who starved herself to death aged 38, making her sound debut. RB

Douglas Fairbanks Jr *Jay Rountree* • Jeanette Loff *Ellen Powell* • Judith Barrie *Leeda Cather* • Marie Prevost *Diana Hoster* • John St Polis *John Rountree* • Lucien Prival *Paul Nucast* ■ *Dir* Victor Halperin • *Scr* Monte Katterjohn, George Draney, Victor Halperin, from their story, from the novel *Dangerous Business* by Edwin Balmer

Party Girl ★★

Crime drama 1958 · US · Colour · 98mins

On the surface, this has everything going for it: a tough and glossy MGM gangster melodrama starring a mature Robert Taylor as a corrupt lawyer and leggy Cyd Charisse, directed by Nicholas Ray. Trouble is, it doesn't quite come off, sabotaged by an over-the-top performance from chief villain Lee J Cobb and an uncertainty of tone, not helped by Charisse's relentlessly non-acting performance and an awkward, subdued Taylor. TS

Robert Taylor (1) *Thomas Farrell* • Cyd Charisse *Vicki Gaye* • Lee J Cobb *Rico Angelo* • John Ireland *Louis Canetto* • Kent Smith *Jeffery Stewart* • Claire Kelly *Genevieve* • Corey Allen *Cookie* ■ *Dir* Nicholas Ray • *Scr* George Wells, from a story by Leo Katcher

Party Girl ★★

Comedy drama 1994 · US · Colour · 94mins

Parker Posey is a flighty 20-something who is puzzled by that pervasive Generation X question: "What should I do with my life?" Bored during the day and drawn to the bright Manhattan lights at night, she ends up getting nicked for hosting an illegal party. She asks her godmother (played by the director's mother) for the bail money and has to work the debt off as a clerk in a library. Lightweight and skinny like its star but mildly fun. FL

Parker Posey *Mary* • Omar Townsend *Mustafa* • Sasha von Scherler *Judy Lindendorf* • Guillermo Diaz *Leo* • Anthony DeSando *Derrick* • Donna Mitchell *Rene* • Liev Schreiber *Nigel* • Nicole Bobbitt *Venus* ■ *Dir* Daisy von Scherler Mayer • *Scr* Daisy von Scherler Mayer, Harry Birckmayer, from a story by Daisy von Scherler Mayer, Harry Birckmayer, Sheila Gaffney

Party Line ★ 18

Thriller 1988 · US · Colour · 86mins

A sleazy schlocker about phone party-liners who, looking for love on the telephone lines, find they've dialled M for murder instead. A tough cop and the assistant DA join forces to track down the deadly brother and sister duo responsible for the slayings. Richard Roundtree and Richard Hatch star, along with short-lived 1970s teen heart-throb Leif Garrett, who plays one of the killers. A film best described as "don't call us, we'll call you". DA

Richard Hatch *Dan* • Leif Garrett *Seth* • Shawn Weatherly *Stacy* • Greta Blackburn *Angelina* • Richard Roundtree *Captain Barnes* ■ *Dir* William Webb • *Scr* Richard Brandes, from a story by Tom Byrnes

Party Monster ★★★ 18

Crime drama based on a true story
2003 · US/Neth · Colour · 94mins

Macaulay Culkin returns to the screen after a nine-year absence in this colourful, true-story drama. The former child sensation slaps on glitter and lip gloss to portray late-1980s nightclub promoter Michael Alig. The toast of Manhattan, flamboyant Alig and his Club Kid pals turned dance floors into living art installations, only for drugs, in-fighting and murder to shatter their hedonistic dreams. Having already presented the sensational story in a 1998 documentary, directors Fenton Bailey and Randy Barbato vividly capture the wild and superficial glamour of these Warhol-inspired youngsters. The dialogue is wonderfully witty too, giving extra sparkle to this exhilarating portrait. SF DVD

Macaulay Culkin *Michael Alig* • Seth Green *James St James* • Chloë Sevigny *Gitsie* • Natasha Lyonne *Brooke* • Wilmer Valderrama *Keoki* • Wilson Cruz *Angel Melendez* • Diana Scarwid *Elke Alig* • Dylan McDermott *Peter Gatien* • Marilyn Manson *Christina* ■ *Dir* Fenton Bailey, Randy Barbato • *Scr* Fenton Bailey, Randy Barbato, from the non-fiction book *Disco Bloodbath* by James St James

Party Party ★ 18

Comedy 1983 · UK · Colour · 97mins

This charmless comedy shambles is set around a New Year's Eve celebration, and only early glimpses of now-familiar TV faces make the hard slog worthwhile. Directed by film-school graduate Terry Winsor and co-scripted by *Comic Strip* regular Daniel Peacock (who also stars), this expanded student short will have everyone congregating in the kitchen in double-quick time. AJ

Daniel Peacock *Toby* • Karl Howman *Johnny* • Perry Fenwick *Larry* • Sean Chapman *Sam Diggins* • Phoebe Nicholls *Rebecca* • Gary Olsen *Terry* • Clive Mantle *Bobby* • Caroline Quentin *Shirley* ■ *Dir* Terry Winsor • *Scr* Terry Winsor, Daniel Peacock

The Party's Over ★

Drama 1965 · UK · BW · 93mins

This bizarre study in necrophilia was shot in 1963 and banned outright by the British film censor. When it was re-edited and then released in 1965, producer Anthony Perry and director Guy Hamilton took their names off the credits. While one admires their integrity, the movie is a real stinker. Set in Chelsea in the Swinging Sixties, it's about the daughter of an American industrialist who falls in with a crowd of beatniks, led by a menacing Oliver Reed. The poor girl goes to the party, ends up dead and is then ravished. AT

Oliver Reed *Moise* • Clifford David *Carson* • Ann Lynn *Libby* • Catherine Woodville *Nina* • Louise Sorel *Melina* ■ *Dir* Guy Hamilton • *Scr* Marc Behm

Pas sur la Bouche ★★★★ PG

Musical romantic comedy
2003 · Fr/Swi · Colour · 116mins

Alain Resnais's remarkable career as a director hits another peak with this delicious adaptation of André Barde's 1925 musical comedy. The farcical plot has Parisian socialite Sabine Azéma trying to prevent her high-principled husband Pierre Arditi from discovering that his new American business partner, Lambert Wilson, is her ex-husband. Enacted on a stylised period set by a cast singing all the songs live, the action could have resembled an upmarket amateur operatics production. However, the sparkling musical numbers and the polished performances ensure that Resnais's mischievous satire is wholly cinematic and hugely enjoyable. DP. In French with English subtitles.

Sabine Azéma *Gilberte Valandray* • Isabelle Nanty *Arlette Poumaillac* • Audrey Tautou *Huguette Verberie* • Pierre Arditi *Georges Valandray* • Darry Cowl *Madame Foin* • Jalil Lespert *Charley* • Daniel Prévost *Faradel* • Lambert Wilson *Eric Thomson* ■ *Dir* Alain Resnais • *Scr* From the operetta by André Barde, Maurice Yvain

Pascali's Island ★★★★ 15

Period drama 1988 · UK · Colour · 98mins

Helen Mirren is the prime suspect for acting honours in this adaptation of the Barry Unsworth novel about treachery and betrayal. Set in the year 1908, she's the painter torn between bogus archaeologist Charles Dance and spy Ben Kingsley, the Pascali of the title. Her love and loyalty are as divided as Nisi, the Turkish-occupied Greek island, part of the Ottoman empire which is crumbling around them. Pascali's sexual ambiguity is beautifully observed by Ben Kingsley, but it's the observed beauty of Helen Mirren which upstages languid atmospherics and lyrical vistas. TH

Ben Kingsley *Basil Pascali* • Charles Dance *Anthony Bowles* • Helen Mirren *Lydia Neuman* • George Murcell *Herr Gesing* • Sheila Allen *Mrs Marchant* • Nadim Sawalha *Pasha* • TP McKenna *Dr Hogan* • Danielle Allan *Mrs Hogan* ■ *Dir* James Dearden • *Scr* James Dearden, from the novel by Barry Unsworth • *Cinematographer* Roger Deakins

Pass the Ammo ★★

Comedy satire 1988 · US · Colour · 97mins

This is a frantic, somewhat over-the-top comedy targetting TV evangelism. Reverend Tim Curry and his wife Annie Potts have earned millions for their mission from donations made via the small screen but in actuality they are just con artists. When Bill Paxton and Linda Kozlowski try to retrieve the money extorted from her grandmother they set in motion a train of events which culminate in a live-TV hostage taking. DF

Bill Paxton *Jesse* • Linda Kozlowski *Claire* • Annie Potts *Darla* • Glenn Withrow *Arnold Limpet* • Dennis Burkley *Big Joe Becker* • Tim Curry *Rev Ray Porter* ■ *Dir* David Beaird • *Scr* Neil Cohen, Joel Cohen

The Passage ★

Second World War drama
1978 · UK · Colour · 98mins

This ludicrous war movie has Anthony Quinn as a Basque shepherd who guides James Mason and his family to safety over the Pyrenees. Trotting out his usual Zorba act, Quinn's "life force" is exhausting while Malcolm McDowell camps it up as the SS sadist who wears a swastika on his jock strap and treats Michael Lonsdale's fingertips as a gourmet snack. Laughable and repellent. AT

Anthony Quinn *The Basque* • James Mason *Professor John Bergson* • Malcolm McDowell *Captain Von Berkow* • Patricia Neal *Ariel Bergson* • Kay Lenz *Leah Bergson* • Christopher Lee *Head Gypsy* • Michael Lonsdale [Michel Lonsdale] *Renoudot* ■ *Dir* J Lee Thompson • *Scr* Bruce Nicolaysen, from his novel *The Perilous Passage*

The Passage ★★

Supernatural drama
1986 · Fr · Colour · 100mins

Alain Delon stars as the pacifist animator who, following a car crash, is offered a deal by the physical personification of Death: unless Delon transforms his next film into a rallying cry for mass destruction, both he and his young son will die.This might have made for compelling viewing, but once Delon discovers the passage between existence and the afterlife, the emphasis shifts predictably on to abrasive action. DP. French dialogue dubbed into English.

Alain Delon *Jean Diaz* • Christine Boisson *Catherine* • Alan Musey *David Diaz* • Jean-Luc Moreau *Patrick* • Alberto Lomeo *"The Surgeon"* ■ *Dir/Scr* René Manzor

Passage Home ★★

Drama 1955 · UK · BW · 102mins

Thirty men and one woman sail from South America to London in 1931. Tensions run high among the superstitious crew because of the presence of a woman passenger, played by sultry Diane Cilento. Captain Peter Finch turns to the bottle when she rebuffs him; first mate Anthony Steel saves her from the captain but fancies his chances. Never more than a B-movie, this recycles old material with a modicum of style. AT

Anthony Steel *First Mate Vosper* • Peter Finch *Captain Lucky Ryland* • Diane Cilento *Ruth Elton* • Cyril Cusack *Bohannon* • Geoffrey Keen *Ike* • Hugh Griffith *Pettigrew* • Duncan Lamont *Llewellyn* • Gordon Jackson *Burne* • Bryan Forbes *Shorty* • Patrick McGoohan *McIsaacs* ■ *Dir* Roy Ward Baker • *Scr* William Fairchild, from the novel by Richard Armstrong

A Passage to India ★★★★★ PG

Period drama 1984 · UK · Colour · 156mins

Nominated for 11 Academy Awards, David Lean's final feature trespasses on territory usually reserved for Merchant Ivory and EM Forster. But Lean was the master of the stately epic and, in this lusciously photographed picture, the 75-year-old director showed that none of his powers had waned. Stripping away the sheen of Raj life, he exposes the tensions, prejudices and snobberies of imperialism with a satirical blade every bit as sharp as Forster's. Oscar-winning Peggy Ashcroft garnered the acting headlines, but she is surpassed by Judy Davis as the outsider whose disregard for the rules of the game shatters the calm of this Indian Eden. DP DVD

Judy Davis *Adela Quested* • Victor Banerjee *Dr Aziz* • Peggy Ashcroft *Mrs Moore* • James Fox *Richard Fielding* • Nigel Havers *Ronny Heaslop* • Alec Guinness *Professor Godbole* • Richard Wilson *Turton* • Antonia Pemberton *Mrs Turton* • Michael Culver *McBryde* • Art Malik *Mahmoud Ali* • Saeed Jaffrey *Hamidullah* ■ *Dir* David Lean • *Scr* David Lean, from the play by Santha Rama Rau, from the novel by EM Forster • *Cinematographer* Ernest Day

Passage to Marseille ★★★ PG

Second World War drama
1944 · US · BW · 104mins

Despite the efforts of the eminently watchable Humphrey Bogart, Sydney Greenstreet, Peter Lorre and Claude Rains, this is tiresome and hard to follow. As the girl in the flashbacks, Michèle Morgan doesn't really register and Bogart is strangely cast as a French journalist leading an escape from a penal colony to join the French Resistance. But director Michael Curtiz does what he can, and he's aided by great camerawork from James Wong Howe and a superb score by Max Steiner. TS

Humphrey Bogart *Matrac* • Claude Rains *Captain Freycinet* • Michèle Morgan *Paula* • Philip Dorn *Renault* • Sydney Greenstreet *Major Duval* • Peter Lorre *Marius* • George Tobias *Petit* • Victor Francen *Captain Patain Malo* • Helmut Dantine *Garou* • John Loder *Manning* ■ *Dir* Michael Curtiz • *Scr* Casey Robinson, Jack Moffitt, from the novel *Men without a Country* by Charles Nordhoff, James Norman Hall

Passed Away ★★★ 15

Black comedy 1992 · US · Colour · 92mins

This entertaining comedy grabs the attention thanks to some exceptional ensemble acting, but in the end settles for schmaltz and neatly tied loose ends. Gathering the members of his clan for their father's funeral, Bob Hoskins is nominally the star of the picture, but his midlife crisis is never as interesting as brother William Petersen's problems, sister Pamela Reed's passion for embalmer Peter Riegert or liberated nun Frances McDormand's deadpan marxism. Its quip count remains high throughout, but the script runs out of steam too early. DP DVD

Bob Hoskins *Johnny Scanlan* • Blair Brown *Amy Scanlan* • Tim Curry *Boyd Pinter* • Frances McDormand *Nora Scanlan* • William Petersen [William L Petersen] *Frank Scanlan* • Pamela Reed *Terry Scanlan* • Peter Riegert *Peter Syracusa* • Maureen Stapleton *Mary Scanlan* • Nancy Travis *Cassie Slocombe* • Jack Warden *Jack Scanlan* ■ *Dir/Scr* Charlie Peters

Passenger ★★★★

Drama 1963 · Pol · BW · 60mins

Director Andrzej Munk was partway through his masterpiece when he was killed in a car crash. Yet, although Witold Lesiewicz used a voiceover and an adroit collage of stills to approximate its resolution, its very incompleteness reinforces the powerful message that while the Holocaust may belong to history, its legacy can never be forgotten. Aleksandra Slaska gives a chilling performance as the cruise liner passenger who attempts to reinvent her career as an overseer at Auschwitz following a chance encounter with a survivor she thought long dead. Despite the horror of the camp sequences, there's no bitterness, just aching sadness. DP. In Polish with English subtitles.

Aleksandra Slaska *Liza* • Jan Kreczmar *Walter* • Anna Ciepielewska *Marta* • Irena Malkiewicz *"Ober"* • John Rees *English narrator* ■ *Dir* Andrzej Munk, Witold Lesiewicz • *Scr* Zofia Posmysz-Piasecka, Andrzej Munk

The Passenger ★★★★ PG

Drama 1975 · Fr/It/Sp · Colour · 113mins

Michelangelo Antonioni's movie portrays what happens to burnt-out TV reporter Jack Nicholson who adopts the identity of a dead man, a gun-runner, and loses himself in Africa's civil wars. There are two big themes here – the emptiness of existence and the exploitation of the Third World – and the film's vague style may frustrate those looking for concrete answers. Maria Schneider doesn't do much except look pretty, and the scenes in London with Jenny Runacre are not up to the African ones. However, the film has a wonderful hypnotic atmosphere, mainly due to Nicholson's excellent performance and to the location photography of the Sahara and the Gaudi buildings in Barcelona. AT

Jack Nicholson *David Locke* • Maria Schneider *Girl* • Jenny Runacre *Rachel Locke* • Ian Hendry *Martin Knight* • Steven Berkoff *Stephen* • Ambrose Bia *Achebe* ■ *Dir* Michelangelo Antonioni • *Scr* Mark Peploe, Peter Wollen, Michelangelo Antonioni, from a story by Mark Peploe • *Cinematographer* Luciano Tovoli

Passenger 57 ★★★ 15

Action thriller 1992 · US · Colour · 80mins

This enjoyable airborne thriller stars Wesley Snipes as a security expert who finds himself on the same aeroplane as British master criminal Bruce Payne, temporarily in police custody. Of course, Payne's henchmen have hitched a lift as well and when they duly free him, it's up to Snipes to save the day. Despite the hand-me-down plot and dialogue, director Kevin Hooks wrings the requisite suspense out of some expertly staged action set pieces. JF. Contains violence and swearing. DVD

Wesley Snipes *John Cutter* • Bruce Payne *Charles Rane* • Tom Sizemore *Sly Delvecchio* • Alex Datcher *Marti Slayton* • Bruce Greenwood *Stuart Ramsey* • Robert Hooks *Dwight Henderson* • Elizabeth Hurley *Sabrina Ritchie* ■ *Dir* Kevin Hooks • *Scr* David Loughery, Dan Gordon, from a story by Stewart Raffill, David Gordon

The Passing of the Third Floor Back ★★★ U

Fantasy drama 1935 · UK · BW · 90mins

The German-born actor Conrad Veidt, so often cast in sinister roles, had one of the best parts of his career in this allegorical tale of a mysterious stranger who takes a back room in a boarding house run by a greedy landlord and populated by sad inhabitants. The newcomer profoundly affects their lives before disappearing as swiftly as he arrived. It was co-written by Alma Reville, better known as Mrs Alfred Hitchcock, from a play by Jerome K Jerome. Well observed and intriguing, with an excellent cast. RK

Conrad Veidt *The stranger* • René Ray *Stasia* • Frank Cellier *Wright* • Anna Lee *Vivian Tompkin* • John Turnbull *Major Tompkin* • Cathleen Nesbitt *Mrs Tompkin* ■ *Dir* Berthold Viertel • *Scr* Michael Hogan, Alma Reville, from a play by Jerome K Jerome

Passion ★★ U

Western 1954 · US · Colour · 82mins

Passion is conspicuously missing from this dreary story starring Cornel Wilde as the young hero seeking revenge on the band who have killed his wife and child. With glamorous Yvonne De Carlo as co-star and a great cameraman, John Alton, working with veteran director Allan Dwan, the film looks attractive enough but is slowed down by the ponderous dialogue and predictable development. AE

Cornel Wilde *Juan Obreon* • Yvonne De Carlo *Tonya Melo/Rosa Melo* • Raymond Burr *Captain Rodriguez* • Lon Chaney Jr *Castro* • John Qualen *Gaspar Melo* • Rodolfo Acosta *Salvador Sandro* ■ *Dir* Allan Dwan • *Scr* Beatrice A Dresher, Joseph Leytes, Howard Estabrook, from a story by Beatrice A Dresher, Joseph Leytes, Miguel Padilla

A Passion ★★★★ 12

Drama 1969 · Swe · Colour · 96mins

This ranks among Ingmar Bergman's most powerful, personal and pessimistic statements on the human condition. Utilising forbidding island landscape and the recurrence of dreams to emphasise the isolation of the protagonists, Bergman explores the impossibility of escaping from one's past and finding contentment in an irrational and violent society. Hell is definitely other people in this godless place, especially once Liv Ullmann drags Max von Sydow out of his reclusive self-sufficiency and into confrontation with both his neighbours and her ghosts. Released on DVD as *The Passion of Anna*. DP. In Swedish with English subtitles. DVD

Liv Ullmann *Anna Fromm* • Bibi Andersson *Eva Vergerus* • Max von Sydow *Andreas Winkelman* • Erland Josephson *Elis Vergerus* • Erik Hell *Johann Andersson* ■ *Dir/Scr* Ingmar Bergman • *Cinematographer* Sven Nykvist

Passion ★★ 15

Drama 1982 · Fr/Swi · Colour · 83mins

This marks Jean-Luc Godard's semi-return to a more commercial way of movie-making, reuniting him with Raoul Coutard, the man who photographed all the early, epoch-making films, and using big-name stars of the time. Its central story – about a Polish film director and his crew staying in a hotel – is almost lifted from François Truffaut's *Day for Night*, except in Godard's hands it is fragmented, vague and still experimental. AT. In French with English subtitles.

Isabelle Huppert *Isabelle* • Hanna Schygulla *Hanna* • Jerzy Radziwilowicz *Jerzy* • Michel Piccoli *Michel* • Laszlo Szabo ■ *Dir/Scr* Jean-Luc Godard • *Cinematographer* Raoul Coutard

Passion ★★★★

Musical drama 1996 · US · Colour · 114mins

This film version of Stephen Sondheim's 1994 Tony Award-winning Broadway musical – itself an adaptation of Iginio Ugo Tarchetti's classic novel *Fosca* – contains all the emotional intimacy and dramatic intensity that made the show such a success. In what is basically a *Beauty and the Beast* fable in reverse, Donna Murphy (re-creating her Tony Award-winning role) stars as the plain, mortally ill Fosca who falls for handsome officer Jere Shea and eventually melts his heart. The rich score is one of Sondheim's best, the performances are dazzling and anyone expecting the usual static and stilted approach to such stagebound material is in for a surprise. AJ

Jere Shea *Giorgio* • Marin Mazzie *Clara* • Donna Murphy *Fosca* • Gregg Edelman *Colonel Ricci* • Tom Aldredge *Dr Tambourri* • Francis Ruivivar *Lt Torasso* ■ *Dir* James Lapine • *Scr* James Lapine, from the musical by Stephen Sondheim, from the novel *Fosca* by Iginio Ugo Tarchetti

Passion ★★★

Biographical drama
1999 · Aus/US · Colour · 102mins

Following the success of *Shine*, it was inevitable that the early life of another celebrated Australian pianist would reach the screen – especially one who was a devotee of flagellation and was rumoured to have had an incestuous relationship with his mother. Richard Roxburgh turns in an energetic performance as Percy Grainger, the unconventional maestro who wrote *Country Gardens* and took pre-First World War London by storm, while Barbara Hershey valiantly attempts to capture the eccentricity of his syphilitic mother. But director Peter Duncan's biographical fantasy lacks focus. DP

Richard Roxburgh *Percy Grainger* • Barbara Hershey *Rose Grainger* • Emily Woof *Karen Holten* • Claudia Karvan *Alfhild de Luce* • Simon Burke *Herman Sandby* • Linda Cropper *Mrs Lowery* ■ *Dir* Peter Duncan • *Scr* Don Watson, from the non-fiction book *Percy Grainger* by John Bird, from the play *Percy & Rose* by Rob George

Passion Fish ★★★★ 15

Drama 1992 · US · Colour · 129mins

Trust writer/director John Sayles to lift a theme that's often used in TV movies and transform it into something finer and richer. Mary McDonnell received an Oscar nomination for her performance as May-Alice, a daytime soap opera star who is paralysed after an accident and returns to her family home in Louisiana. Starting off as a "bitch on wheels" and taking to drink and self-pity, her disability and personality undergo a dramatic change with the help of her companion, played by Alfre Woodard. Sayles judges the tone expertly and creates a striking study of courageous individuals within a small community. AT. Contains substance abuse and swearing.

Mary McDonnell *May-Alice* • Alfre Woodard *Chantelle* • David Strathairn *Rennie* • Vondie Curtis-Hall *Sugar LeDoux* • Angela Bassett *Dawn/Rhonda* • Lenore Banks *Nurse Quick* • William Mahoney *Max* ■ *Dir/Scr* John Sayles

A Passion for Murder ★★ 18

Thriller 1992 · US/Can · Colour · 87mins

Joanna Pacula is an undercover CIA agent who, following the death of her politician lover, ends up going on the run with cab driver Michael Nouri while being pursued by assassin Michael Ironside. Silly stuff indeed, but worth watching for bug-eyed Ironside, who seems to have made a career for himself playing mesmerising killers, bad guys and mercenaries. JB. Contains swearing, violence, sex scenes and nudity. DVD

Joanna Pacula *Vanessa* • Michael Nouri *Ben Shorr* • Michael Ironside *Quinn* • Lee J Campbell *Sheriff* ■ *Dir* Neill Fearnley • *Scr* Arne Olsen, John Alan Schwartz

Passion in the Desert ★★★ 12

Period drama 1998 · UK · Colour · 87mins

Lavinia Currier's debut feature is clearly a labour of love. Set against the backdrop of Napoleon's Egyptian campaign, it opens as a treatise on man's disrespect for art, as painter Michel Piccoli and his officer escort Ben Daniels lament the wanton destruction of war. However, once circumstances force Daniels into the wilderness, the emphasis shifts to his primeval relationship with the leopardess that teaches him to survive his breathtaking but treacherous surroundings. Strikingly shot by Russian cinematographer Alexei Rodionov, this is a disconcerting tale. DP. Contains violence and nudity.

Ben Daniels *Augustin Robert* • Michel Piccoli *Jean-Michel Venture de Paradis* • Paul Meston *Grognard* • Kenneth Collard *Officer* • Nadi Odeh *Bedouin bride* ■ *Dir* Lavinia Currier • *Scr* Lavinia Currier, Martin Edmunds, from a novella by Honoré de Balzac

The Passion of Darkly Noon ★★★ 18

Drama 1995 · UK/Ger · Colour · 100mins

Beauty and the Beast meets *Twin Peaks* in an intellectual stalk-and-slasher picture about religion, redemption and repression. Brendan Fraser gives an eerie performance as the titular drifter Darkly Noon, sole survivor of a religious cult, who becomes obsessed with local beauty Ashley Judd. Written and directed by Philip Ridley, this intriguingly warped fairy tale is a challenging, inventive and deeply stylish exploration of forbidden desire. AJ

Brendan Fraser *Darkly Noon* • Ashley Judd *Callie* • Viggo Mortensen *Clay* • Loren Dean *Jude* • Grace Zabriskie *Roxie* • Lou Meyers *Quincey* ■ *Dir/Scr* Philip Ridley

The Passion of Joan of Arc ★★★★★ PG

Classic silent drama 1928 · Fr · BW · 80mins

Based on authentic trial records and drawing on artistic styles from the Renaissance to the avant-garde, Danish director Carl Th Dreyer's film is one of the masterpieces of the silent era. Working with cinematographer Rudolph Maté, Dreyer used all manner of symbolic angles, zooms, tilts and pan shots to capture the dramatic intensity of the action, only for the flow to be interrupted too often by the descriptive captions. In her only screen appearance, Maria Renée Falconetti gives an astonishing performance, filmed almost exclusively in close-up both to convey her personal agony and to contrast her sincerity with the duplicity of her accusers. DP

Mlle Falconetti [Maria Renée Falconetti] *Jeanne* • Eugène Silvain *Bishop Pierre Cauchon* • André Berley *Jean d'Estivet* • Maurice Schultz *Nicolas Loyseleur* • Antonin Artaud *Jean Massieu* • Michel Simon *Jean Lemaître* • Jean d'Yd *Guillaume Erard* • Ravet [Louis Ravet] *Jean Beaupère* ■ *Dir* Carl Th Dreyer • *Scr* Carl Th Dreyer, Joseph Delteil, from a novel by Joseph Delteil

Passion of Mind ★ 12

Romantic fantasy drama
2000 · US · Colour · 100mins

Demi Moore clearly believed the challenge of playing a New York literati and a French single mother existing within the same mental space would finally establish her acting credentials. But what on earth possessed *Ma Vie en Rose* director Alain Berliner to embark on such a debacle? To his credit, he maintains the secret of Moore's true identity until the final reel. An embarrassment. DP

Demi Moore *Marie/Martha Marie "Marty" Talmadge* • Stellan Skarsgård *William Granther* • William Fichtner *Aaron Reilly* • Sinead Cusack *Jessie* • Peter Riegert *Dr Peters* • Joss Ackland *Dr Langer* ■ *Dir* Alain Berliner • *Scr* Ron Bass [Ronald Bass], David Field

The Passion of the Christ ★★★ 18

Religious drama 2004 · US · Colour · 121mins

Compelling yet repetitive, shocking yet plodding, Mel Gibson's labour of love charts the last 12 hours of Jesus's life on Earth, from his betrayal by Judas in the Garden of Gethsemane through to the most punishing depiction of the crucifixion ever mounted. Gibson's commitment to the material is tangible, the much talked about brutality is unflinching and the earthy atmosphere is expertly evoked. But Jim Caviezel's Jesus makes for an impenetrable figure, some of the imagery doesn't quite come off and the narrow focus does little to provide a context to Jesus's teachings and suffering. Gibson subsequently re-released the film as *The Passion: Recut*, deleting six minutes of violence for a new 15 certificate, but the flaws of the original remain. IF. In Aramaic and Latin with English subtitles. Contains violence. DVD

Jim Caviezel *Jesus* • Maia Morgenstern *Mary* • Monica Bellucci *Mary Magdalene* • Mattia Sbragia *Caiphas, the High Priest* • Hristo Naumov Shopov *Pontius Pilate* • Claudia Gerini *Claudia Procles, Pilate's wife* • Luca Lionello *Judas Iscariot* • Hristo Jivkov *John* • Francesco De Vito *Peter* • Toni Bertorelli *Annas* • Sergio Rubini *Dismas* ■ *Dir* Mel Gibson • *Scr* Mel Gibson, Benedict Fitzgerald

The Passionate Friends ★★ PG

Romantic drama 1948 · UK · BW · 86mins

One of three films made by David Lean with Ann Todd, whom he married in 1949. In a stuffy melodrama, Todd is forced to choose between luxury and love. Her cause is not helped by the script, which successfully buries one of HG Wells's more forgettable novels in a welter of confused flashbacks and clipped platitudes. Todd's haughty manner renders her eminently resistible and she is further disadvantaged by comparison with those astute screen actors Trevor Howard and Claude Rains. DP

Ann Todd *Mary Justin* • Claude Rains *Howard Justin* • Trevor Howard *Steven Stratton* • Isabel Dean *Pat* • Betty Ann Davies *Miss Layton* ■ *Dir* David Lean • *Scr* Eric Ambler, David Lean, Stanley Haynes, from the novel by HG Wells

The Passionate Plumber ★

Comedy 1932 · US · BW · 73mins

One of the last, and worst, comedies of the great Buster Keaton, due to MGM's poor choice of script and the studio's decision to combine him with the coarser comedy of Jimmy Durante. Directed with all the subtlety of an overflow by Edward Sedgwick, it has Keaton hired by Parisienne Irene Purcell to pose as her *amour* to make Gilbert Roland jealous. Keaton's own personal problems overwhelmed this underwhelming rubbish. TH

Buster Keaton *Elmer E Tuttle* • Jimmy Durante *Julius J McCracken* • Irene Purcell *Patricia Jardine* • Polly Moran *Albine* • Gilbert Roland *Tony Lagorce* ■ *Dir* Edward Sedgwick • *Scr* Laurence E Johnson, Ralph Spence, from the play *Her Cardboard Lover* by Valerie Wyngate, PG Wodehouse, from the play *Dans Sa Candeur Naïve* by Jacques Deval

The Passionate Stranger ★★

Comedy 1957 · UK · BW and Colour · 97mins

This feeble comedy wastes the talent of Margaret Leighton, playing a a novelist who bases one of her characters on her chauffeur. Marital complications follow when he misunderstands her motives. Part of the film shows the central characters in real life and the rest dramatises sections of her book, but unfortunately the conceit does not work. BB

Ralph Richardson *Roger Wynter/Sir Clement Hathaway* • Margaret Leighton *Judith Wynter/Leonie* • Patricia Dainton *Emily/Betty* • Carlo Giustini *Carlo/Mario* ■ *Dir* Muriel Box • *Scr* Muriel Box, Sydney Box

Passionate Summer ★★ U

Romantic drama
1958 · UK · Colour · 103mins

Noted television producer Rudolph Cartier – best known for the *Quatermass* serials – made a rare foray into features with this hothouse Rank melodrama, set in a sweltering Jamaica. Virginia McKenna is the air hostess who lusts after Carl Mohner, while Bill Travers is in love with McKenna but being seduced by wicked Yvonne Mitchell. Travers and McKenna may have been a real-life couple, but they really are the most unconvincing of screen lovers here. DP

Virginia McKenna *Judy* • Bill Travers *Douglas Lockwood* • Yvonne Mitchell *Mrs Pawley* • Alexander Knox *Mr Pawley* • Carl Mohner *Louis* • Ellen Barrie *Silvia* • Guy Middleton *Duffield* ■ *Dir* Rudolph Cartier • *Scr* Joan Henry, from the novel *The Shadow and the Peak* by Richard Mason

La Passione ★ 15

Musical fantasy 1996 · UK · Colour · 89mins

A young boy's obsession with Ferraris and his hero worship of a German racing driver form the basis of rock star Chris Rea's script for this misfiring drama, set in Yorkshire in the early 1960s. When his idol is killed at Monza, the boy becomes withdrawn and the film resorts to fantasies involving Shirley Bassey. You really want to like this movie, but, like many 1960s sports cars, it looks good and goes wrong a lot. AT

Shirley Bassey • Paul Shane *Papa* • Jan Ravens *Mama* • Carmen Silvera *Grandmother* • Gorden Kaye *PC Keecy* • Sean Gallagher *Jo* • Thomas Orange *Young Jo* • Keith Barron *Roy* ■ *Dir* John B Hobbs • *Scr* Chris Rea

The Passover Plot ★★

Religious drama 1976 · Is · Colour · 108mins

Derived from the Hugh J Schonfield book, this is a controversial account of the life of Jesus Christ, depicting him as a zealot leader who brings about his own crucifixion in order to make a political point against the Roman authorities. Donald Pleasence and Biblical stalwarts Harry Andrews and Hugh Griffith feature in the cast, while Christ is played by Zalman King. The whole production is somewhat pedestrian, making the film's contentious issues rather bland. TH

Harry Andrews *Yohanan the Baptist* • Hugh Griffith *Caiaphas* • Zalman King *Yeshua* • Donald Pleasence *Pontius Pilate* • Scott Wilson *Judah* ■ *Dir* Michael Campus • *Scr* Millard Cohan, Patricia Knop, from the book by Hugh J Schonfield

Passport to Pimlico ★★★★ U

Comedy 1949 · UK · BW · 80mins

The cosiest of the Ealing comedies, this is essentially a one-joke affair that is spun out with masterly skill by that most gifted teller of shaggy dog stories, TEB Clarke, who received an Oscar nomination for his story and screenplay. Once local historian Margaret Rutherford discovers that Pimlico belongs to the Duchy of Burgundy, the scene could have been set for a sniping satire on the state of postwar England. Clarke and director Henry Cornelius's decision to cock only the gentlest of snooks at such bugbears as rationing and the breakdown of wartime camaraderie is slightly disappointing, but the majority of the situations are ingenious, and the cast is top quality. DP DVD

Stanley Holloway *Arthur Pemberton* • Margaret Rutherford *Professor Hatton-Jones* • Basil Radford *Gregg* • Naunton Wayne *Straker* • Hermione Baddeley *Edie Randall* • John Slater *Frank Huggins* • Betty Warren *Connie Pemberton* • Barbara Murray *Shirley Pemberton* ■ *Dir* Henry Cornelius • *Scr* TEB Clarke

Passport to Shame ★★★

Drama 1958 · UK · BW · 92mins

In the late 1950s, the BBFC reluctantly allowed producers to tackle prostitution as long as the films masqueraded as "Awful Warnings". This typical example has poor French waif Odile Versois coming to England and tricked into working for a brothel run by evil Herbert Lom. A cheap, tawdry and fascinating piece of vintage sexploitation. Way down the cast list, Michael Caine plays a bridegroom. DM

Eddie Constantine *Johnny* • Diana Dors *Vicki* • Odile Versois *Malou* • Herbert Lom *Nick* • Brenda de Banzie *Madame* • Robert Brown *Mike* • Elwyn Brook-Jones *Heath* • Cyril Shaps *Willie* • Dennis Shaw [Denis Shaw] *Mac* • Joan Sims *Miriam* • Michael Caine *Bridegroom* ■ *Dir* Alvin Rakoff • *Scr* Patrick Alexander

Passport to Treason ★ U

Mystery 1956 · UK · BW · 83mins

Western star Rod Cameron should never have packed his passport to play the private eye in this dire British B-feature with its sub-Hitchcockian plot about neo-fascists in London concealing their activities within an organisation for world peace. A better actor than granite-jawed Cameron might have breathed some life into the line-up of hackneyed situations. AE

Rod Cameron *Mike O'Kelly* • Lois Maxwell *Diane Boyd* • Clifford Evans *Orlando Sims* • Peter Illing *Giorgio Sacchi* • Marianne Stone *Miss Jones* ■ *Dir* Robert S Baker • *Scr* Norman Hudis, Kenneth R Hayles, from a novel by Manning O'Brine

The Password Is Courage ★★★ U

War drama based on a true story
1962 · UK · BW · 115mins

Rather a forgotten film in Dirk Bogarde's canon, this is a fitfully amusing war offering, based on the true-life exploits of one Charles Coward, a cocky PoW who spent his time humiliating his guards and preparing his colleagues for escape. Writer/director Andrew L Stone occasionally pushes too hard for comic effect and Bogarde is hardly perfect casting, but the story of Coward's attempts to reach the Polish Resistance is fascinating. DP

Dirk Bogarde *Charles Coward* • Maria Perschy *Irena* • Alfred Lynch *Billy Pope* • Nigel Stock *Cole* • Reginald Beckwith *Unteroffizier* • Richard Marner *Schmidt* • Ed Devereaux *Aussie* ■ *Dir* Andrew L Stone • *Scr* Andrew L Stone, from the biography of Charles Coward by John Castle

Pastime ★★★

Sports drama 1991 · US · Colour · 94mins

Set in the 1950s, this appealing low-key film chronicles the friendship of ageing but chipper minor-league baseball player William Russ, and a promising young black pitcher Glenn Plummer who has just joined his floundering team. Both men are used as scapegoats by the other players, who are frustrated at the team's performance. Naturally, the two form a bond in the face of this adversity. A real treat for baseball fans, but some may find Russ's impossibly upbeat personality difficult to tolerate. ST

William Russ *Roy Dean Bream* • Scott Plank *Randy Keever* • Reed Rudy *Spicer* • Ricky

Paull Goldin *Hahn* • Peter Murnik *Simmons* • John Jones *Colbeck* • Glenn Plummer *Tyrone Debray* ■ *Dir* Robin B Armstrong • *Scr* David M Eyre Jr [David Eyre Jr]

Pastor Hall ★★★★

Second World War drama
1940 · UK · BW · 97mins

This highly impressive third feature from the Boulting brothers has been dismissed as a routine wartime flagwaver on the theme of Nazi intolerance. Rather, it is a bold and often stirring tribute to the universal power of faith, courage and personal conviction. The picture is based on the life of the Protestant minister Martin Niemoller who was interned in a concentration camp for failing to preach against either socialism or Judaism. Wilfrid Lawson plays the pastor with great dignity. DP

Wilfrid Lawson *Pastor Hall* • Nova Pilbeam *Christine Hall* • Seymour Hicks *General von Grotjahn* • Marius Goring *Fritz Gerte* • Brian Worth *Werner von Grotjahn* • Percy Walsh *Herr Veit* • Hay Petrie *Nazi Pastor* ■ *Dir* Roy Boulting • *Scr* Leslie Arliss, Anna Reiner, Haworth Bromley, John Boulting, Roy Boulting, Miles Malcolm, from a play by Ernest Toller

Pasty Faces ★★ 15

Crime comedy 2000 · UK · Colour · 83mins

Originally performed at a local arts centre, this is yet another British crime flick that's directed by a novice who's convinced watching lots of movies equips you for making one. David Paul Baker even has the assurance to star as the wannabe actor who abandons his dead-end Glasgow existence for Hollywood. Everything goes belly up and he agrees to participate in a Vegas casino heist. This threatens to hold its own before collapsing into a crass collection of clichés and caricatures. DP [video] DVD

David Baker [David Paul Baker] *Mickey* • Alan McCafferty *Joe* • Gary Cross *Steve* • Martin McGreechin *Bobby* ■ *Dir/Scr* David Baker [David Paul Baker]

Pat and Mike ★★★★ U

Sports comedy 1952 · US · BW · 91mins

A rollicking vehicle for the wonder team of Katharine Hepburn and Spencer Tracy: she's a sportswoman, he's a rugged, cynical sports promoter. The Ruth Gordon/Garson Kanin Oscar-nominated story and screenplay is, frankly, weakish compared with the divine sophistication of other Tracy/Hepburn films. Hepburn is born to play the all-round athlete, but Tracy has, despite his top billing, distinctly the secondary role, and seems uncomfortable at times. TS [video]

Spencer Tracy *Mike Conovan* • Katharine Hepburn *Pat Pemberton* • Aldo Ray *Davie Hucko* • William Ching *Collier Weld* • Charles Buchinski [Charles Bronson] *Hank Tasling* • Sammy White *Barney Grau* • Chuck Connors *Policeman* ■ *Dir* George Cukor • *Scr* Ruth Gordon, Garson Kanin, from their story

Pat Garrett and Billy the Kid ★★★★ 18

Western 1973 · US · Colour · 116mins

Despite studio tinkering, this near-masterpiece from director Sam Peckinpah is almost on a par with *The Wild Bunch*. It's a brooding meditation on violence, honour and loyalty in the last days of the Old West, as gunman-turned-sheriff Garrett (James Coburn) relives the past before taking on his one-time partner Billy (Kris Kristofferson). It becomes an elegy for the father-son relationship that figures in so much American literature, as both men try to live up to their legends. TH. Contains violence, swearing and nudity. [video]

James Coburn *Pat Garrett* • Kris Kristofferson *Billy the Kid* • Bob Dylan *Alias* • Jason Robards *Governor Lew Wallace* • Richard Jaeckel *Sheriff Kip McKinney* • Katy Jurado *Mrs Baker* • Slim Pickens *Sheriff Baker* • Chill Wills *Lemuel* • John Beck *Poe* • Rita Coolidge *Maria* • Jack Elam *Alamosa Bill* • Harry Dean Stanton *Luke* ■ *Dir* Sam Peckinpah • *Scr* Rudolph Wurlitzer • *Music* Bob Dylan

Patch Adams ★★★ 12

Biographical comedy drama
1998 · US · Colour · 110mins

Robin Williams is ideally cast as an irrepressible idealist whose dream of becoming a doctor is threatened by his inability to conform to medical school dictates. Williams's penchant for playing the clowning do-gooder is indulged by director Tom Shadyac, and the pat manipulation of the emotions comes with a high level of saccharin. But anyone who's ever felt aggrieved by impersonal treatment from the medical establishment will enjoy the system-bucking antics. AME. Contains swearing, sexual references. [video] DVD

Robin Williams *Hunter "Patch" Adams* • Daniel London *Truman* • Monica Potter *Carin* • Philip Seymour Hoffman *Mitch* • Bob Gunton *Dean Walcott* • Josef Sommer *Dr Eaton* • Irma P Hall *Joletta* • Frances Lee McCain *Judy* ■ *Dir* Tom Shadyac • *Scr* Steve Oedekerk, from the book *Gesundheit, Good Health Is a Laughing Matter* by Hunter Doherty Adams, Maureen Mylander

A Patch of Blue ★★★

Drama 1965 · US · BW · 105mins

A bit of a weepie, with Elizabeth Hartman as a young blind woman and Sidney Poitier as the man she meets in the park who becomes her closest friend. Hartman is remarkably stable despite her tragic history, while Poitier is as solid as Mount Rushmore. The picture lacks any semblance of subtlety: Shelley Winters as Hartman's monstrous mother goes straight for the jugular, and won an Oscar as best supporting actress. AT

Sidney Poitier *Gordon Ralfe* • Shelley Winters *Rose-Ann D'Arcy* • Elizabeth Hartman *Selina D'Arcy* • Wallace Ford *Ole Pa* • Ivan Dixon *Mark Ralfe* • Elisabeth Fraser *Sadie* ■ *Dir* Guy Green • *Scr* Guy Green, from the novel *Be Ready with Bells and Drums* by Elizabeth Kata • *Cinematographer* Robert Burks

Paternity ★★ 15

Romantic comedy
1981 · US · Colour · 88mins

Burt Reynolds plays the middle-aged manager of Madison Square Gardens who decides he wants an heir to carry on his name. Of course, he doesn't want the wife to go with it. Beverley D'Angelo is a struggling musician waiting tables, so she is more than happy to play surrogate mother to his progeny. An unlovely subject, with a charmless script. FL [video]

Burt Reynolds *Buddy Evans* • Beverly D'Angelo *Maggie Harden* • Norman Fell *Larry* • Paul Dooley *Kurt* • Elizabeth Ashley *Sophia Thatcher* • Lauren Hutton *Jenny Lofton* • Juanita Moore *Celia* • Peter Billingsley *Tad* ■ *Dir* David Steinberg • *Scr* Charlie Peters

Path to War ★★★★ 15

Historical drama
2002 · US · Colour · 157mins

Although made for TV, this final film from director John Frankenheimer is among his most powerful work. A slow-burning look at the political machinery behind America's conflict in Vietnam under Lyndon B Johnson, the feature is brilliantly executed and meticulously detailed. Interweaving original archive footage with believable dramatisation, Frankenheimer turns potentially tedious melodrama into a highly-charged and fascinating exploration of arrogance, ignorance and tragedy. Michael Gambon gives an emotional and finely nuanced performance as the guilt-racked president, outstandingly supported by an electrifying Donald Sutherland as his advisor Clark Clifford. SF. Contains swearing and violence. DVD

Michael Gambon *Lyndon Baines Johnson* • Donald Sutherland *Clark Clifford* • Alec Baldwin *Robert McNamara* • Bruce McGill *George Ball* • James Frain *Dick Goodwin* • Felicity Huffman *Ladybird Johnson* • Frederic Forrest *General Earle "Buzz" Wheeler* • John Aylward *Dean Rusk* • Philip Baker Hall *Everett Dirkson* • Tom Skerritt *General Westmoreland* ■ *Dir* John Frankenheimer • *Scr* Daniel Giat

Pather Panchali ★★★★★ U

Drama 1955 · Ind · BW · 119mins

Translating as *The Song of the Road*, Satyajit Ray's debut as director is one of the masterpieces of world cinema. The first in the acclaimed Apu trilogy, it astounded everyone when it won the Special Jury Prize at Cannes, particularly as it was filmed on weekends and holidays over a four-year period, with Ray having to pawn his wife's jewellery to complete the shoot. Played with restraint by a non-professional cast and influenced by such Italian neorealist features as *Bicycle Thieves*, its story of a young Bengali boy's introduction to the ways of the world is remarkable for its simplicity and humanity. The trilogy was completed with *Aparajito* (1956) and *The World of Apu* (1959). DP. In Bengali with English subtitles. [video] DVD

Kanu Bannerjee *Harihar, the father* • Karuna Bannerjee *Sarbojaya, the mother* • Subir Bannerjee *Apu* • Runki Bannerjee *Durga, as a child* ■ *Dir* Satyajit Ray • *Scr* Satyajit Ray, from a novel by Bibhutibhusan Bannerjee

Pathfinder ★★★★ 15

Adventure drama 1987 · Fin · Colour · 82mins

Described as the very first film to be made in the Lapp language, *Pathfinder* is far more than a curiosity, being a splendid excursion into myth and legend above the Arctic Circle. The first scenes suggest a variant of *Conan*, with a young boy witnessing the massacre of his parents; but instead of growing into a strapping warrior, he remains a boy whose plan for vengeance takes us into a morass of betrayal and cunning in which the leading figure is a mythological reindeer. Set against this bleak and grand landscape, Nils Gaup's picture – a rites of passage saga – has an intense authenticity and exoticism. AT. In Lappish with English subtitles. [video]

Mikkel Gaup *Aigin* • Ingvald Guttorm *Father* • Ellen Anne Buljo *Mother* • Inger Utsi *Sister* ■ *Dir/Scr* Nils Gaup • *Cinematographer* Erling Thurmann-Andersen

Paths of Glory ★★★★★ PG

First World War drama
1957 · US · BW · 83mins

Winston Churchill claimed this film came closest to capturing the atmosphere of the First World War and exposing the workings of the military mind. As the general who orders a hopeless attack on a German position, Adolphe Menjou is a villain not because he is an officer slavishly adhering to the letter of army law, but because he is an arrogant aristocrat, motivated more by fear of the lower classes than by hatred of the enemy. Kirk Douglas and Timothy Carey are outstanding among the troops on the front line, while Kubrick's relentlessly probing camera offers constant evidence of a film-maker at the height of his powers. DP [video] DVD

Kirk Douglas *Colonel Dax* • Ralph Meeker *Corporal Paris* • Adolphe Menjou *General Broulard* • George Macready *General Mireau* • Wayne Morris *Lieutenant Roget* • Richard Anderson *Major Saint-Auban* • Joseph Turkel [Joe Turkel] *Private Pierre Arnaud* • Timothy Carey *Private Ferol* ■ *Dir* Stanley Kubrick • *Scr* Stanley Kubrick, Calder Willingham, Jim Thompson from the novel by Humphrey Cobb • *Cinematographer* Georg Krause

Patlabor: the Mobile Police ★★★ PG

Animated adventure
1989 · Jpn · Colour · 98mins

With *manga* movies, the emphasis is usually on ultra violence and stunning design, but this is a more cerebral affair. The plot revolves around an attempt by the Tokyo police, assisted by advanced robots, to track down a gang of criminals intent on bringing down the city. There are still the trademark scenes of explosive action, but director Mamoru Oshii takes a more measured approach to the tale. A sequel followed in 1993. JF. A Japanese language film. [video] DVD

Dir Mamoru Oshii • *Scr* Kazunori Ito, from a story by Masami Yuuki

The Patricia Neal Story: an Act of Love ★★★★

Drama based on a true story
1981 · US · Colour · 100mins

A well-cast TV movie about the Oscar-winning actress Patricia Neal's recovery from a series of debilitating strokes, benefiting immensely from the sensitive playing of Glenda Jackson as Neal and an intelligent script from Robert Anderson. Although lacking Neal's American ranginess (and accent), Jackson possesses the resolute wilfulness the part needs, and she performs beautifully. Dirk Bogarde plays celebrated children's novelist Roald Dahl, who was married to Neal at the time of the story. TS

Glenda Jackson *Patricia Neal* • Dirk Bogarde *Roald Dahl* • Ken Kercheval *Dr Charles Carton* • Jane Merrow *Val Eaton* • John Reilly *Barry Farrell* • James Hayden *Martin Sheen* ■ *Dir* Anthony Harvey, Anthony Page • *Scr* Robert Anderson, from the book *Pat and Roald* by Barry Farrell

Patrick ★★★ 18

Horror 1978 · Aus · Colour · 107mins

Although it rather loses its way, this Gothic grotesque benefits from the creepy atmosphere director Richard Franklin generates in the hospital ward, where the comatose Robert Thompson develops a passion for nurse Susan Penhaligon that acts as a catalyst for a series of increasingly malevolent telekinetic happenings. Amid the mayhem, there is a delicious performance from ballet maestro Robert Helpmann as a sadistic doctor. DP [video]

Susan Penhaligon *Kathy Jacquard* • Robert Helpmann *Dr Roget* • Rod Mullinar *Ed Jacquard* • Bruce Barry *Dr Brian Wright* • Julia Blake *Matron Cassidy* • Helen Hemingway *Sister Williams* • Robert Thompson *Patrick* ■ *Dir* Richard Franklin • *Scr* Everett de Roche

Patrick the Great ★★ U

Musical comedy 1944 · US · BW · 89mins

This breezy musical has the usual corny showbiz setting, but it allows Donald O'Connor and Peggy Ryan to shine in a few pleasant numbers and gives O'Connor the chance to perform some spectacular tap-dancing. The paper-thin plot has O'Connor and his father (a colourless Donald Cook) as rivals for the same part in a Broadway show. Eve Arden, usually relied on to perk up the dullest screenplay, only has a few wisecracks here. RB

Donald O'Connor *Pat Donahue Jr* • Peggy Ryan *Judy Watkins* • Frances Dee *Lynn Andrews* • Donald Cook *Pat Donahue Sr* • Eve Arden *Jean Mathews* • Thomas Gomez *Max*

P

Wilson ■ *Dir* Frank Ryan • *Scr* Dorothy Bennett, Bertram Millhauser, from a story by Jane Hall, Frederick Kohner, Ralph Block

The Patriot

Silent historical drama
1928 · US · BW · 113mins

Sadly, no prints exist of this now lost film, in which Emil Jannings is the tyrannical Tsar Paul I, in the grip of dangerous insanity, so his trusted confidante Lewis Stone puts aside loyalty to his ruler in an attempt to save his country. This drama was the last silent to be directed by Ernst Lubitsch, here departing from his customary romantic comedies; it was also the first film made during his long and sparklingly successful tenure at Paramount. Jannings, a frequent Lubitsch star in Germany, was nearing the end of his Hollywood sojourn, his thick German accent unsuited to the talkies. Stone, Lubitsch and the picture were all nominated for Oscars, but the only winner was Hans Kräly's screenplay. RK

Emil Jannings *Tsar Paul the First* • Lewis Stone *Count Pahlen* • Florence Vidor *Countess Ostermann* • Neil Hamilton *Crown Prince Alexander* • Harry Cording *Stefan* • Vera Voronina *Mlle Lapoukhine* ■ *Dir* Ernst Lubitsch • *Scr* Hans Kräly, Julian Johnson, from the novel *Der Patriot: Drama in 5 Akten* by Alfred Neumann, from its stage adaptation by Ashley Dukes, from the story *Paul I* by Dimitri Merejkowski

The Patriot ★ 15

Action drama 1986 · US · Colour · 88mins

This apology for a movie is unmitigated rubbish, with dire production levels, a non-plot and an unintentionally camp air. Gregg Henry stars as a burned-out Vietnam vet redeeming his dignity by attempting to save the western world from nuclear annihilation. AJ. Contains violence and nudity.

Gregg Henry *Lieutenant Matt Ryder* • Simone Griffeth *Sean* • Michael J Pollard *Howard* • Jeff Conaway *Mitchell* • Stack Pierce *Atkins* • Leslie Nielsen *Admiral Frazer* ■ *Dir* Frank Harris • *Scr* Andy Ruben, Katt Shea Ruben

The Patriot ★★ 18

Action adventure 1998 · US · Colour · 86mins

Martial arts specialist Steven Seagal stars as a rancher and doctor in Montana whose neighbour is a militant extremist with a biological weapon that threatens human existence on Earth. Seagal's peaceful, eco-friendly message sits beside a further message about native Americans and is sorted out with lashings of violence. The best thing about the picture is its magnificent landscapes, beautifully caught under the direction of Dean Semler, the Oscar-winning cameraman of *Dances with Wolves*. AT. Contains swearing and violence. DVD

Steven Seagal *Wesley McClaren* • Gailard Sartain *Floyd Chisholm* • LQ Jones *Frank* • Silas Weir Mitchell *Pogue* • Dan Beene *Dr Richard Bach* • Damon Collazo *Lieutenant Johnson* • Brad Leland *Big Bob* • Molly McClure *Molly* ■ *Dir* Dean Semler • *Scr* M Sussman, John Kingswell, from a story by M Sussman, from the novel *The Last Canadian* by William Heine • *Cinematographer* Stephen Windom

The Patriot ★★★ 15

Period war drama
2000 · US · Colour · 157mins

Mel Gibson stars in this action drama set during the American War of Independence. He's living peacefully in South Carolina who, along with his gung-ho son Heath Ledger, comes out fighting against the English army. The battle scenes are ferociously well-staged, but some may baulk at the almost pantomimic villainy of Jason Isaacs's cruel Colonel Tavington and the historically inaccurate atrocities he is seen to commit. TH. Contains violence and swearing. DVD

Mel Gibson *Benjamin Martin* • Heath Ledger *Gabriel Martin* • Joely Richardson *Charlotte Selton* • Tcheky Karyo *Major Jean Villeneuve* • Jason Isaacs *Colonel William Tavington* • Tom Wilkinson *General Cornwallis* • Chris Cooper *Colonel Harry Burwell* ■ *Dir* Roland Emmerich • *Scr* Robert Rodat

Patriot Games ★★★ 15

Thriller 1992 · US · Colour · 111mins

Harrison Ford takes over from Alec Baldwin as CIA analyst Jack Ryan in this follow-up to box-office hit *The Hunt for Red October*. Director Phillip Noyce has the now former agency man rescuing peer James Fox from an IRA attack in London and being hounded for his trouble by psychotic renegade terrorist Sean Bean. But, apart from one brilliant sequence showing a remote-controlled desert massacre, Noyce's thriller (based on the novel by Tom Clancy) never gets its act together to provide the direct appeal that all good action movies should have. TH. Contains swearing. DVD

Harrison Ford *Jack Ryan* • Anne Archer *Dr Cathy Ryan* • Patrick Bergin *Kevin O'Donnell* • Sean Bean *Sean Miller* • Thora Birch *Sally Ryan* • James Fox *Lord Holmes* • Samuel L Jackson *Robby Jackson* • Polly Walker *Annette* • James Earl Jones *Admiral James Greer* • Richard Harris *Paddy O'Neil* ■ *Dir* Phillip Noyce • *Scr* W Peter Iliff, Donald Stewart, Steve Zaillian, from the novel by Tom Clancy

Patriots 

Thriller 1994 · Fr · Colour · 80mins

Eric Rochant's in-depth investigation into the methodology of modern espionage has been painstakingly researched and staged. Yvan Attal plays the young Parisian Ariel, who joins the Mossad and is dispatched to obtain the blueprints of a French nuclear power plant. But for all the character's idealism and eventual disillusionment, he simply gets lost in the works. Interminably long and only fitfully interesting. DP. In French with English subtitles.

Yvan Attal *Ariel* • Yossi Banai *Yossi* • Sandrine Kiberlain *Marie-Claude* • Richard Masur *Jeremy Pelman* • Nancy Allen *Catherine Pelman* • Allen Garfield *Eagleman* • Christine Pascal *Laurence* ■ *Dir/Scr* Eric Rochant

The Patsy ★★★

Silent comedy drama
1928 · US · BW · 64mins

King Vidor's silent showcases the not inconsiderable comedic talents of Marion Davies. The unimportant plot concerns the efforts of Davies to overcome her position as the family "patsy" and captivate her sister's boyfriend. The high point has Davies, for no particular reason, doing very funny impersonations of silent stars Mae Murray, Lillian Gish and the exotic Pola Negri. RK

Marion Davies *Patricia Harrington* • Orville Caldwell *Tony Anderson* • Marie Dressler *Ma Harrington* • Dell Henderson *Pa Harrington* • Lawrence Gray *Billy* • Jane Winton *Grace Harrington* ■ *Dir* King Vidor • *Scr* Agnes Christine Johnston, Ralph Spence (titles), from the play by Barry Connors

The Patsy ★★★ U

Comedy 1964 · US · Colour · 101mins

A very black premise indeed from Jerry Lewis, whose adulation by French cineastes is sometimes regarded with puzzlement here. Judge for yourself, as co-writer/director Lewis casts star Jerry as the bellboy who stumbles upon a group of desperate showbiz types who have lost their meal ticket and who groom Lewis to replace the noted comedian killed in a plane crash. Tasteless, but also clever and very funny, with a marvellous cast. It may be a one-gag sketch stretched to feature length, but it works for the brilliant Lewis. TS DVD

Jerry Lewis *Stanley Belt* • Ina Balin *Ellen Betz* • Everett Sloane *Caryl Fergusson* • Keenan Wynn *Harry Silver* • Peter Lorre *Morgan Heywood* • John Carradine *Bruce Alden* • Phil Harris *Chic Wymore* • Hans Conried *Dr Mulerrr* ■ *Dir* Jerry Lewis • *Scr* Jerry Lewis, Bill Richmond

Patterns ★★★

Drama 1956 · US · BW · 83mins

This exposé of unethical American big business is a remake of a live television play. In Rod Serling's strong script Van Heflin portrays the new business executive who is being groomed by the Machiavellian company head, Everett Sloane, to replace the ageing and likeable Ed Begley. Shooting in New York, director Fielder Cook extracts fine performances from the cast and the ending is not quite what you'd expect. AE

Van Heflin *Fred Staples* • Everett Sloane *Walter Ramsey* • Ed Begley *William Briggs* • Beatrice Straight *Nancy Staples* • Elizabeth Wilson *Marge Fleming* • Joanna Roos *Miss Lanier* ■ *Dir* Fielder Cook • *Scr* Rod Serling, from his TV play

Patti Rocks ★★★ 18

Comedy 1987 · US · Colour · 83mins

Karen Landry is a man-wary Minnesotan who tells her chauvinist boyfriend Chris Mulkey she's pregnant. Unfortunately, Mulkey is married with children and doesn't know how he's going to break it to her. An incisive look at masculine double-standards and hypocrisy, David Burton Morris's fiercely independent feature digs down deep and isn't afraid to get dirty doing it. Tough-talking and adult. AJ

Chris Mulkey *Billy Regis* • John Jenkins *Eddie Hassit* • Karen Landry *Patti Rocks* • David L Turk *Barge worker* • Stephen Yoakam *Bartender* ■ *Dir* David Burton Morris • *Scr* David Burton Morris, Chris Mulkey, John Jenkins, Karen Landry, from characters created by Victoria Wozniak in the film *Loose Ends*

Patton ★★★★★ PG

Biographical drama
1970 · US · Colour · 163mins

Released while US forces were still in Vietnam, this can be viewed as both a tribute to the indomitability of the fighting man and a satire on the myth of the American hero. The screenplay, by Francis Ford Coppola and Edmund H North, received one of the picture's seven Oscars, while director Franklin J Schaffner took another, thanks to the horrific majesty of the battle sequences. But the bedrock of this biopic is the performance in the title role of George C Scott, who became the first actor in Oscar history to refuse his award. Combining blimpish bluster with moments of monstrous ego and unexpected humanity, Scott makes this unforgettable. DP. Contains swearing. DVD

George C Scott *General Patton* • Karl Malden *General Bradley* • Michael Bates *Field Marshal Montgomery* • Stephen Young *Captain Hansen* • Michael Strong *Brig Gen Carver* • Cary Loftin *General Bradley's driver* • Albert Dumortier *Moroccan minister* • Frank Latimore *Lt Col Davenport* ■ *Dir* Franklin J Schaffner • *Scr* Francis Ford Coppola, Edmund H North, from the books *Patton: Ordeal and Triumph* by Ladislas Farago and *A Soldier's Story* by General Omar N Bradley

Patty Hearst ★★ 18

Biographical drama
1988 · US/UK · Colour · 103mins

The career low of writer/director Paul Schrader. Inspired by Patricia Hearst's autobiography, this was meant to be a bold cinematic experiment to re-create the deprivations and sensations that transformed her from want-for-nothing press heiress into committed terrorist. Yet Schrader's use of darkness, dazzling light and off-screen voices fails to convey the fearful disorientation, and the Symbionese Liberation Army propaganda soon has the attention wandering. DP. Contains violence, swearing, nudity. DVD

Natasha Richardson *Patricia Campbell Hearst* • William Forsythe *Teko* • Ving Rhames *Cinque* • Frances Fisher *Yolanda* • Jodi Long *Wendy Yoshimura* • Olivia Barash *Fahizah* • Dana Delany *Gelina* ■ *Dir* Paul Schrader • *Scr* Nicholas Kazan, from the autobiography *Every Secret Thing* by Patricia Campbell Hearst, Alvin Moscow

Paul and Michelle ★

Romantic drama
1974 · Fr/UK · Colour · 102mins

Lewis Gilbert directs this sequel to his own tale of teenage romance, *Friends* (1971). Yet, in his long career, he never missed his step as badly as this. Every emotion and every romantic interlude rings false, as Sorbonne student Sean Bury seeks to lure Anicée Alvina away from pilot Keir Dullea. The performances are insufferably inept and Claude Renoir's cloying soft-focus photography only makes things worse. DP

Anicée Alvina *Michelle Latour* • Sean Bury *Paul Harrison* • Keir Dullea *Garry* • Ronald Lewis *Sir Robert Harrison* • Catherine Allégret *Joanna* ■ *Dir* Lewis Gilbert • *Scr* Angela Huth, Vernon Harris, from a story by Lewis Gilbert

Paulie ★★★ U

Comedy adventure
1998 · US · Colour · 87mins

Voiced by Jay Mohr, Paulie is a blue-crown conure parrot who lives in the basement of an animal study institute. How he got there and why he's so desperate to find the little girl he helped cure of a stammer form the basis of the story, as told to the building's Russian janitor, Tony Shalhoub. Refreshingly free of gratuitous pyrotechnics and sentimental moralising, this fine-feathered film has longueurs, but mostly flies by. DP DVD

Gena Rowlands *Ivy* • Tony Shalhoub *Misha* • Cheech Marin [Richard "Cheech" Marin] *Ignacio* • Bruce Davison *Dr Reingold* • Jay Mohr *Paulie/Benny* • Trini Alvarado *Adult Marie* • Buddy Hackett *Artie* • Hallie Kate Eisenberg *Marie* ■ *Dir* John Roberts • *Scr* Laurie Craig

Pauline & Paulette ★★★★ PG

Comedy drama
2001 · Bel/Neth/Fr · Colour · 74mins

Tackling such sensitive issues as age, sibling responsibility and self-sacrifice with a frankness that belies the film's "chocolate-box" visual style, director Lieven Debrauwer's cosily caustic study of relative values is a delight. As the gaudy boutique owner who has to care for an elderly sister – with the mental age of a child – to claim her share of an inheritance, Ann Petersen achieves the perfect blend of kitsch and bitch that makes Dora van der Groen's infantile dottiness seem both harmless and harrowing. With Hilde Duyck's picture-book art direction reinforcing the fairy-tale atmosphere, this is disarmingly droll and endlessly endearing. DP. In Flemish with English subtitles. DVD

Ann Petersen *Paulette* • Dora van der Groen *Pauline* • Rosemarie Bergmans *Cécile* • Idwig Stéphane *Albert* • Julienne de Bruyn *Martha* • Camilia Blereau *Butcher's wife* ■ *Dir* Lieven Debrauwer • *Scr* Lieven Debrauwer, Jaak Boon

Pauline at the Beach

★★★★ 15

Comedy drama 1983 · Fr · Colour · 90mins

Earning Eric Rohmer the Best Director prize at Berlin, this was originally conceived in the 1950s, with Brigitte Bardot in the role of the flirtatious divorcee that was eventually taken by Arielle Dombasle. Considerably racier than Rohmer's earlier outings, but just as witty and eloquent, the film is light enough to be blown away on the same sea breeze which fans the flames of holiday lust felt by Dombasle and her cousin, Amanda Langlet, as they dally between a trio of willing men. Sparklingly played, sunnily photographed and staged with a master's touch. DP. In French with English subtitles. VIDEO DVD

Amanda Langlet *Pauline* • Arielle Dombasle *Marion* • Pascal Greggory *Pierre* • Feodor Atkine *Henry* • Simon de la Brosse *Sylvain* ■ *Dir/Scr* Eric Rohmer • *Cinematographer* Nestor Almendros

Pavilion of Women

★★ 15

Period drama
2000 · Chi/US · Colour · 111mins

Set in southern China in the late 1930s, Ho Yim's grandiose adaptation concerns the domestic trials of Yan Luo, whose husband and son both fall in love with concubine Yi Ding, while Yan becomes enamoured of Willem Dafoe, the American missionary she has hired to educate wayward offspring John Cho. Packing in the epic incidents as though they had to be ticked off some historical checklist, Ho certainly achieves a sense of time and place, but he seems detached from his characters. DP. In Mandarin and English with subtitles. Contains violence, sex scenes. VIDEO DVD

Willem Dafoe *Father Andre* • Yan Luo *Madame Wu* • Sau Shek *Mr Wu* • John Cho *Wu Fengmo* • Yi Ding *Chiuming* • Koh Chieng Mun *Ying* ■ *Dir* Ho Yim • *Scr* Yan Luo, Paul R Collins, from the novel by Pearl S Buck

Paw

★★★

Drama 1959 · Den · Colour · 93mins

Denmark received its first Oscar nomination for this popular picture. Working from her own script, director Astrid Henning-Jensen draws on the documentary experience gained in partnership with her husband, Bjarne. There's a pleasing authenticity to this tale of a West Indian orphan billeted on his Danish aunt, and Jimmy Sterman's disillusion with his racist schoolmates is as convincing as his delight in the local wildlife. The drama may be naive in both message and staging, but the intentions are admirable. DP

Jimmy Sterman *Paw* • Edvin Adolphson *Anders Nilsson* • Ninja Tholstrup *Aunt Frieda* • Asbjørn Andersen *Yvonne* ■ *Dir* Astrid Henning-Jensen • *Scr* Astrid Henning-Jensen, Bjarne Henning-Jensen, from the story *Paw, der Indianerjunge* by Torry Gredsted

The Pawnbroker

★★★★★ 12

Psychological drama
1965 · US · BW · 110mins

Rod Steiger established his credentials as an actor of international standing with this complex psychological portrait of a Holocaust survivor. He's a Jewish refugee in New York who has tried to withdraw from life into the small fortress of the Harlem pawn shop where he works, but is inescapably haunted by his memories of the concentration camp. Director Sidney Lumet treats his material with solemnity and compassion, and the tone is sensitively enhanced by an evocative jazz score from first-time film composer Quincy Jones. AME VIDEO

Rod Steiger *Sol Nazerman* • Geraldine Fitzgerald *Marilyn Birchfield* • Brock Peters *Rodriguez* • Jaime Sanchez *Jesus Ortiz* • Thelma Oliver *Ortiz's girl* • Marketa Kimbrell *Tessie* • Baruch Lumet *Mendel* ■ *Dir* Sidney Lumet • *Scr* David Friedkin, Morton Fine, from the novel by Edward Lewis Wallant

The Pawnshop

★★★★ U

Silent comedy 1916 · US · BW · 20mins

One of the first of the dozen short films that Charlie Chaplin made for Mutual, this is a slight, but extremely effective comedy with Chaplin as an assistant in a pawnbroker's shop "where the depressed poor come to try to redeem their pledges". There is some remarkable knockabout as Chaplin battles with his colleague John Rand and abuses his customers, but also more subtle moments such as the sequence in which the star tries to wash dishes by pushing them through a clothes wringer, repeats the process to dry them and then cleans his hands in the same way. For lovers of happy endings, the ever-loving Edna Purviance is in there along with the jokes. TH VIDEO

Charles Chaplin *Pawnshop assistant* • Edna Purviance *Daughter* • John Rand *Clerk* • Henry Bergman *Pawnbroker* • Albert Austin *Customer* ■ *Dir/Scr* Charles Chaplin

Paws

★★★ U

Comedy adventure
1997 · UK/Aus · Colour · 80mins

This good-natured comedy is about a computer literate Jack Russell terrier called PC who speaks with the aid of a microchip voice implant. Though the main story is pretty standard – a missing fortune, a recently bereaved teenager – director Karl Zwicky whisks the slapstick humour, technical gimmickry, outrageous action and appealing animal whimsy into a subtle soufflé packed with emotional warmth. Billy Connolly is brilliant as PC's voice. AJ VIDEO

Billy Connolly *PC* • Nathan Cavaleri *Zac Feldman* • Emilie François *Samantha Arkwright* • Joe Petruzzi *Stephen Feldman* • Caroline Gillmer *Susie Arkwright* • Rachael Blake *Amy Feldman* ■ *Dir* Karl Zwicky • *Scr* Harry Cripps, from a story by Harry Cripps, from a story by Karl Zwicky, Stephen Dando-Collins

Pay Day

★★★ U

Silent comedy 1922 · US · BW · 22mins

This was the last of Charlie Chaplin's short films, coming just after *The Kid* (1921) and before his non-starring drama, *A Woman of Paris* (1923). It's about what happens when a pay check finally arrives in a working-class home and stars Chaplin as a construction worker struggling to avoid the wrath of his nagging wife. There are some inventive sight gags, but also some sour social significance – it shows the lengths the needy will go to for money. TH VIDEO

Charles Chaplin *Worker* • Phyllis Allen *His wife* • Mack Swain *The foreman* • Edna Purviance *Foreman's daughter* • Sydney Chaplin [Syd Chaplin] *Friend* ■ *Dir/Scr* Charles Chaplin

Pay It Forward

★★ 12

Comedy drama 2000 · US · Colour · 118mins

When asked to come up with a way of making the world a better place as part of a class project, schoolboy Haley Joel Osment concocts the notion of carrying out random acts of kindness to strangers, who then pay the favour forward to new beneficiaries rather than back to the giver. This notion brings together the youngster's emotionally scarred, alcoholic mum (Helen Hunt) and physically scarred schoolteacher (Kevin Spacey), both in need of companionship. Reasonable performances in stereotyped roles sustain interest during the early part of film, but the sentimentality may prove hard to stomach. DA VIDEO DVD

Kevin Spacey *Eugene Simonet* • Helen Hunt *Arlene McKinney* • Haley Joel Osment *Trevor McKinney* • Jay Mohr *Chris Chandler* • James Caviezel [Jim Caviezel] *Jerry* • Jon Bon Jovi *Ricky* • Angie Dickinson *Grace* ■ *Dir* Mimi Leder • *Scr* Leslie Dixon, from a novel by Catherine Ryan Hyde

Pay or Die

★★★

Crime drama based on a true story
1960 · US · BW · 111mins

From the opening religious ceremony in New York's Little Italy in which the evil force of the "Black Hand" cuts down a girl dressed as an angel, this is a powerful study, based on fact, of a community living in fear. Relishing the opportunity to play a heroic role, Ernest Borgnine gives a vivid and rounded performance as the tough and incorruptible cop who heads a special force to fight the Mafia's secret terror organisation. Director Richard Wilson brings a fresh look to familiar situations helped by a supporting cast of little-known players. AE

Ernest Borgnine *Lt Joseph Petrosino* • Zohra Lampert *Adelina Saulino* • Alan Austin *Johnny Viscardi* • Robert F Simon *Commissioner* • Renata Vanni *Mama Saulino* • Bruno Della Santina *Papa Saulino* ■ *Dir* Richard Wilson • *Scr* Richard Collins, Bertram Millhauser, from the short story *Pay-Off in Sicily* by Burnett Hershey

Payback

★★ 15

Drama 1997 · US · Colour · 83mins

In this TV movie, Mary Tyler Moore plays a shop owner who one night witnesses a gang of policemen beat a robbery suspect half to death. Reluctantly, she agrees to testify against them, only to find a campaign of harassment being launched against her entire family. Moore and her forner sitcom co-star Edward Asner deliver capable performances but are let down by the plodding direction of Ken Cameron. JF. Contains violence and some swearing. VIDEO DVD

Mary Tyler Moore *Kathryn Stanfill* • Edward Asner *Lt Jack Patkanis* ■ *Dir* Ken Cameron • *Scr* Dennis Nemec

Payback

★★★ 18

Action crime thriller
1998 · US · Colour · 96mins

The source material that provided Lee Marvin with an unforgettable role in *Point Blank* is here recycled for the solid directing debut of *LA Confidential* writer Brian Helgeland (though he refused to re-shoot some scenes and has effectively disowned the result). Mel Gibson stars as violent antihero Porter, a professional thief who seeks revenge when his wife and crime partner double-cross him during a successful hold-up of some Chinese gangsters and leave him for dead. AJ. Contains violence, some swearing and sex scenes. VIDEO DVD

Mel Gibson *Porter* • Gregg Henry *Val* • Maria Bello *Rosie* • David Paymer *Stegman* • Bill Duke *Detective Hicks* • Deborah Kara Unger *Lynn* • John Glover *Phil* • William Devane *Carter* • Kris Kristofferson *Bronson* • James Coburn *Fairfax* ■ *Dir* Brian Helgeland • *Scr* Brian Helgeland, Terry Hayes, from the novel *The Hunter* by Richard Stark [Donald E Westlake]

Paycheck

★★ 12

Science-fiction action thriller
2003 · US · Colour · 113mins

Electronics genius Ben Affleck undertakes the last in a series of lucrative, top-secret corporate projects that require a memory-wipe on completion. Emerging with no recollection of the three years that have passed, including a relationship with biologist Uma Thurman, he's baffled to discover he's forfeited his pay in favour of an envelope of apparently worthless items. Director John Woo's vision of the future is an uninspiring, under-stylised twist on the present. SF VIDEO DVD

Ben Affleck *Michael Jennings* • Aaron Eckhart *Rethrick* • Uma Thurman *Rachel Porter* • Paul Giamatti *Shorty* • Colm Feore *Wolfe* • Joe Morton *Agent Dodge* • Michael C Hall *Agent Klein* ■ *Dir* John Woo • *Scr* Dean Georgaris, from the short story by Philip K Dick

Payday

★★★★

Drama 1972 · US · Colour · 103mins

Rip Torn gives the definitive performance of a fading country-and-western star in this magnificently grim but sadly overlooked film that uncompromisingly captures the music business gone sour. Torn – cruel, self-centred and as empty as the bottle he is always holding – has never been better. The film follows his last 36 hours as he ping-pongs from one low-life honky-tonk bar to another, portraying the booze, the groupies, the hangers-on and the pay-offs in a manner as far away from rhinestones and fringes as it is possible to get. FL

Rip Torn *Maury Dann* • Ahna Capri *Mayleen* • Elayne Heilveil *Rosamond* • Michael C Gwynne *Clarence* ■ *Dir* Daryl Duke • *Scr* Don Carpenter

Paydirt

★★ 15

Crime comedy 1992 · US · Colour · 84mins

Jeff Daniels, a prison psychiatrist, is beset by a run of bad luck which sees him lose his house and his girlfriend. Salvation comes in the dying statement of one of the prisoners, who tells him of a huge amount of loot stashed away in the basement of a house in Cherry Hill, New Jersey. This exchange is overheard by two other prisoners, who break out of jail with the intention of beating Daniels to the loot. Thin but amiable. DF VIDEO

Jeff Daniels *Willis Embry* • Rhea Perlman *Lydia* • Dabney Coleman *Jeffrey* • Catherine O'Hara *Jessie* • Hector Elizondo *Norman* ■ *Dir/Scr* Bill Phillips

Payment Deferred

★★★

Murder drama 1932 · US · BW · 80mins

Charles Laughton is brilliant, despite some pretty hokey dialogue, as a poverty-stricken bank teller, with a wife (Dorothy Peterson) and daughter (Maureen O'Sullivan) to support, who resorts to poisoning his wealthy nephew (a young, almost unrecognisable, Ray Milland). Directed by Lothar Mendes, who perfectly captures the grimly claustrophobic atmosphere of an ugly, constantly rain-drenched suburban house and the bleak lives of its inhabitants, this is a curiously intriguing little piece. RK

Charles Laughton *William Marble* • Neil Hamilton *Gordon Holmes* • Maureen O'Sullivan *Winnie Marble* • Dorothy Peterson *Annie Marble* • Verree Teasdale *Mme Collins* • Ray Milland *James Medland* • Billy Bevan *Hammond* ■ *Dir* Lothar Mendes • *Scr* Ernest Vajda, Claudine West, from the play by Jeffrey Dell

Payment on Demand

★★★

Melodrama 1951 · US · BW · 90mins

Bette Davis is stunned when husband Barry Sullivan announces he loves Frances Dee and wants a divorce. At first she turns vindictive, until she realises her own contribution to the breakdown of her marriage. Curtis Bernhardt's movie eschews the more obvious clichés of the genre and charts the course of the central relationship in flashback. The first of Davis's films as a freelance following her rupture with Warner Bros after 18 years under contract, it was made

P

before the hugely successful *All About Eve*, but released after. RK

Bette Davis *Joyce Ramsey* • Barry Sullivan *David Ramsey* • Jane Cowl *Mrs Hedges* • Kent Taylor *Robert Townsend* • Betty Lynn *Martha Ramsey* • Frances Dee *Eileen Benson* • Peggie Castle *Diana Ramsey* ■ *Dir* Curtis Bernhardt • *Scr* Bruce Manning, Curtis Bernhardt

Payroll ★★ PG

Crime drama 1961 · UK · BW · 102mins

Sidney Hayers is one of the forgotten journeymen of 1960s British cinema. This is a solidly crafted crime story in which the perfect blag begins to unravel as the gang lies low. Michael Craig is on surprisingly good form as the gang leader, but it's Billie Whitelaw, as the widow of a murdered security van guard, who commands centre stage as she risks her own life to snare the culprits. DP

Michael Craig *Johnny Mellors* • Françoise Prévost *Katie Pearson* • Billie Whitelaw *Jackie Parker* • William Lucas *Dennis Pearson* • Kenneth Griffith *Monty* • Tom Bell *Blackie* ■ *Dir* Sidney Hayers • *Scr* George Baxt, from the novel by Derek Bickerton

The Peace Game ★★★

Futuristic satire 1969 · Swe · Colour · 91mins

Made four years after the BBC banned his Oscar-winning holocaust masterpiece, *The War Game*, Peter Watkins sought to wreak revenge on the Establishment by holding it up to ridicule in this futuristic satire. Comfortably predating the millennial vogue for actuality TV, the premise posits that warfare has been outlawed and that the global hierarchy is now decided by a cynical updating of the ancient gladiatorial games, which are more a means of mass repression than a celebration of national prowess. Cinematographer Peter Suschitzky achieves some memorable images, but Watkins's message is lost in the imprecision of his protest. DP

Arthur Pentelow *British general* • Frederick Danner *British staff officer* • Hans Bendrik *Capt Davidsson* • Daniel Harle *French officer* • Hans Berger *West German officer* • Rosario Gianetti *American officer* ■ *Dir* Peter Watkins • *Scr* Nicholas Gosling, Peter Watkins

The Peacekeeper ★★★ 15

Action thriller 1997 · Can · Colour · 94mins

Any resemblance to the George Clooney/Nicole Kidman vehicle *The Peacemaker* is, of course, completely intentional! Actually, this suspense thriller gives that post-Cold War adventure a good run for its money, as maverick air force major Dolph Lundgren gets in the way of a sinister plot to nuke Washington. An exciting roof-top car chase and an explosive attack on Mount Rushmore make up for the two-dimensional acting from Lundgren in this better-than-average flag-waver. AJ. Contains swearing and violence. DVD

Dolph Lundgren *Major Frank Cross* • Montel Williams *Lt Col Northrop* • Michael Sarrazin *Lt Col Douglas Murphy* • Roy Scheider *President Robert Baker* • Christopher Heyerdahl *Hettinger* ■ *Dir* Frederic Forestier • *Scr* Robert Geoffrion, James H Stewart

Peacemaker ★★★ 18

Science-fiction action thriller
1990 · US · Colour · 87mins

Despite an at times quite noticeable low budget this exhilarating sci-fi thriller really delivers the goods for action fans. A well-worn theme for sure – alien cop tracking down alien villain – but the twist comes when they crash-land on Earth and both claim to be the good guy. Cue a virtual non-stop montage of chases, explosions and shoot-outs. Kevin S Tenney keeps you engrossed, while Robert Forster and Lance Edwards as the humanoid and virtually indestructible aliens make it fun guessing who's who. RS

Robert Forster *Yates* • Lance Edwards *Townsend* • Hilary Shepard *Dori Caisson* • Robert Davi *Sergeant Frank Ramos* • Bert Remsen *Doc* • John Denos *Reeger* • Wally Taylor *Moses* ■ *Dir/Scr* Kevin S Tenney

The Peacemaker ★★★ 15

Action thriller 1997 · US · Colour · 118mins

George Clooney and Nicole Kidman attempt to save Manhattan from nuclear destruction in his pacey thriller. When a Russian train is blown up to disguise the theft of a nuclear warhead, the stage is set for a nailbiting countdown. Kidman isn't entirely convincing as a government scientist, but Clooney gives a confident lead performance as a Special Forces officer. This failed to ignite at the box office, but action fans will enjoy the irresistible combination of explosions, car crashes and shots of the ticking bomb. AT. Contains violence, swearing. DVD

George Clooney *Thomas Devoe* • Nicole Kidman *Julia Kelly* • Armin Mueller-Stahl *Dimitri Vertikoff* • Marcel Iures *Dusan Gavrich* • Alexander Baluev *Alexsander Kodoroff* • Rene Medvesek *Vlado Mirich* • Randall Batinkoff *Ken* ■ *Dir* Mimi Leder • *Scr* Michael Schiffer, from an article by Leslie Cockburn, Andrew Cockburn

Peaches ★★ 15

Comedy 2000 · Ire · Colour · 82mins

In Nick Grosso's adaptation of his own 1994 play, peaches are pretty girls and the obsession of likely lads Matthew Rhys, Justin Salinger and Matthew Dunster. Rhys is the focus of attention, discovering that he would actually like his girl "friend", Kelly Reilly, to be rather more than a "chick for chats", but is at a complete loss as to how to woo her. Salinger and Dunster are mere two-dimensional cut-outs with a crass *Loaded* mentality and little else. LH DVD

Matthew Rhys *Frank* • Kelly Reilly *Cherry* • Justin Salinger *Johnny* ■ *Dir* Nick Grosso • *Scr* Nick Grosso, from his play

The Peanut Butter Solution ★★★ PG

Fantasy drama 1985 · Can · Colour · 90mins

A Roald Dahl-style children's fantasy from Canada, also known as *Michael's Fright*. After losing all his hair, young Mathew Mackay is given a special type of peanut butter which is supposed to help his hair grow back. Unfortunately, he uses too much and is soon rivalling Samson in the long tresses department. A fun tale that will delight most children. JB

Mathew Mackay *Mathew Baskin* • Siluck Saysanasy *Connie* • Alison Podbrey *Suzie* • Michael Hogan (3) *Billy* • Michael Maillot *Signor* ■ *Dir/Scr* Michael Rubbo

Pearl Harbor ★★ 12

Second World War romantic drama
2001 · US · Colour · 175mins

The surprise bombing of Pearl Harbor on 7 December 1941 is a major event in US history and who better to capture it on-screen than the big-thinking producer/director team of Jerry Bruckheimer and Michael Bay? Perhaps unsurprisingly, the actual attack, which forms the middle act of the film's bloated three hours, is an amazing spectacle. But sheer cinematic power is undermined by our total lack of empathy for any of the cardboard cut-out characters. Weaknesses of plot are only amplified by the film's unwieldy size, while the script is toe-curling. AC. Contains some violence. DVD

Ben Affleck *Rafe McCawley* • Josh Hartnett *Danny Walker* • Kate Beckinsale *Evelyn Johnson* • Cuba Gooding Jr *Doris "Dorie" Miller* • Tom Sizemore *Earl Sistern* • Jon Voight *President Franklin D Roosevelt* • Colm Feore *Admiral Kimmel* • Alec Baldwin *Gen James H Doolittle* • Dan Aykroyd *Captain Thurman* ■ *Dir* Michael Bay • *Scr* Randall Wallace • *Cinematographer* John Schwartzman

The Pearl of Death ★★★ PG

Mystery 1944 · US · BW · 68mins

Basil Rathbone and Nigel Bruce did pick 'em! This is the one in which Rondo Hatton creeps out of the crypt of bad dreams as homicidal sidekick to jewel thief Miles Mander. Not only is he encumbered with a zombie-lumbering walk and a nasty ability to break backs, but also an unhealthy obsession with Evelyn Ankers that results in the villain's comeuppance – a nightmare for us, but an elementary deduction for Holmes, if not Watson. TH DVD

Basil Rathbone *Sherlock Holmes* • Nigel Bruce *Dr Watson* • Evelyn Ankers *Naomi Drake* • Dennis Hoey *Inspector Lestrade* • Miles Mander *Giles Conover* • Rondo Hatton *"Creeper"* ■ *Dir* Roy William Neill • *Scr* Bertram Millhauser, from the story *The Adventure of the Six Napoleons* by Sir Arthur Conan Doyle

Pearl of the South Pacific ★★ U

Adventure 1955 · US · Colour · 84mins

This piece of tosh is immensely enjoyable if you're unsophisticated, aged under ten, or both. There's a great deal of period charm in the Technicolored tale for fans of both the exotic and of cheesy interior set dressing trying to look like authentic locations, but, although Virginia Mayo is just about adequate in the lead, her co-stars, Dennis Morgan and David Farrar, are well past their primes. TS

Virginia Mayo *Rita Delaine* • Dennis Morgan *Dan Merrill* • David Farrar *Bully Hayes* • Lance Fuller *George* • Murvyn Vye *Halemano* ■ *Dir* Allan Dwan • *Scr* Talbot Jennings, Jesse Lasky Jr, from a story by Anna Hunger

La Peau Douce ★★★★ PG

Comedy 1964 · Fr · BW · 112mins

The influence of Alfred Hitchcock is apparent in this darkly comic and wonderfully observed tale of *femmes fatales* and *crimes passionels*. François Truffaut depicts air hostess Françoise Dorléac (Catherine Deneuve's sister) as a blonde ice maiden whose passing fancy for intellectual Jean Desailly has a life-shattering effect. There are also touches of Jean Renoir's humanism and echoes of Jacques Tati's despair at the mechanised world in what was wrongly considered to be a coolly cynical melodrama. An overlooked gem. DP. In French with English subtitles. DVD

Jean Desailly *Pierre Lachenay* • Françoise Dorléac *Nicole Chomette* • Nelly Benedetti *Franca Lachenay* ■ *Dir* François Truffaut • *Scr* François Truffaut, Jean-Louis Richard

The Pebble and the Penguin ★★ U

Animation 1995 · US · Colour · 70mins

This undistinguished offering from the Don Bluth studio owes little to nature and too much to the kind of clawing sentimentality that spoils so many animated features. The story of Hubie, the shy bird whose hopes of romance are dashed by the dastardly Drake, is further disadvantaged by the poor voiceovers of Martin Short, James Belushi and Tim Curry and the dreadful songs of Barry Manilow. DP

Shani Wallis *Narrator* • Martin Short *Hubie* • James Belushi *Rocko* • Tim Curry *Drake* • Annie Golden *Marina* • Scott Bullock *Chubby/Gentoo* ■ *Dir* Don Bluth • *Scr* Rachel Korestsky, Steve Whitestone • *Music* Barry Manilow • *Lyrics* Bruce Sussman

Pecker ★★★ 15

Satirical comedy 1998 · US · Colour · 86mins

John Waters movies don't come more sweet and adorable than this portrait of a young and ingenuous Baltimore photographer (a rather low-key Edward Furlong) who becomes an instant "art star" after winning over New York's jaded establishment with his neighbourhood snaps. The scanty story charts Pecker's rise to fame and the subsequent attempts to pluck him from his proletarian backwater. Waters gently – though at times didactically – satirises the vampiric art world as a frame for a comparatively sympathetic picture of his B-list Maryland home town. DM. Contains nudity, sexual references and swearing. DVD

Edward Furlong *Pecker* • Christina Ricci *Shelley* • Bess Armstrong *Dr Klompus* • Mark Joy *Jimmy* • Mary Kay Place *Joyce* • Martha Plimpton *Tina* • Brendan Sexton III *Matt* • Mink Stole *Precinct captain* • Lili Taylor *Rorey* • Patricia Hearst *Lynn Wentworth* • Brigid Berlin [Brigid Polk] *Super market rich lady* ■ *Dir/Scr* John Waters (2)

The Pedestrian ★★★

Drama 1974 · W Ger · Colour · 97mins

Austrian-born actor/director Maximilian Schell wrote, directed and starred in this film, influenced by his own experience of fleeing with his family to Switzerland in 1938. Through the story of a wealthy German industrialist – a former Nazi officer, who is exposed in the press – Schell examines the nature of collective guilt and was subsequently coolly received in Germany. BB. A German language film.

Gustav Rudolf Sellner *Heinz Alfred Giese* • Ruth Hausmeister *Inge Maria Giese* • Peter Hall *Rudolf Hartmann* • Maximilian Schell *Andreas Giese* • Gila Von Weitershausen *Karin* • Alexander May *Alexander Markowitz* • Peggy Ashcroft *Lady Gray* • Elisabeth Bergner *Frau Lilienthal* • Lil Dagover *Frau Eschenlohr* • Françoise Rosay *Frau Dechamps* ■ *Dir/Scr* Maximilian Schell

Pee-wee's Big Adventure ★★★ U

Comedy 1985 · US · Colour · 87mins

A film built around a cult children's TV character may seem a strange place for Tim Burton to start his feature career, but, actually, it's not that big a leap from Pee-Wee Herman to Edward Scissorhands, Batman or Ed Wood. At the centre of this cartoonish comedy, Paul Reubens is wonderful as the curious little chap whose world falls apart when his precious bicycle is stolen. But some of the gags are spectacularly unfunny and Pee-Wee's nervous prattling can become irritating. A bold attempt to do something dazzlingly original. DP

Paul Reubens *Pee-wee Herman* • Elizabeth Daily *Dottie* • Mark Holton *Francis* • Diane Salinger *Simone* • Judd Omen *Mickey* • Monte Landis *Mario* • Damon Martin *Chip* • Daryl Roach *Chuck* ■ *Dir* Tim Burton • *Scr* Phil Hartman, Paul Reubens, Michael Varhol, from the character created by Paul Reubens

Peeper ★★ PG

Detective comedy
1975 · US · Colour · 83mins

The lovely Natalie Wood and the equally lovely Michael Caine are cast together in this private eye spoof and lift what is otherwise a fairly lame movie. (It was shot under the title *Fat Chance* and lay dormant for a year before 20th Century-Fox allowed it to creep out on release in a heavily edited version.) Detective Caine starts sniffing around a mysterious family, searching for a missing daughter and finding Wood, whose real parentage is the crux of the matter. AT

Michael Caine *Leslie Tucker* • Natalie Wood *Ellen Prendergast* • Kitty Winn *Mianne Prendergast* • Thayer David *Frank Prendergast* • Liam Dunn *Billy Pate* • Dorothy Adams *Mrs Prendergast* ■ *Dir* Peter Hyams • *Scr* WD Richter, from the novel *Deadfall* by Keith Laumer

Peeping Tom ★★★★★ 18

Thriller 1960 · UK · Colour · 101mins

This infamous thriller was director Michael Powell's first solo project after 20 years of collaboration with Emeric Pressburger. A Freudian nightmare about a film technician (Karlheinz Böhm) who photographs the look of terror in the eyes of the women he kills, it was badly received at the time and destroyed Powell in this country. Only in recent years has it been recognised, by directors such as Martin Scorsese (who was instrumental in having the film restored and re-released in the late-1970s), as a risk-all masterpiece from one of our greatest film-makers. Maxine Audley and Moira Shearer are among those who encounter the killer's lethal voyeurism, while Powell himself plays the father who created a monster. TH. Contains violence. DVD

Carl Boehm [Karlheinz Böhm] *Mark Lewis* • Moira Shearer *Vivian* • Anna Massey *Helen Stephens* • Maxine Audley *Mrs Stephens* • Esmond Knight *Arthur Baden* • Bartlett Mullins *Mr Peters* • Shirley Anne Field *Diane Ashley* • Michael Goodliffe *Don Jarvis* • Brenda Bruce *Dora* ■ *Dir* Michael Powell • *Scr* Leo Marks • *Cinematographer* Otto Heller

Peg o' My Heart ★★★

Comedy drama 1933 · US · BW · 86mins

This charts the travails of the unspoilt, uneducated daughter of a widowed Irish fisherman after she inherits two million pounds. She is wrenched away from her beloved father to lodge with a gruesomely awful family in England, upper class but broke, who are being paid to turn her into a lady. Awash in sentimentality, this combines the poignant, the coyly comical and the melodramatic on the way to its fairy-tale climax. RK

Marion Davies *Peg O'Connell* • Onslow Stevens *Sir Jerry Markham* • J Farrell MacDonald *Pat O'Connell* • Juliette Compton *Ethel Chichester* • Irene Browne *Mrs. Chichester* • Tyrrell Davis *Alaric Chichester* • Alan Mowbray *Capt Christopher Brent* ■ *Dir* Robert Z Leonard • *Scr* Francis Marion, Frank R Adams, from the play *Peg O' My Heart* by J Hartley Manners

Peggy Su! ★★

Romantic comedy
1997 · UK · Colour · 94mins

Despite good intentions and some charm, this *My Beautiful Laundrette* clone (same setting, same paternal relationship, same ethnic banter) fails to gel. Instead of letting the slight tale speak for itself, the director, Frances-Anne Solomon, has mistakenly trussed up the film with would-be "style". It's sad when the nicest thing you can say about a film is that the best jokes are in the subtitles. TS. In English and Cantonese with subtitles.

Pamela Oei *Peggy* • Adrian Pang *Gilbert* • Sukie Smith *Rita* • Burt Kwouk *Dad* • Daniel York *Jack* • Daphne Cheung *Jackie* ■ *Dir* Frances-Anne Solomon • *Scr* Kevin Wong

Peggy Sue Got Married ★★★ 15

Comedy fantasy 1986 · US · Colour · 98mins

Francis Ford Coppola's time-travelling fantasy sees the unhappily married Kathleen Turner passing out during her 25th high-school reunion and waking up back in 1960, in the body of her younger self. Her subtle performance beautifully re-creates the traits of teenagehood, and earned an Oscar nomination, while Nicolas Cage (whose performance was originally slated in many quarters) is amazing as the boy she knows will grow up into a slob. It's not Coppola's usual territory, and he overplays the Capra card a little, but he has fashioned a rewarding tale. DP. Contains swearing. DVD

Kathleen Turner *Peggy Sue Bodell* • Nicolas Cage *Charlie Bodell* • Barry Miller *Richard Norvik* • Catherine Hicks *Carol Heath* • Joan Allen *Maddy Nagle* • Kevin J O'Connor *Michael Fitzsimmons* • Barbara Harris *Evelyn Kelcher* • Don Murray *Jack Kelcher* • Maureen O'Sullivan *Elizabeth Alvorg* • Leon Ames *Barney Alvorg* • Helen Hunt *Beth Bodell* • John Carradine *Leo* • Sofia Coppola *Nancy Kelcher* • Jim Carrey *Walter Getz* ■ *Dir* Francis Coppola [Francis Ford Coppola] • *Scr* Jerry Leichtling, Arlene Sarner

Peking Express ★★

Drama 1951 · US · BW · 84mins

This is a typical "Red Menace" yarn, with Chinese villains instead of Russian ones. Aboard the train is UN doctor Joseph Cotten, who is going to perform an operation on a anti-communist leader; there's also Cotten's love interest, a priest and a communist apparatchik. The hefty doses of ideological dialogue make for a rather slow journey, but things liven up when bandits raid the train and take everyone hostage. AT

Joseph Cotten *Michael Bachlin* • Corinne Calvet *Danielle Grenier* • Edmund Gwenn *Father Joseph Murray* • Marvin Miller *Kwon* • Benson Fong *Wong* ■ *Dir* William Dieterle • *Scr* John Meredyth Lucas, Jules Furthman, from a story by Harry Hervey

Peking Opera Blues ★★★★ 18

Period action adventure
1986 · HK · Colour · 104mins

Among the best films made in Hong Kong in the 1980s, this dazzling period adventure will leave you breathless and begging for more. Director Tsui Hark packs so much into the movie that it's hard to know what to praise first – the spectacle, the athleticism, the sprawling storyline, the slapstick or the exhilarating action. Yet there isn't a martial arts hero in sight, as Cherie Chung, Lin Ching Hsia and Sally Yeh take centre stage to challenge the sexist prejudices that survived the republican uprising of 1911. Both brutally balletic and intricately frantic, this colourful picture will have you cheering out loud. DP. In Cantonese with English subtitles. Contains violence.

Lin Ching Hsia [Brigitte Lin] *Tsao Wan* • Mark Cheng *Ling Pak Ho* • Sally Yeh • Cherie Chung • Lin Ching Hsia [Brigitte Lin] ■ *Dir* Tsui Hark • *Scr* To Kwok Wai

The Pelican Brief ★★★★ 12

Thriller 1993 · US · Colour · 135mins

Julia Roberts stars as the aspiring young legal eagle who stumbles upon a massive conspiracy reaching right to the Oval Office. Her only ally is Denzel Washington, a sceptical reporter who finds himself investigating the scoop of a lifetime. The two leads are fine, but the real coup is the depth of talent in the supporting cast: Sam Shepard and John Heard are among those delivering killer cameos, although all are eclipsed by Robert Culp's witty portrayal of a shifty president. The plot combines legal thriller with conspiracy movie, and director Alan J Pakula weaves his way adeptly through the myriad characters and subplots. JF. Contains violence and swearing. DVD

Julia Roberts *Darby Shaw* • Denzel Washington *Gray Grantham* • Sam Shepard *Thomas Callahan* • John Heard *Gavin Verheek* • Tony Goldwyn *Fletcher Coal* • James B Sikking *Denton Voyles* • William Atherton *Bob Gminski* • Robert Culp *President* • Stanley Tucci *Khamel* • Hume Cronyn *Justice Rosenberg* • John Lithgow *Smith Keen* ■ *Dir* Alan J Pakula • *Scr* Alan J Pakula, from the novel by John Grisham

La Pelle ★★★

Second World War drama
1981 · It /Fr · Colour · 131mins

Set during the Allied liberation of Naples in 1943, this captures the moral collapse and social chaos of a decimated nation. Relating stories both shocking and dolorous, Liliana Cavani refuses to shy away from the city's grinding poverty and the desperate measures to which many resorted to survive. Marcello Mastroianni holds the piece together as a liaison officer, while Burt Lancaster is brusque as the head of the US forces. DP. In English, Italian and French with subtitles.

Marcello Mastroianni *Curzio Malaparte* • Burt Lancaster *General Mark Cork* • Claudia Cardinale *Princess Consuelo Caracciolo* • Ken Marshall *Jimmy Wren* • Alexandra King *Deborah Wyatt* ■ *Dir* Liliana Cavani • *Scr* Robert Katz, Liliana Cavani, from the memoirs by Curzio Malaparte

Pelle the Conqueror ★★★★ 15

Period drama
1987 · Den/Swe · Colour · 150mins

Max von Sydow gives a towering performance as the elderly Swede who emigrates to Denmark in the early 20th century with his son Pelle (played by Pelle Hvenegaard) to seek employment. Hvenegaard is also outstanding as the youngster who must grow up quickly when his father finds work on a farm. Director Bille August's adaptation of the first part of Nobel Prize winner Martin Andersen Nexo's four-volume novel is genuine life-affirming drama. So many strands of conflict are unravelled that it's occasionally hard to keep track, but the power of the acting (von Sydow was Oscar nominated) and the dialogue will keep you gripped. TH. A Danish language film. DVD

Max von Sydow *Lasse Karlsson* • Pelle Hvenegaard *Pelle Karlsson* • Erik Paaske *Farm manager* • Kristina Tornqvist *Anna* ■ *Dir* Bille August • *Scr* Bille August, from a novel by Martin Andersen Nexo

The Penalty ★

Crime drama 1941 · US · BW · 80mins

A feeble attempt to resurrect the violent gangster film of the 1930s, this stars burly character actor Edward Arnold as the ruthless and egotistical bank robber whose only soft spot is for his young son, played by Gene Reynolds, whom he grooms for a life of crime. But after the son is exposed to traditional family values on a farm, he turns against his father. Predictable, and Lionel Barrymore grates as the invalid grandfather. AE

Edward Arnold *Martin "Stuff" Nelson* • Lionel Barrymore *"Grandpop" Logan* • Marsha Hunt *Katherine Logan* • Robert Sterling *Edward McCormick* • Gene Reynolds *"Roosty"* • Emma Dunn *"Ma" McCormick* • Veda Ann Borg *Julie* • Phil Silvers ■ *Dir* Harold S Bucquet • *Scr* Harry Ruskin, John Q Higgins, from the play by Martin Berkeley

Pendulum ★★★ 15

Detective crime drama
1969 · US · Colour · 97mins

George Peppard turns in a tough performance in this above-par thriller as a police captain who becomes a murder suspect when his wife (Jean Seberg) and her lover are murdered. Ostracised by his former police colleagues and thrown in prison, he escapes to hunt down the real culprit. There's good support from Robert F Lyons, playing the murderer and rapist Peppard puts away at the outset, but who is then released on a technicality. JG

George Peppard *Captain Frank Matthews* • Jean Seberg *Adele Matthews* • Richard Kiley *Woodrow Wilson King* • Charles McGraw *Deputy Chief Hildebrand* • Madeleine Sherwood *Mrs Eileen Sanderson* • Robert F Lyons *Paul Martin Sanderson* ■ *Dir* George Schaefer • *Scr* Stanley Niss

Penelope ★★ U

Comedy 1966 · US · Colour · 97mins

A glossy comedy with Natalie Wood as the compulsive thief who robs a bank and is then persuaded by her shrink to break into the bank again and put the money back. Heist movies were very big in the mid-1960s and this one certainly has the most gorgeous-looking thief. If only it also had a wittier script, pacier direction and a real leading man to play opposite the vivacious Natalie Wood. AT

Natalie Wood *Penelope Elcott* • Ian Bannen *James B Elcott* • Dick Shawn *Dr Gregory Mannix* • Peter Falk *Lt Bixbee* • Jonathan Winters *Professor Klobb* ■ *Dir* Arthur Hiller • *Scr* George Wells, from the novel by EV Cunningham [Howard Fast]

The Penguin Pool Murder ★★★

Comedy mystery 1932 · US · BW · 65mins

This marvellous RKO B-movie has sleuthing teacher Hildegarde Withers (played by Edna May Oliver) and cigar-chewing cop Oscar Piper (James Gleason) teaming up to investigate a bizarre death in an aquarium. The experience is mesmerising and the two characters end up contemplating marriage. Stuart Palmer's original stories were spun out into six films from 1932 to 1937, but Oliver only graced the first three – a pity, as it's the stars that make this film so watchable. *Murder on the Blackboard* (1934) continued the series. TS

Edna May Oliver *Hildegarde Martha Withers* • James Gleason *Inspector Oscar Piper* • Mae Clarke *Gwen Parker* • Robert Armstrong *Barry Costello* • Donald Cook *Philip Seymour* • Clarence Wilson *Bertrand B Hemingway* ■ *Dir* George Archainbaud • *Scr* Willis Goldbeck, from the novel by Stuart Palmer

P

The Penitent ★★★ 15

Drama 1988 · US · Colour · 90mins

Actor Cliff Osmond turned writer/director with this weird, heavily symbolic tale about an isolated Hispanic village that has an annual religious festival which climaxes with a re-enactment of the Crucifixion. Few survive the ordeal, even though ropes are used instead of nails. The penitent this year is Raul Julia, trapped in a sexless marriage and watching his wife being easily seduced by Armande Assante. AT

Raul Julia *Ramon Guerola* • Armand Assante *Juan Mateo* • Rona Freed *Celia Guerola* • Julie Carmen *Corina* • Lucy Reina *Margarita* ■ *Dir/Scr* Cliff Osmond

Penitentiary ★★★ 18

Blaxploitation prison drama
1979 · US · Colour · 99mins

This late entry in the blaxploitation cycle cleverly mixes gritty prison drama with the boxing movie. Leon Isaac Kennedy is the clichéd innocent inmate who puts his fighting skills to good use competing in a prison boxing tournament where victory offers early parole. As written, directed and produced by Jamaa Fanaka, this is a relatively uncompromising look at daily prison life which dumps the usual blaxploitation stereotypes in a bid for more realistic and deeper characterisations. Successful enough to spawn two sequels. RS

Leon Isaac Kennedy *Too Sweet* • Thommy Pollard *Eugene* • Hazel Spears *Linda* • Wilbur "Hi-Fi" White *Sweet Pea* • Gloria Delaney *Inmate* ■ *Dir/Scr* Jamaa Fanaka

Penn & Teller Get Killed ★

Black comedy 1989 · US · Colour · 89mins

It's hard to figure out why Arthur Penn would direct a goofball comedy starring two magician comedians who are an acquired taste. There is a plot buried somewhere here – a psychopath sets his sights on assassinating one of the duo during their nationwide tour – but the movie makes excuses to show the pair involved with material better suited to one of their talk-show appearances. KB

Penn Jillette *Penn* • Teller • Caitlin Clarke *Carlotta* • Jon Cryer *3rd Frat Boy* • David Patrick Kelly *Fan* • Christopher Durang *Jesus Freak* • Leonardo Cimino *Ernesto* ■ *Dir* Arthur Penn • *Scr* Penn Jillette, Teller

Pennies from Heaven ★★★ U

Musical comedy drama
1936 · US · BW · 80mins

One of a stream of Depression-era movies that consolidated the starpower of crooner Bing Crosby, giving him the chance to warble the title song into posterity and an Oscar nomination. The slight plot and even slighter production values don't really matter, though these days it's hard to take Bing seriously as he befriends an orphaned little girl and wanders through life's incidents with her and her near-dotty grandad, played by the wonderful Donald Meek. TS

Bing Crosby *Larry Poole* • Madge Evans *Susan Sprague* • Edith Fellows *Patsy Smith* • Donald Meek *Gramp Smith* • John Gallaudet *Hart* • Louis Armstrong *Henry* • Tom Dugan *Crowbar* • Nana Bryant *Miss Howard* ■ *Dir* Norman Z McLeod • *Scr* Jo Swerling, from the novel *The Peacock's Feather* by Katherine Leslie Moore

P

Pennies from Heaven ★★★ 15

Musical romantic drama
1981 · US · Colour · 103mins

Dennis Potter's TV serial is given the Hollywood treatment here with Steve Martin starring as a music salesman. Set in Chicago during the Depression, Martin's frustrating marriage spurs him into a dalliance with schoolteacher Bernadette Peters. The drama is offset and enriched by their happy-go-lucky musical numbers – the most enjoyable feature of the film. The cinematography is rich and slick, the leads engaging and Christopher Walken worth seeing in support. LH

Steve Martin *Arthur Parker* • Bernadette Peters *Eileen* • Christopher Walken *Tom* • Jessica Harper *Joan* • Vernel Bagneris *Accordion man* • John McMartin *Mr Warner* • John Karlen *Detective* • Jay Garner *Banker* ■ *Dir* Herbert Ross • *Scr* Dennis Potter, from his TV serial • *Cinematographer* Gordon Willis

Penny Gold ★★

Thriller 1973 · UK · Colour · 90mins

Never trust a twin sister if she looks like Francesca Annis and behaves with such suspicion-inviting self consciousness, especially as her sibling's been found dead. Director Jack Cardiff, taking time off from being one of British cinema's great cameramen, just couldn't come to terms with this thriller about stamp dealing. The film lacks credibility, and the flashback structure would have looked dated even in the 1970s. TH

Francesca Annis *Delphi Emerson* • James Booth *Matthews* • Nicky Henson *Roger* • Una Stubbs *Anna* • Joseph O'Conor *Charles Blachford* • Joss Ackland *Jones* • Richard Heffer *Claude Grancourt* • Sue Lloyd *Model* ■ *Dir* Jack Cardiff • *Scr* David Osborne, Liz Charles-Williams

Penny Paradise ★★ U

Comedy 1938 · UK · BW · 71mins

A Merseyside tugboat captain wins the football pools, celebrates with an uproarious party, and must cope with a grasping aunt and his daughter's unscrupulous suitor who both hope to profit from his good fortune. A simple and oft-told tale makes for a short and straightforward British film, given an authentic background by director Carol Reed, and beautifully played by Welsh character actor Edmund Gwenn, soon to find Hollywood stardom. RK

Edmund Gwenn *Joe Higgins* • Jimmy O'Dea *Pat* • Betty Driver *Betty Higgins* • Maire O'Neill *Widow Clegg* • Jack Livesey *Bert* • Ethel Coleridge *Aunt Agnes* ■ *Dir* Carol Reed • *Scr* Thomas Thompson, Thomas Browne, WL Meade, from a story by Basil Dean

The Penny Pool ★ U

Comedy 1937 · UK · BW · 89mins

Duggie Wakefield was a music-hall comedian who made his living playing dolts who, against all the odds, eventually came good. Released by Mancunian Films, which specialised in broad comedies with a distinctly regional feel, this hopelessly dated picture has our gormless hero getting mixed up with factory worker Luanne Shaw just as her winning pools coupon goes missing. For aficionados only. DP

Duggie Wakefield [Douglas Wakefield] *Duggie* • Billy Nelson *Billy* • Tommy Fields *Tommy Bancroft* • Luanne Shaw *Renee Harland* • Charles Sewell *Henry Bancroft* ■ *Dir* George Black • *Scr* Arthur Mertz

Penny Princess ★★★ U

Comedy 1952 · UK · Colour · 93mins

As a British spoof on the free market – New York girl inherits European principality and invigorates flagging economy – this is so gentle that the satire is scarcely as noticeable as the appearance of a young Dirk Bogarde as star Yolande Donlan's suitor. But Donlan, the wife of writer/director Val Guest, still puts in an effervescent performance despite the rather lacklustre plot. TH

Yolande Donlan *Lindy Smith* • Dirk Bogarde *Tony Craig* • Edwin Styles *Chancellor/Cobbler* • Reginald Beckwith *Finance minister/ Blacksmith* • Kynaston Reeves *Burgomeister/ Policeman* ■ *Dir/Scr* Val Guest

Penny Serenade ★★★★ U

Romantic melodrama
1941 · US · BW · 119mins

In this heartbreaking melodrama, Irene Dunne looks back over the highs and lows of her marriage to Cary Grant as they prepare to part. It's all expertly controlled by master director George Stevens, but don't watch if the deaths of young children are upsetting to you. Grant gives a lesson in screen acting and was rightly Oscar-nominated for a superb, subtly-shaded portrayal that keeps sentimentality at bay. If you can take it, this is quite a viewing experience. TS DVD

Cary Grant *Roger Adams* • Irene Dunne *Julie Gardiner Adams* • Beulah Bondi *Miss Oliver* • Edgar Buchanan *Applejack* • Ann Doran *Dotty* ■ *Dir* George Stevens • *Scr* Morrie Ryskind, from a story by Martha Cheavens

The Pentagon Wars ★★★★ 15

Comedy 1998 · US · Colour · 103mins

A wonderfully biting made-for-TV comedy, with the American defence industry as the target, in particular the gravy train responsible for developing new technology. Cary Elwes is the idealistic officer determined to crack down on dodgy practices. Kelsey Grammer is his adversary. Director Richard Benjamin (who also makes a brief cameo) wisely allows the very funny script to take centre stage. JF. Contains some swearing.

Kelsey Grammer *General Partridge* • Cary Elwes *Colonel Burton* • Viola Davis *Fanning* • John C McGinley *Colonel Bock* • Clifton Powell *Sergeant Benjamin Dalton* • Richard Schiff *Smith* • Tom Wright *Major William Sayers* • Richard Benjamin *Casper Weinberger* ■ *Dir* Richard Benjamin • *Scr* Martyn Burke, Jamie Malanowski, from a non-fiction book by James G Burton

Pentathlon ★★ 18

Action thriller 1994 · US · Colour · 96mins

Dolph Lundgren returns to the sporting arena (he made his name in *Rocky IV*) for this strange action thriller. He plays a top East German athlete who defects to the West only to find himself pursued by his former trainer, David Soul. Made at the time when Lundgren was at the height of his video-star fame, this marked a departure from his usual fare, although the mix of sporting and action heroics is unconvincing. JF. Contains scenes of violence, swearing and drug abuse.

Dolph Lundgren *Eric Brogar* • Renee Coleman [Renée Coleman] *Julie* • Roger E Mosley *Creese* • David Soul *Mueller* • Evan James *Offerman* • Barry Lynch *Horst* ■ *Dir* Bruce Malmuth • *Scr* William Stadiem, Gary MacDonald, Gary Devore, from a story by William Stadiem, Bruce Malmuth

Penthouse ★★★

Crime mystery 1933 · US · BW · 88mins

When lawyer Phillips Holmes is framed for murder by criminal heavy C Henry Gordon, the crime is solved by respectable lawyer/sleuth Warner Baxter, with Myrna Loy co-starring as his helpmate. This Hunt Stromberg production was written by Albert Hackett and Frances Goodrich, who livened the formula up with a good seasoning of wit, directed with excellent judgement for the nuances of comedy-drama by WS Van Dyke. RK

Warner Baxter *Jackson Durant* • Myrna Loy *Gertie Waxted* • Charles Butterworth *Layton* • Mae Clarke *Mimi Montagne* • Phillips Holmes *Tom Siddall* • C Henry Gordon *Jim Crelliman* • Martha Sleeper *Sue Leonard* • Nat Pendleton *Tony Grazotti* ■ *Dir* WS Van Dyke • *Scr* Frances Goodrich, Albert Hackett, from the novel by Arthur Somers Roche

The Penthouse ★

Thriller 1967 · UK · Colour · 96mins

Married estate agent Terence Morgan and his mistress Suzy Kendall are terrorised in their love nest by Tom and Dick (Tony Beckley and Norman Rodway), a knife-wielding pair of villains – Harry turns up later. After tying up the estate agent, they force him to watch them abuse the girlfriend as well as listen to self-justifying monologues and musings on the sad state of the world. The original stage play was probably more effective; the film version, however, comes across as grim, tasteless and pretentious. JG

Suzy Kendall *Barbara Willason* • Terence Morgan *Bruce Victor* • Tony Beckley *Tom* • Norman Rodway *Dick* • Martine Beswick *Harry* ■ *Dir* Peter Collinson • *Scr* Peter Collinson, from the play *The Meter Man* by C Scott Forbes

The People against O'Hara ★★★

Crime drama 1951 · US · BW · 102mins

James Arness may have the title role, but the main interest in this legal potboiler lies in watching longtime buddies Spencer Tracy and Pat O'Brien share the screen for the first time. Unfortunately, their time together is limited, as lawyer Tracy is mostly confined to a courtroom, attempting to disprove DA John Hodiak's murder charge. John Sturges's pacing is often over-deliberate and the jibes made against the judicial system are far from original. Solid, but not Tracy's best. DP

Spencer Tracy *James Curtayne* • Pat O'Brien *Vincent Ricks* • Diana Lynn *Ginny Curtayne* • John Hodiak *Louis Barra* • Eduardo Ciannelli *Knuckles Lanzetta* • James Arness *Johnny O'Hara* • Yvette Duguay [Yvette Dugay] *Mrs Lanzetta* • Jay C Flippen *Sven Norson* • Charles Buchinsky [Charles Bronson] *Angelo Korvac* ■ *Dir* John Sturges • *Scr* John Monks Jr, from the novel by Eleazar Lipsky

People I Know ★★ 15

Thriller 2002 · Ger/US · Colour · 94mins

Al Pacino's acute overacting as a past-his-prime publicist fails to give this disappointing film heavyweight status. Charting a turbulent 24 hours in the murky world of his ailing New York PR veteran, director Daniel Algrant interweaves various social and political intrigues with limited credibility or conviction. The script's tart dialogue and a terrific supporting turn from Téa Leoni as a drugged-up good-time girl lend the film some minor distinction, but this is decidedly low-voltage drama. JC. Contains swearing, drug abuse and sex scenes. DVD

Al Pacino *Eli Wurman* • Kim Basinger *Victoria Gray* • Téa Leoni *Jilli Hopper* • Ryan O'Neal *Cary Launer* • Richard Schiff *Elliot Sharansky* ■ *Dir* Daniel Algrant • *Scr* Jon Robin Baitz

The People Next Door ★★

Drama 1970 · US · Colour · 93mins

A 1950s-style drama about teenage angst and parental despair, starring Eli Wallach and Julie Harris as the married couple and Deborah Winters and Stephen McHattie as their teenage children. It's Winters who's the problem, indulging in drugs, getting close to overdosing and ending up in rehab. The people next door, though, are Hal Holbrook and Cloris Leachman who offer neighbourly coffee and assurance, though their son turns out to be a drug dealer. AT

Eli Wallach *Arthur Mason* • Julie Harris *Gerrie Mason* • Deborah Winters *Maxie Mason* • Stephen McHattie *Artie Mason* • Hal Holbrook *David Hoffman* • Cloris Leachman *Tina Hoffman* • Don Scardino *Sandy Hoffman* • Rue McClanahan *Della* ■ *Dir* David Greene • *Scr* JP Miller, from his TV play

People on Sunday ★★★★★

Documentary drama 1929 · Ger · BW · 89mins

This launched the careers of a number of film-makers who would subsequently make it in Hollywood: the Siodmak brothers (Robert and Curt), Edgar G Ulmer, Billy Wilder and Fred Zinnemann. Predating neorealism by some years, being shot in a free-wheeling style on location with non-professional actors, the film follows 24 hours in the lives of a group of Berliners on a day's outing, among them a bachelor, his married friend, a model and a shopgirl. Still as fresh, romantic and humorous as ever. RB DVD

Dir Robert Siodmark [Robert Siodmak], Edgar G Ulmer • *Scr* Robert Siodmark, Kurt Siodmark [Curt Siodmak], Billy Wilder, from an idea by Kurt Siodmark [Curt Siodmak] • *Production Assistant* Fred Zinnemann • *Cinematographer* Eugen Schüfftan

 U = SUITABLE FOR ALL Uc = SUITABLE FOR ALL, ESPECIALLY FOR YOUNG CHILDREN (VIDEO ONLY) PG = PARENTAL GUIDANCE

The People That Time Forgot ★★ U

Adventure 1977 · UK · Colour · 86mins

In this OK sequel to *The Land That Time Forgot*, missing explorer Doug McClure is traced to an exotic prison on the lost island of Caprona. It's not as trashy as the original Edgar Rice Burroughs adventure, but director Kevin Connor's constipated confection still features ludicrous mechanised dinosaurs and hopeless acting from an interesting cast – John Wayne's son Patrick and Dave Prowse (the original body of Darth Vader). A few shots, composed around celebrated fantasy illustrations, compensate for all the film's shortcomings. AJ DVD

Patrick Wayne *Major Ben McBride* • Doug McClure *Bowen Tyler* • Sarah Douglas *Lady Charlotte "Charly"* • Dana Gillespie *Ajor* • Thorley Walters *Dr Edward Norfolk* • Shane Rimmer *Hogan* • Tony Britton *Captain Lawton* • David Prowse [Dave Prowse] *Executioner* ■ *Dir* Kevin Connor • *Scr* Patrick Tilley, from the novel by Edgar Rice Burroughs

The People under the Stairs ★★★ 18

Horror 1991 · US · Colour · 97mins

Wes Craven was back to nearly his very best with this sly, satirical shocker, a modern-day fable in which the rich are literally feeding off the poor. Young Brandon Adams is the lad from the ghetto who gets trapped in the house owned by mad slum landlords Everett McGill and Wendy Robie, and discovers that he is not the only person to fall victim to the couple. The plot stretches credibility to the limit, but McGill and Robie have a ball as the monstrous duo, while Craven keeps the adrenalin pumping. JF. Contains violence, swearing. DVD

Brandon Adams *"Fool"* • Everett McGill *Man* • Wendy Robie *Woman* • AJ Langer *Alice* • Ving Rhames *LeRoy* • Sean Whalen *Roach* • Bill Cobbs *Grandpa Booker* ■ *Dir/Scr* Wes Craven

The People vs Dr Kildare ★★

Medical drama 1941 · US · BW · 77mins

Moving out of the operating theatre and into the courtroom, MGM's *Dr Kildare* series was showing signs of exhaustion by this seventh instalment (out of nine). Lew Ayres's James Kildare is sued for gross negligence by Bonita Granville's skating star after an emergency operation leaves her with a paralysed leg. Red Skelton makes the first of two appearances in the series, providing some painful comedy relief as an orderly. AE

Lew Ayres *Dr James Kildare* • Lionel Barrymore *Dr Leonard Gillespie* • Laraine Day *Mary Lamont* • Bonita Granville *Frances Marlowe* • Alma Kruger *Molly Byrd* • Red Skelton *Vernon Briggs, janitor* • Diana Lewis *Fay Lennox* • Paul Stanton *Mr Reynolds* ■ *Dir* Harold S Bucquet • *Scr* Willis Goldbeck, from a story by Lawrence P Bachmann, Max Brand, from characters created by Max Brand

The People vs Larry Flynt ★★★★ 18

Biographical drama
1996 · US · Colour · 124mins

America's most notorious and successful pornographer is played with red-blooded bawdiness by Woody Harrelson in this sanitised biopic. Director Milos Forman would have you believe that obscenity is therapy as he charts Larry Flynt's rise from the Kentucky backwoods to run a series of strip clubs and publish explicit nude magazines. But his film was entertaining enough to gain him and Harrelson Oscar nominations. The real tour de force comes from Courtney Love as Flynt's stripper wife, Althea Leasure. TH. Contains swearing, sex scenes, drug abuse, nudity. VIDEO DVD

Woody Harrelson *Larry Flynt* • Courtney Love *Althea Leasure* • Edward Norton *Isaacman* • Brett Harrelson *Jimmy Flynt* • Donna Hanover *Ruth Carter Stapleton* • James Cromwell *Charles Keating* • Crispin Glover *Arlo* • Vincent Schiavelli *Chester* ■ *Dir* Milos Forman • *Scr* Scott Alexander, Larry Karaszewski

People Will Talk ★★★ U

Comedy drama 1951 · US · BW · 105mins

The title is apt indeed: this is one of the talkiest movies Joseph L Mankiewicz ever wrote and directed. On paper, it's a romantic comedy about a doctor (Cary Grant) who treats, then marries already pregnant Jeanne Crain, much to the chagrin of both the academic fraternity and the moral majority. Along the way, Mankiewicz takes pot shots at American sexual morality, tax evasion, the Korean war, the McCarthy witch-hunts and a lot more besides. Though the film is bombastic and visually static, Grant is on top form, while you have to hand it to Mankiewicz for bravery. AT DVD

Cary Grant *Dr Noah Praetorius* • Jeanne Crain *Annabel Higgins* • Finlay Currie *Shunderson* • Hume Cronyn *Professor Elwell* • Walter Slezak *Professor Barker* • Sidney Blackmer *Arthur Higgins* • Margaret Hamilton *Miss Pickett* ■ *Dir* Joseph L Mankiewicz • *Scr* Joseph L Mankiewicz, from the play *Dr Praetorius* by Curt Goetz

Pepe ★

Musical comedy 1960 · US · Colour · 157mins

An atrocious all-star mess, led by the singularly unappealing Mexican actor Cantinflas. It starts in Mexico, where Cantinflas plays a stupido ranch foreman whose beloved white stallion is sold to an American film director. The story then moves to Hollywood, where a mind-boggling array of stars drop in for a look, a line, a song or a scene with the befuddled Cantinflas. The joke might have just passed muster at 80 minutes, but the film originally lasted over three hours, stretching the plot and the audience's patience beyond endurance. AT

Cantinflas *Pepe* • Dan Dailey *Ted Holt* • Shirley Jones *Suzie Murphy* • Carlos Montalban *Auctioneer* • Vicki Trickett *Lupita* • Matt Mattox *Dancer* • Hank Henry *Manager* • Ernie Kovacs *Immigration inspector* • William Demarest *Studio gateman* • Joey Bishop • Maurice Chevalier • Charles Coburn • Bing Crosby • Tony Curtis • Bobby Darin • Sammy Davis Jr • Jimmy Durante • Zsa Zsa Gabor • Judy Garland • Greer Garson • Peter Lawford • Janet Leigh • Jack Lemmon • Dean Martin • Kim Novak • André Previn *André Previn* • Debbie Reynolds • Edward G Robinson • Cesar Romero • Frank Sinatra ■ *Dir* George Sidney (2) • *Scr* Dorothy Kingsley, Claude Binyon, from a story by Leonard Spigelgass, Sonya Levien

Pépé le Moko ★★★★★ PG

Romantic melodrama 1937 · Fr · BW · 90mins

An unmissable French classic, a little bit frayed at the edges but still possessing irresistible Gallic glamour as Jean Gabin's fugitive from justice hangs out in the Algiers Casbah and is only tempted out of his hideaway by romantic love. Photographed like a thriller, with lots of shadows, the film is dominated by Gabin's superb portrayal of the self-sufficient loner – just one look at his sad face, and you know he's haunted by his past and doomed to life as an exile (or worse). A huge hit in France, this influenced a whole range of Hollywood movies, notably *Algiers* (1938) which was a remake of sorts, and, most famous of all, *Casablanca* (1942). AT. In French with English subtitles. VIDEO DVD

Jean Gabin *Pépé le Moko* • Mireille Balin *Gaby Gould* • Line Noro *Inès* • Lucas Gridoux *Inspector Slimane* • Gabriel Gabrio *Carlos* • Fernand Charpin *Régis* ■ *Dir* Julien Duvivier • *Scr* Julien Duvivier, Henri Jeanson, Detective Ashelbe [d'Henri La Barthe], Jacques Constant, from a novel by Detective Ashelbe [d'Henri La Barthe] • *Cinematographer* Jules Krüger, Marc Fossard

Pepi, Luci, Bom... ★★★ 18

Comedy 1980 · Sp · Colour · 77mins

The first full-length movie from Spanish director Pedro Almodóvar set the camp/trash/kitsch seal on his future output. Informed by the Andy Warhol pop art, photo romances and John Waters cult movies of his youth, Almodóvar's zany dissection of what constitutes happiness for people living on the edge is a flawed home-movie in which the flaws dictate a surreal style all their own. Featuring a cast of actual investors in the picture, including friends (and future leading ladies) Carmen Maura and Cecilia Roth, it tells the story of how three Madrid girls bond and set up house. AJ. In Spanish with English subtitles. VIDEO

Carmen Maura *Pepi* • Felix Rotaeta *Policeman* • Olvido "Alaska" Gara *Bom* • Eva Siva *Luci* • Cecilia Roth • Pedro Almodóvar ■ *Dir/Scr* Pedro Almodóvar

Peppermint Frappé ★★★

Drama 1967 · Sp · Colour · 94mins

Although dedicated to Luis Buñuel, the shadows of Alfred Hitchcock and Michelangelo Antonioni fall just as heavily across this tale of repressed sexuality and physical transformation. The film couches its political message in terms of a *Vertigo*-like plot, in which a rural physician transforms his comely nurse into the double of his stunning sister-in-law. That Carlos Saura won the best director prize at Berlin is due in no small measure to his future companion, Geraldine Chaplin, who handles the dual role with a panache that has since eluded her. DP. In Spanish with English subtitles.

Geraldine Chaplin *Elena/Ana* • José Luis Lopez Vazquez *Julian* • Alfredo Mayo *Pablo* ■ *Dir* Carlos Saura • *Scr* Rafael Azcona, Angelino Fons, Carlos Saura

Perceval le Gallois ★★★★ PG

Period adventure
1978 · Fr/W Ger/It/Swi · Colour · 113mins

This adaptation of the 12th-century Arthurian poem is an unexpected film from Eric Rohmer, the anatomist of French modern-day sexual relationships. Yet the episodic story about the naive young Welsh knight's quest for the Holy Grail is observed with much ironic wit. Shot completely in the studio against stylised painted sets, it combines the means of cinema and theatre, with medieval music, mime and verse. It takes a while to adjust to the style and language and, at over two hours, the film needs quite a bit of concentration, but many sensual as well as intellectual pleasures can be gained. RB. A French language film. VIDEO

Fabrice Luchini *Perceval* • André Dussollier *Gauvain* • Marie-Christine Barrault *Queen Guinevere* • Marc Eyraud *King Arthur* ■ *Dir* Eric Rohmer • *Scr* Eric Rohmer, from the poem by Chrétien de Troyes • *Cinematographer* Nestor Almendros

Percy ★ 15

Comedy 1971 · UK · Colour · 96mins

Denholm Elliott clearly revels in the opportunity to perform the world's first penis transplant. Sadly, his wonderfully manic turn is the only reason to catch a film whose awfulness has earned it a certain cult kudos. Phallic gags abound as Hywel Bennett seeks the identity of the donor and becomes wrapped up in his complicated love life. No wonder he refused the equally dreadful sequel, *Percy's Progress*. DP. Contains some swearing, a sex scene and nudity. VIDEO

Hywel Bennett *Edwin Anthony* • Denholm Elliott *Emmanuel Whitbread* • Elke Sommer *Helga* • Britt Ekland *Dorothy Chiltern-Barlow* • Cyd Hayman *Moira Warrington* • Janet Key *Hazel* • Julia Foster *Marilyn* ■ *Dir* Ralph Thomas • *Scr* Hugh Leonard, Terence Feel, from the novel by Raymond Hitchcock

Percy's Progress ★ 15

Comedy 1974 · UK · Colour · 96mins

This sorry sequel to the dire sex comedy *Percy* was surely the career low of all who participated. There's a certain poetic justice in the fact that this limp effort should be about the entire male population of the world being rendered infertile, although infantile would be a better word to describe the dismal contribution of director Ralph Thomas. DP. Contains swearing and sex scenes. VIDEO

Leigh Lawson *Percy Edward Anthony* • Elke Sommer *Clarissa* • Denholm Elliott *Sir Emmanuel Whitbread* • Judy Geeson *Dr Fairweather* • Harry H Corbett *Prime minister* • Vincent Price *Stavos Mammonian* • Adrienne Posta *Iris* • Julie Ege *Miss Hanson* • Barry Humphries *Dr Anderson/Australian TV lady* ■ *Dir* Ralph Thomas • *Scr* Sid Colin, Ian La Frenais, from a story by Harry H Corbett, from the novel by Raymond Hitchcock

Perdita Durango ★★★ 18

Black comedy road movie
1997 · Sp/Mex/US · Colour · 118mins

Rosie Perez gives a flamboyant performance in this insanely violent, amoral black comedy thriller. She teams up with black magic cult leader Javier Bardem to kidnap a couple of young lovers for human sacrifice, then moves on to smuggle a cargo of human foetuses to Las Vegas. Director Alex de la Iglesia sets out to offend just about everybody and pretty much succeeds, but the mix of Latin craziness and ultra-violence is utterly compulsive. JF VIDEO DVD

Rosie Perez *Perdita Durango* • Javier Bardem *Romeo Dolorosa* • Harley Cross *Duane* • Aimee Graham *Estelle* • James Gandolfini *Dumas* • Screamin' Jay Hawkins *Adolfo* • Carlos Bardem *Reggie* • Santiago Segura *Shorty Dee* • Alex Cox *Agent Doyle* ■ *Dir* Alex de la Iglesia • *Scr* Alex de la Iglesia, David Trueba, Jorge Guerricaechevarría, Barry Gifford, from the novel *59 Degrees and Raining: the Story of Perdita Durango* by Barry Gifford

P

The Perez Family ★★ 15

Romantic comedy drama
1995 · US · Colour · 108mins

This disappointing romantic comedy stars Marisa Tomei and Alfred Molina as Cubans, mistaken for husband and wife when they arrive in Miami because they have the same surname, who decide to take advantage of the coincidence. Set against the backdrop of a real-life drama (the 1980 Mariel Boatlift of Cuban refugees), this picks up whenever Anjelica Huston (as Molina's wife, who's been waiting for him in Miami for 20 years) is on screen. JB VIDEO

Marisa Tomei *Dottie Perez* • Anjelica Huston *Carmela Perez* • Alfred Molina *Juan Raul Perez* • Chazz Palminteri *Lieutenant John Pirelli* • Trini Alvarado *Teresa Perez* • Celia Cruz *Luz Paz* • Diego Wallraff *Angel Perez* • Angela Lanza *Flavia* ■ *Dir* Mira Nair • *Scr* Robin Swicord, from a novel by Christine Bell

Perfect ★★ 15

Drama 1985 · US · Colour · 115mins

Writing an exposé of the Californian fitness industry to keep busy while chasing a drug story, *Rolling Stone* reporter John Travolta falls in love with Jamie Lee Curtis, the aerobics guru whose club he intends to destroy in his feature. Director James Bridges's air-head film is one of the prime reasons Travolta fell out of favour before his *Pulp Fiction* rediscovery. AJ. Contains swearing, nudity. [VIDEO] DVD

John Travolta *Adam Lawrence* • Jamie Lee Curtis *Jessica Wilson* • Jann Wenner *Mark Roth* • Anne De Salvo *Frankie* • Stefan Gierasch *Charlie* • John Napierala *City news editor* • Laraine Newman *Linda* • Marilu Henner *Sally* • Carly Simon ■ *Dir* James Bridges • *Scr* Aaron Latham, James Bridges, from articles in *Rolling Stone* by Aaron Latham

Perfect Alibi ★★ 15

Thriller 1994 · US · Colour · 95mins

How perfect can an alibi be if Teri Garr can unravel it with one phone call? Garr plays the nosey friend of Kathleen Quinlan whose doctor husband (Alex McArthur) is having sex with their French au pair (Lydie Denier). Soon people begin to die, and it looks as if the wife is next. The doctor's plan for a perfect crime is so prosaic that the movie seems pointless. ST [VIDEO]

Teri Garr *Laney Tolbert* • Hector Elizondo *Detective Ryker* • Alex McArthur *Keith Bauers* • Lydie Denier *Janine* • Kathleen Quinlan *Melanie Bauers* ■ *Dir* Kevin Meyer • *Scr* Kevin Meyer, from the novel *Where's My Mommy Now?* by Rochelle Majer Krich

Perfect Blue ★★★ 18

Animated adventure
1998 · Jpn · Colour · 81mins

Clearly influenced by Katsuhiro Otomo, who directed that *animé* classic *Akira*, Satoshi Kon's atmospheric visuals disconcertingly mirror the growing paranoia of Mima, the clean-cut pop star whose drastic image change not only alienates her fans, but also puts her life in danger. Superbly drawn and packed with ambitious visuals, this impressive picture only stumbles in the later stages with a surfeit of dream sequences muddling an already unconvincing ending. DP. Japanese dialogue dubbed into English. Contains violence, swearing and nudity.

Ruby Marlowe • Wendee Lee • Gil Starberry • Lia Sargent • Steve Bulen • James Lyon • Frank Buck • David Lucas ■ *Dir* Satoshi Kon • *Scr* Sadayuki Murai, from the novel *Perfect Blue* by Yoshikazu Takeuchi, from characters created by Hisashi Eguchi

The Perfect Catch ★★★ PG

Romantic comedy
2005 · US · Colour · 103mins

It could have been a recipe for disaster, with Farrelly brothers Bobby and Peter remaking *Fever Pitch*, Nick Hornby's autobiographical chronicle of an obsessive sports fan. Moving the action to America, baseball takes the place of football and the Boston Red Sox take over from Arsenal in the affections of the story's protagonist. Jimmy Fallon is the maths teacher with the anorak, while Drew Barrymore is the high-flying executive with whom he strikes up an unlikely romance. The Farrellys rein in their usual excesses, but still produce the laughs, and this is very hard not to like. BP

Drew Barrymore *Lindsey* • Jimmy Fallon *Ben* • James B Sikking *Doug Meeks* • JoBeth Williams *Maureen Meeks* • Willie Garson *Kevin* • Evan Helmuth *Troy* • Ione Skye *Molly* • KaDee Strickland *Robin* • Jack Kehler *Al* • Scott H Severance *Artie* ■ *Dir* Bobby Farrelly, Peter Farrelly • *Scr* Lowell Ganz, Babaloo Mandel, from the non-fiction book *Fever Pitch* by Nick Hornby

A Perfect Couple ★★★

Romantic comedy
1979 · US · Colour · 111mins

Director Robert Altman abandons the scattershot technique that made *Nashville* so memorable to concentrate on an intimate, offbeat love story brought about by computer dating. Paul Dooley plays a strait-laced prude intimidated by his oppressive Greek-American family, who is drawn to Marta Heflin, the member of a rock group. Gently awkward dilemmas and a well-earned happy ending result in a magic that only a fine director can create. TH

Paul Dooley *Alex Theodopoulos* • Marta Heflin *Sheila Shea* • Titos Vandis *Panos Theodopoulos* • Belita Moreno *Eleousa* • Henry Gibson *Fred Bott* ■ *Dir* Robert Altman • *Scr* Robert Altman, Allan Nicholls

Perfect Day ★★★★★ U

Comedy 1929 · US · BW · 19mins

One of the very best of Laurel and Hardy's short comedies, with an alarming soundtrack – a bell is sounded when Stanley is struck on the head. Edgar Kennedy is the sublimely exasperated uncle with a gouty foot which is being continually attacked by the family dog. Our heroes are off on a picnic with wives Isabelle Keith and Kaye Deslys, but a series of incidents keep the car immovable until the end. Lovingly inventive and as cherishable as the duo themselves. TH [VIDEO] DVD

Stan Laurel *Stan* • Oliver Hardy *Ollie* • Edgar Kennedy *Uncle Edgar* • Kay Deslys *Mrs Hardy* • Isabelle Keith *Mrs Laurel* ■ *Dir* James Parrott • *Scr* HM Walker, from a story by Leo McCarey, Hal Roach

Perfect Friday ★★★

Crime comedy 1970 · UK · Colour · 94mins

This sprightly crime caper is hardly the kind of material normally associated with its director, Peter Hall. Stanley Baker stars as the timid banker who teams up with aristocratic wastrel David Warner and his bored wife Ursula Andress for a raid on his own bank. The raid never completely enthrals us, which is as much down to the script as Hall's discomfort with the genre, for, while the scam is smoothly staged, the suspense seems contrived. DP. Contains swearing, sex scenes, brief nudity.

Ursula Andress *Britt* • Stanley Baker *Mr Graham* • David Warner *Nicholas* • Patience Collier *Nanny* • TP McKenna *Smith* • David Waller *Williams* • Joan Benham *Miss Welsh* ■ *Dir* Peter Hall • *Scr* Anthony Greville-Bell, C Scott Forbes, from a story by C Scott Forbes

The Perfect Furlough ★★

Comedy 1958 · US · Colour · 92mins

Tony Curtis and Janet Leigh star in their third film together, and the second Curtis made for director Blake Edwards. It's a sex comedy, with Curtis plucked by lottery from a secret military base in the Arctic and sent to Paris for a little R&R with dream girl Linda Cristal and army shrink Leigh, the idea being that Curtis's tales will raise morale when he gets back to base. This is very much a 1950s movie – glossily made and very coy. AT

Tony Curtis *Corporal Paul Hodges* • Janet Leigh *Lieutenant Vicki Loren* • Linda Cristal *Sandra Roca* • Keenan Wynn *Harvey Franklin* • Elaine Stritch *Liz Baker* • Marcel Dalio *Henri* • Les Tremayne *Colonel Leland* • Jay Novello *René* ■ *Dir* Blake Edwards • *Scr* Stanley Shapiro

The Perfect Gentleman ★★★

Musical comedy drama
1935 · US · BW · 65mins

Cicely Courtneidge strikes up an acquaintance with "perfect gentleman" Frank Morgan during a train journey and invites him to her opening night. Matters don't go quite as planned at the theatre, but Morgan comes to the rescue, paving the way for romance. This piece of insubstantial but sweet-natured nonsense was Hollywood's sole attempt (courtesy of MGM) to popularise the British comedienne in America. That the attempt was unsuccessful is hardly surprising, since the movie is far too insubstantial a vehicle. RK

Frank Morgan *Major Horatio Chatteris* • Cicely Courtneidge *April Maye* • Heather Angel *Evelyn* • Herbert Mundin *Hitch* • Una O'Connor *Harriet* • Richard Waring *John Chatteris* • Tim Whelan *Usher* ■ *Dir* Tim Whelan • *Scr* Edward Childs Carpenter, from his unproduced play, from the short story *The Prodigal Father* by Cosmo Hamilton

The Perfect Husband ★★ PG

Romantic comedy
2003 · US · Colour · 111mins

Writer/director Priya Ruth Paul makes her feature debut with this comedy of marital manners that contrasts traditional family values with the bustle of the modern, northern city of Chandigarth. However, the humour surrounding manipulative matriarch Sinia Duggal's refusal to contemplate either asthmatic daughter Rajeshwari Sachdev's liaison with gentlemanly English visitor William Russell or granddaughter Neha Dubey's romance with doctor Parvin Dabas is far too gentle and formulaic. DP. In English and Hindi with English subtitles.

Neha Dubey *Jaya* • Parvin Dabas *Doctor* • Rajeshwari Sachdev *Uma* • William Randall *William* • Sinia Duggal *Badi Mummy* ■ *Dir/Scr* Priya Ruth Paul

Perfect Match ★★ 15

Romantic comedy
1987 · US · Colour · 92mins

Marc McClure and Jennifer Edwards play a couple who meet through the personal ads. But their relationship gets extremely complicated after both of them lie about their real identities to make themselves more interesting. Both the leads are enjoyable to watch, and the various twists and turns of the plot keep things moving nicely in this lightweight but fun comedy. JB [VIDEO]

Marc McClure *Tim Wainwright* • Jennifer Edwards *Nancy Bryant* • Diane Stilwell *Vicki* ■ *Dir* Mark Deimel • *Scr* Nick Duretta, David Burr, Mark Deimel

The Perfect Murder ★ PG

Murder mystery
1988 · UK/Ind · Colour · 93mins

This is a simply dreadful adaptation of one of HRF Keating's Inspector Ghote yarns. Ghote is played by Naseeruddin Shah, a big star in Bombay talkies, who investigates the murder of a man named Perfect (that's the only clever thing in the picture). Madhur Jaffrey and her real-life daughter Sakeena also appear. Produced by the Merchant Ivory stable, it's badly photographed by Walter Lassally and comes across like nothing more than an amateur dramatics production. AT DVD

Naseeruddin Shah *Inspector Ghote* • Madhur Jaffrey *Mrs Lal* • Stellan Skarsgård *Axel Svensson* • Dalip Tahil *Dilip Lal* • Dinshaw Daji *Mr Perfect* ■ *Dir* Zafar Hai • *Scr* Zafar Hai, HRF Keating, from a novel by HRF Keating

A Perfect Murder ★★ 15

Mystery thriller 1998 · US · Colour · 102mins

Dial M for Murder was not one of Hitchcock's best movies, but this remake isn't even in the same league, despite the appeal of its two stars, Michael Douglas and Gwyneth Paltrow. Douglas plots the demise of his beautiful, wealthy wife, Paltrow, by getting her lover, Viggo Mortensen, to murder her for a $500,000 fee. So far so good, but things quickly come unglued. So, too, does Andrew Davis's direction, which fails to maintain the tension. AT. Contains sex scenes, swearing, violence, nudity. [VIDEO] DVD

Michael Douglas *Steven Taylor* • Gwyneth Paltrow *Emily Bradford Taylor* • Viggo Mortensen *David Shaw* • David Suchet *Detective Mohamed Karaman* • Sarita Choudhury *Raquel Martinez* ■ *Dir* Andrew Davis • *Scr* Patrick Smith Kelly, from the play *Dial M For Murder* by Frederick Knott

The Perfect Score ★★ 12

Comedy 2004 · US/Ger · Colour · 88mins

Stressed-out older kids coping with exam pressure might find a little to identify with in this below-par teen comedy, but everyone else would be advised to give this derivative caper movie a miss. A group of high-schoolers desperate to get into university are led by Chris Evans in a plan to steal the question papers for a vital aptitude test. All the stereotypes are present: the jock, the stoner, the brain... What isn't in evidence is any particular charm. AS. Contains swearing. [VIDEO] DVD

Erika Christensen *Anna* • Chris Evans *Kyle* • Bryan Greenberg *Matty* • Scarlett Johansson *Francesca* • Darius Miles *Desmond* • Leonardo Nam *Roy* • Tyra Ferrell *Desmond's mother* • Matthew Lillard *Larry* ■ *Dir* Brian Robbins • *Scr* Mark Schwahn, Marc Hyman, Jon Zack, from a story by Marc Hyman, Jon Zack

The Perfect Specimen ★★★ U

Comedy 1937 · US · BW · 99mins

Warner Bros gave their resident swashbuckler Errol Flynn a crack at contemporary comedy in this tale of a rich, upper-class young man who has been raised as an over-protected hothouse specimen and kept from any contact with the dangers of reality. Things change when attractive young Joan Blondell crashes her car through his fence and brings love into his life. Flynn, not quite in control of comedy technique, nonetheless is a perfect model of looks and charm and the film, directed by Michael Curtiz, is a pleasing, if not too believable, romantic comedy romp. RK

Errol Flynn *Gerald Beresford Wicks* • Joan Blondell *Mona Carter* • Hugh Herbert *Killigrew Shaw* • Edward Everett Horton *Mr Grattan* • Dick Foran *Jink Carter* • Beverly Roberts *Alicia* • May Robson *Mrs Leona Wicks* • Allen Jenkins *Pinky* ■ *Dir* Michael Curtiz • *Scr* Norman Reilly Raine, Lawrence Riley, Brewster Morse, Fritz Falkenstein, from the novel by Samuel Hopkins Adams

The Perfect Storm ★★★ 15

Action drama based on a true story
2000 · US · Colour · 124mins

This truly tempestuous drama has to be the most waterlogged film since *Titanic*. Based on a true story, it concerns the *Andrea Gail*, a fishing vessel that, while sailing in the North Atlantic in 1991, was caught up in the 20th century's worst storm. A stubbled George Clooney and a smooth-talking Mark Wahlberg, last seen together in *Three Kings*, head the crew, while director Wolfgang Petersen takes a deep breath and plunges audiences in and out of skyscraper-tall waves. TH. Contains violence, swearing. [VIDEO] DVD

George Clooney *Captain Billy Tyne* • Mark Wahlberg *Bobby Shatford* • Diane Lane *Christina Cotter* • John C Reilly *Dale "Murph" Murphy* • William Fichtner *David "Sully" Sullivan* • Mary Elizabeth Mastrantonio *Linda Greenlaw* • Karen Allen *Melissa Brown* ■ *Dir* Wolfgang Petersen • *Scr* Bill Wittliff [William D Wittliff], from the non-fiction book *The Perfect Storm* by Sebastian Junger • *Music* James Horner

Perfect Strangers ★★★

Drama 1945 · UK · BW · 102mins

With the outbreak of the Second World War, a nondescript clerk (Robert Donat) and his dowdy wife (Deborah

Kerr), locked in a staid and indifferent marriage, join the navy and the Wrens respectively. Their separate wartime experiences transform them and their postwar relationship. Adapted from a story by Clemence Dane, and produced and directed by Alexander Korda, this is an interesting, engaging and sympathetic film, guaranteed to please thanks to the presence of its attractive co-stars. The Americans loved it, and gave Dane an Oscar for her story. RK

Robert Donat *Robert Wilson* • Deborah Kerr *Catherine Wilson* • Glynis Johns *Dizzy Clayton* • Ann Todd *Elena* • Roland Culver *Richard* ■ *Dir* Alexander Korda • *Scr* Clemence Dane, Anthony Pelissier, from a story by Clemence Dane

Perfect Strangers ★★

Romantic drama 1950 · US · BW · 88mins

Married Dennis Morgan and divorced Ginger Rogers meet and fall in love while doing jury duty on a love-nest murder case. Sadly, these perfect strangers make for a less than perfect film, which suffers from a woolly script. It aims for romantic comedy in a dramatic setting, but only gets real laughs from Thelma Ritter's splendid performance as a dumb housewife. TH

Ginger Rogers *Terry Scott* • Dennis Morgan *David Campbell* • Thelma Ritter *Lena Fassler* • Margalo Gillmore *Isobel Bradford* • Anthony Ross *Robert Fisher* • Howard Freeman *Timkin* • Alan Reed *Harry Patullo* • Paul Ford *Judge Byron* • Harry Bellaver *Bailiff* ■ *Dir* Bretaigne Windust • *Scr* Edith Sommer, George Oppenheimer, from the play *Ladies and Gentleman* by Ben Hecht, Charles Macarthur, from the play *Twelve in the Box* by Ladislaus Bus-Fekete

The Perfect Woman ★★★ U

Comedy 1949 · UK · BW · 83mins

Patricia Roc was rarely given the chance to show what she could do in starring roles. When she did get her name above the title, she was invariably given a raw deal when it came to dialogue. This frantic comedy of errors is a case in point, for while she handles the role of a scientist's social-climbing niece who poses as a robot with considerable ease, the choicest lines land in the laps of co-stars Stanley Holloway and Nigel Patrick. DP [video]

Patricia Roc *Penelope* • Stanley Holloway *Ramshead* • Nigel Patrick *Roger Cavendish* • Miles Malleson *Professor Belmond* • Irene Handl *Mrs Butter* • Pamela Devis *Olga, the robot* ■ *Dir* Bernard Knowles • *Scr* Bernard Knowles, JB Boothroyd, George Black, from the play by Wallace Geoffrey, Basil John Mitchell

A Perfect World ★★★★ 15

Drama 1993 · US · Colour · 132mins

It should have been perfect: Clint Eastwood was fresh from Oscar-winning success with *Unforgiven*, while Kevin Costner was challenging his heroic status forged in such hits as *The Bodyguard* by playing a bad guy. As it is, the chemistry isn't quite there and the film has to settle for being just very good indeed. Costner is perhaps a little too introspective as the escaped convict who kidnaps a young boy and heads for freedom in Alaska, developing a curious bond with the child en route. Eastwood is the veteran Texas Ranger on his trail, growling his way through some trademark throwaway lines and proving yet again that nobody directs Clint better than himself. JF. Contains violence, swearing and sex scenes. [video] DVD

Kevin Costner *Butch Haynes* • Clint Eastwood *Red Garnett* • Laura Dern *Sally Gerber* • TJ Lowther *Phillip Perry* • Keith Szarabajka *Terry Pugh* • Leo Burmester *Tom Adler* • Paul Hewitt *Dick Suttle* • Bradley Whitford *Bobby Lee* ■ *Dir* Clint Eastwood • *Scr* John Lee Hancock

Perfectly Normal ★★★ 15

Comedy 1990 · Can · Colour · 101mins

This Canadian comedy is so eager to please that it nearly sits up and begs, as a hockey-playing brewery worker (Michael Riley) teams up with an aspiring chef (Robbie Coltrane) to open a restaurant that serves up opera as a special addition to the menu. It means well, but it comes across as rather bizarre, though Coltrane gives a good-natured performance. TH. Contains swearing. [video]

Robbie Coltrane *Alonzo Turner* • Michael Riley *Renzo Parachii* • Deborah Duchene *Denise* • Eugene Lipinski *"Hopeless"* • Kenneth Welsh *Charlie Glesby* • Patricia Gage *Mrs Hathaway* • Jack Nichols *Duane Bickle* ■ *Dir* Yves Simoneau • *Scr* Eugene Lipinski, Paul Quarrington, from a story by Eugene Lipinski

Performance ★★★★★ 18

Drama 1970 · UK · Colour · 101mins

Warner Bros executives reeled in shock when they first saw it, and the censor reached for the smelling salts. This seminal cult classic still has the power to disturb with its examination of the lifestyles of a masochistic gangster (played by James Fox) and a bisexual pop star (Mick Jagger) as they enter into a drugged-out parallel universe of their own creation. With its fragmented narrative, hallucinatory images and arcane literary references, ranging from Jorge Luis Borges to Harold Pinter, this profound study of sexuality and identity remains a sensibility-shattering masterpiece. AJ. Contains violence, swearing, drug abuse, sex scenes and nudity. [video]

James Fox *Chas Devlin* • Mick Jagger *Turner* • Anita Pallenberg *Pherber* • Michèle Breton *Lucy* • Ann Sidney *Dana* • Johnny Shannon *Harry Flowers* • John Bindon *Moody* • Anthony Valentine *Joey Maddocks* ■ *Dir* Nicolas Roeg, Donald Cammell • *Scr* Donald Cammell • *Cinematographer* Nicolas Roeg

Perfume de Violetas ★★★ 15

Drama based on a true story
2001 · Mex/US/Neth · Colour · 88mins

The collapse of the family unit, grinding urban poverty and society's indifference to morality are discussed by Maryse Sistach in this fact-based Mexican story that avoids melodramatics. Ximena Ayala poignantly captures the descent from innocence to introspection, as the tomboyish teenager whose stepbrother, Luis Fernando Peña, allows a bus company colleague to rape her in return for a few pesos. She is matched by the waif-like Nancy Gutiérrez, who plays her best friend, but the incessant intrusion of the pop soundtrack tends to debase the authenticity. DP. In Spanish with English subtitles.

Ximena Ayala *Yessica* • Nancy Gutiérrez *Miriam* • Arcelia Ramírez *Alicia* • Maria Rojo *Yessica's mother* • Luis Fernando Peña *Jorge* ■ *Dir* Maryse Sistach • *Scr* José Buil, Maryse Sistach

Perfume of the Cyclone ★★ 18

Thriller 1989 · US/S Afr · Colour · 85mins

The only surprising thing about this decidedly underwhelming thriller is that it managed to attract performers of the calibre of Kris Kristofferson and Marisa Berenson. This is one of the lower spots in Kristofferson's patchy career. Growling his lines with little enthusiasm, he plays a Chicago cop who uncovers a white slavery racket while searching an exotic island for his missing daughter. DP. Contains swearing and nudity. [video]

Kris Kristofferson *Stan* • Marisa Berenson *Françoise* • Jeff Meek [Jeffrey Meek] *Adam* • Alla Kurot *Angélique* • Bud T Chud [Gerrit Graham] *Lt France* ■ *Dir* David Irving • *Scr* Patrick Lee

The Perils of Pauline ★★★ U

Musical comedy
1947 · US · Colour and BW · 92mins

Borrowing in title only from the twenty-chapter cliffhanger serial of 1914, this frisky period pic is in fact a biographical musical based very loosely on the life of Pearl White, the original peril-encountering Pauline and star of over 100 films before her death in 1938. An amateur performer who serenades her sweatshop co-workers, Betty Hutton hits the national bigtime when film director William Demarest, so impressed by her intrepid kicking of a lion on set, casts her as the star of a serial about a death-defying woman named Pauline. RT

Betty Hutton *Pearl White* • John Lund *Michael Farrington* • Billy De Wolfe *Timmy* • William Demarest *George "Mac" McGuire* • Constance Collier *Julia Gibbs* • Frank Faylen *Joe Gurt* • William Farnum *Western saloon set hero* • Chester Conklin *Chef comic* • Paul Panzer *Drawing room agent* • Snub Pollard *Western set propman* • James Finlayson *Chef comic* • Creighton Hale *Marcelled leading man* ■ *Dir* George Marshall • *Scr* PJ Wolfson, Frank Butler, from a story by PJ Wolfson

The Perils of Pauline ★★★ U

Comedy adventure
1967 · US · Colour · 98mins

The famous 1914 silent cliffhanger serial thrilled cinema audiences and made a star out of action heroine Pearl White. In 1947, a feature film of the same title told White's story, but this 1967 version returns to the original serial for inspiration. Pamela Austin plays Pauline, an orphan who enjoys adventures and escapades on her international travels. Pat Boone is a fellow orphan who romantically pursues her. Terry-Thomas brings an extra dash of class to proceedings, and the whole thing is an enjoyable romp played out to manic piano music from Vic Mizzy. DF

Pat Boone *George* • Terry-Thomas *Sten Martin* • Pamela Austin *Pauline* • Edward Everett Horton *Casper Coleman* • Hamilton Camp *Thorpe* • Doris Packer *Mrs Carruthers* • Kurt Kasznar *Consul General* ■ *Dir* Herbert B Leonard, Joshua Shelley • *Scr* Albert Beich, suggested by the play *The Perils of Pauline; a Drama in One Act* by Charles W Goddard

Period of Adjustment ★★★★

Comedy drama 1962 · US · BW · 111mins

Based on one of Tennessee Williams's most light-hearted and accessible plays, this adult comedy drama receives a delightful screen treatment blessed with a superb cast provided by MGM. Everyone looks like the epitome of 1960s' glamour, including sexy Jane Fonda and talented Jim Hutton as a pair of newlyweds concerned over the marriage troubles of friends Tony Franciosa and the sublime Lois Nettleton, who has the film's best moments. The black-and-white photography enhances the sense of period, and many viewers will find this neglected gem deeply satisfying. TS

Tony Franciosa [Anthony Franciosa] *Ralph Baitz* • Jane Fonda *Isabel Haverstick* • Jim Hutton *George Haverstick* • Lois Nettleton *Dorothea Baitz* • John McGiver *Stewart P Mcgill* • Mabel Albertson *Mrs Alice McGill* • Jack Albertson *Desk sergeant* ■ *Dir* George Roy Hill • *Scr* Isobel Lennart, from the play *A Period of Adjustment* by Tennessee Williams

Permanent Midnight ★★★ 18

Biographical drama
1998 · US · Colour · 84mins

Ben Stiller makes the most of a meaty role in this gripping drugs drama, set in the Hollywood fast lane. It's based on the autobiography of Jerry Stahl, a writer working in television whose career self-destructed when his heroin addiction overtook his life. Stiller plays him warts and all and at times it's actually hard to work up any sympathy for his descent into drugs hell. There are good supporting turns, and even Elizabeth Hurley acquits herself quite well as the naive producer who ends up in a marriage of convenience with Stiller. JF [video] DVD

Ben Stiller *Jerry Stahl* • Elizabeth Hurley *Sandra* • Janeane Garofalo *Jana* • Maria Bello *Kitty* • Owen Wilson *Nicky* • Lourdes Benedicto *Vola* • Jay Paulson *Phoenix Punk* • Jerry Stahl *Dr Murphy* ■ *Dir* David Veloz • *Scr* David Veloz, from the autobiography by Jerry Stahl

Permanent Record ★★★ 15

Drama 1988 · US · Colour · 88mins

An early, and affecting, performance from Keanu Reeves is the sole reason for bothering with this "social issue" movie about what drives teens to suicide. Reeves is the under-achieving best friend of the seemingly perfect pupil (Alan Boyce) who throws himself off a cliff. For what reason is endlessly discussed, although the self-obsessed, angst-ridden traumas of the classmates left behind provide more than enough motive. Only in Reeves's case does such vapid posturing ring heart-breakingly true and appealingly sincere. AJ. Contains swearing. [video]

Alan Boyce *David Sinclair* • Keanu Reeves *Chris Townsend* • Michelle Meyrink *MG* • Jennifer Rubin *Lauren* • Pamela Gidley *Kim* • Michael Elgart *Jake* • Richard Bradford *Leo Verdell* ■ *Dir* Marisa Silver • *Scr* Jarre Fees, Alice Liddle, Larry Ketron

Permanent Vacation ★★★

Drama 1982 · US · Colour · 75mins

Jim Jarmusch signed up to the film programme at New York University, where he was tutored by the great film-maker Nicholas Ray. The dying Ray encouraged Jarmusch in the production of his graduation project, *Permanent Vacation*. The spare, quirky Jarmusch style is already in evidence in this slight story about a disillusioned New Yorker who decides his future lies in Europe. Jarmusch regular John Lurie provides both a typically deadpan performance and a slick score. DP

Chris Parker *Aloysious Parker* • Leila Gastil *Leila* • Maria Duval *Latin girl* • Ruth Bolton *Mother* • Richard Boes *War veteran* • John Lurie *Sax player* ■ *Dir/Scr* Jim Jarmusch

Permission to Kill ★★ 15

Spy thriller
1975 · Austria/UK/US · Colour · 92mins

A decade before he was fitted for 007's tuxedo, Timothy Dalton found himself knee-deep in double-dealing in this humdrum spy thriller. However, Dirk Bogarde headlines as a security chief anxious to prevent Third World exile Bekim Fehmiu from returning to lead his oppressed people in a revolution. The story resolutely fails to gather momentum and Ava Gardner looks decidedly uncomfortable as Fehmiu's mistress. DP [video]

Dirk Bogarde *Alan Curtis* • Ava Gardner *Katin Petersen* • Bekim Fehmiu *Alexander Diakim* • Timothy Dalton *Charles Lord* • Nicole Calfan *Melissa Lascade* • Frederic Forrest *Scott Alexander* ■ *Dir* Cyril Frankel • *Scr* Robin Estridge, from a play by Robin Estridge

P

Persecution ★★★ 15

Psychological thriller
1974 · UK · Colour · 91mins

Lana Turner stars as a rich American widow living in Britain with her oppressed son Ralph Bates, whose dark past is catching up with her. Director Don Chaffey tries hard to make the action sinister and succeeds in promoting a few chills. Adding to the entertainment value is an experienced support cast that includes Trevor Howard. By now, Turner's prolific film career was nearing its end and she only made three more features. TH. Contains violence.

Lana Turner *Carrie Masters* • Ralph Bates *David Masters* • Trevor Howard *Paul Bellamy* • Olga Georges-Picot *Monique Kalfon* ■ *Dir* Don Chaffey • *Scr* Robert B Hutton, Rosemary Wootten, Frederick Warner

Persona ★★★★★ 15

Drama 1966 · Swe · BW · 79mins

Ingmar Bergman devised this ambitious drama while recovering in hospital from debilitating dizziness. Inspired by the physical similarity between Liv Ullmann and Bibi Andersson – playing an actress struck mute and the nurse who treats her – it explores the very nature of art and reality. Everything about this most modern of films is designed to disorientate the viewer – the inclusion of off-screen voices and the paraphernalia of film-making, the sudden melting of the frame, the disjointed structure of the narrative and, finally, the famous melding of Ullmann and Andersson's faces into a single identity. Proclaiming the artist to be both communicator and charlatan, this is audacious, complex and unforgettable. DP DVD

Bibi Andersson *Alma, the nurse* • Liv Ullmann *Elisabeth Vogler* • Margaretha Krook *Doctor* • Gunnar Björnstrand *Herr Vogler* • Jörgen Lindström *Boy* ■ *Dir/Scr* Ingmar Bergman • *Cinematographer* Sven Nykvist

Personal Affair ★★ U

Crime drama 1953 · UK · BW · 78mins

Hollywood beauty Gene Tierney co-stars as the wife of village schoolmaster Leo Genn in this small-scale tale. Teenage pupil Glynis Johns at Genn's school becomes infatuated with him and, after a confrontation with Tierney, disappears. The girl is assumed to be dead and suspicion falls on the luckless schoolmaster. A somewhat overheated and unconvincing drama, this nevertheless illustrates the ease with which relationships in small communities can become damaged by gossip. RK

Gene Tierney *Kay Barlow* • Leo Genn *Stephen Barlow* • Glynis Johns *Barbara Vining* • Pamela Brown *Evelyn* • Walter Fitzgerald *Henry Vining* • Megs Jenkins *Vi Vining* • Thora Hird *Mrs Usher* • Michael Hordern *Headmaster* ■ *Dir* Anthony Pelissier • *Scr* Anthony Pelissier, from the play *A Day's Mischief* by Lesley Storm

Personal Best ★★★ 18

Sports drama 1982 · US · Colour · 122mins

Robert Towne was accused of voyeurism for his depiction of Mariel Hemingway and Patrice Donnelly in this lesbian love story played against the backdrop of the Moscow Olympic Games. In his directorial debut, Towne demonstrates a sure visual sense as he not only chronicles the athletes' romance, but also their physical progress under martinet coach Scott Glenn. The camerawork is occasionally fussy and over-reliant on sporting clichés, but this is still subtle, sensual stuff. DP

Mariel Hemingway *Chris Cahill* • Scott Glenn *Terry Tingloff* • Patrice Donnelly *Tory Skinner* • Kenny Moore *Denny Stites* • Jim Moody *Roscoe Travis* • Kari Gosswiller *Penny Brill* • Jodi Anderson *Nadia "Pooch" Anderson* ■ *Dir/Scr* Robert Towne

Personal Foul ★★ PG

Romantic drama 1987 · US · Colour · 95mins

This intimate, character-driven independent film reaches higher than it can touch. Adam Arkin plays a committed teacher whose disillusionment with the system leads him to hit the road. He meets up with an introverted drifter, David Morse, who lives in a van making and selling paper flowers. Into this equation comes Susan Wheeler Duff, who merely serves to underscore the men's limited emotional capabilities. FL

Adam Arkin *Jeremy* • David Morse *Ben* • Susan Wheeler Duff *Lisa* • F William Parker *Principal* ■ *Dir/Scr* Ted Lichtenheld

Personal Property ★★

Comedy 1937 · US · BW · 88mins

Starry but feeble, this comedy has Robert Taylor as a London playboy given the job of overseeing a house belonging to a penniless American widow (Jean Harlow). A victim of censorship codes, this inoffensive picture dawdles from one non-event to the next, though the female audiences of the time appreciated the lingering shots of Taylor in the bathtub. AT

Robert Taylor (1) *Raymond Dabney* • Jean Harlow *Crystal Wetherby* • Reginald Owen *Claude Dabney* • Una O'Connor *Clara* • EE Clive *Mr Dabney* • Henrietta Crosman *Mrs Dabney* • Cora Witherspoon *Mrs Burns* ■ *Dir* WS Van Dyke II [WS Van Dyke] • *Scr* Hugh Mills, Ernest Vajda, from the play *The Man in Possession* by HM Harwood

Personal Services ★★★ 18

Comedy 1987 · UK · Colour · 100mins

A gently witty, if curiously coy, attempt by director Terry Jones to re-create the odd career of "luncheon voucher madam" Cynthia Payne. Julie Walters is a good choice to portray her droll matter-of-factness about the sexual proclivities of a succession of middle-aged men, but in its jolly, almost seaside postcard approach, the movie loses edge and bite. SH. Contains swearing and nudity. DVD

Julie Walters *Christine Painter* • Alec McCowen *Wing Commander Morton* • Shirley Stelfox *Shirley* • Danny Schiller *Dolly* • Victoria Hardcastle *Rose* • Tim Woodward *Timms* ■ *Dir* Terry Jones • *Scr* David Leland

Personal Velocity ★★★ 15

Portmanteau drama
2001 · US · Colour · 82mins

The second feature from playwright Arthur Miller's writer/director daughter Rebecca may lack the froth commonly associated with "chick flicks", but it's most definitely a woman's film. The drama is split into three inter-connected segments, each dealing with a woman who has reached a turning point in her life. Kyra Sedgwick plays the battered wife who's finally had enough, Parker Posey the married book editor suddenly liberated by her career and a typecast Fairuza Balk is the rebel forced to face adult responsibilities. This is emotionally invigorating, with an articulate script and solid, spirited performances. SF. Contains violence, swearing, sex scenes, nudity. DVD

Kyra Sedgwick *Delia Shunt* • Parker Posey *Greta Herskovitz* • Fairuza Balk *Paula* • John Ventimiglia *Narrator* • Ron Liebman *Avram Herskovitz* • Wallace Shawn *Mr Gelb* • David Warshofsky *Kurt Wurtzle* • Leo Fitzpatrick *Mylert* • Tim Guinee *Lee Schneeweiss* • Patti D'Arbanville *Celia* ■ *Dir* Rebecca Miller • *Scr* Rebecca Miller, from her short story collection

Personality Kid ★★ U

Drama 1946 · US · BW · 67mins

This feelgood film shatters that old maxim about the advisability of working with children and animals. There is something irresistible about critters for young Ted Donaldson and he pleads with his parents to take possession of a donkey. He gets his wish, thanks to older brother Michael Duane, whose decision to quit the soap factory and become a photographer makes the pair famous. DP

Anita Louise *Laura Howard* • Michael Duane *Harry Roberts* • Ted Donaldson *Davey Roberts* • Barbara Brown *Mrs Roberts* • Bobby Larson *Albert Partridge* ■ *Dir* George Sherman • *Scr* Lewis Helmar Herman, William B Sackheim, from a story by Cromwell MacKechnie

The Personals ★★

Romantic comedy
1982 · US · Colour · 90mins

This weak romantic comedy features a middle-aged loser from Minnesota (Bill Schopperty) trying to deal with the loss of both his hair and his wife (she leaves him for another man) and finding life on the dating circuit something of a learning experience. This slight study was the first outing for director Peter Markle, who has spent most of his subsequent career in television. FL

Bill Schoppert *Bill* • Karen Landry *Adrienne* • Paul Eiding *Paul* • Michael Laskin *David* • Vicki Daki *Shelly* • Chris Forth *Jennifer* • Patrick O'Brien *Jay* ■ *Dir/Scr* Peter Markle

Persons Unknown ★★ 18

Thriller 1996 · US · Colour · 94mins

Before it turns into a soppy love story, this cynical thriller is a stylish and innovative take on the usual cops-and-robbers scenario. Joe Mantegna plays an ex-cop-turned-security systems rep who has a one-night stand with Kelly Lynch, who uses the opportunity to steal his files detailing the defences of the local drug dealers. Mantegna then gets involved at a distance, Lynch's handicapped sister (Naomi Watts) arrives to take part in the robbery, and this caper loses its way and slips into bathos. AJ. Contains swearing, violence, sex scenes.

Joe Mantegna *Jim Holland* • Kelly Lynch *Amanda* • JT Walsh *Cake* • Naomi Watts *Molly* • Xander Berkeley *Tosh* • Jon Favreau *Terry* ■ *Dir* George Hickenlooper • *Scr* Craig Smith

Persuasion ★★★★ U

Period romance
1995 · UK/US/Fr · Colour · 102mins

Amanda Root glows as gentle Anne Elliot, past her bloom and thoughtlessly put-upon by her horrid, snobbish family when the once-poor suitor she was persuaded to reject returns in the shape of dashing Captain Wentworth (Ciaran Hinds). Now he's rich, socially desirable and eager to find a wife – just as long as she's not Anne. However, the attentions of a caddish admirer revive the resentful hero's interest. This artful BBC adaptation of Jane Austen's most mature love story is beautifully realised by *Notting Hill* director Roger Michell and a class ensemble who never let the superb period detail intrude on the emotional realism or romantic suspense. AME DVD

Amanda Root *Anne Elliot* • Ciaran Hinds *Captain Wentworth* • Susan Fleetwood *Lady Russell* • Corin Redgrave *Sir Walter Elliot* • Fiona Shaw *Mrs Croft* • John Woodvine *Admiral Croft* • Phoebe Nicholls *Elizabeth Elliot* • Samuel West *Mr Elliot* • Sophie Thompson *Mary Musgrove* • Judy Cornwell *Mrs Musgrove* • Simon Russell Beale *Charles Musgrove* ■ *Dir* Roger Michell • *Scr* Nick Dear, from the novel by Jane Austen

The Pest ★★ 12

Comedy 1997 · US · Colour · 80mins

This aptly-named comedy is about a small-time con artist who owes the "Scottish Mob" $50,000. Offered a "cash scholarship" by Jeffrey Jones, John Leguizamo finds himself the prey in a remake of *The Most Dangerous Game*. The hunt ranges from Jones's private island to the streets of Miami, with Leguizamo cracking wise and spouting pop culture references all the way. ST. Contains swearing, sexual references.

John Leguizamo *Pestario "Pest" Vargas* • Jeffrey Jones *Gustav* • Edoardo Ballerini *Himmel* • Freddy Rodriguez *Ninja* • Tammy Townsend *Xantha Kent* • Aries Spears *Chubby* • Joe Morton *Mr Kent* ■ *Dir* Paul Miller • *Scr* David Bar Katz, from a story by John Leguizamo, David Bar Katz

Pet Sematary ★★★ 18

Horror 1989 · US · Colour · 98mins

Morbid but compulsive horror, adapted by Stephen King from his own novel, about a young couple (Dale Midkiff and Denise Crosby), who discover that corpses buried in the pet cemetery near their new home come back to life. For much of its length, the story, which seems to be yet another re-working of the classic short story *The Monkey's Paw*, provides only the occasional shudder and is interrupted by awkward flashbacks. But those who stick with it are rewarded with a really ghastly climax, cleverly engineered to tweak very raw nerves. DM DVD

Fred Gwynne *Jud Crandall* • Dale Midkiff *Louis Creed* • Denise Crosby *Rachel Creed* • Brad Greenquist *Victor Pascow* • Michael Lombard *Irwin Goldman* • Miko Hughes *Gage Creed* ■ *Dir* Mary Lambert • *Scr* Stephen King, from his novel

Pet Sematary II ★★ 18

Horror 1992 · US · Colour · 100mins

Although it begins unpromisingly with plodding, TV movie-style exposition, this sequel picks up speed when two boys discover the Indian burial ground that brings the dead back to life. The resurrected dog is a spine-chilling creature; later, wicked stepfather Clancy Brown returns from the grave to make love to his widow. The grossness culminates in carnage that almost rivals that of the original film, while the tone throughout is much more tongue-in-cheek than before. DM DVD

Anthony Edwards *Chase Matthews* • Edward Furlong *Jeff Matthews* • Clancy Brown *Gus Gilbert* • Jason McGuire *Drew Gilbert* • Jared Rushton *Clyde Parker* ■ *Dir* Mary Lambert • *Scr* Richard Outten

Pet Shop ★★ U

Comedy fantasy 1995 · US · Colour · 84mins

In the suburb of Cactus Flats, Arizona, a magical pet shop sells pets that are actually fantastic animals in disguise. A Mob family in the witness protection programme end up with some of the magic animals, with supposedly hilarious consequences ensuing. The characters are so stereotypical and the humour so broad that this low-budget kids' movie will probably appeal only to unsophisticated youngsters. ST

Terry Kiser *Joe Yeagher* • Leigh Ann Orsi *Dena Yeagher* • Spencer Vrooman *Mike* • Joanne Baron *Marilyn Yeagher* • David Wagner *Charlie Yeagher* ■ *Dir* Hope Perello • *Scr* Mark Goldstein, Greg Suddeth, Brent Friedman, from an idea by Peter Von Sholly

Pétain ★★★★ 15

Historical war drama
1992 · Fr · Colour · 129mins

With the scars of the Occupation still running deep, it took director Jean Marboeuf six years to find willing collaborators for this meticulously researched history of the Vichy government. Much of the action takes place inside the infamous Hôtel du Parc, which tends to isolate the population at large from the enormity of the deeds carried out in its name by Pétain and his chief minister, Laval. As the Great War hero-cum-figurehead, Jacques Dufilho turns in a momentous display of shabby pride and gullible opportunism. DP. In French with English subtitles.

Jacques Dufilho *Philippe Pétain* • Jean Yanne *Laval* • Jean-Pierre Cassel *Hans Roberto* • Jean-Claude Dreyfus *Dumoulin* • Antoinette Moya *Eugénie Pétain* ■ *Dir* Jean Marboeuf • *Scr* Jean-Pierre Marchand, Marc Ferro, Alain Riou, Jean Marboeuf, from a non-fiction book by Marc Ferro

Pete Kelly's Blues ★★★★ PG

Drama 1955 · US · Colour · 91mins

A marvellous one-off, directed by, produced by and starring *Dragnet*'s Jack Webb: a tale of a Kansas City cornet player that is one of the most sympathetic and understanding movies about jazz. Additionally, the film is superbly designed and photographed in early CinemaScope, deploying that letterbox frame to its best advantage, and perfectly cast. Not just moll Janet Leigh and bootlegger Edmond O'Brien, but also Ella Fitzgerald and Peggy Lee, the latter touching and Oscar-nominated for a performance that includes the affecting *Sing a Rainbow*. The melancholy tone is brilliantly sustained, the attitudes and language resolutely adult. TS

Jack Webb *Pete Kelly* • Janet Leigh *Ivy Conrad* • Edmond O'Brien *Fran McCarg* • Peggy Lee *Rose Hopkins* • Andy Devine *George Tenell* • Lee Marvin *Al Gannaway* • Ella Fitzgerald *Maggie Jackson* ■ *Dir* Jack Webb • *Scr* Richard L Breen

Pete 'n' Tillie ★★★

Romantic comedy
1972 · US · Colour · 100mins

"When you're my age, blind dates are a way of life," says Carol Burnett to Walter Matthau at the start of this romantic comedy. Later, they get married and have a son with a terminal disease. Yes, this is unashamedly manipulative, but its saving grace is the acting: Burnett was making a big screen comeback after a decade's absence, and Matthau is a sheer delight as a character who speaks in puns and riddles and lives for practical jokes. As Burnett's matchmaking friend, Geraldine Page won an Oscar nomination, as did the sudsy script. AT

Walter Matthau *Pete* • Carol Burnett *Tillie* • Geraldine Page *Gertrude* • Barry Nelson *Burt* • René Auberjonois *Jimmy* • Lee H Montgomery [Lee Montgomery] *Robbie* ■ *Dir* Martin Ritt • *Scr* Julius J Epstein, from the novella *Witch's Milk* by Peter De Vries

Peter and Pavla ★★★★

Drama 1964 · Cz · BW · 85mins

Milos Forman made his feature directorial debut with this story about a store detective pressurised by his parents to succeed in life and love. Making atmospheric use of the Bohemian town of Kolin and coaxing wondrously naturalistic, improvised performances from Ladislav Jakim and Pavla Martinkova, Forman began his perpetual fascination with the outsider with a sympathetic wit that would never desert him. DP. In Czech with English subtitles.

Ladislav Jakim *Peter* • Pavla Martinkova *Pavla* ■ *Dir* Milos Forman • *Scr* Milos Forman, Jaroslav Papousek • *Cinematographer* Jan Nemecek

Peter Ibbetson ★★★★

Romantic fantasy drama
1935 · US · BW · 82mins

This Hollywood oddity became a landmark for members of the European surrealist movement in the 1930s, with Gary Cooper and Ann Harding as lovers who communicate their passion in dreams. Off-the-wall casting (Cooper is not very effective) adds to the sense of alienation in this adaptation of George du Maurier's novel and John Nathaniel Raphael's play, while the finale's fulfilment of *l'amour fou* received a rapturous reception from the surrealists. TH

Gary Cooper *Peter Ibbetson* • Ann Harding *Mary, Duchess of Towers* • John Halliday *Duke of Towers* • Ida Lupino *Agnes* • Douglass Dumbrille *Colonel Forsythe* • Virginia Weidler *Mimsey* • Dickie Moore *Gogo* ■ *Dir* Henry Hathaway • *Scr* Vincent Lawrence, Waldemar Young, Constance Collier, John Meehan, Edwin Justus Mayer, from the play by John Nathaniel Raphael, from the novel by George du Maurier • *Cinematographer* Charles Lang

Peter Pan ★★★★ U

Animated fantasy adventure
1953 · US · Colour · 76mins

Although Peter Pan purists disliked the use of Bobby Driscoll's twangy American voice as the leader of JM Barrie's Lost Boys, this is still a well-crafted animated feature from Disney with such great songs by Sammy Cahn and Sammy Fain as *You Can Fly* and *What Makes the Red Man Red?*. The artists based Tinker Bell on Marilyn Monroe, while the ongoing battle between Captain Hook and the crocodile is a delight. TH DVD

Bobby Driscoll *Peter Pan* • Kathryn Beaumont *Wendy* • Hans Conried *Capt Hook/Mr Darling* • Bill Thompson *Mr Smee* • Heather Angel *Mrs Darling* • Paul Collins *Michael Darling* • Tommy Luske *John* • Tom Conway *Narrator* ■ *Dir* Hamilton Luske, Clyde Geronimi, Wilfred Jackson • *Scr* Ted Sears, Bill Peet, Joe Rinaldi, Erdman Penner, Winston Hibler, Milt Banta, Ralph Wright, from the play by JM Barrie

Peter Pan ★★★ PG

Fantasy action adventure
2003 · US/UK/Aus · Colour · 107mins

In searching for a mother, Peter (Jeremy Sumpter) very nearly ends up with a wife. It's no wonder that fairy Tinker Bell (Ludivine Sagnier) occasionally throws a tantrum. Peter and Wendy (Rachel Hurd-Wood) trifle with each others hearts as they tussle with Jason Isaacs's terrifying Captain Hook. PJ Hogan gives this spin on the boy who wouldn't grow up an eye-catching makeover and, despite Sumpter's American accent, retains the essential Englishness of the source text. TH DVD

Jason Isaacs *Captain Hook/Mr Darling* • Jeremy Sumpter *Peter Pan* • Rachel Hurd-Wood *Wendy Darling* • Olivia Williams *Mrs Darling* • Ludivine Sagnier *Tinker Bell* • Richard Briers *Smee* • Lynn Redgrave *Aunt Millicent* • Geoffrey Palmer *Sir Edward Quiller Couch* • Harry Newell *John Darling* • Freddie Popplewell *Michael Darling* ■ *Dir* PJ Hogan • *Scr* PJ Hogan, Michael Goldenberg, from the play by JM Barrie, from the novel *Peter and Wendy* by JM Barrie

Peter's Friends ★★★★ 15

Comedy 1992 · UK · Colour · 97mins

Seeming rather small, smug and insignificant when it first played in the cinema, Kenneth Branagh's engaging ensemble comedy is far more at home (and considerably more enjoyable) on the small screen. The air of "luvvieness" still hangs heavy, but Rita Rudner's script succeeds in being sharp and cosy without ever over-straining for effect, and Branagh's handling of his players is impeccable (if only he could get the hang of camera movement!). DP. Contains swearing and nudity. DVD

Hugh Laurie *Roger* • Imelda Staunton *Mary* • Stephen Fry *Peter* • Emma Thompson *Maggie* • Kenneth Branagh *Andrew* • Alphonsia Emmanuel *Sarah* • Rita Rudner *Carol* • Phyllida Law *Vera* • Alex Lowe *Paul* • Tony Slattery *Brian* ■ *Dir* Kenneth Branagh • *Scr* Martin Bergman, Rita Rudner

Petersen ★★

Drama 1974 · Aus · Colour · 107mins

Infidelity in academia, with a blue-collar worker Down Under securing a university place and seeking solace from his fish-out-of-water feelings in a romance with his stuffy English professor's attractive wife. The romance looks doomed, however, when she lands a teaching post at Oxford. This offbeat love story benefits from a novel setting and nice playing by a cast headed by Aussie film veteran Jack Thompson. DA

Jack Thompson *Tony Petersen* • Jacki Weaver *Suzie Petersen* • Joey Hohenfels *Debbie* • Amanda Hunt *Carol* • George Mallaby *Executive* • Arthur Dignam *Charles Kent* • David Phillips *Heinz* • Helen Morse *Jane* • Wendy Hughes *Patricia Kent* ■ *Dir* Tim Burstall • *Scr* David Williamson

Pete's Dragon ★★ U

Part-animated musical fantasy
1977 · US · Colour · 123mins

The magic largely left the Disney kingdom in the 1970s and this mix of animation and live action is a long way from the likes of *Toy Story*. Sean Marshall plays the lonely youngster who finds an unlikely friend in the shape of a dragon called Elliott (voiced by Charlie Callas). Despite a stellar cast, the special effects pale alongside the sharper technologies of today, and, sadly, the tunes fail to provide much in the way of compensation. JF DVD

Helen Reddy *Nora* • Jim Dale *Dr Terminus* • Sean Marshall *Pete* • Mickey Rooney *Lampie* • Red Buttons *Hoagy* • Shelley Winters *Lena Gogan* • Jean Kean *Miss Taylor* • Jim Backus *Mayor* ■ *Dir* Don Chaffey • *Scr* Malcolm Marmorstein, from a story by Seton I Miller

Petit Con ★★★

Comedy 1984 · Fr · Colour · 90mins

Gérard Lauzier directs this adaptation of his own book. Like all rites of passage pictures, there are hard lessons to be learned about the big bad world. But few teenagers make as many errors of judgement as the resistible Bernard Brieux, as he treats his undeserving father, Guy Marchand, to relentless socialist diatribes and allies with diverse bohemians, hobos and rebels in his rage against bourgeois conformity. An astute portrait of 1980s attitudes. DP. In French with English subtitles.

Bernard Brieux *Michel Choupon* • Guy Marchand *Bob Choupon* • Caroline Cellier *Annie Choupon* • Eric Carlos *Alain Choupon* • Philippe Khorsand *Eric* ■ *Dir* Gérard Lauzier • *Scr* Gérard Lauzier, from his cartoon album *Souvenirs d'un Jeune Homme*

Le Petit Prince A Dit ★★★★ PG

Drama 1992 · Fr/Swi · Colour · 104mins

Although its main protagonist has been diagnosed with an inoperable brain tumour, rather than being a mawkish melodrama, Christine Pascal's unconventional road movie is a joyous celebration of life. While her divorced parents, scientist Richard Berry and actress Anémone, wallow in recrimination and self-pity, ten-year-old Marie Kleiber simply gets on with the business of getting the most out of each day, as Berry whisks her away on an Alpine tour that he desperately hopes will forestall the onset of the disease. Demonstrating wondrous maturity, Kleiber is a revelation, and her rapport with Berry is both persuasive and poignant. DP. In French with English subtitles.

Richard Berry *Adam Leibovich* • Anémone *Melanie* • Marie Kleiber *Violette* • Lucie Phan *Lucie* • Mista Préchac *Minerve* ■ *Dir* Christine Pascal • *Scr* Christine Pascal, Robert Boner

Le Petit Soldat ★★★★ 15

Spy drama 1960 · Fr · BW · 84mins

Jean-Luc Godard's second feature was a controversial dramatisation of the Algerian civil war that was then tearing France apart. Initially banned by the French government for its violence, the film concerns a secret agent sent to Geneva to assassinate a leading member of the Algerian resistance. Godard shoots it like a gangster thriller, with some disturbing sequences of bathroom torture, and achieves a chilling portrait of colonialism's last gasp. The film's heroine is played by Anna Karina, who became his wife and the star of many of his subsequent films. AT. In French with English subtitles. DVD

Michel Subor *Bruno Forestier* • Anna Karina *Véronica Dreyer* • Henri-Jacques Huet *Jacques* • Paul Beauvais *Paul* • Laszlo Szabo *Laszlo* • Georges de Beauregard *Beauregard* • Jean-Luc Godard *Bystander at railway station* ■ *Dir/Scr* Jean-Luc Godard

La Petite Voleuse ★★★

Drama 1988 · Fr · Colour · 105mins

Teenager Charlotte Gainsbourg, abandoned by her mother and living with her aunt and uncle in a small French town, longs for adulthood, freedom and excitement. She looks for it by stealing, working as a maid, losing her virginity to a married man and decamping with a young thief (Simon de la Brosse). Adapted and directed by François Truffaut's one-time assistant Claude Miller, working from a synopsis left by Truffaut who planned to make it before his premature death, the film is well-cast, well-made, accurately observed and hard to fault. However, those who fail to respond to the deeply irritating and fundamentally uninteresting heroine will find the whole thing utterly tedious. RK. In French with English subtitles.

Charlotte Gainsbourg *Janine Castang* • Didier Bezace *Michel Davenne* • Simon de la Brosse *Raoul* • Raoul Billerey *André Rouleau* • Chantal Banlier *Aunt Léa* ■ *Dir* Claude Miller • *Scr* François Truffaut, Claude de Givray

Petites Coupures ★★ 15

Comedy drama
2002 · Fr/UK · Colour · 91mins

Daniel Auteuil struggles valiantly to make an impact as the ageing lothario in this meandering comedy drama of sexual manners. But director Pascal Bonitzer succeeds only in keeping his star shuttling between a variety of transient characters without pausing to let us learn very much about him. This tactic also reduces the performances of wife Emmanuelle Devos and his countless lovers to mere walk-on parts, with only Kristin Scott Thomas registering. Polished but aimlessly superficial. DP. In French with English subtitles. Contains swearing, sex scenes and violence. DVD

Daniel Auteuil *Bruno* • Kristin Scott Thomas *Béatrice* • Ludivine Sagnier *Nathalie* • Pascale Bussières *Mathilde* • Catherine Mouchot *Anne* • Emmanuelle Devos *Gaëlle* • Jean Yanne *Gérard* ■ *Dir* Pascal Bonitzer • *Scr* Pascal Bonitzer, Emmanuel Salinger • *Cinematographer* William Lubtchansky

P

The Petrified Forest ★★★★ PG

Drama 1936 · US · BW · 78mins

This studio-bound adaptation of playwright Robert E Sherwood's Broadway success afforded character actor Humphrey Bogart the star-making role of his life as snarling Duke Mantee, the escaped thug who holds a motley group of travellers at bay as hostages. Star Leslie Howard insisted Bogie play the role, and in gratitude Bogart named his daughter "Leslie". Some of Sherwood's moralising may have dated, but there's no denying the power and conviction of the performances as Howard, Bogie and Bette Davis fire up the screen, setting the style and pace for future Warner Bros melodramas. TS DVD

Leslie Howard *Alan Squier* • Bette Davis *Gabrielle Maple* • Genevieve Tobin *Mrs Chisholm* • Dick Foran *Boze Hertzlinger* • Humphrey Bogart *Duke Mantee* • Joseph Sawyer [Joe Sawyer] *Jackie* • Porter Hall *Jason Maple* • Charley Grapewin *Gramp Maple* ■ *Dir* Archie Mayo • *Scr* Charles Kenyon, Delmer Daves, from the play by Robert E Sherwood

Petticoat Pirates ★ U

Comedy 1961 · UK · Colour · 82mins

In his third tilt at movie stardom, TV comic Charlie Drake again finds himself up a well-known creek without a script. This time, however, he's only got himself to blame, as he co-wrote this woeful comedy, in which he plays a timid stoker ordered to disguise himself as a Wren in order to recover a battleship hijacked by a mutinous all-woman crew. DP

Charlie Drake *Charlie* • Anne Heywood *Anne Stephens* • Cecil Parker *Commander in Chief* • John Turner *Captain Michael Patterson* • Maxine Audley *Superintendent* • Thorley Walters *Lieutenant Jerome Robertson* • Eleanor Summerfield *Mabel* • Victor Maddern *COC Nixon* ■ *Dir* David MacDonald • *Scr* Lew Schwartz, Charlie Drake, from a story by TJ Morrison

The Petty Girl ★★★

Biographical musical comedy
1950 · US · Colour · 87mins

George Petty was a real-life popular mid-century illustrator akin to Vargas and this is a light-hearted depiction of Petty's daily rounds, as portrayed here by affable Robert Cummings. The humour's very dated: he's a pin-up artist, whereas co-star Joan Caulfield is a bit of a prude, but it makes for agreeable viewing. The film is stolen by comedians Elsa Lanchester and the inimitable Mary Wickes, and watch closely for a glimpse of Hitchcock's "discovery" Tippi Hedren, a decade before *Marnie*. TS

Robert Cummings *George Petty* • Joan Caulfield *Victoria Braymore* • Elsa Lanchester *Dr Crutcher* • Melville Cooper *Beardsley* • Audrey Long *Connie* • Mary Wickes *Prof Whitman* • Tippi Hedren *Ice box, Petty girl* ■ *Dir* Henry Levin • *Scr* Nat Perrin, from a story by Mary McCarthy

Petulia ★★★★ 15

Drama 1968 · US/UK · Colour · 100mins

Few directors embraced the technical trickery of the French New Wave with as much enthusiasm as Richard Lester. But the kind of narrative leap-frogging and camera eccentricity that worked a treat on *A Hard Day's Night* is something of a distraction in this Swinging Sixties story in which freewheeling Julie Christie cheats on dullard husband Richard Chamberlain with divorced surgeon George C Scott. The film has dated just a tad, but Christie and Scott make a surprisingly potent couple. DP

Julie Christie *Petulia Danner* • George C Scott *Archie Bollen* • Richard Chamberlain *David Danner* • Arthur Hill *Barney* • Shirley Knight *Polo* • Pippa Scott *May* • Kathleen Widdoes *Wilma* • Joseph Cotten *Mr Danner* • Austin Pendleton *Intern* • René Auberjonois *Salesman* ■ *Dir* Richard Lester • *Scr* Lawrence B Marcus, from the novel *Me and the Arch-Kook Petulia* by John Haase, adapted by Barbara Turner • *Cinematographer* Nicolas Roeg

Peyton Place ★★★★ 15

Drama 1957 · US · Colour · 150mins

This is an excellent rendering of the steamy, sexy small-town novel that was a runaway bestseller for author Grace Metalious. Lana Turner is perfectly cast in this tight, taut film, and she shows what a riveting screen presence she could be, given a passable script. Nothing is crassly overt, but you can feel the tension of people wound-up like coiled springs. To this end, passion tugs at the skirts of hick morality throughout. Fans will enjoy the 1961 sequel, *Return to Peyton Place*. SH DVD

Lana Turner *Constance MacKenzie* • Hope Lange *Selena Cross* • Lee Philips *Michael Rossi* • Lloyd Nolan *Dr Matthew Swain* • Diane Varsi *Allison MacKenzie* • Arthur Kennedy *Lucas Cross* • Russ Tamblyn *Norman Page* ■ *Dir* Mark Robson • *Scr* John Michael Hayes, from the novel by Grace Metalious

Phaedra ★

Drama 1962 · US/Gr/Fr · BW · 115mins

Melina Mercouri, the second wife of Greek shipping tycoon Raf Vallone, falls for her husband's son Anthony Perkins. They embark on a steamy affair in Paris, before continuing to the island of Hydra where all is revealed to Vallone. This overheated updating of a classical Greek tragedy by Mercouri's producer/writer/director husband Jules Dassin is risibly awful. RK

Melina Mercouri *Phaedra* • Anthony Perkins *Alexis* • Raf Vallone *Thanos* • Elizabeth Ercy *Ercy* • Olympia Papadouka *Anna* ■ *Dir* Jules Dassin • *Scr* Jules Dassin, Margarita Liberaki, from a story by Margarita Liberaki, from the play *Hippolytus* by Euripides

Phantasm ★★★ 18

Horror 1978 · US · Colour · 84mins

A fantasy horror with a science-fiction twist, director Don Coscarelli's lurid chiller is as wildly imaginative as it is totally illogical. Angus Scrimm impresses as the memorable celluloid demon who sends human victims into another dimension where they become slave dwarves. Don't even ask! Coscarelli's main concern is to shock you senseless while weaving a powerful primal spell. With the unforgettable flying sphere that drills out brains, a macabre fun-house mortuary and cemetery romance, he easily fulfils that aim. AJ DVD

A Michael Baldwin *Mike* • Bill Thornbury *Jody Pearson* • Angus Scrimm *Tall Man* • Reggie Bannister *Reggie* • Kathy Lester *Lady in lavender* • Lynn Eastman *Sally* ■ *Dir/Scr* Don Coscarelli

Phantasm II ★★ 18

Horror 1988 · US · Colour · 92mins

Director Don Coscarelli waited ten years before making a follow-up to his weirdly different cult classic because he didn't want to be pigeonholed as a horror director. But he ended up merely rehashing the original with an equally gory but far less effective entry that barely carries the story forward. Slickly made, but with all the appeal of an empty crisp packet. RS. Contains violence, swearing, a sex scene and nudity. DVD

James LeGros *Mike Pearson* • Reggie Bannister *Reggie* • Angus Scrimm *Tall Man* • Paula Irvine *Liz* • Samantha Phillips *Alchemy* ■ *Dir/Scr* Don Coscarelli

Phantasm III – Lord of the Dead ★ 18

Horror 1994 · US · Colour · 85mins

This third instalment in the series continues the adventures of Reggie and Mike as they battle the "Tall Man" and his flying silver balls. Director Don Coscarelli tries to make things a little different with the addition of Gloria Lynne Henry as a sexy female fighter, but this is still cheap and slow. *Phantasm IV: Oblivion* followed in 1998. KB. Contains violence, swearing, a sex scene and brief nudity. DVD

Angus Scrimm *The Tall Man* • Reggie Bannister *Reggie* • A Michael Baldwin *Mike Pearson* • Bill Thornbury *Jody Pearson* • Gloria Lynne Henry *Rocky* ■ *Dir/Scr* Don Coscarelli

The Phantom ★★★ 12

Action adventure
1996 · US/Aus · Colour · 96mins

The equivalent of watching ten episodes of a Saturday matinée serial rolled into one *Die Hard* package, director Simon Wincer's pleasure cruise through the comic-book pages of Phantom creator Lee Falk's masked avenger story is a retro fantasy adventure. Billy Zane plays the orphaned jungle "ghost" trying to stop master criminal Treat Williams unlocking the magical powers of three legendary skulls. Wincer's gently self-mocking tone makes this pulp-fiction treasure a slice of exotic escapism. AJ DVD

Billy Zane *The Phantom/Kit Walker* • Kristy Swanson *Diana Palmer* • Treat Williams *Xander Drax* • Catherine Zeta-Jones *Sala* • James Remar *Quill* • Cary-Hiroyuki Tagawa *Kabai Sengh* • Bill Smitrovich *Uncle Dave* ■ *Dir* Simon Wincer • *Scr* Jeffrey Boam, from a character created by Lee Falk

The Phantom Carriage ★★★★ U

Silent fantasy drama
1920 · Swe · BW · 90mins

Victor Sjöström's eerie adaptation of the novel about the feckless husband whose 11th-hour redemption spares him the onerous duty of soul-taking is one of the key films in the development of expressionist cinema. The sermon on the demon power of drink could have come from a DW Griffith short, but Sjöström's inspired use of superimposition and time frames is infinitely more sophisticated. Indeed, it was a little too ingenious, as he was forced to simplify the structure to make the various flashbacks and visions more accessible for contemporary audiences. DP

Victor Sjöström *David Holm* • Hilda Borgström *Mrs Holm* • Tore Svennberg *Georges* • Astrid Holm *Edit* • Lisa Lundholm *Maria* • Olof As *Driver* ■ *Dir* Victor Sjöström • *Scr* Victor Sjöström, from the novel *Körkarlen* by Selma Lagerlöf

Phantom India ★★★★

Documentary 1968 · Fr · Colour · 378mins

In tune with the student rebellion in Paris in 1968, Louis Malle decided to give up fictional films for a while (it was three years, in fact) and embark on a six-month voyage to India to find both himself and the country. It resulted in this TV documentary series in seven 54-minute parts, later shown in theatres. Malle, who narrates, makes it a personal journey, and reveals quite a number of fascinating things about the people and society. The Indian government protested at what they saw as a negative view of their country, complaining that the director had put too much emphasis on the poverty and overcrowding. RB

Louis Malle *Narrator* ■ *Dir/Scr* Louis Malle • *Cinematographer* Etienne Becker

Phantom Lady ★★★★

Film noir 1944 · US · BW · 86mins

This is one of the high points of *film noir*. Based on a Cornell Woolrich novel, it's about businessman Alan Curtis, accused of strangling his wife, and the search for the woman – the phantom lady – who can give him an alibi and save him from the electric chair. Leading the search is Curtis's secretary Ella Raines, a policeman who believes in his innocence and his best friend Franchot Tone. The plot spins into spirals of cross and double-cross, all deliriously decked out by director Robert Siodmak with a dizzying array of camera angles, light and shadows. AT

Franchot Tone *Jack Marlow* • Ella Raines *Carol "Kansas" Richman* • Alan Curtis *Scott Henderson* • Aurora Miranda *Estela Monteiro* • Thomas Gomez *Inspector Burgess* • Fay Helm *Ann Terry* • Elisha Cook Jr *Cliff* ■ *Dir* Robert Siodmak • *Scr* Bernard C Schoenfeld, from the novel by William Irish [Cornell Woolrich] • *Cinematographer* Woody Bredell

The Phantom Light ★ U

Thriller 1934 · UK · BW · 76mins

This has gained a high reputation among Michael Powell's early films because of its good cast, lurid subject matter, continued availability, and tenuous links to later major works. But Powell is really sunk by the atrocious story, more suited to a Will Hay send-up, as new lighthouse keeper Gordon Harker uncovers a shipwreckers' plot. The director tried hard to create atmosphere with his limited location work at Portmadoc and by some dramatic lighting effects but he achieved far more in some of his other B-pictures of the period. AE

Binnie Hale *Alice Bright* • Gordon Harker *Sam Higgins* • Ian Hunter *Jim Pearce* • Donald Calthrop *David Owen* • Milton Rosmer *Dr Carey* • Reginald Tate *Tom Evans* • Mickey Brantford *Bob Peters* ■ *Dir* Michael Powell • *Scr* J Jefferson Farjeon, Austin Melford, Ralph Smart, from the play *The Haunted Light* by Evadne Price, Joan Roy Byford

Phantom of Death ★★ 18

Horror 1988 · It · Colour · 87mins

This marked a welcome return to the Italian horror thriller by director Ruggero Deodato, who was sidetracked by the success of his infamous and controversial *Cannibal Holocaust*. Famous classical pianist Michael York is diagnosed with a rare disease that prematurely ages him and twists his mind to such an extent he doesn't recall committing horrendous murders. An unexpectedly thoughtful production, mainly because York conveys his physical and mental disintegration extremely credibly. AJ. Some dialogue dubbed into English.

Michael York *Robert Domenici* • Donald Pleasence *Inspector Downey* • Edwige Fenech • Mapi Galan • Fabio Sartor ■ *Dir* Ruggero Deodato • *Scr* Gigliola Battagnini, Vincenzo Mannino, Gianfranco Clerici

The Phantom of the Opera ★★★★ PG

Classic silent horror
1925 · US · BW Tinted and Colour · 90mins

This is the influential classic silent first version of Gaston Leroux's novel about a deformed composer living in the Paris Opera House tunnels, who is obsessed by a young soprano (Mary Philbin). Despite outdated acting techniques and staging, this is a must-see for all cinema buffs, as make-up genius Lon Chaney's Phantom is a landmark. New prints restore the famous experimental two-colour section, including the awesome "Masque of the Red Death" sequence. AJ DVD

Lon Chaney *Erik/The Phantom* • Mary Philbin *Christine Daae* • Norman Kerry *Raoul de Chagny* • Snitz Edwards *Florine Papillon* • Gibson Gowland *Simon* • George B Williams *Monsieur Ricard* • Bruce Covington *Monsieur Moncharmin* ■ *Dir* Rupert Julian • *Scr* Raymond Schrock, Elliott J Clawson, Tom Reed, Frank M McCormack, from the novel *Le Fantôme de l'Opéra* by Gaston Leroux

Phantom of the Opera

★★ PG

Horror 1943 · US · Colour · 88mins

Claude Rains plays the Phantom in this remake of the lavish silent film of 1925 that starred Lon Chaney. However, those expecting a horror movie will be disappointed from the outset when Nelson Eddy's name appears in the opening credits. Rains wears the mask and suffers as Eddy and his co-star Susanna Foster sing *Lullaby of the Bells*. Nevertheless, director Arthur Lubin's film won Oscars for its cinematography and art direction, with nominations for its score and sound. AT [video] DVD

Nelson Eddy *Anatole Garron* • Susanna Foster *Christine Dubois* • Claude Rains *Enrique Claudin* • Edgar Barrier *Inspector Raoul de Chagny* • Leo Carrillo *Signor Feretti* • Jane Farrar *Biancarolli* ■ *Dir* Arthur Lubin • *Scr* Eric Taylor, Samuel Hoffenstein, from the novel *Le Fantôme de l'Opéra* by Gaston Leroux, adapted by John Jacoby • *Cinematographer* Hal Mohr, W Howard Greene • *Art Director* Alexander Golitzen, John B Goodman

The Phantom of the Opera

★★★ PG

Horror 1962 · UK · Colour · 80mins

Hammer's film of Gaston Leroux's perennially popular story was treated with polite disdain in 1962, when it was released as one half of a double bill. It still appears a minor contribution to the *Phantom* cycle, and a pale shadow of the 1925 Lon Chaney version. The main problem is the casting, with perfectly competent actors playing at too low a key for the operatic passions. Hammer relocated the action from Paris to London and went to town on the art direction, particularly for the Phantom's subterranean lair – still the film's most impressive aspect. DM [video]

Herbert Lom *The Phantom* • Heather Sears *Christine Charles* • Thorley Walters *Lattimer* • Michael Gough *Lord Ambrose D'Arcy* • Edward De Souza *Harry Hunter* • Martin Miller *Rossi* ■ *Dir* Terence Fisher • *Scr* Anthony Hinds, from the novel *Le Fantôme de l'Opéra* by Gaston Leroux

The Phantom of the Opera

★ 18

Horror 1989 · US · Colour · 88mins

This version of Gaston Leroux's timeless classic finds Robert Englund doing his Freddy Krueger routine and the story reduced to "composer by day, serial killer by night" basics. Coming on strong like a bad British sex farce crossed with junk Hammer horror, the look is heavily Gothic, the acting is hilariously mannered and the gore is shakily pizzicato (with the emphasis on the pits). AJ [video]

Robert Englund *Erik Destler, the Phantom* • Jill Schoelen *Christine* • Alex Hyde-White *Richard* • Bill Nighy *Barton* • Stephanie Lawrence *Carlotta* • Peter Clapham *Harrison* • Terence Harvey *Hawking* ■ *Dir* Dwight H Little • *Scr* Duke Sandefur, Gerry O'Hara, from the novel *Le Fantôme de l'Opéra* by Gaston Leroux

The Phantom of the Opera

★★★ 18

Horror 1998 · It · Colour · 99mins

Italian horror maestro Dario Argento's postmodern version of the classic Gaston Leroux tale is a typically gory, scary and spectacular *Grand Guignol* epic brimming with his trademark rich visual poetry. Rather than the deformed masked composer of old, however, Julian Sands's telepathic Phantom is a handsome orphan raised by sewer rats who resorts to gruesome murder to put ingénue soprano Christine Daae (a touching performance from Asia Argento) centre stage at the Paris Opera House. Although Sands is weak as the obsessed fiend, Argento takes his enigmatic story down refreshingly different dark alleyways. AJ [video] DVD

Julian Sands *The Phantom* • Asia Argento *Christine Daae* • Andrea Di Stefano *Raoul de Chagny* • Nadia Rinaldi *Carlotta* ■ *Dir* Dario Argento • *Scr* Dario Argento, Gérard Brach

The Phantom of the Opera

★★★ 12

Musical romantic drama
2004 · US/UK · Colour · 135mins

Director Joel Schumacher's big-screen take on Andrew Lloyd Webber's hit stage musical is sumptuous to look at and lavishly produced, but suffers from being too faithful (and therefore too flat) an adaptation. An over-familiarity with the story (disfigured sewer dweller falls for ingénue diva) doesn't help, nor do the colourless leads, but at least Minnie Driver has a laugh as demanding Italian prima donna Carlotta. However, the power and theatrical romance of the show often shines thrillingly through. AJ [video] DVD

Gerard Butler *The Phantom* • Emmy Rossum *Christine* • Patrick Wilson *Vicompte Raoul de Chagny* • Miranda Richardson *Madame Giry* • Minnie Driver *Carlotta* • Ciaran Hinds *Richard Firmin* • Simon Callow *Gilles Andre* • Victor McGuire *Piangi* • Jennifer Ellison *Meg Giry* ■ *Dir* Joel Schumacher • *Scr* Joel Schumacher, Andrew Lloyd Webber, from the musical by Andrew Lloyd Webber, from the novel *Le Fantôme de l'Opéra* by Gaston Leroux

Phantom of the Paradise

★★★★ 15

Satirical rock opera
1974 · US · Colour · 87mins

Arguably the best musical comedy fantasy on film after *The Rocky Horror Picture Show*, Brian De Palma's funky retelling of the Faust legend via *The Phantom of the Opera* is a savvy satire on the rock industry, delivering plenty of diabolical chills in the process. Paul Williams may be hard to take as the eternally youthful impresario who lusts after Jessica Harper, but Gerrit Graham is superb as the effeminate glam-rocker Beef. This being a De Palma film, the Hitchcock references are in abundance, including the wittiest *Psycho* shower scene send-up ever. AJ. Contains violence and swearing. DVD

Paul Williams *Swan* • William Finley *Winslow Leach* • Jessica Harper *Phoenix* • George Memmoli *Philbin* • Gerrit Graham *Beef* ■ *Dir* Brian De Palma • *Scr* Brian De Palma

Phantom of the Ritz

★ 15

Horror comedy 1988 · US · Colour · 88mins

A dire horror comedy that finds Peter Bergman buying an old disused cinema in order to put on a 1950s rock show. As surviving members of the Coasters and an Elvis Presley impersonator are subjected to weird "accidents" in the supposedly haunted theatre, the management ask the audience to remain calm as they unmask the perpetrator. A strange mixture of rock revue and ersatz Gaston Leroux, with neither strand being well-served. AJ [video]

Peter Bergman *Ed Blake* • Deborah Van Valkenburgh *Nancy* • Cindy Vincino *Sally* • Joshua Sussman *The Phantom* • Russell Curry *Marcus* • Steve Geng *Detective Lassarde* • Frank Tranchina *Dutch* ■ *Dir* Allen Plone • *Scr* Allen Plone, Tom Dempsey, from the novel *Le Fantôme de l'Opéra* by Gaston Leroux

Phantom of the Rue Morgue

★★

Horror 1954 · US · Colour · 83mins

A fairly naff adaptation of the Edgar Allan Poe yarn about a Paris psychiatrist who hypnotises a gorilla to perform his murders of beautiful women. Whenever the gorilla hears the sound of bells, he goes absolutely ape and embraces whichever pretty girl happens to be close by. Karl Malden is much too nice a guy to play the shrink-on-the-blink, while Claude Dauphin seems far too elegant to play the French detective. What seems to concern the producers most is the 3-D process; without that, the film may seem as flat as a pancake. AT

Karl Malden *Dr Marais* • Patricia Medina *Jeannette Revere* • Claude Dauphin *Inspector Bonnard* • Steve Forrest *Professor Paul Dupin* • Allyn McLerie [Allyn Ann McLerie] *Yvonne* • Veola Vonn *Arlette* • Dolores Dorn *Camille* • Anthony Caruso *Jacques* • Merv Griffin *Georges Brevert* ■ *Dir* Roy Del Ruth • *Scr* Harold Medford, James R Webb, from the story *Murders in the Rue Morgue* by Edgar Allan Poe

The Phantom President

★★ U

Musical comedy 1932 · US · BW · 77mins

George M Cohan is one of the great legends of American showbusiness. A playwright, screenwriter, stage actor, songwriter, singer and dancer who was worshipped by Broadway and radio audiences, and famously portrayed by James Cagney in *Yankee Doodle Dandy*. Here Cohan plays a singing medicine quack commandeered to impersonate and undermine a presidential candidate. The result was a box office disaster, though it does offer a rare and valuable opportunity to see the legend in action. RK

George M Cohan *Theodore K Blair/Peter "Doc" Varney* • Claudette Colbert *Felicia Hammond* • Jimmy Durante *Curly Cooney* • George Barbier *Jim Ronkton* • Sidney Toler *Prof Aikenhead* • Louise Mackintosh *Sen Sarah Scranton* ■ *Dir* Norman Taurog • *Scr* Walter DeLeon, Harlan Thompson, from the novel by George F Worts • *Music/lyrics* Richard Rodgers, Lorenz Hart, George M Cohan

Phantom Raiders

★★★

Detective drama 1940 · US · BW · 70mins

The second of three films (after 1939's *Nick Carter, Master Detective*) made by MGM featuring the private detective created in 1886. All three were updated, given the studio polish that disguised their B-status, and fast-paced enough to overcome fanciful storylines. In this adventure, Walter Pidgeon investigates sabotage in the Panama Canal, and Jacques Tourneur, getting started as a director, efficiently controls the action. *Sky Murder*, also 1940, completed the series. TV

Walter Pidgeon *Nick Carter* • Donald Meek *Bartholomew* • Joseph Schildkraut *Al Taurez* • Florence Rice *Cora Barnes* • Nat Pendleton *"Gunboat" Jacklin* • John Carroll *John Ramsell Jr* • Steffi Duna *Dolores* • Cecil Kellaway *Franklin Morris* ■ *Dir* Jacques Tourneur • *Scr* William R Lipman, from a story by Jonathan Latimer

The Phantom Tollbooth

★★★★ U

Part-animated fantasy
1969 · US · Colour · 85mins

This is what happens when Bugs Bunny and Daffy Duck let Chuck Jones, their favourite artist, out on his own: he becomes a bit solemn and preachy. By and large an animated story, this has a live start and finish, but in between Jones animates the adventures of a bored boy who passes through a magic tollbooth into a wondrous land where he has to rescue Rhyme and Reason from Ignorance Demons. It's likely to be a bit above the heads of very young children. The rest should enjoy it, especially listening to the great Mel Blanc, Toonville's greatest ever voice. TH [video]

Butch Patrick *Milo* • Mel Blanc ■ *Dir* Chuck Jones, Abe Levitow, David Monahan • *Scr* Chuck Jones, Sam Rosen, from the book by Norton Juster

Phantoms

★★ 18

Horror 1998 · US · Colour · 82mins

In a curiously clunky mix of sci-fi and horror Rose McGowan and Joanna Going play sisters who return to their isolated home town and discover that virtually everyone has vanished. Ben Affleck is the puzzled local cop, while Peter O'Toole hams it up as a dotty scientist who holds the key to the mystery. However, despite a script from horror maestro Dean R Koontz (adapting his own novel), this fails in the fright department, with too much talk and not enough gore. JF. Contains violence and swearing. [video] DVD

Peter O'Toole *Timothy Flyte* • Joanna Going *Dr Jennifer Pailey* • Rose McGowan *Lisa Pailey* • Ben Affleck *Sheriff Bryce Hammond* • Liev Schreiber *Deputy Stu Wargle* • Clifton Powell *General Leland Copperfield* • Nicky Katt *Deputy Steve Shanning* • Michael DeLorenzo *Soldier Velazquez* • Rick Otto *Scientist Lockland* ■ *Dir* Joe Chappelle • *Scr* Dean R Koontz, from his novel

Phar Lap

★★★★ PG

Drama 1983 · Aus · Colour · 102mins

This thoroughbred drama tells the story of the Australian horse that dominated world racing during the 1920s and early 1930s. The film follows the horse's career, up to and including its mysterious death in 1932. En route, it also takes a behind-the-scenes look at the cruel practices then prevalent in racehorse training. Impeccably staged and nicely acted, it survives the sort of turn-off title that could have brought it down within the first furlong. DA [video]

Tom Burlinson *Tommy Woodcock* • Martin Vaughan *Harry Telford* • Judy Morris *Bea Davis* • Celia De Burgh *Vi Telford* • Ron Leibman *Dave Davis* • Vincent Ball *Lachlan McKinnon* ■ *Dir* Simon Wincer • *Scr* David Williamson

Pharaoh

★★★

Historical epic 1966 · Pol · Colour · 180mins

This historical epic, based on a classic Polish novel, tells of how the young prince Ramses incurs the wrath of the powerful high priest when he takes a Jewish girl as his mistress. When he becomes Ramses XIII, his battle with the priest continues unabated. More restrained, intelligent and veracious than its Hollywood counterparts, the film is rather pompous and plodding, and George Zelnik, though handsome, is not up to the lead role. RB. In Polish with English subtitles.

George Zelnik *Ramses XIII* • Barbara Brylska *Kama* • Krystyna Mikolajewska *Sarah* • Piotr Pawlowski *Herbor* • Leszek Herdegen *Pentuer* ■ *Dir* Jerzy Kawalerowicz • *Scr* Jerzy Kawalerowicz, Tadeusz Konwicki, from a novel by Boleslaw Prus

Phase IV

★★ PG

Science-fiction thriller
1973 · UK/US · Colour · 79mins

This messy eco-upheaval picture was the first feature directed by title sequence maestro Saul Bass, whose work is notable for its animation and stylised use of colour and caption. Here, he fails to conjure up any sense of suspense. The special effects don't improve matters much, nor do the lacklustre performances of Nigel Davenport and Michael Murphy as scientists who discover that a desert

P

ant colony is preparing to take over the planet. DP [video] DVD

Nigel Davenport *Ernest Hubbs* • Michael Murphy *James Lesko* • Lynne Frederick *Kendra* • Alan Gifford *Eldridge* • Robert Henderson *Clete* • Helen Horton *Mrs Eldridge* ■ *Dir* Saul Bass • *Scr* Mayo Simon

The Phenix City Story ★★★

Crime drama 1955 · US · BW · 86mins

Sensational in its day, this exposé of vice and corruption in an Alabama town was filmed in the wake of the infamous Senator Estes Kefauver investigations into crime across the United States, and expertly directed by Phil Karlson. Co-star Richard Kiley embodies moral uprightness as the returning lawyer, who finds his life dramatically changed by encroaching home-town vice. The movie is brutally unsparing in its depiction of corruption, and the sense of realism is heightened by a non-stellar cast, though both John McIntire and Edward Andrews may seem more familiar to today's movie watchers than at the time. TS

John McIntire *Albert Patterson* • Richard Kiley *John Patterson* • Kathryn Grant *Ellie Rhodes* • Edward Andrews *Rhett Tanner* • Lenka Peterson *Mary Jo Patterson* • Biff McGuire *Fred Gage* • Truman Smith *Ed Gage* ■ *Dir* Phil Karlson • *Scr* Crane Wilbur, Daniel Mainwaring

Phenomenon ★★★ PG

Fantasy drama 1996 · US · Colour · 118mins

A strange light in the sky gives small-town mechanic John Travolta paranormal powers in director Jon Turteltaub's feel-good sci-fi fable. As scientists attempt to evaluate his sudden escalation to genius, Travolta battles against an obvious script to focus all his energies on wooing divorced single mother Kyra Sedgwick. Hidden among the waves of sentiment are some genuinely funny moments, but, for all its well-meaning tear-jerking, this tribute to human potential is less than phenomenal. AJ [video] DVD

John Travolta *George Malley* • Kyra Sedgwick *Lace Pennemin* • Forest Whitaker *Nate Pope* • Robert Duvall *Doc* • David Gallagher *Al* • Ashley Buccille *Glory* • Tony Genaro *Tito* ■ *Dir* Jon Turteltaub • *Scr* Gerald DiPego

P

Phffft! ★★★

Comedy 1954 · US · BW · 88mins

This started as an unproduced play by George Axelrod, rewritten for the movies and specifically for Judy Holliday, who was so good as the dumb blonde in *Born Yesterday*. Like *The Seven Year Itch*, it's a comedy of sexual angst, with Holliday divorcing Jack Lemmon and relishing her freedom. He moves in with grouchy bachelor Jack Carson thereby inspiring *The Odd Couple* and starts to canoodle with Kim Novak. It's all very 1950s, stagey and not particularly funny now, though Holliday was one of a kind and is always a pleasure to watch. AT

Judy Holliday *Nina Tracy* • Jack Lemmon *Robert Tracy* • Jack Carson *Charlie Nelson* • Kim Novak *Janis* • Luella Gear *Mrs Chapman* • Donald Randolph *Dr Van Kessel* • Donald Curtis *Rick Vidal* ■ *Dir* Mark Robson • *Scr* George Axelrod

Philadelphia ★★★★★ 12

Drama 1993 · US · Colour · 120mins

This was the first major Hollywood movie about Aids, and it won Tom Hanks his first best actor Oscar. Hanks plays a homosexual lawyer who takes his employers to court for sacking him. The company bigwigs claim he was dismissed for incompetence, but Hanks suspects the real reason is his Aids-related illness. His counsel is Denzel Washington, who despises homosexuals but worships fair play, while company boss Jason Robards is a bigot whose intolerance is hidden by bluff camaraderie. Hanks portrays the ravaged, dying lawyer as a disabled everyman whose life has lessons for all of us. His passionate crescendo of praise for opera is a tour de force of close-up acting. TH. Contains swearing. [video] DVD

Tom Hanks *Andrew Beckett* • Denzel Washington *Joe Miller* • Jason Robards *Charles Wheeler* • Mary Steenburgen *Belinda Conine* • Antonio Banderas *Miguel Alvarez* • Ron Vawter *Bob Seidman* • Robert Ridgely *Walter Kenton* • Charles Napier *Judge Garnett* • Lisa Summerour *Lisa Miller* • Joanne Woodward *Sarah Beckett* ■ *Dir* Jonathan Demme • *Scr* Ron Nyswaner

The Philadelphia Experiment ★★★ PG

Science-fiction adventure
1984 · US · Colour · 101mins

Michael Paré and Bobby DiCicco play a couple of American sailors from 1943 who are yanked into 1984 when an experiment to render ships invisible to radar backfires. They team up with gung ho Nancy Allen in a bid to get home. The cast delivers their lines with deadpan élan in this enjoyably intriguing slice of sci-fi hokum. The project had been kicking around Hollywood since the late 1970s; by the time it got rolling, Stewart Raffill had replaced original director John Carpenter, who installed himself as executive producer. RS [video] DVD

Michael Paré *David Herdeg* • Nancy Allen *Allison Hayes* • Eric Christmas *Dr James Longstreet* • Bobby DiCicco *Jim Parker* • Kene Holliday *Major Clark* • Joe Dorsey *Sheriff Bates* ■ *Dir* Stewart Raffill • *Scr* William Gray, Michael Janover, from a story by Don Jakoby, Wallace Bennett, from the book by William I Moore, Charles Berlitz

The Philadelphia Experiment 2 ★★ 18

Science-fiction adventure
1993 · US · Colour · 94mins

Brad Johnson steps into the time-travelling shoes vacated by Michael Paré and gets propelled to an alternate 1993 where America has become a military state thanks to Hitler winning the Second World War. Then it's back to Germany, 1943, to set history straight. If you can follow the sometimes bewildering plot, this is a reasonably taut action fantasy, relying perhaps a little too heavily on slow-motion battles, black-and-white newsreel footage and wacky hallucination scenes. AJ. Contains some violence and mild swearing. [video]

Brad Johnson *David Herdeg* • Marjean Holden *Jess* • Gerrit Graham *Mailer/Mahler* • John Christian Graas *Benjamin* • Cyril O'Reilly *Decker* • Geoffrey Blake *Logan* ■ *Dir* Stephen Cornwell • *Scr* Kevin Rock, Nick Paine

Philadelphia, Here I Come ★★ PG

Drama 1975 · US/Ire · Colour · 90mins

The old problem of expanding the themes of a stage play away from their theatrical origins rears its ugly head in this production of Brian Friel's first play. Disappointingly, director John Quested takes the easy way out here and places the emphasis firmly on text and performance rather than imagery. However, he's been well served by Des Cave and Donal McCann, who complement each other admirably playing the public and private sides of Gar, an Irishman preparing to leave his bullying father and provincial life for a fresh start in America. DP. Contains swearing. DVD

Donal McCann *Gareth (public)* • Des Cave *Gareth (private)* • Siobhan McKenna *Madge* • Eamon Kelly *SA O'Donnell* • Fidelma Murphy *Kate Doogan* • Liam Redmond *Senator Doogan* • Mavis Villiers *Liz Sweeney* ■ *Dir* John Quested • *Scr* Brian Friel, from his play

The Philadelphia Story ★★★★★ U

Classic romantic comedy
1940 · US · BW · 112mins

Fans of the musical remake *High Society* who haven't seen the classic, all-talking, no-dancing original might wish to remedy that. In order to reverse her reputation as "box office poison" Katherine Hepburn shrewdly bought the rights to the Broadway play in which she had been a hit (written for her by Philip Barry). She sold it to MGM and was able to hand-pick the cast, together with old pal George Cukor to direct. Her plan worked. The film was huge. In it, her society girl is engaged to John Howard's executive dullard; her boozy ex-husband Cary Grant turns up with information about an imminent press scandal, while a rival publication's reporter James Stewart finds his class-war cynicism melting away as he falls for Hepburn. It's more complicated than that, but just sit back and enjoy the screwball ride. AC [video] DVD

Cary Grant *CK Dexter Haven* • Katharine Hepburn *Tracy Samantha Lord* • James Stewart *Macaulay "Mike" Connor* • Ruth Hussey *Elizabeth Imbrie* • John Howard (1) *George Kittredge* • Roland Young *Uncle Willie* • John Halliday *Seth Lord* • Mary Nash *Margaret Lord* • Virginia Weidler *Dinah Lord* • Henry Daniell *Sidney Kidd* ■ *Dir* George Cukor • *Scr* Donald Ogden Stewart, from the play by Philip Barry

Phobia ★ 15

Murder mystery 1980 · Can · Colour · 86mins

Paul Michael Glaser plays an unorthodox doctor who treats patients suffering from various phobias in eccentric ways. Soon, his patients start getting killed one by one in manners related to their individual phobias. The story is so poor, most viewers will be able to figure out who the killer is even before the first murder occurs. Shoddy. KB [video]

Paul Michael Glaser *Dr Peter Ross* • Susan Hogan *Jenny St Clair* • John Colicos *Inspector Barnes* • Alexandra Stewart *Barbara Grey* • Robert O'Ree *Bubba King* • David Bolt *Henry Owen* • David Eisner *Johnny Venuti* • Lisa Langlois *Laura Adams* ■ *Dir* John Huston • *Scr* Lew Lehman, Jimmy Sangster, Peter Bellwood, from a story by Gary Sherman, Ronald Shusett

Phoenix ★★★ 15

Crime thriller 1998 · US · Colour · 102mins

Though it's obviously influenced by *Pulp Fiction*, this absorbing crime drama manages to do quite a lot on its own. Ray Liotta gives a commendable performance as a cop addicted to gambling who gets involved in a "foolproof" plan to rob a local loan shark. Liotta's self-destructive behaviour is repulsive yet riveting, especially when interacting with a number of other well-developed characters. KB DVD

Ray Liotta *Harry Collins* • Anjelica Huston *Leila* • Anthony LaPaglia *Mike Henshaw* • Daniel Baldwin *James Nutter* • Jeremy Piven *Fred Shuster* • Tom Noonan *Chicago* ■ *Dir* Danny Cannon • *Scr* Eddie Richey

Phone ★★★ 15

Horror 2002 · S Kor · Colour · 102mins

Those who view the mobile phone as one of the evils of modern life will warm to Ahn Byeong-ki's eerie tale of the journalist whose handset brings her into contact with the malevolent spirit of a dead schoolgirl. Ha Ji-won is suitably spooked by the spate of menacing text messages, but it's Eun Seo-woo who steals the show as the young daughter of a friend who becomes possessed. The influence of *Ring* and *The Exorcist* is a little too apparent, but Ahn still springs a surprise or two. DP. In Korean with English subtitles. DVD

Ha Ji-won *Ji-won* • Kim Yu-mi *Ho-jung* • Choi Woo-jae *Chang-hoon* • Choi Ji-yeon *Jin-hie* • Eun Seo-woo *Young-ju* ■ *Dir/Scr* Ahn Byeong-ki

Phone Booth ★★★ 15

Thriller 2002 · US · Colour · 77mins

This lean, innovative thriller has a compelling premise, but is too gimmicky to maintain its grip until the end. Colin Farrell plays an arrogant publicist who is trapped in a New York phone booth by an unseen sniper, apparently as retribution for attempting to start an affair with a client (Katie Holmes). The psychological warfare waged on Farrell by "The Caller" – voiced with malevolence by Kiefer Sutherland – carries a suspenseful charge. Although the two central performances are credible, Larry Cohen's script dials "m" for melodrama, with the arrival of amiable cop Forest Whitaker and the media dissipating much of the tension. JC. Contains violence, swearing. [video] DVD

Colin Farrell (2) *Stu Shepard* • Kiefer Sutherland *The caller* • Forest Whitaker *Captain Ramey* • Radha Mitchell *Kelly Shepard* • Katie Holmes *Pamela McFadden* • Richard T Jones *Sgt Cole* • Keith Nobbs *Adam* ■ *Dir* Joel Schumacher • *Scr* Larry Cohen

Phone Call from a Stranger ★★★ U

Portmanteau drama 1952 · US · BW · 95mins

Portmanteau movies were a fashion in the late 1940s and early 1950s, and this is an excellent example of such multi-chaptered works. A survivor from a plane crash calls the families of the three people with whom he became close on the flight. It's television fodder today, perhaps, but, in the hands of a grade-A 20th Century-Fox team, this is a fine, gripping drama, well acted by Gary Merrill and, especially, Keenan Wynn as the husband of a bedridden Bette Davis, on screen all too briefly. TS

Shelley Winters *Binky Gay* • Gary Merrill *David Trask* • Michael Rennie *Dr Fortness* • Keenan Wynn *Eddie Hoke* • Evelyn Varden *Sally Carr* • Warren Stevens *Marty Nelson* • Bette Davis *Marie Hoke* ■ *Dir* Jean Negulesco • *Scr* Nunnally Johnson, from the story by IAR Wylie

Photographing Fairies ★★★ 15

Fantasy drama 1997 · UK · Colour · 101mins

Made at the same time as *FairyTale: a True Story* and inspired by the same report of two little girls who took photos of fairies at the bottom of their garden, Nick Willing's film stars Toby Stephens as a professional debunker of photographic forgeries who stumbles upon a genuine supernatural phenomenon. Convinced that the pixies caught on camera by two young sisters will allow him to contact his dead wife, Stephens's investigation brings him into conflict with local pastor Ben Kingsley. Imaginatively shot, Willing's fantasy drama is also rather dour and downbeat. JF [video]

Toby Stephens *Charles Castle* • Emily Woof *Linda* • Ben Kingsley *Reverend Templeton* • Frances Barber *Beatrice Templeton* • Phil Davis [Philip Davis] *Roy* • Edward Hardwicke *Sir Arthur Conan Doyle* ■ *Dir* Nick Willing • *Scr* Chris Harrald, Nick Willing, from the book by Steve Szilagyi

Physical Evidence ★★ 18

Thriller 1988 · US · Colour · 95mins

A judicial lark from *Jurassic Park*'s Michael Crichton, directing, in

U = SUITABLE FOR ALL Uc = SUITABLE FOR ALL, ESPECIALLY FOR YOUNG CHILDREN (VIDEO ONLY) PG = PARENTAL GUIDANCE

dinosaur-lumbering fashion, this tough courtroom drama in which ex-cop Burt Reynolds is defended by Theresa Russell for a murder he says he didn't commit. Russell's ability to suggest obsession never matches up to her fatal attractiveness, but Reynolds manages a depressive attitude with real effectiveness. It never works up much tension, but it has its moments. TH. Contains swearing.

Burt Reynolds *Joe Paris* • Theresa Russell *Jenny Hudson* • Ned Beatty *James Nicks* • Kay Lenz *Deborah Quinn* • Ted McGinley *Kyle* • Tom O'Brien *Matt Farley* • Kenneth Welsh *Harry Norton* ■ *Dir* Michael Crichton • *Scr* Bill Phillips, from a story by Steve Ransohoff, Bill Phillips

Pi ★★★ 15

Psychological science-fiction thriller
1997 · US · BW · 80mins

In this original, fascinating thriller, Sean Gullette stars as a reclusive maths genius who becomes obsessed with the notion that everything in the universe can be broken down into mathematics and therefore follows a predictable pattern. This acclaimed feature debut from Darren Aronofsky is filled with complex issues and makes arresting use of disorientating camerawork to depict Gullette's distorted view of the world. JC. Contains swearing, violence. DVD

Sean Gullette *Maximillian Cohen* • Mark Margolis *Sol Robeson* • Ben Shenkman *Lenny Meyer* • Pamela Hart (2) *Marcy Dawson* • Stephen Pearlman *Rabbi Cohen* • Samia Shoaib *Devi* ■ *Dir* Darren Aronofsky • *Scr* Darren Aronofsky, from a story by Sean Gullette, Eric Watson, Darren Aronofsky • *Cinematographer* Matthew Libatique

Piaf: the Sparrow of Pigalle ★★★

Biographical drama
1974 · Fr · Colour · 104mins

Based on the book by Edith Piaf's half-sister, Simone Berteaut, this biopic traces the Little Sparrow's life from her troubled childhood to her first hit song. Born in the gutter and raised in a brothel, Piaf recovered from infant blindness to join her father in performing on the pavements of Paris. However, there was also the tragedy of losing her child to tuberculosis to bear before she finally found fame. Brigitte Ariel is well cast in the title role, but it's a shame that impersonator Betty Mars was used to provide the vocals and not Piaf's original recordings. DP. In French with English subtitles.

Brigitte Ariel *Edith Piaf* • Pascale Christophe *Simone Berteaut* • Guy Tréjan *Lucien Leplée* • Pierre Vernier *Raymond Asso* • Jacques Duby *Julien* • Anouk Ferjac *Madeleine* ■ *Dir* Guy Casaril • *Scr* Guy Casaril, Françoise Ferley, Marc Behm, from the biography *Piaf* by Simone Berteaut

The Pianist ★★★★ 15

Second World War biographical drama
2002 · Fr/Pol/Ger/UK · Colour · 142mins

Evoking his own childhood experiences in the Krakow ghetto, Roman Polanski laid some personal ghosts to rest with this poignant Holocaust drama based on the memoirs of survivor Wladyslaw Szpilman, and won an Oscar as best director in the process. Events are seen through the eyes of Szpilman (Adrien Brody), a Jewish concert pianist who escaped the Warsaw Ghetto as deportations to the death camps began, but witnessed its systematic destruction while in hiding. Although Brody never quite gets under Szpilman's skin, his performance remains admirable. By avoiding the simplistic and manipulative clichés of good and evil usually found in Holocaust films, Polanski has added a new layer of understanding to the cinematic depictions of the period. An emotionally and visually compelling triumph. SF. Contains violence and swearing. DVD

Adrien Brody *Wladyslaw Szpilman* • Thomas Kretschmann *Captain Wilm Hosenfeld* • Frank Finlay *Mr Szpilman* • Maureen Lipman *Mrs Szpilman* • Emilia Fox *Dorota* • Ed Stoppard *Henryk Szpilman* • Julia Rayner *Regina Szpilman* • Jessica Kate Meyer *Halina Szpilman* • Ruth Platt *Janina* ■ *Dir* Roman Polanski • *Scr* Ronald Harwood, from the non-fiction book *Death of a City* by Wladyslaw Szpilman

The Piano ★★★★★ 15

Period drama 1993 · Aus · Colour · 120mins

Director Jane Campion's superbly staged tale of passion and obsession won her an Oscar for best screenplay. Holly Hunter, who chose to stop speaking at the age of six, communicates through her daughter Anna Paquin, and her piano, which she brings with her to New Zealand when she is sent to marry local landowner Sam Neill. Hunter's new husband can read her hurriedly written notes, but he does not appreciate her music and won't take the trouble to learn either her sign language or the local Maori dialect. The illiterate Harvey Keitel, on the other hand, has fully embraced the customs of his adopted home and, belying his uncouth outward appearance, proves to be much more tender and passionate. There's a masterly score by Michael Nyman and splendid photography from Stuart Dryburgh, and Campion coaxes stupendous performances from Hunter and Paquin, who both won Oscars. DP. In English and Maori with subtitles. Contains violence, nudity. DVD

Holly Hunter *Ada* • Harvey Keitel *Baines* • Sam Neill *Stewart* • Anna Paquin *Flora* • Kerry Walker *Aunt Morag* • Geneviève Lemon *Nessie* • Tungia Baker *Hira* • Ian Mune *Reverend* ■ *Dir/Scr* Jane Campion

A Piano for Mrs Cimino ★★★

Drama 1982 · US · Colour · 100mins

This TV movie provided the 74-year-old Bette Davis with another opportunity to demonstrate her vitality and her appetite for scene-stealing. It's hardly a subtle performance, but the story of a widow battling to overturn a court ruling that she's mentally incompetent has a definite feel-good factor. This may be shameless melodrama, but it's also polished, knowingly played and involving. DP

Bette Davis *Esther Cimino* • Penny Fuller *Mrs Polanski* • Alexa Kenin *Karen Cimino* • George Hearn *George Cimino* • Christopher Guest *Philip Ryan* • Keenan Wynn *Barney Fellman* • Leroy Schulz *Harold Cimino* ■ *Dir* George Schaefer • *Scr* John Gay, from the novel by Robert Oliphant

The Piano Teacher ★★★ 18

Drama
2001 · Austria/Fr/Ger · Colour · 125mins

Isabelle Huppert plays the middle-aged tutor who lives at home with a possessive mother in spite of her morbid interest in voyeurism and pornography. No surprise then that the relationship she starts with talented but wayward student Benoît Magimel is a dark and disturbing one. Michael Haneke's adaptation is as much an indictment of modern Austria as a study of the female struggle to make a cultural, political or sexual impact. Yet, for all its thematic fidelity, this often overwrought melodrama falters because of the increasing implausibility of the plot and the problems the two leads have with conveying their anguish. DP. In French with English subtitles. DVD

Isabelle Huppert *Erika Kohut* • Annie Girardot *Mother* • Benoît Magimel *Walter Klemmer* • Susanne Lothar *Mrs Schober* • Udo Samel *Dr Blonskij* • Anna Sigalevitch *Anna Schober* ■ *Dir* Michael Haneke • *Scr* Michael Haneke, from the novel *Die Klavierspielerin* by Elfriede Jelinek

The Picasso Summer ★★

Surreal drama 1969 · US · Colour · 94mins

Astonishingly based on a short story by the great science-fiction Ray Bradbury, this is an account of a young couple (Albert Finney and Yvette Mimieux) so addicted to Picasso's works that they wander through France in the hope of meeting him. Sadly for us, it's more of a dutiful trudge than a pleasurable ramble, though the animated sequence is worth staying awake for. TH

Albert Finney *George Smith* • Yvette Mimieux *Alice Smith* • Luis Miguel Dominguin • Theo Marcuse *The Host* • Jim Connell *The Artist* ■ *Dir* Serge Bourguignon, Robert Sallin • *Scr* Douglas Spaulding [Ray Bradbury], Edwin Boyd, from the short story by Ray Bradbury

Piccadilly ★★ PG

Crime melodrama 1929 · UK · BW · 113mins

Directed by EA Dupont as a British silent, with sound added the following year, this crime melodrama, atmospherically designed by Alfred Junge, was much admired in its day as a stylish piece of work. Now, though, its old-fashioned acting is more likely to cause giggles. The plot has a nightclub owner (Jameson Thomas) fomenting rivalry between his fiancée (Gilda Gray) and his Chinese mistress (Anna May Wong). When the mistress is murdered, the fiancée is accused. Charles Laughton appears in the supporting cast, as does one Raymond (later Ray) Milland. RK DVD

Gilda Gray *Mabel Greenfield* • Jameson Thomas *Valentine Wilmot* • Anna May Wong *Shosho* • King Ho Chang *Jim* • Cyril Ritchard *Victor Smiles* • Hannah Jones *Bessie* • Charles Laughton *Greedy nightclub diner* • Raymond Milland [Ray Milland] ■ *Dir* EA Dupont • *Scr* Arnold Bennett

Piccadilly Incident ★★

Second World War melodrama
1946 · UK · BW · 102mins

Anna Neagle and Michael Wilding co-star in this British tale about a Wren and a Royal Marine who meet during an air raid, fall in love and marry, only for her to go missing, presumed dead, after the fall of Singapore. Producer/director Herbert Wilcox teamed his wife Neagle with Wilding for the first time in this emotional drama of love, war and noble sacrifice. Old-fashioned, occasionally laboured and heavily sentimental. RK

Anna Neagle *Diana Fraser* • Michael Wilding *Capt Alan Pearson* • Michael Laurence (1) *Bill Weston* • Frances Mercer *Joan Draper* • Coral Browne *Virginia Pearson* • Reginald Owen *Judge* • Roger Moore ■ *Dir* Herbert Wilcox • *Scr* Nicholas Phipps, from a story by Florence Tranter

Piccadilly Jim ★★★ U

Comedy 1936 · US · BW · 95mins

PG Wodehouse's story, previously filmed in 1920, glides through London's clubland and has an American cartoonist, Robert Montgomery, as its hero. The main plot has Montgomery converting the life of his sweetheart's family into a cartoon strip but it's the gallery of secondary characters and MGM's idea of what London Town is like that makes this creaky picture still watchable. Eric Blore plays an English butler to perfection. AT

Robert Montgomery *Jim Crocker/Jim Bayliss* • Frank Morgan *Mr James Crocker/Count Olav Osrio* • Madge Evans *Ann Chester* • Eric Blore *Bayliss* • Billie Burke *Eugenia Willis* • Robert Benchley *Bill Macon* • Ralph Forbes *Lord Freddie Priory* • Cora Witherspoon *Nesta Pett* ■ *Dir* Robert Z Leonard • *Scr* Charles Brackett, Edwin Knopf, Lynn Starling, Samuel Hoffenstein, from the novel *Piccadilly Jim* by PG Wodehouse as serialised in *The Saturday Evening Post*

Piccadilly Third Stop ★

Crime thriller 1960 · UK · BW · 90mins

This is a plodding low-budget thriller, with Terence Morgan playing a London low-lifer who dates ambassador's daughter Yoko Tani in order to gain access to the embassy safe. Dennis Price, William Hartnell and Mai Zetterling are among those who obviously needed the work. DP

Terence Morgan *Dominic Colpoys-Owen* • Yoko Tani *Seraphina Yokami* • John Crawford *Joe Preedy* • Mai Zetterling *Christine Preedy* • William Hartnell *Colonel* • Dennis Price *Edward* ■ *Dir* Wolf Rilla • *Scr* Leigh Vance

Pick a Star ★ U

Musical comedy 1937 · US · BW · 66mins

Innocent young hopeful Rosina Lawrence arrives in Hollywood hoping for stardom and, after some disillusion, gets a screen test thanks to Jack Haley. This thoroughly feeble movie was misleadingly presented as a Laurel and Hardy comedy – they appear in only a couple of brief sequences that make for the brightest spots. RK

Patsy Kelly *Nellie Moore* • Jack Haley *Joe Jenkins* • Rosina Lawrence *Cecilia Moore* • Mischa Auer *Rinaldo Lopez* • Stan Laurel *Stan* • Oliver Hardy *Oliver* ■ *Dir* Edward Sedgwick • *Scr* Richard Flournoy, Arthur Vernon Jones, Thomas J Dugan

The Pick-Up Artist ★ 15

Comedy drama 1987 · US · Colour · 77mins

A great cast is stymied by half-baked dialogue and a barely-there plot in cult director James Toback's dating disaster. Serial womaniser Robert Downey Jr puts the make on feisty Molly Ringwald and is amazed when she doesn't respond to his chat-up lines. Wise girl! Downey Jr emits none of his future star charisma. AJ. Contains swearing.

Molly Ringwald *Randy Jensen* • Robert Downey Jr *Jack Jericho* • Dennis Hopper *Flash Jensen* • Danny Aiello *Phil* • Mildred Dunnock *Nellie, Jack's grandmother* • Harvey Keitel *Alonzo* • Brian Hamill *Mike* • Vanessa L Williams *Rae* ■ *Dir/Scr* James Toback

P

Picking Up the Pieces ★ 15

Black comedy 2000 · US · Colour · 91mins

This abysmal religious satire consistently misses the easiest of targets and succeeds only in humiliating a stellar cast. Least besmirched is Woody Allen, as a New Mexico butcher who murders shrewish wife Sharon Stone and dismembers her corpse, only to discover her severed hand is being credited with a series of miracles. So far, so unfunny. But with the arrival of Elliott Gould at the head of a Vatican fact-finding commission, the whole sorry mess spirals into crass, crude, and irreverent misanthropy. DP DVD

Woody Allen *Tex Cowley* • David Schwimmer *Father Leo Jerome* • Maria Grazia Cucinotta *Desi* • Cheech Marin [Richard "Cheech" Marin] *Mayor Machado* • Kiefer Sutherland *Bobo* • Sharon Stone *Candy Cowley* • Elliott Gould *Father LaCage* • Fran Drescher *Sister Frida* • Lou Diamond Phillips *Officer Alfonso* ■ *Dir* Alfonso Arau • *Scr* Bill Wilson

The Pickle ★ 15

Comedy 1993 · US · Colour · 98mins

Danny Aiello plays a film director (whose most recent movie is a sci-fi tale about a giant pickle hence the title) desperately in need of a career boost. Unfortunately, despite an interesting supporting cast, this is virtually unwatchable. It fails to find the appropriate tone and generally misfires on all cylinders. TS

Danny Aiello *Harry Stone* • Dyan Cannon *Ellen Stone* • Clotilde Courau *Françoise* • Shelley Winters *Yetta* • Barry Miller *Ronnie Liebowitz* • Jerry Stiller *Phil Hirsch* • Chris Penn *Gregory Stone* • Little Richard *President* • Griffin Dunne *President's man* • Dudley Moore *Planet Cleveland Man* • Donald Trump ■ *Dir/Scr* Paul Mazursky

Pickpocket ★★★★ PG

Crime drama 1959 · Fr · BW · 72mins

A mesmeric sequence in which a young thief learns the tricks of the trade from a master pickpocket is the highlight of Robert Bresson's exceptional study of obsession, desperation and guilt. Inspired by Dostoyevsky's *Crime and Punishment*, the film follows a theme used several times by Bresson as lonely individuals lay bare their souls in the midst of personal torment. Martin Lassalle gives a performance of chilling restraint as the possessed "dip", but it is Bresson's control over his cast, the Parisian locations and the austere imagery that makes this extraordinary film so compelling. DP. In French with English subtitles. DVD

Martin Lassalle [Martin Lasalle] *Michel* • Marika Green *Jeanne* • Jean Pélégri *Inspector* • Dolly Scal *Michel's mother* • Pierre Leymarie *Jacques* • Kassagi *Accomplice* • Pierre Etaix *Accomplice* • César Gattegno *Detective* ■ *Dir/Scr* Robert Bresson • *Cinematographer* Léonce-Henri Burel

Pickup on South Street ★★ PG

Film noir 1953 · US · BW · 77mins

A pick-up that's a hiccup for petty thief Richard Widmark, pocketing more than he bargained for by stealing Jean Peters's purse, only to find it loaded with espionage plans. Not one of director Sam Fuller's most successful outings – the anti-Communist spiel seems tacked on to cash in on contemporary hysteria – though it's worth a look for Thelma Ritter's acid-drop old lady betraying all to save up for "a plot and a stone". TH DVD

Richard Widmark *Skip McCoy* • Jean Peters *Candy* • Thelma Ritter *Moe* • Murvyn Vye *Captain Dan Tiger* • Richard Kiley *Joey* ■ *Dir* Samuel Fuller • *Scr* Samuel Fuller, from a story by Dwight Taylor

The Pickwick Papers ★★★ U

Comedy 1952 · UK · BW · 104mins

Dickens's sprawling, episodic novel has been reined in by writer/director Noel Langley without sacrificing too much of its jaunty good nature. Brimming over with memorable characters, the film is well served by some solid performances. James Hayter is the embodiment of Pickwick, really hitting his stride during the breach of promise trial. Not all the vignettes come off, but Nigel Patrick is bang on form as the disreputable Mr Jingle, and Kathleen Harrison is ever-excellent. DP

James Hayter *Samuel Pickwick* • James Donald *Mr Winkle* • Alexander Gauge *Mr Tupman* • Lionel Murton *Mr Snodgrass* • Nigel Patrick *Mr Jingle* • Kathleen Harrison *Rachael Wardle* • Joyce Grenfell *Mrs Leo Hunter* • Hermione Gingold *Miss Tomkins* • Donald Wolfit *Sergeant Buzfuz* • Hermione Baddeley *Mrs Bardell* • Hattie Jacques *Mrs Nupkins* ■ *Dir* Noel Langley • *Scr* Noel Langley, from the novel by Charles Dickens

Picnic ★★★ U

Drama 1955 · US · Colour · 108mins

Adapted by Daniel Taradash from William Inge's Pulitzer Prize-winning play, and directed for maximum cinematic effect by Joshua Logan, *Picnic* earned six Oscar nominations for its daringly frank depiction (by 1950s standards) of the emotional havoc wrought on the women of a rustic Kansas town when a sexy itinerant wanders in to their Labor Day picnic. William Holden (not ideal for the role, but giving a polished performance) is the attractive cat among the pigeons. Enjoyable drama with an edge. RK

William Holden (2) *Hal Carter* • Rosalind Russell *Rosemary Sydney* • Betty Field *Flo Owens* • Kim Novak *Madge Owens* • Susan Strasberg *Millie Owens* • Cliff Robertson *Alan* ■ *Dir* Joshua Logan • *Scr* Daniel Taradash, from the play by William Inge

Picnic at Hanging Rock ★★★★ PG

Psychological mystery
1975 · Aus · Colour · 110mins

On St Valentine's Day in 1900 a party of schoolgirls enjoys a day at Hanging Rock, a local beauty spot. But something odd is at work: clocks stop at midday and three girls vanish. Dingo dogs, extraterrestrials, kidnappers or what? Director Peter Weir leaves clues hanging in the air like a glistening spider's web, hears celestial choirs and thrumming insects – he hasn't the foggiest, but he adores ambiguity, mysticism and metaphor. This is a very sexy picture, which stares an enigma straight in the eye. There are fine performances, which, with the outstanding location work, add up to a class act. AT DVD

Rachel Roberts (1) *Mrs Appleyard* • Dominic Guard *Michael Fitzhubert* • Helen Morse *Dianne de Potiers* • Jacki Weaver *Minnie* • Vivean Gray *Miss McCraw* • Kirsty Child *Dora Lumley* • Anne Lambert [Anne Louise Lambert] *Miranda* ■ *Dir* Peter Weir • *Scr* Cliff Green, from the novel by Joan Lindsay • *Cinematographer* Russell Boyd

Picture Bride ★★ 12

Period drama 1994 · US · Colour · 94mins

Set in 1918, Kayo Hatta's debut feature recalls the old custom of using photographs to arrange marriages between Japanese workers in Hawaii and girls back home. The action captures a sense of period and place in spite of financial restraint. But there are few fresh insights into loveless marriage or the trials facing women in a patriarchal society, as 16-year-old Youki Kudoh attempts to escape the elderly husband who tricked her into emigrating. DP. In English and Japanese with subtitles.

Youki Kudoh *Riyo* • Akira Takayama *Matsuji* • Tamlyn Tomita *Kana* • Cary-Hiroyuki Tagawa *Kanzaki* • Toshiro Mifune *The Benshi* • Yoko Sugi *Aunt Sode* ■ *Dir* Kayo Hatta • *Scr* Kayo Hatta, Mari Hatta, Kayo Hatta, Mari Hatta, Diane Mei Lin Mark

Picture Mommy Dead ★★

Horror 1966 · US · Colour · 82mins

Typical 1960s "shocker" with Susan Gordon (daughter of the film's director, Bert I Gordon) haunted by dim memories of her mother's mysterious death. Pure melodrama (wicked stepmother, scarred caretaker, an absurd chain of events) is punctuated by shock effects to enjoyably silly result. A bonus is the cast of veterans trying to retain their dignity. DM

Don Ameche *Edward Shelley* • Martha Hyer *Francene Shelley* • Zsa Zsa Gabor *Jessica* • Susan Gordon *Susan Shelley* • Maxwell Reed *Anthony* • Wendell Corey *Clayborn* • Signe Hasso *Sister Rene* ■ *Dir* Bert I Gordon • *Scr* Robert Sherman

The Picture of Dorian Gray ★★★★

Period horror drama
1945 · US · BW and Colour · 109mins

This big-budget version of Oscar Wilde's only novel was rather a curious venture for a studio that prided itself on its family entertainment. But flamboyant screenwriter/director Albert Lewin turned in a compelling picture that teeters between sophistication and vulgarity. Hurd Hatfield gives a muted performance as Dorian and is thus easily surpassed by Angela Lansbury, who plays the chirpy music-hall singer with whom he falls in lust, and by George Sanders as the languidly witty Lord Henry Wotton. The picture earned supervising art director Cedric Gibbons one of his record 40 Oscar nominations. DP

George Sanders *Lord Henry Wotton* • Hurd Hatfield *Dorian Gray* • Donna Reed *Gladys Hallward* • Angela Lansbury *Sibyl Vane* • Peter Lawford *David Stone* • Lowell Gilmore *Basil Hallward* • Richard Fraser *James Vane* • Douglas Walton *Allen Campbell* ■ *Dir* Albert Lewin • *Scr* Albert Lewin, from the novel *The Picture of Dorian Gray* by Oscar Wilde • *Cinematographer* Harry Stradling

Picture Perfect ★★★ PG

Romantic comedy
1997 · US · Colour · 97mins

Glenn Gordon Caron directs Jennifer Aniston in this good-natured romantic comedy. Aniston is the single girl who discovers she needs a boyfriend to succeed at work. So she invents a fiancé using a photo of her with a complete stranger taken at a wedding. Of course, it's not long before her bosses want to meet the man (Jay Mohr), so she has to track him down, complicating the secret affair she's having with a corporate sleaze (a fun performance from Kevin Bacon). Preposterous, but sweetly done. JB. Contains swearing. DVD

Jennifer Aniston *Kate* • Jay Mohr *Nick* • Kevin Bacon *Sam* • Olympia Dukakis *Rita* • Illeana Douglas *Darcy* • Kevin Dunn *Mr Mercer* • Anne Twomey *Sela* • Faith Prince *Mrs Mercer* ■ *Dir* Glenn Gordon Caron • *Scr* Glenn Gordon Caron, Arleen Sorkin, Paul Slansky, from a story by May Quigley, Arleen Sorkin, Paul Slansky

The Picture Show Man ★★

Comedy drama 1977 · Aus · Colour · 99mins

Rod Taylor returned to his native Australia for a good-natured but rambling account of the early years of cinema, playing a villainous entrepreneur dogging the steps of the film's real hero, played by John Meillon. The two rivals slog their way around the outback drumming up enthusiasm for the picture show among the bemused citizens, and there's enough humour en route to keep the attention from flagging. RSm

Rod Taylor *Palmer* • John Meillon *Mr Pym, "Pop"* • John Ewart *Freddie* • Harold Hopkins *Larry* • Sally Conabere *Lucy* • Patrick Cargill *Fitzwilliam* ■ *Dir* John Power • *Scr* Joan Long

Picture Snatcher ★★★

Crime drama 1933 · US · BW · 74mins

Great title for a terrific James Cagney vehicle from that marvellous period at Warner Bros when pace was everything and dialogue just snapped and crackled its way across the screen. Cagney was making five or six movies a year at this time, his cocky optimism at odds with the downbeat reality of everyday living. He is seldom more dynamic than here, playing a whirlwind photographer, based on a true character, who succeeded in getting published a gruesome photo of a murderess being electrocuted. TS

James Cagney *Danny Kean* • Ralph Bellamy *McLean* • Patricia Ellis *Patricia Nolan* • Alice White *Allison* • Ralf Harolde *Jerry* ■ *Dir* Lloyd Bacon • *Scr* Allen Rivkin, PJ Wolfson, Ben Markson, from a story by Danny Ahearn

Pictures of the Old World ★★★

Documentary 1972 · Cz · Colour · 74mins

The Slovakian director Dusan Hanak had the dubious distinction of having his first three films banned by the Czech authorities. This rural documentary offended the Communist regime for daring to suggest that isolated shepherds and hill farmers had managed to resist Party propaganda and retain their old ways and ideas. It was banned until the late 1980s when the democratically elected government opened up the film vaults. DP. In Czech with English subtitles.

Dir/Scr Dusan Hanak

Pie in the Sky ★★★ 18

Romantic comedy
1995 · US · Colour · 90mins

This quirky romantic comedy neatly avoids the usual slushy clichés. Josh Charles plays an offbeat teen, who was conceived during a traffic jam, and now remains obsessed with gridlock. That is, until the girl next door grows up into beautiful dancer Anne Heche. The two leads are charming, although the film is stolen by a typically larger-than-life performance from John Goodman as a wacky eye in the sky traffic reporter. Bryan Gordon's direction is unobtrusive and, even if it fades a little towards the end, there are plenty of funny moments. JF

Josh Charles *Charlie* • Anne Heche *Amy* • John Goodman *Alan Davenport* • Christine Lahti *Ruby* • Christine Ebersole *Mom Dunlap* • Peter Riegert *Dad Dunlap* • Dey Young *Mrs Tarnell* • Bob Balaban *Mr Entamen* • Wil Wheaton *Jack* ■ *Dir/Scr* Bryan Gordon

A Piece of the Action ★★ 15

Comedy 1977 · US · Colour · 129mins

The third teaming of Sidney Poitier and Bill Cosby (after *Uptown Saturday Night* and *Let's Do It Again*) continues their comic misadventures as two con artists. This time they avoid a jail sentence by volunteering to work with under-privileged kids. It's a well-intentioned, occasionally funny farce, exploiting the easy charm of the two able leads, but Poitier's direction overemphasises the preachy and saccharine elements. AJ

Sidney Poitier *Manny Durrell* • Bill Cosby *Dave Anderson* • James Earl Jones *Joshua Burke* • Denise Nicholas *Lila French* • Hope Clarke *Sarah Thomas* • Tracy Reed *Nikki McLean* • Titos Vandis *Bruno* ■ *Dir* Sidney Poitier • *Scr* Charles Blackwell, from a story by Timothy March

Pieces ★ 18

Horror 1982 · It/Sp · Colour · 81mins

Real-life husband-and-wife team Christopher and Lynda Day George must rue the day they agreed to star in this twisted stalk-and-slash flick. George is a cop hunting down a psycho who chops up college girls for body parts to make a grotesque human jigsaw. Is one really to take Spanish director Juan Piquer Simon's effort seriously, riddled as it is with goofs and inane dialogue? RS

Christopher George *Lieutenant Bracken* • Edmund Purdom *Dean* • Lynda Day George *Mary Riggs* • Paul Smith *Willard* ■ *Dir* Juan Piquer Simon • *Scr* Dick Randall, John Shadow [Aristide Massaccesi]

Pieces of April ★★★ 12

Comedy drama 2002 · US · Colour · 78mins

Katie Holmes plays the grunged-up and scowling April Burns, whose shifting moods reach a crescendo when she decides to host a Thanksgiving meal for her estranged family, including her cancer-stricken mother (Patricia Clarkson). Everything that could go wrong invariably does, leading to moments of bittersweet comedy that are as touching as they are amusing. Holmes excels as the black sheep of the Burns clan, but her heartfelt performance is overshadowed by the Oscar-nominated Clarkson, whose brutal honesty and coldness are poignantly exact. SF. Contains swearing and drug abuse. [VIDEO] DVD

Katie Holmes *April Burns* • Patricia Clarkson *Joy Burns* • Derek Luke *Bobby* • Sean Hayes *Wayne* • Oliver Platt *Jim Burns* • Alison Pill *Beth Burns* • John Gallagher Jr *Timmy Burns* • Alice Drummond *Grandma Dottie* • SisQo [Sisqo] *Latrell* ■ *Dir/Scr* Peter Hedges

Pieces of Dreams ★★

Romantic drama 1970 · US · Colour · 99mins

Despite touching on controversial subjects that challenged the Catholic Church, this adaptation is too melodramatic for any serious examination of doctrinal issues. Disenchanted with his pastoral role, Robert Forster's inner-city priest has to endure a street gang accusing him of being gay as well as bishop Will Geer and his family badgering him to keep the faith. No wonder he comes to question his vocation after falling for wealthy social worker Lauren Hutton. This is a very human crisis, but director Daniel Haller seems more concerned with sin and sensationalism. DP

Robert Forster *Gregory Lind* • Lauren Hutton *Pamela Gibson* • Will Geer *Bishop* • Ivor Francis *Father Paul Schaeffer* • Richard O'Brien *Mgr Francis Hurley* ■ *Dir* Daniel Haller • *Scr* Roger Hirson, from the novel *The Wine and the Music* by William E Barrett

The Pied Piper ★★★ U

Second World War drama
1942 · US · BW · 86mins

The Pied Piper theme is transferred to the Second World War, with Monty Woolley emotionally allergic to children but forced to lead two of them out of Nazi-occupied France. Woolley gives a fine performance, successfully overturning our belief in his pathological state, and helping what could have been a squeakily saccharine offering become an often intensely moving film, sadly spoilt overall by some very dull patches. SH

Monty Woolley *Howard* • Roddy McDowall *Ronnie Cavanaugh* • Anne Baxter *Nicole Rougeron* • Otto Preminger *Major Diessen* • J Carrol Naish *Aristide Rougeron* • Lester Matthews *Mr Cavanaugh* • Jill Esmond *Mrs Cavanaugh* • Ferike Boros *Madame* ■ *Dir* Irving Pichel • *Scr* Nunnally Johnson, from the novel by Nevil Shute

The Pied Piper ★★ PG

Fantasy drama 1971 · UK · Colour · 86mins

From French director Jacques Demy, the master of enchantment, this is a lumpen disappointment. Based on the Grimm brothers' fairy tale and the Robert Browning poem about the medieval minstrel whose music rids the town of Hamelin of its plague of rats, the lead is played by British pop-singer Donovan – in one of his few films, and one can see why. But though prettily olde worlde to look at, it lacks the necessary ingredients of fantasy and appeal. TH [VIDEO]

Donald Pleasence *Baron* • Donovan *The Pied Piper* • Jack Wild *Gavin* • John Hurt *Franz* • Michael Hordern *Melius* • Roy Kinnear *Burgermeister* • Diana Dors *Frau Poppendick* ■ *Dir* Jacques Demy • *Scr* Andrew Birkin, Jacques Demy, Mark Peploe, from the poem by Robert Browning, from the fairy tale by Jacob Grimm, Wilhelm Grimm

Pièges ★★★★

Thriller 1939 · Fr · BW · 115mins

This was Robert Siodmak's last French-made film before his departure for Hollywood, and it is interesting to see how much this thriller, with its police investigation and seedy characters, prefigures the "night city" movies of his American period. The excellent cast includes Maurice Chevalier as a nightclub owner, with Pierre Renoir (Jean's elder brother) and Erich von Stroheim as prime suspects connected with the disappearance of a number of young women. The film was remade in 1947 by Douglas Sirk as *Lured*. RB. A French language film.

Maurice Chevalier *Robert Fleury* • Erich von Stroheim *Pears* • Pierre Renoir *Bremontière* • Marie Déa *Adrienne* • André Brunot *Ténier* ■ *Dir* Robert Siodmak • *Scr* Jacques Companeez, Ernest Neuville, Simon Gantillon

Pierrot le Fou ★★★★★ 15

Drama 1965 · Fr/It · Colour · 105mins

"*Pierrot le Fou* isn't really a film," said director Jean-Luc Godard on its release, "It's an attempt at cinema." Although it was based on Lionel White's novel *Obsession*, the action was nearly all improvised as Godard was inspired by the locations en route from Paris to the south of France. Shot in razor sharp colour by Raoul Coutard, it is a bewildering blend of genres and visual styles, but the over-riding atmosphere is one of despair for both runaways Jean-Paul Belmondo and Anna Karina and for the violent world of the mid-1960s. DP. In French with English subtitles. [VIDEO] DVD

Jean-Paul Belmondo *Ferdinand Griffon, "Pierrot"* • Anna Karina *Marianne Renoir* • Dirk Sanders *Fred, Marianne's brother* • Raymond Devos *Man on pier* • Graziella Galvani *Ferdinand's wife* • Sam Fuller [Samuel Fuller] • Laszlo Szabo *Political exile* • Jean-Pierre Léaud *Young man in cinema* ■ *Dir* Jean-Luc Godard • *Scr* Jean-Luc Godard, from the novel *Obsession* by Lionel White

The Pigeon That Took Rome ★★

Second World War comedy
1962 · US · BW · 101mins

Charlton Heston plays an American army captain smuggled into Rome under the nose of its German occupiers. He makes contact with the partisans – especially Elsa Martinelli – and falls in with a daft spy scheme involving a carrier pigeon. It's all a bit silly, and the American studio interiors make for some ugly joins with the exterior locations. Heston is miscast, though his discomfort proves to be the source of the biggest chuckles. AT

Charlton Heston *Capt Paul MacDougall* • Elsa Martinelli *Antonella Massimo* • Harry Guardino *Sgt Joseph Contini* • Salvatore Baccaloni *Ciccio Massimo* • Marietto *Livio Massimo* ■ *Dir* Melville Shavelson • *Scr* Melville Shavelson, from the novel *The Easter Dinner* by Donald Downes

Piglet's Big Movie ★★★ U

Animated adventure
2003 · US · Colour · 71mins

A juvenile audience will be enchanted by this animated tribute to the diminutive sidekick from *Winnie the Pooh* – and some adults could find enough here to go along with them. Tiny Piglet (voiced by John Fiedler) is feeling very low because he's far too near the ground. He sets off into the woods, wondering how he can gain height to be able to help his friends. Director Francis Glebas and writer Brian Hohlfeld have created a well-crafted fable, while Carly Simon's songs boost the film's charm and moments of poignancy. TH [VIDEO] DVD

John Fiedler *Piglet* • Jim Cummings *Winnie the Pooh/Tigger* • Andre Stojka *Owl* • Kath Soucie *Kanga* • Nikita Hopkins *Roo* • Peter Cullen *Eeyore* • Ken Sansom *Rabbit* • Tom Wheatley *Christopher Robin* ■ *Dir* Francis Glebas • *Scr* Brian Hohlfeld, inspired by the stories by AA Milne • *Music* Carly Simon

A Pig's Tale ★★ U

Comedy 1994 · US · Colour · 89mins

When oddball youngster Joe Flaherty is sent to summer camp, he finds himself sharing a cabin with three other losers. Together they manage to triumph against the odds stacked against them. Juvenile high jinks with the simple message that even misfits can make good. DF [VIDEO]

Joe Flaherty *Milt* • Graham Sack *Andy* • Mike Damus *Frank* • Andrew Harrison Leeds *Beckerwood* • Lisa Jakub *Tiffany* • Jake Beecham *Swackback* • Jimmy Zepeda *Cruz* ■ *Dir* Paul Tassie • *Scr* Charles Ransom, Scott Sandorf, Todd Richardson

Pigskin Parade ★★★ U

Musical comedy 1936 · US · BW · 92mins

A rather silly, if charming, 20th Century-Fox football musical, worth watching today for its cast, including a young Judy Garland in her first feature. Stuart Erwin and Patsy Kelly are the leads in this likeable romp, but keep an eye out for a gauche Tony Martin, Betty Grable a decade before she became Queen of the Fox lot, and don't-blink-or-you'll-miss Alan Ladd, singing with the Yacht Club Boys. TS

Stuart Erwin *Amos Dodd* • Patsy Kelly *Bessie Winters* • Jack Haley *"Slug" Winston Winters* • Johnny Downs *Chip Carson* • Betty Grable *Laura Watson* • Arline Judge *Sally Saxon* • Dixie Dunbar *Ginger Jones* • Judy Garland *Sairy Dodd* • Alan Ladd *Student* • Anthony Martin [Tony Martin] *Tommy Barker* ■ *Dir* David Butler • *Scr* Harry Tugend, Jack Yellen, William Conselman, from a story by Arthur Sheekman, Nat Perrin, Mark Kelly

Pigsty ★★★

Satirical drama
1969 · It/Fr · Colour · 110mins

After great success during the 1960s, Pasolini's controversial career suffered popular decline with three films, including this satire, paralleling a story of cannibalistic soldier Pierre Clémenti roaming a medieval wasteland, with that of the son (Jean-Pierre Léaud) of a former Nazi industrialist. The latter is more enamoured of the pigs, which finally devour him, than of his fiancée. Pasolini appears little interested in the narrative and more concerned with appalling images that parody his work and that of other directors and attacking the capitalist society he despised while experimenting with language and film form. BB. In Italian with English subtitles.

Pierre Clémenti *Young cannibal* • Jean-Pierre Léaud *Julian Klotz* • Ugo Tognazzi *Herdhitze* • Marco Ferreri *Hans Guenther* ■ *Dir/Scr* Pier Paolo Pasolini

The Pilgrim ★★★ U

Silent comedy 1923 · US · BW · 41mins

Charles Chaplin's genius at creating comedy out of desperate situations is well illustrated in this film. He's in hot water as an escaped convict who steals the clothes of a gospel minister and gets roped in to preaching to the congregation of Hell's Hinges, falling for Edna Purviance while bringing a former fellow inmate to justice. Inevitably, the film drew protests from both redneck religionists and the Ku Klux Klan. TH

Charlie Chaplin [Charles Chaplin] *The pilgrim* • Edna Purviance *The girl* • Kitty Bradbury *Her mother* • Mack Swain *The deacon* • Loyal Underwood *The elder* • Dinky Dean *The boy* • Mai Wells *his mother* • Sydney Chaplin [Syd Chaplin] *Her husband* • Chuck Reisner [Charles Reisner] *The crook* ■ *Dir* Charles Chaplin • *Scr* Charles Chaplin

Pilgrimage ★★★

Drama 1933 · US · BW · 96mins

Cruelly possessive mother Henrietta Crosman, wanting to keep her son from the girl (Marian Nixon) he loves, enlists him in the army, resulting in his death on the Western Front. Nixon bears his son, who is also harshly treated by an even more hardened Crosman – until the woman goes on a pilgrimage to the war graves in France. This is uncharacteristic material for John Ford, but it's beautifully shot and a great showcase for the formidable stage actress Crosman. Its themes and incidents seem over-familiar now, but it offers depth, sweep and honest conviction, despite its unrealistic "happy" ending. RK

Henrietta Crosman *Hannah Jessop* • Heather Angel *Suzanne* • Norman Foster *Jim Jessop* • Marian Nixon *Mary Saunders* • Maurice Murphy *Gary Worth* • Lucille La Verne *Mrs Hatfield* • Charley Grapewin *Dad Saunders* • Hedda Hopper *Mrs Worth* ■ *Dir* John Ford • *Scr* Philip Klein, Barry Connors, Dudley Nichols, from the story *Gold Star Mother* by I AR Wylie

Pillars of Society ★★

Drama 1935 · Ger · BW · 82mins

After 20 years in America, Albrecht Schoenhals returns to his native Norway and a reunion with his former business partner Heinrich George. His presence causes upheaval, as he threatens to reveal dark secrets hiding behind the veneer of respectable society. This German adaptation of Ibsen's play never transcends its stage origins and plays out as a rather static and ponderous melodrama. Director Detlef Sierck, however, does display the touch which would bring him fame as Hollywood's Douglas Sirk. RK. A German language film.

Heinrich George *Consul Bernick* • Maria Krahn *Betty, his wife* • Horst Teetzmann *Olaf, his son* • Albrecht Schönhals *Johann Tonnessen* ■ *Dir* Detlef Sierck [Douglas Sirk] • *Scr* Dr Georg C Klaren, Karl Peter Gillman, from the play by Henrik Ibsen

Pillars of the Sky ★★

Western 1956 · US · Colour · 92mins

This handsome-looking CinemaScope western stars two of Universal's smouldering contract icons, Jeff Chandler and Dorothy Malone, in a tale with a decidedly sanctimonious tone (the none-too-subtle British title, *The Tomahawk and the Cross*, says it all). Director George Marshall does what he can with a weak script, but there's a feeling that no one's heart is in tune with the sentiments expressed. TS

Jeff Chandler *First Sergeant Emmett Bell* • Dorothy Malone *Calla Gaxton* • Ward Bond *Doctor Joseph Holden* • Keith Andes *Captain Tom Gaxton* • Lee Marvin *Sergeant Lloyd Carracart* ■ *Dir* George Marshall • *Scr* Sam Rolfe, from the novel *Frontier Fury* by Will Henry

The Pillow Book ★★★★ 18

Erotic drama
1995 · Neth/Fr/UK · Col/BW · 121m

Extraordinary. Ravishing. Preposterous. The usual descriptions of director Peter Greenaway's work can all be applied here in spades. Even more overwrought and over-decorated than his previous films, Greenaway's Hong Kong-set tale of sex and power centres on the fetish of Vivian Wu who enjoys having her flesh written upon, and who takes a dreadful revenge on the homosexual publisher who degraded her father. The split-screen motifs are a wonder to behold but, although it deals with white-hot emotions, the film is as ice-cold as winter. TH. In English and Japanese with subtitles. Contains violence, sex scenes, drug abuse and nudity. [VIDEO] DVD

P

Vivian Wu *Nagiko* • Ewan McGregor *Jerome* • Yoshi Oida *Publisher* • Ken Ogata *Father* • Hideko Yoshida *Aunt/Maid* • Judy Ongg *Mother* • Ken Mitsuishi *Husband* ■ *Dir/Scr* Peter Greenaway

Pillow of Death ★★

Mystery 1945 · US · BW · 66mins

This negligible entry in Universal's *Inner Sanctum* series offers Lon Chaney Jr one of its more interesting challenges. As a lawyer unhappily married to Victoria Horne, he's released due to lack of evidence following her murder. However, as he tries to start again with secretary Brenda Joyce, the killings keep occurring and he's haunted by the voice of his dead spouse. Chaney's mournful bewilderment adds a surprisingly affecting human element to the story, but Wallace Fox's direction is short on both suspense and finesse. DP

Lon Chaney [Lon Chaney Jr] *Wayne Fletcher* • Brenda Joyce *Donna Kincaid* • J Edward Bromberg *Julian Julian* • Rosalind Ivan *Amelia Kincaid* • Clara Blandick *Belle Kincaid* • George Cleveland *Samuel Kincaid* • Victoria Horne *Vivia Fletcher* ■ *Dir* Wallace Fox • *Scr* George Bricker, from a story by Dwight V Babcock

Pillow Talk ★★★★ PG

Romantic comedy
1959 · US · Colour · 98mins

This is the first and most entertaining of the series of comedies Doris Day made for Universal Studios that gave the singing star a career lift and successfully teamed her with the likes of Cary Grant, James Garner and her most popular partner, Rock Hudson. It's ultra-glossy froth, and the smart plot about Day and Hudson sharing a telephone party line won an Oscar for best story and screenplay. Hudson displays a flair for adroit humour, but the funniest material goes to Tony Randall (never better) and the acerbic Thelma Ritter, and both shine through the heavily piled-on glamour. Director Michael Gordon's use of CinemaScope is exemplary. TS DVD

Doris Day *Jan Morrow* • Rock Hudson *Brad Allen* • Tony Randall *Jonathan Forbes* • Thelma Ritter *Alma* • Nick Adams *Tony Walters* • Julia Meade *Marie* ■ *Dir* Michael Gordon • *Scr* Stanley Shapiro, Maurice Richlin, from a story by Russell Rouse, Clarence Greene

P

The Pilot ★★ PG

Drama 1979 · US · Colour · 93mins

Cliff Robertson directs, co-scripts and stars in this worthy drama about a once-lauded pilot's battle with alcoholism. It's a bit dull and, despite a quality supporting cast that includes Dana Andrews and Gordon MacRae, Robertson is clearly overstretched. Nevertheless, the fantastic aerial photography and stirring score help to stave off the ennui. RT

Cliff Robertson *Mike Hagan* • Diane Baker *Pat Simpson* • Frank Converse *Jim Cochran* • Dana Andrews *Randolph Evers* • Milo O'Shea *Dr O'Brian* • Gordon MacRae *Joe Barnes* ■ *Dir* Cliff Robertson • *Scr* Cliff Robertson, Robert P Davis, from the novel by Robert P Davis • *Cinematographer* Walter Lassally • *Music* John Addison

Pilot #5 ★★

Second World War drama
1943 · US · BW · 70mins

Lawyer Franchot Tone is in league with a fascist politician. But then Tone atones for his misjudgment of character by becoming a fighter pilot. Told in a series of flashbacks, this is heavily contrived and rather dully directed by George Sidney, later famous for his musicals. Also famous for musicals was third-billed Gene Kelly, making his second film appearance as Tone's wartime buddy. AT

Franchot Tone *Lt George Braynor Collins* • Marsha Hunt *Freddie Andrews* • Gene Kelly *Vito S Alessandro* • Van Johnson *Everett Arnold* • Alan Baxter *Winston Davis* • Dick Simmons *Henry Willoughby Claven* • Peter Lawford *English soldier* • Ava Gardner *Girl* ■ *Dir* George Sidney (2) • *Scr* David Hertz, from his story

The Pilot's Wife ★★

Romantic drama
2001 · Can/US · Colour · 89mins

The excellent Christine Lahti is certainly not stretched in this romantic TV drama about a loyal wife whose distress at the death of pilot husband John Heard is compounded by the fact that he had been living a double life. Lahti's scenes with her daughter Alison Pill are pure melodrama, but Anita Shreve's adaptation of her own novel descends into soap opera as Lahti arrives in Britain to confront Heard's secret love, Kirsty Mitchell. DP. Contains swearing, sex scenes.

Christine Lahti *Kathryn Lyons* • Campbell Scott *Robert Hart* • Alison Pill *Mattie Lyons* • Kirsty Mitchell *Muire Boland* • John Heard *Jack Lyons* • Nigel Bennett *Dick Somers* ■ *Dir* Robert Markowitz • *Scr* Christine Berardo, Anita Shreve, from the novel by Anita Shreve

Pimpernel Smith ★★★★ U

Second World War spy drama
1941 · UK · BW · 115mins

The screen's greatest Scarlet Pimpernel, Leslie Howard, updates the character to Nazi-occupied Europe in this smashing piece of wartime propaganda. Howard also directs with style, and if the plot is preposterous – archaeologist Howard smuggles refugees out from under the very noses of the Gestapo and then goes back to Berlin to rescue a girl – it awakened the world, and particularly America, to Europe's plight. With this film, and both *The First of the Few* and *The Gentle Sex*, it became clear that Howard was a potent propaganda weapon. TS

Leslie Howard *Prof Horatio Smith* • Francis Sullivan [Francis L Sullivan] *Gen von Graum* • Mary Morris *Ludmilla Koslowski* • Hugh McDermott *David Maxwell* • Raymond Huntley *Marx* • Manning Whiley *Bertie Gregson* • Peter Gawthorne *Sidimir Koslowski* • Allan Jeayes *Dr Beckendorf* • Michael Rennie *Officer at concentration camp* ■ *Dir* Leslie Howard • *Scr* Anatole de Grunwald, Roland Pertwee, Ian Dalrymple, from a story by AG MacDonell, Wolfgang Wilhelm

Pin ★★★★ 18

Psychological thriller
1988 · Can · Colour · 98mins

A first-rate psychological chiller, with David Hewlett giving the performance of his career as a schizophrenic who develops a symbiotic relationship with a medical mannequin called Pin. Broadly in the *Magic* vein, the film was written and directed by Sandor Stern, who also penned *The Amityville Horror*, and provides a truly spooky portrayal of a kid teetering on the tightrope between fantasy and reality. DA

David Hewlett *Leon* • Cyndy Preston *Ursula* • John Ferguson [John Pyper Ferguson] *Stan Fraker* • Terry O'Quinn *Dr Linden* • Bronwen Mantel *Mrs Linden* ■ *Dir* Sandor Stern • *Scr* Sandor Stern, from the novel by Andrew Neiderman

A Pin for the Butterfly ★★

Political drama
1994 · UK/Cz Rep · Colour · 113mins

Despite the excellent use of Prague locations and superb photography from Ivan Slapeta, this film lets itself down by its confused structure and an ill-chosen, but hard-working, British cast. Joan Plowright seems to have cornered the market in European matriarchs, and here her passively benign character is severely underwritten, while Ian Bannen merely reprises *Hope and Glory*'s Grandpa in a Slavonic setting. Most ill-at-ease, though, is Hugh Laurie's subversive uncle. TS

Florence Hoath *Marushka* • Imogen Stubbs *Mother* • Hugh Laurie *Uncle* • Ian Bannen *Grandpa* • Ian Hogg *Great Uncle* • Joan Plowright *Grandma* ■ *Dir/Scr* Hannah Kodicek

Pin Up Girl ★★ U

Musical comedy 1944 · US · Colour · 79mins

In her balmy days at 20th Century-Fox, pin-up queen Betty Grable was usually cushioned with glamorous leading men, zippy tunes and Technicolor to disguise the fact that, in her own words, she was "the original triple threat – couldn't act, couldn't sing, couldn't dance". She might have also added "didn't matter", for her incandescent sheer good-naturedness won over the public's heart. The catchpennny title will attract die-hard fans, but, quite frankly, this one isn't terribly good. TS

Betty Grable *Lorry Jones* • John Harvey *Tommy Dooley* • Martha Raye *Marian* • Joe E Brown *Eddie* • Eugene Pallette *Barney Briggs* ■ *Dir* H Bruce Humberstone • *Scr* Robert Ellis, Helen Logan, Earl Baldwin, from a story by Libbie Block

Piñero ★★ 18

Biographical drama
2001 · US · Colour and BW · 93mins

Born in Puerto Rico, Miguel Piñero endured an abusive upbringing and a spell in jail before finding fame as the Tony-nominated playwright of the semi-autobiographical *Short Eyes*. Yet he succumbed to drug addiction and died derelict in 1988. Benjamin Bratt captures Piñero's pain and unpredictability with affecting power. But in seeking to convey the lyricism of the writing through a flashbacking structure, shaky digi-camerawork, and shifts between monochrome and colour, director Leon Ichaso succeeds only in confusing the issues. DP. Contains swearing and drug abuse.

Benjamin Bratt *Miguel Piñero* • Giancarlo Esposito *Miguel Algarin* • Talisa Soto *Sugar* • Nelson Vasquez *Tito* • Michael Irby *Reinaldo Povod* • Michael Wright *Edgar* • Rita Moreno *Mother* • Jaime Sanchez *Father* • Mandy Patinkin *Joseph Papp* ■ *Dir/Scr* Leon Ichaso

Ping Pong ★★★★ 12

Sports comedy drama
2002 · Jpn · Colour · 113mins

Fumihiko Sori's directorial debut is a stylish hybrid of the high-school buddy movie and the sporting underdog melodrama. This tale of two boys whose friendship is tested by their participation in a local table-tennis tournament gets inside the competitive mind while considering the mechanics of friendship and the transience of glory. The loyalty that the taciturn Arata shows the grandstanding Yosuke Kubozuka is genuinely touching, yet Sori is just as intrigued by the fierce rivalry between the duo and some posh, shaven-headed poseurs. The matches are filmed with grace and panache. DP. In Japanese with English subtitles. Contains violence. DVD

Yosuke Kubozuka *Peco* • Arata *Smile* • Sam Lee *China* • Shido Nakamura *Dragon* • Koji Ohkura *Akuma* ■ *Dir* Sori [Fumihiko Sori] • *Scr* Kankuro Kudo, from the comic book by Taiyou Matsumoto

Pink Cadillac ★★ 15

Comedy drama 1989 · US · Colour · 115mins

One of Clint Eastwood's rare mistakes. Lazily directed by his long-serving associate Buddy Van Horn, it strains for laughs as it follows Eastwood's bounty hunter on the trail of a runaway wife, played by Bernadette Peters. Along the way, Eastwood has to contend with various mentally challenged white supremacists who are part of a counterfeiting ring. The car looks great, even if it does hide a stash of drugs and another endless subplot, and if you blink you may miss the then unknown Jim Carrey. AT. Contains violence and swearing.

Clint Eastwood *Tommy Nowak* • Bernadette Peters *Lou Ann McGuinn* • Timothy Carhart *Roy McGuinn* • John Dennis Johnston *Waycross* • Michael Des Barres *Alex* • Geoffrey Lewis *Ricky Z* • William Hickey *Barton* • Frances Fisher *Dinah* • Jim Carrey *Lounge entertainer* ■ *Dir* Buddy Van Horn • *Scr* John Eskow

Pink Flamingos ★★★★★ 18

Satirical melodrama
1972 · US · Colour · 100mins

The film that not only defined bad taste, but also unashamedly celebrated it. Cult director John Waters's notorious gross-out has upstart perverts David Lochary and Mink Stole trying to wrest the honour of "Filthiest Person Alive" from the tenacious grip of sleaze superstar Divine. Chicken sex, a singing rectum, artificial insemination, lesbian motherhood and the incomparable Edith Massey are paraded before our increasingly appalled eyes in this screamingly funny shocker. Featuring the infamous coda where Divine eats a dog turd (for real), Waters's unique obscenity is the grandfather of midnight movies. AJ. Contains sex scenes, swearing, violence.

Divine *Babs Johnson/Divine* • David Lochary *Raymond Marble* • Mary Vivian Pearce *Cotton* • Mink Stole *Connie Marble* • Danny Mills *Crackers* • Edith Massey *Mama Edie* • Channing Wilroy *Channing* • Cookie Mueller *Cookie* ■ *Dir/Scr* John Waters (2)

Pink Floyd – The Wall ★★ 15

Musical drama 1982 · UK · Colour · 91mins

While undoubtedly lacking in symbolic subtlety – schoolchildren fed into a mincer, the adoration of Bob Geldof's central rock star likened to a Nazi rally, the wall itself (isolation, oppression, yes we get it) – Alan Parker's realisation of Roger Waters' s mega-selling 1979 concept album is not without visual flourish, not least when the pen and ink of Gerald Scarfe is animated into disturbing life. Those who dig the Floyd songs will put up with the pat imagery and Geldof's sleepwalking turn. Unbelievers should walk on by. AC DVD

Bob Geldof *Pink* • Christine Hargreaves *Pink's mother* • James Laurenson *Pink's father* • Eleanor David *Pink's wife* • Kevin McKeon *Young Pink* • Bob Hoskins *Band manager* • David Bingham *Little Pink* • Jenny Wright *American groupie* ■ *Dir* Alan Parker • *Scr* Roger Waters, from the album by Pink Floyd • *Animator* Gerald Scarfe • *Cinematographer* Peter Biziou

The Pink Jungle ★★★ U

Crime caper 1968 · US · Colour · 103mins

James Garner plays a fashion photographer who is stranded in the South American jungle with model Eva Renzi when George Kennedy steals their helicopter in his quest to locate a hidden diamond mine. This is a jolly caper that manages to be tense and spoofish at the same time. Garner is his usual charming self, while Kennedy, who plays everything for laughs, is very amusing. AT

James Garner *Ben Morris* • Eva Renzi *Alison Duquesne* • George Kennedy *Sammy Ryderbeit* • Nigel Green *Crowley* • Michael Ansara *Raul Ortega* ■ *Dir* Delbert Mann • *Scr* Charles Williams, from the novel *Snake Water* by Alan Williams

Pink Narcissus ★★★★ 18

Experimental erotic fantasy
1971 · US · Colour · 64mins

"Seminal" is the only word for this fine and rare example of screen homoerotica. A reinterpretation of the Greek myth of a beautiful youth in love with his own reflection, the film consists of the intercut reveries of a male prostitute, who keeps harsh reality at bay by imagining himself as various romantic characters. The film's meticulously crafted "look" – stagey painted sets and spangly costumes – may now appear plain camp, but it influenced countless other gay film-makers. The sequences were shot on 8mm intermittently and virtually single-handedly from 1965 by photographer James Bidgood. They were assembled in 1971 by Martin Jay Sadoff. Because Bidgood felt unable to take sole credit, the film was released anonymously, thus increasing its mystique. The film was lost from the mid-1970s and did not re-surface until 1987. It was passed uncut by the BBFC in 1993, allegedly because examiners had not noticed the ejaculation shot. DM [video]

Bobby Kendall ■ • *Editor* Martin Jay Sadoff

The Pink Panther ★★★★ PG

Comedy 1963 · US · Colour · 110mins

Peter Sellers went into this film as character support and came out a star. David Niven is the ostensible lead in a rather dull setting-up of the plot, in which the bumbling Inspector Clouseau is called in to prevent the theft of a precious diamond known as the Pink Panther. But Sellers's dud officer was so scene-stealingly comic that director Blake Edwards inserted new scenes. The rest is hysterical history. See it from the beginning: the cartoon title sequence with its Henry Mancini theme is an in-the-pink joy. Sellers took top billing the following year in *A Shot in the Dark*. TH [video] DVD

David Niven *Sir Charles Lytton* • Peter Sellers *Inspector Jacques Clouseau* • Robert Wagner *George Lytton* • Capucine *Simone Clouseau* • Claudia Cardinale *Princess Dala* • Brenda de Banzie *Angela Dunning* • John Le Mesurier *Defence attorney* ■ *Dir* Blake Edwards • *Scr* Maurice Richlin, Blake Edwards • *Title Animator* DePatie-Freleng

The Pink Panther Strikes Again ★★★ PG

Comedy 1976 · UK · Colour · 98mins

The critics were divided on the fourth entry in Blake Edwards's *Pink Panther* series. Some thought that Chief Inspector Dreyfus's increasingly desperate attempts to bump off the incompetent Clouseau were a riot of bawdy humour and inspired slapstick, while others considered the film to be a repetitive rehash. The box-office evidence suggests that the public voted with the "pro" lobby, but there is a shortage of inspiration here. *Revenge of the Pink Panther* continued the series. DP [video] DVD

Peter Sellers *Jacques Clouseau* • Herbert Lom *Dreyfus* • Colin Blakely *Alec Drummond* • Leonard Rossiter *Superintendent Quinlan* • Lesley-Anne Down *Olga* • Bert Kwouk [Burt Kwouk] *Cato* • André Maranne *François* ■ *Dir* Blake Edwards • *Scr* Frank Waldman, Blake Edwards

Pink String and Sealing Wax ★★★

Crime drama 1945 · UK · BW · 95mins

Set in Victorian Brighton, this roaring melodrama takes its title from the way in which pharmacists used to wrap parcels containing poison. There's not an ounce of subtlety in either the acting or in Robert Hamer's direction, but the film is none the worse for that, as restraint would have rendered the whole production ridiculous. The villains have all the fun, with Mervyn Johns unexpectedly severe as the tyrannical father, Garry Marsh on career best form as the brutal husband and Googie Withers gloriously wicked as the landlady leading timid Gordon Jackson astray. DP

Mervyn Johns *Mr Edward Sutton* • Googie Withers *Pearl Bond* • Gordon Jackson *David Sutton* • Sally Ann Howes *Peggy Sutton* • Mary Merrall *Mrs Ellen Sutton* • Catherine Lacey *Miss Porter* • Garry Marsh *Joe Bond* ■ *Dir* Robert Hamer • *Scr* Diana Morgan, Robert Hamer, from the play by Roland Pertwee

The Pink Telephone ★★

Drama 1975 · Fr · Colour · 93mins

Pierre Mondy is a naive, middle-aged provincial industrialist whose business problems lead him to consider selling his factory to an American company. The would-be buyers put him up in a luxury hotel and introduce him to Mareille Darc, with whom he falls in love. The film offers some impeccable acting and the suggestion of insight into ruthless business methods; unfortunately, neither writer nor director seems certain whether this is comedy or drama. Eduoard Molinaro's crude direction only helps to wreck the enterprise. RB. A French language film.

Mireille Darc *Christine* • Pierre Mondy *Benoît Castejac* • Michel Lonsdale *Morrison* • Daniel Ceccaldi *Levêque* • Françoise Prévost *Benoît's wife* ■ *Dir* Edouard Molinaro • *Scr* Francis Veber

Pinky ★★★

Drama 1949 · US · BW · 101mins

This is one of a group of important Hollywood movies that dealt with serious racial issues in the wake of the Second World War. While these films may seem naive and dated to today's audiences, getting them seen and discussed by the general public of the time was little short of miraculous. Here, the white Jeanne Crain gives an affecting performance in the lead, though cast in a role patently requiring a black actress, but the film probably would not have been made otherwise, and Ethel Waters is marvellous as the southern grandmother she visits. Elia Kazan took over the directorial reins from John Ford and the result is extremely moving, despite the unconvincing studio interior sets. TS

Jeanne Crain *Pinky, Patricia Johnson* • Ethel Barrymore *Miss Em* • Ethel Waters *Granny Dysey Johnson* • William Lundigan *Dr Thomas Adams* • Basil Ruysdael *Judge Walker* • Kenny Washington *Dr Canady* ■ *Dir* Elia Kazan • *Scr* Philip Dunne, Dudley Nichols, from the novel *Quality* by Cid Ricketts Sumner

Pinocchio ★★★★★ U

Classic animated fantasy
1940 · US · Colour · 83mins

Some films you think you know well, until you revisit them, and are struck all over again by that sense of wonder that moved you in the first place. This is the case with all of Disney's early feature-length cartoons: they have enthralled us for so long that we take them for granted. There is just such a magic in this tale of the little wooden boy, whose nose grows when he tells a lie and who is instructed to follow his conscience. Jiminy Cricket, Figaro, Geppetto and Monstro the Whale, and even those arch-felons who lead wayward boys to Pleasure Island, have all become a part of 20th-century mythology. The score, which includes the song that became Disney's anthem, *When You Wish upon a Star*, is magnificent, as is the artistic technique and use of early Technicolor. TS [video] DVD

Dickie Jones *Pinocchio* • Cliff Edwards *Jiminy Cricket* • Christian Rub *Geppetto* • Evelyn Venable *The Blue Fairy* ■ *Dir* Ben Sharpsteen, Hamilton Luske • *Scr* Ted Sears, Otto Englander, Webb Smith, William Cottrell, Joseph Sabo, Erdman Penner, Aurelius Battaglia, from the novel *The Adventures of Pinocchio* by Carlo Collodi

Pinocchio ★★

Fantasy adventure
2002 · It · Colour · 105mins

Despite breaking domestic budget records, Roberto Benigni's adaptation has none of the eccentric charm it might have possessed had he realised a lifetime ambition in undertaking the project with Federico Fellini. Much affection has been lavished on the costumes, music and effects, while Dante Spinotti's photography cleverly marries Tuscan landscapes and studio sets. The supporting cast is both pantomimic and literate, but Benigni is too old to play the puppet who comes to life. DP. In Italian with English subtitles.

Roberto Benigni *Pinoccho* • Nicoletta Braschi *Blue Fairy* • Mino Bellei *Medoro* • Carlo Giuffrè *Geppetto* • Peppe Barra *Cricket* ■ *Dir* Roberto Benigni • *Scr* Vincenzo Cerami, Roberto Benigni, from the story by Carlo Collodi

Pinocchio's Revenge ★★

Horror 1996 · US · Colour · 96mins

Despite centering on a wooden doll named Pinocchio, this film has no connection to the classic children's tale. The doll in question, previously owned by a father who murdered his son, comes into the possession of a troubled little girl. But is she or Pinocchio responsible for the "accidents" that befall her enemies soon after? Its ample merits don't prevent it from being a fancily wrapped but fundamentally empty package. KB

Rosalind Allen *Jennifer Garrick* • Lewis Van Bergen *Vincent Gotto* • Brittany Alyse Smith *Zoe Garrick* • Todd Allen *David Kaminsky* • Aaron Lustig *Dr Edwards* ■ *Dir/Scr* Kevin Tenney [Kevin S Tenney]

Pipe Dreams ★★★ U

Drama 1976 · US · Colour · 89mins

Having launched a number of acting careers (including Sylvester Stallone's) in his own co-directing debut *The Lords of Flatbush*, director Stephen Verona focused on a first-time thespian of a different kind for his initial solo venture. Disco diva Gladys Knight acquits herself admirably as a woman who journeys to Alaska to find her husband (Barry Hankerson, to whom she was married in real life) who is working on the pipeline there. The scarcity of women in the frontier town means the only roommate she can find is prostitute Shirley Bain. Slight but sensitively handled. FL

Gladys Knight *Maria Wilson* • Wayne Tippit *Mike Thompson* • Barry Hankerson *Rob Wilson* • Altovise Davis *Lydia* • Bruce French *Duke* • Sylvia Hayes *Sally* ■ *Dir/Scr* Stephen Verona

The Piper's Tune ★★ U

Period adventure 1962 · UK · BW · 62mins

This costume adventure focuses on a gang of children whose attempts to flee the chaos of the Napoleonic Wars are jeopardised by a seemingly kindly doctor. Director Muriel Box valiantly seek to convey the uncertainties of the period, and Frederick Piper shows well as the treacherous spy. But the inexperience of the juveniles, and a lack of finance, fatally undermines their efforts to bring weight and scale to the action. DP

Mavis Ranson *Anna* • Roberta Tovey *Suzy* • Angela White *Maria* • Malcolm Ranson *Thomas* • Brian Wills *Paul* • Graham Wills *Peter* ■ *Dir* Muriel Box • *Scr* Michael Barnes, from a story by Frank Wells

Pippi Longstocking ★★

Adventure 1968 · Swe · Colour · 99mins

This adventure for Astrid Lindgren's popular character was successful enough to warrant two sequels by the same team. Pippi is a super-strong, red-haired nine-year-old who leads a wild, independent life with her pet monkey and horse while her sea captain father is apparently lost at sea. The primitive dubbing may irritate grown-ups, but children will find it cheerful and enjoyable. JG. Swedish dialogue dubbed into English.

Inger Nilsson *Pippi Longstocking* • Maria Persson *Annika* • Paer Sundberg *Tommy* • Oellegard Welton *Mother* • Fredrik Ohlsson *Father* • Hans Alfredson *Konrad* • Margot Trooger *Miss Prusselius* • Beppe Wolgers *Captain Longstocking* ■ *Dir* Olle Hellbom • *Scr* Astrid Lindgren

Pippi Longstocking ★★★ U

Animated musical adventure
1997 · Can/Swe/Ger · Colour · 74mins

Astrid Lindgren's perky heroine comes to the big screen in this lively animated adventure, packed with the uplifting values that characterise her original stories. The strongest girl in the world (appropriately voiced at full belt by Melissa Altro) battles an interfering neighbour and a couple of bungling burglars. Though not up to Disney standards, there's still enough here to keep little girls amused: animation that's full of colour and vitality, a couple of rousing musical numbers and some appealing animals in tow. JF [video] DVD

Melissa Altro *Pippi Longstocking* • Dave Thomas *Thunder-Karlsson* • Catherine O'Hara *Mrs Prysselius* • Gordon Pinsent *Captain Longstocking* • Carole Pope *The Teacher* • Wayne Robson *Bloom* • Richard Binsley *Mr Nilsson/Dog* • Rick Jones *O'Malley* ■ *Dir* Clive Smith • *Scr* Catharina Stackelberg, from the books by Astrid Lindgren

Piranha ★★★ 18

Horror 1978 · US · Colour · 90mins

In this sly, witty cash-in on *Jaws*, director Joe Dante and writer John Sayles dream up a deliriously silly tale about a shoal of killer fish, bred by the army for use in Vietnam, that escapes and munches its way through the waterways of America. Bradford Dillman keeps an admirably straight face as the hero and there are neat supporting turns from Kevin McCarthy, Keenan Wynn, Dick Miller and Barbara Steele. Even at this early stage of his career, Dante embellishes the film with an array of references to other movies, and the laughs and blood flow in equal measure. JF. Contains violence, swearing and nudity. [video] DVD

Bradford Dillman *Paul Grogan* • Heather Menzies *Maggie McKeown* • Kevin McCarthy *Dr Robert Hoak* • Keenan Wynn *Jack* • Dick Miller *Buck Gardner* • Barbara Steele *Dr Mengers* ■ *Dir* Joe Dante • *Scr* John Sayles, from a story by Richard Robinson, John Sayles

Piranha II: the Spawning ★ 18

Horror 1981 · Neth · Colour · 90mins

In this appalling follow-up to Joe Dante's entertaining original, the performances are amateurish (even a young Lance Henriksen lacks conviction), the direction is leaden and the deadly fish are laughably bargain-basement. So it comes as a bit of a shock to find that this was the feature debut of James Cameron. JC [video] DVD

Tricia O'Neil *Anne Kimbrough* • Steve Marachuk *Tyler* • Lance Henriksen *Steve Kimbrough* • Ricky G Paull *Chris Kimbrough* • Ted Richert *Raoul* • Leslie Graves *Allison* ■ *Dir* James Cameron • *Scr* HA Milton

P

Piranhas ★★ 15

Horror 1996 · US · Colour · 86mins

This TV movie is based on the John Sayles script for *Piranha*, the Joe Dante *Jaws* parody. Flesh and ferocity are the order of the day as scientists William Katt and Alexandra Paul accidentally let loose some genetically modified snappers into the tributary running through a holiday resort. But Scott Levy's horror movie remake is devoid of the knowing references that always make Dante's films so much fun. DP. Contains swearing, violence and nudity. DVD

William Katt *Paul Grogan* • Alexandra Paul *Maggie MacNamara* • Mila Kunis *Susie Grogan* • Soleil Moon Frye *Laura* • Kehli O'Byrne *Gina* • Monte Markham *JR Randolph* ■ *Dir* Scott Levy • *Scr* Alex Simon, from the 1978 film

The Pirate ★★★★ U

Musical 1948 · US · Colour · 97mins

This picturesque and largely enjoyable MGM musical swashbuckler was a commercial flop in its day but has since picked up a considerable following. Its latter-day popularity stems more from the Cole Porter songs, opulent sets and lavish choreography than from the story about a sheltered young woman who dreams of escape and adventure with a glamorous pirate. Vincente Minnelli directs his wife Judy Garland and Gene Kelly with gusto and panache. PF

Judy Garland *Manuela* • Gene Kelly *Serafin* • Walter Slezak *Don Pedro Vargas* • Gladys Cooper *Aunt Inez* • Reginald Owen *Advocate* • George Zucco *Viceroy* ■ *Dir* Vincente Minnelli • *Scr* Albert Hackett, Frances Goodrich, from the play by SN Behrman

The Pirate Movie ★★ PG

Adventure 1982 · Aus · Colour · 94mins

A peculiar Australian adaptation of Gilbert and Sullivan's operetta, *The Pirates Of Penzance*, released around the same time as a star-studded American version with Kevin Kline. Kristy McNichol plays a young girl who dreams she's involved in the *Penzance* plot – a leaden rewrite that's hardly helped by Ken Annakin's plodding direction. TH DVD

Kristy McNichol *Mabel* • Christopher Atkins *Frederic* • Ted Hamilton *Pirate King* • Bill Kerr *Major General* • Maggie Kirkpatrick *Ruth* • Garry McDonald *Sergeant Inspector* • Chuck McKinney *Samuel* • Marc Colombani *Dwarf pirate* ■ *Dir* Ken Annakin • *Scr* Trevor Farrant, from the operetta *The Pirates of Penzance* by WS Gilbert, by Arthur Sullivan

Pirates ★ 15

Adventure 1986 · Fr/Tun · Colour · 107mins

Roman Polanski wanted Jack Nicholson to play the lead in what would be a lark, a send-up of Errol Flynn movies and their ilk – a lark, however, that Hollywood wouldn't underwrite. But a dozen years later Polanski found Tunisian backers and shot the picture in the Seychelles with Walter Matthau hiding behind a forest of face-fur, walking on a wooden leg and talking Hollywood-cockney. The waste of money and talent, together with the sub-Python japes, make this a uniquely depressing experience. AT

Walter Matthau *Captain Red* • Cris Campion *Jean-Baptiste, "the Frog"* • Damien Thomas *Don Alfonso* • Olu Jacobs *Boumako* • Ferdy Mayne *Captain Linares* • David Kelly *Surgeon* • Charlotte Lewis *Dolores* • Anthony Peck *Spanish officer* • Anthony Dawson *Spanish officer* • Roy Kinnear *Dutch* ■ *Dir* Roman Polanski • *Scr* Gerard Brach, Roman Polanski, John Brownjohn

The Pirates of Blood River ★★ U

Swashbuckling adventure
1961 · UK · Colour · 94mins

This Hammer swashbuckler is a colourful, action-packed adventure. Kerwin Mathews is a Huguenot who falls into the clutches of pirate king Christopher Lee, a buccaneer complete with eye-patch and hook. There are wenches and scurvy knaves galore, but only tantalising vestiges of the X-rated bloodbath intended, as the film was reduced to U certificate derring-do for the school holidays after long sessions at the censor's office. DM

Christopher Lee *LaRoche* • Kerwin Mathews *Jonathan Standing* • Glenn Corbett *Henry* • Marla Landi *Bess* • Oliver Reed *Brocaire* • Andrew Keir *Jason Standing* • Dennis Waterman *Timothy* ■ *Dir* John Gilling • *Scr* John Gilling, John Hunter, from a story by Jimmy Sangster

The Pirates of Malaysia ★★

Swashbuckling action adventure
1964 · It/W Ger · Colour · 110mins

Former Mr Universe Steve Reeves was coming to the end of his reign as the "sword and sandal" king of Italian movies when he took the lead in *Sandokan the Great* in 1963. He reprises the role in this brash spaghetti swashbuckler, in which he once more does battle with the forces of the British Empire. Director Umberto Lenzi keeps the action fast and, although beginning to look his age, Reeves plays the Tiger of Malaya with suitable vim. DP. Italian dialogue dubbed into English.

Steve Reeves *Sandokan* • Jacqueline Sassard *Princess of Sarawak* • Andrea Bosic *Yanez* • Ananda Kumar *Tuang Olon* ■ *Dir* Umberto Lenzi • *Scr* Fulvio Gicca, Umberto Lenzi

The Pirates of Penzance ★★★ U

Musical 1983 · US · Colour · 107mins

Director Wilford Leach adapted Joseph Papp's famously successful stage production of Gilbert and Sullivan's popular operetta, retaining the original cast plus Angela Lansbury as Ruth. Kevin Kline repeated his rich performance as the Pirate King, with Linda Ronstadt as Mabel and George Rose as "the very model of a model major-general". The familiar and much-loved score was pepped up with a contemporary treatment by William Elliott. The high-spirited energy of the cast, however, can't disguise the show's theatrical origins, and the whole enterprise is somewhat dwarfed by the Panavision screen. RK

Kevin Kline *Pirate King* • Angela Lansbury *Ruth* • Linda Ronstadt *Mabel Stanley* • George Rose *Major-General Stanley* • Rex Smith *Frederic* • Tony Azito *Sergeant* ■ *Dir* Wilford Leach • *Scr* Wilford Leach, from the operetta by WS Gilbert and Arthur Sullivan

Pirates of the Caribbean: the Curse of the Black Pearl ★★★★ 12

Fantasy action adventure
2003 · US · Colour · 137mins

Based on one of Disney's most famous theme-park attractions, this shiver-me-timbers swashbuckler could have been short on plot and long on action. In fact it delivers plenty of both, with brio. This lavish Hollywood voyage into pirate country effortlessly fills its running time as blacksmith Orlando Bloom and governor's daughter Keira Knightley fall foul of cursed buccaneers. The real treasure comes courtesy of Johnny Depp's swaggering, slurring, mascara-wearing rascal Jack Sparrow, a seafaring rock-star type and an irresistible comic hero. Geoffrey Rush also milks his role to the hilt as an archetypal pirate captain, and some superb special effects reveal the skeletal curse of the Black Pearl's crew under moonlight. JC DVD

Johnny Depp *Capt Jack Sparrow* • Geoffrey Rush *Capt Barbossa* • Orlando Bloom *Will Turner* • Keira Knightley *Elizabeth Swann* • Jack Davenport *Commander Norrington* • Kevin R McNally [Kevin McNally] *Joshamee Gibbs* • Zoë Saldana *Anamaria* • Jonathan Pryce *Governor Weatherby Swann* ■ *Dir* Gore Verbinski • *Scr* Ted Elliott, Terry Rossio, from a story by Ted Elliott, Terry Rossio, Stuart Beattie, Jay Wolpert, from the Disney theme-park ride

The Pit and the Pendulum ★★★★ 15

Horror 1961 · US · Colour · 76mins

Roger Corman's seminal series of Edgar Allan Poe adaptations ensures that he can never be dismissed as just a purveyor of schlock. This followed the first in the cycle, *The Fall of the House of Usher*, and boasts an intelligent script from Richard Matheson and another fine performance from Vincent Price. He plays the sinister Nicholas Medina, haunted by his father's tortuous past in the days of the Inquisition. Corman creates a gothic air and works wonders with a limited budget. JF DVD

Vincent Price *Nicholas Medina* • Barbara Steele *Elizabeth Barnard Medina* • John Kerr *Francis Barnard* • Luana Anders *Catherine Medina* • Antony Carbone *Dr Charles Leon* ■ *Dir* Roger Corman • *Scr* Richard Matheson, from the story by Edgar Allan Poe

The Pit and the Pendulum ★★★ 18

Horror 1991 · US · Colour · 92mins

Like the 1961 version, this film pretty much ignores Edgar Allan Poe's original story. The action takes place during the Spanish Inquisition and focuses on Inquisitor-General Torquemada (Lance Henriksen) who, attracted to a baker's wife (Rona De Ricci) accused of witchcraft, makes plans to do away with her husband (Jonathan Fuller). Henriksen hams it up, while director Stuart Gordon gives the torture scenes a gleefully ghoulish edge. KB DVD

Lance Henriksen *Torquemada* • Rona De Ricci *Maria* • Jonathan Fuller *Antonio* • Frances Bay *Esmeralda* • Jeffrey Combs *Francisco* • Oliver Reed *Cardinal* ■ *Dir* Stuart Gordon • *Scr* Dennis Paoli, from the story by Edgar Allan Poe

Pit of Darkness ★ U

Crime drama 1961 · UK · BW · 76mins

William Franklyn had the misfortune to land the lead in this desperate B-feature, as a safe-maker who loses his memory and finds himself implicated in a jewel robbery. With assassination attempts coming thicker than clues, the plot plods along to its predictable conclusion. In spite of the best efforts of writer/director Lance Comfort and a talented cast, this is awful. DP

William Franklyn *Richard Logan* • Moira Redmond *Julie Logan* • Bruno Barnabe *Maxie* • Leonard Sachs *Conrad* • Nigel Green *Jonathan* • Anthony Booth *Ted Mellis* • Nanette Newman *Mary* ■ *Dir* Lance Comfort • *Scr* Lance Comfort, from the novel *To Dusty Death* by Hugh McCutcheon

Pitch Black ★★★★ 15

Science-fiction thriller
1999 · Aus/US · Colour · 103mins

It might start out resembling another assembly-line sci-fi saga, but this visually stunning adventure soon becomes as thrilling as it is imaginatively striking. The setting is a world with three suns, where a tri-solar eclipse allows flesh-hungry creatures to emerge from underground. The motley crew that must traverse this nightmare landscape is led by tough guy Vin Diesel, giving a charismatic performance. With the first half sporting a brilliant desert surrealism and the second loaded with stylised gore, director David Twohy's frightener is a vivid achievement. *The Chronicles of Riddick* is the much less successful sequel. AJ DVD

Radha Mitchell *Fry* • Vin Diesel *Riddick* • Cole Hauser *Johns* • Keith David *Imam* • Lewis Fitz-Gerald *Paris* • Claudia Black *Shazza* ■ *Dir* David Twohy • *Scr* Jim Wheat, Ken Wheat, David Twohy, from a story by Jim Wheat, Ken Wheat • *Cinematographer* David Eggby • *Production Designer* Graham Walker

Pitfall ★★★★

Film noir 1948 · US · BW · 85mins

Bored with his perfect wife and son, an insurance agent falls for a charmer with tragic results in this excellent adult drama, which takes *film noir* into the world of middle-class domesticity. Dick Powell is basically honest, but that doesn't stop his momentary philandering leading to deceit and murder. Lizabeth Scott excels as the seductive adventuress, and Raymond Burr is superbly sleazy as the villain of the piece. Andre De Toth maintains a tense pace in a film with a surprisingly modern view of the American Dream turned sour. TV

Dick Powell *John Forbes* • Lizabeth Scott *Mona Stevens* • Jane Wyatt *Sue Forbes* • Raymond Burr *Mack MacDonald* • John Litel *District Attorney* • Byron Barr *Bill Smiley* • Jimmy Hunt *Tommy Forbes* • Ann Doran *Maggie* ■ *Dir* Andre De Toth • *Scr* Karl Kamb, from the novel by Jay Dratler

Pitfall ★★★★ 15

Crime drama 1962 · Jpn · BW · 96mins

Hiroshi Teshigahara's debut feature draws on the stylised realism he perfected in his early documentary shorts, while anticipating the existential themes of such later collaborations with screenwriter Kobo Abe as *Woman of the Dunes* (1963) and *The Face of Another* (1966). Exploring the moral bankruptcy of postwar Japanese society and the inexplicability of fate, this strikingly photographed film chronicles the travels of miner Hisashi Igawa and his son Kazuo Miyahara, whose discontent and dishonesty culminate in Igawa's murder by white-suited stranger Kunie Tanaka in a ghost town populated soley by sweetshop clerk Sumie Sasaki. DP. In Japanese with English subtitles. Contains swearing, sex scenes and violence. DVD

Hisashi Igawa *Miner* • Kunie Tanaka *Man in white suit* • Kazuo Miyahara *Son* • Sumie Sasaki *Woman* ■ *Dir* Hiroshi Teshigahara • *Scr* Kobo Abe, from his novel • *Cinematographer* Hiroshi Segawa

Pittsburgh ★★

Melodrama 1942 · US · BW · 91mins

John Wayne, Marlene Dietrich and Randolph Scott star in this drama about coal mining in Pittsburgh. Wayne and Scott own the mine but operate it differently: Wayne is the ruthless capitalist, while Scott is more concerned with the health and safety of the workforce. Dietrich is sort of in the middle, though the movie isn't much interested in romance. AT

Marlene Dietrich *Josie Winters* • Randolph Scott *Cash Evans* • John Wayne *Pittsburgh "Pitt" Markham* • Frank Craven *Doc Powers* • Louise Allbritton *Shannon Prentiss* ■ *Dir* Lewis Seiler • *Scr* Kenneth Gamet, Tom Reed, John Twist, from a story by George Owen, from Tom Reed

P

Pixote ★★★★★ 18

Drama 1981 · Bra · Colour · 119mins

The knowledge that Fernando Ramos Da Silva was killed in a shoot-out with the cops just six years after playing a 10-year-old orphan inexorably drawn into a living hell of prostitution, drugs and murder makes Hector Babenco's ultra-realistic picture of São Paulo streetlife all the more chilling. Da Silva genuinely lives a role that stands as an indictment of us all. Adapted from José Louzeiro's novel, the film focuses on the facts of an appalling situation, without offering glib socio-political solutions. DP. In Portuguese with English subtitles. [VIDEO]

Fernando Ramos Da Silva *Pixote* • Marilia Pêra *Sueli* • Jorge Juliao *Lilica* • Gilberto Moura *Dito* • José Nilson Dos Santos *Diego* ■ *Dir* Hector Babenco • *Scr* Hector Babenco, Jorge Duran, from the novel *Infancia dos Mortos* by José Louzeiro

Pizza Man ★★

Comedy 1991 · US · Colour · 90mins

Comedian Bill Maher flexed his satirical muscles in this wacky political comedy about a pizza delivery man who stumbles upon a huge scandal featuring many of the top political figures of the day. A broad sideswipe at policies and personalities from all parties, the film casts its net wide but ends up like a pizza with too many toppings: it looks good on the menu, but it's hard to swallow. DF

Bill Maher *Elmo Bunn* • Annabelle Gurwitch *The Dame* • David McKnight *Vince* • Andy Romano *The Hood* • Bob Delegall *Mayor Bradley* • Bryan Clark *Ronald Reagan* • Cathy Shambley *Geraldine Ferraro* • Ron Darian *Michael Dukakis* ■ *Dir/Scr* JF Lawton

A Place for Annie ★★★★ PG

Drama 1994 · US · Colour · 95mins

The year before she gave such an impressive performance as the HIV-positive Robin in *Boys on the Side*, Mary-Louise Parker produced another powerful portrayal of a young woman with Aids in this deeply affecting TV movie. She is admirably supported by Sissy Spacek as the nurse who wants to adopt the HIV-infected baby Parker has abandoned, and by Joan Plowright and S Epatha Merkerson as, respectively, a nanny and a social worker caught up in the case. This goes to show just what can be done with a true-life drama if it's handled with intelligence rather than sensationalism. DP [VIDEO] DVD

Sissy Spacek *Susan Lansing* • Mary-Louise Parker *Linda Morsten* • Joan Plowright *Dorothy Kilgore* • S Epatha Merkerson *Alice Blakely* • Jack Noseworthy *David Lansing* • David Spielberg *Dr Palmer* ■ *Dir* John Gray • *Scr* Lee Guthrie, Cathleen Young, Nancy Barr

A Place for Lovers ★

Romantic drama
1968 · It/Fr · Colour · 88mins

Italy is the setting for this sudsy film in which American divorcee and fashion designer Faye Dunaway falls in love with engineer Marcello Mastroianni. Well, she would, wouldn't she? She did in reality as well, leading to a well-publicised affair with the archetypal Latin lover. Trash of a low order. AT

Faye Dunaway *Julia* • Marcello Mastroianni *Valerio* • Caroline Mortimer *Maggie* • Karin Engh *Griselda* • Esmeralda Ruspoli ■ *Dir* Vittorio De Sica • *Scr* Vittorio De Sica, Julian Halevy [Julian Zimet], Peter Baldwin, Ennio de Concini, Tonino Guerra, Cesare Zavattini, from a story by Brunello Rondi

A Place in the Sun ★★★★ U

Drama 1951 · US · BW · 115mins

Elizabeth Taylor has never looked lovelier, or the young Montgomery Clift more tortured than in this glossy adaptation of Theodore Dreiser's dour novel *An American Tragedy*, previously filmed by Josef von Sternberg. This film won six Oscars, including best director for George Stevens, whose trademark dissolves are most tellingly displayed as Clift and Taylor meet for the first time. Trouble is, this tale of love across the tracks has dated badly, and today seems rather drawn out. But Clift and Shelley Winters are brilliant, so forget the plot and just revel in what was once Hollywood's idea of classy movie-making. TS [VIDEO] DVD

Montgomery Clift *George Eastman* • Elizabeth Taylor *Angela Vickers* • Shelley Winters *Alice Tripp* • Anne Revere *Hannah Eastman* • Raymond Burr *Marlowe* • Herbert Heyes *Charles Eastman* • Keefe Brasselle *Earl Eastman* ■ *Dir* George Stevens • *Scr* Michael Wilson, Harry Brown, from the play *An American Tragedy* by Patrick Kearney, from the novel *An American Tragedy* by Theodore Dreiser • *Cinematographer* William C Mellor • *Costume Designer* Edith Head

A Place in the World ★★

Drama 1992 · Arg/Urug · Colour · 120mins

An enormous hit with Argentinian audiences, this story about the inhabitants of a small farming village uniting to oppose the forces of grasping capitalism is both naive and long-winded. Director Adolfo Aristarain is clearly determined to say something momentous, but as earnestly as his characters talk, they never come up with anything other than empty aphorisms. DP. In Spanish with English subtitles.

José Sacristan *Hans* • Federico Luppi *Mario* • Cecilia Roth *Ana* • Leonor Benedetto *Nelda* ■ *Dir* Adolfo Aristarain • *Scr* Adolfo Aristarain, Alberto Lecchi

A Place of One's Own ★★★ U

Supernatural drama 1944 · UK · BW · 88mins

A genuinely eerie adaptation of Osbert Sitwell's novel of strange happenings in an English country house. Former cameraman-turned-director Bernard Knowles knows just how to achieve the right spine-chilling touch, keeping the supernatural themes cleverly light in tone. The cast is delightful, with James Mason and Barbara Mullen as the retired homeowners, and lovely Margaret Lockwood as their companion who is the catalyst for the ghostly goings-on. Time has lent this Gainsborough picture a veneer of charm – well worth watching. TS [VIDEO]

Margaret Lockwood *Annette* • James Mason *Mr Smedhurst* • Barbara Mullen *Mrs Smedhurst* • Dennis Price *Dr Selbie* • Helen Haye *Mrs Manning-Tuthorn* • Michael Shepley *Major Manning-Tuthorn* • Dulcie Gray *Sarah* ■ *Dir* Bernard Knowles • *Scr* Brock Williams, from the novel by Osbert Sitwell

A Place to Go ★★

Crime drama 1963 · UK · BW · 88mins

Michael Sarne goes all mean and moody to unfortunately comic effect as he bids to beat the Bethnal Green blues with an ill-conceived factory heist. Rita Tushingham and Bernard Lee do what they can with a dodgy script, while director Basil Dearden captures something of the flavour of the East End. Lacklustre. DP

Bernard Lee *Matt Flint* • Rita Tushingham *Catherine* • Michael Sarne *Ricky Flint* • Doris Hare *Lil Flint* • Barbara Ferris *Betsy* • John Slater *Jack Ellerman* • David Andrews *Jim* • Roy Kinnear *Bunting* ■ *Dir* Basil Dearden • *Scr* Michael Relph, Clive Exton, from the novel *Bethnal Green* by Michael Fisher

Place Vendôme ★★★ 15

Romantic thriller 1998 · Fr · Colour · 112mins

Catherine Deneuve won the best actress prize at Venice for her performance as an alcoholic widow recovering her sense of worth in this mannered thriller from actress-turned-director Nicole Garcia. While her icy detachment and vulnerability are impressive, there's no real sense of danger underlying this tale of duplicitous diamond dealing. Evading industry regulators, Russian mafiosi and the lover who once betrayed her (Jacques Dutronc), Deneuve's attempts to sell the stolen gems left by her husband are not without intrigue, yet the plot sparkles all too rarely. DP. In French with English subtitles. Contains swearing. [VIDEO] DVD

Catherine Deneuve *Marianne* • Jean-Pierre Bacri *Jean-Pierre* • Emmanuelle Seigner *Nathalie* • Jacques Dutronc *Battistelli* • Bernard Fresson *Vincent Malivert* • François Berléand *Eric Malivert* • Philippe Clévenot *Kleiser* ■ *Dir* Nicole Garcia • *Scr* Nicole Garcia, Jacques Fieschi

Places in the Heart ★★★★ PG

Period drama 1984 · US · Colour · 111mins

This beautifully paced and sumptuously shot heart-twanger won Sally Field a best actress Oscar, even if her acceptance speech will go down in the annals of excessive luvviedom. Field is wonderfully moving as the feisty, sorely tried small-town farmer battling the Depression and her emotions, and there's a fine supporting cast including John Malkovich, Danny Glover and Amy Madigan. Written and directed by Robert Benton, who won an Oscar for his screenplay, this is a lovingly crafted homage to the community values of his Texas home town. SH [VIDEO]

Sally Field *Edna Spalding* • Danny Glover *Moze* • John Malkovich *Mr Will* • Lindsay Crouse *Margaret Lomax* • Ed Harris *Wayne Lomax* • Amy Madigan *Viola Kelsey* • Yankton Hatten *Frank Spalding* • Gennie James *Possum Spalding* ■ *Dir/Scr* Robert Benton

Plaff! ★ 15

Black comedy drama
1988 · Cub · Colour · 92mins

This anarchic comedy from Juan Carlos Tabio divides audiences with its farcical portrait of a Cuban household run by the widowed Daisy Granados, and inhabited by her newly married son and liberated wife. It tries, soap-opera style, to be mildly serious in theme while attempting broad comedy, compounded by the overt presence of the film crew. All very exhausting. BB. In Spanish with English subtitles.

Daisy Granados *Concha Perez* • Thais Valdes *Clarita* • Luis Alberto Garcia *José Ramon Perez* • Raul Pomares *Tomas* • Jorge Cao *Contreras* ■ *Dir* Juan Carlos Tabio • *Scr* Daniel Chavarria, Juan Carlos Tabio

The Plague ★★★ 15

Drama
1992 · Fr/UK/Arg/US · Colour · 116mins

The reunion of *Kiss of the Spider Woman* stars William Hurt and Raul Julia is something of a disappointment. Adapted from the Albert Camus novel by director Luis Puenzo, it involves a dedicated doctor (Hurt), a French reporter (Sandrine Bonnaire) and a TV cameraman (Jean-Marc Barr) whose lives become entangled during an outbreak of a lethal pestilence in a South American city. The existentialism of the original is lost in this version, which doesn't make up for it with action or tension. TH. Contains swearing, sex scenes and some violence. [VIDEO] DVD

William Hurt *Dr Bernard Rieux* • Sandrine Bonnaire *Martine Rambert* • Jean-Marc Barr *Jean Tarrou* • Robert Duvall *Joseph Grand* • Raul Julia *Cottard* • Lautaro Murua *Father Paneloux* • Victoria Tennant *Alice Rieux* ■ *Dir* Luis Puenzo • *Scr* Luis Puenzo, from the novel *La Peste* by Albert Camus

The Plague Dogs ★★★ PG

Animated adventure
1982 · US/UK · Colour · 98mins

After *Watership Down*, Martin Rosen went on to adapt another Richard Adams novel, though the film's troubling and downbeat nature possibly explains its comparative lack of success. Two laboratory dogs (voiced by John Hurt and Christopher Benjamin) escape from a British laboratory and seek a canine paradise while trying to avoid recapture. The animation does not reach modern standards, but it's pretty good for the period it was produced and still manages to convey the gritty emotion dictated by the bleak yet absorbing story. The violence and general grimness make it inappropriate for younger viewers. KB [VIDEO] DVD

John Hurt *Snitter* • Christopher Benjamin *Rowf* • James Bolam *The Tod* • Nigel Hawthorne *Dr Robert Boycott* • Warren Mitchell *Tyson/Wag* • Bernard Hepton *Stephen Powell* ■ *Dir* Martin Rosen • *Scr* Martin Rosen, from the novel by Richard Adams

The Plague of the Zombies ★★★★ 15

Horror 1965 · UK · Colour · 86mins

Voodoo rituals in 18th-century Cornwall disguise a savage indictment of the British class system in a superior Hammer horror with a strong plotline. It's John Gilling's best work, and his tight direction and stylish visuals build the tension most effectively. Especially memorable moments include the green-tinted dream sequence, where churchyard corpses are resurrected, and a quite stunning decapitation scene. A vintage bloodcurdler from Hammer's golden era. AJ [VIDEO] DVD

André Morell *Sir James Forbes* • Diane Clare *Sylvia Forbes* • Brook Williams *Dr Peter Tompson* • Jacqueline Pearce *Alice* • John Carson *Clive Hamilton* • Alexander Davion *Denver* • Michael Ripper *Sergeant Swift* • Marcus Hammond *Martinus* ■ *Dir* John Gilling • *Scr* Peter Bryan, John Elder [Anthony Hinds]

Plain Clothes ★★★ PG

Comedy thriller 1988 · US · Colour · 93mins

Some strong, gritty performances, particularly from George Wendt and Robert Stack, lift this workaday thriller above a script that lumbers along like an old car, accompanied by a man with a flag signalling "twist in the plot ahead". We've been undercover before with a disgruntled cop – in this case, he's posing as a student to clear his brother's name – so there is a strong whiff of familiarity about his quest. But this is still professional movie-making. SH. Contains swearing. [VIDEO]

Arliss Howard *Nick Dunbar/Nick Springsteen* • Suzy Amis *Robin Torrence* • George Wendt *Chet Butler* • Diane Ladd *Jane Melway* • Seymour Cassel *Ed Malmburg* • Larry Pine *Dave Hechtor* • Jackie Gayle *Coach Zeffer* • Abe Vigoda *Mr Wiseman* • Robert Stack *Mr Gardner* ■ *Dir* Martha Coolidge • *Scr* A Scott Frank, from a story by A Scott Frank, Dan Vining

The Plainsman ★★★★ U

Western 1936 · US · BW · 111mins

A no-holds-barred spectacle from Cecil B DeMille, impressively capturing the landscape of the Wild West, teeming with hordes of Sioux and Cheyenne Indians, and merrily ignoring historical truths. This western also presents us with a totally fictitious romance between Wild Bill Hickok and Calamity Jane, gloriously glamorised by Gary Cooper and Jean Arthur. A highly enjoyable epic in true DeMille style. RK

Gary Cooper *Wild Bill Hickok* • Jean Arthur *Calamity Jane* • James Ellison *Buffalo Bill Cody* • Charles Bickford *John Latimer* • Porter Hall *Jack McCall* • Helen Burgess *Louisa Cody* • John Miljan *Gen George Armstrong Custer* •

P

Victor Varconi *Painted Horse* • Anthony Quinn *Cheyenne warrior* • Frank McGlynn Sr *Abraham Lincoln* ■ *Dir* Cecil B DeMille • *Scr* Waldemar Young, Harold Lamb, Lynn Riggs, Grover Jones, from the novel *Wild Bill Hickok, the Prince of the Pioneers* by Frank J Wilstach and from stories by Courtney Ryley Cooper

The Plainsman ★★ U

Western 1966 · US · Colour · 91mins

In this pointless remake of Cecil B DeMille's 1936 classic western, a callow Don Murray and a comical Abby Dalton (as Wild Bill Hickok and Calamity Jane) prove no match for the charismatic stars of the original. DeMille's film wasn't noted for its plot, and 30 years on the storyline remains hopelessly old-fashioned and cliché ridden. Even the colour photography is mediocre. AE

Don Murray *Wild Bill Hickock* • Guy Stockwell *Buffalo Bill Cody* • Abby Dalton *Calamity Jane* • Bradford Dillman *Lieutenant Stiles* • Henry Silva *Crazy Knife* • Leslie Nielsen *Col George A Custer* ■ *Dir* David Lowell Rich • *Scr* Michael Blankfort, from the 1936 film

Le Plaisir ★★★★★ PG

Drama 1951 · Fr · BW · 93mins

In the second of his four last masterpieces made in France, Max Ophüls approaches these three tales based on stories by Guy de Maupassant in a virtuoso manner. The first one tells of an old man who finds his youth again by wearing a magic mask; the second accompanies a group of prostitutes on a trip to the country; and the third relates how an artist marries his model after she tries to commit suicide. Each episode has memorable sequences, there is splendid period detail, and the wonderful cast includes Jean Gabin, Simone Simon, Danielle Darrieux and Madeleine Renaud as the madame of the brothel. RB [video]

Claude Dauphin *The doctor* • Jean Galland *Ambroise, "The Mask"* • Daniel Gélin *Jean* • Simone Simon *Josephine* • Madeleine Renaud *Mme Tellier* • Jean Gabin *Joseph Rivet* • Danielle Darrieux *Rosa* • Peter Ustinov *Guy de Maupassant* ■ *Dir* Max Ophüls • *Scr* Max Ophüls, Jacques Natanson, from the stories *The Mask/The House of Madame Tellier/The Model* by Guy de Maupassant

P

Plan 9 from Outer Space ★ PG

Science-fiction thriller
1959 · US · BW · 75mins

Camp aliens attempt to take over the world by reviving the dead in Ed Wood Jr's science-fiction opus, built around a few minutes of footage Bela Lugosi shot days before he died and often cited as the worst movie ever made. There is some unintentional humour to be had from the way Wood desperately incorporates his shots of Lugosi (and a fake body double) into a mess of stock footage, amateur acting, crude special effects and wobbly sets. Tediously depressing. AJ [video] DVD

Gregory Walcott *Jeff Trent* • Bela Lugosi *Ghoul man* • Mona McKinnon *Paula Trent* • Duke Moore *Lieutenant Harper* • Richard Powers [Tom Keene] *Colonel Tom Edwards* • Vampira *Ghoul Woman* • Lyle Talbot *General Roberts* ■ *Dir/Scr* Edward D Wood Jr

Plan 10 from Outer Space ★★

Science-fiction spoof
1995 · US · Colour · 82mins

Why Salt Lake City film-maker Trent Harris would purposely want to invoke the memory of the worst movie ever made is not the only cause of wonderment in this science-fiction spoof. While researching a book about local Mormon history, Stefene Russell finds a plaque which reveals faith founder Brigham Young married an alien queen from the planet Kolob (Karen Black) who's currently plotting a revenge attack on Utah. The chuckles may be few and far between, but good special effects and Black's over-the-top performance add to the eye-rolling bemusement. AJ

Stefene Russell *Lucinda Hall* • Karen Black *Nehor* • Karen Nielson ■ *Dir/Scr* Trent Harris

Planes, Trains and Automobiles ★★★ 15

Comedy 1987 · US · Colour · 88mins

Steve Martin and John Candy give excellent performances as the not-so-good companions desperately trying to get home for Thanksgiving in this amiable comedy, which sends up the vagaries of the whole American transport system. Written and directed by John Hughes, it veers uneasily between slapstick and sentiment. Yet, the cheerfully astute playing by the disaster-prone "little-and-large" leads ensures that the farcical proceedings are always fun to watch. AJ. Contains swearing. [video] DVD

Steve Martin *Neal Page* • John Candy *Del Griffith* • Laila Robbins *Susan Page* • Michael McKean *State trooper* • Kevin Bacon *Taxi racer* • Dylan Baker *Owen* • Carol Bruce *Joy* • Olivia Burnette *Marti* ■ *Dir/Scr* John Hughes

Planet of Blood ★★

Science-fiction horror
1966 · US · Colour · 81mins

This largely unmemorable space opera from the Roger Corman stable is distinguished by an eclectic cast and may be viewed today as a precursor to *Alien* with its tale of a US manned space probe rescuing an alien craft that has ditched on the surface of Mars. Unfortunately, the green-skinned female occupant (Florence Marly) turns out to be a galactic vampire. Filmed in a week for just $65,000, the crude plot was concocted by writer/director Curtis Harrington to fit around cannibalised footage from a big-budget Russian sci-fi movie. RS

Basil Rathbone *Dr Farraday* • John Saxon *Allan* • Dennis Hopper *Paul* • Judi Meredith *Laura* • Florence Marly *Alien queen* ■ *Dir/Scr* Curtis Harrington

Planet of the Apes ★★★★ PG

Science-fiction adventure
1967 · US · Colour · 107mins

Charlton Heston and a team of astronauts crash-land on a desolate planet that is suspiciously reminiscent of Earth – only the apes rule and the humans are the dumb animals. Heston is appropriately square-jawed as the rebellious human, and Roddy McDowall and Kim Hunter shine through the marvellous ape make-up from John Chambers, who received an honorary Oscar for his work. Rod Serling and Michael Wilson provide a sly, clever script, and the twist at the end still delights. A smash hit that was followed by a number of increasingly inferior sequels (beginning with 1969's *Beneath the Planet of the Apes*), plus a rather mundane TV series. JF. Contains violence. [video] DVD

Charlton Heston *George Taylor* • Roddy McDowall *Cornelius* • Kim Hunter *Dr Zira* • Maurice Evans *Dr Zaius* • James Whitmore *President of the assembly* • James Daly *Honorious* • Linda Harrison *Nova* • Robert Gunner *Landon* • Lou Wagner *Lucius* ■ *Dir* Franklin J Schaffner • *Scr* Michael Wilson, Rod Serling, from the novel *La Planète des Singes* by Pierre Boulle

Planet of the Apes ★★★ 12

Science-fiction adventure
2001 · US · Colour · 114mins

Tim Burton's "re-imagining" of the 1967 sci-fi classic begins, like the original, with an astronaut (Mark Wahlberg) crash-landing in the future and being captured by apes on horseback. So far, so similar. What's immediately different is the ape make-up. Though John Chambers's 1967 prosthetic work was ground-breaking, multi-Oscar winner Rick Baker has upgraded it in style, so that the actors can truly emote and express through the latex. That's the good news. The bad news is the story: slight and littered with convenience. AC. Contains violence. [video] DVD

Mark Wahlberg *Captain Leo Davidson* • Tim Roth *Thade* • Helena Bonham Carter *Ari* • Michael Clarke Duncan *Attar* • Paul Giamatti *Limbo* • Estella Warren *Daena* • Cary-Hiroyuki Tagawa *Krull* ■ *Dir* Tim Burton • *Scr* William Broyles Jr, Lawrence Konner, Mark D Rosenthal [Mark Rosenthal], from the novel *La Planète des Singes* by Pierre Boulle

Planet of the Vampires ★★★ 15

Science fiction
1965 · It/Sp/US · Colour · 83mins

Italian horror maestro Mario Bava's only pure science-fiction movie melds the supernatural to space opera with haunting results. Barry Sullivan and Norma Bengell investigate the mysterious planet Aura and discover that its ancient inhabitants are disembodied spirits who await visitors in order to possess them as a means of escaping their dying planet. This is a superb example of how Bava's impressive visual sensibilities disguised a very low budget to depict a convincing alien environment and atmosphere. AJ [video]

Barry Sullivan *Capt Mark Markary* • Norma Bengell *Sanya* • Angel Aranda *Wess* • Evi Marandi *Tiona* • Fernando Villena *Karan* ■ *Dir* Mario Bava • *Scr* Mario Bava, Alberto Bevilacqua, Callisto Cosulich, Antonio Roman, Rafael J Salvia, Louis M Heyward, Ib Melchior, from a story by Ib Melchior, Renato Pestriniero

Planeta Burg ★★★★

Science fiction 1962 · USSR · BW · 74mins

It's likely you've seen this Soviet space odyssey without realising it. Roger Corman acquired the rights and hacked off huge chunks for his own B-movies, Curtis Harrington's *Voyage to the Prehistoric Planet* (1965) and *Voyage to the Planet of Prehistoric Women* (1966). Pavel Klushantsev's film, however, is an original and highly entertaining piece of work, chronicling a three-ship mission to Venus and the encounters of cosmonaut Gennadi Vernov with both the treacherous landscape and various hostile life forms. Colourfully designed and wittily directed, in short, a minor classic. DP. A Russian language film.

Gennadi Vernov *Aloysha* • Vladimir Temelianov *Ilya Vershinin* • Yuri Sarantsev *Scherba* • Georgi Zhonov *Bobrov* • Kyunna Ignatova *Masha* ■ *Dir* Pavel Klushantsev • *Scr* Alexander Kazantsev, Pavel Klushantsev

The Plank ★★★ U

Silent comedy 1967 · UK · Colour · 27mins

A joyously inventive British "silent" comedy from writer/director Eric Sykes about the misadventures of two builders delivering wood to a house. Sykes himself is "Smaller workman" to Tommy Cooper's "Larger workman", and, although not all the jokes are completely fresh, the fun is in the effective sound effects, and the spotting of comedy icons such as Jimmy Edwards, Jimmy Tarbuck and Roy Castle in unfamiliar poses. Music hall on the hoof. TH [video] DVD

Tommy Cooper *Larger workman* • Eric Sykes *Smaller workman* • Jimmy Edwards *Policeman* • Roy Castle *Man covered in garbage* • Graham Stark *Amorous van driver* • Stratford Johns *Station sergeant* • Jim Dale *House painter* • Jimmy Tarbuck *Barman* • Hattie Jacques *Woman with rose* • Johnny Speight *Chauffeur* ■ *Dir/Scr* Eric Sykes

The Planter's Wife ★★

Drama 1952 · UK · BW · 91mins

She's Claudette Colbert, towards the end of her career, in the middle of a then-topical tale about the "troubles" in Malaya, drifting apart from hubby Jack Hawkins and into the arms of Anthony Steel. Then the rebels attack their plantation and the threat to their lives reunites husband and wife. Interestingly, this picture, intended as a tribute to the courage of the rubber planters and their families, inadvertently ends up as a damning indictment of imperialism. Colbert seems uncomfortable, both in the location work and the ill-matched studio interiors. TS

Claudette Colbert *Liz Frazer* • Jack Hawkins *Jim Frazer* • Anthony Steel *Inspector Hugh Dobson* • Ram Gopal *Nair* • Jeremy Spenser *Mat* • Tom Macauley *Jack Bushell* ■ *Dir* Ken Annakin • *Scr* Peter Proud, Guy Elmes, from the novel by SC George

Plastic Jesus ★★★★

Documentary drama
1971 · Yug · Sepia BW and Colour · 76mins

After a decade of unprecedented "novi film" innovation, Yugoslav cinema entered its so-called "black film" phase, in which the anti-socialist rhetoric became increasingly strident and nihilistic. Taking his title from a popular American song, student director Lazar Stojanovic found himself in the vanguard of this movement when he was sentenced to three years imprisonment for making anti-Tito statements in his debut feature, which was immediately banned. Combining newsreel footage challenging the official line on the Second World War and sepia-tinted scenes of a symbolically sexual nature, it's a technically audacious protest, that affects with its visual energy even without in-depth background knowledge. DP. In Serbo-Croat with English subtitles.

Dir/Scr Lazar Stojanovic

Platform ★★★★ 12

Drama
2000 · Chi/HK/Jpn/Fr/Swi · Colour · 148mins

Set in Shanxi province in the 1980s, this is an assured, if occasionally over-elaborate study of China at its socio-economic crossroads. Filmed in long takes that locate the characters in their slowly changing surroundings, the allegorical action focuses on the Fenyang Peasant Culture Group's tortuous transition into the All-Star Rock and Breakdance Electronic Band, as its style of propagandised pop is surpassed by western imports. However, Jia Zhang Ke is careful to leaven the cultural analysis with human interest, as two young couples seek to persuade their intractable elders to accept their modern approach to romance. DP. In Mandarin with English subtitles. [video] DVD

Wang Hong-wei *Minliang* • Zhao Tao *Ruijuan* • Liang Jing-Dong *Chang Jun* • Yang Tian-Yi *Zhong Pin* ■ *Dir/Scr* Jia Zhang Ke

Platinum Blonde ★★★ U

Comedy 1931 · US · BW · 90mins

Jean Harlow is all aglow (and very revealing) in this fast-moving comedy satire. But the real star of the show is leading man Robert Williams (as the reporter who marries debutante Harlow), an inventive, screen-dominating light comedian who tragically died prematurely in the year of this, his greatest hit. The jokes at the expense of high society aren't as funny now, and much of the movie's shooting style has dated badly, but director Frank Capra keeps this zipping along, and the central trio of Harlow, Williams and lovely Loretta Young is a joy to behold. TS

Loretta Young *Gallagher* • Robert Williams *Stew Smith* • Jean Harlow *Anne Schuyler* • Louise Closser Hale *Mrs Schuyler* • Donald Dillaway *Michael Schuyler* • Reginald Owen *Dexter Grayson* ■ *Dir* Frank Capra • *Scr* Jo Swerling, Dorothy Howell, Robert Riskin, from a story by Harry E Chandlee, Douglas W Churchill

Platinum High School ★★

Drama 1960 · US · BW · 93mins

Mickey Rooney stars in this partly interesting, partly nonsensically sensationalist drama, directed by Charles Haas. Rooney is the father, estranged from his son by divorce, who arrives at the military academy where his boy has been killed. There, he realises that the establishment is home to delinquent misfits from wealthy families, suspects foul play in his son's death. RK

Mickey Rooney *Steven Conway* • Terry Moore *Jennifer Evans* • Dan Duryea *Major Redfern Kelly* • Yvette Mimieux *Lorinda Nibley* • Conway Twitty *Billy Jack Barnes* • Jimmy Boyd *Bud Starkweather* • Harold Lloyd Jr *Charley Boy Cable* • Richard Jaeckel *Hack Marlow* • Elisha Cook Jr *Harry Nesbitt* ■ *Dir* Charles Haas • *Scr* Robert Smith, from a story by Howard Breslin

Platoon ★★★★★ 15

War drama 1986 · US · Colour · 114mins

It took ten years for Oliver Stone to get his script made, but when this film finally reached the screen it became a box-office smash and won four Oscars. Unlike other directors who made major Vietnam movies, Stone has the edge in that he was actually there, as a volunteer who fought for patriotic reasons and got wounded before becoming disillusioned. From the scary opening when the new arrivals are greeted by the sight of body bags bound for home, the movie is an authentically messy tour of duty through the paddy fields where two Americans (Willem Dafoe and Tom Berenger) are at war with each other and fight for the soul of rookie Charlie Sheen. A modern classic. AT. Contains violence and swearing. [VIDEO] DVD

Tom Berenger *Sergeant Barnes* • Willem Dafoe *Sergeant Elias* • Charlie Sheen *Chris* • Forest Whitaker *Big Harold* • Francesco Quinn *Rhah* • John C McGinley *Sergeant O'Neill* • Richard Edson *Sal* • Kevin Dillon *Bunny* • Reggie Johnson *Junior* • Keith David *King* • Johnny Depp *Lerner* ■ *Dir/Scr* Oliver Stone • *Cinematographer* Robert Richardson

Play Dead ★ 18

Horror 1981 · US · Colour · 81mins

In her post-*Addams Family* years, Yvonne De Carlo lent dignity to a seemingly unending series of completely worthless scripts. This devilish drivel is yet another waste of her inestimable talents. De Carlo makes a Satanic pact with a Rottweiler to kill off her relatives, all because her late sister married her only true love. Electrocution, strangulation and poisoning are all in the canny canine's canon of carnage, as if anyone cares. Good dog – bad film! AJ [VIDEO]

Yvonne De Carlo *Hester* • Stephanie Dunnam *Audrey* • David Cullinane *Jeff* • Glenn Kezer *Otis* • Ron Jackson *Richard* ■ *Dir* Peter Wittman • *Scr* Lothrop W Jordan

Play Dirty ★★ 15

Second World War drama
1969 · UK · Colour · 113mins

Co-written by Melvyn Bragg at his least cultured and directed by Andre De Toth at his most action-led, this predictable wartime story of inexperienced officer Michael Caine leading a unit to blow up an enemy fuel dump has its moments – especially when roguish Nigel Davenport is around – but not many. It's another take on Robert Aldrich's *The Dirty Dozen* and, though some of the skirmishes do have an impact, this is not in the same class. TH. Contains violence, swearing. [VIDEO]

Michael Caine *Captain Douglas* • Nigel Davenport *Cyril Leech* • Nigel Green *Colonel Masters* • Harry Andrews *Brigadier Blore* • Aly Ben Ayed *Sadok* • Vivian Pickles *German nurse* • Bernard Archard *Colonel Homerton* ■ *Dir* Andre De Toth • *Scr* Lotte Colin, Melvyn Bragg, from a story by George Marton

Play It Again, Sam ★★★★ 15

Comedy 1972 · US · Colour · 81mins

Adapted by Woody Allen from his own 1969 stage play, this is one of the very few entries on his CV that America's leading film auteur has not directed himself. That task fell to Herbert Ross, who adopts an overcautious approach to the story of film buff Allen's tentative relationship with Diane Keaton, the wife of best pal Tony Roberts. But such is the calibre of the playing and the assurance of the writing that it's almost impossible to resist. The more politically correct may feel their hackles rise from time to time, but the one-liners are among Allen's best and the Bogart allusions are priceless. DP [VIDEO] DVD

Woody Allen *Allan Felix* • Diane Keaton *Linda Christie* • Tony Roberts *Dick Christie* • Jerry Lacy *Humphrey Bogart* • Susan Anspach *Nancy Felix* • Jennifer Salt *Sharon* • Joy Bang *Julie* • Viva *Jennifer* ■ *Dir* Herbert Ross • *Scr* Woody Allen, from his play

Play It As It Lays ★★★

Drama 1972 · US · Colour · 98mins

Under-rated director Frank Perry dissects the Hollywood glitterati in this confident adaptation. The story flashes back from Tuesday Weld's convalescence from a suicide bid. It unflinchingly exposes the dog-eat-dog nature of the fame game, as Weld's model-turned-actress falls back on the friendship of troubled producer Anthony Perkins, after she is dumped by husband Adam Roarke (the minor-league director who discovered her) when his own career takes off. It's pure soap, but there are sharp edges beneath the gloss. DP

Tuesday Weld *Maria Wyeth* • Anthony Perkins *BZ* • Tammy Grimes *Helene* • Adam Roarke *Carter Lang* • Ruth Ford *Carlotta* • Eddie Firestone *Benny Austin* • Diana Ewing *Susannah* • Paul Lambert *Larry Kulik* ■ *Dir* Frank Perry • *Scr* John Gregory Dunne, Joan Didion, from the novel by Joan Didion

Play It Cool ★★ U

Comedy drama 1962 · UK · BW · 78mins

A wonderfully nostalgic pre-Beatles teen fest, starring Britain's answer to Elvis, Billy Fury, in a genuine pop musical, as the Liverpool rocker who stops Anna Palk from straying off the straight and narrow – as if the plot matters! It's a real period artefact, with guest appearances from the likes of Bobby Vee, and a batch of splendid English veterans like Dennis Price and Richard Wattis along for the ride. It isn't any good, really, but at least it's fun and moves along briskly. TS [VIDEO]

Billy Fury *Billy Universe* • Michael Anderson Jr *Alvin* • Dennis Price *Sir Charles Bryant* • Richard Wattis *Nervous man* • Anna Palk *Ann Bryant* ■ *Dir* Michael Winner • *Scr* Jack Henry

Play It to the Bone ★★★ 18

Sports comedy drama
2000 · US · Colour · 123mins

Antonio Banderas and Woody Harrelson play second-rate pugilists who get a shot at the big time when they are asked to box each other on the same bill as a Mike Tyson bout. The catch is they have less than 12 hours to get to Vegas, so the two friends hit the road with feisty Lolita Davidovich at the wheel. Too much chat and the aggravating presence of Lucy Liu as a hitch-hiking nymphomaniac make the road trip a long haul, but things pick up during the climactic fisticuffs. NS. Contains swearing, violence, drug abuse, sex scenes and nudity. [VIDEO] DVD

Antonio Banderas *Cesar Dominguez* • Woody Harrelson *Vince Boudreau* • Lolita Davidovich *Grace Pasic* • Tom Sizemore *Joe Domino* • Lucy Liu *Lia* • Robert Wagner *Hank Goody* • Richard Masur *Artie* • George Foreman *HBO commentator* • Rod Stewart • Kevin Costner • James Woods • Drew Carey • Tony Curtis • Wesley Snipes • Natasha Gregson Wagner • Jennifer Tilly ■ *Dir/Scr* Ron Shelton

Play Me Something ★★ 15

Drama 1989 · UK · Colour and BW · 71mins

This highly esoteric "film poem" is based on the work of writer/critic John Berger, who appears as himself, telling a slight tale about romance in Venice to a group of passengers (one of whom is Tilda Swinton) waiting for a flight from Barra, in the Outer Hebrides, to Glasgow. Singer Hamish Henderson, about whom the director subsequently made a documentary, interjects. Fans of folk art may well be enchanted by the experimental blend of words and pictures. Others may wish to avoid. DM

Lucia Lanzarini *Marietta* • Charlie Barron *Bruno* • John Berger (2) *Storyteller* • Hamish Henderson *Electrician* • Tilda Swinton *Hairdresser* • Stewart Ennis *Motorcyclist* • Robert Carr *Salesman* • Liz Lochhead *Pregnant woman* ■ *Dir* Timothy Neat • *Scr* Timothy Neat, John Berger, from a story by John Berger

Play Misty for Me ★★★★ 18

Thriller 1971 · US · Colour · 97mins

Clint Eastwood's fine directorial debut, in which he also stars as a DJ, rejecting fan Jessica Walter after a one-night stand only to discover that she's determined to keep him whatever the cost – and all this 16 years before *Fatal Attraction*. Jealousy is one of the hardest emotions to delineate with any kind of subtlety in cinema, yet Walter is superb as the deranged woman. Eastwood's sideburns and flares lend the movie a period charm today, but its power to grip and chill remains undiminished. Look out for *Dirty Harry* director Don Siegel as Murphy the bartender, and don't watch this one on your own. TS. Contains swearing, drug abuse and brief nudity. [VIDEO] DVD

Clint Eastwood *Dave Garver* • Jessica Walter *Evelyn Draper* • Donna Mills *Tobie Williams* • John Larch *Sergeant McCallum* • James McEachin *Al Monte* • Don Siegel *Murphy the bartender* ■ *Dir* Clint Eastwood • *Scr* Jo Heims, Dean Riesner, from a story by Jo Heims • *Cinematographer* Bruce Surtees

The Playboy of the Western World ★★ PG

Comedy drama 1962 · Ire · Colour · 95mins

Brian Desmond Hurst returned to his roots for this authentic version of the Irish play. However, this theatre-bound work has only a strong cast to recommend it over the other screen versions of Synge's garrulous piece. The playboy is a boastful young man who beguiles the inhabitants of a County Mayo village with stories, perhaps real, perhaps fantasy. Gary Raymond has a field day, but for many viewers the main delight will be seeing one of Ireland's greatest actors, Siobhan McKenna, as one of the women who falls for his charm. BB [VIDEO]

Siobhan McKenna *Pegeen Mike* • Gary Raymond *Christy Mahon* • Elspeth March *Widow Quin* • Michael O'Briain *Shawn Keogh* • Liam Redmond *Michael James* • Niall MacGinnis *Old Mahon* ■ *Dir* Brian Desmond Hurst • *Scr* Brian Desmond Hurst, from the play by John Millington Synge

The Playboys ★★★ PG

Drama 1992 · UK · Colour · 104mins

You wait ages for a film about a single Irish mother who refuses to name the father of her child to turn up, and then, typically, two come along at once. Roddy Doyle's *The Snapper* has the edge over *The Playboys*, although Shane Connaughton cannot be faulted for his part in a script brimming with incident and credible characters. However, a bombastic Albert Finney over-balances the picture in the role of the village policeman, whose jealousy at Robin Wright's romance with Aidan Quinn spills over into violence. DP. Contains violence and swearing. [VIDEO]

Albert Finney *Hegarty* • Aidan Quinn *Tom Casey* • Robin Wright [Robin Wright Penn] *Tara Maguire* • Milo O'Shea *Freddie* • Alan Devlin *Malone* • Niamh Cusack *Brigid* ■ *Dir* Gillies MacKinnon • *Scr* Shane Connaughton, Kerry Crabbe

The Player ★★★★★ 15

Satire 1992 · US · Colour · 119mins

This swingeing satire is easily the best movie about Tinseltown since *Sunset Boulevard*. Director Robert Altman turns the spotlight on the industry hands that feed him and scores a bullseye on each target in Michael Tolkin's deft script. The temptation is to play spot the star, but don't let the galaxy of cameos distract from the gloriously cynical plot and a towering turn from a marvellously oily Tim Robbins. He stars as the high-flying studio executive who is troubled by poison-pen postcards from a discarded scriptwriter, the ambitions of wunderkind Peter Gallagher and the snooping of cop Whoopi Goldberg, who suspects him of murder. This is Hollywood at its worst told by Hollywood at its best. DP. Contains violence, swearing, nudity. [VIDEO] DVD

Tim Robbins *Griffin Mill* • Greta Scacchi *June Gudmundsdottir* • Fred Ward *Walter Stuckel* • Whoopi Goldberg *Detective Susan Avery* • Peter Gallagher *Larry Levy* • Brion James *Joel Levison* • Cynthia Stevenson *Bonnie Sherow* • Vincent D'Onofrio *David Kahane* • Dean Stockwell *Andy Civella* • Richard E Grant *Tom Oakley* • Sydney Pollack *Dick Mellen* ■ *Dir* Robert Altman • *Scr* Michael Tolkin, from his novel

Players ★★ PG

Romantic drama
1979 · US · Colour · 115mins

This charts the rise of a young tennis player who makes it to the Wimbledon final, despite the distractions of a romance with a millionaire's mistress. Dean Paul Martin (Dean's son) stars, with Ali MacGraw as the love interest, in a curate's egg that's very good as a tennis action movie but risibly poor away from the court. But with appearances by Guillermo Vilas, John McEnroe, Ilie Nastase and John Lloyd among others, this is sure to appeal to aficionados of the game. RK [VIDEO]

Ali MacGraw *Nicole* • Dean Paul Martin *Chris* • Maximilian Schell *Marco* • Pancho Gonzalez *Pancho* • Steve Guttenberg *Rusty* • Melissa Prophet *Ann* • Guillermo Vilas ■ *Dir* Anthony Harvey • *Scr* Arnold Schulman

The Players Club ★★★ 18

Crime drama 1998 · US · Colour · 98mins

This is a flawed curiosity, written and directed by rap star/actor Ice Cube (who also pops up in a brief cameo). Newcomer LisaRaye plays an aspiring journalist who takes up stripping to pay

P

her way through college and soon finds herself drawn into the murkier aspects of the business. She delivers a feisty performance, although Bernie Mac steals the show as the motormouth owner of the club where she works. There's an exploitative nature to the whole affair, and both the writing and direction are erratic. RT. Contains violence, swearing, drug abuse, sex scenes and nudity.

LisaRaye *Diana Armstrong/Diamond* • Monica Calhoun *Ebony* • Bernie Mac *Dollar Bill* • Jamie Foxx *Blue* • Chrystale Wilson *Ronnie* • Adele Givens *Tricks* • AJ Johnson [Anthony Johnson] *Li'l Man* • Ice Cube *Reggie* ■ *Dir/Scr* Ice Cube

Playgirl ★★

Drama 1954 · US · BW · 85mins

Old-fashioned melodrama given a 1950s flavour as a simple Nebraska lass (Colleen Miller) arrives in New York to seek fame and fortune. She rapidly finds herself gracing the cover of *Glitter* magazine, incurring the jealousy of her roommate (Shelley Winters); other undesirable consequences include her descent into the sleazy party scene and her implication in a gangster's murder. Acceptable couch-potato fodder. RK

Shelley Winters *Fran Davis* • Barry Sullivan *Mike Marsh* • Colleen Miller *Phyllis Matthews* • Gregg Palmer *Tom Bradley* • Richard Long *Barron Courtney* • Kent Taylor *Ted Andrews* • Dave Barry *Jonathan* • Philip Van Zandt *Lew Martel* ■ *Dir* Joseph Pevney • *Scr* Robert Blees, from a story by Ray Buffum

Playing Away ★★★ 15

Satire 1986 · UK · Colour · 101mins

In Horace Ove's immensely likeable film, Britain's race relations and its imperial hangover are boiled down to a game of cricket, played on a village green between the local side and a team from Brixton. The country lads are confident of victory and are staging the match to raise money for the Third World. The cosy, quaint English movie of the pre-war years has been fondly updated and spiked with razor-sharp social observation. AT

Norman Beaton *Willy Boy* • Robert Urquhart *Godfrey* • Helen Lindsay *Marjorie* • Nicholas Farrell *Derek* • Brian Bovell *Stuart* • Suzette Llewellyn *Yvette* ■ *Dir* Horace Ové • *Scr* Caryl Phillips

Playing by Heart ★★★★ 15

Comedy drama 1998 · US · Colour · 116mins

This beautifully wrought multi-character love story provides great roles for Sean Connery, Ellen Burstyn and Gena Rowlands, and also puts newer Hollywood hopefuls Ryan Phillippe, Gillian Anderson and Angelina Jolie in the spotlight. Director Willard Carroll's glossy ensemble is engaging and emotionally resonant as it cuts between a multitude of stormy confrontations, intriguing trysts and startling dates, and then neatly ties them all off with a bravura conclusion that's clever and satisfying. AJ. Contains swearing. DVD

Gillian Anderson *Meredith* • Angelina Jolie *Joan* • Madeleine Stowe *Gracie* • Anthony Edwards *Roger* • Ryan Phillippe *Keenan* • Gena Rowlands *Hannah* • Sean Connery *Paul* • Dennis Quaid *Hugh* • Ellen Burstyn *Mildred* • Nastassja Kinski *Melanie* ■ *Dir/Scr* Willard Carroll

Playing for Keeps ★ 15

Comedy 1986 · US · Colour · 102mins

An embarrassing attempt to make a youth movie. Having just finished high school, three friends inherit a run-down hotel in the Catskills and decide to turn it into the perfect place for rock-obsessed teenagers. They work hard on the hotel but there are local residents waiting to stop the lads from their dream, including a nefarious industrialist who wants to use the site as a toxic waste dump. A film as awful as it sounds. FL

Daniel Jordano *Danny D'Angelo* • Matthew Penn *Spikes* • Leon W Grant *Silk* • Mary B Ward *Chloe* • Marisa Tomei *Tracy* • Jimmy Baio *Steinberg* • Harold Gould *Rockerfeller* • Kim Hauser *Marie* ■ *Dir* Bob Weinstein, Harvey Weinstein • *Scr* Bob Weinstein, Harvey Weinstein, Jeremy Leven

Playing for Time ★★★★

Drama based on a true story
1980 · US · Colour · 149mins

A highly acclaimed and well-acted TV movie, based on the experiences of a Jewish Holocaust survivor who managed to avoid death by forming an orchestra with fellow captives. Vanessa Redgrave, who caused controversy when she accepted the role owing to her Palestinian sympathies, is as impressive and heartfelt as ever, and she is given memorable support by Jane Alexander and Melanie Mayron. Perhaps too heart-rending for some tastes, this is nonetheless a thought-provoking and moving drama. JB

Vanessa Redgrave *Fania Fenelon* • Jane Alexander *Alma Rose* • Maud Adams *Mala* • Christine Baranski *Olga* • Robin Bartlett *Etalina* • Marisa Berenson *Elzvieta* • Verna Bloom *Paulette* ■ *Dir* Daniel Mann • *Scr* Arthur Miller, from the book by Fania Fenelon

Playing God ★★ 18

Crime thriller 1997 · US · Colour · 93mins

Playing against type, David Duchovny stars as a disgraced surgeon with a drug habit who becomes unofficial physician to slimy mobster Timothy Hutton and his gang. Both Hutton and underworld rival Peter Stormare are flamboyantly over the top, and Angelina Jolie supplies the glamour. The plot is ridiculously far-fetched while the direction is slick but a touch erratic. JF. Contains violence and swearing. DVD

David Duchovny *Dr Eugene Sands* • Timothy Hutton *Raymond Blossom* • Angelina Jolie *Claire* • Michael Massee *Gage* • Peter Stormare *Vladimir* • Andrew Tiernan *Cyril* ■ *Dir* Andy Wilson • *Scr* Mark Haskell Smith

Playmaker ★

Mystery thriller 1994 · US · Colour · 88mins

Casting couch codswallop, with Jennifer Rubin as a wannabe actress willing to do almost anything in her bid for celluloid stardom. Colin Firth co-stars as a manipulative acting coach in a routine sexploitation movie that's far less erotic than it thinks it is. It's also marred by a first hour of appalling pop psychology and irritatingly vague plot development. DA

Colin Firth *Ross* • Jennifer Rubin *Jamie Harris* • John Getz *Eddie* ■ *Dir* Yuri Zeltser • *Scr* Yuri Zeltser, from a story by Darren Block, Kathryn Nemesh, from a screenplay (unproduced) by Michael Schroeder

Playmates ★ U

Musical comedy 1941 · US · BW · 95mins

The last film made by John Barrymore is a bizarrely awful comedy musical starring Kay Kyser and his band, with the usual Kyser appendages such as the comedian Ish Kabibble. The ludicrous plot presents the humiliating spectacle of a self-parodying Barrymore as a washed-up actor trying for a comeback on radio by teaching Shakespeare to Kyser. Adding to the comic chaos (which some might find amusing), is Lupe Velez, once known as the "Mexican Spitfire", exhibiting her particular brand of crude slapstick. RK

John Barrymore • Kay Kyser • Lupe Velez *Carmen Del Toro* • Ginny Simms *Ginny* • May Robson *Grandma* • Patsy Kelly *Lulu Monahan* • Peter Lind Hayes *Peter Lindsey* • Ish Kabibble ■ *Dir* David Butler • *Scr* James V Kern, Arthur Phillips, from a story by James V Kern, MM Musselman

Playtime ★★★★★ U

Satirical comedy 1967 · Fr · Colour · 114mins

It took Jacques Tati close to ten years to realise his greatest achievement, but it left him virtually broke. No wonder. He and his designer Eugène Roman built an ultramodern Paris of steel and glass skyscrapers through which Monsieur Hulot, Tati's marvellous comic creation, continues his battle with mechanical objects. The amiable, bumbling Hulot gets caught up with a group of American tourists, and finds himself at the opening of a nightclub that is far from ready. Ironically, given Tati's technophobe philosophy, his use of stereophonic sound and the 70mm screen has seldom been equalled. Unfortunately, the film, originally 152 minutes long, has mainly been shown since its first release in versions reduced in time and space. RB DVD

Jacques Tati *Monsieur Hulot* • Rita Maiden *Mr Schultz's companion* • Barbara Dennek *Young tourist* • Jacqueline Lecomte *Her friend* • Valérie Camille *Monsieur Luce's secretary* • France Romilly *Woman selling spectacles* • France Delahalle *Shopper in department store* • Billy Kearns *Monsieur Schulz* ■ *Dir* Jacques Tati • *Scr* Jacques Tati, Jacques Lagrange, Art Buchwald (English dialogue)

Plaza Suite ★★★ PG

Comedy 1971 · US · Colour · 109mins

Three Walter Matthaus for the price of one, as he cynically bulldozes his way through three acts of Neil Simon's play about the goings-on in a swank hotel suite. As nervous comedy, it's best when it's most serious (Maureen Stapleton trying to keep husband Matthau from his mistress). Yet the more slapstick episodes (Hollywood producer trying to bed old flame; bemused father trying to coax bride-to-be daughter out of a locked loo) have their moments, even if the top-of-the-voice humour sometimes becomes so strident, it's inaudible. TH

Walter Matthau *Sam Nash/Jesse Kiplinger/Roy Hubley* • Maureen Stapleton *Karen Nash* • Louise Sorel *Miss McCormack* • Barbara Harris *Muriel Tate* • Lee Grant *Norma Hubley* • Jenny Sullivan *Mimsey Hubley* • Tom Carey *Borden Eisler* ■ *Dir* Arthur Hiller • *Scr* Neil Simon, from his play

Pleasantville ★★★★ 12

Fantasy comedy drama
1998 · US · Colour and BW · 119mins

Tobey Maguire and Reese Witherspoon play sparring siblings who, while fighting over the TV remote control, get zapped inside Maguire's favourite soap, a 1950s re-run called "Pleasantville". They find themselves in what is literally a black-and-white world. How the youngsters' progressive attitudes to sex and marriage begin to induce unfamiliar feelings in the show's two-dimensional caricatures forms the basis of this witty and affectionate comedy. And how these new-found emotions are depicted by the gradual encroachment of colour into their monochrome lives is where its brilliance lies. It's a clever concept, although the multiple metaphors do pile up somewhat. DA. Contains swearing. DVD

Tobey Maguire *David* • Reese Witherspoon *Jennifer* • Joan Allen *Betty Parker* • William H Macy *George Parker* • Jeff Daniels *Mr Johnson* • JT Walsh *Big Bob* • Don Knotts *TV repairman* ■ *Dir/Scr* Gary Ross

Please Believe Me ★★★ U

Romantic comedy 1950 · US · BW · 86mins

Efficient acting by an attractive cast turns this run-of-the-mill and somewhat dated romantic comedy into a pleasant diversion. English rose Deborah Kerr stars as an English rose who inherits a large and profitable ranch. Off she goes to Texas, pursued and wooed by layabout Robert Walker, who sees her as the answer to his gambling debts, and womanising millionaire playboy Peter Lawford, looking for a good time. Lawford's shy, respectable lawyer, Mark Stevens, comes along, too. Guess who gets the lady. RK

Deborah Kerr *Alison Kirbe* • Robert Walker *Terence Keath* • Mark Stevens *Matthew Kinston* • Peter Lawford *Jeremy Taylor* • James Whitmore *Vincent Maran* • J Carrol Naish *Lucky Reilly* • Spring Byington *Mrs Milwright* ■ *Dir* Norman Taurog • *Scr* Nathaniel Curtis

Please Don't Eat the Daisies ★★★★ U

Comedy 1960 · US · Colour · 110mins

A brash, colourful and fast-moving MGM comedy based on Jean Kerr's episodic reminiscences about life with hubby, Broadway's ace drama critic Walter Kerr. The couple are delightfully played here by Doris Day and the ever-urbane David Niven. Director Charles Walters maintains a fast pace, as Day and Niven decamp from Manhattan to a country abode. This was one of a series of generally under-rated MGM comedies directed by Walters. TS

Doris Day *Kate Mackay* • David Niven *Larry Mackay* • Janis Paige *Deborah Vaughn* • Spring Byington *Suzie Robinson* • Richard Haydn *Alfred North* • Patsy Kelly *Maggie* ■ *Dir* Charles Walters • *Scr* Isobel Lennart, from the book by Jean Kerr

Please Let the Flowers Live ★★

Drama 1986 · W Ger · Colour · 90mins

Duccio Tessari's weighty, symbolic "second chance" film about a lawyer who vows to reform after he is spared in a plane crash takes itself desperately seriously and is, thus, unintentionally hilarious. DP. German dialogue dubbed into English.

Klaus-Jürgen Wussow *Charles Duhamel* • Birgit Doll • Hannelore Elsner • Gerd Böckmann • Kurt Meisel ■ *Dir* Duccio Tessari • *Scr* Joachim Hammann, from a novel by Johannes Mario Simmel

Please Sir! ★★ PG

Comedy 1971 · UK · Colour · 97mins

Inspired by the Sidney Poitier feature *To Sir with Love*, ITV's often hilarious sitcom ran for four years from 1968. The original class of 5C were all ready to depart for their own series, *The Fenn Street Gang*, when this shambolic film version was made. John Alderton is good as the put-upon form teacher, but the few funny moments belong to Joan Sanderson as the headmaster's formidable assistant. DP DVD

John Alderton *Bernard Hedges* • Deryck Guyler *Norman Potter* • Noel Howlett *Mr Cromwell* • Joan Sanderson *Doris Ewell* • Richard Davies *Mr Price* • Erik Chitty *Mr Smith* ■ *Dir* Mark Stuart • *Scr* John Esmonde, Bob Larbey, from their TV series

Please Teacher ★★ U

Comedy 1937 · UK · BW · 80mins

Believing the will bequeathing him a legacy is hidden in a bust that resides in a country-house girls' school, a young man inveigles himself into the premises by masquerading as the visiting explorer-brother of one of the pupils. Bashful Bobby Howes and waif-like René Ray, both popular stars in 1930s Britain, feature in this *Boys'*

Own farce with songs that's good-natured, inoffensive and belongs firmly to a bygone era. RK

Bobby Howes *Tommy Deacon* • René Ray *Ann Trent* • Wylie Watson *Oswald Clutterbuck* • Bertha Belmore *Agatha Pink* • Vera Pearce *Petunia Trundle* • Aubrey Dexter *Reeves* • Arthur Chesney *Round* ■ *Dir* Stafford Dickens • *Scr* Stafford Dickens, from the play by KRG Browne, RP Weston, Bert Lee

Please Turn Over ★★★

Comedy 1960 · UK · BW · 85mins

Notwithstanding its *Carry On* credentials, this gentle comedy of embarrassment could not be further from the bawdy humour of the celebrated series. Adapted by Norman Hudis, it boasts Leslie Phillips, Joan Sims and Charles Hawtrey among those aghast at the revelations contained in a potboiling novel populated by local luminaries. It's a one-joke affair, but director Gerald Thomas ensures the cast keeps it light and frothy. DP

Ted Ray *Edward Halliday* • Jean Kent *Janet Halliday* • Leslie Phillips *Dr Henry Manners* • Joan Sims *Beryl* • Julia Lockwood *Jo Halliday* • Tim Seely *Robert Hughes* • Charles Hawtrey *Jeweller* • Dilys Laye *Millicent Jones* • Lionel Jeffries *Ian Howard* • Joan Hickson *Saleswoman* ■ *Dir* Gerald Thomas • *Scr* Norman Hudis, from the play *Book of the Month* by Basil Thomas

Pleasure at Her Majesty's ★★★★ 12

Concert comedy documentary
1976 · UK · Colour · 71mins

The first in a long line of celebrity galas featuring major comedy and music stars performing in aid of Amnesty International. Originally screened on TV, then given a theatrical release, this elegantly filmed piece captures the magic of a special night. The Monty Python team dominate the proceedings, but there are wonderful contributions from all the artists involved. This documentary, and the others that followed, provide an invaluable historical (and hysterical) record of many artists at the peak of their powers. DF

John Cleese • Terry Gilliam • Terry Jones • Michael Palin • Graham Chapman • Alan Bennett • Peter Cook • Dudley Moore • John Bird • John Fortune • Eleanor Bron • Tim Brooke-Taylor • Carol Cleveland • Graeme Garden • Barry Humphries ■ *Dir* Roger Graef

The Pleasure Garden ★★★

Silent drama 1925 · UK/Ger · BW · 75mins

Chorus girl Virginia Valli follows new husband Miles Mander to the Tropics. There, she discovers he's really a psychotic alcoholic who's living with a native woman. Made at the UFA studios in Germany as a co-production between Michael Balcon and Erich Pommer, this is a creaky, unconvincing and sometimes tedious silent melodrama. However, it does mark the solo feature directing debut of Alfred Hitchcock and, for all its shortcomings, reveals in embryo several of the master's stylistic devices. A must for students of his work. RK

Virginia Valli *Patsy Brand* • Carmelita Geraghty *Jill Cheyne* • Miles Mander *Levet* • John Stuart *Hugh Fielding* • Nita Naldi *Native girl* ■ *Dir* Alfred J Hitchcock [Alfred Hitchcock] • *Scr* Eliot Stannard, from the novel by Oliver Sandys

The Pleasure Girls ★★

Drama 1965 · UK · BW · 86mins

This attempt to show the problems facing a young model in the Swinging Sixties is an exasperating effort from writer/director Gerry O'Hara, who seems to think that incessant references to sexual freedom are enough to sustain a paper-thin story about the ever-changing relationships of Francesca Annis and her flatmates. The script strains every sinew to be gear and fab. DP

Ian McShane *Keith Dexter* • Francesca Annis *Sally Feathers* • Klaus Kinski *Nikko* • Mark Eden *Prinny* • Tony Tanner *Paddy* • Rosemary Nicols *Marion* ■ *Dir/Scr* Gerry O'Hara

The Pleasure of His Company ★★ U

Romantic comedy
1961 · US · Colour · 113mins

Fred Astaire brings all his easy, debonair charm but not, alas, his twinkling feet to this, the second non-musical of his long career. The film shows what happens when ageing playboy Astaire, long-separated from his family, turns up for his daughter's wedding. Debbie Reynolds is delighted to see her father again; husband-to-be Tab Hunter is bemused; while Astaire's ex-wife Lilli Palmer, now remarried to Gary Merrill, is none too pleased. RK

Fred Astaire *Biddeford "Pogo" Poole* • Debbie Reynolds *Jessica Poole* • Lilli Palmer *Katharine Dougherty* • Tab Hunter *Roger Henderson* • Gary Merrill *James Dougherty* • Charlie Ruggles [Charles Ruggles] *Mackenzie Savage* • Edith Head *Dress designer* ■ *Dir* George Seaton • *Scr* Samuel Taylor, from the play by Samuel Taylor, Cornelia Otis Skinner • *Costume Designer* Edith Head

The Pleasure Principle ★★ 18

Sex comedy 1991 · UK · Colour · 96mins

Peter Firth plays a philandering journalist who beds a succession of women before getting his comeuppance in this curious British sex comedy, very much in the tradition of the saucy romps of the 1970s. It was unpopular with critics, who found its style outmoded in the Aids era. However, the surprisingly literate script does take into account the morals of the early 1990s. The performances are also much more polished than in the rubbish of yore. DM [video]

Peter Firth *Dick* • Lynsey Baxter *Sammy* • Haydn Gwynne *Judith* • Lysette Anthony *Charlotte* • Sara Mair-Thomas *Anne* • Ian Hogg *Malcolm* • Gordon Warnecke *Policeman* ■ *Dir/Scr* David Cohen (2)

The Pleasure Seekers ★★★

Musical romance
1964 · US · Colour · 106mins

A rare example of a successful movie remade by the same director as the original, this is Jean Negulesco's reworking of his own *Three Coins in the Fountain*, this time set in Spain. The cast is exemplary, with sexy Ann-Margret, Pamela Tiffin and Carol Lynley more than a match for their glossy 1950s predecessors. The novelty has worn a bit thin, and Fox's standard "three girls out on the town" plot looks stale, but this fun film is still worth a look. TS

Ann-Margret *Fran Hobson* • Tony Franciosa [Anthony Franciosa] *Emilio Lacaye* • Carol Lynley *Maggie Williams* • Gardner McKay *Pete Stenello* • Pamela Tiffin *Susie Higgins* • Andre Lawrence *Dr Andres Briones* • Gene Tierney *Jane Barton* • Brian Keith *Paul Barton* ■ *Dir* Jean Negulesco • *Scr* Edith Sommer, from the novel *Coins in the Fountain* by John H Secondari

The Pledge ★★★★ 15

Psychological detective drama
2000 · US · Colour · 118mins

In this utterly gripping drama, Jack Nicholson plays a detective on the eve of retirement who just can't let go of a case that begins when a young girl's mutilated body is discovered in a remote snowy forest in Nevada. His fellow cops believe simple-minded ex-con Benicio Del Toro committed the crime. But Nicholson's promise to the girl's parents that he would find the actual murderer leads him to conduct his own investigations, which embroil Robin Wright Penn and her young daughter. The pacing may be languid but this is a movie that continually gets under your skin, thanks to Sean Penn's atmospheric direction and the terrific performances. JB. Contains violence and swearing. [video] DVD

Jack Nicholson *Jerry Black* • Robin Wright Penn *Lori* • Sam Shepard *Eric Pollack* • Aaron Eckhart *Stan Krolak* • Vanessa Redgrave *Annalise Hansen* • Michael O'Keefe *Duane Larsen* • Benicio Del Toro *Toby Jay Wadenah* • Mickey Rourke *Jim Olstad* • Harry Dean Stanton *Floyd Cage* • Helen Mirren *Doctor* ■ *Dir* Sean Penn • *Scr* Jerzy Kromolowski, Mary Olson-Kromolowski, from the novel *Das Versprechen* by Friedrich Dürrenmatt

Pledge Night ★

Horror 1990 · US · Colour · 90mins

This obnoxious horror quickie has a plot so risible and sleazy one must wonder at the sanity of its perpetrators. It's set at an American fraternity house, where an initiation prank ends with luckless new boy Sid being thrown into a vat of acid. Years later, a suitably peeved "Acid Sid" returns to wreak havoc on a new generation of freshmen. RS

Todd Eastland *Bonner* • Shannon McMahon *Wendy* • Will Kempe *Acid Sid* • Joey Belladonna *Young Sidney Snyder* • Dennis Sullivan *Bodine* • Craig Derrick *Cagle* • David Neal Evans *Goodman* • Robert Lentini *Silvera* ■ *Dir* Paul Ziller • *Scr* Joyce Snyder

Plein Soleil ★★★★ PG

Crime drama 1960 · Fr/It · Colour · 113mins

This shimmering and suspenseful *film noir* is based on the Patricia Highsmith novel, *The Talented Mr Ripley*. Rarely has such a sinister tale been told against such a gloriously sunny backdrop, yet the picture-postcard views are every bit as atmospheric as the gloomiest monochrome cityscape. With more than a nod in the direction of Alfred Hitchcock, René Clément makes extensive use of a moving camera to pick up every nuance and detail as the murderous Alain Delon seeks to assume the identity of his well-to-do pal, Maurice Ronet. Stylish, impeccably played and utterly engrossing. DP. In French with English subtitles. [video] DVD

Alain Delon *Tom Ripley* • Marie Laforêt *Marge* • Maurice Ronet *Philippe Greenleaf* • Bill Kearns [Billy Kearns] *Freddy Miles* • Erno Crisa *Inspector Riccordi* • Frank Latimore *O'Brien* ■ *Dir* René Clément • *Scr* René Clément, Paul Gégauff, from the novel *The Talented Mr Ripley* by Patricia Highsmith • *Cinematographer* Henri Decaë

Plenty ★★ 15

Drama 1985 · US · Colour · 119mins

David Hare's trenchant, deeply layered stage plays transfer badly to film and *Plenty* is a prime example of how the requisite small nervy performances, here from Meryl Streep, Charles Dance and Sam Neill, appear affected and over-stylised on screen. As always, Hare does have some interesting points to make, but everything is spelt out laboriously with a glum and squeakily pretentious air. SH. Contains violence, swearing. [video]

Meryl Streep *Susan Traherne* • Charles Dance *Raymond Brock* • Tracey Ullman *Alice Park* • John Gielgud *Sir Leonard Darwin* • Sting *Mick* • Ian McKellen *Sir Andrew Charleson* • Sam Neill *Lazar* • Burt Kwouk *Mr Aung* • Lim Pik Sen *Madame Aung* • André Maranne *Villon* ■ *Dir* Fred Schepisi • *Scr* David Hare, from his play

The Plot against Harry ★★★ PG

Comedy 1969 · US · BW · 80mins

Finally released 20 years after it was filmed, Michael Roemer's pseudo-*cinéma vérité* comedy was clearly ahead of its time. But, by 1989, its determinedly deadpan style had become such a familiar part of the comic landscape in the films of directors such as Jim Jarmusch that its impact was somewhat reduced. Newly sprung from jail, petty mobster Martin Priest is convinced that life has got it in for him. And a series of incidents, including a car accident that leads him to discover that he is the father of a family he never knew he had, seem to uphold his suspicions. DP

Martin Priest *Harry Plotnick* • Ben Lang *Leo Perlmutter* • Maxine Woods *Kay Skolnik* • Henry Nemo *Max* • Jacques Taylor *Jack* • Jean Leslie *Irene* • Ellen Herbert *Mae* • Sandra Kazan *Margie* • Ronald Coralian *Mel Skolnik* • Ruth Roemer *Linda Skolnik* ■ *Dir/Scr* Michael Roemer

The Plot Thickens ★★ U

Mystery 1936 · US · BW · 64mins

ZaSu Pitts took over the role of RKO's schoolmarm sleuth Hildegarde Withers from Helen Broderick, who herself succeeded Edna May Oliver, and was responsible for this more comedic entry in a most likeable series. Her flustery mode of performance isn't ideal for acutely rational detective Withers, but she's nevertheless fun to watch paired opposite series regular irascible James Gleason. As the title indicates, this is a particularly complex mystery, full of humour; Pitts and Gleason were to team again for one more film (*40 Naughty Girls*) which was to be the last of the series. TS

James Gleason *Oscar Piper* • ZaSu Pitts *Hildegarde Withers* • Owen Davis Jr *Robert Wilkins* • Louise Latimer *Alice Stevens* • Arthur Aylesworth *Kendall* • Richard Tucker *John Carter* • Paul Fix *Joe* • Barbara Barondess *Marie* ■ *Dir* Ben Holmes • *Scr* Clarence Upson Young, Jack Townley, from a story by Stuart Palmer

The Plough and the Stars ★★

Drama 1936 · US · BW · 66mins

Barbara Stanwyck is magnificently miscast as the loyal wife fearing for the life of her IRA husband, played by the incredibly dreary Preston Foster, and the supporting cast is so authentically Irish that the two leads seem even more at sea. It's truly dispiriting to watch a major Irish play sink into the Hollywood mire, particularly since John Ford should have known better, and the cheap production values and ill-chosen intercut newsreel clips don't help. TS

Barbara Stanwyck *Nora Clitheroe* • Preston Foster *Jack Clitheroe* • Barry Fitzgerald *Fluther Good* • Denis O'Dea *The Young Covey* • Eileen Crowe *Bessie Burgess* • FJ McCormick *Captain Brennon* • Arthur Shields *Padraic Pearse* ■ *Dir* John Ford • *Scr* Dudley Nichols, from the play by Sean O'Casey

The Ploughman's Lunch ★★★★ 15

Drama 1983 · UK · Colour · 102mins

Well-observed and thought-provoking drama about the way in which the private life of a BBC radio news producer affects his work. The background detail looks absolutely authentic, and the performances, particularly from Jonathan Pryce as the producer and Charlie Dore as the TV researcher he beds, are excellent. The film is a collaboration between novelist Ian McEwan and director Richard Eyre, who went on to head the National Theatre. It's remarkable how a film so

P

critical of the media could wangle location facilities out of the BBC, LWT and even the 1982 Conservative Party conference in Brighton. Slow-starting, but stay with it. DM

Jonathan Pryce *James Penfield* • Tim Curry *Jeremy Hancock* • Rosemary Harris *Ann Barrington* • Frank Finlay *Matthew Fox* • Charlie Dore *Susan Barrington* ■ *Dir* Richard Eyre • *Scr* Ian McEwan

The Plow That Broke the Plains ★★★★

Documentary 1934 · US · BW · 49mins

Sponsored by the United States Resettlement Administration, this piece of New Deal propaganda is usually considered the cornerstone of American documentary film-making. Made on a shoestring, yet filmed with evocative expertise by socialist cinematographers Ralph Steiner, Paul Strand and Leo Hurwitz, ex-critic Pare Lorentz's debut explored the history of the Great Plains and the ecological causes of the Dust Bowl that had made the Depression even more disastrous for the Mid-West's valiant farmers. With a superb score by Virgil Thompson and a rhythmic commentary delivered by Thomas Chalmers, it is emotive, persuasive and powerful, both in its message and its imagery. DP

Thomas Chalmers *Narrator* ■ *Dir/Scr* Pare Lorentz

Plughead Rewired: Circuitry Man II ★ 15

Science-fiction thriller
1994 · US · Colour · 92mins

Dennis Christopher, so good in *Breaking Away*, is wasted in a witless sequel that makes his character look even more foolish and aimless than he was in the original. The film feels like a collection of out-takes from the first *Circuitry Man*, even recycling some of its effects. The incomprehensible plot has something to do with Vernon Wells again setting his sights on capturing Jim Metzler. KB DVD

Vernon Wells *Plughead* • Deborah Shelton *Kyle* • Jim Metzler *Danner* • Dennis Christopher *Leech* • Nicholas Worth *Rock* • Traci Lords *Norma* ■ *Dir/Scr* Steven Lovy, Robert Lovy

P

The Plumber ★★★

Black comedy 1979 · Aus · Colour · 76mins

An early film from director Peter Weir, this black comedy, made on 16mm in just three weeks for Australian television, this is about a coarse plumber who arrives at a middle-class household. He fixes the pipes, but refuses to budge, acting as a catalyst and provoking some very funny but also some scary responses. Behind it all is the evocation of otherness that Weir explores in all his films. AT

Judy Morris *Jill Cowper* • Robert Coleby *Brian Cowper* • Ivar Kants *Max, The Plumber* • Candy Raymond *Meg* ■ *Dir/Scr* Peter Weir

Plunder Road ★★★ U

Crime thriller 1957 · US · BW · 71mins

Veteran players Gene Raymond and Wayne Morris clearly relished the opportunity to star in this cleverly written story of a train hold-up and the robbers' doomed attempts to shift their massive haul of gold ingots. Elisha Cook Jr already knew his loser's part by heart but plays it, as usual, to perfection. Aided by veteran cameraman Ernest Haller, new director Hubert Cornfield makes a visually exciting picture that squeezes every ounce of suspense from the story. AE

Gene Raymond *Eddie* • Jeanne Cooper *Fran* • Wayne Morris *Commando* • Elisha Cook Jr *Skeets* • Stafford Repp *Roly Adams* • Steven Ritch *Frankie* • Nora Hayden *Hazel* ■ *Dir* Hubert Cornfield • *Scr* Steven Ritch, from a story by Jack Charney, Steven Ritch

The Plunderers ★★ U

Western 1948 · US · Colour · 87mins

Joseph Kane was among the most prolific directors of formulaic westerns at Republic Studios, but this is one of his more considered efforts. It's aimed less at the Saturday matinée crowd than at the adherents of the pulp novels. As a result, outlaw Forrest Tucker is a step up from a straightforward black-hatted villain, as army agent Rod Cameron discovers when he infiltrates his gang. That said, the Sioux attack on the fort returns the tale to traditional western values. DP

Rod Cameron *John Druin* • Ilona Massey *Lin Conner* • Adrian Booth [Lorna Gray] *Julie McCabe* • Forrest Tucker *Whit Lacey* • George Cleveland *Sam Borden* • Grant Withers *Tap Lawrence* • Taylor Holmes *Eben Martin* • Paul Fix *Calico* • Francis Ford *Barnaby* ■ *Dir* Joseph Kane • *Scr* Gerald Adams [Gerald Drayson Adams], Gerald Geraghty, from a story by James Edward Grant

Plunkett & Macleane ★★ 15

Period action adventure
1999 · UK · Colour · 97mins

Robert Carlyle and Jonny Lee Miller star as the infamous highwaymen who terrorised high society in 18th-century London in this misfiring adventure, which marked the debut feature of Jake (son of Ridley) Scott. Music and design are both deliberately anachronistic in an attempt to make the larcenous odd couple a hip, English *Butch Cassidy and the Sundance Kid* for the 1990s. Liv Tyler, as Macleane's aristocratic groupie, adds a touch of romance, but this is mostly a chaotic jumble of style over substance. AME. Contains violence and swearing. DVD

Robert Carlyle *Will Plunkett* • Jonny Lee Miller *James Macleane* • Liv Tyler *Lady Rebecca* • Ken Stott *Chance* • Michael Gambon *Lord Gibson* • Alan Cumming *Lord Rochester* ■ *Dir* Jake Scott • *Scr* Robert Wade, Neal Purvis, Charles McKeown, from a screenplay (unproduced) by Selwyn Roberts

Pluto Nash ★ PG

Science-fiction action comedy
2001 · US/Aus · Colour · 90mins

With elaborate special effects substituting for the missing script, director Ron Underwood's alleged sci-fi comedy is a $100 million turkey. An unusually bland Eddie Murphy plays former crook Pluto Nash, who is struggling to keep his moon nightclub from falling under intergalactic mafia control in 2087. Accompanying Murphy on these lunar-tic rambles is his outdated robot bodyguard (a truly asinine Randy Quaid) and wannabe singer Rosario Dawson. A flop of epic proportions. AJ DVD

Eddie Murphy *Pluto Nash* • Randy Quaid *Bruno* • Rosario Dawson *Dina Lake* • Joe Pantoliano *Mogan* • Jay Mohr *Anthony "Tony" Francis* • Luis Guzman *Felix Laranga* • James Rebhorn *Belcher* • Pam Grier *Flura Nash* • John Cleese *James* ■ *Dir* Ron Underwood • *Scr* Neil Cuthbert

Plymouth Adventure ★★ U

Historical drama
1952 · US · Colour · 104mins

Spencer Tracy is the stern skipper of the *Mayflower* as it sets sail for America in 1620. His heavyweight presence is sorely needed in a ponderous rendering of an unwieldy script that is overloaded with history. The special effects, which won an Oscar, and Miklos Rozsa's rousing score are among the few highlights in director Clarence Brown's rather dull depiction of the epic journey. JM

Spencer Tracy *Captain Christopher Jones* • Gene Tierney *Dorothy Bradford* • Van Johnson *John Alden* • Leo Genn *William Bradford* • Dawn Addams *Priscilla Mullins* • Lloyd Bridges *Coppin* • Barry Jones *William Brewster* ■ *Dir* Clarence Brown • *Scr* Helen Deutsch, from a novel by Ernest Gebler

Pocahontas ★★★ U

Animated adventure
1995 · US · Colour · 77mins

Visually stunning but historically botched re-creation of the legendary romance between Indian maid Pocahontas (Irene Bedard) and captain John Smith (Mel Gibson) in the 17th-century New World. The first Disney animation to deal with a factual subject skilfully communicates both its "love conquers all" and ecological messages, although the greedy governor (David Ogden Stiers) is so over-the-top he's practically out of sight. TH DVD

Irene Bedard *Pocahontas* • Mel Gibson *John Smith* • Joe Baker *Lon* • Christian Bale *Thomas* • Billy Connolly *Ben* • Linda Hunt *Grandmother Willow* • David Ogden Stiers *Governor Ratcliffe/Wiggins* ■ *Dir* Mike Gabriel, Eric Goldberg • *Scr* Carl Binder, Susannah Grant, Philip LaZebnik

Pocahontas II: Journey to a New World ★★ U

Animated adventure
1998 · US · Colour · 70mins

An adequate straight-to-video sequel to one of Disney's less memorable recent cartoons, with the Indian princess sailing to England. Predictably, her cute pet hummingbird and raccoon go along for the ride. The script takes the usual liberties with history (though the real-life Pocahontas *did* visit England, and in fact died there), though children will derive a fair amount of fun from the film. DA DVD

Irene Bedard *Pocahontas* • Billy Zane *John Rolfe* • David Ogden Stiers *Governor Ratcliffe* • Jean Stapleton *Mrs Jenkins* • Russell Means *Powhatan* • Linda Hunt *Grandmother Willow* • Donald Gibson *John Smith* ■ *Dir* Bradley Raymond, Tom Ellery • *Scr* Allen Estrin, Cindy Marcus, Flip Kobler

Pocket Money ★★ PG

Western 1972 · US · Colour · 95mins

A tepid latter-day western. After Martin Ritt pulled out, Paul Newman installed his friend Stuart Rosenberg in the director's chair, but he never came to grips with Terrence Malick's rambling screenplay and the result is a directionless, if fitfully amusing, tale in which Newman and Lee Marvin try to round up some cattle for shady beef baron Strother Martin. Laszlo Kovacs's photography is so authentic it leaves you with dust in your eyes, but Newman and Marvin look like they're acting in different movies. DP

Paul Newman *Jim Kane* • Lee Marvin *Leonard* • Strother Martin *Garrett* • Christine Belford *Adelita* • Kelly Jean Peters *Wife* • Fred Graham *Herb* • Wayne Rogers *Stretch Russell* • Hector Elizondo *Juan* ■ *Dir* Stuart Rosenberg • *Scr* Terry Malick [Terrence Malick], John Gay, from the novel *Jim Kane* by JPS Brown

Pocketful of Miracles ★★ U

Comedy 1961 · US · Colour · 131mins

Frank Capra's remake of his 1933 comedy *Lady for a Day* is a disappointing end to his distinguished career. Damon Runyon's yarn worked during the Depression, but here this tale of class envy and economic inequality now seems dated. It has its sentimental moments, but it's too long, and Bette Davis is badly miscast as the apple-seller transformed into a wealthy socialite by a superstitious gangster (Glenn Ford) and his gang of hoodlums. AT DVD

Glenn Ford *Dave the Dude* • Bette Davis *Apple Annie* • Hope Lange *Queenie Martin* • Arthur O'Connell *Count Alfonso Romero* • Peter Falk *Joy Boy* • Thomas Mitchell *Judge Henry G Blake* • Edward Everett Horton *Butler* • Ann-Margret *Louise* • Mike Mazurki *Big Mike* ■ *Dir* Frank Capra • *Scr* Hal Kanter, Harry Tugend, Jimmy Cannon, from the film *Lady for a Day* by Robert Riskin, from the story *Madame La Gimp* by Damon Runyon

Poetic Justice ★★ 15

Drama 1993 · US · Colour · 104mins

After making a big splash with his first film, *Boyz N the Hood*, John Singleton lost his way somewhat with this twee, right-on drama that charts the burgeoning romance between hairdresser and poetess Janet Jackson and postal worker Tupac Shakur as they get to know each other on the road to Oakland. Mawkish and well-intentioned instead of gritty and real, the movie is saved by the acting of the two leads. Incidentally, Maya Angelou wrote the poetry for Jackson's character. AJ. Contains violence, swearing and sex scenes. DVD

Janet Jackson *Justice* • Tupac Shakur *Lucky* • Tyra Ferrell *Jessie* • Regina King *Iesha* • Joe Torry *Chicago* • Roger Guenveur Smith *Heywood* • Lori Petty *Penelope* • Billy Zane *Brad* • Khandi Alexander *Simone* • Maya Angelou *Aunt June* ■ *Dir/Scr* John Singleton

Poil de Carotte ★★★★

Drama 1932 · Fr · BW · 80mins

This is a glorious remake of the touching rites-of-passage drama director Julien Duvivier first attempted as a silent in 1925. Avoiding the sentimentality that tainted so many Hollywood studies of childhood, this is a resolutely grown-up account of the misery endured by red-headed Robert Lynen at the hands of his uncaring mother, Catherine Fontenay. Beautifully filmed by Armand Thirard, the film acquired added poignancy after Lynen's execution while fighting for the Resistance in 1944. DP. In French with English subtitles.

Harry Baur *M Lepic* • Robert Lynen *François, "Poil de Carotte"* • Catherine Fonteney *Mme Lepic* • Christiane Dor *Annette* • Colette Segall *Young Mathilde* • Louis Gauthier *Godfather* ■ *Dir* Julien Duvivier • *Scr* Julien Duvivier, from the play *Poil de Carotte* by Jules Renard, from the novels *Poil de Carotte/La Bigote* by Jules Renard

Point Blank ★★★★★ 18

Thriller 1967 · US · Colour · 87mins

British director John Boorman's US directing debut was this grim, violent, virtually metaphysical thriller. It's a gripping and sexy action movie, with a magnificent performance from Lee Marvin as the revenge-seeking Walker, the ultimate lethal weapon, whose insane quest to retrieve Mob money assumes mythical proportions. With the subtle complexity of the storytelling and Philip H Lathrop's brilliant cinematography, the film is a markedly superior and powerful work. AT. Contains violence and swearing.

Lee Marvin *Walker* • Angie Dickinson *Chris* • Keenan Wynn *Yost* • Carroll O'Connor *Brewster* • Lloyd Bochner *Frederick Carter* • Michael Strong *Stegman* • John Vernon *Mal Reese* • Sharon Acker *Lynne* • James Sikking [James B Sikking] *Hired gun* ■ *Dir* John Boorman • *Scr* Alexander Jacobs, David Newhouse, Rafe Newhouse, from the novel *The Hunter* by Richard Stark [Donald E Westlake] • *Cinematographer* Philip H Lathrop [Philip Lathrop]

Point Blank ★ 18

Action thriller 1997 · US · Colour · 85mins

Mickey Rourke's detractors will have a field day when they see the actor hilariously humiliated in this *Die Hard* rip-off. Rourke stars an ex-Texas Ranger who sneaks into a shopping mall that's been taken over by a gang of escaped convicts; the star is only given about 25 lines of dialogue in the entire movie. The film mixes utter sleaze and graphic violence. KB

Mickey Rourke *Rudy Ray* • Kevin Gage *Joe Ray* • Michael Wright *Sonny* • Danny Trejo *Wallace* • Frederic Forrest *Mac Bradford* ■ *Dir* Matt Earl Beesley • *Scr* James Bannon, Cary Solomon, Chuck Konzelman, Daniel Raskov, from a story by Daniel Raskov, Cary Solomon, Chuck Konzelman

Point Break ★★★★ 18

Thriller 1991 · US · Colour · 122mins

Kathryn Bigelow shows that the action adventure is not just the preserve of the lads in this silly but hugely enjoyable thriller. Keanu Reeves plays the young FBI agent who unsurprisingly makes a very convincing surfing dude when he goes undercover to infiltrate a gang, headed by Patrick Swayze, suspected of carrying out a string of audacious bank robberies. Try to ignore the mystical claptrap and concentrate instead on Bigelow's stunningly conceived action set pieces, as well as some exhilarating sky-diving and surfing scenes. JF. Contains violence, swearing, nudity. DVD

Patrick Swayze *Bodhi* • Keanu Reeves *Johnny Utah* • Gary Busey *Angelo Pappas* • Lori Petty *Tyler* • John C McGinley *Ben Harp* • James LeGros *Roach* • John Philbin *Nathanial* ■ *Dir* Kathryn Bigelow • *Scr* W Peter Iliff, from a story by Rick King, W Peter Iliff

The Point Men ★★ 18

Action thriller
2000 · UK/Fr/Lux · Colour · 86mins

After overseeing Roger Moore's final James Bond appearances and Timothy Dalton's only two 007 contributions, the work all but dried up for John Glen in the 1990s. This finds him back in the director's chair, but even he can't bring much fizz to this tame action thriller. Christopher Lambert is the disgraced Israeli secret agent called back into action when members of his old team start getting bumped off by an old adversary, terrorist Vincent Regan. JF DVD

Christopher Lambert *Tony Eckhardt* • Kerry Fox *Maddy Hope* • Vincent Regan *Amar Kamil* • Cal MacAninch *Horst* • Maryam D'Abo *Francie Koln* ■ *Dir* John Glen • *Scr* Ripley Highsmith, from the novel *The Heat of Ramadan* by Steven Hartov

Point of No Return ★★

Thriller 1993 · US · Colour · 109mins

This serviceable American remake of Luc Besson's *Nikita* is a near scene-for-scene re-tread of the slick, sexy original. Bridget Fonda makes a far less convincing lead than Anne Parillaud, and her metamorphosis from psycho junkie to elegant assassin is much harder to swallow. The strong supporting cast boosts credibility, but there's an oddly cold, detached feeling about director John Badham's re-creation of the original's dynamic action scenes. JC

Bridget Fonda *Maggie* • Gabriel Byrne *Bob* • Dermot Mulroney *JP* • Miguel Ferrer *Kaufman* • Anne Bancroft *Amanda* • Olivia D'Abo *Angela* • Richard Romanus *Fahd Bahktiar* • Harvey Keitel *Victor the cleaner* ■ *Dir* John Badham • *Scr* Robert Getchell, Alexandra Seros, from the film *Nikita* by Luc Besson

Poison ★★★ 18

Drama 1990 · US · Colour and BW · 85mins

Todd Haynes's feature debut showcases his ability to faithfully re-create eras and film styles. Haynes cleverly interweaves three entirely different stories into a quirky and provocative lesson on sexual and social stereotyping: *Hero*, shot like a 1980s TV documentary, records a community's responses to a missing boy who murdered his father; *Horror* portrays a 1950s B-movie-style tale of a scientist whose sexual libido experiments go hideously wrong; while *Homo* plays with the gritty sensual eroticism of gay cinema with its depiction of a prisoner's cruel obsession with a fellow inmate. SF

Edith Meeks *Felicia Beacon* • Millie White *Millie Sklar* • Buck Smith *Gregory Lazar* • Anne Giotta *Evelyn McAlpert* • Lydia Lafleur *Sylvia Manning* ■ *Dir* Todd Haynes • *Scr* Todd Haynes, from the novels *Our Lady of the Flowers, Miracle of the Roses, Thief's Journal* by Jean Genet

Poison Ivy ★★★ 18

Thriller 1992 · US · Colour · 89mins

Drew Barrymore came of age in this alluring tale about a poor girl from the wrong side of the tracks who befriends fellow loner Sara Gilbert and inveigles her way into her wealthy family, with deadly results. There's a touch of music-video style about director Katt Shea Ruben's over-glossy visuals, but she is well-served by the leads, particularly Barrymore, who's a sexy but vulnerable junior *femme fatale*. Look out, too, for Leonardo DiCaprio in one of his earliest roles. JF. Contains violence, swearing, nudity. DVD

Sara Gilbert *Sylvie Cooper* • Drew Barrymore *Ivy* • Tom Skerritt *Darryl Cooper* • Cheryl Ladd *Georgie Cooper* • Alan Stock *Bob* • Jeanne Sakata *Isabelle* • Leonardo DiCaprio *Guy* ■ *Dir* Katt Shea Ruben • *Scr* Katt Shea Ruben, Andy Ruben, from the story by Melissa Goddard , Peter Morgan

Poison Ivy 2 ★ 18

Erotic thriller 1995 · US · Colour · 101mins

The connection to the 1992 *Poison Ivy* comes with repressed college student Alyssa Milano finding Drew Barrymore's old diary. After reading it, she is inspired to transform herself into a sexually liberated woman, confusing her boyfriend and generating lust in her professor (Xander Berkeley). After her transformation, the movie doesn't know what to do, with Berkeley's sudden change in character only occurring to facilitate some kind of climax. Jaime Pressly took over the lead for a second sequel in 1997. KB. Contains violence, swearing, sex scenes and nudity. DVD

Alyssa Milano *Lily* • Xander Berkeley *Donald Falk* • Johnathon Schaech *Gredin* • Belinda Bauer *Angela Falk* • Camilla Belle *Daphne Falk* ■ *Dir* Anne Goursaud • *Scr* Chloe King

Poison Pen ★★★

Psychological drama 1939 · UK · BW · 79mins

Here's an early and powerful working of an intrinsically downbeat subject, as a rash of anonymous letters cause major misery and distress among the inhabitants of an English hamlet. Catherine Lacey's seamstress is wrongly hounded as the likely perpetrator because she's an outsider. Could it possibly be that the saintly spinster sister of the vicar is not all she seems? When she's played by Flora Robson, you have to wonder. AE

Flora Robson *Mary Rider* • Robert Newton *Sam Hurrin* • Ann Todd *Ann Rider* • Geoffrey Toone *David* • Reginald Tate *Rev Rider* • Belle Chrystall *Sucal Hurrin* • Edward Chapman *Len Griffin* • Edward Rigby *Badham* • Catherine Lacey *Connie Fateley* • Wilfrid Hyde White *Postman* ■ *Dir* Paul L Stein • *Scr* Doreen Montgomery, William Freshman, NC Hunter, Esther McCracken, from the play by Richard Llewellyn

Pokémon the First Movie: Mewtwo Strikes Back ★ PG

Animated fantasy adventure
1998 · Jpn · Colour · 72mins

The big-screen debut of the cuddly Japanese monsters of trading card, video game and TV fame could hardly have been worse. The movie actually comprises two films, the first being a virtually plotless short (*Pikachu's Vacation*). In the main feature, genetically modified monster Mewtwo goes on the rampage. The climactic battle is repetitious and boring. DM. Japanese dialogue dubbed into English. DVD

Dir Kunihiko Yuyama, Michael Haigney • *Scr* English adaptation by Norman J Grossfeld, Michael Haigney, John Touhey, from characters created by Satoshi Tajiri • *Chief Animator* Sayuri Ichiishi

Pokémon the Movie 2000 ★★ PG

Animated fantasy adventure
1999 · Jpn · Colour · 97mins

This second big-screen outing for Pikachu and his pals follows the same format as their first film, with a perky 20-minute short film followed by the feature, *The Power of One*. The main story has hero Ash restoring the balance of nature (no less!) after a megalomaniac Pokémon collector pockets the elemental controllers of fire, ice and lightning. Less downbeat and marginally more enjoyable than its predecessor. DA. Japanese dialogue dubbed into English. DVD

Veronica Taylor *Ash Ketchum/Mrs Ketchum* • Rachael Lillis *Misty Williams/Jessie Morgan/* • Ted Lewis *Tracey Sketcher* • Eric Stuart *Brock/James Morgan/Charizard* ■ *Dir* Michael Haigney • *Scr* Takeshi Shudo, adapted by Norman J Grossfeld, Michael Haigney

Pokémon 3: Spell of the Unown ★★ U

Animated fantasy adventure
2001 · Jpn · Colour · 87mins

Pokémon may be a flagging playground phenomenon, but the Japanese keep churning the films out, and the Americans keep dubbing and redistributing them. This is the big-screen formula as before with a 15-minute short preceding the 70-minute main feature, which has Ash and pals confronting Pokémon from the spirit world. There have been a number of further sequels. DA. Japanese dialogue dubbed into English. DVD

Veronica Taylor *Ash Ketchum/Mrs Delia Ketchum* • Eric Stuart *Brock/James* • Rachael Lillis *Misty/Jessie* ■ *Dir* Michael Haigney, Kunihiko Yuyama • *Scr* Michael Haigney, Norman J Grossfeld

Pola X ★★ 18

Drama 1999 · Fr/Ger/Swi · Colour · 128mins

Léos Carax's film takes its acronymic name from the French title of Herman Melville's novel *Pierre, or the Ambiguities*; the "X" refers to the fact that there were ten drafts of the screenplay. Guillaume Depardieu plays the carefree son of wealthy widow Catherine Deneuve whose world is changed irrevocably when he meets a young woman (Katerina Golubeva) who claims to be his illegitimate half-sister. With its nihilistic antihero and unfeeling urban landscape, this bleak film is too dull to engage. NS. In French with English subtitles.

Catherine Deneuve *Marie* • Guillaume Depardieu *Pierre Valombreuse* • Katerina Golubeva *Isabelle* • Delphine Chuillot *Lucie de Boisieux* • Laurent Lucas *Thibault* ■ *Dir* Léos Carax • *Scr* LéosCarax, Jean-Pol Fargeau, Lauren Sedofsky, from the novel *Pierre, or the Ambiguities (Pierre, ou les Ambiguités)* by Herman Melville

Polar ★★★

Thriller 1984 · Fr · Colour · 97mins

This adaptation owes both its atmosphere and its complexity to *The Big Sleep*. However, Jacques Bral's direction lacks the incisiveness of Howard Hawks and Jean-François Balmer is certainly no Bogart, despite delivering his voiceover narrative in a suitably laconic drawl. But, the case is sufficiently twisting and sinister, with Balmer entering the seedy world of skin flicks after being lured by Sandra Montaigu into investigating the death of her roommate. DP. French dialogue dubbed into English.

Jean-François Balmer *Eugène Tarpon* • Sandra Montaigu *Charlotte le Dantec* • Roland Dubillard *Jean-Baptiste Haymann* • Pierre Santini *Insp Coccioli* • Claude Chabrol *Theodore Lyssenko* ■ *Dir* Jacques Bral • *Scr* Jacques Bral, Jean-Paul Leca, Julien Lévi, from the novel *Morgue Pleine* by Jean-Patrick Manchette

The Polar Express ★★★ U

Animated fantasy
2004 · US · Colour · 100mins

In this animated tale, a sceptical boy finds his belief in Father Christmas restored by an incredible journey to the North Pole on board a magical train. Director Robert Zemeckis's fantasy adventure is undoubtedly technically impressive, thanks to the introduction of "Performance Capture" – a new type of CGI that transfers the live actions of actors into a digital format. The process enables star Tom Hanks to take on six different roles. However, as a fast-moving life lesson about faith and hope, the film weaves sentimentality and gentle moralising into every scene. SF

Tom Hanks *Hero boy/Father/Conductor/ Hobo/Scrooge/Santa Claus* • Michael Jeter *Smokey/Steamer* • Nona Gaye *Hero girl* • Peter Scolari *Lonely boy* • Eddie Deezen *Know-it-all* • Charles Fleischer *Elf General* • Steven Tyler *Elf Lieutenant/Elf singer* • Leslie Zemeckis *Sister Sarah/Mother* • Daryl Sabara *Hero boy* ■ *Dir* Robert Zemeckis • *Scr* Robert Zemeckis, William Broyles Jr, from the illustrated children's book by Chris Van Allsburg

Police ★★★★ 15

Crime thriller 1985 · Fr · Colour · 108mins

Sophie Marceau was the wunderkind of French cinema and Maurice Pialat was its most uncompromisingly realistic director, so the off-screen clashes were inevitable, but the tensions are also evident on the screen and they help give this superior crime drama an added charge. The opening sequences, in which bruising cop Gérard Depardieu muscles in on a Tunisian drugs-ring, make for compelling viewing thanks to Pialat's attention to authentic detail, but the erotic duel between Depardieu and the drug-dealing Marceau is less effective, even though sparks certainly fly from this oddly matched pair. Not your average thriller, but a cracking one, nevertheless. DP. Contains violence, swearing and nudity.

Gérard Depardieu *Mangin* • Sophie Marceau *Noria* • Richard Anconina *Lambert* • Pascale Rocard *Marie Vedret* • Sandrine Bonnaire *Lydie* ■ *Dir* Maurice Pialat • *Scr* Maurice Pialat, Catherine Breillat, Sylvie Danton, Jacques Fieschi, from a story by Catherine Breillat

Police Academy ★★★ 15

Comedy 1984 · US · Colour · 92mins

Back in 1984, it's hard to imagine that anyone thought this would go on to spawn six sequels as well as a cartoon series. However, it managed to strike a chord with audiences around the world and made a star (briefly) out of Steve Guttenberg. And, while the follow-ups became increasingly puerile as the series went on, the original film produces its fair share of belly laughs. Guttenberg leads a group of oddballs into police training, where they clash with authority but prove themselves in the end. It's crude and juvenile but

P

fans will be in heaven. JF. Contains swearing, violence, nudity. DVD

Steve Guttenberg *Carey Mahoney* • Kim Cattrall *Karen Thompson* • GW Bailey *Lieutenant Harris* • Bubba Smith *Moses Hightower* • Donovan Scott *Leslie Barbara* • George Gaynes *Commandant Lassard* • Andrew Rubin *George Martin* • David Graf *Tackleberry* • Leslie Easterbrook *Sergeant Callahan* ■ *Dir* Hugh Wilson • *Scr* Neal Israel, Pat Proft, Hugh Wilson, from a story by Neal Israel, Pat Proft

Police Academy 2: Their First Assignment ★ 15

Comedy 1985 · US · Colour · 83mins

The international success of the first movie in the *Police Academy* series meant that new director Jerry Paris wasn't going to mess with a winning formula. This time the misfits get the opportunity to cause chaos on the streets, but, while it features many members of the original cast, this is a lazy replay of the original outing, with grossness substituting for any genuine humour. JF DVD

Steve Guttenberg *Carey Mahoney* • Bubba Smith *Hightower* • David Graf *Tackleberry* • Michael Winslow *Larvell Jones* • Bruce Mahler *Doug Fackler* • Marion Ramsey *Laverne Hooks* • Colleen Camp *Kirkland* • Howard Hesseman *Pete Lassard* • Art Metrano *Lieutenant Mauser* • Bob Goldthwait [Bobcat Goldthwait] *Zed* ■ *Dir* Jerry Paris • *Scr* Barry Blaustein, David Sheffield, from characters created by Neal Israel, Pat Proft

Police Academy 3: Back in Training ★★ PG

Comedy 1986 · US · Colour · 80mins

The title sums up the plot, really, although predictably the lovable losers eventually save the day as rival police academies battle for survival in an era of cutbacks in public spending. It is an improvement of sorts on the first sequel, but by this stage you were either a fan or holding the series up as the prime example of Hollywood puerility. JF. Contains swearing and violence. DVD

Steve Guttenberg *Sergeant Mahoney* • Bubba Smith *Sergeant Hightower* • David Graf *Sergeant Tackleberry* • Michael Winslow *Sergeant Jones* • Marion Ramsey *Sergeant Hooks* • Leslie Easterbrook *Lieutenant Callahan* • Art Metrano *Commandant Mauser* • Bobcat Goldthwait *Cadet Zed* ■ *Dir* Jerry Paris • *Scr* Gene Quintano, from characters created by Neal Israel, Pat Proft

Police Academy 4: Citizens on Patrol ★ PG

Comedy 1987 · US · Colour · 87mins

This sequel is only worth watching for the opportunity to watch a pre-*Basic Instinct* Sharon Stone stranded down the cast list with the thankless role of star Steve Guttenberg's girlfriend. George Gaynes is the feeble-minded commander who finds himself training an even crazier bunch of recruits when citizens are encouraged to become part-time policemen. JF. Contains swearing. DVD

Steve Guttenberg *Mahoney* • Bubba Smith *Hightower* • Michael Winslow *Jones* • David Graf *Tackleberry* • Sharon Stone *Claire Mattson* • George Gaynes *Commandant Lassard* • Bobcat Goldthwait *Zed* • Leslie Easterbrook *Callahan* ■ *Dir* Jim Drake • *Scr* Gene Quintano, from characters created by Neal Israel, Pat Proft

Police Academy 5: Assignment Miami Beach ★ PG

Comedy 1988 · US · Colour · 86mins

What could audiences have possibly done to deserve such torture? As this inane series continues, each episode becomes sillier and more slapdash than the last. There's no Steve Guttenberg in this one (he must have read the script), and all you need to know is that the bumbling cops, as the title suggests, visit Miami for a convention. JB. Contains some swearing. DVD

Matt McCoy *Nick* • Janet Jones *Kate Stratton* • George Gaynes *Commandant Lassard* • GW Bailey *Captain Harris* • René Auberjonois *Tony Stark* • Bubba Smith *Moses Hightower* • David Graf *Eugene Tackleberry* • Michael Winslow *Larvelle Jones* • Leslie Easterbrook *Debbie Callahan* ■ *Dir* Alan Myerson • *Scr* Stephen J Curwick, from characters created by Neal Israel, Pat Proft

Police Academy 6: City under Siege ★ PG

Comedy 1989 · US · Colour · 79mins

Having run out of inventive gags and originality by the final scene of the very first *Police Academy*, the series had overstayed its welcome long before this fifth sequel by stretching a thin premise to breaking point. Aside from the vocal gymnastics of Michael Winslow, this laughter-free zone couldn't even get itself arrested for indecency. AJ. Contains swearing and violence. DVD

Bubba Smith *Hightower* • David Graf *Tackleberry* • Michael Winslow *Jones* • Leslie Easterbrook *Callahan* • Marion Ramsey *Hooks* • Lance Kinsey *Proctor* • Matt McCoy *Nick* • Bruce Mahler *Fackler* ■ *Dir* Peter Bonerz • *Scr* Stephen J Curwick, from characters created by Neal Israel, Pat Proft

Police Academy: Mission to Moscow ★ PG

Comedy 1994 · US · Colour · 79mins

To mark the tenth anniversary of the series, back came George Gaynes and his crew of cockeyed cops to prove once more the law of diminishing sequels. Christopher Lee can never have been in a more terrifying movie – terrifyingly bad, that is. There isn't a single joke worthy of the name in this humiliating farrago. DP DVD

George Gaynes *Commandant Lassard* • Michael Winslow *Sgt Jones* • David Graf *Sgt Tackleberry* • Leslie Easterbrook *Capt Callahan* • GW Bailey *Capt Harris* • Christopher Lee *Commandant Alexander Rakov* • Ron Perlman *Constantine Konali* ■ *Dir* Alan Metter • *Scr* Randolph Davis, Michele S Chodos, from characters created by Neal Israel, Pat Proft

Police Dog ★★ U

Crime drama 1955 · UK · BW · 74mins

This competent quota quickie from Derek Twist is, in all honesty, "mutt ado about nothing". In one of his few movie excursions, Tim Turner plays a bobby who adopts an Alsatian stray and has reason to break out the Bonio when it helps him on the trail of his friend's murderer. It's hardly a baffling mystery – even Scooby Doo would have sussed it! DP

Joan Rice *Pat Lewis* • Tim Turner *Frank Mason* • Sandra Dorne *Blonde* • Charles Victor *Sergeant* • Jimmy Gilbert *Ken Lade* • Nora Gordon *Mrs Lewis* • John Le Mesurier *Inspector* ■ *Dir/Scr* Derek Twist

Police Story ★★

Crime drama 1975 · Fr/It · Colour · 107mins

Based on a real-life case – which explains the 1940s setting – this efficient thriller stars Alain Delon as a French detective and Jean-Louis Trintignant as his quarry, a psychotic killer and robber. Director Jacques Deray is clearly influenced by the work of Jean-Pierre Melville, and there are also traces of a Gallic *Dirty Harry* in Delon's parallel fight against bureaucratic red tape and liberal policies. Otherwise, this is a routine policier that was a big hit at the French box office. AT. A French language film.

Alain Delon *Borniche* • Jean-Louis Trintignant *Buisson* • Renato Salvatori *Le Rital* • Maurice Barrier *Bollec* • André Pousse *Le Nus* ■ *Dir* Jacques Deray • *Scr* Deray Alphonse Boudard, from an autobiography by Roger Borniche

Police Story ★★★ 15

Martial arts comedy thriller
1985 · HK · Colour · 95mins

Jackie Chan became an international superstar on the back of this fast-paced martial arts comedy thriller, in which he plays a Hong Kong police officer on the trail of drug-dealing gangsters. Chan also directs, providing the action with some spectacular set pieces, the best being a car chase through a shantytown and the shopping mall climax. The lightweight story is merely an excuse to display Chan's death-defying agility and his inventive use of scenery and props. TH. Cantonese dialogue dubbed into English. Contains violence and brief nudity. DVD

Jackie Chan *Chan Ka Kui* • Brigitte Lin *Selina Fong* • Maggie Cheung *May* • Yuen Cho *Chu Tao* • Bill Tung *Inspector Wong* ■ *Dir* Jackie Chan • *Scr* Edward Tang

Police Story 2 ★★ 15

Martial arts comedy thriller
1986 · HK · Colour · 101mins

Jackie Chan directs, co-writes and stars as the policeman in this chop-socky sequel. Like many Hong Kong action films, its breathless pace cannot prevent it from becoming a drag, and the soundtrack seems to have been recorded in a cardboard box. AT. Cantonese dialogue dubbed into English. Contains violence and brief nudity. DVD

Jackie Chan *Kevin Chan* • Maggie Cheung *May* • Bill Tung *Inspector Wong* • Lam Kwok Hung *Superintendent Lee* ■ *Dir* Jackie Chan • *Scr* Edward Tang, Jackie Chan

Police Story III: Supercop ★★★ 15

Martial arts comedy thriller
1992 · HK · Colour · 91mins

The best part of this typically lively Jackie Chan outing is the final credit sequence featuring the reckless stunts that failed to make the picture. This is a cracking romp in which Hong Kong cop Chan and Chinese police director Michelle Yeoh team up to infiltrate the gang of a vicious drugs baron. Riotous fun throughout. Michelle Yeoh returned to the role in 1993's *Project S*. DP. Cantonese dubbed into English. Contains violence, swearing. DVD

Jackie Chan *Chen Chia-Chu* • Maggie Cheung *May* • Michelle Yeoh *Inspector Yang* ■ *Dir* Stanley Tong • *Scr* Edward Tang, Filre Ma, Lee Wai Yee

The Police War ★★

Police drama 1979 · Fr · Colour · 102mins

The bent cop is a familiar figure in French commercial cinema, but while Robin Davis manages to draw decent performances from his leading trio, he offers few new insights on the subjects of duty and criminality. Claude Brasseur plays the humane commissioner who is convinced that the detested head of a rival brigade, Claude Rich, is in cahoots with gangster Gérard Desarthe after he bungles an arrest ambush. DP. French dialogue dubbed into English.

Claude Brasseur *Fush* • Marlène Jobert *Marie* • Claude Rich *Ballestrat* • François Périer *Millard* • Rufus *Le Garret* • Gérard Desarthe *Hector Sarlat* ■ *Dir* Robin Davis • *Scr* Jacques Labib, Jean-Marie Guillaume

The Polish Bride ★★★★ 15

Romantic drama
1998 · Neth · Colour · 85mins

This warmly sympathetic chamber-work certainly puts Dutch-based director Karim Traïdia on the map. It's an acute analysis of an oddball relationship: Jaap Spijkers is a near-bankrupt farmer who gives shelter to Monic Hendrickx, a Polish prostitute on the run from abusing city pimps. She becomes his housekeeper and they form a relationship that turns to love. For all its heartache, this is an engrossing affirmation that's a tonic for the spirit. TH. In Dutch, German and Polish with English subtitles. Contains violence and a brief sex scene.

Jaap Spijkers *Henk Woldring* • Monic Hendrickx *Anna Krzyzanowska* • Rudi Falkenhagen *Father* • Roef Ragas *Son* • Hakim Traïdia *Postman* ■ *Dir* Karim Traïdia • *Scr* Kees van der Hulst

Polish Wedding ★★ 15

Romantic comedy
1998 · US · Colour · 101mins

This tale of a Polish-American family in Detroit works quite well, but fails to stir up much emotion in the audience. Claire Danes is the teenager whose actions send her family into a turmoil – though perhaps they should be more alarmed at the casting. Not only are the leads not Polish; they're not even American! (Gabriel Byrne is Irish, while Lena Olin is a Swede.) They handle the accents well enough, but this is one of those slight films that can best be described as "nice". JB. Contains some swearing. DVD

Lena Olin *Jadzia Pzoniak* • Gabriel Byrne *Bolek Pzoniak* • Claire Danes *Hala Pzoniak* • Adam Trese *Russell Schuster* • Mili Avital *Sofie Pzoniak* • Daniel Lapaine *Ziggy Pzoniak* • Rade Serbedzija *Roman* ■ *Dir/Scr* Theresa Connelly

Pollock ★★★★ 18

Biographical drama
2000 · US · Colour · 118mins

Unfettered passion fuelled tormented American artist Jackson Pollock and, watching this remarkable biopic of his life, it would seem this same fervour possessed actor Ed Harris. Assuming the roles of first-time director, co-producer and star, this often under-rated performer turns an obvious labour of love into a respectable addition to Hollywood's "tortured artist" canon. With a keen eye for detail, Harris paints a compelling and passionate portrait of a creative genius consumed by personal demons. Gritty faded visuals and an understated, naturalistic style help focus attention on the plot and characterisation. SF. Contains swearing. DVD

Ed Harris *Jackson Pollock* • Marcia Gay Harden *Lee Krasner* • Amy Madigan *Peggy Guggenheim* • Jennifer Connelly *Ruth Kligman* • Jeffrey Tambor *Clement Greenberg* • Bud Cort *Howard Putzel* • John Heard *Tony Smith* • Val Kilmer *Willem de Kooning* ■ *Dir* Ed Harris • *Scr* Barbara Turner, Susan J Emshwiller, from the book *Jackson Pollock: an American Saga* by Steven Naifeh, and from the book *Jackson Pollock: an American Saga* by Gregory White Smith

Polly of the Circus ★★ U

Romantic drama 1932 · US · BW · 69mins

It took MGM some time to get the measure of their rising star Clark Gable and cast him according to his personality. This romantic drama, a perfect example of studio misjudgment, has Gable playing a man of the cloth who rescues a trapeze artist (a colourless Marion Davies) from physical and moral degradation in the face of disapproval from his bishop (C Aubrey Smith). A thin little film, devoid of sparks, despite Gable's flaming good looks. RK

P

Marion Davies *Polly Fisher* • Clark Gable *Reverend John Hartley* • C Aubrey Smith *Reverend James Northcott* • Raymond Hatton *Downey* • David Landau *Beef* • Ruth Selwyn *Mitzi* • Ray Milland *Rich young man* ■ *Dir* Alfred Santell • *Scr* Carey Wilson, Laurence Johnson, from the play by Margaret Mayo

Pollyanna ★★★★

Silent drama 1920 · US · BW · 60mins

This adaptation of Eleanor H Porter's book is probably Mary Pickford's most sugary confection. "The world's sweetheart" plays an orphan girl whose irresistible good nature converts the hard hearts of Aunt Polly (Katherine Griffith) and her grumpy New England neighbours. (Her final, near-fatal illness is schmaltz with a temperature.) Pickford is wonderful, while director Paul Powell catches the mood of the time, and the town, with casual expertise. TH

Mary Pickford *Pollyanna* • Wharton James *Rev Whittier* • Katherine Griffith *Aunt Polly Harrington* • Herbert Prior *Dr Chilton* • William Courtleigh *John Pendleton* • Helen Jerome Eddy *Nancy* • George Berrell *Tom* ■ *Dir* Paul Powell • *Scr* Frances Marion, from the novel by Eleanor H Porter

Pollyanna ★★★★ U

Drama 1960 · US · Colour · 134mins

Writer/director David Swift made a splendid job of adapting Eleanor H Porter's 1912 children's classic for the screen. Disney spared no expense in re-creating the look and feel of small-town Vermont, and splashed out in no uncertain terms to land such top-line performers as Agnes Moorehead, Karl Malden, Adolphe Menjou and Jane Wyman. They play the cheerless citizens whose lives are transformed by the effervescent orphan Pollyanna (Hayley Mills) and her bottomless supply of "gladness". Mills won a special Oscar for her spirited performance. If there is a fault, it is that it's a bit too long. DP [video] DVD

Hayley Mills *Pollyanna* • Jane Wyman *Aunt Polly Harrington* • Richard Egan *Dr Edmond Chilton* • Karl Malden *Reverend Paul Ford* • Nancy Olson *Nancy Furman* • Adolphe Menjou *Mr Pendergast* • Donald Crisp *Mayor Warren* • Agnes Moorehead *Mrs Snow* ■ *Dir* David Swift • *Scr* David Swift, from the novel by Eleanor H Porter

Poltergeist ★★★★ 15

Horror 1982 · US · Colour · 109mins

Evil spirits enter the home of a typical suburban American family through their possessed television set in this spectacular horror film, co-produced and co-written by Steven Spielberg. After a deceptively cute opening, Tobe Hooper gets down to some serious haunting and piles on the thrilling special effects and grisly moments. Hooper's direction may lack its usual edgy personality – apparently over-ruled by Spielberg's script suggestions – but he puts on a dazzling show. AJ. Contains violence, swearing. [video] DVD

JoBeth Williams *Diane Freeling* • Craig T Nelson *Steve Freeling* • Beatrice Straight *Dr Lesh* • Dominique Dunne *Dana Freeling* • Oliver Robbins *Robbie Freeling* • Heather O'Rourke *Carol Anne Freeling* • Michael McManus (1) *Ben Tuthill* • Virginia Kiser *Mrs Tuthill* • Zelda Rubinstein *Tangina Barrons* ■ *Dir* Tobe Hooper • *Scr* Steven Spielberg, Michael Grais, Mark Victor, from a story by Steven Spielberg

Poltergeist II: the Other Side ★★★ 15

Horror 1986 · US · Colour · 86mins

The haunted Freeling family has moved to Arizona, but the evil spirits aren't giving up their pursuit of the family's daughter, Heather O'Rourke. This sequel does little more than recycle the original story, yet there are enough supernatural visitations and grisly surprises to prevent the ghostly goings-on from getting dull. Julian Beck gives a marvellous fire-and-brimstone performance. AJ. Contains violence. [video] DVD

JoBeth Williams *Diane Freeling* • Craig T Nelson *Steve Freeling* • Heather O'Rourke *Carol Anne Freeling* • Oliver Robins *Robbie Freeling* • Zelda Rubinstein *Tangina Barrons* • Will Sampson *Taylor* • Julian Beck *Reverend Henry Kane* • Geraldine Fitzgerald *Gramma Jess* ■ *Dir* Brian Gibson • *Scr* Mark Victor, Michael Grais

Poltergeist III ★ 15

Horror 1988 · US · Colour · 93mins

"Enough, stop this stupid sideshow!" says the obnoxious psychiatrist in this repetitious and completely unnecessary second sequel. You'll give voice to the same sentiment long before he does in this slack, lifeless sequel. Heather O'Rourke died, at the age of 12, shortly after the film's completion, only adding to the legendary stories about a curse stalking the variable series. AJ. Contains swearing. [video]

Tom Skerritt *Bruce Gardner* • Nancy Allen *Patricia Gardner* • Heather O'Rourke *Carol Anne Freeling* • Zelda Rubinstein *Tangina Barrons* • Lara Flynn Boyle *Donna Gardner* • Kip Wentz *Scott* • Richard Fire *Dr Seaton* ■ *Dir* Gary Sherman • *Scr* Gary Sherman, Brian Taggert

Polyester ★★★★ 18

Satirical melodrama
1981 · US · Colour · 79mins

A fabulously vulgar surburban tale of a materially minded housewife with a perverse and ultimately tragic sense of gentility, *Polyester* brought about a long overdue reunion between director John Waters and Divine. Devoid of any conventional artistry while referencing lurid Hollywood melodrama in its satirical take on the lower-middle classes, the film showcases several other Waters regulars and also features resurrected sun-and-surf heart-throb Tab Hunter. Unmissable for anyone interested in the origins of what are now institutionalised obsessions with trash, kitsch and consumerist America, this candy-coloured, "mainstream" landmark arrived in cinemas with scratch-and-sniff Odorama cards. DM [video]

Divine *Francine Fishpaw* • Tab Hunter *Todd Tomorrow* • Edith Massey *Cuddles Kevinsky* • Mink Stole *Sandra Sullivan* • David Samson *Elmer Fishpaw* • Joni Ruth White *La Rue* • Mary Garlington *Lu-Lu Fishpaw* • Cookie Mueller *Betty Lelinski* ■ *Dir/Scr* John Waters (2) • *Costume Designer* Van Smith

Le Polygraphe ★★★

Thriller 1996 · Can/Fr/Ger · Colour · 99mins

Reduced to its essentials, this is a thriller about an unsolved murder. But, working from his 1987 play, Robert Lepage's main concerns are art and artifice, repression and redemption. Still disturbed by the death of her friend, actress Josée Deschênes decides to make a movie about the case. But film and fiction are soon blurring and coincidence plays an unnerving role in the proceedings. Visually and psychologically complex, this is both intriguing and inventive. DP In French with English subtitles.

Patrick Goyette *François Tremblay* • Marie Brassard *Lucie* • Peter Stormare *Christof Haussman* • Maria de Medeiros *Claude* • Josée Deschênes *Judith* ■ *Dir* Robert Lepage • *Scr* Marie Brassard, Robert Lepage, Michael Mackenzie, Patrick Goyette, from the play by Robert Lepage

The Pompatus of Love ★

Romantic comedy
1995 · US · Colour · 99mins

Four affluent New York males (including co-writers Jon Cryer and Adam Oliensis) are confused about love in the 1990s, regularly meeting to have long-winded discussions about it. There's no plot; just a series of choppily edited, unrelated vignettes of their unsatisfying love lives. All the characters are shallowly written and scripted to utter flip statements and observations that no one in real life would ever say. KB

Jon Cryer *Mark* • Adrian Pasdar *Josh* • Tim Guinee *Runyon* • Adam Oliensis *Phil* • Mia Sara *Cynthia* • Kristin Scott Thomas *Caroline* • Jennifer Tilly *Tarzaan* • Roscoe Lee Browne *Leonard Folder* ■ *Dir* Richard Schenkman • *Scr* Richard Schenkman, Jon Cryer, Adam Oliensis

Ponette ★★★ PG

Drama 1996 · Fr · Colour · 93mins

Four-year-old Victoire Thivisol won the best actress prize at Venice for her remarkable work in this exquisite study of loss and the indomitability of innocence. Bruised and confused after surviving the car crash that killed her mother, she has to cope not only with the shocked anger of her father, but also the conflicting advice of her teachers and playmates on the nature of death and the afterlife. However, director Jacques Doillon undermines the authenticity of Thivisol's pain and bewilderment by tacking on a cosy, contrived ending. DP. In French with English subtitles. [video]

Victoire Thivisol *Ponette* • Matiaz Bureau Caton *Matiaz* • Delphine Schiltz *Delphine* • Léopoldine Serre *Ada* • Luckie Royer *Luce* • Carla Ibled *Carla* • Antoine du Merle *Antoine* • Marie Trintignant *Ponette's mother* ■ *Dir/Scr* Jacques Doillon

Pontiac Moon ★★ 12

Comedy drama 1994 · US · Colour · 102mins

This cloying drama stars Ted Danson as a rural science teacher who decides to take his son (Ryan Todd) on the road to discover the meaning of life on the eve of the Apollo XI Moon mission. Mary Steenburgen and Cathy Moriarty go along for the mawkish ride. Peter Medak's direction errs on the side of the sentimentally mundane and only the good-natured performances make this journey worth following. AJ [video]

Ted Danson *Washington Bellamy* • Mary Steenburgen *Katherine Bellamy* • Ryan Todd *Andy Bellamy* • Eric Schweig *Ernest Ironplume* • Cathy Moriarty *Lorraine* • Max Gail *Jerome Bellamy* • Lisa Jane Persky *Alicia Frook* ■ *Dir* Peter Medak • *Scr* Finn Taylor, Jeffrey Brown, from an idea by Finn Taylor

Pontius Pilate ★★

Biblical drama 1961 · It/Fr · Colour · 100mins

The crucifixion is replayed from the viewpoint of the Roman procurator whose hand-wringing has earned him a place in the Christian faith. French superstar Jean Marais is directed by Hollywood stalwart Irving Rapper, who went to Europe for this concatenation on Pilate's love affairs. The muddled dubbing makes some of the plot almost impenetrable. TH. Italian and French dialogue dubbed into English.

Jean Marais *Pontius Pilate* • Jeanne Crain *Claudia Procula* • Basil Rathbone *Caiaphas* • Leticia Roman *Sarah* • Massimo Serato *Nicodemus* • Riccardo Garrone *Galba* • Livio Lorenzon *Barabbas* • Gianni Garko *Jonathan* • John Drew Barrymore *Jesus/Judas* ■ *Dir* Irving Rapper, Gian Paolo Callegari • *Scr* O Biancolo, Gino DeSantis, Gian Paolo Callegari, from a story by Gino DeSanotis

The Pony Express ★★★

Silent western 1925 · US · BW · 110mins

This major silent western, directed by James Cruze for Paramount to follow up his smash hit, *The Covered Wagon*, was again about an historical aspect of the Old West. Ricardo Cortez plays the gambler turned pony express rider who carries vital news of the election of President Lincoln to California, thereby linking both sides of the huge country. Although overburdened with plot and subsidiary characters, it does have a spectacular climactic attack by Indians and some vivid villainy from George Bancroft. AE

Ricardo Cortez *Jack Weston* • Betty Compson *Molly Jones* • Ernest Torrence *"Ascension" Jones* • Wallace Beery *"Rhode Island" Red* • George Bancroft *Jack Slade* ■ *Dir* James Cruze • *Scr* Walter Woods, from a novel by Henry James Forman, Walter Woods

Pony Express ★★ U

Western 1953 · US · Colour · 101mins

Charlton Heston, always cast in roles where he can lead with his chin, is fuelled by purposeful action, decency and high moral fibre in a western which has all the expected shorthand of the genre. The lightweight plot revolves around the adventures of Heston, as Buffalo Bill Cody, and Forrest Tucker, as Wild Bill Hickok, and the opening of mail routes to California. This is a lumpy stew of lean crackerjack action and rather earnest, talky stretches. JM

Charlton Heston *Buffalo Bill Cody* • Rhonda Fleming *Evelyn* • Jan Sterling *Denny* • Forrest Tucker *Wild Bill Hickok* • Michael Moore (3) *Rance Hastings* • Porter Hall *Bridger* ■ *Dir* Jerry Hopper • *Scr* Charles Marquis Warren, from a story by Frank Gruber

Pony Soldier ★★ U

Western 1952 · US · Colour · 82mins

The Mounties certainly had their day in the early 1950s, what with Alan Ladd in *Saskatchewan* and Howard Keel and Ann Blyth in *Rose Marie*, and here's Tyrone Power sent to don the scarlet as MacDonald of the Canadian Mounties (the film's British title). To be honest, Power looks thoroughly bored and ill-at-ease in this lame adventure. Why Fox didn't even give him a decent leading lady is anyone's guess, though Penny Edwards does her best. TS

Tyrone Power *Duncan MacDonald* • Cameron Mitchell *Konah* • Thomas Gomez *Natayo* • Penny Edwards *Emerald Neeley* • Robert Horton *Jess Calhoun* • Anthony Earl Numkena *Comes Running* • Adeline De Walt Reynolds *White Moon* • Howard Petrie *Inspector Frazer* ■ *Dir* Joseph M Newman • *Scr* John C Higgins, from a story by Garnett Weston in *The Saturday Evening Post*

Poodle Springs ★★ 15

Mystery thriller 1998 · US · Colour · 95mins

Ageing private eye Philip Marlowe, laconically played by James Caan, gets mixed up with blackmail and murder among the elite 1960s in-crowd in director Bob Rafelson's stilted take on Raymond Chandler. Despite a brave and literate attempt by scriptwriter Tom Stoppard to solve the contradictions of a story which existed only in sketch form at the time of the writer's death, this TV *faux film noir* is a thin stylistic oddity. AJ. Contains swearing, nudity and violence. [video] DVD

James Caan *Philip Marlowe* • Dina Meyer *Laura* • David Keith *Larry Victor* • Tom Bower *Arnie Burns* • Julia Campbell *Muffy Blackstone* • Brian Cox *Clayton Blackstone* • Nia Peeples *Angel* ■ *Dir* Bob Rafelson • *Scr* Tom Stoppard, from the novel by Robert B Parker, Raymond Chandler

P

Pooh's Heffalump Movie ★★ U

Animated comedy adventure
2005 · US · Colour · 65mins

Winnie the Pooh and his pals learn valuable lessons about friendship and diversity in Disney's slight and sugary tale, which is clearly aimed at young children. Believing that a mysterious rumbling noise in the Hundred Acre Wood is the sound of a much-feared Heffalump monster, the grown-up animals set out to catch the creature, leaving a disappointed young Roo behind. The 2-D animation is a bit flat and quaint, but the appealing candy colours and overall sweetness of the story help to disguise its shortcomings. SF DVD

Jim Cummings *Winnie the Pooh/Tigger* • John Fiedler *Piglet* • Nikita Hopkins *Roo* • Kath Soucie *Kanga* • Ken Sansom *Rabbit* • Peter Cullen *Eeyore* • Brenda Blethyn *Mama Heffalump* • David Ogden Stiers *Narrator* ■ *Dir* Frank Nissen • *Scr* Brian Hohlfeld, Evan Spiliotopoulos, from characters created by AA Milne

Pool Girl ★★ 15

Romantic comedy drama
1997 · US · Colour · 89mins

The tribulations of an LA pool-cleaner form the basis of this comedy drama, directed by Robert Downey and featuring his son. Alyssa Milano is Hugo, whose thriving business forces her to draft in mum Cathy Moriarty and dad Malcolm McDowell, plagued (respectively) with alcohol and gambling problems. This inadequate pair accompany Hugo on her rounds as she meets the usual assortment of weird customers, including Downey Jr's movie director and Sean Penn's drifter. A disappointing example of talented actors in search of a script. RT DVD

Alyssa Milano *Hugo* • Malcolm McDowell *Henry* • Sean Penn *Strange Hitchhiker* • Robert Downey Jr *Franz* • Cathy Moriarty *Minerva* • Patrick Dempsey *Floyd Gaylen* • Richard Lewis *Chick Chicalini* ■ *Dir* Robert Downey [Robert Downey Sr] • *Scr* Robert Downey, Laura Downey

Pool of London ★★

Crime drama 1950 · UK · BW · 85mins

The thriller elements may be routine, but the mixed-race romance in this Ealing Studios production broke new ground for British cinema. Set in London's Docklands, it's a smuggling yarn involving a black stevedore, his white girlfriend and plenty of double-crosses before the cops close in. Director Basil Dearden makes the most of his eclectic cast. AT

Bonar Colleano *Dan MacDonald* • Susan Shaw *Pat* • Renée Asherson *Sally* • Earl Cameron *Johnny* • Moira Lister *Maisie* • Max Adrian *Vernon* • Joan Dowling *Pamela* • James Robertson-Justice *Trotter* ■ *Dir* Basil Dearden • *Scr* Jack Whittingham, John Eldredge

Poor Cow ★★★ 15

Drama 1967 · UK · Colour · 97mins

Ken Loach made his feature debut with this adaptation of Nell Dunn's social realist (if unashamedly sensationalist) novel. The first of several films with working-class themes made by Loach, this isn't a patch on either his TV plays *Up the Junction* and *Cathy Come Home*, or his follow-up feature, *Kes*. This determinedly grim tale centres on the tangled love life of teenager Carol White, who turns to Terence Stamp after her thieving lover John Bindon is sent to prison. But only Queenie Watts impresses as White's prostitute aunt. Watch out for a debuting Malcolm McDowell. DP DVD

Carol White *Joy* • Terence Stamp *Dave* • John Bindon *Tom* • Kate Williams *Beryl* • Queenie Watts *Aunt Emm* • Geraldine Sherman *Trixie* • James Beckett *Tom's friend* • Billy Murray *Tom's friend* • Malcolm McDowell *Billy* ■ *Dir* Kenneth Loach [Ken Loach] • *Scr* Kenneth Loach, Nell Dunn, the novel by Nell Dunn

Poor Little Rich Girl ★★★ U

Musical comedy 1936 · US · BW · 76mins

She's little Shirley Temple, and it's jolly difficult to care when such an obviously talented, bright-and-shiny youngster feels neglected and runs away from the home of her wealthy widower father. She's befriended by blonde Alice Faye and Tin Man-to-be Jack Haley and turned into a major radio star. Temple was the biggest movie star in the world at this time, and her studio, 20th Century-Fox, was hard-pressed to find suitable vehicles to showcase her talents. It did her proud with this one, and the militaristic finale is mesmerising. TS DVD

Shirley Temple *Barbara Barry* • Alice Faye *Jerry Dolan* • Gloria Stuart *Margaret Allen* • Jack Haley *Jimmy Dolan* • Michael Whalen *Richard Barry* • Sara Haden *Collins* • Jane Darwell *Woodward* • Billy Gilbert *Waiter* ■ *Dir* Irving Cummings • *Scr* Sam Hellman, Gladys Lehman, Harry Tugend, from stories by Eleanor Gates, Ralph Spence

Poor White Trash ★★ 15

Crime comedy 2000 · US · Colour · 85mins

Sean Young is the mom who turns to crime so she can afford to send her son to college in this uneven but occasionally amusing indie film. Unfortunately you won't like her son enough to care either way, but at least director Michael Addis has populated his film with quirky and fun supporting characters, from William Devane as a barking mad lawyer to Jason London as the larcenous mother's young lover. JB DVD

Sean Young *Linda Bronco* • William Devane *Ron Lake* • Jason London *Brian Ross* • Tony Denman *Mike Bronco* • Jacob Tierney *Lennie Lake* • M Emmet Walsh *Judge Pike* ■ *Dir* Michael Addis • *Scr* Michael Addis, from a story by Michael Addis, Tony Urban

Pop & Me ★★★ 12

Documentary 1999 · US · Colour · 88mins

Brandishing a raw honesty that often leaves the viewer feeling like an intruder, this is a relentlessly revealing insight into father-son relationships around the world. The focus falls on Californian graphic designer Chris Roe, who agrees to help his broker father, Richard, through a midlife crisis by reprising the family's 1979 globe-trotting expedition. Starting with Richard's reunion with the alcoholic father he'd not seen for over 30 years, the trip soon opens up fissures in the Roes' affinities. But while the various international tensions are compelling, the real coup is persuading Julian Lennon to speak so candidly about his Beatle dad. DP

Dir Chris Roe • *Scr* Chris Roe, Richard Roe, Erik Arnesen, Jesse Negron, Juliann Jannus, Mark Kornweibel

Popcorn ★★ 15

Horror 1991 · US · Colour · 86mins

This quirky little movie puts too much on its plate, trying to mix a standard slasher tale with attempts to satirise campy old horror movies. The satire is more successful than the slash, with amusing and on-target homages to William Castle and failed cinematic innovations such as "Smell-O-Vision". The sporadic cuts to these segments are nice breaks in an otherwise predictable opus about a university film class sponsoring an all-night horror festival. KB DVD

Jill Schoelen *Maggie* • Tom Villard *Toby* • Dee Wallace Stone *Suzanne* • Derek Rydall *Mark* • Malcolm Danare *Bud* • Elliott Hurst *Leon* ■ *Dir* Mark Herrier • *Scr* Alan Ormsby, from a story by Mitchell Smith

Pope Joan ★★

Period drama 1972 · UK · Colour · 140mins

Before he wrote his Oscar-winning script for *Gandhi*, John Briley penned this mythical tale of a woman who disguises herself as a monk and (to cut a long story short) ends up as pope. The main question is not what it all means, but why Liv Ullmann was such a riveting actress for Ingmar Bergman and such a prissy plum pudding for everyone else. The strong supporting cast pop in and out of the story, while the ninth-century settings are no more than perfunctory. AT

Liv Ullmann *Joan* • Keir Dullea *Dr Stevens* • Maximilian Schell *Adrian* • Olivia de Havilland *Mother Superior* • Lesley-Anne Down *Cecilia* • Trevor Howard *Pope Leo* ■ *Dir* Michael Anderson • *Scr* John Briley

The Pope Must Die ★★★ 15

Comedy 1991 · UK · Colour · 95mins

This feature-length outing for the *Comic Strip* team is a little ragged around the edges, but there are enough sharp gags to make it entertaining. Robbie Coltrane plays the simple, rock 'n' roll-loving priest who is mistakenly elected Pope, only to discover a hot-bed of corruption within the Vatican. Coltrane can do this sort of thing in his sleep, and the best performances come from some canny scene-stealers not normally associated with the TV show. JF. Contains violence, swearing and nudity.

Robbie Coltrane *Dave Albinizi* • Beverly D'Angelo *Veronica Dante* • Herbert Lom *Vittorio Corelli* • Alex Rocco *Cardinal Rocco* • Paul Bartel *Monsignor Vitchie* • Balthazar Getty *Joe Don Dante* • William Hootkins *Cardinal Verucci* • Robert Stephens *Carmelengo* • Annette Crosbie *Mother Superior* • Steve O'Donnell *Rico* • John Sessions *Dino* ■ *Dir* Peter Richardson • *Scr* Peter Richardson, Pete Richens

The Pope of Greenwich Village ★★★ 15

Crime drama 1984 · US · Colour · 115mins

This never once approaches the creatively crazed energy of Martin Scorsese's *Mean Streets*, on whose coat-tails it rather obviously hangs. But what the film lacks in imagination and drive it gains in rich character acting, particularly from those who look as if they've been pushed and pulled by New York life or just spent too long in its gutters. JM. Contains swearing.

Mickey Rourke *Charlie* • Eric Roberts *Paulie* • Daryl Hannah *Diane* • Geraldine Page *Mrs Ritter* • Kenneth McMillan *Barney* • Tony Musante *Pete* • M Emmet Walsh *Burns* • Burt Young *"Bedbug" Eddie* ■ *Dir* Stuart Rosenberg • *Scr* Vincent Patrick, from his novel

Popeye ★★ U

Musical comedy 1980 · US · Colour · 92mins

When Robert Altman fails, he flops from a great height. And this is as high as it gets in terms of failed aspirations as the director tries to turn the comic strip *Popeye* into a live-action musical comedy. Robin Williams raps inarticulately as the heroic sailorman searching for his long-lost Pappy with the help of Shelley Duvall's witless though seductive Olive Oyl. There are compensations – the brilliantly designed town of Sweethaven and Harry Nilsson's songs, for example – but it's all too manic, jittery and overblown. TH DVD

Robin Williams *Popeye* • Shelley Duvall *Olive Oyl* • Ray Walston *Poopdeck Pappy* • Paul L Smith [Paul Smith] *Bluto* • Paul Dooley *Wimpy* • Richard Libertini *Geezil* • Roberta Maxwell *Nana Oyl* • Donald Moffat *Taxman* ■ *Dir* Robert Altman • *Scr* Jules Feiffer, from comic strip characters created by EC Segar

Popi ★★★

Comedy 1969 · US · Colour · 113mins

A hard-working Puerto Rican tries to get his sons out of the New York ghetto by an elaborate hoax. Passing them off as Cuban refugees in Florida, he hopes to have them adopted by richer people. This pleasant and well-made comedy gives good parts to Alan Arkin and Rita Moreno while offering a believable, though ultimately cosy view of the rawer aspects of the American Dream. JG

Alan Arkin *Abraham, "Popi"* • Rita Moreno *Lupe* • Miguel Alejandro *Junior* • Ruben Figueroa [Reuben Figueroa] *Luis* • John Harkins *Harmon* • Joan Tompkins *Miss Musto* ■ *Dir* Arthur Hiller • *Scr* Tina Pine [Tina Rome], Les Pine

Poppy ★★★

Drama 1935 · Jpn · BW · 72mins

This Kenji Mizoguchi adaptation has been somewhat overlooked. At its core lies the contrasting social attitudes of two women: dutiful daughter Yukichi Iwata, who reluctantly accedes to her betrothal to Daijiro Natsukawa, and older, more liberated English student, Kuniko Miyake. The director abandoned his now customary long takes and adopted a traditional Hollywood narrative approach, with editing, not camera movement, creating the rhythm and significance of the action. DP. In Japanese with English subtitles.

Kuniko Miyake *Fujio Kono* • Ichiro Tsukida *Seizo Ono* • Daijiro Natsukawa *Hajime Munechika* • Kazuyoshi Takeda *Kingo Kono* • Yukichi Iwata *Tomotaka Inoue* • Chiyoko Okura *Sayoko Inoue* ■ *Dir* Kenji Mizoguchi • *Scr* Haruo Takayanagi, Daisuke Ito, from the novel *Gubijinso* by Soseki Natsume • *Cinematographer* Minoru Miki

Poppy ★★★★ U

Comedy 1936 · US · BW · 70mins

WC Fields made the role of travelling medicine seller Eustace McGargle his own when he first appeared in Dorothy Donnelly's play back in the early 1920s and in the 1925 silent version, *Sally of the Sawdust*. This film version finds him setting up his stall in a small town where his adopted daughter (Rochelle Hudson) falls in love with the mayor's son. There's more sentimentality than is usual for a Fields movie, but the sour delight of watching him never giving a sucker an even break is still a delight. TH

WC Fields *Prof Eustace McGargle* • Rochelle Hudson *Poppy* • Richard Cromwell *Billy Farnsworth* • Granville Bates *Mayor Farnsworth* • Catherine Doucet *Countess Maggie Tubbs DePuizzi* ■ *Dir* A Edward Sutherland • *Scr* Waldemar Young, Virginia Van Upp, from the play by Dorothy Donnelly

The Poppy Is Also a Flower ★★ PG

Crime thriller 1966 · US · Colour · 95mins

For incurable star-spotters and collectors of 007 trivia, this thriller about two UN agents who go up against the international heroin trade is absolutely unmissable. James Bond author Ian Fleming had the original idea of opening with a shot of a pretty poppy growing in the fields of Iran and following its progress to the ugly streets of Harlem. Among the host of stars, Bond fans will immediately spot Harold Sakata, who played Oddjob in *Goldfinger*. It was first seen on American TV, then released in European cinemas as *Danger Grows Wild*. DP

EG Marshall *Jones* • Trevor Howard *Lincoln* • Gilbert Roland *Marco* • Rita Hayworth *Monique* • Anthony Quayle *Captain* • Angie Dickinson *Linda Benson* • Yul Brynner *Colonel Salem* • Eli Wallach *Locarno* • Harold Sakata *Martin* • Marcello Mastroianni *Inspector Mosca* • Stephen Boyd *Benson* • Omar Sharif *Dr Rad* • Grace Kelly *Introduction* ■ *Dir* Terence Young • *Scr* Jo Eisinger, from an idea by Ian Fleming

Popsy-Pop ★

Crime drama 1970 · Fr · Colour · 88mins

This dreary romantic thriller stars Stanley Baker as an incorruptible cop sent to arrest jewel smuggler Claudia Cardinale as she collects another consignment of stones from her double-crossing partner. Unsurprisingly, the couple fall in lust as their bad-tempered cat-and-mouse game grinds along to its predictable conclusion. DP. French dialogue dubbed into English.

Stanley Baker *Silva* • Claudia Cardinale *Popsy* • Henri Charrière *Marco* • Georges Aminel *Priest* • Ginette Leclerc *Madame* ■ *Dir* Jean Herman • *Scr* Henri Charrière, Jean Herman

Porgy and Bess ★★★ PG

Opera 1959 · US · Colour · 183mins

Producer Samuel Goldwyn bowed out at the age of 75 with this film version of the folk opera about crippled Porgy, his girl Bess and the inhabitants of Catfish Row. The familiar music, given Oscar-winning treatment by André Previn and Ken Darby, is gloriously intact. However, despite a starry cast of principals, the result disappoints. Otto Preminger's direction is heavy-handed, the singing not as good as it should be, and the whole production too lavish to convince as a poignant tale of slum life. RK [video]

Sidney Poitier *Porgy* • Dorothy Dandridge *Bess* • Sammy Davis Jr *Sportin' Life* • Pearl Bailey *Maria* • Brock Peters *Crown* • Leslie Scott *Jake* • Diahann Carroll *Clara* • Ruth Attaway *Serena* ■ *Dir* Otto Preminger • *Scr* N Richard Nash, from the opera by George Gershwin, Ira Gershwin, DuBose Heyward, from the stage play by DuBose Heyward, Dorothy Heyward

Pork Chop Hill ★★★★ PG

War drama 1959 · US · BW · 93mins

This is the definitive Korean War movie from director Lewis Milestone, who dealt with the Second World War impressively in *A Walk in the Sun* and the First World War unforgettably in the classic *All Quiet on the Western Front*. Bleak and grim, it boasts a superb all-male cast, headed by Gregory Peck at his glummest. Watch out for the young Martin Landau and Harry Dean Stanton (billed here as plain Dean Stanton) amid all the shrapnel. As with Milestone's other war films, the action sequences are terrific. TS [video] DVD

Gregory Peck *Lieutenant Clemons* • Harry Guardino *Forstman* • Rip Torn *Lieutenant Russell* • George Peppard *Fedderson* • James Edwards *Corporal Jurgens* • Bob Steele *Kern* • Woody Strode *Franklin* • George Shibita *Lieutenant O'Hashi* • Norman Fell *Sergeant Coleman* • Robert Blake *Velie* • Barry Atwater *Davis* • Martin Landau *Marshall* • Dean Stanton [Harry Dean Stanton] *MacFarland* ■ *Dir* Lewis Milestone • *Scr* James R Webb, from a story by General SLA Marshall

Porky's ★★★ 18

Comedy 1981 · Can · Colour · 94mins

Set in the 1950s, this crude, crass comedy centres around the elaborate revenge plotted by a group of students on the redneck owner of the local bar-cum-whorehouse, Porky's. Director Bob Clark makes a few misguided nods to serious issues such as anti-Semitism. For the most part, though, he sticks to a seamless mix of vulgar sexual gags and spectacular slapstick, which is most definitely not PC but is often hugely entertaining. JF. Contains swearing and nudity. [video] DVD

Dan Monahan *Pee Wee* • Mark Herrier *Billy* • Wyatt Knight *Tommy* • Roger Wilson *Mickey* • Cyril O'Reilly *Tim* • Tony Ganios *Meat* • Kim Cattrall *Honeywell* • Nancy Parsons *Ms Balbricker* • Susan Clark *Cherry Forever* • Chuck Mitchell *Porky* ■ *Dir/Scr* Bob Clark

Porky's II: The Next Day ★★ 18

Comedy 1983 · Can · Colour · 93mins

After the huge success of *Porky's*, all the leads reunited for this continuation of the story. This time the 1950s Florida high school gang are trying to mount an evening of Shakespeare, but face opposition from the Righteous Flock, who deem the Bard obscene, and the KKK, who object to the casting of a Seminole Indian (Joseph Runningfox) as Romeo. A tighter plot than its predecessor, but with the same emphasis on sex – and, like the original, very funny in places. DF. Contains swearing, nudity. [video] DVD

Dan Monahan *Pee Wee* • Wyatt Knight *Tommy* • Mark Herrier *Billy* • Roger Wilson *Mickey* • Cyril O'Reilly *Tim* • Tony Ganios *Meat* • Kaki Hunter *Wendy* • Scott Colomby *Brian* • Nancy Parsons *Ms Balbricker* • Joseph Runningfox *John Henry* ■ *Dir* Bob Clark • *Scr* Roger E Swaybill, Alan Ormsby, Bob Clark

Porky's Revenge ★ 18

Comedy 1985 · Can · Colour · 88mins

This third entry in the series is easily the worst. The energetic vulgarity of the first two films is replaced here by a leering coarseness – which is ironic, as the first two films were unfairly condemned (by those that hadn't seen them) for containing exactly this sort of crudity. The thin plot revolves around our heroes being forced to throw a basketball match by bar owner Chuck Mitchell. DF [video]

Dan Monahan *Pee Wee* • Wyatt Knight *Tommy* • Tony Ganios *Meat* • Mark Herrier *Billy* • Kaki Hunter *Wendy* • Scott Colomby *Brian* • Nancy Parsons *Ms Balbricker* • Chuck Mitchell *Porky Wallace* ■ *Dir* James Komack • *Scr* Ziggy Steinberg, from characters created by Bob Clark

The Pornographer ★★★ 18

Psychological drama
2001 · Fr/Can · Colour · 105mins

The inspired casting of Jean-Pierre Léaud is the key to this thoughtful examination of the strictures of reputation and the increasing difficulty of making meaningful movies. Léaud turns in a pensive portrayal of dejected disillusionment as the one-time porn director whose debts force him to return to an industry in which tastes have coarsened considerably since his 1970s heyday. The hardcore sex scene graphically symbolises his ambivalence, but director Bertrand Bonello wisely places greater emphasis on Léaud's fractured relationship with his student activist son (Jérémie Rénier). DP. In French with English subtitles. [video] DVD

Jean-Pierre Léaud *Jacques Laurent* • Jérémie Rénier *Joseph* • Dominique Blanc *Jeanne* • Catherine Mouchet *Olivia Rochet* • Thibault de Montalembert *Richard* • André Marcon *Louis* ■ *Dir/Scr* Bertrand Bonello

Porridge ★★ PG

Comedy 1979 · UK · Colour · 89mins

The original TV series had been over for two years and Ronnie Barker had even been *Going Straight* before he was talked back into the role of Norman Fletcher for this movie spin-off. He's excellent and this is one of the best of its kind, but, sadly, that's not saying much. What worked in a tightly scripted half-hour falls apart over 90 minutes in a story about a Lags XI v Celebrity All-stars football match set up to cover an escape. DP [video]

Ronnie Barker *Norman Fletcher* • Richard Beckinsale *Lennie Godber* • Fulton Mackay *Mackay* • Brian Wilde *Barrowclough* • Peter Vaughan *"Grouty"* • Julian Holloway *Bainbridge* ■ *Dir* Dick Clement • *Scr* Dick Clement, Ian La Frenais, from their TV series

Port Djema ★★★

War thriller 1997 · Fr/It/Gr · Colour · 96mins

This is a fictionalised version of events that took place in the war-torn, famine-stricken East African country of Eritrea. Director Eric Heumann disconcertingly combines scenes of brutality with moments of pure pathos, as he follows emotionally and intellectually detached doctor Jean-Yves Dubois on a journey into his own heart of darkness, to keep his promise to a murdered friend to find a small boy trapped in spiralling civil unrest. As a thriller it's too deliberate to involve, but its views on post-colonial culpability and political indifference are powerfully expressed. DP. In French with English subtitles.

Jean-Yves Dubois *Pierre Feldman* • Nathalie Boutefeu *Alice* • Christophe Odent *Jerome Delbos* • Edouard Montoute *Ousman* • Claire Wauthion *Sister Marie-Françoise* • Frédéric Pierrot *Antoine Barasse* ■ *Dir* Eric Heumann • *Scr* Eric Heumann, Jacques Lebas, Lam Le

Port of Call ★★★ PG

Drama 1948 · Swe · BW · 93mins

Alienated Nine-Christine Jönsson, recently released from a reformatory and tormented by her relationship with her destructive mother and the puritanical restraints placed on her by social workers, seeks solace in a love affair with simple young sailor Bengt Eklund, who is unable to comprehend her complexities. This interesting early entry from Ingmar Bergman, well-photographed in semi-documentary style on location in the Gothenburg docks, is, as one would expect, depressingly downbeat. It's marred by touches of melodrama, but Jönsson's performance is compelling. RK. In Swedish with English subtitles. DVD

Nine-Christine Jönsson *Berit* • Bengt Eklund *Gösta* • Berta Hall *Berit's mother* • Erik Hell *Berit's father* • Mimi Nelson *Gertrud* ■ *Dir* Ingmar Bergman • *Scr* Ingmar Bergman, from a story by Olle Länsberg

Port of Escape ★★★

Crime drama 1956 · UK · BW · 75mins

The skilled performances of John McCallum and Googie Withers and an atmospheric treatment of the London Docks setting give this modest melodrama a considerable lift. McCallum is the Aussie adventurer who accidentally kills a man while helping his mentally ill American friend (played by Bill Kerr). They commandeer a boat owned by journalist Withers, whose initial hostility gives way to love for the Australian. An obscure director, Anthony Young, lets the pace slacken occasionally, but overall this is an intelligent and offbeat work that deserves to be better known. AE

Googie Withers *Anne Stirling* • John McCallum *Mitchell Gillie* • Bill Kerr *Dinty Missouri* • Joan Hickson *Rosalie Watchett* ■ *Dir* Tony Young [Anthony Young] • *Scr* Barbara Harper, Abby Mann, Tony Young [Anthony Young], from the story *Safe Harbour* by Barbara Harper

Port of Hell ★★

Drama 1954 · US · BW · 79mins

The commies are up to their usual tricks in this minor melodrama, anchoring a freighter in Los Angeles harbour with an atomic bomb on board that will be detonated within hours. Fortunately, Dane Clark's stern harbourmaster is on hand to team up with an old adversary, Wayne Morris, and foil the dastardly plot. The film suggests that, as long as the atomic bomb is exploded out at sea, no real harm will occur. The under-rated Carole Mathews shines as co-star. AE

Dane Clark *Pardee* • Carole Mathews *Julie Povich* • Wayne Morris *Stanley Povich* • Marshall Thompson *Marsh Walker* • Harold Peary *Leo* ■ *Dir* Harold Schuster • *Scr* Tom Hubbard, Gil Doud, Fred Eggers, from a story by Gil Doud, DD Beauchamp

Port of New York ★★

Crime drama 1949 · US · BW · 81mins

The main interest in this minor thriller is the screen debut of Yul Brynner as a New York drug trafficker whose operation is infiltrated by narcotics agents Scott Brady and Richard Rober. Brynner had hair in those days and isn't easily recognisable as the mafioso who smuggles the drugs through the New York docks. Laslo Benedek directs in pseudo-documentary style, revelling in his locations. AT

Scott Brady *Michael "Mickey" Waters* • Richard Rober *Jim Flannery* • KT Stevens *Toni Cardell* • Yul Brynner *Paul Vicola* • Arthur Blake *Dolly Carney* ■ *Dir* Laslo Benedek • *Scr* Eugene Ling, Leo Townsend, from a story by Arthur A Ross, Bert Murray

Port of Seven Seas ★★★

Drama 1938 · US · BW · 80mins

James Whale inherited this project from William Wyler, although neither was exactly suited to adapt Marcel Pagnol's Marseilles classic, *Fanny*. Delivered to the accompaniment of Franz Waxman's twee score, Preston Sturges's dialogue lacks the easy charm of the original. But Wallace Beery and Frank Morgan grow into the roles of the waterfront bar owner and the widower who agrees to marry his daughter, Maureen O'Hara, after she's left pregant by her sailor lover, John Beal. DP

Wallace Beery *Cesar* • Frank Morgan *Panisse* • Maureen O'Sullivan *Madelon* • John Beal *Marius* • Jessie Ralph *Honorine* • Cora Witherspoon *Claudine* • Etienne Girardot *Bruneau* ■ *Dir* James Whale • *Scr* Preston Sturges, from the play *Fanny* by Marcel Pagnol, from the books *Marseilles Trilogy* by Marcel Pagnol

Les Portes de la Nuit ★★★★

Drama 1946 · Fr · BW · 106mins

The film that marked the end of both the fruitful partnership between director Marcel Carné and screenwriter Jacques Prévert and the sombre, poetic-realist tradition of which they formed an important part. The action focuses on a quartet of doomed lovers and a tramp, who is the personification of Destiny. Pretty gloomy, portentous stuff, but it does have a heady, nocturnal 1940s atmosphere, impressive sets by Alexander Trauner and a haunting theme song, known in English as *Autumn Leaves*. The film, which misjudged the postwar mood, failed miserably at the box office. RB. In French with English subtitles.

Nathalie Nattier *Malou* • Yves Montand *Diego* • Pierre Brasseur *Georges* • Saturnin Fabre *Monsieur Senechal* • Raymond Bussières *Raymond Lecuyer* • Serge Reggiani *Guy* ■ *Dir* Marcel Carné • *Scr* Jacques Prévert • *Production Designer* Alexander Trauner [Alexandre Trauner]

Portion d'Eternité ★★

Drama 1989 · Can · Colour · 101mins

Told largely in flashback, Robert Favreau's film starts out as an engrossing human interest story but soon descends into a Michael Crichton-like medical thriller. The opening section is both provocative and moving, as French-Canadian couple Danielle Proulx and Marc Messier explore the artificial

P

insemination options open to them at an expensive clinic when they try to start a family. But once we begin to discover their doctor's murky past and his involvement with corrupt pharmaceutical companies, the plot begins to unravel. DP. In French with English subtitles.

Danielle Proulx *Marie* • Marc Messier *Pierre* • Patricia Nolin *Hélène* • Paul Savoie *Antoine* ■ *Dir/Scr* Robert Favreau

Portnoy's Complaint ★ 18

Comedy drama 1972 · US · Colour · 96mins

For his directing debut, screenwriter Ernest Lehman chose Philip Roth's scandalous novel about the difficulties of being Jewish and the joys of masturbation. Portnoy (a smirking Richard Benjamin) has been a lonely, repressed child who has grown up playing obsessively with himself. Various prostitutes and fashion models try and help Portnoy in this satire that emerges as a limp, unfunny imitation of *The Graduate*. AT

Richard Benjamin *Alexander Portnoy* • Karen Black *Mary Jane Reid/The Monkey* • Lee Grant *Sophie Portnoy* • Jack Somack *Jack Portnoy* • Renee Lippin *Hannah Portnoy* ■ *Dir* Ernest Lehman • *Scr* Ernest Lehman, from the novel by Philip Roth

Portrait from Life ★★

Drama 1948 · UK · BW · 90mins

Terence Fisher's film tackles the then thorny topic of rehabilitating Nazi sympathisers within postwar German society. The cast is first rate, with Mai Zetterling particularly good as the amnesiac forced to explore her association with a high-ranking fascist. However, the dramatic demands of a reconciliation with her father and a romance with Robert Beatty soon swamp the infinitely more fascinating background story. DP

Mai Zetterling *Hildegarde* • Robert Beatty *Campbell Reid* • Guy Rolfe *Major Lawrence* • Herbert Lom *Hendlemann* • Patrick Holt *Ferguson* • Arnold Marlé *Professor Menzel* • Thora Hird *Mrs Skinner* ■ *Dir* Terence Fisher • *Scr* Muriel Box, Sidney Box, Frank Harvey Jr, from a story by David Evans

P

Portrait in Black ★★

Murder mystery 1960 · US · Colour · 112mins

This is tosh, and don't think producer Ross Hunter didn't know it. Lana Turner stars in a film with a plot so full of holes that it's hard to stop the cast falling through them. But Hunter was shrewd enough to know that if it looked good and was cleverly cast you could get away with murder (almost). Trouble is, Turner is too genteel for the hysterics, and director Michael Gordon has a tough time pulling all the threads together. TS

Lana Turner *Sheila Cabot* • Anthony Quinn *Dr David Rivera* • Sandra Dee *Catherine Cabot* • John Saxon *Blake Richards* • Richard Basehart *Howard Mason* • Lloyd Nolan *Matthew Cabot* • Ray Walston *Cob O'Brien* • Virginia Grey *Miss Lee* • Anna May Wong *Tani* ■ *Dir* Michael Gordon • *Scr* Ivan Goff, Ben Roberts, from their play

Portrait of a Hitman ★★

Action adventure 1977 · US · Colour · 85mins

It's a shame that, in later years, Rod Steiger all but erased memories of his quality work with empty gestures or prime ham. Here Steiger is stranded between implausibility and emotional truth as a criminal who pays an assassin (Jack Palance) to bump off the killer's old chum (Bo Svenson), so that pursuer and pursued inhabit an awkward grey area. Furthermore, love arrives as an unlikely intrusion just to add to the fun. Palance looks both sinister and soulful, but the picture is generally a pretty shaky effort. JM. Contains violence and swearing.

Jack Palance *Jim Buck* • Rod Steiger *Max* • Ann Turkel *Kathy* • Bo Svenson *Dr Michaels* • Philip Ahn *Mr Wong* ■ *Dir* Allan A Buckhantz • *Scr* Harold "Yabo" Yablonsky [Yabo Yablonsky]

The Portrait of a Lady ★★★ 12

Period drama
1996 · NZ/UK/US · Colour and BW · 138mins

Nicole Kidman is captivating as Henry James's heroine, an independent, dynamic woman seduced into the machinations of Barbara Hershey and her lover John Malkovich. Caught like a bright bird in their trap, her loss of spirit is the tragedy of the film, but it doesn't make for easy viewing. Jane Campion's film is beautifully shot and captures the spirit of the novel, but you walk away with a troubled brow. LH. Contains brief nudity. DVD

Nicole Kidman *Isabel Archer* • John Malkovich *Gilbert Osmond* • Barbara Hershey *Madame Serena Merle* • Mary-Louise Parker *Henrietta Stackpole* • Martin Donovan (2) *Ralph Touchett* • Shelley Winters *Mrs Touchett* • Richard E Grant *Lord Warburton* • Shelley Duvall *Countess Gemini* • Christian Bale *Edward Rosier* • Viggo Mortensen *Caspar Goodwood* • John Gielgud *Mr Touchett* ■ *Dir* Jane Campion • *Scr* Laura Jones, from the novel by Henry James • *Cinematographer* Stuart Dryburgh • *Costume Designer* Janet Patterson

Portrait of Clare ★★ U

Period drama 1950 · UK · BW · 99mins

British director Lance Comfort had a successful early career, but by the time he came to make this flashback frippery, he had rather lost the knack for this kind of "woman's picture", with its all-too-familiar blend of reminiscence, romance and regret. Australian-born actress Margaret Johnston fails to make much impact as she recounts details of her three marriages to her granddaughter. DP

Margaret Johnston *Clare Hingston* • Richard Todd *Robert Hart* • Robin Bailey *Dudley Wilburn* • Ronald Howard *Ralph Hingston* • Jeremy Spenser *Steven Hingston* • Marjorie Fielding *Aunt Cathie* ■ *Dir* Lance Comfort • *Scr* Leslie Landau, Adrian Arlington, from the novel by Francis Brett Young

Portrait of Hell ★★★ 12

Action drama 1969 · Jpn · Colour · 95mins

Adapted from a story by Ryunosuke Akutagawa (who also wrote *Rashomon*), this is both a piercing plea for racial tolerance and a nightmarish allegory of life on earth. Obsessed by the afterlife following a bloody military campaign, 14th-century ruler Kinnosuke Nakamura kidnaps Korean beauty Yoko Naito to ensure her artist father completes a heavenly mural. However, as Naito is subjected to pitiless torture, Tatsuya Nakadai abuses his commission to reflect the cruelties of Nakamura's regime. Taking stylistic risks to capture the painting's texture, Shiro Toyoda not only generates a sense of evil, but also a fair measure of socio-political indignation. DP. In Japanese with English subtitles. DVD

Tatsuya Nakadai *Yoshihide* • Yoko Naito *Yoshika* • Kinnosuke Nakamura *Lord Hosokawa* ■ *Dir* Shiro Toyoda • *Scr* Toshio Yasumi, from a novel by Ryunosuke Akutagawa

Portrait of Jason ★★★★

Documentary 1967 · US · BW · 105mins

An early example of the confrontational, intrusive style now so commonplace, this long interview was conducted over 12 hours with a black man who calls himself Jason Holliday. It is still a disconcerting experience, making us question the relationship between interviewer and subject. The conversation is at first straightforward, covering Jason's early career; but as he becomes more drunk and stoned, Jason gets maudlin about his homosexuality and his current occupation as a prostitute. Finally, his off-screen interviewers (one of whom is the director) taunt him with abuse to keep his responses more "interesting". How much of what we see was collusion? Given Jason's stated ambition to be a cabaret artist, was he in fact acting? Or, if it was real, what do we learn from watching someone disintegrate in front of our eyes? The viewer is left to answer these questions. DM

Dir Shirley Clarke • *Cinematographer* Jeri Sapanen • *Sound* Francis Daniel

Portrait of Jennie ★★★★ U

Romance 1948 · US · BW and Colour · 86mins

Produced by David O Selznick as a monument to the beauty of his wife-to-be, Jennifer Jones, this is one of Hollywood's best romantic fantasies. A long opening title sequence ponders eternal questions of life, space and death, and then we meet Joseph Cotten as a struggling artist who falls in love with the mystical Jones. The movie has considerable passion and conviction and Jones is simply gorgeous, while Cotten's innate weakness and vulnerability are perfect for his role. With William Dieterle's stylish direction and composer Dimitri Tiomkin plagiarising Debussy, the movie heads into a surreally romantic world of its own. AT DVD

Jennifer Jones *Jennie Appleton* • Joseph Cotten *Eben Adams* • Ethel Barrymore *Miss Spinney* • Cecil Kellaway *Mr Matthews* • David Wayne *Gus O'Toole* • Albert Sharpe *Mr Moore* • Florence Bates *Mrs Jekes* • Lillian Gish *Mother Mary of Mercy* ■ *Dir* William Dieterle • *Scr* Paul Osborn, Peter Berneis, Leonardo Bercovici, from the novel by Robert Nathan

Portrait of Maria ★★★

Drama 1943 · Mex · BW · 101mins

Romanticising the spartan splendour of the Mexican countryside, director Emilio Fernandez and ace cinematographer Gabriel Figueroa came to international attention with this tragic tale of misunderstood motives and patriarchal prejudice. Dolores Del Rio gives a luminous performance as the woman who, like her mother, is stoned by the reactionary inhabitants of pre-revolutionary Xochimilco after they wrongly surmise she has posed nude for painter Alberto Galán. DP. In Spanish with English subtitles.

Dolores Del Rio *Maria Candelaria* • Pedro Armendáriz *Lorenzo Rafael* • Alberto Galán *Pintor* • Margarita Cortés *Lupe* ■ *Dir* Emilio Fernandez • *Scr* Emilio Fernandez, Mauricio Magdaleno

A Portrait of the Artist as a Young Man ★★★★ 15

Drama 1977 · Ire · Colour · 91mins

American director Joseph Strick could never match talent to integrity, so his inability to compromise meant that attempts to film modern classics such as this one by James Joyce never lived up to his expectations. This is one of his most successful, with Bosco Hogan as the young Dubliner in an Ireland that is "the sow that eats her farrow", while John Gielgud preaches the famous hellfire sermon with the power and eloquence Strick wanted for all his films, but which he seldom achieved. TH. Contains sex scenes. DVD

Bosco Hogan *Stephen Dedalus* • TP McKenna *Simon Dedalus* • John Gielgud *Preacher* • Rosaleen Linehan *May Dedalus* • Maureen Potter *Dante* • Cecil Sheehan *Uncle Charles* ■ *Dir* Joseph Strick • *Scr* Judith Rascoe, from the novel by James Joyce

Portraits Chinois ★★★ 15

Drama 1996 · Fr/UK · Colour · 106mins

Set among the young Parisian smart set, this is a slight, but enjoyable comedy from director Martine Dugowson. At the centre of a web of interweaving plot strands is fashion designer Helena Bonham Carter, whose personal and professional contentment is threatened by pushy newcomer Romane Bohringer. Everyone in the ensemble gets their moment in the spotlight, although none can match shopaholic underachiever Elsa Zylberstein's gloriously awful cabaret routine. DP. In French with English subtitles. Contains swearing. DVD

Helena Bonham Carter *Ada* • Romane Bohringer *Lise* • Marie Trintignant *Nina* • Elsa Zylberstein *Emma* • Yvan Attal *Yves* • Sergio Castellitto *Guido* • Jean-Claude Brialy *René Sandre* ■ *Dir* Martine Dugowson • *Scr* Martine Dugowson, Peter Chase

The Poseidon Adventure ★★★★ PG

Disaster movie 1972 · US · Colour · 116mins

In this memorable calamity-at-sea epic from disaster-movie specialist Irwin Allen, an ocean liner turns turtle under a tidal wave and survivors fight their way to the ship's underside in an attempt to find an exit. The religious aspects of Paul Gallico's source novel get buried under a barrage of set pieces as director Ronald Neame cranks up the suspense and minister Gene Hackman leads a group of uptight passengers to what they hope will be their salvation. There are wonderfully poignant performances, but it's always Hackman's movie – not even the remarkable effects can upstage him. TH DVD

Gene Hackman *Reverend Frank Scott* • Ernest Borgnine *Mike Rogo* • Red Buttons *James Martin* • Carol Lynley *Nonnie Parry* • Roddy McDowall *Acres* • Stella Stevens *Linda Rogo* • Shelley Winters *Belle Rosen* • Jack Albertson *Manny Rosen* • Leslie Nielsen *Ship's captain* • Pamela Sue Martin *Susan Shelby* ■ *Dir* Ronald Neame • *Scr* Stirling Silliphant, Wendell Mayes, from the novel by Paul Gallico

Positive ID ★★★ 18

Thriller 1986 · US · Colour · 91mins

Stephanie Rascoe is a young housewife who discovers she cannot live her life as before following an assault. Instead, she takes on a new identity and proceeds to track down her attacker. This interesting thriller certainly has a different twist-in-the-tale from other movies on the same subject, and Rascoe is a convincing victim-turned-avenger. JB

Stephanie Rascoe *Julie Kenner/Bobbie King* • John Davies [John S Davies] *Don Kenner* • Steve Fromholz *Roy* • Laura Lane *Dana* • Gail Cronauer *Melissa* ■ *Dir/Scr* Andy Anderson

The Positively True Adventures of the Alleged Texas Cheerleader-Murdering Mom ★★★ 15

Comedy drama 1993 · US · Colour · 98mins

Director Michael Ritchie has had an erratic career, but here he has created a delightfully sardonic, stranger-than-fiction TV movie. Holly Hunter is the potty mom, who decides the best way to get her daughter on to the cheerleading team is murder. Ritchie exploits the comic potential of the story to the hilt and makes some neat satiric jibes at American family values. Hunter has a ball in the lead role and the talented supporting cast delivers broad comic performances. JF. Contains swearing. DVD

Holly Hunter *Wanda Holloway* • Beau Bridges *Terry Harper* • Swoosie Kurtz *Marla Harper* • Matt Frewer *Troy McKinney* • Fred Koehler [Frederick Koehler] *Shane Holloway* ■ *Dir* Michael Ritchie • *Scr* Jane Anderson

Posse ★★★

Western 1975 · US · Colour · 93mins

A rare assignment behind the cameras for Kirk Douglas, who also stars in this likeably quirky western. Bruce Dern, cast against type, plays a Robin Hood-style bandit being hunted by a marshal (Douglas) who thinks Dern's capture will give his career a much-needed boost. Douglas the director takes a no-nonsense approach to the material and draws able performances from a winning support cast. JF

Kirk Douglas *Marshal Howard Nightingale* • Bruce Dern *Jack Strawhorn* • Bo Hopkins *Wesley* • James Stacy *Hellman* • Luke Askew *Krag* • David Canary *Pensteman* ■ *Dir* Kirk Douglas • *Scr* William Roberts, Christopher Knopf, from a story by Christopher Knopf

Posse ★★★ 15

Western 1993 · US · Colour · 105mins

Mario Van Peebles's ambitious attempt to fuse the spaghetti western with 1990s black consciousness doesn't always work, but it remains a provocative and entertaining addition to the revitalised genre. Van Peebles himself plays the mean and moody leader of a disparate group of black soldiers, plus token white good guy Stephen Baldwin, who find themselves caught between a cruel, racist sheriff (Richard Jordan) and their psychopathic old colonel (Billy Zane). Van Peebles's flashy, hyperactive direction is sometimes at odds with the genre, as is some of the dialogue, but he succeeds with his astonishingly eclectic cast. Followed by *Los Locos* in 1997. JF. Contains violence, swearing and nudity. [VIDEO] DVD

Mario Van Peebles *Jessie Lee* • Stephen Baldwin *Little J* • Charles Lane (3) *Weezie* • Tiny Lister [Tom "Tiny" Lister Jr] *Obobo* • Big Daddy Kane *Father Time* • Billy Zane *Colonel Graham* • Blair Underwood *Sheriff Carver* • Melvin Van Peebles *Papa Joe* • Isaac Hayes *Cable* • Woody Strode *Storyteller* ■ *Dir* Mario Van Peebles • *Scr* Sy Richardson, Dario Scardapane

Posse from Hell ★★

Western 1961 · US · Colour · 85mins

Four convicts break out of jail and go on the rampage in a quiet orderly town called Paradise, killing the sheriff and taking a woman hostage. Local resident Audie Murphy, a former gunfighter, gathers a posse and heads off in pursuit. Not content with being a simple shoot-'em-up, this pitches itself as a deeply moral parable about the value of society and the nature of violence. This means that the action grinds to a halt while Murphy disgorges nuggets of scripted wisdom. AT

Audie Murphy *Banner Cole* • John Saxon *Seymour Kern* • Zohra Lampert *Helen Caldwell* • Ward Ramsey *Marshal Webb* • Vic Morrow *Crip* • Robert Keith (1) *Captain Brown* • Royal Dano *Uncle Billy Caldwell* • Rudolph Acosta [Rodolfo Acosta] *Johnny Caddo* • Paul Carr *Jack Wiley* • Lee Van Cleef *Leo* ■ *Dir* Herbert Coleman • *Scr* Clair Huffaker, from his novel

Les Possédées ★★★

Drama 1955 · Fr/It · BW · 97mins

A meticulous craftsman, who considered text as significant as visual signature, Charles Brabant was one of many French film-makers whose prospects were dimmed by the scathing proponents of auteur theory. This adaptation was lambasted as a typical example of *cinéma du papa*, the polished escapism that relied on literate dialogue and star performance. Yet, such was the animal magnetism of Raf Vallone, as the ugly man who exercises a fatal charm over Madeleine Robinson's household, that it scandalised contemporary audiences with its freakish eroticism. DP. In French with English subtitles.

Madeleine Robinson *Agatha* • Raf Vallone *Angelo* • Magali Noël *Pia* • Dany Carrel *Sylvia* ■ *Dir* Charles Brabant • *Scr* Charles Brabant, Maurice Clavel, from the play *The Island of Goats* by Ugo Betti

Possessed ★★★

Melodrama 1931 · US · BW · 75mins

An MGM melodrama with some hard-edged dialogue and a positively glowing Joan Crawford playing the low-class mistress of aspiring politician Clark Gable. Crawford becomes the most famous courtesan in New York as Gable puts his career on the line in a genuinely witty movie. TS

Joan Crawford *Marian Martin* • Clark Gable *Mark Whitney* • Wallace Ford *Al Mannings* • Richard "Skeets" Gallagher *Wally Stuart* • Frank Conroy *Travers* • Marjorie White *Vernice* ■ *Dir* Clarence Brown • *Scr* Lenore Coffee, from the play *The Mirage* by Edgar Selwyn

Possessed ★★ PG

Melodrama 1947 · US · BW · 103mins

Joan Crawford's second movie with the same title, this dotty study in dementia features a mature Joan deeply disturbed (and over-acting) as a guilt-ridden schizophrenic. It's pretentious psychological piffle, but nevertheless enjoyable for fans of Crawford's remarkable non-acting style. TS [VIDEO]

Joan Crawford *Louise Howell Graham* • Van Heflin *David Sutton* • Raymond Massey *Dean Graham* • Geraldine Brooks *Carol Graham* • Stanley Ridges *Dr Harvey Willard* • John Ridgely *Lieutenant Harker* • Nana Bryant *Pauline Graham* • Moroni Olsen *Dr Ames* ■ *Dir* Curtis Bernhardt • *Scr* Silvia Richards, Ranald MacDougall, from the story *One Man's Secret* by Rita Weiman

Possessed ★★

Thriller 1999 · Den/Nor · Colour · 99mins

Produced by Lars von Trier's Zentropa company, this millennial shocker starts out as a "race against time" contagion movie, in which a flesh-eating virus and an obscure case of arson take on satanic significance. Anders Ronnow-Klarlund ensures Ole Lemmeke's virologist and student girlfriend Kirsti Eline Torhaug are constantly on the move, as they shuttle between Denmark and Romania. But while he judges the jolts well, Ronnow-Klarlund fails to generate a tangible sense of evil, despite the best efforts of Udo Kier as a zodiac-obsessed cultist. DP. In Danish, Romanian and English with subtitles.

Ole Lemmeke *Soren* • Ole Ernst *Bentzon* • Udo Kier *Vincent* • Kirsti Eline Torhaug *Sarah* • Niels Anders Thorn *Jensen* • Jesper Langberg *Lyngfelt* ■ *Dir* Anders Ronnow-Klarlund • *Scr* Anders Ronnow-Klarlund, Ola Saltin

Possessed ★ 15

Horror drama 2000 · US · Colour · 105mins

Based on the "true story" of modern-day America's only documented exorcism (performed in the 1950s), this extraordinarily awful TV horror movie was co-written and directed by successful Hollywood action screenwriter, Stephen E de Souza. Timothy Dalton reaches a career low as a Catholic priest with his own personal demons, who's called upon to investigate the case of a cute child who's showing the full signs of possession. A mess. JC [VIDEO] DVD

Timothy Dalton *Father William Bowden* • Henry Czerny *Father Raymond McBride* • Jonathan Malen *Robbie Mannheim* • Christopher Plummer *Archbishop Hume* • Piper Laurie *Aunt Hanna* ■ *Dir* Steven E de Souza • *Scr* Steven E de Souza, Michael Lazarou, from the non-fiction book *Possessed: the True Story of an Exorcism* by Thomas B Allen

Possession ★★★ 18

Horror drama
1981 · Fr/W Ger · Colour · 118mins

No précis can do justice to the dizzying visuals or eccentricity of its storyline in this horror, in which disgruntled wife, Isabelle Adjani, has an affair with a tentacled fungoid creature and produces a spitting image of her husband, Sam Neill. Any number of interpretations are valid. Or was Andrzej Zulawski simply seeking to disturb with the explosive encounters, sickening blood-letting and the grandest of *Guignol* symbolism? DP. Contains violence, swearing and sex scenes [VIDEO]

Isabelle Adjani *Anna/Helen* • Sam Neill *Marc* • Margit Carstensen *Margie* • Heinz Bennent *Heinrich* ■ *Dir* Andrzej Zulawski • *Scr* Andrzej Zulawski, Frédéric Tuten

Possession ★★ 12

Romantic drama
2002 · US/UK · Colour · 97mins

This wispy, time-shifting romance represents a clumsy change of pace for edgy director Neil LaBute. His adaptation of AS Byatt's 1990 Booker Prize-winning novel evokes neither the poetry nor the passion of its source, while Gwyneth Paltrow and LaBute regular Aaron Eckhart phone in their drippy roles as literary sleuths researching the amorous secrets of bisexual Victorian poet Jennifer Ehle and her married lover Jeremy Northam. Low on mystery and emotional engagement, but high on clichés and chocolate-box settings. AJ [VIDEO] DVD

Gwyneth Paltrow *Maud Bailey* • Aaron Eckhart *Roland Michell* • Jeremy Northam *Randolph Henry Ash* • Jennifer Ehle *Christabel LaMotte* • Lena Headey *Blanche Glover* • Toby Stephens *Dr Fergus Wolfe* • Tom Hickey *Professor Blackadder* • Trevor Eve *Prof Mortimer Cropper* • Tom Hollander *Euan* • Graham Crowden *Sir George Bailey* • Anna Massey *Lady Bailey* ■ *Dir* Neil LaBute • *Scr* David Henry Hwang, Laura Jones, Neil LaBute, from the novel by AS Byatt

The Possession of Joel Delaney ★★★

Supernatural horror
1971 · US · Colour · 107mins

For some, this occult thriller was superior to *The Exorcist*, but time has not been kind and it now feels ponderously slow while its modishly violent climax seems to belong to another film. Through the eyes of his rich bitch sister Shirley MacLaine, we see the gradual disintegration of Perry King, possessed by the spirit of a Puerto Rican psycho with a penchant for decapitation. The horror is dignified by social comment, although the message is garbled, but the script and performances are strong. DM

Shirley MacLaine *Norah Benson* • Perry King *Joel Delaney* • Michael Hordern *Justin Lorenz* • Edmundo Rivera Alvarez *Don Pedro* • Robert Burr *Ted Benson* ■ *Dir* Waris Hussein • *Scr* Matt Robinson, Grimes Grice [Albert Maltz], from the novel by Ramona Stewart

Possible Worlds ★★★ 15

Science-fiction mystery
2000 · Can · Colour · 88mins

A theatrical legend, but yet to convince wholly on film, Québecois Robert Lepage makes his English-language debut with this highly stylised slice of cerebral sci-fi. This adaptation is also an identity drama, a whodunnit and a philosophical romance, so it's easy to lose sight of the complex ideas and intricate scene shifts. Central to the conceit is the murder of Thomas McCamus. But discovering who stole his brain matters less than whether he'll find love – in one of several parallel universes – with the chameleon-like Tilda Swinton. DP [VIDEO] DVD

Tilda Swinton *Joyce* • Tom McCamus *George Barber* • Sean McCann *Inspector Berkley* • Gabriel Gascon *Kleber/Doctor* • Rick Miller *Williams* ■ *Dir* Robert Lepage • *Scr* John Mighton, from his play

Possums ★★★

Sports drama 1998 · US · Colour · 97mins

A charming slice of small-town life that had only a limited release in the States, despite enthusiastic receptions at a number of festivals. Country singer/songwriter Mac Davis stars as the ardent fan of a school football team (the Possums of the title) who are on the brink of being disbanded. Davis starts broadcasting fictitious results on a local radio station, and soon the Possums are blazing an imaginary trail to the top of the league – until reality intervenes. Clever, and handled with a light touch by first-time director J Max Burnett. RT

Mac Davis *Will Clark* • Cynthia Sikes *Elizabeth Clark* • Gregory Coolidge *Jake Malloy* • Andrew Prine *Charlie Lawton* • Dennis Burkley *Orville Moss* • Jerry Haynes *Bob* • Barry Switzer *Prattville Coach* ■ *Dir/Scr* J Max Burnett

Post Mortem ★★

Psychological drama
1999 · Can · Colour · 92mins

This rigidly controlled thriller from Québec made little international impact despite domestic acclaim. Divided into three acts, the story slowly intertwines the seemingly separate lives of lone parent Sylvie Moreau, who feeds her daughter by mugging gullible losers, and Gabriel Arcand, a self-contained morgue assistant with a passion for jazz. But, while debutant director Louis Bélanger's manipulation of audience expectation is assured, the final resolution feels forced. DP. In French with English subtitles.

Gabriel Arcand *Ghislain O'Brien* • Sylvie Moreau *Linda Faucher* • Hélène Loiselle *Madame Faucher* • Sarah Lecompte-Bergeron *Charlotte Faucher* • Ghislain Taschereau *Marc* ■ *Dir/Scr* Louis Bélanger

P

Postcards from America ★★★ 18

Biographical drama
1994 · UK/US · Colour · 87mins

This moving and adroitly made feature is based on the life of New York multi-media artist and Aids activist David Wojnarowicz, who died in 1992. Divided into three segments (with the lead shifting between Olmo and Michael Tighe, and James Lyons), the film moves from his abused childhood, through a period of prostitution and petty crime, to an adulthood of audacious creativity, emotional instability and casual sex. This stylised drama is directed by Wojnarowicz's sometime British collaborator Steve McLean. DP. Contains violence and substance abuse. [VIDEO]

James Lyons *David Wojnarowicz* • Michael Tighe *Teenage David* • Olmo Tighe *Young David* • Michael Imperioli *The hustler* • Michael Ringer *Father* • Maggie Low *Mother* ■ *Dir* Steve McLean • *Scr* Steve McLean, from the books *Close to the Knives* and *Memories That Smell like Gasoline* by David Wojnarowicz

Postcards from the Edge ★★★★ 15

Comedy drama 1990 · US · Colour · 97mins

It bears little resemblance to Carrie Fisher's screamingly funny bestseller, yet director Mike Nichols's grand tour through "Hollywood Babylon" still emerges as a savage showbiz satire.

Meryl Streep is the selfish actress in celebrity detox who moves back home with her overbearing mother (Shirley MacLaine) in this thinly-veiled account of Fisher's own poignant relationship with real-life mother Debbie Reynolds. Both stars rise to the bitchy one-liner occasion and turn on the glitz, glamour and grit. AJ. Contains swearing and drug abuse. DVD

Meryl Streep *Suzanne Vale* • Shirley MacLaine *Doris Mann* • Dennis Quaid *Jack Falkner* • Gene Hackman *Lowell* • Richard Dreyfuss *Dr Frankenthal* • Rob Reiner *Joe Pierce* • Mary Wickes *Grandma* • Conrad Bain *Grandpa* • Annette Bening *Evelyn Ames* • Simon Callow *Simon Asquith* ■ *Dir* Mike Nichols • *Scr* Carrie Fisher, from her novel

Il Postino ★★★★★ U

Romantic drama 1994 · It/Fr · Colour · 103mins

Massimo Troisi stars as a shy postman on an Italian island whose only port of call is the residence of legendary exiled Chilean poet Pablo Neruda (Philippe Noiret). Too timid to talk to the local beauty (Maria Grazia Cucinotta), the postman turns to his new-found friend for poetic assistance to win her heart. Wonderful contrasting performances from the two stars, beautiful scenery and understated direction from British film-maker Michael Radford give this delightfully different international gem the radiance of a Mediterranean *Local Hero*. In a tragic footnote, Troisi died the day after completing this life-affirming movie. JC. In Italian with English subtitles. DVD

Massimo Troisi *Mario* • Philippe Noiret *Pablo Neruda* • Maria Grazia Cucinotta *Beatrice Russo* • Linda Moretti *Donna Rosa* • Renato Scarpa *Telegraph operator* ■ *Dir* Michael Radford • *Scr* Anna Pavignano, Michael Radford, Furio Scarpelli, Giacomo Scarpelli, Massimo Troisi, from a story by Furio Scarpelli, Giacomo Scarpelli, from the novel *Il Postino di Neruda* by Antonio Skarmeta

The Postman ★ 15

Futuristic epic 1997 · US · Colour · 170mins

There's more than a touch of vanity about Kevin Costner's overlong futuristic epic. Costing more than $100 million, it has gone down as one of Hollywood's biggest flops, in which Costner drifts across a post-apocalypse America, claiming to be a postman with 15-year-old mail. A complete dud. AT. Contains violence, swearing, sex scene, nudity. DVD

Kevin Costner *The Postman* • Will Patton *Bethlehem* • Larenz Tate *Ford* • Olivia Williams *Abby* • James Russo *Idaho* • Tom Petty *Bridge City mayor* • Daniel Von Bargen *Sheriff Briscoe* ■ *Dir* Kevin Costner • *Scr* Eric Roth, Brian Helgeland, from the novel by David Brin

The Postman Always Rings Twice ★★★★★ PG

Classic film noir 1946 · US · BW · 108mins

Sweaty and sensuous, this MGM *film noir* remains utterly electrifying today, thanks to the riveting sexual chemistry between its stars, Lana Turner and John Garfield, and Tay Garnett's tense directorial style. Garnett clearly understood the world of James M Cain's original novel, though he was forced to circumvent certain sections because of the censorship demands of the day. Despite competition from several other movies, notably Luchino Visconti's *Ossessione* and Bob Rafelson's 1981 film, this has proved to be the definitive interpretation of the novel, and the Turner/Garfield coupling the most incandescent – their first meeting remains a classic moment of screen desire. TS DVD

Lana Turner *Cora Smith* • John Garfield *Frank Chambers* • Cecil Kellaway *Nick Smith* • Hume Cronyn *Arthur Keats* • Leon Ames *Kyle Sackett* • Audrey Totter *Madge Gorland* ■ *Dir* Tay Garnett • *Scr* Harry Ruskin, Niven Busch, from the novel by James M Cain • *Costume Designer* Irene

The Postman Always Rings Twice ★★★ 18

Crime drama 1981 · US · Colour · 116mins

Following James M Cain's novel more closely than was allowed in the classic 1946 version, Bob Rafelson's take on the murderous morality fable opts for explicit action over extra adulterous tension. Despite luminous performances from Depression drifter Jack Nicholson and young wife Jessica Lange as the plotters-in-lust, the loose ends and even looser ending point to a below par effort from Rafelson, and the final result is not up to the standard of his masterly work with Nicholson on *Five Easy Pieces* and *The King of Marvin Gardens*. AJ. Contains violence, swearing and sex scenes. DVD

Jack Nicholson *Frank Chambers* • Jessica Lange *Cora Papadakis* • John Colicos *Nick Papadakis* • Christopher Lloyd *Salesman* • Michael Lerner *Katz* • John P Ryan *Kennedy* • Anjelica Huston *Madge* • William Traylor *Sackett* ■ *Dir* Bob Rafelson • *Scr* David Mamet, from the novel by James M Cain

Postman's Knock ★ U

Comedy 1961 · UK · BW · 86mins

One of two comedies (the other is *Invasion Quartet*) created for Spike Milligan by John Briley and Jack Trevor Story, talented writers not noted for their eccentric humour. Consequently, the brilliant Goon flounders in the conventional, happy-go-lucky tale of a village postman who is transferred to London and comes up against mail robbers and streamlined sorting equipment. The supporting cast is, disastrously, funnier than the star. DM

Spike Milligan *Harold Petts* • Barbara Shelley *Jean* • John Wood *PC Woods* • Ronald Adam *Fordyce* • Wilfrid Lawson *Postman* • Miles Malleson *Psychiatrist* • Warren Mitchell *Rupert* ■ *Dir* Robert Lynn • *Scr* John Briley, Jack Trevor Story, Spike Milligan, George Barclay [Ronald Kinnoch], from a story by Jack Trevor Story

Postmark for Danger ★★

Murder mystery 1955 · UK · BW · 84mins

This B-movie, derived from a TV serial by Francis Durbridge called *Portrait of Alison*, was originally released under that title in cinemas. Robert Beatty investigates the mysterious death of his brother, a trail that leads to a smuggling ring and another brother, played by William Sylvester. Predictable and only moderately gripping. AT

Terry Moore *Alison Ford* • Robert Beatty *Tim Forrester* • William Sylvester *Dave Forrester* • Josephine Griffin *Jill Stewart* • Geoffrey Keen *Inspector Colby* • Allan Cuthbertson *Henry Carmichael* ■ *Dir* Guy Green • *Scr* Guy Green, Ken Hughes, from the TV series *Portrait of Alison* by Francis Durbridge

Postmortem ★★ 18

Crime thriller 1999 · US/UK · Colour · 105mins

In terms of personnel, this has to go down as one of the oddest Scottish films in recent years. Director Albert Pyun, best known for his straight-to-video martial arts thrillers, here links up with Hollywood bad boy Charlie Sheen for a moody and surprisingly gritty thriller set in and around Glasgow. Sheen plays a boozy American ex-cop, now writing "true crime" books, who finds himself drawn into the hunt for a serial killer playing mind games with the police. JF Contains violence, swearing. DVD

Charles Sheen [Charlie Sheen] *James McGregor* • Michael Halsey *Inspector Balantine* • Stephen McCole *George Statler* • Gary Lewis *Wallace* ■ *Dir* Albert Pyun • *Scr* John Lowry Lamb, Robert McDonnell

Il Posto ★★★★ U

Comedy drama 1961 · It · BW · 99mins

True to his neorealist roots, former documentarist Ermanno Olmi employed a wholly non-professional cast for this vaguely autobiographical insight into the hostile world of work. As the provincial whose delight at finding a job in a Milanese office blinds him to the dehumanising effect of the daily urban grind, the impassive Sandro Panzeri proves himself to be a clown in the Buster Keaton mould as he performs mundane tasks with eager pride in the hope of impressing sympathetic colleague Loredano Detto. Yet it's Olmi's attention to satirical detail and his gentle pacing that make this episodic comedy so engaging. DP. In Italian with English subtitles.

Sandro Panzeri *Domenico* • Loredano Detto *Antonietta* ■ *Dir/Scr* Ermanno Olmi

The Pot Carriers ★★★

Comedy drama 1962 · UK · BW · 84mins

Part social drama, part knockabout comedy, this is an odd but entertaining account of British prison life in the 1950s. It's based on a 1960 TV play by Mike Watts, who used real-life experience for his story of an old lag (Ronald Fraser, the only member of the TV cast to reprise his role) who befriends new inmate Paul Massie and shows him the ropes. The depiction of prison routine still has an impact. DM

Ronald Fraser *Redband* • Paul Massie *James Rainbow* • Carole Lesley *Wendy* • Dennis Price *Smooth Tongue* • Paul Rogers *Governor* ■ *Dir* Peter Graham Scott • *Scr* Mike Watts, TJ Morrison, from the play by Mike Watts

Pot Luck ★★★ 15

Comedy 2002 · Fr/Sp · Colour · 121mins

This mischievous study of the national characteristics that stand in the way of genuine European integration is too often sidetracked by melodramatic subplots. Cédric Klapisch manipulates his ensemble cast with great skill, particularly when the cosmopolitan students sharing a Barcelona apartment set to gossiping and squabbling. But the pace begins to flag once attention shifts to Romain Duris's relationships with Parisian girlfriend Audrey Tautou and neglected housewife Judith Godrèche. DP. In French, Spanish, Catalan, English and Danish with subtitles.

Romain Duris *Xavier* • Judith Godrèche *Anne-Sophie* • Audrey Tautou *Martine* • Cécile de France *Isabelle* • Kelly Reilly *Wendy* • Kevin Bishop *William* • Federico D'Anna *Alessandro* • Barnaby Metschurat *Tobias* • Cristina Brondo *Soledad* • Christian Pagh *Lars* ■ *Dir/Scr* Cédric Klapisch

Pot o' Gold ★★ U

Musical comedy 1941 · US · BW · 85mins

James Stewart sings with Horace Heidt and his Orchestra on his uncle Charles Winninger's radio show, while falling for Mary Gordon's lovely daughter Paulette Goddard. That's all there is to the plot, really, and Stewart later publicly declared this the worst of his films. Viewed today, it has a quaint period charm, though the songs don't exactly light any fires. The title was also the name of a popular long-running radio show featuring bandleader Heidt, and this film was really made to capitalise on his appeal. TS DVD

James Stewart *Jimmy Haskell* • Paulette Goddard *Molly McCorkle* • Charles Winninger *CJ Haskell* • Mary Gordon *Ma McCorkle* • Frank Melton *Jasper* • Jed Prouty *Mr Louderman* • Dick Hogan *Willie McCorkle* ■ *Dir* George Marshall • *Scr* Walter DeLeon, from a story by Monte Brice, Andrew Bennison, Harry Tugend, from an idea by Haydn Roth Evans, Robert Brilmayer

Pound Puppies and the Legend of Big Paw ★★ U

Animated adventure
1988 · US · Colour · 73mins

Following in the pawprints of *The Care Bears Movie* and *My Little Pony*, this cartoon feature was made simply to sell more pups. Clearly not enough time or money was put into the project, with the animation way below the standard you'd expect from a children's TV show. The storyline is quite fun, however, as the cute canines take on a power-crazed villain who's searching for the two halves of a magical bone that will enable him to rule the world. There's a good doo-wop soundtrack, too. DP

George Rose *McNasty* • BJ Ward *Whopper* • Ruth Buzzi *Nose Marie* • Nancy Cartwright *Bright Eyes* ■ *Dir* Pierre DeCelles • *Scr* Jim Carlson, Terrence McDonnell

Pour Rire! ★★★

Comedy 1996 · Fr · Colour · 100mins

Talented Jean-Pierre Léaud has not always chosen his roles with care. However, as the cuckolded husband in Lucas Belvaux's assured comedy of manners, he's given free rein to demonstrate the offbeat amiability that illuminated the *Nouvelle Vague*. In a time of impermanent relationships, Léaud's marriage appears rock solid, until wife Ornella Muti confesses her affair with sports photographer Antoine Chappey. This isn't a visually innovative film, but the humour is sophisticated and the leads make splendid adversaries. DP. A French language film.

Jean-Pierre Léaud *Nicolas* • Ornella Muti *Alice* • Tonie Marshall *Juliette* • Antoine Chappey *Gaspard* ■ *Dir/Scr* Lucas Belvaux

Pourquoi Pas! ★★★

Drama 1977 · Fr · Colour · 93mins

Coline Serreau directs this gently subversive utopian tale, in which she inverts the traditional ménage à trois by having having homemaker Sami Frey, breadwinner Christine Murillo and musician Mario Gonzales take on a fourth member in Nicole Jamet. However, their idiosyncratic idyll is disturbed by the intrusion of police inspector Michel Aumont, whose investigation into an accident results in his having an affair himself. DP. In French with English subtitles.

Sami Frey *Fernand* • Mario Gonzalez *Louis* • Christine Murillo *Alexa* • Nicole Jamet *Sylvie* • Michel Aumont *Inspector* • Alain Salomon *Roger* ■ *Dir/Scr* Coline Serreau

Pourquoi Pas Moi? ★★ 15

Comedy 1999 · Fr/Sp/Swi · Colour · 90mins

A whiff of old-fashioned theatricality pervades this determinedly modern "glad to be gay" comedy. Just about everyone harbours a guilty secret or a pernicious prejudice, as a quartet of comic-book artists and their parents gather for a come-clean dinner date. Sadly, Stéphane Giusti's screenplay is so lacking in wit and surprise that each revelation arrives with a thud of inevitability, and the performances are equally predictable. DP. In French with English subtitles. DVD

Amira Casar *Camille* • Julie Gayet *Eve* • Bruno Putzulu *Nick* • Alexandra London *Ariane* • Carmen Chaplin *Lili* ■ *Dir/Scr* Stéphane Giusti

Powaqqatsi ★★★ U

Documentary 1988 · US · Colour · 98mins

Having censured the old world order for allowing itself to be enslaved by

P

modern technology in *Koyaanisqatsi*, director Godfrey Reggio condemns it for the merciless manner in which it exploits the Third World in this heartfelt eco-documentary, whose title comes from the Hopi language word for "parasite". As in the original, it is an ambitious collage of images (some stunning, some shocking and some straining to make their point), combined with the futuristic music of Philip Glass. Ultimately it's an unsatisfactory exercise, as Reggio too often states the obvious and settles for gloss when grit might have been more effective. DP [VIDEO] DVD

Dir Godfrey Reggio • *Scr* Godfrey Reggio, Ken Richards • *Music* Philip Glass

Powder ★★★★ 12

Fantasy drama 1995 · US · Colour · 107mins

This extremely moving fantasy drama tells the tale of a teenager whose mother was struck by lightning during labour, giving him a ghostly white appearance, an extraordinary intellect and miraculous powers. Sean Patrick Flanery delivers a wonderfully sympathetic central performance as the young misfit whose unique abilities generate feelings of hostility in the small-minded townsfolk. There's fine support , too, from Jeff Goldblum, Mary Steenburgen and an unusually expressive Lance Henriksen. Victor Salva's intelligent script and assured direction take some fairly familiar themes to some quite unexpected places. JC. Contains violence and swearing. [VIDEO] DVD

Mary Steenburgen *Jessie Caldwell* • Sean Patrick Flanery *Jeremy Reed, "Powder"* • Lance Henriksen *Sheriff Barnum* • Jeff Goldblum *Donald Ripley* • Brandon Smith *Duncan* • Bradford Tatum *John Box* • Susan Tyrrell *Maxine* ■ *Dir/Scr* Victor Salva

Powder River ★★ U

Western 1953 · US · Colour · 77mins

This taut little western, made with some style, features a top-notch, albeit second-string, cast. Rory Calhoun is on the right side of the law for once, looking for a killer, and Cameron Mitchell is excellent as the doctor who becomes his pal. Corinne Calvet makes a fetching heroine and Penny Edwards also scores as the other woman in the picture. Director Louis King doesn't get in the way. TS

Rory Calhoun *Chino Bullock* • Corinne Calvet *Frenchie* • Cameron Mitchell *Mitch Hardin* • Penny Edwards *Debbie* • Carl Betz *Loney Hogan* • John Dehner *Harvey Logan* ■ *Dir* Louis King • *Scr* Geoffrey Homes [Daniel Mainwaring], from an idea by Sam Hellman, from a novel by Stuart N Lake

The Power ★★

Science-fiction thriller
1968 · US · Colour · 109mins

A number of B-league players (George Hamilton, Suzanne Pleshette, Michael Rennie) can't invest much conviction or authority in this science-fiction tale about a group of scientists who discover that one of them can kill by willpower alone. Director Byron Haskin adds some clever touches of menace, but authenticity is sorely lacking. TH

George Hamilton *Jim Tanner* • Suzanne Pleshette *Margery Lansing* • Richard Carlson *NE Van Zandt* • Yvonne De Carlo *Sally Hallson* • Earl Holliman *Talbot Scott* • Gary Merrill *Mark Corlane* • Michael Rennie *Arthur Nordlund* ■ *Dir* Byron Haskin • *Scr* John Gay, from the novel by Frank M Robinson • *Music* Miklos Rozsa

Power ★★★ 15

Drama 1986 · US · Colour · 105mins

Not quite as sophisticated or as clever as it thinks it is, this political drama nevertheless has much to recommend it, despite cursory reviews at the time from critics who were snobby about its glamorous media-based theme. Newly greying Richard Gere plays a public relations manipulator, heading for a welcome comeuppance, undeterred by warnings from his alcoholic mentor (another of those seemingly effortless performances from the redoubtable Gene Hackman). This is eminently watchable nonsense, smoothly controlled by director Sidney Lumet, though it sank without trace on its theatrical release. TS [VIDEO]

Richard Gere *Pete St John* • Julie Christie *Ellen Freeman* • Gene Hackman *Wilfred Buckley* • Kate Capshaw *Sydney Betterman* • Denzel Washington *Arnold Billings* • Michael Learned *Governor Andrea Stannard* • JT Walsh *Jerome Cade* ■ *Dir* Sidney Lumet • *Scr* David Himmelstein

The Power and the Glory ★★

Drama 1933 · US · BW · 76mins

This is the movie that made a massive impact on the young Orson Welles, telling the story of a railway magnate's life in a series of non-chronological flashbacks, with different characters revealing different aspects of the great man himself. Sound familiar? Well, *Citizen Kane* this isn't. William K Howard's direction is turgid in the extreme and Preston Sturges's script is underdeveloped. This can't help but seem historically interesting, but it's something of an endurance test. TS

Spencer Tracy *Tom Garner* • Colleen Moore *Sally* • Ralph Morgan *Henry* • Helen Vinson *Eve* • Clifford Jones [Philip Trent] *Tom Garner Jr* • Henry Kolker *Mr Borden* ■ *Dir* William K Howard • *Scr* Preston Sturges

The Power and the Prize ★★

Drama 1956 · US · BW · 98mins

This drama about the ruthless nature of American big business is relatively weak stuff. Robert Taylor is rather too old to convince as the executive being groomed by Burl Ives's tycoon to be his successor. Elisabeth Mueller is unexciting, but there is sterling supporting work from Mary Astor, Charles Coburn and Cedric Hardwicke. AE

Robert Taylor (1) *Cliff Barton* • Elisabeth Mueller *Miriam Linka* • Burl Ives *George Salt* • Charles Coburn *Guy Eliot* • Cedric Hardwicke *Mr Carew* • Mary Astor *Mrs George Salt* ■ *Dir* Henry Koster • *Scr* Robert Ardrey, from the novel by Howard Swiggett

Power of Attorney ★ 18

Crime drama 1994 · US · Colour · 92mins

A preposterous script leaves a talented cast floundering in this botched gangster drama. Elias Koteas plays a lawyer who improbably sells his soul to public enemy number one, the larger-than-life mobster Danny Aiello. It's hard to work up much enthusiasm about whether he will rediscover his conscience in time, while the finale itself beggars belief. JF [VIDEO] DVD

Danny Aiello *Joseph Scassi* • Elias Koteas *Paul Diehl* • Rae Dawn Chong *Joan Armstrong* ■ *Dir* Howard Himelstein • *Scr* Jeff Barmash, George Erschbamer

The Power of One ★★★ 15

Period drama 1991 · US · Colour · 121mins

A solid and gritty adaptation of Bryce Courtenay's rites-of-passage novel set in South Africa in the 1930s and 1940s. Stephen Dorff stars as an outsider whose friendship, as a young boy, with tutor Armin Mueller-Stahl and prisoner Morgan Freeman inspires him to fight against racial injustice. Dorff gives a mature performance, but he struggles to carry the action, while his experienced co-stars never put a foot wrong. John G Avildsen handles the boxing scenes with some skill, but his grasp of political discourse and teenage romance is less assured. DP. Contains violence and swearing. [VIDEO]

Stephen Dorff *P K, aged 18* • Morgan Freeman *Geel Piet* • Armin Mueller-Stahl *Doc* • John Gielgud *Headmaster St John* • Fay Masterson *Maria Marais* ■ *Dir* John G Avildsen • *Scr* Robert Mark Kamen, from the novel by Bryce Courtenay

Power Play ★★ 18

Thriller 1978 · Can/UK · Colour · 97mins

This is a confused thriller in which an international cast struggles to get to grips with an uninspired script about a power struggle in an unnamed country. Peter O'Toole, Donald Pleasence and David Hemmings bring class to the proceedings, but for the most part it is entirely forgettable. JF [VIDEO]

Peter O'Toole *Colonel Zeller* • David Hemmings *Colonel Anthony Narriman* • Donald Pleasence *Blair* • Barry Morse *Dr Jean Rousseau* ■ *Dir* Martyn Burke • *Scr* Martyn Burke, from a novel by Edward N Luttwak

Power Play ★★ 18

Erotic thriller 1998 · US · Colour · 87mins

No one can touch Shannon Tweed when it comes to erotic thrillers. Unlike so many of her younger competitors, she's not simply cast for her physical attributes, and here she brings a Cruella De Vil-like glee to her villainy, as she schemes and seduces her way to ill-gotten – and temporary – wealth. Tweed's gold-digging is rooted in the *femme fatale* tradition of *film noir* and she has long deserved wider recognition. DP [VIDEO]

Shannon Tweed *Jacqueline Knight* • Jim Richer *Steve Ganse* • Danielle Ciardi *Candice Alcott* • Bryan Kent *Benjamin Alcott* • Ron McCoy *Max DeLaine* ■ *Dir* Chris Baugh • *Scr* Chris Baugh, Geri Cudia Barger

Power Trip ★★★★

Documentary
2003 · US/Georgia · Colour · 86mins

In 1999, AES Corp, the American giant owner of power, bought the Georgian electricity distribution company, Telasi. Power had been free in the former Soviet Union and, so, a battle began between the US corporation (which was investing heavily in modernising a crumbling network), the government of Eduard Shevardnadze and the ordinary citizens of Tbilisi who were suddenly faced with monthly bills that far exceeded their average wage. Employing an impressive range of sources, director Paul Devlin deserves enormous credit for exploring this combustible situation with such humour and impartiality, especially as the situation threatens to descend into chaos and violence. DP. In English and Georgian with English subtitles.

Dir Paul Devlin

The Powerpuff Girls ★★★ PG

Animated action comedy
2002 · US · Colour · 70mins

Short and sweet has always been the strength of Cartoon Network's *Powerpuff Girls*. So it's to the credit of director and original series creator Craig McCracken that he has managed to turn a bite-sized animated format into a convincing feature-length cartoon. He does so by making a prequel to the programme, concentrating on the superhero sisters' origins and how they learnt to use their special powers to crack crime and take on lab-monkey-turned-megalomaniac Mojo Jojo. Brought winningly to life with retro-style animation in ice-cream shades, the bubbly confection is easy on the eye and the mind. SF [VIDEO] DVD

Catherine Cavadini [Cathy Cavadini] *Blossom* • Tara Strong [Tara Charendoff] *Bubbles* • EG Daily [Elizabeth Daily] *Buttercup* • Roger L Jackson *Mojo Jojo* • Tom Kane *Professor Utonium* • Tom Kenny *Mayor/Narrator* • Jennifer Hale *Ms Keane* ■ *Dir* Craig McCracken • *Scr* Craig McCracken, Charlie Bean, Lauren Faust, Paul Rudish, Don Shank, from characters created by Craig McCracken

Powwow Highway ★★★ 15

Drama 1988 · UK/US · Colour · 87mins

A film of great warmth and easy-going morality, which follows two men as they travel to New Mexico in an old Buick – one is a philosophical Cheyenne, the other a fiery activist. In the lead roles unknowns Gary Farmer and A Martinez deliver performances of charm and understanding. A courageous film that deserves to be better known, as does its director, Jonathan Wacks. TS. Contains some violence and swearing. [VIDEO]

A Martinez *Buddy Red Bow* • Gary Farmer *Philbert Bono* • Amanda Wyss *Rabbit Layton* • Joanelle Nadine Romero *Bonnie Red Bow* • Sam Vlahos *Chief Joseph* ■ *Dir* Jonathan Wacks • *Scr* Janet Heaney, Jean Stawarz, from the novel by David Seals

Practical Magic ★★ 12

Romantic black comedy
1998 · US · Colour · 99mins

Nicole Kidman and Sandra Bullock star as two sisters who are descended from witches in this uneven romance. Kidman is the wilder sibling, while Bullock is the home-loving store owner who falls for Aidan Quinn, the detective who investigates when Kidman's abusive boyfriend disappears. Director Griffin Dunne ultimately fails to make either a moving comedy romance or a funny romantic comedy. JB. Contains some violence and swearing. [VIDEO] DVD

Sandra Bullock *Sally Owens* • Nicole Kidman *Gillian Owens* • Stockard Channing *Aunt Frances* • Dianne Wiest *Aunt Jet* • Aidan Quinn *Gary Hallet* • Goran Visnjic *Jimmy Angelov* ■ *Dir* Griffin Dunne • *Scr* Robin Swicord, Akiva Goldsman, Adam Brooks, from the novel by Alice Hoffman

Practically Yours ★★ U

Second World War romantic comedy
1944 · US · BW · 89mins

Claudette Colbert and Fred MacMurray co-star for the umpteenth time in what proved an unworthy swansong to the sparkling Colbert's 16-year tenure at Paramount. The tale of a young woman who suffers from a vivid and over-romantic imagination and comes to believe she is the fiancée of a supposedly dead fighter pilot, can be summed up in one word: drivel. It's a tribute to the expertise of the stars that parts are perfectly tolerable. RK

Claudette Colbert *Peggy Martin* • Fred MacMurray *Lt SG Daniel Bellamy* • Gil Lamb *Albert Beagell* • Cecil Kellaway *Marvin P Meglin* • Robert Benchley *Judge Oscar Stimson* • Rosemary DeCamp *Ellen Macy* • Yvonne De Carlo *Employee* ■ *Dir* Mitchell Leisen • *Scr* Norman Krasna,

Praise Marx and Pass the Ammunition ★★★

Political comedy 1968 · UK · Colour · 89mins

Do not be deterred by this formidable-looking piece of political propaganda, made for virtually nothing and originally seen by virtually no one. Although it is part agitprop, with lots of facts and figures on social deprivation, it is, as the title suggests, mostly satire and takes amusing swipes at a Swinging Sixties stereotype, the Marxist-Leninist revolutionary with noble ideals and feet of clay. Partly shot during the Paris student riots, it is a fascinating testament to long-lost hopes. DM

John Thaw *Dom* • Edina Ronay *Lucy* • Louis Mahoney *Julius* • Anthony Villaroel *Arthur* •

P

Helen Fleming *Clara* ■ *Dir* Maurice Hatton • *Scr* Maurice Hatton, from an idea by Michael Wood, Maurice Hatton

The Pram ★★★

Drama 1963 · Swe · Colour · 93mins

Bo Widerberg's feature debut, which drew favourable comparisons with Ingmar Bergman, François Truffaut and Jean-Luc Godard. Inger Taube gives a truly Bergmanesque performance as an aimless young girl unable to decide between a dull, dependable friend and a wannabe pop singer. Using many of the tricks associated with the French New Wave, Widerberg draws us into the heart of his tale, while passing astute asides on Swedish society. DP. In Swedish with English subtitles.

Inger Taube *Britt* • Thommy Berggren *Bjorn* • Lars Passgård *Robban* ■ *Dir/Scr* Bo Widerberg

Prancer ★★★ U

Christmas drama 1989 · US · Colour · 98mins

A charming and disarming family film. Rebecca Harrell plays a nine-year-old girl, recovering from the death of her mother, who finds an injured reindeer and thinks it belongs to Santa Claus. Unfortunately, her grief-stricken father (Sam Elliott) is struggling to save their farm from the bailiffs, and has little patience with his daughter's attempt to nurse the beast. Sentimental without being mawkish, with the grown-ups given as much character as the children, this is lump-in-the-throat stuff from start to finish. TH [video] DVD

Sam Elliott *John Riggs* • Rebecca Harrell *Jessica Riggs* • Cloris Leachman *Mrs McFarland* • Rutanya Alda *Aunt Sarah* ■ *Dir* John Hancock • *Scr* Greg Taylor, from his story • *Music* Maurice Jarre

Prancer Returns ★★ U

Christmas fantasy drama
2001 · Can/US · Colour · 86mins

It's something of a surprise to see veteran hard man Jack Palance getting into the festive spirit, but he lends a certain credibility to this sequel to the 1989 film. Here, a lonely boy believes that the deer he has found in the forest near his home belongs to Santa and vows to return it to the North Pole. Gavin Fink acquits himself well as the misunderstood misfit, but the sense of magic is missing. DP [video] DVD

John Corbett *Tom Sullivan* • Stacy Edwards *Denise Holton* • Michael O'Keefe *Mr Klock* • avin Fink *Charlie Holton* • Jack Palance *Old Man Richards* • Robert Clark *Ryan Holton* ■ *Dir* Joshua Butler • *Scr* Greg Taylor

A Prayer for the Dying ★★★ 15

Crime thriller 1987 · UK · Colour · 103mins

Sadly, those involved in this political thriller could never decide what they wanted to make of Jack Higgins's novel about the moral dilemma of a priest unable to shop an IRA terrorist because he has identified himself in the confessional. The end result works relatively well as a fast-paced action adventure, but it is certainly shallow and melodramatic, and Bob Hoskins is hard to take as the priest. As the terrorist, Mickey Rourke was also unpopular, though his Belfast accent isn't at all bad. DM [video] DVD

Mickey Rourke *Martin Fallon* • Bob Hoskins *Father Da Costa* • Alan Bates *Jack Meehan* • Liam Neeson *Liam Docherty* • Sammi Davis *Anna* ■ *Dir* Mike Hodges • *Scr* Edmund Ward, Martin Lynch, from the novel by Jack Higgins

Prayer of the Rollerboys ★★ 15

Futuristic adventure
1990 · US/Jpn · Colour · 90mins

In a future where the American economy has failed, Los Angeles is run by a group of rollerblading junior fascists known as the Rollerboys. Standing against them is Corey Haim, a pizza delivery boy who used to be a friend of the Rollerboys' leader Christopher Collet. Patricia Arquette plays Haim's love interest, and the action scenes are sometimes exciting. All rather silly. ST [video]

Corey Haim *Griffin* • Patricia Arquette *Casey* • Christopher Collet *Gary Lee* • JC Quinn *Jaworski* • Julius Harris *Speedbagger* • Devin Clark *Miltie* • Mark Pellegrino *Bingo* ■ *Dir* Rick King • *Scr* W Peter Iliff

The Preacher's Wife ★★★ U

Romantic fantasy
1996 · US · Colour · 118mins

This 1990s version of *The Bishop's Wife* has Denzel Washington as the angel sent down to save the marriage of pastor Courtney B Vance and his gospel-singing wife (Whitney Houston), as well as restoring Vance's wavering faith. Unsurprisingly with diva Houston in the cast, there's lots of singing, leaving Oscar-winner Washington and Vance on the sidelines to act as scenery for her musical moments. It tries to be one of those films you watch every holiday season, but ends up a pale imitation of the Cary Grant/ David Niven original. JB [video] DVD

Denzel Washington *Dudley* • Whitney Houston *Julia Biggs* • Courtney B Vance *Henry Biggs* • Gregory Hines *Joe Hamilton* • Jenifer Lewis *Marguerite Coleman* • Loretta Devine *Beverly* ■ *Dir* Penny Marshall • *Scr* Nat Mauldin, Allan Scott, from the film *The Bishop's Wife* by Robert E Sherwood, by Leonardo Bercovici, from the novel *In Barleyfields* by Robert Nathan

Preaching to the Perverted ★★ 18

Sex comedy 1997 · UK · Colour · 99mins

The first film to focus on the London fetish scene is an odd mix of traditional British sex comedy and serious message. It starts well with atmospheric, if glamorised scenes in a fetish club run by sexy Guinevere Turner. Thereafter, it doesn't seem to know where to go, and its story of a government man seduced by the depravity he's investigating is very weak. The result will probably shock the easily shocked and disappoint sensation-seekers hoping for something stronger. DM [video]

Guinevere Turner *Tanya Cheex* • Christien Anholt *Peter Emery* • Tom Bell *Henry Harding* • Julie Graham *Eugenie* • Julian Wadham *Prosecuting lawyer* • Georgina Hale *Miss Wilderspin* • Ricky Tomlinson *Fibbin' Gibbins* ■ *Dir/Scr* Stuart Urban

Predator ★★★★ 18

Science-fiction action thriller
1987 · US · Colour · 106mins

It may not seem much of a compliment, but this is one of Arnold Schwarzenegger's most efficient movies: a stripped-down thriller that cheerfully sacrifices characterisation on the altar of exhilarating action and special effects. Schwarzenegger is the leader of an elite special forces team whose jungle mission is thrown into chaos when they are tracked by a lethal alien game-hunter. As with *Aliens*, much of the fun derives from watching a bunch of macho soldiers crack under pressure. Director John McTiernan ensures the tension is kept at snapping point. JF. Contains violence and swearing. [video] DVD

Arnold Schwarzenegger *Major Alan "Dutch" Schaeffer* • Carl Weathers *Dillon* • Elpidia Carrillo *Anna* • Bill Duke *Mac* • Jesse Ventura *Sergeant Blain* • Sonny Landham *Billy* • Kevin Peter Hall *Predator* ■ *Dir* John McTiernan • *Scr* Jim Thomas, John Thomas

Predator 2 ★★★ 18

Science-fiction action thriller
1990 · US · Colour · 107mins

In Los Angeles in 1997, Danny Glover is the unorthodox cop who can't work out who or what is murdering the city's gangsters, or why sinister government official Gary Busey is so interested. However, it's not long before he realises that the culprit is far from human. The action sequences are ably staged but it lacks the sweaty, claustrophobic tension of the Arnold Schwarzenegger original. JF. Contains swearing and violence. [video] DVD

Danny Glover *Detective Mike Harrigan* • Gary Busey *Peter Keyes* • Rubén Blades *Danny Archuleta* • Maria Conchita Alonso *Leona Cantrell* • Kevin Peter Hall *Predator* • Bill Paxton *Jerry Lambert* ■ *Dir* Stephen Hopkins • *Scr* Jim Thomas, John Thomas

Prefontaine ★★

Sports biography
1997 · US · Colour · 106mins

For his follow-up to his acclaimed documentary, *Hoop Dreams*, writer/ director Steve James made this biography of Steve Prefontaine, the Olympic runner who died in a car crash at the tragically young age of 24. Jared Leto does an excellent job impersonating Prefontaine and keeps a straight face while wearing some of the worst hairstyles the 1970s had to offer. R Lee Ermey plays the running coach. ST. Contains violence and swearing.

Jared Leto *Steve Prefontaine* • R Lee Ermey *Bill Bowerman* • Ed O'Neill *Bill Dellinger* • Breckin Meyer *Pat Tyson* • Lindsay Crouse *Elfriede Prefontaine* ■ *Dir* Steve James (2) • *Scr* Steve James, Eugene Corr

Prehysteria! ★★★ PG

Fantasy 1993 · US · Colour · 80mins

A junior-league *Jurassic Park*, with kids hatching a clutch of pygmy-dino eggs and a comic-book bad guy trying to force the family into handing them over. The dialogue is surprisingly good for a low-budget movie such as this and the diddly dinos, if not exactly state-of-the-art special effects, are cute and cuddly enough to keep younger kids enthralled. DA [video]

Brett Cullen *Frank Taylor* • Colleen Morris *Vicki* • Austin O'Brien *Jerry Taylor* • Tony Longo *Louis* • Stuart Fratkin *Richie* • Stephen Lee *Rico Sarno* ■ *Dir* Charles Band, Albert Band • *Scr* Greg Suddeth, Mark Goldstein, from an idea by Peter Von Sholly

Prejudice ★★ U

Documentary drama
1988 · Aus · Colour · 59mins

This Australian docudrama bites off rather more than it can chew. Writer Pamela Williams wastes director Ian Munro's realistic atmosphere by insisting on using melodramatic situations to prove that, if it is difficult for talented white women to succeed in their chosen professions, then it's next to impossible for those of a different race. The makers care passionately about their material, but they must involve before they can influence, and it's here that this film falls down. DP

Grace Parr *Leticia* • Patsy Stephen *Jessica* ■ *Dir* Ian Munro • *Scr* Pamela Williams

Prelude to a Kiss ★★★ PG

Romantic comedy fantasy
1992 · US · Colour · 98mins

An offbeat, gentle romantic fantasy. Alec Baldwin is the groom who begins to suspect something is up with new wife Meg Ryan, whose personality change may or may not be connected to the appearance of an elderly stranger at their wedding. This certainly isn't the usual romantic fare from Hollywood, but Norman René directs the proceedings with subtlety and summons up a charming, if slightly melancholic, air. JF. Contains swearing. [video] DVD

Alec Baldwin *Peter Hoskins* • Meg Ryan *Rita Boyle* • Kathy Bates *Leah Blier* • Ned Beatty *Dr Boyle* • Patty Duke *Mrs Boyle* • Sydney Walker *Julius, the old man* ■ *Dir* Norman René • *Scr* Craig Lucas, from his play

Prelude to Fame ★★ U

Drama 1950 · UK · BW · 88mins

Films about classical music have nearly always been box-office poison. This uninspired tale about a child prodigy whose tutor is his only refuge from expectation and exploitation was no exception. Adapted from a minor Aldous Huxley story, the film was directed with little flair by Fergus McDonell, who keeps the focus firmly on the sickly soloist, played rather well by Jeremy Spenser. The film was the last made using the ill-fated Independent Frame method, which aimed to cut costs by using back-projected interior scenery. DP

Guy Rolfe *John Morell* • Kathleen Byron *Signora Bondini* • Kathleen Ryan *Catherine Morell* • Jeremy Spenser *Guido* • Rosalie Crutchley *Carlotta* ■ *Dir* Fergus McDonell • *Scr* Robert Westerby, from the story *Young Archimedes* by Aldous Huxley

Prelude to War ★★

Second World War documentary
1943 · US · BW · 53mins

This was the first of director Frank Capra's *Why We Fight* series, which was originally intended for military use only. Theatrical release was the subject of prolonged debate, and only came after President Roosevelt's personal approval. It was one of four documentaries to win an Oscar in 1943. There is little historical or social analysis, and this film simply demonises Hitler, which it does quite efficiently through footage, maps and graphics, with an uncredited voiceover by Walter Huston. AT

Walter Huston *Narrator* ■ *Dir* Ernst Lubitsch, Major Anatole Litvak [Anatole Litvak], Robert Flaherty • *Scr* Eric Knight, Anthony Veiller, Robert Heller • *Music* Alfred Newman

The Premature Burial ★★★

Horror 1962 · US · Colour · 80mins

Originally not intended as one of Roger Corman's unofficial Edgar Allan Poe series – the reason Ray Milland starred instead of Vincent Price – this moody chiller jettisoned any pretence of a plot for an eerie essay on the terrors of being buried alive. Although somewhat starchily written and slightly static in approach, the B-movie master of the macabre still manages to raise the odd claustrophobic spine-tingle or two thanks to graveyard-loads of gloomy atmosphere. AJ

Ray Milland *Guy Carrell* • Hazel Court *Emily Gault* • Richard Ney *Miles Archer* • Heather Angel *Kate Carrell* • Alan Napier *Dr Gideon Gault* ■ *Dir* Roger Corman • *Scr* Charles Beaumont, Ray Russell, from the story by Edgar Allan Poe in *Dollar Newspaper* (31 July 1884)

The Premonition ★★★ 15

Supernatural thriller
1975 · US · Colour · 88mins

A young girl is torn between her foster mother and her real mom, who's nutty as a fruitcake yet determined to regain custody. Shot in Mississipi, Robert Allen Schnitzer's eerie thriller evokes a murky swampland atmosphere and has some nicely spooky moments, while the cast deliver convincing performances. TH [video]

Sharon Farrell *Sheri Bennett* • Richard Lynch *Jude* • Jeff Corey *Detective Mark Denver* • Ellen Barber *Andrea Fletcher* • Edward Bell *Miles Bennett* ■ *Dir* Robert Allen Schnitzer • *Scr* Anthony Mahon, Robert Allen Schnitzer

The Premonition ★★ 18

Thriller 1992 · Swe · Colour · 109mins

If disembowelled cats, teenage sexual fantasies, Peeping Toms, sadomasochistic murder and violent accidents are your idea of a good time, then this overwrought chiller is for you. Director Rumle Hammerich falls over himself to pack his picture with eerie images as schoolgirl Tova Magnusson experiences the premonitions with which she fills her distinctly weird diary. But too much of the symbolism (most of it borrowed from Hitchcock) is contrived and a good deal of it is totally irrelevant to a plot. DP. In Swedish with English subtitles. [video]

Tova Magnusson *Mikaela* • Figge Norling *Joakim* • Björn Kjellman *Max* • Niklas Hjulström *Johan* ■ *Dir* Rumle Hammerich • *Scr* Carina Rydberg

Preppies ★ 18

Comedy 1984 · US · Colour · 79mins

Three rich college kids are threatened with expulsion should they fail upcoming exams. One of them, Dennis Drake invites the others to his country home for some intensive study. Drake's cousin, however, realises he will be disinherited if he's sent down, so hires some call girls to distract the boys. Lame and limp. DF [video] DVD

Dennis Drake *Robert "Chip" Thurston* • Steven Holt *Bayard* • Peter Brady Reardon *Marc* • Nitchie Barrett *Roxanne* • Cindy Manion *Jo* ■ *Dir* Chuck Vincent • *Scr* Rick Marx, Chuck Vincent, from a story by Todd Kessler

Prescription: Murder ★★★★ PG

Detective mystery
1968 · US · Colour · 94mins

This superbly scripted thriller marks the small-screen debut of an American TV legend. Peter Falk is now so associated with the role of shambling Los Angeles detective Lt Columbo that it is impossible to believe that anyone else could have played him. However, Thomas Mitchell was Columbo in Richard Levinson and William Link's stage play, and first choice for the TV series was Bing Crosby, who turned it down because it would interfere with his golf. In the event, Falk made the character his own and here the deceptively haphazard way in which he dismantles the master plan of smug, wife-murdering psychiatrist Gene Barry is a delight to watch. DP [video] DVD

Peter Falk *Lt Columbo* • Gene Barry *Doctor Ray Flemming* • Katherine Justice *Joan Hudson* • Nina Foch *Carol Flemming* • William Windom *Burt Gordon* ■ *Dir* Richard Irving • *Scr* Richard Levinson, William Link, from the play by Richard Levinson, William Link

Presenting Lily Mars ★★ U

Musical comedy 1943 · US · BW · 103mins

Stage-struck singer Judy Garland leaves her small Indiana town to follow young Broadway producer Van Heflin to Manhattan. There, despite falling foul of his temperamental star (Marta Eggerth), she eventually finds stardom and romance. A formula musical in the *Cinderella* vein, is enlivened by Garland's usual high-calibre performance and a climactic appearance from Tommy Dorsey and his Orchestra. AJ

Judy Garland *Lily Mars* • Van Heflin *John Thornway* • Fay Bainter *Mrs Thornway* • Richard Carlson *Owen Vail* • Spring Byington *Mrs Mars* • Marta Eggerth *Isobel Rekay* • Tommy Dorsey ■ *Dir* Norman Taurog • *Scr* Richard Connell, Gladys Lehman, from the novel by Booth Tarkington

The President ★★★

Silent melodrama
1919 · Den · Tinted · 90mins

The tale of three women who are abused, impregnated and abandoned by shiftless, socially superior males, Carl Th Dreyer's directorial debut established several traits that would persist throughout his career. The influence of little-known Danish painter Vilhelm Hammershoi is evident in his austere interiors, while his choice of source material began a lifetime of basing his films on works of little literary merit. This narratively sophisticated and compositionally precise melodrama can now be seen in a lustrous, tinted print . DP

Halvard Hoff *Karl Victor von Sendlingen, president* • Elith Pio *The president's father* • Carl Meyer *The president's grandfather* • Olga Raphael-Linden *Victorine Lippert, president's daughter* • Betty Kirkebye *Hermine Lippert* ■ *Dir* Carl Th Dreyer • *Scr* Carl Th Dreyer, from the novel by Karl Emil Franzos

The President's Analyst ★★★★

Political satire 1967 · US · Colour · 102mins

It may seem dated today, but this clever satire was the ultimate hip trip back in the Swinging Sixties, and it is still very, very funny. Talented iconoclast Theodore J Flicker wrote and directed, and profited from the presence of James Coburn in the lead as the suave psychiatrist earmarked for secret service assassination, only to be saved by other agencies interested in the information they assume has passed between the president and his shrink. Coburn leads them all a merry chase, notably causing international havoc during a hilarious sex romp with hippy Jill Banner. TS. Contains some violence.

James Coburn *Dr Sidney Schaefer* • Godfrey Cambridge *Don Masters* • Severn Darden *Kropotkin* • Joan Delaney *Nan Butler* • Pat Harrington *Arlington Hewes* • Barry McGuire *Old wrangler* • Jill Banner *Snow White* ■ *Dir/ Scr* Theodore J Flicker

The President's Lady ★★★

Biographical drama 1953 · US · BW · 97mins

Charlton Heston takes on one of his iconic roles with this neat portrayal of American president Andrew Jackson and the two loves of his life. One, his country, naturally, in all its early 19th-century tumult and the other, luscious Susan Hayward as the woman with a dodgy past he is determined to marry. Based soundly on Irving Stone's novel rather than historical fact, it allows Heston once again to convey the heavy burden of office with an endearing helping of agonising self-doubt. Like Hayward's stays, however, the whole exercise does creak a bit. SH

Susan Hayward *Rachel Donelson Robards* • Charlton Heston *Andrew Jackson* • John McIntire *Jack Overton* • Fay Bainter *Mrs Donelson* ■ *Dir* Henry Levin • *Scr* John Patrick, from the novel by Irving Stone

The President's Man ★★ 15

Action adventure thriller
2000 · US · Colour · 86mins

Action heroes never die, they just get smaller budgets. Not that Chuck Norris was ever in the Arnold Schwarzenegger league, despite having a cult following among martial arts aficionados. But the penny-pinching shows in this TV effort, in which Norris plays a veteran secret service agent who is forced back into the fray when the wife of the US president is kidnapped by a shady terrorist organisation. DP. Contains violence. [video] DVD

Chuck Norris *Joshua McCord* • Dylan Neal *Deke Slater* • Jennifer Tung *Que* • Ralph Waite *President Matthews* ■ *Dir* Michael Preece, Eric Norris • *Scr* Bob Gookin

The Presidio ★★★ 15

Mystery thriller 1988 · US · Colour · 94mins

Director Peter Hyams is an under-rated master of the high concept action thriller and this effort boasts his usual strengths and weaknesses. On the downside, the plotting – in which San Francisco cop Mark Harmon is paired with an old enemy, military policeman Sean Connery, to solve a murder mystery – is perfunctory to say the least. However, Hyams distracts attention from that with some humdinging action sequences. Meg Ryan is a feisty love interest. JF. Contains swearing, violence. [video] DVD

Sean Connery *Lt Col Alan Caldwell* • Mark Harmon *Jay Austin* • Meg Ryan *Donna Caldwell* • Jack Warden *Sergeant Major Ross Maclure* • Mark Blum *Arthur Peale* ■ *Dir* Peter Hyams • *Scr* Larry Ferguson

Presque Rien ★★★ 18

Romantic drama
2000 · Fr/Bel · Colour · 93mins

Consciously seeking to explore a traumatic train of events in a non-linear fashion, Sébastien Lifshitz provides a perceptive insight into the pain of realising one's sexual identity in this Rohmeresque tale of summer love turned sour. Although he switches time frames to great visual and emotional effect, what is particularly impressive about Lifshitz's direction is the way in which he leaks the snippets of information that link Jérémie Elkaïm's idyllic seaside romance and his desperate attempt to track down his lover, Stéphane Rideau, in the bleakest of midwinters. DP. In French with English subtitles. [video] DVD

Jérémie Elkaïm *Mathieu* • Stéphane Rideau *Cédric* • Marie Matheron *Annick* • Dominique Reymond *Mother* • Laetitia Legrix *Sarah* • Nils Ohlund *Pierre* ■ *Dir* Sébastien Lifshitz • *Scr* Sébastien Lifshitz, Stéphane Bouquet

Press for Time ★ U

Comedy 1966 · UK · Colour · 98mins

After headlining in 14 consecutive films, this was Norman Wisdom's last starring role before his impressive supporting performance in American comedy *The Night They Raided Minsky's* in 1968, and a sorry swansong it makes. He is woefully out of form in this feeble comedy and there is nothing new in his performance as a bungling reporter on a local rag. DP [video] DVD

Norman Wisdom *Norman Shields/Sir Wilfred Shields/Emily Shields* • Derek Bond *Major Bartlett* • Angela Browne *Eleanor* • Tracey Crisp *Ruby Fairchild* • Noel Dyson *Mrs Corcoran* • Derek Francis *Alderman Corcoran* ■ *Dir* Robert Asher • *Scr* Norman Wisdom, Eddie Leslie, from the novel *Yea Yea Yea* by Angus McGill

Pressure ★★★

Drama 1976 · UK · Colour · 136mins

Horace Ové's pioneering feature, which was the first to be released in the United Kingdom by a black director, explores the subject of being black and British. Ové focuses on the limited opportunities offered to young black men in the face of institutional and individual hostility, but he also examines the resentment exhibited by Herbert Norville's own family when he tries to conform. It would be easy to dismiss the film as dated were it not for the fact that little has actually changed. DP

Herbert Norville *Anthony* • Oscar James *Colin* • Frank Singuineau *Lucas* • Lucita Lijertwood *Bopsie* • Sheila Scott-Wilkinson *Sister Louise* • Ed Devereaux *Police inspector* • Norman Beaton *Preacher* ■ *Dir* Horace Ové • *Scr* Horace Ové, Samuel Selvon

Pressure Point ★★★★

Drama 1962 · US · BW · 86mins

Based on a real-life story, this case history about a black prison psychiatrist and his ongoing confrontations with a fascist, racist inmate was considered very controversial in its day. Sidney Poitier, as the doctor, gives a brilliantly controlled performance while singer Bobby Darin – in one of his rare dramatic appearances – is bellowingly obnoxious as the bigoted prisoner. Director Hubert Cornfield stresses the caged claustrophobia of life inside with casual expertise. TH

Sidney Poitier *Doctor* • Bobby Darin *Patient* • Peter Falk *Young psychiatrist* • Carl Benton Reid *Chief medical officer* ■ *Dir* Hubert Cornfield • *Scr* Hubert Cornfield, S Lee Pogostin, from the story *Destiny's Tot* by Robert Mitchell Lindner in *The Fifty-Minute Hour: a Collection of True Psychoanalytic Tales*

Presumed Innocent ★★★★ 18

Thriller 1990 · US · Colour · 121mins

Harrison Ford was at the peak of his popularity when he starred in this glossy, highly polished blockbuster, playing a lawyer assigned to untangle the murder of his former mistress. Based on the multi-million-selling novel by Scott Turow, this could have been a great movie, but, despite being a darn good yarn well told, the essential magic is somehow missing. Quite what turns a competent movie into a classic remains the great Hollywood conundrum – the elements are here, but they're too tightly threaded for this to attain true classic status. SH. Contains swearing, violence, sex scenes and nudity. [video] DVD

Harrison Ford *Rozat "Rusty" Sabich* • Brian Dennehy *Raymond Horgan* • Raul Julia *Alejandro "Sandy" Stern* • Bonnie Bedelia *Barbara Sabich* • Paul Winfield *Judge Larren Lyttle* • Greta Scacchi *Carolyn Polhemus* ■ *Dir* Alan J Pakula • *Scr* Frank Pierson, Alan J Pakula, from the novel by Scott Turow

Pret-a-Porter ★★★ 15

Satirical comedy
1994 · US · Colour · 127mins

Director Robert Altman was always going to struggle to surpass the sprawling perfection of his episodic drama *Short Cuts*, and when this satirical look at the fashion industry opened the backlash really kicked in. Yes, it does lack the bite and subtlety of Altman's best work, but it's not half as bad as some have made it out to be. Setting the action against the backdrop of the French spring fashion shows, Altman characteristically weaves a bewildering number of subplots through the piece, some of which you care about, some of which you don't. There's also a cast to die for – a fascinating failure, but a star-gazer's delight. JF. Contains swearing, drug abuse and nudity. [video] DVD

Julia Roberts *Anne Eisenhower* • Tim Robbins *Joe Flynn* • Stephen Rea *Milo O'Brannagan* •

P

Lauren Bacall *Slim Chrysler* • Marcello Mastroianni *Sergei/Sergio* • Sophia Loren *Isabella de la Fontaine* • Anouk Aimée *Simone Lowenthal* • Lili Taylor *Fiona Ulrich* • Kim Basinger *Kitty Potter* • Sally Kellerman *Sissy Wanamaker* • Tracey Ullman *Nina Scant* • Linda Hunt *Regina Krumm* • Rupert Everett *Jack Lowenthal* • Forest Whitaker *Cy Bianco* • Richard E Grant *Cort Romney, fashion designer* • Danny Aiello *Major Hamilton, retail buyer* • Teri Garr *Louise Hamilton, Major Hamilton's wife* • Lyle Lovett *Clint Lammeraux, Texas cowboy-boot mogul* ■ *Dir* Robert Altman • *Scr* Robert Altman, Barbara Shulgasser

Pretty Baby ★★★ U

Comedy 1950 · US · BW · 91mins

An innocuous Warner Bros crowd-pleaser about, quite simply, what a working girl has to resort to in order to get a seat on the subway. Betsy Drake (Mrs Cary Grant at the time) is perky in the lead, and for once Dennis Morgan's bland performance matches his bland role, so no harm done there. Morgan is no match for sophisticated Zachary Scott, who yet again demonstrates why he was nicknamed "The Eyebrow". *Miracle on 34th Street's* Edmund Gwenn also makes a welcome appearance. TS

Betsy Drake *Patsy Douglas* • Dennis Morgan *Sam Morley* • Zachary Scott *Barry Holmes* • Edmund Gwenn *Cyrus Baxter* ■ *Dir* Bretaigne Windust • *Scr* Everett Freeman, from the book *Gay Deception* by Jules Furthman, John Klorer

Pretty Baby ★★★★ 18

Period drama 1978 · US · Colour · 104mins

"Scandal!" yelled the moralists of the time about the under-age sex theme of director Louis Malle's depiction of brothel life in the New Orleans of 1917. It's a cosier treatment than might have been expected, though, with Brooke Shields as the bordello girl awaiting her 12th birthday – and the official loss of her virginity – while Keith Carradine is the photographer whose candid camera strips the romance from her naive view of life with the women who are the only family she's got. Louis Malle treats the difficult subject with a sensitivity that might offend some, but intrigue others. TH

Keith Carradine *EJ Bellocq* • Susan Sarandon *Hattie* • Brooke Shields *Violet* • Frances Faye *Madame Nell Livingston* • Antonio Fargas *Professor, piano player* • Barbara Steele *Josephine* ■ *Dir* Louis Malle • *Scr* Polly Platt, from a story by Polly Platt, Louis Malle, from the book *Storyville, New Orleans: Being an Authentic Account of the Notorious Redlight District* by Al Rose • *Cinematographer* Sven Nykvist

Pretty Boy Floyd ★★

Crime biography 1960 · US · BW · 101mins

Pretty Boy Floyd was a 1930s gangster who hung out with John Dillinger and Baby Face Nelson and created a vivid legend about himself. His great moment came in 1933 when he took part in the Kansas City Massacre, in which he reputedly machine-gunned to death an FBI agent, three cops and a prisoner they were escorting to jail. The story was first told in *"G" Men* (1935) and touched on in *The FBI Story* (1959), but here Floyd gets his own biography with John Ericson as the flamboyant killer. AT

John Ericson *Pretty Boy Floyd* • Barry Newman *Al Riccardo* • Joan Harvey *Lil Courtney* • Jason Evers *Blackie Faulkner* • Peter Falk *Shorty Walters* ■ *Dir/Scr* Herbert J Leder

Pretty in Pink ★★★ 15

Comedy drama 1986 · US · Colour · 92mins

Molly Ringwald stars in this Brat Pack take on Cinderella, making a game fist of playing a rebellious teenager from the wrong side of the tracks who meets an upmarket designer boy (Andrew McCarthy). Ringwald, all flaming red hair and grungy attire, brings a touch of charisma to the well-worn theme, and she receives sterling support from Harry Dean Stanton as her deadbeat dad. It belts along pleasingly enough, but is too hackneyed to be entirely successful. SH. Contains swearing. DVD

Molly Ringwald *Andie Walsh* • Andrew McCarthy *Blane McDonough* • James Spader *Steff McKee* • Jon Cryer *Phil "Duckie" Dale* • Harry Dean Stanton *Jack Walsh* • Annie Potts *Iona* • Jim Haynie *Donnelly* ■ *Dir* Howard Deutch • *Scr* John Hughes

Pretty Maids All in a Row ★

Black comedy thriller
1971 · US · Colour · 91mins

Roger Vadim made his Hollywood debut with this dire sex satire. It also poses itself as a thriller, starting with a girl found murdered in a high school and suspicion initially falling on a shy, introverted boy. But then Rock Hudson takes the film over, laughingly playing the school counsellor who advises students on their sex lives. Mainly, though, Vadim just wants his cast of starlets to get their clothes off. Tacky and hopelessly dated. AT

Rock Hudson *Michael "Tiger" McDrew* • Angie Dickinson *Miss Smith* • Telly Savalas *Capt Sam Surcher* • John David Carson *Ponce de Leon Harper* • Roddy McDowall *Mr Proffer* • Keenan Wynn *Chief John Poldaski* • James Doohan *Follo* • William Campbell *Grady* ■ *Dir* Roger Vadim • *Scr* Gene Roddenberry, from a novel by Francis Pollini • *Music* Lalo Schifrin

Pretty Poison ★★★ 15

Psychological crime thriller
1968 · US · Colour · 84mins

In of his more subtle variations on his Norman Bates character in *Psycho*, Anthony Perkins plays a young man, just released on parole from reform school, who hooks up with high school cheerleader Tuesday Weld to destroy a polluting factory. Shot on a low budget, and influenced by the French New Wave, Noel Black's first feature remained pretty poisonous at the box office, though it later gained cult status. RB

Anthony Perkins *Dennis Pitt* • Tuesday Weld *Sue Ann Stepanek* • Beverly Garland *Mrs Stepanek* • John Randolph *Azenauer* • Ken Kercheval *Harry Jackson* ■ *Dir* Noel Black • *Scr* Lorenzo Semple Jr, from the novel *She Let Him Continue* by Stephen Geller

Pretty Polly ★★

Comedy drama 1967 · UK · Colour · 99mins

A soft-centred adaptation of Noël Coward's harder-edged short story about the transformation from ugly duckling to swan of diffident young Hayley Mills, thanks to the accidental death of her wealthy aunt (Brenda de Banzie) in the swimming pool of a Singapore hotel. Mills is agreeably fresh, and Guy Green's direction of this pleasantly escapist but unmemorable film is helped by some attractive locations, Trevor Howard as Polly's unconventional uncle, and Indian actor Shashi Kapoor as the romantic interest. RK

Hayley Mills *Polly Barlow* • Trevor Howard *Robert Hook* • Shashi Kapoor *Amaz* • Brenda de Banzie *Mrs Innes-Hook* • Dick Patterson *Rick Preston* • Patricia Routledge *Miss Gudgeon* ■ *Dir* Guy Green • *Scr* Keith Waterhouse, Willis Hall, from the story *Pretty Polly Barlow* by Noël Coward

Pretty Village Pretty Flame ★★★★ 18

War drama 1996 · Ser · Colour · 123mins

Set at the height of the Bosnian conflict, yet continuously flashing back through the 15 years in which Yugoslavia fell apart, this is the sobering story of how the lifelong friendship between a Serb and a Muslim was shattered by civil war. Srdan Dragojević's film was attacked for appearing pro-Serbian, yet, as the Serb's unit is trapped inside the Tito-inspired tunnel that stood for unity and progress, it's clear that no one is immune from blame. Crisply acted and tautly directed, the action is strewn with striking scenes, but nothing can prepare you for the horror of the final image. DP. In Serbo-Croat with English subtitles. Contains violence.

Dragan Bjelogrlic *Milan* • Nikola Kojo *Velja Kozic* • Dragan Maksimovic *Petar aka "Professor"* • Velimir Bata Zivojinovic [Bata Zivojinovic] *Gvozden Maksimovic* • Zoran Cvijanovic *"Speedy"* ■ *Dir* Srdjan Dragojevic • *Scr* Vanja Bulic, Srdjan Dragojevic, Nikola Pejakovic, from a war report by Vanja Bulic as published in *Duga*

Pretty Woman ★★★★ 15

Romantic comedy
1990 · US · Colour · 114mins

Originally meant to be a serious drama (called *$3,000*) about a man buying a prostitute for the night, this turned into a delightful romantic comedy in the hands of Garry Marshall and sent the career of star Julia Roberts into the stratosphere. Co-star Richard Gere didn't do badly either as the tycoon. On screen, they make the "hooker falls for a millionaire in Beverly Hills" Cinderella tale completely plausible, aided by Marshall's glossy direction, the hit-filled soundtrack, a perky script from J F Lawton and hilarious support from Marshall stalwart Hector Elizondo. JB. Contains swearing, nudity and a sex scene. DVD

Richard Gere *Edward Lewis* • Julia Roberts *Vivian Ward* • Ralph Bellamy *James Morse* • Laura San Giacomo *Kit De Luca* • Hector Elizondo *Hotel manager* • Jason Alexander *Philip Stuckey* • Alex Hyde-White *David Morse* ■ *Dir* Garry Marshall • *Scr* JF Lawton

PrettyKill ★ 18

Crime thriller
1987 · US/Can · Colour · 97mins

Pretty awful exploitation thriller about a sleazy cop and his hooker girlfriend trying to track down a serial killer. Director George Kaczender seems to lose interest once the central idea has been set up, while the acting is as convincing as a sex chatline. TH

David Birney *Larry Turner* • Season Hubley *Heather Todd* • Susannah York *Toni* • Yaphet Kotto *Harris* • Suzanne Snyder *Francie* ■ *Dir* George Kaczender • *Scr* Sandra K Bailey

Prey ★ 18

Science-fiction horror
1977 · UK · Colour · 77mins

An alien in human disguise (Barry Stokes) moves in with a lesbian couple (Sally Faulkner, Glory Annen) to ascertain the protein value of human flesh for a possible invasion. Norman J Warren's uninspired direction makes this already padded mix of cannibalism, sexual titillation, madness and shifting relationship dynamics more protracted than need be. A cumbersome, sluggish and gruelling slog. AJ DVD

Barry Stokes *Anders* • Sally Faulkner *Josephine* • Glory Annen *Jessica* • Sandy Chinney *Sandy* ■ *Dir* Norman J Warren • *Scr* Max Cuff, from a story by Quinn Donoghue

A Price above Rubies ★★★ 15

Drama 1997 · US/Fr/UK · Colour · 111mins

This fierce assault on today's orthodox Jewish community in Brooklyn features a sympathetic performance by Renee Zellweger as a young Hassidic woman locked into a world where rules are laid down by men. As feminist propaganda, the film overdoes the hypocrisy and bigotry; as a portrait of a religious community, it is unconvincing and provides little insight; but, as a fictional tale of repression and liberation, it makes you want to cheer. TH. Contains swearing, sex scenes.

Renee Zellweger *Sonia Horowitz* • Christopher Eccleston *Sender* • Allen Payne *Ramon* • Glenn Fitzgerald *Mendel* • Julianna Margulies *Rachel* • Kim Hunter *Rebbitzn* • John Randolph *Rebbe* ■ *Dir/Scr* Boaz Yakin

Price of Glory ★★ 15

Sports drama 2000 · US · Colour · 112mins

Had sportswriter Phil Berger based this screenplay on the bouts he'd witnessed rather than the movies he'd seen, this might have been a contender. But with every pug being a caricature and almost every situation (in and out of the ring) being a cliché, it's hard to go the distance with the story of a nearly man living out his dreams through his kids. Jimmy Smits pulls no punches as the father who makes boxing glory his sole priority and Ron Perlman scores points as a seedy promoter. DP DVD

Jimmy Smits *Arturo Ortega* • Ron Perlman *Nick Everson* • Jon Seda *Sonny Ortega* • Clifton Collins Jr *Jimmy Ortega* • Maria Del Mar *Rita Ortega* ■ *Dir* Carlos Avila • *Scr* Phil Berger

The Price of Milk ★★

Romance 2000 · NZ · Colour · 87mins

Danielle Cormack and Karl Urban run a New Zealand dairy farmstead until love blossoms between them. But just to be sure, Cormack decides she must test Urban before slipping his ring on her finger. Her goal is convoluted by a mystical subplot involving one "Auntie" (Rangi Motu) who instructs her golf-obsessed Maori minions to steal their duvet (don't ask). A discordant mix of fairy tale and muddy romance which never quite explains its cast of 175 cows. LH

Danielle Cormack *Lucinda* • Karl Urban *Rob* • Willa O'Neill *Drosophila* • Michael Lawrence *Bernie* • Rangi Motu *Auntie* ■ *Dir/Scr* Harry Sinclair

The Price of Passion ★★★ 15

Drama 1988 · US · Colour · 100mins

Also known as *The Good Mother*, this is a rather depressing tale about a divorced mother (Diane Keaton) who finds love and sexual fulfilment in the arms of Liam Neeson, only to have her ex-husband sue her for custody of her daughter because he is convinced Neeson is sexually abusing her. There are good performances and it's an interesting subject, but the overall result is rather dreary drama. JB. Contains swearing, nudity. DVD

Diane Keaton *Anna Dunlap* • Liam Neeson *Leo Cutter* • Jason Robards Jr [Jason Robards] *Muth* • Ralph Bellamy *Grandfather* • Teresa Wright *Grandmother* • James Naughton *Brian Dunlap* • Asia Vieira *Molly* • Joe Morton *Frank Williams* ■ *Dir* Leonard Nimoy • *Scr* Michael Bortman, from the novel by Sue Miller

The Price of Vengeance ★★ 15

Crime drama based on a true story
1994 · US · Colour · 88mins

This plodding TV thriller is of primary interest for featuring Dean Stockwell in one of his more grim-faced incarnations. This time round, a policeman seeks revenge following the death of his partner a family man and loyal friend and proceeds to administer justice without bothering about a trial. It's all rather predictable, but if you enjoy police thrillers this one will probably be acceptable entertainment. SH. Contains some violence. DVD

Dean Stockwell *Jack Lowe* • Michael Gross *Tom Williams* • Mary Kay Place *Norma Williams* • Brent Jennings *Johnny Moore* ■ *Dir* Dick Lowry • *Scr* Keith Ross Leckie

Prick Up Your Ears ★★★★★ 18

Biographical drama
1987 · UK · Colour · 105mins

The life of doomed gay British playwright Joe Orton gets a tart, no-holds-barred, sure-handed telling by director Stephen Frears, with Gary Oldman giving a marvellous performance as the promiscuous cheeky chappie. Alan Bennett's wonderful script is full of hilarious one-liners, and is more interesting when focusing on what it meant to be homosexual in the 1960s rather than on Orton's lauded theatrical achievements. Yet, with Alfred Molina also a joy as his jealous lover, this is still British film-making at its finest. AJ. Contains violence, swearing and sex scenes. [video] DVD

Gary Oldman *Joe Orton* • Alfred Molina *Kenneth Halliwell* • Vanessa Redgrave *Peggy Ramsay* • Wallace Shawn *John Lahr* • Lindsay Duncan *Anthea Lahr* • Julie Walters *Elsie Orton* • Frances Barber *Leonie Orton* ■ *Dir* Stephen Frears • *Scr* Alan Bennett, from the biography by John Lahr

Pride and Prejudice ★★★★ U

Period drama 1940 · US · BW · 112mins

This Jane Austen adaptation, co-scripted by novelist Aldous Huxley, is set half a century in advance of the book's period, to take advantage of more glamorous costumes – a very MGM trick. Greer Garson is a sprightly, lively Elizabeth Bennet, but Laurence Olivier, though dashing and handsome, seems slightly uncomfortable as Darcy. The supporting cast, notably Mary Boland's very funny Mrs Bennet and Maureen O'Sullivan as a very sweet-natured Jane, is utterly superb, and the art direction won an Oscar. TS [video]

Greer Garson *Elizabeth Bennet* • Laurence Olivier *Mr Darcy* • Mary Boland *Mrs Bennet* • Edna May Oliver *Lady Catherine de Bourgh* • Maureen O'Sullivan *Jane Bennet* • Ann Rutherford *Lydia Bennet* • Frieda Inescort *Miss Caroline Bingley* • Edmund Gwenn *Mr Bennet* • Karen Morley *Charlotte Lucas* • Heather Angel *Kitty Bennet* • Marsha Hunt *Mary Bennet* • Bruce Lester *Mr Bingley* ■ *Dir* Robert Z Leonard • *Scr* Aldous Huxley, Jane Murfin, from the play by Helen Jerome, from the novel by Jane Austen • *Art Director* Cedric Gibbons, Paul Groesse • *Costume Designer* Adrian

The Pride and the Passion ★★★★ PG

Epic period adventure
1957 · US · Colour · 129mins

Much abused in its day, this is a splendidly calculated spectacle, with a priceless, eye-catching cast, though criticism at the time centred on Frank Sinatra's Spanish accent (excellent) and Cary Grant's British prissiness (unavoidable). Flamenco queen Sophia Loren is gorgeous, and the Franz Planer photography remarkable. No expense was spared by producer/director Stanley Kramer to tell the tale of a guerrilla band dragging a massive cannon across the Iberian Peninsula in 1810 to blow up a French stronghold. Sincere and brutal. TS [video] DVD

Cary Grant *Capt Anthony Trumbull* • Frank Sinatra *Miguel* • Sophia Loren *Juana* • Theodore Bikel *General Jouvet* • John Wengraf *Sermaine* • Jay Novello *Ballinger* • José Nieto *Carlos* ■ *Dir* Stanley Kramer • *Scr* Edna Anhalt, Edward Anhalt, from the novel *The Gun* by CS Forester

The Pride of St Louis ★★★ U

Sports biography 1952 · US · BW · 92mins

One of the most likeable baseball biopics, this is the tale of pitcher Dizzy Dean, a witty and talented player elevated to his sport's Hall of Fame. He is expertly played by the versatile Dan Dailey, an often under-rated, clever and skilful screen actor who is better remembered for his work in musicals, but who began and ended his screen career in dramas. TS

Dan Dailey *Dizzy Dean* • Joanne Dru *Patricia Nash Dean* • Richard Hylton *Johnny Kendall* • Richard Crenna *Paul Dean* • Hugh Sanders *Horst* • James Brown (1) *Moose* ■ *Dir* Harmon Jones • *Scr* Herman J Mankiewicz, from a story by Guy Trosper

Pride of the Blue Grass ★★ U

Drama 1954 · US · Colour · 70mins

Director William Beaudine's career spanned Mary Pickford silents through the television series *Lassie* to such bizarre projects as *Billy the Kid vs Dracula*, and his reputation for efficiency and lack of artistic pretention gained him plenty of work, albeit variable in quality as well as content. This enjoyable, sentimental tale features Lloyd Bridges as a stableman who spots racing potential in a plucky horse owned by Vera Miles. JG

Lloyd Bridges *Jim* • Vera Miles *Linda* • Margaret Sheridan *Helen* • Arthur Shields *Wilson* ■ *Dir* William Beaudine • *Scr* Harold Shumate, from his story

Pride of the Bowery ★★ U

Comedy 1941 · US · BW · 60mins

Also known as *Here We Go Again*, this is a sprightly comedy drama that reunites several of the gang that had first appeared on screen as the Dead End Kids, and would later be known as the Bowery Boys. It's pretty standard B-movie fare, with the kids befriending a boxer while staying at a training camp run by a welfare charity. Wise-cracking series regular Leo Gorcey is as rough and ready as ever, and he's well served by a cast that includes his brother David. DP

Leo Gorcey *Muggs Maloney* • Bobby Jordan *Danny* • Donald Haines *Skinny* • Carleton Young *Norton* • Kenneth Howell *Al* • David Gorcey *Peewee* • Sunshine Morrison ["Sunshine Sammy" Morrison] *Scruno* ■ *Dir* Joseph H Lewis • *Scr* George Plympton, William Lively, from the story by Steven Clensos

The Pride of the Clan ★★★

Silent drama 1917 · US · BW · 84mins

Mary Pickford later admitted her Scottish accent was dreadful, so it's just as well this was a silent. Pickford plays a fisherman's daughter who becomes head of her clan after her father drowns at sea. She and Matt Moore are sweethearts, but their romance is threatened when it turns out he is the son of the countess Kathryn Browne Decker. Maurice Tourneur directs with the kind of conviction that pleased Pickford's legion of fans. TH

Mary Pickford *Marget MacTavish* • Matt Moore *Jamie Campbell* • Warren Cook *Robert, Earl of Dunstable* • Kathryn Browne Decker *Countess of Dunstable* ■ *Dir* Maurice Tourneur • *Scr* Elaine Sterne, Charles E Whittaker

Pride of the Marines ★★

Biographical drama 1945 · US · BW · 119mins

John Garfield gives a convincing performance as real-life marine and war hero Al Schmid who is blinded in the battle against Japanese forces at Guadalcanal in 1942 and dreads going home because he "don't want nobody to be a seeing-eye dog for me". Eleanor Parker is the girlfriend he married on the eve of war and Rosemary DeCamp is the nurse who gets him through the crisis. Designed to give comfort and even inspiration to returning war veterans, it's well meaning and upbeat, but often grossly oversentimental. AT

John Garfield *Al Schmid* • Eleanor Parker *Ruth Hartley* • Dane Clark *Lee Diamond* • John Ridgely *Jim Merchant* • Rosemary DeCamp *Virginia Pfeiffer* • Ann Doran *Ella Merchant* • Warren Douglas *Kebabian* ■ *Dir* Delmer Daves • *Scr* Albert Maltz, Marvin Borowsky, from a story by Roger Butterfield

The Pride of the Yankees ★★★★ U

Sports biography 1942 · US · BW · 122mins

Lou Gehrig played 2,130 consecutive games for the New York Yankees, becoming one of baseball's immortals. Not bad for a tenement kid who only began playing professionally because his mother needed an operation. There's not a lot of sporting action in Sam Wood's movingly inspirational biopic, as the tale concentrates on the romance between Gary Cooper and Teresa Wright, but there's drama aplenty as "Iron Horse" battles the neurological condition that has since become known as Lou Gehrig's disease. Coop gives a typically sympathetic performance. DP [video]

Gary Cooper *Lou Gehrig* • Teresa Wright *Eleanor Gehrig* • Walter Brennan *Sam Blake* • Babe Ruth ■ *Dir* Sam Wood • *Scr* Jo Swerling, Herman J Mankiewicz, from a story by Paul Gallico

Priest ★★★★ 15

Drama 1994 · UK · Colour · 104mins

Antonia Bird's timely and compassionate portrait of a gay priest, struggling to live up to his vows is wryly written by *Cracker* creator Jimmy McGovern, and is a biting indictment of a religion that preaches love and forgiveness yet shuns another human for not conforming. A sensitive, if harrowing, tale of lives needlessly destroyed by hypocrisy, it pulls no punches dealing with the subjects of incest and homosexuality, and contains an unforgettably moving finale. Linus Roache gives an amazing performance as the torn cleric. AJ. Contains sex scenes and nudity. [video]

Linus Roache *Father Greg Pilkington* • Tom Wilkinson *Father Matthew Thomas* • Robert Carlyle *Graham* • Cathy Tyson *Maria Kerrigan* • James Ellis *Father Ellerton* • Lesley Sharp *Mrs Unsworth* • Robert Pugh *Mr Unsworth* ■ *Dir* Antonia Bird • *Scr* Jimmy McGovern

Priest of Love ★★ 15

Biographical drama
1981 · UK · Colour · 94mins

Christopher Miles directs this biopic of the novelist, dealing with Lawrence's early life (in flashback) and the controversy his novels caused in England, bringing about his various exiles – to New Mexico and Provence where he coughs himself to death. The locations are often lavish but the movie feels puny, mainly due to Ian McKellen's pedantic, archly theatrical performance. Janet Suzman plays his German wife and there's a clutch of distracting cameos. AT [video] DVD

Ian McKellen *DH Lawrence* • Janet Suzman *Frieda Lawrence* • Ava Gardner *Mabel Dodge Luhan* • Penelope Keith *Honorable Dorothy Brett* • Jorge Rivero *Tony Luhan* • Maurizio Merli *Angelo Ravagli* • John Gielgud *Herbert G Muskett* • Sarah Miles *Actress* ■ *Dir* Christopher Miles • *Scr* Alan Plater, from the book by Harry T Moore

The Priest's Wife ★★

Comedy 1970 · It/Fr · Colour · 106mins

It's hard to convey to an Anglo-Saxon audience how controversial this title – *La Moglie del Prete* – would be to Italians. Singer Sophia Loren, therefore, should know better than to try to persuade priest Marcello Mastroianni out of his vows in order to wed and bed her. What sounds like a promising sex comedy turns out to be a wordy bore, and quite an unworthy vehicle for the two stars. The couple have little to do but bicker and argue, and what passes for humour falls very flat indeed. For some perverse artistic reason, director Dino Risi filmed this in deliberately muted colours. TS. Italian dialogue dubbed into English.

Sophia Loren *Valeria Billi* • Marcello Mastroianni *Don Mario* • Venantino Venantini *Maurizio* • Jacques Stany *Jimmy Guitar* • Pippo Starnazza *Valeria's father* ■ *Dir* Dino Risi • *Scr* Ruggero Maccari, Bernardino Zapponi, from a story by Ruggero Maccari, Dino Risi, Bernardino Zapponi

Primal Fear ★★★★ 18

Courtroom thriller
1996 · US · Colour · 125mins

When hotshot lawyer Richard Gere takes on the high-profile case of bewildered altar boy Edward Norton, accused of murdering an archbishop, his cut-and-dried life begins to unravel. Having squared up to state prosecutor Laura Linney, who just happens to be his ex-girlfriend, Gere begins to suspect that still waters run deep in his seemingly angelic client. The movie brims with humour and excitement – plus a twist guaranteed to drop jaws – while the performances of Gere and the quite electric Norton crackle with energy until the very last frame. AJ. Contains swearing, violence and a sex scene. [video] DVD

Richard Gere *Martin Vail* • Laura Linney *Janet Venable* • John Mahoney *DA John Shaughnessy* • Alfre Woodard *Judge Miriam Shoat* • Frances McDormand *Dr Molly Arrington* • Edward Norton *Aaron Stampler* • Terry O'Quinn *Assistant DA Bud Yancy* ■ *Dir* Gregory Hoblit • *Scr* Steve Shagan, Ann Biderman, from the novel by William Diehl

Primal Force ★ 15

Science-fiction horror
1999 · US · Colour · 85mins

In this expendable TV movie, Ron Perlman is the brooding guide brought in to save the survivors of a crashed plane on a Mexican island. The members of the supporting cast prove largely anonymous as they're picked off by savage mutant baboons that are obviously stunt performers in monkey suits. DP. Contains violence and swearing. [video]

Ron Perlman *Frank Brodie* • Roxana Zal *Tara Matthews* • Mark Kiely *Scott Davis* • Guillermo Rios *Eddie Mendoza* • Kimberlee Peterson *Kelsey Cunningham* ■ *Dir* Nelson McCormick • *Scr* Michael Thoma (2)

Primary Colors ★★★★ 15

Political comedy drama
1998 · US · Colour · 137mins

John Travolta is convincing as a womanising senator running for president in this smart and witty satire, written by Elaine May and directed by her frequent partner, Mike Nichols. Adapted from a novel by Joe Klein, it has some great, cynical set pieces while, as the combative wife, Emma Thompson gives as good as she gets. Both leads turn in accomplished performances, but they're almost outshone by Kathy Bates as the future president's lesbian hatchet woman. This is politics with an all too human face. TH. Contains swearing. [video] DVD

John Travolta *Governor Jack Stanton* • Emma Thompson *Susan Stanton* • Billy Bob Thornton

Richard Jemmons • Adrian Lester *Henry Burton* • Maura Tierney *Daisy* • Paul Guilfoyle (2) *Howard Ferguson* • Larry Hagman *Governor Fred Picker* • Kathy Bates *Libby Holden* • Diane Ladd *Mamma Stanton* • Rob Reiner *Izzy Rosenblatt* ■ *Dir* Mike Nichols • *Scr* Elaine May, from the novel *Primary Colors: a Novel of Politics* by Anonymous [Joe Klein]

Primary Motive ★★★

Political thriller 1992 · US · Colour · 93mins

A political drama about duplicity and double-dealing in the corridors of power. Now, there's a novelty! However, while it breaks no new ground, this is a well-made film, with a strong central performance from the under-rated Judd Nelson. He plays an inexperienced press secretary who digs up some dirt on his candidate's opponent, and is morally torn as to what to do about it. DA

Judd Nelson *Andrew Blumenthal* • John Savage *Wallace Roberts* • Sally Kirkland *Helen Poulas* • Justine Bateman *Darcy Link* • Frank Converse *John Eastham* • Joe Grifasi *Paul Melton* ■ *Dir* Daniel Adams • *Scr* Daniel Adams, William Snowden

Primary Suspect ★★ 18

Action thriller 2000 · US · Colour · 91mins

This able enough police thriller stars William Baldwin as a cop who goes off the deep end when his wife, a fellow cop, is murdered during a drugs raid that goes wrong. Two years on, he gets the opportunity for a little personal payback, but instead finds himself drawn into a deeper conspiracy. Unremarkable, but the performances are solid. JF DVD

William Baldwin *Christian Box* • Brigitte Bako *Nikki* • Lee Majors *Lt Blake* • Vincent Castellanos *Reuben* ■ *Dir* Jeff Celentano • *Scr* MF McDowell

Prime Cut ★★★ 18

Crime thriller 1972 · US · Colour · 82mins

In director Michael Ritchie's sleazy and irreverent crime thriller, Lee Marvin plays a Chicago Mob enforcer sent to Kansas to teach renegade slaughterhouse owner Gene Hackman a lesson. While the engaging quirkiness initially comes thick and fast, Ritchie is unable to sustain the offbeat style for the duration. However, bloody bursts of violent action and great performances help this skewed movie through its rough patches. Look out for Sissy Spacek in her film debut. AJ. Contains swearing and nudity.

Lee Marvin *Nick Devlin* • Gene Hackman *"Mary Ann"* • Sissy Spacek *Poppy* • Angel Tompkins *Clarabelle* • Gregory Walcott *Weenie* • Bob Wilson *Reaper driver* ■ *Dir* Michael Ritchie • *Scr* Robert Dillon

Prime Evil ★ 18

Horror 1988 · US · Colour · 86mins

Notorious horror/porno director Roberta Findlay has had a hand in some of the most controversial and reprehensible exploitation movies in film history. This dire Satanist drama isn't one of them. A 14th-century devil cult grants the Parkman family eternal life, which explains why they're now scouring contemporary New York for victims to sacrifice in the name of Lucifer. Although as tedious and amateurish as usual, this doesn't have the offensive shock value of Findlay's "best" work. AJ

William Beckwith *Thomas Seaton* • Christine Moore *Alexandra Parkman* • Tim Gail *Bill King* • Max Jacobs *George Parkman* ■ *Dir* Roberta Findlay • *Scr* Ed Kelleher, Harriette Vidal

The Prime Gig ★★★★ 15

Crime drama 2000 · US · Colour · 93mins

Director Gregory Mosher's "cold calling" features an engrossing script plus the high calibre star trio of Vince Vaughn, Ed Harris and Julia Ormond. Vaughn is perfectly cast as a sceptical high-flyer recruited for an organisation selling shares in land containing gold, run by ex-inside trader Harris. Mosher's thoughtful direction makes great use of extended takes to draw us into the tale, Vaughn and Ormond share genuine screen chemistry and Harris, as ever, dominates every moment of screen time. JC DVD

Vince Vaughn *Pendelton "Penny" Wise* • Julia Ormond *Caitlin Carlson* • Ed Harris *Kelly Grant* • Rory Cochrane *Joel* • Wallace Shawn *Gene* • George Wendt *Archie* • Stephen Tobolowsky *Mick* ■ *Dir* Gregory Mosher • *Scr* William Wheeler

The Prime Minister ★★ U

Biographical drama 1940 · UK · BW · 109mins

The Victorian novelist and prime minister Benjamin Disraeli once said, "Never complain and never explain" but one wonders if he would have kept quiet after seeing this dull-as-ditchwater biopic. John Gielgud is plummy of tone, supercilious of manner and always convincing as the writer persuaded to run for parliament who ends up running the nation and the Empire. But it's a stodgy history lesson and soapy domestic drama, made primarily to remind audiences embroiled in the second year of war of what they were fighting for. AT

John Gielgud *Benjamin Disraeli* • Diana Wynyard *Mary Anne Wyndham-Lewis* • Will Fyffe *Agitator* • Stephen Murray *William E Gladstone* • Fay Compton *Queen Victoria* ■ *Dir* Thorold Dickinson • *Scr* Brock Williams, Michael Hogan

The Prime of Miss Jean Brodie ★★★★★ 15

Drama 1969 · UK · Colour · 110mins

Although Vanessa Redgrave was a hit in the West End version of Jay Presson Allen's adaptation of Muriel Spark's novel, few would argue that the part of liberated Edinburgh schoolmarm Jean Brodie now belongs solely to Maggie Smith. Never have such politically incorrect opinions been expressed with such disarming charm or been received with such trusting innocence. While Smith thoroughly deserved her Oscar, it is somewhat surprising that Celia Johnson was overlooked for her superb performance as the disapproving headmistress. Robert Stephens and Gordon Jackson are also on form as the men in Smith's life, and Pamela Franklin impresses as the pupil who turns Judas. *Crème de la crème*, indeed. DP. Contains brief nudity.

Maggie Smith *Jean Brodie* • Robert Stephens *Teddy Lloyd* • Pamela Franklin *Sandy* • Gordon Jackson *Gordon Lowther* • Celia Johnson *Miss Mackay* • Diane Grayson *Jenny* • Jane Carr (2) *Mary McGregor* • Shirley Steedman *Monica* ■ *Dir* Ronald Neame • *Scr* Jay Presson Allen, from her play, from the novel by Muriel Spark

Prime Risk ★★ PG

Action adventure 1985 · US · Colour · 94mins

Two bored kids concoct a scheme to rip off hole-in-the-wall cash machines, but find themselves out of their league when the scam brings them into contact with international baddies engaged in a similar but far more subversive activity. Lee Montgomery and Sam Bottoms are attractive leads, and there's a good baddie from veteran Keenan Wynn. DA

Toni Hudson *Julie Collins* • Lee Montgomery *Michael Fox* • Sam Bottoms *Bill Yeoman* • Clu Gulager *Paul Minsky* • Keenan Wynn *Dr Lasser* ■ *Dir/Scr* Michael Farkas

Prime Target ★★ 15

Action drama 1991 · US · Colour · 86mins

This routine action movie was written, produced and directed by one David Heavener, who positions himself in front of the camera as John Bloodstone, a tough, small town sheriff in the Chuck Norris mould, who's given the job of escorting Mob boss Tony Curtis to a different prison, unaware that it's a set-up. The mess that follows is nothing you haven't seen before, though Curtis – in a new toupee – is watchable as ever. DA

David Heavener *John Bloodstone* • Tony Curtis *Marrietta Copella* • Isaac Hayes *Captain Thompkins* • Andrew Robinson *Commissioner Garth* • Robert Reed *Agent Harrington* ■ *Dir/Scr* David Heavener

Primer ★★

Science-fiction thriller 2004 · US · Colour · 78mins

A pretentious headache of a movie, this ultra-low-budget film requires complete concentration. Self-taught film-maker Shane Carruth directs himself in the role of one of two boffins who spend their leisure time conducting scientific experiments. While tinkering with their latest project the duo accidentally discovers that it has time-shift capabilities. Though well shot, with an attractive, over-exposed look, it's undone by the tedious plot and droning dialogue. SF

Shane Carruth *Aaron* • David Sullivan *Abe* • Anand Upadhyaya *Phillip* • Casey Gooden *Robert* • Carrie Crawford *Kara* ■ *Dir/Scr* Shane Carruth

The Primitives ★★ U

Crime drama 1962 · UK · BW · 69mins

The Primitives are four jewel thieves – three men led by one woman – posing as entertainers, who draw upon their skill with disguises in their nefarious schemes. Jan Holden is Cheta, well named as the female cat burglar of the team, who becomes an inconvenient love interest. When they rob a London jewellers, the British police spot the unusual trapeze quality of the crime and get on their tails. All pretty incredible, yet watchable. JG

Jan Holden *Cheta* • Bill Edwards *Peter* • Rio Fanning *John* • George Mikell *Claude* • Terence Fallon *Sgt Henry* ■ *Dir* Alfred Travers • *Scr* Alfred Travers, Moris Farhi

Primrose Path ★★★

Melodrama 1940 · US · BW · 92mins

Determined to escape from the wrong side of the tracks, where her mother is a woman of easy virtue and her father a drunk, Ginger Rogers finds love and respectability with decent Joel McCrea – until he meets her family, that is. Director Gregory La Cava's film was quite daring within the censorious climate of the time, although it compromises its attempt at dramatic realism with a predictably sentimental, romantic outcome. Interesting, though, thanks to the standard of direction and the convincing cast. RK

Ginger Rogers *Ellie May Adams* • Joel McCrea *Ed Wallace* • Marjorie Rambeau *Mamie Adams* • Henry Travers *Gramp* • Miles Mander *Homer Adams* • Queenie Vassar *Grandma* ■ *Dir* Gregory La Cava • *Scr* Allan Scott, Gregory La Cava, from the play by Robert Buckner, Walter Hart, from the novel *February Hill* by Victoria Lincoln

The Prince & Me ★★ PG

Romantic comedy 2004 · US/Can · Colour · 110mins

Julia Stiles plays a hard-working undergraduate whose dreams of becoming a doctor are threatened when she falls for a fellow student (Luke Mably), unaware that he's actually the Crown Prince of Denmark. Director Martha Coolidge creates a modern fairy tale that's as cautionary as it is frothy. The likeable performances from Stiles and the Prince William-styled Mably give this slushy nonsense a warm feeling. SF

Julia Stiles *Paige Morgan* • Luke Mably *Prince Edward/"Eddie"* • Ben Miller *Soren* • James Fox *King Haraald* • Miranda Richardson *Queen Rosalind* • Alberta Watson *Amy Morgan* • John Bourgeois *Ben Morgan* • Eliza Bennett *Princess Arabella* ■ *Dir* Martha Coolidge • *Scr* Jack Amiel, Michael Begler, Katherine Fugate, from a story by Mark Amin, Katherine Fugate

The Prince and the Pauper ★★★ U

Period adventure 1937 · US · BW · 113mins

A historical romp from the classic period at Warner Bros, this famous version of the much-filmed Mark Twain tale about a street urchin who swaps roles with the young Prince Edward was billed as an Errol Flynn feature, but Flynn doesn't even appear as swashbuckler Miles Hendon until nearly halfway through. The title youngsters are played by the Mauch twins and it's hard to summon up any interest in their adventures. The things that actually give this movie its verve and style are a fabulous score by Erich Wolfgang Korngold and a wonderful supporting cast. TS

Errol Flynn *Miles Hendon* • Claude Rains *Earl of Hertford* • Henry Stephenson *Duke of Norfolk* • Barton MacLane *John Canty* • Billy Mauch *Tom Canty* • Bobby Mauch *Prince Edward Tudor* • Alan Hale *Captain of the Guard* • Eric Portman *First lord* ■ *Dir* William Keighley • *Scr* Laird Doyle, from the play by Catherine Chishold Cushing, from the novel by Mark Twain

The Prince and the Pauper ★★★ U

Period adventure 1962 · US · Colour · 93mins

This is an entertaining American TV-movie version of Mark Twain's classic story about the humble street urchin who trades places with a lookalike prince. The tale had already been told to more lavish effect on the big screen with Errol Flynn and Claude Rains in 1937, and would be made as an extravagant romp with Oliver Reed and Mark Lester in 1977. Here, Donald Houston and company do well enough, while Disney's stamp provides a minimum quality guarantee. PF

Sean Scully *Edward, Prince of Wales/Tom Canty* • Donald Houston *John Canty* • Niall MacGinnis *Father Andrew* • Jane Asher *Lady Jane Grey* • Laurence Naismith *Lord Hertford* ■ *Dir* Don Chaffey • *Scr* Jack Whittingham, from the novel by Mark Twain

The Prince and the Pauper ★★ PG

Period adventure 1977 · Pan/US · Colour · 115mins

Oliver Reed, Charlton Heston and Raquel Welch, following on from the success of Richard Lester's two Musketeers films, don the costumes once again for another historical romp, this one based on Mark Twain's classic story. No expense was spared on production values and the distinguished cast has a fine time hamming things up. Despite the extravagance, it remains a lifeless affair that isn't helped by an unconvincing lead performance from Mark Lester as the prince who swaps places with a beggar. JF

Mark Lester (2) *Tom Canty/Prince Edward* • Oliver Reed *Miles Hendon* • Raquel Welch *Lady Edith* • Ernest Borgnine *John Canty* • George C Scott *Ruffler* • Rex Harrison *Duke of Norfolk* • David Hemmings *Hugh Hendon* • Charlton Heston *Henry VIII* • Harry Andrews *Hertford* ■ *Dir* Richard Fleischer • *Scr* George MacDonald Fraser, Berta Dominguez, Pierre Spengler, from the novel by Mark Twain

The Prince and the Showgirl ★★★ PG

Romantic comedy
1957 · UK · Colour · 111mins

What should have been an explosive pairing of Hollywood's golden girl, Marilyn Monroe, and England's greatest theatre actor, Laurence Olivier, doesn't quite come off, largely owing to the vapidity of the vehicle chosen: a tired Terence Rattigan play, written for the Coronation and already dated before it hit the West End boards. As you would expect, Monroe sparkles, showing a terrific sense of comic timing in a performance of great skill and beauty. Olivier, who also directed, seems overawed, and hampers himself with a Balkan accent that's a cross between Garbo and Bela Lugosi. TS [video] DVD

Marilyn Monroe *Elsie Marina* • Laurence Olivier *Charles, Prince Regent* • Sybil Thorndike *Queen Dowager* • Richard Wattis *Northbrooke* • Jeremy Spenser *King Nicholas* ■ *Dir* Laurence Olivier • *Scr* Terence Rattigan, from his play *The Sleeping Prince* • *Costume Designer* Beatrice Dawson

Prince Jack ★★

Political drama 1984 · US · Colour · 100mins

The prince in question is John F Kennedy, whose life and presidency are portrayed in "mockumentary" style. Starting off with Frank Sinatra singing *High Hopes* – which became JFK's campaign anthem – the movie takes in the major issues of the day. Conspicuous by her absence is Jackie, who was alive when the film was made. As always, the main problem is that the actors don't look like the people they claim to be. AT

Robert Hogan *Jack Kennedy* • James F Kelly *Bobby Kennedy* • Kenneth Mars *Lyndon B Johnson* • Lloyd Nolan *Joseph Kennedy* • Cameron Mitchell *General Walker* • Robert Guillaume *Martin Luther King* • Theodore Bikel *Russian Ambassador* ■ *Dir/Scr* Bert Lovitt

Prince of Darkness ★★ 18

Horror 1987 · US · Colour · 101mins

In what is virtually a supernatural remake of his own *Assault on Precinct 13*, director John Carpenter takes one of his sporadic delves into Nigel Kneale sci-fi/horror territory (he even wrote the script as Martin Quatermass) with tedious results. It's old superstitions versus the computer age in an awkward yarn about a weird container full of green liquid in an LA church that contains pure evil. AJ. Contains violence, swearing. [video] DVD

Donald Pleasence *Priest* • Jameson Parker *Brian* • Victor Wong (2) *Professor Birack* • Lisa Blount *Catherine* • Dennis Dun *Walter* • Susan Blanchard *Kelly* • Alice Cooper *Street people leader* ■ *Dir* John Carpenter • *Scr* Martin Quatermass [John Carpenter]

The Prince of Egypt ★★★★ U

Animation 1998 · US · Colour · 98mins

DreamWorks's animated interpretation of the story of Moses has a visual grandeur that's almost a match for the best of Disney. From its magical opening sequence, showing the baby Moses's journey down the river, to the visually stunning sections involving the parting of the Red Sea and the plagues – the curse on the first born is particularly disturbing – this makes for epic cinema. A host of Hollywood heavyweights provide emotive vocal contributions, enhanced by Stephen Schwartz's stirring, Broadway-style songs (the moving *When You Believe* earned an Oscar). Some may even see it as religious propaganda, but this is still an astonishing achievement. A direct-to-video sequel, *Joseph: King of Dreams*, followed. JC [video] DVD

Val Kilmer *Moses* • Ralph Fiennes *Rameses* • Michelle Pfeiffer *Tzipporah* • Sandra Bullock *Miriam* • Jeff Goldblum *Aaron* • Danny Glover *Jethro* • Patrick Stewart *Pharaoh Seti* • Helen Mirren *The Queen* • Steve Martin *Hotep* • Martin Short *Huy* ■ *Dir* Brenda Chapman, Stephen Hickner, Simon Wells • *Scr* Philip LaZebnik • *Music/lyrics* Stephen Schwartz

Prince of Foxes ★★★

Historical drama 1949 · US · BW · 106mins

This is a lavish historical pageant about the wicked Borgias, with Orson Welles giving a magnificently over-ripe performance as the Machiavellian Cesare Borgia, and Tyrone Power as his loyal aide. Filmed in Florence, Siena, Venice and San Gimignano by Oscar-nominated cameraman Leon Shamroy, the picture looks handsome, and Welles is clearly having a whale of a time. AT

Tyrone Power *Andrea Corsini* • Orson Welles *Cesare Borgia* • Wanda Hendrix *Camilla Verano* • Everett Sloane *Mario Belli* • Marina Berti *Angela Borgia* ■ *Dir* Henry King • *Scr* Milton Krims, from the novel by Samuel Shellabarger

The Prince of Homburg ★★

Historical drama 1997 · It · Colour · 85mins

Although Italian director Marco Bellocchio had built his reputation on uncompromising realism, he resorts to conservative pictorialism for this reworking of Heinrich von Kleist's 19th-century play about loyalty and patriotism. Andrea Di Stefano is suitably stiff as the aristocratic cavalry officer charged with recklessness after he leads a victorious charge against orders. It's a painstakingly crafted film, but the observations on the nature of honour and heroism are as old-fashioned as the imagery. DP. In Italian with English subtitles.

Andrea Di Stefano *Prince of Homburg* • Barbara Bobulova *Natalia* • Toni Bertorelli *Elector* • Anita Laurenzi *Electoress* ■ *Dir* Marco Bellocchio • *Scr* Marco Bellocchio, from the play by Heinrich von Kleist

Prince of Jutland ★ 15

Historical drama
1994 · Den · Colour · 103mins

A basic great cast of British thespians back up Christian Bale in this retelling of Shakespeare's *Hamlet*. More medieval Viking than Danish Royal Court, this is a risible and mucky affair, sticking to the nutshell plot (man murders king, marries queen and father's ghost calls on son to avenge) it flails around mixing poor dialogue, laughable fight sequences and worse cinematography. LH [video] DVD

Christian Bale *Amled* • Helen Mirren *Queen Geruth* • Gabriel Byrne *Fenge* • Kate Beckinsale *Ethel* • Steven Waddington *Ribold* • Brian Cox *Aethelwine, Duke of Lindsey* • Brian Glover *Caedman* ■ *Dir* Gabriel Axel • *Scr* Gabriel Axel, Erik Kjersgaard, from the book *The Denmark Chronicle* by Saxo Grammaticus

The Prince of Pennsylvania ★ 15

Comedy drama 1988 · US · Colour · 89mins

This dreadfully unbelievable small-town movie stars Keanu Reeves as a misunderstood loner, whose father (Fred Ward) harbours dreams of being the King of Pennsylvania. Reeves's problems increase when he discovers his mother Bonnie Bedelia in bed with his father's best friend. He seeks solace in Amy Madigan, on feisty form as the hippy owner of a down-town drive-in. A good cast can't rise above the absurdities of the plot. LH [video]

Keanu Reeves *Rupert Marshetta* • Amy Madigan *Carla Headlee* • Bonnie Bedelia *Pam Marshetta* • Fred Ward *Gary Marshetta* • Jeff Hayenga *Jack Sike* • Jay O Sanders *Trooper Joe* ■ *Dir/Scr* Ron Nyswaner

Prince of Pirates ★★ U

Swashbuckling adventure
1953 · US · Colour · 80mins

A second-rate swashbuckler that used up existing studio costumes and sets (one of the last of its kind) and was tailored for then heart-throb John Derek, later to achieve a sort of notoriety as the photographer/director husband of Ursula Andress and the discoverer (and uncoverer) of Bo. Derek wears the period Franco-Spanish costume well but it's not really much good, and viewers will have to be very indulgent to stay with it. TS

John Derek *Prince Roland of Haagen* • Barbara Rush *Nita Orde* • Carla Balenda *Princess Maria* • Whitfield Connor *Stephan* ■ *Dir* Sidney Salkow • *Scr* John O'Dea, Samuel Newman, from the story by William Copeland, Herbert Kline

Prince of Players ★★★

Biographical drama
1955 · US · Colour · 102mins

A biopic of the American actor Edwin Booth who achieved another sort of notoriety by being the brother of Abraham Lincoln's assassin, John Wilkes Booth. Richard Burton plays Booth the actor and is at his best in the Bardian clips, starting with the time he played Richard III when his father was too drunk to go on. Marriage and extracts from *Hamlet*, *Othello* and *Romeo and Juliet* follow, building up to the Lincoln assassination and the public demonstrations against all actors that apparently followed. AT

Richard Burton *Edwin Booth* • Maggie McNamara *Mary Devlin* • John Derek *John Wilkes Booth* • Raymond Massey *Junius Brutus Booth* • Charles Bickford *Dave Prescott* • Elizabeth Sellars *Asia* ■ *Dir* Philip Dunne • *Scr* Moss Hart, from the biography by Eleanor Ruggles • *Music* Bernard Herrmann

Prince of Shadows ★★ 18

Political thriller 1991 · Sp · Colour · 86mins

This moodily shot political thriller has Terence Stamp as a Spanish exile, sent back to Madrid in the early 1960s to assassinate a traitor to the anti-fascist cause. Nightclub performer Patsy Kensit demonstrates how not to imitate Rita Hayworth, with an ill-advised rendition of *Put the Blame on Mame*. Director Pilar Miró makes it looks splendid but the acting – apart from John McEnery – should face a firing squad. TH [video]

Terence Stamp *Darman* • Patsy Kensit *Rebeca* • José Luis Gómez *Valdivia/Ugarte* • Geraldine James *Rebeca Osorio* • Simon Andreu *Andrade* • [Aleksander Bardini] *Bernal* • John McEnery *Walter* ■ *Dir* Pilar Miró • *Scr* Pilar Miró, Mario Camus, Juan Antonio Porto

Prince of the City ★★★ 15

Crime drama based on a true story
1981 · US · Colour · 160mins

This movie has a marvellously complex plot about a cop who reveals interdepartmental corruption, yet, sadly, it lacks both a star and an audience-friendly running time. Treat Williams, excellent though he is, doesn't have the power to hold the attention, and, despite sterling support from Jerry Orbach and sinister prosecutor James Tolkan, the film's length diminishes its impact. TS. Contains violence and swearing. [video]

Treat Williams *Daniel Ciello* • Jerry Orbach *Gus Levy* • Richard Foronjy *Joe Marinaro* • Don Billett *Bill Mayo* • Kenny Marino *Dom Bando* • Carmine Caridi *Gino Mascone* ■ *Dir* Sidney Lumet • *Scr* Jay Presson Allen, Sidney Lumet, from a book by Robert Daley

The Prince of Thieves ★★ U

Adventure 1948 · US · Colour · 71mins

Rarely has Lincoln Green looked as bilious as in this Cinecolor romp. But then, just about everything in Howard Bretherton's Sherwood adventure is off colour. The action centres on Adele Jurgens's reluctance to marry a suitor selected by her father and Jon Hall's bid to ensure that true love wins out. Hall typifies the film's inadvertent tone, which is compounded by Patricia Morison's anaemic Maid Marian. DP

Jon Hall *Robin Hood* • Patricia Morison *Lady Marian* • Adele Jergens *Lady Christabel* • Alan Mowbray *Friar Tuck* • Michael Duane *Sir Allan Claire* • HB Warner *Gilbert Head* • Syd Saylor *Will Scarlet* ■ *Dir* Howard Bretherton • *Scr* Charles Schnee, Maurice Tombragel

The Prince of Tides ★★★★ 15

Romantic drama
1991 · US · Colour · 126mins

Pat Conroy's epic novel about a dysfunctional Southern family is deftly translated to the screen under the subtle direction of Barbra Streisand, who also stars as the New York psychiatrist helping Nick Nolte to come to terms with his twin sister's attempted suicide. Nolte is superb as he wrestles with his family's demons, and Streisand sensibly stays on the sidelines. Jason Gould (Streisand's son from her marriage to Elliott Gould) also features as Streisand's on-screen son. JB. Contains violence, swearing and sex scenes. [video] DVD

Nick Nolte *Tom Wingo* • Barbra Streisand *Susan Lowenstein* • Blythe Danner *Sallie Wingo* • Kate Nelligan *Lila Wingo Newbury* • Jeroen Krabbé *Herbert Woodruff* • Melinda Dillon *Savannah Wingo* • George Carlin *Eddie Detreville* • Jason Gould *Bernard Woodruff* • Brad Sullivan *Henry Wingo* ■ *Dir* Barbra Streisand • *Scr* Pat Conroy, Becky Johnston, from the novel by Pat Conroy

Prince Valiant ★★ U

Period adventure 1954 · US · Colour · 99mins

This jovial Arthurian spectacle, based on the comic strip by Harold Foster, is in that strange dialect called Hollywood Archaic, a tongue known to no one except Hollywood executives. James Mason plays Sir Brack, a Knight of the Round Table, and Robert Wagner in his first leading role is Valiant, the son of a beleaguered Swedish king who arrives in Camelot seeking assistance in the clanking armour and sword department. Janet Leigh swoons whenever Wagner's around, but goodness knows why considering the terrible wig he had to wear. AT

Robert Wagner *Prince Valiant* • Janet Leigh *Princess Aleta* • James Mason *Sir Brack* • Debra Paget *Ilene* • Sterling Hayden *Sir Gawain* • Victor McLaglen *Boltar* • Donald Crisp *King Aguar* • Brian Aherne *King Arthur* ■ *Dir* Henry Hathaway • *Scr* Dudley Nichols, from the comic strip by Harold R Foster

Prince Valiant ★★ PG

Period adventure
1997 · Ger/UK/Ire/US · Colour · 87mins

Cod-historical hokum derived from the popular US comic strip, in which King Arthur's sword, Excalibur, is stolen by marauding Vikings. Things go from bad to Norse when the legendary British symbol falls into the hands of an evil Euro king with designs on Arthur's seat. Fortunately, the heroic Prince Valiant rides to the sword's rescue. This could have been okay, but obvious cash restraints plus hamfisted editing relegate the film to definite B-movie status. DA [video]

Stephen Moyer *Prince Valiant* • Katherine Heigl *Princess Ilene* • Thomas Kretschmann *Thagnar* • Edward Fox *King Arthur* • Udo Kier *Sligon* • Joanna Lumley *Morgan Le Fey* • Ron Perlman *Boltar* • Warwick Davis *Pechet* ■ *Dir*

P

Anthony Hickox • *Scr* Michael Frost Beckner, Anthony Hickox, Carsten Lorenz., from a story by Michael Frost Beckner, from the comic strip by Harold R Foster

The Prince Who Was a Thief ★★

Adventure 1951 · US · Colour · 88mins

From the days when Tony Curtis was a tousle-haired idol for teenagers, this *Arabian Nights* nonsense showed him at his athletic, if not dramatic, best. He's a royal baby brought up by kindly thieves who then duels his way to his rightful throne. Perhaps most surprising, this fantasy was adapted from a story by Theodore Dreiser. TH

Tony Curtis *Julna* • Piper Laurie *Tina* • Everett Sloane *Yussef* • Betty Garde *Mirna* • Jeff Corey *Mokar* • Peggie Castle *Princess Yasmin* ■ *Dir* Rudolph Maté • *Scr* Gerald Drayson Adams, Aeneas MacKenzie, from a story in the book *Chains* by Theodore Dreiser

Les Princes ★★★ 15

Drama 1982 · Fr · Colour · 99mins

This is the first instalment of Tony Gatlif's Romany trilogy, which was completed by *Latcho Drom* (1993) and *Gadjo Dilo* (1997). The villains of the piece are clearly the gendarmes who harass the despised *gitanes*. But Gatlif isn't blind to the problems caused by the patriarchal conservatism that prompts French Romany Gérard Darmon to disown his wife after discovering she's followed a social worker's advice on birth control. Living in squalor with his octogenarian mother and young daughter, he's bitter and unstable, yet he's every bit as authentic as Jacques Loiseleux's gloomy photography. DP. In French with English subtitles.

Gérard Darmon *Nara* • Muse Dalbray *Nara's grandmother* • Dominique Maurin *Petiton* • Hagop Arslanian *Chico* • Tony Gatlif *Leo* • Tony Librizzi *Tony* • Céline Militon *Zorka* • Concha Tavora *Miralda* ■ *Dir/Scr* Tony Gatlif

Princesa ★★★ 18

Drama 2000 · UK/Ger/It · Colour · 93mins

This touching drama focuses on Ingrid de Souza, a small-town Brazilian transsexual, who is forced to work in Milan as a prostitute to finance gender reassignment surgery. Ignoring the warnings of friend Biba Lerhue and transvestite madame Lulu Pecorari, de Souza falls in love with married man Cesare Bocci, who appears to be her route to dreamed-for domesticity – they set up home and he agrees to pay for her surgery – until the reality of their situation eventually sinks in. Given added authenticity by its reliance on improvisation and meticulous casting, this has an almost documentary feel. DP. In Italian and Portuguese with English subtitles.

Ingrid de Souza *Fernanda* • Cesare Bocci *Gianni* • Lulu Pecorari *Karin* • Biba Lerhue *Charlo* • Mauro Pirovano *Fabrizio* ■ *Dir* Henrique Goldman • *Scr* Ellis Freeman, Henrique Goldman, from a book by Fernanda Farias de Albuquerque, Maurizio Jannelli

The Princess Academy ★★

Comedy 1987 · US/Yug/Fr · Colour · 90mins

Some questionable life values inform this light sex comedy about a girls finishing school which is dedicated to teaching its charges how to find rich husbands. Eva Gabor doesn't need to stretch herself as the girls' elegant lecturer, the Countess. JG

Eva Gabor *Countess* • Richard Paul *Drago* • Carole Davis *Sonia* • Lar Park-Lincoln *Cindy* • Lu Leonard *Fraulein Stickenschmidt* • Britt Helfer *Lulu* ■ *Dir* Bruce A Block • *Scr* Sandra Weintraub, from an idea by Fred Weintraub

The Princess and the Goblin ★★★ U

Animated fantasy adventure
1992 · UK/Hun · Colour · 78mins

This animated feature film will keep most children happy, although even they won't fail to notice that the drawings are way below the standard of Disney features. Princess Irene enlists the help of her magical great-great-grandmother and of a miner's son called Curdi to try to prevent a tribe of goblins from capturing the royal palace. With their ugly faces, hatred of poetry and jealousy of humans (because people have toes and they don't), the goblins easily steal the show. DP

Joss Ackland *King* • Claire Bloom *Irene's great great grandmother* • Roy Kinnear *Mump* • Sally Ann Marsh *Princess Irene* • Rik Mayall *Froglip* • Peggy Mount *Goblin Queen* • Peter Murray *Curdi* • Victor Spinetti *Glump* ■ *Dir* József Gémes • *Scr* Robin Lyons, from the fairy tale by George MacDonald

The Princess and the Pirate ★★★ U

Swashbuckling comedy
1944 · US · Colour · 90mins

One of comedian Bob Hope's better vehicles. He plays the cowardly "Sylvester the Great Man of Seven Faces", an 18th-century variety artist with an aversion to pirates. Hope is surrounded by superb character actors. There's a hilarious turn from Walter Brennan, who seems to have based his part on Disney's cartoon dwarf Dopey. Virginia Mayo partners Hope ably, especially when they do their vaudeville number in the splendidly art-directed Bucket of Blood inn. TS

Bob Hope *Sylvester Crosby/The Great Sylvester* • Virginia Mayo *Princess Margaret* • Walter Brennan *Featherhead* • Walter Slezak *La Roche* • Victor McLaglen *The Hook* • Bing Crosby *Commoner* ■ *Dir* David Butler • *Scr* Don Hartman, Melville Shavelson, Everett Freeman, Allen Boretz, Curtis Kenyon, suggested by a story by Sy Bartlett

The Princess & the Warrior ★★★ 15

Drama 2000 · Ger · Colour · 129mins

Director Tom Tykwer bravely drops the pace and stuffs this intense romantic drama with mysterious symbolism, muddled motivations and unresolved incidents. Despite referencing numerous art house icons, this is actually a highly personal piece, hence the setting is Tykwer's home town, Wuppertal. But he spends too much time demonstrating his technical virtuosity to involve us in the tortuous relationship between psychiatric nurse Franka Potente and widowed ex-soldier Benno Fürmann. With its shifting tone and wayward plot, this isn't an easy watch. DP. In German with English subtitles. DVD

Franka Potente *Sissi* • Benno Fürmann *Bodo* • Joachim Król *Walter* • Lars Rudolph *Steini* • Melchior Beslon *Otto* ■ *Dir/Scr* Tom Tykwer

The Princess Bride ★★★★ PG

Fantasy adventure
1987 · US · Colour · 94mins

Rob Reiner has always been careful to avoid typecasting as a director, so following the warm nostalgia of *Stand by Me* he opted for this curious, but ultimately charming, children's fable. The film opens with Peter Falk reading the story to the young Fred Savage, and this ironic distancing continues throughout the movie. Although the requisite monsters, giants and swordfights are present and correct for the children, Reiner also ensures there are plenty of quiet chuckles for adults, largely thanks to the eclectic cast. A delight for all the family. JF DVD

Cary Elwes *Westley* • Mandy Patinkin *Inigo Montoya* • Chris Sarandon *Prince Humperdinck* • Christopher Guest *Count Rugen* • Wallace Shawn *Vizzini* • André the Giant *Fezzik* • Fred Savage *Grandson* • Robin Wright [Robin Wright Penn] *Buttercup, the Princess Bride* • Peter Falk *Grandfather* • Peter Cook *Impressive clergyman* • Billy Crystal *Miracle Max, the Wizard* • Mel Smith *Albino* ■ *Dir* Rob Reiner • *Scr* William Goldman, from his novel

Princess Caraboo ★★★ PG

Historical romance
1994 · US · Colour · 92mins

Is exotic Phoebe Cates a Javanese princess, washed up on the Devon coastline after escaping from pirates? Or is she really a clever con artist using her suspect credentials to infiltrate the parlours and palaces of 19th-century England? Cates exudes the necessary glamour, but it's Jim Broadbent who nets the biggest laughs, while Kevin Kline (Cates's real-life husband) steals every scene he's in. Based on a true slice of history, co-writer/director Michael Austin's satirical fairy tale is disarming fluff with little more substance than a marshmallow. AJ. Contains swearing.

Phoebe Cates *Princess Caraboo* • Jim Broadbent *Mr Worrall* • Wendy Hughes *Mrs Worrall* • Kevin Kline *Frixos* • John Lithgow *Professor Wilkinson* • Stephen Rea *Gutch* • John Sessions *Prince Regent* • Peter Eyre *Lord Apthorpe* ■ *Dir* Michael Austin • *Scr* Michael Austin, John Wells

The Princess Comes Across ★★★

Romantic comedy mystery
1936 · US · BW · 75mins

Carole Lombard is perfectly cast in this combination of romantic comedy and comedy detective thriller, set on board a transatlantic passenger ship, and directed with appropriate zip by William K Howard. Lombard stars as a Brooklyn showgirl with aspirations to be another Garbo. To this end, she poses as a Swedish princess during a sea voyage, but falls in love with ship's musician Fred MacMurray. Together they get caught up in trying to solve the murder of a blackmailing fellow passenger. Delightfully screwy nonsense, harmoniously played by the winning star combination. RK

Carole Lombard *Princess Olga/Wanda Nash* • Fred MacMurray *King Joe Mantell* • Douglass Dumbrille *Paul Musko/Detective Lorel* • Alison Skipworth *Lady Gertrude "Gertie" Allwyn* • George Barbier *Capt Nicholls* • William Frawley *Benton* ■ *Dir* William K Howard • *Scr* Walter DeLeon, Francis Martin, Don Hartman, Frank Butler, from a story by Philip MacDonald, from the novel *A Halakabin* by Louis Lucien Rogger

The Princess Diaries ★★★ U

Comedy 2001 · US · Colour · 110mins

Despite the regality of the title, this is a downmarket comedy with its box-office intentions very much aimed at the pre-teen market. Julie Andrews projects her usual sweet-faced radiance as Queen Clarisse Renaldi of Genovia in another variation on the *Pygmalion* story. The Eliza Doolittle character here is San Francisco schoolgirl Anne Hathaway, who's so clumsy that she's always at the mercy of cheerleader bullies. But when the gauche geek finds out she's next in line to the throne of a small European country, she receives a royal makeover from her new-found Queen grandmother. A wish-fulfilling romance, featuring a performance of class from Andrews. TH DVD

Julie Andrews *Queen Clarisse Renaldi* • Anne Hathaway *Mia Thermopolis* • Hector Elizondo *Joe* • Heather Matarazzo *Lilly Moscovitz* • Mandy Moore *Lana Thomas* • Caroline Goodall *Mia's mom, Helen* • Robert Schwartzman *Michael Moscovitz* ■ *Dir* Garry Marshall • *Scr* Gina Wendkos, from the novels by Meg Cabot

The Princess Diaries 2: Royal Engagement ★★ U

Romantic comedy
2004 · US · Colour · 108mins

After the cheery feel-good charm of his original rags-to-royal-riches fairy tale, director Garry Marshall should have aimed higher than the feel-okay of this barely amusing follow-up. When Anne Hathaway's grandmother (Julie Andrews) steps down from the Genovian throne, the ancient constitution decrees that Hathaway must be married to be crowned queen. The one undisputed highlight is Andrews singing on screen for the first time since her 1997 throat surgery. AJ DVD

Anne Hathaway *Mia Thermopolis* • Julie Andrews *Queen Clarisse Renaldi* • Hector Elizondo *Joe* • John Rhys-Davies *Viscount Mabrey* • Heather Matarazzo *Lilly Moscovitz* • Chris Pine *Lord Nicholas Devereaux* • Callum Blue *Lord Andrew Jacoby* • Kathleen Marshall *Charlotte Kutaway* ■ *Dir* Garry Marshall • *Scr* Shonda Rhimes, from a story by Gina Wendkos, Shonda Rhimes, from the novel by Meg Cabot

Princess Mononoke ★★★★ PG

Animated action fantasy
1997 · Jpn · Colour · 128mins

A luxuriously animated legend of ancient gods going head to head with mankind and industry over the balance of nature. This boldly surrealistic and starkly experimental cartoon is beautifully drawn, using the inspiration of classic Japanese artwork, and drums home a modern ecological message with a feminist bias. Set in the 14th century, it's a complicated tale of cursed Prince Ashitaka condemned to roam the land looking for a way to lift the malediction that has given him supernatural gifts. AJ. Japanese dialogue dubbed into English. DVD

Claire Danes *San, the Princess Mononoke* • Minnie Driver *Eboshi* • Gillian Anderson *Moro* • Billy Crudup *Ashitaka* ■ *Dir* Hayao Miyazaki • *Scr* Neil Gaiman, Hayao Miyazaki, from a story by Hayao Miyazaki

Princess of the Nile ★★ U

Adventure 1954 · US · Colour · 70mins

This is one of those costume pantomimes that 20th Century-Fox used to churn out as insurance against box-office failure elsewhere. Debra Paget is the medieval Egyptian princess who moonlights as an exotic dancer, a move that doesn't endear her to nasty Bedouin invader Michael Rennie. Fortunately Jeffrey Hunter comes to her rescue. Colourful nonsense that looks good but doesn't bear close analysis. TH

Debra Paget *Princess Shalimar/Taura the Dancer* • Jeffrey Hunter *Prince Haidi* • Michael Rennie *Rama Khan* • Dona Drake *Mirva* • Wally Cassell *Goghi* • Edgar Barrier *Shaman* • Michael Ansara *Captain Kral* • Jack Elam *Basra* ■ *Dir* Harmon Jones • *Scr* Gerald Drayson Adams

Princess O'Hara ★ U

Comedy drama 1935 · US · BW · 80mins

Adapted from the short story by Damon Runyon, but failing to capture his unique language and characterisation, this vapid comedy drama involves a hapless heroine (Jean Parker), a stolen racehorse and a bunch of totally inept Runyonesque protection racketeers. The story was remade as the Abbott and Costello vehicle *It Ain't Hay* in 1943, when it fared little better than this version. RK

Jean Parker *Princess Kitty O'Hara* • Chester Morris *Vic Toledo* • Leon Errol *Louie "Last Card" Schulz* • Henry Armetta *Henry Spidoni, veterinary* • Verna Hillie *Alberta Whitley* ■ *Dir* David Burton • *Scr* Harry Clark, Doris Malloy, Robert C Rothafel, Nat Ferber, from a short story in *Collier's* by Damon Runyon

Princess O'Rourke ★★ U

Comedy 1943 · US · BW · 94mins

When ace flyer Robert Cummings and princess Olivia de Havilland fall in love with one another, they cause consternation at diplomatic levels which requires the intervention of President Franklin D Roosevelt. Writer/director Norman Krasna's screenplay for this frothy wartime romantic comedy won an Academy Award, and it offers a few good laughs and attractive star performances, but is ultimately no more than a pleasant time-waster. RK

Olivia de Havilland *Princess Maria/Mary Williams* • Robert Cummings *Eddie O'Rourke* • Charles Coburn *Uncle* • Jack Carson *Dave* • Jane Wyman *Jean* • Harry Davenport *Supreme court judge* ■ *Dir/Scr* Norman Krasna

The Princess Yang Kwei Fei ★★★

Period romantic drama
1955 · Jpn/HK · Colour · 91mins

This colourful period drama was only undertaken with the greatest reluctance by director Kenji Mizoguchi. However, such was his consummate professionalism, that he overcame artistic misgivings and chronic health problems to fashion a dramatically involving and visually beguiling tale of court intrigue and familial feuding. Machiko Kyo gives a touching display of naivety and self-sacrificing nobility as the servant who marries one of the last T'ang emperors of 8th-century China and remains true to his love from beyond the grave. DP. A Japanese language film.

Machiko Kyo *Yang Kwei Fei* • Masayuki Mori *Emperor Hsuan-tsung* • So Yamamura *An Lu-shan* • Sakae Ozawa [Eitaro Ozawa] *Yang Kuo-chung* ■ *Dir* Kenji Mizoguchi • *Scr* Yoshikata Yoda, T'ao Chin, Matsutaro Kawaguchi, Masashige Narusawa, from the poem *Ch'ang Hen Ko* by T'ien Pai Lo

The Principal ★★ 18

Drama 1987 · US · Colour · 105mins

This adequate reworking of an over-familiar tale stars James Belushi as a "problem" teacher whose career seems to have reached rock bottom when he is made principal of the worst school in the neighbourhood. His new charges are an unwholesome mixture of delinquents and drug addicts. Belushi is lightweight but likeable, but Louis Gossett Jr, as the school's tough-nut security chief, takes the acting honours. The mix of comedy and drama is perhaps hard to take. DA [video]

James Belushi *Rick Latimer* • Louis Gossett Jr *Jake Phillips* • Rae Dawn Chong *Hilary Orozco* • Michael Wright *Victor Duncan* • JJ Cohen *"White Zac"* • Esai Morales *Raymi Rojas* ■ *Dir* Christopher Cain • *Scr* Frank Deese

The Principles of Lust ★ 18

Drama 2002 · UK · Colour · 104mins

Writer/director Penny Woolcock's grimy social melodrama veers between the ludicrous and the obvious with a spectacularly exploitative dreariness. What should jobless drifter Alec Newman do? Stay as househusband to working mum Sienna Guillory and her son? Or join the uninhibited Marc Warren on the road to excess with pub strippers, high-stakes gambling, amphetamine addiction, juvenile bare-knuckle boxing and group sex? AJ. Contains swearing, sex scenes, violence, drug abuse. [video] DVD

Alec Newman *Paul* • Marc Warren *Billy* • Sienna Guillory *Juliette* • Lara Clifton *Hole* • Alexander Popplewell *Harry* • Julian Barratt *Phillip* • Gwyne Hollis *Jude* • Kelli Hollis *Lizzie* ■ *Dir* Penny Woolcock • *Scr* Penny Woolcock, based on the unpublished novel by Tim Cooke

Prison ★★★ 18

Horror 1987 · US · Colour · 98mins

Renny Harlin's classy direction, some startling make-up effects and atmospheric use of jail locations enliven this low-budget horror. This tale of the ghost of a wrongly executed prisoner on a vengeance spree pays unusual attention to its characters – you wouldn't know it was a scary movie for the first half hour – and when the gruesome fireworks begin, they certainly light up the screen. Decent performances from Viggo Mortensen and Lane Smith compensate for the film's unnecessary abundance of prison clichés. JC [video]

Lane Smith *Ethan Sharpe* • Viggo Mortensen *Connie Burke* • Chelsea Field *Katherine Walker* • Lincoln Kilpatrick *Cresus* • André De Shields *Sandor* • Steven Little *Rhino* ■ *Dir* Renny Harlin • *Scr* C Courtney Joyner, from a story by Irwin Yablans

The Prisoner ★★★ U

Psychological drama 1955 · UK · BW · 89mins

Alec Guinness reprises his stage role in this adaptation of Bridget Boland's play about a Catholic cardinal's encounter with an official from the totalitarian government that has arrested him. Frequently shown in close-up, Guinness superbly conveys the humility, isolation and commitment of a man who is fighting as much for his flock as for his own survival. Yet, Peter Glenville's theatrical direction won't do much to persuade those without religious or political convictions to become involved. DP [video]

Alec Guinness *Cardinal* • Jack Hawkins *Interrogator* • Wilfrid Lawson *Cell warder* • Kenneth Griffith *Secretary* • Jeannette Sterke *Girl* • Ronald Lewis *Warder* ■ *Dir* Peter Glenville • *Scr* Bridget Boland, from her play

Prisoner of Honor ★★★★ PG

Historical drama
1991 · US/UK · Colour · 84mins

A dramatisation of the famous Dreyfus case that obsessed France for more than a decade, and already the basis of several films. This one stars Richard Dreyfuss as a French officer, Lieutenant Colonel Picquart, who comes to believe that Dreyfus, a Jewish officer languishing on Devil's Island, was wrongly convicted for treason. Made for cable TV, co-executive produced by Dreyfuss and directed by Ken Russell, it boasts a splendid cast. AT [video]

Richard Dreyfuss *Lt Col Picquart* • Oliver Reed *General Boisdeffre* • Peter Firth *Major Henry* • Jeremy Kemp *General DePellieux* • Brian Blessed *General Gonse* • Peter Vaughan *General Mercier* • Kenneth Colley *Captain Alfred Dreyfus* ■ *Dir* Ken Russell • *Scr* Ron Hutchinson

Prisoner of Rio ★★ 15

Biographical drama
1988 · Bra · Colour · 100mins

The story of the efforts of a British copper (Steven Berkoff) to bring back notorious Great Train Robber Ronnie Biggs (Paul Freeman) from Brazil, has a cheap and cheerful look about it. Biggs had a hand in the screenplay, ensuring that the fugitive is portrayed in a not entirely unsympathetic light. Meanwhile Berkoff, as his would-be captor, comes across as a bungling incompetent as his schemes to trap Biggs meet with disaster. TH [video]

Steven Berkoff *Jack McFarland* • Paul Freeman *Ronald Biggs* • Peter Firth *Clive Ingram* • Florinda Bolkan *Stella* • Desmond Llewelyn *Police commissioner* • José Wilker *Salo* ■ *Dir* Lech Majewski • *Scr* Lech Majewski, Ronald Biggs, Julia Frankel

The Prisoner of Second Avenue ★★★ PG

Comedy 1974 · US · Colour · 93mins

Working from his own play, Neil Simon unusually fails to strike the right balance between wit and pathos in this strained study of midlife crisis. Jack Lemmon pulls out all the stops as the executive who not only has to cope with being sacked after 22 years, but also with the evident delight with which wife Anne Bancroft embraces her new career at the local TV station. Gene Saks provides stiff support as his brother, while Sylvester Stallone pops up as an innocent bystander suspected of theft. DP [video]

Jack Lemmon *Mel* • Anne Bancroft *Edna* • Gene Saks *Harry* • Elizabeth Wilson *Pauline* • Florence Stanley *Pearl* • Maxine Stuart *Belle* • Sylvester Stallone *Youth in park* • F Murray Abraham *Cab driver* • M Emmet Walsh *Doorman* ■ *Dir* Melvin Frank • *Scr* Neil Simon, from his play

The Prisoner of Shark Island ★★★

Historical prison drama
1936 · US · BW · 95mins

Dr Samuel Mudd, a Maryland physician, was sentenced to life imprisonment on Shark Island for complicity in the assassination of Abraham Lincoln. John Ford's film about this unfortunate man is part adventure and part penal drama, beginning with John Wilkes Booth's visit to the theatre, where he shoots Lincoln and is injured escaping. Mudd treats Booth's leg and gets thrown into jail, where he helps fight an outbreak of yellow fever. The film, scripted by Nunnally Johnson, has a well-measured anger at the injustice and Warner Baxter's performance as the doctor penalised for his dedication to saving life is remarkably persuasive. AT

Warner Baxter *Dr Samuel A Mudd* • Gloria Stuart *Mrs Peggy Mudd* • Joyce Kay *Martha Mudd* • Claude Gillingwater *Colonel Dyer* • Douglas Wood *General Ewing* • John Carradine *Sergeant Rankin* ■ *Dir* John Ford • *Scr* Nunnally Johnson

Prisoner of the Mountains ★★★★ 15

War drama 1996 · Rus/Kaz · Colour · 94mins

Inspired by a Tolstoy short story, this was the first fictional film to tackle the Chechen conflict. Having been ambushed on patrol, along with battle-scarred sergeant Oleg Menshikov, rookie private Sergei Bodrov Jr falls for Susanna Mekhralieva, the Muslim warlord's daughter, who is nearly tempted by passion to betray her own people. Exhausting combat stereotypes, director Sergei Bodrov reinforces his pacifist plea by unearthing wit and warmth amid the war's brutal ethnic and political realities. But, even more impressive, are Pavel Lebeshev's photographed mountainscapes. DP. In Russian with English subtitles. Contains swearing, sexual references and violence. [video]

Oleg Menshikov *Sacha Kostylin* • Sergei Bodrov Jr *Ivan "Vania" Zhilin* • Susanna Mekhralieva *Dina* • Dzhemal Sikharulidze *Abdul-Murat* ■ *Dir* Sergei Bodrov • *Scr* Arif Aliev, Sergei Bodrov, Boris Giller, from an idea by Boris Giller, from the short story *Kavkazsky Plennik (Prisoner of the Caucasus)* by Leo Tolstoy • *Cinematographer* Pavel Lebeshev

Prisoner of War ★

War drama 1954 · US · BW · 80mins

Ronald Reagan parachutes behind enemy lines into North Korea and – unbelievably – allows himself to be taken prisoner. His mission is dangerous yet silly: he is there to verify reports that the Communists have been treating their prisoners harshly. A movie as cretinous as Hollywood's "Red Scare" movies ever got. AT

Ronald Reagan *Web Sloane* • Steve Forrest *Corporal Joseph Robert Stanton* • Dewey Martin *Jesse Treadman* • Oscar Homolka *Colonel Nikita Biroshilov* ■ *Dir* Andrew Marton • *Scr* Allen Rivkin

The Prisoner of Zenda ★★★

Silent swashbuckling adventure
1922 · US · BW · 125mins

Rex Ingram directs this silent version of the swashbuckler about the English commoner Rudolf Rassendyll (Lewis Stone), forced to impersonate his lookalike, the kidnapped king of the small kingdom of Ruritania. Not as stalwart or convincing as the later 1937 version, but Alice Terry makes an adorable princess and Stone excels in his dual role. TH

Lewis Stone *Rudolf Rassendyll/King Rudolf* • Alice Terry *Princess Flavia* • Robert Edeson *Col Sapt* • Stuart Holmes *Duke "Black" Michael* • Ramon Samaniegos [Ramon Novarro] *Rupert of Hentzau* ■ *Dir* Rex Ingram (1) • *Scr* Mary O'Hara, from the play by Edward E Rose, from the novel by Anthony Hope • *Cinematographer* John F Seitz

The Prisoner of Zenda ★★★★★

Swashbuckling adventure
1937 · US · BW · 101mins

This is the first sound version of Anthony Hope's famous novel of derring-do in the mythical kingdom of Ruritania. Producer David O Selznick was determined to make a splash and raised a budget of $1.25 million, a more than generous sum at the time. The cast is top drawer, but director John Cromwell was less than happy with his stars, convinced that Ronald Colman didn't know his lines and that Douglas Fairbanks Jr and David Niven were indulging in too many wild nights. Selznick came down in favour of his stars and, with production nearly complete, he removed Cromwell and hired George Cukor to shoot some of the final scenes as well as using WS Van Dyke to do the action sequences, both without credit. There's no evidence of the behind-the-scenes crises, however, as the picture is seamlessly enjoyable, with Colman typically assured in the dual role of king and commoner. But it's Fairbanks Jr's swaggering turn that gives this swashbuckler its five-star status. DP

Ronald Colman *Rudolf Rassendyll/King Rudolf V* • Madeleine Carroll *Princess Flavia* • Douglas Fairbanks Jr *Rupert of Hentzau* • Mary Astor *Antoinette De Mauban* • C Aubrey Smith *Colonel Zapt* • Raymond Massey *Black Michael* • David Niven *Captain Fritz von Tarlenheim* ■ *Dir* John Cromwell • *Scr* John Balderston, Wells Root, Donald Ogden Stewart, from the play by Edward Rose, from the novel by Anthony Hope • *Cinematographer* James Wong Howe • *Editor* James E Newcom • *Art Director* Lyle Wheeler • *Music* Alfred Newman

The Prisoner of Zenda ★★★★ U

Swashbuckling adventure
1952 · US · Colour · 96mins

There are those who prefer the popular 1937 Ronald Colman movie, but the Ruritanian romance cried out for this MGM Technicolor treatment, plus the dashing splendour of an experienced cast. Stewart Granger is simply marvellous in the dual central role, born to fence and carouse, and equally at ease romancing Deborah Kerr. The 1937 score by Alfred Newman is retained, and apparently a Moviola on set ensured that the camera set-ups were also copied. TS [video]

P

Stewart Granger *Rudolf Rassendyll/King Rudolf V* • Deborah Kerr *Princess Flavia* • James Mason *Rupert of Hentzau* • Louis Calhern *Colonel Zapt* • Lewis Stone *Cardinal* ■ *Dir* Richard Thorpe • *Scr* John L Balderston, Noel Langley, Wells Root, Donald Ogden Stewart, from the play by Edward Rose, from the novel by Anthony Hope • *Cinematographer* Joseph Ruttenberg • *Music* Alfred Newman

The Prisoner of Zenda ★★ PG

Comedy adventure
1979 · US · Colour · 103mins

This spoof remake of the oft-filmed classic story stars Peter Sellers as a London cabbie who bears an uncanny likeness to Prince Rudolph of Ruritania. Sellers is conned into acting as a decoy for the Prince, whose throne is under threat. The film was plagued by on-set troubles, most reputedly emanating from Sellers's increasingly bizarre behaviour and superstitious nature. On screen these troubles were all too evident. DF

Peter Sellers *Prince Rudolph/Sydney Frewin/ Old King* • Lynne Frederick *Princess Flavia* • Lionel Jeffries *General Sapt* • Elke Sommer *Countess* • Simon Williams *Fritz* ■ *Dir* Richard Quine • *Scr* Dick Clement, Ian La Frenais, from the novel by Anthony Hope

Prisoners of the Casbah ★

Romance adventure
1953 · US · Colour · 78mins

A threadbare and thoroughly dismal attempt at exotic adventure romance. Gloria Grahame, suitably veiled and gowned in gossamer robes, is a princess who, with her sheik-like suitor, Turhan Bey, hides out in the teeming Casbah to escape the clutches of villain Cesar Romero. This would be good for a laugh if it weren't so wooden and dreary. RK

Gloria Grahame *Princess Nadja* • Cesar Romero *Firouz* • Turhan Bey *Ahmed* • Nestor Paiva *Marouf* ■ *Dir* Richard Bare [Richard L Bare] • *Scr* DeVallon Scott, from a story by William Raynor

Private ★★★★ 15

Drama 2004 · It · Colour · 93mins

The Arab-Israeli conflict is distilled into the struggle for control of one house in former documentarian Saverio Costanzo's gripping feature debut. The home of a middle-class Palestinian family in the occupied zone becomes a prison when Israeli soldiers commandeer the building. As the family is penned in the lounge together, tensions between patriarchal schoolteacher Mohammad Bakri and his wife intensify, and the young troops experience misgivings over their commander's aggressive treatment of their "hosts". However, this is no polemic; the even-handed screenplay ensures both sides are represented by believable, multi-dimensional characters. LF. In Arabic, Hebrew and English with subtitles. Contains swearing.

Lior Miller *Commander Ofer* • Mohammad Bakri *Mohammad B* • Tomer Russo *Private Eial* • Areen Omari *Samiah B* • Hend Ayoub *Mariam B* • Karem Emad Hassan Aly *Karem B* ■ *Dir* Saverio Costanzo • *Scr* Camilla Costanzo, Saverio Costanzo, Alessio Cremonini, Sayed Qashua

The Private Affairs of Bel Ami ★★★★

Period drama
1947 · US · BW and Colour · 112mins

This is based on a novel by Guy de Maupassant and, in return for cutting out the more sordid aspects of the original story, director Albert Lewin gives it an extraordinary visual exoticism. George Sanders is marvellous as the lecherous rake and Angela Lansbury is the young widow he loves all along. It's weird, melodramatic, delirious, in black and white and suddenly colour, and how Lewin sneaked it around the studio's financial bosses is anyone's guess. AT

George Sanders *Georges Duroy* • Angela Lansbury *Clotilde de Marelle* • Ann Dvorak *Madeleine Forestier* • Frances Dee *Marie de Varenne* • John Carradine *Charles Forestier* ■ *Dir* Albert Lewin • *Scr* Albert Lewin, from the story by Guy de Maupassant

Private Benjamin ★★★ 15

Comedy 1980 · US · Colour · 105mins

This high octane tale about a Jewish princess who joins the US Army is basically a one-joke effort, but that joke has Goldie Hawn throwing herself with great gusto into the role of a bewildered spoilt brat who comes good. If only director Howard Zieff had allowed someone else to get a look in – the members of the supporting cast are mere satellites around a perky sun. SH. Contains swearing, sex scenes and brief nudity. DVD

Goldie Hawn *Judy Benjamin* • Eileen Brennan *Captain Doreen Lewis* • Armand Assante *Henri Tremont* • Robert Webber *Colonel Clay Thornbush* • Sam Wanamaker *Teddy Benjamin* • Harry Dean Stanton *Sergeant Jim Ballard* • Albert Brooks *Yale Goodman* ■ *Dir* Howard Zieff • *Scr* Nancy Myers, Charles Shyer, Harvey Miller

Private Buckaroo ★★ U

Second World War musical
1942 · US · BW · 68mins

There is a plot in here somewhere, involving cocky conscript Dick Foran being tamed by veteran's daughter Jennifer Holt. But this is essentially a showcase for guest stars such the Andrews Sisters, who contribute their best-loved song, *Don't Sit under the Apple Tree with Anyone Else but Me.* Also featuring in the boot camp revue are comics Shemp Howard, Joe E Lewis, and Donald O'Connor and Peggy Ryan, who became the studio's equivalent of MGM's Judy Garland and Mickey Rooney. DP

The Andrews Sisters [Maxene Andrews] *Maxene Andrews* • The Andrews Sisters [Patty Andrews] *Patty Andrews* • The Andrews Sisters [Laverne Andrews] *Laverne Andrews* • Dick Foran *Lon Prentice* • Joe E Lewis *Lancelot Pringle McBiff* • Jennifer Holt *Joyce Mason* • Shemp Howard *Sgt "Muggsy" Shavel* • Richard Davies *Lt Mason* • Mary Wickes *Bonnie-Belle Schlopkiss* • Donald O'Connor *Donny* • Peggy Ryan *Peggy* • Huntz Hall *Cpl Anemic* • Harry James *Harry James and His Music Makers* ■ *Dir* Edward F Cline [Edward Cline] • *Scr* Edmond Kelso, Edward James, from a story by Paul Gerard Smith

Private Confessions ★★★

Period drama 1996 · Swe · Colour · 127mins

Ingmar Bergman reunited the key members of his creative family – Liv Ullmann, Sven Nykvist and Max von Sydow – for this concluding episode in the trilogy about his parents that began with *Best Intentions* and *Sunday Children.* Samuel Froler and Pernilla August reprise their roles as the strict pastor and his unhappy wife, whose confession of an affair brings forth several shocking revelations and some long-suppressed emotions. Ullmann directs as inobtrusively as possible to keep Bergman's screenplay to the fore. It's an excruciatingly personal film that dissects human nature with rare skill and almost flagellatory honesty. DP. In Swedish with English subtitles.

Pernilla August *Anna* • Max von Sydow *Jacob* • Samuel Froler *Henrik Bergman* • Kristina Adolphson *Maria* • Anita Björk *Karin Akerblom* ■ *Dir* Liv Ullmann • *Scr* Ingmar Bergman • *Cinematographer* Sven Nykvist

A Private Conversation ★★★ PG

Drama 1983 · USSR · Colour · 93mins

Also known as *Without Witnesses*, this is a two-hander about a divorced man who pays a surprise visit on his ex-wife at her apartment. Gradually they discuss their life together and the reasons for their separation, though his attempts to seduce her are not entirely successful. Strong performances, the constricted setting and the "real time" structure are major virtues, while the twist at the end is likely to surprise everyone. AT. In Russian with English subtitles.

Irina Kupchenko *Woman* • Mikhail Ulyanov *Man* ■ *Dir* Nikita Mikhalkov • *Scr* Nikita Mikhalkov, Sofia Prokofyeva, Ramiz Fataliyev, from the play *A Talk without Witnesses* by Sofia Prokofyeva

The Private Eyes ★★★

Mystery spoof 1980 · US · Colour · 92mins

Another outing for comedy duo Tim Conway and Don Knotts who seemed destined to become the Abbott and Costello of the 1970s and 1980s. This time they're lampooning every private eye flick ever made, in a tall story of a murder investigation set in a 250-room English mansion. Huge amounts of slapstick as is usual with the pairing, but there are plenty of good comic sequences. DF

Tim Conway *Dr Tart* • Don Knotts *Inspector Winship* • Trisha Noble *Mistress Phyllis Morley* • Bernard Fox *Justin* • Grace Zabriskie *Nanny* • Irwin Keyes *Jock* • Suzy Mandel *Hilda* ■ *Dir* Lang Elliott • *Scr* Tim Conway, John Myhers

The Private Files of J Edgar Hoover ★★★

Crime drama 1977 · US · Colour · 110mins

A lurid, enjoyable exploitation flick from horror maestro Larry Cohen, purporting to reveal the truth about America's legendary head of the FBI. As Hoover, a closet homosexual cross-dresser, jowly Broderick Crawford is hard to beat, but Dan Dailey is actually even better as Hoover's long-time partner Clyde Tolson. If it all seems a mite unbelievable, only Hoover himself knew the whole truth, and he took it with him to the grave. Scored, surprisingly, by Miklos Rozsa. TS. Contains swearing and violence.

Broderick Crawford *J Edgar Hoover* • José Ferrer *Lionel McCoy* • Michael Parks *Robert F Kennedy* • Ronee Blakley *Carrie DeWitt* • Rip Torn *Dwight Webb* • Celeste Holm *Florence Hollister* • Michael Sacks *Melvin Purvis* • Dan Dailey *Clyde Tolson* ■ *Dir/Scr* Larry Cohen

A Private Function ★★★★ 15

Comedy 1984 · UK · Colour · 92mins

With its gentle, witty portrait of postwar Britain and its sly digs at bourgeois aspirations, this comedy has the stamp of Ealing about it. Scripted by Alan Bennett, it is an often hilarious mixture of well-observed social comedy and sometimes laborious earthy humour, much of the latter being inspired by the bodily functions of a pig being fattened for a feast to celebrate the 1947 royal wedding. Michael Palin does a nice line in mortified meekness, but he is upstaged by Maggie Smith, as his scheming wife, and Liz Smith, whose eccentric antics and ramblings provide some of the highlights. DP. Contains swearing. DVD

Michael Palin *Gilbert Chilvers* • Maggie Smith *Joyce Chilvers* • Denholm Elliott *Dr Charles Swaby* • Richard Griffiths *Henry Allardyce* • Tony Haygarth *Bernard Sutcliff* • John Normington *Frank Lockwood* • Pete Postlethwaite *Douglas Nuttal* • Bill Paterson *Maurice Wormold* • Liz Smith *Mother* • Alison Steadman *Mrs Allardyce* • Jim Carter *Inspector Howard Noble* • Reece Dinsdale *PC Penny* ■ *Dir* Malcolm Mowbray • *Scr* Alan Bennett, from a story by Alan Bennett, Malcolm Mowbray

Private Hell 36 ★★★

Crime drama 1954 · US · BW · 81mins

Ida Lupino co-wrote and produced this tense thriller with ex-husband Collier Young, co-starred with then husband Howard Duff, and played her love scenes with Steve Cochran. He's the hard-up cop who pockets some loot so that she will marry him, and Howard Duff is the partner who reluctantly goes along with the lapse. The strong cast performs well under director Don Siegel. AE

Ida Lupino *Lilli Marlowe* • Steve Cochran *Cal Bruner* • Howard Duff *Jack Farnham* • Dean Jagger *Captain Michaels* • Dorothy Malone *Francey Farnham* • Bridget Duff *Farnham child* • King Donovan *Burglar* ■ *Dir* Don Siegel • *Scr* Collier Young, Ida Lupino • *Cinematographer* Burnett Guffey

Private Investigations ★★★ 18

Thriller 1987 · US · Colour · 75mins

The film that was meant to make actor Clayton Rohner a star back in 1987 manages to be a watchable if overly-complicated thriller, vaguely in the mould of *The Man Who Knew Too Much.* Rohner plays a Los Angeles architect, who is falsely set up as being privy to a Mob secret and finds himself hunted by hired guns as a consequence. Slickly made, it offers some decent performances, especially by the ever reliable Ray Sharkey as a hapless hitman. DA

Clayton Rohner *Joey Bradley* • Ray Sharkey *Ryan* • Paul Le Mat *Detective Wexler* • Talia Balsam *Jenny Fox* • Phil Morris *Eddie Gordon* • Martin Balsam *Cliff Dowling* ■ *Dir* Nigel Dick • *Scr* John Dahl, David W Warfield, from a story by Nigel Dick

Private Lessons ★★ 18

Erotic drama 1981 · US · Colour · 79mins

Sylvia Kristel takes her notoriety as princess of soft-porn in European erotica such as *Emmanuelle* for an American makeover. But this suggestive fantasy – teenager Eric Brown being sexually initiated by maid Kristel – is the wish-fulfiller much as before, even though it's set in Arizona. A blackmail scheme is the feeble excuse for a plot, backed by a rather good rock soundtrack, but production problems didn't help the dislocated way it's put together. TH

Sylvia Kristel *Nicole* • Howard Hesseman *Lester* • Eric Brown *Philly* • Patrick Piccininni *Sherman* • Ed Begley Jr *Jack Travis* • Pamela Bryant *Joyce* ■ *Dir* Alan Myerson • *Scr* Dan Greenburg, from his novel

Private Life ★★★

Drama 1982 · USSR · Colour · 104mins

Yuli Raizman earned himself an Oscar nomination for best foreign film for this wry parable on the growing detachment between the Communist Party and the People. Overlooked for promotion, Mikhail Ulyanov decides to focus on his family, only to discover that his careerism has alienated him from them, too. Laboured in its symbolism and languorous in its pacing, this is, nevertheless, a sincere, if occasionally sentimental, study in disillusion and redemption. The mournful Ulyanov is well supported by Iya Savvina as his wife and Irina Gubanova as his initially sympathetic former secretary. DP. Russian dialogue dubbed into English.

Mikhail Ulyanov *Sergei Abrikosov* • Iya Savvina *Natalya Ilyinichna* • Irina Gubanova *Nelly Petrovna* ■ *Dir* Yuli Raizman • *Scr* Anatoly Grebnyev, Yuli Raizman

The Private Life of Don Juan ★★ U

Romantic adventure 1934 · UK · BW · 83mins

The marks the rather sad end to the soaring, dynamic career of the original swashbuckler, Douglas Fairbanks. Legendary lover Don Juan, now in middle age, returns to Seville, where he discovers that a young man has been impersonating him. It's directed by the inimitable Alexander Korda, but sadly, Fairbanks is well past his swashbuckling prime, but there are still a few stylish moments to savour. SH

Douglas Fairbanks *Don Juan* • Merle Oberon *Antonia* • Binnie Barnes *Rosita* • Joan Gardner *Carmen* • Benita Hume *Dolores* ■ *Dir* Alexander Korda • *Scr* Frederick Lonsdale, Lajos Biró, Arthur Wimperis, from the play *L'Homme à la Rose* by Henri Bataille

The Private Life of Helen of Troy ★★

Silent historical drama
1927 · US · BW · 87mins

Hardly a serious slice of history, this irreverent dip into Ancient Greece was made during Alexander Korda's Hollywood period. Korda's wife, Maria Corda, stars as Helen, whisked off by Paris (Ricardo Cortez), away from her husband Menelaus (Lewis Stone). It's really a Flapper Era sex comedy in togas. AT

Maria Corda *Helen* • Lewis Stone *Menelaus* • Ricardo Cortez *Paris* • George Fawcett *Eteoneus* ■ *Dir* Alexander Korda • *Scr* Carey Wilson, from the novel by John Erskine and from the play *The Road to Rome, a Play* by Robert Emmet Sherwood [Robert E Sherwood]

The Private Life of Henry VIII ★★★★ U

Biographical drama 1933 · UK · BW · 89mins

This was the British movie that finally cracked the American market: a superb, sexy, roistering biographical drama based on history's most flamboyant monarch. It caused a sensation and started a widespread trend for belching in public and tossing used meat bones over one's shoulder in imitation of the great Charles Laughton, whose subtle and clever portrayal rightly won him the best actor Oscar at the age of 33, the first time a British film had been honoured by the Academy. Director and co-producer Alexander Korda pulls out all the stops, and, although the style looks creaky today, the performances are simply splendid, especially Mrs Laughton, Elsa Lanchester, who is very funny as Anne of Cleves. TS

Charles Laughton *Henry VIII* • Robert Donat *Thomas Culpepper* • Elsa Lanchester *Anne of Cleves* • Merle Oberon *Anne Boleyn* • Binnie Barnes *Katherine Howard* • Wendy Barrie *Jane Seymour* • Everley Gregg *Catherine Parr* ■ *Dir* Alexander Korda • *Scr* Lajos Biró, Arthur Wimperis

The Private Life of Sherlock Holmes ★★★★ PG

Mystery 1970 · UK · Colour · 120mins

Director Billy Wilder here gives an affectionate comic spin to the great detective partnership, casting a wondrously theatrical Robert Stephens as Holmes and a bemusedly stolid Colin Blakely as Dr Watson. Always one of Wilder's favourite films, the director was enraged when studio executives insisted on whittling the proposed four stories in the screenplay down to two. *Holmes in Love* (with Genevieve Page), though, is a sight to behold and *The Adventure of the Mini-Submarine*, featuring Queen Victoria, is bizarre and even wistful fun. The Baker Street set by the great Alexander Trauner is a joy of craftsmanship – an architectural metaphor for the film itself. TH DVD

Robert Stephens *Sherlock Holmes* • Colin Blakely *Dr John H Watson* • Irene Handl *Mrs Hudson* • Christopher Lee *Mycroft Holmes* • Tamara Toumanova *Petrova* • Genevieve Page *Gabrielle Valladon* • Clive Revill *Rogozhin* • Catherine Lacey *Old lady* • Stanley Holloway *First gravedigger* • Mollie Maureen *Queen Victoria* ■ *Dir* Billy Wilder • *Scr* Billy Wilder, IAL Diamond, from characters created by Sir Arthur Conan Doyle • *Music* Miklos Rozsa

Private Lives ★★★

Romantic comedy 1931 · US · BW · 82mins

Norma Shearer and Robert Montgomery star in Noël Coward's most famous and enduring high comedy about divorced couple Amanda and Elyot, who were once "so ridiculously over-in love". They meet again unexpectedly while on their respective honeymoons and run away to start their fiery relationship all over again. Given how deeply English the play is and, with its tight three acts and confined sets, how uncinematic, MGM and director Sidney Franklin did quite well by it. It lacks the brilliance of the original, but Shearer is perfect. RK

Norma Shearer *Amanda Chase Prynne* • Robert Montgomery *Elyot Chase* • Reginald Denny *Victor Prynne* • Una Merkel *Sibyl Chase* • Jean Hersholt *Oscar* ■ *Dir* Sidney Franklin • *Scr* Hans Kräly, Richard Schayer, Claudine West, from the play by Noël Coward

The Private Lives of Adam and Eve ★

Comedy fantasy
1959 · US · BW and Colour · 87mins

Stranded bus passengers have a collective dream in which they become characters in the biblical story of the Creation. In 1959 this satire was condemned as "blasphemous and sacrilegious" by America's Legion of Decency. Universal was obliged to withdraw the film and re-shoot to make the fantasy less ambiguous. This version was released in 1961, but was not seen in Britain until 1988. The Garden-of -Eden comedy was revealed to be an extended revue sketch, racy but naive and witless, despite the many distinguished names involved. DM

Mickey Rooney *Nick Lewis/Devil* • Mamie Van Doren *Evie Simms/Eve* • Fay Spain *Lil Lewis/Lilith* • Mel Tormé *Hal Sanders* • Marty Milner [Martin Milner] *Ad Simms/Adam* • Cecil Kellaway *Doc Bayles* • Tuesday Weld *Vangie Harper* • Paul Anka *Pinkie Parker* ■ *Dir* Albert Zugsmith, Mickey Rooney • *Scr* Robert Hill, from a story by George Kennett

The Private Lives of Elizabeth and Essex ★★★ U

Historical drama
1939 · US · Colour · 102mins

This ridiculous piece of pomp and circumstantial evidence stars Bette Davis as Elizabeth I, who's infatuated with the Earl of Essex, played by Errol Flynn. Unfortunately, without a buckle to swash, Flynn seems stranded in the reams of ripe Hollywood dialogue. Yet the stirring Erich Wolfgang Korngold music and lavish sets almost compensate for the film's travesty of history. Davis herself hated doing the picture and didn't enjoy being cast against Flynn – she wanted Laurence Olivier as Essex – though studio head Jack Warner knew that Davis and Flynn were a marriage made in box-office heaven. AT

Bette Davis *Queen Elizabeth I* • Errol Flynn *Robert Devereaux, Earl of Essex* • Olivia de Havilland *Lady Penelope Gray* • Donald Crisp *Francis Bacon* • Alan Hale *Earl of Tyrone* • Vincent Price *Sir Walter Raleigh* ■ *Dir* Michael Curtiz • *Scr* Norman Reilly Raine, Aeneas MacKenzie, from the play *Elizabeth the Queen* by Maxwell Anderson

A Private Matter ★★★★ PG

Drama based on a true story
1992 · US · Colour · 88mins

Back in the 1960s, Sherri Finkbine presented a children's programme on US TV called *Romper Room*. However, the mother of four made more headlines when she opted for an abortion after discovering that her unborn child had been damaged by the drug thalidomide. Scripted by William Nicholson (of *Shadowlands* fame) and directed with intelligence and sensitivity by Joan Micklin Silver, this intense TV movie explores the storm of media and pressure group controversy that followed her decision. Sissy Spacek excels as Finkbine and Aidan Quinn provides unfussy support as her husband Bob. DP

Sissy Spacek *Sherri Finkbine* • Aidan Quinn *Bob Finkbine* • Estelle Parsons *Mary Chessen* • Sheila McCarthy *Diane Callaghan* ■ *Dir* Joan Micklin Silver • *Scr* William Nicholson

The Private Navy of Sgt O'Farrell ★★ U

Second World War comedy
1968 · US · Colour · 92mins

Bob Hope was an unabashed Republican whose support for the war in Vietnam and Richard Nixon post-Watergate gave him the reputation of a stolid right-winger. Strange then to find him in this shipshape satire with antiwar undertones, co-produced by his own company, about lost beer and a wild and crazy nurse (Phyllis Diller). JG

Bob Hope *Dan O'Farrell* • Phyllis Diller *Nurse Nellie Krause* • Jeffrey Hunter *Lt Lyman Jones* • Gina Lollobrigida *Maria* • Mylène Demongeot *Gaby* • John Myhers *Lt Cdr Snavely* • Mako *Calvin Coolidge Ishimura* • Henry Wilcoxon *R Adm Stokes* • Dick Sargent *Capt Prohaska* ■ *Dir* Frank Tashlin • *Scr* Frank Tashlin, from a story by John L Greene, Robert M Fresco

Private Parts ★★★★ 18

Biographical comedy
1997 · US · Colour · 104mins

This is an enthralling biopic of American "shock jock" Howard Stern, notorious for his sexually explicit media broadcasts and for his bust-ups with just about everybody. Charting his rise from hopeless DJ to America's most outspoken radio celebrity, this presents Stern (playing himself) as a deeply offensive human being, but it also reveals a softer off-air side, particularly in his relationship with Catherine McCormack. Although obviously toned down, this rude, crude and highly entertaining adaptation of Stern's own book doesn't flinch from re-creating many of his raunchier moments. JC. Contains swearing, nudity, sexual references. DVD

Howard Stern • Robin Quivers • Mary McCormack *Alison Stern* • Fred Norris • Paul Giamatti *Kenny* • Gary Dell'Abate *Gary Dell'Abate* • Jackie Martling • Carol Alt *Gloria* • Ozzy Osbourne • Mia Farrow ■ *Dir* Betty Thomas • *Scr* Len Blum, Michael Kalesniko, from the autobiography by Howard Stern

Private Potter ★★ U

War drama 1963 · UK · BW · 88mins

Tom Courtenay is the eponymous soldier whose inexperience causes him to cry out while on a mission, leading to the death of a colleague. In his defence, Courtenay claims that at the critical moment he had a vision of God. This leads to a debate over whether he should be court martialled, the existence of God and a lot of other weighty issues. Courtenay is utterly convincing as the delicate creature who wilts under pressure but Ronald Harwood's script, based on his TV play, is a sermon few actors could survive. Flashy direction doesn't help matters, either. AT

Tom Courtenay *Pte Potter* • Mogens Wieth *Yannis* • Ronald Fraser *Doctor* • James Maxwell *Lt Col Gunyon* • Ralph Michael *Padre* • Brewster Mason *Brigadier* • Eric Thompson *Capt Knowles* • John Graham (1) *Maj Sims* • Frank Finlay *Capt Patterson* ■ *Dir* Casper Wrede • *Scr* Casper Wrede, Ronald Harwood, from the TV play by Ronald Harwood

Private Resort ★★ 18

Sex comedy 1985 · US · Colour · 78mins

A typical 1980s sun, sea, sand and sex movie about the exploits of two friends on the hunt for girls at a Miami resort. The main point of interest in what would otherwise be a forgettable movie is a first starring role for Johnny Depp. Here he plays Jack, who with pal Ben (Rob Morrow from TV's *Northern Exposure*) seeks simple hedonistic pleasure. Even this early in his career Depp shows promise, demonstrating that most important screen attribute: presence. DF

Rob Morrow *Ben* • Johnny Depp *Jack Marshall* • Emily Longstreth *Patti* • Karyn O'Bryan *Dana* • Hector Elizondo *The Maestro* • Dody Goodman *Amanda Rawlings* ■ *Dir* George Bowers • *Scr* Gordon Mitchell, from a story by Ken Segall, Alan Wenkus, Gordon Mitchell

Private School ★ 18

Comedy 1983 · US · Colour · 84mins

Even fans of *Porky's* will loathe this witless teen sex comedy in which a bunch of voyeurs from an all-boy academy try to spy on the girls in the school next door. Sylvia Kristel (*Emmanuelle*) plays sex-education teacher Ms Regina Copuletta, which is about the level of humour to be expected here. FL

Phoebe Cates *Christine Ramsay* • Betsy Russell *Jordan Leigh-Jensen* • Kathleen Wilhoite *Betsy Newhouse* • Matthew Modine *Jim Green* • Ray Walston *Chauncey* • Sylvia Kristel *Ms Regina Copuletta* ■ *Dir* Noel Black • *Scr* Dan Greenburg, Suzanne O'Malley

The Private Secretary ★★ U

Comedy 1935 · UK · BW · 70mins

Fussy, ever-anxious and with an unrivalled gift for mismanagement, Edward Everett Horton was one of the great comic sidekicks of the studio era. However, he had to come to Twickenham Studios for this rare leading role. He plays an amiably muddled vicar who has to fend off the irate creditors on the trail of spendthrift playboy Barry Mackay. Based on a popular German farce, the picture is pretty stagebound, but it trots along smoothly. DP

Edward Everett Horton *Reverend Robert Spalding* • Barry Mackay *Douglas Cattermole* • Judy Gunn *Edith Marsland* • Oscar Asche *Robert Cattermole* • Sydney Fairbrother *Miss Ashford* ■ *Dir* Henry Edwards • *Scr* George Broadhurst, Arthur Macrae, H Fowler Mear, from the play *Der Bibliotheker* by Van Moser

The Private War of Major Benson ★★★ U

Comedy 1955 · US · Colour · 104mins

Charlton Heston knocked off this dated but likeable comedy while on a month-long lay-off during the shooting of DeMille's gargantuan *The Ten Commandments*. Heston plays a hard-nosed army major, who displeases his superiors and winds up drilling the students at a military school run by nuns. Heston's intense physicality is often the source of the comedy, and the Oscar-nominated screenplay delivers the message that in the postwar era the US military needn't be for tough nuts only. AT

Charlton Heston *Major Bernard Benson* • Julie Adams *Dr Kay Lambert* • William Demarest *John* • Tim Considine *Cadet Sergeant Hibler* • Sal Mineo *Cadet Colonel Dusik* ■ *Dir* Jerry

P

Hopper • *Scr* William Roberts, Richard Alan Simmons, from a story by Joe Connelly, Bob Mosher

Private Worlds ★★★

Medical drama 1935 · US · BW · 80mins

Producer Walter Wanger bought Phyllis Bottome's novel because its setting – a mental hospital – had not been featured in an American film before, but both Fredric March and Warner Baxter turned down the male lead. Wanger then hired Charles Boyer, about to return to his native France after finding little success in Hollywood. The film brought him a huge female following and a reputation as "the great lover", and Claudette Colbert, as the doctor who initially encounters prejudice from Boyer, received an Oscar nomination. TV

Claudette Colbert *Dr Jane Everest* • Charles Boyer *Dr Charles Monet* • Joan Bennett *Sally MacGregor* • Helen Vinson *Claire Monet* • Joel McCrea *Dr Alex MacGregor* • Esther Dale *The matron* • Sam Hinds [Samuel S Hinds] *Dr Arnold* ■ *Dir* Gregory La Cava • *Scr* Lynn Starling, Gregory La Cava, Gladys Unger, from the novel by Phyllis Bottome • *Cinematographer* Leon Shamroy

A Private's Affair ★★ U

Comedy 1959 · US · Colour · 92mins

Sal Mineo was neither comedian nor leading man, but he makes a stab at both in this service comedy. Mineo is one of three military cadets who form a vocal trio as part of their basic training. The three kids aren't convincing as cadets at all, the idea being that even rock 'n' roll beatnik types can wear a uniform. Look out for Bing Crosby's son Gary. AT

Sal Mineo *Luigi Maresi* • Christine Carere *Marie* • Barry Coe *Jerry Morgan* • Barbara Eden *Katey* • Gary Crosby *Mike* • Terry Moore *Louise Wright* • Jim Backus *Jim Gordon* • Jessie Royce Landis *Elizabeth T Chapman* ■ *Dir* Raoul Walsh • *Scr* Winston Miller, from a story by Ray Livingston Murphy

Privates on Parade ★★ 15

Comedy drama 1982 · UK · Colour · 107mins

A sort of *Virgin Soldiers* with pretentious knobs on, based on Peter Nichols's play in which a troupe of soldiers put on musical revues in Singapore. The Malay emergency, when communists threatened to topple the British colony, provides the background. In the foreground are John Cleese, Denis Quilley and lots of dodgy racial innuendo. The palm trees are all plastic as the picture was filmed in England, the jokes are a notch above the *Carry On* level and Cleese is an inch away from a nervous breakdown. Not nearly as funny as it should have been. AT. Contains some violence and swearing. DVD

John Cleese *Major Giles Flack* • Denis Quilley *Captain Terri Dennis* • Nicola Pagett *Sylvia Morgan* • Patrick Pearson *Private Steven Flowers* ■ *Dir* Michael Blakemore • *Scr* Peter Nichols, from his play

Private's Progress ★★★★ U

Comedy 1956 · UK · BW · 95mins

This pleasing mix of satire and nostalgia was unusual at the time for suggesting that not every tommy who went to fight in the Second World War was a hero. Ian Carmichael is superbly cast as the hapless Stanley Windrush, whose natural ineptitude is seen as a God-given gift by the roguish Richard Attenborough and Dennis Price. Although the Boulting brothers rather lose track of the plot once Carmichael goes after Nazi art treasures, this is still richly entertaining, not least because of the smashing performance of Terry-Thomas. DP DVD

Richard Attenborough *Private Cox* • Dennis Price *Brigadier Bertram Tracepurcel* • Terry-Thomas *Major Hitchcock* • Ian Carmichael *Stanley Windrush* • Peter Jones *Egan* • William Hartnell *Sergeant Sutton* ■ *Dir* John Boulting • *Scr* John Boulting, Frank Harvey, from the novel by Alan Hackney

Privilege ★★

Satirical drama 1967 · UK · Colour · 102mins

Peter Watkins, who made the chilling atomic warning *The War Game*, directed this uneven satire in which real-life pop star Paul Jones is the rock idol who finds himself manipulated by the Church and the State, who seek to contain the violent instincts of his fans. This entails a change of image that transforms him into a religious leader. It's filled with confidence, but little conviction. Jean Shrimpton, one of the fashion icons of the time, is the singer's girlfriend, but her acting talent doesn't match her looks. TH

Paul Jones *Steve Shorter* • Jean Shrimpton *Vanessa Ritchie* • Mark London *Alvin Kirsch* • Max Bacon *Julie Jordan* • Jeremy Child *Martin Crossley* ■ *Dir* Peter Watkins • *Scr* Norman Bogner, Peter Watkins, from a story by Johnny Speight

Prix de Beauté ★★★

Silent drama 1930 · Fr · BW · 109mins

One for Louise Brooks fans, and a perfect showcase for her specialist gifts as a tragic heroine, this was made as a silent in Paris by Italian director Augusto Genina. Disastrously badly dubbed as sound came into fashion, its American release, as *Miss Europe*, was an understandable failure. In its pure silent version, however, a print of which was rediscovered in Italy and restored, this tale of an ordinary girl of extraordinary beauty, who wins a beauty contest with tragic consequences, is replete with many exquisite images. RK

Louise Brooks *Lucienne Garnier* • Georges Charlia *André* • H Bandini *Antonin* ■ *Dir* Augusto Genina • *Scr* René Clair, Georg Wilhelm Pabst [GW Pabst], Bernard Zimmer, from a story by Augusto Genina, René Clair, Bernard Zimmer, Alessandro de Stefani • *Cinematographer* Rudolf Maté, Louis Née • *Editor* Edmond T Gréville

The Prize ★★★

Spy adventure 1963 · US · Colour · 134mins

The Nobel prizes are handed out in Stockholm, with Paul Newman winning his for literature and Edward G Robinson getting his for physics. But this is the Cold War, Russia is almost next door, and Newman smells a big fat communist conspiracy. Screenwriter Ernest Lehman wrote Hitchcock's classic chase picture *North by Northwest*; here he recycles some of those ideas and cares not a jot about plausibility. A bit long perhaps, but this is still an enjoyable romp that displays a healthy cynicism towards international politics and culture. AT

Paul Newman *Andrew Craig* • Edward G Robinson *Dr Max Stratman* • Elke Sommer *Inger Lisa Andersen* • Diane Baker *Emily Stratman* • Micheline Presle *Dr Denise Marceau* • Gérard Oury *Dr Claude Marceau* ■ *Dir* Mark Robson • *Scr* Ernest Lehman, from the novel by Irving Wallace

The Prize Fighter ★★

Comedy 1979 · US · Colour · 99mins

The regular collaborations between Don Knotts and Tim Conway proved popular to their fans. In this one, Conway plays a dim-witted boxer and Knotts is his dispirited manager. The unsuccessful pair are down on their luck when they get involved with a gangster who promises them some big bucks. Some farcical slapstick and passable comedy sequences, but it's hardly a knockout. DF

Tim Conway *Bags* • Don Knotts *Shake* • David Wayne *Pop Morgan* • Robin Clarke *Mike* • Cisse Cameron *Polly* • Mary Ellen O'Neill *Mama* ■ *Dir* Michael Preece • *Scr* Tim Conway, John Myhers

A Prize of Arms ★★★

Crime thriller 1961 · UK · BW · 104mins

A clever and exciting caper about the heist of army loot, starring Stanley Baker, who was never quite as effective in leading roles as he was playing the supporting villain. Master cameraman and later cult director Nicolas Roeg co-wrote the original story while under-rated Cliff Owen took on the directorial duties. The nail-biting climax is very well handled and there's a terrific co-starring performance from Tom Bell. Good reviews at the time didn't help this film's box office takings, and it became known as just another average British thriller. TS

Stanley Baker *Turpin* • Helmut Schmid *Swavek* • Tom Bell *Fenner* • David Courtenay *Lieutenant Davies* • Tom Adams *Corporal Glenn* • Anthony Bate *Sergeant Reeves* • Rodney Bewes *Private Maynard* ■ *Dir* Cliff Owen • *Scr* Paul Ryder, from a story by Nicolas Roeg, Kevin Kavanagh

A Prize of Gold ★★

Crime adventure
1955 · UK · Colour · 101mins

For reasons never satisfactorily explained, Mai Zetterling wants to take a number of orphaned children from their home in Germany to a new life in South America. Her lover, an American soldier played by Richard Widmark, agrees to help her and decides to steal a load of gold bullion which is being flown from Berlin to London. It's part routine thriller, part soggy melodrama with a lot of winsome kiddies, and Richard Widmark plays a softie! In a word, unconvincing. AT

Richard Widmark *Sergeant Joe Lawrence* • Mai Zetterling *Maria* • Nigel Patrick *Brian Hammell* • George Cole *Sergeant Roger Morris* • Donald Wolfit *Alfie Stratton* ■ *Dir* Mark Robson • *Scr* Robert Buckner, John Paxton, from the novel by Max Catto

The Prizefighter and the Lady ★★★

Sports romance 1933 · US · BW · 101mins

Heavyweight boxing champion Max Baer (displaying enough acting talent to go on to several more films) stars as a fighter who falls for Myrna Loy. He marries her – with the permission of her former lover, gangster Otto Kruger – only to lose her through his own arrogance and womanising. The romantic plot, however, is incidental to the action in the ring, climaxing in a bloody battle with Primo Carnera. WS Van Dyke directed for MGM with his usual pace, enlisting the services of several fighters playing themselves, including Carnera, Jack Dempsey, Jess Willard and Jim Jeffries. RK

Myrna Loy *Belle Morgan* • Max Baer *Steve Morgan* • Primo Carnera • Jack Dempsey • Walter Huston *"Professor" Edwin J Bennett* • Otto Kruger *Willie Ryan* • Vince Barnett *Bugsie* • Jess Willard • Jim Jeffries ■ *Dir* WS Van Dyke • *Scr* John Lee Mahin, John Meehan, from a story by Frances Marion

Prizzi's Honor ★★★★ 15

Black comedy 1985 · US · Colour · 123mins

Director John Huston's penultimate film sees a return to the type of *film noir* with which he made his name in the 1940s, sent up as a black comedy. His daughter Anjelica has an Oscar-nominated supporting role and her then-partner Jack Nicholson is the Oscar-nominated lead. He plays a grizzled Mafia hitman who falls for and marries Kathleen Turner's foxy freelance hitwoman. Their loyalties are tested (he works for the powerful East Coast Prizzi family; she, a West Coast operator, does not) and then shattered when each is tasked with bumping off the other. Complex farce ensues under the steady hand of Huston, and it's all irresistibly dark. AC. Contains nudity, swearing, sex, violence. DVD

Jack Nicholson *Charley Partanna* • Kathleen Turner *Irene Walker* • Anjelica Huston *Maerose Prizzi* • Robert Loggia *Eduardo Prizzi* • William Hickey *Don Corrado Prizzi* • John Randolph *Angelo "Pop" Partanna* • Lee Richardson *Dominic Prizzi* ■ *Dir* John Huston • *Scr* Richard Condon, Janet Roach, from the novel by Richard Condon

Problem Child ★ PG

Comedy 1990 · US · Colour · 81mins

In this dreadful mishmash of a comedy, John Ritter stars as a man who adopts a child so dysfunctional it is a wonder any part of him works at all. Not only is it crude and deeply unfunny, but it also fails to work on the simplest level as an object lesson in giving love and eventually receiving it. There is something offensive about using an unloved and rebellious child as the butt of bad jokes in this way. But, unfortunately, it led to some even more obnoxious sequels. SH. Contains swearing.

John Ritter *Ben Healy* • Jack Warden *"Big" Ben Healy Sr* • Michael Oliver *Junior* • Gilbert Gottfried *Mr Peabody* • Amy Yasbeck *Flo Healy* ■ *Dir* Dennis Dugan • *Scr* Scott Alexander, Larry Karaszewski

Problem Child 2 ★ PG

Comedy 1991 · US · Colour · 85mins

There are those who like nothing better than a full celluloid cacophony of life's more basic bodily functions and, if you find lavatorial humour a must, you will be well served by this execrable film. Continuing where the original film left off, this was justifiably slated on its release. Amazingly, a further, made-for-TV sequel followed in 1995. SH. Contains swearing and violence.

John Ritter *Ben Healy* • Michael Oliver *Junior Healy* • Jack Warden *"Big" Ben Healy* • Laraine Newman *LaWanda Dumore* • Amy Yasbeck *Annie Young* • Ivyann Schwan *Trixie Young* • Gilbert Gottfried *Mr Peabody* • Charlene Tilton *Debbie Claukinski* ■ *Dir* Brian Levant • *Scr* Scott Alexander, Larry Karaszewski

Le Procès de Jeanne d'Arc ★★★★ PG

Drama 1962 · Fr · BW · 61mins

Robert Bresson, a master of minimalist technique, returned to the original trial transcripts to give an authentic feel to this remarkable featurette that deservedly won the Special Jury Prize at Cannes. Florence Carrez seems overawed by the part, but this only helps make Joan's torment all the more credible. The deeply moving final shot will live long in the memory. DP. In French with English subtitles. DVD

Florence Carrez *Jeanne d'Arc* • Jean-Claude Fourneau *Bishop Cauchon* • Marc Jacquier *Jean Lemaître, Inquisitor* • Roger Honorat *Jean Beaupère* • Jean Gillibert *Jean de Châtillon* • André Régnier *d'Estivet* ■ *Dir/Scr* Robert Bresson

Process ★★★

Drama 2004 · Fr/UK · Colour · 94mins

Composed of 29 scenes, each comprised of one unbroken take, this tells in fragmentary form how an unnamed actress (played with guts by Béatrice Dalle) gets to the point of committing suicide after enduring several personal tragedies, including the death of a child, a messy divorce and breast cancer. All this unfolds with virtually no dialogue, and is exceedingly pretentious but also often gorgeous and mesmerising, filmed with rigorous precision. LF. In English and French with subtitles.

Béatrice Dalle *Actress* • Guillaume Depardieu *Husband* • Julia Faure *Actress* • Daniel Duval *Lover* • Sébastien Viala *Young lover* • Françoise Klein *Nurse* • Erik Arnaud *Doctor* • Léos Carax *Doctor* ■ *Dir/Scr* CS Leigh

The Prodigal ★★

Biblical drama 1955 · US · Colour · 112mins

"Two years in the making!" shrieked the gaudily coloured posters for this very studio-bound MGM epic based on the New Testament tale of the prodigal son, but clearly less than two minutes were spent on the script. Director Richard Thorpe was obviously smitten by having hordes of extras, and, regrettably, lets himself linger, tableau-style. Top-billed Lana Turner, though perfectly typecast, is a shade too old for her predatory role, but is mesmerisingly watchable. TS

Lana Turner *Samarra, high priestess of Astarte* • Edmund Purdom *Micah* • Louis Calhern *Nahreeb, high priest of Baal* • Audrey Dalton *Ruth* • James Mitchell *Asham* • Neville Brand *Rhakim* • Walter Hampden *Eli, Micah's father* ■ *Dir* Richard Thorpe • *Scr* Maurice Zimm, Joe Breen Jr, Samuel James Larsen

The Prodigal ★ PG

Religious drama 1983 · US · Colour · 101mins

John Travolta's brother Joey, Scottish actor Ian Bannen and evangelist Billy Graham make for an eclectic mix in the cast of this ultra-conservative spiritual drama. The story follows a family who, pressured by the trials and tribulations of modern existence, are losing their faith and coming close to disintegration. As written and directed by James F Collier, it's squeaky clean and dreadfully dull. FL [VIDEO]

John Hammond *Greg Stuart* • Hope Lange *Anne Stuart* • John Cullum *Elton Stuart* • Morgan Brittany *Sheila Holt-Browning* • Ian Bannen *Riley Wyndham* • Joey Travolta *Tony* • Arliss Howard *Scott Stuart* • Sarah Rush *Laura* • Billy Graham ■ *Dir/Scr* James F Collier

The Prodigal Son ★★★ 18

Martial arts drama
1983 · HK · Colour · 100mins

Yuen Biao and Sammo Hung co-star in this action-packed but nevertheless stylish tale of deception and revenge. With his cheeky grin and flying fists, the irrepressible Yuen is on top form as a disappointed street fighter who joins a Chinese opera company to study under a martial arts master after he discovers that his over-protective father has been rigging all his bouts. The stocky Hung brings a typical touch of good humour. DP. Cantonese dialogue dubbed into English. Contains violence. [VIDEO] DVD

Sammo Hung *Wong Wah Bo* • Yuen Biao *Leung Jan* • Frankie Chan *Lord Ngai* • Lam Ching Ying *Leung Yee Tai* ■ *Dir* Sammo Hung • *Scr* Samo Hung, Wong Bing Yiu

The Producers ★★★★★ PG

Comedy 1968 · US · Colour · 84mins

This triumphantly tasteless affair was Mel Brooks's first feature and it fully deserves its status as a comedy classic. Zero Mostel plays the sweaty, down-on-his-luck Broadway impresario who links up with shy accountant Gene Wilder in a scam to fleece theatrical investors with the worst play of all time: a musical biopic of Adolf Hitler. The two leads are wonderful, as is Dick Shawn as the hippy star who takes the lead role in their production, and, while the gags flow freely throughout, it's the jaw-dropping numbers from *Springtime for Hitler* that cement the film's place in cinema history. JF [VIDEO] DVD

Zero Mostel *Max Bialystock* • Gene Wilder *Leo Bloom* • Kenneth Mars *Franz Liebkind* • Estelle Winwood *"Hold me, touch me" old lady* • Renee Taylor *Eva Braun* • Christopher Hewett *Roger De Bris* • Lee Meredith *Ulla* • Andreas Voutsinas *Carmen Giya* • Dick Shawn *Lorenzo St Du Bois* • Josip Elic *Violinist* • Madlyn Cates *Concierge* • John Zoller *Drama critic* • William Hickey *Drunk in theatre bar* ■ *Dir/Scr* Mel Brooks

The Professional ★★★

Thriller 1981 · Fr · Colour · 105mins

This is an absorbing thriller, with Jean-Paul Belmondo as a French secret service agent sent to assassinate the ruler of a minor African republic. However, a change in his political circumstances prompts the dictator to sue for an alliance. The contract is cancelled, but Belmondo is determined to fulfil his mission and now finds himself at the top of the French government's hit list. Belmondo's vigour elevates this picture above the norm. DP. French dialogue dubbed into English.

Jean-Paul Belmondo *Joss Beaumont* • Robert Hossein *Rosen* • Michel Baune *Valera* ■ *Dir* Georges Lautner • *Scr* Georges Lautner, Michel Audiard, from the novel *La Mort d'une Bête à la Peau Fragile* by Patrick Alexander

A Professional Gun ★★★

Spaghetti western
1968 · It/Sp · Colour · 105mins

This spaghetti western – with Franco Nero as the professional gun, Tony Musante as a workers' liberator and Jack Palance as a sadistic homosexual – lays on the gallows humour with bloodshot zest. That's because director Sergio Corbucci used to be a gag writer, so it's jokier than most of its kind, even if its jokes are as simple-minded as Nero striking a match on a villain's stubble. TH. Some dialogue dubbed into English.

Franco Nero *Sergei Cowalski* • Tony Musante *Eufemio* • Jack Palance *Ricciolo* • Giovanna Ralli *Columba* • Eduardo Fajardo *Alfonso Garcia* ■ *Dir* Sergio Corbucci • *Scr* Luciano Vincenzoni, Sergio Spina, Sergio Corbucci, from a story by Franco Solinas, Giorgio Arlorio

The Professionals ★★★★ PG

Western 1966 · US · Colour · 112mins

Richard Brooks's action western was a box-office smash, repairing the damage that the flop *Lord Jim* had done to his reputation two years before. Burt Lancaster, Lee Marvin, Robert Ryan and Woody Strode are the magnificent four, flawed and fearsome, hired to rescue Claudia Cardinale from the clutches of manic Mexican bandit Jack Palance. Grittily shot in canyon country, bursting with violence and with pit stops for philosophising. AT [VIDEO] DVD

Burt Lancaster *Bill Dolworth* • Lee Marvin *Henry Rico Farden* • Robert Ryan *Hans Ehrengard* • Jack Palance *Captain Jesus Raza* • Claudia Cardinale *Maria Grant* • Ralph Bellamy *JW Grant* • Woody Strode *Jacob Sharp* • Joe De Santis *Ortega* ■ *Dir* Richard Brooks • *Scr* Richard Brooks, from the novel *A Mule for the Marquesa* by Frank O'Rourke

Profile ★

Crime drama 1954 · UK · BW · 65mins

Steel-jawed magazine editor John Bentley is accused of forging a cheque in the name of his publisher, who inconveniently keels over with a heart attack. Meanwhile, the publisher's wife (a totally wasted Kathleen Byron) lusts after Bentley (who's in love with her daughter), but is soon murdered herself. Rubbish? You bet, from Monarch, one of the lowest on the British B-movie totem pole: don't look for style here. TS

John Bentley *Peter Armstrong* • Kathleen Byron *Margot Holland* • Thea Gregory *Susan Holland* • Stuart Lindsell *Aubrey Holland* • Garard Green *Charlie Pearson* ■ *Dir* Francis Searle • *Scr* John Gilling, from a story by John Temple-Smith, Maurice Temple-Smith

The Profound Desire of the Gods ★★★★

Drama 1968 · Jpn · Colour · 167mins

Shohei Imamura embraced the Japanese New Wave's genius for controversy in this head-on collision between tradition and progress. There's seemingly no taboo that Imamura is not willing to tackle here, as engineer Kazuo Kitamura arrives on an isolated island to arrange the water supply for a modern sugar refinery only to find himself embroiled in the incest and insanity of Kanjuro Arashi's eccentric family. With a subplot involving a shamanist shrine, this is a scathingly surreal study of a society about to implode that's made all the more disconcerting by Imamura's typically uncompromising realism. DP. In Japanese with English subtitles. Contains sex scenes.

Rentaro Mikuni *Nekichi Futori, the chained son* • Choichiro Kawarazaki *Kametaro Futori* • Kazuo Kitamura *Engineer Kariya* • Hideko Okiyama *Toriko Futori, the backward daughter* • Yoshi Kato *Ritsugen Ryu* • Yasuko Matsui *Uma Futori, the priestess daughter* • Kanjuro Arashi *Yamamori Futori, the patriarch* ■ *Dir* Shohei Imamura • *Scr* Shohei Imamura, Keiji Hasebe

Progeny ★★★ 18

Science-fiction horror
1998 · US · Colour · 91mins

A interesting change of pace for splatter specialist Brian Yuzna in this *Outer Limits*-style tale of a pregnancy that might not be of this world. Arnold Vosloo isn't exactly leading man material, but he does convey an escalating sense of paranoia with some gusto, while Lindsay Crouse and Brad Dourif provide solid support. Although Yuzna does occasionally betray his roots with dollops of gore and nudity, this is a far more restrained and atmospheric tale than you might expect. JC. Contains violence, nudity, swearing. [VIDEO] DVD

Arnold Vosloo *Dr Craig Burton* • Jillian McWhirter *Sherry Burton* • Brad Dourif *Dr Bert Clavell* • Lindsay Crouse *Dr Susan Lamarche* ■ *Dir* Brian Yuzna • *Scr* Aubrey Solomon, from a story by Stuart Gordon, Aubrey Solomon

The Program ★★ 15

Sports drama 1993 · US · Colour · 107mins

American sporting movies rarely translate well for British audiences and this is no exception, despite its fine cast. James Caan plays the hard-bitten coach (with the obligatory soft heart) who is told to transform the fortunes of his struggling college football team. The playing – both the football and the acting – is the best thing about the movie, with the dependable Caan receiving nice support. But director David S Ward can't resist turning out all the usual clichés. DP. Contains swearing, drug abuse and violence. [VIDEO]

James Caan *Coach Sam Winters* • Halle Berry *Autumn* • Omar Epps *Darnell Jefferson* • Craig Sheffer *Joe Kane* • Kristy Swanson *Camille* • Abraham Benrubi *Bud-Lite* ■ *Dir* David S Ward • *Scr* Aaron Latham, David S Ward

Project A ★★★ 12

Martial arts adventure
1983 · HK · Colour · 100mins

For those who think kung fu is kung-phooey, a chance to be converted by one of the masters. With an overworked soundtrack – thwack! kapow! crunch! – and fight choreography ballet companies would die for, Jackie Chan is a turn-of-the-century coastguard battling pirates. Credibility walks the buccaneers' plank, but the humour-leavened action takes some beating. TH. In Cantonese with English subtitles. [VIDEO] DVD

Jackie Chan *Dragon Ma* • Sammo Hung *Fei* • Yuen Biao *Hung Tin Tze* • Lau Hak Suen *Admiral* ■ *Dir* Jackie Chan • *Scr* Jackie Chan, Edward Tang

Project A: Part II ★★★ 15

Martial arts adventure
1987 · HK · Colour · 100mins

Starting and finishing with the sequences of previous picture highlights and hair-raising set piece out-takes that have become a familiar feature of a Jackie Chan sequel, this rattling chop-socky adventure has all the action and slapstick we've come to expect from this unique star. Corrupt cops, spies, revolutionaries and pirates hurtle across the screen as Chan teams with the rebellious Maggie Cheung to confound bent bobby David Lam. DP. In Cantonese with English subtitles. [VIDEO] DVD

Jackie Chan *Dragon Ma* • Maggie Cheung • David Lam ■ *Dir* Jackie Chan • *Scr* Edward Tang

Project: Alien ★ 15

Science-fiction thriller
1990 · US/Aus/Yug · Colour · 88mins

Michael Nouri plays a journalist who investigates a plane crash and other mysterious events including a meteor shower and unexplained illness among a group of geologists. He enlists the help of bush pilot Darlanne Fluegel but the authorities want everything to be hushed up. The convoluted plot will will soon lose your attention, and even the flight sequences are boring. ST [VIDEO]

Michael Nouri *Jeff Milker* • Charles Durning *Colonel Clancy* • Maxwell Caulfield *George Abbott* • Darlanne Fluegel *Bird McNamara* ■ *Dir* Frank Shields (2) • *Scr* David Peoples

Project: Kill ★★

Spy mystery 1976 · US · Colour · 90mins

Leslie Nielsen plays a kung fu-fighting secret agent who wants out of his way of work, but discovers the only exit door is the one marked "Death". When he goes on the run, friend and fellow agent Gary Lockwood is assigned to track him down. Expect a few unintentional laughs from seeing comedy icon Nielsen playing it straight, but the action's adequate. DA

Leslie Nielsen • Gary Lockwood • Nancy Kwan ■ *Dir* William Girdler • *Scr* Donald G Thompson, from a story by David Sheldon, Donald G Thompson

Project Moonbase ★

Science fiction 1953 · US · BW · 63mins

Science-fiction icon Robert Heinlein co-wrote the script for this talky space odyssey about man conquering the moon (in 1970, nearly right!). The highlights are communists sabotaging all chances of a return to Earth and the first lunar marriage, which is given a female president's blessing. A pseudo-scientific bore cobbled together from an unsold TV series with mind-boggling space outfit designs. AJ

Donna Martell *Col Britels* • Hayden Rorke *Gen Greene* • Ross Ford *Maj Moore* • Larry Johns *Dr Wernher* • Ernestine Barrier *Mme President* ■ *Dir* Richard Talmadge • *Scr* Robert A Heinlein, Jack Seaman

Project X ★★

Science-fiction thriller
1968 · US · Colour · 96mins

As Hollywood's foremost hustler of horror, William Castle was a legend. He directed this science-fiction film after producing *Rosemary's Baby*, but its story of Christopher George, from the next century, time-trapped in the present to discover a humankind destructor, is unlike Castle's usual scary stuff. A low-budget, low-key affair, it's imaginatively thought through, with enough data to convince. What's sadly missing, though, is the kind of gusto he brought to his other work. TH

Christopher George *Hagen Arnold* • Greta Baldwin *Karen Summers* • Henry Jones *Dr Crowther* • Monte Markham *Gregory Gallea* • Harold Gould *Colonel Holt* • Phillip E Pine [Phillip Pine] *Lee Craig* ■ *Dir* William Castle • *Scr* Edmund Morris, from two novels by Leslie P Davies

Project X ★★★ 12

Comedy thriller 1987 · US · Colour · 102mins

There is plenty going on in this pleasing piece of monkey business. Matthew Broderick stars as a cocky USAF pilot who is sent to a strategic weapons unit to care for the chimpanzees being used to test flight simulators. However, when he learns that they are being subjected to radiation, he decides to stop the programme before Virgil, an orphan chimp trained in sign language, is strapped into the hot seat. Helen Hunt proves an able accomplice, but Jonathan Kaplan fails to sustain the suspense. DP

Matthew Broderick *Jimmy Garrett* • Helen Hunt *Teresa "Teri" McDonald* • Bill Sadler [William Sadler] *Dr Lynnard Carroll* • Johnny Ray McGhee *Isaac Robertson* • Jonathan Stark *Sergeant "Kreig" Kreiger* • Robin Gammell *Colonel Niles* • Stephen Lang *Watts* ■ *Dir* Jonathan Kaplan • *Scr* Stanley Weiser, from a story by Stanley Weiser, Lawrence Lasker

The Projected Man ★★ PG

Science-fiction horror
1966 · UK · Colour · 86mins

The special effects here have the look of wobbly cardboard about them, especially when viewed from a post-*Star Wars* vantage point. The story is hardly original either, with a dotty scientist getting his sums wrong in a teleportation experiment and ending up hideously disfigured. However, for all its shortcomings, this still packs a minor punch, largely due to the sense of menace engendered by Ian Curteis's direction and some passable acting. SH

Bryant Halliday *Professor Paul Steiner* • Mary Peach *Dr Pat Hill* • Ronald Allen *Dr Mitchell* • Norman Wooland *Dr Blanchard* • Derek Farr *Inspector Davis* ■ *Dir* Ian Curteis • *Scr* John C Cooper, Peter Bryan, from a story by Frank Quattrocchi

The Projectionist ★★★★

Comedy fantasy 1970 · US · Colour · 84mins

An independent, low-budget pearl from writer/director Harry Hurwitz. Chuck McCann is the lonely projectionist whose job leads him into flights of fantasy in which he is transformed into superhero Captain Flash, clashing with arch-enemy The Bat (Rodney Dangerfield). Film clips from other movies are well used, as McCann's daydreams lead him into adventures with fictional characters from Hollywood classics as well as historical characters. This early effort now enjoys a cult following. TH

Chuck McCann *Projectionist/Captain Flash* • Ina Balin *Girl* • Rodney Dangerfield *Renaldi/The Bat* • Jara Kohout *Candy Man/Scientist* • Harry Hurwitz *Friendly usher* • Robert Staats *TV pitchman* ■ *Dir/Scr* Harry Hurwitz

Prom Night ★★★ 18

Horror 1980 · US · Colour · 88mins

Jamie Lee Curtis cemented her Scream Queen title with this inventively plotted, (relatively) light on gore, entry in the teenagers-in-jeopardy/stalk-and-slash cycle inaugurated by *Halloween*. Four youngsters cause the death of a fifth in the modishly formula opening prologue, and several years later an axe-wielding killer turns up at the school prom seeking belated revenge. A suspenseful chase sequence through the campus and the surprise identity of the masked maniac lift it above average. Three sequels followed. AJ. Contains violence, swearing and some nudity.

Leslie Nielsen *Mr Hammond* • Jamie Lee Curtis *Kim* • Casey Stevens *Nick* • Antoinette Bower *Mrs Hammond* • Eddie Benton [Anne-Marie Martin] *Wendy* • Michael Tough *Alex* • Robert Silverman *Sykes* ■ *Dir* Paul Lynch • *Scr* William Gray, from a story by Robert Guza Jr

La Promesse ★★★★ 15

Drama
1996 · Bel/Fr/Tun/Lux · Colour · 90mins

Borrowing its uncompromising style from the British school of realism, this harrowing rites-of-passage story was partly inspired by Dostoyevsky's *The Brothers Karamazov*. Depicting Europe as a soulless capitalist subjecting the underdeveloped world to a new form of slavery, the film focuses on the feud that develops between an apprentice mechanic and his immigrant-trafficking father over how to help the widow of an African worker. Co-directors Luc and Jean-Pierre Dardenne pull no punches in this grimy study of human misery, saving their fiercest body blow for the very end. DP. In French with English subtitles. DVD

Jérémie Rénier *Igor* • Olivier Gourmet *Roger* • Assita Ouedraogo *Assita* • Rasmane Ouedraogo *Amidou* ■ *Dir/Scr* Jean-Pierre Dardenne, Luc Dardenne

Prometheus ★★ 15

Drama 1998 · UK · Colour · 130mins

Somehow, British poet Tony Harrison raised the cash for this modern interpretation of the Greek myth, filmed all over Europe, with dialogue entirely in rhyming couplets. For those who persevere for more than two hours, there are some dazzling visuals, for example the collapsing cooling towers, but many will find Harrison's ideas either baffling or unoriginal. (The business with redundant Yorkshire miners plays like a throwback to the worthy political theatre of the 1970s). DM. Contains swearing.

Michael Feast *Hermes* • Walter Sparrow *Grandad* • Fern Smith *Mam* • Jonathan Waistnidge *Jack* • Steve Huison *Dad* • Audrey Haggerty *Grandma* ■ *Dir/Scr* Tony Harrison

Promise ★★★★

Drama 1986 · US · Colour · 96mins

Party animal James Garner promises his dying mother that he will take care of his schizophrenic brother (James Woods) in this award-winning, critically acclaimed and heartfelt drama. Remarkably similar to *Rain Man*, made two years later, this emotional roller coaster ride is no less memorable in all artistic departments. A TV movie gem, beautifully written by Richard Friedenberg and shot entirely on location in Oregon. AJ

James Garner *Bob* • James Woods *DJ* • Piper Laurie *Annie* • Peter Michael Goetz *Stuart* • Michael Alldredge *Gibb* • Alan Rosenberg *Dr Pressman* • Mary Marsh *Mrs Post* ■ *Dir* Glenn Jordan • *Scr* Richard Friedenberg, from a story by Richard Friedenberg, Tennyson Flowers, Kenneth Blackwell

The Promise ★★ 15

Romantic drama
1994 · Ger/Fr/Swi · BW and Colour · 110mins

Once one of the most vital forces in New German Cinema, Margarethe von Trotta has been forced into something of a festival backwater of late. The reasons are not hard to identify in this laboured romantic allegory about Germany in the era of the Wall. Initially, there's a certain sweetness about the doomed relationship between young easterners Anian Zollner and Meret Becker. But once she escapes to the West and the couple mature into August Zirner and Corinna Harfouch, the political ironies and cruel coincidences begin to mount up. DP. In German with English subtitles.

Corinna Harfouch *Sophie* • Meret Becker *Sophie, as a young woman* • August Zirner *Konrad* • Anian Zollner *Konrad, as a young man* • Jean-Yves Gautier *Gerard* • Eva Mattes *Barbara* ■ *Dir* Margarethe von Trotta • *Scr* Peter Schneider, Margarethe von Trotta, Felice Laudadio, from an idea by Francesco Laudadio

Promise Her Anything ★

Comedy 1966 · UK · Colour · 96mins

The worst movie of Warren Beatty's career cast him as a porno film-maker redeemed by his relationship with next-door neighbour Leslie Caron and her baby son. Tacky and flashily directed, it is set in New York but was shot entirely in London since Beatty was living there with Caron who was unable to leave because of a court order regarding her children. AT

Warren Beatty *Harley Rummel* • Leslie Caron *Michele O'Brien* • Bob Cummings [Robert Cummings] *Dr Peter Brock* • Hermione Gingold *Mrs Luce* • Lionel Stander *Sam* • Keenan Wynn *Angelo Carelli* • Asa Maynor *Rusty* • Michael Bradley *John Thomas* • Donald Sutherland *Baby's father* ■ *Dir* Arthur Hiller • *Scr* William Peter Blatty, from a story by Arne Sultan, Marvin Worth

Promised a Miracle ★★★★ PG

Drama based on a true story
1988 · US · Colour · 95mins

A classy and highly intelligent TV movie which takes a great moral conundrum and for once gives it the breadth and vision it deserves. Based on the true story of the Parkers, a deeply religious couple who were accused of manslaughter after refusing medical treatment for their diabetic son, it addresses a subject on which most people will have strong views. But, far from portraying the Parkers as negligent nutters, director Stephen Gyllenhaal extracts two wonderfully complex, compassionate performances from Rosanna Arquette and Judge Reinhold. All concerned acquit themselves exceptionally well. SH

Rosanna Arquette *Alice "Lucky" Parker* • Judge Reinhold *Larry Parker* • Tom Bower *Michael Elliott* • Vonni Ribisi [Giovanni Ribisi] *Wesley Parker* • Robin Pearson Rose *Beth* ■ *Dir* Stephen Gyllenhaal • *Scr* David Hill, from the book *We Let Our Son Die* by Larry Parker, Donald Tanner

Promised Land ★★★ 15

Drama 1988 · US · Colour · 101mins

Michael Hoffman marked himself out as a promising young director on the strength of this under-rated coming-of-age drama. There is much to enjoy in this accomplished tale of high school friends discovering that adulthood is not quite what they expected. Kiefer Sutherland gives one of his best performances as the drop-out of the group, who hooks up with misunderstood bad girl Meg Ryan. Meanwhile, back home his old chum Jason Gedrick is now a cop with romantic problems of his own. The interweaving stories don't quite gel, but the cinematography is superb and Hoffman succeeds in summoning up an air of quiet melancholy. JF. Contains swearing and nudity.

Jason Gedrick *Davey Hancock* • Tracy Pollan *Mary Daley* • Kiefer Sutherland *Danny Rivers* • Meg Ryan *Bev* • Googy Gress *Baines* • Deborah Richter *Pammie* • Oscar Rowland *Mr Rivers* • Jay Underwood *Circle K Clerk* ■ *Dir/Scr* Michael Hoffman

Promises ★★★★

Documentary 2001 · US · Colour · 106mins

Filmed in 1995, five years before the Intifada, this documentary is a powerful and moving yet ultimately dispiriting insight into the outlook of children caught up in the Israeli-Palestinian conflict. Co-director BZ Goldberg interviews seven children from different. What hits hardest are not the tales of injury and injustice or the unthinking regurgitation of implacable rhetoric, but how little these innocents know about each other's lifestyles even though they live just a few miles apart. The real tragedy occurs in the postscript: as the children (now five years older) express their powerlessness to influence change, their attitudes still seem irredeemably entrenched. DP. An Arabic/Hebrew/English language film.

Dir Justine Shapiro [Justine Arlin], BZ Goldberg, Carlos Bolado

Promises in the Dark ★★

Drama 1979 · US · Colour · 115mins

This bleak drama focuses unblinkingly on the ravaging effects of cancer and the debilitating results of chemotherapy. Kathleen Beller plays an ailing teenager, Ned Beatty and Susan Clark are her parents, and Marsha Mason is her doctor, a divorcee who is having an affair with radiologist Michael Brandon. A first-time directing effort from Jerome Hellman, the Oscar-winning producer of *Midnight Cowboy* and *Coming Home*. AT. Contains swearing and nudity.

Marsha Mason *Dr Alexandra Kenda* • Ned Beatty *Bud Koenig* • Susan Clark *Fran Koenig* • Michael Brandon *Dr Jim Sandman* • Kathleen Beller *Buffy Koenig* • Paul Clemens *Gerry Hulin* • Donald Moffat *Dr Walter McInerny* ■ *Dir* Jerome Hellman • *Scr* Loring Mandel

Proof ★★★★ 15

Psychological drama
1991 · Aus · Colour · 86mins

An astonishing Australian oddity that should have established the reputation of writer/director Jocelyn Moorhouse, but didn't, this is about a blind photographer (that's right) who relies on others to describe his work and who is lusted after by his cleaner. Rejected, she discovers that her employer has become friends with another young man and from this point the triangular eroticism strikes an even more bizarre note. Hugo Weaving, Genevieve Picot and Russell Crowe as the romantically inclined threesome pursue their outlandish course with skill and humour. TH. Contains swearing and nudity.

Hugo Weaving *Martin* • Genevieve Picot *Celia* • Russell Crowe *Andy* • Heather Mitchell *Martin's mother* • Jeffrey Walker *Young Martin* • Belinda Davey *Doctor* ■ *Dir/Scr* Jocelyn Moorhouse

Proof of Life ★★★ 15

Action drama
2000 · US/UK · Colour · 129mins

Part action movie, part romance and part thriller, Taylor Hackford's efficient kidnap drama is set in a fictional South American country where Meg Ryan's marriage comes under further strain when her engineer husband David Morse is taken hostage by guerrillas. Enter the heroic Russell Crowe, a professional "K&R" (that's kidnap and ransom) man, who agrees to help Ryan. The leads enjoyed a well publicised romance during filming, but any steaminess apparently ended up on the cutting room floor. JB. Contains swearing and violence. DVD

Meg Ryan *Alice Bowman* • Russell Crowe *Terry Thorne* • David Morse *Peter Bowman* • David Caruso *Dino* • Pamela Reed *Janis Goodman* ■ *Dir* Taylor Hackford • *Scr* Tony Gilroy

Prophecy ★★ 15

Horror 1979 · US · Colour · 97mins

One of the earliest of the eco-shockers, this demonstrates the decline of director John Frankenheimer. Doctor Robert Foxworth and his pregnant wife Talia Shire go to investigate a report of mercury poisoning in the Maine backwoods and find themselves battling giant mutants. If only the direction had been as fluid as the mercury. TH [video]

Talia Shire *Maggie* • Robert Foxworth *Rob Vern* • Armand Assante *John Hawks* • Richard Dysart *Isley* • Victoria Racimo *Ramona* • George Clutesi *M'Rai* ■ *Dir* John Frankenheimer • *Scr* David Seltzer

The Prophecy ★★★ 18

Supernatural horror
1994 · US · Colour · 93mins

Priest-turned-cop Elias Koteas gets caught up in an earthly battle between renegade angels Christopher Walken and Eric Stoltz in a strangely ambiguous and slightly pretentious horror fantasy. The wildly imaginative premise and poetic development, along with a solid cast that includes Virginia Madsen and Amanda Plummer, make this often compelling, sometimes corny, chiller a bizarre cult item. Lacking the sort of special effects you would expect from such an apocalyptic notion, this was successful enough to spawn two sequels. AJ. Contains violence and swearing. [video] DVD

Christopher Walken *Angel Gabriel* • Elias Koteas *Thomas Dagget* • Eric Stoltz *Angel Simon* • Virginia Madsen *Katherine* • Moriah Shining Dove Snyder *Mary* • Adam Goldberg *Jerry* • Amanda Plummer *Rachael* • Viggo Mortensen *Lucifer* ■ *Dir/Scr* Gregory Widen

The Prophecy II ★★ 18

Supernatural horror
1997 · US · Colour · 79mins

Carrying on from the first movie, Christopher Walken's archangel Gabriel, angered that God has favoured humans over his kind, returns to hunt down Jennifer Beals, who is pregnant with the saviour of mankind. But where the original boasted some good, offbeat ideas, this degenerates into just another dumb chase movie. RS. Contains swearing, violence and nudity. [video] DVD

Christopher Walken *Gabriel* • Jennifer Beals *Valerie Rosales* • Brittany Murphy *Izzy* • Russell Wong *Danyael* • William Prael *Rafayel* • Danny Strong *Julian* • Glenn Danzig *Samayel* • Eric Roberts *Michael* ■ *Dir* Greg Spence • *Scr* Matt Greenberg, Greg Spence

The Prophecy 3: the Ascent ★★ 15

Supernatural horror
2000 · US · Colour · 80mins

This disappointing climax to the series lacks both narrative ingenuity and visual élan. Returning as the Archangel Gabriel, Christopher Walken isn't given nearly enough to do, as the ambitious Vincent Spano seeks to destroy street preacher Dave Buzzotta (replacing Russell Wong as Danyael, the half-human, half-angel nephilim). It's the unsung Spano who seizes the attention with his quirky display of celestial malevolence. DP [video] DVD

Christopher Walken *Gabriel* • Scott Cleverdon *Pyriel* • Brad Dourif *Zealot* • Vincent Spano *Zophael "Jones"* • Dave Buzzotta *Danyael* ■ *Dir* Patrick Lussier • *Scr* Joel Soisson

Prophet of Evil ★★ 15

Biographical drama
1993 · US · Colour · 88mins

Single-minded investigator William Devane pursues charismatic cult leader Brian Dennehy for whom killing is part of his creed in director Jud Taylor's cliché-ridden TV drama. The two principals offer a winning mix of decency and menace, lending a certain amount of credibility to an otherwise wayward outing. JM [video] DVD

Brian Dennehy *Ervil LeBaron* • William Devane *Dan Fields* • Tracey Needham *Rena Chynoweth* • Philip Abbott *Dr Rulon Allred* • Lucy Butler *Naomi Kane* • Danny Cooksey *Isaac* • Dee Wallace Stone *Jackie Fields* ■ *Dir* Jud Taylor • *Scr* Fred Mills

The Prophet's Game ★★ 18

Thriller 1999 · US · Colour · 103mins

The pairing of Dennis Hopper with clean-cut Stephanie Zimbalist is probably the most imaginative thing about this undemanding serial-killer thriller. Hopper is the retired Seattle detective whose past comes back to haunt him with the seeming reappearance of his old nemesis The Prophet – a killer who likes to confess his crimes to the veteran policeman. As the body count mounts, Zimbalist is the only local cop who believes Hopper's story. The two leads are watchable, but it fails to chill the bones. JF [video] DVD

Dennis Hopper *Vincent Swan* • Stephanie Zimbalist *Det Francis Aldobrandi* • Joe Penny *Walter Motter* • Robert Yocum *Alan Joyce* • Sondra Locke *Adele Highsmith* • Shannon Whirry *Barb* • Michael Dorn *Chief Bob Bowman* ■ *Dir* David Worth • *Scr* Carol Chrest

The Proposal ★★★ 18

Crime thriller 2000 · US · Colour · 86mins

Nick Moran stars with considerable aplomb in this direct-to-video offering. Credibly suggesting the pressures of his perilous situation, he plays an undercover cop whose sting on mobster Stephen Lang is jeopardised by both the divided loyalties of rookie Jennifer Esposito and the heavy-handed tactics of the FBI. Considering this was his directorial debut, Richard Gale sustains the tension without resort to self-conscious flourish and allows the action to turn on character, not contrivance. DP [video]

Nick Moran *Terry Martin* • Jennifer Esposito *Susan Reese* • Stephen Lang *Simon Bacig* • William B Davis *Agent Frank Gruning* ■ *Dir* Richard Gale • *Scr* Maurice Hurley, Richard Gale

The Proposition ★★★ 18

Period romantic drama
1996 · UK/US · Colour · 92mins

This period drama has a plot that sounds like a classic western, but it's actually set in 19th-century Wales around the time of the Napoleonic Wars. Theresa Russell plays a feisty widow who refuses to be forced into a marriage of convenience to local sheriff Richard Lynch, despite her dire financial situation. Instead she opts to save the estate by driving her herd of cattle to market herself – with a little help from Patrick Bergin. It's a strong story, well told, with good use of landscape, and memorable performances from Russell and co-stars Bergin and Lynch. DA

Theresa Russell *Catherine Morgan* • Patrick Bergin *Rhys Williams* • Richard Lynch *Sheriff Williams* ■ *Dir* Strathford Hamilton • *Scr* Paul Matthews

The Proposition ★★★ 12

Romantic crime drama
1998 · US · Colour · 107mins

The plot for this crime film set in Boston in the 1930s is more suited to a lurid soap opera than a major movie, but it's saved by the quality of the acting on show. Director Lesli Linka Glatter's overwrought drama centres on impotent lawyer William Hurt, who "hires" Neil Patrick Harris to impregnate his wife Madeleine Stowe. The trouble starts when Harris falls in love with Stowe, and clergyman Kenneth Branagh arrives on the scene to further confuse matters. TH. Contains swearing and sexual references. [video]

Kenneth Branagh *Father Michael McKinnon* • Madeleine Stowe *Eleanor Barret* • William Hurt *Arthur Barret* • Neil Patrick Harris *Roger Martin* • Robert Loggia *Hannibal Thurman* • Blythe Danner *Syril Danning* • Josef Sommer *Father Dryer* ■ *Dir* Lesli Linka Glatter • *Scr* Rick Ramage

The Proprietor ★★ 12

Drama
1996 · UK/Fr/Tur/US · Colour · 108mins

Ismail Merchant's second solo directorial outing is a middlebrow misfire. Pitted with clumsy flashbacks, the story turns around author Jeanne Moreau's memories of her mother, who was murdered by the Nazis, and her hopes for a screen version of her most famous novel. Romances and reunions provide diversions, but the action too often lapses into kitsch and cultural snobbery. DP. In French and English with subtitles. [video] DVD

Jeanne Moreau *Adrienne Mark* • Sean Young *Virginia Kelly/Sally* • Austin Pendleton *Willy Kunst* • Nell Carter *Milly* • Marc Tissot *Patrice Legendre* • Christopher Cazenove *Elliott Spencer* • Sam Waterston *Harry Bancroft* • Jean-Pierre Aumont *Franz Legendre* ■ *Dir* Ismail Merchant • *Scr* Jean-Marie Besset, George Trow

Prospero's Books ★★★★ 15

Drama
1991 · Neth/Fr/It/UK · Colour · 120mins

Historically important both as a record of John Gielgud's celebrated stage rendition of Prospero, and as the first film to be shot entirely in High Definition Video, this visually stunning fantasy is more than just a straightforward adaptation of *The Tempest*. Focusing on the exiled Duke of Milan's beloved 24-volume library, Peter Greenaway overlays multiple images and textual information in a meditation on the processes of thought and artistic creation, with Gielgud's voicing of all Shakespeare's characters. Viewers may find Greenaway's experiments with non-linear narrative challenging, but those with patience should find it rewarding. TH [video]

John Gielgud *Prospero* • Michael Clark *Caliban* • Michel Blanc *Alonso* • Erland Josephson *Gonzalo* • Isabelle Pasco *Miranda* • Tom Bell *Antonio* • Kenneth Cranham *Sebastian* • Mark Rylance *Ferdinand* • Gérard Thoolen *Adrian* • Pierre Bokma *Francisco* ■ *Dir* Peter Greenaway • *Scr* Peter Greenaway, from the play *The Tempest* by William Shakespeare • *Music* Michael Nyman

The Protector ★★★ 18

Martial arts action drama
1985 · US · Colour · 90mins

This was one of Jackie Chan's early American productions, an efficient action movie tinged with 007-style hardware. He plays a tough cop battling bad guys in New York before being sent on assignment with Danny Aiello to Hong Kong to track down a drug kingpin. As usual with Chan movies, the plot and dialogue are forgettable but the all-out action scenes dazzle the eye. RS [video]

Jackie Chan *Billy Wong* • Danny Aiello *Danny Garoni* • Sandy Alexander *Gang leader* • Roy Chiao *Mr Ko* • Victor Arnold *Police Captain* ■ *Dir/Scr* James Glickenhaus

Proteus ★★★ 18

Science-fiction horror
1995 · UK · Colour · 92mins

This typical monsters-on-the-loose movie is creepy all the way, floundering only slightly in its pacing and acting. A group of inept yuppies-turned-amateur drug-runners stumble upon a seemingly abandoned research rig in mid-ocean. The few people left seem terrified of something, but they never stick around long enough to say what. The dark industrial setting makes for good atmosphere, but it's still just a monster movie. ST. Contains swearing and violence. [video] DVD

Craig Fairbrass *Alex* • Toni Barry *Linda* • William Marsh *Mark* • Jennifer Calvert *Rachel* • Robert Firth *Paul* • Margot Steinberg *Christine* ■ *Dir* Bob Keen • *Scr* John Brosnan, from the novel *Slimer* by Harry Adam Knight [John Brosnan]

Protocol ★★★ PG

Comedy 1984 · US · Colour · 90mins

Hardly A-grade Goldie Hawn, but a charming enough comedy all the same. She plays, unsurprisingly, a dizzy blonde, thrown into the world of intrigue in Washington when she saves the life of a Middle Eastern politician. The engaging cast struggles valiantly with an uneven script from writer Buck Henry, but director Herbert Ross puts sufficient energy into his task to paper over the creative cracks. JF. Contains violence and swearing. [video]

Goldie Hawn *Sunny Davis* • Chris Sarandon *Michael Ransome* • Richard Romanus *Emir of Ohtar* • Andre Gregory *Nawaf Al Kabeer* • Gail Strickland *Mrs St John* • Cliff De Young *Hilley* • Ed Begley Jr *Hassler* ■ *Dir* Herbert Ross • *Scr* Buck Henry, from a story by Charles Shyer, Nancy Meyers, Harvey Miller

The Proud and Profane ★★

Second World War romance
1956 · US · BW · 111mins

William Holden stars in this war melodrama, as an officer who romances widow Deborah Kerr. She becomes pregnant and then finds out Holden's married – a sort of "From Here to Maternity". Drivel, but watchable. AT

William Holden (2) *Lt Col Colin Black* • Deborah Kerr *Lee Ashley* • Thelma Ritter *Kate Connors* • Dewey Martin *Eddie Wodcik* • William Redfield *Chaplain Holmes* • Ross Bagdasarian *Louie* • Adam Williams *Eustace Press* • Marion Ross *Joan* ■ *Dir* George Seaton • *Scr* George Seaton, from the novel *The Magnificent Bastards* by Lucy Herndon Crockett

The Proud and the Damned ★★

Western action adventure
1972 · US · Colour · 94mins

A routine western, differentiated from a thousand others only by its use of slightly more exotic locales than usual. The plot centres on a wild bunch of mercenaries and ex-Civil War soldiers who get caught up in a revolution while way south of the border, down Latin America way. The action sequences are OK, but dire dialogue and dead direction speedily consign the film to the celluloid equivalent of Boot Hill. DA

Chuck Connors *Will* • Aron Kincaid *Ike* • Cesar Romero *Alcalde* • José Greco *Ramon* • Henry Capps *Hank* • Peter Ford *Billy* ■ *Dir/Scr* Ferde Grofe Jr

The Proud Ones ★★★

Drama 1953 · Fr/Mex · BW · 94mins

It's difficult to accept that this simmering Mexican melodrama was adapted from a Jean-Paul Sartre novel. But, while it's deficient in the psychological department, Yves Allégret's tale of damaged souls and redemption through love and sacrifice

P

has many other things going for it, not least the atmospheric photography of Alex Phillips, who captures the stifling desperation of a small coastal town at the height of a meningitis epidemic. Michèle Morgan has rarely combined vulnerability and eroticism to better effect, as the stranded widow who rouses doctor Gérard Philipe from his alcoholic haze. DP. French dialogue dubbed into English.

Michèle Morgan *Nellie* • Gérard Philipe *Georges* • Victor Manuel Mendoza *Don Rodrigo* • Carlos Lopez Moctezuma *Doctor* • Michèle Cordoue *Anna* ■ *Dir* Yves Allégret • *Scr* Jean Aurenche, Yves Allégret, from the novel *Typhus* by Jean-Paul Sartre

The Proud Ones ★★★ U

Western 1956 · US · Colour · 94mins

Robert Ryan, so good at being bad, was in heroic mould for this minor-league western with some high-impact moments. As a sheriff, hampered by disability but psyching himself up for a showdown with a mixed bag of outlaws, his vulnerability is as credible as his courage. It's his performance that makes this modest suspenseful tale better than average. TH

Robert Ryan *Marshal Cass Silver* • Virginia Mayo *Sally Kane* • Jeffrey Hunter *Thad Anderson* • Robert Middleton *Honest John Barrett* • Walter Brennan *Jake* • Arthur O'Connell *Jim Dexter* ■ *Dir* Robert D Webb • *Scr* Edmund H North, Joseph Petracca, from the novel *The Proud Ones* by Verne Athanas

The Proud Rebel ★★★★ U

Western 1958 · US · Colour · 99mins

Alan Ladd's finest achievement from the years following *Shane* carries echoes of that film, particularly in the prominence of a small boy. Ladd plays father to his own son, David, who's mute since witnessing his mother's death in the Civil War. It's about the search for a cure, the boy's beloved dog, Olivia de Havilland's kindly spinster farmer, and an evil brood of sheep farmers that includes a young Harry Dean Stanton. Exquisitely photographed, beautifully acted and directed with quiet mastery by Michael Curtiz, it's that rare breed of family film which entrances kids and adults alike. AE

Alan Ladd *John Chandler* • Olivia de Havilland *Linnett Moore* • Dean Jagger *Harry Burleigh* • David Ladd *David Chandler* • Cecil Kellaway *Dr Enos Davis* • James Westerfield *Birm Bates* • Henry Hull *Judge Morley* • Dean Stanton [Harry Dean Stanton] *Jeb Burleigh* ■ *Dir* Michael Curtiz • *Scr* Joseph Petracca, Lillie Hayward, from the story *Journal of Linnett Moore* by James Edward Grant • *Cinematographer* Ted McCord

P

The Proud Valley ★★

Drama 1940 · UK · BW · 76mins

This rather dated parable on the need for community unity in the face of wartime tragedy was one of six films Paul Robeson made in Britain, and it gave him the rare opportunity to escape from typecasting as a tribal African. However, his presence is the only thing not to ring true in this well-crafted tale about a mining disaster in a small Welsh village, as he is more prone to melodrama than the solid supporting cast. DP

Paul Robeson *David Goliath* • Edward Chapman *Dick Parry* • Simon Lack *Emlyn Parry* • Rachel Thomas *Mrs Parry* • Dilys Thomas *Dilys* • Edward Rigby *Bert Rigby* ■ *Dir* Penrose Tennyson [Pen Tennyson] • *Scr* Roland Pertwee, Louis Goulding, Jack Jones, Penrose Tennyson, from a story by Herbert Marshall, Alfredda Brilliant

Providence ★★★★★ 15

Drama 1977 · Fr/Swi · Colour · 102mins

Alain Resnais's English-language debut was voted the film of the 1970s by an international panel of film-makers and critics. As ever playing intricate games with time and memory, the director has constructed a typically complex film that leaves you unsure whether the action is a flashback to a real event or a figment of the imagination of dying novelist John Gielgud. Intensifying the illusion, David Mercer's script is a perfect pastiche of the kind of florid dialogue found in purple fiction. Gielgud is outstanding, but Dirk Bogarde and Ellen Burstyn also give fine performances. Wonderful cinema from a true master of the art. DP. Contains swearing.

John Gielgud *Clive Langham* • Dirk Bogarde *Claude Langham* • Ellen Burstyn *Sonia Langham* • David Warner *Kevin Woodford* • Elaine Stritch *Helen Weiner/Molly Langham* • Denis Lawson *Dave Woodford* • Cyril Luckham *Dr Mark Eddington* ■ *Dir* Alain Resnais • *Scr* David Mercer • *Music* Miklos Rozsa

The Prowler ★★★ U

Film noir 1951 · US · BW · 92mins

While investigating a prowler in the neighbourhood, embittered policeman Van Heflin meets Evelyn Keyes whose sterile husband Emerson Treacy is a night-duty disc jockey. Cop and wife then embark on an affair that leads to murder. A taut, bleak *film noir*, well-handled by director Joseph Losey, and by the cast, notably Van Heflin. RK

Van Heflin *Webb Garwood* • Evelyn Keyes *Susan Gilvray* • John Maxwell *Bud Crocker* • Katherine Warren *Mrs Crocker* • Emerson Treacy *William Gilvray* • Madge Blake *Martha Gilvray* ■ *Dir* Joseph Losey • *Scr* Dalton Trumbo, Hugo Butler, from a story by Robert Thoren, from a story by Hans Wilhelm

Prudence and the Pill ★★ 15

Comedy 1968 · UK · Colour · 88mins

David Niven and Deborah Kerr's marriage has degenerated into separate bedrooms and lovers. When their niece Judy Geeson steals her mother Joyce Redman's contraceptive pills, substituting aspirin, and Redman gets pregnant, Niven tries the same trick on Kerr, hoping she'll get pregnant by lover Keith Michell and give him grounds for divorce. Topical at the time with the coming of the pill, this British-made farce was directed by Ronald Neame (taking over from Fielder Cook). The polished expertise of Niven and Kerr more or less holds this witless farrago together. RK

Deborah Kerr *Prudence Hardcastle* • David Niven *Gerald Hardcastle* • Robert Coote *Henry Hardcastle* • Irina Demick *Elizabeth* • Joyce Redman *Grace Hardcastle* • Judy Geeson *Geraldine Hardcastle* • Keith Michell *Dr Alan Hewitt* • Edith Evans *Lady Roberta Bates* ■ *Dir* Fielder Cook, Ronald Neame • *Scr* Hugh Mills, from his novel

Psych-Out ★★ 18

Drama 1968 · US · Colour · 85mins

After Jack Nicholson wrote the pro-LSD movie *The Trip*, he appeared in this other druggie epic, set in San Francisco's Haight-Ashbury district where deaf girl Susan Strasberg searches for her freaked-out brother, Bruce Dern, who think's he's Jesus Christ. As a relic of the flower power era, this takes some beating – and some watching, too – but Nicholson completists should get a buzz from seeing him as a rock musician and as the film's romantic lead. AT DVD

Susan Strasberg *Jennie* • Dean Stockwell *Dave* • Jack Nicholson *Stoney* • Bruce Dern *Steve* • Adam Roarke *Ben* • Max Julien *Elwood* • Henry Jaglom *Warren* • IJ Jefferson *Pandora* ■ *Dir* Richard Rush • *Scr* E Hunter Willett [Betty Tusher], Betty Ulius, from a story by E Hunter Willett [Betty Tusher]

Psyche '59 ★★

Drama 1964 · UK · BW · 94mins

An intriguing though slightly over-the-top melodrama about the blind wife (Patricia Neal) of a businessman, who is forced to see (yes, her illness is psychosomatic) when her sister Samantha Eggar, fresh from a divorce, comes to stay. You've seen it all before, and the cod psychology may be a bit irritating, but the cast is strong and the movie is glossily photographed. JG

Curt Jurgens *Eric Crawford* • Patricia Neal *Allison Crawford* • Samantha Eggar *Robin* • Ian Bannen *Paul* • Beatrix Lehmann *Mrs Crawford* • Elspeth March *Mme Valadier* • Sandra Lee *Susan* ■ *Dir* Alexander Singer • *Scr* Julian Halevy [Julian Zimet], from the novel *Psyché 58* by Françoise des Ligneris

Psychic Killer ★★ 18

Horror thriller 1975 · US · Colour · 85mins

This sensationalist low-budget thriller rips off *Psycho* so blatantly it's surprising that Hitchcock never sued. We have the gothic house, the mummy's boy, even a murder in a shower. Its story tells of a psychiatrist who unwittingly secures the release of a mental patient, who then uses psychic powers to revenge himself against those who wronged him in the past. Director Ray Danton crudely mixes comedy with scenes of brutal murder, while Jim Hutton makes for a chilling killer. RS

Paul Burke *Detective Morgan* • Jim Hutton *Arnold* • Julie Adams *Laura* • Nehemiah Persoff *Dr Gubner* • Neville Brand *Lemonowski* • Aldo Ray *Anderson* • Stack Pierce *Emilio* • Whit Bissell *Dr Taylor* • Della Reese *Mrs Gibson* ■ *Dir* Ray Danton • *Scr* Ray Danton, Greydon Clark, Mike Angel

Psycho ★★★★★ 15

Classic horror 1960 · US · BW · 108mins

Containing the most famous montage sequence since *The Battleship Potemkin*, this is easily the most shocking film produced by the "Master of Suspense". Yet Alfred Hitchcock always maintained it was a black comedy. Working with a TV crew, he completed the picture for a mere $800,000. But the California Gothic tale of the Bates Motel went on to become his greatest commercial success. The opening segment, involving Janet Leigh and an envelope of stolen cash, is the biggest "MacGuffin" in Hitchcock's career. His most audacious achievement, however, was in getting us to side with Anthony Perkins's serial killer against the authorities, Leigh's lover and sister, and his incessantly shrewish mother. DP DVD

Anthony Perkins *Norman Bates* • Janet Leigh *Marion Crane* • Vera Miles *Lila Crane* • John Gavin *Sam Loomis* • Martin Balsam *Milton Arbogast* • John McIntire *Sheriff Chambers* • Simon Oakland *Dr Richmond* ■ *Dir* Alfred Hitchcock • *Scr* Joseph Stefano, from the novel by Robert Bloch • *Cinematographer* John L Russell • *Music* Bernard Herrmann • *Editor* George Tomasini

Psycho ★ 15

Horror 1998 · US · Colour · 99mins

Gus Van Sant must have been a little mad when he agreed to direct this near word-for-word, scene-for-scene impersonation of Hitchcock's most celebrated movie. It simply doesn't work, because every major character is horribly miscast – Anne Heche plays Marion Crane as a kooky cutie and Vince Vaughn's Norman is an effeminate hunk. The pointlessness of watching a stagey, badly acted replica of one of cinema's true masterpieces cannot be ignored. JC. Contains violence and brief nudity. DVD

Vince Vaughn *Norman Bates* • Anne Heche *Marion Crane* • Julianne Moore *Lila Crane* • Viggo Mortensen *Sam Loomis* • William H Macy *Milton Arbogast* • Robert Forster *Dr Simon* • Philip Baker Hall *Sheriff Chambers* • Anne Haney *Mrs Chambers* • Chad Everett *Tom Cassidy* ■ *Dir* Gus Van Sant • *Scr* Joseph Stefano, from the 1960 film

Psycho II ★★★ 18

Horror 1983 · US · Colour · 107mins

Two decades after the motel murders, Norman Bates is released from the asylum and returns to the scene of his crimes but has "Mother" come too? Of course, this isn't Hitchcock, but it's a highly credible, nicely creepy and well paced sequel, and Anthony Perkins reprises his most famous role with no visible signs of ennui, and several other enjoyable and gritty performances, most notably from original cast member Vera Miles and Dennis Franz. SH. Contains violence, swearing and nudity. DVD

Anthony Perkins *Norman Bates* • Vera Miles *Lila Loomis* • Meg Tilly *Mary* • Robert Loggia *Dr Raymond* • Dennis Franz *Toomey* • Hugh Gillin *Sheriff Hunt* • Claudia Bryar *Mrs Spool* ■ *Dir* Richard Franklin • *Scr* Tom Holland, from characters created by Robert Bloch

Psycho III ★★ 18

Horror 1986 · US · Colour · 88mins

Anthony Perkins stars in and directs a rather mean-spirited second sequel to the Hitchcock classic in which Norman falls in love with a suicidal nun, poignantly played by Diana Scarwid. Filled with overwrought in-jokes (the *Vertigo*-influenced opening), flashbacks to the original film (Janet Leigh's face turning into Scarwid's) and copious blood-letting (the studio added extra gore), Perkins goes for the jugular in a melodramatic, somewhat vulgar, way with the accent on sleazy humour and viciousness. AJ. Contains swearing and violence. DVD

Anthony Perkins *Norman Bates* • Diana Scarwid *Maureen Coyle* • Jeff Fahey *Duane Duke* • Roberta Maxwell *Tracy Venable* • Hugh Gillin *Sheriff Hunt* • Lee Garlington *Myrna* • Robert Alan Browne *Statler* ■ *Dir* Anthony Perkins • *Scr* Charles Edward Pogue, from characters created by Robert Bloch

Psycho IV: the Beginning ★★ 18

Horror 1990 · US · Colour · 92mins

The Norman Bates saga came to an end in this sorry made-for-TV finale. It's a shame because the plot at least offers up an intriguing twist: as the now rehabilitated Norman (Anthony Perkins, again excellent) discusses his fears over a radio phone-in, we flash back to the young Norman (played here by *ET's* Henry Thomas) and his troubled relationship with his mother. However, this is sloppily executed and the climax is just plain silly. JF. Contains violence and nudity. DVD

Anthony Perkins *Norman Bates* • Henry Thomas *Young Norman* • Olivia Hussey *Norma Bates* • CCH Pounder *Fran Ambrose* • Warren Frost *Dr Leo Richmond* • Donna Mitchell *Connie Bates* ■ *Dir* Mick Garris • *Scr* Joseph Stefano, from characters created by Robert Bloch

Psychomania ★★

Murder mystery 1964 · US · BW · 93mins

Not, unfortunately, the delirious zombie biker flick of 1972 starring George Sanders and Beryl Reid, but an altogether more conventional affair. Lee Philips is an ex-serviceman and painter of nude women who becomes prime suspect in a serial murder case involving college girls. With the help of lawyer James Farentino, he attempts to clear his name. JG

Lee Philips *Elliot Freeman* • Shepperd Strudwick *Adrian Benedict* • Jean Hale *Carol Bishop* • Lorraine Rogers *Alice St Clair* • Margot Hartman *Lynn Freeman* • Kaye Elhardt *Dolores Martello* • James Farentino *Charlie Perone* • Richard Van Patten [Dick Van Patten] *Palmer* • Sylvia Miles *Silvia* ■ *Dir* Richard Hilliard [Richard L Hilliard] • *Scr* Robin Miller

Psychomania ★★★

Horror 1972 · UK · Colour · 90mins

This British horror cheapie is so ridiculous it works. For much of the time this psychedelic zombie biker frightener is utter drivel, but director Don Sharp throws in some cracking scenes, notably the one in which leader of the gang Nicky Henson rises from the grave, bike and all. Henson has a hoot as the Angel from Hell, and he is superbly supported by Beryl Reid as his devil-worshipping mum and George Sanders as her ghoulish butler. Sanders committed suicide shortly after this film was made. DP

Nicky Henson *Tom Latham* • Beryl Reid *Mrs Latham* • George Sanders *Shadwell* • Mary Larkin *Abby* • Roy Holder *Bertram* • Robert Hardy *Chief Inspector Hesseltine* • Patrick Holt *Sergeant* • Denis Gilmore *Hatchet* ■ *Dir* Don Sharp • *Scr* Arnaud D'Usseau, Julian Halevy [Julian Zimet]

The Psychopath ★ 18

Horror thriller 1966 · UK · Colour · 90mins

Hammer's main rival, Amicus, produced some highly original shockers but, despite a screenplay by Robert Bloch, author of *Psycho*, this isn't one of them. Once again, a psychopath murders his enemies one by one, leaving a model of the victim next to each body, and it doesn't take much imagination to work out who the culprit is. Talented horror director Freddie Francis rather uncharacteristically creates little atmosphere, while Margaret Johnston overplays almost to the point of burlesque. DM

Patrick Wymark *Inspector Holloway* • Margaret Johnston *Mrs Von Sturm* • John Standing *Mark Von Sturm* • Alexander Knox *Frank Saville* • Judy Huxtable *Louise Saville* ■ *Dir* Freddie Francis • *Scr* Robert Bloch

P'Tang, Yang, Kipperbang ★★★★ PG

Comedy 1982 · UK · Colour · 76mins

This surreal phrase chanted by 14-year-old schoolboys illustrates the gentle, oddball comedy of this story by TV playwright Jack Rosenthal. John Albasiny has a crush on the prettiest girl in class (Abigail Cruttenden) but a host of obstacles are put in the way of his declaration of passion. Directed by Michael Apted, it's a wry and highly comic look at teenage lust with some splendid performances. TH

John Albasiny *Alan Duckworth* • Abigail Cruttenden *Ann* • Maurice Dee *Geoffrey* • Alison Steadman *Estelle Land* • Mark Brailsford *Abbo* • Chris Karallis *Shaz* • Frances Ruffelle *Eunice* • Robert Urquhart *Headmaster* ■ *Dir* Michael Apted • *Scr* Jack Rosenthal

Pterodactyl Woman from Beverly Hills ★

Comedy 1996 · US · Colour · 99mins

"A perfect Beverly Hills housewife by day – a prehistoric flying reptile by night", ran the ad line, which just about sums up the plot of this miserably unfunny comedy. Hovering somewhere between a satire of affluent American suburbia and a plain old monster movie spoof, it fails at both. Beverly D'Angelo plugs away gamely but to little effect, hampered as she is by pricelessly naff dialogue and cheesy effects. RS

Beverly D'Angelo *Pixie Chandler* • Brad Wilson *Dick Chandler* • Brion James *Salvador Dali/Sam* • Barry Humphries *Bert/Lady shopper/manager* • Moon Zappa *Susie* • Aron Eisenberg *Tommy Chandler* • Sharon Martin *Jenny Chandler* ■ *Dir/Scr* Philippe Mora

Puberty Blues ★★ 15

Drama 1981 · Aus · Colour · 82mins

Here two young Aussie women (Nell Schofield and Jad Capelja) try to break into the male bastion of the surfing set, experiencing all the frustrations and rejections that you'd expect. It's sensitively handled, if ultimately a little weak. Not one of director Bruce Beresford's finest moments by any means. FL

Nell Schofield *Debbie Vickers* • Jad Capelja *Sue Knight* • Geoff Rhoe *Garry* • Tony Hughes *Danny* • Sandy Paul *Tracy* ■ *Dir* Bruce Beresford • *Scr* Margaret Kelly, from the novel by Kathy Lette, Gabrielle Carey

Public Access ★★★★ 18

Thriller 1993 · US · Colour · 85mins

Clean-cut Ron Marquette starts a show on public access cable TV in the small town of Brewster. Marquette encourages his viewers to call in and sound off about the problems in their town, stirring up antipathy. But what is his motive for getting people to reveal their grievances? This was Bryan Singer's first feature film as writer/director, and you can already see his propensity for camera tricks and intelligent scripts. Ron Marquette is arresting as the mild-mannered Whiley and probably had an interesting career ahead, but he committed suicide in 1995. ST DVD

Ron Marquette *Whiley Pritcher* • Dina Brooks *Rachel* • Burt Williams *Bob Hodges* • Larry Maxwell *Jeff Abernathy* • Charles Kavanaugh *Mayor Breyer* • Brandon Boyce *Kevin Havey* ■ *Dir* Bryan Singer • *Scr* Christopher McQuarrie, Michael Feit Dugan, Bryan Singer

The Public Enemy ★★★★★ PG

Classic crime drama 1931 · US · BW · 80mins

This is the film that transformed James Cagney from a sparky song-and-dance man into the world's favourite gangster. But it was not his brutal bootlegging methods, his machine-gun delivery of threats and wisecracks or his ruthless rubbing out of his enemies that secured his tough-guy image, but the shoving of a grapefruit into moll Mae Clarke's face. Cagney makes the most of his chance, giving a performance of raw power. Action expert William A Wellman keeps the story racing along at the speed of a getaway car, setting a style for Warner Bros (fast pace, crackling dialogue, unsentimental scripting and playing) that glamorised the gangster in the 1930s and inadvertently helped pave the way to the Hays Code and film censorship. DP DVD

James Cagney *Tom Powers* • Jean Harlow *Gwen Allen* • Edward Woods *Matt Doyle* • Joan Blondell *Mamie* • Beryl Mercer *Ma Powers* • Donald Cook *Mike Powers* • Mae Clarke *Kitty* • Mia Marvin *Jane* • Leslie Fenton *"Nails" Nathan* • Robert Emmett O'Connor *Paddy Ryan* ■ *Dir* William A Wellman • *Scr* Kubec Glasmon, John Bright, Harvey Thew, from the story *Beer and Blood* by John Bright, Kubec Glasmon

Public Enemy ★★★ 18

Action drama 2002 · S Kor · Colour · 138mins

A maverick cop and a cold-blooded financier utterly lacking in scruple lock horns in this compelling South Korean character study. But director Kang Woo-seok is in no hurry to bring shambolic ex-boxer Seol Gyeong-gu and preening yuppie Lee Seong-jae together, even after the latter murders his parents to prevent them from blowing a deal. Consequently, we're left to stew as Seol is demoted for his reckless tactics before Kang finally rewards us with a satisfying showdown. Littered with moments of violence and hilarity, this is a no-nonsense exercise in macho posturing and sinister style. DP. In Korean with English subtitles. DVD

Seol Gyeong-gu *Kang Cheol-gu* • Lee Seong-jae *Jo Kyo-hwan* • Kang Shin-il *Eom Ban-jeong* • Kim Jeong-hak *Detective Kim Hyeong-sa* ■ *Dir* Kang Woo-seok • *Scr* Gaek Seung-jae, Jung Yoon-seup, Kim Hyun-jung, Chae Yoon-suk, from a story by Gu Bon-han

The Public Eye ★★★ 15

Period crime drama
1992 · US · Colour and BW · 94mins

Joe Pesci is a 1940s tabloid crime photographer who secretly dreams of being recognised as an artist. When wealthy widow Barbara Hershey offers to help him create a book of his photographs in return for some information, he is pulled into her world which involves a war between opposing Mob families. Although this looks great – dark shadows and moody lighting aplenty – the *film noir* style needs a stronger script, and the final product, clearly inspired by real-life photographer Weegee, is rather tedious. JB. Contains swearing.

Joe Pesci *Leon Bernstein* • Barbara Hershey *Kay Levitz* • Stanley Tucci *Sal Minetto* • Jerry Adler *Arthur Nabler* • Jared Harris *Danny the doorman* • Gerry Becker *Conklin* • Richard Riehle *Officer O'Brien* ■ *Dir/Scr* Howard Franklin • *Cinematographer* Peter Suschitzky

Public Hero No 1 ★★

Crime drama 1935 · US · BW · 88mins

Rapped over the knuckles for glorifying the American gangster, Hollywood obligingly promoted the forces of law and order. They're represented here by G-man Chester Morris who is planted in a cell with gangster Joseph Calleia and escapes with him to help bring his gang to justice. This minor film has a major plot contrivance introducing the always delightful Jean Arthur as the gangster's sister. It gives lead billing to Lionel Barrymore, heavy going in the role of an alcoholic doctor. AE

Lionel Barrymore *Dr Josiah Glass* • Chester Morris *Jeff Crane* • Jean Arthur *Theresa O'Reilly* • Paul Kelly (1) *Duff* • Lewis Stone *Warden Alcott* • Joseph Calleia *Sonny Black* • Walter Brennan *Farmer* ■ *Dir* J Walter Ruben • *Scr* Wells Root, from a story by J Walter Ruben, fWells Root

Pucker Up and Bark like a Dog ★

Romantic comedy
1989 · US · Colour · 94mins

Robert Culp and Paul Bartel make appearances in this romantic comedy about a shy and isolated artist living in LA who finds love and with it the confidence to exhibit his work. It tries to be offbeat but ends up being only slightly less daft than its name. FL

Jonathan Gries *Max* • Lisa Zane *Taylor* • Robert Culp *Gregor* • Sal Lopez *Carlos* • Phyllis Diller *Mrs Frasco* • Wendy O Williams *Butch* • Paul Bartel *Director* ■ *Dir* Paul S Parco • *Scr* Mel Green, Gary Larimore, Jude Jansen, Walter Josten, Patricia Bando Josten

Puckoon ★★★ PG

Period comedy
2002 · Ire/UK/Ger · Colour · 80mins

For an hour, this adaptation of Spike Milligan's cult comic novel comes close to capturing the anarchic dexterity of the ex-Goon's matchless wit. The cockamamie characters – whose village is rent asunder by the 1924 border division of Ireland – are brought vividly to life. Yet once writer/director Terence Ryan turns his attention to the increasingly fraught narrative, the offbeat quips and surreal happenstance are replaced by contrived confusions and knockabout farce. It's all enjoyable, but Milligan's sublime, literate lunacy belongs on the page. DP DVD

Sean Hughes *Dan Madigan* • Elliott Gould *Dr Goldstein* • Richard Attenborough *Writer/Director* • Daragh O'Malley *Father Rudden* • John Lynch *O'Brien* • Griff Rhys Jones *Colonel Stokes* • Nickolas Grace *Foggerty* • BJ Hogg *Rafferty* ■ *Dir* Terence Ryan • *Scr* Terence Ryan, from the novel by Spike Milligan

Puerto Escondido ★★★ 15

Comedy 1992 · It · Colour · 106mins

Gabriele Salvatores's follow-up to the Oscar-winning *Mediterraneo* was coolly received by the critics, who couldn't believe that the director capable of such quiet observation could now produce a work of such broad comedy and cack-handedness. However, Diego Abatantuono turns in a splendid performance as the Milan bankteller who is shot during a robbery by deranged police commissioner Renato Carpentieri and hides out in a Mexican backwater to avoid the corrupt copper's wrath. Slow in places, manic in others, but mostly entertaining. DP. In Italian with English subtitles.

Diego Abatantuono *Mario* • Valeria Golino *Anita* • Claudio Bisio *Alex* • Renato Carpentieri *Commissario Viola* • Antonio Catania *Di Gennaro* ■ *Dir* Gabriele Salvatores • *Scr* Enzo Monteleone, Diego Abatantuono, Gabriele Salvatores, from a novel by Pino Cacucci

Pufnstuf ★★ U

Fantasy 1970 · US · Colour · 94mins

An unoriginal, uninspired children's musical about the adventures of a young boy, led by his talking flute to a land where he encounters creatures, including a dragon and several witches. Based on an US TV series, it stars Jack Wild, a bunch of life-size puppets and Martha Raye as the leader of a witches' convention. Highlight of a forgettable score is Mama Cass, another witch, belting out a number called *Different*. RK

Jack Wild *Jimmy* • Billie Hayes *Witchiepoo* • Martha Raye *Boss Witch* • "Mama" Cass Elliot *Witch Hazel* • Billy Barty *Googy Gopher* ■ *Dir* Hollingsworth Morse • *Scr* John Fenton Murray, Si Rose

P

Pull My Daisy ★★★★

Experimental drama 1959 · US · BW · 27mins

Directed by Alfred Leslie and by Robert Frank, this delightful 27-minute short is the only film the Beat writers of the 1950s actually created themselves. Largely a spontaneous experiment, it hovers around a slim storyline that's based on an incident in the life of Neal Cassady and his wife, when they invited a respectable neighbourhood bishop over for dinner with their unrespectable Beat friends, among them poets Allen Ginsberg, Gregory Corso and artist Larry Rivers. With the daddy of them all, Jack Kerouac, providing voiceover, it offers a fascinating glimpse into the lives of the major Beat writers, when they were still capable of just having fun. RB

Allen Ginsberg *Allen* • Gregory Corso *Gregory* • Peter Orlovsky *Peter* • Larry Rivers *Milo* • Delphine Seyrig *Milo's wife* • David Amram *Mez McGillicuddy* • Jack Kerouac *Narrator* ■ *Dir* Alfred Leslie, Robert Frank • *Scr* Jack Kerouac

Pulp ★★★ 12

Comedy thriller 1972 · UK · Colour · 91mins

One of the more interesting teams in the British post-New Wave period was that of the three Michaels – star Caine, writer/director Hodges, producer Klinger – who failed to hit their former *Get Carter* pay dirt with this, their second outing. Nevertheless, the sheer knowing coolness of this bizarre original bears watching. The central theme involving the hiring of a ghostwriter is explored with wit and style, as Hodges deploys his camera cleverly through Maltese locations, and the uncompromising plot makes excellent use of Hollywood icons Mickey Rooney and Lizabeth Scott. TS. Contains violence and swearing. DVD

Michael Caine *Mickey King* • Mickey Rooney *Preston Gilbert* • Lionel Stander *Ben Dinuccio* • Lizabeth Scott *Princess Betty Cippola* • Nadia Cassini *Liz Adams* • Al Lettieri *Miller* • Dennis Price *Mysterious Englishman* ■ *Dir/Scr* Michael Hodges [Mike Hodges]

Pulp Fiction ★★★★★ 18

Crime drama 1994 · US · Colour · 147mins

While not as abrasive or compelling as *Reservoir Dogs*, Quentin Tarantino's follow-up not only confirmed his genius for writing hard-boiled comic dialogue, but also demonstrated a control over a wealth of characters and crossplots that was simply astonishing for a film-maker still, essentially, in the process of learning his trade. The picture went on to scoop the Palme d'Or at the Cannes film festival and win Oscars for Tarantino and his co-writer Roger Avary. Scorching though the writing is, it needed a high-calibre cast to carry it off. Uma Thurman, Bruce Willis, Maria de Medeiros and Christopher Walken are excellent, but the revitalised John Travolta and the then largely unknown Samuel L Jackson are unforgettable. As much pop as pulp, this is exhilarating stuff and clearly one of the best films of the 1990s. DP. Contains violence, swearing, sex scenes, drug abuse and nudity. DVD

John Travolta *Vincent Vega* • Samuel L Jackson *Jules Winnfield* • Uma Thurman *Mia Wallace* • Harvey Keitel *The Wolf* • Tim Roth *Pumpkin* • Amanda Plummer *Honey Bunny* • Maria de Medeiros *Fabienne* • Ving Rhames *Marsellus Wallace* • Eric Stoltz *Lance* • Rosanna Arquette *Jody* • Christopher Walken *Captain Koons* • Bruce Willis *Butch Coolidge* • Quentin Tarantino *Jimmie* • Steve Buscemi *Surly Buddy Holly Waiter* • Stephen Hibbert *The Gimp* • Peter Greene *Zed* ■ *Dir* Quentin Tarantino • *Scr* Quentin Tarantino, Roger Avary, from their stories • *Cinematographer* Andrzej Sekula

Pulse ★★★ 18

Science-fiction horror
1988 · US · Colour · 86mins

A quirky little horror tale that makes up for what it lacks in blood and gore with a neat line in suspense. Cliff De Young is the puzzled suburbanite who can't work out why all the appliances in the house are beginning to turn on their owners. Writer/director Paul Golding pokes some fun at life in the 'burbs, and makes ingenious use of the rogue electrical machines. JF

Cliff De Young *Bill* • Roxanne Hart *Ellen* • Joey Lawrence *David* • Matthew Lawrence *Stevie* • Charles Tyner *Old man* ■ *Dir/Scr* Paul Golding

Pummaro ★★★

Drama 1990 · It · Colour · 102mins

Actor Michele Placido made his directorial debut with this heartfelt drama in which a young Ghanaian comes to Naples in search of his brother. In the course of his travels, he witnesses racial prejudice, the exploitation of immigrant labour, the threat of organised crime and the contrasts between the two Italys – the impoverished south and the affluent north. In painting this picture of a nation coming to terms with its disparate ethnic make-up, Placido offers no easy answers and is careful to avoid sensationalism. DP. In Italian with English subtitles.

Thywill Ak Amenya *Kua Ku* • Pamela Villoresi *Eleonora* • Jacqueline Williams *Nanou* • Gerardo Scala *Professor* ■ *Dir* Michele Placido • *Scr* Sandro Petraglia, Stefano Rulli, Michele Placido, Vilko Filac

Pump Up the Volume ★★★ 15

Drama 1990 · US · Colour · 97mins

Christian Slater has been involved in some of the more thought-provoking teen movies to venture out of Hollywood and he hardly puts a foot wrong here. He plays a quiet high-school student who metamorphoses into an anarchic radio shock jock, who enrages the authorities but becomes a cult hero to his fellow students. Director Allan Moyle shows a sensitive feel for adolescent angst, Samantha Mathis is impressive in an early role and the music is a cut above the FM pap that normally inhabits American teen movies. JF. Contains swearing, drug abuse and nudity. DVD

Christian Slater *Mark Hunter* • Samantha Mathis *Nora Diniro* • Ellen Greene *Jan Emerson* • Scott Paulin *Brian Hunter* • Cheryl Pollak *Paige* • Andy Romano *Murdock* • Mimi Kennedy *Marta Hunter* ■ *Dir/Scr* Allan Moyle

Pumping Iron ★★★★ PG

Documentary 1976 · US · Colour · 81mins

The real centre of attention in this entertaining tour of the body building world is an Austrian man-mountain by the name of Arnold Schwarzenegger, who is aiming to retain his Mr Olympia title. Big Arnie's personality is as overdeveloped as any of the biceps on display here, and whether he's explaining the sexual pleasure he gets from lifting weights or psyching-out an opponent over breakfast, it's clear that you're witnessing a star in the making. And you'll never guess who wins! JC DVD

Charles Gaines *Narrator* ■ *Dir* George Butler, Robert Fiore • *Scr* George Butler, from the non-fiction book by Charles Gaines, George Butler

Pumping Iron II: the Women ★★★★ PG

Documentary 1984 · US · Colour · 102mins

The sequel to the film that made Arnold Schwarzenegger a star, this may be a little more contrived than some fly-on-the-wall documentaries, but it's still hugely entertaining and highly revealing of how so many men view the female form. Concentrating on the 1983 Caesar's Cup contest, director George Butler not only sets out to justify the sport of women's bodybuilding, but also proves that most of the competitors can intellectually knock spots off he-men and beauty queens alike. DP

Dir George Butler • *Scr* Charles Gaines, George Butler, from their book *Pumping Iron II: the Unprecedented Woman*

The Pumpkin Eater ★★★★

Drama 1964 · UK · BW · 119mins

This study of a marriage is based on Penelope Mortimer's novel, with Anne Bancroft as the mother of several screaming brats and the wife of adulterous screenwriter husband Peter Finch. She suffers a nervous collapse in Harrods, undergoes psychoanalysis, then a hysterectomy. Bancroft and Finch deliver blockbuster performances and the supporting cast is equally impressive. There's also beautifully modulated direction from Jack Clayton but scriptwriter Harold Pinter's acidulated signature is all over it, for this British movie is so arty and so alienating it almost needs subtitles. AT

Anne Bancroft *Jo Armitage* • Peter Finch *Jake Armitage* • James Mason *Bob Conway* • Cedric Hardwicke *Mr James, Jo's father* • Richard Johnson *Giles* • Maggie Smith *Philpot* • Eric Porter *Psychiatrist* ■ *Dir* Jack Clayton • *Scr* Harold Pinter, from the novel by Penelope Mortimer

Pumpkinhead ★★★ 18

Horror 1988 · US · Colour · 82mins

For his directorial debut Oscar-winning special effects genius Stan Winston stayed on safe ground with this EC Comic inspired dark horror morality tale. Well-cast Lance Henriksen invokes an ancient witch curse to resurrect the demon Pumpkinhead to take vengeance on the vacationing bikers who killed his son. The smoky backwoods ambience and several plot twists paper over some plodding and under-characterised exposition, and the gore murders are of a standard issue nature. But Winston's creature is as awesomely frightening and brilliantly constructed and offers more than enough feral scream-lined chills to thrill along to. The sequel *The Revenge of Pumpkinhead – Blood Wings* followed in 1994. AJ DVD

Lance Henriksen *Ed Harley* • Jeff East *Chris* • John DiAquino *Joel* • Kimberly Ross *Kim* • Joel Hoffman *Steve* • Cynthia Bain *Tracy* • Kerry Remsen *Maggie* • Tom Woodruff Jr *Pumpkinhead* ■ *Dir* Stan Winston • *Scr* Mark Patrick Carducci, Gary Gerani, from a story by Mark Patrick Carducci, Stan Winston, Richard C Weinman, from a poem by Ed Justin

The Punch and Judy Man ★★ U

Comedy 1962 · UK · BW · 88mins

Cast adrift from his regular scriptwriters Ray Galton and Alan Simpson for the first time in a decade studded with radio and TV triumphs, Tony Hancock comes unstuck in this glum comedy. This tale about a seaside showman driven to distraction by the petty dictates of the local authorities and the social ambitions of his grasping wife (Sylvia Syms) is overwhelmed by moments of unrelieved melancholy. Hancock's lack of finesse allows the despondency to descend into bathos. DP DVD

Tony Hancock *Wally Pinner* • Sylvia Syms *Delia Pinner* • Ronald Fraser *Mayor Palmer* • Barbara Murray *Lady Jane Caterham* • John Le Mesurier *Charles the Sandman* • Hugh Lloyd *Edward Cox* • Mario Fabrizi *Nevil Shanks* ■ *Dir* Jeremy Summers • *Scr* Tony Hancock, Phillip Oakes, from a story by Tony Hancock

Punch-Drunk Love ★★★★ 15

Romantic comedy drama
2002 · US · Colour · 91mins

Adam Sandler stars as the head of a bathroom novelties company who collects air-mile coupons in his spare time, is prone to uncontrollable rages and is mercilessly bullied by his seven sisters. In the first five minutes of the movie a car flips over outside his office, an old harmonium is abandoned and Emily Watson appears from nowhere and asks him to look after her car. Then things start to get really strange. Much has been made of low-brow favourite Sandler teaming up with art house darling Paul Thomas Anderson, but the curious combination works. Sandler's antisocial persona is given a surprising, touching twist, and he handles the movie's moments of slapstick and pathos with equal ease. StH DVD

Adam Sandler *Barry Egan* • Emily Watson *Lena Leonard* • Philip Seymour Hoffman *Dean Trumbell* • Luis Guzman *Lance* • Mary Lynn Rajskub *Elizabeth* • Lisa Spector *Susan* • Hazel Mailloux *Rhonda* ■ *Dir/Scr* Paul Thomas Anderson

Punchline ★★★ 15

Comedy drama 1988 · US · Colour · 117mins

David Seltzer's look at the laughter-makers has wise-cracking performances by Tom Hanks, as a disorientated entertainer, and Sally Field, as a housewife with comic ambitions. But, in trying to escape the humdrum, they just create new restraints on their personalities. It's slow in places, but both stars make this a thoughtful study as to why professional humour is no joke. TH. Contains swearing. DVD

Sally Field *Lilah Krytsick* • Tom Hanks *Steven Gold* • John Goodman *John Krytsick* • Mark Rydell *Romeo* • Kim Greist *Madeline Urie* • Paul Mazursky *Arnold* ■ *Dir/Scr* David Seltzer

The Punisher ★★ 18

Action crime thriller
1989 · US/Aus · Colour · 84mins

The Marvel Comics vigilante is brought to the screen in the guise of square-jawed giant Dolph Lundgren. He's no superhero though, merely a leather-clad man on a motorbike avenging the murder of his family by the New York mob. Lundgren certainly looks every inch the comic book hero, plus there's better-than-average support from Louis Gossett Jr and Jeroen Krabbé, but the lack of visual style, repetitive action scenes and a lifeless script place this in the second division of comic book adaptations. JC

Dolph Lundgren *Frank Castle/The Punisher* • Louis Gossett Jr *Jake Berkowitz* • Jeroen Krabbé *Gianni Franco* • Barry Otto *Shake* • Bryan Marshall *Dino Moretti* • Kim Miyori *Lady Tanaka* ■ *Dir* Mark Goldblatt • *Scr* Robert Mark Kamen, Boaz Yakin, from a story by Boaz Yakin, from the Marvel comicbook character created by Gerry Conway, John Romita Sr, Ross Andru

The Punisher ★★★ 18

Action crime thriller
2004 · US/Ger · Colour · 118mins

This more faithful take on Marvel Comic's character obliterates the 1989 Dolph Lundgren version. It's loud, fast and extremely vicious. Tom Jane stars as former FBI special agent Frank Castle, who turns vigilante when his family is gunned down on Florida Mob boss John Travolta's orders. Jane has the cool air of a super-human rock star as he orchestrates the darkest of revenge. There's no let up to the destruction and violence, nor is there any semblance of reality. SF. Contains violence. DVD

Tom Jane [Thomas Jane] *Frank Castle/The Punisher* • John Travolta *Howard Saint* • Rebecca Romijn-Stamos *Joan* • Will Patton *Quentin Glass* • Roy Scheider *Frank Castle Sr* • Laura Harring *Livia Saint* • Ben Foster *Spacker Dave* • Samantha Mathis *Maria Castle* • James Carpinello *John Saint/Bobby Saint* • Russell Andrews *Jimmy Weeks* ■ *Dir* Jonathan Hensleigh • *Scr* Jonathan Hensleigh, Michael France, from the Marvel comic book character created by Gerry Conway, John Romita Sr, Ross Andru

Punishment Park ★★★★

Documentary drama
1971 · US · Colour · 88mins

The best of the socio-political fantasies made by documentary film-maker Peter Watkins whose *Privilege* and *The War Game* also interpreted present ills through reconstructions of the future. Draft dodgers who oppose America's Indo-China war are put in detention camps where they must chose between a three-day ordeal in "Punishment Park" to win their freedom or a long jail sentence. Watkins plays the leader of a British documentary film unit observing one group of dissenters as they take the former option and run for their lives across a desert. Powerful and depressing, this is an outstanding indictment of repression and insidious state bullyboy tactics. AJ

Jim Bohan *Captain, Dheriff's Department* • Van Daniels *County Sheriff* • Frederick Franklyn *Professor Daly* • Carmen Argenziano *Jay Kaufman* • Stan Armsted *Charles Robbins* • Gladys Golden *Mrs Jergens* • Sanford Golden *Sen Harris* • Patrick Boland *Defendant* • Peter Watkins *Documentarist* ■ *Dir/Scr* Peter Watkins

The Punk ★★ 15

Romantic drama 1993 · UK · Colour · 92mins

This punk-induced ode to Romeo and Juliet, set on the streets of Notting Hill, features 1960s star Jess Conrad as the father of a rich girl who falls for a local punk, much to the disgust of parents and the like. Director Michael Sarne turns out something approaching a modern fairy tale. FL. Contains swearing, violence and sex scenes. [video]

Charlie Creed-Miles *David* • Vanessa Hadaway *Rachel* • David Shawyer *David's father* • Jess Conrad *Rachel's father* • Jacqueline Skarvellis *David's mother* • Yolanda Mason *Rachel's stepmother* • Alex Mollo *Stray Cat* ■ *Dir* Mike Sarne [Michael Sarne] • *Scr* Michael Sarne, from the novel by Gideon Sams

The Punk Rock Movie ★★★ 15

Music documentary 1978 · UK · Colour · 79mins

An 8mm-blown-up-to-35mm record of the London punk scene just as it was exploding globally to shake up the moribund music world irrevocably . Filmed by Don Letts, the road manager for various Brit-punk bands, this technically haphazard chronicle covers all the bases – tiny hothouse venues, cramped recording studios, road tours, pogo rituals (featuring a young Shane McGowan), razor blade fashions and drug-taking. Filmed mostly at London's Roxy Club, this is a simply presented but valuable history lesson. AJ [video]

Dir Don Letts

Puppet Master ★★ 18

Horror 1989 · US · Colour · 86mins

The first of a long series of horror films about the puppets given life by their creator, Toulon. A group of highly unlikely psychic researchers, including Paul Le Mat, are terrorised in a hotel by the murderous marionettes. Director David Schmoeller, veteran of much low-grade horror, does little with the formulaic script, which is slow to get going, but finally delivers the gory goods. The puppets are cleverly animated by special effects expert David Allen. DM [video] DVD

Paul Le Mat *Alex* • Irene Miracle *Dana Hadley* • Matt Roe *Frank* • Kathryn O'Reilly *Clarissa* • Robin Frates *Megan Gallagher* • Merrya Small [Marya Small] *Theresa* • Jimmie F Scaggs *Neil* • William Hickey *Toulon* ■ *Dir* David Schmoeller • *Scr* Joseph G Collodi, from a story by Charles Band, Kenneth J Hall

The Puppet Masters ★★ 15

Science-fiction drama 1994 · US · Colour · 104mins

This dumb incarnation of Robert Heinlein's excellent short novel takes liberties with the story in such a way that Heinlein might have objected. If you've seen Donald Sutherland's other alien invasion flick, 1978's *Invasion of the Body Snatchers*, you've already got a pretty good idea of what's in store here when there's hidden menace in a meteorite strike in rural Iowa. While technically competent, it offers little in the way of plot. ST [video] DVD

Donald Sutherland *Andrew Nivens* • Eric Thal *Sam Nivens* • Julie Warner *Mary Sefton* • Yaphet Kotto *Ressler* • Keith David *Holland* • Will Patton *Graves* • Richard Belzer *Jarvis* • Tom Mason *President Douglas* ■ *Dir* Stuart Orme • *Scr* David S Goyer, Ted Elliot, Terry Rossio, from the novel by Robert A Heinlein

Puppet on a Chain ★★ 15

Thriller 1970 · UK · Colour · 93mins

Director Geoffrey Reeve is saddled with Swedish actor Sven-Bertil Taube, whose charmless playing makes involvement in the Alistair MacLean based-plot almost impossible. However, his performance serves to make the final speedboat chase along the canals of Amsterdam (a sequence directed by Don Sharp) even more thrilling. DP. Contains violence and some swearing. [video]

Sven-Bertil Taube *Paul Sherman* • Barbara Parkins *Maggie* • Alexander Knox *Colonel de Graaf* • Patrick Allen *Inspector Van Gelder* • Vladek Sheybal *Meegeren* • Ania Marson *Astrid Leman* ■ *Dir* Geoffrey Reeve • *Scr* Alistair MacLean, Paul Wheeler, Don Sharp, from the novel by Alistair MacLean

The Puppetmaster ★★★ 15

Biographical drama
1993 · Tai · Colour · 136mins

Steeped in the folklore of his beloved Taiwan, this hypnotic account of puppetmaster Li Tianlu's first 36 years features fleeting appearances from Li himself. Taking us from Li's troubled childhood in what was still essentially a feudal society to the liberation of the island from the Japanese at the end of the Second World War, the film is enlivened throughout by some compelling dramatic sequences and several wonderful displays of puppetry. Yet director Hou Hsiao-Hsien's sometimes heavy-handed symbolism and his decision to adopt such a funereal pace occasionally counts against the intrigue of the story. DP. In Mandarin, Taiwanese and Japanese with English subtitles. [video]

Li Tianlu • Lim Giong [Lin Qiang] *Li Tianlu, young adult* • Chen Kuizhong *Li Tianlu, teenager* • Zuo Juwei *Li Tianlu, child* ■ *Dir* Hou Xiaoxian [Hou Hsiao-Hsien] • *Scr* Wu Nianzhen, Zhu Tianwen, from the book *Ximeng Rensheng* by Li Tianlu Li, Hou Xiaoxian [Hou Hsiao-Hsien], Zheng Yumen

The Purchase Price ★★★

Melodrama 1932 · US · BW · 66mins

Manhattan torch singer Barbara Stanwyck, eager to escape the clutches of her gangster lover, Lyle Talbot, becomes a mail order bride to North Dakota farmer George Brent. How the couple, especially Stanwyck, cope with adjusting to their unlikely alliance, and the series of dramatic incidents that attends them, is the stuff of this full-blooded melodrama. Director William A Wellman extracts as much humour as possible from clichéd secondary characters, while squeezing some credibility from the bizarre incidents. The sublime Stanwyck rises, as always, above the material. RK

Barbara Stanwyck *Joan Gordon* • George Brent *Jim Gilson* • Lyle Talbot *Ed Fields* • Hardie Albright *Don* • David Landau *Bull McDowell* • Murray Kinnell *Spike Forgan* ■ *Dir* William A Wellman • *Scr* Robert Lord, from the story *The Mud Lark* by Arthur Stringer

Pure ★★★★ 18

Drama 2002 · UK · Colour · 92mins

An exceptional performance from Harry Eden, John de Borman's unflinching images of a West Ham housing estate and director Gillies MacKinnon's courageous reclamation of the subject of drug crime from soap sensationalism give this drama a sobering power that recalls a bygone era of British social realism. The despair and degradation of the addict's existence is laid bare by Molly Parker as a widowed mother so dependent on dealer David Wenham that she can no longer care for her young sons. But the real drama lies in 10 year-old Harry Eden's gradual realisation of her plight (which eventually prompts him to try crack himself). Starkly touching and shockingly authentic. DP [video] DVD

Molly Parker *Mel* • David Wenham *Lenny* • Harry Eden *Paul* • Geraldine McEwan *Nanna* • Kate Ashfield *Helen* • Gary Lewis *Det Insp French* • Marsha Thomason *Vicki* • Karl Johnson *Granddad* ■ *Dir* Gillies MacKinnon • *Scr* Alison Hume

Pure Country ★★ PG

Drama 1992 · US · Colour · 107mins

"Pure Corn" might have been a better title for this slice of country-and-western hokum. Your opinion of this tale of a troubled superstar will depend on your reaction to George Strait. There's no denying he's handy with a tune, but dialogue proves more difficult for him. It's a shame we couldn't spend more time with his tacky manager, played by Lesley Ann Warren. Rory Calhoun is also wasted in an undemanding supporting role. DP [video]

George Strait *Dusty Wyatt Chandler* • Lesley Ann Warren *Lula Rogers* • Isabel Glasser *Harley Tucker* • Kyle Chandler *Buddy Jackson* • John Doe *Earl Blackstock* • Rory Calhoun *Ernest Tucker* • Molly McClure *Grandma Ivy Chandler* ■ *Dir* Christopher Cain • *Scr* Rex McGee

A Pure Formality ★★ 12

Psychological mystery drama
1994 · It/Fr · Colour · 106mins

Director Giuseppe Tornatore had a hit with *Cinema Paradiso*, a near hit with *The Legend of 1900* and a big miss here. Gérard Depardieu stars as a famous French writer fleeing from a mysterious gunshot. The movie centres round his interrogation by inspector Roman Polanski in a wet, seedy shed in the middle of a dank forest. These two film giants cannot pull together a ponderous plot and meandering monologues. LH. In French with English subtitles. [video] DVD

Gérard Depardieu *Onoff* • Roman Polanski *Inspector* • Sergio Rubini *Andre, the young policeman* • Nicola DiPinto *The captain* • Paolo Lombardi *The warrant officer* • Tano Cimarosa *The old attendant* ■ *Dir* Giuseppe Tornatore • *Scr* Giuseppe Tornatore, Pascal Quignard, from a story by Giuseppe Tornatore

The Pure Hell of St Trinian's ★★ U

Comedy 1960 · UK · BW · 90mins

Bereft of Alastair Sim, the third film in the St Trinian's series (that began with *The Belles of St Trinian's*) has its moments, but sadly all too few of them. With the school reduced to smouldering ashes, mysterious child psychologist Cecil Parker takes charge of the tearaways, in league with white-slaving sea captain Sid James. Woefully short on mayhem, the film spends too much time in the company of eventual castaways Parker and Joyce Grenfell. Followed by *The Great St Trinian's Train Robbery*. DP [video]

Cecil Parker *Professor Canford* • Joyce Grenfell *Sergeant Ruby Gates* • George Cole *Flash Harry* • Thorley Walters *Butters* • Eric Barker *Culpepper-Brown* • Irene Handl *Miss Harker-Packer* • Sidney James *Alphonse O'Reilly* • Dennis Price *Gore-Blackwood* ■ *Dir* Frank Launder • *Scr* Frank Launder, Val Valentine, Sidney Gilliat, from the drawings by Ronald Searle

Pure Luck ★★ PG

Comedy 1991 · US · Colour · 91mins

A limp attempt to find life in the corpse of the buddy-buddy movie, this stars Danny Glover as a gumshoe and Martin Short as his idiotic sidekick who go shooting off to Mexico in search of a missing heiress. This lazy wheeze, which abandons any pretence at a decent script at an early stage, relies for the odd outbreak of energy on Short, who is required to shore up the film with a volley of pratfalls. JM. Contains swearing. [video]

Martin Short *Eugene Proctor* • Danny Glover *Raymond Campanella* • Sheila Kelley *Valerie Highsmith* • Sam Wanamaker *Mr Highsmith* • Scott Wilson *Grimes* • Harry Shearer *Monosoff* • Jorge Russek *Inspector Segura* ■ *Dir* Nadia Tass • *Scr* Herschel Weingrod, Timothy Harris

Purely Belter ★★★ 15

Comedy 2000 · UK · Colour · 98mins

This "social comedy" from Mark Herman is an acceptable addition to the growing roster of feel-good British underdog films. It's set in football-mad Newcastle upon Tyne, where cash-strapped Chris Beattie and Greg McLane are two Toon Army tykes desperate to raise the necessary money for season tickets. As the underprivileged but enterprising pair pursue their goal by fair means and foul, Herman fashions some telling social commentary from the slight tale. An amusing script and likeable performances make this an interesting diversion. DA. Contains swearing and drug abuse. [video] DVD

Chris Beattie *Gerry McCarten* • Greg McLane *Sewell* • Charlie Hardwick *Mrs McCarten* • Tim Healy *Mr McCarten* • Roy Hudd *Mr Sewell* • Kevin Whately *Mr Caird* • Jody Baldwin *Gemma* • Alan Shearer ■ *Dir* Mark Herman • *Scr* Mark Herman, from the novel *The Season Ticket* by Jonathan Tulloch

Purgatory ★ 18

Prison drama 1988 · US · Colour · 89mins

This boring "women in prison" saga contains all the usual clichés, but not many of the needed lip-smacking exploitation elements to make it endearing to fans of the genre. Peace Corps worker Tanya Roberts gets locked up on a phoney drugs charge while pounding her South African beat and discovers her fellow inmates are being used as prostitutes by the wardens. Utter tosh. AJ [video] DVD

Tanya Roberts *Carly Arnold* • Julie Pop *Melanie* • Hal Orlandini *Bledsoe* • Rufus Swart *Paul Cricks* ■ *Dir* Ami Artzi • *Scr* Felix Kroll, Paul Aratow

Purgatory ★★★ 15

Western 1999 · US · Colour · 90mins

This barmy but richly enjoyable western fable stars Eric Roberts as a bank robber who holes up with his gang in a sleepy, weapons-free village south of the border. One of the young gang members (Brad Rowe) realises that this is Purgatory for legends of the West – Billy the Kid (Donnie Wahlberg), Doc Holliday (Randy Quaid), Jesse James (JD Souther) and Wild Bill Hickock (Sam Shepard). But if they take up arms against the newcomers, will they be refused their place in heaven? JF. Contains sexual references, violence, swearing. [video]

Sam Shepard *Sheriff Forest* • Eric Roberts *Blackjack* • Randy Quaid *Director* • Peter Stormare *Cavin* • Brad Rowe *Sonny* • Donnie Wahlberg *Deputy Glen* • JD Souther *Brooks* ■ *Dir* Uli Edel • *Scr* Gordon Dawson

Purple Haze ★★ 18

Drama 1982 · US · Colour · 96mins

Another *American Graffiti*-inspired clone focusing on the summer of 1968 and the hippy antics of college drop-out Peter Nelson and his drugged-out best friend Chuck McQuary. Parental conflicts, the threat of the draft and the usual round of chemically fuelled parties are the familiar signposts in this not very insightful look at the turbulent late 1960s. A great Golden Oldie soundtrack eases the bumps along director David Burton Morris's familiar nostalgia ride. AJ

Peter Nelson *Matt Caulfield* • Chuck McQuary *Jeff Maley* • Bernard Baldan *Derek Savage* • Susanna Lack *Kitty Armstrong* • Bob Breuler *Walter Caulfield* • Joanne Bauman *Margaret Caulfield* ■ *Dir* David Burton Morris • *Scr* Victoria Wozniak, from a story by Tom Kelsey, David Burton Morris, Victoria Wozniak

P

The Purple Heart ★★★

Second World War drama
1944 · US · BW · 100mins

An unashamed wartime propaganda movie directed by Lewis Milestone, the man responsible for some of the greatest war films ever. Here, a group of US air force personnel are falsely accused of war atrocities after being captured by the Japanese. When they refuse to admit to the charges, they face a terrible ordeal. This isn't one of Milestone's best, mainly because every character seems such an obvious stereotype, despite the fact that the tragic events depicted are based on fact. TS

Dana Andrews *Captn Harvey Ross* • Richard Conte *Lt Angelo Canelli* • Farley Granger *Sgt Howard Clinton* • Kevin O'Shea *Sgt Jan Skvoznik* • Donald Barry *Lt Peter Vincent* ■ *Dir* Lewis Milestone • *Scr* Jerome Cady, from a story by Melville Crossman [Darryl F Zanuck]

Purple Hearts ★★ 15

War drama 1984 · US · Colour · 110mins

In this Vietnam romance, former *Charlie's Angel* Cheryl Ladd is the nurse who falls for doctor Ken Wahl during the war, intending to spend the rest of her medical career by his side. It's tosh, of course, but not unenjoyable, with a *Romeo and Juliet*-style series of endings, as you wonder who's been killed, or not. Watch out for former military drill instructor Lee Ermey, appearing in a Vietnam feature three full years before *Full Metal Jacket*. TS. Contains swearing.

Ken Wahl *Don Jardian* • Cheryl Ladd *Deborah Solomon* • Stephen Lee *Wizard* • David Harris *Hanes* • Cyril O'Reilly *Zuma* • Lane Smith *Commander Markel* • Lee Ermey [R Lee Ermey] *Gunny* ■ *Dir* Sidney J Furie • *Scr* Rick Natkin, Sidney J Furie

The Purple Mask ★★ U

Period adventure 1955 · US · Colour · 81mins

A Napoleonic frolic with Tony Curtis in historical mode – that is to say, adding adenoidal timbre and generally camping it up. The plot is some nonsense about Napoleon and those irritating Royalists who keep losing their heads on the guillotine. Curtis sports a mask and waves his rapier at arch rival, Dan O'Herlihy. Angela Lansbury is a milliner whose shop is also a cover for the Resistance, while the love interest is Colleen Miller. AT

Tony Curtis *Rene* • Colleen Miller *Laurette* • Gene Barry *Capt Laverne* • Dan O'Herlihy *Brisquet* • Angela Lansbury *Madame Valentine* • George Dolenz *Marcel Cadonal* • John Hoyt *Rochet* ■ *Dir* H Bruce Humberstone • *Scr* Oscar Brodney, from the play *Le Chevalier aux Masques* by Paul Armont, Jean Manoussi, adapted by Charles Latour

The Purple People Eater ★★★ U

Musical fantasy 1988 · US · Colour · 90mins

Thirty years after Sheb Wooley had a hit with the song of the title in 1958, this daft little movie attempted to rekindle the spirit of a time when aliens were synonymous with communists and rock 'n' roll was considered the Devil's music. There's something irresistible about seeing Ned Beatty and Shelley Winters playing helpless pensioners, while Neil Patrick Harris co-stars as the lad who brings the eponymous alien to Earth by playing Wooley's hit. DP

Ned Beatty *Grandpa* • Neil Patrick Harris *Billy Johnson* • Shelley Winters *Rita* • Peggy Lipton *Mom* • James Houghton *Dad* • Thora Birch *Molly Johnson* • John Brumfield *Mr Noodle* • Little Richard *Mayor* • Chubby Checker *Singer* ■ *Dir* Linda Shayne • *Scr* Linda Shayne, from the song by Sheb Wooley

The Purple Plain ★★★

Second World War drama
1954 · UK · Colour · 101mins

In this romantic adventure, Gregory Peck plays the Canadian Second World War pilot, haunted by the death of his wife, who regains his confidence via a love affair and a bungled combat mission in Burma. Adapted by Eric Ambler from the novel by HE Bates, this is quite a classy production, directed by Robert Parrish and impressively shot by Geoffrey Unsworth in the jungles of Ceylon. AT

Gregory Peck *Squadron Leader Forrester* • Than Min Win *Anna* • Bernard Lee *Dr Harris* • Maurice Denham *Blore* • Brenda de Banzie *Miss McNab* • Ram Gopal *Mr Phang* • Lyndon Brook *Carrington* • Anthony Bushell *Commander Aldridge* • Jack McNaughton *Sergeant Brown* • Harold Siddons *Navigator Williams* ■ *Dir* Robert Parrish • *Scr* Eric Ambler, from the novel by HE Bates

Purple Rain ★★★ 15

Musical drama 1984 · US · Colour · 106mins

The first and easily the best of pint-sized rock star Prince's forays into film. Breathtakingly egotistical, it follows the adventures of struggling rock singer "The Kid" as he battles to the top of the pop tree, despite the underhand tactics of his rivals. The less said about the lead performances the better although Morris Day eclipses the star with a charismatic turn. Prince and the Revolution were at the height of their powers and their hits are memorably captured by director Albert Magnoli. A sequel of sorts, *Graffiti Bridge*, followed in 1990. JF. Contains violence, sex scenes and nudity. DVD

Prince *The Kid* • Apollonia Kotero *Apollonia* • Morris Day *Morris* • Olga Karlatos *Mother* • Clarence Williams III *Father* • Jerome Benton *Jerome* • Billy Sparks *Billy* • Jill Jones *Jill* ■ *Dir* Albert Magnoli • *Scr* Albert Magnoli, William Blinn

The Purple Rose of Cairo ★★★★ PG

Fantasy romantic comedy
1985 · US · Colour and BW · 78mins

In Woody Allen's short story *The Kugelmass Episode*, an academic is transported into the bedroom of the literary character Madame Bovary. *The Purple Rose of Cairo* is a film inversion of this idea, with Mia Farrow as a brutalised waitress who wins the heart of a character in her favourite movie (played by Jeff Daniels) who steps out of the screen to court her. Farrow and Daniels are charming and writer/director Allen poignantly recalls the importance of Hollywood dreams to people weighed down by the cares of the 1930s. Technically polished and ingenious. DP DVD

Mia Farrow *Cecilia* • Jeff Daniels *Tom Baxter/Gil Shepherd* • Danny Aiello *Monk* • Dianne Wiest *Emma* • Van Johnson *Larry* • Zoe Caldwell *Countess* • John Wood *Jason* • Milo O'Shea *Father Donnelly* ■ *Dir/Scr* Woody Allen • *Cinematographer* Gordon Willis

The Purple Taxi ★★★

Drama 1977 · Fr/It/Ire · Colour · 107mins

The multinational producers and cast give this curio a strange cross-cultural edge. The drama centers on several moneyed expats of widely varying backgrounds who cross paths in the west of Ireland after escaping their previous lives. Doctor Fred Astaire drives the purple taxi, millionaire Edward Albert searches for traces of his Irish ancestry, while the sexy wife of a German prince, Charlotte Rampling, tries to seduce a terminally ill patient. Offbeat and watchable. JG

Charlotte Rampling *Sharon* • Philippe Noiret *Philippe* • Agostina Belli *Anne Taubelman* • Peter Ustinov *Taubelman* • Fred Astaire *Dr Scully* • Edward Albert *Jerry* • Mairin O'Sullivan *Colleen* • Jack Watson *Sean* ■ *Dir* Yves Boisset • *Scr* Yves Boisset, Michel Déon, from a novel by Michel Déon

Pursued ★★★★ PG

Western 1947 · US · BW · 101mins

Not as well-known as *High Noon*, *The Searchers* or *Red River*, this was one of the first "psychological westerns" and has the same sort of story, theme and flashback structure usually found in the urban *film noir*. Robert Mitchum plays a tortured soul who was adopted as a child, murders his half-brother and then marries his brother's wife. It has the feel of a classical tragedy, with Mitchum superb as the brooding hero who journeys back into his past. Critics have laid all the praise at the door of the director, Raoul Walsh, but it's largely the creation of screenwriter Niven Busch. AT

Robert Mitchum *Jeb Rand* • Teresa Wright *Thorley Callum* • Judith Anderson *Mrs Medora Callum* • Dean Jagger *Grant Callum* • Alan Hale *Jake Dingle* • John Rodney *Adam Callum* • Harry Carey Jr *Prentice McComber* ■ *Dir* Raoul Walsh • *Scr* Niven Busch • *Cinematographer* James Wong Howe • *Music* Max Steiner

The Pursuers ★★

Crime thriller 1961 · UK · BW · 63mins

The arrest and trial of Adolph Eichmann made the pursuit of Nazi war criminals a fitting topic for thrillers such as this. The plot resembles any fugitive on-the-run yarn, with the Nazi hiding out in a nightclub singer's flat in London, hunted by a German organisation and unable to flee the country because he's damaged his passport. Never more than a B-movie, it's worth seeing for its treatment of its subject and for the performance of Cyril Shaps. AT

Cyril Shaps *Karl Luther* • Francis Matthews *David Nelson* • Susan Denny *Jenny Walmer* • Sheldon Lawrence *Rico* • George Murcell *Freddy* ■ *Dir* Godfrey Grayson • *Scr* Brian Clemens, David Nicholl

The Pursuit of DB Cooper ★★ 15

Comedy crime drama
1981 · US · Colour · 96mins

A thriller that begins with Treat Williams jumping out of a plane with a bag containing $200,000. Amazingly, this airborne robbery, with its James Bond-style stunt, really happened and DB Cooper vanished into myth. This is where fiction takes over, conjuring up Cooper's subsequent life and the attempts of a former Green Beret (Robert Duvall) to track him down. Sadly, the picture bungles a nifty idea and it's rarely more than routine. AT. Contains violence.

Robert Duvall *Gruen* • Treat Williams *Meade* • Kathryn Harrold *Hannah* • Ed Flanders *Brigadier* • Paul Gleason *Remson* • RG Armstrong *Dempsey* ■ *Dir* Roger Spottiswoode • *Scr* Jeffrey Alan Fiskin, from the book *Free Fall* by JD Reed

The Pursuit of Happiness ★

Drama 1971 · US · Colour · 93mins

Robert Mulligan directs this clichéd, hopelessly dated story of a disenchanted hippy who rejects the life style of his affluent Manhattan family. Michael Sarrazin's life goes wrong – he kills someone in an auto accident, goes to jail and then thinks he should escape and hop over the Canadian border. Barbara Hershey is his girlfriend and there's a song, repeated often, by Randy Newman. AT

Michael Sarrazin *William Popper* • Barbara Hershey *Jane Kauffman* • Arthur Hill *John Popper* • Ruth White *Mrs Popper* • EG Marshall *Daniel Lawrence* • Robert Klein *Melvin Lasher* • William Devane *Pilot* ■ *Dir* Robert Mulligan • *Scr* Jon Boothe, George L Sherman, from a novel by Thomas Rogers

Pursuit to Algiers ★★ U

Mystery 1945 · US · BW · 65mins

Basil Rathbone and Nigel Bruce just cruise through this, one of the worst of the Sherlock Holmes series from Universal Studios. They're aboard an ocean liner, escorting an imperilled prince to safety. Despite being a royalist loyalist, Holmes looks decidedly sniffy about the whole affair, probably lamenting the poor production values and sets which look like *Crossroads* on a bad day. TH

Basil Rathbone *Sherlock Holmes* • Nigel Bruce *Dr John H Watson* • Marjorie Riordan *Sheila Woodbury, singer* • Rosalind Ivan *Agatha Dunham* • Martin Kosleck *Mirko* • John Abbott *Jodri* • Frederick Worlock *Prime Minister* • Morton Lowry *Sanford, ship's steward* ■ *Dir* Roy William Neill • *Scr* Leonard Lee, from characters created by Sir Arthur Conan Doyle

Pusher ★★★ 18

Crime drama 1996 · Den · Colour · 105mins

Although debuting Danish director Nicolas Winding Refn gives as his references such American indie icons as Quentin Tarantino and Abel Ferrara, the grungy handheld visuals, improvised dialogue and dark sense of humour mean this feels more like a European art house movie. In keeping with drug dealer Kim Bodnia's occupational ducking and diving, the action becomes increasingly claustrophobic as his options run out. This is a sobering, often violent drama; but even though Bodnia's problems are of his own making, it's impossible not to empathise with him. DP. In Danish with English subtitles. DVD

Kim Bodnia *Frank* • Zlatko Buric *Milo* • Laura Drasbaek *Vic* • Slavko Labovic *Radovan* ■ *Dir* Nicolas Winding Refn • *Scr* Nicolas Winding Refn, Jens Dahl

Pushing Hands ★★★

Comedy drama
1991 · Tai/US · Colour · 100mins

The title of this early gem from director Ang Lee refers to the Oriental t'ai chi exercise during which you keep your balance while unbalancing your opponent. This is an apt metaphor for the narrative about retired martial arts expert Lung Sihung, whose life is turned upside down when he moves in with his son and his American wife in a New York suburb. While not as assured as his later works, Lee's subtle observations are worth watching as the older man struggles to fit in with his hostile daughter-in-law (Deb Snyder). LH. In English and Mandarin with subtitles.

Lung Sihung *Mr Chu* • Wang Lai *Mrs Chen* • Bo Z Wang *Alex Chu* • Deb Snyder *Martha Chu* • Lee Haan *Jeremy Chu* ■ *Dir* Ang Lee • *Scr* Ang Lee, James Schamus

Pushing Tin ★★★ 15

Comedy drama 1999 · US · Colour · 123mins

This uneven but fascinating comedy drama looks at the air-traffic controllers who guide planes in and out of New York's airspace. Mike Newell's film focuses on two in particular: super-cool John Cusack and Zen-like Billy Bob Thornton, who challenges Cusack's claim to be the best controller in town. It's not only Cusack's ego that is bruised by his rivalry with Thornton; their wives (Cate Blanchett and Angelina Jolie) also get caught in the crossfire. Overly dramatic in places, this boasts superb performances from Thornton and Cusack. JB. Contains swearing and a sex scene. DVD

John Cusack *Nick Falzone* • Billy Bob Thornton *Russell Bell* • Cate Blanchett *Connie Falzone* • Angelina Jolie *Mary Bell* • Jake Weber *Barry Plotkin* ■ *Dir* Mike Newell • *Scr* Glen Charles, Les Charles, from the article *Something's Got to Give* by Darcy Frey

Pushover ★★★

Crime drama 1954 · US · BW · 87mins

A smart and unpredictable thriller with Fred MacMurray as the cop who puts a bank robber's girlfriend (Kim Novak) under surveillance, only to fall in love with her himself. Novak's glamorous and glacial presence, not to mention the easy-going charm of MacMurray, makes this movie a sort of forerunner to Hitchcock's *Vertigo*. The basic idea was reprised three decades later in the comedy *Stakeout*. AT

Fred MacMurray *Paul Sheridan* • Kim Novak *Lona McLane* • Phil Carey [Philip Carey] *Rick McAllister* • Dorothy Malone *Ann* • EG Marshall *Lt Carl Eckstrom* ■ *Dir* Richard Quine • *Scr* Roy Huggins, from a story and novel by Thomas Walsh, from the novel *Rafferty* by William S Ballinger

Putney Swope ★★

Satire 1969 · US · BW and Colour · 85mins

American independent film-maker Robert Downey had a modest hit with this satirical swipe at corporate America. Arnold Johnson plays the token black man on the board of directors of a Madison Avenue advertising agency. When the chairman keels over, Johnson surprisingly takes over and overturns the racial pecking order. Unfortunately, Johnson's regime makes enemies of some of his staff, while his politically correct business policies arouse the suspicions of the pot-smoking US President. AT

Arnold Johnson *Putney Swope* • Antonio Fargas *Arab* • Laura Greene *Mrs Swope* • Eric Krupnik *Mark Focus* • Pepi Hermine *United States President* • Ruth Hermine *First Lady* • Lawrence Wolf *Mr Borman Six* • Stan Gottlieb *Nathan* • Mel Brooks *Mr Forget It* ■ *Dir/Scr* Robert Downey Sr

Puzzle of a Downfall Child ★★

Drama 1970 · US · Colour · 104mins

A once-famous fashion model (Faye Dunaway), now in a state of disintegration as a result of her less than savoury lifestyle, retires to a beach house. There, she recounts her sordid past (in flashback) to photographer Barry Primus. Former fashion photographer Jerry Schatzberg made his directing debut with this visually excellent movie in which Dunaway, looking stunning, gives a good account of herself. RK

Faye Dunaway *Lou Andreas Sand* • Barry Primus *Aaron Reinhardt* • Viveca Lindfors *Pauline Galba* • Barry Morse *Dr Galba* • Roy Scheider *Mark* • Ruth Jackson *Barbara Casey* • John Heffernan *Dr Sherman* ■ *Dir* Jerry Schatzberg • *Scr* Adrien Joyce [Carole Eastman], from a story by Jerry Schatzberg, Adrien Joyce [Carole Eastman]

Pygmalion ★★★★★ U

Comedy 1938 · UK · BW · 94mins

A superb rendering of George Bernard Shaw's most popular play, for which Shaw himself was awarded a special Academy Award for his contribution (the embassy ball scene) to the screenplay. The film actually won Oscars for the adaptors of the screenplay. Leslie Howard was never better as Henry Higgins (a role Shaw wanted to go to Charles Laughton) and both he and Wendy Hiller (quite brilliant as Eliza Doolittle) were unlucky not to win Oscars themselves. Although Howard took a co-directing credit, Anthony Asquith handled most of the action, acquiring himself an unrivalled reputation for stage adaptation in the process. DP [VIDEO]

Leslie Howard *Professor Henry Higgins* • Wendy Hiller *Eliza Doolittle* • Wilfrid Lawson *Alfred Doolittle* • Marie Lohr *Mrs Higgins* • Scott Sunderland *Colonel Pickering* • Jean Cadell *Mrs Pearce* • David Tree *Freddy Eynsford-Hill* • Everley Gregg *Mrs Eynsford-Hill* ■ *Dir* Anthony Asquith, Leslie Howard • *Scr* George Bernard Shaw, from his play, adapted by WP Lipscomb, Cecil Lewis, Ian Dalrymple • *Editor* David Lean

Pyrates ★★ 18

Comedy 1991 · US · Colour · 91mins

In this oddity, real-life husband-and-wife leads Kevin Bacon and Kyra Sedgwick play a young couple with a fiery love life, literally – when the pair get together, buildings tend to go up in smoke. It's an unusual concept, with the two stars giving it their best shot, but director Noah Stern doesn't take the original idea anywhere interesting and it's far too self-consciously wacky for its own good. JF. Contains swearing, sex scenes, nudity. [VIDEO]

Kevin Bacon *Ari* • Kyra Sedgwick *Sam* • Bruce Martyn Payne [Bruce Payne] *Liam* • Kristin Dattilo *Pia* • Buckley Norris *Dr Weiss* • Deborah Falconer *Rivkah* • David Pressman *Carlton* ■ *Dir/Scr* Noah Stern

A Pyromaniac's Love Story ★★ PG

Romantic comedy
1995 · US · Colour · 90mins

Love-starved workers at Armin Mueller-Stahl's bakery try to find romance while dealing with a mystery arsonist in this witless comedy directed by Joshua Brand, the creator of *Northern Exposure*. Each of the game cast wants to be known as the pyromaniac responsible for the fire so they can say their motive was love. Despite some cute turns, this incomprehensible farce raises little heat and is too quirky for its own good. AJ [VIDEO] DVD

William Baldwin *Garet* • John Leguizamo *Sergio* • Sadie Frost *Hattie* • Erika Eleniak *Stephanie* • Michael Lerner *Perry* • Joan Plowright *Mrs Linzer* • Armin Mueller-Stahl *Mr Linzer* • Richard Crenna *Businessman* ■ *Dir* Joshua Brand • *Scr* Morgan Ward

Python ★★ 15

Horror 2000 · US · Colour · 95mins

The 130ft snake really should be the star of this 1950s-style horror movie, yet the abysmal effects make this genetically engineered python feel about as terrifying as an earthworm. Still, it does have a sense of humour, typified by genre regular Robert Englund's knowing performance as a verbose reptile expert. In fact, it is mainly of note to genre fans for its cast, but if you're watching this for decent shocks, laughs or effects, beware. JC [VIDEO] DVD

Casper Van Dien *Special Agent Bart Parker* • Robert Englund *Dr Anton Rudolph* • Frayne Rosanoff *John Cooper* • Wil Wheaton *Tommy* • Sara Mornell *Theresa* • Chris Owens *Brian Cooper* ■ *Dir* Richard Clabaugh • *Scr* Chris Neal, Gary Hershberger, Paul JM Bogh, from a story by Phillip Roth [Phillip J Roth]

Q

Q & A ★★★ 18

Crime drama 1990 · US · Colour · 127mins

Sidney Lumet, who was once described as New York's Charles Dickens, chronicles yet another case of civic corruption and bigotry. Nick Nolte stars as a dedicated, if brutal, cop who is suspected of killing a drug pusher. Seeking the truth behind the murder is Timothy Hutton, a squeaky-clean kid from upstairs. It is best appreciated now as a showcase for Nolte's explosive talent. AT. Contains violence, swearing, nudity. [VIDEO] DVD

Nick Nolte *Lieutenant Mike Brennan* • Timothy Hutton *Al Reilly* • Armand Assante *Bobby Texador* • Patrick O'Neal *Kevin Quinn* • Lee Richardson *Leo Bloomenfeld* • Luis Guzman *Luis Valentin* • Charles S Dutton *Sam Chapman* • Jenny Lumet *Nancy Bosch* ■ *Dir* Sidney Lumet • *Scr* Sidney Lumet, from the novel by Edwin Torres

Q Planes ★★★ U

Second World War spy drama
1939 · UK · BW · 78mins

Laurence Olivier (as a test pilot) and Ralph Richardson (as a Scotland Yard officer) co-star in this terrific Irving Asher/Alexander Korda produced espionage romp. Richardson is especially good value as the policeman trying to discover just how planes are disappearing off the coast of Cornwall and it's rare to find light-heartedness working so well in a British film of the period. DP [VIDEO]

Laurence Olivier *Tony McVane* • Valerie Hobson *Kay Hammond* • Ralph Richardson *Charles Hammond* • George Curzon *Jenkins* • George Merritt *Barrett* ■ *Dir* Tim Whelan • *Scr* Ian Dalrymple, from a story by Jack Whittingham, Brock Williams, Arthur Wimperis

Q – the Winged Serpent ★★★★ 15

Fantasy horror 1982 · US · Colour · 92mins

The ancient Aztec god Quetzacoatl, a giant flying serpent-bird, is reincarnated by a Manhattan cult and decapitates New Yorkers from its nest atop the Chrysler Building. As detectives David Carradine and Richard Roundtree try to make sense of the myth, petty crook Michael Moriarty holds the Big Apple to ransom. Larry Cohen's classic B picture is part wonderfully entertaining cop thriller, part old-fashioned monster movie. AJ. Contains violence, swearing and nudity. DVD

Michael Moriarty *Jimmy Quinn* • David Carradine *Detective Shepard* • Candy Clark *Joan* • Richard Roundtree *Sgt Powell* • James Dixon *Lt Murray* • Malachy McCourt *Police commissioner* ■ *Dir/Scr* Larry Cohen • *Special Effects* David Allen

Quackser Fortune Has a Cousin in the Bronx ★★★

Comedy drama 1970 · US · Colour · 90mins

The dreadful title apart, this is a charming Irish fable with Gene Wilder cast as Quackser Fortune – his duck imitations earn him the nickname – who shovels horse manure for a living, selling it to housewives all over Dublin. A know-all American student, Margot Kidder, distracts him romantically and patronises him intellectually, until the cousin in the Bronx brings about an ironic conclusion. Cameraman Gilbert Taylor turns the city's glistening Georgian buildings and cobbled streets into a tourist agent's dream. AT

Gene Wilder *Quackser Fortune* • Margot Kidder *Zazel Pierce* • Eileen Colgan *Betsy Bourke* • Seamus Ford *Mr Fortune* • May Ollis *Mrs Fortune* • Liz Davis *Kathleen Fortune* ■ *Dir* Waris Hussein • *Scr* Gabriel Walsh

Quadrophenia ★★★★ 18

Musical drama 1979 · UK · Colour · 114mins

The Who's *My Generation* musical tribute to Mods and Rockers in pre-1960s England is a near-perfect integration of cinematic story and rousing pop. It specifically focuses on the antics of parka-clad Phil Daniels, whose alienation is fuelled by pill-popping, scooter rave-ups and seaside battles in Brighton. Director Franc Roddam evokes the budding Swinging Sixties and the teenage sense of frustration and disillusionment with a lively precision. Sting makes his acting debut in this musical milestone crackling with energy and great performances. AJ. Contains swearing, violence and sex scenes. [VIDEO] DVD

Phil Daniels *Jimmy Michael Cooper* • Leslie Ash *Steph* • Philip Davis *Chalky* • Mark Wingett *Dave* • Sting *Ace Face* • Raymond Winstone [Ray Winstone] *Kevin* • Garry Cooper *Peter* • Toyah Willcox *Monkey* ■ *Dir* Franc Roddam • *Scr* Dave Humphries, Martin Stellman, Franc Roddam

Le Quai des Brumes ★★★★★ PG

Romantic melodrama 1938 · Fr · BW · 86mins

As war clouds gathered, French poetic realism grew increasingly pessimistic. None expressed this despondency more poignantly than Marcel Carné and screenwriter Jacques Prévert, who collaborated on this mist-shrouded waterfront tale of doomed romance. Confining the action entirely to the sublime studio sets designed by Alexandre Trauner and evocatively shot by Eugen Schüfftan, Carné was able to control every detail of his meticulous compositions and, thus, make the plight of army deserter Jean Gabin and waif Michèle Morgan all the more allegorically tragic. Pure melancholic magic. DP. In French with English subtitles. [VIDEO]

Jean Gabin *Jean* • Michèle Morgan *Nelly* • Michel Simon *Zabel* • Pierre Brasseur *Lucien* • Robert Le Vigan *Michel Krauss* ■ *Dir* Marcel Carné • *Scr* Jacques Prévert, from the novel by Pierre MacOrlan [Pierre Dumarchais]

Quai des Orfèvres ★★★★

Thriller 1947 · Fr · BW · 102mins

The title of this wonderfully atmospheric thriller refers to the French equivalent of Scotland Yard. The story revolves around a seedy music hall, where singer Suzy Delair thinks she has committed a murder for which her husband becomes a suspect. The director Henri-Georges Clouzot portrays a Paris teeming with life and mystery in which he observes human frailty with wit and compassion. Outstanding is Louis Jouvet as a police inspector, part cynic, part sentimentalist. It was Clouzot's first film for four years because his previous picture, *The Raven* (*Le Corbeau*), had been accused of being anti-French propaganda. RB. In French with English subtitles.

Simone Renant *Dora* • Suzy Delair *Jenny Lamour* • Bernard Blier *Maurice Martineau* • Charles Dullin *Brignon the industrialist* • Louis Jouvet *Inspector Antoine* ■ *Dir* Henri-Georges Clouzot • *Scr* Henri-Georges Clouzot, Jean Ferry, from the novel *Légitime Défense* by Stanislas-André Steeman

Quake! ★

Disaster movie 1992 · US · Colour · 83mins

An earthquake hits San Francisco, but this film is too cheap to show us more than a few flimsy models and a lot of falling plaster. Rather than the usual disaster movie clichés, *Quake!* follows a beautiful attorney (Erika Anderson) who is kidnapped by obsessed Steve Railsback when he is supposed to be rescuing her from an unstable building. Railsback manages a performance that is slightly less restrained than the one he gave as Charles Manson in the TV mini-series *Helter Skelter*. ST

Steve Railsback *Kyle* • Erika Anderson *Jenny* • Eb Lottimer *David* • Burton Gilliam *Willie* • Richard Dean [Rick Dean] *Young tough* ■ *Dir* Louis Morneau • *Scr* Mark Evan Schwartz

Quality Street ★★ U

Comedy drama 1937 · US · BW · 82mins

JM Barrie's now hopelessly dated whimsy came to the screen as a vehicle for Katharine Hepburn in a last-ditch – and unsuccessful – attempt by RKO to arrest her box-office decline. She's in love with the dashing Franchot Tone, who goes off to the Napoleonic Wars for several years without declaring his intentions. Amid studio-bound Toytown sets, George Stevens directs at a deadly pace for the first half, and the star's stagey and hysterical performance is more deranged Southern belle than genteel Englishwoman. RK

Katharine Hepburn *Phoebe Throssel* • Franchot Tone *Dr Valentine Brown* • Fay Bainter *Susan Throssel* • Eric Blore *Recruiting Sergeant* • Cora Witherspoon *Patty the Maid* • Joan Fontaine *Charlotte Parratt* ■ *Dir* George Stevens • *Scr* Mortimer Offner, Allan Scott, from the play by JM Barrie

Quantez ★★

Western 1957 · US · Colour · 80mins

This is distinguished by its location photography and the tough performance of Dorothy Malone. Unfortunately, Malone is paired with an ageing – though still top-billed – Fred MacMurray and callow John Gavin to little advantage in this slow-paced tale about a group journeying to Mexico through Apache territory. TS

Fred MacMurray *Gentry/John Coventry* • Dorothy Malone *Chaney* • James Barton *Minstrel* • Sydney Chaplin *Gato* • John Gavin *Teach* • John Larch *Heller* ■ *Dir* Harry Keller • *Scr* R Wright Campbell, from a story by R Wright Campbell, Anne Edwards

Q

Quantrill's Raiders ★★ U

Western 1958 · US · Colour · 70mins

This CinemaScope western programme filler is made interesting not by the presence of star Steve Cochran, but by Leo Gordon as the legendary William Quantrill himself, whom this movie kills off during the raid on an ammunitions dump at Lawrence, Kansas, and not, as actually happened, two years later in Kentucky. The thickset Gordon specialised in psychotic villains, and eventually found a natural haven in Europe. Here, as Quantrill, his psychoses are given free rein. TS

Steve Cochran *Westcott* • Diane Brewster *Sue* • Leo Gordon *Quantrill* • Gale Robbins *Kate* • Will Wright *Judge* • Kim Charney *Joel* ■ *Dir* Edward Bernds • *Scr* Polly James

Quarantine ★ 15

Science-fiction thriller
1989 · Can · Colour · 91mins

Schlock Canadian horror, in which a deadly disease leads to the overthrow of democracy and the installation of a dictatorship that confines everyone to death camps. Cheap and shoddy, with subplots glued on, the film fires off metaphors and allegories and makes no sense at all. AT. Contains swearing and violence.

Beatrice Boepple *Ivan Joad* • Garwin Sanford *Spencer Crown* • Jerry Wasserman *Senator Edgar Ford* • Michele Goodger *Berlin Ford* ■ *Dir/Scr* Charles Wilkinson

The Quare Fellow ★★★ 15

Drama 1962 · Ire · Colour · 86mins

Patrick McGoohan stars in this anti-capital punishment treatise, a gloomily sincere adaptation of Brendan Behan's renowned play. He's the novice prison warder who has his hanging convictions severely shaken after meeting the wife of one "Quare Fellow", Irish slang for a criminal on death row. And they're rattled again when another reprieved murderer takes his own life. The claustrophobic prison atmosphere is expertly conjured up in a well-intentioned, if downbeat, protest movie. AJ

Patrick McGoohan *Thomas Crimmin* • Sylvia Syms *Kathleen* • Walter Macken *Regan* • Dermot Kelly *Donnelly* • Jack Cunningham *Chief warder* • Hilton Edwards *Holy Healy* ■ *Dir* Arthur Dreifuss • *Scr* Arthur Dreifuss, Jacqueline Sundstrom, from the play by Brendan Behan

Quartet ★★★ PG

Portmanteau drama
1948 · UK · BW · 114mins

With W Somerset Maugham introducing the four vignettes based on his celebrated short stories, an air of literary portentousness hangs over this portmanteau picture, but, each tale is told with refreshing lightness. In *The Facts of Life*, Jack Watling enjoys the attentions of Monte Carlo gold-digger Mai Zetterling; *The Alien Corn* sees Dirk Bogarde driven to despair by his ambition to become a concert pianist; nerdy inventor George Cole is caught between wife Susan Shaw and hectoring mother, Hermione Baddeley in *The Kite*; while in *The Colonel's Lady*, Cecil Parker frets about the contents of a slim volume of love poems published by his wife, Nora Swinburne. DP

Basil Radford *Henry Garnet* • Jack Watling *Nicky* • Mai Zetterling *Jeanne* • Dirk Bogarde *George Bland* • Honor Blackman *Paula* • George Cole *Herbert Sunbury* • Hermione Baddeley *Beatrice Sunbury* • Susan Shaw *Betty* • Cecil Parker *Colonel Peregrine* • Nora Swinburne *Mrs Peregrine* ■ *Dir* Ralph Smart, Harold French, Arthur Crabtree, Ken Annakin • *Scr* RC Sherriff, from stories by W Somerset Maugham

Quartet ★★★ 18

Drama 1981 · UK/Fr · Colour · 96mins

Based on the novel by Jean Rhys, this is a typically classy piece of film-making from director James Ivory. In 1920s Paris, Isabelle Adjani takes refuge with married couple Alan Bates and Maggie Smith after her husband (Anthony Higgins) is jailed. She eventually submits to the advances of Bates at the expense of his rather sad bullied wife, as the film explores with subtlety an upper-class lifestyle beset with moral corruption. LH DVD

Isabelle Adjani *Marya Zelli* • Anthony Higgins *Stephan Zelli* • Maggie Smith *Lois Heidler* • Alan Bates *HJ Heidler* • Pierre Clémenti *Theo the pornographer* • Daniel Mesguich *Pierre Schlamovitz* ■ *Dir* James Ivory • *Scr* Ruth Prawer Jhabvala, from the novel *Quartet* by Jean Rhys

Quartier Mozart ★★★

Drama 1992 · Cameroon · Colour · 80mins

Set in modern-day Cameroon, this is a scathing insight into the ways that poverty and cultural conservatism are coupled with violence to maintain macho hegemony in a patriarchal society. Determined to beat the system, a young girl is turned into a swaggering man by a sorceress; she/he then discovers the harsh realities of sexual and economic exploitation. Made for just $30,000, Jean-Pierre Bekolo's film is as visually ambitious as it is politically daring. DP. In French with English subtitles.

Serge Amougou *Montype* • Sandrine Ola'a *Samedi* • Jimmy Biyong *Chien Mechant* • Essindi Mindja *Atango* • Atebass *Capo* ■ *Dir/Scr* Jean-Pierre Bekolo

Quatermass II ★★★★ 12

Science-fiction thriller
1957 · UK · BW · 81mins

The second in Hammer's *Quatermass* trilogy is a potent, low-budget roller coaster ride through government conspiracies and alien invasions, set against the chilling backdrop of postwar new town paranoia. Great writing by Nigel Kneale (based on his original BBC TV serial), superb direction by Val Guest and Gerald Gibbs's stark black-and-white photography make this British classic one of the best science-fiction allegories of the 1950s. AJ DVD

Brian Donlevy *Quatermass* • John Longden *Inspector Lomax* • Sidney James *Jimmy Hall* • Bryan Forbes *Marsh* • William Franklyn *Brand* • Vera Day *Sheila* • Charles Lloyd Pack *Dawson* • Michael Ripper *Ernie* ■ *Dir* Val Guest • *Scr* Val Guest, Nigel Kneale, from the TV serial by Nigel Kneale • *Cinematographer* Gerald Gibbs

Quatermass and the Pit ★★★ 15

Science-fiction thriller
1967 · UK · Colour · 93mins

This remains the most popular of the movies taken from Nigel Kneale's acclaimed BBC TV serial. Although the Deluxe Color dissipates some of the atmosphere and mystery, the story of the Martian spaceship uncovered in a London tube station retains much of its intrigue and sense of disquiet thanks to Roy Ward Baker's careful direction and special effects that never attempt to exceed their technical or budgetary limitations. As well as providing a generous helping of shocks, Kneale's script gives his complex themes and theories plenty of space, and both action and argument are neatly judged. DP DVD

James Donald *Dr Matthew Roney* • Andrew Keir *Professor Bernard Quatermass* • Barbara Shelley *Barbara Judd* • Julian Glover *Colonel Breen* • Duncan Lamont *Sladden* ■ *Dir* Roy Ward Baker • *Scr* Nigel Kneale, from his TV serial

The Quatermass Conclusion ★★★ 15

Science-fiction thriller
1979 · UK · Colour · 101mins

After *Quatermass and the Pit*, the Professor returned to television in a four-part serial that was generally regarded as a failure. This cut-down feature film was released to cinemas abroad and on video in the UK. As author Nigel Kneale correctly observed, the serial was too long and the film too short. Nevertheless, the story, which uses a favourite Kneale theme, the re-emergence of old fears and religions, begins and ends well. Quatermass (a creditable stab at the role by John Mills) gradually realises that aliens are harvesting humans from places of congregation. DM DVD

John Mills *Professor Bernard Quatermass* • Simon MacCorkindale *Joe Kapp* • Barbara Kellerman *Clare Kapp* • Margaret Tyzack *Annie Morgan* • Brewster Mason *Gurov* ■ *Dir* Piers Haggard • *Scr* Nigel Kneale, from his TV serial.

The Quatermass Xperiment ★★★ PG

Science-fiction thriller
1955 · UK · BW · 78mins

Hammer's film of Nigel Kneale's ground-breaking television serial was a huge success, encouraging the studio to concentrate on the production of horror films; in that regard, it can truly be said to have changed the course of British film history. The story, of an astronaut who returns to Earth only to mutate gradually into a vegetable, was subsequently much emulated. Veteran director Val Guest detested the casting of American actor Brian Donlevy, though his portrayal of Quatermass was generally well-received at the time. DM DVD

Brian Donlevy *Professor Bernard Quatermass* • Jack Warner *Inspector Lomax* • Margia Dean *Judith Carroon* • Richard Wordsworth *Victor Carroon* • David King-Wood *Dr Gordon Briscoe* • Thora Hird *Rosie* • Gordon Jackson *TV producer* • Lionel Jeffries *Blake* ■ *Dir* Val Guest • *Scr* Val Guest, Richard Landau, from the TV serial by Nigel Kneale

Que la Bête Meure ★★★★ 15

Thriller 1969 · Fr/It · Colour · 107mins

Adapted from a novel by Nicholas Blake (pseudonym of former poet laureate Cecil Day Lewis), this is one of Claude Chabrol's most accomplished pictures. Starting out as a whodunnit – as widower Michel Duchaussoy seeks the hit-and-run driver who killed his son – the film turns into a psychological thriller. Duchaussoy inveigles himself into the culprit's family, only to decide that his planned revenge would be inappropriate. While exploring such themes as guilt, justice and moral responsibility, Chabrol mischievously muddies the waters by allowing Jean Yanne to portray the killer as an oaf who, despite alienating his own boy, is somehow grotesquely engaging. DP. In French with English subtitles.

Michel Duchaussoy *Charles Thenier* • Caroline Cellier *Helene Lanson* • Jean Yanne *Paul Decourt* • Anouk Ferjac *Jeanne* • Marc DiNapoli *Philippe Decourt* • Maurice Pialat *Police inspector* ■ *Dir* Claude Chabrol • *Scr* Paul Gegauff, Claude Chabrol, from the novel *The Beast Must Die* by Nicholas Blake [Cecil Day Lewis]

Queen Bee ★★★ PG

Melodrama 1955 · US · BW · 90mins

Joan Crawford virtually breathes fire as the power-crazed woman who marries into an unhappy Southern family and then ruins their lives. Crawford is perfectly cast in her Tennessee Williams-style role and acts up a storm in one fabulous hostess gown after another, while expertly cutting the rest of the cast down to size. An overblown extravaganza much beloved by Crawford fans and lovers of glossy Hollywood melodramas in the grand tradition. AJ

Joan Crawford *Eva Phillips* • Barry Sullivan *John Avery Phillips* • Betsy Palmer *Carol Lee Phillips* • John Ireland *Judson Prentiss* • Fay Wray *Sue McKinnon* ■ *Dir* Ranald MacDougall • *Scr* Ranald MacDougall, from the novel by Edna Lee

Queen Christina ★★★★

Historical romantic drama
1933 · US · BW · 99mins

Greta Garbo stars as a 17th-century queen of Sweden who falls in inappropriate love with the Spanish ambassador sent to deliver a marriage proposal from his king. Garbo is quintessentially Garboesque in one of her most famous roles, while John Gilbert, her crony from silent days, is the ambassador, a role he played only at her insistence, after she had failed to warm to Laurence Olivier. The action is better when Garbo is travelling the kingdom dressed as a man than when she is weighed down by the worries of her throne. PF

Greta Garbo *Queen Christina* • John Gilbert (1) *Don Antonio de la Prada* • Ian Keith *Magnus* • Lewis Stone *Chancellor Oxenstierna* ■ *Dir* Rouben Mamoulian • *Scr* HM Harwood, Salka Viertel, SN Behrman, from a story by Salka Viertel, Margaret Levin • *Cinematographer* William Daniels [William H Daniels]

Queen Kelly ★★★ PG

Silent romantic melodrama
1928 · US · BW · 99mins

Despite Erich von Stroheim's legendary profligacy, Gloria Swanson hired him to direct this silent tale of the waif who is mistreated by both a Teutonic aristocrat and a mad Ruritanian monarch, in the hope he could turn a simmering melodrama into a sophisticated masterpiece. However, on learning her character would inherit a chain of brothels in German East Africa, Swanson pulled the plug and cobbled together a save-face version that included a musical number to cash in on the talkie boom. Von Stroheim evidently forgave her, as together they watch clips from this visual feast in *Sunset Boulevard*. DP

Gloria Swanson *Patricia Kelly, an orphan* • Walter Byron *Prince "Wild" Wolfram Von Hohenberg Falsenstein* • Seena Owen *Queen Regina V, his cousin and fiancée* • Sidney Bracey *Prince Wolfram's valet* • William von Brincken *Adjutant to Wolfram* ■ *Dir/Scr* Erich von Stroheim • *Cinematographer* Paul Ivano

Queen of Hearts ★★★★ PG

Drama 1989 · UK · Colour · 107mins

In Italy, sometime after the Second World War, Anita Zagaria breaks off her engagement to fierce Vittorio Amandola, and runs off to London with her lover, Joseph Long. But has she seen the last of her ex-fiancé? No chance. In later life, her ten-year-old son tells the whole magical tale. Jon Amiel debuts as director with a smashing mixture of vivid reality and dream-like surrealism. He introduces us to a world where people fly out of towers, where pigs dispense wisdom like Greek oracles, and where espresso machines puff out steam like mechanical dragons. Add terrific period atmosphere, and engaging performances from a largely unknown cast, and you've a terrific piece of offbeat entertainment that can be thoroughly recommended. DA [video]

Vittorio Duse *Nonno* • Joseph Long *Danilo* • Anita Zagaria *Rosa* • Eileen Way *Mama Sibilla* • Vittorio Amandola *Barbariccia* • Jimmy Lambert *Bruno* • Anna Pernicci *Angelica* ■ *Dir* Jon Amiel • *Scr* Tony Grisoni

Queen of Outer Space ★ U

Science-fiction adventure
1958 · US · Colour · 79mins

A serious contender for the worst film ever made list, this idiotic would-be sexy sci-fi movie stars Zsa Zsa Gabor, who rescues our astronaut heroes, headed by Eric Fleming, who should have known better than to land on Venus, anyway. The colour gives the film an illusion of expense, but most British prints have faded to pink. TS

Zsa Zsa Gabor *Talleah* • Eric Fleming *Patterson* • Laurie Mitchell *Queen Yllana* • Paul Birch *Professor Konrad* • Barbara Darrow *Kaeel* ■ *Dir* Edward Bernds • *Scr* Charles Beaumont, from a story by Ben Hecht

The Queen of Spades ★★★★

Supernatural drama 1948 · UK · BW · 95mins

Set in Imperial Russia, this is the definitive film version of Pushkin's short story about an army captain who takes on more than he bargained for when he tries to discover the secret of an old countess's success at cards. Director Thorold Dickinson creates what is generally regarded as his best film: a handsomely mounted and highly atmospheric ghost story which still chills the blood. In her first major film, Edith Evans was heavily made up to add decades to her true age of 60. Surprisingly, Dickinson directed only two more films before retirement. DM

Anton Walbrook *Herman Savorin* • Edith Evans *Countess Ranevskaya* • Yvonne Mitchell *Lizavetta Ivanova* • Ronald Harwood *Andrei* • Mary Jerrold *Old Varvarushka* • Anthony Dawson *Fyodor* ■ *Dir* Thorold Dickinson • *Scr* Rodney Ackland, Arthur Boys, from a short story by Alexander Pushkin • *Cinematographer* Otto Heller • *Music* Georges Auric

Queen of the Damned ★★ 15

Horror 2002 · US/Aus · Colour · 97mins

Camp and often silly, this is an adaptation of another Anne Rice novel, and as such is a sort of sequel to 1994's *Interview with the Vampire*. Stuart Townsend takes over from Tom Cruise in the role of the vampire Lestat, here woken from centuries of slumber by the lure of rock music. Fanged temptress Akasha (Aaliyah) wants him to join her in a confused scheme to take over the world. R 'n' B star Aaliyah's performance is rather wooden; sadly, she was killed in a plane crash shortly after the production wrapped. TH. Contains violence and swearing. [video] DVD

Stuart Townsend *Lestat* • Marguerite Moreau *Jesse Reeves* • Aaliyah *Akasha* • Vincent Perez *Marius* • Paul McGann *David Talbot* • Lena Olin *Maharet* ■ *Dir* Michael Rymer • *Scr* Scott Abbott, Michael Petroni, from the novel *The Vampire Chronicles: Queen of the Damned* by Anne Rice

Queen of the Pirates ★★ U

Action adventure
1960 · It/W Ger · Colour · 79mins

A good-looking adventure which is blighted by an overloaded script. There's tyranny, piracy, romance and tales of capture and recapture. The dull acting doesn't help, and the already inadequate package is further let down by a weak ending. Amazingly, there was more in store with a sequel called *Tiger of the Seven Seas*. NF. Italian dialogue dubbed into English.

Gianna Maria Canale *Sandra* • Massimo Serato *Count Cesare* • Scilla Gabel *Isabella* • Paul Muller *Duke Zulian* ■ *Dir* Mario Costa • *Scr* Nino Stresa, from a story by Kurt Nachmann, Rolf Olsen

The Queen's Guards ★

Drama 1960 · UK · Colour · 110mins

"The most inept piece of film-making that I have ever produced or directed", said Michael Powell of this wearisome slice of pomp and circumstance. It's a family drama about two brothers, one of whom dies at Tobruk leaving the other to maintain the family tradition by joining the Guards and fighting for the Empire in some fly-blown Arab state. Raymond Massey plays the father, Daniel Massey the son and it's all jolly well British, a sort of belated reaction to the humiliation of Suez. AT

Daniel Massey *John Fellowes* • Robert Stephens *Henry Wynne-Walton* • Raymond Massey *Captain Fellowes* • Ursula Jeans *Mrs Fellowes* • Judith Stott *Ruth Dobbie* ■ *Dir* Michael Powell • *Scr* Roger Milner, from a idea by Simon Harcourt-Smith

Queens Logic ★★★ 15

Comedy drama 1991 · US · Colour · 108mins

As in *The Big Chill*, a group of old friends are brought together by a life-changing event – in this case the impending marriage of Ken Olin and Chloe Webb. Gathering for the bachelor party (in Queens, of course) are Joe Mantegna, a fishmonger married to Linda Fiorentino, a gay but celibate John Malkovich and Kevin Bacon, now living in Hollywood. The film provides a gritty and thoroughly watchable group, but is essentially a series of well-written sketches. LH [video]

Kevin Bacon *Dennis* • Linda Fiorentino *Carla* • John Malkovich *Eliot* • Joe Mantegna *Al* • Ken Olin *Ray* • Tony Spiridakis *Vinny* • Chloe Webb *Patricia* • Tom Waits *Monte* • Jamie Lee Curtis • Helen Hunt ■ *Dir* Steve Rash • *Scr* Tony Spiridakis, from a story by Joseph W Savino, Tony Spiridakis

Quentin Durward ★★★★ U

Period drama 1955 · US · Colour · 116mins

This marvellous romp gave a new lease of life to the mature Robert Taylor and his career. Based on Sir Walter Scott's novel, and clearly an attempt to emulate the success of *Ivanhoe* (same star, same director, same fiery climax), this is deliberately more tongue-in-cheek. Taylor is charmingly witty as the noble Durward, dignified by a moustache and a trimmed beard, and is the only American in a prestige, mainly British cast. The leading lady is Kay Kendall, and she and the fabulous location shooting in the chateaux of the Loire valley are reasons enough to watch. TS

Robert Taylor (1) *Quentin Durward* • Kay Kendall *Isabelle Countess of Marcoy* • Robert Morley *King Louis XI* • Alec Clunes *Charles, Duke of Burgundy* • Marius Goring *Count Philip de Creville* • Wilfrid Hyde White *Master Oliver* • Ernest Thesiger *Lord Crawford* • George Cole *Hayraddin* ■ *Dir* Richard Thorpe • *Scr* Robert Ardrey, George Froeschel, from the novel by Sir Walter Scott

Querelle ★★★ 18

Erotic drama
1982 · W Ger/Fr · Colour · 104mins

Rainer Werner Fassbinder didn't live to see the release of this long-cherished adaptation of Jean Genet's once-banned novel. By consistently deflecting away from the drama and by having the cast recite lines rather than give performances, Fassbinder was able to explore the cinematic quality of non-action. Moreover, his use of blatantly theatrical sets emphasises the unreality of the events that follow sailor Brad Davis's arrival at Jeanne Moreau's waterfront brothel. It's a despondent wallow in a world full of drugs, murder, alienation and suppressed emotion and is, therefore, more valuable as a final self-portrait than as a work of art. DP. In German with English subtitles. [video] DVD

Brad Davis *Querelle* • Franco Nero *Lieutenant Seblon* • Jeanne Moreau *Lysiane* • Günther Kaufmann *Nono* • Laurent Malet *Roger Bataille* ■ *Dir* Rainer Werner Fassbinder • *Scr* Rainer Werner Fassbinder, Burkhard Driest, from the novel *Querelle de Brest* by Jean Genet

The Quest ★★★ 18

Martial arts action adventure
1996 · US · Colour · 90mins

Jean-Claude Van Damme made his directorial debut with this adventure, and he also stars as a small-time street criminal in 1920s New York who finds himself a stowaway on a ship headed for the South China Sea. Following an attack by pirates, Van Damme meets Roger Moore, and soon the two are scheming to enter Van Damme in the "ultimate fighting match" with its winning prize of a solid gold dragon statue. Remarkably better than his usual films. ST. Contains violence and swearing. [video] DVD

Jean-Claude Van Damme *Chris Dubois* • Roger Moore *Lord Edgar Dobbs* • James Remar *Maxie Devine* • Janet Gunn *Carrie Newton* ■ *Dir* Jean-Claude Van Damme • *Scr* Steven Klein, Paul Mones, from a story by Frank Dux, Jean-Claude Van Damme

Quest for Fire ★★ 15

Prehistoric drama
1981 · Fr/Can · Colour · 95mins

The accepted wisdom is that cavemen movies don't work. Even if you dress them up with anthropological significance and call upon experts like Desmond Morris and Anthony Burgess to design the diverse gestures and grunts, the action will still be limited by the spartan simplicity of the prehistoric lifestyle. To his credit, Jean-Jacques Annaud succeeds in locating the characters within their hostile environment (Canada, Scotland, Iceland and Kenya) and explores the primitive intelligence of the questing Ulams without patronising them or the less civilised Ivakas. But it's still a trying experience. DP [video]

Everett McGill *Naoh* • Ron Perlman *Amoukar* • Nameer El-Kadi *Gaw* • Rae Dawn Chong *Ika* • Gary Schwartz *Rouka* ■ *Dir* Jean-Jacques Annaud • *Scr* Gerard Brach, from the novel *La Guerre du Feu* by JH Rosny Sr

Quest for Love ★★★ PG

Science-fiction drama
1971 · UK · Colour · 87mins

Before *Dynasty* became her destiny, Joan Collins made many attempts at acting, including this beguiling British science-fiction idea from *Carry On* producer Peter Rogers and *Doctor in the House* director Ralph Thomas. Tom Bell co-stars as a physicist who, after an explosion, finds himself in an alternative universe where his girlfriend Collins is dying. Bell is believably bemused. And Collins? A moving performance minus the power-shoulders. TH [video]

Joan Collins *Ottilie* • Tom Bell *Colin Trafford* • Denholm Elliott *Tom Lewis* • Laurence Naismith *Sir Henry Lanstein* • Lyn Ashley *Jennifer* • Juliet Harmer *Geraldine Lambert* • Ray McAnally *Jack Kahn* ■ *Dir* Ralph Thomas • *Scr* Terence Feely, from the short story *Random Quest* by John Wyndham

Quest for Love ★★★ 15

Drama 1988 · S Afr · Colour · 90mins

Helen Nogueira became the first South African woman to direct a feature with this confident combination of political thriller and lesbian love story. Set in the fictional state of Mozania, shortly after black independence, the yacht-board action focuses on a romantic triangle comprising journalist Jana Cilliers, her passionate friend, Sandra Prinsloo, and her flighty lover, Joanna Weinberg. The film is primarily concerned with breaking with the stereotypical depiction of lesbian sensuality, but Cilliers's relationship with terrorist Wayne Bowman (and graphic scenes of torture) reinforce the political dimension. DP [video]

Jana Cilliers *Alex* • Sandra Prinsloo *Dorothy* • Joanna Weinberg *Mabel* • Wayne Bowman *Michael* • Lynn Gaines *Isabella* ■ *Dir* Helen Nogueira • *Scr* Helen Nogueira, from the novel *QED* by Gertrude Stein

Quest of the Delta Knights ★

Action fantasy adventure
1993 · US · Colour · 97mins

This lame addition to the sword-and-sorcery genre is notable for its threadbare production values. In the Dark Ages, young Corbin Allred is sold into slavery, bought by mysterious beggar David Warner, and trained to become one of the Delta Knights, a secret order whose mission is to help humanity. The direction is almost as shaky as the sets. AJ

David Warner *Lord Vultare/Raydoor* • Corbin Allred *Tee* • David Kriegel *Leonardo* • Brigid Conley Walsh *Thena* • Richard Kind *Wamthool* • Olivia Hussey *Mannerjay* ■ *Dir* James Dodson • *Scr* Redge Mahaffey

A Question of Silence

★★★★ 15

Crime drama 1982 · Neth · Colour · 95mins

Without any prior film-making experience, Marleen Gorris received state funding for this highly controversial debut, which posits that patriarchal capitalism exists solely to exploit, repress and abuse women. One of the angriest (yet most lucid and undogmatic) feminist statements ever committed to celluloid, it uses cleverly contrasting flashbacks to chart court psychiatrist Cox Habbema's gradual appreciation of the motives that drove housewife Edda Barends, waitress Nelly Frijda and secretary Henriette Tol to beat to death a smug male boutique owner. Compelling and provocative. DP. In Dutch with English subtitles.

Edda Barends *Christine M* • Nelly Frijda *Waitress* • Henriette Tol *Secretary* • Cox Habbema *Dr Janine Van Den Bos* • Eddy Brugman *Rudd* ■ *Dir/Scr* Marleen Gorris

Quick

★★ 18

Action crime drama
1993 · US · Colour · 94mins

Unremarkable shoot-em up action filler notable for the performance of Teri Polo. She outshines the material as a hit woman in Los Angeles who does favours for her corrupt cop boyfriend Jeff Fahey. Things really hot up when she's asked to kidnap a government witness Martin Donovan and a relationship to develop between them. It's a plot thinner than a negligee but there is adequate action and snappy dialogue. RS

Jeff Fahey *Muncie* • Teri Polo *Quick* • Robert Davi *Davenport* • Tia Carrere *Janet* • Martin Donovan (2) *Herschel Brewer* ■ *Dir* Rick King • *Scr* Frederick Bailey

The Quick and the Dead

★★★ 15

Western 1995 · US · Colour · 103mins

Sharon Stone stars as a mysterious stranger, riding Clint Eastwood-style into a town called Redemption to take part in a gunfighting competition presided over by the evil Gene Hackman. This homage to the spaghetti-western style of Sergio Leone is as daft as they come. *Evil Dead* director Sam Raimi smacks his lips in every OTT scene, but today this wacky movie will draw an entirely new audience because it also stars Russell Crowe and Leonardo DiCaprio. AT. Contains violence, swearing and sex scenes. DVD

Sharon Stone *Ellen* • Gene Hackman *John Herod* • Russell Crowe *Cort* • Leonardo DiCaprio *Kid* • Tobin Bell *Dog Kelly* • Lance Henriksen *Ace Hanlon* • Gary Sinise *Marshall* ■ *Dir* Sam Raimi • *Scr* Simon Moore

Quick, before It Melts

★★

Comedy 1965 · US · Colour · 97mins

Steady Delbert Mann wasn't the best choice for this scattershot adaptation of Philip Benjamin's Cold War comedy. Despatched to Antarctica to report on American efforts to protect the Pole from Communist incursion, timid journalist Robert Morse soon finds himself out of his depth, as he's seduced by Anjanette Comer, falls foul of brass hat James Gregory, is corrupted by womanising photographer George Maharis and can't find a bad word to say about the only Russian he can find, Michael Constantine. Frantic – but unfunny – anarchy. DP

George Maharis *Peter Santelli* • Robert Morse *Oliver Cromwell Cannon* • Anjanette Comer *Tiare Marshall* • James Gregory *Vice admiral* • Michael Constantine *Mikhail Drozhensky* ■ *Dir* Delbert Mann • *Scr* Dale Wasserman, from the novel by Philip Benjamin

Quick Change

★★★ 15

Crime comedy 1990 · US · Colour · 84mins

Bill Murray chose an offbeat, small-scale project for his directorial debut, and the result is a warm, slightly melancholic comedy. Murray also stars, playing a reluctant robber who pulls off the perfect bank raid dressed as a clown but who is driven to despair trying to leave the city with partners in crime Geena Davis and Randy Quaid. The three leads are great and there is fine support, too, from Jason Robards Jr as the cop on their trail. The source novel was filmed earlier, in 1985, as *Hold-Up*, starring Jean-Paul Belmondo. JF. Contains swearing, violence.

Bill Murray *Grimm* • Geena Davis *Phyllis* • Randy Quaid *Loomis* • Jason Robards Jr [Jason Robards] *Chief Rotzinger* • Dale Grand *Street barker* • Bob Elliott *Bank guard* ■ *Dir* Howard Franklin, Bill Murray • *Scr* Howard Franklin, from the novel by Jay Cronley

Quick, Let's Get Married

★

Comedy 1964 · US · Colour · 100mins

The great Ginger Rogers bowed out of films in the 1950s but returned briefly in the 1960s to make two new movies, this one and later a biopic *Harlow*. Rogers features here as the madam of a brothel and this was supposed to be the first of a new string of Rogers comedies produced by her ex-husband William Marshall. No further titles were made and this film itself wasn't released until 1971. DF

Ginger Rogers *Mme Rinaldi* • Ray Milland *Mario Forni* • Barbara Eden *Pia* • Walter Abel *The thief* • Elliott Gould *The mute* • Michael Ansara *Mayor* ■ *Dir* William Dieterle • *Scr* Allan Scott

Quick Millions

★★ U

Crime drama 1931 · US · BW · 61mins

Spencer Tracy plays a truck driver who organises a protection racket and becomes a mobster, almost against his will since he really craves respectability. His bodyguard is played by George Raft. Boasting much less action than others of the genre, it is directed by the combative left-winger, Rowland Brown. AT

Spencer Tracy *Daniel J "Bugs" Raymond* • Marguerite Churchill *Dorothy Stone* • John Wray *Kenneth Stone* • George Raft *Jimmy Kirk* ■ *Dir* Rowland Brown • *Scr* Courtney Terrett, Rowland Brown

Quicker than the Eye

★★ PG

Action drama
1989 · Swi/Fr/W Ger · Colour · 88mins

What on earth is Jean Yanne, one of French cinema's most bitingly satirical directors and veteran actor of classy French features, doing in a cornball cheapie like this? That's not to say this ambitious story of a magician who uses his powers to confound a gang of killers is not without its merits. Ben Gazzara obviously enjoys the sleights of hand, but Mary Crosby wanders through the action as if someone has put her in a trance. DP. Some dialogue dubbed into English. Contains violence and swearing

Ben Gazzara *Ben Norrell* • Mary Crosby *Mary Preston* • Catherine Jarrett *Catherine Lombard* • Jean Yanne *Inspector Sutter* • Wolfram Berger *Kurt* ■ *Dir* Nicolas Gessner • *Scr* Joseph Morhaim, Nicolas Gessner, from the novel by Claude Cueni

Quicksand

★★★

Crime drama 1950 · US · BW · 79mins

This excellent but forgotten little programme-filler features a well-cast Mickey Rooney as a car mechanic who's got the hots for no-good *femme fatale* Jeanne Cagney (James's real-life sister). Rooney is superb, and his demented persona is admirably suited to this underlit half-world. Even better, however, is sleazy Peter Lorre in one of his finer depictions of screen menace as a penny arcade owner. Director Irving Pichel cleverly puts all the elements together to produce an undervalued *film noir*. TS

Mickey Rooney *Dan Brady, auto mechanic* • Jeanne Cagney *Vera Novak, cafe cashier* • Barbara Bates *Helen* • Peter Lorre *Nick Dramoshag, penny arcade owner* • Art Smith *Mackey, garage owner* ■ *Dir* Irving Pichel • *Scr* Robert Smith

Quicksand: No Escape

★★★ PG

Thriller 1992 · US · Colour · 88mins

This effective thriller stars Donald Sutherland as a detective hired by an architect's wife who suspects her husband of having an affair. From this conventional opening, the plot spins some clever webs of intrigue, but this TV movie's main attraction is Sutherland, whose character has some of the weird, repressed spookiness of his earlier creation, John Klute. AT

Donald Sutherland *Doc* • Tim Matheson *Scott Reinhardt* • Jay Acovone *Ted Herman* • Timothy Carhart *Charlie* • John Joseph Finn [John Finn] *Ken Griffith* • Felicity Huffman *Joanna Reinhardt* ■ *Dir* Michael Pressman • *Scr* Peter Baloff, Dave Wollert

Quicksilver

★★ 15

Drama 1986 · US · Colour · 101mins

The mind boggles at how films like this ever get the money to be made. Imagine the pitch to the studio: "OK, there's this hotshot financial whizzkid who drops out of the Wall Street rat race to become – wait for it – a bicycle messenger. But heh, I see bicycle messengers as America's new cowboys, wheels instead of hoofs, get it? Still not sold? How about roping in your usual 1980s music soundtrack suspects. It could be another *Flashdance* or *Footloose*. Heh, that gives me a great idea, let's cast Kevin Bacon!" "Sounds great kid, here's $7 million, go make it!!!" RS

Kevin Bacon *Jack Casey* • Jami Gertz *Terri* • Paul Rodriguez *Hector Rodriguez* • Rudy Ramos *Gypsy* • Andrew Smith *Gabe Kaplan* • Larry Fishburne [Laurence Fishburne] *Voodoo* ■ *Dir* Tom Donnelly [Thomas Michael Donnelly] • *Scr* Thomas Michael Donnelly

The Quiet American

★★★ PG

Period political drama
1958 · US · BW · 116mins

America's most decorated Second World War soldier was baby-faced Audie Murphy, who carved out a screen career with a gun in his hand, notably in a stream of support westerns, until his tragic death in 1971. Following the filming of his own autobiography *To Hell and Back*, Murphy became a major star for a short while, and was ideally cast as the naive American in this worthy but, unfortunately, rather dull adaptation of Graham Greene's novel about Saigon politics in the pre-Vietnam era. He is well cast, and actually very good, but at the time the critics over-praised co-star Michael Redgrave and, as ever, under-rated Murphy. An interesting failure. TS

Audie Murphy *The American* • Michael Redgrave *Fowler* • Giorgia Moll *Phuong* • Claude Dauphin *Inspector Vigot* • Kerima *Miss Hei* • Bruce Cabot *Bill Granger* ■ *Dir* Joseph L Mankiewicz • *Scr* Joseph L Mankiewicz, from the novel by Graham Greene

The Quiet American

★★★★ 15

Political drama
2002 · US/Ger · Colour · 96mins

Graham Greene's classic 1955 novel – about the political rumblings in Indo-China that would eventually lead to the Vietnam War – gets a more faithful, elegant and resonant adaptation in director Philip Noyce's version than in the abridged 1958 film. A love triangle between disillusioned journalist Michael Caine (a commanding, yet beautifully restrained performance), mysterious American aid worker Brendan Fraser and young Vietnamese woman Do Thi Hai Yen is all the narrative hook Noyce needs to explore assuredly the complex issues surrounding Vietnam's fight for independence from French colonial rule, and make it a powerful and provocative drama. This is a remarkably penetrating and vivid account of the naivety and blunderings of US foreign policy. AJ DVD

Michael Caine *Thomas Fowler* • Brendan Fraser *Alden Pyle* • Do Thi Hai Yen *Phuong* • Rade Sherbedgia [Rade Serbedzija] *Inspector Vigot* • Ma Tzi *Hinh* • Robert Stanton *Joe Tunney* • Holmes Osborne *Bill Granger* ■ *Dir* Phillip Noyce • *Scr* Christopher Hampton, Robert Schenkkan, from the novel by Graham Greene

Quiet Cool

★ 18

Action thriller 1986 · US · Colour · 77mins

The only thing this movie has that differentiates it from other dreary action films (apart from characters actually running out of ammo in the shoot-outs) is the Pacific Northwest setting, though even that manages to look as grungy as the cast members. James Remar is the New York cop who travels there to help a former girlfriend living in a community under the thumb of violent marijuana growers, led by Nick Cassavetes. KB

James Remar *Joe Dillon* • Nick Cassavetes *Valence* • Jared Martin *Mike Prior* • Adam Coleman Howard *Joshua Greer* • Daphne Ashbrook *Katy Greer* ■ *Dir* Clay Borris • *Scr* Clay Borris, Susan Vercellino

Quiet Days in Clichy

★★ 18

Biographical comedy
1969 · Den · BW · 99mins

The French New Wave meets the Danish skin flick in this wild adaptation of Henry Miller's novel. Badly showing its age, it now stands as a fascinating tribute both to the freewheeling spirit of Miller's sexual odyssey and to the technical excess that was hailed as progressive film-making in the 1960s. Played out to the eccentric folk music of Country Joe McDonald, the amorous adventures of a lusty American in Paris are punctuated by jump cuts, captions, speech bubbles and moments of soft-core sex and actorly incompetence. DP. In Danish with English subtitles. Contains sex scenes. DVD

Paul Valjean *Joey* • Louise White *Surrealist* • Wayne John Rodda *Carl* • Ulla Lemvigh-Mueller *Nys* ■ *Dir* Jens Jørgen Thorsen • *Scr* Jens Jørgen Thorsen, from the novel by Henry Miller

The Quiet Earth

★★★ 15

Science-fiction thriller
1985 · NZ · Colour · 87mins

A scientist awakes one morning only to realise he may be the only person left alive on Earth after an experiment goes wrong. It's an intriguing if not altogether original concept. Bruno Lawrence gives a beguiling central performance as someone who is suddenly able to live out his fantasies, to enjoy the empty city without guilt or interference. Shot against stunning Auckland backdrops, the early section develops a strong sense of mystery, but after Lawrence discovers two other

Q

survivors, one male, one female, the script follows an all too predictable path. RS DVD

Bruno Lawrence *Zac Hobson* • Alison Routledge *Joanne* • Pete Smith *Api* • Anzac Wallace *Api's mate* • Norman Fletcher *Perrin* • Tom Hyde *Scientist* ■ *Dir* Geoff Murphy • *Scr* Bill Baer, Bruno Lawrence, Sam Pillsbury, from the novel by Craig Harrison

The Quiet Family ★★★

Black comedy thriller
1998 · S Kor · Colour · 98mins

Shades of *Arsenic and Old Lace* colour this dark South Korean romp. No sooner has the "Misty Lodge" opened its doors than the bodies start to pile up and the garden begins to resemble a cemetery. But there's worse to come when a murderous businessman lures his detested stepmother to the isolated hilltop cottage and the government announces plans for a new road – right past the front gate. This is a wickedly anarchic comedy of errors. DP. A Korean language film.

Choi Min-sik • Mun-hee Na • Park In-hwan • Song Kang-ho ■ *Dir/Scr* Kim Ji-woon

The Quiet Man ★★★★★ U

Romantic comedy drama
1952 · US · Colour · 129mins

John Ford won his fourth best director Oscar for this immensely popular chunk of old blarney, much of it shot on location in the west of Ireland. John Wayne is, of course, splendid as the boxer returning to his roots, with feisty Maureen O'Hara more than a match for him. Victor Young's lilting score is also very enjoyable, while Winton Hoch and Archie Stunt's Techincolor photography deservedly won the film a second Oscar. If you're in the right mood, *The Quiet Man* will make you laugh and cry, but only if you're receptive to blarney. TS DVD

John Wayne *Sean Thornton* • Maureen O'Hara *Mary Kate Danaher* • Barry Fitzgerald *Michaeleen Flynn* • Ward Bond *Father Peter Lonergan* • Victor McLaglen *"Red" Will Danaher* ■ *Dir* John Ford • *Scr* Frank S Nugent (uncredited), Richard Llewellyn, from the story by Maurice Walsh • *Cinematographer* Winton C Hoch • *Music* Victor Young

Quiet Please, Murder ★★

Detective drama 1942 · US · BW · 70mins

An interesting little programme-filler starring the suave George Sanders. He plays a master forger, passing off his imitations as First Folio Shakespeare, in a clever and relatively sophisticated blend of romance and murder. His female co-star is Gail Patrick, who later went on to produce the *Perry Mason* TV series. Virtually unknown director John Larkin doesn't get in the way of some cleverish writing, though budgetary limitations don't help. TS

George Sanders *Fleg* • Gail Patrick *Myra Blandy* • Richard Denning *Hal Mcbyrne* • Lynne Roberts *Kay Ryan* • Sidney Blackmer *Martin Cleaver* ■ *Dir* John Larkin • *Scr* John Larkin, from a story by Lawrence G Blochman

Quiet Wedding ★★★

Comedy 1940 · UK · BW · 80mins

Based on a very successful stage play, this delightful British romantic comedy stars a fresh and charming Margaret Lockwood in her pre-*Wicked Lady* days. The escalation of wedding plans – culminating in the arrival of an army of objectionable relatives – overwhelm Lockwood's bride-to-be, causes tension with hapless groom Derek Farr and threatens not only to scupper their entire relationship, but also the wedding itself. Stylishly directed by Anthony Asquith, the movie benefits from a standout cast of supporting players. It was remade as *Happy Is the Bride* in 1957 with Janette Scott and Ian Carmichael. See below for the less successful sequel. RK

Margaret Lockwood *Janet Royd* • Derek Farr *Dallas Chaytor* • Marjorie Fielding *Mildred Royd, Janet's mother* • AE Matthews *Arthur Royd, Janet's father* • Athene Seyler *Aunt Mary Jarrow* • Jean Cadell *Aunt Florence Bute* • Peggy Ashcroft *Flower Lisle* ■ *Dir* Anthony Asquith • *Scr* Terence Rattigan, Anatole de Grunwald, from the play by Esther McCracken

Quiet Weekend ★★ U

Comedy 1946 · UK · BW · 90mins

As anyone familiar with Anthony Asquith's classic comedy of manners *Quiet Wedding* will know, the title of this disappointing sequel is ironic in the extreme. The screenplay lacks the crisp chaos of the original co-written by Terence Rattigan. Consequently, the romantic tangles of Derek Farr and the poaching misadventures of George Thorpe and magistrate Frank Cellier fail to deliver the laughs deserving of such whole-hearted playing. DP

Derek Farr *Denys Royd* • Frank Cellier *Adrian Barrasford* • Marjorie Fielding *Mildred Royd* • George Thorpe *Arthur Royd* • Barbara White *Miranda Bute* • Helen Shingler *Rowena Hyde* ■ *Dir* Harold French • *Scr* Warwick Ward, Victor Skutezky, Stephen Black , TJ Morrison, from the play by Esther McCracken

The Quiet Woman ★ U

Crime thriller 1950 · UK · BW · 70mins

Writer/director John Gilling was a vital cog in the conveyor belt that churned out quota quickie-style films in the 1950s. Jane Hylton stars in this feeble thriller as the woman whose fresh start is threatened when her jailbird ex-husband arrives on her doorstep. Romance and a smuggling subplot can't save the picture from sinking deservedly into the mire. DP

Derek Bond *Duncan Mcleod* • Jane Hylton *Jane Foster* • Dora Bryan *Elsie* • Michael Balfour *Lefty* • Dianne Foster *Helen* ■ *Dir* John Gilling • *Scr* John Gilling

Quigley Down Under ★★★ 15

Western 1990 · US · Colour · 114mins

Entertaining attempt to transplant the western genre Down Under with a grizzled Tom Selleck as the laid-back sharpshooter who rebels against Australian land baron Alan Rickman, who wants him for a little Aborigine genocide. Director Simon Wincer makes full use of the grand Australian locations. Selleck is likeable enough in the title role, but unwittingly joins the list of Hollywood stars who have been effortlessly upstaged by Rickman, who delivers another wonderfully villainous performance. JF DVD

Tom Selleck *Matthew Quigley* • Laura San Giacomo *Crazy Cora* • Alan Rickman *Elliott Marston* • Chris Haywood *Major Ashley Pitt* • Ron Haddrick *Grimmelman* • Tony Bonner *Dobkin* ■ *Dir* Simon Wincer • *Scr* John Hill

The Quiller Memorandum ★★★★ PG

Spy thriller 1966 · UK · Colour · 100mins

The menace of Harold Pinter's script is marvellously sustained by director Michael Anderson in this under-rated thriller, with George Segal giving one of his finest performances as the secret agent investigating a neo-Nazi movement in 1960s Berlin. Alec Guinness and Max von Sydow excel as the British spy chief and his evil Nazi counterpart, and, for once, a woman (Senta Berger) plays a formidable part in an ambiguous role, the true nature of which is only revealed in the final shots. TH DVD

George Segal *Quiller* • Alec Guinness *Pol* • Max von Sydow *Oktober* • Senta Berger *Inge* • George Sanders *Gibbs* • Robert Helpmann *Weng* ■ *Dir* Michael Anderson • *Scr* Harold Pinter, from the novel *The Berlin Memorandum* by Adam Hall [Elleston Trevor]

Quills ★★★★★ 18

Biographical drama
2000 · US/Ger · Colour · 118mins

This is either a remarkable testimony to the importance of artistic freedom or the debauched tale of a devilish man: either way it's a considerable cinematic achievement. Geoffrey Rush is perfect as the unrepentant Marquis de Sade, confined to a mental institution and smuggling his "smut" to a publisher care of laundry maid Kate Winslet. When hard-line Michael Caine is sent to oversee the liberal regime of priest Joaquin Phoenix, de Sade has to use all his ingenuity to continue writing. Director Philip Kaufman's multilayered exploration of cruelty, repression and hypocrisy celebrates de Sade's indomitable spirit, while reminding us of the corruptive power of his imagination. LH. Contains violence, swearing, sex scenes and nudity. DVD

Geoffrey Rush *Marquis de Sade* • Kate Winslet *Madeleine* • Joaquin Phoenix *Abbé Coulmier* • Michael Caine *Dr Royer-Collard* • Billie Whitelaw *Madame LeClerc* • Patrick Malahide *Delbène* • Amelia Warner *Simone* • Jane Menelaus *Renée Pelagie* ■ *Dir* Philip Kaufman • *Scr* Doug Wright, from his play • *Production Designer* Martin Childs • *Costume Designer* Jacqueline West • *Set Designer* Jill Quertier • *Cinematographer* Rogier Stoffers

Quilombo ★★★

Historical drama
1984 · Bra · Colour · 114mins

Carlos Diegues here compares conditions in the 17th-century utopian settlement of Quilombo de Palmares with those in modern-day Brazil. The narrative, divided into three acts, involves a rebellion of plantation slaves and the establishing of a tolerant and prosperous community with an elected leader. Also embracing the persecuted indigenous people and Jews fleeing the Inquisition, the community ultimately collapses through colonial brutality and internal division. This is an overly stylised, but engagingly powerful tract. DP. In Portuguese with English subtitles.

Antonio Pompeo *Zumbi* • Zeze Motta *Dandara* • Toni Tornado *Ganga Zumba* • Vera Fischer *Ana de Ferro* ■ *Dir/Scr* Carlos Diegues

The Quince Tree Sun ★★★★ U

Documentary 1991 · Sp · Colour · 132mins

You'll get a whole new angle on the phrase "as interesting as watching paint dry" after seeing this wonderful documentary by the Spanish director Victor Erice. The film focuses on Antonio Lopez's meticulous execution of a painting of the quince tree in his garden. While this provides fascinating insights into the creative process, what is even more compelling is the artist's interaction both with the camera and the numerous visitors who drop in to see him. Best known for the haunting *Spirit of the Beehive*, Erice allows events to dictate the pace and what emerges is a mesmerising portrait. DP. In Spanish with English subtitles.

Dir Victor Erice • *Scr* Victor Erice, Antonio López, from an idea by Victor Erice, Antonio López Garcia

Quintet ★★ 15

Science-fiction drama
1979 · US · Colour · 113mins

One of Robert Altman's more forgettable films, made during a spell when he was out of favour with critics and audiences alike (see also *Popeye*). An uncomfortable looking Paul Newman heads a largely European cast in a slow-moving and pretentious piece of post-apocalyptic sci-fi, about a deadly survival game played out in a deep-frozen future city. Everyone looks cold and watching it has a similar effect on the viewer. DA

Paul Newman *Essex* • Vittorio Gassman *St Christopher* • Fernando Rey *Grigor* • Bibi Andersson *Ambrosia* • Brigitte Fossey *Vivia* • Nina Van Pallandt *Deuca* ■ *Dir* Robert Altman • *Scr* Robert Altman, Frank Barhydt, Patricia Resnick, from a story by Lionel Chetwynd, Robert Altman, Patricia Resnick

Quiz Show ★★★★ 15

Drama based on a true story
1994 · US · Colour · 127mins

Intelligently crafted by director Robert Redford, this is a riveting account of a true-life scandal in 1950s America, in which the winning contestant of the popular *Twenty-One* television game show was exposed as a fraud. Week after week, millions of viewers tuned in to watch a debonair professor (another memorable performance from Ralph Fiennes) flex his intellectual muscle, but it was later revealed he was given the answers in advance by a corrupt network seeking sponsorship dollars. John Turturro matches Fiennes as the show's deposed champion, while Rob Morrow plays the lawyer investigating the scam. AJ. Contains swearing. DVD

John Turturro *Herbie Stempel* • Rob Morrow *Dick Goodwin* • Ralph Fiennes *Charles Van Doren* • Paul Scofield *Mark Van Doren* • David Paymer *Dan Enright* • Hank Azaria *Albert Freedman* ■ *Dir* Robert Redford • *Scr* Paul Attanasio, from the book *Remembering America: a Voice from the Sixties* by Richard N Goodwin

Quo Vadis ★★★ PG

Historical epic 1951 · US · Colour · 161mins

Long and bloated, Mervyn LeRoy's film shows both the best and worst of depicting religious fervour in the Hollywood epic style. Alongside too-lengthy scenes of po-faced piety involving pallid hero Robert Taylor and wan Deborah Kerr, there is Peter Ustinov revelling in his role as the Emperor Nero. He pouts, simpers and fiddles while Rome burns, ad-libs to perfection and sends Christians to the lions in some spectacular arena scenes. Superbly cast against him is Leo Genn as Petronius, arbiter of fashion, whose speech before he opens his veins ("Do not mutilate the arts") is a veiled attack on the communist witch-hunts. AT

Deborah Kerr *Lygia* • Robert Taylor (1) *Marcus Vinicius* • Peter Ustinov *Nero* • Leo Genn *Petronius* • Patricia Laffan *Poppaea* • Finlay Currie *Peter* • Abraham Sofaer *Paul* • Elizabeth Taylor ■ *Dir* Mervyn LeRoy • *Scr* John Lee Mahin, Sonya Levien, SN Behrman, from the novel by Henryk Sienkiewicz

Q

RKO 281 ★★★★ 15

Drama based on a true story 1999 · US · Colour · 83mins

When Orson Welles embarked upon his directorial debut, he described RKO as the biggest train set a boy could ever have. However, there was nothing juvenile about project 281, as *Citizen Kane* was to become the most critically lauded film of all time. Its production was anything but untroubled, though, as this stylish TV movie demonstrates. The feuds with co-scenarist Herman J Mankiewicz and media tycoon William Randolph Hearst are fully explored in this splendidly cast drama. DP DVD

Liev Schreiber *Orson Welles* • James Cromwell *William Randolph Hearst* • Melanie Griffith *Marion Davies* • John Malkovich *Herman Mankiewicz* • Brenda Blethyn *Louella Parsons* • Roy Scheider *George Schaefer* • David Suchet *Louis B Mayer* • Fiona Shaw *Hedda Hopper* ■ *Dir* Benjamin Ross • *Scr* John Logan, from the original documentary script for *The Battle over Citizen Kane* by Richard Ben Cramer, Thomas Lennon

RPM – Revolutions per Minute ★

Political drama 1970 · US · Colour · 91mins

This woeful effort tries to evoke the era of student protest – hence the silly title. It stars Anthony Quinn as a campus professor, Ann-Margret as his mistress and Gary Lockwood as the student who organises a takeover of the university's admin offices. Stanley Kramer, never the subtlest of directors, gets heavy with empty parallels to the student riots in Chicago and at Kent State University. AT

Anthony Quinn *Perez* • Ann-Margret *Rhoda* • Gary Lockwood *Rossiter* • Paul Winfield *Dempsey* • Graham Jarvis *Thatcher* ■ *Dir* Stanley Kramer • *Scr* Erich Segal

R-Point ★★★ 15

Supernatural war horror 2004 · S Kor · Colour · 107mins

South of Saigon lies the strategically important island region R-Point. That's where a South Korean platoon is sent to investigate mysterious radio transmissions from a supposedly dead squadron in this slow-burning psychological horror. With the Vietnam War making an excellent backdrop to all the atmospheric creepiness, the accent is more on allegory than the gory. Too drawn out and often hilariously over-acted, this does benefit from strong, beautifully photographed images and some truly haunting moments. AJ. In Korean with English subtitles.

Kam Woo-seong *First Lieutenant Choi Tae-In* • Son Byung-ho • Oh Tae-kyung • Park Won-sang • Lee Seon-gyun ■ *Dir/Scr* Kong Su-chang

Raaz ★★★ 15

Horror thriller 2001 · Ind · Colour · 151mins

Bollywood's master of suspense Vikram Bhatt directs this teasing psychological thriller. Supermodel Bipasha Basu shows to advantage as the unhappy wife who hopes to save her marriage by returning to the isolated hill station where she first fell in love. But she becomes increasingly fraught as she starts to believe that the house is haunted. Dino Morea is lumpen as her husband, while Ashutosh Rana chomps the scenery as an eccentric academic, but the movie still exerts a strong grip until its formulaic plotting forces a slipshod resolution. DP. In Hindi with English subtitles. Contains swearing and violence. DVD

Dino Morea *Aditya* • Bipasha Basu *Sanjana* • Malini Sharma *Malini* • Shruti Ulfat *Priya* • Ashutosh Rana *Professor Agni* • Mink [Mink Singh] *Nisha* ■ *Dir* Vikram Bhatt • *Scr* Mahesh Bhatt

Rabbit-Proof Fence ★★★ PG

Period drama based on a true story 2002 · Aus/UK · Colour · 89mins

Though rather worthy, director Philip Noyce's superbly photographed true-life drama is not without impact as it throws light on a shameful period in Australia's past. In 1931, 14-year-old Molly (Everlyn Sampi) is interned by the Australian government as part of its policy to forcibly integrate "half-caste" Aborigines into white society. Molly escapes with her younger sister and cousin, and walks the 1,200 miles back home. The children are wonderfully natural, Kenneth Branagh and David Gulpilil are excellent, but Noyce's predictable direction fails to engage us emotionally. AJ DVD

Everlyn Sampi *Molly Craig* • Tianna Sansbury *Daisy Craig* • Laura Monaghan *Gracie Fields* • David Gulpilil *Moodoo* • Kenneth Branagh *Mr AO Neville* • Deborah Mailman *Mavis* • Jason Clarke *Constable Riggs* • Ningali Lawford *Molly's mother* ■ *Dir* Phillip Noyce • *Scr* Christine Olsen, from the biography *Follow the Rabbit-Proof Fence* by Doris Pilkington Garimara

Rabbit, Run ★★ 18

Drama 1970 · US · Colour · 90mins

With its open discussion of fellatio and sodomy, Howard B Kreitsek's adaptation of John Updike's novel was one of the most daring dramas to emerge from a Hollywood newly liberated from the Production Code. Director Jack Smight, who was so disgruntled with the final edit that he attempted to have his name removed from the credits, allows James Caan to overdo the self-pity as the washed-up former teenage basketball star who abandons pregnant wife Carrie Snodgress for mistress Anjanette Comer. DP

James Caan *Rabbit Angstrom* • Carrie Snodgress *Janice Angstrom* • Anjanette Comer *Ruth* • Jack Albertson *Marty Tothero* • Arthur Hill *Reverend Jack Eccles* ■ *Dir* Jack Smight • *Scr* Howard B Kreitsek, from the novel by John Updike

Rabid ★★★★ 18

Horror 1976 · Can · Colour · 90mins

This is another formative exercise in fear and loathing of the human body from director David Cronenberg, which takes up the themes of his first "mainstream" success, *Shivers*. This time a plague is let loose after accident victim Marilyn Chambers becomes the unwitting carrier of a rabid disease which turns people into bloodsuckers. This disturbing film lacks the claustrophobia of *Shivers*, but is an altogether slicker affair, and the spiralling, random violence still shocks. JF DVD

Marilyn Chambers *Rose* • Frank Moore *Hart Read* • Joe Silver *Murray Cypher* • Howard Ryshpan *Dr Dan Keloid* • Patricia Gage *Dr Roxanne Keloid* • Susan Roman *Mindy Kent* ■ *Dir/Scr* David Cronenberg

Rabid Grannies ★ 18

Comedy horror 1989 · Bel · Colour · 88mins

This badly-made Belgian splatter movie is both boring and offensive. A waft of smoke from a satanist turns two wealthy old aunts into slobbering, blood-crazed zombies during their birthday party. The guests are all obvious stereotypes who end up being savagely slaughtered. AJ. French dialogue dubbed into English. DVD

Catherine Aymerie *Helen* • Caroline Braekman *Suzie* • Danielle Daven *Elisabeth Remington* • Richard Cotica *Gilbert* • Raymond Lescot *Reverend Father* ■ *Dir/Scr* Emmanuel Kervyn

Race against Time ★★

Futuristic thriller 2000 · US · Colour · 86mins

This unoriginal TV thriller fulfils its purpose with clunking efficiency. In 2018, construction worker Eric Roberts is forced on the run from Chris Sarandon's organ-harvesting corporation after it refuses to cancel the contract that Roberts signed too late to save his son. Cary Elwes is in snarling pursuit, while bounty hunter Sarah Wynter is having misgivings about her mission. The plot and characterisation are as flimsy as the computer-generated special effects. DP. Contains swearing and violence.

Eric Roberts *James Gabriel* • Cary Elwes *Burke* • Sarah Wynter *Alex* • Chris Sarandon *Dr Anton Stofeles* • Diane Venora *Dr Helen Steele* • Michael Greyeyes *Johnny Black Eagle* ■ *Dir* Geoff Murphy • *Scr* Cary Solomon, Chuck Konzelman

Race for Glory ★★ 15

Sports drama 1989 · US · Colour · 102mins

Peter Berg and Alex McArthur play friends from a small town who find their relationship under strain when one of them decides he wants to become an international motorcycling champion. Despite a well-known cast that includes Ray Wise and Burt Kwouk, this never rises above the average. JB. Contains swearing.

Alex McArthur *Cody Gifford* • Peter Berg *Chris Washburn* • Pamela Ludwig *Jenny Eastman* • Ray Wise *Jack Davis* • Oliver Stritzel *Klaus Kroeter* • Burt Kwouk *Yoshiro Tanaka* ■ *Dir* Rocky Lang • *Scr* Scott Swanton

Race for Your Life, Charlie Brown ★★ U

Animation 1977 · US · Colour · 72mins

The *Peanuts* people leave the familiar neighbourhood for a summer camp in this third feature-length outing for Charles M Schulz's enduring creations. As usual, Charlie Brown is the goat all the other kids mock as he fails hopelessly at each activity, with Peppermint Patty adding the kind of scathing encouragement only she can. However, the little round-headed kid finally proves his worth during a white-water raft race. There are plenty of the customarily witty observations on life, but the pace is slack. DP

Duncan Watson *Charlie Brown* • Greg Felton *Schroeder* • Stuart Brotman *Peppermint Patty* • Gail Davis *Sally* • Liam Martin *Linus Van Pelt* ■ *Dir* Bill Melendez, Phil Roman • *Scr* Charles M Schulz, from his comic strip

Race the Sun ★★ PG

Comedy 1996 · US · Colour · 95mins

Disadvantaged Hawaiian high school students, inspired by their teacher Halle Berry, build a solar-powered vehicle and enter it into a race across Australia. Along the way they get to prove they aren't quitters, and show up evil corporations and arrogant foreigners. This features a number of young actors who would go on to greater success. ST

Halle Berry *Sandra Beecher* • James Belushi *Frank Machi* • Bill Hunter *Commissioner Hawkes* • Casey Affleck *Daniel Webster* • Eliza Dushku *Cindy Johnson* • Kevin Tighe *Jack Fryman* • Steve Zahn *Hans Kooiman* ■ *Dir* Charles T Kanganis • *Scr* Barry Morrow

Race with the Devil ★★ 15

Thriller 1975 · US · Colour · 84mins

Easy Rider was both a triumph and a millstone for its star and producer, Peter Fonda, who lurched from one *Easy Rider* rip-off to the next. The bad guys are satanists from the back of Texas beyond, but this is a studio concoction and the characters are taken straight off the shelf. Director Jack Starrett keeps things moving and Fonda's co-star, Warren Oates, is always worth watching. AT. Contains swearing.

Peter Fonda *Roger* • Warren Oates *Frank* • Loretta Swit *Alice* • Lara Parker *Kelly* • RG Armstrong *Sheriff Taylor* ■ *Dir* Jack Starrett • *Scr* Wes Bishop, Lee Frost

The Racers ★★

Sports drama 1955 · US · Colour · 91mins

Set around Europe but shot on the backlot at 20th Century-Fox with an overworked back projection machine, this motor-racing saga stars Kirk Douglas as the reckless driver who trashes his car and kills a dog whose owner, Bella Darvi, falls in love with him and finances his new car. Polish-born Darvi was a compulsive gambler and then the mistress of studio boss Darryl F Zanuck. Mrs Zanuck had her banished from Hollywood, and she later committed suicide. AT

Kirk Douglas *Gino* • Bella Darvi *Nicole* • Gilbert Roland *Dell 'Oro* • Lee J Cobb *Maglio* ■ *Dir* Henry Hathaway • *Scr* Charles Kaufman, from a novel by Hans Ruesch

Rachel and the Stranger ★★★

Romantic western 1948 · US · BW · 92mins

This utterly charming quasi-western is distinguished by one of Robert Mitchum's most likeable, deceptively throwaway roles, as the itinerant tracker who momentarily comes between husband and wife William Holden and Loretta Young. Mitchum's vocal talents are given full rein here; indeed, he had a hit record of sorts in the duet he performs with youngster Gary Gray, *Just Like Me*. Sadly, its fame, as so often happens, outlived the film from which it came. TS

Loretta Young *Rachel* • William Holden (2) *Big Davey Harvey* • Robert Mitchum *Jim Fairways* • Gary Gray *Little Davey* • Tom Tully *Parson Jackson* ■ *Dir* Norman Foster • *Scr* Waldo Salt, from the stories *Rachel and Neighbor Sam* by Howard Fast

The Rachel Papers ★★ 18

Comedy drama 1989 · UK · Colour · 90mins

Writer/director Damian Harris is responsible for this misfiring adaptation of Martin Amis's novel. Dexter Fletcher does well enough as the lovesick youngster who keeps a record of former girlfriends to aid future seductions, but the fact that he spends so much time talking directly to camera (in a clumsy bid to reproduce the book's first-person perspective) says a good deal about Harris's uninspired direction. DP. Contains swearing and nudity.

Dexter Fletcher *Charles Highway* • Ione Skye *Rachel Seth-Smith* • Jonathan Pryce *Norman* • James Spader *DeForest* • Bill Paterson *Gordon Highway* • Shirley Anne Field *Mrs Seth-Smith* • Michael Gambon *Dr Knowd* • Amanda De Cadenet *Yvonne* • Aubrey Morris *Sir Herbert* ■ *Dir* Damian Harris • *Scr* Damian Harris, from the novel by Martin Amis

Rachel, Rachel ★★★★

Drama 1968 · US · Colour · 101mins

This may have been Paul Newman's directorial debut, but it's the performance of his wife Joanne Woodward that makes it such a moving and memorable drama. As the bashful teacher for whom returning childhood friend James Olson presents the last chance of romance, she brilliantly conveys the timidity born of a frustrated life spent in the service of others. Woodward's quiet power also comes to Newman's rescue when his inexperience allows the tone and tempo to slip. Their daughter Nell Potts plays the young Rachel. DP

Joanne Woodward *Rachel Cameron* • James Olson *Nick Kazlik* • Kate Harrington *Mrs Cameron* • Estelle Parsons *Calla Mackie* • Donald Moffat *Niall Cameron* • Terry Kiser *Preacher* • Nell Potts *Rachel as a child* ■ *Dir* Paul Newman • *Scr* Stewart Stern, from the novel *A Jest of God* by Margaret Laurence

Rachel's Man ★★

Religious drama 1975 · Is · Colour · 111mins

A reverent, hushed version of the Biblical love story between Jacob (Leonard Whiting) and Rachel (Michal Bat-Adam). Filmed in Israel by Moshe Mizari, it also features Rita Tushingham as Rachel's older sister, Lea, and Mickey Rooney as the father of the two girls. But the film is let down by a script which brooks no conflict in its characterisation. TH

Mickey Rooney *Laban* • Rita Tushingham *Lea* • Leonard Whiting *Jacob* • Michal Bat-Adam *Rachel* • Avner Hiskiyahu *Isaac* • Dalia Cohen *Zilpah* • Robert Stevens *Narrator* ■ *Dir* Moshe Mizrahi • *Scr* Moshe Mizrahi, Rachel Fabien

Racing Stripes ★★ U

Part-animated comedy adventure
2004 · US/S Afr · Colour · 101mins

Take one unsophisticated *Babe* clone, add a dollop of *Seabiscuit* sentiment, stir in a positive message and you have *Racing Stripes*. Director Frederik Du Chau's comedy uses the trick of live animals with CGI mouths to lip-synch the broad one-liners, but this yarn tries too hard to appeal to all members of the family. Although well served by its human actors and voice cast, this remains a charmless and predictable confection. AJ

Bruce Greenwood *Nolan Walsh* • Hayden Panettiere *Channing Walsh* • M Emmet Walsh *Woodzie* • Wendie Malick *Clara Dalrymple* • Frankie Muniz *Stripes* • Mandy Moore *Sandy* • Michael Clarke Duncan *Clydesdale* • Jeff Foxworthy *Reggie* • Joshua Jackson *Trenton's Pride* • Joe Pantoliano *Goose* • Snoop Dogg *Lightning* • Dustin Hoffman *Tucker* • Whoopi Goldberg *Franny* ■ *Dir* Frederik Du Chau • *Scr* David F Schmidt, from a story by David F Schmidt, Steven P Wegner, Kirk DeMicco, Frederik Du Chau

Racing with the Moon ★★★ 15

Second World War romantic drama
1984 · US · Colour · 103mins

Considering it was written by Steve Kloves when in his 20s and features such stars in the making as Sean Penn, Elizabeth McGovern and Nicolas Cage, this is a curiously old-fashioned rites-of-passage romance. The atmosphere of a wartime Christmas has been deftly achieved without undue nostalgia by director Richard Benjamin, who artfully masks the story's comparative lack of incident by allowing his cast to explore their characters fully. Slight, but charmingly authentic. DP [video] DVD

Sean Penn *Henry "Hopper" Nash* • Elizabeth McGovern *Caddie Winger* • Nicolas Cage *Nicky* • John Karlen *Mr Nash* • Rutanya Alda *Mrs Nash* • Max Showalter *Mr Arthur* ■ *Dir* Richard Benjamin • *Scr* Steven Kloves

The Rack ★★

Drama 1956 · US · BW · 100mins

In this early starring role, Paul Newman plays the previously heroic army captain on trial for having collaborated with the enemy while a captive in Korea. This big-screen version of a TV drama by Rod Serling is an intelligent but overlong examination of the Newman character's psychological make-up and what brought him to the breaking point. Unfortunately, Newman's performance is mostly boorish and monotonous. AE

Paul Newman *Capt Edward W Hall Jr* • Wendell Corey *Maj Sam Moulton* • Walter Pidgeon *Col Edward W Hall Sr* • Edmond O'Brien *Lt Col Frank Wasnick* • Lee Marvin *Capt John R Miller* • Cloris Leachman *Caroline* ■ *Dir* Arnold Laven • *Scr* Stewart Stern, from the TV play by Rod Serling

The Racket ★★★

Silent crime drama 1928 · US · BW · 60mins

Long unseen, this was a notable entry in the silent gangster cycle of the late 1920s, directed with considerable flair by Lewis Milestone. The film's exposé of crooked cops and politicians was daring for its time and it was widely banned in the United States. There would be more pressure to revive it had the star of the original Broadway play, Edward G Robinson, repeated his role as the big bootlegger; instead the film cast Louis Wolheim. The 1951 remake with Robert Mitchum was updated and conventionalised. AE

Thomas Meighan *Capt McQuigg* • Marie Prevost *Helen Hayes, an entertainer* • Louis Wolheim *Nick Scarsi, bootleg king* • George Stone [George E Stone] *Joe Scarsi* • John Darrow *Ames, a cub reporter* ■ *Dir* Lewis Milestone • *Scr* Harry Behn, Del Andrews, Eddie Adams, Bartlett Cormack, from the play by Bartlett Cormack

The Racket ★★★

Crime drama 1951 · US · BW · 88mins

Robert Mitchum plays an honest cop who goes up against gangster Robert Ryan. Despite being made by RKO for peanuts, this tough film has some decent action scenes and car chases, and co-directors John Cromwell and Nicholas Ray lace the rather hackneyed story with a welcome dash of political cynicism. RKO was owned at the time by Howard Hughes and this is a remake of a 1928 film that Hughes produced. AT

Robert Mitchum *Captain McQuigg* • Lizabeth Scott *Irene* • Robert Ryan *Nick Scanlon* • William Talman *Johnson* • Ray Collins *Welch* • Joyce MacKenzie *Mary McQuigg* • Robert Hutton *Ames* ■ *Dir* John Cromwell, Nicholas Ray • *Scr* William Wister Haines, WR Burnett, from the play by Bartlett Cormack

Racket Busters ★★

Crime drama 1938 · US · BW · 65mins

Humphrey Bogart relishes an early starring role as the racketeer muscling in on the fruit and produce market in this crisp but forgettable Warner Bros crime drama. By contrast, George Brent is duller than usual, miscast as the honest trucker who eventually stands up to Bogart. Allegedly based on the crime-busting exploits of New York district attorney Thomas E Dewey, this is a lesser example of the studio's penchant in the 1930s for headline-based stories. AE

Humphrey Bogart *John Martin* • George Brent *Denny Jordan* • Gloria Dickson *Nora Jordan* • Allen Jenkins *Skeets Wilson* • Walter Abel *Hugh Allison* • Henry O'Neill *Governor* • Penny Singleton *Gladys* ■ *Dir* Lloyd Bacon • *Scr* Robert Rossen, Leonardo Bercovici

Radiance ★★

Comedy drama 1998 · Aus · Colour · 83mins

It's easy to imagine Louis Nowra's play making a squirmingly disconcerting night at the theatre, but unpersuasive performances and indifferent direction mean that much of its intensity and passion are missing from this earnest, but unfocused, adaptation. Making her feature debut, Aborigine director Rachel Perkins captures the prejudice and simmering despair of small-town Queensland. Sadly, she also makes too many basic errors in tone and continuity to sustain the tension, as three estranged sisters reunite for their mother's funeral. DP

Rachel Maza *Cressy* • Deborah Mailman *Nona* • Trisha Morton-Thomas *Mae* ■ *Dir* Rachel Perkins • *Scr* Louis Nowra, from his play

Radio ★ PG

Drama based on a true story
2003 · US · Colour · 104mins

This true-life feel-good tale starring Cuba Gooding Jr may be marginally better than his dire *Boat Trip*, but it's still a mawkish slushfest. Set in the South Carolina of the 1970s, Gooding plays – or, rather overplays – "Radio", a mentally challenged kid who's made team mascot by Ed Harris's high-school football coach. Radio's new-found status arouses the hostility of the town's narrow-minded locals, making Harris's mentoring of Gooding problematic. DA DVD

Cuba Gooding Jr *James Robert "Radio" Kennedy* • Ed Harris *Coach Harold Jones* • Alfre Woodard *Principal Daniels* • S Epatha Merkerson *Maggie Kennedy* • Brent Sexton *Honeycutt* • Chris Mulkey *Frank Clay* • Sarah Drew *Mary Helen Jones* • Riley Smith *Johnny Clay* • Debra Winger *Linda Jones* ■ *Dir* Mike Tollin • *Scr* Mike Rich, from the *Sports Illustrated* magazine article "Someone to Lean On" by Gary Smith

Radio City Revels ★★ U

Musical comedy 1938 · US · BW · 89mins

This can be recommended only to die-hard musical fans, since the plot, about a composer who only functions when he is asleep, is not only skimpy but becomes tiresome as Milton Berle and Jack Oakie desperately try to get Bob Burns to nap in their presence so that they can steal his creations. Amid the dross, however, are some sparkling musical moments. TV

Bob Burns *Lester Robin* • Jack Oakie *Harry Miller* • Kenny Baker (1) *Kenny* • Ann Miller *Billie Shaw* • Victor Moore *Paul Plummer* • Milton Berle *Teddy Jordan* • Helen Broderick *Gertie Shaw* • Jane Froman *Jane* ■ *Dir* Ben Stoloff • *Scr* Eddie Davis, Matt Brooks, Anthony Veiller, Mortimer Offner, from a story by Matt Brooks

Radio Days ★★★★ PG

Period comedy 1987 · US · Colour · 84mins

An under-rated entry in the Woody Allen canon, this is an intelligent and endlessly delightful examination of childhood and the process of memory. Although it is subtly directed and played to a nicety by a splendid ensemble cast, the film stands and falls on the wit and insight of the script and the minute period detail of the production design, and both Allen and production designer Santo Loquasto deserved more than just Oscar nominations. Cutting effortlessly from the crowded family home in Brooklyn to the empty glamour of Radioland, this celluloid scrapbook is evocative and irresistible. DP. Contains swearing and brief nudity. [video] DVD

Mia Farrow *Sally White* • Julie Kavner *Mother* • Michael Tucker *Father* • Seth Green *Little Joe* • Dianne Wiest *Aunt Bea* • Josh Mostel *Uncle Abe* • Danny Aiello *Rocco* • Diane Keaton *New Year's singer* • Woody Allen *Narrator* ■ *Dir/Scr* Woody Allen

Radio Flyer ★★★ PG

Fantasy drama 1992 · US · Colour · 109mins

The importance of belief in the impossible is the central theme of director Richard Donner's difficult yet delicate fantasy about two boys who escape the physical abuse of their stepfather via their toy red wagon, the *Radio Flyer*. Reconciling the children's battered background with their desperate need for release, Donner punctuates his affecting fable with surreal and mystical twists that weave a powerful spell. Well acted by an excellent cast (Tom Hanks is the uncredited narrator). AJ [video]

Lorraine Bracco *Mary* • John Heard *Daugherty* • Adam Baldwin *The King* • Elijah Wood *Mike* • Joseph Mazzello *Bobby* • Ben Johnson *Geronimo Bill* • Sean Baca *Fisher* • Tom Hanks *Narrator* ■ *Dir* Richard Donner • *Scr* David Mickey Evans

Radio On ★★★ 18

Road movie 1979 · UK/W Ger · BW · 99mins

In this striking British road movie, David Beames plays the disc jockey who drives haphazardly from London to Bristol to find out why his brother died, only to reach a dead end of existential despair. Much influenced by German director Wim Wenders (who acts as associate producer), director Christopher Petit casts a bleak eye over the British countryside, but any attempt to construct a multilayered narrative is undercut by wooden acting. Yet its use of pop music and landscape make this a captivating, if cryptic, experience. TH [video]

David Beames *Robert* • Lisa Kreuzer *Ingrid* • Sandy Ratcliff *Kathy* • Andrew Byatt *Deserter* • Sue Jones-Davies *Girl* • Sting *Just Like Eddie* • Sabina Michael *Aunt* ■ *Dir* Christopher Petit • *Scr* Christopher Petit, Heidi Adolph

Radioactive Dreams ★★ 18

Science-fiction fantasy comedy
1986 · US/Mex · Colour · 94mins

Two little boys are taken into a bomb shelter just as World War III breaks out and grow up reading the works of Raymond Chandler. As adults (Michael Dudikoff and John Stockwell), they rename themselves after Phillip Marlowe, take on the personality of the hero of Chandler's novels and set out on a journey across the wastelands. However, Albert Pyun settles for a routine story concerning the heroes trying to stop some villains from getting their hands on a remaining nuclear bomb. KB [video]

John Stockwell *Phillip* • Michael Dudikoff *Marlowe* • Lisa Blount *Miles* • George Kennedy *Spade Chandler* • Don Murray *Dash Hammer* • Michele Little [Michelle Little] *Rusty Mars* • Norbert Weisser *Sternwood* ■ *Dir/Scr* Albert Pyun

Radioland Murders ★★ PG

Comedy thriller 1994 · US · Colour · 103mins

After his success with *The Tall Guy*, comic-turned-director Mel Smith was courted by Hollywood. He ended up with this misfire. Intended as a salute to the golden age of radio, this finds Brian Benben and Mary Stuart Masterson overacting frantically as they attempt to find out who is dispatching the employees of a radio station in 1939 Chicago. Well choreographed slapstick by Smith cannot compensate for the chaotic whole. JF [video]

Brian Benben *Roger* • Mary Stuart Masterson *Penny Henderson* • Ned Beatty *General Whalen* • George Burns *Milt Lackey* • Scott Michael Campbell *Billy* • Michael McKean *Rick Rochester* • Christopher Lloyd *Zoltan* ■ *Dir* Mel Smith • *Scr* Willard Huyck, Gloria Katz, Jeff Reno, Ron Osborne, from a story by George Lucas

Rafferty and the Gold Dust Twins ★★ 15

Comedy road movie
1974 · US · Colour · 87mins

A slow and meandering road movie that takes the same route as *Easy Rider* – from LA to New Orleans – but tries to mirror the working class ambience of *Alice Doesn't Live Here Anymore*. Alan Arkin is an army veteran

R

and drifter who is implausibly kidnapped by two vagrant women – a wannabe singer (wacky Sally Kellerman) and an orphaned, teenage runaway (Mackenzie Phillips). The plot twists and is easily seduced down secondary roads, but compensations include the southwest scenery and the amazingly funky conveyance. AT

Alan Arkin *Rafferty* • Sally Kellerman *Mac Beachwood* • Mackenzie Phillips *Frisbee* • Alex Rocco *Vinnie* • Charles Martin Smith *Alan* • Harry Dean Stanton *Billy Winston* ■ *Dir* Dick Richards • *Scr* John Kaye

The Raffle ★★

Romantic comedy adventure
1994 · Can · Colour · 100mins

An obvious shoestring budget continually undercuts the initially intriguing premise of this light Canadian affair about two down-on-their-luck men devising a money-making scheme to find the world's most beautiful woman and then setting up a raffle where the first prize is a date with her. A good cast, headlined by Nicholas Lea, works wonders with the schematic plot. AJ

Nicholas Lea *David Lake* • Bobby Dawson *Frank Palmer* • Jennifer Clement *Margo Miller* • Teri-Lynn Rutherford *Anya Monroe* • Mark Hamill *Bernard Wallace* ■ *Dir* Gavin Wilding • *Scr* John Fairley

Raffles ★★★

Romantic crime adventure
1930 · US · BW · 70mins

Villainy is all very well if you can carry it off with a smile, smooth out misunderstandings with a mellifluous voice and look as handsome as Ronald Colman does here playing the elusive AJ Raffles. This urbane adaptation makes the toff thief amusingly likeable, a rogue with charm – unless you're his victim, of course. The result is a fascinating curio from a gentler age. TH

Ronald Colman *AJ Raffles* • Kay Francis *Lady Gwen Manders* • Bramwell Fletcher *Bunny Manders* • Frances Dade *Ethel Crowley* • David Torrence *McKenzie* • Alison Skipworth *Lady Kitty Melrose* • Frederick Kerr *Lord Harry Melrose* ■ *Dir* Harry d'Abbadie D'Arrast • *Scr* George Fitzmaurice, Sidney Howard, from the play *Raffles, the Amateur Cracksman* by Ernest William Hornung, Eugene Wiley Presbrey, from the novel *The Amateur Cracksman* by Ernest William Hornung

Raffles ★★★ U

Romantic crime adventure
1939 · US · BW · 68mins

A pleasant but mindless remake by producer Samuel Goldwyn of his 1930 film, with debonair David Niven lacking the suave charm of Ronald Colman's famed gentleman thief incarnation. Olivia de Havilland is lovely, however, and more than makes up for Niven's over-casual approach. What is truly amazing is that this film is particularly strong on English mores and atmosphere, yet not a frame was shot outside Hollywood – all credit to under-rated co-director Sam Wood. TS

David Niven *AJ Raffles* • Olivia de Havilland *Gwen Manders* • Douglas Walton *Bunny Manders* • Dudley Digges *Inspector McKenzie* • Dame May Whitty *Lady Kitty Melrose* • Lionel Pape *Lord Harry Melrose* ■ *Dir* Sam Wood, William Wyler • *Scr* John Van Druten, Sidney Howard, F Scott Fitzgerald, from the novel *The Amateur Cracksman* by Ernest William Hornung

Rag Doll ★★

Drama 1960 · UK · BW · 66mins

A starring vehicle for would-be British heart-throb and teen idol Jess Conrad, perhaps best remembered for making some of the worst pop records ever, notably *This Pullover*. He's a singing burglar, really, who gets involved with teenage runaway Christina Gregg in this cheapie, directed without much flair by Lance Comfort. Conrad's bravado makes this watchable. TS

Jess Conrad *Joe Shane* • Christina Gregg *Carol Flynn* • Hermione Baddeley *Princess Sophia* • Kenneth Griffith *Mort Wilson* • Patrick Magee *Flynn* • Patrick Jordan *Wills* ■ *Dir* Lance Comfort • *Scr* Brock Williams, Derry Quinn, from a story by Brock Williams

Ragan ★ 15

Action adventure
1967 · Sp/It · Colour · 84mins

Set in an unnamed South American republic, this goes some way to explaining why director Sidney Pink was entrusted with only five bad B-movies in his brief career and why the handsome Ty Hardin eventually became a preacher. Hired to spring an anti-Junta general from an inaccessible prison, Hardin and accomplice Jack Stewart play second fiddle to the stunning mountain scenery. The action looks stagey and the dubbed dialogue is embarrassing. DP. Some dialogue dubbed into English.

Ty Hardin *Ragan* • Antonella Lualdi *Janine* • Jack Stewart *Kohler* • Dick Palace *Flower* ■ *Dir* Sidney Pink • *Scr* Howard Berk, Sidney Pink, from a story by Howard Berk

Rage ★★★ 15

Drama 1966 · US/Mex · Colour · 99mins

Glenn Ford is the resident medico at a construction site in the wilds of Mexico. One day he's bitten by his pet dog which turns out to have rabies, so Ford has two days in which to get to a proper hospital and have the serum pumped into him before he starts foaming at the mouth. Instead of rushing, he tends to a pregnant woman who goes into labour; then his jeep breaks down; then Stella Stevens, as a tart with a heart, takes a shower, delaying things still further. AT

Glenn Ford *Reuben* • Stella Stevens *Perla* • David Reynoso *Pancho* • Armando Silvestre *Antonio* • Ariadna Welter *Blanca* • José Elias Moreno *Fortunato* ■ *Dir* Gilberto Gazcon • *Scr* Teddi Sherman, Gilberto Gazcon, Fernando Mendez, from a story by Jesus Velazquez, Guillermo Hernandez, Gilberto Gazcon

Rage ★★ 15

Drama 1972 · US · Colour · 95mins

Rancher George C Scott and his son Nicolas Beauvy, are accidentally caught in the spray of what turns out to be a deadly nerve gas. When the boy dies, Scott learns the truth about the chemical and takes revenge by destroying the company where the gas was made. What might have been developed as a provocative social conscience drama emerges as thin and uninteresting melodrama. Actor Scott made his feature directing debut with the film, and might have been better advised to concentrate on one job or the other. RK

George C Scott *Dan Logan* • Richard Basehart *Dr Caldwell* • Martin Sheen *Major Holliford* • Barnard Hughes *Dr Spencer* • Nicolas Beauvy *Chris Logan* ■ *Dir* George C Scott • *Scr* Philip Friedman, Dan Kleinman

Rage ★★ 15

Crime drama 1999 · UK · Colour · 96mins

Newton I Aduaka's rites-of-passage debut feature falls into all the familiar traps, as it equates *vérité* camerawork with dramatic realism. But there's an honesty about his attempt to portray the limited options open to mixed-race teenager Fraser Ayres and his mates, Shaun Parkes and John Pickard, as they resort to desperate measures in order to fund their hip-hop recording ambitions. As much about dreams and friendship as gangsta rap and crime, this smacks of authenticity, yet ultimately succumbs to street clichés and violence. DP. Contains swearing, violence and drug abuse DVD

Fraser Ayres *Jamie, "Rage"* • Shaun Parkes *Godwin, "G"* • John Pickard *Thomas, "T"* • Shango Baku *Marcus* • Wale Ojo *Pin* ■ *Dir/Scr* Newton I Aduaka

Rage at Dawn ★★ U

Western 1955 · US · Colour · 82mins

Handsome-looking but lethargic western in which special agent Randolph Scott goes undercover to trap one of the earliest bands of outlaws, that of the Reno brothers who committed the first train hold-up in 1866. The Renos also have an attractive sister (Mala Powers), which naturally complicates matters for Scott. The rage at dawn refers to the historically accurate conclusion in which a lynch mob plucks the Renos from jail. AE DVD

Randolph Scott *James Barlow* • Forrest Tucker *Frank Reno* • Mala Powers *Laura Reno* • J Carrol Naish *Sim Reno* • Edgar Buchanan *Judge Hawkins* • Myron Healey *John Reno* • Richard Garland *Bill Reno* • Denver Pyle *Clint Reno* ■ *Dir* Tim Whelan • *Scr* Horace McCoy, from a story by Frank Gruber

The Rage: Carrie 2 ★ 18

Horror 1999 · US · Colour · 107mins

A belated sequel to Brian De Palma's terrifying masterpiece *Carrie*, this abysmal travesty goes through the same narrative motions as the 1976 classic, even using clips as redundant flashbacks. Yet it repeatedly stomps on the memory of that class Stephen King act with utterly routine direction, tired gore and a complete lack of pathos. AJ DVD

Emily Bergl *Rachel Lang* • Jason London *Jesse Ryan* • Dylan Bruno *Mark* • J Smith-Cameron *Barbara Lang* • Zachery Ty Bryan *Eric* • Amy Irving *Sue Snell* ■ *Dir* Katt Shea [Katt Shea Ruben] • *Scr* Rafael Moreu, Howard A Rodman, from characters created by Stephen King

A Rage in Harlem ★★★★ 18

Crime thriller
1991 · UK/US · Colour · 103mins

In this stylish, fast-moving and often humorous thriller, Robin Givens looks every inch the sex siren. She arrives in 1950s Harlem with a bag full of stolen gold. As she tries to exchange the booty for cash, various seedy characters get involved in her scheming, as does an innocent undertaker's assistant (played with charm and naivety by the ever-dependable Forest Whitaker). The cast is enjoyable to watch as the twisting tale unfolds, but the squeamish should beware: there is quite a lot of violence. JB. Contains swearing, nudity.

Forest Whitaker *Jackson* • Gregory Hines *Goldy* • Robin Givens *Imabelle* • Zakes Mokae *Big Kathy* • Danny Glover *Easy Money* • Badja Djola *Slim* • John Toles-Bey *Jodie* ■ *Dir* Bill Duke • *Scr* John Toles-Bey, Bobby Crawford, from the novel by Chester Himes

Rage in Heaven ★★

Drama 1941 · US · BW · 84mins

The English heir to a fortune (Robert Montgomery) returns home to his mother Lucile Watson after an absence in France where, unbeknown to her, he has been in a mental hospital. He marries his mother's social secretary (Ingrid Bergman), but his psychosis soon surfaces in unfounded jealousy of his wife and his friend (George Sanders), leading to violent and melodramatic events. WS Van Dyke directed this overheated nonsense and was unable to rescue Montgomery from an unconvincing parody of a mad Englishman. RK

Robert Montgomery *Philip Monrell* • Ingrid Bergman *Stella Bergen* • George Sanders *Ward Andrews* • Lucile Watson *Mrs Monrell* • Oscar Homolka *Dr Rameau* ■ *Dir* WS Van Dyke • *Scr* Christopher Isherwood, Robert Thoeren, from the novel by James Hilton

The Rage in Placid Lake ★★ 15

Comedy drama
2002 · Aus/UK · Colour · 89mins

Australian teenager Placid Lake (played by musician Ben Lee) is no ordinary rebel. The bullied son of two ageing hippies, Lee decides to try to fit in with the straight world by getting a job in insurance. Sketching a ruthless corporate world where hearts and souls are swapped for executive perks, this quirky Aussie satire is worthy yet rarely witty. Lee charms in the lead role, yet not even he can make Placid's calculated plans for acceptance seem anything more than a lazy contrivance. JR. Contains swearing, sexual references.

Ben Lee *Placid Lake* • Rose Byrne *Gemma Taylor* • Miranda Richardson *Sylvia Lake* • Garry McDonald *Doug Lake* • Christopher Stollery *Joel* • Nicholas Hammond *Bill Taylor* • Francis McMahon *Anton* • Saskia Smith *Jane* ■ *Dir* Tony McNamara • *Scr* Tony McNamara, from his play *The Cafe Latte Kid*

The Rage of Paris ★★★

Romantic comedy 1938 · US · BW · 78mins

This amoral, sophisticated romantic comedy was made at Universal as a vehicle for French star Danielle Darrieux, making her Hollywood debut. Directed with a light touch by Henry Koster, the movie has Darrieux as a casino girl who, finding herself unemployed, turns model, and then, with the collusion and encouragement of two friends, gold-digger. These are the bare bones of an intricate plot that involves suspicions of blackmail and an unexpected love affair. The wildly glamorous Darrieux sparkles in this outrageous flim-flam. RK

Danielle Darrieux *Nicole de Cortillon* • Douglas Fairbanks Jr *Jim Trevor* • Mischa Auer *Mike* • Louis Hayward *Bill Jerome Duncan* • Helen Broderick *Gloria Patterson* • Charles Coleman *Rigley* ■ *Dir* Henry Koster • *Scr* Bruce Manning, Felix Jackson, from their story

Rage to Kill ★★ 18

Action drama 1988 · US · Colour · 88mins

Despite all the questions that have been asked about the rights and wrongs of American involvement in Grenada, this jingoistic exercise in exploiting the conflict now seems more than a little dated. James Ryan is the beefcake hero who's caught up in a military takeover while visiting his student brother. Pretty poor timing, particularly as the bad guy is Oliver Reed playing a hostage-taking Marxist general. A tedious exercise out of the straight-to-video abyss. TH

James Ryan *Blaine Striker* • Oliver Reed *General Turner* • Cameron Mitchell *Miller* • Maxine John *Trishia Baker* ■ *Dir* David Winters • *Scr* David Winters, Ian Yule

A Rage to Live ★★

Drama 1965 · US · Colour · 101mins

Rich young nymphomaniac Suzanne Pleshette goes through a succession of men, beginning with her brother's best friend, and progressing through a hotel employee to a desperate marriage until infidelity (with Ben Gazzara) takes over and her husband Bradford Dillman leaves her. This superficial, watered-down account of John O'Hara's bestselling novel is rendered even more uninteresting by the casting of the inadequate Pleshette. Walter Grauman's dreary direction doesn't help either. RK

Suzanne Pleshette *Grace Caldwell* • Bradford Dillman *Sidney Tate* • Ben Gazzara *Roger Bannon* • Peter Graves (2) *Jack Hollister* • Bethel Leslie *Amy Hollister* ■ *Dir* Walter Grauman • *Scr* John T Kelley, from the novel by John O'Hara

Raggedy Ann and Andy

★★ U

Animation 1977 · US · Colour · 85mins

Somnolent cartoon musical about toys coming to life when their owners are away. Hailed as the adventures of "America's favourite dolls" and directed by Richard Williams, it succumbs to some songs – written by Joe Raposo – which stultify the action even more. The characters have appeal but no story that will interest children above the age of five. TH

Didi Conn *Raggedy Ann* • Mark Baker *Raggedy Andy* • Fred Stuthman *Camel with the wrinkled knees* • Niki Flacks *Babette* • George S Irving *Captain Contagious* ■ *Dir* Richard Williams • *Scr* Patricia Thackray, Max Wilk, from characters created by Johnny Gruelle

Raggedy Man ★★★ 15

Drama 1981 · US · Colour · 89mins

Sissy Spacek is a wartime divorcee who falls in love with a sailor played by Eric Roberts. This causes problems with her two children as well as the local predatory men, including Sam Shepard. Spacek had just won an Oscar for *Coal Miner's Daughter* and produces another trademark backwoods performance, heavy on the Texan accent and the wistful look. Her real-life husband, former art director Jack Fisk, directs the show with sensitivity, though the violent ending seems misjudged. AT

Sissy Spacek *Nita Longley* • Eric Roberts *Teddy* • Sam Shepard *Bailey* • William Sanderson *Calvin* • Tracey Walter *Arnold* • RG Armstrong *Rigby* • Henry Thomas *Harry* ■ *Dir* Jack Fisk • *Scr* William D Wittliff

The Raggedy Rawney

★★★ 15

Period drama 1987 · UK · Colour · 98mins

Much maligned on its original release, Bob Hoskins's directorial debut is undeniably ragged in places, but there is still much to admire in this plea for toleration and peace set in an unidentified war-torn European country at the turn of the century. Once you've accepted the premise that Dexter Fletcher (a deserter who has disguised himself as a woman) could be mistaken for a "rawney", a gypsy with magical powers, then this intriguing venture into the mysterious Romany world has many rewards. The different rituals and customs are handled with great reverence by Hoskins, whose efforts behind the camera are more impressive than his disappointing performance. DP. Contains violence, swearing and nudity.

Bob Hoskins *Darky* • Dexter Fletcher *Tom* • Zoe Nathenson *Jessie* • Zoë Wanamaker *Elle* • Dave Hill *Lamb* • Ian Dury *Weazel* • Ian McNeice *Stanley, the farmer* ■ *Dir* Bob Hoskins • *Scr* Bob Hoskins, Nicole de Wilde

Raging Bull ★★★★★ 18

Biographical sports drama
1980 · US · BW and Colour · 128mins

Critics and film-makers are always being asked to reel off their desert island films: this, without question, is one such great. Director Martin Scorsese makes no concession to character likeability as he portrays Jake La Motta's downward slide from arrogant prizefighter to frustrated, hateful dropout. Robert De Niro, who piled on the pounds to play the latter-day La Motta, proves he is the ultimate Method actor, both utterly convincing in the ring (the brutal fight sequences are spectacularly staged) and as the empty barrel abusing everyone (including his wife, Cathy Moriarty, and brother, Joe Pesci) at home. Scorsese effortlessly fuses top-drawer acting (De Niro rightly won a best actor Oscar for his efforts), pumping narrative drive and blitzkrieg camera technique to deliver a giddy, claustrophobic classic. JM. Contains violence and swearing. DVD

Robert De Niro *Jake La Motta* • Cathy Moriarty *Vickie La Motta* • Joe Pesci *Joey La Motta* • Frank Vincent *Salvy* • Nicholas Colasanto *Tommy Como* • Theresa Saldana *Lenore* • Johnny Barnes *"Sugar" Ray Robinson* ■ *Dir* Martin Scorsese • *Scr* Paul Schrader, Mardik Martin, from the non-fiction book by Jake La Motta, Joseph Carter, Peter Savage • *Editor* Thelma Schoonmaker • *Cinematographer* Michael Chapman

The Raging Moon ★★★ PG

Romantic drama
1970 · UK · Colour · 106mins

The suggestion that disabled people might enjoy a sexual relationship was still shocking when this romance in wheelchairs appeared, offering invaluable insight into a previously closed world. Malcolm McDowell is the young buck embittered by his crippling illness until he meets Nanette Newman, who is better adjusted to her fate. Director Bryan Forbes (Newman's husband in real life) tends to overdo everything, particularly the sentimentality, but the leads are sympathetic. DM

Malcolm McDowell *Bruce Pritchard* • Nanette Newman *Jill* • Georgia Brown *Sarah Charles* • Bernard Lee *Uncle Bob* • Gerald Sim *Reverend Corbett* • Michael Flanders *Clarence Marlow* ■ *Dir* Bryan Forbes • *Scr* Bryan Forbes, from the novel by Peter Marshall

The Ragman's Daughter

★★★

Romantic drama 1972 · UK · Colour · 94mins

Written by Alan Sillitoe from his own story, this is an intelligent, romantic drama that has unfortunately been tagged with the "kitchen sink" label. It features an ingenious thief (Simon Rouse) who falls for the astonishingly beautiful daughter (Victoria Tennant) of a rich rag-and-bone man. Beautifully acted and stylishly executed, this British independent feature marked the directorial debut of Harold Becker (*Sea of Love*). A little gem. FL

Simon Rouse *Tony Bradmore* • Victoria Tennant *Doris Randall* • Patrick O'Connell *Tony, aged 35* • Leslie Sands *Doris's father* • Rita Howard *Doris's mother* • Brenda Peters *Tony's mother* • Brian Murphy *Tony's father* • Sydney Livingstone *Prison officer* ■ *Dir* Harold Becker • *Scr* Alan Sillitoe, from his story

Ragtime ★★★ 15

Period drama 1981 · US · Colour · 148mins

EL Doctorow's novel was a publishing sensation and producer Dino De Laurentiis spent $27 million on re-creating (at Shepperton Studios) New York in 1906. But the novel is almost unfilmable, a chaotic bundle of characters and situations that relies solely on Doctorow's flashy wordplay. However, Milos Forman grabs bits and bobs of plot and relies on dazzling sets and photography. Plus there's James Cagney (back on the screen after a 20-year retirement) and Norman Mailer as Stanford White, the real-life architect murdered by millionaire Harry K Thaw (played here by Robert Joy). AT. Contains swearing and nudity.

James Cagney *Police commissioner Waldo* • Brad Dourif *Younger brother* • Moses Gunn *Booker T Washington* • Elizabeth McGovern *Evelyn Nesbit* • Kenneth McMillan *Willie Conklin* • Pat O'Brien *Delmas* • Mandy Patinkin *Tateh* • Norman Mailer *Stanford White* • Robert Joy *Harry K Thaw* ■ *Dir* Milos Forman • *Scr* Michael Weller, from the novel by EL Doctorow

The Raid ★★★ U

Historical war drama
1954 · US · Colour · 82mins

This little-known Civil War drama, about a group of escaped Confederate soldiers who lay vengeful siege to a town near the Canadian border, has much to commend it: a tight construction, bursts of action, strong characters and a great cast. The script plays like an allegory of a wider conflict, while Hugo Fregonese (an Argentinian director who deserved greater public recognition) keeps the tension bubbling. AT

Van Heflin *Major Neal Benton* • Anne Bancroft *Katy Bishop* • Richard Boone *Captain Foster* • Lee Marvin *Lieutenant Keating* • Tommy Rettig *Larry Bishop* • Peter Graves (2) *Captain Dwyer* ■ *Dir* Hugo Fregonese • *Scr* Sydney Boehm, from the story by Francis Cockrell, from the article *Affair at St Albans* by Herbert Ravenal Sass

Raid on Entebbe ★★★ PG

Drama based on a true story
1977 · US · Colour · 120mins

This TV movie is the pick of three films about the Israeli commando mission in Uganda in 1976 to save the passengers of a plane hijacked by Palestinian terrorists. Peter Finch, in his last screen role, heads a distinguished cast as Israeli prime minister Yitzhak Rabin, and he's given fine support by Charles Bronson, Martin Balsam and Jack Warden. Director Irvin Kershner doesn't get carried away with the *Boys' Own* heroics and builds the tension nicely to its explosive climax. JF

Peter Finch *Yitzhak Rabin* • Martin Balsam *Daniel Cooper* • Horst Buchholz *Wilfrid Boese* • John Saxon *Maj Gen Benny Peled* • Sylvia Sidney *Dora Bloch* • Jack Warden *Lt Gen Mordechai Gur* • Yaphet Kotto *President Idi Amin* • Charles Bronson *Brig Gen Dan Shamron* ■ *Dir* Irvin Kershner • *Scr* Barry Beckerman

Raid on Rommel ★★ 15

Second World War drama
1971 · US · Colour · 93mins

It says a lot for Richard Burton that he was able to plumb the depths in dreary Second World War action movies such as this one, about a British officer releasing prisoners to attack Tobruk, without doing any apparent damage to his career. Even the usually dependable director Henry Hathaway falters in this flawed effort that was originally meant for TV. TH DVD

Richard Burton *Captain Foster* • John Colicos *MacKenzie* • Clinton Greyn *Major Tarkington* • Danielle De Metz *Vivi* • Wolfgang Preiss *General Rommel* ■ *Dir* Henry Hathaway • *Scr* Richard Bluel

The Raiders ★★ U

Western 1964 · US · Colour · 75mins

This western drama stars the forceful Brian Keith as leader of impoverished Texas ranchers whose desperate actions bring them into conflict with the US Army. In a spurious attempt to add interest, the film ropes in Wild Bill Hickok (Robert Culp), Buffalo Bill Cody (James McMullan) and Calamity Jane (Judi Meredith). Stock action footage from better pictures is crudely inserted and there are many dull stretches. AE

Robert Culp *James Butler "Wild Bill" Hickok* • Brian Keith *John G McElroy* • Judi Meredith *Martha "Calamity Jane" Canary* • James McMullan [Jim McMullan] *William F "Buffalo Bill" Cody* • Alfred Ryder *Captain Benton* • Simon Oakland *Sgt Austin Tremaine* ■ *Dir* Herschel Daugherty • *Scr* Gene L Coon

Raiders of the Lost Ark

★★★★★ PG

Action adventure
1981 · US · Colour · 110mins

Executive producer George Lucas and director Steven Spielberg minted fresh excitement from the cliffhanger serials of their youth in this breathless fantasy extravaganza. Archaeologist Indiana Jones (a part that fits Harrison Ford like a glove) searches the Holy Land for the fabled Ark of the Covenant, and finds himself up to his neck in booby-trapped caves, snake chambers, Nazi spies, religious demons, damsels in distress and even a spot of romance. The brilliantly evocative 1930s-set saga uses all the old clichés as if they've just been newly minted and dazzling special effects to craft a wonderful action yarn that rattles along with wit, invention and the raw spirit of true adventure. No surprise then that one of the four Oscars this fabulous production picked up was for visual effects. Two sequels followed, *Indiana Jones and the Temple of Doom* and *Indiana Jones and the Last Crusade*. AJ. Contains violence. DVD

Harrison Ford *Indiana Jones* • Karen Allen *Marion Ravenwood* • Paul Freeman *Belloq* • Ronald Lacey *Toht* • John Rhys-Davies *Sallah* • Denholm Elliott *Brody* • Wolf Kahler *Dietrich* • Anthony Higgins *Gobler* • Alfred Molina *Satipo* • Vic Tablian *Barranca/Monkey man* ■ *Dir* Steven Spielberg • *Scr* Lawrence Kasdan, from a story by George Lucas, Philip Kaufman • *Cinematographer* Douglas Slocombe • *Editor* Michael Kahn • *Music* John Williams • *Special Effects* Richard Edlund, Kit West, Joe Johnston, Bruce Nicholson • *Production Designer* Norman Reynold • *Art Director* Leslie Dilley

Raiders of the Seven Seas

★★ U

Swashbuckling adventure
1953 · US · Colour · 88mins

Red-bearded pirate John Payne commandeers a prison ship and takes on all-comers in this lively swashbuckler filmed in lush Technicolor. The love interest is supplied by Donna Reed who, as is often the way in these by-the-book high-seas adventures, is won over by our dashing hero's charms. TS

John Payne *Barbarossa* • Donna Reed *Alida* • Gerald Mohr *Salcedo* • Lon Chaney Jr *Peg Leg* ■ *Dir* Sidney Salkow • *Scr* John O'Dea, from a story by John O'Dea, Sidney Salkow

Railroaded ★★★

Crime melodrama 1947 · US · BW · 72mins

Anthony Mann brings a sure touch to this low-budget crime B-movie. Innocent youngster Ed Kelly is framed for murder by psychopathic professional John Ireland, whose penchant is spraying bullets with perfume before discharging them into his victims. Although formula stuff, it's taut, coolly violent and very tough, particularly in its treatment of female characters. RK

John Ireland *Duke Martin* • Sheila Ryan *Rosa Ryan* • Hugh Beaumont *Mickey Ferguson* • Jane Randolph *Clara Calhoun* • Ed Kelly *Steve Ryan* ■ *Dir* Anthony Mann • *Scr* John C Higgins, from a story by Gertrude Walker

The Railrodder ★★★★ U

Comedy 1965 · Can · Colour · 24mins

A whimsical, poetic farewell to an elderly Buster Keaton in director Gerald Potterton's short film, a diminutive view of Keaton's *The General*, in which Keaton makes his way across Canada on a railway trolley. The solo slapstick is sweet-natured, the adoration of the director for his star is obvious and Buster Keaton recalls his silent days – by not saying a word, which makes it all the more poignant. TH

Buster Keaton *The Railrodder* ■ *Dir/Scr* Gerald Potterton

Rails into Laramie ★★ U

Western 1954 · US · Colour · 81mins

This routine western is given distinction by a snarling study in black-hearted villainy by Dan Duryea, who is trying to stop the railroad from reaching Laramie for his own devious purpose. Meanwhile, sexy Mari Blanchard aims to rustle up an all-female jury to put Duryea away. All this would be interesting were it not for the presence of John Payne, past his prime and looking ill-at-ease. TS

John Payne *Jefferson Harder* • Mari Blanchard *Lou Carter* • Dan Duryea *Jim Shanessy* • Joyce MacKenzie *Helen Shanessy* • Barton MacLane *Lee Graham* • Lee Van Cleef *Ace Winton* ■ *Dir* Jesse Hibbs • *Scr* DD Beauchamp, Joseph Hoffman

The Railway Children ★★★★★ U

Classic period drama 1970 · UK · Colour · 104mins

Directed by Lionel Jeffries, this adaptation of E Nesbit's much-loved novel is simply the finest children's film ever made in this country. Told with quiet intelligence and wry humour, the story follows three Edwardian siblings as they relocate to Yorkshire with their mother (Dinah Sheridan), following their father's wrongful arrest for treason. The set pieces are equally memorable – whether it's the prevention of a train wreck, the rescue of a schoolboy trapped in a tunnel, or the collection of birthday gifts for the proud but kindly stationmaster (winningly played by Bernard Cribbins). Jenny Agutter's magnificent performance as Bobbie stands out. It perfectly balances a child's passion for adventure with a growing sense of responsibility as she comes to understand her family's predicament. DP DVD

Jenny Agutter *Bobbie* • Sally Thomsett *Phyllis* • Gary Warren *Peter* • Dinah Sheridan *Mother* • Bernard Cribbins *Perks* • William Mervyn *Old gentleman* • Iain Cuthbertson *Father* • Peter Bromilow *Doctor* ■ *Dir* Lionel Jeffries • *Scr* Lionel Jeffries, from the novel by E Nesbit

Rain ★★★ PG

Drama 1932 · US · BW · 93mins

Somerset Maugham's tale of a hellfire-and-damnation church missionary's lust for a prostitute who fetches up at a trading post on a rain-drenched South Sea island was a steamy shocker in its day, and has attracted three film versions and three major actresses. Gloria Swanson starred in the silent *Sadie Thompson* (1928), earning a best actress nomination in the first ever Oscars; Rita Hayworth was a Technicolored (and terrific) *Miss Sadie Thompson*, in 1953. Here Joan Crawford, dressed and made-up to kill, gives her considerable all in a much under-rated performance that failed to please the customers in 1932. Co-star Walter Huston is hammy, while the screenplay and direction fail to hit the right note. RK DVD

Joan Crawford *Sadie Thompson* • Walter Huston *Rev Alfred Davidson* • William Gargan *Sgt "Handsome" O'Hara* • Guy Kibbee *Joe Horn* • Walter Catlett *Quartermaster Hal Bates* ■ *Dir* Lewis Milestone • *Scr* Maxwell Anderson, from the play by John Colton, Clemence Randolph, from the short story by W Somerset Maugham

Rain ★★★★ 15

Drama 2001 · NZ/US · Colour · 87mins

A haunting, dreamy tale of a young girl entering adolescence, the debut feature of award-winning New Zealand commercials director Christine Jeffs marks her out as a major talent. A 13-year-old girl (a stunning turn from newcomer Alicia Fulford-Wierzbicki) travels with her younger brother and parents for a traditional sleepy summer holiday by the beach. However, the cracks in their idyllic life soon begin to appear. The marriage of her parents (Sarah Peirse and Alistair Browning) is falling apart, while both mother and daughter find themselves drawn to charismatic photographer Marton Csokas. Jeffs's measured direction, along with the hazy cinematography of John Toon, make the tragic finale compelling. JF DVD

Alicia Fulford-Wierzbicki *Janey* • Sarah Peirse *Kate* • Marton Csokas *Cady* • Alistair Browning *Ed* • Aaron Murphy *Jim* ■ *Dir* Christine Jeffs • *Scr* Christine Jeffs, from the novel by Kirsty Gunn

Rain Man ★★★★★ 15

Drama 1988 · US · Colour · 127mins

While everyone remembers this film about an autistic man as Dustin Hoffman's Oscar-winning triumph, it is equally Tom Cruise's. As a wheeler-dealer living out the 1980s dream, he learns that not only is he out of his father's will (save for a 1949 Buick), he also has an institutionalised elder brother (Hoffman). This is a classic road movie, with the two siblings crossing country to California in the Buick. Hoffman's savant is one of modern cinema's great triumphs: believable, unsentimental, often hilarious. But without Cruise, whose emotional journey runs from confused and impatient to understanding, protective and eventually loving, there is no film. Director Barry Levinson handles the whole thing beautifully. AC. Contains swearing. DVD

Dustin Hoffman *Raymond Babbitt* • Tom Cruise *Charlie Babbitt* • Valeria Golino *Susanna* • Jerry Molen *Dr Bruner* • Jack Murdock *John Mooney* • Michael D Roberts *Vern* ■ *Dir* Barry Levinson • *Scr* Ronald Bass, Barry Morrow, from a story by Barry Morrow

Rain or Shine ★★

Comedy drama 1930 · US · BW · 90mins

A very early, too early, Frank Capra-directed peek beneath the big top, with a trio of clowns (Joe Cook, Dave Chasen and Tom Howard) attempting a lacklustre stab at the hackneyed "tears behind the greasepaint" scenario. The movie's problems stem from an overindulgence in leering acrobats and acres of sawdust at the expense of a plot and characterisation. A depressing experience. SH

Joe Cook *Smiley* • Louise Fazenda *Frankie* • Joan Peers *Mary* • William Collier Jr *Bud* • Tom Howard *Amos* • David Chasen *Dave* ■ *Dir* Frank Capra • *Scr* Jo Swerling, Dorothy Howell, from the play by James Gleason

The Rain People ★★

Drama 1969 · US · Colour · 101mins

This early outing from director Francis Ford Coppola is certainly not without interest today, but its 1960s attitudes have dated badly. Nevertheless, it is fascinating to see James Caan and Robert Duvall at a stage of their careers prior to *The Godfather*, and there's a superb performance from Shirley Knight in the leading role as the neurotic pregnant housewife who takes life on the lam. Uneven and slackly paced, this remains a moderate curiosity. TS. Contains swearing.

James Caan *Jimmie "Killer" Kilgannon* • Shirley Knight *Natalie Ravenna* • Robert Duvall *Gordon* • Marya Zimmet *Rosalie* • Tom Aldredge *Mr Alfred* • Laurie Crewes *Ellen* ■ *Dir/Scr* Francis Ford Coppola

The Rainbow ★★ 15

Drama 1988 · UK · Colour · 106mins

Director Ken Russell takes a further dip after *Women in Love* into the DH Lawrence lucky bag, but to decidedly lacklustre effect. All clichés are alive and thrashing, including monosyllabic but "deeply meaningful" dialogue interspersed with heaving bosoms and frantic copulation by crashing waterfalls. Only Sammi Davis's portrayal of the feisty, no-nonsense Ursula lifts the unleavened load. SH. Contains swearing, nudity. DVD

Sammi Davis *Ursula Brangwen* • Paul McGann *Anton Skrebensky* • Amanda Donohoe *Winifred Inger* • Christopher Gable *Will Brangwen* • David Hemmings *Uncle Henry* • Glenda Jackson *Anna Brangwen* • Dudley Sutton *MacAllister* • Jim Carter *Mr Harby* ■ *Dir* Ken Russell • *Scr* Ken Russell, Vivian Russell, from the novel by DH Lawrence

Rainbow ★★ PG

Fantasy comedy adventure 1995 · UK/Can · Colour · 94mins

Four kids go searching for the end of the rainbow in the second feature directed by Bob Hoskins. Unfortunately, when they find it in New Jersey, one of them takes pieces of gold from the spectrum causing all colour to drain from the real world and a crime wave to break out. One of the first features to be shot on Digital High Definition, the results are not entirely successful. Hoskins doesn't have the feather-light touch such hokum demands as the whimsy he aims for never quite comes into focus. AJ

Bob Hoskins *Frank Bailey* • Dan Aykroyd *Sheriff Wyatt Hampton* • Willy Lavendal *Mike* • Saul Rubinek *Sam Cohen* ■ *Dir* Bob Hoskins • *Scr* Ashley Sidaway, Robert Sidaway

Rainbow Bridge ★★ 18

Documentary drama 1971 · US · Colour · 73mins

Although it captures the mood of the late 1960s, director Chuck Wein's mixture of hippy fact and impenetrable fiction is a rambling and tedious artefact from the era. Centred around model Pat Hartley making a pilgrimage to the Rainbow Bridge Occult Research Meditation Centre on the Hawaiian island of Maui, this disjointed mess is only worth watching to see Jimi Hendrix play a short concert by the side of the Haleakala volcano three months before his death. AJ

Dir/Scr Chuck Wein

The Rainbow Jacket ★★ PG

Crime drama 1958 · UK · Colour · 96mins

Screenwriter TEB Clarke was the brains behind many of the Ealing comedies. Yet he also had a well-developed social conscience, as he proves in this unconvincing racing drama. As the disgraced jockey who saves his protégé from a bribes scandal, Bill Owen has one of his meatiest screen roles. However, this is a workmanlike film, with some suitably downbeat photography from Otto Heller and neat cameos from Sid James and Wilfrid Hyde White. DP

Robert Morley *Lord Logan* • Kay Walsh *Barbara Crain* • Edward Underdown *Geoffrey Tyler* • Bill Owen *Sam Lilley* • Honor Blackman *Monica Tyler* • Wilfrid Hyde White *Lord Stoneleigh* • Sidney James *Harry* ■ *Dir* Basil Dearden • *Scr* TEB Clarke

Rainbow on the River ★★ U

Period melodrama 1936 · US · BW · 88mins

A vehicle for boy soprano Bobby Breen. Always smiling in the face of on-screen adversity, this male answer to Shirley Temple, with a voice and repertoire to rival Deanna Durbin, was a relatively short-lived but popular and profitable phenomenon, whose fans were willing to overlook the dire sentimentality of scripts. This one has little orphan Bobby, poor but happy, ensconced down South in the care of his beloved "mammy" (Louise Beavers), only to be whipped away to his rich grandmother (May Robson) and a bunch of vile cousins in New York. RK

Bobby Breen *Philip* • May Robson *Mrs Ainsworth* • Charles Butterworth *Barrett, butler* • Louise Beavers *Toinette* • Alan Mowbray *Ralph Layton* • Benita Hume *Julia Layton* ■ *Dir* Kurt Neumann • *Scr* Earle Snell, Harry Chandlee, William Hurlbut, Clarence Marks, from the story *Toinnette's Philip* by Mrs CV Jamison

The Rainbow Thief ★★★

Fantasy 1990 · UK · Colour · 91mins

Alexandro Jodorowsky's most ardent fans will enjoy this obscure, whimsical fable about a man and his servant, played by Peter O'Toole and Omar Sharif. O'Toole is the eccentric who lives in the city sewers with Sharif, his servant who scavenges for food. Christopher Lee plays O'Toole's uncle who leaves his fortune to his dogs and his whores. AT

Peter O'Toole *Prince Meleagre* • Omar Sharif *Dima* • Christopher Lee *Uncle Rudolf* • Berta Dominguez D *Tiger Lily* ■ *Dir* Alexandro Jodorowsky • *Scr* Berta Dominguez D

Raincoat ★ PG

Romantic drama 2004 · Ind · Colour · 117mins

Ajay Devgan and former Miss World Aishwarya Rai play the star-crossed lovers who meet after six years apart in this dull drama. The couple trudge through their pasts, indulging in meaningless chatter that fails to light up the gloomy room of the dilapidated house in which the film is primarily set. Genuinely cringe-worthy. OA. In Hindi with English subtitles.

Ajay Devgan *Manu* • Aishwarya Rai *Neeru* • Annu Kapoor *The visitor* • Mouli Ganguli *The friend's wife* • Surekha Sikri ■ *Dir/Scr* Rituparno Ghosh

Raining Stones ★★★★★ 15

Comedy drama 1993 · UK · Colour · 86mins

The genius of director Ken Loach lies in his ability to point out the comic ironies and absurdities of existence while exposing the prejudices and injustices of working-class life. While a touch uneven, this is one of his most effective films, showing the desperate measures an unemployed man is willing to take in order to raise the cash for his daughter's Communion dress. Bruce Jones occasionally loses his way, but mostly he conveys the stubborn pride and determination of his character with considerable skill. Julie Brown shows up well as his wife, while Ricky Tomlinson steals scenes as his mate. DP. Contains violence, swearing. DVD

Bruce Jones *Bob Williams* • Julie Brown *Anne Williams* • Gemma Phoenix *Coleen Williams* • Ricky Tomlinson *Tommy* • Tom Hickey *Father Barry* • Mike Fallon *Jimmy* • Ronnie Ravey *Butcher* ■ *Dir* Ken Loach • *Scr* Jim Allen

The Rainmaker ★★★

Comedy drama 1956 · US · Colour · 121mins

Burt Lancaster only made *Gunfight at the OK Corral* on condition that he star in this period comedy drama. Based on a Broadway play, the story is set in Kansas, 1913, with Lancaster as the conman who promises he will bring an end to a serious drought, while also finding time to charm local spinster Katharine Hepburn. Director Joseph Anthony staged the original play and clearly has a reverential ear for dialogue, but while Lancaster is solid, Hepburn is miscast. AT

Burt Lancaster *Starbuck* • Katharine Hepburn *Lizzie Curry* • Wendell Corey *File* • Lloyd Bridges *Noah Curry* • Earl Holliman *Jim Curry* • Wallace Ford *Sheriff Thomas* ■ *Dir* Joseph Anthony • *Scr* N Richard Nash, from his play

The Rains Came ★★★

Romantic melodrama
1939 · US · BW · 104mins

Torrid stuff from 1939, Hollywood's *annus mirabilis*, and generally overlooked among the welter of great films on display. This is major tosh, set in a very 20th Century-Fox India with classy Myrna Loy chasing a turbaned Tyrone Power, face-darkened by make-up as a Hindu doctor. The flood effects, tame by today's standards, won an Oscar. Author Louis Bromfield's novel was ruthlessly pared by the censorship of the time. TS

Myrna Loy *Lady Edwina Esketh* • Tyrone Power *Major Rama Safti* • George Brent *Tom Ransome* • Brenda Joyce *Fern Simon* • Nigel Bruce *Albert, Lord Esketh* ■ *Dir* Clarence Brown • *Scr* Philip Dunne, Julien Josephson, from the novel by Louis Bromfield

The Rains of Ranchipur ★★

Romantic drama
1955 · US · Colour · 103mins

A widescreen remake of the 1939 movie hit *The Rains Came*, this time with Richard Burton in ludicrous brown make-up as the Indian doctor Lana Turner decides to seduce. The Oscar-nominated special effects are pathetic by today's standards, while co-stars Fred MacMurray, Joan Caulfield and Michael Rennie look particularly lost, as well they might, for director Jean Negulesco struggles to overcome the underdeveloped subplots. TS

Lana Turner *Edwina Esketh* • Richard Burton *Dr Safti* • Fred MacMurray *Tom Ransome* • Joan Caulfield *Fern Simon* • Michael Rennie *Lord Esketh* • Eugenie Leontovich *Maharani* ■ *Dir* Jean Negulesco • *Scr* Merle Miller, from the novel *The Rains Came* by Louis Bromfield

Raintree County ★★★★

Period drama 1957 · US · Colour · 166mins

MGM's follow-up to its masterpiece *Gone with the Wind* failed to meet with much critical or public approval in its day. Such lack of enthusiasm now seems unfair and unwarranted, as this is a stunning, complex epic, dealing with issues and themes way ahead of its time. It's superbly cast and benefits from a particularly emotive and evocative vocal from Nat "King" Cole. This is the movie for which Elizabeth Taylor should have got her Oscar, as it contains some of the finest screen work she has ever done. TS

Montgomery Clift *John Wickliff Shawnessy* • Elizabeth Taylor *Susanna Drake* • Eva Marie Saint *Nell Gaither* • Nigel Patrick *Professor Jerusalem Webster Stiles* • Lee Marvin *Orville "Flash" Perkins* • Rod Taylor *Garwood B Jones* • Agnes Moorehead *Ellen Shawnessy* ■ *Dir* Edward Dmytryk • *Scr* Millard Kaufman, from the novel by Ross Lockridge Jr

Raise the Red Lantern ★★★★★ PG

Drama 1991 · Chi · Colour · 119mins

Although a lesser film than the stunning *Ju Dou*, this is still one of the jewels of recent Chinese cinema. Once again making exceptional use of bright colour, symbolic compositions, stylised sets and the breathtaking rural landscape, director Zhang Yimou has fashioned a compelling and at times erotic story about the repression of women in 1920s' China. Gong Li excels as the teenager who is forced to abandon her studies to become the fourth wife of a nobleman, but He Caifei, as the usurped third wife, matches her throughout their struggle for the right to the red lantern that signifies the master's favour. DP. In Mandarin with English subtitles. Contains violence. [VIDEO]

Gong Li *Songlian* • Ma Jingwu *Chen Zuoqian* • He Caifei *Meishan* • Cao Cuifeng *Zhuoyun* • Jin Shuyuan *Yuru* • Kong Lin *Yan'er* • Ding Weimin *Mother Song* • Cui Zhigang *Doctor Gao* ■ *Dir* Zhang Yimou • *Scr* Ni Zhen, from the short story by Su Tong

Raise the Titanic ★ PG

Adventure 1980 · US · Colour · 108mins

One of Lew Grade's most memorable flops, this adventure cost a fortune, was touted as a major blockbuster and then proceeded to sink faster than the world famous liner. Jason Robards and Richard Jordan are among the unfortunate actors trying to raise the ship, believed to have a store of precious cargo in its hold, while Alec Guinness pops up as a crusty member of the *Titanic's* original crew. A clunker. JB. Contains swearing. [VIDEO] DVD

Jason Robards *Admiral James Sandecker* • Richard Jordan *Dirk Pitt* • David Selby *Dr Gene Seagram* • Anne Archer *Dana Archibald* • Alec Guinness *John Bigalow* • M Emmet Walsh *Vinnie Giordino* ■ *Dir* Jerry Jameson • *Scr* Adam Kennedy, from the novel by Clive Cussler

Raise Your Voice ★★ PG

Drama 2004 · US · Colour · 102mins

Small-town girl Hilary Duff makes her singing dreams come true in this sprightly but predictable romantic drama. Aimed squarely at pre-teens, it's a feel good romp-cum-life lesson as Duff is forced to conquer her fears and insecurities during a summer at a highly competitive performing arts school in Los Angeles. While older viewers may scoff at the contrived and often cheesy plot, younger girls will respond to its positive messages and frothy atmosphere. SF [VIDEO] DVD

Hilary Duff *Terri Fletcher* • Oliver James *Jay Corgan* • David Keith *Simon Fletcher* • Rita Wilson *Francis Fletcher* • Rebecca De Mornay *Aunt Nina* • John Corbett *Mr Torvald* • Dana Davis *Denise Gilmore* ■ *Dir* Sean McNamara • *Scr* Sam Schreiber, from a story by Mitch Rotter

A Raisin in the Sun ★★ PG

Drama 1961 · US · BW · 122mins

Lorraine Hansberry's play opened on Broadway in 1959 and became a smash hit, showing white audiences what it was like to be black, working-class and living in a Chicago tenement. Within that social framework lies a melodrama of family life, built around a son's struggle to achieve some sort of status and independence away from his dominant mother and sister. For the film version, Daniel Petrie slavishly follows every last syllable of dialogue and stage direction. Though inherently and unavoidably theatrical, it should be viewed in the context of the developing civil rights movement. AT [VIDEO] DVD

Sidney Poitier *Walter Lee Younger* • Claudia McNeil *Lena Younger* • Ruby Dee *Ruth Younger* • Diana Sands *Beneatha Younger* • Ivan Dixon *Asagai* • John Fiedler *Mark Lindner* • Louis Gossett [Louis Gossett Jr] *George Murchison* ■ *Dir* Daniel Petrie • *Scr* Lorraine Hansberry, from her play

Raising a Riot ★★ U

Comedy 1955 · UK · Colour · 94mins

Left to cope with three unruly children during his wife's absence in Canada, naval officer Kenneth More takes his offspring to his father's converted windmill and institutes a strictly ordered regime. Of course, chaos ensues. An inconsequential comedy, kept moving by the polished More, but old-fashioned and rather flat. RK

Kenneth More *Tony* • Shelagh Fraser *Mary* • Mandy Miller *Anne* • Gary Billings *Peter* • Fusty Bentine *Fusty* • Ronald Squire *Grampy* • Olga Lindo *Aunt Maud* • Michael Bentine *Museum official* ■ *Dir* Wendy Toye • *Scr* Ian Dalrymple, Hugh Perceval, James Matthews, from the novel by Alfred Toombs

Raising Arizona ★★★★ 12

Comedy 1987 · US · Colour · 90mins

A delirious mix of slapstick, surrealism and sentimentality, this film by Joel and Ethan Coen remains one of their warmest, most complete works. Nicolas Cage and Holly Hunter are the couple who decide to kidnap one of a set of famous Arizona quintuplets when they discover they can't have children, only to find themselves pursued by the lone biker of the apocalypse. Cage and Hunter (in her breakthrough role) are superb, and there are winning supporting performances from John Goodman and William Forsythe as two cons on the run. However, in the end it is the dazzling invention of the Coen brothers that shines through. JF. Contains some violence and swearing. [VIDEO] DVD

Nicolas Cage *Hi McDonnough* • Holly Hunter *Edwina* • Trey Wilson *Nathan Arizona Sr* • John Goodman *Gale* • William Forsythe *Evelle* • Frances McDormand *Dot* ■ *Dir* Joel Coen • *Scr* Ethan Coen, Joel Coen

Raising Cain ★★★★ 15

Thriller 1992 · US · Colour · 87mins

After the mauling he received for his disastrous adaptation of *The Bonfire of the Vanities*, director Brian De Palma went back to the disturbing Hitchcockian territory he knows so well. The result was his best movie in years: a sly, witty thriller in which the tortuous plot takes a back seat to a virtuoso display of cinematic technique. John Lithgow, getting into the grisly, over-the-top spirit of the piece, plays a suspect in a series of kidnappings, Lolita Davidovich is his unfaithful wife, and there's solid support from Steven Bauer, Frances Sternhagen and Gregg Henry. JF. Contains swearing. [VIDEO] DVD

John Lithgow *Carter/Cain/Dr Nix/Josh/Margo* • Lolita Davidovich *Jenny* • Steven Bauer *Jack* • Frances Sternhagen *Dr Waldheim* • Gregg Henry *Lieutenant Terri* • Tom Bower *Sergeant Cally* ■ *Dir/Scr* Brian De Palma

Raising Helen ★★★ PG

Romantic comedy drama
2004 · US · Colour · 114mins

Kate Hudson stars as a hip, carefree Manhattan modeling agent who gains an instant family when her sister is killed in a car crash. The three children pose problems enough, but adding to Hudson's woes is her mumsy elder sister Joan Cusack, who resents the fact that the kids were not entrusted to her. Helen Mirren features as Hudson's boss, while John Corbett plays the pastor who's the potential love in her life. The material is saved from slush by spirited performances from Hudson and the ever-reliable Cusack. DA [VIDEO] DVD

Kate Hudson *Helen Harris* • John Corbett *Pastor Dan Parker* • Joan Cusack *Jenny Portman* • Hector Elizondo *Mickey Massey* • Helen Mirren *Dominique* • Hayden Panettiere *Audrey Davis* • Spencer Breslin *Henry Davis* • Abigail Breslin *Sarah Davis* • Felicity Huffman *Lindsay Davis* ■ *Dir* Garry Marshall • *Scr* Jack Amiel, Michael Begler, from a story by Patrick J Clifton, Beth Rigazio

Raising Heroes ★★ 18

Crime drama 1995 · US · Colour · 85mins

A refreshing, if not entirely successful attempt to subvert the formula action/buddy/thriller genre by giving it a gay twist. An all-male couple, in the process of adopting a child, have their lives turned upside down when one of them witnesses a Mob hit. Although painfully amateur in execution, this isn't just a limp-wristed *Lethal Weapon*, as director Douglas Langway's straight-to-video exercise delivers all the punch and predictability of the Hollywood mainstream but with its own fresh voice. It's just a shame the production values don't equal its often side-splitting hilarity. AJ. Contains swearing and violence. [VIDEO]

Troy Sostillio *Josh* • Henry White *Paul* • Greg Bodkin ■ *Dir* Douglas Langway • *Scr* Douglas Langway, Edmond Sorel, Henry White

Raising the Wind ★★★ U

Comedy 1961 · UK · Colour · 87mins

Leslie Phillips stars in this laboured but likeable Gerald Thomas comedy as a penniless music student whose talent for writing pop songs while drunk jeopardises his scholarship at a top classical academy until gruff tutor James Robertson-Justice unexpectedly comes to his rescue. These accomplished funnymen go through their usual paces with aplomb, but the film belongs to the delightful Esma Cannon as a deaf landlady, Kenneth Williams as a toffee-nosed swot and Sid James as the publisher behind Phillips's predicament. DP [VIDEO]

James Robertson-Justice *Sir Benjamin* • Leslie Phillips *Mervyn* • Sidney James *Sid* • Paul Massie *Malcolm* • Kenneth Williams *Harold* • Eric Barker *Morgan Rutherford* • Liz Fraser *Miranda* • Esma Cannon *Mrs Deevens* • Jim Dale *Bass trombone player* ■ *Dir* Gerald Thomas • *Scr* Bruce Montgomery

Raising Victor Vargas ★★★ 15

Drama 2002 · US/Fr · Colour · 84mins

Director Peter Sollet makes a creditable debut with this tale of first love in New York's Lower East Side. The result of extensive workshopping, the performances of the juvenile cast are touchingly authentic, with Victor Rasuk swaggering in the title role as he disses his siblings and seeks to impress neighbour Judy Marte, who is as much amused as seduced by his tactics. However, the standout is Altragracia Guzman, the grandmother who keeps threatening her charges with social services to keep them in line. The ending's a touch too cute, but the overall tone is one of restrained realism. DP [VIDEO] DVD

Victor Rasuk *Victor Vargas* • Judy Marte *"Juicy" Judy Ramirez* • Melonie Diaz *Melonie* • Altagracia Guzman *Grandma* • Silvestre Rasuk *Nino Vargas* • Krystal Rodriguez *Vicki Vargas* • Kevin Rivera *Harold* ■ *Dir* Peter Sollett • *Scr* Peter Sollett, from a story by Peter Sollett, Eva Vives

R

Raja Hindustani ★★ PG

Romantic drama
1996 · Ind · Colour · 170mins

This box-office smash from director Dharmesh Dharshan propelled Aamir Khan and Karishma Kapoor into superstardom. It's actually a rather slight, almost fairy-tale, affair, in which an impoverished taxi driver is kept from his wealthy beloved by the machinations of her grasping stepmother. However, it was Nadeem Sharavan's music and the beauty of the stars that pulled in the audiences rather than the prospect of narrative complexity or social commentary. DP. In Hindi with English subtitles. [VIDEO]

Aamir Khan *Raja Hindustani* • Karishma Kapoor *Aarti* • Suresh Oberoi *Sehgal* • Farida Jalal *Chachi* • Johnny Lever *Balwant Singh* ■ *Dir/Scr* Dharmesh Dharshan

The Rake's Progress ★★★ U

Drama 1945 · UK · BW · 115mins

The first film produced by Frank Launder and Sidney Gilliat for their

Individual Pictures company is a brisk comedy drama that, if not as elegant and sophisticated as it would have us believe, perfectly suits the debonair style of Rex Harrison. His exploits, first as a student at Oxford and then among the upper reaches of polite society, have a jaunty air and provide a nostalgic glimpse of Britain between the wars. Although some of its feel-good aura has diminished, the film still entertains. DP

Rex Harrison *Vivian Kenway* • Lilli Palmer *Rikki Krausner* • Godfrey Tearle *Colonel Kenway* • Griffith Jones *Sandy Duncan* ■ *Dir* Sidney Gilliat • *Scr* Frank Launder, Sidney Gilliat, from a story by Val Valentine

Rally 'round the Flag, Boys! ★★ PG

Comedy 1958 · US · Colour · 102mins

When the citizens of a nice, leafy town learn they are to have a nuclear missile silo built nearby, local busybody Joanne Woodward sends her husband, Paul Newman, off to lobby Washington. This forgotten satire of the Cold War era strains for importance but fails to generate much humour, apart from Joan Collins's performance as the town flirt. AT

Paul Newman *Harry Bannerman* • Joanne Woodward *Grace Bannerman* • Joan Collins *Angela Hoffa* • Jack Carson *Capt Hoxie* • Tuesday Weld *Comfort Goodpasture* ■ *Dir* Leo McCarey • *Scr* Leo McCarey, Claude Binyon, from the novel by Max Shulman

Rambling Rose ★★★ 15

Romantic comedy drama
1991 · US · Colour · 106mins

A neat, rather eccentric movie that shines for a while but ends up being rather aptly named. Laura Dern is very good as the sexually precocious girl with a big heart who arrives to work for a rich Southern family surrounded by 1930s' poverty. Director Martha Coolidge does play the "whale I do deeclare" card a mite too often, but the movie is saved from parody by Robert Duvall's consummate performance as the clan's kindly patriarch. Dern and her real-life mother Diane Ladd were both rewarded with Oscar nominations. SH DVD

Laura Dern *Rose* • Robert Duvall *Daddy Hillyer* • Diane Ladd *Mother Hillyer* • Lukas Haas *Buddy Hillyer* • John Heard *Willcox "Buddy" Hillyer* • Kevin Conway *Doctor Martinson* • Robert Burke *Police Chief Dave Wilkie* • Lisa Jakub *Doll Hillyer* ■ *Dir* Martha Coolidge • *Scr* Calder Willingham, from his novel

Rambo: First Blood, Part II ★★★ 15

Action drama 1985 · US · Colour · 91mins

This explosive action sequel to 1982's *First Blood* is entertaining, if implausible. Sylvester Stallone flexes his muscles for some cartoon-like heroics, rescuing American prisoners in Vietnam but discovering that he's considered as expendable as the men he's trying to save. All this might be thought laughable, but it comes across as deadly serious and, therefore, rather scary. A bit of a come-down for James Cameron after directing the previous year's massive sleeper hit, *The Terminator*. TH. Contains violence and swearing. DVD

Sylvester Stallone *John Rambo* • Richard Crenna *Colonel Trautman* • Charles Napier *Marshall Murdock* • Steven Berkoff *Lieutenant Podovsky* • Julia Nickson [Julia Nickson-Soul] *Co Bao* ■ *Dir* George Pan Cosmatos • *Scr* Sylvester Stallone, James Cameron, from a story by Kevin Jarre, from characters created by David Morrell

Rambo III ★★ 18

Action drama 1988 · US · Colour · 97mins

Sylvester Stallone transforms from slightly confused loner to the Free World's white knight. Reluctantly giving up his blissfully mystic life in Thailand (hilariously parodied in *Hot Shots! Part Deux*) to go on one more mission, he seemingly takes on the entire Soviet army in Afghanistan when his old boss (Richard Crenna) is taken prisoner. There's cartoon action by the bucketful, but the mindless celebration of carnage leaves a nasty taste in the mouth. JF. Contains violence and swearing. DVD

Sylvester Stallone *John Rambo* • Richard Crenna *Colonel Trautman* • Marc de Jonge *Colonel Zaysen* • Kurtwood Smith *Griggs* • Spiros Focas *Masoud* ■ *Dir* Peter MacDonald • *Scr* Sylvester Stallone, Sheldon Lettich, from characters created by David Morrell

Rampage ★★

Adventure 1963 · US · Colour · 94mins

One of Robert Mitchum's lesser movies, a hunting saga involving the search for an elusive big cat, with Elsa Martinelli providing the human quarry. Mitchum virtually sleepwalks through the picture, as does his co-star Jack Hawkins, who has to sweat a lot and go mad when his mistress Martinelli switches her affections. Claiming to be set in Malaya, it was actually shot in Hawaii and at the San Diego zoo. Sabu makes his penultimate screen appearance. AT

Robert Mitchum *Harry Stanton* • Elsa Martinelli *Anna* • Jack Hawkins *Otto Abbot* • Sabu *Talib* • Cely Carrillo *Chep* • Emile Genest *Schelling* • Stefan Schnabel *Sakai chief* ■ *Dir* Phil Karlson • *Scr* Robert I Holt, Marguerite Roberts, from the novel by Alan Caillou

Rampage ★★ 18

Crime drama 1987 · US · Colour · 96mins

This is a story that actually seems to advocate the application of the death penalty – in some cases. Michael Biehn is a prosecutor who desperately wants to get an obviously psychotic killer (Alex McArthur) into the electric chair. Despite his flair for controversy, director William Friedkin doesn't address the complexities of the issue of legal insanity, which forms the basis of the killer's defence. ST

Michael Biehn *Anthony Fraser* • Alex McArthur *Charles Reece* • Nicholas Campbell *Albert Morse* • Deborah Van Valkenburgh *Kate Fraser* ■ *Dir* William Friedkin • *Scr* William Friedkin, from the novel by William P Wood

Ramparts of Clay ★★★

Drama 1969 · Fr/Alg · Colour · 83mins

Jean-Louis Bertucelli made his feature debut with this adaptation of Jean Duvignaud's book, *Chebika*. By filming in almost documentary fashion, Bertucelli achieves a rare immediacy that is underscored by the personal liberation of Leila Schenna, the young Tunisian girl who comes to appreciate the harsh realities of so-called civilisation when the owner of a stone quarry calls in the troops to confront his striking workers. DP. In French and Arabic with English subtitles.

Leila Schenna *Rima* ■ *Dir* Jean-Louis Bertucelli • *Scr* Jean Duvignaud, from his book *Chebika (Change at Shebika)* • *Cinematographer* Andréas Winding

Ramrod ★★★ U

Western 1947 · US · BW · 94mins

War on the range, as sultry ranch owner Veronica Lake stakes her personal claim to land owned by her weak-willed father Charlie Ruggles, who's selling out to baddie Preston Foster. Joel McCrea's the titular ramrod (or ranch foreman) in this tense and violent western directed by Lake's then husband, the talented Andre De Toth. The stark black-and-white photography, the presence of disenfranchised characters and Lake's *femme fatale*-like portrayal lend this the look of a western *film noir*. TS

Veronica Lake *Connie Dickason* • Joel McCrea *Dave Nash* • Ian MacDonald *Walt Shipley* • Charles Ruggles *Ben Dickason* • Preston Foster *Frank Ivey* • Arleen Whelan *Rose* • Lloyd Bridges *Red Cates* ■ *Dir* Andre De Toth • *Scr* Jack Moffitt, Graham Baker, Cecile Kramer, from a story by Luke Short

Ran ★★★★★ 15

Epic drama 1985 · Jpn/Fr · Colour · 153mins

Having reworked *Macbeth* in *Throne of Blood*, Akira Kurosawa tackled another Shakespearean tragedy, *King Lear*, in this majestic epic, in which a ruler's decision to partition his realm between his sons plunges his realm into civil war. There is so much to admire here, but special mention must be made of Kurosawa's genius as a storyteller and his masterly movement of the camera (particularly in the stunning battle sequences), the remarkable performances of Tatsuya Nakadai as the repentant monarch and Mieko Harada as his Machiavellian daughter-in-law, and the sumptuous use of colour and period detail by production designers Yoshiro and Shinobu Muraki. A true classic. DP. In Japanese with English subtitles. DVD

Tatsuya Nakadai *Lord Hidetora* • Akira Terao *Taro* • Jinpachi Nezu *Jiro* • Daisuke Ryu *Saburo* • Mieko Harada *Lady Kaede* • Peter *Kyoami The Fool* • Hisashi Igawa *Kurogane* • Masayuki Yui *Tango* • Yoshiko Miyazaki *Lady Sué* ■ *Dir* Akira Kurosawa • *Scr* Akira Kurosawa, Hideo Oguni, Masato Ide, from the play *King Lear* by William Shakespeare

Rancho Deluxe ★★★ 15

Comedy western 1975 · US · Colour · 89mins

Not so much a modern buddy-buddy western as a younger generation nose-thumbing at the traditions of the range, with Jeff Bridges and Sam Waterston as disdainful young cattle rustlers who rightly end up behind bars but for the wrong reasons. Director Frank Perry's overwrought style is tightly reined in this time to make the most of the humour and the heroes, while cowboy specialist Thomas McGuane's screenplay is a joy. TH. Contains swearing and nudity.

Jeff Bridges *Jack McKee* • Sam Waterston *Cecil Colson* • Elizabeth Ashley *Cora Brown* • Charlene Dallas *Laura Beige* • Clifton James *John Brown* • Slim Pickens *Henry Beige* • Harry Dean Stanton *Curt* ■ *Dir* Frank Perry • *Scr* Thomas McGuane

Rancho Notorious ★★★ PG

Western 1952 · US · Colour · 85mins

This ridiculously over-the-top western has developed quite a cult following. There is pleasure to be had from watching Marlene Dietrich past her prime, running a hole in the wall called "Chuck-a-Luck" and being romanced by louche Mel Ferrer. But director Fritz Lang's hand falls heavy on the proceedings, and the cheap studio settings don't help. The dialogue occasionally sparkles and writer Daniel Taradash knows how to create and embellish a legend. TS DVD

Marlene Dietrich *Altar Keane* • Arthur Kennedy *Vern Haskell* • Mel Ferrer *Frenchy Fairmont* • Gloria Henry *Beth* • William Frawley *Baldy Gunder* • Jack Elam *Geary* • George Reeves *Wilson* ■ *Dir* Fritz Lang • *Scr* Daniel Taradash, from the story *Gunsight Whitman* by Sylvia Richards

Rancid Aluminium ★ 18

Comedy thriller 1999 · UK · Colour · 87mins

James Hawes brings his own cult novel to the screen with unengaging characters and incoherent plotting to match the unappetising title. Rhys Ifans is so preoccupied with his low sperm count and broody girlfriend (Sadie Frost), he's unsuspicious when scheming buddy Joseph Fiennes embroils them in a deadly partnership with a pair of cartoonish Russian gangsters (Steven Berkoff and Tara FitzGerald). This coarse, cluttered caper has lots of nudity and sex but little wit. AME. Contains violence, swearing, drug abuse. DVD

Joseph Fiennes *Sean Deeny* • Rhys Ifans *Pete Thompson* • Tara FitzGerald *Masha* • Sadie Frost *Sarah* • Steven Berkoff *Mr Kant* • Keith Allen *Dr Jones* • Dani Behr *Charlie* • Andrew Howard *Trevor* ■ *Dir* Ed Thomas • *Scr* James Hawes, from his novel

Random Harvest ★★★★ U

Romance 1942 · US · BW · 126mins

This is, rightly, one of the best-loved and best-remembered movies of all time, teaming two of MGM's most romantic stars, Ronald Colman and Greer Garson, in a superb James Hilton story. Genuinely moving under Mervyn LeRoy's masterly direction, and produced with all the wartime gloss MGM could muster, this film regularly seduces generation after cynical generation. If you're not totally hooked when Colman doesn't return to Garson after his trip to Liverpool, you've no soul. This is clever, gracious and superbly satisfying. TS

Ronald Colman *Charles Rainier* • Greer Garson *Paula* • Philip Dorn *Dr Jonathan Benet* • Susan Peters *Kitty* • Reginald Owen *Biffer* • Henry Travers *Dr Sims* • Edmund Gwenn *Prime Minister* • Margaret Wycherly *Mrs Deventer* ■ *Dir* Mervyn LeRoy • *Scr* Claudine West, George Froeschel, Arthur Wimperis, from the novel by James Hilton

Random Hearts ★★★ 15

Romantic drama
1999 · US · Colour · 128mins

When Washington cop Harrison Ford and Republican congresswoman Kristin Scott Thomas discover that their respective spouses have died together in a plane crash, the couple are drawn together over the realisation that their partners were having an affair. Sydney Pollack directs with real skill, convincingly portraying the emotional complications of middle-aged passion, and is aided by the marvellous performances of Ford and Scott Thomas, though the action sequences often seem out of tune with the romance. TH. Contains violence, swearing and a sex scene. DVD

Harrison Ford *Dutch Van Den Broeck* • Kristin Scott Thomas *Kay Chandler* • Charles S Dutton *Alcee* • Bonnie Hunt *Wendy Judd* • Dennis Haysbert *Detective George Beaufort* • Sydney Pollack *Carl Broman* • Peter Coyote *Cullen Chandler* • M Emmet Walsh *Bartender at Billy's* ■ *Dir* Sydney Pollack • *Scr* Kurt Luedtke, from the novel by Warren Adler

Randy Rides Alone ★★ U

Western 1934 · US · BW · 52mins

One of the more entertaining of John Wayne's Monogram Studio westerns, featuring not only the Duke singing (well, pretending to: he's dubbed by cowboy crooner Smith Ballew) but also starting on a chilling note – Wayne rides into a deserted town and finds a saloon full of dead men. The mystery is quite well sustained for what is no more than a B-western. TS DVD

John Wayne *Randy Bowers* • Alberta Vaughn *Sally Rogers* • George "Gabby" Hayes *Matt the Mute/Marvin Black* • Yakima Canutt *Spike* • Earl Dwire *Sheriff* ■ *Dir* Harry Fraser • *Scr* Lindsley Parsons, from his story

Rangeela ★★★ U

Drama 1995 · Ind · Colour · 149mins

A former tennis pro who followed his producer father and director uncle to Bollywood, Aamir Khan has made dozens of movies. Capable of a greater psychological depth than many of his contemporaries, he demonstrates his famed sense of comic timing in this romantic triangle, in which he plays a ticket tout who competes for the affections of a wannabe actress with the star who can grant her wishes. A typical mix of music and melodrama. DP. In Hindi with English subtitles. [video]

Jackie Shroff *Rajkamal* • Aamir Khan *Muna* • Urmila Matondkar *Mili* • Gulshan Grover *Steven Grover* ■ *Dir* Ram Gopal Varma

Ransom! ★★★

Crime drama 1956 · US · BW · 109mins

During the 1950s Glenn Ford averaged three films a year. Mainly westerns and thrillers, they gave the stern-faced star angst-ridden roles on both sides of the law. Here he is in trouble as the wealthy father of a boy who has been kidnapped. In a novel idea for the period, he contacts the abductors on television, offering the ransom for their capture and threatening to kill them if they harm his son. Originally made for television, it's the inspiration for Mel Gibson's 1996 film. BB

Glenn Ford *David G Stannard* • Donna Reed *Edith Stannard* • Leslie Nielsen *Charlie Telfer* • Juano Hernandez *Jesse Chapman* • Robert Keith (1) *Chief Jim Backett* • Mabel Albertson *Mrs Partridge* ■ *Dir* Alex Segal • *Scr* Cyril Hume, Richard Maibaum

Ransom ★ PG

Action drama 1975 · UK · Colour · 89mins

This lamely directed and badly written drama about international terrorism is a rare dud from Sean Connery. He plays a security chief tackling a ransom demand for a kidnapped British ambassador while also dealing with a hijacked plane. Confusion reigns for most of the time, and that's just among the cast – so the audience will have virtually no chance of following the plot. AT [video]

Sean Connery *Nils Tahlvik* • Ian McShane *Petrie* • Norman Bristow *Captain Denver* • John Cording *Bert* • Robert Harris *Gerald Palmer* • Isabel Dean *Mrs Palmer* ■ *Dir* Casper Wrede • *Scr* Paul Wheeler

Ransom ★★★ 18

Action thriller 1996 · US · Colour · 116mins

In this entertaining remake of a 1956 Glenn Ford thriller, Mel Gibson stars as a maverick tycoon who must decide whether to pay a $2 million ransom for his kidnapped son or take the law into his own hands. There are no prizes for guessing the *Die Hard*-style avenue Gibson takes, but his method of action is an interesting one. The film suffers overall under Ron Howard's unusually starchy direction and Rene Russo is wasted as Gibson's concerned wife, but Gary Sinise gives his villainous role a few wry twists. AJ [video] DVD

Mel Gibson *Tom Mullen* • Rene Russo *Kate Mullen* • Gary Sinise *Jimmy Shaker* • Brawley Nolte *Sean Mullen* • Delroy Lindo *Agent Lonnie Hawkins* • Lili Taylor *Maris Connor* • Liev Schreiber *Clark Barnes* ■ *Dir* Ron Howard • *Scr* Richard Price, Alexander Ignon, from the 1956 film

Ransom for a Dead Man ★★★ PG

Detective mystery
1971 · US · Colour · 91mins

Four years after he first played Lieutenant Columbo in the TV movie *Prescription: Murder*, Peter Falk reprised the role in this pilot for the long-running TV series (which was released theatrically in the UK). Based on a story by William Link and Richard Levinson, who created the original character, the tale sees the perceptive detective on the trail of a lawyer who has passed off her rich husband's murder as a kidnap plot. Lee Grant was rewarded with an Emmy nomination for her bravura performance as the lawyer, and Falk is typically sly as he seemingly stumbles towards the solution. DP [video]

Peter Falk *Lieutenant Columbo* • Lee Grant *Leslie Williams* • John Fink *Michael Clarke* • Harold Gould *Carlson* • Patricia Mattick *Margaret Williams* ■ *Dir* Richard Irving • *Scr* Dean Hargrove, from a story by Richard Levinson, William Link

Rapa Nui ★ 12

Drama 1994 · US · Colour · 102mins

The *moai*, the huge stone faces that dominate the landscape of Easter Island, make a hugely tempting topic for a film-maker. How did they get there? Who made them? What purpose did they serve? Kevin Reynolds succumbed to the temptation of the tale, but the result is an insulting concoction. Crass and ridiculous. DP. Contains violence and nudity. [video]

Jason Scott Lee *Noro* • Esai Morales *Make* • Sandrine Holt *Ramana* • Emilio Tuki Hito *Messenger* • Gordon Hatfield *Riro* • Faenza Reuben *Heke* ■ *Dir* Kevin Reynolds • *Scr* Tim Rose Price, Kevin Reynolds, from a story by Reynolds

The Rape of Aphrodite ★★★

Drama 1985 · Cyp · Colour · 150mins

This sweeping study of 30 years of the country's turbulent history was one of the first Cypriot films to attract international attention. Costas Timvios stars as a former member of the Greek Cypriot terrorist group EOKA, who dedicates his life to searching for his wife and child who vanished during the 1974 Turkish invasion that resulted in the island being partitioned. It's obviously an emotive story and the film is full of dramatic incident and provocative insight, but director Andreas Pantzis doesn't always keep far enough back from his subject. DP. In Greek with English subtitles.

Costas Timvios *Evagoras* • Thalia Argiriou *Aphrodite* • Ilias Aletras *Taxi driver* ■ *Dir/Scr* Andreas Pantzis

The Rape of Richard Beck ★★★★ 18

Drama 1985 · US · Colour · 91mins

Director Karen Arthur has built a reputation for producing powerful films about women who draw on hidden resources to overcome all manner of ailments and abuses. That's why she was the ideal choice for this compelling TV movie in which macho cop Richard Crenna comes to appreciate the hell female sexual assault victims go through when he himself is raped. Crenna won an Emmy for his wonderfully aware performance. DP. Contains violence. [video]

Richard Crenna *Richard Beck* • Meredith Baxter Birney [Meredith Baxter] *Barbara McKay* • Pat Hingle *Chappy Beck* • Frances Lee McCain *Caroline Beck* • Cotter Smith *Lieutenant Hugo* • George Dzundza *Blastig* ■ *Dir* Karen Arthur • *Scr* James G Hirsch

Rapid Fire ★★★ 18

Martial arts thriller
1992 · US · Colour · 91mins

Brandon Lee may have lacked the martial arts grace of his father, but there was no denying his charisma, and this serviceable action thriller offered him the opportunity to make the transition from straight-to-video star to a man with genuine box-office appeal. There's not much subtlety involved in this story of a college student who finds himself on the run from villainous Nick Mancuso, but the production values are a notch above the usual B-movie action adventures. JF. Contains swearing, sex scenes and nudity. [video] DVD

Brandon Lee *Jake Lo* • Powers Boothe *Mace Ryan* • Nick Mancuso *Antonio Serrano* • Raymond J Barry *Agent Stuart* • Kate Hodge *Karla Withers* • Ma Tzi *Kinman Tau* ■ *Dir* Dwight H Little • *Scr* Alan McElroy, from the story by Cindy Cirile, Alan McElroy

Rappin' ★ PG

Drama 1985 · US · Colour · 88mins

One of the many exploitation films released in the aftermath of the rap, break-dancing and hip-hop explosion, in which ex-con Mario Van Peebles takes on a crooked property baron who has recruited a gang to bully and evict the tenants from a run-down Pittsburgh ghetto. Van Peebles puts his rhyming skills to good use in this absurdly unrealistic social thriller teeming with offensive action and ludicrous stereotypes. AJ [video]

Mario Van Peebles *John Hood* • Tasia Valenza *Dixie* • Charles Flohe *Duane* • Leo O'Brien *Allan* • Eriq La Salle *Ice* • Richie Abanes *Richie* ■ *Dir* Joel Silberg • *Scr* Robert Litz, Adam Friedman

The Rapture ★★★ 18

Drama 1991 · US · Colour · 96mins

Mimi Rogers reminds us what a fine actress she can be with a bravura performance as a bored LA telephone operator and part-time swinger who joins a fundamentalist religious movement that believes the end of the world is nigh. Michael Tolkin makes a striking directorial debut with this admittedly imperfect but also ambitious, challenging and intelligent offering that perfectly captures the conspiratorial creepiness of such zealous religious sects. RS [video]

Mimi Rogers *Sharon* • David Duchovny *Randy* • Patrick Bauchau *Vic* • Kimberly Cullum *Mary* • Will Patton *Sheriff Foster* • Terri Hanauer *Paula* ■ *Dir/Scr* Michael Tolkin

The Rare Breed ★★★ U

Western 1966 · US · Colour · 92mins

In this warm-hearted, sprawling western, widow Maureen O'Hara imports a prize Hereford bull to the Old West for breeding purposes. The pleasure's really in watching the languid by-play between O'Hara, lovable drifter James Stewart and rugged cattle baron Brian Keith, and enjoying a supporting cast that looks as if it stepped out of a John Ford movie. Director Andrew V McLaglen brings out the best in his actors, and if it is all a bit jovial and sub-Ford, well, that's no bad thing. TS DVD

James Stewart *Sam Burnett* • Maureen O'Hara *Martha Price* • Brian Keith *Alexander Bowen* • Juliet Mills *Hilary Price* • Don Galloway *Jamie Bowen* • David Brian *Charles Ellsworth* • Jack Elam *Deke Simons* ■ *Dir* Andrew V McLaglen • *Scr* Ric Hardman

A Rare Breed ★

Drama 1981 · US · Colour · 94mins

A horse-racing story, filmed in 1981 but left in the stables until 1984. The story is really *National Velvet* in different silks, about a teenage girl who falls in love with the horse which becomes a champion racer and is then kidnapped for ransom, much like Shergar. Set in Italy but shot in North Carolina, it can be safely recommended to horse fanciers. AT

George Kennedy *Nathan Hill* • Forrest Tucker *Jess Cutler* • Tracy Vaccaro *Anne Cutler* • Tom Hallick *Luigi Nelson* ■ *Dir* David Nelson • *Scr* Garner Simmons, from a story by Stanley S Canter

Rashomon ★★★★★ 12

Drama 1950 · Jpn · BW · 86mins

Showered with prizes at festivals worldwide, this was the film that introduced western audiences to Japanese cinema. Exploring the relativity of truth, Akira Kurosawa presents four equally credible accounts of the woodland encounter between a wealthy married couple and a bandit that results in the husband's death. The endlessly moving camera, the stylised composition of the shots and the subtly shifting performances enable Kurosawa to challenge the notion that the camera never lies. Machiko Kyo as the wife and Toshiro Mifune as the bandit are superb, but it's Kurosawa's control that makes this exercise in emphasis and atmosphere so mesmerising. Hollywood remade this as *The Outrage* in 1964, starring Paul Newman. DP. In Japanese with English subtitles. [video] DVD

Toshiro Mifune *Tajomaru* • Machiko Kyo *Masago* • Masayuki Mori *Takehiro* • Takashi Shimura *Firewood dealer* • Minoru Chiaki *Priest* ■ *Dir* Akira Kurosawa • *Scr* Shinobu Hashimoto, Akira Kurosawa, from the short story *Yabu no Naka* and the novel *Rasho-Mon* by Ryunosuke Akutagawa

Rasputin ★★★★ 15

Biographical drama
1996 · US · Colour · 100mins

An Emmy and Golden Globe-winning biopic made for cable by HBO. As far from staid costume television drama as you can get, Alan Rickman is dangerously dynamic as the Mad Monk and spiritual adviser to Russia's royals on the brink of dissolution. He's well matched by Greta Scacchi as Tsarina Alexandra and Ian McKellen as Tsar Nicholas II. This was a huge hit Stateside and while there are historical inaccuracies, it captures the flavour of this often told tale of the enigmatic royals confronting the onset of revolution. LH [video] DVD

Alan Rickman *Rasputin* • Greta Scacchi *Tsarina Alexandra* • Ian McKellen *Tsar Nicholas* • David Warner *Dr Botkin* • John Wood *Stolypin* • James Frain *Prince Yussoupov* ■ *Dir* Uli Edel • *Scr* Peter Pruce

Rasputin and the Empress ★★

Historical drama 1932 · US · BW · 93mins

A trio of Barrymores is on display: Lionel as the demonic monk, Ethel as the tsarina and John as the nobleman who puts an end to Rasputin's sinister influence. Ethel had not made a picture for 13 years, and, in an effort to please her, Louis B Mayer hired Charles Brabin, who immediately became embroiled in sibling rivalry and John's excessive drinking. After a month of delays, Brabin was replaced by Richard Boleslawski. The resulting overlong stodge caused fireworks at MGM's legal department when surviving members of Russia's aristocracy claimed they were misrepresented in the film. AT

John Barrymore *Prince Paul Chegodieff* • Ethel Barrymore *Empress Alexandra* • Lionel Barrymore *Rasputin* • Ralph Morgan *Emperor Nikolai* • Diana Wynyard *Natasha* • Tad Alexander *Alexis* • C Henry Gordon *Grand Duke Igor* ■ *Dir* Richard Boleslawski • *Scr* Charles MacArthur

Rasputin, the Mad Monk ★★★ 15

Horror 1965 · UK · Colour · 87mins

Christopher Lee's commanding presence is splendidly suited to his role here as the lecherous mystic who dominated the Romanov court of pre-revolutionary Russia and carved a debauched path through its ladies-in-waiting. But, although it was an

R

intriguing change of pace for Hammer, with stylish studio regular Barbara Shelley present and correct as a different sort of scream queen, the tale eventually degenerates into wild-eyed hysteria. TH DVD

Christopher Lee *Rasputin* • Barbara Shelley *Sonia* • Richard Pasco *Dr Zargo* • Francis Matthews *Ivan* • Suzan Farmer *Vanessa* • Joss Ackland *Bishop* ■ *Dir* Don Sharp • *Scr* John Elder [Anthony Hinds]

Rat ★★★ PG

Fantasy comedy
2000 · UK/US · Colour · 87mins

In this barbed Irish fantasy, Dubliner Pete Postlethwaite metamorphoses into a rodent. Had the focus remained on the socio-political circumstances that wrought this astonishing transformation, the film might have been even sharper. But there's still much to amuse and contemplate, as journalist David Wilmot tempts Imelda Staunton into exploiting her husband's unexpected celebrity. Slight, but mischievously satirical. DP DVD

Imelda Staunton *Conchita Flynn* • Pete Postlethwaite *Hubert Flynn* • David Wilmot *Phelim Spratt* • Frank Kelly *Uncle Matt* • Ed Byrne *Rudolph* • Geoffrey Palmer *Doctor* ■ *Dir* Steve Barron • *Scr* Wesley Burrowes

The Rat Pack ★★★ 15

Biographical drama
1998 · US · Colour · 114mins

Ray Liotta as Frank Sinatra, Joe Mantegna as Dean Martin, Don Cheadle as Sammy Davis Jr and Angus MacFadyen as Peter Lawford. You don't really believe it's them until they go on stage at one of JFK's fundraisers and sing *High Hopes* and the movie snaps into gear. The pulse of the era is beautifully evoked in this TV film that explores Sinatra's twin links to the Mob and to Jack and Robert Kennedy. AT DVD

Ray Liotta *Frank Sinatra* • Joe Mantegna *Dean Martin* • Don Cheadle *Sammy Davis Jr* • Angus MacFadyen *Peter Lawford* • William L Petersen *John F Kennedy* • Zeljko Ivanek *Bobby Kennedy* • Bobby Slayton *Joey Bishop* ■ *Dir* Rob Cohen • *Scr* Kario Salem

Rat Pfink a Boo Boo ★★ 18

Spoof comedy thriller
1965 · US · BW · 69mins

A typically incoherent effort from cult trash film maker Ray Dennis Steckler. Steckler intended this film as a "roughie" (a sexploitation picture with violence) in which hoodlums kidnap the girlfriend (Steckler's real-life wife Carolyn Brandt) of rock singer Vin Saxon (alias real-life rock singer Ron Haydock). This, the first section of the film, is an adequate melodrama. Then, inexplicably, Saxon and his gardener (Titus Moede) turn into comic-book superheroes and the plot disentegrates into a desperately unfunny spoof of *Batman*. Famously, the title came about when "Rat Pfink and Boo Boo" was accidentally misspelled. DM

Vin Saxon [Ron Haydock] *Lonnie Lord/Rat Pfink* • Titus Moede *Titus Twimbly/Boo Boo* • Carolyn Brandt *Cee Bee Beaumont* • George Caldwell *Linc* • Mike Kannon *Hammer* • James Bowie *Benjie* ■ *Dir* Ray Dennis Steckler • *Scr* Ronald Haydock, from a story by Ray Dennis Steckler

The Rat Race ★★

Comedy 1960 · US · Colour · 105mins

Saxophone player Tony Curtis arrives from the sticks in New York, moves into a run-down tenement boarding house, and tries to make a career in the sleazy nightclub run by Don Rickles. He's just an inch away from crime and a bit closer to Debbie Reynolds, a dance-hall "hostess". This is Hollywood's idea of what a Beat movie should be like; the settings are picturesquely drab and Elmer Bernstein contributes a racy score but Curtis and Reynolds are much too clean-looking to be convincing. AT

Tony Curtis *Peter Hammond Jr* • Debbie Reynolds *Peggy Brown* • Jack Oakie *Mac* • Kay Medford *Soda* • Don Rickles *Nellie* • Joe Bushkin *Frankie* ■ *Dir* Robert Mulligan • *Scr* Garson Kanin, from his play

Rat Race ★★★ 12

Comedy 2001 · US/Can · Colour · 107mins

This is an infectiously silly comedy packed with celebrities and gags. John Cleese – complete with the maddest set of dentures ever seen on film – is the billionaire casino owner who decides to give his high-rolling gamblers something unusual to bet on: the outcome of a race from Las Vegas to a locker a few hundred miles away in New Mexico that just happens to contain $2 million. A group of ordinary people are given the chance to get their hands on the loot – the only rule being that whoever gets there first, gets the cash. A fun, old-fashioned chase movie. JB DVD

Whoopi Goldberg *Vera Baker* • John Cleese *Donald Sinclair* • Cuba Gooding Jr *Owen Templeton* • Rowan Atkinson *Enrico Pollini* • Jon Lovitz *Randy Pear* • Kathy Najimy *Beverly Pear* • Amy Smart *Tracy Faucet* ■ *Dir* Jerry Zucker • *Scr* Andy Breckman

Rat-Trap ★★★

Drama 1981 · Ind · Colour · 121mins

Considered by some critics to be the legitimate heir to Satyajit Ray, Adoor Gopalakrishnan concedes there is an autobiographical element to this weighty political drama, focusing on the slow emergence of the Kerala region of south-western India. With every action and gesture of his performance laced with symbolism, Karamana is compelling as the increasingly paranoid head of a redundant family of rent collectors, caught between the inevitable collapse of the traditional order and the caprices of his three sisters. DP. In Malayalam with English subtitles.

Karamana *Unni* • Sarada *Rajamma* • Jalaja *Sridevi* • Rajam K Nair *Janamma* ■ *Dir/Scr* Adoor Gopalakrishnan

Ratboy ★★ PG

Drama 1986 · US · Colour · 99mins

Sondra Locke directs and stars in yet another tale of an exploited misfit. This time it's a half boy, half rat creature (SL Baird) and again we have the archetypal outsider being exposed and promoted as a weird commercial fairground attraction. Plucked from the comfort of his Hollywood rubbish dump into a media circus, Ratboy is "rescued" by Locke, who has her own plans to exploit her protégé. LH

Sondra Locke *Nikki Morrison* • Robert Townsend *Manny* • Christopher Hewett *Acting coach* • Larry Hankin *Jewell* • Sydney Lassick *"Dial-a-Prayer"* • SL Baird *Ratboy* ■ *Dir* Sondra Locke • *Scr* Rob Thompson

Ratcatcher ★★★★ 15

Drama 1999 · UK · Colour · 89mins

Lynne Ramsay made her feature debut with this unsentimental portrait of growing up in Glasgow in the 1970s. Achieving a lyrical realism that often recalls Jean Vigo's 1934 classic *L'Atalante*, Ramsay manages to turn a rundown housing estate at the height of a refuse strike into fertile ground for the imagination of 12-year-old William Eadie (giving a remarkably natural performance), as a neglected scallywag forced to bear the burden of accidentally drowning his friend in the canal. Assured and affecting. DP. Contains swearing, nudity. DVD

William Eadie *James* • Tommy Flanagan *Da* • Mandy Matthews *Ma* • Michelle Stewart *Ellen* • Lynne Ramsay Jr *Anne Marie* • Leanne Mullen *Margaret Anne* • John Miller *Kenny* ■ *Dir/Scr* Lynne Ramsay

Rated X ★★ 18

Biographical drama
2000 · US · Colour · 109mins

Emilio Estevez's fact-mangling odyssey through the sleazy showbiz excesses of the 1970s has all the class and conviction of a teleplay. Yet, there's a ghoulish fascination in watching him and brother Charlie Sheen portray Jim and Artie Mitchell, the feuding, drug-addled siblings who transformed the American porn industry with their "sophisticated" soft core. This untidy film leaves you hoping the story will eventually be revisited by a steadier hand. DP DVD

Charlie Sheen *Artie Mitchell* • Emilio Estevez *Jim Mitchell* • Tracy Hutson *Marilyn Chambers* • Megan Ward *Meredith* • Terry O'Quinn *JR Mitchell* • Danielle Brett *Adrienne* • Nicole de Boer *Karen Mitchell* ■ *Dir* Emilio Estevez • *Scr* David Hollander, Anne Meredith, Norman Snider, from the non-fiction book *X-Rated: The Mitchell Brothers, a True Story of Sex, Money and Death* by David McCumber

The Rats ★★★

Drama 1955 · W Ger · BW · 97mins

Hollywood exile and *film noir* expert Robert Siodmak returned to his native Germany to make this drama about a refugee from the East who gives her newborn baby to a childless woman from the West. As an allegory, it may now seem exceptionally crude but in 1955, when the still bombed-out Berlin was divided into four militarised zones, it carried enormous weight – indeed, the film won the main prize at the Berlin Film Festival. AT. A German language film.

Curt Jurgens *Bruno Mechelke* • Maria Schell *Pauline Karka* • Heidemarie Hatheyer *Anna John* • Gustav Knuth *Karl John* ■ *Dir* Robert Siodmak • *Scr* Jochen Huth, from a play by Gerhart Hauptmann

A Rat's Tale ★★

Fantasy adventure
1998 · US/Ger · Colour · 90mins

This is an unusual story for younger children, made all the more intriguing by the marionettes from Germany's celebrated Augsburger Puppet Theatre. Our hero is Monty Mad-Rat Jr, an artist romancing politician's daughter Isabella Noble-Rat, who allies with Jean-Paul Canalligator to prevent a property developer from poisoning their underground metropolis. Lauren Hutton, Beverly D'Angelo and Jerry Stiller play sporting foils to the puppets, which aren't exactly cuddly, but are full of character. DP

Beverly D'Angelo *Mrs Dollart* • Jerry Stiller *Professor Plumpingham* • Josef Ostendorf *Lou Dollart* • Lauren Hutton *Evelyn Jellybelly* • Steffen Wink *Assistant Nick McRafferty* • Andreas Herder *Assistant Tom O'Dooley* • Lynsey Bartilson *Isabella Noble-Rat* • Donald Arthur *John-Paul Canalligator* ■ *Dir* Michael F Huse • *Scr* Werner Morgenrath, Peter Scheerbaum, from the book by Tor Seidler

Rattle of a Simple Man ★★ 15

Comedy drama 1964 · UK · BW · 91mins

Harry H Corbett strays into Norman Wisdom territory in this disappointing comedy from the husband-and-wife team of Sydney and Muriel Box. In adapting his play for the big screen, Charles Dyer so overdoes the pathos that what few laughs there are seem rather cruel and out of place. As the innocent following his football team to Wembley, Corbett is unconvincingly wide-eyed, although his scenes with prostitute Diane Cilento have a certain sweetness about them. DP

Harry H Corbett *Percy Winthram* • Diane Cilento *Cyrenne* • Thora Hird *Mrs Winthram* • Michael Medwin *Ginger* • Charles Dyer *Chalky* • Hugh Futcher *Ozzie* • Brian Wilde *Fred* ■ *Dir* Muriel Box • *Scr* Charles Dyer, from his play

The Raven ★★★★ 15

Horror 1935 · US · BW · 58mins

The second of Universal's horror vehicles to co-star Bela Lugosi and Boris Karloff is an unusually sadistic slice of shock from the Golden Age of *Grand Guignol*. Lugosi plays a crazed surgeon obsessed with the works of Edgar Allan Poe, who builds a dungeon with torture devices inspired by the writer. Karloff is the scarred criminal he promises to fix surgically if he carries out a few murderous tasks. Remarkably scripted, this vintage horror show, combining both the striking imagery and mournfully beautiful poetry of Poe, is brought to startling life by performances of twisted ferocity. AJ

Karloff [Boris Karloff] *Edmond Bateman* • Bela Lugosi *Dr Richard Vollin* • Lester Matthews *Dr Jerry Halden* • Irene Ware *Jean Thatcher* • Samuel S Hinds *Judge Thatcher* ■ *Dir* Louis Friedlander [Lew Landers] • *Scr* David Boehm, from the poem by Edgar Allan Poe

The Raven ★★★★ PG

Mystery thriller 1943 · Fr · BW · 87mins

Such was the hostility levelled at this excoriating study of French provincial life that, on the Liberation, Henri-Georges Clouzot was accused of peddling collaborationist propaganda and banned from directing until 1947. Subsequently, this atmospheric thriller, about a poison-pen campaign that exposes the malicious hypocrisy simmering beneath the respectable surface of a tightly knit community, was reclaimed as an indictment of the paranoia that existed under the Nazi occupation. A riveting whodunnit, thanks to exceptional ensemble playing and Clouzot's claustrophobic staging, this was remade in 1950 by Otto Preminger as *The 13th Letter*. DP. In French with English subtitles. DVD

Pierre Fresnay *Dr Germain* • Ginette Leclerc *Denise Saillens* • Pierre Larquey *Vorzet* • Micheline Francey *Laura Vorzet* ■ *Dir* Henri-Georges Clouzot • *Scr* Louis Chavance, Henri-Georges Clouzot

The Raven ★★★★ PG

Comedy horror 1963 · US · Colour · 84mins

The most flippant of Roger Corman's Edgar Allan Poe cycle, this is, nevertheless, a minor B-movie classic, and a cast containing Vincent Price, Boris Karloff, Peter Lorre and a young Jack Nicholson alone makes it a must-see. There is also a script littered with throwaway one-liners and some unashamedly home-made special effects that add considerably to the charm of this beautifully pitched gothic romp. As the duelling masters of the black arts, Price and Karloff selflessly send up their screen images, but it's Lorre's performance of tipsy comic incompetence that endures. DP DVD

Vincent Price *Dr Erasmus Craven* • Peter Lorre *Dr Adolphus Bedlo* • Boris Karloff *Dr Scarabus* • Hazel Court *Lenore Craven* • Olive Sturgess *Estelle Craven* • Jack Nicholson *Rexford Bedlo* ■ *Dir* Roger Corman • *Scr* Richard Matheson, from the poem by Edgar Allan Poe in *American Review*

Ravenous ★★★★ 18

Period black comedy horror
1999 · US/UK · Colour · 96mins

Priest director Antonia Bird's stunning mix of gut-spilling gore and *Carry On*-style banter is a shocker that you'll either love for its edgy tone, or absolutely hate because it's so in-your-face. Inspired by the tragic Donner Pass disaster of 1846-7, the film stars Robert Carlyle as a devious maneater, decimating the inhabitants of a mountain outpost to keep human flesh on his winter menu. Bird's highly disturbing and thought-provoking film features a couple of impeccable performances. Carlyle etches the strongest portrait of pure evil since Anthony Hopkins in *The Silence of the Lambs*, while Guy Pearce is equally brilliant as the army captain who tries to stop his bloodthirsty exploits. AJ. Contains swearing. [video] DVD

Robert Carlyle *Colqhoun/Ives* • Guy Pearce *Captain John Boyd* • David Arquette *Cleaves* • Jeremy Davies *Private Toffler* • Jeffrey Jones *Colonel Hart* • John Spencer *Gen Slauson* ■ *Dir* Antonia Bird • *Scr* Ted Griffin

Raven's End ★★★

Drama 1963 · Swe · BW · 100mins

Lauded at the time for its realism, Bo Widerberg's Oscar-nominated second feature is actually more notable for the economy of its storytelling. Constantly underplaying or not depicting key events, Widerberg forces us to concentrate on the characters enduring the harsh conditions that existed in Malmö during the 1930s. Thommy Berggren is ingratiatingly feckless as the budding novelist deliberating whether to break for freedom or accept the responsibility to his pregnant girlfriend. But the star turn is Keve Hjelm's drunken, work-shy father. DP. In Swedish with English subtitles.

Thommy Berggren *Anders* • Keve Hjelm *Father* • Emy Storm *Mother* • Ingvar Hirdwall *Sixten* • Christina Frambäck *Elsie* ■ *Dir/Scr* Bo Widerberg

Raw Courage ★

Thriller 1984 · US · Colour · 90mins

Raw courage is what it takes to sit through this dreadful thriller. Three marathon runners (Ronny Cox, Lois Chiles and Art Hindle) are taken prisoner by a citizens' army in the New Mexico desert. The army is commanded by M Emmet Walsh which gives them a distinct edge in terms of acting, but Robert L Rosen directs with a leaden-footed lack of momentum. TH

Ronny Cox *Pete Canfield* • Lois Chiles *Ruth* • Art Hindle *Roger Bower* • M Emmet Walsh *Colonel Crouse* ■ *Dir* Robert L Rosen • *Scr* Ronny Cox, Mary Cox

Raw Deal ★★★★

Film noir 1948 · US · BW · 78mins

A smashing, low-budget thriller, photographed by John Alton so as to disguise the lack of money for sets by plunging whole areas of the screen into mysterious, menacing blackness. In and out of these voids stalk and flee some desperate characters – including gangster Dennis O'Keefe on the run from jail and aiming to kill the man who framed him, Raymond Burr. Marsha Hunt is his hostage and Claire Trevor is O'Keefe's girlfriend who helped him escape and who narrates the movie like an ode to the dead. A masterly exercise in atmospherics and tension from Anthony Mann. AJ

Dennis O'Keefe *Joe Sullivan* • Claire Trevor *Pat Regan* • Marsha Hunt *Ann Martin* • John Ireland *Fantail* • Raymond Burr *Rick Coyle* ■ *Dir* Anthony Mann • *Scr* Leopold Atlas, John C Higgins, from a story by Arnold B Armstrong, Audrey Ashley

Raw Deal ★★★ 18

Action thriller 1986 · US · Colour · 101mins

This entertaining exercise in crash-bang policing comes from John Irvin, whose only previous action assignment was the less-than-inspiring *Dogs of War*. Fresh from the critically panned *Red Sonja*, Arnold Schwarzenegger was probably keen to get back to the old routine and here stars as an ex-FBI agent who goes undercover to nail a mobster (Sam Wanamaker). The film is populated with stereotypes and Arnie dispatches a great many bad guys with his usual lack of expression – suspend your disbelief and have a ball. DP. Contains violence, swearing. [video] DVD

Arnold Schwarzenegger *Mark Kaminski* • Kathryn Harrold *Monique* • Sam Wanamaker *Luigi Patrovita* • Paul Shenar *Rocca* • Robert Davi *Max* ■ *Dir* John Irvin • *Scr* Gary M DeVore, Norman Wexler, from a story by Luciano Vincenzoni, Sergio Donati

Raw Edge ★★★

Western 1956 · US · Colour · 76mins

One of those splendid Universal programme fillers produced by *Touch of Evil's* Albert Zugsmith, this time in lurid colour and boasting an equally lurid plot about a gang of ranch hands trying to kill Herbert Rudley so they can lay claim to his wife, Yvonne De Carlo. There's no direction to speak of from John Sherwood, but who cares? TS

Rory Calhoun *Tex Kirby* • Yvonne De Carlo *Hannah Montgomery* • Mara Corday *Paca* • Rex Reason *John Randolph* • Herbert Rudley *Gerald Montgomery* ■ *Dir* John Sherwood • *Scr* Harry Essex, Robert Hill, from a story by William Kozlenka, James Benson Nablo

Raw Nerve ★★★ 18

Thriller 1991 · US · Colour · 91mins

Hollywood legends often made late career appearances in movies they'd have been well advised to steer clear of. Who can forget Joan Crawford in *Trog*? Glenn Ford, though, star of *The Blackboard Jungle* and *Gilda* fares rather better in this thriller about a racing driver who's having nightmares about a local killer in action. Schlock it may be, but it's superior schlock, made with an understanding of genre conventions. DA [video] DVD

Glenn Ford *Captain Gavin* • Jan-Michael Vincent *Lieutenant Ellis* • Sandahl Bergman *Gloria Freeman* • Randall "Tex" Cobb *Blake Garrett* • Traci Lords *Gina Clayton* ■ *Dir* David A Prior • *Scr* David A Prior, Lawrence L Simeone

Raw Wind in Eden ★

Romantic drama 1958 · US · Colour · 93mins

Her bathing beauty days at MGM over, Esther Williams ventured into romantic drama at Universal, and found herself as a fashion model who lands up on a remote island when her playboy escort Carlos Thompson's plane crashes. The location allows her to take a dip, while falling in love with island inhabitant Jeff Chandler. Thompson conveniently departs, leaving Esther and Jeff to an affair that was rather more dramatic than this, back in Hollywood when filming was over. RK

Esther Williams *Laura* • Jeff Chandler *Mark Moore/Scott Moorehouse* • Rossana Podesta *Costanza* • Carlos Thompson *Wally Tucker* ■ *Dir* Richard Wilson • *Scr* Richard Wilson, Elizabeth Wilson, from a story by Dan Lundberg, Elizabeth Wilson

Rawhead Rex ★★ 18

Horror 1986 · UK · Colour · 85mins

This was only the second Clive Barker script to be filmed and could have dealt a fatal blow to his career. No wonder the horror master practically disowned George Pavlou's movie. Beautifully shot in southern Ireland, the slender tale concerns a village farmer smashing an ancient Celtic monument, thus unleashing an age-old demon who terrorises the country, taking chunks out of people. This low-budget horror is derivative of every bad monster movie you've ever seen, complete with requisite unconvincing rubber-suited creature. RS [video] DVD

David Dukes *Howard Hallenbeck* • Kelly Piper *Elaine Hallenbeck* • Ronan Wilmot *Declan O'Brien* • Niall Toibin *Reverend Coot* • Niall O'Brien *Detective Inspector Gissing* • Heinrich von Schellendorf *Rawhead Rex* ■ *Dir* George Pavlou • *Scr* Clive Barker, from his short story

Rawhide ★★★

Western 1951 · US · BW · 86mins

Initially evoking the romance of running a stagecoach line, this quickly turns into a superior suspense drama that happens to be set in the Old West, with the outlaws behaving rather like gangsters. Tyrone Power is too mature to play the young stageline trainee who becomes the captive of a hold-up gang, while Susan Hayward, as a passenger mistaken for his wife and imprisoned with him, has more to do at the climax. The villains are well characterised, with Hugh Marlowe as their businesslike leader and Jack Elam as a lecherous henchman. AE

Tyrone Power *Tom Owens* • Susan Hayward *Vinnie Holt* • Hugh Marlowe *Zimmerman* • Dean Jagger *Yancy* • Edgar Buchanan *Sam Todd* • Jack Elam *Tevis* • George Tobias *Gratz* ■ *Dir* Henry Hathaway • *Scr* Dudley Nichols

The Rawhide Years ★★

Western 1956 · US · Colour · 84mins

Universal used up sets and props from *The Mississippi Gambler* to decorate this vehicle for its young star Tony Curtis. The plot's a bit of a hand-me-down as well, but the supporting cast is good value, particularly Arthur Kennedy. Not very good, but watchable in parts. TS

Tony Curtis *Ben Mathews* • Colleen Miller *Zoe* • Arthur Kennedy *Rick Harper* • William Demarest *Brand Comfort* • William Gargan *Marshal Sommers* • Peter Van Eyck *Andre Boucher* ■ *Dir* Rudolph Maté • *Scr* Earl Felton, Robert Presnell Jr, DD Beauchamp, from the novel by Norman A Fox

Ray ★★★★ 15

Musical biographical drama
2004 · US · Colour · 146mins

Sex, drugs and rock 'n' roll (or, in Ray Charles's case, soul, gospel, blues and even a little bit of country) are the basic ingredients for a biopic. Throw in childhood poverty, tragedy, racial prejudice and blindness and you are in danger of producing an indigestible mixture of cliché and sentimentality. Taylor Hackford's movie avoids that trap, with Charles emerging as a hugely original talent (his recordings are used throughout the film) and a sympathetic human being, despite his heroin addiction and serial adultery. This is thanks to the assured script and direction, and to Oscar-winning star Jamie Foxx, who's Ray is not just an uncanny impersonation, but a great performance. BP. Contains drug abuse. [video] DVD

Jamie Foxx *Ray Charles* • Kerry Washington *Della Bea Robinson* • Regina King *Margie Hendricks* • Clifton Powell *Jeff Brown* • Aunjanue Ellis *Mary Ann Fisher* • Harry Lennix *Joe Adams* • Terrence Dashon Howard *Gossie McKee* • Larenz Tate *Quincy Jones* • Bokeem Woodbine *Fathead Newman* ■ *Dir* Taylor Hackford • *Scr* James L White, from a story by Taylor Hackford, James L White

Razor Blade Smile ★ 18

Erotic action horror
1998 · UK · Colour and BW · 97mins

A terminally trendy take on a tired theme, director Jake West's erotic popcorn vampire movie gives trash a bad name. *Femme fatale* Eileen Daly is made immortal in 1850 after a visit from aristocratic vampire Christopher Adamson. In modern London, she becomes a leather cat-suit clad assassin with a coffin full of weapons in her bedroom. Derivative, not even unintentionally funny, and technically inept. AJ. Contains swearing, violence and sex scenes. [video] DVD

Eileen Daly *Lilith Silver* • Christopher Adamson *Sir Sethane Blake* • Jonathan Coote *Detective Inspector Ray Price* • Kevin Howarth *Platinum* ■ *Dir/Scr* Jake West

Razorback ★★ 18

Horror 1984 · Aus · Colour · 90mins

Partly inspired by the dingo baby case that became the basis of the Meryl Streep drama *A Cry in the Dark*, this black horror tale about a giant wild pig terrorising the Australian outback borrows, too, from *The Texas Chain Saw Massacre* in its depiction of sick and depraved backwoods yokels. Making his directorial debut, Russell Mulcahy dishes up too rich a visual feast for what is a meandering man-against-nature storyline; the creature, when it finally appears, is also a big letdown. RS [video] DVD

Gregory Harrison *Carl Winters* • Arkie Whiteley *Sarah Cameron* • Bill Kerr *Jake Cullen* • Chris Haywood *Benny Baker* ■ *Dir* Russell Mulcahy • *Scr* Everett DeRoche, from the novel by Peter Brennan

The Razor's Edge ★★★ PG

Drama 1946 · US · BW · 144mins

Tyrone Power plays a First World War veteran who, after a tragic love affair in Paris, goes to India for spiritual renewal. Based on W Somerset Maugham's novel (the author himself is played by Herbert Marshall), this big-budget melodrama bursts with incident and was pitched as Power's return to the screen after distinguished war service. Gene Tierney and Anne Baxter tug on Power's heartstrings. AT. Contains swearing. [video]

Tyrone Power *Larry Darrell* • Gene Tierney *Isabel Bradley* • John Payne *Gray Maturin* • Anne Baxter *Sophie MacDonald* • Clifton Webb *Elliott Templeton* • Herbert Marshall *W Somerset Maugham* • Elsa Lanchester *Miss Keith* ■ *Dir* Edmund Goulding • *Scr* Lamar Trotti, from the novel by W Somerset Maugham

The Razor's Edge ★★ 15

Drama 1984 · US · Colour · 123mins

Another attempt to film W Somerset Maugham's novel, relating how an American First World War survivor takes stock of his life as those close to him go through historically based personal crises. Comedian Bill Murray thought the *Gump*-like soap opera would open up a whole new dramatic career. Theresa Russell livens things up as a drunken hooker in Paris, but there's little else to enjoy. AJ. Contains swearing. [video]

Bill Murray *Larry Darrell* • Theresa Russell *Sophie* • Catherine Hicks *Isabel* • Denholm Elliott *Elliot Templeton* • James Keach *Gray Maturin* • Peter Vaughan *Mackenzie* • Saeed Jaffrey *Raaz* ■ *Dir* John Byrum • *Scr* Bill Murray, John Byrum, from the novel by W Somerset Maugham

Razzia sur la Chnouf ★★★★

Crime drama 1955 · Fr · BW · 105mins

This is a gripping exposé of the criminal underworld in mid-1950s France, with the inimitable Jean Gabin taking centre stage, as the hard-nosed narcotics expert hired by insidious dealer Marcel Dalio to run his Paris operation, only for vital information to begin falling into the hands of the police. Henri Decoin reveals his hand early, but expertly keeps the audience sweating on the outcome. Gabin is outstanding, but Lila Kedrova's junkie and Lino Ventura and Albert Rémy's heavies are also superb. DP. A French language film.

R

Jean Gabin *Henri Ferré* • Magali Noël *Lisette* • Marcel Dalio *Liski* • Lino Ventura *Le Catalan* • Albert Rémy *Bibi* • Pierre Louis *Leroux* • Lila Kedrova *Lea* • Alain Nobis *Decharme* ■ *Dir* Henri Decoin • *Scr* Henri Decoin, Maurice Griffe, from a novel by Auguste Le Breton

Reach for Glory ★★★

Drama 1962 · UK · BW · 86mins

A strange, haunting study of a family of Second World War evacuees and the young son who feels shamed by his conscientious objector brother and his shanghaied father. Joining up with a local gang of kids, he turns into a fervent nationalist who persecutes the local Jewish immigrant boy, then befriends him, before the ritualistic tragedy that lies ahead. This drama poses some disturbing questions and is well worth seeking out. AT

Harry Andrews *Capt Curlew* • Kay Walsh *Mrs Curlew* • Michael Anderson Jr *Lewis Craig* • Oliver Grimm *Mark Stein* • Martin Tomlinson *John Curlew* ■ *Dir* Philip Leacock • *Scr* John Kohn, Jud Kinberg, John Rae, from the novel *The Custard Boys* by John Rae

Reach for the Sky ★★★★ U

Second World War biographical drama 1956 · UK · BW · 130mins

While many of Hollywood's tales about heroism during the Second World War were tainted by smug patriotism and unwelcome sentiment, postwar British cinema tended to handle the events of the conflict with fidelity and dignity. This inspiring tale of courage is one of the finest in a proud tradition. Lewis Gilbert masterfully makes the drama as compelling as the action sequences, and Kenneth More gives the performance of his career as Douglas Bader, who overcame the loss of his legs in a pre-war flying accident to become one of the RAF's most decorated heroes. DP DVD

Kenneth More *Douglas Bader* • Muriel Pavlow *Thelma Bader* • Lyndon Brook *Johnny Sanderson* • Lee Patterson *Stan Turner* • Alexander Knox *Mr Joyce* • Dorothy Alison *Nurse Brace* • Michael Warre *Harry Day* ■ *Dir* Lewis Gilbert • *Scr* Lewis Gilbert, Vernon Harris, from the biography *Story of Douglas Bader* by Paul Brickhill

Read My Lips ★★★ 15

Thriller 2001 · Fr · Colour · 113mins

Director Jacques Audiard shrewdly manipulates both sound and audience expectation in this compelling critique of gender politics. However, he then opts for systematic thrills rather than concentrating on the meticulously established psychological intrigue between deaf secretary Emmanuelle Devos and thuggish parolee Vincent Cassel. Her ruthless pursuit of both professional advancement and personal revenge against those who have spurned her is realised in a chilling display of outward humility and simmering self-belief. DP. In French with English subtitles. DVD

Vincent Cassel *Paul Angeli* • Emmanuelle Devos *Carla Behm* • Olivier Gourmet *Marchand* • Olivia Bonamy *Annie* • Olivier Perrier *Masson* • Bernard Alane *Morel* ■ *Dir* Jacques Audiard • *Scr* Tonino Benacquista, Jacques Audiard

Ready to Rumble ★★ 15

Sports comedy 2000 · US · Colour · 106mins

David Arquette and Scott Caan play two obsessed wrestling fans who are determined to resurrect the career of their favourite fighter, Jimmy King, when he "loses" his world title after falling out with his manager. This suffers from crass dialogue, limp gags and predictable plot twists. That the film still grows on you is thanks mainly to the endearing performances of the two young leads. However, Oliver Platt (as King) is very obviously too puny to be king of the ring, and his trademark extra-large acting only makes some amends for any physical deficiencies. JF. Contains violence, swearing

David Arquette *Gordie Boggs* • Oliver Platt *Jimmy King* • Scott Caan *Sean Dawkins* • Bill Goldberg • Rose McGowan *Sasha* • Diamond Dallas Page • Martin Landau *Sal* ■ *Dir* Brian Robbins • *Scr* Steven Brill, from World Championship Wrestling characters

The Real Blonde ★★★ 15

Romantic comedy 1997 · US · Colour · 101mins

The pursuit of perfection in the shallow world of film, fashion and advertising lies at the core of writer/director Tom DiCillo's bright and breezy showbiz exposé. Matthew Modine is an idealistic aspiring actor in his mid-30s, who draws everyone he meets into interlocking morality tales about sexism and image obsession that overlap in increasingly comic and complex ways. A wonderful cast makes the most of the shrewd observations, even though the satire does meander at times. AJ. Contains swearing and sex scenes. DVD

Matthew Modine *Joe* • Catherine Keener *Mary* • Daryl Hannah *Kelly* • Maxwell Caulfield *Bob* • Elizabeth Berkley *Tina* • Christopher Lloyd *Ernst* • Kathleen Turner *Dee Dee Taylor* • Denis Leary *Doug* • Steve Buscemi *Nick* ■ *Dir/Scr* Tom DiCillo

Real Genius ★★★ 15

Comedy 1985 · US · Colour · 101mins

Enjoyable, if at times slightly silly, screwball comedy, moulded by some of the same minds that brought *Police Academy* and *Bachelor Party* to the screen. Val Kilmer plays one of a gang of scientific prodigies holed up in an institute for young boffins. But, while the youngsters are supposed to be expanding technology, and might be exploring the moral responsibilities of the post-nuclear arms race, they are far keener on getting up to fiendish japes in the corridor. No real genius here, but still fun. PF DVD

Val Kilmer *Chris Knight* • Gabe Jarret *Mitch Taylor* • Michelle Meyrink *Jordan Cochran* • William Atherton *Professor Jerome Hathaway* • Patti D'Arbanville *Sherry Nugil* ■ *Dir* Martha Coolidge • *Scr* Neal Israel, Pat Proft, Peter Torokvei, from a story by Neal Israel, Pat Proft

The Real Glory ★★★ PG

War adventure 1939 · US · BW · 92mins

Intended to be a Spanish-American War rerun of the previously successful Gary Cooper/Henry Hathaway collaboration *The Lives of a Bengal Lancer*, this Philippines-based saga stints on nothing, and the action sequences are particularly well staged and suitably bloody. Only an actor of Cooper's integrity could bring off a character so utterly brilliant at problem-solving, and he does so with aplomb. TS

Gary Cooper *Dr Bill Canavan* • David Niven *Lt Terrence McCool* • Andrea Leeds *Linda Hartley* • Reginald Owen *Capt Steve Hartley* • Broderick Crawford *Lt Swede Larson* • Kay Johnson *Mabel Manning* ■ *Dir* Henry Hathaway • *Scr* Jo Swerling, Robert R Presnell, from the novel by Charles L Clifford

The Real Howard Spitz ★★★ PG

Comedy 1998 · UK/Can · Colour · 97mins

Kelsey Grammer is perfectly cast as a reclusive writer struggling to get his Raymond Chandler-esque pulp novels published in this comic winner. He finds success with his new Crafty Cow children's detective books, but goes to insane lengths to avoid public engagements. Grammer gives an accomplished performance as the curmudgeon with a well-hidden heart, and the droll script offers amusing dialogue and cynical charm. JC DVD

Kelsey Grammer *Howard Spitz* • Genevieve Tessier *Samantha* • Joseph Rutten *Lou* • Amanda Donohoe *Laura* • Kay Tremblay *Theodora Winkle* • Cathy Lee Crosby *Librarian* • Gary Levert *Allen* ■ *Dir* Vadim Jean • *Scr* Jurgen Wolff

Real Life ★★★ PG

Satirical comedy 1979 · US · Colour · 88mins

In 1973 on US TV, docusoap *An American Family* shocked audiences with its voyeuristic chronicling of the everyday life of an average US family – including on-screen divorce and the revelation that one of the kids was gay. For his directorial debut, Albert Brooks effectively spoofed the series and film documentaries in general. Brooks (as a darker version of himself) is the director filming the lives of an average family just at the point when the family is going into meltdown. Brooks even involved his own relatives in the film to make sure it had an authentic look. A fine debut from a strangely under-appreciated comic talent. DF

Dick Haynes *Councilman Harris* • Albert Brooks • Matthew Tobin *Dr Howard Hill* • JA Preston *Dr Ted Cleary* • Mort Lindsey • Joseph Schaffler *Paul Lowell* • Phyllis Quinn *Donna Stanley* • James Ritz *Jack from Cincinnati* ■ *Dir* Albert Brooks • *Scr* Albert Brooks, Monica Johnson, Harry Shearer

Real Life ★★ PG

Crime drama 1983 · UK · Colour · 88mins

In his debut feature, Rupert Everett works hard to convey the whimsicality of the fantasist whose claims that a valuable Rembrandt has been stolen coincide with a genuine attempt on the painting. However, he fails to gel with Cristina Raines, as the smarter older woman who not only extricates him from his dilemma, but also helps him make up with exasperated girlfriend, Catherine Rabett. DP

Rupert Everett *Tim* • Cristina Raines *Laurel* • Catherine Rabett *Kate* • James Faulkner *Robin* • Isla Blair *Anna* • Norman Beaton *Leon McDonald* • Warren Clarke *Gerry* • Lynsey Baxter *Jackie* ■ *Dir* Francis Megahy • *Scr* Francis Megahy, Bernie Cooper

The Real McCoy ★★ 15

Crime thriller 1993 · US · Colour · 90mins

Kim Basinger stars as a reformed thief who is forced back into crime in this fair comic thriller. To make matters worse, Basinger is also saddled with a klutzy partner played by Val Kilmer. Mulcahy's cinematic eye for detail is on vivid show once more but the handsome stars have little to do except pose in front of his eye-popping electric backdrops. AJ. Contains some swearing. DVD

Kim Basinger *Karen McCoy* • Val Kilmer *JT Barker* • Terence Stamp *Jack Schmidt* • Gailard Sartain *Gary Buckner* • Zach English *Patrick* • Raynor Scheine *Baker* • Deborah Hobart *Cheryl Sweeney* • Pamela Stubbart *Kelly* ■ *Dir* Russell Mulcahy • *Scr* William Davies, William Osborne

Real Men ★★ 15

Spy comedy 1987 · US · Colour · 82mins

James Belushi is the hotshot CIA agent, John Ritter is the shy insurance clerk he's forced to recruit as a courier. It's that mismatched-buddy/fish-out-of-water concept again, which can work so well but all too often falls decidedly flat. Despite some moments of inventive farce, this spy comedy belongs in the latter category as it fails to gel under Dennis Feldman's overactive direction. AJ

James Belushi *Nick Pirandello* • John Ritter *Bob Wilson* • Barbara Barrie *Mom* • Bill Morey *Cunard* • Iva Andersen *Dolly* • Gail Berle *Sherry* ■ *Dir/Scr* Dennis Feldman

Real Women Have Curves ★★★ 12

Comedy drama 2002 · US · Colour · 82mins

Newcomer America Ferrera is impressive as the headstrong Ana, a Mexican-American high-school graduate who constantly challenges tradition after her overbearing mother (a ripely humorous Lupe Ontiveros) forces her to give up dreams of college for a job at her sister's dress-making factory. Essentially a warm and sassy chick flick infused with world cinema sensibilities, the film hits back at preconceived notions of class, race and beauty. SF DVD

Lupe Ontiveros *Carmen* • America Ferrera *Ana* • Ingrid Oliu *Estela* • George Lopez *Mr Guzman* • Brian Sites *Jimmy* • Soledad St Hilaire *Pancha* • Lourdes Perez *Rosali* • Jorge Cervera Jr *Raul* ■ *Dir* Patricia Cardoso • *Scr* George Lavoo, Josefina Lopez, from the play by Josefina Lopez

Reality Bites ★★★ 12

Comedy drama 1994 · US · Colour · 94mins

Ben Stiller made his directorial debut with this Generation X comedy, which wouldn't know reality if it jogged its arm during a showy but superficial hand-held camera movement. Strip away the attitude and you'll find an old-fashioned romantic comedy, in which Winona Ryder can't make up her mind between geek Stiller and tuned-in drop-out Ethan Hawke. For all its faults, this still has moments of hip charm. DP. Contains some swearing and drug abuse. DVD

Winona Ryder *Lelaina Pierce* • Ethan Hawke *Troy Dyer* • Janeane Garofalo *Vickie Miner* • Steve Zahn *Sammy Gray* • Ben Stiller *Michael Grates* • Swoosie Kurtz *Charlane McGregor* • Harry O'Reilly *Wes McGregor* • Susan Norfleet *Helen Anne Pierce* • Joe Don Baker *Tom Pierce* • Renee Zellweger *Tami* ■ *Dir* Ben Stiller • *Scr* Helen Childress

Re-Animator ★★★★ 18

Black comedy horror 1985 · US · Colour · 83mins

A ground-breaking horror black comedy that reintroduced HP Lovecraft to a new generation, and set a new level as to how far on-screen outrageousness could go. It also introduced cult star Jeffrey Combs, excellent as the funny and scary borderline-mad medical student working on a formula that brings the dead back to life. However, the dead don't come back in either tip-top or co-operative shape. First-time director Stuart Gordon constantly pushes the limits with the gory antics, but also shows an absurd side to such sequences. Followed in 1990 by *Bride of Re-Animator*. KB. Contains violence and sex scenes. DVD

Jeffrey Combs *Herbert West* • Bruce Abbott *Dan Cain* • Barbara Crampton *Megan Halsey* • Robert Sampson *Dean Halsey* • David Gale *Dr Carl Hill* • Gerry Black *Mace* • Peter Kent *Melvin, the Re-animated* ■ *Dir* Stuart Gordon • *Scr* Dennis Paoli, William J Norris, Stuart Gordon, from the story *Herbert West – the Re-Animator* by HP Lovecraft

Reap the Wild Wind ★★★ PG

Drama 1942 · US · Colour · 123mins

This lurid melodrama seems to take an interminable amount of time to reach its famous Oscar-winning climax with a giant squid unless, of course, you happen to care whether it's John Wayne or a miscast Ray Milland that ends up with southern belle Paulette Goddard. If that little bit of romance isn't enough for Mills and Boon fans, there's another involving Susan Hayward and Robert Preston. The

U = SUITABLE FOR ALL Uc = SUITABLE FOR ALL, ESPECIALLY FOR YOUNG CHILDREN (VIDEO ONLY) PG = PARENTAL GUIDANCE

beginning and end are spectacular, but this maritime vessel does get very watery amidships. TS [video]

John Wayne *Captain Jack Stuart* • Ray Milland *Stephen Tolliver* • Paulette Goddard *Loxi Claiborne* • Raymond Massey *King Cutler* • Robert Preston *Dan Cutler* • Lynne Overman *Captain Phillip Philpott* • Susan Hayward *Drusilla Alston* ■ *Dir* Cecil B DeMille • *Scr* Alan LeMay, Charles Bennett, Jesse Lasky Jr, Jeanie Macpherson (uncredited), from a story by Thelma Strabel • *Special Effects* Gordon Jennings, Faricot Edouart, William L Pereira, Louis Mesenkop

Rear Window ★★★★★ PG

Classic thriller 1954 · US · Colour · 107mins

Like his earlier *Rope*, this masterpiece from director Alfred Hitchcock began as a technical stunt: Hitchcock wondered if he could make a film on just one set, from one single vantage point. James Stewart plays a photojournalist with a broken leg and a high society girlfriend, Grace Kelly. Confined to his apartment, he whiles away the time gazing out of the window through his telephoto lens and becomes convinced that a neighbour opposite (Raymond Burr) has murdered his wife and chopped her into disposable pieces. Hitchcock's "stunt" became a classic study of voyeurism – all those windows, shaped like movie screens, each containing a mini-drama of their own – and the tension builds brilliantly, complemented by the sexy repartee between Stewart and Kelly, and the cynical humour provided by nurse Thelma Ritter. This extraordinary achievement has never been equalled. AT [video] DVD

James Stewart *LB "Jeff" Jeffries* • Grace Kelly *Lisa Carol Fremont* • Wendell Corey *Detective Thomas J Doyle* • Thelma Ritter *Stella* • Raymond Burr *Lars Thorwald* • Judith Evelyn *Miss Lonely Hearts* • David Seville [Ross Bagdasarian] *Songwriter* • Georgine Darcy *Miss Torso* • Sara Berner *Woman on fire escape* ■ *Dir* Alfred Hitchcock • *Scr* John Michael Hayes, from the short story *It Had to Be Murder* by Cornell Woolrich • *Cinematographer* Robert Burks

Rear Window ★★★

Thriller 1998 · US · Colour · 89mins

It takes a brave man to remake one of Alfred Hitchcock's finest films, and director Jeff Bleckner was always going to be on a hiding to nothing with this made-for-TV update. This does score, however, with the presence of Christopher Reeve in the lead role of a wheelchair-bound architect. Reeve's own condition adds an extra dimension to the role, as does the range of hi-tech equipment at his disposal. JF. Contains violence and swearing.

Christopher Reeve *Jason Kemp* • Daryl Hannah *Claudia Henderson* • Robert Forster *Detective Charlie Moore* • Ruben Santiago-Hudson *Antonio* ■ *Dir* Jeff Bleckner • *Scr* Larry Gross, Eric Overmyer, from a short story by Cornell Woolrich

A Reasonable Man ★★

Courtroom drama
1999 · Fr/S Afr · Colour · 103mins

In Gavin Hood's directorial debut set in post-apartheid South Africa, he also stars as a lawyer defending Kwazulu herd boy Loyiso Gxwala, who insists he bludgeoned a baby to death because it was possessed by evil spirits. Disappointingly, in the courtroom battle that ensues before judge Nigel Hawthorne, Gxwala's belief in traditional "tikoloshe" matters less than Hood's memories of his tour of duty in Angola, when he killed a black youth. DP

Gavin Hood *Sean Raine* • Nigel Hawthorne *Judge Wendon* • Janine Esler *Jennifer Raine* • Vusi Kunene *Prosecutor Linde* • Loyiso Gxwala *Sipho Mbombela* ■ *Dir/Scr* Gavin Hood

Rebecca ★★★★★ PG

Classic romantic thriller
1940 · US · BW · 130mins

Director Alfred Hitchcock's first Hollywood film is a sumptuous and suspenseful adaptation of author Daphne du Maurier's romantic novel, produced by David O Selznick, immaculately played and rightly awarded the Oscar for best picture. Laurence Olivier as Maxim de Winter is superb, but it's mousey Joan Fontaine who is a revelation as the second Mrs de Winter. Lovers of lesbian subtexts will have a field day with Judith Anderson's sinister housekeeper, Mrs Danvers, as Hitchcock circumvents the censors who forced plot changes to the original story to accommodate the Hays Code. TS [video] DVD

Laurence Olivier *Maxim de Winter* • Joan Fontaine *Mrs de Winter* • George Sanders *Jack Favell* • Judith Anderson *Mrs Danvers* • Nigel Bruce *Major Giles Lacy* • Reginald Denny *Frank Crawley* • C Aubrey Smith *Colonel Julyan* • Gladys Cooper *Beatrice Lacy* • Florence Bates *Mrs Edythe Van Hopper* • Melville Cooper *Coroner* • Leo G Carroll *Dr Baker* • Leonard Carey *Ben* ■ *Dir* Alfred Hitchcock • *Scr* Robert E Sherwood, Joan Harrison, Philip MacDonald, Michael Hogan, Barbara Keon, from the novel by Daphne du Maurier • *Cinematographer* George Barnes • *Editor* Hal C Kern • *Art Director* Lyle Wheeler • *Music* Franz Waxman

Rebecca of Sunnybrook Farm ★★★

Silent drama 1917 · US · BW · 78mins

The first screen adaptation of the novel and play by Kate Douglas Wiggin stars "America's Sweetheart" Mary Pickford in one of the most famous of her perennial little girl roles. This silent version of the tale of Rebecca, who is sent away to live with stern aunts, displays Pickford at her sympathetic, amusing best, as she matures from childish rebellion to young adulthood and romance under Marshall Neilan's direction. But only silent movie fans are likely to stay with it. RK

Mary Pickford *Rebecca Randall* • Eugene O'Brien *Adam Ladd* • Helen Jerome Eddy *Hannah Randall* • Charles Ogle *Mr Cobb* • Marjorie Daw *Emma Jane Perkins* • ZaSu Pitts ■ *Dir* Marshall Neilan • *Scr* Frances Marion, from the play by Kate Douglas Wiggin, Charlotte Thompson, from the novel by Kate Douglas Wiggin

Rebecca of Sunnybrook Farm ★★ U

Musical comedy 1938 · US · BW · 77mins

Unable to get Shirley Temple a break in radio, her stepfather deposits her down on the farm to live with her rigid, puritanical, anti-show biz aunt, Helen Westley. Fate intervenes when new neighbour Randolph Scott who, entranced by the child, also turns out to be a radio executive. The classic tale was totally remodelled as a vehicle for the all-singing, all-dancing moppet, a veteran at 10. RK [video]

Shirley Temple *Rebecca Winstead* • Randolph Scott *Anthony Kent* • Jack Haley *Orville Smithers* • Gloria Stuart *Gwen Warren* • Phyllis Brooks *Lola Lee* • Helen Westley *Aunt Miranda Wilkins* • Slim Summerville *Homer Busby* • Bill Robinson *Aloysius* ■ *Dir* Allan Dwan • *Scr* Karl Tunberg, Don Ettlinger, from the novel by Kate Douglas Wiggin

Rebecca's Daughters ★★★ 15

Historical comedy
1991 · UK/Ger · Colour · 92mins

Based on a screenplay by Dylan Thomas, this is inspired by the somewhat surreal events of the 1840s Rebecca Riots in which the Welsh poor, fed up with toll charges and taxes, and starving while the English landowners were getting fat, began rioting, disguised as women. Each leader was known as Rebecca and followers were "her daughters", a reference from Genesis. Peter O'Toole hams it up as the drunken Lord Sarn and Paul Rhys is Anthony Raine, a liberal from the landowning class, who incites the rioters. FL [video]

Paul Rhys *Anthony Raine* • Joely Richardson *Rhiannon* • Peter O'Toole *Lord Sarn* • Dafydd Hywel *Rhodri* • Sue Roderick *Sarah Hughes* • Simon Dormandy *Captain Marsden* • Clive Merrison *Sir Henry* • Keith Allen *Davy* ■ *Dir* Karl Francis • *Scr* Guy Jenkin, from a screenplay (unproduced) by Dylan Thomas

The Rebel ★★★ U

Comedy 1960 · UK · Colour · 100mins

Tony Hancock's first star vehicle is no masterpiece, but it is a fascinating misfire. Written by regular collaborators Ray Galton and Alan Simpson, the film has all the touches that made *Hancock's Half-Hour* so popular, although they seem a little strained over the course of a feature-length film. Happier in surburbia using landlady Irene Handl as a model for "Aphrodite by the Waterhole" than he is fooling the pretentious Parisians of the Left Bank, Hancock is his usual deluded, pompous self, while George Sanders's suave shiftiness is as watchable as ever. DP [video] DVD

Tony Hancock *Anthony Hancock* • George Sanders *Sir Charles Brouard* • Paul Massie *Paul* • Margit Saad *Margot Carreras* • Grégoire Aslan *Aristotle Carreras* • Dennis Price *Jim Smith* • Irene Handl *Mrs Crevatte* • John Le Mesurier *Office manager* • Liz Fraser *Waitress* ■ *Dir* Robert Day • *Scr* Ray Galton, Alan Simpson, from the story by Ray Galton, Alan Simpson, Tony Hancock

Rebel ★★

Thriller drama 1973 · US · Colour · 84mins

Sylvester E Stallone, as he is credited here, takes his first leading screen role in this conspiracy thriller about a group of antiwar hippies who are infiltrated by an FBI *agent provocateur* and encouraged to blow up a New York skyscraper. A straightforward paranoia drama which gives little kudos to America's political institutions. Contains violence and bad haircuts. JG

Anthony Page *Tommy* • Sylvester E Stallone [Sylvester Stallone] *Jerry* • Vickey Lancaster *Estelle* • Dennis Tate *Ray* • Barbara Lee Govan *Marlena* ■ *Dir* Robert Allen Schnitzer • *Scr* Robert Allen Schnitzer, Larry Beinhart

Rebel ★★ 15

Musical drama 1985 · Aus · Colour · 89mins

This wildly ill-conceived curiosity from Australia is an obscure must for Matt Dillon fans, although he seems understandably ill at ease in a musical drama set in the Second World War. Dillon's a troubled American GI who goes AWOL in Sydney and hides out with nightclub singer Debbie Byrne, who has a dance routine for every melodramatic development. Lots of flashy production numbers fail utterly to evoke the right era or further the scanty plot. AME [video]

Matt Dillon *Rebel* • Debbie Byrne *Kathy* • Bryan Brown *Tiger* • Bill Hunter *Browning* • Ray Barrett *Bubbles* • Julie Nihill *Joycie* • John O'May *Bernie* • Kim Deacon *Hazel* ■ *Dir* Michael Jenkins • *Scr* Michael Jenkins, Bob Herbert, from the play *No Names … No Packdrill* by Bob Herbert

Rebel in Town ★★★

Western 1956 · US · BW · 78mins

This post-American Civil War drama takes as its starting point the accidental shooting of the small son of a former Union officer by a member of a Confederate family passing through a small town. Going on to explore the divisions that emerge within the killer's family, as well as the response of the parents (played by John Payne and Ruth Roman), it is more thoughtful than most westerns, with veteran character actor J Carrol Naish scoring as the bearded Confederate patriarch. AE

John Payne *John Willoughby* • Ruth Roman *Nora Willoughby* • J Carrol Naish *Bedloe Mason* • Ben Cooper *Gray Mason* • John Smith *Wesley Mason* ■ *Dir* Alfred Werker • *Scr* Danny Arnold

Rebel Rousers ★★ 15

Drama 1967 · US · Colour · 73mins

This is a low-budget trough, but most of the young hopefuls have become today's stars. Here's Bruce Dern and Diane Ladd the year after they had daughter Laura, and here's Dean Stanton before he added the Harry. The nominal lead is Cameron Mitchell, and the truly tasteless plot involves a drag race organised to offer Mitchell's pregnant girlfriend to the champion dragster. The release of this movie was delayed until after Nicholson had scored in *Easy Rider*. TS. Contains some violence and swearing. [video] DVD

Cameron Mitchell *Mr Collier* • Jack Nicholson *"Bunny"* • Bruce Dern *"J J"* • Diane Ladd *Karen* • Dean Stanton [Harry Dean Stanton] ■ *Dir* Martin B Cohen • *Scr* Abe Polsky, Michael Kars, Martin B Cohen

The Rebel Set ★★

Crime drama 1959 · US · BW · 72mins

Three malcontents who hang out in a Beat Generation Hollywood coffee house – an unemployed actor, an unpublished novelist and a film star's delinquent son – are recruited to carry out an ingenious hold-up. Once shed of its beatnik trappings, this turns into an engrossing crime drama with character player Edward Platt given a rare chance to stand out as its rather devilish criminal mastermind. As his dupes, Gregg Palmer, John Lupton and Don Sullivan give solid performances. AE

Gregg Palmer *John Mapes* • Kathleen Crowley *Jeanne Mapes* • Edward Platt *Mr Tucker* • John Lupton *Ray Miller* • Ned Glass *Sidney Horner* • Don Sullivan *George Leland* ■ *Dir* Gene Fowler Jr • *Scr* Louis Vittes, Bernard Girard

Rebel without a Cause ★★★★★ PG

Classic drama 1955 · US · Colour · 106mins

The theme of the teenager as an alienated victim of family and society has never been done better. James Dean gives a superb performance as a frustrated youth from a well-to-do family, who rebels against his weak father and shrewish mother with such delinquent behaviour as boozing, knife-fighting and racing hot rods in hazardous games of "chicken". Natalie Wood and Sal Mineo also stand out in an excellent, youthful cast that's wonderfully controlled by director Nicholas Ray, but it's Dean who remains most memorable, and his heartfelt portrayal epitomised his tragically short career. TH [video] DVD

James Dean *Jim* • Natalie Wood *Judy* • Jim Backus *Jim's father* • Ann Doran *Jim's mother* • William Hopper *Judy's father* • Rochelle Hudson *Judy's mother* • Corey Allen *Buzz* • Sal Mineo *Plato* • Dennis Hopper *Goon* ■ *Dir* Nicholas Ray • *Scr* Stewart Stern, from the story *The Blind Run* by Dr Robert M Lindner, adapted by Irving Shulman

Rebellion ★★★★

Period action drama
1967 · Jpn · BW · 120mins

Rivalling any of Akira Kurosawa's more famous samurai dramas, *Rebellion* stars the great Toshiro Mifune as a dishonoured samurai searching for revenge. In fact, it's the usual samurai stuff, given hardly any new twists, and

R

seemingly influenced by Sergio Leone's *Dollars* films. But what is remarkable is Masaki Kobayashi's magnificent evocation of a vanished era in Japanese history and his stunning images, shot in the traditional black-and-white Scope format. Mifune's intensity is something to marvel at. AT. In Japanese with English subtitles.

Toshiro Mifune *Isaburo Sasahara* • Go Kato *Yogoro Sasahara* • Tatsuyoshi Ehara *Bunzo Sasahara* • Michiko Otsuka *Suga Sasahara* • Yoko Tsukasa *Ichi Sasahara* ■ *Dir* Masaki Kobayashi • *Scr* Shinobu Hashimoto, from the story *Hairyo Zuma Shimatsu Yori* by Yasuhiko Takiguchi • *Cinematographer* Kazuo Yamada

Rebels of the Neon God ★★★★

Drama 1992 · Tai/HK · Colour · 106mins

Establishing what would come to be trademark preoccupations with water, confined spaces and disaffected youth, Taiwanese minimalist Tsai Ming-liang presents a dispiriting, yet often amusing insight into inner-city *ennui* in this hugely impressive debut. A homoerotic charge crackles throughout the drama, as college dropout Lee Kang-sheng is caught between admiration and revenge when he starts stalking Chen Chao-jung, the petty crook who smashed the wing-mirror on his father's taxi. Tsai explores the human cost of the techno era with a compassion that's matched only by his idiosyncratic wit. DP. In Mandarin and Hokkien with English subtitles.

Chen Chao-jung *Ah-Tze* • Wang Yu-wen *Ah-Kuei* • Lee Kang-sheng *Hsiao-Kang* • Jen Ch'ang-pin *Ah-Bing* ■ *Dir/Scr* Tsai Ming-liang

Recess: School's Out ★★★ U

Animated comedy
2001 · US · Colour · 79mins

Yet another big-screen spin-off from a popular children's TV animation. Young TJ Detweiler and chums must save their school (and the world's weather system) from dastardly forces who plan to put an end to their six weeks of freedom. Brightly if basically cartooned, the real plus point here is subject matter that kids everywhere can identify with. DA [video] DVD

Ricky D'Shon Collins *Vince* • Jason Davis *Mikey* • Ashley Johnson *Gretchen* • Andy Lawrence *TJ* • Courtland Mead *Gus* • Pamela Segall *Spinelli* • Dabney Coleman *Principal Prickly* • Robert Goulet *Mikey* • Melissa Joan Hart *Becky* • Peter MacNicol *Fenwick* • James Woods *Benedict* • Dan Castellaneta *First guard* • Robert Stack *Superintendent* ■ *Dir* Chuck Sheetz • *Scr* Jonathan Greenberg, from a story by Joe Ansolabehere, Paul Germain, Jonathan Greenberg

Reckless ★★★

Romantic musical 1935 · US · BW · 96mins

A wildly unbelievable MGM vehicle for blonde bombshell Jean Harlow, which was reportedly based on the notorious shooting scandal involving real-life torch singer Libby Holman. Harlow plays a Broadway actress and she's ably backed up by Franchot Tone (their third film together) and suave, debonair William Powell, who actually fell for Harlow off-screen and left flowers on her grave for many years after her death in 1937. Glossy and contrived, but very watchable. TS

Jean Harlow *Mona Leslie* • William Powell *Ned Riley* • Franchot Tone *Bob Harrison* • May Robson *Granny* • Ted Healy *Smiley* • Nat Pendleton *Blossom* • Robert Light *Paul Mercer* • Rosalind Russell *Josephine* • Henry Stephenson *Harrison* • Louise Henry *Louise* ■ *Dir* Victor Fleming • *Scr* PJ Wolfson, from the story *A Woman Called Cheap* by Oliver Jeffries [David O Selznick], Victor Fleming

Reckless ★★

Black comedy 1995 · US · Colour · 91mins

This strange, nightmarish comedy thriller stars Mia Farrow, suitably gauche and naive, as a woman who discovers her husband has hired a hitman to knock her off on Christmas Eve. Escaping into the snow, Farrow begins a bizarre journey and has a series of encounters in which no one is what they seem. All a bit too *Twilight Zone* in the final analysis. LH

Mia Farrow *Rachel* • Scott Glenn *Lloyd* • Mary-Louise Parker *Pooty* • Tony Goldwyn *Tom* • Eileen Brennan *Sister Margaret* • Giancarlo Esposito *Game show host* • Stephen Dorff *Tom Jr* ■ *Dir* Norman René • *Scr* Craig Lucas, from his play

Reckless Kelly ★★ PG

Comedy 1993 · Aus · Colour · 76mins

The spirit of Aussie outlaw Ned Kelly is alive and well and dwelling in director/star Yahoo Serious in this frantic and not particularly funny crime comedy. It begins well, as Yahoo's island idyll is threatened by evil banker Hugo Weaving and his explosive sidekick, Alexei Sayle. But, from the moment he arrives in the US intent on robbing banks to save his home, the gags begin to fall flat. DP. Contains violence and swearing. [video]

Yahoo Serious *Reckless Kelly* • Melora Hardin *Robin Banks* • Alexei Sayle *Major Wimp* • Hugo Weaving *Sir John* • Kathleen Freeman *Mrs Delance* • John Pinette *Sam Delance* • Bob Maza *Dan Kelly* ■ *Dir* Yahoo Serious • *Scr* Yahoo Serious, Warwick Ross, Lulu Serious, David Roach

The Reckless Moment ★★★

Thriller 1949 · US · BW · 81mins

Short, sharp and to the point, this pitches anxious mother Joan Bennett against James Mason after her gauche daughter Geraldine Brooks has an affair with older married man Shepperd Strudwick. Paying less attention than usual to set detail and ornate camera movement, ultra-sophisticated German director Max Ophüls directs with a cool detachment. But, while this allows Bennett to suffer and scheme without the histrionics of a Joan Crawford, it prevents Mason from trying out any new tricks as a blackmailing cad. DP

James Mason *Martin Donnelly* • Joan Bennett *Lucia Harper* • Geraldine Brooks *Beatrice Harper* • Henry O'Neill *Mr Harper* • Shepperd Strudwick *Ted Darby* ■ *Dir* Max Ophüls • *Scr* Henry Garson, Robert W Soderberg, Mel Dinelli, Robert E Kent, from the story *The Blank Wall* by Elisabeth Sanxay Holding

The Reckoning ★★★

Drama 1969 · UK · Colour · 111mins

A tough but troubled businessman is forced to deal with the chip on his shoulder when he learns his father is dying. Returning to Liverpool and his roots, he decides to take revenge on the teenager who attacked his father. An adult drama about class in Britain, it's held together with a muscular performance from Nicol Williamson as the dislikeable hero. JG

Nicol Williamson *Michael Marler* • Ann Bell *Rosemary Marler* • Lilita De Barros *Maria* • Tom Kempinski *Brunzy* ■ *Dir* Jack Gold • *Scr* John McGrath, from the play *The Harp That Once* by Patrick Hall

The Reckoning ★★★ 15

Period murder mystery
2001 · UK/Sp · Colour · 105mins

This medieval murder-mystery play follows a troupe of travelling players who drop their religious repertoire to expose the corruption hiding under the Church's righteous protection. Paul Bettany, playing a young priest on the run from an adulterous past, joins a group of itinerant actors led by Willem Dafoe. Arriving in a town where Elvira Minguez has been sentenced to death for the murder a young boy, the company decides to tell the story of the killing in the form of a production for the local townsfolk. Director Paul McGuigan maintains a mood as dark as the plague-ridden times, but lapses into theatricality. TH. Contains violence and sex scenes. [video] DVD

Willem Dafoe *Martin* • Paul Bettany *Nicholas* • Gina McKee *Sarah* • Brian Cox *Tobias* • Ewen Bremner *Simon Damian* • Vincent Cassel *Robert de Guise* • Simon McBurney *Stephen* • Tom Hardy *Straw* • Elvira Minguez *Martha* ■ *Dir* Paul McGuigan • *Scr* Mark Mills, from the novel *Morality Play* by Barry Unsworth

Recollections of the Yellow House ★★★ 18

Drama 1989 · Por · Colour · 122mins

Strewn with references to silent classics such as *Greed, The Cabinet of Dr Caligari* and *Nosferatu*, this is a frustrating, yet persistently fascinating study on self-obsession and misery. Exercising rigid control over both the *mise-en-scène* and his elliptical storyline, writer/director João César Monteiro turns in a seedily antiheroic performance, as the academic whose growing sense of dissatisfaction with life in general and his desolate Lisbon boarding house in particular results in an assault that sees him consigned to an asylum. This is often as funny as it is despondent. DP. In Portuguese with English subtitles.

João César Monteiro *Joao De Deus* • Manuela De Freitas *Dona Violeta* • Sabina Sacchi *Mimi* • Teresa Calado *Menina Julieta* • Ruy Furtado *Señor Armando* • Henrique Viana *Police Captain* ■ *Dir/Scr* João César Monteiro

Reconstruction ★★★ 12A

Romantic drama
2003 · Den /Swe/Ger · Colour · 91mins

Danish director Christoffer Boe explores the relationship between cinema and literature in this teasingly *film noir*-like mystery. Tempted into a fling with novelist Krister Henriksson's glamorous wife, photographer Nikolaj Lie Kaas awakes in a seemingly alternative universe, where neither friends nor family know him and he suspects he's being manipulated by a higher force. Playing fast and loose with the rules of storytelling, Boe delights in misleading the viewer, a conceit made easier by the fact that both the women in Kaas's life are played by the bewitching Maria Bonnevie. DP. In Danish with English subtitles. Contains swearing.

Nikolaj Lie Kaas *Alex David* • Maria Bonnevie *Aimee Holm/Simone* • Krister Henriksson *August Holm* • Nicolas Bro *Leo Sand* • Peter Steen *Mel David* • Ida Dwinger *Monica* ■ *Dir* Christoffer Boe • *Scr* Christoffer Boe, Mogens Rukov

Record of a Tenement Gentleman ★★★★ PG

Drama 1947 · Jpn · BW · 71mins

Recalling the visual style and emotional tone of pre-War Japanese social cinema, Yasujiro Ozu's delicate character drama combines unsentimental nostalgia and contemporary comment to poignant effect. Self-contained widow Choko Iida slowly becomes fond of abandoned, bed-wetting urchin Hohi Aoki, whose tenacious desire to belong awakens Iida's suppressed maternal instincts. Cleverly using camera angles to create a sense of place and parallel motifs to unify the action, Ozu reveals his directorial genius. DP. In Japanese with English subtitles. DVD

Chishu Ryu *Tashiro, the fortune teller* • Choko Iida *Otane* • Takeshi Sakamoto *Kihachi* • Eitaro Ozawa *Kohei's father* ■ *Dir* Yasujiro Ozu • *Scr* Yasujiro Ozu, Tadao Ikeda

The Recruit ★★ 12

Spy thriller 2002 · US · Colour · 110mins

Al Pacino gives another gruff, seen-it-all performance here, as a veteran CIA agent who recruits cocksure computer whizzkid Colin Farrell. The same could be said about the plot of this thriller from director Roger Donaldson. Most of the action takes place in "The Farm", a CIA training facility where would-be agents are taught hi-tech espionage and survival skills, and where Farrell meets and falls for enigmatic rival Bridget Moynahan. Predictable. AJ. Contains violence, swearing, sex scenes. [video] DVD

Al Pacino *Walter Burke* • Colin Farrell (2) *James Clayton* • Bridget Moynahan *Layla* • Gabriel Macht *Zack* • Karl Pruner *Dennis Slayne* • Eugene Lipinski *Husky man* ■ *Dir* Roger Donaldson • *Scr* Roger Towne, Kurt Wimmer, Mitch Glazer

The Red and the White ★★★

Historical war drama
1967 · Hun/USSR · BW · 90mins

Made to celebrate the 50th anniversary of the Bolshevik Revolution, this is ostensibly a tribute to the Hungarian volunteers who fought with the Red Army against the pro-Tsarist Whites. But Miklos Jancso clearly has an ironic agenda. Employing lateral tracking shots and meticulously composed widescreen images of the sweeping plains, he suggests the changing fortunes of the two armies and the enormity of the stakes for which they were fighting. DP. A Hungarian language film.

Jozsef Madaras *Hungarian commander* • Tibor Molnar *Andras* • Andras Kozak *Laszlo* • Jacint Juhasz *Istvan* ■ *Dir* Miklos Jancso • *Scr* Georgiy Mdivani, Gyula Hernadi, Miklos Jancso

The Red Badge of Courage ★★★★ U

War drama 1951 · US · BW · 66mins

Apart from the brilliance of individual scenes, John Huston's American Civil War epic is also famous for having been butchered by the studio. Audie Murphy, America's most decorated soldier in the Second World War, plays the young recruit who is given a baptism of fire and emerges a hero, his experiences on the battlefield captured in some remarkable documentary-style, black-and-white photography. Although a shadow of the film Huston intended (James Whitmore's narration fills in the gaps created by MGM's scissor-happy editors), this is still a powerful study of the waste of war. AT [video] DVD

Audie Murphy *Henry Fleming, the youth* • Bill Mauldin *Tom Wilson, the loud soldier* • Douglas Dick *Lieutenant* • Royal Dano *Tattered soldier* • John Dierkes *Jim Conlin, the tall soldier* • Arthur Hunnicutt *Bill Porter* • Andy Devine *Talkative soldier* • James Whitmore *Narrator* ■ *Dir* John Huston • *Scr* John Huston, from the novel by Stephen Crane, adapted by Albert Band • *Cinematographer* Harold Rosson

Red Ball Express ★★★ U

Second World War drama
1952 · US · BW · 83mins

Alfred Hitchcock's favourite screenwriter of the 1950s, John Michael Hayes was perhaps an odd choice to pen a war picture. But he manages to inject enough tension into this routine story about the problems facing a transportation unit as it accompanies General Patton on his push to Paris. By giving sergeant Alex Nicol a chip on his shoulder and corporal Sidney Poitier a sense of racial injustice, he makes unit leader Jeff Chandler seem a very human hero. Intriguing and under-rated. DP

Jeff Chandler *Lieutenant Chick Campbell* • Alex Nicol *Sergeant Ernest Kalleck* • Charles Drake *Private Ronald Partridge* • Judith Braun *Joyce McClellan* • Hugh O'Brian *Private Wilson* • Jacqueline Duval *Antoinette DuBois* • Sidney Poitier *Corporal Andrew Robertson* ■ *Dir* Budd Boetticher • *Scr* John Michael Hayes, from the story by Marcel Klauber, Billy Grady Jr

Red Balloon ★★★★ U

Fantasy 1956 · Fr · Colour · 33mins

The first dialogue-less film to receive an Oscar nomination for its screenplay since the silent era (it went on to win), Albert Lamorisse's simple fable about the unique friendship between a lonely boy and a vibrant red balloon remains one of the most enchanting children's films ever made. Responding with adorable naturalism to his father's direction, Pascal Lamorisse seems lost in awe at the mischievous balloon's ingenuity as it follows him across Paris and into his classroom. The triumph of loyalty and love over envy and cruelty is a weighty message for such a slight tale, but Lamorisse carries it off magnificently with a joyous balloon-filled finale. DP

Pascal Lamorisse *Little boy* • Sabine Lamorisse *Little girl* ■ *Dir/Scr* Albert Lamorisse

Red Beard 

Period drama 1965 · Jpn · BW · 172mins

The plot is simple: an ageing doctor (Toshiro Mifune) persuades his younger, rather feckless assistant to dedicate himself to work among the disadvantaged in 19th-century Japan. But what (almost) justifies the film's three-hour running time is Akira Kurosawa's wider interest in Japan's transition from its feudal past to its future as a modern industrialised society. Perhaps too slow for modern tastes, and too obscure for western audiences, it's a major work from a major director. AT. In Japanese with English subtitles. DVD

Toshiro Mifune *Doctor Kyojo "Akahige" Niide* • Yuzo Kayama *Doctor Noboru Yasumoto* • Yoshio Tsuchiya *Doctor Handayu Mori* • Tatsuyoshi Ehara *Genzo Tsugawa* ■ *Dir* Akira Kurosawa • *Scr* Akira Kurosawa, Ryuzo Kikushima, Hideo Oguni, Masato Ide, from the novel *Akahige Shinryo Tan* by Shugoro Yamamoto

The Red Beret ★★★ U

Second World War drama
1953 · UK · Colour · 88mins

Wags recall that a trench was dug at Shepperton for the action sequences, but the diminutive Alan Ladd was too small to use it. However, the star puts in an excellent performance as a guilt-racked American who joins the famous parachute battalion. An interesting note for film historians: this rip-roaring film was co-produced by "Cubby" Broccoli, co-written by Richard Maibaum and directed by Terence Young, the same team responsible for the first Bond movie, *Dr No*, nine years later. TS

Alan Ladd *Canada MacKendrick* • Leo Genn *Major Snow* • Susan Stephen *Penny Gardner* • Harry Andrews *RSM* • Donald Houston *Taffy* • Anthony Bushell *General Whiting* • Stanley Baker *Breton* ■ *Dir* Terence Young • *Scr* Richard Maibaum, Frank S Nugent, from the book by Hilary St George Saunders, adapted by Sy Bartlett

Red Canyon ★★★ U

Western 1949 · US · Colour · 82mins

A charming western based on Zane Grey's novel *Wildfire*, with former radio actor Howard Duff playing a drifter trying to tame a wild stallion and falling for Ann Blyth, daughter of horse breeder George Brent. Blyth is particularly good, and there's an interesting supporting cast of western veterans such as Edgar Buchanan and Chill Wills, plus a youthful Lloyd Bridges. The Utah locations are beautifully shot by cinematographer Irving Glassberg. TS

Ann Blyth *Lucy Bostell* • Howard Duff *Lin Slone/Cordt* • George Brent *Mathew Boatel* • Edgar Buchanan *Jonah Johnson* • John McIntire *Floyd Cordt* • Chill Wills *Brackton* • Jane Darwell *Aunt Jane* • Lloyd Bridges *Virgil Cordt* ■ *Dir* George Sherman • *Scr* Maurice Geraghty, from the novel *Wildfire* by Zane Grey

The Red Circle ★★

Crime drama 1960 · W Ger · BW · 84mins

The crime movie is one of the staples of German cinema and this Scotland Yard mystery is one of three films featuring Fritz Rasp, a veteran from the golden age of German silents, who spent much of his later years in thrillers based on the novels of Edgar Wallace. How does he fit into the case of a serial killer who leaves his victims with a curious circular mark on their necks? You'll have to join inspector Karl Saebisch to find out. DP. German dialogue dubbed into English.

Karl Saebisch *Inspector Parr* • Renate Ewert *Thalia Drummond* • Klaus-Jürgen Wussow *Derrik Yale* • Thomas Alder *Jack* • Fritz Rasp *Ulrich Berger* ■ *Dir* Jürgen Roland • *Scr* Trygve Larsen, Wolfgang Menge, from a novel by Edgar Wallace

The Red Circle ★★★★ PG

Thriller 1970 · Fr/It · Colour · 136mins

Before he began writing *The Red Circle*, Jean-Pierre Melville made a list of his favourite thriller situations and came up with 19, noting that the only film to use them all was *The Asphalt Jungle*. Thus *The Red Circle* is a sort of condensation of all thrillers, with the sort of fully developed characters, ambiguities, betrayals, tense scenes and intricate plotting one expects from the best of them. It's about a robbery, of course, near the Ritz in Paris, immaculately performed by some of France's top male stars. Avoid seeing the English-dubbed version, which is cut by some 45 minutes; the four stars are for the original. AT. In French with English subtitles. DVD

Alain Delon *Corey* • Yves Montand *Jansen* • Bourvil *Inspector Mattei* • Gian Maria Volonté *Vogel* • André Eykan *Rico* • François Périer *Santi* ■ *Dir/Scr* Jean-Pierre Melville

Red Corner ★★ 15

Courtroom thriller
1997 · US · Colour · 117mins

In this courtroom thriller set in Beijing, something of the terror of being trapped in the machinery of a foreign legal system comes across, as Richard Gere's smarmy American TV executive finds himself relying on a Chinese female lawyer, Bai Ling, to defend him on a fraudulent murder charge. Yet, for all its Zen idealism, the film lacks tension and focus. DP. In English and Mandarin with subtitles. Contains some violence, swearing and a sex scene. DVD

Richard Gere *Jack Moore* • Bai Ling *Shen Yuelin* • Bradley Whitford *Bob Ghery* • Byron Mann *Lin Dan* • Peter Donat *David McAndrews* • Robert Stanton *Ed Pratt* ■ *Dir* Jon Avnet • *Scr* Robert King

The Red Dance ★★★★

Romantic drama 1928 · US · BW · 103mins

The influence of European art films affected even no-nonsense action directors such as Raoul Walsh, whose control of this novelettish excursion into the Russian Revolution – starring Charles Farrell and Dolores Del Rio – makes it a joy to look at. Camerawork is by Charles Clark and John Marta, and overall art direction by Ben Carrie. The story and action are incidental to the visuals, which makes it remarkable entertainment for its time. TH

Charles Farrell *The Grand Duke Eugen* • Dolores Del Rio *Tasia* • Ivan Linow *Ivan Petroff* • Boris Charsky *Agitator* • Dorothy Revier *Princess Varvara* • Andrés De Segurola *General Tanaroff* • Demetrius Alexis *Rasputin* ■ *Dir* Raoul Walsh • *Scr* James Ashmore Creelman, Pierre Collings (adaptation), Philip Klein (adaptation), from a story by Eleanor Browne, from the novel *The Red Dancer of Moscow* by Henry Leyford Gates

The Red Danube ★★

Period drama 1949 · US · BW · 118mins

American army officers Walter Pidgeon and Peter Lawford, stationed in Allied-occupied Vienna after the Second World War, are involved in the repatriation of Russians as a result of which, it is implied, they will suffer the cruel retribution of the Communist state. Janet Leigh is a ballerina loved by Lawford, which doesn't save her, and Ethel Barrymore a nun. Directed by George Sidney, this is heavy-handed drama, cashing in on the anti-Red climate of the times. Despite a large cast of authentic Europeans, it's ineffectual and unpersuasive. RK

Walter Pidgeon *Colonel Michael "Jokey" Nicobar* • Ethel Barrymore *Mother Superior* • Peter Lawford *Major John "Twingo" McPhimister* • Angela Lansbury *Audrey Quail* • Janet Leigh *Maria Buhlen* • Louis Calhern *Colonel Piniev* • Francis L Sullivan *Colonel Humphrey "Blinker" Omicron* ■ *Dir* George Sidney (2) • *Scr* Gina Kaus, Arthur Wimperis, from the novel *Vespers in Vienna* by Bruce Marshall

Red Dawn ★★ 15

Action drama 1984 · US · Colour · 109mins

A small band of American teenagers wages guerrilla warfare against Russian and Cuban troops staging an invasion of their small town in a ludicrously gung-ho fantasy. Some of Hollywood's finest struggle with some highly unconvincing dialogue to justify the bombastic militarism, and the result is a scrambled action adventure smothered by political insensitivity. AJ. Contains violence and swearing.

Patrick Swayze *Jed* • C Thomas Howell *Robert* • Lea Thompson *Erica* • Charlie Sheen *Matt* • Darren Dalton *Daryl* • Jennifer Grey *Toni* • Brad Savage *Danny* • Doug Toby *Aardvark* • Ben Johnson *Mason* • Harry Dean Stanton *Mr Eckert* • Powers Boothe *Andy* ■ *Dir* John Milius • *Scr* John Milius, Kevin Reynolds, from the novel by Kevin Reynolds

Red Desert ★★ 15

Drama 1964 · Fr/It · Colour · 116mins

Here, Michelangelo Antonioni has almost exhausted his theme of urban alienation and simply rehashes it in colour, taking his symbolism to artistic extremes as streets are repainted and a room changes hue. The story, though, is opaque – Monica Vitti plays a manic depressive who sleeps with her husband's friend (Richard Harris). Vitti is, as ever, convincingly neurotic, but Harris is totally miscast, dubbed and barely a presence. Most viewers will regard this as pretentious twaddle, no matter how beautiful the photography. AT. In Italian with English subtitles. DVD

Monica Vitti *Giuliana* • Richard Harris *Corrado Zeller* • Carlo Chionetti *Ugo* • Xenia Valderi *Linda* • Rita Renoir *Emilia* • Aldo Grotti *Max* ■ *Dir* Michelangelo Antonioni • *Scr* Michelangelo Antonioni, Tonino Guerra, from a story by Michelangelo Antonioni, Tonino Guerra • *Cinematographer* Carlo Di Palma

The Red Dragon ★★

Mystery 1945 · US · BW · 64mins

Sidney Toler's 18th Charlie Chan series outing was also the seventh to be released by Poverty Row studio Monogram, after it took over the franchise from 20th Century-Fox. By now the cases were becoming mundane affairs and, although Toler is suitably inscrutable as Earl Derr Biggers's sleuth, Benson Fong's Tommy Chan is nowhere near as effective as Keye Luke's "Number One Son". Moreover, Fortunio Bonanova is given too little to do as the police inspector left in Chan's wake as he searches for stolen plans. DP

Sidney Toler *Charlie Chan* • Fortunio Bonanova *Inspector Luis Carvero* • Benson Fong *Tommy Chan* • Robert E Keane [Robert Emmett Keane] *Alfred Wyans* • Willie Best *Chattanooga Brown* • Carol Hughes *Marguerite Fontan* ■ *Dir* Phil Rosen • *Scr* George Callahan, from his story, from characters created by Earl Derr Biggers

Red Dragon ★★★ 15

Thriller 2002 · US/Ger · Colour · 119mins

In this remake of Michael Mann's revered *Manhunter* (the first version of Thomas Harris's novel *Red Dragon* filmed in 1986), ex-FBI agent Edward Norton investigates a series of killings committed by a tattooed Ralph Fiennes, known only as "The Tooth Fairy". To get inside the killer's head, Norton has to consult his arch-nemesis – and the man he put behind bars – Dr Lecter (Anthony Hopkins). Closer to *The Silence of the Lambs* than *Hannibal* in tone and tension, this is a classier, less campy outing for the gourmet doctor, who is well matched in the psycho stakes by Fiennes's killer. TH. Contains violence, swearing and nudity. DVD

Anthony Hopkins *Dr Hannibal Lecter* • Edward Norton *Will Graham* • Ralph Fiennes *Francis Dolarhyde* • Harvey Keitel *Jack Crawford* • Emily Watson *Reba* • Mary-Louise Parker *Molly Graham* • Philip Seymour Hoffman *Freddy Lounds* • Anthony Heald *Dr Chilton* • Frankie Faison *Barney* • Lalo Schifrin *Conductor* • Ellen Burstyn *Grandmother Dolarhyde* ■ *Dir* Brett Ratner • *Scr* Ted Tally, from the novel by Thomas Harris

Red Dust ★★★★ PG

Romantic drama 1932 · US · BW · 79mins

Love in a hot climate is the theme of this melodrama, directed by Victor Fleming, which today risks looking clichéd, if not over-the-top. The film was a hit in its time, thanks not just to Fleming's direction, but also to sultry stylish performances by Clark Gable, as the macho boss of a rubber plantation in the tropics, and Jean Harlow and Mary Astor as the two very different women after whom he lusts. John Ford directed the 1953 re-make, *Mogambo*. PF

Clark Gable *Dennis Carson* • Jean Harlow *Vantine* • Mary Astor *Barbara Willis* • Gene Raymond *Gary Willis* • Donald Crisp *Guidon* • Tully Marshall *McQuarg* • Forrester Harvey *Limey* ■ *Dir* Victor Fleming • *Scr* John Mahin, from the play by Wilson Collison

Red Firecracker, Green Firecracker ★★★ 15

Romantic drama
1993 · HK/Chi · Colour · 111mins

The story of an artist's forbidden love for the female head of a firework manufacturing family is right out of the ordinary. In a country where women are permitted to have only one child, this study of repressed sexuality takes on a whole new meaning. However, Da Ying's cumbersome screenplay and Ning Jing's unsubtle portrayal of the cross-dressing heiress undermine the beauty of He Ping's direction and the irrepressible performance of Wu Gang. DP. In Cantonese with English subtitles. Contains nudity.

Ning Jing *Chun Zhi* • Wu Gang *Niu Bao, painter* • Zhao Xiaorui *Mr Mann* • Gai Yang *Mr Zhao* • Xu Zhengyun *Mr Xu* ■ *Dir* He Ping • *Scr* Ying Da, Feng Jicai

R

Red Garters ★★★ U

Western musical comedy
1954 · US · Colour · 90mins

Set in the fictional town of Paradise Lost, the action revolves around sharp-shooting cowboy Guy Mitchell out to avenge his brother's death, sassy saloon singer Rosemary Clooney and lawyer Jack Carson on whom her sights are set. The neither-here-nor-there plot, unremarkable script and hit-free score undermine an adventurously stylised production (the art direction was Oscar-nominated), lively performances and some genuinely funny upending of every heroic western cliché in the book. RK

Rosemary Clooney *Calaveras Kate* • Jack Carson *Jason Carberry* • Guy Mitchell *Reb Randall* • Pat Crowley *Susana Martinez De La Cruz* • Joanne Gilbert *Sheila Winthrop* • Gene Barry *Rafael Moreno* ■ *Dir* George Marshall • *Scr* Michael Fessier

Red-Headed Woman ★★★

Romantic drama 1932 · US · BW · 79mins

Infamously banned by the British censors at the time of its release, audiences here didn't have sight of this raunchy little opus until its TV bow some decades ago, and only then realised what all the fuss was about. This is a torrid tale that positively glorifies husband-stealing, and the electric Jean Harlow leaves no doubt where her sympathies lie. There's a sexual candour in the telling that provoked the pro-censorship lobby, but it's that startling erotic charge that makes this movie so electrifyingly watchable today. Look out for a young Charles Boyer, impressive as Harlow's uniformed chauffeur. TS

Jean Harlow *Lil Andrews* • Chester Morris *Bill Legendre Jr* • Lewis Stone *William Legendre Sr* • Leila Hyams *Irene Legendre* • Una Merkel *Sally* • Henry Stephenson *Gaersate* • May Robson *Aunt Jane* • Charles Boyer *Albert* • Harvey Clark *Uncle Fred* ■ *Dir* Jack Conway • *Scr* Anita Loos, from the novel by Katherine Brush

Red Heat ★★ 18

Prison drama
1985 · W Ger/US · Colour · 101mins

This is routine "bras behind bars" stuff, about an American woman in West Germany who is mistakenly arrested as a spy and tossed into a prison packed with sadistic guards and even more unmentionable inmates. The film is most notable for co-starring *The Exorcist*'s Linda Blair and Emmanuelle herself, Sylvia Kristel, both of whom were, after their first big breaks, quickly reduced to making quickie tosh like this. DA

Linda Blair *Christine Carlson* • Sylvia Kristel *Sofia* • Sue Kiel *Dr Hedda Kliemann* • William Ostrander *Michael Grainger* • Albert Fortell *Ernst* • Elisabeth Volkmann *Warden Einbech* ■ *Dir* Robert Collector • *Scr* Robert Collector, Gary Drucker

Red Heat ★★★ 18

Action thriller 1988 · US · Colour · 99mins

This routine thriller from director Walter Hill offered Arnold Schwarzenegger one of his more interesting action roles before he became a superstar. Playing a stony, monosyllabic Soviet cop poses no real acting problems for the big man, and in James Belushi he has an agreeably foul-mouthed foil, as the pair team up to hunt for an escaped Russian drug dealer. Hill stages a series of entertainingly violent and increasingly silly set pieces. JF. Contains violence, swearing, a sex scene and nudity. DVD

Arnold Schwarzenegger *Captain Ivan Danko* • James Belushi *Det Sgt Art Ridzik* • Peter Boyle *Lou Donnelly* • Ed O'Ross *Viktor Rostavili* • Larry Fishburne [Laurence Fishburne] *Lieutenant Stobbs* • Gina Gershon *Catherine Manzetti* ■ *Dir* Walter Hill • *Scr* Harry Kleiner, Walter Hill, from a story by Troy Kennedy Martin, Walter Hill

The Red House ★★★

Mystery thriller 1947 · US · BW · 100mins

A splendid thriller with grand passions and Freudian undertones, which has grown in reputation. Now often described as *noir*, it is closer in style to the psychological horror of the 1960s. Edward G Robinson has a meaty role as the tormented, crippled farmer, who warns juveniles Allene Roberts and Lon McCallister to keep away from the Red House, and hires hunky Rory Calhoun to make sure they do. There are longueurs during the build-up to the awful truth, but compensation is provided by the beautiful Sierra Nevada locations and Miklos Rozsa's score. DM

Edward G Robinson *Pete Morgan* • Lon McCallister *Nath Storm* • Judith Anderson *Ellen Morgan* • Allene Roberts *Meg Morgan* • Julie London *Tibby* • Rory Calhoun *Teller* ■ *Dir* Delmer Daves • *Scr* Delmar Daves, from the novel by George Agnew Chamberlain

Red Light ★★

Crime drama 1949 · US · BW · 83mins

This turgid crime drama from director Roy Del Ruth is not helped by the low-key performance of its star, the past-his-prime George Raft, here playing a businessman searching (seemingly interminably) for the killer of his army chaplain brother. What sexy Virginia Mayo sees in the gloomy Raft is a mystery known only to the casting department. It's redeemed only by its black-and-white photography and some sterling support. TS

George Raft *John Torno* • Virginia Mayo *Carla North* • Raymond Burr *Nick Cherney* • Gene Lockhart *Warni Hazard* • Barton MacLane *Strecker* • William "Bill" Phillips *Ryan* ■ *Dir* Roy Del Ruth • *Scr* George Callahan • *Cinematographer* Bert Glennon

Red Lights ★★★★ 15

Thriller 2003 · Fr · Colour · 101mins

Once again a Georges Simenon story provides exceptional cinematic material, as Cédric Kahn combines sly comedy with controlled suspense in this revisionist road movie. Alternating between resentment, penitence and distraction, Jean-Pierre Darroussin is outstanding as the everyman made to pay an extreme price for the uncharacteristic lapse in judgement that prompts wife Carole Bouquet to storm off in the middle of a cross-country car journey and promptly disappear. Tense, mischievous and darkly optimistic. DP. In French with English subtitles. Contains swearing and violence. DVD

Jean-Pierre Darroussin *Antoine Dunan* • Carole Bouquet *Hélène* • Vincent Deniard *Man on the run* • Charline Paul *Waitress* • Jean-Pierre Gos *Inspector Levet* ■ *Dir* Cédric Kahn • *Scr* Cédric Kahn, Laurence Ferreira Barbosa, Gilles Marchand, from the novel *Feux Rouges* by Georges Simenon

Red Line 7000 ★★

Action drama 1965 · US · Colour · 110mins

Director Howard Hawks returns to territory that he'd first tackled in 1932's *The Crowd Roars*, but somehow this racetrack movie doesn't quite measure up. The Technicolor is particularly fine, with that Paramount gloss much in evidence, but new boy James Caan is a woeful lead, and the process shots are poor, making the whole look rather like an Elvis Presley movie with fewer songs. TS

James Caan *Mike Marsh* • Laura Devon *Julie Kazarian* • Gail Hire *Holly MacGregor* • Charlene Holt *Lindy Bonaparte* • John Robert Crawford *Ned Arp* • Marianna Hill *Gabrielle Queneau* • James Ward *Dan McCall* • George Takei *Kato* ■ *Dir* Howard Hawks • *Scr* George Kirgo, from a story by Howard Hawks • *Cinematographer* Milton Krasner

Red Mountain ★★

Western 1951 · US · Colour · 84mins

One of those Civil War dramas transposed to the Wild West, where the scenery is more dramatic and where the Indians turn the dilemma of the Confederates and the Unionists into a "trilemma". Alan Ladd, a Confederate captain, kills a man, and another Southerner, Arthur Kennedy, gets blamed, but is saved from a lynch mob. Meanwhile, John Ireland has abandoned "The Cause" and is organising Indians and mercenaries for a war of his own. There's a decent moral, bright-as-a-button Technicolor and a rousing finale. AT

Alan Ladd *Captain Brett Sherwood* • Lizabeth Scott *Chris* • Arthur Kennedy *Lane Waldron* • John Ireland *Quantrell* • Jeff Corey *Skee* • James Bell *Dr Terry* • Bert Freed *Randall* ■ *Dir* William Dieterle • *Scr* John Meredyth Lucas, George Slavin, George W George, from a story by George Slavin

Red Planet ★★ 12

Science-fiction action horror
2000 · US/Aus · Colour · 102mins

It's 2050 and Val Kilmer, Tom Sizemore, Carrie-Anne Moss and a hammier-than-ever Terence Stamp are sent to investigate when long-range efforts to make Mars habitable run into problems. Vital equipment is damaged in a crash-landing and the survivors are forced to depend on one another to survive in the inhospitable terrain. Director Antony Hoffman's feel-bad fantasy can't be faulted technically, but the plot lacks dramatic drive. AJ. Contains violence, swearing and brief nudity. DVD

Val Kilmer *Gallagher* • Tom Sizemore *Burchenal* • Carrie-Anne Moss *Kate Bowman* • Benjamin Bratt *Santen* • Simon Baker *Pettengil* • Terence Stamp *Chantilas* ■ *Dir* Antony Hoffman • *Scr* Chuck Pfarrer, Jonathan Lemkin, from a story by Chuck Pfarrer • *Cinematographer* Peter Suschitzky

Red Planet Mars ★★ U

Science-fiction drama
1952 · US · BW · 87mins

One of the oddest science-fiction movies ever made and worth sitting through every unwatchable preachy moment and ludicrous plot twist just to feel your jaw drop at various junctures. Could utopian Mars really be ruled by God? It's really a Nazi plot, run by Soviet agents, to destroy the world's economy. What can Earth do? Easy. Draft religious revolutionaries into Russia to overthrow the Communist government. This simple-minded slice of po-faced seriousness is sci-fi's most explicit anti-Communist tract. AJ

Peter Graves (2) *Chris Cronyn* • Andrea King *Linda Cronyn* • Orley Lindgren *Steward Cronyn* • Bayard Vellier *Roger Cronyn* • Walter Sande *Admiral Carey* • Marvin Miller *Arjenian* • Herbert Berghof *Franz Calder* • Willis Bouchey *President* ■ *Dir* Harry Horner • *Scr* Anthony Veiller, John L Balderson, from the play *Red Planet* by John L Balderson, John Hoare

The Red Pony ★★ PG

Drama 1949 · US · Colour · 84mins

John Steinbeck's tale of a boy and his horse is an awkward blend of children's picture and social realist drama, and it isn't really good enough in either department. However, while Myrna Loy seems miscast as the boy's mum, Robert Mitchum is impressive as the ranch hand. The most impressive thing here is the fine "outdoor" score by Aaron Copland, who also wrote the music for Milestone's earlier Steinbeck adaptation, *Of Mice and Men*. AT

Robert Mitchum *Billy Buck* • Myrna Loy *Alice Tiflin* • Louis Calhern *Grandpa* • Shepperd Strudwick *Fred Tiflin* • Peter Miles *Tom Tiflin* • Beau Bridges *Beau* • Margaret Hamilton *Teacher* ■ *Dir* Lewis Milestone • *Scr* John Steinbeck, from his story

Red Riding Hood ★★ PG

Fantasy 1987 · US · Colour · 77mins

Here the rather stolid Craig T Nelson gets to play twin brothers, one good, one bad, in a somewhat drawn-out "full" version of the Brothers Grimm original. It's all a bit uneven, and the musical numbers in particular are uninspired, but Isabella Rossellini is as graceful as ever playing the good twin's wife-in-jeopardy. RT

Craig T Nelson *Godfrey/Percival* • Isabella Rossellini *Lady Jeanne* • Amelia Shankley [Amelia Curtis] *Linet aka Red Riding Hood* • Rocco Sisto *Dagger the Wolf* • Linda Kaye *Badger Kate* • Helen Glazary *Nanny Bess* ■ *Dir* Adam Brooks • *Scr* Carole Lucia Satrina, from the fairy tale by the Brothers Grimm

Red River ★★★★★ U

Classic western 1948 · US · BW · 127mins

This magnificent cattle-driving western is one of the greatest achievements of American cinema. Basing his film on co-screenwriter Borden Chase's novel, producer/director Howard Hawks created a rich masterpiece. Hawks is aided by arguably John Wayne's finest performance (as cattle boss Tom Dunson), and Wayne's matched by young Montgomery Clift (as Dunson's ward). This is Hollywood film-making at its highest level, with music by Dimitri Tiomkin and photography by Russell Harlan that enhances and embellishes the text. Not to be missed, and ideally watched on the biggest screen available. Inexplicably remade as a TV movie in 1988. TS DVD

John Wayne *Thomas Dunson* • Montgomery Clift *Matthew Garth* • Joanne Dru *Tess Millay* • Walter Brennan *Groot Nadine* • Coleen Gray *Fen* • John Ireland *Cherry Valance* • Noah Beery Jr *Buster McGee* • Harry Carey Sr [Harry Carey] *Mr Melville* • Harry Carey Jr *Dan Latimer* • Shelley Winters *Dance-hall girl* ■ *Dir* Howard Hawks • *Scr* Borden Chase, Charles Schnee, from the novel *The Chisholm Trail* by Borden Chase

Red River Range ★★ U

Western 1938 · US · BW · 55mins

This "Three Mesquiteers" B-western, starring John Wayne takes less than an hour to trot out its modern-day story of the trio (Wayne, Ray Corrigan, Max Terhune) catching highly organised cattle rustlers. Veteran comedian Polly Moran takes a supporting role. AE

John Wayne *Stony Brooke* • Ray "Crash" Corrigan *Tucson Smith* • Max Terhune *Lullaby Joslin* • Polly Moran *Mrs Maxwell* • Lorna Gray *Jane Mason* • Kirby Grant *Tex Reilly* ■ *Dir* George Sherman • *Scr* Luci Ward, Stanley Roberts, Betty Burbridge, from a story by Luci Ward, from characters created by William Colt MacDonald

Red Rock West ★★★★ 15

Black comedy thriller
1992 · US · Colour · 94mins

The Last Seduction was the film that finally made people stand up and take notice of director John Dahl, but this *film noir* thriller is almost its equal. Nicolas Cage, this time in a non-comic variation on his innocent dupe persona, is the hapless drifter who is mistaken for a hitman by JT Walsh and is sent to murder Walsh's wife Lara Flynn Boyle. Things go from bad to worse when the real assassin (the demonic Dennis Hopper) turns up. The plot twists and turns deliciously, and Dahl's direction strikes a deft balance between knowing humour and genuine suspense. JF. Contains violence and swearing. DVD

Nicolas Cage *Michael Williams* • Lara Flynn Boyle *Suzanne Brown* • Dennis Hopper *Lyle* • JT Walsh *Wayne Brown* • Craig Reay *Jim* • Vance Johnson *Mr Johnson* ■ *Dir* John Dahl • *Scr* John Dahl, Rick Dahl

Red Salute ★★ U

Romantic comedy 1935 · US · BW · 79mins

General's daughter Barbara Stanwyck falls for a Communist and her father sends her to Mexico, where she meets a young soldier. Ensuing complications have them both on the run. Made when the radical movement in American universities was strong, this is basically a road comedy, with the spoiled daughter having to see the error of her leftist enthusiasms. At its premiere, students picketed and critics either condemned it as propaganda or felt it burlesqued the "American Way". Discounting the politics, it's diverting enough, with a particularly disarming performance by Stanwyck. TV

Barbara Stanwyck *Drue Van Allen* • Robert Young (1) *Jeff* • Hardie Albright *Leonard Arner* • Ruth Donnelly *Mrs Edith Rooney* • Cliff Edwards *PJ Rooney* • Gordon Jones *Lefty* • Paul Stanton *Louis Martin* ■ *Dir* Sidney Lanfield • *Scr* Humphrey Pearson, Manuel Seff, from a story by Humphrey Pearson

Red Scorpion ★ 15

Action adventure
1989 · US · Colour · 100mins

Dolph Lundgren stars in this awful action adventure as a Soviet agent who is sent to a warring African state to take out a resistance leader. Inexplicably, this was a big hit on video, perhaps because there's loads of mindless mass destruction, but the script and the performances make Rambo look positively Wildean. Lundgren didn't return for the 1995 sequel. JF [VIDEO] DVD

Dolph Lundgren *Lt Nikolai* • M Emmet Walsh *Dewey Ferguson* • Al White *Kallunda* • TP McKenna *General Vortek* • Carmen Argenziano *Zayas* • Alex Colon *Mendez* • Brion James *Krasnov* ■ *Dir* Joseph Zito • *Scr* Arne Olsen, from a story by Robert Abramoff, Jack Abramoff

The Red Shoes ★★★★★ U

Romantic dance drama
1948 · UK · Colour · 127mins

In her film debut, Moira Shearer stars as the ballerina whose life is torn between a career with a manipulative impresario (Anton Walbrook) and marriage to a young composer (Marius Goring). This is arguably the best-loved dance film of all time, enabling the team of Michael Powell and Emeric Pressburger to ponder the power and nature of the subject matter with some extravagant, exuberant dance sequences and a riot of Oscar-winning Technicolor designs. Shearer and Walbrook give impeccable portrayals of innocence and tragedy at the service of art. AT [VIDEO] DVD

Anton Walbrook *Boris Lermontov* • Moira Shearer *Victoria Page* • Marius Goring *Julian Craster* • Léonide Massine *Grischa Ljubov* • Robert Helpmann *Ivan Boleslawsky* • Albert Basserman *Sergei Ratov* • Esmond Knight *Livy* • Ludmilla Tcherina *Irina Boronskaja* ■ *Dir* Michael Powell, Emeric Pressburger • *Scr* Michael Powell, Emeric Pressburger, Keith Winter • *Cinematographer* Jack Cardiff • *Editor* Reginald Mills • *Music* Brian Easdale • *Art Director* Hein Heckroth, Arthur Lawson • *Choreographer* Robert Helpmann

Red Skies of Montana ★★

Adventure drama 1952 · US · Colour · 89mins

Richard Widmark and Richard Boone just about make this old-time action adventure worth watching. Both charismatic tough guys, they play firefighters in the Rockies who parachute into forest fires and either hose them down or create corridors over which the flames can't jump. You can't do this for an entire movie so various subplots are trumped up, with Widmark haunted by the death of a colleague while his wife (Constance Smith) gazes lovingly at him. AT

Richard Widmark *Cliff Mason* • Constance Smith *Peg* • Jeffrey Hunter *Ed Miller* • Richard Boone *Dryer* • Warren Stevens *Steve* • James Griffith *Boise* • Joe Sawyer *Pop Miller* • Charles Buchinsky [Charles Bronson] *Neff* ■ *Dir* Joseph M Newman • *Scr* Harry Kleiner, from a story by Art Cohn

Red Sky at Morning ★★

Drama 1971 · US · Colour · 112mins

Left to his own devices in a strange New Mexico town, Richard Thomas struggles to come to terms with mother Claire Bloom's despairing fling after his father Richard Crenna is killed while serving with the navy. In contrast to this domestic bombast, James Goldstone tackles both Thomas's friendship with Desi Arnaz Jr and his hesitant romance with Catherine Burns with an overweening sensitivity that's punctuated only by monstrously unsubtle symbolism. Vilmos Zsigmond's photography threatens to capture life, but not often enough. DP

Richard Thomas *Josh Arnold* • Catherine Burns *Marcia Davidson* • Desi Arnaz Jr *Steenie Moreno* • Richard Crenna *Frank Arnold* • Claire Bloom *Ann Arnold* • John Colicos *Jimbob Buel* • Harry Guardino *Romeo Bonino* ■ *Dir* James Goldstone • *Scr* Marguerite Roberts, from the novel by Richard Bradford

Red Sonja ★★ 15

Fantasy adventure
1985 · US · Colour · 84mins

Brigitte Nielsen stars as a leather bikini-clad warrior who aims to avenge the death of her family by confronting wicked queen Sandahl Bergman. But it's Arnold Schwarzenegger who is the real star here, showing off his bulging biceps while trying to retain his dignity in a loincloth as the grunting hero who helps her. This is a sword-and-sorcery adventure for those who like their action fast, their dialogue ropey and their acting filled with more ham than a butcher's shop. JB. Contains violence and brief nudity [VIDEO] DVD

Brigitte Nielsen *Red Sonja* • Arnold Schwarzenegger *Kalidor* • Sandahl Bergman *Queen Gedren* • Paul Smith *Falkon* • Ernie Reyes Jr *Prince Tarn* • Ronald Lacey *Ikol* ■ *Dir* Richard Fleischer • *Scr* Clive Exton, George MacDonald Fraser, from the character created by Robert E Howard

Red Sorghum ★★★★★ 15

Drama 1987 · Chi · Colour · 87mins

Having made his name as a cinematographer on such pictures as Chen Kaige's *Yellow Earth*, Zhang Yimou established himself as one of the most important Chinese film-makers with this, his directorial debut. The start of his collaboration with then-partner Gong Li and the winner of the Golden Bear at Berlin, *Red Sorghum* has a visual bravura that has since become Zhang's trademark, making majestic use of colour and setting the scene with stunning long-shots of buildings or breathtaking landscapes. He is also a natural storyteller, switching with great skill from the cosiness of a simple family drama to the brutality of a heroic resistance struggle. A true modern classic. DP. In Mandarin with English subtitles. Contains violence. [VIDEO]

Gong Li *Nine, "my grandma"* • Jiang Wen *Yu, "my grandpa"* • Teng Rujun *Liu Luohan* • Liu Ji *Douguan "my dad"* • Qian Ming *Nine's father* • Ji Chunhua *Bandit Sanpao* • Zhai Chunhua *Hu Er* ■ *Dir* Zhang Yimou • *Scr* Chen Jianyu, Zhu Wei, Mo Yan, from the short stories by Mo Yan

The Red Squirrel ★★★★ 18

Comedy drama 1993 · Sp · Colour · 109mins

Exploring such sundry themes as identity and memory, female intuition, male boorishness and Basque nationalism, this is a typically inventive and beguiling outing from director Julio Medem. The frantic pace and dazzling technique complement the endlessly diverging train of events that follows suicidal musician Nancho Novo's chance encounter with runaway amnesiac Emma Suarez. Unconventionally comic, yet deftly passionate in its themes, this virtuoso picture not only benefits from storming lead performances, but also from inspired character turns. DP. In Spanish with English subtitles. Contains violence, sex scenes and swearing. [VIDEO] DVD

Nancho Novo *Jota* • Emma Suarez *Lisa* • Maria Barranco *Carmen* • Carmelo Gomez *Felix* ■ *Dir/Scr* Julio Medem

Red Sun ★★★ 15

Western 1971 · Fr/It/Sp · Colour · 108mins

Toshiro Mifune teams up with gunslinger Charles Bronson to recover a golden, ceremonial sword, stolen by black-clad Alain Delon from the Japanese Ambassador to the US. Ursula Andress and Capucine add glamour to a yarn that's always entertaining and full of heavily stylised violence. Because the spaghetti western owed its origins to the samurai movie, this is a clever example of fusion cinema, but it lacks cultural insights and wit. AT [VIDEO]

Charles Bronson *Link* • Toshiro Mifune *Kuroda – samurai bodyguard* • Alain Delon *Gauche* • Ursula Andress *Cristina* • Capucine *Pepita* • Satoshi Nakamura *Ambassador* ■ *Dir* Terence Young • *Scr* Laird Koenig, Denne Bart Petitclerc, William Roberts, Lawrence Roman, from a story by Laird Koenig

Red Sun Rising ★★★ 18

Martial arts action
1994 · US · Colour · 99mins

In the 1990s, Don "The Dragon" Wilson was consigned mainly to straight-to-video fodder, but his charismatic skills marked him out as a name to watch. Sadly he faded from sight but this remains one of his stronger efforts, boasting a better than average script that still finds room for plenty of astonishing fight sequences. Here, Wilson plays a cop who comes up against his most lethal enemy in the shape of a black-hearted Japanese master (James Lew). JF [VIDEO] DVD

Don "The Dragon" Wilson *Thomas Hoshino* • Terry Farrell *Karen Ryder* • Michael Ironside *Captain Meisler* • Mako *Buntoro Iga* ■ *Dir* Francis Megahy • *Scr* David S Green, from a story by David S Green, Neva Friedden, Paul Maslak

Red Sundown ★★★ U

Western 1956 · US · Colour · 81mins

A terrific Universal co-feature, this western stars the excellent Rory Calhoun as a former gunslinger strapping on his guns one more time to thwart an evil cattle baron. Not terribly original but given zest by understanding director Jack Arnold and produced by exploitation king Albert Zugsmith of *Touch of Evil* fame. Martha Hyer gives a fine performance as a frontier woman, and veterans Dean Jagger and Robert Middleton lend supporting class. TS

Rory Calhoun *Alec Longmire* • Martha Hyer *Caroline Murphy* • Dean Jagger *Sheriff Jade Murphy* • Robert Middleton *Rufus Henshaw* • Grant Williams *Chet Swann* • Lita Baron *Maria* • James Millican *Purvis* ■ *Dir* Jack Arnold • *Scr* Martin Berkeley, from the novel *Black Trail* by Lewis B Patten

Red Surf ★ 18

Crime drama 1990 · US · Colour · 98mins

A relentlessly predictable, dumber-than-average thriller that has some interest value because it stars Hollywood heart-throb George Clooney in an early role. He plays a surfer dude, who together with best friend Doug Savant, deals drugs to make ends meet. Deciding to make one last big score, they involve their friend Doug McKeon in the plan. But when he gets arrested, he quickly names the local drug kingpin, who seeks revenge for the betrayal. A hokey, derivative exercise featuring Gene Simmons from the band *Kiss* as the surfers' mentor. AJ [VIDEO]

George Clooney *Remar* • Doug Savant *Attila* • Gene Simmons *Doc* • Dedee Pfeiffer *Rebecca* • Rick Najera *Calavera* • Philip McKeon *True Blue* ■ *Dir* H Gordon Boos • *Scr* Vincent Robert, from a story by Brian Gamble, Jason Hoffs, Vincent Robert

Red Team ★★ 18

Crime thriller 1999 · Can · Colour · 90mins

It's a nifty premise – a serial killer who specialises in murdering fellow serial killers. But sadly director Jeremy Haft fails to make the most of the opportunity and the result is routine police thriller. Patrick Muldoon and Cathy Moriarty are the FBI agents who have a crisis of conscience when they cotton on to the fact that someone else is doing their job for them – and that the killer may actually be one of their own. JF [VIDEO] DVD

Patrick Muldoon *Jason Chandler* • Cathy Moriarty *Agent Stephanie Dobson* • Tim Thomerson *William Heywood* • Fred Ward *Randall Brooks* • C Thomas Howell *JB Gaines* ■ *Dir* Jeremy Haft • *Scr* Alexander Metcalf

The Red Tent ★★★ U

Historical adventure
1969 · It/USSR · Colour · 120mins

This ran at over four hours in Russia but was half that length in Europe and the United States. The movie deals with the dramatic rescue in 1928 of an Italian expedition to the Arctic. Playing the leader of the expedition, Peter Finch had to endure the entire 16-month shoot – a near record – while Sean Connery's role, as Roald Amundsen, was added later in the hope of boosting the film's box-office appeal. As a survivalist epic, it has its moments and the authentic locations are often spectacular. Finch, too, is always excellent and there's an Ennio Morricone score as a bonus. AT. Some dialogue dubbed into English.

Sean Connery *Roald Amundsen* • Claudia Cardinale *Nurse Valeria* • Hardy Kruger *Aviator Lundborg* • Peter Finch *General Umberto Nobile* • Massimo Girotti *Romagna, rescue coordinator* • Luigi Vannucchi *Captain Zappi* • Mario Adorf *Biagi, radio operator* • Edward Marzevic *Finn Malmgren, meteorologist* ■ *Dir* Mikhail K Kalatozov [Mikhail Kalatozov] • *Scr* Ennio De Concini, Richard Adams, Robert Bolt (uncredited)

The Red Violin ★★★ 15

Drama 1998 · Can/It/UK · Colour · 130mins

Spanning 300 years, three continents and five languages, François Girard's musical chain letter looks and sounds superb. But, with locale and narrative carrying more weight than character, it's difficult to identify with any of the temporary owners of the violin, dyed red with the blood of the maker's dead family. Cursed by its maker's obsessive pursuit of perfection, the instrument passes on down the centuries, bringing ill-fortune to Austrian child prodigy Christoph Koncz, English virtuoso Jason Flemyng and Chinese student Sylvia Chang, although, intriguingly, we're left unsure whether crooked antiquarian Samuel L

R

Jackson will suffer the same fate. DP. Contains some sex scenes. DVD

Samuel L Jackson *Charles Morritz* • Greta Scacchi *Victoria Byrd* • Eva Marie Bryer *Sara* • Jason Flemyng *Frederick Pope* • Sylvia Chang *Xiang Pei* • Colm Feore *Auctioneer* • Carlo Cecchi *Nicolo Bussotti* ■ *Dir* François Girard • *Scr* François Girard, Don McKellar

Redemption ★★★ 15

Biographical crime drama
2004 · US · Colour · 91mins

Jamie Foxx flexes his serious acting muscles in this powerful made-for-TV movie. It's based on the story of Stan "Tookie" Williams, who has been on Death Row in the United States since 1981, and who has become a crusader against gang violence. Lynn Whitfield plays the sceptical journalist who ends up helping him write a bestselling series of children's books designed to deter kids from the gang lifestyle. Although the script lacks substance, Foxx delivers a nicely understated performance, and director Vondie Curtis-Hall mostly succeeds in avoiding the usual clichés. JF. Contains violence, swearing. DVD

Jamie Foxx *Stan "Tookie" Williams* • Lynn Whitfield *Barbara Becnel* • CCH Pounder *Winnie Mandela* • Brenden Jefferson *Young Stan Williams* • Lee Thompson Young *Charles Becnel* ■ *Dir* Vondie Curtis-Hall • *Scr* JT Allen

The Redhead and the Cowboy ★★★

Wartime western 1950 · US · BW · 82mins

A strong trio of leading players – Glenn Ford, Rhonda Fleming and Edmond O'Brien – make this plot-heavy Civil War story watchable enough for western buffs, although the title cries out for Technicolor. Fleming is the redheaded messenger for the South, O'Brien the undercover Union officer on her trail, and Ford the cowboy she mistakes for a contact. The film only falls apart when Alan Reed as a renegade Confederate officer starts chewing up the scenery. AE

Glenn Ford *Gil Kyle* • Edmond O'Brien *Dunn Jeffers* • Rhonda Fleming *Candace Bronson* • Alan Reed *Lamartine* • Morris Ankrum *Sheriff* ■ *Dir* Leslie Fenton • *Scr* Jonathan Latimer, Liam O'Brien, from a story by Charles Marquis Warren

The Redhead from Wyoming ★★★ U

Western adventure
1953 · US · Colour · 80mins

If ever anybody deserved to be filmed in colour, it was green-eyed, red-headed Irish beauty Maureen O'Hara, whose Hollywood career was as historic as it was colourful. Besides doing terrific work for John Ford, she invariably starred in swashbucklers and westerns that perfectly showcased her talents. In this movie, she falls for a sheriff while supposedly taking care of a rancher. The story is pure fluff, of course, but when O'Hara's on the screen the weaknesses in the plot aren't important. TS

Maureen O'Hara *Kate Maxwell* • Alex Nicol *Stan Blaine* • William Bishop *Jim Averell* • Robert Strauss *"Knuckles" Hogan* • Alexander Scourby *Reece Duncan* • Jack Kelly *Sandy* • Jeanne Cooper *Myra* ■ *Dir* Lee Sholem • *Scr* Polly James, Herb Meadow, from the story by Polly James

Redheads ★★ 15

Thriller 1992 · Aus · Colour · 102mins

When she discovers she's videotaped the murder of her lover, a corrupt lawyer in the Justice Commission, Claudia Karvan goes on the run, only to be arrested for damaging a police car. Will she manage to convince her sceptical counsel, Catherine McClements, that she's in danger? Unfortunately, it's not too difficult to work out that one, or the identity of the culprit. DP

Claudia Karvan *Lucy Darling* • Catherine McClements *Diana Ferraro* • Alexander Petersons *Simon* • Sally McKenzie *Warden Zeida* • Anthony Phelan *Inspector Quigley* • Mark Hembrow *Brewster* • Jennifer Flowers *Carolyn* ■ *Dir* Danny Vendramini • *Scr* Danny Vendramini, from the play *Say Thank You to the Lady* by Rosie Scott

Redneck Zombies ★★

Horror 1988 · US · Colour · 83mins

Shot on videotape, this concerns a drum of radioactive waste lost during a military transport through redneck country. Some locals find the drum and use it to repair their broken still, contaminating the moonshine they make and distribute. As a result, the area's residents become flesh-eating zombies. Aside from the plentiful (and extremely graphic) gore sequences, this is characterised by production values that hit a new low and a script that grabs every opportunity to use stereotypes and sophomoric humour. KB. Contains violence.

Lisa DeHaven *Lisa Dubois* • WE Benson *Jed "Pa" Clemson* • William W Decker • James Housely *Wilbur* ■ *Dir/Scr* Pericles Lewnes

Reds ★★★★★ 15

Epic biographical drama
1981 · US · Colour · 186mins

It took Warren Beatty's ferocious energy to even attempt this chronicle of the Russian Revolution, focused through a radical love affair, and come up with a final product that is close to the project's original intentions. In telling the story of American journalist John Reed – who wrote *Ten Days That Shook the World*, regarded by many as the definitive account of the revolution – and his on-off romance with left-wing activist Louise Bryant (Diane Keaton), Beatty surrounded himself with massive talent: British writer Trevor Griffiths, cinematographer Vittorio Storaro, composer Stephen Sondheim, the great editor Dede Allen and a scene-stealing Jack Nicholson as playwright Eugene O'Neill. Beatty won a well-deserved Oscar for best direction. TH. Contains swearing.

Warren Beatty *John Reed* • Diane Keaton *Louise Bryant* • Jack Nicholson *Eugene O'Neill* • Edward Herrmann *Max Eastman* • Jerzy Kosinski *Grigory Zinoviev* • Maureen Stapleton *Emma Goldman* • Gene Hackman *Pete Van Wherry* • Paul Sorvino *Louis Fraina* • Nicolas Coster *Paul Trullinger* • M Emmet Walsh *Speaker at Liberal club* • Ian Wolfe *Mr Partlow* • Bessie Love *Mrs Partlow* ■ *Dir* Warren Beatty • *Scr* Warren Beatty, Trevor Griffiths

Reed: Insurgent Mexico ★★★★

Historical drama
1971 · Mex · Sepia · 106mins

Long before he reported on the ten days that shook the world in 1917, American journalist John Reed witnessed the Mexican Revolution of 1910. Paul Leduc may not have enjoyed the vast resources utilised by Warren Beatty's Reed opus *Reds*, but his modest film is a fine example of how depicting the past need not be as dry as a history lesson. The Mexican director's use of a sepia tint to convey both the time of the events and their authenticity is extremely shrewd, while his ability to put across factual information without swamping the human drama is most impressive. DP. In Spanish with English subtitles.

Claudio Obregon *John Reed* • Eduardo Lopez Rojas *General Tomas Urbina* • Ernesto Gómez Cruz *Captain Pablo Seanez* • Juan Angel Martinez *Lieutenant Julian Reyes* • Carlos Castanon *Fidencio Soto* • Victor Fosado *Isidro Amaya* ■ *Dir* Paul Leduc • *Scr* Paul Leduc, Juan Tovar, from the book *Insurgent Mexico* by John Reed

Reefer and the Model ★★★ 15

Comedy thriller 1988 · UK · Colour · 89mins

This spiky, acerbic tale of a small-time criminal and his involvement with a junkie "model", veers alarmingly at times between winsome charm and outré violence. It wins out in the end through sheer bravura of characterisation as director Joe Comerford cuts to the core of his cast's motivations. London's underbelly is exposed in all its visceral glory, the narrative occasionally roves all over the shop, but it's worth sticking with this unusually energetic thriller that contains just enough cutting wit and dark humour. SH

Ian McElhinney *Reefer* • Carol Scanlan *Teresa, the model* • Eve Watkinson *Reefer's mother* • Sean Lawlor *Spider* • Ray McBride *Badger* • Birdy Sweeney *"Instant Photo"* ■ *Dir/Scr* Joe Comerford

Reefer Madness ★★ 15

Cult drama 1936 · US · BW · 59mins

Initially released as *The Burning Question* and later retitled *Tell Your Children*, this exploitation classic emerged from decades of obscurity to become a campus classic in the early 1970s. In this hilariously misinformed exposé of the perils of smoking dope, exhortation comes a poor second to sensationalism, as Dave O'Brien tempts his classmates into toking on the weed. DP DVD

Dorothy Short *Mary Lane* • Kenneth Craig *Bill Harper* • Lillian Miles *Blanche* • Dave O'Brien *Ralph Wiley* • Thelma White *Mae Colman* • Carleton Young *Jack Perry* • Warren McCollum *Jimmy Lane* ■ *Dir* Louis Gasnier • *Scr* Arthur Hoerl and Paul Franklin, from an original story by Lawrence Meade

The Reflecting Skin ★★ 15

Drama 1990 · UK · Colour · 91mins

The directorial debut of Philip Ridley is a wilfully perverse affair centred on a child (Jeremy Cooper) whose confused perceptions of the adults and events in his 1950s American farming community make for a disturbing vision of childhood. Ridley has a bad case of David Lynchitis, populating a striking rural landscape with weirdos, paedophiles and murderous kids. Cooper's cruellest fantasies are fixed on reclusive widow Lindsay Duncan, whose liaison with the boy's hero-brother (Viggo Mortensen) inspires the child to connive at her ruin. Heavy portents and deep symbolism abound to absurd effect. AME

Viggo Mortensen *Cameron* • Lindsay Duncan *Dolphin Blue* • Jeremy Cooper *Seth* • Sheila Moore *Ruth* • Duncan Fraser *Luke* ■ *Dir/Scr* Philip Ridley • *Cinematographer* Dick Pope

A Reflection of Fear ★★★★ 18

Horror 1973 · US · Colour · 85mins

This weird thriller was very unpopular in its day but its unnervingly sinister atmosphere will repay another look. Strange teenager Sondra Locke lives with her mother Mary Ure, her grandmother Signe Hasso and her dolls. Then, when her absentee father (Robert Shaw, Ure's husband in real life) appears out of the blue, she goes completely off the rails, and the film leads to a truly mind-boggling ending. Director William A Fraker creates chills by never quite revealing the menace; primarily a cinematographer, everything looks great. Performances are also strong, especially from the ethereal-looking Locke. DM

Robert Shaw *Michael* • Sally Kellerman *Anne* • Mary Ure *Katherine* • Sondra Locke *Marguerite* • Signe Hasso *Julia* • Mitchell Ryan *Inspector McKenna* ■ *Dir* William A Fraker • *Scr* Edward Hume, Lewis John Carlino, from the novel *Go to Thy Deathbed* by Stanton Forbes

Reflections in a Golden Eye ★★★ 15

Drama 1967 · US · Colour · 104mins

A weird John Huston effort, with Marlon Brando as the US Army officer and latent homosexual married to Elizabeth Taylor. Brian Keith is having an affair with Taylor because his wife, Julie Harris, performed a partial mastectomy on herself after the birth of her child. All this emanates from a novel by Carson McCullers, and very steamy it is, too. Cameraman Aldo Tonti strikes some interesting angles and colour combinations, but it's hideously overblown and unintentionally funny. AT. Contains swearing.

Elizabeth Taylor *Leonora Penderton* • Marlon Brando *Maj Weldon Penderton* • Brian Keith *Lt Col Morris Langdon* • Julie Harris *Alison Langdon* • Zorro David *Anacleto* • Gordon Mitchell (1) *Stables sergeant* • Irvin Dugan *Captain Weincheck* • Fay Sparks *Susie* • Robert Forster *Private Williams* • Douglas Stark *Dr Burgess* ■ *Dir* John Huston • *Scr* Chapman Mortimer, Gladys Hill, from the novel by Carson McCullers

Reflections on a Crime ★★★

Psychological drama
1994 · US · Colour · 84mins

Although he will always be remembered for cult low-budget B-movies, Roger Corman sometimes took a chance on artier fare, such as this intriguing movie. Mimi Rogers puts in a mesmerising performance as a woman on death row for the murder of her husband, who reluctantly reveals her story in flashback to prison guard Billy Zane. It's too talky for its own good, but director/writer Jon Purdy still delivers some chilling insights into domestic hell. JF. Contains violence, swearing and nudity.

Mimi Rogers *Regina* • Billy Zane *Colin* • John Terry *James* • Kurt Fuller *Howard* • Lee Garlington *Tina* • Nancy Fish *Ellen* ■ *Dir/Scr* Jon Purdy

Reform School Girl ★ 12

Prison crime drama 1957 · US · BW · 70mins

In this trashy exploitation picture aimed at the youth market, Gloria Castillo is the kind of well-developed teenager who has only to iron a dress in her underwear to be propositioned by her uncle. Sent to reform school after refusing to squeal on her car-thief boyfriend, she is victimised and almost murdered before settling down to a more wholesome future. AE DVD

Gloria Castillo *Donna Price* • Edward Byrnes [Edd Byrnes] *Vince* • Ross Ford *David Lindsay* • Ralph Reed *Jackie* • Yvette Vickers *Roxy* • Helen Wallace *Mrs Trimble* • Donna Jo Gribble *Cathy* • Luana Anders *Josie* • Sally Kellerman *Girl* ■ *Dir/Scr* Edward Bernds

Reform School Girl ★★ 18

Drama 1994 · US · Colour · 79mins

Based loosely on a 1950s flick of the same name, this TV movie features Aimee Graham as a sulky teen rebel who finds herself way out of her depth when she is sent to reform school after being implicated in a case of manslaughter. The young cast which includes a pre-*Friends* Matt Le Blanc gives its all, but director Jonathan Kaplan treats the premise too seriously, and exploitation fans are likely to be disappointed. JF. Contains swearing and nudity.

Aimee Graham *Donna* • Teresa DiSpina *Maria* • Carolyn Seymour *Mrs Turnbull* • Eleanor

O'Brien *Dink* • Matt LeBlanc *Vince* • Ashley Lister *Kathy Graham* • Harry Northrop *Uncle Charlie* ■ *Dir* Jonathan Kaplan • *Scr* Bruce Meade

Reform School Girls ★★ 18

Prison spoof 1986 · US · Colour · 90mins

Director Tom DeSimone had a string of enjoyably trashy pictures including porn to his credit, before making this "women behind bars" spoof. Youngster Linda Carol is sent to a harsh reform school where she has to deal with the usual unsympathetic female warden and a lesbian gang leader, played by one-time rock singer Wendy O Williams. Amusing and campy in spots, with plenty of nudity and gratuitous underwear. JG [video]

Sybil Danning *Sutter* • Wendy O Williams *Charlie* • Linda Carol *Jenny* • Pat Ast *Edna* • Charlotte McGinnis *Dr Norton* • Sherri Stoner *Lisa* • Denise Gordy *Claudie* • Laurie Schwartz *Nicky* ■ *Dir/Scr* Tom DeSimone

Regarding Henry ★★★ 15

Drama 1991 · US · Colour · 102mins

What looked like a sure-fire winner on paper – ruthless high-flying lawyer Harrison Ford fights back from brain injury and becomes a better person in the process – in fact emerged as a rather cold, lacklustre affair. Ford, who can be unnervingly emotionless on screen, was simply the wrong choice for the role, and director Mike Nichols invests the action with so much gloss and polish you feel as if your brain is swimming in an oil slick. Annette Bening looks lovely and gives one of the film's better performances, but from the start it's hard to sympathise with the family and their plight. SH. Contains some swearing. [video] DVD

Harrison Ford *Henry Turner* • Annette Bening *Sarah Turner* • Bill Nunn *Bradley* • Mikki Allen *Rachel Turner* • Donald Moffat *Charlie* • Aida Linares *Rosella* • Elizabeth Wilson *Jessica* • Robin Bartlett *Phyllis* • Bruce Altman *Bruce* • Rebecca Miller *Linda Palmer* ■ *Dir* Mike Nichols • *Scr* Jeffrey Abrams

Regeneration ★★★★

Silent drama 1915 · US · BW · 74mins

Bowery hoodlum Owen Kildare published his memoir *My Mamie Rose: the Story of My Regeneration* in 1903 and a play duly followed. Writing with half-brother Carl Harbaugh, Raoul Walsh changed some names and tinkered with the odd fact to produce this vivid crime movie that also provides an invaluable portrait of inner-city slum life in America. Rockliffe Fellowes and Anna Q Nilsson are aptly teamed as the orphan-gone-bad and the selfless socialite whose happiness is thwarted by Harbaugh's crusading DA. The story is affecting, the acting functional, but the images achieved by Walsh and cameraman Georges Benoit are indelible. DP

Rockliffe Fellowes *Owen Conway* • Anna Q Nilsson *Marie Deering* • William Sheer *Skinny* • Carl Harbaugh *District Attorney Ames* • James A Marcus *Jim Conway* • Maggie Weston *Maggie Conway* ■ *Dir* RA Walsh [Raoul Walsh] • *Scr* RA Walsh [Raoul Walsh], Carl Harbaugh, from the play by Owen Kildare, Walter Hackett, from the memoir *My Mamie Rose: the Story of My Regeneration* by Owen Kildare

Regeneration ★★★★ 15

First World War drama
1997 · UK/Can · Colour · 108mins

Four shell-shocked men help each other come to terms with their shared horrific First World War experiences in director Gillies MacKinnon's compelling, if sometimes highly romanticised, adaptation of the first book in Pat Barker's trilogy. How they cope in a military psychiatric hospital – Siegfried Sassoon and Wilfred Owen (James Wilby and Stuart Bunce) wrote their most famous poetry in such institutions to exorcise their feelings – makes for a grim, intelligent drama suffused with haunting and harrowing images, none more so than the opening aerial shot of no man's land strewn with the casualties of war. AJ. Contains swearing, nudity. [video] DVD

Jonathan Pryce *Dr William Rivers* • James Wilby *Siegfried Sassoon* • Jonny Lee Miller *Billy Prior* • Stuart Bunce *Wilfred Owen* • Tanya Allen *Sarah* • David Hayman *Dr Bryce* • Dougray Scott *Robert Graves* • John Neville *Dr Yealland* ■ *Dir* Gillies MacKinnon • *Scr* Allan Scott, from the novel by Pat Barker

Regina ★★★

Psychological drama
1982 · Fr/It · Colour · 95mins

Was ever a control freak so glamorous? Ava Gardner is the mother who dominates her husband (Anthony Quinn) and son (Ray Sharkey) to such an extent that, when the boy wants to marry, mum refuses, then takes to her bed with a psychosomatic illness. This rarely seen performance by Ava Gardner is one of her very best and director Jean-Yves Prate has contrived an atmosphere as morbid as the central character herself. TH

Ava Gardner *Mother* • Anthony Quinn *Father* • Anna Karina *Daughter* • Ray Sharkey *Son* ■ *Dir* Jean-Yves Prate • *Scr* from the play by Pierre Rey

La Règle du Jeu ★★★★★ PG

Comedy drama 1939 · Fr · BW · 101mins

This complex comedy of manners from director Jean Renoir was such a box-office turkey on its first release in 1939 that it was not allowed out again at its original length until the late 1950s. It was then promptly acclaimed as a masterpiece, going on a few years later to selection by an international poll of critics as the third greatest film of all time. Focusing on an up-market country house party, the film is a sophisticated, poignant and often funny study of social mores and the games people play. Renoir stars, directs and co-writes. PF. In French with English subtitles. [video] DVD

Marcel Dalio *Robert la Chesnaye* • Nora Gregor *Christine* • Jean Renoir *Octave* • Roland Toutain *Jurieu* • Mila Parely *Genevieve de Marras* • Paulette Dubost *Lisette* • Carette [Julien Carette] *Marceau* • Gaston Modot *Schumacher* ■ *Dir/Scr* Jean Renoir

Reign of Fire ★★ 12

Futuristic fantasy adventure
2001 · US/UK/Ire · Colour · 97mins

If it weren't for the dragons, this far-fetched fantasy would have drowned in its own mediocrity. A skeletal, anti-climactic mess from Rob Bowman, it relies totally on its mythological flying fire-breathers to carry the film. These scaly monsters have overrun the world after London Underground workers inadvertently unleashed a slumbering ancestor. The performances range from hammy (Christian Bale) to simply wooden (Gerard Butler). SF. Contains violence and swearing. [video] DVD

Christian Bale *Quinn Abercromby* • Matthew McConaughey *Denton Van Zan* • Izabella Scorupco *Alex Jensen* • Gerard Butler *Dave Creedy* • Scott James Moutter *Jared Wilke* • David Kennedy *Eddie Stax* • Alexander Siddig *Ajay* • Ned Dennehy *Barlow* ■ *Dir* Rob Bowman • *Scr* Gregg Chabot, Kevin Peterka, Matt Greenberg, from a story by Gregg Chabot, Kevin Peterka

Reign of Terror ★★★★

Historical drama 1949 · US · BW · 89mins

A visually exhilarating, ingeniously-plotted political thriller about Robespierre's plot to become dictator after the French Revolution, this even extracts passable performances from usually limp Robert Cummings and insipid but beautiful Arlene Dahl in the starring roles. Richard Basehart makes a superbly malevolent Robespierre and supporting actor Arnold Moss has his finest moment as a sly opportunist. The Machiavellian intrigue unfolds in vivid *film noir* style as the powerful team of director Anthony Mann and cameraman John Alton is joined by the great art director William Cameron Menzies (taking credit only as the producer). The imagery conveys the terror and uncertainty of the period, while the pace overrides the script's contrivances. Heady stuff indeed. AE

Robert Cummings *Charles D'Aubigny* • Richard Basehart *Maximilien Robespierre* • Richard Hart *François Barras* • Arlene Dahl *Madelon* • Arnold Moss *Police chief Fouché* • Norman Lloyd *Tallien* • Charles McGraw *Sergeant* • Beulah Bondi *Grandma* ■ *Dir* Anthony Mann • *Scr* Philip Yordan, Aeneas MacKenzie, from a story by Philip Yordan, Aeneas MacKenzie

The Reincarnation of Peter Proud ★★★ 18

Horror mystery 1975 · US · Colour · 101mins

Slated in its time, this has become almost a cult movie since. Director J Lee Thompson treated Max Ehrlich's adaptation of his own novel with a seriousness it didn't deserve – but his approach worked. Michael Sarrazin is the history professor who dreams his way back to the past and makes some discoveries about previous lives and loves. The plot never gets it together, but the mood and atmosphere are spot on. TH [video]

Michael Sarrazin *Peter Proud* • Jennifer O'Neill *Ann Curtis* • Margot Kidder *Marcia Curtis* • Cornelia Sharpe *Nora Hayes* • Paul Hecht *Dr Samuel Goodman* • Norman Burton *Dr Frederick Spear* ■ *Dir* J Lee Thompson • *Scr* Max Ehrlich, from his novel

La Reine Margot ★★

Historical drama
1954 · Fr/It · Colour · 93mins

Catherine de Medici (Françoise Rosay) rules France through her son, Charles IX (Robert Porte), and hopes to avoid civil war between the Protestants and the Catholics by arranging a marriage between her daughter Margot (Jeanne Moreau) and a handsome count. Dumas's novel was originally adapted by Abel Gance, the director of the legendary silent epic *Napoléon*, but the film that finally emerged was much more of a bodice-ripper and it suffered cuts for the American and British markets. AT. A French language film.

Jeanne Moreau *Marguerite de Valois, Queen Margot* • Françoise Rosay *Catherine de Medici* • Armando Francioli *Joseph Peyrac de la Mole* • Robert Porte *Charles IX* • Henri Génès *Annibal de Coconas* • André Versini *Henri de Navarre* ■ *Dir* Jean Dréville • *Scr* Abel Gance, from the novel by Alexandre Dumas

La Reine Margot ★★★ 18

Historical drama
1994 · Fr/Ger/It · Colour · 155mins

One of the dangers of historical film-making is that there is so much information available that the pace becomes fatally slow. Patrice Chéreau avoids this by taking the events described in the novel by Alexandre Dumas at such a furious lick, that the action becomes incomprehensible unless you pay keen attention. Isabelle Adjani won her fourth César as the Catholic Marguerite de Valois, who was married by her scheming mother Catherine de Médici (a César-winning Virna Lisi) to the Protestant leader Henri de Navarre (Daniel Auteuil). The illicit romance with Vincent Perez is deadly dull, but Jean-Hugues Anglade is outstanding as the deranged Charles IX. DP. In French with English subtitles. Contains violence, sex scenes and nudity. [video] DVD

Isabelle Adjani *Marguerite de Valois (Margot)* • Daniel Auteuil *Henri de Navarre* • Jean-Hugues Anglade *Charles IX* • Vincent Perez *La Môle* • Virna Lisi *Catherine de Médici* • Dominique Blanc *Henriette de Nevers* ■ *Dir* Patrice Chéreau • *Scr* Danièle Thompson, Patrice Chéreau, from the novel by Alexandre Dumas

Re-inventing Eddie ★★ 15

Drama 2002 · UK · Colour · 94mins

John Lynch puts passion aplenty into this low-budget film about mistaken child abuse, but his character acts so daftly he never elicits the sympathy he needs. He plays a doting dad who is determined to bring up his children in an open and honest environment. But, after his daughter's impromptu playground sex-education lesson comes to the attention of the school authorities, the social services visit. It's the start of a downward spiral that threatens him with the loss both his children and his wife. Though well acted and decently enough made, this is overwrought and underdeveloped. DA. Contains sexual references.

John Lynch *Eddie Harris* • Geraldine Somerville *Jeanie Harris* • John Thomson *Cliff* • Ian Mercer *Dougie* • John McCardle *Donald* • Judith Barker *Sheila* • Sidney Livingstone *Arthur* • Lauren Crook *Katie Harris* • Ben Thompson *Billy Harris* ■ *Dir* Jim Doyle • *Scr* Jim Doyle, Ian Brady, from the play *One Fine Day* by Dennis Lumborg

The Reivers ★★★★ PG

Period comedy drama
1969 · US · Colour · 106mins

Steve McQueen is well cast here as the ne'er-do-well guiding youngster Mitch Vogel through the minefield of adolescence in turn-of-the-century Mississippi. McQueen plays a hired hand working for Vogel's grandfather, Will Geer, who makes use of his employer's new car to take the lad on an adventure that includes a brothel and a racetrack. Mark Rydell directs with a gentle pace, while Burgess Meredith tightens it all up as narrator. There's also a scene-stealing, Oscar-nominated performance by Rupert Crosse. TH [video] DVD

Steve McQueen *Boon Hogganbeck* • Sharon Farrell *Corrie* • Will Geer *Boss McCaslin* • Michael Constantine *Mr Binford* • Rupert Crosse *Ned McCaslin* • Mitch Vogel *Lucius McCaslin* • Lonny Chapman *Maury McCaslin* • Juano Hernandez *Uncle Possum* • Clifton James *Butch Lovemaiden* • Ruth White *Miss Reba* • Dub Taylor *Dr Peabody* • Diane Ladd *Phoebe* • Burgess Meredith *Narrator* ■ *Dir* Mark Rydell • *Scr* Irving Ravetch, Harriet Frank Jr, from the novel by William Faulkner

The Rejuvenator ★★★ 18

Horror 1988 · US · Colour · 84mins

Ageing actress Jessica Dublin is financing demented doctor John Mackay's experiments in eternal youth. When he finally creates a serum from human brains to make her young again, she pretends to be her actress niece in order to revive her film career. But sex makes her mutate into a giant-headed monster with huge claws, which she uses to decapitate victims before eating their brains. Well made and oddly affecting, this is also oppressively creepy. AJ [video]

Vivian Lanko *Elizabeth Warren/Monster* • John MacKay *Dr Gregory Ashton* • James Hogue *Wilhelm* • Katell Pleven *Dr Stella Stone* • Marcus Powell *Dr Germaine* • Jessica Dublin *Ruth Warren* • Roy MacArthur *Hunter* • Louis F Homyak *Tony* ■ *Dir* Brian Thomas Jones • *Scr* Simon Nuchtern, Brian Thomas Jones, from a story by Simon Nuchtern

Relative Values ★★★ PG

Satirical comedy 2000 · UK · Colour · 85mins

Julie Andrews makes a big-screen comeback in Eric Styles's brittle adaptation of Noël Coward's comedy.

R

Andrews uses all her feminine wiles to prevent her son Edward Atterton from marrying glamorous Hollywood starlet Jeanne Tripplehorn, who is, in fact, the sister of Andrews's personal maid Sophie Thompson, and arrives with her hell-raising boyfriend William Baldwin in hot pursuit. Styles can't make Coward's creaky characters breathe on film, but Colin Firth and Stephen Fry play supporting roles with élan, while Andrews never puts a foot wrong. NS DVD

Julie Andrews *Felicity* • Sophie Thompson *Moxie* • Edward Atterton *Nigel* • Jeanne Tripplehorn *Miranda* • William Baldwin *Don Lucas* • Colin Firth *Peter* • Stephen Fry *Crestwell* ■ *Dir* Eric Styles • *Scr* Paul Rattigan, Michael Walker, from the play by Noël Coward

Relatives ★★ 15

Drama 1985 · Aus · Colour · 83mins

Languishing on the shelves for five years before it was finally released on video, Anthony Bowman's tale of deep-seated resentments and emotional outbursts follows along all-too-familiar dysfunctional family lines. As Bill Kerr's kinfolk gather for his 80th birthday party at his rundown Sydney estate, there's only one thing on the minds of all and sundry as they jockey for largess. Every tired feud imaginable is dusted down and pushed into service. Brisk and abrasive. DP

Bill Kerr *Grandfather* • Rowena Wallace *Nancy* • Alyson Best *Clare* • Ray Barrett *Geoffrey* • Brett Climo *Ross* • Michael Aitken *Peter* • Norman Kaye *Ed* ■ *Dir* Anthony Bowman [Antony J Bowman] • *Scr* Anthony Bowman

Relax... It's Just Sex ★★ 18

Comedy 1998 · US · Colour · 105mins

The emphasis in this comedy of sexual manners is on same sex relationships, but the action is spiced up by the intervention of straight characters whose tangles add to the overall tone of insecurity and confusion. Notwithstanding the verbosity of the script, Jennifer Tilly is boisterously maternal as the cement keeping the disparate acquaintances together and she's well supported by veterans Seymour Cassel, Paul Winfield and Susan Tyrrell. However, the sitcomedic mood is undermined by a brutal male rape scene. DP DVD

Mitchell Anderson *Vincey Sauris* • Jennifer Tilly *Tara Ricotto* • Cynda Williams *Sarina Classer* • Seymour Cassel *Emile Pillsbury* • Susan Tyrrell *Alicia Pillsbury* • Serena Scott Thomas *Megan Pillsbury* • Paul Winfield *Auntie Mahalia* • Lori Petty *Robin Moon* ■ *Dir/Scr* PJ Castellaneta

R

Relentless ★★★

Western 1948 · US · Colour · 92mins

Robert Young enjoys an offbeat role as an intelligent cowboy while desert settings in gorgeous Technicolor and a more realistic than usual storyline turn this into an above average western. Wrongly accused of murder, Young stays one jump ahead of a sheriff's posse as he attempts to clear himself with the aid of Marguerite Chapman's travelling saleswoman. That inveterate scene stealer, Akim Tamiroff, upstages surly Barton MacLane in the villainy department. AE

Robert Young (1) *Nick Buckley* • Marguerite Chapman *Luella Purdy* • Willard Parker *Jeff Moyer* • Akim Tamiroff *Joe Faringo* • Barton MacLane *Tex Brandow* • Mike Mazurki *Jake* • Robert Barrat *Ed Simpson* ■ *Dir* George Sherman • *Scr* Winston Miller, from the story *Three Were Thoroughbreds* by Kenneth Perkins

Relentless ★★ 18

Thriller 1989 · US · Colour · 88mins

This movie spawned three sequels and no one can quite understand why. Judd Nelson turns in the greatest performance of his career so far as a serial killer who makes Jack the Ripper seem a dilettante. Apart from Nelson acting his socks off, this is a very ho hum effort which is only passable fare if you're in an undemanding mood. SH DVD

Judd Nelson *Buck Taylor* • Robert Loggia *Bill Malloy* • Leo Rossi *Sam Dietz* • Meg Foster *Carol Dietz* • Patrick O'Bryan *Todd Arthur* • Ken Lerner *Arthur* • Mindy Seger *Francine* • Angel Tompkins *Carmen* • Beau Starr *Ike Taylor* • Harriet Hall *Angela Taylor* ■ *Dir* William Lustig • *Scr* Jack TD Robinson [Phil Alden Robinson]

Relentless 2: Dead On ★★★ 18

Thriller 1991 · US · Colour · 89mins

This is a rarity in sequels, being an improvement over the original, and also the best entry in the four-part series. Leo Rossi returns as LA detective Sam Dietz, estranged from his wife (Meg Foster), and tracking down another serial killer, a surprisingly effective Miles O'Keeffe. When FBI agent Ray Sharkey starts to interfere, it becomes clear the killer isn't just another random slasher. Forget about the two further inferior sequels. KB

Miles O'Keeffe *Gregor* • Sven-Ole Thorsen *Mechanic* • Leo Rossi *Sam Dietz* • Meg Foster *Carol Dietz* • Dawn Mangrum *Reporter* • Ray Sharkey *Kyle Valsone* • Leilani Jones *Belinda Belos* ■ • *Scr* Mark Sevi

The Relic ★★★ 15

Horror 1996 · US · Colour · 105mins

Director Peter Hyams pulls out all the stops in this unpretentious, super-slick gothic horror. An ancient Amazonian beast is creeping around Chicago's natural history museum on the night of a gala opening party. Can feisty scientist Penelope Ann Miller or detective Tom Sizemore overcome their fears to battle the blood-lusting demon of superstition? Hardly earth-shattering, a glossy veneer on the time-worn clichés and harum-scarum jolts keep the suspense simmering. AJ DVD

Penelope Ann Miller *Dr Margo Green* • Tom Sizemore *Lt Vince D'Agosta* • Linda Hunt *Dr Ann Cuthbert* • James Whitmore *Dr Albert Frock* • Clayton Rohner *Detective Hollingsworth* ■ *Dir* Peter Hyams • *Scr* Amy Holden Jones, John Raffo, Rick Jaffa, Amanda Silver, from the novel by Douglas Preston, Lincoln Child

La Religieuse ★★★★

Religious drama 1965 · Fr · Colour · 139mins

Jacques Rivette's austere allegory was, initially, banned in France for its anti-clerical content. Rejected by her family, Anna Karina is forced to take the veil, only to be subjected to deprivations and beatings by mother superior, Micheline Presle, and then sexually harassed by the lesbian head (Liselotte Pulver) of her new convent. Not even the priest (Francisco Rabal) who rescues her acts out of pure motives. However, this visually rigorous film is more about freedom of conscience than the severity or hypocrisy of religious celibacy and proves as provocative as it's tragic. DP. In French with English subtitles.

Anna Karina *Suzanne Simonin* • Liselotte Pulver *Mme de Chelles* • Micheline Presle *Mme de Moni* • Christine Lenier *Mme Simonin* • Francine Bergé *Sister St Christine* • Francisco Rabal *Dom Morel* ■ *Dir* Jacques Rivette • *Scr* Jacques Rivette, Jean Gruault, from the novel *Memoirs of a Nun* by Denis Diderot

The Reluctant Astronaut ★★ U

Comedy 1967 · US · Colour · 101mins

Don Knotts's gormless comic style always polarised audiences, with some lapping it up and others unable to bear him. Here he plays a timid chap afraid of heights who is bullied by his father into going for a job at the Nasa space centre. He ends up working as a trainee janitor. But as the Russians prepare to launch a man into space, US scientists bring forward their plans and urgently need a volunteer. DF

Don Knotts *Roy Fleming* • Leslie Nielsen *Major Fred Gifford* • Joan Freeman *Ellie Jackson* • Jesse White *Donelli* • Jeanette Nolan *Mrs Fleming* • Frank McGrath *Plank* ■ *Dir* Edward J Montagne • *Scr* Jim Fritzell, Everett Greenbaum, from an idea by Don Knotts

The Reluctant Debutante ★★★ U

Comedy 1958 · US · Colour · 95mins

This soft-centred dig at the London "season" was outmoded the moment it was made. A not very convincing change was the casting of two American teen idols, Sandra Dee, in the title role, and John Saxon, as her drum-playing sweetheart. Thankfully, Dee's father and stepmother were played delightfully by (recently married) Rex Harrison and Kay Kendall. The nicely designed film was shot in Paris, because Harrison couldn't enter England for tax reasons. RB

Rex Harrison *Jimmy Broadbent* • Kay Kendall *Sheila Broadbent* • John Saxon *David Parkson* • Sandra Dee *Jane Broadbent* • Angela Lansbury *Mabel Claremont* • Peter Myers *David Fenner* • Diane Clare *Clarissa Claremont* ■ *Dir* Vincente Minnelli • *Scr* William Douglas Home, from his play

The Reluctant Dragon ★★ U

Documentary 1941 · US · BW and Colour · 73mins

American humorist Robert Benchley fronts this documentary about the Walt Disney studios, which takes its name from the 25-minute short that concludes the picture. Never more than a blatant plug for the studio, it encouraged the trade paper *Variety* to opine: "Dr Goebbels couldn't do a better propaganda job to show the workers in Disney's pen-and-ink factory as a happy and contented lot." In fact, the workers were on strike when the film was released in 1941. The demonstrations of the then up-to-date techniques, though, should interest historians of animation. AT

Dir Alfred Werker, Hamilton Luske, Jim Handley, Ford Beebe, Erwin Verity, Jasper Blystone • *Scr* Ted Sears, Al Perkins, Larry Clemmons, Bill Cottrell

The Reluctant Saint ★★ U

Biographical drama 1962 · US/It · BW · 114mins

Maximilian Schell stars in this portrait of St Joseph of Cupertino. Considered to be an idiot by his village, the future Franciscan brother apparently entered a monastery as protection from the outside world and then studied successfully – despite lacking a formal education – to become a priest. Director Edward Dmytryk's earnest chronicle follows his progress until his declaration of sainthood, as the result of his exemplary life. This movie was a case of good intentions overwhelming the material. BB

Maximilian Schell *Giuseppe Desa* • Ricardo Montalban *Father Raspi* • Lea Padovani *Francesca Desa* • Akim Tamiroff *Bishop Durso* • Harold Goldblatt *Father Giovanni* ■ *Dir* Edward Dmytryk • *Scr* John Fante, Joseph Petracca

The Reluctant Widow ★★ U

Period drama 1950 · UK · BW · 82mins

Romance, espionage and villainy during the Napoleonic Wars unfold at an English country estate inherited by former governess Jean Kent on the death of her wealthy husband. The widow finds herself surrounded by French spies and British traitors, all after some vital documents secreted in the house, but she foils them all. A good-looking but rather muddled and unsatisfactory adaptation of a novel by Georgette Heyer, which entertains in fits and starts. RK

Jean Kent *Elinor* • Peter Hammond *Eustace Cheviot* • Guy Rolfe *Lord Carlyon* • Paul Dupuis *Lord Nivelle* • Kathleen Byron *Mme de Chevreaux* ■ *Dir* Bernard Knowles • *Scr* JB Boothroyd, Gordon Wellesley, from the novel by Georgette Heyer

The Remains of the Day ★★★★★ U

Period drama 1993 · UK/US · Colour · 128mins

An impeccable adaptation of Kazuo Ishiguro's Booker Prize-winning novel, with Anthony Hopkins as the emotionally repressed butler and Emma Thompson as the housekeeper he possibly loves. Framed in flashbacks, the story is an English twist on Jean Renoir's classic *La Règle du Jeu*, a broad view of a narrow class of aristocrats on the verge of self-destruction. Co-starring James Fox as a fascistic English lord and Christopher Reeve as an American diplomat (the past and present owners of Darlington Hall), it is as much a study in power and politics as it is Hopkins's blinkered view of the world from behind the gleaming silver salvers. The 1930s and 1940s settings are immaculately staged, and James Ivory's direction is alive to every nuance and chink of the sherry glasses. AT DVD

Anthony Hopkins *Stevens* • Emma Thompson *Miss Kenton* • James Fox *Lord Darlington* • Christopher Reeve *Lewis* • Peter Vaughan *Father* • Hugh Grant *Cardinal* • Michael Lonsdale [Michel Lonsdale] *Dupont D'Ivry* • Tim Pigott-Smith *Benn* • John Haycraft *Auctioneer* • Caroline Hunt *Landlady* • Paula Jacobs *Mrs Mortimer* • Ben Chaplin *Charlie* • Steve Dibben *George* ■ *Dir* James Ivory • *Scr* Ruth Prawer Jhabvala, from the novel by Kazuo Ishiguro

Remains to Be Seen ★★

Comedy mystery 1953 · US · BW · 88mins

Van Johnson, drum-playing manager of a Park Avenue block, finds a wealthy tenant mysteriously dead in his apartment. His discovery leads to romance with the corpse's niece, band-singer June Allyson, en route to which the pair outwit the evil, scheming Angela Lansbury. Despite a pretty silly, unconvincing plot, this romantic comedy mystery moves along good-naturedly and comes to life with stars duetting a couple of lively numbers and Dorothy Dandridge (as herself) singing *Taking a Chance on Love*. RK

June Allyson *Jody Revere* • Van Johnson *Waldo Williams* • Louis Calhern *Benjamin Goodwin* • Angela Lansbury *Valeska Chauvel* • John Beal *Dr Glenson* • Dorothy Dandridge ■ *Dir* Don Weis • *Scr* Sidney Sheldon, from the play by Howard Lindsay, Russel Crouse

The Remarkable Mr Pennypacker ★★★ U

Period comedy 1959 · US · Colour · 87mins

Clifton Webb is the son of sausage manufacturer Charles Coburn, for whom he works, and married to Dorothy McGuire in 1890s Harrisburg, Pennsylvania. Forced to spend much time at his father's Philadelphia plant, lonely Webb takes a second wife, happily runs two families and fathers a total of 17 children before the truth is revealed. Scripted by Walter Reisch from a successful play and directed by Henry Levin, this is a good-natured, nicely observed period comedy, to which the polished and very "correct" Webb is ideally suited. RK

Clifton Webb *Pa Pennypacker* • Dorothy McGuire *Ma Pennypacker* • Charles Coburn *Grampa* • Jill St John *Kate Pennypacker* • Ron Ely *Wilbur Fielding* • Ray Stricklyn *Horace Pennypacker III* • David Nelson *Henry Pennypacker* ■ *Dir* Henry Levin • *Scr* Walter Reisch, from the play by Liam O'Brien

Rembrandt ★★★ U

Biographical drama 1936 · UK · BW · 80mins

One of the prestige productions that brought dignity to the British film industry, this distinguished film stars Charles Laughton in a remarkably affecting performance. His tendency to ham is brought under control by producer/director Alexander Korda, whose brother Vincent provides some particularly well-designed studio sets, quaintly converting Denham's sound stages to Rembrandt van Rijn's Amsterdam. A rare screen performance from co-star Gertrude Lawrence reveals why this great lady of the stage wasn't loved by the movie camera. TS [video]

Charles Laughton *Rembrandt Van Rijn* • Gertrude Lawrence *Geertje Dirx* • Elsa Lanchester *Hendrickje Stoffels* • Edward Chapman *Fabrizius* • Walter Hudd *Banning Cocq* • Roger Livesey *Beggar Saul* • John Bryning *Titus Van Rijn* • Allan Jeayes *Dr Tulp* ■ *Dir* Alexander Korda • *Scr* Carl Zuckmayer, Lajos Biró, June Head, Arthur Wimperis • *Cinematographer* Georges Périnal • *Art Director* Vincent Korda

Remember? ★

Romantic comedy 1939 · US · BW · 83mins

Lew Ayres introduces his fiancée Greer Garson to his best friend Robert Taylor over lunch, whereupon friend sweeps her away and marries her, setting in train a series of events encompassing everything from divorce to amnesia-inducing potions. This must surely be one of the most witless romantic comedies ever dreamed up. RK

Robert Taylor (1) *Jeff Holland* • Greer Garson *Linda Bronson* • Lew Ayres *Sky Ames* • Billie Burke *Mrs Bronson* • Reginald Owen *Mr Bronson* • George Barbier *Mr McIntyre* • Henry Travers *Judge Milliken* • Richard Carle *Mr Piper* ■ *Dir* Norman Z McLeod • *Scr* Corey Ford, Norman Z McLeod

Remember Last Night? ★★★

Comedy mystery 1935 · US · BW · 76mins

Universal assigned their star horror movie director James Whale and a first-rate cast, headed by Robert Young, Constance Cummings and Edward Arnold, to this offbeat comedy thriller, in which a group of socialites wake up with hangovers after a party, to find that one of their number has been murdered. A witty, sophisticated and suspenseful puzzler, the film combines, and parodies, a number of styles and genres to fascinating (if occasionally confusing) effect. RK

Edward Arnold *Danny Harrison* • Robert Young (1) *Tony Milburn* • Constance Cummings *Carlotta, his wife* • George Meeker *Vic Huling* • Sally Eilers *Bette, his wife* • Reginald Denny *Jack Whitridge* • Louise Henry *Penny, his wife* • Gregory Ratoff *Faronea* • Robert Armstrong *Fred Flannagan* • Monroe Owsley *Billy Arliss* ■ *Dir* James Whale • *Scr* Harry Clork, Doris Malloy, Dan Totheroh, Murray Roth, from the novel *Hangover Murders* by Adam Hobhouse

Remember Me ★★★

Thriller 1985 · Aus · Colour · 95mins

One of Australia's finest actresses, Wendy Hughes is given the chance to indulge in a little hysterical excess, as the return of her mentally disturbed ex-husband jeopardises both her new career and her second marriage. Torn between lingering passion and growing terror, Hughes brings some credibility to a potboiler that is otherwise played at fever pitch by Richard Moir and Richard Grubb. Unsubtle, but there's tension and tragedy in the finale. DP

Wendy Hughes *Jenny* • Richard Moir *Howard* • Robert Grubb *Geoff* • Carol Raye *Jenny's mother* • Peter Gwynne *Jenny's father* • Celia de Burgh *Barbara* • Sandy Gore *Adele* ■ *Dir* Lex Marinos • *Scr* Anne Brooksbank

Remember Me? ★ PG

Comedy 1996 · UK · Colour · 77mins

Although the producers claimed this as a latter-day Ealing comedy, it's actually a single-pace, single-joke farce that leaves an expert cast floundering amid a myriad of clumsy plot contrivances. Yet Michael Frayn's tired script is only part of the problem, as Nick Hurran's direction is rendered even more leaden by the painfully slow editing, which at times delays the reactions of the cast so long, it makes them look like amateur theatricals. DP [video]

Robert Lindsay *Jamie* • Rik Mayall *Ian* • Imelda Staunton *Lorna* • Brenda Blethyn *Shirley* • James Fleet *Donald* • Haydn Gwynne *Jamie's wife* ■ *Dir* Nick Hurran • *Scr* Michael Frayn

Remember My Name ★★★

Drama 1978 · US · Colour · 93mins

Written and directed by Alan Rudolph and produced by his mentor Robert Altman, this is a film full of fine moments, but, because of Rudolph's tendency to over-complicate, those moments ultimately add up to an unsatisfying whole. Returning from prison to make life hell for ex-husband Anthony Perkins, Geraldine Chaplin gives a scorching performance, but even she gets bogged down in the subplots involving shopkeeper Jeff Goldblum and landlord Moses Gunn. DP. Contains swearing.

Geraldine Chaplin *Emily* • Anthony Perkins *Neil Curry* • Berry Berenson *Barbara Curry* • Moses Gunn *Pike* • Jeff Goldblum *Mr Nudd* • Timothy Thomerson [Tim Thomerson] *Jeff* • Alfre Woodard *Rita* • Marilyn Coleman *Teresa* ■ *Dir/Scr* Alan Rudolph

Remember the Day ★★★ U

Drama 1941 · US · BW · 86mins

What usually brought a tear to the eye of tough studio boss Darryl F Zanuck invariably worked with audiences worldwide, and this small-town soap opera is no exception. Claudette Colbert is cast against type as a schoolteacher who, in flashback, tells of her influence on a particular pupil, who grows up to be a presidential candidate. Meanwhile, Colbert falls for dull-but-worthy sports master John Payne. It's all professionally done and, if you like this sort of thing and can enjoy Colbert in a rare straight role, a fair slice of entertainment. TS

Claudette Colbert *Nora Trinell* • John Payne *Dan Hopkins* • John Shepperd [Shepperd Strudwick] *Dewey Roberts* • Ann E Todd *Kate Hill* • Douglas Croft *Dewey as a boy* • Jane Seymour (1) *Mrs Roberts* ■ *Dir* Henry King • *Scr* Tess Slesinger, Frank Davis, Allan Scott, from the play by Philo Higley, Philip Dunning

Remember the Night ★★★★

Romantic comedy drama
1940 · US · BW · 94mins

Barbara Stanwyck and Fred MacMurray, both at the top of their form and perfect foils for one another, co-star in this romantic comedy, written by Preston Sturges and directed by Mitchell Leisen. The action concerns a shoplifter (Stanwyck) whose trial is delayed by the Christmas holiday, leaving her somewhat adrift. Sympathetic, assistant district attorney MacMurray takes pity on her and brings her home to his family's snowbound country home for Christmas. An absolute delight, combining warmth and charm with a little sentimentality and humour. RK

Barbara Stanwyck *Lee Leander* • Fred MacMurray *John Sargent* • Beulah Bondi *Mrs Sargent* • Elizabeth Patterson *Aunt Emma* • Willard Roberton *Francis X O'Leary* • Sterling Holloway *Willie* • Charles Waldron *Judge – New York* • Paul Guilfoyle (1) *District attorney* ■ *Dir* Mitchell Leisen • *Scr* Preston Sturges

Remember the Titans ★★★ PG

Sports drama based on a true story
2000 · US · Colour · 108mins

Denzel Washington tackles the potentially explosive combination of football and racial desegregation in 1970s America. When two Virginia high schools are combined, Washington supersedes his white counterpart Will Patton as head coach of the Titans football team. This causes friction between them and among the players, as they try to overcome hostility and prejudice in the pursuit of sporting glory. Washington gives a typically solid performance, but it's Patton who steals the show. DA [video] DVD

Denzel Washington *Coach Herman Boone* • Will Patton *Coach Bill Yoast* • Donald Adeosun Faison *Petey Jones* • Wood Harris *Julius "Big Ju" Campbell* • Ryan Hurst *Gerry Bertier* • Ethan Suplee *Lewis Lastik* ■ *Dir* Boaz Yakin • *Scr* Gregory Allen Howard

Remo – Unarmed and Dangerous ★★★ 15

Action adventure
1985 · US · Colour · 110mins

A solid, unpretentious little action thriller, which is notable mainly for the presence of Joel Grey the Oscar-winning MC of *Cabaret*, making a rare return to the big screen. The Remo of the title is Fred Ward, a no-nonsense policeman who is transformed into a super agent by a wise old Oriental (Grey). Director Guy Hamilton probably would have preferred to have the same sort of budgets that were afforded him for his Bond movies, but he still keeps the action roaring along. JF [video]

Fred Ward *Remo Williams* • Joel Grey *Chiun* • Wilford Brimley *Harold Smith* • JA Preston *Conn MacCleary* • George Coe *General Scott Watson* • Charles Cioffi *George S Grove* • Kate Mulgrew *Major Rayner Fleming* ■ *Dir* Guy Hamilton • *Scr* Christopher Wood, from characters in *The Destroyer*,series by Richard Sapir, Warren Murphy

Remote Control ★★ 15

Science-fiction comedy
1988 · US · Colour and BW · 84mins

Kevin Dillon is good as a video-store clerk who stumbles into an alien conspiracy involving a video release of a cheesy 1950s movie called *Remote Control*. Viewers of the tape are hypnotised into committing violent psychotic acts. The black-and-white movie-within-a-movie is amusing, but although this is ostensibly a sci-fi comedy, the entire enterprise is frequently stuck awkwardly between being funny and being serious. KB [video]

Kevin Dillon *Cosmo* • Deborah Goodrich *Belinda* • Jennifer Tilly *Allegra* • Christopher Wynne *Georgie* • Frank Beddor *Victor* • Kaaren Lee *Patricia* • Bert Remsen *Bill Denver* ■ *Dir/Scr* Jeff Lieberman

Renaissance Man ★★ 12

Comedy 1994 · US · Colour · 122mins

Penny Marshall directs this misconceived high-concept movie, which just about gets by on the quality of its cast. Danny DeVito, as the unemployed advertising executive called up to teach English to stroppy army recruits, does his best to counteract the sentimentality that keeps rising to the surface, and he is ably supported by some top-line players. Ultimately, however, the film is just too nice for its own good. JF. Contains some swearing. [video] DVD

Danny DeVito *Bill Rago* • Gregory Hines *Sergeant Cass* • Cliff Robertson *Colonel James* • James Remar *Captain Murdoch* • Lillo Brancato Jr [Lillo Brancato] *Donnie Benitez* • Stacey Dash *Miranda Myers* • Kadeem Hardison *Jamaal Montgomery* • Richard T Jones *Jackson Leroy* • Khalil Kain *Roosevelt Hobbs* • Marky Mark [Mark Wahlberg] *Tommy Lee Haywood* • Ed Begley Jr *Jack Markin* ■ *Dir* Penny Marshall • *Scr* Jim Burnstein

Rendez-vous ★★★

Erotic drama 1985 · Fr · Colour · 83mins

Former critic and film teacher André Téchiné has certainly practiced what he formerly preached, having emerged as one of the more highly regarded French directors of the past three decades. This is an atmospheric, backstage drama in which Juliette Binoche plays a girl from the provinces who wants to become a star. She goes to Paris and decides that one way to success and home comfort is to sleep with the young men she meets. But when she gets a part in a production of *Romeo and Juliet*, it is director Jean-Louis Trintignant, an older man, who becomes her salvation. Far from profound, but seldom boring. BB. In French with English subtitles.

Juliette Binoche *Nina Larrieu* • Lambert Wilson *Quentin* • Wadeck Stanczak *Paulot* • Jean-Louis Trintignant *Scrutzler* • Dominique Lavanant *Gertrude* ■ *Dir* André Téchiné • *Scr* André Téchiné, Olivier Assayas

Les Rendez-vous d'Anna ★★★

Drama
1978 · Fr/Bel/W Ger · Colour · 127mins

Made by Belgian film director Chantal Akerman, this follows the meanderings of Anna (Aurore Clément), a young Belgian film director as she travels to several European cities to publicise her latest film. The overtly autobiographical element makes it an uncomfortable film to watch, especially in the long scene when she admits to her mother that she is in love with a woman. Some may find Akerman's minimalist cinema coolly captures the modern malaise, while others might suffer from a sense of malaise while watching it. RB. In French with English subtitles.

Aurore Clément *Anna Silver* • Helmut Griem *Heinrich* • Magali Noël *Ida* • Lea Massari *Anna's mother* ■ *Dir/Scr* Chantal Akerman

Les Rendez-vous de Paris ★★★★ PG

Romantic drama 1995 · Fr · Colour · 94mins

Alighting on his favourite themes of pursuit and evasion, Eric Rohmer fashions three bittersweet vignettes in this fond tribute to capricious youth and the hidden beauties of Paris. As narcissistic as they are garrulous, each protagonist is a choice Rohmer archetype – whether it's the girl trying to catch her boyfriend in his infidelity in *The Seven O'Clock Rendezvous*, the student toying with an affair, while summoning the courage to break her engagement, in *The Benches of Paris*, or the artist in *Mother and Child, 1907*, who is gently rebuffed by a recently married woman. Minor perhaps, but still irresistible. DP. In French with English subtitles. [video]

Clara Bellar *Esther* • Antoine Basler *Horace* • Aurore Rauscher *Her* • Serge Renko *Him* • Michaël Kraft *Painter* • Bénédicte Loyen *Young woman* ■ *Dir/Scr* Eric Rohmer

R

Rendezvous ★★★ U

Spy comedy 1935 · US · BW · 94mins

Puzzle expert William Powell, aching to see frontline action in France during the First World War, is reluctantly seconded to the American war ministry as a code-breaker to rescue a critical situation. He finds himself involved with a spy-ring and the assistant secretary of war's glamorous but dizzy niece (Rosalind Russell). An unusual, even daring, mixture of light – almost screwball – romantic comedy and espionage thriller, this features polished performances and atmospheric, well-judged direction from William K Howard. RK

William Powell *Lt Bill Gordon/Anson Meridan* • Rosalind Russell *Joel Carter* • Binnie Barnes *Olivia Karloff* • Lionel Atwill *Maj Charles Brennan* • Cesar Romero *Capt Nikki Nikolajeff* • Samuel S Hinds *John Carter, Assistant Secretary of War* ■ *Dir* William K Howard • *Scr* Bella Spewack, Samuel Spewack, PJ Wolfson, George Oppenheimer, from the novel *American Black Chamber* by Herbert O Yardley

Rendezvous with Annie ★★★

Wartime romantic comedy 1946 · US · BW · 89mins

American director Allan Dwan notched up over 400 feature credits in a career that spanned from Douglas Fairbanks's silent epics to RKO co-features in the 1950s. This long-forgotten gem is frantic, fast and extremely entertaining especially for its glimpses of a very Hollywood England – as likeable GI Eddie Albert goes AWOL to check up on his stateside wife. Jolly good fun. TS

Faye Marlowe *Annie Dolan* • Gail Patrick *Dolores Starr* • Philip Reed *Lt Avery* • C Aubrey Smith *Sir Archibald Clyde* • Raymond Walburn *Everett Thorndyke* ■ *Dir* Allan Dwan • *Scr* Richard Sale, Mary Loos

Renegade ★★★ 18

Spaghetti western 1987 · It · Colour · 95mins

This amiable latter day western gets off to an amusing start as Terence Hill (a drifter who makes a living by repeatedly selling a horse with a homing instinct) hits the road with Ross Hill, the young son of a jailed buddy. Their encounters with truckers, bikers, flirts and a crooked knife thrower are all good value, but the picture falls away when villainous Robert Vaughn comes on the scene to steal the boy's farm in order to build a base for his drug business. DP. Some dialogue dubbed into English.

Terence Hill *"Renegade"* • Robert Vaughn *Tycoon* • Ross Hill • Norman Bowler • Beatrice Palme • Donald Hodson • Cyros Elias ■ *Dir* EB Clucher [Enzo Barboni] • *Scr* Marco Tullio Barboni, Mario Girotti [Terence Hill], Sergio Donati

Renegades ★★★

Adventure 1930 · US · BW · 90mins

Warner Baxter stars as an officer who leads a small group of Foreign Legionnaires against a band of warlike heathens in the desert and becomes a hero. Lots of blood and thunder, famous horror-star-to-be Bela Lugosi as The Marabout and the distracting, and disruptive, presence of female spy Myrna Loy contribute to a respectable early sound entry in the "exotic heroic adventure melodrama" genre. The movie, directed by Victor Fleming, does, however, suffer from a narrative confusion. RK

Warner Baxter *Deucalion* • Myrna Loy *Eleanore* • Noah Beery Sr [Noah Beery] *Machwurth* • Gregory Gaye *Vologuine* • George Cooper *Bilox* • C Henry Gordon *Capt Mordiconi* • Colin Chase *Sgt Maj Olson* • Bela Lugosi *The Marabout* • Victor Jory *Young officer* ■ *Dir* Victor Fleming • *Scr* Jules Furthman, from the novel *Le Renégat* by André Armandy

Renegades ★★ 18

Action thriller 1989 · US · Colour · 101mins

This mindless, if energetic, thriller would have benefited considerably from a decent script. As it is, the endless action only serves to highlight that a single, scrawny idea is being stretched to breaking point, and the attempts at "serious" dialogue between the set pieces are just embarrassing. Kiefer Sutherland and Lou Diamond Phillips were better employed in *Young Guns*. JM. Contains swearing and violence.

Kiefer Sutherland *Buster* • Lou Diamond Phillips *Hank* • Jami Gertz *Barbara* • Rob Knepper [Robert Knepper] *Marino* • Bill Smitrovich *Finch* • Floyd Westerman [Floyd Red Crow Westerman] *Red Crow* • Joe Griffin *Matt* ■ *Dir* Jack Sholder • *Scr* David Rich

Rent-a-Cop ★★ 15

Action comedy 1988 · US · Colour · 92mins

This lacklustre thriller was the second teaming of stars Burt Reynolds and Liza Minnelli (remember *Lucky Lady*?). Reynolds is an ex-cop with a seriously visible rotten toupee, and Minnelli's a flashy call girl working for ace madam Dionne Warwick. Say goodbye to credibility right there. TS. Contains swearing and some violence.

Burt Reynolds *Tony Church* • Liza Minnelli *Della Roberts* • James Remar *Dancer* • Richard Masur *Roger* • Dionne Warwick *Beth* • Bernie Casey *Lemar* • Robby Benson *Pitts* • John Stanton *Alexander* ■ *Dir* Jerry London • *Scr* Dennis Shryack, Michael Blodgett

Rent-a-Kid ★★★ U

Comedy 1992 · Can · Colour · 85mins

This is a children's film that doesn't patronise its audience by resorting to slapstick for its comedy or sentimentality for its message. Leslie Nielsen crops up in a showy cameo as the father of an orphanage owner, who rents out three children, unwilling to have their family broken up, to a couple who can't decide whether parenting is for them. Although the antiques shop subplot and the final resolution are a tad corny, the scenes in which the couple try to please the threesome are good fun. DP

Leslie Nielsen *Harry* • Christopher Lloyd *Lawrence Kady* • Matt McCoy *Russ Syracuse* • Sherry Miller *Val Syracuse* • Tabitha Lupien *Molly Ward* • Amos Crawley *Brandon Ward* • Cody Jones *Kyle Ward* • Tony Rosato *Cliff Haber* ■ *Dir* Fred Gerber • *Scr* Paul Bernbaum

Rentadick ★ PG

Comedy 1972 · UK · Colour · 89mins

This woeful private eye spoof started out as a project for *Monty Python* team members John Cleese and Graham Chapman, who wrote the original screenplay, but then disowned the film and had their names removed from the credits. John Wells and John Fortune were drafted in as replacements, but couldn't avert a disaster. DP

James Booth *Hamilton* • Richard Briers *Gannet* • Julie Ege *Utta* • Ronald Fraser *Upton* • Donald Sinden *Armitage* • Kenneth Cope *West* • John Wells *Owltruss* • Richard Beckinsale *Hobbs* • Michael Bentine *Hussein* • Derek Griffiths *Henson* • Spike Milligan *Customs Officer* • Penelope Keith *Madge* ■ *Dir* Jim Clark • *Scr* John Wells, John Fortune • *Producer* Ned Sherrin

Repentance ★★★★ PG

Political drama 1984 · USSR · Colour · 150mins

Not filmed for three years after it was written and then not released for another three after its completion, this was the first Soviet feature to be openly critical of Stalin and is one of the most daring films ever made in the former USSR. Ostensibly a black comedy about the repeated exhumation of the mayor of a small Georgian town, it is a defiant assault on revisionist history, that shows, through a series of harrowing flashbacks, that the crimes of the past cannot simply be buried and forgotten. Exceptionally played and unflinchingly directed. DP. In Georgian with English subtitles. Contains some violence, swearing and brief nudity.

Avtandil Makharadze *Varlam Aravidze/Abel Aravidze* • Zeinab Botsvadze *Keti Barateli* • Ia Ninidze *Guliko Aravidze* • Merab Ninidze *Tornike Aravidze* • Ketevan Abuladze *Nino Barateli* • Edisher Giorgobiani *Sandro Barateli* ■ *Dir* Tengiz Abuladze • *Scr* Nana Janelidze, Tengiz Abuladze, Rezo Kveselava

The Replacement Killers ★★★ 18

Action thriller 1998 · US · Colour · 83mins

Forget the fact there's no plot whatsoever and focus on the high-energy action and you'll enjoy this dumb, noisy and enjoyable thriller with Hong Kong superstar Chow Yun-Fat making his American debut. When he refuses to assassinate an assigned target Stateside, conscientious hitman Chow puts his family in danger back in China. Fiery Mira Sorvino is the expert passport forger who helps him out. Don't think, just thrill to the wild gunplay and slick stunts. AJ. Contains violence and some swearing. DVD

Mira Sorvino *Meg Coburn* • Chow Yun-Fat *John Lee* • Michael Rooker *Stan "Zeedo" Zedkov* • Kenneth Tsang *Terence Wei* • Jürgen Prochnow *Michael Kogan* • Til Schweiger *Ryker* • Danny Trejo *Collins* ■ *Dir* Antoine Fuqua • *Scr* Ken Sanzel

The Replacements ★★ 15

Sports comedy based on a true story 2000 · US · Colour · 113mins

This stale and hackneyed sports comedy about a bunch of has-beens and no-hopers replacing striking professional American football players has quite an impressive cast for its type. While it has some funny touches, all the characters are purely one-dimensional, with even Gene Hackman failing to achieve anything with his veteran coach role. JC DVD

Keanu Reeves *Shane Falco* • Gene Hackman *Jimmy McGinty* • Brooke Langton *Annabelle Farrell* • Orlando Jones *Clifford Franklin* • Jon Favreau *Daniel Bateman* • Jack Warden *Edward O'Neil* • Rhys Ifans *Nigel "The Leg" Gruff* ■ *Dir* Howard Deutch • *Scr* Vince McKewin

Replicant ★★ 18

Science-fiction action thriller 2001 · US · Colour · 95mins

Jean-Claude Van Damme gets a dual role, again, as serial killer and his confused clone in an otherwise perfunctory thriller. While it has the makings of a departure for the "Muscles from Brussels", with his sympathetic, naive good guy used and abused by both his villainous "brother" and grizzled cop Michael Rooker, his awkwardness sits uncomfortably with his kick-boxing prowess. JC. Contains violence, a sex scene, swearing, nudity. DVD

Jean-Claude Van Damme *The Torch/Replicant* • Michael Rooker *Jake Riley* • Catherine Dent *Angie* • Ian Robison *Stan Reisman* ■ *Dir* Ringo Lam • *Scr* Lawrence Riggins, Les Weldon

Repo Man ★★★★ 18

Science-fiction thriller 1984 · US · Colour · 88mins

Despite poor reviews on its initial release, Alex Cox's darkly satirical swipe at American urban low life mutated into one of the 1980s greatest cult movies. Emilio Estevez plays a novice car repossession man in Los Angeles, learning the tricks of the trade from veteran Harry Dean Stanton, while coming into contact with aliens and drug pushers. The film is a winning blend of sci-fi, social commentary and *film noir*, with lots of quotable dialogue. The characters exist on the fringes of society and it's a world that's beautifully captured by Wim Wenders's regular cinematographer Robby Müller. RS. Contains violence, swearing. DVD

Emilio Estevez *Otto* • Harry Dean Stanton *Bud* • Tracey Walter *Miller* • Olivia Barash *Leila* • Sy Richardson *Lite* • Susan Barnes *Agent Rogersz* • Fox Harris *J Frank Parnell* • Tom Finnegan *Oly* • Del Zamora *Lagarto* • Eddie Velez *Napo* ■ *Dir/Scr* Alex Cox

Report to the Commissioner ★★★ PG

Crime drama 1975 · US · Colour · 112mins

Michael Moriarty stars as the idealistic rookie detective involved in the killing of an undercover cop, then embroiled in a vast cover-up. A solid script and some crisp action sequences, including a shoot-out in the Saks department store, make this eminently watchable, though most eyes now will be on Richard Gere, making his screen debut as a pimp. AT

Michael Moriarty *Beauregard "Bo" Lockley* • Yaphet Kotto *Richard "Crunch" Blackstone* • Susan Blakely *Patty Butler* • Hector Elizondo *Captain d'Angelo* • Tony King *Thomas "Stick" Henderson* • Michael McGuire *Lt Hanson* • Edward Grover *Captain Strichter* • Dana Elcar *Chief Perna* • Robert Balaban [Bob Balaban] *Joey Egan* • William Devane *Assistant District Attorney Jackson* • Stephen Elliott *Police commissioner* • Richard Gere *Billy* ■ *Dir* Milton Katselas • *Scr* Abby Mann, Ernest Tidyman, from the novel by James Mills

Repossessed ★ 15

Horror spoof 1990 · US · Colour · 80mins

It must have seemed a good idea at the time. Give *The Exorcist* the *Airplane!* treatment, get Linda Blair to reprise her infamous head-turning/pea-soup-vomit role, cast *The Naked Gun's* Leslie Nielsen as Max von Sydow and wait for the laughs to come thick and fast. Sadly, they come thin and slow in this lame-brained, mistimed fiasco. AJ. Contains swearing. DVD

Linda Blair *Nancy Aglet* • Leslie Nielsen *Father Jedidiah Mayii* • Ned Beatty *Ernest Weller* • Anthony Starke *Father Luke Brophy* • Thom J Sharp *Braydon Aglet* • Lana Schwab *Fanny Weller* ■ *Dir/Scr* Bob Logan

The Reptile ★★★ 15

Horror 1966 · UK · Colour · 86mins

Hysteria hits a 19th-century Cornish village when murder victims turn up with fang marks on their necks. Could sultry Jacqueline Pearce be the victim of a Malayan curse doomed to writhe the night away? A splendidly spooky vintage Hammer horror featuring an endearingly 1950s-style monster, remarkably atmospheric art direction and taut, stylish direction by John Gilling. AJ

Noel Willman *Dr Franklyn* • Jennifer Daniel *Valerie* • Ray Barrett *Harry* • Jacqueline Pearce *Anna* • Michael Ripper *Tom Bailey* • John Laurie *Mad Peter* • Marne Maitland *Malay* • David Baron *Charles Spalding* • Charles Lloyd Pack *Vicar* • Harold Goldblatt *Solicitor* ■ *Dir* John Gilling • *Scr* John Elder [Anthony Hinds]

Repulsion ★★★★ 18

Psychological thriller 1965 · UK · BW · 100mins

Director Roman Polanski takes us on a deeply disturbing, hallucinatory trip into Catherine Deneuve's mental breakdown in this British psychological thriller, his first film in English. As Swinging London parties in the background, repressed Belgian manicurist Deneuve unsheathes her claws with deadly results. There are shades of Buñuel and Cocteau, but Polanski puts his personal stamp on the violent visuals (the killing of a boyfriend and landlord) and the terrifying soundtrack (the buzzing of flies, a slashing knife). TH. Contains violence. [VIDEO] DVD

Catherine Deneuve *Carol Ledoux* • Ian Hendry *Michael* • John Fraser *Colin* • Patrick Wymark *Landlord* • Yvonne Furneaux *Helen Ledoux* • Renee Houston *Miss Balch* • Roman Polanski *Spoons player* ■ *Dir* Roman Polanski • *Scr* Roman Polanski, Gerard Brach, David Stone • *Cinematographer* Gilbert Taylor

Requiem ★★

Fantasy drama
1998 · Swi/Fr/Por · Colour · 100mins

Alain Tanner uses Lisbon as a stifling backdrop to this slow-moving treatise on memory and regret. The film is intended as a tribute to the Portuguese author Fernando Pessoa, who puts in a guest appearance as one of the mysterious characters Francis Frappat encounters while awaiting a meeting with a ghost from his past. A pall of impossible sophistication hangs over the piece, which wears its intellectual credentials on its sleeve. DP. A French language film.

Francis Frappat *Paul* • André Marcon *Pierre* ■ *Dir* Alain Tanner • *Scr* Bernard Comment, Alain Tanner, from a novel by Antonio Tabucchi

Requiem for a Dream ★★★★ 18

Drama 2000 · US · Colour · 96mins

Junk TV shows, diet pills and Class A drugs are the life blood of these doomed characters: Ellen Burstyn is the widowed mother hooked on game shows and sweet foods; her heroin addict son Jared Leto and his friend Marlon Wayans pawn the TV for drugs money, while Leto's girlfriend Jennifer Connelly degrades herself at stag parties. Making stylish use of the split-screen technique, huge close-ups and exaggerated sound effects, Darren Aronofsky depicts the highs and lows of drug-taking to chilling effect. TH. Contains swearing, violence, sex scenes and drug abuse. [VIDEO] DVD

Ellen Burstyn *Sara Goldfarb* • Jared Leto *Harry Goldfarb* • Jennifer Connelly *Marion Silver* • Marlon Wayans *Tyrone C Love* • Christopher McDonald *Tappy Tibbons* • Louise Lasser *Ada* • Keith David *Little John* ■ *Dir* Darren Aronofsky • *Scr* Hubert Selby Jr, Darren Aronofsky, from a novel by Hubert Selby Jr

Requiem for a Heavyweight ★★★

Sports drama 1962 · US · BW · 86mins

Based on an American live TV production written by Rod Serling, this stars Anthony Quinn as an over-the-hill boxer. He has to continue fighting, risking permanent blindness, in order to pay off debts to the Mafia run up by his manager Jackie Gleason, while Mickey Rooney is his devoted trainer In the ring (and on the moral message front) this is a bloody, brutal big-hitter of a movie and Quinn gives a committed performance. AT

Anthony Quinn *Mountain Rivera* • Jackie Gleason *Maish Rennick* • Mickey Rooney *Army* • Julie Harris *Grace Miller* • Stanley Adams *Perelli* • Madame Spivy *Ma Greeny* • Herbie Faye *Bartender* • Jack Dempsey • Cassius Clay [Muhammad Ali] *Ring opponent* ■ *Dir* Ralph Nelson • *Scr* Rob Serling, from his TV play

Requiem for Dominic ★★★

Historical political thriller
1990 · Austria · Colour · 88mins

Set in Ceausescu's Romania on the eve of the 1989 revolution, this intelligent film from Austria follows exile Felix Mitterer, in his quest to prove that his childhood friend August Schmölzer was not responsible for the murder of 80 factory workers in the town of Timisoara. Director Robert Dornhelm based his film on the experiences of his own friend, Dominic Paraschiv, a member of the notorious Securitate who was branded "the Butcher of Timisoara". Making studied use of news footage and fictional material, he has fashioned an engrossing, violent, political thriller that lays bare the soul of a troubled land. DP. In German with English subtitles.

Felix Mitterer *Paul Weiss* • August Schmolzer *Dominic Paraschiv* • Viktoria Schubert *Clara* • Angelica Schutz *Codrata Paraschiv* • Antonia Rados *Antonia* ■ *Dir* Robert Dornhelm • *Scr* Michael Kohlmeier, Felix Mitterer

The Rescue ★★ PG

Action adventure 1988 · US · Colour · 92mins

A daft drama with Kevin Dillon as one of a group of teenagers who mount a rescue mission when they discover the US government isn't going to help their dads, a group of Navy SEALS who have been captured behind enemy lines. JB. Contains swearing and violence. [VIDEO]

Kevin Dillon *JJ Merrill* • Christina Harnos [Christine Harnos] *Adrian Phillips* • Marc Price *Max Rothman* • Ned Vaughn *Shawn Howard* • Ian Giatti *Bobby Howard* • Charles Haid *Commander Howard* • Edward Albert *Commander Merrill* ■ *Dir* Ferdinand Fairfax • *Scr* Jim Thomas, John Thomas

Rescue Me ★★ 15

Action comedy 1991 · US · Colour · 94mins

In this silly spoof of the action adventure genre, Stephen Dorff is a high-school nerd who suffers from unrequited love for teen-queen Ami Dolenz. Obsessed with cameras (Dorff is a collector of vintage cameras in real life), he takes pictures of Dolenz just as she is being kidnapped instead of rescuing her. He teams up with hard man Michael Dudikoff (taking the mickey out of his screen persona) to rescue his fair maiden. FL [VIDEO]

Michael Dudikoff *Daniel "Mac" MacDonald* • Stephen Dorff *Fraser Sweeney* • Ami Dolenz *Ginny Grafton* • Peter DeLuise *Rowdy* • William Lucking *Kurt* • Dee Wallace Stone *Sarah Sweeney* • Liz Torres *Carney* • Danny Nucci *Todd* ■ *Dir* Arthur Allan Seidelman • *Scr* Mike Snyder

The Rescuers ★★★★ U

Animated adventure
1977 · US · Colour · 75mins

A thoroughly delightful Disney cartoon, this is about the all-mouse Rescue Aid Society and bids by its leading lights, Bernard and Miss Bianca, to free a little girl held hostage by hiss-boo baddie Madam Medusa. Bob Newhart, Eva Gabor and George C Scott are among the voice artists in a well-told tale with memorable characters. This was one of the animated features that indicated a return to form by Disney after a lengthy spell of cartoon mediocrity. DA [VIDEO] DVD

Bob Newhart *Bernard* • Eva Gabor *Miss Bianca* • Michelle Stacy *Penny* • Geraldine Page *Madame Medusa* • Joe Flynn *Mr Snoops* ■ *Dir* Wolfgang Reitherman, John Lounsbery, Milt Kahl, Art Stevens • *Scr* Larry Clemmons, Ken Anderson, Vance Gerry, David Michener, Burny Mattinson, Frank Thomas, Fred Lucky, Ted Berman, Dick Sebast, from the books *The Rescuers* and *Miss Bianca* by Margery Sharp

The Rescuers Down Under ★★★ U

Animated adventure
1990 · US · Colour · 80mins

This acceptable enough Disney animation is a sequel that came such a long time after *The Rescuers* (1977) that it could be forgiven for having lost the plot, because introductions to the "rescue mice" Miss Bianca and Bernard had to be made all over again. This time they're called to Australia to help a boy and golden eagle in danger from a fearsome trapper. It's likeable enough and the crocodile-snapping climax is exciting stuff. Bob Newhart and Eva Gabor are great as the voices of Bernard and Bianca. TH [VIDEO] DVD

Bob Newhart *Bernard* • Eva Gabor *Miss Bianca* • John Candy *Wilbur* • George C Scott *Percival McLeach* ■ *Dir* Hendel Butoy, Mike Gabriel • *Scr* Jim Cox, Karey Kirkpatrick, Byron Simpson, Joe Ranft, from the characters created by Margery Sharp

Reservoir Dogs ★★★★★ 18

Crime drama 1991 · US · Colour · 94mins

"Robbery, blood, violence, torture all in the comfort of your own home". The film that many consider the most influential of the 1990s was shot in just five weeks on a tight $1.5-million budget. Its runaway success came as something of a surprise even to its debuting writer/director Quentin Tarantino, who was hoping for a cult hit rather than a phenomenon that would inspire countless wannabes. Working wonders with Tarantino's pacey, attitude-laced dialogue, the ensemble cast is uniformly excellent, with Michael Madsen's sadistic, ear-slashing Mr Blonde and Steve Buscemi's exasperated Mr Pink particularly outstanding. Brash, abrasive and unrelenting. DP. Contains violence, swearing. [VIDEO] DVD

Harvey Keitel *Mr White (Larry)* • Tim Roth *Mr Orange (Freddy)* • Michael Madsen *Mr Blonde (Vic Vega)* • Chris Penn *Nice Guy Eddie* • Steve Buscemi *Mr Pink* • Lawrence Tierney *Joe Cabot* • Randy Brooks *Holdaway* • Kirk Baltz *Marvin Nash* • Eddie Bunker [Edward Bunker] *Mr Blue* • Quentin Tarantino *Mr Brown* ■ *Dir/Scr* Quentin Tarantino • *Cinematographer* Andrzej Sekula

Resident Alien ★★★

Documentary 1990 · US · Colour · 85mins

Having become a celebrity because of John Hurt's portrayal in *The Naked Civil Servant*, Quentin Crisp moved to New York where he quickly became the darling of the cultural poseurs and a TV talk-show standby. In this thorough profile, Crisp exercises his wit and wisdom – "John Hurt played me and then played Caligula which is me in a sheet" – and is joined by Hurt, Sting and others who ruminate on the man who wore his camp credentials on his ruffled sleeves. We learn many nuggets of trivia (such as Crisp's deleted cameo in *Fatal Attraction*) and gain some deeper insights into this perpetual exile. AT

Dir/Scr Jonathan Nossiter

Resident Evil ★★★ 15

Science-fiction action horror
2002 · Ger/UK/Fr · Colour · 96mins

Paul Anderson makes amends for his lacklustre *Mortal Kombat* with another video game adaptation. A single-minded tale of genetic research facility workers accidentally turned into ravenous zombies, it's a relentless throat-grabber. Milla Jovovich and her commandos move through progressively more dangerous levels to wipe out the undead. There's no enduring substance here, but the nerve-jangling score, co-composed by shock rocker Marilyn Manson, gives it an extra frenetic edge. SF [VIDEO] DVD

Milla Jovovich *Alice* • Michelle Rodriguez *Rain* • Eric Mabius *Matt* • James Purefoy *Spence* • Martin Crewes *Kaplan* • Colin Salmon *One* ■ *Dir* Paul WS Anderson [Paul Anderson] • *Scr* Paul WS Anderson [Paul Anderson], from a story by Alan McElroy, Paul WS Anderson [Paul Anderson], from the video game

Resident Evil: Apocalypse ★ 15

Science-fiction action horror
2004 · US/Can/UK/Fr · Colour · 89mins

First-timer Alexander Witt picks up the directorial reins from Paul Anderson for this limp sequel. Continuing from where the original left off, it sees the zombies break out from the Umbrella Corporation's underground research facility to wreak havoc on the quarantined city above. Though once again written by Anderson, the film lacks his visual flair and breakneck pacing, resulting in an unbelievable and uninspired shoot-'em-up. SF. Contains swearing, violence. [VIDEO] DVD

Milla Jovovich *Alice* • Sienna Guillory *Jill Valentine* • Oded Fehr *Carlos Olivera* • Thomas Kretschmann *Major Cain* • Jared Harris *Dr Charles Ashford* • Mike Epps *L J* • Sandrine Holt *Terri Morales* • Sophie Vavasseur *Angie Ashford* ■ *Dir* Alexander Witt • *Scr* Paul WS Anderson [Paul Anderson]

Respiro ★★★ 12

Drama 2002 · It/Fr · Colour · 91mins

Unable to cope with wife Valeria Golino's mood swings, Vincenzo Amato bows to communal pressure and agrees to have her committed to an institution on the mainland. However, Golino is protected in her beach hideaway by teenage son Francesco Casisa, who admires her free spirit, even though he doesn't understand it. By contrasting the island of Lampedusa's natural beauty with its inhabitants' struggle to survive, Emanuele Crialese's drama avoids rose-tinted realism and focuses on landscape and character. DP. In Italian with English subtitles. [VIDEO] DVD

Valeria Golino *Grazia* • Vincenzo Amato *Pietro* • Francesco Casisa *Pasquale* • Veronica D'Agostino *Marinella* • Filippo Pucillo *Filippo* • Emma Loffredo *Nonna* • Elio Germano *Pier-Luigi* ■ *Dir/Scr* Emanuele Crialese

Restaurant ★★ 18

Romantic comedy drama
1998 · US · Colour · 102mins

Set agains the backdrop of an upmarket restaurant, this ensemble piece focuses on a group of 20-somethings, most of whom seem to be waiting for the big break to come in the world of arts or music. The story centres on troubled writer Adrien Brody, who is agonising over his first off-Broadway production, his inability to commit to a relationship and his own racist upbringing. He's good, as are the rest of the young cast, but unless you're looking to make your way in the entertainment industry, it is hard to work up much sympathy for this self-obsessed gang. JF [VIDEO]

Adrien Brody *Chris Calloway* • Elise Neal *Jeanine* • David Moscow *Reggae* • Simon Baker-Denny *Kenny* • Catherine Kellner *Nancy* • Malcolm-Jamal Warner *Steven* • Lauryn Hill *Leslie* ■ *Dir* Eric Bross • *Scr* Tom C Cudworth

Resting Place ★★★★ PG

Drama 1986 · US · Colour · 98mins

Tautly scripted by Walter Halsey Davis and impeccably paced by director John Korty, this is one of the best TV movies ever made in America. Combining the themes of racial prejudice and military cover-up, this engrossing drama shuttles back and forth between Georgia and Vietnam as army officer John Lithgow seeks to discover why a black war hero has been denied burial in his home-town cemetery. Morgan Freeman and CCH Pounder also excel as the boy's proud parents. DP [VIDEO]

John Lithgow *Major Kendall Laird* • Morgan Freeman *Luther Johnson* • Richard Bradford *General Willard P Hauer* • CCH Pounder *Ada Johnson* • GD Spradlin *Sam Jennings* •

R

Frances Sternhagen *Mrs Eudora McAlister* • M Emmet Walsh *Sarge* ■ *Dir* John Korty • *Scr* Walter Halsey Davis

The Restless Breed ★★ U

Western 1957 · US · Colour · 83mins

This is veteran director Allan Dwan's last western, a cripplingly low-budgeted colour B-movie starring deadpan Scott Brady in a routine tale, as a lawyer trying to unmask his father's killer, helped by a cast which includes Anne Bancroft and Jim Davis. TS

Scott Brady *Mitch Baker* • Anne Bancroft *Angelita* • Jay C Flippen *Marshal Steve Evans* • Rhys Williams *Ed Newton* • Jim Davis *Reverend Simmons* • Leo Gordon *Cherokee* ■ *Dir* Allan Dwan • *Scr* Steven Fisher

Restless Natives ★★ PG

Comedy 1985 · UK · Colour · 85mins

Two Scottish lads become modern-day Robin Hoods, robbing tourists and giving the proceeds to the poor. Soon they are local, then international, heroes. The trouble is that much of the comedy is a parody of the work of the then-popular Scottish director Bill Forsyth, and jokes that were considered feeble in their day now seem even more obscure. A treat, however, for lovers of the Scottish countryside, and an effective career spur for director Michael Hoffman, who went on to make more sophisticated comedies in Hollywood. DM DVD

Joe Mullaney *Ronnie* • Vincent Friell *Will* • Ned Beatty *Bender* • Robert Urquhart *Det Insp Baird* • Teri Lally *Margot* • Bernard Hill *Will's Father* • Mel Smith *Pyle* • Bryan Forbes *Man in Car* • Nanette Newman *Woman in Car* ■ *Dir* Michael Hoffman • *Scr* Ninian Dunnett • *Music* Stuart Adamson

The Restless Years ★★

Drama 1958 · US · Colour · 85mins

Family traumas abound in a conservative suburban community where Teresa Wright's major goal in life is to protect her teenage daughter Sandra Dee from the knowledge and stigma of illegitimacy, while John Saxon's young life is complicated by the reappearance of his long-absent failure of a father, James Whitmore. As a vehicle for teen stars when teen culture was on the way up, this outmoded drama of small-town life was a curious choice. RK

John Saxon *Will Henderson* • Sandra Dee *Melinda Grant* • Teresa Wright *Elizabeth Grant* • James Whitmore *Ed Henderson* • Luana Patten *Polly Fisher* • Margaret Lindsay *Dorothy Henderson* • Virginia Grey *Miss Robson* • Alan Baxter *Alex Fisher* ■ *Dir* Helmut Kautner [Helmut Käutner] • *Scr* Edward Anhalt, from the play *Teach Me How to Cry* by Patricia Joudry

Restoration ★★★★ 15

Period drama 1995 · US · Colour · 112mins

Michael Hoffman's adaptation of Rose Tremain's novel is a period movie that treats the past as something very, very strange. Filmed at Forde Abbey and other historic sites, the Oscar-winning design is astonishing. The court of Charles II resembles Nero's and the picture subversively suggests that the foppish king lit the Great Fire of London to purge the plague and build a new capital. The casting is as weird as the settings: Sam Neill as the cholic King; Robert Downey Jr as a womanising medic; Hugh Grant as a splendidly pompous artist; but what on earth is Meg Ryan doing as a traumatised patient? A flawed picture with flashes of crazy brilliance. AT. Contains nudity.

Robert Downey Jr *Robert Merivel* • Sam Neill *King Charles II* • David Thewlis *John Pearce* • Polly Walker *Celia* • Meg Ryan *Katherine* • Ian McKellen *Will Gates* • Hugh Grant *Finn* • Ian McDiarmid *Ambrose* ■ *Dir* Michael Hoffman • *Scr* Rupert Walters, from the novel by Rose Tremaine

Resurrected ★★★★ 15

Drama 1989 · UK · Colour · 88mins

This is a sombre, unsettling account of a soldier who goes AWOL in the Falklands War and returns to his North Country village, with cruelly ironic consequences. Directed by former documentarist Paul Greengrass, it depicts the combat in First World War terms, but with the political complexity of a Vietnam. He imbues the story with a wealth of religious imagery – walking on water, cruciform poses, resurrection – while examining a flagging nation's regeneration and the attendant jingoism. AT

David Thewlis *Kevin Deakin* • Tom Bell *Mr Deakin* • Rita Tushingham *Mrs Deakin* • Rudi Davies *Julie* • Michael Pollitt *Gregory Deakin* • William Hoyland *Capt Sinclair* • Ewan Stewart *Cpl Byker* • Christopher Fulford *Slaven* • David Lonsdale *Hibbert* • Peter Gunn *Bonner* ■ *Dir* Paul Greengrass • *Scr* Martin Allen

The Resurrected ★★★

Horror mystery 1992 · US · Colour · 106mins

Director Dan O'Bannon is to be commended for this successful adaptation of the classic story *The Case of Charles Dexter Ward*, since most attempts to film the works of HP Lovecraft have proved to be directorial failures. The focus here is on mystery and atmosphere instead of gore, which makes the occasional necessary forays into blood and guts more repulsive and shocking. The story's progression is cleverly constructed, always tantalising the viewer with more questions as each answer is given. John Terry is adequate as the private detective investigating Chris Sarandon. KB

John Terry *John March* • Jane Sibbett *Claire Ward* • Chris Sarandon *Charles Dexter Ward/ Joseph Curwin* • Richard Romanus *Lonnie Peck* • Laurie Briscoe *Holly Tender* • Ken Cameroux *Captain Ben Szandor* ■ *Dir* Dan O'Bannon • *Scr* Brent V Friedman, from the novel by HP Lovecraft

Resurrection ★★★ 15

Fantasy drama 1980 · US · Colour · 98mins

After nearly dying in a car crash, Ellen Burstyn glimpses the "Gates of Heaven" and becomes endowed with healing powers. Is she Christ reborn? That's what neurotic preacher's son Sam Shepard thinks, leading to a provocative and tear-jerking climax. Superb scripting, a terrific cast and Daniel Petrie's heartfelt direction make this rural tale of faith and spirituality a rewarding experience. Burstyn is a revelation as the modest woman who soon realises how much of a burden her "gift" truly is. An under-rated moral fantasy. AJ

Ellen Burstyn *Edna McCauley* • Sam Shepard *Cal Carpenter* • Richard Farnsworth *Esco* • Roberts Blossom *John Harper* • Clifford David *George* • Pamela Payton-Wright *Margaret* ■ *Dir* Daniel Petrie • *Scr* Lewis John Carlino

Resurrection ★★

Psychological drama
1999 · US · Colour · 120mins

Dana Delany assumes the role created by Ellen Burstyn in this redundant remake of Daniel Petrie's 1980 study of blind faith and spiteful retribution. The focus in this TV movie is more on the reaction of Delany's family and friends to the healing powers she acquires following her husband's death in a car crash. Nevertheless, Brenda Fricker and Rita Moreno show well in support. DP

Dana Delany *Clare Miller* • Nick Chinlund *Dr Jake Sandler* • Rita Moreno *Mimi* • Mitchell Kosterman *Joe* • Brenda Fricker *Clare's mother* • Maggie Gyllenhaal *Mary* ■ *Dir* Stephen Gyllenhaal • *Scr* Peachy Markowitz, from the film by Lewis John Carlino

Resurrection ★★

Thriller 1999 · US · Colour · 108mins

Christopher Lambert stars in this serviceable thriller, in which a religious fanatic spends Lent constructing a corpse to host what he believes will be Christ's resurrection. There's a half-hearted attempt at saying something significant about the modern world, but the emphasis is firmly on action and the various dismemberments. Cinematographer Jonathan Freeman achieves some nice visual effects through the rain and it's directed with bravado. DP. film.

Christopher Lambert *John Prudhomme* • Rick Fox *Detective Scholfield* • James Kidnie *Walter Chibley* • Leland Orser *Detective Andrew Hollingworth* ■ *Dir* Russell Mulcahy • *Scr* Brad Mirman, from a story by Brad Mirman, Christopher Lambert

Resurrection Man ★★★ 18

Political crime drama
1997 · UK · Colour · 97mins

With the troubles in Northern Ireland providing a background, this thriller effectively creates an atmosphere of warfare and shows how the situation can affect – and even apparently excuse – the actions of psychopathic killer Stuart Townsend, who leads a gang of Loyalists on a killing spree. Director Marc Evans favours the bloody and the obvious, over defining events and motives, but this is still an engrossing account of humankind's inhumanity. TH. Contains violence, swearing, sex scenes. DVD

Stuart Townsend *Victor Kelly* • Geraldine O'Rawe *Heather Graham* • James Nesbitt *Ryan* • John Hannah *Darkie Larche* • Brenda Fricker *Dorcas Kelly* • James Ellis *Ivor Coppinger* • Sean McGinley *Sammy McLure* • Derek Thompson *Herbie Ferguson* ■ *Dir* Marc Evans • *Scr* Eoin McNamee, from his novel

The Resurrection of Zachary Wheeler ★★

Science-fiction thriller
1971 · US · Colour · 100mins

Playboy presidential hopeful Bradford Dillman is brought back from the dead thanks to organ transplants from synthetic zombies, which have been bred for the purpose by mad doctor James Daly. Reporter Leslie Nielsen uncovers the grisly manufacturing plant in New Mexico. This suffers from too much Cold War philosophy and stodgy chase footage of Nielsen, which get in the way of the intriguing plot. AJ

Leslie Nielsen *Harry Walsh* • Bradford Dillman *Senator Zachary Wheeler* • James Daly *Dr Redding* • Angie Dickinson *Dr Layle Johnson* • Robert J Wilke *Hugh Fielding* • Jack Carter *Dwight Childs* • Don Haggerty *Jake* ■ *Dir* Robert Wynn • *Scr* Jay Simms, Tom Rolf

Retreat, Hell! ★★

War drama 1952 · US · BW · 94mins

Cult B-movie director Joseph H Lewis turns in a conventional combat movie, set during the Korean War. All the clichés are firmly in place: the training routines, the heroic commanding officer; the platoon leader worried about the wife and kids he has left behind; the frayed nerves; and the camaraderie of the men as they are picked off by communist snipers. Made while the Korean War was actually being fought, this was shot on a low budget and isn't a patch on later films with the same theme. AT

Frank Lovejoy *Steve Corbett* • Richard Carlson *Paul Hansen* • Rusty Tamblyn [Russ Tamblyn] *Jimmy McDermid* • Anita Louise *Ruth Hansen* ■ *Dir* Joseph H Lewis • *Scr* Milton Sperling, Ted Sherdeman

Return ★

Mystery 1985 · W Ger/US · Colour · 82mins

A ponderous and talky chiller revolving around hypnotic regression and dark family secrets. Karlene Crockett wants to know how her grandfather died 20 years ago and discovers that gardener John Walcutt could be his reincarnation and the key to unravelling the bizarre mystery. A disappointing adaptation that squanders its few decent ideas through weak direction and over-earnest performances. AJ

Karlene Crockett *Diana Stoving* • John Walcutt *Day Whittaker* • Lisa Richards *Ann Stoving* • Frederic Forrest *Brian Stoving* • Anne Lloyd Francis [Anne Francis] *Eileen Sedgely* • Lenore Zann *Susan* • Thomas Rolapp *Lucky* ■ *Dir* Andrew Silver • *Scr* Andrew Silver, from the novel *Some Other Place, the Right Place* by Donald Harrington

The Return ★★★ U

Drama 1994 · Viet · Colour · 40mins

Already established among his country's most important film-makers, Nhat Minh Dang sampled more festival success with this astute study of how Vietnam's past impinges on its present. At the centre of events is Nguyen Thu Hien, an unhappily married schoolteacher, who is forced to reassess her life on the unexpected return of her first love, who fled three years earlier as one of the infamous "boat people". DP. In Vietnamese with English subtitles.

Nguyen Thu Hien • Tran Luc ■ *Dir/Scr* Nhat Minh Dang

The Return ★★★★ 12

Drama 2003 · Rus · Colour · 105mins

Director Andrey Zvyagintsev's debut feature is an enigmatic rite of passage, in which brothers Vladimir Garin and Ivan Dobronravov are taken on a fishing trip when their missing father (Konstantin Lavronenko) returns to his home in northern Russia after many unexplained years away. Lavronenko tries gruffly to re-establish a relationship with his sons, but their tense journey to a remote island has an ulterior motive, and attempted bonding quickly turns to paranoia and violence. Atmospheric, meditative and drained of warmth by cinematographer Mikhail Kritchman's blue palette, this chilly film refuses to colour in the blanks where backstory might be, and the result is a stunningly beautiful puzzle that brilliantly captures the boys' confusion. AC. In Russian with English subtitles. DVD

Vladimir Garin *Andrey* • Ivan Dobronravov *Ivan* • Konstantin Lavronenko *Father* • Natalia Vdovina *Mother* ■ *Dir* Andrey Zvyagintsev • *Scr* Alexander Novototsky, Vladimir Moiseenko

Return from the Ashes ★★★

Crime thriller 1965 · UK/US · BW · 103mins

An extraordinary picture from British director J Lee Thompson in which a Jewish woman, Ingrid Thulin, returns to Paris from the Dachau concentration camp with her face and mind deeply scarred, so she has plastic surgery. Her husband Maxmilian Schell, a chess master, is now in love with his stepdaughter and at first believes Thulin is a "double" whom he can exploit for compensation money. This bizarre tale at times plumbs depths of awfulness yet rises to the giddiest heights of melodrama. AT

Maximilian Schell *Stanislaus Pilgrin* • Samantha Eggar *Fabienne* • Ingrid Thulin *Dr Michele Wolf* • Herbert Lom *Dr Charles Bovard* • Talitha Pol *Claudine* ■ *Dir* J Lee Thompson • *Scr* Julius J Epstein, from the novel *Le Retour des Cendres* by Hubert Monteilhet

R

Return from the River Kwai ★★ 15

Second World War action adventure
1988 · UK · Colour · 97mins

There's no link between this and David Lean's 1957 classic film, and it doesn't come close in terms of acting or direction, but is still a tough, grim action movie. Set two years after Alec Guinness's bridge-building antics, this recounts with a certain level of realism PoW life in the Far East during the last days of the war. NF [video] DVD

Edward Fox *Benford* • Denholm Elliott *Colonel Grayson* • Chris Penn *Crawford* • George Takei *Tanaka* • Timothy Bottoms *Miller* • Richard Graham (2) *Perry* ■ *Dir* Andrew V McLaglen • *Scr* Sargon Tamimi, Paul Mayersberg

Return from Witch Mountain ★★★★ U

Science-fiction adventure
1978 · US · Colour · 89mins

Bette Davis is in her element here, giving a scene-stealing performance as henchwoman to Christopher Lee's mad scientist. Lee is seeking world domination by gaining control of two extraterrestrial kids, who possess all kinds of strange powers (telekinesis, anti-gravity, cute expressions). A sequel to *Escape to Witch Mountain*, it's a Disney fantasy in which the usual blandness has been spiked with an interesting touch of colour, courtesy of the film's legendary star. TH [video] DVD

Bette Davis *Letha Wedge* • Christopher Lee *Dr Victor Gannon* • Kim Richards *Tia Malone* • Ike Eisenmann *Tony Malone* • Jack Soo *Mr Yokomoto* • Anthony James *Sickle* • Dick Bakalyan [Richard Bakalyan] *Eddie* • Ward Costello *Mr Clearcole* • Christian Juttner *Dazzler* • Poindexter *Crusher* • Brad Savage *Muscles* • Jeffrey Jacquet *Rocky* • Stu Gilliam *Dolan* ■ *Dir* John Hough • *Scr* Malcolm Marmorstein, from characters created by Alexander Key

Return Home ★★★★

Drama 1989 · Aus · Colour · 87mins

Carefully directed by former cinematographer Ray Argall, this is a thoughtful treatise on family loyalty and the passing of traditional values. Dennis Coard turns in an impressive performance as a Melbourne stockbroker who reluctantly returns to his Adelaide roots to renew the ties he has allowed to lapse with his brother (Frankie J Holden), a small-time garage owner caught in the swell of consumerism. Unusual in its positive portrait of suburban life, this is a most pleasant surprise. DP

Dennis Coard *Noel McKenzie* • Frankie J Holden *Steve McKenzie* • Micki Camilleri [Mickey Camilleri] *Judy McKenzie* • Ben Mendelsohn *Gary Wilson* • Rachel Rains *Wendy* • Alan Fletcher *Barry Marshall* ■ *Dir/Scr* Ray Argall

The Return of a Man Called Horse ★★★ 15

Western 1976 · US · Colour · 118mins

This sequel – just as good as the original – has Richard Harris as the peer-turned-native, travelling from England to right the wrongs done to his adopted Sioux tribe. Sadomasochistic rituals such as the Sun Vow ceremony usually result in near-skinning alive, but director Irvin Kershner keeps it relevant to the story, while Gale Sondergaard, everyone's favourite female villain, breathes vengeful fire. Followed in 1983 by *Triumphs of a Man Called Horse*. TH. Contains violence. [video] DVD

Richard Harris *John Morgan* • Gale Sondergaard *Elk Woman* • Geoffrey Lewis *Zenas Morro* • Bill Lucking [William Lucking] *Tom Gryce* • Jorge Luke *Running Bull* • Claudio Brook *Chemin D'Fer* • Enrique Lucero *Raven* • Jorge Russek *Blacksmith* • Ana De Sade *Moonstar* • Pedro Damien *Standing Bear* ■ *Dir* Irvin Kershner • *Scr* Jack DeWitt, from characters created by Dorothy M Johnson

Return of a Stranger ★★

Crime drama 1937 · UK · BW · 63mins

In this creaky melodrama, a scientist disfigured in an explosion returns to London to clear his name, identify a killer and reclaim his girl. The plot is now a cliché, of course, but this remains mesmerisingly watchable because of its period production values and the sheer gall of the finale. Griffith Jones and Rosalyn Boulter are the lacklustre, but remarkably well-spoken leads. TS

Griffith Jones *James Martin* • Rosalyn Boulter *Carol* • Ellis Jeffreys *Lady Wall* • Athole Stewart *Sir Patrick Wall* • Cecil Ramage *John Forbes* • Constance Godridge *Esme* • Sylvia Marriott *Mary* • James Harcourt *Johnson* ■ *Dir* Victor Hanbury • *Scr* Akos Tolnay, Reginald Long, from a play by Rudolph Lothar

The Return of Bulldog Drummond ★

Detective mystery adventure
1934 · UK · BW · 74mins

Based on a real Guards officer (Gerald Fairlie), the character of Bulldog Drummond was conceived by Fairlie's friend "Sapper" or, more correctly, H C McNeile and subsequently developed in novels and films. Drummond is a precursor to many sleuths and gentlemanly detectives. He enjoyed various incarnations including the urbane Jack Buchanan, but here Ralph Richardson takes the part. Neither the role, nor the film, involving the kidnapping of Drummond's wife (Ann Todd) by a secret society, proved worthy of the great actor. BB

Ralph Richardson *Hugh Drummond* • Ann Todd *Phyllis Drummond* • Francis L Sullivan *Carl Peterson* • Claud Allister *Algy Longworth* • H Saxon-Snell *Zadowa* • Spencer Trevor *Sir Bryan Johnstone* • Charles Mortimer *Inspector McIver* ■ *Dir* Walter Summers • *Scr* Walter Summers, from the novel *The Black Gang* by HC "Sapper" McNeile

The Return of Captain Invincible ★★ PG

Spoof adventure 1983 · Aus · Colour · 87mins

Intermittently enjoyable comic book spoof starring Alan Arkin as a down-and-out, alcoholic superhero dragged from his dazed retirement to save the world one last time. Christopher Lee rises to the occasion as an evil megalomaniac in a cheaply-made Australian comedy fantasy, peppered with songs by *Rocky Horror Show* creator Richard O'Brien. Director Philippe Mora tries hard to combine all genres, but the film doesn't quite have the courage of his convictions. AJ [video]

Alan Arkin *Captain Invincible* • Christopher Lee *Mr Midnight* • Michael Pate *US President* • Graham Kennedy *Australian PM* • Kate Fitzpatrick *Patty Patria* ■ *Dir* Philippe Mora • *Scr* Steven E de Souza, Andrew Gaty

The Return of Count Yorga ★★★

Horror 1971 · US · Colour · 96mins

Robert Quarry dons the black cape once more in this polished picture that is superior to the original *Count Yorga, Vampire*, the sexploitation movie that became a cult horror flick. This time he's developed a passion for Mariette Hartley, the daughter of the principal of the orphanage close to his Los Angeles home. But before he can have his wicked way with her he has to overcome her dogged boyfriend Roger Perry. Everything's been done a dozen times before, but Bob Kelljan conjures up a few chills and Quarry turns on the menacing charm with some skill. DP

Robert Quarry *Count Yorga* • Mariette Hartley *Cynthia Nelson* • Roger Perry *Dr David Baldwin* • Yvonne Wilder *Jennifer* • Tom Toner *Reverend Thomas* ■ *Dir* Bob Kelljan • *Scr* Bob Kelljan, Yvonne Wilder

The Return of Dr Fu Manchu ★★

Mystery thriller 1930 · US · BW · 73mins

Swedish character actor Warner Oland stars as Sax Rohmer's insidious Chinese villain, struggling with Scotland Yard's Nayland Smith for world domination. In this slow, but atmospheric film, the Oriental madman, having used a secret drug that induces catalepsy to fake his death, comes back to get revenge on those responsible for killing his wife and son in the Boxer Rebellion. Oland shines in the star role, one he made his own before becoming the screen's most popular Charlie Chan. AJ

Warner Oland *Dr Fu Manchu* • Neil Hamilton *Dr Jack Petrie* • Jean Arthur *Lila Eltham* ■ *Dir* Rowland V Lee • *Scr* Florence Ryerson, Lloyd Corrigan, from the novel by Sax Rohmer

The Return of Dr Mabuse ★★

Crime thriller
1961 · Fr/It/W Ger · BW · 88mins

Shortly after Fritz Lang had released *The Thousand Eyes of Dr Mabuse* and announced his disinterest in continuing the series, Harald Reinl jumped on the bandwagon with this unofficial sequel. Wolfgang Preiss reprises the role of the master criminal, who seemingly returns from the dead to hatch another plan for world domination, this time based in Chicago and involving a nuclear reactor. Preiss would return in *The Invisible Dr Mabuse*. DP. A German language film.

Gert Fröbe *Inspector Lohmann* • Lex Barker *Joe Como* • Daliah Lavi *Maria Sabrehm* • Wolfgang Preiss *Dr Mabuse* • Fausto Tozzi *Prison governor* ■ *Dir* Harald Reinl • *Scr* Ladislaus Fodor [Ladislas Fodor], Marc Behm, from the character created by Norbert Jacques

The Return of Dr X ★★

Horror mystery 1939 · US · BW · 62mins

With Humphrey Bogart in a clichéd role as a murderous monster, this is a conventional account of a vampire terrorising a city. An attempt by Warner Bros to appeal to horror fans, it's notable for the inclusion of many members of the studio's acting B-league, including Dennis Morgan and Rosemary Lane. Only two years later, Bogart became a major star – and wisely steered clear of horror films for the rest of his career. TH

Humphrey Bogart *Marshall Quesne/Dr Maurice J Xavier* • Rosemary Lane *Joan Vance* • Wayne Morris *Walter Barnett* • Dennis Morgan *Michael Rhodes* • John Litel *Dr Francis Flegg* • Lya Lys *Angela Merrova* • Huntz Hall *Pinky* ■ *Dir* Vincent Sherman • *Scr* Lee Katz, from the story *The Doctor's Secret* by William J Makin

The Return of Dracula ★★

Horror 1958 · US · BW and Colour · 77mins

Dracula turns up in California masquerading as a refugee Transylvanian artist and starts his nasty nocturnal habits among the homely community. Released in the same year as Hammer's *Dracula*, this modern gothic thriller lost out in the vampire sweepstakes for being drearily highbrow in comparison. But undead Francis Lederer turning into a wolf, a bat and a curl of mist (hence the loony British retitling *The Fantastic Disappearing Man*) plus other nifty camera tricks, lift it above the average B-movie rut. Mainly for devotees who will find the more intelligent use of horror clichés a surprising bonus. AJ

Francis Lederer *Bellac* • Norma Eberhardt *Rachel* • Ray Stricklyn *Tim* • Jimmy Baird *Mickey* • Greta Granstedt *Cora* • Virginia Vincent *Jennie* • John Wengraf *Merriman* • Gage Clark [Gage Clarke] *Reverend* • John McNamara *Sheriff Bicknell* ■ *Dir* Paul Landres • *Scr* Pat Fielder

The Return of Frank James ★★★ U

Western 1940 · US · Colour · 92mins

Henry Fonda had played Frank to Tyrone Power's Jesse in the superb *Jesse James*, and in this disappointing follow-up he spends all his time searching for brothers Charles and, in particular, Bob Ford (John Carradine), the "dirty little coward" who shot his own brother. But, unfortunately, Hank has neither benefit of a decent script nor a sympathetic director, as Austrian émigré Fritz Lang makes heavy going of this lightweight material, dragging the pace to the point of boredom. Notable mainly for the movie debut of the beautiful Gene Tierney. TS [video]

Henry Fonda *Frank James/Ben Woodson* • Gene Tierney *Eleanor Stone* • Jackie Cooper *Clem/Tom Grayson* • Henry Hull *Major Rufus Cobb* • John Carradine *Bob Ford* • Charles Tannen *Charles Ford* • J Edward Bromberg *Runyon* • Donald Meek *McCoy* ■ *Dir* Fritz Lang • *Scr* Sam Hellman

The Return of Godzilla ★★ PG

Monster horror 1984 · Jpn · Colour · 87mins

After a decade in hibernation, the King of the Monsters returned as the villain to cause an international Cold War incident after trashing a Soviet submarine. Russia and America want the outsized nuisance destroyed, and Tokyo is nearly razed to the ground for the umpteenth time. Raymond Burr pops up as an intrepid reporter, just as he did in the original 1954 movie, in footage added for western markets. Elsewhere, it's business as usual – thin plot, inane dialogue, daft dubbing and cheap special effects. AJ. A Japanese language film with both dubbed and subtitled versions. [video]

Raymond Burr *Steve Martin* • Keiju Kobayashi *Prime Minister Mitamura* • Ken Tanaka *Goro Maki* • Yasuko Sawaguchi *Naoko Okumura* • Shin Takuma *Hiroshi Okumura* • Eitaro Ozawa *Finance Minister Kanzaki* • Taketoshi Naito *Chief Cabinet Secretary Takegami* • Nobuo Kaneko *Home Affairs Minister Isomura* ■ *Dir* Kohji Hashimoto, RJ Kizer • *Scr* Shuichi Nagahara, Lisa Tomei, from a story by Tomoyuki Tanaka

The Return of Josey Wales ★ 15

Western 1986 · US · Colour · 87mins

Josey's back! But this time he ain't Clint Eastwood – so who cares? Josey is now played by Michael Parks. This sequel is mainly just a series of shoot-outs. Parks also directs and he shot it in Mexico with an eye to the Latino market – much of the dialogue is in Spanish and the styling is reminiscent of those paella westerns of the 1970s. AT. In English and Spanish with subtitles. [video]

Michael Parks *Josey Wales* • Rafael Campos *Chato* • Bob Magruder *Ten Spot* • Paco Vela *Paco* • Everett Sifuentes *Escobedo* • Charlie McCoy *Charlie* ■ *Dir* Michael Parks • *Scr* Forrest Carter, Ro Taylor, from the novel *Vengeance Trail of Josey Wales* by Forrest Carter

The Return of Martin Guerre ★★★★ 15

Historical drama 1982 · Fr · Colour · 106mins

Infinitely superior to its Hollywood remake, *Sommersby*, Daniel Vigne's suspenseful riddle of identity is a fascinating study of the blind faith, superstition and prejudice that governed most rural communities in the mid-16th century. Gérard Depardieu typically imposes himself on proceedings as the farmer who returns a changed man after nine years at war. But just how changed is he? The winner of a César for its screenplay, this highly literate film benefits from some meticulous historical research and a sensitive performance from Nathalie Baye as the unquestioning wife. DP. In French with English subtitles. DVD

Gérard Depardieu *Martin Guerre* • Bernard-Pierre Donnadieu *Martin Guerre* • Nathalie Baye *Bertrande de Rols* • Roger Planchon *Jean de Caros* • Maurice Jacquemont *Judge Rieux* • Isabelle Sadoyan *Catherine Boere* ■ *Dir* Daniel Vigne • *Scr* Daniel Vigne, Jean-Claude Carrière

The Return of Mr Moto ★

Detective drama 1965 · UK · BW · 68mins

More than a quarter of a century after Peter Lorre made the last of his eight films as John Philip Marquand's Oriental sleuth, Fox released this bizarre coda to the series. Henry Silva took the title role, but assumed a Japanese disguise only to conclude the case. Stationed in London to protect petroleum magnate Gordon Tanner, Silva's Interpol agent is soon on the trail of Martin Wyldeck, a former Nazi who plans world domination. Crude is the only word to describe this opportunistic, ineptly played revival. DP

Henry Silva *Mr Moto* • Terence Longdon *Jonathan Westering* • Suzanne Lloyd *Maxine Powell* • Marne Maitland *Wasir Hussein* • Martin Wyldeck *Dargo* ■ *Dir* Ernest Morris • *Scr* Fred Eggers, from a story by Randall Hood, from the character created by John Phillip Marquand

The Return of October ★★

Comedy drama 1948 · US · Colour · 89mins

October's a racehorse, but he's also the reincarnation of Terry Moore's Uncle Willie – or so she believes in this whimsical comedy bolstered by Technicolor and an ingratiating performance by Glenn Ford, as the professor of psychology who writes a book about the girl's strange belief. Director Joseph H Lewis shows some talent for comedy, but seems happiest shooting the racetrack sequences – although the races themselves are made up of stock shots from 1938's *Kentucky*,. AE

Glenn Ford *Prof Bentley Bassett Jr* • Terry Moore *Terry Ramsey* • Albert Sharpe *Vince, the Tout* • James Gleason *Uncle Willie* • Dame May Whitty *Aunt Martha* • Henry O'Neill *President Hotchkiss* ■ *Dir* Joseph H Lewis • *Scr* Melvin Frank, Norman Panama, from a story by Connie Lee, Karen De Wolf

The Return of Peter Grimm ★★★

Fantasy 1935 · US · BW · 81mins

The theme of returning from the dead to see how the living are coping has always fascinated dramatists, and this adaptation has Lionel Barrymore as a crusty millionaire allowed after his death to see what a mess he made of things. Though the film suffers from an uncertain tone, with director George Nichols Jr not sure how seriously to treat the story, the performances are strong and the tale's premise remains intriguing and involving. TV

Lionel Barrymore *Peter Grimm* • Helen Mack *Catherine* • Edward Ellis *Dr Andrew MacPherson* • Donald Meek *Mr Batholomew* • George Breakston *William Van Dam* • Allen Vincent *Frederik* • James Bush *James* ■ *Dir* George Nichols Jr • *Scr* Francis Edwards Faragoh, from the play by David Belasco

The Return of Swamp Thing ★★ 15

Spoof science-fiction thriller
1989 · US · Colour · 83mins

Louis Jourdan returns as evil genius Dr Arcane, back in melodramatic Dr Moreau mode, and still gene-splitting to halt the ageing process. Soap queen Heather Locklear is his stepdaughter searching for the truth behind her mother's death, but how and why she falls for Swampy has to be seen to be believed. It's a moss-eaten slice of splat-stick packed with laboured in-jokes (Jourdan's pet parrot is called "Gigi"). AJ

Louis Jourdan *Dr Anton Arcane* • Heather Locklear *Abby Arcane* • Sarah Douglas *Dr Lana Zurrell* • Dick Durock *Swamp Thing* • Ace Mask *Dr Rochelle* • Joey Sagal *Gunn* ■ *Dir* Jim Wynorski • *Scr* Derek Spencer, Grant Morris, from the DC Comics character

Return of the Bad Men ★★

Western 1948 · US · BW · 90mins

Stuff enough famous western desperadoes into one film to keep the action crowd happy and you don't have to worry too much about plot or characterisation. There's the Youngers, the Daltons, Wild Bill Doolin and Billy the Kid all spoiling for a fight, but the real villainy comes from Robert Ryan's vicious Sundance Kid and the only man who can stop him is Randolph Scott's marshal. AE

Randolph Scott *Vance* • Robert Ryan *Sundance Kid* • Anne Jeffreys *Cheyenne* • George "Gabby" Hayes *John Pettit* • Jacqueline White *Madge Allen* • Steve Brodie *Cole Younger* • Richard Powers [Tom Keene] *Jim Younger* • Robert Bray *John Younger* • Lex Barker *Emmett Dalton* • Walter Reed *Bob Dalton* • Michael Harvey *Grat Dalton* • Dean White *Billy the Kid* • Robert Armstrong *Wild Bill Doolin* ■ *Dir* Ray Enright • *Scr* Charles O'Neal, Jack Natteford, Luci Ward, from a story by Jack Natteford, Luci Ward

The Return of the Cisco Kid ★★★ U

Western 1939 · US · BW · 70mins

Matinée idol Warner Baxter stars as author O Henry's dashing Mexican hero for the third time her. He received the first talkie best actor Oscar for the role in the 1929 film *In Old Arizona*, and did well commercially in the absurdly heroic 1931 sequel *The Cisco Kid*. But this time, eight long years later, Baxter's drinking, a substandard director and a makeshift plot make for a disappointing outing, which proved to be Baxter's last as the Kid. This led to a Cisco Kid movie series, starring Cesar Romero (beginning with *The Cisco Kid and the Lady*). TS

Warner Baxter *Cisco Kid* • Lynn Bari *Ann Carver* • Cesar Romero *Lopez* • Henry Hull *Colonel Jonathan Bixby* • Kane Richmond *Alan Davis* • C Henry Gordon *Mexican Captain* • Robert Barrat *Sheriff McNally* ■ *Dir* Herbert I Leeds • *Scr* Milton Sperling, from the characters created by O Henry

Return of the Fly ★★ 15

Horror 1959 · US · BW · 76mins

The sequel to the original 1958 horror hit is a more standard B-movie retelling of the same story, with Brett Halsey playing Al Hedison's son, repeating his father's teleportation tinkering with similarly disastrous results. Thankfully Vincent Price is back, again playing the concerned uncle, and goes a long way towards keeping things buzzing along. But, aside from a few horrific moments in a mortuary and the sick guinea pig experiment, director Edward Bernds sadly stresses plot gimmicks, at the expense of an involving story. *Curse of the Fly* completed the trilogy. AJ DVD

Vincent Price *François Delambre* • Brett Halsey *Phillipe Delambre* • David Frankham *Alan Hinds* • John Sutton *Inspector Charas* • Dan Seymour *Max Berthold* • Danielle De Metz *Cecile Bonnard* ■ *Dir* Edward Bernds • *Scr* Edward Bernds, from a story by George Langelaan

Return of the Idiot ★★★★

Drama 1999 · Cz Rep/Ger · Colour · 99mins

This is the deceptively intricate tale of a seemingly simple man. Visiting distant relatives after a lengthy spell in an asylum, Pavel Liska is the epitome of innocence abroad as he artlessly dismantles the web of romantic deceit spun by a couple of small-town brothers and their adversarial sister lovers. The humour is as precise as it is gentle, although there are also some priceless moments of slapstick and some unexpectedly surreal imagery in Liska's nightmares. DP. In Czech with English subtitles.

Pavel Liska *The Idiot/Frantisek* • Anna Geislerova *Anna* • Tatiana Vilhelmova *Olga* • Jiri Langmajer *Emil* • Jiri Machacek *Robert* ■ *Dir* Sasa Gedeon • *Scr* Sasa Gedeon, from the novel by Fyodor Dostoyevsky

Return of the Killer Tomatoes ★ 15

Horror comedy 1988 · US · Colour · 94mins

As *Attack of the Killer Tomatoes* was a big video rental (solely because of its catchy title), a belated sequel was commissioned and it is even worse. Professor Gangrene (John Astin) turns a tomato into a sexy babe by playing music at it and plans to take over the world with a bevy of similarly exposed red fruits. John DeBello's charmless wonder is only notable for an early appearance by future heart-throb George Clooney. AJ DVD

Anthony Starke *Chad* • Karen Mistal *Tara* • George Clooney *Matt* • Steve Lundquist *Igor* • John Astin *Professor Gangrene* ■ *Dir* John DeBello • *Scr* Constantine Dillon, John DeBello, John Stephen Peace [Steve Peace]

Return of the Living Dead ★★★ 18

Comedy horror 1984 · US · Colour · 86mins

This enjoyable horror comedy marked the directorial debut of long-time sci-fi scribe Dan O'Bannon. This semi-sequel to George A Romero's 1968 cult classic *Night of the Living Dead* is like an DC comic come alive, in that it'll make you laugh and squirm – often at the same time. "They're back. They're hungry. And they're not vegetarian," blared the poster. O'Bannon cleverly makes the zombies the real stars of this movie and, unlike the Romero variety, these can speak, though they're mostly limited to spouting, "Brains, more brains!" A must for horror fans, this was followed by two sequels. RS DVD

Clu Gulager *Burt* • James Karen *Frank* • Don Calfa *Ernie* • Thom Mathews *Freddy* • Beverly Randolph *Tina* • John Philbin *Chuck* • Jewel Shepard *Casey* ■ *Dir* Dan O'Bannon • *Scr* Dan O'Bannon, from a story by Judy Ricci, John Russo, Russell Streiner

Return of the Living Dead Part II ★★ 18

Comedy horror 1988 · US · Colour · 85mins

The emphasis here is on humour at the expense of horror – most of it, it must be said, unintentional. Once again small-town America is overrun by brain-eating zombies, the by-products of toxic waste from bacteriological warfare, which has seeped into a local graveyard with familiar results. And it's up to the usual motley crew of teens to sort it out. This predictable sequel is dull and repetitive. RS DVD

James Karen *Ed* • Thom Mathews *Joey* • Dana Ashbrook *Tom Essex* • Marsha Dietlein *Lucy Wilson* • Philip Bruns *Doc Mandel* • Michael Kenworthy *Jesse Wilson* • Suzanne Snyder *Brenda* • Thor Van Lingen *Billy* • Jason Hogan *Johnny* ■ *Dir/Scr* Ken Wiederhorn

Return of the Living Dead III ★★★ 18

Horror 1993 · US · Colour · 92mins

After the risible *Return of the Living Dead Part II*, the series got back on track with this splatter fest from Brian Yuzna. Dispensing with the spoof elements of its predecessors, this is a darker and surprisingly intelligent mix of gore, special effects and tragic romance. J Trevor Edmond is the lovelorn teen who uses the zombie gas that caused such chaos in the earlier movies to resurrect his girlfriend, after she is killed in a motorcycle accident, with predictable results. RS DVD

Mindy Clarke [Melinda Clarke] *Julie* • J Trevor Edmond *Curt Reynolds* • Kent McCord *Colonel John Reynolds* • Basil Wallace *Riverman* ■ *Dir* Brian Yuzna • *Scr* Jon Penney

The Return of the Musketeers ★★ PG

Swashbuckling comedy adventure
1989 · UK/Fr/Sp · Colour · 101mins

Fifteen years after the success of his sparkling version of Alexandre Dumas's swashbuckling favourite, Richard Lester reunited the musketeers in this bid to save Charles I of England from the executioner's axe. Roy Kinnear's tragic death following a riding accident obviously sapped everyone's enthusiasm for the project. The Dumas book, on which the story is based, inspired the marginally more successful Bertrand Tavernier 1994 film *D'Artagnan's Daughter*. DP. Contains swearing and violence.

Michael York *D'Artagnan* • Oliver Reed *Athos* • Frank Finlay *Porthos* • C Thomas Howell *Raoul* • Kim Cattrall *Justine* • Geraldine Chaplin *Queen Anne* • Roy Kinnear *Planchet* • Christopher Lee *Rochefort* • Philippe Noiret *Cardinal Mazarin* • Richard Chamberlain *Aramis* ■ *Dir* Richard Lester • *Scr* George MacDonald Fraser, from the novel *Vingt Ans Après* by Alexandre Dumas

The Return of the Pink Panther ★★★ PG

Comedy 1974 · UK · Colour · 107mins

Peter Sellers repeatedly returned to his Inspector Clouseau role, and everyone should be thankful. This is Blake Edwards and Sellers working together at their best, producing memorable moments of film comedy. Clouseau's attempts to woo Catherine Schell with his Bogart-style chat-up lines had even his co-star in fits of laughter, which they thankfully kept on screen. Not as good as the first, but still great fun. Followed by *The Pink Panther Strikes Again* in 1976. NF DVD

Peter Sellers *Inspector Clouseau* • Christopher Plummer *Sir Charles Litton* • Catherine Schell *Claudine* • Herbert Lom *Chief Inspector Dreyfus* • Peter Arne *Colonel Sharki* • Peter Jeffrey *General Wadafi* • Grégoire Aslan *Chief of Lugash Police* • David Lodge *Mac* • Graham Stark *Pepi* • Eric Pohlmann *Fat man* • André Maranne *François* • Burt Kwouk *Cato* ■ *Dir* Blake Edwards • *Scr* Frank Waldman, Blake Edwards, from a character created by Blake Edwards, Maurice Richlin

The Return of the Scarlet Pimpernel ★★ U

Period adventure 1937 · UK · BW · 74mins

Leslie Howard had such a hit with *The Scarlet Pimpernel* in 1934 that Alexander Korda immediately ordered a sequel – for far less than the budget of the original. After Howard turned the part down to play in a little something called *Gone with the Wind*, the role of Sir Percy Blakeney went to Barry K Barnes, a stage actor who made his

R

screen debut. Being a Korda production, it looks handsome, but that's the best one can say. AT

Barry K Barnes *Sir Percy Blakeney/The Scarlet Pimpernel* • Sophie Stewart *Marguerite Blakeney* • Margaretta Scott *Theresa Cabarrus* • James Mason *Jean Tallien* • Francis Lister *Chauvelin* • Anthony Bushell *Sir Andrew Ffoulkes* • Patrick Barr *Lord Hastings* • David Tree *Lord Harry Denning* • Henry Oscar *Maximilien de Robespierre* ■ *Dir* Hans Schwartz [Hanns Schwarz] • *Scr* Lajos Biró, Arthur Wimperis, Adrian Brunel, from the novel by Baroness Orczy

Return of the Secaucus Seven ★★★★

Drama 1980 · US · Colour · 109mins

John Sayles's directing debut was shot for a mere $60,000 and deals with the reunion of seven friends, all of whom were part of the student protest movement of the 1960s and are now definitely older, richer and perhaps wiser. There's a teacher, a singer, a doctor and so on and they talk, attend a play, talk some more, have sex, get arrested and go their separate ways. It has the density of a novel and the non-starry cast is simply marvellous, each creating a real character, yet none making too big a show of it. This is a real ensemble piece that is often regarded as superior to the very similar, big-budgeted *The Big Chill*. AT

Bruce MacDonald (1) *Mike* • Adam LeFevre *JT* • Gordon Clapp *Chip* • Karen Trott *Maura* • David Strathairn *Ron* • Marisa Smith *Carol* • Carolyn Brooks *Meg* • John Sayles *Howie* ■ *Dir/Scr* John Sayles

Return of the Seven ★★★ PG

Western 1966 · US/Sp · Colour · 90mins

Only Yul Brynner actually returns for this sequel to *The Magnificent Seven*. Of the newcomers, trusty tough guys Warren Oates and Claude Akins alone cut the mustard as Brynner and his band attempt to liberate a Mexican village from the slavery imposed by a megalomaniac father, grieving for his dead son. Director Burt Kennedy could always be depended upon to grind out robust westerns, but Larry Cohen's derivative script gives him too little to get his teeth into. Another sequel, *Guns of the Magnificent Seven* followed in 1969. DP DVD

Yul Brynner *Chris* • Robert Fuller *Vin* • Julian Mateos *Chico* • Warren Oates *Colbee* • Jordan Christopher *Manuel* • Claude Akins *Frank* • Virgilio Teixeira *Luis* • Emilio Fernandez *Lorca* • Rudy Acosta [Rodolfo Acosta] *Lopez* • Elisa Montés *Petra* • Fernando Rey *Priest* ■ *Dir* Burt Kennedy • *Scr* Larry Cohen

The Return of the Soldier ★★★ PG

Period drama 1982 · UK · Colour · 98mins

Alan Bates is in the trenches, leaving wife, Julie Christie emotionally frozen in limbo and cousin, Ann-Margret worried sick and heaving with desire for him. Then Bates returns – shellshocked and an amnesiac, he may as well be dead. Instead he runs off with an old flame – dour Glenda Jackson, nursing a big social chip on her shoulder. This is an impeccably mounted costume drama in which every class division and every unsaid emotion knows its place. AT

Alan Bates *Captain Chris Baldry* • Ann-Margret *Jenny* • Glenda Jackson *Margaret Grey* • Julie Christie *Kitty Baldry* • Jeremy Kemp *Frank* • Edward De Souza *Edward* • Frank Finlay *William Grey* • Ian Holm *Dr Anderson* • Pauline Quirke *Girl searching in hospital* • Kevin Whately *Hostile soldier's mate* ■ *Dir* Alan Bridges • *Scr* Hugh Whitemore, from a novel by Rebecca West

The Return of the Vampire ★

Second World War horror
1943 · US · BW · 68mins

Playing a vampire for the first time since *Dracula* in 1931, Bela Lugosi is Armand Tesla (because Universal wouldn't let Columbia use its copyright name), a blood-sucker revived when a German bomb hits a cemetery during the Blitz. Our ill-humoured hero is then doomed to wander around foggy wartime London with a werewolf minion in tow to execute an aimless revenge plot. Crude and cornball. AJ

Bela Lugosi *Armand Tesla/Dr Hugo Bruckner* • Frieda Inescort *Lady Jane Ainsley* • Nina Foch *Nicki Saunders* • Miles Mander *Sir Frederick Fleet* • Roland Varno *John Ainsley* • Matt Willis *Andreas Obry* • Ottola Nesmith *Elsa* • Gilbert Emery *Prof Walter Saunders* ■ *Dir* Lew Landers • *Scr* Griffin Jay, Randall Faye, from an idea by Kurt Neumann

Return to Glennascaul ★★★ U

Supernatural drama
1951 · US · Colour and BW · 23mins

Orson Welles was in the middle of his interminable *Othello* shoot when he cameoed in this diverting Irish ghost story, as a favour to writer/director Hilton Edwards, whom he'd known since their days at Dublin's Gate Theatre. However, the brunt of the action is carried by Michael Laurence, who relates the LeFanu-style tale of his midnight encounter with a long-deceased mother and daughter. Views of the isolated house, both in its baroque cosiness and its eerie desolation, are stylishly achieved. DP

Orson Welles • Michael Laurence (1) *Sean Merriman* • Sheila Richards *Mrs Campbell* • Helena Hughes *Lucy Campbell* ■ *Dir/Scr* Hilton Edwards

Return to Macon County ★★ 15

Drama 1975 · US · Colour · 85mins

This disappointing follow-up to the cult hit *Macon County Line*, is distinguished only by the casting of Nick Nolte and Don Johnson in early roles. This is really a sequel in name and setting only. Where the original focused on the horrors and violence of backwoods America, this goes down the *American Graffiti* route of a jukebox-friendly soundtrack for a tale of teen sex and hot-rod racing. Nolte and Johnson spend most of the movie driving fast and being chased by a vengeful cop. RS

Nick Nolte *Bo Hollinger* • Don Johnson *Harley McKay* • Robin Mattson *Junell* • Eugene Daniels *Tom* • Matt Greene *Pete* • Devon Ericson *Betty* • Ron Prather *Steve* • Robert Viharo *Sergeant Whittaker* ■ *Dir/Scr* Richard Compton

Return to Me ★★ PG

Romantic comedy drama
2000 · US · Colour · 111mins

Recently widowed architect David Duchovny falls in love with waitress Minnie Driver. The catch is that she got his late wife's heart in a transplant. It's a rather grisly premise for an otherwise lightweight affair. The Chicago locations are well used, and a colourful cast deftly hints at the city's broad ethnic mix. Duchovny, however, is a dour leading man, while Driver is strangely subdued as his love interest. NS DVD

David Duchovny *Bob Rueland* • Minnie Driver *Grace Briggs* • Carroll O'Connor *Marty O'Reilly* • Robert Loggia *Angelo Pardipillo* • Bonnie Hunt *Megan Dayton* • David Alan Grier *Charlie Johnson* • Joely Richardson *Elizabeth Rueland* • Eddie Jones *Emmett McFadden* • James Belushi *Joe Dayton* ■ *Dir* Bonnie Hunt • *Scr* Bonnie Hunt, Don Lake, from a story by Bonnie Hunt, Don Lake, Andrew Stern, Samantha Goodman

Return to Never Land ★★★ U

Animated musical adventure
2002 · US · Colour · 69mins

Disney's recycling of JM Barrie's main themes from their classic animated feature *Peter Pan* is surprisingly effective, although the animation is occasionally a little flat and the snatches of new songs are rather unnecessary. Now married with two children of her own, Wendy Darling has never stopped believing in "The Boy Who Would Never Grow Up". Her daughter Jane has no time for such piffle, until she's kidnapped by Captain Hook. Cleverly set during the Blitz, this is a heartfelt paean to childhood innocence and the power of imagination. AJ DVD

Harriet Owen *Jane/Young Wendy* • Blayne Weaver *Peter Pan* • Corey Burton *Captain Hook* • Jeff Bennett *Smee/Pirates* • Kath Soucie *Wendy* • Roger Rees *Edward* ■ *Dir* Robin Budd • *Scr* Temple Mathews, from characters created by JM Barrie

Return to Oz ★★★ PG

Fantasy 1985 · US · Colour · 105mins

Disney recaptures the dark side of L Frank Baum's *Oz* stories in this exciting sequel to the 1939 classic. Fairuza Balk is wonderful as Dorothy, who ends up back in a ruined Oz facing the evil Nome King and Princess Mombi with her friends Pumpkinhead, Tik Tok the clockwork man and a talking chicken. Sombre in tone it may be, but director Walter Murch's non-musical is imaginative and hugely appealing. Will Vinton's Claymation process animates the rock faces as part of the colourful special-effects extravaganza. AJ DVD

Fairuza Balk *Dorothy Gale* • Nicol Williamson *Dr Worley/Nome King* • Jean Marsh *Nurse Wilson/Princess Mombi* • Piper Laurie *Aunt Em* • Matt Clark *Uncle Henry* • Michael Sundin *Tik Tok* • Sean Barrett (2) *Tik Tok* • Stewart Larange *Jack Pumpkinhead* • Brian Henson *Jack Pumpkinhead* • Steve Norrington *Gump* • Justin Case *Scarecrow* ■ *Dir* Walter Murch • *Scr* Walter Murch, Gill Dennis, from the books by L Frank Baum • *Cinematographer* David Watkin • *Art Director* Norman Reynolds

Return to Paradise ★★

Romance 1953 · US · Colour · 100mins

Gary Cooper, pursuing a peaceable devil-may-care beachcombing existence on a South Seas paradise, has a love affair with island girl Roberta Haynes and clashes with puritanical missionary Barry Jones. Haynes dies in childbirth and Cooper leaves, only to return during the Second World War when he meets his now grown-up daughter. The film beguiles with its authentic atmosphere and flavour, but is too erratic to be fully satisfying. RK

Gary Cooper *Mr Morgan* • Roberta Haynes *Maeva* • Barry Jones *Pastor Corbett* • Moira MacDonald *Turia* • John Hudson (1) *Harry Faber* ■ *Dir* Mark Robson • *Scr* Charles Kaufman, from the short story *Mr Morgan* by James A Michener • *Cinematographer* Winton C Hoch

Return to Paradise ★★★★ 15

Drama 1998 · US · Colour · 107mins

Would you let a friend die in a Malaysian prison for an offence you committed? That's the dilemma facing Vince Vaughn and David Conrad when lawyer Anne Heche tells them Joaquin Phoenix will hang unless they go back to Asia and serve their part of his prison sentence. Director Joseph Ruben weaves a wrenching tragedy out of the awesome predicament, mining every ounce of indignation and empathy. Acted with anguished conviction, Ruben's crisis-of-conscience thriller doesn't take any easy options and the result casts a singularly provocative spell. AJ. Contains swearing, drug abuse and violence.

Vince Vaughn *Sheriff* • Anne Heche *Beth* • Joaquin Phoenix *Lewis* • David Conrad *Tony* • Vera Farmiga *Kerrie* • Nick Sandow *Ravitch* • Jada Pinkett Smith *MJ Major* • Ming Lee *Mr Chandran* ■ *Dir* Joseph Ruben • *Scr* Wesley Strick, Bruce Robinson

Return to Peyton Place ★★★

Drama 1961 · US · Colour · 121mins

A sequel to the hit 1957 feature film *Peyton Place*, this offers the same sensational mix as before and needs little comment for devotees of its predecessor, the original bestselling novel, or the long-running TV soap. Carol Lynley is Allison Mackenzie, who provokes outrage in her home town when she publishes her first novel, a thinly veiled exposé of the town's inhabitants. Utterly predictable glossy tosh, it showcases the then relative newcomer Tuesday Weld and offers a standout performance from Mary Astor. RK

Carol Lynley *Allison MacKenzie* • Jeff Chandler *Lewis Jackman* • Eleanor Parker *Connie Rossi* • Mary Astor *Roberta Carter* • Robert Sterling *Mike Rossi* • Luciana Paluzzi *Raffaella Carter* • Tuesday Weld *Selena Cross* • Brett Halsey *Ted Carter* ■ *Dir* José Ferrer • *Scr* Ronald Alexander, from the novel by Grace Metalious

A Return to Salem's Lot ★★★ 18

Horror 1987 · US · Colour · 96mins

In this genuine treat for undead cultists, Larry Cohen pitches his tone a long way from the original Stephen King book for a loose semi-sequel. Michael Moriarty plays an anthropologist arriving, with son Ricky Addison Reed, in the infamous title locale to take over an inherited farmhouse, only to find the vampire population want him to set down their venerable history for posterity. Watch for veteran director Samuel Fuller, who steals the show as a single-minded vampire hunter. AJ

Michael Moriarty *Joe Weber – Dad* • Richard Addison Reed *Jeremy Weber* • Andrew Duggan *Judge Axel* • Samuel Fuller *Dr Van Meer* • June Havoc *Aunt Clara* • Ronee Blakley *Sally* • Evelyn Keyes *Mrs Axel* ■ *Dir* Larry Cohen • *Scr* Larry Cohen, James Dixon, from a story by Larry Cohen, from the novel *Salem's Lot* by Stephen King

Return to Snowy River ★★

Adventure 1988 · Aus · Colour · 97mins

Brian Dennehy steals the limelight in a role first played in 1982 by Kirk Douglas in this below-par sequel to *The Man from Snowy River*, the tale of feuding Australian ranchers. Tom Burlinson, who left Snowy River to make his fortune, now wants to come back to his former girlfriend. Burlinson and Sigrid Thornton reprise the roles they played better in George Miller's original film, but the spectacular scenery is some compensation for an unfocused story with and underdeveloped characters. SG

Tom Burlinson *Jim Craig* • Sigrid Thornton *Jessica Harrison* • Brian Dennehy *Harrison* • Nicholas Eadie *Alistair Patton* • Mark Hembrow *Seb* • Bryan Marshall *Hawker* ■ *Dir* Geoff Burrowes • *Scr* John Dixon, Geoff Burrowes

R

Return to the Blue Lagoon ★ 15

Romantic adventure
1991 · US · Colour · 97mins

While 1980's *The Blue Lagoon* had a certain grimly humorous value, this sequel lacks even that, as Brian Krause, playing the son of Brooke Shields's character from the original, and Milla Jovovich experience puberty and nudity on a deserted island. Contains bad acting, an appalling script and some of the most unconvincing love scenes ever committed to film. JB. Contains nudity. DVD

Milla Jovovich *Lilli* • Brian Krause *Richard* • Lisa Pelikan *Sarah Hargrave* • Courtney Phillips *Young Lilli* • Garette Patrick Ratliff *Young Richard* ■ *Dir* William A Graham • *Scr* Leslie Stevens, from the novel *The Garden of God* by Henry de Vere Stacpoole

Return to Treasure Island ★★ U

Adventure 1954 · US · Colour · 75mins

In this desperate updating of Robert Louis Stevenson's classic adventure, pirate descendant Dawn Addams is joined in her bid to find Captain Flint's treasure by archaeology student Tab Hunter (a feeble forerunner of Indiana Jones), who relies on a little brawn to outwit bogus professor Porter Hal. Meagre fare. DP

Tab Hunter *Clive Stone* • Dawn Addams *Jamesina Hawkins* • Porter Hall *Maximillian Harris* • James Seay *Felix Newman* • Harry Lauter *Parker* • William Cottrell *Cookie* • Henry Rowland *Williams* • Lane Chandler *Cardigan* ■ *Dir* EA Dupont • *Scr* Aubrey Wisberg, Jack Pollexfen, from their story

Return to Yesterday ★★ U

Drama 1940 · UK · BW · 69mins

English actor Clive Brook, who enjoyed some success in Hollywood, stars in this British film about an English actor who has found success in Hollywood. Yearning for the simplicity of his past, however, he buys his way into a season with a humble British rep company. Directed by Robert Stevenson, a pacifist who publicised his resentment of British film-makers escaping the war by fleeing to Hollywood, this is a mediocre and technically inadequate film. RK

Clive Brook *Robert Maine* • Anna Lee *Carol Sands* • Dame May Whitty *Mrs Truscott* • Hartley Power *Regan* • Milton Rosmer *Sambourne* • David Tree *Peter Thropp, playwright* • Olga Lindo *Grace Sambourne* ■ *Dir* Robert Stevenson • *Scr* Robert Stevenson, Margaret Kennedy, Roland Pertwee, Angus MacPhail, from the play *Goodness How Sad!* by Robert Morley

R

Reuben, Reuben ★★★ 15

Comedy 1983 · US · Colour · 95mins

Tom Conti was Oscar nominated for his tour de force as an impossible, alcoholic, womanising, flamboyantly verbose Scottish poet – a character shamelessly but affectionately inspired by Welsh icon Dylan Thomas and Ireland's Brendan Behan – who trades on his fading literary celebrity to scrounge off the generous hospitality of thrilled female admirers in a sleepy American university town. Inspiration to pull himself together comes in the shape of winsome young student Kelly McGillis (in her screen debut). The old-fashioned, but witty script by the venerable Julius J Epstein and charming performances give this lightweight throwback appeal. AME

Tom Conti *Gowan McGland* • Kelly McGillis *Geneva Spofford* • Roberts Blossom *Frank Spofford* • Cynthia Harris *Bobby Springer* • E Katherine Kerr *Lucille Haxby* • Joel Fabiani *Dr Haxby* • Lois Smith *Mare Spofford* ■ *Dir* Robert Ellis Miller • *Scr* Julius J Epstein, from a novel by Peter DeVries, from the play *Spofford* by Herman Shumlin

Reunion ★★★ 15

Historical drama
1989 · Fr/W Ger/UK · Colour · 105mins

Samuel West and Christien Anholt give mature performances and Jason Robards turns in a dignified cameo in this thought-provoking drama, about the interracial implications of Hitler's rise to power and the pain of coming to terms with the past. But it's the behind-the-camera credits that make this co-production so fascinating. Jerry Schatzberg directs steadily from a Harold Pinter script, while the stylish sets were created by the veteran Alexandre Trauner, who had designed some of the most famous French films during his 60-year career. DP

Jason Robards *Henry Strauss* • Christien Anholt *Hans Strauss* • Samuel West *Konradin Von Lohenburg* • Françoise Fabian *Countess Grafin Von Lohenburg* • Maureen Kerwin *Lisa, Henry's daughter* • Barbara Jefford *Madame Strauss* ■ *Dir* Jerry Schatzberg • *Scr* Harold Pinter, from a novel by Fred Uhlman

Reunion at Fairborough ★★★

Romantic drama
1985 · US · Colour · 110mins

Over a quarter of a century after they made *Heaven Knows, Mr Allison*, Robert Mitchum and Deborah Kerr teamed up for the fourth time in this burnished tale of reunions and revelations. Originally made for American television but also given a cinema release, Herbert Wise's verbose melodrama centres on ex-GI Mitchum's return to the village where he'd been based during the war to discover that he not only fathered Kerr's child, but is also now a grandfather. Tony Imi's photography romanticises the rural locations, but the key is the rapport of the leads. DP

Robert Mitchum *Carl Hostrup* • Deborah Kerr *Sally Wells* • Red Buttons *Jiggs Quealy* • Judi Trott *Sheila* • Barry Morse *Dr "Ski" Barsky* • Shane Rimmer *Joe Szyluk* ■ *Dir* Herbert Wise • *Scr* Albert Ruben

Reunion in France ★★★★ U

Second World War romantic drama
1942 · US · BW · 99mins

Joan Crawford stars as a vain, thoughtless, wealthy French woman, interested only in her lover Philip Dorn and her wardrobe, who undergoes a transformation after the Nazi occupation of France. Believing that wealthy industrialist Dorn is a high-level collaborator, she develops a new awareness and a sense of patriotism, which is further fuelled by her accidental involvement with American airman John Wayne who is fleeing the Gestapo. Directed with a European sensibility and a hard edge by Jules Dassin, this under-rated war drama is – despite some mawkish moments, mainly involving Wayne, and the odd lapse into melodrama – interesting, taut and compelling. RK

Joan Crawford *Michele de la Becque* • John Wayne *Pat Talbot* • Philip Dorn *Robert Cortot* • Reginald Owen *Schultz/Pinkum* • Albert Basserman *Gen Hugo Schroeder* • John Carradine *Ulrich Windler* • Ava Gardner *Marie, salesgirl* ■ *Dir* Jules Dassin • *Scr* Jan Lustig, Marvin Borowsky, Marc Connelly, Charles Hoffman, from a story by Ladislaus Bus-Fekete

Reunion in Vienna ★★

Romantic comedy 1933 · US · BW · 97mins

Former lovers Diana Wynyard and John Barrymore meet after ten years, at a monarchists' party in Vienna. Wynard is now married to a famous psychoanalyst (Frank Morgan), while Barrymore, the dethroned Hapsburg archduke, is now a taxi driver. He is determined to rekindle the flame: she is equally determined to resist. This is a largely tedious conversation piece, with Barrymore charmless and hammy for two-thirds of the action. Wynyard, however, is wonderful, as are the sets and clothes. RK

John Barrymore *Rudolf* • Diana Wynyard *Elena* • Frank Morgan *Anton* • Henry Travers *Father Krug* • May Robson *Frau Lucher* • Eduardo Ciannelli *Poffy* • Una Merkel *Isle* ■ *Dir* Sidney Franklin • *Scr* Ernest Vajda, Claudine Westt, from the play by Robert E Sherwood

Reveille with Beverly ★★★ U

Musical 1943 · US · BW · 77mins

One of many B-movies churned out by super-hoofer Ann Miller during her career with Columbia, this light-hearted musical was based on the life and career of a real-life female disc jockey. Miller is fabulous, bringing her customary warm-heartedness and tap-dancing skills to this insubstantial film. Watch for a pre-film fame Frank Sinatra, Duke Ellington and Count Basie, and the Mills Brothers, too. A collector's item. TS

Ann Miller *Beverly Ross* • William Wright *Barry Lang* • Dick Purcell *Andy Adams* • Franklin Pangborn *Vernon Lewis* • Tim Ryan *Mr Kennedy* • Larry Parks *Eddie Ross* • Adele Mara *Evelyn Ross* • Frank Sinatra ■ *Dir* Charles Barton • *Scr* Howard J Green, Jack Henley, Albert Duffy

Revelation ★★ 15

Supernatural horror thriller
2001 · UK · Colour · 106mins

No one could accuse writer/director Stuart Urban's complex quest movie of not having ideas or ambition but, unfortunately, this saunter across Europe in search of a valuable relic is too ponderous and repetitious to appeal. Bland James D'Arcy and Natasha Wightman follow the convoluted trail of the "Loculus", an ancient box also sought by demonic immortal, Udo Kier. There are moments of visual panache, but the journey to enlightenment is grindingly dull. JC DVD

James D'Arcy *Jake Martel* • Natasha Wightman *Mira* • Terence Stamp *Magnus Martel* • Udo Kier *The Grand Master* • Derek Jacobi *The Librarian* • Liam Cunningham *Father Ray Connolly* • Celia Imrie *Harriet Martel* • Ron Moody *Sir Isaac Newton* ■ *Dir* Stuart Urban • *Scr* Stuart Urban, from an idea by Frank Falco

Revenge ★★

Thriller 1971 · UK · Colour · 92mins

It was British films like this that encouraged Joan Collins and James Booth to flee to Hollywood. The glamorous pair play a suburban couple who turn vigilantes and become involved in the kidnap and imprisonment of the man (Kenneth Griffith) whom they believe raped and murdered their daughter. What begins as a serious examination of a growing social problem becomes increasingly melodramatic, ending in a blaze of hysterical stabbing. Enjoyable for all the wrong reasons. DM

Joan Collins *Carol Radford* • James Booth *Jim Radford* • Ray Barrett *Harry* • Kenneth Griffith *Seely* • Sinead Cusack *Rose* • Tom Marshall *Lee Radford* • Zuleika Robson *Jill Radford* ■ *Dir* Sidney Hayers • *Scr* John Kruse

Revenge ★★ 18

Thriller 1990 · US · Colour · 118mins

This daft drama has retired navy pilot Kevin Costner going down to Mexico to visit old friend Anthony Quinn, only to incur the latter's wrath when he goes off with his wife, Madeleine Stowe. It all gets exceedingly silly, and overacting abounds as Costner and Stowe flee the understandably irate Quinn. Laboriously directed by the normally fluent action aficionado Tony Scott. JB. Contains swearing, violence and sex scenes.

Kevin Costner *Cochran* • Anthony Quinn *Tiburon Mendez* • Madeleine Stowe *Miryea* • Tomas Milian *Cesar* • Joaquin Martinez *Mauro* • James Gammon *Texan* • Jesse Corti *Medero* • Sally Kirkland *Rock star* ■ *Dir* Tony Scott • *Scr* Jim Harrison. Jeffrey Fiskin, from the novella by Jim Harrison

Revenge of Billy the Kid ★ 18

Horror 1991 · UK · Colour · 86mins

This tasteless, low-budget, British offering is directed by Jim Groom, who plays this more for laughs than chills, but succeeds in raising neither. Michael Balfour is the perverted yeoman, whose nocturnal couplings result in the birth of a goat-headed dwarf, who embarks on a murderous rampage, only to be terminated by a chain saw. DP

Michael Balfour *Gyles MacDonald* • Samantha Perkins *Ronnie MacDonald* • Jackie D Broad *Gretta MacDonald* • Trevor Peake *Ronald MacDonald* • Bryan Heeley *Ronald MacDonald* • Julian Shaw *Billy T Kid* • Norman Mitchell *Mr Allott* ■ *Dir* Jim Groom • *Scr* Richard Mathews, James Groom, Tim Dennison

The Revenge of Frankenstein ★★★ 15

Horror 1958 · UK · Colour · 86mins

Hammer's first sequel to *The Curse of Frankenstein*, has the baron rescued from execution, changing his name to Dr Stein and continuing his body-part experiments in a charity hospital. The usual first-rate performances, excellent production values and gothic atmosphere are permeated by a macabre sense of humour in this superior spine-chiller, crisply directed by Terence Fisher. The second sequel was the slightly disappointing *Evil of Frankenstein*. AJ DVD

Peter Cushing *Dr Victor Stein* • Francis Matthews *Dr Hans Kleve* • Eunice Gayson *Margaret* • Michael Gwynn *Karl* • John Welsh *Bergman* • Lionel Jeffries *Fritz* • Oscar Quitak *Karl* • Richard Wordsworth *Patient* • Charles Lloyd Pack *President* ■ *Dir* Terence Fisher • *Scr* Jimmy Sangster, H Hurford Janes, from characters created by Mary Shelley

The Revenge of Pumpkinhead – Blood Wings ★★★ 18

Horror 1994 · US · Colour · 83mins

The engaging return of the monster from *Pumpkinhead* dispenses with the previous story elements to create a mystery. This time, small-town sheriff Andrew Robinson must deduce the monster's reasons for picking particular victims. Pumpkinhead is used to good effect, although no explanation is given as to why a thunderstorm follows the monster wherever he goes. Look out for amusing bit-part turns by American presidential sibling Roger Clinton and Soleil Moon Frye. ST

Andrew Robinson *Sean Braddock* • Ami Dolenz *Jenny Braddock* • J Trevor Edmond *Danny Dixon* • Mark McCracken *Creature* • Gloria Hendry *Delilah Pettibone* • Alexander Polinsky *Paul* • Soleil Moon Frye *Marcie* • Roger Clinton *Mister Bubba* ■ *Dir* Jeff Burr • *Scr* Steve Mitchell, Craig W Van Sickle

Revenge of the Creature ★★★

Horror 1955 · US · BW · 81mins

Almost as enjoyable as the original, director Jack Arnold's follow-up to *Creature from the Black Lagoon* has the "Gill-Man" (Ricou Browning)

recaptured and taken to a sea-world park in Florida. There, ichthyologists John Agar and Lori Nelson try to teach him to speak, before the primeval monster goes on the rampage and drags Nelson back to his Everglades hideaway. Look out for Clint Eastwood, in his first screen role, playing a laboratory technician. Though this was made in 3-D like the original, very few saw it projected that way after its initial release. A disappointing second sequel, *The Creature Walks among Us*, followed in 1956. AJ

John Agar *Clete Ferguson* • Lori Nelson *Helen Dobson* • John Bromfield *Joe Hayes* • Robert B Williams *George Johnson* • Nestor Paiva *Lucas* • Grandon Rhodes *Foster* • Dave Willock *Gibson* • Charles Cane *Captain of Police* • Clint Eastwood *Lab technician* • Ricou Browning *Gill-Man* ■ *Dir* Jack Arnold • *Scr* Martin Berkeley, from a story by William Alland

Revenge of the Nerds ★ 18

Comedy 1984 · US · Colour · 86mins

In this puerile campus comedy, Anthony Edwards is one of the nerds of the title who decide to fight back against the bullying jocks at school. Amazingly, this dire mix of lavatorial humour and tasteless slapstick spawned three sequels. JF. Contains swearing and nudity.

Robert Carradine *Lewis* • Anthony Edwards *Gilbert* • Timothy Busfield *Poindexter* • Andrew Cassese *Wormser* • Curtis Armstrong *"Booger"* • Larry B Scott *Lamar* • Brian Tochi *Takashi* • Julie Montgomery *Betty Childs* • Michelle Meyrink *Judy* • Ted McGinley *Stan Gable* ■ *Dir* Jeff Kanew • *Scr* Steve Zacharias, Jeff Buhai, from a story by Tim Metcalfe, Miguel Tejada-Flores, Steve Zacharias, Jeff Buhai

Revenge of the Pink Panther ★★★ PG

Comedy 1978 · US · Colour · 94mins

There are so many comedy turns hanging from a slender plotline in this immoderate helping of Inspector Clouseau that it tends to sag in places. But there are still plenty of laughs to be had as Clouseau goes on the trail of drug smugglers. Peter Sellers is well supported by Dyan Cannon, as a drug dealer's girlfriend, and by Bert Kwouk, as the valet. This may lack coherence, but if you accept it as just a vehicle for Seller's comic genius you won't be disappointed. The depressing *Trail of the Pink Panther* concluded Sellers's Clouseau series. TH DVD

Peter Sellers *Chief Inspector Clouseau* • Herbert Lom *Chief Inspector Dreyfus* • Dyan Cannon *Simone Legree* • Robert Webber *Philippe Douvier* • Bert Kwouk [Burt Kwouk] *Cato* • Paul Stewart *Scallini* • Robert Loggia *Marchione* • Graham Stark *Dr Auguste Balls* • André Maranne *François* • Sue Lloyd *Claude Russo* ■ *Dir* Blake Edwards • *Scr* Frank Waldman, Ron Clark, Blake Edwards, from a story by Blake Edwards

Revenge of the Radioactive Reporter ★ 18

Comedy horror 1990 · Can · Colour · 80mins

This Canadian attempt to emulate the kind of movies the Troma studio is famous for, specifically the *Toxic Avenger* films, has none of the mayhem, outrageousness and cynicism for which Troma movies are famous. In fact, it frequently takes itself quite seriously, completely missing the point of its premise. Like *The Toxic Avenger*, the plot concerns an unlucky hero forced into toxic waste by his enemies, then later coming back in a hideously mutated form for revenge. KB

David Scammell *Mike R Wave* • Kathryn Boese *Richelle Darlington* • Derrick Strange *Richard Swell* • Randy Pearlstein *Joe Wave Junior* ■ *Dir* Craig Pryce • *Scr* Craig Pryce, David Wiechorek

The Revengers ★★

Western 1972 · US · Colour · 108mins

William Holden sets out to find and destroy the band of Comanches who killed his wife and children. Obviously he can't do this alone, so he springs six condemned men from prison. The movie provides the requisite number of bloody gunfights, but Daniel Mann's direction is slack and easily diverted by flimsy subplots, including a longish dalliance with a frontier nurse played by Susan Hayward. It would prove to be her final feature film. AT

William Holden (2) *John Benedict* • Susan Hayward *Elizabeth* • Ernest Borgnine *Hoop* • Woody Strode *Job* • Roger Hanin *Quiberon* • René Koldehoff *Zweig* • Jorge Luke *Chamaco* • Scott Holden *Lieutenant* ■ *Dir* Daniel Mann • *Scr* Wendell Mayes, from a story by Steven W Carabatsos

The Revengers' Comedies ★★★

Black comedy 1997 · UK/Fr · Colour · 86mins

Alfred Hitchcock's *Strangers on a Train* receives another reworking in this adept amalgamation of two Alan Ayckbourn plays. Meeting on Tower Bridge, Sam Neill and Helena Bonham Carter agree to abandon thoughts of suicide and do away with the other's chief tormentor instead. However, he soon discovers his co-conspirator's true nature after he becomes besotted with his intended victim, Kristin Scott Thomas. The main asset of this unfairly overlooked Britpic is its stellar cast, but Malcolm Mowbray's direction lacks subtlety. DP. Contain violence, swearing.

Sam Neill *Henry Bell* • Helena Bonham Carter *Karen Knightly* • Kristin Scott Thomas *Imogen Staxton-Billing* • Rupert Graves *Oliver Knightly* • Martin Clunes *Anthony Staxton-Billing* • Steve Coogan *Bruce Tick* • John Wood *Colonel Marcus* • Liz Smith *Winnie* ■ *Dir* Malcolm Mowbray • *Scr* Malcolm Mowbray, from two plays by Alan Ayckbourn

Revengers Tragedy ★ 15

Black comedy 2002 · US · Colour · 105mins

Director Alex Cox makes a bid to become Britain's answer to Baz Luhrmann with this interpretation of Thomas Middleton's 17th-century play about family, loyalty and vengeance. Christopher Eccleston returns to his home city after a ten-year absence to avenge the murder of his wife, killed on their wedding day by dastardly duke, Derek Jacobi. Eccleston displays a wry wit and gleeful dementia, but he is drowned out by a glut of hammy supporting performances. Cox adds to the mess with a profusion of flashy camera techniques and clichéd imagery. SF DVD

Christopher Eccleston *Vindici* • Eddie Izzard *Lussurioso* • Derek Jacobi *Duke* • Diana Quick *Duchess* • Carla Henry *Castiza* • Andrew Schofield *Carlo* • Anthony Booth *Lord Antonio* • Margi Clarke *Hannah* • Sophie Dahl *Imogen* ■ *Dir* Alex Cox • *Scr* Frank Cottrell Boyce, from the play by Thomas Middleton

Reversal of Fortune ★★★★ 15

Biographical drama
1990 · US · Colour · 106mins

Jeremy Irons won an Oscar for his portrayal of millionaire Claus von Bulow, who was found guilty of the attempted murder of his wife Sunny (Glenn Close), but acquitted on appeal. Even though there's no surprise about the outcome of this real-life story, this is a thoroughly absorbing and beautifully scripted drama, with events leading to the trial told in flashback and Close's comatose character bringing us up to date by a clever narration. Director Barbet Schroeder shoots with a documentary eye and gives the picture a sense of irony, a quality enhanced by Irons's superb performance as the haughty, European aristocrat defended by a Jewish lawyer. AT. Contains violence, swearing. DVD

Jeremy Irons *Claus von Bulow* • Glenn Close *Martha "Sunny" von Bulow* • Ron Silver *Alan Dershowitz* • Annabella Sciorra *Sarah* • Uta Hagen *Maria* • Fisher Stevens *David Marriott* • Jack Gilpin *Peter Macintosh* • Christine Baranski *Andrea Reynolds* • Stephen Mailer *Elon Dershowitz* • Christine Dunford *Ellen* ■ *Dir* Barbet Schroeder • *Scr* Nicholas Kazan, from the book by Alan Dershowitz

The Revolt of Mamie Stover ★★★

Drama 1956 · US · Colour · 86mins

Great title for a strictly B-grade melodrama, dressed up with A-movie trappings by 20th Century-Fox, including filming on location in exotic Hawaii. But there's no disguising the fact that this movie really belongs to an earlier decade. Jane Russell is, to be kind, a little past her prime. Joan Leslie looks slightly weary, and Richard Egan, a leading man once touted as the new Clark Gable proves to be all brawn and little else. Still, there's much fun to be had by guessing the real professions of these characters, hidebound as they were by 1950s censorship. TS

Jane Russell *Mamie Stover* • Richard Egan *Jim* • Joan Leslie *Annalea* • Agnes Moorehead *Bertha Parchman* • Jorja Curtright *Jackie* • Michael Pate *Harry Adkins* • Richard Coogan *Eldon Sumac* ■ *Dir* Raoul Walsh • *Scr* Sydney Boehm, from the novel by William Bradford Huie

Revolution ★★★ PG

Historical war drama
1985 · UK/Nor · Colour · 120mins

Hugh Hudson's look at the American War of Independence was a famous mega-flop, sealing the fate of the already over-extended Goldcrest production house. It is the story of a father and son, and the way history intrudes on their relationship. On the plus side: the battle scenes, brilliantly filmed with a handheld camera; a remarkable portrayal of a sadistic English officer by a deeply in period Donald Sutherland; and clever art direction which turns King's Lynn into New York. On the debit side is Al Pacino's ludicrous performance and laughable accent. AT

Al Pacino *Tom Dobb* • Nastassja Kinski *Daisy McConnahay* • Donald Sutherland *Sergeant Major Peasy* • Joan Plowright *Mrs McConnahay* • Dave King *Mr McConnahay* • Steven Berkoff *Sergeant Jones* • Annie Lennox *Liberty Woman* • Dexter Fletcher *Ned Dobb* • Sid Owen *Young Ned* • John Wells *Corty* • Richard O'Brien *Lord Hampton* ■ *Dir* Hugh Hudson • *Scr* Robert Dillon

The Revolutionary ★★★

Political drama
1970 · UK/US · Colour · 101mins

A compelling portrayal by Jon Voight of a political subversive makes this worth the effort of watching. He moves from handing out revolutionary leaflets at college to an attempted assassination, in a moral tale that's too one-track for its own good, but which poses hard questions for would-be revolutionaries who could become terrorists – for the best possible reasons. Writer Hans Koningsberger and director Paul Williams highlight the way that anything can be excused by strongly held belief. TH

Jon Voight *A* • Jennifer Salt *Helen Peret* • Seymour Cassel *Leonard* • Robert Duvall *Despard* • Collin Wilcox-Horne *Anne* • Lionel Murton *Professor* ■ *Dir* Paul Williams • *Scr* Hans Koningsberger, from the novel by Hans Koningsberger

The Revolving Doors ★★★ U

Drama 1988 · Can/Fr · Colour · 101mins

This absorbing drama shows that the coming of sound to cinema meant the end of a unique form of entertainment, the silent movie, complete with its atmospheric piano accompaniment. As the pianist who leaves the dream palaces to find fame in the jazz joints of New York, Monique Spaziani gives an engaging performance. Francis Mankiewicz directs neatly and there's a solid performance from French actress Miou-Miou. DP. In French with English subtitles.

Monique Spaziani *Céleste Beaumont* • Gabriel Arcand *Blaudelle* • Miou-Miou *Lauda* • Jacques Penot *Pierre Blaudelle* • François Méthé *Antoine* • Françoise Faucher *Simone Blaudelle* ■ *Dir* Francis Mankiewicz • *Scr* Jacques Savoie

The Reward ★★★

Drama 1965 · US · Colour · 90mins

This slow, elegiac, contemporary western is one of the most interesting failures. A motley cast, headed by glum import Max von Sydow, spends a lot of time sitting around in the desert, very slowly motivated by greed to seek a bigger share of the title pay-out. It's not uninteresting, and is intelligently cast, but French director Serge Bourguignon is well out of his *métier*, and the result, though fascinating, is not enjoyable. TS

Max von Sydow *Scott Swanson* • Yvette Mimieux *Sylvia* • Efrem Zimbalist Jr *Frank Bryant* • Gilbert Roland *Captain Carbajal* • Emilio Fernandez *Sargento Lopez* • Henry Silva *Joaquin* • Rafael Lopez *Indian Boy* ■ *Dir* Serge Bourguignon • *Scr* Serge Bourguignon, Oscar Milland, from the novel by Michael Barrett

Rhapsody ★★★ U

Romantic drama
1954 · US · Colour · 115mins

Beautiful heiress Elizabeth Taylor is in love with classical violinist Vittorio Gassman, but leaves him – via a broken-hearted suicide attempt when he puts ambition first – for concert pianist John Ericson, who makes her his priority. There's much flitting back and forth between the two men and across Europe, before the final fade. An essentially hollow and old-fashioned romantic soap opera, this is given a cultural gloss by the outpouring of music. Taylor is good and at her loveliest, and the location photography in Technicolor and CinemaScope is eye-catching. RK

Elizabeth Taylor *Louise Durant* • Vittorio Gassman *Paul Bronte* • John Ericson *James Guest* • Louis Calhern *Nicholas Durant* • Michael Chekhov *Professor Schuman* • Barbara Bates *Effie Cahill* • Richard Hageman *Bruno Furst* • Richard Lupino *Otto Krafft* • Stuart Whitman *Dove* ■ *Dir* Charles Vidor • *Scr* Fay Kanin, Michael Kanin, Ruth Goetz, Augustus Goetz, from the novel *Maurice Guest* by Henry Handel Richardson • *Cinematographer* Robert Planck

Rhapsody in August ★★ U

Drama 1990 · Jpn · Colour · 93mins

This is comfortably the worst film made by the late Akira Kurosawa during his 50-year career. There is a certain charm in the interaction between Sachiko Murase and the four grandchildren, who spend the summer with her, but the storyline is weak and Richard Gere looks distinctly out of place. DP. In Japanese with English subtitles. DVD

Sachiko Murase *Kane* • Hisashi Igawa *Tadao* • Narumi Kayashima *Machiko* • Tomoko Ohtakara *Tami* • Mitsunori Isaki *Shinjiro* • Toshie Negishi *Yoshie* • Richard Gere *Clark* ■ *Dir* Akira Kurosawa • *Scr* Akira Kurosawa, from the novel *Nabe-no-Naka* by Kiyoko Murata

R

Rhapsody in Blue ★★★ U

Biographical drama 1945 · US · BW · 139mins

This splendid tosh, purporting to be the life story of composer George Gershwin, is actually an enjoyable epic which embraces every single cliché of the Lower East Side, Jewish-kid-makes-good, rags-to-riches saga, and almost brings it off. Robert Alda lacks star power as Gershwin, and Herbert Rudley is undercast as his brother Ira, but there's a wealth of fabulous support, including Al Jolson as himself and the great Oscar Levant, who performs both *Concerto in F* and *Rhapsody in Blue*. TS

Robert Alda *George Gershwin* • Joan Leslie *Julie Adams* • Alexis Smith *Christine Gilbert* • Charles Coburn *Max Dreyfus* • Julie Bishop *Lee Gershwin* • Albert Basserman *Professor Frank* • Morris Carnovsky *Poppa Gershwin* • Rosemary DeCamp *Momma Gershwin* • Anne Brown *Bess* • Herbert Rudley *Ira Gershwin* ■ *Dir* Irving Rapper • *Scr* Howard Koch, Elliott Paul, from a story by Sonya Levien

Rhinestone ★★ PG

Comedy 1984 · US · Colour · 106mins

Sylvester Stallone does have the knack for comedy, albeit in a light form. However, he frequently lacks the ability to judge if a script is good, especially if he's involved in its writing. Country star Dolly Parton takes a bet on whether she can turn cab driver Stallone into a country singer and the results, as far as both the wager and their interest in each other are concerned, are as expected, but not funny. KB

Sylvester Stallone *Nick* • Dolly Parton *Jake* • Richard Farnsworth *Noah* • Ron Leibman *Freddie* • Tim Thomerson *Barnett* • Steven Apostlee Peck *Father* ■ *Dir* Bob Clark • *Scr* Phil Alden Robinson, Sylvester Stallone, from the story by Phil Alden Robinson, from the song *Rhinestone Cowboy* by Larry Weiss

Rhino! ★★

Adventure 1964 · US · Colour · 91mins

Unlike other big game adventures, this one at least has the benefit of a conservationist message, as Hunter Harry Guardino and scientist Robert Culp go in search of a pair of white rhino that are threatened with extinction. Director Ivan Tors makes the most of his South African locations and the majestic wildlife, but his handling of the dramatic sequences is uncertain. DP

Harry Guardino *Alec Burnett* • Shirley Eaton *Edith Arleigh* • Robert Culp *Dr Jim Hanlon* • Harry Mekela *Jopo* • George Lane *Haragay* ■ *Dir* Ivan Tors • *Scr* Art Arthur, Arthur Weiss, from a story by Art Arthur

R

Rhinoceros ★★★ PG

Surreal comedy 1974 · US · Colour · 99mins

The allegorical material of Eugène Ionesco's absurdist play *Rhinoceros* has always been seen as self-defeating, and actors as distinguished as Laurence Olivier and Orson Welles, among others, have fallen foul of it. Here, the leads from *The Producers*, Zero Mostel and Gene Wilder, are reunited under the iconoclastic direction of Tom O'Horgan, and the result, though fascinating, is very much an acquired taste. TS DVD

Zero Mostel *John* • Gene Wilder *Stanley* • Karen Black *Daisy* • Robert Weil *Carl* • Joe Silver *Norman* • Marilyn Chris *Mrs Bingham* ■ *Dir* Tom O'Horgan • *Scr* Julian Barry, from the play by Eugène Ionesco

Rhodes of Africa ★★★

Biographical adventure
1936 · UK · BW · 89mins

Walter Huston stars as Cecil John Rhodes in a superior, literate and informative biopic, much of it shot on location. While the film waters down Rhodes's ruthless streak and is a little stolid and worthy in tone, it does do justice to the story of the diamond magnate, visionary, empire-builder and politician, who endowed the famed Rhodes scholarship scheme and died at the age of 49. Huston is excellent playing one of the most significant figures in an eventful era of Southern African history, and there's a good supporting cast. RK

Walter Huston *Cecil Rhodes* • Oscar Homolka *Kruger* • Basil Sydney *Jameson* • Frank Cellier *Barney Barnato* • Peggy Ashcroft *Anna Carpenter* • Renee De Vaux *Mrs Kruger* • Bernard Lee *Cartwright* ■ *Dir* Berthold Viertel • *Scr* Leslie Arliss, Michael Barringer, Miles Malleson, from the book *Rhodes* by Sarah Gertrude Millin

Rhubarb ★★★ PG

Comedy 1951 · US · BW · 94mins

The second-best cat movie ever and it's only a whisker behind the greatest, *Harry and Tonto*. Rhubarb is a fiery alley cat who inherits a baseball team. Although he brings the team luck, he poses a triple headache for Ray Milland, the marketing man charged with caring for the new manager/ mascot, for not only does Rhubarb insist on living on his own terms, but Milland's girlfriend Jan Sterling is allergic to him and a jilted benefactor is out to prove in the courts that he is an impostor. It's slight and silly, but there are plenty of laughs. DP

Ray Milland *Eric Yeager* • Jan Sterling *Polly Sickles* • Gene Lockhart *Thaddeus J Banner* • William Frawley *Len Sickles* • Elsie Holmes *Myra Banner* • Taylor Holmes *P Duncan Munk* ■ *Dir* Arthur Lubin • *Scr* Dorothy Reid, Francis Cockrell, David Stern, from the novel by H Allen Smith

Rhythm on the Range ★★ U

Western musical comedy
1936 · US · BW · 85mins

Bing Crosby is the star of this musical western romance in which he sings a song to a mightily large Hereford bull, as well as winning the hand of a rebellious heiress Frances Farmer. The movie's main interest now, and extraordinary box-office success then, is down to motor-mouthed comedian and songstress Martha Raye, who makes her screen debut and delivers an all-stops-out rendition of *Mr Paganini*. RK

Bing Crosby *Jeff Larrabee* • Frances Farmer *Doris Halloway* • Bob Burns *Buck* • Martha Raye *Emma Mazda* • Samuel S Hinds *Robert Halloway* • Lucille Webster Gleason *Penelope "Penny" Ryland* • Warren Hymer *Big Brain* ■ *Dir* Norman Taurog • *Scr* John C Moffitt, Sidney Salkow, Walter DeLeon, Francis Martin, from a story by Mervin J Houser

Rhythm on the River ★★★

Musical drama 1940 · US · BW · 92mins

With Bing Crosby and Mary Martin as the leads and a screenplay co-written by Billy Wilder, it's no surprise that this amiable musical was a great hit on release. The third star is Basil Rathbone, taking time off from being Sherlock Holmes to play a composer who finds inspiration lacking and employs Bing and Mary to ghost write his work. They realise that they would be better off writing for themselves, only to discover that without the composer's name their talent is unacknowledged. BB

Bing Crosby *Bob Summers* • Mary Martin *Cherry Lane* • Basil Rathbone *Oliver Courtney* • Oscar Levant *Charlie Starbuck* • Oscar Shaw *Charlie Goodrich* • Charley Grapewin *Uncle Caleb* • Lillian Cornell *Millie Starling* • William Frawley *Westlake* ■ *Dir* Victor Schertzinger • *Scr* Dwight Taylor, from a story by Billy Wilder, Jacques Thery • *Music Director* Victor Young

Rhythm Serenade ★★ U

Romantic musical 1943 · UK · BW · 87mins

During the Second World War, a schoolteacher does her bit for the war effort by opening a nursery school next door to a munitions factory so that the children's mothers can work. Directed by Gordon Wellesley for the British arm of Columbia, this sentimental and unremarkable film combines patriotic flag-waving with romance, some humour and a few songs, as a vehicle for "Forces' Sweetheart" Vera Lynn, who does her best. RK

Vera Lynn *Ann Martin* • Peter Murray Hill *John Drover* • Julien Mitchell *Mr Jimson* • Charles Victor *Mr Martin* • Jimmy Jewel *Jimmy Martin* • Ben Warriss *Ben Martin* • Irene Handl *Mrs Crumbling* • Jimmy Clitheroe *Joey* ■ *Dir* Gordon Wellesley • *Scr* Marjorie Deans, Basil Woon, Margaret Kennedy, Edward Dryhurst, from a story by Marjorie Deans

Rhythm Thief ★★★ 18

Drama 1994 · US · BW · 83mins

An extremely impressive no-budget film from the grubbier side of New York, revealing the sure hand of new director Matthew Harrison at the tiller. Much applauded at the 1994 World Film Festival in Montreal, it tells the story of a small-time hustler whose inner emptiness is filtered through his unfocused life of peanut butter scoffing and noisy neighbours, and whose hidden feelings are ignited by the arrival of an odd young girl. Harrison makes good use of his admirable cast, balancing the film's vital spark with a high degree of thoughtfulness. All this in a movie that took 11 days to shoot. JM. Contains violence, swearing.

Jason Andrews *Simon* • Eddie Daniels *Marty* • Kimberly Flynn *Cyd* • Kevin Corrigan *Fuller* • Sean Hagerty *Shayme* ■ *Dir* Matthew Harrison • *Scr* Matthew Harrison, Christopher Grimm

Rice People ★★★ PG

Drama
1994 · Camb/Fr/Swi/Ger · Colour · 129mins

Cambodian director Rithy Panh – an exile in France since the genocidal regime of Pol Pot came to power in 1975 – returns to his roots and builds an entire film around a rice harvest. It's a harvest beset by nature's adversity and human nightmare – the father has visions of the Khmer Rouge and then a thorn infects his foot while the mother is menaced by a cobra. It's a bit of a slog at two hours, but connoisseurs of movies from the developing world should still find plenty to admire here. AT. In Khmer with English subtitles.

Peng Phan *Yim Om, mother* • Mom Soth *Vong Poeuv, father* • Chhim Naline *Sakha, eldest daughter* ■ *Dir* Rithy Panh • *Scr* Rithy Panh, Eve Deboise, from a novel by Shahnon Ahmad

Rich and Famous ★★ 18

Comedy drama 1981 · US · Colour · 111mins

The last film from director George Cukor is a disappointingly ho-hum remake of 1943's *Old Acquaintance*. Jacqueline Bisset and Candice Bergen step into roles Bette Davis and Miriam Hopkins made their own, as childhood friends who become rivals in their writing careers and in love. Playing spot the celeb is more entertaining than their tiresome jealous, bitchy confrontations or Bisset's crisis with a younger lover. Teenaged Meg Ryan, cute as a button, makes her film debut as Bergen's daughter. AME

Jacqueline Bisset *Liz Hamilton* • Candice Bergen *Merry Noel Blake* • David Selby *Doug Blake* • Hart Bochner *Chris Adams* • Steven Hill *Jules Levi* • Meg Ryan *Debby, aged 18* • Matt Lattanzi *Jim* ■ *Dir* George Cukor • *Scr* Gerald Ayres, from the play *Old Acquaintance* by John Van Druten

Rich and Strange ★★

Comedy drama 1932 · UK · BW · 92mins

Alfred Hitchcock made this curious, often rather cruel and tiresome comedy when his career was in the doldrums. Henry Kendall and Joan Barry (too sophisticated for their roles) star as the young married couple who spend an inheritance on a world cruise during which their relationship comes under strain, particularly when they become shipwrecked in the Far East. Hitchcock's stylistic touches provide the main interest of the film today but even they are rather exaggerated for such slight subject matter. AE

Henry Kendall *Fred Hill* • Joan Barry *Emily Hill* • Percy Marmont *Commander Gordon* • Betty Amann *Princess* ■ *Dir* Alfred Hitchcock • *Scr* Val Valentine, Alma Reville, Alfred Hitchcock, from a novel by Dale Collins

The Rich Are Always with Us ★★★★

Romance 1932 · US · BW · 71mins

The brilliant Broadway actress Ruth Chatterton is at the centre of this tale about an unusual and inordinately wealthy society hostess who resists the overtures of handsome young novelist George Brent – until she discovers her husband's infidelity. Meanwhile, a very young Bette Davis sets her sights on Brent; the actor would later become her future and frequent co-star. Polished acting, surprise twists and a dialogue studded with archly witty gems make this period piece entertaining from start to finish – a sophisticated reflection of a bygone era, with a satirical thrust and a bittersweet edge. RK

Ruth Chatterton *Caroline Grannard* • George Brent *Julian Tierney* • Adrienne Dore *Allison Adair* • Bette Davis *Malbro* • John Miljan *Greg Grannard* ■ *Dir* Alfred E Green • *Scr* Austin Parker, from the novel by Mrs Arthur Somers Roche [E Petit]

Rich in Love ★★ PG

Drama 1992 · US · Colour · 100mins

Jill Clayburgh walks out on Albert Finney, leaving him with their daughter, Kathryn Erbe, and a lot of excess emotional baggage. Among the supporting cast, Kyle MacLachlan is the "other man" who causes even more angst, and Piper Laurie plays a traditional Southern crackpot. Slow to start, slower to finish, it's nevertheless worth watching for Finney's heavily accented display of pique. AT

Albert Finney *Warren Odom* • Jill Clayburgh *Helen Odom* • Kathryn Erbe *Lucille Odom* • Kyle MacLachlan *Billy McQueen* • Piper Laurie *Vera Delmage* • Ethan Hawke *Wayne Frobiness* • Suzy Amis *Rae Odom* • Alfre Woodard *Rhody Poole* ■ *Dir* Bruce Beresford • *Scr* Alfred Uhry, from the novel by Josephine Humphreys

Rich Kids ★★★

Comedy drama 1979 · US · Colour · 96mins

At the centre of the picture is 12-year-old Trini Alvarado, who gradually comes to realise that her parents are about to get divorced; her friend Jeremy Levy, who has already gone through the process, has an endless stream of advice for her on how to deal with the impending split. A rather heavy-handed message movie, this features good performances all round but it's never quite the film it could have been. DF

Trini Alvarado *Franny Philips* • Jeremy Levy *Jamie Harris* • Kathryn Walker *Madeline Philips* • John Lithgow *Paul Philips* • Terry Kiser *Ralph Harris* • David Selby *Steve Sloan* • Roberta Maxwell *Barbara Peterfreund* • Paul Dooley *Simon Peterfreund* ■ *Dir* Robert M Young • *Scr* Judith Ross

The Rich Man's Wife ★★ 18

Mystery thriller 1996 · US · Colour · 90mins

Halle Berry is convincing as an unhappily married woman, whose flippant asides to a man she meets in a bar (Peter Greene) result in said man murdering her husband. Berry becomes a key suspect – she, is after all, the black widow of a white man. But, all is not as it seems and, despite strong acting and a tight script, the balloon bursts all over the place at the end. DP. Contains swearing, sexual references, violence. [video] DVD

Halle Berry *Jane Potenza* • Christopher McDonald *Tony Potenza* • Clive Owen *Jake Golden* • Peter Greene *Cole Wilson* • Charles Hallahan *Dan Fredricks* • Frankie Faison *Ron Lewis* ■ *Dir/Scr* Amy Holden Jones

Rich, Young and Pretty ★★★ U

Musical 1951 · US · Colour · 94mins

A sweet soufflé of an MGM musical. Produced by musical supremo Joe Pasternak, it stars Jane Powell as a Texan girl whose sophisticated mother Danielle Darrieux fled the ranch for the delights of Europe many years earlier. Powell's father Wendell Corey takes her on a trip to Paris where she sees the sights, parties, falls in love with Mr Right (crooner Vic Damone, in his film debut) and meets up with her mother. This is full of fun, romantic innocence and vintage songs. RK

Jane Powell *Elizabeth Rogers* • Danielle Darrieux *Marie Devarone* • Wendell Corey *Jim Stauton Rogers* • Vic Damone *Andre Milan* • Fernando Lamas *Paul Sarnac* • Marcel Dalio *Claude Duval* • Una Merkel *Glynnie* ■ *Dir* Norman Taurog • *Scr* Dorothy Cooper, Sidney Sheldon, from a story by Dorothy Cooper

Richard Pryor: Live on the Sunset Strip ★★★ 18

Comedy concert 1982 · US · Colour · 77mins

Richard Pryor can be an acquired taste, and his concert films are variable, but on form there are few more astute comedians. In this, culled from two one-man shows at the Hollywood Palladium, he is in subdued mood. The Mafia, his drug abuse and his trip to Africa are among the diverse subjects covered, and he even picks up on some of the sick humour directed at his own accident, when he set himself alight while on a cocaine binge. Honest and funny. JG [video]

Richard Pryor ■ *Dir* Joe Layton • *Scr* Richard Pryor

Richard III ★★★★ U

Historical drama
1955 · UK · Colour · 150mins

After turning *Henry V* into wartime propaganda and *Hamlet* into *film noir* on the battlements, Laurence Olivier made *Richard III* as outright melodrama. Olivier's stage portrayal of Richard was legendary and the film serves principally as a record of that triumph and as such less of a movie than its two predecessors. Olivier's hunchback scowls and lurches around the sets like Charles Laughton's Quasimodo. While Ralph Richardson, John Gielgud and Claire Bloom give performances of great distinction and emotion, Olivier's is more a display of cold technique. AT [video] DVD

Laurence Olivier *Richard III* • Ralph Richardson *Buckingham* • Claire Bloom *Lady Anne* • John Gielgud *Clarence* • Cedric Hardwicke *King Edward IV* • Mary Kerridge *Queen Elizabeth* • Pamela Brown *Jane Shore* • Alec Clunes *Hastings* • Stanley Baker *Henry Tudor* • Michael Gough *Dighton* ■ *Dir* Laurence Olivier • *Scr* Alan Dent, Laurence Olivier, Colley Cibber, David Garrick, from the play by William Shakespeare • *Production Designer* Roger Furse [Roger K Furse] • *Art Director* Carmen Dillon • *Cinematographer* Otto Heller

Richard III ★★★★ 15

Historical drama
1995 · UK/US · Colour · 99mins

Sir Ian McKellan authoritatively revisits one of the greatest roles in the English language in Richard Loncraine's daring, flashy reworking of the acclaimed National Theatre production, in which Richard was styled as a 1930s fascist dictator. The excellent cast includes Maggie Smith and Kristin Scott Thomas's drug-addicted Lady Anne, with Annette Bening and a scene-stealing Robert Downey Jr, as an American arriviste queen and her brother. Although the artifice is dispassionately cold, the splashy nods to modern cinemagoers' frame of reference – sex, violence, explosions – do pep up the appeal without condescension or gutting the text. AME. Contains violence and sex scenes. [video] DVD

Ian McKellen *Richard III* • Annette Bening *Queen Elizabeth* • Robert Downey Jr *Earl Rivers* • Nigel Hawthorne *Clarence* • Maggie Smith *Duchess of York* • Jim Broadbent *Duke of Buckingham* • Kristin Scott Thomas *Lady Anne* ■ *Dir* Richard Loncraine • *Scr* Ian McKellen, Richard Loncraine, from the stage production by Richard Eyre of the play by William Shakespeare

The Richest Girl in the World ★★★

Romantic comedy 1934 · US · BW · 74mins

Desperate to find true romance and be loved for herself rather than her money, heiress Miriam Hopkins, whom nobody can recognise since there are no pictures of her and few are privileged to meet her, swaps identities with her best-friend-cum-secretary Fay Wray to test the worth of Joel McCrea. Henry Stephenson and Reginald Denny join the conspiracy under William A Seiter's direction of Norman Krasna and Leona D'Ambry's Oscar-nominated screenplay. Sweetly sparkling, with Hopkins on delightful form. RK

Miriam Hopkins *Dorothy Hunter* • Joel McCrea *Tony Travers* • Fay Wray *Sylvia Lockwood* • Henry Stephenson *John Connors* • Reginald Denny *Phillip Lockwood* • Beryl Mercer *Marie* • George Meeker *Donald* ■ *Dir* William A Seiter • *Scr* Norman Krasna, Leona D'Ambry, from a story by Norman Krasna

Richie Rich ★★ PG

Comedy 1994 · US · Colour · 90mins

Based on the US comic strip, this features Macaulay Culkin as a boy who has unlimited wealth but longs for a normal life. His wish is granted when he takes up with a ragbag gang of kids to foil nasty John Larroquette, who is trying to cheat Culkin out of his fortune. All the usual clichés are present and correct, with Jonathan Hyde as the obligatory British butler. Children will lap up the juvenile slapstick. A straight-to-video sequel, *Richie Rich's Christmas Wish*, followed in 1998, minus Culkin. JF [video]

Macaulay Culkin *Richie Rich* • John Larroquette *Van Dough* • Edward Herrmann *Mr Rich* • Christine Ebersole *Mrs Rich* • Jonathan Hyde *Cadbury* • Michael McShane [Micheal McShane] *Professor Keenbean* ■ *Dir* Donald Petrie • *Scr* Tom S Parker, Jim Jennewein, from a story by Neil Tolkin, from the Harvey Comics characters

Ricochet ★★★ 18

Action crime drama
1991 · US · Colour · 97mins

This enjoyable, totally over-the-top action thriller has Denzel Washington's cop being systematically persecuted by John Lithgow's deranged killer, whom he had arrested years earlier in front of enraptured TV viewers. Director Russell Mulcahy keeps the energy levels high and the camera just about active enough to disguise the ridiculousness of the story. Lithgow shows why he is one of modern cinema's premier psycho performers, but Washington's acting skills are somewhat wasted. JC [video] DVD

Denzel Washington *Nick Styles* • John Lithgow *Earl Talbot Blake* • Ice-T *Odessa* • Kevin Pollak *Larry Doyle* • Lindsay Wagner *Priscilla Brimleigh* • Victoria Dillard *Alice* ■ *Dir* Russell Mulcahy • *Scr* Steven E de Souza, from the story by Fred Dekker, Menno Meyjes

The Riddle of the Sands ★★★ U

Action adventure 1978 · UK · Colour · 98mins

Despite the riotous action contained in the original Erskine Childers adventure classic, this brave attempt to pin down the novel's narrative never quite succeeds, because it's too reverent for its own good. Michael York and Simon MacCorkindale are the yachtsmen discovering a fiendish pre-emptive strike against England by the Germans, way ahead of the First World War. Tony Maylam's direction strives to make the most of authentic locations, but the glossiness of the production makes it unconvincing. TH. In English and German with subtitles. [video]

Michael York *Charles Carruthers* • Jenny Agutter *Clara* • Simon MacCorkindale *Arthur Davies* • Alan Badel *Dollmann* • Jurgen Andersen *Commander Von Brüning* • Michael Sheard *Böhme* ■ *Dir* Tony Maylam • *Scr* Tony Maylam, John Bailey, from the novel by Erskine Childers

Ride ★★ 15

Comedy road movie
1998 · US · Colour · 80mins

This cheap and cheerful hip-hop comedy thriller was made by the team behind *House Party*. Melissa DeSouza plays an aspiring film-maker who gets a job with a top music promo director and is given the task of chaperoning a rap group on their way from New York to Miami. Unbeknown to her, one of the number has stolen money from a local gangster, prompting a cross-country chase. Loud and brash, with a pumping hip-hop soundtrack. JF [video]

Malik Yoba *Poppa* • Julia Garrison *Blacke* • Guy Torry *Indigo* • Melissa DeSouza *Leta* • John Witherspoon *Roscoe* • Cedric the Entertainer *Bo* • Fredro Starr *Geronimo* • Snoop Doggy Dogg [Snoop Dogg] *Mente* • Dr Dre *Eight* ■ *Dir/Scr* Millicent Shelton

Ride a Crooked Trail ★★★ U

Western 1958 · US · Colour · 87mins

The series of westerns made by Universal starring baby-faced war hero Audie Murphy was extremely variable in quality, but it nevertheless made Murphy a household name. This is one of the better examples, using a basic mistaken identity plot from Borden Chase. Director Jesse Hibbs keeps things moving along and there's also a marvellous supporting cast, including a pre-stardom Walter Matthau is a drunken judge. Don't expect too much and you'll be pleasantly surprised. TS

Audie Murphy *Joe Maybe* • Gia Scala *Tessa Milotte* • Walter Matthau *Judge Kyle* • Henry Silva *Sam Teeler* • Joanna Moore *Little Brandy* • Eddie Little [Eddie Little Sky] *Jimmy* • Mary Field *Mrs Curtis* • Leo Gordon *Sam Mason* • Mort Mills *Pecos* ■ *Dir* Jesse Hibbs • *Scr* Borden Chase, from a story by George Bruce

Ride a Wild Pony ★★★ U

Period drama 1976 · US · Colour · 85mins

A highly moralistic and sentimental tale of love and jealousy adapted from the James Aldridge novel. Set in 18th-century Australia, Robert Bettles plays a poor, farm schoolboy battling over the ownership of a prize horse with the rich, but polio-stricken, Eva Griffith. Typical Disney fare directed with compassion by Don Chaffey. AJ [video]

Robert Bettles *Scott Pirie* • Eva Griffith *Josie Ellison* • Alfred Bell *Angus Pirie* • Melissa Jaffer *Angus' Wife* • Michael Craig *James Ellison* • Lorraine Bayly *Mrs Ellison* • Graham Rouse *Bluey Waters* ■ *Dir* Don Chaffey • *Scr* Rosemary Anne Sisson, from the novel *A Sporting Proposition* by James Aldridge

Ride beyond Vengeance ★★★

Western 1966 · US · Colour · 100mins

A bartender tells a census taker a local story from the 1880s: as he returns to a wife he hasn't seen for 11 years, hunter Chuck Connors is mistaken for a rustler, sadistically branded and robbed. When he's rescued by the real rustler, he plans his revenge. A tough, brutal western, featuring a number of TV stalwarts. JG

James MacArthur *Delahay, the census taker* • Arthur O'Connell *Narrator* • Ruth Warrick *Aunt Gussie* • Chuck Connors *Jonas Trapp* • Michael Rennie *Brooks Durham* • Kathryn Hays *Jessie* • Joan Blondell *Mrs Lavender* • Gloria Grahame *Bonnie Shelley* • Gary Merrill *Dub Stokes* • Bill Bixby *Johnsy Boy Hood* ■ *Dir* Bernard McEveety • *Scr* Andrew J Fenady, from the novel *The Night of the Tiger* by Al Dewlen

Ride Clear of Diablo ★★ U

Western 1954 · US · Colour · 80mins

Audie Murphy's up against a crooked sheriff and a corrupt lawyer, responsible for the murder of his rancher father and kid brother. With the help of Dan Duryea's likeable badman, he gains his revenge in this well-written but essentially by-the-numbers western. Susan Cabot plays the nice girl, while Abbe Lane is the far more interesting saloon singer. Duryea's rich performance steals the film from the ever stolid Murphy. AE

Audie Murphy *Clay O'Mara* • Dan Duryea *Whitey Kincade* • Susan Cabot *Laurie* • Abbe Lane *Kate* • Russell Johnson *Ringer* • Paul Birch *Sheriff Kenyon* • Jack Elam *Tim* ■ *Dir* Jesse Hibbs • *Scr* George Zuckerman, DD Beauchamp, from a story by Ellis Marcus

Ride 'em Cowboy ★★★★ U

Musical comedy 1942 · US · BW · 85mins

Among the very best Abbott and Costello vehicles, made when the team's routines were still fresh and funny, this is given top-flight treatment by their studio, with some great music providing strong support in between the team's antics, including Ella Fitzgerald singing her hit version of *A Tisket, a Tasket*. The Don Raye and Gene DePaul songs include the classic *I'll Remember April*, given class-A treatment with a moonlit setting and a lovely choral arrangement backing the singer Dick Foran. TV

Bud Abbott *Duke* • Lou Costello *Willoughby* • Anne Gwynne *Anne Shaw* • Samuel S Hinds *Sam Shaw* • Dick Foran *Bronco Bob Mitchell* • Richard Lane *Peter Conway* • Ella Fitzgerald *Ruby* • Dorothy Dandridge ■ *Dir* Arthur Lubin • *Scr* True Boardman, John Grant, Harold Shumate, from a story by Edmund L Hartmann

Ride Him, Cowboy ★★ U

Western 1932 · US · BW · 56mins

The first of six B-westerns, largely based on old Ken Maynard silents, that a young John Wayne made for Warner Bros in the early 1930s. This cost the same as a mere two-reeler, but doesn't look it. The plot gives prominence to the white horse, Duke, with whom Wayne shares top billing. The steed is framed by the villains and sentenced to death until Wayne comes to his rescue. AE

John Wayne *John Drury* • Ruth Hall *Ruth Gaunt* • Henry B Walthall *John Gaunt* • Otis Harlan *Judge Jones* ■ *Dir* Fred Allen • *Scr* Scott Mason, from a story by Kenneth Perkins, from the novel by Kenneth Perkins

R

Ride in the Whirlwind ★★ PG

Western 1966 · US · Colour · 77mins

Made back-to-back with *The Shooting*, this Jack Nicholson–Monte Hellman western is a loose remake of an Italian film they both admired called *Bandits of Orgosolo*. Three cowpokes, including Nicholson, stumble upon a gang of outlaws hiding out in a mountain shack. Invited to wet their whistles, the cowpokes stay the night and then find themselves surrounded by a gang of vigilantes. It's not as good as the existentialist *Shooting* and is let down by scrappy photography and wooden acting, but the plot still has a symbolic and moral power. AT

Cameron Mitchell *Vern* • Jack Nicholson *Wes* • Tom Filer *Otis* • Millie Perkins *Abby* • Katherine Squire *Catherine* • George Mitchell *Evan* • Brandon Carroll *Sheriff* • Rupert Crosse *Indian Joe* • Harry Dean Stanton *Blind Dick* ■ *Dir* Monte Hellman • *Scr* Jack Nicholson

Ride Lonesome ★★★★ U

Western 1959 · US · Colour · 72mins

Director Budd Boetticher and executive producer and star Randolph Scott made a short cycle of fine westerns, unequalled in their classic simplicity and under-appreciated on their first release. This is one of the best. The finely tuned Burt Kennedy screenplay wastes not a moment as craggy-featured bounty hunter Scott goes after a young killer (the giggling James Best), ostensibly for the cash reward, but really to flush out his brother, the snarling Lee Van Cleef. Fine western stuff, with brilliantly taut, terse dialogue. Watch out for James Coburn's movie debut. TS

Randolph Scott *Ben Brigade* • Karen Steele *Carrie Lane* • Pernell Roberts *Sam Boone* • James Best *Billy John* • Lee Van Cleef *Frank* • James Coburn *Wid* • Dyke Johnson *Charlie* • Boyd Stockman *Indian chief* ■ *Dir* Budd Boetticher • *Scr* Burt Kennedy

Ride the High Country ★★★★ PG

Western 1962 · US · Colour · 90mins

Director Sam Peckinpah proved his magisterial talent with this, his second movie (and many think his finest), a gentle requiem to the Old West, co-starring two icons of the genre, sturdy Joel McCrea and craggy Randolph Scott (in his last role). The casting provides constant delights as the two veterans bicker and cuss their way through a plot about a gold shipment, and should it be stolen or not. The action is superbly photographed by the great Lucien Ballard in eye-filling CinemaScope and Metrocolor, and there are marvellous supporting performances. There's also a knockout vignette from Edgar Buchanan as a drunken judge. A deeply satisfying, mature movie. TS

Randolph Scott *Gil Westrum* • Joel McCrea *Steve Judd* • Mariette Hartley *Elsa Knudsen* • Ronald Starr *Heck Longtree* • RG Armstrong *Joshua Knudsen* • Edgar Buchanan *Judge Tolliver* • John Anderson *Elder Hammond* • LQ Jones *Sylvus Hammond* • Warren Oates *Henry Hammond* • James Drury *Billy Hammond* • John Davis Chandler *Jimmy Hammond* ■ *Dir* Sam Peckinpah • *Scr* NB Stone Jr

Ride the Man Down ★★ U

Western 1952 · US · Colour · 89mins

Republic put more than enough stalwarts of the genre into this Trucolor western to keep undemanding fans happy. Rod Cameron is the heroic foreman who holds a cattle empire together when, after the death of its owner, Forrest Tucker and Brian Donlevy try to move in. It should add up to more, but a congested screenplay and indifferent direction rob it of dramatic impact. AE

Brian Donlevy *Bide Marriner* • Rod Cameron *Will Ballard* • Ella Raines *Celia Evarts* • Forrest Tucker *Sam Danfelser* • Barbara Britton *Lottie Priest* • Chill Wills *Ike Adams* • J Carrol Naish *Joe Kneen* • Jim Davis *Red Courteen* • Paul Fix *Ray Cavanaugh* • Roy Barcroft *Russ Schultz* ■ *Dir* Joseph Kane • *Scr* Mary McCall Jr, from a story by Luke Short first published in *The Saturday Evening Post*

Ride the Wild Surf ★★ U

Comedy drama 1964 · US · Colour · 101mins

A colourful and exuberant teen movie about three beach-bum pals who head for Hawaii for the surfing. However, though all three find romance, their new girlfriends (including Barbara Eden of *I Dream of Jeannie* fame) try to persuade them to change their ways. The characters are as flat as their surfboards, but the film is fun and well-made, and the surfing sequences eminently watchable. JG

Fabian *Jody Wallis* • Shelley Fabares *Brie Matthews* • Tab Hunter *Steamer Lane* • Barbara Eden *Augie Poole* • Peter Brown *Chase Colton* ■ *Dir* Don Taylor • *Scr* Jo Napoleon, Art Napoleon

The Ride to Hangman's Tree ★★★ U

Western 1967 · US · Colour · 89mins

This is an evocative title for a minor Universal western, utilising the studio's contract players and existing sets. It isn't bad, with Jack Lord (a year before he hit the TV big time with *Hawaii Five-O*) and the ever-excellent James Farentino and Don Galloway playing a trio of outlaws vaguely reminiscent of those cowboy stars whose adventures enthralled young audiences at the Saturday morning pictures. This begins with a cleverly directed and well-staged robbery: stick with it, it's fun. TS

Jack Lord *Guy Russell* • James Farentino *Matt Stone* • Don Galloway *Nevada Jones* • Melodie Johnson *Lillie Malone* • Richard Anderson *Steve Carlson* • Robert Yuro *Jeff Scott* • Ed Peck *Sheriff Stewart* • Paul Reed *Corbett* ■ *Dir* Alan Rafkin • *Scr* Luci Ward, Jack Natteford, William Bowers, from a story by Luci Ward, Jack Natteford

Ride, Vaquero! ★★ U

Western 1953 · US · Colour · 90mins

This poorly written western arouses interest from MGM's offbeat casting of the three stars: Robert Taylor, as the quiet but deadly right-hand man of a Mexican bandit; Howard Keel, in a non-singing role as a foolhardy rancher; and Ava Gardner, as the rancher's virtuous wife. Only Anthony Quinn, playing the flamboyant, egotistical Mexican bandit chief who attacks the American ranchers invading his domain, seems cast to type – and he walks away with the picture. AE

Robert Taylor (1) *Rio* • Ava Gardner *Cordelia Cameron* • Howard Keel *King Cameron* • Anthony Quinn *Jose Esqueda* • Kurt Kasznar *Father Antonio* • Ted De Corsia *Sheriff Parker* • Charlita *Singer* • Jack Elam *Barton* ■ *Dir* John Farrow • *Scr* Frank Fenton, John Farrow

Ride with the Devil ★★★★★ 15

Period war drama
1999 · US · Colour · 132mins

Director Ang Lee turns in another handsome, moving and unmissable piece of cinema, this time set against the backdrop of the American Civil War. Skeet Ulrich and Tobey Maguire are two members of the "Bushwhackers" – southern guerrillas who secretly ambush Yankee platoons along the Missouri backroads. When they have to hide out for the winter, the pair and two fellow irregulars – one an ex-slave – hole up in a cave cut out of a hill, where they are sent food and water by a beautiful young widow (singer Jewel). It's an epic yet intimate portrait of relationships and war, boasting superb performances from the cast and a compelling script by writer/producer James Schamus. JB. Contains violence. DVD

Skeet Ulrich *Jack Bull Chiles* • Tobey Maguire *Jacob Friedel Roedel, "Dutchman"* • Jewel *Sue Lee Shelley* • Jeffrey Wright *Daniel Holt* • Simon Baker *George Clyde* • Jonathan Rhys Meyers *Pitt Mackeson* • James Caviezel [Jim Caviezel] *Black John* • Tom Guiry *Riley Crawford* • Tom Wilkinson *Orton Brown* ■ *Dir* Ang Lee • *Scr* James Schamus, from the novel *Woe to Live On* by Daniel Woodrell

Rider from Tucson ★ U

Western 1950 · US · BW · 60mins

One of seven Tim Holt B-westerns released in 1950, this has a competent cast but is sunk by the usual idiotic script and plot in which, as a stagecoach driver notes, the villains steal his passenger but ignore the strongbox. Amid its mechanical storytelling, a chance glimpse of a cat fleeing the hooves of a heavy's mount is refreshingly natural. The only character of interest is Veda Ann Borg's hard-boiled villainess. AE

Tim Holt *Dave* • Richard Martin (1) *Chito Rafferty* • Elaine Riley *Jane* • Douglas Fowley *Rankin* • Veda Ann Borg *Gypsy* • Robert Shayne *Avery* ■ *Dir* Lesley Selander • *Scr* Ed Earl

Rider on the Rain ★★★ 18

Thriller 1970 · Fr/It · Colour · 109mins

Marlène Jobert kills the man who rapes her and then tries to cover it up, but she's thwarted by Charles Bronson, who starts sniffing around while keeping his identity a mystery. A solid piece of work from veteran director René Clément, who orchestrates subplots galore, this is a sharp portrait of life in a French seaside town, with echoes of Hitchcock in its concern with the burden of guilt. AT. French dialogue dubbed into English.

Marlène Jobert *Mellie* • Charles Bronson *Colonel Harry Dobbs* • Jean Gaven *Inspector Toussaint* • Corinne Marchand *Tania* • Jill Ireland *Nicole* • Annie Cordy *Juliette* ■ *Dir* René Clément • *Scr* Sébastien Japrisot, Lorenzo Ventavoli

Riders in the Sky ★★ U

Western 1949 · US · BW · 69mins

One of an interminable series of Gene Autry programme fillers, this film allows the singing cowboy to break into the hit song *Ghost Riders in the Sky*. The plot, grafted on to the song, is the usual one about freeing someone framed for murder, but the structure is interesting for this type of production-line fare: a flashback within a flashback that's certainly original and quite amusing. TS

Gene Autry • Gloria Henry *Ann Lawson* • Pat Buttram *Chuckwalla Jones* • Mary Beth Hughes *Julie Steward* • Robert Livingston *Rock McCleary* • Steve Darrell *Ralph Lawson* • Alan Hale Jr *Marshal Riggs* ■ *Dir* John English • *Scr* Gerald Geraghty, from a story by Herbert A Woodbury

Riders of Destiny ★★ U

Western 1933 · US · BW · 49mins

Historically important, and prophetically titled, this is the first of a dozen or so B-westerns made by John Wayne for Monogram Pictures under producer Paul Malvern's Lone Star trademark. Here Wayne plays "Singin' Sandy", a government agent sent a-hunting villains, who (are you ready for this?) sings as he guns them down. The villain of the piece is played by stuntman Yakima Canutt, and this is a movie where, to establish the character's black heart, he actually kicks a dog on his entrance. This style of baddie was therefore known as a "dog heavy", and was a popular cliché in westerns. TS DVD

John Wayne *Singin' Sandy Saunders* • Cecilia Parker *Fay Denton* • George Hayes [George "Gabby" Hayes] *Sheriff Denton* • Forrest Taylor *Kincaid* • Lafe McKee *Sheriff* • Fern Emmett *Farm woman* • Yakima Canutt ■ *Dir* Robert North Bradbury [Robert N Bradbury] • *Scr* Robert North Bradbury

Riders of the Purple Sage ★★★★

Silent western 1925 · US · BW · 56mins

Tom Mix, the most famous cowboy-star of his time, rides tall in the saddle for this engrossing yarn, from the novel by western writer Zane Grey. Texas Ranger Mix pursues his sister (Beatrice Burnham) and niece, who have been kidnapped by the evil Warner Oland. Lots of fine "head 'em off at the pass" stuff. The definitive version of this much filmed novel. TH

Tom Mix *Jim Lassiter* • Beatrice Burnham *Millie Erne* • Arthur Morrison *Frank Erne* • Seesel Ann Johnson *Bess Erne as a child* • Warner Oland *Lew Walters/Judge Dyer* • Fred Kohler *Metzger* ■ *Dir* Lynn Reynolds • *Scr* Edfrid Bingham, from the novel by Zane Grey

Riders of the Purple Sage ★★

Western 1931 · US · BW · 58mins

Zane Grey's huge popularity as a western novelist made his name the principal selling point of Fox's third filming of his first bestseller, dating from 1912. Early in his career as a series cowboy star, George O'Brien follows Tom Mix as the laconic westerner, seeking the man who killed his sister. Superbly photographed by George Schneiderman and – outside of stilted dialogue sequences – briskly directed by Hamilton MacFadden. AE

George O'Brien *Lassiter* • Marguerite Churchill *Jane Withersteen* • Noah Beery *Judge Dyer* • Yvonne Pelletier *Bess* • James Todd *Venters* • Stanley Fields *Oldring* • Lester Dorr *Judkins* • Shirley Nails *Fay* • Frank McGlynn Sr *Jeff Tull* ■ *Dir* Hamilton MacFadden • *Scr* John F Goodrich, Philip Klein, Barry Connors, from the novel by Zane Grey

Riders of the Purple Sage ★★ U

Western 1941 · US · BW · 65mins

Here it's poker-faced George Montgomery who's wrestling with the multiple twists and turns of the complex plot, though Zane Grey's story has been simplified this time around. The bleak, nihilistic ending still works, proving quite a startling climax to what is basically an ordinary 20th Century-Fox B-western. TS

George Montgomery *Jim Lassiter* • Mary Howard *Jane Withersteen* • Robert Barrat *Judge Frank Dyer* • Lynne Roberts *Bess* • Kane Richmond *Adam Dyer* • Patsy Patterson *Fay Larkin* • Richard Lane *Steve Oldring* • Oscar O'Shea *Noah Judkins* • James Gillette *Venters* • Frank McGrath *Pete* • LeRoy Mason *Jerry Card* ■ *Dir* James Tinling • *Scr* William Bruckner, Robert Metzler, from the novel by Zane Grey

Riders of the Storm ★★ 15

Satirical comedy
1986 · UK · Colour · 100mins

A group of Vietnam veterans start up a pirate radio station to hound right-wing senators in this limp satire on American politics. All the offbeat elements are present and correct – weirdo duo Dennis Hopper and Michael J Pollard doing their "wacky" thing, the presidential candidate etched as a full-blown drag queen, the station situated inside an old B-52 bomber – but the whole strange enterprise doesn't gel or elicit much laughter. AJ

Dennis Hopper *Captain* • Michael J Pollard *Doc* • Eugene Lipinski *Ace* • James Aubrey

R

Claude • Al Matthews *Ben* • William Armstrong *Jerry* • Nigel Pegram *Sen Willa Westinghouse* • Michael Ho *Minh* • Josie Lawrence *Guerillette* • Ozzy Osbourne ■ *Dir* Maurice Phillips • *Scr* Scott Roberts

Ridicule ★★★★ 15

Historical drama 1996 · Fr · Colour · 97mins

Winner of four Césars and the Bafta for best foreign language film, Patrice Leconte's insight into life at Louis XVI's Versailles sends an icy chill through the cosy corridors of the costume picture. The rapiers in Remi Waterhouse's script may not be tipped with venom, but there's enough sophistication in the repartee to produce a slyly credible vision of a world founded solely on ambition and indolence. Entering this mausoleum of mordant wit, Charles Berling's country Jekyll turns courtly Hyde, as he seeks to outwit influential black widow Fanny Ardant and her provocative priest, Bernard Giraudeau. An acute, acerbic delight. DP. In French with English subtitles. Contains violence, sex scenes and nudity. [video]

Charles Berling *Ponceludon de Malavoy* • Jean Rochefort *Marquis de Bellegrade* • Fanny Ardant *Madame de Blayac* • Judith Godèrche *Mathilde de Bellegarde* • Bernard Giraudeau *L'Abbé de Vilecourt* • Bernard Dhéran *Monsieur de Montalieri* ■ *Dir* Patrice Leconte • *Scr* Remi Waterhouse, Michel Fessler, Eric Vicaut

Riding Giants ★★★★ 12A

Documentary 2004 · US/Fr · Colour · 100mins

This second excellent documentary feature from ex-skateboard star Stacy Peralta (*Dogtown and Z-Boys* charted the development of vertical skateboarding) examines the development of big-wave surfing from its origins in Hawaii in the 1950s through to the new style of jet-ski assisted surfing that gives adrenalin junkies access to what were impossibly huge waves only a few years ago. Peralta uses archive footage and personal reminiscences to chart the development of the sport, and he's aided by top-notch editing as well as a cracking soundtrack. But it's the obvious passion that Peralta has for his subject matter that gives this superb documentary its abundant energy. AS

Dir Stacy Peralta • *Scr* Stacy Peralta, Sam George • *Cinematographer* Peter Pilafian

Riding High ★★ U

Musical western 1943 · US · Colour · 88mins

Crooner Dick Powell is out west, as the owner of a silver mine that's not paying. Enter burlesque queen Dorothy Lamour who does her act at a dude ranch, run by shrieking singer Cass Daley, to help Powell and his partner – the whiny Victor Moore – pay off the mortgage on the mine. Pretty forgettable, with unmemorable songs. Released as *Melody Inn* in the UK. RB

Dorothy Lamour *Ann Castle* • Dick Powell *Steve Baird* • Victor Moore *Mortimer J Slocum* • Gil Lamb *Bob "Foggy" Day* • Cass Daley *Tess Connors* • Bill Goodwin *Chuck Stuart* • Rod Cameron *Sam Welch* ■ *Dir* George Marshall • *Scr* Walter DeLeon, Arthur Phillips, Art Arthur, from the play *Ready Money* by James Montgomery

Riding High ★★★

Musical comedy 1950 · US · BW · 112mins

Director Frank Capra remakes his 1934 hit *Broadway Bill* as a Bing Crosby vehicle, incorporating stock footage from the original – watch closely! – and even recasting some of the same actors. The result is charming and the slight plot changes are an improvement (the hero is now engaged to the heroine, not married to her), but it lacks the sheer goodwill of the original. The added songs though, don't hurt the narrative and Crosby's real-life affection for horse racing is evident. TS

Bing Crosby *Dan Brooks* • Coleen Gray *Alice Higgins* • Charles Bickford *JL Higgins* • William Demarest *Happy McGuire* • Frances Gifford *Margaret Higgins* • Raymond Walburn *Professor Pettigrew* • James Gleason *Racing Secretary* • Ward Bond *Lee* • Clarence Muse *Whitey* • Percy Kilbride *Pop Jones* ■ *Dir* Frank Capra • *Scr* Robert Riskin, Nelville Shavelson, Jack Rose, from the story *Broadway Bill* by Mark Hellinger

Riding in Cars with Boys ★★★ 12

Biographical comedy drama 2001 · US · Colour · 125mins

Drew Barrymore ages from teenager to 30-something – she manages 15 but 35 is less convincing – in this drama based on the memoirs of underage mother Beverly Donofrio. As Beverly, Barrymore has a baby while still at school, marries the dim-witted but well-meaning father (a superb performance from Steve Zahn) and moans that all hopes of going to college and having a writing career are now lost to her. If it wasn't for Barrymore's likeable performance, this would be irritating rather than enjoyable. JB [video] DVD

Drew Barrymore *Beverly Donofrio* • Steve Zahn *Ray Hasek* • Brittany Murphy *Fay Forrester* • Adam Garcia *Jason, aged 20* • Lorraine Bracco *Mrs Donofrio* • James Woods *Mr Donofrio* • Sara Gilbert *Tina* • Rosie Perez *Shirley* ■ *Dir* Penny Marshall • *Scr* Morgan Upton Ward, from the autobiography by Beverly Donofrio

Riding Shotgun ★★ U

Western 1954 · US · Colour · 74mins

Throughout the 1950s, western fans were well-served by colour programme fillers, invariably featuring either baby-faced Audie Murphy or craggy Randolph Scott. Eventually Scott managed to fashion his co-features into a remarkable series of westerns, the Ranown cycle. Prior to that, however, Randy rode a tall saddle, invariably directed by Warners hack-of-all-trades, the one-eyed Andre De Toth, of whose work this is a prime example. The plot is the usual one of Scott attempting to clear his name. Nothing spectacular, but still reasonably undemanding entertainment. TS

Randolph Scott *Larry Delong* • Wayne Morris *Tub Murphy* • Joan Weldon *Orissa Flynn* • Joe Sawyer *Tom Biggert* • James Millican *Dan Maraday* • Charles Buchinski [Charles Bronson] *Pinto* ■ *Dir* Andre De Toth • *Scr* Tom Blackburn, from the story *Riding Solo* by Kenneth Perkins

Rien à Faire ★★★

Drama 1999 · Fr · Colour · 105mins

This intimate, realist study of an accidental love affair drifts into ennui after an impressive start. The gradual enamourment of Valéria Bruni-Tedeschi's unskilled housewife and Patrick Dell'Isola's equally unemployed executive is charmingly played (particularly by the former), and gains in atmosphere from Marion Vernoux's edgy use of handheld camera and insistent close-up. DP. In French with English subtitles.

Valéria Bruni-Tedeschi *Marie* • Patrick Dell'Isola *Pierre* • Sergi Lopez *Luis* • Florence Thomassin *Sophie* ■ *Dir* Marion Vernoux • *Scr* Marion Vernoux, Santiago Amigorena

Rien Ne Va Plus ★★★★ 15

Comedy thriller 1997 · Fr/Swi · Colour · 101mins

Claude Chabrol's 50th movie is a smashing comedy thriller about a pair of con artists, played by Isabelle Huppert and Michel Serrault. Criss-crossing France in search of victims, Huppert and Serrault are exuberant partners in crime, who nearly come unstuck when Huppert sets her sights on a business executive with a suitcase bursting with Mob money. The mood swings wonderfully from comedy to romance, to occasionally shocking violence. AT. In French with English subtitles. [video]

Isabelle Huppert *Elisabeth/"Betty"* • Michel Serrault *Victor* • François Cluzet *Maurice Biagini* • Jean-François Balmer *Monsieur K* • Jackie Berroyer *Robert Châtillon* • Thomas Chabrol *Hotel Waldhaus bellboy* ■ *Dir/Scr* Claude Chabrol

Rien sur Robert ★★★ 18

Comedy drama 1998 · Fr · Colour · 106mins

Hamstrung by highbrow pomposity and crippling self-doubt, trapped within a circle of friends vying to become his severest critic, Fabrice Luchini gives a wonderful performance of bourgeois neuroticism in this assured satire from writer/director Pascal Bonitzer. Lacing Rohmer-esque discourses with wisecracks Woody Allen would be proud of, the literate screenplay is seized upon by an excellent cast. It's just a shame the picture loses momentum as it approaches its disappointingly flat finale. DP. In French with English subtitles.

Fabrice Luchini *Didier Temple* • Sandrine Kiberlain *Juliette Sauvage* • Valentina Cervi *Aurélie Coquille* • Michel Piccoli *Lord Ariel Chatwick-West* • Bernadette Lafont *Madame Sauvage* • Laurent Lucas *Jérôme Sauveur* ■ *Dir/Scr* Pascal Bonitzer

Riff-Raff ★★

Adventure 1947 · US · BW · 80mins

Cinematographer Ted Tetzlaff turned full-time director with this dynamic thriller down Panama way. This is more a comedy adventure than a suspense mystery, with shamus Pat O'Brien and the murderous Walter Slezak going hell for leather to find a map revealing the site of untapped oil reserves. With Percy Kilbride chipping in as a wisecracking cabbie and Anne Jeffreys providing sultry duplicity as a nightclub chanteuse, it's brisk, brash entertainment. DP

Pat O'Brien *Dan Hammer* • Walter Slezak *Molinar* • Anne Jeffreys *Maxine* • Percy Kilbride *Pop* • Jerome Cowan *Walter Gredson* • George Givot *Rues* • Jason Robards [Jason Robards Sr] *Dominguez* ■ *Dir* Ted Tetzlaff • *Scr* Martin Rackin

Riff-Raff ★★★★ 15

Drama 1991 · UK · Colour · 95mins

Ken Loach's film about life on a London building site gave Robert Carlyle his first shot at stardom, which he seized with both hands. Working from a script by Bill Jesse, who died before the film was finished, this exploration of a gang of ethnically diverse labourers as they work on a closed-down hospital, is lighter in mood than many Loach movies, though Carlyle's romantic dalliance with Emer McCourt never quite convinces. It also features one of Ricky Tomlinson's first screen performances. TH [video] DVD

Robert Carlyle *Stevie* • Emer McCourt *Susan* • Jimmy Coleman *Shem* • George Moss *Mo* • Ricky Tomlinson *Larry* • David Finch *Kevin* ■ *Dir* Ken Loach • *Scr* Bill Jesse

Riffraff ★★★

Drama 1936 · US · BW · 94mins

This is an MGM major feature about a pair of fisherfolk who end up on the wrong side of the law. At any other studio this would be a potboiler, but here it earns its place in posterity thanks to luminous star performances from blonde bombshell Jean Harlow (disguised in a brown wig) and her likeable co-star, dependable Spencer Tracy. Their scenes together reveal an easy camaraderie that's very pleasant to watch, a sort of "hey we know the plot's not up to much but we're having a good time anyway" quality which gives the movie a distinction that rises above J Walter Ruben's pallid direction and an uneasiness of tone. TS

Jean Harlow *Hattie* • Spencer Tracy *Dutch Miller* • Joseph Calleia *Nick Appopolis* • Una Merkel *Lil* • Mickey Rooney *Jimmy* • Victor Kilian *Flytrap* • J Farrell MacDonald *Brains* • Roger Imhof *Pops* • Baby Jane "Juanita" Quigley [Juanita Quigley] *Rosie* ■ *Dir* J Walter Ruben • *Scr* Frances Marion, HW Hanemann, Anita Loos, from a story by Frances Marion

Rififi ★★★★ 12

Classic crime caper 1955 · Fr · BW · 117mins

Little did Jules Dassin know, as he sent Jean Servais and his gang into a Rue de Rivoli jewellery store, that he was giving birth to that ever-popular sub-genre, the caper movie. However, no one since has matched the tension and cinematic mastery of the near 30-minute robbery sequence, which is executed in the minutest detail and without resort to dialogue or ambient score. The change of pace, as rival mobster Marcel Lupovici moves in for an undeserved cut, is also neatly accomplished. But there's precious little happening beneath the dazzling surface. Incidentally, that's Dassin playing César, under the pseudonym, Perlo Vita. DP. In French with English subtitles. [video] DVD

Jean Servais *Tony le Stephanois* • Carl Mohner *Jo le Suedois* • Robert Manuel *Mario* • Perlo Vita [Jules Dassin] *César* • Marie Sabouret *Mado* • Janine Darcey *Louise* • Claude Sylvain *Ida* • Marcel Lupovici *Pierre Grutter* • Magali Noël *Viviane* ■ *Dir* Jules Dassin • *Scr* Jules Dassin, René Wheeler, Auguste Le Breton, from a novel by Auguste Le Breton • *Production Designer* Trauner [Alexandre Trauner]

Right Bank, Left Bank ★★

Drama 1984 · Fr · Colour · 105mins

A much-amended, yet still muddled script and inexact casting undermine this lightweight melodrama. Divorced publicist Nathalie Baye (who has just quit her job because of sexual harassment) slowly comes to trust smooth media lawyer Gérard Depardieu as he regains his principles through her influence. DP. French dialogue dubbed into English.

Gérard Depardieu *Paul Senanques* • Nathalie Baye *Sacha Vernakis* • Bernard Fresson *President* • Charlotte De Turckheim *Catherine* • Robert Bruce (2) *Bobby* • Marcel Bozonnet *Michel Monblanc* ■ *Dir* Philippe Labro • *Scr* Philippe Labro, Françoise Labro

Right Cross ★★★ U

Sports drama 1950 · US · BW · 89mins

Mexican Ricardo Montalban has a chip on his shoulder about his racial origins, but faces a real problem when injury to his hand prevents him from boxing. There's a love triangle involving Montalban, June Allyson and sports writer Dick Powell, and Lionel Barrymore features as the fight manager. The movie does capture the flavour of the boxing world, but the introduction of a racial theme seems to be an attempt to provide depth to an otherwise unremarkable plot. Look out for the brief, unbilled appearance of Marilyn Monroe. RK

June Allyson *Pat O'Malley* • Dick Powell *Rick Gavery* • Ricardo Montalban *Johnny Monterez* • Lionel Barrymore *Sean O'Malley* • Teresa Celli *Marian Monterez* • Barry Kelley *Allan Goff* • Tom Powers *Robert Balford* • Marilyn Monroe *Blonde* ■ *Dir* John Sturges • *Scr* Charles Schnee

The Right Stuff ★★★★ 15

Historical drama
1983 · US · Colour · 184mins

Tom Wolfe's bestseller about the training of the first American astronauts here becomes an exhilarating, sprawling, Oscar-winning chronicle of the race to put a man into space. The point of director Philip Kaufman's visually dazzling epic is to ally the early test pilots, such as Chuck Yeager (stoically played by Sam Shepard), who clearly have the "right stuff" for the job, with the pioneering heroes of the Old West. Borrowing a great deal from the work of maverick director John Ford in terms of mythological scope and story structuring, Kaufman's drama documentary is a great tribute to the space race. It's packed with terrific performances, thought-provoking satire, nail-biting aerial scenes and emotional resonance. AJ [video] DVD

Sam Shepard *Chuck Yeager* • Scott Glenn *Alan Shepard* • Ed Harris *John Glenn* • Dennis Quaid *Gordon Cooper* • Fred Ward *Gus Grissom* • Barbara Hershey *Glennis Yeager* • Kim Stanley *Pancho Barnes* • Veronica Cartwright *Betty Grissom* • Pamela Reed *Trudy Cooper* • Lance Henriksen *Walter Schirra* • Donald Moffat *Lyndon B Johnson* ■ *Dir* Philip Kaufman • *Scr* Philip Kaufman, from the book by Tom Wolfe • *Cinematographer* Caleb Deschanel • *Music* Bill Conti

Rigoletto ★★★ U

Opera 1946 · It · BW · 104mins

Inspired by Victor Hugo's play, *Le Roi S'Amuse*, Verdi's opera is adapted with reverence by veteran director Carmine Gallone. Celebrated baritone Tito Gobbi stars as Rigoletto, the acerbic crookbacked jester of the dilettante Duke of Mantua who, labouring under the curse of an abused count, unknowingly participates in the kidnapping of his own daughter, Gilda. The decor is undeniably theatrical, but the music and the performances (with Lina Pagliughi voicing Marcella Govini's Gilda) are admirable. DP. An Italian language film.

Tito Gobbi *Rigoletto* • Mario Filippeschi *Duke of Mantua* • Marcella Govoni *Gilda* • Lina Pagliughi *Gilda* • Anna Maria Canali *Maddalena* • Giulio Neri *Sparafucile* • Marcello Giorda *Monterone* ■ *Dir* Carmine Gallone • *Scr* from the opera by Giuseppe Verdi

Rigoletto ★★

Drama 1995 · US · Colour · 98mins

This isn't a version of Verdi's classic work, but a tacky melodrama that should never have been allowed to use the revered title. The full-throated Joseph Paur stars as the mean-spirited mystery man whose heart is melted by a young girl so moved by the story of Rigoletto that she will do anything to become a diva. Utterly lacking in finesse. DP

Joseph Paur *Ribaldi* • Ivey Lloyd *Bonnie* • Tracey Williams *Gabriella* • Frank Gerrish *Papanickolas* ■ *Dir/Scr* Leo Paur

Rikky and Pete ★★

Comedy drama 1988 · Aus · Colour · 103mins

There's nothing intriguing about the sister-and-brother act of geologist Nina Landis and inventor Stephen Kearney, whether they're taunting blustering Melbourne cop Bill Hunter or putting their offbeat talents to more constructive use in the backwater mining town of Mount Isa. Dorothy Alison and Bruno Lawrence provide some serviceable support, but there's a rehashed feel to the storyline, the characters and the comedy. DP

Stephen Kearney *Pete* • Nina Landis *Rikky* • Tetchie Agbayani *Flossie* • Bill Hunter *Sergeant Whitstead* • Bruno Lawrence *Sonny* • Bruce Spence *Ben* • Dorothy Alison *Mrs Menzies* ■ *Dir* Nadia Tass • *Scr* David Parker, from his story

Rikyu ★★★★

Biographical drama
1989 · Jpn · Colour · 135mins

This is a stately, allegorical study of 16th-century ritual and intrigue, directed by Hiroshi Teshigahara after a 17-year feature film-making hiatus. Befitting Teshigahara's status as a master flower arranger, every image is laden with precise symbolism and the clash between coarse warrior-turned-ruler, Tsutomu Yamazaki, and culturally refined Buddhist monk, Rentaro Mikuni, is as much about a proposed invasion of China, as the niceties of the tea ceremony. DP. A Japanese language film.

Rentaro Mikuni *Sen-no Rikyu* • Tsutomu Yamazaki *Hideyoshi Toyotomi* • Yoshiko Mita *Riki, Rikyu's wife* ■ *Dir* Hiroshi Teshigahara • *Scr* Hiroshi Teshigahara, Genpei Akasegawa, from a novel by Yaeko Nogami

The Ring ★★★ U

Silent drama 1927 · UK · BW · 109mins

Alfred Hitchcock's silent feature concerns a champion fairground boxer (Carl Brisson), the girl he loves (Lillian Hall-Davies), and the Australian fighter (Ian Hunter) who almost tempts her away. On the surface, a routine drama, but watch it closely and it reveals the psychological undertow, signalled in carefully chosen images, that are the hallmarks of the Master's later films. The very word ring, for example, alludes not only to the men's occupation, but the circular artefacts of the fairground (the tents, the carousel), the bracelet Hunter gives the girl, the wedding ring Brisson places on her finger, and the circular emotional journey of the protagonists. RK [video]

Carl Brisson *Jack Sander* • Lillian Hall-Davis *Nelly* • Ian Hunter *Bob Corby* ■ *Dir* Alfred Hitchcock • *Scr* Alfred Hitchcock, Alma Reville, from a story by Alfred Hitchcock

The Ring ★★★ U

Drama 1952 · US · BW · 79mins

This little-known but interesting drama about racial discrimination concerns a young Mexican-American who tries to earn the respect of whites by succeeding as a prizefighter. The film is refreshingly small scale, the story sensibly rather than sensationally resolved with an excellent script by Irving Shulman and careful direction by Kurt Neumann, which develops a documentary-like atmosphere. AE

Gerald Mohr *Pete* • Rita Moreno *Lucy* • Lalo Rios *Tommy* • Robert Arthur *Billy Smith* • Robert Osterloh *Freddy* • Martin Garralaga *Vidal* • Jack Elam *Harry Jackson* ■ *Dir* Kurt Neumann • *Scr* Irving Shulman, from the novel *Cry Tough* by Irving Shulman

Ring ★★★★ 15

Horror 1997 · Jpn · Colour · 91mins

This adaptation of Koji Suzuki's bestseller has rightly gained an international cult following. Structured like a diary, the plot resembles an old-fashioned detective story, propelled by chance clues and gradual realisations. Yet its emphasis on the paranormal recalls both David Cronenberg's brand of body horror and *The X Files*. Artfully mixing footage formats to achieve a visual texture commensurate with both the tone of the story and Kinji Kawai's eerie score, director Hideo Nakata inexorably builds the suspense right up to the moment when he springs the cursed video cassette's hideous secret. DP. In Japanese with English subtitles. [video] DVD

Nanako Matsushima *Reiko Asakawa* • Miki Nakatani *Mai Takano* • Hiroyuki Sanada *Ryuji Takayama* • Yuko Takeuchi *Tomoko Oishi* • Hitomi Sato *Masami Kurahashi* ■ *Dir* Hideo Nakata • *Scr* Hiroshi Takahashi, from the novel by Koji Suzuki

The Ring ★★★ 15

Horror thriller 2002 · US · Colour · 110mins

The words "Hollywood remake" may fill film fans with dread but director Gore Verbinski's version of Hideo Nakata's Japanese horror classic is a surprisingly good effort that retains much of the unnerving, creepy atmosphere of the original. An unlabelled videotape is in circulation, bringing death after seven days to anyone who watches it. One of its victims is the niece of journalist Naomi Watts, who decides to uncover the source of the tape and find out whether this "curse" is real, a quest that's given added urgency after Watts chooses to view the video herself. Verbinski makes a couple of inventive additions, but the spine-chilling terror of the original is muted by the overuse of CGI. AS [video] DVD

Naomi Watts *Rachel Keller* • Martin Henderson *Noah* • David Dorfman *Aidan* • Brian Cox *Richard Morgan* • Jane Alexander *Dr Grasnik* • Lindsay Frost *Ruth* ■ *Dir* Gore Verbinski • *Scr* Ehren Kruger, from the 1997 film, from the novel by Koji Suzuki

Ring 2 ★★ 12

Horror 1998 · Jpn · Colour · 95mins

Hideo Nakata's *Ring* (1997) has acquired something of a cult status in Japan, where it also achieved record box-office grosses. Pop star Miki Nakatani returns for this less critically admired sequel, which spends too much time tying up its predecessor's loose ends and not enough developing its own storyline. The cursed video cassette is still causing mayhem, but the strict linearity of the narrative removes much of the unease that made the original so chilling. Followed by *Ring 0* in 2000. DP. In Japanese with English subtitles. [video] DVD

Miki Nakatani *Mai Takano* • Rikiya Otaka *Yoichi Asakawa* • Nanako Matsushima *Reiko Asakawa* • Hitomi Sato *Masami Kurahashi* • Kenjiro Ishimaru *Omuta* • Kyoko Fukada *Kanae Sawaguchi* • Hiroyuki Sanada *Ryuji Takayama* ■ *Dir* Hideo Nakata • *Scr* Koji Suzuki, Hiroshi Takahashi, from the *Ring,series of novels by Koji Suzuki*

The Ring Two ★★ 15

Horror thriller 2004 · US · Colour · 109mins

In Hideo Nakata's sequel to the US remake of his Japanese horror, Naomi Watts and her son have moved from Seattle to Oregon to escape the nightmare of the cursed videotape, but the vengeful ghost of Samara follows. Bearing no relation to the convoluted Japanese sequel *Ring 2*, and dropping its urban legend hook far too quickly, this illogical and long-winded story ends up as a soggy mess, despite Nakata's elegantly choreographed shocks. AJ

Naomi Watts *Rachel Keller* • Simon Baker *Max Rourke* • David Dorfman *Aidan Keller* • Elizabeth Perkins *Dr Emma Temple* • Gary Cole *Martin Savide* • Sissy Spacek *Evelyn* • Ryan Merriman *Jake* • Emily Vancamp *Emily* ■ *Dir* Hideo Nakata • *Scr* Ehren Kruger, from the *Ring,series of novels by Koji Suzuki*

Ring 0 ★★★ 15

Horror 2000 · Jpn · Colour and BW · 98mins

It doesn't match the clever conceit, haunting atmosphere or visual chill of *Ring* but director Norio Tsuruta's second sequel to that Japanese horror sensation is far better than *Ring 2*. This spookily atmospheric, if confusing, episode charts the reasons why the demon Sadako now terrorises Tokyo teens' videotapes. The slow-building suspense does test the patience at times. AJ. In Japanese with English subtitles. [video] DVD

Yukie Nakama *Sadako Yamamura* • Seiichi Tanabe *Hiroshi Toyama* • Yoshiko Tanaka *Akiko Miyaji* • Atsuko Takahata *Kaoru Arima* • Kumiko Asou *Etsuko Tachihara* • Takeshi Wakamatsu *Shigemori Isamu* ■ *Dir* Norio Tsuruta • *Scr* Hiroshi Takahashi, from the short story *Lemon Heart* by Koji Suzuki

Ring of Bright Water ★★★ U

Drama 1969 · UK · Colour · 102mins

Born Free stars Bill Travers and Virginia McKenna yet again allow themselves to be upstaged by an adorable creature in this delightful adaptation of Gavin Maxwell's bestseller. While Mij the otter hasn't the majestic presence of Elsa the lioness, he'll still win the hearts of children with his mischievous escapades, whether careering around a cramped city-flat, splashing in his private swimming tank or romping in the snow. There's even room for a few tears. DP [video] DVD

Bill Travers *Graham Merrill* • Virginia McKenna *Mary MacKenzie* • Peter Jeffrey *Colin Clifford* • Roddy McMillan *Bus driver* • Jameson Clark *Storekeeper* • Jean Taylor-Smith *Sarah Chambers* • Helena Gloag *Flora Elrich* ■ *Dir* Jack Couffer • *Scr* Jack Couffer, Bill Travers, from the book by Gavin Maxwell

A Ring of Endless Light ★★

Drama 2002 · US · Colour · 88mins

This amiable but bland Disney adaptation of Madeleine L'Engle's bestseller stars Mischa Barton as a teenage wannabe poet who spends the summer looking after her dying grandfather. Well-heeled Jared Padalecki and marine biologist Ryan Merriman provide a distraction from her family duty, as does her communication with the dolphins who warn her about an illegal drift-net fishing operation. The concentration on human sentiment eventually works against this TV movie. DP

Mischa Barton *Victoria Austin* • James Whitmore *Grandfather* • Ryan Merriman *Adam* • Jared Padalecki *Zach* • Scarlett Pomers *Suzy* • Soren Fulton *Rob* ■ *Dir* Greg Beeman • *Scr* Bruce Graham, Marita Giovanni, from the novel by Madeleine L'Engle

Ring of Fire ★★★

Action adventure 1961 · US · Colour · 90mins

David Janssen stars as an Oregon deputy sheriff who arrests and is then kidnapped by three juvenile delinquents. While the plot's twists and turns take some believing, the pace is fast enough and the action spectacular enough to make such considerations redundant. Directed, produced, written and edited by Andrew and Virginia Stone, a husband-and-wife team whose work still awaits critical "rediscovery", the picture has the old-fashioned virtues of a gutsy outdoor adventure. AT

David Janssen *Sergeant Steve Walsh* • Joyce Taylor *Bobbie Adams* • Frank Gorshin *Frank Henderson* • Joel Marston *Deputy Pringle* • James Johnson *Roy Anderson* • Ron Myron *Sheriff Niles* ■ *Dir/Scr* Andrew L Stone

Ring of Fire ★★ 18

Martial arts drama
1991 · US · Colour · 92mins

Don "The Dragon" Wilson plays Johnny Wu, a young medical intern with great martial arts skills who falls in love with a Caucasian woman (Maria Ford), to the disapproval of her friends. After all the fights are done, will these star-crossed lovers be together? More good-natured and endearing than most films of this type. ST [video] DVD

Don "The Dragon" Wilson *Johnny Wu* • Eric Lee *Kwong* • Dale Edmund Jacoby *Brad* • Steven Vincent Leigh *Terry* • Maria Ford *Julie* ■ *Dir* Richard W Munchkin • *Scr* Richard W Munchkin, Jake Jacobs

Ring of Spies ★★★

Spy drama based on a true story
1963 · UK · BW · 90mins

Throughout his career, Frank Launder proved himself to be just as capable of turning out a nail-biting thriller as he was of crafting a chortle-worthy comedy. For once, separated from his usual partner Sidney Gilliatt (although the latter's brother Leslie acted as producer), Launder and co-writer Peter Barnes capably retell the story of the Portland spy ring, whose activities prompted "Reds under the bed" scare stories in the popular press. The docudramatic style rather undermines director Robert Tronson's attempts to build suspense. DP

Bernard Lee *Henry Houghton* • William Sylvester *Gordon Lonsdale* • Margaret Tyzack *Elizabeth Gee* • David Kossoff *Peter Kroger* • Nancy Nevinson *Helen Kroger* • Thorley Walters *Commander Winters* • Gillian Lewis *Marjorie Shaw* • Brian Nissen *Lieutenant Downes* ■ *Dir* Robert Tronson • *Scr* Frank Launder, Peter Barnes

Ring of Steel ★★ 15

Martial arts action
1994 · US · Colour · 89mins

A disgraced fencing champion joins an illegal swordfighting club – the Ring of Steel. Lots of fights follow and the champion finds out that the Ring exacts a price from its combatants that's too high to pay. The plot is simple and fairly compelling, even if much of the acting is sub-par. A touch of surrealism is added to the proceedings by the casting of beefy Joe Don Baker as the Man in Black, who runs the show. ST [video] DVD

Joe Don Baker *Man in Black* • Carol Alt *Tanya* • Robert Chapin *Alex Freyer* • Darlene Vogel *Elena* • Gary Kasper *Jack* • Jim Pirri *Brian* ■ *Dir* David Frost • *Scr* Robert Chapin

Ring of the Musketeers ★★ 15

Action adventure 1994 · US · Colour · 82mins

Umpteen generations on, the descendents of the old swashbucklers get together for an "all for one, and one for all" bid to rescue a boy from a Mob boss. Either the makers couldn't afford, or couldn't interest, any A-list stars. So, instead, there's David Hasselhoff, Alison Doody, Richard "Cheech" Marin and John Rhys-Davies, all having fun in a mildly entertaining piece of hokum. DA [video]

David Hasselhoff *John Smith D'Artagnan* • Thomas Gottschalk *Peter Porthos* • Corbin Bernsen *Harry* • Alison Doody *Anne-Marie* • John Rhys-Davies *Maurice Treville* • Richard "Cheech" Marin *Burt Aramis* • Catherine E Coulson *Lina* ■ *Dir* John Paragon • *Scr* John Paragon, Joel Surnow

Ringmaster ★ 18

Comedy 1998 · US · Colour · 86mins

In this contrived and uninvolving comedy, Jerry Springer plays a talk-show host Jerry Farrelly, a cool observer of the low-lifes who appear as his guests. But everything rings hollow in this thinly disguised *Jerry Springer Show*, from the bed-hopping antics of Molly Hagan's trailer-trash family to Wendy Raquel Robinson's problems with shiftless boyfriend Michael Jai White. DP [video] DVD

Jerry Springer *Jerry Farrelly* • Jaime Pressly *Angel Zorzak* • William McNamara *Troy Davenport* • Molly Hagan *Connie Zorzak* • John Capodice *Mel Riley* • Wendy Raquel Robinson *Starletta* • Michael Jai White *Demond* ■ *Dir* Neil Abramson • *Scr* Jon Bernstein

Ringo and His Golden Pistol ★★ U

Spaghetti western 1966 · It · Colour · 87mins

Sergio Corbucci spent much of his career in the shadow of spaghetti western master Sergio Leone. Lacking Leone's storytelling gifts, Corbucci was prone to fall back on violence and camera trickery when short on plot inspiration. Here, he is content to enliven this unremarkable, but occasionally explosive, tale of banditry and bounty-hunting with ideas borrowed from other contemporary (and far superior) offerings. DP. Italian dialogue dubbed into English.

Mark Damon *Ringo* • Valeria Fabrizi *Margie* • Ettore Manni *Sheriff Norton* • Giulia Rubini *Norton's wife* ■ *Dir* Sergio Corbucci • *Scr* Adriano Bolzoni, Franco Rossetti

Rings on Her Fingers ★★★ U

Comedy 1942 · US · BW · 86mins

After the popular and critical success of *The Lady Eve*, Henry Fonda's portrayal of naivety was used again as the springboard for a wily female's confidence trick, only this time beautiful Gene Tierney is the fleecer who falls for her victim. There's a regrettable coldness about the Fonda/Tierney partnership, but Laird Cregar and Spring Byington are very watchable as Tierney's crooked partners, and the movie is funny and absorbing in its first half. Unfortunately, it runs out of steam as Tierney reforms her ways. TS

Henry Fonda *John Wheeler* • Gene Tierney *Susan Miller* • Laird Cregar *Warren* • John Shepperd [Shepperd Strudwick] *Tod Fenwick* • Spring Byington *Mrs Maybelle Worthington* • Frank Orth *Kellogg* • Henry Stephenson *Colonel Prentice* ■ *Dir* Rouben Mamoulian • *Scr* Ken Englund, from a story by Robert Pirosh, Joseph Schrank

The Rink ★★★★ U

Silent action comedy
1916 · US · BW · 20mins

In his eighth short for Mutual, Charles Chaplin plays both waiter and skater in this celebration of the roller-skating craze that swept Europe and America during the late 19th/early 20th centuries. At once victim and dominant force, he evades heavy Eric Campbell to win the hand of Edna Purviance with a ferocious cascade of pratfalls and near-miss pirouettes. This typically hilarious piece of sophisticated slapstick was based on a routine dating back to his vaudeville days with Fred Karno. TH [video] DVD

Charles Chaplin *A waiter, posing as Sir Cecil Seltzer* • Edna Purviance *The girl* • James T Kelley *Her father* • Eric Campbell *Mr Stout* ■ *Dir/Scr* Charles Chaplin

Rio Bravo ★★★★★ PG

Western 1959 · US · Colour · 135mins

Under-rated at the time of its release, this majestically paced western is one of the finest achievements of the genre, and stands as a career-best for many of its participants, its longer length and simplistic plot mask a work of depth and artistry. Originally intended by director Howard Hawks as a riposte to the liberal *High Noon*, the quality and class of this movie owe little to what had gone before, save some dialogue lifted from Hawks's earlier *To Have and Have Not*. This is a definitive study of male camaraderie, particularly in the wordless opening sequence as John Wayne attempts to preserve the drunken Dean Martin's dignity. The casting is perfect and the sense of fun contagious. Superb Technicolor photography and a Dimitri Tiomkin score provide the icing on a very impressive cake. TS [video] DVD

John Wayne *John T Chance* • Dean Martin *Dude* • Ricky Nelson *Colorado Ryan* • Angie Dickinson *Feathers* • Walter Brennan *Stumpy* • Ward Bond *Pat Wheeler* • John Russell *Nathan Burdette* ■ *Dir* Howard Hawks • *Scr* Jules Furthman, Leigh Brackett, from a story by Barbara Hawks McCampbell • *Cinematographer* Russell Harlan

Rio Conchos ★★

Western 1964 · US · Colour · 106mins

This is a violent near remake (uncredited) of *The Comancheros*, a reasonable hit for 20th Century Fox in 1961, sadly this time without John Wayne, though Richard Boone is a sturdy, if stolid, substitute. It is competently handled by veteran director Gordon Douglas, and is interesting for the feature film debut of American football star Jim Brown. TS

Richard Boone *Lassiter* • Stuart Whitman *Captain Haven* • Tony Franciosa [Anthony Franciosa] *Rodriguez* • Wende Wagner *Sally* • Edmond O'Brien *Colonel Theron Pardee* • Warner Anderson *Colonel Wagner* • Jim Brown *Sgt Ben Franklyn* ■ *Dir* Gordon Douglas • *Scr* Joseph Landon, Clair Huffaker, from the novel *Guns of the Rio Conchos* by Clair Huffaker

Rio Grande ★★★★★ U

Western 1950 · US · BW · 104mins

This great western – the third film in John Ford's cavalry trilogy, following *Fort Apache* and *She Wore a Yellow Ribbon* – tells the story of a daring off-the-record solution to Indian raids from across the border. It also features a powerful romantic relationship between John Wayne and Maureen O'Hara as the fort commander and his long-separated wife. O'Hara was the strongest leading lady Wayne ever had and almost his match in stubborn pride (they co-starred in four more films). Here, she re-enters Wayne's life seeking to protect their son (Claude Jarman Jr), a private sent out west to serve under him. Once again, Ford creates a stirring picture of the Old West – if this wasn't the way it was, it's the way it should have been. AE [video] DVD

John Wayne *Lt Colonel Yorke* • Maureen O'Hara *Mrs Yorke* • Ben Johnson *Trooper Tyree* • Claude Jarman Jr *Trooper Jeff Yorke* • Harry Carey Jr *Trooper Boone* • Chill Wills *Dr Wilkins* • J Carrol Naish *General Sheridan* • Victor McLaglen *Quincannon* ■ *Dir* John Ford • *Scr* James Kevin McGuinness

Rio Lobo ★★★ PG

Western 1970 · US · Colour · 109mins

It may be a mite saddle-weary, but John Wayne's last film with director Howard Hawks has a wonderful sense of western occasion, together with a sardonic humour that lights up a listless story. Jorge Rivero and Robert's son, Chris Mitchum, play the Confederate looters snatching Union gold, and Wayne is the colonel trying to find the traitor who's feeding information to the robbers. Meanwhile, wild-eyed Jack Elam looks askance at the whole business. It's leisurely, but the characters and circumstance make a real impression. TH [video] DVD

John Wayne *Colonel Cord McNally* • Jennifer O'Neill *Shasta Delaney* • Jack Elam *Phillips* • Chris Mitchum [Christopher Mitchum] *Sergeant Tuscarora* • Jorge Rivero *Captain Pierre Cordona* • Victor French *Ketcham* ■ *Dir* Howard Hawks • *Scr* Leigh Brackett, Burton Wohl, from a story by Burton Wohl

Rio Rita ★★★

Musical revue
1929 · US · BW and Colour · 140mins

Little more than canned theatre, with a static camera filming the spectacular Ziegfeld show of the 1920s, this early film musical, which took 24 days to shoot, is, nevertheless, of historical interest. The slim plot has dashing John Boles as a Texas ranger on the trail of a notorious bandit. He loves Bebe Daniels, in the title role, but boy loses girl (temporarily), when he suspects her brother of being the outlaw. Tiresome Bert Wheeler and Robert Woolsey provide what is called "comic relief". The numbers are good and the finale is in pleasing two-strip Technicolor. RB

Georges Renavent *Gen Ravinoff* • Eva Rosita *Carmen* • Bebe Daniels *Rita Ferguson* • John Boles *Capt Jim Stewart* • Don Alvarado *Roberto Ferguson* • Dorothy Lee *Dolly* • Bert Wheeler *Chick* • Robert Woolsey *Lovett* ■ *Dir* Luther Reed • *Scr* Luther Reed, Russell Mack, from the musical by Guy Bolton, Fred Thompson

Rio Rita ★★ U

Wartime musical comedy
1942 · US · BW · 90mins

MGM borrowed Abbott and Costello from Universal and placed them in this remake of the 1929 film. The updated version, featuring Nazis and saboteurs, was a bit of an odd fish and didn't serve Abbott and Costello too well – the pair find themselves squeezing their comedy routines in between the love story of John Carroll and Kathryn Grayson. Predictably the film's best moments come when the boys do their stuff. DF

Bud Abbott *Doc* • Lou Costello *Wishy* • Kathryn Grayson *Rita Winslow* • John Carroll *Ricardo Montera* • Patricia Dane *Lucille Brunswick* • Tom Conway *Maurice Craindall* ■ *Dir* S Sylvan Simon • *Scr* Richard Connell, Gladys Lehman, John Grant

Riot ★★

Prison drama 1969 · US · Colour · 96mins

Produced by master of schlock William Castle, this jailhouse drama was filmed inside Arizona State Prison, with the real warden and real prisoners appearing as extras. While the warden's away, Gene Hackman leads a revolt and takes over the prison's isolation wing, holding several guards hostage. Jim Brown is a prisoner who thinks Hackman has made a big mistake. Strong performances from the leads and a half-decent script place this film a notch above similar exploitation fare. AT

Jim Brown *Cully Briston* • Gene Hackman *Red Fletcher* • Ben Carruthers *Surefoot* • Mike Kellin *Bugsy* • Gerald S O'Loughlin *Grossman* ■ *Dir* Buzz Kulik • *Scr* James Poe, from the novel *The Riot* by Frank Elli

Riot in Cell Block 11 ★★★★ 15

Prison drama 1954 · US · BW · 80mins

Don Siegel emerged as more than just a Hollywood journeyman director with this hard-hitting, realistic prison picture, which presents a credible account of the riot and the conditions that caused it. Warden Emile Meyer could be accused of being overly sympathetic to the inmates' demands and Frank Faylen is far too dogmatic as the uncompromising senator. But, otherwise, the characters ring true, with Neville Brand's ringleader-turned-scapegoat particularly well realised. Russell Harlan's brooding photography heightens both the tension and the realism, and this remains a powerful indictment of the dehumanising effects of the penal system. DP [video]

Neville Brand *Dunn* • Emile Meyer *Warden* • Frank Faylen *Haskell* • Leo Gordon *Carnie* • Robert Osterloh *Colonel* • Paul Frees *Monroe* • Don Keefer *Reporter* • Alvy Moore *Gator* • Dabbs Greer *Schuyler* • Whit Bissell *Snader* ■ *Dir* Don Siegel • *Scr* Richard Collins

R

Ripe ★

Drama 1996 · US · Colour · 93mins

Monica Keena and Daisy Eagan are adolescent twin sisters who go on the run after their parents get killed in a car crash. Somehow, they end up living with a handyman on an army base, where they learn about sex and violence. This coming-of-age story is often distasteful and unrealistic. ST

Monica Keena *Violet* • Daisy Eagan *Rosie* • Gordon Currie *Pete* • Ron Brice *Ken* • Karen Lynn Gorney *Janet Wyman* • Vincent Laresca *Jimmy* • Scott Sowers *Colonel Wyman* • Eric Jensen *Dave* ■ *Dir/Scr* Mo Ogrodnik

The Ripening Seed ★★★★

Romantic drama 1953 · Fr · BW · 110mins

Condemned by the Catholic Church and banned in various parts of the world, this adaptation of Colette's erotic novel may have seemed daring back in 1953. But today it stands simply as a delicate – and often touching – account of a young man's initiation into the delights of physical love. Under Claude Autant-Lara's watchful eye, Pierre-Michel Beck is suitably bashful as the 16-year-old, who exploits a seaside holiday to spare his childhood sweetheart (Nicole Berger) the humiliation of untutored lovemaking. However, it's Edwige Feuillère's exquisite performance, as the ethereal woman in white, that gives the film its soul. DP. In French with English subtitles.

Nicole Berger *Vinca* • Pierre-Michel Beck *Phil* • Edwige Feuillère *Madame Dalleray* ■ *Dir* Claude Autant-Lara • *Scr* Pierre Bost, Jean Aurenche, Claude Autant-Lara, from the novel by Colette

Ripley's Game ★★★ 15

Crime thriller
2002 · It/UK/US · Colour · 105mins

John Malkovich portrays charming sociopath Tom Ripley in this languid adaptation of the Patricia Highsmith novel. Ripley is now living a cultured, comfortable life in Italy, procuring rare art for collectors by rather dubious methods. When a boorish British associate (Ray Winstone, in an undemanding performance) asks him to bump off a troublesome rival, Malkovich sets himself a diverting challenge: to recruit terminally ill picture-framer Dougray Scott to be the assassin. Despite Malkovich's silky smooth performance, the film doesn't completely succeed due to implausible plotting and the ineffectual direction. JC DVD

John Malkovich *Tom Ripley* • Dougray Scott *Jonathan Trevanny* • Ray Winstone *Reeves* • Lena Headey *Sarah Trevanny* • Chiara Caselli *Luisa Ripley* ■ *Dir* Liliana Cavani • *Scr* Charles McKeown, Liliana Cavani, from the novel by Patricia Highsmith

Riptide ★★★

Romantic drama 1934 · US · BW · 92mins

The unusual meeting of British aristocrat Herbert Marshall and Park Avenue party girl with a past Norma Shearer leads to an idyllic love affair, then marriage and a child. However, when the wife is caught up in a scandal in Cannes, through the drunken antics of an old flame (Robert Montgomery), the husband is consumed with jealousy and wants a divorce. The film is an intriguing, but sometimes uneasy, mix of romance, farce, arch comedy of manners and moral dilemma. Shearer carries it off superbly, Montgomery (as so often) irritates. Very 1930s. RK

Norma Shearer *Lady Mary Rexford* • Robert Montgomery *Tommy Trent* • Herbert Marshall *Lord Philip Rexford* • Mrs Patrick Campbell *Lady Hetty Riversleigh* • Richard "Skeets" Gallagher *Erskine* • Ralph Forbes *David Fenwick* • Lilyan Tashman *Sylvia* • Arthur Jarrett *Percy* ■ *Dir/Scr* Edmund Goulding

The Rise and Fall of Legs Diamond ★★★★ PG

Biographical crime drama
1960 · US · BW · 97mins

A sharply observed and crisply photographed attempt by Warner Bros to revive its gangster cycle. Budd Boetticher, better known for his Randolph Scott westerns, does a terrific job of directing the ice-cold Ray Danton in the leading role, and of sustaining a thoroughly amoral atmosphere on a tight schedule and a very low budget. The black-and-white cinematography by Lucien Ballard is also a major plus. Watch out for an early appearance by Warren Oates and a glimpse of Dyan Cannon. TS

Ray Danton *Jack "Legs" Diamond* • Karen Steele *Alice Shiffer* • Elaine Stewart *Monica Drake* • Jesse White *Leo Bremer* • Simon Oakland *Lieutenant Moody* • Robert Lowery *Arnold Rothstein* • Judson Pratt *Fats Walsh* • Warren Oates *Eddie Diamond* • Dyan Cannon *Dixie* ■ *Dir* Budd Boetticher • *Scr* Joseph Landon • *Cinematographer* Lucien Ballard

The Rise and Rise of Michael Rimmer ★★

Satirical political comedy
1970 · UK · Colour · 102mins

Having played a minor role in Kevin Billington's debut feature, *Interlude*, John Cleese reteamed with the director for this patchy political satire. In addition to co-starring, Cleese and fellow Python, Graham Chapman contributed to the script, which charts the meteoric rise of efficiency expert Peter Cook, who bluffs his way into high office. Although the gags gradually fall flat, there are several scathing swipes at the British character and the nature of power. DP

Peter Cook *Michael Rimmer* • Denholm Elliott *Peter Niss* • Ronald Fraser *Tom Hutchinson* • Arthur Lowe *Ferret* • Vanessa Howard *Patricia Cartwright* • George A Cooper *Blackett* • Graham Crowden *Bishop of Cowley* • Harold Pinter *Steven Hench* • James Cossins *Crodder* • Richard Pearson *Wilting* • Ronnie Corbett *Interviewer* • Dennis Price *Fairburn* • John Cleese *Pumer* • Julian Glover *Col Moffat* ■ *Dir* Kevin Billington • *Scr* Peter Cook, John Cleese, Graham Chapman, Kevin Billington

The Rise of Catherine the Great ★★ U

Historical drama 1934 · UK · BW · 84mins

British-based movie mogul Alexander Korda produced this historical saga, hoping it would repeat the transatlantic success of *The Private Life of Henry VIII*. But it's all rather stuffy and lacks the humour of the previous year's royal romp. The director is Paul Czinner, whose wife, Elisabeth Bergner, plays the Tsarina rather glumly, and Douglas Fairbanks Jr is the rakish Grand Duke who quickly goes off his troika. AT

Elisabeth Bergner *Catherine II* • Douglas Fairbanks Jr *Grand Duke Peter* • Flora Robson *Empress Elizabeth* • Gerald du Maurier *Lecocq* • Irene Vanbrugh *Princess Anhalt-Zerbst* • Griffith Jones *Grigory Orlov* ■ *Dir* Paul Czinner • *Scr* Marjorie Deans, Arthur Wimperis, from the play *The Czarina* by Lajos Biró, Melchior Lengyel

The Rise to Power of Louis XIV ★★★★

Historical drama 1966 · Fr · BW · 100mins

Achieving the ingenious illusion of historical contemporaneity, Roberto Rossellini explores the intrigues of Louis XIV's court, without once threatening to turn this docudrama into a stylised history lesson. Employing tracks and zooms to animate the elaborate tableaux, he reveals how the Sun King tamed his treacherous nobility and turned the uncertainties of his regency into a regal dictatorship based at Versailles. This engrossing film (which was originally made for TV) is the perfect riposte to those who denounce costume dramas for their empty spectacle. DP. In French with English subtitles.

Jean-Marie Patte *Louis XIV* • Raymond Jourdan *Colbert* • Silvagni *Cardinal Mazarin* • Katharina Renn *Anne of Austria* • Dominique Vincent *Mme du Plessis* • Pierre Barrat *Fouquet* ■ *Dir* Roberto Rossellini • *Scr* Jean Gruault, Philippe Erlanger

Rising Damp ★★★ PG

Comedy 1980 · UK · Colour · 94mins

The absence of Richard Beckinsale does much to sap the enjoyment of this decent movie version of the enduring television sitcom. Eric Chappell, who wrote the series and the original stage play about Rigsby the scheming landlord, overwrites to compensate and the film suffers from too many padded scenes and too few hilarious situations. Newcomer Denholm Elliott looks a tad out of place alongside regulars Frances de la Tour and Don Warrington, but he makes a solid foil for the magnificent Leonard Rossiter. DP. Contains swearing. DVD

Leonard Rossiter *Rigsby* • Frances de la Tour *Miss Jones* • Don Warrington *Philip* • Christopher Strauli *John* • Denholm Elliott *Seymour* • Carrie Jones *Sandra* • Glynn Edwards *Cooper* • John Cater *Bert* ■ *Dir* Joe McGrath [Joseph McGrath] • *Scr* Eric Chappell, from his TV series

The Rising of the Moon ★★

Comedy drama 1957 · Ire · BW · 81mins

A minor late offering from John Ford, this anthology of three stories was made in Ireland, scene of his own ancestral roots. More a collection of sketches, paying largely comic but occasionally poignant homage to a vanishing way of life, the movie is played with uninhibited gusto by an A-list of Irish actors. Dated, and too whimsical for an era when both Irish history and its cinematic treatment have moved on, the film still evokes a strong sense of place and culture. RK

Tyrone Power *Introduction* • Cyril Cusack *Inspector Michael Dillon* • Noel Purcell *Dan O'Flaherty the old man* • Jack MacGowran *Mickey J, the poteen maker* • Jimmy O'Dea *Porter* • Tony Quinn *Station master* • Paul Farrell *Engine driver* • Denis O'Dea *The police sergeant* • Eileen Crowe *His wife* ■ *Dir* John Ford • *Scr* Frank S Nugent, from the following three sources: the short story *The Majesty of the Law* by Frank O'Connor, the play *A Minute's Wait* by Martin J McHugh, the play by Lady Augusta Gregory

Rising Sun ★★★ 18

Thriller 1993 · US · Colour · 124mins

Michael Crichton's novel caused a stir for its portrait of Japan as a tentacular monster, devouring every American corporation in its path. Sean Connery brings his inimitable presence to the cop investigating a politically sensitive murder in the offices of a Japanese company in Los Angeles. Connery's sidekick is played by Wesley Snipes, and there's quirky character support from Harvey Keitel. Often exciting, occasionally brutal and kinky, but still a bit of a letdown. AT. Contains violence, swearing, sex scenes, nudity. DVD

Sean Connery *John Connor* • Wesley Snipes *Web Smith* • Harvey Keitel *Tom Graham* • Cary-Hiroyuki Tagawa *Eddie Sakamura* • Kevin Anderson *Bob Richmond* • Mako *Yoshida-San* • Ray Wise *Senator John Morton* • Stan Egi *Ishihara* • Stan Shaw *Phillips* • Tia Carrere *Jingo Asakuma* • Steve Buscemi *Willy "The Weasel" Wilhelm* ■ *Dir* Philip Kaufman • *Scr* Philip Kaufman, Michael Crichton, Michael Backes, from the novel by Michael Crichton

Risk ★★

Romantic drama 1993 · US · Colour · 85mins

The "lovers on the run" genre is a popular one for independent films, but this effort, by first-time film-maker Deirdre Fishel, fails to do anything special with it. Karen Sillas is a painter's model who falls for petty criminal and big-time loser David Ilku, after meeting him on a New York bus. Later, on the spur of the moment, the pair steal a car and drive out to see Ilku's sister in Connecticut, where they encounter a heap of trouble related to his past. A film full of good intentions, but ultimately a bit disappointing. FL

Karen Sillas *Maya* • David Ilku *Joe* • Molly Price *Nikki* • Jack Gwaltney *Karl* • Christie MacFadyen *Alice* • Barry Snider *Phil* • David Lansing *Todd* • Gloria Maddox *Mrs Thompson* ■ *Dir/Scr* Deirdre Fishel

Risk ★★★ 18

Crime drama 2000 · Aus · Colour · 89mins

Director Allan White adds a little dark humour and saucy seduction to this thriller, giving it a distinctly *noir*ish feel. The insurance scam is sketchily outlined and the breakneck chase finale feels tacked on, but Tom Long again impresses (after *The Dish*) as another eager milquetoast, only here he rapidly develops a backbone, as he counters the corrupt schemes of boss Bryan Brown and his shady lawyer lover, Claudia Karvan. DP DVD

Bryan Brown *John Kriesky* • Tom Long *Ben Madigan* • Claudia Karvan *Louise Roncoli* • Jason Clarke *Chris* ■ *Dir* Alan White • *Scr* John Armstrong, Steve Wright, from the short story *The Adjuster* by Tracy Kidder

Risky Business ★★★★ 18

Comedy 1983 · US · Colour · 94mins

Tom Cruise stars as the teenager who turns his parents' home into a brothel after an encounter with Rebecca De Mornay's entrepreneurial hooker. Writer/director Paul Brickman has honed a sharp satire on American go-getting here, as Cruise – parents away, with the use of their Porsche – starts making money out of his sexually frustrated friends. The danger, though, comes when a killer-pimp arrives on the scene ("never muck with a man's business"); that's when this comedy of embarrassment becomes a near-tragedy of class collisions. TH. Contains swearing and sex scenes. DVD

Tom Cruise *Joel Goodson* • Rebecca De Mornay *Lana* • Joe Pantoliano *Guido* • Richard Masur *Rutherford* • Bronson Pinchot *Barry* • Curtis Armstrong *Miles* • Nicholas Pryor *Joel's father* • Janet Carroll *Joel's mother* • Shera Danese *Vicki* • Raphael Sbarge *Glenn* ■ *Dir/Scr* Paul Brickman

Rita, Sue and Bob Too ★★★★ 18

Comedy 1987 · UK · Colour · 88mins

Adapted by Andrea Dunbar from two of her controversial plays, this caused a right old rumpus on its release. Although much of the shock value has been distilled by seeing so much of the same on weekly soaps nowadays, this still makes you squirm as you find yourself unable to decide who is exploiting whom, where the blame lies and how to respond to jokes that are uproariously funny despite their political incorrectness. It is to the credit of Michelle Holmes, Siobhan Finneran and George Costigan that they pitch their performances so perfectly. DP. Contains swearing, sex scenes. DVD

R

Siobhan Finneran *Rita* • Michelle Holmes *Sue* • George Costigan *Bob* • Lesley Sharp *Michelle* • Willie Ross *Sue's father* • Patti Nicholls *Sue's mother* ■ *Dir* Alan Clarke • *Scr* Andrea Dunbar, from her plays *The Arbour* and *Rita, Sue and Bob Too*

The Rite ★★★★ 15

Drama 1969 · Swe · BW · 72mins

Initially made for television, but awarded a cinema release, this intense drama subjects a self-contained community (in this case an acting troupe) to the pressures of the real world. When their show is banned because of an allegedly obscene sketch, Gunnar Björnstrand, Ingrid Thulin and Anders Ek are given a humiliating grilling by the aptly named judge, Erik Hell, whose inquisition not only exposes their own artistic and personal insecurities, but also his own hypocrisy. Stiflingly photographed by Sven Nykvist and unconditionally played, this is Bergman at his most self-denigratingly pessimistic. DP. In Swedish with English subtitles. DVD

Ingrid Thulin *Thea Winkelmann* • Anders Ek *Albert Emanuel Sebastian Fischer* • Gunnar Björnstrand *Hans Winkelmann* • Erik Hell *Judge Abramson* • Ingmar Bergman *Clergyman* ■ *Dir/Scr* Ingmar Bergman

Rites of Passage ★★★

Drama 1999 · US · Colour · 95mins

Dean Stockwell takes an associate producer credit as well as the lead in this explosive look at familial bonding and male pride. Retreating to a mountain cabin to repair his relationship with his son Robert Keith, Stockwell finds himself having to confront his other son's homosexuality (a powerful performance by Jason Behr). Very much written as an actors' showcase, Victor Salva's drama has the intensity and constraint of a stage play. DP. Contains swearing.

Dean Stockwell *Del Farraday* • James Remar *Frank Dabbo* • Jason Behr *Campbell Farraday* • Robert Glen Keith *DJ Farraday* • Jaimz Woolvett *Red Tenney* ■ *Dir/Scr* Victor Salva

The Ritz ★★ 15

Comedy 1976 · US · Colour · 86mins

Richard Lester directs this tasteless camp comedy in which straight Jack Weston takes refuge in a New York gay bath-house. Hiding from his gangster father-in-law (George Coulouris) and brother-in-law (Jerry Stiller), Weston encounters Rita Moreno, who is superb as a talentless singer entertaining the patrons. Terrence McNally's script keeps the clichés flowing. TH. Contains violence and swearing. [video]

Jack Weston *Gaetano Proclo* • Rita Moreno *Googie Gomez* • Jerry Stiller *Carmine Vespucci* • Kaye Ballard *Vivian Proclo* • F Murray Abraham *Chris* • Paul B Price *Claude* • Treat Williams *Michael Brick* • John Everson *Tiger* ■ *Dir* Richard Lester • *Scr* Terrence McNally, from the play by Terrence McNally

The River ★★★★★ U

Documentary 1937 · US · BW · 31mins

Much more cinematically accomplished than its rough-and-ready predecessor, *The Plow That Broke the Plains* (1934), Pare Lorentz's second keystone documentary was sponsored by the Tennessee Valley Authority to expound the significance of its conservation policies. Following a prologue recalling Walt Whitman's poetry, Lorentz charts the history and ecological importance of the Mississippi and its tributaries, with an audiovisual harmony that compensates for its sentimental New Deal liberalism. With clips from *Come and Get It* (1936) and *Show Boat* (1936) juxtaposed with Einsteinian montage sequences, it was widely admired, although Walt Disney vetoed its Oscar nomination; however, it won the Best Documentary at Venice. DP

Thomas Chalmers *Narrator* ■ *Dir/Scr* Pare Lorentz • *Music* Virgil Thomson

The River ★★★ U

Romantic drama
1951 · US/Ind · Colour · 98mins

After his creatively stifling years in Hollywood, the celebrated French director Jean Renoir, venturing into Technicolor for the first time, filmed Rumer Godden's semi-autobiographical novel in India. The focus is on the adolescent longings of Patricia Walters, the eldest daughter of an English family, and her friends, sophisticated Adrienne Corri and Eurasian Radha, all hankering after a handsome, embittered American pilot Thomas E Breen, who has lost a leg in the war. Exquisitely photographed by Claude Renoir, it's more travelogue than narrative entertainment. RK

Nora Swinburne *Mother* • Esmond Knight *Father* • Arthur Shields *Mr John* • Thomas E Breen *Captain John* • Suprova Mukerjee *Nan* • Patricia Walters *Harriet* • Radha *Melanie* • Adrienne Corri *Valerie* ■ *Dir* Jean Renoir • *Scr* Rumer Godden, Jean Renoir

The River ★★ 15

Drama 1984 · US · Colour · 118mins

Rural couple Mel Gibson and Sissy Spacek battle against nature and the machinations of a local landowner (Scott Glenn) in Mark Rydell's well shot, but fairly inconsequential drama. Besides the pretty scenery, the film is chiefly of interest for a pre-super stardom Gibson, taking the kind of unsympathetic role that would give studios heartburn nowadays. He offers a strong performance, but is hampered by a superficial script that gives the protagonists an unlikely "love rivals" back story. JC [video] DVD

Mel Gibson *Tom Garvey* • Sissy Spacek *Mae Garvey* • Scott Glenn *Joe Wade* • Billy Green Bush *Harve Stanley* • Shane Bailey *Lewis Garvey* • Becky Jo Lynch *Beth Garvey* • James Tolkan *Simpson* • Jack Starrett *Swick* • Barry Primus *Roy* • Amy Rydell *Betty Gaumer* ■ *Dir* Mark Rydell • *Scr* Robert Dillon, Julian Barry, from a story by Robert Dillon

The River ★★★★ 18

Drama 1997 · Tai · Colour · 113mins

This is an alarming study of familial dysfunction in Taiwan. When Li Kangsheng contracts a mysterious neck ailment, after working as an extra for film-maker (Ann Hui), neither of his parents can break their routine to tend to him – father Miao Tien frequents gay saunas, while mother Lu Xialin panders to a lover who pirates porn videos. Tsai Ming-liang shoots the almost wordless action in lingering long takes, which make the final incidence of incest all the more shocking. DP. A Mandarin language film. Contains sex scenes. [video]

Miao Tien *Father* • Li Kangsheng *The boy* • Lu Xiaolin *Mother* • Ann Hui *Film director* • Chen Xiangqi *The boy's girlfriend* • Chen Zhaorong *Young man at sauna* • Lu Shiao-Lin *Mother's lover* ■ *Dir* Tsai Ming-liang • *Scr* Tsai Ming-Liang, Yang Pi-Ying, Tsai Yi-Chun

The River and Death ★★★

Drama 1954 · Mex · BW · 90mins

Considering the author of the source novel for this soap-operatic plains western was Luis Buñuel's longtime friend, career diplomat Miguel Alvarez Acosta, this was a surprisingly disharmonious project. The main bone of contention was Buñuel's open contempt for the key idea that higher education was the panacea to the ills of this intemperate, macho society. Denied the chance to alter the ending, Buñuel had to content himself with sly digs at the duplicity of the Catholic Church and the ignorance of the peasant nobility. DP. In Spanish with English subtitles.

Columba Dominguez *Mercedes* • Miguel Torruco *Felipe Anguiano* • Joaquin Cordero *Gerardo Anguiano* • Jaime Fernandez *Romulo Menchaca* • Victor Alcocer *Polo Menchaca* ■ *Dir* Luis Buñuel • *Scr* Luis Buñuel, Luis Alcoriza, from the novel *Muro Blanco en Roca Negra* by Miguel Alvarez Acosta

River Beat ★★ U

Crime drama 1954 · UK · BW · 70mins

Hollywood's Phyllis Kirk gives a dash of much needed class to this minor British thriller. She plays the radio operator on an American freighter docked in the Thames, who's caught with diamonds hidden in her cigarettes. It helps in such circumstances to have an inspector in the river police for a boyfriend. Leading cinematographer Guy Green switched over to direction for the first time and proved he could do an efficient job. AE

Phyllis Kirk *Judy Roberts* • John Bentley *Inspector Dan Barker* • Robert Ayres *Captain Watford* • Glyn Houston *Charlie Williamson* • Leonard White *Sergeant Mcleod* • Ewan Roberts *Customs Officer Blake* • Harold Ayer *Al Gordon* • Charles Lloyd Pack *Hendrick* ■ *Dir* Guy Green • *Scr* Rex Rienits

The River Niger ★★★

Drama 1976 · US · Colour · 105mins

An overflow of compassion and self-understanding makes this story of life in a black ghetto an intelligent and moving movie. Based on a 1972 Tony Award-winning play about a family trying to get it together in a world which seems geared against them, it's directed by Krishna Shah and features remarkable portrayals by James Earl Jones and Cicely Tyson. TH

Cicely Tyson *Mattie Williams* • James Earl Jones *Johnny Williams* • Louis Gossett Jr *Dr Dudley Stanton* • Glynn Turman *Jeff Williams* • Roger E Mosley *Big Moe Hayes* • Jonelle Allen *Ann Vanderguild* ■ *Dir* Krishna Shah • *Scr* Joseph A Walker, from a play by Joseph A Walker

River of Death ★ 15

Action adventure 1989 · US · Colour · 97mins

Adventurer Michael Dudikoff travels up the "river of death" in search of a woman and a Nazi scientist. Accompanying him on his quest is (a toupee-wearing) Donald Pleasence and a bunch of other people who all have their own agendas. This extremely violent and unpleasant action film, includes too many of the modern jungle movie clichés and the ending is particularly pointless. ST [video]

Michael Dudikoff *John Hamilton* • Robert Vaughn *Wolfgang Manteuffel* • Donald Pleasence *Heinrich Spaatz* • Herbert Lom *Colonel Ricardo Diaz* • LQ Jones *Hiller* • Sarah Maur-Thorp *Anna Blakesley* ■ *Dir* Steve Carver • *Scr* Andrew Deutsch, Edward Simpson, from the novel by Alistair MacLean

River of No Return ★★★ PG

Western 1954 · US · Colour · 87mins

Robert Mitchum mumbles away to Marilyn Monroe and shows what a great job two stars can do with a creaking script and poor dialogue. This is an "event" movie, in that we do not really believe in Mitchum and Monroe cast adrift in the glorious scenery of the Canadian Rockies, but we enjoy seeing them do it. In his only western, Otto Preminger directs with enough sense to let the actors shine within the confines of a far-fetched adventure tale. It's good entertainment as long as you suspend your critical faculties and let the star charisma suffice. SH [video] DVD

Robert Mitchum *Matt Calder* • Marilyn Monroe *Kay Weston* • Rory Calhoun *Harry Weston* • Tommy Rettig *Mark Calder* • Murvyn Vye *Dave Colby* • Douglas Spencer *Sam Benson* • Ed Hinton *Gambler* ■ *Dir* Otto Preminger • *Scr* Frank Fenton, from a story by Louis Lantz

The River Rat ★★★ 15

Drama 1984 · US · Colour · 88mins

In this drama set in the eerie swamps of Mississippi, Tommy Lee Jones plays an ex-con who meets his teenage daughter (Martha Plimpton) for the first time after serving a long prison sentence for murder. Determined to go straight and be the perfect dad, Jones's plans unravel when his parole officer, Brian Dennehy, turns nasty. Jones is well cast as the returning father and Plimpton gives a good account of herself in her first major role. AT. Contains some violence, swearing. [video]

Tommy Lee Jones *Billy* • Martha Plimpton *Jonsy* • Brian Dennehy *Doc* • Shawn Smith *Wexel* • Nancy Lea Owen *Vadie* • Norman Bennett *Sheriff Cal* • Frank Tony *Poley* • Angie Bolling *Joyce* ■ *Dir/Scr* Tom Rickman

A River Runs through It ★★★★ PG

Drama 1992 · US · Colour · 118mins

This shows us how to fly-fish and live in a state of grace, harmoniously with the land and water. Set in Montana in the early part of the century, the story focuses on the relationships between stern Presbyterian clergyman, Tom Skerritt and his two sons, Craig Sheffer and Brad Pitt, who grow increasingly apart aside from their common love of fly-fishing. Philippe Rousselot's exquisite photography deservedly won an Oscar. AT. Contains swearing, nudity. [video] DVD

Craig Sheffer *Norman Maclean* • Brad Pitt *Paul Maclean* • Tom Skerritt *Reverend Maclean* • Brenda Blethyn *Mrs Maclean* • Emily Lloyd *Jessie Burns* • Edie McClurg *Mrs Burns* • Stephen Shellen *Neal Burns* ■ *Dir* Robert Redford • *Scr* Richard Friedenberg, from the novella by Norman Maclean

River Street ★★★

Comedy drama 1996 · Aus · Colour · 88mins

Aden Young stars as a ruthless, unfeeling estate agent who is sentenced to community service after he hits a policeman. He is assigned to work at a centre for the homeless and, realising immediately that the building has enormous potential, cons the owner into selling it to him cheaply. However, encounters with a homeless teenager and Essie Davis, the caring woman who runs the centre, lead to a change of heart. Predictable but endearing. DF

Aden Young *Ben Egan* • Bill Hunter *Vincent Pierce* • Essie Davis *Wendy Davis* • Tammy McIntosh *Sharon Pierce* • Sullivan Stapleton *Chris* • Joy Smithers *Marcia* ■ *Dir* Tony Mahood • *Scr* Philip Ryall

The River Wild ★★★★ 12

Adventure thriller
1994 · US · Colour · 106mins

This excellent thriller has Meryl Streep and family white-water rafting. Their enjoyable break soon turns into a nightmare when armed robbers, Kevin Bacon and John C Reilly, hitch a ride on the raft with $250,000 of stolen loot. Directed by Curtis Hanson, this is a real roller-coaster ride, filled with hair-raising action scenes (shot in Montana and Oregon) and some equally tense moments on the river bank. The incredible action and Streep's performance more than compensate for any shortcomings. AT. Contains swearing, violence and brief nudity. [video] DVD

R

Meryl Streep *Gail Hartman* • Joseph Mazzello *Roarke Hartman* • David Strathairn *Tom Hartman* • Kevin Bacon *Wade* • John C Reilly *Terry* • William Lucking *Frank* • Benjamin Bratt *Ranger Johnny* ■ *Dir* Curtis Hanson • *Scr* Denis O'Neill

Rivers and Tides ★★★

Documentary
2001 · Ger/UK/Fin · Colour · 90mins

Scottish sculptor Andy Goldsworthy is renowned for landscape pieces whose natural fragility means they rarely outlive their creation by more than a few hours. Indeed, his unique achievement is almost solely known through photographic representation. This documentary seeks to rectify that situation by presenting the artist at work with the ice, twigs, rocks and other rural debris that form his materials. While never quite as transfixing as, say, Bernard Dufour's sketching in *La Belle Noiseuse*, this is still an experience that repays patience, with Thomas Riedelsheimer's inspired use of time-lapse techniques providing a welcome distraction from Goldsworthy's laudable, but verbose, environmental musings. DP

Dir Thomas Riedelsheimer

The River's Edge ★★★

Comedy adventure
1957 · US · Colour · 87mins

What looks at first glance like a routine action film actually has some surprisingly ironic twists up its sleeve and delivers a rather bleak moral message. Ray Milland is a bank robber on the run who forces Anthony Quinn and his wife, Debra Paget, to guide him and his stolen dollars across the mountainous border to Mexico. An avalanche, the pouting Paget and sundry other inconveniences hinder their progress. Although Milland is slightly miscast, Quinn delivers his usual ethnic exuberance and veteran director Allan Dwan. AT

Ray Milland *Nardo Denning* • Anthony Quinn *Ben Cameron* • Debra Paget *Meg Cameron* • Harry Carey Jr *Chet* • Chubby Johnson *Whiskers* • Byron Foulger *Barry* ■ *Dir* Allan Dwan • *Scr* Harold Jacob Smith, James Leicester, from the story *The Highest Mountain* by Harold Jacob Smith

River's Edge ★★★★ 18

Drama
1987 · US · Colour · 95mins

This is the chilling chronicle of the differing reactions of a group of teenagers when a friend shows them the body of the girl he murdered. A vivid study of alienation and moral vacuity, Tim Hunter's confident direction underlines the bleakness of the sorry tale, based on a true incident. Keanu Reeves scores as the decent guy who doesn't think the killing should go unpunished, but the standout performance comes from Crispin Glover as the speed-freak friend of the killer whose own sorry life is given pathetic meaning by the slaying. AJ DVD

Crispin Glover *Layne* • Keanu Reeves *Matt* • Ione Skye *Clarissa* • Daniel Roebuck *Samson "John" Tollette* • Dennis Hopper *Feck* • Joshua Miller *Tim* • Josh Richman *Tony* ■ *Dir* Tim Hunter • *Scr* Neal Jimenez

Road ★★ 15

Thriller
2002 · Ind · Colour · 134mins

This road thriller may feel a touch formulaic to western audiences, but at least attempts something different from the usual Bollywood fare. That said, the action still pauses for the obligatory song-and-dance routines, which fatally dissipate the tension of the chase sequences that follow hitcher Manoj Bajpai's abduction of eloping beauty, Antara Mali. Vivek Oberoi cuts a dash as the pursuing hero, while Makrand Deshpande's trucker provides some much-needed comic relief. DP. In Hindi with English subtitles. Contains violence and sexual references. DVD

Manoj Bajpai *Babu* • Vivek Oberoi *Arvind* • Antara Mali *Lakshmi* • Makrand Deshpande *Inderpal* • Rajpal Yadav *Bhanwar Singh* ■ *Dir* Rajat Mukherjee • *Scr* Rajnish Thakur

Road Agent ★★ U

Western
1941 · US · BW · 59mins

Crooning cowboy star Dick Foran went to Universal for this western, having made his name at Warner Bros. Although Foran and co-stars Leo Carrillo and Andy Devine look good together and do their own hard ridin', they can't change the plot, which is fast-moving nonsense about the wrongly accused threesome being let out of jail to prove their own innocence. It's enjoyable enough for fans of B westerns. TS

Dick Foran *Duke Masters* • Leo Carrillo *Pancho* • Andy Devine *Andy* • Anne Gwynne *Patricia Leavitt* • Samuel S Hinds *Sam Leavitt* • Anne Nagel *Lola* ■ *Dir* Charles Lamont • *Scr* Morgan Cox, Arthur Strawn, Maurice Tombragel, from a story by Sherman Loew, Arthur St Claire

The Road Builder ★★★

Psychological horror
1971 · UK · Colour · 100mins

The script for this subtle British psycho-thriller was written by famous children's author Roald Dahl. Handsome Nicholas Clay (making his film debut) is a serial killer who buries his victims under a road construction site. How the homicidal handyman sexually manipulates frustrated spinster Patricia Neal (Dahl's then wife) and fools her blind mother Pamela Brown is the thrust of this obsessively dark look at the demented grotesquerie lurking beneath suburban normality. It's a brave, stark and sympathetic study in neuroses and madness that ultimately becomes too restricted by its horror trappings. AJ

Patricia Neal *Maura Prince* • Pamela Brown *Mrs Prince* • Nicholas Clay *Billy Jarvis* • Jean Anderson *Mrs McMurtrey* • Graham Crowden *Mr Bolton* • Yootha Joyce *Mrs Palafax* • Peter Sallis *Rev Palafox* ■ *Dir* Alastair Reid • *Scr* Roald Dahl, from the novel *Nest in a Falling Tree* by Joy Crowley

Road Games ★★ 15

Thriller
1981 · Aus · Colour · 96mins

Stacy Keach plays a truck driver who picks up hitch-hiker Jamie Lee Curtis during a journey across the Australian outback. When she later disappears, Keach becomes the prime suspect. The classic themes of Hitchcock are here: an innocent man on the run, people placed in inescapable danger and an emphasis on suspense over actual violence. However, the paucity of action makes it hard for director Richard Franklin to maintain the tension. KB. Contains violence and swearing.

Stacy Keach *Patrick Quid* • Jamie Lee Curtis *Pamela Rushworth/"Hitch"* • Marion Edward *Madeleine "Sunny" Day/Frita Frugal* • Grant Page *"Smith or Jones"* • Thaddeus Smith *Abbott* • Stephen Millichamp *Costello* ■ *Dir* Richard Franklin • *Scr* Everett DeRoche

The Road Home ★ 15

Drama
1989 · US · Colour · 111mins

Hugh Hudson directs this story of teenage angst, starring Beastie Boy Adam Horovitz as an institutionalised youth and Donald Sutherland as his shrink. Set in Los Angeles, it tries hard to mirror *Rebel without a Cause*, but fails dismally in all departments. The clichéd script, wooden performances and contrived ending are dispiriting to watch. AT. Contains swearing, nudity and violence.

Donald Sutherland *Dr Charles Loftis* • Adam Horovitz *Tim Doolan* • Amy Locane *Cheryl Anderson* • Don Bloomfield *Andy Doolan* • Celia Weston *Felicia Marks* • Graham Beckel *Richard Doolan* • Patricia Richardson *Mrs Anderson* • Ron Frazier *Barton Marks* ■ *Dir* Hugh Hudson • *Scr* Michael Weller

The Road Home ★★★

Adventure
1995 · US · Colour · 90mins

Two sons of Irish immigrants are orphaned and then separated when the younger brother is adopted. The older brother then absconds with his sibling and together they make for the one place they imagine they can be together – Boys Town. This never strays far from the established stereotypes you usually find in this kind of movie but it's still touching. In an ironic bit of casting, Mickey Rooney, who as a teenager appeared in the most famous film version of *Boys Town*, appears in this TV movie. ST

Danny Aiello *Duke* • Will Estes *Michael* • Kris Kristofferson *Davis* • Keegan Macintosh *John* • Sheila Patterson *Sister Elizabeth* • Mickey Rooney *Father Flanagan* • Dee Wallace Stone *Mrs Bastian* ■ *Dir* Dean Hamilton • *Scr* Keith O'Leary

The Road Home ★★★★ U

Drama
1999 · Chi · Colour and BW · 85mins

Prompted by a son returning for his father's funeral, this is ostensibly a touching love story shot through with painstaking attention to the detail of everyday life in a 1950s rural community. But Zhang Yimou also extols virtues forgotten in modern consumerist China, such as loyalty, faith and permanence, which is why he shoots the present-day book ends in sombre monochrome and the romance between the teenage Zhang Ziyi and the village's new teacher, Zheng Hao, in vibrantly warm colour. Lyrical and nostalgic, but shrewd. DP. In Mandarin with English subtitles. DVD

Zhang Ziyi *Zhao Di as a young woman* • Sun Honglei *Luo Yusheng* • Zheng Hao *Luo Changyu* • Zhao Yuelin *Zhao Di, elderly* • Li Bin (1) *Grandmother* ■ *Dir* Zhang Yimou • *Scr* Bao Shi, from his novel *Remembrance*

Road House ★★★★

Crime melodrama
1948 · US · BW · 94mins

Blues singer Ida Lupino gets a job at Richard Widmark's joint, but ill-advisedly falls for his general manager, Cornel Wilde. Lupino plays the floozy to perfection, her unsmoked cigarettes burning lines in the piano, as she plays and sings her tragic ballads. As the rejected lover, Widmark gives one of his trademark psychotic performances. Not one of the great *film noirs*, but still a very gripping movie. AT. Contains strong language.

Ida Lupino *Lily Stevens* • Cornel Wilde *Pete Morgan* • Celeste Holm *Susie Smith* • Richard Widmark *Jefty Robbins* • OZ Whitehead *Arthur* • Robert Karnes *Mike* • George Beranger *Lefty* ■ *Dir* Jean Negulesco • *Scr* Edward Chodorov, from a story by Margaret Gruen, Oscar Saul

Road House ★★★ 18

Action drama
1989 · US · Colour · 109mins

This gloriously brainless, modern-day western is a treat from start to finish and possibly the only time that a bouncer will ever get the full Hollywood hero treatment. Patrick Swayze, with a commendable straight face, plays the softly spoken doorman who brings order and just a little karma to the unruly Double Deuce bar, which is under threat from unsavoury characters and local hoodlums. Kelly Lynch plays the token love interest, but the best roles go to Sam Elliott, as Swayze's old buddy, and Ben Gazzara, as the villain of the piece. JF. Contains swearing, violence, sex scenes, drug abuse, nudity. DVD

Patrick Swayze *Dalton* • Kelly Lynch *Dr Elizabeth "Doc" Clay* • Sam Elliott *Wade Garrett* • Ben Gazzara *Brad Wesley* • Marshall Teague *Jimmy* • Julie Michaels *Denise* • Red West *Red Webster* • Sunshine Parker *Emmet* • Jeff Healey *Cody* • Kevin Tighe *Tilghman* ■ *Dir* Rowdy Herrington • *Scr* David Lee Henry, Hilary Henkin, from a story by David Lee Henry

Road Show ★★★ U

Comedy
1941 · US · BW · 87mins

Millionaire John Hubbard, committed to a lunatic asylum by a vengeful woman, becomes friendly with fellow inmate Adolphe Menjou, who is the inventor of a camera that takes no pictures. Together, they escape and join a carnival owned by Carole Landis, where Hubbard becomes a lion tamer and the carnival runs into riotous (in both senses of the word) trouble. Zany, manic, broad farce. RK

Adolphe Menjou *Col Carleton Carraway* • Carole Landis *Penguin Moore* • John Hubbard *Drogo Gaines* • Charles Butterworth *Harry Whitman* • Patsy Kelly *Jinx* • George E Stone *Indian* • Margaret Roach *Priscilla* ■ *Dir* Gordon Douglas • *Scr* Arnold Belgard, Harry Langdon, Mickell Novak, from the novel by Eric Hatch

Road to Bali ★★★ U

Musical comedy
1952 · US · Colour · 90mins

A wonderfully wacky and surreal entry in Paramount's *Road* series. This was the penultimate of the seven made and the only one in colour. Alongside Bing Crosby, Bob Hope and Dorothy Lamour (whose camaraderie was by now honed to perfection), there are a variety of star cameos and a number of enjoyable special effects, from materialisation by a snake charmer's flute to volcanic eruption, all done with a warmth missing from today's digital wizardry. TS DVD

Bob Hope *Harold Gridley* • Bing Crosby *George Cochran* • Dorothy Lamour *Lalah* • Murvyn Vye *Ken Arok* • Peter Coe *Gung* • Ralph Moody *Bhoma Da* ■ *Dir* Hal Walker • *Scr* Frank Butler, Hal Kanter, William Morrow, from a story by Frank Butler, Harry Tugend

The Road to Corinth ★★★

Crime thriller
1967 · Fr/Gr/It · Colour · 84mins

Claude Chabrol was in playful, commercial mood with a thriller made just before his greatest period. Jean Seberg plays the wife of a NATO security officer who is killed. Accused of his murder, she sets out to prove her innocence. Some wonderful Greek locations (and Chabrol in a small role) help the caper along. Though hardly a serious movie, this deserved better than the dubbing and various cuts that led to alternate versions appearing and its silly American title, *Who's Got the Black Box?* BB. French dialogue dubbed into English.

Jean Seberg *Shanny* • Maurice Ronet *Dex* • Christian Marquand *Robert Ford* • Michel Bouquet *Sharps* • Claude Chabrol *Alcibiades* ■ *Dir* Claude Chabrol • *Scr* Claude Brulé, Daniel Boulanger, from the novel *La Route de Corinthe* by Claude Rank

The Road to Denver ★ U

Western
1955 · US · Colour · 90mins

No wonder John Payne looks more morose than ever – he's reduced to playing in a Republic western and his part requires him to be upstaged by his younger brother's wild behaviour, when he's not stationed at a sink washing dishes. Skip Homeier is convincingly hot-headed as the youngster, but veteran Joseph Kane's direction is tepid and the script is as dull as dishwater. AE

John Payne *Bill Mayhew* • Skip Homeier *Sam Mayhew* • Mona Freeman *Elizabeth Sutton* • Lee J Cobb *Jim Donovan* • Ray Middleton *John Sutton* • Andy Clyde *Whipsaw* • Lee Van Cleef *Pecos Larry* ■ *Dir* Joseph Kane • *Scr* Horace McCoy, Allen Rivkin, from the novel *Man from Texas* by Bill Gulick

The Road to El Dorado ★★★ U

Animated adventure
2000 · US · Colour · 85mins

The third animated feature from DreamWorks – following *Antz* and *The Prince of Egypt* – features Kevin Kline and Kenneth Branagh, voicing a duo of rascally 16th-century Spaniards who stumble on the fabled South American city of gold. Mistaken for gods, the two must fake divinity long enough to run off with the loot, but evil High Priest Amand Assante has other ideas. The film starts and finishes strongly, and boasts at least two terrific action set pieces, while the talky in-between sequences noticeably drag on. The mix of conventional animation and computer graphics is good, but the voices carry the day. DA [video] DVD

Elton John *Narrator* • Kevin Kline *Tulio* • Kenneth Branagh *Miguel* • Rosie Perez *Chel* • Armand Assante *Tzekel-Kan* • Edward James Olmos *Chief* • Jim Cummings *Cortes* • Frank Welker *Altivo* • Tobin Bell *Zaragoza* ■ *Dir* Eric "Bibo" Bergeron, Don Paul • *Scr* Ted Elliott, Terry Rossio • *Music* Elton John • *Lyrics* Tim Rice

The Road to Glory ★★

First World War drama
1936 · US · BW · 102mins

Howard Hawks recycles ideas from another of his films, *The Dawn Patrol*, changing the focus from the war in the air, to the war in the trenches. And that wasn't the only instance of recycling. Fox studio boss Darryl F Zanuck had bought a 1932 French movie, *Les Croix des Bois*, but decided not to release it in the US. Instead Zanuck took all the battle footage from the French movie and got Hawks to graft a plot onto it and glue Hollywood actors around it. AT

Fredric March *Lt Michel Denet* • Warner Baxter *Capt Paul Laroche* • Lionel Barrymore *Papa Laroche* • June Lang *Monique* • Gregory Ratoff *Bouffiou* • Victor Kilian *Regnier* • Paul Stanton *Relief Captain* • John Qualen *Duflous* ■ *Dir* Howard Hawks • *Scr* Joel Sayre and William Faulkner, from the film *Les Croix des Bois* by Raymond Bernard, André Lang, from the novel by Roland Dorgèles

The Road to Hollywood ★★★ U

Biographical compilation
1947 · US · BW · 53mins

Although it's been cheaply cobbled together, this survey of Bing Crosby's early screen appearances is a must for fans of the man who made crooning cool. Although the story starts in 1925, Bing had to wait for the talkies to make a movie impact, when he landed his first solo spot (albeit ninth on the bill) in *Reaching for the Moon* (1930). However, the real pleasure of this compendium are clips from the two-reelers Crosby made for slapstick king, Mack Sennett in the early 1930s: *I Surrender Dear, One More Chance, Billboard Girl* and *Dream House*. Producer/director Bud Pollard provides the connecting narration for the clips. DP [video] DVD

Bud Pollard *Narrator* • Bing Crosby ■ *Dir* Bud Pollard

The Road to Hong Kong ★★ U

Musical comedy 1962 · US/UK · BW · 87mins

Bing Crosby and Bob Hope reteamed ten years after *Road to Bali* for the seventh and last in a once fabulously funny series. Sadly, by now the spark had gone from the relationship and the English locations and parsimonious filming in black and white make the movie look shabby. Worse is the graceless demoting of Dorothy Lamour to "guest star", with the co-starring role being taken by an ill-suited Joan Collins. There's super work from some distinguished supporting players – especially Peter Sellers – but this is neither funny nor attractive. TS DVD

Bing Crosby *Harry Turner* • Bob Hope *Chester Babcock* • Joan Collins *Diane* • Dorothy Lamour • Robert Morley *The Leader* • Walter Gotell *Dr Zorbb* • Roger Delgado *Jhinnah* • Felix Aylmer *Grand Lama* • Peter Madden *Lama* • Peter Sellers • Frank Sinatra • Dean Martin • David Niven • Zsa Zsa Gabor ■ *Dir* Norman Panama • *Scr* Norman Panama, Melvin Frank

The Road to Mandalay ★★★

Silent melodrama 1926 · US · BW

Lon Chaney, the master of disguise, created a grotesque white cataract in his eye with the skin of an eggshell to play the villainous Chinese owner of a Singapore dive. The evil character has sent his daughter Lois Moran to a convent in Mandalay and kidnaps her sweetheart Owen Moore. As eerily atmospheric as the other collaborations between Chaney (another riveting performance) and director Tod Browning, who shared the star's taste for the macabre, it is by today's standards, an overripe melodrama and strictly non-PC. RB

Lon Chaney *Singapore Joe* • Lois Moran *Joe's daughter* • Owen Moore *The Admiral* • Henry B Walthall *Father James* ■ *Dir* Tod Browning • *Scr* Elliott Clawson, Joe Farnham [Joseph Farnham], from a story by Tod Browning, Herman Mankiewicz [Herman J Mankiewicz]

Road to Morocco ★★★★ U

Musical comedy 1942 · US · BW · 78mins

"Like Webster's Dictionary, we're Morocco-bound,", sing Bob Hope and Bing Crosby in arguably one of the best – and certainly the funniest – of their zany *Road* series for Paramount. There's much to cherish here: Dorothy Lamour and *Moonlight Becomes You*; Anthony Quinn as a villainous Arab; the delectable Dona Drake as a slave girl and the talking camels. These comedies may have dated – and certainly they remain unfashionable – but for sheer inventiveness and innate good humour they're hard to beat. In these postmodern times, they're simply full of surreal cinematic in-jokes. TS [video] DVD

Bing Crosby *Jeff Peters* • Bob Hope *Orville "Turkey" Jackson* • Dorothy Lamour *Princess Shalmar* • Anthony Quinn *Mullay Kasim* • Dona Drake *Mihirmah* • Mikhail Rasumny *Ahmed Fey* • Vladimir Sokoloff *Hyder Khan* ■ *Dir* David Butler • *Scr* Frank Butler, Don Hartman

Road to Nhill ★★★

Comedy 1997 · Aus · Colour · 95mins

This award-winning art house movie takes a whimsical look at the effect of a road accident on the inhabitants of an Australian country town. When a car containing four lady bowlers from Pyramid Hill overturns on the Nhill road, an escalating comedy of errors is put into motion. The local emergency services spring into action, but set off in the wrong destination, while the townsfolk contemplate what the accident may mean to their lives. An absorbing, warm and gentle comedy on the theme of fate and destiny, it features wonderful performances. However, the intrusive presence of the "Voice of God" grates. DF

Patricia Kennedy *Jean* • Monica Maughan *Nell* • Lois Ramsey *Carmel* • Lynette Curran *Margot* • Phillip Adams *Voice of God* ■ *Dir* Sue Brooks • *Scr* Alison Tilson

Road to Perdition ★★★★ 15

Period crime drama
2002 · US · Colour · 112mins

Director Sam Mendes here follows up his superlative Oscar winner *American Beauty* with another riveting, intelligent drama imbued with lyrical imagery. Set during the Depression era, it features Tom Hanks as a feared hitman working for Irish-American Mob boss Paul Newman, the man who raised him as a son. Professional and familial loyalties become blurred when Hanks's own family is targeted, forcing him to take to the road with his eldest son, as he embarks on a systematic course of revenge against his betrayers. This evocative gangster movie boasts superb photography, production design and score, which utterly transport the audience back to moody 1930s Chicago. JC. Contains violence and swearing. [video] DVD

Tom Hanks *Michael Sullivan* • Paul Newman *John Rooney* • Jude Law *Maguire* • Jennifer Jason Leigh *Annie Sullivan* • Tyler Hoechlin *Michael Sullivan Jr* • Stanley Tucci *Frank Nitti* • Daniel Craig *Connor Rooney* • Liam Aiken *Peter Sullivan* ■ *Dir* Sam Mendes • *Scr* David Self, from the graphic novel by Max Allan Collins, Richard Piers Rayner

Road to Rio ★★★★ U

Musical comedy 1947 · US · BW · 100mins

The fifth of the seven *Road* movies was also one of the best, even though the formula remained much as before – entertainers Bing Crosby and Bob Hope, on the run, fall for Dorothy Lamour, become rivals for her love and land in hot water. This time, Dorothy is being hypnotised by her guardian (the delightfully wicked Gale Sondergaard) so that she'll marry the guardian's brother, who is after Dorothy's estate. "I find myself saying things and I don't know why I say them," says Dot. "Why don't you just run for Congress," Hope quips. Added attractions are the Andrew Sisters singing *You Don't Have to Know the Language* with Bing, and the zany Weire Brothers doing their famous hat routine. RB [video] DVD

Bing Crosby *"Scat" Sweeney* • Bob Hope *"Hot Lips" Barton* • Dorothy Lamour *Lucia Maria de Andrade* • Gale Sondergaard *Catherine Vail* • Frank Faylen *Trigger* • Joseph Vitale *Tony* • Frank Puglia *Rodrigues* • Nestor Paiva *Cardoso* ■ *Dir* Norman Z McLeod • *Scr* Edmund Beloin, Jack Rose

Road to Ruin ★★ 15

Romantic comedy
1992 · US/Fr · Colour · 90mins

Peter Weller rather improbably stars in this Parisian frippery. The city looks glorious, thanks to cinematographer Jean-Yves LeMener, but Erick Anjou's script is right out of the bottom drawer, taking ludicrous turns to prove to Weller's wealthy exile that model Carey Lowell loves him for more than his money. There's little spark between them and, as the elaborate scams come thick and fast, you're left wondering how anyone so harebrained came to be so rich. DP. Contains swearing and sex scenes. [video]

Peter Weller *Jack Sloan* • Carey Lowell *Jessie Taylor* • Michel Duchaussoy *Julien Boulet* • Rebecca Pauly *Arabella* • Sylvie Laguna *Sarah* • Takashi Kawahara *Toshi* ■ *Dir* Charlotte Brandstrom • *Scr* Erick Anjou, from the story by Richard Gitelson, Eric Freiser

Road to Salina ★

Drama 1969 · Fr/It · Colour · 97mins

The last years of Rita Hayworth's life were saddened by illness and films made towards the end of her career, including this co-production, were of little or no merit. It achieves what interest it has from Hayworth's portrayal of the mother to Mimsy Farmer who gets very involved with the young and wayward Robert Walker Jr. Not much problem there you might think, except that Walker could possibly be Hayward's son. There's more incident than plot in this rather trashy movie, with a couple of killings and some fairly explicit sex. BB

Mimsy Farmer *Billie* • Robert Walker [Robert Walker Jr] *Jonas* • Rita Hayworth *Mara* • Ed Begley *Warren* • Bruce Pecheur *Charlie* ■ *Dir* Georges Lautner • *Scr* Georges Lautner, Pascal Jardin, Jack Miller, from the novel *Sur la Route de Salina* by Maurice Cury

Road to Singapore ★★★ U

Musical comedy 1940 · US · BW · 81mins

Not the best of the *Road* series, but the first, originally intended as a vehicle for a sarong-clad Dorothy Lamour. Several other stars were mooted, notably Jack Oakie with a number of partners, but eventually crooner Bing Crosby and comedian Bob Hope were recruited to team with Lamour in a script which, by then, was nearly ten years old. The public loved the resultant comedy and seeming ad-libs, although the tone of the series (Bing and Bob moon over Lamour, or money, or both) wasn't really established until the second, *Road to Zanzibar*. TS [video] DVD

Bing Crosby *Josh Mallon* • Bob Hope *Ace Lannigan* • Dorothy Lamour *Mima* • Charles Coburn *Joshua Mallon IV* • Judith Barrett *Gloria Wycott* • Anthony Quinn *Caesar* • Jerry Colonna *Achilles Bombanassa* • Johnny Arthur *Timothy Willow* • Pierre Watkin *Morgan Wycott* ■ *Dir* Victor Schertzinger • *Scr* Don Hartman, Frank Butler, from a story by Harry Hervey

Road to Utopia ★★★★ PG

Musical comedy 1945 · US · BW · 85mins

Sadly, they really don't make them like this any more. Released 20 months after it was completed, this is among the best of a much-loved series, with Bing Crosby and Bob Hope as down-at-heel entertainers posing as hardened prospectors in order to get their hands on a Klondike gold map. Told as an elongated flashback and blessed with a mocking commentary by Robert Benchley, the film contains a wealth of insider gags that were a trademark of these freewheeling comedies. Complete with obligatory squabble over Dorothy Lamour, talking animals and the "pat-a-cake" fight sequence. DP [video] DVD

Bing Crosby *Duke Johnson* • Bob Hope *Chester Hooton* • Dorothy Lamour *Sal Van Hoyden* • Hillary Brooke *Kate* • Douglass Dumbrille *Ace Larson* • Jack LaRue *Lebec* • Robert Barrat *Sperry* • Robert Benchley *Narrator* ■ *Dir* Hal Walker • *Scr* Norman Panama, Melvin Frank

The Road to Wellville ★★ 18

Black comedy 1994 · US · Colour · 114mins

Director Alan Parker comes unstuck with this tasteless farce about early 20th century health habits. Anthony Hopkins is all wavering accent and buckteeth as Dr John Harvey Kellogg (yes, he of cornflakes fame), who ran a notorious sanatorium in Battle Creek, Michigan, where idle rich Americans flocked to have enemas, salt scrubs, yogurt therapy and bowel inspections. Matthew Broderick turns up with chronic constipation, his sexually frustrated wife Bridget Fonda in tow, to indulge in numerous *Carry On*-style shenanigans among the handsome period detailing and gorgeous spa sets. AJ. Contains swearing, sex scenes, nudity. [video] DVD

Anthony Hopkins *Dr John Harvey Kellogg* • Bridget Fonda *Eleanor Lightbody* • Matthew

R

Broderick *Will Lightbody* • John Cusack *Charles Ossining* • Dana Carvey *George Kellogg* • Michael Lerner *Goodloe Bender* • Colm Meaney *Dr Lionel Badger* • John Neville *Endymion Hart-Jones* • Lara Flynn Boyle *Ida Muntz* • Traci Lind *Nurse Irene Graves* ■ *Dir* Alan Parker • *Scr* Alan Parker, from the novel by T Coraghessan Boyle

The Road to Yesterday ★★★

Silent romantic drama
1925 · US · BW · 136mins

Lively reincarnation fantasy in which spectacle-specialist Cecil B DeMille transports two unhappily-married modern-day couples into the past to teach them a lesson for the future. Unconscious following a train crash, the crotchety quartet find themselves back in 16th century England, where their bigotry and unkindness backfire horribly. DeMille proves once again what a crowd-pleaser he is with this agreeable slice of hokum. TH

Joseph Schildkraut *Kenneth Paulton* • Jetta Goudal *Malena Paulton* • Vera Reynolds *Beth Tyrell* • William Boyd (1) *Jack Moreland* ■ *Dir* Cecil B De Mille [Cecil B DeMille] • *Scr* Beulah Marie Dix, Jeanie Macpherson, from a story by Beulah Marie Dix, from the play by Evelyn Greenleaf Sutherland

Road to Zanzibar ★★★ PG

Musical comedy 1941 · US · BW · 87mins

The first two *Road* pictures (this is the second after Singapore) seem somewhat disappointing now in light of the wonderful three that followed (Morocco, Utopia and Rio), but this still has Bob Hope, Bing Crosby and Dorothy Lamour, some zany gags and some catchy tunes, so it more than gets by. Bing and Bob are carnival performers, on the run from a gangster to whom they sold a phoney diamond mine, and their ensuing trek through the jungle with Lamour and Una Merkel cues some great satire on jungle pictures in general. TV

Bob Hope *"Fearless" Frazier* • Bing Crosby *Chuck Reardon* • Dorothy Lamour *Donna Latour* • Una Merkel *Julia Quimby* • Eric Blore *Charles Kimble* ■ *Dir* Victor Schertzinger • *Scr* Frank Butler, Don Hartman, from the story *Find Colonel Fawcett* by Don Hartman, Sy Bartlett

Road Trip ★★ 15

Comedy 2000 · US · Colour · 93mins

There are some raunchy and hilarious moments as student Breckin Meyer races from New York to Texas with his friends to avert a disaster that could ruin his relationship with his girlfriend, but the movie is still a jumbled mess. Several lengthy and redundant subplots keep diverting attention from the central story, and the characters come across as stereotypes, sharing the same "wild college guy" persona. The exception is Tom Green, whose insane character is hilarious. KB DVD

Breckin Meyer *Josh* • Seann William Scott *E L* • Amy Smart *Beth* • Paulo Costanzo *Rubin* • DJ Qualls *Kyle* • Rachel Blanchard *Tiffany* ■ *Dir* Todd Phillips • *Scr* Todd Phillips, Scot Armstrong

Roadblock ★★★

Crime thriller 1951 · US · BW · 73mins

Playing against type, square-jawed Charles McGraw gives a surprisingly layered performance in this claustrophobic *film noir*. McGraw is a hard-working insurance investigator, who becomes involved in a million-dollar mail robbery in order to finance new wife Joan Dixon's expensive tastes. Cinematographer Nicholas Musuraca's dank cityscapes give the film both its atmosphere and its sense of middle-class malaise. DP

Charles McGraw *Joe Peters* • Joan Dixon *Diane* • Lowell Gilmore *Kendall Webb* • Louis Jean Heydt *Harry Miller* • Milburn Stone *Egan* • Joseph Crehan *Thompson* • Joe Forte *Brissard* ■ *Dir* Harold Daniels • *Scr* Steve Fisher, George Bricker, from a story by Richard Landau, Geoffrey Holmes

Roadflower ★★★ 18

Thriller 1994 · US · Colour · 85mins

This intriguing action thriller boasts a high quality, if eclectic, cast. Christopher Lambert is the head of a family driving across the Nevada desert who find themselves locked in combat with a gang of psychos led by Craig Scheffer. Lambert is a tad unconvincing as the humble businessman, but there are unlikely, if solid, supporting performances. JF. Contains violence and swearing.

Christopher Lambert *Jack* • Craig Sheffer *Cliff* • David Arquette *Bobby* • Joseph Gordon-Levitt *Richie* • Adrienne Shelly *Red* • Michelle Forbes *Helen* • Josh Brolin *Tom* • Christopher McDonald *Glen* • Alexondra Lee *Ashley* ■ *Dir* Deran Sarafian • *Scr* Tedi Sarafian

Roadhouse 66 ★★ 18

Comedy drama 1984 · US · Colour · 89mins

A youth movie, set over Labor Day weekend on the mythical Route 66. Willem Dafoe plays a cool dude who hitches a ride with University dropout Judge Reinhold. When their car collapses in a one-horse Arizona town, they hang out with the locals, cause some trouble, play pool and finally enter a drag race. Almost every cliché of the youth movie is tossed into the blender, together with a non-stop soundtrack of jukebox faves. AT

Willem Dafoe *Johnny Harte* • Judge Reinhold *Beckman Hallsgood Jr* • Kaaren Lee *Jesse Duran* • Kate Vernon *Melissa Duran* • Stephen Elliott *Sam* • Alan Autry *Hoot* ■ *Dir* John Mark Robinson • *Scr* Galen Lee, George Simpson, from a story by Galen Lee

The Roadhouse Murder ★★★

Crime drama 1932 · US · BW · 71mins

This terrific idea for a movie has journalist Eric Linden deciding to incriminate himself as a killer for a series of newspaper articles, only to find that it's not that easy to extricate himself from the morass of his own making. B-feature stuff, of course, but co-written by real-life journalist Gene Fowler who brings plenty of life and colour to the proceedings. Linden is an acceptably harassed hero and Dorothy Jordan a fine hapless heroine. TS

Eric Linden *Chick Brian* • Dorothy Jordan *Mary Agnew* • Bruce Cabot *Fred Dykes* • Phyllis Clare *Louise Rand* ■ *Dir* J Walter Ruben • *Scr* J Walter Ruben, Gene Fowler, from the play *Lame Dog Inn* by Ladislaus Bus-Fekete, from a novel by Maurice Level

Roadie ★★ 12

Music comedy 1980 · US · Colour · 102mins

The biggest novelty in this movie is the inspired casting of pop melodramatist Meat Loaf as a wide-eyed innocent lost in the corruptible world of rock 'n' roll. Meat Loaf brings an engaging credibility to the role of a Texas mechanic-turned-roadie, who strikes up an unlikely friendship with a groupie who's been saving herself for Alice Cooper. Robert Altman protégé Alan Rudolph punctuates this straightforward tale with tiresome bar-room brawls and noisy knockabout comic moments made bearable only by the occasional celebrity cameo. RS DVD

Meat Loaf *Travis W Redfish* • Kaki Hunter *Lola Bouilliabase* • Art Carney *Corpus C Redfish* • Gailard Sartain *BB Muldoon* • Don Cornelius *Mohammed Johnson* • Rhonda Bates *Alice Poo* • Richard Marion *George* • Sonny Davis [Sonny Carl Davis] *Bird* • Joe Spano *Ace* ■ *Dir* Alan Rudolph • *Scr* Big Boy Medlin, Michael Ventura, from a story by Big Boy Medlin, Michael Ventura, Zalman King, Alan Rudolph

Roadkill ★★★

Road movie 1989 · Can · BW · 80mins

In this road movie with a difference, Valerie Buhagiar does remarkably well in the role of a naive assistant sent by an unscrupulous promoter to find a rock band that's gone missing on tour. En route, she encounters a taxi driver who bores everyone with tales of his days as a roadie, an eccentric documentary-maker and a maniac who wants to put Canadian serial killing on the map. The episodic structure hinders character development, but it also prevents any situation from outstaying its welcome. DP

Valerie Buhagiar *Ramona* • Gerry Quigley *Roy Seth* • Larry Hudson *Buddie* • Bruce McDonald *Bruce Shack* • Shaun Bowring *Matthew* • Don McKellar *Russel* • Mark Tarantino *Luke* ■ *Dir* Bruce McDonald • *Scr* Don McKellar

Roadkill ★★★ 15

Road movie thriller
2001 · US · Colour · 93mins

College kid Paul Walker is on a road trip to pick up pal Leelee Sobieski, after taking a detour to bail his reckless brother (Steve Zahn) out of jail. Unfortunately, a late night prank with their CB radio gets the brothers on the wrong side of an unseen trucker, and it's not long before the boys realise they're being chased by the clearly unhinged driver. This is a nicely paced and suspenseful teen movie, with a smart script and solid performances. JB DVD

Steve Zahn *Fuller Thomas* • Paul Walker *Lewis Thomas* • Leelee Sobieski *Venna* • Jessica Bowman *Charlotte* • Stuart Stone *Danny* • Basil Wallace *Car salesman* ■ *Dir* John Dahl • *Scr* Clay Tarver, JJ Abrams [Jeffrey Abrams]

Roadracers ★★ PG

Action drama 1958 · US · BW · 73mins

Journeyman Arthur Swerdloff unfussily directs this car-racing action film for American International Pictures, the byword for exploitation cinema in the 1950s. Hot-rodder Joel Lawrence is forced to pursue his ambitions in Europe after his father bans him from the track for causing a death through reckless driving. However, he's soon back Stateside to take on Skip Ward to secure both Grand Prix glory and his true love. DP DVD

Joel Lawrence *Rob* • Marian Collier *Liz* • Skip Ward *Greg* • Sally Fraser *Joanie* • Mason Alan Dinehart [Alan Dinehart III] *Kit* • Irene Windust *Alice* • John Shay *Harry* ■ *Dir* Arthur Swerdloff • *Scr* Stanley Kallis, Edward J Lakso

Roadracers ★★ 15

Drama 1994 · US · Colour · 89mins

Made as part of a series of TV remakes of teen B-movies from the 1950s, Robert Rodriguez keeps his tongue firmly in his cheek as he recounts the story of cool singer David Arquette, who finds himself caught between a tough gang leader and a cruel detective. It's a tad indulgent and the film's kitsch appeal begins to fade, but it's enthusiastically played and Rodriguez never lets the pace slacken. JF. Contains swearing.

David Arquette *Dude Delaney* • Salma Hayek *Donna* • John Hawkes *Nixer* • Jason Wiles *Teddy* • William Sadler *Sarge* • O'Neal Compton *J T* ■ *Dir* Robert Rodriguez • *Scr* Robert Rodriguez, Tommy Nix

Roads to Koktebel ★★★★ 12

Drama 2003 · Rus · Colour · 102mins

Lovingly photographed by Shandor Berkeshi, the feature debut of co-directors Boris Khlebnikov and Alexei Popogrebsky is a cross between a folkloric road movie and a post-Communist critique of a once proud nation's struggle to come to terms with the realities of freedom. An eccentric encounter with a drunken hermit and a romantic interlude with a kindly doctor punctuate aviation engineer Igor Chernevich and Gleb Puskepalis's journey south to the Crimea. But it's the taciturn father-son relationship that proves most intriguing, especially once the 11-year-old Puskepalis begins to appreciate that promises are made to be broken. Measured, evocative and melancholic. DP. In Russian with English subtitles. DVD

Igor Chernevich *Father* • Gleb Puskepalis *Boy* • Agrippina Steklova *Doctor* • Alexander Ilyin *Truck driver* • Vladimir Kucherenko *Dacha owner* ■ *Dir/Scr* Boris Khlebnikov, Alexei Popogrebsky

Roads to the South ★★

Political drama
1978 · Fr/Sp · Colour · 100mins

This downbeat drama about the growing disillusionment of an old-style socialist comes across as an old man's lament for past times and missed opportunities. Originally intended for the small screen, Joseph Losey's film has touching moments, particularly when Yves Montand and his young lover, Miou-Miou, head back to Spain on the death of Franco. But, mostly, it's an interminably polemical picture, which offers few historical or contemporary insights. DP. In French with English subtitles.

Yves Montand *Larrea* • Miou-Miou *Julia* • France Lambiotte *Eve* • Laurent Malet *Laurent* ■ *Dir* Joseph Losey • *Scr* Joseph Losey, Patricia Losey, Jorge Semprun

Roadside Prophets ★★★ 15

Road movie comedy drama
1992 · US · Colour · 92mins

Ultra-hip road movie, with many of the leading roles acted out by cutting-edge rock, rap and folk musicians. John Doe, of LA punk band X, and Beastie Boy rapper Adam Horovitz play bikers who hit the highway to deliver a dead friend's ashes for scattering in a remote Nevada town. En route, they encounter deadbeats, philosophers, fighters and loose women. The eclectic cast also includes psychedelia guru Timothy Leary, folk singer Arlo Guthrie, and actors John Cusack and David Carradine. Highly rated by US critics, this manic ride of a movie maybe doesn't push quite the same buttons on this side of the Atlantic. DA

John Doe *Joe Mosely* • Adam Horovitz *Sam* • Arlo Guthrie *Harvey* • David Carradine *Othello Jones* • John Cusack *Caspar* • David Anthony Marshall *Dave Coleman* • Don Cheadle *Happy Days manager* • Timothy Leary *Salvadore* ■ *Dir* Abbe Wool • *Scr* Abbe Wool, from an idea by David Swinson

Roar ★★★ PG

Adventure 1981 · US · Colour · 96mins

The title refers to the lions who star in this sadly self-conscious travelogue featuring wild animals and film-maker Noel Marshall. He's a biological researcher who sends for his family – including his real-life then-wife Tippi Hedren – to come stay at his ranch in the African Bush. That's about all, apart from the yelps of delight from the young humans as they communicate with the oh-so-friendly beasts. Cameraman Jan De Bont went on to direct both *Speed* and *Twister* TH

R

Noel Marshall *Hank* • Tippi Hedren *Madeleine* • John Marshall *John* • Jerry Marshall *Jerry* • Melanie Griffith *Melanie* • Kyalo Mativo *Mativo* • Frank Tom *Frank* ■ *Dir/Scr* Noel Marshall

The Roaring Twenties ★★★★ PG

Crime drama 1939 · US · BW · 101mins

Despite its plentiful shoot-outs, this is not so much a gangster movie but a morality story about a First World War veteran who tries to go straight, then yields to the lure of bootlegging and other crimes. James Cagney is on terrific form as the good guy turned bad and Humphrey Bogart is a vicious hoodlum. Raoul Walsh skilfully creates a convincing Prohibition world of smoky speakeasies and gleaming black cars parked in dark alleys, a world of endless opportunity and rampant corruption, though the script is a typical Warner Bros blend of slang and sermon. AT DVD

James Cagney *Eddie Bartlett* • Humphrey Bogart *George Hally* • Jeffrey Lynn *Lloyd Hart* • Priscilla Lane *Jean Sherman* • Gladys George *Panama Smith* • Frank McHugh *Danny Green* ■ *Dir* Raoul Walsh • *Scr* Jerry Wald, Richard Macaulay, Robert Rossen, from a story by Mark Hellinger

Rob Roy ★★★★ 15

Biographical adventure
1995 · US · Colour · 132mins

Mel Gibson may have grabbed the Oscar glory for *Braveheart*, but this rip-snorting early 18th-century tartan romp is a lot more fun. Liam Neeson plays the principled Robert MacGregor, who becomes the reluctant rebel Rob Roy when his money is stolen and his wife (Jessica Lange) is raped by evil English aristocrat Tim Roth. Neeson is suitably heroic, but Roth is a diabolical delight, and he's matched by fellow villains John Hurt and Brian Cox. Scottish-born director Michael Caton-Jones makes striking use of the rugged locations and stages the action sequences with robust glee. Terrific stuff. JF. Contains violence and swearing. DVD

Liam Neeson *Robert MacGregor* • Jessica Lange *Mary of Comar* • John Hurt *Marquis of Montrose* • Tim Roth *Archie Cunningham* • Eric Stoltz *McDonald* • Andrew Keir *Argyll* • Brian Cox *Killearn* • Brian McCardie *Alasdair* • Gilbert Martin *Guthrie* • Vicki Masson *Betty* ■ *Dir* Michael Caton-Jones • *Scr* Alan Sharp

Rob Roy, the Highland Rogue ★★ U

Historical adventure
1953 · UK/US · Colour · 81mins

Heavy on starch and lacing, this stiff biographical account of the 18th-century Scots clansman is a reminder of the days when Disney would travel to these shores, re-write a bit of history, and provide work for half the British film industry in the process. Richard Todd and Glynis Johns head a cast which also includes anyone who was anyone in 1950s British cinema. DA

Richard Todd *Rob Roy MacGregor* • Glynis Johns *Helen Mary MacGregor* • James Robertson-Justice *Duke of Argyll* • Michael Gough *Duke of Montrose* • Jean Taylor-Smith *Lady Glengyll* • Geoffrey Keen *Killearn* • Finlay Currie *Hamish MacPherson* • Archie Duncan *Dougal MacGregor* ■ *Dir* Harold French • *Scr* Lawrence E Watkin

Robbery ★★★ PG

Crime drama 1967 · UK · Colour · 109mins

Following the Great Train Robbery of 1963, several film projects were announced, but this is the only British production to have got off the ground. It never fulfils the promise of its opening car chase, during which one vehicle mows down a policeman and a procession of schoolchildren. Thereafter, the plotting and execution of the robbery seems rather trite, and the fictitious characters are not half as colourful as the real-life Ronnie Biggs and company. But there is more action towards the end, enough to impress Hollywood, who summoned Peter Yates to direct *Bullitt*. DM

Stanley Baker *Paul Clifton* • Joanna Pettet *Kate Clifton* • James Booth *Inspector Langdon* • Frank Finlay *Robinson* • Barry Foster *Frank* • William Marlowe *Dave* ■ *Dir* Peter Yates • *Scr* Edward Boyd, Peter Yates, George Markstein, from a story by Gerald Wilson

Robbery under Arms ★★ U

Crime adventure 1957 · US · Colour · 99mins

This screen-telling of Rolf Boldrewood's popular tale about bushranger Captain Starlight is saved only by Peter Finch in the lead and the panoramic photography of Harry Waxman. Away from the savage beauty of the Australian wilderness, former documentary film-maker Jack Lee drains all the drama from the round of robberies, escapes and betrayals that engulf brothers, David McCallum and Ronald Lewis. DP

Peter Finch *Captain Starlight* • Ronald Lewis *Dick Marston* • David McCallum *Jim Marston* • Maureen Swanson *Kate Morrison* • Laurence Naismith *Ben Marston* • Jill Ireland *Jean* • Jean Anderson *Ma* ■ *Dir* Jack Lee • *Scr* WP Lipscomb, Alexander Baron, from the novel by Rolf Boldrewood

Robbie Williams: Nobody Someday ★★ 15

Concert documentary
2001 · UK · Colour and BW · 94mins

This routine documentary of Robbie Williams's last European tour delivers no great musical moments, particularly as the sound is so flat and processed. And it offers no great insights into a rock 'n' roller's life on the road. So what makes it just about worth watching? In a nutshell, Williams himself. The cameras catch him shortly after he cleaned up his act. Free from drink and drugs, the singer's sole remaining demon seems to be his own self-doubt as he agonises over whether he really wants to be a rock star. The remaining footage charts the petulant pop star's mood swings and his eventual realisation that maybe being a girl-mobbed multimillionaire isn't that bad after all. DA DVD

Dir/Scr Brian Hill • *Cinematographer* Simon Niblett, Michael Timney

The Robe ★★★ U

Religious drama 1953 · US · Colour · 133mins

Best known as the first film to be released in CinemaScope, this is a plodding, pious epic, with Richard Burton as the Roman officer who wins Christ's robe in a game of dice during the Crucifixion. The torn and bloody piece works its magic and, before long, Burton and Jean Simmons are hauled before the crazed Roman emperor Caligula. It's awkwardly directed by Henry Koster and scripted as if by a committee anxious not to offend any race or creed. But there are compensations: Burton is handsome in a mini-skirt and Jay Robinson makes an unforgettably melodramatic Caligula. Victor Mature was called on for the sequel, *Demetrius and the Gladiators*. AT DVD

Richard Burton *Marcellus Gallio* • Jean Simmons *Diana* • Victor Mature *Demetrius* • Michael Rennie *Peter* • Jay Robinson *Caligula* • Dean Jagger *Justus* • Torin Thatcher *Senator Gallio* • Richard Boone *Pilate* • Betta St John *Miriam* • Ernest Thesiger *Emperor Tiberius* ■ *Dir* Henry Koster • *Scr* Albert Maltz (uncredited), Philip Dunne, from the novel by Lloyd C Douglas, adapted by Gina Kaus • *Costume Designer* Charles LeMaire, Emile Santiago • *Cinematographer* Leon Shamroy

Robert Altman's Jazz '34: Remembrances of Kansas City Swing ★★★★

Music documentary
1996 · US · Colour · 72mins

Director Robert Altman's 1996 film, *Kansas City* – a jazz-tinged melodrama about a corrupt politician and a gangster – was notable if only for some remarkable 1930s music as arranged by the innovative John Cale. This documentary is the offspring of that movie, featuring sessions recorded on the set of the earlier film. With *Jazz '34*'s pumping, grinding blues all set to elevate the spirits, it's a shame that Altman hadn't done a better job on the original move. TH

Harry Belafonte *Narrator* ■ *Dir* Robert Altman • *Production Designer* Stephen Altman

Robert et Robert ★★★

Comedy drama 1978 · Fr · Colour · 105mins

Often dismissed for promoting style over content, Claude Lelouch is still capable of producing hugely entertaining films. While this odd couple comedy may not have anything resounding to say about the modern French male, it's still full of good-natured humour and spirited performances. The pairing of Charles Denner and Jacques Villeret, as the eponymous bachelors who embark on a series of comic misadventures, is inspired, with the former's outgoing cabbie contrasting splendidly with the latter's timid everyman. DP. In French with English subtitles.

Charles Denner *Robert Goldman* • Jacques Villeret *Robert Villiers* • Jean-Claude Brialy *Manager* • Germaine Montero *Madame Goldman* • Régine *Madame Villiers* • Macha Méril *Agathe* ■ *Dir/Scr* Claude Lelouch

Roberta ★★★ U

Musical romantic comedy
1935 · US · BW · 102mins

Fred Astaire and Gingers Rogers and Jerome Kern's ravishing 18-carat score are the attractions of this otherwise quite silly musical, adapted from the Broadway show. The plot, such as it is, has he-man footballer, Randolph Scott inheriting a chic, Paris fashion house. Designer Irene Dunne (who renders *Smoke Gets in Your Eyes* most touchingly) falls for him. But it's the musical numbers performed by Fred and Ginger on the verge of mega-stardom that has kept the film alive. The rich cornucopia of ballads also includes the Oscar-nominated and enduring *Lovely to Look At* from which the 1952 remake took its name. RK

Irene Dunne *Princess Stephanie* • Fred Astaire *Huck Haines* • Ginger Rogers *Comtesse "Tanka" Scharwenka aka Lizzie Gatz* • Randolph Scott *John Kent* • Helen Westley *Roberta aka Minnie* • Victor Varconi *Prince Ladislaw* • Claire Dodd *Sophie Teale* • Luis Alberni *Alexander Petrovich Moskovitch Voyda* • Lucille Ball *Model* ■ *Dir* William A Seiter • *Scr* Jane Murfin, Sam Mintz, Allan Scott, from the musical by Jerome Kern, Otto Harbach, from the novel *Gowns by Roberta* by Alice Duer Miller

Roberto Succo ★★★★ 15

Crime drama based on a true story
2000 · Fr/Swi · Colour · 119mins

The young man who murdered his parents while still a teenager and later embarked on a random killing spree in southern France during the 1980s is shown in a harsh light, but this compelling adaptation refrains from total condemnation of its protagonist. Making exemplary use of the often hostile terrain and its small-town locales, director Cédric Kahn's only misjudgment is in lingering on detective Patrick Dell'Isola's manhunt when the main fascination lies in the psychological instability of the mercurial Stefano Cassetti (an utterly mesmerising performance) and his fumbling relationship with his adoring teenage lover, Isild le Besco. DP. In French and Italian with English subtitles. Contains violence and swearing. DVD

Stefano Cassetti *"Kurt"/Roberto Succo* • Isild Le Besco *Léa* • Patrick Dell'Isola *Major Thomas* • Vincent Deneriaz *Denis* • Aymeric Chauffert *Delaunay* ■ *Dir* Cédric Kahn • *Scr* Cédric Kahn, from the non-fiction book *Je Te Tu – Histoire Vrai de Roberto Succo* by Pascale Froment

Robin and Marian ★★★★ PG

Adventure 1976 · UK · Colour · 102mins

An older and disillusioned Robin Hood returns from the Crusades to find Sherwood empty of outlaws, Marian in a nunnery and the Sheriff of Nottingham still fiddling the books. James Goldman's script has a wonderful way with satire and myth-mongering, while Richard Lester has the sharpest eye for historical detail. Audrey Hepburn was lured out of retirement to play Marian and she is exquisite, but it's Sean Connery's gruff, greybeard performance that ennobles, rather than dominates the picture. Great support, too, from Robert Shaw's Sheriff and Ronnie Barker's perfectly judged "heavy relief" as Friar Tuck. What a pity this gorgeous, masterly elegy for a vanished age of chivalry flopped at the box-office. AT DVD

Sean Connery *Robin Hood* • Audrey Hepburn *Maid Marian* • Robert Shaw *Sheriff of Nottingham* • Richard Harris *King Richard* • Nicol Williamson *Little John* • Denholm Elliott *Will Scarlett* • Kenneth Haigh *Sir Ranulf* • Ronnie Barker *Friar Tuck* • Ian Holm *King John* • Bill Maynard *Mercadier* • Esmond Knight *Old defender* ■ *Dir* Richard Lester • *Scr* James Goldman • *Cinematographer* David Watkin

Robin and the 7 Hoods ★★★★ U

Comedy 1964 · US · Colour · 117mins

This musical crime comedy from veteran director Gordon Douglas was the final fling of Frank Sinatra's Rat Pack. It's Robin Hood in Prohibition-era Chicago, with gangsters battling for control of the city. Sinatra introduces *My Kind of Town (Chicago Is ...)*, Bing Crosby and Dean Martin join him in *Style*, and Peter Falk, Barbara Rush (as Marian) and Edward G Robinson, no less, decorate the fringes. Funny, irreverent and very enjoyable, this movie is a warm-hearted treat. TS

Frank Sinatra *Robbo* • Dean Martin *Little John* • Sammy Davis Jr *Will* • Bing Crosby *Allen A Dale* • Peter Falk *Guy Gisborne* • Barbara Rush *Marian* • Edward G Robinson *Big Jim* • Victor Buono *Sheriff Potts* • Hank Henry *Six Seconds* • Allen Jenkins *Vermin* • Jack LaRue *Tomatoes* ■ *Dir* Gordon Douglas • *Scr* David R Schwartz, from his story

R

Robin Hood ★★★★ PG

Silent romantic adventure
1922 · US · BW · 117mins

One of the showiest (and slowest) of all the epics starring the actionman of the silents, Douglas Fairbanks. The crowds are imaginitavely handled by director Allan Dwan, with Fairbanks as the eponymous, ever-grinning Robin, swashbuckling his way around Sherwood Forest at the behest of Enid Bennett's Maid Marian. And while Wallace Beery weighs in heavily as Richard the Lion-Hearted, it's Sam De Grasse as Prince John who gives the film's best performance. TH DVD

Douglas Fairbanks *The Earl of Huntington/ Robin Hood* • Wallace Beery *Richard the Lion-Hearted* • Sam De Grasse *Prince John* • Enid Bennett *Lady Marian Fitzwalter* • Paul Dickey *Sir Guy of Gisbourne* • William Lowery *The High Sheriff of Nottingham* • Roy Coulson *The King's Jester* • Willard Louis *Friar Tuck* • Alan

Hale *Little John* ■ *Dir* Allan Dwan • *Scr* Lotta Woods, from a story by Elton Thomas [Douglas Fairbanks] • *Costume Designer* Mitchell Leisen

Robin Hood ★★★★ U

Animated adventure
1973 · US · Colour · 79mins

This Disney cartoon may not have the heart or the memorable songs of the studio's classics, but the result is still a pleasant and entertaining diversion for children. Here, it's Robin Hood and his Merry Men-agerie, as all the legendary Nottingham characters have been drawn as animals in a delightful retelling of the "rob from the rich, give to the poor" Sherwood Forest tale. Villainous Prince John (voiced by Peter Ustinov) and slimy Sir Hiss (Terry-Thomas) provide the funniest moments, while the archery contest-turned-American football match is an action highlight. AJ DVD

Brian Bedford *Robin Hood* • Phil Harris *Little John* • Monica Evans *Maid Marian* • Peter Ustinov *Prince John* • Terry-Thomas *Sir Hiss* • Andy Devine *Friar Tuck* ■ *Dir* Wolfgang Reitherman • *Scr* Larry Clemmons, from a story and the characters created by Ken Anderson

Robin Hood ★★★★ PG

Adventure 1990 · UK/US · Colour · 99mins

This version of the classic tale had the misfortune to come out around the same time as Kevin Costner's epic and unsurprisingly was overshadowed by that Hollywood blockbuster. It's a shame because this, in many ways, is a better film. Patrick Bergin sparkles in the title role, doing battle with an enjoyable trio of baddies (Jeroen Krabbé, Jurgen Prochnow and Edward Fox), while Uma Thurman makes for a rather sympathetic Maid Marian. Director John Irvin authentically re-creates the murky medieval settings, while staging some grand action sequences and rousing swordfights. JF. Contains some violence.

Patrick Bergin *Robert Hode/"Robin Hood"* • Uma Thurman *Maid Marian* • Jürgen Prochnow *Sir Miles Folcanet* • Edward Fox *Prince John* • Jeroen Krabbé *Baron Daguerre* • Owen Teale *Will Redding "Will Scarlett"* • David Morrissey *Little John* • Alex Norton *Harry* • Gabrielle Reidy *Lily* • Jeff Nuttall *Friar Tuck* ■ *Dir* John Irvin • *Scr* Mark Allen Smith, John McGrath

R

Robin Hood: Men in Tights ★★ PG

Comedy 1993 · US · Colour · 99mins

While it's sad that Mel Brooks has hung up his megaphone, there's a certain sense of merciful release, as his last pictures veered from poor to downright awful. This Sherwood spoof has the occasional flash of vintage Brooks and wonderfully po-faced performances from Cary Elwes as Robin and Amy Yasbeck as Marian. On the down side are Roger Rees's ghastly Sheriff of Rottingham, the untidy structure and the fact that the bawdy gags are more notable for their antiquity than their quality. DP. Contains swearing. DVD

Cary Elwes *Robin Hood* • Richard Lewis *Prince John* • Roger Rees *Sheriff of Rottingham* • Amy Yasbeck *Marian* • Mark Blankfield *Blinkin* • Dave Chappelle *Achoo* • Isaac Hayes *Asneeze* • Megan Cavanagh *Broomhilde* • Eric Allan Kramer *Little John* • Matthew Poretta *Will Scarlet O'Hara* • Tracey Ullman *Latrine* • Patrick Stewart *King Richard* • Dom DeLuise *Don Giovanni* • Mel Brooks *Rabbi Tuckman* ■ *Dir* Mel Brooks • *Scr* Mel Brooks, Evan Chandler, J David Shapiro, from a story by J David Shapiro, Evan Chandler

The Robin Hood of El Dorado ★★★

Biographical drama 1936 · US · BW · 85mins

Spurred by the success of *Viva Villa!*, its biopic of Pancho Villa, MGM turned out this vigorous account of the life and death in early California of another legendary figure, Joaquin Murrieta. He is depicted as the peaceful farmer who is branded a bandit, after avenging the death of his wife at the hands of four gringos. Former Cisco Kid Warner Baxter takes the role and William A Wellman's typically uneven direction veers from hard-hitting action, to poetic lyricism and sheer sentimentality. At least 11 writers toiled on the script (only three were credited). AE

Warner Baxter *Joaquin Murrieta* • Ann Loring *Juanita de la Cuesta* • Bruce Cabot *Bill Warren* • Margo *Rosita* • J Carrol Naish *Three fingered Jack* • Soledad Jimenez [Soledad Jiminez] *Madre Murrieta* • Carlos de Valdez *Jose Murrieta* • Edgar Kennedy *Sheriff Judd* ■ *Dir* William A Wellman • *Scr* William A Wellman, Joseph Calleia, Melvin Levy, from a novel by Walter Noble

Robin Hood: Prince of Thieves ★★★★ PG

Action adventure
1991 · US · Colour · 148mins

Buckles are truly swashed and derring-do effectively done in Kevin Reynolds's 12th-century adventure, which simply sets out to entertain handsomely and does so with a great deal of dash, flash and panache. Alan Rickman is a joy to behold as the panto-styled Sheriff of Nottingham, while Morgan Freeman's cultured Moor (Robin's early saviour) is a commanding, if unlikely, medieval presence. Kevin Costner is more "Indiana Hood" than the Locksley lad of yore in this popcorn epic of romp and circumstance. Director Reynolds deserves the most praise for disguising such overfamiliar events with imaginative staging and a roving camera. AJ. Contains swearing, violence and brief nudity. DVD

Kevin Costner *Robin of Locksley/Robin Hood* • Mary Elizabeth Mastrantonio *Maid Marian* • Alan Rickman *Sheriff of Nottingham* • Morgan Freeman *Azeem* • Christian Slater *Will Scarlett* • Geraldine McEwan *Mortianna* • Micheal McShane *Friar Tuck* • Brian Blessed *Lord Locksley* • Michael Wincott *Guy of Gisborne* • Nick Brimble *Little John* • Soo Drouet *Fanny* • Sean Connery *King Richard* ■ *Dir* Kevin Reynolds • *Scr* Pen Densham, John Watson, from a story by Pen Densham

Robinson Crusoe on Mars ★★★★ U

Science-fiction drama
1964 · US · Colour · 105mins

Once you get passed the ridiculous title this is a wholly satisfactory and intelligent slice of pulp sci-fi from Byron Haskin, director of *The War of the Worlds*. Shot in the bleak hostility of California's Death Valley, this is an innovative retelling of the classic Defoe tale, centering on astronaut Paul Mantee's survival challenges following a crash-landing that leaves him stranded on the red planet. Haskin wisely bypasses flashy effects to concentrate on the human element, notably the growing relationship between Mantee and the alien he rescues from a slave ship. RS

Paul Mantee *Cmdr Christopher "Kit" Draper* • Vic Lundin *Friday* • Adam West *Col Dan McReady* ■ *Dir* Byron Haskin • *Scr* John C Higgins, Ib Melchior, from the novel *The Life and Strange Surprising Adventures of Robinson Crusoe* by Daniel Defoe • *Cinematographer* William C Hoch • *Special Effects* Lawrence W Butler

Robinson in Space ★★★★ PG

Documentary drama
1997 · UK · Colour · 78mins

Patrick Keiller was inspired to make this follow-up to 1994's *London* by the closure of the old Morris Motors works in Oxford. Visiting factories and ports the length and breadth of the country, he seeks to gauge the impact of 18-years of Tory rule on Britain's traditional manufacturing industries and assess how far we have become a service economy. Complete with a voiceover from Paul Scofield that blends socio-economic data, literary references and the quirky opinions of his fictional companion, Robinson, the film has more of a political agenda than its predecessor, but is every bit as compelling. DP DVD

Paul Scofield *Narrator* ■ *Dir/Scr* Patrick Keiller

RoboCop ★★★★★ 18

Satirical science-fiction thriller
1987 · US · Colour · 102mins

Hi-tech meets *High Noon* in Dutch director Paul Verhoeven's deft science-fiction masterpiece, amply delivering on both violent action and satirical fronts. Peter Weller gives a great mime performance as the Detroit cop of the near future resurrected as a cyborg, who goes head-hunting the sadistic gang responsible for his plight as his human memory begins to return. But it's Verhoeven's scabrous dissection of American social issues, trashy sitcom culture and corporate greed that makes this a subversive and thought-provoking edge-of-the-seat epic. AJ. Contains violence, swearing, drug abuse, brief nudity. DVD

Peter Weller *Murphy/RoboCop* • Nancy Allen *Officer Anne Lewis* • Daniel O'Herlihy [Dan O'Herlihy] *Old man* • Ronny Cox *Dick Jones* • Kurtwood Smith *Clarence Boddicker* • Miguel Ferrer *Robert Morton* • Robert DoQui *Sergeant Reed* • Ray Wise *Leon* ■ *Dir* Paul Verhoeven • *Scr* Edward Neumeier, Michael Miner

RoboCop 2 ★★★ 18

Science-fiction thriller
1990 · US · Colour · 116mins

Peter Weller returns as the cyborg policeman patrolling the mean streets of Detroit. Daniel O'Herlihy, ostensibly the good tycoon from the first film, becomes the bad guy this time around, teaming up with psycho Tom Noonan to destroy his company's creation. It's once again a spectacularly violent affair and the satirical news items still provide a chuckle or two, but it lacks the original's gloriously black excess. JF. Contains swearing, violence. DVD

Peter Weller *RoboCop* • Nancy Allen *Officer Anne Lewis* • Belinda Bauer *Dr Juliette Faxx* • Daniel O'Herlihy [Dan O'Herlihy] *Old man* • Tom Noonan *Cain* • Gabriel Damon *Hob* • Willard Pugh *Mayor Kuzak* • Stephen Lee *Duffy* ■ *Dir* Irvin Kershner • *Scr* Frank Miller, Walon Green, from a story by Frank Miller, from characters created by Edward Neumeier, Michael Miner

RoboCop 3 ★★★ 15

Science-fiction thriller
1993 · US · Colour · 104mins

Robert Burke replaces Peter Weller as the unstoppable cyborg cop in this more comedy driven, and far less violent, futuristic fantasy from director Fred Dekker. The mechanised flatfoot this time defends the downtrodden homeless when an amoral Japanese magnate decides to clean up downtown Detroit in order to build a luxury apartment complex. Well directed and written with a firm eye on the family TV series the concept eventually became. AJ. Contains violence and swearing. DVD

Robert John Burke [Robert Burke] *RoboCop/Alex J Murphy* • Nancy Allen *Officer Anne Lewis* • Rip Torn *Merrit W Morton, CEO* • John Castle *Paul McDaggett* • Jill Hennessy *Dr Marie Lazarus* • CCH Pounder *Bertha* • Mako *Kanemitsu* ■ *Dir* Fred Dekker • *Scr* Frank Miller, Fred Dekker, from a story by Frank Miller, from the characters created by Edward Neumeier, Michael Miner

Robot Jox ★★ 15

Science-fiction action
1989 · US · Colour · 80mins

In a post-nuclear world of banished warfare, nations settle scores with one another via televised games, in which representative heroes battle it out while inside hulking, transformer-like robots. The fascinating premise is sadly let down by a scrawny budget and script to match. While the robot miniature work is effective, the rest of the film has a shoddy, cheap look. RS

Gary Graham *Achilles* • Anne-Marie Johnson *Athena* • Paul Koslo *Alexander* • Robert Sampson *Commissioner Jameson* • Danny Kamekona *Doctor Matsumoto* • Hilary Mason *Professor Laplace* • Michael Alldredge *Tex Conway* ■ *Dir* Stuart Gordon • *Scr* Joe Haldeman, from a story by Stuart Gordon

Robot Monster ★ U

Science fiction 1953 · US · BW · 62mins

After *Plan 9 from Outer Space*, this is the best known bad movie in the science-fiction genre. The last six human survivors in existence struggle against the dreaded Ro-Man (a man dressed in a gorilla suit and a plastic diving helmet), whose race has destroyed the planet with their "calcinator ray". Made for next-to-nothing in four days, and padded out with bizarre stock footage montages, this legendary trash masterpiece is hilariously threadbare. AJ

George Nader *Roy* • Claudia Barrett *Alice* • Selena Royle *Mother* • Gregory Moffett *Johnny* • John Mylong *Professor* • Pamela Paulson *Carla* • George Barrows *Ro-Man* ■ *Dir* Phil Tucker • *Scr* Wyott Ordung

Robot Wars ★ PG

Science-fiction western
1993 · US · Colour · 69mins

This dire, futuristic tale may be set in 2041, but it's got the production values of 1970. The stop-frame animation of the giant robot vehicles is passable, but the acting and dialogue ("You're way too negative. You're a walking minus sign.") is beyond bad. Don Michael Paul's Han Solo-esque robot pilot barely has a pulse. Chuck in a co-pilot called Stumpy and some of the shoddiest back projection work ever seen and you have a film of considerable awfulness. JC

Don Michael Paul *Captain Drake* • Barbara Crampton *Dr Leda Fannon* • James Staley *Stumpy* ■ *Dir* Albert Band • *Scr* Jackson Barr, from an idea by Charles Band

Robots ★★★ U

Animated comedy adventure
2005 · US · Colour · 91mins

This visually inventive romp through a world populated entirely by robots uses inspired computer animation to revitalise a familiar story. Leading an eclectic voice cast, Ewan McGregor gives boyish charm to an idealistic small-town robot who journeys to the big city to make his fortune as an inventor. In a crisply created environment that bursts with colour and visual texture, the sci-fi style of the 1950s rubs shoulders with more contemporary designs and landscapes, giving the movie a very attractive sheen. While the comedy is both light and mischievous, some of the movie's in-jokes and references will be too obscure for younger viewers. SF

Ewan McGregor *Rodney Copperbottom* • Halle Berry *Cappy* • Robin Williams *Fender* • Greg Kinnear *Phineas T Ratchet* • Mel Brooks *Bigweld* • Drew Carey *Crank* • Jim Broadbent *Madame Gasket* • Amanda Bynes *Piper* • Jennifer Coolidge *Aunt Fanny* • Stanley Tucci *Herb Copperbottom* • Dianne Wiest *Mrs Copperbottom* ■ *Dir* Chris Wedge, Carlos Saldanha • *Scr* David Lindsay-Abaire, Lowell Ganz, Babaloo Mandel, from a story by Ron Mita, Jim McClain, David Lindsay-Abaire

Rocco and His Brothers ★★★ 15

Drama 1960 · Fr/It · BW · 170mins

A grimly naturalistic subject – peasant family from southern Italy moves to the corrupting urban jungle of Milan – gets the grand operatic treatment from Luchino Visconti, whose initial restraint should have been maintained throughout. Instead, he goes for empty flourishes of over-the-top despair with which Alain Delon seems somewhat uncomfortable. This may be a long haul, but is certainly worth seeing for Renato Salvatori as the brutish elder brother and the accomplished black-and-white photography of Giuseppe Rotunno. TH. In Italian with English subtitles. [VIDEO] DVD

Alain Delon *Rocco Parondi* • Renato Salvatori *Simone Parondi* • Annie Girardot *Nadia* • Katina Paxinou *Rosaria Parondi* • Roger Hanin *Morini* • Paolo Stoppa *Boxing impresario* • Suzy Delair *Luisa* • Claudia Cardinale *Ginetta* ■ *Dir* Luchino Visconti • *Scr* Luchino Visconti, Vasco Pratolini, Suso Cecchi D'Amico, Pasquale Festa Campanile, Massimo Franciosa, Enrico Medioli, Claude Brulé, from a story by Luchino Visconti, Vasco Pratolini, Suso Cecchi D'Amico, from the novel *I Segretti di Milano: il Ponte della Ghisolfa* by Giovanni Testori

Rocinante ★★ PG

Political drama 1986 · UK · Colour · 92mins

After a meaningful conversation about film narrative with an ex-projectionist, recluse John Hurt leaves the derelict cinema where he has been hiding out and hitches a ride to Dartmoor in a truck named Rocinante (a reference to Don Quixote's horse). On his aimless quest he meets political activist Maureen Douglass who, inspired by the 1984 miners' strike, is intent on industrial sabotage. The resulting blend of road movie, British folklore and the Don Quixote myth is a mind-boggling, often inaccessible slice of pretentious art. AJ

John Hurt *Bill* • Maureen Douglass *Jess* • Ian Dury *Jester* • Carol Gillies *Molly* • Jimmy Jewel *Projectionist* ■ *Dir/Scr* Ann Guedes, Eduardo Guedes

The Rock ★★★★ 15

Action thriller 1996 · US · Colour · 140mins

The setting is Alcatraz, which has been taken over by disenchanted general Ed Harris and his crack team of marines, who are threatening to launch deadly poison-gas rockets to contaminate San Francisco. In desperation, the FBI pair chemical warfare expert Nicolas Cage with jailed former SAS man Sean Connery, who – as the only man to ever escape from the notorious island prison – is seen as their best option to break in. Director Michael Bay's boyish enthusiasm for outlandish stunts and carefree destruction is contagious and even the most cynical of viewers will find it difficult not to feel rushes of adrenalin. JF. Contains violence, swearing and a sex scene. [VIDEO] DVD

Sean Connery *John Patrick Mason* • Nicolas Cage *Stanley Goodspeed* • Ed Harris *General Francis X Hummel* • John Spencer *FBI Director Womack* • David Morse *Major Tom Baxter* • William Forsythe *Ernest Paxton* • Michael Biehn *Commander Anderson* • Vanessa Marcil *Carla Pestalozzi* • John C McGinley *Marine Captain Hendrix* ■ *Dir* Michael Bay • *Scr* David Weisberg, Mark Rosner, Douglas S Cook, from a story by David Weisberg, Douglas S Cook

Rock-a-Bye Baby ★★ U

Comedy 1958 · US · Colour · 106mins

A famous movie star (Marilyn Maxwell), whose marriage has been kept secret in order to preserve her glamorous image, gives birth to triplets, another event that needs hushing up, and turns to a lifelong besotted fan, a bachelor, to take care of the infant trio. He is Jerry Lewis, pursuing his post-Dean Martin, solo career and calling on his full repertoire of frenzied lunacy. The effect, without Martin as foil, is akin to being hit on the head with a sandbag, but Lewis addicts should be happy with that. RK

Jerry Lewis *Clayton Poole* • Marilyn Maxwell *Carla Naples* • Connie Stevens *Sandy Naples* • Reginald Gardiner *Harold Herman* • Baccaloni [Salvatore Baccaloni] *Salvatore Naples* • Hans Conried *Mr Wright* • Isobel Elsom *Mrs Van Cleve* • James Gleason *Dr Simkins* ■ *Dir* Frank Tashlin • *Scr* Frank Tashlin, from the play *The Miracle of Morgan's Creek* by Preston Sturges.

Rock-a-Doodle ★★ U

Animated musical
1990 · US · Colour · 71mins

So-so animation from Don Bluth which isn't really a patch on Disney fare or even Bluth's own *Land Before Time* series. It's the tale of Chanticleer, a rooster who accidentally neglects his duty of heralding the arrival of the dawn and so, humiliated, decides to leave his farmyard home. Bizarrely, he ends up in a city, much like Las Vegas and embarks on a career as an Elvis impersonator – events which are unlikely to impress younger viewers a great deal. Misjudged. JB [VIDEO] DVD

Glen Campbell *Chanticleer* • Eddie Deezen *Snipes* • Sandy Duncan *Peepers* • Charles Nelson Reilly *Hunch* • Ellen Greene *Goldie* • Phil Harris *Patou* • Christopher Plummer *The Duke* • Toby Scott Ganger *Edmond* ■ *Dir* Don Bluth • *Scr* David N Weiss, David Steinberg, from a story by Don Bluth, John Pomeroy, TJ Kuenster, Gary Goldman

Rock All Night ★★ PG

Crime drama 1957 · US · BW · 62mins

Fresh from a supporting role in Corman's *Not of This Earth*, Dick Miller landed the lead in this trashy teen crime drama, about a couple of killers who besiege the Cloud Nine rock 'n' roll club. For once playing the good guy, Miller is great value as the nerdy barman who saves the day. The Platters, in their original line-up with Tony Williams and Zola Taylor and at the height of their fame, make the screen sizzle, despite the economy of footage used to film them. A real curio, shot in under a week. DP DVD

Dick Miller *Shorty* • Abby Dalton *Julie* • Robin Morse *Al* • Richard H Cutting *Steve* • Bruno VeSota *Charley* • Chris Alcaide *Angie* ■ *Dir* Roger Corman • *Scr* Charles B Griffith, from the story by David P Harmon

Rock around the Clock ★★★ U

Musical 1956 · US · BW · 74mins

A low-budget movie, directed by Fred F Sears (hardly a name to conjure with) in which disc jockey, Alan Freed discovers a rock band in a village in the faraway hills, and promotes them in New York. And that would be that, except for the fact that the band is Bill Haley and the Comets, and this little film is now history for the effect they had on teen audiences worldwide and on the music business. Boasting an abundance of hits, this rock-pop fest features numerous other artists, including The Platters. RK

Bill Haley *Bill Haley and the Comets* • Alan Freed • Johnny Johnston *Steve Hollis* • Alix Talton *Corinne* • Lisa Gaye *Lisa Johns* • John Archer *Mike Dennis* ■ *Dir* Fred F Sears • *Scr* Robert E Kent, James B Gordon

Rock Hudson's Home Movies ★★★

Documentary 1992 · US · Colour · 63mins

A hip, smart and sassy probe into the uneasy synthesis of homosexuality and the Hollywood star system. Director Mark Rappaport's camp delight features a Rock Hudson look-alike who takes the viewer on a *That's Entertainment*-style journey of cleverly edited film clips from the heart-throb's life, hilariously underlining their gay connotations. Although tinged with a melancholic sadness over the matinée idol's subsequent Aids-related death in 1985, Rappaport's take on Hudson is a far more militant version of the ageing closeted star who, in this post-Queerdom incarnation, never fails to slyly point out an ultra-modern way of assessing his *Pillow Talk* persona. AJ

Eric Farr *Rock Hudson* ■ *Dir/Scr* Mark Rappaport

Rock 'n' Roll Cop ★★★

Police thriller 1994 · HK · Colour · 93mins

Kirk Wong's acclaimed cop film is a touch more thought-provoking than the average "chop socky" movie. When a triad gang decimates a Kowloon gambling joint, unconventional Hong Kong islander, Anthony Wong, crosses to the mainland in pursuit of mobster Yu Wing-Kwong. The film makes little advance on the usual crime drama themes, and there is nothing new about a cop and a villain harbouring a passion for the same girl (Carrie Ng). But there are plenty of insights into Sino-colonial relations and some spirited action sequences. DP. In Cantonese with English subtitles.

Anthony Wong (1) *Inspector Hung* • Wu Hsing-Kuo *Wang Jun* • Carrie Ng *Hou-yee* • Yu Wing-Kwong *Shum Chi-hung* • Chan Ming-Yuan *Singer* ■ *Dir* Che Kirk Wong [Kirk Wong] • *Scr* Winky Wong

Rock 'n' Roll High School ★★★ 15

Musical comedy 1979 · US · Colour · 87mins

A punk homage to the high-school rock 'n' roll films of the 1950s and 1960s, trailing cult credits like a pair of ripped bondage pants. Roger Corman is the executive producer, Joe Dante co-wrote the story with director Allan Arkush and The Ramones appear live and contribute to the score. There is an excuse of a teenage romance plot but the meat has PJ Soles, a Ramones fan, at war with rock-hating high-school principal Mary Woronov. A scorchingly brilliant soundtrack, a great deal of ludicrous fun, comic-book humour and an explosive ending make this head and shoulders above all other teenage music films, including the miserable 1991 follow-up. FL [VIDEO] DVD

PJ Soles *Riff Randell* • Vincent Van Patten *Tom Roberts* • Clint Howard *Eaglebauer* • Dey Young *Kate Rambeau* • Mary Woronov *Evelyn Togar* • Dick Miller *Police Chief Klein* • Paul Bartel *Mr McGree* ■ *Dir* Allan Arkush • *Scr* Richard Whitley, Russ Dvonch, Joseph McBride, from a story by Allan Arkush, Joe Dante

Rock, Pretty Baby ★★ U

Musical 1956 · US · BW · 89mins

This was made strictly for a teenage audience at the time, and is still likely to appeal mostly to those who were growing up in the 1950s, though fans of the era's music (shockingly radical at the time but amazingly tame-sounding now) will appreciate seeing the stars of the day performing their hits. The slight plot has John Saxon as the leader of a high-school band, intent on winning a major contest against the wishes of his father. TV

Sal Mineo *Angelo Barrato* • John Saxon *Jimmy Daley* • Luana Patten *Joan Wright* • Edward C Platt [Edward Platt] *Thomas Daley Sr* • Fay Wray *Beth Daley* • Rod McKuen *"Ox" Bentley* • John Wilder *"Fingers" Porter* • Alan Reed Jr *"Sax" Lewis* ■ *Dir* Richard Bartlett • *Scr* Herbert Margolis, William Raynor • *Music* Henry Mancini

Rock, Rock, Rock! ★★ U

Musical 1956 · US · BW · 85mins

This cheap quickie is very much a period piece for aficionados. Featuring the man who actually coined the phrase "rock 'n' roll", Alan Freed, the wafer-thin plot hinges on whether teenager Tuesday Weld (songs dubbed by Connie Francis) will get the prom dress of her dreams , set against the backdrop of America's latest novelty craze. Production values? Plot? Acting? It didn't matter then, Daddy-O, and it still doesn't. TS [VIDEO] DVD

Tuesday Weld *Dori* • Jacqueline Kerr *Gloria* • Ivy Schulman *Baby* • Fran Manfred *Arabella* • Jack Collins *Father* • Carol Moss *Mother* • Eleanor Swayne *Miss Silky* • Lester Mack *Mr Bimble* • Bert Conway *Mr Barker* ■ *Dir* Will Price • *Scr* Milton Subotsky, from a story by Milton Subotsky, Phyllis Coe

Rock School ★★★ 15

Music documentary
2004 · US · Colour · 93mins

It would be easy to compare the subject of this documentary, Paul Green, a Philadelphia rock musician-turned-rock-music teacher, to Jack Black's fictional character in *The School of Rock*. This film follows Green, who, using a volatile mix of two parts foul-mouthed abuse to one part gentle encouragement, schools a mixed bag of teen and pre-teen prodigies and relative no-hopers for what turns out to be a very creditable performance of some complex rock music at a Frank Zappa festival in Germany. Stylistically, this isn't the most sparkling of documentaries, but the kids are compulsively watchable, as is their terrifying teacher, so this just about transcends the shortcomings of the film-making. DA. Contains swearing.

Dir Don Argott

Rock Star ★★★ 15

Comedy drama based on a true story
2001 · US · Colour · 101mins

This rags-to-riches morality lesson is little more than a leather-pants clad *Cinderella*. Inspired by the real-life story of rock group Judas Priest, it centres on tribute band vocalist Mark Wahlberg who learns life's harshest truths when he joins his rock heroes as their new lead singer. Coloured acid-bright with a series of boisterous vignettes plucked from documented rock history, the film is a wild and often hilarious trip, with a romantic soft centre. The pervasive old-school metal soundtrack is intoxicating enough to help distract from Jennifer Aniston's miscasting as the rock chick girlfriend. SF [VIDEO] DVD

Mark Wahlberg *Chris Cole* • Jennifer Aniston *Emily Poule* • Dominic West *Kirk Cuddy* • Timothy Spall *Mats* • Timothy Olyphant *Rob Malcolm* • Dagmara Dominczyk *Tania* • Jason Flemyng *Bobby Beers* ■ *Dir* Stephen Herek • *Scr* John Stockwell

Rockabye ★

Drama 1932 · US · BW · 66mins

The overwrought tale of an actress who has clawed her way to the top, only to torment herself over her children and sacrifice her lover, this catastrophe stars the stylish and restrained Constance Bennett in a role to which she is totally unsuited. George Fitzmaurice, a veteran of several silents, was wheeled in to direct, and Phillips Holmes was cast as Bennett's leading man. The resulting film was so awful that Joel McCrea was bundled in to replace Holmes and George Cukor called in to direct a slew of retakes. RK

Constance Bennett *Judy Carroll* • Joel McCrea *Jacobs "Jake" Van Riker Pell* • Paul Lukas *Antoine "Tony" de Sola* • Jobyna Howland *"Snooks" Carroll* • Walter Pidgeon *Commissioner Al Howard* • Clara Blandick *Brida* ■ *Dir* George Cukor, George Fitzmaurice • *Scr* Jane Murfin, Kubec Glasmon, from the play by Lucia Bonder, from the short story *Our Judy* by Lucia Bonder

Rockers ★★★ 15

Action comedy 1978 · Jam · Colour · 99mins

This story of a young Rastafarian trying to drum his way into the music business may well have a see-through story, but it's also high on fruitcake whimsy and meandering charm. Even though the film invites the audience into a world of Rasta ritual and peer-group activity, it always does so with plenty of nimbleness, wit and grace. A relevant and classy soundtrack is provided by the Mighty Diamonds, Peter Tosh et al. JM [video] DVD

Leroy Wallace *Horsemouth* • Richard Hall *Dirty Harry* • Monica Craig *Madgie* • Marjorie Norman *Sunshine* • Jacob Miller *Jakes* • Gregory Isaacs *Jah Tooth* • Winston Rodney *Burning Spear* ■ *Dir/Scr* Theodoros Bafaloukos

Rocket Gibraltar ★★★ PG

Drama 1988 · US · Colour · 94mins

A family gathers on Long Island to celebrate the 77th birthday of its patriarch, Burt Lancaster. There are the customary resentments and jealousies to exercise and/or exorcise. In this case, the only daughter is a sex addict, while the sons are a faded baseball pitcher and a dried-up, stand-up comedian. Grandpa Lancaster is a former blacklisted writer and general egghead. This offers exceptional future-star spotting: Bill Pullman, Kevin Spacey and even Macaulay Culkin in his screen debut. AT [video]

Burt Lancaster *Levi Rockwell* • Suzy Amis *Aggie Rockwell* • Patricia Clarkson *Rose Black* • Frances Conroy *Ruby Hanson* • Sinead Cusack *Amanda "Billi" Rockwell* • John Glover *Rolo Rockwell* • Bill Pullman *Crow Black* • Kevin Spacey *Dwayne Hanson* • Macaulay Culkin *Cy Blue Black* ■ *Dir* Daniel Petrie • *Scr* Amos Poe

The Rocket Man ★ U

Science fiction 1954 · US · Colour · 79mins

For a film written by the celebrated and notorious satirist Lenny Bruce, and featuring the same Klaatu robot costume from *The Day the Earth Stood Still*, this is nothing more than a minor message comedy. A spaceman gives orphan George Winslow a ray gun which, when fired at human targets, makes them tell the truth. Justice of the Peace Spring Byington adopts him as honesty sweeps through the community eventually leading to villain Emory Parnell halting all plans of taking over the local orphanage. AJ

Charles Coburn *Mayor Ed Johnson* • Spring Byington *Justice Amelia Brown* • George Winslow *Timmy* • Anne Francis *June Brown* • John Agar *Tom Baxter* • Emory Parnell *Big Bill Watkins* ■ *Dir* Oscar Rudolph • *Scr* Lenny Bruce, Jack Henley, from a story by George W George, George F Slavin

Rocketeer ★★★★ PG

Fantasy adventure
1991 · US · Colour · 104mins

Based on a cult graphic novel blending Second World War adventure and superhero thrills, director Joe Johnston's vastly entertaining swashbuckler will jet-propel you back to your most cherished childhood fantasies. This brilliant ode to those corny 1930s movie serials has an added Art Deco sheen that enhances the sophisticated nostalgia. Starring Bill Campbell, it also benefits from Timothy Dalton's hissably slimy Nazi agent, masquerading as a devil-may-care, Errol Flynn-inspired matinée idol. AJ. Contains violence. [video] DVD

Bill Campbell *Cliff Secord* • Alan Arkin *Peevy* • Jennifer Connelly *Jenny* • Timothy Dalton *Neville Sinclair* • Paul Sorvino *Eddie Valentine* • Terry O'Quinn *Howard Hughes* • Ed Lauter *Fitch* • James Handy *Wooly* • Tiny Ron *Lothar* ■ *Dir* Joe Johnston • *Scr* Danny Bilson, Paul DeMeo, from a story by Danny Bilson, Paul DeMeo, William Dear, from the graphic novel by Dave Stevens

Rocketman ★★★ PG

Science-fiction comedy
1997 · US · Colour · 89mins

Computer genius Harland Williams finally gets his chance to be an astronaut. Unfortunately, he's a bit too eccentric for his Nasa colleagues, who are treated to a touch more slapstick chaos than they'd bargained for. This goofy comedy is really a vehicle for the antics of Williams, but credit must be given to William Sadler, who does a slow burn while the star inadvertently spoils his dreams. ST [video] DVD

Harland Williams *Fred Z Randall* • Jessica Lundy *Mission Specialist Julie Ford* • William Sadler *Comdr "Wild Bill" Overbeck* • Jeffrey DeMunn *Chief Flight Director Paul Wick* • James Pickens Jr *Ben Stevens* • Beau Bridges *Bud Nesbitt* • Shelley Duvall *Mrs Randall* ■ *Dir* Stuart Gillard • *Scr* Craig Mazin, Greg Erb, from a story by Oren Aviv

Rockets Galore ★★ U

Comedy 1958 · UK · Colour · 91mins

Made a decade after Ealing's classic comedy *Whisky Galore!*, this sequel (albeit adapted from another novel by Compton Mackenzie) was on a hiding to nothing, for no matter how good it might be, it would never be favourably compared with its predecessor. In the event, it is an undeniably feeble follow-up, with only a handful of the original Todday islanders remaining, and the story of their battle to prevent the construction of a missile base lacking both charm and satirical bite. DP

Jeannie Carson [Jean Carson] *Janet MacLeod* • Donald Sinden *Hugh Mander* • Roland Culver *Captain Waggett* • Noel Purcell *Father James McAllister* • Ian Hunter *Air Commodore Watchorn* • Duncan Macrae *Duncan Ban* • Gordon Jackson *George Campbell* • Ronnie Corbett *Drooby* ■ *Dir* Michael Relph • *Scr* Monja Danischewsky, from the novel by Compton Mackenzie

The Rockford Files ★★★ PG

Crime mystery 1974 · US · Colour · 95mins

Spawning more than 100 episodes, the *Rockford* series was devised for *Maverick* star James Garner. Garner later won an Emmy for his portrayal of the private investigator whose wrongful detention in San Quentin prompted him to plump for cases the police had abandoned. In this pilot for the first series, subtitled *Backlash of a Hunter*, Lindsay Wagner wants to trace the killer of her hobo father. As with many pilots, there's a certain amount of scene-setting involved, but Garner's self-depreciating style is fully formed. Both ex-cellmate Stuart Margolin and Joe Santos returned for the series proper, though Noah Beery would replace Robert Donley as Garner's opinionated father. DP [video]

James Garner *Jim Rockford* • Lindsay Wagner *Sara Butler* • Robert Donley *Joseph Rockford* • William Smith *Jerry Grimes* ■ *Dir* Richard T Heffron • *Scr* Stephen J Cannell, John Thomas James [Roy Huggins]

The Rocking Horse Winner ★★★★ PG

Drama 1949 · UK · BW · 87mins

A largely unsung, but truly terrific British feature based on a story from D H Lawrence about a young boy with the gift of picking racetrack winners. The imaginative story leaves plenty of space for director Anthony Pelissier's aptitude for surprise and emotional complexity. He elicits measured, insightful performances from John Mills and Valerie Hobson, and wrings the last ounce of pathos from an intriguing, thought-provoking tale. A film that has always been a favourite among critics and deserves wider recognition. SH [video]

Valerie Hobson *Hester Grahame* • John Howard Davies *Paul Grahame* • Ronald Squire *Oscar Cresswell* • John Mills *Bassett* • Hugh Sinclair *Richard Grahame* • Charles Goldner *Mr Tsaldouris* • Susan Richards *Nannie* • Cyril Smith *Bailiff* ■ *Dir* Anthony Pelissier • *Scr* Anthony Pelissier, from the story by DH Lawrence

Rockshow ★★★

Concert movie 1979 · US · Colour · 103mins

Paul McCartney spreading his Wings with a filmed concert tour featuring his first post-Beatles band. The line-up includes wife Linda, ex-Moody Blues man Denny Laine and former Thunderclap Newman sidekick Jimmy McCullough. The filming is simple and straightforward (no director is credited). Originally recorded in Dolby stereo, it's best seen in cinemas or on a decent home system. DA [video]

• *Cinematographer* Jack Priestly • *Editor* Robin Clarke, Paul Stein

Rockula ★★ PG

Musical comedy horror
1989 · US · Colour · 86mins

Dean Cameron is a teenage vampire and Tawny Fere, in a multitude of reincarnations, is the true love he is doomed to court and lose every 22 years to murderous pirates in this affable musical comedy. Director/co-writer Luca Bercovici aims for camp *Rocky Horror* heights but overstretches the madcap mark with relentless zaniness. It's all too much, yet not enough. AJ [video]

Dean Cameron *Ralph* • Toni Basil *Phoebe* • Thomas Dolby *Stanley* • Tawny Fere *Mona* • Susan Tyrrell *Chuck the Bartender* • Bo Diddley *Axman* ■ *Dir* Luca Bercovici • *Scr* Luca Bercovici, Christopher Verwiel

Rocky ★★★★ PG

Sports drama 1976 · US · Colour · 114mins

Dusting down the classic Hollywood story of the little man winning big, this triple-Oscar-winning boxing drama is shot through with genuine impassioned commitment, born of the fact that Sylvester Stallone realised that this was his best shot at stardom. The notion, then, of success hanging by a thread unites both the character of boxer Rocky Balboa and of Stallone himself. Sly is highly convincing as a mumbling Philadelphia no-hoper who is makes the most of his opportunities and ends up having a crack at the heavyweight champion of the world, Apollo Creed (Carl Weathers, by way of Muhammad Ali). Sly also wrote the script and was rewarded with an Oscar nomination. JM. Contains violence, swearing. [video] DVD

Sylvester Stallone *Rocky Balboa* • Talia Shire *Adrian* • Burt Young *Paulie* • Carl Weathers *Apollo Creed* • Burgess Meredith *Mickey* • Thayer David *Jergens* • Joe Spinell *Gazzo* • Joe Frazier ■ *Dir* John G Avildsen • *Scr* Sylvester Stallone • *Editor* Richard Halsey • *Music* Bill Conti

Rocky II ★★★ PG

Sports drama 1979 · US · Colour · 114mins

Sylvester Stallone, as writer, director and star, took his cue from those B-pictures set in the inner city where decency and success were able to triumph in the midst of adversity. Taking a clutch of simple ideas and comic-strip characters, he creates a giddy whirlwind of sentiment and fisticuffs. Having gone the distance with the heavyweight champ in the first bout, and now married to the love of his life (Talia Shire), Stallone is contemplating a return to the ring. The big-fight finale is executed with skill, passion and glee. JM [video] DVD

Sylvester Stallone *Rocky Balboa* • Talia Shire *Adrian* • Burt Young *Paulie* • Carl Weathers *Apollo Creed* • Burgess Meredith *Mickey* • Tony Burton *Apollo's trainer* • Joe Spinell *Gazzo* • Sylvia Meals *Mary Anne Creed* ■ *Dir/Scr* Sylvester Stallone

Rocky III ★★ PG

Sports drama 1982 · US · Colour · 95mins

By now the formula was starting to look stale, although two further sequels were still to follow this tired effort. The opponent here is Mr T, who takes Sylvester Stallone's championship crown; Rocky then battles to reclaim it. The story is predictable and it all goes a little flat outside the ring. JF. Contains violence and swearing. [video] DVD

Sylvester Stallone *Rocky Balboa* • Carl Weathers *Apollo Creed* • Mr T *Clubber Lang* • Talia Shire *Adrian Balboa* • Burt Young *Paulie* • Burgess Meredith *Mickey* • Ian Fried *Rocky Jr* • Hulk Hogan *Thunderlips* ■ *Dir/Scr* Sylvester Stallone

Rocky IV ★★ PG

Sports drama 1985 · US · Colour · 87mins

Sylvester Stallone returns to the *Rocky* road with decidedly less success than before. Nobody boxes clever in this lazy third sequel, also directed by Stallone, which introduced Dolph Lundgren to the movie world, though Brigitte Nielsen easily outstrips Lundgren in the stone-faced acting stakes. It's impossible not to root for his climactic victory, but the mawkish montages accompanied by blaring music are no substitute for plot. AJ. Contains swearing. [video] DVD

Sylvester Stallone *Rocky Balboa* • Talia Shire *Adrian Balboa* • Burt Young *Paulie* • Carl Weathers *Apollo Creed* • Brigitte Nielsen *Ludmilla* • Tony Burton *Duke* • Michael Pataki *Nicoli Koloff* • Dolph Lundgren *Drago* • James Brown (2) *Godfather of Soul* ■ *Dir/Scr* Sylvester Stallone

Rocky V ★★ PG

Sports drama 1990 · US · Colour · 99mins

Despite John G Avildsen being back as director (he did the first *Rocky*, with Stallone himself directing the intervening rounds), the emotional clout of the original has now given way to simple gestures and acting-by-numbers. It would be impossible to surprise with such a prescriptive format, and the only real spark comes courtesy of Sly's own offspring (Sage Stallone) as his screen son. JM. Contains violence, swearing. [video] DVD

Sylvester Stallone *Rocky Balboa* • Talia Shire *Adrian Balboa* • Burt Young *Paulie* • Sage Stallone *Rocky Jr* • Burgess Meredith *Mickey* • Tommy Morrison *Tommy Gunn* • Richard Gant *George Washington Duke* • Tony Burton *Tony* ■ *Dir* John G Avildsen • *Scr* Sylvester Stallone

The Rocky Horror Picture Show ★★★★ 15

Cult musical satire
1975 · UK · Colour · 95mins

This witty and wickedly naughty Queen Mother of cult movies is a campy, vampy, kinky musical send-up of old horror flicks. Revealing what happens when strait-laced Brad and Janet get stranded at the weird castle of Frank N Furter – Tim Curry wringing every ounce of deranged humour from his glam-rock role in a landmark performance – it cleverly satirises *Frankenstein*, haunted-house mysteries, science-fiction clichés and *Carry On* sexual identity confusion. The score is justifiably famous; the formula didn't work for the now-forgotten follow-up film, *Shock Treatment* (1981). AJ. Contains swearing, nudity. [VIDEO] DVD

Tim Curry *Dr Frank N Furter* • Susan Sarandon *Janet Weiss* • Barry Bostwick *Brad Majors* • Richard O'Brien *Riff Raff* • Patricia Quinn *Magenta* • Little Nell [Nell Campbell] *Columbia* • Jonathan Adams *Dr Everett V Scott* • Peter Hinwood *Rocky Horror* • Meat Loaf *Eddie* • Charles Gray *The Criminologist* • Christopher Biggins *Transylvanian* ■ *Dir* Jim Sharman • *Scr* Jim Sharman, Richard O'Brien, from the musical by Richard O'Brien • *Music Director* Richard Hartley • *Costume Designer* Richard Pointing, Gillian Dods

Rocky Mountain ★★ U

Western 1950 · US · BW · 82mins

This was really the last of Errol Flynn's mainstream Hollywood movies, and it received a lot of publicity at the time as Flynn married his leading lady, Patrice Wymore, just after shooting ended. It's a western, with Flynn as a Confederate leader trying to forge an alliance with outlaws in California. Indians soon scupper that plan. AT

Errol Flynn *Lafe Barstow* • Patrice Wymore *Johanna Carter* • Scott Forbes *Lt Rickey* • Guinn "Big Boy" Williams *Pap Dennison* • Dick Jones [Dickie Jones] *Jim Wheat* • Howard Petrie *Cole Smith* • Slim Pickens *Plank* ■ *Dir* William Keighley • *Scr* Alan LeMay, Winston Miller, from the story by Alan LeMay

Rodan ★★★

Science-fiction thriller
1956 · Jpn · Colour · 70mins

Two years after Ishiro Honda launched the "creature feature" with *Godzilla*, he moved into colour production with this all-action tale of the Cretaceous pterodactyl, which was hatched in a coal mine and gains its powers from consuming giant dragonflies. The atomic theme is once more to the fore, with the seismic shocks created by Rodan's supersonic speeds capable of reducing cities to rubble. But there's also a tragic element, as Rodan seeks to protect its brooding mate from prying scientists. DP. Japanese dialogue dubbed into English.

Kenji Sahara *Shigeru* • Yumi Shirakawa *Kiyo* • David Duncan *Narrator* ■ *Dir* Ishiro Honda [Inoshiro Honda] • *Scr* Takeshi Kimura, Takeo Murata, from a story by Takashi Kuronuma • *Special Effects* Eiji Tsuburaya

Rodgers & Hammerstein's Cinderella ★★★ U

Musical fantasy 1997 · US · Colour · 84mins

This fanciful, multiracial remake of the 1957 and 1965 TV musicals has a lovely score from Broadway's incomparable songwriting team. Superstar Whitney Houston plays the Fairy Godmother, with singer/actress Brandy Norwood donning a glass slipper for the title role. Under director Robert Iscove's skilful handling, the talented cast sings and dances with just enough gusto, turning this timeless fairy tale with its evil stepmother, odious stepsisters and dashing prince into a delightful family film. MC [VIDEO]

Brandy Norwood [Brandy] *Cinderella* • Whitney Houston *The Fairy Godmother* • Jason Alexander *Lionel* • Victor Garber *King* • Whoopi Goldberg *Queen Constantina* • Bernadette Peters *Wicked Stepmother* • Veanne Cox *Stepsister* • Natalie Desselle *Stepsister* • Paolo Montalban *Prince* ■ *Dir* Robert Iscove • *Scr* Robert L Freedman, Oscar Hammerstein II, Richard Rodgers, from the story by Charles Perrault

Roe vs Wade ★★★★

Drama 1989 · US · Colour · 92mins

This Emmy-winning TV film tackles the heated subject of abortion rights in the United States. Academy Award winner Holly Hunter stars as Ellen "Jane Roe" Russell, the destitute unwed mother at the centre of the historic Supreme Court case, with Amy Madigan as her novice attorney. Complex layered performances highlight this ground-breaking film, which deservingly provided Hunter with an Emmy. The script manages to promote a balanced point of view, while the sensitive direction by Gregory Hoblit further enhances this excellent TV drama. MC

Holly Hunter *Ellen Russell aka Jane Roe* • Amy Madigan *Sarah Weddington* • James Gammon *Jimmy Russell* • Terry O'Quinn *Jay Floyd* • Dion Anderson *Bob Flowers* • Kathy Bates *Jessie* • Micole Mercurio *Ida Russell* • Chris Mulkey *Ron Weddington* • Annabella Price *Linda Coffey* • Stephen Tobolowsky *Daryl Horwood* ■ *Dir* Gregory Hoblit • *Scr* Alison Cross

Roger & Me ★★★★★ 15

Satirical documentary
1989 · US · Colour · 86mins

This is a glorious "one off", refusing to fit neatly into any celluloid category, which considerably irked some nit-picking critics at the time. A wonderfully intrusive Michael Moore spent three years roaming his Michigan home town after General Motors chairman, Roger Smith, announced his cold-hearted plan to close down operations, thus decimating its working population. Moore's keen eye for truthful quirky detail shines through via the vivid cast of characters with whom we become instantly involved. Roger deserves everything he gets – with interest – and Moore supplies it with a compelling mixture of impish nerve and investigative flair. SH [VIDEO] DVD

Dir/Scr Michael Moore (2)

Roger Dodger ★★★★ 15

Black comedy drama
2002 · US · Colour · 101mins

Campbell Scott's sharp-tongued advertising copywriter isn't easy to like. Intelligent and attractive, yet cynical and manipulative, he gets a kick out of dispensing his blunt wisdom to unguarded women in Manhattan bars. What begins as a sardonic one-man show receives an original, irresistible twist as Scott's sweet, naive teenage nephew (newcomer Jesse Eisenberg) shows up in town, calling on uncle's supposed skills with the opposite sex to help lose his virginity. The scenes in which Eisenberg's boyish charm wins over out-of-his-league Elizabeth Berkley and Jennifer Beals (both terrific), are beautifully done. An elegantly filmed and impressively performed debut from writer/director Dylan Kidd. JC. Contains swearing and sex scenes. DVD

Campbell Scott *Roger Swanson* • Jesse Eisenberg *Nick* • Isabella Rossellini *Joyce* • Elizabeth Berkley *Andrea* • Jennifer Beals *Sophie* • Ben Shenkman *Donovan* • Mina Badie *Donna* ■ *Dir/Scr* Dylan Kidd

RoGoPaG ★★ PG

Portmanteau drama
1962 · It/Fr · Colour · 117mins

This contemporary critique is one of the least satisfying of the 1960s portmanteau pictures. Roberto Rossellini's *Virginity* is the dull tale of a passenger's obsession with an air hostess. Anticipating the futuristic *Alphaville*, Jean-Luc Godard's *The New World* chronicles a doomed post-apocalyptic romance, while Pier Paolo Pasolini received a four-month suspended sentence for defamation for *Cream Cheese*, in which an actor in Orson Welles's religious epic dies on the cross during an orgiastic shoot. The weakest episode, however, is *The Range-Grown Chicken*, Ugo Gregoretti's take on aggressive marketing, which lacks satirical bite. DP. In Italian with English subtitles. [VIDEO]

Rosanna Schiaffino *Anna Maria* • Bruce Balaban *Joe* • Alexandra Stewart *Alexandra* • Jean-Marc Bory *Narrator* • Jean-Luc Godard *Pill-popping pedestrian* • Orson Welles *The Director* • Mario Cipriani *Stracci* • Laura Betti *The Star* • Ugo Tognazzi *Togni* • Lisa Gastoni *His wife* ■ *Dir/Scr* Roberto Rossellini, Jean-Luc Godard, Pier Paolo Pasolini, Ugo Gregoretti

Rogue Cop ★★★

Crime drama 1954 · US · BW · 92mins

Robert Taylor plays a cop on the take from the Mob, led by George Raft. But following the murder of his brother and fellow cop, Taylor sees the error of his ways and goes after Raft and his murderous henchmen. The script is at its sharpest when dealing with Taylor's moral quagmire: is he avenging his brother, redeeming himself or on a suicide mission? Director Roy Rowland maintains a sprint throughout and offers the usual barrage of *film noir* shadows and doomy ambience. AT

Robert Taylor (1) *Christopher Kelvaney* • Janet Leigh *Karen Stephanson* • George Raft *Dan Beaumonte* • Steve Forrest *Eddie Kelvaney* • Anne Francis *Nancy Corlane* ■ *Dir* Roy Rowland • *Scr* Sydney Boehm, from a novel by William P McGivern

The Rogue Song

Musical romance
1930 · US · Colour · 115mins

One of the things the Hollywood studios did in the early years of sound was sign as many Broadway actors or singers as they could. One of MGM's catches was Lawrence Tibbett, star of the New York Met and described as one of the world's greatest baritones. *The Rogue Song* (sadly, no prints exist of this lost film) was his Oscar-nominated debut, an operatic showcase about a Russian bandit who kidnaps a princess. Apparently the public flocked to see this all-talking, all-singing, all-Technicolor concoction, lured by the voice of Tibbett and by Laurel and Hardy who provided some laughs between arias and plotting. AT

Lawrence Tibbett *Yegor* • Catherine Dale Owen *Princess Vera* • Judith Vosselli *Countess Tatiana* • Nance O'Neil *Princess Alexandra* • Stan Laurel *Ali-Bek* • Oliver Hardy *Murza-Bek* • Florence Lake *Nadja* • Lionel Belmore *Ossman* ■ *Dir* Lionel Barrymore • *Scr* Frances Marion, John Colton, from the operetta *Gypsy Love* by Franz Lehár, AM Willner, Robert Bodansky

Rogue Trader ★★ 15

Biographical drama
1998 · UK/US · Colour · 97mins

You'd think the true story of how Watford wide boy, Nick Leeson brought about the collapse of Barings Merchant Bank, one of the oldest financial institutions in the City, would make a cracking movie brimming with personal intrigues and trader insights. Sadly, under James Dearden's lacklustre direction, the tabloid tale is reduced to the level of a bland TV movie with its futures-market setting and bewildering jargon making it wilfully obscure to the point of abject disinterest. AJ [VIDEO] DVD

Ewan McGregor *Nick Leeson* • Anna Friel *Lisa Leeson* • Yves Beneyton *Pierre Beaumarchais* • Betsy Brantley *Brenda Granger* • Caroline Langrishe *Ash Lewis* • Nigel Lindsay *Ron Baker* • Tim McInnerny *Tony Hawes* • Irene Ng *Bonnie Lee* ■ *Dir* James Dearden • *Scr* James Dearden, from the non-fiction book by Nick Leeson, Edward Whitley

Rogues of Sherwood Forest ★★ U

Swashbuckling adventure
1950 · US · Colour · 79mins

Those men in Lincoln-green tights are at it again, this time with John Derek as Robin Hood's son, battling to get anti-democratic villain George Macready to sign the Magna Carta. It's another example of how Hollywood used to rewrite history, though the meagre script couldn't plump out its entertainment with much value. TH

John Derek *Robin, Earl of Huntingdon* • Diana Lynn *Lady Marianne* • George Macready *King John* • Alan Hale *Little John* • Paul Cavanagh *Sir Giles* • Lowell Gilmore *Count of Flanders* • Billy House *Friar Tuck* • Lester Matthews *Alan-a-Dale* ■ *Dir* Gordon Douglas • *Scr* George Bruce, from a story by Ralph Bettinson

Rogue's Yarn ★★

Crime drama 1956 · UK · BW · 83mins

When Derek Bond is persuaded by his mistress Nicole Maurey to murder his rich invalid wife, he concocts a seemingly waterproof alibi by appearing to be in charge of his yacht on a Channel crossing at the time of her demise. But the scheme proves full of holes under the close inspection of Elwyn Brook-Jones's Scotland Yard inspector. Co-written and directed by Vernon Sewell, it was a watchable enough thriller in its day. AE

Nicole Maurey *Michele Carter* • Derek Bond *John Marsden* • Elwyn Brook-Jones *Insp Walker* • Hugh Latimer *Sgt Adams* • John Serret *Insp Lefarge* ■ *Dir* Vernon Sewell • *Scr* Vernon Sewell, Ernie Bradford

Le Roi Danse ★★★ 15

Historical drama
2000 · Fr/Ger/Bel · Colour · 113mins

Director Gérard Corbiau's use of authentic period trappings and glorious music has more than mere aesthetic purpose, as it echoes the Sun King's inspirational exploitation of opulence to dazzle his potentially troublesome courtiers into submission. However, the focus on the latent sexual tension between the young Louis (Benoît Magimel) and his free-spirited court composer, Lully (Boris Terral). Devised with the help of fellow courtier Molière (Tcheky Karyo), the Baroque masques are stunningly staged but tip the tone too far towards kitsch. DP. In French with English subtitles.

Benoît Magimel *Louis XIV* • Boris Terral *Jean-Baptiste Lully* • Tcheky Karyo *Molière* • Colette Emmanuelle *Queen Mother, Anne of Austria* • Cécile Bois *Madeleine* • Claire Keim *Julie* • Johan Leysen *Cambert* • Idwig Stéphane *Conti* ■ *Dir* Gérard Corbiau • *Scr* Eve de Castro, Andrée Corbiau, Gérard Corbiau, Didier Decoin, from the novel *Lully ou le Musicien du Soleil* by Philippe Beaussant

Roja ★★★ PG

Political drama 1992 · US · Colour · 132mins

Even with a solid understanding of the complexities of Indian politics, this is a labyrinth of sensibilities. A colossal and controversial hit on its release, the film recounts the true story of a wife who battles almost single-handedly for the release of her husband, after he is kidnapped by

R

Kashmiri rebels demanding the liberation of their leader. Director Mani Rathnam is so vehement in his support for the Tamil couple that the film provoked a wave of anti-Muslim feeling in parts of the subcontinent, while Hindus resented his stance in the wake of Rajiv Gandhi's assassination by Tamil terrorists. DP. In Hindi with English subtitles.

Arvind Swamy *Rishi Kumar* • Madhubala *Roja* • Pankaj Kapur *Liaqat* ■ *Dir/Scr* Mani Rathnam

Roller Boogie ★

Musical drama 1979 · US · Colour · 103mins

This quasi-amateurish mishmash about roller disco fans ganging together to stop the closure of the local boogie centre is virtually unwatchable. Linda (*The Exorcist*) Blair lurched from one cheapo exploiter to another, and she's usually much better than the movies in which she found herself. TS

Linda Blair *Terry Barkley* • Jim Bray *Bobby James* • Beverly Garland *Lillian Barkley* • Roger Perry *Roger Barkley* • Jimmy Van Patten [James Van Patten] *Hoppy* • Kimberly Beck *Lana* • Rick Sciacca *Complete Control Conway* ■ *Dir* Mark L Lester • *Scr* Barry Schneider, from a story by Irwin Yablans

Rollerball ★★★ 15

Futuristic action drama
1975 · US · Colour · 119mins

In the Big Business-run world of 2018, anti-social activity and political unrest are kept in check by the gladiatorial spectator sport Rollerball, a lethal mix of hockey, roller-derby, motorbike racing and gang warfare. But when loner champion James Caan bucks the system, one requiring the eventual violent death of its star players, after a ten-year display of provocative individual heroism, cynical corporate patriarch John Houseman attempts to kill him by changing the rules. Although the Rollerball sequences are excitingly staged, director Norman Jewison's over-inflated fable is dull when it leaves the arena. AJ. Contains violence and brief nudity. DVD

James Caan *Jonathan E* • John Houseman *Bartholomew* • Maud Adams *Ella* • John Beck *Moonpie* • Moses Gunn *Cletus* • Pamela Hensley *Mackie* • Barbara Trentham *Daphne* • Ralph Richardson *Librarian* ■ *Dir* Norman Jewison • *Scr* William Harrison, from his story *Rollerball Murders*

Rollerball ★ 15

Futuristic drama
2001 · US/Ger/Jpn · Colour · 94mins

Turgid, spiritless and excitement free, this remake is like an optical lobotomy. Magnifying the original's weaknesses to excruciating levels, it compounds its brain-numbing banality with wooden performances, risible dialogue and an emotionally bankrupt plot. Chris Klein lacks charisma as the sporting hotshot who uncovers global conspiracy, while female lead Rebecca Romijn-Stamos is just an athletic clothes horse. SF DVD

Chris Klein *Jonathan Cross* • Jean Reno *Petrovich* • LL Cool J *Marcus Ridley* • Rebecca Romijn-Stamos *Aurora* • Naveen Andrews *Sanjay* • Oleg Taktarov *Denekin* • David Hemblen *Serokin* ■ *Dir* John McTiernan • *Scr* Larry Ferguson, John Pogue, from the 1975 film by William Harrison

Rollercoaster ★★★ PG

Disaster movie 1977 · US · Colour · 113mins

Universal Studios, cleverly promoting its studio tour while knocking rival attractions, came up with this disaster movie in which a terrorist (Timothy Bottoms), targets popular theme parks, planting bombs on the giant rides of the title. The strain of tracking him down prevents George Segal's safety inspector from quitting smoking and makes Richard Widmark twitch uncontrollably. One of the better 1970s disaster movies, this was originally released in Sensurround, a short-lived process that made cinema seats shake at appropriate moments. AT. Contains violence, swearing.

George Segal *Harry Calder* • Richard Widmark *Hoyt* • Timothy Bottoms *Young man* • Henry Fonda *Simon Davenport* • Harry Guardino *Keefer* • Susan Strasberg *Fran* • Helen Hunt *Tracy Calder* • Dorothy Tristan *Helen* • Harry Davis *Benny* • Stephen Pearlman *Lyons* ■ *Dir* James Goldstone • *Scr* Richard Levinson, William Link, from a story by Sanford Sheldon, Richard Levinson, William Link

Rollercoaster ★★★

Drama 1999 · Can · Colour · 90mins

A Canadian teenage gang break into a dilapidated fairground in order to get high on drugs and alcohol and fool around on the rides. But when the security guard catches them, his outwardly friendly demeanour hides a twisted sexual agenda of his own. A thought-provoking, compelling and disturbing look at hot sexual issues and the protection of the innocent, director Scott Smith's moral fable is made all the more potent by his cool approach to the controversial subject matter, his disarming visuals and an expert cast of unknowns. Many will find this ultimate teen nightmare an upsetting viewing experience. AJ

Brendan Fletcher *Stick* • Kett Turton *Darrin* • Crystal Buble *Chloe* • Brent Glenen *Justin* • Sean Amsing *Sanj* • David Lovgren *Ben* ■ *Dir/Scr* Scott Smith

The Rolling Stones Rock and Roll Circus ★★

Concert movie 1995 · UK · Colour · 65mins

Intended for American television, but vetoed by Mick Jagger, this legendary 1968 concert, set in a circus tent, surfaced on bootleg video in 1995. Ringmaster Jagger cracks the whip under the big-top set, as the Rolling Stones perform several songs in costume and John Lennon and Yoko On, Jethro Tull, the Who, Marianne Faithfull, Eric Clapton and Taj Mahal also do turns. Accompanied by a full orchestra and assorted animal and juggling acts, the psychedelic melange also features Lennon leading an all-star jam of *Yer Blues*. AJ

Dir Michael Lindsay-Hogg

Rolling Thunder ★★ 18

Drama 1977 · US · Colour · 95mins

Paul Schrader who wrote *Taxi Driver* and *Raging Bull* is usually a disciplined screenwriter, but runs amok with this story of embittered Vietnam vet William Devane, who returns home to an ungrateful society and thankless wife Lisa Richards who's fallen for another man. If director John Flynn had been more in control, we might care. As it is, despite fine acting from Devane and Tommy Lee Jones as his Vietnam buddy, we don't. TH. Contains swearing and violence.

William Devane *Major Charles Rane* • Tommy Lee Jones *Johnny Vohden* • Linda Haynes *Linda Forchet* • Lisa Richards *Janet* • Dabney Coleman *Maxwell* • James Best *Texan* • Cassie Yates *Candy* ■ *Dir* John Flynn • *Scr* Paul Schrader, Heywood Gould

Rollover ★★★ 15

Thriller 1981 · US · Colour · 110mins

Before the National Lottery made "rollover" a buzz word for millions, it is out of reach for most audiences, set as it is in the rarefied world of international high finance, and this was an attempt to explain it in dramatic terms. Jane Fonda is the film star widow of a murdered financier, confronted with the news that the Arab world is threatening to withhold monetary reserves, thus putting the global economy at risk. Alan J Pakula's political thriller lays on too much romance, while Kris Kristofferson in widow-wooing mode trys to convince that mercantile mayhem could ensue. TH. Contains violence, swearing.

Jane Fonda *Lee Winters* • Kris Kristofferson *Hub Smith* • Hume Cronyn *Maxwell Emery* • Josef Sommer *Roy Lefcourt* • Bob Gunton *Sal Naftari* • Macon McCalman *Mr Fewster* • Ron Frazier *Gil Hovey* ■ *Dir* Alan J Pakula • *Scr* David Shaber, from a story by David Shaber, Howard Kohn, David Weir

Roman Holiday ★★★★★ U

Romantic comedy 1953 · US · BW · 113mins

This sublime and charming fable rightly secured a best actress Oscar for Audrey Hepburn (in a role originally intended for Jean Simmons) and resulted in both Audrey and Rome (not to mention motor scooters) becoming the epitome of postwar chic. The film could be viewed merely as a love story about princess who falls for a reporter, but, not intending to detract from the charm of the story, the background is perhaps more interesting. The script was written by the uncredited, blacklisted Dalton Trumbo, a fact not revealed for almost 40 years, and actually deals in some depth with personal freedom and responsibilities, the setting and characters distancing the tale far from the witch-hunts in America. Immaculately directed by William Wyler and written and played with style and grace, this is a film to treasure. TS DVD

Audrey Hepburn *Princess Anne* • Gregory Peck *Joe Bradley* • Eddie Albert *Irving Radovich* • Hartley Power *Mr Hennessy* • Margaret Rawlings *Countess Vereberg* • Harcourt Williams *Ambassador* • Laura Solari *Mr Hennessy's secretary* • Tullio Carminati *General Provno* • Paolo Carlini *Mario Delani* ■ *Dir* William Wyler • *Scr* Ian McLellan Hunter, John Dighton, from a story by Ian McLellan Hunter (front for Dalton Trumbo) • *Costume Designer* Edith Head • *Cinematographer* Henri Alekan, Franz Planer • *Music* Georges Auric

Roman Scandals ★★★ PG

Musical comedy 1933 · US · BW · 87mins

Producer, Samuel Goldwyn's six Eddie Cantor vehicles were great fun, and here, Cantor falls asleep and finds himself back in pre-censorship ancient Rome. Naked Goldwyn Girls in long blond wigs besport themselves in a wonderfully lewd Busby Berkeley production number. Cantor is an acquired taste, but he's very amusing as food-taster to emperor Edward Arnold. TS

Eddie Cantor *Eddie* • Ruth Etting *Olga* • Gloria Stuart *Princess Sylvia* • David Manners *Josephus* • Verree Teasdale *Empress Agrippa* • Edward Arnold *Emperor Valerius* • Alan Mowbray *Major-Domo* ■ *Dir* Frank Tuttle • *Scr* William Anthony McGuire, George Oppenheimer, Arthur Sheekman, Nat Perrin, from a story by George S Kaufman, Robert E Sherwood

The Roman Spring of Mrs Stone ★★★

Drama 1961 · US/UK · Colour · 104mins

Making her penultimate screen appearance, Vivien Leigh is superbly cast as a fading beauty who uses her wealth to lure the young lover who will make her life worthwhile. Warren Beatty, in his second film, is equally impressive as her conquest, while Lotte Lenya thoroughly merited her Oscar nomination as a calculating matchmaker. But this adaptation of Tennessee Williams's one and only novel is somewhat bungled by Gavin Lambert's precious dialogue and the plodding direction of the inexperienced Jose Quintero. DP

Vivien Leigh *Karen Stone* • Warren Beatty *Pablo di Leo* • Lotte Lenya *Contessa Magda Terribili-Gonzales* • Coral Browne *Meg* • Jill St John *Bingham* • Jeremy Spenser *Young man* • Stella Bonheur *Mrs Jamison-Walker* • Josephine Brown *Lucia* • Cleo Laine *Singer* ■ *Dir* Jose Quintero • *Scr* Gavin Lambert, Jan Read, from the novel by Tennessee Williams

Romance ★★

Romantic drama 1930 · US · BW · 62mins

Bishop Gavin Gordon relives in flashback his ill-fated love affair with opera star Greta Garbo, who is the mistress of rich businessman Lewis Stone. The amazing idea of making Garbo an operatic soprano – Italian to boot – boggles the imagination; added to which the film's plot is flimsy and uninteresting. But who cares? The usual rules of judgement don't apply to Garbo movies, beyond recognising that some are better than others. This is worse than several, but the star (Oscar-nominated) transcends the material. RK

Greta Garbo *Rita Cavallini* • Lewis Stone *Cornelius Van Tuyl* • Gavin Gordon *Tom Armstrong* • Elliott Nugent *Harry* • Florence Lake *Susan Van Tuyl* • Clara Blandick *Miss Armstrong* ■ *Dir* Clarence Brown • *Scr* Bess Meredyth, Edwin Justus Mayer, from the play *Signora Cavallini* by Edward Sheldon • *Cinematographer* William H Daniels

Romance ★★ 18

Psychological drama
1998 · Fr · Colour · 94mins

A woman's sexuality is explored in gynaecological detail in Catherine Breillat's boundary-pushing drama. It's a dull, emotionless movie in which Caroline Ducey isn't getting "the full monty" from her man. So she wanders aimlessly from one bed to another, having pretentious, penetrative thoughts. Supposedly a feminist tale, Breillat's frank film reveals little (apart from Ducey's flesh) and seems to be saying that sex between men and women is passionless and mechanical. JC. In French with English subtitles. Contains nudity, sex scenes. DVD

Caroline Ducey *Marie* • Sagamore Stevenin *Paul* • François Berléand *Robert* • Rocco Siffredi *Paolo* • Reza Habouhossein *Man in the stairs* • Ashley Wanninger *Ashley* • Emma Colberti *Charlotte* • Fabien de Jomaron *Claude* ■ *Dir* Catherine Breillat • *Scr* Catherine Breillat, Severine Siaut

Romance in Manhattan ★★★ U

Drama 1934 · US · BW · 76mins

Ginger Rogers was desperately anxious to prove that she wasn't just Fred Astaire's screen dance partner, and in 1934 made seven features, only one of which co-starred the great Fred. This little gem has Ginger opposite debonair foreign import Francis Lederer. Ironically, he's an illegal alien who's helped by our Ginger, playing a soubrette from the chorus line. Director Stephen Roberts treats this lightweight nonsense with respect, ensuring a polished and charming romantic movie, a little sub-Capra, maybe, but none the worse for that. TS

Ginger Rogers *Sylvia Dennis* • Francis Lederer *Karel Novak* • Arthur Hohl *Attorney* • Jimmy Butler *Frank Dennis* ■ *Dir* Stephen Roberts • *Scr* Jane Murfin, Edward Kaufman, from a story by Norman Krasna, Don Hartman

Romance of a Horse Thief ★★

Comedy drama
1971 · US/Yug · Colour · 78mins

This movie gave French-based English actress Jane Birkin one of her first starring roles, as a Jewish woman who returns from education in France to urge her Polish peasant community to fight back against their Cossack oppressors, led by Yul Brynner. A well-meaning but at times plodding drama. PF

Yul Brynner *Stoloff* • Eli Wallach *Kifke* • Jane Birkin *Naomi* • Oliver Tobias *Zanvill Kradnik* • Lainie Kazan *Estusha* • David Opatoshu *Schloime Kradnik* • Serge Gainsbourg *Sigmund* ■ *Dir* Abraham Polonsky • *Scr* David Opatoshu, from a story by Joseph Opatoshu

A Romance of the Redwoods ★★

Silent western 1917 · US · BW

In the same year that she played the title child in *Rebecca of Sunnybrook Farm*, Mary Pickford scored a success in this early Cecil B DeMille western, filmed on location in California's redwood country and set against a background of the 1849 gold rush. Pickford is a young woman who, having lost her father in an Indian attack, falls in love with outlaw Elliott Dexter and saves him from the full force of the law by pretending to be pregnant by him. Good enough in its day, but of purely historical interest now. RK

Mary Pickford *Jenny Lawrence* • Elliott Dexter *"Black" Brown* • Charles Ogle *Jim Lyn* • Tully Marshall *Sam Sparks* • Raymond Hatton *Dick Roland* • Walter Long *Sheriff* • Winter Hall *John Lawrence* ■ *Dir* Cecil B DeMille • *Scr* Jeanie Macpherson, Cecil B DeMille

Romance on the High Seas ★★★

Romantic musical
1948 · US · Colour · 98mins

The sudden withdrawal of Betty Hutton (who had herself replaced Judy Garland) is the most significant thing about this breezy Warners musical, as it gave big band singer Doris Day the chance to take her first featured role. The stars of this Caribbean cruise confection were supposed to be Jack Carson and Janis Paige, but time hangs heavy between Day's all-too-brief appearances. Versatile though he was, director Michael Curtiz was never totally comfortable with the musical genre, which explains why Busby Berkeley was brought back to handle the dance routines. DP

Jack Carson *Peter Virgil* • Janis Paige *Elvira Kent* • Don DeFore *Michael Kent* • Doris Day *Georgia Garrett* • Oscar Levant *Oscar Farrar* • Fortunio Bonanova *Plinio* • Eric Blore *Ship's doctor* ■ *Dir* Michael Curtiz • *Scr* Julius J Epstein, Philip G Epstein, IAL Diamond, from the story *Romance in High C* by S Pondal Rios, Carlos A Olivari

Romancing the Stone ★★★★★ PG

Adventure comedy
1984 · US · Colour · 100mins

In this cracker of a roller-coaster ride, director Robert Zemeckis spices up a deliberately old-fashioned matinée adventure with tongue-in-cheek gags, unpredictably clever touches and top-of-the-range action. Kathleen Turner gives an exhilarating performance as the New York novelist who forsakes her cosy Manhattan lifestyle to rescue her sister in the jungles of Colombia. Turner dazzles in a role that proved a career turning point, and there's a wonderful chemistry between her and world-weary co-star Michael Douglas. Followed in 1985 by *The Jewel of the Nile*. AJ. Contains swearing and violence. [video] DVD

Michael Douglas *Jack Colton* • Kathleen Turner *Joan Wilder* • Danny DeVito *Ralph* • Zack Norman *Ira* • Alfonso Arau *Juan* • Manuel Ojeda *Zolo* • Holland Taylor *Gloria* • Mary Ellen Trainor *Elaine* ■ *Dir* Robert Zemeckis • *Scr* Diane Thomas

Romanoff and Juliet ★★★ U

Comedy 1961 · US · Colour · 102mins

Written and directed by Peter Ustinov from his stage play, this is one of those wish-fulfilling fables which blunts its Cold War satire with queasy romanticism. The Americans and Russians are being held to atomic ransom by the tiny nation of Concordia, ruled over by Ustinov. But, while vocal warfare goes on, the kids of the US and Soviet ambassadors (Sandra Dee and John Gavin) fall in love. Charming, but far too simplistic. TH

Peter Ustinov *The General* • Sandra Dee *Juliet Moulsworth* • John Gavin *Igor Romanoff* • Akim Tamiroff *Vadim Romanoff* • Alix Talton *Beulah Moulsworth* • John Phillips (1) *Hooper Moulsworth* • Tamara Shayne *Evdokia Romanoff* ■ *Dir* Peter Ustinov • *Scr* Peter Ustinov, from the play by Peter Ustinov

The Romantic Age ★

Romantic comedy 1949 · UK · BW · 93mins

Schoolgirl Mai Zetterling, feeling put down by her friend's father Hugh Williams, takes revenge by seducing him, but he eventually manages to extricate himself and hold on to his wife and family. The stars of this British film, directed by Edmond T Greville, must really have been desperate for work in 1949. This combination of prurience and coyness is an embarrassment. RK

Mai Zetterling *Arlette* • Hugh Williams *Arnold Dickson* • Margot Grahame *Helen Dickson* • Petula Clark *Julie Dickson* • Carol Marsh *Patricia* • Raymond Lovell *Hedges* • Paul Dupuis *Henri Sinclair* • Margaret Barton *Bessie* • Adrienne Corri *Nora* • Jean Anderson ■ *Dir* Edmond T Gréville • *Scr* Edward Dryhurst, Peggy Barwell, from the novel *Lycee des Jeunes Filles* by Serge Weber

Romantic Comedy ★★ 15

Comedy 1983 · US · Colour · 97mins

Two Broadway playwrights, Dudley Moore and Mary Steenburgen, enjoy a fruitful professional partnership. Their working relationship keeps threatening to teeter over the edge into romance, except that it's never the right time. Each marries someone else, but that doesn't stop them wondering what might have been. A weak script and storyline contributed to Moore's rapid post-*Arthur* (1981) decline. FL [video]

Dudley Moore *Jason Carmichael* • Mary Steenburgen *Phoebe Craddock* • Frances Sternhagen *Blanche* • Janet Eilber *Allison St James* • Robyn Douglass *Kate Mallory* • Ron Leibman *Leo* ■ *Dir* Arthur Hiller • *Scr* Bernard Slade, from his play

The Romantic Englishwoman ★★ 15

Comedy drama
1975 · UK/Fr · Colour · 111mins

Thomas Wiseman wrote the preposterous novel on which this is based, and here he tries to make sense of it with the help of co-scriptwriter Tom Stoppard and director Joseph Losey. They don't succeed. Glenda Jackson goes on an emotional bender with drug-dealer Helmut Berger at Baden-Baden, and husband Michael Caine amazingly invites him to their English country home. The result is high-falutin', puddle-shallow soap opera giving itself airs. TH. Contains swearing, sex scenes, nudity. [video]

Glenda Jackson *Elizabeth Fielding* • Michael Caine *Lewis Fielding* • Helmut Berger *Thomas* • Marcus Richardson *David Fielding* • Kate Nelligan *Isabel* • Rene Kolldehof [Reinhard Kolldehoff] *Herman* • Michael Lonsdale [Michel Lonsdale] *Swan* • Béatrice Romand *Catherine* • Anna Steele *Annie* • Nathalie Delon *Miranda* ■ *Dir* Joseph Losey • *Scr* Tom Stoppard, Thomas Wiseman, from the novel by Thomas Wiseman

Rome Adventure ★★★

Romantic drama
1962 · US · Colour · 118mins

Back in the 1960s, teenage heart-throbs Troy Donahue and Suzanne Pleshette had their every move detailed in America's fan magazines. In this lush and soapy tale they are co-stars, though they did not marry until 1964. Librarian Pleshette is vacationing in Rome and can't choose between callow but good-looking architect Donahue, and sophisticated foreign roué Rossano Brazzi. Angie Dickinson gets all the best lines as Donahue's other woman, Max Steiner contributes one of his most romantic later scores, and director Delmer Daves knows just how far to go with his material. TS

Troy Donahue *Don Porter* • Angie Dickinson *Lyda* • Rossano Brazzi *Roberto Orlandi* • Suzanne Pleshette *Prudence Bell* • Constance Ford *Daisy* • Al Hirt *Al* • Chad Everett *Young man* ■ *Dir* Delmer Daves • *Scr* Delmer Daves, from the novel by Irving Fineman

Rome Express ★★★★ U

Crime drama 1932 · UK · BW · 86mins

A wonderfully entertaining Gaumont-British melodrama featuring a rich variety of passengers (including an art thief, double-crossed accomplices, an American film star, a philanthropist, adulterous lovers and a French police inspector) on a train journey between Paris and Rome. This set the pattern for dozens of later pictures using the same confined setting. The splendid cast includes Conrad Veidt in his first British film. Walter Forde directed it on the cramped sound stages of Shepherd's Bush, cleverly maintaining a sense of continual movement and foreign atmosphere. AE [video]

Esther Ralston *Asta Marvelle* • Conrad Veidt *Zurta* • Hugh Williams *Tony* • Donald Calthrop *Poole* • Joan Barry *Mrs Maxted* • Harold Huth *Grant* • Gordon Harker *Tom Bishop* • Eliot Makeham *Mills* • Cedric Hardwicke *Alistair McBane* ■ *Dir* Walter Forde • *Scr* Clifford Grey, Sidney Gilliat, Frank Vosper, Ralph Stock, from the story by Clifford Grey

Rome, Open City ★★★★★ 15

Second World War drama
1945 · It · BW · 97mins

Roberto Rossellini came to international prominence with this emotive resistance drama, which formed part of a wartime trilogy that was completed by *Paisà* (1946) and *Germany, Year Zero* (1947). Based on actual events, this is set during the last days of the Nazi occupation of Rome and was shot on location using fragments of painstakingly spliced film stills. It's a landmark of neorealist cinema, despite the melodramatic storyline, montage structure and star performances (from Aldo Fabrizi and Anna Magnani at the head of a primarily non-professional cast) somewhat undermining the social commitment, visual authenticity and technical rigour demanded by the movement's intellectual founder, Cesare Zavattini. DP. In Italian with English subtitles. [video] DVD

Anna Magnani *Pina* • Aldo Fabrizi *Don Pietro Pellegrini* • Marcello Pagliero *Giorgio Manfredi, AKA Luigi Ferraris* • Maria Michi *Marina Mari* • Harry Feist *Maj Bergmann* ■ *Dir* Roberto Rossellini • *Scr* Sergio Amidei, Federico Fellini, Roberto Rossellini, from a story by Sergio Amidei, Alberto Consiglio

Romeo and Juliet ★★★★ U

Romantic tragedy 1936 · US · BW · 124mins

This is Shakespeare as a star vehicle for Norma Shearer and the too-mature Leslie Howard as the doomed lovers. Made at the instigation of MGM boss Irving Thalberg, the film contains hugely enjoyable performances from studio regulars Basil Rathbone and Edna May Oliver, plus a breathtaking, scenery-chewing turn from John Barrymore as Mercutio. George Cukor directs with a reverent eye for the text and period detail, and it's all worth seeing as a superb example of Hollywood studio kitsch. TH

Norma Shearer *Juliet* • Leslie Howard *Romeo* • John Barrymore *Mercutio* • Basil Rathbone *Tybalt* • Edna May Oliver *Nurse* • C Aubrey Smith *Lord Capulet* ■ *Dir* George Cukor • *Scr* Talbot Jennings, from the play by William Shakespeare

Romeo and Juliet ★★★★ U

Romantic tragedy
1954 · UK/It · Colour · 141mins

This adaptation of Shakespeare's tragedy of star-crossed lovers tends to be forgotten in the shuffle between George Cukor's all-star 1930s version, Franco Zeffirelli's exquisite 1968 film and Baz Luhrmann's exciting modern take. But, Renato Castellani's classically elegant production, beautifully shot on location in Italy with jewel-bright design inspired by Renaissance paintings, did win the Golden Lion at the Venice Film Festival and can boast attractive, textbook performances. AME

Laurence Harvey *Romeo* • Susan Shentall *Juliet* • Flora Robson *Nurse* • Mervyn Johns *Friar Laurence* • Bill Travers *Benvolio* • Enzo Fiermonte *Tybalt* • Aldo Zollo *Mercutio* • Giovanni Rota *Prince of Verona* • John Gielgud *Chorus* ■ *Dir* Renato Castellani • *Scr* Renato Castellani, from the play by William Shakespeare

Romeo and Juliet ★★★ U

Ballet 1966 · UK · Colour · 127mins

A filmed performance of the Kenneth MacMillan-choreographed ballet that, if nothing else, acts as archive footage of the greatest dance partnership of the last century. Although Margot Fonteyn was 46 at the time, hardly appropriate for the 14-year-old Juliet, her astonishing technicality and musical sense soon overcome any credibility gap. Rudolf Nureyev was always at his best with Fonteyn and their chemistry is almost captured in this stage-bound production. With the stately and beautiful score by Prokofiev, the ballet is enjoyable even for non-balletomanes. FL

Rudolf Nureyev *Romeo* • Margot Fonteyn *Juliet* • David Blair *Mercutio* • Desmond Doyle *Tybalt* • Anthony Dowell *Benvolio* • Derek Rencher *Paris* • Michael Somes *Lord Capulet* • Julia Farron *Lady Capulet* ■ *Dir* Paul Czinner • *Scr* from the ballet by Sergei Prokofiev, from the play by William Shakespeare • *Choreographer* Kenneth MacMillan

Romeo and Juliet ★★★ PG

Romantic tragedy
1968 · UK/It · Colour · 132mins

Franco Zeffirelli's bold adaptation was notorious for jettisoning almost half the text and its chaste use of nudity, but it's tame indeed beside Baz Luhrmann's scintillating update in *William Shakespeare's Romeo + Juliet*. Olivia Hussey and Leonard Whiting might have met the age criteria required to play Verona's star-crossed lovers, but neither can hold a candle to their latter-day counterparts, Leonardo DiCaprio and Claire Danes. They're bailed out, to some extent, by the support playing of John McEnery, Michael York and Milo O'Shea, as well as by Pasquelino De Santis's Oscar-winning photography. DP [video] DVD

Leonard Whiting *Romeo* • Olivia Hussey *Juliet* • Laurence Olivier *Narrator* • Milo O'Shea *Friar Laurence* • Michael York *Tybalt* • John McEnery *Mercutio* • Pat Heywood *Nurse* • Natasha Parry *Lady Capulet* ■ *Dir* Franco Zeffirelli • *Scr* Franco Zeffirelli, from the play by William Shakespeare, adapted by Franco Brusati, Masolino D'Amico

Romeo Is Bleeding ★★★★ 18

Thriller 1992 · US · Colour · 104mins

A deliriously bonkers black comedy thriller that makes little sense but is powered along by a sheer disregard for anything approaching good taste and some wonderfully over-the-top performances. Gary Oldman is the corrupt cop whose life falls apart completely when he encounters psychotic Lena Olin. Don't worry too much about the niceties of the plot, just sit back and enjoy Olin's whirlwind performance as the *femme fatale* from hell. Oldman is equally good and there are fine turns from an exceptional supporting cast. The *film noir* and comic elements don't always gel, but director Peter Medak ensures that it's always an exhilarating ride. JF. Contains violence, swearing, sex scenes and nudity. DVD

Gary Oldman *Jack Grimaldi* • Lena Olin *Mona Demarkov* • Annabella Sciorra *Natalie Grimaldi* • Juliette Lewis *Sheri* • Roy Scheider *Don Falcone* • Michael Wincott *Sal* • Ron Perlman *Jack's attorney* • Dennis Farina *Nick Gazzara* • David Proval *Scully* • Will Patton *Martie Cuchinski* ■ *Dir* Peter Medak • *Scr* Hilary Henkin

Romeo Must Die ★★ 15

Romantic action drama
2000 · US · Colour · 109mins

Jet Li takes his first starring role in a US movie, as an ex-cop convict who flees to America to avenge the death of his brother and gets entangled in a Mob war. During his investigation, he continually mixes with the daughter (played by singer Aaliyah) of the rival gang's head thug. Even for an American movie, the martial arts sequences are very badly choreographed, and there is far more hip-hop music and lingo than either plot or action. KB DVD

Jet Li *Han Sing* • Aaliyah *Trish O'Day* • Isaiah Washington *Mac* • Russell Wong *Kai* • DM X *Silk* • Delroy Lindo *Isaak O'Day* • Henry O *Ch'u Sing* • DB Woodside *Colin* • Anthony Anderson *Maurice* ■ *Dir* Andrzej Bartkowiak • *Scr* Eric Bernt, John Jarrell, Jerrold E Brown, from a story by Mitchell Kapner

Romero ★★★ 15

Political biographical drama
1989 · US · Colour · 100mins

Powerful biopic of Oscar Romero, the El Salvadoran archbishop who, during the late 1970s, voiced the Roman Catholic Church's opposition to his country's ruling repressive regime, and was subsequently assassinated for his outspokenness. The first film ever funded by officials of the US Roman Catholic Church, this is very much a message movie, but its tendency towards heavy-handedness is offset by an understated and dignified performance by Raul Julia. DA

Raul Julia *Archbishop Oscar Romero* • Richard Jordan *Father Rutilio Grande* • Ana Alicia *Arista Zalada* • Eddie Velez *Lieutenant Columa* • Alejandro Bracho *Father Alfonzo Osuna* • Tony Plana *Father Manuel Morantes* • Harold Gould *Francisco Galedo* • Lucy Reina *Lucia* ■ *Dir* John Duigan • *Scr* John Sacret Young

Romper Stomper ★★★ 18

Drama 1992 · Aus · Colour · 88mins

Russell Crowe stars as the leader of a racist gang that preys on Australia's immigrant population in writer/director Geoffrey Wright's unsettling portrait of neo-Nazi thugs. Unflinching in its depiction of the lifestyle of the protagonists, the film caused a *Clockwork Orange*-style controversy Down Under when it was released. Much of the film's power comes from the bruising, raw performances of Crowe, best friend Daniel Pollock and lover Jacqueline McKenzie. Although some may find the violent subject matter a major turn-off, Wright's stylised camerawork and pacey editing make this more than just an exercise in screen brutality. JC DVD

Russell Crowe *Hando* • Daniel Pollock *Davey* • Jacqueline McKenzie *Gabe* • Alex Scott (2) *Martin* • Leigh Russell *Sonny Jim* • Daniel Wyllie [Dan Wyllie] *Cackles* • James McKenna *Bubs* ■ *Dir/Scr* Geoffrey Wright

Romuald et Juliette ★★★ PG

Romantic comedy
1989 · Fr · Colour · 111mins

This cultured romantic comedy features Daniel Auteuil as a yoghurt-company boss who's framed for a food-poisoning scandal, and finds that the only person who can help him, commercially and emotionally, is his company's black cleaning lady (Firmine Richard). Directed with skill and style by Coline Serreau and played with aplomb by the two leads, this is lightweight French film-making at its most likeable best. DA. In French with English subtitles.

Daniel Auteuil *Romuald* • Firmine Richard *Juliette Bonaventure* • Pierre Vernier *Blache* • Maxime Leroux *Cloquet* • Gilles Privat *Paulin* • Muriel Combeau *Nicole* • Catherine Salviat *Françoise* ■ *Dir/Scr* Coline Serreau

Romy and Michele's High School Reunion ★★★ 15

Comedy 1997 · US · Colour · 88mins

This fun comedy stars Mira Sorvino and Lisa Kudrow as the two dim-witted, down-on-their-luck blondes of the title, who pretend they are high-powered businesswomen at their high school reunion to impress those ex-school mates who once made fun of them. It's a simple enough premise that is enlivened by two infectious performances from the leads as well as slick support from Janeane Garofalo and Alan Cumming. JB. Contains swearing, sexual references. DVD

Mira Sorvino *Romy* • Lisa Kudrow *Michele* • Janeane Garofalo *Heather* • Alan Cumming *Sandy Frink* • Julia Campbell *Christie* • Mia Cottet *Cheryl* • Kristin Bauer *Kelly* • Elaine Hendrix *Lisa* • Vincent Ventresca *Billy* • Justin Theroux *Cowboy* ■ *Dir* David Mirkin • *Scr* Robin Schiff

La Ronde ★★★★★ PG

Drama 1950 · Fr · BW · 88mins

The Arthur Schnitzler play on which this is based was a metaphor for the spread of venereal disease. However, director Max Ophüls buried this message beneath a surface elegance and sophistication that characterised his 1950s style. From the dazzling opening sequence, in which master of ceremonies Anton Walbrook flits between studio sets to start this carousel of careless caresses, Ophüls keeps his prying camera on the move in time to the waltz music of Oscar Straus. Each tryst is played to perfection by the remarkable cast. DP. In French with English subtitles.

Anton Walbrook *Storyteller* • Simone Signoret *Leocadie, the prostitute* • Serge Reggiani *Franz, the soldier* • Simone Simon *Marie, the maid* • Daniel Gélin *Alfred, the young man* • Danielle Darrieux *Emma Breitkopf, the wife* • Fernand Gravey [Fernand Gravet] *Charles, Emma's husband* ■ *Dir* Max Ophüls • *Scr* Jacques Natanson, Max Ophüls, from the play *Reigen* by Arthur Schnitzler

La Ronde ★★

Drama 1964 · Fr/It · Colour · 110mins

The first of the four films Jane Fonda made with one-time husband Roger Vadim, this suffers in every aspect on comparison with Max Ophüls's 1950 version. Switching the action to Paris on the eve of the Great War, Vadim makes stylish use of Henri Decaë's widescreen imagery. But, the screenplay is surprisingly coarse considering it was written by acclaimed playwright Jean Anouilh, while many of the cast seem to misread their characters. DP. A French language film.

Marie Dubois *Prostitute* • Claude Giraud *Soldier* • Anna Karina *Maid* • Valérie Lagrange *Maid's friend* • Jean-Claude Brialy *Young man* • Jane Fonda *Married woman* • Maurice Ronet *Husband* • Catherine Spaak *Midinette* • Francine Bergé *Maximillienne de Poussy* ■ *Dir* Roger Vadim • *Scr* Jean Anoilh, from the play *Reigen* by Arthur Schnitzler

Ronin ★★★★ 15

Action thriller 1998 · US · Colour · 116mins

Resembling a 1970s European espionage caper in atmosphere and style, director John Frankenheimer's deliberately retro thriller bounds along at a cracking pace. In an engrossing action adventure with a sobering political slant, Robert De Niro travels to Paris to join an international gang of criminals (including the always watchable Jean Reno) who have been hired by Irish revolutionary Natascha McElhone to steal an important briefcase. No excuse is missed for a frenzied car chase in the *Bullitt* tradition, or the chance to add a menacing hard edge to the deliciously convoluted plot. AJ. Contains violence and swearing. DVD

Robert De Niro *Sam* • Jean Reno *Vincent* • Natascha McElhone *Deirdre* • Stellan Skarsgård *Gregor* • Sean Bean *Spence* • Skipp Sudduth *Larry* • Michael Lonsdale [Michel Lonsdale] *Jean-Pierre* • Jan Triska *Dapper gent* • Jonathan Pryce *Seamus* ■ *Dir* John Frankenheimer • *Scr* JD Zeik, Richard Weisz [David Mamet], from a story by JD Zeik

Rooftops ★★ 15

Romantic drama 1989 · US · Colour · 90mins

Twenty-eight years after winning an Oscar for *West Side Story*, director Robert Wise returns to broadly similar turf. This time around, though, the results are decidedly less spectacular. This is a routine urban musical about the forbidden love between a white boy and a Hispanic girl. Wise structured his film around its footwork – a form of combat dancing that's like kung fu but without the contact. The dance form quickly got the chop, and the film died at the box office. DA

Jason Gedrick *T* • Troy Beyer *Elana* • Eddie Velez *Lobo* • Tisha Campbell *Amber* • Alexis Cruz *Squeak* • Allen Payne *Kadim* • Steve Love *Jackie-Sky* • Rafael Baez *Raphael* • Jaime Tirelli *Rivera* ■ *Dir* Robert Wise • *Scr* Terence Brennan, from a story by Allan Goldstein, Tony Mark

Rookery Nook ★★

Farce 1930 · UK · BW · 107mins

This, probably the most famous Aldwych farce, was the second to be filmed, but the first talkie. British audiences originally found it thrilling to hear favourite comedians speaking on screen but this appeal has dimmed considerably. Director/star Tom Walls is a lifeless actor and doesn't seem to have considered re-takes important: three fluffed lines are kept in. Walls's regular partner Ralph Lynn is much more fun in his perennial silly-ass role, here a meek husband, who gives lovely runaway Winifred Shotter a room in his country house and then has to explain her presence to his family. DM

Tom Walls *Clive Popkiss* • Ralph Lynn *Gerald Popkiss* • Winifred Shotter *Rhoda Marley* • Robertson Hare *Harold Twine* • Mary Brough *Mrs Leverett* • Ethel Coleridge *Mrs Twine* • Griffith Humphreys *Mr Putz* • Doreen Bendix *Poppy Dickey* • Margot Grahame *Clara Popkiss* ■ *Dir* Tom Walls • *Scr* Ben Travers, WP Lipscomb, from the play by Ben Travers

The Rookie ★★ 18

Action thriller 1990 · US · Colour · 115mins

As both a talented director and actor, Clint Eastwood manages to maintain a spirit of lethargic cynicism when working on formula fare such as this all-action buddy movie. For fans, there's plenty of Clint as a firecracker cop, here part of a double act with Charlie Sheen, but Clint the director makes little effort to freshen up plot, character or car chase. JM. Contains swearing, violence, sex scenes.

Clint Eastwood *Nick Pulovski* • Charlie Sheen *David Ackerman* • Raul Julia *Strom* • Sonia Braga *Liesl* • Tom Skerritt *Eugene Ackerman* • Lara Flynn Boyle *Sarah* • Pepe Serna *Lieutenant Ray Garcia* ■ *Dir* Clint Eastwood • *Scr* Boaz Yakin, Scott Spiegel

The Rookie ★★★ U

Sports drama based on a true story
2002 · US · Colour · 122mins

This is a true story that is, sadly, hampered by some signposted plot developments and undernourished characters. However, it does contain a poignant performance by Dennis Quaid as Jimmy Morris, a former pro-ball player who pledges to try out again for the major leagues if the school team he coaches makes the play-offs. The versatile Rachel Griffiths offers stoic support in the clichéd role of his supportive wife. However, this is a bit too long and has too many dull stretches for what aspires to be a feel-good family film. TH DVD

Dennis Quaid *Jimmy Morris* • Rachel Griffiths *Lorri Morris* • Jay Hernandez *Joaquin "Wack" Campos* • Beth Grant *Olline, Jimmy's mother* • Angus T Jones *Hunter* • Brian Cox *James Morris Sr* • Rick Gonzalez *Rudy Bonilla* • Chad Lindberg *Joe David West* ■ *Dir* John Lee Hancock • *Scr* Mike Rich

Rookie of the Year ★★★ PG

Sports comedy 1993 · US · Colour · 99mins

With a few honourable exceptions (*Bull Durham* and *Major League* among them), the British have never really warmed to baseball movies and this one slipped by virtually unnoticed in the UK. It's a slight but affectionate family comedy that follows the adventures of a youngster (Thomas Ian Nicholas) who, after breaking his arm, becomes a wonder pitcher. Director Daniel Stern plays down the cute aspects of the story, while Nicholas is helped by sterling support from Gary Busey, Dan Hedaya and Stern himself. JF DVD

Thomas Ian Nicholas *Henry Rowengartner* • Gary Busey *Chet Steadman* • Albert Hall *Martinella* • Amy Morton *Mary Rowengartner* • Dan Hedaya *Larry "Fish" Fisher* • Bruce Altman *Jack Bradfield* • Eddie Bracken *Bob Carson* ■ *Dir* Daniel Stern • *Scr* Sam Harper

Room at the Top ★★★★★ 15

Drama 1958 · UK · BW · 112mins

This gritty, trenchant film burst upon the late 1950s and stirred a hornet's nest of controversy for its treatment of sex as passionate rather than a merely procreative exercise. Laurence Harvey is at his slit-eyed, manipulative, lizard-like best as the ambitious antihero, with Simone Signoret, glorious and sexy as his ill-fated mistress. For once, the North is portrayed as a shade more complicated than previous "flat cap and whippet" outings had shown, in a movie which perfectly captures the gradual demise of Victorian morality and traditional class culture. Seven years later Harvey returned in *Life at the Top*. SH DVD

Laurence Harvey *Joe Lampton* • Simone Signoret *Alice Aisgill* • Heather Sears *Susan Brown* • Donald Wolfit *Mr Brown* • Ambrosine Philpotts *Mrs Brown* • Donald Houston *Charles Soames* • Raymond Huntley *Mr Hoylake* • John Westbrook *Jack Wales* • Allan

R

Cuthbertson *George Aisgill* • Mary Peach *June Samson* • Hermione Baddeley *Elspeth* ■ *Dir* Jack Clayton • *Scr* Neil Paterson, from the novel by John Braine

Room for One More ★★★ U

Comedy drama 1952 · US · BW · 94mins

Cary Grant brings much-needed charm to this peculiar comedy drama, in which his then real-life wife Betsy Drake plays his spouse, a woman with a compulsive need to adopt. It's somewhat surprisingly based on a true story and is quite watchable, especially when Grant is pitted against that formidable child actor, the deadpan George "Foghorn" Winslow. TS

Cary Grant *"Poppy" Rose* • Betsy Drake *Anna Rose* • Lurene Tuttle *Miss Kenyon* • Randy Stuart *Mrs Foreman* • John Ridgely *Harry Foreman* • Irving Bacon *Mayor* • Mary Lou Treen [Mary Treen] *Mrs Roberts* • Hayden Rorke *Doctor* • Iris Mann *Jane* • George "Foghorn" Winslow [George Winslow] *Teensie* • Clifford Tatum Jr *Jimmy-John* • Gay Gordon *Trot* • Malcolm Cassell *Tim* ■ *Dir* Norman Taurog • *Scr* Jack Rose, Melville Shavelson, from the autobiography by Anna Perrott Rose

A Room for Romeo Brass ★★★★ 15

Comedy drama
1999 · UK/Can · Colour · 86mins

This is a risky, difficult and very impressive little movie about two 12-year-old mates – the spirited Andrew Shim and the sickly Ben Marshall – who are befriended by likeable, albeit peculiar, loner Paddy Considine. Beginning as an earthy but light-hearted study of adolescent friendship, the film takes a sharp turn into quite shocking drama once Considine reveals his darker side. Although the sudden shift in tone won't please everyone, this unsentimental movie offers many insights into the weirdness of human relationships. JC. Contains swearing. DVD

Andrew Shim *Romeo Brass* • Ben Marshall *Gavin "Knock Knock" Woolley* • Paddy Considine *Morell* • Frank Harper *Joseph Brass* • Julia Ford *Sandra Woolley* • James Higgins *Bill Woolley* • Vicky McClure *Ladine Brass* • Ladene Hall *Carol Brass* • Bob Hoskins *Steven Laws* • Shane Meadows *Fish and chip shop man* ■ *Dir* Shane Meadows • *Scr* Paul Fraser, Shane Meadows

Room Service ★★ U

Comedy 1938 · US · BW · 74mins

This oddity in the careers of the Marx Brothers sees a little of their well-established humour applied to a hit Broadway farce. The anarchic personalities of Groucho, Harpo and Chico are fatally weakened by being tied to a situation comedy plot and Groucho is the only brother with a real part, as a penniless Broadway producer trying to put on a new play. There are some inspired moments, but far too few of them. AE

Groucho Marx *Gordon Miller* • Chico Marx *Binelli* • Harpo Marx *Faker Englund* • Lucille Ball *Christine Marlowe* • Ann Miller *Hilda Manny* ■ *Dir* William A Seiter • *Scr* Morrie Ryskind, Glenn Tryon, Philip Loeb, from a play by Allan Boretz, John Murray

Room to Let ★★

Crime thriller 1949 · UK · Colour · 65mins

Hammer Films took a step towards its future speciality with this early B-feature from a radio play by mystery writer Margery Allingham. Is Valentine Dyall's creepy Victorian lodger a missing mental patient or possibly even Jack the Ripper? Jimmy Hanley headlines the cast playing a reporter, while Constance Smith, as his girlfriend and landlady's daughter. Modest, but enjoyable. AE

Jimmy Hanley *Curley Minter* • Valentine Dyall *Dr Fell* • Christine Silver *Mrs Musgrave* • Merle Tottenham *Alice* • Charles Hawtrey *Mike Atkinson* • Constance Smith *Molly Musgrave* ■ *Dir* Godfrey Grayson • *Scr* John Gilling, Godfrey Grayson, from the radio play by Margery Allingham

Room to Rent ★★★ 15

Comedy drama
2000 · UK/Fr · Colour · 91mins

Directed by an Anglophile Egyptian, this British film stars the French-born Moroccan Saïd Taghmaoui as a student from Egypt struggling to become a successful screenwriter before the expiry of his visa. Essentially a series of encounters with characters Taghmaoui meets as he flits in and out of a succession of rented London rooms, this combination of drama, comedy and tinges of the fantastical does not really gel. However vibrant performances and the realistic location shooting just about shade things in its favour. DA DVD

Saïd Taghmaoui *Ali* • Juliette Lewis *Linda* • Rupert Graves *Mark* • Anna Massey *Sarah Stevenson* • Karim Belkhadra *Ahmed* ■ *Dir/Scr* Khaled El Hagar

A Room with a View ★★★★ PG

Period drama 1985 · UK · Colour · 111mins

This is the first of the Merchant Ivory adaptations of EM Forster. While *Howards End* was the one that scooped the major international awards, this is, in many ways, a more vibrant and more influential picture, as it confirmed the marketability of the "heritage" film that was, until recently, this country's most profitable movie export. Everything about the production proclaims its class: Ruth Prawer Jhabvala's script is witty and erudite, Tony Pierce-Roberts's images of Florence and the English countryside are breathtaking and the performances are of masterclass quality. There are longueurs, but the air of Edwardian charm is irresistible. DP. Contains nudity. DVD

Maggie Smith *Charlotte Bartlett* • Helena Bonham Carter *Lucy Honeychurch* • Denholm Elliott *Mr Emerson* • Julian Sands *George Emerson* • Daniel Day-Lewis *Cecil Vyse* • Simon Callow *Reverend Arthur Beebe* • Judi Dench *Miss Eleanor Lavish* • Rosemary Leach *Mrs Honeychurch* • Rupert Graves *Freddy Honeychurch* ■ *Dir* James Ivory • *Scr* Ruth Prawer Jhabvala, from the novel by EM Forster

The Roommate ★★★★ PG

Comedy 1984 · US · Colour · 92mins

This is a superior TV adaptation of John Updike's story, *The Christian Roommates*, about university students in the 1950s. Lance Guest is an unworldly undergrad who finds himself sharing a room with disruptive Bohemian Barry Miller, an early exponent of the sort of alternative lifestyle that would be embraced wholesale throughout the second half of the following decade. DF

Lance Guest *Orson Ziegler* • Barry Miller *Henry "Hub" Palamountain* • Elmer Two Crow *Lester* • Melissa Ford *Emily* ■ *Dir* Nell Cox • *Scr* Neal Miller, from the story *The Christian Roommates* by John Updike

Roommates ★★ 12

Comedy drama 1995 · US · Colour · 104mins

Peter Falk stars as an elderly baker who adopts his grandson to prevent him from being sent to an orphanage. With the help of Oscar-nominated make-up, the film chronicles their relationship over the next three decades. They come to blows when little Michael, played by DB Sweeney, is an adult and studying medicine. Grandad, now over a hundred, is at odds with Sweeney's Chinese roommates and girlfriend Julianne Moore. Daft and overlong, this twaddle is bearable if only for the conviction of Falk's performance. LH

Peter Falk *Rocky* • DB Sweeney *Michael Holczek* • Julianne Moore *Beth* • Ellen Burstyn *Judith* • Jan Rubes *Bolek Krupa* ■ *Dir* Peter Yates • *Scr* Max Apple, Stephen Metcalfe, from the autobiography *Roommates: My Grandfather's Story* by Max Apple

Rooney ★★★ U

Comedy 1958 · UK · BW · 87mins

Ah, the blarney overflows in this very Pinewood version of Catherine Cookson's novel of an Irish dustman in love. Liverpool-born John Gregson makes a likeable stab at the title role, but sadly lacks grit alongside the more authentic Marie Kean, Jack MacGowran, Noel Purcell, Liam Redmond and bedridden Barry Fitzgerald. And if they're all a little too much for you, then so be it, but the result is really quite charming. TS

John Gregson *James Ignatius Rooney* • Muriel Pavlow *Maire Hogan* • Barry Fitzgerald *Grandfather* • June Thorburn *Doreen O'Flynn* • Noel Purcell *Tim Hennessy* • Marie Kean *Mrs O'Flynn* • Liam Redmond *Mr Doolan* • Jack MacGowran *Joe O'Connor* ■ *Dir* George Pollock • *Scr* Patrick Kirwan, from the novel *Rooney* by Catherine Cookson

Rooster Cogburn ★★★ U

Western 1975 · US · Colour · 102mins

A memorable collaboration between John Wayne and Katharine Hepburn, with Wayne reprising his Oscar-winning role in *True Grit* and Hepburn playing the same kind of Bible-punching spinster she portrayed in *The African Queen*. Here, Hepburn is the missionary who tames the truculence of one-eyed Wayne as they search for her father's killers. The performances are wonderful, but the film relies too much on its elderly stars and is fatally flawed by Stuart Millar's sluggish direction. However, it remains eminently watchable, as great stars go through their paces. TH DVD

John Wayne *Rooster Cogburn* • Katharine Hepburn *Eula Goodnight* • Anthony Zerbe *Breed* • Richard Jordan *Hawk* • John McIntire *Judge Parker* • Richard Romancito *Wolf* • Strother Martin *McCoy* ■ *Dir* Stuart Millar • *Scr* Martin Julien, from the character created by Charles Portis in his novel *True Grit*

Roosters ★★

Drama 1993 · US · Colour · 93mins

A who's who of Hispanic acting talent, with the likes of Edward James Olmos, Sonia Braga and Maria Conchita Alonso teaming up for a heavy-handed poetic tale of poultry and patriarchy. Olmos plays an ex-con who returns home to reclaim his place as head of a poverty-line household and raise fighting cocks. The quality of the cast ensures some passionate acting, but this weighs in too lightly on subtlety and too heavily on pretentious dialogue and symbolism. DA

Edward James Olmos *Gallo Morales* • Sonia Braga *Juana* • Maria Conchita Alonso *Chata* • Danny Nucci *Hector* • Sarah Lassez *Angela* • Valente Rodriguez *Adan* ■ *Dir* Robert M Young • *Scr* Milcha Sanchez-Scott, from her play

The Root of All Evil ★★

Drama 1946 · UK · BW · 110mins

Attempting to break from her wholesome image, Phyllis Calvert here found herself in a role much more suited to her *Man in Grey* co-star, Margaret Lockwood. Her transformation from fresh-faced farm girl to scheming oil tycoon, by way of a breach of promise suit against fiancé Hubert Gregg, is totally implausible, and the harder she tries to be wicked, the more ludicrous the action becomes. Without the costumes to provide a distraction, however, this is one of Gainsborough's lesser outings. DP

Phyllis Calvert *Jeckie Farnish* • Michael Rennie *Charles Mortimer* • John McCallum *Joe Bartle* • Brefni O'Rorke *Mr Farnish* • Arthur Young *George Grice* • Hubert Gregg *Albert Grice* • Pat Hicks *Lucy Grice* ■ *Dir* Brock Williams • *Scr* Brock Williams, from the novel by JS Fletcher

The Roots of Heaven ★★

Drama 1958 · US · Colour · 131mins

Seven years after *The African Queen*, John Huston had another gruelling location adventure shooting in French Equatorial Africa for this drama. With Errol Flynn and Trevor Howard in the cast, it was a boozy set, and the movie rather staggers and lurches along. Howard is in Africa to save the elephant from ivory poachers and extinction. Flynn supports Howard's campaign and as does TV reporter Orson Welles. It's sadly muddled and the raddled Flynn looks more endangered than any elephant. AT

Errol Flynn *Major Forsythe* • Juliette Greco *Minna* • Trevor Howard *Morel* • Eddie Albert *Abe Fields* • Orson Welles *Cy Sedgewick* • Paul Lukas *Saint Denis* • Herbert Lom *Orsini* • Grégoire Aslan *Habib* ■ *Dir* John Huston • *Scr* Romain Gary, Patrick Leigh-Fermor, from the novel by Romain Gary

Rope ★★★ PG

Thriller 1948 · US · Colour · 76mins

Alfred Hitchcock here places a pair of homosexual student murderers (Farley Granger and John Dall) in a fashionable New York apartment, where they give a party for academic James Stewart and relatives of the young victim, whose body is present in a trunk from which they serve the drinks. Curiously devoid of suspense, the film is more of an intriguing cerebral exercise, famous as an experiment in the technique of the continuous take than a characteristic Hitchcockian entertainment or character study. Based on the real-life Leopold and Loeb case, it remains historically interesting, but nowadays disappoints. RK DVD

James Stewart *Rupert Cadell* • John Dall *John Brandon* • Farley Granger *Phillip Morgan* • Sir Cedric Hardwicke [Cedric Hardwicke] *Mr Kentley* • Joan Chandler *Janet Walker* • Constance Collier *Mrs Atwater* • Edith Evanson *Mrs Wilson* ■ *Dir* Alfred Hitchcock • *Scr* Arthur Laurents, Hume Cronyn, Ben Hecht (uncredited), from the play by Patrick Hamilton

R

Rope of Sand ★★

Adventure drama 1949 · US · BW · 104mins

In an improbable Hollywood version of South Africa, heroic big-game hunter Burt Lancaster foils the nefarious activities of gem seekers and rescues the lady caught in the complicated plot. Directed by William Dieterle with Claude Rains as a suave schemer, Paul Henreid a chilling sadist and Peter Lorre a whining opportunist on the edge of things, this gathering of half the cast of *Casablanca*, plus French actress Corinne Calvet making a less than persuasive Hollywood debut, is a nonsensical adventure. RK

Burt Lancaster *Mike Davis* • Paul Henreid *Commandant Paul Vogel* • Claude Rains *Arthur Fred Martingale* • Peter Lorre *Toady* • Corinne Calvet *Suzanne Renaud* • Sam Jaffe *Dr Francis "Doc" Hunter* • John Bromfield *Thompson, guard* ■ *Dir* William Dieterle • *Scr* Walter Doniger, John Paxton, from a story by Walter Doniger

Rosa Luxemburg ★★★★ PG

Biographical drama
1986 · W Ger · Colour · 123mins

Despite her surname, Rosa Luxemburg was actually born in Poland, resident in Germany and widely considered one of the most dangerous women of her age: a revolutionary, internationalist, pacifist, Jew and troublemaker and probably vegetarian to boot. Award-winning actress Barbara Sukowa was rightly rewarded for for portraying her in this praised German film. An intelligent biopic, of historical, personal and dramatic interest. PF. In German with English subtitles.

Barbara Sukowa *Rosa Luxemburg* • Daniel Olbrychski *Leo Jogiches* • Otto Sander *Karl Liebknecht* • Adelheid Arndt *Luise Kautsky* • Jürgen Holtz *Karl Kautsky* ■ *Dir/Scr* Margarethe von Trotta

Rosalie ★★ U

Musical comedy 1937 · US · BW · 124mins

Nelson Eddy teams with tap-dancer Eleanor Powell in this crass and kitschy cross between operetta and college musical. Nelson is a West Point cadet in love with Powell, playing Princess Rosalie of Romanza, who is studying at Vassar The best song in the so-so Cole Porter score is *In the Still of the Night*, while the gigantic title number (hated by its composer) had Powell in a frothy tutu and a cast of thousands. RB

Nelson Eddy *Dick Thorpe* • Eleanor Powell *Rosalie* • Ray Bolger *Bill Delroy* • Frank Morgan *King* • Ilona Massey *Brenda* • Edna May Oliver *Queen* • Billy Gilbert *Oloff* • Reginald Owen *Chancellor* • William Demarest *Army's coach* ■ *Dir* WS Van Dyke • *Scr* William Anthony McGuire, from the musical by William Anthony McGuire, by Guy Bolton

Rosalie Goes Shopping ★★★ 15

Comedy 1989 · W Ger · Colour · 89mins

Critics at the time considered German director Percy Adlon's follow-up to the cult favourite *Bagdad Café* to have been something of a disappointment. Yet, in many ways, this is a more assured piece of film-making, largely because Adlon's grasp of modern American mores was much firmer. This is a stinging satire on the consumerist boom that occurred during the Reagan presidency, when acquisition made life worthwhile and payment was an inconvenience. Adlon regular Marianne Sägebrecht gives a beguiling performance as the shopaholic of the title, while Brad Davis provides solid support as her crop-dusting husband. DP. Contains swearing. [video]

Marianne Sägebrecht *Rosalie Greenspace* • Brad Davis *Ray Greenspace, "Liebling"* • Judge Reinhold *Priest* • Erika Blumberger *Rosalie's mum* • Willy Harlander *Rosalie's dad* ■ *Dir* Percy Adlon • *Scr* Percy Adlon, Eleonore Adlon, Christopher Doherty

R

The Rosary Murders ★★★ 18

Murder mystery 1987 · US · Colour · 100mins

The sometimes mildly threatening Donald Sutherland makes an unlikely Detroit priest, but his fine, controlled performance in this dark, unsettling film lifts its rather plodding pace. Sutherland is the recipient of every priest's occupational nightmare, the serial killer who picks his church to confess in. We witness a neat tussle of conscience, as victims are felled like ninepins for most of the film. One of those promising efforts which starts out at a decent lick but ends up running out of steam and ideas. SH. Contains violence and swearing. [video]

Donald Sutherland *Father Bob Koesler* • Charles Durning *Father Ted Nabors* • Josef Sommer *Lieutenant Walt Koznicki* • Belinda Bauer *Pat Lennon* • James Murtaugh *Javison* ■ *Dir* Fred Walton • *Scr* Elmore Leonard, Fred Walton, from the novel by William X Kienzle

The Rose ★★ 15

Musical drama 1979 · US · Colour · 128mins

Trapped by the usual conventions of rock-star biopics – drugs, booze and blues – Bette Midler, playing a singer loosely based on Janis Joplin, is only really effective during her raunchy concert numbers. For the rest of the film she's at the mercy of a script as ridiculous as the hairstyles. Alan Bates gives a skilful performance that makes his ruthless manager a plausible man, but Midler just muddles through. TH. Contains swearing, nudity. [video] DVD

Bette Midler *Rose* • Alan Bates *Rudge* • Frederic Forrest *Dyer* • Harry Dean Stanton *Billy Ray* • Barry Primus *Dennis* • David Keith *Mal* ■ *Dir* Mark Rydell • *Scr* Bo Goldman, William Kerby, Michael Cimino, from the story by William Kerby

The Rose Garden ★★ 15

Courtroom drama based on a true story
1989 · W Ger/US · Colour · 108mins

Winner of the best foreign film Oscar for his 1986 movie *The Assault*, Dutch director Fons Rademakers returned to the subject of the Second World War with this study of memory and guilt. Set in modern-day Germany, the story of Maximilian Schell's prosecution for attacking the former commandant of the concentration camp where his sister died eschews the cheap sentimentality that blights so many films about the Holocaust. However, it also mistakes slowness for sincerity and spends too much time exploring lawyer Liv Ullmann's relationship with her estranged husband, Peter Fonda. DP [video]

Liv Ullmann *Gabriele Schlueter-Freund* • Maximilian Schell *Aaron Reichenbach* • Peter Fonda *Herbert Schlueter* • Jan Niklas *George Paessler* • Katarina Lena Muller *Tina* ■ *Dir* Fons Rademakers • *Scr* Paul Hengge

Rose Marie ★★★★ U

Musical romantic comedy
1936 · US · Colour · 111mins

The phenomenally successful 1930s musicals of "America's Sweethearts" Jeanette MacDonald and Nelson Eddy creak mightily now, but there is still abundant fun in this loose adaptation of the popular operetta combined here with a manhunt melodrama. Opera singer MacDonald falls in love with Canadian Mountie Nelson while trying to shield her ne'er-do-well fugitive kid brother James Stewart from the lawman's dogged pursuit. Watch for a brief appearance by newcomer David Niven as MacDonald's would-be suitor. AME

Jeanette MacDonald *Marie de Flor* • Nelson Eddy *Sgt Bruce* • James Stewart *John Flower* • Reginald Owen *Myerson* • George Regas *Boniface* • Robert Greig *Cafe manager* • Una O'Connor *Anna* • James Conlin [Jimmy Conlin] *Joe, the piano player* • Lucien Littlefield *Storekeeper* • Mary Anita Loos *Corn Queen* • David Niven *Teddy* ■ *Dir* WS Van Dyke II [WS Van Dyke] • *Scr* Frances Goodrich, Albert Hackett, Alice Duer Miller, from the operetta by Otto A Harbach [Otto Harbach], Oscar Hammerstein II, Rudolf Friml, Herbert Stothart

Rose Marie ★★★ U

Musical romantic comedy
1954 · US · Colour · 99mins

MGM's remake of its phenomenally successful 1936 vehicle for Jeanette MacDonald and Nelson Eddy is the first colour CinemaScope musical and takes advantage of locations in the Canadian Rockies, but is nowhere near as beguiling as its predecessor. It stars Ann Blyth, Howard Keel as the Mountie, "Latin Lover" Fernando Lamas as an unlikely fur trapper, and Joan Taylor as the daughter of a tribal chief and a new character in the reworked plot of the operetta. RK [video]

Ann Blyth *Rose Marie Lemaitre* • Howard Keel *Mike Malone* • Fernando Lamas *James Severn Duval* • Bert Lahr *Barney McCorkle* • Marjorie Main *Lady Jane Dunstock* • Joan Taylor *Wanda* ■ *Dir* Mervyn LeRoy • *Scr* Ronald Millar, George Froeschel, from the operetta by Otto A Harbach [Otto Harbach], Oscar Hammerstein II, Rudolf Friml, Herbert Stothart • *Choreographer* Busby Berkeley

Rose of Cimarron ★★ U

Western 1952 · US · Colour · 72mins

Mala Powers is an orphan brought up by native Americans who is seeking revenge for the death of her parents. Powers's co-star is Jack Buetel, but it's up to western veterans such as Jim Davis, Bill Williams and old hand Bob Steele to keep this production on its feet. Incidentally, this was published as a one-off comic book in the 1950s with a knockout cover: mint copies are now much prized by collectors. TS

Jack Buetel *Marshal Hollister* • Mala Powers *Rose of Cimarron* • Bill Williams *George Newcomb* • Jim Davis *Willie Whitewater* • Dick Curtis *Clem Dawley* • Tom Monroe *Mike Finch* • William Phipps *Jeb Dawley* • Bob Steele *Rio* ■ *Dir* Harry Keller • *Scr* Maurice Geraghty

Rose of Washington Square ★★★

Musical 1939 · US · BW · 86mins

Alice Faye plays Rose in a very thinly disguised biopic of Ziegfeld headliner Fanny Brice, later more memorably incarnated by Barbra Streisand in the show and movie *Funny Girl* (and its sequel). Here, Faye falls for handsome but no-good, and severely underwritten, gambler Tyrone Power, and is inspired by him to sing Brice's theme song *My Man*. But the real treat of the movie is the appearance of the great Al Jolson, who sings a batch of his own hits. TS

Tyrone Power *Bart Clinton* • Alice Faye *Rose Sargent* • Al Jolson *Ted Cotter* • William Frawley *Harry Long* • Joyce Compton *Peggy* • Hobart Cavanaugh *Whitey Boone* • Moroni Olsen *Buck Russell* ■ *Dir* Gregory Ratoff • *Scr* Nunnally Johnson, from a story by John Larkin, Jerry Horwin

The Rose Tattoo ★★★

Drama 1955 · US · BW · 116mins

Anna Magnani goes wild with desire for Burt Lancaster who has a tattoo on his chest like that of her virile dead husband. Magnani's daughter, who sets a sailor's pulse racing, adds another layer of smouldering compost to this already earthy tale which could only have come from the pen of Tennessee Williams. Williams wrote the play for Magnani but she chickened out of doing it on stage; however on film, she carted off an Oscar, a Bafta and a New York Film Critics Circle award, though a more OTT performance would be hard to find. AT

Anna Magnani *Serafina Delle Rose* • Burt Lancaster *Alvaro Mangiacavallo* • Marisa Pavan *Rosa Delle Rose* • Ben Cooper *Jack Hunter* • Virginia Grey *Estelle Hohengarten* • Jo Van Fleet *Bessie* ■ *Dir* Daniel Mann • *Scr* Tennessee Williams, Hal Kanter, from the play by Tennessee Williams

Roseanna McCoy ★★★ PG

Romantic drama 1949 · US · BW · 84mins

The bucolic Ozark mountain feuds between rival family factions have barely been touched on in cinema, and neither this movie nor the later *Lolly Madonna War* really conveyed what internecine warfare over moonshine and sex must've really been like. Producer Samuel Goldwyn used the famous Hatfield–McCoy feud to feature his young contract stars Farley Granger and Joan Evans, but the two leads look far too urbane. TS [video]

Farley Granger *Johnse Hatfield* • Joan Evans *Roseanna McCoy* • Charles Bickford *Devil Anse Hatfield* • Raymond Massey *Old Randall McCoy* • Richard Basehart *Mounts Hatfield* ■ *Dir* Irving Reis • *Scr* John Collier, from the novel by Alberta Hannum

Roseanna's Grave ★★★ 12

Romantic comedy
1996 · US/UK · Colour · 93mins

The delightful Jean Reno stars in this spry comedy as a bistro proprietor whose beloved, dying wife Roseanna (Mercedes Ruehl) has her weak heart set on being buried in the village churchyard, next to their daughter. The problem is there are only a few plots left, so Reno embarks on a frantic mission to secure a cemetery space by rescuing the ailing and concealing inconvenient corpses. Reno and Ruehl give heart-warming performances in this lightweight, genial lark, which may sometimes skitter uncertainly between gentle whimsy and laboured farce, but has undeniable charm. AME. Contains swearing and some sex scenes. [video]

Jean Reno *Marcello Beatto* • Mercedes Ruehl *Roseanna Beatto* • Polly Walker *Cecilia* • Mark Frankel *Antonio* • Trevor Peacock *Iaccoponi* • Fay Ripley *Francesca* ■ *Dir* Paul Weiland • *Scr* Saul Turteltaub

Les Roseaux Sauvages ★★★★ 15

Drama 1994 · Fr · Colour · 109mins

For all its shimmering images of the beautiful French countryside and its painstaking attention to period detail, this magnificent rites-of-passage drama tackles such complex themes as war, class, sexuality, the age gap and civic responsibility with an intelligence and a naturalism that one has come to expect of director André Téchiné. Rather than delivering a rose-tinted lament for the lost innocence of youth, he takes the emotions, opinions and confusions of teenagers seriously and is rewarded with exceptional performances from the members of his young cast. DP. In French with English subtitles. [video]

Frédéric Gorny *Henri* • Gaël Morel *François* • Elodie Bouchez *Maïté* • Stéphane Rideau *Serge* • Michèle Moretti *Madame Alvarez* • Laurent Groulout *The photographer* • Jacques Nolot *Monsieur Morelli* ■ *Dir* André Téchiné • *Scr* André Téchiné, Gilles Taurand, Olivier Massart

Rosebud ★★ 15

Political action thriller
1975 · US · Colour · 121mins

A depressing bloom, indeed, from director Otto Preminger in which PLO terrorists kidnap five women who are holidaying aboard a yacht. Intercutting between the women's plight and what's being done to help them slows the idea down to stasis, despite the efforts of CIA agent Peter O'Toole, Richard Attenborough and Adrienne Corri to salvage it. TH. Contains violence and swearing. [video]

Peter O'Toole *Larry Martin* • Richard Attenborough *Sloat* • Cliff Gorman *Hamlekh* • Claude Dauphin *Fargeau* • John V Lindsay *United States Senator Donovan* • Peter Lawford *Lord Carter* • Raf Vallone *George Nikolaos* • Adrienne Corri *Lady Carter* • *Dir* Otto Preminger • *Scr* Erik Lee Preminger, from a novel by Joan Hemingway, Paul Bonnecarrere

Roseland ★★★★ PG

Dance drama 1977 · US · Colour · 103mins

Merchant Ivory's American films are less celebrated than their famously lovely English and Indian literary adaptations, but the American James Ivory is also at his least cosy exploring his homeland. This bittersweet collection of tales set in New York's Roseland ballroom sees a marvellous ensemble of lonely hearts trip the light fantastic reminiscing about life and love. Making one of her rare screen appearances after a premature 1959 retirement, Teresa Wright is moving as the widow with a new lease of life after striking up a dance partnership with

Lou Jacobi. Christopher Walken (a trained dancer early in his career) makes an oily impression as a dancehall predator. AME DVD

Teresa Wright *May* • Lou Jacobi *Stan* • Don DeNatale *Master of Ceremonies* • Louise Kirtland *Ruby* • Hetty Galen *Red-haired lady* • Geraldine Chaplin *Marilyn* • Christopher Walken *Russel* • Lilia Skala *Rosa* ■ *Dir* James Ivory • *Scr* Ruth Prawer Jhabvala • *Executive Producer* Ismail Merchant

Roselyne and the Lions ★★★ PG

Drama 1989 · Fr · Colour · 136mins

It's hard to fathom exactly what director Jean-Jacques Beineix was up to with this too-leisurely parable on the theme of creation and the ever-present spectre of death. As the couple whose desire to tame lions leads to passion, Pasco and Gérard Sandoz look good enough, and the hours of off-screen training they put in with the big cats fully pays off. But the tensions that arise once Pasco is encouraged by a lustful German circus owner are nowhere near as interesting as the tentative manoeuvres of the opening scenes in the Marseille zoo. DP. In French with English subtitles. [video]

Isabelle Pasco *Roselyne* • Gérard Sandoz *Thierry* • Philippe Clevenot *Bracquard* • Günter Meisner *Klint* • Wolf Harnisch *Koenig* • Gabriel Monnet *Frazier* • Jacques Le Carpentier *Markovitch* ■ *Dir* Jean-Jacques Beineix • *Scr* Jean-Jacques Beineix, Jacques Forgeas

Rosemary's Baby ★★★★★ 18

Horror 1968 · US · Colour · 131mins

Ira Levin's bestseller about Antichrist cultism in Manhattan is impeccably and faithfully brought to the screen by director Roman Polanski in this genuinely horrifying chiller that quietly builds unbearable tension. Mia Farrow is the perfect satanic foil in a supernatural classic of conspiratorial evil meshed with apocalyptic revelations, and Ruth Gordon won a deserved Oscar for her busy-body portrayal of eccentric menace. It's one of the most powerful films ever made about Devil worship because Polanski expertly winds up the paranoia with spooky atmospherics and morbid humour. AJ. Contains nudity. [video] DVD

Mia Farrow *Rosemary Woodhouse* • John Cassavetes *Guy Woodhouse* • Ruth Gordon *Minnie Castevet* • Sidney Blackmer *Roman Castevet* • Maurice Evans *Hutch* • Ralph Bellamy *Dr Sapirstein* • Tony Curtis *Donald Baumgart* ■ *Dir* Roman Polanski • *Scr* Roman Polanski, from the novel by Ira Levin

Rosencrantz and Guildenstern Are Dead ★★★★ PG

Comedy 1990 · US · Colour · 112mins

Tom Stoppard's screen version of his own hit play, beginning with a splendid long shot of Rosencrantz and Guildenstern making their way to Elsinore, has largely been dismissed by the critics, who disapproved both of his opening out what had been a delightful theatrical experience and his audacity in penning new material. They were also pretty scathing of the performances by Gary Oldman and Tim Roth. Yet, combining verbal dexterity with precise slapstick timing, they capture the boredom and bewilderment of these two *Hamlet* also-rans with disarming charm. Richard Dreyfuss as the Player and Ian Richardson as Polonius also score. DP [video] DVD

Gary Oldman *Rosencrantz* • Tim Roth *Guildenstern* • Richard Dreyfuss *Player* • Joanna Roth *Ophelia* • Iain Glen *Prince Hamlet* • Donald Sumpter *King Claudius* • Joanna Miles *Queen Gertrude* • Ian Richardson *Polonius* ■ *Dir/Scr* Tom Stoppard

Rosetta ★★★ 15

Drama 1999 · Bel/Fr · Colour · 90mins

Inspired by Kafka and booed on winning the Palme d'Or at Cannes, Luc and Jean-Pierre Dardenne's starkly realistic insight into life on the lowest rung makes for difficult viewing. However, as the debuting Emilie Dequenne clings to the soul-destroying routine she hopes will land the job she needs for self-esteem as much as pay, the film begins to grip. Spurning both the optimism of American "trailer trash" pictures and the politicking of British social realism, this film makes no commercial concessions and is all the better for it. DP. In French with English subtitles. [video]

Emilie Dequenne *Rosetta* • Fabrizio Rongione *Riquet* • Anne Yernaux *Rosetta's mother* • Olivier Gourmet *Boss* ■ *Dir/Scr* Luc Dardenne, Jean-Pierre Dardenne

Rosewood ★★★ 18

Period drama based on a true story 1997 · US · Colour · 136mins

This powerful historical drama from director John Singleton re-creates with shocking intensity a 1920s atrocity that was hushed up until a journalist came across the story by chance in the early 1980s. A false charge of rape leads to the annihilation of a black settlement by a mob of Florida rednecks in 1923. Singleton reconstructs the incident with care, but the intervention of Ving Rhames's fictional American Civil War hero and the unconvincing repentance of adulterous shopkeeper Jon Voight undermine this otherwise noble attempt. DP [video]

Jon Voight *John Wright* • Ving Rhames *Mann* • Don Cheadle *Sylvester Carrier* • Bruce McGill *Duke Purdy* • Loren Dean *James Taylor* • Esther Rolle *Aunt Sarah* • Elise Neal *Scrappie* ■ *Dir* John Singleton • *Scr* Gregory Poirier

Rosie! ★ U

Comedy drama 1967 · US · Colour · 97mins

The grasping daughters of a wealthy, off-the-wall widow with an overdeveloped penchant for spending her money, have her committed to a spartan "rest home" in order to curb her extravagance. Naturally, mother emerges as the heroine after a court case. Rosalind Russell, giving her considerable all as a cut-price version of Auntie Mame, is unable to rescue this unspeakable rubbish adapted, for no good reason, from a failed Broadway play by Ruth Gordon. RK

Rosalind Russell *Rosie Lord* • Sandra Dee *Daphne* • Brian Aherne *Oliver Stevenson* • Audrey Meadows *Mildred* • James Farentino *David* • Vanessa Brown *Edith* • Leslie Nielsen *Cabot* • Margaret Hamilton *Mae* ■ *Dir* David Lowell Rich • *Scr* Samuel Taylor, from the play *A Very Rich Woman* by Ruth Gordon, from the play *Les Joies de la Famille* by Philippe Hériat

Rosie Dixon: Night Nurse ★ 18

Sex comedy 1978 · UK · Colour · 84mins

It should give you some idea of the mire into which the British film industry had plunged itself during the 1970s when you read such names as Beryl Reid, John Le Mesurier and Liz Fraser on the cast list of this bawdy hospital comedy. Debbie Ash (sister of Leslie) suffers countless indignities in the title role, but it's Arthur Askey who stoops the lowest, as he resorts to pinching uniformed bottoms to get the cheapest of laughs. DP [video]

Beryl Reid *Matron* • John Le Mesurier *Sir Archibald MacGregor* • Debbie Ash *Rosie Dixon* • Arthur Askey *Mr Arkwright* • Liz Fraser *Mrs Dixon* • John Junkin *Mr Dixon* ■ *Dir* Justin Cartwright • *Scr* Justin Cartwright, Christopher Wood

Rosie the Riveter ★★ U

Wartime comedy 1944 · US · BW · 74mins

A wartime tribute to the women working in the factories (retitled *In Rosie's Room* in the UK, where few knew what a riveter was), this B-movie is best remembered for its popular title tune. Jane Frazee plays Rosie, who has to share an apartment with three other factory workers (two of them men) due to the housing shortage. TV

Jane Frazee *Rosalind "Rosie" Warren* • Frank Albertson *Charlie Doran* • Vera Vague [Barbara Jo Allen] *Vera Watson* • Frank Jenks *Kelly Kennedy* • Maude Eburne *Grandma Quill* • Lloyd Corrigan *Clem Prouty* ■ *Dir* Joseph Santley • *Scr* Jack Townley, Aleen Leslie, from the story *Room for Two* by Dorothy Curnow Handley

Rosita ★★

Silent period romance 1923 · US · BW

King of Spain Holbrook Blinn wants guitar-strumming dancing girl Mary Pickford for his mistress, but she loves dashing nobleman George Walsh (director Raoul Walsh's brother) who is under sentence of death for treason. This romantic period melodrama, set in 18th-century Toledo, marked Pickford's failed bid to transform herself from America's "Little Mary" into a tempestuous romantic star. More importantly, it marked the Hollywood debut of director Ernst Lubitsch, whom Pickford imported from Germany for the occasion. They didn't hit it off and the film was completed amid a multitude of disagreements. RK

Mary Pickford *Rosita* • Holbrook Blinn *The King* • Irene Rich *The Queen* • George Walsh *Don Diego* • Charles Belcher *The Prime Minister* ■ *Dir* Ernst Lubitsch • *Scr* Edward Knoblock, from a story by Norbert Falk, Hans Kräly, from the play *Don César de Bazan* by Adolphe Philippe Dennery, Philippe François Pinel

The Rossiter Case ★

Crime mystery 1950 · UK · BW · 75mins

This obscure melodrama from Hammer's early B-movie days never escapes its stage origins. Helen Shingler stars as the wife who's paralysed after a car accident, only to discover that her sister (Sheila Burrell) is having an affair with her husband (Clement McCallin). A quarrel leads to the shooting of one sister and the husband's arrest for murder. AE

Helen Shingler *Liz Rossiter* • Clement McCallin *Peter Rossiter* • Sheila Burrell *Honor* • Frederick Leister *Sir James Ferguson* • Henry Edwards *Dr Bendix* ■ *Dir* Francis Searle • *Scr* Kenneth Hyde, John Gilling, Francis Searle, from the play by Kenneth Hyde

Roswell ★★★★ 12

Science-fiction drama 1994 · US · Colour and BW · 87mins

The year is 1947, and Kyle MacLachlan is the military intelligence officer who begins investigating what appears to be the crash-landing of a flying saucer and starts to suspect a cover-up. MacLachlan is convincing as the officer, there are neat supporting turns in this TV movie from Martin Sheen and country singer Dwight Yoakam, and director Jeremy Kagan summons up an air of paranoia that Mulder and Scully would have felt quite at home with. JF. [video]

Kyle MacLachlan *Major Jesse Marcel* • Martin Sheen *Townsend* • Dwight Yoakam *Mac Brazel* • Xander Berkeley *Sherman Carson* • Bob Gunton *Frank Joyce* • Kim Greist *Vy Marcel* • Peter MacNicol *Lewis Rickett* ■ *Dir* Jeremy Kagan [Jeremy Paul Kagan] • *Scr* Arthur Kopit, from a story by Paul Davids, Jeremy Kagan [Jeremy Paul Kagan], from the book *UFO Crash at Roswell* by Donald R Schmitt, Steven Poster

Rothschild's Violin ★★★ U

Biographical drama
1996 · Fr/Swi/Fin/Hun · Colour · 101mins

Argentinian-born director Edgardo Cozarinsky explores the theme of state intervention in the arts in this astute re-creation of a little-known episode in Stalinist history. The composer Shostakovich sought to make a stand by performing the unfinished opera of his disciple Benjamin Fleischmann, a Jew who had died in the siege of Leningrad. Cozarinsky first combines archive footage and re-enacted material to explore Soviet classical music in the 1930s, before presenting a full performance of *Le Violon de Rothschild* and a scathing assessment of Stalin's rule. Difficult, but rewarding. DP. In Russian with English subtitles.

Sergei Makovetsky *Dmitri Shostakovich* • Dainius Kazlauskus *Benjamin Fleischmann* • Miklos B Szekely *Bronze* • Mari Torocsik *Marfa* • Sandor Zsoter *Rothschild* • Ferenc Javori *Chakhkes* ■ *Dir/Scr* Edgardo Cozarinsky

Rotten to the Core ★★

Crime comedy 1965 · UK · BW · 89mins

Everywhere you looked during the early 1960s, there was a comic criminal mastermind planning an audacious raid that was doomed to failure because his gang were paid-up members of Dolts Anonymous. Anton Rodgers is the great brain here, posing as a top-ranking general in order to rob an army camp. Charlotte Rampling is slinkily amusing as the moll, but what few laughs there are come from Eric Sykes. Fitfully funny. DP

Eric Sykes *Hunt* • Ian Bannen *Vine* • Dudley Sutton *Jelly* • Kenneth Griffith *Lenny* • James Beckett *Scapa* • Avis Bunnage *Countess* • Anton Rodgers *Duke* • Charlotte Rampling *Sara* • Victor Maddern *Anxious* ■ *Dir* John Boulting • *Scr* John Warren, Len Heath, Jeffrey Dell, Roy Boulting, from their story, from an idea by John Warren, Len Heath

La Roue ★★★★★

Silent tragedy 1923 · Fr · BW · 303mins

Even before he made *Napoleon* (1927), Abel Gance was considered the Griffith of France; on seeing this masterpiece, Jean Cocteau opined: "There is cinema before and after *La Roue* as there is painting before and after Picasso." The story concerns the suffering of railway engineer Séverin-Mars and his violin-making son Gabriel de Gravone over the marriage of adopted family member Ivy Close to ageing inspector Pierre Magnier. Shot on location over 16 months and originally running some nine hours, it was eventually released by Pathé at just 144 minutes. Yet, even in truncated form the audacious blend of realism and romanticism achieved by superbly-controlled accelerated and associative montage is clearly evident. A restored 303-minute version was completed by Marie Epstein in 1980. DP. With French titles and simultaneous English translation.

Séverin-Mars *Sisif* • Gabriel de Gravone *Elie* • Pierre Magnier *Jacques de Hersan, the engineer* • Ivy Close *Norma* • Georges Terof *Mâchefer* ■ *Dir/Scr* Abel Gance

Rouge ★★★★ 15

Fantasy romance 1987 · HK · Colour · 92mins

This ghost story-cum-satire oozes quality, from the sublime photography of Bill Wong to the outstanding performance of Anita Mui as the troubled spirit of a 1930s courtesan, condemned to wander the streets of Hong Kong until she meets the lover with whom she entered into a suicide pact. Perfectly re-creating the decadent elegance of the 1930s and gently mocking the consumerism of the 1980s, Stanley Kwan tells his story

R

(co-adapted by Li Bihua from her own novel) with a lightness of touch few modern directors can rival. DP. In Cantonese with English subtitles. Contains drug abuse.

Anita Mui *Fleur* • Leslie Cheung *Chan Chen-Pang* • Alex Man *Yuen* • Emily Chu *Ah Chor* • Irene Wan *Suk-Yin* ■ *Dir* Stanley Kwan • *Scr* Li Bihua, Qiu-Dai Anping, from the novel by Li Bihua

Rouge Baiser ★★★ 15

Drama based on a true story
1985 · Fr · Colour · 108mins

With its faithful re-creation of the atmosphere of Parisian jazz clubs in the early 1950s, its perceptive insights into the emotional and intellectual naivety of teenagers, and its inch-perfect performances, this neatly observed film should have been a joy. Charlotte Valandrey plays her heart out as the 15-year-old Communist whose world comes tumbling down with the onset of romance and disturbing news from inside Stalin's empire. But director Véra Belmont spoils it all with an overindulgence in flashy camerawork. DP. In French with English subtitles.

Charlotte Valandrey *Nadia* • Lambert Wilson *Stéphane* • Marthe Keller *Bronka* • Günter Lamprecht *Herschel* • Laurent Terzieff *Moische* ■ *Dir* Véra Belmont • *Scr* Véra Belmont, Guy Konopnicki, David Milhaud

Le Rouge et le Noir ★★★

Period romantic drama
1954 · Fr · Colour · 153mins

Gérard Philipe plays the Stendahl anti-hero in this pictorialist adaptation of his 1830 novel. Claude Autant-Lara was frequently accused by such critics as François Truffaut for producing *cinéma du papa* or traditionalist narratives that were more literary than filmic. Certainly, for all the surface sheen, a paucity of visual imagination was expended on this tale of the young man who seduces his way up the socio-political ladder. But there's little of the book's biting irony, either. DP. In French with English subtitles.

Gérard Philipe *Julien Sorel* • Danielle Darrieux *Mme Louise de Renal* • Antonella Lualdi *Mathilde de la Mole* • Jean Martinelli *M de Renal* • Antoine Balpêtré *Abbé Pirard* • Anna-Maria Sandri *Elisa* • Jean Mercure *Marquis de la Mole* • André Brunot *Abbé Chelan* ■ *Dir* Claude Autant-Lara • *Scr* Jean Aurenche, Pierre Bost, from the novel by Stendhal

R

The Rough and the Smooth ★★

Erotic thriller 1959 · UK · BW · 99mins

Hollywood director Robert Siodmak, a *film noir* specialist, brought his talents to Britain for this thriller that trades on its steamy sex scenes. Tony Britton stars as an archeologist who has a fling with shady lady Nadja Tiller, who plays secretary to rich and ugly William Bendix. A trademark hammy Donald Wolfit represents the gutter press, to which the sordid story is leaked. It's intended to show the decadence and corruption that lies at the heart of the British establishment. AT

Nadja Tiller *Ila Hansen* • Tony Britton *Mike Thompson* • William Bendix *Reg Barker* • Natasha Parry *Margaret Goreham* • Norman Wooland *David Fraser* • Donald Wolfit *Lord Drewell* • Tony Wright *Jack* • Adrienne Corri *Jane Buller* • Joyce Carey *Mrs Thompson* ■ *Dir* Robert Siodmak • *Scr* Audrey Erskine-Lindop, Dudley Leslie, from the novel *The Rough and the Smooth* by Robin Maugham

Rough Cut ★★★ PG

Crime comedy 1980 · US · Colour · 106mins

Burt Reynolds does his Cary Grant impersonation in a stylish caper comedy where even the criminals have a touch of class. It's a mellow throwback to those elegant light entertainments of the 1950s, and director Don Siegel injects irony and droll humour into a breezy script that gives charming gentleman burglar Reynolds every opportunity to shine. Rather an atypical movie from action man Siegel who was, in fact, fired and rehired during filming. AJ. Contains swearing.

Burt Reynolds *Jack Rhodes* • Lesley-Anne Down *Gillian Bromley* • David Niven *Chief Inspector Cyril Willis* • Timothy West *Nigel Lawton* • Patrick Magee *Ernst Mueller* • Al Matthews *Ferguson* • Susan Littler *Sheila* • Joss Ackland *Inspector Vanderveld* • Isabel Dean *Mrs Willis* ■ *Dir* Don Siegel • *Scr* Francis Burns [Larry Gelbart], from the novel *Touch the Lion's Paw* by Derek Lambert

Rough Diamonds ★★ PG

Romantic comedy
1994 · Aus · Colour · 84mins

Angie Milliken leaves her successful lawyer husband and takes to the Australian outback road with her daughter to find herself. What she finds instead is cattleman Jason Donovan struggling to make ends meet on the ranch he inherited from his parents. Will his prize bull win the cash jackpot in the Brisbane championship and solve his financial problems? Prize bull indeed, but harmless enough even though the script is devoid of humour or character development. AJ.

Jason Donovan *Mike Tyrrell* • Angie Milliken *Chrissie Bright* • Peter Phelps *Dozer Brennan* • Max Cullen *Magistrate Roy* • Haley Toomey *Sam Tyrrell* • Jocelyn Gabriel *Lisa Bright* • Kit Taylor *Les Finnigan* ■ *Dir* Donald Crombie • *Scr* Donald Crombie, Christopher Lee

Rough Magic ★★ 12

Fantasy road movie romance
1995 · Fr/UK · Colour · 100mins

Director Clare Peploe wrestles with a mix of genres in the quirky tale of magician's assistant and runaway bride Bridget Fonda, who flees 1950s LA for Mexico, pursued by various men including cynical detective Russell Crowe hired by her peeved millionaire fiancé. En route she discovers her genuine magical powers. It's an oddball road movie, gumshoe romance and fantasy of magic realism whose clumsy peculiarity doesn't best serve its engaging stars. AME. Contains swearing and violence.

Bridget Fonda *Myra Shumway* • Russell Crowe *Alex Ross* • Kenneth Mars *Magician* • DW Moffett *Cliff Wyatt* • Jim Broadbent *Doc Ansell* • Paul Rodriguez *Diego* ■ *Dir* Clare Peploe • *Scr* Clare Peploe, William Brookfield, Robert Mundy, from the novel *Miss Shumway Waves a Wand* by James Hadley Chase

Rough Night in Jericho ★★

Western 1967 · US · Colour · 103mins

Surprisingly violent (for its day), this Universal western stars an unlikely Dean Martin as the baddie who owns the town of the title and is bent on owning Jean Simmons's stagecoach line and tying up the territory. Ex-marshal George Peppard ain't gonna let him, though. Although expertly directed by Arnold Laven, both Martin and Peppard look far too urbane for this kind of savage western, and there's really little to recommend here. TS. Contains violence.

Dean Martin *Alex Flood* • George Peppard *Dolan* • Jean Simmons *Molly Lang* • John McIntire *Ben Hickman* • Slim Pickens *Yarbrough* • Don Galloway *Jace* • Brad Weston *Torrey* ■ *Dir* Arnold Laven • *Scr* Sydney Boehm, Marvin H Albert, from the novel *The Man in Black* by Marvin H Albert

Rough Riders' Roundup ★★

Western 1939 · US · BW · 58mins

One of eight starring vehicles for Roy Rogers released by Republic in 1939, his second year as a western lead, this features the singing cowboy as a former rough rider in the Spanish-American war who joins the border patrol. Between musical interludes, he and sidekicks Raymond Hatton and Eddie Acuff put an end to a spate of gold bullion robberies. AE

Roy Rogers *Roy* • Mary Hart [Lynne Roberts] *Dorothy* • Raymond Hatton *Rusty* • Eddie Acuff *Tommy* • William Pawley *Arizona Jack* • Dorothy Sebastian *Rose* • George Meeker *Lanning* • Jack Rockwell *Harrison* • Glenn Strange *Henchman* ■ *Dir* Joe Kane [Joseph Kane] • *Scr* Jack Natteford, Duncan Renaldo

Rough Shoot ★★★ U

Spy thriller 1952 · UK · BW · 86mins

A postwar lull in Joel McCrea's career found him relegated, as happened to most ageing male stars, to co-feature westerns. He still found time, however, to make this interesting thriller in England, based on a Geoffrey Household spy story scripted by Eric Ambler. It actually has one of the oldest western plots: the hero believes that he has killed someone accidentally. The English period setting affords much pleasure today, with a cast of West End veterans offering sterling support. TS

Joel McCrea *Lt Col Robert Taine* • Evelyn Keyes *Cecily Taine* • Herbert Lom *Peter Sandorski* • Marius Goring *Hiart* • Roland Culver *Randall* • Frank Lawton *Richard Hassingham* • Patricia Laffan *Magda Hassingham* ■ *Dir* Robert Parrish • *Scr* Eric Ambler, from the novel by Geoffrey Household

Roughly Speaking ★★★

Biographical drama 1945 · US · BW · 117mins

This likeable, sprawling account of the life of the engagingly eccentric Louise Randall Pierson, an early exponent of women's lib, covers 40 years of her life in episodic fashion. There are many fine moments here, but Warner Bros possibly erred in allowing Pierson to adapt her own autobiography, for she was by all accounts reluctant to leave anything out. Giving great performances are Rosalind Russell, loaded with grit as the determined wife and mother, and Jack Carson, as her quixotic husband obsessed with get-rich-quick schemes. Michael Curtiz directs, and there's a charming score by Max Steiner. TV

Rosalind Russell *Louise Randall* • Jack Carson *Harold Pierson* • Robert Hutton *John, aged 20-28* • Jean Sullivan *Louise Jr, aged 18-26* • Donald Woods *Rodney Crane* • Alan Hale *Mr Morton* • Andrea King *Barbara, aged 21-29* • Ann Doran *Alice Abbott* ■ *Dir* Michael Curtiz • *Scr* Louise Randall Pierson, from her autobiography

Roughshod ★★★

Western 1949 · US · BW · 88mins

A likeable western made with unusual care and intelligence, this is also a curiously modest, small-scale undertaking which failed to make a star out of its leading man, Robert Sterling. With the help of kid brother Claude Jarman Jr, Sterling directs a herd of thoroughbred horses, rescues a troupe of saloon girls, and has a run-in with three vicious outlaws. Gloria Grahame plays the leading floozie with her customary panache while John Ireland makes for a mean killer. AE

Robert Sterling *Clay Phillips* • Gloria Grahame *Mary Wells* • John Ireland *Lednov* • Claude Jarman Jr *Steve Phillips* • Jeff Donnell *Elaine Wyatt* • Myrna Dell *Helen Carter* • Martha Hyer *Marcia* • George Cooper *Jim Clayton* • Jeff Corey *Jed Graham* ■ *Dir* Mark Robson • *Scr* Geoffrey Homes [Daniel Mainwaring], Hugo Butler, from a story by Peter Viertel

Roujin Z ★★★★ 15

Animated thriller 1991 · Jpn · Colour · 80mins

Written by Katsuhiro Otomo, who made perhaps the best-known *manga* movie, *Akira*, this animated feature concentrates more on character than on the futuristic concepts and designer violence that tends to dominate the genre. Translating roughly as "Old Man Z", this is primarily a "people versus the powers that be" picture, with a student nurse siding with the elderly when they discover that a luxury bed experiment is the front for more sinister activities. However, it's also a mischievously romantic ghost story and an ironic study of male-female hegemony, while for action fans there's a storming finale. DP. Japanese dialogue dubbed into English.

Dir Hiroyuki Kitakubo • *Scr* Katsuhiro Otomo, from his story

'Round Midnight ★★★★ 15

Musical drama
1986 · US/Fr · Colour · 125mins

According to cinematic formula, when they're not living in poverty until the world finally tunes in to their unique style, jazz musicians are on the skids, playing great music through a drug or booze-induced haze. Bertrand Tavernier's superb film is of this school, but has none of the glib clichés of the Hollywood jazz movie. This is a harrowing and truthful study of talent suffocating under the pressures of creativity. Film debutant and jazz veteran Dexter Gordon earned an Oscar nomination for his remarkable performance, while Herbie Hancock's Oscar-winning soundtrack will send shivers down your spine. DP. Contains swearing.

Dexter Gordon *Dale Turner* • François Cluzet *Francis Borier* • Gabrielle Haker *Bérangère* • Sandra Reaves-Phillips *Buttercup* • Lonette McKee *Darcey Leigh* • Christine Pascal *Sylvie* • Herbie Hancock *Eddie Wayne* ■ *Dir* Bertrand Tavernier • *Scr* Bertrand Tavernier, David Rayfiel, based on incidents in the lives of Francis Paudras, Bud Powell

Round Trip to Heaven ★★ 15

Comedy adventure
1992 · US · Colour · 92mins

Corey Feldman and Zach Galligan play two lazy chums who get into all sorts of trouble when they borrow a Rolls-Royce belonging to villain Ray Sharkey for a weekend break. There's a lot of mindless slapstick and the usual obsession with beer and babes, none of which raises more than the occasional chuckle. JF

Corey Feldman *Larry* • Ray Sharkey *Stoneface* • Zach Galligan *Steve* • Julie McCullough *Lucille* • Rowanne Brewer *April* • Lloyd Battista *Mike* • Joey Travolta *Ed* • Shuki Levy *2nd Man* ■ *Dir* Alan Roberts • *Scr* Shuki Levy, Winston Richards

The Round-Up ★★★★★

Historical drama 1966 · Hun · BW · 84mins

Set during the 1848 revolution against Hapsburg imperialism, Miklos Jancso's depiction of the mechanics of power and the vulnerability underlying even the most heroic resistance has powerful contemporary resonance. Just as no concession is made by the sadistic police to the peasants trapped inside an isolated stockade, so none is made to the viewer, who is presented with geometrical arrangements of oppressors and victims instead of tangible heroes and villains. The rebels' refusal to surrender testifies to the indomitability of the human spirit, but the film's chilling conclusion is that totalitarianism can be ruthlessly effective. DP. In Hungarian with English subtitles.

Janos Görbe *Janos Gajdor* • Tibor Molnar *Kabai* • Istvan Avar *1st interrogator* • Lajos Oze *2nd interrogator* ■ *Dir* Miklos Jancso • *Scr* Gyula Hernádi

The Rounders ★★★

Comedy drama 1965 · US · Colour · 84mins

An amiable comedy western, pairing two of the screen's most watchable veterans, Glenn Ford and Henry Fonda, with a determined horse. The film is basically a series of incidents, affectionately directed by cowboy specialist Burt Kennedy and featuring a nice line in very 1960s risqué humour. In the UK this went out as a co-feature, but, although MGM did little to promote it, the movie proved to be a nice little earner for the studio. No great surprises, but very pleasant viewing. TS. Contains some swearing.

Glenn Ford *Ben Jones* • Henry Fonda *Howdy Lewis* • Sue Anne Langdon [Sue Ane Langdon] *Mary* • Hope Holiday *Sister* • Chill Wills *Jim Ed Love* • Edgar Buchanan *Vince Moore* • Kathleen Freeman *Agatha Moore* • Joan Freeman *Meg Moore* • Denver Pyle *Bull* • Barton MacLane *Tanner* ■ *Dir* Burt Kennedy • *Scr* Burt Kennedy, from the novel by Max Evans

Rounders ★★★ 15

Drama 1998 · US · Colour · 115mins

Matt Damon plays a legal student-turned-poker player who, after losing his life savings, promises his girlfriend (Gretchen Mol) he'll give up the game. But the lure of the tables proves strong when a friend and fellow gambler (Edward Norton) comes out of jail with a pressing need to pay off a debt. Damon and Norton give accomplished performances, and director John Dahl imbues this with a downbeat atmosphere that atones for the sketchily drawn characters and familiar plot. TH. Contains swearing, violence and a sex scene. DVD

Matt Damon *Mike McDermott* • Edward Norton *Worm* • John Turturro *Joey Kinish* • Gretchen Mol *Jo* • Famke Janssen *Petra* • John Malkovich *Teddy KGB* • Martin Landau *Abe Petrovsky* • Josh Mostel *Zagosh* ■ *Dir* John Dahl • *Scr* David Levien, Brian Koppelman

The Roundup ★★★

Western 1941 · US · BW · 90mins

This is a fascinating western from Lesley Selander, one of the genre's great unsung directors (whose credits number over a hundred). Primarily a melodrama based on a hoary premise about an interrupted wedding, this could have done with a little more blood and thunder in the styling. It's interesting from the off, though, with Patricia Morison's former fiancé Preston Foster turning up when she is about to marry Richard Dix. TS

Richard Dix *Steve* • Patricia Morison *Janet* • Preston Foster *Greg* • Don Wilson *Slim* • Ruth Donnelly *Polly* • Betty Brewer *Mary* • Douglass Dumbrille *Captain Lane* ■ *Dir* Lesley Selander • *Scr* Harold Shumate, from a story by Edmund Day

Roustabout ★★★ U

Musical 1964 · US · Colour · 95mins

Elvis films are unashamed fluff, containing songs and girls with curiously pointed breasts. This sticks firmly to tradition with Elvis playing the role of a mean, moody general handyman, embittered orphan and karate expert with a very large motorcycle. Barbara Stanwyck plays the fairground owner as if on autopilot, and this time the perky boobs belong to Joan Freeman as her deeply smitten daughter. Very daft, very immature and great fun. SH DVD

Elvis Presley *Charlie Rogers* • Barbara Stanwyck *Maggie Morgan* • Joan Freeman *Cathy Lean* • Leif Erickson *Joe Lean* • Sue Ann Langdon [Sue Ane Langdon] *Madame Mijanou* • Pat Buttram *Harry Carver* • Joan Staley *Marge* • Raquel Welch ■ *Dir* John Rich • *Scr* Paul Nathan, Anthony Lawrence, Allan Weiss, from a story by Allan Weiss

Route 9 ★★ 15

Crime drama 1998 · US · Colour · 101mins

Two backwoods cops discover several corpses and a bag containing $1.5 million. When one of the bodies proves to be somewhat lively, they finish him off and bury the loot. While the convolutions of the script are admirable, this TV thriller really needs gutsier direction and a better cast: Kyle MacLachan's glacial personality is a drawback here. AT DVD

Kyle MacLachlan *Booth Parker* • Peter Coyote *Dwayne Hogan* • Amy Locane *Sally Hogan* • Roma Maffia *Ellen Marks* ■ *Dir* David Mackay • *Scr* Brendan Broderick, Rob Kerchner

The Rover ★★

Period war drama 1967 · It · Colour · 103mins

This slow adventure, based on Joseph Conrad's minor novel, finds Anthony Quinn as a piratical rebel in the Napoleonic Wars. He is drawn to a mentally ill young woman, but she is fond of an officer in the French navy. Not lively enough in the action sequences and not intelligent enough in the dialogue, but it's unusual enough to be watchable. Directed by Shanghai-born British director Terence Young between his hits *Thunderball* and *Wait until Dark*. JG

Anthony Quinn *Peyrol* • Rosanna Schiaffino *Arlette* • Rita Hayworth *Aunt Caterina* • Richard Johnson *Real* • Ivo Garrani *Scevola* ■ *Dir* Terence Young • *Scr* Luciano Vincenzoni, Jo Eisinger, from the novel by Joseph Conrad

Rover Dangerfield ★★ U

Animated comedy
1991 · US · Colour · 70mins

Did somebody really think the world needed a movie that featured a cartoon dog with the voice and likeness of Rodney Dangerfield? And if such a movie had to be made, whose idea was it to let Dangerfield sing? Somebody threw a fair amount of money at this animated story of a wise-cracking Las Vegas dog named Rover who is separated from his showgirl owner and forced to live on a farm. But the animation is nothing special and Dangerfield's schtick doesn't get any funnier just because it's coming from a canine. RT

Rodney Dangerfield *Rover* • Susan Boyd *Daisy* • Dana Hill *Danny* • Sal Landi *Rocky* • Ned Luke *Raffles* ■ *Dir* James George, Robert Seeley • *Scr* Rodney Dangerfield, from a story by Rodney Dangerfield, Harold Ramis

A Row of Crows ★★ 15

Thriller 1991 · US · Colour · 98mins

It's mismatched policemen again in this tough mystery thriller, as big city cop Steven Bauer gets sent to Arizona to team up with local sheriff John Beck. As they squabble about various police matters, they have to try to solve the murder of a young woman who is found decapitated in the desert. Fairly standard crime fare, boasting a ropey script and an unusual role for Katharine Ross as a hard-drinking coroner. JB. Contains sex scenes, swearing, violence, nudity.

John Beck *Kyle Shipp* • Katharine Ross *Grace Hines* • Mia Sara *Elise Shipp* • Steven Bauer *Paul McGraw* • Dedee Pfeiffer *Donna* • John Diehl *Wayne Paris* ■ *Dir/Scr* JS Cardone

Rowing with the Wind ★★

Romantic melodrama
1987 · Sp/Nor · Colour · 126mins

The double-act of Hugh Grant and Elizabeth Hurley has shared many a tabloid headline since this somewhat dazed account of how *Frankenstein* came to be written. Grant is at his least flustered and thus most convincing in this peculiar production, as Mary Shelley recalls events from a ship sailing around the Arctic. Director Gonzalo Suarez takes a sometimes surreal advantage of a situation that was more gruesomely exploited by Ken Russell's *Gothic*. TH

Hugh Grant *Lord Byron* • Lizzy McInnerny *Mary Shelley* • Elizabeth Hurley *Claire Clairmont* • Valentine Pelka *Percy Bysshe Shelley* • José Luis Gómez *Polidori* • Virginia Mataix *Elisa* • Ronan Vibert *Fletcher* • Jose Carlos Rivas *Creature* ■ *Dir/Scr* Gonzalo Suarez

Roxanne ★★★★ PG

Romantic comedy
1987 · US · Colour · 102mins

Nimbly adapted by star Steve Martin (for which he won the American Writers' Guild prize) from the celebrated Edmond Rostand play *Cyrano de Bergerac*, this is romantic comedy as it used to be, with Martin playing the nasally gifted fire chief who falls for stargazer Daryl Hannah. This is remarkably faithful to the original, cleverly transplanting the action from 17th-century Paris to present-day small-town America, and imbuing the sensitive Martin with considerable duelling skills. From the moment he swashbuckles with a tennis racket, it's clear Martin is on peak form, excelling himself during the hilarious nose-jokes sequence. DP DVD

Steve Martin *CD Bales* • Daryl Hannah *Roxanne Kowalski* • Rick Rossovich *Chris* • Shelley Duvall *Dixie* • John Kapelos *Chuck* • Fred Willard *Mayor Deebs* • Max Alexander *Dean* • Michael J Pollard *Andy* ■ *Dir* Fred Schepisi • *Scr* Steve Martin, from the play *Cyrano de Bergerac* by Edmond Rostand

Roxie Hart ★★★★

Crime comedy 1942 · US · BW · 74mins

Ginger Rogers is terrifically hard-boiled and funny in this film based on Maurine Watkins's famous play *Chicago*. There's a crackling script, a magnificent picture-stealing performance from Adolphe Menjou and some super by-play from the supporting cast. Rogers simply scintillates as the on-trial heroine of the title, and, if William A Wellman's direction isn't quite spot-on, or if George Montgomery is a colourless leading man, it doesn't really matter. A minor classic. TS

Ginger Rogers *Roxie Hart* • Adolphe Menjou *Billy Flynn* • George Montgomery *Homer Howard* • Lynne Overman *Jake Callahan* • Nigel Bruce *E Clay Benham* • Phil Silvers *Babe* • Sara Allgood *Mrs Morton* • William Frawley *O'Malley* • Spring Byington *Mary Sunshine* ■ *Dir* William Wellman [William A Wellman] • *Scr* Nunnally Johnson, from the play *Chicago* by Maurine Watkins

Royal Affairs in Versailles ★★★

Historical drama 1953 · Fr · Colour · 165mins

In its day, this was one of the most lavish and expensive French films ever made, a three-hour, all-star evocation of the reigns of three men named Louis – XIV, XV and XVI – and their little cottage outside Paris called Versailles. The director, Sacha Guitry – an alleged Nazi collaborator – himself plays Louis XIV and gets the lion's share of scenes, supported by a gallery of French stars who perform with a lot of pomp and pompadour. AT. In French with English subtitles.

Claudette Colbert *Madame de Montespan* • Sacha Guitry *Louis XIV* • Orson Welles *Benjamin Franklin* • Jean-Pierre Aumont *Cardinal de Rohan* • Edith Piaf *Woman of the People* • Gérard Philipe *D'Artagnan* • Micheline Presle *Madame du Pompadour* • Jean Marais *Louis XV* • Gilbert Boka *Louis XVI* • Brigitte Bardot *Mademoiselle de Rosille* ■ *Dir/Scr* Sacha Guitry

The Royal Family of Broadway ★★ U

Comedy 1930 · US · BW · 106mins

Said to be loosely modelled on the Barrymore dynasty, this once relevant attempt at some kind of satirical comedy is now largely a monumental bore. Fredric March was Oscar-nominated for his performance as the wayward matinée idol son of dowager trouper Henrietta Crosman, but that honour should have gone to Ina Claire as his actress sister who, like her own daughter, is briefly torn between career and personal happiness. Although intermittently amusing, it's painfully stagey, with snail's-pace direction. RK

Ina Claire *Julia Cavendish* • Fredric March *Tony Cavendish* • Mary Brian *Gwen Cavendish* • Henrietta Crosman *Fanny Cavendish* • Charles Starrett *Perry Stewart* • Arnold Korff *Oscar Wolff* ■ *Dir* George Cukor, Cyril Gardner • *Scr* Herman Mankiewicz, Gertrude Purcell, from the play by George S Kaufman, Edna Ferber

Royal Flash ★★ 15

Comedy adventure
1975 · UK · Colour · 97mins

Author George MacDonald Fraser's series of novels featuring a grown-up Harry Flashman, the bully from *Tom Brown's Schooldays*, were fun, but the character doesn't survive the transition to film. As Flashman, Malcolm McDowell lacks the necessary public school veneer and, despite effective support from the likes of Alan Bates (who would have been better cast in the lead role) and Oliver Reed (ditto), it's really hard to care what happens to him. TS

Malcolm McDowell *Captain Harry Flashman* • Alan Bates *Rudi von Starnberg* • Florinda Bolkan *Lola Montez* • Oliver Reed *Otto von Bismarck* • Britt Ekland *Duchess Irma of Strakenz* • Lionel Jeffries *Kraftstein* • Tom Bell *de Gautet* • Joss Ackland *Sapten* • Christopher Cazenove *Eric Hansen* • Roy Kinnear *Old roué* • Alastair Sim *Mr Greig* • Michael Hordern *Headmaster* ■ *Dir* Richard Lester • *Scr* George MacDonald Fraser, from his novel

The Royal Hunt of the Sun ★★★ U

Historical drama
1969 · UK/US · Colour · 121mins

Peter Shaffer's play is made over into a duet for two egoes as Spanish conquistador Pizarro (Robert Shaw) embarks on his South American trek to conquer the Inca god-king, Atahualpa (Christopher Plummer) for the gold he thinks the Incas have. Directed by Irving Lerner, this is surprisingly stagey and static although the acting is extraordinarily powerful. TH

Robert Shaw *Francisco Pizarro* • Christopher Plummer *Atahualpa* • Nigel Davenport *Hernando De Soto* • Leonard Whiting *Young Martin* • Michael Craig *Estete* • Andrew Keir *Valverde* • James Donald *King Carlos V* • *Dir* Irving Lerner • *Scr* Philip Yordan, from the play by Peter Shaffer

A Royal Scandal ★★

Period comedy 1945 · US · Colour · 93mins

Young soldier William Eythe, passionately loyal to Catherine the Great (Tallulah Bankhead), arrives at court as her self-appointed protector, but finds himself dangerously out of his depth when the empress falls for his charms. A sporadically entertaining but silly and antediluvian period comedy, produced by Ernst Lubitsch but directed by Otto Preminger without any of the sophisticated Lubitsch touches it badly needs. Released as *Czarina* in the UK. RK

Tallulah Bankhead *Tsarina Catherine the Great* • Charles Coburn *Chancellor Nicolai Ilyitch* • Anne Baxter *Countess Anna Jaschikoff* • William Eythe *Lt Alexei Chernoff* • Vincent

Price *Marquis de Fleury* • Mischa Auer *Captain Sukov* • Sig Ruman *General Ronsky* ■ *Dir* Otto Preminger • *Scr* Edwin Justis Mayer, Bruno Frank, from the play *The Czarina* by Lajos Biró, Melchior Lengyel

The Royal Tenenbaums ★★★★★ 15

Comedy drama 2001 · US · Colour · 105mins

Produced and directed by the hugely talented Wes Anderson, this is about a gifted, but dysfunctional, New York family that is reunited when estranged patriarch Gene Hackman feigns terminal illness. An ambitiously original ensemble comedy, it is related in an episodic, storybook format with off-screen narration from Alec Baldwin. This stylised presentation suggests that the interlocking subplots involving the various Tenenbaums will be resolved in a detached fashion, without warmth or the audience's empathy. That is not so. As the narrative builds, the atmosphere thaws and something like poetry unfolds. Immaculately written and brilliantly performed, this extraordinary fable restores one's faith in American cinema. AC DVD

Gene Hackman *Royal Tenenbaum* • Anjelica Huston *Etheline Tenenbaum* • Ben Stiller *Chas Tenenbaum* • Gwyneth Paltrow *Margot Tenenbaum* • Owen Wilson *Eli Cash* • Bill Murray *Raleigh St Clair* • Danny Glover *Henry Sherman* • Luke Wilson *Richie Tenenbaum* • Alec Baldwin *Narrator* ■ *Dir* Wes Anderson • *Scr* Wes Anderson, Owen Wilson

Royal Wedding ★★★ U

Musical comedy 1951 · US · Colour · 89mins

Here's a totally delightful oddity: a topical MGM musical, timed to chime in with the wedding of then Princess Elizabeth and Prince Philip, and actually incorporating library footage. Choreographer-turned-director Stanley Donen makes the most of his solo directing debut, despite an over-dependence on English stereotypes and fake fog. Donen has the benefit of the great Fred Astaire in the leading role, who furnishes his director with the movie's highlight, an incredible routine in which he dances effortlessly up the walls and on the ceiling of his room. TS DVD

Fred Astaire *Tom Bowen* • Jane Powell *Ellen Bowen* • Peter Lawford *Lord John Brindale* • Sarah Churchill *Anne Ashmond* • Keenan Wynn *Irving Klinger/Edgar Klinger* • Albert Sharpe *James Ashmond* ■ *Dir* Stanley Donen • *Scr* Alan Jay Lerner

Rubin & Ed ★★★

Road movie comedy drama
1991 · UK · Colour · 82mins

This unconventional road movie features one of cinema's oddest characters, Rubin Farr (Crispin Glover), a recluse who spends most of his life in a motel room mourning the loss of his cat, whose body lies frozen in the icebox. Glover meets up with salesman Howard Hesseman, who is trying to bring in clients for an upcoming sales seminar. He agrees to accompany Hesseman to the seminar, but only if the two journey via the desert, where Rubin can bury his beloved cat. Of course things start to go haywire once they hit the road. Decidedly odd but with a certain twisted appeal. DF

Crispin Glover *Rubin Farr* • Howard Hesseman *Ed Tuttle* • Karen Black *Rula* • Michael Greene *Mr Busta* • Brittney Lewis *Poster girl* ■ *Dir/Scr* Trent Harris

Ruby ★★ 15

Horror 1977 · US · Colour · 163mins

Piper Laurie plays an ex-torch singer, now owner of a drive-in movie theatre, whose deaf-mute daughter seems to be linked to a series of mystifying and chilling deaths. It's mainly a mindless muddle, partly owing to a story cobbled together from numerous chiller clichés and also to director Curtis Harrington's replacement during production by Stephanie Rothman. However, Laurie still manages to hold the 1950s-set bijou blood bath together by the sheer force of her acting ability. AJ. Contains violence.

Piper Laurie *Ruby Claire* • Stuart Whitman *Vince Kemper* • Roger Davis *Doc Keller* • Janit Baldwin *Leslie Claire* • Crystin Sinclaire *Lila June* • Paul Kent *Louie* • Len Lesser *Barney* ■ *Dir* Curtis Harrington, Stephanie Rothman • *Scr* George Edwards, Barry Schneider, from a story by Steve Krantz

Ruby ★★★★ 15

Crime drama 1992 · US · Colour · 105mins

Danny Aiello, one of America's best big-screen brooders, leaps at the complexity of Jack Ruby, the man who shot alleged Kennedy assassin Lee Harvey Oswald, and so creates maximum energy from Ruby's insecurity, arrogance and morose, haunted nature. John MacKenzie sensibly skews his film in the direction of a character piece, which helps it transcend the largely fictionalised and sometimes fuzzy plot. This is an interesting take on events, made as it was just before the 30th anniversary of Kennedy's death. JM. Contains violence and swearing.

Danny Aiello *Jack Ruby* • Sherilyn Fenn *Sheryl Ann Dujean/"Candy Cane"* • Frank Orsatti (2) *Action Jackson* • Jeffrey Nordling *Hank* • Jane Hamilton *Telephone Trixie* • Maurice Bernard *Diego* • Joe Cortese *Louie Vitali* • Marc Lawrence (1) *Santos Alicante* • Arliss Howard *Maxwell* • David Duchovny *Officer Tippit* ■ *Dir* John Mackenzie • *Scr* Stephen Davis, from his play *Love Field*

Ruby and Rata 

Comedy drama 1990 · NZ · Colour · 111mins

Yvonne Lawley and Vanessa Rare turn in spirited performances as, respectively, the elderly Auckland suburbanite and the Maori dole scrounger whose feud takes an unexpected turn thanks to Rare's tearaway son, Lee Mete-Kingi. Originally conceived by director Gaylene Preston as a TV series, the film suffers slightly from some underdrawn secondary characters. However, it doesn't hold back in its consideration of such topics as middle-class snobbery, the iniquities of the social security system and anti-Maori prejudice. DP. Contains swearing.

Yvonne Lawley *Ruby* • Vanessa Rare *Rata* • Lee Mete-kingi *Willie* • Simon Barnett *Buckle* ■ *Dir* Gaylene Preston • *Scr* Graeme Tetley

Ruby Cairo ★★ 15

Mystery 1992 · US/Jpn · Colour · 105mins

Director Graeme Clifford seems convinced that all he has to do to keep us on the edge of our seats is to whisk Andie MacDowell across three continents in search of the clues that will explain the disappearance of errant husband Viggo Mortensen. This is never a dull film, with MacDowell conveying both vulnerability and tenacity, but you can't quite believe in her love for either naughty Morty or hunky charity worker Liam Neeson. DP. Contains swearing and nudity.

Andie MacDowell *Bessie Faro* • Liam Neeson *Fergus Lamb* • Jack Thompson *Ed* • Viggo Mortensen *Johnny* • Paul Spencer *Young Johnny* • Chad Power *Niles Faro* • Monica Mikala *Alexandria Faro* ■ *Dir* Graeme Clifford • *Scr* Robert Dillon, Michael Thomas, from a story by Robert Dillon

Ruby Gentry ★★★ PG

Melodrama 1952 · US · BW · 82mins

A hot 'n' steamy southern melodrama, with Jennifer Jones on seductive form, setting her cap at Charlton Heston and marrying Karl Malden to spite him. Unintentionally hilarious or totally turgid depending on your point of view, but Jones is amazingly sexy, clad in the clingiest of jeans, while Heston looks more perplexed than enamoured. For lovers of Hollywood at its most baroque, this is a real one-off. TS

Jennifer Jones *Ruby Gentry* • Charlton Heston *Boake Tackman* • Karl Malden *Jim Gentry* • Tom Tully *Jud Corey* • Bernard Phillips *Dr Saul Manfred* • James Anderson (2) *Jewel Corey* • Josephine Hutchinson *Letitia Gentry* ■ *Dir* King Vidor • *Scr* Sylvia Richards, from a story by Arthyr Fitz-Richard

Ruby in Paradise ★★★ 15

Drama 1993 · US · Colour · 114mins

A gentle, if at times bordering on the comatose, little elegy to finding oneself, starring Ashley Judd in a debut performance of engaging clarity. Writer/director Victor Nunez does a sterling job with a tiny budget, neatly blending Judd's home territory of Tennessee with the laid-back freedoms of her chosen Florida beach community without resorting to either redneck or post-hippie clichés. As usual with such small American independent movies, this suffered from lack of marketing and undeservedly disappeared without trace. SH. Contains swearing, sex scenes and nudity.

Ashley Judd *Ruby Lee Gissing* • Todd Field *Mike McCaslin* • Bentley Mitchum *Ricky Chambers* • Allison Dean *Rochelle Bridges* • Dorothy Lyman *Mildred Chambers* • Betsy Douds *Debrah Ann* • Felicia Hernandez *Persefina* ■ *Dir/Scr* Victor Nunez

Rude ★★★ 18

Drama 1995 · Can · Colour · 85mins

The enigmatically titled *Rude* follows the indy-spirited route of intertwined tales of urban angst. Writer/director Clément Virgo's Toronto-set drama finds a woman trying to come to terms with a break-up, an athlete with doubts about his sexuality, and an ex-con resisting temptations to get back in the drug dealing business. The low-profile cast does justice to this nicely directed effort. DA

Maurice Dean Wint *The General* • Rachael Crawford *Maxine* • Clark Johnson *Reece* • Richard Chevolleau *Jordan* • Sharon M Lewis *Rude* • Melanie Nicholls-King *Jessica* ■ *Dir/Scr* Clément Virgo

Rude Awakening ★★ 15

Comedy 1989 · US · Colour · 96mins

One of a series of Rip Van Winkle comedies made in recent years. Here, Eric Roberts and Cheech Marin haven't exactly been sleeping between the 1960s and the 1980s – they've been living in a South American commune. When they return to America, they discover life has moved on and – shock, horror– their former pals are yuppies. Nice idea, but this is silly rather than comical, and the jokes are hammered home far too hard. JB. Contains some swearing.

Eric Roberts *Fred* • Richard "Cheech" Marin *Hesus* • Petra Hagerty *Julie* • Robert Carradine *Sammy* • Buck Henry *Lloyd* • Louise Lasser *Ronnie* • Cindy Williams *June* • Cliff De Young *Brubaker* ■ *Dir* Aaron Russo, David Greenwalt • *Scr* Neil Levy, Richard LaGravenese, from a story by Neil Levy

Rude Boy ★★ 18

Music documentary drama
1980 · UK · Colour · 127mins

A muddled blend of documentary footage and part-improvised, part-scripted scenes, this concert drama revolves around the trials and tribulations of sex shop salesman Ray Gange employed by the Clash as their roadie in Scotland around the time of their second album *Give 'Em Enough Rope*. The well-staged performances make this anti-establishment comic book more memorable than it deserves to be. AJ DVD

Ray Gange *Ray* • John Green [Johnny Green (2)] *Road manager* ■ *Dir* Jack Hazan, David Mingay • *Scr* Jack Hazan, David Mingay, Ray Gange

Rudolph the Red-Nosed Reindeer ★★ U

Animated seasonal fantasy
1998 · US · Colour · 83mins

Don't expect the excruciating ditties in this otherwise harmless cartoon to go down in folklore. There are seven altogether and they disrupt a storyline that already struggles for momentum, as Rudolph's run of misfortunes culminates in his confrontation with evil ice-queen Stormella (Whoopi Goldberg). John Goodman provides a jovial voice as Santa, but cameos from Eric Idle and Bob Newhart are less successful. DP DVD

John Goodman *Santa Claus* • Whoopi Goldberg *Stormella, the Evil Ice Queen* • Debbie Reynolds *Mrs Claus* • Bob Newhart *Leonard the Polar Bear* • Richard Simmons *Boone* • Eric Idle *Slyly the Fox* ■ *Dir* Bill Kowalchuk • *Scr* Michael Aschner

Rudolph the Red-Nosed Reindeer and the Island of the Misfit Toys ★★ U

Animated seasonal fantasy
2001 · US · Colour · 74mins

The title pretty much sums up the story of this animated children's Christmas tale, which sees Santa's most famous sledge-puller rescuing presents from the sinister Toy Taker. The vocal performances of villain Rick Moranis, snowman-narrator Richard Dreyfuss and hippo-queen Jamie Lee Curtis are less than special, but what really lets this production down is the choppy, cheap-looking computer animation. JC DVD

Rick Moranis *The Toy Taker/Mr Cuddles the Teddy Bear* • Jamie Lee Curtis *Queen Camilla* • Richard Dreyfuss *Scoop the Snowman* • Kathleen Barr *Rudolph the Red Nosed Reindeer/Mrs Claus/Dolly* • Scott McNeil *Hermey the Elf/DDS/Yukon Cornelius/Coach Comet* • Garry [Gary Chalk] *Santa Claus* ■ *Dir* Bill Kowalchuk • *Scr* Michael Aschner

Rudy ★★ PG

Sports biography
1993 · US · Colour · 109mins

Director David Anspaugh made his name with the gritty basketball drama *Hoosiers*, and he's back batting for the underdog in this less than convincing American football feature that's based on a true story. Sean Astin plays the pint-sized gridiron fanatic who is determined to play for a college team, despite the lack of encouragement. Astin is adequate, but this is sentimental and unintentionally funny. JF. Contains swearing.

Sean Astin *Rudy* • Jon Favreau *D-Bob* • Ned Beatty *Daniel* • Greta Lind *Mary* • Scott Benjaminson *Frank* • Mary Ann Thebus *Betty* • Charles S Dutton *Fortune* • Lili Taylor *Sherry* ■ *Dir* David Anspaugh • *Scr* Angelo Pizzo

Rue Cases Nègres ★★★★ PG

Period drama 1983 · Fr · Colour · 101mins

Euzhan Palcy's feature debut is remarkable for her total immersion in its environment and her complete understanding of its characters. Set in a 1930s Martinique shantytown abutting a French-run sugar cane plantation, this is no mere rites of passage picture, but an affirmation of the vital part love plays in childhood, even (perhaps especially) in the midst of oppression and poverty. Winner of the best actress prize at Venice, Darling Legitimus is superb as the proud woman who sacrifices everything for her grandson's education. DP. In French with English subtitles. [video]

Garry Cadenat *Jose* • Darling Legitimus *M'Man Tine* • Douta Seck *Medouze* • Joby Bernabe *Monsieur Saint-Louis* • Francisco Charles *Le Gereur* ■ *Dir* Euzhan Palcy • *Scr* Euzhan Palcy, from the novel by Joseph Zobel

Ruggles of Red Gap ★★★

Silent comedy 1923 · US · BW · 89mins

This earlier version of the classic comedy known best for its 1935 outing features Edward Everett Horton as the quintessential British valet whose services are won in a game of poker but who is then whisked away from Europe to the Wild Western town of Red Gap, where he's introduced to the locals as a colonel. Horton is wonderfully funny here, with James Cruze directing the story adapted from Henry Leon Wilson's novel. Bob Hope was to star in yet another version, *Fancy Pants* (1950). TH

Edward Horton [Edward Everett Horton] *"Colonel" Ruggles* • Ernest Torrence *Cousin Egbert Floud* • Lois Wilson *Kate Kenner* • Fritzi Ridgeway *Emily Judson* • Charles Ogle *Jeff Tuttle* • Louise Dresser *Mrs Effie Floud* • Anna Lehr *Mrs Belknap-Jackson* • Thomas Holding *Earl of Brinstead* ■ *Dir* James Cruze • *Scr* Walter Woods, Anthony Coldeway, from the novel by Harry Leon Wilson

Ruggles of Red Gap ★★★★★ U

Comedy 1935 · US · BW · 89mins

Charles Laughton is Ruggles, an English butler of impeccable credentials and phlegmatic rectitude, who is sold by his titled employer Roland Young to a visiting American couple at the insistence of the pretentious wife Mary Boland. He is taken out west charged with, among other things, making a gentleman out of his employer's husband (Charlie Ruggles). Once there, events take a surprising turn. A brilliant, hilarious and fondly satirical look at Anglo-American relations and culture gaps, faultlessly directed by Leo McCarey with Laughton in masterly form – magnificently suffering the vulgarities that offend his dignity while slowly learning to profit from another way of life and even falling in love (with ZaSu Pitts). Nobody else could have played it, and the Oscar-nominated film itself could never have emerged with such nuanced perfection in any other era. RK

Charles Laughton *Colonel Marmaduke "Bill" Ruggles* • Mary Boland *Effie Floud* • Charlie Ruggles [Charles Ruggles] *Egbert "Sourdough" Floud* • ZaSu Pitts *Mrs Prunella Judson* • Roland Young *Earl of Burnstead* • Leila Hyams *Nell Kenner* • Maude Eburne *"Ma" Pettingill* • Lucien Littlefield *Charles Belknap-Jackson* ■ *Dir* Leo McCarey • *Scr* Walter DeLeon, Harlan Thompson, Humphrey Pearson, from the novel by Harry Leon Wilson

Rugrats Go Wild ★★ U

Animated comedy adventure
2003 · US · Colour · 77mins

Nickelodeon's decision to marry together *Rugrats* and *The Wild Thornberrys* proves a qualified success. The cartoon romp is a fast-moving carnival of primary colours, in which the vacationing Rugrats are stranded on an apparently deserted island, unaware that the Thornberry clan are shooting a nature documentary there. The absence of a strong plot exposes the film's lame humour and nauseating songs. SF [video] DVD

Bruce Willis *Spike the Dog* • Chrissie Hynde *Siri the Leopard* • Nancy Cartwright *Chuckie Finster* • Kath Soucie *Philip Deville/Lillian Deville/Betty Deville* • Cheryl Chase *Angelica Pickles* • EG Daily [Elizabeth Daily] *Tommy Pickles* • Tara Strong [Tara Charendoff] *Dil Pickles* • Melanie Chartoff *Didi Pickles* ■ *Dir* Norton Virgien, John Eng • *Scr* Kate Boutilier, from characters created by Arlene Klasky, Gabor Csupo, Paul Germain, Steve Pepoon, David Silverman, Stephen Sustarsic

Rugrats in Paris: the Movie ★★★ U

Animated comedy adventure
2000 · US/Ger · Colour · 75mins

This sequel takes TV's adventurous babies to Paris. They invade a Japanese-owned amusement park, where one of the robot movie monsters is malfunctioning. Susan Sarandon supplies the voice of the park's manager, Coco La Bouche, a careerist whose promotion prospects depend on her ability to acquire a ready-made family. Children will enjoy the thrills and spills, all viewed through the Rugrats' eyes. DM [video] DVD

EG Daily [Elizabeth Daily] *Tommy Pickles* • Tara Charendoff *Dil Pickles* • Cheryl Chase *Angelica Pickles* • Christine Cavanaugh *Chuckie Finster* • Cree Summer Franck *Susie Carmichael* • Kath Soucie *Philip Deville/Lillian Deville/Betty Deville* • Michael Bell *Drew Pickles/Chas Finster* • Tress MacNeille *Charlotte Pickles* • Casey Kasem *Wedding DJ* • Debbie Reynolds *Lulu Pickles* ■ *Dir* Stig Bergqvist, Paul Demeyer • *Scr* Kate Boutilier, Jill Gorey, Barbara Herndon, J David Stern, David N Weiss, from characters created by Arlene Klasky, Gabor Csupo, Paul Germain

The Rugrats Movie ★★★ U

Animated comedy adventure
1998 · US · Colour · 76mins

Nickelodeon TV favourites the Rugrats get their own movie in this fun feature-length adventure. Whoopi Goldberg, Tim Curry and David Spade are among the celebrities lending their voices, as cute toddler Tommy Pickles persuades his pals to help him return his new-born brother, Dil, to the hospital so that he can have his parents all to himself again. Of course, their journey doesn't go as planned, and the group end up in a scary forest. There are messages about bravery and friendship here, but they're woven into the fun in a way that won't spoil the enjoyment for the kiddies. JB [video] DVD

EG Daily [Elizabeth Daily] *Tommy Pickles* • Christine Cavanaugh *Chuckie Finster* • Kath Soucie *Philip Deville/Lillian Deville/Betty Deville* • Melanie Chartoff *Didi Pickles/Minka* • Phil Proctor [Philip Proctor] *Howard Deville/Igor* • Cree Summer *Susie Carmichael* • Busta Rhymes *Reptar Wagon* • Iggy Pop *Newborn baby* • Tim Curry *Rex Pester* • Whoopi Goldberg *Ranger Margaret* • David Spade *Ranger Frank* ■ *Dir* Norton Virgien, Igor Kovalyov • *Scr* J David Stem, David N Weiss, from characters created by Arlene Klasky, Gabor Csupo, Paul Germain

Rulers of the Sea ★★★ U

Historical drama 1939 · US · BW · 96mins

Glasgow-born Frank Lloyd, a master craftsman who directed the Academy Award-winning *Mutiny on the Bounty* in 1935, returned to the world of ships to make this excellent, reasonably exciting adventure about the building and maiden voyage of the first steamship. Genuine Scotsman Will Fyffe made a rare excursion into Hollywood, while another import – England's Margaret Lockwood, not yet the nation's favourite wicked lady – was paired with Douglas Fairbanks Jr to supply the romantic subplot that leavens the action. A young, unknown Alan Ladd is in the cast. RK

Douglas Fairbanks Jr *Gillespie* • Margaret Lockwood *Mary Shaw* • Will Fyffe *John Shaw* • George Bancroft *James Oliver* • Montagu Love *Malcolm Grant* • Vaughan Glaser *Junius Smith* • David Torrence *Donald Fenton* • Lester Matthews *Lieutenant Commander Roberts* • Alan Ladd *Colin Farrell* ■ *Dir* Frank Lloyd • *Scr* Talbot Jennings, Frank Cavett, Richard Collins

The Rules of Attraction ★★ 18

Romantic thriller
2002 · US/Ger · Colour · 106mins

A superficial interpretation of Bret Easton Ellis's cult novel, this is an arrogant combination of social satire and 1980s teen comedy. The film centres on three New England college students: drug-dealing waster James Van Der Beek, bisexual party boy Ian Somerhalder and the virginal Shannyn Sossamon. The stereotypical trio flounder through a devil's playground of sex, drugs and violence. Despite an impertinent edge, this falls down by trying too hard to be hip. SF [video] DVD

James Van Der Beek *Sean Bateman* • Shannyn Sossamon *Lauren Hynde* • Ian Somerhalder *Paul Denton* • Jessica Biel *Lara* • Kip Pardue *Victor* • Thomas Ian Nicholas *Mitchell* • Kate Bosworth *Kelly* • Fred Savage *Marc* • Eric Stoltz *Mr Lance Lawson* • Faye Dunaway *Mrs Denton* • Swoosie Kurtz *Mrs Jared* ■ *Dir* Roger Avary • *Scr* Roger Avary, from the novel by Bret Easton Ellis

Rules of Engagement ★★ 15

Courtroom drama
2000 · US · Colour · 122mins

William Friedkin's courtroom melodrama revolves around colonel Samuel L Jackson's decision to fire on a crowd of Arabs storming the US embassy in Yemen. Tommy Lee Jones reluctantly defends him at his court martial, knowing only too well that Jackson has a tendency to buckle under pressure. A terrific cast is wasted as the two leads duke it out with tough prosecution attorney Guy Pearce. Alas, the film is scuppered by unsavoury stereotypes and a Vietnam flashback that suggests the stars have not aged a day in 30 years. NS. Contains violence, swearing. [video] DVD

Tommy Lee Jones *Col Hays Hodges* • Samuel L Jackson *Col Terry Childers* • Guy Pearce *Maj Mark Biggs* • Bruce Greenwood *National Security Adviser William Sokal* • Blair Underwood *Captain Lee* • Philip Baker Hall *Gen H Lawrence Hodges* • Anne Archer *Mrs Mourain* • Ben Kingsley *Ambassador Mourain* ■ *Dir* William Friedkin • *Scr* Stephen Gaghan, from a story by James Webb

Rules of Obsession ★★

Erotic thriller 1994 · US · Colour · 93mins

In this predictable thriller, Scott Bakula plays a psychiatrist whose best friend (John Getz) returns from a cruise with a new wife (Bakula's real-life wife, Chelsea Field). When she starts acting strangely, Getz asks Bakula to talk to her about her problems, but the doctor finds himself seduced by his patient's charms. Then Getz turns up dead ... Only one tiny twist interrupts the pat progress of this routine offering. ST

Scott Bakula *Dr David Lawson* • Chelsea Field *Diana Chamberlain* • Sheila Kelley *Beth* • John Getz *Jerry Chamberlain* ■ *Dir* Rick King • *Scr* William Delligan

The Ruling Class ★★★ 15

Black comedy 1972 · UK · Colour · 123mins

A black-hearted assault on British social institutions and the class system, this boasts moments of cruel comedy and real anger thanks to Peter Medak's inspired direction of Peter Barnes's play. Peter O'Toole stars as the madman who inherits the title of the Earl of Gurney. His relatives – played by a flurry of great character actors – then bury their snouts in the trough of expected riches, but O'Toole fools them all: he switches from being Jesus Christ to Jack the Ripper. The film is dated in its approach, though it still has the power to shock. TH. Contains swearing and nudity. DVD

Peter O'Toole *Jack* • Alastair Sim *Bishop Lampton* • Arthur Lowe *Tucker* • Harry Andrews *13th Earl of Gurney* • Coral Browne *Lady Claire Gurney* • Michael Bryant *Dr Herder* • Nigel Green *McKyle* • William Mervyn *Sir Charles Gurney* • Carolyn Seymour *Grace Shelley* • James Villiers *Dinsdale Gurney* • Hugh Burden *Matthew Peake* • Graham Crowden *Truscott* • Kay Walsh *Mrs Piggot-Jones* • Patsy Byrne *Mrs Treadwell* ■ *Dir* Peter Medak • *Scr* Peter Barnes, from his play

Rumba ★★

Romance 1935 · US · BW · 70mins

A moneyed New York society girl meets a Broadway dancer as a result of a duplicated lottery ticket, falls for him and, predictably, steps in to the big number of his new show when his regular partner lets him down. Paramount's shamelessly recycled version of the previous year's hugely successful *Bolero*, once again starring George Raft and Carole Lombard lacks both the novelty and the enjoyable melodramatics of its predecessor. RK

George Raft *Joe Martin* • Carole Lombard *Diane Harrison* • Lynne Overman *Flash* • Margo *Carmelita* • Gail Patrick *Patsy* • Iris Adrian *Goldie Allen* • Clara Lou Sheridan [Ann Sheridan] *Dance girl* ■ *Dir* Marion Gering • *Scr* Howard J Green, Harry Ruskin, Frank Partos, from an idea by Guy Endore, Seena Owen

Rumble Fish ★★★★ 18

Drama 1983 · US · BW and Colour · 90mins

In the second of Francis Ford Coppola's youth problem pictures adapted from SE Hinton's popular novels, Matt Dillon stars as a vulnerable teenager who idolises his elder brother, Mickey Rourke, a former gang leader. Unlike Coppola's more conventional *The Outsiders*, this alienated teen allegory finds him pulling out all the stylistic stops. The drama is extremely mannered, and the symbolism a mite overdone, but it's a visually startling knockout, brilliantly filmed in moody black and white with some dashes of colour. Stewart Copeland composed the brooding score. AJ. Contains swearing. [video] DVD

Matt Dillon *Rusty-James* • Mickey Rourke *Motorcycle Boy* • Diane Lane *Patty* • Dennis Hopper *Father* • Diana Scarwid *Cassandra* • Vincent Spano *Steve* • Nicolas Cage *Smokey* • Christopher Penn [Chris Penn] *BJ Jackson* • Larry Fishburne [Laurence Fishburne] *Midget* • Tom Waits *Benny* ■ *Dir* Francis Ford Coppola • *Scr* SE Hinton, Francis Ford Coppola, from the novel by SE Hinton • *Cinematographer* Stephen H Burum

Rumble in the Bronx ★★★ 15

Martial arts crime drama
1996 · HK/US · Colour · 85mins

Clumsily dubbed and with Vancouver standing in for New York, this is a typical Jackie Chan outing, as he joins his uncle and the new owner of his market stall in seeing off a gang of doltish villains. Anita Mui and Françoise Yip are big stars back in Hong Kong, but they are given little room for manoeuvre in this lightweight adventure. As ever, there's plenty of thrilling action, but as always Chan invests his set-pieces with an element of balletic humour. DP. Cantonese dialogue dubbed into English. Contains violence and swearing. [video] DVD

Jackie Chan *Keung* • Anita Mui *Elaine* • Bill Tung *Uncle Bill* • Françoise Yip *Nancy* ■ *Dir* Stanley Tong • *Scr* Edward Tang, from a story by Stanley Tong

A Rumor of Angels ★★

Drama 2000 · US · Colour · 106mins

Director Peter O'Fallon's follow-up to his under-rated black comedy *Suicide Kings* is a sentimental and far-fetched story about a boy struggling to come to terms with his mother's death. While on vacation at a summer beach house, young Trevor Morgan rebels against his distant father Ray Liotta and unsympathetic stepmother Catherine McCormack by hanging out with dotty local recluse Vanessa Redgrave. LH

Vanessa Redgrave *Maddy Bennett* • Ray Liotta *Nathan Neubauer* • Catherine McCormack *Mary Neubauer* • Trevor Morgan *James Neubauer* • Ron Livingston *Uncle Charlie* ■ *Dir* Peter O'Fallon • *Scr* Peter O'Fallon, Jamie Horton, James Eric, from the novel *Thy Son Liveth: Messages from a Soldier to His Mother* by Grace Duffie Boylan

Rumpelstiltskin ★ U

Fantasy 1986 · US · Colour · 80mins

The bad news is that this dire film based on the Brothers Grimm story was intended as the first of a series of such adaptations aimed at children. The good news is that others in the dozen or so mooted failed to materialise. Both the adaptation and direction by David Irving are undernourished and he has tried to compensate by over-the-top performances from an international cast (it was filmed in Israel) who flail around in search of a style. BB

Amy Irving *Katie* • Clive Revill *King Mezzer* • Billy Barty *Rumpelstiltskin* • Priscilla Pointer *Queen Grizelda* • Robert Symonds *Victor, Katie's father* • John Moulder-Brown *Prince* ■ *Dir* David Irving • *Scr* David Irving, from the fairy tale by Wilhelm Grimm, Jacob Grimm

Rumpelstiltskin ★ 18

Horror 1995 · US · Colour · 87mins

With this fairy-tale horror monstrosity, Mark Jones, director of the cheerfully inept *Leprechaun*, proved that he hadn't learned from his mistakes. Here, the imprisoned dwarf Rumpelstiltskin is released into modern-day Los Angeles, grants an unwitting Kim Johnston Ulrich her wish, and pursues her into the desert to claim his payment, which is, of course, her baby. KB

Max Grodenchik *Rumpelstiltskin* • Kim Johnston Ulrich *Shelley Stewart* • Tommy Blaze *Max Bergman* • Allyce Beasley *Hildy* ■ *Dir* Mark Jones (2) • *Scr* Mark Jones, Joe Ruby

Run ★★ 15

Action thriller 1991 · US · Colour · 87mins

Patrick Dempsey is a young college student who inadvertently incurs the wrath of a small-town crime lord and then spends the rest of the film running from assorted hitmen and bent policemen. Director Geoff Burrowes appears to be aiming for some sort of cross between a crime thriller and a yuppie-in-peril drama but the end result is convincing as neither, even though he does engineer some slick action sequences. JF. Contains violence.

Patrick Dempsey *Charlie Farrow* • Kelly Preston *Karen Landers* • Ken Pogue *Matt Halloran* • Alan C Peterson *Denny Halloran* • James Kidnie *Sammy* • Sean McCann *Marv* ■ *Dir* Geoff Burrowes • *Scr* Dennis Shryack, Michael Blodgett

Run ★★ 15

Romantic drama
2004 · Ind · Colour · 133mins

Having served as cinematographer on the original Tamil hit of the same name, Jeeva takes over the directorial reins for this Bollywood remake. Abhishek Bachchan and Bhoomika Chawla star as the couple whose romance is jeopardised by her gangster brother (Mahesh Manjrekar). It's pretty much a two-act affair. In the first, boy meets girl; in the second, boy bashes brother. Jeeva's experience behind the camera shows in the confident visuals, but his pacing lacks variation. DP. In Hindi with English subtitles. Contains violence. DVD

Abhishek Bachchan *Siddharth* • Bhoomika Chawla *Jhanavi* • Mahesh Manjrekar *Ganpat* • Ayesha Jhulka *Shivani* ■ *Dir* Jeeva

Run, Angel, Run ★★

Drama 1969 · US · Colour · 94mins

This William Smith motorcycle movie gets off to a good start, with turncoat biker Smith fleeing into hiding with his girlfriend after he rats out the gang to a magazine. Once they settle down on a sheep farm, the movie then focuses on their new and tedious ordinary lives, occasionally cutting back to Smith's ex-gang searching for him. The multi-image sequences and some of the camerawork date this more than other motorcycle movies of the period. KB

William Smith *Angel* • Valerie Starrett *Laurie* • Gene Shane *Ron* • Lee DeBroux *Pappy* • Eugene Cornelius *Space* • Paul Harper *Chic* • Earl Finn *Turk* • William Bonner *Duke* ■ *Dir* Jack Starrett • *Scr* Jerome Wish, VA Furlong, from a story by Richard Compton

Run for Cover ★★★ U

Western 1955 · US · Colour · 92mins

A wistful, almost elegiac western from director Nicholas Ray which pits an ageing Jimmy Cagney against youthful John Derek. The themes are those of a thousand traditional cowboy films – old man teaches young pup new tricks, young pup goes to the bad – but it's handled so sensitively that one forgets its hackneyed origins. Cagney is understated and effective, Derek holds his own and a fine supporting cast provides sound ballast. SH

James Cagney *Mat Dow* • Viveca Lindfors *Helga Swenson* • John Derek *Davey Bishop* • Jean Hersholt *Mr Swenson* • Grant Withers *Gentry* • Jack Lambert *Larsen* • Ernest Borgnine *Morgan* • Ray Teal *Sheriff* ■ *Dir* Nicholas Ray • *Scr* Winston Miller, from a story by Harriet Frank Jr, Irving Ravetch

Run for the Roses ★★ PG

Drama 1978 · US · Colour · 89mins

This is a shamelessly sentimental story about a boy and his horse. Veteran performers Vera Miles and Stuart Whitman were somehow lured into it – she's a horse fancier whose nephew is a 12-year-old Puerto Rican boy with a lame horse, while Whitman is the boy's stepfather, who beams with pride when the horse is nursed back to health and entered for the Kentucky Derby. Henry Levin, an old-time studio hack, hung up his megaphone after this effort. AT

Vera Miles *Clarissa* • Stuart Whitman *Charlie* • Sam Groom *Jim* • Panchito Gomez *Juanito* • Theodore Wilson [Teddy Wilson] *Flash* • Lisa Eilbacher *Carol* ■ *Dir* Henry Levin • *Scr* Joseph G Prieto, Mimi Avins

Run for the Sun ★★

Adventure thriller 1956 · US · Colour · 99mins

In yet another remake of *The Most Dangerous Game*, disillusioned author Richard Widmark and journalist Jane Greer are the human prey hunted down in the jungle by Nazis Trevor Howard and Peter Van Eyck. British director Roy Boulting – making one of his few Hollywood films – piles on the tension with a skilful hand, but this is fairly negligible compensation. TH

Richard Widmark *Mike Latimer* • Trevor Howard *Browne* • Jane Greer *Katy Connors* • Peter Van Eyck *Van Anders* • Carlos Henning *Jan* ■ *Dir* Roy Boulting • *Scr* Dudley Nichols, Roy Boulting, from the story *The Most Dangerous Game* by Richard Connell

A Run for Your Money ★★ U

Comedy 1949 · UK · BW · 83mins

Directed by Charles Frend, this is one of the weakest comedies produced by Ealing Studios. Chronicling the misadventures of Welsh miners Donald Houston and Meredith Edwards after they win a day out in London, it is nothing more than a string of cheap jokes at the expense of the naive boys from the Valleys lost in the urban jungle. More galling than the patronising humour is the waste of Alec Guinness as their guide. DP

Donald Houston *Dai Jones* • Moira Lister *Jo* • Alec Guinness *Whimple* • Meredith Edwards *Twm Jones* • Hugh Griffith *Huw Price* • Clive Morton *Editor* • Leslie Perrins *Barney* • Joyce Grenfell *Mrs Pargiter* ■ *Dir* Charles Frend • *Scr* Charles Frend, Leslie Norman, Richard Hughes, Diana Morgan, from a story by Clifford Evans

Run Lola Run ★★★★ 15

Crime drama 1998 · Ger · Colour · 80mins

This breathtakingly enjoyable German film is faster than a speeding bullet, with a mind-boggling pace that seizes audiences by the scruff of the neck and forces them along with ruthless momentum. Franka Potente receives a phone call from boyfriend Moritz Bleibtreu, who's left the money he owes the Mob on the subway. If it's not delivered, he'll be killed. Can she either find the loot or scrounge it in the time he has left? Director Tom Tykwer pushes cinema to superhuman limits – jump cuts and replays, colour turning to monochrome, action sped to a blur. Not so much a movie as an obstacle course. TH. In German with English subtitles. Contains swearing and violence. DVD

Franka Potente *Lola* • Moritz Bleibtreu *Manni* • Herbert Knaup *Lola's father* • Armin Rohde *Mr Schuster* • Ludger Pistor *Herr Meier* • Suzanne von Borsody *Frau Jäger* • Sebastian Schipper *Mike* • Heino Ferch *Ronnie* ■ *Dir/Scr* Tom Tykwer

Run of the Arrow ★★★★ PG

Western 1957 · US · Colour · 81mins

This was Rod Steiger's least favourite film because he didn't get on with director Samuel Fuller, but the personality clash sparked one of his greatest performances. He plays the bigoted southerner who, after the American Civil War, joins the Sioux tribe as a way of getting back at the Yankees. Surviving the torturous initiation rite, he manages to reveal the macho ethic at its most dangerous, while at the same time investing an unlikeable character with a certain naive dignity. TH

Rod Steiger *O'Meara* • Sarita Montiel *Yellow Moccasin* • Brian Keith *Captain Clark* • Ralph Meeker *Lieutenant Driscoll* • Jay C Flippen *Walking Coyote* • Charles Bronson *Blue Buffalo* • Olive Carey *Mrs O'Meara* ■ *Dir/Scr* Samuel Fuller

The Run of the Country ★★★ 15

Drama 1995 · Ire · Colour · 104mins

Albert Finney gives a towering performance as an Irish policeman trying to cope with his wayward son Matt Keeslar in director Peter Yates's moving drama. Unfortunately, the film's glowing portrayal of the Irish countryside rather softens the rites-of-passage roots of the drama, in which Keeslar is taught a few hard lessons in life when he falls for Victoria Smurfit, a girl from north of the border. Politics rarely intrude, with Yates more content to explore how a mundane existence in rural Ireland effects the young. It's beautiful to look at, but ultimately too nice for its own good. TH

Albert Finney *Father* • Matt Keeslar *Danny* • Victoria Smurfit *Annagh* • Anthony Brophy *Prunty* • David Kelly *Father Gaynor* • Dearbhla Molloy *Mother* ■ *Dir* Peter Yates • *Scr* Shane Connaughton, from his novel

Run, Rebecca, Run ★★★

Adventure 1981 · Aus · Colour · 80mins

Short, sharp action adventure, about a young girl who falls into the hands of an illegal immigrant hiding out on a remote Australian island. Captive becomes captivated, and she winds up working with him to persuade the Aussie authorities to let him legally enter the country. Director Peter Maxwell shows early signs of skill. DA

Simone Buchanan *Rebecca Ann Porter* • Henri Szeps *Manuel Cortes* • Adam Garnett *Rod* • John Stanton *Bob Porter* • Mary Anne Severne *Jean Porter* ■ *Dir* Peter Maxwell • *Scr* Charles Stamp

Run Silent, Run Deep ★★★★ U

Second World War drama
1958 · US · BW · 88mins

One of the best submarine movies, this is a terse, brilliantly directed study in revenge, as commander Clark Gable returns to the dreaded Bongo Straits where he had previously lost a sub and his men. Of course, second-in-command Burt Lancaster isn't happy, feeling that he should be in charge, and his reticence and the resentfulness of the crew make for fine drama in a confined space. The opening, pre-title sequence of this film is a classic example of movie storytelling. Even if you don't like the genre, this film merits watching for its star power alone. TS DVD

Clark Gable *Commander Richardson* • Burt Lancaster *Lieutenant Jim Bledsoe* • Jack Warden *Mueller* • Brad Dexter *Cartwright* • Don Rickles *Ruby* • Nick Cravat *Russo* ■ *Dir* Robert Wise • *Scr* John Gay, from a novel by Commander Edward L Beach

Run Wild, Run Free ★★★ U

Drama 1969 · UK · Colour · 94mins

This rural fable owes much to the earthy evocation of the wild beauty of Dartmoor. Complete with a tense finale and directed with old-fashioned care by Richard C Sarafian, the story of the timid boy whose love of a free-spirited horse brings him out of his shell should appeal to more discriminating youngsters. Mark Lester has few problems looking vulnerable, while John Mills provides seasoned support as the retired colonel who provides the affection denied by parents Sylvia Syms and Gordon Jackson. DP

John Mills *The Moorman* • Gordon Jackson *Mr Ransome* • Sylvia Syms *Mrs Ransome* • Mark Lester (2) *Philip Ransome* • Bernard Miles *Reg* • Fiona Fullerton *Diana* ■ *Dir* Richard C Sarafian • *Scr* David Rook, from the novel *The White Colt* by David Rook • *Cinematographer* Wilkie Cooper

Runaway! ★★

Action drama 1973 · US · Colour · 85mins

Made for American TV but released to cinemas in Britain as *The Runaway Train*, this hokey disaster movie stars Ben Johnson as the driver whose locomotive runs out of control down a mountain and across a field of the corniest clichés. Aboard the train are 200 passengers; they're all carrying lots of emotional baggage, of course, which fills the gap between brake failure and climactic buffers. AT. Contains swearing and violence.

Ben Johnson *Holly Gibson* • Ben Murphy *Les Reaver* • Ed Nelson *Nick Staffo* • Darleen Carr *Carol Lerner* • Lee H Montgomery [Lee Montgomery] *Mark Shedd* • Martin Milner *John Shedd* • Vera Miles *Ellen Staffo* ■ *Dir* David Lowell Rich • *Scr* Gerald DiPego

Runaway ★★ 15

Futuristic action thriller
1984 · US · Colour · 95mins

Tom Selleck stars in this silly futuristic thriller, written and directed by *Jurassic Park* creator Michael Crichton. Selleck is a cop who suffers from vertigo and the villain is Gene Simmons, leader of the rock group Kiss, who has an army of deadly spider-like robots at his command. Apart from some amusing romantic banter between Selleck and his police partner Cynthia Rhodes and a fairly exciting climax, it's routinely made. AT. Contains swearing, violence and brief nudity.

Tom Selleck *Jack Ramsay* • Cynthia Rhodes *Karen Thompson* • Gene Simmons *Dr Charles Luther* • Kirstie Alley *Jackie Rogers* • Stan Shaw *Marvin* • GW Bailey *Chief* • Joey Cramer *Bobby Ramsay* • Chris Mulkey *Johnson* ■ *Dir/Scr* Michael Crichton

Runaway Bride ★★★ PG

Romantic comedy
1999 · US · Colour · 116mins

Julia Roberts, Richard Gere and their *Pretty Woman* director Garry Marshall reunite for this predictable but well-played romantic comedy. Roberts is the small-town girl who has left a trio of heartbroken men at the altar, while Gere is the cynical columnist keen to see if she will actually go through with it on her fourth attempt. Of course, you'll have worked out the ending before you reach the last line of this review. However, thanks to Roberts's deft comedic touch, a zippy script and some nice support, this is a sweet romance that will warm the cockles of wedding fanatics everywhere. JB. Contains swearing. DVD

Julia Roberts *Maggie Carpenter* • Richard Gere *Ike Graham* • Joan Cusack *Peggy* • Hector Elizondo *Fisher* • Rita Wilson *Ellie* • Paul Dooley *Walter* • Christopher Meloni *Coach Bob* • Reg Rogers *George* • Laurie Metcalf *Mrs Trout* ■ *Dir* Garry Marshall • *Scr* Josann McGibbon, Sara Parriott

The Runaway Bus ★★ U

Comedy thriller 1954 · UK · BW · 76mins

This comedy thriller proved the ideal debut vehicle for Frankie Howerd. Never totally at home on film, he wisely follows Bob Hope's lead in combining cowardice and wisecracks as he substitutes for the driver of an airport shuttle bus, blissfully unaware that on this foggy night he has a stash of stolen gold on board. However, he is roundly upstaged by both that expert scene-stealer Margaret Rutherford and the under-rated Belinda Lee. DP

Frankie Howerd *Percy Lamb* • Margaret Rutherford *Cynthia Beeston* • Petula Clark *Lee Nichols* • George Coulouris *Edward Schroeder* • Belinda Lee *Janie Grey* • Reginald Beckwith *Collector* ■ *Dir/Scr* Val Guest

Runaway Car ★★ PG

Action comedy based on a true story
1997 · US · Colour · 90mins

In this TV movie, Judge Reinhold delivers another in a long line of pleasant but undistinguished performances, playing a computer programmer trapped in the passenger seat – along with Leon and a young baby – when goofy nurse Nina Siemaszko's brakes decide to pack in. Although the tale is supposedly inspired by a true incident, it doesn't really add up. RT DVD

Nina Siemaszko *Jenny Todd* • Judge Reinhold *Ed Lauter* • Brian Hooks *Dex* • Leon *Isaiah Beaufort* • Alec Murdock *Dr Mason* ■ *Dir* Jack Sholder • *Scr* Paul F Edwards

Runaway Daughters ★★ PG

Drama 1956 · US · BW · 91mins

Although American International Pictures was synonymous with juvenile rebellion, Edward L. Cahn's B-movie has something of a moral backlash to it. Marla English might despise Anna Sten and John Litel's affluent affectations, but she soon learns that real life is even less palatable, as do Mary Ellen Kay and Gloria Castillo. Today's teenagers might be surprised by how little adolescent angst has changed over the years, but dramatic styles are drastically different and it's hard to overlook how badly this melodrama has dated. DP DVD

Marla English *Audrey Barton* • Mary Ellen Kay *Mary Rubeck* • Gloria Castillo *Angela Forrest* • Lance Fuller *Tony Forrest* • Adele Jergens *Dixie* • Anna Sten *Ruth Barton* • John Litel *George Barton* ■ *Dir* Edward L Cahn • *Scr* Lou Rusoff

Runaway Jury ★★★ 12

Courtroom thriller
2003 · US · Colour · 122mins

A New Orleans woman files a suit against the gun industry (the tobacco conglomerates in John Grisham's original source novel) after her husband is murdered during a madman's shooting spree. Unfortunately for the widow and her idealistic lawyer Dustin Hoffman, the firearms lobby has hired ruthless "jury consultant" Gene Hackman to ensure the people chosen are predisposed to the "right" verdict. Into the mix comes John Cusack as a juror who is not at all what he seems. Well-crafted entertainment, despite the odd implausible plot point and simplistic central message. JA DVD

John Cusack *Nick Easter* • Gene Hackman *Rankin Fitch* • Dustin Hoffman *Wendall Rohr* • Rachel Weisz *Marlee* • Bruce Davison *Durwood Cable* • Bruce McGill *Judge Harkin* • Jeremy Piven *Lawrence Green* • Nick Searcy *Doyle* • Jennifer Beals *Vanessa Lembeck* ■ *Dir* Gary Fleder • *Scr* Brian Koppelman, David Levien, Rick Cleveland, Matthew Chapman, from the novel by John Grisham

Runaway Train ★★★★ 18

Action adventure
1985 · US · Colour · 105mins

This is a fast-paced thriller based on a screenplay co-written by celebrated Japanese director Akira Kurosawa, which takes it a notch above the average action film. Escaping convicts Jon Voight and Eric Roberts have far more depth than your typical gung-ho hero – both landed Oscar nominations, as did Henry Richardson, whose dynamic editing gives Andrei Konchalovsky's superior direction the breakneck pace that will keep you on the edge of your seat. DP. Contains swearing, violence. DVD

Jon Voight *Manny* • Eric Roberts *Buck* • Rebecca De Mornay *Sara* • Kyle T Heffner *Frank Barstow* • John P Ryan *Ranken* • TK Carter *Dave Prince* • Kenneth McMillan *Eddie MacDonald* ■ *Dir* Andrei Konchalovsky • *Scr* Djordje Milicevic, Paul Zindel, Edward Bunker, from a screenplay (unproduced) by Akira Kurosawa, Ryuzo Kikushima, Hideo Oguni

The Runestone ★★ 15

Horror 1991 · US · Colour · 98mins

An archaeologist uncovers a Norse artefact which turns him into a murderous hairy beast in this old-fashioned monster movie with a few good scares. Highly regarded in some genre quarters for its eerie atmosphere, graphic blood-letting and neat acting turns by Peter Riegert and Lawrence Tierney as hard-nosed NYPD cops, writer/director Willard Carroll unfortunately drags the excitement down with elongated passages of pretentious mumbo-jumbo. AJ

Alexander Godunov *Clockmaker* • Peter Riegert *Fanducol* • Joan Severance *Marla Stewart* • William Hickey *Lars Hagstron* • Tim Ryan *Sam Stewart* • Mitchell Laurance *Martin Almquist* • Lawrence Tierney *Chief Richardson* ■ *Dir* Willard Carroll • *Scr* Willard Carroll, from a novella by Mark E Rogers

The Runner ★★★★ PG

Drama 1984 · Iran · Colour · 86mins

Amir Naderi's film furthers the Iranian cinematic tradition of viewing the world through the eyes of disadvantaged children. Living alone in an abandoned boat in the port of Abadan, Majid Nirumand struggles to compete with the bigger lads in the scramble for redeemable bottles carried on the tide. While this neorealist study of post-revolutionary conditions could have been hopelessly pessimistic, Naderi invests it with startling exhilaration through the joyful thrill this waif derives from running. DP. In Farsi with English subtitles.

Majid Nirumand *Amiro* • A Gholamzadeh *Uncle Gholam* • Musa Torkizadeh *Musa* • Reza Ramezani *Ramezan* ■ *Dir* Amir Naderi • *Scr* Amir Naderi, Behruz Gharibpur

The Runner ★★★ 15

Crime drama 1999 · US · Colour · 89mins

Ron Eldard is the Las Vegas loser who becomes a runner for gangster John Goodman. Eldard places bets all over the neon city, falling in love with cocktail waitress Courteney Cox and buying her an engagement ring with Goodman's money. There are some fairly macabre twists in store and Goodman is superbly menacing as the man who has reduced everything in life to a matter of chance. Cox is alluring in a low-rent sort of way, but the weakness is Eldard who hasn't quite got the required charisma. AT DVD

Ron Eldard *Edward Harrington* • Courteney Cox *Karina* • Bokeem Woodbine *477* • John Goodman *Deep Throat* • Joe Mantegna *Rocco* • David Arquette *Bartender* ■ *Dir* Ron Moler • *Scr* Anthony E Zuiker

The Runner Stumbles ★

Drama 1979 · US · Colour · 88mins

Stanley Kramer is Hollywood's big game hunter. He tracks down the weightiest issues of the day and turns them into corny melodramas. This one stars Dick Van Dyke, of all people, as a priest accused in the 1920s of killing a nun he lusted after. There is hardly a line, let alone a scene, that rings true as Kramer bludgeons us with a new moral dilemma every minute. AT

Dick Van Dyke *Father Rivard* • Kathleen Quinlan *Sister Rita* • Maureen Stapleton *Mrs Shandig* • Ray Bolger *Monsignor Nicholson* • Tammy Grimes *Erna* • Beau Bridges *Toby* ■ *Dir* Stanley Kramer • *Scr* Milan Stitt, from a play by Milan Stitt

Runners ★★★ 15

Drama 1983 · UK · Colour · 102mins

With his teenage daughter on the disappearance list for two years, James Fox refuses to accept that she's dead and sets out on a journey to London to find her. He meets Jane Asher, the member of a support group who has lost her son, and his search turns from a contemporary social issue drama into a fully blown cryptic thriller. Idiosyncratically written by Stephen Poliakoff, directed with an accent on documentary realism by Charles Sturridge and well performed by the sympathetic Fox, this drama succeeds in engaging the attention. AJ

Kate Hardie *Rachel* • James Fox *Tom* • Jane Asher *Helen* • Eileen O'Brien *Gillian* • Ruti Simon *Lucy* ■ *Dir* Charles Sturridge • *Scr* Stephen Poliakoff

Running ★★ PG

Drama 1979 · Can · Colour · 96mins

In a typical tale of "The American Dream", Michael Douglas is an unemployed father of two who tries to sort out all of his domestic problems by bidding to join the Olympic marathon team. Not really illustrative of Douglas's subsequent career, this is an obvious attempt to cash in on the running craze of the late 1970s, but fails to get off the starting blocks. NF DVD

Michael Douglas *Michael Andropolis* • Susan Anspach *Janet Andropolis* • Lawrence Dane *Coach Walker* • Eugene Levy *Richard Rosenberg* • Charles Shamata [Chuck Shamata] *Howard Grant* ■ *Dir/Scr* Steven Hilliard Stern

Running Cool ★★ 18

Action drama 1993 · US · Colour · 101mins

An uninspired low-budget movie that tells the predictable story of a pair of bikers who get caught up in a battle against an evil property magnate. Andrew Divoff is the nominal star, although Paul Gleason (as the tycoon) is probably the best known name in the cast, while Dedee Pfeiffer pops up in a supporting role. It's written and directed by exploitation specialists Ferd and Beverly Sebastian. JF. Contains violence, swearing and brief nudity.

Andrew Divoff *Bone* • Tracy Sebastian *Blue Hogg* • Dedee Pfeiffer *Michele* • Paul Gleason *Calvin Hogg* • Arlen Dean Snyder *Sheriff* ■ *Dir/Scr* Beverly Sebastian, Ferd Sebastian

Running Free ★★★ U

Period drama 1999 · US · Colour · 80mins

This equine collaboration between producer Jean-Jacques Annaud, director Sergei Bodrov and the screenwriter of *The Black Stallion*, Jeanne Rosenberg, promised much. But the decision to employ Lukas Haas to articulate the thoughts of Lucky, the colt who survives copper mines, the Namibian wilderness and the rivalry of an older horse to lead his herd to safety at the height of the First World War, doesn't work. A shame, as the young cast, the animals and the scenery are first-rate. DP DVD

Chase Moore *Young Richard* • Jan Decleir *Boss Man* • Arie Verveen *Adult Richard* • Maria Geelbooi *Nyka* • Lukas Haas *Narrator (Lucky)* ■ *Dir* Sergei Bodrov • *Scr* Jeanne Rosenberg, from a story by Jeanne Rosenberg, Jean-Jacques Annaud

Running Hot ★★★ 18

Crime drama 1983 · US · Colour · 88mins

Eric Stoltz plays a young man, wrongfully convicted of murdering his father, who is then sentenced to death. After a hasty escape from a squad car, Stolz hooks up with Monica Carrico, a prostitute, who is drawn to him by a sense of *déjà vu*. Stolz then blunders across the country with Carrico in tow, killing several people who get in his way. A bit long and bleak, but well acted. ST

Monica Carrico *Charlene Andrews* • Eric Stoltz *Danny Hicks* • Stuart Margolin *Officer Trent* • Virgil Frye *Ross, the pimp* • Richard Bradford *Tom Bond* ■ *Dir/Scr* Mark Griffiths

The Running, Jumping and Standing Still Film ★★★ U

Silent comedy 1959 · UK · Sepia · 11mins

Having worked with ex-Goons Peter Sellers and Spike Milligan on three TV series, Richard Lester was the perfect choice to direct this anarchic short, which marked his cinematic debut. Shot in two days for just £700, using Sellers's new 16mm camera, it boasts such bizarre images as a field receiving a good scrubbing, a man playing a record on a tree stump and Graham Stark getting carried away by his kite before being punched on the nose by Leo McKern wearing a single boxing glove. Nominated for an Oscar,

R

it lost out to Jacques-Yves Cousteau's *The Golden Fish*. DP

Peter Sellers • Spike Milligan • Leo McKern • Graham Stark • Mario Fabrizi • David Lodge • Bruce Lacey ■ *Dir* Dick Lester [Richard Lester] • *Scr* Peter Sellers, Spike Milligan, Mario Fabrizi, Dick Lester [Richard Lester]

The Running Man ★★★★

Crime drama 1963 · UK · Colour · 108mins

This is one of those cinematic sleights of hand that only exceptional film-makers can hope to pull off. Armed with a clever script by John Mortimer (of Rumpole fame), director Carol Reed turns a thoroughly run-of-the-mill potboiler into a hugely entertaining three-handed thriller, thanks to his unerring ability to conjure up atmosphere, the striking photography of Robert Krasker and the canny performances of his splendid cast. Laurence Harvey is gleefully extravagant as a cocky conman, Alan Bates doggedly decent as the insurance assessor on his trail, and Lee Remick beguiling as the "widow" caught between them. DP

Laurence Harvey *Rex Black* • Lee Remick *Stella Black* • Alan Bates *Stephen Maddox* • Felix Aylmer *Parson* • Eleanor Summerfield *Hilda Tanner* • Allan Cuthbertson *Jenkins* • Harold Goldblatt *Tom Webster* ■ *Dir* Carol Reed • *Scr* John Mortimer, from the novel *The Ballad of the Running Man* by Shelley Smith

The Running Man ★★★ 18

Science-fiction action thriller
1987 · US · Colour · 96mins

Given TV's increasingly desperate search for new programme formats, this futuristic blockbuster about a game show where a pumped-up audience bays for the blood of convicts on a lethal combat course isn't so far-fetched. Arnold Schwarzenegger is the former police helicopter pilot who is forced into the game of death when he rebels against his totalitarian superiors. Schwarzenegger gets to do what he does best – destroying baddies with a quip – and director Paul Michael Glaser handles the action sequences with panache. JF. Contains swearing and violence. [video] DVD

Arnold Schwarzenegger *Ben Richards* • Maria Conchita Alonso *Amber Mendez* • Yaphet Kotto *Laughlin* • Jim Brown *Fireball* • Jesse Ventura *Captain Freedom* • Erland Van Lidth *Dynamo* • Marvin J McIntyre *Weiss* • Gus Rethwisch *Buzzsaw* • Richard Dawson *Damon Killian* ■ *Dir* Paul Michael Glaser • *Scr* Steven E DeSouza, from the novel *The Running Man* by Richard Bachman [Stephen King]

R

Running on Empty ★★★★ 15

Drama 1988 · US · Colour · 111mins

This interesting twist on the effect the 1960s really had on America is also a sad reminder of the late River Phoenix's talents as an actor. He plays Danny, a teenager who leads an unusual life – he and his parents (Judd Hirsch and Christine Lahti) have been on the run from the FBI for 17 years since the couple bombed a university research centre, blinding a janitor in the blast. But now Phoenix wants a more settled existence, and the film focuses on the family's attempts to keep together. Director Sidney Lumet keeps the drama subtle instead of dissolving into mush. JB. Contains swearing and drug abuse. [video]

Christine Lahti *Annie Pope* • River Phoenix *Danny Pope* • Judd Hirsch *Arthur Pope* • Martha Plimpton *Lorna Phillips* • Jonas Abry *Harry Pope* • Ed Crowley *Mr Phillips* • LM Kit Carson *Gus Winant* ■ *Dir* Sidney Lumet • *Scr* Naomi Foner

Running Out of Luck ★ 18

Music drama 1985 · UK · Colour · 86mins

An obscure musical drama, directed by Julien Temple and made to accompany a Mick Jagger album, it's basically a feature-length music video with an incredibly bizarre plot filling in the gaps between songs. Its self-reflexive start has Jagger, partner Jerry Hall and Dennis Hopper filming a music video in Rio, but the shoot breaks up and somehow Jagger finds himself being beaten up by transvestites and forced into sex slavery on a banana plantation with Rae Dawn Chong. It may sound intriguing, but it's not. DA [video]

Mick Jagger • Jerry Hall • Dennis Hopper *Video director* • Rae Dawn Chong *Slave girl* • Jim Broadbent ■ *Dir* Julien Temple • *Scr* Julien Temple, Mick Jagger

Running Scared ★★★ 15

Action comedy thriller
1986 · US · Colour · 102mins

This enjoyable buddy-buddy cop thriller was comic Billy Crystal's breakthrough movie. Both he and Gregory Hines play streetwise Chicago cops, firing wisecracks like bullets, who've decided to retire to Florida. The only problem is they have to work out a month's notice and underworld boss Jimmy Smits is determined to rub them out. Hines and Crystal make an endearing screen partnership although their stream of funny one-liners and the set-piece spectacles director Peter Hyams is noted for sit uneasily with the gritty look of the production. RS. Contains violence, swearing, nudity. [video] DVD

Billy Crystal *Danny Costanzo* • Gregory Hines *Ray Hughes* • Steve Bauer [Steven Bauer] *Frank* • Darlanne Fluegel *Anna Costanzo* • Joe Pantoliano *Snake* • Dan Hedaya *Capt Logan* • Jimmy Smits *Julio Gonzales* ■ *Dir* Peter Hyams • *Scr* Gary DeVore, Jimmy Huston, from a story by Gary DeVore

Running Wild ★★

Silent comedy 1927 · US · BW · 68mins

Fresh from *So's Your Old Man*, WC Fields and director Gregory La Cava re-teamed on this unofficial reworking of the Will Rogers comedy, *One Glorious Day*. As the henpecked milquetoast, whose only friend at the toy shop where he works is a nodding donkey, Fields is given little room for manoeuvre by a substandard script. However, the vaudeville sequence, in which he's hypnotised into becoming a world-beater, provides a perfect showcase for his pantomimic skills. DP

WC Fields *Elmer Finch* • Mary Brian *Elizabeth* • Claud Buchanan *Jerry Harvey* • Marie Shotwell *Mrs Finch* • Barney Raskle *Junior* ■ *Dir* Gregory La Cava • *Scr* Roy Briant, from a story by Gregory La Cava

Running Wild ★★

Crime drama 1955 · US · BW · 81mins

Keenan Wynn runs a gang of young car thieves. William Campbell is a cop who disguises himself as a teenager and infiltrates the gang, while Mamie Van Doren acts with her chest and plays the gang's swoon centre. Aimed exclusively at the teen market, it features several rock 'n' roll numbers which belt out of the nearest jukebox. The major flaw is that none of the cast look young or thuggish enough. AT

William Campbell *Ralph Barclay* • Mamie Van Doren *Irma Bean* • Keenan Wynn *Ken Osanger* • Kathleen Case *Leta Novak* • Jan Merlin *Scotty Cluett* • John Saxon *Vince Pomeroy* ■ *Dir* Abner Biberman • *Scr* Leo Townsend, from a novel by Ben Benson

Running Wild ★★★ U

Drama 1973 · US · Colour · 96mins

Set in charming and beautiful scenery, this pleasant family drama concerns a news photographer whose horror at the treatment of wild mustangs inspires an exposé. Classy Dina Merrill makes a welcome big-screen return in the pivotal leading role, while gritty veterans Lloyd Bridges, Gilbert Roland, and RG Armstrong give her staunch company. This is a strong and intelligently written piece with its heart in the right place. TS [video]

Lloyd Bridges *Jeff Methune* • Dina Merrill *Whit Colby* • Pat Hingle *Quentin Hogue* • Morgan Woodward *Crug Crider* • Gilbert Roland *Chief Tomacito* • Fred Betts *Cap Methune* • RG Armstrong *Bull* ■ *Dir/Scr* Robert McCahon

Running Wild ★★

Drama documentary
1992 · US · Colour · 98mins

Having dedicated 12 years of his life to making a wildlife documentary about an endangered female cat on the Londolozi game reserve, it seems odd that African naturalist and film-maker John Varty should choose to add a fictional element to its sequel. Viewers will be far more interested in the fate of her orphaned cubs, than in the Tinseltown subplot involving producer Martin Sheen, film-maker Brooke Shields and her obstructive colleague David Keith. Unfortunately for the actors, the focus on the leopards makes the movie business seem all the more redundant. DP

Brooke Shields *Christine Shaye* • Martin Sheen *Dan Walker* • David Keith *Jack Hutton* • Renée Estevez *Aimee* • John Varty ■ *Dir* Duncan McLachlan • *Scr* Duncan McLachlan, Andrea Buck, John Varty

La Rupture ★★★★ 18

Thriller 1970 · Fr/It/Bel · Colour · 119mins

Part of Claude Chabrol's absorbing "Hélène cycle" of films, featuring his wife, the seductive Stéphane Audran, this is another of the director's attacks on the bourgeois family. Here, Audran is less scheming than usual as a woman fighting to gain custody of her child from her drug addict husband and nasty father-in-law. Chabrol's terse and suspenseful style works to great advantage in this neat thriller. The excellent cast includes Jean-Pierre Cassel as a seedy detective and, as the father-in-law, Chabrol favourite Michel Bouquet. RB. In French with English subtitles. [video]

Jean-Pierre Cassel *Paul* • Stéphane Audran *Hélène* • Annie Cordy *Mme Pinelli* • Michel Bouquet *Ludovic Regnier* ■ *Dir* Claude Chabrol • *Scr* Claude Chabrol, from the novel *The Balloon Man* by Charlotte Armstrong

Rush ★★★ 18

Thriller 1991 · US · Colour · 115mins

It's rare these days to hear Eric Clapton music that smacks of commitment. And yet it's his sensitive soundtrack which contributes to the intensity of a movie that successfully captures the unnerving world of the drug addict. Debut director Lili Fini Zanuck sustains the right air of stifling claustrophobia, while Jennifer Jason Leigh and Jason Patric, as two narcotics cops who get hooked, go on their downward spiral with a great deal of force. JM. Contains violence, swearing and drug abuse. [video] DVD

Jason Patric *Jim Raynor* • Jennifer Jason Leigh *Kristen Cates* • Sam Elliott *Larry Dodd* • Max Perlich *Walker* • Gregg Allman *William Gaines* • Tony Frank *Police Chief Nettle* • William Sadler *Monroe* ■ *Dir* Lili Fini Zanuck • *Scr* Pete Dexter, from the book by Kim Wozencraft

Rush Hour ★★★★ 12

Martial arts action comedy
1998 · US · Colour · 93mins

Hong Kong action superstar Jackie Chan teams up with loudmouth American comedian Chris Tucker for this blockbuster thriller. It's essentially an east-meets-west buddy movie about two cops trying to solve an international kidnapping, but director Brett Ratner allows plenty of time for character development between the spectacular set pieces, and Chan and Tucker's inspired double act elevates it above the norm. Equally adept at comic martial arts, Chaplin-esque displays and near-superhuman stunts, Chan has never been more engaging. AJ. Contains swearing, violence and drug abuse. [video] DVD

Jackie Chan *Detective Inspector Lee* • Chris Tucker *Detective James Carter* • Tom Wilkinson *Griffin/Juntao* • Chris Penn *Clive* • Elizabeth Peña *Tania Johnson* • Rex Linn *Agent Whitney* • Philip Baker Hall *Captain Diel* ■ *Dir* Brett Ratner • *Scr* Ross LaManna, Jim Kouf, from a story by Ross LaManna

Rush Hour 2 ★★★ 12

Martial arts action comedy
2001 · US · Colour · 86mins

Pint-sized action star Jackie Chan reteams with motormouth Chris Tucker for this sequel. It's the same hit formula, only this time the two chalk-and-cheese cops find themselves in Hong Kong battling a murderous triad gang, but with the added spice that head man John Lone was involved in the death of Jackie's dad. There's also the opportunity to see *Crouching Tiger, Hidden Dragon* star Zhang Ziyi make her American debut as Lone's beautiful but deadly henchwoman. DA. Contains violence and swearing. [video] DVD

Jackie Chan *Detective Inspector Lee* • Chris Tucker *Detective James Carter* • John Lone *Ricky Tan* • Zhang Ziyi *Hu Li* • Roselyn Sanchez *Agent Isabella Molina* • Alan King *Steven Reign* ■ *Dir* Brett Ratner • *Scr* Jeff Nathanson, from characters created by Ross LaManna

Rush to Judgment ★★★

Documentary 1967 · US · BW · 98mins

A more thought-provoking than polemical documentary about the assassination of John F Kennedy and its aftermath, not only of interest to conspiracy buffs. Using witness interviews and footage, the Warren Commission's lone assassin conclusions are challenged and the conspiracy theory of Mark Lane's landmark article is presented. Director Emile de Antonio made several interesting documentaries on aspects of American politics. JG

Mark Lane (1) *Narrator* ■ *Dir* Emile de Antonio • *Scr* Mark Lane, from his article *Rush to Judgement: a Critique of the Warren Commission Inquiry into the Murder of President John F Kennedy, Officer JD Tippit and Lee Harvey Oswald*

Rushmore ★★★★ 15

Black comedy drama
1998 · US · Colour · 89mins

Director Wes Anderson and his co-writer Owen Wilson – who first caught the eye with their low-budget debut *Bottle Rocket* – score again with this unusual black comedy, which centres around an extremely unconventional teen hero. Jason Schwartzman plays one of the least popular pupils at Rushmore Academy, who nonetheless runs just about every club and school activity in a megalomaniacal effort to further himself. Schwartzman gives a superbly nerdy performance, but Bill Murray – playing a depressed millionaire – steals every scene in this quirky, edgy and very funny tale of an outsider who just might end up leading all those who laugh at him. JB. Contains swearing. [video] DVD

Jason Schwartzman *Max Fischer* • Bill Murray *Herman Blume* • Olivia Williams *Rosemary Cross* • Brian Cox *Dr Guggenheim* • Seymour Cassel *Bert Fischer* • Mason Gamble *Dirk Calloway* • Owen Wilson *Edward Applebee* ■ *Dir* Wes Anderson • *Scr* Wes Anderson, Owen Wilson

The Russia House ★★★★ 15

Spy drama 1990 · US · Colour · 117mins

Adapted by Tom Stoppard from John le Carré's novel, this espionage thriller is a class act in every respect, not least in its clever use of authentic Russian locations. Sean Connery is a tweedy, irascible British publisher and reluctant spy who goes to Russia to check out the truth behind a potentially explosive manuscript. Michelle Pfeiffer is his contact and her moving performance is simply astonishing, with a wholly convincing accent that never comes across as studied. It's a tense, often puzzling picture, subtly directed by Fred Schepisi and with a great supporting cast. AT. Contains swearing. VIDEO DVD

Sean Connery *Barley Blair* • Michelle Pfeiffer *Katya* • Roy Scheider *Russell* • James Fox *Ned* • John Mahoney *Brady* • Klaus Maria Brandauer *Savelev/"Dante"* • Ken Russell *Walter* • JT Walsh *Quinn* • Michael Kitchen *Clive* • David Threlfall *Wicklow* • Martin Clunes *Brock* • Ian McNeice *Merrydew* ■ *Dir* Fred Schepisi • *Scr* Tom Stoppard, from the novel by John le Carré

Russian Ark ★★★★★ U

Experimental drama
2002 · Rus/Ger · Colour · 95mins

This compelling compendium of historical incident and cultural ideas will thrill anyone with a passion for film. The manner in which director Aleksandr Sokurov has choreographed Tilman Büttner's single-take Steadicam waltz around St Petersburg's Hermitage Museum is pure cinematic poetry. This ingenuity is matched by the variety of rhythms the action accomplishes, as the HDV camera hurries between rooms or mingles with revellers at a court ball, pauses to consider the symbolism of a Van Dyck painting or observe the cosy domesticity of Tsar Nicholas II taking tea with his family. A masterclass in content and form. DP. In Russian with English subtitles. VIDEO DVD

Sergei Dreiden [Sergei Dontsov] *Marquis de Custine, the stranger* • Maria Kuznetsova *Catherine the Great* • Leonid Mozgovoy *Spy* • David Giorgobiani *Orbeli* • Alexander Chaban *Boris Piotrovsky* • Maxim Sergeyev *Peter the Great* ■ *Dir* Aleksandr Sokurov • *Scr* Anatoly Nikiforov, Aleksandr Sokurov, Boris Khaimsky, Svetlana Proskurina

The Russians Are Coming, the Russians Are Coming ★★★★ U

Comedy 1966 · US · Colour · 120mins

Norman Jewison's comedy – an Oscar nominee for best picture – now seems funnier than ever and survives, along with Stanley Kubrick's *Dr Strangelove*, as a key artefact of the Cold War era. The story is simple: Russian Alan Arkin grounds his submarine on the American coast, goes ashore for help and panic ensues. It's a little long and there's some rather sticky moralising as well, but these are minor flaws when set beside the general level of comic invention. AT VIDEO DVD

Carl Reiner *Walt Whittaker* • Eva Marie Saint *Elspeth Whittaker* • Alan Arkin *Rozanov* • Brian Keith *Link Mattocks* • Jonathan Winters *Norman Jonas* • Theodore Bikel *Russian captain* • Paul Ford *Fendall Hawkins* ■ *Dir* Norman Jewison • *Scr* William Rose, from the novel *The Off-Islanders* by Nathaniel Benchley

Russkies ★★ PG

Comedy drama 1987 · US · Colour · 98mins

Back in the days when he was still known as Leaf, Joaquin Phoenix plays a Florida youngster whose gang stumbles across stranded Russian sailor Whip Hubley and decides to shelter him from the authorities. Predictable grown-up interference and adolescent heroism become increasingly contrived and saccharin as this well-intentioned but hopelessly clunky rite-of-passage picture proceeds. DP. Contains violence, swearing. VIDEO

Whip Hubley *Mischa* • Leaf Phoenix [Joaquin Phoenix] *Danny* • Peter Billingsley *Adam* • Stefan DeSalle *Jason* • Susan Walters *Diane* • Patrick Kilpatrick *Raimy* • Vic Polizos *Sulock* • Summer Phoenix *Candi* ■ *Dir* Rick Rosenthal • *Scr* Michael Nankin, Alan Jay Glueckman, Sheldon Lettich, from a story by Alan Jay Glueckman, Sheldon Lettich

Rustler's Rhapsody ★★★ PG

Western spoof 1985 · US · Colour · 84mins

A fun spoof of the popular "singing cowboy" films of the 1930s, 1940s and 1950s. Tom Berenger plays the cowboy crooner here, and has the hunky good looks to carry it off. The parody suffers, though, from the fact that the singing cowboy genre never took itself too seriously in the first place, and that anyone under 50 will have probably never seen one. DA VIDEO

Tom Berenger *Rex O'Herlihan* • Marilu Henner *Miss Tracy* • GW Bailey *Peter* • Fernando Rey *Railroad colonel* • Andy Griffith *Colonel Ticonderoga* ■ *Dir/Scr* Hugh Wilson

Ruthless ★★★ PG

Drama 1948 · US · BW · 100mins

This splendid chunk of Hollywood B-movie tosh stars Zachary Scott as the man who ruins everyone in his path. Dames he two-times, men he just destroys. Better enjoyed as cheap junk than taken seriously, it was directed by cult maestro Edgar G Ulmer, a man who knew how to stretch a budget and a schedule. The screenplay is somewhat clumsy, but the cast here is better than expected. TS VIDEO

Zachary Scott *Horace Woodruff Vendig* • Louis Hayward *Vic Lambdin* • Diana Lynn *Martha Burnside/Mallory Flagg* • Sydney Greenstreet *Buck Mansfield* • Lucille Bremer *Christa Mansfield* • Martha Vickers *Susan Dunne* • Raymond Burr *Peter Vendig* ■ *Dir* Edgar G Ulmer • *Scr* Alvah Bessie (uncredited), SK Lauren, Gordon Kahn, from the novel *Prelude to Night* by Dayton Stoddart

Ruthless People ★★★★ 18

Comedy 1986 · US · Colour · 90mins

Airplane! partners Jim Abrahams, Jerry Zucker and David Zucker teamed up again for this fun comedy about a pair of bumbling kidnappers – Helen Slater and Judge Reinhold – who snatch wealthy Bette Midler, to discover that her husband Danny DeVito doesn't want her back. The movie twists and turns as a whole host of other people get involved (including Anita Morris as DeVito's mistress and a young Bill Pullman as her mentally challenged lover). DeVito and Midler are superb in their roles as the greedy philanderer and his overbearing other half. JB. Contains swearing, nudity. VIDEO DVD

Danny DeVito *Sam Stone* • Bette Midler *Barbara Stone* • Judge Reinhold *Ken Kessler* • Helen Slater *Sandy Kessler* • Anita Morris *Carol* • Bill Pullman *Earl* • William G Schilling *Police commissioner* • Art Evans *Lieutenant Bender* • Clarence Felder *Lieutenant Walters* ■ *Dir* Jim Abrahams, David Zucker, Jerry Zucker • *Scr* Dale Launer

The Rutles – All You Need Is Cash ★★★★ 15

Spoof comedy
1978 · UK/US · Colour · 70mins

The career of this mop-topped Liverpudlian band echoes that of a rather more famous quartet, in a witty documentary parody of the Fab Four's career. The brainchild of stars Eric Idle (who writes, co-directs and narrates) and Neil Innes (responsible for music, lyrics and a killer John Lennon impersonation), this cleverly incorporates multiple film stocks and varied musical re-creations to send-up the iconic rise of The Beatles. There's inspired fake newsreel footage, interviews with both invented and real celebrities, elaborate movie clips and brilliantly imitated live performances, using Innes's spot-on pastiches of classic tracks. JC VIDEO DVD

Eric Idle *Dirk McQuickley/Narrator/Stanley Krammerhead III Jr* • Neil Innes *Ron Nasty* • John Halsey *Barry Wom* • Ricky Fataar *Stig O'Hara* • Michael Palin *Eric Manchester* • Bianca Jagger *Martini McQuickley* • George Harrison *The interviewer* • John Belushi *Ron Decline* ■ *Dir* Eric Idle, Gary Weis • *Scr* Eric Idle

Ryan's Daughter ★★★★★ 15

Romantic epic 1970 · UK · Colour · 186mins

Released five years after *Doctor Zhivago*, this romantic epic from David Lean was not so much roasted by the critics as incinerated. The story of a dreamy girl who marries a stolid village teacher and then has an affair with a shell-shocked British officer, it began as a script of Flaubert's *Madame Bovary* that Robert Bolt had written for his wife, Sarah Miles. Set in a bleak Irish village in 1916, it co-stars a courageously cast Robert Mitchum as the teacher. Stories about the year-long making of the picture have duly entered movie legend; as an overblown romance it has no equal and now looks like a masterwork. Freddie Young's Oscar-winning images of the wild Dingle Peninsula need to be seen on the big screen. AT. Contains a sex scene and brief nudity. VIDEO

Robert Mitchum *Charles Shaughnessy* • Sarah Miles *Rosy* • Trevor Howard *Father Collins* • John Mills *Michael* • Christopher Jones *Major Randolph Doryan* • Leo McKern *Thomas Ryan* • Barry Foster *Tim O'Leary* • Arthur O'Sullivan *Mr McCardle* • Marie Kean *Mrs McCardle* • Evin Crowley *Moureen* ■ *Dir* David Lean • *Scr* Robert Bolt • *Music* Maurice Jarre

SFW ★★★ 18

Satirical drama 1994 · US · Colour · 95mins

It's beginning to show its age, but this satirical drama remains a topical dissection of the American fascination with the cult of the non-celebrity. Stephen Dorff is the angry young man who is among a group taken hostage by camcorder-wielding anarchists. They force the networks to broadcast their tapes, but it's the rebellious Dorff who soon becomes the star attraction, making him, unwillingly, the hottest thing on TV. Dorff is suitably surly as the man fighting against his 15 minutes of fame and there's good support from a pre-fame Reese Witherspoon and Jake Busey. JF. Contains violence, swearing, nudity. VIDEO DVD

Stephen Dorff *Cliff Spab* • Reese Witherspoon *Wendy Pfister* • Jake Busey *Morrow Streeter* • Joey Lauren Adams *Monica Dice* • Pamela Gidley *Janet Streeter* ■ *Dir* Jefery Levy • *Scr* Jefery Levy, Danny Rubin, from the novel by Andrew Wellman

SLC Punk! ★★★ 15

Comedy drama 1999 · US · Colour · 97mins

As Salt Lake's only hardcore punks, Matthew Lillard and Michael Goorjian have a take on rednecks, posing cultists and the all-pervading influence of Mormonism. How can you be an anarchist, though, when you have good grades, ambitious parents and a social conscience? Writer/director James Merendino's decision to let Lillard address the audience directly personalises the overly familiar teen-pic tropes. The stomping soundtrack and some archly designed threads can't forestall the inevitable triumph of conventionality. DP. Contains swearing, violence and drug abuse.

Matthew Lillard *Stevo* • Michael Goorjian *Bob* • Annabeth Gish *Trish* • Jennifer Lien *Sandy* • Christopher McDonald *Father* • Devon Sawa *Sean* • Jason Segel *Mike* • Summer Phoenix *Brandy* ■ *Dir/Scr* James Merendino

SOB ★★★

Comedy 1981 · US · Colour · 121mins

You don't expect this sort of vitriol from Blake Edwards, creator of the amiable, if idiotic, Inspector Clouseau, especially when Edwards's wife Julie Andrews is the star. Yet this attack on Hollywood values is one of the crudest satires ever made at the expense of Tinseltown, as Richard Mulligan, playing a director, decides to turn his art-movie stinker into a soft-porn success, with screen-wife Andrews in the leading role. As the showbiz in-fighting gets worse, it's obvious that Edwards is paying off old, rancorous scores, but such personal venom slows down the pace and the point. TH. Contains swearing and nudity.

Julie Andrews *Sally Miles* • William Holden (2) *Tim Culley* • Richard Mulligan *Felix Farmer* • Larry Hagman *Dick Benson* • Robert Loggia *Herb Maskowitz* • Stuart Margolin *Gary Murdock* • Marisa Berenson *Mavis* • Robert Preston *Dr Irving Finegarten* • Craig Stevens *Willard Gaylin* • Loretta Swit *Polly Reed* • Robert Vaughn *David Blackman* • Robert Webber *Ben Coogan* • Shelley Winters *Eva Brown* • Jennifer Edwards *Lila* • Rosanna Arquette *Babs* ■ *Dir/Scr* Blake Edwards

S

SOS Iceberg ★★

Adventure drama 1933 · Ger · BW · 77mins

A German crew under Dr Arnold Fanck, shot 58 hours of Arctic footage; Hollywood director Tay Garnett then went to Berlin to help devise a dual-language drama using some of this material, which included a glacier exploding into thousands of icebergs. On a frozen Swiss lake they shot a formula story of a scientific expedition in trouble, the few survivors sheltering on an ice floe to await rescue. The natural spectacle dwarfs the cast. AE

Rod La Rocque *Dr Carl Lawrence* • Leni Riefenstahl *Ellen Lawrence* • Sepp Rist *Dr Johannes Brand* • Gibson Gowland *John Dragan* • Dr Max Holzboer [Max Holzboer] *Dr Jan Matushek* ■ *Dir* Tay Garnett • *Scr* Tom Reed, Edwin H Knopf, from a story by Dr Arnold Fanck [Arnold Fanck]

SOS Pacific ★★★

Action drama 1959 · UK · BW · 90mins

The secret of a good disaster movie is to ensure that the victims hardly have chance to draw breath after one crisis, before another follows hot on its heels. In this Rank adventure, a plane crash-lands on an island, only for the survivors to discover that it is the site for an imminent atomic test. Considering there is only one outcome, director Guy Green sustains the suspense remarkably well, helped in no small measure by a sound cast led by Richard Attenborough, Pier Angeli and Eddie Constantine. DP

Eddie Constantine *Mark Reisener* • Pier Angeli *Teresa* • Richard Attenborough *Whitey* • John Gregson *Jack Bennett* • Eva Bartok *Maria* • Jean Anderson *Miss Shaw* ■ *Dir* Guy Green • *Scr* Robert Westerby, from a story by Gilbert Travers

SOS Titanic ★★ PG

Historical drama 1979 · US · Colour · 97mins

Originally made for American TV, but released in cinemas over here, this detailed account of the famous shipping disaster mixes fact and fiction as uneasily as it mixes its Anglo-American cast. Director William Hale's grip on the drama is rather tenuous, and the result is regrettably rather low key and cheap looking. Still, Helen Mirren, Ian Holm, Harry Andrews, David Warner, David Janssen and Susan Saint James suffer nobly. TS [video]

David Janssen *John Jacob Astor* • Cloris Leachman *Molly Brown* • Susan Saint James *Leigh Goodwin* • David Warner *Laurence Beesley* • Ian Holm *J Bruce Ismay* • Helen Mirren *May Sloan* • Harry Andrews *Captain Edward J Smith* • Beverly Ross *Madeline Astor* • Ed Bishop *Henry Harris* ■ *Dir* William Hale • *Scr* James Costigan

S

S21: the Khmer Rouge Killing Machine ★★★

Documentary 2003 · Fr · Colour · 101mins

Cambodian artist Vann Nath was one of only three of the 17,000 prisoners detained at the notorious Tuol Sleng interrogation centre to survive their ordeal. The pain is evident in his work. But his courage remains undiminished, as he returns to the former school buildings to confront the Khmer Rouge guards who carried out Pol Pot's hideous policy of genocide. The re-enactment of the daily routines and the inspection of the jail's ghoulishly detailed records are chilling. But director Rithy Panh's unflinching focus may feel a little narrow to those unfamiliar with the historical background to the Killing Fields. DP. In Khmer with English subtitles.

Dir Rithy Panh

Saadia ★★ U

Drama 1953 · US · Colour · 87mins

Albert Lewin was assistant to Irving Thalberg during the great years of MGM. A former critic for the *Jewish Tribune*, he was an intelligent, literate man, who latterly directed six interesting features, including *The Picture of Dorian Gray*, which grew increasingly mediocre as he chased his special muse – *Saadia* was the penultimate, and by far the most preposterous. Mysticism and religiosity obscure a simple Moroccan love story, as Cornel Wilde and Mel Ferrer slug it out for love of dancer Rita Gam. TS

Cornel Wilde *Si Lahssen* • Mel Ferrer *Henrik* • Rita Gam *Saadia* • Michel Simon *Bou Rezza* • Cyril Cusack *Khadir* • Wanda Rotha *Fatima* • Marcel Poncin *Moha* • Anthony Marlowe *Captain Sabert* ■ *Dir* Albert Lewin • *Scr* Albert Lewin, from the novel *Echeck au Destin* by Francis D'Autheville

Saajan ★★★ U

Romantic drama
1991 · Ind · Colour · 173mins

Salman Khan, the hunky pin-up of both India's gay community and the nation's teenage girls, stars here as a playboy on one side of a love triangle in Lawrence D'Souza's amiable Bollywood romance. But, unusually for a masala ménage à trois, he and impoverished poet Sanjay Dutt appear more than willing to see each other's merits and leave poor old Madhuri Dixit feeling rather neglected. DP. In Punjabi with English subtitles. [video] DVD

Salman Khan *Akash* • Sanjay Dutt *Aman/Sagar* • Madhuri Dixit *Pooja* ■ *Dir* Lawrence D'Souza • *Scr* Reema Rakeshnath

Saathiya ★★★ 12

Romantic drama
2002 · Ind · Colour · 134mins

With composer AR Rahman and lyricist Gulzar collaborating on the score and Shah Rukh Khan lending stellar support, Mani Ratnam's longtime assistant Shaad Ali has every chance of establishing his solo credentials. Rani Mukerji stars as the dedicated Mumbai medical student whose life is transformed when she falls for fellow commuter Vivek Oberoi. But, no sooner are they married than capricious fate tears them apart and a heart-tugging journey begins. This is very much the polished article we've come to expect from producer Yash Chopra. DP. In Hindi with English subtitles. [video]

Vivek Oberoi *Aditya Sehgal* • Rani Mukerji [Rani Mukherji] *Suhani Sharma* • Sandhya Mridul *Dina, Suhani's sister* • Tanuja *Shobhana, Suhani's mother* • Sharat Saxena *Chandraprakash, Suhani's father* • Satish Shah *Om, Aditya's father* ■ *Dir* Shaad Ali • *Scr* Mani Ratnam

Sabata ★★★ 12

Spaghetti western
1969 · It · Colour · 102mins

Having established his spaghetti credentials with *Sartana* (1968), Gianfranco Parolini embarked on a trilogy of violent westerns directed under the pseudonym Frank Kramer. Lee Van Cleef is dangerously deadpan as the gunman who becomes the target of Franco Ressel, after he realises the corrupt town elder was behind a daring raid on a shipment of army gold. Packed with gimmicky gadgetry and eccentric set pieces, this is superior to both *Adios, Sabata* (in which Yul Brynner replaced Van Cleef in the title role) and *The Return of Sabata*. DP. Italian dialogue dubbed into English. [video]

Lee Van Cleef *Sabata* • William Berger *Banjo* • Pedro Sanchez [Ignazio Spalla] *Carrincha* • Nick Jordan [Aldo Canti] *Indio* • Franco Ressel *Stengel* • Anthony Gradwell [Antonio Gradoli] *Ferguson* • Linda Veras *Jane* ■ *Dir* Frank Kramer [Ginafranco Parolini] • *Scr* Ginafranco Parolini, Renato Izzo

Sabotage ★★★★ PG

Mystery thriller 1936 · UK · BW · 73mins

There was no such thing as accepted behaviour for suspense master Alfred Hitchcock, and his nonconformity was never more apparent than in the unnerving scene from this movie in which a small boy (Desmond Tester) carries a time-bomb aboard a bus. Movie-goers suddenly had to confront the unexpected (a Hitchcock trademark) in this adaptation of Joseph Conrad's novel *The Secret Agent*, in which terrorist Oscar Homolka, uses his marriage to submissive Sylvia Sidney and his business as a cinema owner as front for his subversive activities. Hitchcock later described the film as "playful" but, as usual for him, it is, in fact, a deadly game with cruel conclusions. TH [video]

Sylvia Sidney *Sylvia Verloc* • Oscar Homolka *Carl Verloc* • John Loder *Sergeant Ted Spencer* • Desmond Tester *Steve* • Joyce Barbour *Renee* • Matthew Boulton *Superintendent Talbot* ■ *Dir* Alfred Hitchcock • *Scr* Charles Bennett, Ian Hay, Alma Reville, Helen Simpson and EVH Emmett, from the novel *The Secret Agent* by Joseph Conrad

Saboteur ★★★★ PG

Spy thriller 1942 · US · BW · 104mins

Dorothy Parker contributed to the screenplay of this cracking Hitchcock thriller, which cleverly served the dual purpose of warning Americans against Fifth Columnists and providing much needed escapism. Although Hitch was unhappy with the stars chosen for him by Universal (Robert Cummings and Priscilla Lane), he clearly enjoyed hurtling them around deserts, ghost towns and luxury mansions. The Statue of Liberty finale is the film's best known set piece, but the encounter with a circus troupe and the Radio City Music Hall shoot-out are bang on the money. DP [video] DVD

Robert Cummings *Barry Kane* • Priscilla Lane *Patricia Martin* • Otto Kruger *Charles Tobin* • Alan Baxter *Freeman* • Clem Bevans *Neilson* • Norman Lloyd *Frank Fry* • Alma Kruger *Mrs Henrietta Sutton* ■ *Dir* Alfred Hitchcock • *Scr* Peter Viertel, Joan Harrison, Dorothy Parker

The Saboteur, Code Name Morituri ★★★★

Spy drama 1965 · US · BW · 123mins

Despite the clashing egos on the set of *Mutiny on the Bounty*, Marlon Brando and Trevor Howard signed on for another shipboard drama. A Second World War spy drama, Brando plays a German pacifist recruited by British agent Howard to destroy a German supply vessel, skippered by Yul Brynner. While Brynner is far from being a card-carrying Nazi, Brando impersonates an SS officer, setting up a complex relationship based on moral deception. Taking place almost entirely aboard the ship, this is a claustrophobic, often very tense movie that deserves to be better known. AT

Marlon Brando *Robert Crain* • Yul Brynner *Captain Mueller* • Janet Margolin *Esther* • Trevor Howard *Colonel Statter* • Martin Benrath *Kruse* • Hans Christian Blech *Donkeyman* • Wally Cox *Dr Ambach* ■ *Dir* Bernhard Wicki • *Scr* Daniel Taradash, from a novel by Werner Jorg Luddecke

Sabrina ★★★★★ U

Romantic comedy 1954 · US · BW · 108mins

Ignore the critics who say this is one of Billy Wilder's minor works. It is a major movie, a masterpiece of romantic comedy. This a Cinderella story about a chauffeur's daughter (Audrey Hepburn) and two brothers, Humphrey Bogart as the workaholic zillionaire and William Holden as the playboy. Because Hepburn's infatuation with Holden is unwittingly wrecking a business deal, Bogart decides to divert her – with predictable results. For a film that is so funny, so sophisticated and so technically polished, it comes as a surprise to learn that the production was a difficult one. The performances are impeccable, with Hepburn radiant, Holden showing real star quality and Bogart perfectly cast against his tough-guy image so that his entry into a new age of innocence is all the more funny and all the more moving. AT [video] DVD

Humphrey Bogart *Linus Larrabee* • Audrey Hepburn *Sabrina Fairchild* • William Holden (2) *David Larrabee* • Walter Hampden *Oliver Larrabee* • John Williams *Thomas Fairchild* • Martha Hyer *Elizabeth Tyson* • Joan Vohs *Gretchen Van Horn* • Marcel Dalio *Baron* • Marcel Hillaire *The professor* • Nella Walker *Maude Larrabee* ■ *Dir* Billy Wilder • *Scr* Billy Wilder, Samuel Taylor, Ernest Lehman, from the play by Samuel Taylor • *Costume Designer* Edith Head

Sabrina ★★★ PG

Romantic comedy
1995 · US · Colour · 121mins

Sydney Pollack must have known before he embarked on this remake of Billy Wilder's 1954 comedy classic, that the ghosts of Humphrey Bogart, Audrey Hepburn and William Holden would be hovering over his production. Yet, with canny casting and some subtle updating, he succeeded in coming up with a charming variation on this Cinderella story, in which the chauffeur's daughter romances the billionaire boss. Julia Ormond and Harrison Ford take a while to settle into their roles, unlike Greg Kinnear, who gives a vibrant debut performance as Ford's brattish brother. Pollack achieves a sparkle to match the picture's polish. DP [video] DVD

Harrison Ford *Linus Larrabee* • Julia Ormond *Sabrina Fairchild* • Greg Kinnear *David Larrabee* • Nancy Marchand *Maude Larrabee* • John Wood *Fairchild* • Richard Crenna *Patrick Tyson* • Angie Dickinson *Ingrid Tyson* • Lauren Holly *Elizabeth Tyson* ■ *Dir* Sydney Pollack • *Scr* Barbara Benedek, David Rayfiel, from the 1954 film, from the play by Samuel Taylor

Sacco and Vanzetti ★★★★

Historical drama
1971 · It/Fr · Colour · 123mins

Based on the real lives and true deaths of two American political martyrs, this drama pulls out all the stops of sympathy to support the two Italian immigrants – and acknowledged anarchists – who were caught between a Communist witch hunt and legal negligence in the 1920s; they were wrongfully arrested and then executed. Directed by Giuliano Montaldo, and featuring Gian Maria Volonté and Riccardo Cucciolla, it won the best film at Cannes in 1971. TH

Gian Maria Volonté *Bartolomeo Vanzetti* • Riccardo Cucciolla *Nicola Sacco* • Cyril Cusack *Frederick Katzmann* • Rosanna Fratello *Rosa Sacco* • Geoffrey Keen *Judge Webster Thayer* ■ *Dir* Giuliano Montaldo • *Scr* Fabrizio Onofri, Giuliano Montaldo, Ottavio Jemma

Sacred Flesh ★ 18

Erotic drama 2000 · UK · Colour · 72mins

Three years after he finally lost his long struggle to reverse the BBFC's decision to withhold video certification from his film, *Visions of Ecstasy*, on the grounds of blasphemy, Nigel Wingrove returns with another assault on the taboos surrounding the depiction of Christianity on screen. Many will proclaim this as a courageous affirmation of free speech, but it's nothing more than porn in wimples, posing as a treatise on the mental, physical and spiritual dangers of chastity. DP [video] DVD

Sally Tremaine *Sister Elizabeth, the Mother Superior* • Moyna Cope *The Abbess* • Simon Hill *Father Henry, The Abbott* • Kristina Bill *Mary Magdalene* • Rachel Taggart *Catechism* • Eileen Daly *Repression* • Daisy Weston *Sister Brigitte* ■ *Dir/Scr* Nigel Wingrove

Sacred Ground ★★

Drama 1983 · US · Colour · 100mins

Charles B Pierce is a genuine maverick director and invariably makes independently financed films with unusual casts or themes. This native American drama concerns a frontiersman with an Apache wife and mixed-race baby, homesteading on sacred Paiute burial grounds, and it generates more issues than it can comfortably cope with. Tim McIntyre is good as the troubled mountain man, and Jack Elam offers strong support, but the film's good intentions are let down by weaker performances from the female cast members. TS

Tim McIntire *Matt* • Jack Elam *Witcher* • LQ Jones *Tolbert* • Ty Randolph *Wannetta* • Eloy Casados *Prairie Fox* • Serene Hedin *Little Doe* • Vernon Foster *Wounded Leg* ■ *Dir/Scr* Charles B Pierce

The Sacrifice ★★★★ PG

Drama
1986 · Fr/Swe · Colour and BW · 142mins

With its location (Faro), themes (alienation, faith and death), cinematographer (Sven Nykvist) and star (Erland Josephson) all primarily associated with Ingmar Bergman, his influence is all-pervasive throughout Andrei Tarkovsky's final film. But the Soviet visionary's tormented lyricism is also very much in evidence, both as he suggests the horror of nuclear war through retired intellectual Josephson's desperate, Faustian reaction to the terrible news broadcast, and as he presents the possibility of redemption, through the intercession of mystical mailman Allan Edwall. DP. In Swedish with English subtitles. [video] DVD

Erland Josephson *Alexander* • Susan Fleetwood *Adelaide* • Allan Edwall *Otto* • Sven Wollter *Victor* ■ *Dir/Scr* Andrei Tarkovsky,

Sacrificed Youth ★★★★ PG

Drama 1985 · Chi · Colour · 95mins

Having waited 20 years from film school graduation to directing her first feature, Zhang Nuanxin emerged as a key member of the Fourth Generation directors. Although Chinese cinema was changing rapidly, this partly autobiographical tale of a city girl's rural re-education owes much to the post-revolutionary humanist tradition, as Li Fengxu learns more about life from the people around her, than from political dictates. Sent to a collective farm in Yunnan during the Cultural Revolution, Li's medical student also matures as a woman, giving the film a subtle eroticism. DP. In Mandarin with English subtitles.

Li Fengxu • Yu Da • Fen Yuanzheng ■ *Dir* Zhang Nuanxin • *Scr* Zhang Nuanxin, from the novel *You Yige Meilide Difang (There Was a Beautiful Place)* by Zhang Manling

The Sad Horse ★★★ U

Adventure drama 1959 · US · Colour · 77mins

A late entry in the seemingly unending series of 20th Century-Fox family films about a boy/girl and his/her horse/dog which included *Kentucky* and *My Friend Flicka*, this story (filmed on location) benefits from sympathetic direction of former Fox film editor James B Clark. Alan Ladd's son David plays the leading role here, and firm support comes from the ever-reliable Chill Wills, sturdy Rex Reason and Patrice Wymore. TS

David Ladd *Jackie Connors* • Chill Wills *Captain Connors* • Rex Reason *Bill MacDonald* • Patrice Wymore *Leslie MacDonald* • Gregg Palmer *Bart Connors* • Leslie Bradley *Jonas* ■ *Dir* James B Clark • *Scr* Charles Hoffman, from a story by Zoe Akins

The Sad Sack ★★★ U

Comedy 1957 · US · BW · 98mins

After making 17 films with Dean Martin, Jerry Lewis took his unique brand of comedy shtick with him and went solo in 1957. In this effort, surrounded by a notable supporting cast that includes Peter Lorre, Jerry inflicts his screwy antics on the armed forces. He plays an unwilling army recruit with a photographic memory who, in addition to the predictable disasters that befall a misfit, gets himself caught up with spies and an Arab conspiracy. Only fitfully funny, but under veteran George Marshall's direction, there's enough here to keep Lewis addicts happy. RK

Jerry Lewis *Bixby* • David Wayne *Dolan* • Phyllis Kirk *Major Shelton* • Peter Lorre *Abdul* • Joe Mantell *Private Stan Wenaslawsky* • Gene Evans *Sergeant Pulley* • George Dolenz *Ali Mustapha* ■ *Dir* George Marshall • *Scr* Edmund Beloin, Nate Monaster

The Saddest Music in the World ★★★ 15

Fantasy musical drama
2003 · Can · BW and Colour · 96mins

Cult director Guy Maddin's love affair with German Expressionist styling continues in this beguiling musical drama set in snowbound Winnipeg during the Great Depression. Beautifully shot in black and white with occasional flashes of colour, the dream-like film blends fantasy and reality into an atmospheric whole. In a wonderfully eccentric turn, a sternly enigmatic Isabella Rossellini plays a double amputee and brewery owner who launches a contest to find the world's most melancholy melody. What follows is a surreal carnival of love, betrayal and revenge. SF. Contains violence and sex scenes. DVD

Isabella Rossellini *Lady Helen Port-Huntly* • Mark McKinney *Chester Kent* • Maria de Medeiros *Narcissa* • David Fox *Fyodor Kent* • Ross McMillan *Roderick Kent/Gavrillo the Great* • Louis Negin *Blind seer* • Darcy Fehr *Teddy* ■ *Dir* Guy Maddin • *Scr* Guy Maddin, George Toles, from the screenplay (unproduced) by Kazuo Ishiguro

Saddle the Wind ★★★

Western 1958 · US · Colour · 84mins

Robert Taylor (Hollywood professional) and John Cassavetes (New York king of improvisation) star as a rancher and no-good brother, heading for their last showdown. The clash of acting styles makes for some decently intriguing drama, directed with flair by Robert Parrish, but this is a film with added rarity value because it's the only western to have been written by *The Twilight Zone*'s Rod Serling, early television's greatest fantasist. TH

Robert Taylor (1) *Steve Sinclair* • Julie London *Joan Blake* • John Cassavetes *Tony Sinclair* • Donald Crisp *Mr Deneen* • Charles McGraw *Larry Venables* • Royal Dano *Clay Ellison* ■ *Dir* Robert Parrish • *Scr* Rod Serling, from a story by Thomas Thompson

Saddle Tramp ★★★ U

Western 1950 · US · Colour · 76mins

This engaging western stars the laconic Joel McCrea as a cowboy who takes care of four orphaned children, trying to keep them a secret from his child-hating boss. Made as a family film, but director Hugo Fregonese keeps the sentimentality in check. The Technicolor location photography by Charles Boyle is particularly attractive, and Wanda Hendrix (Mrs Audie Murphy at the time) makes a perky heroine. Very appealing. TS

Joel McCrea *Chuck Conner* • Wanda Hendrix *Della* • John Russell *Rocky* • John McIntire *Jess Higgins* • Jeanette Nolan *Ma Higgins* • Russell Simpson *Pop* • Ed Begley *Mr Hartnagle* ■ *Dir* Hugo Fregonese • *Scr* Harold Shumate

Sadgati ★★★

Drama 1981 · Ind · Colour · 50mins

A short rural drama from India's most respected director, Satyajit Ray, that tells the simple, but cruel story of a high-caste bully who forces a low-caste labourer to work to his death. It is one of Ray's most politically militant films, not only attacking the prejudices of the caste system, but also protesting about the socio-economic hardships faced by the sub-continent's poorest people. Om Puri gives a performance of great strength and dignity as the repressed bonded labourer, and the final scene is heart-rending. DP. In Hindi with English subtitles.

Om Puri *Dukhi* • Smita Patil *Dukhi's wife* • Mohan Agashe *Brahmin* ■ *Dir/Scr* Satyajit Ray

Sadhna ★★★ U

Drama 1958 · Ind · BW · 136mins

Sunil Dutt made his name playing clean-cut heroes in the late 1950s and here, he is perfectly cast as a college lecturer who pretends that he is going to be married to please his ailing mother, Leia Chitnis. His ruse backfires when he discovers that his "intended" is really a prostitute, but when his proud family throws her into the street in disgust he finds his vehement opposition to marriage beginning to crumble. Although typical of director BR Chopra's influential blend of social comment and stylish entertainment, this *masala* melodrama is not regarded as one of his more significant pictures. DP. In Hindi with English subtitles. [video]

Vyjayanthimala • Sunil Dutt • Radia Krishna • Nandini ■ *Dir* BR Chopra • *Scr* Mukhram Sharma, from a story by Mukhram Sharma

Sadie McKee ★★

Melodrama 1934 · US · BW · 90mins

A typical rags-to-riches melodrama, with maid Joan Crawford embarking on another romantic roller-coaster ride as she tries to climb the social ladder. Crawford virtually carries this entertaining Cinderella saga single-handedly through star charisma alone – only Edward Arnold's performance as her drunken husband survives Crawford's bid to obliterate her co-stars from the spotlight. AJ

Joan Crawford *Sadie McKee* • Gene Raymond *Tommy Wallace* • Franchot Tone *Michael Alderson* • Esther Ralston *Dolly* • Edward Arnold *Jack Brennon* ■ *Dir* Clarence Brown • *Scr* John Meehan, from the story *Pretty Sadie McKee* by Vina Delmar

Sadie Thompson ★★★

Silent drama 1928 · US · BW · 90mins

This silent version of W Somerset Maugham's *Rain*, about a prostitute marooned on a South Seas island where she is almost destroyed by a reforming religious zealot, whose attraction to her undoes him in the end, is the first and most interesting of three attempts to film it (see 1932's *Rain* and 1953's *Miss Sadie Thompson*). Directed by Raoul Walsh, it stars Gloria Swanson (who produced it) and Lionel Barrymore, and it's worth sitting through the now tedious, somewhat heavy-handed first half-hour for the powerful melodrama that follows. Claustrophobic and atmospheric, with Barrymore frightening and Swanson mesmerising in her beauty and commitment. RK

Gloria Swanson *Sadie Thompson* • Lionel Barrymore *Alfred Atkinson* • Raoul Walsh *Sgt Tim O'Hara* • Blanche Frederici *Mrs Atkinson* • Charles Lane (1) *Dr McPhail* • Florence Midgely *Mrs McPhail* • Will Stanton *Quartermaster Bates* ■ *Dir* Raoul Walsh • *Scr* Raoul Walsh, C Gardner Sullivan (titles), from the play *Rain; a Play in Three Acts* by John Colton, Clemence Randolph, from the short story *Rain* by W Somerset Maugham

The Sadist ★★★★ 15

Cult thriller 1963 · US · BW · 92mins

Baby-faced Arch Hall Jr starred in several exploitation pictures in the early 1960s, and this powerful drama is by far the best of them. Hall gives a literally lip-smacking but dynamic performance as a juvenile delinquent who terrorises three teachers whose car has broken down. Although cheaply made with a small cast in one location, the film has a high class gloss (courtesy of the great cameraman Vilmos Zsigmond) and several of its scenes still pack a shocking punch. The anti-authoritarian theme was unacceptable to British censors until 1999, when the video was finally passed uncut. DM [video]

Arch Hall Jr *Charley Tibbs* • Helen Hovey *Doris Page* • Richard Alden *Ed Stiles* • Marilyn Manning *Judy Bradshaw* • Don Russell *Carl Oliver* ■ *Dir/Scr* James Landis

Safari ★★★

Action adventure 1956 · US · Colour · 90mins

A marvellously batty African adventure romp from Warwick Films, photographed, to its credit, on genuine locations and in CinemaScope. There's a real sense of the terror of the Mau Maus – *Simba* and *Something of Value* were the only other mainstream features to deal with this subject. Victor Mature plays the hero and Janet Leigh is at her most beguiling, whether terrorised by snakes or taking a bath in the jungle. *Dr No* director Terence Young was very good at this sort of thing, and it shows. TS

Victor Mature *Ken Duffield* • Janet Leigh *Linda Latham* • John Justin *Brian Sinden* • Roland Culver *Sir Vincent Brampton* • Orlando Martins *Jerusalem* ■ *Dir* Terence Young • *Scr* Anthony Veiller, from a story by Robert Buckner

[Safe] ★★★★ 15

Drama 1995 · US · Colour · 118mins

This claustrophobic study of a dysfunctional Californian housewife who becomes allergic to the chemical by-products of the 20th century casts an eerie spell with its hypnotic camerawork and unusual soundtrack. From cult director Todd Haynes, it's a modern-day psychological horror story, that's made even more harrowing by the intense and impressive performance by Julianne Moore as a woman personally and medically devastated by her surroundings. AJ. Contains swearing, nudity. [video] DVD

Julianne Moore *Carol White* • Xander Berkeley *Greg White* • Peter Friedman *Peter Dunning* • Kate McGregor-Stewart *Claire* • Mary Carver *Nell* • Susan Norman *Linda* • Steven Gilborn *Dr Hubbard* • Ronnie Farer *Barbara* • James LeGros *Chris* ■ *Dir/Scr* Todd Haynes

Safe at Home ★★ U

Sports comedy drama
1962 · US · BW · 84mins

The subject of baseball has always been considered anathema to British audiences, so it is not surprising that this movie was barely shown in the UK. The sentimental tale of a "Little League" youngster who brags that he and his dad are close friends of New York Yankees heroes Mickey Mantle and Roger Maris, then has to make good his boast, makes no claims to

S

subtlety. William Frawley adds a touch of grit as a grouchy coach. TV

Mickey Mantle • Roger Maris • William Frawley *Bill Turner* • Patricia Barry *Johanna Price* • Don Collier *Ken Lawton* • Bryan Russell *Hutch Lawton* • Eugene Iglesias *Mr Torres* • Flip Mark *Henry* ■ *Dir* Walter Doniger • *Scr* Robert Dillon, from a story by Tom Naud, Steve Ritch

Safe Men ★★ 15

Crime comedy 1998 · US · Colour · 84mins

Yet another comedy based around the cobweb-covered "incompetent guys mistaken for experienced criminals" premise. This one is given a lift by two very watchable leads in Steve Zahn and Sam Rockwell and an enjoyably caricatured supporting cast which includes Michael Lerner and Harvey Fierstein as OTT Jewish gangsters. It's a shame then that the material is so run-of-the-mill as this pair of dumb, fifth-rate musicians find themselves forced into cracking a safe. The plot is paper thin, as is the humour. JC. Contains swearing.

Sam Rockwell *Samuel* • Steve Zahn *Eddie* • Mark Ruffalo *Frank* • Josh Pais *Mitchell* • Paul Giamatti *Veal Chop* • Michael Schmidt *Bernie Jr* • Christina Kirk *Hannah* • Raymond Serra *Barber* • Harvey Fierstein *Good Stuff Leo* • Michael Lerner *Big Fat Bernie Gayle* ■ *Dir/Scr* John Hamburg

Safe Passage ★★ 15

Drama 1994 · US · Colour · 93mins

Susan Sarandon gives yet another stunning performance, here playing a frustrated mother of seven boys who struggles to cope with her husband Sam Shepard's bouts of seemingly psychosomatic blindness. Sadly, Sarandon's portrayal is the only thing worth noting in director Robert Allan Ackerman's bland drama. The formula is stale and predictable. LH

Susan Sarandon *Mag Singer* • Sam Shepard *Patrick Singer* • Robert Sean Leonard *Alfred Singer* • Nick Stahl *Simon Singer* • Jason London *Gideon Singer* • Marcia Gay Harden *Cynthia* • Matt Keeslar *Percival Singer* • Sean Astin *Izzy Singer* ■ *Dir* Robert Allan Ackerman • *Scr* Deena Goldstone, from the novel by Ellyn Bache

A Safe Place ★★ PG

Experimental fantasy drama
1971 · US · Colour · 94mins

This fantasy is wildly incoherent or poetically experimental, depending on your tastes. Tuesday Weld plays a vulnerable woman who escapes the pressures of New York life into a dream world, courtesy of a magician (Orson Welles). There's a low-budget feel to this, director Henry Jaglom's first release, and indeed it was filmed at his parent's flat, with the cast largely made up of his pals. However, it gives the impression of having been a labour of love. Jack Nicholson is good value as Weld's old lover. JG

Tuesday Weld *Susan/Noah* • Orson Welles *Magician* • Jack Nicholson *Mitch* • Phil Proctor [Philip Proctor] *Fred* • Gwen Welles *Bari* • Dov Lawrence *Dov* • Fanny Birkenmaier *Maid* ■ *Dir/Scr* Henry Jaglom

The Safecracker ★★ U

Second World War thriller
1958 · UK · BW · 96mins

Ray Milland directs himself in this lightly entertaining Second World War drama, playing the criminal whose digital dexterity comes in useful to the Allies as he's persuaded to join a Commando unit and prise open a Nazi safe in a Belgian castle. At times, it's rather too apt to recall better movies, but it does, in its own modest way, foreshadow *The Dirty Dozen*. AE

Ray Milland *Colley Dawson* • Barry Jones *Bennett Carfield* • Jeannette Sterke *Irene* • Ernest Clark *Major Adbury* • Melissa Stribling *Angela* • Victor Maddern *Morris* • Cyril Raymond *Inspector Frankham* • Barbara Everest *Mrs Dawson* ■ *Dir* Ray Milland • *Scr* Paul Monash, from the book *The Willie Gordon Story* by Rhys Davies, Bruce Thomas

Safety Last ★★★★★ U

Classic silent comedy
1923 · US · BW · 73mins

The film that best illustrates the thrill-comedy of Harold Lloyd with his climactic clock-hanging bravado. Lloyd is the country boy who suggests a high-rise climber as a publicity stunt for the big city store that employs him, and then finds he has to substitute for the original daredevil. No wonder Mildred Davis loves him. As a feature-length expansion of his remarkable acrobatic skills displayed in earlier shorts, it's a movie chock full of incidents to make audiences laugh – and gasp. TH

Harold Lloyd *Boy* • Mildred Davis *Girl* • Bill Strother *Pal* • Noah Young *Law* • Westcott B Clarke *Floorwalker* ■ *Dir* Fred C Newmeyer, Sam Taylor • *Scr* Hal Roach, Tim Whelan, Sam Taylor

The Safety of Objects ★★ 15

Drama 2001 · US/UK · Colour · 115mins

Like Robert Altman's *Short Cuts*, writer/director Rose Troche's film is based on disparate short stories that have been cleverly woven into a cohesive whole. There, sadly, the similarities end. As four neighbouring families go about the everyday business of their misery and pain, a tragedy from the past awaits its big flashback. Despite a fair cast, the film never takes flight, remaining a string of well-trodden vignettes. AC DVD

Glenn Close *Esther Gold* • Dermot Mulroney *Jim Train* • Patricia Clarkson *Annette Jennings* • Joshua Jackson *Paul Gold* • Moira Kelly *Susan Train* • Robert Klein *Howard Gold* • Timothy Olyphant *Randy* • Mary Kay Place *Helen Christianson* • Kristen Stewart *Sam Jennings* ■ *Dir* Rose Troche • *Scr* Rose Troche, from stories by AM Homes

The Saga of Anatahan ★★★★

Drama based on a true story
1953 · Jpn · BW · 91mins

In Josef von Sternberg's curious final film, the director shows what can be done with a simple studio set and lighting. Narrated by Sternberg himself, it tells the true story of a group of Japanese merchant seamen shipwrecked on the island of Anahatan in 1944 who believed, seven years after the war had ended, that Japan was still fighting. Von Sternberg, who was the cinematographer as well, shot the film on a sound stage in a Japanese studio, using synthetic sets made of cellophane and papier maché, sprayed with aluminium paint, making it look as artificial as possible. The acting of the cast, consisting of members of the Kabuki theatre, add to the stylisation of the whole picture. RB. A Japanese/English language film.

Akemi Negishi *Keiko, the "Queen Bee"* • Tadashi Suganuma *Kusakabe, the "King"* • Josef von Sternberg *Narrator* ■ *Dir* Josef von Sternberg • *Scr* Josef von Sternberg, from the story *Anatahan* by Michiro Maruyama and an article in *Life* magazine

The Saga of Hemp Brown ★★★ U

Western 1958 · US · Colour · 77mins

In this under-rated Universal western, Rory Calhoun stars as a disgraced cavalry officer seeking to clear his name with the help of medicine man Fortunio Bonanova. Behind the camera is actor-turned-director Richard Carlson, best known for battling with 3-D monsters in movies such as *Creature from the Black Lagoon*. Calhoun's co-star is cult favourite Beverly Garland, and if this is nothing special, it is competently done. TS

Rory Calhoun *Hemp Brown* • Beverly Garland *Mona Langley* • John Larch *Jed Givens* • Russell Johnson *Hook* • Fortunio Bonanova *Serge Bolanos, medicine man* • Allan "Rocky" Lane [Allan Lane] *Sheriff* • Morris Ankrum *Bo Slauter* ■ *Dir* Richard Carlson • *Scr* Bob Williams, from a story by Bernard Girard

Sagebrush Trail ★★ U

Western 1934 · US · BW · 53mins

This is John Wayne's second Monogram Studios western, and is really only of interest to B-western fans: the plot's average, the direction plods and the cast is unremarkable. What really brings it to life are the stunts, planned and carried out by the incredible Yakima Canutt. Watch out for Canutt doubling for Wayne and hiding underwater. TS DVD

John Wayne *John Brant* • Nancy Shubert *Sally Blake* • Lane Chandler *Bob Jones* • Yakima Canutt *Ed Walsh* ■ *Dir* Armand Schaefer • *Scr* Lindsley Parsons

Sahara ★★★ PG

Second World War action adventure
1943 · US · BW · 93mins

Humphrey Bogart spent most of the war years playing loners in civilian clothes, who stuck their necks out for no one until Lauren Bacall or Ingrid Bergman forced him to take sides. It is something of a surprise, then, to find him here as a resourceful army sergeant, leading a bunch of no-hopers across the desert in a dilapidated tank, dodging Nazis as they search for water. Directed by Zoltan Korda, co-written by John Howard Lawson (later blacklisted in the communist witch-hunt), shot by Rudolph Maté and scored by Miklos Rozsa, there's solid talent behind the camera and a lot of derring-do in front of it. AT DVD

Humphrey Bogart *Sergeant Joe Gunn* • Bruce Bennett *Waco Hoyt* • Lloyd Bridges *Fred Clarkson* • Rex Ingram (2) *Sergeant Tambul* • J Carrol Naish *Giuseppe* • Dan Duryea *Jimmy Doyle* • Richard Nugent *Captain Jason Halliday* ■ *Dir* Zoltan Korda • *Scr* John Howard Lawson, Zoltan Korda, James O'Hanlon, from a story by Philip MacDonald

Sahara ★ PG

Adventure 1983 · US · Colour · 106mins

After her father dies, flapper Brooke Shields disguises herself as a man and takes his place in the 1920s trans-Sahara automobile race, somehow ending up as the wife of dashing desert sheik Lambert Wilson. A pathetic bodice-ripper that tries to emulate the atmosphere and heated eroticism of Rudolph Valentino silent epics, but ends up as a badly plotted and shoddily produced *Mills and Boon*, setting a new low standard for period romances. AJ

Brooke Shields *Dale Gordon* • Lambert Wilson *Jaffar* • John Rhys-Davies *Rasoul* • Horst Buchholz *Von Glessing* • Perry Lang *Andy* • Cliff Potts *String* • John Mills *Cambridge* ■ *Dir* Andrew V McLaglen • *Scr* James R Silke, from a story by Menahem Golan

Sahara ★★★ 12A

Action adventure comedy
2004 · US/Sp · Colour · 123mins

Matthew McConaughey stars as author Clive Cussler's creation Dirk Pitt, an adventurer and salvage expert who stumbles upon evidence that a long-lost American Civil War battleship may have ended up in the desert in West Africa. Along for the ride are sidekick Steve Zahn and Penélope Cruz as a World Health Organisation doctor. The plot is convoluted and at times incomprehensible, but the action sequences are impressive, the locations and villains suitably exotic, and the whole thing remains good fun. BP. Contains violence.

Matthew McConaughey *Dirk Pitt* • Steve Zahn *Al Giordino* • Penélope Cruz *Dr Eva Rojas* • Lambert Wilson *Massarde* • Glynn Turman *Dr Hopper* • Delroy Lindo *Carl* • William H Macy *Admiral Sandecker* • Rainn Wilson *Rudi Gunn* • Patrick Malahide *Ambassador Polidori* ■ *Dir* Breck Eisner • *Scr* Thomas Dean Donnelly, Joshua Oppenheimer, John C Richards, James V Hart from the novel by Clive Cussler

Saigon ★★

Drama 1948 · US · BW · 94mins

Ex-army pilot Alan Ladd washes up in Saigon with one healthy buddy and another, terminally ill, but not knowing he's got a month left to live. The three guys go out on the town – but without that song – and rope Veronica Lake into joining them on a caper that goes more than slightly wrong. This sort of malarkey lives or dies on the charm of its stars and Ladd and Lake were never in the Bogart–Bacall league. Saigon appears on the back projection screen while the foreground is pure studio backlot. AT

Alan Ladd *Maj Larry Briggs* • Veronica Lake *Susan Cleaver* • Douglas Dick *Capt Mike Perry* • Wally Cassell *Sgt Pete Rocco* • Luther Adler *Lt Keon* ■ *Dir* Leslie Fenton • *Scr* PJ Wolfson, Arthur Sheekman, from a story by Julian Zimet

Saigon ★★★ 18

Action thriller 1988 · US · Colour · 97mins

Despite its pretensions, this is no more than a variant of *Lethal Weapon*'s "white cop, black cop" formula transposed to *Apocalypse Now* territory. Willem Dafoe and Gregory Hines are gripping as army cops tracking down a serial killer – who may or may not be military top brass – among the sleazy back alleys of Saigon circa 1968. It's undeniably well crafted, with much macho posturing, and debut director Christopher Crowe offers plenty of twists and turns amid the well-staged action scenes. RS

Willem Dafoe *Buck McGriff* • Gregory Hines *Albaby Perkins* • Fred Ward *Dix* • Amanda Pays *Nicole* • Scott Glenn *Colonel Armstrong* • Lim Kay Tong *Lime Green* • Keith David *Maurice* ■ *Dir* Christopher Crowe • *Scr* Christopher Crowe, Jack Thibeau

Sail a Crooked Ship ★★ U

Comedy 1961 · US · BW · 87mins

This wacky heist comedy has ex-Navy man Robert Wagner re-fitting a ship for leisure purposes, but tricked into sailing it to Boston with a dubious skipper (Ernie Kovacs) and a crew of criminals intent on robbing a bank. Perpetually caught somewhere in the charm and macho league between Cary Grant and Paul Newman (with a dash of Rock Hudson), Wagner sails through effortlessly, trading sexy banter with Carolyn Jones and coping well with the almost slapstick antics of the stormy sea crossing. AT

Robert Wagner *Gilbert Barrows* • Dolores Hart *Elinor Harrison* • Carolyn Jones *Virginia* • Ernie Kovacs *Bugsy F Foglemeyer* • Frankie Avalon *Rodney* • Frank Gorshin *George Wilson* ■ *Dir* Irving Brecher • *Scr* Ruth Brooks Flippen, Bruce Geller, from a novel by Nathaniel Benchley

Sailing Along ★ U

Romantic musical 1938 · UK · BW · 90mins

One of the many substandard – not to say dire – films in which the adored British musical comedy star Jessie Matthews found herself during the 1930s. Directed (and co-written) by her then husband, actor Sonnie Hale, it finds Matthews as a female bargee with aspirations to become a stage star, while her co-worker Barry Mackay dreams of being a financier. RK

S

Jessie Matthews *Kay Martin* • Barry Mackay *Steve Barnes* • Jack Whiting *Dicky Randall* • Roland Young *Anthony Gulliver* • Noel Madison *Windy* • Frank Pettingell *Skipper Barnes* • Alastair Sim *Sylvester* ■ *Dir* Sonnie Hale • *Scr* Lesser Samuels, Sonnie Hale, from a story by Selwyn Jepson

Sailor Beware ★★ U

Comedy 1951 · US · BW · 103mins

The fifth film pairing of Dean Martin and Jerry Lewis is easily one of their worst. You are either a fan or you can't bear to be in the same room as the duo who took American showbiz by storm in the late 1940s. Putting the comic style to one side, what really makes this hard to take are the smug references to their fame, as the boys do a stint in the navy. Minor consolations are an uncredited guest appearance by Betty Hutton and a blink-and-miss bit for James Dean. DP

Jerry Lewis *Melvin Jones* • Dean Martin *Al Crowthers* • Corinne Calvet *Guest Star* • Marion Marshall *Hilda Jones* • Robert Strauss *Lardoski* • Vincent Edwards [Vince Edwards] *Blayden* • Leif Erickson *Commander Lane* • James Dean *Sailor* • Dan Willis *Sailor* • Betty Hutton ■ *Dir* Hal Walker • *Scr* James Allardice, Martin Rackin, from a play by Kenyon Nicholson

Sailor Beware! ★★ U

Comedy 1956 · UK · BW · 80mins

This politically incorrect comedy established Peggy Mount in the booming shrew persona that was to make her such a hit in TV series such as *George and the Dragon*. Here she terrorises hubby Cyril Smith and prospective son-in-law Ronald Lewis on the eve of daughter Shirley Eaton's wedding. However, while Mount dominates the proceedings, the peerless Esma Cannon steals every scene. DP

Peggy Mount *Emma Hornett* • Cyril Smith *Henry Hornett* • Shirley Eaton *Shirley Hornett* • Ronald Lewis *Albert Tufnell* • Esma Cannon *Edie Hornett* • Joy Webster *Daphne* • Gordon Jackson *Carnoustie Bligh* • Thora Hird *Mrs Lack* • Geoffrey Keen *Reverend Purefoy* • Jack MacGowran *Toddy* • Michael Caine ■ *Dir* Gordon Parry • *Scr* Philip King, Falkland L Cary

The Sailor from Gibraltar ★

Romantic drama 1967 · UK · BW · 90mins

One of the two grandiose flops Tony Richardson made with Jeanne Moreau (the other being 1966's *Mademoiselle*), of whom he was much enamoured at the time. Based on a Marguerite Duras novel, adapted by Christopher Isherwood, it's an insufferably arty exercise in alienation with Ian Bannen as the bored office clerk who has an affair with the La Moreau, who sails around exotic Arabian ports, consorting and philosophising with the likes of Orson Welles. Movies come no more pretentious than this. AT

Jeanne Moreau *Anna* • Ian Bannen *Alan* • Vanessa Redgrave *Sheila* • Orson Welles *Louis of Mozambique* • Zia Mohyeddin *Noori* • Hugh Griffith *Llewellyn* • Umberto Orsini *Postcard vendor* ■ *Dir* Tony Richardson • *Scr* Christopher Isherwood, Don Magner, Tony Richardson, from the novel *Le Marin de Gibraltar* by Marguerite Duras

A Sailor-Made Man ★★★★ U

Silent comedy 1921 · US · BW · 36mins

Yet another Harold Lloyd movie, in which he's the bespectacled wimp who redeems himself by an unexpected show of guts and bravery. Here, he's a wealthy playboy who's told to get a job by the father of the girl (Mildred Davis) he loves – so he joins the Navy. Initially the enemy of tough crew mate Noah Young, they soon become best friends and team-up to save Davis from the lecherous intentions of a maharajah. An entertaining swimming pool dip and a marriage proposal via semaphore contribute towards a very enjoyable Lloyd outing. TH

Harold Lloyd *The Boy* • Mildred Davis *The Girl* • Noah Young *Rough-House O'Rafferty* • Dick Sutherland *Maharajah* ■ *Dir* Fred C Newmeyer • *Scr* Hal Roach, Sam Taylor, HM Walker (titles), Jean Havez

Sailor of the King ★★★ U

Second World War drama 1953 · UK · BW · 84mins

Originally released in the UK as *Single-Handed*, this is a rather good second screen version of author CS Forester's novel *Brown on Resolution* (the earlier one being the weakish 1935 film *Forever England* starring John Mills). Hollywood heart-throb Jeffrey Hunter is impressive as the courageous Brown, descended from a long line of seafarers, his unlikely parents being Michael Rennie and Wendy Hiller. TS

Jeffrey Hunter *Seaman Andrew Brown* • Michael Rennie *Captain Richard Saville* • Wendy Hiller *Lucinda Bentley* • Bernard Lee *Petty Officer Wheatley* • Peter Van Eyck *Kapitan von Falk* • Victor Maddern *Signalman Earnshaw* ■ *Dir* Roy Boulting • *Scr* Valentine Davies, from the novel *Brown on Resolution* by CS Forester

The Sailor Takes a Wife ★★

Comedy 1945 · US · BW · 90mins

June Allyson and Robert Walker star in this lightweight version of Chester Erskine's play. Director Richard Whorf makes the most of the limited laughs that follow the whirlwind courtship, leaving our newlyweds with nothing but illusions to be shattered. Discharged from the navy, Walker struggles to make an impact on anyone other than Audrey Totter, whose ditzy vamping enlivens the proceedings. DP

Robert Walker *John* • June Allyson *Mary* • Hume Cronyn *Freddie* • Audrey Totter *Lisa* • Eddie "Rochester" Anderson *Harry* • Reginald Owen *Mr Amboy* • Gerald Oliver Smith *Butler* ■ *Dir* Richard Whorf • *Scr* Chester Erskine, Anne Morrison Chapin, Whitfield Cook, from a play by Chester Erskine

The Sailor Who Fell from Grace with the Sea ★★★ 18

Drama 1976 · UK · Colour · 100mins

This is a weird, sometimes disturbing, sometimes downright laughable adaptation of a novel by the Japanese writer Yukio Mishima – who formed his own right-wing army, committed ritual suicide and became the subject of the brilliant Paul Schrader biopic, *Mishima*. This story is about a sensual widow whose teenage son is a member of a strange secret society. Experts felt that the core elements of Mishima's novel went AWOL in the transition from Japan to England, but there's no denying the strangeness of the story, the sexually charged atmosphere or the power of Sarah Miles's emotionally naked performance. AT [VIDEO]

Sarah Miles *Anne Osborne* • Kris Kristofferson *Jim Cameron* • Jonathan Kahn *Jonathan Osborne* • Margo Cunningham *Mrs Palmer* ■ *Dir* Lewis John Carlino • *Scr* Lewis John Carlino, from the novel by Yukio Mishima

The Sailor's Return ★★

Period drama 1978 · UK · Colour · 112mins

Tom Bell stars in this Victorian tragedy about an English sailor whose return from the sea in the company of a black bride (Shope Shodeinde) scandalises the local community. The period settings are pretty , but nothing much goes on and bigger issues are left unexplored. This was one of several disappointments from director Jack Gold. DM

Tom Bell *William Targett* • Shope Shodeinde *Tulip* • Mick Ford *Tom* • Paola Dionisotti *Lucy* • George Costigan *Harry* • Clive Swift *Reverend Pottock* • Ray Smith *Fred Leake* • Ivor Roberts *Molten* • Bernard Hill *Carter* ■ *Dir* Jack Gold • *Scr* James Saunders, from the novel by David Garnett

Sailors Three ★★ U

Comedy 1940 · UK · BW · 83mins

Who on earth thought that wisecracking Tommy Trinder, silly ass Claude Hulbert and smoothie Michael Wilding would make a winning comedy team? Frankly, even the Ritz Brothers were funnier. Yet, as with most flag-waving pictures made during the Second World War, the aim was to raise morale and not make masterpieces. In that light, this is an effective enough piece of nonsense from Ealing, with our trio of tars taking on the Nazi navy after a boozy shore leave in a South American port. A follow-up film, *Fiddlers Three*, appeared in 1944. DP [VIDEO]

Tommy Trinder *Tommy Taylor* • Claude Hulbert *Admiral* • Michael Wilding *Johnny* • Carla Lehmann *Jane* • Jeanne de Casalis *Mrs Pilkington* • James Hayter *Hans* • Henry Hewitt *Professor Pilkington* ■ *Dir* Walter Forde • *Scr* Angus MacPhail, John Dighton, Austin Melford

The Saint ★ 12

Action thriller 1997 · US · Colour · 111mins

This empty, lumbering spectacular turns author Leslie Charteris's gallant law-breaker into a cat-burgling James Bond clone. Both Val Kilmer, in the title role, and Elisabeth Shue are miscast in a mundane tale about a Russian billionaire who's trying to discover a way to glean energy from tap water. Director Phillip Noyce's misjudged fiasco is sloppily plotted, unexciting and laughable. AJ. Contains violence and swearing. [VIDEO] DVD

Val Kilmer *Simon Templar* • Elisabeth Shue *Dr Emma Russell* • Rade Serbedzija *Ivan Tretiak* • Valery Nikolaev *Ilya Tretiak* • Henry Goodman *Dr Lev Botvin* • Alun Armstrong *Chief Inspector Teal* ■ *Dir* Phillip Noyce • *Scr* Jonathan Hensleigh, Wesley Strick, from a story by Jonathan Hensleigh, from the character created by Leslie Charteris

St Elmo's Fire ★★★ 15

Drama 1985 · US · Colour · 103mins

A Brat Pack movie that most of the cast would probably like to forget, this is now a great example of the excesses of the 1980s. Ally Sheedy, Emilio Estevez, Rob Lowe, Andrew McCarthy and Judd Nelson – all of whose careers have never been the same again – are the college pals trying to make their way in the world while wrestling with problems such as drug abuse, a teenage marriage, unrequited love and hidden sexuality. This is glossy and glib like so much else from the decade it represents, but it's also a fascinating record of that generation. JB. Contains swearing and drug abuse. [VIDEO] DVD

Emilio Estevez *Kirby* • Rob Lowe *Billy* • Demi Moore *Jules* • Andrew McCarthy *Kevin* • Judd Nelson *Alec* • Ally Sheedy *Leslie* • Mare Winningham *Wendy* • Martin Balsam *Mr Beamish* • Andie MacDowell *Dale Biberman* ■ *Dir* Joel Schumacher • *Scr* Joel Schumacher, Carl Kurlander

The Saint in London ★★★ PG

Crime adventure 1939 · UK/US · BW · 72mins

Mention the name Simon Templar nowadays and many will think of Roger Moore, some Ian Ogilvy, and a few Val Kilmer. But the finest Saint of them all was undoubtedly George Sanders, who inherited the role from Louis Hayward in 1939. This tale has our hero pitted against a ruthless counterfeit gang with only dizzy deb Sally Gray in his corner. This was Sanders's second outing as the debonair detective and a rattlingly good yarn it is, too. DP [VIDEO]

George Sanders *Simon Templar "The Saint"* • Sally Gray *Penelope Parker* • David Burns *Dugan* • Gordon McLeod *Inspector Teal* • Henry Oscar *Bruno Lang* • Ralph Truman *Kussella* ■ *Dir* John Paddy Carstairs • *Scr* Lynn Root, Frank Fenton, from the novel *The Million Pound Day* by Leslie Charteris

The Saint in New York ★★ PG

Crime adventure 1938 · US · BW · 72mins

The first film in RKO's resolutely low-budget nine-film series has Louis Hayward perfectly cast as the haloed hero. This was rumoured to be one of the movies that Alfred Hitchcock was offered for his US directing debut. Subsequent Saints were George Sanders and Hugh Sinclair, but Hayward returned for the last film *The Saint's Girl Friday* made in 1954; the next time the Saint appeared on screen was in the guise of smoothie Roger Moore in the 1960s TV series. However, no other adaptation followed Charteris's source material as closely as this one. TS [VIDEO]

Louis Hayward *Simon Templar "The Saint"* • Sig Rumann [Sig Ruman] *Hutch Rellin* • Kay Sutton *Fay Edwards* • Jonathan Hale *Inspector Fernack* • Jack Carson *Red Jenks* • Paul Guilfoyle (1) *Hymie Fanro* ■ *Dir* Ben Holmes • *Scr* Charles Kaufman, Mortimer Offner, from the novel by Leslie Charteris

The Saint in Palm Springs ★★★

Crime adventure 1941 · US · BW · 65mins

George Sanders bade farewell to the role of Simon Templar after this, his fifth outing as Leslie Charteris's suave troubleshooter. There's a pronounced end-of-term feel to the story, in which Sanders crosses swords with a gang intent on preventing him from delivering some rare stamps to their rightful owner. It's not as dull as Sanders's weary expression would have you believe, with director Jack Hively (handling his third Templar adventure) keeping the action brisk, and there is a surprisingly high body count for what was supposed to be a pretty light-hearted series. DP

George Sanders *Simon Templar "The Saint"* • Wendy Barrie *Elna* • Paul Guilfoyle (1) *Pearly Gates* • Jonathan Hale *Fernack* • Linda Hayes *Margaret Forbes* ■ *Dir* Jack Hively • *Scr* Jerry Cady [Jerome Cady], from a story by Leslie Charteris

St Ives ★★ 15

Thriller 1976 · US · Colour · 90mins

This rather silly, if glossy, thriller stars an improbable Charles Bronson as a writer embroiled in a murder plot. Veteran director J Lee Thompson ensures that it all moves along at a reasonable pace and looks technically proficient. Jacqueline Bisset has nothing to do but look lovely, but keep a sharp eye out for Jeff Goldblum and Robert Englund in early roles. Little to get excited about. TS [VIDEO]

Charles Bronson *Raymond St Ives* • John Houseman *Abner Procane* • Jacqueline Bisset *Janet Whistler* • Maximilian Schell *Dr John Constable* • Harry Guardino *Detective Deal* • Elisha Cook [Elisha Cook Jr] *Eddie the bell boy* • Daniel J Travanti *Johnny Parisi* • Robert Englund *Hood* • Mark Thomas *Hood* • Jeff Goldblum *Hood* ■ *Dir* J Lee Thompson • *Scr* Barry Beckerman, from the novel *The Procane Chronicle* by Oliver Bleeck

Saint Jack ★★★

Drama 1979 · US · Colour · 115mins

One of director Peter Bogdanovich's least known movies, based on Paul Theroux's novel, this drama is an effective character study of American Ben Gazzara (in fine form), a well-educated Korean War hero who pimps and wheeler-deals throughout

S

Singapore in the early 1970s. Needing a big cash injection, he accepts an offer to secretly photograph a visiting senator (George Lazenby) with a male prostitute. But will his sense of moral decency actually allow him to carry out the scheme? An evocative and whimsical portrait of sleazy Singapore during the Vietnam era. AJ

Ben Gazzara *Jack Flowers* • Denholm Elliott *William Leigh* • James Villiers *Frogget* • Joss Ackland *Yardley* • Rodney Bewes *Smale* • Mark Kingston *Yates* • Peter Bogdanovich *Eddie Schuman* • George Lazenby *Senator* ■ *Dir* Peter Bogdanovich • *Scr* Howard Sackler, Paul Theroux, Peter Bogdanovich, from the novel by Paul Theroux

Saint Joan ★★★ U

Drama 1957 · US · BW · 110mins

This is one of Hollywood's celebrated disasters, panned by the critics at the time and seen by almost no one. Loosely based on George Bernard Shaw's play, the script is by none other than Graham Greene and, instead of hiring a major star, director Otto Preminger took a huge gamble with a then unknown young actress called Jean Seberg, who was the right age to play France's great heroine. "Poor Jean Seberg wasn't up to it," said Greene later. "Anyway, I got a few laughs that were not in Bernard Shaw; at least I can claim that." Flops are rarely as fascinating as this one. AT

Jean Seberg *Joan* • Richard Widmark *Charles the dauphin* • Richard Todd *Dunois* • Anton Walbrook *Cauchon, Bishop of Beauvais* • John Gielgud *Earl of Warwick* • Felix Aylmer *Inquisitor* • Harry Andrews *John de Stogumber* • Barry Jones *De Courcelles* • Finlay Currie *Archbishop of Rheims* • Bernard Miles *Master executioner* ■ *Dir* Otto Preminger • *Scr* Graham Greene, from the play by George Bernard Shaw

St Louis Blues ★★ U

Musical biography 1958 · US · BW · 95mins

Nat King Cole stars as the legendary and influential blues composer WC Handy in this disappointing biopic, which deals with Handy's pursuit of his calling in the face of his Bible-punching father's disapproval, and his relationships with the two women in his life (Eartha Kitt, Ruby Dee). The movie is a sadly wasted opportunity, unimaginatively directed and dramatically dull, with Cole woodenly unconvincing. There is compensation, however, in a cast that includes Pearl Bailey, Mahalia Jackson, Cab Calloway and, as herself, Ella Fitzgerald. RK

Nat King Cole *WC Handy* • Eartha Kitt *Gogo Germaine* • Pearl Bailey *Aunt Hagar* • Cab Calloway *Blade* • Ella Fitzgerald • Mahalia Jackson *Bessie May* • Ruby Dee *Elizabeth* ■ *Dir* Allen Reisner • *Scr* Robert Smith, Ted Sherdeman

St Martin's Lane ★★★

Melodrama 1938 · UK · BW · 86mins

This prestigious British melodrama was meticulously designed – to the extent that the extras who formed the theatre queues were cast in descending order of height. Yet, for all this preparation, the film was mauled by the critics and flopped at the box office. There's no denying it's a sentimental tale, but it presents a fascinating portrait of theatre land and, while Vivien Leigh overdoes it as the waif yearning for stardom, Charles Laughton is superb as the busker who supports her. DP

Charles Laughton *Charles Saggers* • Vivien Leigh *Libby* • Rex Harrison *Harley Prentiss* • Larry Adler *Constantine* • Tyrone Guthrie *Gentry* • Gus McNaughton *Arthur Smith* • Bart Cormack *Strang* ■ *Dir* Tim Whelan • *Scr* Clemence Dane, from her story

The Saint Meets the Tiger ★

Crime adventure 1943 · US/UK · BW · 78mins

After a two-year gap, RKO continued its wildly inconsistent Saint series with this feeble story of smuggled ingots and worthless gold-mine shares. Hugh Sinclair is simply dreadful as Simon Templar in this cheapskate mystery directed by Paul Stein. DP

Hugh Sinclair *Simon Templar "The Saint"* • Jean Gillie *Pat Holmes* • Gordon McLeod *Inspector Teal/Professor Kahn* • Clifford Evans *Tidmarsh* • Wylie Watson *Horace* ■ *Dir* Paul Stein [Paul L Stein] • *Scr* Leslie Arliss, Wolfgang Wilhelm, James Seymour, from the novel *Meet the Tiger* by Leslie Charteris

The Saint of Fort Washington ★★ 15

Drama 1993 · US · Colour · 99mins

A well-meaning, but self-conscious social drama, which tackles the rather unfashionable (well, for Hollywood at least) subject of homelessness. Matt Dillon is the mentally disabled young man who finds himself on the streets; salvation comes in the shape of Vietnam veteran Danny Glover. The two leads deliver moving performances, and the good support cast includes Ving Rhames and Nina Siemaszko. JF. Contains violence.

Danny Glover *Jerry* • Matt Dillon *Matthew* • Rick Aviles *Rosario* • Nina Siemaszko *Tamsen* • Ving Rhames *Little Leroy* • Joe Seneca *Spits* • Robert Beatty Jr *Ex-pharmacist* ■ *Dir* Tim Hunter • *Scr* Lyle Kessler

St Patrick: the Irish Legend ★★

Historical drama
2000 · US · Colour · 100mins

Kidnapped by pirates as a youth and sold into slavery in Ireland before making his escape after six years, the Welsh-born Patrick returned in around AD 432 to convert his Irish captors and was ultimately canonised as their patron saint. Directed by Robert Hughes with an unconvincing mix of high melodrama, spiritual intensity and SFX miracles, this worthy, but laborious, historical TV drama at least manages to capture the difficulties inherent in Patrick's mission. DP

Patrick Bergin *Patrick* • Malcolm McDowell *Bishop Quentin* • Alan Bates *Calpornius* • Susannah York *Concessa* • Luke Griffin *Young Patrick* ■ *Dir* Robert Hughes • *Scr* Robert Hughes, Martin Duffy

The Saint Strikes Back ★★★

Crime adventure 1939 · US · BW · 64mins

Super-suave George Sanders stepped into the shoes of Simon Templar for this sprightly mystery. Here, Sanders takes on the San Francisco underworld in order to prove the innocence of Wendy Barrie's cop father. Jonathan Hale also joins the series in the recurring role of Inspector Fernack, who starts every case by putting Templar at the top of the list of suspects. Briskly directed by John Farrow, the film boasts atmospheric sets by Van Nest Polglase, who designed the Astaire/Rogers musicals as well as *Citizen Kane*. DP

George Sanders *Simon Templar "The Saint"* • Wendy Barrie *Valerie Travers* • Jonathan Hale *Henry Fernack* • Jerome Cowan *Cullis* • Neil Hamilton *Allan Breck* • Barry Fitzgerald *Zipper Dyson* • Robert Elliott *Webster* ■ *Dir* John Farrow • *Scr* John Twist, from the novel *Angels of Doom* by Leslie Charteris

The Saint Takes Over ★★★

Crime adventure 1940 · US · BW · 69mins

RKO had to borrow George Sanders back from 20th Century-Fox for this entry in the ever-popular *Saint* series. Scripted by Frank Fenton and Lynn Root, it was the first not to be based on a Leslie Charteris story, but the tale of racetrack hoods who implicate Inspector Fernack (Jonathan Hale) in their race-rigging scam is packed with incident and taken at a fair gallop by director Jack Hively. Paul Guilfoyle makes his debut as Simon Templar's light-fingered assistant. DP

George Sanders *Simon Templar "The Saint"* • Wendy Barrie *Ruth* • Jonathan Hale *Inspector Henry Fernack* • Paul Guilfoyle (1) *Clarence "Pearly" Gates* • Morgan Conway *Sam Reese* • Robert Emmett Keane *Leo Sloan* • Cyrus W Kendall [Cy Kendall] *Max Bremer* • James Burke *Mike* ■ *Dir* Jack Hively • *Scr* Lynn Root, Frank Fenton, from characters created by Leslie Charteris

The St Valentine's Day Massacre ★★★

Crime drama 1967 · US · Colour · 99mins

The most authentic documentary-style account – complete with narration giving precise time and location details – of the Chicago gang wars between crime lords Al Capone (Jason Robards) and Bugs Moran (Ralph Meeker), that led to the infamous 1929 massacre. Offbeat casting, lots of bloody action and cult director Roger Corman working for a major studio – and with a decent budget for the first time – make for a compelling and always fascinating throwback to the quick-fire gangster movies of the 1930s. AJ. Contains violence and swearing.

Jason Robards *Al Capone* • George Segal *Peter Gusenberg* • Ralph Meeker *George "Bugsy" Moran* • Jean Hale *Myrtle Nelson* • Clint Ritchie *"Machinegun Jack" McGurn* • Frank Silvera *Nicholas Sorello* • Joseph Campanella *Al Weinshank* • Bruce Dern *John May* • Jack Nicholson *Gino* ■ *Dir* Roger Corman • *Scr* Howard Browne

The Sainted Sisters ★★

Period crime comedy
1948 · US · BW · 89mins

In 1895 Maine, sexy con-women Veronica Lake and Joan Caulfield have the misfortune to come up against broth of a boy Barry Fitzgerald, who has a sneaky method of showing them the error of their ways. An appealing idea is ploddingly developed by William D Russell, a no-count director who moved swiftly to television. The contrivances and folksy comedy make the going tough. DM

Veronica Lake *Letty Stanton* • Joan Caulfield *Jane Stanton* • Barry Fitzgerald *Robbie McCleary* • William Demarest *Vern Tewilliger* • George Reeves *Sam Stoaks* • Beulah Bondi *Hester Rivercomb* • Chill Wills *Will Twitchell* ■ *Dir* William D Russell • *Scr* Harry Clork, Richard Nash [N Richard Nash], Mindret Lord, from the play by Elisa Bialk, Alden Nash, from the story *Sainted Sisters of Sandy Creek* by Elisa Bialk

The Saint's Double Trouble ★★

Crime adventure 1940 · US · BW · 67mins

Perhaps the least accomplished film in RKO's popular B series, this entry, nevertheless, has the added bonus of George Sanders pursuing himself, as he plays both Simon Templar and a criminal mastermind called "The Boss". The scene in which Templar, posing as his criminal double, meets "The Boss" impersonating Templar, is a classic example of back-projected trickery. The film also has the distinction of being one of Bela Lugosi's final bids to prove he was capable of more than just horror, but here, his Egyptian smuggler makes little impact. DP

George Sanders *Simon Templar "The Saint"/ " The Boss"* • Helene Whitney *Anne* • Jonathan Hale *Fernack* • Bela Lugosi *Partner* ■ *Dir* Jack Hively • *Scr* Ben Holmes, from a story by Leslie Charteris

The Saint's Vacation ★★

Crime adventure 1941 · US/UK · BW · 78mins

Hugh Sinclair assumed the role of Simon Templar for this tame thriller, made in Britain by RKO. Although co-scripted by Leslie Charteris from his own story, it's hardly a mystery, with Sinclair racing ruthless Nazi agents to a musical box that contains a vital code. Switzerland has never looked quite so much like a series of hurriedly built studio sets. DP

Hugh Sinclair *Simon Templar " The Saint"* • Sally Gray *Mary Langdon* • Arthur Macrae *Monty Hayward* • Cecil Parker *Rudolph Hauser* • Leueen MacGrath *Valerie* • Gordon McLeod *Inspector Teal* • John Warwick *Gregory* • Ivor Barnard *Emil* • Manning Whiley *Marko* • Felix Aylmer *Charles Leighton* ■ *Dir* Leslie Fenton • *Scr* Jeffry Dell, Leslie Charteris, from the novel *Getaway* by Leslie Charteris

La Saison des Hommes ★★★ 12

Drama 2000 · Fr/Tun · Colour · 122mins

Contrasting the experiences of neglected carpet weaver Rabiaa Ben Abdallah and those of her 20-something daughters Ghalia Ben Ali and Hend Sabri, Moufida Tlatli's second feature makes few structural or thematic advances on her 1994 directorial debut, *The Silences of the Palace*. Yet again the action skips between time frames and imposing environments to demonstrate the lowly status of women, while her predilection for lengthy, leisurely takes serves to emphasise the isolation and frustration they must endure in the absence of their men-folk. DP. In Arabic and French with English subtitles.

Rabiaa Ben Abdallah *Aicha* • Sabah Bouzouita *Zeineb* • Ghalia Ben Ali *Meriem* • Hend Sabri *Emna* ■ *Dir* Moufida Tlatli • *Scr* Moufida Tlatli, Nouri Bouzid

Salaam Bombay! ★★★★ 15

Drama 1988 · Ind/Fr/UK · Colour · 109mins

Dickensian in its empathy with the poor, uncompromising in its realism and ambitious in both scope and technique, Mira Nair's debut feature is one of the most arresting studies of street life ever made. Shot on location after numerous workshops had drawn together a cast made up mostly of homeless kids, the tale of a runaway's assimilation into the dangerous world of petty crime, drugs and prostitution draws on Nair's documentary experience. But it also demonstrates her skill in coaxing a performance of disarming naturalism from Shafiq Syed as the 11-year-old whose indomitability prevents the film from becoming too painful or sentimental. DP. In Hindi with English subtitles. Contains sex scenes, violence, swearing. DVD

Shafiq Syed *Krishna/Chaipau* • Raghubir Yadav [Raghuvir Yadav] *Chillum* • Aneeta Kanwar *Rekha* • Nana Patekar *Baba* • Hansa Vithal *Manju* ■ *Dir* Mira Nair • *Scr* Sooni Taraporevala, from a story by Mira Nair, Sooni Taraporevala

Salaam Cinema ★★★★

Drama documentary
1995 · Iran · Colour · 75mins

In 1995, Moshen Makhmalbaf issued a casting call for Iran's contribution to the celebration of cinema's centenary. An amazing 5,000 movie wannabes arrived at his office and, after a near-riot, he decided to film their auditions to demonstrate how potent the allure of the silver screen remains in even a strictly regulated theocracy. There's a suspicion that the occasional scene in this fascinating experiment has been stage-managed, but the majority of the hopefuls prove to be natural performers, as they try to persuade the director that they're artists in the making. DP. In Farsi with English subtitles.

Dir/Scr Mohsen Makhmalbaf

The Salamander ★ 15

Thriller 1981 · US/It /UK · Colour · 97mins

Morris West's novel becomes a heavy-handed drama about a failed right-wing coup in Italy, with Franco Nero as a spy and Anthony Quinn as a millionaire businessman, who also hunts down war criminals. First time director Peter Zinner (whose editing of *The Deer Hunter* won him an Oscar) gets bogged down in plot and then wastes time on travelogue material, reducing the impressive cast to bystanders. AT [video]

Anthony Quinn *Bruno Manzini* • Franco Nero *Dante Matucci* • Martin Balsam *Stefanelli* • Sybil Danning *Lili Anders* • Christopher Lee *Director Baldassare* • Claudia Cardinale *Elena* • Cleavon Little *Major Malinowski* • Eli Wallach *Leporello* ■ *Dir* Peter Zinner • *Scr* Robert Katz, from the novel by Morris West

Salem's Lot ★★★ 18

Horror 1979 · US · Colour · 105mins

More blood and stronger horror was added to the spooky theatrical version of the truncated television miniseries based on Stephen King's bestseller. Novelist David Soul moves to the New England town to research a new book and finds the place troubled by vampirism after mysterious James Mason moves into the sinister house on the hill. Director Tobe Hooper plunders *Psycho* and *Nosferatu* to good effect in a brisk bloodsucker saga featuring the very creepy looking Reggie Nalder as the undead nemesis. Larry Cohen directed the 1987 sequel, *A Return to Salem's Lot.* AJ [video]

David Soul *Ben Mears* • James Mason *Richard K Straker* • Bonnie Bedelia *Susan Norton* • Lance Kerwin *Mark Petrie* • Lew Ayres *Jason Burke* • Ed Flanders *Dr Bill Norton* • Geoffrey Lewis *Mike Ryerson* • Kenneth McMillan *Parkins Gillespie* • Reggie Nalder *Kurt Barlow* ■ *Dir* Tobe Hooper • *Scr* Paul Monash, from the novel by Stephen King

Salesman ★★★★

Documentary 1969 · US · BW · 91mins

Documentarian brothers Albert and David Maysles' cinéma verité slice of American life almost seems like a time capsule now, capturing an all-but-vanished way of doing business: door-to-door salesmanship. The shifty main protagonist here is Paul Brennan, a middle-aged plodder with a sharp suit and a wit to match, who makes his living going round working-class homes, peddling Bibles from referrals from local churches, mostly to housewives too polite to refuse. Around him swirls a fascinating cast of fellow salesman and customers in the 1960s East Coast, where cars, hair and the salesmen's ambitions are big, but the margins are small. Poignant and funny, its rhythms may seem stately to viewers used to the wham-bam style of current documentary film-making, but this is a classic. LF

Dir Albert Maysles, David Maysles

Sallah ★★★ U

Comedy 1964 · Is · BW · 104mins

In 1948, Topol, his wife and seven children arrive in Israel – only to be housed in a transit camp rather than the roomy flat they were expecting. Needing £1,000 to jump the queue and secure the flat, he throws himself into a number of dodgy schemes to raise the money. Warm-hearted satire with Topol playing Sallah like an early, Jewish version of *Minder*'s "Arfur" Daley. Perhaps a bit overburdened with local colour and characters, but still a pleasant enough time-passer. DF

Chaim Topol [Topol] *Sallah Shabati* • Geula Noni *Habbubah Shabati* • Gila Almagor *Bathsheva Sosialit* • Arik Einstein *Ziggi* • Shraga Friedman *Neuman* ■ *Dir* Ephraim Kishon • *Scr* Ephraim Kishon, from a story by Ephraim Kishon

Sally in Our Alley ★

Romantic musical drama
1931 · UK · BW · 75mins

Of interest only to historians or those addicted to "Our Gracie", this worse-than-mediocre film made Gracie Fields a star and gave her her lifelong signature song, *Sally.* Directed by Maurice Elvey and co-starring Ian Hunter, the plot has Gracie as a teashop entertainer who believes her boyfriend has been killed in the war. Of course he hasn't been. RK

Gracie Fields *Sally Winch* • Ian Hunter *George Miles* • Florence Desmond *Florrie Small* • Ivor Barnard *Tod Small* • Fred Groves *Alf Cope* ■ *Dir* Maurice Elvey • *Scr* Miles Malleson, Alma Reville, Archie Pitt, from the play *The Likes of 'Er* by Charles McEvoy

Sally, Irene and Mary ★★

Silent comedy drama
1925 · US · BW · 58mins

The salutary experiences of three chorus girls on the make. Edmund Goulding directs Constance Bennett as the most worldly of the trio; Sally O'Neil, sprightly and cheerful, who wisely relinquishes the bright lights in favour of her faithful beau; and Joan Crawford who comes to a horrible end. The kind of tale that has been done to death over the decades, this film version of a stage musical inevitably lost much in its transfer to the silent screen and offers little interest now, apart from its leading ladies. RK

Constance Bennett *Sally* • Joan Crawford *Irene* • Sally O'Neil *Mary* • William Haines *Jimmy Dugan* ■ *Dir* Edmund Goulding • *Scr* Edmund Goulding, from the play by Edward Dowling, Cyrus Wood

Sally, Irene and Mary ★★★ U

Musical comedy 1938 · US · BW · 85mins

Borrowing the title, but nothing else of an early stage musical, this musical comedy stars Alice Faye and her then husband Tony Martin. It's movie jam-packed with plot, action, songs, and a cast that includes Jimmy Durante, Fred Allen, Gregory Ratoff and, as a middle-aged moneybags widow with her sights set on Martin, Louise Hovick – better known as stripper Gypsy Rose Lee. This genial nonsense begin with three girls (Faye, Joan Davis, Marjorie Weaver), working as manicurists while looking for the big break into showbiz . RK

Alice Faye *Sally Day* • Tony Martin *Tommy Reynolds* • Fred Allen *Gabriel "Gabby" Green* • Jimmy Durante *Jefferson Twitchell* • Gregory Ratoff *Baron Zorka* • Joan Davis *Irene Keene* • Marjorie Weaver *Mary Stevens* • Louise Hovick [Gypsy Rose Lee] *Joyce Taylor* ■ *Dir* William A Seiter • *Scr* Harry Tugend, Jack Yellen, from a story by Karl Tunberg, Don Ettinger, from the play by Edward Dowling, Cyrus Wood

Sally of the Sawdust ★★ U

Silent comedy 1925 · US · BW · 86mins

After the death of her mother, who was disowned for marrying a circus performer, Carol Dempster is raised by juggler and conman WC Fields. When she's grown up, Fields decides to find her grandparents, and sets a multiplicity of complications into motion. Adapted from the play *Poppy*, under which title it was remade in 1936 with Fields again starring, this was the only feature-length comedy made by DW Griffith. RK [video] DVD

Carol Dempster *Sally* • WC Fields *Prof Eustace P McGargle* • Alfred Lunt *Peyton Lennox* ■ *Dir* DW Griffith • *Scr* Forrest Halsey, from the play *Poppy* by Dorothy Donnelly

Salmonberries ★★★ 15

Drama 1991 · Ger · Colour · 90mins

Deprived of star Marianne Sägebrecht after a trio of pictures, Percy Adlon seemed to lose his way with this story set in the frozen wastes of Alaska and the newly unified Berlin. Ultimately, it's an optimistic film about the true nature of love and coming to terms with the past, but from its confused opening this is hard to engage with, for all the efforts of kd lang as an Inuit trying to conceal her sexual identity and Rosel Zech as the shy German unsure how best to love her. Some moving moments, but lacking in pace. DP. Contains swearing and nudity [video]

kd lang *Kotzebue* • Rosel Zech *Roswitha* • Chuck Connors *Bingo Chuck* • Jane Lind *Noayak* • Oscar Kawagley *Butch* • Wolfgang Steinberg *Albert* ■ *Dir* Percy Adlon • *Scr* Percy Adlon, Felix O Adlon

Salo, or the 120 Days of Sodom ★★★★ 18

Political drama
1975 · It/Fr · Colour · 111mins

Relocating the Marquis de Sade's infamous novel to wartime Italy, this film has become synonymous with sexual deviance and bestial violence. Yet, the soon-to-be-murdered Pier Paolo Pasolini had loftier ambitions than simply shocking the complacent who thought his work obscene. Each of the libertines committing the unspeakably heinous acts represents a social pillar that had delivered the nation into the hands of the Fascists – the law, the merchants, the aristocracy and the church. By depicting their crimes from a distance and by cutting away at the most distasteful moments, he reveals the culpability of the viewer for their passive reponse to the barbarism. Devastating. DP. In Italian with English subtitles. Contains graphic violence, sex scenes. [video] DVD

Paolo Bonacelli *The Duke* • Giorgio Cataldi *The Bishop* • Uberto Paulo Quintavalle *Chief Magistrate* • Caterina Boratto *Signora Castelli* • Hélène Surgère *Signora Vaccari* ■ *Dir* Pier Paolo Pasolini • *Scr* Pier Paolo Pasolini, Sergio Citti, from the novel *Les 120 Journées de Sodome* by Marquis de Sade

Salome ★★

Silent drama 1922 · US · BW · 38mins

Hailed as America's first art film, silent movie star Alla Nazimova lost a personal fortune producing this extravagant version of Oscar Wilde's controversial play, which re-created Aubrey Beardsley's sumptuous text illustrations for the screen. Nazimova plays the lead in this ornate, if stagey, reading of the biblical story of King Herod and his unbridled passion for his adolescent stepdaughter Salome, who demands the head of her own lust object Jokanaan (John the Baptist), in return for the Dance of the Seven Veils. All the sets and costumes were designed by the future Mrs Rudolph Valentino, Natacha Rambova, and the entire cast and crew were allegedly homosexual in homage to Wilde. AJ

Nazimova [Alla Nazimova] *Salome* • Rose Dione *Herodias* • Mitchell Lewis *Herod* • Nigel de Brulier *Jokaanan* ■ *Dir* Charles Bryant • *Scr* Peter M Winters [Natacha Rambova], from the play by Oscar Wilde

Salome ★★★ PG

Biblical drama 1953 · US · Colour · 98mins

This superbly cast tosh from Columbia is directed at a deathly pace by veteran William Dieterle, and given credence only by Alan Badel's sincere portrayal of John the Baptist. But credence isn't what this film's about. You watch it for the stars; the dashing Stewart Granger, flexing his armoured torso for the benefit of ravishing Rita Hayworth, while Charles Laughton chews the scenery as Herod. TS [video]

Rita Hayworth *Princess Salome* • Stewart Granger *Commander Claudius* • Charles Laughton *King Herod* • Judith Anderson *Queen Herodias* • Sir Cedric Hardwicke [Cedric Hardwicke] *Caesar Tiberius* • Alan Badel *John the Baptist* • Basil Sydney *Pontius Pilate* ■ *Dir* William Dieterle • *Scr* Harry Kleiner, from a story by Jesse L Lasky Jr [Jesse Lasky Jr], from a story by Harry Kleiner

Salome, Where She Danced ★★

Wartime spy melodrama
1945 · US · BW · 90mins

The sultry Yvonne De Carlo is Salome, a Viennese dancer who teams up with American newsman Rod Cameron during the Franco-Prussian war to out-manoeuvre Bismarck's lot. Forced to flee Europe, she ends up in an Arizona desert town and then San Francisco, attracting adulation and becoming involved in several adventures along the way. This period melodrama has a script that is so bad and acting that's so variable as to make it absolutely hilarious. Indeed, more than half a century after it was made, it has acquired a certain cult status. RK

Yvonne De Carlo *Salome/Anna Maria* • Rod Cameron *Jim Steed* • David Bruce *Cleve "Stagecoach" Blunt* • Walter Slezak *Colonel Ivan Dimitrioff* • Albert Dekker *Count Erik Von Bohlen* • Marjorie Rambeau *Madam Europe* ■ *Dir* Charles Lamont • *Scr* Laurence Stallings, from a story by Michael J Phillips

Salome's Last Dance ★ 18

Drama 1988 · UK · Colour · 85mins

Ken Russell's career continued to slide downwards with this execrable re-working of Oscar Wilde's banned play, as an end of the pier show acted by some of his pals. The whole grossly over-the-top farrago shrieks excess and truly abominable acting, particularly from Russell himself, who bounces around the small enclosed set as a leering, ruddy-faced photographer. Worth watching only for Stratford Johns's ability to invest a tiresome Herod with a wry, mischievous air. SH. Contains swearing, nudity. [video]

Glenda Jackson *Herodias/Lady Alice* • Stratford Johns *Herod/Alfred Taylor* • Nickolas Grace *Oscar Wilde* • Douglas Hodge *Lord Alfred Douglas/John the Baptist* • Imogen Millais-Scott *Salome/Rose* • Denis Ull *Tigellenus/Chilvers* • Ken Russell *Kenneth* ■ *Dir* Ken Russell • *Scr* Ken Russell, from the play *Salomé* by Oscar Wilde

Salon Kitty ★★ 18

Erotic period drama
1976 · It/W Ger · Colour · 133mins

In independent director Giovanni Tinto Brass's trashy tale of fascist decadence in Berlin in 1939, young women are trained to entertain Nazi officers with degrading perversions in the famous high-class brothel of the title. A wild mix of graphic sex, fetishistic art direction, heavy-handed political statements and gore, this spawned a rash of nasty Nazi exploitation flicks. AJ. In Italian with English subtitles. [video] DVD

Helmut Berger *Captain Helmut Wallenberg* • Ingrid Thulin *Kitty Kellermann* • Teresa Ann Savoy *Margherita* • Bekim Fehmiu *Captain Hans Reiter* ■ *Dir* Giovanni Tinto Brass [Tinto Brass] • *Scr* Ennio De Concini, Maria Pia Fusco, Giovanni Tinto Brass

S

Saloon Bar ★★★

Crime mystery 1940 · UK · BW · 75mins

Gordon Harker was a familiar face in British thrillers during the 1930s, his mournful expression and throaty cockney accent enabled him to play characters on either side of the law. In this engaging Ealing whodunnit, he has a fine old time as a bookie playing detective in his local. Director Walter Forde makes effective use of the claustrophobic set to build tension, and he is well served by an efficient cast of suspects. DP

Gordon Harker *Joe Harris* • Elizabeth Allan *Queenie* • Mervyn Johns *Wickers* • Joyce Barbour *Sally* • Anna Konstam *Ivy* • Cyril Raymond *Harry Small* • Judy Campbell *Doris* • Al Millen *Fred* • Norman Pierce *Bill Hoskins* • Alec Clunes *Eddie Graves* ■ *Dir* Walter Forde • *Scr* Angus MacPhail, John Dighton, from a play by Frank Harvey Jr

Salsa ★ PG

Musical romantic drama
1988 · US · Colour · 93mins

Miserable effort to give a Latin spin to the successful dance flicks phenomenon. Unfortunately, Boaz Davidson forgot to make the plot, about a grease monkey going for the King of Salsa crown, remotely involving. Yet, despite the pluses of Kenny Ortega's choreography and Tito Puente's soundtrack, it's still low-rent and pedestrian. FL

Bobby Rosa *Rico* • Rodney Harvey *Ken* • Magali Alvarado *Rita* • Miranda Garrison *Luna* • Moon Orona *Lola* • Loyda Ramos *Mother* ■ *Dir* Boaz Davidson • *Scr* Boaz Davidson, Tomas Benitez, Shepard Goldman, from a story by Eli Tabor, Boaz Davidson

Salt & Pepper ★★★

Comedy 1968 · UK · Colour · 102mins

Sinatra clan members, Sammy Davis Jr and Peter Lawford came to Britain to make this amiable, though strictly routine, comedy crime caper. They play Soho club-owners involved in a series of murders that turn out to be part of an international conspiracy. The attempt to jump on the "Swinging London" bandwagon, pathetic at the time, now has high camp value and some of the lines are still funny. Although loathed by the press and eventually released as a second-feature, it produced a sequel (*One More Time*) in 1970. DM

Sammy Davis Jr *Charles Salt* • Peter Lawford *Christopher Pepper* • Michael Bates *Inspector Crabbe* • Ilona Rodgers *Marianne Renaud* • John Le Mesurier *Colonel Woodstock* • Graham Stark *Sergeant Walters* • Ernest Clark *Colonel Balsom* • Jeanne Roland *Mai Ling* ■ *Dir* Richard Donner • *Scr* Michael Pertwee

S

Salt of the Earth ★★★★★

Drama 1954 · US · BW · 94mins

Probably the most left-wing movie ever made in America, this represents an extraordinary act of defiance against McCarthyism and the Hollywood blacklist. Its subject is a miners' strike, but the picture opens a Pandora's box of themes, ranging from immigrant workers, racism, the rights of women and the way that America's postwar economic boom passes these people by. Director Herbert J Biberman, producer Paul Jarrico, Oscar-winning writer Michael Wilson, composer Sol Kaplan and actor Will Geer were all blacklisted at the time and the film, financed by the Miners Union, was subject to constant FBI harassment and barely shown in cinemas. A milestone in the political history of the cinema, it's also riveting. JG

Rosaura Revueltas *Esperanza Quintero* • Juan Chacon *Ramon Quintero* • Will Geer *Sheriff* • David Wolfe *Barton* • Melvin Williams *Hartwell* • David Sarvis *Alexander* • Henrietta Williams *Teresa Vidal* ■ *Dir* Herbert J Biberman • *Scr* Michael Wilson

Salt on Our Skin ★★ 18

Romantic drama
1992 · Ger/Can/Fr · Colour · 106mins

This tale of attracting opposites provides Greta Scacchi with another opportunity to indulge in a little steamy romance. As the globetrotting feminist whose principles founder on the rippling torso of Scottish fisherman Vincent D'Onofrio, she is a touch too glamorous to convince. But then nothing about Andrew Birkin's drama is particularly credible, especially the manner in which the lovers keep running into each other. DP

Greta Scacchi *George* • Vincent D'Onofrio *Gavin* • Anaïs Jeanneret *Frederique* • Claudine Auger *George's mother* • Rolf Illig *George's father* • Shirley Henderson *Mary* • Charles Berling *Roger* ■ *Dir* Andrew Birkin • *Scr* Bee Gilbert, from the novel *Les Vaisseaux du Coeur* by Benoîte Groult

The Salton Sea ★★★ 18

Crime thriller 2002 · US · Colour · 99mins

A rock star-styled Val Kilmer plays it hip as a low-life pretender hunting for his wife's killers in this eccentric and atmospheric crime thriller. Shot like a frenetic *film noir* within the murky world of LA's crystal meth users, it marks director DJ Caruso's first non-TV feature. Kilmer is on top form as the jazz player masquerading as an addict, while Vincent D'Onofrio steals the show as a big-time dealer whose own habit has worn away his nose. Sophisticated yet irreverent, intelligent yet bizarre, this is left-field viewing with a seriously cool veneer. SF. Contains violence, swearing, drug abuse and sex scenes. DVD

Val Kilmer *Danny/Tom* • Vincent D'Onofrio *Pooh-Bear* • Adam Goldberg *Kujo* • Luis Guzman *Quincy* • Doug Hutchison *Morgan* • Anthony LaPaglia *Garcetti* • Glenn Plummer *Bobby* ■ *Dir* DJ Caruso • *Scr* Tony Gayton

Saltwater ★★★ 15

Comedy drama
1999 · Ire/UK/Sp · Colour · 95mins

Conor McPherson's feature debut is a darkly comic study of the internal strains threatening a tightly knit family in an isolated Irish seaside town. Young Laurence Kinlan gets involved with a dangerous new friend, while potential brother-in-law Conor Mullen has sexual and intellectual problems at the college where he teaches. But the focus falls primarily on café-owner Brian Cox's eldest son, Peter McDonald, who resorts to robbery to repay his father's debt to local loan shark Brendan Gleeson. The narrative is somewhat disjointed, but it's solidly made and played. DP. Contains violence and swearing.

Peter McDonald *Frank Beneventi* • Brian Cox *George Beneventi* • Conor Mullen *Dr Raymond Sullivan* • Laurence Kinlan *Joe Beneventi* • Brendan Gleeson *"Simple" Simon McCurdie* ■ *Dir/Scr* Conor McPherson

Salty O'Rourke ★★★★

Sports comedy drama
1945 · US · BW · 97mins

Alan Ladd is on top form as a likeable heel in this brightly written racetrack story. A gambler in debt to gangsters, Ladd recruits an obnoxious but talented young jockey, convincingly played by Stanley Clements, to ride a vital race for him. Ladd then has to charm Gail Russell's schoolteacher into tolerating the youth's classroom insolence, as expulsion would bar him from racing. It's a delight from start to finish, thanks to Walsh's polished direction, excellent casting and – most particularly – the original screenplay by Milton Holmes, which gained an Academy Award nomination. AE

Alan Ladd *Salty O'Rourke* • Gail Russell *Barbara Brooks* • William Demarest *Smitty* • Stanley "Stash" Clements [Stanley Clements] *Johnny Cates* • Bruce Cabot *Doc Baxter* • Spring Byington *Mrs Brooks* • Rex Williams *The Babe* • Darryl Hickman *Sneezer* ■ *Dir* Raoul Walsh • *Scr* Milton Holmes

Saludos Amigos ★★★ U

Animation 1943 · US · Colour · 40mins

Produced to support the United States' "Good Neighbour" policy towards Latin America and to prevent its nations from allying with the Axis powers during the Second World War, *Saludos Amigos* and its 1944 companion *The Three Caballeros* are among the least seen Disney films. While perhaps better propaganda than entertainment, this short feature still has plenty to enjoy. Donald Duck's tour of Peru includes a hilarious meeting with a pesky llama, while Goofy comes a cropper on the pampas. DP

Dir Bill Roberts, Jack Kinney, Hamilton Luske, Wilfred Jackson

Salut Cousin! ★★★ 15

Comedy drama
1996 · Fr/Bel/Alg/Lux · Colour · 102mins

Returning to France after a sojourn in his native Algeria, Merzak Allouache opted for a droll approach in relating this sly variation on the town-and-country-mouse theme. In Paris to pick up some clothing, rag-trade gofer Gad Elmaleh accepts the hospitality of his cousin Mess Hattou, who has adapted to the Parisian lifestyle in a way that both shocks and intrigues Elmaleh. An accessible character comedy. DP. In French with English subtitles. Contains swearing and nudity.

Gad Elmaleh *Alilo* • Mess Hattou *Mokrane "Mok" Bensalem* • Magaly Berdy *Fatoumata* • Ann-Gisel Glass *Laurence* • Jean Benguigui *Maurice* ■ *Dir* Merzak Allouache • *Scr* Merzak Allouache, Caroline Thivel

The Salute of the Jugger ★★ 18

Science-fiction action adventure
1989 · US/Aus · Colour · 91mins

This lame post-apocalyptic action adventure resembles TV's *Gladiators* on the cheap. Rutger Hauer stars as a veteran player of a savage future sport that combines rugby, basketball and gratuitous violence, who's reduced to leading a ragbag outfit of semi-pros from village to village to take on all comers. That is, until ambitious apprentice Joan Chen spurs him towards a return to the big city. Trite and dull. RS. Contains violence, swearing and nudity.

Rutger Hauer *Sallow* • Joan Chen *Kidda* • Vincent Phillip D'Onofrio [Vincent D'Onofrio] *Young Gar* • Delroy Lindo *Mbulu* • Anna Katarina *Big Cimber* • Gandhi MacIntyre *Gandhi* • Justin Monju *Dog Boy* • Max Fairchild *Gonzo* • Hugh Keays-Byrne *Lord Vile* ■ *Dir/Scr* David Peoples [David Webb Peoples]

Salute to the Marines ★★

Second World War comedy drama
1943 · US · Colour · 101mins

MGM pays tribute to the US Marine Corps by casting plug-ugly star Wallace Beery as the marine who has spent 30-odd years without seeing active duty. Hitting the bottle – and then some merchant seamen – he ends up in the brig, much to the dismay of his pacifist wife. A physical and emotional wreck, Beery is thrown out of the service. Then the Japanese invade the Philippines and, naturally, Beery is on hand to help with the evacuation. Audiences today will find Beery's self-pity easy to resist. AT

Wallace Beery *Sgt Major Bailey* • Fay Bainter *Jennie Bailey* • Reginald Owen *Mr Caspar* • Ray Collins *Col Mason* • Keye Luke *"Flashy" Logaz* • Marilyn Maxwell *Helen Bailey* ■ *Dir* S Sylvan Simon • *Scr* George Bruce, Wells Root, from a story by Robert D Andrews

Salvador ★★★★ 18

Biographical war drama
1986 · US · Colour · 116mins

In his third feature, director Oliver Stone showed us what he was made of with this indignant, frenetic, politically candid drama. Instead of reflecting the brutality and CIA-supported chaos of the guerrilla war in Central America by making his protagonist the film's moral compass, Stone throws in a cynical, drug-taking, burnt-out foreign correspondent (James Woods), in search of Hunter S Thompson-like kicks with his DJ sidekick James Belushi. It is through Woods, as the scales fall from his eyes and he marries a local girl (Elpidia Carrillo) in order to get her out of the country, that we come to appreciate what's happening. AC. Contains violence, swearing, drug abuse, nudity. DVD

James Woods *Richard Boyle* • James Belushi *Dr Rock* • Michael Murphy *Ambassador Thomas Kelly* • John Savage *John Cassady* • Elpidia Carrillo *Maria* • Tony Plana *Major Max* • Colby Chester *Jack Morgan* • Cynthia Gibb *Cathy Moore* ■ *Dir* Oliver Stone • *Scr* Oliver Stone, Richard Boyle

Salvation! Have You Said Your Prayers Today? ★★ 18

Comedy 1987 · US · Colour · 76mins

Beth B and her husband Scott B were at the vanguard of the New York Super 8 movement of the 1980s, crossing B-movie sensibility with *film noir* and punk rock attitude. Beth B's first solo feature is a raucous satire on TV evangelism, at the same time as the real-life Bakker scandal was hitting the broadcasters of religious television. It's a wild, undisciplined production utilising contrasting techniques and acting styles with the result an intriguing, but chaotic mix that doesn't quite gel. Bonus points, however, for a cutting edge soundtrack. DF

Stephen McHattie *Reverend Edward Randall* • Dominique Davalos *Lenore Finley* • Exene Cervenka *Rhonda Stample* • Viggo Mortensen *Jerome Stample* ■ *Dir* Beth B • *Scr* Beth B, Tom Robinson

The Salvation Hunters ★★★★

Silent drama 1925 · US · BW

Though often ponderous and pretentious –"Our aim has been to photograph thought" – this dockyard drama was a remarkable first film by Josef von Sternberg, who produced, directed, wrote and edited. Shot rapidly in actual locations, with a cast and crew of semi-amateurs, it deals with the world of waterfront derelicts in a detached and stylised way. Sternberg got Charles Chaplin, Mary Pickford and Douglas Fairbanks to watch it, they bought it for more than it cost to make (a paltry $6000) and released it through United Artists, although it was more prestigious than profitable. RB

George K Arthur *The boy* • Georgia Hale *The girl* • Bruce Guerin *The child* ■ *Dir/Scr* Josef von Sternberg

Salvatore Giuliano ★★★★

Historical crime drama
1961 · It · BW · 123mins

Francesco Rosi won the best director prize at Berlin for this documentary-style account of the rise and fall of the eponymous mobster, who was gunned down by disillusioned members of his own gang in Sicily in 1950. Just as the cast comprises a mixture of full-time and non-professional performers, so the elliptical narrative style is a combination of flashbacks, reconstructions and interviews seeking to explore the influence of a corrupt, violent and deeply divided homeland on this self-styled Robin Hood. DP. An Italian language film.

Frank Wolff *Gaspare Pisciotta* • Salvo Randone *President of Viterbo Assize Court* • Federico Zardi *Pisciotta's Defense Counsel* • Pietro Cammarata *Salvatore Giuliano* ■ *Dir* Francesco Rosi • *Scr* Francesco Rosi, Suso Cecchi D'Amico, Enzo Provenzale, Franco Solinas

The Salzburg Connection ★★ PG

Spy drama 1972 · US · Colour · 89mins

This is a convoluted, if scenic spy yarn set in Austria. The plot turns on a chest found by Anna Karina's husband, who is bumped off early on. Seems that the chest contains the names of Nazi collaborators and this sends everyone into a spin, resulting in the kidnapping of Karina and the torture of her brother (Klaus Maria Brandauer in his screen debut). AT

Barry Newman *William Mathison* • Anna Karina *Anna Bryant* • Klaus Maria Brandauer *Johann Kronsteiner* • Karen Jensen *Elissa Lang* • Joe Maross *Chuck* • Wolfgang Preiss *Felix* • Helmut Schmid *Grell* • Udo Kier *Anton* ■ *Dir* Lee H Katzin • *Scr* Oscar Millard, from the novel by Helen MacInnes

Sam Whiskey ★★

Comedy western 1969 · US · Colour · 96mins

Amiability covers a multitude of sins, as Burt Reynolds narrows his eyes and widens his smile to try to distract us from this misfiring story about a gambler hired to recover loot from a Colorado river. The movie surrounds him with a trio of western icons (Clint Walker, Ossie Davis and Angie Dickinson) in an effort to beef up the thin tale, but all it succeeds in being is, well, amiable. TH

Burt Reynolds *Sam Whiskey* • Angie Dickinson *Laura Breckenridge* • Clint Walker *OW Bandy* • Ossie Davis *Jed Hooker* • Rick Davis *Fat Henry Hobson* ■ *Dir* Arnold Laven • *Scr* William W Norton, from his story

Samar ★★

Prison adventure 1962 · US · Colour · 89mins

George Montgomery showed enterprise by producing, directing and writing (as well as starring in) some passably entertaining, low-budget pictures, shot in the Philippines with the help of local film-maker Ferde Grofe Jr. In this story of Spanish oppression in the 1870s, Gilbert Roland is the humane administrator of a colony for political prisoners, who responds to criticism of his methods by leading the inmates to a new life in a remote valley. AE

George Montgomery *Dr John Saunders* • Gilbert Roland *Colonel Salazar* • Ziva Rodann *Ana* • Joan O'Brien *Cecile Salazar* • Nico Minardos *De Guzman* ■ *Dir* George Montgomery • *Scr* Ferde Grofe Jr, George Montgomery

Samaritan Girl ★★★★

Comedy drama 2004 · S Kor · Colour · 94mins

South Korean writer/director *provocateur* Kim Ki-Duk provides another piercing insight into contemporary attitudes in this riveting three-act drama. The first segment sees Gwak Ji-min loyally supporting classmate Seo Min-jung, as she works as a prostitute to raise funds for a European holiday. But when Seo is hospitalised, Gwak seeks out her clients to return their money – unaware that her cop father (Lee Eol) is tracking her every misguided move. Resisting the easy softcore option, Kim devotes more time to the girls' tender friendship than their sexual misdemeanours. He subtly shifts gear from teenpic to quirky comedy to tense domestic morality play, giving the film its fascination and power. DP. In Korean with English subtitles.

Lee Eol *Yeong-gi* • Gwak Ji-min *Yeo-jin* • Seo Min-jung *Jae-yeong* • Gweon Hyeon-min *Censor seller No 1* • Oh Yong *Musician* • Lee Jeong-gil *Lucky guy* ■ *Dir/Scr* Kim Ki-Duk

Samba Traore ★★★ U

Drama 1992 · Burkina Faso · Colour · 85mins

Tracing the misfortunes that befall a decent man when he is prompted by poverty to steal money to open a bar in his home village, this is a remarkable merger of the African social drama and the Hollywood genre film by the Burkinabe director Idrissa Ouedraogo. Anxious to create a picture with an indigenous setting and a universal theme, Ouedraogo has produced what amounts to the first sub-Saharan *film noir*, even though it retains the brilliant outdoor lighting typical of most of the region's films. DP. In Bambara with English subtitles.

Bakary Sangare *Samba* • Mariam Kaba *Saratou* • Abdoulaye Komboudri *Salif* • Irene Tassembedo *Binta* ■ *Dir* Idrissa Ouedraogo • *Scr* Idrissa Ouedraogo, Jacques Arhex, Santiago Amigorena

Same Time, Next Year ★★★★ 15

Romantic comedy drama
1978 · US · Colour · 113mins

This cosy apologia for adultery has all you'd expect from a smash Broadway play brought faithfully to the screen. It tells the story of a married (not to each other) couple who meet every year until the silver anniversary of their coupling, to revive their first, fine, careless rapture. Alan Alda and Ellen Burstyn give superb performances under the sensitive direction by Robert Mulligan; affection and sentimentality are in glorious abundance, but there are few insights into the emotional trauma involved in such a relationship. TH. Contains swearing.

Ellen Burstyn *Doris* • Alan Alda *George* • Ivan Bonar *Chalmers* • Bernie Kuby *Waiter* • Cosmo Sardo *Second waiter* • David Northcutt *First pilot* ■ *Dir* Robert Mulligan • *Scr* Bernard Slade, from his play

Sammy and Rosie Get Laid ★★ 18

Drama 1987 · UK · Colour · 96mins

In this follow-up to *My Beautiful Laundrette*, a retired Pakistani government torturer (Shashi Kapoor) comes to England to stay with his son (Ayub Khan Din) and daughter-in-law (Frances Barber), and anti-Thatcher messages get spelled out in riots and sexual promiscuity. Well-acted, but the characters are totally unsympathetic, except for Claire Bloom as the old man's former mistress. TH

Frances Barber *Rosie Hobbs* • Ayub Khan Din *Sammy* • Shashi Kapoor *Rafi Rahman* • Claire Bloom *Alice* • Roland Gift *Danny/Victoria* • Wendy Gazelle *Anna* • Suzette Llewellyn *Vivia* • Meera Syal *Rani* ■ *Dir* Stephen Frears • *Scr* Hanif Kureishi

Sammy Going South ★★★ U

Period adventure
1963 · UK · Colour · 128mins

Coming between *Mandy* and *A High Wind in Jamaica*, this is the weakest of Alexander Mackendrick's bittersweet trio of films in which the foibles of the adult world are exposed to the gaze of an artless child. Ten-year-old Fergus McClelland heads for South Africa after he is orphaned during the Suez crisis, but the film's episodic structure prevents it from picking up pace. However, McClelland is a likeable lad and his scenes with wizened diamond smuggler Edward G Robinson are of a very high order. DP

Edward G Robinson *Cocky Wainwright* • Fergus McClelland *Sammy Hartland* • Constance Cummings *Gloria Van Imhoff* • Harry H Corbett *Lem* • Paul Stassino *Spyros Dracondopolous* • Zia Mohyeddin *Syrian* • Zena Walker *Aunt Jane* ■ *Dir* Alexander Mackendrick • *Scr* Denis Cannan, from the novel by WH Canaway

Sammy Stops the World ★

Musical 1978 · US · Colour · 105mins

A stage production crudely put on film, this version of the Anthony Newley–Leslie Bricusse musical *Stop the World – I Want to Get Off*, starring Sammy Davis Jr and "updated", is dire stuff and an unworthy record of the great performer. Quickly made, with cameras placed rigidly at the front of the stage (and two focused on the audience), it highlights all the deficiences of the show and its production. TV

Sammy Davis Jr *Littlechap* • Dennis Daniels *Baton Twirler* • Donna Lowe *Schoolgirl* • Marian Mercer *Evie* ■ *Dir* Melvin Shapiro • *Scr* Leslie Bricusse, Anthony Newley

Sammy, the Way Out Seal ★★★ U

Comedy 1962 · US · Colour · 85mins

A Disney animal feature that was originally made for TV in the 1960s, this has found a new lease of life on video in the States. It's very much of its time (check out the title, man), but still is entertaining thanks to the talent of its watery-eyed star. Two young brothers (Michael McGreevey and Bill Mumy) find the injured seal and hide him from parents Robert Culp and Patricia Barry, only for the slippery one to escape from the beach-house and wreck cute havoc around town. RT

Robert Culp *Father* • Patricia Barry *Mother* • Michael McGreevey *Arthur Loomis* • Billy Mumy [Bill Mumy] *Petey Loomis* • Jack Carson *Harold Sylvester* • Elisabeth Fraser *Lovey* • Ann Jillian *Rocky* ■ *Dir/Scr* Norman Tokar

Le Samouraï ★★★★★ PG

Thriller 1967 · Fr/It · Colour · 100mins

Alain Delon excels in this ultra-stylish study of the ultimate professional. The way in which director Jean-Pierre Melville sets up hitman Delon's next job is mesmerising, attending to each part of the preparation with the detailed eye of a true craftsman. Yet, as in every good *film noir*, there is a *femme fatale* waiting in the shadows to tempt the hero away from his purpose, and Cathy Rosier is about as chic as an angel of doom could be. Almost devoid of dialogue, the film owes everything to the subtlety of the acting, the sinister beauty of Henri Decaë's photography and the intricacy of Melville's direction. DP. In French with English subtitles.

Alain Delon *Jef Costello* • François Périer *Inspector* • Nathalie Delon *Jane Lagrange* • Cathy Rosier *Valerie* ■ *Dir* Jean-Pierre Melville • *Scr* Jean-Pierre Melville, from the novel *The Ronin* by Joan McLeod

Sam's Son ★★★ 15

Biographical drama
1984 · US · Colour · 107mins

Michael Landon is no stranger to sentiment, but he reins in the schmaltz in this neglected drama that is as much a tribute to his stern father, as an account of his own transformation from high school athlete to Hollywood hopeful. In addition to writing and directing, Landon also appears in a cameo as the returning prodigal, leaving Timothy Patrick Murphy to impress as the young Gene Orowitz (Landon's real surname) and real-life couple Eli Wallach and Anne Jackson to steal the picture as his parents. DP. Contains swearing.

Eli Wallach *Sam Orowitz* • Anne Jackson *Harriet* • Timothy Patrick Murphy *Gene* • Hallie Todd *Cathy Stanton* • Alan Hayes *Robert Woods* • Jonna Lee *Bonnie Barnes* • Michael Landon *Gene Orman* • Howard Witt *Cy Martin* ■ *Dir/Scr* Michael Landon

Sam's Song ★

Drama 1969 · US · Colour · 92mins

In 1980, Cannon Films tried to cash in on Robert De Niro's fame by re-releasing an obscure 1969 independent movie, in which he stars as a film editor spending the weekend on Long Island. Although it was a total flop, Cannon still thought it had commercial value and reworked the De Niro footage into a newly shot film. In the re-edited version, flashbacks show De Niro getting killed while editing a porno movie. Ten years later his ex-con brother Anthony Charnota searches for his murderer. A dull disaster. AJ

Robert De Niro *Sam* • Jennifer Warren *Erica* • Jered Mickey *Andrew* • Terrayne Crawford *Carol* • Martin Kelley *Mitch* • Phyllis Black *Marge* • Viva *Girl with the hourglass* • Anthony Charnota *Vito* ■ *Dir* John Shade [Jordan Leondopoulos], John C Broderick

Samson and Delilah ★★★ U

Biblical epic 1949 · US · Colour · 122mins

Scooping Oscars for its sets and costumes, this epic prompted veteran American critic Pauline Kael to suggest that Cecil B DeMille considered God to be his co-director. Victor Mature stars as the biblical hero, while Hedy Lamarr brings a gorgeous woodenness to the role of the Philistine, whose jealousy over Samson's fondness for Angela Lansbury leads to treachery. The fight with the lion is so lousy it's brilliant, while the oily villainy of George Sanders provides the only acting highlight. DP

Victor Mature *Samson* • Hedy Lamarr *Delilah* • George Sanders *Saran of Gaza* • Angela Lansbury *Semadar* • Henry Wilcoxon *Ahtur* • Olive Deering *Miriam* • Fay Holden *Hazelelponit* • Julia Faye *Hisham* • Russell Tamblyn [Russ Tamblyn] *Saul* ■ *Dir* Cecil B DeMille • *Scr* Vladimir Jabotinsky, Harold Lamb, Jesse L Lasky Jr [Jesse Lasky Jr], Frederic M Frank, from the book *Judge and Fool* by Vladimir Jabotinsky • *Costume Designer* Edith Head, Dorothy Jeakins, Elois Jenssen, Gile Steele, Gwen Wakeling

Samurai ★★★ PG

Period action adventure
1954 · Jpn · Colour · 300mins

Hiroshi Inagaki was no stranger to the *Meiji-mono*, or historical drama, and he sought to recapture the purity of the genre with this mammoth, colour retelling of his own 1941 trilogy. It opens by exploring the humble origins and reckless youth of Musashi Miyamoto, the 17th-century peasant who rose to become the finest swordsman of his generation. Depicting the samurai's rigorous training and explaining the significance of the bushido code, the film was initially released in the US with narration from William Holden. The three films (which won the Honorary Oscar for Best Foreign Film) possess an elegiac quality that atones for their lack of authenticity. DP. In Japanese with English subtitles. DVD

Toshiro Mifune *Takeso/Miyamoto Musashi* • Kaoru Yachigusa *Otsu* • Rentaro Mikuni *Matahachi* • William Holden (2) *Narrator* ■ *Dir* Hiroshi Inagaki • *Scr* Tokuhei Wakao, Hiroshi Inagaki, Hideji Hojo, from the novel *Miyamoto Musashi* by Eiji Yoshikawa

S

San Antonio ★★ PG

Western 1945 · US · Colour · 104mins

A bloated Errol Flynn western, boasting lovely Technicolor and the high production values of a big-budget Warner Bros feature, but lacking a decent script. Alexis Smith co-stars as the dance hall singer working for villain Paul Kelly, while Flynn sports some fancy outfits including holsters specially designed to give him a lightning-fast draw. The climactic shoot-out is well worth catching. AE

Errol Flynn *Clay Hardin* • Alexis Smith *Jeanne Starr* • SZ Sakall *Sacha Bozic* • Victor Francen *Legare* • Florence Bates *Henrietta* ■ *Dir* David Butler • *Scr* Alan LeMay, WR Burnett

San Demetrio London ★★★ PG

Second World War drama
1943 · UK · BW · 93mins

Thanks to a fine ensemble cast and the authenticity of the action, this Second World War drama about an oil tanker struggling to cross the Atlantic after being attacked by a German battleship not only did its bit in boosting Britain's morale, but also played a key role in the evolution of Ealing studios. Based on a true story, it served as an allegory for the nation's fortunes since 1939 – the ship may have been damaged, but its gallant crew successfully salvaged it and brought it into port ready to fight another day. Although Charles Frend is credited as sole director, he was indisposed for much of the production and co-writer/producer Robert Hamer actually called the shots. DP

Walter Fitzgerald *Chief Engineer Charles Pollard* • Ralph Michael *Second Officer Hawkins* • Frederick Piper *Bosun WE Fletcher* • Gordon Jackson *John Jamieson* • Mervyn Johns *Greaser John Boyle* • Robert Beatty *"Yank" Preston* ■ *Dir* Charles Frend • *Scr* Robert Hamer, Charles Frend, from a story by F Tennyson Jesse

San Francisco ★★★★ U

Disaster movie 1936 · US · BW · 110mins

MGM's classic disaster epic is driven by sheer star power. Clark Gable's cynical saloon keeper, Jeanette MacDonald's showgirl and Spencer Tracy's priest battle for one another's souls until San Francisco gets clobbered by the earthquake of 1906. The quake, itself a magnificent testimony to the studio's special effects department, remains one of the most elaborate and exciting action sequences ever filmed, and it's well worth enduring the 90-minute wait while the three heroes squabble over love and life. DW Griffith reportedly directed one of the scenes. AT

Clark Gable *Blackie Norton* • Jeanette MacDonald *Mary Blake* • Spencer Tracy *Father Tim Mullin* • Jack Holt *Jack Burley* • Jessie Ralph *Maisie Burley* • Ted Healy *Mat* • Shirley Ross *Trixie* ■ *Dir* WS Van Dyke II [WS Van Dyke] • *Scr* Anita Loos, Erich von Stroheim (uncredited), from a story by Robert Hopkins • *Special Effects* A Arnold Gillespie, James Basevi

The San Francisco Story ★★

Drama 1952 · US · BW · 79mins

Hunky Joel McCrea, plays a miner who opposes corrupt politician Sidney Blackmer's plans to take over the city and the state of California. It all ends with a preposterous duel on horseback, by which the point of dispute isn't political morality, but the fairly blatant charms of Yvonne De Carlo. There's a lot of rough-house stuff , and every interior set is so overdressed it makes San Francisco in the 1850s look like a bordello. AT

Joel McCrea *Rick Nelson* • Yvonne De Carlo *Adelaide McCall* • Sidney Blackmer *Andrew Cain* • Richard Erdman *Shorty* • Florence Bates *Sadie* • Onslow Stevens *Jim Martin* • John Raven *Lessing* ■ *Dir* Robert Parrish • *Scr* DD Beauchamp, from the novel *Vigilante* by Richard Summers

San Quentin ★★★

Prison drama 1937 · US · BW · 71mins

A highly enjoyable Warner Bros prison melodrama – with absolutely no redeeming social significance – that revolves around Humphrey Bogart as a hardened young hoodlum who goes inside. His sister (Ann Sheridan) is dating the fair-minded new captain of the prison yard. O'Brien is the nominal star of the picture, but broody Bogart and perky young Sheridan are the centre of interest. AE

Pat O'Brien *Capt Stephen Jameson* • Humphrey Bogart *Joe "Red" Kennedy* • Ann Sheridan *May Kennedy* • Barton MacLane *Lt Druggin* • Joseph Sawyer [Joe Sawyer] *"Sailor Boy" Hansen* • Veda Ann Borg *Helen* • James Robbins *Mickey Callahan* • Joseph King (1) *Warden Taylor* ■ *Dir* Lloyd Bacon • *Scr* Peter Milne, Humphrey Cobb, from a story by Robert Tasker, John Bright

San Quentin ★★

Crime drama 1946 · US · BW · 66mins

Claiming social significance with a filmed introduction by Lewis E Lawes, the reform-minded ex-warden of Sing Sing prison, this is an energetic RKO crime thriller with ideas above its station. Barton MacLaine is the prisoner who has completed a San Quentin reform programme and does a bunk on the way to address a press club. A fully rehabilitated ex-con, Lawrence Tierney, steps in to save the reputation of the governor and his scheme – cue for a well handled, documentary-style manhunt. AE

Lawrence Tierney *Jim Rolands* • Barton MacLane *Nick Taylor* • Marian Carr *Betty* • Harry Shannon *Warden Kelly* • Carol Forman *Ruthie* • Richard Powers [Tom Keene] *Schaeffer* • Joe Devlin *Broadway* ■ *Dir* Gordon M Douglas [Gordon Douglas] • *Scr* Lawrence Kimble, Arthur A Ross, Howard J Green

Sanctimony ★★ 18

Detective thriller
2000 · US/Ger · Colour · 82mins

American Psycho revisited – without the style, satire or savage wit. Casper Van Dien is the arrogant, egotistical financial wizard who becomes the prime suspect in the hunt for the Monkey Maker, a serial killer who has cops Michael Paré and Jennifer Rubin baffled. Writer/director Uwe Boll serves up the occasional jolting image but no real shocks, while the psychological mind games never ring true. JF DVD

Casper Van Dien *Tom Gerrick* • Michael Pare(acute) *Detective Jim Renart* • Eric Roberts *Lieutenant Mann* • Catherine Oxenberg *Susan Renart* • Jennifer Rubin *Dorothy Smith* ■ *Dir/Scr* Uwe Boll

Sanctuary ★★

Melodrama 1961 · US · BW · 89mins

High drama in the Greek tradition reduced to swamp melodrama in the Tennessee Williams tradition, though the source is William Faulkner's novel of the same title. Directed by Tony Richardson and starring Lee Remick, it concerns a Mississippi governor's daughter who is raped by a bootlegger. She goes to live in a New Orleans brothel with him and her black maid Odetta which, of course, leads to several tragedies. An opaque, turgid and unsuccessful attempt to bring Faulkner to the screen. RK

Lee Remick *Temple Drake* • Yves Montand *Candy Man* • Bradford Dillman *Gowan Stevens* • Harry Townes *Ira Bobbitt* • Odetta *Nancy Mannigoe* • Howard St John *Governor* ■ *Dir* Tony Richardson • *Scr* James Poe, from the play *Requiem for a Nun* by Ruth Ford, from the novels *Sanctuary* and *Requiem for a Nun* by William Faulkner

Sanctuary ★★ 18

Action thriller 1997 · US · Colour · 99mins

This is what happens when you take the retired assassin premise of *The Long Kiss Goodnight* and replace the amnesiac housewife with a hunky clergyman. It may sound far-fetched, but Tibor Takacs is no mug when it comes to action, so there are plenty of shoot-outs and explosions to occupy Mark Dacascos and Jaimz Woolvett. Basic, but crudely effective. DP. Contains swearing, violence and sex scenes. DVD

Mark Dacascos *Luke Kovak* • Kylie Travis *Rachel Malcolm* • Jaimz Woolvett *Dominic Grace* • Alan Scarfe *William Dyson* • Monika Schnarre *Colette Fortier* • Nigel Bennett *Senator Stephen Macguire* ■ *Dir* Tibor Takacs • *Scr* Michael Stokes

The Sand Castle ★★★ U

Part-animated fantasy drama
1961 · US · BW and Colour · 65mins

A curious and charming feature from writer/director Jerome Hill, this follows a young boy whose elaborate sand castle attracts a diverse range of admirers during the course of a day on the beach. The action is shot in black and white (originally on 16mm), shifting to colour for an animated sequence in which the boy imagines his castle inhabited by the people he has met. This effect is created with the use of 19th-century-style paper cut-outs. The end result is surprisingly beguiling. RT

Barry Cardwell *Boy* • Laurie Cardwell *Girl* • George Dunham *Artist* • Alec Wilder *Fisherman* • Maybelle Nash *Shade lady* • Erica Speyer *Sun lady* ■ *Dir/Scr* Jerome Hill

The Sand Pebbles ★★★ 15

War drama 1966 · US · Colour · 174mins

Set on a US gunboat patrolling the Yangtze River in 1926, this blend of action and melodrama was something of a surprise hit in its day, earning itself no fewer than eight Oscar nominations (although it won none). Part of the reason for its success can be found in its thinly veiled apology for American intervention in Vietnam, but there are some more enduring plus points, too. Steve McQueen and Richard Attenborough both turn in pleasing performances and Joseph MacDonald's cinematography is outstanding. DP DVD

Steve McQueen *Jake Holman* • Richard Attenborough *Frenchy Burgoyne* • Richard Crenna *Captain Collins* • Candice Bergen *Shirley Eckert* • Marayat Andriane *Maily* • Mako *Po-Han* • Larry Gates *Jameson* • Charles Robinson *Ensign Bordelles* ■ *Dir* Robert Wise • *Scr* Robert W Anderson, from the novel by Richard McKenna

Sanders of the River ★★★ U

Adventure 1935 · UK · BW · 84mins

A famous title in its day, this Alexander Korda production looks patronising and imperialistic to modern eyes. The titular Sanders (Leslie Banks), is a police commissioner in colonial Nigeria, but the real interest here is the performance of the great African-American bass Paul Robeson, as the escaped convict Bosambo (the film's American title), and the "native" chants which greatly enhanced the film's popularity and lead to an infinite number of Robeson impressions in the music halls. The movie still impresses, but it's really best viewed as a fascinating historic document. TS

Leslie Banks *RG Sanders* • Paul Robeson *Bosambo* • Nina Mae McKinney *Lilongo* • Robert Cochran *Tibbets* • Martin Walker *Ferguson* • Richard Grey *Hamilton* • Tony Wane *King Mofolaba* ■ *Dir* Zoltan Korda • *Scr* Lajos Biró, Jeffrey Dell, from the stories by Edgar Wallace

The Sandlot ★★★ PG

Comedy adventure
1993 · US · Colour · 96mins

An adult does occasionally intrude upon the world of baseball, lifeguards and savage dogs described in this pleasing rites-of-passage picture. However, this enchanted summer really belongs to the kids, in particular Tom Guiry, the pre-teen who makes Charlie Brown look like Babe Ruth. Although the games on the sandlot provide the focus, this isn't just another sports movie. It's about self-discovery and learning how to deal with the scuffed knees of life. DP DVD

Tom Guiry *Scotty Smalls* • Mike Vitar *Benjamin Franklin Rodriguez* • Patrick Renna *Hamilton "Ham" Porter* • Chauncey Leopardi *Michael "Squints" Palledorous* • Marty York *Alan "Yeah-Yeah" McClennan* • Brandon Adams *Kenny DeNunez* • Denis Leary *Bill* • Karen Allen *Mom* • James Earl Jones *Mr Mertle* ■ *Dir* David Mickey Evans • *Scr* David Mickey Evans, Robert Gunter

Sandokan against the Leopard of Sarawak ★ U

Adventure 1964 · It · Colour · 88mins

Ray Danton had a variable career with plenty of duff patches. Here, in one of the duffest, he plays the "Tiger", the famous Malaysian warrior, played by Steve Reeves in the earlier *Sandokan the Great*. A somewhat unengaging action adventure, but with some virile skirmishes. JG. Italian dialogue dubbed into English.

Ray Danton *Sandokan* • Guy Madison • Franca Bettoja • Mario Petri ■ *Dir* Luigi Capuano • *Scr* Luigi Capuano, Arpad DeRiso, from a novel by Emilio Salgari

Sandokan Fights Back ★★ PG

Action adventure 1964 · It · Colour · 86mins

Italian director Luigi Capuano was churning them out back in 1964, so he could be forgiven for running out of steam by the time he shot this, one of two sequels to Umberto Lenzi's swashbuckling adventure, *Sandokan the Great*. Ray Danton returns in the title role, while Guy Madison again provides the villainy, as he steals the throne of Sarawak. The sets look as if they could fall down at any second but, for a spot of mindless escapism, you could do a lot worse. DP. Italian dialogue dubbed into English.

Ray Danton *Sandokan* • Guy Madison *Yanez* • Franca Bettoja • Mino Doro ■ *Dir* Luigi Capuano • *Scr* Luigi Capuano, Arpad DeRiso, from a novel by Emilio Salgari

Sandokan the Great ★★ U

Adventure 1963 · Fr/It/Sp · Colour · 109mins

A sturdy adventure set in Victorian Borneo. When British forces begin wiping out East Indian villagers, a band of rebels led by warrior Sandokan take on the colonists, kidnapping the commander's niece. Steve Reeves doesn't get to flash as much musculature as in his "sword and sandal" epics, but he makes an athletic lead and there are enough colourful action sequences to hold the interest. Reeves returned for the 1964 sequel, *The Pirates of Malaysia*. JG. Italian dialogue dubbed into English.

Steve Reeves *Sandokan* • Geneviève Grad *Mary Ann* • Andrea Bosic *Yanez* • Maurice Poli *Giro Batol* • Rik Battaglia *Sambigliong* ■ *Dir*

Umberto Lenzi • *Scr* Umberto Lenzi, Fulvio Gicca, Victor A Catena, from the novel *Le Tigri di Mompracem* by Emilio Salgari

The Sandpiper ★ 15

Romantic drama
1965 · US · Colour · 112mins

This truly terrible movie was made by the great Vincente Minnelli. It's a full-blown example of the Elizabeth Taylor/Richard Burton vehicle, and as mindless and inept as it comes. Of course, its sheer awfulness and desperate pretension create a numbing watchability: you have been warned. The California coastline at Big Sur and Charles Bronson emerge with some credit, but Eva Marie Saint is totally wasted. TS [VIDEO]

Richard Burton *Dr Edward Hewitt* • Elizabeth Taylor *Laura Reynolds* • Eva Marie Saint *Claire Hewitt* • Charles Bronson *Cos Erickson* • Peter O'Toole ■ *Dir* Vincente Minnelli • *Scr* Dalton Trumbo, Michael Wilson, Irene Kamp, Louis Kamp, from a story by Martin Ransohoff

Sands of Iwo Jima ★★★ PG

Second World War drama
1949 · US · BW · 109mins

John Wayne leads his marines to hell and back and they love him for it, every bloodsoaked, heroic foot of the way. Apparently, Kirk Douglas was in line for the role, but, according to the film's producer, Wayne wanted the role so badly "he could taste it." If you believe Wayne's son, though, the Duke worried about the script and only relented when war veterans lobbied him to play the part. The result was a gung-ho classic, made on the cheap, often risible, but it's still eminently watchable and the Duke nabbed his first Oscar nomination to boot. AT [VIDEO]

John Wayne *Sergeant Stryker* • John Agar *Private Peter Conway* • Forrest Tucker *Corporal Al Thomas* • Adele Mara *Allison Bromley* • Wally Cassell *Private Benny Ragazzi* • James Brown (1) *Private Charlie Bass* • Richard Webb *Private Shipley* ■ *Dir* Allan Dwan • *Scr* Harry Brown, Edward James Grant, from a story by Harry Brown

Sands of the Desert ★ U

Comedy 1960 · UK · Colour · 88mins

Poor old Charlie Drake. To call his flirtation with film fame an unmitigated disaster, would be understating the extent to which he failed to translate his stage, radio and TV success to the big screen. Director John Paddy Carstairs also co-wrote this silly story in which travel agent Drake sets out to uncover the saboteur at a holiday camp. Better than his other efforts, but that's not saying much. DP [VIDEO]

Charlie Drake *Charlie Sands* • Peter Arne *Sheikh El Jabez* • Sarah Branch *Janet Brown* • Raymond Huntley *Bossom* • Peter Illing *Sheikh Ibrahim* • Harold Kasket *Abdullah* • Marne Maitland *Sheikh's advisor* • Neil McCarthy *Hassan* ■ *Dir* John Paddy Carstairs • *Scr* John Paddy Carstairs, Charlie Drake, from a story by Robert Hall, Anne Burnaby, Stafford Byrne

Sands of the Kalahari ★★★

Action drama 1965 · UK · Colour · 119mins

The team behind *Zulu* converge upon South Africa for another gritty adventure. It's a well-cast survival picture, in which a charter plane is grounded by a plague of locusts, leaving the United Nations of passengers to bicker, rape, kill and generally abuse each other in the desert. It's an allegory showing how, given half a chance, humans will regress to ape-like behaviour, with Stuart Whitman taking on the role of the prime primate. It's not in the class of Endfield's previous epic, but it has a raw intensity all of its own thanks to some excellent performances and imposing locations. AT

Stuart Whitman *O'Brien* • Stanley Baker *Bain* • Susannah York *Grace Monckton* • Harry Andrews *Grimmelman* • Theodore Bikel *Dr Bondarahkai* • Nigel Davenport *Sturdevant* • Barry Lowe *Detjens* ■ *Dir* Cy Endfield • *Scr* Cy Endfield, from the novel by William Mulvihill

The Sandwich Man ★★ U

Comedy 1966 · UK · Colour · 91mins

Known as the Goon that got away, and as the genius behind *Potty Time*, Michael Bentine was yet another British comedian who failed to repeat his TV and/or radio success on the big screen. This virtually silent comedy was politely considered "ahead of its time" on its release, but, over 30 years later, this euphemism for "not very good" still applies. The cast is all-star, but the film's few pleasures come from Bentine's often inspired mime as he wanders the streets of London with his sandwich board. DP [VIDEO]

Michael Bentine *Horace Quilby* • Dora Bryan *Mrs de Vere* • Harry H Corbett *Stage doorkeeper* • Bernard Cribbins *Photographer* • Diana Dors *Billingsgate woman* • Ian Hendry *Motorcyle cop* • Stanley Holloway *Gardener* • Wilfrid Hyde White *Lord Uffingham* • Michael Medwin *Sewer man* • Ron Moody *Coach* • Anna Quayle *Billingsgate woman* • Terry-Thomas *Scoutmaster* • Norman Wisdom *Father O'Malley* • Suzy Kendall *Sue* • Alfie Bass *Yachtsman* • John Le Mesurier *Sandwich man* • Peter Jones *Escapologist* • Warren Mitchell *Gypsy Syd* ■ *Dir* Robert Hartford-Davis • *Scr* Robert Hartford-Davis, Michael Bentine

Sangam ★★★ U

Melodrama 1964 · Ind · Colour · 213mins

This sprawling tale of star-crossed love and heroic sacrifice was Raj Kapoor's first colour film and is one of the earliest Bollywood pictures to utilise European locations. It has a decidedly homoerotic tone as Kapoor and his socially superior buddy, Rajendra Kumar, become involved in a tug-of-war for the affections of Vyjayanthimala, though she is the one finding it difficult to pierce their long-standing exclusivity. Surprisingly suggestive in its approach to sex, yet also subtly insistent in its avowal that women get a raw deal in Indian society, this tragic melodrama also has more than its share of memorable musical routines. DP. In Hindi with English subtitles. [VIDEO]

Raj Kapoor *Sunder* • Rajendra Kumar *Gopal* • Vyjayanthimala *Radha* ■ *Dir* Raj Kapoor • *Scr* Inder Raj

Sanjuro ★★★ 12

Period action drama 1962 · Jpn · BW · 91mins

Following the success of *Yojimbo*, Akira Kurosawa was persuaded (somewhat against his better judgement) to make a further adventure featuring the self-seeking samurai who uses his own guile and the efforts of others to achieve his ends. Toshiro Mifune returns as Sanjuro, who joins forces with a band of eager warriors to rescue a kidnapped landowner. Until the final eruption of violence, Kurosawa plays the film for laughs, sending up the conventions of the *jidai-geki* (or period costume drama) with an unerring eye, while Mifune bestrides the action with gleeful gravitas. DP. In Japanese with English subtitles. [VIDEO] DVD

Toshiro Mifune *Sanjuro* • Tatsuya Nakadai *Muroto* • Takashi Shimura *Kurofuji* • Yuzo Kayama *Iori Izaka* • Reiko Dan *Koiso, the Chamberlain's daughter* • Masao Shimizu *Kikui* ■ *Dir* Akira Kurosawa • *Scr* Ryuzo Kikushima, Akira Kurosawa, Hideo Oguni, from the short story *Hibi Heian* by Shugoro Yamamoto

Sans Soleil ★★★★ 15

Documentary 1982 · Fr · Colour · 99mins

Still most widely known for his sci-fi short *La Jetée*, Chris Marker emerged in the 1960s as a key practitioner of the *cinéma vérité* documentary style. This is tantamount to a postcard from "a life", as Marker tries to convey his impressions and recollections of cultures as far afield as Africa, Iceland and Japan. Exploiting what was then the latest in video and imaging technology, the film is an exhilarating collage of sights and sounds. Unlike many documentarists, Marker doesn't force his views upon you, but, like a good guide, draws your attention to what you might otherwise have missed. DP [VIDEO] DVD

Alexandra Stewart *English narration* ■ *Dir/Scr* Chris Marker

Sanshiro Sugata ★★★

Adventure drama 1943 · Jpn · BW · 80mins

An intriguing work, as the first film directed by the legendary Japanese director Akira Kurosawa, who went on to international fame with *The Seven Samurai*. Made in the latter part of the war, when he was in his early 30s, it was inevitably influenced by the authorities, which may have accounted for its economical and straightforward storytelling. This concerns Sugata, who in the late 19th century develops the art of Judo, showing its superiority over the martial art of Ju-Jitsu. There was a second part to the story made a couple of years later. BB. In Japanese with English subtitles.

Susumu Fujita *Sanshiro Sugata* • Denjiro Okochi *Shogoro Yano* • Takashi Shimura *Hansuke Murai* • Yukiko Todoroki *Sayo, his daughter* ■ *Dir* Akira Kurosawa • *Scr* Akira Kurosawa, from the novel *Sugata Sanshiro* by Tsuneo Tomita

Sansho the Bailiff ★★★★★ PG

Epic period drama 1954 · Jpn · BW · 118mins

One of the masterworks of Japanese cinema, this powerful, poignant period drama discusses tyranny, liberalism and the psychological differences between the sexes. Reworking a traditional folk tale, Kenji Mizoguchi considers how someone can be driven to barbarism simply to survive, with kidnap victim Yoshiaki Hanayagi's collusion with the barbarous bailiff, Eitaro Shindo, contrasting sharply with the idealism that condemned his father to exile, his mother to prostitution and his sister to death, while contriving his escape. Shooting primarily in long takes from a withdrawn, fluid camera, Mizoguchi conveys a sense of intimacy through flashbacks and the performances of his superlative cast. DP. In Japanese with English subtitles. [VIDEO]

Kinuyo Tanaka *Tamaki* • Yoshiaki Hanayagi *Zushio* • Kyoko Kagawa *Anju* • Masao Shimizu *Tairano no Masauji* • Eitaro Shindo *Sansho Dayu* • Akitake Kono *Taro* • Ryosuke Kagawa *Ritsushi Kumotake* ■ *Dir* Kenji Mizoguchi • *Scr* Yahiro Fuji, Yoshikata Yoda, from a famous legend as related by Ogai Mori in the magazine *Chuo Koron* • *Cinematographer* Kazuo Miyagawa

Santa Claus ★★ U

Seasonal comedy
1985 · UK/US · Colour · 107mins

Dudley Moore plays the elf who loses his job with Santa and decides to sell his former employer's secrets to evil toy manufacturer John Lithgow in this rather daft family comedy. It boasts a great opening, but gets bogged down with infantile humour, a silly script and plot twists that a five-year-old would find insulting. JB [VIDEO] DVD

Dudley Moore *Patch* • John Lithgow *B Z* • David Huddleston *Claus* • Burgess Meredith *Ancient elf* • Judy Cornwell *Anya* • Jeffrey Kramer *Towzer* • Christian Fitzpatrick *Joe* ■ *Dir* Jeannot Szwarc • *Scr* David Newman, from a story by David Newman, Leslie Newman

Santa Claus Conquers the Martians ★ U

Science-fiction comedy drama
1964 · US · Colour · 77mins

One of the all-time great movie titles is, surprise, surprise, also one of cinema's great howlers. Preparing for another busy Christmas our Santa (John Call) is kidnapped by Martians who want to exploit Santa's happiness in order to lift the spirits of their planet's listless, automated youth. Directed on schmaltz overload by Nicholas Webster and further enhanced by amateurish production values and acting, it has garnered unworthy cult status among bad-movie lovers over the years. RS [VIDEO] DVD

John Call *Santa Claus* • Leonard Hicks *Kimar* • Vincent Beck *Voldar* • Victor Stiles *Billy* • Donna Conforti *Betty* • Pia Zadora *Girmar* ■ *Dir* Nicholas Webster • *Scr* Glenville Mareth, from an idea by Paul L Jacobson

The Santa Clause ★★★ U

Seasonal fantasy
1994 · US · Colour · 105mins

Tim Allen gets off rather lightly in this engaging Yuletide comedy, and his feature debut brims over with good ideas. The only trouble is, they are all stocking-fillers when what the action really needs is a couple of huge gift-wrapped set pieces. However, as the sceptic bound by the Claus clause, the *Home Improvement* star slips from Scrooge into Santa with some skill and amiability. DP [VIDEO] DVD

Tim Allen *Scott Calvin* • Judge Reinhold *Neal* • Wendy Crewson *Laura* • Eric Lloyd *Charlie* • David Krumholtz *Bernard* • Larry Brandenburg *Detective Nunzio* ■ *Dir* John Pasquin • *Scr* Leo Benvenuti, Steve Rudnick

The Santa Clause 2 ★★ U

Seasonal fantasy comedy
2002 · US · Colour · 100mins

This lacklustre sequel to the amiable 1994 film is a sugary confection of festive clichés, half-baked jokes and blatant product placement – the celluloid equivalent of an expensively wrapped box filled with junk. Superficially the film has its charm, thanks largely to a likeable performance from Tim Allen, who now has to bag the perfect Mrs Claus or lose his job. SF [VIDEO] DVD

Tim Allen *Scott Calvin/Santa/Toy Santa* • Elizabeth Mitchell *Carol Newman* • David Krumholtz *Bernard* • Eric Lloyd *Charlie Calvin* • Judge Reinhold *Neal Miller* • Wendy Crewson *Laura Miller* • Spencer Breslin *Curtis* • Liliana Mumy *Lucy Miller* • Kevin Pollak *Cupid* ■ *Dir* Michael Lembeck • *Scr* Don Rhymer, Cinco Paul, Ken Daurio, Ed Decter, John Strauss, from a story by Leo Benvenuti, Steve Rudnick, based on their characters

S

Santa Fe ★★ U

Western 1951 · US · Colour · 86mins

Made virtually back-to-back with *Man in the Saddle* (same year, star, producer and writer), this is a much more routine western. This time Confederate soldier Randolph Scott is involved in unseemly sibling rivalry at the end of the Civil War, as his brothers turn against him when he decides to work for the railroad of the title. Irving Pichel's colourless direction and Janis Carter's uninspiring leading lady don't help this over-familiar tale. TS

Randolph Scott *Britt Canfield* • Janis Carter *Judith Chandler* • Jerome Courtland *Terry Canfield* • Peter M Thompson *Tom Canfield* • John Archer *Clint Canfield* • Warner Anderson *Dave Baxter* ■ *Dir* Irving Pichel • *Scr* Kenneth Gamet, from a story by Louis Stevens, from the novel by James Marshall

Santa Fe Passage ★★ U

Western 1955 · US · Colour · 90mins

This average second-division western is given moderate interest by its trio of stars, well past their primes but still able to hold the attention. John Payne plays an ostracised wagon-train scout battling former B-hero Rod Cameron (here cast against type) for the hand of mixed-race Faith Domergue. TS

John Payne *Kirby Randolph* • Faith Domergue *Aurelie St Clair* • Rod Cameron *Jess Griswold* • Slim Pickens *Sam Beekman* • Irene Tedrow *Ptewaquin* • George Keymas *Satank* ■ *Dir* William Witney • *Scr* Lillie Hayward, from a short story by Clay Fisher

Santa Fe Stampede ★★ U

Western 1938 · US · BW · 55mins

The Three Mesquiteers grubstake an old miner, who strikes it rich and summons them to share in his good fortune. A pre-*Stagecoach* John Wayne is the star of this routine B-western, along with Ray Corrigan and Max Terhune. Silent star William Farnum plays the old-timer, who is killed off by the bad guys who then try to pin the blame on Wayne. AE

John Wayne *Stony Brooke* • Ray "Crash" Corrigan *Tucson Smith* • Max Terhune *Lullaby Joslin* • William Farnum *Dave Carson* • June Martel *Nancy Carson* • LeRoy Mason *Gil Byron* ■ *Dir* George Sherman • *Scr* Luci Ward, Betty Burbridge, from a story by Luci Ward, from characters created by William Colt MacDonald

Santa Fe Trail ★★ U

Period action adventure
1940 · US · BW · 109mins

One of the weakest of the Errol Flynn/Olivia de Havilland series at Warners, this rambling saga concerns the attempts of future Civil War cavalryman Flynn to nail the great abolitionist John Brown (a ranting Raymond Massey). As history, this is wild fiction, even for Hollywood, and, despite a watchable supporting cast including Ronald Reagan as George Armstrong Custer, there's precious little going on here. TS DVD

Errol Flynn *Jeb Stuart* • Olivia de Havilland *Kit Carson Halliday* • Raymond Massey *John Brown* • Ronald Reagan *George Armstrong Custer* • Alan Hale *Tex Bell* • Guinn "Big Boy" Williams *Windy Brody* • Van Heflin *Rader* ■ *Dir* Michael Curtiz • *Scr* Robert Buckner

Santa Sangre ★★★ 18

Surreal horror drama
1989 · It/Mex · Colour · 118mins

Alexandro Jodorowsky's cross-cultural collage of ideas and images borrows freely from Freud, Fellini and Ferrara, de Milo, Marceau and *Psycho*. Using the circus as a microcosm, Jodorowsky combines the sacred and the psychedelic, the psychological and the symbolic, as a magician (played variously by the director's sons, Adan and Axel) goes on a murderous rampage to avenge the aerialist mother whose arms were severed by the knife-throwing husband she caught *in flagrante delicto* with the tattooed lady. DP DVD

Axel Jodorowsky *Fenix* • Blanca Guerra *Concha* • Guy Stockwell *Orgo* • Thelma Tixou *Tattooed woman* • Sabrina Dennison *Alma* • Adan Jodorowsky *Young Fenix* ■ *Dir* Alexandro Jodorowsky • *Scr* Alexandro Jodorowsky, Roberto Leoni, Claudio Argento, from a story by Roberto Leoni, Alexandro Jodorowsky

Santa Who? ★★ U

Seasonal comedy 2000 · US · Colour · 88mins

Leslie Nielsen plays Santa Claus with pantomimic brio in this cheerful Disney made-for-TV film. Blown off course by turbulence, he crashes his sleigh into Scrooge-like TV reporter Steven Eckholdt's car. However, it takes young Max Morrow to realise the implications of Santa's amnesia and the race to save the festivities begins. As you'd expect of a Hollywood yule movie, it's awash with sentimentality, but William Dear has too much experience to let it descend into mush. DP DVD

Leslie Nielsen *Santa Claus* • Steven Eckholdt *Peter Albright* • Robyn Lively *Claire Dreyer* • Max Morrow *Zack* • Tommy Davidson *Max* ■ *Dir* William Dear • *Scr* Debra Frank, Steve L Hayes, from a story by Chad Hoffman, Robert Schwartz

Santa with Muscles ★★

Comedy action adventure
1996 · US · Colour · 97mins

The main gag here is that arrogant health-food millionaire Hulk Hogan loses his memory and adopts the role of Santa to protect a local church orphanage. We're supposed to laugh as he submits himself to various indignities in the name of doing good. The problem with this joke is that a guy named "Hulk" doesn't have any dignity to begin with. ST

Hulk Hogan *Blake Thorne* • Ed Begley Jr *Ebner Frost* • Don Stark *Lenny* • Robin Curtis *Leslie* • Garrett Morris *Clayton* • Clint Howard *Hinkley* ■ *Dir* John Murlowski • *Scr* Jonathan Bond, Fred Mata, Dorrie Krum Raymond

Santee ★★★ 15

Western 1973 · US · Colour · 86mins

Glenn Ford is a bounty hunter, long embittered by the memory of his son who was gunned down by a gang he hunts still. In a twist of fate he becomes the surrogate father to another boy – whose father he has killed – and still the ironies pile upon Ford, turning him into a figure from Greek tragedy. While this does not even approach the westerns that Anthony Mann made with James Stewart, its similar classical references and tormented hero make for an immensely satisfying drama. AT

Glenn Ford *Santee* • Michael Burns *Jody* • Dana Wynter *Valerie* • Jay Silverheels *John Crow* • Harry Townes *Sheriff Carter* • John Larch *Banner* • Robert Wilke [Robert J Wilke] *Deake* ■ *Dir* Gary Nelson • *Scr* Tom Blackburn, from a story by Brand Bell

Santiago ★★★

Adventure drama 1956 · US · Colour · 91mins

A cracking script by Martin Rackin and John Twist goes some way to redeeming this period bunkum about gunrunners Alan Ladd and Lloyd Nolan paddle-boating rifles to Cuban revolutionaries fighting Spanish oppression. Gordon Douglas's dull direction backs it all into Cliché Corner, but the writing quite often forces a way out. TH

Alan Ladd *Cash Adams* • Rossana Podesta *Isabella* • Lloyd Nolan *Clay Pike* • Chill Wills *Sidewheel* • Paul Fix *Trasker* • LQ Jones *Digger* ■ *Dir* Gordon Douglas • *Scr* Martin Rackin, John Twist, from the novel *The Great Courage* by Martin Rackin

Los Santos Inocentes ★★★★

Drama 1984 · Sp · Colour · 108mins

Although centred on the brutalised existence of one particular peasant family, this epic commentary reflects life in Franco's Spain during the 1960s in broad political terms. Mario Camus, a brilliant and prolific writer/director has consistently displayed social concerns and his scathing sense of the injustice endured is leavened by a mordant wit and surreal moments. The protagonists are a couple, burdened with a mentally handicapped child and backbreaking work, whose only hope is that their older children might escape the feudal system binding them to uncaring landowners. Superbly photographed against imposing landscapes, this compassionate work deserves a wide audience. BB. In Spanish with English subtitles.

Alfredo Landa *Paco* • Francisco Rabal *Azarias* • Terele Pávez *Regula* • Belen Ballesteros *Nieves* • Juan Sachez *Quirce* • Juan Diego *Master Ivan* • Agustín González *Don Pedro* ■ *Dir* Mario Camus • *Scr* Mario Camus, Antonio Larreta, Manuel Matji, from the novel by Miguel Delibes • *Cinematographer* Hans Burmann

The Saphead ★★★

Silent comedy 1920 · US · BW · 77mins

Buster Keaton's first feature was for Metro who, having lost Fatty Arbuckle, didn't quite know what to do with Buster, so installed him in a Fatty-prepared vehicle. Buster plays the naive son of a rich father, devoted to his father's ward (Carol Holloway). Determined to be "bad", in fact his goodness ensures that he takes the blame for another stockbroker's error. A bit of a letdown for fans, but the character was the basis for many of his later creations. TH

Buster Keaton *Bertie Van Alstyne* • William H Crane *Nicholas Van Alstyne* • Irving Cummings *Mark Turner* • Carol Holloway *Rose Turner* • Beulah Booker *Agnes Gates* ■ *Dir* Herbert Blaché • *Scr* June Mathis, from the play *The New Henrietta* by Winchell Smith, Victor Mapes, Bronson Howard

Sapnay ★★★ U

Romantic drama
1997 · Ind · Colour · 147mins

Director Rajiv Menon's deft camerawork and sense of dramatic tension are well to the fore in this engaging love triangle drama. The well-travelled and dashing Arvind Swamy falls for teenager Kajol, who has unfortunately decided to enter a convent. Matters are not helped when Swamy employs Prabhu Deva, the local honey-tongued barber, to plead his cause, little suspecting that he too will succumb to Kajol's charms. RT. In Hindi with English subtitles. DVD

Kajol *Priya* • Arvind Swamy *Thomas/Mr Dancing Shoes* • Prabhu Deva *Deva* ■ *Dir* Rajiv Menon • *Scr* VC Guhanathan, Rajiv Menon

Sapphire ★★★

Murder mystery 1959 · UK · Colour · 91mins

A young woman's murder leaves many questions unanswered in this intriguing detective tale. The relatively innovative racial element – the victim is a young black woman who has been passing as white – adds to the historical interest, and gives the search for the murderer a wider resonance. Yvonne Mitchell was nominated for best actress at that year's British Academy Awards, while the film itself scooped the Best British Film award. RT

Nigel Patrick *Detective Superintendent Hazard* • Michael Craig *Detective Inspector Learoyd* • Yvonne Mitchell *Mildred* • Paul Massie *David Harris* • Bernard Miles *Mr Harris* • Olga Lindo *Mrs Harris* • Earl Cameron *Dr Robbins* • Gordon Heath *Paul Slade* ■ *Dir* Basil Dearden • *Scr* Janet Green, Lukas Heller

Saps at Sea ★★ U

Comedy 1940 · US · BW · 57mins

This inconsistent comedy was Laurel and Hardy's last film for Hal Roach, and the first of the highly derivative features with which they saw out their distinguished careers. Driven bonkers by honking horns at work, Ollie is prescribed a tranquil sea voyage, during which he and Stan are shanghaied by a fugitive killer. The opening sections are fast and furious, but the action becomes becalmed the moment the boys are afloat. DP

Stan Laurel *Stan* • Oliver Hardy *Ollie* • James Finlayson *Dr JH Finlayson* • Ben Turpin *Mixed-up plumber* • Rychard Cramer [Richard Cramer] *Nick Grainger* • Charlie Hall *Apartment desk clerk* ■ *Dir* Gordon Douglas • *Scr* Charles Rogers, Felix Adler, Gil Pratt [Gilbert W Pratt], Harry Langdon, from their story

Saraband ★★★

Drama 2003 · Swe · Colour · 107mins

Ingmar Bergman closed one of cinema's most significant careers with this sequel to *Scenes from a Marriage* (1973). Divided into ten, book-ended chapters, this made-for-TV film starts off focusing on Liv Ullmann's long-overdue reunion with ex-husband Erland Josephson. But it soon shifts to the tensions between Josephson's son from an earlier marriage, Börje Ahlstedt, and his teenage cellist granddaughter, Julia Dufvenius. Shooting in high-definition video, the auteur reins in his camera, not only to avoid exposing the obviously theatrical backdrops, but also to emphasise the powerful performances of a cast that makes the occasionally stilted dialogue seem sharp and wounding. DP. In Swedish with English subtitles.

Erland Josephson *Johan* • Liv Ullmann *Marianne* • Börje Ahlstedt *Henrik* • Julia Dufvenius *Karin* • Gunnel Fred *Martha* ■ *Dir/Scr* Ingmar Bergman

Saraband for Dead Lovers ★★★ U

Romantic historical drama
1948 · UK · Colour · 91mins

Audiences wanted colour, upholstery and royalty in the postwar era, and this sumptuous British movie about a claim to the Hanoverian throne of England has all the ingredients. Joan Greenwood plays the king's wife, but she fancies Stewart Granger, a Swedish count of indifferent pedigree and accent, who was previously involved with Flora Robson, who goes into a fit of jealous rage. It's a shame that Basil Dearden and Michael Relph directed it with straight faces, but no one, thankfully, could suppress Greenwood in full flounce. AT

Stewart Granger *Count Philip Konigsmark* • Joan Greenwood *Sophie Dorothea* • Françoise Rosay *Electress Sophie* • Flora Robson *Countess Platen* • Frederick Valk *Elector Ernest Augustus* • Peter Bull *Prince George-Louis* • Anthony Quayle *Durer* • Megs Jenkins *Frau Busche* • Michael Gough *Prince Charles* ■ *Dir* Basil Dearden, Michael Relph • *Scr* John Dighton, Alexander Mackendrick, from the novel by Helen Simpson

Sarafina! ★★★ 15

Musical drama
1992 · S Afr/US/UK/Fr · Colour · 111mins

Based on the anti-apartheid Broadway musical, this traces the transformation of a schoolgirl in the South African townships of the 1970s from innocent teenage dreamer to political activist. In her school there is only one teacher (Whoopi Goldberg) who refuses to toe the white-endorsed party line and pays a terrible price for her courage. The upbeat musical numbers are invigorating but seem sometimes at odds with the theme. Miriam Makeba, the singer/actress and *grande dame* of the anti-apartheid movement is in a supporting role. DA

Whoopi Goldberg *Mary Masombuka* • Leleti Khumalo *Sarafina* • Miriam Makeba *Angelina* • John Kani *School principal* • Dumisani Diamini *Crocodile* ■ *Dir* Darrell James Roodt • *Scr* William Nicholson, Mbongeni Ngema, from the musical by Mbongeni Ngema • *Music* Stanley Meyers

The Saragossa Manuscript ★★★★★

Fantasy drama 1964 · Pol · BW · 124mins

This is a complex and exhilarating film that ranks among the most remarkable achievements of 1960s European cinema. Beginning in the Peninsular War, the action shifts, via the pages of a gloriously illustrated tome, to a dazzling compendium of interweaving stories. Zbigniew Cybulski's Walloon guardsman meets with two Muslim princesses, a hermit, a possessed lunatic, a cabalist, a rationalist philosopher, a gypsy and an Inquisitor. Played to the haunting strains of Krzysztof Penderecki's score, this is a highly stylised, darkly surreal exploration of such themes as the capriciousness of nature, authority and, above all, love. DP. In Polish with English subtitles.

Zbigniew Cybulski *Capt Alfons van Worden* • Kazimierz Opalinski *Hermit* • Iga Cembrzynska *Princess Emina* • Joanna Jedryka *Princess Zibelda* • Slawomir Linder *van Worden's father* • Miroslawa Lombardo *van Worden's mother* ■ *Dir* Wojciech Has • *Scr* Tadeusz Kwiatkowski, from the novel *Manuscrit Trouvé à Saragosse* by Jan Potocki

Sarah and Son ★★★

Drama 1930 · US · BW · 86mins

Following her success in *Madame X* as a mother deprived of her child as punishment for her infidelity, Ruth Chatterton returned in this tear-sodden variation on the theme. Here, she is a woman wronged by her cad of a husband who sells their baby to a wealthy couple. The rest of the film is spent with Chatterton as she searches for her lost son while managing to become an opera star. Directed with requisite feeling by Dorothy Arzner, and well-played by the polished Chatteron (Oscar-nominated) and Fredric March, it is predictable but effective. RK

Ruth Chatterton *Sarah Storm* • Fredric March *Howard Vanning* • Fuller Mellish Jr *Jim Gray* • Gilbert Emery *John Ashmore* • Doris Lloyd *Mrs Ashmore* • William Stack *Cyril Belloc* • Philippe De Lacy *Bobby* ■ *Dir* Dorothy Arzner • *Scr* Zoe Akins, from a novel by Timothy Shea

Saratoga ★★★

Comedy 1937 · US · BW · 92mins

This robust racetrack romance had its back broken by the tragic and untimely death (during filming) of its star, blond bombshell Jean Harlow. Her demise cast a pall over the production and resulted in the movie being finished by the necessary use of a none-too-clever double (stand-in Mary Dees) in certain scenes, voice-matched and photographed back-to-camera. The morbidly curious will be able to spot the non-Harlow sections easily. For the rest, it's one of those intelligently crafted, glossy movies from MGM's golden era, with Clark Gable at his most dashing and Lionel Barrymore at his most crusty. Harlow sparkles, sadly for the last time. TS

Jean Harlow *Carol Clayton* • Clark Gable *Duke Bradley* • Lionel Barrymore *Grandpa Clayton* • Walter Pidgeon *Hartley Madison* • Frank Morgan *Jesse Kiffmeyer* • Una Merkel *Fritzi O'Malley* • Cliff Edwards *Tip O'Brien* ■ *Dir* Jack Conway • *Scr* Anita Loos, Robert Hopkins

Saratoga Trunk ★★

Melodrama 1945 · US · BW · 135mins

A lavish film of Edna Ferber's novel which reunited Ingrid Bergman, Gary Cooper, and Sam Wood, the stars and director of *For Whom the Bell Tolls*. Bergman plays a half-Creole beauty, resentful of her illegitimacy, and Cooper is a gambler who fancies her while she sets her sights on a tycoon. Among the embarrassments is Oscar nominee Flora Robson as a maid, blacked up like Hattie McDaniel. AT

Gary Cooper *Colonel Clint Maroon* • Ingrid Bergman *Clio Dulaine* • Flora Robson *Angelique Buiton* • Jerry Austin *Cupidon* • John Warburton *Bartholomew Van Steed* • Florence Bates *Mrs Coventry Bellop* ■ *Dir* Sam Wood • *Scr* Casey Robinson, from the novel by Edna Ferber

Sardar ★★★ 15

Biographical drama
1993 · Ind · Colour · 134mins

An eclectic director associated with the "middle cinema" tradition between the staple masala musicals and the social realism of "parallel cinema", Ketan Mehta helms this controversial biopic focuses on the career of the man who was prime minister Nehru's deputy, and also the minister responsible for domestic affairs in India in the days after Partition. Paresh Rawal does sterling work in the title role, but it's Mehta's frank exploration of the policies and prejudices that still divide the peoples of the subcontinent that makes this so engrossing. DP. In Hindi with English subtitles. [video]

Paresh Rawal *Sardar* • Annu Kapoor ■ *Dir* Ketan Mehta • *Scr* Vijay Tendulkar

Sarraouina ★★★★

Historical drama
1986 · Fr/Burkina Faso · Colour · 120mins

Both a celebration of African culture and a warning against perpetuating the divisions that delivered much of the continent into European rule, Med Hondo's epic account of the battles waged by Sarraounia (Aï Këta), the 19th-century warrior queen of the Aznas, is both inspiring and impressively cinematic. While Guy Famechon's photography conveys the enormity of the Lugu region, Hondo concentrates on the personal problems besetting Këta's resistance to a local tribe and the marauding French. A landmark in Third World Cinema. DP. In French with English subtitles.

Ai Keta *Sarraounia* • Jean-Roger Milo *Captain Voulet* • Feodor Atkine *Captain Chanoine* • Didier Sauvegrain *Doctor Henric* ■ *Dir* Med Hondo • *Scr* Med Hondo, Abdul War

Sartana ★★★ 15

Spaghetti western 1968 · It · Colour · 91mins

A no-nonsense spaghetti western from Gianfranco Parolini, directing under the name of Frank Kramer. John Garko is the eponymous gunfighter who is forced to draw on all his experience and cunning to clear his name after he is accused of masterminding a bank robbery. Parolini has a firm grasp of the conventions of the genre, switching between passages of terse dialogue and outbursts of stylised violence with some aplomb. Garko looks the part, but he is outshone by co-stars Klaus Kinski and William Berger. DP. Italian dialogue dubbed into English. [video]

John Garko [Gianni Garko] *Sartana* • Klaus Kinski • William Berger ■ *Dir* Frank Kramer [Gianfranco Parolini]

Sartana, Angel of Death ★★

Spaghetti western 1969 · It · Colour · 92mins

After the success of *Sartana*, Gianni Garko and Klaus Kinski were reteamed the following year for this unremarkable sequel. It follows the gunfighter as he tries to discover who's behind a series of vicious bank robberies. Whereas Gianfranco Parolini kept the action swift and simple in the original picture, director Giuliano Carnimeo allows this to meander. DP. Italian dialogue dubbed into English.

Gianni Garko *Sartana* • Frank Wolff • Klaus Kinski ■ *Dir* Anthony Ascott [Giuliano Carnimeo] • *Scr* Tito Carpi, Enzo Dell'Aquila

Saskatchewan ★★ U

Western 1954 · US · Colour · 87mins

An under-rated actor, Alan Ladd seemed content to make formula pictures rather than stretch himself. His first western after the memorable *Shane* was this routine story of cavalry versus Indians – only this time the troops are Mounties and the location is Canada. Ladd's the Indian-raised officer who defies his superior officer to deal with hostile Sioux crossing the border. Shelley Winters is thrown in as the woman prisoner of Hugh O'Brian's marshal. The uninvolved direction of veteran Raoul Walsh doesn't help. AE

Alan Ladd *Sergeant O'Rourke* • Shelley Winters *Grace Markey* • J Carrol Naish *Batoche* • Hugh O'Brian *Marshal Smith* • Robert Douglas *Inspector Benton* • Jay Silverheels *Cajou* ■ *Dir* Raoul Walsh • *Scr* Gil Doud

Sasquatch ★ U

Adventure 1978 · US · Colour · 101mins

Of all the monsters that cinema has unleashed, Bigfoot, supposed inhabitant of the North American forests, seems to be one of the most benign. He's even more harmless in this semi-documentary about an expedition that goes in search of the creature. Some blurred photos are supposed to strike a chill, but they are risible – as is the film. TH

George Lauris *Chuck Evans* • Steve Boergadine *Hank Parshall* • Jim Bradford *Barney Snipe* • Ken Kenzle *Josh Bigsby* • William Emmons *Dr Paul Markham* • Joe Morello *Techka Blackhawk* ■ *Dir* Ed Ragozzini • *Scr* Edward H Hawkins, from a story by Ronald B Olson

The Satan Bug ★★★ PG

Science-fiction thriller
1965 · US · Colour · 109mins

Compared to the more straightforward heroics of other Alistair MacLean hits such as *The Guns of Navarone* and *Where Eagles Dare*, this is an altogether more subtle affair, with George Maharis searching for the madman who is threatening to unleash a deadly virus. There's a solid supporting cast, and director John Sturges never lets the suspense slip for a minute. JF. [video]

George Maharis *Lee Barrett* • Richard Basehart *Dr Hoffman/Ainsley* • Anne Francis *Ann* • Dana Andrews *The General* • Edward Asner *Veretti* • Frank Sutton *Donald* • John Larkin *Michaelson* ■ *Dir* John Sturges • *Scr* James Clavell, Edward Anhalt, from the novel by Ian Stuart [Alistair MacLean]

Satan in High Heels ★★

Thriller 1962 · US · BW · 89mins

Great title, shame about the movie! Burlesque dancer Meg Myles robs her junkie boyfriend, heads for New York and quickly becomes a cabaret club owner's mistress, in a typical exploitation item from the early 1960s featuring very little strip but lots of tease. Aside from a standout sequence where Myles sings *More Deadly Than the Male* wearing full leather and brandishing a riding crop, this is strictly routine trash. AJ

Meg Myles *Stacey Kane* • Grayson Hall *Pepe* • Mike Keene *Arnold Kenyon* • Robert Yuro *Laurence Kenyon* • Sabrina (1) *Sabrina* • Nolia Chapman *Felice* • Earl Hammond *Rudy* • Del Tenney *Paul* ■ *Dir* Jerald Intrator • *Scr* John T Chapman [John Chapman], from a story by Harold Bennett, John T Chapman [John Chapman]

Satan Met a Lady ★

Crime comedy drama
1936 · US · BW · 75mins

A reworked version of Dashiell Hammett's *The Maltese Falcon*, this was clearly intended as a sophisticated spoof but emerged as a clumsy, unfunny bore. There is some interest to be had in identifying the worked-over characters – for Madame Barabbas read Sidney Greenstreet, for example – and plot points – several questionable characters are after an ancient ivory horn filled with jewels – but that's about it. Bette Davis regarded the movie as one of the low points in her career. RK

Bette Davis *Valerie Purvis* • Warren William *Ted Shayne* • Alison Skipworth *Mme Barabbas* • Arthur Treacher *Anthony Travers* • Winifred Shaw *Astrid Ames* • Marie Wilson *Murgatroyd* • Porter Hall *Mr Ames* • Maynard Holmes *Kenneth* ■ *Dir* William Dieterle • *Scr* Brown Holmes, from the novel *The Maltese Falcon* by Dashiell Hammett

Satan Never Sleeps ★★

Period drama
1962 · US/UK · Colour · 126mins

This Catholics v Communists saga is a cross between *The Left Hand of God* and director Leo McCarey's own Oscar-winning whimsy *Going My Way*. With British scenery approximating the Chinese landscape, the film has a rugged look in keeping with its often brutal subject matter. Too much time is spent setting the scene, and not enough on the dramatic events that overwhelm the mission run by the William Holden and Clifton Webb. Devout and dour. DP

William Holden (2) *Father O'Banion* • Clifton Webb *Father Bovard* • France Nuyen *Siu Lan* • Athene Seyler *Sister Agnes* • Martin Benson *Kuznietsky* • Edith Sharpe *Sister Theresa* • Burt Kwouk *Ah Wang* ■ *Dir* Leo McCarey • *Scr* Claude Binyon, Leo McCarey, from the novel *Satan Never Sleeps* by Pearl S Buck

The Satanic Rites of Dracula ★★ 18

Horror 1973 · UK · Colour · 83mins

Christopher Lee gives a disappointing final appearance as Dracula, masquerading as a mysterious Howard Hughes-style business mogul, plotting to control the world with a vampire virus. It's lacking in Hammer's usual Gothic flavour and detail, and Alan Gibson's careless direction proved to be the final nail in the Dracula coffin, despite the indefatigable Peter Cushing performing his usual miracle as a descendant of the original Van Helsing, with Joanna Lumley as his daughter. AJ. Contains nudity. [video]

Christopher Lee *Count Dracula* • Peter Cushing *Van Helsing* • Michael Coles *Inspector Murray* • William Franklyn *Torrence* • Freddie Jones *Professor Keeley* • Joanna Lumley *Jessica* • Richard Vernon *Mathews* • Patrick Barr *Lord Carradine* ■ *Dir* Alan Gibson • *Scr* Don Houghton, from the character created by Bram Stoker

Satan's Brew ★★★

Black comedy
1976 · W Ger · Colour · 112mins

Rainer Werner Fassbinder is at his most scathingly anti-bourgeois in this portrayal of a worthless world. His pessimistic conclusion is that all relationships are based on power and that sado-masochism, blind fealty and financial gain have replaced emotion. Playing the burned-out poet capable only of expressing himself in acts of cruelty or self-loathing, Kurt Raab exhibits no redeeming features as a character Fassbinder clearly invests with autobiographical disgust. Fassbinder makes no concessions towards the viewer, who is left to experience either anger or guilt. DP. In German with English subtitles.

Kurt Raab *Walter Kranz* • Margit Carstensen *Andrée* • Helen Vita *Luise Kranz* • Volker Spengler *Ernst* • Ingrid Caven *Lilly* • Marquard Bohm *Rolf* • Ulli Lommel *Lauf* ■ *Dir/Scr* Rainer Werner Fassbinder

Satan's Cheerleaders ★

Horror 1977 · US · Colour · 92mins

A bunch of cheerleaders on their way to a football game are kidnapped by backwood Satanists eager for a virgin

S

sacrifice, in this bottom-of-the-barrel horror movie. So why choose cheerleaders? Luckily one of the girls happens to be descended from a witch and her tormentors get more than they bargained for. Despite the inspired title this is in no way funny or horrific enough to be truly effective. RS

John Ireland *Sheriff Bub/High Priest* • Yvonne De Carlo *Emm Bub, Sheriff's wife/High Priestess* • Jack Kruschen *Billy the janitor* • John Carradine *Bum* • Sydney Chaplin *Mond* • Jacqueline Cole *Ms Johnson* ■ *Dir* Greydon Clark • *Scr* Greydon Clark, Alvin L Fast

Satan's Harvest ★

Detective thriller
1965 · S Afr · Colour · 104mins

American detective George Montgomery inherits a ranch in South Africa, only to discover it's being used as the centre for an international drug-smuggling operation. A slow and banal thriller, set against a spectacular backdrop and featuring a rare screen turn by crooner Matt Monro. This potboiler was kept on the shelf until 1970. Easy to see why. AJ

George Montgomery *Cutter Murdock* • Tippi Hedren *Marla Oaks* • Matt Monro *Bates* • Davy Kaye • Brian O'Shaughnessy *Andrew* ■ *Dir/Scr* George Montgomery

Satan's Slave ★★★ 18

Horror 1976 · UK · Colour · 83mins

Director Norman J Warren lays on the nudity and gore in this obscure, lurid tale of devil worship and ancestral evil. Candace Glendenning plays the girl coming up to her 20th birthday, whose visit to her eccentric uncle (played by Michael Gough) coincides with the violent death of her parents and an attempt to resurrect a witch. Cinematographer Les Young's intense use of colour is matched by Gough's gregarious performance, but Warren overindulges in horror clichés and garish set pieces. DP [video] DVD

Michael Gough *Alexander Yorke* • Candace Glendenning *Catherine Yorke* • Martin Potter *Stephen Yorke* • Barbara Kellerman *Frances* • Michael Craze *John* • James Bree *Malcolm Yorke* • Celia Hewitt *Elizabeth Yorke* • David McGillivray *Priest* ■ *Dir* Norman J Warren • *Scr* David McGillivray

Satellite in the Sky ★★ U

Science fiction 1956 · UK · Colour · 84mins

This full-throttled, but hopelessly inadequate space opera stars Kieron Moore as the commander of an orbital mission to test a tritonium bomb. Lois Maxwell displays none of Miss Moneypenny's sang-froid as a stowed-away pacifist reporter. But no one stands a chance of making much impression alongside Donald Wolfit's risibly bombastic inventor. DP

Kieron Moore *Cmdr Michael Haydon* • Lois Maxwell *Kim Hamilton* • Donald Wolfit *Prof Merrity* • Bryan Forbes *Jimmy Wheeler* • Jimmy Hanley *Larry* • Thea Gregory *Barbara Noble* ■ *Dir* Paul Dickson • *Scr* Edith Dell, John Mather, JT McIntosh

Satisfaction ★★ 15

Drama 1988 · US · Colour · 89mins

Justine Bateman, Julia Roberts, Trini Alvarado and Britta Phillips are the four girls in a rock band who spend the summer playing music at a resort and trying to find eligible men. Club owner Liam Neeson is the older man Bateman falls for in this mediocre teenage tale, notable mainly for a cameo from Blondie singer Debbie Harry, and a chance to see a pre-stardom Roberts and Neeson. You know it's time these girls had their instruments confiscated when you hear Bateman's rendition of *(I Can't Get No) Satisfaction*. JB [video]

Justine Bateman *Jennie Lee* • Liam Neeson *Martin Falcon* • Julia Roberts *Daryle Shane* • Trini Alvarado *May "Mooch" Stark* • Britta Phillips *Billy Swan* • Scott Coffey *Nickie Longo* • Deborah Harry *Tina* ■ *Dir* Joan Freeman • *Scr* Charles Purpura

Saturday Night and Sunday Morning ★★★★★ PG

Classic drama 1960 · UK · BW · 85mins

Arthur Seaton was the only "kitchen sink" hero to accept that, while life was nasty, brutish and short, you had to make the best of it. And there was no one better to convey that complex mix of cynicism, laddishness and resignation than Albert Finney. Both he and Rachel Roberts won British Film Academy awards, while the film itself took the best British picture honour. Author Alan Sillitoe draws on his own experiences of factory life which are given a truly authentic ring by director Karel Reisz. For the first time, the working classes were treated with respect, not condescension. Finney's belligerence towards authority is as convincing as his touching tenderness towards the married woman (Roberts) he seduces, and, while he may not always live by his words – "What I want is a good time. The rest is all propaganda" – the film's affirmation that he can never really be beaten survives. DP [video] DVD

Albert Finney *Arthur Seaton* • Shirley Anne Field *Doreen Gretton* • Rachel Roberts (1) *Brenda* • Hylda Baker *Aunt Ada* • Norman Rossington *Bert* • Bryan Pringle *Jack* • Robert Cawdron *Robboe* ■ *Dir* Karel Reisz • *Scr* Alan Sillitoe, from his novel

Saturday Night at the Palace ★★★

Drama 1987 · S Afr · Colour · 88mins

Precious little South African cinema reaches this country, so Paul Slabolepszy's adaptation of his own much-praised play is all the more welcome. Unfortunately, the story of a broken-down footballer, whose drunken antics result in tragedy at an out-of-town burger bar, is a thoroughly predictable affair that rarely breaks out of its stage confines. Yet, there's undoubted power in the anti-apartheid rhetoric, and Slabolepszy himself gives a chilling performance revealing the ignorance and intolerance of the racist. DP. Contains violence and swearing.

Bill Flynn *Forcie* • John Kani *September* • Paul Slabolepszy *Vince* ■ *Dir* Robert Davies • *Scr* Paul Slabolepszy, Bill Flynn, from a play by Paul Slabolepszy

Saturday Night Fever ★★★★★ 18

Musical drama 1977 · US · Colour · 118mins

John Travolta's role here as Tony Manero, the bum from Brooklyn who becomes king of the New York disco scene, turned him from a B-list TV actor into, for a time, the hottest movie star in the world and a pop culture icon. Party-poopers may find the whole thing a cringeworthy period piece and a reminder that the 1970s really were the naffest decade. But most will sit back and enjoy the snazzy dancing (much of it with co-star Karen Lynn Gorney), the memorable soundtrack – featuring classic songs from the Bee Gees, Tavares and KC and the Sunshine Band – and the all-round, high energy entertainment. By contrast, the 1983 sequel, *Staying Alive*, is a near career-low for Travolta. PF. Contains violence, swearing, sex scenes and brief nudity. [video] DVD

John Travolta *Tony Manero* • Karen Lynn Gorney *Stephanie* • Barry Miller *Bobby C* • Joseph Cali *Joey* • Paul Pape *Double J* • Donna Pescow *Annette* • Bruce Ornstein *Gus* • Julie Bovasso *Flo* ■ *Dir* John Badham • *Scr* Norman Wexler, from the article *Tribal Rites of the New Saturday Night* by Nik Cohn • *Choreographer* Lester Wilson

The Saturday Night Kid ★★

Romantic comedy 1929 · US · BW · 62mins

With her scandalous off-screen antics escalating, Paramount's megastar Clara Bow would soon receive her exit visa from the studio. But she survived the transition to sound and here she is a department store assistant. Jean Arthur, playing Clara's sister, is the bigger vamp of the two and both girls have their sights set on James Hall. The script offers some snappy one-liners as well as the attraction of the leading ladies. Future sex symbol Jean Harlow has a bit part. RK

Clara Bow *Mayme* • James Hall *Bill* • Jean Arthur *Janie* • Charles Sellon *Lem Woodruff* • Ethel Wales *Ma Woodruff* • Frank Ross *Ken* • Edna May Oliver *Miss Streeter* • Jean Harlow *Hazel* ■ *Dir* A Edward Sutherland • *Scr* Lloyd Corrigan, Ethel Doherty, Edward E Paramore Jr, from the play *Love 'em and Leave 'em* by George Abbott, John VA Weaver

Saturday Night Out ★★★

Adventure 1963 · UK · BW · 96mins

This gritty, low-budget, black-and-white exploitation film was very daring in its day but wouldn't cause a stir now. The plot is negligible: five merchant seamen and their passenger spend a long day's leave in London, but it's the location charm and period cast that keep the movie watchable today. The nominal stars are the lovely sweet-faced Heather Sears, and that venerable old grouch Bernard Lee (James Bond's "M"). Francesca Annis and Colin Campbell also impress. TS

Heather Sears *Penny* • Bernard Lee *George Hudson* • Erika Remberg *Wanda* • Francesca Annis *Jean* • John Bonney *Lee* • Colin Campbell *Jamie* • Nigel Green *Paddy* • Vera Day *Arlene* • Freddie Mills *Joe* • David Lodge *Arthur* ■ *Dir* Robert Hartford-Davis • *Scr* Donald Ford, Derek Ford

Saturday the 14th ★ 15

Spoof horror 1981 · US · Colour · 72mins

Despite its title, this childish parody is more a monster-movie spoof than a send-up of slasher movies. Richard Benjamin and Paula Prentiss move into a haunted house where their son Kevin Brando opens an ancient book and a horde of monsters, aliens and vampires pop out eager to take up residence. There are some flashes of humour – a *Creature from the Black Lagoon* in the bubble bath – but for the most part this is a crudely produced rag-bag of sketches. AJ [video]

Richard Benjamin *John* • Paula Prentiss *Mary* • Severn Darden *Van Helsing* • Jeffrey Tambor *Waldemar* • Kari Michaelsen *Debbie* • Kevin Brando *Billy* • Rosemary DeCamp *Aunt Lucille* ■ *Dir* Howard R Cohen • *Scr* Howard R Cohen, from a story by Jeff Begun

Saturday the 14th Strikes Back ★ PG

Spoof horror 1988 · US · Colour · 75mins

Director Howard R Cohen clearly didn't learn from the mistakes of his original sub-standard spoof as this sequel is an even more pitiful parody. This time husband and wife Avery Schreiber and Patty McCormack move into a haunted house built over the entrance to Hell which cracks open and unleashes yet another surfeit of monsters, vampires and werewolves. Footage lifted from bad Roger Corman B-movies replaces the arch-satire of the first movie but with the same poor result. AJ [video]

Jason Presson *Eddie Baxter* • Ray Walston *Gramps* • Avery Schreiber *Frank* • Patty McCormack *Kate* • Julianne McNamara *Linda* • Rhonda Aldrich *Alice* • Daniel Will-Harris *Bert* ■ *Dir/Scr* Howard R Cohen

Saturday's Children ★★★

Drama 1940 · US · BW · 101mins

Young inventor John Garfield meets obstacles to his plans and dreams: marriage to ambitious Anne Shirley and the devastating effects of the Depression. Directed by Vincent Sherman with an excellent cast that includes Claude Rains, this was Garfield's successful bid to break out of the slum boy/crime movie mould. Its social concerns are clear but, like the era it explores, the movie is downbeat and depressing. RK

John Garfield *Rimes Rosson* • Anne Shirley *Bobby Halevy* • Claude Rains *Mr Halevy* • Lee Patrick *Florrie Sands* • George Tobias *Herbie Smith* • Roscoe Karns *Willie Sands* • Dennie Moore *Gertrude Mills* ■ *Dir* Vincent Sherman • *Scr* Julius J Epstein, Philip G Epstein, from the play by Maxwell Anderson

Saturn 3 ★★ 15

Science-fiction thriller
1980 · UK · Colour · 83mins

Kirk Douglas and Farrah Fawcett live an idyllic Adam and Eve existence in a synthetic food-making factory on Titan, the third moon of Saturn. Then along comes snake Harvey Keitel, a psychopath on the run from Earth, and his equally disturbed robot Hector. It was directed for two weeks by *Star Wars/Superman* production designer John Barry before Stanley Donen took over, but no amount of futuristic hardware or fantastic sets can improve the mass of contrivance. AJ [video] DVD

Farrah Fawcett *Alex* • Kirk Douglas *Adam* • Harvey Keitel *Benson* • Douglas Lambert *Captain James* • Ed Bishop *Harding* ■ *Dir* Stanley Donen • *Scr* Martin Amis, from a story by John Barry

Satyamev Jayate ★★★ 15

Crime thriller 1987 · Ind · Colour · 148mins

Director Raj Sippy's epic crime thriller follows the trials and tribulations of a dedicated police officer, who's desperately trying to pick up the pieces of his life following the accidental killing of a young boy. Vinay Shukla's screenplay remains faithful to the genre and, as a result, contains few surprises. RT. In Hindi with English subtitles. [video] DVD

Vinod Khanna • Meenakshi Seshadri • Madhavi ■ *Dir* Raj Sippy • *Scr* Vinay Shukla

Satyricon ★★★★ 18

Historical fantasy drama
1969 · Fr/It · Colour · 124mins

Federico Fellini received an Oscar nomination for best director for this deliriously surreal moving fresco of ancient Rome. This is *La Dolce Vita* out of Petronius by way of Pasolini and DeMille, with the antics of Nero's empire being used to comment on contemporary godlessness. The adventures of squabbling hedonists Martin Potter and Hiram Keller don't matter a fig beside the debauchery and depravity, which for all their excess are not that divorced from historical reality. Over-indulgence, indiscipline and sexual immaturity are the usual accusations hurled at this hellish vision, but few film-makers would have had the courage to make it. DP. In Italian with English subtitles. [video] DVD

Martin Potter *Encolpius* • Hiram Keller *Ascyltus* • Salvo Randone *Eumolpus* • Max Born *Giton* • Fanfulla *Vernacchio* • Mario Romagnoli *Trimalchio* • Capucine *Tryphaena* • Alain Cuny *Lichas* ■ *Dir* Federico Fellini • *Scr* Federico Fellini, Bernardino Zapponi, Brunello Rondi, from the novel by Gaius Petronius

The Savage ★★ U

Western 1953 · US · Colour · 94mins

Charlton Heston was the sole star of his fourth Hollywood film. He makes a sturdy job of portraying the white man

S

raised by the Sioux who becomes an army scout, trusted by neither side. As conflict threatens, he has to decide where his loyalties lie. Blandly directed by George Marshall, the western is far too long and the way the Heston character is handled at the end smacks of box-office compromise. AE

Charlton Heston *Warbonnet/Jim Ahern* • Susan Morrow *Tally Hathersall* • Peter Hanson *Lt Weston Hathersall* • Joan Taylor *Luta* • Richard Rober *Capt Arnold Vaugant* ■ *Dir* George Marshall • *Scr* Sydney Boehm, from the novel *The Renegade* by LL Foreman

Savage Dawn ★ 18

Action drama 1985 · US · Colour · 98mins

It's an unwritten rule among film critics that movies with titles that start with the word "savage" are invariably awful. *Savage Dawn* confirms it beyond any reasonable doubt. Ploughing the same furrow as a thousand other B-movies, it's the violent, foul-mouthed tale of a biker gang that takes over a small desert town. The major mystery is how such tosh managed to attract a half-decent cast. DA [video]

George Kennedy *Tick Rand* • Richard Lynch *Reverend Romano* • Karen Black *Rachel* • Lance Henriksen *Ben Stryker* • Claudia Udy *Kate Rand* • Bill Forsythe [William Forsythe] *Pigiron* • Leo Gordon *Sheriff* ■ *Dir* Simon Nuchtern • *Scr* William P Milling

The Savage Eye ★★

Drama documentary 1959 · US · BW · 66mins

This part-documentary offers a sour and biased view of urban American life, built around Barbara Baxley as a new arrival in a big city, alone and unhappy in a hostile environment. Individual sequences provide a depressing picture of people on their worst behaviour – watching wrestlers and strippers – or at their most gullible and ridiculous, flocking to faith healers and undergoing cosmetic surgery and beauty treatments. Overlaid on the visuals is a pretentious dialogue between the woman and a poet (voiced by Gary Merrill). Made over four years – often with hidden cameras – this gained a wide art house release. AE

Barbara Baxley *Judith McGuire* • Gary Merrill *The poet* • Herschel Bernardi *Kirtz* ■ *Dir/Scr* Ben Maddow, Sidney Myers, Joseph Strick

Savage Harvest ★★★ 15

Adventure drama 1981 · US · Colour · 82mins

This Kenyan-set adventure has an intriguing premise: Michelle Phillips and children are cornered on a plantation by a group of starving lions, but these are no ordinary lions, they exhibit seemingly preternatural intelligence in their tactics. Safari guide (and Phillips ex-husband) Tom Skerritt comes to the rescue. The film never fully capitalises on the potential offered, but it has its moments. RT [video]

Tom Skerritt *Casey* • Michelle Phillips *Maggie* • Shawn Stevens *Jon* • Anne-Marie Martin *Wendy* • Derek Partridge *Derek* • Arthur Malet *Dr MacGruder* • Tana Helfer *Kristie* ■ *Dir* Robert Collins • *Scr* Robert Collins, Robert Blees, from a story by Ralph Helfer, Ken Noyle

The Savage Innocents ★★

Adventure drama
1960 · It /Fr/UK · Colour · 107mins

What started out as a sort of *Nanook of the North*-style look at Inuit culture, with Anthony Quinn in fur and full ethnic mode, was apparently plagued by production problems. These included Peter O'Toole's Mountie sporting his original nose but not his original voice, which was dubbed against the actor's wishes. Quinn makes a creditable attempt at portraying the harsh Inuit lifestyle – hunting, fishing, watching polar bears – but even he can't save this oddity from director Nicholas Ray. AT

Anthony Quinn *Inuk* • Yoko Tani *Asiak* • Marie Yang *Powtee* • Peter O'Toole *First Trooper* • Carlo Giustini *Second Trooper* • Kaida Horiuchi *Imina* ■ *Dir* Nicholas Ray • *Scr* Nicholas Ray, Hans Ruesch, Franco Solinas, from the novel *Top of the World* by Hans Ruesch

The Savage Is Loose ★

Adventure drama
1974 · US · Colour · 115mins

Directed, produced by and starring George C Scott, this is a tale of incest between mother and son after they've been stranded on a desert island with father for some years. Trish Van Devere (Scott's then wife) and John David Carson feature in a story that plumbs the shallows rather ineptly and does Scott's reputation no good. TH

George C Scott *John* • Trish Van Devere *Maida* • John David Carson *David* • Lee H Montgomery [Lee Montgomery] *Young David* ■ *Dir* George C Scott • *Scr* Max Ehrlich, Frank De Felitta

Savage Islands ★★ PG

Swashbuckling adventure
1983 · US/NZ · Colour · 95mins

This has to be a low point in the rollercoaster career of Tommy Lee Jones, who didn't get real recognition until his award-winning turn as the US marshal hunting Harrison Ford in *The Fugitive*. Belonging to the bygone age of Saturday morning pictures, this bloodless romp has Jones as a crusty rogue helping missionary Michael O'Keefe to rescue fiancée Jenny Seagrove from the pirates who've kidnapped her. It's a case of all buckle and no swash. DA [video]

Tommy Lee Jones *Captain "Bully" Hayes* • Michael O'Keefe *Nathaniel Williamson* • Jenny Seagrove *Sophie* • Max Phipps *Ben Pease* • Grant Tilly *Count Von Rittenberg* • Peter Rowley *Louis Beck* • Bill Johnson *Reverend Williamson* ■ *Dir* Ferdinand Fairfax • *Scr* John Hughes, David Odell, from a screenplay (unproduced) by David Odell and a story by Lloyd Phillips

Savage Messiah ★★★

Romantic drama 1972 · UK · Colour · 96mins

After the excesses of *The Music Lovers* and *The Devils*, director Ken Russell handled the platonic love affair between sculptor Henri Gaudier and his muse Sophie Brzeska, with pleasing restraint (apart from a couple of unnecessary song and dance numbers). Set in Paris and London prior to the First World War, Dorothy Tutin and newcomer Scott Antony give superb, impassioned performances as the seemingly ill-matched couple. DM

Dorothy Tutin *Sophie Brzeska* • Scott Antony *Henri Gaudier-Brzeska* • Helen Mirren *Gosh Smith-Boyle* • Lindsay Kemp *Angus Corky* • Peter Vaughan *Louvre attendant* • Michael Gough *Mons Gaudier* ■ *Dir* Ken Russell • *Scr* Christopher Logue, from a book by HS Ede • *Production Designer* Derek Jarman

Savage Sam ★★ PG

Western 1963 · US · Colour · 103mins

This is a hugely disappointing sequel to the popular doggy tale, *Old Yeller*. The story focuses on Yeller's son, Savage Sam, who leads Brian Keith to the Indian camp where brothers Tommy Kirk and Kevin Corcoran and their neighbour Marta Kristen, are being held hostage. The brutal battle at the end of the film might be a little strong for younger children, but most parents will be slightly concerned at the stereotypical depiction of the native Americans. DP [video]

Brian Keith *Uncle Beck Coates* • Tommy Kirk *Travis Coates* • Kevin Corcoran *Arliss Coates* • Dewey Martin *Lester White* • Jeff York *Bud Searcy* • Marta Kristen *Lisbeth Searcy* ■ *Dir* Norman Tokar • *Scr* Fred Gipson, William Tunberg, from a book by Fred Gipson

Savage Streets ★★ 18

Action drama 1984 · US · Colour · 80mins

Following her appearance in *The Exorcist*, Linda Blair made a career out of trashy exploitation flicks. She stars as a typical LA girl who turns into "Charles Bronson in a dress" when her deaf mute sister is raped by a gang of lowlife punks. Linda leads her all-girl gang against those responsible, armed with such niceties as bear traps and a crossbow. Blair's not bad, but she is swamped by the vulgar dialogue and gratuitous violence. RS [video]

Linda Blair *Brenda* • John Vernon *Principal Underwood* • Robert Dryer *Jake* • Johnny Venocur *Vince* • Sal Landi *Fargo* • Scott Mayer *Red* ■ *Dir* Danny Steinmann • *Scr* Norman Yonemoto, Danny Steinmann

Savages ★★ 15

Satirical comedy
1972 · US · Colour, Sepia and BW · 101mins

James Ivory returned to his native America for this heavy-handed Buñuelian parable on the thin line between savagery and sophistication. The arch nature of the enterprise – in which human-sacrificing primitives are guided by a croquet ball into a country manor, where they briefly assume the trappings of gentility – is only emphasised by Walter Lassally's decision to photograph the Mud People's progression and inevitable regression in monochrome, sepia and lavish colour. The cast works hard and the attempt to encapsulate the history of civilisation in the various antics and anecdotes is laudable. DP [video] DVD

Lewis J Stadlen *Julian Branch* • Anne Francine *Carlotta* • Thayer David *Otto Nurder* • Susan Blakely *Cecily* • Russ Thacker *Andrew* • Salome Jens *Emily Penning* • Margaret Brewster *Lady Cora* • Neil Fitzgerald *Sir Harry* ■ *Dir* James Ivory • *Scr* James Ivory, Michael O'Donoghue, George Swift Trow, from an idea by James Ivory

Savannah Smiles ★★ PG

Comedy drama 1982 · US · Colour · 99mins

Bridgette Andersen runs away from her uncaring politician father and makes the mistake of hiding in the car of two not-so-bright crooks. The duo decide to hold her to ransom, but gradually become more like surrogate parents than opportunistic kidnappers as the police close in. Written by co-star Mark Miller, this winsome comedy thriller throws some fresh comic twists into the plot to stop it becoming too mechanical and manipulative. AJ [video]

Mark Miller *Alvie* • Donovan Scott *Boots* • Bridgette Andersen *Savannah Driscoll* • Peter Graves (2) *Harland Dobbs* • Chris Robinson *Richard Driscoll* • Michael Parks *Lt Savage* • Barbara Stanger *Joan Driscoll* ■ *Dir* Pierre DeMoro • *Scr* Mark Miller

Save the Green Planet! ★★★ 18

Science-fiction comedy drama
2003 · S Kor · Colour · 117mins

Although it adopts a magpie approach to its visuals and plumps for a plot twist that undoes much of its early good work, Jang Jun-hwan's ambitious debut is still a crafty combination of offbeat comedy, B-movie sci-fi and macabre thriller. Shin Ha-gyun excels as the movie-mad crank whose conviction that Earth is about to be invaded by aliens from Andromeda prompts him to kidnap industrial tycoon Baek Yun-shik. But, as eccentric cop Lee Jae-yong begins to investigate the abduction, an alternative motive for Shin's actions emerges and the tone becomes increasingly sombre. DP. In Korean with English subtitles. Contains violence. DVD

Shin Ha-gyun *Lee Byeong-Gu* • Baek Yun-shik *Kang Man-Shik* • Hwang Jeong-min *Su-ni* • Lee Jae-yong *Inspector Choo* • Lee Ju-hyeon *Inspector Kim* ■ *Dir/Scr* Jang Jun-hwan

Save the Last Dance ★★★ 12

Musical drama 2000 · US · Colour · 108mins

Julia Stiles is the aspiring ballerina who gives up her ambitions after her beloved mother dies in a car crash while speeding to an important audition. She goes to live with her estranged jazz musician father on Chicago's depressed South Side, where she finds herself part of the minority in a mainly black school, coping with racial slurs when she starts dating model student Sean Patrick Thomas. With its optimistic view of ghetto life, this is fantasy melodrama pure and simple. AJ. Contains swearing, violence. [video] DVD

Julia Stiles *Sara Johnson* • Sean Patrick Thomas *Derek* • Kerry Washington *Chenille* • Fredro Starr *Malakai* • Terry Kinney *Roy* • Bianca Lawson *Nikki* ■ *Dir* Thomas Carter • *Scr* Duane Adler, Cheryl Edwards, from a story by Duane Adler

Save the Tiger ★★★

Drama 1973 · US · Colour · 100mins

Jack Lemmon stars as a struggling Los Angeles garment manufacturer who contemplates burning down his factory in order to claim the insurance and pay off his debts. This drama about the consumer rat race is bludgeoning rather than hard-hitting, and Lemmon's role seems very much in the tradition of Arthur Miller's Willy Loman in *Death of a Salesman*. Though it won Lemmon a best actor Oscar, he has given far better performances in films such as *The Apartment*. AT. Contains swearing.

Jack Lemmon *Harry Stoner* • Jack Gilford *Phil Greene* • Laurie Heineman *Myra* • Norman Burton *Fred Mirrell* • Patricia Smith *Janet Stoner* • Thayer David *Charlie Robbins* • William Hansen *Meyer* ■ *Dir* John G Avildsen • *Scr* Steve Shagan

Saved! ★★★ 12

Comedy 2004 · US · Colour · 88mins

All the high-school stereotypes may be present in this teen movie, but the setting makes it an original. American Eagle High is a strict Christian school with a trendy preacher as principal, where discovering that you're pregnant or gay will get you sent for moral re-education or "degayification". Brian Dannelly's debut movie is, for its first two thirds at least, a scabrous look at the intolerance and hypocrisy of some fundamentalists. The cast is uniformly likeable and the screenplay delivers sharp dialogue and a host of good jokes, but it pulls its punches at the end. AS [video] DVD

Jena Malone *Mary* • Mandy Moore *Hilary Faye* • Macaulay Culkin *Roland* • Patrick Fugit *Patrick* • Heather Matarazzo *Tia* • Eva Amurri *Cassandra* • Martin Donovan (2) *Pastor Skip* • Mary-Louise Parker *Lillian* ■ *Dir* Brian Dannelly • *Scr* Brian Dannelly, Michael Urban

Saving Grace ★★ PG

Comedy drama 1985 · US · Colour · 106mins

The essential decency of Tom Conti just about holds this fragile fable together. As a Pope who slips out of the Vatican to minister to people who truly need him, he wrinkles his brow and smiles sadly with a concern that convinces in a situation that doesn't. Director Robert M Young shoots the southern Italian countryside with the glossy eye of a postcard photographer, while Joaquin Montana's script is overly dependent on easy solutions and glib platitudes. For all its good

S

intentions, this is more of a penance than a pleasure. DP

Tom Conti *Pope Leo XIV* • Fernando Rey *Cardinal Stefano Biondi* • Erland Josephson *Monsignor Francesco Ghezzi* • Giancarlo Giannini *Abalardi* • Donald Hewlett *Monsignor Colin McGee* • Edward James Olmos *Ciolino* ■ *Dir* Robert M Young • *Scr* Joaquin Montana, from the novel by Celia Gittelson

Saving Grace ★★ PG

Comedy 2000 · UK · Colour · 88mins

Brenda Blethyn is the eponymous Grace, a recently widowed housewife whose late husband has left her with a mountain of debts to pay. The only way to keep her beautiful Cornish mansion is to grow marijuana with the aid of her Scottish handyman, Craig Ferguson. The screenplay is more juvenile than risqué and makes tittering pot-shots at the expense of characterisation and plot development. NS DVD

Brenda Blethyn *Grace* • Craig Ferguson *Matthew* • Martin Clunes *Dr Bamford* • Tcheky Karyo *Jacques* • Jamie Foreman *China* • Bill Bailey (2) *Vince* • Valerie Edmond *Nicky* • Diana Quick *Honey* • Leslie Phillips *Vicar* ■ *Dir* Nigel Cole • *Scr* Craig Ferguson, Mark Crowdy, from a story by Mark Crowdy

Saving Private Ryan ★★★★ 15

Second World War drama
1998 · US · Colour · 162mins

With this Oscar-winning attempt to reshape the past through fiction, Steven Spielberg comes closer than ever before to depicting historical truth. The action opens brutally with a wrenching re-creation of the Second World War D-Day landing on Omaha beach. Spielberg and cinematographer Janusz Kaminski succeed in capturing the terrifying and bewildering chaos of the encounter. Yet, away from the fighting, this occasionally lapses into combat picture cliché, but this is still well-meaning, strongly acted and slickly mounted. DP. Contains violence, language and horror. DVD

Tom Hanks *Captain Miller* • Tom Sizemore *Sergeant Horvath* • Edward Burns *Private Reiben* • Barry Pepper *Private Jackson* • Adam Goldberg *Private Mellish* • Vin Diesel *Private Caparzo* • Giovanni Ribisi *T/4 Medic Wade* • Jeremy Davies *Corporal Upham* • Matt Damon *Private Ryan* • Ted Danson *Captain Hamill* • Kathleen Byron *Old Mrs Ryan* ■ *Dir* Steven Spielberg • *Scr* Robert Rodat • *Editor* Michael Kahn

Savior ★★★★ 18

War drama 1997 · US · Colour · 99mins

This Yugoslavian-set tale of cruelty still carries a haunting and shocking impact. Mercenary Dennis Quaid joins the Foreign Legion after his wife and child are killed by Islamic terrorists. While fighting on the Serbian side against the Muslims, circumstances throw him together with a pregnant rape victim and he begins to regain his humanity in the face of Bosnian atrocities. Serbian director Peter Antonijevic draws on his personal experiences to devastating effect and comes up with a grim, but poignant end product of rare emotional depth. AJ. Contains swearing, violence. DVD

Dennis Quaid *Joshua Rose/Guy* • Nastassja Kinski *Maria Rose* • Stellan Skarsgård *Peter* • Natasa Ninkovic *Vera* • Pascal Rollin *Paris Priest* ■ *Dir* Peter Antonijevic • *Scr* Robert Orr • *Producer* Oliver Stone

Saviors of the Forest ★★★

Documentary 1992 · US · Colour · 75mins

Taking their cue from Michael Moore, those self-styled "video warriors", director Bill Day and writer Terry Schwartz cast a satirical eye over the world of eco-politics in this mischievous, yet still highly perceptive investigation into the battle to save the Ecuadorian rainforest. Wryly exploring the paradoxes inherent in environmental crusading, the "camera Guys" unashamedly throw in their lot with the local "colonos", whose agricultural needs often bring them into conflict with both big business and the green lobby. They also highlight the culpability of Hollywood, which shoots impassioned eco-dramas on sets built from rainforest timber. DP

Dir Bill Day • *Scr* Terry Schwartz

Saw ★★★★ 18

Horror thriller 2004 · US · Colour · 98mins

This well-acted thriller chillingly questions how far an individual will go to stay alive. Leigh Whannell (who also wrote the screenplay) and Cary Elwes become the latest playthings of a game-obsessed psychopath, finding themselves chained to opposite walls in a crumbling, subterranean bathroom, with no recollection of how they got there. With its jerky, grainy cinematography and nerve-jangling industrial soundtrack, the film is more disturbing than terrifying. However, just when you think you've got it sussed, the movie throws in some audacious twists. SF. Contains violence and swearing. DVD

Cary Elwes *Dr Lawrence Gordon* • Leigh Whannell *Adam* • Danny Glover *Detective David Tapp* • Monica Potter *Alison Gordon* • Dina Meyer *Kerry* • Tobin Bell *John* • Michael Emerson *Zep Hindle* ■ *Dir* James Wan • *Scr* Leigh Whannell, from a story by James Wan, Leigh Whannell

Sawdust and Tinsel ★★★★

Drama 1953 · Swe · BW · 94mins

This symbolic circus drama is now recognised as a landmark in Ingmar Bergman's film career. While the narrative seems similarly fractured (with its bleached out flashback to clown Anders Ek's humiliation before a platoon of mocking soldiers and a Freudian dream sequence), there is an artistic unity about this tale of ageing ringmaster, Ake Grönberg, whose encounter with the wife he deserted, almost costs him the love of his mistress, Harriet Andersson. DP. In Swedish with English subtitles.

Harriet Andersson *Anne* • Ake Grönberg *Albert Johansson* • Hakke Ekman *Frans* • Anders Ek *Frost* • Annika Tretow *Agda, Albert's wife* ■ *Dir/Scr* Ingmar Bergman • *Cinematographer* Sven Nykvist, Bladh Hilding

The Saxon Charm ★★★

Drama 1948 · US · BW · 88mins

Stage producer Robert Montgomery, an arrogant, amoral egomaniac and bully, causes misery to all who come into his orbit – particularly writer John Payne, whose play he is preparing to stage, Payne's wife Susan Hayward, his own girlfriend Audrey Totter and wealthy backer Harry Von Zell. Reputedly based on Broadway's notoriously unpleasant Jed Harris, this is interesting niche-market stuff for backstage aficionados; it carries an alarming ring of truth, but it's lacking in edge. RK

Robert Montgomery *Matt Saxon* • Susan Hayward *Janet Busch* • John Payne *Eric Busch* • Audrey Totter *Alma Wragg* • Henry Morgan [Harry Morgan] *Hermy* • Harry Von Zell *Zack Humber* • Cara Williams *Dolly Humber* • Chill Wills *Captain Chatham* • Heather Angel *Vivian Saxon* ■ *Dir* Claude Binyon • *Scr* Claude Binyon, from the novel by Frederic Wakeman

Say Anything... ★★★ 15

Comedy drama 1989 · US · Colour · 96mins

Not deemed worthy of a UK cinema release, this little gem from Cameron Crowe is a cleverly formatted teenage romance in which nothing is quite as it seems. John Cusack stars as an underachieving student who falls for Ione Skye, "Miss Priss", the brain of the class, but meets opposition from her divorced dad (John Mahoney). TS. Contains swearing. DVD

John Cusack *Lloyd Dobler* • Ione Skye *Diane Court* • John Mahoney *James Court* • Lili Taylor *Corey Flood* • Amy Brooks *D C* • Pamela Segall *Rebecca* • Jason Gould *Mike Cameron* • Bebe Neuwirth *Mrs Evans* • Eric Stoltz *Vahlere* ■ *Dir/Scr* Cameron Crowe

Say Hello to Yesterday ★

Comedy 1971 · UK · Colour · 91mins

The beautiful and witty Jean Simmons is the only reason to watch this dreadful, Swinging Sixties effort. Simmons plays a bored housewife from the stockbroker belt who takes the train to London and is hounded by a young dropout (Leonard Whiting). This is *Brief Encounter* in the style of *Blow-Up*, taking a tourist's-eye view of London before settling down to its chaste sex scene and Antonioni-esque finale of cold alienation. AT

Jean Simmons *Woman* • Leonard Whiting *Boy* • Evelyn Laye *Woman's mother* • John Lee *Woman's husband* • Jack Woolgar *Boy's father* • Constance Chapman *Boy's mother* • Gwen Nelson *Char* ■ *Dir* Alvin Rakoff • *Scr* Alvin Rakoff, Peter King, from a story by Ray Mathew, Alvin Rakoff

Say It Isn't So ★ 15

Romantic comedy
2001 · US · Colour · 91mins

The Farrelly brothers, though only producers here, have finally gone too far. This is a gratuitously graphic and unwelcome addition to the type of crude comedy that has been so successful for them in recent years. Chris Klein and Heather Graham, both misused here, play a pair of lovers whose affair is halted by speculation that they are brother and sister. This goes beyond decency, which is one thing, but it's not even funny. LH. Contains swearing. DVD

Chris Klein *Gilbert "Gilly" Noble* • Heather Graham *Josephine "Jo" Wingfield* • Orlando Jones *Dig McCaffey* • Sally Field *Valdine Wingfield* • Richard Jenkins *Walter Wingfield* • John Rothman *Larry Falwell* • Jack Plotnick *Leon Pitofsky* ■ *Dir* JB Rogers [James B Rogers] • *Scr* Peter Gaulke, Gerry Swallow

Say It with Songs ★★

Musical drama 1929 · US · BW · 95mins

Soon after the sound-breaking *The Jazz Singer*, Al Jolson embarked on this miscalculated musical drama, co-written by Darryl F Zanuck. Jolson plays a radio singer imprisoned for manslaughter and yearning for his wife and small boy. It's obvious lump-in-the-throat stuff but almost ends up as a joke with the song *Little Pal* trying to be another *Sonny Boy*. TH

Al Jolson *Joe Lane* • Davey Lee *Little Pal* • Marian Nixon *Katherine Lane* • Fred Kohler *Joe's cellmate* • Holmes Herbert *Dr Robert Merrill* • John Bowers *Surgeon* ■ *Dir* Lloyd Bacon • *Scr* Joseph Jackson, from a story by Darryl F Zanuck, Harvey Gates

Say One for Me ★★ U

Musical comedy 1959 · US · BW · 119mins

As his film career faded, ageing crooner Bing Crosby here plays a cleric in charge of a Broadway church for showbiz folk. Alas, this overlong and thinly-scripted affair bears no comparison with Crosby's earlier hits playing a priest, and Frank Tashlin was the wrong man to direct. Debbie Reynolds, like Crosby, has to struggle with both the script and weak musical material, as well as a colourless romantic partner in Robert Wagner. TV

Bing Crosby *Father Conroy* • Debbie Reynolds *Holly LaMaise* • Robert Wagner *Tony Vincent* • Ray Walston *Phil Stanley* • Les Tremayne *Harry LaMaise* • Connie Gilchrist *Mary Manning* • Frank McHugh *Jim Dugan* ■ *Dir* Frank Tashlin • *Scr* Robert O'Brien

Sayonara ★★★ PG

Drama 1957 · US · Colour · 141mins

Marlon Brando's electric acting, not to mention sturdy contributions from Miyoshi Umeki and Red Buttons (both of whom scooped Oscars), forms an almost other-worldly contrast to the travelogue blandness of Joshua Logan's direction. With Brando capably holding centre screen as the Korean War soldier in Japan, and in love, Logan's scenic tendencies are occasionally interrupted by some proper art direction, the quality of which also merited an Oscar. The lovely theme song by Irving Berlin is haunting. JM DVD

Marlon Brando *Major Lloyd "Ace" Gruver* • Ricardo Montalban *Nakamura* • Red Buttons *Joe Kelly* • Patricia Owens *Eileen Webster* • Martha Scott *Mrs Webster* • James Garner *Captain Mike Bailey* • Miyoshi Umeki *Katsumi* ■ *Dir* Joshua Logan • *Scr* Paul Osborn, from the novel by James A Michener • *Art Director* Ted Haworth • *Set Designer* Robert Priestley

Scalawag ★

Adventure 1973 · US/It · Colour · 92mins

For his first film as a director, Kirk Douglas chose to remodel *Treasure Island* as a landlocked yarn. Set in Mexico, Douglas is the one-legged pirate, trying to get his hands on treasure hidden by his former colleagues. Mark Lester is the cute kid who brings out his paternal qualities, and Danny DeVito has a small part. A catastrophe. AT

Kirk Douglas *Peg* • Mark Lester (2) *Jamie* • Neville Brand *Brimstone/Mudhook* • Lesley-Anne Down *Lucy-Ann* • Don Stroud *Velvet* • Danny DeVito *Flyspeck* • Mel Blanc *Barfly the parrot* ■ *Dir* Kirk Douglas • *Scr* Albert Maltz, Sid Fleischman, from the story by Robert Louis Stevenson

The Scalphunters ★★★ PG

Comedy western 1968 · US · Colour · 99mins

Released at the height of civil rights awareness in America, this is an intelligent and highly enjoyable western. If director Sydney Pollack presses home his points about racial tolerance with a heavy hand, he nevertheless coaxes spirited performances from his big-name cast. Trapper Burt Lancaster and runaway slave Ossie Davis play off each other to good effect, but the real sparks fly when scalphunter Telly Savalas and his mistress Shelley Winters are on the screen. DP DVD

Burt Lancaster *Joe Bass* • Shelley Winters *Kate* • Telly Savalas *Jim Howie* • Ossie Davis *Joseph Winfield Lee* • Armando Silvestre *Two Crows* • Dan Vadis *Yuma* • Dabney Coleman *Jed* ■ *Dir* Sydney Pollack • *Scr* William Norton, from his story

The Scamp ★★

Drama 1957 · UK · BW · 88mins

Having made his name in the Australian-set drama *Smiley*, contemporary critics had high hopes for ten-year-old Colin Petersen. He tries hard in this well intentioned story of a delinquent given a second chance, but he never convinces either as the urchin son of alcoholic music-hall actor Terence Morgan or as the confused kid cajoled by teacher Richard Attenborough and his wife Dorothy Alison. Attenborough overdoes the bourgeois benevolence. DP

Richard Attenborough *Stephen Leigh* • Colin Petersen *Tod Dawson* • Dorothy Alison *Barbara Leigh* • Terence Morgan *Mike Dawson* • Jill Adams *Julie Dawson* • Maureen Delaney *Mrs Perryman* • Margaretta Scott *Mrs Blundell*

• David Franks *Eddie* ■ *Dir* Wolf Rilla • *Scr* Wolf Rilla, from the play *Uncertain Joy* by Charlotte Hastings

Scandal ★★★ 18

Drama based on a true story
1988 · UK · Colour · 108mins

This is a by-the-numbers reconstruction of the Profumo affair, a scandal that contributed to the downfall of the Conservative government in 1964. Joanne Whalley-Kilmer makes a fine Christine Keeler and John Hurt a suitably shallow Stephen Ward. But it's Bridget Fonda who steals the show with her spot-on impersonation of Mandy Rice-Davies. Rather tame in the sleaze department, despite all the hype over the "orgy" scenes, but the Swinging Sixties era is neatly evoked. AJ. Contains violence, swearing, sex scenes and nudity.

John Hurt *Stephen Ward* • Joanne Whalley-Kilmer [Joanne Whalley] *Christine Keeler* • Bridget Fonda *Mandy Rice-Davies* • Ian McKellen *John Profumo* • Leslie Phillips *Lord Astor* • Britt Ekland *Mariella Novotny* • Daniel Massey *Mervyn Griffith-Jones* • Roland Gift *Johnnie Edgecombe* • Jean Alexander *Mrs Keeler* • Jeroen Krabbé *Eugene Ivanov* ■ *Dir* Michael Caton-Jones • *Scr* Michael Thomas, from the book *Nothing But* by Christine Keeler, Sandy Fawkes; the book *Mandy* by Mandy Rice-Davies, Shirley Flack; the book *Stephen Ward Speaks* by Warwick Charlton; the book *The Profumo Affair: a Summing Up* by Judge Sparrow; and the book *Scandal '63* by Clive Irving, Ron Hall, Jeremy Wallington

Scandal at Scourie ★★ U

Drama 1953 · US · Colour · 89mins

Walter Pidgeon, leading political, business and religious light of the Protestant community at Scourie – a small town in Canada – reluctantly allows his childless wife Greer Garson to adopt a little girl from a Catholic orphanage that has burnt down. The nuns extract a promise that the child (Donna Corcoran) will be raised a Catholic, and the situation is used as ammunition by Pidgeon's political rivals to discredit him. Directed by Jean Negulesco, this over-plotted, simplistic, anti-bigotry morality tale was the last outing for the once potent Pidgeon–Garson partnership. RK

Greer Garson *Mrs Patrick J McChesney* • Walter Pidgeon *Patrick J McChesney* • Donna Corcoran *Patsy* • Agnes Moorehead *Sister Josephine* • Arthur Shields *Father Reilly* ■ *Dir* Jean Negulesco • *Scr* Norman Corwin, Leonard Spigelgass, Karl Tunberg, from a story by Mary McSherry

Scandalous ★ 15

Comedy thriller 1983 · US · Colour · 88mins

As a TV reporter up to his neck in murder, Robert Hays shows flashes of the talent that made him such a hit in the *Airplane!* spoofs, but he doesn't stand a chance with a script so utterly bereft of ideas. John Gielgud does little for his reputation as a master of disguise, but what's most scandalous is that this unfunny mess was shot by cinematographer Jack Cardiff. DP. Contains nudity and swearing.

Robert Hays *Frank Swedlin* • John Gielgud *Uncle Willie* • Pamela Stephenson *Fiona Maxwell Sayle* • M Emmet Walsh *Simon Reynolds* • Nancy Wood *Lindsay Manning* • Conover Kennard *Francine Swedlin* ■ *Dir* Rob Cohen • *Scr* Rob Cohen, John Byrum, from a story by Larry Cohen, Rob Cohen, John Byrum

Scandalous John ★★★ U

Comedy western
1971 · US · Colour · 109mins

Nice nostalgia piece, with grizzled Brian Keith excellent as an eccentric rancher who is wild about the west. He is touchingly trying to keep to cowboy ways in a world that's long since consigned them to history, and even cattle-drives a single steer. Predictably, though, engaging pottiness brings him into conflict with the authorities. Elegiac and moving, with more than a few laughs, the film also benefits from familiar cowboy-film faces among the supporting cast. DA

Brian Keith *John McCanless* • Alfonso Arau *Paco Martinez* • Michele Carey *Amanda McCanless* • Rick Lenz *Jimmy Whittaker* • Harry Morgan *Sheriff Pippin* • Simon Oakland *Barton Whittaker* • Bill Williams *Sheriff Hart* • Christopher Dark *Card dealer* • John Ritter *Wendell* ■ *Dir* Robert Butler • *Scr* Bill Walsh, Don DaGradi, from a book by Richard Gardner

Scanner Cop ★★★ 18

Science-fiction horror
1994 · US · Colour · 90mins

The fourth entry in the *Scanners* series gets a boost with its change in locale (moving from Canada to LA) and introduces a new psychic hero, who happens to be a police officer. Scanner cop Daniel Quinn is on the trail of bad guy Richard Lynch, a scientist with a grudge against policemen. Lynch is fun as usual, hypnotising innocent people into killing cops in his usual hammy fashion, and the whole movie is executed with zip. A further sequel, know both as *Scanner Cop 2* and *Scanners: the Showdown*, was released in 1995. KB

Daniel Quinn *Samuel Staziak* • Darlanne Fluegel *Dr Joan Alden* • Richard Lynch *Glock* • Hilary Shepard *Zena* • Richard Grove *Commander Peter Harrigan* ■ *Dir* Pierre David • *Scr* George Saunders, John Bryant

Scanners ★★★★ 18

Science-fiction horror
1980 · Can · Colour · 102mins

Evil Michael Ironside and derelict Stephen Lack are the leaders of two rival groups of telepaths in this modern horror classic from David Cronenberg. The Canadian director seamlessly blends science fiction and conspiracy thriller into an exhilarating ride and, while the stunning (and occasionally stomach-churning) set pieces and the final apocalyptic battle will delight genre fans, it's Cronenberg's fascination with the horrors lurking within the human body and our inability to control them that provides the real interest in this landmark movie. JF. Contains violence. DVD

Stephen Lack *Cameron Vale* • Jennifer O'Neill *Kim Obrist* • Patrick McGoohan *Dr Paul Ruth* • Lawrence Dane *Braedon Keller* • Charles Shamata [Chuck Shamata] *Gaudi* • Adam Ludwig *Arno Crostic* • Michael Ironside *Darryl Revok* • Victor Desy *Dr Gatineau* ■ *Dir/Scr* David Cronenberg

Scanners II: The New Order ★★ 18

Science-fiction horror
1991 · Can · Colour · 99mins

This lacks the thought-provoking script of Cronenberg's original *Scanners*, opting for a more conventional and exploitable story. David Hewlett is the naive "scanner" recruited by police chief Yvan Ponton on the pretext of helping out the city. Director Christian Duguay (in his movie debut) brings more style and a much slicker look to the movie, and never allows the pacing to falter for long. KB

David Hewlett *David Kellum* • Deborah Raffin *Julie Vale* • Yvan Ponton *Commander John Forrester* • Isabelle Mejias *Alice Leonardo* • Tom Butler *Doctor Morse* • Raoul Trujillo *Drak* • Vlasta Vrana *Lieutenant Gelson* ■ *Dir* Christian Duguay • *Scr* BJ Nelson, from characters created by David Cronenberg

Scanners III: the Takeover ★★★ 18

Science-fiction horror
1992 · Can/US · Colour · 96mins

The second sequel finds Liliana Komorowska experimenting with a new mind-blowing drug. The result is a serious personality change from sweet young thing to psychotic megalomaniac with an ability to scan through TV airwaves and sway the masses to her ruthless power trip. The only person in her way is brother Steve Parrish who returns from a sojourn in a monastery to give her a piece of his own expanding mind. Canadian director Christian Duguay handles the more knockabout action with flair and wit (Komorowska's delightfully campy villain helps enormously). AJ

Liliana Komorowska *Helena Monet* • Valerie Valois *Joyce Stone* • Steve Parrish *Alexa Monet* • Colin Fox *Dr Elton Monet* ■ *Dir* Christian Duguay • *Scr* BJ Nelson, Rene Malo, David Preston, Julie Richard, from characters created by David Cronenberg

The Scapegoat ★★

Crime mystery 1959 · UK · BW · 119mins

Robert Hamer and Alec Guinness made one of the blackest, greatest comedies of all time – *Kind Hearts and Coronets* – but they can't quite repeat that magic here. Guinness restricts his talents to just two roles – the French count who wants to murder his wife and his double, the meek English teacher who might be tricked into doing it. A hammy Bette Davis plays his mother and Irene Worth is the inconvenient spouse. Co-scripted by Gore Vidal, it's fitfully amusing. AT

Alec Guinness *Jacques De Gue/John Barrett* • Bette Davis *Countess* • Nicole Maurey *Bella* • Irene Worth *Françoise De Gue* • Pamela Brown *Blanche* • Annabel Bartlett *Marie-Noël* • Geoffrey Keen *Gaston* ■ *Dir* Robert Hamer • *Scr* Gore Vidal, Robert Hamer, from the novel by Daphne du Maurier

The Scar ★★★ PG

Drama 1976 · Pol · Colour · 101mins

Krzysztof Kieslowski's debut feature was the first of only two pictures not to be based on an original idea. Yet, ironically, the Polish maestro blamed himself for adding characters and situations to the story uncovered by journalist and co-scenarist Romuald Karas. His documentary background stood him in good stead, however, as minor government official Franciszek Pieczka's brushes with both the locals whose rural community is destroyed by the construction of a factory and the Party bigwigs dissatisfied with his management style has an ominous ring of authenticity. Intriguing, but occasionally heavy handed. DP. In Polish with English subtitles. DVD

Franciszek Pieczka *Bednarz* • Mariusz Dmochowski • Jerzy Stuhr • Jan Skotnicki • Stanislaw Igar • Stanislaw Michalski ■ *Dir* Krzysztof Kieslowski • *Scr* Krzysztof Kieslowski, Romauld Karas

Scaramouche ★★★★

Silent swashbuckling romance
1923 · US · BW · 124mins

Lavishly produced by Metro, which later became MGM, this adaptation of Rafael Sabatini's novel is more an historical pageant than a true swashbuckler. Director Rex Ingram spent months researching the French Revolutionary period so that every detail – from palace to periwig – was as authentic as possible. Yet, while he was keen to ground the adventure in political fact, he was also aware of the spectacular possibilities in law-student-turned-circus-clown Ramon Novarro's feud with pitiless aristocrat Lewis Stone, and the romantic intensity of the heroic swordsman's passion for Alice Terry. The result is a silent film of rare grace and panache. DP

Ramon Novarro *André Moreau/Scaramouche* • Alice Terry *Aline de Kercadiou* • Lewis Stone *Marquis de la Tour d'Azyr* • Lloyd Ingraham *Quintin de Kercadiou* • Julia Swayne Gordon *Countess Thérèse de Plougastel* ■ *Dir* Rex Ingram (1) • *Scr* Willis Goldbeck, from the novel *Scaramouche: a Romance of the French Revolution* by Rafael Sabatini

Scaramouche ★★★★ U

Swashbuckling adventure
1952 · US · Colour · 114mins

Rafael Sabatini's rousing adventure was first filmed in 1923 by the master of the silent swashbuckler, Rex Ingram. This colourful version has been pared down to the bone by its writers, so that only the feuding, flirting and fencing remain of the classic novel's vivacious and complex portrait of Revolutionary France. Stewart Granger exudes charm in his scenes with Janet Leigh and cuts a dash as the mysterious swordsman on the trail of arrogant aristocrat Mel Ferrer. The final duel has the distinction of being the longest in movie history. DP

Stewart Granger *Andre Moreau/Scaramouche* • Eleanor Parker *Lenore* • Janet Leigh *Aline de Gavrillac* • Mel Ferrer *Noel, Marquis de Maynes* • Henry Wilcoxon *Chevalier de Chambrillaine* • Nina Foch *Marie Antoinette* • Richard Anderson *Philippe de Valmorin* • Robert Coote *Gaston Binet* ■ *Dir* George Sidney (2) • *Scr* Ronald Millar, George Froeschel, from the novel *Scaramouche: a Romance of the French Revolution* by Rafael Sabatini

The Scarecrow ★★★★

Silent comedy 1920 · US · BW · 17mins

After comedian Fatty Arbuckle's scandal, Buster Keaton took on many of his projects and this was one of the first silent movies for Buster Keaton Productions. The film is filled with sight gags, concentrating on the domestic set-up enjoyed by him and Joe Roberts: a gramophone converts into a stove, all table items are lowered on strings and the table itself – with plates attached – is hung up for washing. As the caption proclaims: "What is home without a mother?!" TH

Buster Keaton • Sybil Seely • Joe Keaton *Her father* • Joe Roberts *Rival* • Eddie Cline [Edward Cline] *Truck driver* ■ *Dir/Scr* Buster Keaton, Eddie Cline [Edward Cline]

Scarecrow ★★★ 18

Road movie drama
1973 · US · Colour · 107mins

Ex-con Gene Hackman and drifter Al Pacino hook up in California and travel east together, with the latter hoping to reconcile with the wife and child he abandoned in Detroit. On the journey they meet numerous other social misfits who regale them with various life lessons. This arty road movie can't quite harmonise its bleak realism with its glossy Hollywood approach to suffering, but both leads are excellent, even if Pacino – in an underwritten role – can't match Hackman. The film won the Palme d'Or at the 1973 Cannes festival. AJ

Gene Hackman *Max* • Al Pacino *Lion* • Dorothy Tristan *Coley* • Ann Wedgeworth *Frenchy* • Richard Lynch *Riley* • Eileen Brennan *Darlene* • Penny Allen [Penelope Allen] *Annie* • Richard Hackman *Mickey* ■ *Dir* Jerry Schatzberg • *Scr* Garry Michael White

The Scarecrow ★★ 15

Comedy thriller 1982 · NZ · Colour · 84mins

Hollywood horror veteran John Carradine stars in a 1950s-set thriller that mixes the mystical and the mundane in its tale of a New Zealand teen battling both his local bully and a crazed killer. The film's opening, with the mystery disappearance of some chickens setting in motion a spooky chain of events, grabs the attention. Ultimately, though, it never quite sustains this momentum. DA

John Carradine *Hubert Salter* • Tracy Mann *Prudence Poindexter* • Jonathan Smith *Ned Poindexter* • Daniel McLaren *Les Wilson* •

S

Denise O'Connell *Angela Potroz* • Anne Flannery *Mrs Poindexter* ■ *Dir* Sam Pillsbury • *Scr* Michael Heath, Sam Pillsbury, from a novel by Ronald Hugh Morrieson

Scared Stiff ★★★ U

Musical comedy 1953 · US · BW · 107mins

Comic teams always get around to a haunted house vehicle and this is the one from Dean Martin and Jerry Lewis. It's a remake of *The Ghost Breakers*, one of Bob Hope's funniest films, and though not as good as the earlier version, it is entertaining fare from the dynamic duo with veteran director George Marshall neatly combining genuine chills with the laughter. Brazilian bombshell Carmen Miranda makes her final film appearance, cueing an impersonation by Jerry Lewis, which is not very good. TV

Dean Martin *Larry Todd* • Jerry Lewis *Myron Mertz* • Lizabeth Scott *Mary Carroll* • Carmen Miranda *Carmelita Castina* • George Dolenz *Mr Cortega* • Dorothy Malone *Rosie* • William Ching *Tony Warren* • Paul Marion *Carriso Twins* • Jack Lambert *Zombi* • Bob Hope • Bing Crosby ■ *Dir* George Marshall • *Scr* Herbert Baker, Walter DeLeon, Ed Simmons, Norman Lear, from the play *Ghost Breakers* by Paul Dickey, Charles W Goddard

Scared to Death ★★ U

Horror 1947 · US · Colour · 67mins

Bela Lugosi made his sole credited appearance in colour in this low-budget chiller from the once promising silent-era director, Christy Cabanne. It opens intriguingly, with Molly Lamont's voiceover explaining how she came to be lying on a mortuary slab. But once she begins discussing how Lugosi's sinister hypnotist threatened to expose the past misdeeds of her father-in-law (the ever-malevolent George Zucco), the action veers between tepid haunted house antics and the misjudged comic interventions of dumbbell detective Nat Pendleton and dizzy blonde Joyce Compton. DP DVD

Bela Lugosi *Professor Leonide* • George Zucco *Dr Josef Van Ee* • Nat Pendleton *Bill "Bull" Raymond* • Molly Lamont *Laura Van Ee* • Joyce Compton *Jane* • Douglas Fowley *Terry Lee* • Angelo Rossitto *Indigo* • Roland Varno *Ward Van Ee* ■ *Dir* Christy Cabanne • *Scr* Walter Abbott

Scared to Death ★★ 18

Science-fiction horror
1980 · US · Colour · 87mins

In this earthbound *Alien* rip-off, top secret genetic experiments produce a lethal killing machine organism that stalks the sewers of Los Angeles. John Stinson stars as a tough cop turned bestselling author whose job it is to hunt it down. This substandard debut feature from William Malone offers nothing fresh to the actor-in-a-rubber-suit genre save the usual high body count and gruesome gore. An unofficial sequel entitled *Syngenor* followed in 1990. RS DVD

John Stinson *Ted Lonergan* • Diana Davidson *Jennifer Stanton* • Jonathan David Moses *Lou Capell* • Toni Jannotta *Sherry Carpenter* • Kermit Eller *Syngenor* ■ *Dir/Scr* William Malone

S

The Scarf ★★★

Thriller 1951 · US · BW · 93mins

This features John Ireland as the man on the run from an insane asylum who can't remember whether or not he strangled a woman with a scarf. The ever-watchable Mercedes McCambridge plays a singing waitress with a very similar scarf; Emlyn Williams appears as the doctor with some very odd mannerisms; and James Barton portrays a tiresome turkey-farming philosopher. Director EA Dupont indulges in some ripe expressionistic effects, while the screenplay comfortingly demonstrates that psychiatrists can be even crazier than their patients. AE

John Ireland *John Barrington* • Mercedes McCambridge *Connie Carter* • Emlyn Williams *David Dunbar* • James Barton *Ezra Thompson* • Lloyd Gough *Dr Gordon* ■ *Dir* EA Dupont • *Scr* EA Dupont, from a story by IG Goldsmith, EA Rolfe, from the novel by Robert Bloch

Scarface ★★★★★ PG

Crime drama 1932 · US · BW · 89mins

This is one of the great gangster movies of the 1930s. Producer Howard Hughes told director Howard Hawks to make it "as realistic, as exciting, as grisly as possible". Hawks happily obliged, though Hollywood's moral watchdog, the Hays Office, later insisted the ending was softened and a subtitle was added – *Shame of the Nation*. The story is a thinly-disguised biography of Al Capone, with Paul Muni as a monster who lusts after his own sister, Ann Dvorak, yet whose business acumen embodies the American Dream. It's filled with moments that define the gangster genre – terrific shoot-outs, psychotic characters and George Raft spinning a coin. *Scarface* remains a bracingly violent and subversive tragicomedy that says crime pays and that mowing people down is fun. AT

Paul Muni *Tony Camonte* • Ann Dvorak *Cesca Camonte* • Karen Morley *Poppy* • Osgood Perkins *Johnny Lovo* • C Henry Gordon *Inspector Guarino* • George Raft *Guino Rinaldo* • Vince Barnett *Angelo* • Boris Karloff *Gaffney* • Howard Hawks *Man on bed* ■ *Dir* Howard Hawks • *Scr* Ben Hecht, Seton I Miller, John Lee Mahin, WR Burnett, Fred Pasley, from the novel by Armitage Trail

Scarface ★★★★ 18

Crime thriller 1983 · US · Colour · 162mins

Director Brian De Palma's scorching update of Howard Hawks's 1932 classic relocates events to Miami and follows the rapid rise and violent fall of a Cuban refugee turned cocaine-smuggling kingpin. Al Pacino is the ruthless criminal pursuing the American dream, and he gets top support from Michelle Pfeiffer as his wife, Steven Bauer as his partner in crime and Mary Elizabeth Mastrantonio as his sister. The accurate, if four-letter-word heavy, dialogue and sharp wit contained in Oliver Stone's script and the vivid cinematography of John A Alonzo help make De Palma's urban shocker a modern-day classic. AJ. Contains violence, swearing, sex scenes and nudity. DVD

Al Pacino *Tony Montana* • Steven Bauer *Manny Ray* • Michelle Pfeiffer *Elvira* • Mary Elizabeth Mastrantonio *Gina* • Robert Loggia *Frank Lopez* • Miriam Colon *Mama Montana* • F Murray Abraham *Omar* ■ *Dir* Brian De Palma • *Scr* Oliver Stone, from the 1932 film

The Scarlet and the Black ★★★★ PG

Second World War drama
1983 · US/It · Colour · 137mins

Gregory Peck made his TV-movie debut in this true story of wartime hide-and-seek. Although it's far too long, it is certainly one of the more impressive efforts made for the small screen. In addition to a cameo from John Gielgud as Pope Pius XII, the film boasts photography by Giuseppe Rotunno and a score by the great Ennio Morricone. Peck's character is a sort of Oskar Schindler in vestments, who gives sanctuary to Jews and other persecuted peoples prior to smuggling them to safety. Christopher Plummer is villainous as the Nazi who can't pin down the elusive priest. DP DVD

Gregory Peck *Monsignor Hugh O'Flaherty* • Christopher Plummer *Colonel Herbert Kappler* • John Gielgud *Pope Pius XII* • Raf Vallone *Father Vittorio* • Kenneth Colley *Captain Hirsch* ■ *Dir* Jerry London • *Scr* David Butler, from the non-fiction book *The Scarlet Pimpernel of the Vatican* by JP Gallagher

Scarlet Angel ★★★ U

Period adventure 1952 · US · Colour · 80mins

Saloon girl Yvonne De Carlo, displaced by the Civil War, takes off for San Francisco. There she masquerades as the widow of a wealthy society type and cons her way into the social register. Everything goes swimmingly and her future prospects are looking good until her past re-enters in the shape of hunky Rock Hudson. With a storyline more redolent of films of the 1930s or early 1940s, this romantic adventure is nonetheless well put together and very enjoyable. RK

Yvonne De Carlo *Roxy McClanahan* • Rock Hudson *Frank Truscott* • Richard Denning *Malcolm Bradley* • Bodil Miller *Linda Caldwell* • Amanda Blake *Susan Bradley* • Henry O'Neill *Morgan Caldwell* ■ *Dir* Sidney Salkow • *Scr* Oscar Brodney

The Scarlet Blade ★★ U

Swashbuckling drama
1963 · UK · Colour · 84mins

Oliver Reed is on form here as a renegade swordsman with an eye for the ladies in this period drama from Hammer set during the English Civil War. Swordfights abound as sadistic Cromwellian colonel Lionel Jeffries discovers his daughter has Royalist sympathies. But writer/director John Gilling was on surer ground with later horror films such as *The Plague of the Zombies*. TH

Lionel Jeffries *Colonel Judd* • Oliver Reed *Sylvester* • Jack Hedley *Edward* • June Thorburn *Clare* • Michael Ripper *Pablo* • Harold Goldblatt *Jacob* ■ *Dir/Scr* John Gilling

The Scarlet Claw ★★★★ PG

Mystery 1944 · US · BW · 73mins

Here's the greatest of all Sherlocks (Basil Rathbone) and the most bumbling of all Watsons (Nigel Bruce) in possibly the best of the Universal Studios series, with the pair in Canada investigating ghostly and ghastly murders. The under-rated Roy William Neill causes consternation with some memorably uneasy visuals: a dead woman's hand clutching a bell-rope, a luminous "monster" stalking Holmes across a marsh and the fog that just avalanches down. TH DVD

Basil Rathbone *Sherlock Holmes* • Nigel Bruce *Dr John H Watson* • Gerald Hamer *Potts* • Paul Cavanagh *Lord William Penrose* • Arthur Hohl *Emile Journet* • Kay Harding *Marie Journet* ■ *Dir* Roy William Neill • *Scr* Roy William Neill, Edmund L Hartmann, from a story by Paul Gangelin, Brenda Weisberg, from characters created by Sir Arthur Conan Doyle

The Scarlet Clue ★★ PG

Mystery 1945 · US · BW · 62mins

The fifth Charlie Chan mystery produced by the Poverty Row Studio, Monogram, is a lively affair that sees Sidney Toler on the track of the sinister boss who ordered the assassination of an Axis spy intent on stealing government radar plans. Much of the action takes place in a building that not only houses a research laboratory, but also a radio station that conveniently employs the majority of the suspects. As ever, director Phil Rosen allows Mantan Moreland a comedy spot. DP DVD

Sidney Toler *Charlie Chan* • Benson Fong *Tommy Chan* • Mantan Moreland *Birmingham Brown* • Helen Devereaux *Diane Hall* • Robert E Homans [Robert Homans] *Captain Flynn* • Virginia Brissac *Mrs Marsh* • Jack Norton *Willie Rand* ■ *Dir* Phil Rosen • *Scr* George Callahan, from characters created by Earl Derr Biggers

The Scarlet Coat ★★ U

Historical spy drama
1955 · US · Colour · 100mins

An espionage drama set during the American War of Independence, dealing with the famous traitor Benedict Arnold. Playing the hero is Cornel Wilde, an American who becomes a double agent and joins the British in order to expose Arnold's treachery. This being a Hollywood movie, there is some romantic intrigue as well as a fairly cavalier treatment of historical fact. A very camp George Sanders steals every scene he's in. AT

Cornel Wilde *Major John Bolton* • Michael Wilding *Major John Andre* • George Sanders *Dr Jonathan Odell* • Anne Francis *Sally Cameron* • Robert Douglas *Benedict Arnold* • John McIntire *General Robert Howe* • Rhys Williams *Peter* • John Dehner *Nathanael Greene* ■ *Dir* John Sturges • *Scr* Karl Tunberg

Scarlet Dawn ★★

Period drama 1932 · US · BW · 58mins

The dawn here is the colour of the Russian Revolution. In the thick of it is Douglas Fairbanks Jr, an aristocrat from St Petersburg who has no truck with Lenin and instead runs off to Constantinople with Nancy Carroll. He marries her, leaves her for one of his own class and then returns. Made when Hollywood was just discovering that movies could talk and that Fairbanks Jr had charm aplenty but somewhat less talent. AT

Douglas Fairbanks Jr *Baron Nikiti Krasnoff* • Nancy Carroll *Tanyusha* • Lilyan Tashman *Vera Zimina* • Guy Kibbee *Murphy* • Sheila Terry *Marjorie Murphy* • Earle Fox *Boris* • Ivan Linow *Ivan* ■ *Dir* William Dieterle • *Scr* Niven Busch, Edwin Gelsey, Douglas Fairbanks Jr, from the novel *Revolt* by Mary McCall Jr

The Scarlet Empress ★★★★★ 12

Historical drama 1934 · US · BW · 98mins

This is more fun than you could ever imagine, more suggestive than you'd thought possible, even in those days prior to the imposition of the Hays Production Code. Director Josef von Sternberg fills the screen with typically lustrous images and staggeringly rich art direction. This movie, which does have its detractors, was influential on Russian director Sergei Eisenstein. More than just a vehicle for Marlene Dietrich, the film conveys a real sense of the lusts and intrigues of the court of Catherine the Great. TS

Marlene Dietrich *Sophia Frederica, Catherine II* • Gerald Fielding *Lieutenant Dmitri* • John Lodge *Count Alexei* • Sam Jaffe *Grand Duke Peter* • Louise Dresser *Empress Elizabeth* • C Aubrey Smith *Prince August* • Gavin Gordon *Gregory Orloff* • Ruthelma Stevens *Countess Elisabeth* • Hans von Twardowski *Ivan Shuvolov* ■ *Dir* Josef von Sternberg • *Scr* Manuel Komroff, from a diary of Catherine II • *Cinematographer* Bert Glennon • *Costume Designer* Travis Banton • *Set Designer* Hans Dreier, Peter Ballbusch, Richard Kollorsz

The Scarlet Letter ★★★★

Silent drama 1926 · US · BW · 80mins

Lillian Gish gives here what many regard as her finest performance. The fifth screen version of Nathaniel Hawthorne's novel, this is by far the finest adaptation of any era. With Hendrik Sartov's photography bringing a painterly austerity to the already puritanical setting, Hester Prynne's adultery with Pastor Dimmesdale assumes a social enormity that is often disregarded by those concentrating on the story's human aspects. Yet director Victor Sjöström is not blind to the tragedy of the couple's disgrace, as he locates beauty and sensitivity amid the bigotry. DP

Lillian Gish *Hester Prynne* • Lars Hanson *The Reverend Arthur Dimmesdale* • Henry B

Walthall *Roger Prynne* • Karl Dane *Giles* • William H Tooker *The governor* • Marcelle Corday *Mistress Hibbins* ■ *Dir* Victor Seastrom [Victor Sjöström] • *Scr* Frances Marion, from the novel by Nathaniel Hawthorne

The Scarlet Letter ★★ 15

Period drama 1995 · US · Colour · 129mins

In this absurd version of Nathaniel Hawthorne's classic novel, Demi Moore gives a confused performance as the 17th-century wife who has an affair and is ostracised by the community. Gary Oldman is ludicrously over the top as the preacher with whom Moore has a passionate fling, while Robert Duvall, as her cuckolded husband, gives a performance that is totally out of place with the period. TH. Contains some violence, sex scenes and nudity. [VIDEO] DVD

Demi Moore *Hester Prynne* • Gary Oldman *Arthur Dimmesdale* • Robert Duvall *Roger Prynne* • Lisa Joliff-Andoh *Mituba* • Edward Hardwick [Edward Hardwicke] *John Bellingham* • Robert Prosky *Horace Stonehall* • Roy Dotrice *Thomas Cheever* • Joan Plowright *Harriet Hibbons* • Jodhi May *Pearl* ■ *Dir* Roland Joffé • *Scr* Douglas Day Stewart, from the novel by Nathaniel Hawthorne

The Scarlet Pimpernel ★★★ U

Period adventure 1934 · UK · BW · 93mins

Leslie Howard stars as Sir Percy Blakeney, master of disguise, outwitting Raymond Massey's evil Chauvelin during the French Revolution and fooling his wife, Merle Oberon, who thinks he's just a boorish fop. Its chief virtues are Howard's portrait of strength masquerading as superciliousness and some lavish production design. But it seems rather creaky nowadays, mainly because of the stagey direction from Harold Young (with uncredited assistance from Rowland Brown and Korda). It was a big success in its day, though, and Howard played the role again in the updated 1941 sequel, *Pimpernel Smith*. AT [VIDEO]

Leslie Howard *Sir Percy Blakeney/The Scarlet Pimpernel* • Merle Oberon *Lady Marguerite Blakeney, formerly Marguerite St Just* • Raymond Massey *Chauvelin* • Nigel Bruce *Prince of Wales (HRH the Prince Regent)* • Bramwell Fletcher *Priest* • Anthony Bushell *Sir Andrew Ffoulkes* • Joan Gardner *Suzanne de Tournay* • Walter Rilla *Armand St Just* ■ *Dir* Harold Young • *Scr* SN Behrman, Robert Sherwood [Robert E Sherwood], Arthur Wimperis, Lajos Biró, from the novel by Baroness Orczy • *Production Designer* Vincent Korda

The Scarlet Pimpernel ★★★★ PG

Period adventure 1982 · UK/US · Colour · 135mins

In this superior TV movie, director Clive Donner makes the most of the period plushness to fashion a lively swashbuckler that's true to the spirit of the novels of Baroness Orczy. Anthony Andrews is on form as Sir Percy Blakeney, the foppish English noble who risks all to rescue French aristocrats from the guillotine during the Reign of Terror. Jane Seymour also surpasses herself as the neglected Lady Marguerite, while Ian McKellen has a ripe old time as the villainous Chauvelin. DP [VIDEO] DVD

Anthony Andrews *Sir Percy Blakeney/The Scarlet Pimpernel* • Jane Seymour (2) *Marguerite St Just* • Ian McKellen *Paul Chauvelin* • James Villiers *Baron de Batz* • Eleanor David *Louise Lenjean* • Malcolm Jamieson *Armand St Just* • Julian Fellowes *Prince Regent* ■ *Dir* Clive Donner • *Scr* William Bast, from the novel by Baroness Orczy

Scarlet Street ★★★ PG

Film noir 1945 · US · BW · 101mins

Edward G Robinson stars (brilliantly) as a diffident cashier with a termagant wife (Rosalind Ivan) and limited means, whose only pleasure is painting in his spare time. He falls in love with Joan Bennett who, under the sway of her sadistic boyfriend Dan Duryea, leads him into a tangle of deceptions, embezzlement and murder. An effective *noir* drama, directed by Fritz Lang, a master of the genre, the movie is grim, downbeat and well-played, with some imaginative and unusual plot developments and an audacious ending. The script, though, does strain credibility at times. RK [VIDEO] DVD

Edward G Robinson *Christopher Cross* • Joan Bennett *Kitty March* • Dan Duryea *Johnny Prince* • Margaret Lindsay *Millie* • Rosalind Ivan *Adele Cross* • Jess Barker *Janeway* • Arthur Loft *Dellarowe* ■ *Dir* Fritz Lang • *Scr* Dudley Nichols, from the novel *La Chienne* by Georges de la Fouchardiere, from the play *La Chienne* by Georges de la Fouchardière, André Mouëzy-Eon

The Scarlet Thread ★★

Crime thriller 1951 · UK · BW · 84mins

This downbeat British crime drama gains some modest interest from being an early effort of director Lewis Gilbert with Laurence Harvey in one of his early leading roles. Harvey is convincingly unpleasant as the skirt-chasing spiv and petty criminal who panics and kills a bystander during a jewel robbery. He then uses his sleazy charm on the love-starved daughter of a Cambridge University professor (Kathleen Byron, trying hard to look plain and desperate) in order to gain refuge. The twist in the tale is more implausible than ironic. AE

Kathleen Byron *Josephine* • Laurence Harvey *Freddie* • Sydney Tafler *Marcon* • Arthur Hill *Shaw* • Dora Bryan *Maggie* • Eliot Makeham *Jason* ■ *Dir* Lewis Gilbert • *Scr* Ar Rawlinson, from the play *The Scarlet Thread* by AR Rawlinson, Moie Charles

The Scarlet Tunic ★★★ 12

Period drama 1997 · UK · Colour · mins

Minimally budgeted, this British period drama Concerns the ill-starred romance between a rich man's daughter and a foreign mercenary who's about to set off to fight Napoleon. The melodramatic crunch comes when the soldier has to do a *High Noon* and choose between love and duty. Emma Fielding and Jean-Marc Barr play the lovers while Simon Callow chews the scenery as Barr's brutal military commander. DA. Contains some violence and sexual situations. DVD

Jean-Marc Barr *Sergeant Matthaus Singer* • Emma Fielding *Frances Elizabeth Groves* • Simon Callow *Captain John Fairfax* • Jack Shepherd *Dr Edward Groves* • John Sessions *Humphrey Gould* ■ *Dir* Stuart St Paul • *Scr* Stuart St Paul, Mark Jenkins, Colin Clements, from the story *The Melancholy Hussar* by Thomas Hardy

Scarred City ★★ 18

Action thriller 1998 · US · Colour · 92mins

This unexceptional action thriller boasts a cast that doesn't deserve the film's video-dustbin status. Stephen Baldwin stars as a cop facing investigation after killing some criminal suspects in rather dubious circumstances. Police lieutenant Chazz Palminteri offers him a way out with his very secret squad, although it soon transpires that this force takes neither prisoners nor witnesses. JF. Contains violence, swearing, nudity. [VIDEO] DVD

Stephen Baldwin *John Trace* • Chazz Palminteri *Lieutenant Laine Devon* • Tia Carrere *Candy* • Michael Rispoli *Sam Bandusky* • Gary Dourdan *Sergeant Creedy* • Bray Poor *Zero* ■ *Dir/Scr* Ken Sanzel

The Scars of Dracula ★★★ 18

Horror 1970 · UK · Colour · 91mins

Christopher Lee thinks this is his weakest *Dracula* sequel, but Hammer horror fans like it because the Count has more screen time here than in any other episode. There's also a dark fairy-tale atmosphere achieved by director Roy Ward Baker as Dracula tries sinking his fangs into naive Transylvanian travellers Dennis Waterman and Jenny Hanley. Propping up the formula vampire tale are a memorable death-by-lightning climax, and more blood, sadism and rubber bats than ever before. AJ [VIDEO] DVD

Christopher Lee *Count Dracula* • Dennis Waterman *Simon Carlson* • Christopher Matthews *Paul Carlson* • Jenny Hanley *Sarah Framsen* • Patrick Troughton *Klove* • Michael Gwynn *Priest* • Wendy Hamilton *Julie* • Anouska Hempel *Tania* ■ *Dir* Roy Ward Baker • *Scr* John Elder [Anthony Hinds], from characters created by Bram Stoker

Scary Movie ★★★ 18

Horror spoof 2000 · US · Colour · 88mins

Director Keenen Ivory Wayans spoofs 1990s teenage horror movies, which seems a bit of a redundant exercise when you consider that *Scream* was itself a dig at the horror genre. Luckily, Wayans and family (among the writers are his brothers Shawn and Marlon, who also star) get some good laughs in along the way. The film includes in-jokes and send-ups, plus a superb spoof of *The Matrix* that will have fans chuckling in the aisles. Instantly forgettable, but fun. JB. Contains swearing, violence, drug abuse and sex scenes. [VIDEO] DVD

Anna Faris *Cindy Campbell* • Shannon Elizabeth *Buffy Gilmore* • Regina Hall *Brenda Meeks* • Jon Abrahams *Bobby Prinze* • Lochlyn Munro *Greg Phillippe* • Shawn Wayans *Ray Jones* • Marlon Wayans *Shorty Meeks* • Carmen Electra *Drew Decker* ■ *Dir* Keenen Ivory Wayans • *Scr* Shawn Wayans, Marlon Wayans, Buddy Johnson, Phil Beauman, Jason Friedberg, Aaron Seltzer

Scary Movie 2 ★ 18

Horror spoof 2001 · US · Colour · 78mins

It wasn't a classic or particularly well made but at least *Scary Movie* was good for a few honest *Scream*-inspired laughs.This uninspired sequel is barely competent on any technical or artistic level. Once past the opening where *The Exorcist* is amusingly sent up by James Woods in a cameo appearance as a priest (a role originally earmarked for Marlon Brando), it descends rapidly into a shoddy satire. AJ [VIDEO] DVD

Shawn Wayans *Ray Jones* • Marlon Wayans *Shorty Meeks* • Anna Faris *Cindy Campbell* • Regina Hall *Brenda Meeks* • Chris Masterson *Buddy* • Kathleen Robertson *Theo* • James Woods *Father McFeely* • Tim Curry *Professor Oldman* • Veronica Cartwright *Mrs Voorhees, Megan's mother* ■ *Dir* Keenen Ivory Wayans • *Scr* Marlon Wayans, Shawn Wayans, Craig Wayans, Alyson Fouse, Greg Grabianski, Dave Polsky, Michael Anthony Snowden, from characters created by Marlon Wayans, Shawn Wayans, Buddy Johnson, Phil Beauman, Jason Friedberg, Aaron Seltzer

Scary Movie 3 ★★ 15

Horror spoof 2003 · US · Colour · 80mins

David Zucker directs this third entry in the horror-spoof franchise, which, though not as good as the original, is certainly an improvement on the second. This time around, television reporter Anna Faris investigates a planned alien invasion of a farm owned by Charlie Sheen, while a mysterious video kills all who watch it. All kinds of references are dragged kicking and screaming into the bedraggled plot, but this is not as funny as it thinks it is. There are some inspired moments, however, and Leslie Nielsen is always a joy. TH [VIDEO] DVD

Anna Faris *Cindy Campbell* • Anthony Anderson *Mahalik* • Leslie Nielsen *President Harris* • Camryn Manheim *Trooper Champlin* • Simon Rex *George* • George Carlin *The Architect* • Queen Latifah *The Oracle* • Charlie Sheen *Tom* ■ *Dir* David Zucker • *Scr* Craig Mazin, Pat Proft, from characters created by Marlon Wayans, Shawn Wayans, Buddy Johnson, Phil Beauman, Jason Friedberg, Aaron Seltzer

Scavenger Hunt ★★

Comedy 1979 · US · Colour · 116mins

It's a Mad, Mad, Mad, Mad World was an honourable but failed attempt to make the "comedy to end all comedies". *Scavenger Hunt* treads a similar path with its star-studded cast involved in a frantic hunt for a hidden fortune. Mad games inventor Vincent Price leaves a will which stipulates that his relatives have to participate in a grand scavenger hunt, with the winner inheriting his millions. Even wider of the mark than its illustrious predecessor, this is, at least, a lot shorter. DF

Richard Benjamin *Stuart Selsome* • James Coco *Henri* • Scatman Crothers *Sam* • Cloris Leachman *Mildred Carruthers* • Cleavon Little *Jackson* • Roddy McDowall *Jenkins* • Robert Morley *Bernstein* • Richard Mulligan *Marvin Dummitz* • Tony Randall *Henry Motley* • Dirk Benedict *Jeff Stevens* • Vincent Price *Milton Parker* • Arnold Schwarzenegger *Lars* ■ *Dir* Michael Schultz • *Scr* Steven A Vail, Henry Harper, John Thompson, Gerry Woolery, from a story by Steven A Vail

A Scene at the Sea ★★★

Sports drama 1991 · Jpn · Colour · 102mins

This entertaining surfing odyssey marks a change of pace for Takeshi Kitano. The story revolves around a deaf garbage collector (Kurodo Maki) who finds a discarded surfboard and, after reconditioning it, battles to conquer the waves. Kitano's proclivity for slapstick is very much in evidence: Maki repeatedly comes a cropper as he masters the basic skills of surfing and then competes in local championships before the supportive gaze of his deaf girlfriend, Hiroko Oshima. DP. In Japanese with English subtitles.

Kurodo Maki *Shigeru* • Hiroko Oshima *Takako* • Sabu Kawahara *Tamukai, garbage truck driver* • Toshizo Fujiwara *Nakajima, owner of surfing goods shops* ■ *Dir/Scr* Takeshi Kitano

Scene of the Crime ★★

Crime drama 1949 · US · BW · 94mins

Van Johnson is Los Angeles detective, Mike Conovan, investigating the murder of one of his colleagues. Part of the late 1940s fad for documentary realism and police procedure, the movie spends much time depicting our hero's dogged, dedicated work as well as his blissfully ordinary home life with Arlene Dahl. But a movie about routine inevitably becomes routine. AT

Van Johnson *Mike Conovan* • Gloria De Haven [Gloria DeHaven] *Lili* • Tom Drake *CC Gordon* • Arlene Dahl *Gloria Conovan* • Leon Ames *Captain AC Forster* • John McIntire *Fred Piper* • Norman Lloyd *Sleeper* • Donald Woods *Herkimer* ■ *Dir* Roy Rowland • *Scr* Charles Schnee, from the story *Smashing the Bookie Gang Marauders* by John Bartlow Martin

The Scene of the Crime ★★★

Thriller 1986 · Fr · Colour · 90mins

Catherine Deneuve heads a quality cast in this fine French thriller from director André Téchiné. The action takes place over an eventful four-day period, in which a run-in between a 13-year-old boy and two escaped convicts leads to murder, and to the forging of an unlikely alliance between the killer

S

and the boy's mother. DA. In French with English subtitles.

Catherine Deneuve *Lili* • Danielle Darrieux *Grandmother* • Nicolas Giraudi *Thomas* • Wadeck Stanczak *Martin* • Victor Lanoux *Maurice* • Jean Bousquet *Grandfather* ■ *Dir* André Téchiné • *Scr* André Téchiné, Pascal Bonitzer, Olivier Assayas

Scenes from a Mall ★★★ 15

Comedy 1991 · US · Colour · 83mins

The notion of Woody Allen and Bette Midler playing a smugly successful couple whose marriage begins to crumble as they go shopping must have brought a big smile to the faces of the producers. Unfortunately, director Paul Mazursky reduces the satirical potential to a torrent of words. Woody's lines, unsurprisingly the best, are not matched by the dialogue or performance of the too-loud Midler, and the added irony of a marriage teetering at Christmas is too corny. But despite the leaden weight of the script, there are some fine moments. JM. Contains swearing.

Bette Midler *Deborah Fifer* • Woody Allen *Nick Fifer* • Bill Irwin *Mime* • Daren Firestone *Sam* • Rebecca Nickels *Jennifer* • Paul Mazursky *Dr Hans Clava* ■ *Dir* Paul Mazursky • *Scr* Paul Mazursky, Roger L Simon

Scenes from a Marriage ★★★★ 15

Drama 1973 · Swe · Colour · 162mins

Originally a six-part TV series, this was edited for feature release by writer/director Ingmar Bergman. Mostly shot in tight close-ups to enhance the tensions between the protagonists, this is not easy viewing: some of the insights seem too blatant for a film-maker of Bergman's intellect to be bothered with. However, when the rambling gives way to fierce infighting and wounding insults, the film exerts a much firmer grip. Liv Ullmann as the betrayed wife, Erland Josephson as the philandering husband and Bibi Andersson as the other woman are all quite superb. DP. In Swedish with English subtitles. DVD

Liv Ullmann *Marianne* • Erland Josephson *Johan* • Bibi Andersson *Katarina* • Jan Malmsjö *Peter* • Anita Wall *Interviewer* ■ *Dir/Scr* Ingmar Bergman

Scenes from the Class Struggle in Beverly Hills ★★★★ 18

Comedy 1989 · UK · Colour · 99mins

Jacqueline Bisset gets a juicy role as a recently widowed soap star who invites her neighbour and her son to stay while their house is being defumigated. Joining them are a hilarious mix of the rich and famous that reaches across sexual and racial divides, and into areas such as body fascism, freak diets and weird sex. A guest spot is reserved for Paul Mazursky, director of both *Bob & Carol & Ted & Alice* and *Down and Out in Beverly Hills*, touchstones for Paul Bartel's subversive brand of humour that sets out to offend everyone. AT DVD

Jacqueline Bisset *Clare Lipkin* • Ray Sharkey *Frank* • Robert Beltran *Juan* • Mary Woronov *Lisabeth Hepburn-Saravian* • Ed Begley Jr *Peter* • Wallace Shawn *Howard Saravian* • Arnetia Walker *To-bel* • Paul Mazursky *Sidney Lipkin* ■ *Dir* Paul Bartel • *Scr* Bruce Wagner, from a story by Paul Bartel, Bruce Wagner

Scent of a Woman ★★★

Comedy drama 1974 · It · Colour · 103mins

Somewhat overlooked since Al Pacino's Oscar-winning remake, Dino Risi's adaptation boasts a similarly show-stopping performance from Vittorio Gassman. He won the best actor prize at Cannes for his portrayal of the blind army captain with a stubborn streak to match his simmering sense of resentment. However, that's where the similarities end, as Gassman journeys from Turin to Naples to enter into a suicide pact with a soldier disfigured in the accident that disabled him. There's sly humour in his relationship with rookie escort Alessandro Momo, but the romantic reunion with Agostina Belli is cringingly sentimental. DP. An Italian language film.

Vittorio Gassman *Fausto* • Alessandro Momo *Ciccio* • Agostina Belli *Sara* • Moira Orfei *Mirka* • Franco Ricci *Raffaele* • Elena Veronese *Michelina* ■ *Dir* Dino Risi • *Scr* Ruggero Maccari, Dino Risi, from the novel *Il Buio e il Miele* by Giovanni Arpino

Scent of a Woman ★★★★ 15

Drama 1992 · US · Colour · 149mins

This lengthy melodrama is kept vibrantly alive and out of the clutches of sickly sentimentality by a towering Oscar-winning performance from Al Pacino. He plays the blind ex-soldier who heads for New York to sample once more life's little luxuries over the Thanksgiving weekend. As his unworldly teenage escort, Chris O'Donnell is quietly impressive, but it's Pacino's picture, whether waltzing with Gabrielle Anwar, berating O'Donnell's schoolmates or barking his famous "hoo-ha" cough. DP. Contains swearing, sex scenes. DVD

Al Pacino *Lt Col Frank Slade* • Chris O'Donnell *Charlie Simms* • James Rebhorn *Mr Trask* • Gabrielle Anwar *Donna* • Philip S Hoffman [Philip Seymour Hoffman] *George Willis Jr* • Richard Venture *WR Slade* • Bradley Whitford *Randy* ■ *Dir* Martin Brest • *Scr* Bo Goldman, suggested by a character from *Profuma di Donna (Scent of a Woman)* by Ruggero Maccari and Dino Risi, based on the novel *Il Buio e il Miele* by Giovanni Arpino

The Scent of Green Papaya ★★★★★ U

Drama 1993 · Fr · Colour · 99mins

Set in pre-Vietnam War Saigon, this is the leisurely, minutely observed and thoroughly involving story of a servant girl and the relationships she develops with her employers and a handsome family friend. The opening segment is quite captivating, thanks to the guileless performance of Man San Lu as the ten-year-old maid, but the intensity of the drama as it moves into the 1960s compensates for the mannered innocence of Tran Nu Yen-Khe as the older Mui. A delightful study, it won director Tran Anh Hung the Camera d'Or at Cannes for best debut feature. DP. In Vietnamese with English subtitles. DVD

Tran Nu Yen-Khe *Mui, aged 20* • Man San Lu *Mui, aged 10* • Thi Loc Truong *Mother* • Anh Hoa Nguyen *Old Thi* • Hoa Hoi Vuong *Khuyen* • Ngoc Tran Trung *Father* ■ *Dir/Scr* Tran Anh Hung

Scent of Mystery ★★ U

Mystery 1960 · US · Colour · 132mins

The only film ever shot in "smell-o-vision " – a process which squirted appropriate odours at the audience. Denholm Elliott wanders through Spain and finds he has to protect Beverly Bentley who's being menaced by such classy heavies as Peter Lorre and Paul Lukas. Produced by the American showman Mike Todd, who liked gimmicks, the smellier the better. Not exactly a stinker, but nearly. TH

Denholm Elliott *Oliver Larker* • Beverly Bentley *The Decoy Sally* • Peter Lorre *Smiley, chauffeur* • Paul Lukas *Baron Saradin* • Diana Dors *Winifred Jordan* • Liam Redmond *Johnny Gin, derelict* • Elizabeth Taylor *The Real Sally Kennedy* ■ *Dir* Jack Cardiff • *Scr* William Rose, from a story by Kelley Roos

Schindler's List ★★★★★ 15

War drama based on a true story
1993 · US · BW and Colour · 187mins

Steven Spielberg's outstanding Holocaust drama won seven Oscars and tells the story of Second World War entrepreneur Oskar Schindler (played by Liam Neeson), whose operation to supply the German war effort led him to be the unexpected saviour of more than 1,000 Jewish factory workers in Poland. Spielberg uses stark, brutal realism to put over his powerful points, and the stunning black-and-white photography and gritty hand-held camera footage give it a potent documentary style. Ralph Fiennes invokes an awesome mixture of revulsion and sympathy as the inhuman Nazi commandant, and Neeson matches him with a heartfelt performance. Ben Kingsley is also superb as Schindler's Jewish accountant and conscience. AJ. Contains violence, swearing, sex scenes and nudity. DVD

Liam Neeson *Oskar Schindler* • Ben Kingsley *Itzhak Stern* • Ralph Fiennes *Amon Goeth* • Caroline Goodall *Emilie Schindler* • Jonathan Sagalle *Poldek Pfefferberg* • Embeth Davidtz *Helen Hirsch* • Andrzej Seweryn *Julian Scherner* ■ *Dir* Steven Spielberg • *Scr* Steven Zaillian, from the novel *Schindler's Ark* by Thomas Keneally • *Cinematographer* Janusz Kaminski • *Music* John Williams • *Editor* Michael Kahn

Schizo ★★ 18

Horror 1976 · UK · Colour · 103mins

This tepid gore thriller exhibits little of the down-and-dirty histrionic style that built director Pete Walker's cult appeal. Ice skating star Lynne Frederick has the days before her marriage disturbed by the attentions of a brutal assassin provoked to kill by memories of earlier matricide. One slashed psychiatrist, a mutilated medium, one hacked-up housekeeper and a *Psycho* shower scene rip-off later, the maniac's obvious identity is revealed. AJ

Lynne Frederick *Samantha* • John Leyton *Alan Falconer* • Stephanie Beacham *Beth* • John Fraser *Leonard Hawthorne* • Jack Watson *William Haskin* • Queenie Watts *Mrs Wallace* ■ *Dir* Pete Walker • *Scr* David McGillivray

Schizopolis ★★ 15

Experimental comedy drama
1996 · US · Colour · 96mins

An inspired surrealist swipe at the American mainstream or a vanity project gone off the rails? The answer lies somewhere in between these verdicts on Steven Soderbergh's ambitious satire on language, identity, fidelity, advertising, self-help and dentistry. Writer/director Soderbergh also stars as a speech writer, whose wife (Betsy Brantley) is having an affair with a dentist (also played by Soderbergh). Mixing the absurd with the autobiographical, this is a riot of ideas but not enough of them come off. DP DVD

Steven Soderbergh *Fletcher Munson/Dr Jeffrey Korchek* • Betsy Brantley *Mrs Munson/Attractive woman No 2* • David Jensen (2) *Elmo Oxygen* • Eddie Jemison *Nameless Numberheadman* • Scott Allen *Right hand man* • Mike Malone *T Azimuth Schwitters* ■ *Dir/Scr* Steven Soderbergh

Schlock ★

Science-fiction horror spoof
1971 · US · Colour · 77mins

Director John Landis donned an ape suit in his debut as a director. The monkey-suited title character – a thawed prehistoric missing link – runs amok in a small town, and leaves a trail of banana skins in his murderous wake. Nothing more than a poor excuse to lampoon Kubrick's *2001*, this is a game, but lame, student effort. Future Oscar winner Rick Baker designed the hairy costume. AJ

John Landis *The Schlockthropus* • Saul Kahan *Detective/Sgt Wino* • Joseph Piantadosi *Prof Shlibovitz* • Eliza Garrett *Mindy Binerman* • Eric Allison *Joe Puzman* • Enrica Blankey *Mrs Binerman* ■ *Dir/Scr* John Landis

School Daze ★★ 18

Musical comedy 1988 · US · Colour · 120mins

In attempting to present campus life as a microcosm of African-American society, Spike Lee succeeds in raising many points without reaching any conclusions. He attacks the conventions of college life without exploring any alternatives and takes pot shots at sexism, racism and the age and class divides without steadying his aim. Laurence Fishburne gives a steady performance, but, overall, this is a disjointed and disappointing satire. DP. Contains swearing and nudity.

Larry Fishburne [Laurence Fishburne] *Vaughn "Dap" Dunlap* • Giancarlo Esposito *Julian "Big Brother Almighty" Eaves* • Tisha Campbell *Jane Toussaint* • Kyme *Rachel Meadows* • Joe Seneca *President McPherson* • Ellen Holly *Odrie McPherson* • Art Evans *Cedar Cloud* • Ossie Davis *Coach Odom* • Bill Nunn *Grady* • Branford Marsalis *Jordan* • Spike Lee *Half-Pint* • Samuel L Jackson ■ *Dir/Scr* Spike Lee

School for Postmen ★★★★

Comedy 1947 · Fr · BW · 18mins

Returning behind the camera for the first time since the mid-1930s, Jacques Tati here tried out the routines that would form the core of his feature debut, *Jour de Fête*. A winner on the festival circuit, this hilarious short introduces the character of François, the work-shy postman, as well as containing two scenes – a hilarious tutorial and an eccentric dance – which didn't make the feature. Bearing the influence of Max Linder, Buster Keaton and Charlie Chaplin, the film showcases the athletic slapstick style honed over many years in the French music hall, but it also demonstrates an innate understanding of the cinematic medium. DP. A French language film.

Jacques Tati *Postman* • Paul Demange *Head Postman* ■ *Dir/Scr* Jacques Tati

School for Scoundrels ★★★ U

Comedy 1960 · UK · BW · 90mins

Based on Stephen Potter's popular one-upmanship books, this hit-and-miss comedy just about passes muster thanks to the willing performances of Ian Carmichael and Terry-Thomas. There are some amusing moments as Carmichael learns how to "confound a bounder" under the tutelage of Alastair Sim, but director Robert Hamer handles the subtle humour with a heavy hand and fails to knit the various sketches into a convincing whole. DP DVD

Ian Carmichael *Henry Palfrey* • Terry-Thomas *Raymond Delauney* • Alastair Sim *Stephen Potter* • Janette Scott *April Smith* • Dennis Price *Dunstan Dorchester* • Peter Jones *Dudley Dorchester* • Edward Chapman *Gloatbridge* • John Le Mesurier *Head waiter* • Irene Handl *Mrs Stringer* • Hattie Jacques *First instructress* ■ *Dir* Robert Hamer • *Scr* Hal E Chester, Patricia Moyes, Peter Ustinov, from the books by Stephen Potter

School for Secrets ★★★

Wartime drama 1946 · UK · BW · 107mins

After the war the RAF and the Ministry of Defence wanted to boast about their invention of radar and the job of producing, directing and writing the account went to the 25-year-old Peter Ustinov. Ralph Richardson plays the

S

boffin and there are some half-hearted action scenes and mini-melodramas to flesh out the reams of technospeak. Fortunately, Ustinov's refusal to make a blatant back-slapper suffuses the film with both a distorted attitude to heroism and a cartoonish wit. AT

Ralph Richardson *Prof Heatherville* • Richard Attenborough *Jack Arnold* • Raymond Huntley *Prof Laxton-Jones* • John Laurie *Dr McVitie* • Ernest Jay *Dr Dainty* • David Tomlinson *Mr Watlington* • Finlay Currie *Sir Duncan Wilson Wills* • Norman Webb *Dr Wainwright* • Michael Hordern *Lt Cdr Lowther* • Alvar Liddell *BBC announcer* ■ *Dir/Scr* Peter Ustinov

School for Seduction ★★★ 12

Romantic comedy drama
2004 · UK/Ger · Colour · 100mins

Director Sue Heel's debut movie comes across as a sort of distaff version of *The Full Monty*, as a beautiful Italian woman fetches up in Newcastle upon Tyne and, through her own brand of sex education, tries to help some local ladies put the heat back in their cooling relationships. In her first starring role, former TV presenter Kelly Brook is certainly alluring enough to play a voluptuous bombshell, although her ability to sustain an air of mystery recedes pretty rapidly. On the other hand, supporting players Emily Woof, Dervla Kirwan and Margi Clarke are exceptionally good as the women who learn how to live through Brook's sensual instruction. KK. Contains sexual references. DVD

Kelly Brook *Sophia Rosselini* • Dervla Kirwan *Clare* • Neil Stuke *Craig Hughes* • Tim Healy *Derek* • Margi Clarke *Irene* • Emily Woof *Kelly* • Jessica Johnson *Donna* • Ben Porter *Toni* • Daymon Britton *Mark* ■ *Dir* Sue Heel • *Scr* Sue Heel, Martin Herron

The School of Flesh ★★

Romantic drama 1998 · Fr · Colour · 105mins

Divorced, middle-aged fashion executive Isabelle Huppert is aided in her pursuit of bisexual hustler Vincent Martinez by transvestite Vincent Lindon. Instead of tension, tantrums and tempestuous sex, it's chat and heartache, as her manipulative strategies misfire. In transferring Yukio Mishima's tale of sexual obsession to a chic Parisian setting, director Benoît Jacquot and screenwriter Jacques Fieschi have dissipated the novel's reckless passion by coating it with a sheen of empty sophistication. DP. A French language film.

Isabelle Huppert *Dominique* • Vincent Martinez *Quentin* • Vincent Lindon *Chris* • Marthe Keller *Madame Thorpe* • François Berléand *Soukaz* • Danièle Dubroux *Domonique's friend* • Bernard Le Coq *Cordier* • Jean-Claude Dauphin *Louis-Guy* ■ *Dir* Benoît Jacquot • *Scr* Jacques Fieschi, from the novel *Nikutai no Gakko* by Yukio Mishima

The School of Rock ★★★★ PG

Musical comedy
2003 · US/Ger · Colour · 104mins

Jack Black is outstanding as an unemployed rock guitarist who passes himself off as a supply teacher and enlightens the pupils of a posh private school with the joys of rock and roll. Joan Cusack provides excellent comic support as the school's headmistress who is twitchily uptight but by no means unsympathetic. Director Richard Linklater deftly avoids the saccharine schmaltz that can easily ruin these kind of films and he extracts natural performances from his precocious young cast. Expertly crafted escapism and a great family movie. AS [video] DVD

Jack Black *Dewey Finn* • Joan Cusack *Principal Rosalie Mullins* • Mike White *Ned Schneebly* • Sarah Silverman *Patty Di Marco* • Joey Gaydos Jr *Zack* • Maryam Hassan *Tomika* • Miranda Cosgrove *Summer* • Kevin Clark *Freddy* ■ *Dir* Richard Linklater • *Scr* Mike White

School Spirit ★ 15

Comedy 1985 · US · Colour · 86mins

Tom Nolan is a dislikeably sex-mad high school kid who is killed in a car crash, but returns in spirit form for one last day of trying to get it on with the girls. Post-mortem powers give him a ghost of a chance. Far less haunting than Nolan is, the film mixes slapstick and sexism to unfunny and unpleasant effect. Audiences "exorcised" their right to stay away in droves. DA [video]

Tom Nolan *Billy Batson* • Elizabeth Foxx *Judy Hightower* • Roberta Collins *Mrs Grimshaw* • John Finnegan *Pinky Batson* • Larry Linville *President Grimshaw* ■ *Dir* Alan Holleb • *Scr* Geoffrey Baere

School Ties ★★★ PG

Drama 1992 · US · Colour · 102mins

Although responsible and challenging, *School Ties* isn't just a sermon sugared by the forceful presence of Chris O'Donnell and Brendan Fraser. The film is a mix of *Gentleman's Agreement* and the code-of-honour subplot of *Scent of a Woman*, as aspiring American footballer Fraser hides his Judaism to ensure that he succeeds at an exclusive school where racist remarks are part of polite conversation. Not all the pitfalls are avoided, but the performances are impressive. DP. Contains some swearing and brief nudity. [video] DVD

Brendan Fraser *David Greene* • Matt Damon *Charlie Dillon* • Chris O'Donnell *Chris Reece* • Randall Batinkoff *Rip Van Kelt* • Andrew Lowery *McGivern* • Cole Hauser *Jack Connors* • Ben Affleck *Chesty Smith* • Anthony Rapp *McGoo* • Amy Locane *Sally Wheeler* • Kevin Tighe *Coach McDevitt* • Ed Lauter *Alan Greene* ■ *Dir* Robert Mandel • *Scr* Dick Wolf, Darryl Ponicsan, from a story by Dick Wolf

Schtonk! ★★ 15

Satire 1992 · Ger · Colour · 106mins

Named after a word spluttered by Charlie Chaplin during one of Adenoid Hynkel's speeches in *The Great Dictator*, this German farce cashed in on the "Hitler Diaries" fiasco and was a huge domestic hit. However, it fared less well abroad, where the satirical digs at modern German ambivalence towards the Nazi past meant little to the average overseas viewer. Uwe Ochsenknecht, as the forger of Hitler memorabilia, and Götz George as the journalist who seizes on the diaries to make his reputation, give it everything they've got, but a little restraint would not have gone amiss. DP. In German with English subtitles. [video]

Götz George *Hermann Willié* • Uwe Ochsenknecht *Fritz Knobel* • Christiane Hörbiger *Freya von Hepp* • Rolf Hoppe *Karl Lentz* • Dagmar Manzel *Biggi* ■ *Dir* Helmut Dietl • *Scr* Helmut Dietl, Ulrich Limmer

Scissors ★★ 18

Psychological thriller
1991 · US · Colour · 90mins

Sharon Stone stars in this little known thriller as a sexually traumatised woman suffering from nightmares and illusions which are in fact a bold plot to drive her insane. Stone gives the part her all and there's creepy support from Steve Railsback in a dual role as her neighbour and his disabled brother. But the leaden direction stifles the life out of what could have been a decent little thriller. RS. Contains violence, swearing and nudity. [video]

Sharon Stone *Angie* • Steve Railsback *Alex/Cole* • Ronny Cox *Dr Carter* • Michelle Phillips *Ann* • Vicki Frederick *Nancy* • Leonard Rogel *Red Beard* ■ *Dir* Frank De Felitta • *Scr* Frank De Felitta, from a story by Joyce Selznick

Scooby-Doo ★★ PG

Mystery comedy adventure
2002 · US · Colour · 82mins

Hanna-Barbera's much-loved teen sleuths make their live-action debut in director Raja Gosnell's colourful but misjudged rendition of the popular cartoon series. It attempts to please knowing adults who remember the TV series from their youth with coded drug references and post-modernism, while delivering gags along the lines of a flatulence duel to satisfy otherwise baffled kids. James Gunn's screenplay stays true to the cartoon, but the CGI Scooby is so charmless he sucks the life out of the film. SF [video] DVD

Freddie Prinze Jr *Fred Jones* • Sarah Michelle Gellar *Daphne Blake* • Matthew Lillard *Norville "Shaggy" Rogers* • Linda Cardellini *Velma Dinkley* • Rowan Atkinson *Emile Mondavarious* • Miguel A Nunez Jr *Voodoo maestro* • Isla Fisher *Mary Jane* • Steven Grives *N'Goo Tuana* • Neil Fanning *Scooby-Doo* ■ *Dir* Raja Gosnell • *Scr* James Gunn (2), from a story by James Gunn (2), Craig Titley, from characters created by William Hanna, Joseph Barbera

Scooby-Doo 2: Monsters Unleashed ★★★ PG

Mystery comedy adventure
2004 · US · Colour · 88mins

The cast and director of 2002's disappointing cartoon adaptation reunite for this superior sequel. Sensibly focusing on Mystery Inc's most popular duo – Shaggy and Scooby – the film follows the newly disgraced team as they try to unmask a villain whose monster machine is re-creating all their classic foes. Although some of the effects are ropey, the decision to up the excitement levels with multiple spooky creatures is a prudent one. The enjoyable visual overload makes it easier to ignore the insubstantial plot, but the CGI Scooby still doesn't work. SF [video] DVD

Freddie Prinze Jr *Fred Jones* • Sarah Michelle Gellar *Daphne Blake* • Matthew Lillard *Norville "Shaggy" Rogers* • Linda Cardellini *Velma Dinkley* • Seth Green *Patrick Wisely* • Peter Boyle *Jeremiah "Old Man" Wickles* • Tim Blake Nelson *Dr Jonathan Jacobo* • Alicia Silverstone *Heather Jasper-Howe* • Neil Fanning *Scooby-Doo* ■ *Dir* Raja Gosnell • *Scr* James Gunn (2), from characters created by William Hanna, Joseph Barbera

Scooby-Doo and the Alien Invaders ★★★ U

Animated comedy adventure
2000 · US · Colour · 69mins

This cartoon adventure is the best of a spate of feature-length spin-offs from the much-loved TV series. In an action-packed story, the intrepid sleuths find themselves stranded in a spooky desert town that's apparently being invaded by extraterrestrials. Apart from Shaggy's musical interlude and a soppy romantic subplot, this brings back fond memories of the original series. The cast includes Mark Hamill, and there's the added attraction of Jennifer Love Hewitt performing the theme tune. DP [video] DVD

Scott Innes *Scooby Doo/Norville "Shaggy" Rogers* • Mary Kay Bergman *Daphne* • Frank Welker *Fred* • BJ Ward *Velma* • Jeff Glen Bennett [Jeff Bennett] *Lester* • Jennifer Hale *Dottie* • Mark Hamill *Steve* ■ *Dir* Jim Stenstrum • *Scr* Lance Falk, Davis Doi, from a story by Davis Doi, Glenn Leopold

Scorchers ★ 18

Drama 1991 · US · Colour · 77mins

An unusually strong cast, including Faye Dunaway and James Earl Jones, rants and raves to little effect in a philosophical tale of sex and southern girl Emily Lloyd who would rather hide under the bed than be in it on her wedding night. She plays Splendid and her name is the only thing that is in a tepid Tennessee Williams inspired, high-decibel shouting match barely held together by globs of blue bayou mysticism. AJ. Contains swearing and sex scenes. [video]

Faye Dunaway *Thais* • Denholm Elliott *Howler* • Emily Lloyd *Splendid* • James Earl Jones *Bear* • Jennifer Tilly *Talbot* • James Wilder *Dolan* • Anthony Geary *Preacher* • Leland Crooke *Jumper* • Luke Perry *Ray Ray* ■ *Dir* David Beaird • *Scr* David Beaird, from his play

Scorchy ★★

Crime action 1976 · US · Colour · 97mins

This forgettable action film is a mid-career low for Connie Stevens, better known for her earlier roles in a slew of dumb-but-fun 1960s beach flicks. Here she's an undercover cop tackling a high-profile drugs ring in Seattle. Heavy on the violence, and light on anything else – such as plot and characters. Stevens and a solid supporting cast do little more than carry the film from one shoot-out to the next. DA

Connie Stevens *Sergeant Jackie Parker* • Cesare Danova *Philip Bianco* • William Smith *Carl Henrich* • Norman Burton *Chief Frank O'Brien* • John Davis Chandler *Nicky* • Joyce Jameson *Mary Davis* ■ *Dir/Scr* Howard Avedis

The Score ★★★ 15

Crime thriller
2001 · US/Ger · Colour · 118mins

Arguably the three finest screen actors of their respective generations – Marlon Brando, Robert De Niro and Edward Norton – combine to flesh out what might have been a bog-standard one-last-job heist movie were it not for two things: one, it's set in Montreal (and not the familiar, over-used cities of Chicago or LA); two, hardly any computer hardware is on display when the attempted heist of a priceless sceptre from Montreal's Customs House takes place. Brando is bizarrely compelling, De Niro is stoic, operating here in a low gear, while Norton walks away with the film as an arrogant young turk. AC [video] DVD

Robert De Niro *Nick Wells* • Edward Norton *Jack "Jackie" Teller/Brian* • Angela Bassett *Diane* • Marlon Brando *Max Baron* • Gary Farmer *Burt* • Jamie Harrold *Steven* • Paul Soles *Danny* ■ *Dir* Frank Oz • *Scr* Kario Salem, Lem Dobbs, Scott Marshall Smith, from a story by Daniel E Taylor, Kario Salem

Scorpio ★★★ 15

Spy thriller 1973 · US · Colour · 109mins

All the ingredients are here for a presentable thriller – treachery, murder, intrigue and a handful of foreign locations – but a garbled script and Michael Winner's rather slipshod direction undoes much of the good work put in by his admirable cast. As the CIA agent suspected of having double standards, Burt Lancaster combines the fear of the fugitive with toughness and resourcefulness. Alain Delon does a solid job of blending duty and doubt. DP [video] DVD

Burt Lancaster *Cross* • Alain Delon *Laurier* • Paul Scofield *Zharkov* • John Colicos *McLeod* • Gayle Hunnicutt *Susan* • JD Cannon *Filchock* ■ *Dir* Michael Winner • *Scr* David W Rintels, Gerald Wilson, from a story by David W Rintels

Scorpio Rising ★★★★ 18

Erotic parody 1963 · US · Colour · 28mins

One of the most famous American underground films and a seminal force in gay cinema, Kenneth Anger's orgiastic study of leather bike boys, was banned as obscene in places as far apart as California and Belgium. Anger injects black humour into the homoeroticism, such as intercutting the action with sequences of Marlon Brando in *The Wild One* and of Christ from Cecil B DeMille's religious epic *King of Kings*. There's also Nazi

S

symbolism, occultism and 13 rock songs on the soundtrack. Tasteless, self-indulgent and juvenile at times, the brilliantly-edited film still has some fascination. RB

Bruce Byron *Scorpio* • Johnny Sapienza *Taurus* • Frank Carifi *Leo* • Bill Dorfman *The Back* • John Palone *Pin* • Ernie Allo *Joker* ■ *Dir/Scr* Kenneth Anger

The Scorpion King ★★★ 12

Action adventure fantasy
2002 · US/Ger · Colour · 87mins

Director Chuck Russell's spin-off from *The Mummy Returns* is entertaining, escapist hokum. The plot is hardly original: an evil warlord (Steven Brand), who has conquered and enslaved half the tribes in the desert, is opposed by The Rock (in an imposing, star-making performance), who unites the remaining warring factions and leads them against the common oppressor. There might not be much sense or depth amid the noisy, but not terribly gory, violence, yet the spirited action makes for an unpretentious, enjoyable adventure. AJ DVD

The Rock *Mathayus, the Scorpion King* • Michael Clarke Duncan *Balthazar* • Steven Brand *Memnon* • Kelly Hu *Cassandra* • Bernard Hill *Philos* • Grant Heslov *Arpid* • Peter Facinelli *Prince Takmet* ■ *Dir* Chuck Russell • *Scr* Stephen Sommers, Will Osborne [William Osborne], David Hayter, from a story by Stephen Sommers, Jonathan Hales

Scorpion Spring ★★★ 18

Road movie thriller
1995 · US · Colour · 85mins

Quentin Tarantino has a lot to answer for. His slick genre pastiches have inspired a whole slew of imitations of his imitations. Here's one of the better ones: a sweaty Tex-Mex border yarn about a cross-country driver who's daft enough to give a ride to a couple of drug runners. Though ultimately it lacks a genuine sting in its tale, the plot is twisty and violent enough to hold the interest. DA. Contains violence, drug abuse and swearing. DVD

Alfred Molina *Denis Brabant* • Patrick McGaw *Zac Cross* • Esai Morales *Astor* • Angel Aviles *Nadia* • Rubén Blades *Sam Zaragosa* • Kevin Tighe *Rawley Gill* • Matthew McConaughey *El Rojo* ■ *Dir/Scr* Brian Cox

La Scorta ★★★ 15

Crime thriller 1993 · It · Colour · 91mins

This involving Mafia thriller centres on the story of a mainland judge sent to Sicily to smash Mob control of the water supply. The film has a gritty semi-documentary look, which is reinforced by the episodic nature of the action and the naturalistic performances. The *carabinieri* detailed to escort the judge may be sketchily drawn macho types, but their petty problems soon come to matter as much as the success of the racket-busting mission. DP. In Italian with English subtitles. Contains violence, swearing and nudity.

Claudio Amendola *Angelo Mandolesi* • Enrico Lo Verso *Andrea Corsale* • Carlo Cecchi *Judge Michele de Francesco* • Ricky Memphis *Fabio Muzzi* • Leo Gullotta *Policeman* • Tony Sperandeo *Raffaele Frasca* • Angelo Infanti *Judge Barresi* ■ *Dir* Ricky Tognazzi • *Scr* Graziano Diana, Simona Izzo, from an idea by Stefano Sudrie, Giovanni Romoli

Scotland Yard Mystery ★★★

Mystery 1933 · UK · BW · 75mins

At the heart of this macabre mixture of medicine and malice aforethought is Home Office pathologist George Curzon, who defrauds an insurance company out of a small fortune by sending several of its wealthiest clients into a zomboid trance. Considering the budgetary contraints, this is quite an atmospheric little chiller, with Curzon's ingenuity only being matched by the arrogance and greed that plays right into inspector Gerald du Maurier's hands. DP

Gerald du Maurier *Inspector Stanton* • George Curzon *Dr Masters* • Belle Chrystall *Mary Stanton* • Grete Natzier *Irene* • Leslie Perrins *John* ■ *Dir* Thomas Bentley • *Scr* Frank Miller, from the play by Wallace Geoffrey

Scott Joplin ★★

Musical biography
1977 · US · Colour · 96mins

Motown produced this biopic of another great black musical star, after the success of *Lady Sings the Blues* which also starred Billy Dee Williams. Shot quickly as a TV movie, it was given a limited theatrical release. It traces the career of the ragtime pianist who created a nationwide craze from his struggle for recognition to his death. Great performances and terrific music do not always a great movie make, but it's not a bad shot. FL

Billy Dee Williams *Scott Joplin* • Clifton Davis *Louis Chauvin* • Margaret Avery (2) *Belle Joplin* • Eubie Blake *Will Williams* • Godfrey Cambridge *Tom Turpin* • Seymour Cassel *Dr Jaelki* ■ *Dir* Jeremy Paul Kagan • *Scr* Christopher Knopf

Scott of the Antarctic ★★★★ U

Historical drama
1948 · UK · Colour · 105mins

This is a documentary-like account of the ill-fated British expedition to the South Pole that ended in 1912. Although sticking closely to Scott's journal, it plays down his probable errors of judgement in order to concentrate on his reckless courage and the unswerving loyalty of his men. Using many of the team's actual possessions to increase the authenticity, the cast is only rarely allowed to demonstrate the humanity behind the stiff upper lips. John Mills is splendidly British in the title role, although he nearly came a cropper when he fell through the snow while filming in the Alps. DP DVD

John Mills *Captain Scott* • Derek Bond *Captain Oates* • Harold Warrender *Dr Wilson* • Diana Churchill *Kathleen Scott* • Anne Firth *Oriana Wilson* • Reginald Beckwith *Lieutenant Bowers* • James Robertson-Justice *Taffy Evans* • Kenneth More *Teddy Evans* ■ *Dir* Charles Frend • *Scr* Ivor Montagu, Walter Meade, Mary Hayley Bell

The Scoundrel ★★★

Drama 1935 · US · BW · 73mins

Noël Coward considered this to be his screen debut, though he had appeared briefly in DW Griffith's *Hearts of the World* in 1918. Written and directed jointly by Ben Hecht and Charles MacArthur, this is a fantasy about a publisher who comes back from the dead bearing a bunch of seaweed which he claims will guarantee him true love. Coward liked the idea and was also lured by the promise that his co-star would be Helen Hayes, but she dropped out at the last minute and was replaced by Julie Haydon. AT

Noël Coward *Anthony Mallare* • Julie Haydon *Cora Moore* • Stanley Ridges *Paul Decker* • Rosita Moreno *Carlotta* • Martha Sleeper *Julia Vivian* • Hope Williams *Maggie* • Ernest Cossart *Jimmy Clay* • Ben Hecht *Flophouse bum* • Charles MacArthur *Flophouse bum* • Burgess Meredith ■ *Dir* Ben Hecht, Charles MacArthur • *Scr* Ben Hecht, Charles MacArthur, from their story

The Scout ★★★★ 12

Sports comedy drama
1994 · US · Colour · 97mins

Engaging human comedy, with Albert Brooks excellent as a struggling talent scout for big-league baseball teams, and Brendan Fraser likeable as ever as an unsigned super-pitcher whom Brooks discovers on a scouting trip down Mexico way. Trouble is, Fraser gets "moundfright", and can't pitch straight when crowds are watching. So Brooks turns for help to psychiatrist Dianne Wiest. Very watchable. DA

Albert Brooks *Al Percolo* • Brendan Fraser *Steve Nebraska* • Dianne Wiest *Doctor Aaron* • Anne Twomey *Jennifer* • Lane Smith *Ron Wilson* • Michael Rapaport *Tommy Lacy* ■ *Dir* Michael Ritchie • *Scr* Andrew Bergman, Albert Brooks, Monica Johnson, from an article by Roger Angell

Scram! ★★★★ U

Comedy 1932 · US · BW · 20mins

A title that could only be appplied to Laurel and Hardy, whose disreputable appearance ensures they are ordered out of town because they might spoil the town's chances of winning a civic prize. However, several adventures later, they find a judge's wife on their side and it all ends in a lengthy laughfest. A short from producer Hal Roach, the small-town hypocrisy is never punctured as it should be, but the mythic laughmakers are at their most sweet-hearted and endearing. TH DVD

Stan Laurel *Stanley* • Oliver Hardy *Oliver* • Arthur Housman *Drunk* • Vivien Oakland *Mrs Beaumont* • Richard Cramer *Judge Beaumont* ■ *Dir* Ray McCarey • *Scr* HM Walker

Scratch ★★★ 15

Music documentary
2001 · US · Colour · 87mins

Following a survey of the Seattle grunge scene, Doug Pray fixes his aim on the art of DJing in this episodic but energetic documentary. Having explored the differences between rap and hip-hop and charted the latter's history from the 1970s, Pray concentrates on the turntable techniques – and such unsung labours as digging through mounds of obscure vinyl for samples – that make today's DJs more like musical visionaries than record collections for hire. Encounters with genuine characters such as Jazzy Jay and Qbert punctuate the plentiful performance footage. DP. Contains swearing. DVD

Dir Doug Pray • *Cinematographer* Robert Bennett • *Editor* Doug Pray

Scream ★★★★★ 18

Horror comedy 1996 · US · Colour · 106mins

The 1990s horror revival started here, with director Wes Craven's intelligent reinvention of the slasher genre. Gleefully exploring the relationship between gore movies and their core audience, while paying clever homage to such key titles as *Halloween* and *Friday the 13th*, the elaborate script subversively keeps things scary even when sinister events are at their funniest. A sick maniac on the loose in a small suburban town murdering anyone who gets horror trivia questions wrong is all Craven needs to expose the genre's knee-jerk devices in this terrific shocker that has gasps galore and a genuinely surprising denouement. AJ. Contains swearing and violence. DVD

Neve Campbell *Sidney Prescott* • Courteney Cox *Gale Weathers* • David Arquette *Deputy Dwight "Dewey" Riley* • Skeet Ulrich *Billy Loomis* • Drew Barrymore *Casey Becker* • Matthew Lillard *Stuart* • Liev Schreiber *Cotton Weary* • Jamie Kennedy *Randy* • Rose McGowan *Tatum Riley* • Lawrence Hecht *Mr Prescott* • Linda Blair *Obnoxious reporter* • Henry Winkler *Principal Himbry* • Wes Craven *Fred, the janitor* ■ *Dir* Wes Craven • *Scr* Kevin Williamson

Scream 2 ★★★ 18

Horror comedy 1997 · US · Colour · 115mins

The body count increases in this easily digestible sequel from director Wes Craven. But the scare factor is considerably diluted in this reheated outing that picks up on events two years after the notorious Woodsboro murders. Although once more cleverly twisting the genre rules, this lacks the satirical originality of the first recursive nightmare and coasts, rather than builds, on the shrewd achievements of the far superior first film. AJ. Contains violence and swearing DVD

David Arquette *Dwight "Dewey" Riley* • Neve Campbell *Sidney Prescott* • Courteney Cox *Gale Weathers* • Sarah Michelle Gellar *Casey "Cici" Cooper* • Jamie Kennedy *Randy Meeks* • Laurie Metcalf *Debbie Salt* • Elise Neal *Hallie* • Jerry O'Connell *Derek* • Jada Pinkett [Jada Pinkett Smith] *Maureen Evans* • Omar Epps *Phil Stevens* • Liev Schreiber *Cotton Weary* • David Warner *Gus Gold* ■ *Dir* Wes Craven • *Scr* Kevin Williamson

Scream 3 ★★ 18

Horror comedy 1999 · US · Colour · 111mins

The *Scream* trilogy ends, not with a bang, but a whimper in director Wes Craven's unconvincing wrap-up to the franchise. With the surviving cast members of the previous episodes now merely going through the expected self-referential motions, the worst thing about *Scream 3* is that it makes you forget how original and inventive the first outing was in slicing and dicing slasher movie conventions. Despite a reasonably surprising ending, the film runs out of steam and becomes exactly what the first *Scream* so smartly sent up. AJ DVD

David Arquette *Dwight "Dewey" Riley* • Neve Campbell *Sidney Prescott* • Courteney Cox Arquette [Courteney Cox] *Gale Weathers* • Patrick Dempsey *Mark Kincaid* • Parker Posey *Jennifer Jolie* • Scott Foley *Roman Bridger* • Lance Henriksen *John Milton* • Matt Keeslar *Tom Prinze* • Jenny McCarthy *Sarah Darling* • Liev Schreiber *Cotton Weary* • Carrie Fisher *Bianca* • Kevin Smith (2) *Silent Bob* • Roger L Jackson *"The Voice"* • Roger Corman *Studio executive* ■ *Dir* Wes Craven • *Scr* Ehren Kruger, from characters created by Kevin Williamson

Scream and Scream Again ★★★ 18

Science-fiction horror mystery
1969 · UK · Colour · 90mins

A highly regarded, but confusing, sci-fi horror tale tinged with political allegory. Vincent Price is a scientist creating an artificial super-race via gruesome transplant surgery for a foreign fascist power. Peter Cushing is an ex-Nazi and Christopher Lee a British agent in veteran genre director Gordon Hessler's imaginative blood-curdler, but the three leads' highly publicised (at the time) teaming is a cheat, as they have virtually no scenes together. Price lends dignity and class to some credible chills. AJ. Contains violence, swearing and some nudity.

Vincent Price *Dr Browning* • Christopher Lee *Fremont* • Peter Cushing *Major Benedek Heinrich* • Judy Huxtable *Sylvia* • Alfred Marks *Superintendent Bellaver* • Anthony Newlands *Ludwig* • Peter Sallis *Schweitz* • David Lodge *Det Insp Strickland* ■ *Dir* Gordon Hessler • *Scr* Christopher Wicking, from the novel *The Disorientated Man* by Peter Saxon

Scream Blacula Scream ★★ 15

Blaxploitation horror
1973 · US · Colour · 91mins

Blacula was one of the more outrageous novelties of the

S

blaxploitation era, further distinguished by its tongue-in-cheek approach. This flat sequel is merely a routine vampire yarn in which the characters happen to be black. William Marshall returns to his role of the African prince bitten in the 18th century by Dracula. He is resuscitated with an incantation and joins forces with voodoo priestess Pam Grier. There is some appeal in the film's depiction of the swinging Los Angeles scene. DM [video]

William Marshall (2) *Manuwalde* • Don Mitchell *Justin* • Pam Grier *Lisa* • Michael Conrad *Sheriff Dunlop* • Richard Lawson *Willis* • Lynne Moody *Denny* • Janee Michelle *Gloria* ■ *Dir* Bob Kelljan • *Scr* Joan Torres, Raymond Koenig, Maurice Jules, from a story by Raymond Koenig, Joan Torres

Scream of Stone ★★★ 15

Drama 1991 · Can/Ger/Fr · Colour · 102mins

The "mountain film" has been a key German genre since the silent era, but Werner Herzog's film lacks the dramatic drive to match its stunning photography. It's as if he's dissipated his trademark intensity by dividing the obsession that motivates nearly all his protagonists between two characters, mountaineer Vittorio Mezzogiorno and indoor climbing champion, Stefan Glowacz, whose race to scale El Toro in Patagonia (sponsored by TV reporter Donald Sutherland) is intensified by a rivalry for the affections of Mathilda May. DP DVD

Mathilda May *Katharina* • Vittorio Mezzogiorno *Roccia* • Stefan Glowacz *Martin* • Donald Sutherland *Ivan* • Brad Dourif *"Fingerless"* ■ *Dir* Werner Herzog • *Scr* Hans-Ulrich Klenner, Walter Saxer, Robert Geoffrion, from an idea by Reinhold Messner • *Cinematographer* Rainer Klausmann

Screamers ★★ 18

Science-fiction thriller
1995 · Can/US/Jpn · Colour · 103mins

This dingy adaptation of a Philip K Dick short story is only a moderate success. Peter Weller plays the soldier brokering peace with his futuristic enemies, who comes up against the eponymous deadly defence units, which have evolved into increasingly sophisticated adversaries. Although there are decently mounted action sequences and the post-nuclear production design is nicely realised, there are too many lulls. JC [video] DVD

Peter Weller *Colonel Hendricksson* • Andy Lauer [Andrew Lauer] *Ace* • Roy Dupuis *Becker* • Charles Powell *Ross* • Jennifer Rubin *Jessica* • Ron White *Elbarak* ■ *Dir* Christian Duguay • *Scr* Dan O'Bannon, Miguel Tejada-Flores, from the short story *Second Variety* by Philip K Dick

Screaming Mimi ★★

Thriller 1958 · US · BW · 77mins

This would-be lurid and sexy thriller, filmed in gritty black and white and directed by Gerd Oswald, falls far short of expectation. A tortuous and virtually incomprehensible plot, and an almost unwatchable hero played by an expressionless Phil Carey are the main culprits. Anita Ekberg is splendidly awful as an assault victim, and there's a palpable sexual tension whenever she's on screen. For 1950s freaks, fans of the bizarre and anyone interested in that late *film noir* style when all the streets were wet ones. TS

Anita Ekberg *Virginia Wilson* • Phil Carey [Philip Carey] *Bill Sweeney* • Gypsy Rose Lee *Joann Mapes* • Harry Townes *Dr Greenwood* • Linda Cherney *Ketti* • Romney Brent *Charlie Wilson* • Alan Gifford *Captain Bline* ■ *Dir* Gerd Oswald • *Scr* Robert Blees, from the book by Frederic Brown

Screw Loose ★ 12

Comedy 1999 · It · Colour · 84mins

Mel Brooks co-stars as a colourful mental patient sought as the final wish of a dying man, in a dreadful, near plotless comedy. Italian star/producer/director Ezio Greggio carries out his duties on both sides of the camera with staggering ineptness, not aided by the unmistakable feeling that the cast are making this up as they go along, not least a manic, unbridled Brooks. Excruciating. JC [video] DVD

Ezio Greggio *Bernardo Puccini* • Mel Brooks *Jake Gordon* • Julie Condra *Dr Barbara Collier* • Gianfranco Barra *Guido Puccini* • Randi Ingerman *Sofia* • John Karlsen *Dr Caputo* ■ *Dir* Ezio Greggio • *Scr* Rudy DeLuca, Steve Haberman

Screwballs ★ 18

Comedy 1983 · US/Can · Colour · 76mins

Five high school students on detention blame the school's last remaining virgin, Purity Busch, for their predicament, and plan revenge by contriving to see her ample breasts. This is a leering, juvenile slice of limp titillation that spawned an equally naff sequel. DF [video] DVD

Peter Keleghan *Rick McKay* • Lynda Speciale *Purity Busch* • Alan Deveau *Howie Bates* • Kent Deuters *Brent Van Dusen III* • Jason Warren *Melvin Jerkovski* • Linda Shayne *Bootsie Goodhead* ■ *Dir* Rafal Zielinski • *Scr* Linda Shayne, Jim Wynorski

Screwed ★ 15

Comedy 2000 · US · Colour · 78mins

Scott Alexander and Larry Karaszewski fell flat on their faces in directing this black comedy, which owes more to the Farrellys than Milos Forman. Norm MacDonald gives a totally lackadaisical performance as the aggrieved factotum whose bid to kidnap his uppity employer's dog goes predictably wrong. Regardless of what they're doing in such an undeserving mediocrity, Danny DeVito, Elaine Strich and Daniel Benzali provide some typically accomplished support. DP [video] DVD

Norm MacDonald *Willard Fillmore* • Dave Chappelle *Rusty P Hayes* • Danny DeVito *Grover Cleaver* • Elaine Stritch *Miss Crock* • Daniel Benzali *Detective Tom Dewey* • Sherman Hemsley *Chip Oswald* ■ *Dir/Scr* Scott Alexander, Larry Karaszewski

Scrooge ★★ U

Fantasy drama 1935 · US · BW · 77mins

Seymour Hicks plays the old curmudgeon and Donald Calthrop is Bob Cratchit in the first talking version of Dickens's *A Christmas Carol*. Viewers who expect something deeply sentimental and technically creaky will not be disappointed but it should not really be compared to the classic Alastair Sim version of 1951. AT [video]

Seymour Hicks *Ebenezer Scrooge* • Donald Calthrop *Bob Cratchit* • Robert Cochran *Fred* • Mary Glynne *Belle* • Garry Marsh *Belle's husband* • Oscar Asche *Spirit of Christmas Present* • Marie Ney *Spirit of Christmas Past* • CV France *Spirit of Christmas Future* ■ *Dir* Henry Edwards • *Scr* Seymour Hicks, H Fowler Mear, from the story *A Christmas Carol* by Charles Dickens

Scrooge ★★★★★ U

Christmas drama 1951 · UK · BW · 86mins

Released in the US under Dickens's original title, *A Christmas Carol*, this is easily the best screen version of the much-loved yuletide tale. Alastair Sim is impeccable as the miser who comes to see the error of his ways through the promptings of the spirits of Christmas Past, Present and Future. Michael Hordern makes a splendid Jacob Marley and Mervyn Johns a humble Bob Cratchit, while George Cole does well as the younger, carefree Scrooge. Beautifully designed by Ralph Brinton and directed with finesse by Brian Desmond Hurst, this is not to be missed. DP [video] DVD

Alastair Sim *Scrooge* • Kathleen Harrison *Mrs Dilber* • Jack Warner *Mr Jorkins* • Michael Hordern *Jacob Marley* • Mervyn Johns *Bob Cratchit* • Hermione Baddeley *Mrs Cratchit* • John Charlesworth *Peter Cratchit* • Glynn Dearman *Tiny Tim* • George Cole *Scrooge as young man* • Rona Anderson *Alice* • Carol Marsh *Fan, Scrooge's sister* • Brian Worth *Fred, Scrooge's nephew* • Hattie Jacques *Mrs Fezziwig* • Patrick Macnee *Young Marley* ■ *Dir* Brian Desmond Hurst • *Scr* Noel Langley, from the story *A Christmas Carol* by Charles Dickens

Scrooge ★★ U

Musical 1970 · UK · Colour · 108mins

This adaptation of the Dickens tale stars an overly made-up Albert Finney, who gives the impression he'd be happier somewhere other than on the palpably phoney Shepperton sets. Only Alec Guinness really registers, and director Ronald Neame oversees matters with the heaviest of hands. There is some compensation in watching fine twilight-year performances from Dame Edith Evans and Kenneth More. TS [video] DVD

Albert Finney *Ebenezer Scrooge* • Alec Guinness *Jacob Marley's Ghost* • Edith Evans *Ghost of Christmas Past* • Kenneth More *Ghost of Christmas Present* • Michael Medwin *Scrooge's nephew* • Laurence Naismith *Fezziwig* • David Collings *Bob Cratchit* • Anton Rodgers *Tom Jenkins* • Suzanne Neve *Isabel* • Roy Kinnear *Portly gentleman* • Gordon Jackson *Nephew's friend* ■ *Dir* Ronald Neame • *Scr* Leslie Bricusse, from the story *A Christmas Carol* by Charles Dickens • *Music/lyrics* Leslie Bricusse

Scrooged ★★★ PG

Seasonal comedy 1988 · US · Colour · 96mins

For the opening quarter, this is a joyously black Christmas treat with Bill Murray at his sour-faced best as a monstrous TV executive preparing for the festive break by sacking staff, planning a season of violence and ordering mini antlers to be stapled on the heads of mice. But it's not long before sentimentality starts seeping in, as Murray is shown what a heel he is by unconventional ghosts John Forsythe, Carol Kane and David Johansen. A missed opportunity, but some of the gags still hit the mark. JF. Contains swearing. [video] DVD

Bill Murray *Frank Cross* • Karen Allen *Claire Phillips* • John Forsythe *Lew Hayward* • Bobcat Goldthwait *Eliot Loudermilk* • Robert Mitchum *Preston Rhinelander* • Carol Kane *Ghost of Christmas Present* • John Glover *Brice Cummings* • David Johansen *Ghost of Christmas Past* • Alfre Woodard *Grace Cooley* ■ *Dir* Richard Donner • *Scr* Mitch Glazer, Michael O'Donoghue, from the story *A Christmas Carol* by Charles Dickens

Scrubbers ★★★ 15

Drama 1982 · UK · Colour · 88mins

Bursting at the seams with all manner of GBH and blaspheming, director Mai Zetterling's moderately successful attempt at showing the gritty and depressing underbelly of life in a girls' borstal and beyond was highly controversial. Utilising inventive moody camerawork and incisive editing, Zetterling does well in portraying the problems facing her two main protagonists, who emote like fury in realistic performances, but this is dreadfully depressing. SH. Contains some violence and swearing. [video] DVD

Amanda York *Carol* • Chrissie Cotterill *Annetta* • Elizabeth Edmonds *Kathleen* • Kate Ingram *Eddie* • Debbie Bishop *Doreen* • Dana Gillespie *Budd* • Camille Davis *Sharon* • Amanda Symonds *Mac* • Kathy Burke *Glennis* • Robbie Coltrane • Pam St Clement ■ *Dir* Mai Zetterling • *Scr* Mai Zetterling, Roy Minton, Jeremy Watt

Scum ★★★ 18

Prison drama 1979 · UK · Colour · 96mins

Originally written for the BBC's *Play for Today* series, Roy Minton's stark, bruising drama about conditions inside a juvenile detention centre was banned by the BBC in 1978. Minton persuaded director Alan Clarke to make a cinema version on a shoestring budget the following year. Minton presents an uncompromising picture of borstal life, made all the more shocking by Clarke's docudramatic approach, with the scenes of sexual and physical violence still having the power to revolt and arouse anger. DP. Contains violence and swearing. [video] DVD

Ray Winstone *Carlin* • Mick Ford *Archer* • John Judd *Sands* • Phil Daniels *Richards* • John Blundell *Banks* • Ray Burdis *Eckersly* • Julian Firth *Davis* • Alrick Riley *Angel* ■ *Dir* Alan Clarke • *Scr* Roy Minton

The Sea Chase ★★★ U

Second World War adventure
1955 · US · Colour · 112mins

John Wayne stars as a German sea captain in this Second World War adventure. However, the real villain of the piece is first mate Lyle Bettger, whose murder of some defenceless fishermen prompts British naval officer David Farrar to pursue Wayne's freighter across the Pacific. Director John Farrow adopts a no-nonsense approach, but Wayne's dalliance with sultry passenger Lana Turner slows up the action. However, the rivalry between the Duke and Farrar gives the picture extra edge. DP [video]

John Wayne *Captain Karl Ehrlich* • Lana Turner *Elsa Keller* • David Farrar *Commander Napier* • Lyle Bettger *Kirchner* • Tab Hunter *Cadet Wesser* • James Arness *Schlieter* • Richard Davalos *Cadet Walter Stemme* ■ *Dir* John Farrow • *Scr* James Warner Bellah, John Twist, from the novel by Andrew Geer

Sea Devils ★★

Action drama 1937 · US · BW · 87mins

A highly predictable sea drama, this is a star vehicle for the expansive personality of Victor McLaglen, playing the petty officer in the US Coastguard who wants his precious daughter Ida Lupino to marry Donald Woods's decent but dull seaman while she prefers Preston Foster's man of the world. McLaglen has Foster under his command and tries to break him at sea. AE

Victor McLaglen *Medals Malone* • Preston Foster *Mike O'Shay* • Ida Lupino *Doris Malone* • Donald Woods *Steve Webb* • Helen Flint *Sadie* • Gordon Jones *Puggy* ■ *Dir* Ben Stoloff • *Scr* Frank Wead, John Twist, PJ Wolfson

Sea Devils ★★ U

Period adventure
1952 · UK/US · Colour · 86mins

One-eyed, macho action maestro Raoul Walsh directs this routine seafaring yarn. The svelte Yvonne De Carlo plays a spy for George III who slips into France to try to uncover Napoleon's invasion plans. Rock Hudson, sporting designer stubble, is a smuggler from Guernsey who, after being duped by her, becomes a patriotic hero. Filmed in the Channel Islands and Brittany, the picture often looks good, but still falls well below Walsh's usually high standards. AT [video]

Yvonne De Carlo *Drouette* • Rock Hudson *Gilliatt* • Maxwell Reed *Rantaine* • Denis O'Dea *Lethierry* • Michael Goodliffe *Ragan* • Bryan Forbes *Willie* • Jacques Brunius *Fouche* • Gérard Oury *Napoleon* ■ *Dir* Raoul Walsh • *Scr* Borden Chase, from the novel *The Toilers of the Sea* by Victor Hugo

Sea Devils ★★

Period adventure 1982 · Sp · Colour · 84mins

Based on a Jules Verne novel, this frantic adventure does provide a few thrills amid the endless spills. Six youngsters, heading for reunions with their parents in Australia, fall foul of pirates, storms and an unfriendly whale. But that's nothing compared to the African flesh-eating ants that await them when they encounter old sea dog and slave trader Frank Brana. DP. Spanish dialogue dubbed into English. Contains violence.

Ian Sera *Mark* • Patty Shepard *Mrs Waldom* • Frank Brana *Van Hassel* • Flavia Zarzo *Jenny* • Gaby Jiminez *Dick Sand* • Aldo Sambrell *Negoro* ■ *Dir* J Piquer Simon [Juan Piquer Simon] • *Scr* Joaquin Grau, J Piquer Simon, from the novel *A Fifteen Years Old Captain* by Jules Verne

Sea Fury ★★★

Adventure 1958 · UK · BW · 97mins

After the success of *Hell Drivers*, star Stanley Baker and writer/director Cy Endfield teamed up again for this modest but strangely effective action movie set in Spain. Baker plays a drifter who gets a job aboard Victor McLaglen's salvage vessel. The pair end up competing for local siren Luciana Paluzzi. A study in macho posturing, failing sexuality and the virility of the weather: a heady brew that also features an early role for Robert Shaw. AT

Stanley Baker *Abel Hewson* • Victor McLaglen *Captain Bellew* • Luciana Paluzzi *Josita* • Grégoire Aslan *Fernando* • David Oxley *Blanco* • Robert Shaw *Gorman* • Dermot Walsh *Kelso* • Barry Foster *Vincent* ■ *Dir* C Raker Endfield [Cy Endfield] • *Scr* C Raker Endfield [Cy Endfield], John Kruse

The Sea Gull ★★★

Drama 1968 · UK · Colour · 141mins

Solid if unsensational version of the Chekhov play about life, loves and hates on a 19th-century Russian estate. Director Sidney Lumet clearly likes filming plays: he'd done *Long Day's Journey into Night* six years earlier, and would later make *Equus*. But it's the cast that really catches the eye here: a veritable who's who of 1960s British cinema. DA

James Mason *Trigorin* • Vanessa Redgrave *Nina* • Simone Signoret *Arkadina* • David Warner *Konstantin* • Harry Andrews *Sorin* • Ronald Radd *Shamraev* • Eileen Herlie *Polina* • Kathleen Widdoes *Masha* • Denholm Elliott *Dorn* ■ *Dir* Sidney Lumet • *Scr* Moura Budberg, from the play by Anton Chekhov

The Sea Gypsies ★★ U

Adventure 1978 · US · Colour · 97mins

Robert Logan enjoyed a brief period of fame at the end of the 1970s in a string of family films, most of which found him battling against the elements. In this one, he and his family find themselves trapped on the Alaskan coast when their ship sinks. All the usual clichés are present and correct, but children will lap it up and the scenery looks great. JF

Robert Logan *Travis Maclaine* • Mikki Jamison-Olsen *Kelly* • Heather Rattray *Courtney* • Cjon Damitri Patterson *Jesse* • Shannon Saylor *Samantha* ■ *Dir/Scr* Stewart Raffill

The Sea Hawk ★★★★

Silent swashbuckling adventure
1924 · US · BW · 129mins

Rivalling anything produced by Douglas Fairbanks, this thrilling adventure sweeps from Georgian England to the Algerian bazaar, in pursuit of baronet, Milton Sills as he seeks revenge on his treacherous half-brother Wallace MacDonald. Frank Lloyd is most heavily indebted to art director Stephen Goosson, whose sets for everything from a country manor to a desert palace, a Spanish galleon to a Moorish pirate ship give the action a splendour to match its zest. The performances are also top notch, with Sills's clean-cut hero complemented by Enid Bennett's chaste beloved and Wallace Beery's scowling villain. DP

Milton Sills *Sir Oliver Tressilian, the Sea Hawk* • Enid Bennett *Rosamund Godolphin* • Lloyd Hughes *Master Lionel Tressilian* • Wallace MacDonald *Master Peter Godolphin* • Marc MacDermott *Sir John Killigrew* • Wallace Beery *Jasper Leigh, a freebooter* ■ *Dir* Frank Lloyd • *Scr* JG Hawks, Walter Anthony, from a novel by Rafael Sabatini

The Sea Hawk ★★★★ U

Classic swashbuckling adventure
1940 · US · BW · 121mins

This rip-roaring adventure yarn was made at lavish expense, and, as they say, it all shows up there on the screen. Directed by Michael Curtiz, who was soon to make *Casablanca*, and starring Errol Flynn in his swashbuckling prime, it's stronger in its scenes of derring-do and Spanish galleons on the high seas than it is when detailing the political intrigue at the court of Elizabeth I. But, all in all, it even improves on the rousing 1924 silent movie of the same name, of which it is a remake – and that's praise indeed. PF

Errol Flynn *Captain Geoffrey Thorpe* • Claude Rains *Don Jose Alvarez de Cordoba* • Brenda Marshall *Doña Maria Alvarez de Cordoba* • Donald Crisp *Sir John Burleson* • Flora Robson *Queen Elizabeth I* • Alan Hale *Carl Pitt* • Henry Daniell *Lord Wolfingham* • Una O'Connor *Martha, Miss Latham* ■ *Dir* Michael Curtiz • *Scr* Seton I Miller, Howard Koch

The Sea Inside ★★★★★ PG

Drama based on a true story
2004 · Sp/Fr/It · Colour · 120mins

The controversial and emotive subject of euthanasia presents film-makers with ample opportunities to pile on the melodrama and manipulate the audience. Fortunately, Spanish director Alejandro Amenábar keeps this true-story drama funny and free of sentiment, while never sacrificing emotional integrity. Javier Bardem gives an amazing performance as quadriplegic Ramón Sampedrobe, who became famous in 1990s Spain for waging a one-man war against religious leaders, family members and the authorities for the right to die with dignity. It's clear where Amenábar's sympathies lie, but he presents both sides of the complex argument and his heartfelt human drama is all the better for this balanced view. Enormously touching and relevant. AJ. Spanish with English subtitles. DVD

Javier Bardem *Ramón Sampedro* • Belén Rueda *Julia* • Lola Duenas *Rosa* • Mabel Rivera *Manuela* • Celso Bugallo *José* • Clara Segura *Gené* • Joan Dalmau *Joaquín* ■ *Dir* Alejandro Amenábar • *Scr* Alejandro Amenábar, Mateo Gil

The Sea Is Watching ★★★ 15

Romantic drama
2002 · Jpn · BW and Colour · 114mins

Under-rated director Kei Kumai assumed control of this tale set in a 19th-century brothel on the death of Akira Kurosawa. An air of what might have been under Kurosawa's direction hangs heavy over the story of geisha Nagiko Tohno's encounters with disreputable samurai Hidetaka Yoshioka and Masatoshi Nagase. While Kumai ably re-creates the atmosphere within Tokyo's infamous Okabasho district and conceives some affecting monochrome flashbacks to Nagase's childhood, he's saddled with parallel plots that are only resolved by a dismayingly gauche contrivance. DP. In Japanese with English subtitles. Contains sex scenes and nudity. DVD

Misa Shimizu *Kikuno* • Nagiko Tohno *Oshin* • Masatoshi Nagase *Ryosuke* • Hidetaka Yoshioka *Fusanosuke* • Eiji Okuda *Ginji* • Renji Ishibashi *Zenbei* • Michiko Kawai *Osono* • Miho Tsumiki *Okichi* ■ *Dir* Kei Kumai • *Scr* Akira Kurosawa, from short stories by Shugoro Yamamoto

The Sea of Grass ★★

Western 1947 · US · BW · 123mins

This New Mexico-set western wasn't one of the more interesting vehicles for the stellar partnership of Katharine Hepburn and Spencer Tracy. Tracy is the steely cattle rancher who becomes increasingly ruthless in his efforts to protect his livelihood from the influx of homesteaders. Hepburn is his wife, who finds herself driven into the arms of Melvyn Douglas. Despite the high-powered cast, director Elia Kazan fails to engender any interest. AJ

Spencer Tracy *Col Jim Brewton* • Katharine Hepburn *Lutie Cameron* • Melvyn Douglas *Brice Chamberlain* • Robert Walker *Brock Brewton* • Phyllis Thaxter *Sara Beth Brewton* • Edgar Buchanan *Jeff* • Harry Carey *Doc Reid* • Ruth Nelson *Selina Hall* ■ *Dir* Elia Kazan • *Scr* Marguerite Roberts, Vincent Lawrence, from the novel by Conrad Richter

Sea of Love ★★★★ 18

Erotic thriller 1989 · US · Colour · 108mins

There's a real sexual charge to this tough thriller, with New York cop Al Pacino and chief murder suspect Ellen Barkin conveying a highly plausible erotic tension. It's a rather lurid story about Manhattan men being killed after advertising in the lonely-hearts columns, with a screenplay by Richard Price that's as serrated as a dozen *Jagged Edges*. The film is effectively directed by Harold Becker, who gives it an air of realism that only adds to the suspense. The title record (playing at the scene of each murder) is a bit of an irrelevance, but is still a treat to listen to. TH. Contains nudity and sex scenes. DVD

Al Pacino *Frank Keller* • Ellen Barkin *Helen* • John Goodman *Sherman Touhey* • Michael Rooker *Terry* • Lorraine Bracco *Denise* • William Hickey *Frank Keller Sr* • Richard Jenkins *Gruber* • Paul Calderon *Serafino* ■ *Dir* Harold Becker • *Scr* Richard Price

Sea of Sand ★★ U

Second World War action adventure
1958 · UK · BW · 94mins

Guy Green was a leading British cameraman (*Great Expectations*, *Oliver Twist*) who, when he became a director, lost his way nearly as badly as this desert patrol of British stalwarts (Richard Attenborough, John Gregson, Michael Craig) out to blow up an Axis fuel dump before the battle of El Alamein. Green handles the macho element with credibility, but the sentimentality that finally consigned him to directing weepie movies proves to be an irritating distraction. TH

Richard Attenborough *Trooper Brody* • John Gregson *Captain Williams* • Michael Craig *Captain Cotton* • Vincent Ball *Sergeant Nesbitt* • Percy Herbert *Trooper White* • Barry Foster *Corporal Matheson* • Ray McAnally *Sergeant Hardy* ■ *Dir* Guy Green • *Scr* Robert Westerby, from a story by Sean Fielding

The Sea Shall Not Have Them ★★ U

Second World War adventure
1954 · UK · BW · 91mins

Lewis Gilbert fails to generate much excitement with this stiff wartime tale of pluck and endurance, about a plane-load of heroes pitching into the briny. The calamities are utterly predictable, and there is no palpable tension between the castaways (clichés to a man). Each member of the stellar cast is seemingly more preoccupied with holding his own in such august company than contributing to the ensemble effort. DP

Michael Redgrave *Air Commodore Waltby* • Dirk Bogarde *Flight Sergeant Mackay* • Anthony Steel *Flying Officer Treherne* • Nigel Patrick *Flight Sergeant Slingsby* • Bonar Colleano *Sergeant Kirby* • Jack Watling *Flying Officer Harding* ■ *Dir* Lewis Gilbert • *Scr* Lewis Gilbert, Vernon Harris, from the novel by John Harris

Sea Wife ★★ PG

Second World War romantic adventure
1957 · UK · Colour · 81mins

This doesn't quite come off, mainly owing to a change of directors mid-production. Richard Burton, Joan Collins, Basil Sydney and Cy Grant play the only survivors of a ship wrecked off the coast of Singapore during the evacuation in 1942. Director Bob McNaught – he took over from Roberto Rossellini – makes a fair job of it, but the characters are predictable types and not even a shark attack can enliven the chatty lifeboat sequences. DP

Joan Collins *Sea Wife* • Richard Burton *Biscuit* • Basil Sydney *Bulldog* • Cy Grant *Number four* • Ronald Squire *Teddy* • Harold Goodwin (2) *Daily Telegraph clerk* • Joan Hickson *Scribe* ■ *Dir* Bob McNaught • *Scr* George K Burke, from the novel *Sea Wyf and Biscuit* by JM Scott

The Sea Wolf ★★★★ PG

Adventure drama 1941 · US · BW · 84mins

This exciting nautical melodrama from director Michael Curtiz is based on the classic Jack London tale. Edward G Robinson is terrific as the tormented skipper, trading intellectual barbs with rescued novelist Alexander Knox. John Garfield and Ida Lupino are both wasted in relatively minor roles, and their shipboard romance takes clear second place to the captain's fiendish desire to break the spirits of his crew members. TS

Edward G Robinson *Wolf Larsen* • John Garfield *George Leach* • Ida Lupino *Ruth Webster* • Alexander Knox *Humphrey van Weyden* • Gene Lockhart *Dr Louie Prescott* • Barry Fitzgerald *Cooky* • Stanley Ridges *Johnson* ■ *Dir* Michael Curtiz • *Scr* Robert Rossen, from the novel by Jack London

The Sea Wolves ★★ PG

Second World War drama
1980 · UK/US/Swi · Colour · 115mins

Starring a trio of venerable old sea dogs, the exploits are headed up by Gregory Peck, attempting a most ill-advised English accent, which is especially disturbing when pitched, literally, alongside Roger Moore and David Niven, with whom he once stormed the cliffs at Navarone. This tosh was directed with some verve by Andrew V McLaglen, but there's little point in pretending this has any real merit. It's not boring, though, for all sorts of strange reasons. TS

Gregory Peck *Lt Col Lewis Pugh* • David Niven *Colonel Bill Grice* • Roger Moore *Captain Gavin Stewart* • Trevor Howard *Jack Cartwright* • Barbara Kellerman *Mrs Cromwell* • Patrick Macnee *Major "Yogi" Crossley* • Patrick Allen *Colin Mackenzie* ■ *Dir* Andrew V McLaglen • *Scr* Reginald Rose, from the novel *Boarding Party* by James Leasor

Seabiscuit ★★★ PG

Period drama based on a true story
2003 · US · Colour · 134mins

Three broken men came together to own (Jeff Bridges), train (Chris Cooper) and ride (Tobey Maguire) a no-hoper racehorse named Seabiscuit, turning him into an inspirational winner that lifted the spirits of Depression-era America. Gary Ross may be unsubtle in his direction at times but the emotional core of this heart-warming story remains true and the races are grippingly executed. The three leads give superb performances, as does William H Macy, who, as the track announcer, provides some much-needed comic relief in this overly sentimental, yet thoroughly absorbing drama. AJ DVD

Tobey Maguire *Johnny "Red" Pollard* • Jeff Bridges *Charles Howard* • Chris Cooper *Tom Smith* • Elizabeth Banks (2) *Marcela Howard* • Gary Stevens *George "The Iceman" Woolf* • William H Macy *"Tick-Tock" McGlaughlin* • Kingston DuCoeur *Sam* • Eddie Jones *Samuel Riddle* • Ed Lauter *Charles Strub* • David McCullough *Narrator* ■ *Dir* Gary Ross • *Scr* Gary Ross, from the non-fiction book *Seabiscuit: an American Legend* by Laura Hillenbrand

Seagulls over Sorrento ★★★ U

Second World War drama
1954 · UK · BW · 91mins

One of the stranger products of the Cold War, this stage hit was "opened out" considerably by the Boultings for this film version. In a weird bit of casting, Gene Kelly plays an American navy scientist working on torpedo research on a Scottish island. The British boffins have already blown themselves to bits when the Yanks arrive, thus sparking a lot of transatlantic rivalry and resentment. An enjoyable and often quirky drama about the "Special Relationship". AT

Gene Kelly *Lieutenant Bradville, USN* • John Justin *Lieutenant Wharton* • Bernard Lee *Lofty Turner* • Jeff Richards *Butch Clelland, USN* • Sidney James *Charlie Badger* • Patric Doonan *PO Herbert* ■ *Dir* John Boulting, Roy Boulting • *Scr* Frank Harvey, Roy Boulting, from the play by Hugh Hastings

Sealed Cargo ★★ U

Second World War drama
1951 · US · BW · 89mins

Dana Andrews plays a Newfoundland fisherman who comes across a sailing ship with its hold full of guns, bombs and torpedoes. Manned by Nazis in disguise, led by the urbane but miscast Claude Rains, it's actually the mother ship for a German U-boat invasion of the USA. RKO gave Andrews sideburns and Carla Balenda as his leading lady, neither of which makes this film convincing. TS

Dana Andrews *Pat Bannon* • Claude Rains *Skalder* • Carla Balenda *Margaret McLean* • Philip Dorn *Conrad* • Onslow Stevens *McLean* • Skip Homeier *Steve* • Eric Feldary *Holger* ■ *Dir* Alfred Werker • *Scr* Dale Van Every, Oliver HP Garrett, Roy Huggins, from the novel *The Gaunt Woman* by Edmund Gilligan

Seance on a Wet Afternoon ★★★ 

Drama 1964 · UK · BW · 111mins

Kim Stanley gives a compelling, Oscar-nominated performance as an unbalanced medium in this engrossing and imaginative drama. She orders her brow-beaten husband Richard Attenborough to kidnap a wealthy industrialist's daughter so she can enhance her reputation as a spiritualist by "finding" the youngster. The tension screws are chillingly turned when Attenborough realises his wife will go to any lengths to achieve celebrity status. Director Bryan Forbes skilfully conjures up suspenseful uncertainty as the ghastly implications of Stanley's plan unfold. AJ DVD

Kim Stanley *Myra Savage* • Richard Attenborough *Billy Savage* • Mark Eden *Charles Clayton* • Nanette Newman *Mrs Clayton* • Judith Donner *Amanda Clayton* • Patrick Magee *Supt Walsh* • Gerald Sim *Sergeant Beedle* ■ *Dir* Bryan Forbes • *Scr* Bryan Forbes, from the novel by Mark McShane

The Search ★★★★ U

Drama 1948 · US · BW · 103mins

Although Montgomery Clift had already made his first movie *Red River*, protracted delays kept that film off the screen until after *The Search* had premiered, giving movie-goers their first sight of the actor who was the forerunner of the Method style of acting. This semi-documentary won an Oscar for best motion picture story, but Clift largely improvised his own dialogue for his portrayal of a soldier in postwar Germany, who befriends a nine-year-old homeless boy. Clift gives a casual, unaffected performance, and Ivan Jandl, as the boy, was awarded a special juvenile Oscar. TS

Montgomery Clift *Ralph "Steve" Stevenson* • Aline MacMahon *Mrs Murray* • Wendell Corey *Jerry Fisher* • Jarmila Novotna *Mrs Hanna Malik* • Mary Patton *Mrs Fisher* • Ewart G Morrison *Mr Crookes* • William Rogers *Tom Fisher* • Ivan Jandl *Karel Malik* ■ *Dir* Fred Zinnemann • *Scr* Richard Schweizer, David Wechsler, Paul Jarrico

Search and Destroy ★★ 15

Action drama 1978 · US · Colour · 89mins

This potboiler is indistinguishable from the hundreds of other movies that have been made for the lucrative and undemanding video market. The plot involves a Vietnamese officer who, after the war, seeks violent revenge against the American GIs who crossed him. You'd expect the likes of George Kennedy and Don Stroud to pop up in something like this: they do. DA

Perry King *Kip Moore* • Don Stroud *Buddy Grant* • Tisa Farrow *Kate* • Park Jong Soo *Assassin* • George Kennedy *Anthony Fusqua* • Tony Sheer *Frank Malone* ■ *Dir* William Fruet • *Scr* Don Enright

Search and Destroy ★★ 18

Black comedy drama
1995 · US · Colour · 87mins

This hopelessly misconceived would-be black comedy was the disappointing debut feature from controversial New York visual artist David Salle. Griffin Dunne stars as a Florida film producer, his business and private life down the tubes, whose last throw of the dice is putting together a film deal with kooky TV guru Dennis Hopper. Salle has assembled a dream cast that only partially redeems this poorly directed film, which relies too heavily on its weird assortment of characters and events to sustain the thin narrative. RS. Contains swearing, nudity, sexual references and some violence.

Griffin Dunne *Martin Mirkheim* • Illeana Douglas *Marie Davenport* • Christopher Walken *Kim Ulander* • Dennis Hopper *Dr Luther Waxling* • John Turturro *Ron* • Rosanna Arquette *Lauren Mirkheim* • Ethan Hawke *Roger* • Martin Scorsese *The accountant* ■ *Dir* David Salle • *Scr* Michael Almereyda, from the play by Howard Korder

Search for Danger ★★

Detective mystery 1949 · US · BW · 66mins

The Falcon's 16th and last assignment is a double-murder mystery, with the suave sleuth in pursuit of the gambler who's left Albert Dekker and Ben Welden out of pocket to the tune of $100,000. His task is not made easier, however, by the devious distraction provided by Myrna Dell. Considering he was making his third appearance as Michael Waring, professional magician John Calvert still looks uncomfortable, and he handed over to Charles McGraw for the ensuing TV series. DP

John Calvert *The Falcon/Michael Waring* • Albert Dekker *Kirk* • Myrna Dell *Wilma Rogers* • Ben Welden *Gregory* • Douglas Fowley *Inspector* • Michael Mark *Perry* ■ *Dir* Jack Bernhard • *Scr* Don Martin, from a story by Jerome Epstein, from the character created by Michael Arlen

The Search for John Gissing ★★★

Comedy 2001 · US · Colour · 91mins

Moments of inspired situation comedy are swamped by a growing desperation to sustain the madcap momentum in this increasingly contrived office farce. Arriving in London to assume his new post, American executive Mike Binder is sabotaged at every turn by Alan Rickman, the man he's been hired to replace. Rickman's genius for teetering on the brink of excess enables him to steal the show from Binder, who is also frequently upstaged by long-suffering wife, Janeane Garofalo. Fun, but wildly inconsistent. DP

Mike Binder *Matthew Barnes* • Janeane Garofalo *Linda Barnes* • Alan Rickman *John Gissing* • Juliet Stevenson *Gwyneth Moore* ■ *Dir/Scr* Mike Binder

The Search for One-Eye Jimmy ★★ 15

Comedy 1996 · US · Colour · 84mins

Holt McCallany is an aspiring film-maker who decides to shoot a movie documenting life in his own South Brooklyn neighbourhood. While conducting interviews with various colourful local characters he stumbles across a mystery – the disappearance of "One-Eye" Jimmy. He's convinced his film will break him into the big time if he can follow (and solve) the mystery. A valiant low-budget attempt at character comedy with well-known faces in caricature roles, it's too meandering for its own good. DF. Contains swearing. DVD

Nick Turturro [Nicholas Turturro] *Junior* • Steve Buscemi *Ed Hoyt* • Michael Badalucco *Joe Head* • Ray "Boom Boom" Mancini [Ray Mancini] *Lefty* • Holt McCallany *Les* • Anne Meara *Holly Hoyt* • John Turturro *Disco Bean* • Samuel L Jackson *Colonel Ron* • Jennifer Beals *Ellen* • Tony Sirico *The Snake* ■ *Dir/Scr* Sam Henry Kass

The Search for Signs of Intelligent Life in the Universe ★★★

Comedy drama 1991 · US · Colour · 106mins

The filmed version of comedian-turned-movie star Lily Tomlin's hit one-woman Broadway show. The bare stage is transformed with colourful sets to reflect the history of each individual, purposely breaking the seamless stand-up illusion. All of Tomlin's familiar characters do a turn, including Lyn, who's going through a midlife crisis. It's a sustained monologue by Lyn – where all her 1960s hippy and feminist revolutionary dreams are catalogued with despair – which ends this engrossing record of Tomlin's talent for accents and mimicry. AJ

Lily Tomlin ■ *Dir* John Bailey • *Scr* Jane Wagner, from her play

The Searchers ★★★★★ U

Classic western 1956 · US · Colour · 113mins

Like Monument Valley, where it was filmed, John Ford's masterpiece western of revenge and reconciliation is massive and unmissable. It touches the heart of racist darkness and cleanses itself in the process. As John Wayne's Ethan sets out to kill both the "redskin" butcher of his brother's family and the abducted niece who, in his eyes, has turned native, his five-year quest becomes a search for his own soul. Jeffrey Hunter is the conscience along for the ride, but it's the complexity of Ethan – as the antihero being redeemed – that reveals him as a rootless pioneer, forever framed in the doorways of family homesteads of which he can never become part. Ford's great allegory is of a people lost and found. TH DVD

John Wayne *Ethan Edwards* • Jeffrey Hunter *Martin Pawley* • Vera Miles *Laurie Jorgensen* • Ward Bond *Sam Clayton* • Natalie Wood *Debbie Edwards* • John Qualen *Lars Jorgensen* • Olive Carey *Mrs Jorgensen* • Henry Brandon *Chief Scar* • Ken Curtis *Charlie McCorry* • Harry Carey Jr *Brad Jorgensen* ■ *Dir* John Ford • *Scr* Frank S Nugent, from the novel by Alan LeMay • *Cinematographer* Winton C Hoch

The Searching Wind ★★★

Drama 1946 · US · BW · 107mins

A high-toned – in both content and production – exploration of political and ideological issues as represented by an American career diplomat (Robert Young) of vacillating opinions. Set in the 1930s, with the spectre of war hovering over it, the screenplay was written by Lillian Hellman from her own Broadway play, and is directed with gravity by William Dieterle. It's well-played by Young, and an excellent cast, but the literate material is more suited to its stage origins. RK

Robert Young (1) *Alex Hazen* • Sylvia Sidney *Cassie Bowman* • Ann Richards *Emily Hazen* • Dudley Digges *Moses* • Albert Basserman *Count Von Stammer* • Dan Seymour *Torrone* • Douglas Dick *Sam* ■ *Dir* William Dieterle • *Scr* Lillian Hellman, from her play

The Seashell and the Clergyman ★★★★

Silent experimental classic
1928 · Fr · BW · 29mins

Although dismissed by the Surrealist group at the time, this is generally accepted as the first Surrealist film. The cryptic scenario was written by Antonin Artaud, but the avant-garde theorist, writer and actor, who had intended to direct it and play the lead, later repudiated it – perhaps because it was directed by a woman. Germaine Dulac brought her technical skill to bear on the plotless film which shows, by automatic association, the dreams of a frustrated and celibate clergyman. An interesting, but fruitless attempt at "pure cinema", free from the influence of literature, the theatre and other visual arts. RB.

Alex Allin *The clergyman* • Génica Athanasiou *The woman* ■ *Dir* Germaine Dulac • *Scr* Antonin Artaud

Season of Dreams ★ PG

Drama 1987 · US · Colour · 90mins

A disappointing coming-of-age drama which milks the golden hues of rural America for all their worth but sinks under an uninvolving script. Megan Follows plays the troubled young teenager, but not even the presence of such charismatic performers as Christine Lahti, Frederic Forrest, Jason Gedrick and Peter Coyote can rescue this dud. JF. Contains swearing.

Christine Lahti *Kathleen Morgan* • Frederic Forrest *Buster McGuire* • Megan Follows *Anna Mae Morgan* • Jason Gedrick *Gary Connaloe* • Peter Coyote *Photographer* ■ *Dir* Martin Rosen • *Scr* Victoria Jenkins

Season of Fear ★

Thriller 1989 · US · Colour · 89mins

A young man visits his famous inventor father in the Midwestern heartland to rekindle their relationship after a 20-year estrangement and becomes romantically entangled with his sexy new stepmother. It all ends very badly with a shoot-out and much writhing in dirt. Completely fatuous and dragged out beyond belief, writer/director Doug Campbell's odd erotic thriller could almost pass as avant-garde because it's so confused and affected. AJ

S

Michael Bowen *Mick Drummond* • Ray Wise *Fred Drummond* • Clancy Brown *Ward* • Clare Wren *Sarah Drummond* • Michael J Pollard *Bob* • Heather Jane MacDonald *Penny* • Dean Fortunato *David* ■ *Dir* Doug Campbell • *Scr* Doug Campbell, from a story by Scott J Mulvaney, Doug Campbell

Season of Passion ★★★

Romantic drama 1960 · Aus · BW · 94mins

This willing Australian melodrama slowly creeps under the skin thanks to the fascinating contrasts in the acting styles of its star quartet. John Mills and Ernest Borgnine are cleverly cast as chalk-and-cheese sugar cane cutters in Sydney for their annual holiday, while Anne Baxter and Angela Lansbury are their feisty sheilas who refuse to tolerate their rough and ready notions of romance any longer. Director Leslie Norman showcases the performances, but occasionally lets the authentic Aussie atmosphere slip. DP

Ernest Borgnine *Roo* • John Mills *Barney* • Anne Baxter *Olive* • Angela Lansbury *Pearl* • Vincent Ball *Dowd* • Ethel Gabriel *Emma* • Janette Craig *Bubba* ■ *Dir* Leslie Norman • *Scr* John Dighton, from the play *Summer of the Seventeenth Doll* by Ray Lawler

Season of the Witch ★★ 18

Horror 1972 · US · Colour · 104mins

Between his classic *Night of the Living Dead* and its sequel, *Dawn of the Dead*, cult director George A Romero experimented with feminist fright in this tedious horror, in which bored suburban housewife Jan White dabbles in black magic, casting a spell that will lead to murder. Apart from some mildly interesting dream sequences, this dated and slow psychological study is unexcitingly presented and for Romero completists only. AJ [video]

Jan White *Joan* • Ray Laine *Gregg* • Ann Muffly *Shirley* • Joedda McClain *Nikki* • Bill Thunhurst *Jack* • Virginia Greenwald *Marion* ■ *Dir/Scr* George A Romero

Seasons of the Heart ★★

Period drama 1993 · US · Colour · 100mins

It's rather unusual to find a tale about pioneering folk that focuses on the female characters. Here, as the wagon-train wife attempting to come to terms with the loss of her two daughters, Leigh Lombardi manages an affecting display of grief. Sadly, she simply resorts to petulence when husband Sam Hennings tries to persuade her to accept orphan Logan Hall as her own. Deborah Hofstedt's script proficiently demonstrates the strength of maternal feeling, but the Christmas-time finale is overly sentimental. DP

Leigh Lombardi *Martha Richards* • Sam Hennings *Jed Richards* • Claude Akins *William Clay* • Logan Hall *Daniel Merriss* • Yvonne De Carlo *Older Martha* ■ *Dir* TC Christensen • *Scr* Deborah Hofstedt, from a story by Lael J Littke

S

Sebastian ★★★

Comedy thriller 1968 · UK · Colour · 99mins

This semi-spoof of Swinging Sixties spy stories ends up packing so much plot into the final third that its careful characterisation and smart satire go out of the window. The tensions within John Gielgud's eavesdropping unit are far more intriguing than spymaster Ronald Fraser's attempts to compromise codebuster Dirk Bogarde, and the cast seems more at ease with the knowing humour and hushed tones of this opening segment than it does with the blaring muzak and trippy dreams of the finale. DP

Dirk Bogarde *Sebastian* • Susannah York *Becky Howard* • Lilli Palmer *Elsa Shahn* • John Gielgud *Head of Intelligence* • Janet Munro *Carol* • Margaret Johnston *Miss Elliott* • Nigel Davenport *General Phillips* • Ronald Fraser *Toby* • Donald Sutherland *American* • Alan Freeman *TV disc jockey* ■ *Dir* David Greene • *Scr* Gerald Vaughan-Hughes, from a story by Leo Marks • *Music* Jerry Goldsmith

Sebastiane ★★ 18

Historical drama 1976 · UK · Colour · 81mins

Sebastian was a favourite at the court of Roman Emperor Diocletian and Derek Jarman's explicit biopic details his death at the hands of fellow soldiers while in naked exile. Shot on a semi-improvisational basis, with a largely non-professional cast, Jarman explores with frank honesty why Renaissance artists found this gay hero to be the perfect vehicle to depict homoeroticism in their paintings. A must for gay viewers, but others may find it rather a hard slog. AJ. In Latin with English subtitles. [video]

Leonardo Treviglio *Sebastian* • Barney James *Severus* • Neil Kennedy *Max* • Richard Warwick *Justin* • Donald Dunham *Claudius* • Ken Hicks *Adrian* ■ *Dir* Derek Jarman, Paul Humfress • *Scr* Derek Jarman, James Waley, Jack Welch (Latin translation)

Second Best ★★★ 12

Drama 1993 · US · Colour · 100mins

This largely overlooked drama perfectly illustrates the genius for restraint that is the basis of William Hurt's acting talent. As the shy Welsh postmaster who decides to adopt a son, he brilliantly exposes the mixed emotions of a lonely, self-contained 40-something trying to break with the habits of a lifetime and start anew. Director Chris Menges nearly loses control in the scenes featuring Miles's disturbed dad, Keith Allen, but mostly gets the tone right. DP. Contains some violence and swearing [video]

William Hurt *Graham* • John Hurt *Uncle Turpin* • Chris Cleary Miles *James* • Nathan Yapp *Jimmy* • Keith Allen *John* • Jane Horrocks *Debbie* • Prunella Scales *Margery* ■ *Dir* Chris Menges • *Scr* David Cook, from his novel

Second Chance ★★★

Romantic crime drama 1953 · US · Colour · 82mins

Originally shown in 3-D, this relies on the potency of its starpower, as laconic boxer Robert Mitchum falls for lovely gangster's moll Linda Darnell, who is on the run from killer Jack Palance. Director Rudolph Maté keeps this moving along, and the Mexican scenery is striking. This is very much a product of RKO under its new boss Howard Hughes, featuring good-looking stars in exotic locations. TS

Robert Mitchum *Russ Lambert* • Linda Darnell *Clare Shepperd* • Jack Palance *Cappy Gordon* ■ *Dir* Rudolph Maté • *Scr* Oscar Millard, Sydney Boehm, DM Marshman Jr, from a story by DM Marshman Jr

Second Chance ★★★

Drama 1976 · Fr · Colour · 99mins

Charged as an accessory to murder, a young woman gives birth to a baby while in prison. Freed many years later, she is reunited with her teenage son, who falls in love with her friend from prison, while she herself finds happiness with the boy's teacher. This glossy, glamorised and superficial melodrama was written and directed by Claude Lelouch, and is undemanding viewing for the romantically minded. RK. In French with English subtitles.

Catherine Deneuve *Catherine Berger* • Anouk Aimée *Sarah Gordon* • Charles Denner *Lawyer* • Francis Huster *Patrick* • Niels Arestrup *Henri Lano* • Colette Baudot *Lucienne Lano* • Jean-Jacques Briot *Simon Berger* ■ *Dir/Scr* Claude Lelouch • *Music* Francis Lai

Second Chorus ★★★ U

Musical comedy 1940 · US · BW · 84mins

Playing an undergraduate at the age of 41, Fred Astaire considered this the worst film he ever made. But an off-form Fred is still worth watching, even though his dancing style is undeniably cramped by Paulette Goddard, who is the subject of his romantic rivalry with Burgess Meredith. Goddard (then Mrs Charlie Chaplin) married Meredith in 1942. Artie Shaw earned an Oscar nomination for best score and shared another with Johnny Mercer for the song *Love of My Life*. DP [video] DVD

Fred Astaire *Danny O'Neill* • Paulette Goddard *Ellen Miller* • Burgess Meredith *Hank Taylor* • Charles Butterworth *Mr Chisholm* • Frank Melton *Stu* ■ *Dir* HC Potter • *Scr* Frank Cavett, Elaine Ryan, Johnny Mercer, Ian McLellan Hunter, from a story by Frank Cavett

The Second Civil War ★★★

Political satire 1997 · US · Colour · 97mins

America finds itself on the brink of another civil war when the US president (Phil Hartman) allows a group of refugee children to settle in Idaho. Governor Beau Bridges has other ideas and decides to close the state borders. Media frenzy escalates the conflict as the nation takes sides over the controversial issue. Bridges won an Emmy for his performance and he's well supported by James Coburn, Joanna Cassidy and James Earl Jones in this wicked TV satire. MC

Beau Bridges *Governor Jim Farley* • Joanna Cassidy *Helena Newman* • James Coburn *Jack Buchan* • Kevin Dunn *Jimmy Cannon* • Phil Hartman *The President* • Dan Hedaya *Mel Burgess* • James Earl Jones *Jim Calla* ■ *Dir* Joe Dante • *Scr* Martyn Burke

The Second Coming of Suzanne ★

Fantasy drama 1974 · US · Colour · 90mins

Pretentious blip in the early career of Richard Dreyfuss. He plays a frustrated film-maker obsessed with the idea that Christ was a woman. He tries to film his vision, with Sondra Locke as the sex-swapped Messiah. Just about as bad as it sounds, the film was reportedly inspired by the lyrics of the Leonard Cohen song, *Suzanne*, which features on the soundtrack. DA

Sondra Locke *Suzanne* • Paul Sand *Artist* • Jared Martin *Film-maker* • Richard Dreyfuss *Clavius* • Gene Barry *TV commentator* ■ *Dir/Scr* Michael Barry

Second Fiddle ★★★ U

Musical comedy 1939 · US · BW · 86mins

You'd be forgiven if you couldn't tell one Sonja Henie vehicle from the next, but this is the one with the Irving Berlin score, where Tyrone Power plays the Hollywoodite who starts off promoting a romance for La Henie, but ends up falling for her himself. The 20th Century-Fox production values are all high gloss, and the ever-professional director Sidney Lanfield keeps the fluffy proceedings running smoothly. Also on hand, for nostalgia buffs, are the delightful Rudy Vallee and Edna May Oliver. TS

Sonja Henie *Trudi Hovland* • Tyrone Power *Jimmy Sutton* • Rudy Vallee *Roger Maxwell* • Edna May Oliver *Aunt Phoebe Hovland* • Mary Healy *Jean Varick* • Lyle Talbot *Willie Hogger* • Alan Dinehart *George "Whit" Whitney* ■ *Dir* Sidney Lanfield • *Scr* Harry Tugend, from a story by George Bradshaw • *Music/lyrics* Irving Berlin

Second Generation ★★ 15

Comedy thriller 1999 · UK · Colour · 80mins

Shot on digital video amid the disparate Asian communities of London's East End, Shane O'Sullivan's ambitious feature is a misfiring comedy thriller which suffers from an uncertainty of tone and some am-dram acting. Shigetomo Yutani and pop star Hanayo are more willing than able as the hapless Japanese detective and the runaway Hong Kong bride he's sent to track down. But, at least there's an honesty about their work that is surprisingly lacking from Saeed Jaffrey's pantomimic turn. DP. In English, Hindi and Japanese with subtitles.

Hanayo *Lili* • Shigetomo Yutani *Go* • Nitin Chandra Ganatra *Jamal* • Adrian Pang *Jimmy* • Saeed Jaffrey *Saeed Mian* ■ *Dir/Scr* Shane O'Sullivan

The Second Jungle Book ★★ PG

Adventure 1997 · US · Colour · 85mins

Loosely based on the Rudyard Kipling original, and most definitely nothing to do with Disney, this live-action family film has jungle boy Mowgli and bear-friend Baloo driven deep into the interior by the unwanted attentions of a talent scout for PT Barnum's circus. There, they stumble on a lost city whose sole inhabitant is deranged British soldier Roddy McDowall. This offers some fun for kids, but grown-ups will wonder why the animal sequences look like they've been spliced in from another film altogether. DA [video] DVD

Jamie Williams *Mowgli* • William Campbell [Bill Campbell] *Harrison* • Roddy McDowall *King Murphy* • David Paul Francis *Chuchundra* • Dyrk Ashton *Karait* • Cornelia Hayes O'Herlihy *Emily Reece* ■ *Dir* Duncan McLachlan • *Scr* Matthew Horton, Bayard Johnson, from the books by Rudyard Kipling

Second Serve ★★★★ 15

Biographical drama 1986 · US · Colour · 90mins

On paper it has all the signs of a tacky hagiography, but a towering performance from Vanessa Redgrave and a taut, insightful script make this a TV movie of unusual depth and sensitivity. The true story of transsexual surgeon-turned-tennis star Renee Richards is adapted by director Anthony Page into an intriguing, multi-layered look at the agonies and resourcefulness of a truly extraordinary personality. Redgrave plays both Richards's male and female personae wonderfully. SH [video]

Vanessa Redgrave *Richard Radley/Renee Richards* • Martin Balsam *Dr Stone* • William Russ *Josh* • Alice Krige *Gwen* • Kerrie Keane *Meriam* ■ *Dir* Anthony Page • *Scr* Stephanie Liss, Gavin Lambert, from the autobiography by Renee Richards, John Ames

Second Sight ★★ PG

Comedy 1989 · US · Colour · 80mins

Few would give this lame cop comedy a second glance. It's one of those "everything but the kitchen sink" movies that throws in any plot device it can think of, the most prominent of which is partnering ex-cop John Larroquette and psychic Bronson Pinchot as dumb detectives in search of laughs. Larroquette once again fails to set the big screen alight. RT [video]

John Larroquette *Willis* • Bronson Pinchot *Bobby* • Bess Armstrong *Sister Elizabeth* • Stuart Pankin *Dr Preston Pickett* • John Schuck *Manoogian* ■ *Dir* Joel Zwick • *Scr* Tom Schulman, Patricia Resnick

Second Skin ★★★ 18

Romantic drama 2000 · Sp · Colour · 104mins

The evergreen eternal triangle plot is given a modern twist in director Gerardo Vera's absurdly gripping Spanish melodrama. Jordi Molla is apparently happily married to Ariadna Gil, but her discovery of a hotel bill in his pocket leads to accusations of an affair with another woman. The truth is, he's having a relationship with another man, Javier Bardem. That's really the starting point for Vera's study in fluctuating sexuality, as Molla struggles to come to terms with his double life and Gil with the reality of her failed marriage. AJ. In Spanish with English subtitles. Contains swearing and sex scenes.

Javier Bardem *Diego* • Jordi Mollà *Alberto Garcia* • Ariadna Gil *Elena* • Cecilia Roth *Eva* • Javier Albala *Rafael* • Adrian Sac *Manuel* ■ *Dir* Gerardo Vera • *Scr* Angeles Gonzalez-Sinde, from an idea by Gerardo Vera

Second Thoughts ★ 15

Melodrama 1982 · US · Colour · 93mins

Second thoughts are what you should have before deciding to view this turkey. Lucie Arnaz (Lucille Ball for mum and Desi Arnaz for dad) is a bored attorney who swaps her stuffy hubby for hippy misfit Craig Wasson in an attempt to spice up her life. The relationship founders but not before she gets pregnant. From there on the film descends into a right-to-life debate that is neither informative nor insightful. Unpleasant. FL

Lucie Arnaz *Amy Ash* • Craig Wasson *Will Thorson* • Ken Howard *John Michael Tombs* • Anne Schedeen *Janis* • Arthur Rosenberg *Dr Eastman* • Peggy McCay *Dr Martha Carpenter* • Joe Mantegna *Orderly* ■ *Dir* Lawrence Turman • *Scr* Steve Brown, from a story by Terry Louise Fisher, Steve Brown

The Second Time Around ★★ U

Comedy western 1961 · US · Colour · 98mins

Debbie Reynolds stars as a young widow from the east who moves to an Arizona frontier town to start life afresh. Unfazed by the culture shock, she labours in the mud as a humble ranch-hand (for the always admirable Thelma Ritter) before becoming sheriff and ridding the town of its lawless elements. The spirited Reynolds is the attraction of this innocuous but pleasant movie, which can't decide whether it's a western, a comedy, a romance or a drama. RK

Debbie Reynolds *Lucretia Rogers* • Steve Forrest *Dan Jones* • Andy Griffith *Pat Collins* • Juliet Prowse *Rena* • Thelma Ritter *Aggie* • Ken Scott *Sheriff John Yoss* • Isobel Elsom *Mrs Rogers* ■ *Dir* Vincent Sherman • *Scr* Oscar Saul, Cecil Dan Hansen, from the novel *Star in the West* by Richard Emery Roberts

The Second Victory ★★ 15

Period action drama
1986 · UK · Colour · 98mins

Adapted from his own novel by Morris West, this is a drama set in Austria shortly after the Second World War. Anthony Andrews is the bold soldier in pursuit of the sniper who shot and killed his sergeant. From there on in, it's strictly action fare, with Andrews looking ill-at-ease, having to tote a gun and look vengeful at the same time. Nice scenery, though. JB

Anthony Andrews *Major Hanlon* • Max von Sydow *Dr Huber* • Helmut Griem *Karl Fischer* • Mario Adorf *Dr Sepp Kunzli* • Birgit Doll *Anna Kunzli* • Wolfgang Reichmann *Max Holzinger* • Renée Soutendijk *Traudi Holzinger* • Immy Schell *Liesl Holzinger* ■ *Dir* Gerald Thomas • *Scr* Morris West, from his novel

The Second Woman ★★

Thriller 1951 · US · BW · 91mins

This minor melodrama explains why Robert Young's architect suffers from blackouts and memory loss and is driven to attempt suicide. More usually it's a female who is being victimised in the psychological thrillers of this period, but here it's girlfriend Betsy Drake who exposes the villain who is out to deprive Young of his sanity. The best feature is the photography by Hal Mohr, which aims at a *film noir* moodiness. AE

Robert Young (1) *Jeff Cohalan* • Betsy Drake *Ellen Foster* • John Sutton *Keith Ferris* • Henry O'Neill *Ben Sheppard* • Florence Bates *Amelia Foster* • Morris Carnovsky *Dr Hartley* ■ *Dir* James V Kern • *Scr* Robert Smith, Mort Briskin

Secondhand Lions ★★★ 12

Period comedy drama
2003 · US · Colour · 104mins

Haley Joel Osment plays a teenager who is sent to stay with his yarn-spinning great-uncles (Michael Caine and Robert Duvall), two cranky old men who, rumour has it, have a legendary stash of loot hidden on their remote Texan homestead. Caine and Duvall succeed in creating a sense of mystery and mischief, but this is unfortunately dissipated each time director Tim McCanlies flashes back to their all-action past. The comedy is corny and the suspense is rarely sustained, but this is still enjoyable. DP. Contains violence. DVD

Michael Caine *Garth McCann* • Robert Duvall *Hubbard "Hub" McCann* • Haley Joel Osment *Walter* • Kyra Sedgwick *Mae* • Nicky Katt *Stan* • Emmanuelle Vaugier *Princess Jasmine* • Christian Kane *Young Hub* • Kevin Haberer *Young Garth* ■ *Dir/Scr* Tim McCanlies

Seconds ★★★★

Cult science-fiction thriller
1966 · US · BW · 105mins

Dealing with the uncomfortable subject of spiritual rebirth, this brilliant social science-fiction movie from seminal 1960s director John Frankenheimer is years ahead of its time in both theme and style. X-rated on its original release, the frightening premise is intensified by cameraman James Wong Howe's use of stark black-and-white photography and distorting fish-eye lenses. Under-rated star Rock Hudson gives one of his best performances as the deeply disturbed recipient of life-changing plastic surgery. TS

Rock Hudson *Antiochus "Tony" Wilson* • Salome Jens *Nora Marcus* • John Randolph *Arthur Hamilton* • Will Geer *Old man* • Jeff Corey *Mr Ruby* • Richard Anderson *Dr Innes* ■ *Dir* John Frankenheimer • *Scr* Lewis John Carlino, from the novel by David Ely

Le Secret ★★★ 18

Drama 2000 · Fr · Colour · 104mins

Having co-scripted Erick Zonca's acclaimed drama, *The Dream Life of Angels*, Virginie Wagon reunited with the talented Frenchman for her directorial debut. Anne Coësens is creditably vulnerable as the married encyclopedia saleswoman who disregards husband Michel Bompoil's suggestion of a second child to indulge in a fling with house-sitting American dancer Tony Todd. With a caustic wit complementing its psychological intensity and the graphic sexuality, this is very much an adult film, and only the cosy ending feels forced. DP. In French and English with subtitles.

Anne Coësens *Marie* • Michel Bompoil *François* • Tony Todd *Bill* • Quentin Rossi *Paul* ■ *Dir* Virginie Wagon • *Scr* Virginie Wagon, Erick Zonca

Secret Admirer ★ 15

Comedy 1985 · US · Colour · 93mins

An unsigned love letter leads the unwary into a repulsive comedy of errors that verges on the insulting to both teenagers and adults alike. Fred Ward and Dee Wallace Stone do what they can as the parents and C Thomas Howell and Lori Loughlin try to elevate it above the level of farcical teen-sex comedy but ultimately fail. FL

C Thomas Howell *Michael Ryan* • Lori Loughlin *Toni* • Kelly Preston *Deborah Anne Fimple* • Dee Wallace Stone *Connie Ryan* • Cliff De Young *George Ryan* • Fred Ward *Lou Fimple* • Leigh Taylor-Young *Elizabeth Fimple* • Casey Siemaszko *Roger Despard* ■ *Dir* David Greenwalt • *Scr* Jim Kouf, David Greenwalt

The Secret Adventures of Tom Thumb ★★ 12

Animated fantasy 1993 · UK · Colour · 57mins

An adult animated version of the Grimm tale that you won't be taking the kids to. Into a surreal landscape of mutants and insects is born poor Tom. His parents fail to protect him from kidnappers who conduct a series of bizarre medical experiments on our hero. Escaping, Tom befriends a giant who inadvertently kills him, releasing him into an afterlife that is not harps, clouds and angels. Director Dave Borthwick's ten-minute short has been expanded into a full length feature but not everyone will enjoy his nightmarish vision. LH

Nick Upton *Pa Thumb* • Deborah Collard *Ma Thumb* • Frank Passingham *Man/Giant* • John Schofield *Man/Giant* ■ *Dir/Scr* Dave Borthwick

A Secret Affair ★★ 12

Romantic drama 1999 · US · Colour · 84mins

Arriving in Venice on business, bride-to-be Janine Turner falls under the city's spell in this mediocre romantic TV drama. Unfortunately, there's nothing new in the voyage of self-discovery that Turner's would-be artist takes after meeting Paudge Behan's Irish TV reporter. Director Bobby Roth leaves a talented supporting cast fumbling in the background. DP DVD

Janine Turner *Vanessa Stewart* • Paudge Behan *Bill Fitzgerald* • Fionnula Flanagan *Drucilla Fitzgerald* • Robert Mailhouse *Stephen Rocken* • Gia Carides *Mimi* ■ *Dir* Bobby Roth • *Scr* Carole Real, from the novel by Barbara Taylor Bradford

Secret Agent ★★★★ U

Spy thriller 1936 · UK · BW · 82mins

John Gielgud might not be everyone's ideal Hitchcock hero, and critics were quick to point out his lack of derring-do, but he acquits himself admirably in this engaging thriller. A script based on a play that was itself adapted from a clutch of Somerset Maugham's *Ashenden* stories was bound to have more than its fair share of loose ends, particularly by Robert Young and the amazing Peter Lorre, and the director's genius for generating suspense out of ordinary situations and locations, that they scarcely seem to matter. DP DVD

John Gielgud *Edgar Brodie/Richard Ashenden* • Madeleine Carroll *Elsa Carrington* • Peter Lorre *The General* • Robert Young (1) *Robert Marvin* • Percy Marmont *Caypor* • Florence Kahn *Mrs Caypor* • Lilli Palmer *Lilli* ■ *Dir* Alfred Hitchcock • *Scr* Charles Bennett, Ian Hay, Jesse Lasky Jr, Alma Reville, from the play by Campbell Dixon, from the *Ashenden,stories by W Somerset Maugham*

The Secret Agent ★★ 12

Period spy thriller
1996 · US/UK · Colour · 90mins

This slow-moving adaptation of Joseph Conrad's spy tale stars Bob Hoskins as an anarchist living in London at the end of the 19th century who becomes involved in a terrorist attack on the Greenwich Observatory. There's a good performance from Patricia Arquette and an accomplished supporting cast, but Christopher Hampton adheres too slavishly to Conrad's text and the film never really gets off the ground. JB. Contains swearing, violence.

Bob Hoskins *Adolph Verloc* • Patricia Arquette *Winnie Verloc* • Gérard Depardieu *Tom "Alexander" Ossipon* • Jim Broadbent *Chief Inspector Heat* • Christian Bale *Stevie Verloc* • Eddie Izzard *Vladimir* • Elizabeth Spriggs *Winnie's mother* • Peter Vaughan *The driver* • Robin Williams *The professor* ■ *Dir* Christopher Hampton • *Scr* Christopher Hampton, from the novel by Joseph Conrad

The Secret Agent Club ★ PG

Action comedy 1995 · US · Colour · 86mins

Secret agent Hulk Hogan is kidnapped by arms dealers and spends most of the movie under sedation. His young son gets his friends to help track him down, dodging bullets and killers while having a jolly good time. Reprehensible for its attitude towards violence while children are present, this also contains blatant racist stereotypes. It's a pity the audience couldn't be as unconscious as Hogan was throughout this travesty. KB DVD

Hulk Hogan *Ray* • Lesley-Anne Down *Eve* • Barry Bostwick *Vincent Scarletti* • Mathew McCurley *Jeremy* • Edward Albert *Max* • Richard Moll *Wrecks* • Lyman Ward *SHADOW General* • Jack Nance *Doc* ■ *Dir* John Murlowski • *Scr* Rory Johnston

Secret Ballot ★★★★ U

Satirical comedy
2001 · It/Ir/Can/Swi/Neth · Colour · 100mins

Arriving on an isolated Iranian island, the zealous, chador-clad Nassim Abdi is ferried around by sceptical soldier Cyrus Abidi in a bid to persuade locals to vote in a presidential election. Exploring everything from military inertia and rural ignorance to political idealism and the changing role of women, this is a deliciously absurdist satire on a country where remoteness and indifference are as much a hindrance to reform as doctrine and tradition. Babak Payami reinforces his gently mocking message through the cautious byplay between his non-professional leads. DP. In Farsi with English subtitles. DVD

Nassim Abdi *Girl* • Cyrus Abidi *Soldier* ■ *Dir* Babak Payami • *Scr* Babek Payami, inspired by the short film *Testing Democracy* by Mohsen Makhmalbaf

Secret beyond the Door ★★ PG

Thriller melodrama 1948 · US · BW · 93mins

A woman marries an architect whose house contains his painstaking re-creations of rooms in which brutal murders were committed. Furthermore, there's a first wife she never knew about and a jealous secretary. Director Fritz Lang's third collaboration with Joan Bennett, this is visually accomplished, but Michael Redgrave lacks any romantic appeal as the architect. The complicated flashback structure and a climax that combines lurid melodrama with Freudian explanations make this heavy going and pretentious. AE

Joan Bennett *Celia Lamphere* • Michael Redgrave *Mark Lamphere* • Anne Revere *Caroline Lamphere* • Barbara O'Neil *Miss Robey* • Natalie Schafer *Edith Potter* • Paul Cavanagh *Rick Barrett* ■ *Dir* Fritz Lang • *Scr* Silvia Richards, from the story *Museum Piece No.13* by Rufus King

The Secret Bride ★

Political drama 1934 · US · BW · 76mins

Attorney general Warren William and governor's daughter Barbara Stanwyck marry in secret but, about to break the happy news to her father, they learn that he is to be impeached for taking a bribe. A nonsensical farrago involving political corruption, murder and a frame-up, typical of the kind of rubbish the peerless Stanwyck was so often forced to endure. Even she can't rise above the comically bad dialogue. RK

Barbara Stanwyck *Ruth Vincent* • Warren William *Robert Sheldon* • Glenda Farrell *Hazel Normandie* • Grant Mitchell *Willie Martin* • Arthur Byron *Gov Vincent* • Henry O'Neill *Jim*

S

Lansdale • Douglass Dumbrille *Dave Bredeen* ■ *Dir* William Dieterle • *Scr* Tom Buckingham, F Hugh Herbert, Mary McCall Jr, from a play by Leonard Ide

Secret Ceremony ★★

Drama 1968 · UK/US · Colour · 109mins

A typically bitter, twisted and pretentious morality tale from cerebral director Joseph Losey. This moody mistaken-identity melodrama quickly becomes a macabre muddle of daft sexual psychosis and suspect psychology when nympho Mia Farrow adopts prostitute Elizabeth Taylor as her surrogate mother after a meeting on a London bus. The return of Farrow's stepfather Robert Mitchum provides this meandering morsel of Swinging Sixties Gothic with a suitably off-the-wall climax. AJ

Elizabeth Taylor *Leonora* • Mia Farrow *Cenci* • Robert Mitchum *Albert* • Peggy Ashcroft *Hannah* • Pamela Brown *Hilda* • Michael Strong *Dr Walter Stevens* • Robert Douglas *Sir Alex Gordon* ■ *Dir* Joseph Losey • *Scr* George Tabori, from the short story *Ceremonia Secreta* by Marco Denevi

Secret Command ★★

Second World War spy drama
1944 · US · BW · 81mins

Pat O'Brien is a naval intelligence agent who goes undercover to prevent a Nazi sabotage operation. Chester Morris runs the shipyard under threat, and since he happens to be O'Brien's brother, he's understandably bewildered by O'Brien's sudden arrival with a wife and two children in tow. In fact, the FBI have drafted in another agent, Carole Landis, to play O'Brien's imaginary wife. You can guess what happens to them in between all the fist fights and propaganda. AT

Pat O'Brien *Sam Gallagher* • Carole Landis *Jill McCann* • Chester Morris *Jeff Gallagher* • Ruth Warrick *Lea Damaron* • Barton MacLane *Red Kelly* • Tom Tully *Brownell* • Wallace Ford *Miller* ■ *Dir* A Edward Sutherland • *Scr* Roy Chanslor, from the story *The Saboteurs* by John Hawkins, Ward Hawkins

Secret Defense ★★★ PG

Mystery drama
1997 · Fr/Swi/It · Colour · 173mins

Jacques Rivette continues his career-long preoccupation with the nature of real-screen time and the concept of plot as conspiracy in this leisurely, but still intriguing anti-thriller. Investigating the murder of her father, scientist Sandrine Bonnaire becomes embroiled in a cover-up of her own after an accidental shooting. With a subplot involving the mysterious death of Bonnaire's sister (Laure Marsac, who also plays the woman Bonnaire kills), this is more a study of motives, methods and responses than a tension-packed nailbiter, but it still exercises a slow-burning fascination. DP. In French with English subtitles.

Sandrine Bonnaire *Sylvie Rousseau* • Jerzy Radziwilowicz *Walser* • Laure Marsac *Véronique Lukachevski/Ludivine Lukachevski* • Grégoire Colin *Paul Rousseau* ■ *Dir* Jacques Rivette • *Scr* Jacques Rivette, Pascal Bonitzer, Emmanuelle Cuau

The Secret Diary of Sigmund Freud ★

Comedy 1984 · US · Colour · 99mins

A game cult cast is wasted in this painful comedy based on the early life and psychoanalytical theories of Doctor Sigmund Freud, performed by Bud Cort in his typical deadpan manner. Carroll Baker plays his mother, Klaus Kinski the doctor she has an affair with, and Carol Kane his lisping nurse. Each are primarily there to take turns at being the butt of pretty pathetic gags. Comedian Dick Shawn puts in a marvellous turn, but the lethargic pace and annoying script would put anyone in therapy. AJ

Bud Cort *Sigmund Freud* • Carol Kane *Martha Bernays* • Klaus Kinski *Dr Max Bauer* • Marisa Berenson *Emma Herrmann* • Carroll Baker *Mama Freud* • Dick Shawn *Ultimate patient* • Ferdy Mayne *Herr Herrmann* ■ *Dir* Danford B Greene • *Scr* Roberto Mitrotti, Linda Howard

Secret Friends ★★★ 15

Fantasy drama
1991 · UK/US · Colour · 93mins

Dennis Potter was one of Britain's greatest TV playwrights, but this directorial debut – an adaptation of his novel, *Ticket to Ride* – is an embittered mess about sex and the violent impulses that drive his hero Alan Bates to amnesia and beyond, with Gina Bellman as the sexual catalyst. Compelling enough, but the love-making is sleazy and the intercutting flashbacks make an already muddled narrative even more murky. TH

Alan Bates *John* • Gina Bellman *Helen* • Frances Barber *Angela* • Tony Doyle *Martin* • Joanna David *Kate* • Colin Jeavons *Vicar* ■ *Dir* Dennis Potter • *Scr* Dennis Potter, from his novel *Ticket to Ride*

The Secret Garden ★★★ U

Drama 1949 · US · BW and Colour · 88mins

This solid adaptation of Frances Hodgson Burnett's delightful children's classic is mounted on a lavish scale. Margaret O'Brien makes a spirited Mary Lennox, the orphan whose mischievous optimism brightens up life at her morbid uncle's mansion, and Elsa Lanchester is typically splendid as the kindly maid. Unfortunately Gladys Cooper overdoes the tyranny as the housekeeper and Herbert Marshall is a damp squib as the uncle. DP

Margaret O'Brien *Mary Lennox* • Herbert Marshall *Archibald Craven* • Dean Stockwell *Colin Craven* • Gladys Cooper *Mrs Medlock* • Elsa Lanchester *Martha* • Brian Roper *Dickon* • Reginald Owen *Ben Weatherstaff* ■ *Dir* Fred M Wilcox • *Scr* Robert Ardrey, from the novel by Frances Hodgson Burnett

The Secret Garden ★★★★ U

Period drama 1993 · US · Colour · 97mins

Frances Hodgson Burnett's enchanting children's classic is given a new lease of life in this imaginative adaptation by Polish film-maker Agnieszka Holland. Always a skilled director of children, she draws a spirited performance out of Kate Maberly as the orphan who sweeps away the cobwebs from Misselthwaite Manor. Scripted by Caroline Thompson – who wrote *Edward Scissorhands* – the film retains the gothic atmosphere of the book and looks amazing, thanks to Roger Deakins's photography. Stealing the show is Maggie Smith as the beastly housekeeper. DP DVD

Kate Maberly *Mary Lennox* • Heydon Prowse *Colin Craven* • Andrew Knott *Dickon* • Maggie Smith *Mrs Medlock* • Laura Crossley *Martha* • John Lynch *Lord Craven* • Walter Sparrow *Ben Weatherstaff* • Irène Jacob *Mary's mother/Lilas Craven* ■ *Dir* Agnieszka Holland • *Scr* Caroline Thompson, from the novel by Frances Hodgson Burnett

The Secret Heart ★★

Drama 1946 · US · BW · 96mins

Widowed by the suicide of the alcoholic husband she married and in spite of loving another man (Walter Pidgeon), Claudette Colbert has devotedly cared for her stepchildren. Now she faces problems with her psychologically traumatised stepdaughter June Allyson. Robert Z Leonard directs this attempt to make a serious domestic drama out of a soap opera, but the material stubbornly refuses to budge. RK

Claudette Colbert *Lee Addams* • Walter Pidgeon *Chris Matthews* • June Allyson *Penny Addams* • Lionel Barrymore *Dr Rossiger* • Robert Sterling *Chase Addams Jr* • Marshall Thompson *Brandon Reynolds* • Elizabeth Patterson *Mrs Stover* • Richard Derr *Larry Addams Sr* ■ *Dir* Robert Z Leonard • *Scr* Whitfield Cook, Anne Morrison Chapin, Rose Franken, from a story by Rose Franken, William Brown Meloney

Secret Honor ★★★★ 15

Biographical political drama
1984 · US · Colour · 86mins

Maverick director Robert Altman's stunning portrayal of a drunken President Richard Milhous Nixon features Philip Baker Hall as Tricky Dicky. Set after his ignominious resignation, he rants and raves about his contemporaries in his White House study, comparing his "secret honour with his public shame". Altman's prowling camera keeps this one-character drama cinematic and on its toes, and ensures that the man's insane, bigoted mediocrity has a certain vivid poignancy. TH

Philip Baker Hall *Richard M Nixon* ■ *Dir* Robert Altman • *Scr* Donald Freed, Arnold M Stone, from the play *Secret Honor, The Last Will and Testament of Richard M Nixon* by Donald Freed

The Secret Invasion ★★★ PG

Second World War action drama
1964 · US · Colour · 93mins

Cult director Roger Corman's snappily-paced action/adventure bears a strikingly similarity to *The Dirty Dozen*, but lacks the powerhouse cast. British Intelligence officer Stewart Granger leads five hardened criminals into Dubrovnik during the Second World War to rescue an Italian general from the Nazis. Although cheaply produced, the veteran cast wrings every ounce of conviction from a routine script. AJ

Stewart Granger *Maj Richard Mace* • Raf Vallone *Roberto Rocca* • Mickey Rooney *Terence Scanlon* • Edd Byrnes *Simon Fell* • Henry Silva *John Durrell* • Mia Massini [Spela Rozin] *Mila* • William Campbell *Jean Saval* ■ *Dir* Roger Corman • *Scr* R Wright Campbell

The Secret Laughter of Women ★★ 15

Romantic comedy
1998 · UK/Can · Colour · 95mins

There's little love and even less humour in this stiffly staged Riviera story of a Nigerian single mother's encounter with an exiled English writer of comic books. Nia Long struggles to suppress her American accent as the former, while Colin Firth mistakes monotone for laconicism as the latter. Even less well-defined is the ex-pat community that tries to force Long into marrying Ariyon Bakare. DP

Colin Firth *Matthew Field* • Nia Long *Nimi Da Silva, "Big Eyes"* • Dan Lett *John* • Joke Silva *Nene* • Ariyon Bakare *Reverend Fola* ■ *Dir* Peter Schwabach • *Scr* OO Sagay

The Secret Life of an American Wife ★★

Comedy 1968 · US · Colour · 92mins

Here, Anne Jackson plays a housewife who, thinking she's lost her sexual charm, impersonates a hooker and sets out to seduce a big movie star, Walter Matthau – whose agent happens to be Jackson's husband. While the playing is a constant delight, the sets are like amateur rep and the dialogue, thought to be very risqué in 1968, will seem very dated indeed. AT

Walter Matthau *The Movie Star* • Anne Jackson *Victoria Layton* • Patrick O'Neal *Tom Layton* • Edy Williams *Suzie Steinberg* • Richard Bull *Howard* • Paul Napier *Herb Steinberg* • Gary Brown *Jimmy* • Albert Carrier *Jean-Claude* ■ *Dir/Scr* George Axelrod

The Secret Life of Walter Mitty ★★★★ U

Comedy 1947 · US · Colour · 105mins

James Thurber's short story becomes a marvellous Technicolored cavalcade for Danny Kaye, who plays both the daydreaming Mitty and the amazingly heroic characters of his fantasies. Kaye's on top form here, as a surgeon performing a near-impossible operation, an ace gunslinger (the "Perth Amboy Kid") and a pernickety RAF pilot, among others. The energetic star is not so popular today, but this is generally acknowledged to be his finest screen performance and is certainly his most endearing. There's marvellous support from the great Boris Karloff as a homicidal psychiatrist. TS

Danny Kaye *Walter Mitty* • Virginia Mayo *Rosalind van Hoorn* • Boris Karloff *Dr Hugo Hollingshead* • Fay Bainter *Mrs Mitty* • Ann Rutherford *Gertrude Griswold* • Thurston Hall *Bruce Pierce* • Konstantin Shayne *Peter van Hoorn* • Florence Bates *Mrs Griswold* • Gordon Jones *Tubby Wadsworth* • Reginald Denny *RAF colonel* ■ *Dir* Norman Z McLeod • *Scr* Ken Englund, Everett Freeman, from the story by James Thurber

The Secret Lives of Dentists ★★★★

Fantasy comedy drama
2002 · US · Colour · 101mins

This marks a masterful return to form for Alan Rudolph, so long the nearly-man of American independent cinema. Dentist Campbell Scott (terrific) is having a mental meltdown after becoming convinced his wife (and fellow dentist) Hope Davis is having an affair. Working from a wry, yet acidic script by Craig Lucas, Rudolph beautifully juxtaposes the banalities of domestic life with increasingly bizarre fantasy sequences, most of them revolving around caustic patient Denis Leary, who becomes Scott's imaginary alter-ego. A bleakly funny – and occasionally creepy – examination of modern marriage. JF

Campbell Scott *David Hurst* • Denis Leary *Slater* • Robin Tunney *Laura* • Peter Samuel *Larry* • Hope Davis *Dana Hurst* • Jon Patrick Walker *Mark* • Gianna Beleno *Lizzie Hurst* • Lydia Jordan *Stephanie Hurst* • Cassidy Hinkle *Leah Hurst* ■ *Dir* Alan Rudolph • *Scr* Craig Lucas, from the novella *The Age of Grief* by Jane Smiley

The Secret Mark of D'Artagnan ★★ U

Adventure 1962 · Fr/It · Colour · 92mins

Yet another film from the Musketeers industry, this time from Italy with American actor George Nader swordfighting against those would do do down Louis XIII and Richelieu. The plot is several blades short of a scabbard, but director Siro Marcellini moves it at enough of a pace to cover that inadequacy. TH. French/Italian dialogue dubbed into English.

George Nader *D'Artagnan* • Magali Noël *Carlotta, maid* • Georges Marchal *Duke of Montserrant* • Mario Petri *Porthos* • Alessandra Panaro *Diana* • Massimo Serato *Cardinal Richelieu* ■ *Dir* Siro Marcellini • *Scr* Ottario Poggi, Milton Krims, Siro Marcellini, from characters created by Alexandre Dumas

Secret Mission ★★ U

Second World War spy drama
1942 · UK · BW · 89mins

It's hard to see how this flag-waver could have raised anyone's spirits during the darkest days of the Second World War. There's a modicum of excitement in the attempt by Michael Wilding, Hugh Williams and Roland Culver, along with their French guide James Mason, to glean information about Nazi invasion plans. But the comic subplot involving Wilding and his French wife, and the romance that

S

develops between Williams and Mason's sister (Carla Lehmann), are embarrassing. Unremarkable. DP

Hugh Williams *Peter Garnett* • Carla Lehmann *Michele de Carnot* • James Mason *Raoul de Carnot* • Roland Culver *Red Gowan* • Michael Wilding *Nobby Clark* • Nancy Price *Violette* • Herbert Lom *Medical officer* • Stewart Granger *Sub-lieutenant Jackson* ■ *Dir* Harold French • *Scr* Anatole de Grunwald, Basil Bartlett, from a story by Shaun Terence Young

The Secret Nation ★★★★

Drama 1989 · Bol · Colour · 125mins

Although the theme of this remarkable study in existential angst is atonement, Jorge Sanjines is also keen to highlight the marginalisation of Bolivia's indigenous Aymara peoples, who have been consigned to shanties on the edge of the major cities by the European descendants, who continue to resist full national integration. Recalling Miklos Jancso with his use of lingering long takes, Sanjines employs a flashback structure to explain why Reynaldo Yujra, a man whose life has been one long act of betrayal, is returning to his village on the altiplano to perform a ritual cleansing dance that will end in his death. DP. In Bolivian dialect with English subtitles.

Reynaldo Yujra *Sebastian* • Delfina Mamani *Basilia* • Orlando Huanca *Vicente* • Roque Salgado *Clarividente* ■ *Dir* Jorge Sanjines

The Secret of Blood Island ★★

Second World War drama 1964 · UK · Colour · 83mins

Secret agent Barbara Shelley has to go into hiding after her plane is shot down on a Japanese-occupied island during the Second World War. A lurid but fairly enjoyable jungle-bound war movie from Quentin Lawrence, director of *The Trollenberg Terror*, this is a sequel to 1958's *The Camp on Blood Island*. RT

Barbara Shelley *Elaine* • Jack Hedley *Sergeant Crewe* • Charles Tingwell *Major Dryden* • Bill Owen *Bludgin* • Peter Welch *Richardson* • Lee Montague *Levy* ■ *Dir* Quentin Lawrence • *Scr* John Gilling

The Secret of Convict Lake ★★★

Western 1951 · US · BW · 83mins

In this routine melodrama set in 19th-century California, escaped prisoners take over a town populated just by women, while the menfolk are away prospecting. The studio boosted the hackneyed plot by putting in top-class players such as Glenn Ford, Gene Tierney, Ethel Barrymore and Zachary Scott, and their presence helps make the rather predictable scenario much more enjoyable. TH

Glenn Ford *Canfield* • Gene Tierney *Marcia Stoddard* • Ethel Barrymore *Granny* • Zachary Scott *Greer* • Ann Dvorak *Rachel* • Barbara Bates *Barbara Purcell* • Cyril Cusack *Limey* ■ *Dir* Michael Gordon • *Scr* Oscar Saul, Victor Trivas, from a story by Anna Hunger, Jack Pollexfen

The Secret of Dr Kildare ★★★

Medical drama 1939 · US · BW · 84mins

The relationship between Lew Ayres's idealistic young Dr Kildare and Lionel Barrymore's curmudgeonly old Dr Gillespie was beginning to mature in the third of MGM's popular series. Kildare, concerned for Gillespie's health, tries to get his superior to take a holiday. At the same time, he cures a woman with psychosomatic blindness. All the regulars are on hand, including nurse Mary Lamont (Laraine Day), who provides Kildare with some romance. RB

Lew Ayres *Dr James Kildare* • Lionel Barrymore *Dr Leonard Gillespie* • Lionel Atwill *Paul Messenger* • Laraine Day *Mary Lamont* • Helen Gilbert *Nancy Messenger* • Nat Pendleton *Joe Wayman* • Samuel S Hinds *Dr Stephen Kildare* ■ *Dir* Harold Bucquet [Harold S Bucquet] • *Scr* Willis Goldbeck, Harry Ruskin, from the story by Max Brand

The Secret of Madame Blanche ★★★

Period melodrama 1933 · US · BW · 78mins

Respectable musical actress Irene Dunne is swept off her feet by Phillips Holmes, a charming but weak upper class idler. She marries him and falls pregnant, but when his cruel and rigid father Lionel Atwill refuses to acknowledge the union, Holmes kills himself. She is stranded in France with her newborn son, whose grandfather steals the baby away. An 18-carat weepie, this is a wonderful wallow, though Dunne – enchanting as the young woman – is less successful as middle-aged "Madame Blanche". RK

Irene Dunne *Sally Sanders St John/Madame Blanche* • Lionel Atwill *Aubrey St John* • Phillips Holmes *Leonard St John* • Una Merkel *Ella* • Douglas Walton *Leonard St John Jr* ■ *Dir* Charles Brabin • *Scr* Frances Goodrich, Albert Hackett, from the play *The Lady* by Martin Brown

The Secret of My Success ★★

Black comedy 1965 · UK · Colour · 107mins

Yet another in the seemingly endless parade of lacklustre British comedies, this features James Booth as a naive, garrulous mother's boy who starts the film as a PC and ends up unwittingly helping to overthrow a foreign dictator, becoming a hero in the process. The film owes much to Voltaire's *Candide* but it's just not very funny, though Booth is worth watching, and Lionel Jeffries gets to play four roles. JG

Shirley Jones *Marigold Marado* • Stella Stevens *Violet Lawson* • Honor Blackman *Baroness von Lukenberg* • James Booth *Arthur Tate* • Lionel Jeffries *Inspector Hobart/ Baron von Lukenberg/President Esteda/Earl of Aldershot* • Amy Dolby *Mrs Tate* ■ *Dir/Scr* Andrew L Stone

The Secret of My Success ★★★ PG

Comedy 1987 · US · Colour · 105mins

Another tailor-made Michael J Fox role in which he plays a mailroom boy who tries to make his way to the top by spending half his day impersonating an executive. Lots of pratfalls ensue, and Fox is reasonably engaging as he runs around frantically trying to keep up the charade. Margaret Whitton, as the scheming boss's wife, steals the show, however, and makes this rather basic comedy worth watching. JB DVD

Michael J Fox *Brantley Foster* • Helen Slater *Christy Wills* • Richard Jordan *Howard Prescott* • Margaret Whitton *Vera Prescott* • John Pankow *Fred Melrose* • Christopher Murney *Barney Rattigan* • Gerry Bamman *Art Thomas* • Mercedes Ruehl *Sheila* ■ *Dir* Herbert Ross • *Scr* Jim Cash, Jack Epps, AJ Carothers, from a story by AJ Carothers

The Secret of NIMH ★★★ U

Animated fantasy 1982 · US · Colour · 78mins

Animator Don Bluth rebelled against the mighty Mouse and set out to remind a then-struggling Disney about the glory days of animation. He largely succeeded (the sentimentality that would cloud his *An American Tail* and *The Land before Time* is the only drawback) with this story of a proud mouse who strikes up an unlikely friendship with the rat branch of Mensa. The animation is lovingly rendered and there is a pedigree cast providing voices. JF DVD

Derek Jacobi *Nicodemus* • Elizabeth Hartman *Mrs Brisby* • Arthur Malet *Mr Ages* • Dom DeLuise *Jeremy* • Hermione Baddeley *Auntie Shrew* • John Carradine *Great Owl* • Peter Strauss *Justin* • Paul Shenar *Jenner* • Shannen Doherty *Teresa* ■ *Dir* Don Bluth • *Scr* John Pomeroy, Gary Goldman, Don Bluth, Will Finn, from the novel *Mrs Frisby and the Rats of NIMH* by Robert C O'Brien

The Secret of NIMH II: Timmy to the Rescue ★ U

Animated adventure 1998 · US · Colour · 65mins

This made-for-video sequel to animator Don Bluth's one good movie makes his other wretched efforts look like masterpieces. The screenplay here freely ignores or alters key characters and events from the previous movie in this tale of now grown-up mouse Timmy traveling to Thorn Valley to save his furry friends from the returning menace of NIMH. This is blighted by poor animation and art design, plus a surprisingly grim tone. JF DVD

Dom DeLuise *Jeremy* • Andrew Ducote *Timmy, aged 10* • Eric Idle *Martin* • Harvey Korman *Floyd* • Ralph Macchio *Timmy, aged 19* • Peter MacNicol *Narrator* ■ *Dir* Dick Sebast • *Scr* Sam Graham, Chris Hubbell, from characters created by Robert C O'Brien

The Secret of Roan Inish ★★★★ PG

Period fantasy 1993 · US · Colour · 97mins

This is a gem of a film from talented writer/director John Sayles. Without sentiment and accompanied by stunning cinematography from veteran Haskell Wexler, Sayles spins a tale of ten-year-old Fiona living in 1940s Ireland who believes her family are descendants from selkies: half-seal, half-human creatures from the island of Roan Inish. While staying with her grandparents near the now-deserted island, the youngster starts to uncover her true heritage. The result is a mythical, magical and entertaining film. LH

Jeni Courtney *Fiona Coneelly* • Mick Lally *Hugh Coneelly, Fiona's Grandfather* • Eileen Colgan *Tess Coneelly, Fiona's Grandmother* • Richard Sheridan *Eamon* • John Lynch *Tadhg Coneelly* • Cillian Byrne *Jamie* • Susan Lynch *Selkie* ■ *Dir* John Sayles • *Scr* John Sayles, from the novel *The Secret of the Ron Mor Skerry* by Rosalie K Fry

The Secret of Santa Vittoria ★★★★

Second World War comedy 1969 · US · Colour · 139mins

This under-rated film is based on a supposedly true incident during the Second World War, when the population of a small village in the Italian hills secreted its stocks of wine to prevent them from falling into the hands of the Germans. Producer/director Stanley Kramer has crafted an irresistible game of cat and mouse as town drunk-cum-mayor Anthony Quinn and Nazi officer Hardy Kruger try to outsmart each other. Quinn and fiery Anna Magnani make a dynamic duo and you'll be hard pressed to choose between tears and cheers. DP

Anthony Quinn *Italo Bombolini* • Anna Magnani *Rosa Bombolini* • Virna Lisi *Caterina Malatesta* • Hardy Kruger *Sepp Von Prum, German Commander* • Sergio Franchi *Tufa* ■ *Dir* Stanley Kramer • *Scr* William Rose, Ben Maddow, from the novel by Robert Crichton

Secret of the Incas ★★★ U

Adventure 1954 · US · Colour · 104mins

Charlton Heston and Thomas Mitchell play the rivals engaged in a perilous search for a fabled Inca icon in this adventure yarn from director Jerry Hopper. There's romance and Cold War intrigue, so fashionable in 1954, but what distinguishes the film are the location shots of the fabled Inca city of Machu Picchu, which sits swathed in Andean clouds. AT

Charlton Heston *Harry Steele* • Nicole Maurey *Elena Antonescu* • Robert Young (1) *Dr Stanley Moorehead* • Thomas Mitchell *Ed Morgan* • Glenda Farrell *Jane Winston* • William Henry *Phillip Lang* ■ *Dir* Jerry Hopper • *Scr* Ranald MacDougall, Sydney Boehm, from the story *Legend of the Incas* by Sydney Boehm

The Secret of the Purple Reef ★ U

Murder mystery 1960 · US · Colour · 79mins

An early role for Peter Falk and the screen debut of Richard Chamberlain may be the sole reasons to watch this seaborne schlock. The plot has Jeff Richards and brother Chamberlain looking into the death of another brother who went down in his fishing sloop in the Caribbean. The weather is good, the acting less so, the script scrapes the bottom, and there are any number of suspects, notably local heavy Falk, whose girlfriend, Margia Dean, switches sides in mid-drama. AT

Jeff Richards *Mark Christopher* • Margia Dean *Rue Amboy* • Peter Falk *Tom Weber* • Richard Chamberlain *Dean Christopher* • Robert Earle *Tobias* • Terence DeMarney *Ashby* ■ *Dir* William Witney • *Scr* Harold Yablonsky [Yabo Yablonsky], Gene Corman, from a serial in *The Saturday Evening Post* by Dorothy Cottrell

Secret of Treasure Mountain ★★ U

Western adventure 1956 · US · BW · 67mins

The moral of this routine western must be that if you're going to bury some treasure, don't do it on Indian land. Snarling villain Raymond Burr and Valerie French lead the desultory crew looking for some gold buried by the Spanish and now protected by a particularly potent Apache curse. AT

Valerie French *Audrey Lancaster* • Raymond Burr *Cash Larsen* • William Prince *Robert Kendall* • Lance Fuller *Juan Alvarado* • Susan Cummings *Tawana* • Pat Hogan *Vahoe* ■ *Dir* Seymour Friedman • *Scr* David Lang

Secret of Treasure Mountain ★★

Adventure 1993 · US · Colour · 80mins

The sequel to *The Butter Cream Gang* finds the eager band of do-gooders on the horns of a dilemma. Do they pocket the proceeds of a treasure map or do they help a neighbour who's about to be made homeless? Of course, there are the small matters of locating the concealed crypt in a derelict monastery, escaping from a mountain cave and confounding a trio of desperadoes before thoughts turn to sharing out the loot all of which should keep the pre-teens entertained. DP

Brandon Blaser *Eldon* • Jason Glenn *Lanny* • Jason Johnson *Scott* • Rick Macy *Almodovar* • Frank Gerrish *Mugfat* ■ *Dir* Scott Swofford • *Scr* Carter Burch, Leo D Paur

The Secret Partner ★★★

Crime drama 1961 · UK · BW · 91mins

In this implausible but ingenious British thriller, a hooded man forces a dentist to drug a shipping executive during an appointment so that he will reveal the combination of his company's strongroom. It remains watchable thanks to some skilful characterisation and the strong performances of Stewart Granger as the executive, Norman Bird as the dentist and Bernard Lee as the dogged, chain-smoking policeman. AE

Stewart Granger *John Brent* • Haya Harareet *Nicole Brent* • Bernard Lee *Det Supt Hanbury*

S

• Hugh Burden *Charles Standish* • Lee Montague *Det Inspector Henderson* • Norman Bird *Ralph Beldon, dentist* ■ *Dir* Basil Dearden • *Scr* David Pursall, Jack Seddon

The Secret People ★

Crime drama 1951 · UK · BW · 95mins

Given carte blanche by Ealing Studios, director Thorold Dickinson set out to make a polemical film about the ethics of political assassination, and encouraged the young Lindsay Anderson to write a book documenting its production. Sadly, the result was a wordy, pretentious and boring picture, too coldly characterised, too unspecific in detail, too cerebral by far. Its sole interest lies in Audrey Hepburn, in one of her earliest roles. AE

Valentina Cortesa [Valentina Cortese] *Maria Brentano* • Serge Reggiani *Louis* • Charles Goldner *Anselmo* • Audrey Hepburn *Nora Brentano* • Angela Fouldes *Nora as a child* • Megs Jenkins *Penny* • Irene Worth *Miss Jackson* • Reginald Tate *Inspector Eliot* • Bob Monkhouse *Barber* ■ *Dir* Thorold Dickinson • *Scr* Thorold Dickinson, Wolfgang Wilhelm, Christianna Brand, from a story by Thorold Dickinson, Joyce Carey

Secret Places ★★ 15

Drama 1984 · UK · Colour · 94mins

In the claustrophobic atmosphere of an all-girl's school at the beginning of the Second World War, two disparate pupils (Marie-Theres Relin and Tara MacGowran) strike up a friendship which is so close, the other schoolgirls and teachers (including Jenny Agutter) suspect "something is going on". Warm, low-key and somewhat lacking in drama. FL [video]

Marie-Theres Relin *Laura Meister* • Tara MacGowran *Patience* • Claudine Auger *Sophy Meister* • Jenny Agutter *Miss Lowrie* • Cassie Stuart *Nina* • Ann-Marie Gwatkin *Rose* • Pippa Hinchley *Barbara* ■ *Dir* Zelda Barron • *Scr* Zelda Barron, from the novel by Janice Elliott

The Secret Policeman's Ball ★★★★ 15

Comedy concert 1980 · UK · Colour · 91mins

This recording of the comedy fundraiser for Amnesty International enjoyed a theatrical release (in a much longer form) following its TV screening. A brilliant cast of comedians and performers (including John Cleese, Peter Cook, Clive James, Rowan Atkinson, Billy Connolly, Pete Townshend), and some wonderful sketches provide guaranteed entertainment. The same formula was repeated with *The Secret Policeman's Other Ball* which had a theatrical debut as well as the *Third Ball* in 1987. All feature wonderful moments from some of the most popular comedians of the last 35 years. DF [video] DVD

Dir Roger Graef

The Secret Policeman's Other Ball ★★★ 15

Comedy concert 1982 · UK · Colour · 90mins

Combining footage from benefits staged in aid of Amnesty International, this movie is more a souvenir than great cinema. Directors Roger Graef and Julien Temple's video images are murky and jerky, and while they work for such memorable musical slots as Sting's *Message in a Bottle* and the blues teaming of guitar legends Eric Clapton and Jeff Beck, they distract from the comedy without conveying any audience excitement. However, Alan Bennett and John Fortune's dialogue, the Pythons' immortal "Four Yorkshiremen" sketch and the End of the World routine featuring Peter Cook and Rowan Atkinson, all survive the edgy camerawork. DP [video] DVD

Dir Julien Temple, Roger Graef

The Secret Policeman's Third Ball ★★★ 15

Comedy concert 1987 · UK · Colour · 86mins

The fourth charity bash – before the three Balls there was *Pleasure at Her Majesty's* – performed over four evenings at the London Palladium in March 1987. Regulars like Alan Bennett, Rowan Atkinson and Billy Connolly are notable absentees, though John Cleese strides on to receive an award from Stephen Fry and Hugh Laurie. Lenny Henry plays a clapped out blues singer, Ben Elton outstays his welcome and there are songs by the likes of Bob Geldof, Duran Duran and Peter Gabriel. Ruby Wax sends herself up and *Spitting Image* contributes a scabrous dialogue between Larry Olivier and Johnny Gielgud. Blessings, as they say, are mixed. AT [video] DVD

Dir Kevin O'Neill

The Secret Rapture ★★★★ 15

Drama 1993 · UK · Colour · 96mins

Writer David Hare can veer from nuance to crassness in one giddy swoop. Here, for once, he has merged the personal and the political without letting us see too much of the join. Set on the cusp of the shark-toothed 1980s and the more introspective 1990s, this tale of sisterly rivalry is shot through with fine acting, particularly from Juliet Stevenson and Penelope Wilton as the sisters, Joanne Whalley-Kilmer as the stepmother and Neil Pearson as the boyfriend. JM

Juliet Stevenson *Isobel Coleridge* • Joanne Whalley-Kilmer [Joanne Whalley] *Katherine Coleridge* • Penelope Wilton *Marion French* • Neil Pearson *Patrick Steadman* • Alan Howard *Tom French* • Robert Stephens *Max Lopert* • Hilton McRae *Norman* • Robert Glenister *Jeremy* ■ *Dir* Howard Davies • *Scr* David Hare, from his play

A Secret Sin ★★ 15

Period drama 1997 · US · Colour · 120mins

Set in the 1950s, this family melodrama appears dated, despite the up-to-the-minute casting of Vince Vaughn, Ashley Judd and Paul Rudd. Kate Capshaw stars as a sultry widow who spends her spare time bedding her farm hands to the detriment of her emotionally damaged son Jeremy Davies. Drifter Vaughn appears in town and soon becomes involved with Judd; there are dark secrets to be revealed on the way to a suitably dramatic climax. The gothic tone and certain masterful moments transform it from bad to not uninteresting. LH [video]

Kate Capshaw *Delilah Ashford Potts* • Jessica Capshaw *Patsy* • Vince Vaughn *Clay Hewitt* • Ashley Judd *Kitty* • Jeremy Davies *Flyboy* • Daniel Meyer *Joel* • Paul Rudd *Earl* ■ *Dir/Scr* John Patrick Kelley

The Secret Six ★★

Crime drama 1931 · US · BW · 83mins

Bootlegger Wallace Beery rises to gangland supremo, only to be brought down by a six-man consortium of influential men, with a little help from newspaperman Clark Gable (in a supporting role). Slow to start, this is a serviceable, though superficially characterised, gangster movie. George Hill directed, with Lewis Stone excellent as a crooked attorney and, in small but key parts, John Mack Brown and Jean Harlow. RK

Wallace Beery *Louis Scorpio* • Lewis Stone *Richard Newton* • John Mack Brown [Johnny Mack Brown] *Hank Rogers* • Jean Harlow *Anne Courtland* • Marjorie Rambeau *Peaches* • Paul Hurst *Nick Mizoski the Gouger* • Clark Gable *Carl Luckner* • Ralph Bellamy *Johnny Franks* ■ *Dir* George W Hill [George Hill] • *Scr* Frances Marion, from her story

Secret Things ★★★

Comedy drama 2002 · Fr · Colour · 115mins

Although Marilyn Monroe, Betty Grable and Lauren Bacall shared Coralie Revel and Sabrina Seyvecou's gold-digging aspirations, they never resorted to these lusty tactics in *How to Marry a Millionaire*. As the exotic dancer and naive barmaid whose plan of attack includes frequent bouts of graphic coupling, Revel and Seyvecou give courageous displays of naked ambition, while also exhibiting a delicious sense of fun. Writer/director Jean-Claude Brisseau also stays just the right side of exploitation by making men the target of his most barbed satire, although he also has justified pops at class, consumerism and the corporate mentality. DP. In French with English subtitles.

Sabrina Seyvecou *Sandrine* • Coralie Revel *Nathalie* • Roger Mirmont *Delacroix* • Fabrice Deville *Christophe* • Blandine Bury *Charlotte* • Olivier Soler *Cadene* ■ *Dir/Scr* Jean-Claude Brisseau

The Secret War of Harry Frigg ★★★ U

Second World War comedy
1967 · US · Colour · 109mins

Paul Newman was never fully convincing as a comedian, though he makes a fair stab at it here, as a deadbeat private whose one gift is the ability to escape from military prisons. Given the temporary rank of full general, he is sent to Italy to engineer the escape of five Allied generals, who are enjoying their imprisonment in a lavish villa owned by Countessa Sylva Koscina. This is a jolly jape, lifted by some lovely turns from the supporting cast, notably John Williams as one of the two terribly English generals. AT

Paul Newman *Harry Frigg* • Sylva Koscina *Countess di Montefiore* • Andrew Duggan *General Armstrong* • Tom Bosley *General Pennypacker* • John Williams *General Mayhew* • Charles Gray *General Cox-Roberts* ■ *Dir* Jack Smight • *Scr* Peter Stone, Frank Tarloff, from a story by Frank Tarloff

The Secret Ways ★★★

Spy thriller 1961 · US · BW · 111mins

A Cold War drama with the always watchable Richard Widmark as an American soldier-of-fortune helping a noted Hungarian intellectual and anti-communist escape from behind the Iron Curtain. The tone wavers between realism and satire, the result of a dispute between Widmark and director Phil Karlson, who wanted to do it tongue in cheek. AT

Richard Widmark *Michael Reynolds* • Sonja Ziemann *Julia* • Charles Regnier *The Count* • Walter Rilla *Jansci* • Howard Vernon *Colonel Hidas* • Senta Berger *Elsa* • Heinz Moog *Minister Sakenov* ■ *Dir* Phil Karlson • *Scr* Jean Hazlewood, from a novel by Alistair MacLean

Secret Wedding ★★★★

Romantic political drama
1989 · Arg/Neth/Can · Colour · 95mins

Argentinian director Alejandro Agresti provides a fascinating insight into the problems facing the "disappeared", imprisoned under the junta, and now released back into society with the restoration of democracy. From the moment we find him naked on the streets of Buenos Aires, Tito Haas dominates the action, whether coming to terms with the years he has lost, attempting to win back the love of Mirtha Busnelli, or coping with the suspicions of his new neighbours. Ricardo Rodriguez's photography is superb, complementing the unusual camera angles favoured by Agresti. DP. In Spanish with English subtitles.

Tito Haas *Fermin Garcia* • Mirtha Busnelli *Tota* • Sergio Poves Campos *Pipi* • Nathan Pinzon *Priest* • Floria Bloise *Dona Patricia* • Elio Marchi *Leandro* ■ *Dir/Scr* Alejandro Agresti

Secret Window ★★ 12

Thriller 2004 · US · Colour · 91mins

Movie history is littered with poor attempts to exploit literary cash cow Stephen King, and this lacklustre psychological thriller joins them. Johnny Depp stars as a successful author whose writer's block is nothing compared to the hell that he encounters when psychotic stranger John Turturro accuses him of plagiarism. While Depp's emotional seesawing and Turturro's furrow-browed intensity are entertaining in themselves, director David Koepp signposts all the twists. SF. Contains violence. [video] DVD

Johnny Depp *Mort Rainey* • John Turturro *John Shooter* • Maria Bello *Amy Rainey* • Timothy Hutton *Ted Milner* • Charles S Dutton *Ken Karsch* • Len Cariou *Sheriff Dave Newsome* ■ *Dir* David Koepp • *Scr* David Koepp, from the novella *Secret Window, Secret Garden* by Stephen King

Secretary ★★★ 18

Comedy drama 2001 · US · Colour · 106mins

Love stories don't come much more bizarre than this strangely touching tale of a sadomasochistic relationship. Maggie Gyllenhaal plays a troubled young woman recently released from a mental hospital, whose obsessive self-harming is a concern to friends and parents alike. Taking a job at a legal firm, Lee comes under the control of her boss (James Spader), who has extremely unorthodox attitudes to office discipline. Both Gyllenhaal and Spader are excellent, and although the (relatively tame) sadomasochistic scenes may be too much for more sensitive viewers, this curious story delivers the optimistic message that there really is somebody out there for everyone. AS. Contains sex, nudity and swearing. [video] DVD

James Spader *E Edward Grey* • Maggie Gyllenhaal *Lee Holloway* • Jeremy Davies *Peter* • Patrick Bauchau *Dr Twardon* • Stephen McHattie *Burt Holloway* • Oz Perkins *Jonathan* • Jessica Tuck *Tricia O'Connor* • Amy Locane *Theresa Holloway* • Lesley Ann Warren *Joan Holloway* ■ *Dir* Steven Shainberg • *Scr* Erin Cressida Wilson, from the short story in the collection *Bad Behavior* by Mary Gaitskill

Secrets ★

Period drama 1933 · US · BW · 84mins

This was Mary Pickford's last film and made for an ignominious end to her long career as "America's Sweetheart". Pickford cast herself as a pioneering woman bravely enduring hardships and tragedy – and nobly standing by her philandering husband through 50 years of marriage. Leslie Howard, not surprisingly, is uncharacteristically ill at ease as the wayward spouse in a creaky melodrama that had already passed its sell-by date in the 1930s. RK

Mary Pickford *Mary Marlowe/Mary Carlton* • Leslie Howard *John Carlton* • C Aubrey Smith *Mr William Marlowe* • Blanche Frederici *Mrs Martha Marlowe* • Doris Lloyd *Susan Channing* • Herbert Evans *Lord Hurley* • Ned Sparks *"Sunshine"* ■ *Dir* Frank Borzage • *Scr* Frances Marion, Salisbury Field, Leonard Praskins, from the play by Rudolf Besier

Secrets ★★ 18

Drama 1971 · US · Colour · 82mins

This terribly ordinary romantic drama follows a disenchanted married couple (Jacqueline Bisset and Robert Powell) as they each have separate adventures in London. Powell's encounter with Shirley Knight is frankly laughable, but Bisset at least seems

S

more comfortable during her fling with Per Oscarsson – her orgasm was, by its sheer length, the screen's most famous until Meg Ryan erupted in the deli in *When Harry Met Sally...* But it is their young daughter's unpredictable story which is the most memorable, and this surely cannot have been the intention. DM

Jacqueline Bisset *Jacky* • Per Oscarsson *Raoul* • Shirley Knight Hopkins [Shirley Knight] *Beatrice* • Robert Powell *Allan* • Tarka Kings *Josy* ■ *Dir* Philip Saville • *Scr* Rosemary Davies, from a story by Philip Saville

Secrets & Lies ★★★★★ 15

Drama 1995 · UK · Colour · 141mins

Acclaimed director Mike Leigh finally scored a resounding box-office hit with this bittersweet snoop into the nooks and crannies of family life. The winner of the Palme d'Or at Cannes, this is a return to the familiar battleground of suburbia, but without the caricature that occasionally undermines Leigh's razor-sharp social observation. The teasing statements on the original poster best sum up the film's labyrinthine relationships: "Roxanne drives her mother crazy. Maurice never speaks to his niece. Monica can't talk to her husband. Hortense has never met her mother. Cynthia has a shock for her family." But even the secrets and lies themselves are of less significance than how the different characters respond to the revelations. Brenda Blethyn's café scene with fellow Oscar nominee Marianne Jean-Baptiste is a highlight. DP. Contains swearing. DVD

Timothy Spall *Maurice* • Brenda Blethyn *Cynthia* • Marianne Jean-Baptiste *Hortense* • Phyllis Logan *Monica* • Claire Rushbrook *Roxanne* • Elizabeth Berrington *Jane* • Michele Austin *Dionne* • Lee Ross *Paul* • Lesley Manville *Social worker* • Ron Cook *Stuart* ■ *Dir/Scr* Mike Leigh

Secrets d'Alcove ★★★

Portmanteau comedy
1954 · Fr/It · BW · 110mins

A bed links this amusing collection of short stories, told by a trio of diplomats and their chauffeur. In Henri Decoin's *Le Billet de Logement* Richard Todd parachutes into occupied France and helps Jeanne Moreau deliver a baby; Vittorio De Sica has to spend a night with professional co-respondent, Dawn Addams, in Gianni Franciolini's *Le Divorce*; the mysteries of the night haunt trucker Marcel Mouloudji when he stops to help the stranded François Périer in Ralph Habib's *Riviera-Express*, while Martine Carol seeks verification of the bed's historical importance in Jean Delannoy's *Le Lit de la Pompadour*. DP. In English and French with subtitles.

Jeanne Moreau *Mother* • Richard Todd *Soldier* • Martine Carol *Agnes* • Bernard Blier *President* • François Périer *Alfred* • Vittorio De Sica *Bob* • Dawn Addams *Janet* • Mouloudji [Marcel Mouloudji] *Ricky* ■ *Dir* Henri Decoin, Jean Delannoy, Ralph Habib, Gianni Franciolini • *Scr* Maurice Auberge, Jean Delannoy, Roland Laudenbach, Sergio Amidei, Antoine Blondin, Janet Wolf, Jacques Fano, Niccolo Theodoli, Paul Andreota, Richard Todd

Secrets of a Soul ★★★★

Silent psychological drama
1926 · Ger · BW · 56mins

Co-scripted with two of Freud's associates, Hans Neumann and Colin Ross, this was something of a departure for GW Pabst, who was better known for street realism than pure silent expressionism. However, there's no denying the technical ingenuity behind the symbolic dreams experienced by chemistry professor Werner Krauss, as he wrestles with the combined effects of his own sexual inadequacy and his jealous response to wife Ruth Weyher's infatuation with cousin Jack Trevor. Predominantly shot in the camera, the multiple superimpositions have lost none of their extraordinary potency, although Freud, apparently, wasn't impressed. DP

Werner Krauss *Martin Fellman* • Ruth Weyher *Fellman's wife* • Ilka Grüning *Mother* • Jack Trevor *Erich* • Pawel Pawlow *Dr Charles Orth* ■ *Dir* GW Pabst • *Scr* Colin Ross, Hans Neumann • *Cinematographer* Guido Seeber, Curt Oertel, Walter Robert Lach

Secrets of the Heart ★★★ 12

Fantasy drama
1997 · Sp/Fr/Por · Colour · 104mins

Admirers of Victor Erice's *The Spirit of the Beehive* will be intrigued by this Oscar-nominated tale of childhood innocence and the lure of the unknown. Set in the Basque country around Pamplona in the 1960s, the film doesn't overplay its allegorical hand, even though the symbolism of the abandoned house, with its locked rooms and buried secrets, is pretty blatant. Instead, Montxo Armendáriz focuses on the curiosity and incomprehension of nine-year-old Andoni Erburu, who is more interested in rumours that whispering ghosts inhabit the basement than in the relationship between his widowed mother and his uncle. DP. In Spanish with English subtitles. DVD

Andoni Erburu *Javi – Javier Zabalza* • Carmelo Gomez *Uncle* • Maria Charo Lopez *Aunt* • Silvia Munt *Mother* • Vicky Peña *Aunt Rosa* ■ *Dir/Scr* Montxo Armendáriz

Secrets of the Phantom Caverns ★ 15

Action thriller 1984 · UK · Colour · 87mins

Robert Powell's presence is so negligible as to be negative in this lost-world fantasy. Director Don Sharp, who could usually turn out high action from low budgets, never got to grips with this story of an albino tribe discovered in South American caves. With the quality of acting from Lisa Blount and Richard Johnson, besides the pathetic Powell, a stranglehold wouldn't have been enough. TH

Robert Powell *Wolfson* • Timothy Bottoms *Major Stevens* • Lisa Blount *Leslie Peterson* • Richard Johnson *Ben Gannon* • Anne Heywood *Frida Shelley* • Jackson Bostwick *Hunter* ■ *Dir* Don Sharp • *Scr* Christy Marx, Robert Vincent O'Neil, from a story by Ken Barnett

The Sect ★★★ 18

Horror 1991 · It · Colour · 111mins

Fans of spaghetti shockers will lap up this offering from Dario Argento acolyte Michele Soavi who established himself as a horror stylist in his own right with this highly atmospheric fantasy about a coven of devil worshippers carrying out ritualistic killings in modern-day Frankfurt. It's less a story than a succession of surreal and bravura set pieces; Soavi holds back on the gore (for the most part) emphasising suspense instead and succeeds in coming up with a good deal of genuine frights. He wrings good performances from Kelly Leigh Curtis as a schoolteacher caught up in the murders and, most notably, from Herbert Lom as the cult leader. RS. Italian dialogue dubbed into English.

Kelly Leigh Curtis [Kelly Curtis] *Miriam* • Herbert Lom *Gran Vecchio* • Maria Angela Giordano *Kathryn* • Tomas Arana *Damon* • Erica Sinisi *Sara* • Donald O'Brien *Jonathan* • Michel Hans Adatte *Franz* ■ *Dir* Michele Soavi • *Scr* Dario Argento, Giovanni Romoli, Michele Soavi, from a story by Dario Argento, Giovanni Romoli, Michele Soavi

Security Risk ★★

Action spy drama 1954 · US · BW · 69mins

While FBI agent John Ireland is on holiday at a ski resort, an atomic scientist is murdered by his assistant – who plans to sell secret papers to the KGB. Ireland's girlfriend, Dolores Donlon, witnesses the crime and takes the papers, intending to sell them herself. The bodies pile up before Ireland saves the day. An unremarkable example of the Red Scare movies that were a dime a dozen in Hollywood in the 1950s. AT

John Ireland *Ralph Payne* • Dorothy Malone *Donna Weeks* • Keith Larsen *Ted* • John Craven *Dr Lanson* • Joe Bassett *Malone* • Murray Alper *Mike* ■ *Dir* Harold Schuster • *Scr* Jo Pagano, Frank McDonald, John Rich, from a story by John Rich

Seduced ★★ 15

Crime thriller 1985 · US · Colour · 90mins

A good cast – including Cybill Shepherd, Ray Wise and Adrienne Barbeau – makes the most of this average made-for-television thriller about a district attorney trying to track down the murderer of the wealthy businessman husband of his former mistress. José Ferrer and his namesake Mel also give some edge to the tale, but the chances are you'll have guessed whodunnit well before the end credits. JB DVD

Gregory Harrison *Michael Riordan* • Cybill Shepherd *Vicki Orloff* • José Ferrer *James Killian* • Michael C Gwynne *Keith Fitzgibbons* • Ray Wise *Bartecki* • Adrienne Barbeau *Barbara Orloff* • Mel Ferrer *Arthur Orloff* ■ *Dir* Jerrold Freedman • *Scr* Charles Robert Carner

Seduced and Abandoned ★★★

Comedy drama 1964 · Fr/It · BW · 117mins

Less subtle than its predecessor, *Divorce – Italian Style*, Pietro Germi's scattershot assault on the Sicilian code of honour is deflected in its satirical purpose by the broad ebullience of its situation comedy. Depicting island society as archaic, prejudicial, superstitious and sex-ridden, Germi relies on caricature to expose the patriarchal tyranny that still claims proprietorial right over its womenfolk. This is a bitterly realistic film, with Aldo Puglisi impregnating his fiancée's teenage sister, Stefania Sandrelli, only to discard her because she's no longer a virgin. Yet, it's also scurrilously funny, with hypocritical father Saro Urzi thoroughly meriting his best actor prize at Cannes. DP. In Italian with English subtitles.

Stefania Sandrelli *Agnese Ascalone* • Aldo Puglisi *Peppino Califano* • Saro Urzi *Vincenzo Ascalone* • Lando Buzzanca *Antonio Ascalone* • Leopoldo Trieste *Baron Rizieri* ■ *Dir* Pietro Germi • *Scr* Pietro Germi, Luciano Vincenzoni, Age, Furio Scarpelli, from an idea by Pietro Germi, Luciano Vincenzoni

The Seduction of Joe Tynan ★★★ 15

Political drama 1979 · US · Colour · 102mins

You always get the feeling with this portrait of American political life that it has more than a ring of truth about it. Unfortunately, the echo has a hollowness that undermines the satire. Alan Alda's performance is superior to his script, capturing the glib, Kennedy-like charm that can still win votes, and Meryl Streep is convincing as a ruthless lawyer. However, some of the Senate scenes seem far-fetched, while the melodramatic finale is a shoddy way to end an otherwise well-constructed drama. DP. Contains swearing and brief nudity.

Alan Alda *Joe Tynan* • Barbara Harris *Ellie Tynan* • Meryl Streep *Karen Traynor* • Rip Torn *Senator Hugh Kittner* • Melvyn Douglas *Senator Birney* • Charles Kimbrough *Francis* • Carrie Nye *Althena Kittner* ■ *Dir* Jerry Schatzberg • *Scr* Alan Alda

The Seduction of Mimi ★★★

Satire 1972 · It · Colour · 92mins

Remade in 1977 as the Richard Pryor vehicle *Which Way Is Up?* (1977), Lina Wertmuller's third collaboration with actor Giancarlo Giannini earned her best director kudos at Cannes. A study in sexual hypocrisy and political expediency, it stars Giannini as Mimi, a Sicilian labourer who manages to alienate both the Mob and the communists, lose his wife and his mistress, and impregnate the spouse of the man who cuckolded him. Wertmuller is scarcely more sympathetic in her depiction of the female characters. DP. Italian dialogue dubbed into English.

Giancarlo Giannini *Mimi* • Mariangela Melato *Fiore* • Agostina Belli *Rosalia* • Elena Fiore *Amelia* • Turi Ferro *Tricarico* • Luigi Diberti *Pippino* ■ *Dir/Scr* Lina Wertmuller

Seduction: the Cruel Woman ★★★ 18

Drama 1985 · W Ger · Colour · 84mins

This lesbian *ménage à trois* combines sadomasochism, fetishism and erotic fantasy to explore everything from Germany's relationship with the USA, to consumerism, bourgeois hypocrisy and the battle of the sexes. Udo Kier gives a Calibanesque performance as the slave of dominatrix Mechthild Grossmann, who divides her time between running a taboo-shattering cabaret and disciplining her lovers, shoe seller Carola Regnier and naive American Sheila McLaughlin. DP. In German with English subtitles.

Mechthild Grossmann *Wanda* • Udo Kier *Gregor* • Sheila McLaughlin *Justine* • Carola Regnier *Caren* ■ *Dir* Elfi Mikesch, Monika Treut • *Scr* Elfi Mikesch, Monika Treut, from the novel *Venus in Furs* by Leopold von Sacher-Masoch

See Here, Private Hargrove ★★★

Second World War comedy drama
1944 · US · BW · 101mins

This is a pleasant enough boot-camp tale, with Robert Walker doing well as the hapless private, infuriating his senior officers in much the same way as he drove his editor up the wall during his civilian career as a reporter. There's echoes of Sergeant Bilko, as Walker schemes a way to visit his girlfriend in New York, but the picture lacks the commanding comic presence of a Phil Silvers. However, it's well directed by Wesley Ruggles – plus an uncredited Tay Garnett, who handled the tacked-on upbeat ending. RT

Robert Walker *Pte Marion Hargrove* • Donna Reed *Carol Holliday* • Robert Benchley *Mr Holliday* • Keenan Wynn *Pte Mulvehill* • Bob Crosby *Bob* • Ray Collins *Brody S Griffith* • Chill Wills *First Sgt Cramp* ■ *Dir* Wesley Ruggles • *Scr* Harry Kurnitz, from the book by Marion Hargrove

See How They Fall ★★★★ 18

Drama 1993 · Fr · Colour · 95mins

The inspiration for this frankly homoerotic crime drama is hard-boiled French *film noir* as practised by director Jacques Audiard's screenwriter father, Michel. Stripping down motives to loyalty and survival, the story follows two distinct avenues, which, through the supremely controlled, convoluted structure, eventually coincide with explosive consequences. Ageing conman Jean-Louis Trintignant and reckless rookie Mathieu Kassovitz encounter Jean Yanne, a travelling salesman whose life has fallen apart

S

through his obsessional crusade to avenge the death of the undercover cop to whom he'd become attached. DP. In French with English subtitles. Contains swearing, violence, sex scenes.

Jean-Louis Trintignant *Marx* • Jean Yanne *Simon* • Mathieu Kassovitz *Johnny* • Bulle Ogier *Louise* • Christine Pascal *Sandrine* • Yvon Back *Mickey* ■ *Dir* Jacques Audiard • *Scr* Alain Le Henry, Jacques Audiard, from the novel *Triangle* by Teri White

See No Evil, Hear No Evil ★ 15

Comedy 1989 · US · Colour · 97mins

An original comic talent, Richard Pryor has the dubious distinction of appearing in a plethora of truly execrable movies. The man has a homing instinct for a dreadful script and this is certainly one of them. The two-handed comedy – Gene Wilder is Pryor's partner in puerile nonsense in their third movie together – manages to waste both men's ability. Boring and deeply offensive. SH. Contains violence and swearing. DVD

Gene Wilder *Dave Lyons* • Richard Pryor *Wally Karew* • Joan Severance *Eve* • Kevin Spacey *Kirgo* • Alan North *Captain Braddock* • Anthony Zerbe *Sutherland* • Louis Giambalvo *Gatlin* • Kirsten Childs *Adele* ■ *Dir* Arthur Hiller • *Scr* Earl Barret, Arne Sultan, Eliot Wald, Andrew Kurtzman, Gene Wilder, from a story by Earl Barret, Arne Sultan, Marvin Worth

See Spot Run ★★★ PG

Comedy 2001 · US/Aus · Colour · 93mins

This tells the tale of an FBI supermutt who teams up with a postman to thwart an attempt by the Mob on the dog's life. Toss into the mix a cute little kid and two hitmen, and it all sounds like the recipe for a right dog's dinner. The film has its fair share of boring sequences and third-rate scatological humour, yet David Arquette gives an enthusiastic performance as the postman, and there are some nice supporting performances. DA DVD

David Arquette *Gordon* • Michael Clarke Duncan *Agent Murdoch* • Leslie Bibb *Stephanie* • Joe Viterelli *Gino* • Angus T Jones *James* • Steven R Schirripa *Arliss* • Paul Sorvino *Sonny* ■ *Dir* John Whitesell • *Scr* George Gallo, Gregory Poirier, Danny Baron, Chris Faber, from a story by Andrew Deane, Michael Alexander Miller, George Gallo

See You in the Morning ★★ 15

Romantic drama
1989 · US · Colour · 113mins

This is one of those intense relationship dramas in which everyone behaves like an adult – including the children. Jeff Bridges keeps the film on the rails, as a psychiatrist who spends so much time analysing his motives it's a wonder he's got any time left for living. Lukas Haas and Drew Barrymore are very subdued as Bridges's stepchildren, but they are certainly more interesting than their mother (Alice Krige). Heavygoing. DP

Jeff Bridges *Larry Livingston* • Alice Krige *Beth Goodwin* • Farrah Fawcett *Jo Livingston* • Drew Barrymore *Cathy Goodwin* • Lukas Haas *Petey Goodwin* • David Dukes *Peter Goodwin* • Frances Sternhagen *Neenie* • George Hearn *Martin* ■ *Dir/Scr* Alan J Pakula

Seed of Chucky ★★★ 15

Horror spoof 2004 · US · Colour · 86mins

Screenwriter Don Mancini, who created killer doll Chucky, makes his directorial feature debut with this, the fifth entry in the franchise. Here, Chucky (voiced, as always, by Brad Dourif) and his bride, Tiffany (breathlessly vocalised by Jennifer Tilly), are brought back to life by their gender-bending offspring Glen/Glenda (Billy Boyd) on the set of the Hollywood film chronicling their murderous exploits. The terrible toys then attempt to transfer their souls into the movie's director (real-life rapper Redman) and Tiffany's favourite star, Jennifer Tilly (playing herself). Genuinely sick and fitfully funny. AJ

Jennifer Tilly *Jennifer Tilly/Tiffany* • Brad Dourif *Chucky* • Billy Boyd *Glen/Glenda* • Redman • Hannah Spearritt *Joan* • John (2) Waters *Pete Peters* • Keith-Lee Castle *Psychs* • Jason Flemyng *Santa* ■ *Dir* Don Mancini • *Scr* Don Mancini, from his characters

The Seed of Man ★★★★

Science-fiction drama
1969 · It · Colour · 101mins

Director Marco Ferreri, dubbed "The Italian Master of Bad Taste" by critics, adapts his coolly sardonic gender-specific observations to the sci-fi genre in this superior work. After global warfare, plagues and catastrophes have virtually wiped out mankind, Marco Margine and Anne Wiazemsky (then married to Jean-Luc Godard) survive together on a deserted beach. But the post-nuclear Adam and Eve can't agree on having kids; he wants a son but she doesn't want to repopulate the self-destructive planet. Then maternally willing Annie Giradot enters the equation. Ferreri's engrossing fable, heightened by stunningly surreal art direction and sunny photography, ends suitably bleakly. AJ. An Italian language film.

Marco Margine *Ciro* • Anne Wiazemsky *Dora* • Annie Girardot *Anna* ■ *Dir* Marco Ferreri • *Scr* Sergio Bazzini, Marco Ferreri • *Cinematographer* Mario Vulpiani

Seeds of Doubt ★★

Thriller 1996 · US · Colour

Crusading journalist Alberta Watson risks her reputation on a series of articles proclaiming artist Joe Lando innocent of the murder of his model in this so-called thriller. Her campaign is successful, but former lover, detective Peter Coyote, is far from convinced and installs Lando as prime suspect when a killing coincides with Lando's release. There are few surprises in store, but that's due as much to the cast's overplaying as to the predictability of the screenplay or Peter Foldy's laboured direction. DP

Alberta Watson *Jennifer Kingsley* • Joe Lando *Raymond Crawford* • Peter Coyote *Police Lieutenant Henry Dexter* • Sten Eirik *Joe Bly* ■ *Dir* Peter Foldy • *Scr* David Wiechorek

Seeing Double ★★ PG

Musical comedy
2003 · UK/Sp · Colour · 87mins

Chirpy British popstars S Club sought to exploit their popularity with pre-teen audiences with this shameful but effective mass-marketing exercise. Wooden, unimaginative and with the feel of an extended pop promo, this nutrient-free nonsense makes *Spice World* look like an epic. It features not one, but two S Clubs, after an evil celebrity-obsessed scientist decides to clone Rachel, Hannah and the gang and send the doppelgängers out on a world tour. SF DVD

Bradley McIntosh *Bradley* • Rachel Stevens *Rachel* • Hannah Spearritt *Hannah* • Jo O'Meara *Jo* • Tina Barrett *Tina* • Jon Lee *Jon* • Joseph Adams *Alistair, the manager* • David Gant *Victor, the clonemaster* • Gareth Gates *Clone Gareth Gates* ■ *Dir* Nigel Dick • *Scr* Kim Fuller, Paul Alexander

Seeing Red ★★★

Political documentary
1983 · US · BW and Colour · 100mins

This Oscar-nominated documentary about American Marxists examines their beliefs, their efforts to transform American society, their victimisation at the hands of ambitious politicians and their responses to political developments in Soviet Russia. It makes for fascinating viewing, and the film's only real weakness is that none of the politicians of the time – such as future presidents Nixon and Reagan – are interviewed. While we get plenty of retrospective thought from the persecuted, it would have been nice to have had some thoughts from their persecutors as well. AT

Dir James Klein, Julia Reichert

The Seekers ★★

Period adventure 1954 · UK · Colour · 90mins

This costume adventure from director Ken Annakin is set in 19th-century New Zealand and boasts striking photography by Geoffrey Unsworth. The major influence on this story of colonial expansion at the expense of the Maoris is undoubtedly the Hollywood western and, consequently, it is hardly the most enlightened interpretation of the colonial spirit ever committed to film. Jack Hawkins cuts a dash as the leader of the expedition, however. DP

Jack Hawkins *Philip Wayne* • Glynis Johns *Marion Southey* • Noel Purcell *Paddy Clarke* • Inia Te Wiata *Hongi Tepe* • Kenneth Williams *Peter Wishart* • Laya Raki *Moana* ■ *Dir* Ken Annakin • *Scr* William Fairchild, from the novel by John Gutherie

Seems like Old Times ★★ PG

Screwball comedy
1980 · US · Colour · 97mins

Despite the presence of stars Goldie Hawn, Chevy Chase and Charles Grodin, plus a screenplay by Neil Simon, this tribute to the heyday of screwball comedy falls as flat as a pancake under the leaden hand of Jay Sandrich, making his film-directing debut. Some sharp lines pass muster, but the plot is limp and witless, while the ending is spectacularly pointless. TS. Contains swearing. DVD

Goldie Hawn *Glenda* • Chevy Chase *Nick* • Charles Grodin *Ira* • Robert Guillaume *Fred* • Harold Gould *Judge* • George Grizzard *Governor* • Yvonne Wilder *Aurora* • TK Carter *Chester* ■ *Dir* Jay Sandrich • *Scr* Neil Simon

Seizure ★★★

Horror 1974 · US · Colour · 94mins

For a long time after he hit the Hollywood big time, Oliver Stone refused to acknowledge this low-budget horror movie as his directorial debut. If it was bad, one could understand it. But it isn't. In fact, it's an unusually gripping gem starring ex-*Dark Shadows* vampire Jonathan Frid as a demented writer dreaming up three characters (Queen of Evil Martine Beswick, evil dwarf Herve Villechaize and towering Henry Baker) who spring to life to do his murderous bidding. Gory and scary, this is easily recognisable as a talented debut. AJ

Jonathan Frid *Edmund Blackstone* • Martine Beswick *Queen of Evil* • Joseph Sirola *Charlie* • Christina Pickles *Nicole Blackstone* • Herve Villechaize *The Spider* • Anne Meacham *Eunice* • Roger De Koven *Serge* • Troy Donahue *Mark* • Henry Baker [Henry Judd Baker] *Jackal* ■ *Dir* Oliver Stone • *Scr* Edward Mann, Oliver Stone

Sélect Hôtel ★★★ 18

Drama 1996 · Fr · Colour · 81mins

Laurent Bouhnik's debut feature attempts to achieve a visual edginess to match the marginalisation of its characters. It's a rough-and-ready, 1990s version of that poetic realist classic *Hôtel du Nord* (hence the dedication to Arletty), with prostitute Julie Gayet caught between her thieving, junkie brother (Jean-Michel Fête) and her scheming pimp (Marc Andréoni). Bouhnik's empathy with the disenfranchised otherwise seems authentic. DP. In French with English subtitles. Contains swearing, sex scenes and some violence.

Julie Gayet *Nathalie* • Jean-Michel Fête *Tof* • Serge Blumenthal *Pierre* • Marc Andréoni *Denis* • Sabine Bail *Clémentine* ■ *Dir/Scr* Laurent Bouhnik

Selena ★★★ PG

Biographical musical drama
1997 · US · Colour · 122mins

Virtually unknown outside the Latino community, Selena Quintanilla was a major figure in Tejano music until, on the very brink of her crossover into mainstream pop charts, she was murdered by the president of her fan club. This glossy, slick and predictable biography centres on her relationship with her father (Edward James Olmos) and her determination to hit the big time. The perfect vehicle for Jennifer Lopez, who was nominated for a Golden Globe. FL DVD

Jennifer Lopez *Selena Quintanilla* • Edward James Olmos *Abraham Quintanilla* • Jon Seda *Chris Perez* • Jackie Guerra *Suzette Quintanilla* • Constance Marie *Marcela Quintanilla* • Jacob Vargas *Abie* ■ *Dir/Scr* Gregory Nava

A Self-Made Hero ★★★★ 15

Drama 1995 · Fr · Colour · 101mins

Brilliantly exploiting the confusion precipitated by the liberation of France in the Second World War, this fascinating film from director Jacques Audiard ventures into the "forbidden" territory of Nazi collaboration. Mathieu Kassovitz plays the son of a collaborator who so credibly reinvents his past that he is invited to join a crack war-crimes unit. Kassovitz gives a nerve-end portrayal of an opportunist whose very survival depends on his addiction to deception, while Audiard's direction slyly captures the chilling postwar atmosphere. DP. In French with English subtitles. Contains swearing.

Mathieu Kassovitz *Young Albert Dehousse* • Anouk Grinberg *Servane* • Sandrine Kiberlain *Yvette* • Albert Dupontel *Dionnet* • Jean-Louis Trintignant *Old Albert Dehousse* ■ *Dir* Jacques Audiard • *Scr* Jacques Audiard, Alain Le Henry, from the novel *Un Héros Très Discret* by Jean-François Deniau

The Sellout ★★★

Crime drama 1951 · US · BW · 83mins

Using one of the most common themes in American films, this crime drama has small-town decency once more opposing corruption in high places. Even though the film is a touch predictable, it gains considerably from the performance of Walter Pidgeon as a crusading newspaper editor and from its short, sharp style, created by director Gerald Mayer. JM

Walter Pidgeon *Haven D Allridge* • John Hodiak *Chick Johnson* • Audrey Totter *Cleo Bethel* • Paula Raymond *Peggy Stauton* • Thomas Gomez *Sheriff Kellwin C Burke* • Cameron Mitchell *Randy Stauton* • Karl Malden *Buck Maxwell, policeman* • Everett Sloane *Nelson S Tarsson, attorney* ■ *Dir* Gerald Mayer • *Scr* Charles Palmer, from a story by Matthew Rapf

The Sellout ★★ 15

Spy drama 1975 · UK/It · Colour · 96mins

Before his premature death in 1980, British director Peter Collinson achieved a certain notoriety with a ragbag of action adventures like this one, set and filmed in Israel. It's not surprising to find Oliver Reed and Gayle Hunnicutt on hand, since they tended to prop up international co-productions on attractive locations, but sad to see the great Richard Widmark slumming it. This would-be thriller about spies brings credit to no one, and the film's pace is leaden. TS

Richard Widmark *Sam Lucas* • Oliver Reed *Gabriel Lee* • Gayle Hunnicutt *Deborah* • Sam Wanamaker *Sickles* • Vladek Sheybal *The Dutchman* • Ori Levy *Major Benjamin* • Assaf Dayan [Assi Dayan] *Lieutenant Elan* • Shmuel Rodensky *Zafron* ■ *Dir* Peter Collinson • *Scr* Murray Smith, Judson Kinberg, from a story by Murray Smith • *Cinematographer* Arthur Ibbetson

Semi-Tough ★★★ 15

Sports comedy 1977 · US · Colour · 103mins

Good-natured and often very funny, this is set around the world of American football. Burt Reynolds is the star player who finds himself competing with team-mate and good pal Kris Kristofferson for the attentions of Jill Clayburgh, whose dad owns the team. Reynolds and Kristofferson exude an easy-going charm and there is some expert comic support from the likes of Richard Masur and Robert Preston. JF. Contains swearing [video]

Burt Reynolds *Billy Clyde Puckett* • Kris Kristofferson *Marvin "Shake" Tiller* • Jill Clayburgh *Barbara Jane Bookman* • Robert Preston *Big Ed Bookman* • Bert Convy *Friedrich Bismark* • Roger E Mosley *Puddin* • Lotte Lenya *Clara Pelf* • Richard Masur *Phillip Hooper* • Carl Weathers *Dreamer Tatum* • Brian Dennehy *TJ Lambert* • Ron Silver *Vlada* ■ *Dir* Michael Ritchie • *Scr* Walter Bernstein, from the novel by Dan Jenkins

Seminole ★★ U

Western 1953 · US · Colour · 86mins

This otherwise effective western from Universal Studios is hobbled by a combination of its own earnestness and a weak leading performance by Rock Hudson. Nevertheless, it's beautifully filmed (with Technicolor photography by Russell Metty) and has a striking turn from Hugh O'Brian. Anthony Quinn, however, is as unlikely as an Indian chief as Hudson is as a West Point veteran, and a stronger script would have helped. TS

Rock Hudson *Lieutenant Lance Caldwell* • Barbara Hale *Revere Muldoon* • Anthony Quinn *Osceola/John Powell* • Richard Carlson *Major Harlan Degan* • Hugh O'Brian *Kajeck* • Russell Johnson *Lieutenant Hamilton* • Lee Marvin *Sergeant Magruder* ■ *Dir* Budd Boetticher • *Scr* Charles K Peck Jr

The Senator Was Indiscreet ★★★ U

Comedy 1947 · US · BW · 81mins

This interesting satire on Capitol Hill stars a very tongue-in-cheek William Powell as the senator with an interest in more than just the latest crop sharers' bill. This Universal comedy is unusual for its time, in that it pokes very obvious fun at political institutions when other movies were considerably less direct. Inexplicably, this was the only directorial outing for playwright George S Kaufman, who acquits himself well. Perhaps his brand of no-holds-barred satire was a little too strong for 1940s Hollywood. SH

William Powell *Senator Melvin G Ashton* • Ella Raines *Poppy McNaughton* • Peter Lind Hayes *Lew Gibson* • Arleen Whelan *Valerie Shepherd* • Ray Collins *Houlihan* • Allen Jenkins *Farrell* • Charles D Brown *Dinty* • Hans Conried *Waiter* • Myrna Loy *Mrs Ashton* ■ *Dir* George S Kaufman • *Scr* Charles MacArthur, from a story by Edwin Lanham

Send for Paul Temple ★★

Mystery 1946 · UK · BW · 83mins

Francis Durbridge's novelist-cum-troubleshooter had been a popular radio character (played by Hugh Morton) for many years before making his big-screen debut in this undistinguished thriller from that den of British movie mediocrity, the Butcher's Exchange. Anthony Hulme assumes the title role, as he poses as a police inspector to help reporter Joy Shelton expose the diamond thieves who murdered her brother. John Argyle directs with a rough proficiency. Three more films featuring Paul Temple followed, as did a TV series in the late 1960s. DP

Anthony Hulme *Paul Temple* • Joy Shelton *Steve Trent* • Tamara Desni *Diana Thornley* • Jack Raine *Sir Graham Forbes* • Beatrice Varley *Miss Marchmont* • Hylton Allen *Dr Milton* ■ *Dir* John Argyle • *Scr* Francis Durbridge, John Argyle, from characters created by Francis Durbridge

Send Me No Flowers ★★★★ U

Romantic black comedy
1964 · US · Colour · 95mins

Riotously funny or extraordinarily tasteless, depending on your point of view, this stars Rock Hudson as a hypochondriac who's convinced he's dying. Doris Day is his put-upon wife and Tony Randall the friend who takes the news of Hudson's impending demise badly. This is sophisticated stuff, the last of the Day/Hudson collaborations, and it's shot through with a mordant wit that may chime better with today's audience than it did with movie-goers back in the 1960s. Hudson was invariably under-rated as a performer, but here he's excellent, lending grace to a difficult role and imbuing his character with sly, winning humour. TS [video] DVD

Rock Hudson *George Kimball* • Doris Day *Judy Kimball* • Tony Randall *Arnold Nash* • Paul Lynde *Mr Akins* • Hal March *Winston Burr* • Edward Andrews *Dr Ralph Morrissey* • Patricia Barry *Linda Bullard* • Clint Walker *Bert Power* ■ *Dir* Norman Jewison • *Scr* Julius J Epstein, from the play by Norman Barasch, Carroll Moore

The Sender ★★★ 18

Science-fiction thriller
1982 · UK · Colour · 87mins

Former art director Roger Christian's directorial debut was this piece of metaphysical sci-fi, in which psychiatrist Kathryn Harrold pieces together the bizarre circumstances of amnesiac Zeljko Ivanek's condition. At times extremely disturbing, and regularly punctuated by set pieces highlighting Nick Allder's special effects, this mystery keeps one constantly alert and on the edge of one's seat. Too bad about the many loose ends. DM [video]

Kathryn Harrold *Gail Farmer* • Zeljko Ivanek *Sender* • Shirley Knight *Jerolyn* • Paul Freeman *Dr Denman* • Sean Hewitt *Messiah* • Harry Ditson *Dr Hirsch* • Olivier Pierre *Dr Erskine* • Marsha A Hunt *Nurse Jo* ■ *Dir* Roger Christian • *Scr* Thomas Baum

Senior Prom ★★ U

Musical 1958 · US · BW · 81mins

Passing itself off as a campus musical, the college girl-meets-boy-then meets-another-boy wisp of a plotline serves only as an excuse for stringing together 20 unmemorable musical numbers. Five of the songs spotlight the girl at the centre (Jill Corey). The boys between whom Corey's affections travel – if anyone cares – are rich Tom Laughlin (who picked up some fame in the 1970s for *Billy Jack*) and penniless Paul Hampton. RK

Jill Corey *Gay Sherridan* • Paul Hampton *Tom Harper* • Jimmie Komach *Dog* • Barbara Bostock *Flip* • Tom Laughlin *Carter Breed III* • Frieda Inescort *Mrs Sherridan* • Selene Walters *Caroline* • Marvin Miller *Narrator* • Louis Prima • Keely Smith • Ed Sullivan • Mitch Miller • Connee Boswell • Bob Crosby ■ *Dir* David Lowell Rich • *Scr* Hal Hackady

The Seniors ★★

Comedy 1978 · US · Colour · 87mins

Screenwriter Stanley Shapiro (a co-Oscar winner for *Pillow Talk*) turned his hand to the frat-pack genre here, with uneven results. A young Dennis Quaid is one of a group of students who set up a phony sex clinic, only for the prank to turn into a multi-million-dollar concern. This is too tame to provoke and too lame to amuse. RT

Dennis Quaid *Alan* • Jeffrey Byron *Larry* • Gary Imhoff *Ben* • Lou Richards *Steve* • Priscilla Barnes *Sylvia* • Rockey Flinterman *Arnold* • Alan Reed *Professor Helgner* • Edward Andrews *Banker* • Ian Wolfe *Mr Bleiffer* ■ *Dir* Rod Amateau • *Scr* Stanley Shapiro

La Señora ★★ 18

Drama 1987 · Sp · Colour · 103mins

This is what happens when a director trespasses on Buñuel territory, without having the wit, insight or film-making skills to prevent a dark story and a couple of slick scenes from descending into a pretentious mess. Catalan director Jordi Cadena is so fascinated by the cruel sexual games played by Silvia Tortosa (a gripping performance) and her paranoid husband that he never delves deeply enough into his socio-political themes. DP. In Spanish with English subtitles.

Silvia Tortosa *Teresa* • Hermann Bonnin *Don Nicolau* • Luis Merlo *Rafael* • Fernando Guillen-Cuervo *Josep* • Jeannine Mestre *Aina* ■ *Dir* Jordi Cadena • *Scr* Jordi Cadena, Silvia Tortosa, from the novel by Antoni Mus

Sensations ★★★ U

Musical 1944 · US · BW · 85mins

This is one of those of those musicals with a mouthwatering cast list that promises much more than it delivers. Director Andrew Stone also produced and co-wrote the script so must take most of the blame. Top-billed Eleanor Powell had been MGM's brightest dancing star, but was freelancing when she made this modest affair. She could still dance up a storm and her numbers are the best things in the movie. Her efforts to obtain publicity make up the wispy plot, welcome relief from which is provided by the guest spot of WC Fields (in his last film appearance). TV

Eleanor Powell *Ginny Walker* • Dennis O'Keefe *Junior Crane* • C Aubrey Smith *Dan Lindsay* • Eugene Pallette *Gus Crane* • Mimi Forsythe *Julia Westcott* • Lyle Talbot *Randall* • Hubert Castle *The Great Gustafson* • WC Fields ■ *Dir* Andrew L Stone • *Scr* Dorothy Bennett, Andrew L Stone, from a story by Frederick Jackson, Andrew L Stone

Sense and Sensibility ★★★★★ U

Period romantic drama
1995 · US · Colour · 130mins

The decision to hire Taiwan's Ang Lee to direct this adaptation of Jane Austen's first novel was truly inspired. Avoiding the chocolate-box visuals that cheapen so many British costume dramas, Lee brings a refreshing period realism to this tale of two sisters that allows Emma Thompson's respectful Oscar-winning script to flourish. Kate Winslet's spirited Marianne stands out from a solid display of ensemble acting, but the mystery remains why Lee, who became the first director to win Berlin's Golden Bear twice, was not among the film's seven Oscar nominations. DP [video] DVD

Emma Thompson *Elinor Dashwood* • Kate Winslet *Marianne Dashwood* • Alan Rickman *Colonel Brandon* • Hugh Grant *Edward Ferrars* • Greg Wise *John Willoughby* • Gemma Jones *Mrs Dashwood* • Imogen Stubbs *Lucy Steele* • Elizabeth Spriggs *Mrs Jennings* • Tom Wilkinson *Mr Dashwood* • Harriet Walter *Fanny Dashwood* • James Fleet *John Dashwood* • Emilie François *Margaret Dashwood* • Robert Hardy *Sir John Middleton* • Imelda Staunton *Charlotte Palmer* • Hugh Laurie *Mr Palmer* ■ *Dir* Ang Lee • *Scr* Emma Thompson, from the novel by Jane Austen

A Sense of Loss ★★

Documentary
1972 · US/Swi · Colour · 132mins

Marcel Ophüls's fatally flawed investigation into the Troubles in Northern Ireland was considered sufficiently inflammatory by the BBC for them to ban it. However, such is the evident bias in his assessment of the situation that it has precious little value, either as reportage or propaganda. His presentation of key Protestant apologists such as Ian Paisley is so dismissive that, rather than exposing the prejudice in their polemic, he succeeds only in ridiculing them, thus making the pronouncements of the Republican cause seem wholly acceptable. DP

Dir Marcel Ophüls

Senseless ★ 15

Comedy 1998 · US · Colour · 89mins

This poor man's imitation of a Jim Carrey movie is weak on all fronts. Marlon Wayans stars as a student so desperate to get a junior analyst's job that he agrees to take a sense-enhancing potion. Inevitably this lends him super senses that soon spiral out of control. Not worth the eyestrain. LH. Contains swearing and brief nudity. [video]

Marlon Wayans *Darryl Witherspoon* • Matthew Lillard *Tim LaFlour* • Rip Torn *Randall Tyson* • David Spade *Scott Thorpe* • Brad Dourif *Dr Wheedon* ■ *Dir* Penelope Spheeris • *Scr* Greg Erb, Craig Mazin • *Music* Yello

Senso ★★★ PG

Period drama 1954 · It · Colour · 116mins

A full-blown melodrama from Luchino Visconti about an Italian countess, trapped in a sexless marriage, falling in love with a dashing Austrian cavalry officer who is invading Italy. As usual with Visconti, there is a welter of baroque effects and an acute sense of history, as the countess betrays her country and her social class for the sake of passion. AT. Italian dialogue dubbed into English. [video]

Alida Valli *Contessa Livia Serpieri* • Farley Granger *Lieut Franz Mahler* • Massimo Girotti *Marquis Roberto Ussoni* • Heinz Moog *Count Serpieri* • Rina Morelli *Laura* ■ *Dir* Luchino Visconti • *Scr* Luchino Visconti, Suso Cecchi D'Amico, Giorgio Prosperi, Carlo Alianello, Giorgio Bassani, from the *Senso: Nuove Storielle Vane* by Camillo Boito

Sentimental Journey ★★ U

Melodrama 1946 · US · BW · 94mins

A stage actress (Maureen O'Hara) with a heart condition adopts an orphan child so that, if she succumbs, her husband, John Payne, won't be left alone. Weepies don't come much weepier than this offering, which is crassly manipulative and the sort of emotional rollercoaster that American audiences responded to immediately after the Second World War. There have been two remakes: with Lauren Bacall in 1958 as *The Gift of Love* and a 1984 TV-movie with Jaclyn Smith. AT

John Payne *Bill* • Maureen O'Hara *Julie* • William Bendix *Donnelly* • Cedric Hardwicke *Dr Miller* • Glenn Langan *Judson* • Mischa Auer *Lawrence Ayres* ■ *Dir* Walter Lang • *Scr* Samuel Hoffenstein, Elizabeth Reinhardt, from a story by Nelia Gardner White

The Sentinel ★★ 18

Horror 1977 · US · Colour · 87mins

Michael Winner is one of our most frequently disparaged directors, and it isn't difficult to see why on the evidence of this risible attempt to jump on *The Exorcist's* demonic band wagon. Cristina Raines moves into a stately old Brooklyn mansion, is menaced by ghastly apparitions and finds the place is built over a gateway to hell. Even those disposed to find Winner's direction enjoyably trashy – as opposed to clumsy and sensationalist – will be shocked by his decision to use genuinely handicapped people in one scene. RS

Chris Sarandon *Michael Lerman* • Cristina Raines *Alison Parker* • Martin Balsam *Professor* • John Carradine *Father Halliran* • José Ferrer *Robed figure* • Ava Gardner *Miss Logan* • Arthur Kennedy *Franchino* • Burgess Meredith *Chazen* • Eli Wallach *Gatz* • Christopher Walken *Rizzo* • Jerry Orbach *Director* • Beverly D'Angelo *Sandra* • Tom Berenger *Man at end* • Jeff Goldblum *Jack* ■ *Dir* Michael Winner • *Scr* Michael Winner, Jeffrey Konvitz, from the novel by Jeffrey Konvitz

Separate Lives ★ 18

Thriller 1995 · US · Colour · 97mins

James Belushi and Linda Hamilton are consigned to B-movie hell in a limp psychological thriller from David Madden. Belushi plays a former detective who is persuaded by his college lecturer (Hamilton) to watch her for signs of a murderous multiple personality. Tedious, predictable and awful. JB. Contains, violence, sex scenes and swearing. DVD

James Belushi *Tom Beckwith* • Linda Hamilton *Lauren Porter/Lena* • Vera Miles *Dr Ruth Goldin* • Elisabeth Moss *Ronnie Beckwith* • Drew Snyder *Robert Porter* • Mark Lindsay Chapman *Keno Sykes* • Marc Poppel *Detective Joe Gallo* ■ *Dir* David Madden • *Scr* Steven Pressfield

Separate Tables ★★★★ PG

Drama 1958 · US · BW · 95mins

David Niven won an Oscar as the retired "major" whose libido gets the better of him in this wonderfully cast version of Terence Rattigan's play. Wendy Hiller is the proprietor of a Bournemouth boarding house, presiding over a small group of paying guests whose neuroses start to unravel. Deborah Kerr's mother-dominated mousiness is too insistent, but Burt Lancaster's Hemingwayesque turn is great fun and Rita Hayworth, as his ex-wife, is marvellously convincing as a woman who knows that time and her beauty are running out. Delbert Mann's film is both moving and entertaining.There was a TV movie remake in 1983 starring Julie Christie and Alan Bates. TH DVD

Rita Hayworth *Ann Shankland* • Deborah Kerr *Sibyl Railton-Bell* • David Niven *Major Pollock* • Burt Lancaster *John Malcolm* • Wendy Hiller *Miss Pat Cooper* • Gladys Cooper *Mrs Railton-Bell* • Cathleen Nesbitt *Lady Matheson* • Rod Taylor *Charles* ■ *Dir* Delbert Mann • *Scr* Terence Rattigan, John Gay, from the play by Terence Rattigan

S

Separate Vacations ★★ 18

Comedy 1986 · Can · Colour · 87mins

David Naughton stars in this comedy, but it's a shame the material isn't more deserving of his talents. He plays a child-harried husband who opts out of the family skiing holiday in favour of a business trip to Mexico, with hopes of a bit of sauce on the side. This is a mildly "swinging" comedy that attempts to hide its intrinsic tackiness behind a moralistic theme of marital strife. RT

David Naughton *Richard Moore* • Jennifer Dale *Sarah Moore* • Mark Keyloun *Jeff Ferguson* • Laurie Holden *Karen* • Blanca Guerra *Alicia* • Suzie Almgren [Susan Almgren] *Helen Gilbert* • Lally Cadeau *Shelley* • Jackie Mahon *Annie Moore* ■ *Dir* Michael Anderson • *Scr* Robert Kaufman, from the novel by Eric Webber

Separate Ways ★

Romantic drama 1981 · US · Colour · 92mins

This is an uninspired drama about an upper middle-class couple having to re-evaluate their relationship in the wake of non-blissful domesticity. Karen Black starts an affair with a student at her community college just as her relationship with her former racing-driver husband Tony LoBianco, who is also having it on the side, goes into the pits. A real non-starter. FL

Karen Black *Valentine Colby* • Tony LoBianco *Ken Colby* • Arlene Golonka *Annie* • David Naughton *Jerry* • Sharon Farrell *Karen* • Jack Carter *Barney* • William Windom *Huey* • Robert Fuller *Woody* ■ *Dir* Howard Avedis • *Scr* Leah Appet, from a story by Leah Appet, Howard Avedis, Marlene Schmidt

La Séparation ★★★ PG

Drama 1994 · Fr · Colour · 84mins

Although a masterclass in actorly restraint, the agonisingly slow deterioration of Isabelle Huppert and Daniel Auteuil's relationship makes for painful viewing. It would have been much more effective with a more balanced presentation of emotions and events – by siding with Auteuil's character, director Christian Vincent makes Huppert's Anne seem unnecessarily callous and allows Auteuil to become increasingly pathetic. The political subtext, on how radicals conform with time, is much more engaging than the detached melodrama. DP. In French with English subtitles. DVD

Isabelle Huppert *Anne* • Daniel Auteuil *Pierre* • Jerôme Deschamps *Victor* • Karin Viard *Claire* • Laurence Lerel *Laurence* • Louis Vincent *Loulou* • Nina Morato *Marie* ■ *Dir* Christian Vincent • *Scr* Christian Vincent, Dan Franck, from the novel by Dan Franck

September ★★★★ PG

Drama 1987 · US · Colour · 171mins

Woody Allen's autumnal film has a story straight out of Chekhov, as relationships fray between intellectuals in a Vermont mansion and Mia Farrow, Denholm Elliott, Dianne Wiest and Sam Waterston vent their frustrations on each other. One of Allen's "serious" pieces, without his angst-prone presence, this was originally filmed with Maureen O'Sullivan (Farrow's real-life mother), Sam Shepard and Charles Durning. Allen was so unsure about its balance that he largely re-shot it and was forced to find alternative actors because of the cast's other commitments. The result is wonderfully stylish and beautifully shot, but not a barrel of laughs. TH DVD

Denholm Elliott *Howard* • Dianne Wiest *Stephanie* • Mia Farrow *Lane* • Elaine Stritch *Diane* • Sam Waterston *Peter* • Jack Warden *Lloyd* • Ira Wheeler *Mr Raines* • Jane Cecil *Mrs Raines* ■ *Dir/Scr* Woody Allen • *Cinematographer* Carlo Di Palma

September Affair ★★★

Romantic drama 1950 · US · BW · 105mins

Set in various Italian locations, this soapy romance might have been more appealing in colour. What it does have, however, are two likeable leads in Joseph Cotten and Joan Fontaine and Kurt Weill's *September Song*, sung by Walter Huston on the soundtrack. The contrived plot has Fontaine, a concert pianist, and wealthy married Cotton falling in love when they miss their plane back to the USA. The plane crashes and they are listed among the dead. Now they can start a new life together. Or can they? Thankfully William Dieterle's direction avoids oversentimentality. RB

Joan Fontaine *Manina Stuart* • Joseph Cotten *David Lawrence* • Françoise Rosay *Maria Salvatini* • Jessica Tandy *Catherine Lawrence* • Robert Arthur *David Lawrence Jr* • James Lydon *Johnny Wilson* ■ *Dir* William Dieterle • *Scr* Robert Thoeren, from a story by Fritz Rotter • *Music* Victor Young

September 30, 1955 ★★★

Drama 1977 · US · Colour · 107mins

The title is the date on which James Dean crashed his Porsche and turned himself into a legend. This film's hero, Richard Thomas, is a Dean-obsessed student in Arkansas, who hears the news of his idol's death and with other students stages an elaborate pagan-style ceremony which ends in a terrible accident. Moodily shot by Gordon Willis and scored by veteran Leonard Rosenman, this is an effective meditation on the power of celebrity and its impact on youth culture. AT

Richard Thomas *Jimmy J* • Susan Tyrrell *Melba Lou* • Deborah Benson *Charlotte* • Lisa Blount *Billie Jean* • Tom Hulce *Hanley* • Dennis Quaid *Frank* • Dennis Christopher *Eugene* ■ *Dir/Scr* James Bridges

Serena ★★★ U

Crime drama 1962 · UK · BW · 62mins

Rising well above the usual quota-quickie standards, this entertaining little whodunnit shoehorns about two hours of plot into its short running time. Directed at a fair lick by Peter Maxwell, it revolves around the complicated sex life of smoothie artist Emrys Jones, who wants to leave his wife for his model mistress. When the body of an unknown woman is found in a country cottage, inspector Patrick Holt is called in to investigate. DP

Patrick Holt *Inspector Gregory* • Emrys Jones *Howard Rogers* • Honor Blackman *Ann Rogers* • Bruce Beeby *Sergeant Conway* • John Horsley *Mr Fisher* • Robert Perceval *Bank manager* ■ *Dir* Peter Maxwell • *Scr* Edward Abraham, Reginald Hearne, from a story by Edward Abraham, Valerie Abraham

Serenade ★★★★ U

Musical drama 1956 · US · Colour · 121mins

This film version of James M Cain's steamy novel about a singer who has a homosexual relationship with his patron seems an unlikely vehicle for Hollywood's top tenor Mario Lanza. Even with the book's plot substantially changed (the patron is now a woman), this is compulsive viewing thanks to director Anthony Mann's skill, the urbane villainy of Vincent Price and the sheer soap-opera pleasure of watching cool Joan Fontaine and sultry Sarita Montiel vie for Lanza. The Warner Bros production values are top-notch, but it's a bit long. TS

Mario Lanza *Damon Vincenti* • Joan Fontaine *Kendall Hale* • Sarita Montiel *Juana Montes* • Vincent Price *Charles Winthrop* • Joseph Calleia *Maestro Marcatello* • Harry Bellaver *Monte* • Vince Edwards *Marco Roselli* ■ *Dir* Anthony Mann • *Scr* Ivan Goff, Ben Roberts, John Twist, from the novel by James M Cain

Serendipity ★★★ PG

Romantic comedy
2001 · US · Colour · 87mins

John Cusack and Kate Beckinsale are the two Christmas shoppers who meet in Bloomingdales. In spite of both being involved with other people, they share a couple of hot chocolates and then, on her insistence, leave the chance that they could make a cute twosome to the fickle hands of fate. Years later, when they're about to go down the aisle with their respective partners, they try to find each other to see if it was really true love. Cusack's winning performance saves this sweet (if occasionally sickly) romantic whimsy. JB DVD

John Cusack *Jonathan Trager* • Kate Beckinsale *Sara Thomas* • Molly Shannon *Eve* • Jeremy Piven *Dean Kansky* • John Corbett *Lars Hammond* • Bridget Moynahan *Halley Buchanan* • Eugene Levy *Bloomingdale's salesman* ■ *Dir* Peter Chelsom • *Scr* Marc Klein

The Sergeant ★★★

Drama 1968 · US · Colour and BW · 108mins

Rod Steiger boldly goes where few actors have dared to go, even in the liberated Swinging Sixties, by portraying a homosexual character. As a US Army sergeant serving in postwar Paris he finds a love-object in young private John Phillip Law, though it takes a long time for him to realise why the hands-off relationship means so much to him. John Flynn directs with ponderous seriousness, but Steiger is believably vulnerable as the man caught up in a system that won't allow him to reveal his sexuality. TH

Rod Steiger *Master Sergeant Albert Callan* • John Phillip Law *Private Tom Swanson* • Ludmila Mikael *Solange* • Frank Latimore *Captain Loring* • Elliott Sullivan *Pop Henneken* • Ronald Rubin *Corporal Cowley* • Phillip Roye *Aldous Brown* ■ *Dir* John Flynn • *Scr* Dennis Murphy, from his novel

Sgt Bilko ★★ PG

Comedy 1996 · US · Colour · 90mins

Steve Martin must have known the comparisons with Phil Silvers were not going to be favourable when he took on this tepid spin-off, but he combines elements of Silvers's character with his own comic personality. Andy Breckman's script is strongest in its double-talk, but the plot – about a top-secret hover-tank – is less than involving and the feud between Martin and Phil Hartman is overcooked. Mediocre, but not a total disaster. DP. Contains swearing. DVD

Steve Martin *Master Sgt Ernest G Bilko* • Dan Aykroyd *Colonel Hall* • Phil Hartman *Major Thorn* • Glenne Headly *Rita Robbins* • Daryl Mitchell *Wally Holbrook* • Max Casella *Dino Paparelli* • Eric Edwards *Duane Doberman* • Dan Ferro *Tony Morales* ■ *Dir* Jonathan Lynn • *Scr* Andy Breckman, from the TV series *The Phil Silvers Show* by Nat Hiken

Sergeant Deadhead ★★ U

Musical comedy 1965 · US · Colour · 88mins

One-time pop star Frankie Avalon plays a dual role in this watchable, if rowdy, musical comedy. Sergeant OK Deadhead is the kind of nervous, Jerry Lewis-style klutz the US Air Force doesn't need when it's about to launch a top-secret rocket. Deadhead is accidentally blasted off into space with a chimpanzee and, on his return, temporarily becomes a crazed rebel. Buster Keaton, in one of his final movies, supplies some quieter visual humour as a mad electrician. JG

Frankie Avalon *Sgt OK Deadhead/Sgt Donovan* • Deborah Walley *Col Lucy Turner* • Fred Clark *Gen Rufus Fogg* • Cesar Romero *Adm Stoneham* • Gale Gordon *Capt Weiskopf* • Harvey Lembeck *Pte McEvoy* • John Ashley *Pte Filroy* • Buster Keaton *Pte Blinken* ■ *Dir* Norman Taurog • *Scr* Louis M Heyward

Sgt Kabukiman NYPD ★★★ 18

Action comedy adventure
1991 · US/Jpn · Colour · 100mins

Gleefully disregarding trifles such as quality and taste, Troma has produced some of the most delirious B-movies of recent times. However, none can rival the silliness of this comic-book caper. Doltish cop Rick Gianasi is possessed by the spirit of a kabuki actor and masters the heat-seeking chopsticks and suffocating sushi rolls that will prevent the Evil One from taking over the world. While mercilessly mocking the superhero tradition, directors Michael Herz and Lloyd Kaufman resort too readily to stereotypes and socko slapstick. DP DVD

Rick Gianasi *Harry Griswold/Sergeant Kabukiman* • Susan Byun *Lotus* • Bill Weeden *Reginald Stuart* • Thomas Crnkovich *Rembrandt* • Larry Robinson *Reverend Snipes* • Noble Lee Lester *Captain Bender* • Brick

Bronsky *Jughead* ■ *Dir* Lloyd Kaufman, Michael Herz • *Scr* Lloyd Kaufman, Andrew Osborne, Jeffrey W Sass

Sergeant Madden ★★

Drama 1939 · US · BW · 82mins

Josef von Sternberg, under contract to MGM to make two films, was forced to take on this typical sentimental Wallace Beery vehicle after being removed from *I Take This Woman* with Hedy Lamarr. The director was not happy, either with the screenplay or his pug-ugly star, with whom he had many a row. The result was a mediocre crime melodrama about an Irish cop (Beery), whose son goes wrong. RB

Wallace Beery *Shaun Madden* • Tom Brown *Al Boylan Jr* • Alan Curtis *Dennis Madden* • Laraine Day *Eileen Daly* • Fay Holden *Mary Madden* • Marc Lawrence (1) *"Piggy" Ceders* • Marion Martin *Charlotte* • David Gorcey *"Punchy"* ■ *Dir* Josef von Sternberg • *Scr* Wells Root, from the story *A Gun in His Hand* by William A Ullman Jr

Sgt Pepper's Lonely Hearts Club Band ★★ PG

Musical 1978 · US · Colour · 106mins

This is a daft attempt to conceptualise the classic Beatles album by linking its songs via a contrived connective storyline. Some sequences are OK, but others are embarrassing. Some interest resides in its pick 'n' mix cast of musicians and actors. Musicians include The Bee Gees, soul band Earth Wind & Fire, and 1970s pin-up Peter Frampton. Actors in the cast include Steve Martin, George Burns, Donald Pleasence and Frankie Howerd. DA [video]

Peter Frampton *Billy Shears* • Barry Gibb *Mark Henderson* • Robin Gibb *Dave Henderson* • Maurice Gibb *Bob Henderson* • Frankie Howerd *Mr Mustard* • Paul Nicholas *Dougie Shears* • Donald Pleasence *BD Brockhurst* • Steve Martin *Dr Maxwell Edison* • Alice Cooper *Father Sun* • Billy Preston *Sgt Pepper* • George Burns *Mr Kite* ■ *Dir* Michael Schultz • *Scr* Henry Edwards

Sergeant Rutledge ★★★ PG

Western drama 1960 · US · Colour · 106mins

John Ford directs this rather static courtroom drama about a black cavalry officer accused of rape and murder. Daring in its time, it's still powerful today. Woody Strode gets the role of a lifetime as Rutledge, and the sequence where he sings *Captain Buffalo* (the film's original title) and crosses the River Pecos was one of the most significant in Hollywood's treatment of blacks in cinema to that date. Carleton Young is also impressive, but nominal stars Jeffrey Hunter and Constance Towers are inadequate. TS [video]

Jeffrey Hunter *Lt Thomas Cantrell* • Woody Strode *Sgt Braxton Rutledge* • Constance Towers *Mary Beecher* • Willis Bouchey *Colonel Fosgate* • Billie Burke *Mrs Fosgate* • Carleton Young *Captain Shattuck* • Judson Pratt *Lieutenant Mulqueen* • Juano Hernandez *Sgt Skidmore* ■ *Dir* John Ford • *Scr* Willis Goldbeck, James Warner Bellah, from the novel *Captain Buffalo* by James Warner Bellah

Sergeant Ryker ★★ U

Courtroom drama 1968 · US · Colour · 85mins

Military prosecutor Bradford Dillman is persuaded that bitter, convicted traitor Lee Marvin, who is awaiting execution, may not have received a fair hearing, and he agrees to a retrial. As it was originally an extended TV play and not intended as a film, the courtroom drama jars occasionally, but the intelligent writing and supporting cast make it worth watching. JG

Lee Marvin *Sergeant Paul Ryker* • Bradford Dillman *Captain David Young* • Vera Miles *Ann Ryker* • Peter Graves (2) *Major Whitaker* • Lloyd Nolan *General Amos Bailey* • Norman Fell *Sergeant Max Winkler* • Walter Brooke *Colonel Arthur Merriam* ■ *Dir* Buzz Kulik • *Scr* Seeleg Lester, William D Gordon, from a story by Seeleg Lester

Sergeant York ★★★★ U

Biographical war drama
1941 · US · BW · 128mins

Nominated for 11 Oscars and winning Gary Cooper his first best actor statuette, this is a model of biopic making. As decent and determined as ever, Cooper is a Tennessee backwoodsman who swears off violence after lightning strikes his rifle during a land dispute, only to become a national hero after single-handedly killing 20 Germans and capturing 132 more during a First World War offensive. Director Howard Hawks handles the action sequences with customary confidence, but he also creates several fully fledged supporting characters, who are convincingly played by Joan Leslie and Oscar nominees Walter Brennan and Margaret Wycherly. DP [video]

Gary Cooper *Alvin C York* • Walter Brennan *Pastor Rosier Pile* • Joan Leslie *Gracie Williams* • George Tobias *"Pusher" Ross* • Stanley Ridges *Major Buxton* • Margaret Wycherly *Mother York* • Ward Bond *Ike Botkin* ■ *Dir* Howard Hawks • *Scr* Abem Finkel, Harry Chandlee, Howard Koch, John Huston, from the *War Diary of Sergeant York* by Alvin C York and edited by Sam K Cowan, and the biographies *Sergeant York and His People* by Sam K Cowan and *Sergeant York – Last of the Long Hunters* by Tom Skeyhill • *Cinematographer* Sol Polito, Arthur Edeson • *Music* Max Steiner

Sergeants 3 ★★★ U

Western comedy
1962 · US · Colour · 112mins

Following on from *Ocean's Eleven*, this rambunctious on-screen get-together of the "Rat Pack" – Frank Sinatra, Dean Martin, Peter Lawford, Sammy Davis Jr, Joey Bishop – finds the first three as brawling cavalry officers out to repulse marauding Indians, which they succeed in doing with the help of bugle-blowing ex-slave Davis. Directed by John Sturges from a WR Burnett script that transposes *Gunga Din* to the American west and spoofs that film's heroics, this romp only entertains in parts. RK

Frank Sinatra *1st Sergeant Mike Merry* • Dean Martin *Sgt Chip Deal* • Sammy Davis Jr *Jonah Williams* • Peter Lawford *Sgt Larry Barrett* • Joey Bishop *Sgt Major Roger Boswell* • Henry Silva *Mountain Hawk* • Ruta Lee *Amelia Parent* • Buddy Lester *Willie Sharpknife* ■ *Dir* John Sturges • *Scr* WR Burnett

Sergei Eisenstein: Mexican Fantasy ★★★★

Documentary 1998 · Rus · BW · 98mins

Que Viva Mexico!, Sergei Eisenstein's first (and only) non-Soviet venture was dogged throughout by authorial disputes. Spurned by Paramount in 1930, he received sufficient sponsorship from left-wing novelist Upton Sinclair to shoot some 50 hours of footage, only for it to be delivered to Hollywood producer Sol Lesser, who used it for the bowdlerised feature *Thunder over Mexico* (1933). Eisenstein's biographer Marie Seton and former student Jay Leyda both reworked the material (the former as co-writer of 1939's *Time in the Sun*), as is related in this fascinating documentary on the travelogue that turned into a tract on the colonial abuses that instilled revolutionary fervour into a land of stark beauty and cultural complexity. DP. A Russian language film.

Alexandra Scheff *Narrator* ■ *Dir/Scr* Oleg Kovalov • *Cinematographer* Yevgeny Shermergor, Edouard Tissé

Serial ★★★ 18

Satirical comedy 1980 · US · Colour · 88mins

Christopher Lee plays a gay Hell's Angel in an under-rated satire about the worst excesses in 1970s America. Bizarre religious cults, ludicrous fashions, absurd self-help groups, marital fidelity and love affairs with poodle-parlour workers all come under the social mores microscope, in a scattershot spoof. Lee rises to the occasion and the rest of the eclectic cast – including Tuesday Weld, Martin Mull and Sally Kellerman – make their oddball moments count. AJ [video]

Martin Mull *Harvey* • Tuesday Weld *Kate* • Jennifer McAlister *Joan* • Sam Chew Jr *Bill* • Sally Kellerman *Martha* • Anthony Battaglia *Stokeley* • Nita Talbot *Angela* • Bill Macy *Sam* • Christopher Lee *Luckman/Skull* • Pamela Bellwood *Carol* ■ *Dir* Bill Persky • *Scr* Rich Eustis, Michael Elias, from the novel by Cyra McFadden

Serial Killer ★★★ 18

Thriller 1996 · Can · Colour · 90mins

Here's a film that states its intentions up front. Tobin Bell is the serial killer, recently escaped from captivity and out to exact revenge on Kim Delaney, the FBI psychological profiler who put him away. The film's only real attractions are the unusual method of revenge Bell has in mind for his former captor and the gleam of menace in his eye. Pam Grier appears as the police captain, and while this is no *Silence of the Lambs*, it does have a definite twist. ST [video]

Kim Delaney *Selby Younger* • Gary Hudson *Cole Grayson* • Tobin Bell *William Lucian Morrano* • Pam Grier *Capt Maggie Davis* • Marco Rodriguez *Manny Ramirez* • Joel Polis *Jack Blund* • Andrew Prine *Perry Jones* ■ *Dir* Pierre David • *Scr* Mark Sevi

Serial Mom ★★★ 18

Black comedy 1994 · US · Colour · 89mins

Kathleen Turner is the archetypal cheerful mother – until someone disrupts her orderly life. Then she turns into the homicidal housewife from hell. Didn't rewind your videotape? Wearing white shoes after Labour Day? Watch out! Cult director John Waters's darkly funny look at the murderer-as-celebrity phenomenon trashes American family values and sends up splatter movies, mining each target for maximum screwball outrage. While not as perverse as some of Waters's previous bad-taste epics, this "Doris Day goes *Psycho*" comedy still retains his trademark shocking edge. AJ. Contains violence, swearing and sex scenes. [video] DVD

Kathleen Turner *Beverly Sutphin, Mom* • Sam Waterston *Eugene Sutphin, Dad* • Ricki Lake *Misty Sutphin* • Matthew Lillard *Chip Sutphin* • Scott Wesley Morgan *Detective Pike* • Walt MacPherson *Detective Gracey* • Justin Whalin *Scotty* • Patricia Dunnock *Birdie* • Lonnie Horsey *Carl* • Mink Stole *Dottie Hinkle* • Mary Jo Catlett *Rosemary Ackerman* • Traci Lords *Carl's date* • Suzanne Somers • Patricia Hearst *Juror No 8* • Mary Vivian Pearce *Book buyer* ■ *Dir/Scr* John Waters (2)

Series 7: the Contenders ★★ 18

Satire 2001 · US · Colour · 87mins

First-time writer/director Daniel Minahan began developing this low-budget, no-star project – a game show in which contestants must kill the others to win – at Sundance in 1997, so there's a degree of prescience (or luck) about the timing, as "reality TV" shows proliferate. Presented in *vérité* style as edited segments of a TV show (*The Contenders*), this is a one-idea film, whose central gimmick soon palls. It's hard to care about any of the promising characters in such a deliberately unreal format. AC [video] DVD

Brooke Smith *Dawn* • Marylouise Burke *Connie* • Glenn Fitzgerald *Jeff* • Michael Kaycheck *Tony* • Richard Venture *Franklin* • Merritt Wever *Lindsay* • Donna Hanover *Sheila* • Angelina Phillips *Doria* ■ *Dir/Scr* Daniel Minahan

Serious Charge ★★★ PG

Drama 1959 · UK · BW · 95mins

Anthony Quayle plays a former army vicar who arrives in a new town (an early Milton Keynes) to run a youth club. Sarah Churchill throws herself at him but Quayle prefers football. Then a local teddy boy accuses Quayle of sexual assault. The movie is especially good at subverting British movie decorum – people exchanging mild gossip over cups of tea – by focusing on the sterility of life in the New Britain of purpose-built towns. All this, plus Cliff Richard making his screen debut. AT [video]

Anthony Quayle *Howard Phillips* • Sarah Churchill *Hester Peters* • Andrew Ray *Larry Thompson* • Irene Browne *Mrs Phillips* • Percy Herbert *Mr Thompson* • Noel Howlett *Mr Peters* • Cliff Richard *Curley Thompson* ■ *Dir* Terence Young • *Scr* Mickey Delamar, Guy Elmes, from the play by Philip King

The Serpent ★★

Spy drama
1972 · Fr/It/W Ger · Colour · 121mins

As well as an outstanding cast, this boasts exemplary technical credits, with Claude Renoir behind the camera and Ennio Morricone composing the score. Alas, it turns out to be a distinctly muted cloak-and-dagger affair. Yul Brynner is a top Russian diplomat whose defection to the west is complicated by a series of deaths. The whole production is given a glossy look by director Henri Verneuil and his set pieces display a fine eye for detail, but the overly complicated story never grips the viewer. RS

Yul Brynner *Vlassov* • Henry Fonda *Allan Davies* • Dirk Bogarde *Philip Boyle* • Philippe Noiret *Lucien Berthon* • Michel Bouquet *Tavel* • Farley Granger *Computer chief* • Virna Lisi *Annabel Lee* ■ *Dir* Henri Verneuil • *Scr* Henri Verneuil, Gilles Perrault, Tom Rowe, from the novel *Le Suicide* by Pierre Nord

The Serpent and the Rainbow ★★★ 18

Horror 1987 · US · Colour · 98mins

Inspired by Wade Davis's non-fiction account of scouring Haiti for authentic "zombie powder" on behalf of a pharmaceutical company wanting to market a new anaesthetic, director Wes Craven turns his intriguing quest into nothing more than a high-tone fright flick. However, while paying scant attention to the role political terror plays in some parts of the West Indies, this is well appointed in the creepy atmosphere department, veering from chilling fact to hallucinatory horror via Craven's sure-handed shock tableaux. AJ. Contains violence and swearing. [video] DVD

Bill Pullman *Dennis Alan* • Cathy Tyson *Dr Marielle Duchamp* • Zakes Mokae *Dargent Peytraud* • Paul Winfield *Lucien Celine* • Brent Jennings *Mozart* • Conrad Roberts *Christophe* • Badja Djola *Gaston* • Theresa Merritt *Simone* • Michael Gough *Schoonbacher* ■ *Dir* Wes Craven • *Scr* Richard Maxwell, AR Simoun, from the book by Wade Davis

Serpent of the Nile ★ U

Historical drama 1953 · US · Colour · 81mins

If Perry Mason is your idea of Mark Antony, this risible historical drama is for you. For, verily, Raymond Burr plays the noble Roman, with red-headed Rhonda Fleming as Queen Cleopatra, seducing him and heading for a suicide

S

pact. Made on a budget that would only have paid for a day's linguini lunches on the Burton/Taylor *Cleopatra*, this effort from director William Castle is lamentable. AT

Rhonda Fleming *Cleopatra* • William Lundigan *Lucilius* • Raymond Burr *Mark Antony* • Jean Byron *Charmion* • Michael Ansara *Florus* ■ *Dir* William Castle • *Scr* Robert E Kent

The Serpent's Egg ★★★ 18

Drama 1977 · W Ger/US · Colour · 119mins

The critics have been unkind to this film, attacking it for its noise, its depiction of pain and prejudice and its echoes of the portrait of Germany painted in *Cabaret*. Admittedly, this is one of Ingmar Bergman's lesser pictures – he wasn't used to working in English, his knowledge of the period was somewhat limited and he was still nursing the hurt caused by his brush with the Swedish inland revenue that had driven him into temporary exile. But, occasionally, this bold experiment in style throws up some striking images that capture the mix of decadence and danger of life in the Weimar Republic. DP. Contains some violence and swearing. DVD

Liv Ullmann *Manuela Rosenberg* • David Carradine *Abel Rosenberg* • Gert Fröbe *Inspector Bauer* • Heinz Bennent *Doctor Hans Vergerus* • James Whitmore *Priest* • Toni Berger *Mr Rosenberg* • Christian Berkel *Student* ■ *Dir/Scr* Ingmar Bergman

The Serpent's Kiss ★ 15

Period mystery
1997 · Fr/Ger/UK · Colour · 105mins

Given Ewan McGregor's popularity, it's a sure sign of a bad movie that this sank into obscurity. McGregor plays a landscape architect hired by wealthy Pete Postlethwaite to design a garden for his wife (Greta Scacchi). Not surprisingly, McGregor becomes embroiled in a plot by scheming Richard E Grant to bankrupt Postlethwaite. LH DVD

Greta Scacchi *Juliana* • Ewan McGregor *Meneer Chrome* • Pete Postlethwaite *Thomas Smithers* • Richard E Grant *James Fitzmaurice* • Carmen Chaplin *Thea* ■ *Dir* Philippe Rousselot • *Scr* Tim Rose Price

Serpent's Path ★★★

Psychological thriller
1998 · Jpn · Colour · 85mins

Completed in just a fortnight, Kiyoshi Kurosawa's stark yakuza drama presents a far more credible insight into the murky world of snuff movies than commercially minded offerings such as *Mute Witness* or *8mm*. However, while it eschews cheap sensationalism, the film doesn't shy away from the depiction of pitiless violence, as astrophysics expert Sho Aikawa subjects various underlings to savage beatings in order to discover who was responsible for the rape and murder of the eight-year-old daughter of unstable gangster Teruyuki Kagawa. Considerably more downbeat than its companion piece, *Eyes of the Spider*. DP. In Japanese with English subtitles.

Sho Aikawa *Nijima* • Teruyuki Kagawa *Miyashita* ■ *Dir* Kiyoshi Kurosawa • *Scr* Hiroshi Takahashi

Serpico ★★★★ 18

Police thriller based on a true story
1973 · US · Colour · 124mins

Al Pacino gives an outstanding, Oscar-nominated performance as real-life cop Frank Serpico, who helped expose corruption in the New York Police Department in the early 1970s. Director Sidney Lumet shows in fascinating detail how hush-money and bribes were a way of life for Serpico's colleagues and how the idealistic young officer refused to toe the line. After years of watching partners take backhanders, Serpico agreed to testify against a fellow officer and became a marked man. Even though Lumet revisited similar territory, he never found a better purveyor of idealism than Pacino. TH. Contains violence, swearing. DVD

Al Pacino *Frank Serpico* • John Randolph *Sidney Green* • Jack Kehoe *Tom Keough* • Biff McGuire *McClain* • Barbara Eda-Young *Laurie* • Cornelia Sharpe *Leslie* • Tony Roberts *Bob Blair* • John Medici *Pasquale* ■ *Dir* Sidney Lumet • *Scr* Waldo Salt, Norman Wexler, from the book by Peter Maas

The Servant ★★★★ 15

Drama 1963 · UK · BW · 110mins

This claustrophobic tale of envy and manipulation sees James Fox descend from a champagne lifestyle into a decadent dependence upon his servant, Dirk Bogarde. The snarling story is handled with great insight by director Joseph Losey, who had keenly studied the British class system since being exiled from Hollywood in 1951 during the Communist witch-hunt. Sarah Miles and Wendy Craig impress as the women caught in the powerplay, but this is essentially a two-hander, with Fox admirable as a latter-day Sebastian Flyte and Bogarde (finally nailing his matinée reputation) chilling as the mercenary valet. DP DVD

Dirk Bogarde *Hugo Barrett* • Sarah Miles *Vera* • Wendy Craig *Susan* • James Fox *Tony* • Catherine Lacey *Lady Mounset* • Richard Vernon *Lord Mounset* • Ann Firbank *Society woman* • Harold Pinter *Society man* ■ *Dir* Joseph Losey • *Scr* Harold Pinter, from the novel by Robin Maugham • *Cinematographer* Douglas Slocombe • *Music* John Dankworth

Serving Sara ★★ 12

Comedy 2002 · US/Ger · Colour · 95mins

Elizabeth Hurley plays the British trophy wife of Bruce Campbell's unfaithful Texan millionaire. When she receives divorce papers from acerbic process server Matthew Perry, Hurley sets out for financial revenge. Though Perry can't seem to escape his *Friends* persona, his strong chemistry with Hurley and the story's gentle absurdity keep proceedings buoyant. The leads may not be excellent actors, but they are fun to watch, and – like the film itself – don't take themselves too seriously. SF DVD

Matthew Perry *Joe Tyler* • Elizabeth Hurley *Sara Moore* • Bruce Campbell *Gordon Moore* • Amy Adams *Kate* • Vincent Pastore *Tony* • Cedric "The Entertainer" [Cedric the Entertainer] *Ray Harris* • Terry Crews *Vernon* • Jerry Stiller *Milton the cop* ■ *Dir* Reginald Hudlin • *Scr* Jay Scherick, David Ronn

Sesame Street Presents: Follow That Bird ★★★ U

Comedy 1985 · US · Colour · 84mins

Fans of *Sesame Street* will be thrilled with this adventure, which features everyone's favourite resident, Big Bird. The yellow-feathered one has been evicted from the street, so he goes off on a long adventure, making new friends along the way while his friends back home desperately search for him. It's strictly for the under-fives, but adults will nonetheless be entertained by celebrity cameos from such luminaries as Sandra Bernhard, Chevy Chase and John Candy. JB

Carroll Spinney *Big Bird/Oscar* • Jim Henson *Kermit the Frog/Ernie* • Frank Oz *Cookie Monster/Bert/Grover* • Paul Bartel *Grouch cook* • Sandra Bernhard *Grouch waitress* • John Candy *State trooper* • Chevy Chase *Newscaster* • Joe Flaherty *Sid Sleaze* ■ *Dir* Ken Kwapis • *Scr* Tony Geiss, Judy Freudberg

Session 9 ★★★★ 15

Horror thriller 2001 · US · Colour · 95mins

Brilliantly scripted, atmospherically chilling and seat-edged suspenseful right up to its masterful shock ending, this hard-hitting psychological horror concerns a group of workers hired to clear an abandoned insane asylum of asbestos in one week. As the crew, all harbouring dark secrets of their own, is drawn deeper into the mysteries surrounding the imposing building, the gruelling pressures mount to complete their assignment. Evocatively shot on High Definition Digital Video and graced by superb ensemble performances, director Brad Anderson's cautionary tale of psyche-infection is a stunning success on every character-driven, grimly realistic and spine-tingling front. AJ DVD

David Caruso *Phil* • Stephen Gevedon *Mike* • Paul Guilfoyle (2) *Bill Griggs* • Josh Lucas *Hank* • Peter Mullan *Gordon Fleming* • Brendan Sexton III *Jeff* ■ *Dir* Brad Anderson • *Scr* Brad Anderson, Stephen Gevedon

Set It Off ★★★ 18

Action crime drama
1996 · US · Colour · 117mins

Four down-on-their-luck African-American women from Los Angeles band together to pull off a string of bank robberies. The subplots are numerous, resulting in romance, statements about ghetto life and thrilling bullet-strewn action scenes being crammed together, yet they still manage to grab the attention. Jada Pinkett does well in the lead, but it's Queen Latifah who has the acting ability and personality to stand out, though Blair Underwood gives a nice supporting performance. KB DVD

Jada Pinkett [Jada Pinkett Smith] *Stony* • Queen Latifah *Cleo* • Vivica A Fox *Frankie* • Kimberly Elise *Tisean* • John C McGinley *Detective Strode* • Blair Underwood *Keith* • Dr Dre *Black Sam* ■ *Dir* F Gary Gray • *Scr* Kate Lanier, Takashi Bufford, from a story by Takashi Bufford

The Set-Up ★★★★ PG

Sports drama 1949 · US · BW · 68mins

This bruising boxing drama is a knockout production from the great days of RKO studios. It was among the first to show the crippling confrontation between good and evil in the ring, when an over-the-hill boxer is sold out by his manager, and then has to face the consequences of his gangster connections. The usually villainous Robert Ryan is wonderful and plausibly decent as the fighter, though Audrey Totter as his wife is miscast. Director Robert Wise controversially depicts the ringside audience as sadists lusting for blood. And there is plenty of it, as Milton Krasner's camera darts around in a flurry of action to create boxing scenes of brain-jarring ferocity. TH

Robert Ryan *Bill "Stoker" Thompson* • Audrey Totter *Julie* • George Tobias *Tiny* • Alan Baxter *Little Boy* • Wallace Ford *Gus* • Percy Helton *Red* ■ *Dir* Robert Wise • *Scr* Art Cohn, from a poem by Joseph Moncure March

The Set Up ★★★★ 18

Thriller 1995 · US · Colour · 89mins

This superior TV movie benefits from a tightly plotted story and a stellar cast led by Billy Zane and featuring thriller icon James Coburn. Zane gives a dogged performance as a cat burglar whose plans to go straight are waylaid by ex-con James Russo, who threatens to kill Zane's girlfriend unless he dismantles the security system he has installed at Coburn's bank. The boxing scene is strong meat, but stick with it because the finale is a belter. DP. Contains violence and sex scenes.

Billy Zane *Charlie Thorpe* • Mia Sara *Gina Sands* • James Russo *Kliff* • James Coburn *Jeremiah Cole* • Louis Mandylor *Pauly* • Tiny "Zeus" Lister [Tom "Tiny" Lister Jr] *Leon* • Mark Rolston *Ray Harris* • Margaret Avery (2) *Olivia Dubois* ■ *Dir* Strathford Hamilton • *Scr* Michael Thoma, from the book *My Laugh Comes Last* by James Hadley Chase

The Settlement ★★★

Drama 1982 · Aus · Colour · 91mins

Bill Kerr and John Jarratt arrive in an outback town looking to hustle a few quid, but when they hook up with barmaid Lorna Lesley, they incur the wrath of the conservative locals. Without forcing the issue, director Howard Rubie succeeds in celebrating individuality rather than sniping at the muddled morality of the Australian majority. His only false step is in allowing Catholic cop's wife Katy Wild to be so shrill in whipping up animosity. The performances of May-December lovers Lesley and Kerr and the guileless Jarratt are spot-on. DP

Bill Kerr *Kearney* • John Jarratt *Tommy Martin* • Lorna Lesley *Joycie* • Tony Barry *Sgt Crowe* • Alan Cassell *Lohan* • Katy Wild *Mrs Crowe* ■ *Dir* Howard Rubie • *Scr* Ted Roberts

Seul contre Tous ★★★★ 18

Drama 1998 · Fr · Colour · 88mins

Setting out to rouse the lethargic cinema establishment, Gaspar Noé succeeds in turning a barrage of shocking images, abrasive captions and jarring sounds into a grotesquely credible portrait of furious misery that enervates and repels in equal measure. Whether spouting self-pitying, misanthropic bile or assaulting his pregnant mistress and handicapped daughter, butcher Philippe Nahon (in an alarmingly courageous performance) still commands our pity, as a victim of poverty, injustice and his own twisted logic. DP. In French with English subtitles. Contains violence, sex scenes and swearing.

Philippe Nahon *The butcher* • Blandine Lenoir *His daughter, Cynthia* • Frankye Pain *His mistress* • Martine Audrain *Mother-in-law* ■ *Dir/Scr* Gaspar Noé

Seven ★★★ 18

Action comedy 1979 · US · Colour · 96mins

Director Andy Sidaris carved out a niche for himself making enjoyable low-budget action films destined for video, rather than big-screen exposure. This is such a film. Veteran hunk William Smith stars as the leader of a seven-strong team of experts assembled by a government agent to combat a syndicate of seven gangsters planning mayhem in Hawaii. Lots of fisticuffs, gunplay and female flesh comes as no surprise for fans of this genre. DF

William Smith *Drew* • Barbara Leigh *Alexa* • Guich Koock *Cowboy* • Art Metrano *Kinsella* • Martin Kove *Skip* • Richard LePore *Professor* ■ *Dir* Andy Sidaris • *Scr* William Driskill, Robert Baird, from a story by Andy Sidaris

Se7en ★★★★★ 18

Thriller 1995 · US · Colour · 126mins

Director David Fincher's brilliant postmodern *film noir* is a grim and disturbing tale about a vicious serial killer. Intelligently scripted by Andrew Kevin Walker, it is a work of extraordinary style, power and narrative daring. It also boasts fine performances from Morgan Freeman as a disillusioned detective on the brink of retirement and Brad Pitt as his enthusiastic replacement. With only seven days left on the job, Freeman finds himself drawn to a puzzling case of a psychopath who murders his victims in a gruesome manner to atone for the sins he deems them to have committed. Draining his landscapes of colour, and setting all the tense action

S

against rain-washed streets and underlit interiors, Fincher evokes a nightmarish atmosphere. AJ. Contains swearing, violence. [video] DVD

Brad Pitt *Detective David Mills* • Morgan Freeman *Lieutenant William Somerset* • Gwyneth Paltrow *Tracy Mills* • Richard Roundtree *Talbot* • John C McGinley *California* • R Lee Ermey *Police captain* • Kevin Spacey *John Doe* • Daniel Zacapa *Detective Taylor* ■ *Dir* David Fincher • *Scr* Andrew Kevin Walker • *Cinematographer* Darius Khondji

Seven Alone ★ [U]

Western adventure based on a true story
1974 · US · Colour · 97mins

This is the tale of the Sager children who were orphaned in the American northwest of the 1840s during a wagon train journey to Oregon. The seven children, lead by oldest child Stewart Petersen, make the rest of the journey by themselves, encountering various low-budget dangers along the way. Based on his performance, Petersen must have secured his role in this "family values" movie only because he had the same Mormon background as the producers. KB

Dewey Martin *Henry Sager* • Aldo Ray *Dr Dutch* • Anne Collings *Naome Sager* • Dean Smith *Kit Carson* • James Griffith *Billy Shaw* • Stewart Petersen *John Sager* • Dehl Berti *White Elk* ■ *Dir* Earl Bellamy • *Scr* Douglas Stewart, Eleanor Lamb, from the book *On to Oregon* by Honore Morrow

Seven Angry Men ★★ [U]

Historical drama 1955 · US · BW · 91mins

Raymond Massey takes centre stage as the fanatical abolitionist John Brown. The verbose script by Daniel B Ullman and the heavy-handed direction by Charles Marquis Warren concentrate on Brown's increasingly savage campaign in Kansas to abolish slavery, culminating in his attack on Harper's Ferry. Jeffrey Hunter, as one of Brown's six sons, conducts a romance with Debra Paget in a subplot that's an uninspired attempt to appeal to younger audiences. AE

Raymond Massey *John Brown* • Debra Paget *Elizabeth* • Jeffrey Hunter *Owen* • Larry Pennell *Oliver* • Leo Gordon *White* • John Smith *Frederick* • James Best *Jason* • Dennis Weaver *John Jr* • Guy Williams *Salmon* ■ *Dir* Charles Marquis Warren • *Scr* Daniel B Ullman

Seven Beauties ★★★★ [18]

Satirical war drama
1976 · It · Colour · 111mins

This really is a film with something to offend everyone. A sizzling satire on the political naivety and military incompetence of the Italian male, it also passes scathing comment on such sensitive issues as obesity, female emancipation, the Mafia and concentration camps. Not all of the jokes come off. But Lina Wertmuller, who received Oscar nominations for both her writing and direction, takes events at a ferocious pace and gets a superb performance from her regular collaborator Giancarlo Giannini, who is the everyman struggling to survive the war and feed his indolent family. DP. In Italian with English subtitles. Contains violence and sex scenes. [video]

Giancarlo Giannini *Pasqualino Settebellezze* • Fernando Rey *Pedro* • Shirley Stoler *Hilde* • Elena Fiore *Concetta* • Piero Di Iorio *Francesco* ■ *Dir/Scr* Lina Wertmuller

Seven Brides for Seven Brothers ★★★★★ [U]

Musical 1954 · US · Colour · 101mins

Rightly a sensational commercial success in its day, especially in Britain, this joyous romp remains one of the freshest and most satisfying of movie musicals. A screen original, it was fashioned by director Stanley Donen and choreographer Michael Kidd into an exciting, heart-warming and technically accomplished (though perhaps a shade politically incorrect) musical. The central barn dance is magnificent, and the early use of CinemaScope is as exquisite as the beautifully stylised MGM interiors. Although generally cleverly cast, the movie gains strength from the two leading performances. TS [video] DVD

Howard Keel *Adam Pontipee* • Jane Powell *Milly* • Russ Tamblyn *Gideon* • Jeff Richards *Benjamin* • Tommy Rall *Frank* • Marc Platt *Daniel* • Matt Mattox *Caleb* • Jacques d'Amboise *Ephraim* • Howard Petrie *Pete Perkins* ■ *Dir* Stanley Donen • *Scr* Albert Hackett, Frances Goodrich, Dorothy Kingsley, from the story *The Sobbin' Women* by Stephen Vincent Benet • *Music/lyrics* Gene De Paul, Johnny Mercer • *Cinematographer* George Folsey • *Music Director* Adolph Deutsch, Saul Chaplin

Seven Chances ★★★

Silent farce
1925 · US · BW and Colour · 56mins

Made immediately after three Keaton masterpieces, culminating with *The Navigator*, this enjoyable comedy has been somewhat neglected, partly because the highlight is in the last reel. Buster plays his usual doleful character who discovers that he has been left seven million dollars, provided he marries within the day. There are soon plenty of hopefuls and the climax of the film finds him pursued first by would-be brides and then by an avalanche of rocks. BB

Buster Keaton *Jimmie Shannon* • Ruth Dwyer *Mary Jones* • T Roy Barnes *Billy Meekin, Jimmie's partner* • Snitz Edwards *Lawyer* • Frankie Raymond *Mary's mother* • Jules Cowles *Hired hand* • Jean Arthur *Miss Jones, switchboard operator at country club* • Erwin Connelly *Clergyman* • Jean Havez *Man on the landing* ■ *Dir* Buster Keaton • *Scr* Jean Havez, Clyde Bruckman, Joseph Mitchell, from the play *Seven Chances: a Comedy in Three Acts* by Roi Cooper Megrue

Seven Cities of Gold ★★ [U]

Period adventure
1955 · US · Colour · 102mins

It's the late 18th century, and Richard Egan and Anthony Quinn ride out from Mexico in an attempt to load their saddlebags with gold. In their way stands pious and pompous Michael Rennie, bent on bringing Christianity to the land and converting the Indians. Although pitched as an action drama, the historical context of Spanish colonialism, in which the church and army are sidekicks, is not ignored. AT

Richard Egan *Jose* • Anthony Quinn *Captain Portola* • Michael Rennie *Father Junipero Serra* • Jeffrey Hunter *Matuwir* • Rita Moreno *Ula* • Eduardo Noriega (1) *Sergeant* • Leslie Bradley *Galvez* ■ *Dir* Robert D Webb • *Scr* Richard L Breen, John C Higgins, Joseph Petracca, from the novel *The Nine Days of Father Serra* by Isabelle Gibson Ziegler • *Cinematographer* Lucien Ballard

Seven Days in May ★★★★ [U]

Political thriller 1964 · US · BW · 113mins

This outlandish conspiracy thriller is made credible thanks to its outstanding cast that includes Burt Lancaster, Fredric March, Kirk Douglas and Ava Gardner. It follows the machinations of a military group that is trying to topple the US president (March) because he has signed a nuclear disarmament treaty with the Soviet Union. Director John Frankenheimer uses all the mechanical tricks of the surveillance trade – TV monitors, hidden cameras and electronic devices – to suggest the omnipresent miltary machine, but it's the magnificent performances of the stars that keep you watching. TH [video]

Burt Lancaster *General James M Scott* • Kirk Douglas *Colonel Martin "Jiggs" Casey* • Fredric March *President Jordan Lyman* • Ava Gardner *Eleanor Holbrook* • Edmond O'Brien *Senator Raymond Clark* • Martin Balsam *Paul Girard* • George Macready *Christopher Todd* • Whit Bissell *Senator Prentice* • Hugh Marlowe *Harold McPherson* ■ *Dir* John Frankenheimer • *Scr* Rod Serling, from the novel by Fletcher Knebel, Charles Waldo Bailey II

Seven Days' Leave ★★★ [U]

Wartime musical comedy
1942 · US · BW · 87mins

This endearing RKO romp effectively teams a pre-*I Love Lucy* Lucille Ball and handsome hunk Victor Mature, both of whom seem to be having a jolly good time and manage to convey that pleasure to the audience. The plot's a clunker, with army private Mature inheriting $100,000 if he can marry socialite Ball. There's fun and frolics along the way, plus some terrific music from top bands of the era. TS

Victor Mature *Johnny Grey* • Lucille Ball *Terry* • Harold Peary *Great Gildersleeve* • Mapy Cortes *Mapy* • Ginny Simms *Ginny* • Marcy McGuire *Mickey* • Peter Lind Hayes *Jackson* • Walter Reed *Ralph Bell* • Wallace Ford *Sergeant Mead* ■ *Dir* Tim Whelan • *Scr* William Bowers, Ralph Spence, Curtis Kenyon, Kenneth Earl

7 Days to Live ★ [15]

Supernatural horror
2000 · Ger · Colour · 92mins

A very dull haunted house of shamelessly derivative horrors directed by Sebastian Niemann as if he were in a coma. Struggling novelist Sean Pertwee and his freaked-out wife Amanda Plummer move to a creepy country home to get over the death of their son. Eerie things start happening, but you won't stick around long enough to find out the answers in this muddled bore. Not terrifying, just terrible. AJ [video]

Amanda Plummer *Ellen Shaw* • Sean Pertwee *Martin Shaw* • Nick Brimble *Carl Farrell* • Amanda Walker *Elizabeth Farrell* • Gina Bellman *Claudia* • Eddie Cooper *Tommy Shaw* ■ *Dir* Sebastian Niemann • *Scr* Dirk Ahner

Seven Days to Noon ★★★★

Thriller 1950 · UK · BW · 96mins

Doomsday movies were everywhere in the early 1950s, as the Cold War chill began to bite. This is the finest British contribution to that sub-genre. Although the threat of an atomic explosion in London makes for compelling viewing, the true power of the picture comes from a magnificent performance by Barry Jones as the professor driven to suicidal despair by the misappropriation of his work. Thanks to Jones and cinematographer Gilbert Taylor's eerie images of the capital, this Boulting brothers film maintains an unbearable tension. DP

Barry Jones *Professor Willingdon* • Olive Sloane *Goldie* • André Morell *Superintendent Folland* • Sheila Manahan *Ann Willingdon* • Hugh Cross *Stephen Lane* • Joan Hickson *Mrs Peckett* ■ *Dir* John Boulting, Roy Boulting • *Scr* Roy Boulting, Frank Harvey, from a story by Paul Dehn, James Bernard

The Seven Deadly Sins ★★★

Portmanteau drama
1952 · Fr/It · BW · 155mins

Gérard Philipe introduces each of these tales with more charm than they really merit. The main interest in these modern parables – five of them in French and two in Italian – is how much they reveal about the attitude to sex in the early 1950s. Inevitably there are a few duds in the collection, with the best being Roberto Rossellini's *Envy*, based on a story by Colette, about a woman becoming more attached to her cat than her husband. Yves Allégret's *Lust* effectively reveals the difference between puppy and adult love, and Carlo Rim's *Gluttony* tells how a piece of cheese comes between a man and a woman. RB. A French/Italian language film.

Eduardo De Filippo *Eduardo* • Jacqueline Plessis *Laziness* • Frank Villard *Ravila* • Francette Vernillat *Chantel* • Gérard Philipe *Master of Ceremonies* • Noël-Noël *The Director* • Michèle Morgan *Anne-Marie* ■ *Dir* Eduardo De Filippo, Jean Dréville, Yves Allégret, Roberto Rossellini, Carlo Rim, Claude Autant-Lara, Georges Lacombe • *Scr* Charles Spaak, Carlo Rim, Pierre Bost, Jean Aurenche, Roberto Rossellini, Carlo Rim, Pierre Bost, Jean Aurenche, Claude Autant-Lara, Pierre Bost, Jean Aurenche

The Seven Deadly Sins ★★★

Portmanteau drama
1961 · Fr/It · BW · 115mins

It must have seemed a good idea at the time to get several of the New Wave French directors to give their slant on the seven deadly sins. But the result is a hit-and-miss affair, as with so many portmanteau films, with a mixture of good, average and awful. Among the better episodes are Philipe de Broca's *Gluttony*, Roger Vadim's *Pride*, Jacques Demy's *Lust*, and Jean-Luc Godard's *Sloth* – about a film star (Eddie Constantine) who is too lazy to have sex even when offered to him on a plate. The other three sins were committed by Claude Chabrol (*Greed*), Edouard Molinaro (*Envy*) and Sylvain Dhomme (*Anger*). RB. In French with English subtitles.

Danièle Barraud *Suzon* • Jacques Charrier *Antoine* • Nicole Mirel *Starlet* • Eddie Constantine *Eddie* • Micheline Presle *Mother* • Jean-Louis Trintignant *Paul* • Michèle Girardon *La maîtrese* • Marcelle Arnold *The wife* • Georges Wilson *Valentin* • Perrette Pradier *TV announcer* • Marie-José Nat *Young wife* ■ *Dir* Claude Chabrol, Edouard Molinaro, Jean-Luc Godard, Jacques Demy, Roger Vadim, Philippe de Broca, Sylvain Dhomme • *Scr* Félicien Marceau, Claude Chabrol, Claude Mauriac, Jean-Luc Godard, Roger Peyrefitte, Jacques Demy, Félicien Marceau, Daniel Boulanger, Eugène Ionesco

711 Ocean Drive ★★

Crime drama 1950 · US · BW · 101mins

This features Edmond O'Brien as a telephone engineer lured into organised crime by the Mob. At first he just fixes the phone lines that link the racetracks, but then he gets a taste for power and starts cutting people off at the neck. It's a little moral tale, which says that crime doesn't pay – except that the Mob are still in control after the spectacular climax on the Hoover Dam. AT

Edmond O'Brien *Mal Granger* • Joanne Dru *Gail Mason* • Donald Porter [Don Porter] *Larry Mason* • Sammy White *Chippie Evans* • Dorothy Patrick *Trudy Maxwell* • Barry Kelley *Vince Walters* • Otto Kruger *Carl Stephans* ■ *Dir* Joseph M Newman • *Scr* Richard English, Frances Swan

7 Faces of Dr Lao ★★★ [U]

Fantasy western drama
1963 · US · Colour · 99mins

This odd, almost surrealistic, fantasy western hit a nerve at the time and became a major success largely because of the mesmerising performance of Tony Randall, who plays the titular doctor and no less than six other roles. This is the classic tale of a strange travelling circus, which arrives in town puts the fear of God into the locals and teaches them a few of life's lessons along the way. What distinguishes this intriguing movie is the glorious make-up, which won William Tuttle an Oscar. SH

Tony Randall *Dr Lao/Merlin the Magician/Medusa/Apollonius of Tyana/Pan/The Abominable Snowman/Giant Serpent* • Arthur

S

O'Connell *Clint Stark* • John Ericson *Ed Cunningham* • Barbara Eden *Angela Benedict* • Kevin Tate *Mike Benedict* • Noah Beery Jr *Tim Mitchell* • Lee Patrick *Mrs Howard T Cassan* ■ *Dir* George Pal • *Scr* Charles Beaumont, from the novel *The Circus of Dr Lao* by Charles G Finney

Seven Hills of Rome ★★ U

Musical 1957 · US · Colour · 103mins

Tenor Mario Lanza's insatiable appetite coupled with appalling manners made him hard both to cast and to like. Although his robust voice was undeniably attractive, his screen persona became awkward and contrived. Here, under the expert directorial hand of Roy Rowland, his performance is a little more mellow – but when those lungs open, nothing seems able to contain him. This film is really for fans only. TS

Mario Lanza *Marc Revere* • Renato Rascel *Pepe Bonelli* • Marisa Allasio *Rafaella Marini* • Peggie Castle *Carol Ralston* • Clelia Matania *Beatrice* • Rossella Como *Anita* • Amos Davoli *Carlo* • Guido Celano *Luigi* ■ *Dir* Roy Rowland • *Scr* Art Cohn, Giorgio Prosperi, from a story by Giuseppi Amato

Seven Hours to Judgment ★★★ 15

Thriller 1988 · US · Colour · 89mins

Beau Bridges directs and stars in this revenge thriller, playing a judge who's forced to acquit a gang of killer thugs on a technicality. The victim's husband (Ron Leibman) blames Beau, kidnaps the judge's wife and forces him to run the gauntlet through the gang's tough home turf. The direction is a bit twitchy and Beau is far too baby-faced to be credible in a role that requires a lot more visual gravitas. This nevertheless remains a solid and watchable if preposterous action thriller. DA

Beau Bridges *John Eden* • Ron Leibman *David Reardon* • Julianne Phillips *Lisa Eden* • Tiny Ron Taylor [Tiny Ron] *Ira* • Al Freeman Jr *Danny Larwin* • Reggie Johnson *Chino* ■ *Dir* Beau Bridges • *Scr* Walter Davis, Elliot Stephens, from a story by Walter Davis

Seven Keys to Baldpate ★★ U

Comedy mystery 1935 · US · BW · 69mins

Across four decades, film-makers were drawn to this story from a novel by Earl Derr Biggers. A writer who needs peace and quiet to finish a book in 24 hours, takes himself off to the remote Baldpate Inn, only to find himself in the hub of activity involving a constant stream of mysterious strangers chasing $200,000 worth of illicit cash. The tale was adapted for the stage by George M Cohan who, in 1917, starred in the first of two silent versions. Here, Gene Raymond does his usual uninspired best, but the intriguing aspects of the movie take second place to the creaking tedium. RK

S

Gene Raymond *Magee* • Margaret Callahan *Mary* • Eric Blore *Bolton* • Erin O'Brien-Moore *Myra* • Moroni Olsen *Cargan* • Walter Brennan *Station agent* ■ *Dir* William Hamilton, Edward Killy • *Scr* Wallace Smith, Anthony Veiller, from the play by George M Cohan, from the novel by Earl Derr Biggers

Seven Keys to Baldpate ★★

Comedy mystery 1947 · US · BW · 68mins

Yet another remake of the cold, dark house mystery about a novelist who, forced to finish a book to a 24-hour deadline, seeks refuge in the isolated Baldpate Inn, but is disturbed by the arrival of thieves come to split the proceeds of a heist. It's directed by Lew Landers at programme-filler length, and there are a couple of minor variations in the convoluted plot, but it's really hard to understand why RKO returned to this dated material. RK

Phillip Terry *Magee* • Jacqueline White *Mary* • Eduardo Ciannelli *Cargan* • Margaret Lindsay *Connie Lane* • Arthur Shields *Bolton* • Jimmy Conlin *Hermit* ■ *Dir* Lew Landers • *Scr* Lee Loeb, from the play by George M Cohan, from the novel by Earl Derr Biggers

Seven Little Foys ★★★ U

Musical biography
1955 · US · Colour · 92mins

In one of his straighter roles, Bob Hope plays real-life comedian Eddie Foy who, after the early death of his wife, trained his seven children to join him in his vaudeville act. The trouble is that Hope's character is hard to like, and the musical routines are lacklustre, apart from one memorable sequence featuring guest star James Cagney. Reprising his portrayal of George M Cohan from *Yankee Doodle Dandy*, Cagney joins Hope in a song-and-soft-shoe routine to two Cohan favourites, momentarily lifting the film into a classier category. TV DVD

Eddie Foy Jr *Narrator* • Bob Hope *Eddie Foy* • Milly Vitale *Madeleine Morando* • George Tobias *Barney Green* • Angela Clarke *Clara* • Herbert Heyes *Judge* • James Cagney *George M Cohan* ■ *Dir* Melville Shavelson • *Scr* Melville Shavelson, Jack Rose

Seven Men from Now ★★★★

Western 1956 · US · Colour · 77mins

John Wayne's production company made this modestly budgeted Randolph Scott western and it turned out so well that the Duke wished he'd starred in it himself. Burt Kennedy's lean script has Scott grimly tracking down the seven men who killed his wife during a hold-up, with Lee Marvin's gunman following close behind hoping to grab the loot they've hidden. Wayne gave his former co-star Gail Russell the female lead. Director Budd Boetticher makes terrific use of outdoor settings. AE

Randolph Scott *Ben Stride* • Gail Russell *Annie Greer* • Lee Marvin *Masters* • Walter Reed *John Greer* • John Larch *Pate Bodeen* • Donald Barry *Clete* ■ *Dir* Budd Boetticher • *Scr* Burt Kennedy, from his story • *Cinematographer* William H Clothier [William Clothier]

Seven Miles from Alcatraz ★★★

Second World War spy drama
1942 · US · BW · 62mins

As befits someone with Edward Dmytryk's political convictions (he was later one of the Hollywood Ten), he invests this wartime flagwaver with plenty of anti-Nazi fervour. However, the decision of escaped convicts James Craig and Frank Jenks to sacrifice their liberty for the greater good is anything but patriotic propaganda. Indeed, there's a decidedly cynical aspect to Craig's initial refusal to help imprisoned lighthouse keeper George Cleveland warn the San Francisco authorities of an imminent U-boat attack. His change of heart might have been more persuasive had it not been partly inspired by his interest in Cleveland's daughter, Bonita Granville. DP

James Craig *Champ Larkin* • Bonita Granville *Anne Porter* • Frank Jenks *Jimbo* • Cliff Edwards *Stormy* • George Cleveland *Captain Porter* ■ *Dir* Edward Dmytryk • *Scr* Joseph Krumgold, from the unpublished story *Sou'West Pass* by John D Klorer

The Seven Minutes ★★

Courtroom drama 1971 · US · Colour · 93mins

This adaptation of Irving Wallace's pornography-on-trial tale – about a man accused of rape who claims reading a dirty book incited him to do it – is a real hoot. It's chiefly notable as the only "straight" film of director Russ Meyer, better known as the purveyor of mega-bosomed babes in such cult "classics" as *Faster Pussycat! Kill! Kill!*. Although the cast is populated by fine character actors, with an early appearance by Tom Selleck, there's no *Magnum* force here. DA

Wayne Maunder *Mike Barrett* • Yvonne De Carlo *Constance Cumberland* • Marianne McAndrew *Maggie Russell* • Philip Carey *Elmo Duncan* • Jay C Flippen *Luther Yerkes* • Edy Williams *Faye Osborn* • Lyle Bettger *Frank Griffith* • Charles Drake *Sgt Kellog* • John Carradine *Sean O'Flanagan* • Harold J Stone *Judge Upshaw* • Tom Selleck *Phil Sanford* ■ *Dir* Russ Meyer • *Scr* Richard Warren Lewis, from the novel by Irving Wallace

Seven Minutes ★★★★ 15

Second World War thriller
1989 · W Ger · Colour · 91mins

This is an intelligent, auspicious directorial debut from Klaus Maria Brandauer, who also stars as a determined, methodical would-be assassin of one Adolf Hitler. Brandauer's strong, impressive performance overlays a thriller that intrigues and grips in equal measure. The cast is excellent, with the always watchable Brian Dennehy chilling but understated as a Gestapo chief. Celebrated cinematographer Lajos Koltai gives the film a suitably dense, atmospheric air. SH

Klaus Maria Brandauer *Elser* • Rebecca Miller *Anneliese* • Brian Dennehy *Wagner* • Nigel Le Vaillant *Mayer* • Maggie O'Neill *Berta* • Roger Ashton-Griffiths *Watchman* ■ *Dir* Klaus Maria Brandauer • *Scr* Stephen Sheppard, from his novel *The Artisan*

Seven Nights in Japan ★ PG

Romantic drama
1976 · UK/Fr · Colour · 99mins

Michael York looks far less embarrassed than he should be, as the British prince who evades his bodyguards to indulge in a spot of romance with tour guide Hidemi Aoki. As toffs such as James Villiers and Charles Gray fret patriotically, we are treated to cinematographer Henri Decaë's postcard vistas and the delirious efforts of York and Aoki to look besotted. DP

Michael York *Prince George* • Hidemi Aoki *Somi* • Charles Gray *Ambassador Hollander* • Ann Lonnberg *Jane Hollander* • Eléonore Hirt *Mrs Hollander* • James Villiers *Finn* ■ *Dir* Lewis Gilbert • *Scr* Christopher Wood

The Seven-Per-Cent Solution ★★ 15

Mystery 1976 · US · Colour · 108mins

Sherlock Holmes's fans will immediately recognise that the title refers to the sleuth's preferred mixture of cocaine, but that's as clever as it gets. The spoof plot is a simple one involving a mystery kidnapping. Although the cast is impressive – Nicol Williamson and Robert Duvall as Holmes and Watson, Alan Arkin, Laurence Olivier and Vanessa Redgrave (as the damsel in distress) – the solution is rather less so. AT

Nicol Williamson *Sherlock Holmes* • Robert Duvall *Dr Watson* • Alan Arkin *Sigmund Freud* • Laurence Olivier *Professor Moriarty* • Vanessa Redgrave *Lola Deveraux* • Joel Grey *Lowenstein* • Samantha Eggar *Mary Watson* • Jeremy Kemp *Baron von Leinsdorf* ■ *Dir* Herbert Ross • *Scr* Nicholas Meyer, from his novel, from the characters created by Sir Arthur Conan Doyle

Seven Samurai ★★★★★ PG

Classic action drama
1954 · Jpn · BW · 190mins

One of the undisputed masterpieces of world cinema, Akira Kurosawa's epic was inspired by the westerns of John Ford and had the compliment repaid with John Sturges's classic reworking, *The Magnificent Seven*. Showered with international awards, the film is a mesmerising combination of historical detail, spectacular action and poignant humanism. Over 18 months in production, it has been described as "a tapestry of motion", with the final battle standing out for its audacious use of moving camera, telephoto lenses, varied film speeds and precision editing. Takashi Shimura and Toshiro Mifune are the pick of an excellent cast, but it's the director's genius that leaves an impression. DP. In Japanese with English subtitles. Contains violence. DVD

Takashi Shimura *Kambei* • Toshiro Mifune *Kikuchiyo* • Yoshio Inaba *Gorobei* • Seiji Miyaguchi *Kyuzo* • Minoru Chiaki *Heihachi* • Daisuke Kato *Shichiroji* • Isao Kimura *Katsushiro* • Kamatari Fujiwara *Manzo* ■ *Dir* Akira Kurosawa • *Scr* Akira Kurosawa, Shinobu Hashimoto, Hideo Oguni • *Cinematographer* Asakasu Nakai • *Editor* Akira Kurosawa

Seven Seas to Calais ★★★ U

Swashbuckling adventure
1962 · It/US · Colour · 101mins

Swashbucklers don't come more buckled than this, with Rod Taylor chasing Spanish treasure as Sir Francis Drake. Keith Michell and Irene Worth articulate the "prithee-avast" language with clarity, but director Rudolph Maté, who had made some great *films noirs*, was in decline, and this movie follows that downhill trend in lacking tension and credibility. TH

Rod Taylor *Sir Francis Drake* • Keith Michell *Malcolm Marsh* • Irene Worth *Queen Elizabeth I* • Anthony Dawson *Burleigh* • Basil Dignam *Walsingham* • Mario Girotti [Terence Hill] *Babington* ■ *Dir* Rudolph Maté, Primo Zeglio • *Scr* Filippo Sanjust, George St George, Lindsay Galloway

Seven Sinners ★★★

Detective drama 1936 · UK · BW · 69mins

This brisk British mystery was something of a transatlantic affair, with Edmund Lowe and Constance Cummings lending some Hollywood zing to Michael Balcon's typically efficient production. It doesn't take long to work out who's behind a series of train smashes or what their motive might be, but director Albert de Courville is as much concerned with the banter between Lowe's cocky American detective and Cummings's sassy insurance investigator as he is with the crimes. DP

Edmund Lowe *Harwood* • Constance Cummings *Caryl Fenton* • Thomy Bourdelle *Paul Turbe* • Henry Oscar *Axel Hoyte* • Felix Aylmer *Sir Charles Webber* ■ *Dir* Albert de Courville • *Scr* L du Garde Peach, Sidney Gilliat, Frank Launder, Austin Melford, from the play *The Wrecker* by Arnold Ridley, Bernard Merivale

Seven Sinners ★★★

Drama 1940 · US · BW · 86mins

Marlene Dietrich is a sultry cabaret singer who arrives on a South Sea island to perform at the Seven Sinners Café. There, her erotic presence inflames every man in sight and captures the heart of navy lieutenant John Wayne. He wants to marry her, but she's wise enough to know that's a bad idea. Dietrich, giving a knowing, self-mocking parody of a Shanghai Lil stereotype, sings (if that's the right word) three numbers and inflames a climactic bar-room brawl in this rumbustious nonsense. RK

Marlene Dietrich *Bijou Blanche* • John Wayne *Lieutenant Dan Brent* • Broderick Crawford *"Little Ned", Edward Patrick Finnegan* • Mischa Auer *Sasha* • Albert Dekker *Dr Martin* • Billy Gilbert *Tony* • Oscar Homolka *Antro* • Anna Lee *Dorothy Henderson* • Reginald Denny *Captain Church* • Samuel S Hinds

Governor ■ *Dir* Tay Garnett • *Scr* John Meehan, Harry Tugend, from a story by Ladislaus Fodor [Ladislas Fodor], Laslo Vadnay

Seven Thieves ★★★

Crime drama 1960 · US · BW · 101mins

Three Hollywood veterans – star Edward G Robinson, producer/writer Sydney Boehm and director Henry Hathaway – try to breathe life into a caper plot that itself had seen better days. Edward G does manage to add a certain validity to the story of an ageing criminal planning a last assault on a Monte Carlo casino and his acting meshes surprisingly well with that of comparative newcomer and Method actor Rod Steiger. TH

Edward G Robinson *Theo Wilkins* • Rod Steiger *Paul Mason* • Joan Collins *Melanie* • Eli Wallach *Poncho* • Michael Dante *Louis* • Alexander Scourby *Raymond Le May* • Berry Kroeger *Hugo Baumer* ■ *Dir* Henry Hathaway • *Scr* Sydney Boehm, from the novel *Lions at the Kill* by Max Catto

Seven Thunders ★★ PG

Wartime horror 1957 · UK · BW · 96mins

James Robertson-Justice plays a French physician, ostensibly helping escaped PoWs including Stephen Boyd, who in reality is mass-poisoning refugees for their money and goods. Sadly, Robertson-Justice is like a whale out of water away from his much loved Sir Lancelot in the light-hearted *Doctor* movies. Based on a real-life killer, the character he plays here was more fully realised in the 1990 French film *Docteur Petiot*, which had Michel Serrault playing the title role to chillingly merciless effect. TH

Stephen Boyd *Dave* • James Robertson-Justice *Dr Martout* • Kathleen Harrison *Madame Abou* • Tony Wright *Jim* • Anna Gaylor *Lise* • Eugene Deckers *Emile Blanchard* • Rosalie Crutchley *Therese Blanchard* • Katherine Kath *Madame Parfait* ■ *Dir* Hugo Fregonese • *Scr* John Baines, from the novel by Rupert Croft-Cooke

The Seven-Ups ★★★ 15

Police drama 1973 · US · Colour · 98mins

The nerve-scraping car-chase in this fast-moving New York police thriller is quite the equal of those pacey pile-ups in *Bullitt* and *The French Connection*. It's not surprising, really, as the producer of those movies, Philip D'Antoni, directs here. Roy Scheider stars as an undercover cop in an unorthodox unit, whose chief informant uses Scheider's criminal lists for his own purposes. It's one of those movies in which you can't tell the good guys from the bad guys, and character development is given the elbow in favour of violent action. TH. Contains some violence and swearing.

Roy Scheider *Buddy Manucci* • Tony LoBianco *Vito Lucia* • Larry Haines *Max Kalish* • Ken Kercheval *Ansel* • Richard Lynch *Moon* • Victor Arnold *Barilli* • Jerry Leon *Mingo* • Bill Hickman *Bo* • Lou Polan *Coltello* ■ *Dir* Philip D'Antoni • *Scr* Albert Ruben, Alexander Jacobs, from a story by Sonny Grosso

Seven Waves Away ★★★

Drama 1957 · UK · Colour · 99mins

Also known as *Abandon Ship!*, this drama has Tyrone Power in charge of a lifeboat filled to the gunwhales with people who survive the sinking of a liner in the South Atlantic. Power decides that the injured and helpless must be thrown overboard and this makes him a hero until a rescue ship appears, when everyone feels guilty at what has happened. Like Hitchcock's earlier *Lifeboat*, it's set entirely at sea, with moral problems floating like flotsam among the cast of familiar British stalwarts. AT

Tyrone Power *Alec Holmes* • Mai Zetterling *Julie* • Lloyd Nolan *Frank Kelly* • Stephen Boyd *Will McKinley* • Moira Lister *Edith Middleton* • James Hayter *"Cookie" Morrow* • Marie Lohr *Mrs Knudson* • Noel Willman *Aubrey Clark* • Gordon Jackson *John Merritt* • Clive Morton *Maj Gen Barrington* • Laurence Naismith *Captain Darrow* • John Stratton *"Sparks" Clary* • Victor Maddern *Willie Hawkins* ■ *Dir/Scr* Richard Sale

Seven Ways from Sundown ★★★ U

Western 1960 · US · Colour · 86mins

In this satisfying western, Audie Murphy stars as a Texas Ranger bringing in a killer, played by the ever-excellent Barry Sullivan, who gives Murphy more than a run for his money in the acting stakes. There's a nice wryness running through this feature, with a cast of western veterans to lend credibility. Although Murphy would continue filming big-screen westerns, this was his last one of any real merit. TS

Audie Murphy *Seven Jones* • Barry Sullivan *Jim Flood* • Venetia Stevenson *Joy Karrington* • John McIntire *Sergeant Hennessy* • Kenneth Tobey *Lieutenant Herly* • Mary Field *Ma Kerrington* • Ken Lynch *Graves* • Suzanne Lloyd *Lucinda* ■ *Dir* Harry Keller • *Scr* Clair Huffaker, from his novel

7 Women 

Period drama 1966 · US · Colour · 86mins

The last movie from great American director John Ford is, as one might expect, a transplanted western. It's set in Manchuria in 1935, where a group of remarkably resolute women missionaries are threatened by the local Mongolian warlord (a cleverly cast Mike Mazurki). Ford has the benefit of a superb cast, headed by Anne Bancroft as a cynical physician who ends up risking everything to protect the mission. This may seem unlikely Ford material on the surface, but the old maestro certainly makes it his own, treating such skilled performers as Flora Robson, Margaret Leighton and Sue Lyon as though they were members of the US cavalry. TS

Anne Bancroft *Dr Cartwright* • Sue Lyon *Emma Clark* • Margaret Leighton *Agatha Andrews* • Flora Robson *Miss Binns* • Mildred Dunnock *Jane Argent* • Betty Field *Florrie Pether* • Anna Lee *Mrs Russell* • Eddie Albert *Charles Pether* • Mike Mazurki *Tunga Khan* • Woody Strode *Lean warrior* ■ *Dir* John Ford • *Scr* Janet Green, John McCormick, from the novel *Chinese Finale* by Norah Lofts

The Seven Year Itch ★★★★ PG

Comedy 1955 · US · Colour · 100mins

One of the great moments from this film, when Marilyn Monroe lets the updraft from a subway ventilation shaft lift her skirt, has passed into movie legend; true cineastes will delight in noting that the sequence is divided into two horizontal cuts, since the film was one of Fox's early CinemaScope productions, and director Billy Wilder made it all look so seamless. In the more prudish 1950s this film was very risqué indeed, the title giving a catch phrase to the nation and a new insight into marriage. The film is still very funny, and beautifully played by Monroe and Tom Ewell. Make allowances for the period and enjoy yourself. TS DVD

Marilyn Monroe *The Girl* • Tom Ewell *Richard Sherman* • Evelyn Keyes *Helen Sherman* • Sonny Tufts *Tom McKenzie* • Robert Strauss *Mr Kruhulik* • Oskar Homolka [Oscar Homolka] *Dr Brubaker* • Marguerite Chapman *Miss Morris* • Victor Moore *Plumber* ■ *Dir* Billy Wilder • *Scr* Billy Wilder, George Axelrod, from the play by George Axelrod • *Cinematographer* Milton Krasner • *Music* Alfred Newman

Seven Years in Tibet ★★★ PG

Biographical adventure drama 1997 · US/UK · Colour · 130mins

Jean-Jacques Annaud's magnificently photographed Dalai Lama drama is strong on visual appeal and spiritual ambience, but makes one fatal error – the miscasting of Brad Pitt as real-life Austrian mountaineer Heinrich Harrer, whose eventful life was capped by a lengthy stay in Tibet. The camera loves him, but his catalogue model looks and ropey Teutonic accent undermine the whole movie. David Thewlis, however, is excellent as his climbing partner, as is Annaud's feeling for time and place. JC DVD

Brad Pitt *Heinrich Harrer* • David Thewlis *Peter Aufschnaiter* • BD Wong *Ngawang Jigme* • Mako *Kungo Tsarong* • Danny Denzongpa *Regent* • Victor Wong (2) *Chinese "Amban"* ■ *Dir* Jean-Jacques Annaud • *Scr* Becky Johnston, from the memoirs of Heinrich Harrer • *Music* John Williams • *Cinematographer* Robert Fraisse

Seventh Cavalry ★★★ U

Western 1956 · US · Colour · 76mins

Randolph Scott played a key role in the emergence of the psychological western in the late 1950s, in which motives mattered more than action. This disjointed picture does manage to combine excitement and emotion, as Scott seeks to disprove a charge of cowardice by leading a cavalry detail to reclaim the dead after the Battle of the Little Bighorn. The skirmishes are solidly staged by B-movie specialist Joseph H Lewis. DP

Randolph Scott *Captain Tom Benson* • Barbara Hale *Martha Kellogg* • Jay C Flippen *Sergeant Bates* • Jeanette Nolan *Mrs Reynolds* • Frank Faylen *Krugger* • Leo Gordon *Vogel* • Denver Pyle *Dixon* • Harry Carey Jr *Corporal Morrison* • Michael Pate *Captain Benteen* ■ *Dir* Joseph H Lewis • *Scr* Peter Packer, from a story by Glendon F Swarthout

The Seventh Coin ★★

Mystery thriller 1993 · US · Colour · 92mins

On holiday in old Jerusalem, American teenager Alexandra Powers hangs out with an Arab boy who steals a precious coin that once belonged to King Herod. Soon the duo are being pursued by dotty Peter O'Toole, who believes that he is the reincarnation of the ancient monarch and the coin is his. This is a mild-mannered family thriller, high on lush visuals, but low on basic action and adventure trappings. O'Toole goes hilariously over the top. AJ

Alexandra Powers *Ronnie Segal* • Navin Chowdhry *Salim Zouabi* • Peter O'Toole *Emil Saber* • John Rhys-Davies *Captain Galil* • Ally Walker *Lisa* ■ *Dir* Dror Soref • *Scr* Dror Soref, Michael Lewis

The Seventh Continent ★★★★

Surreal drama
1989 · Austria · Colour · 90mins

Echoes of Robert Bresson, Chantal Akerman and Rainer Werner Fassbinder reverberate through Michael Haneke's stark, but deeply affecting study of the mechanised, antiseptic inertia blighting modern Austria. The ritualistic, almost robotic existence endured by Dieter Berner and Birgit Doll is briefly disturbed by the punishment meted out to daughter Leni Tanzer after she feigns blindness. But rather than shake the family from its torpor, it persuades the bourgeois parents to begin their meticulous preparations for suicide. Haneke's use of repetition and fragmentation, coupled with his attention to detail and rigorous pacing, makes this a dislocating and dispiriting, yet relentlessly provocative, experience. DP. In German with English subtitles.

Dieter Berner *Georg* • Birgit Doll *Anna* • Leni Tanzer *Eva* • Udo Samel *Alexander* ■ *Dir/Scr* Michael Haneke

The Seventh Cross ★★★

Drama 1944 · US · BW · 111mins

Seven inmates escape from a concentration camp in pre-Second World War Germany, but only one (Spencer Tracy), against all the odds, evades capture and execution. This is a gripping story that evokes the poisonous atmosphere of threat and terror and the dangers and difficulties for the Resistance in Nazi Germany. Directed with full command by Austrian émigré Fred Zinnemann and played by Tracy as you would expect, there's also excellent support from the Oscar-nominated Hume Cronyn. RK

Spencer Tracy *George Heisler* • Signe Hasso *Toni* • Hume Cronyn *Paul Roeder* • Jessica Tandy *Liesel Roeder* • Agnes Moorehead *Mme Marelli* • Herbert Rudley *Franz Marnet* ■ *Dir* Fred Zinnemann • *Scr* Helen Deutsch, from the novel *Das Siebte Kreuz* by Anna Seghers

The 7th Dawn ★

Drama 1964 · UK · Colour · 125mins

This dismal melodrama stars William Holden as an engineer who finds himself at odds with a former comrade in post-Second World War Malaya. Lewis Gilbert directs the film at a funereal pace and it's packed with clichéd characters who pompously spout political platitudes and entangle themselves in shabby love affairs. Looking uncomfortable in the clinches with Capucine and Susannah York, a grumpy Holden gives one of his worst performances. DP

William Holden (2) *Ferris* • Susannah York *Candace* • Capucine *Dhana* • Tetsuro Tamba *Ng* • Michael Goodliffe *Trumphey* • Allan Cuthbertson *Cavendish* • Maurice Denham *Tarlton* • Beulah Quo *Ah Ming* ■ *Dir* Lewis Gilbert • *Scr* Karl Tunberg, from the novel *The Durian Tree* by Michael Koen

7th Heaven ★★★★

Silent romantic drama
1927 · US · BW · 110mins

Poor, lonely, and religious Parisian sewer worker Charles Farrell takes in Janet Gaynor off the streets. They fall in love and marry, he is sent to the the First World War battlefront, and she, hearing that he has been killed, loses her faith in God. This classic tearjerker is an effective drama about love triumphing over adversity and still has the power to draw tears. With its impressive battle scenes and atmospheric production, the film featured large in the first ever Academy Awards, winning Oscars for Frank Borzage, Gaynor, and Benjamin Glazer's script, and nominations for best picture and Harry Oliver's art direction. RK

Janet Gaynor *Diane* • Charles Farrell *Chico* • Ben Bard *Colonel Brissac* • David Butler *Gobin* • Marie Mosquini *Mme Gobin* • Albert Gran *Boul* ■ *Dir* Frank Borzage • *Scr* Benjamin Glazer, Katherine Hilliker (titles), HH Caldwell (titles), from the play by Austin Strong

Seventh Heaven ★★★

Romantic drama 1937 · US · BW · 102mins

This is a serviceable remake of the 1927 silent film. It tells of the love affair, tested by war and tragedy, between a Parisian sewer worker (James Stewart) and a homeless girl. Gale Sondergaard plays the heartless sister who throws Simone Simon out onto the streets, while Hollywood's resident screen medic Jean Hersholt exchanges his stethoscope for a priest's dog-collar. Reworked in certain areas (the hero starts out as an atheist, the heroine is a prostitute), it dilutes the sugar quotient of the

S

original, but fails to achieve its dreamlike poignancy. RK

Simone Simon *Diane* • James Stewart *Chico* • Gale Sondergaard *Nana* • Gregory Ratoff *Boul* • Jean Hersholt *Father Chevillon* • J Edward Bromberg *Aristide* ■ • *Scr* Melville Baker, from the play by Austin Strong

The Seventh Seal ★★★★★ PG

Period drama 1957 · Swe · BW · 92mins

This is an undoubted masterpiece of world cinema. It tells of a crusader knight (Max von Sydow) who refuses to accompany Death (Bengt Ekerot) until he has found a flicker of hope in a world stricken by plague, corruption and fear. While this is a highly personal film, in which director Ingmar Bergman (the son of the chaplain of the Swedish royal family) resolves his own doubts about the existence of God, its conclusions will leave even the most cynical filled with optimism. DP. In Swedish with English subtitles. VIDEO DVD

Max von Sydow *Antonius Block, the knight* • Gunnar Björnstrand *Jons, Block's squire* • Bengt Ekerot *Death* • Nils Poppe *Jof* • Bibi Andersson *Mia* ■ *Dir* Ingmar Bergman • *Scr* Ingmar Bergman, from his play *Tramalning, (Sculpture in Wood)*

The Seventh Sign ★★ 15

Supernatural horror thriller 1988 · US · Colour · 96mins

Great! Demi Moore is given the opportunity to save the world. As blood rains from the sky and earthquakes shake cities, Moore is more worried about having a successful pregnancy. But with a weirdo reading Hebrew in her garage and CNN broadcasting apocalyptic bulletins on the hour, having the baby and saving humanity become synonymous. Moore is good but the rest of the movie is a marvellous mess. LH VIDEO DVD

Demi Moore *Abby Quinn* • Michael Biehn *Russell Quinn* • Jürgen Prochnow *David the Boarder* • Peter Friedman *Father Lucci* • Manny Jacobs *Avi* • John Taylor (2) *Jimmy* • John Heard *Reverend* ■ *Dir* Carl Schultz • *Scr* WW Wicket, George Kaplan

The Seventh Veil ★★★ PG

Melodrama 1945 · US · BW · 89mins

The Oscar-winning screenplay for this all-stops-out melodrama was written by the husband-and-wife team of Sydney and Muriel Box. But, whichever way you slice it, there's no escaping the fact that, for all its aspirations to musical and psychological gravity, this is nothing more than home-cured ham. Ann Todd is at her drippiest as a persecuted pianist whose love-hate relationship with crippled guardian James Mason is founded on romantic clichés that first appeared in Victorian penny-dreadfuls. Nontheless, it's still irresistible entertainment, done with considerable style. DP VIDEO

James Mason *Nicholas* • Ann Todd *Francesca Cunningham* • Herbert Lom *Dr Larson* • Hugh McDermott *Peter Gay* • Albert Lieven *Maxwell Leyden* • Yvonne Owen *Susan Brook* • David Horne *Dr Kendal* ■ *Dir* Compton Bennett • *Scr* Sydney Box, Muriel Box

The Seventh Victim ★★

Horror 1943 · US · BW · 70mins

The directing debut of former editor Mark Robson is an underwritten but atmospheric and creepy tale about a sect of Satanists who live in deepest Greenwich Village. Tom Conway is a pallid lead, out-performed by Kim Hunter, who screams on cue with considerable conviction. If the main set looks vaguely familiar, it's because it was originally built the previous year for Orson Welles's *The Magnificent Ambersons*. AT

Kim Hunter *Mary Gibson* • Tom Conway *Dr Louis Judd* • Jean Brooks *Jacqueline Gibson* • Isabel Jewell *Frances Fallon* • Evelyn Brent *Natalie Cortez* • Erford Gage *Jason Hoag* • Ben Bard *Brun* • Hugh Beaumont *Gregory Ward* ■ *Dir* Mark Robson • *Scr* DeWitt Bodeen, Charles O'Neal • *Cinematographer* Nicholas Musuraca

The 7th Voyage of Sinbad ★★★★ U

Fantasy adventure 1958 · US · Colour · 88mins

The first Sinbad adventure saga from stop-motion genius Ray Harryhausen is still the best. Sokurah the Magician (Torin Thatcher) demands that Sinbad (Kerwin Matthews) find a magic lamp that is being guarded by an ingenious gallery of monsters – brought to fabulous life by Harryhausen's expertise and Bernard Herrmann's rousing score. A 30-foot-tall cyclops, a two-headed bird, a fire-breathing dragon and a warrior skeleton combine with swashbuckling spectacle and thrilling escapism under Nathan Juran's sure-handed direction. The result is a fantastic family favourite. Followed by *The Golden Voyage of Sinbad*. AJ VIDEO DVD

Kerwin Mathews *Captain Sinbad* • Kathryn Grant *Princess Parisa* • Richard Eyer *Barroni the Genie* • Torin Thatcher *Sokurah the Magician* • Alec Mango *Caliph* • Danny Green *Karim* • Harold Kasket *Sultan* ■ *Dir* Nathan Juran • *Scr* Kenneth Kolb

71 Fragments of a Chronology of Chance ★★★

Experimental drama 1994 · Austria/Ger · Colour · 96mins

As its title suggests, this is a masterly mosaic of a movie, in which a combination of fate and caprice causes the lives of disparate Viennese citizens to be touched by tragedy. Flashing back from a teenage student's seemingly unprovoked Christmas Eve gun rampage, the film assembles various story snippets that are linked together by the desperate pleadings of a homeless Romanian refugee. It's the kind of controlled, cerebral affair we've now come to expect from Michael Haneke. Compelling, if cool and calculating. DP

Gabriel Cosmin Urdes *Romanian boy* • Lukas Miko *Max, student* • Otto Grünmandl *Tomek, old man* • Anne Bennent *Inge Brunner* • Udo Samel *Paul Brunner* ■ *Dir/Scr* Michael Haneke

A Severed Head ★★★

Black comedy 1970 · UK · Colour · 99mins

Though not a patch on Iris Murdoch's 1961 novel, nor its subsequent stage adaptation, this is still an amusing, sophisticated comedy which, in its highly polished way, recalls Ross Hunter's Hollywood films of the 1950s and 1960s. Screenwriter Frederic Raphael was obviously writing about people he knew – academics and posh folk indulging in a mad charade of partner-swapping. In his first screen lead, Ian Holm is the harassed wine merchant juggling a wife and mistresses. DM

Lee Remick *Antonia Lynch-Gibbon* • Richard Attenborough *Palmer Anderson, psychiatrist* • Ian Holm *Martin Lynch-Gibbon, wine merchant* • Claire Bloom *Honor Klein* • Jennie Linden *Georgie Hands* • Clive Revill *Alexander Lynch-Gibbon* • Ann Firbank *Rosemary Lynch-Gibbon* ■ *Dir* Dick Clement • *Scr* Frederic Raphael, from the play by Iris Murdoch, JB Priestley, from the novel by Iris Murdoch

Sex and Lucia ★★★ 18

Drama 2001 · Sp/Fr · Colour · 122mins

Exploring such perennial themes as identity, coincidence and sexual psychology, this has all the visual bravura and narrative complexity one would expect of writer/director Julio Medem. There's technical assurance and dramatic intensity to spare as the fractured storyline subtly reveals how waitress Paz Vega (the eponymous Lucia), scuba-diver Daniel Freire and nanny Elena Anaya are all bound into novelist Tristan Ulloa's tortuous existence. It's chic and seductive, but its fascination lies solely on the surface. DP. In Spanish with English subtitles. VIDEO DVD

Paz Vega *Lucia* • Tristan Ulloa *Lorenzo* • Najwa Nimri *Elena* • Daniel Freire *Carlos/Antonio* • Elena Anaya *Belen* ■ *Dir/Scr* Julio Medem

Sex and the Other Man ★★★

Comedy 1995 · US · Colour · 89mins

In this blackish comedy, Ron Eldard, suffering from impotence, is shocked when he catches his girlfriend Kari Wuhrer in bed with her boss Stanley Tucci. But this scene has a positive affect on Eldard's libido, and he and Wuhrer then hold Tucci captive while they work out their sexual frustrations. This off-centre farce is lifted by the brilliant performance of Tucci. DF

Ron Eldard *Billy* • Stanley Tucci *Arthur* • Kari Wuhrer *Jessica* ■ *Dir* Karl Slovin • *Scr* Karl Slovin, from the play *Captive* by Paul Weitz

Sex and the Single Girl ★★★

Satirical comedy 1964 · US · Colour · 119mins

Tony Curtis and Natalie Wood make an attractive couple in this comedy, which was regarded as very risqué in 1964. It's based on an enormous bestseller by Helen Gurley Brown, the legendary editor of *Cosmopolitan*. Warner's paid a reputed $200,000 for the rights, then realised it didn't have a story, so Joseph Heller (*Catch-22*), wrote the script as a satire on sex therapy in general and Brown's book in particular. Wood played Miss Brown as a virginal sexologist and Curtis is the journalist who interviews her, posing as a man with deep sexual problems, which leads to a lot of in-jokes. AT

Tony Curtis *Bob Weston* • Natalie Wood *Dr Helen Brown* • Henry Fonda *Frank Broderick* • Lauren Bacall *Sylvia Broderick* • Mel Ferrer *Rudy DeMeyer* • Fran Jeffries *Gretchen* • Leslie Parrish *Susan* • Edward Everett Horton *The Chief* • Larry Storch *Motorcycle cop* ■ *Dir* Richard Quine • *Scr* Joseph Heller, David R Schwartz, from the story by Joseph Hoffman, from the book by Helen Gurley Brown

Sex and Zen ★★★ 18

Period sex comedy 1992 · HK · Colour · 86mins

This is the best-known example of the soft-core genre known in Hong Kong as Category III. Although the scenes involving concubine-wife Amy Yip have a high erotic content, director Michael Mak largely plays the film for laughs. Envious scholar Lawrence Ng undergoes a transplant of equine proportions and, after many energetic misadventures, comes to repent at leisure at a Buddhist monastery. A frantic mixture of morality tale and bedroom farce. Two less successful sequels followed. DP. A Cantonese language film. Contains sex scenes, violence. VIDEO

Kent Cheng *Doctor* • Lo Lieh *Choi Run Lun* • Amy Yip *Yuk Heung* • Isabella Chow *Kuen's wife* • Lawrence Ng *Mei Yang* • Elvis Tsui *Kuen* ■ *Dir* Michael Mak • *Scr* Lee Ying Kit, from the book *Yu Ou Tuan (The Carnal Prayer Mat)* by Li Yu

Sex, Drugs, Rock & Roll ★★★

Satirical comedy 1991 · US · Colour · 96mins

Filmed at Boston's Wilbur Theatre, this record of comic performance artist Eric Bogosian's hit Broadway one-man show is directed to hilarious perfection by John McNaughton. Bogosian offers up an assortment of unpleasant characters to laugh at uncontrollably, including a drug-addled youth remembering a debauched stag night, an entertainment lawyer driven by success, and an ageing English rock star about to play a benefit concert for Amazon Indians. Often surreal, always outrageous and very funny. AJ

Eric Bogosian ■ *Dir* John McNaughton • *Scr* Eric Bogosian

Sex Is Comedy ★★★ 18

Comedy drama 2002 · Fr · Colour · 90mins

Catherine Breillat's intriguing satire considers the problems a woman faces not only in directing a sex scene, but also in imposing her authority upon a largely male crew. Anne Parillaud adeptly conveys the doubts and frustrations of the auteur struggling to secure the co-operation of arrogant, yet insecure actor Grégoire Colin in coupling convincingly with teenage co-star Roxane Mesquida for their ironically titled movie, *Intimate Scenes*. But while Breillat frequently captures the political import of the various on-set tensions and alliances, some of Parillaud's artistic pronouncements ring luvvily hollow. DP. In French with English subtitles. VIDEO DVD

Anne Parillaud *Jeanne* • Grégoire Colin *The actor* • Roxane Mesquida *The actress* • Ashley Wanninger *Léo* • Dominique Colladant *Willy* ■ *Dir/Scr* Catherine Breillat

Sex Kittens Go to College ★★ 15

Sex comedy 1960 · US · BW · 103mins

The pneumatic charms of Mamie Van Doren adds an extra *frisson* to nostalgic viewings of such fare. Van Doren plays a brilliant science teacher whose previous incarnation as a stripper catches up with her. Corny dialogue and inept slapstick abound. Tuesday Weld, Jackie Coogan and John Carradine are also present in this sexploitation flick, which – in its truncated form at least – cannot quite live up to its lurid title. DF VIDEO

Mamie Van Doren *Dr Mathilda West* • Tuesday Weld *Jody* • Mijanou Bardot *Suzanne* • Mickey Shaughnessy *Boomie* • Louis Nye *Dr Zorch* • Pamela Mason [Pamela Kellino] *Dr Myrtle Carter* • Marty Milner [Martin Milner] *George Barton* • Jackie Coogan *Wildcat MacPherson* • John Carradine *Professor Watts* • Vampira *Etta Toodie* • Conway Twitty ■ *Dir* Albert Zugsmith • *Scr* Robert F Hill [Robert Hill], from a story by Albert Zugsmith

sex, lies, and videotape ★★★★ 18

Drama 1989 · US · Colour · 95mins

The winner of the Palme d'Or at Cannes, Steven Soderbergh's debut feature was made for just $1.2 million. Although it took an uncompromisingly adult approach to sex, it wasn't explicit nudity (of which there is none) that made this intelligent film so controversial, but the intimacy of the drama and the frankness of the dialogue. Peter Gallagher is a lawyer having an affair with his sister-in-law (Laura San Giacomo), who has always resented the prissiness of her perfect sibling (Andie MacDowell). However, we never really discover anything about James Spader, the long-lost friend who forces the other three to re-examine their motives and desires. It's this ambiguity that makes Spader's character the most fascinating of the

S

quartet. DP. Contains swearing and sex scenes. [video] DVD

James Spader *Graham Dalton* • Andie MacDowell *Ann Millaney* • Peter Gallagher *John Millaney* • Laura San Giacomo *Cynthia Bishop* • Ron Vawter *Therapist* • Steven Brill *Barfly* ■ *Dir/Scr* Steven Soderbergh

Sex Lives of the Potato Men ★ 18

Comedy 2003 · UK · Colour · 79mins

The title more or less tells the whole story of this thoroughly British "smutfest", as Johnny Vegas and Mackenzie Crook play Brummie potato deliverers whose amorous adventures could be summed up as soft-paw corn "comedy". Andy Humphries's film is less a coherent whole than a loosely connected series of sketches. Unfunny and unambitious. DA. Contains swearing. [video] DVD

Johnny Vegas *Dave* • Mackenzie Crook *Ferris* • Mark Gatiss *Jeremy* • Dominic Coleman *Tolly* • Julia Davis *Shelley* • Lucy Davis *Ruth* • Kate Robbins (2) *Joan* • Nicolas Tennant *Phil* ■ *Dir/Scr* Andy Humphries

The Sex Monster ★★ 15

Sex comedy 1998 · US · Colour · 93mins

Writer/director Mike Binder as a wealthy Californian who wants to spice up his sex life and talks his wife, Mariel Hemmingway, into a threesome with another woman. Although initially reluctant to satisfy this clichéd male fantasy, Hemmingway finds herself increasingly intrigued by lesbianism, and before long Binder has unleashed a bisexual monster on the LA swingers scene. This is an amiable, if unsophisticated, farce that dabbles in political incorrectness and wonky gay sensibilities with glee. AJ [video] DVD

Mariel Hemingway *Laura Barnes* • Mike Binder *Marty* • Renee Humphrey *Didi* • Missy Crider *Diva* ■ *Dir/Scr* Mike Binder

Sex, Shame and Tears ★★

Romantic comedy
1999 · Mex · Colour · 107mins

In reworking his own play for the screen, Mexican director Antonio Serrano has been unable to take the staginess out of either the acting or the narrative, and the entire cast seems to be projecting to the back of an auditorium. An impotent would-be intellectual is piqued by the arrival of his wife's flashy photographer ex, while across the street the long-suffering wife of a philandering executive finally reaches boiling point with the entry of his smouldering old flame. DP. A Spanish language film.

Demian Bichir *Tomas* • Susana Zabaleta *Ana* • Monic Dionne *Maria* • Jorge Salinas *Miguel* • Cecilia Suárez *Andrea* • Victor Hugo Martin *Carlos* ■ *Dir* Antonio Serrano • *Scr* Antonio Serrano, from his play *Sexo, Pudor y Lagrimas*

Sex: the Annabel Chong Story ★★★ 18

Documentary 1999 · US · Colour · 85mins

Grace Quek, the Singaporean student who re-created herself as porn queen Annabel Chong, may believe she set a world record for having sexual intercourse in the name of feminism. However, as Gough Lewis's documentary discloses, it was just another act of self-loathing by a fiercely intelligent but deeply confused innocent abroad in a world of frauds and exploiters. With on-screen acts of self-mutilation undermining the hard-core antics and aggressive psychobabble, this is a film that prompts one to question both the director's motives and those of his convent-educated star. DP [video] DVD

Dir Gough Lewis

Sextette ★★ PG

Musical comedy 1978 · US · Colour · 84mins

They don't come any stranger than this too-late vehicle for the octogenarian (and virtually embalmed) Mae West. The musical exists in its own inspired limboland, where salaciousness and dated vulgarity ineptly combine to render it mesmerisingly, appallingly, watchable. Interspersed with what attempts to pass for a plot, the movie is padded with some bizarre London locations. The cast is truly astonishing: you'll shudder for their collective embarrassment. TS [video]

Mae West *Marlo Manners* • Timothy Dalton *Sir Michael Barrington* • Dom DeLuise *Dan Turner* • Tony Curtis *Alexei Karansky* • Ringo Starr *Laslo Karolny* • George Hamilton *Vance* • Alice Cooper *Waiter* • Rona Barrett • Keith Moon *Dress designer* • George Raft ■ *Dir* Ken Hughes • *Scr* Herbert Baker, from the play by Mae West

Sexton Blake and the Hooded Terror ★★

Crime drama 1938 · UK/US · BW · 68mins

Unlike so many other suave English sleuths, Sexton Blake has never really come to life on the big screen. Tod Slaughter is admittedly below par as the master crook, but the film's failure lies squarely at the door of George Curzon in the title role. He lacks the necessary looks and charm, while AR Rawlinson's script lacks the zip of Hal Meredith's original story. This is considered the best of the three films in which Curzon starred as Blake. Two more films, in the 1940s, also featured the sleuth (played then by David Farrar). AT

George Curzon *Sexton Blake* • Tod Slaughter *Michael Larron* • Greta Gynt *Mademoiselle Julie* • Charles Oliver *Max Fleming* • Tony Sympson *Tinker* • Marie Wright *Mrs Bardell* ■ *Dir* George King • *Scr* AR Rawlinson, from the novel by Pierre Quiroule, from the character created by Hal Meredith [Harry Blyth]

The Sexual Life of the Belgians 1950-1978 ★★★ 18

Satirical comedy drama
1994 · Bel · Colour · 78mins

Prior to this semi-autobiographical satire, director Jan Bucquoy's greatest claim to fame was as the curator of Belgium's National Museum of Underpants. Whether his intention was to chart his own voyage of sexual discovery or expose every guilty secret in Belgian culture, Bucquoy only partially fulfils his ambitions. In spite of a bravura performance by Jean-Henri Compère as the director's alter ego, the personal side of the story too often finds itself suffocating under the bedclothes or wallowing in the bottom of a glass. The social observations, however, are often very amusing. DP. In Flemish with English subtitles. Contains swearing. [video]

Jean-Henri Compère *Jan Bucquoy* • Noé Francq *Jan as a child* • Isabelle Legros *Noella Bucquoy* • Sophie Schneider *Thérèse* • Pascale Binneri *Ariane Bucquoy* • Michele Shor *Aunt Martha* ■ *Dir/Scr* Jan Bucquoy

Sexual Magic ★★

Erotic drama 2001 · US · Colour · 85mins

Jacy Andrews plays the college student who moves in with a quartet of rapacious occultists, and gradually becomes aware that she's being lined up as the fifth point of a witches' pentangle. The development also bodes ill for her boyfriend, Jared Lincoln, who becomes the target of a mysterious blonde. This erotic thriller is hardly edifying viewing, but not particularly stimulating either. DP

Jacy Andrews *Nina* • Jared Lincoln *Vincent* • Teanna Kai [Teanara Kai] *Kate* • Nikki Fairchild *Judy* ■ *Dir* Edward R Holzman [Edward Holzman]

Sexual Predator ★★ 18

Erotic thriller 2001 · US · Colour · 83mins

Former *Baywatch* star Angie Everhart features here as an parole officer getting down and dirty with kinky photographer Richard Grieco. The hard-faced Everhart does have a well toned body and well groomed hair, as does Grieco, but this is simply ticking items off the list. JC [video] DVD

Angie Everhart *Beth Spinella* • Richard Grieco *JC Gale* • Kevin Fry *Joe* • Elizabeth Barondes *Caroline* ■ *Dir* Robert Angelo, Rob Spera • *Scr* Ed Silverstein

Sexy Beast ★★★★ 18

Crime drama
2000 · UK/Sp/US · Colour · 84mins

Ray Winstone is in relatively restrained mode as a retired crook, now living the life of Riley on the Costa del Crime. He's content to play second fiddle to a terrifying and transfixing performance from Ben Kingsley as the psychopathic hardman sent to "persuade" him back to Blighty for one last job. Debuting director Jonathan Glazer made his name in advertising – he was the man behind the "Swimmer" and "Surfer" Guinness commercials – and his visual flair is evident here. The idyllic Spanish settings nicely counterpoint the growing sense of menace as cat-and-mouse games spiral toward an inevitable act of violence. DA. Contains swearing, violence and sexual references. [video] DVD

Ray Winstone *Gary "Gal" Dove* • Ben Kingsley *Don "Malky" Logan* • Ian McShane *Teddy Bass* • Amanda Redman *DeeDee* • Cavan Kendall *Aitch* • Julianne White *Jackie* • James Fox *Harry* ■ *Dir* Jonathan Glazer • *Scr* Louis Mellis, David Scinto

Shack Out on 101 ★★★

Drama 1955 · US · BW · 80mins

Lee Marvin delivers the standout performance in this Cold War melodrama centred around a remote roadside café near a top-secret research station. Marvin relishes the part of the dimwitted cook who's not all that he seems. Frank Lovejoy plays the nuclear scientist who romances Terry Moore's waitress and is apparently willing to sell secrets to the other side. Directed on a low budget by Edward Dein, it's an unconventional picture that holds the interest. AE

Terry Moore *Kotty, the waitress* • Frank Lovejoy *Professor* • Keenan Wynn *George* • Lee Marvin *Slob, the cook* • Whit Bissell *Eddie* • Jess Barker *Artie* • Donald Murphy *Pepe* • Frank De Kova *Dillon* ■ *Dir* Edward Dein • *Scr* Edward Dein, Mildred Dein

Shades of Fear ★★

Mystery comedy romance
1993 · UK/US · Colour · 92mins

Director Beeban Kidron and writer Jeanette Winterson failed to repeat the success of *Oranges Are Not the Only Fruit* with this disappointing TV movie set in the 1950s. Aspiring pilot Rakie Ayola finds herself on a cruise ship bound for England in the company of bizarre set of characters, including (perhaps) a forger and a murderer. Unfortunately, the mixture of romance and mystery doesn't work and even the combined acting talents of Vanessa Redgrave, Jonathan Pryce, John Hurt and Dorothy Tutin can't save it. LH

Vanessa Redgrave *Dr Angela Bead* • John Hurt *Rex Goodyear* • Jonathan Pryce *Duncan Stewart* • Dorothy Tutin *Gwendolyn Quinn* • Rakie Ayola *Gabriel Angel* ■ *Dir* Beeban Kidron • *Scr* Jeanette Winterson

Shadey ★ 15

Black comedy 1985 · UK · Colour · 102mins

The idea is a good one – a clairvoyant, who can transfer his precognitions to film, is exploited by big business and British Intelligence – and the production values are glossy. But the treatment is a mystifying mishmash of transexualism, incest, insanity and ESP. Described as black comedy, it is indulgent in the extreme. DM [video]

Antony Sher *Oliver Shadey* • Patrick Macnee *Sir Cyril Landau* • Leslie Ash *Carol Landau* • Bernard Hepton *Capt Amies* • Katherine Helmond *Lady Landau* • Larry Lamb *Dick Darnley* • Billie Whitelaw *Dr Cloud* ■ *Dir* Philip Saville • *Scr* Snoo Wilson

The Shadow ★

Murder mystery 1936 · UK · BW · 75mins

A hooded figure is murdering the inhabitants of a rambling mansion in this creaky chiller, which has nothing in common with the American radio serial of the same name, made famous by Orson Welles. Director George A Cooper's musty "old dark house" yawn adds nothing to the fear formula you've all seen before. Others more cognisant of the rules of the genre have done it far better. AJ

Henry Kendall *Reggie Ogden/The Shadow* • Elizabeth Allan *Sonya Bryant* • Jeanne Stuart *Moya Silverton* • Felix Aylmer *Sir Richard* • Cyril Raymond *Silverton* • Viola Compton *Mrs Bascomb* • John Turnbull *Inspector* • Sam Livesey *Sir Richard Bryant* ■ *Dir* George A Cooper • *Scr* H Fowler Mear, Terence Egan, from a play by Donald Stuart

The Shadow ★★★

Psychological murder mystery
1956 · Pol · BW · 95mins

This thriller was something of a change of pace for Jerzy Kawalerowicz and announced him as a versatile and highly individual talent. Set during and immediately after the Second World War, the film is comprised of three separate episodes which are linked by a mysterious villain, who first acts as a Nazi informer and then as an anti-Communist saboteur. An already involved political scenario is further complicated by the enigmatic editing. DP. In Polish with English subtitles.

Zygmunt Kestowicz *Dr Knyszyn* • Adolf Chronicki *Karbowski, security officer* • Emil Karewicz *Jasiczka, his colleague* • Tadeusz Jurasz *Mikula, a young miner* • Ignacy Machowski *Shadow* ■ *Dir* Jerzy Kawalerowicz • *Scr* Aleksander Scibor-Rylski, from his stories

S

The Shadow ★★★ 12

Action adventure
1994 · US · Colour · 102mins

"Who knows what evil lurks in the hearts of men?". Alec Baldwin does, here playing both wealthy socialite Lamont Cranston and his mysterious alter ego, the Shadow, who uses psychic powers to render himself invisible at will. The famous 1930s' pulp crime-fighter takes on a descendant of Genghis Khan who's out to conquer the world in director Russell Mulcahy's comic-strip fantasy. It's stuffed with fun clichés of the genre, but the flashy production values rather overshadow the performances, while the plot rarely grips. AJ. Contains swearing and violene. [video]

Alec Baldwin *Lamont Cranston/The Shadow* • John Lone *Shiwan Khan* • Penelope Ann Miller *Margo Lane* • Peter Boyle *Moe Shrevnitz* • Ian McKellen *Reinhardt Lane* • Tim Curry *Farley Claymore* • Jonathan Winters *Wainwright Barth* • Sab Shimono *Dr Tam* ■ *Dir* Russell Mulcahy • *Scr* David Koepp, from the characters created by Walter Gibson

Shadow Conspiracy ★★★ 15

Political action thriller
1996 · US · Colour · 98mins

An A-minus cast makes a good fist of this conspiracy thriller that is never less than gripping. Charlie Sheen is a presidential adviser whose life is on the line when he stumbles upon a top-level White House plot. Linda Hamilton is the political journalist in peril who teams up with Sheen, while Donald Sutherland is a high-ranking official whose motives may not be as pure as they seem. One set piece follows another at a cracking pace as Sheen is hunted by a merciless killer intent on silencing him before he can blow the whistle. JF. Contains violence and swearing. DVD

Charlie Sheen *Bobby Bishop* • Linda Hamilton *Amanda Givens* • Donald Sutherland *Conrad* • Stephen Lang *The Agent* • Sam Waterston *The President* • Ben Gazzara *Vice President Saxon* • Nicholas Turturro *Grasso* • Theodore Bikel *Professor Pochenko* • Gore Vidal *Congressman Page* ■ *Dir* George Pan Cosmatos • *Scr* Adi Hasak, Ric Gibbs

Shadow Hours ★★★ 18

Drama 2000 · US · Colour · 87mins

A pair of first-rate performances from Balthazar Getty and Peter Weller fuel Isaac H Heaton's snappy urban *noir*. Getty is a recovering drug addict and alcoholic driven to distraction by his night time service station job. Rich, unconventional writer Weller takes him under his wing, but an initially invigorating tour of hedonistic night-spots begins to takes its toll. Sharp direction and energetic music add further atmosphere, but there is a major flaw, with a significant murder subplot that's never resolved satisfactorily. JC DVD

Balthazar Getty *Michael Holloway* • Peter Weller *Stuart Chappell* • Rebecca Gayheart *Chloe Holloway* • Peter Greene *Det Steve Adrianson* • Frederic Forrest *Sean* • Brad Dourif *Roland Montague* • Michael Dorn *Det Thomas Greenwood* • Corin Nemec *Vincent* ■ *Dir/Scr* Isaac H Eaton

Shadow Magic ★★★

Period drama
2000 · Ger/US/Chi/Tai · Colour · 112mins

Raised in China during the Cultural Revolution, but since based in the States, Ann Hu returns home for her feature debut, which recalls the pioneering era of indigenous movie-making in the early 1900s. As much exploring the imperial state's resistance to outside influence as the ambitions of Beijing photographer Xia Yu and his Occidental partner Jared Harris, this is very much an allegorical drama, which suggests that East-West collaboration would prove globally beneficial. DP. In English and Mandarin with subtitles.

Jared Harris *Raymond Wallace* • Xia Yu *Liu Jinglun* • Xing Yufei *Ling* • Liu Peiqi *Master Ren* • Lu Liping *Madame Ren* • Wang Jingming *Old Liu* • Li Yusheng *Lord Tan* ■ *Dir* Ann Hu • *Scr* Ann Hu, Huang Dan, Tang Louyi, Kate Raisz, Bob McAndrew

Shadow Makers ★★ PG

Drama 1989 · US · Colour · 121mins

While it's enjoyable to have Paul Newman as a nastily punctilious army officer, this account of the secret project that developed the first American atom bomb never detonates into real drama. There is conflict between the by-the-book soldiers and off-the-wall scientists, and also among the scientists themselves but, despite a quality cast, the story comes to life only when there's the threat of illness on the base. TH DVD

Paul Newman *General Leslie R Groves* • Dwight Schultz *J Robert Oppenheimer* • Bonnie Bedelia *Kitty Oppenheimer* • John Cusack *Michael Merriman* • Laura Dern *Kathleen Robinson* • Ron Frazier *Peer de Silva* • John C McGinley *Richard Schoenfield* • Natasha Richardson *Jean Tatlock* ■ *Dir* Roland Joffé • *Scr* Roland Joffé, Bruce Robinson, from a story by Bruce Robinson

Shadow of a Doubt ★★★★★ PG

Classic thriller 1942 · US · BW · 103mins

Early on in Alfred Hitchcock's personal favourite of his own movies, a train, belching out a cloud of ominous black smoke, pulls into Santa Rosa, California. Joseph Cotten has arrived and is met by his adoring niece, Teresa Wright. Both are called "Charlie". She is pumpkin-pie innocence; but is he really a suave killer, wanted back east for relieving widows of their wealth and their lives? Although Hitchcock blurs the line between good and evil, the two Charlies are inevitably pitched against each other, as suspicion increases and the police start nosing around. The movie may lack the show-off set pieces that Hitchcock turned into his trademark, yet its tension never falters. AT DVD

Teresa Wright *Young Charlie Newton* • Joseph Cotten *Uncle Charlie Oakley/Mr Spencer/Mr Otis* • Macdonald Carey *Jack Graham* • Henry Travers *Joseph Newton* • Patricia Collinge *Emma Spencer Oakley Newton* • Hume Cronyn *Herbie Hawkins* • Wallace Ford *Fred Saunders* • Edna May Wonacott *Ann Newton* ■ *Dir* Alfred Hitchcock • *Scr* Thornton Wilder, Sally Benson, Alma Reville, from a story by Gordon McDonell

Shadow of a Man ★★

Crime drama 1954 · UK · BW · 69mins

Thanks to Geoffrey Faithfull's seedy seaside cinematography, this British crime drama has more atmosphere than most of the period. When Bill Nagy is found dead after a nightclub brawl, novelist Paul Carpenter refuses to believe that his friend died from heart failure. Carpenter isn't the most winning of heroes, but Michael McCarthy directs steadily and comes up with a truly original solution. DP

Paul Carpenter *Gene Landers* • Rona Anderson *Linda Bryant* • Jane Griffiths *Carol Seaton* • Tony Quinn *Inspector Gates* • Bill Nagy *Paul Bryant* ■ *Dir* Michael McCarthy • *Scr* Paul Erickson

A Shadow of Doubt ★★★★ 15

Psychological thriller
1992 · Fr · Colour · 101mins

When 11-year-old Alexandrine (Sandrine Blancke) accuses her father of molestation, no one believes her except social worker, Josiane Balasko. It would have been easy to have turned this situation into a grimly effective melodrama. But, director Aline Issermann allows the doubt to linger, exploring both the torment of the suspected father and the loneliness of a child trapped in the misery and fear of incest. Staged without sensationalism or sermonising, this impeccably played picture has an emotional messiness that owes everything to life, not the movies. DP. In French with English subtitles.

Mireille Perrier *Marie LeBlanc* • Alain Bashung *Jean LeBlanc* • Sandrine Blancke *Alexandrine LeBlanc* • Emmanuelle Riva *Grandma* • Michel Aumont *Grandpa* • Josiane Balasko *Sophia* ■ *Dir* Aline Issermann • *Scr* Aline Issermann

Shadow of Doubt ★ 15

Courtroom thriller
1998 · US · Colour · 106mins

In this highly contrived courtroom drama, Melanie Griffith is the attorney defending a rap star against murder charges from prosecutor and ex-lover Tom Berenger. The proceedings are so jam-packed with wild plot twists, subplots, and unnecessary details that it comes close to being entertaining in its badness. KB DVD

Melanie Griffith *Kitt Devereux* • Tom Berenger *Jack Campioni* • Huey Lewis *Al Gordon* • Nina Foch *Sylvia Saxon* • Kimberley Kates *Bridget* • Wade Dominguez *Bobby Medina* ■ *Dir* Randal Kleiser • *Scr* Myra Byanka, Raymond DeFelitta

Shadow of Evil ★★ U

Spy thriller 1964 · Fr/It · Colour · 92mins

That James Bond wannabe, OSS 117 (Kerwin Mathews) dons the superspy's gunbelt to thwart Robert Hossein's insane scheme to wipe out what he considers "inferior races" in order to head a perfect world. Although the subject matter is decidedly unpleasant for such a tongue-in-cheek romp, director André Hunebelle knows enough about swashbucklers to keep the action moving along. AT. French dialogue dubbed into English.

Kerwin Mathews *OSS 117/Hubert Barton* • Robert Hossein *Dr Sinn* • Pier Angeli *Lila* • Dominique Wilms *Eva Davidson* ■ *Dir* André Hunebelle • *Scr* André Hunebelle, Pierre Foucaud, Raymond Borel, Michel Lebrun, Richard Caron, Patrice Rondard, from the novel *Lila de Calcutta* by Jean Bruce

Shadow of Fear ★★ U

Spy drama 1963 · UK · BW · 60mins

Paul Maxwell stars in this risible thriller from the Butcher's B-movie factory. When he agrees to deliver a secret message, Maxwell and his girlfriend get caught up in an effort to catch enemy agents operating in Britain. Ernest Morris directs with little enthusiasm, but this does benefit from South Coast locations. DP

Paul Maxwell *Bill Martin* • Clare Owen *Barbara* • Anita West *Ruth* • Alan Tilvern *Warner* • John Arnatt *Sharp* • Eric Pohlmann *Spiroulos* • Reginald Marsh *Oliver* ■ *Dir* Ernest Morris • *Scr* Ronald Liles, James O'Connolly, from the novel *Decoy Be Damned* by TF Fotherby

The Shadow of the Cat ★★

Horror 1961 · UK · BW · 78mins

Hammer removed their credit from director John Gilling's bizarre curiosity for legal quota reasons. But this tale of a manic moggy exacting a terrible revenge on those who conspired to kill its mistress is only a serviceable melodrama at best, despite the addition of House of Horror heroine Barbara Shelley. Notable for the way Gilling shows the deaths of the terrified murderers through the eyes of the feline, but not much else. AJ

André Morell *Walter Venable* • Barbara Shelley *Beth Venable* • William Lucas *Jacob* • Freda Jackson *Clara* • Conrad Phillips *Michael Latimer* ■ *Dir* John Gilling • *Scr* George Baxt

Shadow of the Eagle ★★ U

Period swashbuckling drama
1950 · UK · BW · 95mins

This is typical of the clutch of second-rate swashbucklers made by Sidney Salkow during a mid-career crisis. The grim monochrome doesn't help conjure up the grandeur of 18th-century Venice, but it is Salkow's pedestrian direction that prevents us becoming caught in the web of intrigue surrounding Russian diplomat Richard Greene and intended royal kidnap victim Valentina Cortese. DP

Richard Greene *Count Alexei Orloff* • Valentina Cortesa [Valentina Cortese] *Princess Tarakanova* • Greta Gynt *Countess Camponiello* • Binnie Barnes *Empress Catherine* • Charles Goldner *General Korsakov* • Walter Rilla *Prince Radziwill* ■ *Dir* Sidney Salkow • *Scr* Doreen Montgomery, Hagar Wilde, from the story by Jacques Companeez

Shadow of the Past ★★★

Drama 1995 · US · Colour · 105mins

This showcase role for country superstar Dwight Yoakam has him as a former top rodeo clown reluctant to re-enter the ring. Yoakam is laid back but effective in this moving tale that follows him as he attempts to tackle the hang-ups from his past before he can settle comfortably back in the saddle. An offbeat and likeable character study, with sturdy support by the likes of Bo Hopkins, Cindy Pickett and John Getz. Watch out for a cameo appearance from Peter Fonda. DA

Dwight Yoakam *Virgil Kidder* • Michelle Joyner *Katelin* • Kiersten Warren *Teresa* • Cindy Pickett *Sadie* • John Getz *Sheriff Gil Acuff* • Bo Hopkins *Brownie* • Peter Fonda ■ *Dir* Terry Benedict • *Scr* Terry Benedict, Stan Bertheaud

Shadow of the Thin Man ★★

Detective comedy 1941 · US · BW · 96mins

While Nick and Nora Charles (William Powell and Myrna Loy), now the proud parents of a baby son, are at the races, a jockey is murdered. Nick gets involved when a reporter is also bumped off. By this fourth entry in the popular series, quality was on the decline, with the original sharp wit lessened by injections of broader comedy and more convoluted plotting. But Powell and Loy's polish is undimmed. The series continued with *The Thin Man Goes Home*. RK

William Powell *Nick* • Myrna Loy *Nora* • Barry Nelson *Paul* • Donna Reed *Molly* • Sam Levene *Lieutenant Abrams* • Alan Baxter *"Whitey" Barrow* ■ *Dir* Major WS Van Dyke II [WS Van Dyke] • *Scr* Irving Brecher, Harry Kurnitz, from a story by Harry Kurnitz, from characters created by Dashiell Hammett

Shadow of the Vampire ★★★ 15

Horror
2000 · UK/US/Lux · BW and Colour · 87mins

John Malkovich and Willem Dafoe gleefully sink their teeth into a couple of juicy roles in director E Elias Merhige's film about German Expressionist director FW Murnau. Malkovich plays Murnau in this curiously comic reconstruction of the making of his classic vampire film *Nosferatu, a Symphony of Horrors* (1922). Eschewing historical accuracy, the film portrays the director as a fanatic, who hires a real bloodsucker (Dafoe) to portray the vampire. This starts promisingly but has fewer grand ideas up its sleeve than it thinks. TH. Contains violence, swearing, drug abuse and brief nudity. DVD

John Malkovich *FW Murnau* • Willem Dafoe *Max Schreck, Count Orlok* • Cary Elwes *Fritz Arno Wagner, cameraman* • Aden Gillett *Henrick Galeen, the screenwriter* • Eddie Izzard *Gustav von Wangerheim, Hutter* • Udo Kier *Albin Grau, producer/art director* • Catherine McCormack *Greta Schröder, Ellen* ■ *Dir* E Elias Merhige • *Scr* Steven Katz

Shadow of the Wolf ★★ 15

Historical drama
1992 · Can/Fr · Colour · 107mins

This costly wilderness epic about the conflict between the Inuit and encroaching whites in the Arctic of the 1930s proves to be an insipid watch. Lou Diamond Phillips stars as a young Inuit hunter banished from his tribe only to be hunted down for murder by Donald Sutherland's cop. Director Jacques Dorfmann allows his narrative to become convoluted and cluttered with mystical mumbo jumbo, though there are some moments of pictorial beauty, courtesy of Oscar-winning cinematographer Billy Williams. RS

Lou Diamond Phillips *Agaguk* • Toshiro Mifune *Ramook* • Jennifer Tilly *Iriook* • Donald

S

Sutherland *Henderson* • Bernard-Pierre Donnadieu *Brown* • Qalingo Tookalak *Tulugak* • Harry Hill *McTavish* ■ *Dir* Jacques Dorfmann • *Scr* Rudy Wurlitzer, Evan Jones, from the novel *Agaguk* by Yves Theriault

Shadow Play ★★ 15

Supernatural thriller
1986 · US · Colour · 93mins

In this routine haunted house tale, a New York playwright (Dee Wallace Stone) becomes so obsessed by her dead lover that, on returning to the island where he died, she ends up playing host to his ghost. Unfortunately for the audience, the spirit helps her ghost-write some pretty awful poetry. And that's about it. DA

Dee Wallace Stone *Morgan Hanna* • Cloris Leachman *Millie Crown* • Ron Kuhlman *John Crown* • Barry Laws *Jeremy Crown* • Al Strobel *Byron* ■ *Dir/Scr* Susan Shadburne

Shadow Run ★★ 15

Heist thriller 1998 · US · Colour · 91mins

Michael Caine is a ruthless bank robber, recruited by dodgy toff James Fox to rob a top secret van transporting the paper used to produce British currency from a sleepy country town. However, complications ensue when his actions draw the attention of a young schoolboy. There's plenty of familiar TV faces on show, but it's let down badly by diffident direction and a weak script. JF DVD

Michael Caine *Haskell* • Kenneth Colley *Larcombe* • James Fox *Landon Higgins* • Leslie Grantham *Liney* • Christopher Cazenove *Melchior* • Tim Healy *Daltry* ■ *Dir* Geoffrey Reeve • *Scr* Desmond Lowden

Shadowlands ★★★★★ U

Romantic biographical drama
1993 · UK/US · Colour · 125mins

This intimate drama set far from the world stage remains one of director Richard Attenborough's best pictures to date. It charts the tragic love affair between the author CS Lewis and an American poet, Joy Gresham. Anthony Hopkins and Debra Winger give performances that you dream about but rarely see, and the tone is set by Winger's entrance into Oxford's Randolph Hotel: "Anyone here named Loowis?" she rasps, upsetting the decorum of academe and rattling Hopkins's tea cup. Thereafter, Hopkins's life as an emotionally frigid bachelor is transformed. With its immaculate 1950s setting, the film creates a totally convincing world and Attenborough gets beneath the skin of his characters as never before. AT

Anthony Hopkins *CS "Jack" Lewis* • Debra Winger *Joy Gresham* • John Wood *Christopher Riley* • Edward Hardwicke *Warnie Lewis* • Joseph Mazzello *Douglas Gresham* • Julian Fellowes *Desmond Arding* • Roddy Maude-Roxby *Arnold Dopliss* • Michael Denison *Harry Harrington* • Peter Firth *Doctor Craig* ■ *Dir* Richard Attenborough • *Scr* William Nicholson, from his play

Shadowman ★★★★★

Mystery adventure
1973 · Fr/It · Colour · 87mins

This movie spin-off from Georges Franju's TV serial *Nuits Rouges* was inspired by the novels of Pierre Souvestre and Marcel Allain, one of which was brought to the screen by silent maestro Louis Feuillade, whose visual style is evident in almost every frame. Feuillade's grandson Jacques Champreux plays the antiheroic lead attempting to track down the outlawed Knights Templar in order to steal their golden horde. With every street secreting a hidden passage, each character a perfectly observed archetype and no opportunity missed to glory in a futuristic gadget or gimmick, this is comic book with class. DP. In French with English subtitles.

Jacques Champreux *The Man* • Gayle Hunnicut *The Woman* • Gert Fröbe *Sorbier* • Josephine Chaplin *Martine* • Ugo Pagliani *Paul* • Patrick Préjean *Seraphin* • Clément Harari *Dutreuil* • Henry Lincoln *Prof Petri* ■ *Dir* Georges Franju • *Scr* Jacques Champreux

Shadows ★★★ PG

Drama 1959 · US · BW · 77mins

This format-breaking social drama was the first film from actor-turned-director John Cassavetes. It's the mainly improvised story of three black siblings – Lelia Goldoni, Ben Carruthers and Hugh Hurd – who are making their way in Manhattan. Goldoni, who passes for white, begins a love affair with a white man, which gives Cassavetes plenty of scope for interracial discussion, while jazz trumpeter Hurd finds life full of sour notes. Cassavetes's style of ad-lib acting and situations became a benchmark for future independent film-making. TH

Hugh Hurd *Hugh* • Lelia Goldoni *Lelia* • Ben Carruthers *Ben* • Anthony Ray *Tony* • Dennis Sallas *Dennis* • Tom Allen *Tom* • David Pokitillow *David* ■ *Dir* John Cassavetes • *Music* Charlie Mingus

Shadows and Fog ★★★ 15

Period comedy drama
1991 · US · BW · 81mins

Reworking his 1972 one-act play *Death*, Woody Allen originally intended this esoteric drama to be a homage to German expressionism. However, he opted for a look owing more to Universal's pre-war horror movies and, thus, deprived an already slight premise of some visual power. As the nobody who is co-opted into the search for a strangler in an eastern European town, Allen is typically twitchy amid a galaxy of guest stars. Short on humour, perhaps, but this curio is laced with ideas that took on a new relevance when news broke of his split with Mia Farrow. DP. Contains some violence. DVD

Woody Allen *Kleinman* • Mia Farrow *Irmy* • John Malkovich *Clown* • Madonna *Marie* • Donald Pleasence *Doctor* • Kathy Bates *Prostitute* • Jodie Foster *Prostitute* • Lily Tomlin *Prostitute* • John Cusack *Student Jack* • Julie Kavner *Alma* ■ *Dir/Scr* Woody Allen • *Music* Kurt Weill

Shadows of Our Forgotten Ancestors ★★★★★ 12

Drama 1964 · USSR · Colour and BW · 91mins

A radical departure from his previous films, Sergei Paradjanov's masterpiece sought to challenge accepted notions of narrative and visual representation. This expressionist variation on the Tristan and Isolde theme is not just cinematically subversive, but also politically contentious, through its bold assertion of Ukrainian heritage. Nothing can be taken at face value in this psychologically dense exercise in deconstruction. The hallucinatory effects achieved through camera movement, lens manipulation and cutting, the brilliant "dramaturgy of colour" and the disorientating use of sound all ran counter to existing norms in Soviet art and made its director a marked man. DP. In Russian with English subtitles.

Ivan Mikolaychuk *Ivan* • Larisa Kadochnikova *Marichka* • Tatyana Bestayeva *Palagna* • Spartak Bagashvili *Yurko the Sorcerer* ■ *Dir* Sergei Paradjanov • *Scr* Sergei Paradzhanov, Ivan Chendey, from the novelette *Tini Zabutykh Predkiv* by Mikhaylo Mikhaylovich Kotsyubinsky

Shadows of the Peacock ★★

Drama 1987 · Aus · Colour · 92mins

Before decamping for Hollywood, Australian director Phillip Noyce signed off with this uneven drama. Wendy Hughes is the mother trying to rebuild her life after discovering her husband has been cheating on her and finding romance in Thailand with John Lone. It looks glorious and is superbly played by the talented cast, although the suspicion remains that there is less going on here than meets the eye. JF

Wendy Hughes *Maria McEvoy* • John Lone *Raka* • Steven Jacobs [Steve Jacobs] *George McEvoy* • Peta Toppano *Judy* ■ *Dir* Phillip Noyce • *Scr* Jan Sharp, Anne Brooksbank

Shadows on the Stairs ★

Mystery 1941 · US · BW · 63mins

One of those irritating thrillers that explain away an implausible plot through a cheat ending. Murder is committed in the Bloomsbury boarding house run by Frieda Inescort and Miles Mander and investigated by a resident, Bruce Lester's budding playwright. Turhan Bey plays a shady Asian businessman in one of his earliest screen appearances. AE

Paul Cavanagh *Mr Reynolds* • Heather Angel *Sylvia* • Turhan Bey *Ram Singh* • Frieda Inescort *Mrs Armitage* • Miles Mander *Mr Armitage* • Bruce Lester *Bromilow* • Phyllis Barry *Lucy* • Lumsden Hare *Inspector* • Mary Field *Miss Snell* ■ *Dir* D Ross Lederman • *Scr* Anthony Coldeway, from the play *Murder on the 2nd Floor* by Frank Vosper

Shadowzone ★★★ 18

Science-fiction horror
1990 · US · Colour · 84mins

In this intriguing and competent low-budget shocker, a team of scientists working in an isolated underground complex investigates the mysteries of dreams and long-term sleep but accidentally unleashes a shape-shifting monster from another dimension. An *Alien* rip-off it may be, but writer/director JS Cardone heightens the sense of foreboding inherent within the claustrophobic situation and pumps up the suspense. RS DVD

Louise Fletcher *Dr Erhardt* • Miguel A Nunez Jr *Wiley* • David Beecroft *Captain Hickock* • Lu Leonard *Mrs Cutter* • James Hong *Dr Van Fleet* • Shawn Weatherly *Dr Kidwell* • Frederick Flynn *Tommy Shivers* ■ *Dir/Scr* JS Cardone

Shaft ★★★ 15

Blaxploitation crime thriller
1971 · US · Colour · 100mins

The film that firmly established the blaxploitation genre in the early 1970s is nothing more than an urban ghetto, James Bond-style thriller. But ex-male model Richard Roundtree brings a casual charm to the vicious proceedings as the private dick ("a sex machine to all the chicks") enlisted to find a Harlem racketeer's kidnapped daughter, and director Gordon Parks gives it a fast and furious style. Isaac Hayes won an Oscar for the landmark theme song that laid down the ground rules for all the funky, satin-sheet sounds that followed. AJ. Contains violence, swearing and brief nudity. DVD

Richard Roundtree *John Shaft* • Moses Gunn *Bumpy Jonas* • Charles Cioffi *Lieutenant Vic Androzzi* • Christopher St John *Ben Buford* • Gwenn Mitchell *Ellie Moore* • Lawrence Pressman *Sergeant Tom Hannon* • Victor Arnold *Charlie* • Sherri Brewer *Marcy* ■ *Dir* Gordon Parks • *Scr* Ernest Tidyman, John DF Black, from the novel by Ernest Tidyman

Shaft ★★★★ 18

Crime thriller 2000 · US/Ger · Colour · 95mins

Samuel L Jackson has the necessary presence to carry off John Singleton's slick homage to the icon of 1970s blaxploitation. This Shaft is the nephew of the original (Richard Roundtree), and he's one mad, mean mother, especially when wealthy creep Christian Bale gets away with a brutal, racially motivated murder. Jeffrey Wright is brilliant as his drugs lord nemesis, while Isaac Hayes's Oscar-winning theme song once again gets the pulse pumping for some maliciously funny twists and heavy violence. AME. Contains violence, swearing and some nudity. DVD

Samuel L Jackson *John Shaft* • Vanessa Williams [Vanessa L Williams] *Carmen Vasquez* • Jeffrey Wright *Peoples Hernandez* • Christian Bale *Walter Wade Jr* • Busta Rhymes *Rasaan* • Dan Hedaya *Jack Roselli* • Toni Collette *Diane Palmieri* • Richard Roundtree *Uncle John Shaft* ■ *Dir* John Singleton • *Scr* Richard Price, John Singleton, Shane Salerno, from a story by John Singleton, Shane Salerno, from the 1971 film

Shaft in Africa ★★★ 18

Blaxploitation thriller
1973 · US · Colour · 107mins

Richard Roundtree's portrayal of the supercool black private eye is still, in this sequel, the film's most persuasive quality. With a screenplay by Stirling Silliphant, this tale has Shaft lured out of his ghetto domain to break Frank Finlay's slave-smuggling racket. The film gets across its message with some cracking dialogue and bursts of violent skulduggery, with British director John Guillermin showing an eye for sadistic detail. TH. Contains nudity, violence, swearing. DVD

Richard Roundtree *John Shaft* • Frank Finlay *Amafi* • Vonetta McGee *Aleme* • Neda Arneric *Jazar* • Debebe Eshetu *Wassa* • Cy Grant *Emir Ramila* • Spiros Focas *Sassari* ■ *Dir* John Guillermin • *Scr* Stirling Silliphant, from the characters created by Ernest Tidyman

Shaft's Big Score! ★★★ 15

Blaxploitation thriller
1972 · US · Colour · 100mins

Richard Roundtree and Moses Gunn return in the sequel to the huge blockbuster *Shaft*, which kicked off the early 1970s blaxploitation craze. This time the private eye hero acts more like a hip James Bond than a retro Sam Spade, in a routine social conscience tale that finds him avenging the murder of a friend while retrieving money stolen by warring gangsters. It's not as tightly directed by Gordon Parks as the first movie, but the New York harbour ending is memorably exciting. AJ DVD

Richard Roundtree *John Shaft* • Moses Gunn *Bumpy Jonas* • Drew Bundini Brown *Willy* • Joseph Mascolo *Gus Mascola* • Kathy Imrie *Rita* • Wally Taylor *Kelly* • Julius W Harris [Julius Harris] *Captain Bollin* • Rosalind Miles *Arna Asby* ■ *Dir* Gordon Parks • *Scr* Ernest Tidyman, from his characters

Shag ★★★ 15

Comedy 1988 · UK/US · Colour · 95mins

This unfortunately titled (it's a dance) youth movie is directed by former continuity girl Zelda Barron. The film features an attractive American cast plus Britain's own Shirley Anne Field, but nobody has anything significant to do. Phoebe Cates is on the verge of matrimony, and her buddies decide to throw her one last fling at Myrtle Beach. Since it's 1963 and the Yanks have yet to discover the Beatles and the Pill, not much happens. Slight and undemanding, but fun in places. TS. Contains swearing.

Phoebe Cates *Carson McBride* • Scott Coffey *Chip Guillyard* • Bridget Fonda *Melaina Buller* • Annabeth Gish *Caroline "Pudge" Carmichael* • Page Hannah *Luanne Clatterbuck* • Robert Rusler *Buzz Ravenel* • Tyrone Power Jr *Harley Ralston* • Shirley Anne Field *Mrs Clatterbuck*

S

■ *Dir* Zelda Barron • *Scr* Robin Swicord, Lanier Laney, Terry Sweeney, from a story by Lanier Laney, Terry Sweeney

The Shaggy DA ★★★ U

Comedy 1976 · US · Colour · 87mins

A belated follow-up to Disney's 1959 hit, *The Shaggy Dog*, finds lawyer Dean Jones turning into a pooch at the slightest provocation. Unfortunately, this peculiar canine condition occurs just as he's up for election as district attorney against the unscrupulous Keenan Wynn. Notable for a juicy scene involving some cherry pies and an ingenious breakout from the dog pound, this is one of those rare occasions when the sequel is superior to the original. DP

Dean Jones *Wilby Daniels* • Suzanne Pleshette *Betty Daniels* • Keenan Wynn *District Attorney John Slade* • Tim Conway *Tim* • Jo Anne Worley *Katrinka Muggelberg* • Dick Van Patten *Raymond* ■ *Dir* Robert Stevenson • *Scr* Don Tait, from the novel *The Hound of Florence* by Felix Salten

The Shaggy Dog ★★★ U

Fantasy comedy 1959 · US · BW · 100mins

This was the first of Disney's contemporary slapstick fantasies and typifies the generally reviled genre. It was a big success and led to a belated sequel. With his usual aplomb, Fred MacMurray plays the troubled *paterfamilias* whose son turns into a sheepdog, while Jean Hagen has a thankless role as mom. Disney regulars Annette Funicello and Tommy Kirk head the support cast, but today's audience might still be disappointed with this tale. TS

Fred MacMurray *Wilson Daniels* • Jean Hagen *Frieda Daniels* • Tommy Kirk *Wilby Daniels* • Annette Funicello *Allison D'Allessio* • Tim Considine *Buzz Miller* • Kevin Corcoran *Moochie Daniels* • Cecil Kellaway *Professor Plumcutt* • Alexander Scourby *Doctor Mikhail Andrassy* ■ *Dir* Charles Barton • *Scr* Bill Walsh, Lillie Hayward, from the novel *The Hound of Florence* by Felix Salten

Shaheed ★★★

Political melodrama
1948 · Ind · BW · 164mins

Set in the final days of the Raj, this outspoken drama focuses on the tensions placed on the already strained relationship between a mandarin in the imperial civil service and his freedom fighter son, when the latter is charged with a political killing. Director Ramesh Saigal tackles the thorny subject of divided loyalties with restraint, considering that he had been forced to abandon his native Punjab the previous year after it became part of Pakistan. The intelligent performances of matinée idol Dilip Kumar and Chandra Mohan ensure the action never descends into melodrama. DP. In Urdu and Hindi with English subtitles.

Dilip Kumar • Kamini Kaushal • Chandra Mohan ■ *Dir* Ramesh Saigal • *Scr* Ramesh Saigal, Qamar Jalalabadi, from a story by Ramesh Saigal

Shai'r ★★★ U

Comedy 1949 · Ind · BW · 135mins

Fuelled by caprice, confusion and coincidence, the *masala* musical melodramas produced by the studios of Bombay (Bollywood) are something of an acquired taste. But if you can forgive the plot contrivances and cope with the highly individual musical style, there is much to enjoy in lively extravaganzas like this popular story about a poet who loves a singer, unaware of the effect he has on an innocent country girl. It may not be one of the best films made by future pin-up Dev Anand or former child star Suraiya, but it's a fair starting point for the uninitiated. DP. In Urdu and Hindi with English subtitles.

Dev Anand • Kamini Kashai • Suraiya ■ *Dir* Chawla

Shake Hands with the Devil ★★★

Political drama 1959 · Ire/US · BW · 110mins

A distinguished cast of British and Irish actors, plus American Don Murray, bolster James Cagney in this somewhat grim and melodramatic but well-made mix of politics, romance, and violence. Cagney is a professor of medicine in 1921 Dublin, whose respectability is a cover for his IRA activities. When his student Murray, an Irish-American, is beaten up by British officers, a vengeful Cagney abducts the daughter (Dana Wynter) of a British functionary. A provocative, if undeveloped proposition. RK

James Cagney *Sean Lenihan* • Don Murray *Kerry O'Shea* • Dana Wynter *Jennifer Curtis* • Glynis Johns *Kitty Brady* • Michael Redgrave *The General* • Sybil Thorndike *Lady Fitzhugh* • Cyril Cusack *Chris Noonan* • Marianne Benet *Mary Madigan* ■ *Dir* Michael Anderson • *Scr* Ben Roberts, Marian Thompson, Ivan Goff, from the novel by Rearden Conner

Shake, Rattle and Rock! ★★★ PG

Drama 1957 · US · BW · 75mins

Quintessential viewing for rock 'n' roll fans and a key film of its era. Plotwise it's the usual stuff about a town's parents at odds with the new music craze. What makes it worth watching is the music. Highlights include the legendary Joe Turner performing *Lipstick, Powder and Paint* and the great Fats Domino belting out *I'm in Love Again* and the fabulous *Ain't That a Shame*. The cast is headed by Touch Connors, who as Mike Connors achieved stardom of sorts in the TV series *Mannix*. TS DVD

Touch Connors [Mike Connors] *Garry Nelson* • Lisa Gaye *June* • Sterling Holloway *Axe* • Margaret Dumont *Georgianna* • Douglass Dumbrille *Eustace* ■ *Dir* Edward L Cahn • *Scr* Lou Rusoff

Shake, Rattle and Rock ★★★ PG

Drama 1994 · US · Colour · 79mins

Part of a series of TV remakes of 1950s B-movies, this is a slight but affectionate take on that old staple, the teen musical. Howie Mandel has a ball as a rebel with a cause allowing teenagers to get down to the rock 'n' roll music hated by their conservative elders. The eclectic cast includes Renee Zellweger, Roger Corman regular Dick Miller, singer Ruth Brown and cult icon Mary Woronov. Director Allan Arkush keeps his tongue firmly in his cheek and conjures up the atmosphere of cheerful irreverence. JF. Contains some swearing.

Renee Zellweger *Susan Doyle* • Patricia Childress *Cookie* • Max Perlich *Tony* • Howie Mandel *Danny Klay* • Latanyia Baldwin *Sireena Cooper* • Mary Woronov *Joyce* • Stephen Furst *Frank* • Dick Miller *Officer Miller* • Ruth Brown *Ella* • PJ Soles *Evelyn* ■ *Dir* Allan Arkush • *Scr* Trish Soodik

Shakedown ★★

Crime drama 1950 · US · BW · 80mins

Howard Duff stars as the ambitious and unscrupulous newspaper photographer who uses his skills to blackmail a gangster and, in a neat touch, ends up recording his own downfall. Brian Donlevy and Lawrence Tierney play feuding big shots, with French actress Anne Vernon as Donlevy's loving wife. Former actor Joseph Pevney makes a solid job of directing his first film and also appears very briefly as a reporter. Rock Hudson can be glimpsed in a bit part. AE

Howard Duff *Jack Early* • Brian Donlevy *Nick Palmer* • Peggy Dow *Ellen Bennett* • Lawrence Tierney *Colton* • Bruce Bennett *David Glover* • Anne Vernon *Lita Palmer* • Rock Hudson ■ *Dir* Joe Pevney [Joseph Pevney] • *Scr* Alfred Lewis Levitt, Martin Goldsmith, from a story by Nat Dallinger, Don Martin

The Shakedown ★★

Crime drama 1959 · UK · BW · 91mins

Terence Morgan plays a photographer with an eye for extortion in this film that sets out to shock with sleazy settings and sensationalist suggestions of nudity. However, few of the misdemeanours from this period piece would raise even a blush today. Director John Lemont forgets to concentrate on the storyline, which grinds to its inevitable conclusion. DP

Terence Morgan *Augie Cortona* • Hazel Court *Mildred* • Donald Pleasence *Jessel* • Bill Owen *Spettigue* • Robert Beatty *Inspector Jarvis* • Harry H Corbett *Gollar* • Gene Anderson *Zena* • Eddie Byrne *George* ■ *Dir* John Lemont • *Scr* John Lemont, Leigh Vance

Shaker Run ★★ 15

Thriller 1985 · NZ · Colour · 86mins

Lush New Zealand landscape emphasises the clichéd inanity and inadequacy of this car-chase melodrama in whch Cliff Robertson and Leif Garrett are two American stunt drivers helping a naive girl (Lisa Harrow) transport a deadly virus cross-country. Crashes and pursuits are beautifully shot by director Bruce Morrison, but otherwise, it's totally predictable. TH

Cliff Robertson *Judd Pierson* • Leif Garrett *Casey Lee* • Lisa Harrow *Dr Christine Rubin* • Shane Briant *Paul Thoreau* • Peter Hayden *Michael Connolly* ■ *Dir* Bruce Morrison • *Scr* James Kouf Jr, Henry Fownes, Bruce Morrison

Shakes the Clown ★★ 18

Comedy 1991 · US · Colour · 82mins

Stand-up comedian Bobcat Goldthwait exploits the sinister side of the classic circus clown, writing, directing and starring in this bizarre, harsh fantasy. Set in the mythical town of Palukaville, Goldthwait is the eponymous Shakes, an alcoholic clown and regular barfly. When his boss, the clown dispatcher, is found murdered Shakes is the prime suspect. In the end, this is more funny peculiar than funny ha-ha. DF. Contains swearing and drug abuse.

Bobcat Goldthwait *Shakes the Clown* • Julie Brown *Judy* • Bruce Baum *Ty the Rodeo Clown* • Blake Clark *Stenchy the Clown* • Paul Dooley *Owen Cheese* • Marty Fromage [Robin Williams] *Mime Jerry* • Florence Henderson *The Unknown Woman* • Tom Kenny *Binky the Clown* • Sydney Lassick *Peppy the Clown* • Adam Sandler *Dink the Clown* ■ *Dir/Scr* Bobcat Goldthwait

Shakespeare in Love ★★★★★ 15

Period romantic comedy
1998 · US · Colour · 118mins

Taking the writing process behind Shakespeare's *Romeo and Juliet* as its inspiration, John Madden's film combines contemporary humour with a convincing 16th-century setting. Young Will (Joseph Fiennes) falls for the soon-to-be-married Viola (Gwyneth Paltrow) and casts her, disguised as a boy, as his Romeo. As their love affair unfolds, so does the play in a film that is passionate, intelligent and hysterically funny in turns. Fiennes and Paltrow are supported by an outstanding cast that includes Geoffrey Rush, Tom Wilkinson and Colin Firth, while Judi Dench delivers an Oscar-winning portrayal of Elizabeth I. LH. Contains sex scenes. DVD

Gwyneth Paltrow *Viola De Lesseps* • Joseph Fiennes *Will Shakespeare* • Colin Firth *Lord Wessex* • Geoffrey Rush *Philip Henslowe* • Judi Dench *Queen Elizabeth* • Tom Wilkinson *Hugh Fennyman* • Ben Affleck *Ned Alleyn* • Simon Callow *Tilney, Master of the Revels* • Jim Carter *Ralph Bashford* • Martin Clunes *Richard Burbage* • Imelda Staunton *Nurse* • Rupert Everett *Christopher Marlowe* ■ *Dir* John Madden • *Scr* Marc Norman, Tom Stoppard • *Cinematographer* Richard Greatrex • *Costume Designer* Sandy Powell • *Art Director* Martin Childs, Jill Quertier • *Music* Stephen Warbeck

Shakespeare Wallah ★★★ PG

Romantic drama 1965 · Ind · BW · 122mins

With its gentle pacing and keen eye for atmospheric detail, anyone seeing this delightful film for the first time could be forgiven for thinking it had been directed by Satyajit Ray. But while he provided both the score and the cinematographer (Subrata Mitra), this tale of strolling players was, in fact, the second collaboration between Merchant Ivory and screenwriter Ruth Prawer Jhabvala. Based on their own experiences performing the Bard around the subcontinent, Geoffrey and Felicity Kendal effortlessly avoid condescension, while Shashi Kapoor is suitably dashing as Felicity's culture-crossed lover. But no one stands a chance alongside Madhur Jaffrey's hilarious Bollywood bitch. DP DVD

Shashi Kapoor *Sanju* • Felicity Kendal *Lizzie Buckingham* • Madhur Jaffrey *Manjula* • Geoffrey Kendal *Tony Buckingham* • Laura Liddell *Carla Buckingham* • Utpal Dutt *The Maharajah* ■ *Dir* James Ivory • *Scr* Ruth Prawer Jhabvala, James Ivory • *Producer* Ismail Merchant

The Shakiest Gun in the West ★★ U

Comedy western
1967 · US · Colour · 100mins

Don Knotts steps into the shoes first worn by Bob Hope in this feeble reworking of that classic comedy western *The Paleface*. Never one to underplay when some shameless mugging will do, the ever-nervous Knotts overcooks every gag. However, this story of the dentist mistaken for a gunfighter isn't entirely as painful as root-canal surgery. DP.

Don Knotts *Jesse W Haywood* • Barbara Rhoades *Penelope Cushings* • Jackie Coogan *Matthew Basch* • Don "Red" Barry [Donald Barry] *Reverend Zachary Grant* • Ruth McDevitt *Olive* • Frank McGrath *Mr Remington* ■ *Dir* Alan Rafkin • *Scr* Jim Fritzell, Everett Greenbaum, from the film *The Paleface* by Frank Tashlin, Edmund Hartmann [Edmund L Hartmann]

Shaking the Tree ★★ 15

Drama 1990 · US · Colour · 102mins

A retread of over-familiar territory, as a bunch of Chicago pals, all from differing backgrounds and circumstances, come together to make the collective transition from wild youth to responsible adulthood. There are the usual trials and tribulations en route – getting married, paying off gambling debts, adultery – and it's well enough acted, but a po-faced approach does the film no favours. DA. Contains swearing.

Arye Gross *Barry* • Gale Hansen *John "Sully" Sullivan* • Doug Savant *Michael* • Steven Wilde *Terry "Duke" Keegan* • Courteney Cox *Kathleen* • Christina Haag *Michelle* ■ *Dir* Duane Clark • *Scr* Duane Clark, Steven Wilde

Shakti – the Power ★★★ 15

Musical drama 2002 · Ind · Colour · 174mins

The Sally Field vehicle, *Not without My Daughter*, is the inspiration for Krishna Vamsi's tale of clashing cultures, which calls into question the validity of

S

including musical numbers in even the most politically charged Bollywood features. Granted, rising superstar Aishwarya Rai excels in her dance routine and Shah Rukh Khan makes an impact with his heroic cameo appearance. But the songs undoubtedly distract from Karishma Kapoor's plight, as she seeks to return to California with her young son after discovering, while on a visit to India, that husband Sanjay Kapoor's family are involved in terrorism. DP. In Hindi with English subtitles. [video] DVD

Karishma Kapoor *Nandini* • Nana Patekar *Narsimha* • Sanjay Kapoor *Shekhar* • Shah Rukh Khan *Guide* • Deepti Naval *Narsimha's wife* • Aishwarya Rai ■ *Dir/Scr* Krishna Vamsi

Shalako ★★ PG

Western 1968 · UK · Colour · 112mins

Sean Connery and Brigitte Bardot are screen icons well adrift out west in this would-be epic western, though geographically they are not so far from their respective manors since it was filmed entirely in Spain. Despite director Edward Dmytryk in the saddle, this is a slow-moving, high-camp fiasco. Connery (playing a cowboy) and Bardot (an aristocrat) are not alone in being oddly cast, as British actors Jack Hawkins and Eric Sykes also look like fish out of water. TS [video] DVD

Sean Connery *Shalako* • Brigitte Bardot *Countess Irina Lazaar* • Stephen Boyd *Bosky Fulton* • Jack Hawkins *Sir Charles Daggett* • Peter Van Eyck *Frederick von Hallstatt* • Honor Blackman *Lady Julia Daggett* • Woody Strode *Chato* • Eric Sykes *Mako* • Alexander Knox *Henry Clarke* • Valerie French *Elena Clarke* ■ *Dir* Edward Dmytryk • *Scr* JJ Griffith, Hal Hopper, Scot Finch, from a story by Clarke Reynolds, from the novel by Louis L'Amour

Shall We Dance ★★★ U

Musical comedy 1937 · US · BW · 103mins

This is a particularly silly Fred Astaire/ Ginger Rogers movie, with him chasing her across the Atlantic. He's a Russian ballet dancer, and there's a chorus of cardboard Ginger cut-outs at the finale. Forget the daftness and enjoy the wonderful George and Ira Gershwin score, especially *They Can't Take That Away from Me*. TS [video]

Fred Astaire *Petrov/Pete Peters* • Ginger Rogers *Linda Keene* • Edward Everett Horton *Jeffrey Baird* • Eric Blore *Cecil Flintridge* • Jerome Cowan *Arthur Miller* • Ketti Gallian *Lady Tarrington* ■ *Dir* Mark Sandrich • *Scr* Allan Scott, Ernest Pagano, PJ Wolfson, from the story *Watch Your Step* by Lee Loeb, Harold Buchman

Shall We Dance? ★★★★ PG

Romantic comedy drama
1995 · Jpn · Colour · 114mins

Koji Yakusho exudes a salaryman dignity worthy of Chishu Ryu in this acute study of social embarrassment, Japanese style. Having established the tyranny of national reserve, Masayuki Suo presents Tamiyo Kusakari's ballroom dancing studio as a foreign sanctuary, in which inhibition succumbs to the illicit sensuality and liberating grace of the rhythm. Making a delicious contrast to the timid Yakusho and the melancholic Kusakari (who once lost a big competition in Blackpool) is Naoto Takenaka, the office nobody who is transformed into a rumba monster by his macho wig and tight duds. DP. In Japanese with English subtitles. [video] DVD

Koji Yakusho *Shohei Sugiyama* • Tamiyo Kusakari *Mai Kishikawa* • Naoto Takenaka *Tomio Aoki* • Eriko Watanabe *Toyoko Takahashi* ■ *Dir/Scr* Masayuki Suo

Shall We Dance ★★ 12

Romantic comedy drama
2004 · US/Can · Colour · 101mins

In westernising Masayuki Suo's 1995 dance-floor delight, this insipid remake loses the warmth and wry social observation that gave the original its appeal. To his credit, Richard Gere makes a charming lead, playing a jaded Chicago lawyer who secretly takes up ballroom dancing lessons. Unfortunately, the casting of Jennifer Lopez as his dance instructor is where the film falls down. Her miserable demeanour is a real downer in a tale that's meant to be light and frothy. SF. Contains swearing. [video] DVD

Richard Gere *John Clark* • Jennifer Lopez *Paulina* • Susan Sarandon *Beverly Clark* • Stanley Tucci *Link Peterson* • Bobby Cannavale *Chic* • Lisa Ann Walter *Bobbie* • Omar Miller [Omar Benson Miller] *Vern* • Richard Jenkins *Devine* ■ *Dir* Peter Chelsom • *Scr* Audrey Wells, from the film by Masayuki Suo

Shallow Grave ★★★★★ 18

Black comedy 1994 · UK · Colour · 88mins

This incredibly slick and inventive and, at times, gruesome thriller, owes a great deal to the Coen brothers' *Blood Simple*. It starts with a dead body and a stash of money lying in a huge flat. The deceased man's flatmates decide to dismember and dispose of the corpse. Things go slightly haywire after that. Director Danny Boyle's picture bursts with energy and springs some deliciously macabre surprises. Especially brilliant are the use of the cavernous flat and city locations and the performances from Kerry Fox, Christopher Eccleston and Ewan McGregor who are all outwardly ordinary, inwardly strange. Deservedly a box-office smash everywhere, it gave a much-needed shot in the arm to a British film industry preoccupied by Jane Austen. AT. Contains violence, swearing and nudity. [video] DVD

Kerry Fox *Juliet Miller* • Christopher Eccleston *David Stephens* • Ewan McGregor *Alex Law* • Ken Stott *Detective Inspector McCall* • Keith Allen *Hugo* • Colin McCredie *Cameron* ■ *Dir* Danny Boyle • *Scr* John Hodge

Shallow Ground ★★ 18

Horror 2004 · US · Colour · 96mins

A naked boy covered in blood carrying a knife appears at a rural American police station on the eve of it closing down for good. Has Sheriff Timothy V Murphy finally discovered the serial killer who has haunting his time in office? Something much more supernaturally sinister is going on and that's the problem with director Sheldon Wilson's micro-budget shocker. Initially keenly atmospheric, his chiller over-reaches itself without the resources to do its "Big Idea" justice. AJ. Contains violence and nudity.

Timothy V Murphy *Sheriff Jack Sheppard* • Stan Kirsch *Deputy Stuart Dempsey* • Lindsey Stoddart *Deputy Laura Russell* • Patty McCormack *Helen Reedy* • Rocky Marquette *The Boy* • Natalie Avital *Darby Owens* • Steve Easton *Detective Russell* • John Kapelos *LeRoy Riley* ■ *Dir/Scr* Sheldon Wilson

Shallow Hal ★★★ 12

Romantic comedy
2001 · US/Ger · Colour · 109mins

Gwyneth Paltrow dons a fat suit in this comedy from the Farrelly Brothers. Prepare to be mildly offended (and intermittently amused) as Jack Black plays a man who only goes for the most attractive of gals, which in his mind means the slender, supermodel type. That is until he's hypnotised by motivational speaker Tony Robbins into only seeing a woman's inner beauty. Black then finds himself falling for sweet-natured but hefty Paltrow. Surprisingly tame, this is more romance than comedy. JB. Contains swearing. [video] DVD

Gwyneth Paltrow *Rosemary Shanahan* • Jack Black *Hal Larson* • Jason Alexander *Mauricio* • Joe Viterelli *Steve Shanahan* • Rene Kirby *Walt* • Bruce McGill *Reverend Larson* • Tony Robbins ■ *Dir* Bobby Farrelly, Peter Farrelly • *Scr* Sean Moynihan, Bobby Farrelly, Peter Farrelly

Shame ★★★★ 12

Drama 1968 · Swe · BW · 98mins

Apolitical concert violinists Max von Sydow and Liv Ullmann take refuge on a remote island but are dragged back into society when civil war soldiers arrive in huge numbers. As loyalties shift around a corrupt, quisling colonel (Gunnar Björnstrand), Ullmann's strength and tenderness come to the fore, while von Sydow turns into a selfish, immature, treacherous coward. Rigorously played and staged as a hideously realistic nightmare, this is a chilling vision of a world without beauty, trust or love. DP. In Swedish with English subtitles. DVD

Liv Ullmann *Eva Rosenberg* • Max von Sydow *Jan Rosenberg* • Gunnar Björnstrand *Colonel Jacobi* • Sigge Furst *Filip* • Birgitta Valberg *Mrs Jacobi* ■ *Dir/Scr* Ingmar Bergman

Shame ★★★★ 15

Drama 1987 · Aus · Colour · 89mins

Released in the same year as the more sensationalised *The Accused*, this is a more down-to-earth, responsible and raw look at the subject of gang rape. Deborra-Lee Furness is the barrister whose bike breaks down in the Australian outback, where she meets rape victim Simone Buchanan. Standing up against the male-led community who believe the girl asked for it, the lawyer takes on her case, battling not only the criminal who must be brought to justice but the prejudices of the town. Excellent, restrained performances turn this into a powerful piece of cinema. Remade in 1992 as an American TV movie, followed by a sequel, starring Amanda Donohoe. JB [video]

Deborra-Lee Furness *Asta Cadell* • Tony Barry *Tim Curtis* • Simone Buchanan *Lizzie Curtis* • Gillian Jones *Tina Farrel* • Peter Aanensen *Sergeant Wal Cuddy* • Margaret Ford *Norma Curtis* ■ *Dir* Steve Jodrell • *Scr* Beverly Blankenship, Michael Brindley

Shampoo ★★★ 18

Comedy 1975 · US · Colour · 105mins

This one-time *succès de scandale* grossed more than $60 million at the box office in its day. While it is delightfully amoral, producer, co-writer and star Warren Beatty never quite pulled his themes together. Nevertheless, there are striking moments, not least of which is Julie Christie's now classic appearance at a memorable dinner table. The model for Beatty's crimper was widely believed to be Jon Peters, but was actually Jay Sebring, who was killed in the Sharon Tate massacre. TS. Contains swearing and nudity. [video] DVD

Warren Beatty *George Roundy* • Julie Christie *Jackie Shawn* • Goldie Hawn *Jill* • Lee Grant *Felicia Carr* • Jack Warden *Lester Carr* • Tony Bill *Johnny Pope* • Carrie Fisher *Lorna Carr* • Jay Robinson *Norman* ■ *Dir* Hal Ashby • *Scr* Warren Beatty, Robert Towne

Shamus ★★★ 18

Comedy thriller 1973 · US · Colour · 94mins

Violent (by 1970s standards), fast-moving, if not very original, this Burt Reynolds vehicle was stylishly directed on New York locations by thriller specialist Buzz Kulik. Reynolds is well cast here as the tough-as-nails Brooklyn private eye who gets called in by a tycoon to find some stolen diamonds. There's some terrific character work along the way and Dyan Cannon is particularly fine as the moll in the tale. TS. Contains swearing. [video]

Burt Reynolds *Shamus McCoy* • Dyan Cannon *Alexis Montaigne* • John Ryan [John P Ryan] *Colonel Hardcore* • Joe Santos *Lieutenant Promuto* • Giorgio Tozzi *Il Dottore* • Ron Weyland *EJ Hume* • Larry Block *Springy* ■ *Dir* Buzz Kulik • *Scr* Barry Beckerman

Shane ★★★★★ PG

Classic western 1953 · US · Colour · 112mins

A marvellous distillation of all that is fine about Hollywood cinema, this is a revelation, sweeping you up via magnificent editing and Loyal Griggs's Technicolor photography into a tale of a man, a woman and, especially, a boy, whose lives are changed by the man dressed in buckskin who rides on to their farm. Alan Ladd gives the performance of a lifetime in the title role, and the rest of the cast is also impeccable, notably Jean Arthur as the married woman whose relationship with Shane is subtly understated. Victor Young's majestic main theme lingers long after the movie is over. Directed by the great George Stevens, this is one of the finest American motion pictures, brilliantly constructed and beautifully filmed. TS [video] DVD

Alan Ladd *Shane* • Jean Arthur *Marion Starrett* • Van Heflin *Joe Starrett* • Brandon de Wilde *Joey Starrett* • Jack Palance *Wilson* • Ben Johnson *Chris* • Edgar Buchanan *Lewis* • Emile Meyer *Ryker* • Elisha Cook Jr *Torrey* • Douglas Spencer *Mr Shipstead* • John Dierkes *Morgan* • Ellen Corby *Mrs Torrey* ■ *Dir* George Stevens • *Scr* AB Guthrie Jr, Jack Sher, from the novel by Jack Schaefer • *Cinematographer* Loyal Griggs

The Shanghai Cobra ★★ PG

Mystery 1945 · US · BW · 62mins

Cobra venom in a jukebox proves the key to this case of a murdered banker. But before Sidney Toler can nab a killer he first encountered a decade earlier, he must first risk the nation's radium supply. Phil Karlson brings an effective *noir*ish feel to proceedings that had increasingly become sidetracked by the antics of Mantan Moreland's chauffeur and "Number Three Son", Benson Fong. Addison Richards and Arthur Loft lend better than usual support. DP DVD

Sidney Toler *Charlie Chan* • Mantan Moreland *Birmingham Brown* • Benson Fong *Tommy Chan* • James Cardwell *Ned Stewart* • Joan Barclay *Paula* • Addison Richards *John Adams/Jan Van Horn* • Arthur Loft *Bradford Harris* ■ *Dir* Phil Karlson • *Scr* George Callahan, George Wallace Sayre, from a story by George Callahan, from characters created by Earl Derr Biggers

S

Shanghai Express ★★★★ PG

Romantic drama 1932 · US · BW · 88mins

The fourth collaboration between Marlene Dietrich and director Josef von Sternberg, this arch melodrama divides audiences. Fans love its exotic lighting (cinematographer Lee Garmes won an Oscar) and its clever, intimate use of confined space; detractors laugh at its high camp histrionics and its ludicrous (but stylish) plot and satirically ridiculous dialogue. This 1930s hokum is immensely enjoyable, as notorious hooker Dietrich is amazingly reunited with her former true love Clive Brook (characteristically wooden but well cast) aboard the titular train that's hijacked by brigand Warner Oland. TS [video]

Marlene Dietrich *Shanghai Lily* • Clive Brook *Captain Donald "Doc" Harvey* • Anna May Wong *Hui Fei* • Warner Oland *Henry Chang* • Eugene Pallette *Sam Salt* • Lawrence Grant *Reverend Carmichael* • Louise Closser Hale *Mrs Haggerty* • Gustav von Seyffertitz *Eric*

Baum • Emile Chautard *Major Lenard* ■ *Dir* Josef von Sternberg • *Scr* Jules Furthman, from a story by Harry Hervey

The Shanghai Gesture ★★★★★

Melodrama 1941 · US · BW · 98mins

Gene Tierney is at her loveliest as the spoilt rich girl who, using an alias, enters a Shanghai casino and is seduced by its "incredibly evil" atmosphere, unaware that her entrepreneur dad (Walter Huston) is intent on closing down the iniquitous establishment, domain of the glacial "Mother" Gin Sling (Ona Munson in a series of lacquered, Medusa-like wigs). Director Josef von Sternberg was forced to sanitise his adaptation of John Colton's stage play, but his vision suggestively offers more than the salacious detail he was forced to cut from the script. The film's masterful use of musical rhythms, stylised dialogue and close-ups makes it a high point from the studio age. DO

Gene Tierney *Victoria Charteris/Poppy Smith* • Walter Huston *Sir Guy Charteris* • Victor Mature *Doctor Omar* • Ona Munson *"Mother" Gin Sling* • Phyllis Brooks *Dixie Pomeroy, the chorus girl* • Albert Basserman *Commissioner* • Maria Ouspenskaya *Amah* • Eric Blore *Caesar Hawkins, the bookkeeper* • Mike Mazurki *Coolie* • Marcel Dalio *Master of the spinning wheel* ■ *Dir* Josef von Sternberg • *Scr* Josef von Sternberg, Geza Herczeg, Jules Furthman, Kurt Vollmoeller, from the play by John Colton • *Cinematographer* Paul Ivano

Shanghai Knights ★★★ 12

Period action comedy
2002 · US · Colour · 109mins

Jackie Chan's Chinese sheriff and Owen Wilson's slacker outlaw reteam and relocate to what is meant to be Victorian London (actually Prague) for this spry sequel to the immensely successful action comedy *Shanghai Noon*. After a brisk intro involving the theft of an Imperial seal and the murder of Chan's father, the action slows a little so they can plod through some unimaginative gags about the English. However, Chan's action sequences are as spectacularly inventive and meticulously choreographed as ever. AS DVD

Jackie Chan *Chon Wang* • Owen Wilson *Roy O'Bannon* • Aaron Johnson *Charlie* • Thomas Fisher *Artie Doyle* • Aidan Gillen *Lord Rathbone* • Fann Wong *Chon Lin* • Donnie Yen *Wu Chan* ■ *Dir* David Dobkin • *Scr* Alfred Gough, Miles Millar, from their characters

Shanghai Madness ★★

Adventure 1933 · US · BW · 64mins

Adrift in Shanghai after being dishonorably dismissed from the US Navy, former lieutenant Spencer Tracy finds work on a boat carrying guns to the Mandarin government. This ship is also transporting stowaway Fay Wray whose life Tracy saved ashore and who has taken a fancy to him. The boat is attacked by Communists, allowing Tracy the requisite heroics to rescue his reputation. An undemanding but efficient enough formula adventure. RK

Spencer Tracy *Lt Pat Jackson* • Fay Wray *Wildeth Christie* • Ralph Morgan *Li Po Chang* • Eugene Pallette *Capt Lobo Lornegan* • Herbert Mundin *Third Officer Jones* • Reginald Mason *William Christie* • Arthur Hoyt *Van Emery* ■ *Dir* John Blystone [John G Blystone] • *Scr* Austin Parker, from the short story by Frederick Hazlitt Brennan

Shanghai Noon ★★★ 12

Western action comedy
2000 · US · Colour · 105mins

Visually authentic and deliciously anachronistic, this period western from martial arts maestro Jackie Chan is a hugely enjoyable combination of buddy comedy and adventure. Sent to the States to rescue kidnapped princess Lucy Liu, Chan's Imperial Palace guard hooks up with outlaw Owen Wilson, who proves to be his equal in the fish-out-of-water stakes. Using antlers, sheriff's badges and horseshoes to prise himself out of a tight corner, Chan is pure slapstick poetry in motion: falling off horses, getting drunk and confusing slave-owning louse Roger Yuan and corrupt sheriff Xander Berkeley. DP DVD

Jackie Chan *Chon Wang* • Owen Wilson *Roy O'Bannon* • Lucy Liu *Princess Pei Pei* • Brandon Merrill *Indian wife* • Roger Yuan *Lo Fong* • Xander Berkeley *Van Cleef* • Walton Goggins *Wallace* • Jason Connery *Andrews* ■ *Dir* Tom Dey • *Scr* Miles Millar, Alfred Gough

The Shanghai Story ★★

Spy drama 1954 · US · BW · 90mins

Edmond O'Brien is an American doctor imprisoned with other foreigners in a Shanghai hotel by Marvin Miller's police chief who's seeking to identify a western spy believed to be among them. As the mysterious woman who's friendly with both sides, Ruth Roman fails to add any spice to the drawn-out proceedings. AE

Ruth Roman *Rita King* • Edmond O'Brien *Dr Dan Maynard* • Richard Jaeckel *"Knuckles" Greer* • Barry Kelley *Ricki Dolmine* • Whit Bissell *Paul Grant* • Basil Ruysdael *Reverend Hollingsworth* • Marvin Miller *Colonel Zorek* ■ *Dir* Frank Lloyd • *Scr* Seton I Miller, Steve Fisher, from a story by Lester Yard

Shanghai Surprise ★ 15

Period adventure 1986 · UK · Colour · 92mins

Madonna is ludicrously miscast here, playing a peroxide-blonde missionary looking for stolen opium in pre-Second World War China (to put to good use in hospitals, of course). Her then husband Sean Penn is OK as the rogue salesman she hires to help her acquire the vast stash. Otherwise, director Jim Goddard's heavy-handed and over-inflated screwball adventure is desperately seeking laughs at every vulgar turn and is woefully short of the madcap antics that go to define the genre. A witless embarrassment. AJ. Contains swearing and brief nudity.

Sean Penn *Glendon Wasey* • Madonna *Gloria Tatlock* • Paul Freeman *Walter Faraday* • Richard Griffiths *Willie Tuttle* • Philip Sayer *Justin Kronk* • Clyde Kusatsu *Joe Go* • Lim Kay Tong *Mei Gan* • Sonserai Lee *China Doll* • Michael Aldridge *Mr Burns* • George Harrison *Night club singer* ■ *Dir* Jim Goddard • *Scr* John Kohn, Robert Bentley, from the novel *Faraday's Flowers* by Tony Kenrick

Shanghai Triad ★★★ 15

Crime drama 1995 · HK/Fr · Colour · 103mins

Longtime companions Gong Li and Zhang Yimou parted during the production of this, their seventh collaboration. As a result, perhaps, this is their least effective picture, with the plot allowed to ramble when swift, *noir*ish strokes would have heightened the tension. But the stunning beauty of both Li and director Zhang's imagery give this an allure. In particular, the teasing sensuality of Li's musical numbers and the sudden realisation that her gangster lover has discovered her deceptions are unforgettable. DP. In Mandarin with English subtitles. Contains violence.

Gong Li *Xiao Jinbao, "Jewel"* • Wang Xiaowing *Shuisheng* • Li Baotian *Gangster* • Li Xuejian *Uncle Liu* ■ *Dir* Zhang Yimou • *Scr* Bi Feiyu, from the novel *Men Gui [Gang Law]* by Li Xiao

Shanks ★★

Horror comedy 1974 · US · Colour · 93mins

An extremely offbeat horror-comedy, this is the last film directed by William Castle, a showman often attracted to horror, comedy and gimmicks, but never with such bizarre results as here. It marked virtually the beginning and end of Marcel Marceau's screen career. The world's most famous mime doesn't speak in his role as a puppeteer bequeathed a gadget that brings the dead back to life. The section where Marceau learns how to animate corpses (played by other mime artists) is very funny, but much of the rest looks contrived. DM

Marcel Marceau *Malcolm Shanks/Old Walker* • Tsilla Chelton *Mrs Barton* • Philippe Clay *Mr Barton* • Cindy Eilbacher *Celia* • Larry Bishop *Napoleon* • William Castle *Grocer* ■ *Dir* William Castle • *Scr* Ranald Graham

Shannon's Deal ★★★★

Drama 1989 · US · Colour · 95mins

Writer/director John Sayles generally adds flavour to even his smallest characters and creates the power of suggestion through dialogue. Writing for director Lewis Teague, Sayles transforms what could so easily have been a trawl through inanity and cliché into a work of edgy, dramatic clout. He takes the gumshoe genre and puts his own spin on events, and lifts it considerably. The insinuating, unnerving score by Wynton Marsalis for this TV pilot perfectly matches the psychology of the key character. JM

Jamey Sheridan *Jack Shannon* • Elizabeth Peña *Lucy Acosta* • Jenny Lewis *Neala Shannon* • Miguel Ferrer *Todd Snyder* • Stefan Gierasch *Klaus* ■ *Dir* Lewis Teague • *Scr* John Sayles

Shaolin Soccer ★★★ 12

Sports action comedy
2001 · HK/Chi/US · Colour · 85mins

Stephen Chow turns to football in this cartoonish underdog comedy, which broke box-office records in his native Hong Kong. The action centres on the efforts of Ng Man Tat's disgraced, disabled ex-pro teaming with Chow's Shaolin monk to coach a side capable of defeating Patrick Tse's team of ruthless over-achievers. The action is everything here, although Chow also tosses in some ingenious effects, the odd movie parody and several throwaway in-jokes. The result is fast, furious fun. DP. Cantonese dialogue dubbed into English. DVD

Stephen Chow *Sing* • Vicki Zhao [Zhao Wei] *Mui* • Ng Man Tat *Golden Leg Fung* • Patrick Tse *Hung* • Wong Yat Fei *Iron Head* ■ *Dir* Stephen Chow • *Scr* Stephen Chow, Tsang Kan-Cheung

The Shape of Things ★★ 15

Drama 2003 · US/Fr/UK · Colour · 92mins

Misanthropy and psychological violence have been Neil LaBute's stock in trade ever since his impressive debut, *In the Company of Men*. This serves up yet another helping of the formula, but sadly the result is not so much shocking as silly. Paul Rudd plays a geeky student given a makeover by his radical artist girlfriend Rachel Weisz, but her intentions are not what they seem. The mind games that ensue drag in Rudd's friends Gretchen Mol and Frederick Weller and expose tensions in their relationship. The theatricality of the dialogue is a distraction from the frankly implausible plot. AS DVD

Gretchen Mol *Jenny* • Paul Rudd *Adam* • Rachel Weisz *Evelyn* • Frederick Weller *Philip* ■ *Dir* Neil LaBute • *Scr* Neil LaBute, from his play

Sharaz ★★

Adventure 1968 · Sp/It · Colour · 92mins

This spot of Eastern delight in a Spanish setting is so teeth-grindingly awful that it becomes well worth watching for a laugh. Take one son of the Sultan of Granada, one dastardly interloper, one flashing female genie, a loyal slave who badly needs to raise his political consciousness and stew well with a phalanx of Spanish extras all dressed to the nines and bumping into each other. SH. Spanish dialogue dubbed into English.

Jeff Cooper *Omar* • Luciana Paluzzi *Sharaz* • Raf Vallone *Hixem* • Perla Cristal *"Favourite"* ■ *Dir* Joe Lacy

Shark! ★ 15

Action drama
1969 · US/Mex · Colour · 88mins

This watery tale about underwater treasure that cast barely a ripple – except for a public row between the producers and director Sam Fuller who wanted his name removed from the credits, claiming the film had been re-edited against his will. Fuller's army of fans accepted this, overlooking the fact that in 1967 Fuller was reduced to making dime-budget stuff in Mexico to pay the rent. The movie spent three years on the shelf only seeing the light of day when Burt Reynolds became a major box-office draw. AT DVD

Burt Reynolds *Caine* • Barry Sullivan *Mallare* • Arthur Kennedy *Doc* • Silvia Pinal *Anna* • Enrique Lucero *Barok* ■ *Dir* Samuel Fuller • *Scr* Samuel Fuller, John Kingsbridge, from the novel *His Bones Are Coral* by Victor Canning

Shark Attack ★★★ 15

Horror thriller 1999 · US · Colour · 91mins

Investigating a series of shark attacks, marine biologist Casper Van Dien discovers something fishy in the waters off the coast of Africa. This video fodder is a very long way from the expertly created suspense of its ultimate inspiration, *Jaws*. But, for a B picture, it is ambitious – fast moving, packed with spectacular shark effects and shot on rarely seen, picturesque South African locations. It has spawned two sequels to date. DM DVD

Casper Van Dien *Steven McKray* • Ernie Hudson *Laurence Rhodes* • Bentley Mitchum *Dr Miles Craven* • Jenny McShane *Corinne DeSantis* • Tony Caprari *Mani* ■ *Dir* Bob Misiorowski • *Scr* Scott Devine, William Hooke

Shark Tale ★★★ U

Animated comedy adventure
2004 · US · Colour · 86mins

A thinly disguised morality lesson, this family comedy from DreamWorks tells the tale of a celebrity-obsessed fish (voiced by Will Smith) who masquerades as a shark-killing hero with the aid of a vegetarian great white (Jack Black). The film is kept buoyant by irreverent humour and some adult-friendly movie skits. The sea life looks rather charmless, but the voice casting shows more imagination, with Robert De Niro's Mafioso shark and Martin Scorsese's crooked puffer fish both delightfully memorable. SF DVD

Will Smith *Oscar* • Robert De Niro *Don Lino* • Renée Zellweger [Renee Zellweger] *Angie* • Jack Black *Lenny* • Angelina Jolie *Lola* • Martin Scorsese *Sykes* • Peter Falk *Don Brizzi* • Michael Imperioli *Frankie* ■ *Dir* Eric "Bibo" Bergeron, Vicky Jenson, Rob Letterman • *Scr* Michael J Wilson, Rob Letterman

Shark's Treasure ★★ PG

Adventure 1975 · US · Colour · 91mins

For all its trendy references to *Jaws*, this feels like a relic of those deadly dull deep-sea diving movies of the 1950s. Apart from the odd shark, the camera only has eyes for Cornel Wilde, which is hardly surprising, considering he also wrote and directed this hokum about a man who sacrifices his beloved boat in the hope of finding buried treasure. Yaphet Kotto provides burly support and Al Giddings's underwater photography is fine. DP

Cornel Wilde *Jim* • Yaphet Kotto *Ben* • John Neilson *Ron* • Cliff Osmond *Lobo* • David Canary *Larry* ■ *Dir/Scr* Cornel Wilde

Sharky's Machine ★★★ 18

Crime thriller 1981 · US · Colour · 116mins

As both director and star, Burt Reynolds proves just a bit too ambitious. His vice cop on the tail of some nasties is not only packed with bull-necked aggression but also has a sensitive interest in woodcarving, while his direction similarly moves abruptly from the overbearing to the light'n'easy and back again. Neither character nor situation is built up enough to obscure the crude joins. However, Burt-the-director has a nifty way with the boisterous action set pieces, in which Burt-the-star is at his best. JM. Contains violence, swearing.

Burt Reynolds *Sharky* • Vittorio Gassman *Victor* • Brian Keith *Papa* • Charles Durning *Friscoe* • Earl Holliman *Hotchkins* • Bernie Casey *Arch* • Henry Silva *Billy Score* • Richard Libertini *Nosh* • Rachel Ward *Dominoe* ■ *Dir* Burt Reynolds • *Scr* Gerald Di Pego, from the novel by William Diehl

Shatter ★

Martial arts action thriller
1974 · UK · Colour · 90mins

When Hammer's horror movies started to bomb at the box-office, the studio forged a short-lived partnership with Hong Kong studios and made kung fu action films, though they stopped short of calling the company Hammer and Tongs. What everyone failed to appreciate was that while Bruce Lee could invade the west, it was a one-way traffic. AT

Stuart Whitman *Shatter* • Peter Cushing *Rattwood* • Ti Lung *Tai Pah* • Anton Diffring *Hans Leber* • Yemi Ajibade *M'Goya* • Huang Pei-Chi *Bodyguard* ■ *Dir* Michael Carreras, Monte Hellman • *Scr* Don Houghton

Shattered ★★★ 15

Thriller 1991 · US · Colour · 93mins

Modern directors show no sign of losing their desire to pay their respects to Alfred Hitchcock, and this intriguing thriller from Wolfgang Petersen succeeds better than most. Tom Berenger wakes up after a horrific car accident with amnesia and attempts to put his life back together again with the help of a private detective (Bob Hoskins); Greta Scacchi is the *femme fatale* who may or may not be trying to kill him. There's a very neat twist at the end, but there are so many bluffs and double bluffs it becomes quite exhausting to follow. JF. Contains swearing, violence and nudity.

Tom Berenger *Dan Merrick* • Bob Hoskins *Gus Klein* • Greta Scacchi *Judith Merrick* • Joanne Whalley-Kilmer [Joanne Whalley] *Jenny Scott* • Corbin Bernsen *Jeb Scott* • Debi A Monahan *Nancy Mercer* ■ *Dir* Wolfgang Petersen • *Scr* Wolfgang Petersen, from the novel *The Plastic Nightmare* by Richard Neely

Shattered Family ★★ PG

Drama based on a true story
1993 · US · Colour · 88mins

This made-for-TV drama traces the court battle in which 12-year-old Tom Guiry attempts to sever his ties with his uncaring biological family. Richard Crenna plays the caring family man who wants to adopt the young lad and helps him in his fight. The storyline will keep viewers hooked, but the direction is strictly routine. JF DVD

Richard Crenna *George Russ* • Rhea Perlman *Jerri Blair* • Linda Kelsey *Liz Russ* • Thomas Guiry [Tom Guiry] *Gregory Kingsley/Shawn Russ* • Cyril O'Reilly *Ralph Kingsley* • Cotter Smith *Mike Caldwell* ■ *Dir* Sandy Smolan • *Scr* Blair Ferguson

Shattered Glass ★★★ 12

Drama based on a true story
2003 · US/Can · Colour · 89mins

Hubris is at the heart of this true story about a high-flying young magazine journalist whose scoops turn out to be figments of his imagination. Hayden Christensen is unexpectedly excellent as a wheedling star reporter who manipulates his colleagues into helping him with his writing and defending him against his unpopular but rigorous editor, played with equal skill by Peter Sarsgaard. Debut director Billy Ray keeps the story rattling along and support is uniformly good, particularly from Steve Zahn and Hank Azaria. If there is a flaw, it's the screenplay's failure to provide any real explanation for Glass's motives. AS. Contains swearing. DVD

Hayden Christensen *Stephen Glass* • Peter Sarsgaard *Charles "Chuck" Lane* • Chloë Sevigny *Caitlin Avey* • Rosario Dawson *Andy Fox* • Melanie Lynskey *Amy Brand* • Steve Zahn *Adam Penenberg* • Hank Azaria *Michael "Mike" Kelly* ■ *Dir* Billy Ray • *Scr* Billy Ray, from the *Vanity Fair* article by Buzz Bissinger

Shattered Image ★★ 18

Thriller mystery 1998 · US · Colour · 90mins

Schizophrenic after a brutal rape, hit woman Anne Parillaud finds herself drifting in and out of reality. The action flips between Seattle and Jamaica and as fantasy begins to take hold, Parillaud must decide what's real: Is she a pitiless revenge-killer of men, or a happy wife on holiday with new husband William Baldwin? Then again, maybe she's a bit of both. A solidly made psychodrama that just about keeps you watching. Director Raúl Ruiz's first American film. DA

William Baldwin *Brian* • Anne Parillaud *Jessie* • Lisanne Falk *Paula/Laura* • Graham Greene (2) *Conrad/Mike* • Billy Wilmott *Lamond* • O'Neil Peart *Simon* • Bulle Ogier *Mrs Ford* ■ *Dir* Raúl Ruiz • *Scr* Duane Poole

Shattered Trust ★★ 15

Drama 1993 · US · Colour · 88mins

Melissa Gilbert plays a high-flying attorney whose world comes tumbling down when a courtroom incident releases long-suppressed memories of childhood abuse at the hands of her father. While director Bill Corcoran allows melodrama to get the better of restraint in this TV movie, he handles the family feuds and Gilbert's crusade with care. DP DVD

Melissa Gilbert *Shari Karney* • Ellen Burstyn *Joan Delvecchio* • Kate Nelligan *Stephanie Crawford* • Dick Latessa *Jack Karney* ■ *Dir* Bill Corcoran • *Scr* Susan Nanus

Shattering the Silence ★★ 15

Drama 1992 · US · Colour · 87mins

This is a well-meaning but soporific TV examination of the tricky subject of child abuse. Joanna Kerns plays the seemingly content woman who starts behaving strangely following the birth of her first child. When it becomes apparent that her behaviour may be connected to her own upbringing, subsequent revelations start to tear the family apart. Director Linda Otto lays on the melodrama with a shovel. JF DVD

Joanna Kerns *Veronica Ricci* • Michael Brandon *Ted Ricci* • Shelley Hack *Becky Worth* • Richard Gilliland *Tom Worth* • Dina Merrill *Clair Worth* ■ *Dir* Linda Otto • *Scr* Joe Cacaci, Michael Love, Martin Salinas

Shaun of the Dead ★★★★ 15

Comedy horror
2004 · UK/US/Fr · Colour · 95mins

On the day north London slacker Shaun (Simon Pegg) decides to get his aimless life together, the capital becomes Zombie Central as the dead rise to eat the living. If you like Pegg and director Edgar Wright's cult Channel 4 series *Spaced*, you'll enjoy this deadpan blend of undergraduate humour and hardcore horror. It may seem like a one-joke conceit but you do actually care about the characters, which sustains the narrative. Shaun's mates are all played by familiar TV faces, but the real stars are his mum, the magnificent Penelope Wilton, and stepdad, Bill Nighy, who move the splatter farce into more resonant areas. AJ. Contains violence and swearing. DVD

Simon Pegg *Shaun* • Kate Ashfield *Liz* • Nick Frost *Ed* • Dylan Moran *David* • Lucy Davis *Dianne* • Penelope Wilton *Barbara* • Bill Nighy *Philip* • Jessica Stevenson *Yvonne* ■ *Dir* Edgar Wright • *Scr* Edgar Wright, Simon Pegg

The Shawshank Redemption ★★★★★ 15

Prison drama 1994 · US · Colour · 136mins

Re-released on its tenth anniversary, this deeply moving version of a Stephen King story from first-time director Frank Darabont is one of the best adaptations of the novelist's work. Tim Robbins plays a Maine banker sent to Shawshank State Prison for murdering his wife and her lover. Regularly brutalised by the inmates and the penal system in general, his existence improves when he befriends fellow lifer and prison fixer Morgan Freeman. Under Darabont's inspired direction, Robbins and Freeman both rise to the challenge of portraying world-weary dignity against the odds, while the severity of the prison system is underlined in the poignant performance of James Whitmore as a veteran convict trying to make it on parole, but ill-equipped to do so. AJ. Contains violence, swearing and nudity. DVD

Tim Robbins *Andy Dufresne* • Morgan Freeman *Ellis Boyd "Red" Redding* • Bob Gunton *Warden Norton* • William Sadler *Heywood* • Clancy Brown *Captain Hadley* • Gil Bellows *Tommy* • Mark Rolston *Bogs Diamond* • James Whitmore *Brooks Hatlen* ■ *Dir* Frank Darabont • *Scr* Frank Darabont, from the short story *Rita Hayworth and Shawshank Redemption* by Stephen King

She ★★

Fantasy adventure 1935 · US · BW · 94mins

The first talkie verison of H Rider Haggard's romantic adventure about the explorer lured by a woman who, having bathed in the Flame of Life, becomes immortal, provides only short-lived interest. Randolph Scott is a grim-jawed explorer, Helen Gahagan a rather muted siren and the story is transferred from Africa to the Arctic Circle. The result is as frozen as the setting. TH

Helen Gahagan *Hash-A-Mo-Tep, "She"* • Randolph Scott *Leo Vincey* • Helen Mack *Tanya Dugmore* • Nigel Bruce *Archibald Holly* • Gustav von Seyffertitz *Prime Minister Billali* • Samuel S Hinds *John Vincey* • Noble Johnson *Amahagger chief* • Lumsden Hare *Dugmore* ■ *Dir* Irving Pichel, Lansing C Holden • *Scr* Ruth Rose, Dudley Nichols, from the novel by H Rider Haggard

She ★★★ U

Fantasy adventure
1965 · UK · Colour · 101mins

Swiss-born Ursula Andress acquits herself better than you might expect in this adaptation of H Rider Haggard's much-filmed fantasy. Indeed, she looks in great shape for a 2,000-year-old queen of a lost kingdom, who is still yearning for the embrace of a lover she killed centuries ago. The jungle backdrops are easily matched by Andress's own brand of exotic beauty and, while there's plenty to criticise, there's also much to enjoy. *The Vengeance of She* followed three years later, minus Andress. PF DVD

Ursula Andress *Ayesha* • John Richardson *Leo Vincey* • Peter Cushing *Major Horace Holly* • Bernard Cribbins *Job* • Rosenda Monteros *Ustane* • Christopher Lee *Billali* ■ *Dir* Robert Day • *Scr* David T Chantler, from the novel by H Rider Haggard

The She Beast ★★★

Horror 1965 · UK/It · Colour · 75mins

Cult director Michael Reeves made his feature debut with this painfully cheap shocker that nevertheless revealed the powerful use of horrific imagery he would harness to perfection in his masterpiece, *Witchfinder General*. Honeymooners Barbara Steele and Ian Ogilvy visit modern-day Transylvania, only to crash their car in the lake where vengeful witch Vardella was tortured to death in the 18th century. Steele transforms into the decrepit hag and goes on a murder spree in this amalgam of stark terror and facile humour. AJ. Some Italian dialogue dubbed into English.

Barbara Steele *Veronica/Vardella* • Ian Ogilvy *Philip* • John Karlsen *Count von Helsing* ■ *Dir* Michael Reeves • *Scr* Michael Byron

The She-Creature ★★

Cult horror 1956 · US · BW · 80mins

Chester Morris hypnotises sexy Marla English back to prehistoric times, and has her reptilian alter ego materialise in the present to help him and money-grabbing promoter Tom Conway con the police. He predicts a murder and the scaly, large-breasted amphibian carries it out. One of those bonkers 1950s sci-fi quickies that are so awful they become irresistibly compelling. Incidentally, the monster is an impressive work of trash art. AJ

Chester Morris *Carlo Lombardi* • Marla English *Andrea* • Tom Conway *Timothy Chappel* • Cathy Downs *Dorothy* • Lance Fuller *Ted Erickson* ■ *Dir* Edward L Cahn • *Scr* Lou Rusoff, from his play

She Creature ★★ 15

Period horror 2001 · US · Colour · 85mins

This first in a new series of "Creature Feature" TV remakes from Stan Winston's effects studio is a strange choice, given that Edward L Cahn's 1956 sci-fi quickie isn't exactly held in the highest regard. Set in the early 20th century, Rufus Sewell plays the owner of a fake freak show who stumbles across the existence of a genuine mermaid and tries to transport her across sea to make his fortune. Decent production values and cast fail to compensate for a stagnant script that takes itself far too seriously, while the gore and nudity don't sit easily with the period feel. JC DVD

Rufus Sewell *Angus Shaw* • Carla Gugino *Lillian* • Jim Piddock *Capt Dunn* • Reno Wilson *Bailey* • Mark Aiken *Gifford* • Fintan McKeown *Shelly* ■ *Dir/Scr* Sebastian Gutierrez

She Dances Alone ★★★

Documentary drama
1981 · US/Austria · Colour · 87mins

This intriguing blend of fact and fiction has Bud Cort as a director trying to make an objective documentary about the legendary dancer Nijinsky. Unfortunately he's blocked at every turn by Nijinsky's daughter, Kyra. Well over 60 years old at the time, Kyra is a huge presence in the film in every sense, and it is as much about her

S

strong-willed desire to make her own career with the burden/blessing of such a famous father as it is about the great man himself. To blur the edges even further, Max von Sydow plays himself and is the voice reading Nijinsky's diary. FL

Max von Sydow *Voice of Nijinsky* • Jon Bradshaw *Narrator* • Bud Cort *Director* • Patrick Dupond *Dancer* ■ *Dir* Robert Dornhelm • *Scr* Paul Davids, from an idea by Robert Dornhelm

She Demons ★

Horror 1958 · US · BW · 79mins

They don't come any more ludicrously inept than this Z-movie trash about a Nazi war criminal turning gorgeous shipwreck survivors into ugly monsters on his uncharted island, in an effort to restore beauty to his wife's scarred face. Connoisseurs will enjoy the wobbly sets, a ritual jungle dance and a volcanic eruption climax. AJ

Irish McCalla *Jerrie Turner* • Tod Griffin *Fred Maklin* • Victor Sen Yung *Sammy Ching* • Rudolph Anders *Herr Osler* • Gene Roth *Egore* ■ *Dir* Richard E Cunha • *Scr* Richard E Cunha, HE Barrie, from their story

She-Devil ★★ 15

Comedy 1989 · US · Colour · 95mins

Fay Weldon's dark, acerbic tale of rejection and revenge receives the full Hollywood treatment, reducing its saturnine charm to frothy candyfloss. The whole farrago is hopelessly miscast with a wet and vapid Meryl Streep as the vamp novelist, a cardboard cut-out Ed Begley Jr as the errant husband she snares, and, most disappointing of all, Roseanne Barr as a curiously weak and woolly She-Devil. Watching this makes you appreciate once more the celebrated BBC TV adaptation. SH. Contains swearing, sex scenes and brief nudity. [video] DVD

Meryl Streep *Mary Fisher* • Roseanne Barr *Ruth Patchett* • Ed Begley Jr *Bob Patchett* • Linda Hunt *Nurse Hooper* • Sylvia Miles *Francine Fisher* • Elisebeth Peters *Nicolette Patchett* • Bryan Larkin *Andy Patchett* • Robin Leach ■ *Dir* Susan Seidelman • *Scr* Barry Strugatz, Mark R Burns, from the novel *The Life and Loves of a She-Devil* by Fay Weldon

She-Devils on Wheels ★★ 18

Action thriller 1968 · US · Colour · 79mins

After *Blood Feast*, this tawdry tale of chopper chicks on the rampage is splatter pioneer Herschell Gordon Lewis's most popular drive-in exploiter. The domineering Man-Eaters battle a bunch of male hot-rodders for use of the abandoned airport runway where they hold their weekly Harley races. Ritual humiliation, decapitation, kidnap, torture and the hilarious "stud-line" – the race winner gets to choose which man to sexually abuse – are the main focus of Lewis's Hells Angels in high heels plodder. AJ [video] DVD

Betty Connell *Queen* • Pat Poston *Whitey* • Nancy Lee Noble *Honey-Pot* • Christie Wagner *Karen* • Rodney Bedell *Ted* • Ruby Tuesday *Terry* ■ *Dir* Herschell Gordon Lewis • *Scr* Louise Downe

She Done Him Wrong ★★★★

Comedy 1933 · US · BW · 66mins

Probably *the* classic Mae West movie and a perfect opportunity to make the acquaintance of "the finest woman that ever walked the streets". The truly outrageous West is today mainly regarded as a camp icon. The predatory creature known as Lady Lou in this opus was once West's infamous "Diamond Lil" in her own play, but the requirements of both national and local censors caused the modification of nickname and dialogue for the movie. Young Cary Grant is the person she asks to "come up sometime and see me", a phrase that is now well established as part of cinema iconography. TS

Mae West *Lady Lou* • Cary Grant *Captain Cummings* • Owen Moore *Chick Clark* • Gilbert Roland *Serge Stanieff* • Noah Beery Sr [Noah Beery] *Gus Jordan* • David Landau *Dan Flynn* ■ *Dir* Lowell Sherman • *Scr* Mae West, Harvey Thew, John Bright, from the play *Diamond Lil* by Mae West

She Freak ★ 15

Cult horror 1967 · US · Colour · 79mins

Director Byron Mabe lets this redneck freak tale slip from promising camp trash into complete ineptitude. While the story – an ambitious greasy spoon waitress marries the owner of a seedy side show with gruesome results – is not without its moments, you can see the money drain away from the micro-budget as this grade Z flick staggers to its rip-off climax. AJ [video]

Claire Brennen *Jade Cochran* • Lee Raymond *Blackie Fleming* • Lynn Courtney *Pat Mullins* • Bill McKinney *Steve St John* • Van Teen *Babcock* • Felix Silla *Shortie* ■ *Dir* Byron Mabe • *Scr* David F Friedman

She Hate Me ★★ 15

Comedy drama 2004 · US/Fr · Colour · 132mins

Director Spike Lee's messy comedy drama is excruciatingly clichéd and so unconventionally constructed that it plays like a handful of genre movies all competing for supremacy. Suave Anthony Mackie goes into unofficial business by impregnating rich lesbians after being sacked as a whistle-blower from a corporation pushing a defective Aids vaccine. There are some very funny moments, but the feature's increasing ludicrousness and Lee's insistence on pandering to crude male fantasies undermine any serious messages. SF. Contains swearing and sex scenes. DVD

Anthony Mackie *John Henry "Jack" Armstrong* • Kerry Washington *Fatima Goodrich* • Ellen Barkin *Margo Chadwick* • Monica Bellucci *Simona Bonasera* • Jim Brown *Geronimo Armstrong* • Ossie Davis *Judge Buchanan* • Brian Dennehy *Chairman Church* • Woody Harrelson *Leland Powell* • Bai Ling *Oni* • John Turturro *Don Angelo Bonasera* • Chiwetel Ejiofor *Frank Wills* ■ *Dir* Spike Lee • *Scr* Michael Genet, Spike Lee, from a story by Michael Genet

She Loves Me Not ★★★

Musical comedy 1934 · US · BW · 80mins

Showgirl Miriam Hopkins, fleeing from mobsters, hides out in a boys' college in this enjoyable early musical starring Bing Crosby. Though Hopkins is basically miscast as a burlesque queen, the complications as she is forced to masquerade as a male are fun, and Crosby oozes affable charm. Kitty Carlisle has her best screen role, and gets to introduce with Crosby *Love in Bloom*, which reached number one in the hit parade. TV

Bing Crosby *Paul Lawton* • Miriam Hopkins *Curly Flagg* • Kitty Carlisle *Midge Mercer* • Edward Nugent *Buzz Jones* • Henry Stephenson *Dean Mercer* • Warren Hymer *Mugg Schnitzel* • Lynne Overman *Gus McNeal* ■ *Dir* Elliott Nugent • *Scr* Benjamin Glazer, from the play by Lindsay Howard. from the novel by Edward Hope

She Married Her Boss ★★★ U

Screwball comedy 1935 · US · BW · 88mins

Claudette Colbert shines under the deft and witty direction of Gregory La Cava, with a screenplay by Columbia's arch-sophisticate Sidney Buchman. Melvyn Douglas is the titular "boss", and Colbert has to cope with his awful daughter (Edith Fellows) and his drama queen of a sister (Katherine Alexander). The movie is genuinely funny but runs out of comedic steam towards the end. Nevertheless, there are some wonderful performances, most notably Raymond Walburn as a squiffy butler. TS

Claudette Colbert *Julia Scott* • Michael Bartlett *Lonnie Rogers* • Melvyn Douglas *Richard Barclay* • Raymond Walburn *Franklin* • Jean Dixon *Martha* • Katherine Alexander *Gertrude* • Edith Fellows *Annabel* ■ *Dir* Gregory La Cava • *Scr* Sidney Buchman, from the story by Thyra Samter Winslow

She Wore a Yellow Ribbon ★★★★★ PG

Western 1949 · US · Colour · 99mins

This first-class cavalry western from director John Ford contains some of John Wayne's finest screen moments. Wayne is marvellously in character as retiring commander Nathan Brittles, a performance that even those vehemently anti-Wayne, and all he stood for, feel forced to admire. This is one of the great Technicolor movies, justly winning an Oscar for cinematography that expertly captures Ford's favourite Monument Valley locations. There's also a stirring, majestic soundtrack and a mighty fine supporting cast that includes Ben Johnson, Harry Carey Jr and the lovely Joanne Dru – ignore the slightly ludicrous Irish whimsy involving Victor McLaglen. This is a deeply satisfying work by one of cinema's greatest film-makers. TS [video] DVD

John Wayne *Captain Brittles* • Joanne Dru *Olivia* • John Agar *Lieutenant Cohill* • Ben Johnson *Tyree* • Harry Carey Jr *Lieutenant Pennell* • Victor McLaglen *Sergeant Quincannon* • Mildred Natwick *Mrs Allshard* • Arthur Shields *Dr O'Laughlin* • Harry Woods *Toucey Rynders* ■ *Dir* John Ford • *Scr* Frank Nugent, Laurence Stallings, from the stories *War Party* and *The Big Hunt* by James Warner Bellah • *Cinematographer* Winton Hoch [Winton C Hoch]

Sheena ★★ 15

Romantic adventure 1984 · US/UK · Colour · 111mins

Tanya Roberts is hopelessly miscast as the orphan raised by African natives in this lacklustre adaptation of the 1930s jungle woman comic strip. Roberts learns how to talk to animals and use mystical powers to protect her people against political intrigue and an intrusive newsreel crew. John Guillermin directs the colourful adventure yarn with a straight face and completely avoids the campy tone such exotica cries out for. AJ [video]

Tanya Roberts *Sheena* • Ted Wass *Vic Casey* • Donovan Scott *Fletcher* • Elizabeth of Toro *Shaman* • France Zobda *Countess Zanda* • Trevor Thomas *Prince Otwani* • Clifton Jones *King Jabalani* ■ *Dir* John Guillermin • *Scr* David Newman, Lorenzo Semple Jr • *Music* Richard Hartley

The Sheep Has Five Legs ★★★

Comedy 1954 · Fr · BW · 107mins

Seizing the opportunity to demonstrate his genius for comic characterisation, Fernandel takes on six roles in this engaging family album, compiled by Henri Verneuil. In addition to playing the disapproving vintner father, he also essays the five sons, who are reunited on their 40th birthday. The vignettes involving the prissy beautician and the Parisian agony aunt are unremarkable, but Fernandel excels as the hypochondriac window cleaner feuding with a grasping undertaker, the old salt reduced to betting on flies landing on sugar lumps, and the priest weary of being reminded he resembles Don Camillo (a part the star made famous). DP. In French with English subtitles.

Fernandel *Papa Saint Forget* • Delmont [Edouard Delmont] *Dr Bollene* • Louis De Funès *Pilate, the undertaker* ■ *Dir* Henri Verneuil • *Scr* Albert Valentin

The Sheepman ★★★★ U

Comedy western 1958 · US · Colour · 85mins

Directed with wit and style by veteran George Marshall, this wonderful Glenn Ford comedy western co-stars a splendidly raucous and unusually sympathetic Shirley MacLaine. The opening is a real humdinger and sets the style for the rest of the movie, as Ford's milk-drinking sheep farmer picks a fight with local character Mickey Shaughnessy, proving that he's not a man to trifle with. This is a reminder that Ford was not only Hollywood's most popular star of this period, but one of America's finest. TS

Glenn Ford *Jason Sweet* • Shirley MacLaine *Dell Payton* • Leslie Nielsen *Johnny Bledsoe* • Mickey Shaughnessy *Jumbo McCall* • Edgar Buchanan *Milt Masters* • Willis Bouchey *Mr Payton* • Pernell Roberts *Choctaw* • Slim Pickens *Marshal* ■ *Dir* George Marshall • *Scr* William Bowers, James Edward Grant, William Roberts, from a story by James Edward Grant

The Sheik ★★★★ PG

Silent adventure melodrama 1921 · US · BW · 86mins

Rudolph Valentino achieved iconic status with his performance as the dashing Ahmed Ben Hassan in this overheated desert melodrama. Female fans swooned as he delivered Agnes Ayres from the clutches of the lascivious Walter Long, while their dates looked on in disbelief at his effete heroics and impassioned wooing. There were even those who demanded the film should be banned for its dubious morality and acceptance of miscegenation. Yet, for all its surface glamour and romantic abandon, the story hurtles towards a rather traditional conclusion. DP DVD

Agnes Ayres *Diana Mayo* • Rudolph Valentino *Sheik Ahmed Ben Hassan* • Adolphe Menjou *Raoul de Saint Hubert* • Walter Long *Omair* • Lucien Littlefield *Gaston* ■ *Dir* George Melford • *Scr* Monte M Katterjohn, from the novel by Edith Maude Hull

Sheila Levine Is Dead and Living in New York ★★

Comedy 1975 · US · Colour · 113mins

A pathetic conversion of Gail Parent's bestselling comic novel about a spoilt girl trying to make it in New York, with Jeannie Berlin as the Jewish Princess fighting prejudice and her own nature. Director Sidney J Furie blots his copybook by failing to grasp the comedy and squeezing too hard on the social significance. TH

Jeannie Berlin *Sheila* • Roy Scheider *Sam* • Rebecca Dianna Smith *Kate* • Janet Brandt *Bernice* • Sid Melton *Manny* • Charles Woolf *Wally* • Noble Willingham *School Principal* ■ *Dir* Sidney J Furie • *Scr* Kenny Solms, from the novel by Gail Parent

Shelf Life ★★★

Comedy drama 1993 · US · Colour · 83mins

On the day President Kennedy is assassinated, a suburban 1960s family retreat to their bomb shelter and stay there for 30 years. When their parents die of food poisoning, the three children resort to acting out scenes from their favourite TV shows to stay sane. Based on their play, the stars – Jim Turner, O-Lan Jones and Andrea Stein – wrote the script that was filmed on one claustrophobic set by cult director Paul Bartel. Much surreal fun is had when the trio indulge in cultural rituals based upon the famous sitcoms of the era. AJ

Andrea Stein *Pam/Mrs St Cloud* • O-Lan Jones *Tina* • Jim Turner *Scotty/Mr St Cloud* •

S

Paul Bartel *Various Apparitions* ■ *Dir* Paul Bartel • *Scr* Jim Turner, O-Lan Jones, Andrea Stein, from their play

She'll Be Wearing Pink Pyjamas ★★ 15

Comedy drama 1984 · UK · Colour · 86mins

All talk and no trousers, pyjama or otherwise, in this tiresome natter-fest about a bunch of women who go on a wilderness survival course as part of a company "bonding" scheme. Julie Walters stars and, as always, gives it her all. But neither she nor the supporting girls are particularly well served by the tedious dialogue and aimless plotting. The awful title doesn't help. DA [video] DVD

Julie Walters *Fran* • Anthony Higgins *Tom* • Jane Evers *Catherine* • Janet Henfrey *Lucy* • Paula Jacobs *Doreen* • Penelope Nice *Ann* • Maureen O'Brien *Joan* • Alyson Spiro *Anita* ■ *Dir* John Goldschmidt • *Scr* Eva Hardy

She'll Have to Go ★★ U

Comedy 1961 · UK · BW · 89mins

Known in the States as *Maid for Murder*, this mediocre comedy was something of a family affair. The Asher brothers co-produced the picture, with Robert also directing and his younger sibling, Jack, as cinematographer. They might have been better off having a crack at the script, too, as John Waterhouse's adaptation is so slipshod that not even Hattie Jacques can bring it to life. But most sympathy goes to Jean-Luc Godard's then wife Anna Karina, who looks lost fighting off gold-digging brothers Bob Monkhouse and Alfred Marks. DP

Bob Monkhouse *Francis Oberon* • Alfred Marks *Douglas Oberon* • Hattie Jacques *Miss Richards* • Anna Karina *Toni* • Dennis Lotis *Gilbert* • Graham Stark *Arnold* • Clive Dunn *Chemist* ■ *Dir* Robert Asher • *Scr* John Waterhouse, from the play *We Must Kill Toni* by Ian Stuart Black

Shelter ★★ 18

Crime thriller 1997 · US · Colour · 95mins

Aside from the novelty of being centred around the Greek Mafia rather than the more familiar Italian or Russian outfits, this lukewarm thriller has little to recommend it. The wooden John Allen Nelson is a good cop who stands up against his department's corruption, saving the life of head mafiosi Peter Onorati and earning himself a new job as his security chief. Brenda Bakke shines in a sympathetic role as the maltreated wife who turns to Nelson for affection, but script and direction are strictly of a "join the dots" standard. JC [video] DVD

John Allen Nelson *Martin Roberts* • Brenda Bakke *Helena* • Peter Onorati *Dimitri* • Costas Mandylor *Nikos* • Charles Durning *Captain Landis* • Linden Ashby *Jimmy Parker* ■ *Dir* Scott Paulin • *Scr* Max Strom

The Sheltering Sky ★★★ 18

Drama 1990 · UK/It · Colour · 132mins

Bernardo Bertolucci directs this immensely ambitious film of Paul Bowles's strange, mystical, metaphysical novel. The tale concerns an American married couple (John Malkovich and Debra Winger) and a friend (Campbell Scott) touring North Africa in 1947 in search of the mystery that is the desert. Filmed in arduous conditions in Algeria and Niger, the movie tries to be bookish and introspective yet full of vast landscapes. Despite Winger's committed, intensely physical performance, it remains a rather soulless and aloof experience. AT. Contains swearing, violence, sex scenes and nudity. [video] DVD

Debra Winger *Kit Moresby* • John Malkovich *Port Moresby* • Campbell Scott *George Tunner* • Jill Bennett *Mrs Lyle* • Timothy Spall *Eric Lyle* • Eric Vu-An *Belqassim* • Paul Bowles *Narrator* ■ *Dir* Bernardo Bertolucci • *Scr* Mark Peploe, Bernardo Bertolucci, from the novel by Paul Bowles • *Cinematographer* Vittorio Storaro

Shenandoah ★★★★ PG

Western 1965 · US · Colour · 100mins

This marvellous and moving late western features a superb performance from James Stewart as a widower trying to ignore the Civil War until the tide of history washes over his whole family. Unusually, the deliberate sentimentality does work, and the scene where Stewart offers a moving soliloquy beside his wife's grave was so popular that it was released on record. Director Andrew V McLaglen (Victor's son) achieves a real sense of scale here, and the supporting cast, including many veterans from John Ford's repertory company, is particularly well chosen. TS [video] DVD

James Stewart *Charlie Anderson* • Doug McClure *Sam* • Glenn Corbett *Jacob* • Patrick Wayne *James* • Phillip Alford *Boy* • Katharine Ross *Ann* • Rosemary Forsyth *Jennie* • Charles Robinson *Nathan* • George Kennedy *Colonel Fairchild* ■ *Dir* Andrew V McLaglen • *Scr* James Lee Barrett

The Shepherd of the Hills ★★★

Adventure 1941 · US · Colour · 97mins

The heavyweight presence of John Wayne helps make this one of the best adaptations of Harold Bell Wright's Missouri-set novel. Wayne stars as the backwoods boy who blames his absent father for the death of his mother and spends his days plotting revenge. Betty Field plays the girl who won't marry Wayne while he's consumed with hate. Director Henry Hathaway just stands back and lets the splendid cast get on with it. NF

John Wayne *Young Matt Matthews* • Betty Field *Sammy Lane* • Harry Carey *Daniel Howitt* • Beulah Bondi *Aunt Mollie* • James Barton *Old Matt* • Samuel S Hinds *Andy Beeler* • Marjorie Main *Granny Becky* • Ward Bond *Wash Gibbs* ■ *Dir* Henry Hathaway • *Scr* Grover Jones, Stuart Anthony, from the novel by Harold Bell Wright

Shepherd on the Rock ★★

Drama 1995 · Can · Colour · 100mins

Bernard Hill stars as a Scottish shepherd who takes on a cabal of shiftless property developers. But Bob Keen's film is less interested in environmental issues than the "us and them" tension of the similarly themed *Local Hero*, as Hill's pastoral principles frustrate the ambitions of his neighbours. The scenery's sublime, the performances polished, but the plot is a touch too predictable. DP

Bernard Hill *Tam Ferrier* • John Bowles *Ewan* • Betsy Brantley *Jean* • Doug Bradley *James Culzean* • Mark McKenna *Andy Murray* • Oliver Parker *Simon McIntyre* ■ *Dir* Bob Keen

The Sheriff of Fractured Jaw ★★★★ U

Comedy western
1958 · UK · Colour · 103mins

This is the first western shot in Spain, its standing set later used for Sergio Leone's *Dollars* trilogy. The title role in this super spoof is played by British actor Kenneth More at his most diffident, and the director is the great Raoul Walsh, who films in the grand tradition of the genre. 1950s sex symbol Jayne Mansfield provides the love interest and there's a touching musical interlude in which she croons *In the Valley of Love*, dubbed by Connie Francis. The film's soundtrack is especially witty, and there's the added value of an entertaining Anglo-American supporting cast. TS

Kenneth More *Jonathan Tibbs* • Jayne Mansfield *Kate* • Henry Hull *Mayor Masters* • William Campbell *Keno* • Bruce Cabot *Jack* • Robert Morley *Uncle Lucius* • Ronald Squire *Toynbee* • David Horne *James* ■ *Dir* Raoul Walsh • *Scr* Arthur Dales [Howard Dimsdale], from a short story by Jacob Hay • *Music* Robert Farnon

Sheriff of Sage Valley ★★ U

Western 1942 · US · BW · 55mins

Buster Crabbe was an Olympic swimmer who played hero figures Tarzan, Flash Gordon and Buck Rogers in series and serials throughout the 1930s that are still recalled with affectionate nostalgia today. But Crabbe was no actor, and he soon became a leading man in B-westerns, of which this is a typical example: skimpy-on-plot but action-packed. TS

Buster Crabbe [Larry "Buster" Crabbe] *Billy The Kid/Kansas Ed* • Al St John *Fuzzy Jones* • Tex O'Brien *Jeff* • Maxine Leslie *Janet* ■ *Dir* Sherman Scott [Sam Newfield] • *Scr* George W Sayre, Milton Raison

Sherlock Holmes ★★★

Mystery 1932 · US · BW · 62mins

Call it "the Case of the Clueless Sleuth". Before Basil Rathbone put his definitive imprint on Conan Doyle's famous private detective, matinée idol Clive Brook was a refined and far too discreet Holmes, with Reginald Owen as a very ineffectual Dr Watson. The film loses a lot of gaslight appeal as Chicago gangsters, brought in by the monstrous Moriarty, invade a bewildered London. Holmes's nemesis is given such a wonderfully OTT presence by Ernest Torrence that, in the end, you almost hope he'll win. TH

Clive Brook *Sherlock Holmes* • Ernest Torrence *Professor Moriarty* • Reginald Owen *Dr Watson* • Miriam Jordan *Alice Faulkner* • Howard Leeds *Little Billy* • Alan Mowbray *Gore-King* ■ *Dir* William K Howard • *Scr* Bertram Milhauser, from a play by William Gillette, from stories by Sir Arthur Conan Doyle

Sherlock Holmes and the Deadly Necklace ★ 12

Mystery 1962 · W Ger/Fr/It · BW · 82mins

Hammer stars Christopher Lee and Thorley Walters and acclaimed Hammer director Terence Fisher, went to Germany to make this Holmes adventure. The plot of this badly edited hotch-potch of clichéd nonsense revolves around Professor Moriarty's theft of a priceless necklace. Both English and German versions were released, but Lee disowned the whole unpalatable affair because his Holmes was abysmally dubbed in both with high-pitched, nasal vocals. A dreadful disaster. AJ [video] DVD

Christopher Lee *Sherlock Holmes* • Thorley Walters *Dr Watson* • Senta Berger *Ellen Blackburn* • Hans Söhnker *Professor Moriarty* • Hans Nielsen *Inspector Cooper* • Ivan Desny *Paul King* • Leon Askin *Chauffeur Charles* • Wolfgang Lukschy *Peter Blackburn* ■ *Dir* Terence Fisher, Frank Winterstein • *Scr* Curt Siodmak, from the story *The Valley of Fear* by Sir Arthur Conan Doyle

Sherlock Holmes and the Secret Code ★★ U

Mystery 1946 · US · BW · 71mins

Sherlock Holmes sets out to track down three music boxes containing stolen Bank of England engraving plates in this mystery, which was Basil Rathbone's final outing as the great detective. Patricia Morison does well as the villainess, but she doesn't have the evil presence of Moriarty. Luckily, Nigel Bruce is on form as Dr Watson, and his bumbling joviality lightens up the dour atmosphere. Released on video in the UK as *Dressed to Kill*. TH [video] DVD

Basil Rathbone *Sherlock Holmes* • Nigel Bruce *Dr Watson* • Patricia Morison *Hilda Courtney* • Edmond Breon [Edmund Breon] *Gilbert Emery* • Frederick Worlock *Colonel Cavanaugh* • Carl Harbord *Inspector Hopkins* ■ *Dir* Roy William Neill • *Scr* Leonard Lee, Frank Gruber, from a story by Sir Arthur Conan Doyle

Sherlock Holmes and the Secret Weapon ★★★ PG

Mystery 1942 · US · BW · 68mins

The Nazis stood no chance once they knew they were up against the Allies' own secret weapon, Basil Rathbone as Holmes, ably assisted as always by Nigel Bruce as Dr Watson. This modernised, morale-boosting story drew only a fraction of its plot (the "dancing men" code) from Conan Doyle, as Holmes searches for a unique bombsight. As the baleful Moriarty, Lionel Atwill walks the corridors of glower with real malevolence, and the film was the first in the series to be directed by Roy William Neill. TH [video] DVD

Basil Rathbone *Sherlock Holmes* • Nigel Bruce *Dr Watson* • Kaaren Verne *Charlotte Eberli* • Lionel Atwill *Professor Moriarty* • William Post Jr *Dr Franz Tobel* • Dennis Hoey *Inspector Lestrade* ■ *Dir* Roy William Neill • *Scr* Edward T Lowe, Scott Darling, Edmund L Hartmann, from the story *The Dancing Men* by Sir Arthur Conan Doyle

Sherlock Holmes and the Spider Woman ★★★ U

Mystery 1944 · US · BW · 59mins

The serene elegance of Basil Rathbone as Holmes is just a tad ruffled when he's set up in a shooting gallery by the great Gale Sondergaard – as vicious a foe as Holmes has faced in a film as effective as any in the series. The only fly, or flaw, in the web is that Nigel Bruce's Dr Watson is at his most boringly bumbling. TH [video] DVD

Basil Rathbone *Sherlock Holmes* • Nigel Bruce *Dr Watson* • Gale Sondergaard *Andrea Spedding* • Dennis Hoey *Inspector Lestrade* • Vernon Downing *Norman Locke* • Alec Craig *Radlik* • Arthur Hohl *Adam Gilflower* ■ *Dir* Roy William Neill • *Scr* Bertram Millhauser, from the story *The Sign of the Four* by Sir Arthur Conan Doyle

Sherlock Holmes and the Voice of Terror ★★ U

Mystery 1942 · US · BW · 62mins

This was the first of Universal's 11-film series featuring Basil Rathbone and Nigel Bruce as the slender sleuth and his rotund sidekick, though the two actors had already played the roles in two films for 20th Century-Fox. The wartime plot is simplistic, with Holmes searching for the traitor in the government supplying a Nazi broadcaster with information. Laborious. TH [video] DVD

Basil Rathbone *Sherlock Holmes* • Nigel Bruce *Dr Watson* • Evelyn Ankers *Kitty* • Reginald Denny *Sir Evan Barham* • Montagu Love *General Jerome Lawford* • Henry Daniell *Anthony Lloyd* • Thomas Gomez *RF Meade* ■ *Dir* John Rawlins • *Scr* Lynn Riggs, John Bright, Robert Andrews, from the story *His Last Bow* by Sir Arthur Conan Doyle

Sherlock Holmes Faces Death ★★★ U

Mystery 1943 · US · BW · 65mins

One of the best of the Basil Rathbone/Nigel Bruce movies, in which a clock strikes 13 and murder comes in triplicate. For once Dr Watson is the plot's prime mover, in charge of an army officers' convalescent home at Musgrave Manor where shell-shocked patients are the cover for misdeeds in a hidden cellar. It's one of the most old-fashioned of the series, which explains the craftsmanlike grip it exerts. TH DVD

Basil Rathbone *Sherlock Holmes* • Nigel Bruce *Dr Watson* • Dennis Hoey *Inspector Lestrade* • Arthur Margetson *Dr Sexton* • Hillary Brooke *Sally Musgrave* • Halliwell Hobbes *Brunton, the butler* • Minna Phillips *Mrs Howells* ■ *Dir* Roy William Neill • *Scr* Bertram Millhauser, from the story *The Musgrave Ritual* by Sir Arthur Conan Doyle

Sherlock Holmes in New York ★★★ U

Mystery 1976 · US · Colour · 98mins

Roger Moore as Sherlock Holmes, Patrick Macnee as Dr Watson and John Huston as Professor Moriarty enliven this TV movie outing for Conan Doyle's inimitable hero, which involves Huston messing with the world's gold supply. Having already created one of the modern cinema's great villains – Noah Cross in *Chinatown* – Huston slips into Moriarty's wardrobe with ease and dominates this enjoyable movie. AT

Roger Moore *Sherlock Holmes* • John Huston *Professor James Moriarty* • Patrick Macnee *Dr John Watson* • Gig Young *Mortimer McGraw* • Charlotte Rampling *Irene Adler* • David Huddleston *Inspector Lafferty* • Signe Hasso *Fraulein Reichenbach* • Jackie Coogan *Hotel Haymarket proprietor* ■ *Dir* Boris Sagal • *Scr* Alvin Sapinsley, from characters created by Sir Arthur Conan Doyle

Sherlock Holmes in Washington ★★ U

Mystery 1943 · US · BW · 68mins

Sherlock Holmes (Basil Rathbone) smokes a cigarette while Dr Watson (Nigel Bruce) puffs on his pipe in the first of the series not connected, however tenuously, to a story by Arthur Conan Doyle. A weakish update of the character, Holmes is after a microfilm passed to the wrong stranger on a train and a prime target for nasty Nazis. Holmes gets to quote Winston Churchill and waxes paternal about democracy. TH DVD

Basil Rathbone *Sherlock Holmes* • Nigel Bruce *Dr Watson* • Marjorie Lord *Nancy Partridge* • Henry Daniell *William Easter* • George Zucco *Stanley* • John Archer *Lt Peter Merriam* • Gavin Muir *Bart Lang* ■ *Dir* Roy William Neill • *Scr* Bertram Millhauser, Lynn Riggs, from a story by Bertram Millhauser, from characters created by Sir Arthur Conan Doyle

Sherlock Junior ★★★★★ U

Silent comedy 1924 · US · BW · 45mins

One of Buster Keaton's finest comedies, certainly his most inventive and technically audacious. He plays an amateur detective and cinema projectionist who dreams himself into the movie he is showing and, hopefully, into the arms of the girl he loves. As early as 1924 Keaton recognised the cinema's role as escapism in society, and constructed an entire film about it (although the early sequences were directed by Roscoe Arbuckle). The result is richly romantic and oddly educational: audiences were shown all the tricks of the trade, notably editing, back projection and other special effects. But mostly it works as a brilliant comedy, full of the clever bits of business and ambitious stunts one associates with Keaton. AT

Buster Keaton *Projectionist* • Kathryn McGuire *His fiancée* • Joseph Keaton [Joe Keaton] *Her father* • Ward Crane *Rival* • Erwin Connelly *Handyman/butler* ■ *Dir* Buster Keaton • *Scr* Clyde Bruckman, Jean Havez, Joseph Mitchell

She's All That ★★★ 12

Romantic comedy
1999 · US · Colour · 95mins

This preposterous but fun comedy has Rachael Leigh Cook as the gawky teen who gets a makeover from popular soccer star Freddie Prinze Jr. He's made a secret bet with his pals that he can turn even the most unlikely girl into a prom queen. Both the leads are enjoyable, but equally worth catching are the supporting stars, especially Matthew Lillard as an egotistical oaf, Anna Paquin as Prinze's sister and Kieran Culkin as Cook's gutsy younger brother. JB. Contains swearing. DVD

Freddie Prinze Jr *Zack Siler* • Rachael Leigh Cook *Laney Boggs* • Matthew Lillard *Brock Hudson* • Paul Walker *Dean Sampson* • Jodi Lyn O'Keefe *Taylor Vaughan* • Kevin Pollak *Wayne Boggs* • Kieran Culkin *Simon Boggs* • Anna Paquin *Mackenzie Siler* ■ *Dir* Robert Iscove • *Scr* R Lee Fleming Jr

She's Gotta Have It ★★★★ 18

Comedy drama
1986 · US · BW and Colour · 80mins

Spike Lee's directorial debut hasn't lost any of its vitality over the years and remains his most genuinely entertaining work, refreshingly free of much of the political rhetoric which occasionally overcomes his other projects. Tracy Camila Johns is the strong willed young woman who not only has to have it, but also refuses to be tied down to one of three suitors out to tame her. Lee has plenty of fun deflating the macho egos on parade, grabbing many of the best lines for himself as the irritatingly persistent Mars Blackmon. Vividly shot in black and white apart from one lovely colour sequence at the end. JF. Contains swearing and nudity.

Tracy Camila Johns *Nola Darling* • Tommy Redmond Hicks *Jamie Overstreet* • John Canada Terrell *Greer Childs* • Spike Lee *Mars Blackmon* • Raye Dowell *Opal Gilstrap* • Joie Lee *Clorinda Bradford* • Epatha Merkinson [S Epatha Merkerson] *Dr Jamison* • Bill Lee *Sonny Darling* ■ *Dir/Scr* Spike Lee • *Cinematographer* Ernest Dickerson [Ernest R Dickerson]

She's Having a Baby ★★ 15

Comedy 1988 · US · Colour · 101mins

This rather humdrum look at young love turning into disgruntled parenthood stars a highly believable Kevin Bacon and a less rooted-in-reality Elizabeth McGovern. There are some neat jokes about bulges, nappies and loss of freedom, and Bacon's terror at the impending event is palpable. But the movie fails to break any new ground and there is a familiar jaded ring to every hackneyed scenario. SH. Contains swearing. DVD

Kevin Bacon *Jefferson "Jake" Briggs* • Elizabeth McGovern *Kristy Briggs* • Alec Baldwin *Davis McDonald* • Isabel Lorca *Fantasy girl* • William Windom *Russ Bainbridge* ■ *Dir/Scr* John Hughes

She's Out of Control ★★ 15

Comedy 1989 · US · Colour · 94mins

Tony Danza here plays a single father worried about his daughter's burgeoning sexuality who becomes embroiled in a number of increasingly embarrassing situations as he tries to curb her romantic liaisons. This is all in vain, however, as daughter Ami Dolenz is a level-headed sort who can manage perfectly without dad's over-attentiveness. A 1950s story in 1980s clothes. DF

Tony Danza *Doug Simpson* • Catherine Hicks *Janet Pearson* • Ami Dolenz *Katie Simpson* • Wallace Shawn *Dr Fishbinder* • Dick O'Neill *Mr Pearson* • Laura Mooney *Bonnie Simpson* ■ *Dir* Stan Dragoti • *Scr* Seth Winston, Michael J Nathanson

She's So Lovely ★★★ 15

Romantic drama 1997 · US · Colour · 92mins

At one time Nick Cassavetes looked as if he would be just another actor with a more famous relative. However, he has successfully reinvented himself as a director and, although the influences of his independent film-maker father John are clear to see, this affectingly offbeat drama stands up in its own right. Sean Penn is a mentally troubled young man who is locked away in a psychiatric hospital. Ten years later he is released and sets out to find his wife (Robin Wright Penn) who has divorced him and married John Travolta. It's a slight tale, but the performances are finely judged. JF. Contains swearing, violence. DVD

Sean Penn *Eddie* • Robin Wright [Robin Wright Penn] *Maureen* • John Travolta *Joey* • Harry Dean Stanton *Shorty* • Debi Mazar *Georgie* • Gena Rowlands *Miss Green* • James Gandolfini *Kiefer* ■ *Dir* Nick Cassavetes • *Scr* John Cassavetes

She's the One ★★ 15

Romantic comedy
1996 · US · Colour · 92mins

Two brothers, Edward Burns and Mike McGlone, banter about love and marriage: one still smarts from an ex-fiancée's infidelity, the other happily plays away from his wife without conscience. John Mahoney stars as their father, with Cameron Diaz and Jennifer Aniston as the women in question. Witty and well observed by Burns, both directing and starring, the problem is that though it's instantly entertaining, it's also instantly forgettable. LH. Contains swearing and sexual references. DVD

Jennifer Aniston *Renee* • Edward Burns *Mickey Fitzpatrick* • Cameron Diaz *Heather* • Mike McGlone *Francis Fitzpatrick* • Maxine Bahns *Hope* • John Mahoney *Mr Fitzpatrick* ■ *Dir/Scr* Edward Burns

She's Working Her Way through College ★★★ U

Musical comedy 1952 · US · Colour · 101mins

An attractive Warner Bros musical version of James Thurber and Elliott Nugent's stage play *The Male Animal*, filmed previously in 1942 with Henry Fonda. Here Ronald Reagan is the college professor who makes a stand for freedom of expression, and it's not often that you get to see a future US president watching voluptuous Virginia Mayo perform saucy dance routines! The generally under-rated Mayo is super as the showgirl determined to improve her mind, and there's nice back-up from hoofer Gene Nelson. TS

Virginia Mayo *Angela Gardner/"Hot Garters Gertie"* • Ronald Reagan *John Palmer* • Gene Nelson *Don Weston* • Don DeFore *Shep Slade* • Phyllis Thaxter *Helen Palmer* • Patrice Wymore *Ivy Williams* • Roland Winters *Fred Copeland* ■ *Dir* H Bruce Humberstone • *Scr* Peter Milne, from the play *The Male Animal* by James Thurber, Elliott Nugent

Shield for Murder ★★

Crime drama 1954 · US · BW · 82mins

Edmond O'Brien co-directs and stars in this meaty drama of a city cop "gone sour", a veteran of the force who hankers after the good life in suburbia. Killing a crook for the loot he's carrying, the cop then tries to deal with the complications. O'Brien's sweaty performance is better than his uneven direction, but there are tense moments and the climax is forceful. AE

Edmond O'Brien *Barney Nolan* • Marla English *Patty Winters* • John Agar *Mark Brewster* • Emile Meyer *Captain Gunnarson* • Carolyn Jones *Girl at bar* • Claude Akins *Fat Michaels* ■ *Dir* Edmond O'Brien, Howard W Koch • *Scr* Richard Alan Simmons, John C Higgins, from the novel by William P McGivern

Shikaar – the Musical Thriller ★★ 15

Musical thriller 2004 · Ind · Colour · 139mins

This Bollywood whodunnit is essentially a tale of two crooks. Danny Denzongpa is a murderous mobster, while Jas Pandher is a charming conman who marries hotelier Kanishka in order to defraud her of her property. However, Darshan Bagga drags out the action over two decades before finally getting down to the mystery of who killed one of Denzongpa's henchmen. This consistently fails to live up to its billing, for while it contains some solid song-and-dance routines, the thrills are harder to find. DP. In Hindi with English subtitles. DVD

Jas Pandher *Vijay Sanyal* • Kanishka *Madhu* • Danny Denzongpa *Damania* • Raj Babbar *ACP Sumed Singh* • Shakti Kapoor • Ashish Vidhyarthi [Ashish Vidyarthi] • Sapru *Tej* • Shweta Menon • Prem Chopra ■ *Dir* Darshan Bagga

Shiloh ★★★★ U

Drama 1996 · US · Colour · 86mins

In a first-rate family entertainment, a boy befriends a hunting dog that's being cruelly treated by its owner, a neighbouring farmer. The boy's dad reckons it's the neighbour's business, and that he shouldn't get involved. But, convinced by a kindly shopkeeper that a boy's gotta do what a boy's gotta do, the kid takes the paw into his own hands and fights doggedly to become the beagle's new owner. Refreshingly unsentimental and impeccably acted, *Shiloh* is a minor treat for kids and grown-ups alike. A sequel followed in 1999. DA DVD

Michael Moriarty *Ray Preston* • Rod Steiger *Doc Wallace* • Blake Heron *Marty Preston* • Scott Wilson *Judd Travers* • Bonnie Bartlett *Mrs Wallace* • Ann Dowd *Louise Preston* ■ *Dir* Dale Rosenbloom • *Scr* Dale Rosenbloom, from a novel by Phyllis Reynolds Naylor

Shinbone Alley ★★

Animated musical comedy
1971 · US · Colour · 83mins

This less-than-animated animation features the characters archy and mehitabel – a love-struck cockroach and the happy-go-lucky cat who's the object of his affection. Created by Don Marquis and originally adapted into a stage musical by Joe Darion and Mel Brooks, Eddie Bracken and Carol Channing take up the big-screen vocal roles and breathe some much needed life into this listless cartoon. TH

Carol Channing *mehitabel* • Eddie Bracken *archy* • Alan Reed *Big Bill Sr* • John Carradine *Tyrone T Tattersall* ■ *Dir* John David Wilson • *Scr* Joe Darion, from the musical by Mel Brooks, Joe Darion, from characters created by Don Marquis

Shine ★★★★★ 12

Biographical drama
1996 · Aus/UK · Colour · 107mins

Although reservations have been expressed about the accuracy of the "facts" in this film based on the life of gifted but deeply troubled Australian pianist David Helfgott, the resulting drama is still an exhilarating and uplifting screen experience. While it was Geoffrey Rush who took many of the plaudits, including the best actor Oscar, it's the acumen of Scott Hicks that prevents this often harrowing story from turning into a melodramatic mush. From the over-looked Noah Taylor as the young Helfgott, Googie Withers as the writer who launched Helfgott's career through to Lynn Redgrave as the future wife who saved him, the performances are of an extraordinary quality, with an astonishing screen debut from stage star Rush. DP. Contains swearing and brief nudity. DVD

S

Geoffrey Rush *David as an adult* • Armin Mueller-Stahl *Peter* • Noah Taylor *David as an adolescent* • Lynn Redgrave *Gillian* • John Gielgud *Cecil Parkes* • Googie Withers *Katharine Susannah Prichard* • Sonia Todd *Sylvia* ■ *Dir* Scott Hicks • *Scr* Jan Sardi, from a story by Scott Hicks

Shine On, Harvest Moon ★★ U

Western 1938 · US · BW · 55mins

This is an early Roy Rogers western, made when Rogers was beginning a challenge to Gene Autry's popularity that would culminate in 1942 when Autry joined up and Rogers officially became "King of the Cowboys". Veteran western director Joseph Kane made dozens of these B-movies with both Autry and Rogers, and knew how to keep the action swift and the running time short. TV

Roy Rogers *Roy* • Mary Hart [Lynne Roberts] *Claire* • Stanley Andrews *Jackson* • William Farnum *Brower* ■ *Dir* Joseph Kane • *Scr* Jack Natteford

Shine On, Harvest Moon ★★★ U

Musical biography
1944 · US · BW and Colour · 112mins

This is a lively vehicle for sexy and talented "Oomph Girl" Ann Sheridan. She plays Broadway star Nora Bayes in one of those Warner Bros biopics that owes little to the truth but includes a load of period songs. Dennis Morgan is terrific as songwriter Jack Norworth – also Nora's husband – and there are telling contributions from Warners regulars SZ "Cuddles" Sakall and Jack Carson. If you want the sordid truth about the Bayes/Norworth vaudeville-to-Broadway affair, this isn't the place to look, but it's still a jolly enjoyable movie. TS

Ann Sheridan *Nora Bayes* • Dennis Morgan *Jack Norworth* • Jack Carson *The Great Georgetti* • Irene Manning *Blanche Mallory* • SZ Sakall *Poppa Karl* ■ *Dir* David Butler • *Scr* Sam Hellman, Richard Weil, Francis Swan, James Kern, from the story by Richard Weil

Shiner ★★★ 18

Crime drama 2000 · UK · Colour · 95mins

This is so nearly a great film. So nearly a gem from the punch-drunk British gangster genre. Michael Caine is in cracking form as a small-time boxing promoter, pinning his ego on one big fight involving his son "Golden Boy" (Matthew Marsden) and an American rival. Yet all around him is rotten and while he blinds himself to betrayals from his daughter Frances Barber and others in his coterie, the police are closing in on the illegal prizefighting scene. Director John Irvin has shot the film through with a steely grey dampness, but this is small-screen subject matter. LH [VIDEO] DVD

Michael Caine *Billy "Shiner" Simpson* • Martin Landau *Frank Spedding* • Frances Barber *Georgie* • Frank Harper *Stoney* • Andy Serkis *Mel* • Claire Rushbrook *Ruth* • Danny Webb [Daniel Webb] *Karl* ■ *Dir* John Irvin • *Scr* Scott Cherry

The Shining ★★★★★ 18

Horror 1980 · US/UK · Colour · 114mins

Based on Stephen King's novel, Stanley Kubrick's horror show stars Jack Nicholson, Shelley Duvall and young Danny Lloyd as the family who are invited to look after a remote mountain hotel when it's closed for the winter. It's not long before Nicholson becomes unhinged as a series of apparitions, hallucinations and time-warps begin to affect his sanity. Trust Kubrick to be different: this horror film chills rather than shocks, works by stealth and provides nothing but eerie discomfort. Filmed on an amazing set built at Elstree (the opening aerial scenes were shot by Kubrick's daughter at the Timberline Lodge in Oregon) and using a gliding Steadicam throughout, the technique is as overpowering as Nicholson's performance, which is both hammy and deeply disturbing. AT. Contains violence, swearing, nudity. [VIDEO] DVD

Jack Nicholson *Jack Torrance* • Shelley Duvall *Wendy Torrance* • Danny Lloyd *Danny* • Scatman Crothers *Dick Hallorann* • Barry Nelson *Ullman* • Philip Stone *Grady* • Joe Turkel *Lloyd* • Anne Jackson *Doctor* ■ *Dir* Stanley Kubrick • *Scr* Stanley Kubrick, Diane Johnson, from the novel by Stephen King • *Cinematographer* John Alcott

The Shining Hour ★★★

Drama 1938 · US · BW · 76mins

Ultra-wealthy landowner Melvyn Douglas, ignoring the disapproval of his brother Robert Young and his possessive, embittered sister Fay Bainter, marries nightclub dancer with a past Joan Crawford. Emotional havoc is unleashed as Young, adored by his wife Margaret Sullavan, falls for his sister-in-law. Director Frank Borzage's film is highly entertaining, marked by committed performances, lots of atmosphere and a luminous portrayal from Sullavan. RK

Joan Crawford *Olivia Riley* • Margaret Sullavan *Judy Linden* • Robert Young (1) *David Linden* • Melvyn Douglas *Henry Linden* • Fay Bainter *Hannah Linden* • Allyn Joslyn *Roger Franklin* • Hattie McDaniel *Belvedere* ■ *Dir* Frank Borzage • *Scr* Jane Murfin, Ogden Nash, from the play by Keith Winters

Shining Through ★★ 15

Second World War spy drama
1992 · US · Colour · 127mins

This should have won the award for the "most hilarious miscasting in a movie ever". Melanie Griffith stars as the half-Jewish, German-speaking American who goes to work for US agent Michael Douglas and volunteers to risk her life by going to Berlin to spy on debonair Nazi Liam Neeson. There's some tension as Griffith runs the risk of being caught, but the 1990s dialogue, ludicrous plot twists and Griffith spoil the film. JB. Contains violence, swearing, sex scenes. [VIDEO] DVD

Michael Douglas *Ed Leland* • Melanie Griffith *Linda Voss* • Liam Neeson *Franze-Otto Dietrich* • Joely Richardson *Margrete Von Eberstien* • John Gielgud *Konrad Friedrichs, "Sunflower"* • Francis Guinan *Andrew Berringer* • Stanley Beard *Linda's father* • Sylvia Syms *Linda's mother* ■ *Dir* David Seltzer • *Scr* David Seltzer, from the novel by Susan Isaacs • *Cinematographer* Jan De Bont

Shining Victory ★★

Drama 1941 · US · BW · 79mins

An adaptation of AJ Cronin's play, *Jupiter Laughs*, in which every character seems to be a doctor and every scene is a crisis of some sort. James Stephenson plays a research scientist who is forced out of Hungary and washes up in a Scottish sanatorium. There his theories of psycho-biology are swallowed whole, especially by Geraldine Fitzgerald. AT

James Stephenson *Dr Paul Venner* • Geraldine Fitzgerald *Dr Mary Murray* • Donald Crisp *Dr Drewett* • Barbara O'Neil *Miss Leeming* • Montagu Love *Dr Blake* • Sig Ruman *Professor Herman Von Reiter* ■ *Dir* Irving Rapper • *Scr* Howard Koch, Anne Froelick, from the play *Jupiter Laughs* by AJ Cronin

Ship Ahoy ★★★ U

Musical comedy 1942 · US · BW · 94mins

Forget the silly story of this spy spoof, which culminates with dancer Eleanor Powell sending a morse code message in taps, and enjoy her sensational dancing, including one of her greatest routines – a breathtaking ship-board tap dance. The first-rate songs include the plaintive *Poor You*, sung by a skinny vocalist with Tommy Dorsey's orchestra – Frank Sinatra. Comics Red Skelton and Bert Lahr are among others contributing to the above-average entertainment quotient. TV

Eleanor Powell *Tallulah Winters* • Red Skelton *Merton K Kibble* • Bert Lahr *Skip Owens* • Virginia O'Brien *Fran Evans* • William Post Jr *HU Bennett* • James Cross *Stump* • Eddie Hartman *Stumpy* • Frank Sinatra ■ *Dir* Edward N Buzzell [Edward Buzzell] • *Scr* Harry Clork, Harry Kurnitz, Irving Brecher, from a story by Matt Brooks, Bradford Ropes, Bert Kalmar

Ship of Fools ★★★

Drama 1965 · US · BW · 149mins

This big, bloated and often boring drama marked the final screen appearance of Vivien Leigh. The story concerns a group of refugees – exiles, Jews, aristocrats, and oddballs – who leave Mexico for Germany in 1933, just as Hitler was lying in wait for them. It's a giant allegory that takes itself very seriously indeed. Leigh's performance as a lonely divorcee is absolutely riveting to watch, and there's an amazing supporting cast. AT

Vivien Leigh *Mary Treadwell* • Simone Signoret *La Condesa* • José Ferrer *Rieber* • Lee Marvin *Tenny* • Oskar Werner *Dr Schumann* • Elizabeth Ashley *Jenny* • George Segal *David* • José Greco *Pepe* • Werner Klemperer *Lieutenant Heebner* ■ *Dir* Stanley Kramer • *Scr* Abby Mann, from the novel by Katherine Anne Porter • *Cinematographer* Ernest Laszlo • *Art Director* Robert Clatworthy, Joseph Kish

The Ship of Lost Men ★★★

Silent drama 1929 · Ger · BW · 121mins

The last silent movie made by Marlene Dietrich before *The Blue Angel* sent her star soaring. The future Hollywood legend plays an heiress who crash-lands during a transatlantic flight and is secretly picked up by a good doctor (British Robin Irvine) and a gentle cook (Vladimir Sokoloff). Although contrived at times, the characters are convincing, the plot is skilfully developed and director Maurice Tourneur's striking visuals and moody atmosphere keep the high seas adventure on an even keel. AJ

Fritz Kortner *Captain Fernando Vela* • Marlene Dietrich *Ethel Marley* • Gaston Modot *Morain* • Robin Irvine *William Cheyne* • Vladimir Sokoloff *Grischa* ■ *Dir* Maurice Tourneur • *Scr* Maurice Tourneur, from the novel by Franzos Keremen

The Ship That Died of Shame ★★ PG

Drama 1955 · UK · BW · 88mins

This is one of the more peculiar civvy street pictures made in the decade after the war. It lurches uncomfortably between comedy, social drama and thriller as it follows the fortunes of the washed-up crew of a motor torpedo boat, who recondition the old tub and turn to smuggling because Britain no longer has anything to offer its one-time heroes. Richard Attenborough is the star of the show, but the uncertainty of tone finally gets the better of him. DP [VIDEO]

Richard Attenborough *Hoskins* • George Baker *Bill* • Bill Owen *Birdie* • Virginia McKenna *Helen* • Roland Culver *Fordyce* • Bernard Lee *Customs officer* • Ralph Truman *Sir Richard* ■ *Dir* Michael Relph, Basil Dearden • *Scr* Michael Relph, Basil Dearden, John Whiting, from the novel by Nicholas Monsarrat

A Ship to India ★★★

Drama 1947 · Swe · BW · 98mins

Set on the Stockholm waterfront, Ingmar Bergman's third feature begins with a happy ending, from which the action flashes back to chronicle the rivalry between captain Holger Lowenadler (whose dreams of seeing the world have been dashed by incipient blindness) and his hunchbacked son, Birger Malmsten, for the affections of dance-hall waif Gertrud Fridh. The structure allows the intensity to wane and the handling is decidedly melodramatic. DP. In Swedish with English subtitles.

Holger Lowenadler *Captain Alexander Blom* • Anna Lindahl *His wife* • Birger Malmsten *Johannes* • Gertrud Fridh *Sally* • Naemi Briese *Selma* • Hjordis Petterson *Sofie* ■ *Dir* Ingmar Bergman • *Scr* Ingmar Bergman, from the play *Skepp till India land* by Martin Söderhjelm

Shipmates Forever ★★ U

Musical 1935 · US · BW · 111mins

Continuing the string of Dick Powell–Ruby Keeler musicals that had served them so wonderfully well with *42nd Street, Gold Diggers of 1933, Footlight Parade* and *Dames*, Warner Bros came up with this slender tale about an admiral's son who would rather be a song and dance man than join the Navy. However, without Busby Berkeley on hand to lift the wafer-thin plot and entirely forgettable score, this is no more than inoffensively nondescript entertainment that doesn't stand comparison with its predecessors. RK

Dick Powell *Richard John Melville III* • Ruby Keeler *June Blackburn* • Lewis Stone *Admiral Melville* • Ross Alexander (1) *Sparks Brown* • Dick Foran *Gifford* ■ *Dir* Frank Borzage • *Scr* Delmer Daves, from a story by Delmer Daves

The Shipping News ★★★ 15

Drama 2001 · US · Colour · 106mins

The icy mists, haunting sounds and shadows of the Newfoundland shores imbue this with a bleak sadness that the intriguing storyline and strong performances fail to dispel. A miscast Kevin Spacey stars as a dull, uninspired man who is seduced into marriage and fatherhood by the sluttish Cate Blanchett, then deserted and widowed in short order. Aunt Judi Dench invites him and his daughter to return with her to the family home in a Newfoundland fishing village. There he lands a job writing the shipping news on the local paper and begins a tentative love affair with widow Julianne Moore. LH [VIDEO] DVD

Kevin Spacey *Quoyle* • Julianne Moore *Wavey Prowse* • Judi Dench *Agnis Hamm* • Cate Blanchett *Petal Bear* • Pete Postlethwaite *Tert Card* • Scott Glenn *Jack Buggit* • Rhys Ifans *Beaufield Nutbeem* • Gordon Pinset *Billy Pretty* ■ *Dir* Lasse Hallström • *Scr* Robert Nelson Jacobs, from the novel by E Annie Proulx

S

Ships with Wings ★

Second World War action drama
1942 · UK · BW · 105mins

An hour could easily be cut from this endless flagwaver designed to glorify the aircraft carrier *Ark Royal* and the men of the Fleet Air Arm. No one doubts their bravery, but did they really deserve this awful mess of soap opera and derring-do? John Clements is the hero who almost turns himself into a kamikaze pilot, his suicidal tactics reportedly worrying Churchill who wanted the film shelved. AT

John Clements *Lt Dick Stacey* • Leslie Banks *Admiral Wetherby* • Jane Baxter *Celia Wetherby* • Ann Todd *Kay Gordon* • Basil Sydney *Captain Fairfax* • Edward Chapman *Papadopoulos* • Michael Wilding *Lt Grant* ■ *Dir* Sergei Nolbandov • *Scr* Patrick Kirwan, Austin Melford, Diana Morgan, Sergei Nolbandov

Shipwrecked ★★★ U

Period adventure 1990 · US · Colour · 89mins

Scandinavian cinema has an international reputation for children's films, a renown recognised by the

Disney studio, who hired Norwegian Nils Gaup to make this lively action tale. There are calm waters to wade through between the swashbuckling, but Gabriel Byrne shivers the odd timber as the pirate captain and Stian Smestad impresses as the cabin boy embarking on the adventure of a lifetime. DP

Stian Smestad *Haakon Haakonsen* • Gabriel Byrne *Lieutenant Merrick* • Louisa Haigh *Mary* • Trond Peter Stamso Munch *Jens* • Bjorn Sundquist *Mr Haakonsen* • Eva Von Hanno *Mrs Haakonsen* • Kjell Stormoen *Captain Madsen* ■ *Dir* Nils Gaup • *Scr* Nils Gaup, Bob Foss, Greg Dinner, Nick Thiel, from the novel *Haakon Haakonsen* by OV Falck-Ytter

Shipyard Sally ★★★ U

Comedy drama 1939 · UK · BW · 79mins

Gracie Fields bade farewell to British cinema with this clarion call for the rights of the working class. Considering the international situation, a film that dared to criticise Westminster for leaving Clydeside shipyards idle and poked open fun at our self-satisfied system of government was rather bold. However, it all ends on a note of rousing patriotism, as Gracie's barmaid returns from impersonating a major American star in London in time to belt out *Land of Hope and Glory*. Another song, *Wish Me Luck As You Wave Me Goodbye* became an embarkation favourite during the Second World War. DP

Gracie Fields *Sally Fitzgerald* • Sydney Howard *Major Fitzgerald* • Morton Selten *Lord Randall* • Norma Varden *Lady Patricia* • Oliver Wakefield *Forsyth* • Tucker McGuire *Linda Marsh* ■ *Dir* Monty Banks • *Scr* Don Ettinger, Karl Tunberg, from a story by Gracie Fields, Tom Geraghty, Val Valentine

The Shiralee ★★★

Adventure drama 1957 · UK · BW · 99mins

One of several features Ealing Studios made in Australia, *The Shiralee* stars genuine Aussie Peter Finch as a poacher who finds his wife shacked up with another man. Consequently, he leaves for a life on the road with his daughter, who becomes his shiralee – an aboriginal word for "burden". The result is a captivating double-act between Finch and the bright-as-a-button Dana Wilson as each of them realises they have a lot to learn. The location photography is incredible, though attempts to inject some humour with cameos from Sid James and Tessie O'Shea backfire. AT

Peter Finch *Jim Macauley* • Elizabeth Sellars *Marge Macauley* • Dana Wilson *Buster Macauley* • Rosemary Harris *Lily Parker* • Tessie O'Shea *Bella* • Sidney James *Luke* • George Rose *Donny* ■ *Dir* Leslie Norman • *Scr* Leslie Norman, Neil Paterson, from the novel by D'Arcy Niland • *Cinematographer* Paul Beeson

S

The Shiralee ★★★★

Adventure drama 1986 · Aus · Colour · 120mins

The edited feature film version of the top-rated Australian television mini-series loses a few subplots but still remains an emotionally moving look at father-daughter relationships. Bryan Brown is a swagman, odd-jobbing his way through 1940s Australia looking for permanent work, who gets landed with his daughter Rebecca Smart when he returns to Adelaide and finds his boozy, unfaithful wife romancing the town bookie. On the road the two bond through illness, separation and the final hurdle of his wife's threat to get Smart back. High-class comfort viewing, superbly acted. AJ

Bryan Brown *Macauley* • Noni Hazlehurst *Lily* • Rebecca Smart *Buster* • Lewis Fitz-Gerald *Tony* • Lorna Lesley *Marge* • Ned Manning *Jim* ■ *Dir* George Ogilvie • *Scr* Tony Morphett, from the novel by D'Arcy Niland

Shiri ★★★ 18

Romantic action thriller
1999 · S Kor · Colour · 120mins

Taking its title from a tropical fish whose survival depends on its ability to swim against the tide – a symbol of the reunification aspirations of Koreans on either side of the 38th Parallel – director Kang Je-gyu's no-holds-barred blockbuster slickly combines political intrigue and explosive action. The identity of the terrorist co-ordinating an audacious bid to assassinate the leaders of the North and South Korean states at a football match is never in doubt. But what is impressive is the way that Kang finds time to explore security agent Han Suk-kyu's emotions during a breakneck race against the clock. Generic film-making perhaps, but executed with intelligence and panache. DP. In Korean with English subtitles. DVD

Han Suk-kyu *Ryu Jung-won* • Choi Min-sik *Park Mu-young* • Song Kang-ho *Lee Jung-gil* • Kim Yun-jin *Lee Myung-hyun/Hee* • Yun Ju-sang *Ko Jung-suk* ■ *Dir* Kang Je-gyu • *Scr* Park Je-hyun, Paek Woon-hak, Jeon Yoon-soo, from a story by Kang Je-gyu

Shirley Valentine ★★★★ 15

Comedy 1989 · US/UK · Colour · 104mins

This is the movie that gladdened a generation of women's hearts and brought cinema stardom to Pauline Collins at an age when actresses are often resigned to sitcom suburbia. Collins's performance as the long-suffering housewife who decamps to a Greek island and Tom Conti is quite sublime and carefully crafted. Director Lewis Gilbert manages to retain the best of Willy Russell's theatrical devices – Collins talking to the kitchen wall, for instance – while opening out the action to embrace a big-screen atmosphere. The supporting cast, particularly Bernard Hill as Collins's Neanderthal husband, is equally convincing, with only the hammy Conti striking a momentary false note. SR. Contains swearing, nudity. DVD

Pauline Collins *Shirley Valentine* • Tom Conti *Costas Caldes* • Julia McKenzie *Gillian* • Alison Steadman *Jane* • Joanna Lumley *Marjorie* • Sylvia Syms *Headmistress* • Bernard Hill *Joe Bradshaw* • George Costigan *Dougie* ■ *Dir* Lewis Gilbert • *Scr* Willy Russell, from his play

Shiver of the Vampires ★★ 18

Horror 1970 · Fr · Colour · 90mins

French director Jean Rollin is the latest eccentric personality to be lionised by exploitation genre fans. His banal poverty row output from the early 1970s is now considered chic thanks to its up-front sexual content and hallucinatory visuals streaked with eerie sadism. This honeymooners-meet-hippy-vampires saga verges on boredom, but ranks as one of his better efforts, occasionally throwing up the odd surreal image and macabre moment of delirium. AJ. In French with English subtitles. Contains violence, nudity. DVD

Dominique *Isolde* • Sandra Julien • Jean-Marie Durand • Nicole Nancel • Michel Delahaye ■ *Dir/Scr* Jean Rollin

Shivers ★★★★ 18

Horror 1975 · Can · Colour · 84mins

David Cronenberg's first important horror film may now look a little crude, but the obsessions that would colour his later works are already apparent. The story is centred around a vaguely futuristic apartment complex where a parasite is gradually working its way through the occupants, transforming them into sex-obsessed zombies. It's not exactly subtle, but Cronenberg delights in some stomach-churning imagery and the stark, chilling design would later be revisited in films such as *Dead Ringers* and *The Fly*. JF. Contains swearing, violence. DVD

Paul Hampton *Roger St Luc* • Joe Silver *Rollo Linsky* • Lynn Lowry *Forsythe* • Allan Migicovsky *Nicholas Tudor* • Susan Petrie *Janine Tudor* • Barbara Steele *Betts* ■ *Dir/Scr* David Cronenberg

Shoah ★★★★★ PG

Documentary 1985 · Fr · Colour · 565mins

Claude Lanzmann spent over a decade shooting the 350 hours of interviews and location footage – he purposely did not use archive material – that were distilled into this cinematic monument to those who perished in the death camps and ghettos of the Second World War. Several decades on, the ruins of Auschwitz, Chelmno and the rest still induce revulsion, as do the remorseless recollections of the Polish peasants who remain tainted with the hatred that made the Holocaust possible. Yet this is also a testament to the survivors who refused to let their spirit be broken by the daily horrors. Putting a face on inhuman misery, this remarkable achievement demonstrates film's unique power. DP. In French with English subtitles.

Dir Claude Lanzmann

Shock Corridor ★★★★ 15

Psychological drama
1963 · US · BW and Colour · 95mins

The characters talk in slogans, the idea verges on the outrageous, but Sam Fuller's direction barrels us through discrepancies in this film's plot with a gut-punching style that flattens objections. Journalist Peter Breck has himself committed to a mental hospital to find a killer and discovers more than he bargained for. Pitting himself against many ideas of good taste, Fuller creates a film that has the stifling grip of a straitjacket. TH DVD

Peter Breck *Johnny Barrett* • Constance Towers *Cathy* • Gene Evans *Boden* • James Best *Stuart* • Harry Rhodes *Trent* • Larry Tucker *Pagliacci* • William Zuckert *Swanee* • Philip Ahn *Dr Fong* ■ *Dir* Samuel Fuller • *Scr* Samuel Fuller, from his treatment

A Shock to the System ★★★ 15

Black comedy 1990 · US · Colour · 84mins

This adaptation of one of novelist Simon Brett's superb tales lacks forceful direction, but Michael Caine gives a terrific performance as the cold-blooded advertising executive who realises that he can get away with anything, even murder, in his ruthless climb to the top. There are a few fair swipes at some obvious targets. TS. Contains swearing.

Michael Caine *Graham Marshall* • Elizabeth McGovern *Stella Anderson* • Peter Riegert *Robert Benham* • Swoosie Kurtz *Leslie Marshall* • Will Patton *Lieutenant Laker* • Jenny Wright *Melanie O'Connor* • Samuel L Jackson *Ulysses* ■ *Dir* Jan Egleson • *Scr* Andrew Klavan, from the novel by Simon Brett

Shock Treatment ★★

Mystery drama 1964 · US · Colour · 94mins

This is the unpleasant story of an actor, played by Stuart Whitman, who has himself committed to a mental hospital and undergoes electro-therapy while seeking a fortune hidden by Roddy McDowall's apparently crazed murderer. True to cliché, Lauren Bacall's psychiatrist proves to be nuttier than any of her patients. AE

Stuart Whitman *Dale Nelson* • Carol Lynley *Cynthia* • Roddy McDowall *Martin Ashly, gardener* • Lauren Bacall *Dr Edwina Beighley* • Olive Deering *Mrs Mellon* • Ossie Davis *Capshaw* • Douglass Dumbrille *Judge* ■ *Dir* Denis Sanders • *Scr* Sydney Boehm, from the novel by Winfred Van Atta

Shock Treatment ★★★

Horror 1973 · Fr/It · Colour · 90mins

A short sequence of Alain Delon and Annie Girardot frolicking stark naked gained this film a notoriety that detracted from its value as a Frankensteinian chiller. Girardot has checked into a clifftop clinic to rebuild her self-esteem after a fractured love affair. However, following a friend's death, she deduces the source of Delon's miraculous rejuvenation treatment. With its sinister antiseptic interiors, brutal Darwinian logic, satirical undercurrent, and twist ending, Alain Jessua's third feature is a much more than mere exploitation fodder. DP. French dialogue dubbed into English.

Alain Delon *Dr Devilers* • Annie Girardot *Hélène Masson* • Michel Duchaussoy *Dr Bernard* • Robert Hirsch *Gérôme Savignat* ■ *Dir/Scr* Alain Jessua

Shock Treatment ★★ PG

Musical satire 1981 · UK · Colour · 91mins

Typical teenagers Brad and Janet reappear in this calamitous and now largely forgotten sequel to *The Rocky Horror Picture Show*, in which life resembles not a B-movie but a TV game show. In the small American town of Denton, everyone participates in 24-hour television in some way. The idea has potential; once again Brad and Janet are the victims of a megalomaniac, but this time a confusing and unfunny story goes nowhere. Wonderful visuals were not enough to provide another cult hit for author Richard O'Brien. DM

Cliff De Young *Farley Flavors/Brad Majors* • Jessica Harper *Janet Majors* • Patricia Quinn *Nation McKinley* • Richard O'Brien *Cosmo McKinley* • Charles Gray *Judge Oliver Wright* • Nell Campbell *Nurse Ansalong* • Ruby Wax *Betty Hapschatt* • Barry Humphries *Bert Schnick* • Rik Mayall *"Rest Home" Ricky* ■ *Dir* Jim Sharman • *Scr* Richard O'Brien, Jim Sharman, Brian Thomson • *Music/lyrics* Richard O'Brien

Shock Waves ★★★ 15

Horror drama 1975 · US · Colour · 84mins

Survivors of a shipwreck are washed up on a tropical island where fugitive Gestapo officer Peter Cushing is busy re-animating drowned Nazi soldiers to form a zombie army. Relying more on atmosphere and tension than gore or jolts, Ken Wiederhorn's directorial debut is an eerie cult favourite featuring a fine performance from Cushing as evil personified. The sub-aqueous undead marching along the ocean floor in jackboots is one of the creepiest sequences in this Florida-shot independent. AJ

Peter Cushing *Scar, SS Commander* • John Carradine *Captain Ben* • Brooke Adams *Rose* • Fred Buch *Chuck* • Jack Davidson *Norman* • Luke Halpin *Keith* • DJ Sidney *Beverly* • Don Stout *Dobbs* ■ *Dir* Ken Wiederhorn • *Scr* John Harrison, Ken Wiederhorn

Shocker ★ 18

Horror thriller 1989 · US · Colour · 104mins

This dud from Wes Craven charts the murderous exploits of an electrocuted maniac television repair man who can appear wherever someone switches on a set. Confusing and tedious, it's a shame such a neat concept was wasted by Craven in his worst movie. AJ DVD

Michael Murphy *Lt Don Parker* • Peter Berg *Jonathan Parker* • Mitch Pileggi *Horace Pinker* • Cami Cooper [Camille Cooper] *Alison* • Heather Langenkamp *Victim* • Richard Brooks *Rhino* ■ *Dir/Scr* Wes Craven

U = SUITABLE FOR ALL Uc = SUITABLE FOR ALL, ESPECIALLY FOR YOUNG CHILDREN (VIDEO ONLY) PG = PARENTAL GUIDANCE

The Shocking Miss Pilgrim ★★★ U

Musical 1947 · US · Colour · 84mins

This was a rare box-office dud in Betty Grable's series of hit movies for 20th Century-Fox. Today, though, this looks like courageous casting on Fox's part, with Grable as a feisty suffragette in strait-laced 19th-century Boston, and there's a Gershwin brothers score to enjoy as well. Particularly pleasing is co-star Dick Haymes, whose mastery of the romantic ballad does not prevent him having fun with Grable during the up-tempo numbers. Despite all that, a horde of disgruntled fans wrote in pleading for Grable to get back to the garish flicks that made her name. TS

Betty Grable *Cynthia Pilgrim* • Dick Haymes *John Pritchard* • Anne Revere *Alice Pritchard* • Allyn Joslyn *Leander Woolsey* • Gene Lockhart *Saxon* • Elizabeth Patterson *Catherine Dennison* ■ *Dir* George Seaton • *Scr* George Seaton, from the story by Ernest Maas, Frederica Maas

Shockproof ★★★

Film noir 1949 · US · BW · 79mins

This deliciously tense *film noir* has parole officer Cornel Wilde is drawn into the tangled past of ex-convict Patricia Knight. Unfortunately here, director Douglas Sirk's initial pace and stylishness run out of steam, and the denouement can only be described as a cop-out. However, although the final destination is a disappointment, you can still luxuriate in the journey. SR

Cornel Wilde *Griff Marat* • Patricia Knight *Jenny Marsh* • John Baragrey *Harry Wesson* • Esther Minciotti *Mrs Marat* • Howard St John *Sam Brooks* • Russell Collins *Frederick Bauer* • Charles Bates *Tommy Marat* ■ *Dir* Douglas Sirk • *Scr* Helen Deutsch, Samuel Fuller

The Shoes of the Fisherman ★★★ U

Drama 1968 · US · Colour · 146mins

Anthony Quinn, in one of his best performances, plays a Russian priest, a political prisoner for many years, who is suddenly elected to be Pope at a time of superpower instability. Director Michael Anderson and screenwriters John Patrick and James Kennaway make a decent fist of translating Morris West's bestseller, even if there is a tendency towards awe at Vatican bureaucracy when it should be inspecting it for story interest. A celebrity cast adds to the gravitas, but Quinn is the reason to view. TH

Anthony Quinn *Kiril Lakota* • Laurence Olivier *Piotr Ilyich Kamenev* • Oskar Werner *Father David Telemond* • David Janssen *George Faber* • Barbara Jefford *Dr Ruth Faber* • Leo McKern *Cardinal Leone* • Vittorio De Sica *Cardinal Rinaldi* • John Gielgud *Elder Pope* • Clive Revill *Vucovich* ■ *Dir* Michael Anderson • *Scr* John Patrick, James Kennaway, from the novel by Morris L West

Shoeshine ★★★★★

Drama 1946 · It · BW · 91mins

The recipient of the first best foreign film Oscar (albeit honorary), Vittorio De Sica's unblinking (and, at the time, controversial) portrait of postwar Italian society has none of the sentimentality that would coat his other neorealist classics, *Bicycle Thieves* and *Umberto D*. Co-scripted by the movie's co-founder, Cesare Zavattini, the fall from innocence of street scamps Rinaldo Smordoni and Franco Interlenghi is clearly allegorical. But, even bearing in mind the prominence of their longed-for white horse, the symbolism is as unforced as the performances. DP. In Italian with English subtitles.

Rinaldo Smordoni *Giuseppe* • Franco Interlenghi *Pasquale* • Aniello Mele *Raffaele* • Bruno Ortensi *Arcangeli* • Pacifico Astrologo *Vittorio* ■ *Dir* Vittorio De Sica • *Scr* Cesare Zavattini, Sergio Amidei, Adolfo Franci, Cesare Giulio Viola, Vittorio De Sica

Shogun Warrior ★★★ PG

Period action adventure
1991 · Jpn · Colour · 101mins

Boasting a fine cast and some rousing action, it's hard to see why this period adventure went straight to video in America. Sho Kosugi (best known for the *Enter the Ninja* movies) stars as a 17th-century samurai who leaves behind the ravages of a Japanese civil war only to find himself plunged into a rebellion against the Spanish king (Christopher Lee). This is swashbuckling entertainment, martial arts style. DP. Contains violence and brief nudity. [VIDEO] DVD

Sho Kosugi *Mayeda* • David Essex *Don Pedro* • Kane Kosugi *Yorimune* • Christopher Lee *King Philip* • Polly Walker *Cecilia* • Norman Lloyd *Father Vasco* • Ronald Pickup *Captain Crawford* • John Rhys-Davies *El Zaidan* • Toshiro Mifune *Lord Akugawa Leyasu* ■ *Dir* Gordon Hessler • *Scr* Nelson Gidding, from the story by Nelson Gidding, Sho Kosugi

Sholay ★★★★ 15

Adventure 1975 · Ind · Colour · 155mins

In making what is considered to be a classic of Indian cinema, director Ramesh Sippy combines elements of Bollywood music, comedy and romance with the spaghetti western genre, creating a technically lauded, as well as massively popular, adventure movie. Told as a couple of extended flashbacks that lead to an all-action finale, the story concerns the rivalry between Amjad Khan's fabled bandit and Sanjeev Kumar, a courageous former policeman, who hires Amitabh Bachchan and Dharmendra to avenge his murdered family. The performances are impressive, especially that of Khan. DP. In Hindi with English subtitles. [VIDEO] DVD

Sanjeev Kumar *Thakur Baldev Singh* • Dharmendra *Veeru* • Amitabh Bachchan *Jaidev* • Amjad Khan *Gabbar Singh* ■ *Dir* Ramesh Sippy • *Scr* Salim-Javed, from his story

Shoot ★

Action drama 1976 · Can · Colour · 92mins

Cliff Robertson, Henry Silva and Ernest Borgnine find themselves deep in *Deliverance* territory in this little-known Canadian movie. It starts well as they go into the woods to hunt and find themselves in a shoot-out with a group of hostile hunters. The rest of the movie focuses on their complex, deadly and increasingly improbable plans to wreak revenge on the attackers. Things pick up towards the end, but it's too little and too late. KB

Cliff Robertson *Major Rex Jeanette* • Ernest Borgnine *Lou* • Henry Silva *Zeke Springer* • James Blendick *Pete* • Larry Reynolds *Bob* • Les Carlson *Jim* • Helen Shaver *Paula* ■ *Dir* Harvey Hart • *Scr* Dick Berg, from the novel by Douglas Fairbairn

Shoot Out ★★

Western 1971 · US · Colour · 94mins

Henry Hathaway goes to the Rocky Mountains with Gregory Peck for this disappointing revenge western. Peck plays the "good" bad guy, a bank robber who comes out of jail swearing vengeance on the members of the gang who betrayed him. The violence is of the fashionable, post-*Wild Bunch* school, with all the blood but none of the resonance. AT. Contains swearing.

Gregory Peck *Clay Lomax* • Pat Quinn [Patricia Quinn] *Juliana Farrell* • Robert F Lyons *Bobby Jay* • Susan Tyrrell *Alma* • Jeff Corey *Trooper* • James Gregory *Sam Foley* • Rita Gam *Emma* • Dawn Lyn *Decky* • Pepe Serna *Pepe* ■ *Dir* Henry Hathaway • *Scr* Marguerite Roberts, from the book *The Lone Cowboy* by Will James

Shoot-Out at Medicine Bend ★★ U

Western 1957 · US · BW · 86mins

A standard Randolph Scott revenge western is given a fresh suit of clothes as three ex-soldiers dress up and talk like Quakers to bring about the downfall of James Craig's ruthless town boss. Scott leads the trio and James Garner, working his way toward stardom, plays one of Randy's two sidekicks in his usual ingratiating manner. On the other hand, Angie Dickinson can do little with the undemanding role of Scott's gal. AE

Randolph Scott *Cap Devlin* • James Craig *Clark* • Angie Dickinson *Priscilla* • Dani Crayne *Nell* • James Garner *Maitland* ■ *Dir* Richard L Bare • *Scr* John Tucker Battle, DD Beauchamp

Shoot the Moon ★★★★ 15

Drama 1982 · US · Colour · 118mins

In this alarming story of marital collapse, Albert Finney – demonstrating what accomplished screen acting credentials he has – plays a writer parting from housebound wife Diane Keaton and their four children. Creating a character more sympathetic than you'd expect, you can almost hear the ticking timebomb of his enraged personality and, although the photography does Keaton no favours, she is less quirky than in her Woody Allen pictures. One of Alan Parker's most interesting essays in intimate drama, it has an uneven, but literate, script by Bo Goldman. TH. Contains violence, swearing and nudity. [VIDEO]

Albert Finney *George Dunlap* • Diane Keaton *Faith Dunlap* • Peter Weller *Frank Henderson* • Karen Allen *Sandy* • Dana Hill *Sherry* • Viveka Davis *Jill* • Tracey Gold *Marianne* ■ *Dir* Alan Parker • *Scr* Bo Goldman

Shoot the Pianist ★★★★★ 15

Crime drama 1960 · Fr · BW · 77mins

Coming between *The 400 Blows* and *Jules et Jim*, this is François Truffaut's forgotten masterpiece. It is a knowing homage to Hollywood *films noirs*, with Charles Aznavour excelling as the pianist whose descent from the classical stage to a seedy Parisian bar culminates in his involvement with some unforgiving gangsters. A grab bag of fond memories, both cinematic and personal, this is Truffaut at his most exuberant, with the stylistic flourishes of the *nouvelle vague* enhancing the romantic melancholy of this tragicomic tale. Endlessly inventive and bustling with life. DP. In French with English subtitles. Contains violence, swearing, nudity. [VIDEO] DVD

Charles Aznavour *Charlie Kohler/Edouard Saroyan* • Marie Dubois *Léna* • Nicole Berger *Thérésa* • Michèle Mercier *Clarisse* • Albert Rémy *Chico Saroyan* • Jacques Aslanian *Richard Saroyan* • Richard Kanayan *Fido Saroyan* • Claude Mansard *Momo* ■ *Dir* François Truffaut • *Scr* François Truffaut, Marcel Moussy, from the novel *Down There* by David Goodis • *Cinematographer* Raoul Coutard

The Shooter ★★ 18

Thriller
1994 · US/UK/Sp/Cz Rep · Colour · 100mins

The unmistakeable whiff of a Euro-pudding hangs over this fairly dim addition to the Dolph Lundgren canon. Playing a US marshal, Lundgren finds himself mixed up in all sorts of intrigue when he hunts for a glamorous hit woman (Maruschka Detmers) at a major Cuban/American summit in Prague. The film fails because of the needlessly complicated plotting. JF. Contains swearing and violence. [VIDEO]

Dolph Lundgren *Michael Dane* • Maruschka Detmers *Simone Rosset* • Assumpta Serna *Marta* • John Ashton *Alex Reed* • Gavan O'Herlihy *Dick Powell* ■ *Dir* Ted Kotcheff • *Scr* Billy Ray, Meg Thayer, from a story by Yves Andre Martin

Shooters ★★ 18

Crime drama
2000 · Neth/US/UK · Colour · 91mins

Surely you've heard the one about the ex-con who tries to go straight but ends up getting dragged into a dangerously dodgy deal by his loose cannon of a pal? Of course, the underworld's seedy opportunism and latent violence underpin the action. Things might have improved had directors Colin Teague and Glenn Durfort focused on honour and responsibility instead of packing in the double-crosses. But it's unlikely. DP [VIDEO] DVD

Adrian Dunbar *Max Bell* • Andrew Howard *J* • Louis Dempsey *Gilly* • Gerard Butler *Jackie Junior* • Jason Hughes *Charlie Franklin* • Matthew Rhys *Eddie* • Ioan Gruffudd *Freddy Guns* ■ *Dir* Glenn Durfort, Colin Teague • *Scr* Gary Young, Howard Andrew, Louis Dempsey

The Shooting ★★★ PG

Western 1967 · US · Colour · 71mins

A weird, legendary western whose existentialism and minimalism is as much the result of having no budget as the philosophical inclinations of its director, Monte Hellman, and its star, Jack Nicholson. Shot in the empty deserts of Utah, it has Nicholson as a grinning hired killer involved with bounty hunters and a mysterious woman in a journey into the real or imaginary past. A puzzle picture that's either intentionally metaphorical or just ineptly made. Hellman and Nicholson made a second western, *Ride in the Whirlwind*, on the same trip. AT [VIDEO]

Jack Nicholson *Billy Spear* • Millie Perkins *Woman* • Warren Oates *Willett Gashade* • Will Hutchins *Coley* • BJ Merholz *Leland Drum* ■ *Dir* Monte Hellman • *Scr* Adrien Joyce [Carole Eastman]

Shooting Elizabeth ★★ 15

Black comedy 1992 · Fr · Colour · 91mins

This is an eminently resistible black comedy. Even if nagging wife Mimi Rogers had been grotesquely shrewish, it would have been difficult to snigger along with Jeff Goldblum's inept attempts to dispose of her on a second honeymoon, but the details of their relationship are actually too black for the unsubtle comic elements to work smoothly. Rogers retains her poise in a thankless role, but Goldblum flounders hopelessly in this increasingly distasteful farce. DP [VIDEO]

Jeff Goldblum *Harold Pigeon* • Mimi Rogers *Elizabeth Pigeon* • Burt Kwouk *Father Chu/Mad Mountaineer* • Juan Echanove *Detective* ■ *Dir* Baz Taylor • *Scr* Robbie Fox

Shooting Fish ★★★ 12

Romantic comedy
1997 · UK · Colour · 107mins

Director Stefan Schwartz's daft, yet endearing, romantic comedy sees two friends – American Dan Futterman and Briton Stuart Townsend – trying to pull off a series of money-making scams. From selling bogus voice-recognition computers to nonexistent loft insulation, the boys are doing well until mutual love interest Kate Beckinsale sets them at odds. This is an Ealing comedy-style caper in a contemporary setting with both a high cuteness factor and some imaginative gags. LH. Contains swearing. [VIDEO] DVD

Dan Futterman *Dylan* • Stuart Townsend *Jez* • Kate Beckinsale *Georgie* • Nickolas Grace *Mr Stratton-Luce* • Claire Cox *Floss* • Ralph Ineson *Mr Ray* • Dominic Mafham *Roger* • Peter Capaldi *Mr Gilzean* • Annette Crosbie *Mrs Cummins* ■ *Dir* Stefan Schwartz • *Scr* Stefan Schwartz, Richard Holmes

S

The Shooting Party ★★★★ 15

Period drama 1984 · UK · Colour · 92mins

On target with regard to upper-class attitudes just prior to the First World War, James Mason's penultimate feature film casts him as the aristocratic organiser of a weekend shoot at his country mansion, where class exploitation and numerous infidelities are also on the menu. Similar to Renoir's *La Règle du Jeu* in its theme of a disintegrating social order, it has a cast to die for; connoisseurs of British television drama may have seen it all before, but this still has acting class in abundance. TH

James Mason *Sir Randolph Nettleby* • Edward Fox *Lord Gilbert Hartlip* • Dorothy Tutin *Lady Minnie Nettleby* • John Gielgud *Cornelius Cardew* • Gordon Jackson *Tom Harker* • Cheryl Campbell *Lady Aline Hartlip* • Robert Hardy *Lord Bob Lilburn* • Rupert Frazer *Lionel Stephens* • Judi Bowker *Lady Olivier Lilburn* ■ *Dir* Alan Bridges • *Scr* Julian Bond, from the novel by Isabel Colegate

Shooting the Moon ★★★★

Drama 1998 · It · Colour · 90mins

Rome emerges as a soulless city in Francesca Archibugi's unflinching yet warm-hearted study of brotherly love and innocent determination. Niccolo Senni carries the film as the teenage son of heroin-addict Valeria Golina, who so distrusts the adults around him that when his half-sister accidentally pricks herself on one of their mother's needles, he assumes the responsibility of having her Aids-tested. Francesca di Giovanni is also impressively natural as his toddling co-star, which speaks volumes for Archibugi's unforced yet eminently sympathetic direction. DP. An Italian language film.

Valeria Golino *Silvia* • Sergio Rubini *Massimo* • Stefano Dionisi *Roberto* • Niccolo Senni *Siddharta* • Francesca di Giovanni *Domitilla* ■ *Dir/Scr* Francesca Archibugi

The Shootist ★★★★ PG

Western 1976 · US · Colour · 94mins

This was John Wayne's last movie and it turned out to be a fitting tribute to a great talent. Director Don Siegel was not a man to dwell on the maudlin, and this fine western plays like a *Shane* for the 1970s. The Duke stars as a retired gunfighter dying of cancer, with Ron Howard as the wide-eyed innocent to Wayne's Alan Ladd. There's also superb support from the likes of James Stewart, Lauren Bacall and, especially, the under-used Hugh O'Brian. The opening titles form a touching montage to an outstanding career; how often does a star of Wayne's magnitude leave the stage with such dignity? TS DVD

John Wayne *John Bernard Books* • Lauren Bacall *Bond Rogers* • James Stewart *Dr Hostetler* • Ron Howard *Gillom Rogers* • Richard Boone *Sweeney* • Hugh O'Brian *Pulford* • Bill McKinney *Cobb* • Harry Morgan *Marshall Thibido* • John Carradine *Beckum* • Sheree North *Serepta* ■ *Dir* Don Siegel • *Scr* Miles Hood Swarthout, Scott Hale, from the novel by Glendon Swarthout

The Shop around the Corner ★★★★ U

Romantic comedy drama
1940 · US · BW · 98mins

Based on Nikolaus Laszlo's play *Parfumerie*, this is a truly wonderful film, deftly directed by the great Ernst Lubitsch and containing a delightful performance by Margaret Sullavan, full of grace and warmth. The plot, about pen pals who fall in love after realising they work together, is paper-thin, but charm is there in abundance, and the young James Stewart is a portrait in perfection. Judy Garland starred in the 1949 musical remake, *In the Good Old Summertime*, and it was also remade in 1998 as *You've Got Mail*, with Tom Hanks and Meg Ryan. TS

James Stewart *Alfred Kralik* • Margaret Sullavan *Klara Novak* • Frank Morgan *Hugo Matuschek* • Joseph Schildkraut *Ferencz Vadas* • Sara Haden *Flora* • Felix Bressart *Pirovitch* • William Tracy *Pepi Katona* • Inez Courtney *Ilona* ■ *Dir* Ernst Lubitsch • *Scr* Samson Raphaelson, from the play *Parfumerie* by Nikolaus Laszlo

The Shop at Sly Corner ★★★

Crime drama 1946 · UK · BW · 94mins

This is a splendid showcase for that master of malevolence, Oscar Homolka. With an accent thicker than his eyebrows, he is suitably shifty as an antiques dealer who not only trades in stolen goods but is also a fugitive from Devil's Island. However, he is occasionally in serious danger of having the picture filched from under his nose by Kenneth Griffith, who is revoltingly effective as a blackmailer who threatens to ruin the musical career of Homolka's daughter. DP

Oscar Homolka *Descius Heiss* • Derek Farr *Robert Graham* • Muriel Pavlow *Margaret Heiss* • Kenneth Griffith *Archie Fellowes* • Manning Whiley *Corder Morris* • Kathleen Harrison *Mrs Catt* • Garry Marsh *Major Elliot* ■ *Dir* George King • *Scr* Katherine Strueby, from a play by Edward Percy

The Shop on the High Street ★★★★ 15

Second World War drama
1965 · Cz · BW · 119mins

Winner of the 1965 Oscar for best foreign film, Czech writer/director Jan Kadar's intimate portrait of two simple people destroyed by the Nazi occupation is exquisitely sensitive, brilliantly played and utterly heartbreaking. Ida Kaminska gives a miraculous performance as an old Jewish woman who owns a little button shop where a humble carpenter (a superb Jozef Kroner) is appointed "Aryan comptroller" by the occupiers. He discovers that Kaminska's stock of buttons is depleted almost to nothing, and that she's totally deaf and quite unaware of the war. His growing affection for her leads Kroner into muddled efforts to protect her, with tragic results for both of them. RK. In Czech with English subtitles.

Ida Kaminska *Rozalie Lautmannova* • Jozef Kroner *Tono Brtko* • Frantisek Zvarik *Markus Kolkocky* • Hana Slivkova *Evelyna Brtkova* ■ *Dir* Jan Kadar, Elmar Klos • *Scr* Jan Kadár, Elmar Klos

Shopping ★★★ 18

Drama 1993 · UK · Colour · 102mins

Paul Anderson's first feature is a slick, superficial exercise that doesn't quite reach the heights of the Hollywood blockbusters to which he aspires, but is still a riveting ride. Jude Law is the adrenalin freak who, along with Sadie Frost, gets his kicks by joyriding and ram raiding. His nihilistic lifestyle is threatened by the forces of law and order and rival rider Sean Pertwee, who views Law's hobby as a profession. The two leads are unconvincing, but Pertwee excels as the villain. JF. Contains violence, swearing. DVD

Sadie Frost *Jo* • Jude Law *Billy* • Sean Pertwee *Tommy* • Fraser James *Be Bop* • Sean Bean *Venning* • Marianne Faithfull *Bev* • Jonathan Pryce *Conway* • Danny Newman *Monkey* ■ *Dir/Scr* Paul Anderson

Shopworn ★★

Melodrama 1932 · US · BW · 68mins

The plot is as shopworn as Barbara Stanwyck's notorious showgirl in this perfunctory melodrama. She starts out as a waitress loved by a college student. Framed on morals charges by his wealthy, disapproving mother, she is sent to reform school. Heavy censorship trimmed the details of her subsequent rise in showbusiness, but Stanwyck's terrific performance makes it enjoyable. AE

Barbara Stanwyck *Kitty Lane* • Regis Toomey *Dave Livingston* • ZaSu Pitts *Dot* • Lucien Littlefield *Fred* ■ *Dir* Nicholas Grinde [Nick Grinde] • *Scr* Jo Swerling, Robert Riskin, from a story by Sarah Y Mason

The Shopworn Angel ★★★

Silent romantic drama
1928 · US · BW · 82mins

Innocent young Texan Gary Cooper, about to be shipped off to France with the army, meets showgirl Nancy Carroll. To the displeasure of her wealthy lover (Paul Lukas), she befriends the young man, who falls passionately in love with her. A superior romantic drama, this is still worth watching, though it's now understandably superceded by the better-known 1938 remake. The coming of sound allowed Carroll to burst effectively into song at the end of this silent version. RK

Nancy Carroll *Daisy Heath* • Gary Cooper *William Tyler* • Paul Lukas *Bailey* • Emmett King *The chaplain* • Mildred Washington *Daisy's maid* • Roscoe Karns *Dance director* ■ *Dir* Richard Wallace • *Scr* Howard Estabrook, Albert Shelby Le Vino, Tom Miranda (titles), from the story *Private Pettigrew's Girl* by Dana Burnet

The Shopworn Angel ★★★★

Wartime romantic drama
1938 · US · BW · 84mins

Benefiting from sound, technical advance and dream casting, this triumphantly successful remake offers the always magical pairing of James Stewart and Margaret Sullavan. With his youthful, gawky attractiveness, Stewart is perfect as the naive and idealistic soldier in love, while Sullavan is exemplary as the self-centred, kept showgirl whose hard-boiled exterior hides a soft heart buried by life's knocks. The stars are marvellous in their scenes together, resolutely unsentimental and extracting every shred of truth from the tale. RK

Margaret Sullavan *Daisy Heath* • James Stewart *Bill Pettigrew* • Walter Pidgeon *Sam Bailey* • Nat Pendleton *Dice* • Hattie McDaniel *Martha the maid* • Charley Grapewin *Wilson the caretaker* • Charles D Brown *Mr Gonigle the stage manager* ■ *Dir* HC Potter • *Scr* Waldo Salt, from the short story *Private Pettigrew's Girl* by Dana Burnet

Shoreditch ★★ 15

Romantic mystery drama
2002 · UK · Colour · 100mins

Shane Richie and Joely Richardson head the cast list of this modest British drama set in London's clubland. A couple in the present day inherit an old Shoreditch warehouse that they discover also contains a bricked-up club and a skeleton. The film unfolds the mystery by flitting back and forth between today and the club's pre-War heyday, when it was a jazz dive. The acting is decent enough, but the ending is contrived, and overall there's little to distinguish it. DA. Contains swearing, sex scenes and drug abuse.

Joely Richardson *Butterfly* • Shane Richie *Thomas Hickman* • Glen Murphy *Albert Challis* • John Standing *Jenson Thackery* • Natasha Wightman *Maisie Hickman* • Jonathan Coy *Karl* • Adam Ross *Tom Hickman* ■ *Dir/Scr* Malcolm Needs

Short Circuit ★★★ PG

Fantasy comedy 1986 · US · Colour · 94mins

Youngsters will love this hip spoof on hardware movies, in which a government robot called Number Five gets struck by lightning, goes AWOL and takes on hilarious human characteristics. As Steve Guttenberg's goofy inventor tries to locate his missing model, the cute cyborg befriends vegetarian animal lover Ally Sheedy and has a series of misadventures. John Badham directs with the lightest of touches, and funny moments include the runaway robot's mimicry of John Wayne, the Three Stooges and John Travolta. AJ. Contains swearing. DVD

Ally Sheedy *Stephanie Speck* • Steve Guttenberg *Newton Crosby* • Fisher Stevens *Ben Jabituya* • Austin Pendleton *Howard Marner* • GW Bailey *Skroeder* • Brian McNamara *Frank* • Tim Blaney *Number Five* ■ *Dir* John Badham • *Scr* SS Wilson, Brent Maddock

Short Circuit 2 ★★ PG

Fantasy comedy 1988 · US · Colour · 105mins

Yet another attempt to humanise technology, this sequel about the former military robot Number Five, now Johnny Five, has several moments of humour, but too many minutes of tedium as it wonders whether to be social satire or pratfall parody. Fisher Stevens returns as the Indian co-inventor of the robot, and again his clichéd character is infuriating. TH. Contains swearing. DVD

Fisher Stevens *Ben Jahrvi* • Michael McKean *Fred Ritter* • Cynthia Gibb *Sandy Banatoni* • Jack Weston *Oscar Baldwin* • Dee McCafferty *Saunders* • David Hemblen *Jones* • Don Lake *Manic Mike* ■ *Dir* Kenneth Johnson • *Scr* SS Wilson, Brent Maddock

Short Cut to Hell ★

Crime drama 1957 · US · BW · 89mins

Look in vain for any sign of the vitality you'd expect from the directing debut of James Cagney. He himself appears only in a very brief prologue to introduce two newcomers, Robert Ivers and Georgann Johnson, as the stars of this updated remake of *This Gun for Hire*. In 1942 it did wonders for the careers of Alan Ladd and Veronica Lake, but not here. AE

Robert Ivers *Kyle* • William Bishop *Stan* • Georgann Johnson *Glory Hamilton* • Jacques Aubuchon *Bahrwell* • Peter Baldwin *Adams* • Yvette Vickers *Daisy* • Murvyn Vye *Nichols* ■ *Dir* James Cagney • *Scr* Ted Berkman, Raphael Blau, from the film *This Gun for Hire* by Albert Maltz, WR Burnett, from the novel *A Gun for Sale* by Graham Greene

Short Cuts ★★★★★ 18

Drama 1993 · US · Colour · 187mins

Admirers of Raymond Carver, whose stories inspired *Short Cuts*, were less than impressed by Robert Altman's reworking and interweaving of his tales into this tapestry of southern Californian mores. But, for those less wedded to or ignorant of the originals, this is a superbly controlled piece of film-making that invites comparison with Altman's own *Nashville*. The only discordant note is provided by the sole non-Carver story, involving jazz singer Annie Ross and her daughter Lori Singer. The rest, however, are engaging in their own right and spellbinding when taken as a whole. In a brilliant ensemble cast, Lily Tomlin, Tim Robbins, Jennifer Jason Leigh and Andie MacDowell give the stand-out performances, but the real star is Altman. DP. Contains violence, swearing, sex scenes and nudity.

Andie MacDowell *Ann Finnigan* • Bruce Davison *Howard Finnigan* • Jack Lemmon *Paul Finnigan* • Julianne Moore *Marian Wyman* • Matthew Modine *Dr Ralph Wyman* • Anne

S

Archer *Claire Kane* • Fred Ward *Stuart Kane* • Jennifer Jason Leigh *Lois Kaiser* • Chris Penn *Jerry Kaiser* • Robert Downey Jr *Bill Bush* • Madeleine Stowe *Sherri Shepard* • Tim Robbins *Gene Shepard* • Lily Tomlin *Doreen Piggot* • Tom Waits *Earl Piggot* • Peter Gallagher *Stormy Weathers* • Frances McDormand *Betty Weathers* • Annie Ross *Tess Trainer* • Lori Singer *Zoe Trainer* ■ *Dir* Robert Altman • *Scr* Robert Altman, Frank Barhydt, from stories by Raymond Carver

A Short Film about Killing ★★★★★ 18

Crime drama 1988 · Pol · Colour · 84mins

Krzysztof Kieslowski, arguably Poland's greatest contemporary director, made a series of television films about the Ten Commandments called *Dekalog*. This harrowing full-length entry in the series won the Special Jury Prize at Cannes. Powerful precisely because of its subdued, matter-of-fact approach, this judgement on murder (be it illegal or state-sanctioned) concerns a youth who kills a cab driver and must face the consequences. Kieslowski was a true master of narrative construction, and many of his thoughtful compositions linger long in the memory. JM. In Polish with English subtitles. DVD

Miroslaw Baka *Yatzek* • Krzysztof Globisz *Lawyer* • Jan Tesarz *Taxi driver* ■ *Dir* Krzysztof Kieslowski • *Scr* Krzysztof Kieslowski, Krzysztof Piesiewicz

A Short Film about Love ★★★ 15

Drama 1988 · Pol · Colour · 83mins

From its bitingly ironic title to its downbeat conclusion, this is one of the most damning pictures of modern city life ever made. Expanding on the seventh part of the *Dekalog* series he made for TV, director Krzysztof Kieslowski revisits the themes of obsession and voyeurism touched on by Alfred Hitchcock in *Rear Window* and Michael Powell in *Peeping Tom*. But his main preoccupation here is with the impossibility of love and the breakdown of community. Impressive and provocative. DP. In Polish with English subtitles. Contains sex scenes and nudity. DVD

Grazyna Szapolowska *Magda* • Olaf Lubaszenko *Tomek* • Stefania Iwinska *Gospodyni* • Piotr Machalica *Roman* • Artur Barcis *Mlody Mezczyzna* ■ *Dir* Krzysztof Kieslowski • *Scr* Krzysztof Kieslowski, Krzysztof Piesiewicz

The Short Night of the Glass Dolls ★★★★

Thriller 1971 · It/W Ger/Yug · Colour · 92mins

Aldo Lado may not be the biggest name in *giallo*, but he created one of the genre's minor masterpieces with this superbly controlled tale of paranoia and political persecution. Complete with a haunting score by Ennio Morricone, it makes eerie use of the grey beauty of Prague to chronicle to the abstract, but increasingly terrifying recollections of Jean Sorel, an American journalist whose search for missing lover Barbara Bach leaves him cataleptic in the city morgue. Ingrid Thulin and Mario Adorf provide superior support, but it's Lado's rejuvenation of such tired symbolism as impaled butterflies that makes this so chillingly memorable. DP. Italian dialogue dubbed into English.

Jean Sorel *Gregory Moore* • Ingrid Thulin *Jessica* • Mario Adorf *Jacques* • Barbara Bach *Mira* ■ *Dir/Scr* Aldo Lado

Short Time ★★★ 15

Comedy drama 1990 · US · Colour · 93mins

A rare leading role for that accomplished comedy actor Dabney Coleman. He plays a cop on the verge of retirement who discovers that not only is he dying, but that the insurers will pay out only if he dies in the line of duty. To the astonishment of partner Matt Frewer, Coleman is then transformed into the craziest risk-taking policeman since Mel Gibson. It's an intriguing concept and Coleman milks it for all it is worth, but director Gregg Champion doesn't look entirely comfortable juggling the action and comedy. JF. Contains violence and swearing. DVD

Dabney Coleman *Burt Simpson* • Matt Frewer *Ernie Dills* • Teri Garr *Carolyn Simpson* • Barry Corbin *Captain* • Joe Pantoliano *Scalese* • Xander Berkeley *Stark* ■ *Dir* Gregg Champion • *Scr* John Blumenthal, Michael Berry

The Shot ★★ 15

Satirical comedy 1996 · US · Colour · 84mins

A little seen but enthusiastic satire on Hollywood, notable mainly for a cameo appearance by Dana Carvey. Yet it is another actor from *Wayne's World*, Dan Bell, who stars here, as well as serving as writer/director. Bell plays a jobless actor who hits upon an insane scheme to hold a blockbuster film to ransom. Sadly, this lacks the satirical precision of similarly themed major-league films. JF. Contains violence, swearing.

Dan Bell *Dern Reel* • Michael Rivkin *Patrick St Patrick* • Ted Raimi *Detective Corelli* • Michael DeLuise *Bob Mann* • Jude Horowitz *Anna* • Vincent Ward *Smith* • Mo Gaffney *Sheila Ricks* • Dana Carvey ■ *Dir* Dan Bell • *Scr* Dan Bell, from his play

A Shot at Glory ★★ 15

Sports drama 2000 · US · Colour · 110mins

What with all the sectarian rivalry, family feuding and boardroom machinations, it's a wonder there's any room left at all for football in this mid-table misfire. Robert Duvall plays the manager of a Scottish club struggling to survive in the lower divisions until new American owner Michael Keaton decides to bring in star forward, played by real-life footballer Ally McCoist. But his on-going battle with ex-son-in-law and wasted talent McCoist soon become tiresome; much of the problem lies with the falsity of the action sequences. DP DVD

Robert Duvall *Gordon McLeod* • Michael Keaton *Peter Cameron* • Ally McCoist *Jackie McQuillan* • Libby Langdon • Brian Cox *Martin Smith* ■ *Dir* Michael Corrente • *Scr* Denis O'Neill

A Shot in the Dark ★★

Mystery 1933 · UK · BW · 53mins

This typically mediocre British "quota quickie" thriller is full of unlikely coincidences and false clues. A Bromley Davenport plays an aged recluse, always fearful of being murdered, who apparently commits suicide. OB Clarence, as the local clergyman, suspects foul play and uses the gathering of the family for the reading of the will to get the truth. AE

Dorothy Boyd *Alaris Browne* • OB Clarence *Rev John Malcolm* • Jack Hawkins *Norman Paul* • Russell Thorndike *Dr Stuart* • Michael Shepley *Vivian Waugh* • Davy Burnaby *Colonel Browne* • A Bromley Davenport *Peter Browne* ■ *Dir* George Pearson • *Scr* H Fowler Mear, from a novel by Gerard Fairlie

A Shot in the Dark ★★★★ PG

Comedy mystery 1964 · US · Colour · 98mins

This was the movie in which Peter Sellers first headed the cast as Clouseau (after stealing every scene from nominal stars David Niven and Capucine in *The Pink Panther* the year before). He mingles accents and mangles motives with his usual skill, producing some of the most hilarious moments in the series. The self-righteous buffoon investigates a murder at a millionaire's Paris apartment, with suave George Sanders as the wealthy resident and saucy chambermaid Elke Sommer the prime suspect. Ten years later he returned to the role in *The Return of the Pink Panther*. TH DVD

Peter Sellers *Inspector Jacques Clouseau* • Elke Sommer *Maria Gambrelli* • George Sanders *Benjamin Ballon* • Herbert Lom *Chief Inspector Charles Dreyfus* • Tracy Reed *Dominique Ballon* • Graham Stark *Hercule Lajoy* • Bert Kwouk [Burt Kwouk] *Kato* ■ *Dir* Blake Edwards • *Scr* Blake Edwards, William Peter Blatty, from the plays *A Shot in the Dark* by Harry Kurnitz and *L'Idiote* by Marcel Achard

Shotgun ★★

Western 1955 · US · Colour · 80mins

A well-cast western that was, for its time, rather brutal and violent. Yvonne De Carlo is splendidly sultry as a mixed-race woman staked out in a snake trap by Apaches and left to die. Rescued by Sterling Hayden, she tags along with him as he pursues a killer. The harsh landscape is striking in Technicolor and the characters are strongly etched in a screenplay co-written by actor Rory Calhoun. AE

Sterling Hayden *Clay* • Yvonne De Carlo *Abby* • Zachary Scott *Reb* • Guy Prescott *Thompson* • Robert Wilke [Robert J Wilke] *Bentley* • Angela Greene *Aletha* • Paul Marion *Delgadito* • Harry Harvey Jr *Davey* ■ *Dir* Lesley Selander • *Scr* Clark E Reynolds, Rory Calhoun, John C Champion

Shoulder Arms ★★★ U

Silent comedy drama
1918 · US · BW · 29mins

How Charles Chaplin could find comedy in desperate situations is once again illustrated in this short film. But this film also drew howls of protests, as Chaplin dares make fun of conditions for men in the trenches of the First World War. He co-stars with vermin, a sniper, flooding rain, mud and fear, proving he could laugh in the face of the most horrifying extremes. TH

Charles Chaplin *Recruit* • Edna Purviance *French girl* • Sydney Chaplin [Syd Chaplin] *The American sergeant/The Kaiser* • Loyal Underwood *Short German officer* ■ *Dir/Scr* Charles Chaplin

The Shout ★★★ 15

Horror drama 1978 · UK · Colour · 82mins

Robert Graves's weird story becomes a weird movie, directed by Polish émigré Jerzy Skolimowski and starring Alan Bates as the mysterious interloper who claims to have murdered his family in Australia and is the custodian of various aboriginal curses. Chief of these is the ability to shout so loudly that it can kill. John Hurt and Susannah York are among those reaching for their earplugs. Obscurity is at the heart of the matter, but there is some tension in waiting for the moment when Bates lets his larynx rip. AT. Contains swearing. DVD

Alan Bates *Charles Crossley* • Susannah York *Rachel Fielding* • John Hurt *Anthony Fielding* • Robert Stephens *Chief medical officer* • Tim Curry *Robert* • Julian Hough *Vicar* • Carol Drinkwater *Cobbler's wife* • Nick Stringer *Cobbler* ■ *Dir* Jerzy Skolimowski • *Scr* Jerzy Skolimowski, Michael Austin, from a story by Robert Graves

Shout ★★ 15

Drama 1991 · US · Colour · 197mins

Until his rebirth as the master of cool in *Pulp Fiction*, John Travolta was sunk by embarrassments such as this. He plays a music teacher at a tough school who just loves rock 'n' roll (what a surprise) and, on the run himself, reaches out naturally to rebel pupil James Walters. Lumpy direction of the first order is enlivened by occasional unexpected charm. JM. Contains some swearing.

John Travolta *Jack Cabe* • James Walters [Jamie Walters] *Jesse Tucker* • Heather Graham *Sara Benedict* • Richard Jordan *Eugene Benedict* • Linda Fiorentino *Molly* ■ *Dir* Jeffrey Hornaday • *Scr* Joe Gayton, from his story

Shout at the Devil ★★ 15

Action adventure
1976 · UK · Colour · 114mins

Mixing the rough (Lee Marvin) with the smooth (Roger Moore) wasn't such a good idea, even if their oddball partnership was supposed to be for king and country in the First World War. Based on a Wilbur Smith novel, the tale follows the undynamic duo as they set out to sabotage a German cruiser berthed in an East African delta. Lots of action, but, as neither hero is very likeable, you really don't care. TH. Contains swearing. DVD

Lee Marvin *Flynn* • Roger Moore *Sebastian Oldsmith* • Barbara Parkins *Rosa* • Ian Holm *Mohammed* • Rene Kolldehoff [Reinhard Kolldehoff] *Commissioner Fleischer* • Maurice Denham *Mr Smythe* • Jean Kent *Mrs Smythe* • George Coulouris *El Keb* ■ *Dir* Peter Hunt • *Scr* Wilbur Smith, Stanley Price, Alastair Reid, from the novel by Wilbur Smith

Shout Loud, Louder... I Don't Understand ★★

Comedy 1966 · It · Colour · 100mins

Marcello Mastroianni is a timid chap with a vivid imagination who suffers from flights of fantasy. When he sees his neighbours commit a murder, he is unsure whether this is real or another fantasy. But when the beautiful Raquel Welch supports his story, Mastroianni realises they are both in very real danger. A typically wacky 1960s Italian comedy with Welch turning in another eye-catching performance. DF. An Italian language film.

Marcello Mastroianni *Alberto Saporito* • Raquel Welch *Tania Mottini* • Guido Alberti *Pasquale Cimmaruta* • Leopoldo Tieste *Carlo Saporito* • Tecla Scarano *Aunt Rosa Cimmaruta* • Eduardo De Filippo *Uncle Nicola* ■ *Dir* Eduardo De Filippo • *Scr* Eduardo De Filippo, Suso Cecchi D'Amico, from the play *Le Voci di Dentro* by Eduardo De Filppo

The Show ★★ 15

Music documentary
1995 · US · Colour and BW · 89mins

This adequate hip-hop documentary features talk and squawk from all the leading exponents of the musical genre, including Dr Dre, Naughty by Nature, Run-DMC, Wu-Tang Clan and Snoop Doggy Dogg. Aren't any of them just called Bob or Jeff? Billed on release as the first "rapumentary", the film could frustrate hip-hop fans by being overlong on talk, and overshort on actual hip-hopping. DA

Dir Brian Robbins

Show Boat ★★★★★ U

Musical 1936 · US · BW · 114mins

Arguably the finest creation of the Broadway musical theatre, this Jerome Kern/Oscar Hammerstein II stage masterpiece has been blessed by two equally fine talkie versions. This one is aided by a screenplay from Hammerstein himself, and by the appearances of the great bass Paul Robeson as Joe, who gets to sing *Ol' Man River*, and torch singer Helen Morgan. Irene Dunne is fine, strutting and cakewalking as though to the manner born, but Allan Jones is nowhere near as dashing as Howard Keel in the 1951 Technicolor remake. However, there's little to choose between the versions: both are splendid and well worthy of their superb source material. TS

S

Irene Dunne *Magnolia Hawks* • Allan Jones *Gaylord Ravenal* • Charles Winninger *Captain Andy Hawks* • Helen Westley *Parthy Hawks* • Paul Robeson *Joe* • Helen Morgan (1) *Julie* • Donald Cook *Steve* • Sammy White *Frank Schultz* • Queenie Smith *Ellie* ■ *Dir* James Whale • *Scr* Oscar Hammerstein II, from the musical by Oscar Hammerstein II, Jerome Kern, from the novel by Edna Ferber

Show Boat ★★★★★ U

Musical 1951 · US · Colour · 103mins

A magnificent musical achievement, and unquestionably one of the finest MGM Technicolor features, this triumph from producer Arthur Freed and director George Sidney is supremely satisfying. The cast couldn't be bettered, with Ava Gardner hitting a career high as Julie LaVerne, never more moving than in the scene where she's left on the river bank to the strains of William Warfield singing *Ol' Man River*. The show was, and is, Broadway at its peak, and here the Kern–Hammerstein score receives a definitive rendering. The plot, with its themes of miscegenation and compulsive gambling, is adult, while the opening sequence of the show boat's arrival is a superb marriage of music, style and colour. TS

Kathryn Grayson *Magnolia Hawks* • Ava Gardner *Julie LaVerne* • Howard Keel *Gaylord Ravenal* • Joe E Brown *Captain Andy Hawks* • Marge Champion *Ellie May Shipley* • Gower Champion *Frank Schultz* • Robert Sterling *Stephen Baker* • Agnes Moorehead *Parthy Hawks* • William Warfield *Joe* ■ *Dir* George Sidney (2) • *Scr* John Lee Mahin (uncredited), George Wells, Jack McGowan, from the musical by Oscar Hammerstein II, Jerome Kern, from the novel by Edna Ferber

Show Business ★★★ U

Musical 1944 · US · BW · 92mins

After 35 years in showbusiness, saucer-eyed comedian Eddie Cantor decided to produce a film based on his early days in vaudeville. The result was a cliché-packed musical, beginning in 1914, about the ups and downs of two contrasting couples – hoofer George Murphy and singer Constance Moore (almost broken up by vamp Nancy Kelly), and Cantor and the tiresomely madcap Joan Davis. But there are a lot of good old tunes, including *It Had To Be You*, and Cantor favourites such as *Making Whoopee*. RB

Eddie Cantor *Eddie Martin* • Joan Davis *Joan Mason* • George Murphy *George Doane* • Nancy Kelly *Nancy Gaye* • Constance Moore *Constance Ford* • Don Douglas *Charles Lucas* ■ *Dir* Edwin L Marin • *Scr* Joseph Quillan, Dorothy Bennett, Irving Elinson, from a story by Bert Granet

S

The Show Goes On ★★ U

Musical 1937 · UK · BW · 94mins

Gracie Fields has the dubious distinction here of starring in a *film à clef* about her own rise to showbiz fame. As the chorus girl who becomes the darling of the music halls, Gracie shows occasional flashes of her unique Lancastrian charm. But director Basil Dean stifles her exuberance by saddling her with some woefully unsuitable material. The backstage details ring false, while the film has a shoddiness that would have been unthinkable in Hollywood. DP

Gracie Fields *Sally Scowcroft* • Owen Nares *Martin Fraser* • John Stuart *Mack* • Horace Hodges *Sam Bishop* • Edward Rigby *Mr Scowcroft* • Amy Veness *Mrs Scowcroft* ■ *Dir* Basil Dean • *Scr* Austin Melford, Anthony Kimmins, EG Valentine, from a story by Basil Dean

Show Me Love ★★★ 15

Comedy drama 1998 · Swe · Colour · 85mins

A colossal hit in its native Sweden, this charming rite of passage picture marks the feature debut of acclaimed poet and short film-maker, Lukas Moodysson. However, its treatment of alienated adolescence, provincial ennui and sexual confusion is every bit as superficial as the numerous American indies that have tackled the subject of lesbian first love. Rebecca Liljeberg's performance as the 15-year-old outsider who falls for school stunner Alexandra Dahlström brims with anti-parental resentment and repressed longing. Alas, such perspicacity is absent from the depiction of more peripheral characters. DP. In Swedish with English subtitles. DVD

Alexandra Dahlström *Elin* • Rebecca Liljeberg *Agnes* • Erica Carlson *Jessica* • Mathias Rust *Johan Hult* ■ *Dir/Scr* Lukas Moodysson

A Show of Force ★★ 15

Political thriller 1990 · US · Colour · 88mins

This movie from Brazilian director Bruno Barreto is loosely based on a supposedly true event, when some Puerto Rican student activists were shot as terrorists during an action instigated by a renegade FBI agent. Unfortunately, Barreto's film takes a potentially interesting and controversial subject and turns it into a rather tedious and violent political thriller. However, it does feature a strong cast, including Andy Garcia, Robert Duvall, Kevin Spacey and Amy Irving. JB

Amy Irving *Kate Melendez* • Andy Garcia *Luis Angel Mora* • Robert Duvall *Howard* • Lou Diamond Phillips *Jesus Fuentes* • Kevin Spacey *Frank Curtin* • Erik Estrada *Machado* • Juan Fernandez *Captain Correa* ■ *Dir* Bruno Barreto • *Scr* Evan Jones, John Strong, from the non-fiction book *Murder under Two Flags* by Anne Nelson

The Show of Shows ★★★

Musical revue 1929 · US · BW · 128mins

An early, technically primitive forerunner of the studio star-parade revues that would remain in the repertoire over the next 15 years, filmed entirely as a stage show and compèred by languid, quirky, deadpan comedian Frank Fay. Basically an experimental PR exercise to showcase Warners contract artists, it demonstrates how rapidly and radically tastes in humour, music and performing styles change. On the one hand a lengthy exercise in indescribable tedium, which only the dedicated will endure; on the other hand, a unique and fascinating social-historical document. RK

Frank Fay *Master of ceremonies/Mexican general* • William Courtenay *The Minister* • HB Warner *The Victim* • Hobart Bosworth *The Executioner* • Myrna Loy *Floradora girl/Chinese fantasy girl* • Douglas Fairbanks Jr *Ambrose* • John Barrymore *Duke of Gloucester* ■ *Dir* John G Adolfi • *Scr* Frank Fay, J Keirn Brennan

Show People ★★★★★ U

Silent satirical comedy
1928 · US · BW · 84mins

Here's a wonderful chance to see Marion Davies, the mistress of billionaire William Randolph Hearst as well as the model for Susan Alexander in *Citizen Kane*. How Orson Welles wronged her! In truth, she was a highly intelligent comedian, here playing a young hopeful in Hollywood who graduates from Keystone Kops custard pies to a Gloria Swanson-style *femme fatale*. Hearst didn't want to entrust any old director with Marion, so chose his old friend, King Vidor, who makes an appearance in the film-within-a-film at the end. A sparkling satire. TH

Marion Davies *Peggy Pepper* • William Haines *Billy Boone* • Dell Henderson *Colonel Pepper* • Paul Ralli *André* • Charles Chaplin • Douglas Fairbanks • John Gilbert (1) *John Gilbert* ■ *Dir* King Vidor • *Scr* Wanda Tuchock, Agnes Christine Johnston, Laurence Stallings, Ralph Spence

Showdown ★★★

Western 1963 · US · BW · 78mins

Baby-faced Audie Murphy and bluff Charles Drake star as escaped convicts who become involved in a robbery. There's a marvellous supporting cast of western regulars, and director RG Springsteen tells the tale tersely and tautly. Unusually for a Murphy western, it's in grim black and white. TS

Audie Murphy *Chris Foster* • Kathleen Crowley *Estelle* • Charles Drake *Bert Pickett* • Harold J Stone *Lavalle* • Skip Homeier *Calson* • LQ Jones *Foray* • Strother Martin *Charlie Reeder* ■ *Dir* RG Springsteen • *Scr* Bronson Howitzer

Showdown ★★ PG

Western 1973 · US · Colour · 94mins

This unremarkable western stars Rock Hudson as a sheriff and Dean Martin as a train robber. Both were the closest of childhood friends until Hudson went into crime and married Martin's sweetheart, Susan Clark, who has to stand referee while these two movie stars slug it out and reach a compromise. There are times when the script scratches around for a classical allusion, though mostly it's a matter of furrowed brows, running sweat and New Mexican vistas. AT

Dean Martin *Billy* • Rock Hudson *Chuck* • Susan Clark *Kate* • Donald Moffat *Art Williams* • John McLiam *PJ Wilson* • Charles Baca *Martinez* • Jackson D Kane *Clem* • Ben Zeller *Perry Williams* • Ed Begley Jr *Pook* ■ *Dir* George Seaton • *Scr* Theodore Taylor, from a story by Hank Fine

Showdown at Abilene ★★

Western 1956 · US · Colour · 80mins

Jock Mahoney is no more than adequate playing the American Civil War veteran who refuses to carry a gun as sheriff of Abilene. Much better is Lyle Bettger, who gives a typically intense performance as the one-armed cattle king who has taken Mahoney's girl (Martha Hyer) and wants him dead. Producer Howard Christie liked the story so much he re-made it 11 years later as *Gunfight in Abilene*. AE

Jock Mahoney *Jim Trask* • Martha Hyer *Peggy Bigelow* • Lyle Bettger *Dave Mosely* • David Janssen *Verne Ward* • Grant Williams *Chip Tomlin* • Ted De Corsia *Dan Claudius* ■ *Dir* Charles F Haas [Charles Haas] • *Scr* Bernie Giler, from the novel *Gun Shy* by Clarence Upson Young

Showdown at Boot Hill ★★★

Western 1958 · US · BW · 71mins

Charles Bronson plays a US marshal who rides into a strange town, kills the man he has been pursuing, and is then thwarted by the local residents who regarded the deceased as a respectable citizen. Denied his bounty money, Bronson turns all moody and reflective, pondering the ethics of his line of work. Within the conventions of the B-western, this develops into a fairly complex character study, using the townspeople with imagination. AT

Charles Bronson *Luke Welsh* • Robert Hutton *Sloane* • John Carradine *Doc Weber* • Carole Mathews *Jill* • Paul Maxey *Judge* • Thomas Browne Henry *Con Maynor* • Fintan Meyler *Sally* ■ *Dir* Gene Fowler Jr • *Scr* Louis Vittes

Showdown in Little Tokyo ★★ 18

Martial arts action adventure
1991 · US · Colour · 75mins

This brainless martial arts kickabout teams Dolph Lundgren with a pre-*Crow* Brandon Lee as cops hunting down a vicious yakuza gang operating in Los Angeles. Mark L Lester packs in enough shoot-outs and fights to keep undemanding fans of the genre happy, while Tia Carrere crops up as a singer in the gangster's nightclub. But the best thing about this movie is the short running time. RS. Contains violence, swearing, drug abuse, a sex scene and nudity. DVD

Dolph Lundgren *Detective Chris Kenner* • Brandon Lee *Johnny Murata* • Cary-Hiroyuki Tagawa *Yoshida* • Tia Carrere *Minako Okeya* • Toshishiro Obata *Sato* • Philip Tan *Tanaka* ■ *Dir* Mark L Lester • *Scr* Stephen Glantz, Caliope Brattlestreet

Shower ★★★ 12

Comedy drama 1999 · Chi · Colour · 90mins

Zhang Yang is among China's most contentious indie directors. However, he's in a less abrasive mood with this obvious but amiable allegory, in which the nation's current obsession with consumerism is symbolised by the imminent closure of a traditional Beijing bath-house to make way for a soulless shopping mall. City slicker Pu Quanxin's gradual conversion to his father and slow-witted brother's viewpoint hardly makes for incisive politicking. Yet Zhang treats us to a gallery of engaging elderly eccentrics who drink, gamble and gossip their days away. DP. In Mandarin with English subtitles. DVD

Xu Zhu *Mr Liu* • Pu Quanxin *Liu Daming* • Wu Jiang *Liu Erming* ■ *Dir* Zhang Yang • *Scr* Zhang Yang, Liu Fendou, Huo Xin, Diao Yinan, Cai Xiangjun

Showgirls ★ 18

Erotic drama 1995 · US · Colour · 125mins

According to director Paul Verhoeven, his controversial and much-reviled showbiz exposé is an incisive look at sleazy Las Vegas life. To almost everyone else, it was a posh sexploitation flick charting the rise of small-town girl Elizabeth Berkley from tawdry lap dancer to famed topless revue headliner. Practically nothing works in this tacky sashay through unerotic burlesque. AJ. Contains violence, swearing, drug abuse, sex scenes, nudity. DVD

Elizabeth Berkley *Nomi Malone* • Kyle MacLachlan *Zack Carey* • Gina Gershon *Cristal Connors* • Glenn Plummer *James Smith* • Robert Davi *Al Torres* • Alan Rachins *Tony Moss* ■ *Dir* Paul Verhoeven • *Scr* Joe Eszterhas

Showtime ★★ 12

Action comedy
2002 · US/Aus · Colour · 91mins

The pairing of Robert De Niro and Eddie Murphy probably looked better on paper than it proves to be on screen in this so-so action comedy. De Niro is typically tough and taciturn as a serious undercover cop while Murphy's motor-mouthed persona suits his ambitious patrolman with thespian aspirations. The comedy kicks in when the chalk-and-cheese duo are teamed up by a TV producer (an underused Rene Russo) for a new reality cop show. An action subplot, involving the hunt for an illegal supergun, serves simply to bridge the funny bits. DA. Contains violence, swearing. DVD

Robert De Niro *Mitch Preston* • Eddie Murphy *Trey Sellars* • Rene Russo *Chase Renzi* • Frankie R Faison [Frankie Faison] *Captain Winship* • William Shatner • Rachel Harris *Teacher* ■ *Dir* Tom Dey • *Scr* Keith Sharon, Alfred Gough, Miles Millar, from a story by Jorge Saralegui

Shrek ★★★★ U

Animated fantasy comedy
2001 · US · Colour · 86mins

This is an irreverent, occasionally scatological fairy tale whose state-of-the-art computer-generated technique almost steals a march on *Toy Story*. Almost. Shrek is an ugly, antisocial green ogre (variable Scottish accent by Mike Myers) who must rescue a human princess (Cameron Diaz) in order to appease evil Lord Farquaad (John Lithgow) and rid his swamp of an infestation of traditional fairy-tale characters. *Shrek*'s animators achieve a startling level of reality but it's the characters who carry what is a slight beauty/beast story. Eddie Murphy's Donkey steals the film. AC DVD

Mike Myers *Shrek/Blind mouse* • Eddie Murphy *Donkey* • Cameron Diaz *Princess Fiona* • John Lithgow *Lord Farquaad* • Vincent Cassel *Monsieur Hood* • Peter Dennis *Ogre hunter* • Kathleen Freeman *Old woman* ■ *Dir* Andrew Adamson, Vicky Jenson • *Scr* Ted Elliott, Terry Rossio, Joe Stillman, Roger SH Schulman, from a book by William Steig

Shrek 2 ★★★★ U

Animated fantasy comedy
2004 · US · Colour · 88mins

This welcome follow-up is every bit as cute, clever and funny as the original. The sequel picks up after the marriage of Shrek (voiced by Mike Myers) and Fiona (Cameron Diaz) and follows their trip to her homeland of Far Far Away. If Fiona's parents, King Harold (John Cleese) and Queen Lillian (Julie Andrews), are shocked to discover she's an ogre, that's nothing compared to Harold's reaction to her new husband. The king wants Fiona to marry the foppish Prince Charming (Rupert Everett), so he hires assassin Puss-in-Boots (marvellously voiced by Antonio Banderas) to kill his new son-in-law. The parodies, pop references and Hollywood send-ups are hilarious, as is Eddie Murphy, who's on great form as Donkey. AJ DVD

Mike Myers *Shrek* • Eddie Murphy *Donkey* • Cameron Diaz *Princess Fiona* • Julie Andrews *Queen Lillian* • Antonio Banderas *Puss-in-Boots* • John Cleese *King Harold* • Rupert Everett *Prince Charming* • Jennifer Saunders *Fairy Godmother* ■ *Dir* Andrew Adamson, Kelly Asbury, Conrad Vernon • *Scr* Andrew Adamson, Joe Stillman, J David Stern, David N Weiss, from a story by Andrew Adamson, from a book by William Steig

Shriek If You Know What I Did Last Friday the 13th ★ 15

Horror parody 2000 · US · Colour · 82mins

Spoofing a spoof is a risky business, if only because the jokes are already third-hand before the cameras start to roll. This straight-to-video, threadbare rattlebag of slapstick, skit and smut chronicles the crimes of yet another high school serial killer by way of an excuse for tossing in gags about every element of American juvenilia. Infantile in the extreme. DP DVD

Julie Benz *Barbara* • Harley Cross *Dawson* • Tom Arnold *Doughy* • Tiffani-Amber Thiessen *Hagitha Utslay* • Majandra Delfino *Martina* • Danny Strong *Boner* • Coolio *Principal* ■ *Dir* John Blanchard • *Scr* Sue Bailey, Joe Nelms

The Shrike ★★

Drama 1955 · US · BW · 88mins

José Ferrer made his directing debut with this record of his stage performance in Joseph Kramm's play about a Broadway director who suffers a nervous breakdown and then starts to have flashbacks in a mental hospital. Ferrer acts his socks off, as does June Allyson as his wife, who resents her husband's success and makes sure he never gets to read his good reviews. As a depiction of Broadway's egotism and bitchery, it may be quite accurate but as an entertainment it's gloomy. AT

José Ferrer *Jim Downs* • June Allyson *Ann Downs* • Joy Page *Charlotte Moore* • Kendall Clark *Dr Bellman* • Isabel Bonner *Dr Barrow* • Jay Barney *Dr Kramer* • Edward Platt *Harry Downs* ■ *Dir* José Ferrer • *Scr* Ketti Frings, from the play by Joseph Kramm

The Shrimp on the Barbie ★★

Comedy 1990 · NZ/US · Colour · 87mins

Crocodile Dundee made Down Under flavour of the month for a while and this co-production planned to cash in on the craze. The film mirrored the Paul Hogan smash hit by having a fish-out-of-water type thrown together with his perceived opposite. Rich heiress Emma Samms is going out with a chunky Aussie, much to the chagrin of her father. Although directed by Michael Gottlieb, the film is credited to Alan Smithee – usually an indication of unrest behind the scenes. DF

Richard "Cheech" Marin *Carlos* • Emma Samms *Alexandra Hobart* • Bruce Spence *Wayne* • Vernon Wells *Bruce Woodley* • Carole Davis *Dominique* • Terence Cooper *Sir Ian Hobart* • Jeanette Cronin *Maggie* ■ *Dir* Alan Smithee [Michael Gottlieb] • *Scr* Grant Morris, Ron House, Alan Shearman

The Shrink Is In ★★ 15

Romantic comedy
2000 · US · Colour · 86mins

Executively produced by its star Courteney Cox, this misguided goofball comedy also features an equally wasted performance from her real-life husband David Arquette. Although Arquette's eccentricity has a certain wacky charm, Cox is annoying as an anxiety-ridden travel writer masquerading as a psychiatrist to win over her dream man. Director Richard Benjamin confuses slapstick with stupidity at every turn. SF. Contains swearing, drug abuse. DVD

Courteney Cox *Samantha Crumb* • David Arquette *Henry Popopolis* • David James Elliott *Michael* • Carol Kane *Dr Louise Rosenberg* • Kimberley Davies *Isabelle* • Viola Davis *Robin* ■ *Dir* Richard Benjamin • *Scr* Joanna Johnson, from a story by Alison Balian

Shrunken Heads ★ 18

Horror comedy 1994 · US · Colour · 82mins

Three New York teenagers are killed by hoodlums and brought back to life by voodoo-practising news vendor Julius Harris as severed, shrunken heads eager to wreak revenge and turn other street gangs into zombie monsters. Aside from a few flashes of inspired goreand Meg Foster as a lesbian gangster, this interminable horror comedy has shrunken thrills and sense to match its cranial capacity. AJ. Contains violence and swearing

Aeryk Egan *Tommy* • Becky Herbst *Sally* • Meg Foster *Big Moe* • Julius Harris *Mr Sumatra* • AJ Damato *Vinnie* ■ *Dir* Richard Elfman • *Scr* Matthew Bright, from an idea by Charles Band • *Music* Danny Elfman

The Shuttered Room ★★★

Horror 1967 · UK · Colour · 99mins

This superior tale of the supernatural was based on a short story by August Derleth and HP Lovecraft. Twenty years after she was driven away from her childhood home by a series of sinister happenings, Carol Lynley returns with her new husband, Gig Young. But the old mill is as daunting as ever and deliriously malevolent cousin Oliver Reed and his gang of New England delinquents are far from the ideal welcoming committee. David Greene leaks the secret of the room at the top of the stairs early on, but he still conveys a genuine sense of evil. DP

Gig Young *Mike Kelton* • Carol Lynley *Susannah Kelton* • Oliver Reed *Ethan* • Flora Robson *Aunt Agatha* • William Devlin *Zebulon Whateley* • Bernard Kay *Tait* ■ *Dir* David Greene • *Scr* DB Ledrov, Nathaniel Tanchuk, from a story by HP Lovecraft, August Derleth

Shuttlecock ★★★

Drama 1991 · UK/Fr · Colour · 99mins

Director Andrew Piddington struggles to bring to life Graham Swift's complex tale of a son investigating his father's sudden nervous breakdown, the roots of which lie in the father's wartime activities under the code-name "Shuttlecock". Lambert Wilson is intense as the son whose own sanity begins to shatter in his quest for the truth; Alan Bates simmers as the war hero repressing a grim secret. But the film – though absorbing – fails to match the source novel's intricate layering of past and present. RT

Alan Bates *Major James Prentis VC* • Lambert Wilson *John Prentis* • Kenneth Haigh *Dr Quinn* • Jill Meager *Marian* • Gregory Chisholm *Martin* • Beatrice Buccholz *Beatrice Carnot* ■ *Dir* Andrew Piddington • *Scr* Tim Rose Price, from the novel by Graham Swift

Shy People ★★★ 15

Drama 1987 · US · Colour · 114mins

Russian director Andrei Konchalovsky succeeds in coming up with an intriguing, if flawed, variation on the swamp melodrama. Jill Clayburgh is the snooty New Yorker who sets out on a *Roots*-style journey to the bayous, sulky teenage daughter Martha Plimpton in tow, to locate some long-lost relatives, headed up by Barbara Hershey. The ensuing culture clash is a tad predictable, but Konchalovsky does well in invoking a spooky gothic atmosphere. JF

Jill Clayburgh *Diana* • Barbara Hershey *Ruth* • Martha Plimpton *Grace* • Merritt Butrick *Mike* • John Philbin *Tommy* • Don Swayze *Mark* • Pruitt Taylor Vince *Paul* • Mare Winningham *Candy* ■ *Dir* Andrei Konchalovsky • *Scr* Gerard Brach, Andrei Konchalovsky, Marjorie David, from a story by Andrei Konchalovsky • *Cinematographer* Chris Menges

Siam Sunset ★★★ 15

Comedy road movie
1999 · Aus/UK · Colour · 91mins

A distraught widower's quest to create the perfect paint colour takes him on a wild adventure through the Australian outback in John Polson's quirky road movie. Linus Roache is dogged by disaster – his wife was killed by a refrigerator unit that fell from a passing jumbo – and catastropes occur wherever he goes. Salvation comes in the shape of Danielle Cormack, a free-spirited young woman who's as accident-prone as he is. While there are laughs aplenty, the movie's biggest achievement is to make us really care about these bizarre characters and their off-kilter universe. NS

Linus Roache *Perry* • Danielle Cormack *Grace* • Ian Bliss *Martin* • Roy Billing *Bill* • Alan Brough *Stuart* • Rebecca Hobbs *Jane* • Terry Kenwrick *Arthur* ■ *Dir* John Polson • *Scr* Max Dann, Andrew Knight

Siberia ★★★ 18

Black comedy
1998 · Neth/Fr · BW and Colour · 83mins

This bouncy Dutch black comedy set in Amsterdam is about two friends and flatmates who seduce female backpackers of all nationalities and keep a page from their passport as a memento. Driven by a soundtrack by techno band Junkie XL, this immoral low-budget game of sexual rivalry is full of free-spirited, bed-hopping zeal and has a couple of winning actors in Hugo Metsers and Roeland Fernhout. When Vlatca Simac shows up as the spunky, enigmatic Lara, a dark and dirty *ménage à trois* ensues, but the film retains its cynical anti-romantic stance to the very end. JC. In Dutch and English with subtitles.

Hugo Metsers *Hugo* • Roeland Fernhout *Goof* • Nicole Eggert *Kristy* • Vlatca Simac *Lara* • Johnny Lion *Freddy* ■ *Dir* Robert Jan Westdijk • *Scr* Jos Driessen, Robert Jan Westdijk

Sibiriada ★★★

Epic drama 1979 · USSR · Colour · 275mins

Running over four hours and covering events from the Tsarist era to the middle of the Cold War, Andrei Konchalovsky's powerfully played, panoramic epic is tantamount to the Soviet *Birth of a Nation*. However, there are also echoes of *Gone with the Wind* and *Giant*, as family feuds, thwarted romances and industrial conflicts dominate the action. The film fleetingly considers the impact of history on the individual, but the melodrama holds sway, as the oil prospecting son of a humble peasant accompanies his father to the scene of both his humiliation and his lost love. Imposing, but obtuse. DP. In Russian with English subtitles.

Nikita Mikhalkov *Alexei* • Vitaly Solomin *Nikolai* • Lyudmila Gurchenko *Taia* • Sergei Shakurov *Spiridou* • Natalya Andreichenko *Anastassia* • Yevgeni Petrov *Yerofei* ■ *Dir* Andrei Mikhalkov-Konchalovsky [Andrei Konchalovsky] • *Scr* Valentin Yezhov, Andrei Mikhalkov-Konchalovsky [Andrei Konchalovsky]

Sibling Rivalry ★★★ 15

Black comedy 1990 · US · Colour · 83mins

This movie contains a highly ingenious plotline, with some subtle twists and turns that are negotiated skilfully by the likes of Kirstie Alley and Carrie Fisher. They are supported by several familiar American TV faces, who throw themselves wholesale into the frantic, vulgar action with varying degrees of success. It's all pulled together by the stylish direction of Carl Reiner, but the result still disappoints. SH. Contains swearing and sex scenes. DVD

Kirstie Alley *Marjorie Turner* • Bill Pullman *Nick Meany* • Jami Gertz *Jeanine* • Carrie Fisher *Iris Turner-Hunter* • Scott Bakula *Harry Turner* • Sam Elliott *Charles Turner Jr* • Ed O'Neill *Wilbur Meany* • Frances Sternhagen *Rose Turner* ■ *Dir* Carl Reiner • *Scr* Martha Goldhirsh

The Sicilian ★★ 18

Crime drama 1987 · US · Colour · 109mins

This is a plodding and sententious account of the postwar Sicilian rebel Salvatore Giuliano, whose mania for independence from Italy inspired him to a career of murder and pillage. Christopher Lambert stars as a remarkably uncharismatic Giuliano, who nonetheless charms his way into the hearts of the Sicilian people and even the Mafia (in the person of the sinister Joss Ackland). Director Michael Cimino lets the action swing between huge messy gunfights and tedious moralising from Lambert. RT. Contains swearing, violence, nudity. DVD

Christopher Lambert *Salvatore Giuliano* • John Turturro *Aspanu Pisciotta* • Terence Stamp *Prince Borsa* • Joss Ackland *Don Masino Croce* • Richard Bauer *Professor Hector Adonis* • Ray McAnally *Minister Trezza* ■ *Dir* Michael Cimino • *Scr* Steve Shagan, from the novel by Mario Puzo

The Sicilian Clan ★★★ 15

Crime drama 1969 · Fr · Colour · 113mins

The teaming of charismatic threesome – Alain Delon, Jean Gabin and Lino Ventura – alone guaranteed this film's success at the box office in France and abroad. Delon is a Mafia hitman, sprung from jail by godfather Gabin who's planning to heist some jewellery. Ventura is the dogged cop on the case. It's an old-fashioned thriller, expertly made and boasting a score by

S

Ennio Morricone. AT. A French language film. [video]

Jean Gabin *Vittorio Manalese* • Alain Delon *Roger Sartet* • Lino Ventura *Inspector Le Goff* • Irina Demick *Jeanne Manalese* • Amedeo Nazzari *Tony Nicosia* ■ *Dir* Henri Verneuil • *Scr* Henri Verneuil, José Giovanni, Pierre Pelegri, from the novel *Le Clan des Siciliens* by Auguste Le Breton

The Sicilian Cross ★★

Thriller 1976 · It · Colour · 101mins

It's a double-cross obviously, considering the country of origin of this very conventional Mafia thriller. The only novelty is the pairing of Stacy Keach and Roger Moore as a racing driver and half-Sicilian lawyer who probe the disappearance of a consignment of heroin. Amazingly, it took six writers to come up with such a humdrum idea. Mind you, the shock of watching Moore play a Mafia mouthpiece is a stunning enough concept in itself. TH. Italian dialogue dubbed into English.

Roger Moore *Ulysses* • Stacy Keach *Charlie* • Ivo Garrani *Salvatore Francesco* • Fausto Tozzi *Nicoletta* ■ *Dir* Maurizio Lucidi • *Scr* Maurizio Lucidi, Ernest Tidyman, Gianfranco Bucceri, Randal Kleiser, Roberto Leoni, Nicola Badalucco, from a story by Gianfranco Bucceri, Roberto Leoni

The Sicilians ★★ U

Crime thriller 1964 · UK · BW · 69mins

Known for his brisk approach to shooting and his no-nonsense style, Ernest Morris was able to make even the flimsiest of crime thrillers watchable, including this one about a dancer and a diplomat who search for a mafioso's kidnapped son. Robert Hutton is the imported Hollywood has-been and, even though he was never more than a second division star, he is streets ahead of this material. DP

Robert Hutton *Calvin Adams* • Reginald Marsh *Inspector Webb* • Ursula Howells *Madame Perrault* • Alex Scott (1) *Henri Perrault* • Susan Denny *Carole Linden* • Robert Ayres *Angelo di Marco* • Eric Pohlmann *Inspector Bressin* • Patricia Hayes *Passenger* • Warren Mitchell *O'Leary* ■ *Dir* Ernest Morris • *Scr* Ronald Liles, Reginald Hearne

Sick: the Life and Death of Bob Flanagan, Supermasochist ★★★★ 18

Documentary 1997 · US · Colour · 85mins

This is an excruciatingly painful documentary about the extraordinary life and dying days of Californian comedian and performance artist Bob Flanagan, who used his own sexual masochism as a means of articulating the suffering caused by cystic fibrosis. His partner, Sheree Rose, at first objected to the intrusion of director Kirby Dick's camera into their private practices, but came to terms with it as Flanagan approached death. The result, though not for the squeamish, is sad and very moving. TH [video] DVD

Dir Kirby Dick

Sid and Nancy ★★★★ 18

Biographical drama
1986 · UK · Colour · 108mins

This punk love story is an authentic, uncompromising insight into the obsession of Sid Vicious, who played bass guitar for the Sex Pistols, with drug addict groupie Nancy Spungen, and their inexorable descent into death. It brilliantly recaptures the rage, cynicism and self-destructiveness of the late 1970s punk scene, while never setting up the rock 'n' roll lifestyle as a blissful idyll. Alex Cox directs with an eye for the age and its absurdities, mixing gritty realism with moments of charming romance and black comedy. Gary Oldman and Chloe Webb are outstanding as the lovers. DP. Contains violence, swearing, sex scenes, drug abuse, nudity. [video] DVD

Gary Oldman *Sid Vicious* • Chloe Webb *Nancy Spungen* • Andrew Schofield *Johnny Rotten* • David Hayman *Malcolm McLaren* • Debby Bishop [Debbie Bishop] *Phoebe* • Tony London *Steve* • Courtney Love *Gretchen* ■ *Dir* Alex Cox • *Scr* Alex Cox, Abbe Wool

Siddhartha ★★

Drama 1972 · US · Colour · 89mins

Herman Hesse's 1922 novel is brought to the screen with the reverence of a true devotee by American writer/director Conrad Rooks. However, such is the unquestioning dogmatism of the screenplay, the lushness of Sven Nykvist's Indian landscapes and the stylised earnestness of Bollywood icon Shashi Kapoor in the title role that instead of a moving journey to spiritual enlightenment, this comes across as a glossy promo for Buddhism, in which self-discovery is trampled under foot by clumsy symbolism. An airless adaptation of an obdurate text. DP

Shashi Kapoor *Siddhartha* • Simi Garewal *Kamala* • Romesh Sharma *Govinda* • Pincho Kapoor *Kamaswami* • Zul Vellani *Vasudeva* ■ *Dir* Conrad Rooks • *Scr* Conrad Rooks, from the novel by Hermann Hesse

Side by Side ★★

Comedy 1975 · UK · Colour · 83mins

Who'll win the only nightclub licence in town? Old-timer Terry-Thomas at the Golden Nugget, or those groovy new kids on the block at Sound City? Glam rockers Mud and the Rubettes are joined by 1970s sensations Kenny, Fox and Stephanie De Sykes for this candyfloss movie directed by none other than Bruce Beresford, of *Driving Miss Daisy* fame. Barry Humphries also appears in what must rank as one of the strangest musical comedies. AJ

Barry Humphries *Rodney* • Terry-Thomas *Max Nugget* • Stephanie De Sykes *Julia* • Billy Boyle *Gary* • Dave Mount *Flip* • Frank Thornton *Inspector Crumb* ■ *Dir* Bruce Beresford • *Scr* Garry Chambers, Ron Inkpen, Peter James, Bruce Beresford

Side Out ★★ 15

Sports drama 1990 · US · Colour · 99mins

This poor attempt to cash in on the largely American craze for beach volleyball became yet another turkey for former Brat Packer C Thomas Howell. He plays a naive young law student who comes to California to work for his uncle and gets mixed up with a dropout volleyball star (Peter Horton). It apparently features appearances from the real-life stars of the sport, but that won't mean much to audiences here, and it ends up largely resembling an extended trailer for *Baywatch*. JF. Contains nudity. [video]

C Thomas Howell *Monroe Clark* • Peter Horton *Zack Barnes* • Courtney Thorne-Smith *Samantha* • Harley Jane Kozak *Kate Jacobs* • Christopher Rydell *Wiley Hunter* ■ *Dir* Peter Israelson • *Scr* David Thoreau

Side Street ★★★

Thriller 1950 · US · BW · 82mins

An absolutely first-rate MGM co-feature, one of those super programme-fillers that's not quite a main feature, but far above the average B-movie. The studio's customary production gloss and intelligence is here provided by masterly director Anthony Mann, not long before he hit his stride as one of the finest ever western directors. The film is a virtual *film noir* about a postman (Farley Granger) whose solitary act of theft changes the shape of his life forever. TS

Farley Granger *Joe Norson* • Cathy O'Donnell *Ellen Norson* • James Craig *Georgie Garsell* • Paul Kelly (1) *Captain Walter Anderson* • Edmon Ryan *Victor Backett* • Paul Harvey *Emil Lorrison* • Jean Hagen *Harriet Sinton* • Charles McGraw *Stanley Simon* ■ *Dir* Anthony Mann • *Scr* Sydney Boehm, from his story

Side Streets ★★ 15

Drama 1998 · US · Colour · 130mins

Director/co-writer Tony Gerber's debut depicts New York as a city of self-contained immigrant conclaves that only interact through necessity. While this makes an important sociological point, it doesn't help the structure of this meandering collection of short cuts. Of the five stories, the tragedy of faded Bollywood star Shashi Kapoor has the most heart, while fashion wannabe Valeria Golino's encounter with the pinball of fate offers both satire and slapstick. DP. Contains swearing and sex scenes. [video]

Valeria Golino *Sylvie Otti* • Shashi Kapoor *Vikram Raj* • Leon *Errol Boyce* • Art Malik *Bipin Raj* • Shabana Azmi *Chandra Raj* • Mirjana Jokovic *Elena Iscovescu* • Miho Nikaido *Yuki Shimamura* ■ *Dir* Tony Gerber • *Scr* Lynn Nottage, Tony Gerber • *Executive Producer* Ismail Merchant

Sidekicks ★★ PG

Martial arts comedy
1993 · US · Colour · 92mins

As a bullied asthmatic teenager who constantly dreams of fighting beside Chuck Norris, Jonathan Brandis is likeable and sympathetic. Joe Piscopo is outrageous as a lunk-headed karate instructor, though Mako counter-balances that with a nice little performance as another tutor. Outrageous portrayals and unoriginality apart, the main quibble is that this frequently comes across as a commercial for Norris . KB [video]

Chuck Norris • Jonathan Brandis *Barry Gabrewski* • Beau Bridges *Jerry Gabrewski* • Joe Piscopo *Kelly Stone* • Mako *Mr Lee* • Julia Nickson-Soul *Noreen Chan* ■ *Dir* Aaron Norris • *Scr* Donald G Thompson

The Sidelong Glances of a Pigeon Kicker ★★

Drama 1970 · US · Colour · 86mins

A little late for the psychedelic 1960s, this self-satisfied and barely screened little movie was a rare US feature outing for talented theatre and opera director John Dexter, whose main claim to cinematic fame was the dire but popular *The Virgin Soldiers*. Manhattan, as ever, looks good, and the cast of Broadway ladies is not without interest, but Jordan Christopher is wholly inadequate as a forerunner to Travis Bickle in *Taxi Driver*. TS. Contains swearing.

Jordan Christopher *Jonathan* • Jill O'Hara *Jennifer* • Robert Walden *Winslow Smith* • Kate Reid *Mother* • William Redfield *Father* • Lois Nettleton *Mildred* • Boni Enten *Naomi* • Elaine Stritch *Tough lady* ■ *Dir* John Dexter • *Scr* Ron Whyte, from the novel by David Boyer

Sidewalk Stories ★★★★ 15

Silent drama 1989 · US · BW · 100mins

Written, directed, produced by and starring Charles Lane, this remarkable tribute to the art of Charlie Chaplin is virtually without dialogue. As a struggling Greenwich Village artist, Lane pays his debt to the Little Tramp in a knockabout scene that recalls a dozen stand-offs between Chaplin and bushy-browed Eric Campbell. In keeping with the homage there's pathos as well as slapstick, as Lane takes in an abandoned child (played by his own daughter, Nicole Alysia). Rarely has the modern city looked less sinister than in Bill Dill's stylish black-and-white images, while Marc Marder's score is almost a character in itself. DP. Contains nudity.

Charles Lane (3) *Artist* • Nicole Alysia *Child* • Sandye Wilson *Young woman* • Darnell Williams *Father* • Trula Hoosier *Mother* • George Riddick *Street partner* • Tom Hoover *Portrait artist* ■ *Dir/Scr* Charles Lane (3)

Sidewalks of New York ★★★ 15

Romantic comedy
2000 · US · Colour · 103mins

Writer/director/actor Edward Burns tries to emulate Woody Allen with this romantic comedy that doubles as an ode to the city of New York. It follows the interrelated romantic liaisons of six individuals. Stanley Tucci is suitably sleazy as the philandering husband having a relationship with Brittany Murphy while his wife Heather Graham considers a romance of her own with a TV producer (played by Burns himself). Charming in places, this never quite gels into a captivating story, despite a memorable turn from Dennis Farina as an ageing lothario. JB [video] DVD

Edward Burns *Tommy* • Rosario Dawson *Maria* • Dennis Farina *Carpo* • Heather Graham *Annie* • David Krumholtz *Ben* • Brittany Murphy *Ashley* • Stanley Tucci *Griffin* ■ *Dir/Scr* Edward Burns

Sideways ★★★★★ 15

Romantic comedy drama
2004 · US · Colour · 121mins

Director Alexander Payne's dissection of American social mores is his finest movie to date. Middle-aged mates Paul Giamatti and Thomas Haden Church take a trip to California's wine country to celebrate the latter's upcoming wedding. But Giamatti's wine-tasting plans get sidelined by Church's desperation for a last fling and his attempts to set his friend up with an equally grape-savvy waitress (Virginia Madsen). Thanks to astonishing performances from Giamatti (a rumpled bundle of nervous self-loathing), Church (a deliciously deadpan but fading Casanova) and the Oscar-nominated Madsen, Payne's richly rewarding comedy is of the best vintage. It takes oblique glances at the buddy flick and road movie by skewering both with poignancy, truth and wit to give a fresh vitality to each well-worn genre. AJ. Contains swearing, sex scenes. [video] DVD

Paul Giamatti *Miles Raymond* • Thomas Haden Church *Jack Lopate* • Virginia Madsen *Maya* • Sandra Oh *Stephanie* • Marylouise Burke *Miles's mother* • Jessica Hecht *Victoria* • Missy Doty *Cammi* • MC Gainey *Cammi's husband* ■ *Dir* Alexander Payne • *Scr* Alexander Payne, Jim Taylor, from the novel by Rex Pickett

Sidewinder One ★

Sports action drama
1977 · US · Colour · 96mins

Fans of motocross (the fancy name for scrambling) won't find much to enjoy in this 1970s action drama featuring Susan Howard as the wealthy owner of a company specialising in stripped-down racing bikes. When not wandering the tracks between the interminable, identical-seeming runs, she enjoys the attentions of biker Michael Parks. Parks's buddy is played by the oddly repellent Marjoe Gortner, the real-life evangelist turned actor. AT

Marjoe Gortner *Digger* • Michael Parks *JW Wyatt* • Susan Howard *Chris Gentry* • Alex Cord *Packard Gentry* • Charlotte Rae *Mrs Holt* ■ *Dir* Earl Bellamy • *Scr* Nancy Voyles Crawford, Thomas A McMahon

The Siege ★★ 15

Political action thriller
1998 · US · Colour · 111mins

Denzel Washington and Annette Bening play rival agents in this muddled thriller that can't decide whether it's a message movie or an action adventure. Islamic terrorists are attacking New York and different Government agencies are competing to deal with the violent outbreak. Listlessly directed by Edward Zwick and understated in key plot areas, this routine potboiler lacks suspense. AJ. Contains swearing, violence. [video] DVD

Denzel Washington *Anthony "Hub" Hubbard* • Annette Bening *Elise Kraft/Sharon Bridger* • Bruce Willis *General William Devereaux* • Tony Shalhoub *Frank Haddad* • Sami Bouajila *Samir Nazhde* • Ahmed Ben Larby *Sheik Ahmed Bin Talal* ■ *Dir* Edward Zwick • *Scr* Lawrence Wright, Menno Meyjes, Edward Zwick, from a story by Lawrence Wright

The Siege at Red River ★★★ U

Western 1954 · US · Colour · 85mins

A routine programme filler from producer Leonard Goldstein, who cleverly hijacked the colour climax of an earlier western (1944's *Buffalo Bill*) and used it virtually intact in this movie, inserting new close-ups of his principal players. The cast is headed by the ever interesting, and once hugely popular, Van Johnson. Director Rudolph Maté keeps the film moving, and the 1950s Technicolor, along with the appearance of Joanne Dru make it still worth watching today. TS

Van Johnson *Jim Farraday* • Joanne Dru *Nora Curtis* • Richard Boone *Brett Manning* • Milburn Stone *Benjy* • Jeff Morrow *Frank Kelso* • Craig Hill *Lieutenant Braden* ■ *Dir* Rudolph Maté • *Scr* Sydney Boehm, from a story by J Robert Bren, Gladys Atwater

The Siege of Pinchgut ★★ U

Thriller 1959 · UK · BW · 106mins

Ealing Studios had already made several films in Australia, including *Bitter Springs* and *The Shiralee*. Among the company's last productions was this muddled crime drama about an escaped prisoner who wants a new trial, holding captives on the tiny island of Pinchgut in the middle of Sydney Harbour. Aldo Ray was uninspired casting for the central role, and the resolution is rather unsatisfactory. At least the picture gains a strong documentary look from director Harry Watt's use of the locations. AE

Aldo Ray *Matt Kirk* • Heather Sears *Ann Fulton* • Neil McCallum *Johnny Kirk* • Victor Maddern *Bert* • Carlo Justini *Luke* • Alan Tilvern *Supt Hanna* • Barbara Mullen *Mrs Fulton* ■ *Dir* Harry Watt • *Scr* Inman Hunter, Lee Robinson, Harry Watt, John Cleary, from a story by Inman Hunter, Lee Robinson

The Siege of Sidney Street ★★

Historical drama 1960 · UK · BW · 93mins

Alfred Hitchcock drew on this famous piece of Edwardian history for *The Man Who Knew Too Much*, but this reconstruction sticks a mite closer to the facts. The East End locale looks rather thrown together and the early scenes get bogged down in background information. But once the Russian anarchists have barricaded themselves in, the action begins to come to life. Donald Sinden plods along as the inspector on the trail of Peter Wyngarde and his compatriots, Kieron Moore and Leonard Sachs. DP

Peter Wyngarde *Peter the Painter* • Donald Sinden *Inspector John Mannering* • Nicole Berger *Sara* • Kieron Moore *Yoska* • Godfrey Quigley *Blakey* • Angela Newman *Nina* • TP McKenna *Lapidos* • Leonard Sachs *Svaars* ■ *Dir* Robert S Baker, Monty Berman • *Scr* Jimmy Sangster, Alexander Baron, from a story by Jimmy Sangster

The Siege of Syracuse ★★

Period adventure epic
1959 · It · Colour · 97mins

Heart-throb Rossano Brazzi stars this rather ridiculous sword-and-sandal adventure. He manages to keep a straight face as Archimedes, the mathematician and engineer who is torn between duty and ambition during a war between Rome and Carthage. If all the intrigue and treachery weren't enough, there is also a romantic triangle involving a dancer, a Roman consul and a son Brazzi didn't know he had. The destruction of the Roman fleet with giant mirrors is a stroke of bargain basement brilliance. DP. In Italian with English subtitles.

Rossano Brazzi *Archimedes* • Tina Louise *Diana* • Sylva Koscina *Clio* • Enrico Maria Salerno *Gorgia* • Gino Cervi *Gerone* ■ *Dir* Pietro Francisci • *Scr* Pietro Francisci, Giorgio Graziosi, Ennio De Concini

The Siege of the Saxons ★★ U

Period adventure 1963 · UK · Colour · 85mins

Second-rate British thespians clank around in chain mail while women blush demurely in this Arthurian tosh. The sword Excalibur is still the weapon of choice, sought after by outlaw hero Ronald Lewis, the wooden Mark Dignam as King Arthur himself, and Jerome Willis as a villain with a dodgy leg. Chief damsel is Janette Scott, the daughter of Thora Hird and a leading British starlet of the day. Several knights short of a round table. AT

Ronald Lewis *Robert Marshall* • Janette Scott *Katherine* • Ronald Howard *Edmund of Cornwall* • Mark Dignam *King Arthur* • John Laurie *Merlin* • Jerome Willis *Limping man* • Richard Clarke (3) *Saxon Prince* • Charles Lloyd Pack *Doctor* ■ *Dir* Nathan Juran • *Scr* Jud Kinberg, John Kohn

Sierra ★★ U

Western 1950 · US · Colour · 82mins

America's most decorated war hero, Audie Murphy, was just settling into his western stride when he starred in this Technicolor remake of a forgotten 1938 film called *Forbidden Valley*, in which Murphy accompanies his wrongly accused father Dean Jagger into hiding. He also had a decent director in Alfred E Green to help him, but the result was still routine. TS

Wanda Hendrix *Riley Martin* • Audie Murphy *Ring Hassard* • Burl Ives *Lonesome* • Dean Jagger *Jeff Hassard* • Richard Rober *Big Matt* • Anthony Curtis [Tony Curtis] *Brent Coulter* • James Arness *Little Sam* ■ *Dir* Alfred E Green • *Scr* Edna Anhalt, Milton Gunzberg, from the novel by Stuart Hardy

Sierra Baron ★★ U

Western 1958 · US · Colour · 79mins

A standard western plot is moved to the early California of 1848 as Brian Keith's gunslinger is hired to kill Rick Jason's young Spanish rancher by Steve Brodie's Yankee landgrabber. Rita Gam, as the Spaniard's beautiful sister, is instrumental in making Keith change sides. Brian Keith does well in one of his first leading roles. Mexican locations stand in for California and are outstandingly well photographed by Alex Phillips under the direction of former editor James B Clark. AE

Brian Keith *Jack McCracken* • Rick Jason *Miguel Delmonte* • Rita Gam *Felicia Delmonte* • Mala Powers *Sue Russell* • Steve Brodie *Rufus Bynum* ■ *Dir* James B Clark • *Scr* Houston Branch, from a novel by Thomas Wakefield Blackburn

Siesta ★ 18

Psychological drama
1987 · US · Colour · 92mins

An interesting cast flounders in a plotless scenario which lands (with skydiver Ellen Barkin!) in steamy Spain. There, Barkin's murder and rape fantasies entwine as ineffectually as a soft porn movie while the film explores her sexual history. One is left feeling conned by an array of stars all purporting to be in something far more interesting than this actually is. LH [video]

Ellen Barkin *Claire* • Gabriel Byrne *Augustine* • Julian Sands *Kit* • Isabella Rossellini *Marie* • Martin Sheen *Del* • Alexei Sayle *Cabbie* • Grace Jones *Conchita* • Jodie Foster *Nancy* • Anastassia Stakis *Desdra* ■ *Dir* Mary Lambert • *Scr* Patricia Louisianna Knop, from the novel by Patrice Chaplin • *Music* Miles Davis

Sign o' the Times ★★ 15

Music concert 1987 · US · Colour · 81mins

Prince's filmed treatment of his 1987 European concert tour, with short scenes filmed in his Paisley Park studios linking together the live tracks, which were shot in Rotterdam. His Royal Purpleness androgynously bumps and grinds his way through one limp MTV-inspired sexual fantasy after another, all of which run the gaudy gamut between laughable machismo and arch feminism. Sheena Easton and Sheila E puncture his posing with their nifty musical contributions, but this isn't in the same class as *Purple Rain*. AJ. Contains swearing. [video]

Dir Prince

The Sign of Four ★★★ U

Mystery 1932 · UK · BW · 76mins

The first sound adaptation of Sir Arthur Conan Doyle's second novel marked Arthur Wontner's third outing as Sherlock Holmes. Much of the focus of this version falls on Watson's obsession with a young woman who has recently been sent some pearls that were part of an Indian treasure trove discovered by her murdered father. Ian Hunter invests the good doctor's fascination with Isla Bevan with precisely the right blend of well-mannered attentiveness and stiff military dignity. DP

Arthur Wontner *Sherlock Holmes* • Isla Bevan *Mary Morstan* • Ian Hunter *Dr Watson* • Gilbert Davis *Athelney Jones* • Graham Soutten *Jonathan Small* ■ *Dir* Rowland V Lee, Graham Cutts • *Scr* WP Lipscomb, from the novel *The Sign of Four* by Sir Arthur Conan Doyle

The Sign of Four ★★★ PG

Mystery 1983 · UK/US · Colour · 103mins

Ian Richardson gives a sly performance as Sherlock Holmes in director Desmond Davis's entertaining version of Conan Doyle's novel. Davis invests the material with a keen sense of atmosphere and mystery as Holmes is called in to investigate events at Pondicherry Lodge, and soon finds himself embroiled in a case of murder and betrayal. By choosing to focus on Holmes's brusqueness and his insufferable vanity rather than his powers of deduction, Davis brings a fresh slant to the genre. DP [video] DVD

Ian Richardson *Sherlock Holmes* • David Healy *Dr Watson* • Thorley Walters *Major John Sholto* • Terence Rigby *Inspector Layton* • Joe Melia *Jonathan Small* • Cherie Lunghi *Mary Morstan* • Clive Merrison *Bartholomew Sholto* ■ *Dir* Desmond Davis • *Scr* Charles Pogue, from the novel by Sir Arthur Conan Doyle

The Sign of Leo ★★★★ PG

Drama 1959 · Fr · BW · 98mins

Eric Rohmer was the editor of the influential French film magazine *Cahiers du Cinéma* when he made his first feature in 1956, which was only released three years later. It told of a 40-year-old American in Paris, borrowing money on the expectation of an inheritance. However, when it is not forthcoming, he becomes a tramp begging outside cafés. The film, which gives little indication as to the direction Rohmer was to take, is an insightful portrait of a good-natured but hopelessly irresponsible man slowly disintegrating in the face of reality. RB. In French with English subtitles. [video]

Jess Hahn *Pierre Wesselrin* • Van Doude *Jean-Francois Santeuil* • Michèle Girardon *Dominique* • Jean Le Poulain *The clochard* • Stéphane Audran *Concierge at Hotel de Seine* • Jean-Luc Godard *Man listening to gramophone at party* ■ *Dir/Scr* Eric Rohmer

The Sign of the Cross ★★★★

Historical epic 1932 · US · BW · 118mins

Anyone unsure why Cecil B DeMille's name is synonymous with epic showmanship must see this. The territory is familiar: ancient Rome under the rule of the deranged, debauched Nero (Charles Laughton) and his wife Poppaea (Claudette Colbert), and the hunting down of Christians to throw to the lions. The narrative is pegged to a doomed love between Nero's chief prefect (Fredric March) and a young Christian convert (Elissa Landi), but this is secondary to the opulence, decadence, and graphic cruelty of the climactic sequences in the gladiatorial arena. RK

Fredric March *Marcus Superbus* • Elissa Landi *Mercia* • Claudette Colbert *Empress Poppaea* • Charles Laughton *Emperor Nero* • Ian Keith *Tigellinus* • Vivian Tobin *Dacia* • Harry Beresford *Flavius* • Ferdinand Gottschalk *Glabrio* ■ *Dir* Cecil B DeMille • *Scr* Waldemar Young, Sidney Buchman, from the play by Wilson Barrett • *Cinematographer* Karl Struss

The Sign of the Gladiator ★

Period epic drama
1958 · Fr/ W Ger/It · Colour · 84mins

A trashy sword-and-sandal epic about Queen Zenobia, a wanton Syrian beauty whose desert stronghold, Palmyra, is a thorn in Rome's side until they send in the heavy mob to rape and pillage. Zenobia is taken as a slave and loves happily ever after. Released around the same time as *Ben-Hur*, this pathetic effort is crude in every department, with wobbly sets, wonky swords and wooden acting. AT. In Italian with English subtitles. [video]

Anita Ekberg *Zenobia, Queen Of Palmyra* • Georges Marchal *Marcus Valerius, Roman general* • Folco Lulli *Semanzio* • Chelo Alonso *Erica, slave dancer* • Jacques Sernas *Julian* • Lorella De Luca *Bathsheba* ■ *Dir* Guido Brignone • *Scr* Francesco De Feo, Antonio Thellung, Roberti Sergio Leone [Sergio Leone], Giuseppe Mangione

S

Sign of the Pagan ★★★ U

Historical epic 1954 · US · Colour · 92mins

Jack Palance has a whale of a time playing the ferocious Attila, king of the Huns. His bold attempt to sack Rome is only halted by a welter of plot contrivances, but Jeff Chandler's centurion seems no real match for the ruthless barbarian. Lustily staged by director Douglas Sirk and strikingly photographed in early CinemaScope by Russell Metty (who would later shoot *Spartacus*), this is that rarity, an epic with a short running time that doesn't overstay its welcome. AE

Jeff Chandler *Marcian* • Jack Palance *Attila* • Ludmilla Tcherina *Princess Pulcheria* • Rita Gam *Kubra* • Jeff Morrow *Paulinus* • George Dolenz *Theodosius* • Eduard Franz *Astrologer* • Allison Hayes *Ildico* ■ *Dir* Douglas Sirk • *Scr* Oscar Brodney, Barre Lyndon, from a story by Oscar Brodney

Signal 7 ★★★

Comedy drama 1983 · US · Colour · 92mins

This movie is surely dedicated to the patron saint of experimental low-budget drama, John Cassavetes. He would doubtless have approved of the episodic structure, improvisational acting techniques and recording on videotape and transferring to film stock to cut costs. The casual viewer, however, might struggle to identify with Bill Ackridge and Dan Leegant, the taxi drivers whose opinions, concerns and aspirations are the focus of this talkative drama. DP. Contains swearing.

Bill Ackridge *Speed* • Dan Leegant *Marty* • John Tidwell *Johnny* • Herb Mills *Steve* • Don Bajema *Roger* • Phil Polakoff *Phil* ■ *Dir/Scr* Rob Nilsson

La Signora di Tutti ★★★

Drama 1934 · It · BW · 89mins

Made during the nomadic phase of his career, Max Ophüls's sole Italian venture bears the slight influence of the glossy "white telephone" pictures then dominating the local industry. However, this is very much an Ophüls picture, giving early glimpses of the structural fragmentation and visual fluidity that characterises his best work. Told in a series of flashbacks, as actress Ise Miranda undergoes surgery following a suicide attempt, this melodrama reveals the price she has paid for her brush with fame. DP. In Italian with English subtitles.

Isa Miranda *Gabriella Murge, "Gaby Doriot"* • Memo Benassi *Leonardo Nanni* • Tatiana Pawlova *Alma Nanni* • Federico Benfer *Roberto Nanni* • Nelly Corradi *Anna* ■ *Dir* Max Ophüls • *Scr* Max Ophüls, Hans Wilhelm, Curt Alexander, from a novel by Salvator Gotta

La Signora senza Camelie ★★★

Drama 1953 · It · BW · 105mins

Michelangelo Antonioni's third feature continues to explore the alienating effects of modern society in what was originally conceived as a vehicle for Gina Lollobrigida. Instead, Lucia Bosé shoulders the burden of a faintly improbable storyline, in which her naive shopgirl is transformed into a starlet, only for her to be destroyed through a combination of limited ability, media pressure and the self-seeking ambition of her producer husband, Andrea Checchi, who pushes her into a doomed Joan of Arc project. DP. An Italian language film.

Lucia Bosé *Clara Manni* • Andrea Checchi *Gianni Granchi* • Gino Cervi *Ercole "Ercolino" Bora* • Ivan Desny *Nardo Rusconi* • Alain Cuny *Lodi* • Enrico Glori *Director* ■ *Dir* Michelangelo Antonioni • *Scr* Suso Cecchi D'Amico, Francesco Maselli, PM Pasinetti, from a story by Michelangelo Antonioni

Signpost to Murder ★★

Thriller 1964 · US · BW · 77mins

This is a well acted but relentlessly stagey opus, made by MGM in black and white when they still felt the need to produce co-features, and based on a one-set West End play of no particular distinction. Joanne Woodward makes it watchable, and Irish-born Edward Mulhare surfaces in one of his few screen roles. TS

Joanne Woodward *Molly Thomas* • Stuart Whitman *Alex Forrester* • Edward Mulhare *Dr Mark Fleming* • Joyce Worsley *Mrs Barnes* • Leslie Denison *Supt Bickley* ■ *Dir* George Englund • *Scr* Sally Benson, from the play by Monte Doyle

Signs ★★★ 12

Science-fiction fantasy thriller
2002 · US · Colour · 102mins

Writer/director M Night Shyamalan here once again deals with extraordinary events from an intimate perspective. He scores highly with the edgy, apprehensive atmosphere that he builds up, as Mel Gibson's Pennsylvanian farmer (a former minister who's lost his faith) discovers crop circles in his wheat field, leading him to believe that an alien invasion is imminent. Credible performances from Gibson and Joaquin Phoenix, as his brother, combine with a spooky ambience and some very effective, old-fashioned jolts to lead us into what should have been an enthralling final act. However, mawkish sentimentality and creaky flashbacks blunt the suspense. JC [video] DVD

Mel Gibson *Graham Hess* • Joaquin Phoenix *Merrill Hess* • Cherry Jones *Officer Caroline Paski* • Rory Culkin *Morgan Hess* • Abigail Breslin *Bo Hess* • Patricia Kalember *Colleen Hess* • M Night Shyamalan *Ray Reddy* ■ *Dir/Scr* M Night Shyamalan

Signs of Life ★★★

Second World War drama
1968 · W Ger · BW · 91mins

Inspired by an event that occurred during the Seven Years' War, Werner Herzog's feature debut incorporates many of the themes that would preoccupy him throughout his career. Peter Brogle is impressively distracted as the Nazi trooper detailed to guard an arms dump on the Greek island of Kos with his wife and two comrades. Using the hostile landscape to explore his psychological state, Herzog contrives a brooding study of an outsider whose sanity ebbs away as isolation, paranoia and the pressures of combat close in on him. Never wholly convincing, but disturbing. DP. In German with English subtitles.

Peter Brogle *Stroszek* • Wolfgang Reichmann *Meinhard* • Athina Zacharopoulou *Nora* • Wolfgang von Ungern-Sternberg *Becker* • Wolfgang Stumpf *Captain* • Henry van Lyck *Lieutenant* • Julie Pinheiro *Gypsy* ■ *Dir/Scr* Werner Herzog

The Silence ★★★★ 15

Drama 1963 · Swe · BW · 91mins

The early work of Swedish director Ingmar Bergman is very much an acquired taste, and this enigmatic contemplation on loneliness and obsessive desire is one of his most obscure passion plays. It symbolically explores the bleak lives of two sisters as they embark on individual odysseys to find emotional warmth and tenderness. The overt sexuality caused censorship problems at the time, but now it's hard to see what all the fuss was about. AJ. In Swedish with English subtitles. [video] DVD

Ingrid Thulin *Ester* • Gunnel Lindblom *Anna* • Jörgen Lindström *Johan* • Håken Jahnberg *Hotel waiter* ■ *Dir/Scr* Ingmar Bergman

Silence between Two Thoughts ★★★★ PG

Drama 2003 · Iran/Swi · Colour · 95mins

Smuggled out of Iran on video, this political parable may look a little rough around the edges, but Farzad Jodat's precise camera movements capture the sombre landscape, while reinforcing the studious pacing. Indeed, director Babak Payami's technical and dramatic ingenuity consistently shine through, as he returns to the assault on patriarchal society that made his 2001 satire, *Secret Ballot*, so compelling. This time, condemned prisoner Maryam Moghaddam causes executioner Kamal Naroui to rethink his unquestioning allegiance to Islamic tradition after he's ordered to marry and deflower her before carrying out his duties – if she dies a virgin, she will go to heaven. A provocative study of gender, poverty and religious authority. DP. In Farsi with English subtitles.

Kamal Naroui *The executioner* • Maryam Moghaddam *The virgin* ■ *Dir/Scr* Babak Payami

Le Silence de la Mer ★★★★★

Drama 1947 · Fr · BW · 86mins

Filmed using non-union labour and without the rights to Jean Vercors's clandestine tribute to the Resistance, Jean-Pierre Melville's debut feature is a masterclass in nuance and gesture. Employing camera angles derived from Carl Theodor Dreyer, Melville conveys the impact on a patriotically silent uncle and niece of the cultured nostalgia and political idealism espoused by a convalescing Nazi officer, whose essential decency has been blunted by indoctrination. Howard Vernon delivers the monologues to perfection, but the dramatic power comes from the heroic stoicism of Jean-Marie Robain and Nicole Stéphane. DP. A French language film.

Howard Vernon *Werner von Ebrennac* • Nicole Stéphane *Niece* • Ami Aaroé *Werner's fianceé* • Jean-Marie Robain *Uncle* ■ *Dir* Jean-Pierre Melville • *Scr* Jean-Pierre Melville, from the novel by Jean Vercors

Silence like Glass ★★

Drama 1989 · W Ger · Colour · 105mins

Jami Gertz heads a cracking cast in a routine disease-of-the-month movie, a contrived three-hanky tear-jerker about a ballet dancer struck down by cancer. With a cast of the calibre of Martha Plimpton, George Peppard, Rip Torn and Gayle Hunnicutt, you'd expect better. But even their combined talents can't transcend a formula film and an especially clichéd screenplay. DA

Jami Gertz *Eva* • Martha Plimpton *Claudia* • George Peppard *Eva's father* • Bruce Payne *Dr Burton* • Rip Torn *Dr Markowitz* • Gayle Hunnicutt *Eva's mother* ■ *Dir* Carl Schenkel • *Scr* Carl Schenkel, Bea Hellmann

The Silence of the Hams ★ 15

Spoof horror 1993 · It/US · Colour · 78mins

Possibly the worst film spoof ever made and it's not hard to identify the guilty party: step forward one Ezio Greggio, who not only gets top billing but also wrote, directed and produced this tripe. Character names such as Jo Dee Fostar and Dr Animal Cannibal Pizza illustrate the supposed target, but more tellingly demonstrate the crass level of the humour. JF [video]

Ezio Greggio *Antonio Motel* • Dom DeLuise *Dr Animal Cannibal Pizza* • Billy Zane *Jo Dee Fostar* • Joanna Pacula *Lily* • Charlene Tilton *Jane* • Martin Balsam *Detective Balsam* • Shelley Winters *The mother* • Phyllis Diller *Old secretary* ■ *Dir/Scr* Ezio Greggio

The Silence of the Lambs ★★★★★ 18

Psychological thriller
1991 · US · Colour · 113mins

This multi-Oscar-winning classic, adapted from Thomas Harris's bestseller, was responsible for giving cinematic serial killers a better image. So what if Hannibal Lecter was an incarcerated cannibal? Portrayed by the masterful Anthony Hopkins, he enthralled cinema audiences. Hopkins won an Oscar for his performance, as did Jodie Foster for her role as fledgeling FBI agent Clarice Starling, who is drawn into a disturbingly close relationship with Lecter as she hunts for serial killer "Buffalo Bill". With a track record for directing quirky comedies, director Jonathan Demme made a seemingly effortless switch to terror, summoning up a magnificent air of gothic gloom. This modern masterpiece was followed by the disappointing sequel, *Hannibal* (2001), and a more successful prequel, *Red Dragon* (2002). JF. Contains violence, swearing and nudity. [video] DVD

Jodie Foster *Clarice Starling* • Anthony Hopkins *Dr Hannibal Lecter* • Scott Glenn *Jack Crawford* • Ted Levine *Jame Gumb* • Anthony Heald *Dr Frederick Chilton* • Kasi Lemmons *Ardelia Mapp* • Chris Isaak *Swat commander* ■ *Dir* Jonathan Demme • *Scr* Ted Tally, from the novel by Thomas Harris

Silence of the North ★★ PG

Historical adventure
1981 · Can · Colour · 89mins

Based on a true story, this woman-and-wilderness drama from documentary film-maker Allan King zeroes in on the trials and tribulations that befall a trapper, his soon-to-be-widowed wife and their family in the Canadian wilds in 1919. Ellen Burstyn stars as Olive Fredrickson, who raises her family alone and in harsh conditions before succumbing to a second marriage. The scenery is stunning. FL [video]

Ellen Burstyn *Olive Fredrickson* • Tom Skerritt *Walter Reamer* • Gordon Pinsent *John Fredrickson* • Jennifer McKinney *Little Olive* • Donna Dobrijevic *Vala Reamer* • Jeff Banks *Lewis Reamer* ■ *Dir* Allan King • *Scr* Patricia Knop, from a non-fiction book by Ben East, Olive Fredrickson

Silence... We're Rolling ★★★

Musical comedy
2001 · Egy/Fr · Colour · 102mins

Combining – and even lampooning – elements from Bollywood musicals and Hollywood screwball comedies, this represents a change of pace for veteran Egyptian director Youssef Chahine. Yet he still manages to slip a few pertinent comments about prejudice into the story of movie icon Latifa's seduction by Ahmed Wafik's smooth-operating wannabe. The mix of styles in the studio sequences is inspired, but the subplots are overly strained. DP. In Arabic with English subtitles.

Latifa *Malak* • Ahmed Bedir *Alphi* • Ahmed Wafik *Lamei* • Magda Al Khattib *Grandmother* ■ *Dir/Scr* Youssef Chahine

The Silencer ★★ 18

Action thriller 1999 · Can · Colour · 92mins

Video star Michael Dudikoff, who can usually give Chuck Norris a run for his money in the woodenness stakes, gives something close to a performance in this OK-ish crime thriller. Dudikoff is the hitman who takes Brennan Elliott under his wing, without realising that he is in fact an undercover government agent. The performances are adequate and there are a few nice plot twists, but it's not ground-breaking. JF [video] DVD

Michael Dudikoff *Quinn Simmons* • Brennan Elliott *Jason Black/Jason Wells* • Terence Kelly *Neal* • Peter LaCroix *Rodeski* • Gabrielle Miller *Jill Martin* ■ *Dir* Robert Lee • *Scr* John A Curtis

The Silencers ★★★ PG

Action comedy 1966 · US · Colour · 97mins

A quintessential 1960s spy spoof, this is the first (and best) of four colourful Matt Helm features, with debonair Dean Martin cleverly cast as the womanising smoothie. The attitudes may have dated, but the women continue to delight, especially Stella Stevens as a divine klutz. Also making an impact are former Miss Israel Daliah Lavi and one-time MGM siren Cyd Charisse, whose title song is a highlight. If you care, the plot's about Helm trying to divert a Chinese-aimed missile to avoid global warfare. *Murderers' Row* was the next outing for Martin's spy. TS [video] DVD

Dean Martin *Matt Helm* • Stella Stevens *Gail* • Daliah Lavi *Tina Batori* • Victor Buono *Tung-Tze* • Arthur O'Connell *Wigman* • Robert Webber *Sam Gunther* • James Gregory *MacDonald* • Cyd Charisse *Sarita* ■ *Dir* Phil

Karlson • *Scr* Oscar Saul, from the novels *The Silencers* and *Death of a Citizen* by Donald Hamilton • *Music* Elmer Bernstein

The Silences of the Palace ★★★★ 12

Drama 1994 · Fr/Tun · Colour · 123mins

Moufida Tlatli's directorial debut is a slow, multilayered drama set during the reign of Tunisia's last king, Sidi Ali. Life within his palace is so cloistered that the mounting protests against royal collaboration with the French barely intrude upon the life of a young servant girl, whose talent for music sparks a bitter rivalry between her mother and the king's barren wife. Well served by a fine ensemble cast, Tlatli superbly contrasts the shabby grandeur of the palace and the rigid protocol of a decaying system with the young girl's innocent beauty and the subtle simplicity of the music. DP. In Arabic with English subtitles.

Ahmel Hedhili *Khedija* • Hend Sabri *Young Alia* • Najia Ouerghi *Khalti Hadda* • Ghalia Lacroix *Adult Alia* ■ *Dir/Scr* Moufida Tlatli

Silent Assassins ★ 18

Action 1988 · US · Colour · 86mins

A group of hired killers eccentric enough to be at home in a *Batman* comic book kidnap a scientist who has invented some sort of biological weapon. The only person who can rescue him is Sam Jones, a standard issue cop on the edge whose partners were, of course, victims of these same assassins. Even by action movie standards, this scrapes the bottom of the barrel. ST

Sam J Jones [Sam Jones] *Sam Kettle* • Linda Blair *Sara* • Jun Chong *Jun Kim* • Phillip Rhee *Bernard* • Bill Erwin *Dr London* • Gustav Vintas *Kendrick* • Mako *Oyama* ■ *Dir* Doo-yong Lee, Scott Thomas • *Scr* Will Gates, Ada Lin, from a story by John Bruner

The Silent Bell ★★★

Period drama 1944 · US · Colour · 69mins

In one of the least known of Val Lewton's low-budget productions for RKO, Simone Simon plays a common laundress in an adaptation of two Guy de Maupassant stories. Set during the Prussian invasion of France in the 1870s (paralleling the Nazi occupation of France during the Second World War), the story enables Simon to display real patriotism that shames her aristocratic fellow passengers on a coach journey. AE

Simone Simon *Elizabeth Rousset* • John Emery *Jean Cornudet* • Kurt Kreuger *Lt von Eyrick, "Mademoiselle Fifi"* • Alan Napier *Count de Breville* • Helen Freeman *Countess de Breville* • Jason Robards [Jason Robards Sr] *Wine wholesaler* ■ *Dir* Robert Wise • *Scr* Josef Mischel, Peter Ruric, from the short stories *Mademoiselle Fifi* and *Boule de Suif* by Guy de Maupassant

Silent Conflict ★★ U

Western 1948 · US · BW · 61mins

The long-running Hopalong Cassidy series was on its last legs when William Boyd saddled up once more to help a chum who had been hypnotised into a life of crime. Despite the presence of regulars Andy Clyde and Rand Brooks, this entry is long on talk and low on action. JF

William Boyd (1) *Hopalong Cassidy* • Andy Clyde *California Carlson* • Rand Brooks *Lucky Jenkins* • Virginia Belmont *Rene Richards* • Earle Hodgins *Doc Richards* • James Harrison *Speed Blaney* • Forbes Murray *Randall* ■ *Dir* George Archainbaud • *Scr* Charles Belden, from characters created by Clarence E Mulford

Silent Dust ★

Drama 1948 · UK · BW · 81mins

Adapted by Michael Pertwee from the play he co-wrote with his father Roland, this is supposed to be a provocative treatise on the nature of heroism, but is nothing more than a mawkish drama with a shamelessly sentimental performance by Stephen Murray, whose rose-tinted image of his son is tarnished by the truth. DP

Sally Gray *Angela Rawley* • Stephen Murray *Robert Rawley* • Derek Farr *Maxwell Oliver* • Nigel Patrick *Simon Rawley* • Beatrice Campbell *Joan Rawley* ■ *Dir* Lance Comfort • *Scr* Michael Pertwee, from the play *The Paragon* by Michael Pertwee, Roland Pertwee • *Music* Georges Auric

The Silent Enemy ★★★ PG

Second World War biographical drama
1958 · UK · BW · 107mins

This distinguished war film celebrates the exploits of celebrated Royal Navy frogman Lt Lionel "Buster" Crabb, played here by Laurence Harvey, whose explosive temperament is a perfect match for the volatile character he plays. The underwater shooting (by Egil Woxholt) is well done, and the plot has more excitement than many fictional tales. The saga is shot through with a rich vein of humour, a credit to the film's writer/director William Fairchild. TS DVD

Laurence Harvey *Lieutenant Lionel Crabb* • Dawn Addams *Third Officer Jill Masters* • Michael Craig *Leading Seaman Knowles* • John Clements *The Admiral* • Sidney James *Chief Petty Officer Thorpe* • Alec McCowen *Able Seaman Morgan* • Nigel Stock *Able Seaman Fraser* ■ *Dir* William Fairchild • *Scr* William Fairchild, from the non-fiction book *Commander Crabb* by Marshall Pugh

Silent Fall ★★★ 15

Psychological thriller
1994 · US · Colour · 96mins

Director Bruce Beresford is one of Hollywood's safer pairs of hands and he hardly misses a beat with this absorbing, if somewhat predictable thriller. Richard Dreyfuss is the retired child psychologist called in to help unlock the memory of an autistic child who holds the key to the murder of his parents. Ben Faulkner is movingly believable as the boy and Dreyfuss is as dependable as ever, even though John Lithgow and JT Walsh steal every scene they're in. Look out to for a charismatic debut from Liv Tyler. JF. Contains violence and swearing.

Richard Dreyfuss *Jake Rainer* • Linda Hamilton *Karen Rainer* • John Lithgow *Doctor Harlinger* • JT Walsh *Sheriff Mitch Rivers* • Ben Faulkner *Tim Warden* • Liv Tyler *Sylvie Warden* ■ *Dir* Bruce Beresford • *Scr* Akiva Goldsman

The Silent Flute ★★★ 18

Martial arts fantasy adventure
1978 · US · Colour · 91mins

Based on a story Bruce Lee was writing (with James Coburn) before his death, director Richard Moore's beguiling mystical martial arts fantasy tells of arena fighter Jeff Cooper and his quest for the Book of Enlightenment. A series of trials with bizarre opponents stands between him and its Keeper, Christopher Lee. On his travels (through exquisite Israeli locations) he keeps chancing on a blind man (David Carradine, in one of four roles) who plays a silent flute and teaches him the meaning of life. Although Cooper is a weak protagonist, this Oriental fable has a haunting musical score and is too strange and too interesting to dismiss. AJ

David Carradine *Blind man/Jungar/Death/Changsha* • Jeff Cooper *Cord* • Roddy McDowall *White Robe* • Eli Wallach *Man in oil* • Christopher Lee *Zetan* • Erica Creer *Tara* ■ *Dir* Richard Moore • *Scr* Stirling Silliphant, Stanley Mann, from a story by Bruce Lee, James Coburn, Stirling Silliphant

Silent Grace ★★★ 15

Prison drama based on a true story
2001 · Ire/UK · Colour · 86mins

Set against the backdrop of the IRA's dirty protest and the hunger strikes of the early 1980s, Maeve Murphy's feature debut efficiently conveys the determination of those women incarcerated within Armagh prison who actively supported their brothers in arms. Yet, the director is more interested in exploring how women bond together *in extremis*. The rapport between loudmouthed joyrider Cathleen Bradley and Orla Brady's charismatic activist is established rather too conveniently, but the performances have a conviction that commands attention. DP. Contains swearing.

Orla Brady *Eileen* • Cathleen Bradley *Aine* • Cara Seymour *Margaret* • Dawn Bradfield *Geraldine* • Conor Mullen *Cunningham* • Robert Newman (2) *Father McGarry* • Patrick Bergin *Peter, IRA man* ■ *Dir* Maeve Murphy • *Scr* Maeve Murphy, from the play *Now and at the Hour of Our Death* by Maeve Murphy, theatre company Trouble and Strife

Silent Movie ★★★ PG

Comedy 1976 · US · Colour · 87mins

In a (virtually) dialogue-free movie, Mel Brooks plays film director Mel Funn who plans to make a modern-day silent movie in an attempt to save ailing film corporation Big Picture Studios. Aided by his henchmen Marty Feldman and Dom DeLuise, Brooks sets out to shoot his masterpiece and on the way runs into a number of well-known movie faces in cameo roles. There's some well-honed slapstick and a number of fair gags, but the film is always more of a Brooks comedy than a homage to the silent era. DF

Mel Brooks *Mel Funn* • Marty Feldman *Marty Eggs* • Dom DeLuise *Dom Bell* • Bernadette Peters *Vilma Kaplan* • Sid Caesar *Studio Chief* • Harold Gould *Engulf* • Ron Carey *Devour* ■ *Dir* Mel Brooks • *Scr* Mel Brooks, Ron Clark, Rudy DeLuca, Barry Levinson, by Ron Clark

Silent Night, Bloody Night ★★

Horror 1972 · US · Colour · 88mins

The much under-rated Patrick O'Neal plays a lawyer sent to a small provincial American town to sell off an old mansion which used to be an insane asylum. It transpires that the inmates were released and now form the bulk of the townsfolk, who are being bumped off by a mystery killer. Director Theodore Gershuny delivers a few atmospheric chills but not enough to lift this above the humdrum. RS

Patrick O'Neal *Carter* • John Carradine *Towlman* • James Patterson *Jeffrey Butler* • Walter Abel *Mayor* • Mary Woronov *Diane Adams* • Candy Darling ■ *Dir* Theodore Gershuny • *Scr* Theodore Gershuny, Jeffrey Konvitz, Ami Artzi, Ira Teller

Silent Night, Deadly Night ★★

Horror 1984 · US · Colour · 79mins

This routine stalk-and-slasher movie gained notoriety when American parents protested about the effect that portraying Father Christmas as a mad murderer would have on children. Billy sees his parents slain at Christmas by someone dressed as Santa. Not surprisingly, he grows up hating the festive season. Working in a department store, he's forced into a Santa outfit by his boss and goes on a homicidal rampage. Undistinguished, shallow and depressing. Four sequels followed. AJ

Lilyan Chauvin *Mother Superior* • Gilmer McCormick *Sister Margaret* • Toni Nero *Pamela* • Robert Brian Wilson *Billy aged 18* ■ *Dir* Charles E Sellier Jr • *Scr* Michael Hickey, from a story by Paul Caimi

The Silent One ★★★

Spy thriller 1973 · Fr/It · Colour · 117mins

Nobody did the chase thriller better than Alfred Hitchcock and on the evidence of this stylish, suspenseful espionage story, Claude Pinoteau had clearly been taking notes. From the moment Soviet nuclear scientist Lino Ventura is revealed to be a kidnapped Frenchman, nothing can be taken for granted, apart from the excellence of the star whose mournful response to freedom is very much that of a spy coming in from the cold with the greatest reluctance. Both intelligent and entertaining. DP. French dialogue dubbed into English.

Lino Ventura *Tibère* • Lea Massari *Maria* • Suzanne Flon *Jeanne* • Leo Genn *Man from MI5* • Robert Hardy *MI5 assistant* ■ *Dir* Claude Pinoteau • *Scr* Jean-Loup Dabadie, Claude Pinoteau, from the novel *Drôle de Pistolet* by Francis Ryck

The Silent One ★★★

Fantasy 1984 · NZ · Colour · 95mins

This charming children's film is about an abandoned boy who's washed up on a remote South Pacific island. He can't hear or speak, but the islanders discover he can communicate with the local sea turtles. Shot on location in the Cook Islands, with many of the locals taking supporting roles, this overturns conventional notions of family entertainment, being just about as exotic as you can get. DA

Telo Malese *Jonasi* • George Henare *Paui Te Po* • Pat Evison *Luisa* • Anzac Wallace *Tasiri* ■ *Dir* Yvonne Mackay • *Scr* Ian Mune, from the novel by Joy Cowley

The Silent Partner ★★★

Crime caper 1978 · Can · Colour · 105mins

This thriller boasts a sort of retro 1960s cast and an ingenious script by Curtis Hanson, who later won an Oscar for his adaptation of *LA Confidential*. It's about a bank, which is robbed by Christopher Plummer dressed as Santa Claus, though part of his potential haul is stolen by devious bank clerk Elliott Gould. Both the male leads are in fine fettle but Susannah York has too little to do. It sounds like a comedy but the tone is actually quite dark with some casual violence. AT

Susannah York *Julie Carver* • Christopher Plummer *Harry Reikle* • Elliott Gould *Miles Cullen* • Celine Lomez *Elaine* • Michael Kirby *Charles Packard* • Ken Pogue *Detective Willard* • John Candy *Simonsen* ■ *Dir* Daryl Duke • *Scr* Curtis Hanson, from the novel *Think of a Number* by Anders Bodelsen

Silent Rage ★ 18

Action drama 1982 · US · Colour · 95mins

Chuck Norris doesn't say much in his movies, which is just as well given scripts like this one. As a former karate champion turned actor he lets his feet do the talking. Here we discover him in one of those ubiquitous small Texas towns that seem to have, and need, sheriffs like Chuck, especially when an axe killer (Brian Libby) he's already dealt with is back in town. Norris looks bemused in a preposterously silly film which is less fun than it should be. BB

Chuck Norris *Dan Stevens* • Ron Silver *Dr Tom Halman* • Steven Keats *Dr Philip Spires* • Toni Kalem *Alison Halman* • William Finley *Dr Paul Vaughn* • Brian Libby *John Kirby* • Stephen Furst *Charlie* ■ *Dir* Michael Miller (2) • *Scr* Joseph Fraley

S

Silent Running ★★★★ U

Science-fiction drama
1971 · US · Colour · 85mins

Special-effects ace Douglas Trumbull (of *2001* fame) turned director with this ecologically based thriller about the last of Earth's plant-life preserved on the *Valley Forge* spaceship, lovingly cared for by space ranger Bruce Dern and his three cute "drone" robots. Dern mutinies when orders arrive to destroy the precious cargo. Although the film may seem rather hippy-influenced now (those syrupy Joan Baez ballads), Trumbull's gentle direction highlights a sensitive performance by Dern. Imaginative and much admired. AJ DVD

Bruce Dern *Freeman Lowell* • Cliff Potts *Wolf* • Ron Rifkin *Barker* • Jesse Vint *Keenan* ■ *Dir* Douglas Trumbull • *Scr* Deric Washburn, Mike Cimino, Steve Bocho

Silent Scream ★★ 15

Biographical drama
1989 · UK · Colour · 81mins

Extremely powerful in parts, director David Hayman's heartfelt biographical drama, based on the life of convicted murderer Larry Winters, is very much a mixed blessing. Iain Glen gives a marvellous performance as the manic-depressive Winters, jailed for killing a barman, recalling his life while dying from a drugs overdose in prison. But Hayman drenches his potent polemic in an earnest and inappropriately fractured style. AJ. Contains swearing and drug abuse.

Iain Glen *Larry Winters* • Paul Samson *Jimmy* • Andrew Barr *Shuggie* • Kenneth Glenaan *Rab* • Steve Hotchkiss *Mo* • John Murtagh *Ken Murray* • Robert Carlyle *Big Woodsy* ■ *Dir* David Hayman • *Scr* Bill Beech, Jane Beech, from the life and writings of Larry Winters

Silent Tongue ★★ 12

Supernatural western
1993 · US · Colour · 97mins

This western, written and directed by Sam Shepard for French television, has a bizarre cast headed by two survivors of 1960s British cinema, Alan Bates and Richard Harris, and dysfunctional former child star River Phoenix in his final credited screen appearance. Bates plays the drunken proprieter of a mystical, crazy Wild West show in the wilderness. Years before, Bates sold Harris his half-American Indian baby daughter, who later married Harris's son Phoenix. But the girl has died in childbirth and Phoenix has become insane. Most viewers will wonder what the heck it all means. AT

Richard Harris *Prescott Roe* • Sheila Tousey *Awbonnie/Ghost* • Alan Bates *Eamon McCree* • River Phoenix *Talbot Roe* • Dermot Mulroney *Reeves McCree* • Jeri Arredondo *Velada McCree* • Tantoo Cardinal *Silent Tongue* ■ *Dir/Scr* Sam Shepard

The Silent Touch ★★★ 15

Romantic comedy
1992 · UK /Pol/Den · Colour · 91mins

A complex display of frustrated creativity, simmering fury and manipulative cunning from Max von Sydow dominates this intense study of the sacrifices art demands of life. Roused from his reclusive ennui by Polish musicologist Lothaire Bluteau, von Sydow's exiled composer battles the bottle, physical pain and his emotional demons to complete his masterpiece, a snatch of which had lingered elusively in the mind of his mystical visitor. This turbulent relationship is delineated with care by director Krzysztof Zanussi. DP

Max von Sydow *Henry Kesdi* • Lothaire Bluteau *Stefan Bugajski* • Sarah Miles *Helena Kesdi* • Sofie Grabol *Annette Berg* • Aleksander Bardini *Professor Jerzy Kern* ■ *Dir* Krzysztof Zanussi • *Scr* Peter Morgan, Mark Wadlow, from a story by Krzysztof Zanussi, Edward Zebrowski

Silent Trigger ★★ 18

Action thriller
1996 · UK/Can · Colour · 89mins

Dolph Lundgren and Gina Bellman play a pair of hired killers, waiting in an eerie building for their next target, in a sleep-inducing thriller. This is considered one of Lundgren's better outings, but the competition isn't that stiff. Here his role isn't mere beefcake but demands emotional depth, but he's still guilty of delivering dialogue like a foreign exchange student. RS. Contains violence, swearing, drug abuse and nudity. DVD

Dolph Lundgren *Shooter* • Gina Bellman *Spotter* • Conrad Dunn *Supervisor* • Christopher Heyerdahl *O'Hara* • Emma Stevens *Target woman* ■ *Dir* Russell Mulcahy • *Scr* Sergio Altieri

Silhouette ★★ 15

Thriller 1994 · US · Colour · 86mins

This TV thriller has a familiar plot about a stranger suddenly appearing and recognising a murder victim as his wife. The cast performs with conviction, but it would be nice to see the likes of Stephanie Zimbalist (playing the victim) and JoBeth Williams (her musician sister) back on the big screen in decent roles. TS

JoBeth Williams *Nancy Parkhurst* • Corbin Bernsen *Mark Reichard* • Stephanie Zimbalist *Ann Parkhurst* • Winston Rekert *Paul Gatlin* ■ *Dir* Eric Till • *Scr* Karol Ann Hoeffner

Silk Stockings ★★★ U

Musical comedy 1957 · US · Colour · 112mins

A musical remake of *Ninotchka* with a Cole Porter score might have seemed a good idea at the time, but this MGM CinemaScope special is more than a little heavy-handed under the arthritic direction of veteran Rouben Mamoulian. Nevertheless, the splendid cast and choreography keep it all eminently watchable, even if the anti-Russian jokes and the anti-rock 'n' roll number leave a sour taste in the mouth. The commissars, headed by Peter Lorre, are funny, but it lacks the sparkle of MGM's best. TS

Fred Astaire *Steve Canfield* • Cyd Charisse *Ninotchka* • Janis Paige *Peggy Dainton* • Peter Lorre *Brankov* • Jules Munshin *Bibinski* • Joseph Buloff *Ivanov* • George Tobias *Commissar Vassili Markovich* ■ *Dir* Rouben Mamoulian • *Scr* Leonard Gershe, Leonard Spigelgass, Harry Kurnitz, from the musical by George S Kaufman, Leueen McGrath [Leueen MacGrath], Abe Burrows, from the film *Ninotchka* by Charles Brackett, Billy Wilder, Walter Reisch, from a story by Melchior Lengyel • *Choreographer* Hermes Pan

The Silken Affair ★★ U

Comedy 1957 · UK · BW · 95mins

David Niven is the accountant who goes off the rails when he decides to indulge in a spot of creative book-keeping in this frivolous comedy. His ill-gotten gains are used to fund a romantic spree with French girl Genevieve Page (appearing in her first British film). Lots of well-known faces feature in the supporting cast. DM

David Niven *Roger Tweakham/New accountant* • Genevieve Page *Genevieve Gerard* • Ronald Squire *Marberry* • Beatrice Straight *Theora* • Wilfrid Hyde White *Sir Horace Hogg* • Howard Marion-Crawford *Baggott* • Dorothy Alison *Mrs Tweakham* • Miles Malleson *Mr Blucher* ■ *Dir* Roy Kellino • *Scr* Robert Lewis Taylor, from an idea by John McCarten

Silkwood ★★★★ 15

Biographical drama
1983 · US · Colour · 125mins

This moving film is based on a true story about a female nuclear power plant worker who died under mysterious circumstances on her way to a meeting with the press, at which she intended to show them proof of improprieties at her workplace. Meryl Streep is charismatic and convincing in the lead and there's strong support from Cher and Kurt Russell. Unfortunately, the interesting premise, particularly topical at the time of its release, is let down by a lack of tension and director Mike Nichols's tendency to digress into the romantic subplot. Thought-provoking and still relevant. LH DVD

Meryl Streep *Karen Silkwood* • Kurt Russell *Drew Stephens* • Cher *Dolly Pelliker* • Craig T Nelson *Winston* • Diana Scarwid *Angela* • Fred Ward *Morgan* • Ron Silver *Paul Stone* ■ *Dir* Mike Nichols • *Scr* Nora Ephron, Alice Arlen

Silver Bears ★ PG

Comedy crime caper
1977 · US · Colour · 107mins

Michael Caine has made some odd choices in his career, but none as peculiar as this caper in which he sets up a bank in Switzerland for gangster Martin Balsam and becomes involved in a scam involving an Iranian silver mine. There's an elegant cast (Louis Jourdan, Cybill Shepherd, Stéphane Audran), but hardly any sympathetic characters. TH

Michael Caine *Doc Fletcher* • Cybill Shepherd *Debbie Luckman* • Louis Jourdan *Prince di Siracusa* • Stéphane Audran *Shireen Firdausi* • David Warner *Agha Firdausi* • Martin Balsam *Joe Fiore* • Jay Leno *Albert Fiore* • Joss Ackland *Henry Foreman* • Tom Smothers *Donald Luckman* ■ *Dir* Ivan Passer • *Scr* Peter Stone, from the novel by Paul E Erdman

The Silver Brumby ★★★★ U

Adventure 1992 · Aus · Colour · 91mins

Less sentimental than most family films, this will transfix those teenagers who are obsessed with all things equine. Shooting both the landscape and the fabulous horses with a genuine passion, director John Tatoulis forgoes the easy rites-of-passage clichés as Ami Daemion learns the lessons contained in her mother Caroline Goodall's book about a wild stallion, the "brumby" of the title. Russell Crowe cuts a dash as the cattleman intent on possessing the beast. DP

Caroline Goodall *Elyne* • Russell Crowe *The man* • Ami Daemion [Amiel Daemion] *Indy* ■ *Dir* John Tatoulis • *Scr* Elyne Mitchell, John Tatoulis, Jon Stephens, from the novel by Elyne Mitchell

Silver Bullet ★★ 18

Horror 1985 · US · Colour · 90mins

Scripted by Stephen King from his own story *Cycle of the Werewolf*, this half-hearted horror is a tired sheep in werewolf's clothing. Disabled Corey Haim (his wheelchair is the silver bullet of the title) knows there's a werewolf on the prowl in his small town and convinces his sister (Megan Fellows) and their alcoholic uncle (Gary Busey) to help him unmask its human identity. First-time director Daniel Attias draws credible performances from his able cast but the irony-rich murders draw more laughter than terror. AJ DVD

Gary Busey *Uncle Red* • Corey Haim *Marty Coslaw* • Megan Follows *Jane Coslaw* • Everett McGill *Reverend Lowe* • Terry O'Quinn *Sheriff Joe Haller* • Lawrence Tierney *Owen Knopfler* ■ *Dir* Daniel Attias • *Scr* Stephen King, from his story *Cycle of the Werewolf*

The Silver Chalice ★★ U

Religious drama 1954 · US · Colour · 143mins

This biblical epic focuses on a Greek slave, freed from bondage to design and make a chalice to hold the silver cup used at the Last Supper, this was the film that launched the career of Paul Newman. Unfortunately, the underdeveloped script gave him no chance to display his considerable acting gifts. Despite William V Skall's Oscar-nominated CinemaScope photography, which made the most of the visual spectacle, and Franz Waxman's sweeping score (also nominated), the dreary writing and Victor Saville's lifeless direction make for a movie that's too long by half. RK

Virginia Mayo *Helena* • Pier Angeli *Deborra* • Jack Palance *Simon* • Paul Newman *Basil* • Walter Hampden *Joseph* • Joseph Wiseman *Mijamin* • Alexander Scourby *Luke* • Lorne Greene *Peter* • Natalie Wood *Helena as a child* ■ *Dir* Victor Saville • *Scr* Lesser Samuels, from the novel by Thomas B Costain

Silver City ★★ 15

Romantic drama 1984 · Aus · Colour · 97mins

Recalled in flashback, the romantic triangle involving aspiring teacher Gosia Dobrowolska, lawyer Ivar Kants and his put-upon wife, Anna Jemison, develops along all-too-predictable lines, wasting both the unusual backdrop (an immigrant camp nicknamed Silver City on account of its dehumanising corrugated huts) and the inevitable culture clashes between the refugee Poles and the local Australians. Earnestly acted, yet mediocre and disappointingly flat. DP

Gosia Dobrowolska *Nina* • Ivar Kants *Julian* • Anna Jemison *Anna* • Steve Bisley *Viktor* • Debra Lawrance *Helena* • Ewa Brok *Mrs Bronowska* ■ *Dir* Sophia Turkiewicz • *Scr* Sophia Turkiewicz, Thomas Keneally

Silver City ★★ 15

Political satire 2004 · US · Colour · 127mins

Dickie Pilager (Chris Cooper) is the tongue-tied, "user-friendly" candidate for Colorado governor (blatantly modelled on George W Bush), and his family's dodgy links with corporate mogul Kris Kristofferson drive what is actually an old-fashioned detective story. Disappointingly, Cooper fades into the background as Danny Huston's down-at-heel investigator risks all to join the corrupt dots. In the end, John Sayles's liberal indignation hobbles this political satire and, while admirable and full of great supporting performances, the plot is baggy and the tone moralising. AC. Contains swearing..

Chris Cooper *Richard "Dickie" Pilager* • Richard Dreyfuss *Chuck Raven* • Daryl Hannah *Maddy Pilager* • Maria Bello *Nora Allardyce* • Danny Huston *Danny O'Brien* • Thora Birch *Karen Cross* • Tim Roth *Mitch Paine* • Michael Murphy *Senator Jud Pilager* • Mary Kay Place *Grace Seymour* ■ *Dir/Scr* John Sayles

The Silver Cord ★★★

Drama 1933 · US · BW · 75mins

Although this adaptation of a play by Sidney Howard retains the style, atmosphere, small cast of characters and theatrical speeches that betray its origins, it is nonetheless one of the most frightening and powerful studies of poisonously destructive mother-love you are likely to see. Laura Hope Crews delivers something of a tour de force as the selfish, manipulative and unhealthily possessive mother of two adult sons, bent on destroying the engagement of one (Eric Linden) and the marriage of the other (Joel McCrea). Irene Dunne delivers a shining performance. RK

Irene Dunne *Christina Phelps* • Joel McCrea *David Phelps* • Frances Dee *Hester Phelps* •

S

Eric Linden *Robert Phelps* • Laura Hope Crews *Mrs Phelps* • Helen Cromwell *Delia* ■ *Dir* John Cromwell • *Scr* Jane Murfin, from the play by Sidney Howard

The Silver Darlings ★★ U

Drama 1947 · UK · BW · 93mins

The silver darlings are the herrings that provide a precarious living for the fishermen of the Hebrides in the mid-19th century. This Scottish enterprise was a work of love, made over a two-year span by writer/director Clarence Elder in collaboration with leading actor and associate director Clifford Evans. A pity, then, that the location footage not only overwhelms the commonplace narrative but is too often back-projected behind actors in the studio. Evans's Welsh accent and Helen Shingler's English one are a hindrance to cultivating an authentic tone. AE

Clifford Evans *Roddy* • Helen Shingler *Catrine* • Carl Bernard *Angus* • Norman Shelley *Hendry* • Jean Shepherd *Mrs Hendry* • Simon Lack *Don* • Norman Williams *Tormad* • Phyllis Morris *Tormad's mother* ■ *Dir* Clarence Elder, Clifford Evans • *Scr* Clarence Elder, from a novel by Neil M Gunn

Silver Dream Racer ★★ 15

Action drama 1980 · UK · Colour · 106mins

Whatever happened to David Essex? Here he is, near the end of his heyday, racing motorbikes, dressing in leather, trying to be James Dean and keeping Brylcreem in business. He wrote the music, too. The plot kicks in when Essex is given the mean machine of the title, a space-age ride designed to leave American ace rider Beau Bridges on the starting grid. A vanity project from beginning to end, it tries hard to be a British *Electra Glide in Blue*, but rarely rises above the level of a clapped out Vespa. AT [video] DVD

David Essex *Nick Freeman* • Beau Bridges *Bruce McBride* • Cristina Raines *Julie Prince* • Clarke Peters *Cider Jones* • Harry H Corbett *Wiggins* • Diane Keen *Tina* • Lee Montague *Jack Freeman* ■ *Dir/Scr* David Wickes

The Silver Fleet ★★★ U

Second World War drama
1943 · UK · BW · 84mins

This British wartime flag-waver boasts the magic names of Michael Powell and Emeric Pressburger, but they were only producers – it was actually written and directed by Vernon Sewell and Gordon Wellesley. Their influence may well account for the too-stately progress of the tale, in which shipping engineer Ralph Richardson poses as a traitor in Nazi-occupied Holland in order to destroy the U-boat he's just had built. Richardson's performance is never less than convincing and neither is the story once it gets going. TH [video]

Ralph Richardson *Jaap Van Leyden* • Googie Withers *Helene Van Leyden* • Esmond Knight *Von Schiller* • Beresford Egan *Krampf* • Frederick Burtwell *Captain Muller* • Willem Akkerman *Willem Van Leyden* • Dorothy Gordon *Janni Peters* • Charles Victor *Bastiaan Peters* ■ *Dir/Scr* Vernon Campbell Sewell [Vernon Sewell], Gordon Wellesley

Silver Lode ★★★

Western 1954 · US · Colour · 80mins

John Payne is accused of murder on his wedding day and has to go on the run from a posse led by Dan Duryea. Many critics regard this tale as an allegory about the political witch-hunts of the time. Tightly directed by Allan Dwan and nicely photographed by John Alton, this is one of many RKO productions that belies its dime budget, producing some distinctive sequences, even though Payne makes for a rather colourless hero. AT

John Payne *Dan Ballard* • Lizabeth Scott *Rose Evans* • Dan Duryea *McCarty* • Dolores Moran *Dolly* • Emile Meyer *Sheriff Woolley* • Robert Warwick *Judge Cranston* • John Hudson (1) *Mitch Evans* • Harry Carey Jr *Johnson* ■ *Dir* Allan Dwan • *Scr* Karen De Wolfe

Silver River ★★★ U

Western 1948 · US · BW · 104mins

After *Gentleman Jim* and *They Died with Their Boots On*, director Raoul Walsh and Errol Flynn renewed their parnership in this run-of-the-mill Warner Bros western, not even considered worthy of shooting in colour. Still, movie fans today will find much to enjoy, since the film shows the Hollywood system in fine fettle. Flynn's the former soldier turned gambler who'll stop at nothing to win the affection of Ann Sheridan. TS [video]

Errol Flynn *Capt Mike McComb* • Ann Sheridan *Georgia Moore* • Thomas Mitchell *John Plato Beck* • Bruce Bennett *Stanley Moore* • Tom D'Andrea *Pistol Porter* • Barton MacLane *Banjo Sweeney* • Monte Blue *Buck Chevigee* • Jonathan Hale *Maj Spencer* ■ *Dir* Raoul Walsh • *Scr* Stephen Longstreet, Harriet Frank Jr, from a novel by Stephen Longstreet

Silver Streak ★★★★ PG

Comedy thriller 1976 · US · Colour · 108mins

Gene Wilder and Richard Pryor star in a spectacular comedy thriller set aboard the Los Angeles-Chicago *Silver Streak* train. Publisher Wilder witnesses a murder and thief Pryor helps to hide him as Patrick McGoohan and his gang of villains close in. It harks back to those British thrillers of the 1930s, with some screwball antics thrown in for good measure, plus Jill Clayburgh sorting out the men from the boys. With such an endearing trio of characters, it makes you wonder why there wasn't a sequel, though it paved the way for Wilder and Pryor's 1980 collaboration, *Stir Crazy*. TH [video]

Gene Wilder *George Caldwell* • Jill Clayburgh *Hilly Burns* • Richard Pryor *Grover Muldoon* • Patrick McGoohan *Roger Devereau* • Ned Beatty *Sweet* • Clifton James *Sheriff Chauncey* • Ray Walston *Mr Whiney* • Richard Kiel *Reace* • Scatman Crothers *Ralston* ■ *Dir* Arthur Hiller • *Scr* Colin Higgins

Silverado ★★★★ PG

Western 1985 · US · Colour · 127mins

Billed as the movie that was going to revive the ailing western, this film merely performed a little resuscitation before Clint Eastwood's *Unforgiven* proved there was life in the old genre yet. Just as Steven Spielberg plundered the Saturday serial for his *Raiders* trilogy, so this rousing tale rustles ideas from virtually every B-western ever made. While this makes for an invigorating adventure, it's also rather untidy. Nevertheless, Kevin Kline, Kevin Costner, Danny Glover and Scott Glenn make attractive heroes, Brian Dennehy is a hissable villain and John Cleese enjoys his cameo as an English lawman. DP. Contains some swearing. [video] DVD

Kevin Kline *Paden* • Scott Glenn *Emmett* • Kevin Costner *Jake* • John Cleese *Sheriff Langston* • Brian Dennehy *Cobb* • Danny Glover *Mal* • Jeff Goldblum *Slick* • Linda Hunt *Stella* • Rosanna Arquette *Hannah* ■ *Dir* Lawrence Kasdan • *Scr* Lawrence Kasdan, Mark Kasdan

Silverlake Life: the View from Here ★★★★

Documentary
1992 · US · Colour and BW · 99mins

After *Longtime Companion*, this is the best movie made about the Aids experience. A profoundly moving and multi-award-winning documentary charting the lives of gay lovers Tom Joslin and Mark Massi as they enter the final stages of the disease. Using home-movie footage of their 20-odd years living happily together in the gay-friendly Silverlake area of Los Angeles, intercut with the harsh reality of their present situation, this is an incredibly thought-provoking tribute to the agony, pain and candid self-revelation of two fascinating and brave individuals. Often unbearably distressing to watch, it's their humanity and spirit in the face of adversity you will remember. AJ

Dir Tom Joslin, Peter Friedman

Simba ★★

Drama 1955 · UK · Colour · 99mins

Simba is the Swahili word for lion, though this is no wildlife adventure frolic. It's a drama about the Mau Mau troubles in Kenya, but it reduces a complex political crisis to a feeble love story and colonial posturings on the verandah, while a back-projected Africa wobbles in the distance. Dirk Bogarde was then in his matinée idol period, while Donald Sinden and Virginia McKenna are pretty lightweight in support. AT

Dirk Bogarde *Alan Howard* • Donald Sinden *Inspector Tom Drummond* • Virginia McKenna *Mary Crawford* • Basil Sydney *Mr Crawford* • Marie Ney *Mrs Crawford* • Joseph Tomelty *Dr Hughes* ■ *Dir* Brian Desmond Hurst • *Scr* John Baines, Robin Estridge, from a novel by Anthony Perry

The Simian Line ★★

Supernatural romantic drama
2000 · US · Colour · 106mins

With whispered voiceovers constantly striving to impart psychological depth to scenes of banal domesticity, this ensemble drama takes itself so seriously that it feels like an intrusion to look in on such self-obsession. It all starts when crazed clairvoyant Tyne Daly senses the ghostly presence of William Hurt and Samantha Mathis at the Halloween party thrown by Lynn Redgrave and toyboy lover, Harry Connick Jr. Verbose, precious and dripping with faux significance. DP

Harry Connick Jr *Rick* • Cindy Crawford *Sandra* • Tyne Daly *Arnita* • William Hurt *Edward* • Monica Keena *Marta* • Samantha Mathis *Mae* • Lynn Redgrave *Katharine* • Jamey Sheridan *Paul* • Eric Stoltz *Sam* • Dylan Bruno *Billy* ■ *Dir* Linda Yellen • *Scr* Gisela Bernice [Linda Yellen and the cast], from a story by Linda Yellen, from a story by Michael Leeds

Simon ★★ PG

Comedy 1980 · US · Colour · 93mins

This half-baked satirical comedy from Woody Allen associate Marshall Brickman (the pair shared *Annie Hall's* best screenplay Oscar) is too clever by half. In truth, it's not funny where it's meant to be, and tiresomely long. But there's some compensation in Alan Arkin's strong central performance as a professor of psychology who's brainwashed into thinking he's an alien, and clever support from a cast hand-picked for their eccentricity. TS. Contains swearing. [video]

Alan Arkin *Simon Mendelssohn* • Madeline Kahn *Cynthia* • Austin Pendleton *Becker* • Judy Graubart *Lisa* • Wallace Shawn *Van Dongen* • Max Wright *Hundertwasser* • Fred Gwynne *Korey* • Adolph Green *Commune leader* ■ *Dir/Scr* Marshall Brickman

Simon and Laura ★★

Comedy 1955 · UK · Colour · 90mins

Simon and Laura (Peter Finch and Kay Kendall) are a husband-and-wife acting team, publicly celebrated, privately bankrupt and one step from the divorce court. But the BBC, no less, comes to the rescue, offering them a series in which they play a happily married couple. Oh, the irony. Directed by Muriel Box, this starts out as a brisk satire on celebrity, emancipation and cinema's enemy, television. It goes soft by the end, of course, and now looks terribly dated. AT

Peter Finch *Simon Foster* • Kay Kendall *Laura Foster* • Muriel Pavlow *Janet Honeyman* • Hubert Gregg *Bertie Burton* • Maurice Denham *Wilson* • Ian Carmichael *David Prentice* • Richard Wattis *Controller* • Thora Hird *Jessie* ■ *Dir* Muriel Box • *Scr* Peter Blackmore, from the play by Alan Melville

Simon Birch ★★★ PG

Drama 1998 · US · Colour · 113mins

This sentimental drama is set in a Norman Rockwell-esque small town in the 1950s and 60s, and tells of the friendship between the illegitimate, pre-adolescent Joseph Mazzello and Ian Michael Smith, a dwarf with an answer for everything and a question for everyone. The story, narrated by Jim Carrey, describes how the boys cope with their disadvantages and what they hope for in the future. The action is predictable, but the acting makes it worthwhile. TH [video] DVD

Ian Michael Smith *Simon Birch* • Joseph Mazzello *Joe Wenteworth* • Ashley Judd *Rebecca Wenteworth* • Oliver Platt *Ben Goodrich* • David Strathairn *Reverend Russell* • Dana Ivey *Grandmother Wenteworth* ■ *Dir* Mark Steven Johnson • *Scr* Mark Steven Johnson, from the novel *A Prayer for Owen Meany* by John Irving

Simon Magus ★ PG

Romantic fantasy
1998 · UK/Ger/It/Fr · Colour · 106mins

Opening with a pseudo-silent movie view of 19th-century Silesia, Ben Hopkins's feature debut quickly descends into costume melodramatics as he loses control of both his multinational cast and his folkloric tale of progress, prejudice and superstition. As the titular village outcast who's convinced he's in the thrall of Satan, Noah Taylor partially conveys the incomprehending resentment that prompts him to spy for anti-Semitic aristocrat, Sean McGinley. DP

Noah Taylor *Simon* • Stuart Townsend *Dovid* • Embeth Davidtz *Leah* • Sean McGinley *Hase* • Rutger Hauer *Squire* • Ian Holm *Sirius* ■ *Dir/Scr* Ben Hopkins

Simon of the Desert ★★★ 12

Religious drama 1965 · Mex · BW · 43mins

Winner of the special jury prize at the Venice Film Festival in 1965, this is one of Luis Buñuel's least strident assaults on Roman Catholicism. How much this was influenced by a consciously playful mood or by having to make do when funds dried up after only 25 days (hence its short running time) is open to conjecture. Based loosely on the story of the 5th-century saint, Simeon Stylites, the film is packed with ribald comments on the improbability of miracles, the hypocrisy of the faithful and the impossibility of holiness. Stylishly photographed, it's a minor film, but it's still evidently the work of a master. DP. In Spanish with English subtitles. [video]

Claudio Brook *Simon* • Silvia Pinal *The Devil* • Hortensia Santovena *Simon's mother* • Jesus Fernandez *Goatherd* • Enrique Alvarez Felix *Brother Matias* ■ *Dir* Luis Buñuel • *Scr* Luis Buñuel, Julio Alejandro • *Cinematographer* Gabriel Figueroa

Simon Sez ★ 12

Action comedy adventure
1999 · Bel/Ger · Colour · 81mins

The producer of *Double Team* (1997) didn't learn his lesson with the casting of basketball pro Dennis Rodman in that movie, casting him again in this action comedy that actually seems to be an unofficial sequel. Actually, except for being in one of the most unintentionally funny sex scenes ever filmed, Rodman actually looks good when compared to his sidekick Dane

S

Cook, who comes across as Jim Carrey on cocaine. KB

Dennis Rodman *Simon* • Dane Cook *Nick* • Natalia Cigliuti *Claire* • Filip Nicolic *Michael* • John Pinette *Macro* ■ *Dir* Kevin Elders • *Scr* Andrew Miller, Andrew Lowery, from a story by Moshe Diamant, Rudy Cohen

Simon, Simon ★★ U

Comedy 1970 · UK · Colour · 31mins

Unsung character actor Graham Stark made his debut as the writer and director of this fond, if laboured tribute to the silent slapstick style of the Keystone Kops. Comedy stars crop up in cameo roles, as does movie star Michael Caine. But the main focus falls on the rivalry between Stark's council workman and fireman Norman Rossington, as they woo typist Julia Foster. The mugging mime and the excessive crane shots soon become wearisome, but it's still fun. DP

Graham Stark *First workman* • John Junkin *Second workman* • Julia Foster *Typist* • Norman Rossington *Fireman* • Peter Sellers • Michael Caine • Eric Morecambe • Ernie Wise • Bob Monkhouse *Photographer* • Bernie Winters ■ *Dir/Scr* Graham Stark

S1MØNE ★★ PG

Satirical comedy drama
2002 · US · Colour · 112mins

This interesting failure from Andrew Niccol is about a computer-generated film star. She's the creation of director Al Pacino, who's fired from a film after his prima donna star walks off set. He "re-versions" the movie, replacing his leading lady with a virtual woman, a computer programme called S1mØne, billed as "Simone". Nobody twigs that she's not for real and Simone becomes an international phenomenon. The idea doesn't quite work on screen because Simone is clearly a pixelated mannequin and it's hard to believe that anyone would be fooled for long. StH

Al Pacino *Viktor Taransky* • Catherine Keener *Elaine Christian* • Pruitt Taylor Vince *Max Sayer* • Jay Mohr *Hal Sinclair* • Jason Schwartzman *Milton* • Winona Ryder *Nicola Anders* • Stanley Anderson *Frank Brand* • Simone [Rachel Roberts (2)] *Simone* ■ *Dir/Scr* Andrew Niccol

Simpatico ★★ 15

Drama 1999 · US/Fr · Colour · 101mins

A great cast and impeccable credentials still make for an awkward drama. The first film from stage director Matthew Warchus, it tells of millionaire racehorse owner Jeff Bridges, who answers an SOS from former friend Nick Nolte. The alcoholic Nolte has a precarious hold over Bridges: they used to fix races together, a scam which ended in the ruin of course official Albert Finney. Both men are still in love with Sharon Stone, but her appearance seems merely gratuitous. TH

Nick Nolte *Vincent "Vinnie" T Webb* • Jeff Bridges *Lyle Carter* • Sharon Stone *Rosie Carter* • Catherine Keener *Cecilia Ponz* • Albert Finney *Simms* ■ *Dir* Matthew Warchus • *Scr* Matthew Warchus, David Nicholls, from a play by Sam Shepard

The Simple Life of Noah Dearborn ★★★

Drama 1999 · US · Colour · 87mins

Screen icon Sidney Poitier makes a rare small-screen appearance in this TV tale of quiet determination and inner strength. An elderly small-town craftsman/farmer refuses to sell his land to a greedy developer, who then tries to get his psychiatrist girlfriend (Mary Louise Parker) to declare the man mentally incompetent. An observant screenplay, sensitive direction and compelling performances paint a vivid picture of innocent dignity under siege. MC

Sidney Poitier *Noah Dearborn* • Dianne Wiest *Sarah McClellan* • Mary-Louise Parker *Valerie Crane* • George Newbern *Christian Nelson* • Bernie Casey *Silas* ■ *Dir* Gregg Champion • *Scr* Sterling Anderson

Simple Men ★★★★ 15

Comedy drama
1992 · US/UK · Colour · 100mins

This is one of the most accessible of writer/director Hal Hartley's oddball accounts of his slightly-skewed world. This begins mid-robbery and then follows a white-collar crook Robert Burke and his younger brother William Sage as they search for their father, a former baseball star and suspected bomber who's been on the run for years. Along the way there's a fight between a nun and a cop, romantic interludes and musings on the meaning of life. The usual Hartley repertory company respond as to a puppeteer's twitch. TH

Robert Burke *Bill McCabe* • William Sage [Bill Sage] *Dennis McCabe* • Karen Sillas *Kate* • Elina Lowensohn *Elina* • Martin Donovan (2) *Martin* • Chris Cooke *Vic* ■ *Dir/Scr* Hal Hartley

The Simple-Minded Murderer ★★★★

Drama 1982 · Swe · Colour · 107mins

Winning international awards for writer/director Hans Alfredson and star Stellan Skarsgård, this is a chilling period piece with a slow-burning fuse. Alfredson, who co-stars, gives a performance of terrifying brutality as the vicious landowner whose persecution of Skarsgård's village idiot ends in inevitable tragedy. With its persuasive evocation of rural life in the 1930s and its perceptive insights into the prejudices of enclosed communities, this is a disturbing film that is all the more effective for its sedate pacing and restrained playing. DP. In Swedish with English subtitles.

Stellan Skarsgård *The Idiot* • Hans Alfredson *Hoglund* • Maria Johansson *Anna* • Per Myrberg *Andersson* • Lena-Pia Bernhardsson *Mrs Andersson* ■ *Dir* Hans Alfredson • *Scr* Hans Alfredson, from his novel *En ond man*

A Simple Plan ★★★★ 15

Thriller
1998 · US/UK/Jpn/Ger/Fr · Colour · 116mins

Shallow Grave meets *Fargo* in director Sam Raimi's change-of-pace thriller about the corrupting influence of greed. Three men find a crashed plane in thick snow containing over $4 million and hesitantly decide to split the loot once they are sure they won't be suspected. Of course, everything that could go wrong does. In this grim fairy tale, Raimi comes up with a poetic suspense film that delves unassumingly into the cryptic regions of human nature, and the uneasy mood is underscored by two marvellous performances from Bill Paxton and Billy Bob Thornton as the two brothers in the pledge triangle. AJ. Contains violence and swearing.

Bill Paxton *Hank Mitchell* • Billy Bob Thornton *Jacob Mitchell* • Bridget Fonda *Sarah Mitchell* • Gary Cole *Baxter* • Brent Briscoe *Lou* • Becky Ann Baker *Nancy* • Chelcie Ross *Carl* • Jack Walsh *Tom Butler* ■ *Dir* Sam Raimi • *Scr* Scott B Smith, from his novel

A Simple Twist of Fate ★★★ PG

Drama 1994 · US · Colour · 101mins

Steve Martin likes to have an audience on his side, and nowhere is that more evident than in this personally-scripted drama, updated from George Eliot's *Silas Marner*. Martin plays a reclusive cabinet-maker who "adopts" the illegitimate toddler of local magnate Gabriel Byrne when the child's mother dies in the snow near his isolated home. The Victorian poignancy of the tale still grips, even in modern-day dress, but Martin unfortunately comes across as a bit of a wimp. Still very watchable, however. TH

Steve Martin *Michael McMann* • Gabriel Byrne *John Newland* • Laura Linney *Nancy Newland* • Catherine O'Hara *Mrs Simon* • Alana Austin *Mathilda McCann aged ten* • Alyssa Austin *Mathilda McCann aged five* • Stephen Baldwin *Tanny Newland* • Byron Jennings *Keating* ■ *Dir* Gillies MacKinnon • *Scr* Steve Martin, from the novel *Silas Marner* by George Eliot

A Simple Wish ★★★ U

Fantasy comedy 1997 · US · Colour · 85mins

Martin Short stars as a fumbling fairy godmother who gets into all sorts of trouble when he tries to grant little Mara Wilson's wish that her actor dad (Robert Pastorelli) finally finds success. More interesting, though, is the conflict the fairy godmothers (including Teri Garr and Ruby Dee) are facing against struck-off fairy-turned-witch Kathleen Turner, who chews up the scenery and spits it out with hilarious venom in a deliciously evil turn. It's gets a bit flabby towards the middle, but still a fun family romp. JB

Martin Short *Murray* • Kathleen Turner *Claudia* • Mara Wilson *Anabel* • Robert Pastorelli *Oliver* • Amanda Plummer *Boots* • Francis Capra *Charlie Greening* • Ruby Dee *Hortense* • Teri Garr *Rena* ■ *Dir* Michael Ritchie • *Scr* Jeff Rothberg

Simply Irresistible ★ PG

Supernatural romantic comedy
1999 · US · Colour · 91mins

Sarah Michelle Gellar stars as the mediocre chef of a small New York bistro who suddenly discovers she can magically make wonderful food that affects people's emotions. Sean Patrick Flanery plays the Manhattan businessman who offers her a culinary opportunity and possible romance. Unfortunately, the pair have no chemistry whatsoever, and this is virtually unwatchable. JB. Contains sexual references and swearing.

Sarah Michelle Gellar *Amanda Shelton* • Sean Patrick Flanery *Tom Bartlett* • Patricia Clarkson *Lois McNally* • Dylan Baker *Jonathan Bendel* • Christopher Durang *Gene O'Reilly* • Larry Gilliard Jr *Nolan Traynor* • Betty Buckley *Aunt Stella* ■ *Dir* Mark Tarlov • *Scr* Judith Roberts

Sin ★★ 15

Romantic drama 1972 · US · Colour · 86mins

An incredibly daft 1970s drama from director George Pan Cosmatos, who went on to make the more impressive *Tombstone*. Raquel Welch, looking stunning (of course), gets involved in some serious passion, Mills and Boon style, in a case of forbidden love on a Mediterranean island, which you just know is going to end in tears. Never mind, because both the scenery and Miss Welch look beautiful. JB

Raquel Welch *Elena* • Richard Johnson *Orestes* • Frank Wolff *Hector* • Flora Robson *Antigone* • Jack Hawkins *Father Nicholas* ■ *Dir/Scr* George Pan Cosmatos

Sin City ★★★★ 18

Crime drama
2005 · US · BW and Colour · 124mins

Frank Miller's neo-*noir* comic book comes to spectacular life here, meticulously re-creating three interlinked stories. In each segment, cops, criminals and *femmes fatales* collide in love, lust or gory conflict. Bruce Willis brings poignancy as the disgraced ex-cop shielding dancer Jessica Alba, while tough private eye Clive Owen's brutal clash with rival suitor Benicio Del Toro adds a streak of gallows humour. However, Mickey Rourke steals the show, playing a soft-hearted ex-con out to avenge his sweetheart's murder. Stylistically, the movie is a masterpiece, with its astonishing visuals papering over a repetitious plot and some corny dialogue. This directorial collaboration with Robert Rodriguez (with Quentin Tarentino as "guest director") is not for every taste, but genre fans will be blown away. SF. Contains violence.

Jessica Alba *Nancy Callahan* • Benicio Del Toro *Jackie Boy* • Brittany Murphy *Shellie* • Clive Owen *Dwight* • Mickey Rourke *Marv* • Bruce Willis *Hartigan* • Elijah Wood *Kevin* • Rosario Dawson *Gail* • Carla Gugino *Lucille* • Josh Hartnett *The Man* • Michael Madsen *Bob* • Jaime King *Goldie/Wendy* • Nick Stahl *Roark Jr/Yellow Bastard* • Powers Boothe *Senator Roark* • Rutger Hauer *Cardinal Roark* ■ *Dir* Frank Miller, Robert Rodriguez • *Scr* Robert Rodriguez, Frank Miller, from the *Sin City* graphic novel stories *The Hard Goodbye*, *The Big Fat Kill*, *That Yellow Bastard* by Frank Miller

The Sin Eater ★★ 15

Horror thriller
2002 · US/Ger · Colour · 98mins

This religious farrago suffers from a terminal case of farcical script. Brian Helgeland has constructed what might be called a *roman policier* about young priest Heath Ledger who's sent to Rome with Shannyn Sossamon to investigate the suspicious death of his mentor. The film's candle-lit goings on, familiar religious trappings and diabolical dialogue diminish the occasional moments of ecclesiastical high thinking. TH. Contains swearing and violence.

Heath Ledger *Father Alex Bernier* • Shannyn Sossamon *Mara Sinclair* • Benno Fürmann *William Eden* • Mark Addy *Father Thomas Garrett* • Peter Weller *Cardinal Driscoll* • Francesco Carnelutti *Father Dominic* • Mattia Sbragia *Apathetic Bishop* ■ *Dir/Scr* Brian Helgeland

The Sin of Madelon Claudet ★★★★

Drama 1931 · US · BW · 74mins

Broadway legend Helen Hayes, who walked off with an Oscar for her performance as the unfortunate heroine, plays an innocent French country girl who elopes to Paris with an American artist, is deserted and left pregnant. How she sacrifices herself for the child who thinks she's dead (shades of *Madame X*) is the stuff of an archetypal five-handkerchief weepie. Lewis Stone is splendid as Madelon's protector-lover, while Jean Hersholt is the mentor of her "orphan" son. RK

Helen Hayes *Madelon Claudet* • Lewis Stone *Carlo Boretti* • Neil Hamilton *Larry* • Robert Young (1) *Dr Jacques Claudet* • Cliff Edwards *Victor* • Jean Hersholt *Dr Dulac* • Marie Prevost *Rosalie* • Alan Hale *Claudet* ■ *Dir* Edgar Selwyn • *Scr* Charles Macarthur, Ben Hecht (uncredited), from the play *The Lullaby* by Edward Knoblock

The Sin of Nora Moran ★★★

Murder mystery melodrama
1933 · US · BW · 67mins

This sentimental melodrama from B-movie veteran Phil Goldstone stars Zita Johann as a poor orphaned girl who gets into a terrible fix after a romantic entanglement with ambitious politician Paul Cavanagh. The film was one of many that disappeared, virtually written out of the history books. In 2000 it was rediscovered, restored and hailed as "maybe the best Hollywood B-movie of the 1930s". Its appeal lies in the non-linear construction; the narrative jumps backwards and forwards and there is even a flashback within a flashback. The treatment does increase our curiosity about poor Nora Moran's fate, but it's debatable

S

whether this really is the best of its kind. DM

Zita Johann *Nora Moran* • Alan Dinehart *District Attorney John Grant* • Paul Cavanagh *Governor Dick Crawford* • Claire DuBrey *Edith Crawford* • Cora Sue Collins *Nora Moran as a child* ■ *Dir* Phil Goldstone, Howard Christy • *Scr* Frances Hyland, from a play by Willis Maxwell Goodhue

The Sin Ship ★

Crime drama 1931 · US · BW · 65mins

Louis Wolheim not only starred in this lurid drama but made his directing debut. Dead from stomach cancer before it opened, he was spared the bad reviews. His hard-boiled skipper of a cargo ship takes on board Ian Keith and Mary Astor, a fleeing bank robber and his moll posing as a church minister and wife. Wolheim falls heavily for Astor and becomes a reformed character while she, unbelievably, is attracted to him. AE

Louis Wolheim *Captain Sam McVeigh* • Mary Astor *"Frisco" Kitty* • Ian Keith *Marsden* • Hugh Herbert *Charlie* ■ *Dir* Louis Wolheim • *Scr* Hugh Herbert, from a story by Keane Thompson, Agnes Brand Leahy

Sin Town ★★

Western 1942 · US · BW · 73mins

An average little western, kept moving at a rate of knots by one of those unsung heroes of the studio system, director Ray Enright. There's a certain gritty realism in the script, Broderick Crawford is good, but it's the ever elegant Constance Bennett who sweeps up the acting honours. The film packs a surprising amount into its short running time, but sadly little that is above programme-filler standard. TS

Constance Bennett *Kye Allen* • Broderick Crawford *Dude McNair* • Anne Gwynne *Laura Kirby* • Patric Knowles *Wade Crowell* • Andy Devine *Judge Eustace Vale* • Leo Carrillo *Angelo Colina* • Ward Bond *Rock Delaney* ■ *Dir* Ray Enright • *Scr* W Scott Darling, Gerald Geraghty, Richard Brooks

Sinbad and the Eye of the Tiger ★★★ U

Fantasy adventure
1977 · UK/US · Colour · 112mins

Not up to the previous two *Sinbad* adventures from the Ray Harryhausen fantasy factory – it's too long and Patrick Wayne is a charisma-free hero. As you'd expect, special effects wizard Harryhausen enhances this romantic exotica with his distinctive brand of visual thrills. It all helps to pass the time away agreeably between the frothy *Arabian Nights* nonsense standing in for the plot. AJ [video] DVD

Patrick Wayne *Sinbad* • Taryn Power *Dione* • Jane Seymour (2) *Princess Farah* • Margaret Whiting *Zenobia* • Patrick Troughton *Melanthius* • Kurt Christian *Rafi* • Nadim Sawalha *Hassan* ■ *Dir* Sam Wanamaker • *Scr* Beverley Cross, from a story by Beverley Cross, Ray Harryhausen

Sinbad: Legend of the Seven Seas ★★★ U

Animated comedy adventure
2003 · US · Colour · 81mins

This enjoyable mix of swashbuckling action and *Arabian Nights*-style fantasy demonstrates that there's still plenty of mileage in good old-fashioned storytelling. Scallywag Sinbad (voiced by Brad Pitt) and his crew try to retrieve the powerful Book of Peace from conniving goddess Eris (a fabulously sinister Michelle Pfeiffer). Although some of the animation, like the plotline, is a tad basic, the stops are pulled out for the set pieces. Catherine Zeta-Jones's stowaway is strong and sassy. SF [video] DVD

Brad Pitt *Sinbad* • Catherine Zeta-Jones *Marina* • Michelle Pfeiffer *Eris* • Joseph Fiennes *Proteus* • Dennis Haysbert *Kale* • Timothy West *King Dymas* • Adriano Giannini *Rat* ■ *Dir* Tim Johnson, Patrick Gilmore • *Scr* John Logan

Sinbad the Sailor ★★★ U

Swashbuckling adventure
1947 · US · Colour · 111mins

In this splendid Technicolor romp, Douglas Fairbanks Jr ably follows in the dashing footsteps of his father. He stars as the swashbuckling hero who searches for hidden treasure and falls for Maureen O'Hara. The costumes lack flair (as does the plot), and the whole thing's very juvenile, but there's no denying the film's sense of *joie de vivre*. The right tone is defined from the opening: this is great fun. TS [video]

Douglas Fairbanks Jr *Sinbad* • Maureen O'Hara *Shireen* • Walter Slezak *Melik* • Anthony Quinn *Emir* • George Tobias *Abbu* • Jane Greer *Pirouze* • Mike Mazurki *Yusuf* ■ *Dir* Richard Wallace • *Scr* John Twist, from a story by John Twist, George Worthing

Since Otar Left ★★★★ 15

Drama 2003 · Fr/Bel · Colour · 98mins

Julie Bertuccelli's debut feature is a moving study of family loyalty amid societal decay. With Tbilisi facing economic meltdown, nonagenarian Esther Gorintin heads for Paris with her daughter (Nino Khomassouridze) and grandchild (Dinara Droukarova), unaware that her beloved work-away son Otar has been killed. Although afflicted by arthritis, Gorintin is anything but an object of pity, whether she's feistily championing Georgia's Soviet past or facing the truth about her son's fate. Gorintin is superbly supported by her co-stars, as well as an intelligent screenplay and sensitive direction. DP. In French, Georgian and Russian with English subtitles. Contains swearing. DVD

Esther Gorintin *Eka* • Nino Khomassouridze *Marina* • Dinara Droukarova *Ada* • Temour Kalandadze *Tenguiz* • Roussoudan Bolkvadze *Roussiko* • Sacha Sarichvili *Alexo* • Douta Skhirtladze *Niko* • Mzia Eristavi *Dora* ■ *Dir* Julie Bertuccelli • *Scr* Julie Bertuccelli, Bernard Renucci, Roger Bohbot

Since You Went Away ★★★ U

Wartime drama 1944 · US · BW · 163mins

Everything is absolutely certain in this vision of wartime middle-class America. Claudette Colbert waits faithfully, keeping the home fires burning, while husband Neil Hamilton (his only appearance in the film is in a photograph) and family friend Joseph Cotten are off saving everyone from Hitler. Marriage is wonderful, children are dreamboats and democracy rules OK. It's all syrupy nonsense, of course, but the wonderful cast (the brilliant Agnes Moorehead is particularly noteworthy) makes it very watchable. SH [video]

Claudette Colbert *Anne Hilton* • Jennifer Jones *Jane Hilton* • Shirley Temple *Bridget Hilton* • Joseph Cotten *Lieutenant Anthony Willett* • Monty Woolley *Colonel Smollett* • Robert Walker *Corporal William G Smollett II* • Lionel Barrymore *Clergyman* • Hattie McDaniel *Fidelia* • Agnes Moorehead *Emily Hawkins* ■ *Dir* John Cromwell • *Scr* David O Selznick, Margaret Buell Wilder, from the novel *Together* by Margaret Buell Wilder

Sincerely Yours ★ U

Drama 1955 · US · Colour · 120mins

This is an ill-judged, ineptly updated and ludicrous remake of *The Man Who Played God*, the unusual, fantastical and rather powerful 1932 melodrama. Liberace takes the role of a concert pianist who goes deaf, learns to lip-read and anonymously helps people in trouble on whose conversations he "eavesdrops" through binoculars. This would be funny if it weren't so awful. RK

Liberace *Anthony Warrin* • Joanne Dru *Marion Moore* • Dorothy Malone *Linda Curtis* • Alex Nicol *Howard Ferguson* • William Demarest *Sam Dunne* • Lori Nelson *Sarah Cosgrove* • Lurene Tuttle *Mrs McGinley* • Richard Eyer *Alvie Hunt* ■ *Dir* Gordon Douglas • *Scr* Irving Wallace, from the play *The Man Who Played God* by Jules Eckert Goodman

Sinful Davey ★★

Period comedy adventure
1969 · UK · Colour · 94mins

John Hurt is Scot Davey Haggart, who deserts the British army and, like his father before him, becomes a highwayman, always just an inch away from the hangman's noose. John Huston included this extremely lightweight and modestly enjoyable romp among his failures. Filmed in Ireland, where Huston owned an estate for many years, it boasts some nice camerawork by Freddie Young, a cute performance by Pamela Franklin and the fleeting screen debut of the director's daughter, Anjelica. AT

John Hurt *Davey Haggart* • Pamela Franklin *Annie* • Nigel Davenport *Constable Richardson* • Ronald Fraser *MacNab* • Robert Morley *Duke of Argyll* • Maxine Audley *Duchess of Argyll* • Fionnuala Flanagan [Fionnula Flanagan] *Penelope* • Anjelica Huston ■ *Dir* John Huston • *Scr* James R Webb, from the autobiography *The Life of David Haggart* by David Haggart

A Sinful Life ★★

Comedy 1989 · US · Colour · 90mins

This low-budget comedy finds Anita Morris opting for single motherhood, having once danced for Sonny and Cher. When the authorities threaten to take away her unusual daughter Blair Tefkin, she enters the arena of domestic respectabilty, complete with dutiful husband. Actor/director William Schreiner's comedy is a nice, if slight vehicle for Morris's talents. FL

Anita Morris *Claire* • Rick Overton *Janitor Joe* • Dennis Christopher *Nathan Flowers* • Blair Tefkin *Baby* • Mark Rolston *Teresa Tremaine* ■ *Dir* William Schreiner • *Scr* Melanie Graham, from her play *Baby Bump and the Last of the Pom Pom Girls*

Sing ★★★ 15

Musical romance 1989 · US · Colour · 94mins

A teen romance that's as corny as Kansas in August, September *and* October, but that's so sweet and disingenuous it's hard to dislike it, however clichéd. Richard Baskin's musical drama is set in a Brooklyn high school where the students take part in an annual "Sing" contest. Participating bad boy Peter Dobson and nice Jewish girl Jessica Steen share a certain talent for each other, while empathetic teacher Lorraine Bracco must shield the kids from the nasty education authorities, who want to shut the school down. DA [video]

Lorraine Bracco *Miss Lombardo* • Peter Dobson *Dominic* • Jessica Steen *Hannah* • Louise Lasser *Rosie* • George DiCenzo *Mr Marowitz* • Patti LaBelle *Mrs DeVere* • Susan Peretz *Mrs Tucci* • Laurnea Wilkerson *Zena* ■ *Dir* Richard Baskin • *Scr* Dean Pitchford

Sing as We Go ★★★ U

Musical comedy 1934 · UK · BW · 74mins

Gracie Fields is the life and soul of this dated but spirited musical comedy, as she makes for the bright lights of Blackpool after the small-town mill that she works in is forced to close. JB Priestley's source story may not be one of his most original or complex, but Gracie's attempts to hold down a variety of seaside jobs and her encounter with benevolent tycoon Lawrence Grossmith are both amusing and politically astute. DP [video]

Gracie Fields *Gracie Platt* • John Loder *Hugh Phillips* • Dorothy Hyson *Phyllis Logan* • Stanley Holloway *Policeman* • Frank Pettingell *Murgatroyd Platt* • Lawrence Grossmith *Sir William Upton* • Morris Harvey *Cowboy* • Arthur Sinclair *Maestro* ■ *Dir* Basil Dean • *Scr* Gordon Wellesley, from a story by JB Priestley

Sing, Baby, Sing ★★★★

Musical comedy 1936 · US · BW · 87mins

A fast-moving musical comedy which set Alice Faye on the road to becoming 20th Century-Fox's top singing star. Appearing with a softened, more alluring hairstyle, Faye is a nightclub singer who attracts the attentions of a drunken Shakespearean actor. Adolphe Menjou is hilarious in this role, which is obviously based on that great tippler John Barrymore. The film marked the debut of the Ritz Brothers, who have a few funny moments. The singer with the band is Tony Martin, recently married to Alice Faye, who sings the Oscar-nominated song *When Did You Leave Heaven*. RB

Alice Faye *Joan Warren* • Adolphe Menjou *Bruce Farraday* • Gregory Ratoff *Nicky* • Ted Healy *Al Craven* • Patsy Kelly *Fitz* • Montagu Love *Robert Wilson* • The Ritz Brothers [Al Ritz] • The Ritz Brothers [Jimmy Ritz] • The Ritz Brothers [Harry Ritz] ■ *Dir* Sidney Lanfield • *Scr* Milton Sperling, Jack Yellen, Harry Tugend, from a story by Milton Sperling, Jack Yellen

Sing, Boy, Sing ★★

Musical drama 1958 · US · BW · 90mins

Tommy Sands, singing idol of the rock 'n' roll era, had a chequered career, but his screen debut in this adaptation of a television play was impressive and promised better things. The story has teen idol Sands being manipulated by a ruthless manager (Edmond O'Brien) while being torn between his love of pop music and his obligation to succeed his grandfather as a preacher. The tale has too much angst and too little originality to be more than mildly entertaining. TV

Tommy Sands *Virgil Walker* • Lili Gentle *Leora Easton* • Edmond O'Brien *Joseph Sharkey* • John McIntire *Reverend Walker* • Nick Adams *CK Judd* • Diane Jergens *Pat* • Josephine Hutchinson *Caroline Walker* • Jerry Paris *Fisher* ■ *Dir* Henry Ephron • *Scr* Claude Binyon, from the TV play *The Singin' Idol* by Paul Monash

Singapore ★★

Adventure drama 1947 · US · BW · 79mins

Pearl-smuggling sailor Fred MacMurray returns to Singapore after the Second World War to retrieve a valuable bag of pearls he left hidden in his hotel room. In flashback, he relives his romance with Ava Gardner, apparently killed in the Japanese invasion which coincided with their wedding. Back in present time, he discovers her alive but suffering total amnesia and married to wealthy Roland Culver. This much-derided piece of nonsensical escapism is really quite entertaining. RK

Fred MacMurray *Matt Gordon* • Ava Gardner *Linda* • Roland Culver *Michael Van Leyden* • Richard Haydn *Chief Inspector Hewitt* • Thomas Gomez *Mr Mauribus* • Spring Byington *Mrs Bellows* • Porter Hall *Mr Bellows* • George Lloyd *Sascha Barda* ■ *Dir* John Brahm • *Scr* Seton I Miller, Robert Thoeren, from a story by Seton I Miller

Singapore Sling ★★★

Black comedy horror
1990 · Gr · BW · 114mins

Apparently inspired by *Laura*, this is appropriately shot in handsome *film noir* style. The story has something to do with a mother, her daughter and the stranger who comes calling, but there is really no plot and instead torture, gorging, vomiting and urination are dwelt upon to a perplexing degree. A minor *succès de scandale* on the festival and art house circuit, this is strictly for those on the lookout for the truly bizarre. DM

Meredyth Herold *Daughter/Laura* • Michele Valley *Mother* • Panos Thanassoulis *Singapore Sling* ■ *Dir/Scr* Nikos Nikolaidis

The Singer Not the Song ★★ U

Western 1960 · UK · Colour · 132mins

With Dirk Bogarde strutting around a small Mexican town in the tightest black leather trousers the censors would allow and John Mills spouting Catholic dogma in an abominable Irish accent, this has all the makings of a cult classic. Sadly, the story is so dull that your mind is soon numbed to the actorly excesses of the stars. Director Roy Ward Baker doesn't help matters with his leaden pacing and over-deliberate staging. DP

Dirk Bogarde *Anacleto* • John Mills *Father Keogh* • Mylène Demongeot *Locha* • Laurence Naismith *Old uncle* • John Bentley *Chief of police* • Leslie French *Father Gomez* • Eric Pohlmann *Presidente* ■ *Dir* Roy Ward Baker • *Scr* Nigel Balchin, from the novel by Audrey Erskine Lindop

Singin' in the Rain ★★★★★ U

Classic musical 1952 · US · Colour · 102mins

Never, in the whole history of the American cinema, has such a collection of talents come together at the peak of their abilities to generate such an enjoyable and clever movie. Not only is this utterly irrepressible, but the story also beautifully evokes the excitement and pleasure of making motion pictures. Gene Kelly was responsible in his lifetime for providing enormous pleasure for movie audiences, and his joyous rendition of the title song in this film stands as a lasting tribute. For those who don't know, this film is an affectionate parody of the days when sound came to Hollywood in the wake of *The Jazz Singer*, and every incident wittily referred to in Betty Comden and Adolph Green's sparkling screenplay actually happened. TS DVD

Gene Kelly *Don Lockwood* • Debbie Reynolds *Kathy Selden* • Donald O'Connor *Cosmo Brown* • Jean Hagen *Lina Lamont* • Millard Mitchell *RF Simpson* • Rita Moreno *Zelda Zanders* • Douglas Fowley *Roscoe Dexter* • Cyd Charisse *Dancer* ■ *Dir* Gene Kelly, Stanley Donen • *Scr* Adolph Green, Betty Comden • *Cinematographer* Harold Rosson • *Music/lyrics* Nacio Herb Brown • *Music Director* Lennie Hayton

S

The Singing Detective ★★ 15

Period musical drama
2003 · US · Colour · 104mins

Dennis Potter's excellent 1980s amalgam of psychological drama, detective thriller and musical fantasy gets hung, drawn and quartered by this ill-advised Hollywood remake. Replacing Michael Gambon as the bitter, psoriasis-afflicted writer, Robert Downey Jr overplays every scene. Truncating the key childhood flashback scenes, the film is more interested in sterile musical numbers and sleazy *film noir* fragments. Aside from some striking, if theatrical, lighting, the only plus point is Mel Gibson's cameo as Downey Jr's psychiatrist. JC DVD

Robert Downey Jr *Dan Dark* • Robin Wright Penn *Nicola/Nina/Blonde* • Jeremy Northam *Mark Binney* • Katie Holmes *Nurse Mills* • Carla Gugino *Betty Dark/Hooker* • Adrien Brody *First hood* • Jon Polito *Second hood* • Mel Gibson *Dr Gibbon* ■ *Dir* Keith Gordon • *Scr* Dennis Potter, from his TV series

The Singing Fool ★★

Musical drama 1928 · US · BW · 105mins

Al Jolson's follow-up to *The Jazz Singer*, was even more popular and was Hollywood's most financially successful sound film until *Gone with the Wind* in 1939. Its blatant assault on the tear ducts and Jolson's performance take a lot of swallowing now, and its appeal rests purely on its important place in Hollywood history. Jolson plays a singer/composer who loses his wife and small son, the demise of the latter prompting the film's most famous sequence, as Jolson sings *Sonny Boy*. TV

Al Jolson *Al Stone* • Betty Bronson *Grace* • Josephine Dunn *Molly Winton* • Reed Howes *John Perry* • Edward Martindel *Louis Marcus* • Arthur Housman *Blackie Joe* • Davey Lee *Sonny Boy* ■ *Dir* Lloyd Bacon • *Scr* Joseph Jackson, C Graham Baker, from a story by Leslie S Barrows

The Singing Kid ★★★ U

Musical comedy 1936 · US · BW · 85mins

If ever a musical was saved by its songs, this is it. Though Al Jolson had been the saviour of Warner Bros when he starred in *The Jazz Singer*, the studio was happy to terminate his contract by the time this film was released. Tastes had changed and Jolson's extrovert style was going out of fashion. Mundane scripts like this one did not help, with Jolson a stage star who loses his voice and goes to the country to convalesce. Fortunately, the songs by Harold Arlen and EY Harburg crop up often enough to provide some adrenalin. TV

Al Jolson *Al Jackson* • Allen Jenkins *Joe Eddy* • Lyle Talbot *Bob Carey* • William B Davidson *Barney Hammond* • Frank Mitchell *Dope* • Edward Keane *Potter* • Sybil Jason *Sybil Haines* • Edward Everett Horton *Davenport Rogers* ■ *Dir* William Keighley • *Scr* Warren Duff, Pat C Flick, from a story by Robert Lord

The Singing Nun ★★ U

Musical drama 1966 · US · Colour · 96mins

Audiences in the mid-1960s must have had sweet teeth for this mawkish musical biopic to be a box-office success. Piously pert Debbie Reynolds plays Soeur Sourire, the guitar-strumming Belgian nun who composed the song *Dominique*, written for a motherless boy, which ended up as an international hit. Greer Garson pours more syrup over it as the Mother Prioress. Schmaltzy. RB

Debbie Reynolds *Sister Ann* • Ricardo Montalban *Father Clementi* • Greer Garson *Mother Prioress* • Agnes Moorehead *Sister Cluny* • Chad Everett *Robert Gerarde* • Katharine Ross *Nicole Arlien* • Juanita Moore *Sister Mary* • Ed Sullivan ■ *Dir* Henry Koster • *Scr* Sally Benson, John Furia Jr, from a story by John Furia Jr

The Singing, Ringing Tree ★★★ U

Fantasy 1957 · E Ger · Colour · 71mins

This unassuming fairy tale has captivated three generations. First seen on British television in 1964 (when it was shown in three parts on the BBC series *Tales from Europe*), this colourful fantasy was later rediscovered by London's National Film Theatre, where it became one of the audience's favourite films. The simple story is about a prince who sets out to find the eponymous tree to win the love of a beautiful but arrogant princess. Although slow-paced by modern standards, it is shot on surprisingly large sets and has the charm of a picture book come to life. DM. In German with English subtitles. DVD

Christel Bodenstein *Thousand-Beauty/Princess* • Charles Hans Vogt *King* • Eckart Dux *Prince/Bear* • Richard Krüger *Dwarf* • Dorothea Thiessing *Nurse* • Fredy Barten *Minister* ■ *Dir* Francesco Stefani • *Scr* Francesco Stefani, Anne Geelhaar, inspired by episodes in stories collected by Jacob Grimm, Wilhelm Grimm

The Singing Sheriff ★★ U

Comedy western 1944 · US · BW · 62mins

Intended as a satire on westerns, this works better today as a vehicle for bandleader Bob Crosby (brother of Bing) playing a Broadway cowboy finding himself out in the real Wild West. Much of the spoofing is heavy-handed, but some of it does work and it's all good-natured stuff with Crosby a likeable lead. TS

Bob Crosby *Bob Richards* • Fay McKenzie *Caroline* • Fuzzy Knight *Fuzzy* • Iris Adrian *Lefty* • Samuel S Hinds *Seth* • Edward Norris *Vance* ■ *Dir* Leslie Goodwins • *Scr* Henry Blankfort, Eugene Conrad, from a story by John Grey

Single Room Furnished ★★

Drama 1968 · US · Colour · 93mins

Like *Game of Death*, this is a salvage job, cobbled together after the death of its star. Her career on the skids, Jayne Mansfield met and married Italian stage director Matteo Ottaviano, later known as Matt Cimber. He found a play about the occupant of a single room, a young woman picked up and dropped by a succession of men, and developed it as a vehicle for his wife. Halfway through shooting, she flounced off the set and was killed in a car crash. Cimber had the script re-written, shot a framing story with new characters, and further padded the running time by adding a prologue in which journalist Walter Winchell pays tribute to Mansfield. Depressingly cheap and tawdry. DM

Jayne Mansfield *Johnnie/Mae/Eilene* • Dorothy Keller *Flo* • Fabian Dean *Charley* • Billy M Greene *Pop* • Terri Messina *Maria Adamo* ■ *Dir* Matteo Ottaviano [Matt Cimber] • *Scr* Michael Musto

The Single Standard ★★★

Silent romantic drama
1929 · US · BW · 73mins

Greta Garbo's last film with Nils Asther presents her in the familiar mix of convention-defying free spirit and penitent coming to her senses. She plays a San Francisco socialite who jaunts off on a yacht for an affair with Asther, a macho sailor-turned-artist. When he has second thoughts, she returns home to find herself a social outcast. Soft-edged stuff, directed with almost puritan discretion by John S Robertson. RK

Greta Garbo *Arden Stuart* • Nils Asther *Packy Cannon* • John Mack Brown [Johnny Mack Brown] *Tommy Hewlett* • Dorothy Sebastian *Mercedes* • Lane Chandler *Ding Stuart* • Robert Castle *Anthony Kendall* ■ *Dir* John S Robertson • *Scr* Josephine Lovett, from a story by Adela Rogers St Johns

Single White Female ★★★★ 18

Thriller 1992 · US · Colour · 103mins

Jennifer Jason Leigh plays the lodger from hell who makes nice Bridget Fonda's life a misery in this ludicrous but hugely enjoyable thriller from director Barbet Schroeder. Based on John Lutz's novel, this has Fonda as a chic Manhattanite looking for a roommate, and Leigh as the shy, frumpy "perfect" candidate. That is, until she starts dressing like Fonda and tries to steal her boyfriend. Yes, you may be able to guess the end from the first five minutes, but that doesn't make this any less enthralling. JB. Contains violence, swearing, sex scenes and nudity. DVD

Bridget Fonda *Allison Jones* • Jennifer Jason Leigh *Hedra Carlson* • Steven Weber *Sam Rawson* • Peter Friedman *Graham Knox* • Stephen Tobolowsky *Mitchell Myerson* • Frances Bay *Elderly neighbour* ■ *Dir* Barbet Schroeder • *Scr* Don Roos, from the novel *SWF Seeks Same* by John Lutz

Singles ★★★★ 15

Romantic comedy
1992 · US · Colour · 95mins

Former rock journalist Cameron Crowe directs this interesting romantic comedy, a wonderfully funny look at love among Seattle's 20-somethings. Matt Dillon is the self-centred grunge rocker in love with Bridget Fonda, while Campbell Scott and Kyra Sedgwick are the couple too scared of commitment because of past experiences. They head an exemplary cast involved in the sort of dating rituals that recall the acerbic wit of early Woody Allen, but appealingly countered with a touching sweetness. AJ. Contains swearing and sex scenes. DVD

Bridget Fonda *Janet Livermore* • Campbell Scott *Steve Dunne* • Kyra Sedgwick *Linda Powell* • Sheila Kelley *Debbie Hunt* • Jim True *David Bailey* • Matt Dillon *Cliff Poncier* • Bill Pullman *Dr Jamison* • James LeGros *Andy* ■ *Dir/Scr* Cameron Crowe

Sink or Swim ★★★

Period adventure 1971 · Fr · Colour · 98mins

Jean-Paul Rappeneau likened this rousing costume adventure to a collaboration between Mozart and bullish Hollywood director Raoul Walsh. Certainly, there's plenty of Walsh brio about the proceedings, which see anti-royalist Jean-Paul Belmondo return from New World exile to revolutionary France to secure the divorce he needs to marry an American heiress. He's soon entangled in the schemes of his duplicitous wife Marlène Jobert. Smartly satirising period politics, this keeps the action light and furious. DP. In French with English dialogue.

Jean-Paul Belmondo *Nicolas* • Marlène Jobert *Charlotte* • Laura Antonelli *Pauline* • Michel Auclair *Prince* • Sami Frey *Marquis* • Pierre Brasseur *Gosselin* ■ *Dir* Jean-Paul Rappeneau • *Scr* Daniel Boulanger, Jean-Paul Rappeneau, Claude Sautet, Maurice Clavel

Sink the Bismarck! ★★★★ U

Second World War drama
1960 · UK · BW · 97mins

The postwar British film industry relied heavily on "now the story can be told" accounts of engagements that helped turn the Second World War in favour of the Allies. Too many were smug action adventures that devalued the true heroism of the exploits they depicted, but this fine film fully captures the tensions, dangers and complexities of battle by concentrating on the unsung back-room planners as much as on the combatants themselves. There are caricatures on both sides, but at the same time there is a respect for the enemy that is missing in many previous flag-wavers. DP DVD

Kenneth More *Captain Jonathan Shepard* • Dana Wynter *Anne Davis* • Carl Mohner *Captain Lindemann* • Laurence Naismith *First Sea Lord* • Geoffrey Keen *ACNS* • Karel Stepanek *Admiral Lutjens* • Michael Hordern *Commander on King George V* • Maurice Denham *Commander Richards* ■ *Dir* Lewis Gilbert • *Scr* Edmund H North, from the non-fiction book by CS Forester

Sinners in Paradise ★

Drama 1938 · US · BW · 64mins

Scraping the bottom of the barrel of stories about strangers thrown together by unusual and unfortunate circumstances, this is the plane crash version. Here the passengers are stranded on a remote tropical island, seemingly deserted until escaped convict John Boles shows himself.

Happily, it only takes 64 minutes for their dreary skeletons to come rattling out of the cupboard. RK

Madge Evans *Anne Wesson* • John Boles *Jim Taylor* • Bruce Cabot *Robert Malone/"The Torpedo"* • Marion Martin *Iris Compton* • Gene Lockhart *Senator Corey* • Charlotte Wynters *Thelma Chase/Doris Bailey* ■ *Dir* James Whale • *Scr* Lester Cole, Harold Buckley, Louis Stevens, from the story *Half Way to Shanghai* by Harold Buckley

Sinners in Silk ★★★

Silent romantic fantasy
1924 · US · BW · 68mins

Louis B Mayer personally produced this high-society melodrama, which was given a whisper of sensationalism by its incestuous undertone. Little attention is paid to the scientific process by which Jean Hersholt relieves ageing roué Adolphe Menjou of 20 years. Instead, director Hobart Henley concentrates on the fact that Menjou and his dashing son, Conrad Nagel, are in competition for the affections of the ravishing Eleanor Boardman. The sudden resolution leaves all sorts of unsatisfactory loose ends, but it's expertly performed. DP

Adolphe Menjou *Arthur Merrill* • Eleanor Boardman *Penelope Stevens* • Conrad Nagel *Brock Farley* • Jean Hersholt *Dr Eustace* • Edward Connelly *Bates* • Jerome Patrick *Jerry Hall* • Hedda Hopper *Mrs Stevens* ■ *Dir* Hobart Henley • *Scr* Carey Wilson, from a story by Benjamin Glazer

Sinners in the Sun ★★

Romance 1932 · US · BW · 60mins

Dress-shop model Carole Lombard and mechanic Chester Morris, madly in love, part after a difference of opinion about their planned marriage. She becomes the kept mistress of wealthy Walter Byron; he graduates from chauffeur to husband of rich socialite Adrienne Ames. Paramount's sophisticated house style is only celluloid deep, a surface cover for a clichéd and simplistic demonstration that money doesn't buy happiness. RK

Carole Lombard *Doris Blake* • Chester Morris *Jimmie Martin* • Adrienne Ames *Claire Kinkaid* • Alison Skipworth *Mrs Blake* • Cary Grant *Ridgeway* • Walter Byron *Eric Nelson* • Rita La Roy *Lil* ■ *Dir* Alexander Hall • *Scr* Waldemar Young, Samuel Hoffenstein, Vincent Lawrence, from the short story *The Beachcomber* by Mildred Cram

The Sins of Rachel Cade ★★★

Wartime melodrama
1960 · US · Colour · 122mins

Almost single-handedly, Warner Bros cut a melodramatic swathe through the late 1950s and 1960s with a series of star-studded colourful dramas, tackling "adult" themes and featuring their contract players. Here, missionary nurse Angie Dickinson sweats it out with Peter Finch in the Belgian Congo, while Roger Moore looks on in lust. Director Gordon Douglas understands the quintessential trashiness of the material and does well by it. TS

Angie Dickinson *Rachel Cade* • Peter Finch *Colonel Henri Derode* • Roger Moore *Paul Wilton* • Errol John *Kulu, Rachel's assistant* • Woody Strode *Muwango* • Juano Hernandez *Kalanumu* • Scatman Crothers *Musinga* ■ *Dir* Gordon Douglas • *Scr* Edward Anhalt, from the novel *Rachel Cade* by Charles E Mercer

Sioux City ★★ 15

Mystery thriller 1994 · US · Colour · 97mins

Lou Diamond Phillips decided – after starring in a number of movies – that he wanted to direct. He also takes the lead as the Sioux who has been adopted by an affluent Jewish couple and become a busy doctor in Beverly Hills. He then discovers that his real mother has died mysteriously. His search for his identity parallels a crime story that lapses into melodrama. Well intentioned rather than gripping. BB [video]

Lou Diamond Phillips *Jesse Rainfeather Goldman* • Ralph Waite *Chief Drew McDermott* • Melinda Dillon *Leah Goldman* • Salli Richardson *Jolene Buckley* • Adam Roarke *Blake Goldman* • Tantoo Cardinal *Dawn Rainfeather* ■ *Dir* Lou Diamond Phillips • *Scr* L Virginia Browne

Sir Henry at Rawlinson End ★★ 15

Surreal comedy 1980 · UK · Sepia · 67mins

A mercifully brief British oddity, with Trevor Howard as an eccentric, boozy aristocrat at odds with an army of characters seemingly left over from other comedies. *The Goon Show* it isn't, though it would like to be. The fault lies firmly at the door of former Bonzo Dog (Doo Dah) Band member Vivian Stanshall, who wrote the film and contributed the music. TH [video]

Trevor Howard *Sir Henry Rawlinson* • Patrick Magee *Reverend Slodden* • JG Devlin *Old Scrotum* • Sheila Reid *Florrie* • Denise Coffey *Mrs E* • Harry Fowler *Buller Bullethead* • Vivian Stanshall *Hubert Rawlinson* • Jeremy Child *Peregrine Maynard* ■ *Dir* Steve Roberts • *Scr* Vivian Stanshall, Steve Roberts, from the radio series by Vivian Stanshall

Siren of Atlantis ★★

Fantasy adventure 1948 · US · BW · 75mins

Only camp followers of sultry 1940s star Maria Montez will put up with this inept fantasy showing the "Cobra Woman" posturing, pouting and slinking her way through a cobbled-together slice of exotica. La Montez stars as the cruel ruler of the lost kingdom of Atlantis, discovered by French Legionnaires Jean-Pierre Aumont (Montez's husband) and Dennis O'Keefe. Shoddy stuff. AJ

Maria Montez *Queen Antinea* • Jean-Pierre Aumont *Andre St Avit* • Dennis O'Keefe *Jean Morhange* • Morris Carnovsky *Le Mesge* • Henry Daniell *Blades* ■ *Dir* Gregg G Tallas [Gregg Tallas] • *Scr* Rowland Leigh, Robert Lax, Thomas Job, from the novel *L'Atlantide* by Pierre Benoit

Sirens ★★ 15

Erotic comedy
1994 · Aus/UK/Ger · Colour · 90mins

Hugh Grant stars as a prudish clergyman whose first task in his new Australian parish is to prevent bohemian artist Sam Neill from exhibiting both his models and his portraits of them. Director John Duigan contents himself with a few gentle barbs and elegant *bons mots*, but rather loses his way once Grant's less inhibited wife, Tara FitzGerald, joins Elle Macpherson and her fellow poseurs. DP. Contains swearing, sex scenes and nudity. [video] DVD

Hugh Grant *Anthony Campion* • Tara FitzGerald *Estella Campion* • Sam Neill *Norman Lindsay* • Elle Macpherson *Sheela* • Portia de Rossi *Giddy* • Kate Fischer *Pru* • Pamela Rabe *Rose Lindsay* ■ *Dir/Scr* John Duigan

Sirocco ★★★ PG

Spy drama 1951 · US · BW · 94mins

This pretty blatant imitation of *Casablanca* was made by Humphrey Bogart's own production company, Santana. Set in Syria in the 1920s, this was by his own admission not one of Bogart's best pictures, but it's still a moodily gripping yarn about gunrunners, political commitment and various other intrigues. What it sadly lacks is a decent heroine though Lee J Cobb is excellent. AT [video] DVD

Humphrey Bogart *Harry Smith* • Marta Toren *Violette* • Lee J Cobb *Colonel Feroud* • Everett Sloane *General LaSalle* • Gerald Mohr *Major Leon* • Zero Mostel *Balukjian* • Nick Dennis *Nasir Aboud* ■ *Dir* Curtis Bernhardt • *Scr* AI Bezzerides, Hans Jacoby, from the novel *Coup de Grace* by Joseph Kessel

Sister Act ★★★★ PG

Comedy 1992 · US · Colour · 96mins

Ghost may have won Whoopi Goldberg an Oscar, but it was *Sister Act* that turned her into a huge Hollywood star. Whoopi is the Reno lounge singer who witnesses lover Harvey Keitel killing a man, so she accepts a police offer of protection that entails hiding out in a convent. That's about it for plot in this comedy from the Disney stable, while the remainder of the movie follows our heroine as she tries to bring the nuns and Maggie Smith's strict Mother Superior into the 20th century. Relying on some great songs and a superb cast (including Kathy Najimy as sunny Sister Mary Patrick), this gets past the slight story to become a hugely enjoyable, very funny comedy. JB. Contains some swearing. [video] DVD

Whoopi Goldberg *Deloris Van Cartier* • Maggie Smith *Mother Superior* • Kathy Najimy *Sister Mary Patrick* • Wendy Makkena *Sister Mary Robert* • Mary Wickes *Sister Mary Lazarus* • Harvey Keitel *Vince LaRocca* • Bill Nunn *Eddie Souther* • Robert Miranda *Joey* ■ *Dir* Emile Ardolino • *Scr* Joseph Howard

Sister Act 2: Back in the Habit ★★★ PG

Musical comedy 1993 · US · Colour · 102mins

Las Vegas cabaret singer Whoopi Goldberg dons her Sister Mary Clarence habit again to teach music to a bad-attitude class at a run-down high school in this OK sequel. Goldberg delivers the good-education/family-values/follow-your-dream messages with likeable charm, even if the familiar concept is treated in a heavy-handed fashion. Still, the musical sequences are lively and Maggie Smith gives sterling support. AJ [video] DVD

Whoopi Goldberg *Deloris Van Cartier/Sister Mary Clarence* • Kathy Najimy *Sister Mary Patrick* • Barnard Hughes *Father Maurice* • Mary Wickes *Sister Mary Lazarus* • James Coburn *Mr Crisp* • Michael Jeter *Father Ignatius* • Wendy Makkena *Sister Mary Robert* • Maggie Smith *Mother Superior* • Lauryn Hill *Rita Watson* • Jennifer Love Hewitt *Margaret* ■ *Dir* Bill Duke • *Scr* James Orr, Jim Cruickshank, Judi Ann Mason, from characters created by Joseph Howard

Sister Kenny ★★★★

Biographical drama 1946 · US · BW · 116mins

In this engrossing and moving biographical drama, Rosalind Russell stars as Australian nurse Elizabeth Kenny, who fought the medical establishment to gain acceptance for her pioneering work with polio sufferers. In possibly her finest film performance, the Oscar-nominated Russell totally eschews the maudlin and banal to give a deep portrayal of a woman compelled to battle a feared and potentially fatal disease. Russell dominates the screen and aficionados of the star will probably be able to quote much of the film's dialogue. SH

Rosalind Russell *Elizabeth Kenny* • Alexander Knox *Dr McDonnell* • Dean Jagger *Kevin Connors* • Philip Merivale *Dr Brack* • Beulah Bondi *Mary Kenny* • Charles Dingle *Michael Kenny* ■ *Dir* Dudley Nichols • *Scr* Dudley Nichols, Alexander Knox, Mary McCarthy, Milton Gunzburg (uncredited), from the autobiography *And They Shall Walk* by Elizabeth Kenny, Martha Ostenso

Sister My Sister ★★★ 15

Historical crime drama
1994 · UK · Colour · 85mins

In 1933, two French maids murdered their employer and her daughter. This brutal act gave rise to Jean Genet's classic play *The Maids* and, decades later, also inspired American playwright Wendy Kesselman to write *My Sister in This House* on which director Nancy Meckler based this strange but haunting little oddity. Joely Richardson and Jodhi May are the pair who allow their repressions to surface when in the service of Julie Walters. Tautly directed by Meckler, this sinister portrait of corrupted innocence and sisterly love beyond the norm is quite a chilling curiosity. AJ. Contains violence and sex scenes. [video]

Julie Walters *Madame Danzard* • Joely Richardson *Christine* • Jodhi May *Lea* • Sophie Thursfield *Isabelle Danzard* • Amelda Brown *Visitor* • Lucita Pope *Visitor* • Kate Gartside *Sister Veronica* ■ *Dir* Nancy Meckler • *Scr* Wendy Kesselman, from her play *My Sister in This House*

The Sisterhood of the Traveling Pants ★★★ PG

Comedy drama 2005 · US · Colour · 118mins

A shared pair of thrift-shop jeans becomes a powerful friendship talisman for four teenage girls in this feel-good drama. With the young women retaining the jeans for a week each, the clothing acts as a spiritual linking device between their very different experiences during their first summer apart. Unfortunately, while director Ken Kwapis expertly weaves together the storylines, he gives greater weight to the least interesting strands. Alexis Bledel's Greek holiday romance and the boy-chasing Blake Lively are clichéd and flimsy. Where the film excels is in America Ferrera and Amber Tamblyn's raw and poignant segments. SF

Amber Tamblyn *Tibby* • America Ferrera *Carmen* • Blake Lively *Bridget* • Alexis Bledel *Lena* • Bradley Whitford *Al* • Nancy Travis *Lydia Rodman* • Rachel Ticotin *Carmen's mother* • Jenna Boyd *Bailey* ■ *Dir* Ken Kwapis • *Scr* Delia Ephron, Elizabeth Chandler, from the novel by Ann Brashares

The Sisters ★★★

Drama 1938 · US · BW · 98mins

Sisters be damned! This costume drama is all about how far poor Bette Davis can fall after she's abandoned by drunken husband Errol Flynn. Admittedly, director Anatole Litvak drops in on Anita Louise and Jane Bryan from time to time to see how they're getting along, but Davis dominates the action, whether eloping with sports reporter Flynn, surviving the San Francisco earthquake or flitting around an Oakland bordello. Orry-Kelly's costumes are a delight and Max Steiner's soundtrack neatly captures the feel of the period and the melodramatics of the plot. DP

Bette Davis *Louise Elliott* • Errol Flynn *Frank Medlin* • Anita Louise *Helen Elliott* • Jane Bryan *Grace Elliott* • Ian Hunter *William Benson* • Henry Travers *Ned Elliott* • Beulah Bondi *Rose Elliott* • Susan Hayward *Telephone operator* ■ *Dir* Anatole Litvak • *Scr* Milton Krims, from the novel by Myron Brinig

Sisters ★★★★ 18

Psychological thriller
1973 · US · Colour · 88mins

The first foray into fully-fledged fright by director Brian De Palma is a masterful Hitch-cocktail of the sinister and the satirical. De Palma established his flashy style in this well-choreographed shocker about journalist Jennifer Salt who's compelled to investigate when she witnesses her neighbour Margot Kidder appear to commit murder. To some extent a modified version of *Psycho* dealing with duality and psychosis in an insightful way, this *Peeping Tom* nightmare is a well-tuned slice of cinematic frenzy. AJ [video]

Margot Kidder *Danielle Breton* • Jennifer Salt *Grace Collier* • Charles Durning *Larch* • William Finley *Emil Breton* • Lisle Wilson *Phillip*

S

Woode • Barnard Hughes *Mr McLennen* • Mary Davenport *Mrs Collier* ■ *Dir* Brian De Palma • *Scr* Louisa Rose, Brian De Palma, from a story by Brian De Palma

Sisters of the Gion ★★★★★

Drama 1936 · Jpn · BW · 70mins

Two Japanese geisha sisters differ in their outlook: the elder (Yoko Umemura) subscribes to tradition, while the younger (Isuzu Yamada) embraces a more modern view of life. Both come to grief at the hands of men, one physically abused by a jealous ex-lover, the other deserted by the man she has loved. An acknowledged masterpiece from Kenji Mizoguchi, one of the truly great directors in world cinema, this restrained, beautifully composed film, replete with gentle sadness and a touch of humour, well demonstrates the film-maker's empathy with women, and his implied critique of society's treatment of them. RK. A Japanese language film.

Isuzu Yamada *Omocha* • Yoko Umemura *Umekichi* • Benkei Shiganoya *Shinbee Furusawa* • Eitaro Shindo *Kudo* • Taizo Fukami *Kimura* • Fumio Okura *Jurakudo, the antiques dealer* ■ *Dir* Kenji Mizoguchi • *Scr* Yoshikata Yoda, Kenji Mizoguchi, from the novel *Yama* by Alexandr Ivanovich Kuprin

Sisters, or the Balance of Happiness ★★★★ 15

Drama 1979 · W Ger · Colour · 95mins

Margarethe von Trotta considered this study of sibling misunderstanding to be a "soul painting", in which the personalities of the protagonists took priority over the political climate that created them. However, the fact that mollycoddling elder sister Jutta Lampe is an efficient secretary and Gudrun Gabriel a depressive biology student suggests that a pronounced socio-feminist vein still runs through the piece. With the *mise en scène* taking on symbolic significance, this is both cinematically accomplished and psychologically intriguing. DP. In German with English subtitles.

Jutta Lampe *Maria* • Gudrun Gabriel *Anna* • Jessica Früh *Miriam* • Konstantin Wecker *Robert* • Rainer Delventhal *Maurice* ■ *Dir* Margarethe von Trotta • *Scr* Margarethe von Trotta, Luisa Francia, Martje Grohmann, from the story *Traumprotokolle* by Wolfgang Bachler

Sitcom ★★★★ 18

Comedy horror fantasy
1997 · Fr · Colour · 80mins

François Ozon's send-up of soap opera conventions is raunchy, kitsch and hilariously funny. In this John Waters-tilted farcical fantasy, a bourgeois family's existence is disrupted when the head of the household brings home a pet rat. How this outsider's evil influence causes them all to jettison their sexual inhibitions and embark on a round robin of escalating perversion is ultra camp and very cutting edge. AJ. In French with English subtitles. Contains sex scenes. DVD

Evelyne Dandry *Hélène, the mother* • François Marthouret *Jean, the father* • Marina de Van *Sophie, the daughter* • Adrien de Van *Nicolas, the son* • Stéphane Rideau *David* ■ *Dir/Scr* François Ozon

Sitting Bull ★ U

Western 1954 · US · Colour · 105mins

Superficially spectacular, this independent production relied on early use of CinemaScope and on hordes of Mexican extras to fill its wide screen. Something went wrong with the colour, however, while the routine story takes forever to unfold. There's Douglas Kennedy is the usual glory-seeking Custer, Dale Robertson is the honest cavalry major trying to bring about lasting peace, and J Carrol Naish is the dignified Chief Sitting Bull. AE

Dale Robertson *Parrish* • Mary Murphy *Kathy* • J Carrol Naish *Sitting Bull* • Iron Eyes Cody *Crazy Horse* • John Litel *General Howell* • Bill Hopper *Wentworth* • Douglas Kennedy *Colonel Custer* ■ *Dir* Sidney Salkow • *Scr* Jack DeWitt, Sidney Salkow

Sitting Ducks ★★★★

Comedy caper 1979 · US · Colour · 87mins

Michael Emil and Zack Norman rip off a cool $724,000 from their mobster bosses and flee New York. The pair find themselves hitting the road and en route they pick up genial gas-station attendant Richard Romanus and two girls, Patrice Townsend and Irene Forrest. An enjoyable mix of oddball comedy and romance follows. The sadly under-rated Henry Jaglom, a great exponent of improvisation, hits pay dirt here with a thoughtful, constantly amusing road movie. DF

Michael Emil *Simon* • Zack Norman *Sidney* • Patrice Townsend *Jenny* • Irene Forrest *Leona* • Richard Romanus *Moose* • Henry Jaglom *Jenny's friend* ■ *Dir/Scr* Henry Jaglom

Sitting in Limbo ★★★ 15

Drama 1986 · Can · Colour · 38mins

This is a well-intentioned drama about the limited opportunities available to African-American teenagers living in Montreal. Aiming for a hard-hitting but freewheeling realism, director John N Smith casts engaging non-professionals Fabian Gibbs and Pat Dillon in the leading roles and uses rough-and-ready, documentary-style camera techniques to capture the transient joys and incessant despairs of their hand-to-mouth existence. DP. Contains swearing.

Pat Dillon *Pat* • Fabian Gibbs *Fabian* • Sylvie Clarke *Sylvie* • Debbie Grant *Debbie* • Compton McLean *John* ■ *Dir* John N Smith • *Scr* John N Smith, David Wilson

Sitting Pretty ★★★

Musical comedy drama
1933 · US · BW · 80mins

Jack Oakie and Jack Haley, an aspiring Tin Pan Alley songwriting team, are advised by their music publisher and their rehearsal pianist – Mack Gordon and Harry Revel respectively, who also composed the movie's song score – to try their luck in Hollywood. Which they do, finding fame, fortune and lunch-room waitress Ginger Rogers. "Cheerful" is the word for this musical, zippily played and directed by Harry Joe Brown from a script co-written by humorist SJ Perelman that offers some nice Hollywood-satirising-Hollywood comedy. RK

Jack Oakie *Chick Parker* • Jack Haley *Pete Pendleton* • Ginger Rogers *Dorothy* • Gregory Ratoff *Tannenbaum* • Thelma Todd *Gloria Duval* • Lew Cody *Jules Clark* • Harry Revel *Pianist* • Mack Gordon *Song publisher* ■ *Dir* Harry Joe Brown • *Scr* Jack McGowan, SJ Perelman, Lou Breslow, from a story by Harry Stoddard, suggested Nina Wilcox Putnam

Sitting Pretty ★★★ U

Comedy 1948 · US · BW · 84mins

Clifton Webb stars in this popular comedy hit as the self-centred, pompous Mr Belvedere. Webb takes a job as a baby-sitter to Hummingbird Hill parents Robert Young and Maureen O'Hara, and the memorable scene where the toddler pours porridge over Webb's head was not only used as the film's poster motif, but also became part of the cultural imagery of postwar America. Two sequels, *Mr Belvedere Goes to College* and *Mr Belvedere Rings the Bell*, followed. TS

Robert Young (1) *Harry* • Clifton Webb *Lynn Belvedere* • Maureen O'Hara *Tacey* • Richard Haydn *Mr Appleton* • Louise Allbritton *Edna Philby* • Randy Stuart *Peggy* • Ed Begley *Hammond* • Larry Olsen *Larry* ■ *Dir* Walter Lang • *Scr* F Hugh Herbert, from the novel *Belvedere* by Gwen Davenport

Sitting Target ★★★ 18

Crime thriller 1972 · US/UK · Colour · 90mins

Oliver Reed gets to brutalise and barnstorm as a convicted murderer who escapes from jail in order to bump off his wife, Jill St John (she's been putting herself about a bit and now has some other man's bun in the oven). A splendid supporting cast of TV familiars and peculiars make this a juicy and none too subtle excursion into the underworld. AT

Oliver Reed *Harry Lomart* • Jill St John *Pat Lomart* • Ian McShane *Birdy Williams* • Edward Woodward *Inspector Milton* • Frank Finlay *Marty Gold* • Freddie Jones *MacNeil* • Jill Townsend *Maureen* ■ *Dir* Douglas Hickox • *Scr* Alexander Jacobs, from a novel by Laurence Henderson

Situation Hopeless – but Not Serious ★★★

Second World War comedy
1965 · US · BW · 97mins

This maverick, oddball film version of actor Robert Shaw's novel is about two Allied airmen who think they are taking refuge but are actually imprisoned in a comfortable cellar for seven years by a meek little shop assistant. It's mildly allegorical, faintly satirical and almost funny. A nearly movie, then, but worth seeing for Alec Guinness's performance as Herr Frick, whose demure exterior conceals a card-carrying Nazi on the verge of emotional meltdown. At times, Guinness makes the movie seem like an Ealing comedy with an umlaut. Notable for an early appearance by Robert Redford as one of the unwitting kidnap victims. AT

Alec Guinness *Herr Wilhelm Frick* • Michael Connors [Mike Connors] *Lucky Finder* • Robert Redford *Hank Wilson* • Anita Hoefer *Edeltraud* • Mady Rahl *Lissie* • Paul Dahlke *Herr Neusel* • Frank Wolff *QM Master Sergeant* • John Briley *Sergeant* ■ *Dir* Gottfried Reinhardt • *Scr* Silvia Reinhardt, Jan Lustig, from the novel *The Hiding Place* by Robert Shaw

Six Black Horses ★★

Western 1962 · US · Colour · 80mins

Originally intended for Randolph Scott, this ended up as a vehicle for baby-faced cowboy star Audie Murphy. It's good to see snarling Dan Duryea in his element, and the plot – determined Joan O'Brien hires Murphy and Duryea to apprehend her husband's killer – is unusually seasoned with humour. TS

Audie Murphy *Ben Lane* • Dan Duryea *Frank Jesse* • Joan O'Brien *Kelly* • George Wallace [George D Wallace] *Boone* • Roy Barcroft *Mustanger* • Phil Chambers *Undertaker* ■ *Dir* Harry Keller • *Scr* Burt Kennedy

Six Bridges to Cross ★★★

Crime drama 1955 · US · BW · 95mins

Sal Mineo made his screen debut here playing a juvenile delinquent and recidivist who grows into a criminal big shot, despite the best efforts of kindly cop George Nader. As the years pass by, Mineo metamorphoses into Tony Curtis (spot the join) who carries the movie across its various moral hurdles. Inspired by Boston's notorious Brinks Robbery of 1950, the film was scipted by noted crime scenarist Sydney Boehm. AT

Tony Curtis *Jerry Florea* • Julie Adams *Ellen Gallagher* • George Nader *Edward Gallagher* • Jay C Flippen *Vincent Concannon* • Ken Clark *Sanborn* • Sal Mineo *Jerry as a boy* ■ *Dir* Joseph Pevney • *Scr* Sydney Boehm, from the story *They Stole $2,000,000 and Got Away With It* by Joseph Dineen

Six Cylinder Love ★★ U

Comedy 1931 · US · BW · 72mins

Newly married Sidney Fox and Lorin Raker cause a stir with the purchase of an expensive new car. How they sort themselves out when they have a crash and incur thousands of dollars worth of damage passes for a plot in this inconsequential comedy. The movie is interesting only in reminding us that cars were once considered a privilege and for the chance to see that future great star Spencer Tracy as a car salesman. RK

Spencer Tracy *Donroy* • Sidney Fox *Marilyn Sterling* • Edward Everett Horton *Monty Winston* ■ *Dir* Thornton Freeland • *Scr* William Conselman, Norman Houston, from the play by William Anthony McGuire • *Cinematographer* Ernest Palmer

Six Days Seven Nights ★★★ 12

Romantic comedy adventure
1998 · US · Colour · 97mins

This adventure comedy stars Anne Heche as a New York fashion magazine journalist who sets out on a romantic island trip with her fiancé (David Schwimmer) but ends up stranded on an even more remote island with drunken local pilot Harrison Ford. Unfortunately, director Ivan Reitman decides that pirates and ludicrous plot twists are more intriguing than exploring the far more interesting chemistry between the two leads. Enjoyable, thanks to the stars' attractive screen presence, but it could have been so much better. JB. Contains swearing, sexual references and some violence. DVD

Harrison Ford *Quinn Harris* • Anne Heche *Robin Monroe* • David Schwimmer *Frank Martin* • Jacqueline Obradors *Angelica* • Temuera Morrison *Jager* • Allison Janney *Marjorie* • Amy Sedaris *Robin's secretary* ■ *Dir* Ivan Reitman • *Scr* Michael Browning

Six Days, Six Nights ★★

Drama 1994 · Fr/UK · Colour · 90mins

The naturalistic style and keen, witty social insights for which Diane Kurys is renowned are notably absent from this disappointing outing. Indeed, there's a distinct shortage of tension and sexual ambiguity in this otherwise carefully constructed tale of female rivalry, as Béatrice Dalle abandons her family in a bid to destroy artist Anne Parillaud's romance with Patric Aurignac. An intriguing premise, undermined by the slack scripting and inconsistent acting. DP. In French with English subtitles. Contains violence, sex scenes, nudity.

Anne Parillaud *Alice* • Béatrice Dalle *Elsa* • Patric Aurignac *Franck* • Bernard Verley *Sanders* • Alain Chabat *Thomas* ■ *Dir* Diane Kurys • *Scr* Diane Kurys, Antoine Lacomblez • *Music* Michael Nyman

Six Degrees of Separation ★★★★ 15

Drama 1993 · US · Colour · 108mins

In this bourgeois satire, Will Smith displays the talents that were to elevate him to the superstar stratosphere. As the young man who talks his way into the rich New York household of liberal-minded art dealer Donald Sutherland and his wife Stockard Channing by purporting to be the friend of their student children, Smith is as busy as a gadfly. Fred Schepisi's direction is too safe for a real sarcastic sting, but Smith's performance shines above these limitations, transcending the too-glib spelling-out of the gulf between integrity and hypocrisy. TH. Contains swearing and nudity. DVD

Stockard Channing *Ouisa Kittredge* • Will Smith *Paul* • Donald Sutherland *Flan Kittredge* • Ian McKellen *Geoffrey* • Mary Beth Hurt *Kitty*

S

U = SUITABLE FOR ALL Uc = SUITABLE FOR ALL, ESPECIALLY FOR YOUNG CHILDREN (VIDEO ONLY) PG = PARENTAL GUIDANCE

• Bruce Davison *Larkin* • Richard Masur *Doctor Fine* • Anthony Michael Hall *Trent* • Heather Graham *Elizabeth* ■ *Dir* Fred Schepisi • *Scr* John Guare, from his play

6.5 Special ★★ U

Musical 1958 · UK · BW · 78mins

Here's the film version of one of BBC TV's much-loved nostalgic teenfests, a programme that grew out of the need to fill the Saturday slot between children's telly and early evening viewing. It was hosted by Josephine Douglas and Pete Murray, both on hand here, and became a key showcase for British pop music in the pre-Beatles era. Ignore the wisp of a plot about two girls taking the titular train to London to crash showbiz; this is a real period treat. TS [video]

Josephine Douglas • Pete Murray ■ *Dir* Alfred Shaughnessy • *Scr* Norman Hudis

The Six Million Dollar Man ★★★ U

Science-fiction adventure
1973 · US · Colour · 70mins

This is the appealing feature-length pilot for the popular series that ran for 102 episodes during its five-year history. Lee Majors headlines as the pilot who receives a bionic makeover after crashing an experimental plane, with Martin Balsam as the scientist surgeon who rebuilds him and Darren McGavin as his operations chief. The exploration of Majors's emotions is sophisticatedly handled by director Richard Irving, making this a cut above the usual pilot. DP [video]

Lee Majors *Colonel Steve Austin* • Barbara Anderson *Jean Manners* • Martin Balsam *Dr Rudy Wells* • Darren McGavin *Oliver Spencer* • Dorothy Green *Mrs McKay* ■ *Dir* Richard Irving • *Scr* Henri Simoun [Howard Rodman], from the novel *Cyborg* by Martin Caidin

Six of a Kind ★★★★

Comedy 1934 · US · BW · 62mins

Director Leo McCarey was a wiz where comedy was concerned and triumphed whether the theme was slapstick, screwball or, as in this case, sheer anarchy. Here he has a dream comedy cast, and an unruly Great Dane, fizzing together on a crazy car trip. WC Fields and Alison Skipworth appear late in the film but still manage to steal it from the other two double acts, Charles Ruggles and Mary Boland, and George Burns and Gracie Allen. Fields gets to perform his famous "billiards" routine, a miniature masterpiece in itself. DF

Charles Ruggles *J Pinkham Whinney* • Mary Boland *Flora Whinney* • WC Fields *Sheriff "Honest" John Hoxley* • George Burns *George* • Gracie Allen *Gracie Devore* • Alison Skipworth *Mrs K Rumford* ■ *Dir* Leo McCarey • *Scr* Walter DeLeon, Harry Ruskin, from a story by Keene Thompson, Douglas MacLean

Six Pack ★★

Action comedy 1982 · US · Colour · 107mins

After proving his worth as an actor in a number of TV roles (most famously *The Gambler*), Kenny Rogers made his big-screen debut in this middle-of-the-road tale of an ex-stock car driver and six orphaned youngsters. The car-crazy kids help Rogers in his attempts to make a comeback in the sport. DF

Kenny Rogers *Brewster Baker* • Diane Lane *Breezy* • Erin Gray *Lilah* • Barry Corbin *Sheriff* • Terry Kiser *Terk* • Bob Hannah *Diddler* ■ *Dir* Daniel Petrie • *Scr* Mike Marvin, Alex Matter

633 Squadron ★★★ PG

Second World War action drama
1964 · UK/US · Colour · 93mins

This film suffers in comparison with that other tribute to the Royal Air Force, *The Dam Busters*. The mission is less audacious, the casting is less precise (Cliff Robertson as an American in the RAF and George Chakiris as a Norwegian Resistance fighter) and the theme tune is far harder to sing along to. The flying sequences are, undeniably, more thrilling (particularly the Scottish Highlands training exercises), but they cannot compensate for the dullness of the Norwegian-set scenes. DP [video] DVD

Cliff Robertson *Wing Commander Roy Grant* • George Chakiris *Lieutenant Erik Bergman* • Maria Perschy *Hilde Bergman* • Harry Andrews *Air Marshal Davis* • Donald Houston *Wing Commander Tom Barrett* • Michael Goodliffe *Squadron Leader Bill Adams* ■ *Dir* Walter E Grauman [Walter Grauman] • *Scr* James Clavell, Howard Koch, from the novel by Frederick E Smith

Six Ways to Sunday ★★★ 18

Drama 1997 · US · Colour · 93mins

A bleak, bitter and very brutal American drama which went straight to video in Britain. Norman Reedus plays a sociopathic teenager with an unhealthily close relationship with his mother (an almost unrecognisable Deborah Harry), who gets involved with mobsters impressed with his capacity of violence. Finely performed by the eclectic cast and directed with seedy style by Adam Bernstein. JF. Contains swearing, nudity, violence. [video] DVD

Norman Reedus *Harry Odum* • Deborah Harry *Kate Odum* • Elina Lowensohn *Iris* • Adrien Brody *Arnie Finklestein* • Isaac Hayes *Bill Bennet* • Jerry Adler *Louis Varga* • Peter Appel *Abie "The Bug" Pinkwise* ■ *Dir* Adam Bernstein • *Scr* Adam Bernstein, Marc Gerald, from the novel *Portrait of a Young Man Drowning* by Charles Perry

Six Weeks ★ PG

Drama 1982 · US · Colour · 107mins

Distinctly yucky, TV movie-style fodder dressed up as tear-jerking drama. The cancer-stricken daughter of Mary Tyler Moore melts the heart of Congressional candidate Dudley Moore, who helps the girl win a role in a ballet. At this point, you'll be either blubbing helplessly or sneering at the crass contrivances of the plot. A manipulative monstrosity. AT

Dudley Moore *Patrick Dalton* • Mary Tyler Moore *Charlotte Dreyfus* • Katherine Healy *Nicole Dreyfus* • Shannon Wilcox *Peg Dalton* • Bill Calvert *Jeff Dalton* • John Harkins *Arnold Stillman* • Joe Regalbuto *Bob Crowther* ■ *Dir* Tony Bill • *Scr* David Seltzer, from a novel by Fred Mustard Stewart • *Music* Dudley Moore

Sixteen Candles ★★★ 15

Comedy drama 1984 · US · Colour · 88mins

John Hughes made his directorial debut as the master of the teen pic with this sharp comedy, which not only has a keen ear for the idiom of teenspeak, but also a genuine sympathy with its various geeks, jocks, seniors and girls next door. Molly Ringwald is the personification of the sulky, sweet 16-year-old whose birthday goes from bad to worse as her parents forget the occasion and the school pest begins showing off her underwear to his classmates. Beaming through his braces, Anthony Michael Hall is nigh-on perfect as the nerd trying too hard to impress. DP. Contains swearing and brief nudity [video]

Molly Ringwald *Samantha* • Justin Henry *Mike Baker* • Michael Schoeffling *Jake* • Haviland Morris *Caroline* • Gedde Watanabe *Long Duk Dong* • Anthony Michael Hall *Ted, the geek* • John Cusack *Bryce* • Joan Cusack *First geek girl* ■ *Dir/Scr* John Hughes

16 Years of Alcohol ★★★ 18

Drama 2003 · UK · Colour · 100mins

Richard Jobson's debut feature draws inspiration from both a semi-autobiographical novel and *A Clockwork Orange*. Kevin McKidd and his little gang of sociopaths even dress like the droogs in Kubrick's film. McKidd has grown up in a world where life revolves largely around the pub and drinking. As a youth he develops problems not just with alcohol but also with violence, and attempts to change his ways after meeting art student Susan Lynch. Jobson's film teeters on pretentiousness at times, but is rescued by a towering performance from McKidd and a surprisingly assured visual style. BP. Contains swearing. [video] DVD

Kevin McKidd *Frankie Mac* • Laura Fraser *Helen* • Susan Lynch *Mary* • Stuart Sinclair Blyth *Miller* • Jim Carter *Director* • Ewen Bremner *Jake* ■ *Dir* Richard Jobson • *Scr* Richard Jobson, from his novel

Sixth and Main ★★

Comedy drama 1977 · US · Colour · 103mins

Leslie Nielsen stars in this indie production about life on Skid Row – or Skid Drive as it's known in Beverly Hills. Playing a once-famous writer, Nielsen lives in a trailer crammed with unpublished manuscripts, which are uncovered by Beverly Garland while researching a book on LA's derelicts. Nielsen is celebrated as an author of genius, but his friends on Skid Row carry on living on the rubbish heap. AT

Leslie Nielsen *John Doe* • Roddy McDowall *Skateboard* • Beverly Garland *Monica* • Leo Penn *Doc* • Joe Maross *Peanut* • Bard Stevens *Carlsburg* • Sharon Thomas *Tina* ■ *Dir/Scr* Christopher Cain

The 6th Day ★★★★ 15

Science-fiction action thriller
2000 · US/Can · Colour · 118mins

Director Roger Spottiswoode's futuristic thriller is fast-paced fare, and provides another satisfying slice of science-fiction action for star Arnold Schwarzenegger. When ex-fighter pilot Schwarzenegger discovers he has been illegally cloned, he embarks on a turbo-charged mission to get his identity back and expose the corrupt organisation behind the experiment. Even if the plot doesn't bear close scrutiny, the movie packs some surprise twists and builds to a chilling climax. This is what sci-fi film-making should be about – dark speculation, a sense of wonder and ace special effects. AJ. Contains violence, swearing and brief nudity. [video] DVD

Arnold Schwarzenegger *Adam Gibson* • Michael Rapaport *Hank Morgan* • Tony Goldwyn *Michael Drucker* • Michael Rooker *Robert Marshall* • Sarah Wynter *Talia Elsworth* • Rod Rowland [Rodney Rowland] *Wiley* • Terry Crews *Vincent* • Ken Pogue *Speaker Day* • Colin Cunningham *Tripp* • Robert Duvall *Dr Griffin Weir* ■ *Dir* Roger Spottiswoode • *Scr* Cormac Wibberley, Marianne Wibberley

Sixth Happiness ★★★ 12

Biographical drama
1997 · UK · Colour · 94mins

Firdaus Kanga not only wrote the screenplay for this moving drama from his autobiographical novel, but he also turns in a riveting performance in this extraordinary account of what it's like being gay, Parsee and disabled in 1970s Bombay. With the endless round of suicides, betrayals and doomed relationships going on around him, it almost seems as though being born with osteoporosis is the least of Kanga's problems. The film suffers slightly from the fussy direction, but remains a brave attempt to convey true courage. DP. Contains nudity. DVD

Firdaus Kanga *Brit Kotwal* • Souad Faress *Sera Kotwal* • Khodus Wadia *Sam Kotwal* • Nina Wadia *Dolly Kotwal* • Ahsen Bhatti *Cyrus* ■ *Dir* Waris Hussein • *Scr* Firdaus Kanga, from his autobiography *Trying to Grow*

The 6th Man ★★ 12

Sports comedy 1997 · US · Colour · 103mins

Judging from its first half-hour, this could be a touching drama about two brothers with hoop dreams. When the older brother dies, the younger one is lost without him. Lost, that is, until older bro shows up as a ghost with a wacky sense of humour and a drive to win the college basketball championships! Unless you're a huge fan of poltergeist comedy or basketball, this Marlon Wayans vehicle probably won't score too many points. ST. Contains some swearing and sexual references. [video] DVD

Marlon Wayans *Kenny Tyler* • Kadeem Hardison *Antoine Tyler* • David Paymer *Coach Pederson* • Michael Michele *RC St John* • Kevin Dunn *Mikulski* ■ *Dir* Randall Miller • *Scr* Christopher Reed, Cynthia Carle

The Sixth Sense ★★★★★ 15

Supernatural drama
1999 · US · Colour · 102mins

M Night Shyamalan has fashioned a modern classic here, a chilly, intelligent, emotional ghost story that relies not on gore and knifeplay for its many shocks but on glimpses of an afterlife that's anything but angels and harps. Bruce Willis is it quiet and reflective as the child psychologist attempting to get inside the head of Haley Joel Osment, who sees dead people. Toni Collette is equally convincing as the boy's troubled mum and, though the film's initial impact hinged on chatter about its knockout twist ending, in truth it's the controlled pace of Shyamalan's direction and the simplicity of his storytelling that make it so watchable. AC. Contains violence, swearing. [video] DVD

Bruce Willis *Malcolm Crowe* • Haley Joel Osment *Cole Sear* • Toni Collette *Lynn Sear* • Olivia Williams *Anna Crowe* • Donnie Wahlberg *Vincent Gray* • Glenn Fitzgerald *Sean* • Mischa Barton *Kyra Collins* • Trevor Morgan *Tommy Tammisimo* • M Night Shyamalan *Doctor Hill* ■ *Dir/Scr* M Night Shyamalan

Sixty Glorious Years ★★★ U

Historical drama 1938 · UK · Colour · 91mins

Following the success of *Victoria the Great* starring his wife Anna Neagle, producer/director Herbert Wilcox continued the saga up to and including Victoria's death. Peopled with a cast of dignified upper-crust actors such as C Aubrey Smith and Felix Aylmer, the film has Neagle presiding regally, and sometimes touchingly, over events personal, political and public – among them her wedding to Albert (Anton Walbrook), the opening of the Great Exhibition, Albert's death and the Diamond Jubilee. RK [video]

Anna Neagle *Queen Victoria* • Anton Walbrook *Prince Albert* • C Aubrey Smith *Duke of Wellington* • Walter Rilla *Prince Ernst* • Charles Carson *Sir Robert Peel* • Felix Aylmer *Lord Palmerston* ■ *Dir* Herbert Wilcox • *Scr* Charles de Grandcourt, Miles Malleson, Robert Vansittart

61* ★★★

Sports drama based on a true story
2001 · US · Colour · 129mins

Billy Crystal's passion for baseball informs every frame of this sporting biopic, which recalls the summer of 1961 when New York Yankees team-mates Mickey Mantle and Roger Maris went head to head to break Babe Ruth's home run record. With Haskell Wexler's crisp photography helping him avoid overt nostalgia and Hank Steinberg's teleplay providing him with a rousing, intelligent drama, Crystal adroitly combines diamond action with character study. DP

S

Thomas Jane *Mickey Mantle* • Barry Pepper *Roger Maris* • Anthony Michael Hall *Whitey Ford* • Richard Masur *Milt Kahn* • Bruce McGill *Ralph Houk* ■ *Dir* Billy Crystal • *Scr* Hank Steinberg

Sizzle Beach, USA ★★ 18

Sex comedy 1974 · US · Colour · 83mins

The history of this creaky soft-core sexploitation movie is of far more interest than the story it tries to tell. The film details the sexual adventures of a trio of girls who share a Malibu beach house. One of their conquests is the young Kevin Costner (making his screen debut). Years later this appearance returned to haunt him when the schlock horror film company Troma acquired the rights and cheekily touted it round the Cannes Film Festival as Costner's latest flick. DF

Terry Congie *Janice* • Leslie Brander *Sheryl* • Roselyn Royce *Dit* • Kevin Costner *John Logan, horse trainer* ■ *Dir* Richard Brander • *Scr* Craig Kusaba

Skagerrak ★★

Comedy drama
2003 · Den/UK · Colour · 104mins

Søren Kragh-Jacobsen directs this unconvincing combination of romantic drama and realist fairy tale. Iben Hjejle and Bronagh Gallagher banter effectively as the 20-something oil-rig cleaners who lose their money shortly after landing at a Scottish port. But once Hjejle agrees to surrogate for the wealthy but childless Scott Handy and Helen Baxendale, the storyline loses its freewheeling unpredictability and settles for melodramatic cosiness. DP. Contains swearing.

Iben Hjejle *Marie* • Martin Henderson *Ian/Ken* • Bronagh Gallagher *Sophie* • Ewen Bremmer *Gabriel* • Simon McBurney *Thomas* • Gary Lewis *Willy* • Helen Baxendale *Stella* • James Cosmo *Sir Robert Lumley* • Scott Handy *Roman* ■ *Dir* Søren Kragh-Jacobsen • *Scr* Søren Kragh-Jacobsen, Anders Thomas Jensen

Skateboard ★

Sports drama 1978 · US · Colour · 95mins

Owing money to everyone from his ex-wife to the Mob, talent agent Allen Garfield organizes several neighborhood kids and teenagers into a touring skateboard team, promising them fame but with dreams of big bucks in his heart. Made during the height of the skateboard craze in the late 1970s, there is surprisingly little boarding, and what there is looks boring. Incompetent and shallow. KB

Allen Garfield *Manny Bloom* • Kathleen Lloyd *Millicent Broderick* • Leif Garrett *Brad Harris* • Richard Van Der Wyk *Jason Maddox* • Tony Alva *Tony Bluetile* ■ *Dir* George Gage • *Scr* Richard A Wolf, George Gage, from a story by Richard A Wolf

The Skateboard Kid ★

Fantasy 1993 · US · Colour · 83mins

Foisted on an undeserving public by Roger Corman's Concorde-New Horizons company, this film featuring a talking skateboard marks a new low in teen movies. Trevor Lissauer is the charmless kid who brings a little life to the hick town of Mill Creek by taking on a gang of bullies, matchmaking his widowed father and finding treasure. A sequel followed. DP

Timothy Busfield *Frank Tyler* • Trevor Lissauer *Zack Tyler* • Bess Armstrong *Maggie* • Dom DeLuise *Rip* ■ *Dir* Larry Swerdlove • *Scr* Larry Swerdlove, Gary Stuart Kaplan

Skatetown, USA ★★

Comedy 1979 · US · Colour · 98mins

The first to hop on the minor roller-disco bandwagon that pulled up at the fag end of the 1970s, this brainless little comedy has good guy Greg Bradford in a roller-skating dance duel with bullying nasty Patrick Swayze. A period curiosity at best, it features not only Patrick Swayze's movie debut but also a roll call of fading American TV stars. Further down the cast list is Playboy playmate Dorothy Stratten, who appeared in a tiny handful of films before her murder in 1980. FL

Scott Baio *Richie* • Flip Wilson *Harvey Ross* • Ron Palillo *Frankey* • Ruth Buzzi *Elvira* • Greg Bradford *Stan* • Patrick Swayze *Ace* • Dorothy Stratten *Girl who orders pizza* ■ *Dir* William A Levey • *Scr* Nick Castle

The Skeleton Key ★★★

Supernatural thriller 2005 · US · Colour

A decrepit Louisiana mansion holds terrifying secrets in this flimsy yet effective slice of southern gothic horror. Kate Hudson plays a live-in nurse who's hired by elderly Gena Rowlands to look after her ailing husband (an under-used John Hurt). But after discovering a hidden attic room crammed with hoodoo paraphernalia, the inquisitive carer soon realises that all is not what it seems in the foreboding house. It's weakly plotted, though hugely atmospheric, with good performances and a dark and exciting finale. SF

Kate Hudson *Caroline* • Gena Rowlands *Violet* • Peter Sarsgaard *Luke* • Joy Bryant *Jill* • John Hurt *Ben* ■ *Dir* Iain Softley • *Scr* Ehren Kruger

Skeletons ★★★ 15

Thriller 1996 · US · Colour · 86mins

After a heart attack, journalist Ron Silver and his family move out to the country for a year of rest and relaxation, and are welcomed by the surprisingly friendly small town residents, but when Silver starts investigating the case surrounding a local resident accused of murder, the town's mood turns ugly. The big revelation at the end, while a little unlikely, is still reasonably believable, and much of the credit for the movie's success goes to the cast for their excellent performances. KB. Contains violence and swearing. DVD

Ron Silver *Peter Crane* • Christopher Plummer *Reverend Carlyle* • Dee Wallace Stone *Heather Crane* • Kyle Howard *Zach Crane* • James Coburn *Frank Jove* • Arlene Golonka *Melanie Jove* ■ *Dir* David DeCoteau • *Scr* Joshua Michael Stern

Ski Party ★★ U

Musical comedy 1965 · US · Colour · 79mins

This amiable, if vastly inferior take on *Some Like it Hot*, is set in a ski resort where college chums Frankie Avalon and Dwayne Hickman do what any red-blooded American males would do on discovering their girlfriends fancy another man – dress up in drag. Predictably, the cross-dressed students then become the focus for male interest. James Brown gets to perform his classic *I Got You (I Feel Good)*, probably the best thing here. JG

Frankie Avalon *Todd Armstrong/Jane* • Dwayne Hickman *Craig Gamble/Nora* • Deborah Walley *Linda Hughes* • Yvonne Craig *Barbara Norris* • Robert Q Lewis *Donald Pevney* • Bobbi Shaw *Nita* • Lesley Gore • Annette Funicello ■ *Dir* Alan Rafkin • *Scr* Robert Kaufman

Ski Patrol ★★ PG

Comedy 1989 · US · Colour · 87mins

Owner of the Snowy Peaks ski lodge, Ray Walston has maintained a safely run operation in his 40 years in the business. But now he has a rival, Martin Mull, who schemes to sabotage the safety record in order to take over the resort himself. It's up to the motley Ski Patrol team to save the day. Fairly standard, but enlivened by some spectacular ski stunts. DF

Roger Rose *Jerry* • Yvette Nipar *Ellen* • TK Carter *Iceman* • Leslie Jordan *Murray* • Paul Feig *Stanley* • Sean Gregory Sullivan *Suicide* • Ray Walston *Pops* • Martin Mull *Maris* ■ *Dir* Rich Correll [Richard Correll] • *Scr* Steven Long Mitchell, Craig W Van Sickle, from a story by Wink Roberts, Steven Long Mitchel, Craig W Van Sickle

Ski School ★★ 18

Comedy 1991 · Can · Colour · 84mins

Having discovered the public's appetite for teenage sex-themed comedies with such fare as *Porky's* and *Screwballs*, the Canadian film industry continued to mine this lucrative vein. *Ski School* provides a similar mix of sexy high-jinks and laughs. Set around a ski school at Vancouver's Whistler Mountain, the film squeezes in the usual quota of wild parties, practical jokes and acres of female flesh. Although relentlessly par for the course, it was successful enough to spawn a sequel in 1995. DF. Contains swearing and nudity.

Mark Thomas Miller *Reid* • Tom Breznahan *Johnny* • Dean Cameron *Dave* • John Pyper-Ferguson *Erich* • Spencer Rochfort *Derek* • Patrick Labyorteaux *Ed* • Stuart Fratkin *Fitz* ■ *Dir* Damian Lee • *Scr* David Mitchell

Skidoo ★

Comedy 1968 · US · Colour · 97mins

A rack of top-line comedy stars, not to mention a good score by Harry Nilsson, is wasted in this bizarre and unfunny satire. Reformed gangster Jackie Gleason is bullied out of retirement by gang boss "God" (Groucho Marx, in his final picture) for an unwanted job: to get sent to jail, murder Mickey Rooney, then escape. But within those walls he discovers the alleged joys of LSD. Among the most misguided movies ever made. JG

Jackie Gleason *Tony Banks* • Carol Channing *Flo Banks* • Frankie Avalon *Angie* • Fred Clark *Tower Guard* • Michael Constantine *Leech* • Frank Gorshin *Man* • John Phillip Law *Stash* • Peter Lawford *Senator* • Burgess Meredith *Warden* • George Raft *Captain Garbaldo* • Mickey Rooney *"Blue Chips" Packard* • Groucho Marx *"God"* ■ *Dir* Otto Preminger • *Scr* Doran William Cannon, Elliott Baker (uncredited), Stanley Ralph Ross (uncredited), from a story by Erik Kirkland

Skin Deep ★ 18

Comedy 1989 · US · Colour · 96mins

An ugly and deeply unappealing sex comedy from Blake Edwards. John Ritter is the womaniser attempting to win back his ex-wife but finding old habits die hard. The fact that its most memorable gag involves fluorescent condoms is an indication of the level of the humour. As infantile as his *Pink Panther* movies but not nearly as funny. JF. Contains swearing.

John Ritter *Zach Hutton* • Vincent Gardenia *Barney* • Alyson Reed *Alex Hutton* • Joel Brooks *Jake* • Julianne Phillips *Molly* • Chelsea Field *Amy* • Peter Donat *Sparky* • Don Gordon *Curt* ■ *Dir/Scr* Blake Edwards

The Skin Game ★★

Drama 1931 · UK · BW · 88mins

Alfred Hitchcock enjoyed the challenge of the seemingly theatrical confines of restricted space, creating works of extraordinary fluidity. But the actual theatre pieces which dominated his early British career defeated even his genius and this adaptation of Galsworthy's London success is inevitably dated. It concerns a wealthy family, the Hillcrests, dominated by the aristocratic mother (Helen Haye in the film's best performance) which is at loggerheads with a neighbouring builder who wants to replace farms with factories. BB

Phyllis Konstam *Chloe Hornblower* • Edmund Gwenn *Mr Hornblower* • John Longden *Charles Hornblower* • Frank Lawton *Rolf Hornblower* • CV France *Mr Hillcrest* • Jill Esmond *Jill Hillcrest* • Edward Chapman *Dawker* • Helen Haye *Mrs Hillcrest* ■ *Dir* Alfred Hitchcock • *Scr* Alfred Hitchcock, Alma Reville, from the play by John Galsworthy

Skin Game ★★★ PG

Comedy western 1971 · US · Colour · 97mins

An enjoyable comedy western which teams James Garner and Lou Gossett as conmen in the years before the Civil War. Their scam is an ingenious and contentious one: Garner poses as a slave trader who sells Gossett for big bucks, only for Gossett to escape and rejoin Garner at the next town where someone else is cheated. Garner trades heavily on his *Maverick* persona, Gossett skilfully transforms himself from a free man to a "Stepin Fetchit" menial, and Ed Asner impresses as a slave dealer. AT

James Garner *Quincy* • Lou Gossett [Louis Gossett Jr] *Jason* • Susan Clark *Ginger* • Brenda Sykes *Naomi* • Edward Asner *Plunkett* • Andrew Duggan *Calloway* • Henry Jones *Sam* ■ *Dir* Paul Bogart • *Scr* Pierre Marton [Peter Stone]

Skin of Man, Heart of Beast ★★★

Drama 1999 · Fr · Colour · 96mins

An atmosphere of latent violence pervades this uncompromising study of domestic disaffection. Set in southern France, the small-town scenario centres on the tensions between returning prodigal Bernard Blancan, his wastrel younger brother Pascal Cervo and older sibling Serge Riaboukine, a short-fused cop on a break from his duties. But what makes Hélène Angel's debut feature so unpredictable – and occasionally melodramatic – is that Angel views events through the eyes of Riaboukine's alienated adolescent daughter, Virginie Guinand, and her trusting little sister, Cathy Hinderchied. DP. In French with English subtitles. Contains violence and swearing.

Serge Riaboukine *Francky Pujol* • Bernard Blancan *Coco Pujol* • Maaike Jansen *Marthe* • Pascal Cervo *Alex Pujol* • Jean-Louis Richard *Tac Tac* • Guilaine Londez *Annie* • Cathy Hinderchied *Aurélie Pujol* • Virginie Guinand *Christelle Pujol* ■ *Dir* Hélène Angel • *Scr* Hélène Angel, Agnes de Sacy, Jean-Claude Janer

Skip Tracer ★★★

Crime thriller 1977 · Can · Colour · 94mins

A smashing Canadian indie production, shot for around $150,000, *Skip Tracer* made quite an impact at international film festivals with its story of a debt collector who's determined to be the best in the business. But the repossession of a car goes slightly wrong when the owner, who has legitimately paid for it, turns bad-tempered and has murder on his mind. Directed by first-timer Zale Dalen and acted out by a cast of Vancouver stage performers, this is a tough, witty and gloriously quirky thriller. AT

David Peterson *John Collins* • John Lazarus *Brent Solverman* • Rudy Szabo *Leo Gabrowski* ■ *Dir/Scr* Zale Dalen

Skippy ★★★ U

Comedy drama 1931 · US · BW · 85mins

Drawing its idea from a comic strip, this wholesome, successful entertainment for all the family recounts the tale of how two youngsters (Jackie Cooper, Robert Coogan) set about earning enough money to buy their mutt back from the neighbourhood dog-catcher. Co-written by Joseph L Mankiewicz and Norman Z McLeod, this simple little movie garnered Oscar nominations for story, script and Cooper, and won Taurog the director's statuette. RK

Jackie Cooper *Skippy Skinner* • Robert Coogan *Sooky* • Mitzi Green *Eloise* • Jackie Searl [Jackie Searle] *Sidney* • Willard Robertson *Dr Herbert Skinner* • Enid Bennett *Mrs Ellen Skinner* • David Haines *Harley Nubbins* • Helen Jerome Eddy *Mrs Wayne* ■ *Dir* Norman Taurog • *Scr* Joseph L Mankiewicz, Norman McLeod [Norman Z McLeod], Don Marquis, Sam Mintz, from the comic strip and novel by Percy Crosby

Skirts Ahoy! ★★★ U

Musical 1952 · US · Colour · 109mins

It's three girls rather than boys in the navy for a change in this musical which puts Esther Williams, Vivian Blaine and Joan Evans into uniform . Evans is not really happy with song and dance (she replaced Sally Forrest, reputedly because Forrest's hair colour was too similar to Williams) and Blaine, fresh from her Broadway triumph in *Guys and Dolls*, is not given enough opportunity, but the film is pleasant escapist fare. TV

Esther Williams *Whitney Young* • Joan Evans *Mary Kate Yarbrough* • Vivian Blaine *Una Yancy* • Barry Sullivan *Lt Cmdr Paul Elcott* • Keefe Brasselle *Dick Hallson* • Billy Eckstine • Dean Miller *Archie O'Conovan* • Debbie Reynolds • Bobby Van ■ *Dir* Sidney Lanfield • *Scr* Isobel Lennart

Skokie ★★★★ PG

Drama based on a true story
1981 · US · Colour · 120mins

Head and shoulders above the majority of fact-based television dramas, this award-winning reconstruction of the stand-off between the citizens of Skokie, Illinois, and a gang of militant neo-Nazis is a sobering reminder that anti-Semitism did not end with the defeat of Hitler. In his only TV movie, Danny Kaye gives a genuinely moving performance as the Holocaust survivor refusing to be intimidated by the bully boys. But then everyone in this stellar cast is totally credible, including acting guru Lee Strasberg in what proved to be his last role. DP [video] DVD

Danny Kaye *Max Feldman* • John Rubinstein *Herb Lewisohn* • Carl Reiner *Abbot Rosen* • Kim Hunter *Bertha Feldman* • Eli Wallach *Bert Silverman* • Lee Strasberg *Morton Weisman* • Brian Dennehy *Chief Arthur Buchanan* • George Dzundza *Frank Collin* ■ *Dir* Herbert Wise • *Scr* Ernest Kinoy

The Skull ★★

Horror 1965 · UK · Colour · 83mins

Horror stars Peter Cushing and Christopher Lee are strongly cast in Freddie Francis's disappointing adaptation of Robert Bloch's story about the strange properties of the Marquis de Sade's skull. There are some good moments and impressive special effects, though, while Francis's direction has panache. AJ

Peter Cushing *Professor Christopher Maitland* • Patrick Wymark *Marco* • Christopher Lee *Sir Matthew Phillips* • Jill Bennett *Jane Maitland* • Nigel Green *Inspector Wilson* • Michael Gough *Auctioneer* • George Coulouris *Dr Londe* • Patrick Magee *Police doctor* ■ *Dir* Freddie Francis • *Scr* Milton Subotsky, from the story *The Skull of the Marquis de Sade* by Robert Bloch

Skullduggery ★★

Adventure 1969 · US · Colour · 105mins

Burt Reynolds managed to rise above unworthy material with a good-natured charm and skill in the early days of his film career, and this weak adventure is a good example of that ability. Reynolds plays an adventurer who accompanies archaeologist Susan Clark to New Guinea. There they discover a tribe that could be a clue to human evolution, but evil scientist Paul Hubschmid forces them to take their find to the courts. TH

Burt Reynolds *Doug Temple* • Susan Clark *Dr Sybil Greame* • Roger C Carmel *Otto Kreps* • Paul Hubschmid *Vancruysen* • Chips Rafferty *Father "Pop" Dillingham* • Alexander Knox *Buffington* • Pat Suzuki *Topazia* • Edward Fox *Bruce Spofford* • Wilfrid Hyde White *Eaton* ■ *Dir* Gordon Douglas, Richard Wilson • *Scr* Nelson Gidding, from the novel *Les Animaux Denaturés (You Shall Know Them)* by Vercours [Jean Marcel Brewer]

The Skulls ★★★ 15

Thriller 2000 · US · Colour · 102mins

Joshua Jackson stars in this preposterous but entertaining thriller about a college secret society called the Skulls, which counts politicians and rich businessmen among its alumni and offers them flash benefits. Jackson plays a non-wealthy student who is given the opportunity to join. Shortly after his initiation his best friend (who's been investigating the group) suspiciously commits suicide, leaving Jackson to choose between his jet set pals or Doing The Right Thing. An initially tense set-up gets increasingly daft, but Jackson holds your interest until the end. Two sequels followed. JB [video] DVD

Joshua Jackson *Luke McNamara* • Paul Walker *Caleb Mandrake* • Hill Harper *Will Beckford* • Leslie Bibb *Chloe* • Christopher McDonald *Martin Lombard* • Steve Harris *Detective Sparrow* • William Petersen [William L Petersen] *Senator Ames Levitt* • Craig T Nelson *Litten Mandrake* ■ *Dir* Rob Cohen • *Scr* John Pogue

The Sky above, the Mud below ★★★

Documentary
1960 · Bel/Fr/Neth · Colour · 90mins

Considering it only had the official Rome Olympics film as competition, it was no surprise that Pierre-Dominique Gaisseau's ethnographical exercise won the feature documentary Oscar. Although it could now be accused of patronising its subjects, this study of life in Dutch New Guinea, as seen during a seven-month Franco-Dutch expedition, at least provides a valuable record of tribal customs – cannibalism, headhunting and so on – and the region's flora and fauna. A version with English-language narration also exists. DP. A French language film.

William Peacock *Narrator* ■ *Dir/Scr* Pierre-Dominique Gaisseau • *Cinematographer* Gilbert Sarthre

Sky Blue ★★ 15

Animated science-fiction adventure
2003 · S Kor/US · Colour · 85mins

South Korea jumps onto the dystopian animé bandwagon with this visually arresting slice of future *noir*. Reportedly Korea's most expensive animated movie ever, the hi-tech blend of line-drawn and CGI animation is certainly distinctive. The same can't be said for its eco-friendly storyline in which heroine Jay battles a band of revolutionaries, led by her childhood friend Shua, who are intent on sabotaging the domed city of Ecoban. This feels like a plodding, cheap facsimile of better animated movies. JR. In Korean and English language versions. Contains violence.

Catherine Cavadini *Jay* • Marc Worden *Shua* • Kirk Thornton *Cade* • David Naughton *Commander Locke/Dr Noah* • Karl Wiedergott *Moe* • Rebecca Wink *Woody* ■ *Dir* Kim Moon Sang, Park Sunmin • *Scr* Kim Moon Sang, Park Jun Yong, Park Sunmin, Park Sunmin (English version), Howard Rabinowitz (English version), Jeffrey Winter (English version)

Sky Captain and the World of Tomorrow ★★★ PG

Science-fiction action adventure
2004 · US/UK/It · Colour · 102mins

Writer/director Kerry Conran uses the latest digital technology to create a hymn to the heroes of cliffhanger serials. In some curiously imprecise era, people work in skyscrapers, ride in airships, and only one man can save the world when leading scientists start disappearing and cities are attacked by enormous robots – Jude Law, aka Sky Captain, accompanied by erstwhile girlfriend and ace reporter Gwyneth Paltrow. What is most impressive is the way in which Conran has created the future as it was perceived back in the 1930s. However, despite being breathtakingly clever, this lacks warmth and charm. BP [video] DVD

Jude Law *Joe "Sky Captain" Sullivan* • Gwyneth Paltrow *Polly Perkins* • Angelina Jolie *Franky Cook* • Giovanni Ribisi *Dex* • Michael Gambon *Editor Morris Paley* • Bai Ling *Mysterious Woman* • Omid Djalili *Kaji* ■ *Dir/Scr* Kerry Conran

Sky Murder ★

Second World War detective drama
1940 · US · BW · 72mins

Nick Carter, one of the 20th century's earliest pulp fiction detectives and the focus of some early French silent movies, finally made it to the American screen in 1939 with *Nick Carter, Master Detective*. However, only two more movies followed before the series died and this last instalment explains why. The plot concerns killer spies and a millionaire, but the action quotient is almost nil. RK

Walter Pidgeon *Nick Carter* • Donald Meek *Bartholomew* • Karen Verne [Kaaren Verne] *Pat Evens* • Edward Ashley *Cortland Grand* • Joyce Compton *Christina Cross* • Tom Conway *Andrew Hendon* • George Lessey *Senator Monrose* • Dorothy Tree *Kathe* ■ *Dir* George B Seitz • *Scr* William R Lipman

Sky Pirates ★★ PG

Science-fiction adventure
1986 · Aus · Colour · 83mins

John Hargreaves does his best as the pilot flying into a time warp in this Australian attempt to recapture the excitement and adventure of the old Saturday morning serials. The secret of remaking old B-movies for modern audiences is to apply A-movie polish and production values, but this effort struggles to rise above C-movie standards. PF [video]

John Hargreaves *Flight Lieutenant Harris* • Meredith Phillips *Melanie Mitchell* • Max Phipps *Squadron Leader Savage* • Bill Hunter *O'Reilly* • Simon Chilvers *Reverend Kenneth Mitchell* • Alex Scott (2) *General Hackett* ■ *Dir* Colin Eggleston • *Scr* John Lamond

Sky Riders ★★ PG

Action adventure
1976 · US/Gr · Colour · 86mins

In Greece, the family of an American businessman Robert Culp is kidnapped by a terrorist group and taken to a monastery on top of a mountain. To the rescue comes a group of hang-gliding freaks led by soldier-of-fortune James Coburn. Coburn is as emotionless as a cold fish, but the hang-gliding stunts are excellent. TH [video]

James Coburn *Jim McCabe* • Susannah York *Ellen Bracken* • Robert Culp *Jonas Bracken* • Charles Aznavour *Inspector Nikolidis* • Werner Pochath *No 1, terrorist leader* • Zouzou *No 6, female terrorist* • Kenneth Griffith *Wasserman* ■ *Dir* Douglas Hickox • *Scr* Jack DeWitt, Stanley Mann, Garry Michael White, from a story by Hall T Sprague, Bill McGaw

Sky West and Crooked ★★★

Drama 1965 · UK · Colour · 105mins

John Mills's sole assignment behind the camera is something of a family affair: it was co-scripted by his novelist wife, Mary Hayley Bell, and stars their daughter Hayley Mills. Intended to help Hayley distance herself from her kiddie roles at Disney, the film is a variation on DH Lawrence's *The Virgin and the Gypsy*, with Hayley's slightly touched teen falling for romantic Romany Ian McShane. It's all somewhat melodramatic, but Mills Sr directs with a steady hand. DP

Hayley Mills *Brydie White* • Ian McShane *Roibin* • Laurence Naismith *Edwin Dacres* • Geoffrey Bayldon *Philip Moss* • Annette Crosbie *Mrs White* • Norman Bird *Cheeseman* ■ *Dir* John Mills • *Scr* Mary Hayley Bell, John Prebble, from a story by Mary Hayley Bell

Skyjacked ★★★ PG

Disaster movie 1972 · US · Colour · 96mins

Before he made the mother of all disaster movies, *The Towering Inferno*, John Guillermin worked out with this aerial jeopardy epic which cashed in on the rash of terrorist hijackings as well as the box-office success of *Airport*. Charlton Heston is the stoical pilot, Yvette Mimieux the plucky stewardess, and James Brolin the psychotic hijacker who orders Heston to head for Moscow. Passengers either stay calm or go bonkers, the Russians launch their jet fighters and Heston worries about running out of gas. AT [video]

Charlton Heston *Captain O'Hara* • Yvette Mimieux *Angela Thacher* • James Brolin *Jerome K Weber* • Claude Akins *Sgt Ben Puzo* • Jeanne Crain *Mrs Shaw* • Susan Dey *Elly Brewster* • Roosevelt Grier [Rosey Grier] *Gary Brown* • Walter Pidgeon *Senator Arne Lindner* ■ *Dir* John Guillermin • *Scr* Stanley R Greenberg, from the novel *Hijacked* by David Harper

Skylark ★★

Comedy 1941 · US · BW · 94mins

After five years of marriage to Ray Milland, Claudette Colbert is fed up with her wifely role as second fiddle to her husband's career. When charming Brian Aherne appears on the scene, he offers just the diversion she's seeking. This is a standard comedy of the period, played with style and given the Paramount studio gloss. Profiting from the attractive personalities of the stars, it amuses but is nothing special. RK

Claudette Colbert *Lydia Kenyon* • Ray Milland *Tony Kenyon* • Brian Aherne *Jim Blake* • Binnie Barnes *Myrtle Vantine* • Walter Abel *George Gore* • Grant Mitchell *Frederick Vantine* ■ *Dir* Mark Sandrich • *Scr* Zion Myers, Allan Scott, from the play and novel by Samson Raphaelson

S

The Sky's the Limit ★★ U

Musical comedy 1943 · US · BW · 86mins

The most forgettable – and largely forgotten – of Fred Astaire's musicals pairs him with Joan Leslie in a wafer-thin romance about a flying hero (Astaire) on leave in New York where, to escape adulation, he pretends to be an idle civilian. Leslie is the news photographer more interested in the war effort than his attempts to woo her. The movie yielded a couple of great songs, including *One For My Baby*, and the dance routines staged by the star aren't bad. RK [video]

Fred Astaire *Fred Atwell* • Joan Leslie *Joan Manyon* • Robert Benchley *Phil Harriman* • Robert Ryan *Reginald Fenton* • Elizabeth Patterson *Mrs Fisher* • Eric Blore *Jasper* • Marjorie Gateson *Canteen lady* • Peter Lawford *Naval commander* ■ *Dir* Edward H Griffith • *Scr* Frank Fenton, Lynn Root, from their story *A Handful of Heaven*

Skyscraper Souls ★★★

Melodrama 1932 · US · BW · 80mins

Working to the same formula as that year's major hit *Grand Hotel*, MGM came up with a New York skyscraper as the location for a group of characters whose personal dramas are interconnected by their location. At the centre of the action is Warren William as the owner of the building and a man as uncompromising with women as he is in his ruthless business deals. The colourful Gregory Ratoff, later to become a leading director, and future scourge of the stars Hedda Hopper are among the supporting cast. Decent entertainment, despite a melodramatic climax. RK

Warren William *David Dwight* • Maureen O'Sullivan *Lynn Harding* • Gregory Ratoff *Vinmont* • Anita Page *Jenny LeGrande* • Verree Teasdale *Sarah Dennis* • Norman Foster *Tom* • Jean Hersholt *Jake Sorenson* • Hedda Hopper *Ella Dwight* ■ *Dir* Edgar Selwyn • *Scr* C Gardner Sullivan, Elmer Harris, from the novel *Skyscraper* by Faith Baldwin

The Slab Boys ★★★ 15

Drama 1997 · UK · Colour · 97mins

John Byrne's love of 1950s rock 'n' roll shone through his superb TV series *Tutti Frutti* and it also forms a musical background to this flawed but quirkily entertaining drama. Based on two of Byrne's plays, it's a coming-of-age tale about three young lads employed in a carpet factory who dream of escape from their bleak working-class surroundings. Byrne draws out fine performances from a largely unknown cast and lovingly evokes the era. The superb soundtrack mixes Little Richard and Chuck Berry with Scottish contemporary artists Edwyn Collins and the Proclaimers. JF

Robin Laing *Phil McCann* • Russell Barr *George "Spanky" Farrell* • Bill Gardiner *Hector McKenzie* • Louise Berry *Lucille Bentley* • Julie Wilson Nimmo *Bernadette Rooney* • Duncan Ross *Alan Downie* • Tom Watson *Willie Curry* • Anna Massey *Miss Elsie Walkinshaw* ■ *Dir* John Byrne • *Scr* John Byrne, from his plays *The Slab Boys* and *Cuttin' a Rug*

Slacker ★★★★ 15

Cult comedy 1989 · US · Colour · 96mins

Director Richard Linklater made his name with this offbeat, low-budget effort, whose title was taken up by the bored 20-somethings of 1990s America. There's no plot to speak of, with Linklater instead taking a rather hazy ramble through the lives of a large number of eccentrics living in Austin, Texas. It's an occasionally over-indulgent affair, but the natural performances and dizzying number of barmy conspiracy theories and philosophies win you over in the end. JF. Contains swearing. DVD

Richard Linklater *Should have stayed at the bus station* • Rudy Basquez *Taxi driver* • Jean Caffeine *Roadkill* • Jan Hockey *Jogger* • Stephan Hockey *Running late* • Mark James *Hit-and-run son* ■ *Dir/Scr* Richard Linklater

S

Slackers ★★★ 15

Comedy 2001 · US · Colour · 83mins

This agreeable campus comedy is given an injection of quirky humour by the brilliant Jason Schwartzman (*Rushmore*) who adds another eccentric nerd to his CV. He plays a creepy obsessive who uncovers evidence that three "slackers" – Devon Sawa, Michael Maronna and Jason Segel – have lied, cheated and manipulated their way through the education system. To stop him blowing the whistle, Sawa reluctantly agrees to set him up with brainy beauty Jaime King. This wants to have its *American Pie* and eat it, aiming to be both crudely offensive and sweetly soft-centred. JC. Contains swearing and sex scenes. DVD

Devon Sawa *Dave* • Jason Schwartzman *Ethan* • Jaime King *Angela* • Jason Segel *Sam* • Michael Maronna *Jeff* • Mamie Van Doren *Mrs Van Graaf* • Leigh Taylor-Young *Valerie Patton* • Cameron Diaz ■ *Dir* Dewey Nicks • *Scr* David H Steinberg

Slade in Flame ★★★ PG

Musical drama 1974 · UK · Colour · 86mins

The usual rags-to-riches-to-bitching rock 'n' roll saga is given a gritty, thoughtful and far more realistic patina by director Richard Loncraine. After forming the group Flame circa 1967 and having a monster hit, the band members suffer managerial manipulation and financial fraud before acrimoniously breaking up in this somber account of the downsides to the music industry. This is well written, well made and well performed by Slade and Tom Conti. AJ

Noddy Holder *Stoker* • Jim Lea *Paul* • Dave Hill *Barry* • Don Powell *Charlie* • Tom Conti *Seymour* ■ *Dir* Richard Loncraine • *Scr* Andrew Birkin

Slam ★★★ 15

Prison drama 1998 · US · Colour · 99mins

Unusual film about the redemptive power of poetry, with a small-time drug dealer discovering his true calling courtesy of an arts course he signs up for while in prison. Back on the outside, he becomes a leading light of Washington's black rap-poetry scene. Preachy but powerful, the film makes extensive use of handheld cameras to give it a genuine feel of the real. Performances are in-your-face and convincing, but the subject matter won't appeal to all tastes. DA. Contains swearing, sex scene.

Saul Williams *Ray Joshua* • Bonz Malone *Hopha* • Sonja Sohn *Lauren Bell* • Beau Sia *Jimmy Huang* • Lawrence Wilson *Big Mike* • Andre Taylor *China* ■ *Dir* Marc Levin • *Scr* Marc Levin, Richard Stratton, Saul Williams, Sonja Sohn, Bonz Malone, from a story by Marc Levin, Richard Stratton

Slam Dance ★★★ 15

Thriller 1987 · US · Colour · 95mins

Director Wayne Wang shows his versatility with this intriguing excursion into the thriller genre. Tom Hulce is the harassed cartoonist who finds himself suspected of murder after a brief liaison with Virginia Madsen. Wang cleverly uses the device of Hulce being hounded by both cops and the violent Don Opper to invoke a disturbing atmosphere of individual paranoia and general psychosis. There are many delicious surprises and red herrings are scattered around like confetti. SH. Contains swearing.

Tom Hulce *CC Drood* • Mary Elizabeth Mastrantonio *Helen Drood* • Adam Ant *Jim Campbell* • Don Opper *Buddy* • John Doe *Gilbert* • Harry Dean Stanton *Detective Smiley* • Robert Beltran *Frank* • Virginia Madsen *Yolanda Caldwell* • Millie Perkins *Bobby Nye* ■ *Dir* Wayne Wang • *Scr* Don Opper

Slam Dunk Ernest ★ U

Comedy 1995 · US · Colour · 92mins

The consistently unfunny Jim Varney returns as Ernest P Worrell in another edition in the film series about the madcap adventures of a trouble-prone simpleton. When the dumber than dumb Ernest comes into possession of a pair of magic basketball shoes, he and his work colleagues come up against the professionals of the game. Puerile humour is interspersed with the usual lashings of childish slapstick and sentimentality. JF

Jim Varney *Ernest P Worrell* • Kareem Abdul-Jabbar *Archangel* • Jay Brazeau *Mr Moloch* ■ *Dir* John Cherry [John R Cherry III] • *Scr* John R Cherry III, Daniel Butler

The Slams ★★ 18

Prison drama 1973 · US · Colour · 86mins

No-brain prison drama, with athlete-turned-actor Jim Brown the star behind bars. He finds himself under pressure from fellow inmates to reveal where he's hidden a heroin-and-cash stash. The film starts off as a drama, but oddly transmutes into something resembling a comedy. Yet it's neither particularly exciting, nor particularly funny. DA

Jim Brown *Curtis Hook* • Judy Pace *Iris Daniels* • Roland "Bob" Harris *Stambell* • Paul Harris *Jackson Barney* • Frank De Kova *Capiello* • Ted Cassidy *Glover* ■ *Dir* Jonathan Kaplan • *Scr* Richard L Adams

Slap Her, She's French! ★★ 12

Comedy 2001 · Ger/US/UK · Colour · 87mins

A cultural exchange visit descends into a teen twist on *Single White Female* in this Texas-set comedy. And the movie's magpie nature doesn't end with that little lift, as director Melanie Mayron was clearly taking copious notes while watching *Legally Blonde* as well. Yet, despite its derivative nature, this still comes across as an entertaining farce thanks to Jane McGregor's vivacious turn as the shallow overachiever whose life is sabotaged by seemingly harmless French gamine Piper Perabo. DP DVD

Piper Perabo *Genevieve LePlouff* • Jane McGregor *Starla Grady* • Trent Ford *Ed Mitchell* • Michael McKean *Monsieur Duke* • Julie White *Bootsie Grady* • Brandon Smith *Arnie Grady* • Jesse James *Randolph Grady* • Nicki Aycox [Nicki Lynn Aycox] *Tanner Jennings* ■ *Dir* Melanie Mayron • *Scr* Damon Lamar, Robert Lee King

Slap Shot ★★★ 18

Comedy drama 1977 · US · Colour · 117mins

Paul Newman is reunited with his *Butch Cassidy* director George Roy Hill for this sharp, satirical look at unethical tactics in professional ice hockey. Fashioned as a series of deliberately crude epithets by scriptwriter Nancy Dowd, the film follows the fortunes of a minor-league team that is encouraged to play dirty to win by ambitious coach Newman. Unfortunately, the relentless violence and profanity that provide the film with its great strength are usually toned down in TV versions, with much of the locker-room language removed. A belated, made-for-video sequel followed in 2002. TS DVD

Paul Newman *Reggie Dunlop* • Strother Martin *Joe McGrath* • Michael Ontkean *Ned Braden* • Jennifer Warren *Francine Dunlop* • Lindsay Crouse *Lily Braden* • Jerry Houser *"Killer" Carlson* • Andrew Duncan *Jim Carr* ■ *Dir* George Roy Hill • *Scr* Nancy Dowd

Slapstick of Another Kind ★★ PG

Science-fiction comedy 1982 · US · Colour · 80mins

A would-be satirical comedy about the birth of huge, hideously ugly twins (Jerry Lewis and Madeline Kahn) who in reality are super-intelligent beings from another planet, the film widely misses the mark. A strong cast ensure that some good moments survive but all in all it demonstrates the difficulty certain idiosyncratic novelists such as Kurt Vonnegut have with their on-screen adaptations. DF DVD

Jerry Lewis *Wilbur Swain/Caleb Swain* • Madeline Kahn *Eliza Swain/Letitia Swain* • Marty Feldman *Sylvester* • John Abbott *Dr Frankenstein* • Jim Backus *United States President* • Samuel Fuller *Colonel Sharp* • Merv Griffin *Anchorman* • Pat Morita *Ambassador Ah Fong* • Orson Welles *Alien Father* ■ *Dir* Steven Paul • *Scr* Steven Paul, from the novel *Slapstick* by Kurt Vonnegut Jr

Slate, Wyn & Me ★★ 18

Crime drama 1987 · Aus · Colour · 87mins

An intriguing title for this watchable, violent and foul-mouthed Australian drama which concerns two brothers who rob a bank, kill a cop and take hostage the eponymous "Me", a girl witness. The ensuing triangle creates various roadblocks in the getaway process. Don McLennan's crime drama is strong for the first 30 minutes, but doesn't quite know how to fulfil its early potential, yet there's a quirkiness to it that sustains interest. DA

Sigrid Thornton *Blanche McBride* • Simon Burke *Wyn Jackson* • Martin Sacks *Slate Jackson* • Tommy Lewis *Morgan* • Lesley Baker *Molly* • Harold Baigent *Sammy* • Michelle Torres *Daphne* • Murray Fahey *Martin* ■ *Dir* Don McLennan • *Scr* Don McLennan, from a novel by Georgia Savage

Slattery's Hurricane ★★★

Disaster drama 1949 · US · BW · 83mins

Pilot Richard Widmark's post-Second World War career has included flying for a front company for the Mob and an affair with the boss's girlfriend, Veronica Lake. Various complications result in Widmark taking old mate John Russell's place on a dangerous assignment into the eye of a hurricane. This forgettable drama, told in flashback, is not to be taken seriously, but the storm-tossed aerial sequences are entertaining. RK

Richard Widmark *Willard Francis Slattery* • Linda Darnell *Aggie Hobson* • Veronica Lake *Dolores Greeves* • John Russell *Lt FJ "Hobby" Hobson* • Gary Merrill *Comdr ET Kramer* • Walter Kingsford *RJ Milne* ■ *Dir* Andre De Toth • *Scr* Herman Wouk, Richard Murphy, from a story by Herman Wouk

Slaughter ★★ 18

Blaxploitation crime drama
1972 · US · Colour · 88mins

This piece of blaxploitation tries to cash in on the supercool black avenger image institutionalised by *Shaft* (1971), but it's set at such a fast pace by director Jack Starrett that you scarcely feel the potholes of the plot. Jim Brown is the former Green Beret on a trigger-happy vendetta against the underworld mob responsible for killing his parents. It has the ruthless efficiency of a well-oiled automatic weapon – and about as much characterisation. TH

Jim Brown *Slaughter* • Stella Stevens *Ann* • Rip Torn *Dominick* • Cameron Mitchell *Price* • Don Gordon *Harry* • Marlene Clark *Kim* • Norman Alfe *Mario* ■ *Dir* Jack Starrett • *Scr* Mark Hanna, Don Williams

Slaughter on Tenth Avenue ★★★

Crime drama 1957 · US · BW · 102mins

Three years after *On the Waterfront*, this formula movie discovered the waterfront racket all over again. Craftily directed by Arnold Laven, it has assistant District Attorney Richard Egan at war with the crime around the docks, and finding true love with longshoreman's widow Jan Sterling. Dan Duryea is the heavy. TH

Richard Egan *William Keating* • Jan Sterling *Madge Pitts* • Dan Duryea *John Jacob Masters* • Julie Adams *Dee* • Walter Matthau *Al Dahlke* • Charles McGraw *Lieutenant Anthony Vosnick* ■ *Dir* Arnold Laven • *Scr* Lawrence Roman, from the memoirs *The Man Who Rocked the Boat* by William J Keating, Richard Carter

Slaughter Trail ★★ U

Western 1951 · US · Colour · 76mins

A small band of outlaws disturbs the peace between Navajos and whites in this Cinecolor western, which is enlivened by the pre-*Cat Ballou* novelty of a commentary which is sung at intervals by guitar-strumming cavalrymen. Gig Young also makes the principal villain colourful. The film's release was delayed by the blacklisting of actor Howard Da Silva, as RKO's owner, Howard Hughes, insisted that all Da Silva's scenes as the cavalry commander were re-shot with Brian Donlevy in the role. AE

Brian Donlevy *Captain Dempster* • Gig Young *Vaughn* • Virginia Grey *Lorabelle Larkin* • Andy Devine *Sgt McIntosh* • Robert Hutton *Lt Morgan* ■ *Dir* Irving Allen • *Scr* Sid Kuller

Slaughter's Big Rip-Off ★★★

Blaxploitation crime drama
1973 · US · Colour · 90mins

Black Vietnam vet/urban warrior Jim Brown returns to avenge the murder of his mother and father by gangsters, led this time around by Ed McMahon. Jim Brown goes in for a lot of violent confrontations but is really too good for this blaxploitation fix. A hint of humour would have helped. TH

Jim Brown *Slaughter* • Ed McMahon *Duncan* • Brock Peters *Reynolds* • Don Stroud *Kirk* • Gloria Hendry *Marcia* • Richard Williams *Joe Creole* • Judy Brown [Judith Brown] *Norji* ■ *Dir* Gordon Douglas • *Scr* Charles Johnson, from a character created by Don Williams

Slaughterhouse ★ 18

Comedy horror 1987 · US · Colour · 79mins

This features a graphic opening montage of farmyard pigs being killed for real. The tired plot concerns local authorities about to foreclose on the rural homestead-cum-slaughterhouse of Don Barrett and his hog-loving son Joe Barton. Psycho Barton axes anyone who tries to evict them including the usual bunch of witless teens using the property to shoot a low-budget horror movie. A derivative gore bore. Julianne Moore made her feature debut in the 1988 sequel. AJ

Joe Barton *Buddy* • Don Barrett *Lester Bacon* • Sherry Bendorf *Liz Borden* • William Houck *Sheriff* • Jeffrey Grossi *Buzz* ■ *Dir/Scr* Rick Roessler

Slaughterhouse-Five ★★★★ 15

Science-fiction satire
1972 · US · Colour · 98mins

Kurt Vonnegut's science-fiction masterpiece is done marvellous justice in director George Roy Hill's wildly complex, truly bizarre and poignant commentary on the absurdity of human existence. In this postmodern *Pilgrim's Progress*, Michael Sacks is Billy Pilgrim, a man "unstuck in time" who constantly leaves the present to either return to the past, when he was a prisoner of war in Dresden, or flit to the future, where his existence with half-naked actress Valerie Perrine is viewed under glass by aliens. A wry, intelligent and thought-provoking parable with a surreal quality. AJ

Michael Sacks *Billy Pilgrim* • Ron Leibman *Paul Lazzaro* • Eugene Roche *Derby* • Sharon Gans *Valencia* • Valerie Perrine *Montana Wildhack* • Roberts Blossom *Wild Bob Cody* • Sorrell Booke *Lionel Merble* • Kevin Conway *Weary* ■ *Dir* George Roy Hill • *Scr* Stephen Geller, from the novel by Kurt Vonnegut Jr

Slave Girl ★ U

Period comedy adventure
1947 · US · Colour · 79mins

A less than charismatic George Brent stars as an American diplomat who is sent off to Tripoli to buy back a group of sailors held hostage by a cruel potentate. En route, the ransom money is stolen and exotic dancing girl Yvonne De Carlo is saved by Brent from a dreadful fate. With its miscasting, ridiculous plot and hackneyed slapstick jokes, the movie falls flat on its face. RK

Yvonne De Carlo *Francesca* • George Brent *Matt Claibourne/Pierre* • Broderick Crawford *Chips Jackson* • Albert Dekker *Pasha* • Lois Collier *Aleta* • Andy Devine *Ben* • Arthur Treacher *Thomas "Liverpool" Griswald* ■ *Dir* Charles Lamont • *Scr* Michael Fessier, Ernest Pagano

A Slave of Love ★★★

Period drama 1976 · USSR · Colour · 92mins

Such is the status of silent Soviet cinema that it's easy to overlook the sophistication of film-making in the late-Tsarist era. Unsurprisingly, Nikita Mikhalkov is only able to pay passing tribute to those forgotten masters in this bitingly satirical drama, in which a cash-strapped unit shooting in Odessa gradually becomes aware of the Bolshevik Revolution. The story sees haughty diva Elena Solovei rally to the cause after the death of cameraman-lover Rodion Nakhapetov, who's been secretly filming propaganda footage of White Guard atrocities. DP. In Russian with English subtitles.

Elena Solovei *Olga Voznesenskaya* • Rodion Nakhapetov *Victor Pototsky* • Aleksandr Kalyagin *Kalyagin* • Oleg Basilashvili *Yuzhakov* • Konstantin Grigoryev *Fedotov* ■ *Dir* Nikita Mikhalkov • *Scr* Friedrich Gorenstein, Andrei Mikhalkov-Konchalovsky [Andrei Konchalovsky]

Slave Ship ★★★

Adventure 1937 · US · BW · 90mins

Warner Baxter should really have known better than to buy a "blood ship" called the *Albatross*, for no sooner has he sworn to cease slave trading than he has a mutiny on his hands. Wallace Beery plays his trademark soft-centred sourpuss with typical gusto, and he's ably supported by George Sanders as the chief mutineer and Mickey Rooney as a cheeky cabin boy. But the soggy performance of Baxter as the Captain Bligh of the piece makes it almost impossible for director Tay Garnett to keep the wind in the sails of this otherwise boisterous picture. DP

Warner Baxter *Jim Lovett* • Wallace Beery *Jack Thompson* • Elizabeth Allan *Nancy Marlowe* • Mickey Rooney *Swifty* • George Sanders *Lefty* • Jane Darwell *Mrs Marlowe* • Joseph Schildkraut *Danelo* ■ *Dir* Tay Garnett • *Scr* Sam Hellman, Lamar Trotti, Gladys Lehman, from a story by William Faulkner, from the novel *The Last Slaver* by George S King

Slavers ★ 18

Drama 1977 · W Ger · Colour · 94mins

In this bloody, repellent mess, Trevor Howard and Ray Milland are slumming, playing Victorian-era slave traders. Howard owns the trading post, while Milland is browned-up as a shifty Arab, Hassan, who shoots his slaves as target practice (which doesn't make very sound economic sense). Britt Ekland introduces some love interest, while Zimbabwe (then Rhodesia) provides the scenery. AT

Trevor Howard *Alec MacKenzie* • Ron Ely *Steven Hamilton* • Britt Ekland *Anna von Erken* • Jürgen Goslar *Max von Erken* • Ray Milland *Hassan* • Don Jack Rousseau *Mazu* • Helen Morgan (2) *Malika* ■ *Dir* Jürgen Goslar • *Scr* Henry Morrisson, Nathaniel Kohn, Marcia MacDonald

Slaves ★★★

Drama 1969 · US · Colour · 105mins

Herbert J Biberman, the blacklisted director of *Salt of the Earth* (1954), had to wait 15 years for his next film, a study of slavery. Ossie Davis plays the hero who is sold to Stephen Boyd, a Mississippi landowner who keeps a black mistress, played by singer Dionne Warwick in her screen debut. While Davis and Warwick are fairly conventional archetypes, Boyd has the best material, playing a satisfyingly complex character – brutal yet haunted by a religious upbringing which draws him to the Christian-motivated Davis. The director's wife Gale Sondergaard – herself both an Oscar winner and a blacklist victim – appears in the New Orleans sequence. It was her first film since 1949. AT

Stephen Boyd *Nathan MacKay* • Dionne Warwick *Cassy* • Ossie Davis *Luke* • Robert Kya-Hill *Jericho* • Barbara Ann Teer *Esther* • Marilyn Clark *Mrs Bennett* • Gale Sondergaard *New Orleans lady* ■ *Dir* Herbert J Biberman • *Scr* Herbert J Biberman, John O Killens, Alida Sherman

Slaves of New York ★★ 15

Comedy drama 1989 · US · Colour · 119mins

The genteel style of James Ivory and Ismail Merchant sits uneasily on a series of interrelated short stories about middle-class 30-somethings in a district of New York. The abiding relationship is that between kooky hat designer Bernadette Peters and self-centred artist Adam Coleman Howard, but that's as doomed to fail as the rest of the characters. TH. Contains swearing, sex scenes and brief nudity.

Bernadette Peters *Eleanor* • Chris Sarandon *Victor Okrent* • Mary Beth Hurt *Ginger Booth* • Madeleine Potter *Daria* • Adam Coleman Howard *Stash Stotz* • Nick Corri *Marley Mantello* • Mercedes Ruehl *Samantha* • Steve Buscemi *Wilfredo* • Tama Janowitz *Abby* • Anthony LaPaglia *Henry* • Stanley Tucci *Darryl* ■ *Dir* James Ivory • *Scr* Tama Janowitz, from her stories • *Producer* Ismail Merchant

Slayground ★★ 18

Thriller 1983 · UK · Colour · 84mins

Not a horror film, despite the lurid title, but a tepid thriller based on a hard-boiled novel by Richard Stark (crime writer Donald E Westlake). The hero of the book was a tough-nut criminal, but for the film, he's been softened into a whiny petty thief. This sweetening of his character does the film no favours; neither does the dreary plot, which sees the crook on the run from a contract killer. Peter Coyote stars, while other familiar faces include Billie Whitelaw and Mel Smith. DA

Peter Coyote *Stone* • Mel Smith *Terry Abbatt* • Billie Whitelaw *Madge* • Philip Sayer *Costello* • Bill Luhrs *Joe Sheer* • Marie Masters *Joni* • Clarence Felder *Orzel* ■ *Dir* Terry Bedford • *Scr* Trevor Preston, from a novel by Richard Stark [Donald E Westlake]

Sleep, My Love ★★ PG

Psychological melodrama
1948 · US · BW · 92mins

Shades of that old favourite *Gaslight* haunt this psycho-melodrama, which pairs one-time romantic comedy team Claudette Colbert and Don Ameche. Colbert is the wealthy wife of Ameche, for once swapping his debonair persona to play the impassive, cold husband systematically sending Colbert mad so he can inherit her money and marry siren Hazel Brooks. Robert Cummings is the hero figure in a plot too familiar for surprises, but still somewhat suspenseful. RK

Claudette Colbert *Alison Courtland* • Robert Cummings *Bruce Elcott* • Don Ameche *Richard Courtland* • Rita Johnson *Barby* • George Coulouris *Charles Vernay* • Queenie Smith *Mrs Vernay* • Ralph Morgan *Dr Rhinehart* • Keye Luke *Jimmie* • Raymond Burr *Lt Strake* • Hazel Brooks *Daphne* ■ *Dir* Douglas Sirk • *Scr* St Clair McKelway, Leo Rosten, Cyril Endfield [Cy Endfield], Decla Dunning, from a novel by Leo Rosten

Sleep with Me ★★★ 18

Romantic comedy
1994 · US · Colour · 82mins

Suggested by Eric Stoltz and director Rory Kelly, this is a fascinating experiment in film-making. Six writers each penned a different episode; if the end result is a little uneven, the shifts in tone give the picture vibrance and variety. Though the narrative focus is on the twists and trysts involving Stoltz, Meg Tilly and Craig Sheffer, it's the incidentals that stand out, notably Quentin Tarantino's wonderful party piece and Adrienne Shelly's unerring talent for social gaffs. Hilarious when it hits the mark, but never less than amiable. DP. Contains swearing, sex scenes and nudity.

Eric Stoltz *Joseph* • Meg Tilly *Sarah* • Craig Sheffer *Frank* • Todd Field *Duane* • Susan Traylor *Deborah* • Dean Cameron *Leo* • Quentin Tarantino *Sid* • Adrienne Shelly *Pamela* ■ *Dir* Rory Kelly • *Scr* Duane Dell'Amico, Roger Hedden, Neal Jimenez, Joe Keenan, Rory Kelly, Michael Steinberg

Sleeper ★★★★ PG

Science-fiction comedy
1973 · US · Colour · 83mins

In this silly but often hilarious comedy, Woody Allen is a jazz musician who comes round from what he thinks was a minor operation only to discover that he has been in cryogenic suspension for 200 years. What follows is partly inspired by *1984* (Allen gets involved with revolutionaries opposing the totalitarian government), but is mainly a homage to great screen comedians of the past. The sight gags (particularly Allen disguised as a robot) include some of the funniest things Allen has ever done. There is also a rich quota of brilliantly witty lines throughout, with Diane Keaton making a fine foil. DM. Contains swearing. DVD

Woody Allen *Miles Monroe* • Diane Keaton *Luna Schlosser* • John Beck *Erno Windt* • Marya Small *Dr Nero* • Bartlett Robinson *Dr Orva* • Mary Gregory *Dr Melik* • Chris Forbes *Rainer Krebs* ■ *Dir* Woody Allen • *Scr* Woody Allen, Marshall Brickman

Sleepers ★★★ 18

Drama 1996 · US · Colour · 140mins

With its powerhouse cast and an A-list director, this is long and exudes importance and integrity. So why does it come across as bogus? Though based on an autobiography, the plot mechanism and its moral stance – that violent revenge is fully justified – is not totally believable. The story concerns four teenagers who are brought up by a priest. When a foolish prank causes a near-fatal accident, the youths are sent to jail where they are repeatedly abused by the guards. Years later, they plot revenge. Director Barry Levinson vividly evokes the hothouse atmosphere of New York's Hell's Kitchen. AT. Contains violence and swearing. DVD

Kevin Bacon *Sean Nokes* • Robert De Niro *Father Bobby* • Dustin Hoffman *Danny Snyder* • Jason Patric *Lorenzo "Shakes"* • Brad Pitt *Michael* • Billy Crudup *Tommy* • Ron Eldard *John* • Vittorio Gassman *King Benny* • Minnie Driver *Carol Martinez* ■ *Dir* Barry Levinson • *Scr* Barry Levinson, from the autobiography by Lorenzo Carcaterra

Sleeping Beauty ★★★ U

Animated fantasy 1959 · US · Colour · 71mins

This was Disney's most expensive cartoon to date, yet despite its many charms and technical mastery it barely made its money back at the box office in 1959. Unhelpfully compared at the time to *Cinderella* and *Snow White* by critics, it has been re-evaluated by successive audiences. The score, based on Tchaikovsky's *Sleeping Beauty* ballet, was Oscar-nominated.

S

Technical wizardry apart, it's the supporting characters that make the difference, in this case the trio of plump guardians Flora, Fauna and Merryweather, and, in terms of iconic villainy, Maleficent the wicked fairy. The battle royale between Maleficent and Prince Phillip is one of Disney's best climaxes. AC DVD

Eleanor Audley *Maleficent* • Verna Felton *Flora* • Vera Vague [Barbara Jo Allen] *Fauna* • Barbara Luddy *Merryweather* • Taylor Holmes *King Stefan* • Bill Thompson *King Hubert* • Candy Candido *Goons* • Mary Costa *Princess Aurora* • Bill Shirley *Prince Phillip* ■ *Dir* Clyde Geronimi, Eric Larson, Wolfgang Reitherman, Les Clark • *Scr* Erdman Penner, from the fairy tale by Charles Perrault

The Sleeping Car Murders ★★★

Crime thriller 1965 · Fr · BW · 91mins

After years assisting René Clair and Jacques Demy, the Greek-born film-maker Constantin Costa-Gavras finally made his feature debut with this teasing whodunnit. The members of the all-star cast fall like flies as police inspector Yves Montand tries to discover who killed a woman on the Marseille-Paris express. In addition to a grotesquely lecherous Michel Piccoli, the limelight is hogged by Simone Signoret, whose daughter Catherine Allégret also appears. Costa-Gavras takes the picture at a fast pace and keeps the clues well hidden. DP. In French with English subtitles.

Yves Montand *Inspector Grazzi* • Simone Signoret *Eliane Darrès* • Pierre Mondy *Commissioner* • Catherine Allégret *Bambi* • Pascale Roberts *Georgette Thomas* • Michel Piccoli *Cabourg* • Jean-Louis Trintignant *Eric* ■ *Dir* Costa-Gavras • *Scr* Costa-Gavras, Sébastien Japrisot, from the novel *Compartiment Tueurs* by Sébastien Japrisot

Sleeping Car to Trieste ★★ PG

Spy drama 1948 · UK · BW · 91mins

While 1932's *Rome Express* was a sleek, fast-moving turbo of a crime drama, this unnecessary remake is something of a branch-line diesel that director John Paddy Carstairs insists on stopping at every country halt. The story remains basically the same as before, with Albert Lieven and Jean Kent as thieves in pursuit of a diary packed with state secrets, which passes from one shifty passenger to another. Comparisons are inevitable, if slightly unfair, but none of the cast improves on the original characterisations. DP

Jean Kent *Valya* • Albert Lieven *Zurta* • Derrick de Marney *George Grant* • Paul Dupuis *Jolif* • Rona Anderson *Joan Maxted* • David Tomlinson *Tom Bishop* • Finlay Currie *Alastair MacBain* ■ *Dir* John Paddy Carstairs • *Scr* Allan MacKinnon, from the story *Rome Express* by Clifford Grey

The Sleeping City ★★★

Crime drama 1950 · US · BW · 83mins

Critics at the time thought this documentary-style thriller was heavily derived from the 1948 drama *The Naked City*. Set in a New York hospital, it weaves together several strands of narrative and the deaths of two interns who have been stealing drugs to pay off gambling debts. George Sherman's film was one of the earliest Hollywood movies to confront the drug problem and it doesn't stint on the grim details. AT

Richard Conte *Fred Rowan* • Coleen Gray *Ann Sebastian* • Peggy Dow *Kathy Hall* • John Alexander *Inspector Gordon* • Alex Nicol *Dr Bob Anderson* • Richard Taber *Pop Ware* ■ *Dir* George Sherman • *Scr* Jo Eisinger

The Sleeping Tiger ★★★★ U

Crime drama 1954 · UK · BW · 85mins

This highly charged melodrama was made in England by Hollywood blacklistees, director Joseph Losey (hiding behind the name of the film's actual producer, Victor Hanbury) and co-writer Carl Foreman (under the alias Derek Frye). An important film, it brought together for the first time one of British cinema's most accomplished pairings in director Losey and star Dirk Bogarde, who would create a stunning body of work including *The Servant* and *Accident*. Losey seemed able to tap Bogarde's smouldering sexual and social ambivalence, and his scenes here with Alexis Smith are electric. The plot, about a psychiatrist taking a known criminal into his home, is reminiscent of Hollywood at its battiest. TS

Dirk Bogarde *Frank Clements* • Alexis Smith *Glenda Esmond* • Alexander Knox *Dr Clive Esmond* • Hugh Griffith *Inspector Simmons* • Patricia McCarron *Sally* • Maxine Audley *Carol* • Glyn Houston *Bailey* • Harry Towb *Harry* • Billie Whitelaw *Receptionist* ■ *Dir* Victor Hanbury [Joseph Losey] • *Scr* Derek Frye [Harold Buchman, Carl Foreman], from the novel by Maurice Moiseiwitsch

Sleeping Together ★★

Romantic comedy
1997 · US · Colour · 87mins

Cameron Bancroft and Caprice Benedetti are the mismatched couple – he's starchy and strait-laced, she's a wacky, free-spirited gal – who fall in and out of love in this insubstantial romantic comedy. The two young actors put in pleasing performances, although the honours are stolen by Elizabeth Ashley as Benedetti's equally offbeat mum. Writer/director Hugh Bush keeps it moving along nicely enough, though his script is a little on the predictable side. JF

Cameron Bancroft *Bruce* • Caprice Benedetti *Suzanne* • Manny Perez *Carlos* • Amber Smith *Cathy* • Debra Wilson *Wendy* • Elizabeth Ashley *Mrs Tuccinini* ■ *Dir/Scr* Hugh Bush

Sleeping with the Enemy ★★★ 15

Thriller 1991 · US · Colour · 94mins

Julia Roberts is the abused spouse who stages her own death to escape her marriage from hell with Patrick Bergin. She begins her life anew and meets nice Kevin Anderson but her crazed husband is never far behind. This was Roberts's bid for grittier material and she acquits herself well, while Bergin relishes his role as the bad guy. Director Joseph Ruben manages some chilling sequences. JF. Contains violence, sex scenes and swearing. DVD

Julia Roberts *Laura Burney/Sara Waters* • Patrick Bergin *Martin Burney* • Kevin Anderson *Ben Woodward* • Elizabeth Lawrence *Chloe* • Kyle Secor *Fleishman* • Claudette Nevins *Dr Rissner* • Tony Abatemarco *Locke* • Marita Geraghty *Julie* ■ *Dir* Joseph Ruben • *Scr* Ronald Bass, from the novel by Nancy Price

Sleepless in Seattle ★★★★ PG

Romantic comedy
1993 · US · Colour · 100mins

Nora Ephron, the writer of *When Harry Met Sally...*, comes up trumps again as co-writer and director of this gloriously old-fashioned romantic comedy. Tom Hanks, recently widowed, moves to a new home in Seattle where he just grieves and grieves. His young son (Ross Malinger), concerned over his dad's state of mind, calls a radio phone-in and when Hanks himself takes the phone, he pours his heart out. Meg Ryan, a Baltimore journalist who hears the broadcast, recognises a kindred lonely heart and starts tracking Hanks down. For nearly two hours, Ephron keeps her marvellous stars apart, a potentially dangerous tactic that works superbly. AT DVD

Tom Hanks *Sam Baldwin* • Meg Ryan *Annie Reed* • Ross Malinger *Jonah Baldwin* • Rosie O'Donnell *Becky* • Rob Reiner *Jay* • Bill Pullman *Walter* • Rita Wilson *Suzy* • Victor Garber *Greg* • David Hyde Pierce *Dennis Reed* ■ *Dir* Nora Ephron • *Scr* Nora Ephron, David S Ward, Jeff Arch, from a story by Jeff Arch

Sleepover ★ PG

Comedy 2004 · US/Can · Colour · 85mins

Flatulence jokes, grating stereotypes and an avalanche of female neuroses feature in this unappealing adolescent comedy. In a sadly wasted performance, Alexa Vega (*SPYkids*) plays an uncool 14-year-old, whose sleepover is turned on its head when the trendiest girls in school challenge her and her guests to a risky scavenger hunt. Lazily scripted and shoddily executed. SF DVD

Alexa Vega *Julie* • Mika Boorem *Hannah* • Jane Lynch *Gabby* • Sam Huntington *Ren* • Sara Paxton *Staci* • Brie Larson *Liz* • Scout Taylor-Compton *Farrah* • Sean Faris *Steve* ■ *Dir* Joe Nussbaum • *Scr* Elisa Bell

Sleepstalker ★★ 18

Horror 1995 · US · Colour · 102mins

A serial killer whose calling card is pouring sand in his victims' eyes is sent to the gas chamber and ritually resurrected as a demon by the evil Preacher (Michael D Roberts) and his albino acolytes. The Sandman must then kill journalist Jay Underwood, who is investigating Los Angeles' street gangs, to avoid eternal torment. This has good special effects work, but the often tiresomely conventional plot gets in the way. AJ. Contains violence and swearing. DVD

Jay Underwood *Griffin Davis* • Kathryn Morris *Megan* • Michael Harris (2) *The Sandman* • Michael D Roberts *Rev Jonas, preacher* ■ *Dir* Turi Meyer • *Scr* Turi Meyer, Al Septien

Sleepwalkers ★ 18

Fantasy horror 1992 · US · Colour · 85mins

Hailed as the first Stephen King story expressly written for the screen, this minor horror entry revolves around the gory small-town exploits of of shape-shifting, incestuous, psychic vampires. Director Mick Garris tries to inject life into the pathetic script by gyrating the camera, adding some neat computer-generated transformations and flashily accenting what little action there is, but this underdeveloped material is so poor he's fighting a losing battle. AJ DVD

Brian Krause *Charles Brady* • Mädchen Amick *Tanya Robertson* • Alice Krige *Mary Brady* • Jim Haynie *Sheriff Ira* • Cindy Pickett *Mrs Robertson* • Ron Perlman *Captain Soames* • John Landis *Lab technician* • Joe Dante *Lab assistant* • Stephen King *Cemetery caretaker* • Clive Barker *Forensic technician* • Tobe Hooper *Forensic technician* ■ *Dir* Mick Garris • *Scr* Stephen King

Sleepy Hollow ★★★★ 15

Gothic horror fantasy
1999 · US · Colour · 100mins

An alchemic combination of visual splendour, dreamy bloodthirstiness and sly humour, this supernatural Gothic whodunnit is another beautifully crafted offering from eccentric maestro Tim Burton. With a cast milking every sinister nuance, his clever revision of Washington Irving's timeless tale of terror enlists the classic retro look of Hammer's golden horror era to great effect. Johnny Depp, sporting a clipped English accent, is brilliant as radical-thinking police constable Ichabod Crane, sent to the small Dutch community of Sleepy Hollow to investigate three mysterious beheadings the locals are blaming on the ghost of the legendary Headless Horseman. AJ DVD

Johnny Depp *Ichabod Crane* • Christina Ricci *Katrina Van Tassel* • Miranda Richardson *Lady Van Tassel/Crone* • Michael Gambon *Baltus Van Tassel* • Casper Van Dien *Brom Van Brunt* • Jeffrey Jones *Reverend Steenwyck* • Richard Griffiths *Magistrate Philipse* • Christopher Walken *Hessian Horseman* ■ *Dir* Tim Burton • *Scr* Andrew Kevin Walker, from a story by Kevin Yagher, Andrew Kevin Walker, from the story *The Legend of Sleepy Hollow* by Washington Irving • *Cinematographer* Emmanuel Lubezki • *Production Designer* Rick Heinrichs • *Set Decorator* Peter Young

The Slender Thread ★★★

Drama 1965 · US · BW · 98mins

Sidney Poitier stars in this tense little thriller as a volunteer social worker trying to locate Anne Bancroft who's taken a drugs overdose. Based upon an actual incident, what led this wife and mother to take such desperate steps is told in flashback. In his feature debut, director Sydney Pollack concentrates on the telephoned interchange between the two principals, and the suspense that the conversation generates keeps this race against time engrossing. TH

Sidney Poitier *Alan Newell* • Anne Bancroft *Inga Dyson* • Telly Savalas *Dr Coburn* • Steven Hill *Mark Dyson* • Indus Arthur *Marion* • Greg Jarvis *Chris Dyson* • Edward Asner *Det Judd Ridley* • Dabney Coleman *Charlie* ■ *Dir* Sydney Pollack • *Scr* Stirling Silliphant, from the story *Decision To Die* in *Life* magazine by Shana Alexander

Sleuth ★★★★ 15

Mystery 1972 · UK · Colour · 138mins

Both leading players in this mystery were nominated for the best actor Oscar. Neither Michael Caine nor Laurence Olivier won, but they surely had their reward in the fun they had in making this engrossing sleight of hand from playwright Anthony Shaffer. As theatrical duplicity inevitably packs more of a punch than its cinematic counterpart, the impact of the elaborate role-playing is weakened by its translation to the screen. However, the corkscrew plot and the delicious hamming of the leads ensure that it still remains a thundering good watch. DP. Contains some swearing and sexual references. DVD

Laurence Olivier *Andrew Wyke* • Michael Caine *Milo Tindle* ■ *Dir* Joseph L Mankiewicz • *Scr* Anthony Shaffer, from his play

Sliding Doors ★★★ 15

Romantic fantasy comedy
1997 · UK/US · Colour · 95mins

If you could live your life again, would you do it differently? In this lightweight British comedy directed by Peter Howitt, Gwyneth Paltrow plays out two different scenarios after she misses/doesn't miss a Tube train home. In one reality she finds out her boyfriend is a two-timing louse, so she leaves him and gets a cute new haircut. In her parallel world the hair is long and boring – very much like her life. Paltrow handles her English accent with ease, and she gets some nice support from John Hannah and John Lynch, but the movie never quite gels. JB. Contains swearing. DVD

Gwyneth Paltrow *Helen* • John Hannah *James* • John Lynch *Gerry* • Jeanne Tripplehorn *Lydia* • Zara Turner *Anna* • Douglas McFerran *Russell* • Paul Brightwell *Clive* • Nina Young *Claudia* • Virginia McKenna *James's mother* ■ *Dir/Scr* Peter Howitt

S

A Slight Case of Murder ★★★ U

Crime comedy 1938 · US · BW · 86mins

This terrific fast-paced Warner Bros movie, provides a knockout role for Edward G Robinson as the bootlegging hood left high and dry at the end of Prohibition. Robinson hogs the picture, though there's a very funny climax during which four corpses have all the best moments. This was based on a popular Broadway play by Damon Runyon and Howard Lindsay, and the theatrical structure does show through at times, but the marvellous cast doesn't let you dwell on it for a second. The studio remade this in 1952 as *Stop! You're Killing Me.* TS

Edward G Robinson *Remy Marko* • Jane Bryan *Mary Marko* • Willard Parker *Dick Whitewood* • Ruth Donnelly *Nora Marko* • Allen Jenkins *Mike* • John Litel *Post* • Eric Stanley *Ritter* • Margaret Hamilton *Mrs Cagle* ■ *Dir* Lloyd Bacon • *Scr* Earl Baldwin, Joseph Schrank, from the play by Damon Runyon, Howard Lindsay

A Slight Case of Murder ★★★ 15

Detective comedy thriller
1999 · US · Colour · 89mins

William H Macy stars as a film critic seeking to conceal his involvement in the accidental death of his lover. Having tailored the tale (as co-writer) to his own strengths, Macy turns in a splendidly astute performace. Shifting from speeches to camera to lectures on the conventions of *film noir*, he manipulates everyone around him, including blackmailing private eye James Cromwell and cop Adam Arkin. Occasionally glib and self-satisfied, this TV movie is never anything less than intriguing and entertaining. DP [video]

William H Macy *Terry Thorpe* • Adam Arkin *Det Fred Stapelli* • Felicity Hoffman *Kit Wannamaker* • James Cromwell *John Edgerson* • Julia Campbell *Patricia Stapelli* ■ *Dir* Steven Schachter • *Scr* William H Macy, Steven Schachter, from a novel by Donald E Westlake

Slightly Dangerous ★★ U

Comedy 1943 · US · BW · 94mins

At this point in her career, Lana Turner had already successfully co-starred with Clark Gable and Robert Taylor, and could afford to relax in this tosh about a waitress who lies about her origins. MGM was preparing the definitive waitress movie for Turner, but in the end it was Judy Garland who made *The Harvey Girls*, leaving Turner to find everlasting notoriety with *The Postman Always Rings Twice*. TS

Lana Turner *Peggy Evans/Carol Burden/Narrator* • Robert Young (1) *Bob Stuart* • Walter Brennan *Cornelius Burden* • Dame May Whitty *Baba* • Eugene Pallette *Durstin* • Alan Mowbray *English gentleman* • Florence Bates *Mrs Roanoke-Brooke* • Howard Freeman *Mr Quill* ■ *Dir* Wesley Ruggles • *Scr* Charles Lederer, George Oppenheimer, from a story by Ian McLellan Hunter, Aileen Hamilton

Slightly French ★★

Musical comedy 1949 · US · BW · 81mins

In this take on *Pygmalion*, a Brooklyn hoochy-cooch dancer (Dorothy Lamour) is given a crash-course in conduct by film director Don Ameche, who digs himself out of a hole by passing her off as a quality French actress. Smoothly directed by Douglas Sirk and played with pleasing nonchalance by the stars, it's a slightly good idea, slightly amusing, and bears a slight resemblance to *Let's Fall in Love* (1934) – hardly surprising, since it's a makeover of that film's story. RK

Dorothy Lamour *Mary O'Leary/Rochelle Olivier* • Don Ameche *John Gayle* • Janis Carter *Louisa Gayle* • Willard Parker *Douglas Hyde* • Adele Jergens *Yvonne La Tour* • Jeanne Manet *Nicolette* ■ *Dir* Douglas Sirk • *Scr* Karen De Wolf, from a story by Herbert Fields

Slightly Honorable ★★

Mystery 1939 · US · BW · 85mins

Suspected of murder, lawyer Pat O'Brien determines to track down the real killer. He eventually does so with the help of Broderick Crawford and uncovers the villainy of corrupt politician Edward Arnold. Heavily populated with corpses, suspects and jokes – several of them delivered by ace wisecracker Eve Arden – this comedy thriller veers uncertainly between laughter and suspense, with the former winning to the detriment of the latter. Tay Garnett directs, with a large cast of supporting players. RK

Pat O'Brien *John Webb* • Edward Arnold *Vincent Cushing* • Broderick Crawford *Russ Sampson* • Ruth Terry *Ann Seymour* • Claire Dodd *Alma Brehmer* ■ *Dir* Tay Garnett • *Scr* Ken Englund, John Hunter Lay, Robert Tallman, from the novel *Send Another Coffin* by Frank G Presnell

Slightly Scarlet ★★★

Crime drama 1956 · US · Colour · 92mins

In the dying days of RKO following Howard Hughes's ownership, producer Benedict Bogeaus mounted a series of westerns and melodramas using up leftover sets and contract artists, glossily directed by the talented veteran Allan Dwan. This is one of the better examples, a crime drama about a guy (John Payne) involved with a pair of redheaded sisters (Rhonda Fleming and Arlene Dahl), hence the title. The corruption of power theme is well handled, and Dahl is terrific as the slightly sozzled sister. TS

John Payne *Ben Grace* • Rhonda Fleming *June Lyons* • Arlene Dahl *Dorothy Lyons* • Kent Taylor *Frank Jansen* • Ted De Corsia *Sol Caspar* • Lance Fuller *Gauss* • Buddy Baer *Lenhardt* ■ *Dir* Allan Dwan • *Scr* Robert Blees, from the novel *Love's Lovely Counterfeit* by James M Cain

Slim ★★★

Drama 1937 · US · BW · 86mins

A young Henry Fonda is a farm boy who realises his dream of becoming an electric lineman when hardened expert Pat O'Brien makes him his protégé (later his partner) and exposes him to the addiction of a dangerous and wandering life on the pylons. Ray Enright directs this tightly made movie that holds the attention, despite a beginning that plays like a propaganda film for the men who risk their lives. RK

Pat O'Brien *Red Blayd* • Henry Fonda *Slim* • Margaret Lindsay *Cally* • Stuart Erwin *Stumpy* • J Farrell MacDonald *Pop Traver* • Jane Wyman *Stumpy's girlfriend* ■ *Dir* Ray Enright • *Scr* William Wister Haines, from his novel

Sling Blade ★★★★ 15

Drama 1995 · US · Colour · 129mins

This shockingly moving drama brought debutant director Billy Bob Thornton to international attention. In addition to winning an Oscar for his screenplay, he also drew a best actor nomination for his mesmerising performance as the hesitant, seemingly harmless handyman who befriends a lonely boy on being released from the secure hospital where he'd been held for 25 years after murdering his mother and her beau. With unseen sparks flying around an emotional powder keg, this is darkly comic, superbly acted and utterly compelling. DP. Contains violence and swearing.

Billy Bob Thornton *Karl Childers* • Dwight Yoakam *Doyle Hargraves* • JT Walsh *Charles Bushman* • John Ritter *Vaughan Cunningham* • Lucas Black *Frank Wheatley* • Natalie Canerday *Linda Wheatley* • James Hampton *Jerry Woolridge* • Jim Jarmusch *Dairy Queen boy* ■ *Dir/Scr* Billy Bob Thornton

The Slingshot ★★★ 12

Biographical drama
1993 · Swe · Colour · 98mins

Touching upon such topics as sex, sibling rivalry, poverty, royalty and anti-Semitism, this evocation of growing up in 1920s Stockholm is an incredibly busy film. Stellan Skarsgård contributes some uncompromising support and Jesper Salen looks suitably put-upon as the incomprehending son of a lame socialist and the punchbag brother of an aspiring boxer. But Ake Sandgren's episodic approach to his fact-based material means that the action never really gains momentum. DP. In Swedish with English subtitles. [video]

Jesper Salen *Roland Schutt* • Stellan Skarsgård *Fritiof Schutt* • Basia Frydman *Zipa Schutt* • Niclas Olund *Bertil Schutt* ■ *Dir* Ake Sandgren • *Scr* Ake Sandgren, from the autobiography by Roland Schutt

The Slipper and the Rose ★★ U

Musical fantasy 1976 · UK · Colour · 136mins

The story of Cinderella is blown out of all proportion in this lavish British musical that has neither the magic nor the songs to turn it into the extravaganza that director Bryan Forbes obviously had in mind. Gemma Craven has the voice but not the allure to give Cinders a fairy-tale sheen, and Richard Chamberlain looks a little long in the tooth to play the prince. However, Edith Evans and Kenneth More steal scenes with ease and Annette Crosbie is a wonderfully world-weary fairy godmother. DP [video] DVD

Richard Chamberlain *Prince* • Gemma Craven *Cinderella* • Annette Crosbie *Fairy Godmother* • Edith Evans *Dowager Queen* • Christopher Gable *John* • Michael Hordern *King* • Margaret Lockwood *Stepmother* • Kenneth More *Lord Chamberlain* ■ *Dir* Bryan Forbes • *Scr* Bryan Forbes, Robert B Sherman, Richard M Sherman

Slippery When Wet ★★★

Documentary 1958 · US · Colour · 43mins

Having been suitably impressed by an 8mm short that Bruce Brown had shot while stationed on a submarine in Hawaii, Californian surfboard salesman Dale Velzy presented the 20-year-old lifeguard with $5,000 to make a full-length surfing movie. Armed with a 16mm camera and 50 reels of film, Brown flew five buddies to Oahu to launch a career that was to do as much for riding the waves as the Beach Boys. While Brown's self-edited footage is rough 'n' ready, it still has that endless summer feel. DP [video] DVD

Dir Bruce Brown

Slipstream ★★ PG

Science-fiction adventure
1989 · US/UK · Colour · 87mins

The forgotten man of *Star Wars*, Mark Hamill, attempted to get his career airborne again with a return to the sci-fi genre. However, this muddled affair barely got off the ground itself. The concept – a post-apocalyptic world where the favoured form of transportation is the glider – has potential, but director Steven Lisberger never makes up his mind whether this is an escapist fantasy or a more cerebral affair. JF [video]

Mark Hamill *Tasker* • Bob Peck *Byron* • Bill Paxton *Matt Owen* • Kitty Aldridge *Belitski* • Tony Allen *Bartender* • Susan Leong *Abigail* • F Murray Abraham *Cornelius* • Ben Kingsley *Avatar* ■ *Dir* Steven Lisberger • *Scr* Tony Kayden, Charles Pogue, Steven Lisberger, from a story by Bill Bauer

Slither ★★★ 15

Comedy thriller 1973 · US · Colour · 92mins

Easy Rider, *Vanishing Point* and *Two-Lane Blacktop* started a vogue for counterculture road movies. *Slither* took it to extremes, a comedy thriller that has the frenetic absurdity of a *Roadrunner* cartoon and a stash of stolen loot as the reason for it all. MGM, wanting out of its cosy middle-American image, hired the combustible James Caan and surrounded him with oddball characters from the likes of Peter Boyle and Sally Kellerman. Played largely deadpan and set in mobile home parks and bingo parlours, it's a charming mess. AT [video]

James Caan *Dick Kanipsia* • Peter Boyle *Barry Fenaka* • Sally Kellerman *Kitty Kopetzky* • Louise Lasser *Mary Fenaka* • Allen Garfield *Vincent J Palmer* • Richard B Shull *Harry Moss* ■ *Dir* Howard Zieff • *Scr* WD Richter

Sliver ★★★ 18

Erotic thriller 1993 · US · Colour · 103mins

Sharon Stone consolidated her reputation as Hollywood's hottest sex symbol in another steamy thriller from the pen of Joe Eszterhas, who also scripted her breakthrough hit *Basic Instinct*. Stone is the rather unlikely book editor who moves into an apartment block where the tenants have a worrying habit of moving to the morgue rather than new residences. She's then pursued by two of her neighbours, the oafish author Tom Berenger and the mysterious William Baldwin, either one of whom could be a murderer or a voyeur. Director Phillip Noyce cranks up the tension, and there are some pretty raunchy sex scenes. JF [video]

Sharon Stone *Carly Norris* • William Baldwin *Zeke Hawkins* • Tom Berenger *Jack Lansford* • Polly Walker *Vida Jordan* • Colleen Camp *Judy* • Amanda Foreman *Samantha* • Martin Landau *Alex* • CCH Pounder *Lieutenant Victoria Hendrix* ■ *Dir* Phillip Noyce • *Scr* Joe Eszterhas, from the novel by Ira Levin

Slogans ★★★

Satirical political drama
2001 · Albania/Fr · Colour · 90mins

At the height of prime minister Enver Hoxha's tyranny, cinema had little part to play in Albanian life. So the medium exacts its revenge here with this gentle satire on the crudity of propaganda in a Stalinist state. While openly mocking the petty bureaucrats who imposed the policy of constructing hillside slogans out of whitewashed stones, director Gjergj Xhuvani commends the spirit of those who did the donkey work and applauds those who questioned the usefulness of the enterprise. DP. In Albanian with English subtitles.

Artur Gorishti *Andre* • Birce Hasko *Sabaf* • Niko Kanxheri *Selman* ■ *Dir* Gjergj Xhuvani • *Scr* Alicka Ylljet, Yves Hanchar

Slow Dancing in the Big City ★

Drama 1978 · US · Colour · 110mins

Journalist Paul Sorvino falls in love with ballerina Anne Ditchburn while performing his Good Samaritan act on an eight-year-old street urchin. Connoisseurs of the soap-opera-as-social-tract won't be surprised to learn that Ditchburn's dancing days are numbered and that the kid has a drug problem. The tear-jerking bathos gets piled on in ever increasing measures until the absolutely breathtaking ending. You have been warned. AJ

Paul Sorvino *Lou Friedlander* • Anne Ditchburn *Sarah Gantz* • Nicolas Coster *David Fillmore* •

Anita Dangler *Franny* • Thaao Penghlis *Christopher* • Linda Selman *Barbara Bass* ■ *Dir* John G Avildsen • *Scr* Barra Grant

Slow Motion ★★★ 18

Drama 1980 · Fr/Swi · Colour · 84mins

This was Godard's first bona fide movie for ten years, the previous decade having been dedicated to increasingly impoverished and experimental video, documentary and TV work. There is nod to the autobiographical – a character who's a washed-up film-maker called Godard – but it's also about the director's pet themes of prostitution, exploitation and cultural politics. No Godard movie is ever conventional, and this one isn't either, but the presence of major stars is oddly reassuring and shows the respect Godard enjoys among the French film community. AT. In French with English subtitles. [VIDEO] DVD

Isabelle Huppert *Isabelle Rivière* • Jacques Dutronc *Paul Godard* • Nathalie Baye *Denise Rimbaud* • Anna Baldaccini *Isabelle's sister* • Fred Personne *1st client* • Roland Amstutz *2nd client* • Nicole Jacquet *Woman* ■ *Dir* Jean-Luc Godard • *Scr* Jean-Luc Godard, Jean-Claude Carrière, Anne-Marie Miéville

The Slugger's Wife ★ 15

Romantic comedy
1985 · US · Colour · 99mins

Any cinematic expectations that might be raised by the combination of Neil Simon and baseball are quickly dispelled in this dismal comedy that fails to provide either laughs or romance. Rebecca De Mornay looks jaded in the role of a rock singer who (inexplicably) falls for the crude charms of baseball star Michael O'Keefe. They marry and are soon beset by career conflicts, not to mention ridiculous baseball double entendres. A waste of a good cast and director. LH [VIDEO]

Michael O'Keefe *Darryl Palmer* • Rebecca De Mornay *Debby Palmer* • Martin Ritt *Burly DeVito* • Randy Quaid *Moose Granger* • Cleavant Derricks *Manny Alvarado* • Lisa Langlois *Aline Cooper* • Loudon Wainwright III *Gary* ■ *Dir* Hal Ashby • *Scr* Neil Simon

Slumber Party '57 ★★

Comedy drama 1976 · US · Colour · 88mins

Six high school girls at a slumber party recount how they lost their virginity via some variable flashbacks – the best revolving around making a movie. Sloppy direction and continuity matches the Golden Oldie soundtrack which is mainly comprised of sixties hits. Debra Winger makes an inauspicious film debut, appearing topless and suggestively eating a banana. A mess, but not devoid of entertainment value. AJ

Noelle North *Angie* • Bridget Holloman *Bonnie May* • Debra Winger *Debbie* • Mary Ann Appleseth *Jo Ann* • Cheryl Smith *Sherry* • Janet Wood *Smitty* ■ • *Scr* Frank Farmer, from a story by William A Levey

The Slumber Party Massacre ★ 18

Horror 1982 · US · Colour · 76mins

Given the feminist credentials of author Rita Mae Brown and director Amy Jones, the most shocking thing about this addition to the stalk-and-slash cycle is that it's just as crass and exploitative as most other low-budget entries. Student Michele Michaels is holding a slumber party at her house while her parents are away. Homicidal gate-crasher Michael Villela spoils the fun, decimating her friends. Gory, stupid and sexist. AJ

Michele Michaels *Trish Devereaux* • Robin Stille *Valerie* • Michael Villela *Russ Thorn* • Andree Honore *Jackie* • Debra Deliso *Kim* ■ *Dir* Amy Jones [Amy Holden Jones] • *Scr* Rita Mae Brown

Slums of Beverly Hills ★★★★ 15

Comedy drama 1998 · US · Colour · 87mins

Writer/director Tamara Jenkins made her feature debut with this quirky comedy drama about the bizarreness of growing up. The Abramowitz family live on the slum fringes of Beverly Hills, and we see their problematic existence through the eyes of daughter Natasha Lyonne, who has to deal with her two brothers and a dad (Alan Arkin, superb as usual) trying hard to keep it all together. While all the family and their various acquaintances are both funny and well-realised, the film belongs to Lyonne, who gives a terrific turn as the girl finding pubescent life a very strange experience indeed. JB. Contains swearing, sex scenes and nudity. [VIDEO] DVD

Alan Arkin *Murray Abramowitz* • Natasha Lyonne *Vivian Abramowitz* • Kevin Corrigan *Eliot* • Jessica Walter *Doris* • Rita Moreno *Belle* • David Krumholtz *Ben Abramowitz* • Eli Marienthal *Rickey Abramowitz* • Carl Reiner *Mickey Abramowitz* • Marisa Tomei *Rita* • Mena Suvari *Rachel* ■ *Dir/Scr* Tamara Jenkins

Smack and Thistle ★★★

Crime drama 1989 · UK · Colour · 90mins

This intelligent thriller provides a perceptive (and often depressing) analysis of Britain at the end of the 1980s. In the light of recent revelations about sleaze in high places, this story about an ex-con who stumbles across a briefcase full of dodgy deals has an added pertinence, with the camera lens almost turning into a crystal ball. However, writer/director Tunde Ikoli might have resisted a sensationalist romantic subplot that slows down the action without making any telling social point. DP

Charlie Caine *Abel* • Rosalind Bennett *Elizabeth* • Patrick Malahide *Dirk-Brown* • Geoffrey Palmer *Sir Horace Wimbol* • John Elmes *Edward Tulip* • James Saxon *Henry Wilks* • Connie Booth *Ms Kane* ■ *Dir/Scr* Tunde Ikoli

The Small Back Room ★★★ PG

Second World War drama
1949 · UK · BW · 102mins

After the sumptuous theatrics of *Black Narcissus* and *The Red Shoes*, Michael Powell and Emeric Pressburger returned to the muted naturalism of their earlier collaborations for this adaptation of Nigel Balchin's novel about scientists feeling the strain in wartime. The pair were obviously uninspired by the lengthy passages of chat in which the backroom boffins bicker about their latest inventions, but their masterful use of camera angles and cutting gives the finale an unbearable tension. DP [VIDEO] DVD

David Farrar *Sammy Rice* • Kathleen Byron *Susan* • Jack Hawkins *RB Waring* • Leslie Banks *Colonel Holland* • Cyril Cusack *Corporal Taylor* • Robert Morley *Minister* • Emrys Jones *Joe* • Renée Asherson *ATS Corporal* ■ *Dir* Michael Powell, Emeric Pressburger • *Scr* Michael Powell, Emeric Pressburger, from the novel by Nigel Balchin

Small Change ★★ PG

Drama 1976 · Fr · Colour · 102mins

François Truffaut's anecdotal return to the charmed world of childhood suffers from protracted bouts of mawkishness and inconsequence. The linked episodes involving Geory Desmouceaux (a boy caring for his disabled father) and Philippe Goldman (a tearaway beaten by his parents) are the best developed, but even these are tainted by the moralising of their teacher, Jean-François Stévenin. DP. A French language film. DVD

Geory Desmouceaux *Patrick* • Philippe Goldman *Julien* • Claudio Deluca *Mathieu Deluca* • Franck Deluca • Richard Golfier • Laurent Devlaeminck *Laurent Riffle* • Jean-François Stévenin *Jean-François Richet* ■ *Dir* François Truffaut • *Scr* François Truffaut, Suzanne Schiffman

A Small Circle of Friends ★★

Drama 1980 · US · Colour · 112mins

In an unremarkable period drama, three bosom buddies live and love their way through the campus unrest of an American college during the 1960s. Karen Allen, Brad Davis and Shelley Long lead a strong cast, but there's little they can really do with patchy material that never quite gels. DA

Brad Davis *Leonardo Da Vinci Rizzo* • Karen Allen *Jessica Bloom* • Jameson Parker *Nick Baxter* • Shelley Long *Alice* • John Friedrich *Alex Haddox* • Gary Springer *Greenblatt* • Harry Caesar *Jimmy* • Nan Martin *Mrs Baxter* ■ *Dir* Rob Cohen • *Scr* Ezra Sacks

Small Faces ★★★★ 15

Drama 1995 · UK · Colour · 104mins

Gillies MacKinnon's excellent memoir of late-1960s Glasgow was co-written with his producer brother, Billy. Iain Robertson is absolutely superb as the razor-sharp teenager unsure which of his brothers is the best role model – emotionally stunted hardcase JS Duffy or art student Joseph McFadden. Whether running with street gangs, suffering the agonies of a family get-together or driving mother Clare Higgins to distraction, Robertson never fails to convince, which can't always be said for some of the period details. DP. Contains violence, swearing and nudity. [VIDEO] DVD

Iain Robertson *Lex Maclean* • Joseph McFadden *Alan Maclean* • JS Duffy *Bobby Maclean* • Laura Fraser *Joanne MacGowan* • Garry Sweeney *Charlie Sloan* • Clare Higgins *Lorna Maclean* • Kevin McKidd *Malky Johnson* ■ *Dir* Gillies MacKinnon • *Scr* Gillies MacKinnon, Billy MacKinnon

Small Hotel ★★ U

Comedy 1957 · UK · BW · 59mins

Belligerent Cockney character Gordon Harker plays a waiter refusing to be dismissed from his job at the hotel of the title. In this, his penultimate film, japes with guests and other staff make do for the plot. This is a pared-down, low-budget film version of a stage farce (in which Harker also starred), which is no great shakes as comedy, but interesting as a vehicle built around a much-loved British star at the end of his career. DM

Gordon Harker *Albert* • Marie Lohr *Mrs Samson-Fox* • John Loder *Mr Finch* • Irene Handl *Mrs Gammon* • Janet Munro *Effie* • Billie Whitelaw *Caroline Mallet* ■ *Dir* David MacDonald • *Scr* Wilfred Eades, from a play by Rex Frost

Small Soldiers ★★★ PG

Fantasy action adventure
1998 · US · Colour · 105mins

Action Man-type figures fitted with deadly microprocessors go on menacing manoeuvres in director Joe Dante's *Gremlins*-meets-*Toy Story* war fantasy. The slick professionalism and technical brilliance keep the awkward mixture of comedy and carnage from becoming too uncomfortable an experience. Crafty nods to classic war films such as *Patton*, the creepy Gwendy Doll sequence and the GI Joes being voiced by the likes of Tommy Lee Jones, Ernest Borgnine and Bruce Dern also help maintain the interest for adults as well as youngsters. AJ. Contains violence, swearing. [VIDEO] DVD

Denis Leary *Gil Mars* • Kirsten Dunst *Christy Fimple* • Gregory Smith *Alan Abernathy* • Ann Magnuson *Irene Abernathy* • Phil Hartman *Phil Fimple* • Frank Langella *Archer* • Tommy Lee Jones *Major Chip Hazard* • Ernest Borgnine *Kip Killagin* • Bruce Dern *Link Static* • George Kennedy *Brick Bazooka* • Clint Walker *Nick Nitro* • Sarah Michelle Gellar *Gwendy doll* • Christina Ricci *Gwendy doll* ■ *Dir* Joe Dante • *Scr* Gavin Scott, Adam Rifkin, Ted Elliott, Terry Rossio

Small Time ★★★ 18

Crime drama 1990 · US · BW · 58mins

Structured as a five-act morality play, this is an uncompromising study of New York street life. There were so many movies about inner-city problems in the early 1990s that the abrasive attitudes of the participants became as clichéd as having rap hits on the soundtrack. But here writer/director Norman Loftis plays fast and loose with a variety of styles to produce a compelling portrait of Richard Barboza, a kid driven to crime to survive and now suffering the consequences of his errant lifestyle. DP. Contains violence and swearing. [VIDEO]

Richard Barboza *Vince Williams* • Carolyn Kinebrew *Vicki* ■ *Dir/Scr* Norman Loftis

Small Time Crooks ★★★ PG

Comedy 2000 · US · Colour · 94mins

Woody Allen drops a couple of social rungs to lampoon his hermetically sealed Manhattan surroundings in this throwback to his earlier wisecracking comedies. There's much to enjoy in Tracey Ullman's splendid performance as the *nouveau riche* cookie tycoon who seeks acceptance by taking a culture crash-course with highbrow Hugh Grant. Allen's inverted snobbery is strewn with entertainingly sulky acid drops and Elaine May's ditzy turn as Ullman's cousin is priceless. It's a shame, however, that Allen the director adopts such a patronising approach to his proletarian characters while aiming to expose the pretensions of the chattering classes. DP [VIDEO] DVD

Woody Allen *Ray Winkler* • Tracey Ullman *Frenchy Winkler* • Hugh Grant *David* • Elaine May *May* • Tony Darrow *Tommy* • George Grizzard *George Blint* • Jon Lovitz *Benny* • Michael Rapaport *Denny* • Elaine Stritch *Chi Chi Potter* ■ *Dir/Scr* Woody Allen

Small Time Obsession ★★ 15

Crime drama 2000 · UK · Colour · 103mins

Refusing to run his dad's Polish deli, greyhound-fancying Alex King drifts into villainy with his Mob-connected mucker, Jason Merrells, who also happens to have impregnated Juliette Caton, the girl King has always secretly adored. First-time writer/director Piotr Szkopiak may have found an unusual backdrop for this journey down south London's mean streets, but best buddies have been falling out over crime and women since the silent days, and much more interestingly than this. The dialogue is delivered as badly as it's written and the action is clumsily staged. DP [VIDEO] DVD

Alex King *Michael* • Juliette Caton *Ali* • Jason Merrells *Chris* • Oliver Young *Steve* • Richard Banks *John* ■ *Dir/Scr* Piotr Szkopiak

Small Town Girl ★★

Drama 1936 · US · BW · 105mins

Robert Taylor had scored so well as a wastrel turned brain surgeon in *Magnificent Obsession* that he was obvious casting for the role in this romantic drama of a wealthy surgeon who marries Janet Gaynor's small-town girl while drunk. Jean Harlow, originally cast, would have given the proceedings more zest and it's a rising young actor called James Stewart who stands out

S

in the thankless part of Gaynor's beau. Director William A Wellman, who fell out with Gaynor, brings no particular distinctiveness to the picture. AE

Janet Gaynor *Kay Brannan* • Robert Taylor (1) *Bob Dakin* • Binnie Barnes *Priscilla* • James Stewart *Elmer* • Lewis Stone *Dr Dakin* • Elizabeth Patterson *Ma Brannan* • Frank Craven *Pa Brannan* ■ *Dir* William A Wellman • *Scr* John Lee Mahin, Edith Fitzgerald, Frances Goodrich, Albert Hackett, from the novel by Ben Ames Williams

A Small Town in Texas ★★ 15

Action drama 1976 · US · Colour · 92mins

A car chase flick, directed by Jack Starrett the previous year crossed the chase movie with *The Exorcist* and came up with *Race with the Devil*. Timothy Bottoms plays an ex-con, returning home to his white trash girlfriend, Susan George, and their baby son. Bottoms also swears revenge on the redneck cop who busted him, Bo Hopkins, which results in a lot of revving up and wasted gasoline. AT

Timothy Bottoms *Poke* • Susan George *Mary Lee* • Bo Hopkins *Duke* • Art Hindle *Boogie* • John Karlen *Lenny* • Morgan Woodward *CJ Crane* • Patrice Rohmer *Trudy* ■ *Dir* Jack Starrett • *Scr* William Norton

The Small Voice ★★★

Thriller 1948 · UK · BW · 83mins

Howard Keel made his screen debut in this tense adaptation. Although he eventually proves to have a streak of decency, Keel is imposingly menacing as a convict who exploits the charity of James Donald and Valerie Hobson to hold them and a couple of children hostage until he and confederates David Greene and Michael Balfour can make good their escape. His performance led to a contract with MGM and typecasting as a singing hunk that would prevent him from playing an equally challenging role for many years. DP

Valerie Hobson *Eleanor Byrne* • James Donald *Murray Byrne* • Harold Keel [Howard Keel] *Boke* • David Greene *Jim* • Michael Balfour *Frankie* • Joan Young *Potter* • Angela Fouldes *Jenny* • Glynn Dearman *Ken* ■ *Dir* Fergus McDonell • *Scr* George Barraud, Derek Neame, Julian Orde, from the novel by Robert Westerby

The Small World of Sammy Lee ★★

Comedy drama 1963 · UK · BW · 108mins

This fast-moving drama, expanded from a BBC TV play, finds Anthony Newley as a smart-aleck strip-show compère, spending a frantic night trying to raise cash to pay off his gambling debts. Newley was involved with several offbeat and nearly forgotten projects, but this is worth seeing for a string of appearances by familiar British TV faces. The black-and-white photography makes the suitably grim Soho locations even grimmer. JG

Anthony Newley *Sammy Lee* • Julia Foster *Patsy* • Robert Stephens *Gerry* • Wilfrid Brambell *Harry* • Warren Mitchell *Lou* • Miriam Karlin *Milly* • Roy Kinnear *Lucky Dave* ■ *Dir* Ken Hughes • *Scr* Ken Hughes, from his TV play *Sammy*

The Smallest Show on Earth ★★★★ U

Comedy 1957 · UK · BW · 82mins

In praise of fleapits everywhere, this charming comedy will bring back happy memories for anyone who pines for the days when going to the pictures meant something more than being conveyor-belted in and out of a soulless multiplex. Fondly scripted by John Eldridge and William Rose and deftly directed by Basil Dearden, it stars Bill Travers and Virginia McKenna as a couple who inherit a crumbling cinema. The cast alone makes the movie a must-see, and the sequence in which projectionist Peter Sellers, pianist Margaret Rutherford and doorman Bernard Miles relive the glories of the silent era is adorable. DP DVD

Virginia McKenna *Jean Spenser* • Bill Travers *Matt Spenser* • Peter Sellers *Percy Quill* • Margaret Rutherford *Mrs Fazackalee* • Leslie Phillips *Robin Carter* • Bernard Miles *Old Tom* • Sidney James *Mr Hogg* ■ *Dir* Basil Dearden • *Scr* William Rose, John Eldridge, from a story by William Rose

Smalltime ★★★ 18

Comedy drama
1996 · UK · Colour and BW · 58mins

It was *TwentyFourSeven* that propelled Nottingham director Shane Meadows into the mainstream, but this earlier work, made on half a shoestring, is a welcome introduction to his raw, gritty and amusing universe. By turns amateurish and professional, funny and depressing, it follows the lives of a bunch of small-time crooks (all wearing the most ridiculous cheap wigs) whose botched attempts at crime make an art form out of incompetence. A sweet-and-sour suburban satire that's touching in a grotesque way. AJ. Contains swearing.

Mat Hand *Malc* • Dena Smiles *Kate* • Shane Meadows *Jumbo* • Gena Kawecka *Ruby* • Jimmy Hynd *Willy* • Leon Lammond *Bets* • Tim Cunningham *Lenny the Fence* • Dominic Dillon *Mad Terrance* ■ *Dir/Scr* Shane Meadows

Smart Blonde ★★★

Detective comedy drama
1936 · US · BW · 59mins

This is the first in Warner Bros nine-film franchise inspired by the crime stories of magazine writer Frederick Nebel, in which the intrepid reporter was actually a man. But Glenda Farrell sparks as the wiseacre news ace who seems to solve every case before lieutenant Barton MacLane (who's also her fiancée) and his doltish sidekick, Tom Kennedy. Lola Lane and Paul Kelly assumed the roles for *Torchy Blane in Panama*, while the series finale teamed Jane Wyman and Allen Jenkins. But the original, about the killing of a nightclub boss, was the best. DP

Glenda Farrell *Torchy Blane* • Barton MacLane *Steve McBride* • Winifred Shaw *Dolly Ireland* • Addison Richards *Fitz Mularkay* • David Carlyle [Robert Paige] *Louie Friel* • Craig Reynolds *Tom Carney* • Jane Wyman *Dixie* • Tom Kennedy *Gahagan* ■ *Dir* Frank McDonald • *Scr* Kenneth Gamet, Don Ryan, from a story by Frederick Nebel

Smart Money ★★★

Crime drama 1931 · US · BW · 83mins

This is as tough as they come, and, incidentally, the only movie to co-star those two gangster heavyweights James Cagney and Edward G Robinson. Robinson plays a lucky small-time barber who hits it big, and Cagney is his mate. Both actors knew one another from the New York stage, and their naturalistic delivery owes much to their theatre background. Directed by Alfred E Green, this gambling-racket crime drama also features Boris Karloff. TS

Edward G Robinson *Nick Venezelos* • James Cagney *Jack* • Evalyn Knapp *Irene Graham* • Ralf Harolde *Sleepy Sam* • Noel Francis *Marie* • Margaret Livingston *District attorney's girl* • Maurice Black *Greek barber* • Boris Karloff *Sport Williams* ■ *Dir* Alfred E Green • *Scr* Kubec Glasmon, John Bright, Lucien Hubbard, Joseph Jackson, from the story *The Idol* by Lucien Hubbard, Joseph Jackson

Smart Woman ★★

Drama 1948 · US · BW · 93mins

Constance Bennett's last fling as a star provided her with this last leading role as a resourceful defence lawyer pitted against Brian Aherne's special prosecutor – her lover – in an election fraud trial. Bennett chose cameraman Stanley Cortez for the glamour lighting he had given Susan Hayward in *Smash-Up, the Story of a Woman* but most of the budget seems to have gone on her wardrobe by Adrian. AE

Brian Aherne *Robert Larrimore* • Constance Bennett *Paula Rogers* • Barry Sullivan *Frank McCoy* • Michael O'Shea *Johnny Simons, Reporter* • James Gleason *Sam Corkle* ■ *Dir* Edward A Blatt • *Scr* Alvah Bessie, Louis Morheim, Herbert Margolis, Adela Rogers St Johns, from the story by Leon Gutterman, Edwin V Westrate

Smash and Grab ★★ U

Detective comedy drama
1937 · UK · BW · 73mins

Jack Buchanan's name is prominent in the credits of this crime comedy as producer and star, but he tries too hard with a confection that exerts little appeal today. He and his frequent musical comedy co-star Elsie Randolph play an investigator and his wife. Randolph does most of the work by gaining employment with the principal suspects behind a spate of jewel robberies, while Buchanan stays in his flat practising jujitsu with the butler. AE

Jack Buchanan *John Forrest* • Elsie Randolph *Alice Forrest* • Arthur Margetson *Malvern* • Antony Holles *Palino* • Edmund Willard *Cappellano* • David Burns *Bellini* ■ *Dir* Tim Whelan • *Scr* Ralph Spence, from a story by Tim Whelan

Smash Palace ★★★★ 18

Drama 1981 · NZ · Colour · 108mins

Among the films that put New Zealand cinema on the map, this is an engrossing study of one man's retreat into despair. Bruno Lawrence gives a painfully truthful performance as the one-time Grand Prix hero whose idyllic life as a mechanic in the middle of nowhere drives his French wife, Anna Jemison, to adultery. Equally impressive is 10-year-old Greer Robson, as the daughter who becomes a pawn in her parents' increasingly bitter wrangle. This deeply disturbing drama was directed by Roger Donaldson, who has yet to achieve anything of comparable power since his arrival in Hollywood. DP. Contains violence, swearing and nudity.

Bruno Lawrence *Al Shaw* • Anna Jemison *Jacqui Shaw* • Greer Robson *Georgie Shaw* • Keith Aberdein *Ray Foley* • Desmond Kelly *Tiny* ■ *Dir* Roger Donaldson • *Scr* Roger Donaldson, Peter Hansard, Bruno Lawrence

Smash Up – the Story of a Woman ★★★

Drama 1947 · US · BW · 103mins

Adapted from a story co-written by the estimable Dorothy Parker, this overblown melodrama seems to have been concocted by putting *A Star Is Born* and *The Lost Weekend* in a cocktail mixer and shaking well. Susan Hayward received an Oscar nomination for her performance as a singer who begins to view the world through the bottom of a glass at the same time as her shiftless husband's showbiz stock begins to rise. Lee Bowman is out of his depth as Hayward's husband, but it's still worth a watch. DP

Susan Hayward *Angie Evans Conway* • Lee Bowman *Ken Conway* • Marsha Hunt *Martha Gray* • Eddie Albert *Steve Anderson* • Carl Esmond *Dr Lorenz* • Carleton Young *Mr Elliott* • Charles D Brown *Mike Dawson* ■ *Dir* Stuart Heisler • *Scr* John Howard Lawson, Lionel Wiggam, from a story by Dorothy Parker, Frank Cavett

Smash-Up Alley ★★ U

Action sports drama
1972 · US · Colour · 77mins

With its fender-bending, full-throttled action, stock-car racing should make excellent movie material. But as everything from *Fireball 500* to *Days of Thunder* proves, it doesn't matter what happens on the track if the dramatic sequences stink. Richard Petty (playing himself) may be an ace behind the wheel, but in front of a camera he looks like a rabbit dazzled by headlights. Darren McGavin adds a touch of steel as his father, but the rest of the cast is suffering from a case of *dramatis mortis*. DP

Darren McGavin *Lee Petty* • Richard Petty • Kathy Brown [Kathie Browne] *Elizabeth Petty* • Noah Beery Jr *Uncle Julie* • Pierre Jalbert *Curtis Cross* • Lynne Marta *Lynda Petty* • LQ Jones *Koler* ■ *Dir/Scr* Edward J Lakso

The Smashing Bird I Used to Know ★★★

Drama 1969 · UK · Colour · 96mins

This prison drama provides an opportunity to see the youthful early careers of Dennis Waterman and Maureen Lipman. It's a rather bizarre tale concerning the murder of Madeline Hinde's mother's boyfriend and the attendant mayhem wreaked on several relationships and individual psyches. They used to crank them out in this mould by the cartload in the 1960s, and this is not the worst example of the genre by any means. Additional interest may come from spotting today's middle-aged sitcom stars. DP

Madeline Hinde *Nicki Johnson* • Renée Asherson *Anne Johnson* • Dennis Waterman *Peter* • Patrick Mower *Harry Spenton* • Faith Brook *Dr Sands* • Maureen Lipman *Sarah* • Derek Fowlds *Geoffrey* • Sheila Steafel *Gilda* • Megs Jenkins *Matron* ■ *Dir* Robert Hartford-Davis • *Scr* John Peacock

Smashing the Rackets ★★

Crime drama 1938 · US · BW · 68mins

This efficient, if undistinguished crime drama was the result of a conscious effort by RKO executives to produce the kind of topical, if sensationalist, fare known as "exploitation". Loosely based on the career of New York DA Thomas E Dewey, this fast-talking insight into underworld machinations and corruption in high places makes racket-busting look easy, as every illegal operation crumbles at the sight of Chester Morris and his team. DP

Chester Morris *Jim Conway* • Frances Mercer *Susan Lane* • Bruce Cabot *Steve Lawrence* • Rita Johnson *Letty Lane* • Donald Douglas [Don Douglas] *Spaulding* • Ben Welden *Whitey Clark* • Edward Pawley *Chin Martin* • Frank M Thomas *Judge Wend* ■ *Dir* Lew Landers • *Scr* Lionel Houser, from a story by Forrest Davis

Smashing Time ★★

Comedy 1967 · UK · Colour · 96mins

The fact that some of the character names come from the poems of Lewis Carroll provides the clue that this Swinging Sixties comedy is trying too hard to be both clever and cool. It's scripted as satire by George Melly, with Lynn Redgrave and Rita Tushingham as the iconoclastic northern lasses trying to gate-crash the fame game. Director Desmond Davis draws some knowing cameos, but seems ill at ease with the slapstick excesses. DP

Rita Tushingham *Brenda* • Lynn Redgrave *Yvonne* • Michael York *Tom Wabe* • Anna Quayle *Charlotte Brilling* • Irene Handl *Mrs Gimble* • Ian Carmichael *Bobby Mome-Rothlan*

• Jeremy Lloyd *Jeremy Tove* • Toni Palmer *Toni* • Arthur Mullard *Café boss* ■ *Dir* Desmond Davis • *Scr* George Melly

Smile ★★★★

Satire 1975 · US · Colour · 112mins

Michael Ritchie's picture records the run-up to and the staging of the horrendous Young American Miss competition in Santa Rosa, California, in which 33 wide-eyed girls subject themselves to personality interviews, dance sessions, photo calls and every other cringe-making ritual known to man. Ritchie's camera is unblinking: it's like a documentary, but it isn't. Bruce Dern is the chief judge, a car salesman, and among the hopefuls are Melanie Griffith and Annette O'Toole. A minor masterpiece of wit and observation. AT. Contains swearing.

Bruce Dern *"Big Bob" Freelander* • Barbara Feldon *Brenda DiCarlo* • Michael Kidd *Tommy French* • Geoffrey Lewis *Wilson Shears* • Nicholas Pryor *Andy DiCarlo* • Colleen Camp *Connie Thompson, "Miss Imperial County"* • Annette O'Toole *Doria Houston, "Miss Anaheim"* • Melanie Griffith *Karen Love, "Miss Simi Valley"* ■ *Dir* Michael Ritchie • *Scr* Jerry Belson

A Smile like Yours ★★ 12

Romantic comedy
1997 · US · Colour · 93mins

Greg Kinnear and Lauren Holly are both miscast here, playing a couple whose happy marriage comes under fire when they realise they can't have children. Their troubles are compounded when Holly suspects Kinnear of beginning an affair. Sadly, their lack of chemistry is palpable. Cameos from Joan Cusack and Shirley MacLaine are entertaining, but the direction is unfocused. LH. Contains swearing and sexual references. [video]

Greg Kinnear *Danny Robertson* • Lauren Holly *Jennifer Robertson* • Joan Cusack *Nancy Tellen* • Jay Thomas *Steve Harris* • Jill Hennessy *Lindsay Hamilton* • Christopher McDonald *Richard Halstrom* • Shirley MacLaine *Jennifer's mother* ■ *Dir* Keith Samples • *Scr* Kevin Meyers, Keith Samples

Smiles of a Summer Night ★★★★★ PG

Romantic comedy 1955 · Swe · BW · 104mins

Ingmar Bergman's sprightly comedy of sexual manners has a distinguished lineage, inspired as it is by Shakespeare's *A Midsummer Night's Dream*, the operas of Mozart, the plays of Marivaux and Mauritz Stiller's film *Erotikon*. Its progeny includes Stephen Sondheim's musical *A Little Night Music* and Woody Allen's *A Midsummer Night's Sex Comedy*. Bergman's comedies can be laboured and precious, but here he strikes exactly the right note of levity. Led by Eva Dahlbeck as the actress who assembles a weekend party of past, present and prospective lovers, the cast is excellent. DP. In Swedish with English subtitles. [video] DVD

Gunnar Björnstrand *Fredrik Egerman* • Eva Dahlbeck *Desirée Armfeldt* • Ulla Jacobsson *Anne Egerman* • Margit Carlquist [Margit Carlqvist] *Charlotte Malcolm* • Harriet Andersson *Petra the maid* • Birgitta Valberg *Actress* • Bibi Andersson *Actress* ■ *Dir/Scr* Ingmar Bergman

Smiley ★★ U

Adventure drama 1956 · UK · Colour · 96mins

A British movie made entirely in Australia that shows life in an outback town. Smiley is a small boy obliged to become independent because his mum is a washer woman and his dad is a drunken stockman who spends months in the bush. So Smiley rings the church bells for the local vicar (Ralph Richardson no less), innocently gets involved with drug smugglers and yearns to own a bicycle. It's a rather sickly affair that trades on stereotypes which modern Australian viewers may regard as the clincher in the debate about becoming a republic. AT

Ralph Richardson *Rev Lambeth* • John McCallum *Rankin* • Chips Rafferty *Sgt Flaxman* • Colin Petersen *Smiley Greevins* • Jocelyn Hernfield *Miss Workman* ■ *Dir* Anthony Kimmins • *Scr* Moore Raymond, Anthony Kimmins, from the novel by Moore Raymond

Smiley Gets a Gun ★★ U

Comedy drama 1959 · UK · Colour · 89mins

Smiley was a huge hit with British family audiences, many of whom were queuing up to emigrate Down Under to escape the grimness of the British economy and weather. This sequel retains writer/director Anthony Kimmins but exchanges one grand thespian (Ralph Richardson) for another, namely Dame Sybil Thorndike. The story has the local copper, Chips Rafferty, promising to give Smiley a gun if he can catch the man who stole Thorndike's horde of gold. AT

Sybil Thorndike *Granny McKinley* • Chips Rafferty *Sgt Flaxman* • Keith Calvert *Smiley Greevins* • Bruce Archer *Joey* • Margaret Christensen *Ma Greevins* • Reg Lye *Pa Greevins* ■ *Dir* Anthony Kimmins • *Scr* Anthony Kimmons, Rex Rienits, from the novel by Moore Raymond

Smilin' Through ★★★★

Melodrama 1932 · US · BW · 98mins

The famous and much-loved stage play *Smilin' Through* was filmed as a silent with Norma Talmadge in 1922. This first sound version, Oscar-nominated for best picture, showcases Norma Shearer – en route to mega-stardom – with Fredric March and Leslie Howard under the polished direction of Sidney Franklin. Set in England and spanning the years from 1868 to 1918, the complicated plot involves Howard, reclusive and bitter after his adored bride (Shearer) was shot at the altar by a jealous suitor (March), his orphaned niece who is the spitting image of his dead beloved, and the anguish suffered by all when she falls in love with the killer's son. RK

Norma Shearer *Moonyean Clare/Kathleen* • Fredric March *Kenneth Wayne/Jeremy Wayne* • Leslie Howard *John Carteret* • OP Heggie *Dr Owen* • Ralph Forbes *Willie Ainley* • Beryl Mercer *Mrs Crouch* • Margaret Seddon *Ellen* ■ *Dir* Sidney Franklin • *Scr* Ernest Vajda, Claudine West, Donald Ogden Stewart, James Bernard Fagan, from the play by Jane Cowl, Jane Murfin, Langdon McCormick

Smilin' Through ★★

Musical drama 1941 · US · Colour · 100mins

The second sound version of this romantic drama stars Jeanette MacDonald in the dual role of the dead wife and niece of bereaved husband Brian Aherne, and accordingly works in several songs. Director Frank Borzage hits new heights in treacly sentimentality here; MacDonald acts well, as does Aherne, but Gene Raymond (the star's real-life husband) is an unattractive disaster as a drunken jealous suitor and his son. RK

Jeanette MacDonald *Kathleen Clare/ Moonyean Clare* • Brian Aherne *Sir John Carteret* • Gene Raymond *Kenneth Wayne/ Jeremy Wayne* • Ian Hunter *Rev Owen Harding* • Frances Robinson *Ellen* • Patrick O'Moore *Willie* • Eric Lonsdale *Charles* ■ *Dir* Frank Borzage • *Scr* Donald Ogden Stewart, John Balderston, from the play by Jane Cowl, Jane Murfin, Langdon McCormick

The Smiling Lieutenant ★★★★★

Musical comedy 1931 · US · BW · 82mins

Nowhere is director Ernst Lubitsch's famous "touch" more frequently in evidence than in this delicious trifle adapted from the stage operetta *A Waltz Dream*, its charming score given witty lyrics by Clifford Grey. Maurice Chevalier plays a sexy Viennese guards officer enjoying a love affair with Claudette Colbert, the fiddle-playing leader of a ladies' café orchestra, who attracts the attention of the prim and dowdy daughter (Miriam Hopkins) of a visiting monarch. Assigned, at her request, as official aide to the visitors, he is then ordered to marry her. The plot serves as a foundation on which to build a breathless series of heavenly encounters, alternating between the risqué, the romantic, the hilarious and the poignant. RK

Maurice Chevalier *Niki* • Claudette Colbert *Franzi* • Miriam Hopkins *Princess Anna* • George Barbier *King Adolf* • Charles Ruggles *Max* • Hugh O'Connell *Orderly* ■ *Dir* Ernst Lubitsch • *Scr* Ernest Vajda, Samson Raphaelson, Ernst Lubitsch, from the operetta *A Waltz Dream* by Leopold Jacobson, Felix Doermann, from the novel *Nux der Prinzgemahl* by Hans Müller

Smilla's Feeling for Snow ★★ 15

Mystery thriller
1996 · Ger/Den/Swe · Colour · 116mins

Fans of the bestselling book will be disappointed by this plodding adaptation by Bille August. Julia Ormond doesn't have the depth or experience to carry the film as the scientist investigating the death of a young boy who plunges from the roof of her Copenhagen apartment building. While occasionally moody in places, this thriller never quite pushes you to the edge – or even the middle – of your seat, and Ormond is overshadowed at every turn by her impressive co-stars. JB. Contains violence and swearing. [video]

Julia Ormond *Smilla Jasperson* • Gabriel Byrne *Mechanic* • Richard Harris *Tork* • Vanessa Redgrave *Elsa Lubing* • Robert Loggia *Moritz Johnson* • Jim Broadbent *Lagermann* • Bob Peck *Ravn* ■ *Dir* Bille August • *Scr* Ann Biderman, from the novel *Miss Smilla's Feeling for Snow* by Peter Høeg

Smith! ★★ U

Western comedy drama
1969 · US · Colour · 97mins

This is a solidly crafted Disney western about a rancher who tries to prevent the execution of a young American Indian in the custody of a racist sheriff. Glenn Ford is happily married to Nancy Olson and oozes decency and liberal values while Keenan Wynn pushes every button marked "hiss" or "villain". This also marked the screen debut of Chief Dan George, whose next film, *Little Big Man*, would earn him an Oscar nomination. AT [video]

Glenn Ford *Smith* • Nancy Olson *Norah Smith* • Dean Jagger *Judge* • Keenan Wynn *Vince Heber* • Warren Oates *Walter Charlie* • Chief Dan George *Ol' Antoine* • Frank Ramirez *Gabriel Jimmyboy* • John Randolph *Mr Edwards* ■ *Dir* Michael O'Herlihy • *Scr* Louis Pelletier, from the novel *Breaking Smith's Quarter Horse* by Paul St Pierre

Smithereens ★★★ 15

Drama 1982 · US · Colour · 93mins

A low-budget movie packing an adrenalin-charged punch. It features a raucously poignant portrayal by Susan Berman of a punkish, working-class girl trying to make it in the rock 'n' roll world of Manhattan's Lower East Side. The debut film of director Susan Seidelman, this has a terrific soundtrack, and what it lacks in production values it makes up for in verve and gaiety. TH [video]

Susan Berman *Wren* • Brad Rinn *Paul* • Richard Hell *Eric* • Nada Despotovich *Cecile* • Roger Jett *Billy* ■ *Dir* Susan Seidelman • *Scr* Ron Nyswaner, Peter Askin, from a story by Ron Nyswaner, Susan Seidelman

Smoke ★★★★ 15

Drama 1995 · US · Colour and BW · 107mins

Novelist Paul Auster's first original screenplay is clearly the product of a literary mind, as the dialogue hangs on the air like the aroma of a good cigar. But without director Wayne Wang's insouciant control and the nuanced performances, this episodic roundelay about the inevitability of chance and coincidence would have seemed stiff and unconvincing. Instead, it's a vibrant portrait of the small community that congregates around Harvey Keitel's Brooklyn cigar shop, whose customers meet fortune and tragedy alike with equanimity. DP [video] DVD

Harvey Keitel *Auggie Wren* • William Hurt *Paul Benjamin* • Harold Perrineau *Rashid* • Forest Whitaker *Cyrus* • Stockard Channing *Ruby* • Ashley Judd *Felicity* • Giancarlo Esposito *Tommy* • José Zuniga *Jerry* ■ *Dir* Wayne Wang • *Scr* Paul Auster, from his short story *Auggie Wren's Christmas Story*

Smoke Signal ★★ U

Western 1955 · US · Colour · 87mins

Dana Andrews leads the survivors of an Indian massacre to safety in a very routine western, distinguished only by its majestic Grand Canyon setting. Piper Laurie is the only woman in the cast, which includes Universal's handsome heart-throb Rex Reason and veteran Milburn Stone. TS

Dana Andrews *Brett Halliday* • Piper Laurie *Laura Evans* • Rex Reason *Lieutenant Wayne Ford* • William Talman *Captain Harper* • Gordon Jones *Corporal Rogers* • Milburn Stone *Sergeant Miles* • Douglas Spencer *Garode* ■ *Dir* Jerry Hopper • *Scr* George Slavin, George W George

Smoke Signals ★★★

Road movie 1998 · US · Colour · 89mins

A double winner at the Sundance Festival, this is the first US feature to be written, directed and performed solely by native Americans. Adapted by Sherman Alexie from stories in his own collection, it follows Adam Beach and Evan Adams on their trek to Phoenix to collect the ashes of Gary Farmer, the abusive father Beach despises and the hero who pulled Adams out of the fire that killed his parents. Chris Eyre's debut may be a cinematic landmark, but with its sharp, self-deprecating humour, it's also a warm, vibrant and totally human story. DP

Adam Beach *Victor Joseph* • Evan Adams *Thomas Builds-the-Fire* • Irene Bedard *Suzy Song* • Gary Farmer *Arnold Joseph* • Tantoo Cardinal *Arlene Joseph* • Cody Lightning *Young Victor Joseph* • Simon Baker *Young Thomas Builds-the-Fire* ■ *Dir* Chris Eyre • *Scr* Sherman Alexie, from his stories *The Lone Ranger and Tonto Fistfight in Heaven*

Smokescreen ★★★ U

Thriller 1964 · UK · BW · 65mins

This above-average programme filler is kept moving swiftly and painlessly by director Jim O'Connolly. Adultery, embezzlement and murder are all taken in his stride by Peter Vaughan as the insurance claims inspector who suspects that there is more to a blazing car wreck than meets the eye. While all around him give typically second-division performances, Vaughan plays with a dogged determination that is efficient, engaging and quite at odds with the more sinister characters he would essay later in his career. DP

Peter Vaughan *Ropey Roper* • John Carson *Trevor Baylis* • Yvonne Romain *Janet Dexter* • Gerald Flood *Graham Turner* • Glynn Edwards *Inspector Wright* ■ *Dir/Scr* Jim O'Connolly

S

Smokey and the Bandit ★★★★ PG

Comedy 1977 · US · Colour · 91mins

A smash hit in its day, this is a marvellously good-natured chase movie, as Burt Reynolds ("Bandit") carts a rather too obviously product-placed truckload of Coors beer across the state lines, outpacing Sheriff Jackie Gleason ("Smokey" in the local lingo) by way of a variety of spectacular stunts. Unsurprising, since the movie is the directorial debut of former stuntman Hal Needham. Several sequels were spawned, but none captured the freshness and charm of this terrific original, which greatly benefits from the real-life, as well as on-screen, sexual chemistry between co-stars Burt Reynolds and the vivacious Sally Field. TS [video] DVD

Burt Reynolds *Bandit* • Sally Field *Carrie* • Jackie Gleason *Sheriff Buford T Justice* • Jerry Reed *Cledus Snow* • Mike Henry *Junior Justice* • Paul Williams *Little Enos Burdette* • Pat McCormick *Big Enos Burdette* ■ *Dir* Hal Needham • *Scr* James Lee Barrett, Charles Shyer, Alan Mandel, from a story by Hal Needham, Robert L Levy

Smokey and the Bandit II ★★★ PG

Comedy 1980 · US · Colour · 96mins

Not so much of a chase comedy as the first film, this battle of wits between trucker Burt Reynolds and dogged cop Jackie Gleason is more a series of sight gags that pile up like a motorway collision. The tone is set from the beginning when Reynolds emerges from behind a huge heap of beer cans. Reynolds has always been capable of much more than this genial, show-off role, but it's what he obviously likes best. TH. Contains swearing. [video] DVD

Burt Reynolds *Bandit* • Jackie Gleason *Sheriff Buford T Justice/Reginald Van Justice/Gaylord Van Justice* • Jerry Reed *Cledus* • Dom DeLuise *Doc* • Sally Field *Carrie* • Paul Williams *Little Enos* • David Huddleston *John Conn* ■ *Dir* Hal Needham • *Scr* Jerry Belson, Brock Yates, from a story by Michael Kane, from characters created by Hal Needham, Robert L Levy

Smokey and the Bandit III ★ 18

Comedy 1983 · US · Colour · 81mins

Jerry Reed (Burt Reynolds's sidekick from the first two movies) takes over as the number one bandit, once again setting off on a cross-country trek and being pursued by the moronic police force. Dick Lowry takes over the directorial reins, but he simply throws car crash after car crash at the screen in a desperate fashion. Dire. JF. Contains swearing, nudity. [video] DVD

Jackie Gleason *Buford T Justice* • Jerry Reed *Cletus/Bandit* • Paul Williams *Little Enos Burdette* • Pat McCormick *Big Enos* • Mike Henry *Junior* • Colleen Camp *Dusty Trails* • Faith Minton *Tina* • Burt Reynolds *The Real Bandit* ■ *Dir* Dick Lowry • *Scr* Stuart Birnbaum, David Dashev, from characters created by Hal Needham, Robert L Levy

Smokey and the Good Time Outlaws ★★ U

Comedy adventure
1978 · US · Colour · 89mins

When in doubt over the plot, have a car crash. That seems to be the attitude of the producers of this comedy adventure about two aspiring country and western singers who travel to Nashville to seek fame, fortune and fist fights. Despite a title that cashes in on the *Smokey and the Bandit* series, this rang no box-office bells. TH

Jesse Turner *JD Todd* • Dennis Fimple *Salt Flat Kid* • Slim Pickens *Sheriff Leddy* • Dianne Sherrill *Sandy* • Marcie Barkin *Linda* • Hope Summers *Marcie* ■ *Dir* Alex Grasshoff • *Scr* Frank Dobbs, Robert Walsh, Jesse Turner, from a story by Jesse Turner

Smoking/No Smoking ★★★★ PG

Drama 1993 · Fr · Colour · 292mins

The eight plays in Alan Ayckbourn's *Intimate Exchanges* cycle are presented in an unashamedly theatrical manner by Alain Resnais in this mammoth two-part adaptation. It takes a while to get used to hearing the clichéd expressions of the English middle classes in colloquial French, but the exceptional performances of Sabine Azéma and Pierre Arditi will soon have you hooked. It is worth trying to watch in one sitting as the interweaving between the two films is ingenious. DP. In French with English subtitles. Contains swearing.

Sabine Azéma *Celia Teasdale/Rowena Coombes/Sylvie Bell/Irene Pridworthy/Josephine Hamilton* • Pierre Arditi *Toby Teasdale/Miles Coombes/Lionel Hepplewick/Joe Hepplewick* ■ *Dir* Alain Resnais • *Scr* Alan Ayckbourn, Agnès Jaoui, Jean-Pierre Bacri, from the plays *Intimate Exchanges* by Alan Ayckbourn

Smoky ★★★ U

Western 1946 · US · Colour · 84mins

This heartbreaking tale of a horse will bring a lump to the hardiest of throats. Based on the once-popular Will James story, the adventures of Smoky put *Black Beauty* to shame. This version is well photographed in glorious 1940s Technicolor and sympathetically directed by Louis King, lesser-known younger brother of veteran Henry King. Fred MacMurray and Anne Baxter are eminently likeable, but the real scene-stealer, making his movie debut here, is "Big Daddy" Burl Ives. TS

Fred MacMurray *Clint Barkley* • Anne Baxter *Julie Richards* • Burl Ives *Bill* • Bruce Cabot *Frank* • Esther Dale *Gram* • Roy Roberts *Jeff* ■ *Dir* Louis King • *Scr* Lillie Hayward, Dwight Cummins, Dorothy Yost, from the novel *Smoky, the Cowhorse* by Will James

Smooth Talk ★★★ 15

Drama 1985 · US · Colour · 87mins

This American coming-of-age movie features Laura Dern as a gauche teenager unable to relate to her mother (Mary Kay Place), who unfavourably compares the 15-year-old to her peaches and cream sister. Rebelling, Dern hangs out with her girlfriends and gets up to mischief, finally biting off more than she can chew when she encounters the charismatic but sexually aggressive Treat Williams. It's a well-judged piece by director Joyce Chopra, with Dern excelling in the lead role. LH [video]

Treat Williams *Arnold Friend* • Laura Dern *Connie* • Mary Kay Place *Katherine* • Levon Helm *Harry* • Sara Inglis [Sarah Inglis] *Jill* • Margaret Welsh *Laura* ■ *Dir* Joyce Chopra • *Scr* Tom Cole, from the short story *Where Are You Going, Where Have You Been* by Joyce Carol Oates

Smorgasbord ★★ PG

Comedy 1983 · US · Colour · 85mins

Consisting of a number of skits, it's linked by the story of failure related to a psychiatrist by hapless loser Jerry Lewis. The same year *Smorgasbord* finally saw the light of day, Lewis made a triumphant comeback in Scorsese's *King of Comedy*, and reputedly the director is also a fan of this film. However many people simply hate it, citing it as an unfunny, self-indulgent mess. The French had no doubts, though, and the influential magazine *Cahiers du Cinéma* named it as their joint tenth best film of 1983. DF [video]

Jerry Lewis *Warren Nefron/Dr Perks* • Herb Edelman *Dr Jonas Pletchick* • Zane Busby *Waitress* • Foster Brooks *Pilot* • Buddy Lester *Passenger* • Milton Berle *Female patient* • Sammy Davis Jr *Mr Billings* ■ *Dir* Jerry Lewis • *Scr* Jerry Lewis, Bill Richmond

The Snail's Strategy ★★★

Comedy 1993 · Col · Colour · 116mins

Sergio Cabrera's sympathy for the common people is evident in this genial comedy, in which the squatters in a Bogota mansion vacillate between legal stalling and direct action to prevent an avaricious capitalist reclaiming his lapsed rights to ownership. Frank Ramirez's opportunist attorney and Fausto Cabrera's Spanish Civil War veteran standout in an ensemble whose travails reflect the nation's plights and characteristics. It's a typical scenario, but the hilarious house-shifting scam is inspired. DP. In Spanish with English subtitles.

Frank Ramirez • Humberto Dorado • Florina Lemaitre • Gustavo Angarita • Vicky Hernandez • Fausto Cabrera ■ *Dir* Sergio Cabrera • *Scr* Humberto Dorado, from a screenplay (unproduced) by Sergio Cabrera, Ramon Jimeno

Snake Eyes ★★★ 15

Mystery thriller 1998 · US · Colour · 94mins

The US Secretary of Defence is assassinated in full view of a huge audience gathered in an Atlantic City casino for a boxing championship. Can supercharged detective Nicolas Cage use his own recollections and those of key witnesses to find out whodunnit and unravel an ever-widening conspiracy? Although a stunning visual tour de force by director Brian De Palma, this jigsaw murder mystery lacks suspense and disappoints as a thriller, with the expected slam-bang finale never materialising. AJ. Contains violence and some swearing. [video] DVD

Nicolas Cage *Rick Santoro* • Gary Sinise *Kevin Dunne* • John Heard *Gilbert Powell* • Carla Gugino *Julia Costello* • Stan Shaw *Lincoln Tyler* • Kevin Dunn *Lou Logan* ■ *Dir* Brian De Palma • *Scr* David Koepp, from a story by Brian De Palma, David Koepp • *Cinematographer* Stephen H Burum

A Snake of June ★★★★ 18

Drama 2002 · Jpn · BW · 76mins

Although there's a metallic sheen to the monochrome imagery, there is little of the industrial dehumanisation that characterised Shinya Tsukamoto's *Tetsuo* pictures in this sinister, stylish and highly disconcerting rain-saturated study of sexual frustration and the torment of isolation. Decay remains a key theme, however, as both Tsukamoto's manipulative stalker and victim Asuka Kurosawa are suffering from malevolent illnesses. Yet notwithstanding the humiliation Kurosawa endures as Tsukamoto puts her through acts of public exhibitionism and the beating that her complacent husband Yuji Koutari sustains, the story ends on an unexpected note of optimism as the couple re-ignite their long-dormant passion. DP. In Japanese with English subtitles. [video] DVD

Asuka Kurosawa *Rinko Tatsumi* • Yuji Koutari *Shigehiko Tatsumi* • Shinya Tsukamoto *Michio Iguchi* ■ *Dir/Scr* Shinya Tsukamoto

The Snake Pit ★★★★ 12

Psychological drama
1948 · US · BW · 103mins

In its day, this was a truly harrowing and extremely controversial adaptation of Mary Jane Ward's semi-autobiographical novel about life in a mental institution. In Britain, the film was perceived to be so disturbing that it suffered from over-zealous censor cuts. The film still retains its power to shock and, although the medical department may seem slightly antiquated, the performances of the women inmates are still incredibly moving, particularly Olivia de Havilland in the lead, and Celeste Holm, Beulah Bondi and a young Betsy Blair in support. Anatole Litvak's direction may seem on the strident side, but this still has impact. TS DVD

Olivia de Havilland *Virginia Stuart Cunningham* • Mark Stevens *Robert Cunningham* • Leo Genn *Dr Mark Kirk* • Celeste Holm *Grace* • Glenn Langan *Dr Terry* • Helen Craig *Miss Davis* • Leif Erickson *Gordon* • Beulah Bondi *Mrs Greer* ■ *Dir* Anatole Litvak • *Scr* Frank Partos, Millen Brand, from the novel by Mary Jane Ward

Snakes & Ladders ★★ 15

Comedy 1996 · Ire/Ger · Colour · 92mins

Things go downhill rather rapidly in this would-be wacky comedy from Trish McAdam. Pom Boyd and Gina Moxley share a flat in Dublin harbouring dreams that someone will see them performing on the city streets and whisk them off to cabaret celebrity. However, their friendship comes under threat when Boyd's indolent boyfriend Sean Hughes pops the question. This doggedly alternative romp might have passed muster as a sitcom subplot, but it's woefully short of charm and ideas to work as a feature. DP [video]

Pom Boyd *Jean* • Gina Moxley *Kate* • Sean Hughes *Martin* • Paudge Behan *Dan* ■ *Dir/Scr* Trish McAdam

Snapdragon ★ 18

Erotic thriller 1993 · US · Colour · 94mins

This dire erotic thriller has Pamela Anderson playing an amnesiac who has dreams about killing the men she has sex with. Steven Bauer co-stars as the police psychologist who takes an awful long time to figure it all out. There is a twist in the tale, but don't expect too much in the way of a quality plot or decent acting. ST [video]

Steven Bauer *David* • Chelsea Field *Sergeant Peckham* • Pamela Anderson *Felicity* • Matt McCoy *Bernie* • Kenneth Tigar *Captain* • Irene Tsu *Hua* ■ *Dir* Worth Keeter • *Scr* Gene Church

The Snapper ★★ 15

Comedy drama 1993 · UK · Colour · 90mins

Adapted by Roddy Doyle from his own novel, this sassy comedy drama was something of a disappointment after his earlier slice of working-class Dublin life, *The Commitments*. Sometimes funny, sometimes touching, the film benefits from a few snorting one-liners and some solid ensemble playing, although the cast occasionally gets carried away during the very stagey shouting matches. The main problem, however, is that director Stephen Frears too often allows the comedy to slip into sitcom and the drama to come across as something from a social-conscience soap opera. *The Van*, the final part of the trilogy, was released in late 1996. DP

Tina Kellegher *Sharon Curley* • Colm Meaney *Dessie Curley* • Ruth McCabe *Kay Curley* • Eanna MacLiam *Craig Curley* • Peter Rowen *Sonny Curley* • Joanne Gerrard *Lisa Curley* • Colm O'Byrne *Darren Curley* • Brendan Gleeson *Lester* ■ *Dir* Stephen Frears • *Scr* Roddy Doyle, from his novel

Snatch ★★★ 18

Comedy crime drama
2000 · US/UK · Colour · 102mins

One would've thought that Guy Ritchie would have shied away from replicating *Lock, Stock and Two Smoking Barrels* after the current glut of British gangster movies. Sadly not. Although *Snatch* has its merits – among them originality and the talents of Brad Pitt,

S

Benicio Del Toro, and Jasons Statham and Flemyng – the diamond heist and East End Mob plot are just more of the same. Gangs, cheeky chappies, bare-knuckle boxing and cameos from Vinnie Jones and Mike Reid merge into a "seen it all before" mix. Ritchie can direct, but perhaps it's time he got someone else to write the material. LH DVD

Benicio Del Toro *Franky Four Fingers* • Dennis Farina *Avi* • Vinnie Jones *Bullet Tooth Tony* • Brad Pitt *Mickey One Punch O'Neill* • Rade Serbedzija *Boris the Blade* • Jason Statham *Turkish* • Alan Ford *Brick Top* • Mike Reid *Doug the Head* • Ewen Bremner *Mullet* • Jason Flemyng *Darren* ■ *Dir/Scr* Guy Ritchie

Sneakers ★★★★ 15

Comedy thriller 1992 · US · Colour · 120mins

This is a smart and snappy caper that is blessed with a sparkling script and an outstanding ensemble cast. Robert Redford, graciously sending himself up a little, plays the former student radical who now makes a living heading a team that is paid to break into hi-tech buildings to show up lapses in security systems. However, his past returns to haunt him when he is blackmailed into stealing the ultimate codebreaker. Ignore the holes in plot logic and savour the relaxed and unselfish comic interplay. JF. Contains violence, swearing. DVD

Robert Redford *Martin Bishop* • Dan Aykroyd *"Mother"* • Ben Kingsley *Cosmo* • Mary McDonnell *Liz* • River Phoenix *Carl* • Sidney Poitier *Crease* • David Strathairn *Whistler* • Timothy Busfield *Dick Gordon* • James Earl Jones *Bernard Abbott* ■ *Dir* Phil Alden Robinson • *Scr* Phil Alden Robinson, Lawrence Lasker, Walter F Parkes

The Sniper ★★★★

Crime drama 1952 · US · BW · 87mins

An excellent psychological exploration of what drives one man to shoot at random with no apparent thought or feeling. The man in question has a deep grudge against women and the camera follows his gun as if we, the audience, are his eyes, the effect of this visual trick being both eerie and strangely compelling. Arthur Franz gives a powerful performance as the madman and this is neither a eulogy to violence, nor a total condemnation of society, but an intelligent movie that poses many complex questions. SH

Adolphe Menjou *Lieutenant Kafka* • Arthur Franz *Eddie Miller* • Gerald Mohr *Sergeant Ferris* • Marie Windsor *Jean Darr* • Frank Faylen *Inspector Anderson* • Richard Kiley *Dr James G Kent* ■ *Dir* Edward Dmytryk • *Scr* Harry Brown, from a story by Edward Anhalt, Edna Anhalt

Sniper ★★★ 15

Action thriller 1992 · US · Colour · 94mins

Though it doesn't quite come off, this is an intelligent spin on the action thriller. Tom Berenger is a marksman on a covert mission to terminate a Panamanian rebel leader. However, he soon discovers he has more than enough on his plate dealing with his twitchy new partner, Billy Zane. The pair's claustrophobic relationship generates plenty of jungle-bound tension and the action set pieces are stylishly staged by director Luis Llosa. Two sequels to date. JF. Contains swearing, violence. DVD

Tom Berenger *Tom Beckett* • Billy Zane *Richard Miller* • Aden Young *Doug Papich* • Ken Radley *El Cirujano* • JT Walsh *Chester Van Damme, Beckett's senior officer* • Reinaldo Arenas [Reynaldo Arenas] *Cacique* ■ *Dir* Luis Llosa • *Scr* Michael Frost Beckner, Crash Leyland

Snoopy, Come Home ★★★ U

Animation 1972 · US · Colour · 76mins

Second in the series of feature-length *Peanuts* adventures. Charles M Schulz's beagle takes centre stage, vowing that life *isn't* going to the dogs, and, with bird-brained buddy Woodstock in tow, heading off in search of something better. Cutely animated, and packed with all the gentle charm and humour of the *Peanuts* comic strip, this can still delight the kids. DA DVD

Chad Webber *Charlie Brown* • Robin Kohn *Lucy Van Pelt* • Stephen Shea *Linus Van Pelt* • David Carey *Schroeder* • Bill Melendez *Snoopy* ■ *Dir* Bill Melendez • *Scr* from the comic strip by Charles M Schulz

Snow Day ★★ PG

Comedy 2000 · US/Ger · Colour · 85mins

A "snow day" is that special day in America, when a freak blizzard causes an unexpected break from school. Mark Webber uses the opportunity to make a play for the glamorous Emmanuelle Chriqui, while his younger sister Zena Grey tries to keep the Snow-plowman (Chris Elliott) occupied so that her school remains closed. Director Chris Koch piles on the teen movie clichés with all the lumbering tenacity of a plough, but this is still good-natured and energetic. TH DVD

Chris Elliott *Snow-plowman* • Mark Webber *Hal Brandston* • Jean Smart *Laura Brandston* • Schuyler Fisk *Lane Leonard* • Iggy Pop *Mr Zellweger* • Pam Grier *Tina* • John Schneider *Chad Symmonz* • Chevy Chase *Tom Brandston* • Zena Grey *Natalie Brandston* • Emmanuelle Chriqui *Claire Bonner* ■ *Dir* Chris Koch • *Scr* Will McRobb, Chris Viscardi

Snow Dogs ★★ PG

Comedy adventure
2002 · US · Colour · 95mins

A reconciliation between estranged father and son – a familiar Hollywood staple – provides the basis for this comedy adventure, sadly lacking in both thrills and jokes. Cuba Gooding Jr plays a successful Miami dentist who discovers he's adopted but has been left an Alaskan cabin and a pack of sled dogs by his real mother. Travelling to the small town of Tolketna, Gooding Jr also encounters his white biological father, the unwelcoming James Coburn. Dogged – but dull. TH DVD

Cuba Gooding Jr *Ted Brooks* • James Coburn *Thunder Jack* • Sisqo *Dr Rupert Brooks* • Nichelle Nichols *Amelia Brooks* • M Emmet Walsh *George* • Brian Doyle-Murray *Ernie* ■ *Dir* Brian Levant • *Scr* Jim Kouf, Tommy Swerdlow, Michael Goldberg, Mark Gibson, Philip Halprin, from the non-fiction book *Winterdance: the Fine Madness of Running the Iditarod* by Gary Paulsen

Snow Falling on Cedars ★★★★ 15

Courtroom drama
1999 · US · Colour · 121mins

It's rare to experience an adaptation of a novel as true to the spirit of the original as director Scott Hicks's follow-up to the Oscar-winning *Shine*. David Guterson's book is vivid, poetic and sensual, qualities this film, about prejudice within a small fishing community in the years following the Second World War, shares in abundance. Ethan Hawke plays a local journalist fascinated by the trial of a Japanese-American war hero accused of murdering a fellow fisherman. The trial becomes the focus for fear and scapegoating in a mixed-race community torn apart by Pearl Harbor. Hicks sacrifices narrative thrust for atmosphere, resulting in a slow but very beautiful film. LH DVD

Ethan Hawke *Ishmael Chambers* • Youki Kudoh *Hatsue Miyamoto* • Reeve Carney *Young Ishmael Chambers* • Anne Suzuki *Young Hatsue Imada* • Rick Yune *Kazuo Miyamoto* • Max von Sydow *Nels Gudmundsson* • James Rebhorn *Alvin Hooks* • James Cromwell *Judge Fielding* • Sam Shepard *Arthur Chambers* ■ *Dir* Scott Hicks • *Scr* Ron Bass [Ronald Bass], Scott Hicks, from the novel by David Guterson

Snow Job ★★

Crime drama 1972 · US · Colour · 90mins

In this vehicle for the former Olympic ski champion Jean-Claude Killy, the beauty of the Alpine scenery and Killy's sporting prowess are plain for all to see, but so is the fact that this crime caper is just no good. As the ski instructor who robs the local bank, Killy falls flat on his face every time he comes off the piste. The sole bright spot is provided by legendary director Vittorio De Sica, whose sly cameo shows why he was such a matinée idol in the 1930s and 1940s. DP

Jean-Claude Killy *Christian Biton* • Danièle Gaubert *Monica Scotti* • Cliff Potts *Bob Skinner* • Vittorio De Sica *Enrico Dolphi* • Lelio Luttazzi *Bank manager* • Delia Boccardo *Lorraine Borman* ■ *Dir* George Englund • *Scr* Ken Kolb, Jeffrey Bloom, from the story *$125,000 Ski Bum Holdup* by Richard Gallagher

The Snow Queen ★★★

Part-animated fantasy
1959 · USSR · Colour · 54mins

Live-action, directed by Phil Patton and featuring Art Linkletter with Tammy Marihugh, bookends an animated feature from the Soviet Union, based on the Hans Christian Andersen story of the ice-bound queen, thawed by true love. Lev Atamanov directed the animation in 1955, though the voice-overs (including Sandra Dee and Tommy Kirk) are American. TH

Sandra Dee *Gerda* • Tommy Kirk *Kay* • Patty McCormack *Angel* • Louise Arthur *The Snow Queen* • Paul Frees *Ol' Dreamy/The Raven* ■ *Dir* Phil Patton • *Scr* Alan Lipscott, Bob Fisher, from a fairy tale by Hans Christian Andersen • *Tbc* Art Linkletter, Tammy Marihugh

Snow White ★★★

Fantasy 1989 · Cz/W Ger · Colour · 90mins

Such is the hold of Walt Disney's 1937 animated adaptation on the imagination of generations of young viewers, that it is easy to forget other versions exist. Markedly less lavish, this Czech-German co-production is a solid reworking of the dark Brothers Grimm tale, which, like many other eastern European children's films, entertains without ever talking down to its audience. DP. German dialogue dubbed into English.

Natalie Minko *Snow White* • Gudrun Landgrebe *Queen* • Alessandro Gassman *Court Jester* • Eberhard Feik *Priest* • Dietmar Schönherr *King* • Sandor Koleseri *Black Knight* ■ *Dir* Ludvik Raza • *Scr* Bernd Fiedler, from a fairy tale by Jacob Grimm, Wilhelm Grimm

Snow White ★★ PG

Fairy tale 2001 · Can/US · Colour · 84mins

Director Caroline Thompson here attempts to put the Grimm back into a story that has become surprisingly unfamiliar since Disney's fanciful cartoon became the standard version. Consequently, Snow White is imperilled by a wicked stepmother who has gained control of her grieving father through the machinations of a green-eyed genie. Like Sigourney Weaver before her, Miranda Richardson revels in the beauty-fixated queen's venomous villainy, but Kristin Kreuk's inanimate performance makes her a dull heroine. DP DVD

Miranda Richardson *Elspeth* • Kristin Kreuk *Snow White* • Tom Irwin *John* • Clancy Brown *Grandfather of Wishes* • José Zuniga *Hector* • Tyron Leitso *Prince Alfred* • Michael Gilden *Monday* • Mark J Trombino *Tuesday* • Vincent Schiavelli *Wednesday* • Penny Blake *Thursday* • Martin Klebba *Friday* • Warwick Davis *Saturday* • Michael J Anderson *Sunday* ■ *Dir* Caroline Thompson • *Scr* Caroline Thompson, Julie Hickson, from the fairy tale by Wilhelm Grimm, Jacob Grimm

Snow White: a Tale of Terror ★★★ 15

Gothic horror 1996 · UK/US · Colour · 96mins

Director Michael Cohn puts the grim back in to the Grimm Brothers dark fairy tale. All Disney expectation is turned on its head as the sexual tensions and bloody obsessions are accentuated in this highly sinister fable with a richly textured Hammer horror look. The dwarfs are barbaric outcasts in this intriguing revision (scarred, simple-minded, branded) that's too sombre for kids, but too light in the fright department for adults. However, Sigourney Weaver gives the performance of her career as the wicked stepmother. AJ. Contains swearing and violence. DVD

Sigourney Weaver *Claudia Hoffman* • Sam Neill *Frederick Hoffman* • Gil Bellows *Will* • Taryn Davis *Little Lilli* • Brian Glover *Lars* • David Conrad *Peter Gutenberg* • Monica Keena *Lilli Hoffman* • Anthony Brophy *Rolf* ■ *Dir* Michael Cohn • *Scr* Tom Szollosi, Deborah Serra, from the fairy tale by Jacob Grimm, Wilhelm Grimm

Snow White and the Seven Dwarfs ★★★★★ U

Classic animated fantasy
1937 · US · Colour · 81mins

Disney's first animated feature pushed the art form in thrilling new directions, completely redrawing a much-loved fairy tale of bad stepmothers, forest glades and handsome princes that previously existed only on the printed page. (Indeed it opens with a storybook, a respectful nod that has been oft-repeated.) In places, it's cuter than the Brothers Grimm template – the much-loved dwarfs with their pratfalls – but scenes with the Wicked Queen and the poisoned apple achieve a high new level of terror. Its ability to invoke German expressionism on one hand while keeping the gallery entertained with Dopey's antics and *Whistle While You Work* on the other is why this classic has enduring appeal for all ages. AC DVD

Adriana Caselotti *Snow White* • Harry Stockwell *Prince Charming* • Lucille La Verne *The queen/The witch* • Moroni Olsen *Magic Mirror* • Billy Gilbert *Sneezy* • Pinto Colvig *Sleepy/Grumpy* • Otis Harlan *Happy* • Scotty Mattraw *Bashful* • Roy Atwell *Doc* ■ *Dir* David Hand • *Scr* Ted Sears, Richard Creedon, Otto Englander, Dick Rickard, Earl Hurd, Merrill De Maris, Dorothy Ann Blank, Webb Smith, from the fairy tale *Sneewittchen* in *Kinder und Haus-Marchen*, collected by Jacob Grimm, Wilhelm Grimm • *Music* Leigh Harline

Snowball Express ★★★ U

Comedy 1972 · US · Colour · 93mins

Beating a retreat from the city is many a suburbanite's dream. This comedy shows that dream turning sour, when Manhattan family man Dean Jones inherits a ski-resort hotel in the Rockies and tries to make a go of it with wife Nancy Olson. Being a Disney confection that aims to please, the bad succumbs to the beautiful, with lots of ski sequences and a snowmobile race, and the tales of financial hardship tend to get buried under a pile of slush. TH

Dean Jones *Johnny Baxter* • Nancy Olson *Sue Baxter* • Harry Morgan *Jesse McCord* • Keenan Wynn *Martin Ridgeway* • Johnny Whitaker *Richard Baxter* • Michael McGreevey

Wally Perkins ■ *Dir* Norman Tokar • *Scr* Don Tait, Jim Parker, from the novel *Chateau Bon Vivant* by Frankie O'Rear, John O'Rear

Snowbound ★★★ U

Adventure 1948 · UK · BW · 81mins

An Alpine adventure that too often betrays its pulp novel roots among resolutely studio-bound snow. Nevertheless, the cast is splendid, with Dennis Price and Robert Newton positively outdoing each other for the (over-) acting honours: the former plays a film extra-cum-scriptwriter sent by the latter, a film director, to write a script in the Dolomites, knowing full well there's Nazi gold in them there Alps. It becomes slightly less ludicrous when the snow traps everybody, and director David MacDonald ploughs through the tosh, achieving a fine sense of claustrophobia. TS [video]

Robert Newton *Derek Engles* • Dennis Price *Neil Blair* • Herbert Lom *Keramikos* • Marcel Dalio *Stefan Valdini* • Stanley Holloway *Joe Wesson* • Guy Middleton *Gilbert Mayne* ■ *Dir* David MacDonald • *Scr* David Evans, Keith Campbell, from the novel *The Lonely Skier* by Hammond Innes

The Snows of Kilimanjaro ★★★ PG

Romantic drama
1952 · US · Colour · 109mins

This prettified 20th Century-Fox film version of Ernest Hemingway's novella is almost totally wrecked by the miscasting of Gregory Peck. He is much too nice to play the hard-drinking, macho-obsessed, animal-hunting hero suffering from flashback syndrome, as wrong here as he was in the later *Moby Dick*. But Ava Gardner, Hildegarde Neff and Susan Hayward are right, seductively rivalling the African and Riviera landscapes and making Peck's life a misery. AT [video]

Gregory Peck *Harry* • Susan Hayward *Helen* • Ava Gardner *Cynthia* • Hildegarde Neff *Countess Liz* • Leo G Carroll *Uncle Bill* • Torin Thatcher *Johnson* • Ava Norring *Beatrice* • Helene Stanley *Connie* ■ *Dir* Henry King • *Scr* Casey Robinson, from the short story by Ernest Hemingway

Snuff ★ 18

Horror 1976 · US/Arg · Colour · 76mins

Rarely has a film been so mendaciously mythologised as this fifth-rate slasher. It began life in 1971 as a Manson murder cash-in called *Slaughter*, which was shot on a shoestring in Argentina by Michael and Roberta Findlay. It resurfaced under its new title five years later, featuring a gruesome four-minute insert, purporting to depict a real-life disembowelling (but which was actually shot in a Manhattan loft by one Simon Nuchtern using animal entrails). Opportunist distributor Allan Shackleton even launched a bogus morality campaign to garner extra publicity and the movie made a packet. Yet it remains amateurish, incoherent and unpleasant. DP. Contains swearing, nudity, violence and drug abuse.

Ana Carro • Roberta Findlay • Alfredo Iglesias • Aldo Mayo ■ *Dir* Michael Findlay, Roberta Findlay, Simon Nuchtern • *Scr* Michael Findlay, Roberta Findlay

So Big ★★★ U

Period drama 1932 · US · BW · 81mins

Barbara Stanwyck stars as the woman of indomitable character who becomes a schoolteacher in rural Illinois, marries a farmer and has a son, but is widowed and left to care for the land and her difficult child. This is the second of three feature versions of a Pulitzer Prize-winning novel, first filmed as a silent with Colleen Moore in 1924. This one benefits from solid direction by William A Wellman and the all-encompassing commitment of the great Stanwyck. Note the young Bette Davis in a small role. RK

Barbara Stanwyck *Selina Peake* • George Brent *Roelf Pool* • Dickie Moore *Dirk as a boy, "So Big"* • Bette Davis *Dallas O'Mara* • Mae Madison *Julie Hemple* • Hardie Albright *Dirk, adult* ■ • *Scr* J Grubb Alexander, Robert Lord, from the novel by Edna Ferber

So Big ★★★ U

Period drama 1953 · US · BW · 101mins

Jane Wyman, a huge star after her Oscar for *Johnny Belinda*, stars here as Edna Ferber's New Holland schoolmistress bringing up her son Steve Forrest against all odds. The Warner Bros gloss is not too intrusive, and there are nicely honed performances from big Sterling Hayden and lovely Nancy Olsen in support. TS

Jane Wyman *Selina Dejong* • Sterling Hayden *Pervus Dejong* • Nancy Olson *Dallas O'Mara* • Steve Forrest *Dirk Dejong* • Elisabeth Fraser *Julie Hempel* • Martha Hyer *Paula Hempel* ■ *Dir* Robert Wise • *Scr* John Twist, from the novel by Edna Ferber

So Close ★★★ 15

Science-fiction action
2002 · HK · Colour · 106mins

Despite opening with a stunning office sequence (in which Shu Qi redefines the term "computer virus") and closing with a spectacular rooftop swordfight, Corey Yuen's girlpower actioner loses its way in the interim amid a wealth of exposition and a tiresome romantic subplot. Clearly it helps to know why Shu and techno savvy sister Zhao Wei team up with cop Karen Mok to confound a malevolent tycoon. But it's much more fun watching them get on with the job. DP. In Cantonese and Mandarin with English subtitles. [video] DVD

Shu Qi *Lynn* • Zhao Wei *Sue* • Karen Mok *Hong Yat Hong* • Song Seoung Heon *Yan* • Michael Wei *Mark* • Yasuaki Kurata *Master* ■ *Dir* Corey Yuen • *Scr* Jeff Lau

So Close to Life ★★★

Drama 1957 · Swe · BW · 84mins

Ingrid Thulin, Eva Dahlbeck and Bibi Andersson shared the best actress prize at the 1958 Cannes Film Festival, but it's not just the performances that makes this significant. This is the film that signalled Ingmar Bergman's shift towards what are usually called "Chamber Dramas", intense conversation pieces that take place in symbolically confined spaces (in this case, a maternity ward). Bergman hedges his bets about the wisdom of bringing a child into such a troubled world but, for all its purple passages and cosy conclusions, the film leaves you with plenty to think about. DP. In Swedish with English subtitles.

Eva Dahlbeck *Stina* • Ingrid Thulin *Cecilia* • Bibi Andersson *Hjordis* • Barbro Hiort Af Ornas *Brita* • Erland Josephson *Anders* • Max von Sydow *Harry* • Gunnar Sjöberg *Doctor* ■ *Dir* Ingmar Bergman • *Scr* Ingmar Bergman, from a story by Ulla Isaksson

So Dark the Night ★★★

Crime drama 1946 · US · BW · 70mins

It's not often that character actors have the chance to play leading roles and Steven Geray, an east European actor usually cast as bartender, foreign agent or small-time criminal, does a splendid job in this outstanding B-feature. Playing a famous French detective on holiday, he finds himself investigating murders in a small village. Although the rest of the cast is little known, the well-written story has a memorably original twist and the setting is skilfully evoked. AE

Steven Geray *Henri Cassin* • Micheline Cheirel *Nanette Michaud* • Eugene Borden *Pierre Michaud* • Ann Codee *Mama Michaud* • Egon Brecher *Dr Boncourt* ■ *Dir* Joseph H Lewis • *Scr* Martin Berkeley, Dwight Babcock, from a story by Audrey Wisberg

So Dear to My Heart ★★★ U

Part-animated musical
1949 · US · Colour · 78mins

The first actor to sign a long-term contract at Disney, Bobby Driscoll won a special Oscar for his work in 1949, although it clearly had more to do with *The Window*, than this slight blend of live-action and animation. Although the nominated song, *Lavender Blue*, was one of Uncle Walt's favourites, today's youngsters will get more enjoyment out of numbers like *Stick-with-it-ivity*, one of the many animated sequences in which farm boy Driscoll learns the lessons of life as he trains his black lamb, Danny, for a country fair. DP [video]

Burl Ives *Uncle Hiram* • Beulah Bondi *Granny Kincaid* • Harry Carey [Harry Carey Jr] *Judge* • Bobby Driscoll *Jeremiah Kincaid* ■ *Dir* Harold Schuster, Hamilton Luske • *Scr* John Tucker Battle, Maurice Rapf, Ted Sears, from the novel *Midnight and Jeremiah* by Sterling North

So Ends Our Night ★★★

Wartime drama 1941 · US · BW · 121mins

Released before the US entered the Second World War, this strong drama relates the experiences of three Germans who flee the rise of Hitler in 1937. Fredric March, an anti-Nazi German, risks danger to return to his dying wife (Frances Dee), while Jewish girl Margaret Sullavan and half-Jewish Glenn Ford make it to safety, falling in love en route. The subject matter can hardly fail to be moving, and this is frequently tense and gripping. No thanks, though, to director John Cromwell, who tends to use a sledgehammer to kill a gnat. RK

Fredric March *Joseph Steiner* • Margaret Sullavan *Ruth Holland* • Frances Dee *Marie Steiner* • Glenn Ford *Ludwig Kern* • Anna Sten *Lilo* • Erich von Stroheim *Brenner* ■ *Dir* John Cromwell • *Scr* Talbot Jennings, from the novel *Flotsam* by Erich Maria Remarque

So Fine ★★★ 15

Comedy 1981 · US · Colour · 87mins

Clever comic writer Andrew Bergman's directorial debut is an absolutely hilarious wacky comedy about the inventor of see-through jeans – yes, really! Although fresh-faced Ryan O'Neal isn't ideal as the intellectual heir of a New York City clothing manufacturer, his bookish quality is well-used, and his reluctance to make a career in the garment jungle is wittily observed, while the whole descends into a delirious farce. TS [video]

Ryan O'Neal *Bobby Fine* • Jack Warden *Jack Fine* • Mariangela Melato *Lire* • Richard Kiel *Mr Eddie* • Fred Gwynne *Chairman Lincoln* • Mike Kellin *Sam Schlotzman* • David Rounds *Prof Dick McCarthy* • Joel Steadman *Prof Yarnell* ■ *Dir/Scr* Andrew Bergman

So Goes My Love ★★★ U

Period biographical comedy
1946 · US · BW · 91mins

This light tale of eccentric family life in the 19th century features young Bobby Driscollm whose parents are inventor Don Ameche and the fussing Myrna Loy. It's not without period charm, but it needed a more forceful director than Frank Ryan. However, one should be thankful that Hollywood could at one time produce movies whose charm alone outweighed their content. TS

Myrna Loy *Jane* • Don Ameche *Hiram Stephen Maxim* • Rhys Williams *Magel* • Bobby Driscoll *Percy Maxim* • Richard Gaines *Mr Josephus* • Molly Lamont *Anty Gannet* ■ *Dir* Frank Ryan • *Scr* Bruce Manning, James Clifden, from the memoir *A Genius in the Family* by Hiram Percy Maxim

So I Married an Axe Murderer ★★★ 15

Comedy 1993 · US · Colour · 89mins

Mike Myers's first stab at flying solo from his *Wayne's World* partner Dana Carvey is a mixed bag. He plays an aspiring poet who always manages to talk himself out of long-term relationships with women. All that seems to change when he falls madly in love with Nancy Travis, until evidence starts mounting that she may be a black widow who has left a trail of dead husbands in her wake. There are some nicely black comic moments, but Myers tries too hard and mugs shamelessly to the camera. JF. Contains swearing, nudity. [video] DVD

Mike Myers *Charlie Mackenzie/Stuart Mackenzie* • Nancy Travis *Harriet Michaels* • Anthony LaPaglia *Tony Giardino* • Amanda Plummer *Rose Michaels* • Brenda Fricker *May Mackenzie* • Matt Doherty *Heed* • Charles Grodin *Comandeered car driver* • Phil Hartman *Park ranger "Vickie"* • Debi Mazar *Tony's girlfriend "Susan"* ■ *Dir* Thomas Schlamme • *Scr* Robbie Fox, Mike Myers, Neil Mullarkey, from a story by Robbie Fox

So Long at the Fair ★★ U

Mystery 1950 · UK · BW · 85mins

Everything's set here for an attention-grabbing little mystery. In addition to David Tomlinson's unexplained disappearance, there's the unique backdrop of the 1889 Great Exhibition in Paris, a solid supporting cast and the exciting prospect of seeing Dirk Bogarde woo Jean Simmons. Yet, somehow, it fails to gel. Definitely a wasted opportunity. DP

Jean Simmons *Victoria Barton* • Dirk Bogarde *George Hathaway* • David Tomlinson *Johnny Barton* • Marcel Poncin *Narcisse* • Cathleen Nesbitt *Madam Herve* • Honor Blackman *Rhoda O'Donovan* • Betty Warren *Mrs O'Donovan* ■ *Dir* Terence Fisher, Anthony Darnborough • *Scr* Hugh Mills, Anthony Thorne, from a novel by Anthony Thorne

So Proudly We Hail ★★★

Second World War drama
1943 · US · BW · 125mins

When major Hollywood stars such as John Wayne, Gary Cooper and James Stewart were winning the Second World War, major Hollywood actresses tended to lose out on heroism and were cast as *femme fatales* or dewy-eyed wives. But this lavish Paramount flag-waver puts Claudette Colbert, Paulette Goddard and Veronica Lake into army nurse uniform and packs them off to the Pacific where they get on in a no-nonsense, "pass the plasma please" way. Each of them has a personal problem to overcome and each of them battles with Miklos Rozsa's music. Overlong, but watchable for the stars on parade. AT

Claudette Colbert *Lt Janet Davidson* • Paulette Goddard *Lt Joan O'Doul* • Veronica Lake *Lt Olivia D'Arcy* • George Reeves *Lt John Summers* • Barbara Britton *Lt Rosemary Larson* • Walter Abel *Chaplain* • Sonny Tufts *Kansas* ■ *Dir* Mark Sandrich • *Scr* Allan Scott

So Red the Rose ★★★ U

Period war romance 1935 · US · BW · 82mins

This is the period movie that convinced Hollywood producers that there was no money to be made in movies about the American Civil War, so they all rejected *Gone with the Wind*, letting it go to independent David O Selznick who turned it into screen history. This isn't at all bad, though, and Margaret Sullavan is particularly touching as she waits for Randolph Scott to return from the war between the states. King Vidor's direction is restrained and

S

masterly, making this a rewarding, if little known movie. TS

Margaret Sullavan *Vallette Bedford* • Walter Connolly *Malcolm Bedford* • Randolph Scott *Duncan Bedford* • Janet Beecher *Sally Bedford* • Elizabeth Patterson *Mary Cherry* • Robert Cummings *Archie Pendleton* • Harry Ellerbe *Edward Bedford* • Dickie Moore *Middleton Bedford* • Charles Starrett *George McGehee* ■ *Dir* King Vidor • *Scr* Laurence Stallings, Edwin Justus Mayer, Maxwell Anderson, from a novel by Stark Young

So This Is Love ★★ U

Biographical musical drama
1953 · US · Colour · 100mins

Kathryn Grayson was undeniably talented, as her career-best work in *Show Boat* and *Kiss Me Kate* for MGM demonstrates. However, in this Warner Bros biopic she is seriously miscast, lacking the class to portray real-life tragic Metropolitan Opera star Grace Moore, whose screen career faded as her weight ballooned. The songs are worthy and the Technicolor is fine to watch, but leading man Merv Griffin (later a chat-show host) is dull, and in truth there's little of substance. TS

Kathryn Grayson *Grace Moore* • Merv Griffin *Buddy Nash* • Joan Weldon *Ruth Obre* • Walter Abel *Colonel Moore* • Rosemary DeCamp *Aunt Laura Stokley* • Jeff Donnell *Henrietta Van Dyke* • Ann Doran *Mrs Moore* ■ *Dir* Gordon Douglas • *Scr* John Monks Jr, from the autobiography *You're Only Human Once* by Grace Moore • *Music* Max Steiner

So This Is New York ★★★

Comedy 1948 · US · BW · 77mins

This attractive vehicle for radio star Henry Morgan is an early effort from director Richard Fleischer. Based on Ring Lardner's autobiographical novel, his recollections, when transferred to film, are so good-natured they ultimately become tiresome. Still, there's no denying young Fleischer's talent behind the camera, and film buffs should note that this was also Hollywood legend Stanley Kramer's first producer credit. TS

Henry Morgan *Ernie Finch* • Virginia Grey *Ella Finch* • Dona Drake *Kate Goff* • Rudy Vallee *Herbert Daley* • Bill Goodwin *Jimmy Ralston* • Hugh Herbert *Mr Trumball* • Leo Gorcey *Sid Mercer* • Jerome Cowan *Francis Griffin* ■ *Dir* Richard O Fleischer [Richard Fleischer] • *Scr* Carl Foreman, Herbert Baker, from the novel *The Big Town* by Ring Lardner

So This Is Paris ★★★

Silent comedy 1926 · US · BW · 74mins

German import Ernst Lubitsch's seventh American film is an elegant, sophisticated and satirical silent comedy, in which the unique Lubitsch touch, spoke as eloquently as any words could. It made a mint for Warner Bros and was voted one of the year's ten best by the *New York Times*. The plot revolves around the light-hearted complications that ensue when a husband-and-wife dance duo (Lilyan Tashman, André Beranger) decide to spice up their relationship by indulging in criss-cross flirtations with a doctor and his wife (Monte Blue, Patsy Ruth Miller). Very "French", very ooh-la-la, and a lot of fun. RK

Monte Blue *Dr Eisenstein* • Patsy Ruth Miller *Rosalind Eisenstein* • Lilyan Tashman *Adela, a dancer* • André Beranger *Alfred, her husband* • Myrna Loy *Maid* ■ *Dir* Ernst Lubitsch • *Scr* Hans Kräly, from the play *Le Réveillon* by Henri Meilhac, Ludovic Halévy

So This Is Paris ★★ U

Musical comedy 1954 · US · Colour · 96mins

This retread of every tired old musical cliché about sailors on the town or Americans in Paris, stars Tony Curtis, Gene Nelson and Paul Gilbert as three mariners on the make in the French capital. The musical numbers are reasonably pleasing, if totally forgettable, but the script hits a level of such mind-numbing imbecility that the sentimental element – Gloria De Haven masquerading as French and dancing in a nightclub to help support a bunch of cute orphans – is actually a welcome relief. RK

Tony Curtis *Joe Maxwell* • Gloria De Haven [Gloria DeHaven] *Colette D'Avril/Jane Mitchell* • Gene Nelson *Al Howard* • Corinne Calvet *Suzanne Sorel* • Paul Gilbert *Davey Jones* • Mara Corday *Yvonne* ■ *Dir* Richard Quine • *Scr* Charles Hoffman, from a story by Ray Buffum

So Well Remembered ★★★★

Second World War drama
1947 · UK · BW · 114mins

Adapted from a novel by James Hilton (who narrates), this weighty and moving drama stars John Mills as a crusading newspaper editor in a depressed northern mill town. Directed with a vivid sense of place by Edward Dmytryk, the film chronicles the class and social problems and the struggling socialist politics of the era. Against this canvas, the crises for Mills, including his disastrous marriage to the mill-owner's ruthless daughter (Martha Scott) which brings personal tragedy, and his friendship with the equally dedicated town doctor (Trevor Howard) are played out. Powerful, gripping, and beautifully acted. RK

John Mills *George Boswell* • Martha Scott *Olivia* • Patricia Roc *Julie* • Trevor Howard *Whiteside* • Richard Carlson *Charles* • Reginald Tate *Mangin* • Juliet Mills *Baby Julie* • James Hilton *Narrator* ■ *Dir* Edward Dmytryk • *Scr* John Paxton, from a novel by James Hilton

Soapdish ★★★★ 15

Comedy 1991 · US · Colour · 92mins

The inside dope on daytime soap, with Sally Field, Carrie Fisher and Whoopi Goldberg among the stars and creators of a ghastly TV show called *The Sun Also Sets*. Actors are written out, has-beens stage comebacks, real life echoes fiction, emotional wreckage piles up, you know the rest. As for the always brilliant Kevin Kline, he's been off the show for years. But, executive producer Robert Downey Jr and Field's co-star and rival (Cathy Moriarty) want him back to induce Field to leave. Despite some longueurs, this farce has genuinely hysterical moments. AT. Contains swearing. DVD

Sally Field *Celeste Talbert* • Kevin Kline *Jeffrey Anderson* • Robert Downey Jr *David Barnes* • Whoopi Goldberg *Rose Schwartz* • Carrie Fisher *Betsy Faye Sharon* • Cathy Moriarty *Montana Moorehead* • Teri Hatcher *Ariel Maloney* • Paul Johansson *Bolt Brennan* • Elisabeth Shue *Lori Craven* • Kathy Najimy *Tawny Miller* ■ *Dir* Michael Hoffman • *Scr* Robert Harling, Andrew Bergman, from a story by Robert Harling

Sobibor: 14 October 1943, 16:00 ★★★

Documentary
2001 · Fr · BW and Colour · 95mins

With its title referring to the only successful concentration camp uprising to occur during the entire Second World War (and only previously dramatised for television in *Escape from Sobibor*), director Claude Lanzmann's documentary may lack the scale of his masterpiece, *Shoah*, but it's still a compelling and provocative memoir of one survivor's extraordinary experiences. Recorded in 1979, the interview with Yehuda Lerner is hindered by the on-screen translation. But his testimony shatters many of the myths about how much European Jews knew about their fate and their supposed passive reaction to it. Moreover, the insertion of new location footage and deeply moving bookend passages gives the story of Alexander Pechersky's audacious wartime revolt both a historical context and a contemporary resonance. DP. In French with English subtitles.

Dir/Scr Claude Lanzmann

Soccer Dog: the Movie ★

Comedy 1999 · US · Colour · 98mins

This is supposed to teach kids about acceptance and fair play, but all it proves is that Hollywood doesn't have a clue about the beautiful game. The simpering ministrations of foster parents James Marshall and Olivia D'Abo are bad enough, but the big match sequences are excruciating, even after the stray dog adopted by square peg Jeremy Foley emerges as the team's star player. DP

James Marshall *Alden* • Olivia D'Abo *Elena* • Jeremy Foley *Clay* • Sam McMurray *Coach Shaw* • Billy Drago *The dog catcher* ■ *Dir* Tony Giglio • *Scr* Daniel Forman

Society ★★★ 18

Horror 1989 · US · Colour · 94mins

A truly unique shocker, this mixture of social comment and splatter horror will definitely not be to everyone's taste. Is Bill Warlock just paranoid about his well-respected Beverly Hills family? Or do they really get up to unspeakable taboo-breaking orgies when he's not around? The answer involves a great deal of special make-up effects, including torso distortion, melting flesh, deviant gender blurring and surreal spectacle. Disturbing and silly in roughly equal amounts, this over-the-top exposé of what the rich are really doing to the poor marked the directing debut of Brian Yuzna. AJ. Contains swearing, nudity. DVD

Billy Warlock *Bill Whitney* • Devin Devasquez *Clarisa* • Evan Richards *Milo* • Ben Meyerson *Ted Ferguson* • Charles Lucia *Jim* • Connie Danese *Nan* ■ *Dir* Brian Yuzna • *Scr* Woody Keith, Rick Fry • *Makeup Special Effects* Screaming Mad George

Sodbusters ★★ 12

Comedy western 1994 · Can · Colour · 94mins

Is there anything more embarrassing than a spoof that isn't funny? Kris Kristofferson, as the battle-scarred gunslinger helping some Colorado farmers keep the railroad off their land, has only been armed with blanks, thanks to the leaden script co-written by director Eugene Levy. The inclusion of a couple of gay cowboys doesn't help this TV movie much, either. AT. Contains violence and swearing. DVD

Kris Kristofferson *Destiny* • John Vernon *Slade Cantrell* • Fred Willard *Clarence Gentry* • Wendel Meldrum *Lilac Gentry* • Steve Landesberg *Gunther Schteuppin* • Max Gail *Tom Partridge* ■ *Dir* Eugene Levy • *Scr* Eugene Levy, John Hemphill

Sodom and Gomorrah ★★★ PG

Biblical epic
1962 · US/Fr/It · Colour · 153mins

Lot (Stewart Granger) leads his people away from Sodom and Gomorrah, the twin cities of sin, just as God lays waste to them both. "Don't look back!" Lot tells his wife, but she does and is turned into a pillar of salt (one of the strangest special effects in movie history). Ridiculous in so many ways, Robert Aldrich's biblical epic has an energy and a knowing hypocrisy that makes it very watchable. Sergio Leone directed the Italian version and some of the action sequences. AT

Stewart Granger *Lot* • Anouk Aimée *Queen Bera* • Stanley Baker *Astaroth* • Rossana Podesta *Shuah* • Pier Angeli *Ildith* ■ *Dir* Robert Aldrich, Sergio Leone • *Scr* Hugo Butler, Giorgio Prosperi

Sofie ★★★ PG

Period drama
1992 · Den/Nor/Swe · Colour · 145mins

Liv Ullmann's full-feature-length directorial debut is a Bergmanesque examination of the pressures placed on women in late 19th-century Denmark. A study in dignified strength amid the ruins of her romantic ideals, Karen-Lise Mynster gives a performance worthy of her director, as the mature Jewish woman, who abandons a passionate Gentile painter to marry her repressed shopkeeping cousin and bear him a rebellious son. With Jorgen Persson's compositions suggesting the rigidity of the period, this is deliberate and theatrical, but heartfelt. DP. In Swedish with English subtitles.

Karen-Lise Mynster *Sofie* • Erland Josephson *Semmy* • Ghita Norby *Frederikke* • Jesper Christensen *Hojby* • Torben Zeller *Jonas* ■ *Dir* Liv Ullmann • *Scr* Liv Ullmann, Peter Poulsen, from the novel *Mendel Philipsen and Son* by Henri Nathansen

Soft Beds, Hard Battles ★★ 12

Second World War comedy
1973 · UK · Colour · 90mins

This film reunited Peter Sellers with the Boulting Brothers who had been responsible for one of his greatest screen triumphs, *I'm All Right Jack*. Alas this X-rated Second World War romp was not in the same class. Sellers plays multiple roles in a story of murder and duplicity set around a Parisian brothel in 1940. The production was reportedly dogged with problems and the cracks are all too evident in the finished film. DF DVD

Peter Sellers *General Latour/Major Robinson/Schroeder/Hitler/Prince Kyoto/President of France/Radio newsreader* • Lila Kedrova *Madame Grenier* • Curt Jurgens *General von Grotjahn* • Béatrice Romand *Marie-Claude* ■ *Dir* Roy Boulting • *Scr* Leo Marks, Roy Boulting

Soft Deceit ★★★ 18

Erotic thriller
1994 · US/Can · Colour · 91mins

Made in Canada by writer/director Jorge Montesi, this erotic thriller is packed to the rafters with clichés and contrivances. Yet, you can't quite pull yourself away from watching undercover cop Kate Vernon struggle with her feelings for slippery crook Patrick Bergin. Every trick is thrown into the mix to keep the plot rattling along and Vernon gives a gutsy performance. TS. Contains swearing, violence, sex.

Patrick Bergin *Adam Trent* • Kate Vernon *Anne Fowler* • John Wesley Shipp *Detective John Hobart* • Nigel Bennett *Ed McCullough* • Ted Dykstra *Don Froese* ■ *Dir/Scr* Jorge Montesi

Soft Fruit ★★ 18

Comedy drama
1999 · Aus/US · Colour · 97mins

Jane Campion's former assistant, Christina Andreef, made her feature debut with this spikey, but unfocused comedy drama about a splintered family coming to terms with a mother's terminal cancer. Always a sympathetic matriarch, Jeanie Drynan provides a warm focus for the reunion of her larger-than-life siblings in the hellhole steel town of Port Kembla. The episodic structure deprives the action of dramatic and emotional unity. DP. Contains violence, swearing, drug abuse and nudity.

Jeanie Drynan *Patsy* • Linal Haft *Vic* • Russell Dykstra *Bo* • Geneviève Lemon *Josie* • Sacha Horler *Nadia* • Alicia Talbot *Vera* • Dion Bilios *Bud* ■ *Dir/Scr* Christina Andreef • *Executive Producer* Jane Campion

Soft Top, Hard Shoulder ★★ 15

Road movie 1992 · UK · Colour · 90mins

From its contrived title downwards, virtually everything about this odd couple comedy (apart from the playing of Peter Capaldi and Elaine Collins) is ill-judged. Capaldi bases his script on a Frank Capra classic, with several situations here reminiscent of scenes from *It Happened One Night*. However, Capaldi not only misfires with the screwball antics, but is also wide of the mark with the Bill Forsyth-style whimsy he is obviously striving for. DP. Contains swearing. DVD

Peter Capaldi *Gavin Bellini* • Elaine Collins *Yvonne* • Frances Barber *Miss Trimble* • Catherine Russell *Animal Rights activist* • Jeremy Northam *John* • Richard Wilson *Uncle Salvatore* • Sophie Hall *Nancy* • Scott Hall *Mr Young* • Simon Callow *Eddie Cherdowski* • Phyllis Logan *Karla* ■ *Dir* Stefan Schwartz • *Scr* Peter Capaldi

Soigne Ta Droite ★★

Experimental fantasy
1986 · Fr/Swi · Colour · 82mins

Jean-Luc Godard appears as the idiot and the prince in this impenetrable in-joke, complete with whispered mock-philosophical narration. There are several main stories, inseparable but unconnected, including one about an airline pilot apparently about to commit suicide in midair. The film has been described as a "metaphysical cartoon", but what it all means is anyone's guess. A cinematic doodle. AT. A French language film.

Jean-Luc Godard *The idiot/The prince* • Jacques Villeret *The individual* • François Périer *The man* • Jane Birkin *The cricket* • Michel Galabru *The admiral* ■ *Dir/Scr* Jean-Luc Godard

Sokhout ★★★★

Drama
1998 · Iran/Tajikistan/Fr · Colour · 77mins

Seen as a way of exploring sensitive issues with a reduced risk of incurring the censor's ire, films about children have become an Iranian movie staple. Set in a Tadjik fishing village, this episodic drama centres on Tahmineh Normativa, a blind ten year-old who tunes instruments for an exploitative boss. Mohsen Makhmalbaf re-creates his experience of the bustling bazaar and the way in which his friend tracks him down by following the sounds she knows will entice him. The result is a pure, sensual cinema that's also sociologically compelling. DP. In Farsi with English subtitles.

Tahmineh Normativa *Khorshid* • Nadereh Abdelahyeva *Nadereh* • Golbibi Ziadalahyeva *Khorshid's mother* ■ *Dir/Scr* Mohsen Makhmalbaf

Sol Madrid ★★

Action drama 1968 · US · Colour · 89mins

David McCallum, then the star of *The Man From UNCLE*, gets a chance to go solo and shine in this feeble thriller. McCallum plays a US narcotics agent on the trail of Rip Torn, whose mistress Stella Stevens has betrayed him. Telly Savalas plays a drug runner while Ricardo Montalban lounges about in some fancy shirts playing the Latin lover. Director Brian G Hutton maintains a breathless pace. AT

David McCallum *Sol Madrid* • Stella Stevens *Stacey Woodward* • Telly Savalas *Emil Dietrich* • Ricardo Montalban *Jalisco* • Rip Torn *Dano Villanova* • Pat Hingle *Harry Mitchell* • Paul Lukas *Capo Riccione* • Michael Ansara *Captain Ortega* ■ *Dir* Brian G Hutton • *Scr* David Karp, from the novel *Fruit of the Poppy* by Robert Wilder

Solar Crisis ★★ 15

Science-fiction thriller
1990 · Jpn/US · Colour · 107mins

This expensive co-production was filled with production problems, including director Richard C Sarafian opting for a pseudonym when the producers dictated additional shooting after the movie bombed in Japan. Despite the new footage, it's easy to see why the movie went straight to video in North America. Though the story of a 21st-century space station crew working to save the broiling Earth by firing a special bomb into the Sun has plenty of impressive special effects, the proceedings are bogged down by a lack of tension. KB DVD

Charlton Heston *Skeet Kelso* • Peter Boyle *Teague* • Tetsuya Bessho *Ken Minami* • Jack Palance *Travis* • Tim Matheson *Steve Kelso* • Annabel Schofield *Alex* • Corin "Corky" Nemec [Corin Nemec] *Mike Kelso* • Brenda Bakke *Claire* ■ *Dir* Alan Smithee [Richard C Sarafian] • *Scr* Joe Gannon, Crispan Bolt [Ted Sarafian], from a novel by Takeshi Kawata

Solarbabies ★ 15

Science-fiction adventure
1986 · US · Colour · 90mins

This feeble futuristic fantasy about roller-skating orphans arrived too late to cash in on the teen market of the 1980s. The orphans, imprisoned by tyrant Richard Jordan, try to bring moisture to a parched universe. Other sci-fi films are ripped off without mercy, and the kids aren't even likeable. TH. Contains violence.

Jami Gertz *Terra* • Jason Patric *Jason* • Lukas Haas *Daniel* • Richard Jordan *Grock* • James LeGros *Metron* • Claude Brooks *Rabbit* • Peter DeLuise *Tug* • Adrian Pasdar *Darstar* • Charles Durning *Warden* • Alexei Sayle *Malice* ■ *Dir* Alan Johnson • *Scr* Walon Green, Douglas Anthony Metrov

Solaris ★★★★ PG

Science-fiction drama
1972 · USSR · Colour · 159mins

For some, director Andrei Tarkovsky's philosophical cult movie is the Soviet equivalent of *2001*; for others, it's an obscure intellectual exercise. Based on Polish writer Stanislaw Lem's 1961 novel, the tale involves astronauts on an alien planet who are confronted by illusions from their subconscious memories (usually their morose girlfriends back on Earth). Tarkovsky's highly influential and cerebral science-fiction epic is ponderous, very talky and contains minimal special effects, but its remote strangeness exerts a compelling hypnotic power that's often extraordinarily potent. AJ. In Russian with English subtitles. DVD

Natalya Bondarchuk *Hari* • Donatas Banionis *Kris Kelvin* • Juri Jarvet *Snow* • Anatoli Solonitsin [Anatoli Solonitsyn] *Sartorius* • Vladislav Dvorjetzki *Burton* ■ *Dir* Andrei Tarkovsky • *Scr* Andrei Tarkovsky, Friedrich Gorenstein, from the novel by Stanislaw Lem

Solaris ★★★ 12

Romantic science-fiction drama
2003 · US · Colour · 94mins

To remake Andrei Tarkovsky's brilliant 1972 film might seem impertinent, but director Steven Soderbergh has crafted an original drama here. George Clooney, showcasing his acting talent, plays a psychologist who is called to a space station orbiting the planet Solaris. Clooney is joined by his wife Natascha McElhone, though she had committed suicide on Earth some time before, but the nature of her presence is enigmatic. As a profound meditation on love, regret and desire, this dares to put dialogue before action. TH. Contains swearing, a sex scene and nudity. DVD

George Clooney *Dr Chris Kelvin* • Natascha McElhone *Rheya* • Jeremy Davies *Snow* • Viola Davis *Gordon* • Ulrich Tukur *Gibarian* ■ *Dir* Steven Soderbergh • *Scr* Steven Soderbergh, from the novel by Stanislaw Lem

Solas ★★★★ 15

Drama 1998 · Sp · Colour · 96mins

What would Hollywood's ageing actresses give for a role like this? Exuding battered dignity and stubborn devotion, Maria Galiana excels as the rural housewife who quietly transforms her unmarried daughter's life while her abusive, alcoholic husband recovers in a Seville hospital. Galiana's relationship with the prickly, pregnant and bibulous Ana Fernández highlights both Spain's fierce conservatism and its shifting attitude to previously sacrosanct values. But it's her hesitant friendship with Carlos Alvarez Novoa's urbane octagenarian neighbour that gives the film its charm. Debuting film-maker Benito Zambrano's sedate pacing is perfect. DP. In Spanish with English subtitles. DVD

Ana Fernández *Maria* • Maria Galiana *Rosa Jimenez Pena, Maria's mother* • Carlos Alvarez Novoa *Neighbour* • Paco de Osca *Maria's father* • Juan Fernandez *Juan* ■ *Dir/Scr* Benito Zambrano

Soldier ★ 18

Science-fiction action thriller
1998 · US · Colour · 94mins

Shane goes to outer space in director Paul (*Event Horizon*) Anderson's depressingly unoriginal slice of science fiction. A near monosyllabic Kurt Russell is the brainwashed army killing machine dumped on a garbage planet when a newer DNA manipulated model is developed. There he finds a forgotten outpost of stranded humans who adopt him as their warrior saviour. A by-the-numbers empty spectacle. AJ. Contains violence. DVD

Kurt Russell *Todd* • Jason Scott Lee *Caine 607* • Connie Nielsen *Sandra* • Gary Busey *Captain Church* • Jason Isaacs *Colonel Mekum* • Sean Pertwee *Mace* ■ *Dir* Paul Anderson • *Scr* David Webb Peoples

Soldier Blue ★★★ 18

Western drama 1970 · US · Colour · 114mins

Very controversial on its release, this dramatisation of the Sand Creek Massacre of 1864 does not stint on the appalling carnage meted out to the Cheyenne by the US Cavalry. Scenes of women and children being raped and mutilated were cut by the British censor and the film was widely condemned for its extreme violence. Candice Bergen is kidnapped by Cheyenne tribesmen and becomes culturally enriched rather than bigoted. The often vilified *Soldier Blue* was considered by many contemporary viewers to be an allegory of the My Lai massacre in Vietnam. AT. Contains violence and swearing. DVD

Candice Bergen *Cresta Marybelle Lee* • Peter Strauss *Private Honus Gant* • Donald Pleasence *Isaac Q Cumber* • Bob Carraway *Lieut John McNair* • Jorge Rivero *Spotted Wolf* • Dana Elcar *Captain Battles* • John Anderson *Colonel Iverson* ■ *Dir* Ralph Nelson • *Scr* John Gay, from the novel *Arrow in the Sun* by Theodore V Olsen

Soldier in the Rain ★★★★ U

Comedy drama 1963 · US · BW · 87mins

This unfashionable film is one of the most neglected in Steve McQueen's filmography. The story of scamming and shirking at an army base is *Bilko* with bitterness and sentiment stirred in to give the comedy its unique flavour. McQueen engagingly blends naivety with nous, as he tries to persuade scheming sergeant Jackie Gleason to quit the service and cut a dash on civvy street. An odd couple, but they work well together and make the most of the accomplished script. DP

Steve McQueen *Supply Sgt Eustice Clay* • Jackie Gleason *Master Sgt Maxwell Slaughter* • Tuesday Weld *Bobby Jo Pepperdine* • Tony Bill *Private Jerry Meltzner* • Tom Poston *Lieutenant Magee* • Paul Hartman *Chief of Police* • Adam West *Captain Blekeley* ■ *Dir* Ralph Nelson • *Scr* Maurice Richlin, Blake Edwards, from the novel by William Goldman

Soldier of Fortune ★★★

Romantic adventure
1955 · US · Colour · 95mins

Clark Gable's first movie as an independent freelancer, away from the shackles of his 25-year stint as "King" of MGM. Twentieth Century-Fox was trying out its new CinemaScope process in a variety of locations, and here Gable finds himself in Hong Kong as a smuggler, hired to locate Susan Hayward's husband Gene Barry, who's either dead or over in Red China. Skilled director Edward Dmytryk makes this melodramatic tosh seem extremely exciting, and Gable and Hayward strike starry sparks from each other. TS

Clark Gable *Hank Lee* • Susan Hayward *Jane Hoyt* • Michael Rennie *Inspector Merryweather* • Gene Barry *Louis Hoyt* ■ *Dir* Edward Dmytryk • *Scr* Ernest K Gann, from his novel

Soldier of Orange ★★★★ 15

Second World War drama
1977 · Neth · Colour · 115mins

Paul Verhoeven's lavish, personal war epic re-creates the Nazi invasion of his native Holland and shows the effects it has on six university students, all but one of whom become involved in the Resistance. Known for his graphic depiction of sex and violence, Verhoeven's approach here is more traditional and boasts two splendid leading performances from Rutger Hauer and Jeroen Krabbé. Edward Fox appears as the head of British military intelligence and Susan Penhaligon is on hand to give both Hauer and Krabbé a squeeze when they escape to Britain. AT. In Dutch with English subtitles. DVD

Rutger Hauer *Erik* • Jeroen Krabbé *Gus* • Peter Faber *Will* • Derek De Lint *Alex* • Edward Fox *Colonel Rafelli* • Susan Penhaligon *Susan* ■ *Dir* Paul Verhoeven • *Scr* Gerard Soeteman, Kees Holierhoek, Paul Verhoeven, from a autobiography by Erik Hazelhoff Roelfzema

A Soldier's Daughter Never Cries ★★★ 15

Drama 1998 · US · Colour · 126mins

James Ivory may have freed himself from the Henry James/EM Forster orbit, but this remains a bookish story about a young girl and her relationship with her mum and novelist dad (loosely based on James Jones, author of *From Here to Eternity*). There are good performances behind that terrible title, though Kris Kristofferson rather overdoes the Hemingway/James Jones routine. AT. Contains swearing.

Kris Kristofferson *Bill Willis* • Barbara Hershey *Marcella Willis* • Leelee Sobieski *Channe, aged 14* • Jesse Bradford *Billy, aged 14* • Dominique Blanc *Candida* • Jane Birkin *Mrs Fortescue* ■ *Dir* James Ivory • *Scr* James Ivory, Ruth Prawer Jhabvala, from the novel by Kaylie Jones • *Producer* Ismail Merchant

A Soldier's Story ★★★★ 15

Mystery drama 1984 · US · Colour · 96mins

Adapted by Charles Fuller from his own Pulitzer Prize-winning play, this is not just a gripping mystery, but also a far-reaching investigation into the widely differing aspirations and expectations that divide, as much as unite, America's black population. Howard Rollins gives a showy performance as the army captain sent to a camp in the Deep South to discover who murdered a black sergeant. Everyone has motive and opportunity and, under Norman

Jewison's tight direction, the supporting cast, led by Denzel Washington and the Oscar-nominated Adolph Caesar, give nothing away. DP DVD

Howard E Rollins Jr *Capt Davenport* • Adolph Caesar *Master Sgt Vernon C Waters* • Art Evans *Pte Wilkie* • David Alan Grier *Cpl Cobb* • David Harris *Pte Smalls* • Dennis Lipscomb *Capt Taylor* • Larry Riley *CJ Memphis* • Robert Townsend *Cpl Ellis* • Denzel Washington *Pte Peterson* • Patti LaBelle *Big Mary* ■ *Dir* Norman Jewison • *Scr* Charles Fuller, from his play

A Soldier's Tale ★★★

Second World War drama
1988 · NZ · Colour · 99mins

This touching, offbeat drama did not even get a video release in the UK. Gabriel Byrne is the British soldier in France in the latter years of the Second World War, who falls for a French girl (Marianne Basler) who may or may not be a collaborator. Although it's a little too downbeat, the two leads deliver moving performances and it's directed with some sensitivity. JF. Contains violence, swearing, nudity.

Gabriel Byrne *Saul* • Marianne Basler *Belle* • Paul Wyett *Charlie* • Judge Reinhold *Yank* ■ *Dir* Larry Parr • *Scr* Grant Hinden Miller, Larry Parr, from the novel by MK Joseph

Soldiers Three ★★★ U

Adventure 1951 · US · BW · 91mins

Several Rudyard Kipling stories have been put through the MGM blender and reduced to pulp in this rumbustious North-West Frontier tale. The soldiers are a likeable bunch; Stewart Granger, Walter Pidgeon and David Niven among them. Whenever the plot stalls, which is often, a horde of Indians appears on the horizon. It's not as funny as *Carry On Up the Khyber*, but it is played for laughs. AT

Stewart Granger *Private Archibald Ackroyd* • Walter Pidgeon *Colonel Brunswick* • David Niven *Captain Pindenny* • Robert Newton *Private Jock Sykes* • Cyril Cusack *Private Dennis Malloy* • Greta Gynt *Crenshaw* • Frank Allenby *Colonel Groat* • Robert Coote *Major Mercer* • Dan O'Herlihy *Sergeant Murphy* • Michael Ansara *Manik Rao* ■ *Dir* Tay Garnett • *Scr* Marguerite Roberts, Tom Reed, Malcolm Stuart Boylan, from the short stories by Rudyard Kipling

The Solid Gold Cadillac ★★★ U

Comedy 1956 · US · BW and Colour · 95mins

A clever idea and perfect casting make a delightful comedy. Judy Holliday is the small shareholder who embarrasses the crooked directors of a big company by innocently questioning their high salaries and is given a meaningless job to keep her quiet. In the tradition of Frank Capra, the little woman eventually triumphs over the pompous bosses. Paul Douglas figures as the former chairman who becomes her ally and romantic interest. Richard Quine ably directes in black-and-white with a flash of colour at the end. AE

Judy Holliday *Laura Partridge* • Paul Douglas *Edward L McKeever* • Fred Clark *Clifford Snell* • John Williams *John T Blessington* • Hiram Sherman *Harry Harkness* • Neva Patterson *Amelia Shotgraven* • Ralph Dumke *Warren Gillie* • Ray Collins *Alfred Metcalfe* • Arthur O'Connell *Jenkins* ■ *Dir* Richard Quine • *Scr* Abe Burrows, from the play by George S Kaufman, Howard Teichmann

Solitaire for 2 ★ 15

Romantic comedy
1994 · UK · Colour · 100mins

This unwatchable romantic comedy that left cinema audiences groaning in droves. Amanda Pays is implausible as a woman who reads minds, aware that all the men she dates are only interested in one thing. Academic philanderer Mark Frankel is determined to conquer Pays and their battle forms the bedrock of a bad film. Utterly ridiculous. LH. Contains swearing and sex scenes.

Mark Frankel *Daniel Becker* • Amanda Pays *Katie* • Roshan Seth *Sandip Tamar* • Jason Isaacs *Harry* • Maryam D'Abo *Caroline* • Helen Lederer *Cop* • Malcolm Cooper *Cop* • Annette Crosbie *Mrs Dwyer* • Neil Mullarkey *Parris* ■ *Dir/Scr* Gary Sinyor

Solo ★★ 18

Science-fiction action thriller
1996 · US/Mex · Colour · 89mins

A pumped-up Mario Van Peebles plays a cyber-soldier who refuses to kill innocent Latin American villagers and becomes their friend, in this derivative, but amiable, sci-fi action thriller. You'll recognise themes, scenes and characters from dozens of other movies – particularly *Terminator 2* – but Van Peebles isn't bad as a low-budget Arnie and the film has much less violence and more heart than you would expect. JC. Contains violence and swearing. DVD

Mario Van Peebles *Solo* • Barry Corbin *General Clyde Haynes* • William Sadler *Colonel Madden* • Jaime Gomez *Lorenzo* • Adrian Brody *Bill Stewart* ■ *Dir* Norberto Barba • *Scr* David Corley, from the novel *Weapon* by Robert Mason

Solo for Sparrow ★★ U

Crime drama 1962 · UK · BW · 56mins

Two years before his career-making performance in *Zulu*, Michael Caine was marking time taking small parts in humdrum crime dramas such as this. The nominal star is Donald Houston, playing a policeman who takes a leave of absence to set up his own detective agency. The film was not seen in America until 1966, when the producers took advantage of Caine's newfound success and released it with his name above the title. RT

Anthony Newlands *Mr Reynolds* • Glyn Houston *Inspector Sparrow* • Nadja Regin *Mrs Reynolds* • Michael Coles *Pin Norman* • Allan Cuthbertson *Chief Supt Symington* • Ken Wayne *Baker* • Jerry Stovin *Lewis* • Michael Caine *Mooney* ■ *Dir* Gordon Flemyng • *Scr* Roger Marshall, from the novel *The Gunner* by Edgar Wallace

Solomon and Gaenor ★★★ 15

Period romance 1998 · UK · Colour · 103mins

Filmed in both Welsh and English, director/writer Paul Morrison's debut feature is a tragic tale of forbidden love. Set in 1911 in the Welsh valleys, the Romeo and Juliet-esque narrative finds chapel-goer Gaenor (Nia Roberts) falling for door-to-door salesman Solomon (Ioan Gruffudd). Yet Solomon has concealed his Jewish identity and, in a heated atmosphere of anti-Semitism, the couple take desperate measures to preserve their love. Both Gruffudd and Roberts are outstanding as the lovers; ultimately, however, this is a grim and sorry tale. LH. In English, Welsh and Yiddish with subtitles. Contains sex scenes, violence.

Ioan Gruffudd *Solomon* • Nia Roberts *Gaenor* • Sue Jones-Davies *Gwen* • William Thomas *Idris* • Mark Lewis Jones *Crad* • Maureen Lipman *Rezl* • David Horovitch *Isaac* • Bethan Ellis Owen *Bronwen* • Adam Jenkins *Thomas* ■ *Dir/Scr* Paul Morrison

Solomon and Sheba ★★ PG

Biblical epic 1959 · US · Colour · 135mins

This generally stodgy epic has a black-wigged Yul Brynner courting scantily clad Gina Lollobrigida in days of Biblical yore. This has all the weaknesses of the genre, notably a script brimming with non sequiturs and inane Americanisms. Despite some eye-catching designs and photography by Freddie Young, the picture was probably doomed when the original star, Tyrone Power, died on set. That disaster, together with a critical drubbing and poor audiences, caused the director, King Vidor, to abandon the movie business for good. AT DVD

Yul Brynner *Solomon* • Gina Lollobrigida *Magda, Queen of Sheba* • George Sanders *Adonijah* • Marisa Pavan *Abishag* • David Farrar *Pharaoh* • John Crawford *Joab* • Laurence Naismith *Hezrai* • José Nieto *Ahab* • Alejandro Rey *Sittar* ■ *Dir* King Vidor • *Scr* Anthony Veillier, Paul Dudley, George Bruce, from a story by Crane Wilbur • *Art Director* Richard Day, Alfred Sweeney

Sombrero ★★

Musical drama 1952 · US · Colour · 103mins

A messy, meandering and overblown attempt to capture the flavour of Mexican life through three different love stories results in a colourfully filmed but bizarre mix of music and melodrama. The first tale, involving Ricardo Montalban and Pier Angeli in a Romeo and Juliet situation aims for comedy; romance between wealthy Vittorio Gassman and peasant Yvonne Carlo is a tearjerker; and the marriage of bullfighter's dancing sister Cyd Charisse to a street trader ends in bloody violence. The last episode has an electrifying display of flamenco dancing by José Greco and a good bullfighting sequence. RK

Ricardo Montalban *Pepe Gonzales* • Pier Angeli *Eufemia Calderon* • Vittorio Gassman *Alejandro Castillo* • Yvonne De Carlo *Maria* • Cyd Charisse *Lola de Torrano* • Rick Jason *Ruben* • Nina Foch *Elena* • José Greco *Gintanillo de Torrano* ■ *Dir* Norman Foster • *Scr* Norman Foster, Josefina Niggli, from the novel *A Mexican Village* by Josefina Niggli

Some Came Running ★★★ PG

Drama 1958 · US · Colour · 130mins

Dismissed in its day as hokum, this can now be fully appreciated for what it is: a highly stylised MGM melodrama from ace director Vincente Minnelli. The fireworks of the finale are exemplary and there is an extraordinarily watchable cast, headed by Frank Sinatra at his most convincing. Perhaps the real acting revelation is Dean Martin as the man who steadfastly refuses to remove his hat, but gals Shirley MacLaine and Martha Hyer are also mighty fine. TS

Frank Sinatra *Dave Hirsh* • Dean Martin *Bama Dillert* • Shirley MacLaine *Ginny Moorhead* • Arthur Kennedy *Frank Hirsh* • Martha Hyer *Gwen French* • Nancy Gates *Edith Barclay* ■ *Dir* Vincente Minnelli • *Scr* John Patrick, Arthur Sheekman, from the novel by James Jones • *Music* Elmer Bernstein

Some Girls ★★ 15

Comedy 1988 · US · Colour · 89mins

Also known as *Sisters*, this has Patrick Dempsey as the student who looks forward to spending Christmas with his girlfriend's family in Canada, only to fall prey to both of her sisters while trying to avoid the watchful eye of her eccentric parents. Directed by Michael Hoffman, this has some moments of hilarity, but not enough to sustain interest in what is supposed to be a funny film. JB. Contains swearing, sex scenes, nudity.

Patrick Dempsey *Michael* • Jennifer Connelly *Gabby* • Sheila Kelley *Irenka* • Andre Gregory *Father* • Ashley Greenfield *Simone* • Florinda Bolkan *Mother* ■ *Dir* Michael Hoffman • *Scr* Rupert Walters

Some Girls ★★★ 18

Romantic comedy drama
1998 · US · Colour · 81mins

This engagingly quirky and often filthily funny 20-something ensemble piece sadly disappeared straight to video over here. The story focuses on a disparate group of friends all looking for love in 1990s Los Angeles, but none with any particular luck. Marissa Ribisi, who also co-wrote it, heads a hot young cast who all deliver exemplary performances. JF

Marissa Ribisi *Claire* • Juliette Lewis *April* • Giovanni Ribisi *Jason* • Jeremy Sisto *Chad* • Pamela Segall Adlon [Pamela Segall] *Jenn* • Kristin Dattilo *Suzanne* • Michael Rapaport *Neal* ■ *Dir* Rory Kelly • *Scr* Marissa Ribisi, Brie Shaffer

Some Girls Do ★★

Spy comedy thriller
1969 · UK · Colour · 93mins

Having played Bulldog Drummond with some aplomb in *Deadlier than the Male* in 1966, Richard Johnson is left high and dry in this risible sequel about a missing supersonic jet. Desperately seeking to spoof James Bond and cash in on the swinging sauciness of the 1960s, the plot is even flimsier than the costumes worn by the bevy of bad beauties. DP

Richard Johnson *Hugh Drummond* • Daliah Lavi *Baroness Helga Hagen* • Beba Loncar *Pandora* • James Villiers *Carl Petersen* • Sydne Rome *Flicky* • Ronnie Stevens *Peregrine Carruthers* • Robert Morley *Miss Mary* • Maurice Denham *Mr Mortimer* ■ *Dir* Ralph Thomas • *Scr* David Osborn, Liz Charles-Williams, from the character created by HC "Sapper" McNeile

Some Kind of Hero ★★ 15

Comedy 1982 · US · Colour · 92mins

Brilliant stand-up comedian Richard Pryor enjoyed mixed fortunes when he swapped the stage for the silver screen. Here he's a Vietnam vet who returns to the USA after six years imprisonment by the Viet Cong to find the life he left behind has disappeared. Jobs are scarce and Pryor is tempted to try crime to survive. It's an uneasy mix of comedy and drama with its worthy sentiments undermined by feeble attempts at humour. DF

Richard Pryor *Eddie Keller* • Margot Kidder *Toni* • Ray Sharkey *Vinnie* • Ronny Cox *Colonel Powers* • Lynne Moody *Lisa* • Olivia Cole *Jesse* • Paul Benjamin *Leon* ■ *Dir* Michael Pressman • *Scr* Robert Boris, James Kirkwood, from a novel by James Kirkwood

Some Kind of Wonderful ★★★★ 15

Romantic drama 1987 · US · Colour · 90mins

Lea Thompson has one of her best roles as the spoilt girl that garage attendant Eric Stoltz falls for, and Mary Stuart Masterson delightful as the tomboy who secretly harbours deeper feelings for her male friend. Stoltz makes an effective leading man, giving a touching performance in what is a genuinely charming film. JB DVD

Eric Stoltz *Keith Nelson* • Mary Stuart Masterson *Watts* • Lea Thompson *Amanda Jones* • Craig Sheffer *Hardy Jenns* • John Ashton *Cliff Nelson* • Elias Koteas *Skinhead* • Molly Hagan *Shayne* • Chynna Phillips *Mia* ■ *Dir* Howard Deutch • *Scr* John Hughes

Some Like It Hot ★★ U

Musical comedy 1939 · US · BW · 64mins

Based on Ben Hecht and Gene Fowler's Broadway flop *The Great Magoo*, this musical comedy was retitled *Rhythm Romance* for US television broadcast to avoid confusing it with Billy Wilder's 1959 cross-dressing classic. In only his sixth feature, Bob Hope ably holds the

U = SUITABLE FOR ALL Uc = SUITABLE FOR ALL, ESPECIALLY FOR YOUNG CHILDREN (VIDEO ONLY) PG = PARENTAL GUIDANCE

action together, as the fairground shyster exploiting girlfriend Shirley Ross's singing talent in the hope of making it big. This is moderate fare, despite being directed with brisk efficiency by journeyman George Archainbaud, but Gene Krupa's drum routine is worth catching. DP

Bob Hope *Nicky Nelson* • Shirley Ross *Lily Racquet* • Una Merkel *Flo Saunders* • Gene Krupa • Rufe Davis *Stoney* • Bernard Nedell *Stephen Hanratty* ■ *Dir* George Archainbaud • *Scr* Lewis R Foster, Wilkie Mahoney, from the play *The Great Magoo* by Gene Fowler, Ben Hecht

Some Like It Hot ★★★★★ U

Classic comedy 1959 · US · BW · 121mins

Tony Curtis and Jack Lemmon are ideally matched in this crackling cross-dressing comedy, as the 1920s musicians who join an all-girl band to escape the Mob after witnessing a St Valentine's Day massacre. Amazingly, Billy Wilder had originally wanted Bob Hope and Danny Kaye, and even considered casting Frank Sinatra instead of Lemmon. Curtis didn't always get along with Marilyn Monroe and compared their embraces to kissing Hitler (ironically, the name she gave the bullying Wilder). Yet sparks fly when she falls for Curtis's bogus oil tycoon – who not only boasts the voice of Cary Grant but also the body language of Grace Kelly! Clearly, the personality clashes both on- and off-screen were crucial to this becoming a true film classic, for, as Joe E Brown famously says in the last line, "Nobody's perfect!" DP [video] DVD

Marilyn Monroe *Sugar Kane* • Tony Curtis *Joe/Josephine* • Jack Lemmon *Jerry/Daphne* • George Raft *Spats Columbo* • Pat O'Brien *Mulligan* • Joe E Brown *Osgood E Fielding III* • Nehemiah Persoff *Little Bonaparte* • Joan Shawlee *Sweet Sue* • Billy Gray *Sig Poliakoff* ■ *Dir* Billy Wilder • *Scr* Billy Wilder, I AL Diamond, from the film *Fanfares of Love* by Robert Thoeren, M Logan • *Costume Designer* Orry-Kelly

Some Mother's Son ★★★★ 15

Political drama
1996 · Ire/US · Colour · 106mins

This, while it touches the raw nerve of Northern Irish politics, shows Helen Mirren's formidable ability; as a widowed mother who discovers her son is involved with the IRA and fighting for him when he is on the prison hunger strike during which ten activists died in the early 1980s. Director Terry George makes no secret of whose side he's on, but Helen Mirren extends propaganda into an unsentimental, but poignant, portrait of motherhood. TH. Contains swearing, violence. [video]

Helen Mirren *Kathleen Quigley* • Fionnula Flanagan *Annie Higgins* • Aidan Gillen *Gerard Quigley* • David O'Hara *Frank Higgins* • John Lynch *Bobby Sands* • Tom Hollander *Farnsworth* • Tim Woodward *Tim Harrington* • Ciaran Hinds *Damny Boyle* ■ *Dir* Terry George • *Scr* Jim Sheridan, Terry George

Some People ★★★

Melodrama 1962 · UK · Colour · 93mins

This coffee bar musical arrived two months before the Beatles, but its moral values are those of the early 1950s: motorbikes and pop music equal juvenile delinquency, and what young tearaways need is spiritual guidance. (The film's profits went to the Duke of Edinburgh's relatively new Award Scheme, which is heavily plugged.) Ray Brooks and David Hemmings are among the boys who are taken under the wing of church organist Kenneth More. Naively charm, with unusual Bristol locations and a bouncy title song. DM

Kenneth More *Mr Smith* • Ray Brooks *Johnnie* • Annika Wills *Anne Smith* • David Andrews *Bill* • Angela Douglas *Terry* • David Hemmings *Bert* • Timothy Nightingale *Tim* • Frankie Dymon Jr *Jimmy* ■ *Dir* Clive Donner • *Scr* John Eldridge

Some Voices ★★★ 15

Comedy drama 2000 · UK · Colour · 96mins

Simon Cellan Jones makes his feature debut with this low-key study of psychiatric instability and its ramifications. The director occasionally allows Joe Penhall's adaptation of his own play to become stagey and soap-operatic, and there's a lack of impact in the conventional relationships the schizophrenic Daniel Craig has with his café-owning brother, David Morrissey, and sassy Scot Kelly Macdonald. Yet Cellan Jones still manages to give an immediacy to the action by using flash-editing techniques to convey Craig's distorted world. An intense, affecting and well-acted film. DP [video] DVD

Daniel Craig *Ray* • David Morrissey *Pete* • Kelly Macdonald *Laura* • Julie Graham *Mandy* • Peter McDonald *Dave* ■ *Dir* Simon Cellan Jones • *Scr* Joe Penhall, from his play

Some Will, Some Won't ★ PG

Comedy 1969 · UK · Colour · 86mins

If this insipid remake of *Laughter in Paradise* is supposed to be a comedy, it's not only an insult to the memory of the original, but it also breaches the Trades Descriptions Act. What makes this an even more depressing experience is the utter waste of fine cast, with Thora Hird, Michael Hordern, Ronnie Corbett and Leslie Phillips as the quartet forced to humiliate themselves to benefit from joker Wilfrid Brambell's will. DP [video]

Ronnie Corbett *Herbert Russell* • Thora Hird *Agnes Russell* • Michael Hordern *Deniston Russell* • Leslie Phillips *Simon Russell* • Barbara Murray *Lucille* • Wilfrid Brambell *Henry Russell* • Dennis Price *Benson* • James Robertson-Justice *Sir Charles Robson* ■ *Dir* Duncan Wood • *Scr* Lew Schwarz, from the film *Laughter in Paradise* by Jack Davies, Michael Pertwee

Somebody Killed Her Husband ★★ PG

Comedy mystery 1978 · US · Colour · 92mins

Farrah Fawcett (in her first starring feature role) turns amateur detective with Jeff Bridges to find out who killed her husband in this lame comedy mystery. Director Lamont Johnson is clearly aiming for a sophisticated caper in the Hitchcock vein, and the engaging climax during the Macy's Thanksgiving Parade almost gets there. The ex-Charlie's Angel isn't bad but she's a little too lightweight to carry the melodramatic load in such inconsequential fluff. AJ [video]

Farrah Fawcett-Majors [Farrah Fawcett] *Jenny Moore* • Jeff Bridges *Jerry Green* • John Wood *Ernest Van Santen* • Tammy Grimes *Audrey Van Santen* • John Glover *Hubert Little* • Patricia Elliott *Helene* • Mary McCarty *Flora* ■ *Dir* Lamont Johnson • *Scr* Reginald Rose

Somebody Loves Me ★★★ U

Musical biography
1952 · US · Colour · 90mins

This typical highly fictionalised musical biopic was Betty Hutton's penultimate picture, and her last for Paramount. When studio executives refused to give in to her demand that her second husband, Charles O'Curran, who choreographed the film, be allowed to direct her subsequent pictures, she left, and her career was almost over. Hutton is as energetic as ever in this rags-to-riches story of vaudeville entertainer Blossom Seeley, and delivers several fine songs in her raucous and sentimental manner. RB

Betty Hutton *Blossom Seeley* • Ralph Meeker *Benny Fields* • Robert Keith (1) *Sam Doyle* • Adele Jergens *Nola Beach* • Billie Bird *Essie* • Henry Slate *Forrest* • Sid Tomack *Lake* • Ludwig Stossel *Mr Grauman* • Jack Benny ■ *Dir/Scr* Irving Brecher

Somebody to Love ★★ 18

Romantic drama 1994 · US · Colour · 98mins

A meandering menagerie of characters merge here in this stream of consciousness, urban drama. Steve Buscemi, Stanley Tucci, Quentin Tarantino and Anthony Quinn all have bizarre cameos in this story of the unrequited love felt by aspiring actress Rosie Perez for down on his luck TV cowboy Harvey Keitel. Perez is the energy and fun in the film, and it needs her. However, though both an interesting and perceptive exercise by director Alexandre Rockwell, Perez just isn't dynamic enough. A strange and slightly nihilistic trip. LH [video]

Rosie Perez *Mercedes* • Harvey Keitel *Harry* • Michael DeLorenzo *Ernesto* • Stanley Tucci *George* • Steve Buscemi *Mickey* • Anthony Quinn *Emilio* • Samuel Fuller *Old man on highway* • Quentin Tarantino *Bartender* ■ *Dir* Alexandre Rockwell • *Scr* Alexandre Rockwell, Sergei Bodrov

Somebody Up There Likes Me ★★★★ PG

Biographical sports drama
1956 · US · BW · 108mins

The role of middleweight champ Rocky Graziano was intended for James Dean, who unfortunately had a date with destiny on the highway. Into the ring stepped Paul Newman, and he became a star overnight. Newman brings to the role a lot of Marlon Brando's Method mannerisms and the script drags in rather too many social issues for comfort. It's very much a product, albeit an important one, from in the 1950s. Watch closely, and you'll catch Steve McQueen making his screen debut. AT [video]

Paul Newman *Rocky Graziano* • Pier Angeli *Norma* • Everett Sloane *Irving Cohen* • Eileen Heckart *Ma Barbella* • Sal Mineo *Romolo* • Harold J Stone *Nick Barbella* • Steve McQueen *Fidel* • Robert Loggia *Frankie Peppo* ■ *Dir* Robert Wise • *Scr* Ernest Lehman, from the autobiography by Rocky Graziano, Rowland Barber • *Cinematographer* Joseph Ruttenberg • *Art Director* Cedric Gibbons, Malcolm Brown

Someone at the Door ★★

Comedy thriller 1936 · UK · BW · 74mins

Contrived only goes part way to describing this creaky thriller, in which a reporter desperate for a scoop stumbles across a real mystery while staging a fake murder. Noah Beery Sr and Edward Chapman add a touch of spice as jewel thieves, but Billy Milton and Aileen Marson are resistible as the hack and his accomplice sister. DP

Billy Milton *Ronald Martin* • Aileen Marson *Sally Martin* • Noah Beery Sr [Noah Beery] *Harry Kapel* • Edward Chapman *Price* • John Irwin *Bill Reid* • Hermione Gingold *Mrs Appleby* • Charles Mortimer *Sergeant Spedding* ■ *Dir* Herbert Brenon • *Scr* Jack Davies, Marjorie Deans, from the play by Dorothy Christie, Campbell Christie

Someone at the Door ★★ U

Crime comedy 1950 · UK · BW · 61mins

A remake of Herbert Brenon's 1936 version of the hit West End play, this is Hammer hokum of the hoariest kind. There isn't a semblance of suspense in the shenanigans that follow journalist Michael Medwin's bizarre decision to make headlines with the fake killing of his sister. Not even the arrival of jewel thieves at the haunted house they've inherited can revive one's fast-fading interest. DP

Michael Medwin *Ronnie Martin* • Garry Marsh *Kapel* • Yvonne Owen *Sally Martin* • Hugh Latimer *Bill Reid* • Danny Green *Price* • Campbell Singer *Inspector Spedding* • John Kelly (2) *PC O'Brien* ■ *Dir* Francis Searle • *Scr* AR Rawlinson, from the play by Dorothy Christie, Campbell Christie

Someone behind the Door ★★

Crime drama 1971 · Fr /UK · Colour · 95mins

The strange pairing of Anthony Perkins and Charles Bronson (and Bronson's wife Jill Ireland) is the most interesting thing about this psychological suspense drama. It's also interesting to see Bronson cast in a different role for a change, playing a lost and befuddled amnesiac who doesn't know he's a fugitive psychotic. When doctor Perkins discovers who he is, he decides to use him as a tool in his plans for revenge against his adulterous wife. The movie drifts along at a pretty slow pace. KB

Charles Bronson *Stranger* • Anthony Perkins *Laurence Jeffries* • Jill Ireland *Frances Jeffries* • Henri Garcin *Paul Damien* • Adriano Magestretti *Andrew* • Agathe Natanson *Lucy* ■ *Dir* Nicolas Gessner • *Scr* Marc Behm, Jacques Robert, Nicolas Gessner, Lorenzo Ventavoli, from the novel *Quelqu'un Derrière la Porte* by Jacques Robert

Someone Else's America ★★★ 15

Comedy drama
1995 · Fr/UK/Ger · Colour · 95mins

Winner of the audience prize at Cannes, this well-meaning drama gave Tom Conti another chance to play a heavily accented Mediterranean type. As the Spanish bar owner living in Brooklyn with his blind mother, Conti gives a heartfelt performance that's matched by Miki Manojlovic as the illegal immigrant from Montenegro who becomes his lodger. Released at a time when the Balkan crisis was front-page news, this gentle, if unfocused, fable takes on a more serious tone when Manojlovic's mother decides to leave Montenegro and head for the promised land of America to reunite her grandchildren with their father. AT. In English and Serbo-Croat with subtitles. Contains swearing. [video]

Tom Conti *Alonso* • Miki Manojlovic *Bayo* • Maria Casarès *Alonso's mother* • Zorka Manojlovic *Bayo's mother* ■ *Dir* Goran Paskaljevic • *Scr* Gordon Mihic

Someone Is Bleeding ★★★

Thriller 1974 · Fr · Colour · 100mins

Mireille Darc plays against type in this engrossing psychological thriller. As the sociopathic drug addict who spells trouble for all the men she encounters, Darc displays an icy detachment that ensnares television writer Claude Brasseur. Although he usually injected a note of levity into his thrillers, Lautner plays this adaptation of Richard Matheson's novel dead straight, casting a wintry pall over the Riviera coastline that not only reflects Darc's cold heart, but also the film's effectively downbeat ending. DP. French dialogue dubbed into English.

Alain Delon *Marc* • Claude Brasseur *Francois* • Mireille Darc *Peggy* • Nicoletta Machiavelli *Jacqueline* • Fiora Altoviti *Denis* ■ *Dir* Georges Lautner • *Scr* Georges Lautner, from the novel by Richard Matheson

Someone like Hodder ★★★

Fantasy comedy drama
2003 · Den · Colour · 80mins

Inspired by a bestselling Danish novel, this family comedy drama marks the feature debut of Henrik Ruben Genz. It takes its audience seriously and tackles subjects such as bereavement and bullying with wistful gravitas.

S

Indeed, Genz is more interested in the everyday problems facing Frederick Christian Johansen than his dead mother's ethereal insistence that he save the world single-handedly. Lars Brygmann and Birthe Neumann provide offbeat support, but it's the imaginative nine-year-old's melancholic intensity that gives the film its charm. DP. In Danish with English subtitles.

Frederick Christian Johansen *Hodder* • Lars Brygmann *Hodder's father* • Birthe Neumann *Asta K* • Trine Appel *Lola* • Anders Lunden Kjeldsen *Filip* • Maurice Blinkenberg *Alex* ■ *Dir* Henrik Ruben Genz • *Scr* Bo Hr Hansen, from the novel by Bjarne Reuter

Someone to Love ★★★ 15

Comedy drama 1987 · US · Colour · 104mins

This discussion of love and loneliness was written and directed by leading independent Henry Jaglom. He also stars, playing a film-maker who seeks to solve his romantic problems by getting his friends to reveal their deepest emotions during a Valentine's party. While there are a few profound insights and the odd smart remark, it's not an easy picture to get involved in. The highlight is Orson Welles making his final film appearance. DP. Contains swearing. [video]

Orson Welles *Danny's friend* • Henry Jaglom *Danny Sapir* • Andrea Marcovicci *Helen Eugene* • Michael Emil *Mickey Sapir* • Sally Kellerman *Edith Helm* ■ *Dir/Scr* Henry Jaglom

Someone to Watch over Me ★★★★ 15

Thriller 1987 · US · Colour · 102mins

This intelligent thriller remains one of Ridley Scott's most quietly satisfying works. Tom Berenger plays a tough police detective who gets to sample the high life when he is assigned to protect beautiful, wealthy Mimi Rogers, the key witness in a murder trial. It may lack the power of the some of Scott's other films, but this is still a beautifully shot, stylish affair. Howard Franklin's clever script touches upon issues of class and voyeurism, while still producing the goods in the suspense stakes. The performances are first rate. JF. Contains swearing, violence, nudity. [video] DVD

Tom Berenger *Mike Keegan* • Mimi Rogers *Claire Gregory* • Lorraine Bracco *Ellie Keegan* • Jerry Orbach *Lieutenant Garber* • John Rubinstein *Neil Steinhart* • Andreas Katsulas *Joey Venza* ■ *Dir* Ridley Scott • *Scr* Howard Franklin • *Cinematographer* Steven Poster

S

Somersault ★★★★ 15

Drama 2004 · Aus · Colour · 101mins

This moving coming-of-age drama deservedly cleaned up at the 2004 AFI awards (the Australian equivalent of the Oscars), bagging a record 13 gongs. Newcomer Abbie Cornish won the best actress award for her superb performance as a teenage girl who flees home after seducing her mother's partner. She ends up in a small town at the foot of a ski resort, where she begins a troubled relationship with a brooding local farmer (the equally good Sam Worthington, who won best actor). The story is familiar enough, but director Cate Shortland sympathetically catches the heartbreak and emotional confusion of her flawed characters, with an eye for quirky detail and fresh, haunting visuals. JF. Contains swearing, violence, sex scenes. DVD

Abbie Cornish *Heidi* • Sam Worthington *Joe* • Lynette Curran *Irene* • Erik Thomson *Richard* • Hollie Andrew *Bianca* • Leah Purcell *Diane* • Olivia Pigeot *Nicole* • Blake Pittman *Karl* ■ *Dir/Scr* Cate Shortland

Something about Love ★★★ 15

Drama 1987 · Can · Colour · 89mins

Resisting the temptation to wallow in nostalgia, this is an engaging variation on the theme of the returning exile. In addition to his starring role, Stefan Wodoslawsky wrote the semi-autobiographical script, in which a Los Angeles TV producer comes home to Nova Scotia to visit his dying father. The Ukrainian background adds to the interest, but there's nothing particularly new about the squabbles between father and son. However, there's a nice strain of humour to leaven the mix of regret and recrimination. DP [video]

Stefan Wodoslawsky *Wally Olynyk* • Jan Rubes *Stan Olynyk* • Jennifer Dale *Bobbie* • Diana Reis *Elaine* ■ *Dir* Tom Berry • *Scr* Tom Berry, Stefan Wodoslawsky

Something about Sex ★★★ 18

Comedy 1998 · US · Colour · 89mins

Differing attitudes towards sexual fidelity are explored with humorous candour by writer/director Adam Rifkin. It may join a long list of contemporary movies in which affluent, attractive characters are handicapped by the hang-ups and neuroses of "ordinary people", but this is truthfully scripted and keenly acted by its young cast. Despite obvious insights, the unexpected sexiness of its bedroom scenes, coupled with some comical fantasy scenes, give the film some minor distinction. JC [video] DVD

Jonathan Silverman *Joel* • Leah Lail *Sophie* • Ryan Alosio *Isaac* • Amy Yasbeck *Claudia* • Patrick Dempsey *Sam* • Christine Taylor *Sammie* • Jason Alexander *Art* ■ *Dir/Scr* Adam Rifkin

something big ★

Comedy western
1971 · US · Colour · 108mins

This is the only other movie alongside *tom thumb* to insist on lower-case lettering in its original publicity – apt, because this would-be comedy western is very lower case indeed. Dean Martin enjoys his post-Matt Helm stardom by offering such a perilously lazy performance that you just want to shut your eyes and nod off. Tasteless and unfunny. TS

Dean Martin *Joe Baker* • Brian Keith *Colonel Morgan* • Honor Blackman *Mary Anna Morgan* • Carol White *Dover MacBride* • Ben Johnson *Jesse Bookbinder* • Albert Salmi *Johnny Cobb* • Don Knight *Tommy MacBride* • Joyce Van Patten *Polly Standall* • Denver Pyle *Junior Frisbee* ■ *Dir* Andrew V McLaglen • *Scr* James Lee Barrett

Something for Everyone ★★★

Black comedy 1970 · US · Colour · 112mins

Celebrated theatre director Harold Prince made his feature debut with this pitch black adaptation. Walter Lassally's images of the Bavarian countryside are splendid, but otherwise Prince opts for a decidedly stagey approach, with the long-held shots designed to draw attention to the excellence of the cast. Michael York adds malevolence to his trademark charm, as the opportunist who attempts to exploit countess Angela Lansbury while serving as her footman. But it's Lansbury and her spiteful daughter, Jane Carr, who take the acting honours in a story notable for the dastardliness of just about every principal character. DP

Angela Lansbury *Countess Herthe von Ornstein* • Michael York *Konrad Ludwig* • Anthony Corlan [Anthony Higgins] *Helmuth von Ornstein* • Heidelinde Weis *Anneliese Pleschke* • Jane Carr *Lotte von Ornstein* • Eva-Maria Meineke *Mrs Pleschke* • John Gill *Mr Pleschke* ■ *Dir* Harold Prince • *Scr* Hugh Wheeler, from the novel *The Cook* by Harry Kressing

Something for Joey ★★★★

Drama based on a true story
1977 · US · Colour · 96mins

A fine screenplay, superior acting and classy direction save this made-for-TV drama – based on the true-life relationship between a US college football star and his kid brother who is dying of leukaemia– from sentimentality. Geraldine Page and Steve Guttenberg both won praise for their performances and went on to greater fame and fortune. However, it is Jeff Lynas's sensitive portrayal of the afflicted brother, that provides the key to making this such a surprisingly effective, moving and uplifting film. PF

Geraldine Page *Anne Cappelletti* • Gerald S O'Loughlin *John Cappelletti Sr* • Marc Singer *John Cappelletti* • Jeff Lynas [Jeffrey Lynas] *Joey Cappelletti* • Linda Kelsey *Joyce Cappelletti/Narrator* • Brian Farrell *Marty Cappelletti* • Kathleen Beller *Jean Cappelletti* • Steve Guttenberg *Mike Cappelletti* ■ *Dir* Lou Antonio • *Scr* Jerry McNeely

Something for the Boys ★★★ U

Musical 1944 · US · Colour · 86mins

Cole Porter's 1943 stage production lost a lot on its transfer to the screen, including Ethel Merman and most of its score. What remains is a typically garish 20th Century-Fox musical, interesting today for the array of talent on display. The plot's about cousins Carmen Miranda, Vivian Blaine and Phil Silvers opening up their inherited southern plantation to army wives, and putting on a show to fund it. Silvers is terrific in a routine that owes much to his vaudeville background, while that new young crooner Perry Como puts over numbers with style and verve. TS

Carmen Miranda *Chiquita Hart* • Michael O'Shea *Staff Sergeant Rocky Fulton* • Vivian Blaine *Blossom Hart* • Phil Silvers *Harry Hart* • Sheila Ryan *Melanie Walker* • Perry Como *Sergeant Laddie Green* • Glenn Langan *Lieutenant Ashley Crothers* ■ *Dir* Lewis Seiler • *Scr* Robert Ellis, Helen Logan, Frank Gabrielson, from a musical comedy by Herbert Fields, Dorothy Fields, Cole Porter

Something in the City ★★ U

Comedy 1950 · UK · BW · 76mins

After 40 years as a circus clown and music-hall comic, Richard Hearne finally found fame on TV as the fumbling old fool, Mr Pastry. But, as is often the case, the performer was less fond of the character to whom he owed his fortune than the public, and Hearne frequently sought to escape from the corny slapstick of his children's shows. Here, he plays a pavement artist who convinces his wife he is a high financier. The cheery street folk simply don't ring true and the pathos makes Chaplin look like a cynic. DP

Richard Hearne *William Ningle* • Garry Marsh *Mr Holley* • Ellen Pollock *Mrs Holley* • Betty Sinclair *Mrs Ningle* • Tom Gill *Richard* • Dora Bryan *Waitress* ■ *Dir* Maclean Rogers • *Scr* HF Maltby

Something in the Wind ★★★ U

Musical romantic comedy
1947 · US · BW · 85mins

Deanna Durbin would make only a couple more pictures after this engaging comedy of errors, but she's on fine form as a radio star who's kidnapped by John Dall, after he becomes convinced that she'd been gold-digging with his wealthy, late grandfather. Romantic twists and entanglements ensue, complicated by the involvement of Dall's livewire cousin, Donald O'Connor. Director Irving Pichel occasionally pads the action, but Durbin's rendition of a Verdi aria (with Metropolitan Opera star Jan Peerce) is splendid, as is O'Connor's athletic parody of pulp thriller clichés. DP [video] DVD

Deanna Durbin *Mary Collins* • Donald O'Connor *Charlie Read* • John Dall *Donald Read* • Charles Winninger *Uncle Chester* • Helena Carter *Clarissa Prentice* • Margaret Wycherly *Grandma Read* • Jan Peerce *Tony* • Jean Adair *Aunt Mary Collins* ■ *Dir* Irving Pichel • *Scr* Harry Kurnitz, William Bowers, from a story by Fritz Rotter, Charles O'Neal

Something Money Can't Buy ★★

Comedy drama 1952 · UK · BW · 83mins

A stalwart of the British documentary tradition, Pat Jackson was obviously uncomfortable with this intractable mix of demob drama and gender comedy. Struggling to adapt to peacetime, war hero Anthony Steel feels so emasculated by the success of wife Patricia Roc's secretarial agency that he determines to set up his own mobile catering business. Steel's misadventures and the couple's domestic disaffection are mildly diverting. But many viewers will be dismayed that this battle of the sexes ends with such a chauvinist truce. DP

Patricia Roc *Anne Wilding* • Anthony Steele *Harry Wilding* • Moira Lister *Diana Haverstock* • AE Matthews *Lord Haverstock* • David Hutcheson *Buster* • Michael Trubshawe *Willy* ■ *Dir* Pat Jackson • *Scr* JL Hodson, Pat Jackson

Something of Value ★★★

Drama 1957 · US · BW · 113mins

Directed by Richard Brooks, who adapted it from Robert Ruark's novel based on the Mau Mau uprisings in Kenya, the film graphically conveys the horror of slaughter. The more personal plot at the centre of the upheaval between white farmers and black tribesman, focuses on Rock Hudson and Sidney Poitier, close friends plunged into conflicting loyalties by the bloody divide with Poitier, excellent in the role, succumbing to tribal allegiance. Vivid East African locations add to the reality of this tale. For all this, a tad dull. RK

Rock Hudson *Peter McKenzie* • Dana Wynter *Holly Keith* • Wendy Hiller *Elizabeth* • Sidney Poitier *Kimani* • Juano Hernandez *Njogu* • William Marshall (2) *Leader* • Robert Beatty *Jeff Newton* • Walter Fitzgerald *Henry McKenzie* ■ *Dir* Richard Brooks • *Scr* Richard Brooks, from a novel by Robert C Ruark

Something Short of Paradise ★★★ 15

Romantic comedy
1979 · US · Colour · 86mins

David Steinberg and Susan Sarandon star as a moviehouse manager and a journalist who fall in love, despite obstacles thrown in their paths by conniving acquaintances. Performances from the two leads are good, though Steinberg's character is perhaps more unlikeable than he needs to be. Film buffs will go ga-ga over the title sequence, which cleverly strings together old movie ads. DA [video]

Susan Sarandon *Madeleine Ross* • David Steinberg *Harris Soane* • Jean-Pierre Aumont *Jean-Fidel Mileau* • Marilyn Sokol *Ruthie Miller* • Joe Grifasi *Barney Collins* ■ *Dir* David Helpern Jr [David Helpern] • *Scr* Fred Barron

Something to Believe In ★ PG

Romantic drama
1997 · UK/Ger · Colour · 108mins

Schmaltz, saccharine and sentimentality overwhelm this melodrama, despite a strong cast of recognisable faces. William McNamara plays a concert pianist off to compete in Naples and en route he encounters terminally ill Las Vegas croupier Maria Pitillo, who's in Italy seeking a miracle cure. The cast flails with this all too "sweet" material, but to no avail. LH. Contains swearing.

William McNamara *Mike* • Maria Pitillo *Maggie* • Tom Conti *Monsignor Calogero* • Maria Schneider *Maria* • Ian Bannen *Don Pozzi* • Robert Wagner *Brad* • Jill St John *Dr Joann Anderson* • Roddy McDowall *Gambler* ■ *Dir* John Hough • *Scr* John Goldsmith, John Hough, from an idea by John Hough, David Purcell

Something to Hide ★

Thriller 1971 · UK · Colour · 106mins

For ten minutes, as Peter Finch and Shelley Winters hurl drunken abuse at each other, this melodrama looks as if it could be a scorcher. But then Winters departs the scene and Finch is left to wallow in what must be the worst movie hangover since Ray Milland had his lost weekend. Finch's encounter with pregnant waif Linda Hayden is utterly unbelievable, and the preposterous dialogue lacks insight, while the images are packed with thick-ear symbolism. DP

Peter Finch *Harry Field* • Shelley Winters *Gabrielle Field* • Colin Blakely *Blagdon* • John Stride *Sergeant Tom Winnington* • Linda Hayden *Lorelei* • Harold Goldblatt *Dibbick* • Rosemarie Dunham *Elsie* • Helen Fraser *Miss Bunyan* • Graham Crowden *Lay preacher* ■ *Dir* Alastair Reid • *Scr* Alastair Reid, from the novel by Nicholas Monsarrat

Something to Live For ★★

Melodrama 1952 · US · BW · 89mins

Seven years after winning his Oscar for playing an alcoholic in *The Lost Weekend*, Ray Milland was involved with booze again in this less ambitious vehicle, produced and directed by George Stevens. As a member of Alcoholics Anonymous, Milland helps actress Joan Fontaine battle the demon drink and falls for her in the process. Teresa Wright plays Milland's wife, and all three stars, though past the peak of their film careers, give excellent performances. Director Stevens, must take the blame for the film's dull tone and turgid progress. TV

Joan Fontaine *Jenny Carey* • Ray Milland *Alan Miller* • Teresa Wright *Edna Miller* • Richard Derr *Tony Collins* • Douglas Dick *Baker* • Herbert Heyes *Mr Crawley* • Harry Bellaver *Billy* • Paul Valentine *Albert* ■ *Dir* George Stevens • *Scr* Dwight Taylor

Something to Sing About ★★ U

Musical comedy 1937 · US · BW · 87mins

As this is one of James Cagney's all too few musicals, we should be grateful even for this mistitled low-budget affair in which he gets to sing and dance his way through a few numbers. (The film was released ten years later with the worse title: *The Battling Hoofer*). Cagney plays a Hollywood star, who discovers that the small print in his contract says that he must remain a bachelor while with the studio, so he can't marry his sweetheart Evelyn Daw. RB

James Cagney *Terry Rooney* • Evelyn Daw *Rita Wyatt* • William Frawley *Hank Meyers* • Mona Barrie *Stephanie Hajos* • Gene Lockhart *Bennett O Regan* ■ *Dir* Victor Schertzinger • *Scr* Austin Parker, from a story by Victor Schertzinger

Something to Talk About ★★ 15

Romantic drama
1995 · US · Colour · 100mins

Reversing the tactics she employed in *Thelma and Louise*, screenwriter Callie Khouri has disgruntled wife Julia Roberts stand and fight rather than take to the road. But it's not much of a contest, as who could possibly have any sympathy for either play-away husband Dennis Quaid or her overbearing father Robert Duvall? It's directed with care, but no flair by Lasse Hallström, while Roberts is outclassed by both Kyra Sedgwick and Gena Rowlands. DP DVD

Julia Roberts *Grace* • Dennis Quaid *Eddie* • Robert Duvall *Wyly King* • Gena Rowlands *Georgia King* • Kyra Sedgwick *Emma Rae* • Brett Cullen *Jamie Johnson* ■ *Dir* Lasse Hallström • *Scr* Callie Khouri

Something Wicked This Way Comes ★★★ PG

Gothic fantasy drama
1983 · US · Colour · 91mins

Generally thought of as a disappointingly crude adaptation by Ray Bradbury of his own novel, this fantasy promises more than it delivers, but is still a good, spooky horror yarn for children with imagination. Jonathan Pryce is suitably evil as the owner of the Pandemonium Carnival, which appears to grant the wishes of the inhabitants of a small American town. Director Jack Clayton piles on the suspense and atmosphere, especially when Pryce goes in search of two young boys who have discovered too many of his secrets. DM

Jason Robards *Charles Halloway* • Jonathan Pryce *Mr Dark* • Diane Ladd *Mrs Nightshade* • Pam Grier *Dust Witch* • Royal Dano *Tom Fury* • Vidal Peterson *Will Halloway* • Shawn Carson *Jim Nightshade* • Arthur Hill *Narrator* ■ *Dir* Jack Clayton • *Scr* Ray Bradbury, from his novel

Something Wild ★★★★ 18

Black comedy drama
1986 · US · Colour · 108mins

Jonathan Demme's oddball "yuppie nightmare" finds meek Jeff Daniels dragged into boozing and bondage after an accidental meeting with flaky *femme fatale* Melanie Griffith, who persuades him to attend her high-school reunion. The film moves up a violent gear when her crazed ex-con husband Ray Liotta kidnaps them both for his own vengeful purposes. Constantly confounding expectations, Demme's jet-black anarchic comedy features a marvellous rock soundtrack and a great performance by Griffith. AJ. Contains violence, swearing and nudity. DVD

Jeff Daniels *Charles Driggs* • Melanie Griffith *Audrey "Lulu" Hankel* • Ray Liotta *Ray Sinclair* • Margaret Colin *Irene* • Tracey Walter *Country squire* • Dana Preu *"Peaches"* • Jack Gilpin *Larry Dillman* • Su Tissue *Peggy Dillman* ■ *Dir* Jonathan Demme • *Scr* E Max Frye

Something's Gotta Give ★★★ 12

Romantic comedy drama
2003 · US · Colour · 122mins

Jack Nicholson and Diane Keaton star in this frothy portrayal of post-menopausal love from director Nancy Meyers. In a role that combines sassy sophistication and emotionally flummoxed charm, Keaton shines as a divorced playwright who thinks affairs of the heart are a folly of youth, until she reluctantly nurses her daughter's ageing lover (Nicholson). Drawn to the arrogant bachelor, she's surprised to find a mutual attraction, despite his assertion he only dates women under 30. While wolfish Nicholson plays to type, it's still thoroughly enjoyable watching the duo interact. SF. Contains swearing. DVD

Jack Nicholson *Harry Sanborn* • Diane Keaton *Erica Barry* • Keanu Reeves *Dr Julian Mercer* • Frances McDormand *Zoe* • Amanda Peet *Marin* • Jon Favreau *Leo* • Paul Michael Glaser *David Klein* • Rachel Ticotin *Dr Martinez* ■ *Dir* Nancy Meyers • *Scr* Nancy Meyers

Sometimes a Great Notion ★★★ 15

Drama 1971 · US · Colour · 109mins

Set in Oregon, Paul Newman's film of Ken Kesey's gargantuan novel tells of a family of lumberjacks who have no truck with the striking loggers' union. However, it's the family itself, led by Henry Fonda, that offers the meatiest bits of the drama, resulting in scenes that vaguely recall Newman's earlier fim, *Hud*. A strong cast and fine location work make this a gripping, if rather solemn effort. Newman took over from director Richard A Colla halfway through shooting. AT

Paul Newman *Hank Stamper* • Henry Fonda *Henry Stamper* • Lee Remick *Viv Stamper* • Michael Sarrazin *Leeland Stamper* • Richard Jaeckel *Joe Ben Stamper* • Linda Lawson *Jan Stamper* ■ *Dir* Paul Newman • *Scr* John Gay, from the novel by Ken Kesey

Sometimes They Come Back ★★ 15

Horror 1991 · US · Colour · 96mins

This is a so-so shocker from the Stephen King horror conveyor belt. Teacher Tim Matheson returns to his home town where he's haunted by the ghosts of the boys responsible for killing his brother 27 years before. Matheson stumbles with suitable dread through the fights with the juvenile delinquents from hell, but while director Tom McLoughlin aims to engross and gross-out in equal measure, the numerous plot inconsistencies scupper the good intentions. AJ DVD

Tim Matheson *Jim Norman* • Brooke Adams *Sally Norman* • Robert Rusler *Lawson* • Chris Demetral *Wayne* • Robert Hy Gorman *Scott Norman* • William Sanderson *Carl Mueller* ■ *Dir* Tom McLoughlin • *Scr* Lawrence Konner, Mark Rosenthal, from the short story by Stephen King

Sometimes They Come Back... Again ★★ 18

Horror 1996 · US · Colour · 94mins

Michael Gross returns to his home town after his mother dies, to take care of her estate, only to find the town absolutely awash with the occult. Alexis Arquette is the demonically powered teenager who has his eyes on Gross's daughter, played by Hilary Swank. Despite being a needless sequel to a movie that was barely based on a Stephen King short story, it's slickly produced. ST DVD

Michael Gross *Jon Porter* • Hilary Swank *Michelle Porter* • Jennifer Elise Cox *Jules Martin* • Alexis Arquette *Tony Reno* ■ *Dir* Adam Grossman • *Scr* Guy Reidel, Adam Grossman, from characters created by Stephen King

Sometimes They Come Back... for More ★★★ 15

Horror 1998 · US · Colour · 85mins

The best of the three movies based on Stephen King's short story, mainly because director Daniel Zelik Berk's addition to the series has really nothing to do with its title source material. This is an effective variation on *The Thing from Another World* (1951). Sent to the Antarctic military ice station Erebus to investigate weird occurrences and unexplained deaths, Clayton Rohner uncovers a satanic power that kills and then revives the corpses. Berk uses the locations with considerable visual flair, but this does peter out as it wends its way to a hokey conclusion. AJ DVD

Faith Ford *Jennifer Wills* • Clayton Rohner *Capt Sam Cage* • Damian Chapa *Dr Karl Schilling* • Max Perlich *Lt Brian Shebanski* • Michael Stadvec *Capt Robert Reynolds* • Chase Masterson *Major Callie O'Grady* ■ *Dir* Daniel Zelik Berk • *Scr* Adam Grossman, Darryl Sollerh, from characters created by Stephen King

Somewhere beyond Love ★★★★

Romantic drama 1974 · It · Colour · 106mins

Boasting performances as authentic as Dante Ferretti's sets and directed without frills or affectation, this unashamedly linear study of Italy's North-South divide and the gulf between men and women is social conscience cinema at its most poignant and persuasive. The basic premise has Sicilian Catholic Stefania Sandrelli and Milanese Communist Giuliano Gemma refuse to allow pride, principle and prejudice to derail their unlikely romance. In confronting them with cruel fate, Luigi Comencini is able to explore the danger in which factory owners place their employees, while also forcing the couple to reassess their priorities. DP. Italian dialogue dubbed into English.

Giuliano Gemma *Nullo* • Stefania Sandrelli *Carmela* ■ *Dir* Luigi Comencini • *Scr* Luigi Comencini, Ugo Pirro, from a story by Ugo Pirro

Somewhere I'll Find You ★★★

Second World War romantic drama
1942 · US · BW · 107mins

The relationship of two brothers (Clark Gable, Robert Sterling), both war correspondents, is upset by their involvement with journalist Lana Turner, who is sent to report in Indochina. She becomes a nurse, they all go to Bataan, and one of them doesn't return. It's a standard romance, but was a huge box-office success in its day. The film is remembered because Gable's wife, Carole Lombard, was killed three days into shooting, becoming an early Hollywood war casualty. A grief-stricken Gable insisted on finishing the picture, but gives an understandably subdued performance. RK

Clark Gable *Jonathan "Johnny" Davis* • Lana Turner *Paula Lane* • Robert Sterling *Kirk Davis* • Reginald Owen *Willie Manning* • Lee Patrick *Eve Manning* • Charles Dingle *George L Stafford* • Van Johnson *Lt Wade Halls* • Keenan Wynn *Sgt Tom Purdy* ■ *Dir* Wesley Ruggles • *Scr* Marguerite Roberts, Walter Reisch, from a story by Charles Hoffman

Somewhere in Europe ★★★★

Drama 1947 · Hun · BW · 104mins

This is a landmark film in that it was Hungary's first international success for decades and led to the Hungarian cinema becoming a nationalised industry. Bela Balazs – the film theorist and author who had returned from exile in the USSR – co-wrote the screenplay which dealt with the bitter realities of postwar Hungary in a direct manner. It involves a band of thieving, begging orphans who take refuge in a castle, where they find a new and better way of life. Despite its subject matter, this is lyrical and optimistic. RB. A Hungarian language film.

Ladislas Horvath *Kuksi* • Arthur Somlay *Peter Simon* • Miklos Gabor *Ossup* • Zsuzsa Banky *The girl* ■ *Dir* Geza von Radvanyi • *Scr* Geza von Radvanyi, Bela Balazs, Judit Fejer, Felix Mariassy

Somewhere in Sonora ★★

Western 1933 · US · BW · 59mins

From early in the period when John Wayne was languishing in B-movies,

S

comes this remake of an old Ken Maynard silent. Wayne is the hero foiling a plot to rob the silver mine owned by the father (Ralph Lewis) of the girl (Ann Fay) he loves. AE

John Wayne *John Bishop* • Henry B Walthall *Bob Leadly* • Shirley Palmer *Mary Burton* • JP McGowan *Monte Black* • Ann Fay *Patsy Ellis* • Ralph Lewis *Burton* • Paul Fix *Bart Leadly* ■ *Dir* Mack V Wright • *Scr* Joseph Anthony Roach, from a story by Will Levington Comfort, from the novel *Somewhere South in Sonora* by Will Levington Comfort

Somewhere in the Night ★★★

Crime mystery 1946 · US · BW · 110mins

US Marine John Hodiak (the poor man's Clark Gable) is discharged from the service suffering from amnesia. The only lead to his past is an address in Los Angeles, where a series of clues involve him with nightclub singer Nancy Guild, club owner Richard Conte, a police detective, and a bruising encounter with a pair of thugs before he discovers the truth about himself. The complicated plot, well handled by Joseph L Mankiewicz, unfolds as a tense and absorbing crime drama, which is well cast but for Guild, making an undistinguished debut to a career that never took off. RK

John Hodiak *George Taylor* • Nancy Guild *Christy Smith* • Lloyd Nolan *Lt Donald Kendall* • Richard Conte *Mel Phillips* • Josephine Hutchinson *Elizabeth Conroy* ■ *Dir* Joseph L Mankiewicz • *Scr* Howard Dimsdale, Joseph L Mankiewicz, Lee Strasberg, from a story by Marvin Borowsky

Somewhere in Time ★★★ PG

Romantic drama 1980 · US · Colour · 98mins

Christopher Reeve stars as a disaffected playwright in this highly schmaltzy love story. Reeve is serviceable and moist-eyed enough, and Jane Seymour sleepwalks her way through a familiar role in a tale with a supernatural twist. This rather charming, old-fashioned love story is an entertaining tear-jerker for those in the mood. SH DVD

Christopher Reeve *Richard Collier* • Jane Seymour (2) *Elise McKenna* • Christopher Plummer *William Fawcett Robinson* • Teresa Wright *Laura Roberts* • Bill Erwin *Arthur* • Victoria Michaels *Maude* • William P O'Hagan *Rollo* ■ *Dir* Jeannot Szwarc • *Scr* Richard Matheson, from his novel

Somewhere on Leave ★★ U

Musical comedy 1942 · UK · BW · 96mins

Of the music hall turns who made films, the Lancashire comedian Frank Randle was among the most successful. His appeal exemplifies the North-South divide and his success was largely confined to home ground. Here, Randle and three of his regular army pals are invited by a fellow private to have some off-duty fun at his stately home. Unsophisticated perhaps, but great fun. BB

Frank Randle *Private Randle* • Harry Korris *Sgt Korris* • Robbie Vincent *Private Enoch* • Dan Young *Private Young* • Toni Lupino *Toni Beaumont* • Pat McGrath *Private Roy Desmond* ■ *Dir* John E Blakeley • *Scr* Roney Parsons, Anthony Toner, Frank Randle

Somewhere Tomorrow ★★

Romantic drama 1983 · US · Colour · 91mins

A likeable curiosity, notable mainly for the appearance of a young Sarah Jessica Parker, eight years before her scene-stealing performance in Steve Martin's *LA Story*. Here, she plays a teenager who strikes up an offbeat friendship with the ghost of youngster Tom Shea, who was killed in an airplane crash. Robert Wiemer's direction is a touch uneven, but Parker shows early promise and it's a good deal less cloying than other similarly themed American films. JF

Sarah Jessica Parker *Lori Anderson* • Nancy Addison *Betty Anderson* • Tom Shea *Terry Stockton* • Rick Weber *Alex Peiski* ■ *Dir/Scr* Robert Wiemer

Somewhere under the Broad Sky ★★★

Melodrama 1954 · Jpn · BW

A low-key *shomin-geki* (or lower-middle-class movie) directed by Masaki Kobayashi and scripted by his sister. Set in the industrial city of Kawasaki, this unflinching melodrama typified the director's detailed style and commitment to the exposure of social injustice that would find its greatest expression in his *Human Condition* trilogy. DP. A Japanese language film.

Keiji Sata • Yoshiko Kuga • Hideko Takamine • Akira Ishihama ■ *Dir* Masaki Kobayashi • *Scr* Yoshiko Kusuda

Sommersby ★★★ 12

Period romantic drama
1993 · US · Colour · 108mins

This is the American reworking of the Gérard Depardieu/Nathalie Baye modern classic *The Return of Martin Guerre*, and it isn't a patch on the original, either in terms of tension, intelligence or performance. Still, there is much to enjoy in the central mystery surrounding the true identity of returning American Civil War veteran Richard Gere, in particular the sensitive playing of Jodie Foster as his confused "widow". Unfortunately, neither Gere nor Bill Pullman, as Foster's embittered suitor, can hold a candle to her. DP. Contains violence, swearing, sex scenes. DVD

Richard Gere *Jack Sommersby* • Jodie Foster *Laurel Sommersby* • Bill Pullman *Orin Meecham* • James Earl Jones *Judge Isaacs* • Lanny Flaherty *Buck* • William Windom *Reverend Powell* • Wendell Wellman *Travis* • Brett Kelley *Little Rob* • Clarice Taylor *Esther* • Frankie Faison *Joseph* • Ronald Lee Ermey [R Lee Ermey] *Dick Mead* ■ *Dir* Jon Amiel • *Scr* Nicholas Meyer, Sarah Kernochan, from a story by Nicholas Meyer, Anthony Schaffer, from the film *The Return of Martin Guerre* by Daniel Vigne, Jean-Claude Carrière

The Son ★★★★ 12

Drama 2002 · Bel/Fr · Colour · 100mins

Belgian film-makers Jean-Pierre and Luc Dardenne apply their brand of social realism to the subject of masculine emotion in this unsettling account of a carpentry teacher's relationship with the teenager responsible for the death of his son. Yet there's also an element of suspense, as Olivier Gourmet's intentions towards student Morgan Marinne appear anything but honourable. Employing an aggressive hand-held camera to reinforce Gourmet's fraught state, the Dardenne brothers explore the nature of pain, forgiveness and redemption. DP. In French with English subtitles. DVD

Olivier Gourmet *Olivier* • Morgan Marinne *Francis* • Isabella Soupart *Magali* • Remy Renaud *Philippo* • Nassim Hassaïni *Omar* • Kevin Leroy *Raoul* • Félicien Pitsaer *Steve* ■ *Dir/Scr* Jean-Pierre Dardenne, Luc Dardenne

Son Frère ★★★ 15

Drama 2003 · Fr · Colour · 88mins

Director Patrice Chéreau here produces an intimate study of emotion in extremis with this adaptation about siblings repairing their strained relationship. Estranged brothers Bruno Todeschini and Eric Caravaca attempt to reconcile after the former is diagnosed with a potentially fatal illness. Caravaca seeks to console their parents and his brother's girlfriend, Nathalie Boutefeu, while dealing with his own rocky liaison with Sylvain Jacques. The intersecting time frames complicate matters unnecessarily. DP. In French with English subtitles. Contains swearing, sex scenes and nudity. DVD

Bruno Todeschini *Thomas* • Eric Caravaca *Luc* • Nathalie Boutefeu *Claire* • Maurice Garrel *Old man* • Catherine Ferran *Head doctor* • Antoinette Moya *Mother* • Sylvain Jacques *Vincent* • Fred Ulysse *Father* ■ *Dir* Patrice Chéreau • *Scr* Patrice Chéreau, Anne-Louise Trividic, from the novel by Philippe Besson

Son in Law ★★ 15

Comedy 1993 · US · Colour · 91mins

Pauly Shore could never be accused of subtlety. The humour in this rustic comedy is as broad as a barn door and twice as creaky, yet he puts so much energy into his manic mugging that no matter how irritating he is, he coaxes at least one smile. This is a hackneyed variation on the town-and-country mouse theme, in which Shore's campus nerd wins over Carla Gugino's folksy family and exposes her despicable boyfriend. DP

Pauly Shore *Crawl* • Carla Gugino *Rebecca* • Lane Smith *Walter Warner* • Cindy Pickett *Connie Warner* • Mason Adams *Walter Sr* • Patrick Renna *Zack* • Dennis Burkley *Theo* • Tiffani-Amber Thiessen *Tracy* ■ *Dir* Steve Rash • *Scr* Shawn Schepps, Fax Bahr, Adam Small, from a story by Patrick J Clifton, Susan McMartin, Peter M Lenkov

Son of a Gunfighter ★★★ U

Western 1964 · US/Sp · Colour · 91mins

In an enjoyable paella western, Russ Tamblyn portrays the title character, a youngster out to kill the man who deserted his mother 20 years earlier. Many of the characters are Mexican, giving an opportunity for Spanish actors (including Fernando Rey as a cattle rancher) to speak English with appropriate accents. The complicated plot features warring American outlaws and Mexican *bandidos*, but the scenery is terrific, the score rousing and the action briskly handled. AE

Russ Tamblyn *Johnny* • Kieron Moore *Deputy Fenton* • James Philbrook *Ketchum* • Fernando Rey *Don Fortuna* • Maria Granada *Pilar* ■ *Dir* Paul Landres • *Scr* Clarke Reynolds

Son of Ali Baba ★★ U

Fantasy adventure
1952 · US · Colour · 74mins

When good looks mattered more than good acting for Tony Curtis, this is the sort of pantomime stuff he appeared in. As Kashma Baba, son of Ali, he must protect the Princess Kiki from an evil caliph, who also wants to get his greedy hands on Baba Sr's treasure. It's a satirical tale of kidnapping, sword crossing and falling in love, but without a genie or flying carpet, it's less than magical. TH

Tony Curtis *Kashma Baba* • Piper Laurie *Kiki* • Susan Cabot *Tala* • William Reynolds *Mustafa* • Hugh O'Brian *Hussein* • Victor Jory *Caliph* • Morris Ankrum *Ali Baba* ■ *Dir* Kurt Neumann • *Scr* Gerald Drayson Adams

The Son of Captain Blood ★★ U

Swashbuckling adventure
1962 · It/Sp/US · Colour · 93mins

This sequel to the 1935 swashbuckler *Captain Blood* features the stunt casting of Errol Flynn's son Sean in the title role. Sadly, while he shares his father's dashing looks, Sean has none of his screen presence. The story rattles along, with a pirate attack and a race against a tidal wave providing the action highlights. But Flynn's scenes with over-protective mother Ann Todd and imperilled passenger Alessandra Panaro are engaging. DP

Sean Flynn *Robert Blood* • Alessandra Panaro *Abbigail* • José Nieto *De Malagon* • Ann Todd *Arabella Blood* • John Kitzmiller *Moses* • Raf Baldassarre *Bruno* ■ *Dir* Tulio Demicheli • *Scr* Casey Robinson, from the character created by Rafael Sabatini

Son of Dracula ★★★

Horror 1943 · US · BW · 79mins

Lon Chaney Jr plays the famous Count under the pseudonym Alucard (Dracula spelt backwards, a device destined to be used in numerous inferior horrors), and recruits vampires in the Deep South because Universal wouldn't pay for Transylvanian sets. It didn't matter. This has atmosphere to spare, super make-up by *Frankenstein* genius Jack Pierce and fun man-to-bat transformations. A neglected highlight from the golden age of horror. AJ

Lon Chaney Jr *Count Alucard* • Robert Paige *Frank Stanley* • Louise Allbritton *Katherine Caldwell* • Evelyn Ankers *Claire Caldwell* • Frank Craven *Dr Harry Brewster* • J Edward Bromberg *Professor Lazlo* • Samuel S Hinds *Judge Simmons* ■ *Dir* Robert Siodmak • *Scr* Eric Taylor, from a story by Curtis Siodmak

Son of Flubber ★★ U

Comedy 1962 · US · BW · 103mins

You will remember that "flubber" was the flying rubber invented by Fred MacMurray in the fun family comedy *The Absent-Minded Professor*. Disney reassembled many of the same cast two years later, but usually reliable director Robert Stevenson could not repeat the winning formula. Keenan Wynn enjoys himself as the villain, but the jokes are tired. DP

Fred MacMurray *Prof Ned Brainard* • Nancy Olson *Betsy Brainard* • Keenan Wynn *Alonzo Hawk* • Tommy Kirk *Biff Hawk* • Elliott Reid *Shelby Ashton* • Joanna Moore *Desiree de la Roche* • Leon Ames *President Rufus Daggett* • Ed Wynn *AJ Allen* • Ken Murray *Mr Hurley* • Charlie Ruggles [Charles Ruggles] *Judge Murdock* • William Demarest *Mr Hummel* • Paul Lynde *Sportscaster* ■ *Dir* Robert Stevenson • *Scr* Bill Walsh, Don DaGradi, from the story *A Situation of Gravity* by Samuel W Taylor, from novels by Jay Williams, Raymond Abrashkin

Son of Frankenstein ★★★★

Horror 1939 · US · BW · 95mins

The third instalment of Universal's classic series features Boris Karloff's last fling as the Monster and is a superior shocker all round. Basil Rathbone (the Baron), Bela Lugosi (Ygor) and Lionel Atwill (the police chief with a noisy artificial arm) all turn in unforgettably eccentric performances along with the ever-imposing Karloff. Add Rowland V Lee's eerie direction and the result is a majestically macabre chiller. After this, the Monster became a stumbling cliché. AJ

Basil Rathbone *Baron Wolf von Frankenstein* • Boris Karloff *The Monster* • Bela Lugosi *Ygor* • Lionel Atwill *Inspector Krogh* • Josephine Hutchinson *Elsa von Frankenstein* • Donnie Dunagan *Peter von Frankenstein* ■ *Dir* Rowland V Lee • *Scr* Willis Cooper, from characters created by Mary Shelley

Son of Fury ★★★ U

Period adventure 1942 · US · BW · 98mins

Historical nonsense set during the reign of George III. Tyrone Power, cheated out of his inheritance by George Sanders, falls in love with Frances Farmer and ends up on a Polynesian island with native girl Gene Tierney. Having cast its most alluring stars, 20th Century-Fox threw money (though not much-needed Technicolor) at the production and the result was big box office. The stars perform well, especially Sanders as a snarling

S

villain, and the supporting cast is worth a look, too. AT

Tyrone Power *Benjamin Blake* • Gene Tierney *Eve* • George Sanders *Sir Arthur Blake* • Frances Farmer *Isabel Blake* • Roddy McDowall *Benjamin as a boy* • John Carradine *Caleb Green* • Elsa Lanchester *Bristol Isabel* ■ *Dir* John Cromwell • *Scr* Philip Dunne

Son of Godzilla ★★ U

Monster horror 1967 · Jpn · Colour · 81mins

Intense heat from Japanese weather experiments causes cute Godzilla offspring, Minya, to hatch. Then mother (and who knew Godzilla was female?) must protect her son from a giant hairy spider, and other insect life enlarged by the atmospheric conditions. The eighth in the Toho monster series is an inept juvenile adventure with comical episodes spliced into the miniature special effects mayhem. AJ. Japanese dialogue dubbed into English. [video]

Tadao Takashima *Dr Kuzumi* • Akira Kubo *Goro* ■ *Dir* Jun Fukuda • *Scr* Shinichi Sekizawa, Kazue Shiba

Son of Kong ★★★

Fantasy adventure 1933 · US · BW · 69mins

Rushed out within a year of its predecessor *King Kong*'s release, the official sequel took a more light-hearted and whimsical approach and was dismissed by critics because of the accent on comedy. Today, it now plays as short, inoffensive and good fun. The ludicrous story has Carl Denham (Robert Armstrong) returning to Skull Island in a hunt for treasure in order to pay off Manhattan's rebuilding costs after Kong's destructive rampage, and finding the giant ape's cute albino offspring stuck in quicksand. AJ

Robert Armstrong *Carl Denham* • Helen Mack *Hilda Peterson* • Frank Reicher *Captain Englehorn* • John Marston *Helstrom* • Victor Wong (1) *Charlie* • Lee Kohlmar *Mickey* • Ed Brady *Red* • Clarence Wilson *Peterson* ■ *Dir* Ernest B Schoedsack • *Scr* Ruth Rose

Son of Lassie ★★★ U

Drama 1945 · US · Colour · 100mins

A sequel to the tremendously popular *Lassie Come Home*, that consolidated the stardom of the most successful canine performer since Rin Tin Tin. It benefits from a fine supporting cast of caring humans, including Peter Lawford and June Lockhart, but is very much of its time, as Lassie's son Laddie accompanies Lawford into Nazi-occupied Norway. TS

Peter Lawford *Joe Carraclough* • Donald Crisp *Sam Carraclough* • June Lockhart *Priscilla* • Nigel Bruce *Duke of Rudling* • William Severn *Henrik* • Leon Ames *Anton* ■ *Dir* S Sylvan Simon • *Scr* Jeanne Bartlett, from characters created by Eric Knight

Son of Monte Cristo ★★★ U

Swashbuckling adventure
1940 · US · BW · 95mins

This long-gestating sequel to the marvellous 1934 *Count of Monte Cristo* features Louis Hayward (replacing Robert Donat, who refused to return) as the swashbuckling son of the famous Edmond Dantes, and Joan Bennett as an imprisoned queen. The plot assumes a deliberate political relevance as it deals with an evil Balkan dictator, suavely played by George Sanders, attempting to conquer her country. TS [video]

Louis Hayward *Count of Monte Cristo* • Joan Bennett *Grand Duchess Zona* • George Sanders *Gurko Lanen* • Florence Bates *Mathilde* • Lionel Royce *Colonel Zimmerman* • Montagu Love *Baron von Neuhoff* ■ *Dir* Rowland V Lee • *Scr* George Bruce

Son of Paleface ★★★★ U

Spoof western 1952 · US · Colour · 94mins

In this very funny follow-up to *The Paleface* (1948), Bob Hope plays his own son, a cowardly dude who gets entangled with Jane Russell, a bandit who sings in a saloon called "The Dirty Shame". Roy Rogers is delightfully self-mocking as himself, particularly when singing *A Four-Legged Friend* to Trigger. All the clichés of the western are here, played for laughs by director Frank Tashlin, a former animator who sets up many of the sequences like a cartoon. RB

Bob Hope *Junior Potter* • Jane Russell *Mike* • Roy Rogers *Roy Barton* • Bill Williams *Kirk* • Harry Von Zell *Stoner* • Douglass Dumbrille *Sheriff McIntyre* • Lyle Moraine *Waverly* • Lloyd Corrigan *Doc Lovejoy* • Cecil B DeMille ■ *Dir* Frank Tashlin • *Scr* Frank Tashlin, Robert L Welch, Joseph Quillan

Son of Robin Hood ★★ U

Adventure 1958 · UK · Colour · 80mins

The son of Sherwood's finest is in fact a girl, played by June Laverick, and she takes over the remnants of her father's outlaw band to fight against the Black Duke (David Farrar) who wants the British throne. All the most hilarious aspects of Hollywood-on-Trent are present in this jolly jape – the Middle Ages dialogue, the classy grovelling, as well as an undercurrent of cross-dressing – and Laverick makes a pleasing heroine. AT

Al Hedison [David Hedison] *Jamie* • June Laverick *Deering Hood* • David Farrar *Des Roches* • Marius Goring *Chester* • Philip Friend *Dorchester* • Delphi Lawrence *Sylvia* • George Coulouris *Alan A Dale* • George Woodbridge *Little John* ■ *Dir* George Sherman • *Scr* George W George, George Slavin

Son of Sinbad ★★ U

Fantasy adventure
1955 · US · Colour · 85mins

Howard Hughes allegedly produced this frothy fantasy nonsense, solely to placate the screen ambitions of all the starlets to whom he'd promised a career. There can be no other explanation for this "forty thieves" exotica. Even Vincent Price, as comical poet Omar Khayham, considered it the worst script ever written. Dale Robertson, playing Sinbad with a Texas accent, seems perfectly in synch with the rest of the camp confection. AJ

Dale Robertson *Sinbad* • Sally Forrest *Ameer* • Vincent Price *Omar Khayham* • Lili St Cyr *Nerissa* • Mari Blanchard *Kristina* • Jay Novello *Jiddah* • Kim Novak ■ *Dir* Ted Tetzlaff • *Scr* Aubrey Wisberg, Jack Pollexfen

Son of the Bride ★★★ 15

Comedy drama
2001 · Arg/Sp · Colour · 125mins

This comedy is both a bustling ensemble piece and a pensive insight into one man's midlife nightmare. Beset by domestic conflicts and the prospect of losing the family restaurant to a soulless chain, Ricardo Darin is the victim of his own errors of judgement. But, with his father determined to renew his marital vows with a wife suffering from Alzheimer's, Darin's presented with an unexpected opportunity to atone for his past and seize his destiny. Expertly marshalling his cast and capturing Buenos Aires's headlong vibrancy, Juan José Campanella's satire is amusing and astute. DP. In Spanish with English subtitles.

Ricardo Darin *Rafael Belvedere* • Héctor Alterio *Nino Belvedere* • Norma Aleandro *Norma Belvedere* • Eduardo Blanco *Juan Carlos* • Natalia Verbeke *Naty* ■ *Dir* Juan José Campanella • *Scr* Juan José Campanella, Fernando Castets

Son of the Mask ★ PG

Fantasy comedy
2004 · US/Ger · Colour · 90mins

Jim Carrey's 1994 hit *The Mask* gets a poor sequel. This time, the magical Nordic relic falls into the hands of an aspiring cartoonist (Jamie Kennedy), who fathers a son while wearing it. The baby is born with all the literally eye-popping powers of Carrey's original character, turning his dad's world upside down with non-stop mayhem. A barrel-scraping cash-in. SF [video] DVD

Jamie Kennedy *Tim Avery* • Alan Cumming *Loki* • Bob Hoskins *Odin* • Traylor Howard *Tonya Avery* • Ben Stein *Dr Arthur Neuman* ■ *Dir* Lawrence Guterman • *Scr* Lance Khazei

Son of the Pink Panther ★ PG

Action comedy 1993 · US · Colour · 88mins

One can understand Blake Edwards's frustration at seeing a successful series stopped in its tracks by the death of Peter Sellers. Yet surely the critical mauling meted out to those cut-and-paste jobs *Trail* and *Curse*, should have clued him in to the fact that the public were simply not interested in Clouseau clones. Here, he puts Italian comic Roberto Benigni through his paces. The kidnapping plot is inane, the slapstick inept and the cast ineffectual. DP [video]

Roberto Benigni *Jacques Gambrelli* • Herbert Lom *Inspector Dreyfus* • Shabana Azmi *The Queen* • Debrah Farentino *Princess Yasmin* • Jennifer Edwards *Yussa* • Robert Davi *Hans* • Burt Kwouk *Cato* • Mark Schneider *Arnon* • Graham Stark *Dr Balls* • Liz Smith *Madame Balls* ■ *Dir* Blake Edwards • *Scr* Blake Edwards, Madeline Sunshine, Steve Sunshine, from a story by Blake Edwards, from characters created by Maurice Richlin, Blake Edwards

The Son of the Sheik ★★★★ U

Silent adventure 1926 · US · BW · 68mins

Abandon all resistance to the technique and conventions of blood-and-sand romance as filmed in the silent era. Remind yourself that there has been no greater male screen idol than Rudolph Valentino, and surrender to this, his last film before his premature death. The star plays two roles, Prince Ahmed, and his father, the all-powerful Sheik. Marvellously photographed by George Barnes, directed by George Fitzmaurice and drawing excellent work from Valentino, this tongue-in-cheek tale, combining passion, violence and swashbuckling action with humour, has lost none of its entertainment value. RK [video]

Rudolph Valentino *Ahmed/The Sheik* • Vilma Banky *Yasmin* • George Fawcett *André* • Montague Love [Montagu Love] *Ghabah* • Karl Dane *Ramadan* ■ *Dir* George Fitzmaurice • *Scr* Frances Marion, Fred De Gresac, George Marion Jr (titles), from the novel *The Sons of the Sheik* by Edith Maude Hull

Sonatine ★★★

Crime drama 1984 · Can · Colour · 91mins

Writer/director Micheline Lanctôt stages this Antonioni-esque study of social alienation as a "small sonata" in three movements. In the first two movements, a series of glances and gestures prompts Pascale Bussières to become distantly enamoured of a married bus driver, while runaway Marcia Pilote shares a brief moment of tenderness on a cargo boat with a Bulgarian sailor before she's handed over to the authorities. Yet there's little in the opening episodes to prepare you for the teenagers' tragic response to the world's neglect. Delicately directed and persuasively played. DP. In French with English subtitles. Contains violence, nudity.

Pascale Bussières *Chantal* • Marcia Pilote *Louisette* • Kliment Demtchev *Sailor* ■ *Dir/Scr* Micheline Lanctôt

Sonatine ★★★★★ 18

Crime drama 1993 · Jpn · Colour · 89mins

This violent gang war thriller is a stunning piece of film-making. Director Takeshi "Beat" Kitano shows a complete understanding of the Hollywood gangster movie and its Japanese counterpart, the yakuza film. Moreover, he demonstrates a mastery of technique in the magnificent beach hideout segment in which he uses trick effects, imaginative camera angles and a range of comic styles to question the value of the yakuza's existence and build tension towards the superb silhouette shoot-out. He also gives a towering performance as a disillusioned hitman. DP. In Japanese with English subtitles. Contains violence and nudity. [video] DVD

"Beat" Takeshi [Takeshi Kitano] *Murakawa* • Aya Kokumai *Miyuki* • Tetsu Watanabe *Uechi* • Masanobu Katsumura *Ryoji* ■ *Dir/Scr* Takeshi Kitano • *Cinematographer* Katsumi Yanagishima

Song for a Raggy Boy ★★ 15

Drama based on a true story
2002 · Ire/UK/Sp/Den · Colour · 93mins

Although less shocking than *The Magdalene Sisters*, Aisling Walsh's adaptation of Patrick Galvin's autobiographical tome exposes similar abuses that scarred religious education in bygone Ireland. As the socialist returning from the Spanish Civil War, Aidan Quinn has a touching influence over his charges at the Catholic reform school ruled by Iain Glen's sadistic cleric. But Walsh never strikes the right balance between cruelty and compassion, especially as Richard Blackford's score drenches the latter in gushing sentiment. DP. Contains swearing and violence.

Aidan Quinn *William Franklin* • Iain Glen *Brother John* • Marc Warren *Brother Mac* • Dudley Sutton *Brother Tom* • Alan Devlin *Father Damian* • Stuart Graham *Brother Whelan* • John Travers *Liam Mercier* • Chris Newman *Patrick Delaney* ■ *Dir* Aisling Walsh • *Scr* Patrick Galvin, Aisling Walsh, Kevin Byron Murphy, from the autobiography by Patrick Galvin

A Song for Beko ★★★★

Wartime drama
1992 · Ger/Arm · Colour · 86mins

A teacher not a fighter, Turkish Kurd Nizamettin Aric goes in search of his rebel brother with a diligence and dignity that characterises his relationship with orphan refugee Bezara Arsen. The first-ever Kurdish feature, Aric's directorial debut is remarkable not just for its courage, but also for the restraint with which it depicts everyday reality and passionately espouses its cause. The flashback-packed storyline contrasts the persistent prejudice of the Turks with Saddam Hussein's pitiless poison gas attack on a village slowly returning to normality after the Iran-Iraq War. DP. In Kurdish with English subtitles.

Nizamettin Aric *Beko* • Bezara Arsen *Zine* ■ *Dir/Scr* Nizamettin Aric

A Song for Europe ★★★

Drama 1985 · UK/W Ger · Colour · 95mins

David Suchet and Maria Schneider head the mostly German cast of this international co-production. It tells the story of how a drug company executive was imprisoned for industrial espionage after taking evidence of his company's malpractice to Common Market officials. Focusing on the injustices suffered by the executive at the hands of the authorities, director

S

John Goldschmidt offers a disturbing indictment of corporate power. DA

David Suchet *Stephen Dyer* • Maria Schneider *Madeline* • Anne-Marie Blanc *Maman* • Reinhard Glemnitz *Weigel* ■ *Dir* John Goldschmidt • *Scr* Peter Prince

A Song Is Born ★★★ PG

Musical comedy 1948 · US · Colour · 119mins

Howard Hawks here remakes his classic *Ball of Fire*, with Danny Kaye in the Gary Cooper role. Cooper played a gauche professor compiling a dictionary of slang; now the plot's updated to a study of jazz, and on hand are some of its greatest exponents, including Benny Goodman, Louis Armstrong, Charlie Barnet and Tommy Dorsey. In Hawks's canon this is a trifle, though it has interest as the director's first film in colour. TS

Danny Kaye *Professor Hobart Frisbee* • Virginia Mayo *Honey Swanson* • Benny Goodman *Professor Magenbruch* • Hugh Herbert *Professor Twingle* • Steve Cochran *Tony Crow* ■ *Dir* Howard Hawks • *Scr* Harry Tugend, from the story *From A to Z* by Thomas Monroe, Billy Wilder

Song o' My Heart ★★

Musical 1930 · US · BW · 85mins

Designed as a vehicle for the film debut of the internationally popular Irish tenor, John McCormack, this blarney was directed by that skilful engineer of sentimentality, Frank Borzage. McCormack plays a singer whose great love (Alice Joyce) is forced to marry another. It allows McCormack to sing a clutch of songs, including *Rose of Tralee*. Ecstatically received in its day, it's all rather maudlin now, but McCormack fans are in for a treat. RK

John McCormack *Sean O'Carolan* • Maureen O'Sullivan *Eileen O'Brien* • John Garrick *Fergus O' Donnell* • JM Kerrigan *Peter Conlon* ■ *Dir* Frank Borzage • *Scr* Tom Barry

The Song of Bernadette ★★★★ U

Biographical drama 1943 · US · BW · 155mins

This desperately sincere slice of now unfashionable Hollywood sermonising still contrives to move audiences, largely because of the amazing story of young Bernadette Soubirous, who, in 1858, saw a vision of the Virgin Mary in a grotto at Lourdes. Jennifer Jones won the best actress Oscar for her openly affecting Bernadette, the Virgin is portrayed by Linda Darnell and an unusually restrained Vincent Price is impeccable. Cynics won't be converted, but sceptics may find the movie posits a sincere argument. Another Oscar went to Arthur Miller's luminous black-and-white photography. TS DVD

Jennifer Jones *Bernadette Soubirous* • William Eythe *Antoine* • Charles Bickford *Peyremaie* • Vincent Price *Dutour* • Lee J Cobb *Dr Dozous* • Gladys Cooper *Sister Vauzous* • Anne Revere *Louise Soubirous* • Roman Bohnen *François Soubirous* • Linda Darnell *Blessed Virgin* ■ *Dir* Henry King • *Scr* George Seaton, from the novel by Franz Werfel

Song of Ceylon ★★★★★ U

Documentary 1934 · UK · BW · 39mins

Although sponsored by the Ceylon Tea Propaganda Board, this extraordinarily beautiful film is far more concerned with the ancient customs and Buddhist heritage of what is now called Sri Lanka. Basil Wright divided his odyssey into four sections and used the 17th-century travelogue of Robert Knox to counterpoint his poetic and ethnographically invaluable images. Tea is only introduced in the third segment and is presented as a corrupting influence on an idyllic scene. Every bit as impressive as, but less celebrated than, *Night Mail* (which Wright co-directed with Harry Watt), this is one of the glories of the British documentary. DP

Lionel Wendt *Narrator* ■ *Dir* Basil Wright • *Scr* John Grierson, Basil Wright, from a travel book by Robert Knox • *Producer* John Grierson • *Cinematographer* Basil Wright

Song of Freedom ★★★★ U

Drama 1936 · UK · BW · 78mins

Paul Robeson unearthed the legend of the singing king while shooting *Sanders of the River*. Even though he had just completed *Show Boat*, he considered this the first film to showcase his talent without demeaning his race. As the London stevedore who is discovered by an operatic impresario, only to cast off his fame to return to the island kingdom from which he was kidnapped years before, Robeson not only gets to sing several fine songs, but also explores such themes as interracial marriage, the evils of superstition and slavery, and the clash between tradition and progress. Dated, but still powerful. DP

Paul Robeson *John Zinga* • Elisabeth Welch *Ruth Zinga* • Esme Percy *Gabriel Donezetti* • Robert Adams *Monty* • Ecce Homo Toto *Mandingo* ■ *Dir* J Elder Wills • *Scr* Fenn Sherie, Ingram D'Abbes, from a story by Claude Wallace, Dorothy Holloway

Song of Love ★★★ U

Musical biography 1947 · US · BW · 118mins

Clara Wieck Schumann's story is not as awful as you might expect, thanks to Katharine Hepburn's portrayal. Hubby is an austere Paul Henreid and close mate Brahms is a beardless Robert Walker. Fictional tosh, certainly, but expertly produced with just the requisite amount of MGM gloss. Director Clarence Brown, who gave us *The Yearling* and stacks of Garbos, seems overawed by his subject, and his usual sureness of touch lapses into a slow pace. TS

Katharine Hepburn *Clara Wieck Schumann* • Paul Henreid *Robert Schumann* • Robert Walker *Johannes Brahms* • Henry Daniell *Franz Liszt* • Leo G Carroll *Prof Wieck* ■ *Dir* Clarence Brown • *Scr* Ivan Tors, Irmgard Von Cube, Allen Vincent, Robert Ardrey, from the play by Bernard Schubert, Mario Silva

Song of Norway ★ U

Musical biography
1970 · US · Colour · 138mins

Let's be honest: this horrendously overlong biopic of composer Edvard Grieg has precious little going for it, except for the magnificent Scandinavian locations. Otherwise, one-time talented director Andrew L Stone has assembled a motley cast to surround the woefully ill-equipped Toralv Maurstad (who?) in this supremely uninteresting saga. TS

Toralv Maurstad *Edvard Grieg* • Florence Henderson *Nina Grieg* • Christina Schollin *Therese Berg* • Frank Porretta *Rikard Nordraak* • Harry Secombe *Bjornsterne Bjornson* • Robert Morley *Berg* • Edward G Robinson *Krogstad* • Elizabeth Larner *Mrs Bjornson* • Oscar Homolka *Engstrand* ■ *Dir* Andrew L Stone • *Scr* Andrew L Stone, from the musical by Milton Lazarus, Robert Wright and George Forrest, from a play by Homer Curran

Song of Scheherazade ★★★

Musical biography
1947 · US · Colour · 105mins

Supposedly a biopic of Rimsky-Korsakov, this is one of the campest of all Universal's gaudy costume pictures. Jean-Pierre Aumont plays the young Russian composer, who meets and falls for sultry dancer Yvonne De Carlo on his way back to Russia. They fall in love, she inspires him to write *Scherherazade* and dances at the premiere in St Petersburg. Eve Arden, only ten years De Carlo's senior, plays her wisecracking mother in this enjoyable nonsense. RB

Yvonne De Carlo *Cara de Talavera/Scheherazade* • Brian Donlevy *Captain Vladimir Gregovich* • Jean-Pierre Aumont *Nikolai Rimsky-Korsakov* • Eve Arden *Mme Conchita de Talavera* • Philip Reed *Prince Mischetsky* ■ *Dir/Scr* Walter Reisch • *Music Director* Miklos Rozsa

The Song of Songs ★★

Comedy drama 1933 · US · BW · 85mins

After disappointing box-office returns for *Blonde Venus*, Paramount engineered a trial separation between Marlene Dietrich and director Josef von Sternberg. Rouben Mamoulian was entrusted with the task of making something of this tale about a German peasant girl who falls in love with a sculptor and becomes his model, but marries a baron, turns café singer, and has several lovers. The stylish and intelligent Mamoulian did what he could, but this tired old material obstinately refused to come to life. RK

Marlene Dietrich *Lily Czepanek* • Brian Aherne *Richard Waldow* • Lionel Atwill *Baron von Merzbach* • Alison Skipworth *Mrs Rasmussen* ■ *Dir* Rouben Mamoulian • *Scr* Leo Birinski, Samuel Hoffenstein, the play by Edward Brewster Sheldon, from the novel *Das Hohe Lied* by Hermann Sudermann, and

Song of Texas ★★ U

Western 1943 · US · BW · 50mins

This comparatively lavish Roy Rogers western gives priority to the songs, and there's also a speciality number from a Mexican dance troupe. A wagon race in the last reel provides the only big action sequence and the plot is an old one: Roy and friends try to help Harry Shannon's impoverished old-timer, fool his visiting daughter Sheila Ryan into thinking he's the ranch owner he's claimed to be. AE

Roy Rogers *Roy* • Sheila Ryan *Sue Bennett* • Barton MacLane *Jim Calvert* • Harry Shannon *Sam Bennett* • Arline Judge *Hildegarde* ■ *Dir* Joseph Kane • *Scr* Winston Miller

Song of the Exile ★★★

Drama 1990 · HK/Tai · Colour · 100mins

Surviving an indifferent start, Ann Hui's semi-autobiographical drama, gradually develops into a moving study of a strained mother-daughter relationship. Returning to Hong Kong in the early 1970s after studying broadcasting in London, Maggie Cheung is resentful of Chang Shwu-Fen's dismissive attitude towards her newly-acquired western ways. Typically revealing the tempest beneath the surface, Hui directs a touch methodically, but the performances, especially Cheung's, are deeply affecting. DP. In Cantonese with English subtitles.

Chang Shwu-Fen • Maggie Cheung • Lu Shao-fen ■ *Dir* Ann Hui • *Scr* Wu Nien-Jen

Song of the Islands ★★★ U

Romantic musical
1942 · US · Colour · 75mins

This entertaining 20th Century-Fox Technicolor romp stars pin-up Betty Grable as a Hawaiian "hula" girl in a sunny musical. Hunk Victor Mature claims her, despite interference from a pair of feudin' fathers. There's some robust comic playing from reliable Jack Oakie, who's involved in some super by-play with Hilo Hattie. Unsurprisingly, this movie was a massive wartime hit, and is still mightily pleasing today. TS

Betty Grable *Eileen O'Brien* • Victor Mature *Jefferson Harper* • Jack Oakie *Rusty Smith* • Thomas Mitchell *Dennis O'Brien* • George Barbier *Harper* • Billy Gilbert *Palola's father* • Hilo Hattie *Palola* ■ *Dir* Walter Lang • *Scr* Joseph Schrank, Robert Pirosh, Robert Ellis, Helen Logan

Song of the Open Road ★★

Musical comedy 1944 · US · BW · 93mins

The only notable thing about this "let's-put-on-a-show" musical, was the screen debut of 15-year-old radio singing star Jane Powell. Virtually a showcase for her vocal talent, it soon led to an MGM contract and blonde hair. Powell plays a juvenile movie star, who runs away from home to work on a youth farm where everyone seems to have a musical gift. RB

Edgar Bergen • Jane Powell • WC Fields • Bonita Granville *Bonnie* • Peggy O'Neill *Peggy* • Jackie Moran *Jack* • Bill Christy *Bill* ■ *Dir* S Sylvan Simon • *Scr* Albert Mannheimer, from a story by Irving Phillips, Edward Verdier

Song of the Road ★★★ U

Drama 1937 · UK · BW · 73mins

John Baxter was one of the most original British film-makers. In addition to some rather clumsy (but surprisingly commercial) regional comedies, he also made a string of socially aware dramas in which the heroes were either everyday workers or outsiders unwilling to march in step with progress. A sobering, if sentimental view of Britain emerging from the Depression, this old-fashioned, but compelling picture follows Bransby Williams and his horse Polly as they tour the country looking for work. Keep an eye out for that inveterate barnstormer Tod Slaughter in a cameo as a travelling showman. DP

Bransby Williams *Old Bill* • Ernest Butcher *Foreman* • Muriel George *Mrs Trelawney* • Davy Burnaby *Mr Keppel* • Tod Slaughter *Showman* • John Turnbull *Bristow* • Edgar Driver *Titch* ■ *Dir* John Baxter • *Scr* John Baxter, from a story by Michael Kent

Song of the South ★★★ U

Part-animated fantasy
1946 · US · Colour · 90mins

This wonderful Disney fantasy was a technical tour de force in its day, blending live action and animation with wit and brilliance, most notably in the now-classic *Zip-a-Dee Doo-Dah* sequence in which James Baskett's Oscar-winning Uncle Remus meets the woodland folk of his tales. Seen now, alas, such quaint simplicity looks patronising, and makes many contemporary viewers squirm. It's best to remember the film's period and attitudes, and thereby enjoy to the full the sheer innocence of the movie. The three animated adventures of Brer Rabbit, Brer Fox and Brer Bear will captivate adults as well as children. TS

Bobby Driscoll *Johnny* • James Baskett *Uncle Remus/Brer Fox* • Ruth Warrick *Sally* • Luana Patten *Ginny* • Lucile Watson *Grandmother* • Hattie McDaniel *Aunt Tempy* ■ *Dir* Wilfred Jackson, Harve Foster • *Scr* Dalton Raymond, Morton Grant, Maurice Rapf, from a story by Dalton Raymond, William Peet, Ralph Wright, George Stallings, from the story collection *Tales of Uncle Remus* by Joel Chandler Harris

Song of the Thin Man ★★★

Detective comedy 1947 · US · BW · 86mins

The sixth and last of the popular *Thin Man* series that started in 1934, this is closer to *film noir* than the earlier films, with the sleuthing couple visiting several jazz clubs in their search for a killer. The sophisticated banter and the blend of screwball comedy and murder mystery survive, however, and the rapport between stars William Powell and Myrna Loy is still palpable (though actor Leon Ames claimed later that they never spoke to each other during the shooting). A satisfying finish to an immensely enjoyable series. TV

William Powell *Nick Charles* • Myrna Loy *Nora Charles* • Keenan Wynn *Clarence "Clinker" Krause* • Dean Stockwell *Nick Charles Jr* • Philip Reed *Tommy Edlon Drake* • Patricia

S

Morison *Phyllis Talbin* • Leon Ames *Mitchell Talbin* ■ *Dir* Edward Buzzell • *Scr* Steve Fisher, Nat Perrin, from a story by Stanley Roberts, from characters created by Dashiell Hammett

The Song Remains the Same ★★★ 15

Concert documentary
1976 · UK · Colour · 136mins

The thunderous rock riffs of Led Zeppelin were a favourite among 1970s acid-droppers and it looks as if the makers of this odd documentary had more than their fair share. Footage of a 1973 New York concert (with the highlight being jukebox giant *Stairway to Heaven*) are interspersed with behind-the-scenes mishaps, trippy effects and ultra-weird fantasy sequences from the heads of Robert Plant, Jimmy Page *et al*, which makes *Tommy* look like social realism. The dated sound quality might bother those with a re-mastered Led Zep CD collection. JC [video] DVD

Dir Peter Clifton, Joe Massot

A Song to Remember ★★★ U

Biographical drama
1945 · US · Colour · 107mins

Hollywood biographies of classical composers are usually fair game for jest, and this account of Chopin's life is no exception. It features some flowery dialogue, a wildly over-the-top performance by Paul Muni as the composer's tutor and Merle Oberon miscast as the trousered George Sand who tells her lover to "Discontinue that so-called *Polonaise* jumble you've been playing for days." But the melodies, gorgeous Technicolor photography, opulent production and the seductive piano playing of José Iturbi (who dubbed for Cornel Wilde in the title role) add up to a lush, irresistible experience. TV [video]

Cornel Wilde *Chopin* • Paul Muni *Joseph Elsner* • Merle Oberon *George Sand* • Stephen Bekassy *Franz Liszt* • Nina Foch *Constantia* • George Coulouris *Louis Pleyel* • George Macready *Alfred de Musset* ■ *Dir* Charles Vidor • *Scr* Sidney Buchman, from a story by Ernst Marischka • *Cinematographer* Tony Gaudio, Allen M Davey

Song without End ★★★ U

Musical biography
1960 · US · Colour · 142mins

Dirk Bogarde made his Hollywood debut playing Franz Liszt in this ultra-glamorous Columbia biopic, turning down the role of Gaston Lachaille in MGM's *Gigi* in the process. Bogarde swiftly returned to European film-making, and no wonder, for excellent though he is, this is preposterous tosh, redeemed only by Jorge Bolet's off-screen piano and the panache of cameraman James Wong Howe. Alas, the soul went out of the project when the original director, Charles Vidor, died and George Cukor took over. TS

Dirk Bogarde *Franz Liszt* • Capucine *Princess Carolyne* • Genevieve Page *Countess Marie* • Patricia Morison *George Sand* • Ivan Desny *Prince Nicholas* • Martita Hunt *Grand Duchess* ■ *Dir* Charles Vidor, George Cukor • *Scr* Oscar Millard

Songcatcher ★★

Period drama 1999 · US · Colour · 109mins

Maggie Greenwald's tendency to melodrama allows stock characters to assume control of the intriguing early 20th-century scenario. Driven from academe by chauvinism, musicologist Janet McTeer's plan to record for posterity the ballads she hears in the remote mountain town where her sister teaches are jeopardised by the incursion of a ruthless mining company. Her relationship with frontiersman Aidan Quinn is more than a novelettish romance, but the story's real interest lies elsewhere. DP

Janet McTeer *Dr Lily Penleric* • Aidan Quinn *Tom Bledsoe* • Pat Carroll *Viney Butler* • Jane Adams (2) *Elna Penleric* • Greg Russell Cook *Fate Honeycutt* ■ *Dir/Scr* Maggie Greenwald

Songs from the Second Floor ★★★★ 15

Drama
2000 · Swe /Den/Nor · Colour · 94mins

Emerging from a 25-year exile, Roy Andersson has produced a virtuoso film that will infuriate as many people as it intrigues. Littered with eccentrics, it's a colliding series of vignettes that effectively conveys the chaos and coldness of modern life. At its centre is Lars Nordh, whose midlife crisis coincides with millennial angst to create a character teetering on the brink of a cockeyed world. Completely improvised, and shot with a disquieteningly static insistence, this astounding study of urban alienation eventually limps home. Yet it more than justifies Andersson's reputation as cinema's "unknown genius". DP. In Swedish with English subtitles. [video]

Lars Nordh *Kalle* • Stefan Larsson *Stefan, Kalle's son* • Bengt CW Carlsson *Lennart* • Torbjörn Fahlström *Pelle Wigert, the manager* • Sten Andersson *Lasse* ■ *Dir/Scr* Roy Andersson

Songs in Ordinary Time ★★★

Period drama 2000 · US · Colour

In this shrewd TV adaptation of Mary McGarry Morris's bestseller, director Rod Holcomb nails the atmosphere of small-town America at the crossroads between the 1950s and 60s. There's something to hide behind the curtains of every home in Atkinson, Vermont, and this takes the melodramatic curse off divorcee Sissy Spacek's self-evidently dangerous liaison with the mysterious Beau Bridges. If there is a problem it's that there's too much going on to let the storylines gel. DP

Sissy Spacek *Marie Fermoyle* • Beau Bridges *Omar Duvall* • Tom Guiry *Norm Fermoyle* • Jordan Warkol *Ben Fermoyle* • Careena Melia *Alice Fermoyle* ■ *Dir* Rod Holcomb • *Scr* Malcolm MacRury, from the novel by Mary McGarry Morris

Songwriter ★★★ 15

Musical comedy drama
1984 · US · Colour · 90mins

Sheer heaven for country music fans, with Willie Nelson and Kris Kristofferson as former singer-songwriter partners, who reunite to take on unscrupulous elements of the country music biz. The usual cocktail of drugs, booze and sleazy industry professionals is enlivened by the requisite musical number. An amiable and entertaining work from Robert Altman protegé Alan Rudolph. DA [video]

Willie Nelson *Doc Jenkins* • Kris Kristofferson *Blackie Buck* • Melinda Dillon *Honey Carder* • Rip Torn *Dino McLeish* • Lesley Ann Warren *Gilda* ■ *Dir* Alan Rudolph • *Scr* Bud Shrake

Sonny ★★ 18

Drama 2002 · US · Colour · 106mins

Nicolas Cage's New Orleans-set melodrama isn't a bad directorial debut, it's just a stale one, competently constructed but clichéd. James Franco is a handsome former gigolo who returns from the army in 1981 hoping to go straight, much to his trashy madam mother Brenda Blethyn's dismay. Though his performance is sympathetic, Blethyn wildly over-acts, while Cage's cameo as a gay pimp is probably his career worst. SF. Contains swearing, violence and sex scenes. [video] DVD

James Franco *Sonny* • Brenda Blethyn *Jewel* • Mena Suvari *Carol* • Harry Dean Stanton *Henry* • Brenda Vaccaro *Meg* • Scott Caan *Jesse* • Seymour Cassel *Albert* • Nicolas Cage *Acid Yellow* ■ *Dir* Nicolas Cage • *Scr* John Carlen

Sons ★★★

Comedy drama 1989 · US · Colour

This is a modest, but intriguing comedy drama about an attempt by three men to take their elderly father back to France to see the woman he fell in love with during the Second World War. While not saying anything particularly new, it benefits from the neat performances by the leads, and look out for appearances from legendary American director Samuel Fuller, French actress Stéphane Audran and *Flashdance's* Jennifer Beals as a transvestite. JF. Contains swearing.

William Forsythe *Mike* • DB Sweeney *Rich* • Robert Miranda *Fred* • Samuel Fuller *Father* • Stéphane Audran *Florence* • William Hickey *Roger* • Jennifer Beals *Transvestite* ■ *Dir* Alexandre Rockwell • *Scr* Alexandre Rockwell, Brandon Cole

Sons and Lovers ★★★

Drama 1960 · UK · BW · 99mins

The great cameraman Jack Cardiff made a directorial outing with this forthright adaptation of DH Lawrence's semi-autobiographical novel, about a boy caught between the Nottinghamshire rock and the hard place of his possessive mother (Wendy Hiller) and miner father (Trevor Howard). The trouble is that Dean Stockwell, as the teenager, is unconvincing in such great acting company. Ironically, the film won an Oscar for Freddie Francis's cinematography, while Cardiff was nominated as director. TH

Trevor Howard *Walter Morel* • Dean Stockwell *Paul Morel* • Wendy Hiller *Mrs Morel* • Mary Ure *Clara Dawes* • Heather Sears *Miriam Lievers* • William Lucas *William* • Conrad Phillips *Baxter Dawes* • Donald Pleasence *Pappleworth* • Ernest Thesiger *Henry Hadlock* ■ *Dir* Jack Cardiff • *Scr* Gavin Lambert, TEB Clarke, from the novel by DH Lawrence

The Sons of Katie Elder ★★★★ U

Western 1965 · US · Colour · 116mins

This terrific western contains a wonderful score from Elmer Bernstein, and has brothers John Wayne and Dean Martin riding out to avenge the death of their father. It's stirring stuff, beautifully photographed, with a fine support cast headed by Martha Hyer, who dignifies the movie by making a heartfelt speech about matriarchal virtue, addressed to the late Katie Elder's empty chair. TS [video] DVD

John Wayne *John Elder* • Dean Martin *Tom Elder* • Michael Anderson Jr *Bud Elder* • Earl Holliman *Matt Elder* • Martha Hyer *Mary Gordon* • George Kennedy *Curley* • Dennis Hopper *Dave Hastings* ■ *Dir* Henry Hathaway • *Scr* Allan Weiss, William H Wright, Harry Essex, from a story by Talbot Jennings • *Cinematographer* Lucien Ballard

Sons of the Desert ★★★★★ U

Comedy 1933 · US · BW · 64mins

This is probably the finest, and fastest, Laurel and Hardy feature film, in which Stan and Ollie "fool" their intimidating wives (Mae Busch and Dorothy Christy) with a story of a recuperative ocean cruise so they can attend the Chicago convention of their fraternity lodge. The ridiculous men-only antics of the lodge are wonderfully exploited, especially by a burpingly bumptious Charley Chase. The international society devoted to Stan and Ollie bears the name of this comedy gem – an indication of how highly it is thought of. TH [video] DVD

Stan Laurel *Stan* • Oliver Hardy *Ollie* • Charley Chase • Mae Busch *Mrs Lottie Chase Hardy* • Dorothy Christy *Mrs Betty Laurel* ■ *Dir* William A Seiter • *Scr* Frank Craven, Byron Morgan

Sons of the Musketeers ★★★ U

Adventure 1951 · US · Colour · 81mins

This gloriously Technicolored hokum imagines that the offspring of the Musketeers are just as nifty with swords as their fathers. One of them is female (Athos's daughter, in fact), and played by Maureen O'Hara, who tosses her red tresses to the wind and buckles a swash as if to the manner born. Co-star Cornel Wilde, a former member of the US Olympic fencing team, is no match for our Maureen in what is splendid fun. TS

Maureen O'Hara *Claire* • Cornel Wilde *D'Artagnan* • Robert Douglas *Lavalle* • Gladys Cooper *Queen* • Dan O'Herlihy *Aramis* • Alan Hale Jr *Porthos* • June Clayworth *Claudine* • Blanche Yurka *Madame Michom* • Nancy Gates *Princess Henriette* ■ *Dir* Lewis Allen • *Scr* Walter Ferris, Joseph Hoffman, from a story by Aubrey Wisberg, Jack Pollexfen

Sons of the Sea ★★★ U

Wartime drama 1939 · UK · Colour · 108mins

This routine spy drama is an early wartime flagwaver that provides a fascinating insight into the nation's mindset at the start of the Second World War. It follows navy commander Leslie Banks as he rallies to the cause when his son (Simon Lack) is accused of collaborating with the enemy from his naval training college. The actual drama is not really up to the propaganda value, but the movie looks great because it was filmed in the pioneering Dufaycolour process. DP

Leslie Banks *Captain Hyde* • Mackenzie Ward *Newton Hulls* • Kay Walsh *Alison Devar* • Simon Lack *Philip Hyde* • Cecil Parker *Commander Herbert* • Ellen Pollock *Margaret Hulls* • Peter Shaw (1) *Lt John Strepte* • Nigel Stock *Rudd* • Charles Eaton *Commander-in-chief* • Kynaston Reeves *Professor Devar* ■ *Dir* Maurice Elvey • *Scr* D William Woolf, Gerald Eliott, Maurice Elvey, from a story by D William Woolf, George Barraud

The Son's Room ★★★★★ 15

Drama 2001 · It/Fr · Colour · 95mins

Rarely has the raw subject of bereavement been so brilliantly portrayed than here in director Nanni Moretti's heart-wrenching account of how a provincial, middle-class family cope with the death of a child. The deserved winner of the 2001 Palme d'Or at Cannes, Moretti's pitch-perfect tragedy is almost unbearably moving and rings undeniably true. On a day he's supposed to spend with his son Giuseppe Sanfelice, psychoanalyst Moretti is called out on a patient emergency; Sanfelice goes scuba diving with friends instead and is accidentally killed. In the aftermath, Moretti introspectively obsesses over his actions on the fateful day, while his wife and daughter also begin to crack under the pressure of their inconsolable anguish. This is a beautifully observed study in melancholia, and a near faultless masterpiece. AJ. In Italian with English subtitles. [video] DVD

Nanni Moretti *Giovanni* • Laura Morante *Paola* • Jasmine Trinca *Irene* • Giuseppe Sanfelice *Andrea* • Silvio Orlando *Oscar* • Claudia Della Seta *Raffaella* ■ *Dir* Nanni Moretti • *Scr* Linda Ferri, Nanni Moretti, Heidrun Schleef

S

Sophie Scholl – The Final Days ★★★★

Second World War biographical drama
2005 · Ger · Colour · 120mins

The activities of Sophie Scholl and the White Rose resistance movement have been filmed twice before, but Marc Rothemund's starkly authentic drama has the advantage of being based on the Gestapo records of Scholl's interrogation, after she was caught distributing defeatist propaganda around Munich University in 1943. Julia Jentsch is sympathetically stoic in the title role, although her courage and conviction are powerfully matched during their intense confrontations by the disgust, disappointment and grudging respect exhibited by criminologist, Alexander Held. Fabian Hinrichs, as Jentsch's co-conspirator brother, and Johanna Gastdorf, as her Communist cellmate, also impress. DP. In German with English subtitles.

Julia Jentsch *Sophie Scholl* • Alexander Held *Robert Mohr* • Fabian Hinrichs *Hans Scholl* • Johanna Gastdorf *Else* ■ *Dir* Marc Rothemund • *Scr* Fred Breinersdorfer

Sophie's Choice ★★★★ 15

Period drama 1982 · US · Colour · 144mins

Meryl Streep confirmed her status as the Queen of Accents with her Oscar-winning performance in this moving adaptation of William Styron's bestselling novel. Yet, for all the significance of the revelations about Sophie's past, it is the interaction between the three central characters that gives the story its strength, and it is quite bewildering that, in spite of the quality of Kevin Kline's temperamental zest and Peter MacNicol's adoring timidity, neither merited even a nomination. Alan J Pakula's direction is much less constricted than his overly reverential script, thanks to the beautiful and evocative photography by Nestor Almendros. DP DVD

Meryl Streep *Sophie Zawistowska* • Kevin Kline *Nathan Landau* • Peter MacNicol *Stingo* • Rita Karin *Yetta Zimmerman* • Stephen D Newman *Larry Landau* • Greta Turken *Leslie Lapidus* • Josh Mostel *Morris Fink* • Marcel Rosenblatt *Astrid Weinstein* • Moishe Rosenfeld *Moishe Rosenblaum* ■ *Dir* Alan J Pakula • *Scr* Alan J Pakula, from the novel by William Styron

Sophiiie! ★★★

Drama 2002 · Ger · Colour · 107mins

Were it not for a compelling performance by Katharina Schüttler, this uncompromising "day in the life" study of a rootless 20-something's descent into despair would be almost unbearable to watch. Whether confronting rednecks in a Hamburg bar, escaping a brutal clip-joint owner or chatting naively with an immigrant cabbie and an impressionable cinema manager, Schüttler projects a reckless bravura that only cracks when she is seeking solace by phone from a total stranger after a traumatic incident. Unfortunately, director Michael Hofmann is not as courageous as his exceptional star and saddles the story with a less than credible ending. DP. In German with English subtitles.

Katharina Schüttler *Sophie* • Alexander Beyer • Ercan Durmaz ■ *Dir/Scr* Michael Hofmann

Sorcerer ★★

Thriller 1977 · US · Colour · 92mins

William Friedkin remakes Henri-Georges Clouzot's 1953 classic *The Wages of Fear*, about two trucks and their desperate crews who take a load of high explosives through the South American jungle, knowing that the slightest jolt will blow them sky-high. Friedkin's insistence on absolute realism took the budget from $3m to $22m and resulted in some simply staggering footage. As an allegory about Third World exploitation it works, often powerfully, but the vital ingredient – tension – is missing. AT

Roy Scheider *Jackie Scanlon/"Dominguez"* • Bruno Cremer *Victor Manzon/"Serrano"* • Francisco Rabal *Nilo* • Amidou *Kassem/"Martinez"* • Ramon Bieri *Corlette* • Peter Capell *Lartigue* ■ *Dir* William Friedkin • *Scr* Walon Green, from the novel *Le Salaire de la Peur (The Wages of Fear)* by Georges Arnaud

The Sorcerers ★★★ 15

Science-fiction horror
1967 · UK · Colour · 81mins

Prior to *Witchfinder General* and his death at the age of 24, Michael Reeves directed this intelligent shocker. Boris Karloff invents a mesmeric machine to control the mind of bored, swinging Londoner Ian Ogilvy, which can absorb and pass on the sensations he experiences. Karloff's wife gets hooked on the voyeuristic thrills, and wills the mod zombie to steal and kill. Cult brilliance on a small budget. AJ DVD

Boris Karloff *Professor Monserrat* • Catherine Lacey *Estelle Monserrat* • Ian Ogilvy *Mike* • Elizabeth Ercy *Nicole* • Victor Henry *Alan* • Susan George *Audrey* ■ *Dir* Michael Reeves • *Scr* Michael Reeves, Tom Baker, from an idea by John Burke

Sorority Boys ★★ 15

Comedy 2002 · US · Colour · 89mins

Sexist frat boys learn valuable lessons about women in this watered-down college comedy that follows a macho trio masquerading as female students after being kicked out of their fraternity house. Though the film is often amusing with some laugh-out-loud sequences, it's too self-conscious to make a lasting impression. Corny innuendo and repetitive sight gags quickly go stale, while some of the subject matter is just bad taste. SF. Contains swearing, nudity and drug abuse. DVD

Barry Watson *Dave/Daisy* • Michael Rosenbaum *Adam/Adina* • Harland Williams *Doofer/Roberta* • Melissa Sagemiller *Leah* • Tony Denman *Jimmy* • Brad Beyer *Spence* • Kathryn Stockwood *Patty* • Heather Matarazzo *Katie* ■ *Dir* Wallace Wolodarsky • *Scr* Joe Jarvis, Greg Coolidge

Sorority Girl ★★ PG

Drama 1957 · US · BW · 61mins

A torrid 1950s teen-flick from schlock-meister Roger Corman, this stars Susan Cabot as a James Dean figure in a dress, rebelling without much cause, blackmailing and pulling the hair of her college colleagues until she's banished to the American equivalent of Coventry. This deeply moral tale was aimed at an undemanding drive-in audience. AT DVD

Susan Cabot *Sabra Tanner* • Dick Miller *Mort* • Barboura O'Neill [Barboura Morris] *Rita Joyce* • June Kenney *Tina* • Barbara Crane *Ellie Marshall* • Fay Baker *Mrs Tanner* • Jeane Wood *Mrs Fessenden* ■ *Dir* Roger Corman • *Scr* Ed Waters, Lou Lieberman

The Sorrow and the Pity ★★★★★

Political documentary
1969 · Fr/Swi/W Ger · BW · 248mins

Divided into two parts – *The Collapse* (PG) and *The Choice* (12A) – Marcel Ophüls's monumental documentary is not just an investigation into what occurred in France during the Nazi Occupation, but how the nation has elected to remember it. Probing the selective memory of his occasionally evasive witnesses (who range from heroes and survivors to traitors and oppressors), he uncovers contradictions among the half-truths, as well as provoking outbursts of bitter fury and expressions of genuine remorse. Topics such as collaboration and co-operation, resistance and indifference are painfully explored. The archive material may be manipulative, but it retains the power to chill and cast doubt. DP. In French, German and English with subtitles. DVD

Dir Marcel Ophüls • *Scr* Marcel Ophüls, André Harris

Sorrowful Jones ★★★ U

Comedy 1949 · US · BW · 88mins

Damon Runyon's warm-hearted story, *Little Miss Marker* – about a tightwad Broadway bookie forced to look after a gambler's child – had been a huge success as a film with Shirley Temple. Paramount then ingeniously adapted it into a Bob Hope vehicle, taking attention away from the moppet. Although well supplied with quips, a restrained Hope brings out the sentimentality inherent in the story. The film proved such a hit, that director and star teamed up for another Runyon adaptation, *The Lemon Drop Kid*. AE

Bob Hope *Sorrowful Jones* • Lucille Ball *Gladys O'Neill* • William Demarest *Regret* • Bruce Cabot *Big Steve Holloway* • Thomas Gomez *Reardon* • Mary Jane Saunders *Martha Jane Smith* ■ *Dir* Sidney Lanfield • *Scr* Melville Shavelson, Edmund Hartmann [Edmund L Hartmann], Jack Rose, from the film *Little Miss Marker* by Gladys Lehman, William R Lipman, Sam Hellman, from the story by Damon Runyon

Sorry, Wrong Number ★★★★

Thriller 1948 · US · BW · 89mins

This taut drama centres on a bedridden heiress who, left alone in her apartment, tries to call her husband and overhears her own murder being planned. Fletcher opened out the screenplay just enough to allow beefy Burt Lancaster to share a crumb of the honours with Barbara Stanwyck, and to heighten the claustrophobia of the victim's bedroom by contrasting it with a murky outside world. Anatole Litvak directed this classic *film noir*, a real nail-biter, which earned Stanwyck an Oscar-nomination for her tour de force as the domineering, neurotically ill Leona. Remade in 1989 as a TV movie, improbably starring Loni Anderson in the Stanwyck role. RK

Barbara Stanwyck *Leona Stevenson* • Burt Lancaster *Henry Stevenson* • Ann Richards *Sally Lord Dodge* • Wendell Corey *Dr Alexander* • Ed Begley *James Cotterell* • Leif Erickson *Fred Lord* • William Conrad *Morano* ■ *Dir* Anatole Litvak • *Scr* Lucille Fletcher, from her radio play

Sorted ★★ 18

Crime drama 2000 · UK · Colour · 98mins

This is an energetic but utterly predictable crime drama from first-time director Alex Jovy, who was Oscar-nominated for his 1998 short film, *Holiday Romance*. Arriving from Scunthorpe to collect his dead brother's belongings, Matthew Rhys is sucked into the London club scene and its sleazy hinterland. Resisting the designer violence that has accompanied recent British gangster flicks, Jovy directs with pace and visual flourish, but his grasp of character is less assured. DP. Contains swearing and scenes of drug use. DVD

Tim Vincent *Justin* • Mary Tamm *School mother* • Matthew Rhys *Carl* • Sienna Guillory *Sunny* • Fay Masterson *Tiffany* • Jason Donovan *Martin* • Tim Curry *Damian Kemp* • Alex Jovy *Club DJ* ■ *Dir* Alex Jovy • *Scr* Nick Villiers, from a story by Alexander Jovy, from a screenplay (unproduced) by Christian Spurrier, Malcolm Campbell

Le Souffle ★★★ 15

Drama 2001 · Fr · Colour · 74mins

Shot in a monochrome that's variously forbidding and fantastical, the events triggered by the drunken feast attended by 15-year-old Pierre-Louis Bonnetblanc ultimately lapse into melodrama in writer/director Damien Odoul's uncompromising rites-of-passage drama. Yet there's an oppressive inevitability about the outcome considering the boorish irresponsibility of the Limousin farmers who serve as the teenager's role models in the absence of his father. The irregular fantasy sequences feel intrusive, even though their fairy-tale undertones are reinforced by the castellated grandeur of girlfriend Laure Magadoux's house. DP. In French with English subtitles. DVD

Pierre-Louis Bonnetblanc *David* • Dominique Chevallier *Jacques* • Maxime Dalbrut *Paul* • Jean-Claude Lecante *John* • Laure Magadoux *Aurore* • Stéphane Terpereau *Stef* ■ *Dir/Scr* Damien Odoul

Le Souffle au Coeur ★★★★ 18

Drama 1971 · Fr/It/W Ger · Colour · 113mins

On hearing the word incest, the moral guardians who delight in blaming cinema for society's ills almost fell over themselves in the rush to condemn this film. Even the critics got caught up in the fuss, and devoted more column space to a brief, tender scene at the end of the film than they did to the fond, very funny portrait of the French middle-classes in the mid-1950s. This is classic rite-of-passage stuff from Louis Malle, with non-actor Benoît Ferreux giving a wonderfully natural performance as the Dijon teenager curious about everything from sex to art forgery. Lea Massari is equally outstanding as his flirtatious mother. DP. In French with English subtitles. Contains sex scenes, nudity.

Lea Massari *Clara Chevalier* • Benoît Ferreux *Laurent Chevalier* • Daniel Gélin *Father* • Marc Winocourt *Marc* • Fabien Ferreux *Thomas* • Michel Lonsdale *Father Henri* • Ave Ninchi *Augusta* ■ *Dir/Scr* Louis Malle

Soul Food ★★★★ 15

Drama 1997 · US · Colour · 110mins

This well-acted and well-made drama focuses, as the title suggests, on the Sunday dinner get-togethers of a large African-American family. Matriarch Irma P Hall's home cooking just about keeps her three grown-up daughters and their partners from each other's throats, until a tragedy forces them to reconcile their differences. This is a terrific ensemble piece, boosted by the unfussy script and direction of George Tillman Jr. JB. Contains swearing and sex scenes. DVD

Vanessa L Williams *Teri* • Vivica A Fox *Maxine* • Nia Long *Bird* • Michael Beach *Miles* • Mekhi Phifer *Lem* • Brandon Hammond *Ahmad* • Jeffrey D Sams *Kenny* ■ *Dir/Scr* George Tillman Jr

Soul in the Hole ★★★★ 15

Sports documentary
1995 · US · Colour · 98mins

Never has the human drama and the simple beauty of the game of basketball been combined with such pace, passion and personality as in Danielle Gardner's documentary. Following the fortunes of "Bed-Stuy" team Kenny's Kings, and particularly its wayward star Ed "Booger" Smith, it may not break stylistic ground with its blend of talking heads and big game highlights. However, with its concentration on character and locale, this clipped, comic film takes a grip, but its real strength is that it never loses sight of life. DP

Dir Danielle Gardner

Soul Man ★★ 15

Comedy 1986 · US · Colour · 100mins

This charade was supposed to be a daring and right-on attempt to explore the prejudices on either side of the American racial divide, from the perspective of a middle-class white boy who is being penalised for not being black! Even though the social comment is totally subservient to the endless round of cheap-shot gags, the critics were inexplicably charitable to the film on its release, pointing to the sly satire and the courageous performance of C Thomas Howell as the kid who gulps down suntan pills in order to win a law school scholarship. Insidious and offensive. DP [video] DVD

C Thomas Howell *Mark Watson* • Arye Gross *Gordon Bloomfield* • Rae Dawn Chong *Sarah Walker* • James Earl Jones *Professor Rutherford Banks* • Melora Hardin *Whitney Dunbar* • Leslie Nielsen *Mr Dunbar* • James B Sikking *Bill Watson* ■ *Dir* Steve Miner • *Scr* Carol Black

Soul of the Game ★★★★ 12

Historical sports drama
1996 · US · Colour · 90mins

A talented cast toplines this historical TV docudrama about the racial integration of American baseball, told from the point of view of three Negro League baseball greats and friends. Kevin Sullivan deftly directs Delroy Lindo, Mykelti Williamson and Blair Underwood in a tale that rises above the sports genre with its intense look at loyalty, racism and morality. Baseball fans will lap it up, but everyone will appreciate its authentic period locations and atmosphere. MC. Contains swearing. [video]

Delroy Lindo *Satchel Paige* • Mykelti Williamson *Josh Gibson* • Blair Underwood *Jackie Robinson* • Edward Herrmann *Branch Rickey* • R Lee Ermey *Wilkie* ■ *Dir* Kevin Rodney Sullivan • *Scr* David Himmelstein, from a story by Gary Hoffman

Soul Plane ★ 18

Comedy 2004 · US · Colour · 88mins

Kevin Hart uses a $100million settlement from an airline to start up his own carrier – one strictly designed for an African-American clientele. Unfortunately, instead of the urban take on comedy classic *Airplane!* that this was presumably intended to be, what we get is an offensive stream of sexual innuendo, drugs humour and "bling" jokes, delivered by a variety of trite homophobic, sexist and racist characters. KK. Contains swearing, sex scenes and drug abuse. DVD

Kevin Hart *Nashawn* • Tom Arnold *Mr Hunkee* • Method Man *Muggsy* • Snoop Dogg *Captain Mack* • KD Aubert *Giselle* • Godfrey *Gaeman* • Brian Hooks *DJ* • DL Hughley *Johnny* ■ *Dir* Jessy Terrero • *Scr* Bo Zenga, Chuck Wilson

Soul Survivors ★★★ 12

Horror thriller 2001 · US · Colour · 81mins

Melissa Sagemiller plays a college girl who survives the car crash that kills her boyfriend, following a wild night out at a club in a spooky old church. But back at school, she rapidly realises there's something wrong. Dead wrong. Her world's just not quite right anymore. And the key to its eerieness are the schoolmates who survived the crash with her. Featuring *Twilight Zone* qualities, some decent production values, and a teen-friendly cast, this teen film puts head-thrills before blood-spills. DA [video] DVD

Melissa Sagemiller *Cassie* • Casey Affleck *Sean* • Wes Bentley *Matt* • Eliza Dushku *Annabel* • Angela Featherstone *Raven* • Luke Wilson *Father Jude* ■ *Dir/Scr* Steve Carpenter [Stephen Carpenter]

Souls at Sea ★★★

Drama 1937 · US · BW · 90mins

This spectacular features Gary Cooper as the strong, silent opponent of slavery, on trial for shooting survivors of a sinking vessel who clung to the oars of his crowded lifeboat. Co-star George Raft revived his flagging career with a winning performance as Cooper's loyal, but slow-witted companion with a ring in his ear. The story is rather awkwardly presented, but Henry Hathaway's direction is swift and incisive, and the period setting is superbly evoked. AE

Gary Cooper *Michael "Nuggin" Taylor* • George Raft *Powdah* • Frances Dee *Margaret Tarryton* • Henry Wilcoxon *Lt Stanley Tarryton* • Harry Carey *Captain* • Olympe Bradna *Babsie* • Robert Cummings *George Martin* • Virginia Weidler *Tina* ■ *Dir* Henry Hathaway • *Scr* Grover Jones, Dale Van Every, Richard Talmadge, from a story by Ted Lesser

The Sound and the Fury ★★★

Drama 1959 · US · Colour · 115mins

Joanne Woodward is the young misfit in this less intense companion piece to the earlier William Faulkner adaptation, *The Long Hot Summer*, by the same director, screenwriters and leading lady. But there's no escaping Jason, played by Yul Brynner (with hair), the cruel-to-be-kind outsider, who bullies a decayed southern family into some semblance of self respect. It's a delightfully played battle of wills between Woodward and Brynner, with a fine supporting cast. AE

Yul Brynner *Jason* • Joanne Woodward *Quentin* • Margaret Leighton *Caddy* • Stuart Whitman *Charles Busch* • Ethel Waters *Dilsey* • Jack Warden *Ben* • Françoise Rosay *Mrs Compson* ■ *Dir* Martin Ritt • *Scr* Irving Ravetch, Harriet Frank Jr, from the novel by William Faulkner

The Sound Barrier ★★★★ U

Drama 1952 · UK · BW · 111mins

Terence Rattigan's script was Oscar-nominated, but the main honours in this David Lean film are shared between the stunning aerial sequences and the fine performance by Ralph Richardson as an aeroplane designer driven to produce the first craft to outstrip the speed of sound. The film is an illustration of the dictum, that history is made by unreasonable people or by those single-minded enough to pursue their visions, regardless of the cost. PF [video] DVD

Ralph Richardson *John Ridgefield* • Ann Todd *Susan Garthwaite* • Nigel Patrick *Tony Garthwaite* • John Justin *Phillip Peel* • Dinah Sheridan *Jess Peel* • Joseph Tomelty *Will Sparks* • Denholm Elliott *Christopher Ridgefield* • Jack Allen *Windy Williams* • Ralph Michael *Fletcher* • Vincent Holman *ATA officer* • Douglas Muir *Controller* • Leslie Phillips *Controller* ■ *Dir* David Lean • *Scr* Terence Rattigan • *Cinematographer* Jack Hildyard

The Sound of Fury ★★★★ PG

Crime drama 1950 · US · BW · 88mins

This extraordinarily stark and uncompromising low-budget drama features Lloyd Bridges as a hardened criminal of the Depression period who recruits an out-of-work family man, played by Frank Lovejoy, as his accomplice in a kidnapping. After their victim dies, a journalist (Richard Carlson) whips up local feeling, leading to a terrifying climax. Only the unnecessary moral comments of an Italian doctor lessen the film's impact. The critical view of American mores contributed to the blacklisting of its director, Cyril Endfield, who moved to Britain. AE [video]

Frank Lovejoy *Howard Tyler* • Lloyd Bridges *Jerry Slocum* • Kathleen Ryan *Judy Tyler* • Richard Carlson *Gil Stanton* • Katherine Locke *Hazel* • Adele Jergens *Velma* ■ *Dir* Cyril Endfield [Cy Endfield] • *Scr* Jo Pagano, from his novel *The Condemned*

Sound of Love ★★

Romantic drama 1977 · US · Colour · 74mins

Struggling at times between the authentic and overemphasised, this is a sometimes touching portrait of the love between two people with hearing difficulties. He's a mechanic rendered deaf through an accident, she's a drifter. John Power rightly opts for uncluttered direction and gives his characters a chance to breathe. John Jarratt and Celia De Burgh portray the hearing-impaired couple without a hint of self-consciousness. JM

John Jarratt *Dave* • Celia De Burgh *Eileen* ■ *Dir* John Power • *Scr* John Power, from a screenplay (unproduced) by Lew Hunter

The Sound of Music ★★★★★ U

Classic musical 1965 · US · Colour · 165mins

At the time, the biggest money-maker in the history of cinema, this is an artful and professionally made crowd-pleaser that reaches out to every generation, thanks to expert and unsentimental handling from director Robert Wise (replacing William Wyler) and a magnificent performance from Julie Andrews. She is perfectly cast as Maria, the reluctant nun who discovers her true calling as governess to a houseful of youngsters. It still looks lovely, in particular the stunning opening panoramic sweep on to the mountain top and the *Do Re Mi* tour around Salzburg, and the Rodgers and Hammerstein score is as refreshing as ever. As fresh and as magical as Andrews's smile. TS [video] DVD

Julie Andrews *Maria* • Christopher Plummer *Captain Von Trapp* • Eleanor Parker *Baroness* • Richard Haydn *Max Detweiler* • Peggy Wood *Mother Abbess* • Charmian Carr *Liesl* • Heather Menzies *Louisa* • Nicholas Hammond *Friedrich* • Duane Chase *Kurt* • Angela Cartwright *Brigitta* • Debbie Turner *Marta* • Kym Karath *Gretl* • Daniel Truhitte *Rolfe* ■ *Dir* Robert Wise • *Scr* Ernest Lehman, from the musical by Richard Rodgers, Oscar Hammerstein II, Howard Lindsay, Russel Crouse • *Cinematographer* Ted McCord • *Production Designer* Boris Leven • *Music Director* Irwin Kostal • *Editor* William Reynolds

The Sound of One Hand Clapping ★★

Drama 1998 · Aus · Colour · 93mins

Richard Flanagan directs this adaptation of his own novel, a study of misunderstood motives, set amid Tasmania's immigrant community. The action opens with pregnant 30-something Kerry Fox returning after a 20-year exile in Sydney and reflecting on the childhood that prompted her to leave and turned her Slovenian father, Kristof Kaczmarek, into an alcoholic. However, the prolonged flashback segment hovers uncertainly between sociological insight and domestic melodrama, as the abandoned Kaczmarek makes several sacrifices to care for his daughter, who repays him with fury at his relationship with orchard owner Essie Davis. DP

Kerry Fox *Sonja Buloh* • Kristof Kaczmarek *Bojan Buloh* • Rosie Flanagan *Sonja, aged 8* • Evelyn Krape *Jenja* • Melita Jurisic *Maria Buloh* • Essie Davis *Jean* ■ *Dir* Richard Flanagan • *Scr* Richard Flanagan, from his novel

Sounder ★★★★ U

Drama 1972 · US · Colour · 105mins

This is a sentimental, but still powerful movie about a family of black sharecroppers in 1930s Depression-hit Louisiana. Beautifully photographed, it boasts fine performances from Paul Winfield as the dad who is snatched from his family for stealing a ham and Cicely Tyson as the mother of three who struggles to carry on the farm without him. Kevin Hooks (who won a Golden Globe for best newcomer and went on to become a director) is the son who embarks on an odyssey to find Winfield. Accompanied by faithful dog Sounder, he meets schoolteacher Jane McLachlan, who irrevocably changes his life. A sequel (*Part 2, Sounder*) followed in 1976. FL

Cicely Tyson *Rebecca Morgan* • Paul Winfield *Nathan Lee Morgan* • Kevin Hooks *David Lee Morgan* • Carmen Mathews *Mrs Boatwright* • Taj Mahal *Ike* • James Best *Sheriff Young* ■ *Dir* Martin Ritt • *Scr* Lonne Elder III, from the novel by William H Armstrong • *Cinematographer* John A Alonzo

Sour Grapes ★ 15

Comedy 1998 · US · Colour · 88mins

Two goombah cousins hit it rich playing slot machines in Atlantic City – or rather, one of them does, using the quarters he borrowed from his relative. His refusal to split the winnings means the end of their friendship and the start of an endless round of recriminations and snappy repartee. Larry David, co-creator of sitcom *Seinfeld*, may be behind this, but even fans of the TV series will have trouble laughing at any of this. ST. Contains swearing and sexual references. [video]

Steven Weber *Evan* • Craig Bierko *Richie* • Karen Sillas *Joan* • Robyn Peterman *Roberta* • Jack Burns *Eulogist* • Viola Harris *Selma* ■ *Dir/Scr* Larry David

Soursweet ★★★ 15

Drama 1988 · UK · Colour · 105mins

Mike Newell directs this sweet and sour drama of immigrant life in London, about a Chinese couple who set up their own small restaurant. It could have been chop phooey, but, with the help of a fine screenplay by Ian McEwan, and thoughtful direction, it becomes a charming and moving character study of one of the many ethnic strands that make up multiracial Britain. DA [video]

Sylvia Chang *Lily* • Danny An-Ning Dun *Chen* • Jodi Long *Mui* • Soon-Teck Oh *Red Cudgel* • William Chow *White Paper Fan* • Jim Carter *Mr Constantinides* ■ *Dir* Mike Newell • *Scr* Ian McEwan, from the novel by Timothy Mo

S

Sous le Soleil de Satan ★★★★ 15

Religious drama 1987 · Fr · Colour · 97mins

Since Robert Bresson had already adapted two Georges Bernanos novels, *Diary of a Country Priest* and *Mouchette*, it was logical that Maurice Pialat should elect to emulate his stark authenticity in relating Bernanos's tale of the village cleric who comes to see Satan as the world's controlling force. Yet, this is clearly the work of an atheist, who considers that Father Gérard Depardieu's relentless self-flagellation is as much an act of pride as saintliness. The elliptical structure brings an intellectual rigour to the emotive exchanges, while the performances of Depardieu and Sandrine Bonnaire are riveting. DP. In French with English subtitles.

Gérard Depardieu *Donissan* • Sandrine Bonnaire *Mouchette* • Maurice Pialat *Menou-Segrais* • Alain Artur *Cadignan* • Yann Dedet *Gallet* • Brigitte Legendre *Mouchette's mother* • Jean-Claude Bourlat *Malorthy* ■ *Dir* Maurice

Pialat • *Scr* Sylvie Danton, Maurice Pialat, from the novel *Sous le Soleil de Satan* by Georges Bernanos

Sous les Toits de Paris ★★★★

Drama 1930 · Fr · BW · 91mins

Deriving much neighbourhood charm from Lazare Meerson's sets and full of memorable songs and pleasing performances, René Clair's sound debut was a fluent delight at a time when everyone else's talkies were little more than animated radio. Indeed, he places so much emphasis on the narrative power of the image, that he mischievously stages conversations where the dialogue simply couldn't be heard. Keeping the camera on the move and the action light, he utterly enchants with the story of Parisian street singer, Albert Préjean, whose beloved, Pola Illery, is also pursued by his best friend, Edmond Gréville, and the lecherous Gaston Modot. DP. In French with English subtitles.

Albert Préjean *Albert* • Pola Illery *Pola* • Gaston Modot *Fred* • Edmond T Gréville *Louis* • Bill Bocket *Bill* ■ *Dir/Scr* René Clair • *Cinematographer* Georges Périnal

South ★★★

Silent documentary 1919 · UK · Tinted · 83mins

A milestone in Britain's documentary history, Frank Hurley's silent account of Sir Ernest Shackleton's doomed Antarctic expedition (1914-16) is heavily reliant on captions that don't always provide adequate information or explanation. Nor does Hurley come clean about the fate of the 70 sled dogs on whom he lavishes so much attention, until they are abandoned when the mission becomes a desperate bid for survival. However, the tinted footage is compelling, with the hauntingly beautiful night shots of the *Endurance* trapped among the ice floes standing out as symbols of our nation's love affair with flawed heroism. DP [video] DVD

Dir Frank Hurley

South American George ★★★ U

Comedy 1941 · UK · BW · 95mins

The first film that ukulele-playing comic George Formby made after he left Ealing Studios and signed with Columbia, gives him a dual role as an opera singer and his double, a stagehand who agrees to take the singer's place then finds himself fleeing gangsters. Sometimes cited as the start of Formby's decline on the screen, this has more plot than usual for a Formby vehicle and although some of his fans missed the "old" George, they still turned out in their millions and maintained his position as Britain's top box-office draw. TV

George Formby *George Butters/Gilli Vanetti* • Linden Travers *Carole Dean* • Enid Stamp-Taylor *Frances Martinique* • Jacques Brown *Enrico Richardo* • Felix Aylmer *Mr Appleby* • Ronald Shiner *Swifty* ■ *Dir* Marcel Varnel • *Scr* Leslie Arliss, Norman Lee, Austin Melford

South Central ★★★ 15

Drama 1992 · US · Colour · 94mins

This stark look at life on the streets of South Central Los Angeles begins in standard *Boyz N the Hood* territory, but then the action takes a dramatic turn when jailed murderer Glenn Plummer discovers Islam. There's something of the Malcolm X story about this transformation, but the struggle for control of his ten-year-old between Plummer and gang leader Byron Keith Minns, and his girlfriend's descent into addiction and prostitution, make for powerful human drama. DP [video]

Glenn Plummer *Bobby Johnson* • Carl Lumbly *Ali* • Byron Keith Minns [Byron Minns] *Ray Ray* • Lexie D Bigham [Lexie Bigham] *Bear* • Vincent Craig Dupree *Loco* • LaRita Shelby *Carole* • Kevin Best *Genie Lamp* ■ *Dir* Steve Anderson • *Scr* Steve Anderson, from the novel *Crips* by Donald Bakeer

South of Algiers ★★★ PG

Drama 1952 · UK · Colour · 86mins

An exciting, richly Technicolored movie about a sun-scorched search in the Sahara for a fabled "golden mask" (the American title). Imaginatively shot by under-rated documentarist Jack Lee, it features sturdy Van Heflin as the archaeologist with a mission and Eric Portman as his rapacious adversary. Stirring stuff, and beautifully filmed by veteran British cameraman Oswald Morris, with some strikingly authentic sequences. TS [video]

Van Heflin *Nicholas Chapman* • Wanda Hendrix *Anne Burnet* • Eric Portman *Dr Burnet* • Charles Goldner *Petris* • Jacques François *Jacques Farnod* • Jacques Brunius *Kress* • Aubrey Mather *Professor Sir Arthur Young* ■ *Dir* Jack Lee • *Scr* Robert Westerby

South of Heaven, West of Hell ★★

Western 2000 · US · Colour · 132mins

Dwight Yoakam adds another hyphenated credit to his CV with this first outing as a writer-director-composer. But, despite its impressive ensemble, there's not much else to applaud in this sprawling western that is very much a tale of two halves. In the first, Yoakam's Arizona lawman turns on the outlaw family who raised him as an orphan, while in the second he returns, having thrown away his badge, to compete with bombastic brigadier Billy Bob Thornton for the affections of Bridget Fonda. DP

Dwight Yoakam *Valentine Casey* • Vince Vaughn *Taylor Henry* • Billy Bob Thornton *Brigadier Smalls* • Bridget Fonda *Adalyne* • Peter Fonda *Shoshone Bill* • Paul Reubens *Arvid Henry* • Bud Cort *Agent Otts* • Bo Hopkins *Doc Angus Dunfries* ■ *Dir* Dwight Yoakam • *Scr* Dwight Yoakam, Stan Bertheaud, from a story by Dwight Yoakam, Dennis Hackin, Otto Felix

South of Pago Pago ★★★ U

Adventure 1940 · US · BW · 96mins

Pago Pago is the main town of American Samoa, where Victor McLaglen runs a pearl-diving operation while dodging hostile Polynesians and watching his divers fail to come up for air. Romance is supplied by the alluring Frances Farmer who catches the eye of native hunk Jon Hall. Exciting action and fine photography keep it above the merely routine. AT

Victor McLaglen *Bucko Larson* • Jon Hall *Kehane* • Frances Farmer *Ruby Taylor* • Olympe Bradna *Malla* • Gene Lockhart *Lindsay* • Douglass Dumbrille *Williams* • Francis Ford *Foster* ■ *Dir* Alfred E Green • *Scr* George Bruce • *Cinematographer* John J Mescall

South of St Louis ★★ U

Western 1949 · US · Colour · 86mins

This relentlessly routine western about three ranchers wasn't particularly memorable in its day, but is worth a look for nostalgic value alone. The three leads –Joel McCrea, Alexis Smith and Zachary Scott – are watchable, their sheer professionalism a delight. Director Ray Enright proves as competent as ever, this time helped by the great cameraman Karl Freund's outdoor Technicolor photography. TS

Joel McCrea *Kip Davis* • Alexis Smith *Rouge de Lisle* • Zachary Scott *Charlie Burns* • Dorothy Malone *Deborah Miller* • Douglas Kennedy *Lee Price* • Alan Hale *Jake Evarts* • Victor Jory *Luke Cottrell* ■ *Dir* Ray Enright • *Scr* Zachary Gold, James R Webb

South Pacific ★★★ U

Musical 1958 · US · Colour · 143mins

This screen version of the fabulous Rodgers and Hammerstein Broadway show has always been better liked by the public than the critics. It has several flaws, not least of which is the bizarre use of colour filters. Wonderful though Mitzi Gaynor is in the big numbers, her character's brashness grows tiresome and one longs for Doris Day's tenderness in the role, while Rossano Brazzi is wooden and the war sequences seem to belong to a different movie. But the score is wonderful, and no one could fail to be carried away by some of the finest songs ever written. TS [video] DVD

Mitzi Gaynor *Nellie Forbush* • Rossano Brazzi *Emile de Becque* • John Kerr *Lieutenant Cable* • Ray Walston *Luther Billis* • Juanita Hall *Bloody Mary* • France Nuyen *Liat* • Russ Brown *Captain Brackett* • Joan Fontaine *Polynesian woman* ■ *Dir* Joshua Logan • *Scr* Paul Osborn, from the musical by Richard Rodgers, Oscar Hammerstein Ii, Joshua Logan, from the novel *Tales of the South Pacific* by James A Michener

South Pacific ★★★

Musical drama 2001 · US · Colour · 129mins

In this small-screen remake of Rodgers and Hammerstein's hit musical, director Richard Pearce dispenses with the visual artiness of Joshua Logan's 1958 version and returns to James A Michener's source stories to re-emphasise the themes of racial prejudice and the human cost of war. But he doesn't neglect the musical interludes and the classic tunes are competently performed. DP

Glenn Close *Nellie Forbush* • Harry Connick Jr *Lieutenant Cable* • Rade Sherbedgia [Rade Serbedzija] *Emile de Beque* • Lori Tan Chinn *Bloody Mary* • Robert Pastorelli *Luther Billis* • Natalie Mendoza *Liat* ■ *Dir* Richard Pearce • *Scr* Lawrence D Cohen, from the musical by Richard Rodgers, Oscar Hammerstein Ii, Joshua Logan, from the novel *Tales of the South Pacific* by James A Michener

South Park: Bigger, Longer & Uncut ★★★★ 15

Animated comedy 1999 · US · Colour · 81mins

Trey Parker and Matt Stone's tasteless animated TV series gets the big-screen treatment in this dark, demented and deliriously funny feature-length tale. Stan, Kyle, Cartman and Kenny go on an outing to see Terrance and Phillip's profanity-laced movie and their resultant change in vocabulary is the catalyst for an escalating bout of moral-guardian madness, culminating in the outbreak of World War Three (well, the USA versus Canada). This sharp, inventive TV spin-off doesn't pad its plot or waste widescreen opportunities. Bad taste at its best. JC. Contains swearing. [video] DVD

Trey Parker *Stan Marsh/Eric Cartman/Mr Garrison/Mr Hat/Officer Barbrady* • Matt Stone *Kyle Broflovski/Kenny McCormick/Pip/Jesus/Jimbo* • Mary Kay Bergman *Mrs Cartman/Sheila Broflovski/Sharon Manson/Mrs McCormick/Wendy Testaburger/Principal Victoria* • Isaac Hayes *Chef* • George Clooney *Doctor Gouache* • Brent Spiner *Conan O'Brien* • Minnie Driver *Brooke Shields* • Eric Idle *Doctor Vosknocker* ■ *Dir* Trey Parker • *Scr* Trey Parker, Matt Stone, Pam Brady

South Riding ★★★

Romantic drama 1938 · UK · BW · 68mins

Victor Saville makes an admirable job of bringing Winifred Holtby's bubbling cauldron of upper-class insanity, misguided philanthropy and council-chamber corruption to the screen. Deftly capturing the sights and sounds of this Yorkshire neverland, he only loses his grasp at the close as sentimentality is allowed to wash away the grit. Ralph Richardson reins in his customary screen excesses to give a sensitive reading of the misguided squire unable to come to terms with his wife's madness. DP

Ralph Richardson *Robert Carne* • Edna Best *Sarah Burton* • Ann Todd *Madge Carne* • Edmund Gwenn *Alfred Huggins* • John Clements *Joe Astell* • Marie Lohr *Mrs Beddows* • Milton Rosmer *Alderman Snaith* • Glynis Johns *Midge Carne* ■ *Dir* Victor Saville • *Scr* Ian Dalrymple, Donald Bull, from the novel by Winifred Holtby

South Sea Woman ★★

Comedy adventure 1953 · US · BW · 98mins

Even stars as big as Burt Lancaster had to serve their Hollywood apprenticeship in tacky movies such as this, in which he's an eager-to-fight marine sparking with sultry Virginia Mayo on a tropical island. Director Arthur Lubin had made six movies about Francis the Talking Mule, so Burt's reported mulish behaviour off-set was forgivably in character. TH

Burt Lancaster *Sergeant James O'Hearn* • Virginia Mayo *Ginger Martin* • Chuck Connors *Davey White* • Barry Kelley *Colonel Hickman* • Hayden Rorke *Lieutenant Fears* • Leon Askin *Marchand* ■ *Dir* Arthur Lubin • *Scr* Edwin Blum, Earl Baldwin, Stanley Shapiro, from a play by William M Rankin

South West Nine ★★★ 18

Drama 2001 · UK/Ire · Colour · 94mins

Low-budget films set in a distinctive London suburb have become a rather stale British sub-genre of late, but this Brixton-based social tapestry has enough energy, personality and multicultural scope to make its own distinctive mark. Charting 24 hours in the lives of an eclectic bunch of local characters, writer/director Richard Parry combines such elements as a mysterious stolen briefcase, some accidentally ingested LSD and a climactic church rave. He also extracts bright, authentic performances from a largely unknown young cast. It's only real shortcoming is the ineffectual attempt to crank up tension with an unnecessary thriller plot. JC [video] DVD

Wil Johnson *Freddy* • Stuart Laing *Jake* • Mark Letheren *Mitch* • Amelia Curtis *Kat* • Orlessa Edwards *Helen* ■ *Dir/Scr* Richard Parry

Southern Comfort ★★★★ 15

Action drama 1981 · US · Colour · 101mins

Nine National Guardsmen – including Keith Carradine and Powers Boothe – are sent on exercises through the Louisiana swamplands and find themselves drawn into a guerrilla war with the local Cajuns. Set in 1973, Walter Hill's movie is evidently an allegorical treatment of the Vietnam conflict, with the Cajuns cast as the shadowy but lethal Vietcong. Few movies are as single-minded as this one: Hill establishes the bayou as a grey, formless labyrinth and creates a purely abstract action movie that's creepy, tense and never remotely comfortable. AT. Contains violence, swearing and drug abuse. [video] DVD

Keith Carradine *Spencer* • Powers Boothe *Hardin* • Fred Ward *Reece* • Franklyn Seales *Simms* • TK Carter *Cribbs* • Lewis Smith *Stuckey* • Les Lannom *Casper* • Peter Coyote *Poole* • Carlos Brown *Bowden* • Brion James *Trapper* ■ *Dir* Walter Hill • *Scr* Michael Kane, Walter Hill, David Glier

Southern Roses ★★ U

Musical comedy 1936 · UK · BW · 80mins

This is a small-scale, long-forgotten, expendable, British, romantic comedy, in which a naval officer is smitten with a musical comedy actress, while his friend is required to pose as her husband. Notable only for the presence of famous musical hall

S

comedian George Robey, known as "the prime minister of mirth". RK

George Robey *Mr Higgins* • Neil Hamilton *Reggie* • Gina Malo *Mary Rowland* • Chili Bouchier *Estrella Estrello* • Vera Pearce *Carrie* • Richard Dolman *Bill Higgins* • Athene Seyler *Mrs Rowland* • DA Clarke-Smith *Senor Estrello* • Sara Allgood *Miss Florence* ■ *Dir* Frederick Zelnik [Fred Zelnik] • *Scr* Ronald Gow, from a play by Rudolph Bernauer

The Southern Star ★★★ PG

Comedy adventure
1969 · Fr/UK · Colour · 101mins

Splendidly photographed African adventure filmed on authentic Senegalese locations, but alas bearing the curse of international co-production. Under-rated editor-turned-director Sidney Hayers tries to pull together the Jules Verne-inspired plot and a cast that verges on the preposterous, headed by George Segal (far too urban for this type of trek), Ursula Andress and Orson Welles, who was obviously in need of the money. This romp isn't sure whether it's comedy or adventure or both, but it looks good nevertheless. TS

George Segal *Dan* • Ursula Andress *Erica Kramer* • Orson Welles *Plankett* • Ian Hendry *Karl* • Harry Andrews *Kramer* ■ *Dir* Sidney Hayers • *Scr* David Pursall, Jack Seddon, Jean Giono, from the novel *L'Etoile du Sud, le Pays des Diamants* by Jules Verne • *Cinematographer* Raoul Coutard

A Southern Yankee ★★★

Comedy 1948 · US · BW · 90mins

Fans of Buster Keaton's *The General* may well recognise an occasional overlap here. That's because not only was Keaton happy for Red Skelton to borrow ideas from that silent classic, he was also in charge of many comic sequences, which unsurprisingly turn out to be those that make the film really sing. Otherwise proceedings oscillate from swirling exuberance to blandness, though Skelton's comic knack, as a foolish Civil War spy, is never in doubt. TS

Red Skelton *Aubrey Filmore* • Arlene Dahl *Sallyann Weatharby* • Brian Donlevy *Curt Devlynn* • George Coulouris *Major Jack Drumman* • Minor Watson *General Watkins* • Lloyd Gough *Captain Steve Lorford* • John Ireland *Captain Jed Calbern* ■ *Dir* Edward Sedgwick • *Scr* Harry Tugend, from a story by Melvin Frank

The Southerner ★★★★★

Drama 1945 · US · BW · 92mins

The only American film by the great French director Jean Renoir to receive critical praise and break even at the box office, the screenplay, on which Renoir was advised by William Faulkner, told of a year in the life of a cotton farmer who has to fight a malicious neighbour, the elements and malnutrition. In order to achieve pictorial splendour and realism, the film was shot almost entirely on location in the San Joaquin valley in California (standing in for Texas) and produced an effective slice of Americana. Zachary Scott, cast against type, gives one of his finest performances. RB

Zachary Scott *Sam Tucker* • Betty Field *Nona Tucker* • J Carrol Naish *Devers* • Beulah Bondi *Granny* • Jean Vanderwilt *Daisy* • Jay Gilpin *Jot* • Percy Kilbride *Harmie* • Blanche Yurka *Ma* • Charles Kemper *Tim* • Norman Lloyd *Finley* • Jack Norworth *Doctor* • Nestor Paiva *Bartender* • Estelle Taylor *Lizzie* ■ *Dir* Jean Renoir • *Scr* Jean Renoir, Hugo Butler, from the novel *Hold Autumn in Your Hands* by George Sessions Perry

Southpaw ★★★★ 15

Sports documentary
1998 · Ire/UK · Colour · 79mins

This documentary charts the rise to fame of Francis Barrett, an Irish boxer and one of a community of Galway travellers. A national hero, he qualified for the Irish Olympic team, carrying his country's flag during the opening ceremony at Atlanta in 1996. Training in a ramshackle gym, under a boxing-addicted barber, he encounters bigotry, but settles into marriage easily – if not celebrity. Liam McGrath directs this hard-hitting account of a real-life fighter who is naturally appealing. TH. Contains swearing.

Dir Liam McGrath

Southwest Passage ★★★ U

Western 1954 · US · Colour · 75mins

An unusual aspect of western history lifts this drama out of the rut: it's the experimental use of pack camels with Arab drivers to create a shorter route across the American desert. Rod Cameron is surprisingly effective as the determined camel enthusiast and his story should have been enough in itself. But there's John Ireland and Joanne Dru doing their best with clichéd roles as the sympathetic bank robber on the run and his gal, who join the caravan. Originally seen in 3-D, the film was shown flat in Britain under the title *Camels West*. AE

Joanne Dru *Lilly* • Rod Cameron *Edward Fitzpatrick Beale* • John Ireland *Clint McDonald* • Guinn "Big Boy" Williams *Tall Tale* • Darryl Hickman *Jeb* • Morris Ankrum *Doc Stanton* ■ *Dir* Ray Nazarro • *Scr* Harry Essex, Geoffrey Homes [Daniel Mainwaring], from a story by Harry Essex

Southwest to Sonora ★★★ PG

Western 1966 · US · Colour · 94mins

Marlon Brando and his much-prized Appaloosa horse become the target for a Mexican bandit chief in this very 1960s western, flashily directed by Sidney J Furie. Brando is at his mumbliest, moodiest and most masochistic. The highlight is an absurd arm-locking duel fought between Brando and John Saxon over a pair of scorpions – the loser gets stung – and the whole movie has an operatic, parodic quality not unlike Sergio Leone's films. Released on video under its original US title, *The Appaloosa*. AT

Marlon Brando *Fletcher* • Anjanette Comer *Trini* • John Saxon *Chuy Medina* • Emilio Fernandez *Lazaro* • Alex Montoya *Squint Eye* • Miriam Colon *Ana* ■ *Dir* Sidney J Furie • *Scr* James Bridges, Roland Kibbee, from the novel by Robert MacLeod

Souvenir ★★ 15

Drama 1987 · UK · Colour · 92mins

Christopher Plummer plays an elderly German, former Second World War soldier, now resident in New York. He returns to France to try to atone for a massacre he was involved in 40 years earlier. Plummer, an excellent actor, is wasted on such predictable and plodding material. Co-stars Catherine Hicks and Christopher Cazenove fare slightly better, perhaps because of one's low expectations of them. Heavy-handed and wordy. DA

Christopher Plummer *Ernst Kestner* • Catherine Hicks *Tina* • Michael Lonsdale [Michel Lonsdale] *Xavier Lorion* • Christopher Cazenove *William Root* • Lisa Daniely *Madame Lorion* • Jean Badin *Henri* ■ *Dir* Geoffrey Reeve • *Scr* Paul Wheeler, from the novel *The Pork Butcher* by David Hughes

Soylent Green ★★★ 15

Science-fiction thriller
1973 · US · Colour · 92mins

Charlton Heston is in serious jaw-jutting mode as the lone honest cop in a polluted and over-populated 21st-century New York, investigating a murder at the company responsible for a new synthetic food product. Harry Harrison's sober novel has been rather ploddingly adapted as a curious update of the private eye genre with grim glimpses of a future consumer society run amok, though director Richard Fleischer still manages to retain the book's anti-utopian sentiments. Edward G Robinson, in his final performance, gives a very poignant turn. AJ. Contains violence, swearing. DVD

Charlton Heston *Detective Thorn* • Leigh Taylor-Young *Shirl* • Chuck Connors *Tab Fielding* • Joseph Cotten *William Simonson* • Brock Peters *Hatcher* • Edward G Robinson *Sol Roth* ■ *Dir* Richard Fleischer • *Scr* Stanley R Greenberg, from the novel *Make Room! Make Room!* by Harry Harrison

Space Cowboys ★★★ PG

Space adventure
2000 · US/Aus · Colour · 125mins

Houston, we have another problem. But, unlike the factual *Apollo 13*, director/producer/star Clint Eastwood's self-deprecating and winningly indulgent cosmic adventure is a complete macho-fuelled fantasy set in the ultra-realistic world of Nasa operations today. With an irresistible premise – four geriatric astronauts finally get the chance to go into orbit 40 years after being sidelined by a monkey – this slice of gung-ho wish-fulfilment is an entertaining feel-good pleasure, but lacks any real thrills or suspense because the outcome is obvious from the start. AJ. Contains some swearing. DVD

Clint Eastwood *Frank D Corvin* • Tommy Lee Jones *Hawk Hawkins* • Donald Sutherland *Jerry O'Neill* • James Garner *Tank Sullivan* • James Cromwell *Bob Gerson* • Marcia Gay Harden *Sara Holland* • William Devane *Eugene Davis* • Loren Dean *Ethan Glance* • Courtney B Vance *Roger Hines* ■ *Dir* Clint Eastwood • *Scr* Ken Kaufman, Howard Klausner

Space Jam ★★★ U

Part-animated fantasy comedy
1997 · US · Colour · 83mins

American basketball star Michael Jordan makes a charismatic big screen acting debut alongside the entire Warner Bros cartoon catalogue. Aliens from an ailing intergalactic theme park want Bugs Bunny, Daffy Duck et al to be their new attraction. In a desperate attempt to keep their freedom, the animated superstars challenge their would-be captors to a basketball game and increase their odds of success by kidnapping Jordan. The humour cleverly mixes typical Looney Tunes gags with references to *Reservoir Dogs*, while Bill Murray provides some hilarious moments. SO DVD

Michael Jordan • Wayne Knight *Stan Podolak* • Danny DeVito *Swackhammer* • Theresa Randle *Juanita Jordan* • Eric Gordon *Marcus Jordan* • Penny Bae Bridges *Jasmine Jordan* • Bill Murray ■ *Dir* Joe Pytka • *Scr* Leo Benvenuti, Steve Rudnick, Timothy Harris, Herschel Weingrod

Space Marines ★★ 18

Science-fiction action
1996 · US · Colour · 89mins

For all its technology and futuristic settings, this is actually a throwback to the gritty war movies of the 1950s. Here a hard-bitten crew of interstellar GIs lines up against an extravagantly evil gang of space terrorists who have kidnapped an important diplomat. Billy Wirth and Edward Albert manage to keep straight faces throughout, and the special effects are actually pretty decent, but no amount of explosions and gunplay can compensate for the formulaic plotting. JF DVD

Billy Wirth *Zake Delano* • Cady Huffman *Dar Mullins* • John Pyper-Ferguson *Colonel Fraser* • Edward Albert *Captain Gray* • Meg Foster *Commodore Lasser* ■ *Dir* John Weidner • *Scr* Robert Moreland

Space Master X 7 ★★

Science-fiction horror
1958 · US · BW · 70mins

Fungus from a space probe mixes with human blood and turns deadly in this prime example of a 1950s copycat chiller. Told in routine, and extremely padded out, semi-documentary style, the presence of Three Stooges funnyman Moe Howard (playing a cab driver), suggests director Edward Bernds thought it was a comedy, too. Unfortunately, the other actors take it all very seriously. AJ

Bill Williams *John Hand* • Lyn Thomas *Lora Greeling* • Robert Ellis *Radigan* • Paul Frees *Charles Palmer* • Joan Nixon Barry *Miss Meyers* • Thomas Browne Henry *Professor West* • Fred Sherman *Morse* • Rhoda Williams *Miss Archer* ■ *Dir* Edward Bernds • *Scr* George Worthing Yates, Daniel Mainwaring

Space Raiders ★★ PG

Science-fiction adventure
1983 · US · Colour · 79mins

Writer/director Howard R Cohen seems to have concocted his tale of a boy who stows away on a ship belonging to a motley band of space mercenaries, merely to fit around special effects footage lifted from producer Roger Corman's own *Battle beyond the Stars*. Even the score by the celebrated James Horner is the same. Still, undemanding kids may find some enjoyment in its strictly limited thrills and cheap gags. RS

David Mendenhall *Peter Tracton* • Vince Edwards *Hawk* • George Dickerson *Arthur Tracton* • Thom Christopher *Flightplan* • Drew Snyder *Alderbarian* • Patsy Pease *Amanda* ■ *Dir/Scr* Howard R Cohen

Space Truckers ★★★ 12

Science-fiction adventure
1996 · US/Ire · Colour · 92mins

A better than expected cast has an intergalactic brush with killer robots, pirates and motorised body parts in this off-the-wall sci-fi romp from *Re-Animator* director Stuart Gordon. Dennis Hopper, Stephen Dorff and Debi Mazar are among those on the receiving end, while Charles Dance's bio-mechanical adversary even out-camps his pantomime *Last Action Hero* villain. A colourful, unpretentious slice of entertaining nonsense. JC

Dennis Hopper *John Canyon* • Stephen Dorff *Mike Pucci* • Debi Mazar *Cindy* • George Wendt *Mr Keller* • Barbara Crampton *Carol* • Charles Dance *Nabel/Macanudo* • Shane Rimmer *EJ Saggs* ■ *Dir* Stuart Gordon • *Scr* Ted Mann, from a story by Stuart Gordon, Ted Mann

Spaceballs ★★ 12

Science-fiction spoof
1987 · US · Colour · 92mins

Mel Brooks seems to think that just by appearing on screen, assembling assorted clowns (Rick Moranis and John Candy among them) and substituting noise for wit, hilarity will somehow ensue. In this limp spoof of *Star Wars* (where the obvious is never avoided), visual gags leap across the screen with manic abandon, but a handful of decent jokes and japes brighten the mundane proceedings. JM. Contains swearing. DVD

Mel Brooks *President Skroob/Yogurt* • John Candy *Barf the Mawg* • Rick Moranis *Lord Dark Helmet* • Bill Pullman *Lone Starr* • Daphne Zuniga *Princess Vespa* • Dick Van

S

Patten *King Roland* • George Wyner *Colonel Sandurz* • Michael Winslow *Radar technician* • Joan Rivers *Dot Matrix (voice only)* • Lorene Yarnell *Dot Matrix* • John Hurt *John Hurt* • Dom DeLuise *Pizza the Hutt* ■ *Dir* Mel Brooks • *Scr* Mel Brooks, Thomas Meehan, Ronny Graham

SpaceCamp ★★ PG

Adventure 1986 · US · Colour · 106mins

This space opera for youngsters brought Kate Capshaw down to earth with something of a bump from the heady heights of *Indiana Jones and the Temple of Doom*. Younger teenagers might well relish the idea of a group of aspiring astronauts who accidentally blast off into orbit, but they will be less forgiving about the cut-price special effects. DP

Lea Thompson *Kathryn* • Tate Donovan *Kevin* • Kelly Preston *Tish* • Larry B Scott *Rudy* • Leaf Phoenix [Joaquin Phoenix] *Max* • Kate Capshaw *Andie Bergstrom* • Tom Skerritt *Zach Bergstrom* • Barry Primus *Brennan* ■ *Dir* Harry Winer • *Scr* WW Wicket, Casey T Mitchell, from a story by Patrick Bailey, Larry B Williams

Spacehunter: Adventures in the Forbidden Zone ★★ 15

Science-fiction adventure
1983 · US · Colour · 86mins

In this messy jump on the science-fiction bandwagon, galactic adventurer Peter Strauss aims to rescue cosmic travellers held prisoner by an evil man-machine on the plague-ridden planet of Terra 11. Directed with a weary eye by Lamont Johnson, the feeble script gives Strauss's bratty sidekick Molly Ringwald nothing to do, but the sheer force of Michael Ironside's personality creates a hissable villain. AJ

Peter Strauss *Wolff* • Molly Ringwald *Niki* • Ernie Hudson *Washington* • Andrea Marcovicci *Chalmers* • Michael Ironside *Overdog McNabb* • Beeson Carroll *Grandma Patterson* ■ *Dir* Lamont Johnson • *Scr* David Preston, Edith Rey, Dan Goldberg, Len Blum, from a story by Stewart Harding, Jean LaFleur

The Spaceman and King Arthur ★★★ U

Adventure 1979 · US/UK · Colour · 89mins

Also known, with delightful Disney whimsy, as *Unidentified Flying Oddball*, this reworking of Mark Twain's *A Connecticut Yankee in King Arthur's Court* has a frantic charm and provides a chance to see the desperately amiable Jim Dale as a baddie. The tale involves Nasa technician Dennis Dugan who, along with his lookalike robot, ends up in aristocratic Camelot with an engagingly elderly King Arthur (Kenneth More) and John Le Mesurier as a hesitant Sir Gawain. TH

S

Dennis Dugan *Tom Trimble* • Jim Dale *Sir Mordred* • Ron Moody *Merlin* • Kenneth More *King Arthur* • John Le Mesurier *Sir Gawain* • Rodney Bewes *Clarence* • Sheila White *Alisande* • Robert Beatty *Senator Milburn* ■ *Dir* Russ Mayberry • *Scr* Don Tait, from the novel *A Connecticut Yankee in King Arthur's Court* by Mark Twain

The Spacemen of St Tropez ★★

Comedy 1978 · Fr · Colour · 96mins

The last entry in the comedy cop series to be completed by writer/director Jean Girault (who died while shooting *The Gendarme Wore Skirts*) borrows its premise from *Invasion of the Body Snatchers* in order to both exploit and satirise the vogue for all things interstellar in the wake of *Star Wars*. However, the action is utterly reliant on broad slapstick, as the bungling Louis De Funès assaults the cream of St Tropez in a bid to expose some aliens. The script is weak, but the cast is willing. DP. French and Italian dialogue dubbed into English.

Louis De Funès *Ludovic Cruchot* • Michel Galabru *Insp Gerber* • Maurice Risch *Beaupied* • Maria Mauban *Josepha* • Guy Crasso *Tricard* • Jean-Pierre Rambal *Taupin* ■ *Dir/Scr* Jean Girault

Spaceways ★ U

Science-fiction fantasy
1953 · UK · BW · 73mins

Why did anybody who read the radio play on which this is based think it was worth doing anything with it other than hurl it across the room? The plot has leads Howard Duff and Eva Bartok blasting off in pursuit of a satellite to prove Duff's innocence following an accusation of double murder. Terence Fisher's funereal pace kills this cheaply-made picture stone dead long before the denouement. DP DVD

Howard Duff *Stephen Mitchell* • Eva Bartok *Lisa Frank* • Alan Wheatley *Smith* • Philip Leaver *Dr Keppler* • Michael Medwin *Toby Andrews* ■ *Dir* Terence Fisher • *Scr* Paul Tabori, Richard Landau, from the radio play by Charles Eric Maine

La Spagnola ★★ 15

Period comedy drama
2001 · Aus · Colour · 86mins

Making his directorial debut, Australian actor Steve Jacobs merits praise for attempting such an ambitious enterprise as this florid melodrama, especially as it's played out almost entirely in Spanish and Italian. However, he errs in allowing Lola Marceli to give a spitfiring performance as the wronged wife whose desire to exact revenge on husband Simon Palomares's Aussie mistress (Helen Thomson) is a source of acute embarrassment to her gawky teenage daughter (Alice Ansara). Bravura stuff, but too brash to engross. DP. In English, Spanish and Italian with subtitles. DVD

Lola Marceli *Lola* • Alice Ansara *Lucia* • Lourdes Bardolomé *Manola* • Alex Dimitriades *Stefano* • Simon Palomares *Ricardo* • Silvio Ofria *Bruno* • Helen Thomson *Wendy* ■ *Dir* Steve Jacobs • *Scr* Anna Maria Monticelli [Anna Jemison]

Spanglish ★★★★ 12

Comedy drama 2004 · US · Colour · 125mins

Spanish and English-speaking cultures collide to poignant effect in this engaging film that's anchored by strong performances. Mexican single mother Paz Vega becomes housekeeper to a rich but troubled Los Angeles couple (played by Adam Sandler and Téa Leoni). At first unable to communicate in English, she's thrown into an alien world, whose emotional mechanics she finds hard to understand. But it's Sandler's turn as the unhappy husband that's the real surprise, as he is both effortlessly natural and quietly charming. SF. Contains swearing and sex scenes. DVD

Adam Sandler *John Clasky* • Téa Leoni *Deborah Clasky* • Paz Vega *Flor* • Cloris Leachman *Evelyn* • Shelbie Bruce *Cristina* • Sarah Steele *Bernice* • Ian Hyland *Georgie* ■ *Dir/Scr* James L Brooks

The Spaniard's Curse ★★ U

Murder mystery 1958 · UK · BW · 79mins

When an innocent man is sentenced to be hanged for murder, he invokes an old Spanish curse on the judge, prosecuting counsel and jury. After deaths begin to take place, suspicion falls on the condemned man but his sudden death only enhances the mystery. Tony Wright has the most colourful part as the judge's wayward son, a crime reporter, but Michael Hordern as the judge gives the sharpest performance. AE

Tony Wright *Charlie Manton* • Lee Patterson *Mark Brett* • Michael Hordern *Judge Manton* • Ralph Truman *Sir Robert Wyvern* • Henry Oscar *Mr Fredericks* • Susan Beaumont *Margaret Manton* ■ *Dir* Ralph Kemplen • *Scr* Kenneth Hyde, from the novel *The Assize of the Dying* by Edith Pargiter

The Spanish Gardener ★★★ U

Drama 1956 · UK · Colour · 91mins

Dirk Bogarde posted notice that he was much more than Rank's "Mr Charm" in this brooding drama. Although it was supposed to be buried safely beneath the surface, the film's homosexual subtext is clearly detectable as diplomat Michael Hordern comes to resent his son's burgeoning relationship with gardener Bogarde. Thanks to Christopher Challis's sultry cinematography, director Philip Leacock is able to convey the rising emotional temperature of the action, while also coaxing a creditable performance from young Jon Whiteley. DP

Dirk Bogarde *Jose* • Jon Whiteley *Nicholas Brande* • Michael Hordern *Harrington Brande* • Cyril Cusack *Garcia* • Maureen Swanson *Maria* • Lyndon Brook *Robert Burton* • Josephine Griffin *Carol Burton* • Bernard Lee *Leighton Bailey* ■ *Dir* Philip Leacock • *Scr* Lesley Storm, John Bryan, from the novel by AJ Cronin

The Spanish Main ★★ U

Swashbuckling adventure
1945 · US · Colour · 95mins

This hopelessly inadequate swashbuckler is partially redeemed by its ravishing 1940s Technicolor, used to best effect when photographing red-headed Maureen O'Hara, who here proves more than a match for leading man Paul Henreid. Walter Slezak makes a splendidly corrupt villain, but director Frank Borzage hasn't a clue how to buckle a swash. TS

Maureen O'Hara *Francisca* • Paul Henreid *Laurent Van Horn, "The Barracuda"* • Walter Slezak *Don Alvarado* • Binnie Barnes *Anne Bonny* • John Emery *Maria Da Bilar* • Barton MacLane *Captain Benjamin Black* • JM Kerrigan *Pillory* ■ *Dir* Frank Borzage • *Scr* George Worthing Yates, Herman J Mankiewicz, from a story by Aeneas MacKenzie

The Spanish Prisoner ★★★★ PG

Mystery thriller 1997 · US · Colour · 105mins

David Mamet returns to the themes of his first film (*House of Games*) in this adroit fable about the simple-mindedness of complex-minded executives. Campbell Scott is the corporation inventor, creator of "the Process", who's concerned about his employer's integrity. Cue a smoothly plausible Steve Martin and an elaborate and totally convincing con trick played on us as well as the hapless Scott. This is a tale told with all the entertaining sleight of hand of a three-card trick: now you see it, now you don't. TH. Contains swearing. DVD

Campbell Scott *Joe Ross* • Steve Martin *Jimmy Dell* • Rebecca Pidgeon *Susan Ricci* • Ben Gazzara *Joe Klein* • Ricky Jay *George Lang* • Felicity Huffman *Pat McCune* ■ *Dir/Scr* David Mamet

Spanking the Monkey ★★★★ 18

Drama 1994 · US · Colour · 95mins

This low-budget cult hit caused a big stir owing to its story of incest between mother and son. It was not so much the subject matter but the movie's sanguine, almost blasé attitude towards its theme that offended many, yet this view profoundly misunderstood an original and daring film. A largely unknown cast brings great assurance and subtlety to an often funny, sometimes moving and always intriguing look at the essential complexities between parent and child. SH. Contains swearing, sex scenes, drug abuse, nudity.

Jeremy Davies *Raymond Aibelli* • Alberta Watson *Susan Aibelli* • Benjamin Hendrickson *Tom Aibelli* • Carla Gallo *Toni Peck* • Matthew Puckett *Nicky* • Zak Orth *Curtis* • Josh Weinstein *Joel* ■ *Dir/Scr* David O Russell

Spare a Copper ★★ U

Second World War comedy
1940 · UK · BW · 78mins

Wartime audiences were grateful for any relief from the conflict and this did very tidy business at the box office, thanks largely to the jokes at the expense of the special constabulary. But the story, in which George Formby confounds a gang of Nazi saboteurs, is too far-fetched, and there were mutterings in high places that the depiction of the enemy as such easily defeated dolts could lull audiences into a false sense of security. DP

George Formby *George Carter* • Dorothy Hyson *Jane Grey* • Bernard Lee *Jake* • John Warwick *Shaw* • Warburton Gamble *Sir Robert Dyer* • John Turnbull *Inspector Richards* • George Merritt *Edward Brewster* ■ *Dir* John Paddy Carstairs • *Scr* Roger Macdougall, Basil Dearden, Austin Melford

Spare Parts ★★★ 15

Drama 2003 · Slovenia · Colour · 86mins

The gross iniquity of people-trafficking should never be diminished, but writer/director Damjan Kozole's bleak drama suggests that otherwise decent individuals can sometimes enter into this desperate trade, from motives other than naked greed. Former Slovenian speedway champion Peter Musevski's fall from grace, for example, followed the death of his wife from cancer. And his young apprentice Aljosa Kovacic demonstrates a compassion that stands in stark contrast to the exploitation of the pitiless thugs who force migrant Aleksandra Balmazovic into prostituting herself. Uncomfortable, but provocative. DP. In Slovenian with English subtitles. Contains swearing.

Peter Musevski *Ludvik* • Aljosa Kovacic *Rudi* • Primoz Petkovsek *Rajc* • Valter Dragan *Drago* • Aleksandra Balmazovic *Angela* • Vladimir Vlaskalic *Geri* • Verica Nedeska *Ilinka* ■ *Dir/Scr* Damjan Kozole

Spare the Rod ★★★

Drama 1961 · UK · BW · 92mins

Although he didn't make many films, Max Bygraves is a surprisingly sympathetic screen presence in this docudramatic story about a benevolent teacher in a tough inner-city school. Of course, he's not in the same league as those old pros Donald Pleasence and Geoffrey Keen, who give completely credible performances as the wishy-washy headmaster and the staffroom tyrant respectively. A young Richard O'Sullivan is his trademark perky self as a cheeky pupil. DP

Max Bygraves *John Saunders* • Donald Pleasence *Mr Jenkins* • Geoffrey Keen *Arthur Gregory* • Betty McDowall *Ann Collins* • Peter Reynolds *Alec Murray* • Jean Anderson *Mrs Pond* • Eleanor Summerfield *Mrs Harkness* • Richard O'Sullivan *Fred Harkness* ■ *Dir* Leslie Norman • *Scr* John Cresswell, from the novel by Michael Croft

Sparrow ★ 12

Period drama 1993 · It/Ger · Colour · 102mins

Franco Zeffirelli's most vilified film is set in the mid-1850s and tells the story of a young girl who enters a convent. A cholera outbreak results in her returning to her father's villa, where she falls in love with handsome young Johnathon Schaech. The plague over, she returns to the convent to battle with her religious calling and her love for Schaech. Zeffirelli lets rip with full-blown theatricals, but the story and the inexperienced leads are not enough to carry the film. BB

Angela Bettis *Maria* • Johnathon Schaech *Nino* • Sinead Cusack *Matilde* • John Castle *Giuseppe* • Vanessa Redgrave *Sister Agata* • Sara-Jane Alexander *Annetta* • Frank Finlay *Father Nunzio* ■ *Dir* Franco Zeffirelli • *Scr* Franco Zeffirelli, Allan Baker, from the novel *A Sparrow's Tale* by Giovanni Verga

Sparrows ★★★★

Silent melodrama 1926 · US · BW · 81mins

A near classic of the silent era featuring 1920s superstar Mary Pickford in her last juvenile role. She plays Molly, the leader of a rag-tag bunch of orphans treated as slaves by evil Mr Grimes on his farm in the Deep South swamplands. When a gang in league with Grimes kidnaps the daughter of a rich man and hides her on his farm, Molly leads her flock out through alligator-infested waters as the police close in. Although the film is poorly paced, Pickford is as touchingly poignant as ever in an American-style Grimm fairy tale. AJ

Mary Pickford *Mama Mollie* • Gustav von Seyffertitz *Grimes* • Roy Stewart *Richard Wayne* • Mary Louise Miller *Doris Wayne* ■ *Dir* William Beaudine • *Scr* C Gardner Sullivan, George Marion Jr (titles), from a story by Winifred Dunn

Sparrows Can't Sing ★ PG

Comedy drama 1962 · UK · BW · 88mins

You can't capture the sights and sounds of East End life simply by packing the cast with cockneys and touting a camera round the streets of Stepney. Colourful phrases in Bow Bells accents might have convinced theatregoers, but on screen this supposed slice of everyday realism has sham written all over it. James Booth is eminently resistible as the sailor searching for wife Barbara Windsor and her bus-driving fancy man, George Sewell. Missing both social statement and fond characterisation, director Joan Littlewood has succeeded only in being patronising. DP

James Booth *Charlie Gooding* • Barbara Windsor *Maggie Gooding* • Roy Kinnear *Fred Gooding* • Avis Bunnage *Bridgie Gooding* • Brian Murphy *Jack* • George Sewell *Bert* ■ *Dir* Joan Littlewood • *Scr* Stephen Lewis, Joan Littlewood, from the play by Stephen Lewis • *Music/lyrics* Lionel Bart

Spartacus ★★★★★ PG

Historical epic 1960 · US · Colour · 186mins

The restored version of this Roman epic about the famous slave revolt has additional blood, more lingering death agonies of Kirk Douglas on the cross and a risible bath scene with Laurence Olivier and Tony Curtis, which was originally cut because of its alleged homosexual innuendo. Despite the film's length and overemphasis in the latter half on wordy speeches from Douglas, the action leading up to the revolt of the gladiators is brilliantly re-created, with Peter Ustinov, Charles Laughton and Olivier addictively greedy scene-stealers. The early sequences, set in the Libyan desert, were directed by Anthony Mann, who was fired by Douglas and replaced by Stanley Kubrick. AT DVD

Kirk Douglas *Spartacus* • Laurence Olivier *Marcus Crassus* • Tony Curtis *Antoninus* • Jean Simmons *Varinia* • Charles Laughton *Gracchus* • Peter Ustinov *Batiatus* • John Gavin *Julius Caesar* • Nina Foch *Helena Glabrus* ■ *Dir* Stanley Kubrick • *Scr* Dalton Trumbo, from the novel by Howard Fast • *Cinematographer* Russell Metty • *Music* Alex North • *Costume Designer* Bill Thomas, Valles

Spartacus and the Ten Gladiators ★★ U

Adventure 1964 · It/Fr/Sp · Colour · 98mins

An Italian co-produced rehash of the Kirk Douglas blockbuster, with the epic-sounding John Heston as the revolting Spartacus, and Dan Vadis as a gladiator hired by the Senate to destroy the slave army. The dubbing is appalling, but some money was obviously spent on several hundred extras and whatever chariots were left over from *Ben-Hur*. AT. Italian dialogue dubbed into English.

Helga Liné *Daria* • John Heston *Spartacus* • Dan Vadis *Roccia* • Ursula Davis *Lydia* • Gianni Rizzo *Varro* ■ *Dir* Nick Nostro • *Scr* Nick Nostro, Simon Sterling

Spartan ★★★ 15

Political thriller
2004 · US/Ger · Colour · 102mins

David Mamet's sharp political thriller is a typically intelligent, yet irritatingly self-conscious film. The set-up is intriguingly simple: the US president's daughter (Kristen Bell) goes missing, and the Secret Service puts relentless hard man Val Kilmer on the case. Though less stylised than usual, the rhythms and cadences in Mamet's dialogue always take some getting used to. These verbal flourishes occasionally come across as po-faced, deflating the film's tension. Visually, however, this is Mamet's best film, with a clean, economical style that fits perfectly with Kilmer's man-on-a-mission intensity. GM. Contains swearing and violence. DVD

Val Kilmer *Robert Scott* • Derek Luke *Curtis* • William H Macy *Stoddard* • Ed O'Neill *Burch* • Kristen Bell *Laura Newton* • Saïd Taghmaoui *Tariq Asani* • Linda Kimbrough *Donny* • Tia Texada *Jackie Black* ■ *Dir/Scr* David Mamet

The Spartan Gladiators ★★ U

Period adventure 1964 · It · Colour · 88mins

A former child actor, Alberto De Martino was as versatile as most Italian B directors. But his eye for detail made him one of the more accomplished, especially where peplum pictures were concerned. Tony Russel is the leader of a motley, rather than magnificent seven, seeking to escape from the tyrannical Spartan ruler and return a precious golden statue to its temple in Athens. The action, whether in the arena or on the battlefield, is staged with as much spectacle as the budget will allow. DP. Italian dialogue dubbed into English.

Tony Russel *Keros* • Helga Liné *Helea* • Massimo Serato *Baxo* • Nando Gazzolo *Milo* • Livio Lorenzon *Nemete* ■ *Dir* Alberto De Martino • *Scr* Alessandro Continenza, Vincenzo Flamini, Giovanni Simonelli, Alberto De Martino, from a story by Alessandro Continenza, Vincenzo Flamini, Giovanni Simonelli, Alberto De Martino

Spawn ★★ 12

Supernatural horror adventure
1997 · US · Colour · 92mins

This live-action comic-book spin-off promised to duplicate the grim and extremely violent images that were the bestselling comic's hallmarks, but ended up being distributed in a toned-down "12" certificate version; a "15" certificate "Director's Cut " followed later. Michael Jai White plays Al Simmons, a special forces assassin betrayed by boss Martin Sheen and left to fry in a burning chemical factory. Passing beyond death, he is revived as Spawn, who becomes caught up in a plot to trigger the apocalypse. Dark in tone and crammed with computer-generated effects, it found a cult popularity and spawned a follow-up animated series. JF DVD

Michael Jai White *Al Simmons/Spawn* • Martin Sheen *Jason Wynn* • John Leguizamo *Clown* • Theresa Randle *Wanda* • Nicol Williamson *Cogliostro* • Melinda Clarke *Jessica Priest* • DB Sweeney *Terry Fitzgerald* ■ *Dir* Mark AZ Dippe • *Scr* Alan McElroy, from a story by Mark AZ Dippé, Alan McElroy, from the comic book by Todd McFarlane

Spawn of the North ★★★

Period adventure drama
1938 · US · BW · 105mins

Henry Fonda stars as the skipper of an American fishing crew in Alaska, circa 1890, whose best buddy (George Raft) deserts him for some villainous Russian poachers, led by Akim Tamiroff. It's an entertaining action adventure, with some high drama, a little romance, satisfying heroics, and a convincing John Barrymore as a heavy-drinking newspaper reporter. A big hit in its day, superbly directed and with the authentic exteriors filmed on location in Alaska. RK

George Raft *Tyler Dawson* • Henry Fonda *Jim Kimmerlee* • Dorothy Lamour *Nicky Duval* • Akim Tamiroff *Red Skain* • John Barrymore *Windy Turlon* • Louise Platt *Dian Turlon* • Lynne Overman *Jackson* • Fuzzy Knight *Lefty Jones* ■ *Dir* Henry Hathaway • *Scr* Jules Furthman, Talbot Jennings, from the novel by Florence Barrett Willoughby

Spawn of the Slithis ★

Science-fiction horror
1978 · US · Colour · 86mins

The title alone cannot convey how silly this is. A mutated form of sea life is squelching around the California coastline, annoyed that it has evolved from a radiation spillage from a local power plant and prepared to ooze over everything in its path. Stephen Traxler, who wrote, produced and directed this daft tale, obviously saw far too many schlock movies while growing up. JB

Alan Blanchard • Judy Motulsky • Dennis Lee Falt • Win Condict • Mello Alexandria • Hy Pyke ■ *Dir/Scr* Stephen Traxler

Speak Easily ★★★★ U

Comedy 1932 · US · BW · 81mins

When Buster Keaton gave up independent production and signed with MGM in 1928 it was a move he later considered the worst of his career. But of the eight sound films he made for the studio, this was his favourite. It features Keaton as a sheltered university professor who decides to see life and becomes involved with a run-down theatrical troupe. Keaton's co-star Jimmy Durante has some fine moments, and though Keaton disliked working with the brash comic, the two became good friends. The film is a hit-and-miss affair but Keaton is superb as the innocent in a world of showbiz sharpies. TV

Buster Keaton *Prof Post* • Jimmy Durante *James* • Ruth Selwyn *Pansy Peets* • Thelma Todd *Eleanor Espere* • Hedda Hopper *Mrs Peets* • William Pawley *Griffo* • Sidney Toler *Stage director* • Lawrence Grant *Dr Bolton* ■ *Dir* Edward Sedgwick • *Scr* Ralph Spence, Laurence E Johnson, from the novel by Clarence Budington Kelland

Speaking Parts ★★ 18

Drama 1989 · Can · Colour · 91mins

Gabrielle Rose watches videos of her dead brother while pursuing a movie project about his life. She gets involved with aspiring actor Michael McManus who, coincidentally, resembles her sibling, and is himself a lust object for lovelorn Arsinée Khanjian. Writer/director Atom Egoyan successfully connects the characters in his strange story, but in focusing on intellectual dissection the director sacrifices the emotional pay-off essential in this story of a three-way relationship. JM. Contains nudity.

Michael McManus (2) *Lance* • Arsinée Khanjian *Lisa* • Gabrielle Rose *Clara* • Tony Nardi *Eddy* • David Hemblen *Producer* • Patricia Collins *Housekeeper* ■ *Dir/Scr* Atom Egoyan

Special Agent ★★

Crime drama 1935 · US · BW · 77mins

"Miss Davis is too valuable a performer to be doing stories such as this one," said *Variety*, slamming this crime drama which Warners "encouraged" her to do. Bette Davis plays the secretary to a mobster, Ricardo Cortez, whose operation is being investigated by plucky newspaper man George Brent. Davis takes a shine to Brent and gives him secrets. AT

Bette Davis *Julie Carston* • George Brent *Bill Bradford* • Ricardo Cortez *Nick Carston* • Joseph Sawyer [Joe Sawyer] *Rich* • Joseph Crehan *Chief of Police* • Henry O'Neill *District Attorney* • Irving Pichel *US District Attorney* ■ *Dir* William Keighley • *Scr* Laird Doyle, Abem Finkel, from an idea by Martin Mooney

A Special Day ★★

Period drama
1977 · It/Can · Colour · 105mins

Marcello Mastroianni earned an Oscar nomination for performing so subtly against type in this contrived romance dressed up as a sweeping statement about the human condition and Italy's Fascist past. It's beautifully set up, with Mastroianni 's suicidal gay radio announcer and Sophia Loren's harassed mother of six meeting in a Roman tenement on the day in 1938 that Mussolini first played host to Hitler. But, for all the evident chemistry between the leads, the symbolism is heavy-handed and the dialogue drips with portentous pronouncements. DP

Sophia Loren *Antonietta* • Marcello Mastroianni *Gabriele* • John Vernon *Emanuele* • Françoise Berd *Concierge* ■ *Dir* Ettore Scola • *Scr* Ettore Scola, Ruggero Maccari, Maurizio Costanzo, from a story by Ettore Scola

Special Delivery ★★ U

Political satirical comedy
1955 · US/W Ger · BW · 86mins

Even when lumbered with a banal script and mediocre performances from everyone but Joseph Cotten, director John Brahm can't help but conjure atmosphere in this story of an American diplomat being assigned behind the Iron Curtain, where he has to cope with an abandoned baby. TH

Joseph Cotten *Jonathan Adams* • Eva Bartok *Sonia* • René Deltgen *Kovak* • Bruni Loebel *Lila* • Niall MacGinnis *Sidney* • Lexford Richards *Wayne* ■ *Dir* John Brahm • *Scr* Philip Reisman Jr, Dwight Taylor, from an idea by Geva Radvanyi

S

Special Delivery ★★★ 15

Crime comedy 1976 · US · Colour · 94mins

Surprisingly, this Bo Svenson vehicle is a neat little caper movie, with Svenson doing a respectable job as a bank robber who stashes his loot in the mail while fleeing the police. But the real star of the movie is Cybill Shepherd, excellent as the woman who witnesses Svenson at the mailbox. The strength of the movie comes from the many interesting interactions the central characters have with other parties, all realistically done. KB

Bo Svenson *Jack Murdock* • Cybill Shepherd *Mary Jane* • Tom Atkins *Zabelski* • Sorrell Booke *Bank Manager Hubert Zane* • Gerrit Graham *Swivot* • Michael C Gwynne *Carl Graff* • Jeff Goldblum *Snake* ■ *Dir* Paul Wendkos • *Scr* Don Gazzaniga, Gil Ralston

The Specialist ★★★ 18

Thriller 1994 · US · Colour · 105mins

James Woods has a knack for spotting mediocre movies with roles that give him the chance to shine when his co-stars are floundering. This is a case in point, as he strides off with Luis Llosa's bomb thriller without even getting his hair mussed. Sylvester Stallone stars as an explosive expert and former colleague of Woods, who is hired by the mysterious Sharon Stone to avenge the death of her parents. The leads generate some sparks, but the film belongs to the supporting cast. DP. Contains swearing, violence, sex scenes and nudity. DVD

Sylvester Stallone *Ray Quick* • Sharon Stone *May Munro* • James Woods *Ned Trent* • Rod Steiger *Joel Leon* • Eric Roberts *Tomas Leon* • Mario Ernesto Sanchez *Charlie* • Sergio Dore Jr *Strongarm* ■ *Dir* Luis Llosa • *Scr* Alexandra Seros, from the novels by John Shirley

The Specials ★ 18

Action fantasy spoof 2000 · US · Colour · 78mins

An abysmal copy of superhero spoof *Mystery Men*, featuring a day in the life of a team of downbeat crime-fighters. The joke is that these heroes, including Rob Lowe's Weevil and Jamie Kennedy's Amok, are less than special, meaning there's absolutely no reason to want to spend time with them. The performances are weak, the profane dialogue is grating, the suburban locations are dreary and there aren't even any visual effects until the final minutes. JC DVD

Rob Lowe *The Weevil* • Jamie Kennedy *Amok* • Thomas Haden Church *The Strobe* • Paget Brewster *Ms Indestructible* • Kelly Coffield *Power Chick* • Judy Greer *Deadly Girl* • James Gunn (2) *Minute Man* ■ *Dir* Craig Mazin • *Scr* James Gunn

Species ★★★ 18

Science-fiction horror 1995 · US · Colour · 103mins

Natasha Henstridge plays the dangerous spawn of combined alien and human DNA in director Roger Donaldson's sexy sci-fi shocker. Ben Kingsley, Michael Madsen and Alfred Molina are among the inept government scientists speaking daft dialogue as they attempt to track down the genetic engineering experiment gone awry. Nifty designs by surrealist HR Giger (who gave the extraterrestrial in *Alien* its incredible look) and some engaging tongue-in-cheek thrills go part way to disguising the fact that this is essentially clichéd B-movie stuff. AJ. Contains violence, swearing, sex scenes and nudity. DVD

Ben Kingsley *Fitch* • Michael Madsen *Press* • Alfred Molina *Arden* • Forest Whitaker *Dan* • Marg Helgenberger *Laura* • Natasha Henstridge *Sil* ■ *Dir* Roger Donaldson • *Scr* Dennis Feldman

Species II ★★★ 18

Science-fiction horror 1998 · US · Colour · 89mins

Head explosions, torso-bursting and computer-generated aliens in heat: it's all here in Peter Medak's science-fiction howler which continues the half-human/half-alien DNA experiment as a sex rampage saga. Far gorier and camper than the original film, this lascivious popcorn treat is a spectacularly lunatic shocker revelling in soft-core sleaze and grisly death. A second, straight-to-video sequel followed in 2004. AJ. Contains sex scenes, swearing, violence. DVD

Michael Madsen *Press Lennox* • Natasha Henstridge *Eve* • Marg Helgenberger *Doctor Laura Baker* • Mykelti Williamson *Dennis Gamble* • George Dzundza *Colonel Carter Burgess Jr* • Myriam Cyr *Anne Sampas* • Justin Lazard *Patrick Ross* ■ *Dir* Peter Medak • *Scr* Chris Brancato, from characters created by Dennis Feldman

Specter of the Rose ★★★

Comedy drama 1946 · US · BW · 90mins

An unusual and ambitious undertaking by Ben Hecht – one of the sharpest writers in Hollywood – this film purports to be based in part on the ballet *Spectre de la Rose*. One suspects, however, that Nijinsky couldn't have been far from Hecht's mind in this tale of a progressively deranged dancer (Ivan Kirov) driven to attempt murder and suicide by the eponymous ballet. Admittedly "arty", the film is also camp, inventive and eccentric. RK

Judith Anderson *Madame La Sylph* • Michael Chekhov *Max "Poli" Polikoff* • Ivan Kirov *Andre Sanine* • Lionel Stander *Lionel Gans* • Ben Hecht *Waiter* ■ *Dir* Ben Hecht • *Scr* Ben Hecht, from his short story

The Spectre ★★

Horror 1963 · It · Colour · 95mins

Inferior sequel to *The Horrible Dr Hichcock* in which the doctor, apparently murdered by his wife, returns as a ghost. Although the story is utterly conventional, with none of the outrageous elements of its predecessor, the film is liked by fans of stylish director Riccardo Freda and vampish horror star Barbara Steele. DM. Italian dialogue dubbed into English.

Barbara Steele *Margaret* • Peter Baldwin *Dr Charles Livingstone* • Leonard Elliott *Dr Hichcock* • Harriet White [Harriet Medin] *Catherine* • Raoul H Newman [Umberto Raho] *Canon* ■ *Dir* Robert Hampton [Riccardo Freda] • *Scr* Robert Hampton [Riccardo Freda], Robert Davidson, from a story by Robert Davidson

Speechless ★★★ 12

Romantic comedy 1994 · US · Colour · 94mins

Bewilderingly, this starry comedy bypassed cinemas and went straight to video in this country. It's a shame, because it's a smart and sassy affair from director Ron Underwood. Michael Keaton and Geena Davis spark off each other nicely, playing a pair of rival political speech writers who fall in and out of love with each other while on the campaign trail. There are excellent supporting turns from Bonnie Bedelia and Christopher Reeve, plus has some gentle fun at the expense of the American political system. JF. Contains swearing. DVD

Michael Keaton *Kevin Vallick* • Geena Davis *Julia Mann* • Christopher Reeve *Bob Freed* • Bonnie Bedelia *Annette* • Ernie Hudson *Ventura* • Charles Martin Smith *Kratz* ■ *Dir* Ron Underwood • *Scr* Robert King

Speed ★★

Sports drama 1936 · US · BW · 65mins

This minor B-movie about motor racing is notable only for the presence of James Stewart. He plays a test-car driver who, when not romancing the boss's daughter (Wendy Barrie), finds time to develop a high-speed carburettor to use in the Indianapolis 500. The film's depiction of an ultra-modern auto-plant in 1936 makes interesting viewing, but there is too much back projection. TV

James Stewart *Terry Martin* • Wendy Barrie *Jane Mitchell* • Ted Healy *Gadget* • Una Merkel *Josephine Sanderson* • Weldon Heyburn *Frank Lawson* • Patricia Wilder *Fanny Lane* • Ralph Morgan *Mr Dean* • Robert Livingston *George Saunders* ■ *Dir* Edwin L Marin • *Scr* Michael Fessier, from a story by Milton Krims, Larry Bachman

Speed ★★★★★ 15

Action thriller 1994 · US · Colour · 111mins

This pure adrenalin-pumping entertainment of the highest order has action man Keanu Reeves and Sandra Bullock trapped on a crowded LA bus that crazed extortionist Dennis Hopper has primed to explode if its speed falls below 50mph. Slipping smoothly into top gear from the nail-biting scene-setting opening, director Jan De Bont's "*Die Hard* on the Buses" moves into the fast lane with a nonstop barrage of nerve-jangling thrills and death-defying stunts. Outrageous, over-the-top and as exciting as can be. AJ. Contains swearing and violence. DVD

Keanu Reeves *Jack Traven* • Dennis Hopper *Howard Payne* • Sandra Bullock *Annie* • Joe Morton *Captain McMahon* • Jeff Daniels *Harry* • Alan Ruck *Stephens* • Glenn Plummer *Jaguar owner* • Richard Lineback *Norwood* ■ *Dir* Jan De Bont • *Scr* Graham Yost

Speed 2: Cruise Control ★★ PG

Action thriller 1997 · US · Colour · 119mins

Director Jan De Bont's listlessly routine sequel to his own powerhouse original is a massive disappointment. Sandra Bullock reprises her role as Annie Porter who, with cop boyfriend Jason Patric, boards a luxury cruise liner for a holiday. Before you can say "Where's Keanu Reeves gone?", disgruntled computer genius Willem Dafoe puts his extortion plan into operation and turns their voyage into a titanic nightmare. AJ. Contains swearing and some violence. DVD

Sandra Bullock *Annie* • Jason Patric *Alex* • Willem Dafoe *Geiger* • Temuera Morrison *Juliano* • Brian McCardie *Merced* • Christine Firkins *Drew* • Michael G Hagerty *Harvey* ■ *Dir* Jan De Bont • *Scr* Randall McCormick, Jeff Nathanson, from a story by Jan DeBont, Randall McCormick, from characters created by Graham Yost

Speedway ★ U

Musical drama 1968 · US · Colour · 90mins

A bland, cheap and hopelessly unhip musical made when both the recording and screen careers of Elvis Presley were at rock bottom. Recently wed to Priscilla Beaulieu, the rock 'n' roll king seems to be going through the motions as a stock car driver pursued by income tax investigator Nancy Sinatra. DM DVD

Elvis Presley *Steve Grayson* • Nancy Sinatra *Susan Jacks* • Bill Bixby *Kenny Donford* • Gale Gordon *RW Hepworth* • William Schallert *Abel Esterlake* • Victoria Meyerink *Ellie Esterlake* • Ross Hagen *Paul Dado* ■ *Dir* Norman Taurog • *Scr* Phillip Shuken

Speedy ★★★ U

Silent comedy 1928 · US · BW · 86mins

Harold Lloyd's silent swansong is something of a disappointment considering the glorious high-risk clowning that had gone before. Still nurturing go-getting ambitions, his baseball-crazy soda jerk takes on some ruthless traffic tycoons after they try to drive the last horse-drawn trolley bus off the road. Naturally, love is at the heart of Harold's heroism, although the romantic outing to Coney Island lacks both the period charm of the New York street scenes and the comic zest of the concluding chase. DP

Harold Lloyd *Harold "Speedy" Swift* • Ann Christy *Jane Dillon* • Bert Woodruff *Pop Dillon* • Brooks Benedict *Steven Carter* • George Herman "Babe" Ruth [Babe Ruth] ■ *Dir* Ted Wilde • *Scr* John Grey, Lex Neal, Howard Emmett Rogers, Jay Howe

The Spellbinder ★★

Crime drama 1939 · US · BW · 69mins

If you're not allergic to Lee Tracy's fast, attention-grabbing performances, there's an ingenious story told in this courtroom melodrama. Tracy is well cast as a defence lawyer whose tricks get murderers off. He doesn't like it one bit, however, when his precious daughter, played by Barbara Read, elopes with a killer, Patric Knowles, whom she believes is innocent because papa's clever tactics persuaded the jury to acquit him. AE

Lee Tracy *Jed Marlow* • Barbara Read *Janet Marlow* • Patric Knowles *Tom Dixon* • Allan Lane *Steve Kendall* • Linda Hayes *Miss Simpson* • Morgan Conway *Carrington* • Robert Emmett Keane *Judge Butler* ■ *Dir* Jack Hively • *Scr* Thomas Lennon, Joseph A Fields, from a story by Joseph Anthony

Spellbinder ★ 18

Thriller 1988 · US · Colour · 94mins

American TV actor Timothy Daly (brother of *Cagney and Lacey's* Tyne) stars in this silly and completely unthrilling chiller about a lawyer who becomes obsessed with a woman (Kelly Preston) on the run from an evil coven. A disaster. JB

Timothy Daly *Jeff Mills* • Kelly Preston *Miranda Reed* • Rick Rossovich *Derek Clayton* • Audra Lindley *Mrs White* • Anthony Crivello *Aldys* • Diana Bellamy *Grace Woods* • Cary-Hiroyuki Tagawa *Lieutenant Lee* ■ *Dir* Janet Greek • *Scr* Tracey Torme

Spellbound ★★★ PG

Psychological thriller 1945 · US · BW · 110mins

In his eagerness to make the first serious film about psychoanalysis, Alfred Hitchcock so diluted the fantastical elements in Francis Beeding's novel *The House of Dr Edwardes*, all that remained was a melodramatic plot and an awful lot of psychobabble. Not even dream sequences designed by Salvador Dali could enliven the turgid script, made all the less palatable by the robotic performance of Gregory Peck as the amnesiac trying to unravel his troubled past with the help of sympathetic shrink, Ingrid Bergman. Hitch himself was disappointed with the picture, but there are enough masterly touches to keep your attention. DP DVD

Ingrid Bergman *Dr Constance Peterson* • Gregory Peck *John Ballantine/Dr Anthony Edwardes* • Michael Chekhov *Dr Alex Brulov* • Leo G Carroll *Dr Murchison* • Rhonda Fleming *Mary Carmichael* • John Emery *Dr Fleurot* ■ *Dir* Alfred Hitchcock • *Scr* Ben Hecht, Angus MacPhail, from the novel *The House of Dr Edwardes* by Francis Beeding

Spellbound ★★★★ U

Documentary 2002 · US · Colour · 92mins

This quirky documentary follows eight teenagers as they compete in the 1999 American National Spelling Bee. While the competition is exciting enough, it's the kids' differing backgrounds that give this film its real heart. From the daughter of Mexican immigrants whose father speaks no English to a gawky farmboy whose parents struggle to understand their talented offspring, this is really a story of the trials and occasional triumphs of what it's like to be young and "different" in America. Although first-time documentary director Jeff Blitz makes the odd forgivable lapse – trying to cover too many children and structuring the film in an unimaginatively linear way – this is still a fascinating account of a little-known slice of Americana. AS DVD

Dir Jeff Blitz

Spencer's Mountain ★★★

Comedy drama 1963 · US · Colour · 119mins

Although it was a commercial success, Henry Fonda loathed this cosy melodrama. With Fonda playing the church-hating head of a Wyoming hill family, it's not immediately apparent that Earl Hamner Jr's novel also provided the inspiration for that enduringly popular TV show, *The Waltons*. The connection becomes clearer as James MacArthur's character Clayboy struggles to choose between his education and his inheritance. As mom and grandpa, Maureen O'Hara and Donald Crisp provide expert support. DP

Henry Fonda *Clay Spencer* • Maureen O'Hara *Olivia* • James MacArthur *Clayboy Spencer* • Donald Crisp *Grandpa Spencer* • Wally Cox *Preacher Goodson* • Mimsy Farmer *Claris Coleman* • Virginia Gregg *Miss Parker* ■ *Dir* Delmer Daves • *Scr* Delmer Daves, from the novel by Earl Hamner Jr

Spendthrift ★★★

Comedy 1936 · US · BW · 77mins

Millionaire playboy Henry Fonda is temporarily out of cash but can't bring himself to break the news to mercenary spouse Mary Brian. Eventually he gets to see how the other half lives when he takes a job as a sports announcer and falls for Pat Paterson. Action director Raoul Walsh has a light enough touch, and the streak of social conscience – very necessary at the time – is eased in almost painlessly. What's so delightfully manipulative about the movie is the way it shows us how the rich live, spiking those lush vistas with Depression era home truths. TH

Henry Fonda *Townsend Middleton* • Pat Paterson *Valerie "Boots" O'Connell* • Mary Brian *Sally Barnaby* • George Barbier *Uncle Morton Middleton* • Edward Brophy *Bill* • Richard Carle *Popsy* • JM Kerrigan *Pop O'Connell* • Spencer Charters *Col Barnaby* ■ *Dir* Raoul Walsh • *Scr* Raoul Walsh, Bert Hanlon, from the novella by Eric Hatch

Spetters ★★★★ 18

Drama 1980 · Neth · Colour · 102mins

Fans of Paul Verhoeven's Hollywood output will be amazed by this garish Dutch take on the teen pic. Punctuated with graphic scenes of straight and gay sex, played to the melodramatic hilt and deliriously overstylised, it owes its greatest debt to Rainer Werner Fassbinder as a trio of dirt-bike dreamers strive to emulate their motocross hero, Rutger Hauer. Meanwhile, hot-dog seller Renée Soutendjik seeks to seduce one of them into delivering her from dead-end hell. You name it, Verhoeven nails it, whether it's religious fanaticism, homophobia, small-town ennui, media manipulation or adolescent lust. DP. In Dutch with English subtitles. [VIDEO]

Hans Van Tongeren *Reen* • Renée Soutendijk *Fientje* • Toon Agterberg *Eve* • Maarten Spanjer *Hans* • Marianne Boyer *Maya* • Rutger Hauer *Gerrit Witkamp* • Jeroen Krabbé *Frans Henkhof* ■ *Dir* Paul Verhoeven • *Scr* Gerard Soeteman

Sphere ★★★ 12

Science-fiction thriller
1998 · US · Colour · 128mins

A submerged spacecraft from the future containing a golden sphere that has the ability to physically manifest the darkest fears of anyone who enters its enigmatic interior is at the centre of director Barry Levinson's cerebral adaptation of Michael Crichton's bestselling novel. Alternating between being genuinely creepy and overly tame, this underwater *Solaris* relies on moody dread rather than cheap thrills to weave its spell. A wittily scripted chamber piece. AJ. Contains swearing and violence. [VIDEO] DVD

Dustin Hoffman *Dr Norman Goodman* • Sharon Stone *Dr Beth Halperin* • Samuel L Jackson *Harry Adams* • Peter Coyote *Harold C Barnes* • Liev Schreiber *Dr Ted Fielding* • Queen Latifah *Fletcher* ■ *Dir* Barry Levinson • *Scr* Stephen Hauser, Paul Attanasio, from the novel by Michael Crichton

The Sphinx ★

Mystery 1933 · US · BW · 62mins

Lionel Atwill has the perfect alibi for murder – he is deaf-mute, and a witness heard the killer speak. However, he has a deaf-mute twin hidden behind a panel. He substitutes his brother in court, but equally clever justice wins the day. A sorry mix of low-grade suspense and comic relief means *The Sphinx* stinks! AJ

Lionel Atwill *Jerome Breen* • Sheila Terry *Jerry Crane, society editor* • Theodore Newton *Jack Burton, reporter* • Paul Hurst *Terrence Hogan* ■ *Dir* Phil Rosen • *Scr* Albert DeMond, from his story

Sphinx ★★ 15

Adventure 1980 · US · Colour · 112mins

Rarely since *The Perils of Pauline* has so much been endured by a heroine as by Lesley-Anne Down here, starring as an Egyptologist who comes up against a gang smuggling artefacts from the Valley of the Kings. After witnessing John Gielgud's demise, she's shot at, nearly raped, attacked by bats, thrown into a dungeon of rotting corpses and has a tomb cave in on her. She screams a lot, though co-star Frank Langella seems not to hear. TH. Contains swearing and violence. [VIDEO]

Lesley-Anne Down *Erica Baron* • Frank Langella *Ahmed Khazzan* • Maurice Ronet *Yvon* • John Gielgud *Abdu Hamdi* • Vic Tablian *Khalifa* • John Rhys-Davies *Stephanos Markoulis* • Nadim Sawalha *Gamal* • Saeed Jaffrey *Selim* ■ *Dir* Franklin J Schaffner • *Scr* John Byrum, from the novel by Robin Cook

Spice World: the Movie ★★ PG

Musical comedy 1997 · UK · Colour · 88mins

The first (and as it transpired only) feature film to exploit the enormous success of pop quintet the Spice Girls, this is an attempt to capture the comedic style of the Beatles films, and not nearly as bad as it might have been. The girls themselves are engaging screen presences, if not much cop at acting, and seasoned TV sitcom director Bob Spiers corrals the parade of cameos with aplomb. AC. Contains swearing. [VIDEO] DVD

Victoria Adams *Posh Spice* • Melanie Brown *Scary Spice* • Emma Bunton *Baby Spice* • Melanie Chisholm *Sporty Spice* • Geraldine Halliwell *Ginger Spice* • Richard E Grant *Clifford* • Alan Cumming *Piers Cuthbertson-Smyth* • George Wendt *Martin Barnfield* ■ *Dir* Bob Spiers • *Scr* Kim Fuller, from an idea by the Spice Girls, Kim Fuller

Spider ★★★★ 15

Psychological drama
2002 · Can/UK/Jpn/Fr · Colour · 94mins

An intense and complex exploration of mental illness, sociopathic existentialism and Freudian symbolism, director David Cronenberg's film combines pain, sadness and the shock of the new with innovative dexterity. It uses a visually emblematic inner monologue device to depict the destitute Spider (Ralph Fiennes in his finest performance) watching his younger self go through the harrowing motions of misunderstanding and misrepresenting his mother's "murder". Set in an East End London cunningly styled as an empty vacuum, Cronenberg's unravelling of Spider's delusional mind is both intellectually demanding and courageous. AJ. Contains violence, swearing, sex scenes and nudity. [VIDEO] DVD

Ralph Fiennes *Spider* • Miranda Richardson *Yvonne/Mrs Cleg* • Gabriel Byrne *Bill Cleg* • Lynn Redgrave *Mrs Wilkinson* • John Neville *Terrence* • Bradley Hall *Young Spider* • Gary Reineke *Freddy* • Philip Craig *John* • Cliff Saunders *Bob* ■ *Dir* David Cronenberg • *Scr* Patrick McGrath, from his novel

Spider & Rose ★★

Comedy 1994 · Aus · Colour · 90mins

This is something of a disappointment from Australian writer/director Bill Bennett. There haven't been too many age-gap road movies and this goes some way to explaining why. Bennett's direction is steady enough, but his script is littered with predictable situations, as a 70-year-old is driven back to her family farm by an aimless young ambulance driver. The relationship between Ruth Cracknell and Simon Bossell occasionally flickers into life, but it's all too obvious how things will turn out once her loathsome son (Lewis Fitz-Gerald) enters the picture. DP. Contains some swearing.

Ruth Cracknell *Rose Dougherty* • Simon Bossell *Spider McCall* • Lewis Fitz-Gerald *Robert Dougherty* ■ *Dir/Scr* Bill Bennett

The Spider and the Fly ★★★★ U

Crime drama 1949 · UK · BW · 90mins

Predating *Father Brown* by five years, this was Robert Hamer's first attempt at depicting the grudging respect that exists between a master thief and a brilliant detective. Evoking the Paris of Louis Feuillade's *Fantomas* serials, Hamer superbly captures the conspiratorial pre-First World War atmosphere, while artfully keeping the tone as light as it is suspenseful, as Eric Portman initially attempts to capture Guy Rolfe and then enlists him to procure some top-secret German plans. A cat-and-mouse thriller of the highest order. DP [VIDEO]

Eric Portman *Maubert* • Guy Rolfe *Philippe* • Nadia Gray *Madeleine* • George Cole *Marc* • Edward Chapman *Minister of War* • Maurice Denham *Col de la Roche* ■ *Dir* Robert Hamer • *Scr* Robert Westerby

Spider Baby ★★★

Cult horror 1964 · US · BW · 80mins

Director Jack Hill's fascinating curio features Lon Chaney Jr in one of his best Z-movie later roles, as chauffeur to the bizarre Merrye family, who have become cannibals because of inbreeding. That news comes as a shock to visiting relatives who must face death games devised by the tainted clan's demented children. Keeping his weird script perfectly balanced between macabre fable and black satire, the tongue-in-cheek aspects never lessen the chills. AJ

Lon Chaney Jr *Bruno* • Carol Ohmart *Emily* • Quinn Redeker *Peter* • Mantan Moreland *Messenger* • Beverly Washburn *Elizabeth* • Mary Mitchel *Ann* • Sid Haig *Ralph* • Jill Banner *Virginia* ■ *Dir/Scr* Jack Hill

Spider-Man ★ U

Fantasy action adventure
1977 · US · Colour · 88mins

Tinseltown's first attempt to bring Marvel Comics' greatest cartoon character to life was an unmitigated disaster, resulting in a charmless, by-the-numbers thriller made worse by shoddy effects. Nicholas Hammond does an adequate job of imitating our hero, alias Peter Parker – bitten by a radioactive spider which gives him superhuman strength – but is hampered by EW Swackhamer's failure to capture the style or character of the original comic book. Actually made as the pilot for a television show but released to theatres in Europe, it spawned two sequels. RS [VIDEO]

Nicholas Hammond *Peter Parker/Spider-Man* • Lisa Eilbacher *Judy Tyler* • David White *J Jonah Jameson* • Michael Pataki *Captain Barbera* • Hilly Hicks *Robbie Robinson* • Thayer David *Edward Byron* ■ *Dir* EW Swackhamer • *Scr* Alvin Boretz, from the comic books *Amazing Fantasy* and *The Amazing Spider-Man* by Stan Lee, Steve Ditko

Spider-Man ★★★★ 12

Fantasy action adventure
2002 · US · Colour · 116mins

Thanks in part to legal battles, Marvel Comics' much-loved superhero took his time to reach the big screen. A self-confessed fan, director Sam Raimi sticks closely to the character's comic book roots with the creation of a colourful, visually inspired frolic that's bubbling with energy and gleefully tongue-in-cheek, yet edged with pathos. Lead actor Tobey Maguire is unusual but inspired casting, exuding boy-next-door charm as the clandestine teen avenger. Indeed, it's his intense likeability that helps paper over the film's minor flaws. As for the all important villain, Willem Dafoe looks the part as the Green Goblin, but lacks charisma. SF [VIDEO] DVD

Tobey Maguire *Peter Parker/Spider-Man* • Willem Dafoe *Green Goblin/Norman Osborn* • Kirsten Dunst *Mary Jane Watson* • James Franco *Harry Osborn* • Cliff Robertson *Ben Parker* • Rosemary Harris *May Parker* • JK Simmons *J Jonah Jameson* ■ *Dir* Sam Raimi • *Scr* David Koepp, from the comic books *Amazing Fantasy/The Amazing Spider-Man* by Stan Lee, Steve Ditko

Spider-Man 2 ★★★★ PG

Fantasy action adventure
2004 · US · Colour · 122mins

Director Sam Raimi harnesses advances in technology to deliver a fantasy adventure sequel that's slicker and more stylish than its predecessor. Two years after events in the original, Tobey Maguire's web-slinger is struggling to cope with the responsibilities his powers bring, a task complicated by the appearance of multi-tentacled villain Doctor Octopus (Alfred Molina). Doc Ock's clashes with Spider-Man are the film's highlights, while the focus on Spidey's feelings for Mary Jane (Kirsten Dunst) adds emotional depth. Quibbles aside, the feature's still the most solid of the recent comic-book adaptations, with wit, charm and imagination. SF Contains violence. [VIDEO] DVD

Tobey Maguire *Peter Parker/Spider-Man* • Kirsten Dunst *Mary Jane Watson* • Alfred Molina *Doc Ock/Dr Otto Octavius* • James Franco *Harry Osborn* • Rosemary Harris *May Parker* • Donna Murphy *Rosalie Octavius* • JK Simmons *J Jonah Jameson* • Elizabeth Banks *Betty Brant* ■ *Dir* Sam Raimi • *Scr* Alvin Sargent, from a story by Alfred Gough, Miles Millar, Michael Chabon, from the comic book *The Amazing Spider-Man* by Stan Lee, Steve Ditko

The Spiders ★★★★

Silent adventure 1919 · Ger · BW · 72mins

Fritz Lang's first commercial success is an adventure melodrama on a theme popular at the time (and soon to become a reality): arch criminals hoping to take over the world. Inspired by the German pulp writer Karl May and the serials of Louis Feuillade, it was made in two parts, but broken up into episodes like a serial. It tells of a hero pitted against an Asian criminal and a gang called the Spiders, who are after a diamond shaped like the head of Buddha. The earliest of Lang's surviving works, it already has many Langian elements: the use of mirrors, hypnosis and underground chambers. RB

Carl de Vogt *Kay Hoog* • Lil Dagover *Naela, Priestess of the Sun* • Ressel Orla *Lio Sha* • Georg John *Dr Telphas* • Rudolph Lettinger [Rudolf Lettinger] *John Terry, the Diamond King* • Edgar Pauly *Four Finger John* ■ *Dir/Scr* Fritz Lang

The Spider's Stratagem ★★★★★ PG

Drama 1970 · It · Colour · 94mins

One of the all-time great movies of Italian cinema, this shows director Bernardo Bertolucci at the zenith of his consummate talent in the days when he excelled at illuminating the effect of cultural differences on the human spirit. His hero, brilliantly played by Giulio Brogi, returns home to find his sense of family shattered by unseen events from the past. As he struggles to attain greater knowledge of his heroic father's assassination, we are taken on a fascinating psychological journey with enormous verve and wit, while Italy's Po valley looks marvellous thanks to the luminous camerawork of Vittorio Storaro. SH. In Italian with English subtitles.

Giulio Brogi *Athos Magnani/His father* • Alida Valli *Draifa* • Tino Scotti *Costa* • Pippo Campanini *Gaibazzi* • Franco Giovanelli *Rasori* ■ *Dir* Bernardo Bertolucci • *Scr* Bernardo Bertolucci, Eduardo De Gregorio, Marilu Parolini, from the story *Theme of the Traitor and the Hero* by Jorge Luis Borges

Spies ★★★★

Silent spy thriller 1928 · Ger · BW · 86mins

Perhaps the most under-rated of Fritz Lang's silent spectacles, this tale of master criminality has all the visceral thrill and visual atmospherics of one of Louis Feuillade's *Fantomas* serials. Many of the *Metropolis* alumni were reunited for the picture, with Karl Vollbrecht and Otto Hunte creating Expressionist sets which added menace to the dastardly deeds laid at the door of the Mabuse-like Rudolf Klein-Rogge by Lang and Thea von Harbou's breathless script. Lang abandons political allegory to place the emphasis on escapism and his genius for the awe-inspiring set piece. DP

Rudolf Klein-Rogge *Haghi* • Gerda Maurus *Sonia Barranikova* • Willy Fritsch *Number 326* ■ *Dir* Fritz Lang • *Scr* Fritz Lang, Thea von Harbou, from their story

Spies like Us ★★ PG

Comedy 1985 · US · Colour · 97mins

This highly resistible spoof is one of John Landis's failures. Paired for the first time in a film, former *Saturday Night Live* alumni Dan Aykroyd and Chevy Chase simply fail to gel, and there's little fun to be had once the boisterous training school gags are exhausted. Cold comfort can be obtained from a brief appearance by Bob Hope, and movie aficionados can while away the time playing spot the famous film-makers in a variety of cameo roles. DP

Chevy Chase *Emmett Fitz-Hume* • Dan Aykroyd *Austin Millbarge* • Steve Forrest *General Sline* • Donna Dixon *Karen Boyer* • Bruce Davison *Mr Ruby* • Bernie Casey *Colonel Rhombus* • William Prince *Mr Keyes* • Tom Hatten *General Miegs* • Bob Hope ■ *Dir* John Landis • *Scr* Dan Aykroyd, Lowell Ganz, Babaloo Mandel, from a story by Dan Aykroyd, Dave Thomas

Spike of Bensonhurst ★★

Sports comedy 1988 · US · Colour · 101mins

Andy Warhol alumnus Paul Morrissey is the unlikely director of this sub-*Rocky* crime and boxing comedy. Sasha Mitchell is a local wide-boy working for the mob and making a living by taking the odd dive in the boxing ring. Life is fine until he makes the mistake of falling for Maria Pitillo, the daughter of local Mafia don Ernest Borgnine. Some charm but certainly no knockout. DF

Sasha Mitchell *Spike Fumo* • Ernest Borgnine *Baldo Cacetti* • Anne De Salvo *Sylvia Cacetti* • Sylvia Miles *Congresswoman* • Geraldine Smith *Helen Fumo* • Maria Pitillo *Angel* • Talisa Soto *India* ■ *Dir* Paul Morrissey • *Scr* Alan Bowne, Paul Morrissey

The Spikes Gang ★★ 15

Western 1974 · US · Colour · 92mins

It's a shame that this was filmed in Spain, for it's the European look and corny Almeria locations that undermine any grit that director Richard Fleischer and star Lee Marvin can bring to this intriguing screenplay. This is a story of awestruck lads out West, who idolise Marvin's Harry Spikes (the film's original title), while he teaches them to rob banks. The then-fashionable dashes of violence don't help. TS

Lee Marvin *Harry Spikes* • Gary Grimes *Will Young* • Ron Howard *Les Richter* • Charlie Martin Smith [Charles Martin Smith] *Tod Mayhew* • Arthur Hunnicutt *Kid White* • Noah Beery Jr *Jack Bassett* • Marc Smith *Abel Young* ■ *Dir* Richard Fleischer • *Scr* Irving Ravetch, Harriet Frank Jr

Spinout ★★ U

Musical comedy 1966 · US · Colour · 89mins

This may not be Elvis Presley's most distinguished movie outing, but it's certainly one of the busiest. In all, three women have designs on the struggling singer, whose real ambition is to race fast cars. But who will be swooning in the final clinch: author Diane McBain; Shelley Fabares, whose millionaire father wants Presley to drive one of his racing cars; or Deborah Walley, who plays drums in the King's combo? Norman Taurog's direction is enthusiastic, but this is strictly for Elvis fans. DP DVD

Elvis Presley *Mike McCoy* • Shelley Fabares *Cynthia Foxhugh* • Diane McBain *Diana St Clair* • Deborah Walley *Les* • Dodie Marshall *Susan* • Jack Mullaney *Curly* ■ *Dir* Norman Taurog • *Scr* Theodore J Flicker, George Kirgo

The Spiral Road ★

Melodrama 1962 · US · Colour · 135mins

American director Robert Mulligan followed this dire religious medical drama with *To Kill a Mockingbird*, thus making both his best and possibly worst films within the same 12 months. This jungle-set drama is disadvantaged from the start in its implausible casting of the amiable Rock Hudson as an aggressively ambitious doctor who, in the mid-1930s, travels to Java to learn and then profit from the ideas of guru physician Burl Ives. BB

Rock Hudson *Dr Anton Drager* • Burl Ives *Dr Brits Jansen* • Gena Rowlands *Els* • Geoffrey Keen *Willem Wattereus* • Neva Patterson *Louise Kramer* • Will Kuluva *Dr Sordjano* • Philip Abbott *Frolick* ■ *Dir* Robert Mulligan • *Scr* John Lee Mahin, Neil Paterson, from the novel by Jan de Hartog

The Spiral Staircase ★★★★ PG

Thriller 1946 · US · BW · 79mins

Thought-provoking and disturbing, this masterly thriller is directed with touches of sheer genius by Robert Siodmak, who beckons us into a voyeuristic nightmare with taut, creeping camerawork that makes the hair on your neck stand up. However, while this is undoubtedly a classic of 1940s Hollywood Gothic, the movie treads a fine line between acceptable menace and uncomfortable sadism with its story of a serial killer murdering maimed and disabled women. That said, this remains a masterwork, with a fine performance from Dorothy McGuire. An embarrassing TV movie remake appeared in 2000. SH DVD

Dorothy McGuire *Helen Capel* • George Brent *Professor Warren* • Ethel Barrymore *Mrs Warren* • Kent Smith *Dr Parry* • Rhonda Fleming *Blanche* • Gordon Oliver *Steve Warren* • Elsa Lanchester *Mrs Oates* • Sara Allgood *Nurse Barker* ■ *Dir* Robert Siodmak • *Scr* Mel Dinelli, from the novel *Some Must Watch* by Ethel Lina White • *Cinematographer* Nicholas Musuraca

The Spirit of St Louis ★★★★ U

Historical drama
1957 · US · Colour · 129mins

One of the greatest achievements of director Billy Wilder, best known for such mordant comedies as *Some Like It Hot* and *Sunset Boulevard*. It is a staggering conceit to film such a seemingly uncinematic tale as Charles A Lindbergh's solo flight across the Atlantic, confined as it is to one man in a small cockpit. Wilder makes it an emotional tour de force, utilising flashbacks and narration with wit and skill, aided by Franz Waxman's superb score and Robert Burks and J Peverell Marley's magnificent photography. James Stewart is a shade too old for Lindbergh, but no other actor could better his unique all-American combination of intensity, tenderness and wry concern. TS

James Stewart *Charles A Lindbergh* • Murray Hamilton *Bud Gurney* • Patricia Smith *Mirror girl* • Bartlett Robinson *BF Mahoney* • Robert Cornthwaite *Knight* • Sheila Bond *Model/dancer* • Marc Connelly *Father Hussman* ■ *Dir* Billy Wilder • *Scr* Billy Wilder, Wendell Mayes, Charles Lederer, from the autobiography by Charles A Lindbergh

The Spirit of the Beehive ★★★★★ PG

Period drama 1973 · Sp · Colour · 93mins

Set in 1940, Victor Erice's remarkable debut is a controlled assault on the indolence into which Spain slipped under Franco, and a biting allegory on the evil of which the seemingly benevolent state could be capable. A vision of trust and gentleness, Ana Torrent is enchanting as the small girl who watches *Frankenstein* and becomes fascinated by the monster, mistakenly believing that its spirit is embodied in the fugitive soldier she has befriended. Told with a disarming realism and simplicity, this charming film is one of the gems of Spanish cinema. DP. In Spanish with English subtitles. DVD

Ana Torrent *Ana* • Isabel Telleria *Isabel* • Fernando Fernán Gómez *Father* • Teresa Gimpera *Mother* • José Villasante *Frankenstein's monster* ■ *Dir* Victor Erice • *Scr* Francisco J Querejeta

Spirit of the Eagle ★★★ U

Adventure 1991 · US · Colour · 88mins

Those who have not had enough of Dan Haggerty in his "Grizzly" Adams incarnation will probably enjoy this good-natured, Great Outdoors adventure. Haggerty is Big Eli, a cartographer who makes the mistake of leaving son Little Eli home alone, only to find that he's been kidnapped. It's a great advertisement for the attractions of Oregon, even though the story itself could do with more hills and valleys, light and shade. Still, this peek into family harmony is affecting, and the sumptuous locations provide the eye with a rich, ready meal. JG

Dan Haggerty *Big Eli McDonaugh* • Bill Smith [William Smith] *One-Eye* • Trever Yarrish *Little Eli* • Jeri Arredondo *Watawna* • Taylor Lacher *Weasel* • Ken Carpenter *Jake* • Don Shanks *Running Wolf* ■ *Dir/Scr* Boon Collins

Spirit of the People ★★★ U

Historical drama 1940 · US · BW · 110mins

Henry Fonda had just played the young Abraham Lincoln in John Ford's movie. Now it was the turn of Raymond Massey, who repeats his stage performance from the popular Robert E Sherwood play. The 30-year span of the story rather lumbers along but Massey conveys the private complexity of the man as well as his public eloquence, though the film was an expensive flop at the box office. Massey played Lincoln again – ever so briefly – in *How the West Was Won*. AT

Raymond Massey *Abraham Lincoln* • Gene Lockhart *Stephen Douglas* • Ruth Gordon *Mary Todd Lincoln* • Mary Howard *Ann Rutledge* • Dorothy Tree *Elizabeth Edwards* • Harvey Stephens *Ninian Edwards* • Minor Watson *Joshua Speed* • Alan Baxter *Billy Herndon* ■ *Dir* John Cromwell • *Scr* Grover Jones, Robert E Sherwood, from the play *Abe Lincoln in Illinois* by Robert E Sherwood

Spirit: Stallion of the Cimarron ★★ U

Animated western
2002 · US · Colour · 80mins

Despite being beautifully animated (a flawless combination of old school hand-drawn animation and dazzling computer graphics), this wild mustang horse opera doesn't match the heart of classic Disney or the slick fun of modern digital efforts. Saddled with an overly moralistic and politically correct story, this is strictly kids stuff with Matt Damon providing the first person narration, and Bryan Adams crooning bland songs that pointlessly underline the action. AJ DVD

Matt Damon *Spirit* • James Cromwell *Colonel* • Daniel Studi *Little Creek* • Chopper Bernet *Sgt Adams* • Jeff LeBeau *Murphy/Railroad foreman* ■ *Dir* Kelly Asbury, Lorna Cook • *Scr* John Fusco

Spirit Trap ★ 15

Horror 2005 · UK · Colour · 91mins

Five students move into a foreboding North London mansion and find themselves supernaturally forced to re-enact a century-old romantic tragedy in this clichéd chiller. The creepy house contains a grandfather clock that traps them in a time-warped suicide pact between a widow and her black servant. Billie Piper merely goes through the motions as Jenny, cursed with the same gift as her late medium mother. A minor mix of psychic dread and clairvoyant claptrap. AJ. Contains violence, swearing, drug abuse and sex scenes.

Billie Piper *Jenny* • Luke Mably *Tom* • Emma Catherwood *Adele* • Sam Troughton *Nick* ■ *Dir* David Smith

Spirited Away ★★★★ PG

Animated fantasy adventure
2001 · Jpn · Colour · 124mins

Having broken box-office records and added an Oscar to its share of Berlin's Golden Bear, Hayao Miyazaki's follow-up to *Princess Mononoke* has become an instant Japanimation classic. The tale of a sulky girl who learns the importance of being true to one's self contains echoes of *Alice in Wonderland* that are reinforced by the gallery of rogues and grotesques that Chihiro encounters after she's trapped inside a fantasy world ruled by twin witches. Miyazaki's insistence on hand-drawn graphics gives the CGI visuals an ethereal charm that ensures the action is always a pleasure to behold, even during its rare moments of inaction. DP. Japanese dialogue dubbed into English. DVD

Daveigh Chase *Chihiro* • Suzanne Pleshette *Yubaba/Zeniba* • Jason Marsden *Haku* • Susan Egan *Lin* • David Ogden Stiers *Kamaji* • Lauren Holly *Chihiro's mother* • Michael Chiklis *Chihiro's father* • John Ratzenberger *Assistant manager* • Tara Strong [Tara Charendoff] *Baby Boh* ■ *Dir* Hayao Miyazaki • *Scr* Hayao Miyazaki; Cindy Davis Hewitt, Donald H Hewitt (English version)

Spiritual Love ★★★ 15

Fantasy 1987 · HK · Colour · 88mins

Inspired by the writings of the 17th-century chronicler of the supernatural, Master Liaozhai, the female ghost story developed into a popular sub-genre of Hong Kong fantasy horror in the 1980s. Made just before the emphasis shifted away from atmosphere and on to special effects, David Lai and Taylor Wong's film also slips in plenty of comedy, notably the bizarre manner in which Chow Yun-Fat's jealous lover, Pauline Wong, is transformed into his "girlfriend". DP. In Cantonese with English subtitles.

Chow Yun-Fat *Pok* • Cherie Chung *Butterfly* • Pauline Wong ■ *Dir* David Lai, Taylor Wong • *Scr* Stephen Shiu

Spite Marriage ★★★

Silent comedy 1929 · US · BW · 76mins

Despite a couple of uproarious scenes, it was clear – in only his second feature for the studio – that MGM was slowly eroding Buster Keaton's creative autonomy and corrupting his comic instincts. Never had Keaton's stone-faced bewilderment been so apposite, as he hurtles through plot contrivances that culminate in him confronting a rum-runner on his yacht. Much more sure-footed are the scenes between his daydreaming dry cleaner and Dorothy Sebastian, the actress who exploits him to get back at her feckless beau. DP

Buster Keaton *Elmer Edgemont* • Dorothy Sebastian *Trilby Drew* • Edward Earle *Lionel Denmore* • Leila Hyams *Ethyle Norcrosse* • William Bechtel *Frederick Nussbaum* • John Byron *Giovanni Scarzi* ■ *Dir* Edward Sedgwick • *Scr* Richard Schayer, Ernest S Pagano, Robert Hopkins, from a story by Lew Lipton

Spitfire ★

Drama 1934 · US · BW · 85mins

This ludicrous melodrama was an early nail in the coffin of Katharine Hepburn's reputation, that would see her labelled as "box-office poison" by the end of the decade. Improbably cast as a badly educated, uncouth mountain girl, she alienates the backwoods community with her faith-healing ideas, and is caught in a dreary and unbelievable love triangle with Robert Young and Ralph Bellamy. The script is dreadful, and the patrician Hepburn is badly miscast. RK

Katharine Hepburn *Trigger Hicks* • Robert Young (1) *John Stafford* • Ralph Bellamy *George Fleetwood* • Martha Sleeper *Eleanor Stafford* ■ *Dir* John Cromwell • *Scr* Jane Murfin, Lula Vollmer, from the play *Trigger* by Lula Vollmer

The Spitfire Grill ★★★ 12

Drama 1996 · US · Colour · 111mins

A mesmerising performance from Alison Elliott (*The Wings of the Dove*) is the highlight of this moving if slightly unbelievable drama. Elliott plays Percy, the young ex-con paroled to a small (and small-minded) Maine town, where she goes to work at the local diner run by worldly-wise Ellen Burstyn. Well played by a cast that includes Marcia Gay Harden and the always watchable Will Patton, and featuring some luscious, rugged scenery, this is tear-jerking, female bonding stuff. JB [video]

Alison Elliott (2) *Percy Talbott* • Ellen Burstyn *Hannah Ferguson* • Marcia Gay Harden *Shelby Goddard* • Will Patton *Nahum Goddard* • Kieran Mulroney *Joe Sperling* ■ *Dir/Scr* Lee David Zlotoff

Spivs ★★ 15

Crime comedy drama
2003 · UK · Colour · 95mins

Ken Stott is on good form here as the ageing leader of a minor-league con team that falls foul of a vicious bunch of people-smugglers. Director Colin Teague's film is topical and pacey enough, but the interesting premise descends into yawn-inducing melodrama as the East End wideboys get sucked into protecting two young refugees from East European heavies. DA. Contains swearing.

Ken Stott *Jack Pike* • Nick Moran *Steve* • Dominic Monaghan *Goat* • Kate Ashfield *Jenny* • Rita Ora *Rosanna* • Christos Zenonos *Anton* • Jack Dee *Nigel* • Linda Bassett *Vee* • Paul Kaye *O'Brien* ■ *Dir* Colin Teague • *Scr* Colin Teague, Gary Young, from a story by Mike Loveday

Splash ★★★★ PG

Romantic fantasy comedy
1984 · US · Colour · 105mins

This charming romantic comedy touched a chord with audiences around the world and propelled its stars, Tom Hanks and Daryl Hannah, along with director Ron Howard, to Hollywood's front rank. Hannah is the innocent mermaid who docks on dry land to locate Hanks, whom she saved from drowning years ago. The two leads make a charismatic pair, although John Candy gets most of the best gags. Howard piles on the good-natured fun and keeps soppiness largely at bay. The film was followed four years later by a dismal TV-movie sequel. JF. Contains swearing, nudity. [video] DVD

Tom Hanks *Allen Bauer* • Daryl Hannah *Madison* • Eugene Levy *Walter Kornbluth* • John Candy *Freddie Bauer* • Dody Goodman *Mrs Stimler* • Shecky Greene *Mr Buyrite* • Richard B Shull *Dr Ross* ■ *Dir* Ron Howard • *Scr* Lowell Ganz, Babaloo Mandel, Bruce Jay Friedman, from a screen story by Bruce Jay Friedman based on a story by Brian Grazer

Splendor ★★★ U

Melodrama 1935 · US · BW · 73mins

Producer Samuel Goldwyn commissioned playwright Rachel Crothers to write this as a vehicle for Miriam Hopkins. Joel McCrea marries poor girl Hopkins, instead of the rich heiress his mother has set her sights on. Hopkins is a take-her-or-leave-her actress, and she can't quite bring off the early stages of the movie, clearly being anything but a naive newlywed. Yet her later scenes with Helen Westley as McCrea's thwarted mother have a ferocity all their own. TS [video]

Miriam Hopkins *Phyllis Manning Lorrimore* • Joel McCrea *Brighton Lorrimore* • Paul Cavanagh *Martin Deering* • Helen Westley *Mrs Emmeline Lorrimore* • Billie Burke *Clarissa* • David Niven *Clancey Lorrimore* ■ *Dir* Elliott Nugent • *Scr* Rachel Crothers, from her story

Splendor ★★★ 15

Romantic comedy
1999 · US · Colour · 88mins

Gregg Araki takes a tilt at the mainstream with this archly postmodern reworking of Noel Coward's *Design for Living*. Reining in his penchant for societal diatribes, he establishes the romantic triangle with sweeping satirical strokes. But once bespectacled rock critic Johnathon Schaech and primal punk drummer Matt Keeslar move in with aspiring actress Kathleen Robertson any finesse seeps away and the action becomes increasingly sitcomic, especially once a rival suitor appears on the scene. There are numerous neat touches and the leads spark brightly. DP. Contains swearing, drug abuse and sexual situations [video]

Kathleen Robertson *Veronica* • Johnathon Schaech *Abel* • Matt Keeslar *Zed* • Kelly Macdonald *Mike* • Eric Mabius *Ernest* ■ *Dir/Scr* Gregg Araki

Splendor in the Grass ★★★★ 15

Drama 1961 · US · Colour · 118mins

Warren Beatty couldn't have had a better start to his movie career than this, with collaborators such as co-star Natalie Wood and director Elia Kazan. Beatty and Wood play star-crossed lovers in playwright William Inge's tragi-romantic screenplay, set in 1920s Kansas. The young couple who spend the film attempting to cross the sexual morality divide are dominated by interfering parents (Audrey Christie, Pat Hingle), so that what should be splendid is seen to be squalid. The psychology may be simplistic, but the portrayals are powerful. TH. Contains sexual references. [video]

Natalie Wood *Wilma Dean Loomis* • Warren Beatty *Bud Stamper* • Pat Hingle *Ace Stamper* • Audrey Christie *Mrs Loomis* • Barbara Loden *Ginny Stamper* • Zohra Lampert *Angelina* • Fred Stewart *Del Loomis* • Sandy Dennis *Kay* ■ *Dir* Elia Kazan • *Scr* William Inge

The Split ★★★

Crime thriller 1968 · US · Colour · 89mins

This gutsy crime thriller boasts a splendid supporting cast of tough guys and a script based on a novel by Richard Stark, who also wrote *Point Blank*. The movie spins around Jim Brown, who plans to rob a football stadium and recruits his team in the manner of *The Dirty Dozen*. It's a formula picture, though director Gordon Flemyng makes the most of his Los Angeles locations. AT

Jim Brown *McClain* • Diahann Carroll *Ellie* • Julie Harris *Gladys* • Ernest Borgnine *Bert Clinger* • Gene Hackman *Lt Walter Brill* • Jack Klugman *Harry Kifka* • Warren Oates *Marty Gough* • Donald Sutherland *Dave Negli* ■ *Dir* Gordon Flemyng • *Scr* Robert Sabaroff, from the novel *The Seventh* by Richard Stark [Donald E Westlake]

Split Image ★★★ 15

Drama 1982 · US · Colour · 106mins

The 1980s were a quiet time for Peter Fonda, but here he delivers a powerful performance that shows a different side to the counterculture hero. He plays a cult leader who ensnares Michael O'Keefe, only to discover that the latter's father (the ever-reliable Brian Dennehy) is not giving up without a fight. The film additionally provides juicy roles for James Woods and Karen Allen, while director Ted Kotcheff lends a dark edge to the proceedings. JF. Contains swearing and nudity. [video]

Michael O'Keefe *Danny Stetson* • Karen Allen *Rebecca* • Peter Fonda *Neal Kirklander* • James Woods *Charles Pratt* • Elizabeth Ashley *Diana Stetson* • Brian Dennehy *Kevin Stetson* • Ronnie Scribner *Sean Stetson* ■ *Dir* Ted Kotcheff • *Scr* Scott Spencer, Robert Kaufman, Robert Mark Kamen, from a story by Scott Spencer

Split Second ★★★

Thriller 1953 · US · BW · 80mins

A cracking thriller from Dick Powell, here making his directorial debut and managing to crank up a fair amount of suspense. Slimy escaped convict Stephen McNally ends up in a Nevada ghost town with a clutch of hostages to keep the law at bay. The catch is that the town is actually part of a nuclear test site. This is clever stuff, particularly well cast. TS

Stephen McNally *Sam Hurley* • Alexis Smith *Kay Garven* • Jan Sterling *Dottie* • Keith Andes *Larry Fleming* • Arthur Hunnicutt *Asa* • Paul Kelly (1) *Bart Moore* • Robert Paige *Arthur Ashton* • Richard Egan *Dr Garven* ■ *Dir* Dick Powell • *Scr* William Bowers, Irving Wallace, from a story by Chester Erskine, Irving Wallace

Split Second ★★ 18

Science-fiction horror thriller
1991 · UK · Colour · 86mins

Rutger Hauer mugs shamelessly in this nonsensical science-fiction effort. He's an on-edge cop in the flooded London of 2008, in search of a monstrous heart-ripping serial killer with Satanic origins with whom he shares a psychic link. Sidekick Neil Duncan and love interest Kim Cattrall take their places for the daft battle denouement in Cannon Street tube station. AJ [video]

Rutger Hauer *Harley Stone* • Kim Cattrall *Michelle* • Neil Duncan *Dick Durkin* • Michael J Pollard *The Rat Catcher* • Pete Postlethwaite *Paulsen* • Ian Dury *Jay Jay* • Roberta Eaton *Robin* • Alun Armstrong *Thrasher* ■ *Dir* Tony Maylam • *Scr* Gary Scott Thompson

Split Wide Open ★★★ 15

Drama 1999 · Ind · Colour · 100mins

Acclaimed for 1994's *English, August*, Dev Benegal launched another scathing attack on contemporary India with this messy, but provocative picture. Laila Rouass stars as a London expatriate whose celebrity rests on her muck-raking TV talk show. She alights on Bombay water-seller Rahul Bose to expose the gulf between the city's classes. But then a more sinister story breaks, as Bose's adopted sister, Farida Hyder Mullah, claims she's being stalked by wealthy paedophile Shivaji Satham. Benegal slyly mocks the flashy trashiness of daytime TV, but lets the narrative slip out of control. DP. In Hindi and English with subtitles.

Rahul Bose *KP* • Laila Rouass *Nandita Mehta* • Ayesha Dharker [Ayesha Dharkar] *Leela* • Farida Hyder Mullah *Didi* ■ *Dir* Dev Benegal

Splitting Heirs ★★ 15

Comedy 1993 · UK · Colour · 83mins

Eric Idle is mistakenly allowed to roam free here as both star and scriptwriter by director Robert M Young, who should have boxed him in tight. Had the other participants been similarly reined in, Young might have been able to deliver a focused comedy. Odd moments do resurrect the barmy surrealism so familiar from Monty Python, but on the whole this is a rather disorganised comedy. JM. Contains some violence, swearing, sex scenes and nudity. [video]

Eric Idle *Tommy* • Rick Moranis *Henry* • Barbara Hershey *Duchess Lucinda* • Catherine Zeta-Jones *Kitty* • John Cleese *Shadgrind* • Sadie Frost *Angela* • Stratford Johns *Butler* • Brenda Bruce *Mrs Bullock* • Eric Sykes *Jobson the doorman* ■ *Dir* Robert Young [Robert M Young] • *Scr* Eric Idle

S

The Spoilers ★★★ PG

Western 1942 · US · BW · 83mins

Saloon keeper Marlene Dietrich reprises the role she played with much greater success in 1939's *Destry Rides Again*. What distinguishes movie versions of this Alaska-set western is the exciting fist-fight between the leading men that marks the story's climax. The macho cuffing here is between stars John Wayne and Randolph Scott, but watch out for a cameo appearance from silent heart-throb Richard Barthelmess, in his penultimate screen role. TS DVD

Marlene Dietrich *Cherry Malotte* • John Wayne *Roy Glennister* • Randolph Scott *McNamara* • Margaret Lindsay *Helen Chester* • Harry Carey *Dextry* • Richard Barthelmess *Bronco Kid* ■ *Dir* Ray Enright • *Scr* Lawrence Hazard, Tom Reed, from the novel by Rex Beach

The Spoilers ★★ U

Western 1955 · US · Colour · 83mins

Another version of Rex Beach's novel about claim jumping during the Alaskan gold rush and the first to be filmed in colour with a new generation of stars. The preceding films have become noted for the climactic fist-fights between hero and villain and this makes a determined effort to compete as Jeff Chandler and Rory Calhoun (and their stunt doubles) slug it out from the floor above the saloon, but the story is tired and the picture is never more than mildly engrossing. AE

Anne Baxter *Cherry Malotte* • Jeff Chandler *Roy Glennister* • Rory Calhoun *Alex McNamara* • Ray Danton *"Bronco" Blackie* • Barbara Britton *Helen Chester* • John McIntire *Dextry* • Carl Benton Reid *Judge Stillman* • Wallace Ford *Flapjack Simms* ■ *Dir* Jesse Hibbs • *Scr* Oscar Brodney, Charles Hoffman, from the novel by Rex Beach

The SpongeBob SquarePants Movie ★★★★ U

Animated comedy adventure
2004 · US · Colour · 83mins

There's never a dull moment in this multi-level extravaganza featuring Nickelodeon's cartoon cult hero. Even those unfamiliar with the undersea fast-food employee will find the trippy action, hip absurdity and self-aware silliness of Stephen Hillenburg's joyful creation a lot more fun that expected. Passed over for promotion at the Krusty Krab restaurant, SpongeBob (voiced by Tom Kenny) and his dumb starfish buddy Patrick (Bill Fagerbakke) set out on a quest to reclaim the crown stolen from King Neptune (Jeffrey Tambor) and protect the Krusty Krab's special Krabby Patty recipe. They're helped by Neptune's daughter (Scarlett Johansson) and hindered by a hitman (Alec Baldwin). AJ DVD

Tom Kenny *SpongeBob* • Bill Fagerbakke *Patrick Star* • Clancy Brown *Mr Eugene H Krabs* • Rodger Bumpass *Squidward Tentacles* • Doug Lawrence *Plankton* • Alec Baldwin *Dennis* • David Hasselhoff • Scarlett Johansson *Mindy* • Jeffrey Tambor *King Neptune* ■ *Dir* Stephen Hillenburg • *Scr* Stephen Hillenburg, Derek Drymon, Tim Hill, Kent Osborne, Aaron Springer, Paul Tibbitt, from a story by Stephen Hillenburg, from characters in the animated TV series by Stephen Hillenburg

Spooks Run Wild ★★ U

Comedy 1941 · US · BW · 64mins

This entry in the East Side Kids series must have seemed something of a comedown for Bela Lugosi. However, an even more surprising credit for this harum-scarum old-dark-house adventure is that of co-scriptwriter Carl Foreman, who later received five Oscar nominations for pictures such as *High Noon*. Lugosi is mildly sinister, the Kids wisecrack like popcorn machines and there's a nice turn from Dave O'Brien. DP

Bela Lugosi *Nardo, the monster* • Leo Gorcey *Muggsy* • Huntz Hall *Glimpy* • Bobby Jordan *Danny* • David Gorcey *Pee Wee* • "Sunshine Sammy" Morrison *Scruno* • Donald Haines *Skinny* ■ *Dir* Phil Rosen • *Scr* Carl Foreman, Charles Marion, Jack Henley

Spooky House ★★★

Adventure 1999 · US · Colour · 107mins

How many children's films can boast a couple of Oscar winners in the leading roles? Well, Ben Kingsley and Mercedes Ruehl headline this entertaining tale of magic and malevolence that should amuse anyone hooked on the exploits of Harry Potter. Kingsley plays a reclusive magician who has shunned the limelight since his wife mysteriously disappeared during his act. A young quintet choose Halloween to seek his help in dealing with the ne'er-do-wells over-running their little town. DP

Ben Kingsley *The Great Zamboni* • Mercedes Ruehl *Boss* • Matt Weinberg *Max* • Jason Fuchs *Yuri* • Ronald Joshua Scott *Beans* • Simon Baker *Prescott* • Myles Ferguson *Mike the Mouth* ■ *Dir* William Sachs • *Scr* William Sachs, Margaret Sachs

Sporting Blood ★★★ U

Comedy drama 1931 · US · BW · 82mins

Top-billed Clark Gable is the only big name in this "biography" of a horse named Tommy Boy, which follows him from a Kentucky stud farm, through the abuse he suffers at the hands of several racehorse owners, to his eventual rescue and triumph as the Derby winner. This unusual movie is part exposé of the ugly elements in the sport of kings, and part tribute to and plea on behalf of dumb animals. RK

Clark Gable *Rid Riddell* • Ernest Torrence *Jim Rellence* • Madge Evans *Ruby* • Lew Cody *Tip Scanlon* • Marie Prevost *Angela* • Hallam Cooley *Ludeking* • J Farrell MacDonald *MacGuire* ■ *Dir* Charles Brabin • *Scr* Wanda Tuchock, from the novel *Horseflesh* by Frederick Hazlitt Brennan

Spotswood ★★★ PG

Comedy drama 1991 · Aus · Colour · 92mins

Director Mark Joffe's appealing feature is similar to an Aussie Ealing comedy. At his most hesitant and human, Anthony Hopkins stars as a time-and-motion man whose dealings with the workers in a suburban moccasin factory cause him to re-evaluate a life dictated by emotional sterility and ruthless efficiency. The satire is gentle, the comedy often delightfully offbeat and the character traits neatly observed. DP

Anthony Hopkins *Wallace* • Ben Mendelsohn *Carey* • Toni Collette *Wendy* • Alwyn Kurts *Mr Ball* • Dan Wyllie *Frank Fletcher* • Bruno Lawrence *Robert* • Rebecca Rigg *Cheryl* • Russell Crowe *Kim Barrett* ■ *Dir* Mark Joffe • *Scr* Max Dann, Andrew Knight

Spring and Port Wine ★★★

Comedy drama 1969 · UK · Colour · 100mins

Any film adaptation of a play in which the critical action takes place around a dining table is likely to be slightly stagebound. That Bill Naughton's screen version of his own generation-gap comedy works as a movie is partly down to its commonplace, but utterly compelling, content and director Peter Hammond's deft opening out of events. However, the key element is the playing of James Mason, Susan George and a host of sitcom celebrities, with Mason both infuriating and endearing as the Lancastrian feuding with daughter George. DP

James Mason *Rafe Crompton* • Susan George *Hilda Crompton* • Diana Coupland *Daisy Crompton* • Rodney Bewes *Harold Crompton* • Hannah Gordon *Florence Crompton* • Len Jones *Wilfred Crompton* • Keith Buckley *Arthur Gasket* ■ *Dir* Peter Hammond • *Scr* Bill Naughton, from his play

Spring in Park Lane ★★★ U

Romantic comedy 1948 · UK · BW · 95mins

Another of those fatuous fantasies about lords pretending to be servants, as wealthy Anna Neagle falls for footman Michael Wilding. Even though Herbert Wilcox's direction tends to be heavy-handed, there are many deft touches, mainly supplied by Nicholas Phipps's light-as-air screenplay. The two leads carry off the plot with some aplomb, and Wilding plays his role of charming wimp surprisingly well. A big hit in postwar Britain. TS

Anna Neagle *Judy Howard* • Michael Wilding *Richard* • Tom Walls *Uncle Joshua Howard* • Peter Graves (1) *Basil Maitland* • Marjorie Fielding *Mildred Howard* • Nicholas Phipps *Marquis of Borechester* ■ *Dir* Herbert Wilcox • *Scr* Nicholas Phipps, from the play *Come Out of the Kitchen* by Alice Duer Miller

Spring Reunion ★★ U

Romantic drama 1957 · US · BW · 79mins

The once raucous, ebullient Hollywood hoyden Betty Hutton made her final screen appearance in this movie, before suffering psychiatric problems and sliding into bankruptcy. In an uncharacteristically subdued role, she is a spinster whose life is changed for the better when she meets up with Dana Andrews, the once golden student has dismally failed to fulfil his promise, at a high-school reunion. Palatable but run-of-the-mill. RK

Dana Andrews *Fred Davis* • Betty Hutton *Maggie Brewster* • Jean Hagen *Barna Forrest* • Sara Berner *Paula Kratz* • Robert F Simon *Harry Brewster* • Laura La Plante *May Brewster* • James Gleason *Mr Collyer* ■ *Dir* Robert Pirosh • *Scr* Elick Moll, Robert Pirosh, from a story by Robert Alan Aurthur

Spring River Flows East ★★★★

Drama 1947 · Chi · BW · 190mins

Arguably the finest director of the pre-communist era, Cai Chusheng and documentarist Zheng Junli teamed for this convoluted account of the chaos and corruption that afflicted Chinese society around the Sino-Japanese war. Parallel narratives chart the diverging fortunes of schoolteacher Tao Jin and Bai Yang, the wife he leaves behind when he volunteers to fight, with his postwar prosperity contrasting with the poverty and despair she endures in various refugee camps and menial jobs. The strongest performances all come from actresses, with Bai's selfless suffering being matched by the loyalty of mother-in-law Wu Yin. DP. A Mandarin language film.

Bai Yang *Sufen* • Tao Jin *Zhang Zhongliang* • Wu Yin *Zhang's mother* • Shu Xiuwen *Wang Lizhen* • Yunzhu Shangguan *He Wenyan* ■ *Dir/Scr* Cai Chusheng, Zheng Junli

Spring, Summer, Autumn, Winter ... and Spring ★★★★★ 15

Drama 2003 · S Kor/Ger · Colour · 98mins

South Korean director Kim Ki-Duk's exquisite meditation on the trials and burdens of life is not one for fans of intrigue, car chases or explosions. A tiny Buddhist hermitage floats on the glassy waters of a beautiful lake. Inside, a monk and a young boy live and contemplate. The boy grows up and leaves; the monk grows old; the boy returns to the temple as a man, and the cycle of life repeats itself. There you have pretty much the whole plot. But this is not a film greatly concerned with story or even dialogue (which is also minimal), but about image, emotional tone, ritual and symbolism, all of which are employed masterfully, leaving Kim's film moving, mysterious – and utterly unmissable. AS. In Korean with English subtitles. Contains sex scenes. DVD

Oh Young-Su *Old monk* • Kim Ki-Duk *Adult monk* • Kim Young-Min *Young monk* • Kim Jong-Ho *Child monk* • Seo Jae-Kyung *Boy monk* • Ha Yeo-Jin *The girl* ■ *Dir/Scr* Kim Ki-Duk

Springfield Rifle ★★ U

Western 1952 · US · Colour · 88mins

In the same year that Gary Cooper won an Oscar for *High Noon* he also starred in this perfunctory Warner Bros western. Directed with some style by *House of Wax's* Andre De Toth, this feature resembles a Randolph Scott programme filler, wherein Cooper instead of Scott rides with a batch of second-string actors to infiltrate a gang. Cooper is a little too old for this kind of lark, but there's a certain pleasure to be gained from watching a great star at work. TS

Gary Cooper *Major "Lex" Kearney* • Phyllis Thaxter *Erin Kearney* • David Brian *Austin McCool* • Paul Kelly (1) *Lt Col Hudson* • Philip Carey *Captain Tennick* • Lon Chaney Jr *Elm* • James Millican *Matthew Quint* • Martin Milner *Olie Larsen* ■ *Dir* Andre De Toth • *Scr* Charles Marquis Warren, Frank Davis, from a story by Sloan Nibley

Springtime in a Small Town ★★★★ PG

Period drama
2002 · Chi/HK/Fr · Colour · 111mins

Fei Mu's 1948 feature was among the last produced in China before the Communist takeover. So much can be read into the fact that this remake marks Tian Zhuangzhuang's return to film-making after a decade of state-proscribed silence. He certainly uses this sedate, yet intense study of a household coming to terms with the aftermath of war to comment on the equally momentous socio-economic transition currently taking place. But the impact of returning doctor Xin Baiqing upon ailing grandee Wu Jun and his wife Hu Jingfan and sister Lu Sisi works just as well as an exquisitely staged Chekhovian chamber drama. DP. In Mandarin with English subtitles. DVD

Hu Jingfan *Yuwen, the wife* • Wu Jun *Dai Liyan, the husband* • Xin Baiqing *Zhang Zhichen, the visitor* • Ye Xiaokeng *Lao Huang, the retainer* • Lu Sisi *Dai Xiu, the sister* ■ *Dir* Tian Zhuangzhuang • *Scr* Ah Cheng, from a story by Li Tianji, from the1948 film *Xiao Cheng zhi Chun* by Fei Mu

Springtime in the Rockies ★★★ U

Musical comedy 1942 · US · Colour · 87mins

Betty Grable and John Payne play a sparring Broadway duo, and the music includes the wonderful Helen Forrest performing Harry Warren and Mack Gordon's *I Had the Craziest Dream*. The supporting cast includes such eccentrics as Carmen Miranda (attempting *Chattanooga Choo Choo*). Grable shows off her slim talents to best effect, and consolidates her stardom on her way to becoming the Forces' "pin-up". TS

Betty Grable *Vicky Lane* • John Payne *Dan Christy* • Carmen Miranda *Rosita Murphy* • Cesar Romero *Victor Prince* • Charlotte Greenwood *Phoebe Gray* • Edward Everett Horton *McTavish* • Jackie Gleason *The commissioner* • Harry James ■ *Dir* Irving Cummings • *Scr* Walter Bullock, Ken Englund, Jacques Thery, from the short story *Second Honeymoon* by Philip Wylie

Springtime in the Sierras ★★

Western 1947 · US · Colour · 75mins

One of the earliest Roy Rogers westerns to be filmed in colour, this has a plotline with an ecological slant. In support of the preservation of wildlife, the "King of the Cowboys" exposes a gang who are killing game out of season. There's a villainess behind it all, played by Stephanie Bachelor who ends up in a fierce tussle with heroine Jane Frazee while Roy is slugging it out with her beefy henchman, Roy Barcroft. AE

Roy Rogers • Jane Frazee *Taffy Baker* • Andy Devine *"Cookie" Bullfincher* • Stephanie Bachelor *Jean Loring* • Hal Landon *Bert Baker* • Roy Barcroft *Matt Wilkes* ■ *Dir* William Witney • *Scr* A Sloan Nibley

Spun ★★★ 18

Crime comedy drama
2002 · US · Colour · 97mins

Swedish music video director Jonas Akerlund's first foray into feature films is a grimy tale of "spun-out" crystal meth users. The action unfolds over three days, during which their dependency pushes them into increasingly bizarre situations. Frenetically shot, with enough jump-cuts and imaginative visuals to give viewers whiplash, the movie has cult cool written all over it. However, its lack of morality, cheap shock tactics and sewer-mouth script mean it really is an acquired taste. SF. Contains violence, swearing, sex scenes, drug abuse and nudity. DVD

Jason Schwartzman *Ross* • John Leguizamo *Spider Mike* • Brittany Murphy *Nikki* • Patrick Fugit *Frisbee* • Mena Suvari *Cookie* • Mickey Rourke *The Cook* • Peter Stormare *Cop number one* • Alexis Arquette *Cop number two* • Deborah Harry *Neighbour* • Eric Roberts *The Man* • Chloe Hunter *April* ■ *Dir* Jonas Akerlund • *Scr* Will De Los Santos, Creighton Vero

Spy Game ★★★ 15

Spy thriller
2001 · US/Ger/Jpn/Fr · Colour · 121mins

Looking for all the world like father and son, cinema's two golden "boys", Robert Redford and Brad Pitt, team up for this daftly implausible but diverting spy yarn from director Tony Scott. Redford's the old pro set to retire from the CIA. Pitt's the boy-wonder protégé banged up in a Chinese hellhole after failing to free old flame Catherine McCormack from custody. The 24 hours prior to Pitt's execution see Redford reminiscing about his partnership before running rings round his oblivious CIA superiors to save his friend's life. DA. Contains violence and swearing. DVD

Robert Redford *Nathan Muir* • Brad Pitt *Tom Bishop* • Catherine McCormack *Elizabeth Hadley* • Stephen Dillane *Charles Harker* • Larry Bryggman *Troy Folger* • Marianne Jean-Baptiste *Gladys Jennip* • David Hemmings *Harry Duncan* • Charlotte Rampling *Anne Cathcart* ■ *Dir* Tony Scott • *Scr* Michael Frost Beckner, David Arata, from a story by Michael Frost Beckner

Spy Hard ★★ PG

Spoof comedy 1996 · US · Colour · 77mins

The blockbuster action thriller genre is ripe for sending up, but this lazy effort has to go down as a miss despite the presence of spoofmeister Leslie Nielsen. The basic story is firmly rooted in James Bond – Nielsen is superagent Dick Steele battling supervillain Andy Griffith – but the cast is defeated by the determinedly juvenile script. JF. DVD

Leslie Nielsen *Dick Steele* • Nicollette Sheridan *Veronique Ukrinsky* • Charles Durning *The Director* • Marcia Gay Harden *Miss Cheevus* • Barry Bostwick *Norman Coleman* • John Ales *Kabul* • Andy Griffith *General Rancor* ■ *Dir* Rick Friedberg • *Scr* Rick Friedberg, Dick Chudnow, Aaron Seltzer, from a story by Jason Friedberg, Aaron Seltzer

The Spy in Black ★★★ U

First World War spy drama
1939 · UK · BW · 78mins

In this bold and atmospheric spy drama set during the First World War, Conrad Veidt turns in a convincing performance as a German submarine commander on a mission to sink the British fleet. Dispatched to the Orkney Islands, Veidt makes contact with a German agent who turns out to be local schoolteacher Valerie Hobson, and is soon wondering whether she's on his side. Strong writing combines with striking cinematography and talented direction to make this a satisfying entertainment, the first collaboration of celebrated film-makers Michael Powell and Emeric Pressburger. PF

Conrad Veidt *Captain Hardt* • Valerie Hobson *Joan, the schoolmistress* • Sebastian Shaw *Commander Davis Blacklock* • Marius Goring *Lieutenant Schuster* • June Duprez *Anne Burnett* • Athole Stewart *Reverend Hector Matthews* • Agnes Lauchlan *Mrs Matthews* • Helen Haye *Mrs Sedley* ■ *Dir* Michael Powell • *Scr* Emeric Pressburger, Roland Pertwee, from the novel by J Storer Clouston • *Cinematographer* Bernard Browne

The Spy in the Green Hat ★★★

Spy adventure 1966 · US · Colour · 92mins

The Man from UNCLE TV show spawned a hit-and-miss series of spin-off movies of which this is arguably the most accomplished. It features the series' best villains in the guise of Jack Palance's pill-popping megalomaniac and his kinky female secretary/assassin, played with delicious malice by Janet Leigh. The plot is even more tongue in cheek than usual with the ever unflappable Napoleon Solo and Illya Kuryakin teaming up with with a pack of stereotypical Italian-American gangsters to thwart THRUSH's latest plan for world domination. Directed with stylish aplomb by Joseph Sargent. RS

Robert Vaughn *Napoleon Solo* • David McCallum *Illya Kuryakin* • Jack Palance *Louis Strago* • Janet Leigh *Miss Diketon* • Letitia Roman [Leticia Roman] *Pia Monteri* • Leo G Carroll *Alexander Waverly* • Eduardo Ciannelli *Arturo "Fingers" Stilletto* • Allen Jenkins *Enzo "Pretty" Stilletto* • Jack La Rue [Jack LaRue] *Frederico "Feet" Stilletto* • Joan Blondell *Mrs "Fingers" Stilletto* • Elisha Cook [Elisha Cook Jr] *Arnold* ■ *Dir* Joseph Sargent • *Scr* Peter Allan Fields

Spy in Your Eye ★★ U

Spy thriller 1965 · It · Colour · 84mins

Partially blinded American agent Brett Halsey has a miniature camera secretly implanted in his false eye when Russians operate on him to supposedly cure him of sight problems. What they really want is for him to find a death ray formula developed by a scientist who, before dying, had it tattooed it on his daughter Pier Angeli's scalp. Vittorio Sala gets some clever mileage out of the voyeuristic concept and the usual glamorous foreign locations provide some visual interest, but routine direction and minimal action ultimately get the upper hand. AJ. Italian dialogue dubbed into English.

Brett Halsey *Bert Morris* • Pier Angeli *Paula Krauss* • Dana Andrews *Col Lancaster* • Gastone Moschin *Boris* ■ *Dir* Vittorio Sala • *Scr* Romano Ferrara, Adriano Baracco, Adriano Bolzoni, from a story by Lucio Marcuzzo

SPYkids ★★★★ U

Fantasy action adventure
2001 · US · Colour · 84mins

Antonio Banderas and Carla Gugino play married spies who get captured by a megalomaniac kids' TV presenter (Alan Cumming) who's seeking world domination. To the rescue come the couple's pleasingly non-precocious kids (Alexa Vega and Daryl Sabara), aided and abetted by a cool array of gizmoes that range from rocket-packs to electromagnetic chewing gum. Smartly and sassily directed by Robert Rodriguez (who quite rightly pitches the film at youngsters, not down to them) and sporting some nifty special effects, this is rollicking family cinema as it should be. DA DVD

Antonio Banderas *Gregorio Cortez* • Carla Gugino *Ingrid Cortez* • Alexa Vega *Carmen Cortez* • Daryl Sabara *Juni Cortez* • Alan Cumming *Fegan Floop* • Tony Shalhoub *Alexander Minion* • Teri Hatcher *Ms Gradenko* • Cheech Marin [Richard "Cheech" Marin] *Felix Gumm* • Danny Trejo *Machete* • Robert Patrick *Mr Lisp* • George Clooney *Devlin* ■ *Dir/Scr* Robert Rodriguez

SPYkids 2: the Island of Lost Dreams ★★★★ U

Fantasy action adventure
2002 · US · Colour · 96mins

Children's action adventures don't come any more sophisticated than director Robert Rodriguez's slick and colourful sequel to his 2001 hit *SPYkids*. This time around, Carmen and Juni (Alexa Vega and Daryl Sabara) are on a mission to investigate the mysterious volcanic island inhabited by a mad scientist (Steve Buscemi) and his hybrid animal creations. In a playful homage to effects specialist Ray Harryhausen's style of stop-motion animation, these mutant monsters add extra excitement to the thrill-packed feature. Rodriguez utilises high production values and rapid pacing to perfection, and this pint-sized espionage caper is as stylish and inventive as a Bond film. SF DVD

Antonio Banderas *Gregorio Cortez* • Carla Gugino *Ingrid Cortez* • Alexa Vega *Carmen Cortez* • Daryl Sabara *Juni Cortez* • Steve Buscemi *Romero* • Mike Judge *Donnagon* • Danny Trejo *Uncle Machete* • Cheech Marin [Richard "Cheech" Marin] *Felix Gumm* • Ricardo Montalban *Grandpa* • Holland Taylor *Grandma* ■ *Dir* Robert Rodriguez • *Scr* Robert Rodriguez, from his characters

SPYkids 3-D: Game Over ★★ U

Fantasy action adventure
2003 · US · Colour · 78mins

Robert Rodriguez's franchise ditches plot sophistication in favour of pure visual spectacle for this second sequel, filmed predominantly in 3-D. In this minutely detailed cyberspace fantasy, young agents Daryl Sabara and Alexa Vega journey into the virtual-reality world of a 3-D video game to save mankind from its megalomaniac creator, Sylvester Stallone. The humorous cameos and witty banter do little to camouflage the limp storyline and weak characters. SF DVD

Antonio Banderas *Gregorio Cortez* • Carla Gugino *Ingrid Cortez* • Alexa Vega *Carmen Cortez* • Daryl Sabara *Juni Cortez* • Ricardo Montalban *Grandpa* • Holland Taylor *Grandma* • Sylvester Stallone *Toymaker* • Mike Judge *Donnagon Giggles* • Cheech Marin [Richard "Cheech" Marin] *Felix Gumm* ■ *Dir/Scr* Robert Rodriguez

The Spy Who Came in from the Cold ★★★★ PG

Spy drama 1965 · UK · BW · 107mins

This gritty adaptation of John Le Carré's gruelling novel finally offered Richard Burton a role worthy of his wonderfully world-weary style. Bitterness seeps from every pore as he goes behind the Iron Curtain for a final showdown with his East German counterpart. With agents trapped behind state secrecy and false identities, this isn't the glitzy neverland of James Bond, but a dangerous reality in which suppressed emotion matters more than derring-do. Martin Ritt's icy direction and Oswald Morris's bleak black-and-white photography make this not just the most authentic Cold War film, but also one of the best. DP

Richard Burton *Alec Leamas* • Claire Bloom *Nan Perry* • Oskar Werner *Fiedler* • Peter Van Eyck *Hans-Dieter Mundt* • Sam Wanamaker *Peters* • Rupert Davies *George Smiley* • Cyril Cusack *Control* ■ *Dir* Martin Ritt • *Scr* Paul Dehn, Guy Trosper, from the novel by John le Carré

The Spy Who Loved Me ★★★★ PG

Spy adventure 1977 · UK · Colour · 120mins

"Nobody Does It Better" than Roger Moore in one of the best post-Connery James Bond adventures. Well-acted (with less reliance on slapstick humour than normal), smartly cast (metal-toothed Jaws, played by Richard Kiel, makes his first appearance) and lavishly directed (by Lewis Gilbert), this exceptional spy escapade is far-fetched mayhem of the highest order, with a welcome accent on character realism rather than just spectacular sets. Barbara Bach is the alluring Russian agent Anya Amasova. AJ. Contains some violence. DVD

Roger Moore *James Bond* • Barbara Bach *Major Anya Amasova* • Curt Jurgens *Karl Stromberg* • Richard Kiel *Jaws* • Caroline Munro *Naomi* • Walter Gotell *General Gogol* • Geoffrey Keen *Minister of Defence* • Bernard Lee *"M"* • Shane Rimmer *Captain Carter* • Bryan Marshall *Commander Talbot* • Desmond Llewelyn *"Q"* • Lois Maxwell *Miss Moneypenny* ■ *Dir* Lewis Gilbert • *Scr* Christopher Wood, Richard Maibaum, from the novel by Ian Fleming

The Spy with a Cold Nose ★★★ U

Comedy 1966 · UK · Colour · 98mins

Ace sitcom writers Ray Galton and Alan Simpson here offer their contribution to the spy boom that was dominating popular cinema in the 1960s. Their sub-Bondian farce stars Laurence Harvey and fine comedy actor Lionel Jeffries in a story of Cold War espionage which features a bulldog with a listening bug grafted to its insides for spying on the Russians. The script was held up as a model of its type but the genius of the words lost a little something in translation, but much mirth remains. DF

Laurence Harvey *Dr Francis Trevellyan* • Lionel Jeffries *Stanley Farquhar* • Daliah Lavi *Princess Natasha Romanova* • Eric Sykes *Wrigley* • Eric Portman *British ambassador* • Colin Blakely *Russian prime minister* • Denholm Elliott *Pond-Jones* ■ *Dir* Daniel Petrie • *Scr* Ray Galton, Alan Simpson

The Spy with My Face ★★★ PG

Spy adventure 1966 · US · Colour · 82mins

The Man from UNCLE was such a cult hit in this country that the seven movie spin-offs were made almost exclusively with the British box office in mind. In this second film in the series, Robert Vaughn's Napoleon Solo is sent to deal with a devilish doppelgänger. As always David McCallum provides the dependable support as Illya Kuryakin, while Senta Berger is the naughty Napoleon's partner in crime. DP DVD

Robert Vaughn *Napoleon Solo* • David McCallum *Illya Kuryakin* • Senta Berger *Serena* • Leo G Carroll *Alexander Waverly* • Michael Evens *Darius Two* • Sharon Farrell *Sandy Wister* • Fabrizio Mioni *Arsena Coria* ■ *Dir* John Newland • *Scr* Clyde Ware, Joseph Caivelli, from a story by Clyde Ware

SPYS ★★ PG

Comedy 1974 · US · Colour · 99mins

Donald Sutherland and Elliott Gould, a great comedy partnership in *MASH* five years earlier, found the magic hard to repeat. This espionage spoof that attempts to cash in on their double act reputation is both clichéd and unfunny. They play CIA agents who mishandle the defection of a Russian ballet dancer and end up on the run from their own side and the KGB. Compared with their first movie this has neither the verve nor the nerve. TH

Elliott Gould *Douglas "Griff" Griffin* • Donald Sutherland *Eric Brulard* • Zouzou *Sybil* • Joss Ackland *Martinson* • Kenneth Griffith *Lippet* ■ *Dir* Irvin Kershner • *Scr* Mal Marmorstein, Laurence J Cohen, Fred Freeman

S

Squanto: the Last Great Warrior ★★★ PG

Historical adventure
1994 · US · Colour · 97mins

Swiss director Xavier Koller, who won a best foreign film Oscar for *Journey of Hope*, came to Disney to make this costume drama. This is far too fanciful in its description of a native American's adventures in 17th-century England. Adam Beach is suitably noble as the warrior who learns the value of life while taking sanctuary in a monastery. Younger viewers, however, will probably prefer his skirmishes with the wicked Michael Gambon to these spiritual asides. DP

Adam Beach *Squanto* • Sheldon Peters Wolfchild *Mooshawset* • Irene Bedard *Nakooma* • Eric Schweig *Epenow* • Leroy Peltier *Pequod* • Michael Gambon *Sir George* • Nathaniel Parker *Thomas Dermer* • Mandy Patinkin *Brother Daniel* • Donal Donnelly *Brother Paul* ■ *Dir* Xavier Koller • *Scr* Darlene Craviotto, Bob Dolman

The Square Circle ★★ 15

Drama 1996 · Ind · Colour · 107mins

Combining Bollywood-style melodrama with passages of stark realism, director Amol Palekar clearly intended this film to entertain as well as provoke. An intriguing study of gender politics set in rural India, it benefits from the splendidly mannered performances of Nirmal Pandey, as an itinerant female impersonator, and Sonali Kulkarni, as the young girl who adopts men's attire after escaping from the brothel thugs. Overcooked. DP. In Hindi with English subtitles. Contains violence.

Nirmal Pandey *The transvestite* • Sonali Kulkarni *The girl* • Faiyyaz *Madam* • Rekha Sahay *Bar owner* • Nina Kulkarni *Widow* ■ *Dir* Amol Palekar • *Scr* Timeri N Murari, Chitra Palekar, Shashank Shanker, Amol Palekar

Square Dance ★★★ 15

Drama 1987 · US · Colour · 107mins

This was Winona Ryder's second film and her scripture-spouting role ultimately proves too much for her. But she is definitely one of the plus points in a film that deals solely with eccentrics. Jason Robards is lazily effective as Ryder's crotchety grandpa and Jane Alexander lets off plenty of steam as her city-corrupted mother. Rob Lowe is unbelievable as the mentally disabled Rory (and seems to belong to another film altogether). DP. Contains swearing.

Jason Robards Jr [Jason Robards] *Dillard* • Jane Alexander *Juanelle* • Winona Ryder *Gemma Dillard* • Rob Lowe *Rory* • Deborah Richter *Gwen* • Guich Koock *Frank* • Elbert Lewis *Beecham* • Charlotte Stanton *Aggie* ■ *Dir* Daniel Petrie • *Scr* Alan Hines, from his novel

The Square Jungle ★★★

Sports drama 1955 · US · BW · 86mins

Tony Curtis stars as a grocery-store clerk who joins the beasts of the "square jungle", otherwise known as the boxing ring, to earn the money to bail out his drunken father (Jim Backus). With Ernest Borgnine as Curtis's trainer, Paul Kelly as the cop who sponsors him, some peripheral romantic interest, and an appearance by heavyweight champ Joe Louis as himself, this is unremarkable but entertaining drama. RK

Tony Curtis *Eddie Quaid/Packy Glennon* • Patricia Crowley [Pat Crowley] *Julie Walsh* • Ernest Borgnine *Bernie Browne* • Paul Kelly (1) *Jim McBride* • Jim Backus *Pat Quaid* • Leigh Snowden *Lorraine Evans* • David Janssen *Jack Lindsay* • Joe Louis ■ *Dir* Jerry Hopper • *Scr* George Zuckerman, from his story

Square of Violence ★★★

Second World War drama
1961 · US/Yug · BW · 95mins

Leonardo Bercovici's crisis of conscience drama avoids the longeurs that blighted so many stellar co-productions about the Second World War. In a rare sympathetic part, Broderick Crawford excels as the Yugoslavian partisan whose unintentionally reckless action prompts Nazi major Branko Plesa to threaten to execute hundreds of hostages unless the perpetrator of a bombing raid surrenders. Exploring the cruel realities of combat, the film eschews cheap heroics – Crawford is placed in an impossible situation that is resolved in the most chilling circumstances. It's a brave conclusion to a consistently challenging picture. DP

Broderick Crawford *Dr Stefan Bernardi* • Valentina Cortese *Erica Bernardi* • Branko Plesa *Major Kohler* • Bibi Andersson *Maria* • Anita Björk *Sophia* • Bert Sotlar *Partisan leader* ■ *Dir* Leonardo Bercovici • *Scr* Eric Bercovici, Leonardo Bercovici, from a story by Eric Bercovici

The Square Peg ★★ U

Second World War comedy
1958 · UK · BW · 85mins

Norman Wisdom's comedy appeals because many in the audience can identify with the situations his "little man" character struggles valiantly to overcome. But here, Norman becomes a war hero by impersonating a top Nazi general, and it misfires because the commonplace is forsaken for the fantastic. It's hard to sympathise, let alone laugh, with him. DP DVD

Norman Wisdom *Norman Pitkin/General Schreiber* • Honor Blackman *Lesley Cartland* • Edward Chapman *Mr Grimsdale* • Campbell Singer *Sergeant Loder* • Hattie Jacques *Gretchen von Schmetterling* • Brian Worth *Henri Le Blanc* • Terence Alexander *Captain Wharton* • John Warwick *Colonel Layton* ■ *Dir* John Paddy Carstairs • *Scr* Jack Davies, Henry E Blyth, Norman Wisdom, Eddie Leslie

The Square Ring ★★ PG

Portmanteau drama 1953 · UK · BW · 79mins

The portmanteau movie meets the boxing film in this clash of the genres. Covering one night at a seedy boxing ring allows this movie to veer off into separate mini-dramas, each dealing with one boxer – ranging from a wide-eyed beginner to a punch-drunk veteran. Inevitably it's uneven, wavering between comedy and tragedy, but given the dangerous nature of the game there's uncertainty about the future of the pugilists. AT

Jack Warner *Danny Felton* • Robert Beatty *Kid Curtis* • Bill Owen *Happy Burns* • Maxwell Reed *Rick Martell* • George Rose *Whitey Johnson* • Bill Travers *Rowdie Rawlings* • Alfie Bass *Frank Forbes* • Ronald Lewis *Eddie Lloyd* • Sidney James *Adams* • Joan Collins *Frankie* • Kay Kendall *Eve Lewis* • Joan Sims *Bunty* ■ *Dir* Michael Relph, Basil Dearden • *Scr* Robert Westerby, Peter Myers, Alec Grahame, from the play by Ralph W Peterson

The Squaw Man ★★

Western 1931 · US · BW · 106mins

His career floundering in the early years of the talkies, Cecil B DeMille made his third screen version of Edwin Milton Royle's smash hit play. It was horribly dated material by this time, resulting in a huge box-office failure, but its strong cast and lavish production values give it some interest. Warner Baxter is the honourable Englishman who makes a new life for himself in Arizona, marries Lupe Velez's American Indian woman, but is then located by his old love, Eleanor Boardman. AE

Warner Baxter *Capt James Wynegate/Jim Carsten* • Lupe Velez *Naturich* • Eleanor Boardman *Lady Diana* • Charles Bickford *Cash Hawkins* • Roland Young *Sir John Applegate Kerhill* • Paul Cavanaugh [Paul Cavanagh] *Henry, Earl of Kerhill* • Raymond Hatton *Shorty* ■ *Dir* Cecil B DeMille • *Scr* Lucien Hubbard, Lenore Coffee, Elsie Janis, from the play by Edwin Milton Royle

The Squeaker ★★★ U

Crime drama 1937 · UK · BW · 73mins

Edmund Lowe reprises his stage role as the methodical Scotland Yard inspector who doggedly pursues arch criminal Sebastian Shaw. Confined within starchy studio sets, William K Howard directs steadily, but the removal of that touch of mystery leaves him with precious little to play with, to the extent that he has to bolster the action with protracted love scenes between Lowe and Ann Todd. Robert Newton and Alastair Sim put in pleasing support appearances. DP

Edmund Lowe *Inspector Barrabal* • Sebastian Shaw *Frank Sutton* • Ann Todd *Carol Stedman* • Tamara Desni *Tamara* • Robert Newton *Larry Graeme* • Allan Jeayes *Inspector Elford* • Alastair Sim *Joshua Collie* ■ *Dir* William K Howard • *Scr* Bryan Wallace, Edward O Berkman, from the novel by Edgar Wallace

The Squeeze ★★★ 18

Crime drama 1977 · UK · Colour · 102mins

Comedian Freddie Starr shows that there's more to him than pratfalls and doubles entendres. He acquits himself surprisingly well as a small-time London crook, but the focus here falls firmly on Stacy Keach as the booze-sodden former cop who is forced to clean up his act when his ex-wife is kidnapped. This is a violent and abrasive thriller – creaky perhaps, but still disturbingly plausible. DP

Stacy Keach *Naboth* • Freddie Starr *Teddy* • Edward Fox *Foreman* • Stephen Boyd *Vic* • David Hemmings *Keith* • Carol White *Jill* • Alan Ford *Taff* • Roy Marsden *Barry* ■ *Dir* Michael Apted • *Scr* Leon Griffiths, from the novel *Whose Little Girl Are You?* by David Craig

The Squeeze ★ 15

Comedy thriller 1987 · US · Colour · 97mins

Beetle Juice was arguably the only Michael Keaton film ever to make full use of its star's prodigious comic talents. This dreary comedy thriller, about a conman who gets caught up in murder and mayhem, is a case in point. Keaton provides a few laughs, but the remainder of this time-filler is a mirth-free zone. DA

Michael Keaton *Harry Berg* • Rae Dawn Chong *Rachel Dobs* • John Davidson *Honest Tom T Murray* • Ric Abernathy *Bouncer* • Danny Aiello III *Ralph Vigo* • Bobby Bass *Poker player* • Leslie Bevis *Gem Vigo* • Jophery Brown *Poker player* ■ *Dir* Roger Young • *Scr* Daniel Taplitz

Squibs ★★ U

Musical 1935 · UK · BW · 77mins

Betty Balfour had been hailed as the English Mary Pickford during the silent era, but by the mid-1930s she was reduced to taking chirpy supports. Here she reprised the role of Squibs, the tousle-haired cockney flower girl she had played several times at the height of her fame. The story of the waif who becomes wealthy overnight was an old theatrical warhorse in the 1920s, and this version has little new to offer. DP

Betty Balfour *Squibs Hopkins* • Gordon Harker *Sam Hopkins* • Stanley Holloway *PC Charley Lee* • Margaret Yarde *Mrs Lee* • Morris Harvey *Inspector Lee* • Michael Shepley *Colin Barrett* ■ *Dir* Henry Edwards • *Scr* Michael Hogan, H Fowler Mear, from the play by Clifford Seyler, George Pearson

Squirm ★★★ 18

Black comedy horror
1976 · US · Colour · 92mins

The worm turns in this cheap but cheerfully repellent horror film. A pylon, struck by lightning, electrifies the earth in typical small town, USA, and the worms go on the offensive. Writer/director Jeff Lieberman, making the most of a limited budget, builds the tension expertly, and limits the shock effects, giving full value to the scenes (created by master of the art Rick Baker) in which worms crawl through human flesh. DM

Don Scardino *Mick* • Patricia Pearcy *Geri* • RA Dow *Roger* • Jean Sullivan *Naomi* • Peter MacLean *Sheriff* • Fran Higgins *Alma* • William Newman *Quigley* ■ *Dir/Scr* Jeff Lieberman • *Special Effects* Rick Baker

Ssssss ★★★

Horror 1973 · US · Colour · 98mins

The marvellously villainous Strother Martin is a mad doctor who wants to turn men into snakes in this outrageous but often nightmarish horror. Playing cleverly on the audience's fear of snakes, it sustains a strange and suspenseful atmosphere virtually throughout, aided by the excellent make-up work of John Chambers, who had won an Oscar for *Planet of the Apes*. It is only towards the end that the temperature falls as the contrivances pile up and the special effects show their age. Still, an effective shocker. DM

Strother Martin *Dr Carl Stoner* • Dirk Benedict *David Blake* • Heather Menzies *Kristine Stoner* • Richard B Shull *Dr Ken Daniels* • Jack Ging *Sheriff Dale Hardison* • Tim O'Connor *Kogen* ■ *Dir* Bernard L Kowalski • *Scr* Hal Dresner, from a story by Dan Striepeke

Stacy's Knights ★★ PG

Drama 1983 · US · Colour · 90mins

Kevin Costner's star did not begin to shine until he played Eliot Ness in *The Untouchables*, but his creative potential and charisma are evident even in this latter-day B-movie. The film has occasional tense moments in between rather too many flat sequences, though it benefits from Costner's lively performance and screenwriter Michael Blake's realistic portrayal of gambling addiction. JM. Contains swearing and violence.

Andra Millian *Stacy* • Kevin Costner *Will* • Eve Lilith *Jean* • Mike Reynolds *Shecky* • Ed Semenza *Kid* • Don Hackstaff *Lawyer* ■ *Dir* Jim Wilson (2) • *Scr* Michael Blake

Stag ★★★ 18

Thriller 1996 · US · Colour · 90mins

A group of pals hold a stag party, but in a haze of booze and drugs one of the strippers they've hired is killed. What do they do? The film chillingly explores what extremes will people go to save themselves. Andrew McCarthy is in fine form as the most unscrupulous of the bunch, though Mario Van Peebles almost pips him. Gavin Wilding's film adopts a dramatically dark narrative and ends up being an ambitious if flawed moral tale. RS. Contains swearing, violence, nudity and drug abuse. DVD

Mario Van Peebles *Michael* • Andrew McCarthy *Peter* • Kevin Dillon *Dan* • William McNamara *Jon* • John Stockwell *Victor* • Ben Gazzara *Frank* • John Henson *Timan* • Taylor Dayne *Serena* • Jerry Stiller *Ted* ■ *Dir* Gavin Wilding • *Scr* Evan Tylor, Pat Bermel, from a story by Jason Schombing

Stage Beauty ★★★ 15

Period romantic comedy drama
2004 · US/UK/Ger · Colour · 105mins

Set in the world of 17th-century London theatre, when female roles were played by men, this has as its protagonist Ned Kynaston (Billy Crudup), once London theatre's most celebrated "leading lady". The toast of society, Kynaston is oblivious to the romantic feelings of his dresser Maria (Claire Danes), who secretly reprises his performance as Desdemona in a small, illegal production of *Othello*. This promises much as an offbeat period romantic drama, but never quite overcomes the central problem of a "leading lady" who doesn't convince as a woman. BP. Contains swearing, sexual references, nudity. DVD

Billy Crudup *Ned Kynaston* • Claire Danes *Maria* • Rupert Everett *King Charles II* • Tom Wilkinson *Thomas Betterton* • Ben Chaplin *George Villiars, Duke of Buckingham* • Hugh Bonneville *Samuel Pepys* • Richard Griffiths *Sir Charles Sedley* • Edward Fox *Sir Edward Hyde* • Zoe Tapper *Nell Gwyn* ■ *Dir* Richard Eyre • *Scr* Jeffrey Hatcher, from his play *Compleat Female Stage Beauty*

Stage Door ★★★★ U

Comedy drama 1937 · US · BW · 90mins

Marvellous adaptation of the witty Edna Ferber/George S Kaufman play, set mainly in a boarding house for theatrical hopefuls. Scintillating casting gives bravura roles to a batch of Hollywood greats, most notably the fabulous Katharine Hepburn and the sassy Ginger Rogers. Points, too, for acerbic Eve Arden, dippy Constance Collier and a teenaged Ann Miller. Only Andrea Leeds in the tragic role isn't up to the demands of the plot or her co-stars. A true joy, especially for stage-struck hopefuls. TS [video]

Katharine Hepburn *Terry Randall Sims* • Ginger Rogers *Jean Maitland* • Adolphe Menjou *Anthony "Tony" Powell* • Gail Patrick *Linda Shaw* • Constance Collier *Miss Catherine Luther* • Andrea Leeds *Kaye Hamilton* • Samuel S Hinds *Henry Sims* • Lucille Ball *Judith Canfield* • Franklin Pangborn *Harcourt* • Jack Carson *Mr Millbanks* • Eve Arden *Eve* • Ann Miller *Annie* ■ *Dir* Gregory La Cava • *Scr* Morrie Ryskind, Anthony Veiller, William Slavens McNutt, from the play by Edna Ferber, George S Kaufman

Stage Door Canteen ★★★ U

Musical 1943 · US · BW · 131mins

New York's Stage Door Canteen was the venue where servicemen on leave during the Second World War would meet, and be entertained by the stars of stage and screen. Producer Sol Lesser's film (directed by Frank Borzage) is a revue-style show, set in the Canteen and populated by countless entertainers giving their services free. A redundant wisp of romantic plot occasionally interrupts the parade of celebrities. RK [video]

Cheryl Walker *Eileen* • William Terry *Ed "Dakota" Smith* • Marjorie Riordan *Jean Rule* • Lon McCallister *"California"* • Judith Anderson • Tallulah Bankhead • Ralph Bellamy • William Demarest • Gracie Fields • Billy Gilbert • Helen Hayes • Katharine Hepburn • Jean Hersholt • Sam Jaffe • Otto Kruger • Gertrude Lawrence • Gypsy Rose Lee • Peggy Lee • Harpo Marx • Yehudi Menuhin • Ethel Merman • Paul Muni • Merle Oberon • George Raft • Ethel Waters • Johnny Weissmuller ■ *Dir* Frank Borzage • *Scr* Delmer Daves

Stage Fright ★★★★ PG

Comedy thriller 1949 · UK · BW · 105mins

Alfred Hitchcock's overlooked and under-rated film stars Jane Wyman as a stage-struck drama student implausibly forced to play a real-life role in order to solve a murder. Marlene Dietrich is decidedly eye-catching as the jaded international singing star, with Richard Todd on the run as Wyman's former boyfriend. The film offers frequent tickling diversions from great supporting players, and it's a comic charade, really – a whodunnit about role-playing and duplicity; even the flashback lies. AT DVD

Jane Wyman *Eve Gill/Doris Tinsdale* • Marlene Dietrich *Charlotte Inwood* • Michael Wilding *Inspector Wilfrid O "Ordinary" Smith* • Richard Todd *Jonathan Cooper* • Alastair Sim *Commodore Gill* • Sybil Thorndike *Mrs Gill* • Kay Walsh *Nellie Goode* • Miles Malleson *Mr Fortesque* • Hector MacGregor *Freddie Williams* • André Morell *Inspector Byard* • Joyce Grenfell *"Lovely Ducks"* • Patricia Hitchcock *Chubby Bannister* • Irene Handl *Mrs Mason, Mrs Gill's maid* ■ *Dir* Alfred Hitchcock • *Scr* Whitfield Cook, Alma Reville, James Bridie, from the stories *Man Running* and *Outrun the Constable* by Selwyn Jepson

Stage Fright – Aquarius ★★★ 18

Horror thriller 1987 · It · Colour · 86mins

Michele Soavi, a former assistant to horror icon Dario Argento, makes his big screen directorial debut with an impressive horror movie which is not only packed with gross-out gore, but also hasn't forgotten how to frighten its audience. Soavi tackles the conventional storyline of an asylum escapee locked in a theatre where a dance company is rehearsing a ballet based on the Jack the Ripper legend in much the same style as Argento would.Horror fans and lovers of Italian exploitation cinema will not want to miss this one. RS. An Italian language film. [video] DVD

David Brandon • Barbara Cupisti • Robert Gligorov • Martin Philips • Mary Sellers ■ *Dir* Michele Soavi • *Scr* Michele Soavi, George Eastman [Luigi Montefiori]

Stage Struck ★★★

Silent comedy 1925 · US · BW and Colour

Gloria Swanson threw off her famous *haute couture* clothes to star as a grease-stained waitress trying to become an actress via mail order lessons in order to hang on to her stage-struck boyfriend (Lawrence Gray). As directed by Allan Dwan, it's knockabout comedy, and even has Gloria at one moment wearing trousers – and dropping them. It was her last major hit for Paramount. RK

Gloria Swanson *Jennie Hagen* • Lawrence Gray *Orme Wilson* • Gertrude Astor *Lillian Lyons* • Marguerite Evans *Hilda Wagner* • Ford Sterling *Waldo Buck* ■ *Dir* Allan Dwan • *Scr* Forrest Halsey, Sylvia La Varre, from a story by Frank R Adams

Stage Struck ★ U

Musical comedy 1936 · US · BW · 93mins

Empty-headed Joan Blondell, with Broadway aspirations but no talent, backs a show but has problems with dance director Dick Powell (her real-life husband at the time). This miserable apology for a backstage musical was directed by Busby Berkeley but suffers from an almost total absence of music or dance numbers. The script is atrocious, and the comedy relief from Frank McHugh pathetic. RK

Dick Powell *George Randall* • Joan Blondell *Peggy Revere* • Warren William *Fred Harris* • Frank McHugh *Sid* • Jeanne Madden *Ruth Williams* • Carol Hughes *Grace* • Craig Reynolds *Gilmore Frost* • Hobart Cavanaugh *Wayne* • Spring Byington *Mrs Randall* ■ *Dir* Busby Berkeley • *Scr* Tom Buckingham, Pat C Flick, Warren Duff, from a story by Robert Lord • *Cinematographer* Byron Haskin

Stage Struck ★★★ U

Drama 1958 · US · Colour · 94mins

Interesting, sophisticated and compulsively watchable remake of *Morning Glory*, cleverly updated to the 1950s Broadway circuit and directed by Sidney Lumet. Susan Strasberg takes the lead, but isn't quite up to the demands of the role. Her distinguished co-stars include the brilliant Joan Greenwood, who has all the best dialogue as the temperamental actress Strasberg replaces. However, Henry Fonda and Christopher Plummer look as though they belong on Broadway, and the authentic use of Manhattan locations helps immensely. TS

Henry Fonda *Lewis Easton* • Susan Strasberg *Eva Lovelace* • Joan Greenwood *Rita Vernon* • Herbert Marshall *Robert Hedges* • Christopher Plummer *Joe Sheridan* • Daniel Ocko *Constantine* • Pat Harrington *Benny* • Frank Campanella *Victor* ■ *Dir* Sidney Lumet • *Scr* Ruth Goetz, Augustus Goetz, from the play *Morning Glory* by Zoe Akins

Stagecoach ★★★★★ U

Classic western 1939 · US · BW · 91mins

Orson Welles prepared for *Citizen Kane* by watching John Ford's masterpiece some 40 times. And why not, because this is textbook film-making by the only cinematic poet Hollywood ever produced. The plot is simplicity itself, but with just a few deft touches screenwriter Dudley Nichols creates a coachload of credible characters whose vices and virtues are not as apparent as they initially seem. Ford's first venture into Monument Valley was also his first picture starring John Wayne, the man with whom he would transform the very nature of the western. From Yakima Canutt's breathtaking stunts (although Wayne did most of his own) to the brilliant support playing, everything about this picture is perfection. DP [video]

John Wayne *Ringo Kid* • Claire Trevor *Dallas* • Thomas Mitchell *Dr Josiah Boone* • Andy Devine *Buck Rickabaugh, stagecoach driver* • John Carradine *Hatfield* • George Bancroft *Sheriff Curly Wilcox* • Louise Platt *Lucy Mallory* • Tim Holt *Lt Blanchard* • Chris-Pin Martin *Chris* • Donald Meek *Mr Samuel Peacock* ■ *Dir* John Ford • *Scr* Dudley Nichols, from the short story *Stage to Lordsburg* by Ernest Haycox • *Cinematographer* Bert Glennon

Stagecoach ★★

Western 1966 · US · Colour · 113mins

This remake of John Ford's revered classic is no masterpiece, but it's not a total disaster, either. The producers shrewdly decided against filming in Monument Valley, electing for the plains and mountains of Colorado instead. Alex Cord is certainly no John Wayne, but Van Heflin and Ann-Margret contribute solid performances. It's also notable as being Bing Crosby's final big-screen appearance. AT

Ann-Margret *Dallas* • Bing Crosby *Doc Boone* • Red Buttons *Mr Peacock* • Alex Cord *Ringo* • Van Heflin *Curly* • Michael Connors [Mike Connors] *Hatfield* • Bob Cummings [Robert Cummings] *Mr Gatewood* • Slim Pickens *Buck* • Stefanie Powers *Lucy Mallory* • Keenan Wynn *Luke Plummer* ■ *Dir* Gordon Douglas • *Scr* Joseph Landon, from the 1939 film by Dudley Nichols

Stagecoach Kid ★★ U

Western 1949 · US · BW · 59mins

A routine western spiced up with a cross-dressing subplot, as a rail magnate's daughter dons stetson and chaps to sneak away from her overbearing father. Actress Jeff (born Jean Marie) Donnell is the young woman in question, falling for stagecoach owner Tim Holt as he tries to keep her from the clutches of two of her father's crooked employees. Holt is an uninspired lead, and journeyman director Lew Landers brings nothing of note to the proceedings. RT

Tim Holt *Dave Collins* • Richard Martin (1) *Chito Rafferty* • Jeff Donnell *Jessie Arnold* • Joe Sawyer *Thatcher* • Thurston Hall *Arnold* • Carol Hughes *Birdie* • Robert Bray *Clint* • Robert B Williams *Parnell* ■ *Dir* Lew Landers • *Scr* Norman Houston, from his story

Stagecoach to Dancer's Rock ★★★

Western 1962 · US · BW · 72mins

An unprepossessing but interesting minor Universal western dealing with a tricky moral issue – the unceremonious dumping of six passengers from a stagecoach when it transpires that one of them has smallpox. Veteran western director Earl Bellamy makes the most of the film's short duration, and he's helped by the excellent performances of the under-rated Warren Stevens, "B" Jody Lawrence and the ineffable Martin Landau. A bigger budget might have helped, though. TS

Warren Stevens *Jess Dollard* • Martin Landau *Dade Coleman* • Jody Lawrence [Jody Lawrance] *Dr Ann Thompson* • Judy Dan *Loi Yan Wu* • Del Moore *Hiram Best* • Don Wilbanks *Major John Southern* • Bob Anderson *Carl Whip Mott* ■ *Dir* Earl Bellamy • *Scr* Kenneth Darling

Staggered ★★★ 15

Comedy 1993 · UK · Colour · 95mins

Martin Clunes's debut as actor/director is packed with neat cameos, tasty situations and well-timed gags. Yet it suffers from the cinematic equivalent of long stretches of motorway without a service station. Deposited on a Scottish island after his riotous stag night by a best man with designs on his bride, Clunes has to thumb his way across the country to make it to the church on time. Clunes is amiable, but the comedy is, occasionally, rather ridiculous. DP. Contains swearing, nudity. [video] DVD

Martin Clunes *Neil Price* • Michael Praed *Gary* • John Forgeham *Inspector Lubbock* • Anna Chancellor *Carmen Sfennipeg* • Sylvia Syms *Mother* • Sarah Winman *Hilary* • Griff Rhys Jones *Graham* • Michele Winstanley *Tina* • Kate Byers *Jackie* ■ *Dir* Martin Clunes • *Scr* Paul Alexander, Simon Braithwaite

Staircase ★

Comedy drama 1969 · UK · Colour · 97mins

The sight of Richard Burton and Rex Harrison – two of the most notorious serial husbands and womanisers in showbusiness – parading about as ageing homosexual hairdressers made for one of the silliest sights in 1960s cinema. Both are desperately miscast and act accordingly, trying hard not to be camp and failing completely. AT

Richard Burton *Harry Leeds* • Rex Harrison *Charlie Dyer* • Cathleen Nesbitt *Harry's mother* • Beatrix Lehmann *Charlie's mother* • Stephen Lewis *Jack* ■ *Dir* Stanley Donen • *Scr* Charles Dyer, from his play

S

Stakeout ★★★ 15

Comedy thriller 1987 · US · Colour · 112mins

The always watchable Richard Dreyfuss elevates this thriller above the norm. For all its attempts to up the comedy content of the *Lethal Weapon* pictures without cutting down on their violence, it manages to be both too abrasive for family viewing and too soft for the six-pack brigade. Emilio Estevez struggles with the verbal ping-pong, but Dreyfuss's scenes with Madeleine Stowe more than atone. Both Dreyfuss and Estevez reprised their roles in the sequel *Another Stakeout*. DP. Contains swearing, violence, sex scenes and nudity. [video] DVD

Richard Dreyfuss *Chris Leece* • Emilio Estevez *Bill Reimers* • Madeleine Stowe *Maria McGuire* • Aidan Quinn *Richard "Stick" Montgomery* • Dan Lauria *Phil Coldshank* • Forest Whitaker *Jack Pismo* • Ian Tracey *Caylor Reese* • Earl Billings *Captain Giles* ■ *Dir* John Badham • *Scr* Jim Kouf

Stakeout on Dope Street ★★

Crime drama 1958 · US · BW · 75mins

Irvin Kershner made his feature debut with this would-be gritty crime drama. Mark Jeffrey's monochrome images of urban decay provide a credible backdrop, but any authenticity the story might have had is sapped by the ponderous performances of Yale Wexler, Jonathan Haze and Morris Miller, as the trio of street kids who come into possession of a stash of heroin, only to be pursued by a drug dealer. Underwhelming. DP

Yale Wexler *Jim* • Jonathan Haze *Ves* • Morris Miller *Nick* • Abby Dalton *Kathy* • Allen Kramer *Danny* • Herman Rudin *Mitch* • Phillip A Mansour *Lenny* • Frank Harding *Captain Allen* ■ *Dir* Irvin Kershner • *Scr* Andrew J Fenady, Irvin Kershner, Irwin Schwartz

Stalag 17 ★★★★ PG

Second World War drama
1953 · US · BW · 115mins

William Holden won the best actor Oscar for his unsympathetic portrayal here of an imprisoned opportunist in a German PoW camp – an emotive subject just eight years after the end of the Second World War. Director Billy Wilder superbly balances elements of drama, satire and comedy, and captures the claustrophobia of camp life, aided by fine performances from inmates Robert Strauss and Harvey Lembeck, both of whom were veterans of the tale's original Broadway run. Director Otto Preminger is mesmerising as a nasty Nazi. TS [video] DVD

William Holden (2) *Sefton* • Don Taylor *Dunbar* • Otto Preminger *Oberst Von Scherbach* • Robert Strauss *Stosh* • Harvey Lembeck *Harry* • Neville Brand *Duke* • Richard Erdman *Hoffy* • Peter Graves (2) *Price* • Gil Stratton Jr [Gil Stratton] *Cookie* • Jay Lawrence *Bagradian* • Sig Rumann [Sig Ruman] *Schultz* ■ *Dir* Billy Wilder • *Scr* Billy Wilder, Edwin Blum, from the play by Donald Bevan, Edmund Trzcinski

Stalingrad ★★★ 15

Second World War drama
1992 · Ger · Colour · 132mins

Produced to coincide with the 50th anniversary of the Soviet rearguard that cost the Nazis all but 6,000 of their besieging army, Joseph Vilsmaier's combat epic makes its points about the barbarity and futility of war through the sheer scale of the enterprise. However, the lack of a human focus for our horror and pity reduces the impact of the impeccably-reconstructed battle sequences. Mightily impressive, but insufficiently involving or cautionary. DP. A German language film. [video] DVD

Thomas Kretschmann *Hans* • Dominique Horwitz *Fritz* • Jochen Nickel *Rollo* • Karel Hermanek *Musk* • Dana Vavrova *Irina* • Sebastian Rudolph *GeGe* • Martin Benrath *General Hentz* • Sylvester Groth *Otto* ■ *Dir* Joseph Vilsmaier • *Scr* Johannes Heide, Jurgen Buscher, Joseph Vilsmaier

Stalker ★★★★ PG

Science-fiction drama
1979 · USSR · Colour and BW · 154mins

Andrei Tarkovsky could always be relied upon for visual lyricism, but the terrain traversed during this gruelling trek is anything but picturesque. Chillingly shot in muted colour by Aleksandr Knyazhinsky, the Zone is an area of the post-meteoric wilderness that can only be crossed by "stalkers" such as Aleksandr Kaidanovsky. He is hired to guide writer Anatoli Solonitsyn and professor Nikolai Grinko to the "Room", a place in which truth and innermost desire can be attained. The metaphysical discussion feels somewhat mundane after what has gone before, but this still leaves you questioning your own beliefs and values. DP. In Russian with English subtitles. [video] DVD

Alexander Kaidanovsky *Stalker* • Anatoly Solonitsin [Anatoli Solonitsyn] *Writer* • Nikolai Grinko *Professor* • Alisa Freindlikh *Stalker's wife* • Natasha Abramova *Stalker's daughter* ■ *Dir* Andrei Tarkovsky • *Scr* Arkady Strugatsky, Boris Strugatsky, from the book *Picnic by the Roadside* by Arkady Strugatsky

Stalking Laura ★★ 15

Thriller based on a true story
1993 · US · Colour · 91mins

In this TV true-story tale Brooke Shields stars as a whizzkid at a California electronics company who becomes an obsession in the fixated mind of a colleague. Shields makes a decent fist of a tricky role and Richard Thomas is sinister as her creepy workmate, but director Michael Switzer, while delivering efficient thrills, never gets a handle on the psychological depths of his characters. JM. Contains violence. DVD

Richard Thomas *Richard Farley* • Brooke Shields *Laura Black* • Viveka Davis *Mary Ann* • William Allen Young *Chris* • Richard Yniguez *Lt Grijalva* • Scott Bryce *Sam Waters* ■ *Dir* Michael Switzer • *Scr* Frank Abatemarco

The Stalking Moon ★★

Western 1968 · US · Colour · 109mins

Charles Lang's Panavision landscape photography is the redeeming feature in this western, but the pacing leaves much to be desired. Gregory Peck is dull as the scout who agrees to lead Eva Marie Saint and her half-Apache son to safety. The boy's father has other ideas. The screenplay fails to convey the threat. TS

Gregory Peck *Sam Varner* • Eva Marie Saint *Sarah Carver* • Robert Forster *Nick Tana* • Noland Clay *Boy* • Russell Thorson *Ned* • Frank Silvera *Major* • Lonny Chapman *Purdue* • Lou Frizzell *Stationmaster* ■ *Dir* Robert Mulligan • *Scr* Alvin Sargent, Wendell Mayes, from the novel by Theodore V Olsen

Stamboul Quest ★★★

First World War spy romance
1934 · US · BW · 86mins

This espionage drama is conducted in shadows courtesy of some moody lighting by the ace cameraman James Wong Howe. Myrna Loy plays a German spy who claims to have ended Mata Hari's career, but in Istanbul she breaks her own rule by falling in love – with US medical student George Brent – right in the middle of the First World War. There's a preposterous ending, but fans of 1930s Hollywood will find much to enjoy. AT

Myrna Loy *Annemarie/Fräulein Doktor/Helena Bohlen* • George Brent *Douglas Beall* • Lionel Atwill *Von Strum* • C Henry Gordon *Ali Bey* • Douglass Dumbrille *General* • Mischa Auer *Ameel* ■ *Dir* Sam Wood • *Scr* Herman Mankiewicz, from a story by Leo Birinski

Stand Alone ★★ 18

Action drama 1985 · US · Colour · 89mins

In an effort to mount a vigilante thriller where the hero doesn't look as if he chews metal as a hobby, director Alan Beattie has made his righteous avenger (Charles Durning) so ordinary and so overweight that he looks incapable of anything other than watching TV. The film never recovers from this grave central flaw. Durning deserves better material, as does his co-star Pam Grier. JM [video]

Charles Durning *Louis Thibido* • Pam Grier *Catherine* • James Keach *Isgro* • Bert Remsen *Paddie* • Barbara Sammeth *Meg* ■ *Dir* Alan Beattie • *Scr* Roy Carlson

Stand and Deliver ★★★★ PG

Drama based on a true story
1988 · US · Colour · 98mins

A real heart-lifter from Edward James Olmos, who stars in this LA *barrio* tale that he also helped power into existence. Based on the true story of teacher Jaime Escalante (Olmos), who transformed a classroom full of disaffected young gang members into such a top-scoring exam team that the examination board refused to believe it and made them sit everything again. Olmos gives an infectious, driven performance that carries everyone else along. SH. Contains swearing. [video]

Edward James Olmos *Jaime Escalante* • Lou Diamond Phillips *Angel* • Rosana De Soto *Fabiola Escalante* • Andy Garcia *Dr Ramirez* • Virginia Paris *Chairwoman Raquel Ortega* • Carmen Argenziano *Principal Molina* • Mark Eliot *Tito* ■ *Dir* Ramon Menendez • *Scr* Ramon Menendez, Tom Musca

The Stand at Apache River ★★ U

Western 1953 · US · Colour · 76mins

A very ordinary Universal western using up stock sets and contract artists with little real distinction. There are colourful support turns from two newcomers who would soon flourish in TV's golden age of westerns, Hugh O'Brian and Jack Kelly, but the leads sheriff Stephen McNally and fiancée Julia (later Julie) Adams just go through the motions, unaided by Lee Sholem's pedestrian direction. TS

Stephen McNally *Sheriff Lane Dakota* • Julia Adams [Julie Adams] *Valerie Kendrick* • Hugh Marlowe *Colonel Morsby* • Jaclynne Greene *Ann Kenyon* • Hugh O'Brian *Tom Kenyon* • Russell Johnson *Greiner* • Jack Kelly *Hatcher* ■ *Dir* Lee Sholem • *Scr* Arthur Ross, from the novel *Apache Landing* by Robert J Hogan

Stand by for Action ★★

Second World War drama
1942 · US · BW · 100mins

Despite being co-written by Herman J Mankiewicz (of *Citizen Kane* fame) and boasting the heavyweight lustre of Charles Laughton, the story of snooty Harvard graduate Robert Taylor coming to terms with the gritty reality of life on an ancient destroyer is as much junk as the ship itself. Sentimentality waterlogs the studio-harboured craft in this soggy drama. TH

Robert Taylor (1) *Lt Gregg Mastermann* • Charles Laughton *Rear Adm Stephan "Iron Pants" Thomas* • Brian Donlevy *Lt Comdr Martin J Roberts* • Walter Brennan *Chief Yeoman Henry Johnson* • Marilyn Maxwell *Audrey Carr* ■ *Dir* Robert Z Leonard • *Scr* George Bruce, John L Balderston, Herman J Mankiewicz, from a story by Capt Harvey Haislip, RC Sherriff, from the story *A Cargo of Innocence* by Laurence Kirk

Stand by Me ★★★★★ 15

Drama 1986 · US · Colour · 84mins

Rob Reiner made his name as a director with his debut feature, the satirical *This Is Spinal Tap*, and proved his versatility two years later with this coming-of-age drama. It's a smart, sensitive, 1950s-set tale taken from the unlikely source of Stephen King's story *The Body*. The rich dialogue and the intelligent performances, from the likes of Wil Wheaton and River Phoenix, are a joy to behold as four school friends set out to find the corpse of a missing boy. JM. Contains violence and swearing. [video] DVD

Wil Wheaton *Gordie Lachance* • River Phoenix *Chris Chambers* • Corey Feldman *Teddy Duchamp* • Jerry O'Connell *Vern Tessio* • Richard Dreyfuss *The writer* • Kiefer Sutherland *Ace Merrill* • Casey Siemaszko *Billy Tessio* • Gary Riley *Charlie Hogan* • Bradley Gregg *Eyeball Chambers* • John Cusack *Denny Lachance* ■ *Dir* Rob Reiner • *Scr* Raynold Gideon, Bruce A Evans, from the story *The Body* by Stephen King

Stand-In ★★★ U

Satirical comedy 1937 · US · BW · 86mins

A funny and perceptive Hollywood-set tale about the dangers of non-film people involving themselves in making movies. Leslie Howard stars as an accountant sent west to audit the books of the fictional Colossal Studios, with the titular stand-in played by Joan Blondell, whose career is being guided by producer Humphrey Bogart. It's an independent satire produced by Walter Wanger, whose views on labour relations in Los Angeles as depicted here are still relevant today. The second half doesn't really live up to the wacky initial premise. TS [video]

Leslie Howard *Atterbury Dodd* • Joan Blondell *Lester Plum* • Humphrey Bogart *Douglas Quintain* • Alan Mowbray *Koslofski* • Marla Shelton *Thelma Cheri* • C Henry Gordon *Ivor Nassau* • Jack Carson *Tom Potts* ■ *Dir* Tay Garnett • *Scr* Gene Towne, Graham Baker, from a story by Clarence Budington Kelland in *The Saturday Evening Post*

Stand Up and Cheer! ★★ U

Musical 1934 · US · BW · 81mins

Broadway theatrical producer Warner Baxter is summoned to Washington by the president of the USA and appointed "Secretary of Entertainment" with a brief to cheer up a Depression-weary nation. This is the excuse for a revue featuring various musical entertainers and comedians, including a performing penguin, but the film is remembered for the attention it brought a four-year-old moppet named Shirley Temple. Relentlessly cheerful and cheerily propagandistic. RK

Warner Baxter *Lawrence Cromwell* • Madge Evans *Mary Adams* • Nigel Bruce *Eustace Dinwiddie* • Stepin Fetchit *Stepin Fetchit/George Bernard Shaw* • Frank Melton *Fosdick* • Lila Lee *Zelda* • Ralph Morgan *Secretary to the President* • Frank Mitchell *Senator Danforth* • Shirley Temple *Shirley Dugan* ■ *Dir* Hamilton MacFadden • *Scr* Lew Brown, Ralph Spence, Rian James, Edward T Lowe Jr, Malcolm Stuart Boylan, Hamilton MacFadden, from an idea by Will Rogers, Philip Klein

Stand Up Virgin Soldiers ★★ 15

Comedy 1977 · UK · Colour · 87mins

Writer Leslie Thomas revisits his Malayan war memoirs but this time the result is more akin to "Confessions of a National Serviceman". Nigel Davenport returns from the original *The Virgin Soldiers*, but Robin Askwith is a crude substitute for Hywel Bennett and the lavatorial humour sits uneasily alongside the stabs at drama. JF [video]

Robin Askwith *Private Brigg* • George Layton *Private Jacobs* • Pamela Stephenson *Bernice* • Lynda Bellingham *Valerie* • Edward Woodward *Sergeant Wellbeloved* • Nigel Davenport *Sergent Driscoll* • John Le Mesurier *Colonel Bromley-Pickering* • Warren Mitchell *Morris Morris* • Irene Handl *Mrs Phillimore* • Miriam Margolyes *Elephant Ethel* ■ *Dir* Norman Cohen • *Scr* Leslie Thomas, from his novel

Stander ★★★ 15

Drama based on a true story
2003 · Can/Ger/S Afr/UK · Colour · 112mins

Thomas Jane stars as Andre Stander, a Johannesburg police captain who, in 1976, suffered a crisis of conscience after killing an unarmed black man during a political protest. Turning his back on the brutal system, Stander turned from cop to crook, committing a string of bold bank robberies and becoming an unlikely anti-establishment hero in the process. The film's sense of time and place is excellent, as is the acting, but it's flawed by sluggish pacing and apparent indecision as to whether this is an action film or a character drama. DA. In English and Afrikaans with subtitles. Contains swearing, sex scenes and violence.

Thomas Jane *Andre Stander* • Dexter Fletcher *Lee McCall* • David Patrick O'Hara [David O'Hara] *Allan Heyl* • Deborah Kara Unger *Bekkie Stander* • Ashley Taylor *Cor Van Deventer* • Marius Weyers *General Stander* • At Botha *General Viljoen* ■ *Dir* Bronwen Hughes • *Scr* Bronwen Hughes, Bima Stagg, from a story by Bima Stagg

Standing in the Shadows of Motown ★★★ PG

Documentary 2002 · US · Colour · 103mins

Packed with anecdote and insight, this documentary pays overdue tribute to the unheralded session musicians who created the unique Tamla Motown sound. What's remarkable about the Funk Brothers is their equanimity towards missing out on the fame and fortune that befell the label's biggest stars. They are also generous in their praise for the contribution of deceased members such as Benny Benjamin and James Jamerson, who were remarkable characters as well as pioneering artists. What doesn't quite ring true, however, is the contention that the musicianship is so impeccable that anyone could sing these legendary 1960s hits, as the disappointing reunion concert testifies. DP DVD

André Braugher *Narrator* • Jack "Black Jack" Ashford • Bob Babbitt • Johnny Griffith • Uriel Jones • Joe Messina • Eddie "Chank" Willis ■ *Dir* Paul Justman • *Scr* Walter Dallas, Ntozake Shange, from the book by Allan "Dr Licks" Slutsky

Standing Room Only ★★ U

Romantic comedy 1944 · US · BW · 82mins

Fred MacMurray is an executive arriving in town in the hope of landing a government contract for his factory. Paulette Goddard is his inept secretary who bungles their accommodation, forcing them to take up work as husband-and-wife servants for somewhere to sleep. The comic highlight is probably MacMurray's efforts – while serving fruit salad – to retrieve a cherry that's dropped into a guest's lap without her noticing. Poorly written and contrived. AE

Paulette Goddard *Jane Rogers* • Fred MacMurray *Lee Stevens* • Edward Arnold *TJ Todd* • Roland Young *Ira Cromwell* • Hillary Brooke *Alice Todd* • Porter Hall *Hugo Farenhall* • Clarence Kolb *Glen Ritchie* ■ *Dir* Sidney Lanfield • *Scr* Darrell Ware, Karl Tunberg, from a story by Al Martin

Stanley & Iris ★★★ 15

Drama 1989 · US · Colour · 100mins

Although virtually unrecognisable from Pat Barker's source novel *Union Street*, this well meaning blue-collar drama is carried by striking performances from Robert De Niro and Jane Fonda. De Niro is the uneducated factory worker who is slowly drawn out of his shell by recently widowed Fonda. Martin Ritt's direction is curiously anonymous and if it weren't for the cast, this would be little more than just another "issue of the week" TV movie. However, the two stars are on top form, as are the supporting players. JF. Contains swearing. DVD

Jane Fonda *Iris King* • Robert De Niro *Stanley Cox* • Swoosie Kurtz *Sharon* • Martha Plimpton *Kelly King* • Harley Cross *Richard* • Jamey Sheridan *Joe* • Feodor Chaliapin [Feodor Chaliapin Jr] *Leonides Cox* • Zohra Lampert *Elaine* ■ *Dir* Martin Ritt • *Scr* Harriet Frank Jr, Irving Ravetch, from the novel *Union Street* by Pat Barker

Stanley and Livingstone ★★★★ U

Historical adventure
1939 · US · BW · 100mins

This is one of the best 20th Century-Fox historical biopics, despite necessary tamperings with history to enable the inclusion of one of the most famous greetings in history. Avoiding any sense of parody whatsoever are the two fine main performances: the redoubtable Spencer Tracy as an obsessed, fever-ridden Henry Morton Stanley, and Cedric Hardwicke, genuinely convincing as Dr Livingstone. Director Henry King is in his element, but he would have been surprised to see much footage from this film in *Monster from Green Hell* nearly 20 years later. TS

Spencer Tracy *Henry M Stanley* • Nancy Kelly *Eve Kingsley* • Richard Greene *Gareth Tyce* • Walter Brennan *Jeff Slocum* • Charles Coburn *Lord Tyce* • Cedric Hardwicke *Dr David Livingstone* • Henry Hull *James Gordon Bennett Jr* • Henry Travers *John Kingsley* ■ *Dir* Henry King • *Scr* Philip Dunne, Julien Josephson, from research and story outline by Hal Long, Sam Hellman

Stanley's Magic Garden ★★ U

Animated musical fantasy
1994 · US · Colour · 72mins

This instantly forgettable animated fantasy from Don Bluth (also known as *A Troll in Central Park*) geared towards a young audience is a sickly sweet tale about a benevolent troll with an overactive green finger who's banished to New York's Central Park. The voice cast is good, though. JC DVD

Dom DeLuise *Stanley* • Cloris Leachman *Queen Gnorga* • Phillip Glasser *Gus* • Tawney Sunshine Glover *Rosie* • Hayley Mills *Hilary* • Jonathan Pryce *Alan* ■ *Dir* Gary Goldman, Don Bluth • *Scr* Stu Krieger

The Star ★★★

Drama 1953 · US · BW · 90mins

The star is Bette Davis, three years after *All about Eve*, in a role with which she clearly identifies, as an over-the-hill movie star. This is a relatively low-budget independent feature, which gains great strength from the casting of Davis and Sterling Hayden, a pillar of integrity as her admirer. There's nice work, too, from a young and precocious Natalie Wood. Despite a few over-the-top scenes this minor movie echoes with a ring of truth. TS

Bette Davis *Margaret Elliot* • Sterling Hayden *Jim Johannson* • Natalie Wood *Gretchen* • Warner Anderson *Harry Stone* • Minor Watson *Joe Morrison* • June Travis *Phyllis Stone* • Katherine Warren *Mrs Morrison* ■ *Dir* Stuart Heisler • *Scr* Katherine Albert, Dale Eunson

Star! ★★ U

Biographical musical
1968 · US · Colour · 165mins

Julie Andrews spends nearly three mind-boggling hours trying to convince us that she is the stage star Gertrude Lawrence. Daniel Massey does a rather better job portraying Noël Coward (his godfather in real life). Some believe Andrews is a deeply under-rated actress while others think she can only portray herself. If you tend towards the latter view, then this is tedious fare, saved only by some spectacular production numbers. SH DVD

Julie Andrews *Gertrude Lawrence* • Richard Crenna *Richard Aldrich* • Michael Craig *Sir Anthony Spencer* • Daniel Massey *Noël Coward* • Robert Reed *Charles Fraser* • Bruce Forsyth *Arthur Lawrence* • Beryl Reid *Rose* • Jenny Agutter *Pamela* ■ *Dir* Robert Wise • *Scr* William Fairchild

The Star Chamber ★★★ 15

Thriller 1983 · US · Colour · 104mins

This gripping thriller revolves around the moral dilemma of a young judge having to free dangerous criminals because of legal technicalities. As a result, he discovers the existence of the "Star Chamber", a legal vigilante committee that takes the law into its own hands. The drawn-out storyline ultimately fails to convince, and Michael Douglas in the leading role is too inexperienced (at that time) as an actor to bring it off. Director Peter Hyams does well enough, despite having to film on confined sets. TS. Contains swearing and violence.

Michael Douglas *Steven R Hardin* • Hal Holbrook *Benjamin Caulfield* • Yaphet Kotto *Detective Harry Lowes* • Sharon Gless *Emily Hardin* • James B Sikking *Dr Harold Lewin* • Joe Regalbuto *Arthur Cooms* ■ *Dir* Peter Hyams • *Scr* Roderick Taylor, Peter Hyams, from a story by Roderick Taylor

Star Dust ★★★ U

Drama 1940 · US · BW · 85mins

Walter Lang directs Linda Darnell in this tale of the struggles and disappointments suffered by an attractive young woman spotted by a Hollywood talent scout, only to be turned down by the studio boss. About to go home, she meets and falls in love with former singing football star John Payne, who pushes her into persevering. A familiar tale to be sure, but well told here with an unromantic air of authenticity that convinces. RK

Linda Darnell *Carolyn Sayres* • John Payne *Bud Borden* • Roland Young *Thomas Brooke* • Charlotte Greenwood *Lola Langdon* • William Gargan *Dane Wharton* • Mary Beth Hughes *June Lawrence* • Mary Healy *Mary Andrews* • Donald Meek *Sam Wellman* ■ *Dir* Walter Lang • *Scr* Robert Ellis, Helen Logan, from a story by Jesse Malo, Kenneth Earl, Ivan Kahn

Star 80 ★★★★ 18

Biographical drama
1983 · US · Colour · 98mins

The true story of Canadian *Playboy* playmate-turned-Hollywood actress Dorothy Stratten who was on the verge of stardom when she was murdered by her small-time hustler husband Paul Snider. Director Bob Fosse's last movie is a disturbing look at the high cost of fame. Stratten is brilliantly portrayed by Mariel Hemingway (complete with breast enlargements), but it's Eric Roberts as her psychotically jealous mentor/spouse who registers the strongest impact. A downbeat and dark fairy tale of Tinseltown's tarnished ethics. AJ

Mariel Hemingway *Dorothy Stratten* • Eric Roberts *Paul Snider* • Cliff Robertson *Hugh Hefner* • Carroll Baker *Dorothy's mother* • Roger Rees *Aram Nicholas* • David Clennon *Geb* • Josh Mostel *Private detective* ■ *Dir* Bob Fosse • *Scr* Bob Fosse, from the story *Death of a Playmate* by Teresa Carpenter

Star in the Dust ★★★★ U

Western 1956 · US · Colour · 80mins

A very fine but generally under-rated western. Produced by *Touch of Evil's* Albert Zugsmith and directed by Charles Haas, this taut film contains its action between twilight and dawn as sheriff John Agar gets ready to hang killer Richard Boone, while Boone's hired guns (at the behest of banker villain Leif Erickson) menace the town. Sultry 1950s icon (and Zugsmith veteran) Mamie Van Doren is Agar's gal and – to add to the plot – Erickson's relation. Watch closely for a very young Clint Eastwood. TS

John Agar *Sheriff Bill Jorden* • Mamie Van Doren *Ellen Ballard* • Richard Boone *Sam Hall* • Coleen Gray *Nellie Mason* • Leif Erickson *George Ballard* • James Gleason *Orval Jones* • Randy Stuart *Nan Hogan* • Clint Eastwood ■ *Dir* Charles Haas • *Scr* Oscar Brodney, from the novel *Law Man* by Lee Leighton

A Star Is Born ★★★★ U

Drama 1937 · US · Colour · 110mins

One of the most famous movie titles of all time in its second incarnation (the first was called *What Price Hollywood?*), with Janet Gaynor as the young star on the way up and Fredric March as the ageing star on the way out in Tinseltown. Gaynor and March are superb and Hollywood itself is well depicted in early three-strip Technicolor. The now classic screenplay by Dorothy Parker and husband Alan Campbell, among others, is still caustic and vibrant, and, of course, contains one of the greatest last lines in all cinema. TS DVD

Janet Gaynor *Esther Blodgett/Vicki Lester* • Fredric March *Norman Maine* • Adolphe Menjou *Oliver Niles* • May Robson *Lettie, Grandmother Blodgett* • Andy Devine *Danny McGuire* • Lionel Stander *Matt Libby* • Owen Moore *Casey Burke* • Peggy Wood *Miss Phillips, Central Casting Corp clerk* • Elizabeth Jenns *Anita Regis* ■ *Dir* William A Wellman • *Scr* Dorothy Parker, Alan Campbell, Robert Carson, William A Wellman, Ring Lardner Jr, Bud Schulberg, John Le Mahin, from a story by Robert Carson, William A Wellman

A Star Is Born ★★★★★ U

Musical drama 1954 · US · Colour · 167mins

One of the most outstanding melodramas in Hollywood's history, this remake contains the greatest ever performance by the lustrous Judy Garland, paired with the brilliant James Mason at the very zenith of their talents. Their portrayals, plus superb direction from George Cukor, ensure that this film enriches more lives each time it is screened. But on first release, the movie was overlong, and was trimmed. In the 1980s some of this missing material was discovered, with other scenes re-created using stills. This "restoration", though of historical value, may alienate a first-time viewer. In any case, this stunner superbly portrays Hollywood at its self-centred best. When Judy Garland lost that year's Oscar to Grace Kelly (for *The Country Girl*), Groucho Marx quipped, "It's the biggest robbery since Brink's!". TS DVD

Judy Garland *Esther Blodgett/Vicki Lester* • James Mason *Norman Maine* • Jack Carson *Matt Libby* • Charles Bickford *Oliver Niles* • Tommy Noonan *Danny McGuire* • Lucy Marlow *Lola Lavery* • Amanda Blake *Susan Ettinger* • Irving Bacon *Graves* • Hazel Shermet *Miss Wheeler* • James Brown (1) *Glenn Williams* ■ *Dir* George Cukor • *Scr* Moss Hart, from the 1937 film • *Cinematographer* Sam Leavitt

A Star Is Born ★★ 15

Musical drama 1976 · US · Colour · 133mins

This remake, starring Barbra Streisand and Kris Kristofferson as the star-crossed lovers on self-destruct, doesn't quite work, They tried to bring the action screechingly up to date with a contemporary rock soundtrack, but there's little finesse as everyone rushes around in 1970s gear that already looked pretty dated on release. The movie's basic problem is that we simply cannot believe that Streisand and Kristofferson are in the throes of a passionate love affair. SH. Contains swearing and brief nudity.

Barbra Streisand *Esther Hoffman* • Kris Kristofferson *John Norman Howard* • Gary Busey *Bobby Ritchie* • Oliver Clark *Gary Danziger* • Marta Heflin *Quentin* • MG Kelly *Bebe Jesus* • Sally Kirkland *Photographer* • Paul Mazursky *Brian* ■ *Dir* Frank Pierson • *Scr* John Gregory Dunne, Joan Didion, Frank Pierson, from the 1937 film

S

Star Kid ★★★ PG

Science-fiction adventure
1997 · US · Colour · 96mins

Joseph Mazzello gives an engaging performance as an ignored and bullied child who isn't having much luck with girls, either. In a scrap yard he comes across a combat-enhancement suit (with its own intelligence) from an alien race. Cyborsuit takes everything Mazzello says literally, providing much amusement, and the rest of the movie serves up enough action to satisfy the kids and their parents. KB

Joseph Mazzello *Spencer Griffith* • Richard Gilliland *Roland Griffith* • Corinne Bohrer *Janet Holloway* • Alex Daniels *Cyborsuit* • Joey Simmrin *Turbo Bruntley* • Ashlee Levitch *Stacey Griffith* • Jack McGee *Hank Bruntley* ■ *Dir/Scr* Manny Coto

The Star Maker ★★ U

Musical drama 1939 · US · BW · 93mins

This minor musical drama stars Bing Crosby as a showman and songwriter, inspired by the career of Gus Edwards (who discovered Eddie Cantor among others). Failed singer Edwards, forced to work as a store salesman, hits on the idea of setting up a vaudeville act with youngsters. Success is cut short when he falls foul of child labour laws, but he then turns to the new medium of radio. Crosby dispenses easy charm and croons a handful of numbers. RK

Bing Crosby *Larry Earl* • Linda Ware *Jane Gray* • Louise Campbell *Mary* • Ned Sparks *"Speed" King* • Walter Damrosch • Laura Hope Crews *Carlotta Salvina* • Thurston Hall *Mr Proctor* ■ *Dir* Roy Del Ruth • *Scr* Frank Butler, Don Hartman, Arthur Caesar, from a story by Arthur Caesar, William A Pierce

Star Maps ★★★★

Drama 1997 · US · Colour · 90mins

This is a sordid, surreal, yet curiously sympathetic study of immigrant exploitation, familial dysfunction and male prostitution. In revealing the flip side of Hollywood life, debut director Miguel Arteta recognises the parallels with the ruthless world of glamour by having Mexican pimp Efrain Figueroa order his boys to sell maps of the stars' houses as a front for their activities, while Figueroa's son, Douglas Spain, an aspiring actor, regards each trick as a Method opportunity. DP

Douglas Spain *Carlos* • Efrain Figueroa *Pepe* • Kandeyce Jorden *Jennifer* • Martha Velez *Teresa* • Lysa Flores *Maria* • Annette Murphy *Letti* • Robin Thomas *Martin* • Vincent Chandler *Juancito* ■ *Dir* Miguel Arteta • *Scr* Miguel Arteta, from a story by Matthew Greenfield

Star of India ★ U

Period swashbuckling adventure
1954 · UK · Colour · 92mins

A virtually unwatchable swashbuckler, with Cornel Wilde as the French nobleman who, stripped of his estates, starts a search for a priceless jewel. Jean Wallace isn't stripped of anything but tags along anyway. Herbert Lom hisses like a panto villain and seems to have an unhealthy relationship with his Siamese cats. AT

Cornel Wilde *Pierre St Laurent* • Jean Wallace *Katrina* • Herbert Lom *Narbonne* • Yvonne Sanson *Madame De Montespan* • John Slater *Emile* • Walter Rilla *Van Horst* • Basil Sydney *King Louis XIV* ■ *Dir* Arthur Lubin • *Scr* Herbert Dalmas, Denis Freeman

Star of Midnight ★★★

Mystery comedy 1935 · US · BW · 89mins

Capitalising on William Powell's success in *The Thin Man*, RKO plagiarised the attributes of both the Nick Charles character and the actor himself, casting him as a witty and debonair lawyer. Nicely directed by Stephen Roberts, this comedy suspenser sees Powell trying to prove himself innocent of the murder of a gossip columnist by turning sleuth, with the assistance of his girlfriend Ginger Rogers. A characteristic 1930s mixture of cops, criminals, and cocktails – sophisticated and entertaining. RK

William Powell *Clay Dalzell* • Ginger Rogers *Donna Mantin* • Paul Kelly (1) *Jimmy Kinland* • Gene Lockhart *Horace Swayne* • Ralph Morgan *Roger Classon* • Leslie Fenton *Tim Winthrop* • J Farrell MacDonald *Inspector Doremus* • Russell Hopton *Tommy Tennant* ■ *Dir* Stephen Roberts • *Scr* Howard J Green, Anthony Veiller, Edward Kaufman, from the novel *Star of Midnight* by Arthur Somers Roche

The Star Packer ★★ U

Western 1934 · US · BW · 53mins

This John Wayne programme filler for Monogram has a ludicrous plot about a mysterious "Shadow" who traverses the town via an underground tunnel is made palatable by sprightly casting: George Hayes, and the friendly Indian, played by ace stuntman Yakima Canutt, usually cast as the heavy in these B-movies. TS DVD

John Wayne *John Travers* • Verna Hillie *Anita Matlock* • George "Gabby" Hayes *Matt Matlock* • Yakima Canutt *Yak* • Earl Dwire *Mason* • Ed Parker [Eddie Parker] *Parker* • George Cleveland *Old Jake* • William Franey *Pete* ■ *Dir/Scr* Robert N Bradbury

Star Spangled Rhythm ★★★ U

Musical comedy 1942 · US · BW · 100mins

One of the better wartime revue-format shows, for which Paramount corralled just about everybody on the payroll. The screwy premise for the musical and comedy extravaganza is the impending visit of a sailor on leave (Eddie Bracken), who believes that his Paramount gateman father (Victor Moore) is really the studio's executive vice-president. Encouraged by switchboard operator Betty Hutton, Moore pretends he is the studio head, whereupon the mighty organisation co-operates in the deception and stages a show for Bracken and his pals. RK

Bing Crosby • Bob Hope *Master of Ceremonies* • Fred MacMurray *Man playing cards* • Ray Milland *Man playing cards* • Franchot Tone *Man playing cards* • Victor Moore *"Pop" Webster/"Bronco Billy"* • Dorothy Lamour • Paulette Goddard • Veronica Lake • Vera Zorina • Mary Martin • Dick Powell • Betty Hutton *Polly Judson* • Eddie Bracken *Johnny Webster* • Alan Ladd *Scarface* • William Bendix *Husband* • Macdonald Carey *Louie the Lug* • Walter Abel *BG De Soto* • Susan Hayward *Genevieve* • Cecil B DeMille • Preston Sturges • Anne Revere *Sarah* ■ *Dir* George Marshall • *Scr* Harry Tugend, Arthur Phillips, George Kaufman, Arthur Ross, Fred Saidy, Norman Panama, Melvin Frank • *Music/lyrics* Harold Arlen, Johnny Mercer

Star Trek: the Motion Picture ★★★ U

Science-fiction adventure
1979 · US · Colour · 138mins

Dubbed "The Slow Motion Picture" when it was first released, it is rather talky, yet the long-delayed big-screen debut of the cult TV series hits epic heights fans can't fail to be moved by. Director Robert Wise purposely went for *2001* grandeur rather than *Star Wars* mock heroics in an effort to give the beloved characters an enduring film career beyond TV repeats. And it worked, as time has shown, despite the plot merely combining *The Changeling* and *The Doomsday Machine* episodes in one glorious space glob. AJ DVD

William Shatner *Admiral James T Kirk* • Leonard Nimoy *Mr Spock* • DeForest Kelley *Dr Leonard "Bones" McCoy* • Stephen Collins *Commander Willard Decker* • Persis Khambatta *Ilia* • James Doohan *Scotty* • George Takei *Sulu* • Nichelle Nichols *Uhura* • Walter Koenig *Chekov* • Majel Barrett *Dr Christine Chapel* ■ *Dir* Robert Wise • *Scr* Harold Livingston, Gene Roddenberry, from a story by Alan Dean Foster, from the TV series created by Gene Roddenberry

Star Trek II: the Wrath of Khan ★★★★ 12

Science-fiction adventure
1982 · US · Colour · 111mins

The big screen sequel to the 1967 TV episode *Space Seed* is truer in spirit to the beloved space opera than the first feature. Here, genetic superman Ricardo Montalban wreaks vengeance against the *Enterprise* crew for sending him to a prison colony. Director Nicholas Meyer stresses the narrative values that made the original series so compelling and vibrantly weaves the thematic motifs of life, loss and adventure together as he expertly continues the saga. Leonard Nimoy has rarely been so moving. AJ. Contains violence. DVD

William Shatner *Admiral James T Kirk* • Leonard Nimoy *Spock* • DeForest Kelley *Dr Leonard "Bones" McCoy* • James Doohan *Scotty* • Walter Koenig *Chekov* • George Takei *Sulu* • Nichelle Nichols *Commander Uhura* • Bibi Besch *Dr Carol Marcus* • Merritt Butrick *David* • Paul Winfield *Captain Terrell* • Kirstie Alley *Saavik* • Ricardo Montalban *Khan* ■ *Dir* Nicholas Meyer • *Scr* Jack B Sowards, from a story by Harve Bennett, Jack B Sowards, from the TV series created by Gene Roddenberry

Star Trek III: the Search for Spock ★★★ PG

Science-fiction adventure
1984 · US · Colour · 100mins

There are no real surprises in this ponderous journey to the final frontier, in which Admiral Kirk hijacks the starship *Enterprise* to help in the rejuvenation of the deceased Spock on the planet Genesis. It's a good character-driven story, marred by Leonard Nimoy's workmanlike direction, a pseudo-mystical ending and an all-pervasive funereal tone. Amazing special effects supply the wonder and emotional charge missing from what is nothing more than a bloated TV episode. AJ DVD

William Shatner *Admiral James T Kirk* • DeForest Kelley *Dr Leonard "Bones" McCoy* • James Doohan *Scotty* • George Takei *Sulu* • Walter Koenig *Chekov* • Nichelle Nichols *Uhura* • Christopher Lloyd *Kruge* • Robin Curtis *Lieutenant Saavik* • Merritt Butrick *David Marcus* • James B Sikking *Captain Styles* • Mark Lenard *Ambassador Sarek* ■ *Dir* Leonard Nimoy • *Scr* Harve Bennett, from the TV series created by Gene Roddenberry

Star Trek IV: the Voyage Home ★★★★ PG

Science-fiction adventure
1986 · US · Colour · 113mins

After three impressive but rather po-faced adventures, the *Enterprise* regulars got the chance to let their hair down a little for this hugely enjoyable trek. The crew has to travel back to 1980s San Francisco to free a couple of whales that can save the Earth from a destructive space probe. While there is little in the way of traditional sci-fi spectacle, the crew has a great time poking fun at the idiosyncrasies of life in modern-day California. JF. Contains swearing. DVD

William Shatner *Captain James T Kirk* • Leonard Nimoy *Spock* • Catherine Hicks *Dr Gillian Taylor* • DeForest Kelley *Dr Leonard "Bones" McCoy* • James Doohan *Scotty* • George Takei *Sulu* • Walter Koenig *Chekov* • Nichelle Nichols *Commander Uhura* • Majel Barrett *Dr Christine Chapel* • Jane Wyatt *Amanda, Spock's mother* • Mark Lenard *Sarek* • Robin Curtis *Lieutenant Saavik* ■ *Dir* Leonard Nimoy • *Scr* Harve Bennett, Steve Meerson, Peter Krikes, Nicholas Meyer, from a story by Leonard Nimoy, Harve Bennett, from the TV series created by Gene Roddenberry

Star Trek V: the Final Frontier ★★★ PG

Science-fiction adventure
1989 · US · Colour · 102mins

With William Shatner in the director's chair, this lacks the wit and panache of its predecessor, but still makes for an enjoyable romp. A messianic figure (Laurence Luckinbill) is holding a distant planet hostage but, in reality, wants to lay his hands on the *Enterprise* and its creaky crew. Aiming for a more mystical plane than usual, the plot is embarrassingly trite at times. In the end it just about gets by, thanks to the interplay between Shatner, Leonard Nimoy and DeForest Kelley, and an action-packed finale. JF. Contains swearing. DVD

William Shatner *Captain James T Kirk* • Leonard Nimoy *Mr Spock* • DeForest Kelley *Dr Leonard "Bones" McCoy* • James Doohan *Scotty* • Walter Koenig *Chekov* • Nichelle Nichols *Lieutenant Uhura* • George Takei *Sulu* • Laurence Luckinbill *Sybok* • David Warner *St John Talbot* • Melanie Shatner *Yeoman* ■ *Dir* William Shatner • *Scr* David Loughery, from a story by William Shatner, Harve Bennett, David Loughery, from the TV series created by Gene Roddenberry

Star Trek VI: the Undiscovered Country ★★★★ PG

Science-fiction adventure
1991 · US · Colour · 108mins

The *Star Trek* movie series goes supernova with an outstanding episode directed by Nicholas Meyer, who also directed *The Wrath of Khan*. Mirroring world news events of the time (the Soviet Union's dissolution), Meyer crafts a near perfect blend of humanistic messages, affectionate lampooning, epic visuals and fairy-tale imagination as the classic *Enterprise* crew encounters treachery during prospective peace negotiations with the Klingons. Clever Shakespearean touches heighten the dramatic agony and ecstasy. AJ DVD

William Shatner *Captain James T Kirk* • Leonard Nimoy *Spock* • DeForest Kelley *Dr Leonard "Bones" McCoy* • James Doohan *Montgomery "Scotty" Scott* • Walter Koenig *Pavel Chekov* • Nichelle Nichols *Nytoba Uhuru* • George Takei *Captain Hikaru Sulu* • Kim Cattrall *Lieutenant Valeris* • Mark Lenard *Sarek* • Christopher Plummer *General Chang* • Iman *Martia* • David Warner *Chancellor Gorkon* • Christian Slater *"Excelsior" crewman* ■ *Dir* Nicholas Meyer • *Scr* Nicholas Meyer, Denny Martin Flinn, from a story by Leonard Nimoy, Lawrence Konner, Mark Rosenthal, from the TV series created by Gene Roddenberry

Star Trek: Generations ★★★★ PG

Science-fiction adventure
1994 · US · Colour · 113mins

Some of the old *Star Trek* cast, led by William Shatner, unite with the *Next Generation* crew, commanded by Patrick Stewart, to stop mad scientist Malcolm McDowell tapping into an energy source that can bring one's most desired fantasies to life. If you can stay with the multi-layered and self-referential plot, this fun saga builds up to warp speed for an exciting climax. A special-effects laden adventure, it trades on fan sentiment and nostalgia as the two much-loved generations of space heroes merge into one space/time continuum. AJ. Contains violence. DVD

Patrick Stewart *Captain Jean-Luc Picard* • Jonathan Frakes *Commander William T Riker* • Brent Spiner *Lt Commander Data* • LeVar Burton *Lt Commander Geordi La Forge* • Michael Dorn *Lt Worf* • Gates McFadden *Dr Beverly Crusher* • Marina Sirtis *Counselor*

Deanna Troi • Malcolm McDowell *Soran* • James Doohan *Scotty* • Walter Koenig *Chekov* • William Shatner *Captain James T Kirk* • Whoopi Goldberg *Guinan* ■ *Dir* David Carson • *Scr* Ronald D Moore, Brannon Braga, from a story by Brannon Braga, Ronald D Moore, Rick Berman, from characters created by Gene Roddenberry

Star Trek: First Contact ★★★★★ 12

Science-fiction adventure
1996 · US · Colour · 106mins

The Borg travel back in time to sabotage that pivotal moment in Earth's destiny when we first made contact with an alien race in this first-rate adventure. What else can Captain Picard do except follow and sort things out? Epic in scope, grandiose in emotional sweep and featuring awesome special effects, this is captivating science fiction packed with ideas, thrills, in-jokes and tense action. It's all expertly marshalled by director Jonathan Frakes (who also plays Commander Riker) with a keen visual eye and an inherent understanding of the history and importance of the series. AJ. Contains violence. VIDEO DVD

Patrick Stewart *Captain Jean-Luc Picard* • Jonathan Frakes *Commander William T Riker* • Brent Spiner *Lt Commander Data* • LeVar Burton *Lt Commander Geordi La Forge* • Michael Dorn *Lt Commander Worf* • Gates McFadden *Dr Beverly Crusher* • Marina Sirtis *Counselor Deanna Troi* • Alice Krige *Borg Queen* • James Cromwell *Zefram Cochrane* • Alfre Woodard *Lily Sloane* • Dwight Schultz *Lt Barclay* • Robert Picardo *Holographic doctor* ■ *Dir* Jonathan Frakes • *Scr* Brannon Braga, Ronald D Moore, from a story by Rick Berman, Brannon Braga, Ronald D Moore, from the TV series created by Gene Roddenberry

Star Trek: Insurrection ★★★ PG

Science-fiction adventure
1998 · US · Colour · 98mins

Ethnic cleansing gets the *Trek* treatment in the ninth feature, which is aimed squarely at the fans. Travelling where *Star Trek* has boldly gone before, with the light-hearted tale of a planet of perpetual youth and the two races who are struggling for the right to use it, there's nothing new in this proficient cocktail of predictable space heroics and *Lost Horizon* homages. Visually impressive (marking the first use of computer digitals for the spaceship sequences), the film also features F Murray Abraham as an unusual villain. AJ VIDEO DVD

Patrick Stewart *Captain Jean-Luc Picard* • Jonathan Frakes *Commander William T Riker* • Brent Spiner *Lt Commander Data* • LeVar Burton *Lt Commander Geordi La Forge* • Michael Dorn *Lt Commander Worf* • Gates McFadden *Dr Beverly Crusher* • Marina Sirtis *Counselor Deanna Troi* • F Murray Abraham *Ru'afo* • Donna Murphy *Anij* • Anthony Zerbe *Dougherty* ■ *Dir* Jonathan Frakes • *Scr* Michael Piller, from a story by Rick Berman, Michael Piller, from the TV series created by Gene Roddenberry

Star Trek: Nemesis ★★★ 12

Science-fiction adventure
2002 · US · Colour · 111mins

The tenth entry in the long-running *Star Trek* franchise sees the crew of the USS *Enterprise* about to split up after the nuptials of Commander Riker (Jonathan Frakes) and Counselor Troi (Marina Sirtis), and Riker's acceptance of his own starship command. However, their plans change when the Romulans offer a suspect peace treaty and Captain Picard (Patrick Stewart) encounters his evil clone twin, Shinzon (Tom Hardy). Like many of the previous big-screen adventures, this action-packed outing resembles a good episode of the TV series stretched to feature-film length. AS VIDEO DVD

Patrick Stewart *Jean-Luc Picard* • Jonathan Frakes *Cmdr William T Riker* • Brent Spiner *Lt Cmdr Data/B-4* • LeVar Burton *Lt Cmdr Geordi La Forge* • Michael Dorn *Lt Cmdr Worf* • Marina Sirtis *Counselor Deanna Troi* • Gates McFadden *Dr Beverly Crusher* • Tom Hardy *Shinzon* • Ron Perlman *Viceroy* • Kate Mulgrew *Admiral Janeway* • Wil Wheaton *Wesley Crusher* • Majel Barrett Roddenberry [Majel Barrett] *Computer* • Whoopi Goldberg *Guinan* ■ *Dir* Stuart Baird • *Scr* John Logan, from a story by John Logan, Rick Berman, Brent Spiner, from the TV series created by Gene Roddenberry

Star Wars Episode I: the Phantom Menace ★★★ U

Science-fiction epic adventure
1999 · US · Colour · 132mins

No matter how hard George Lucas has tried to recapture the magic of the original films, that vital sense of wonder is missing from this first prequel. Instead, Lucas provides a welter of incident, cosmic dilemmas, cryptic forebodings and idiotic dialogue. It's absolutely phenomenal on the visual front, but completely mindless in the story department. Forget the overworked plot about Natalie Portman trying to stop the Trade Federation invading her planet with help from Jedi Knights Liam Neeson and Ewan McGregor; marvel instead at the technical wizardry and fizzing action. AJ VIDEO DVD

Liam Neeson *Qui-Gon Jinn* • Ewan McGregor *Obi-Wan Kenobi* • Natalie Portman *Queen Amidala/Padmé* • Jake Lloyd *Anakin Skywalker* • Ian McDiarmid *Senator Palpatine* • Pernilla August *Shmi Skywalker* • Oliver Ford Davies *Sio Bibble* • Frank Oz *Yoda* • Anthony Daniels *C-3PO* • Kenny Baker (2) *R2-D2* • Terence Stamp *Chancellor Valorum* • Brian Blessed *Boss Nass* • Ray Park *Darth Maul* • Celia Imrie *Fighter Pilot Bravo 5* • Samuel L Jackson *Jedi Knight Mace Windu* • Sofia Coppola *Saché* • Greg Proops *Fode* • Scott Capurro *Beed* • Lindsay Duncan *TC-14* ■ *Dir/Scr* George Lucas • *Music* John Williams

Star Wars Episode II: Attack of the Clones ★★★ PG

Science-fiction epic adventure
2002 · US · Colour · 136mins

This beats the underwhelming first prequel: more action, less politics and better gags. Ewan McGregor relaxes into the role of Obi-Wan Kenobi, playing master rather than pupil now, and combines withering humour with credible superheroics. By cutting between three major plot strands – Anakin Skywalker (Hayden Christensen) and Padmé Amidala (Natalie Portman) fall in love; Obi-Wan confronts bounty hunter Jango Fett (Temuera Morrison); the Jedi prepare for war – Lucas never loses our attention, and the computer-generated imagery is impeccable. AC. Contains violence. VIDEO DVD

Ewan McGregor *Obi-Wan Kenobi* • Natalie Portman *Padmé Amidala* • Hayden Christensen *Anakin Skywalker* • Christopher Lee *Count Dooku* • Samuel L Jackson *Mace Windu* • Frank Oz *Yoda* • Ian McDiarmid *Supreme Chancellor Palpatine* • Pernilla August *Shmi Skywalker* • Temuera Morrison *Jango Fett* • Jimmy Smits *Senator Bail Organa* • Ahmed Best *Jar Jar Binks* • Anthony Daniels *C-3PO* • Kenny Baker (2) *R2-D2* ■ *Dir* George Lucas • *Scr* George Lucas, Jonathan Hales, from a story by George Lucas

Star Wars Episode III: Revenge of the Sith ★★★ 12A

Science-fiction epic adventure
2005 · US · Colour · 139mins

The *Star Wars* saga finally concludes 28 years after the original instalment first hit cinemas. With the story's outcome predetermined, this crucial and much-anticipated segment details how and why dedicated Jedi knight Anakin Skywalker (Hayden Christensen) turned away from good to become the evil Darth Vader. Given that this involves love, loyalty, jealousy and betrayal, you'd expect an emotionally intense film. However, writer/director George Lucas's ridiculous dialogue and unconvincing plot developments play like second-rate soap opera, almost robbing this epic of pathos and tension. Fortunately, the superb visuals save the day, making for a breathtaking spectacle. SF

Ewan McGregor *Obi-Wan Kenobi* • Hayden Christensen *Anakin Skywalker/Lord Darth Vader* • Natalie Portman *Senator Amidala/Padmé Naberrie-Skywalker* • Ian McDiarmid *Supreme Chancellor Palpatine* • Samuel L Jackson *Mace Windu* • Christopher Lee *Count Dooku/Darth Tyrannus* • Anthony Daniels *C-3PO* • Kenny Baker (2) *R2-D2* • Peter Mayhew *Chewbacca* • Frank Oz *Yoda* • James Earl Jones *Darth Vader* • Ahmed Best *Jar Jar Binks* ■ *Dir/Scr* George Lucas

Star Wars Episode IV: a New Hope ★★★★★ U

Science-fiction epic adventure
1977 · US · Colour · 115mins

Endlessly imitated but never rivalled, this first instalment of George Lucas's space opera (originally titled just *Star Wars*) dresses up the timeless tale of good versus evil with ground-breaking special effects and a dazzling array of intergalactic characters. Mark Hamill plays Luke Skywalker, whose dull life on a remote planet is thrown into chaos when he intercepts a distress call from beleaguered Princess Leia (Carrie Fisher). With robots R2-D2 and C-3PO in tow, Luke teams up with an ageing Jedi warrior (Alec Guinness) and a cynical space rogue (a star-making turn from Harrison Ford) to rescue Leia from the clutches of the evil Darth Vader. Breathless action collides with sci-fi theatrics and more than a hint of mysticism to create a new style of cinema that remains unmatched for entertainment value. AJ VIDEO DVD

Mark Hamill *Luke Skywalker* • Harrison Ford *Han Solo* • Carrie Fisher *Princess Leia Organa* • Peter Cushing *Grand Moff Tarkin* • Alec Guinness *Ben (Obi-Wan) Kenobi* • Anthony Daniels *C-3PO* • Kenny Baker (2) *R2-D2* • Peter Mayhew *Chewbacca* • Dave Prowse *Darth Vader* • James Earl Jones *Darth Vader* ■ *Dir/Scr* George Lucas • *Cinematographer* Gilbert Taylor • *Music* John Williams • *Art Director* John Barry (2)

Star Wars Episode V: the Empire Strikes Back ★★★★★ U

Science-fiction epic adventure
1980 · US · Colour · 124mins

Director Irvin Kershner's imaginative supervision of George Lucas's brainchild gives this second part of the first *Star Wars* trilogy a truly epic dimension, adding a mature, philosophical aspect to the nonstop barrage of brilliant special effects. Events take place all over the universe – Darth Vader sends Imperial troops to crush the rebels on the ice planet Hoth, while Luke Skywalker searches out Jedi master Yoda for further instruction in the mysterious ways of "the Force" – and the much-loved characters are developed in intriguing ways. Kershner darkens the imagery of Lucas's vibrant, futuristic fairy tale and deepens its narrative with provocative plot strands, giving this sequel a cynical, harder edge. AJ VIDEO DVD

Mark Hamill *Luke Skywalker* • Harrison Ford *Han Solo* • Carrie Fisher *Princess Leia* • Billy Dee Williams *Lando Calrissian* • Anthony Daniels *C-3PO* • David Prowse [Dave Prowse] *Darth Vader* • James Earl Jones *Voice of Darth Vader* • Peter Mayhew *Chewbacca* • Kenny Baker (2) *R2-D2* • Frank Oz *Yoda* • Alec Guinness *Obi-Wan "Ben" Kenobi* ■ *Dir* Irvin Kershner • *Scr* Leigh Brackett, Lawrence Kasdan, from a story by George Lucas • *Music* John Williams • *Art Director* Norman Reynold

Star Wars Episode VI: Return of the Jedi ★★★★ U

Science-fiction epic adventure
1983 · US · Colour · 131mins

Sequels are usually a case of diminishing returns, but this third instalment of the first *Star Wars* trilogy is still essential viewing. Director Richard Marquand jumps straight in where the *The Empire Strikes Back* finished off with a stunning sequence involving the monstrous Jabba the Hutt and the pace rarely falters from then on, even if the plot is a dash stop-start at times. Mark Hamill still looks more like an enthusiastic schoolboy than an intergalactic hero, but his climactic scenes with Darth Vader work a treat, and, while adults will probably cringe at the cutesy Ewoks, their presence makes this a particular favourite with younger viewers. JF VIDEO DVD

Mark Hamill *Luke Skywalker* • Harrison Ford *Han Solo* • Carrie Fisher *Princess Leia* • Billy Dee Williams *Lando Calrissian* • Anthony Daniels *C-3PO* • Peter Mayhew *Chewbacca* • Sebastian Shaw *Anakin Skywalker* • Ian McDiarmid *Emperor Palpatine* • Frank Oz *Yoda* • David Prowse [Dave Prowse] *Darth Vader* • James Earl Jones *Voice of Darth Vader* • Alec Guinness *Obi-Wan "Ben" Kenobi* • Kenny Baker (2) *R2-D2* ■ *Dir* Richard Marquand • *Scr* Lawrence Kasdan, George Lucas, from a story by George Lucas

Stardom ★★★

Satire
2000 · Can/Fr · Colour and BW · 100mins

Atoning in perception for what it lacks in subtlety, Denys Arcand's sniping satire on the transient cult of celebrity is as brash as the worlds it depicts. Fittingly for a mockumentary about a life lived in the public gaze, the action is made up of clips from news reports, chat shows and actuality profiles, as Jessica Paré goes from small-town nobody to supermodel and cultural icon in the twinkling of a TV set. The writing is scattershot and the performances inconsistent (although Frank Langella and Dan Aykroyd excel). DP

Jessica Paré *Tina Menzhal* • Dan Aykroyd *Barry Levine* • Thomas Gibson *Renny Ohayon* • Charles Berling *Philippe Gascon* • Robert Lepage *Bruce Taylor* • Camilla Rutherford *Toni* • Frank Langella *Blaine de Castillon* ■ *Dir* Denys Arcand • *Scr* Denys Arcand, J Jacob Potashnik

Stardust ★★★ 15

Musical drama 1974 · UK · Colour · 106mins

Singer David Essex reprises his role as Jim MacLaine, the working class boy who wanted to become a pop star in this dated but enjoyable sequel to *That'll Be the Day.* In this follow-up he becomes the biggest rock star in the world – so you just know it's going to all go horribly wrong. Most interesting here – apart from Essex's lame attempts at acting – is the supporting cast of 1960s warblers, including Adam Faith and Marty Wilde. JB VIDEO

David Essex *Jim MacLaine* • Adam Faith *Mike* • Larry Hagman *Porter Lee Austin* • Ines Des Longchamps *Danielle* • Rosalind Ayres *Jeanette* • Marty Wilde *Colin Day* • Edd Byrnes *Television interviewer* • Keith Moon *JD Clover* • Dave Edmunds *Alex* • Paul Nicholas *Johnny* ■ *Dir* Michael Apted • *Scr* Ray Connolly

Stardust ★★

Science-fiction fantasy adventure
1998 · US · Colour · 97mins

Convinced that his employers are going to use his revolutionary bio-chip for evil purposes, boffin Olek Krupa hides it in the family hoover and entrusts 11 year-old Jared Robbins with keeping it out

S

of his enemies' clutches. This all makes for tolerable fun as mum Amanda Donohoe and her machine come to terms with its new powers, but the action becomes ever-more predictable as it descends into a *Home Alone* showdown. DP

Amanda Donohoe *Christine Wasacz* • Giancarlo Esposito *Mr. Peavey* • Jared Robbins *Charlie Wasacz* • Olek Krupa *Karol Wasacz* • Joseph French *Mr Butz* • Anthony Hamilton *Ricky Wing* • David Kanapsky *Billy Butz* ■ *Dir/Scr* Charles F Cirgenski

Stardust Memories ★★★★ 15

Comedy 1980 · US · BW · 84mins

Woody Allen vents his spleen against critics and audiences in this heavily autobiographical, but surprisingly funny comedy. He plays Sandy Bates, a director remarkably like Allen, who wants to break out of the comedy mould and make "serious" movies. Attending a weekend film festival of his work, he runs the gauntlet of fans and critics, and muses on his complicated love life with Charlotte Rampling and Jessica Harper. This two-fingered salute to audiences deserves marks for audacity and is beautifully shot in black and white. TH. Contains sexual references and some swearing.

Woody Allen *Sandy Bates* • Charlotte Rampling *Dorrie* • Jessica Harper *Daisy* • Marie-Christine Barrault *Isobel* • Tony Roberts *Tony* • Helen Hanft *Vivian Orkin* • John Rothman *Jack Abel* ■ *Dir/Scr* Woody Allen

Starflight One ★★ U

Futuristic adventure
1983 · US · Colour · 109mins

Director Jerry Jameson specialised in this type of jeopardy movie in the 1970s and 1980s. Here, Lee Majors deals with a new-fangled jetliner in crisis, having been inadvertently chucked into outer space on its maiden flight. Naturally there's a sturdy cast of watchables on board, while the special effects are courtesy of *Star Wars* wizard John Dykstra, former head of Industrial Light & Magic. TS

Lee Majors *Capt Cody Briggs* • Hal Linden *Josh Gilliam* • Ray Milland *QT Thornwell* • Gail Strickland *Nancy Gilliam* • Lauren Hutton *Erika Hansen* • George DiCenzo *Bowdish* • Robert Englund ■ *Dir* Jerry Jameson • *Scr* Robert Malcolm Young, from a story by Gene Warren, Peter R Brooke

Stargate ★★★★ PG

Science-fiction adventure
1994 · US/Fr · Colour · 115mins

Aliens colonised ancient Egypt through a space-time portal according to this derivative yet hugely enjoyable cosmic adventure. James Spader is terrific as the code-cracking archaeologist who accompanies soldier Kurt Russell across the universe to fight galactic tyrant Jaye Davidson. Simple in execution, yet classic in the nostalgic way it evokes the feel of vintage 1940s serials, director Roland Emmerich combines plot strands from literature and other films of the genre, with some imaginative special effects and impressive visuals. AJ. Contains swearing, violence. DVD

Kurt Russell *Col Jonathan "Jack" O'Neil* • James Spader *Dr Daniel Jackson* • Jaye Davidson *Ra* • Viveca Lindfors *Catherine* • Alexis Cruz *Skaara* • Mili Avital *Sha'uri* • Leon Rippy *General WO West* • John Diehl *Lieutenant Kawalsky* ■ *Dir* Roland Emmerich • *Scr* Roland Emmerich, Dean Devlin • *Cinematographer* Karl Walter Lindenlaub • *Production Designer* Holger Gross

Stark Raving Mad ★★ 15

Heist comedy drama
2002 · US · Colour · 99mins

This highly derivative heist comedy patches together a ragtag assortment of multi-genre clichés, pop culture references and flashy camera techniques. It follows debt-ridden 20-something Seann William Scott and his slacker pals as they struggle to pull off a bank robbery using a nightclub rave as cover. Throw into the mix a vengeful Mob boss (a blond-haired Lou Diamond Phillips), undercover federal agents, Chinese gangsters and even a couple of transvestites, and you've got a moderately engaging, if predictable feature. SF DVD

Seann William Scott *Ben McGewen* • Timm Sharp *Rikki Simms* • Patrick Breen *Jeffrey Jay* • Lou Diamond Phillips *Mr Gregory* • John B Crye *Jake Nealson* • Suzy Nakamura *Betty Shin* • Dave Foley *Roy* ■ *Dir/Scr* Drew Daywalt, Dave Schneider [David Schneider (2)]

Starlight ★

Musical drama 1989 · US · Colour · 78mins

This musical drama will have you cringeing within minutes. It's set in a country camp where a bunch of aspiring city kids brush up their entertainment skills under the tutelage of a venerable vaudevillian. When he takes his final curtain call, the school gets a far less sympathetic principal and the kids begin to wonder if the show will go on. It shouldn't have got off the ground in the first place. DP

Kario Salem *Arthur Hall* • Jean Taylor *Mary* • Pamela Payton-Wright *Louise* • Ciro Barbaro *Dewey* • Kathryn Eames *Evelyn Ruth* • Robert Earl Jones *Joe* • William Hickey *Billy Davis* ■ *Dir* Orin Wechsberg • *Scr* MJ Wells, from a story by Orin Wechsberg, Daniel Gualtieri

Starlight Hotel ★★★ PG

Drama 1987 · NZ · Colour · 93mins

This would-be "rites of passage" drama is a rather cheery, benign but muddle-headed affair. It's the Depression: cue much wearing of depressing undergarments, and young Greer Robson and Peter Phelps tramping the countryside in search of a crust. And that's all there is here apart from some nice shots of New Zealand and a certain winsome charm. SH

Greer Robson *Kate Marshall* • Peter Phelps *Patrick "Pat" Dawson* • Marshall Napier *Detective Wallace* • The Wizard [Ian Brackenbury Channell] *Spooner* ■ *Dir* Sam Pillsbury • *Scr* Grant Hinden Miller, from the novel *The Dream Monger* by Grant Hinden Miller

The Starmaker ★★★ 18

Comedy drama 1994 · It · Colour · 102mins

Giuseppe Tornatore (*Cinema Paradiso*) returns to similarly nostalgic territory with this drama set in the 1950s. Roving conman Sergio Castellitto poses as a movie talent scout who persuades Sicilian villagers to pay for their own screen tests and promises them a bright future. This is a smashing idea – intrinsically funny and flexible enough to combine the dreams and crushed hopes of any number of budding actors. But the film is oddly repetitive, and the touristy photography is a bit much after a while. AT. In Italian with English subtitles.

Sergio Castellitto *Joe Morelli* • Tiziana Lodato *Beata* • Franco Scaldati *Brigadiere Mastropaolo* • Leopoldo Trieste *Mute* ■ *Dir* Giuseppe Tornatore • *Scr* Giuseppe Tornatore, Fabio Rinaudo, from a story by Giuseppe Tornatore

Starman ★★★★ PG

Science-fiction romance
1984 · US · Colour · 110mins

A curious alien responds to the *Voyager* spacecraft's invitation to visit Earth, lands in Wisconsin and takes the form of Karen Allen's late husband in a romantic road movie with a cosmic twist. John Carpenter's religious sci-fi parable has as much heart and emotion as it does special effects, and gives Oscar-nominated Jeff Bridges a real chance to stretch his acting talent as the extraterrestrial eager to learn about the pleasures and pain of human existence. Funny, suspenseful and moving, this engaging space odyssey is one of Carpenter's best efforts. AJ. Contains swearing and violence. DVD

Jeff Bridges *Starman* • Karen Allen *Jenny Hayden* • Charles Martin Smith *Mark Shermin* • Richard Jaeckel *George Fox* • Robert Phalen *Major Bell* • Tony Edwards *Sergeant Lemon* ■ *Dir* John Carpenter • *Scr* Bruce A Evans, Raynold Gideon

Stars ★★★★

Drama 1959 · E Ger/Bul · BW · 93mins

The first East German film to find favour abroad was written by a Bulgarian Jew and directed by a Red Army veteran. The combination of their experiences and a refusal to indulge in easy sentimentality enables director Konrad Wolf and screenwriter Anzel Wagenstein to impart realism, abhorrence and faint optimism to the story of the German soldier who falls in love while transporting Greek Jews from a Bulgarian detention centre. The dramatic onus rests on Jürgen Frohriep, as he realises the enormity of the Nazis' crimes and deserts to join the Partisans. DP. In German with English subtitles.

Sascha Krusharska *Ruth* • Jürgen Frohriep *Walter* • Erik S Klein *Kurt* • Stefan Peichev *Uncle Petko* • Georgi Naumov *Blazhe* • Ivan Kondov *Ruth's father* ■ *Dir* Konrad Wolf, Rangel Vulchanov • *Scr* Angel Wagenstein

Stars and Bars ★ 15

Comedy 1988 · US · Colour · 90mins

It would be nice to recommend this picture and on paper it promises much: Daniel Day-Lewis and Harry Dean Stanton in the main roles, based on a novel by William Boyd and directed by Pat O'Connor, who made *Cal*. Sadly, something went horribly wrong with this comedy about an Englishman's misadventures in the American Deep South. What was quite funny in the novel becomes, in Boyd's script, trite and embarrassing. AT

Daniel Day-Lewis *Henderson Dores* • Harry Dean Stanton *Loomis Gage* • Laurie Metcalf *Melissa* • Martha Plimpton *Bryant* • Kent Broadhurst *Sereno* • Maury Chaykin *Freeborn Gage* • Matthew Cowles *Beckman Gage* • Joan Cusack *Irene Stein* ■ *Dir* Pat O'Connor • *Scr* William Boyd, from his novel

Stars and Stripes Forever ★★★ U

Musical biography
1952 · US · Colour · 89mins

March king John Philip Sousa is waspishly incarnated by Clifton Webb, who portrays a composer desperate to write ballads, not marches. It may or may not be true, but who cares when his fabulous compositions are dispersed through the movie in superb Alfred Newman arrangements? Ruth Hussey makes a tolerant Mrs Sousa, and upcoming Fox stars Robert Wagner and Debra Paget seem to enjoy themselves as the youngsters. TS

Clifton Webb *John Philip Sousa* • Debra Paget *Lily* • Robert Wagner *Willie* • Ruth Hussey *Jennie* • Finlay Currie *Colonel Randolph* • Benay Venuta *Madame Bernsdorff-Mueller* ■ *Dir* Henry Koster • *Scr* Lamar Trotti, Ernest Vajda, from the autobiography *Marching Along* by John Philip Sousa

The Stars Fell on Henrietta ★★★ PG

Drama 1995 · US · Colour · 105mins

Barely released, this Depression-era drama stars Robert Duvall as a down-on-his-luck Texas oilman dreaming of one last big strike. Director James Keach (brother of Stacy) creates a fine atmosphere from the desolate landscape and gets some good performances – Duvall is excellent, as usual, and so are Aidan Quinn and Frances Fisher as the lowly farmers whose land may hold the key to Duvall's fortune. Fisher was the one-time partner of the film's producer, Clint Eastwood, and their daughter, Francesca, plays one of Fisher's daughters in the story. AT

Robert Duvall *Mr Cox* • Aidan Quinn *Don Day* • Frances Fisher *Cora Day* • Brian Dennehy *Big Dave* • Lexi Randall *Beatrice Day* • Kaytlyn Knowles *Pauline Day* • Francesca Ruth Eastwood *Mary Day* • Billy Bob Thornton *Roy* ■ *Dir* James Keach • *Scr* Philip Railsback

Stars in My Crown ★★★

Period religious drama
1950 · US · BW · 89mins

Joel McCrea gives another sterling performance as the new parson appointed to a small Southern town. He proves to be of stern stuff as he encounters epidemics and the menace of the Ku Klux Klan, while shattering the superstitious illusions of the populace. Director Jacques Tourneur was better known for eerie horrors and brooding *films noirs*, but he neatly blends genre convention with period nostalgia to explore themes rarely tackled in the average B-western. DP

Ellen Drew *Harriet Gray* • Dean Stockwell *John Kenyon* • Alan Hale *Jed Isbell* • Lewis Stone *Dr DK Harris Sr* • James Mitchell *Dr DK Harris Jr* • Amanda Blake *Faith Radmore Samuels* • Ed Begley *Lon Backett* • Jim Arness [James Arness] *Rufe Isbell* ■ *Dir* Jacques Tourneur • *Scr* Margaret Fitts, from the novel by Joe David Brown

The Stars Look Down ★★★★ PG

Drama 1939 · UK · BW · 94mins

Carol Reed's well-crafted drama, based on AJ Cronin's novel about life in an English mining town, is a precursor to the gritty northern school of socially conscious British film-making. Michael Redgrave tops the bill as the upwardly mobile son of a miner, while Margaret Lockwood is the woman he marries. The film is strong on detail in its portrayal of mining life and, although it creaks with age in parts, it remains powerful and moving. Novelist and sometime film critic Graham Greene rated this one of the best British movies he'd ever seen. PF DVD

Michael Redgrave *David Fenwick* • Margaret Lockwood *Jenny Sunley* • Emlyn Williams *Joe Gowan* • Nancy Price *Martha Fenwick* • Allan Jeayes *Richard Barras* • Edward Rigby *Robert Fenwick* ■ *Dir* Carol Reed • *Scr* JB Williams, from the novel by AJ Cronin

Stars on Parade ★★ U

Musical 1944 · US · BW · 62mins

The fact that the leads were the relatively unknown and uninteresting Larry Parks and Lynn Merrick, and that no one else in the cast, except for the Nat King Cole Trio, is anyone you've ever heard of, makes the title a misnomer. The almost invisible plot has a group of struggling entertainers putting on a show to prove to Hollywood producers that there is talent in their own back yard. RB

Larry Parks *Danny Davis* • Lynn Merrick *Dorothy Dean* • Ray Walker *Billy Blake* • Jeff Donnell *Mary Brooks* • Robert B Williams *Jerry Browne* • Selmer Jackson *JL Carson* • Edythe Elliott *Mrs Dean* • Mary Currier *Nan McNair* ■ *Dir* Lew Landers • *Scr* Monte Brice

Starship Troopers ★★★★ 18

Satirical science-fiction adventure
1997 · US · Colour · 129mins

Director Paul Verhoeven's ultra-violent adaptation of science-fiction writer

S

U = SUITABLE FOR ALL Uc = SUITABLE FOR ALL, ESPECIALLY FOR YOUNG CHILDREN (VIDEO ONLY) PG = PARENTAL GUIDANCE

Robert A Heinlein's classic 1959 novel – a saga about Earth versus alien bugs – is popcorn exploitation at its lip-smacking, blood-spattered best. Whether portraying the chilling spectacle of millions of ugly giant insects swarming over the planet or the astonishing intergalactic battles, the digitally-created special effects are simply outstanding. It's when Verhoeven cuts to the teenage romance that his sensational cartoon carnage comes unstuck. This enjoyably absurd apocalyptic satire was followed by an inconsequential straight-to-video sequel in 2004. AJ. Contains violence and some swearing. [VIDEO] DVD

Casper Van Dien *Johnny Rico* • Dina Meyer *Dizzy Flores* • Denise Richards *Carmen Ibanez* • Jake Busey *Ace Levy* • Neil Patrick Harris *Carl Jenkins* • Clancy Brown *Sergeant Zim* • Michael Ironside *Jean Rasczak* ■ *Dir* Paul Verhoeven • *Scr* Edward Neumeier, from the novel by Robert A Heinlein

Starsky and Hutch ★★★ 12

Crime drama 1975 · US · Colour · 68mins

David Soul and Paul Michael Glaser racked up 88 episodes as America's hippest cop duo of the 1970s. Ripping round the streets of an anonymous city in a red Ford Torino (with its much-copied go-faster stripes), they were a buddy team that wasn't afraid to get tough, as in this pilot movie, in which they investigate a double homicide. Antonio Fargas also features as Huggy Bear, with Richard Ward as Captain Dobey (played by Bernie Hamilton in the TV series). DP DVD

David Soul *Ken "Hutch" Hutchinson* • Paul Michael Glaser *David Starsky* • Antonio Fargas *Huggy Bear* • Richard Ward *Captain Dobey* • Michael Conrad *Cannell* ■ *Dir* Barry Shear • *Scr* William Blinn

Starsky & Hutch ★★★ 15

Action crime comedy
2004 · US · Colour · 96mins

By cleverly respecting his source material and skewering some much-loved clichés, co-writer/director Todd Phillips nails the big screen version of TV cop show. The casting of Ben Stiller as by-the-book detective Starsky and Owen Wilson as laid-back chancer "Hutch" couldn't be better. Grudgingly paired up, the mismatched duo learn to rely on each other while bringing a drugs lord (Vince Vaughn) to justice. The show's kitsch iconography ensures a good time is had by old fans and newcomers alike. AJ. Contains drug abuse and violence. [VIDEO] DVD

Ben Stiller *Detective David Starsky* • Owen Wilson *Detective Ken "Hutch" Hutchinson* • Vince Vaughn *Reese Feldman* • Juliette Lewis *Kitty* • Snoop Dogg *Huggy Bear* • Fred Williamson *Captain Doby* • Carmen Electra *Staci* • Amy Smart *Holly* • Jason Bateman *Kevin* • Chris Penn *Manetti* ■ *Dir* Todd Phillips • *Scr* Todd Phillips, John O'Brien, Scot Armstrong, from a story by Stevie Long, John O'Brien, from the characters created by William Blinn

Start Cheering ★★★

Musical comedy 1938 · US · BW · 78mins

Slight but bright and entertaining musical comedy about a Hollywood actor who tires of starring in college films and decides to enrol as a student in a real university, much to the lament of his manager, who schemes to get him expelled. The cast includes an array of vaudeville names, including the Three Stooges and, above all, Jimmy Durante as the manager's sidekick, who steals the show and the best laughs with a high-energy performance. PF

Jimmy Durante *Willie Gumbatz* • Walter Connolly *Sam Lewis* • Joan Perry *Jean Worthington* • Charles Starrett *Ted Crosley* • Raymond Walburn *Dean Worthington* • Broderick Crawford *Biff Gordon* ■ *Dir* Albert S Rogell • *Scr* Eugene Solow, Richard E Wormser, Philip Rapp, from the short story *College Hero* by Corey Ford in *The Saturday Evening Post*

Start the Revolution without Me ★★★★ PG

Period farce 1970 · US · Colour · 86mins

In 18th-century France, two sets of identical twins get scrambled at birth thanks to an incompetent doctor, resulting in double helpings of Donald Sutherland and Gene Wilder. One pair of brothers grow up rich and privileged, while their less fortunate counterparts are peasants. Confused? You will be when the mismatched twins find themselves on opposing sides during some Revolutionary skirmishes. There's a *Monty Python* quality to some of the humour, and director Bud Yorkin places the verbal fireworks where they are most needed. TH [VIDEO]

Gene Wilder *Claude Coupé/Philippe Di Sisi* • Donald Sutherland *Charles Coupé/Pierre Di Sisi* • Hugh Griffith *King Louis XVI* • Jack MacGowran *Jacques Cabriolet* • Billie Whitelaw *Queen Marie Antoinette* • Victor Spinetti *Duke d'Escargot* • Orson Welles *Narrator* ■ *Dir* Bud Yorkin • *Scr* Fred Freeman, Lawrence J Cohen, from the story *Two Times Two* by Fred Freeman

Starting Over ★★★ 15

Romantic comedy
1979 · US · Colour · 101mins

Get those tissues out for this romantic comedy in which a non-mustachioed Burt Reynolds – in one of his most sensitive performances – stars as a man coping with his wife (Candice Bergen) leaving him to pursue a singing career. There are some funny and moving moments to be had as he consults his pals and even joins a divorced men's group. There's also much hilarity from Bergen's eye-wincingly awful singing. Nice support from Jill Clayburgh, too, as the commitment-shy teacher with whom Burt attempts a relationship. JB [VIDEO]

Burt Reynolds *Phil Potter* • Jill Clayburgh *Marilyn Holmberg* • Candice Bergen *Jessica Potter* • Charles Durning *Michael "Mickey" Potter* • Frances Sternhagen *Marva Potter* • Austin Pendleton *Paul* • Mary Kay Place *Marie* • MacIntyre Dixon *Dan Ryan* • Jay O Sanders *Larry* ■ *Dir* Alan J Pakula • *Scr* James L Brooks, from the novel by Dan Wakefield

Startup.com ★★★ 15

Documentary 2001 · US · Colour · 102mins

As fly-on-the-wall documentaries go, this account of the rise and fall of an internet business set up by two college buddies is packed with commercial conflicts and human interest. The contrast between Kaleil Isaza Tuzman's ruthless belief in his business acumen and Tom Herman's more reckless approach to the project is fascinating as the ambitious pair build a website to ease everyday local government transactions such as paying taxes or renewing driving licences. But by adhering to a *cinéma vérité* style, directors Chris Hegedus and Jehane Noujaim allow their subjects to set the agenda, which leaves the audience with more questions than answers. There's a suspicion that a more revealing story somehow got away. DP [VIDEO] DVD

Dir Chris Hegedus, Jehane Noujaim • *Producer* DA Pennebaker

State and Main ★★★★ 15

Comedy 2000 · US · Colour · 101mins

Writer/director David Mamet shows his lighter side with this superb comedy about the havoc that results when a Hollywood film crew descends on a small New England town. There's the movie's star (played perfectly by Alec Baldwin) who has a preference for underage girls; the writer (Philip Seymour Hoffman) who is watching his beautiful words being twisted to suit the budget and the producer; and the actress (Sarah Jessica Parker) known for taking her top off, who is refusing to do any more nude scenes. Meanwhile, the harassed director (William H Macy) is trying to hold it all together. In the midst of all this chaos and comedy, there is also a sweet love story between Hoffman and town resident Rebecca Pidgeon (Mamet's real-life wife). Not especially original material, but a surprisingly warm romantic interlude. JB [VIDEO] DVD

Alec Baldwin *Bob Barrenger* • Charles Durning *Mayor George Bailey* • Clark Gregg *Doug MacKenzie* • Philip Seymour Hoffman *Joseph Turner White* • Patti LuPone *Sherry Bailey* • William H Macy *Walt Price* • Sarah Jessica Parker *Claire Wellesley* • Rebecca Pidgeon *Ann Black* • Julia Stiles *Carla Taylor* ■ *Dir/Scr* David Mamet

State Fair ★★★ U

Comedy 1933 · US · BW · 99mins

A day out at the Iowa state fair with the Frake family is the fulcrum for this folksy, good-humoured, idealised and beautifully performed piece of period Americana. Abel Frake (the much-loved Will Rogers) is hoping his prize pig will win the Blue Ribbon; his wife, Louise Dresser, has entered her pickles and mincemeat. The young ones, meanwhile, are alive to romance, with daughter Janet Gaynor finding true love with newspaper reporter Lew Ayres and son Norman Foster faring less well in a fling with Sally Eilers. Delightful and innocent, it was a major hit. RK

Will Rogers *Abel Frake* • Janet Gaynor *Margy Frake* • Lew Ayres *Pat Gilbert* • Sally Eilers *Emily Joyce* • Norman Foster *Wayne Frake* • Louise Dresser *Melissa Frake* ■ *Dir* Henry King • *Scr* Paul Green, Sonya Levien, from the novel by Phil Stong

State Fair ★★★★ U

Musical 1945 · US · BW · 96mins

The second and probably best of the three Hollywood movies inspired by Phil Stong's popular novel of country folk and their simple ways, set in the American Midwest. It takes the same story of pickles, pigs and boy-meets-girl at the country fair, as told in the 1933 movie, but sets it to music with some top-notch numbers by Rodgers and Hammerstein, including *That's for Me* and *It Might As Well Be Spring*, which bagged the Oscar for best song. Entertaining fare. PF [VIDEO] DVD

Jeanne Crain *Margy Frake* • Dana Andrews *Pat Gilbert* • Dick Haymes *Wayne Frake* • Vivian Blaine *Emily Joyce* • Charles Winninger *Abel Frake* • Fay Bainter *Melissa Frake* • Donald Meek *Hippenstahl* • Frank McHugh *McGee* • Percy Kilbride *Miller* ■ *Dir* Walter Lang • *Scr* Oscar Hammerstein II, Sonya Levien, Paul Green, from the novel by Phil Stong

State Fair ★★ U

Musical 1962 · US · Colour · 118mins

A disappointment, this remake of the much-loved musical is shackled by the leaden direction of José Ferrer. Even the legendary Alice Faye, returning to the screen after an absence of 17 years, seems dispirited. The Rodgers and Hammerstein songs are still wonderful, though the five new ones added by Rodgers alone are merely serviceable. Ann-Margret performs a torrid dance number which would have scandalised 1945 audiences. TV

Pat Boone *Wayne Frake* • Bobby Darin *Jerry Dundee* • Pamela Tiffin *Margie Frake* • Ann-Margret *Emily Porter* • Alice Faye *Melissa Frake* • Tom Ewell *Abel Frake* • Wally Cox *Hipplewaite* • David Brandon *Harry* ■ *Dir* José Ferrer • *Scr* Richard L Breen, from the 1945 film, from the novel by Phil Stong

State of Grace ★★★★ 18

Crime thriller 1990 · US · Colour · 128mins

Set in New York's Irish quarter, this glowering thriller makes so many blatant bids to be bracketed with the Mob movies of Martin Scorsese that it could justifiably be nicknamed *O'GoodFellas*. While not up to the Scorsese standard, this is still a cracking crime movie, with gutsy performances from Sean Penn, the under-rated Ed Harris and that master of manic malevolence, Gary Oldman. Robin Wright gets slightly lost in the mêlée and director Phil Joanou might have kept the running time down, but it's violent, vibrant and very impressive. DP. Contains swearing, violence, drug abuse, nudity. [VIDEO] DVD

Sean Penn *Terry Noonan* • Gary Oldman *Jackie Flannery* • Ed Harris *Frankie Flannery* • Robin Wright [Robin Wright Penn] *Kathleen Flannery* • John Turturro *Nick* • John C Reilly *Stevie* • Burgess Meredith *Finn* ■ *Dir* Phil Joanou • *Scr* Dennis McIntyre

State of Siege ★★★ 15

Political thriller
1972 · Fr/US/It/W Ger · Colour · 115mins

Although set in an unnamed state, this is clearly a film about the abduction by Uruguay's Tupamaro guerrillas of Daniel Mitrione. Mitrione was a member of the US Agency for International Development, whose traffic control brief provided a front for his expertise in the interrogation and torture of political prisoners. There was criticism of the casting of Yves Montand as the villain, while others complained that the director's sympathies lay with the kidnappers. Either way, despite re-using the reportage techniques he employed on *Z*, Costa-Gavras is less successful here. DP. A French language film. [VIDEO]

Yves Montand *Santore* • Renato Salvatori *Lopez* • OE Hasse *Ducas* • Jacques Weber *Hugo* • Jean-Luc Bideau *Este* • Evangeline Peterson *Mrs Santore* ■ *Dir* Constantin Costa-Gavras [Costa-Gavras] • *Scr* Constantin Costa-Gavras [Costa-Gavras], Franco Solinas

State of the Union ★★★★

Political drama 1948 · US · BW · 121mins

Originally released in the year of a presidential campaign, this concerns millionaire industrialist Spencer Tracy running for the highest office and unwittingly putting himself and his integrity at the mercy of other people's unprincipled ambition. When the candidate's estranged wife Katharine Hepburn is persuaded to return for a public reunion, there are unexpected consequences. Enthralling and astringently witty, the film boasts top-class supporting performances, while the star duo fires on all cylinders. RK

Spencer Tracy *Grant Matthews* • Katharine Hepburn *Mary Matthews* • Van Johnson *Spike McManus* • Angela Lansbury *Kay Thorndyke* • Adolphe Menjou *Jim Conover* • Lewis Stone *Sam Thorndyke* ■ *Dir* Frank Capra • *Scr* Anthony Veiller, Myles Connolly, from a play by Howard Lindsay, Russel Crouse

The State of Things ★★★★

Drama 1982 · US/Por/W Ger · BW · 121mins

Shot contemporaneously with the interminable production of *Hammett*, Wim Wenders's treatise on the uneasy relationship between the European art film and Hollywood was dubbed by its director as the last of the B-movies. The shifts between narrative and dissertation are superbly achieved, as the cast and crew of a poverty-stricken sci-fi remake are stranded in Portugal and left to cogitate on the ironies of life and illusion as their producer heads for the States in search of funds. Despite dividing the critics (who found it either cold and cynical or astute and acerbic), this cameo-packed

S

film won the Golden Lion award at the Venice Film Festival. DP

Patrick Bauchau *Friedrich "Fritz" Munro, the director* • Isabelle Weingarten *Anna* • Allen Garfield *Gordon* • Samuel Fuller *Joe Corby, the cameraman* • Viva Auder *Kate, the scriptgirl* • Jeffrey Kime *Mark* • Paul Getty III *Dennis, the writer* • Roger Corman *Lawyer* ■ *Dir* Wim Wenders • *Scr* Wim Wenders, Robert Kramer

State Secret ★★★ U

Thriller 1950 · UK · BW · 100mins

A serviceable thriller from Frank Launder and Sidney Gilliat that borrows its blend of comedy and suspense from their own spy caper *Night Train to Munich*. Douglas Fairbanks Jr stars as a surgeon lured to the Balkan state of Vosnia after its dictator is wounded in an assassination attempt. When his patient dies, Fairbanks has to take to the hills with plucky Glynis Johns at his side. Gilliat directs with plenty of panache and the location photography is stunning. DP

Douglas Fairbanks Jr *Dr John Marlowe* • Glynis Johns *Lisa* • Jack Hawkins *Colonel Galcon* • Herbert Lom *Karl Theodor* • Walter Rilla *General Niva* • Karel Stepanek *Dr Revo* • Carl Jaffe *Janovik Prada* ■ *Dir* Sidney Gilliat • *Scr* Sidney Gilliat, from the novel *Appointment with Fear* by Roy Huggins • *Producer* Frank Launder

The Statement ★★ 12

Drama
2003 · Can/Fr/UK/US · Colour · 114mins

This untypical outing from director Norman Jewison stars Michael Caine as an ageing French collaborator. Pursuing him for his involvement in the execution of seven Jews are war-crime investigators Tilda Swinton and Jeremy Northam, but their prey stays one step ahead of them with the help of his high-level friends. Caine gives his usual solid performance, but Swinton and Northam struggle with their flimsy characters and the film can't decide whether it's a chase thriller, a conspiracy yarn or a message movie. DA. Contains violence. DVD

Michael Caine *Pierre Brossard* • Tilda Swinton *Judge Annemarie Livi* • Jeremy Northam *Colonel Roux* • Alan Bates *Armand Bertier* • John Boswall *Father Léo* • Matt Craven *David Manenbaum* • Frank Finlay *Commissaire Vionnet* • Ciaran Hinds *Pochon* • Charlotte Rampling *Nicole* ■ *Dir* Norman Jewison • *Scr* Ronald Harwood, from the novel by Brian Moore

Static ★★★ 15

Satirical drama 1985 · US · Colour · 90mins

In this decidedly odd drama, Keith Gordon plays a guy who invents a TV that can supposedly tune in to heaven. It can't, of course, and simply shows static. But try telling that to spiritually isolated people who desperately need to believe in something bigger and better. By turns moving and amusing, but also drawn-out and dreary, *Static* displays an obvious, if surreal, intelligence. DA

Keith Gordon *Ernie Blick* • Amanda Plummer *Julia Purcell* • Bob Gunton *Frank* • Lily Knight *Patty* • Barton Heyman *Sheriff William Orling* • Reathel Bean *Fred Savins* • Jane Hoffman *Emily Southwick* ■ *Dir* Mark Romanek • *Scr* Keith Gordon, Mark Romanek

The Station Agent ★★★★ 15

Comedy drama 2003 · US · Colour · 85mins

Finbar McBride (Peter Dinklage) seems to have no emotions, he is a dwarf, and his hobbies are model railways and trainspotting. Finbar works in a model shop and when the owner dies, he inherits a disused rural railway station in New Jersey. He shuns attention, but finds himself befriended by Joe (Bobby Cannavale), a gregarious young Cuban who runs his father's fast-food van, and Olivia (Patricia Clarkson), a local artist grieving for a dead son and a dead marriage. A ragbag collection of misfits and losers, they end up sitting, talking and trainspotting together. The script strikes a fine balance between comedy and the pain of living, with the characters beautifully observed. BP. Contains swearing. DVD

Peter Dinklage *Finbar "Fin" McBride* • Patricia Clarkson *Olivia Harris* • Bobby Cannavale *Joe Oramas* • Paul Benjamin *Henry Styles* • Raven Goodwin *Cleo* • Michelle Williams *Emily* • Josh Pais *Carl* ■ *Dir/Scr* Tom McCarthy [Thomas McCarthy]

A Station for Two ★★★ PG

Romantic drama
1983 · USSR · Colour · 133mins

Considering the restrictions placed on Soviet film-makers, Eldar Ryazanov's mild satire is still an acute analysis of the moral and material problems then facing the USSR, with the queues, delays, shortages, drunkenness and racketeering that provide the back story clearly serving a microcosmic purpose. One-time concert pianist Oleg Basilashvili is released from the gulag where he's serving a sentence for manslaughter in order to visit his wife. However, a chance encounter with waitress Lyudmila Gurchenko alters everything. DP. A Russian language film.

Oleg Basilashvili *Platon* • Lyudmila Gurchenko *Vera* • Nikita Mikhalkov *Vera's boyfriend* • Nonna Mordyukova *Waitress* ■ *Dir* Eldar Ryazanov • *Scr* Emil Braginsky, from a story by Eldar Ryazanov

Station Six-Sahara ★★★★

Drama 1962 · UK/W Ger · BW · 101mins

Eroticism isn't something that the British cinema tackles very often, but this 1962 offering does. It's set on an oil pipeline in the middle of the Sahara where the blokes are muscular, sweaty and bad-tempered. Their frustration is palpable. Then out of the blue comes a provocative, unbuttoned Carroll Baker. Directed by former editor Seth Holt and co-written by Bryan Forbes, it makes the most of an intrinsically ridiculous situation, relishing the clichés, laying on the impudent symbolism and wringing out as much sexual tension as possible. AT

Carroll Baker *Catherine* • Peter Van Eyck *Kramer* • Ian Bannen *Fletcher* • Denholm Elliott *Macey* • Hansjörg Felmy *Martin* • Mario Adorf *Santos* • Biff McGuire *Jimmy* • Harry Baird *Sailor* ■ *Dir* Seth Holt • *Scr* Bryan Forbes, Brian Clemens, from the play *Men without a Past* by Jacques Maret

Station West ★★★

Western 1948 · US · BW · 92mins

Former crooner Dick Powell had just carved out a new career for himself as a tough guy in such taut thrillers as *Farewell My Lovely* (1945) and *Johnny O'Clock* (1947) and so brought a new, darker image to this cleverly scripted RKO western about an army investigator trying to sort out a series of gold heists. Jane Greer makes a feisty sparring partner, but what really gives this movie some distinction is the use of clever one-liners. TS

Dick Powell *Lt John Martin Haven* • Jane Greer *Charlie* • Agnes Moorehead *Mrs Mary Caslon* • Burl Ives *Hotel clerk* • Tom Powers *Captain George Iles* • Gordon Oliver *Prince* • Steve Brodie *Lt Stellman* • [Guinn "Big Boy" Williams] *Mick Marion* • Raymond Burr *Mark Bristow* • Regis Toomey *James Goddard* ■ *Dir* Sidney Lanfield • *Scr* Frank Fenton, Winston Miller, from a novel by Luke Short as serialised in *The Saturday Evening Post*

Stavisky ★★★★

Period drama based on a true story
1974 · Fr/It · Colour · 117mins

With Jean-Paul Belmondo in the lead, a famous scandal as its subject, atmospheric art deco sets and a memorable Stephen Sondheim score, this is Alain Resnais's most commercial picture. Yet, with its temporal shifts and deft blend of fact, memory and fallacy, it also serves as a perfect vehicle for Resnais's trademark preoccupations, as he explores the legend grown up around a financial swindle that had the most sinister political implications. It's a technically accomplished film, too, with Resnais using filters to approximate 1930s Technicolor and restricting himself to angles only extant in the period. DP. In French with English subtitles.

Jean-Paul Belmondo *Stavisky* • Charles Boyer *Baron Raoul* • François Périer *Albert Borelli* • Anny Duperey *Arlette Stavisky* • Michel Lonsdale *Dr Mezy* • Claude Rich *Bonny* ■ *Dir* Alain Resnais • *Scr* Jorge Semprun • *Cinematographer* Sacha Vierny

Stay Away, Joe ★★ U

Comedy drama 1968 · US · Colour · 96mins

Shamefully depicting native Americans as dissolute wastrels obsessed with girls and grog, this Elvis Presley romp was uncharacteristically bawdy. Every bit as unenlightened is the chauvinistic story, with Elvis taking a break from flirting with Joan Blondell's teenage daughter to help his shiftless father (Burgess Meredith) pull a cattle scam on the government. Rarely called upon to sing, Presley shambles along as he's upstaged by his veteran co-stars. DP

Elvis Presley *Joe Lightcloud* • Burgess Meredith *Charlie Lightcloud* • Joan Blondell *Glenda Callahan* • Katy Jurado *Annie Lightcloud* • Thomas Gomez *Grandpa* • Jones Henry *Hy Slager* • LQ Jones *Bronc Hoverty* ■ *Dir* Peter Tewksbury • *Scr* Michael A Hoey, from the novel by Dan Cushman

Stay Hungry ★★★★ 18

Drama 1976 · US · Colour · 98mins

Before Arnold Schwarzenegger found muscleman fame and Robert Englund became Elm Street's Freddy, they turned up as characters in Bob Rafelson's culture-clash tale about what happens when Alabama heir Jeff Bridges infiltrates a downtown gym for real-estate reasons and falls for Sally Field. Totally laid-back, this all seems pointlessly unstructured, until you realise that's the way it's supposed to be: an endearing look at barbell bums who may never win through, but have lots of fun trying. TH. Contains violence, swearing, nudity. DVD

Jeff Bridges *Craig Blake* • Sally Field *Mary Tate Farnsworth* • Arnold Schwarzenegger *Joe Santo* • RG Armstrong *Thor Erickson* • Robert Englund *Franklin* • Helena Kallianiotes *Anita* • Roger E Mosley *Newton* • Scatman Crothers *Butler* ■ *Dir* Bob Rafelson • *Scr* Bob Rafelson, Charles Gaines, from the novel by Charles Gaines

Stay Tuned ★★ PG

Comedy fantasy 1992 · US · Colour · 84mins

The central conceit is quite clever: TV-obsessed John Ritter sells his soul to the Devil (Jeffrey Jones) and finds himself literally trapped in the box with wife Pam Dawber. However, the execution is all wrong, and the result is a string of rather lame send-ups of popular television shows. Jones is as reliable as ever, but the two leads are bland and Peter Hyams never really gets a handle on the project. Watch for the splendid animation sequence directed by Chuck Jones. JF

John Ritter *Roy Knable* • Pam Dawber *Helen Knable* • Jeffrey Jones *Spike* • Eugene Levy *Crowley* • David Tom *Darryl Knable* • Heather McComb *Diane Knable* • Michael Hogan (3) *Duane* ■ *Dir* Peter Hyams • *Scr* Tom S Parker, Jim Jennewein, from a story by Tom S Parker, Jim Jennewein, Richard Siegel

Staying Alive ★★ PG

Musical drama 1983 · US · Colour · 92mins

This sequel to *Saturday Night Fever*, the film that launched his career, isn't the lowest point in John Travolta's career, but one he would still probably love to forget. Warning bells should have started ringing over the involvement of Sylvester Stallone, who co-wrote and directed this clunker. The slim plot focuses on Travolta, now a professional dancer, being torn between two women as he prepares for a big show. Stallone's brother Frank, who was responsible for much of the music, is certainly no Bee Gee. JF. Contains swearing. DVD

John Travolta *Tony Manero* • Cynthia Rhodes *Jackie* • Finola Hughes *Laura* • Steve Inwood *Jesse* • Julie Bovasso *Mrs Manero* • Charles Ward *Butler* ■ *Dir* Sylvester Stallone • *Scr* Sylvester Stallone, Norman Wexler, from characters created by Nik Cohn

Staying Together ★★★ 15

Comedy drama 1989 · US · Colour · 87mins

This is a sentimental, if well-intentioned little movie about a small-town family facing radical upheavals. The McDermotts own a fried chicken business and the three boys believe that is where their future lies. But when dad (Jim Haynie) sells the restaurant and dies, the boys have to rethink. This character-driven movie doesn't sound like much, but this is surprisingly engrossing, thanks to sensitive direction from actress Lee Grant. DA

Sean Astin *Duncan McDermott* • Stockard Channing *Nancy Trainer* • Melinda Dillon *Eileen McDermott* • Jim Haynie *Jake McDermott* • Levon Helm *Denny Stockton* • Dinah Manoff *Lois Cook* • Dermot Mulroney *Kit McDermott* • Tim Quill *Brian McDermott* ■ *Dir* Lee Grant • *Scr* Monte Merrick

The Steal ★★ PG

Crime comedy 1994 · UK · Colour · 90mins

This has a strong cast, but the uninspired direction and script leave the talented players floundering. Alfred Molina and Helen Slater are the amateur crooks out to rob a City firm who get mixed up in an increasingly hysterical series of misadventures. The leads give of their best and there are enthusiastic turns from the good supporting cast, yet it must go down as another missed opportunity. JF. Contains swearing.

Alfred Molina *Cliff* • Helen Slater *Kim* • Peter Bowles *Lord Childwell* • Dinsdale Landen *Sir Wilmot* • Heathcote Williams *Jeremiah* • Stephen Fry *Wimborne* • Bryan Pringle *Cecil, bank doorman* • Jack Dee *Wilmot's servant* ■ *Dir/Scr* John Hay

Steal ★★ 15

Action crime drama
2002 · Fr/Can/UK · Colour · 84mins

Featuring the first rollerskating crooks since Jean-Hugues Anglade trundled his way through *Subway*, the plot strives to provide a few novel twists on the last blag scenario. But Stephen Dorff's plan to land $20 million in five farewell raids is doomed to misfire after someone tips off the cops and the gang steal a consignment of Mafia money. The stunt performers merit mention for the high-speed chases, but everything else is overly familiar, right down to Steven Berkoff's scenery-gnawing histrionics. DP

Stephen Dorff *Slim* • Natasha Henstridge *Karen Svenson* • Bruce Payne *Lt Jake MacGruder* • Steven Berkoff *Surtayne* ■ *Dir* Gérard Pirès • *Scr* Mark Ezra, Gérard Pirès

Steal Big, Steal Little ★★ 12

Action comedy 1995 · US · Colour · 108mins

This misguided comedy tale of greed and corruption stars Andy Garcia as

S

the identical twin brothers battling over the estate left by their adoptive mother. As you would expect, one's a really nice guy and the other is a scheming rat. What sounds like a simple tale is in reality a confusing mess of too many plot strands and supporting characters. JC

Andy Garcia *Ruben Partida Martinez/Robert Martin* • Alan Arkin *Lou Perilli* • Rachel Ticotin *Laura Martinez* • Joe Pantoliano *Eddie Agopian* • Holland Taylor *Mona Rowland-Downey* • Ally Walker *Bonnie Martin* • David Ogden Stiers *Judge Winton Myers* ■ *Dir* Andrew Davis • *Scr* Andrew Davis, Lee Blessing, Jeanne Blake, Terry Kahn, from a story by Teresa Tucker-Davies, Frank Ray Perilli, Andrew Davis

Stealing Beauty ★★ 15

Romantic drama
1995 · It/UK/Fr · Colour · 113mins

Accomplished director Bernardo Bertolucci stumbles into bathos with this small-scale romantic drama. Liv Tyler stars as the American teenager who, after her mother's suicide, takes a summer holiday with an expatriate family in Tuscany. Anxious to lose her virginity and discover the identity of her biological father, she encounters a range of eccentric house guests, including Jeremy Irons as a terminally ill playwright and Jean Marais as an art dealer. Pretentiously false. TH. Contains swearing, sex scenes. DVD

Sinead Cusack *Diana Grayson* • Jeremy Irons *Alex Parrish* • Liv Tyler *Lucy Harmon* • Jean Marais *Monsieur Guillaume* • Donal McCann *Ian Grayson* • DW Moffett *Richard Reed* • Stefania Sandrelli *Noemi* • Rachel Weisz *Miranda Fox* • Joseph Fiennes *Christopher Fox* ■ *Dir* Bernardo Bertolucci • *Scr* Susan Minot, from a story by Bernardo Bertolucci

Stealing Harvard ★ 12

Crime comedy 2002 · US · Colour · 81mins

Tom Green applies the kiss of death to yet another film. Here the hugely unfunny comic may only play support to Jason Lee's lead, but he's enough to sink a mediocre movie. Lee plays a none-too-bright nice guy who's reminded of his vow to pay his trailer-trash niece's tuition fees if she gets into a good university – and she's just got a place at Harvard. Unfunny, overplayed and underplotted. DA DVD

Jason Lee *John Plummer* • Tom Green *Walter "Duff" Duffy* • Leslie Mann *Elaine Warner* • Megan Mullally *Patty Plummer* • Dennis Farina *Mr Warner* • Tammy Blanchard *Noreen* • Richard Jenkins *Mr Cook* • Chris Penn *David Loach* • John C McGinley *Detective Charles* • Seymour Cassel *Uncle Jack* ■ *Dir* Bruce McCulloch • *Scr* Peter Tolan, from a story by Peter Tolan, Martin Hynes

Stealing Heaven ★★ 15

Historical romance
1988 · UK/Yug · Colour · 110mins

The true story of medieval star-crossed lovers Abelard and Heloise gets an unsubtle and highly erotic treatment in director Clive Donner's soap-opera confection. Philosophy scholar Abelard, who is supposed to remain celibate, falls for the aristocratic Heloise and they flout both religion and society as they wend their romantic way towards inevitable tragedy. Despite the efforts of a good cast, the film remains resolutely ordinary. AJ

Derek De Lint *Abelard* • Kim Thomson *Heloise* • Denholm Elliott *Canon Fulbert* • Bernard Hepton *Bishop Martin* • Kenneth Cranham *Vice Chancellor Suger* • Patsy Bryne *Agnes* ■ *Dir* Clive Donner • *Scr* Chris Bryant, from the novel by Marion Meade

Stealing Home ★★★ 15

Drama 1988 · US · Colour · 93mins

This should be seen if only for future Oscar-winner Jodie Foster's fine performance as the wild Katie, whose death evokes troubled memories and regrets among her young contemporaries. Told in flashback, this movie is the cinematic autobiography of its two writer/directors (Steven Kampmann and Will Aldis) and was too earnest and personal to achieve a wide release. TS. Contains swearing, sex scenes.

Mark Harmon *Billy Wyatt as an adult* • Jodie Foster *Katie Chandler* • Blair Brown *Ginny Wyatt* • Jonathan Silverman *Alan Appleby as a teenager* • Harold Ramis *Alan Appleby as an adult* • John Shea *Sam Wyatt* • William McNamara *Billy Wyatt as a teenager* ■ *Dir/Scr* Steven Kampmann, Will Aldis [Will Porter]

Stealth Fighter ★★ 15

Action thriller 1999 · US · Colour · 83mins

Ice-T plays a top pilot who steals a top of the range stealth fighter plane and then teams up with a drug baron to extort the US Government for billion of dollars. Costas Mandylor is the naval officer assigned to bring the rogue pilot in, and there are fleeting appearances from an eclectic collection of vaguely familiar faces. However, no one makes an impression, while the action sequences and effects are laughable. JF DVD

Ice-T *Owen Turner* • Costas Mandylor *Ryan Mitchell* • Ernie Hudson *President Westwood* • Andrew Divoff *Robert Menendez* • Erika Eleniak *Erin Mitchell* • William Sadler *Peterson* ■ *Dir* Jay Andrews [Jim Wynorski] • *Scr* Lenny Juliano

Steamboat Bill, Jr ★★★★★ U

Silent comedy 1928 · US · BW · 69mins

The last of Keaton's fully independent films, made just before he signed with MGM and went into a precipitous decline. The story concerns two rival steamboat operators and Keaton, of course, plays the saphead son of one of them, arriving fresh from college and falling in love with the rival's daughter. Keaton achieves an authentic, Mark Twain-style look, although the film was made entirely in California rather than the Deep South. As well as a series of wonderful gags, he also produces the most spectacular and dangerous sequence of his entire career – a cyclone that sweeps up everything in its path. This culminates in an entire house collapsing on our hero, who escapes through a tiny upstairs window. AT DVD

Buster Keaton *William "Willie" Canfield Jr* • Ernest Torrence *William "Steamboat Bill" Canfield Sr* • Tom Lewis *His first mate* • Tom McGuire *John James King, his rival* • Marion Byron *Kitty, his daughter* ■ *Dir* Charles Reisner • *Scr* Carl Harbaugh • *Cinematographer* J Devereaux Jennings, Bert Haines

Steamboat round the Bend ★★★ U

Drama 1935 · US · BW · 77mins

This warm-hearted Will Rogers vehicle was released after his tragic death in a plane crash. With the distance of time, this may require tolerance from the viewer, but it's still fascinating to watch a riverboat battle between America's two folk philosophers of the time, Rogers himself and the garrulous Irvin S Cobb. Director John Ford was always prone to sentimentalise, and this is no exception, but he achieves a sweet, elegiac feel for a more gentle, romantic past. TS DVD

Will Rogers *Dr John Pearly* • Anne Shirley *Fleety Belle* • Eugene Pallette *Sheriff Rufe Jeffers* • John McGuire *Duke* • Berton Churchill *New Moses* • Stepin Fetchit *Jonah* ■ *Dir* John Ford • *Scr* Dudley Nichols, Lamar Trotti, from the novel by Ben Lucian Burman

Steamboat Willie ★★★★★

Animation 1928 · US · BW · 7mins

Walt Disney's third Mickey Mouse cartoon has Mickey as the captain of a steamboat sailing up the Mississippi, and demonstrates Disney's use of music and sound to give additional weight to a production's narrative and structure. (This was the first animated film with sound.) In one memorable moment, a cow's teeth are played like a xylophone, while its udder is used as a bagpipe. The term "Mickey Mouse Music" – with the soundtrack covering all visual events – undoubtedly came from this cartoon, which was the first notable example of the audio-visual orchestration used so effectively in later Disney successes. TH

Walt Disney *Mickey Mouse* ■ *Dir* Walt Disney • *Scr* Walt Disney, Ub Iwerks • *Music* Carl Stalling [Carl W Stalling] • *Animator* Ub Iwerks

Steaming ★★★★ 18

Drama 1985 · UK · Colour · 91mins

If you liked Nell Dunn's breast-beating play about an all-women group at the local Turkish baths, you'll love Joseph Losey's movie, which sticks rigidly to text and scene. It is a tightly drawn, multi-charactered, often insightful look at the female condition, with a last, wonderful performance from Diana Dors as the surrogate mum in charge of the towels. Both achingly sad and funny. SH. Contains nudity.

Vanessa Redgrave *Nancy* • Sarah Miles *Sarah* • Diana Dors *Violet* • Patti Love *Josie* • Brenda Bruce *Mrs Meadows* • Felicity Dean *Dawn Meadows* • Sally Sagoe *Celia* • Anna Tzelniker *Mrs Goldstein* ■ *Dir* Joseph Losey • *Scr* Patricia Losey, from the play by Nell Dunn

Steel ★★ 15

Drama 1980 · US · Colour · 97mins

This melodrama features a race to complete the top nine floors of a skyscraper before the banks close in. Lee Majors stars (and produces) as the construction leader, while Jennifer O'Neill is the company owner, having taken over from her recently deceased father. Like the skyscraper itself, production in Lexington, Kentucky was dogged by problems, including the death of stuntman AJ Bakunis to whom the picture is dedicated. It's a pity the movie itself is so ordinary. AT

Lee Majors *Mike Catton* • Jennifer O'Neill *Cass Cassidy* • Art Carney *Pignose Moran* • Harris Yulin *Eddie Cassidy* • George Kennedy *Lew Cassidy* • Roger E Mosley *Lionel* • Albert Salmi *Tank* ■ *Dir* Steve Carver • *Scr* Leigh Chapman, from a story by Rob Ewing, Peter S Davis, William N Panzer

Steel ★★ PG

Action fantasy 1997 · US · Colour · 92mins

Former basketball star Shaquille O'Neal suits up in a metal overcoat and butts heads with street gangs in this action fantasy that's loosely based on the DC Comics superhero of the same name. As an actor, Shaq makes a great basketball player, and one suspects that he finds remembering dialogue as hard as making free throw shots consistently. ST. Contains violence and swearing.

Shaquille O'Neal *Steel/John Henry Irons* • Annabeth Gish *Susan Sparks* • Judd Nelson *Nathaniel Burke* • Richard Roundtree *Uncle Joe* • Irma P Hall *Grandma Odessa* • Ray J *Martin* • Charles Napier *Colonel David* ■ *Dir* Kenneth Johnson • *Scr* Kenneth Johnson, from the character created by Jon Bogdanove, Louise Simonson

The Steel Bayonet ★★

Second World War drama
1957 · UK · BW · 82mins

Michael Carreras directs rather in the style of an American platoon picture – the title is reminiscent of a Sam Fuller movie – as it deals with Leo Genn and his battle-worn men who are ordered to hold a farmhouse during the Allied assault on Tunis. As in American movies, the men embody a variety of attitudes towards the morality of war, but, this being a British movie, it all comes down to class attitudes. AT

Leo Genn *Major Gerrard* • Kieron Moore *Captain Mead* • Michael Medwin *Lieutenant Vernon* • Robert Brown *Sgt Maj Gill* • Michael Ripper *Private Middleditch* • John Paul *Lt Col Derry* • Michael Caine ■ *Dir* Michael Carreras • *Scr* Howard Clewes

The Steel Helmet ★★★

War drama 1951 · US · BW · 84mins

The first in a long line of Samuel Fuller war movies has Gene Evans as a seasoned sergeant in the thick of the Korean War. He survives a massacre, is saved by an orphan and injects a deep-rooted cynicism into the platoon he adopts as his own. Shot in a mere ten days and sometimes looking like it took only five, the movie has the energy that is so typical of its director. AT

Gene Evans *Sgt Zack* • Robert Hutton *Pte "Conchie" Bronte* • Richard Loo *Sgt "Buddhahead" Tanaka* • Steve Brodie *Lt Driscoll* • James Edwards *Cpl "Medic" Thompson* • Sid Melton *Joe, 2nd GI* • Richard Monahan *Pte Baldy* • William Chun *"Short Round"* • Lynn Stalmaster *2nd Lieutenant* ■ *Dir/Scr* Samuel Fuller

The Steel Key ★★ U

Spy drama 1953 · UK · BW · 70mins

Terence Morgan is effective enough in this uninspired B-movie, trying to rescue a scientist and his formula for super-hardened steel from the clutches of enemy agents. But director Robert Baker's brisk pace can't disguise either the potholes in the plot or the phoneyness of the dialogue. DP

Terence Morgan *Johnny O'Flynn* • Joan Rice *Doreen Wilson* • Raymond Lovell *Insp Forsythe* • Dianne Foster *Sylvia Newman* • Hector Ross *Beroni* • Colin Tapley *Dr Crabtree* • Arthur Lovegrove *Gilchrist* ■ *Dir* Robert S Baker • *Scr* John Gilling, from a story by Roy Chanslor

Steel Magnolias ★★★★ PG

Comedy drama 1989 · US · Colour · 113mins

At a time when muscle-bound action heroes held sway at the box office, this provided juicy roles for some of Hollywood's leading ladies. Sally Field, Daryl Hannah, Olympia Dukakis and Julia Roberts interact so beautifully as they discuss men, the menopause, manicures and marriage in Dolly Parton's kitsch small-town beauty salon that it was something of a surprise that only Roberts scooped an Oscar nomination. A little too dependent on sassy one-liners and awash with sentiment by the end, this is still wonderful entertainment. DP. Contains swearing. DVD

Sally Field *M'Lynn Eatenton* • Dolly Parton *Truvy Jones* • Shirley MacLaine *Ouiser Boudreaux* • Daryl Hannah *Annelle Dupuy Desoto* • Julia Roberts *Shelby Eatenton Latcherie* • Olympia Dukakis *Clairee Belcher* • Tom Skerritt *Drum Eatenton* • Dylan McDermott *Jackson Latcherie* • Sam Shepard *Spud Jones* • Daryl Hannah *Annelle Dupuy Desoto* ■ *Dir* Herbert Ross • *Scr* Robert Harling, from his play

The Steel Trap ★★★ U

Crime comedy 1952 · US · BW · 84mins

Assistant bank manager Joseph Cotten steals money from his employer and attempts to flee to Brazil where there is no extradition treaty, but finds his plans thwarted when he misses his flight. Cotten and Teresa Wright, the uncle and niece from Hitchcock's *Shadow of a Doubt*, are reunited here as husband and wife, and both are excellent. The film is directed from his own screenplay by Andrew L Stone, who would go on to specialise in well-made suspense tales. TS

Joseph Cotten *Jim Osborne* • Teresa Wright *Laurie Osborne* • Eddie Marr *Ken* • Aline Towne *Gail* • Bill Hudson *Raglin* ■ *Dir/Scr* Andrew Stone [Andrew L Stone]

Steelyard Blues ★★★ 15

Comedy 1973 · US · Colour · 89mins

Whatever happened to director Alan Myerson, who announced himself as an offbeat original with this comic irreverence? Strung out attractively between dotty humour and period paranoia, this concerns a bunch of square pegs who plan to revive an abandoned seaplane and escape to a better life. The humour emerges naturally from the situation. JM. Contains swearing.

Donald Sutherland *Jesse Veldini* • Jane Fonda *Iris Caine* • Peter Boyle *Eagle Throneberry* • Howard Hesseman *Frank Veldini* • Garry Goodrow *Duval Jacks* • John Savage *The Kid* • Richard Schaal *Zoo official* ■ *Dir* Alan Myerson • *Scr* David S Ward

Stella ★★★

Comedy mystery 1950 · US · BW · 75mins

This frantic black comedy feels like an inversion of *The Trouble with Harry*, as all the fun stems from an accidental death and the burial of a body. Victor Mature gives a sportingly self-ridiculing performance as the insurance investigator attempting to make sense of the ramblings of Ann Sheridan's eccentric kin as they seek to pass off any old corpse to get their hands on the pay-out, while barking nephew David Wayne tries to recall where he interred his detested uncle. DP

Ann Sheridan *Stella* • Victor Mature *Jeff De Marco* • David Wayne *Carl Granger* • Randy Stuart *Claire Granger* • Marion Marshall *Mary* • Frank Fontaine *Don* • Leif Erickson *Fred Anderson* • Evelyn Varden *Flora Bevins* ■ *Dir* Claude Binyon • *Scr* Claude Binyon, from the novel *Family Skeleton* by Doris Miles Disney

Stella ★★★ PG

Drama 1955 · Gr · BW · 90mins

Michael Cacoyannis's second feature made an instant star of its debuting lead, Melina Mercouri. Mercouri's hall singer is the Greek equivalent of Carmen, as she inflames passions with her smouldering availability and tempestuous spirit. Yet she herself only has eyes for footballer George Foundas – until, that is, she begins to perceive marriage as a trap and not a declaration of love. Despite bringing a raw realism to his depiction of backstreet Athens, Cacoyannis allows Mercouri too much latitude and her exuberance unbalances the narrative. DP. A Greek language film.

Melina Mercouri *Stella* • George Foundas *Milto* • Alekos Alexandrakis *Aleko* • Sophia Vembo *Maria* • Voula Zoumboulaki *Anneta* ■ *Dir* Michael Cacoyannis • *Scr* Michael Cacoyannis, from the play *Stella with the Red Gloves* by Iakovos Kabanellis

Stella ★★ 15

Melodrama 1990 · US · Colour · 104mins

Battling Bette Midler takes on the old Barbara Stanwyck role of working-class mother Stella Dallas and loses. Not only does her character (here renamed Stella Claire) seem horribly politically incorrect in her efforts to get illegitimate daughter Trini Alvarado married to an upper-crust beau, but Midler is also far too feisty for this out-of-date melodrama. Even the starry cast is defeated by this over-sentimental stodge. TH. Contains swearing, drug abuse, nudity.

Bette Midler *Stella Claire* • John Goodman *Ed Munn* • Trini Alvarado *Jenny Claire* • Stephen Collins *Stephen Dallas* • Marsha Mason *Janice Morrison* • Eileen Brennan *Mrs Wilkerson* • Linda Hart *Debbie Whitman* • Ben Stiller *Jim Uptegrove* ■ *Dir* John Erman • *Scr* Robert Getchell, from the novel *Stella Dallas* by Olive Higgins Prouty

Stella Dallas ★★★★

Silent drama 1925 · US · BW · 108mins

Small-town Belle Bennett marries out of her class. When her husband Ronald Colman leaves their hopeless marriage and returns to New York, she lavishes love on their daughter Lois Moran, but later sacrifices the girl to a better life with her father and marriage to Douglas Fairbanks Jr. Down-at-heel Bennett, watching the wedding through a window with tears streaming down her face, gave the cinema of weepie melodrama one of its most famous and enduring images. Directed with taste and sensitivity by Henry King. RK

Ronald Colman *Stephen Dallas* • Belle Bennett *Stella Dallas* • Alice Joyce *Helen Morrison* • Jean Hersholt *Ed Munn* • Beatrix Pryor *Mrs Grovesnor* • Lois Moran *Laurel Dallas* • Douglas Fairbanks Jr *Richard Grovesnor* • Vera Lewis *Miss Tibbets* ■ *Dir* Henry King • *Scr* Frances Marion, from the novel by Olive Higgins Prouty

Stella Dallas ★★★★ U

Melodrama 1937 · US · BW · 101mins

The magnificent Barbara Stanwyck never won a performance Oscar, the Academy making its usual reparation by presenting her with an honorary award in 1981. *Stella Dallas* is the movie for which she deserved the best actress Oscar, but that year the honour went to Luise Rainer in Sidney Franklin's *The Good Earth*. Stella is the ultimate soap-opera queen, a woman who, quite literally, sacrifices everything for her daughter's happiness, and this movie is the definitive version of the tale. Stanwyck is brilliant, her own upbringing as a Brooklyn orphan giving added resonance to the story. TS

Barbara Stanwyck *Stella Martin Dallas* • John Boles *Stephen Dallas* • Anne Shirley *Laurel Dallas* • Barbara O'Neil *Helen Morrison* • Alan Hale *Ed Munn* • Marjorie Main *Mrs Martin* • Edmund Elton *Mr Martin* • Tim Holt *Richard* ■ *Dir* King Vidor • *Scr* Sarah Y Mason, Victor Heerman, from the play by Harry Wagstaff Gribble, Gertrude Purcell, from the novel by Olive Higgins Prouty

Stella Does Tricks ★★★ 18

Drama 1997 · UK · Colour · 94mins

This bittersweet little story about teenage prostitution from director Coky Giedroyc is well-intentioned but ends up being rather voyeuristic. Kelly Macdonald is excellent as the feisty young girl, working for creepy pimp James Bolam, who wants to stop working the streets and go away with drug addict Hans Matheson. The film is not exactly heartening but remains compelling, thanks to Macdonald's winning performance. JB. Contains drug abuse, swearing and violence.

Kelly Macdonald *Stella McGuire* • James Bolam *Mr Peters* • Hans Matheson *Eddie* • Ewan Stewart *McGuire* • Andy Serkis *Fitz* ■ *Dir* Coky Giedroyc • *Scr* AL Kennedy

Stella Maris ★★★★

Silent drama 1918 · US · BW · 84mins

"Two Marys for the price of one!" gloated the poster for this weepie starring "America's Sweetheart", Mary Pickford, in a dual role. As Stella Maris she is a pretty and pampered invalid, and as Unity Blake she is a less attractive orphan girl. Both are in love with Conway Tearle. In order to ensure some sort of happy ending, it's the homely Unity who sacrifices herself for the happiness of the ringleted Stella. Director Marshall A Neilan pumped the tears without mercy, helped by a realistically successful double portrayal by Pickford. TH

Mary Pickford *Stella Maris/Unity Blake* • Conway Tearle *John Risca* • Marcia Manon *Louise Risca* • Ida Waterman *Lady Blount* • Herbert Standing *Sir Oliver Blount* ■ *Dir* Marshall A Neilan [Marshall Neilan] • *Scr* Frances Marion, from the novel by William J Locke

The Stendhal Syndrome ★★★ 18

Horror thriller 1996 · It · Colour · 110mins

Director Dario Argento's daughter, Asia, plays the lead in this deeply disturbing thriller. However, she rarely convinces as the detective whose pursuit of serial rapist Thomas Kretschmann is hindered by the fact she secretly suffers from a condition that causes her to hallucinate in the presence of paintings. Even ignoring all the psychological ramifications, this is not one of the Italian horror maestro's finer hours. There are some bravura camera movements, Rome and Florence look stunning, and Ennio Morricone's score is superb, but the pacing is indifferent. DP. In Italian with English subtitles. DVD

Asia Argento *Anna Manni* • Thomas Kretschmann *Alfredo Grossi* • Marco Leonardi *Marco Longhi* • Luigi Diberti *Inspector Manetti* ■ *Dir* Dario Argento • *Scr* Dario Argento, from the novel *La Sindrome di Stendhal* by Graziella Magherini

Step Lively ★★★ U

Musical comedy 1944 · US · BW · 84mins

Frank Sinatra's last film before his move to MGM is a musical remake of the comedy *Room Service* – also the basis for a Marx Brothers movie. Under the tutelage of Gene Kelly, Sinatra would finally prove that he was more than just the king of the bobbysoxers, but here he occasionally looks a little lost when he's not given some crooning to do. George Murphy is wildly over the top as a theatrical producer who's initially interested in Sinatra's cash rather than his voice. DP

Frank Sinatra *Glen* • George Murphy *Miller* • Adolphe Menjou *Wagner* • Gloria DeHaven *Christine* • Walter Slezak *Gribble* • Eugene Pallette *Jenkins* • Wally Brown *Binion* • Alan Carney *Harry* ■ *Dir* Tim Whelan • *Scr* Warren Duff, Peter Milne, from the play *Room Service* by John Murray, Allen Boretz • *Music/lyrics* Sammy Cahn, Jule Styne

Step Lively, Jeeves ★★

Comedy 1937 · US · BW · 69mins

This sequel to *Thank You, Jeeves* commits the ultimate heresy of featuring the world's most resourceful gentleman's gentleman without the young master himself, one Bertie Wooster. Owing nothing to the genius of creator PG Wodehouse, this is an amiable affair, but too much of the action centres on a couple of American conmen (Alan Dinehart and George Givot) who trick Jeeves (the superb Arthur Treacher) into believing he has come into a fortune. DP

Arthur Treacher *Jeeves* • Patricia Ellis *Patricia Westley* • Robert Kent *Gerry Townsend* • Alan Dinehart *Hon Cedric B Cromwell* • George Givot *Prince Boris Caminov* • Helen Flint *Babe Ross* • John Harrington *Barney Ross* ■ *Dir* Eugene Forde • *Scr* Frank Fenton, from a story by Lynn Root, Frances Hyland, from characters created by PG Wodehouse

The Stepfather ★★★★ 18

Horror 1986 · US · Colour · 85mins

This sardonic and unerringly frightening B-movie classic strips down the American Dream to its maggot-ridden gory glory. Shelley Hack and daughter Jill Schoelen gradually come to realise that the charming, affable man of the house is actually a multiple murderer obsessed with middle-class values and establishing the perfect home. Their failure to live up to his pure vision of domestic bliss earmarks them as additions to his ever-growing list of victims. The acting is uniformly fine, with Terry O'Quinn unforgettable as the maniacal patriarch whose psychotic mood swings tighten the suspense screws. Joseph Ruben's faultless direction sets the mayhem against an unsettling backdrop of painfully mundane normality. AJ DVD

Terry O'Quinn *Jerry Blake/Henry Morrison/Bill Hodgkins* • Jill Schoelen *Stephanie Maine* • Shelley Hack *Susan Blake* • Stephen Shellen *Jim Ogilvie* • Robyn Stevan *Karen* ■ *Dir* Joseph Ruben • *Scr* Donald E Westlake, from a story by Carolyn Lefcourt, Brian Garfield, Donald E Westlake

Stepfather II ★★ 18

Horror 1989 · US · Colour · 87mins

The psychotic super-dad (Terry O'Quinn) escapes from a Washington State mental institution, sets himself up as a marriage counsellor and has another go at perfect family life with real-estate agent Meg Foster in this lacklustre sequel. O'Quinn is as good as ever, yet even he can't make the jokey dialogue seem believable. A made-for-TV second sequel was produced in 1992. AJ DVD

Terry O'Quinn *The Stepfather* • Meg Foster *Carol Grayland* • Caroline Williams *Matty Crimmins* • Jonathan Brandis *Todd Grayland* • Henry Brown *Dr Joseph Danvers* • Mitchell Laurance *Phil Grayland* ■ *Dir* Jeff Burr • *Scr* John Auerbach, from characters created by Carolyn Lefcourt, Brian Garfield, Donald E Westlake

The Stepford Wives ★★★★ 15

Science-fiction thriller 1975 · US · Colour · 114mins

Intelligent scripting and thoughtful direction by Bryan Forbes turn Ira Levin's bestseller about suburban housewives becoming obedient robots into an intriguing frightener highlighting society's increasing obsession with perfection. It unfolds at a measured pace so the suspenseful mystery can exert a chilling grip before it ultimately appals, and Katharine Ross and Paula Prentiss shine as the nonconformist women fighting their animatronic fate. You'll be looking at those Nanette Newman washing-up liquid commercials in a different light after this. Followed by three inferior made-for-TV affairs. AJ. Contains swearing and violence. DVD

Katharine Ross *Joanna* • Paula Prentiss *Bobby* • Peter Masterson *Walter* • Nanette Newman *Carol* • Patrick O'Neal *Dale Coba* • Tina Louise *Charmaine* • Carol Rosson *Dr Fancher* ■ *Dir* Bryan Forbes • *Scr* William Goldman, from the novel by Ira Levin

The Stepford Wives ★★ 12

Science-fiction comedy thriller 2004 · US · Colour · 89mins

Ira Levin's bestselling tale of extreme female makeovers is given a satirical update in this clumsy comedy from director Frank Oz. Matthew Broderick moves his high-powered TV-executive wife (Nicole Kidman) to the pastel-perfect Connecticut community of Stepford for a flawless "fembot" overhaul under the management of mayor Christopher Walken. The black comedy isn't consistent, there's little in the way of tension or character development, and the cast acts below its ability. AJ DVD

Nicole Kidman *Joanna Eberhart* • Matthew Broderick *Walter Kresby* • Bette Midler *Roberta "Bobbie" Markowitz* • Christopher Walken *Mike Wellington* • Roger Bart *Roger Bannister* • Faith Hill *Sarah Sunderson* • Glenn Close *Claire Wellington* • David Marshall Grant *Jerry Harmon* • Jon Lovitz

S

David Markowitz • Lorri Bagley *Charmaine Van Sant* ■ *Dir* Frank Oz • *Scr* Paul Rudnick, from the novel by Ira Levin

Stephen King's The Night Flier ★★★ 18

Horror thriller 1997 · US · Colour · 92mins

Based on one of Stephen King's most peculiar short stories, this involves a vampire who pilots a Cessna plane and leaves a trail of bodies in his wake. Tabloid reporter Miguel Ferrer and young rival Julie Entwisle pursue the mysterious killer. Director Mark Pavia does wonders on a small budget, making the atmosphere genuinely tense and mysterious, and gruesome when it needs to be. KB [VIDEO] DVD

Miguel Ferrer *Richard Dees* • Julie Entwisle *Katherine Blair* • Dan Monahan *Merton Morrison* • Michael H Moss *Dwight Renfield* • John Bennes *Ezra Hannon* • Beverly Skinner *Selida McCamon* ■ *Dir* Mark Pavia • *Scr* Mark Pavia, Jack O'Donnell, from the short story by Stephen King

Stephen King's Thinner ★ 18

Horror 1996 · US · Colour · 88mins

The "thinner" end of the wedge as far as adaptations of Stephen King's books go. Robert John Burke is the grossly overweight lawyer cursed by the King of the Gypsies to fade away to nothing after killing a Romany in a hit-and-run car accident. Nothing convinces in this latex-heavy bust where the nightmare twists cause more yawns than terror. AJ. Contains swearing and violence. [VIDEO]

Robert John Burke [Robert Burke] *Billy Halleck* • Joe Mantegna *Richie Ginelli* • Lucinda Jenney *Heidi Halleck* • Joie Lenz *Linda Halleck* • Time Winters *Prosecutor* • Howard Erskine *Judge Phillips* ■ *Dir* Tom Holland • *Scr* Michael McDowell, Tom Holland, from the novel by Richard Bachman [Stephen King]

Stepkids ★★ PG

Comedy 1992 · US · Colour · 100mins

The problems of trying to survive in an overextended family form the basis of director Joan Micklin Silver's over-long and mawkish comedy. Disgruntled 13-year-old Hillary Wolf decides to run away to stepbrother Dan Futterman's lakeside cabin, following a row at home. Unfortunately, far from escaping her dysfunctional family, Wolf's disappearance makes them converge on the cabin. Despite the presence of Griffin Dunne, this is an overly cute and schematic tale. AJ [VIDEO]

Hillary Wolf *Laura Chartoff* • David Strathairn *Keith Powers* • Margaret Whitton *Melinda Powers* • Griffin Dunne *David Chartoff* • Patricia Kalember *Barbara Chartoff* • Adrienne Shelly *Stephanie Miller* • Dan Futterman *Josh Powers* ■ *Dir* Joan Micklin Silver • *Scr* Frank Mugavero, from a story by Mark Goddard, Melissa Goddard, Frank Mugavero

Stepmom ★★★★ 12

Drama 1998 · US/Ger · Colour · 119mins

This is a touching and sophisticated film about post-divorce family life. As the girlfriend of divorcee Ed Harris, fashion photographer Julia Roberts starts off on the wrong foot when she meets his family. Attempting to woo his two children she finds herself competing with their "perfect" mother Susan Sarandon. However, when Sarandon falls seriously ill, the women must reappraise their priorities. Strong performances, which are not afraid to be unsympathetic, and unpredictable narrative twists make this a superior family drama. LH [VIDEO] DVD

Julia Roberts *Isabel Kelly* • Susan Sarandon *Jackie Harrison* • Ed Harris *Luke Harrison* • Jena Malone *Anna Harrison* • Liam Aiken *Ben Harrison* • Lynn Whitfield *Dr Sweikert* ■ *Dir* Chris Columbus • *Scr* Gigi Levangie, Jessie Nelson, Steven Rogers, Karen Leigh Hopkins, Ron Bass, from a story by Gigi Levangie

Steppenwolf ★★★

Part-animated drama
1974 · US · Colour · 107mins

Since 1927, Herman Hesse's novel has sold millions of copies and is regarded as an intensely personal work in its portrait of the intellectual and emotional crises facing a man nudging 50. Inevitably, the response to director Fred Haines's treatment of a seemingly unfilmable book has concentrated on the success in translating it to the screen, but for most people it will emerge as a very striking film visually, dominated by Max von Sydow's fine performance. BB

Max von Sydow *Harry* • Dominique Sanda *Hermine* • Pierre Clémenti *Pablo* • Carla Romanelli *Maria* • Roy Bosier *Aztec* • Alfred Baillou *Goethe* ■ *Dir* Fred Haines • *Scr* Fred Haines, from the novel by Hermann Hesse • *Cinematographer* Tomaslav Pinter

Stepping Out ★★ PG

Musical drama
1991 · Can/US · Colour · 104mins

Lewis Gilbert's rather humdrum hymn to tap and shuffle stars Liza Minnelli as a Broadway hoofer attempting to transform a bunch of near-hopeless amateurs into a crack dancing troupe. All stereotypes are firmly in place, including Julie Walters as a germ-obsessed housewife and Shelley Winters as the cantankerous pianist. Despite its obviousness, this has pockets of fun. SH. Contains some swearing. [VIDEO]

Liza Minnelli *Mavis Turner* • Shelley Winters *Mrs Fraser* • Julie Walters *Vera* • Ellen Greene *Maxine* • Sheila McCarthy *Andy* • Bill Irwin *Geoffrey* • Carol Woods *Rose* • Robyn Stevan *Sylvia* • Jane Krakowski *Lynne* ■ *Dir* Lewis Gilbert • *Scr* Richard Harris, from his play

Stepping Razor – Red X ★★★ 18

Documentary
1992 · Can · Colour and BW · 99mins

Canadian film-maker Nicholas Campbell does for murdered reggae star Peter Tosh what Oliver Stone did for JFK: he deconstructs his death and puts intriguing new perspectives on it. Officially Tosh, former sidekick to Bob Marley and one of reggae's undisputed greats, was killed by criminals. Campbell reckons the murder may have been politically motivated. It's intriguing stuff, marred occasionally by Campbell's contrived visuals. DA [VIDEO]

Dir/Scr Nicholas Campbell

Steptoe and Son ★★★ PG

Comedy 1972 · UK · Colour · 93mins

This is one of the better sitcom spin-offs, with Ray Galton and Alan Simpson contributing a script that not only has a half-decent story, but also gags that would not have disgraced the original TV series. Wilfrid Brambell and Harry H Corbett reprise their roles to good effect, along with Carolyn Seymour, Corbett's new stripper-bride, whose mercenary intentions threaten the future of the rag-and-bone yard. DP [VIDEO] DVD

Wilfrid Brambell *Albert Steptoe* • Harry H Corbett *Harold Steptoe* • Carolyn Seymour *Zita* • Arthur Howard (2) *Vicar* • Victor Maddern *Chauffeur* • Fred Griffiths *Barman* ■ *Dir* Cliff Owen • *Scr* Ray Galton, Alan Simpson, from their TV series

Steptoe and Son Ride Again ★★ PG

Comedy 1973 · UK · Colour · 94mins

This second movie featuring the nation's favourite junkmen is very much a rags-and-bones affair, with the material stretched to fraying point to justify the running time. Apart from the unnecessary crudeness of its humour, the main problem here is the dilution of the intense, disappointed fondness that made the pair's TV relationship so engaging. DP [VIDEO] DVD

Wilfrid Brambell *Albert Steptoe* • Harry H Corbett *Harold Steptoe* • Diana Dors *Woman in flat* • Milo O'Shea *Doctor Popplewell* • Neil McCarthy *Lennie* • Bill Maynard *George* • George Tovey *Percy* • Sam Kydd *Claude* ■ *Dir* Peter Sykes • *Scr* Ray Galton, Alan Simpson, from their TV series

Stereo ★★

Science fiction 1969 · Can · BW · 65mins

In the near future, experiments in telepathic exchange are being conducted by the Canadian Academy for Erotic Inquiry. The idea is to remove a group of volunteers' power of speech, increase their latent telepathic powers, give them aphrodisiac drugs and ultimately expose sexuality for its "polymorphous perversity". The tests result in antagonism and violence. David Cronenberg's directorial debut is confused and distanced, but quietly disturbing. AJ

Ronald Mlodzik • Iain Ewing • Jack Messinger • Clara Mayer • Paul Mulholland • Arlene Mlodzik ■ *Dir/Scr* David Cronenberg

The Sterile Cuckoo ★★★

Romantic comedy drama
1969 · US · Colour · 107mins

Liza Minnelli gives an Oscar-nominated performance, playing the sort of character who puts the "kook" into cuckoo. She's an insecure near-nutter who ropes a hapless college student into her neurotically self-centred world. Predictably, his grades go all to pot in the process. Wendell Burton beautifully plays the boy; curiously, he's been little heard of since. No such obscurity for Alan J Pakula, here making his directorial debut. The movie was released as *Pookie* in the UK – the name of Minnelli's character. DA

Liza Minnelli *Pookie Adams* • Wendell Burton *Jerry Payne* • Tim McIntire *Charlie Schumacher* • Elizabeth Harrower *Landlady* • Austin Green *Pookie's father* • Sandra Faison [Sandy Faison] *Nancy Putnam* • Chris Bugbee *Roe* • Jawn McKinley *Helen Upshaw* ■ *Dir* Alan J Pakula • *Scr* Alvin Sargent, from the novel *The Sterile Cuckoo* by John Treadwell Nichols [John Nichols]

Stevie ★★★ 15

Biographical drama
1978 · UK · Colour · 101mins

Glenda Jackson is typically terrific in this play-derived drama about a poetess living with her doting but dotty maiden aunt Mona Washbourne, giving Glenda Jackson a run for her money in the scene-stealing stakes. Trevor Howard narrates and co-stars. As a film, *Stevie* never quite escapes its obvious stage origins, but it's an intriguing character study, and worth watching for the quality of the performances alone. DA [VIDEO]

Glenda Jackson *Stevie Smith* • Mona Washbourne *Aunt* • Alec McCowen *Freddy* • Trevor Howard *The Man* • Emma Louise Fox *Stevie as a child* ■ *Dir* Robert Enders • *Scr* Hugh Whitmore, from his play and the works of Stevie Smith

Stick ★ 18

Crime thriller 1985 · US · Colour · 104mins

Elmore Leonard adapted his own novel about a flamboyant ex-con who goes down the vengeance trail after his best buddy is rubbed out. Set in the now familiar Leonard world of loan sharks, drug dealers and Palm Beach slimeballs with terrible taste in shirts and wallpaper, it squanders everything for the sake of making star/director Burt Reynolds a handsome, lovable rogue. Reynolds took all the guts out of the book and reshot the ending, but the result was still a critical pasting and box-office disaster. AT [VIDEO]

Burt Reynolds *Stick* • Candice Bergen *Kyle* • George Segal *Barry* • Charles Durning *Chucky* • José Perez (2) *Rainy* • Richard Lawson *Cornell* • Castulo Guerra *Nestor* ■ *Dir* Burt Reynolds • *Scr* Elmore Leonard, Joseph C Stinson, from the novel by Elmore Leonard

Stickmen ★★★ 18

Comedy drama 2000 · NZ · Colour · 93mins

Very much in the hip comic vein of *Lock, Stock and Two Smoking Barrels*, this Kiwi caper is a slick, likeable affair, in which three pool players get dragged into an underworld competition. As well as having to contend with a wacky collection of pool competitors, they also have to stay one step ahead of a Greek mobster, the excellent Enrico Mammarella. Hamish Rothwell's direction is suitably laddish and he and writer Nick Ward bring a winning collection of trick shots to the table. JF. Contains violence, swearing and sex scenes. [VIDEO] DVD

Robbie Magasiva *Jack* • Paolo Rotondo *Thomas* • Scott Wills *Wayne* • Simone Kessell *Karen* • Anne Nordhaus *Sarah* • Luanne Gordon *Lulu* • Enrico Mammarella *Daddy* ■ *Dir* Hamish Rothwell • *Scr* Nick Ward

Sticks and Stones ★★★

Drama 1996 · US · Colour · 95mins

The misery of being bullied is explored in this well-balanced, if overly contrived, teenpic from writer/director Neil Tolkin. There's a spiky performance from Justin Isfeld, whose ambitions to be a baseball pitcher are mocked by both his older brother and the school bully, Jordan Brower. It's refreshing to see "outsiders" being depicted as something other than geeks, but less persuasive are the adults in the cast. DP

Justin Isfeld *Joey* • Max Goldblatt *Book* • Chauncey Leopardi *Mouth* • Jordan Brower *Hayes* • Gary Busey *Book's dad* • Kirstie Alley *Joey's mum* • Lisa Eichhorn *Book's mum* ■ *Dir/Scr* Neil Tolkin

The Stickup ★★★ 15

Crime thriller
2001 · US/Can · Colour · 92mins

James Spader stars as a cop who quits the city after the death of his partner and heads into the backwoods. There his ambition to start afresh takes an unexpected twist when he falls for nurse Leslie Stefanson and finds himself lured on to the wrong side of the law. With a series of flashbacks deepening the mystery, this is a brisk, slickly plotted crime thriller that proves once again that no one does offbeat quite like Spader. DP. Contains violence, swearing. [VIDEO] DVD

James Spader *Parker* • Leslie Stefanson *Natalie Wright* • David Keith *Ray DeCarlo* • John Livingston *FBI Agent Rick Kendall* • Robert Miano *Lt Vincent Marino* • Alfred E Humphreys [Alf Humphreys] *Mike O'Grady* ■ *Dir/Scr* Rowdy Herrington

Sticky Fingers ★★★ 15

Comedy 1988 · US · Colour · 84mins

There is a wonderful air of naive debauchery and jangling nerves about this story of two flat-sharing musicians who are left holding $91,000 in a holdall. Piles of designer clothes and plentiful wild parties later, the hoods are on their trail. The film boasts lovely performances from Helen Slater and Melanie Mayron and a gloriously zany overview of immaturity and neurosis from debuting director Catlin Adams. SH. Contains some swearing. [VIDEO]

Helen Slater *Hattie* • Melanie Mayron *Lolly* • Eileen Brennan *Stella* • Loretta Devine *Diane* • Christopher Guest *Sam* • Carol Kane *Kitty* • Stephen McHattie *Eddie* ■ *Dir* Catlin Adams • *Scr* Catlin Adams, Melanie Mayron

S

The Sticky Fingers of Time ★★ 15

Science-fiction thriller
1997 · US · Colour and BW · 82mins

The basic premise of Hilary Brougher's first feature is intriguing enough, with 1950s sci-fi novelist Terumi Matthews finding her work taking her in an unexpected direction – 40 years into the future. There she meets fellow writer Nicole Zaray, who shares her mysterious time-travelling abilities and some other disturbing symptoms. However, Brougher's recurring shifts between monochrome and colour, an excess of expository chat and the introduction of other (malevolent) time-travellers make it almost impossible to follow. DP [video] DVD

Terumi Matthews *Tucker* • Nicole Zaray *Drew* • Belinda Becker *Ofelia* • James Urbaniak *Isaac* • Amanda Vogel *Girl in window* • Leo Marks *Dex* • Samantha Buck *Gorge* ■ *Dir/Scr* Hilary Brougher

Stiff Upper Lips ★★★★ 15

Period drama parody
1997 · UK · Colour · 91mins

This is a parody (long overdue, some might feel) of the "white flannel" school of British film-making that produced the likes of *Brideshead Revisited* and *Chariots of Fire*, which are all amusingly ridiculed here by co-writer/director Gary Sinyor. Prunella Scales is delightful as the aristocratic Aunt Agnes, who takes her soppy family on a Grand Tour, on which many awful mishaps occur. A genuinely witty script, and locations in Italy and India, make one forget that the joke could have been done as a TV sketch. DM [video]

Peter Ustinov *Horace* • Prunella Scales *Aunt Agnes Ivory* • Georgina Cates *Emily Ivory* • Samuel West *Edward Ivory* • Sean Pertwee *George* • Brian Glover *Eric* • Frank Finlay *Hudson Junior* ■ *Dir* Gary Sinyor • *Scr* Paul Simpkin, Gary Sinyor

Stigmata ★★ 18

Supernatural thriller
1999 · US · Colour · 97mins

A dumb religious horror, in which Patricia Arquette is the atheist hairdresser who suddenly starts suffering from vicious stigmata – wounds identical to the ones Christ received on the cross. When Vatican priest Gabriel Byrne is sent to investigate, he realises there are more to her gory wounds than meets the eye. A booming soundtrack (from Billy Corgan of the Smashing Pumpkins), flashy images and pop video-style direction add to the film's frenetic feel, while diverting us from some of the less plausible plot twists. JB [video] DVD

Patricia Arquette *Frankie Paige* • Gabriel Byrne *Father Andrew Kiernan* • Jonathan Pryce *Cardinal Daniel Houseman* • Nia Long *Donna Chadway* • Thomas Kopache *Father Durning* • Rade Serbedzija *Marion Petrocelli* • Enrico Colantoni *Father Dario* • Dick Latessa *Father Gianni Delmonico* ■ *Dir* Rupert Wainwright • *Scr* Tom Lazarus, Rick Ramage, from a story by Tom Lazarus

Still Crazy ★★★★ 15

Comedy 1998 · US/UK · Colour · 91mins

Fans of the superb rockumentary *This Is Spinal Tap* will chortle at this 1990s British take on the theme. Ageing rockers Jimmy Nail, Timothy Spall, Stephen Rea and Bill Nighy (along with roadie Billy Connolly) reform the successful 1970s group Strange Fruit to go on the road one more time. There are all the clashing egos, old grudges and bad rock numbers you'd expect, plus a deft script from comedy writers Dick Clement and Ian La Frenais, but the true plaudits should go to the performances from Nighy (as the narcissistic lead singer) and Bruce Robinson (writer/director of *Withnail and I*) in a strangely moving cameo role. JB. Contains swearing. [video] DVD

Stephen Rea *Tony Costello* • Billy Connolly *Hughie* • Jimmy Nail *Les Wickes* • Timothy Spall *Beano Baggot* • Bill Nighy *Ray Simms* • Juliet Aubrey *Karen Knowles* • Helena Bergström *Astrid Simms* • Bruce Robinson *Brian Lovell* • Phil Daniels *Neil Gaydon* • Frances Barber *Woman in black* • Phil Davis [Philip Davis] *Limo driver* • Zoë Ball *Zoë* ■ *Dir* Brian Gibson • *Scr* Dick Clement, Ian La Frenais

Still Crazy like a Fox ★★★

Crime comedy 1987 · US · Colour · 93mins

Released a year after the demise of the genial TV series *Crazy like a Fox*, this TV movie reunites oddball San Francisco sleuth Jack Warden and his strait-laced lawyer son John Rubinstein. Here, they head off to Britain, where they become the prime suspects in a murder mystery. This might have become a chore were it not for Monty Python stalwart Graham Chapman, as the Scotland Yard flatfoot in hot pursuit. DP

Jack Warden *Harry Fox* • John Rubinstein *Harrison J Fox* • Penny Peyser *Cindy Fox* • Catherine Oxenberg *Nancy* • Robbie Kiger *Josh Fox* • Graham Chapman *Inspector Palmer* ■ *Dir* Paul Krasny • *Scr* George Schenck, Frank Cardea

Still Life ★★★★

Drama 1974 · Iran · Colour · 93mins

This measured study of social alienation from influential Iranian director Sohrab Shahid Saless earned him both the Silver Bear at the Berlin Film Festival and the enmity of the Shah that forced him into German exile. The superficially simple drama focuses on a veteran railwayman who is discarded in the interests of progress after uncomplainingly doing his monotonous job in near isolation for 30 years. By presenting the daily routines of Zadour Bonyadi and his carpet-weaving wife in such unfussy detail, Saless speaks volumes about the irrelevance of the individual to Iranian industrialisation. DP. In Farsi with English subtitles.

Zadour Bonyadi *Mohamad Sardari* ■ *Dir/Scr* Sohrab Shahid Saless

Still of the Night ★★★★ 15

Thriller 1982 · US · Colour · 87mins

Occasionally as tense as *Jagged Edge*, with dramatic moments reminiscent of medium-grade Hitchcock, this never quite attains the status of classic suspense. On-the-move Meryl Streep stays around long enough to enthral psychiatrist Roy Scheider, one of whose patients winds up dead, in director Robert Benton's moral tale that proclaims doctors should not mix business and pleasure. For all its plot flaws, this is a sleekly crafted movie with performances to match. TH. Contains some violence. [video]

Roy Scheider *Sam Rice* • Meryl Streep *Brooke Reynolds* • Jessica Tandy *Grace Rice* • Joe Grifasi *Joe Vitucci* • Sara Botsford *Gail Phillips* • Josef Sommer *George Bynum* • Irving Metzman *Murray* ■ *Dir* Robert Benton • *Scr* Robert Benton, from a story by David Newman, Robert Benton

The Sting ★★★★★ PG

Period crime caper
1973 · US · Colour · 123mins

These things rarely come off, but the reteaming of *Butch Cassidy and the Sundance Kid* stars Paul Newman and Robert Redford and their director George Roy Hill proved to be a glorious triumph, and this raced away with seven Oscars. Newman and Redford play conmen who, after the death of an old chum, set about fleecing mobster Robert Shaw out of a fortune. The sting itself is as audacious as it is elaborate, but the real pleasure comes from the easy, charismatic playing of the two leads, the lovingly created 1930s settings and Marvin Hamlisch's inspired reworking of Scott Joplin's music. JF. Contains swearing. [video] DVD

Paul Newman *Henry Gondorff* • Robert Redford *Johnny Hooker* • Robert Shaw *Doyle Lonnegan* • Charles Durning *Lt William Snyder* • Ray Walston *JJ Singleton* • Eileen Brennan *Billie* • Harold Gould *Kid Twist* • John Heffernan *Eddie Niles* ■ *Dir* George Roy Hill • *Scr* David S Ward • *Costume Designer* Edith Head • *Cinematographer* Robert Surtees • *Art Director* Henry Bumstead • *Music* Scott Joplin

The Sting II ★★ PG

Period crime caper
1983 · US · Colour · 97mins

Proof that lightning seldom strikes twice, this was the belated and unnecessary sequel to George Roy Hill's multi-Oscar-winning hit. Robert Redford and Paul Newman's scam on gangster Robert Shaw is reprised as a boxing set-up, with Jackie Gleason and Mac Davis as their inadequate replacements. TH [video]

Jackie Gleason *Gondorff* • Mac Davis *Hooker* • Teri Garr *Veronica* • Karl Malden *Macalinski* • Oliver Reed *Lonnegan* ■ *Dir* Jeremy Paul Kagan • *Scr* David S Ward

Stir Crazy ★★★ 15

Comedy 1980 · US · Colour · 106mins

As Sidney Poitier's direction and a firm script all but vanish beneath the clowning, Richard Pryor and Gene Wilder are, according to your taste, either highly creative or contrived, witty or noisy, inspired or tedious. Relying more on mugging than acting, they play a couple of goons who leave New York for California and are wrongly imprisoned for a bank robbery en route. Prison clichés are cleverly lampooned, and Pryor's chicken scene is one that will last. JM. Contains violence, swearing. [video] DVD

Gene Wilder *Skip Donahue* • Richard Pryor *Harry Monroe* • Georg Stanford Brown *Rory Schultebrand* • JoBeth Williams *Meredith* • Miguel Angel Suarez *Jesus Ramirez* • Craig T Nelson *Deputy Ward Wilson* • Barry Corbin *Warden Walter Beatty* • Charles Weldon *Blade* ■ *Dir* Sidney Poitier • *Scr* Bruce Jay Friedman

Stir of Echoes ★★★ 15

Supernatural thriller
1999 · US · Colour · 95mins

David Koepp's creepy supernatural tale was completely overshadowed by *The Sixth Sense*. However, while it isn't as smart or satisfying, it delivers a handful of extremely frightening moments and a credible performance from Kevin Bacon as a man haunted by startling visions. Using jolting cuts and stylised camerawork to evoke fear, Koepp immerses the audience in a mystery involving psychic powers, a dead girl and Bacon's son, who seems to share his "gift". The film's biggest flaw is an overcooked final half hour, but the last scene is a real chiller. JC [video] DVD

Kevin Bacon *Tom Witzky* • Kathryn Erbe *Maggie Witzky* • Illeana Douglas *Lisa* • Liza Weil *Debbie Kozac, the babysitter* • Kevin Dunn *Frank McCarthy* • Conor O'Farrell *Harry Damon* • Jenny Morrison [Jennifer Morrison] *Samantha* ■ *Dir* David Koepp • *Scr* David Koepp, from the novel by Richard Matheson

A Stitch in Time ★★ U

Comedy 1963 · UK · BW · 90mins

Norman Wisdom relives a little of his youth in this sentimental comedy, as his first job at 13 was as a delivery boy. This was his final film in black and white and also his last big starring success at the box office, for he belonged to a more innocent age. The script sticks closely to the Wisdom formula and he knots his cap in shyness in his attempts to declare his love for a pretty nurse. DP [video] DVD

Norman Wisdom *Norman Pitkin* • Edward Chapman *Grimsdale* • Jeannette Sterke *Janet Haskell* • Jerry Desmonde *Sir Hector Hardcastle* • Jill Melford *Lady Brinkley* • Glyn Houston *Welsh* • Hazel Hughes *Matron* ■ *Dir* Robert Asher • *Scr* Jack Davies, Norman Wisdom, Henry Blyth, Eddie Leslie

Stock Car ★ U

Drama 1955 · UK · BW · 66mins

This road smash of a picture packs in every kind of quota quickie cliché, as plucky garage owner Rona Anderson turns to dashing driving ace Paul Carpenter to help her repulse the threat of a charlatan creditor. The mediocrity is unrelenting, with the race sequences every bit as hackneyed as the risible melodrama. DP

Paul Carpenter *Larry Duke* • Rona Anderson *Katie Glebe* • Harry Fowler *Monty Albright* • Paul Whitsun-Jones *Turk McNeil* • Susan Shaw *Gina* • Robert Rietty *Roberto* • Alma Taylor *Nurse Sprott* ■ *Dir* Wolf Rilla • *Scr* AR Rawlinson, Victor Lyndon

Stockade ★★★ 15

Drama 1991 · US · Colour · 93mins

Sheen family projects tend to be more serious fare than usual (think of 1996's *The War at Home*) and this is no exception. In this gripping but talky drama, dad Martin is in the director's chair and also has a co-starring role, alongside son Charlie. There's even a part for a less well-known member of the family, Ramon Estevez. Sheen Jr plays a reluctant soldier sentenced to a term in a military stockade, where he gets locked into a dangerous battle of wills with a cruel NCO, played by Sheen Sr. This is solid if slightly familiar entertainment. JF. Contains swearing and violence. [video]

Charlie Sheen *Franklin Bean Jr* • Martin Sheen *Sergeant Otis V McKinney* • Larry Fishburne [Laurence Fishburne] *Stokes* • Blu Mankuma *Spoonman (Bryce)* • Michael Beach *Webb* • Harry Stewart *Sweetbread (Crane)* • John Toles-Bey *Lawrence* • James Marshall *Lamar* • Ramon Estevez *Gessner* • F Murray Abraham *Garcia* ■ *Dir* Martin Sheen • *Scr* Dennis Schryack, Martin Sheen, from the novel *Count a Lonely Cadence* by Gordon Weaver

Stoked: the Rise and Fall of Gator ★★★ 15

Documentary 2002 · US · Colour · 80mins

Helen Stickler's study of skateboarding superstar Mark "Gator" Rogowski reveals the depressing extent to which youthful exuberance has been exploited by corporate America. One of the vertical-ramp legends of the 1980s, the Californian teenager had an unrivalled marketability that sustained his celebrity lifestyle. But his failure to make the transition to street skating saw his star plummet until he was given 31 years for raping and murdering his former fiancée's best friend. Stickler never excuses Gator's crime, but her precise evocation of a once-golden age makes his actions more comprehensible. DP. Contains swearing, sexual references. DVD

Dir Helen Stickler

The Stolen Children ★★★★ 15

Drama 1992 · It/Fr/Swe · Colour · 110mins

This heart-warming if occasionally sentimental story was inspired by a newspaper headline. In addition to highlighting a range of social issues, director Gianni Amelio also coaxes a quite remarkable performance from Valentina Scalici, as an 11-year-old Sicilian girl who is sent to an orphanage after her desperate mother sells her into prostitution in Milan. Enrico Lo Verso is equally impressive as the inexperienced cop escorting the girl and her younger brother. DP. In Italian with English subtitles.

Enrico Lo Verso *Antonio* • Valentina Scalici *Rosetta* • Giuseppe Ieracitano *Luciano* • Renato Carpentieri *Marshal* • Vitalba Andrea *Antonio's sister* • Fabio Alessandrini *Grignani* ■ *Dir* Gianni Amelio • *Scr* Sandro Petraglia, Stefano Rulli, Gianni Amelio

Stolen Face ★★ PG

Drama 1952 · UK · BW · 69mins

Take this early Hammer melodrama with a ton of salt and you may enjoy its wild fantasy about sexual obsession and the incredible achievements of plastic surgery. Two 1940s stars, past their prime, were dragged to Britain to boost international sales. Surgeon Paul Henreid falls in love with pianist Lizabeth Scott. Thwarted in his desire, he gives Scott's face to a woman convict (not a good move). Fans may detect in this tosh the themes that director Terence Fisher later developed in his *Frankenstein* films. DM DVD

Paul Henreid *Dr Philip Ritter* • Lizabeth Scott *Alice Brent/Lilly* • André Morell *David* • Mary Mackenzie *Lilly* • John Wood *Dr Jack Wilson* • Susan Stephen *Betty* • Arnold Ridley *Dr Russell* ■ *Dir* Terence Fisher • *Scr* Martin Berkeley, Richard Landau

Stolen Hearts ★★ 15

Romantic comedy
1996 · US · Colour · 91mins

Sandra Bullock has little to do in this romantic comedy caper but look gorgeous, leaving her co-star, American stand-up comedian Denis Leary, with the lion's share of the movie. Unfortunately, Leary's trademark put-downs are not enough to carry the film. He's a petty thief who steals a Matisse painting and goes on the run with his girlfriend (Bullock), holing up in a rich New England neighbourhood where the white-trash twosome stand out like sore thumbs. The film shows some glimmers of sarcastic potential, but co-writer Leary's ego gets in the way. TH. Contains swearing. DVD

Denis Leary *Frank* • Sandra Bullock *Roz* • Stephen Dillane *Evan Marsh* • Yaphet Kotto *O'Malley* • Mike Starr *Fitzie* • Jonathan Tucker *Todd* • Wayne Robson *Beano* • Michael Badalucco *Quinn* ■ *Dir* Bill Bennett • *Scr* Denis Leary, Mike Armstrong, from a story by Denis Leary, Mike Armstrong, Ann Lembeck

Stolen Hours ★★ U

Drama 1963 · UK/US · Colour · 96mins

This glossy British remake of *Dark Victory* is a pale imitation of the Bette Davis classic. Susan Hayward – no stranger to screen hardship – is an American socialite with a terminal illness who falls for doctor Michael Craig. It's a worthy production, but the Davis original is too indelible to forget. Cult jazz trumpeter Chet Baker makes a brief appearance, playing himself. RT

Susan Hayward *Laura Pember* • Michael Craig *Dr John Carmody* • Diane Baker *Ellen Pember* • Edward Judd *Mike Bannerman* • Paul Rogers *Dr Eric McKenzie* • Robert Bacon *Peter* • Chet Baker ■ *Dir* Daniel Petrie • *Scr* Jessamyn West, Joseph Hayes, from the play *Dark Victory* by George Emerson Brewer Jr, Bertram Block

Stolen Innocence ★★ 15

Thriller based on a true story
1995 · US · Colour · 89mins

This made-for-TV road movie has a twist – hitcher Tracey Gold strikes out for freedom, but the trucker she takes a lift with turns out to be a maniac. Shot in Kansas and California, director Bill L Norton's thriller starts well, with sparks flying between Gold and the seemingly charming Thomas Calabro. Once her parents leap into action, however, events rapidly become improbable. DP DVD

Tracey Gold *Stacy Sapp* • Thomas Calabro *Richard Brown* • Bess Armstrong *Becky Sapp* • Terence Knox *Jed Harris* • Nick Searcy *John Sapp* • Matthew Letscher *Eddie Shea* ■ *Dir* Bill L Norton • *Scr* Phil Penningroth

Stolen Kisses ★★★★★ 15

Romantic comedy 1968 · Fr · Colour · 87mins

After *The 400 Blows* and the *Antoine et Colette* episode of *Love at Twenty*, Truffaut catches up with Antoine Doinel as he leaves the army and becomes a private eye. Hired by shoeshop owner Michel Lonsdale to find out why the employees hate him, Doinel falls madly in love with Lonsdale's wife (Delphine Seyrig), while trying to remain faithful to his girlfriend (Claude Jade). Once again, Doinel is played to perfection by Jean-Pierre Léaud. Add some engaging subplots and a bit of Hitchcockian mischief with a man in a raincoat, and you have one of Truffaut's greatest movies, a slight but utterly magical romantic comedy set in the Paris of our dreams. AT. In French with English subtitles. DVD

Jean-Pierre Léaud *Antoine Doinel* • Delphine Seyrig *Fabienne Tabard* • Claude Jade *Christine Darbon* • Michel Lonsdale *Monsieur Tabard* • Harry-Max *Monsieur Henri* • André Falcon *Monsieur Blady* ■ *Dir* François Truffaut • *Scr* François Truffaut, Claude de Givray, Bernard Revon

Stolen Life ★★

Romantic drama 1939 · UK · BW · 90mins

Legendary German actress Elisabeth Bergner stars in this British-made romantic melodrama, directed, as were most of her films, by her husband Paul Czinner. Bergner takes the dual role of identical twin sisters in love with the same man (in this case, Michael Redgrave). He is duped into marrying the wrong sister, who later conveniently drowns in his absence, allowing the other to deceive him by taking her place. And that's not all! Well-acted, and quite pleasing for fans of the genre, but more restrained and dull than the full-blooded Bette Davis version made seven years later. RK

Elisabeth Bergner *Sylvina Lawrence/Martina Lawrence* • Michael Redgrave *Alan McKenzie* • Wilfrid Lawson *Thomas Lawrence* • Mabel Terry Lewis *Aunt Helen* • Richard Ainley *Morgan* ■ *Dir* Paul Czinner • *Scr* Margaret Kennedy, from the novel by KJ Benes [Karel J Benes]

A Stolen Life ★★★

Melodrama 1946 · US · BW · 107mins

The great Bette Davis sometimes struggled to find vehicles worthy of her talent, but even in this relatively creaky melodrama, which is the only film she ever produced, she conveys the marvellous sense of the dramatics that made her a Hollywood great. Her star quality is particularly evident as she plays twins (one good, one bad), but unfortunately the men in the cast aren't up to her standard. Glenn Ford is callow and uninteresting, and both Dane Clark and Bruce Bennett offer period good looks, and do what little the script allows them to do well. TS

Bette Davis *Kate Bosworth/Pat Bosworth* • Glenn Ford *Bill Emerson* • Dane Clark *Karnock* • Walter Brennan *Eben Folgor* • Charles Ruggles *Freddie Lindley* • Bruce Bennett *Jack Talbot* • Peggy Knudsen *Diedra* ■ *Dir* Curtis Bernhardt • *Scr* Catherine Turney, Margaret Buell Wilder, from the novel by Karel J Benes

Stolen Summer ★★

Comedy drama 2002 · US · Colour · 91mins

Having won the Project Greenlight screenwriting contest and endured a documentary about his initiation into movie-making, Pete Jones delivered this sugar-coated paean to childhood and lost innocence. The concept of a 1970s Catholic kid trying to convert a Chicago rabbi's son to please God is not without its controversies. But Jones takes such a superficial approach that he neither offends nor enlightens. Bonnie Hunt rings true as the child's mother, but Aidan Quinn and Kevin Pollak are predictable as the respective fathers of do-gooding Adi Stein and the leukaemia-stricken Michael Weinberg. DP

Aidan Quinn *Joe O'Malley* • Bonnie Hunt *Margaret O'Malley* • Kevin Pollak *Rabbi Jacobsen* • Brian Dennehy *Father Kelly* • Eddie Kaye Thomas *Patrick O'Malley* • Adi Stein *Pete O'Malley* • Mike Weinberg *Danny Jacobsen* ■ *Dir/Scr* Pete Jones

Stolen Youth ★★ 12

Drama 1996 · US · Colour · 83mins

In this almost unbearable melodramatic TV tosh, Brian Austin Green begins an affair with Sharon Lawrence, the best friend of his mum, Harley Jane Kozak, who naturally hits the roof when she learns of the illicit romance. There's a capable supporting cast, but the performances of the leads drip with treacle. RT DVD

Brian Austin Green *Paul Hewitt* • Sharon Lawrence *Nina Talbert* • Harley Jane Kozak *Abby Hewitt* • John Getz *Dennis Hewitt* ■ *Dir* Christopher Leitch • *Scr* JB White, from a story by Hal Sitowitz, JB White

The Stone Boy ★★★★

Drama 1984 · US · Colour · 93mins

Robert Duvall, Frederic Forrest and Glenn Close head the terrific cast of this powerful rural drama. Young Jason Presson accidentally shoots and kills his older brother, then has to cope alone with the trauma of it after his farming family retreat into their own private grief. This is one of those rare films that seems quietly and accurately to convey the emotions of true tragedy. While downbeat, it remains a fine ensemble piece. DA

Robert Duvall *Joe Hillerman* • Jason Presson *Arnold Hillerman* • Frederic Forrest *Andy Jansen* • Glenn Close *Ruth Hillerman* • Wilford Brimley *George Jansen* • Gail Youngs *Lu Jansen* • Cindy Fisher *Amalie* • Dean Cain *Eugene Hillerman* ■ *Dir* Christopher Cain • *Scr* Gina Berriault, from her novel

Stone Cold ★★ 18

Action thriller 1991 · US · Colour · 88mins

Former football player Brian Bosworth started his new thespian career in this bubble-brained action movie that required some cuts before obtaining an R rating in the US. There is still more than enough violence to satisfy action fans, though its frequent heavy-handedness and perversely cruel tone may cause some misgivings. Bosworth is a cop, working undercover with the FBI to infiltrate Lance Henriksen's biker/white militant gang. KB

Brian Bosworth *Joe Huff/John Stone* • Lance Henriksen *Chains Cooper* • William Forsythe *Ice* • Arabella Holzbog *Nancy* • Sam McMurray *Lance* • Richard Gant *Cunningham* ■ *Dir* Craig R Baxley • *Scr* Walter Doniger

The Stone Killer ★★ 18

Action thriller 1973 · US · Colour · 91mins

A Michael Winner film starring Charles Bronson immediately conjures up an image of violence, and both men live up to expectations in this nasty movie. Bronson plays a former New York cop now working in LA, who is almost indistinguishable from the killers he's trying to track down. Stomach-churning and predictable. SG. Contains drug abuse, swearing, violence, nudity.

Charles Bronson *Detective Lou Torrey* • Martin Balsam *Al Vescari* • David Sheiner *Detective Guido Lorenz* • Norman Fell *Detective Les Daniels* • Ralph Waite *Detective Mathews* • Eddie Firestone *George Armitage, the junkie* • Walter Burke *JD* ■ *Dir* Michael Winner • *Scr* Gerald Wilson, from the novel *A Complete State of Death* by John Gardner

Stones for Ibarra ★★★★ PG

Drama 1988 · US · Colour · 96mins

This is a thoughtful and often moving TV drama about a San Francisco couple who move to a small Mexican village to reopen a copper mine, only to have their dreams turn sour when the husband learns he is suffering from cancer. Glenn Close and Keith Carradine give restrained and touching performances; they are well supported by Alfonso Arau, now better known as the director of *Like Water for Chocolate* and *A Walk in the Clouds*. Simple but poignant. JB.

Glenn Close *Sara Everton* • Keith Carradine *Richard Everton* • Alfonso Arau *Chuy Santos* • Ray Oriel *Domingo Garcia* • Trinidad Silva *Basilio Garcia* ■ *Dir* Jack Gold • *Scr* Ernest Kinoy, from the novel by Harriett Doerr

Stonewall ★★ 15

Drama 1995 · UK · Colour · 94mins

The decision to introduce a fictional love story into this re-creation of the infamous 1969 riot at the Stonewall Inn in Greenwich Village was a serious misjudgement. It constantly clouds the issue and deflects from the more serious purpose of examining the penalties and prejudices suffered by the gay community in those pre-liberation days. The cast looks good but, sadly, lacks the necessary acting ability. DP. Contains swearing.

Guillermo Diaz *La Miranda* • Frederick Weller *Matty Dean* • Brendan Corbalis *Ethan* • Duane Boutté *Bostonia* • Bruce MacVittie *Vinnie* • Peter Ratray *Burt* • Dwight Ewell *Helen Wheels* ■ *Dir* Nigel Finch • *Scr* Rikki Beadle Blair, from the book by Martin Duberman

The Stooge ★★★ U

Musical comedy 1951 · US · BW · 100mins

This clever and prescient Dean Martin and Jerry Lewis vehicle sees Martin showing a marked antipathy to his partner – the titular stooge. There is a brilliant character study from Eddie Mayehoff, while Polly Bergen proves an attractive foil. With hindsight, it looks as though reality was intruding on the popular comedy team, as the Dino character learns how important his stooge is to his career. It wasn't until until after *Pardners* (when the pair split) that the paying public became aware of the truth. TS

Dean Martin *Bill Miller* • Jerry Lewis *Ted Rogers* • Polly Bergen *Mary Turner* • Marion Marshall *Frecklehead Tait* • Eddie Mayehoff *Leo Lyman* • Richard Erdman *Ben Bailey* ■ *Dir* Norman Taurog • *Scr* Fred F Finklehoffe, Martin Rackin, Elwood Ullman, from a story by Fred F Finklehoffe, Sid Silvers

Stop Making Sense ★★★★ PG

Concert documentary
1984 · US · Colour · 87mins

Building from an image of a single pair of white sneakers into a sublime, almost surreal display of cerebral rock, this is simply one of the finest concert films ever made. Yet this enviable achievement isn't down to the understated direction of Jonathan Demme or the subtle photography of *Blade Runner* cameraman Jordan Cronenweth. What makes this such a memorable experience is the ingenuity of Talking Heads frontman David Byrne. In addition to writing and giving a mesmerising performance of the 16 songs on the soundtrack, he also designed the show, which includes some wonderfully atmospheric shadow mime sequences, played out on a

S

triptych screen behind the minimalist stage. DP DVD

Dir Jonathan Demme • *Scr* David Byrne

Stop! or My Mom Will Shoot ★ PG

Action comedy 1992 · US · Colour · 87mins

This was the comedy that finally seemed to convince Sylvester Stallone that he wasn't really very funny; after this he was back to the action-adventure genre with *Cliffhanger*. Stallone is the tough detective whose life is ruined when his fussy, dotty mother Estelle Getty turns up to stay with him. Inane and joke-free. JF. Contains swearing, violence. DVD

Sylvester Stallone *Joe Bomowski* • Estelle Getty *Tutti* • JoBeth Williams *Gwen Harper* • Roger Rees *Parnell* • Martin Ferrero *Paulie* • Gailard Sartain *Munroe* • John Wesley *Tony* • Al Fann *Lou* ■ *Dir* Roger Spottiswoode • *Scr* Blake Snyder, William Osborne, William Davies

Stop the World, I Want to Get Off ★★

Musical 1966 · UK · Colour and BW · 99mins

"What kind of fool am I?" bawls Tony Tanner, and what kind of musical is this, you might ask. It's a listless version of the Broadway and West End hit by Anthony Newley and Leslie Bricusse, which turns allegorical as it recounts the ups and downs of its Everyman hero Littlechap (Tanner), and is only kick-started into some sort of life by the delectable Millicent Martin. Too self-pitying for long-term tolerance, it was remade in 1978 as *Sammy Stops the World*, with Sammy Davis Jr. TH. Contains swearing.

Tony Tanner *Littlechap* • Millicent Martin *Evie/Anya/Ara/Ginnie* • Leila Croft *Susan* • Valerie Croft *Jane* • Neil Hawley *Little Littlechap* • Graham Lyons *Father-in-law* ■ *Dir* Philip Saville • *Scr* Anthony Newley, Leslie Bricusse, David Donable, Al Ham, Marilyn Bergman, Alan Bergman, from the play by Anthony Newley, Leslie Bricusse

Stop, You're Killing Me ★★★

Musical comedy 1952 · US · Colour · 86mins

This is an update of a marvellous Damon Runyon/Howard Lindsay play called *A Slight Case of Murder*, which in 1938 became one of Edward G Robinson's most popular film vehicles. Broderick Crawford, though personable, is no substitute for Edward G, and the film certainly doesn't need its musical moments. Nevertheless, this is still amusing and there's a nice piece of casting in the wonderful Margaret Dumont as the unlucky discoverer of the body at the climax. TS

Broderick Crawford *Remy Marko* • Claire Trevor *Nora Marko* • Virginia Gibson *Mary Marko* • Bill Hayes *Chance Whitelaw* • Margaret Dumont *Mrs Whitelaw* • Howard St John *Mahoney* • Charles Cantor *Mike* ■ *Dir* Roy Del Ruth • *Scr* James O'Hanlon, from the play *A Slight Case of Murder* by Damon Runyon, Howard Lindsay

Stopover Forever ★

Thriller 1964 · UK · BW · 59mins

This amateur-hour B-movie stars Ann Bell as an air hostess who becomes convinced that she's the target for a killer when she swaps flights at the last moment and her replacement is murdered. Wandering round Sicily, she suspects everyone and whips herself up into a paranoid frenzy in the process. The acting is distinctly ropey and the final twist can't save a woeful story. DP

Ann Bell *Sue Chambers* • Anthony Bate *Trevor Graham* • Conrad Phillips *Eric Cunningham* • Bruce Boa *Freddie* • Julian Sherrier *Captain Carlos Mordente* ■ *Dir* Frederic Goode • *Scr* David Osborne

Stopover Tokyo ★★ U

Spy drama 1957 · US · Colour · 100mins

Screenwriter Richard Breen directed just one picture, this spy drama about double- and triple-crossing in Tokyo. Robert Wagner is likeable but also a bit lightweight as the counter-espionage agent who may – or may not – be protecting the US Ambassador. He finds time for a romance with Joan Collins but things get rather hard to follow. AT

Robert Wagner *Mark Fannon* • Joan Collins *Tina* • Edmond O'Brien *George Underwood* • Ken Scott *Tony Barrett* • Reiko Oyama *Koko* • Larry Keating *High Commissioner* ■ *Dir* Richard L Breen • *Scr* Richard L Breen, Walter Reisch, from the novel by John P Marquand

Storefront Hitchcock ★★★ 12

Concert movie 1998 · US · Colour · 77mins

A mix of alfresco music and off-the-wall musings from eccentric British songster Robyn Hitchcock. The film is directed by Jonathan Demme, of *The Silence of the Lambs* fame. He's a big Robyn Hitchcock fan, and patently regarded this small-scale spot of whimsy as a welcome change from the high-pressure world of big-bucks Hollywood film-making. Incidentally, new-ager Hitchcock is also one of the UK's leading authorities on ancient stone circles, ley lines and the like. DA

Dir Jonathan Demme

Storia di Piera ★★★

Drama 1983 · It/Fr/W Ger · Colour · 110mins

Hanna Schygulla won the Best Actress prize at Cannes for her performance in Marco Ferreri's characteristically frank adaptation of actress Piera Degli Esposti's autobiography. Isabelle Huppert takes the title role, but it's Schygulla who dominates as the embittered mother who uses promiscuity as a weapon against her neglectful husband, Marcello Mastroianni. This discomforting blend of dark comedy and sordid melodrama is more concerned with the shock treatment meted out to Scygulla after she's committed for nympomania and the family's eccentric sexual practices. DP. An Italian language film.

Hanna Schygulla *Eugenia* • Isabelle Huppert *Piera as an adult* • Bettina Gruhn *Piera as a child* • Marcello Mastroianni *Lorenzo* ■ *Dir* Marco Ferreri • *Scr* Piera Degli Esposti, Dacia Maraini, Marco Ferreri, from the autobiography by Piera Degli Esposti, Dacia Maraini

The Stork Club ★★★ U

Musical comedy 1945 · US · BW · 98mins

A lightweight frivolity that is at once a major plug for the legendary Manhattan nightspot, and a showcase for the energetic talents of Betty Hutton, who sings half-a-dozen made-to-order numbers. The plot has Stork Club hat-check girl Hutton saving a shabby tramp (Barry Fitzgerald) from drowning and being rewarded for her good deed when he turns out to be a millionaire. He sets her up in luxury, which causes a problem with her musician boyfriend (Don DeFore). RK

Betty Hutton *Judy Peabody* • Barry Fitzgerald *JB Bates* • Don DeFore *Danny Wilton* • Robert Benchley *Tom Curtis* • Bill Goodwin *Sherman Billingsley* • Iris Adrian *Gwen* ■ *Dir* Hal Walker • *Scr* BG De Sylva, John McGowan

The Storm ★★

Drama 1938 · US · BW · 75mins

Formula storytelling has Charles Bickford as the burly ship's radio operator who looks out for Tom Brown as his kid brother and gets the wrong idea about his girl, played by Nan Grey. Barton MacLane is the reckless skipper who lets Bickford's pal, Preston Foster, die at sea. It's a short trip, but never dull. AE

Charles Bickford *Bob Roberts* • Barton MacLane *Captain Cogswell* • Preston Foster *Jack Stacey* • Tom Brown *Jim Roberts* • Nan Grey *Peggy Phillips* • Andy Devine *Hansen* • Frank Jenks *Peter Carey* • Samuel S Hinds *Captain Kenny* ■ *Dir* Harold Young • *Scr* Daniel Moore, Hugh King, Theodore Reeves, George Yohalem, from a story by Daniel Moore, Hugh King

Storm ★★ 12

Action thriller 1999 · US · Colour · 86mins

Weather movies rarely fulfil their makers' expectations. Neither *Twister* nor *A Perfect Storm* lived up to the hype about their special effects, so what chance can a low-budget TV thriller such as this have of success? Martin Sheen gives his all as the leader of a government research programme that develops a weather controlling device, but Luke Perry is woefully miscast as the computer whizz who takes to the skies when the device threatens to destroy Los Angeles. DP DVD

Luke Perry *Dr Ron Young* • Martin Sheen *General Roberts* • Robert Knott *Tom Holt* • David Moses *Dr Platt* • Marc McClure *Brian Newmeyer* • Renée Estevez *Andrea* ■ *Dir* Harris Done, Vincent Spano • *Scr* Harris Done, Diane Fine

Storm Boy ★★★

Drama 1976 · Aus · Colour · 88mins

Shot off the coast of South Australia, Henri Safran's movie debut is a kind of *Kes* with pelicans. His handling of the bird sequences and the stunning views of the island seascape cannot be faulted, but Safran has misjudged the pacing of his tale and, fascinating and beautiful though the natural history footage often is, it prevents the narrative from flowing. Greg Rowe gets under your skin as the neglected boy who is befriended by Aboriginal outsider David Gulpilil, giving his customary sound performance. DP

Greg Rowe *Mike* • Peter Cummins *Hide-Away Tom* • David Gulpilil *Fingerbone Bill* • Judy Dick *Miss Walker* • Tony Allison *Ranger* • Michael Moody *Boat master* ■ *Dir* Henri Safran • *Scr* Sonia Berg, from the novel by Colin Thiele

Storm Catcher ★ 18

Action thriller 1999 · US · Colour · 91mins

Faced with a minuscule budget, a few feet of stock aerial footage and a script with dialogue that amounts to an aural assault, director Anthony Hickox has done well to produce a film that's only as bad as this one. Dolph Lundgren is serviceable as the ace pilot who has to recover a top-secret plane that only he and colleague John Pennell can fly, but the supporting performances range from the rank to the ranting. DP DVD

Dolph Lundgren *Major Jack Holloway* • Mystro Clark *Sparks* • John Pennell [Jon Pennell] *Captain Lucas* • Robert Miano *General Jacob* • Yvonne Zima *Nicole* • Kylie Bax *Jessica Holloway* ■ *Dir* Tony Hickox [Anthony Hickox] • *Scr* Bill Gucwa, Ed Masterson

Storm Center ★★★

Drama 1956 · US · BW · 85mins

This is a tremendously courageous subject for its period that is still relevant today, as librarian Bette Davis is fired for refusing to remove a book on communism from the shelves. Unfortunately, the movie is directed by one of the screenwriters (Daniel Taradash) and it lapses too often into cliché and sentiment. Although the theme deserved more than this melodramatic treatment, it's also likely that a better movie would still have met with an uninterested public. TS

Bette Davis *Alicia Hull* • Brian Keith *Paul Duncan* • Kim Hunter *Martha Lockridge* • Paul Kelly (1) *Judge Robert Ellerbe* • Kevin Coughlin *Freddie Slater* • Joe Mantell *George Slater* • Sallie Brophy *Laura Slater* • Howard Wierum *Mayor Levering* ■ *Dir* Daniel Taradash • *Scr* Daniel Taradash, Elick Moll

Storm in a Teacup ★★★

Comedy 1937 · UK · BW · 88mins

When the authoritarian provost of a small Scottish town (Cecil Parker) orders an old lady's dog to be confiscated because she hasn't paid her fines, reporter Rex Harrison picks up the story and creates a national scandal. The furious provost institutes legal proceedings against the journalist, but his daughter Vivien Leigh, who is in love with the young man, intervenes. Well directed by Victor Saville, the film is an oh-so-English, pre-Second World War relic, that's sweet and funny. RK

Vivien Leigh *Victoria Gow* • Rex Harrison *Frank Burden* • Sara Allgood *Mrs Hegarty* • Cecil Parker *Provost Willie Gow* • Ursula Jeans *Lisbet Skirving* • Gus McNaughton *Horace Skirving* ■ *Dir* Victor Saville, Ian Dalrymple • *Scr* Ian Dalrymple, Donald Bull, from James Bridie's adaptation of the play *Sturm in Wasserglas* by Bruno Frank

A Storm in Summer ★★★

Drama 2000 · US · Colour · 94mins

Originally aired in 1970, with Peter Ustinov in the lead, Rod Serling's tele-drama has been respectfully revived by veteran director Robert Wise. Peter Falk assumes the role of the Fairview deli owner whose jaundiced outlook is slowly transformed by the arrival of Aaron Meeks, a young New Yorker afforded the opportunity of an upstate vacation by a charity. The focus falls firmly on the unlikely cross-generational rapport that develops between the embittered outsiders, who have both lost loved ones in war. DP

Peter Falk *Abel Shaddick* • Aaron Meeks *Herman Washington* • Nastassja Kinski *Gloria Ross* • Andrew McCarthy *Stanley Banner* • Ruby Dee *Grandmother* ■ *Dir* Robert Wise • *Scr* Rod Serling

Storm over Asia ★★★★★ PG

Classic silent drama
1928 · USSR · BW · 125mins

The summit of Soviet cinema was reached in the 1920s with the films of Dovzhenko, Eisenstein and Pudovkin, whose last great silent film this was. It concerns nomadic fur-trapper, Blair, who is set up as a puppet monarch by the occupying British interventionist forces in Mongolia in 1918. But, realising his national identity, and believing himself to be a descendent of Genghis Kahn, he rouses the Asian hordes against their oppressors. A film of great visual beauty, dynamic montage, humour and compassion, it also has an ethnographic quality in the detailed depiction of the life of the Mongolian herdsmen. A new version with a sound track was released some 20 years later under Pudovkin's supervision. RB DVD

Valeri Inkishinov *Blair, a mongol huntsman* • I Inkishinov *Blair's father* • A Chistyakov *Commander of a partisan detachment* • A Dedintsev *Commander of the occupation forces* ■ *Dir* Vsevolod I Pudovkin • *Scr* Osip Brik, from a story by I Novokshenov

Storm over the Nile ★★ U

Adventure 1955 · UK · Colour · 102mins

Zoltan Korda makes little effort to disguise the fact that this is a remake of his 1939 classic *The Four Feathers*. Some of the original location footage is also included, distorted to fit the new picture's CinemaScope format. Co-director Terence Young helps bring a touch of pizzazz to the action sequences, yet the story, of an officer who's branded a coward but who proves to have more pluck than his pals, has dated badly. DP

Laurence Harvey *John Durrance* • Anthony Steel *Harry Faversham* • James Robertson-Justice *General Burroughs* • Geoffrey Keen *Dr Sutton* • Ronald Lewis *Peter Burroughs* • Ian Carmichael *Tom Willoughby* • Michael Hordern *General Faversham* • Jack Lambert *Colonel* • Mary Ure *Mary Burroughs* • Christopher Lee *Karaga Pasha* ■ *Dir* Zoltan Korda, Terence Young • *Scr* RC Sherriff, Lajos Biró, Arthur Wimperis, from the novel *The Four Feathers* by AEW Mason

Storm over Wyoming ★★ U

Western 1950 · US · BW · 60mins

One of seven Tim Holt B-westerns cranked out by RKO during 1950 (when such pictures were beginning to lose money), this has more action than most but no other distinguishing features. Tim and his Mexican-Irish sidekick Richard Martin rescue a cowboy from being strung up and are rewarded with jobs as ranch hands. AE

Tim Holt *Dave* • Richard Martin (1) *Chito Rafferty* • Noreen Nash *Chris Marvin* • Richard Powers [Tom Keene] *Tug Caldwell* • Betty Underwood *Ruby* • Bill Kennedy *Rawlins* • Kenneth MacDonald *Scott* • Leo McMahon *Zeke* • Richard Kean *Watson* • Don Haggerty *Marshal* ■ *Dir* Lesley Selander • *Scr* Earl Repp

Storm Warning ★★

Drama 1950 · US · BW · 89mins

Fashion model Ginger Rogers decides to visit her sister Doris Day in a small southern town. Arriving at night, she witnesses a Klan murder, and soon realises that one of the perpetrators is her brother-in-law, Steve Cochran. District attorney Ronald Reagan asks her to testify as a witness to the killing, leading to an agonising clash of loyalties. This punchy and intriguing little social conscience effort is ruined by its descent into crudely obvious melodrama. RK

Ginger Rogers *Marsha Mitchell* • Ronald Reagan *Burt Rainey* • Doris Day *Lucy Rice* • Steve Cochran *Hank Rice* • Hugh Sanders *Charlie Barr* • Lloyd Gough *Cliff Rummel* • Raymond Greenleaf *Faulkner* ■ *Dir* Stuart Heisler • *Scr* Daniel Fuchs, Richard Brooks, from their story *Storm Center*

Stormy ★★ U

Western 1935 · US · BW · 66mins

Noah Beery Jr may take the lead in this western melodrama about a thoroughbred colt that's lost after a train wreck, but his thunder is stolen by the horse in the title role. Among the other supporting humans, J Farrell MacDonald, as the wonderfully named Trinidad Dorn, emerges with dignity. TS

Noah Beery Jr *Stormy* • Jean Rogers *Kerry Dorn* • J Farrell MacDonald *Trinidad Dorn* • Walter Miller *Craig* • James P Burtis *Greasy* • Charles Hunter *The Arizona Wrangler* ■ *Dir* Louis Friedlander [Lew Landers] • *Scr* George H Plympton, Ben G Kohn, from a story by Cherry Wilson

Stormy Monday ★★★ 15

Romantic thriller 1987 · UK · Colour · 88mins

Mike Figgis marked himself out as a director to watch out for with this assured debut, which successfully transplants *film noir* to the unlikely surroundings of Newcastle upon Tyne. Sean Bean is the young innocent who falls for visiting American Melanie Griffith and gets caught between the machinations of sinister American developer Tommy Lee Jones and local jazz club owner Sting. It doesn't always convince, but Figgis summons up a melancholy air of menace, and the performances, particularly Jones's, are memorable. JF. Contains violence, swearing, sex scenes and nudity.

Melanie Griffith *Kate* • Tommy Lee Jones *Cosmo* • Sting *Finney* • Sean Bean *Brendan* • James Cosmo *Tony* • Mark Long *Patrick* • Brian Lewis *Jim* ■ *Dir/Scr* Mike Figgis

Stormy Waters ★★★★

Romantic drama 1941 · Fr · BW · 90mins

Tugboat captain Jean Gabin rescues Michèle Morgan from the sea and falls in love with her. The picture was begun in 1939, but the Nazi Occupation held up production. It was eventually completed in the studio, although director Jean Grémillon had earlier filmed a number of realistic sea scenes on location at Brest. A perceptive but gloomy study of passion and fidelity, the film benefits from the masterly performances of its trio of top stars. RB. In French with English subtitles.

Jean Gabin *André Laurent* • Michèle Morgan *Catherine* • Madeleine Renaud *Yvonne Laurent* • Charles Blavette *Gabriel Tanguy* ■ *Dir* Jean Grémillon • *Scr* Roger Vercel, Charles Spaak, Jacques Prévert, André Cayatte, from the novel *Remorques* by Roger Vercel

Stormy Weather ★★★ U

Musical 1943 · US · BW · 77mins

Little more than an excuse to feature some of the finest black American performers, this expertly made extravaganza may well seem tasteless today. Try to ignore the parade of grinning racial stereotypes, and concentrate instead on the star turns: the great Bill Robinson, Cab Calloway, Fats Waller and, best of all, lovely Lena Horne performing the title number and a wondrous *I Can't Give You Anything but Love, Baby*. The virtually nonexistent plot is trite, with the Horne-Robinson romance particularly unbelievable. TS

Lena Horne *Selina Rogers* • Bill Robinson *Corky* • Cab Calloway • Katherine Dunham • Fats Waller • Ada Brown • Dooley Wilson *Gabe* ■ *Dir* Andrew Stone [Andrew L Stone] • *Scr* Frederick Jackson, Ted Koehler, HS Kraft, from a story by Jerry Horwin, Seymour B Robinson

The Story of a Cheat ★★★★★

Comedy drama 1936 · Fr · BW · 83mins

Though very much a man of the stage who only occasionally made films, Sacha Guitry was still capable of being highly cinematic. Here, for example, the entire story is enacted visually, with only Guitry's voiceover and Adolphe Borchard's score for accompaniment – although Marguerite Moreno does speak in a café scene. An under-acknowledged influence on the New Wave, this is a bravura auteurist exhibition. Guitry stars in this self-scripted picaresque about a cardsharp convinced that fortune can be seduced by deception; as director, he manipulates time and space with a masterly ease that perfectly complements the action's witty amorality. DP. A French language film.

Sacha Guitry *The cheat* • Jacqueline Delubac *Young woman* • Rosine Deréan *The jewel thief* • Marguerite Moreno *The countess* ■ *Dir* Sacha Guitry • *Scr* Sacha Guitry, from the novel *Memoires d'un Tricheur* by Sacha Guitry

Story of a Love Story ★★

Romantic fantasy drama 1973 · Fr · Colour · 110mins

Give director John Frankenheimer a hard-hitting melodrama or a bruising action film and he'll produce a polished picture. However, when confronted with a romantic drama he's likely to be confounded by his own pretensions.That is exactly what has happened here: the film is so preoccupied with the fact or fiction game that the adulterous affair between author Alan Bates and Dominique Sanda is almost secondary. DP. Contains nudity.

Alan Bates *Harry* • Dominique Sanda *Nathalie* • Evans Evans *Elizabeth* • Lea Massari *Woman* • Michael Auclair [Michel Auclair] *Georges* • Laurence De Monaghan *Cleo* ■ *Dir* John Frankenheimer • *Scr* Nicholas Mosley

The Story of Adèle H ★★★ 12

Biographical drama 1975 · Fr · Colour · 96mins

In what was only her fourth feature, the 19-year-old Isabelle Adjani comes remarkably close to conveying the desolation of a passionate older woman broken by her own determination. She plays Victor Hugo's daughter Adèle, who followed a young English soldier (Bruce Robinson) from Nova Scotia to Barbados, despite the fact that her love was unreciprocated. Director François Truffaut relies heavily on Adjani's crestfallen beauty and the oppressive majesty of Nestor Almendros's photography to suggest the heroine's agonising hope and incipient madness. DP. In French with English subtitles. DVD

Isabelle Adjani *Adèle Hugo* • Bruce Robinson *Lt Albert Pinson* • Sylvia Marriott *Mrs Saunders* • Joseph Blatchley *Mr Whistler* • Reuben Dorey *Mr Saunders* • M White *Colonel White* • Cal Hathwell *Lt Pinson's Batman* • Ivry Gitlis *Hypnotist* ■ *Dir* François Truffaut • *Scr* François Truffaut, Jean Gruault, Suzanne Schiffman, from *Le Journal d'Adèle Hugo* by Adèle Hugo, Frances V Guille

The Story of Alexander Graham Bell ★★ U

Biographical drama 1939 · US · BW · 98mins

This biopic of the man who invented the telephone is straightforward, sentimental and slow. Don Ameche, then known as a light comedian and debonair leading man, tried to gain gravitas in the role as he teaches the deaf to communicate, while pioneering his research into transmitting speech over the telegraph wires. His loyal assistant is Henry Fonda, who is far more convincing as a visionary than the miscast Ameche. AT

Don Ameche *Alexander Graham Bell* • Loretta Young *Mrs Bell* • Henry Fonda *Tom Watson* • Charles Coburn *Gardner Hubbard* • Spring Byington *Mrs Hubbard* • Gene Lockhart *Thomas Sanders* ■ *Dir* Irving Cummings • *Scr* Lamar Trotti, from a story by Ray Harris

The Story of Dr Wassell ★★

Second World War drama 1944 · US · Colour · 136mins

Having won an Oscar as the First World War hero in *Sergeant York*, Gary Cooper played another real-life hero, Dr Corydon Wassell, who managed to evacuate nine wounded men from Java and get them safely to Australia, dodging Japanese bombs all the way. Wassell himself was awarded the Navy Cross and was commended in a Presidential radio broadcast. He was reluctant to give his co-operation to Cecil B DeMille's movie, which is overlong, sentimental, self-important and cliché-ridden. AT

Gary Cooper *Dr Corydon M Wassell* • Laraine Day *Madeline* • Signe Hasso *Bettina* • Dennis O'Keefe *"Hoppy" Hopkins* • Carol Thurston *Tremartini* • Carl Esmond *Lt Dirk Van Daal* ■ *Dir* Cecil B DeMille • *Scr* Alan LeMay, Charles Bennett, James Hilton, from the stories by Dr Corydon M Wassell, James Hilton

The Story of Esther Costello ★★★

Drama 1957 · UK · BW · 104mins

Melodrama in the grand Hollywood tradition as wealthy socialite Joan Crawford adopts an Irish girl (Heather Sears) who has lost her sight, speech and hearing as a result of an accident. Unfortunately, Crawford's estranged husband (Rossano Brazzi) turns her charitable deed into a shameless exploitation racket. Crawford adds high emotional gloss to a tailor-made role that successfully tugs the heartstrings and holds the interest. AJ

Joan Crawford *Margaret Landi* • Rossano Brazzi *Carlo Landi* • Heather Sears *Esther Costello* • Lee Patterson *Harry Grant* • Ron Randell *Frank Wenzel* • Fay Compton *Mother Superior* • John Loder *Paul Marchant* • Denis O'Dea *Father Devlin* • Sidney James *Ryan* ■ *Dir* David Miller • *Scr* Charles Kaufman, from the novel by Nicholas Monsarrat

The Story of GI Joe ★★★★

Biographical Second World War drama 1945 · US · BW · 109mins

This salute to the ordinary foot soldier is based on the memoirs of war correspondent Ernie Pyle, who is played by Burgess Meredith. Dealing with the guys who yomped it all the way from North Africa to Rome via Sicily, it was hailed at the time as one of the most authentic war movies ever made. It's crudely manipulative yet often very moving, mainly due to Robert Mitchum's star-building, Oscar-nominated performance as the GI who rises to become the platoon's commander. AT

Burgess Meredith *Ernie Pyle* • Robert Mitchum *Lt Bill Walker* • Freddie Steele *Sgt Steve Warnicki* • Wally Cassell *Pte Dondaro* • Jimmy Lloyd *Pte Spencer* • Jack Reilly *Pte Robert "Wingless" Murphy* • Bill Murphy *Pte Mew* • William Self *"Gawky" Henderson* ■ *Dir* William A Wellman • *Scr* Leopold Atlas, Guy Endore, Philip Stevenson, from the books *Here Is Your War* and *Brave Men* by Ernie Pyle

The Story of Gilbert and Sullivan ★★★ U

Biographical musical drama 1953 · UK · Colour · 111mins

Splendidly Technicolored, though slow-moving, this is a British account of the Tim Rice and Andrew Lloyd Webber team of their day, incarnated by Robert Morley (a rare top-billed appearance as the volatile Gilbert) and Maurice Evans (a rather bloodless Sullivan). Chunks of the comic operettas are ladled out among the petty squabblings that constitute the plot, and music fans will enjoy Martyn Green in an acting role. The movie is stolen by the urbane Peter Finch as the equally urbane Richard D'Oyly Carte. TS

Robert Morley *WS Gilbert* • Maurice Evans *Arthur Sullivan* • Eileen Herlie *Helen Lenoir* • Martyn Green *George Grossmith* • Peter Finch *Richard d'Oyly Carte* • Dinah Sheridan *Grace Marston* • Isabel Dean *Mrs Gilbert* • Wilfrid Hyde White *Mr Marston* ■ *Dir* Sidney Gilliat • *Scr* Sidney Gilliat, Leslie Bailey, Vincent Korda, from the book *The Gilbert and Sullivan Book* by Leslie Bailey

The Story of Louis Pasteur ★★★

Biographical drama 1936 · US · BW · 87mins

Paul Muni won an Oscar and established a formula for Warner Bros biopics with his performance in the lead role of Louis Pasteur. The trick that Sheridan Gibney and Pierre Collings's Oscar-winning script pulls is to make scientific research into sterilisation and rabies interesting, and director William Dieterle pulls another trick by keeping a firm check on the running time. There's some minor love interest, of course, but it's Muni's picture – though today his acting style and the general hagiographic approach seem very old-fashioned. AT

Paul Muni *Louis Pasteur* • Josephine Hutchinson *Mme Pasteur* • Anita Louise *Annette Pasteur* • Donald Woods *Jean Martel* • Fritz Leiber *Dr Charbonnet* • Henry O'Neill

Roux ■ *Dir* William Dieterle • *Scr* Sheridan Gibney, Pierre Collings, from a story by Sheridan Gibney, Pierre Collings

The Story of Mankind ★ U

Historical fantasy drama
1957 · US · Colour · 99mins

Future disaster-movie king Irwin Allen made this portentous rubbish in which the question of whether or not the human race should be allowed to survive is debated in front of a heavenly tribunal. Ronald Colman (in his last film) is the Spirit of Man, advancing the argument in favour of human kind; Vincent Price gleams with wicked delight as the Devil. This is generally, and rightly, acknowledged as one of the worst films ever made. RK

Ronald Colman *Spirit of Man* • Hedy Lamarr *Joan of Arc* • Groucho Marx *Peter Minuit* • Harpo Marx *Isaac Newton* • Chico Marx *Monk* • Virginia Mayo *Cleopatra* • Agnes Moorehead *Queen Elizabeth* • Vincent Price *Devil* ■ *Dir* Irwin Allen • *Scr* Irwin Allen, Charles Bennett, from the book by Hendrik Willem Van Loon

The Story of O ★★★ 18

Erotic drama
1975 · Fr/W Ger · Colour · 92mins

This tale of a woman who becomes a willing slave to the men she loves was banned in the UK for 25 years. Dramatising the controversial sadomasochistic novel by Pauline Réage, director Just Jaeckin takes a dreamy, soft-focus, shampoo commercial approach to the sexual content, though it remains eye-opening. The addition of then-fashionable feminism barely excuses the exploitative tableaux. However, Jaeckin's often unintentionally funny erotic epic still stands as a 1970s landmark. AJ. In French with English subtitles. DVD

Corinne Cléry *O, a photographer* • Udo Kier *René* • Anthony Steel *Sir Stephen H* • Jean Gaven *Pierre, O's valet* • Christiane Minazzoli *Anne-Marie* • Martine Kelly *Thérèse* • Jean-Pierre Andréani *Eric, Master III* ■ *Dir* Just Jaeckin • *Scr* Sébastien Japrisot, from the novel *Histoire d'O* by Pauline Réage [Anne Desclos]

The Story of Qiu Ju ★★★★★ 15

Drama
1992 · HK/Chi · Colour · 96mins

Scooping both the Golden Lion and the best actress award at Venice, this is an impeccable piece of film-making by Zhang Yimou. Gong Li gives an exceptional performance as the tenacious woman who is prepared to go to any lengths to secure justice after her husband is assaulted by the village elder. Exposing the flaws in the Communist legal system and the chasm between urban and rural living standards, this is Zhang's first study of contemporary China. As ever, the engrossing drama, which is underpinned with bitter humour, is tightly handled and the use of colour and landscape is exhilarating. DP. In Mandarin with English subtitles.

Gong Li *Wan Qiu Ju* • Liu Peiqi *Wan Qing Lai* • Yang Liuchun *Meizi* • Lei Laosheng *Wang Shantang, village chief* • Ge Zhijun *Officer Li* ■ *Dir* Zhang Yimou • *Scr* Liu Heng, from the story *Wanjia Susong* by Chen Yuanbin

The Story of Robin Hood and His Merrie Men ★★★ U

Adventure
1952 · UK · Colour · 83mins

This may not hold a candle to the Errol Flynn version, but at around 80 minutes and boasting authentic English locations and fine Technicolor photography, it's excellent family entertainment. Richard Todd enjoys himself as the famous outlaw, but is up against strong competition, with Peter Finch as the wicked Sheriff and the delightful Hubert Gregg cast against type as the evil King John. There's light-hearted humour, a tuneful Allan-a-Dale and some lively swordfights. Briskly directed by the highly professional Ken Annakin. BB

Richard Todd *Robin Hood* • Joan Rice *Maid Marian* • Peter Finch *Sheriff of Nottingham* • James Hayter *Friar Tuck* • James Robertson-Justice *Little John* • Martita Hunt *Queen Eleanor* • Hubert Gregg *Prince John* • Bill Owen *Stutely* • Reginald Tate *Hugh Fitzooth* ■ *Dir* Ken Annakin • *Scr* Lawrence E Watkin

The Story of Ruth ★★ U

Biblical drama
1960 · US · Colour · 131mins

Twentieth Century-Fox was the studio behind this Hollywood makeover of the Old Testament. It's a lengthy and colourful but ultimately static version of the Sunday School favourite. Elana Eden plays Ruth, who renounces false gods in order to worship the true faith of her husband. Familiar faces Stuart Whitman and Tom Tryon are the men in her life. The clichés are strung together by Norman Corwin. TH

Stuart Whitman *Boaz* • Tom Tryon *Mahlon* • Viveca Lindfors *Eleilat* • Peggy Wood *Naomi* • Jeff Morrow *Tob* • Elana Eden *Ruth* • Thayer David *Hedak* ■ *Dir* Henry Koster • *Scr* Norman Corwin

The Story of Seabiscuit ★★ U

Sports drama
1949 · US · Colour · 92mins

Shirley Temple co-stars with the famous American racehorse Seabiscuit in a fictionalised account of its racing success. Temple plays the niece of Seabiscuit's dedicated trainer, Barry Fitzgerald, and her romantic interest is provided by jockey Lon McCallister. Racing historians will enjoy the documentary footage of the great horse in action. Released in the UK as *Pride of Kentucky*. RT

Shirley Temple *Margaret O'Hara* • Barry Fitzgerald *Shawn O'Hara* • Lon McCallister *Ted Knowles* • Rosemary DeCamp *Mrs Charles S Howard* • Donald MacBride *George Carson* • Pierre Watkin *Charles S Howard* ■ *Dir* David Butler • *Scr* John Taintor Foote, from his story

The Story of Sin ★★★ 15

Period drama
1975 · Pol · Colour · 124mins

This picaresque melodrama shares the themes of innocence and experience that informed Walerian Borowczyk's previous outing, *La Bête*. However, this is far less sexually explicit in its chronicling of Grazyna Dlugolecka's pursuit across Europe of her married lover, Olgierd Lukaszewicz, as he seeks to secure a divorce. The plot is packed with bodice-ripping excess, as the naive Dlugolecka resorts to prostitution and murder between erotic encounters, while Borowczyk records every sordid detail with deliciously ironic refinement. DP. In Polish with English subtitles. Contains swearing and sex scenes. DVD

Grazyna Dlugolecka *Ewa* • Jerzy Zelnik *Lukasz* • Olgierd Lukaszewicz *Count* • Marek Walczewski *Plaza-Splawski* • Roman Wilhelmi *Pochron* • Zdzislaw Mrozewski *Ewa's father* • Jadwiga Chojnacka *Leoska* • Mieczyslaw Voit *Cyprian Bodzanta* ■ *Dir* Walerian Borowczyk • *Scr* Walerian Borowczyk, from the novel *Dzieje Grzechu* by Stefan Zeromski

Story of the Late Chrysanthemums ★★★★★

Period melodrama
1939 · Jpn · BW · 142mins

Widely regarded as director Kenji Mizoguchi's finest accomplishment, this is notable for its humanist insight into the role of women in Japanese society. Composed in depth and shot primarily in stately long takes, the story follows the selfless trials of servant Kakuko Mori, as she tries to help the son of a wealthy family achieve his ambition of becoming a kabuki artist. While painting a harsh portrait of life in the 1880s, Mizoguchi warms the heart with his attention to detail and the understated way in which female impersonator Shotaro Hanayagi comes to appreciate his wife's sacrifice. Quite beautiful. DP. In Japanese with English subtitles.

Shotaro Hanayagi *Kikunosuke Onoue* • Kakuko Mori *Otoku* • Gonjuro Kawarazaki *Kikugoro Onoue V* • Kokichi Takada *Fukusuke Nakamura* • Ryotaro Kawanami *Eiju Dayu* • Nobuko Fushimi *Onaka, a geisha* • Benkei Shiganoya *Genshun Anma* • Yoko Umemura *Osato, Kikugoro's wife* ■ *Dir* Kenji Mizoguchi • *Scr* Yoshikata Yoda, Matsutaro Kawaguchi, from a story by Shofu Muramatsu

The Story of the Weeping Camel ★★★★ U

Documentary
2003 · Ger/Mongolia · Colour · 86mins

When Byambasuren Davaa and Luigi Falorni arrived in the Gobi Desert, they had only ten hours of Super-16 film stock. So the fact that this study of a family of Mongolian camel herders is both compelling and charming owes as much to luck as judgement. When a mother camel begins to neglect her new-born white calf, the action becomes increasingly affecting, especially after a local musician is summoned to perform a mystical ritual to bond the intransigent mother and her adorable offspring. But the human side of the story is equally poignant, with the final arrival of satellite television symbolising a threat to this ancient and arduous way of life. DP. In Russian with English subtitles. DVD

Dir Byambasuren Davaa, Luigi Falorni

The Story of Three Loves ★★★★ U

Portmanteau romantic drama
1953 · US · Colour · 121mins

A beautifully shot portmanteau romance, filmed by MGM with all stops out, featuring a marvellously starry cast, impossibly romantic situations and a particularly fine score from Miklos Rozsa. The mood is bittersweet throughout, and the attitudes and settings resolutely Hollywood European, with wonderful resonances for film fans. Here's James Mason as a ballet impresario, touched by *Red Shoes* ballerina Moira Shearer. Here's Kirk Douglas playing a trapeze artist, partnered by tragic Pier Angeli. Best of all, in the weakest segment, is young Ricky Nelson, transformed by magic into Farley Granger. TS

Moira Shearer *Paula Woodward* • James Mason *Charles Coudray* • Agnes Moorehead *Aunt Lydia* • Miklos Rozsa *Conductor* • Ethel Barrymore *Mrs Pennicott* • Leslie Caron *Mademoiselle* • Farley Granger *Thomas Campbell Jr* • Ricky Nelson *Tommy, aged 12* • Pier Angeli *Nina* • Kirk Douglas *Pierre Narval* ■ *Dir* Gottfried Reinhardt, Vincente Minnelli • *Scr* John Collier, Jan Lustig, George Froeschel, John Collier, Jan Lustig, George Froeschel, from the stories by Arnold Phillips, Ladislas Vajda, Jacques Maret

The Story of Us ★★ 15

Romantic comedy
1999 · US · Colour · 91mins

Director Rob Reiner tries to make another *When Harry Met Sally*-style romantic comedy, but clearly forgot to hire someone capable of turning in a funny or moving script. Bruce Willis and Michelle Pfeiffer do their best as an unhappily married couple who opt for a temporary separation when their kids go off to summer camp. However, what could have been a sweet and amusing tale of mid-marriage crisis is a rather one-sided affair. JB. Contains swearing. DVD

Michelle Pfeiffer *Katie Jordan* • Bruce Willis *Ben Jordan* • Rita Wilson *Rachel* • Julie Hagerty *Liza* • Paul Reiser *Dave* • Tim Matheson *Marty* • Colleen Rennison *Erin aged 10* • Jake Sandvig *Josh aged 12* • Red Buttons *Arnie* ■ *Dir* Rob Reiner • *Scr* Alan Zweibel, Jessie Nelson

The Story of Vernon and Irene Castle ★★★★ U

Musical biography
1939 · US · BW · 89mins

This was the last RKO teaming of its incomparable dance duo of Fred Astaire and Ginger Rogers. They are cleverly cast as their great predecessors the Castles, the foremost dance partners of the early 20th century, in a tale that took on new resonances at the outbreak of the Second World War. The finale is almost unbearably moving, but to reveal more would give away the ending. The period songs are spot on, though the ever-sophisticated Astaire and Rogers look nothing like the bunny-hugging Castles (Irene was critical of Ginger's impersonation). The scripting leaves something to be desired, but despite its flaws, Ginger looks swell and Fred dances divinely. TS

Fred Astaire *Vernon Castle* • Ginger Rogers *Irene Castle* • Edna May Oliver *Maggie Sutton* • Walter Brennan *Walter* • Lew Fields • Etienne Girardot *Papa Aubel* • Janet Beecher *Mrs Foote* • Rolfe Sedan *Emile Aubel* ■ *Dir* HC Potter • *Scr* Richard Sherman, Oscar Hammerstein, Dorothy Yost, from the books *My Husband* and *My Memories of Vernon Castle* by Irene Castle

The Story on Page One ★★

Courtroom drama
1959 · US · BW · 123mins

Given that this was written and directed by hard-hitting playwright Clifford Odets, it should have been a cracker, but it's a damp squib, thanks to inept plotting and sloppy assembly. It does have its moments, and Rita Hayworth, though past her sex symbol days, is on excellent acting form. The story concerns the trial of adulterous Rita and her lover Gig Young, accused of murdering her husband and defended by an over-the-top Anthony Franciosa. RK

Rita Hayworth *Jo Morris* • Anthony Franciosa *Victor Santini* • Gig Young *Larry Ellis* • Mildred Dunnock *Mrs Ellis* • Hugh Griffith *Judge Nielsen* ■ *Dir/Scr* Clifford Odets

Storybook ★

Fantasy adventure
1995 · US · Colour · 88mins

This is a dreadfully botched attempt to create a world of wonder similar to CS Lewis's Narnia. Everything about Lorenzo Doumani's film is either derivative or third rate. Set during the Second World War, the story concerns a young boy who is transported to a mythical kingdom through the pages of a magic book, where he teams up with a woodsman, an owl and a boxing kangaroo to wrest the throne from the evil Swoosie Kurtz. DP

Sean Fitzgerald *Brandon* • Swoosie Kurtz *Queen Evilia* • Richard Moll *Woody* • William McNamara *Arthur* • Milton Berle *Illuzor* • Gary Morgan *Pouch* ■ *Dir* Lorenzo Doumani • *Scr* Susan Bowen, Lorenzo Doumani

Storytelling ★★ 18

Black comedy
2001 · US · Colour · 83mins

Todd Solondz's focus here seems less on a coherent story than on satirising the art of storytelling itself. He employs a two-part structure, "Fiction" and "Non-fiction", to mock both the art of the written word (involving student Selma Blair's creative writing course) and documentary-making (Paul Giamatti examines disaffected teenage life), as well as the dark side of suburban folk. The thinly developed characters fail to rouse much interest or empathy, and some witty notions about fiction versus reality are lost among the director's apparent desire to be disturbing, offensive and cruel. JC DVD

John Goodman *Marty Livingston* • Julie Hagerty *Fern Livingston* • Mark Webber *Scooby Livingston* • Paul Giamatti *Toby Oxman* • Selma Blair *Vi* • Jonathan Osser *Mikey Livingston* ■ *Dir/Scr* Todd Solondz

Storyville ★★★ 15

Mystery drama 1992 · US · Colour · 113mins

Mark Frost, David Lynch's unsung partner on the cult TV series *Twin Peaks*, made his directorial debut with this nasty story of dark deeds in the Deep South. As if adultery, corruption, blackmail and murder weren't enough, Frost throws in a little video voyeurism and an upcoming election to keep the plot simmering. James Spader disappoints as the politically ambitious lawyer at the centre of events, but there are some choice performances from Jason Robards, Joanne Whalley-Kilmer and Piper Laurie. Engagingly offbeat, but the action loses its way. DP. Contains violence, sex scenes and swearing.

James Spader *Cray Fowler* • Joanne Whalley-Kilmer [Joanne Whalley] *Natalie Tate* • Jason Robards *Clifford Fowler* • Charlotte Lewis *Lee* • Michael Warren *Nathan LeFleur* • Michael Parks *Michael Trevallian* • Chuck McCann *Pudge Herman* • Charles Haid *Abe Choate* • Woody Strode *Charlie Sumpter* ■ *Dir* Mark Frost • *Scr* Mark Frost, Lee Reynolds, from the book *Juryman* by Frank Galbally, Robert Macklin

Stowaway ★★★★ U

Musical comedy 1936 · US · BW · 86mins

Talented child star Shirley Temple plays the daughter of a slain Chinese missionary, who stows away on a playboy's yacht. This prime vehicle is one of Temple's best, with an excellent cast, just enough plot and some splendid musical moments. She sings, dances and, in one memorable sequence, impersonates Al Jolson, Eddie Cantor and Ginger Rogers. The moppet even converses in Chinese in this entertaining movie, which was one of the biggest box-office hits of its year. TV DVD

Shirley Temple *Ching-Ching, daughter of missionaries* • Robert Young (1) *Tommy Randall* • Alice Faye *Susan Parker* • Eugene Pallette *The Colonel* • Helen Westley *Mrs Hope* • Arthur Treacher *Atkins* • J Edward Bromberg *Judge Booth* ■ *Dir* William A Seiter • *Scr* William Conselman, Arthur Sheekman, Nat Perrin, from the story by Samuel G Engel

La Strada ★★★★ PG

Drama 1954 · It · BW · 103mins

This Fellini classic about a brutal circus strong man and a childlike woman was dismissed in Italy on release, but hailed abroad as a masterpiece, sealing Fellini's reputation as a "great artist". Fellini's wife Giulietta Masina gives a touching perfomance, but viewed today the movie might seem sentimental, its love story between a human animal and a simple waif hardly able to contain all the messages and symbols about humanity that the Italian maestro tosses at it. Combining the neorealism of Fellini's early career and the outright fantasies of his later work, this is well worth seeing, if only for its historical impact and striking influence. AT. In Italian with English subtitles. DVD

Anthony Quinn *Zampano* • Giulietta Masina *Gelsomina* • Richard Basehart *Il Matto/"The Fool"* • Aldo Silvani *Il Signor Giraffa* ■ *Dir* Federico Fellini • *Scr* Federico Fellini, Tullio Pinelli, Ennio Flaiano

Straight out of Brooklyn ★★★ 15

Drama 1991 · US · Colour · 82mins

With its firm grasp of the realities of Brooklyn street life and its uncompromising use of realistic language and violence, this bruising account of what it's like to be black in urban America is all the more remarkable considering its debuting writer/director, Matty Rich, was only 19 when he completed it. There are jagged edges, but, like the rawness of the performances, they only add to the power of the picture. DP. Contains sex scenes and drug abuse.

George T Odom *Ray Brown* • Ann D Sanders *Frankie Brown* • Lawrence Gilliard Jr [Larry Gilliard Jr] *Dennis Brown* • Barbara Sanon *Carolyn Brown* • Reana E Drummond *Shirley* • Matty Rich *Larry Love* • Mark Malone *Kevin* • Ali Shahid Abdul Wahha *Luther* ■ *Dir/Scr* Matty Rich

Straight Shooting ★★★

Silent western 1917 · US · BW · 75mins

Long believed to be lost until it was rediscovered in a Czech film archive in the 1960s, this very early western is part of a series that starred Harry Carey as Cheyenne Harry under the direction of John Ford. During production it crept up to five reels, becoming Ford's first feature. It develops a cattlemen versus homesteaders conflict, with Cheyenne Harry changing sides. Ford's visual style is already often striking. AE

Harry Carey *Cheyenne Harry* • Duke Lee *Thunder Flint* • George Berrell *Sweetwater Sims* • Molly Malone *Joan Sims* • Ted Brooks *Tom Sims* • Hoot Gibson *Danny Morgan* ■ *Dir* Jack Ford [John Ford] • *Scr* George Hively

The Straight Story ★★★★★ U

Road movie based on a true story
1999 · US/Fr/UK · Colour · 106mins

David Lynch is in a mellow mood with this whimsical road movie that slyly dissects middle American mores with disarming precision. Exhibiting dignified self-assurance, Richard Farnsworth gives an Oscar-nominated performance as the Iowa farmer travelling by lawnmower to visit his dying brother in Wisconsin. There's selfless support from Sissy Spacek, as his traumatised daughter, and from the various eccentrics he meets en route. It's hard to imagine a gentler film, yet Lynch exploits the stately pace to gaze fondly upon life's rich pageant. DP DVD

Richard Farnsworth *Alvin Straight* • Sissy Spacek *Rose Straight* • Harry Dean Stanton *Lyle Straight* • Everett McGill *Tom the John Deere dealer* • John Farley *Thorvald Olsen* • Kevin Farley *Harald Olsen* • Jane Galloway Heitz *Dorothy* • Joseph A Carpenter *Bud* ■ *Dir* David Lynch • *Scr* John Roach, Mary Sweeney • *Cinematographer* Freddie Francis • *Music* Angelo Badalamenti

Straight Talk ★★★★ PG

Romantic comedy
1992 · US · Colour · 86mins

Both Dolly Parton and James Woods are perfectly cast as the bogus radio agony aunt and the sleazy reporter investigating her in this fun romantic comedy, which was filmed on location in Chicago. Woods's reporter wants to expose Parton as a sham, but soon finds he wants to get her into bed along the way. What makes this work so well is the sparring double act of the two leads. JB. Contains some swearing. DVD

Dolly Parton *Shirlee Kenyon* • James Woods *Jack Russell* • Griffin Dunne *Alan Riegert* • Michael Madsen *Steve Labell* • Deirdre O'Connell *Lily* • John Sayles *Guy Girardi* • Teri Hatcher *Janice* • Spalding Gray *Dr Erdman* • Jerry Orbach *Milo Jacoby* ■ *Dir* Barnet Kellman • *Scr* Craig Bolotin, Patricia Resnick

Straight Time ★★★ 18

Crime drama 1978 · US · Colour · 109mins

This terrific if sordid little opus was originally begun with the film's star Dustin Hoffman directing himself, but he handed the reins over to Broadway veteran Ulu Grosbard when the strain of juggling both tasks got too much for him. Hoffman is brilliant as a petty hood, and there are marvellous supporting performances. TS. Contains violence, swearing and nudity.

Dustin Hoffman *Max Dembo* • Theresa Russell *Jenny Mercer* • Harry Dean Stanton *Jerry Schue* • Gary Busey *Willy Darin* • M Emmet Walsh *Earl Frank* • Sandy Baron *Manny* • Kathy Bates *Selma Darin* ■ *Dir* Ulu Grosbard • *Scr* Alvin Sargent, Edward Bunker, Jeffrey Boam, from the novel *No Beast So Fierce* by Edward Bunker

Straight to Hell ★ 15

Spoof spaghetti western
1987 · UK · Colour · 82mins

This awful spoof spaghetti western is directed by Alex Cox, who took all his pop star friends to Spain to shoot what is essentially an expensive home movie. Sy Richardson, Joe Strummer and Dick Rude play desperadoes on the run after a bank robbery. The Pogues are the gang who want them out of the one-horse town they control. Stilted and boring. AJ

Sy Richardson *Norwood* • Joe Strummer *Simms* • Dick Rude *Willy* • Courtney Love *Velma* • Zander Schloss *Karl* • Del Zamora *Poncho* • Luis Contreras *Sal* • Dennis Hopper *IG Farben* • Elvis Costello *Hives, the butler* • Grace Jones *Sonya* ■ *Dir* Alex Cox • *Scr* Alex Cox, Dick Rude

Strait-Jacket ★★★

Horror 1963 · US · BW · 92mins

"When the axe swings, the excitement begins!" screamed the original poster for William Castle's showy horror tale. But you'll be screaming louder with laughter watching trampy Joan Crawford playing a rehabilitated convicted murderess who may, or may not, be returning to her old head-severing habits. Scripted by *Psycho's* Robert Bloch, it was the writer's favourite because it was filmed intact. Castle provided restrictive seat belts in cinemas, plus free cardboard axes to wave during the head-rolling mayhem. AJ

Joan Crawford *Lucy Harbin* • Diane Baker *Carol* • Leif Erickson *Bill Cutler* • Howard St John *Raymond Fields* • John Anthony Hayes *Michael Fields* • Rochelle Hudson *Emily Cutler* • George Kennedy *Leo Krause* ■ *Dir* William Castle • *Scr* Robert Bloch

The Straits of Love and Hate ★★★

Drama 1937 · Jpn · BW · 88mins

This is a typically sympathetic study of a woman *in extremis* from master director Kenji Mizoguchi. However, Fumiko Yamaji, who plays the servant who is impregnated by an innkeeper's feckless son and who runs away to join a band of second-rate strolling players, must have felt oppressed herself, as Mizoguchi reportedly made her rehearse one scene 700 times. Yet, the stress was apparently worthwhile, as there is touching resignation in her decision to foreswear romance and settle for the minor consolations of life on the road. DP. In Japanese with English subtitles.

Fumiko Yamaji *Ofumi* • Seizaburo Kawazu *Yoshitaro* • Masao Shimizu *Kenkichi* • Haruo Tanaka *Hirose* • Kumeko Urabe ■ *Dir* Kenji Mizoguchi • *Scr* Yoshikata Yoda, Kenji Mizoguchi, Matsutaro Kawaguchi, from the novel *Resurrection* by Leo Tolstoy

Strand – Under the Dark Cloth ★★★★

Documentary 1989 · Can · Colour · 81mins

Paul Strand was always at the forefront of US artistic innovation. His 1914-15 abstracts introduced Cubism to Stateside photography, while his collaboration with Charles Sheeler, *Manhatta* (1921), launched American avant-garde cinema. He emerged as a key figure in the left-wing documentary group, Frontier Films, thanks to his input to Pare Lorentz's *The Plow That Broke the Plains* (1934) and *Native Land* (1942), which he co-directed with Leo Hurwitz. Covering all aspects of Strand's long, influential career, John Walker's portrait is both accessible and informative. DP

Dir John Walker • *Scr* Seaton Findlay

Stranded ★★ 15

Science-fiction drama
1987 · US · Colour · 77mins

Friendly aliens crash-land and establish contact with an old woman and her granddaughter in a rural area, but the usual movie misunderstandings occur and the local authorities rush in to make a mess of things. Add an alien assassin and some feisty locals into the mix and you've got 80 minutes of science-fiction fun starring Joe Morton as the Sheriff. It looks pretty good and Maureen O'Sullivan adds a nice touch as a grandma. ST

Ione Skye *Deirdre* • Joe Morton *Sheriff McMahon* • Maureen O'Sullivan *Grace Clark* • Susan Barnes *Helen Anderson* • Cameron Dye *Lieutenant Scott* • Michael Greene *Vernon Burdett* • Brendan Hughes *Prince* ■ *Dir* Tex Fuller [Fleming B Fuller] • *Scr* Alan Castle

Stranded ★★ 15

Supernatural thriller
1989 · Can · Colour · 87mins

Deborah Wakeham and Ryan Michael play an unhappily married couple in a lightweight chiller that only delivers a modicum of suspense and mystery. Suspecting that Michael is having an affair, Wakeham books a break on a secluded island in a bid to patch up their relationship, but they soon find themselves at the mercy of the island's violent past. The two leads are bland and director Paul Tucker, saddled with an unremarkable script, struggles to inject any style into the proceedings. JF. Contains some violence and swearing.

Deborah Wakeham *Lynn* • Ryan Michael *Paul* • Stephen E Miller *Boyd* ■ *Dir* Paul Tucker • *Scr* Boon Collins, Dan Vining, from a story by Daniel D Williams

S

The Strange Affair ★★★

Crime drama 1968 · UK · Colour · 104mins

Failed student Michael York becomes a policeman and gets entangled with bent cops, drug dealing and lustful Susan George. This film's swinging London trappings – Indian mystics, flower people, garish decor, circular beds, touristy locations – tend to work against the more traditional underworld elements. On the plus side are some diverting supporting performances and flashes of quirky humour. AT

Michael York *Peter Strange* • Jeremy Kemp *Detective Sgt Pierce* • Susan George *Frederika "Fred" March* • Jack Watson *Daddy Quince* • George A Cooper *Superintendent Kingley* • Barry Fantoni *Charley Small, informer* ■ *Dir* David Greene • *Scr* Stanley Mann, from the novel by Bernard Toms

A Strange Affair ★★★

Psychological drama
1981 · Fr · Colour · 100mins

There's a Capra-esque feel to this drama, which begins with an air of despondent realism only to suddenly soar into flights of inexplicable fantasy. The reason for this sudden change in the fortunes of Gérard Lanvin is Michel Piccoli, who not only takes over the shop where he works, but also insinuates himself into other areas of his life. But such is the lightness of Pierre Granier-Deferre's touch that this transformation has a disarming stealth that prevents the action from becoming tacky or twee. DP. French dialogue dubbed into English.

Michel Piccoli *Bertrand Malair* • Nathalie Baye *Nina Coline* • Gérard Lanvin *Louis Coline* • Jean-Pierre Kalfon *François Lingre* • Jean-François Balmer *Paul Belais* • Madeleine Cheminat *Yette* ■ *Dir* Pierre Granier-Deferre • *Scr* Christopher Frank, Pierre Granier-Deferre

The Strange Affair of Uncle Harry ★★ 15

Mystery drama 1945 · US · BW · 77mins

Released as plain *Uncle Harry* in the USA, this Broadway-based thriller stars George Sanders as a textile designer who lives with his two spinster sisters. When he falls in love with Ella Raines, one of the sisters is consumed with jealousy. While Sanders gives an excellent, multilayered performance, the dreadful studio-imposed ending precipitated the resignation of the producer, Joan Harrison, a regular associate of Hitchcock. AT

George Sanders *Harry Melville Quincy* • Geraldine Fitzgerald *Lettie Quincy* • Ella Raines *Deborah Brown* • Sara Allgood *Nona* • Moyna MacGill *Hester Quincy* • Samuel S Hinds *Dr Adams* ■ *Dir* Robert Siodmak • *Scr* Stephen Longstreet, Keith Winter, from the play *Uncle Harry* by Thomas Job

Strange Alibi ★★

Police drama 1941 · US · BW · 63mins

Arthur Kennedy proved to be a consummate character actor but early in his screen career, under a standard Warner Bros contract, he was tried out as leading man material in some B-pictures. In this one he's the cop who consorts with crooks and deliberately gets a bad reputation in the hope of exposing the mysterious head of a crime syndicate, only to be found out, framed and put behind bars. AE

Arthur Kennedy *Joe Geary* • Joan Perry *Alice Delvin* • Jonathan Hale *Chief Sprague* • John Ridgely *Tex* • Florence Bates *Katie* • Charles Trowbridge *Governor Phelps* • Cliff Clark *Capt Reddick* • Stanley Andrews *Lt Detective Pagle* ■ *Dir* D Ross Lederman • *Scr* Kenneth Gamet, Fred Niblo Jr, from the story *Give Me Liberty* by Leslie T White

Strange Bedfellows ★★★

Romantic comedy
1965 · US · Colour · 98mins

Executive Rock Hudson and his Italian wife Gina Lollobrigida have been separated for five years. When they come across each other in London, it is obvious there is still a spark between them, but after one passionate night they start bickering all over again. Their plans to part are complicated by Gig Young, a PR man determined to keep them together for the sake of Hudson's firm. Old hand Melvin Frank here turns in another smooth but unexceptional romantic comedy, enlivened by the talents of Terry-Thomas and Arthur Haynes. DF

Rock Hudson *Carter Harrison* • Gina Lollobrigida *Toni* • Gig Young *Richard Bramwell* • Edward Judd *Harry Jones* • Terry-Thomas *Assistant mortician* • Arthur Haynes *Carter's taxi driver* • Howard St John *JL Stevens* • David King *Toni's taxi driver* ■ *Dir* Melvin Frank • *Scr* Melvin Frank, Michael Pertwee, from a story by Norman Panama, Melvin Frank

Strange Boarders ★★★

Comedy thriller 1938 · UK · BW · 74mins

The spy thriller meets the bedroom farce in this sprightly suspense comedy. Tom Walls plays an investigator called away from his honeymoon with Renée Saint-Cyr to discover which of the guests at Irene Handl's boarding house has stolen some top-secret blueprints. Walls was never the most understated of screen performers, but he keeps this enjoyable mystery bright and breezy. DP

Tom Walls *Tommy Blythe* • Renée Saint-Cyr *Louise Blythe* • Googie Withers *Elsie* • Ronald Adam *Barstow* • CV France *Colonel Anstruther* • Nina Boucicault *Mrs Anstruther* • Leon M Lion *Luke* • C Denier Warren *Fry* • Irene Handl *Mrs Dewar* ■ *Dir* Herbert Mason • *Scr* A R Rawlinson, Sidney Gilliat, from the novel *The Strange Boarders of Paradise Crescent* by E Phillips Oppenheim

Strange Brew ★★ PG

Comedy 1983 · US · Colour · 86mins

This is of interest chiefly because it marked the first starring role for Rick Moranis, who also shares directorial duties with comic partner Dave Thomas. The film is built around a pair of characters the duo originally created for a Canadian TV sketch show and, consequently, it is episodic and a little uneven. However, Moranis and Thomas make an endearing pair of numbskulls and Max von Sydow has fun as the mad man who is putting something strange in a brewery's beer. AT

Dave Thomas *Doug McKenzie* • Rick Moranis *Bob McKenzie* • Max von Sydow *Brewmeister Smith* • Paul Dooley *Claude Elsinore* • Lynne Griffin *Pam Elsinore* • Angus MacInnes *Jean Larose* • Tom Harvey *Inspector* ■ *Dir* Dave Thomas, Rick Moranis • *Scr* Dave Thomas, Rick Moranis, Steven DeJarnatt

Strange Cargo ★★★

Drama 1940 · US · BW · 113mins

Clark Gable and Joan Crawford's eighth and last picture together is a jungle adventure that turns into a religious parable about redemption. Gable, Paul Lukas and Peter Lorre hack their way through the jungle together with Ian Hunter, Christ's disciple in French Guiana, in a bid to escape from Devil's Island. Crawford, meanwhile, turns in another Sadie Thompson routine. Banned in Boston, when the Catholic Legion of Decency condemned it as blasphemous. Recommended for connoisseurs of studio foliage and general crankiness. AT

Clark Gable *Andre Verne* • Joan Crawford *Julie* • Ian Hunter *Cambreau* • Peter Lorre *Cochon* • Paul Lukas *Hessler* • Albert Dekker *Moll* • J Edward Bromberg *Flaubert* • Eduardo Ciannelli *Telez* ■ *Dir* Frank Borzage • *Scr* Lawrence Hazard, Lesser Samuels, Anita Loos (adaptation), from the book *Not Too Narrow… Not Too Deep* by Richard Sale

Strange Confession ★★

Mystery 1945 · US · BW · 62mins

In this mediocre *Inner Sanctum* entry, novice director John Hoffman fails to seize the attention, despite the urgency with which series regular Lon Chaney Jr starts to relate the events that lead to a murder rap. The opening segment, in which Chaney's chemist endures the bullying of boss J Carrol Naish (who also has designs on his wife, Brenda Joyce), offers the occasional morsel of juicy melodrama. But time hangs heavy during the South American exile sequences. DP

Lon Chaney [Lon Chaney Jr] *Jeff Carter* • Brenda Joyce *Mary Carter* • J Carrol Naish *Roger Graham* • Milburn Stone *Stevens* • Lloyd Bridges *Dave Curtis* ■ *Dir* John Hoffman • *Scr* M Coates Webster, from the play *The Man Who Reclaimed His Head* by Jean Bart

Strange Days ★★★★ 18

Science-fiction action thriller
1995 · US · Colour · 139mins

Ralph Fiennes plays a dealer in virtual reality clips that replicate sensory perceptions in director Kathryn Bigelow's dazzling sci-fi thriller. As New Year's Eve 1999 approaches, he tries to track down a killer recording his crimes for the ultimate "snuff" experience. This controversial, highly imaginative and inventively staged movie is a fascinating look at the moral implications of advanced technology. Using subjective camerawork to place the viewer in the voyeuristic frame, Bigelow reinvents *film noir* for contemporary audiences. AJ. Contains violence, swearing, drug abuse and nudity. DVD

Ralph Fiennes *Lenny Nero* • Angela Bassett *Lornette "Mace" Mason* • Juliette Lewis *Faith Justin* • Tom Sizemore *Max Peltier* • Michael Wincott *Philo Gant* • Vincent D'Onofrio *Burton Steckler* • Glenn Plummer *Jeriko One* ■ *Dir* Kathryn Bigelow • *Scr* James Cameron, Jay Cocks, from a story by James Cameron

The Strange Door ★★ U

Horror 1951 · US · BW · 80mins

A contrived melodrama is heightened in stature by the presence of Boris Karloff and Charles Laughton. The latter is a sadistic French nobleman who imprisons his brother in the basement for marrying a woman they both loved. It's when Laughton tries to marry his brother's daughter to an infamous brigand in revenge that manservant Karloff rebels. More histrionic than horror historic. AJ

Charles Laughton *Sire Alan de Maletroit* • Boris Karloff *Voltan* • Sally Forrest *Blanche de Maletroit* • Richard Stapely *Denis de Beaulieu* • Michael Pate *Talon* • Paul Cavanagh *Edmond de Maletroit* ■ *Dir* Joseph Pevney • *Scr* Jerry Sackheim, from the story *The Sire de Maletroit's Door* by Robert Louis Stevenson

Strange Fits of Passion ★★

Comedy drama 1999 · Aus · Colour · 83mins

Initially, director Elise McCredie's screen debut could be mistaken for just another *Bridget Jones*-alike. But then, she seems to recoil from agonised encounters and gentle insights and veers off in search of a profundity that turns out to be nothing more than a melodramatic contrivance. As the virginal 20-something desperate to find love in a world that has something against her, Michela Noonan pitches a nice line between gauche and misguided. DP

Michela Noonan *She* • Mitchell Butel *Jimmy* • Samuel Johnson *Josh* • Steve Adams *Pablo* • Anni Finsterer *Judy* • Jack Finsterer *Francis* • Nathan Page *Simon* ■ *Dir/Scr* Elise McCredie

Strange Gardens ★★★ 15

Second World War comedy drama
2003 · Fr · Colour · 97mins

Jean Becker's adaptation is perfectly pitched between whimsical nostalgia and genuinely moving human drama. Teacher Jacques Villeret and aristocratic milliner André Dussollier come to appreciate the unexpected moment of human warmth shown them by a Nazi soldier detailed to guard a quartet of hostages after a mischievous act of Resistance escalates into a major incident. This thoughtful film's emphasis is firmly on character and how a seemingly minor moment can change someone's life forever. Impeccably judged and played with restraint. DP. In French with English subtitles. Contains violence.

Jacques Villeret *Jacques Pouzay* • André Dussollier *André Designy* • Thierry Lhermitte *Thierry Plaisance* • Benoît Magimel *Emile Bailleul* • Suzanne Flon *Marie Gerbier* • Isabelle Candelier *Louise* ■ *Dir* Jean Becker • *Scr* Jean Becker, Jean Cosmos, Guillaume Laurant, from the novella *In Our Strange Gardens* by Michel Quint

Strange Holiday ★

Second World War drama
1942 · US · BW · 61mins

One of the more bizarre artefacts to have survived from the Second World War, this propaganda piece was financed by General Motors and stars Claude Rains, who returns from a holiday in the backwoods to find America transformed into a Nazi dictatorship. It was made in 1942 and shelved until 1945 when Rains himself arranged its limited release. AT

Claude Rains *John Stevenson* • Bobbie Stebbins *John Jr* • Barbara Bates *Peggy Lee* • Paul Hilton *Woodrow Jr* • Gloria Holden *Mrs Jean Stevenson* • Milton Kibbee *Sam Morgan* ■ *Dir/Scr* Arch Oboler

Strange Impersonation ★★

Drama 1946 · US · BW · 62mins

Director Anthony Mann had his work cut out here to make a halfway decent picture from such a ridiculous story, on a minuscule budget. Brenda Marshall is a the research scientist, badly scarred in a fire, who returns after plastic surgery with a new identity, seeking to regain her fiancé from the rival who caused the blaze. The director draws good performances from his cast and builds an atmosphere of oppressive tension. AE

Brenda Marshall *Nora Goodrich* • William Gargan *Dr Stephan Lindstrom* • Hillary Brooke *Arline Cole* • George Chandler *JW Rinse* • Ruth Ford *Jane Karaski* • HB Warner *Dr Mansfield* ■ *Dir* Anthony Mann • *Scr* Mindret Lord, from a story by Anne Wigton, Lewis Herman

Strange Interlude ★★★★

Melodrama 1932 · US · BW · 109mins

Norma Shearer, distraught at the death of her beloved in war, makes a self-sacrificing marriage to Alexander Kirkland, but she is forced by circumstance to have her child by Clark Gable and falls in love with him. MGM's attempt to film Eugene O'Neill's complex Pulitzer Prize-winning play was either foolhardy or a brave bid for intellectual respectability. Critics were divided over the merits of the play and few people liked (or saw) the lavish film, which is a heightened, experimental delve into the torment of an idealistic, highly strung and strong woman, and the weak men around her. RK

Norma Shearer *Nina Leeds* • Clark Gable *Ned Darrell* • Alexander Kirkland *Sam Evans* • Ralph Morgan *Charlie Marsden* • Robert Young (1) *Gordon, as a young man* • May Robson *Mrs Evans* • Maureen O'Sullivan *Madeleine* • Henry B Walthall *Prof Leeds* ■ *Dir* Robert Z Leonard • *Scr* Bess Meredyth, C Gardner Sullivan, from the play by Eugene O'Neill

Strange Invaders ★★★★ 12

Science fiction 1983 · US · Colour · 89mins

An affectionate parody of 1950s alien invasion B-movies, this film's simple premise evokes memories of *It Came from Outer Space*, with co-writer/ director Michael Laughlin bringing the genre bang up to date courtesy of the marvellous special effects, warmly comic overtones and a sharply observed script. This recaptures the heady atmosphere and demented imagery of its major inspirations. AJ. Contains swearing.

Paul Le Mat *Charles Bigelow* • Nancy Allen *Betty Walker* • Diana Scarwid *Margaret* • Michael Lerner *Willie Collins* • Louise Fletcher *Mrs Benjamin* • Wallace Shawn *Earl* • Fiona Lewis *Waitress/Avon Lady* • Kenneth Tobey *Arthur Newman* ■ *Dir* Michael Laughlin • *Scr* William Condon, Michael Laughlin

Strange Justice ★★★ 15

Political documentary drama
1999 · US · Colour · 107mins

In 1991, the American legal system was rocked when President Bush's African-American candidate for the Supreme Court, Clarence Thomas, was accused of sexual harassment by Anita Hill during his confirmation hearing. It was a critical and compelling case. In Ernest R Dickerson's made-for-TV reconstruction it's less the morality of the establishment that comes under scrutiny than the advisability of allowing women access to the corridors of power. Delroy Lindo and Regina Taylor impress as the main protagonists, but they're overshadowed by the hissably persuasive performance of Mandy Patinkin as White House spin doctor Kenneth Duberstein. DP [video]

Delroy Lindo *Clarence Thomas* • Mandy Patinkin *Kenneth Duberstein* • Regina Taylor *Anita Hill* • Stephen Young *Senator Danforth* • Paul Windfield *Thurgood Marshall* • Louis Gossett Jr *Vernon Jordan* ■ *Dir* Ernest R Dickerson • *Scr* Jacob Epstein, from the non-fiction book *Strange Justice: the Selling of Clarence Thomas* by Jane Mayer, Jill Abramson

Strange Lady in Town ★★★ U

Western 1955 · US · Colour · 111mins

Doctor Greer Garson is peddling pills to the good citizens of Santa Fe in the late 19th century. Glossily shot by Harold Rosson, this is more melodrama than western, with Garson having trouble with her outcast brother Cameron Mitchell as well as confronting the usual ignorance and prejudice among her patients. As with many of director Mervyn LeRoy's later films, this is polished stuff, but paste rather than a real gem. DP

Greer Garson *Dr Julia Winslow Garth* • Dana Andrews *Rork O'Brien* • Cameron Mitchell *David Garth* • Lois Smith *Spurs O'Brien* • Walter Hampden *Father Gabriel* ■ *Dir* Mervyn LeRoy • *Scr* Frank Butler

The Strange Love of Martha Ivers ★★★★★ PG

Film noir 1946 · US · BW · 115mins

A critical and commercial hit for Barbara Stanwyck, Van Heflin and, making his debut, Kirk Douglas, this high-voltage portrait of evil and greed remains blissfully absorbing and entertaining. Stanwyck plays manipulative millionairess Martha, married to Douglas, a weak-willed district attorney with a drink problem, whom she despises. Enter Van Heflin, Stanwyck's nemesis from the past, and the fun begins. Robert Rossen (who would write and direct the Oscar-winning *The Hustler* in 1961) has a hand in the screenplay, and Lewis Milestone directs for maximum effect. RK [video] DVD

Barbara Stanwyck *Martha Ivers* • Van Heflin *Sam Masterson* • Kirk Douglas *Walter O'Neil* • Lizabeth Scott *Toni Marachek* • Judith Anderson *Mrs Ivers* • Roman Bohnen *Mr O'Neil* • Ann Doran *Secretary* ■ *Dir* Lewis Milestone • *Scr* Robert Rossen, from the story *Love Lies Bleeding* by Jack Patrick

The Strange Love of Molly Louvain ★★

Melodrama 1932 · US · BW · 70mins

Ann Dvorak, abandoned in childhood to the wrong side of the tracks but determined to be respectable, is courted by a wealthy young man. He deserts her, leaving her pregnant. She boards out her daughter, but her liaison with a scumbag (Leslie Fenton) implicates her in a murder. In hiding with Richard Cromwell, long in love with her, she falls for fast-talking newspaperman Lee Tracy who is unaware she's the fugitive. Unbelievable, but not uninvolving. RK

Ann Dvorak *Molly Louvain* • Lee Tracy *Scottie Cornell* • Richard Cromwell *Jimmy Cook* • Guy Kibbee *Pop* • Leslie Fenton *Nicky Grant* • Frank McHugh *Skeets* ■ *Dir* Michael Curtiz • *Scr* Erwin Gelsey, Brown Holmes, from the play *Tinsel Girl* by Maurine Dallas Watkins

The Strange One ★★

Drama 1957 · US · BW · 99mins

A hard-nosed, pulls-no-punches drama for its time. It's about life at a US military academy, ruled by a sadistic cadet leader played by Ben Gazzara, who revels in the name of Jocko De Paris. A sort of landlocked *Caine Mutiny*, it doubtless seems preachy and stagey today, and only James Olson and George Peppard register as Jocko's punching bags. AT

Ben Gazzara *Jocko De Paris* • Pat Hingle *Harold Knoble* • Mark Richman [Peter Mark Richman] *Cadet Colonel Corger* • Arthur Storch *Simmons* • Paul Richards (1) *Perrin McKee* • Larry Gates *Major Avery* • James Olson *Roger Gatt* • Julie Wilson *Rosebud* • George Peppard *Robert Marquales* ■ *Dir* Jack Garfein • *Scr* Calder Willingham, from his novel and play *End as a Man*

A Strange Place to Meet ★★ PG

Drama 1988 · Fr · Colour · 93mins

Catherine Deneuve's enthusiasm provided the impetus behind this minimalist roadside drama, and ultimately earned her a producer's credit on the film. Having impressed with a series of shorts and documentaries, François Dupeyron took something of a risk with his debut feature, as there is precious little story and plenty of inconsequential dialogue involved in the chance encounter between an unworldly doctor attempting to mend his car and a woman who has been dumped in a layby by her exasperated husband. DP. In French with English subtitles. [video]

Catherine Deneuve *France* • Gérard Depardieu *Charles* • André Wilms *Georges* • Nathalie Cardone *Sylvie* • Jean-Pierre Sentier *Pierrot* ■ *Dir* François Dupeyron • *Scr* François Dupeyron, Dominique Faysse

Strange Planet ★★★ 15

Romantic comedy
1999 · Aus · Colour · 91mins

This episodic romantic comedy from Australia is about a year in the love lives of six men and women. Perceptive and engaging, Emma-Kate Croghan's film features a trio of delightful performances from career girl Claudia Karvan, sweet but insecure Naomi Watts and quirky Alice Garner. The male characters are incredibly dull and self-absorbed in comparison. The film loses its perky momentum after a cracking first half. JC. Contains swearing, drug abuse and sex scenes. [video]

Claudia Karvan *Judy* • Naomi Watts *Alice* • Alice Garner *Sally* • Tom Long *Ewan* • Aaron Jeffrey *Joel* • Felix Williamson *Neil* • Hugo Weaving *Steven* • Rebecca Frith *Amanda* ■ *Dir* Emma-Kate Croghan • *Scr* Stavros Kazantzidis, Emma-Kate Croghan

The Strange Vengeance of Rosalie ★

Drama 1972 · US · Colour · 107mins

A pointless, ill-conceived and painfully contrived thriller that revives the old chestnut of the kidnapped falling in love with the kidnapper. In this instance it's travelling salesman Ken Howard who is abducted by young native American girl Bonnie Bedelia. The dumb plot about a stash of gold descends into mass confusion. AJ

Bonnie Bedelia *Rosalie* • Ken Howard *Virgil* • Anthony Zerbe *Fry* ■ *Dir* Jack Starrett • *Scr* Anthony Greville-Bell, John Kohn

The Strange Woman ★★★

Period melodrama 1946 · US · BW · 101mins

This is a rare examples of ace cult director Edgar G Ulmer (*Detour*, *Bluebeard*) working with major stars and he coaxes what is possibly a career-best performance from Hedy Lamarr. Lamarr stars as a social-climbing beauty who ensnares boring Gene Lockhart, suave George Sanders and gauche Louis Hayward during her rise from a deprived childhood. It's enjoyable tosh, glamorous to look at and played to perfection. TS

Hedy Lamarr *Jenny Hager* • George Sanders *John Evered* • Louis Hayward *Ephraim Poster* • Gene Lockhart *Isaiah Poster* • Hillary Brooke *Meg Saladine* • Rhys Williams *Deacon Adams* • June Storey *Lena Tempest* ■ *Dir* Edgar G Ulmer • *Scr* Herb Meadow, from the novel by Ben Ames Williams

The Strange World of Planet X ★★

Science-fiction thriller
1957 · UK · BW · 78mins

Perhaps because the hysterical levels of 1950s Cold War paranoia that swept America did not reach the same heights here, Britain never really went for big insect movies. However, the odd ones did slip out and here Forrest Tucker is the obligatory square-jawed imported American out to stop irradiated bugs taking over the world. Cheap and cheerful fun. JF

Forrest Tucker *Gil Graham* • Gaby André *Michele Dupont* • Martin Benson *Smith* • Hugh Latimer *Jimmy Murray* • Wyndham Goldie *Brigadier Cartwright* • Alec Mango *Dr Laird* ■ *Dir* Gilbert Gunn • *Scr* Paul Ryder, Joe Ambor, from a story by René Ray

The Stranger ★★★ PG

Thriller 1946 · US · BW · 94mins

Orson Welles was said to have had little time for this thriller about the search for a Nazi war criminal in small-town America, but it helped put him back on the Hollywood map after a series of box-office failures. There are some of his characteristic directorial touches on view, as well as some of the actorly excesses that typified the performances he gave when he was jobbing to fund his more personal projects. Russell Metty's stylish, shadowy black-and-white photography is so superb, it beggars belief the film was also released in a colourised version. DP [video] DVD

Edward G Robinson *Wilson* • Loretta Young *Mary Longstreet* • Orson Welles *Professor Charles Rankin/Franz Kindler* • Philip Merivale *Judge Longstreet* • Richard Long *Noah Longstreet* • Byron Keith *Dr Jeff Lawrence* ■ *Dir* Orson Welles • *Scr* Anthony Veiller, John Huston (uncredited), Orson Welles, from a story by Victor Trivas, Decla Dunning

The Stranger ★★

Drama 1967 · Alg/Fr/It · Colour · 104mins

Despite the insistence of the author's widow, Luchino Visconti was totally the wrong director to adapt Albert Camus's stark, existential tale of the outsider whose irrational act of murder lands him on death row. His visuals are too ornate, his grasp of 1930s Franco-Algerian politics too tenuous and his sympathy for the alienated killer too superficial. Yet, he still succeeds in drawing an undervalued performance from Marcello Mastroianni. Fascinating, but a failure nonetheless. DP. An Italian language film.

Marcello Mastroianni *Arthur Meursault* • Anna Karina *Marie Cardona* • Georges Wilson *Examining magistrate* • Bertrand Blier *Defense counsel* • Pierre Bertin *Judge* • Georges Geret *Raymond* • Bruno Cremer *Priest* ■ *Dir* Luchino Visconti • *Scr* Suso Cecchi D'Amico, Georges Conchon, Emmanuel Robles, Luchino Visconti, from the novel *L'Etranger* by Albert Camus • *Cinematographer* Giuseppe Rotunno

The Stranger ★★★

Psychological thriller
1987 · US/Arg · Colour and BW · 89mins

One thing strikes you about this film immediately, and that's how good it looks. But what this intriguing memory-loss thriller gains in style, it loses in construction, as Argentinian director Adolfo Aristarain overdoes the black-and-white flashbacks and too often allows the tension to slacken. However, Bonnie Bedelia is convincing as an amnesiac witness to murder, and Peter Riegert chips in with a decent turn as the doctor she believes she can trust. DP. Contains brief nudity.

Bonnie Bedelia *Alice Kildee* • Peter Riegert *Dr Harris Kite* • Barry Primus *Sergeant Drake* • David Spielberg *Hobby* • Marcos Woinski *Macaw* • Julio DeGrazia *Jay* • Cecilia Roth *Anita* ■ *Dir* Adolfo Aristarain • *Scr* Dan Gurskis • *Cinematographer* Horacio Maira

The Stranger ★★

Drama 1991 · Ind · Colour · 118mins

With a nod towards the story of Martin Guerre, this was Satyajit Ray's final film, but still very much a minor work. Utpal Dutt is suitably ambiguous as the returning prodigal who may or may not be the uncle Mamata Shankar has not seen since 1955. While Ray handles the awkward civilities of the homecoming in his typically unassuming manner, he fails to build the tension as Shankar's husband (Dipankar De) decides to put the stranger to the test. Subtly satirical, allegorically autobiographical, yet disappointingly formal. DP. In Bengali with English subtitles.

Dipankar Dey *Sudhindra Bose* • Mamata Shankar *Anila Bose* • Bikram Bhattacharya *Satyaki/Bablu* • Utpal Dutt *Manmohan Mitra* • Dhritiman Chatterjee *Prithwish Sen Gupta* ■ *Dir/Scr* Satyajit Ray

A Stranger among Us ★★ 15

Crime drama 1992 · US · Colour · 104mins

Released in British cinemas as *Close to Eden*, this is a flop under any name, with Melanie Griffith woefully miscast as a cop investigating a murder in New York's tightknit Hasidic community. Throw in a romantic interest in the form of Eric Thal and you have an uneven thriller from director Sidney Lumet, who has certainly had his share of career ups and downs. JB. Contains some violence and swearing. [video]

Melanie Griffith *Emily Eden* • Eric Thal *Ariel* • John Pankow *Levine* • Tracy Pollan *Mara* • Lee Richardson *Rebbe* • Mia Sara *Leah* • Jamey Sheridan *Nick Kemp* ■ *Dir* Sidney Lumet • *Scr* Robert J Avrech

Stranger at My Door ★★★ U

Western 1956 · US · BW · 84mins

This western adventure stars Skip Homeier as a dangerous outlaw who learns that there is more to life than stealing and killing when he seeks shelter in the home of preacher Macdonald Carey. Good characterisation and plenty of action make this fine family entertainment. RT

Macdonald Carey *Hollis Jarret* • Patricia Medina *Peg Jarret* • Skip Homeier *Clay Anderson* • Stephen Wootton *Dodie Jarret* • Louis Jean Heydt *Sheriff John Tatum* • Howard Wright *Doc Parks* • Slim Pickens *Ben Silas, horse trader* ■ *Dir* William Witney • *Scr* Barry Shipman, from his story

The Stranger Came Home ★

Crime mystery 1954 · UK · BW · 80mins

Paulette Goddard gave up her screen career (apart from one Italian job ten

S

years later) after being reduced to this dreary non-thriller for Hammer Films. Supposedly irresistible as the wife of a vanished businessman, she is favoured by Hollywood-style soft-focus close-ups. Husband William Sylvester reappears with amnesia, seeking to find out which of three former associates had tried to kill him. AE

Paulette Goddard *Angie* • William Sylvester *Philip Vickers* • Patrick Holt *Job Crandall* • Paul Carpenter *Bill Saul* • Alvys Maben *Joan Merrill* • Russell Napier *Inspector Treherne* • David King-Wood *Sessions* ■ *Dir* Terence Fisher • *Scr* Michael Carreras, from the novel *Stranger at Home* by George Sanders

Stranger from Venus ★ [U]

Science fiction 1954 · UK · BW · 74mins

This is directed by Burt Balaban, who adds a mere hint of American zip to the stiff upper lip atmosphere and limited public house setting. After crashing her car, Patricia Neal meets mysterious Helmut Dantine who has travelled from Venus to persuade mankind to abandon their nuclear power experiments. Lacklustre and too restrained. AJ

Patricia Neal *Susan North* • Helmut Dantine *The Stranger* • Derek Bond *Arthur Walker* • Cyril Luckham *Dr Meinard* • Willoughby Gray *Tom* • Marigold Russell *Gretchen* • Arthur Young *Scientist* • Kenneth Edwards *Charles Dixon* ■ *Dir* Burt Balaban • *Scr* Hans Jacoby, from a story by Desmond Leslie

A Stranger in My Arms ★★

Melodrama 1959 · US · BW · 88mins

June Allyson plays a war widow whose husband has been killed in Korea in this not-so-classic melodrama from Ross Hunter, producer of many of Douglas Sirk's best films. She has to deal with her difficult mother-in-law (Mary Astor), a woman ruthlessly intent on seeing that her adored son is posthumously honoured, and with the air force officer (Jeff Chandler) asked to testify to the dead man's heroism. The earnest stars lack the charisma to lift the material, leaving the polished veteran Astor to provide what little spark there is. RK

June Allyson *Christina Beasley* • Jeff Chandler *Pike Yarnell* • Sandra Dee *Pat Beasley* • Charles Coburn *Vance Beasley* • Mary Astor *Mrs Beasley* • Peter Graves (2) *Donald Beasley* • Conrad Nagel *Harley Beasley* • Hayden Rorke *Marcus Beasley* • Reita Green *Bessie Logan* ■ *Dir* Helmut Käutner • *Scr* Peter Berneis, from the novel *And Ride a Tiger* by Robert Wilder

Stranger in the House ★★ [15]

Mystery melodrama
1967 · UK · Colour · 90mins

Also known as *Cop-Out*, the highlight of this melodrama is a solid performance from James Mason as a depressed, drunken ex-barrister who comes out of retirement for a seemingly hopeless murder case involving his daughter's boyfriend. Georges Simenon's novel makes an uneasy transfer to sleepy Hampshire, but reliable British performers are worth picking out in small parts. JG

James Mason *John Sawyer* • Geraldine Chaplin *Angela Sawyer* • Bobby Darin *Barney Teale* • Paul Bertoya *Jo Christophorides* • Ian Ogilvy *Desmond Flower* • Bryan Stanyon *Peter Hawkins* • Pippa Steel *Sue Phillips* • Clive Morton *Col Flower* • Moira Lister *Mrs Flower* • Yootha Joyce *Girl at shooting range* • Rita Webb *Mrs Plaskett* ■ *Dir* Pierre Rouve • *Scr* Pierre Rouve, from the novel *Les Inconnus dans la Maison* by Georges Simenon

Stranger Inside ★★★ [18]

Drama 2001 · US · Colour · 86mins

Pitching itself well above the usual lesbian prison drama by taking time to explore key issues of Afro-American race and the social damage done by incarceration, director Cheryl Dunye's unflinching made-for-cable movie is a worthy if intermittently affecting polemic. Tough young offender Yolanda Ross gets herself transferred to the same prison where her mother is serving a life sentence. As they uneasily bond behind bars, and hardened mother shows long-lost daughter the inside ropes, both must face each others' hurt and dark past secrets. Gritty, realistic and compelling. AJ DVD

Yolanda Ross *Treasure* • Davenia McFadden *Brownie* • Rain Phoenix *Kit* • LaTonya "T" Hagan *Shadow* • Mary Mara *Tanya* • Marc Vann *Nelson* • Conchata Ferrell *Mama Cass* ■ *Dir* Cheryl Dunye • *Scr* Cheryl Dunye, Catherine Crouch

Stranger on Horseback ★★★ [U]

Western 1955 · US · Colour · 65mins

Joel McCrea brings his calm authority to this strong but brief western, playing the circuit judge who dares to arrest Kevin McCarthy, the spoiled killer son of the local land baron (John McIntire) and then has to coax witnesses to testify. The film was shot in Mexico using an unsatisfactory colour process. However, capable director Jacques Tourneur draws effective performances from his cast. AE

Joel McCrea *Rick Thorne* • Miroslava *Amy Lee Bannerman* • Kevin McCarthy *Tom Bannerman* • John McIntire *Josiah Bannerman* • Nancy Gates *Caroline Webb* • John Carradine *Colonel Streeter* • Emile Meyer *Sheriff Nat Bell* ■ *Dir* Jacques Tourneur • *Scr* Herb Meadow, Don Martin, from a story by Louis L'Amour

Stranger on the Run ★★★

Western 1967 · US · Colour · 97mins

This intelligent western drama stars Henry Fonda as an ex-con who finds himself arrested for murder by perverse lawman Michael Parks, who has the habit of releasing drifters into the desert to be chased by his brutal railway posse. This TV movie has a strong cast, workmanlike direction by Don Siegel and an intelligent script that lifts it above the average. JG. Contains violence.

Henry Fonda *Ben Chamberlain* • Anne Baxter *Valverda Johnson* • Michael Parks *Vince McKay* • Dan Duryea *OE Hotchkiss* • Sal Mineo *George Blaylock* • Lloyd Bochner *Mr Gorman* • Michael Burns *Matt Johnson* • Tom Reese *Leo Weed* ■ *Dir* Don Siegel • *Scr* Dean E Riesner, from a story by Reginald Rose

Stranger on the Third Floor ★★★

Thriller 1940 · US · BW · 62mins

Although John Huston's *The Maltese Falcon* is usually regarded as the first authentic *film noir*, this gripping thriller from RKO came out a year earlier. All the requisite *noir* elements are present: the fatalistic, paranoid mood, the corkscrew murder plot and bug-eyed Peter Lorre as the "stranger". The violent story, including knifings and capital punishment, is remarkably compressed by Boris Ingster's direction. But the star of the show is the expressionistic camerawork of maestro Nicholas Musuraca. AT

Peter Lorre *The Stranger* • John McGuire *Michael Ward* • Margaret Tallichet *Jane* • Elisha Cook Jr *Joe Briggs* • Charles Waldron *District attorney* • Charles Halton *Meng* • Ethel Griffies *Mrs Kane* • Cliff Clark *Martin* ■ *Dir* Boris Ingster • *Scr* Frank Partos, from his story

Stranger than Fiction ★★ [18]

Black comedy thriller
1999 · US · Colour · 95mins

A dark comedy thriller that is just a little clever for its own good, this begins intriguingly, but eventually spirals out of control. The plot revolves around a group of young friends who agree to cover up an accidental killing one of their number has committed. However, as they dig themselves deeper and deeper into trouble, it transpires that some of them may have been a little economical with the truth . The attractive young cast delivers solid performances, but the over-elaborate plotting strains credibility. JF DVD

MacKenzie Astin *Jared* • Todd Field *Austin* • Dina Meyer *Emma* • Natasha Gregson Wagner *Violet* ■ *Dir* Eric Bross • *Scr* Tim Garrick, Scott Russell

Stranger than Paradise ★★★★ [15]

Road movie 1984 · US · BW · 85mins

Developed from a 30-minute short and made for a mere $120,000, this chilled-out road movie could be seen as the first slacker picture. Shot in long takes, each ending with a dawdling fade to black, the action (if that's the word) centres on Hungarian immigrant John Lurie, his cousin Eszter Balint and his mate Richard Edson, and their driftings between Cleveland and Florida. The winner of the Caméra d'Or at Cannes, this is a unique and irresistible film, which warned us all that the only thing to expect from Jim Jarmusch is the unexpected. DP. Contains swearing.

John Lurie *Willie* • Eszter Balint *Eva* • Richard Edson *Eddie* • Cecillia Stark *Aunt Lottie* • Danny Rosen *Billy* • Sara Driver *Girl with hat* ■ *Dir/Scr* Jim Jarmusch • *Cinematographer* Tom DiCillo

The Stranger Wore a Gun ★★ [U]

Western 1953 · US · Colour · 78mins

A strong cast comes to the aid of this implausible Randolph Scott western, originally released in 3-D in the United States. One-eyed director Andre De Toth stages a fiery climax in a blazing saloon, that made 3-D audiences feel the heat. Scott plays the man protecting gold shipments from hold-ups, and his adversaries include the ever-hissable George Macready, Alfonso Bedoya's beaming Mexican bandit, and two gunmen played by Lee Marvin and Ernest Borgnine early in their careers. AE

Randolph Scott *Jeff Travis* • Claire Trevor *Josie Sullivan* • Joan Weldon *Shelby Conroy* • George Macready *Jules Mourret* • Alfonso Bedoya *Degas* • Lee Marvin *Dan Kurth* • Ernest Borgnine *Bull Slager* ■ *Dir* Andre De Toth • *Scr* Kenneth Gamet, from the novel *Yankee Gold* by John M Cunningham

Strangers All ★★

Drama 1935 · US · BW · 68mins

The strangers are the members of a family, each so different from the other as to have no common ground. Shopkeeper and family breadwinner Preston Foster is at loggerheads with brothers William Bakewell, an egotistical aspiring actor, and James Bush, a naive socialist radical; daughter Florine McKinney dumps her fiancé and marries another without telling the family; and mother May Robson tries to hold her bickering brood together. Director Charles Vidor tries to keep control with no more than passable results. RK

May Robson *"Mom" Anna Carter* • Preston Foster *Murray Carter* • Florine McKinney *Lily Carter* • William Bakewell *Dick Carter* • James Bush *Lewis Carter* • Samuel S Hinds *Mr Green* • Clifford Jones [Philip Trent] *Pat Gruen* ■ *Dir* Charles Vidor • *Scr* Milton Krims, from the play *Strangers All: or, Separate Lives* by Marie M Bercovici

The Stranger's Hand ★★★ [U]

Spy thriller 1953 · It/UK · BW · 85mins

This intriguing Cold War thriller is most memorable for director Mario Soldati's inspired use of the magic and mystery of Venice. Combining both wide-eyed wonder and growing fear, Richard O'Sullivan impresses as the young boy who goes in search of his kidnapped father, receiving sympathetic support from unlikely hero Richard Basehart and hotel receptionist Alida Valli. Trevor Howard appears all too briefly as the missing major, but author Graham Greene contributes a cameo, as the hand untying the mooring rope of one of the gondolas. DP

Trevor Howard *Major Court* • Alida Valli *Roberta* • Richard Basehart *Joe Hamstringer* • Eduardo Ciannelli *Dr Vivaldi* • Richard O'Sullivan *Roger Court* ■ *Dir* Mario Soldati • *Scr* Guy Elmes, Giorgio Bassani, from the story by Graham Greene

Strangers Kiss ★★★★ [15]

Romantic drama
1983 · US · Colour and BW · 93mins

This cleverly conceived and well-executed drama has as its obvious inspiration Stanley Kubrick's *Killer's Kiss*, but without that film's steely black-and-white photography. Mikhail Suslov's colour shots are more akin to the lush melodramas that Douglas Sirk used to make for producer Ross Hunter. Peter Coyote is outstanding as the obsessive director prepared to endanger the life of his star Victoria Tennant to complete his picture. Intricate, astute and very classy. DP

Peter Coyote *Stanley* • Victoria Tennant *Carol Redding* • Blaine Novak *Stevie Blake* • Dan Shor *Farris* • Richard Romanus *Frank Silva* • Linda Kerridge *Shirley* • Carlos Palomino *Estoban* ■ *Dir* Matthew Chapman • *Scr* Blaine Novak, Matthew Chapman, from a story by Blaine Novak

Strangers May Kiss ★★★

Romantic drama 1931 · US · BW · 83mins

In love with foreign correspondent Neil Hamilton, Norma Shearer is heartbroken when he goes off on an assignment. She dallies with a series of lovers in Europe and finally decides to go home and marry her faithful suitor Robert Montgomery, whereupon Hamilton reappears. Shearer holds the screen in the kind of role she came to play almost peerlessly countless times. An archetypal 1930s romantic drama, this is very good if not quite the very best. RK

Norma Shearer *Lisbeth Corbin* • Robert Montgomery *Steve* • Neil Hamilton *Alan* • Marjorie Rambeau *Geneva* • Irene Rich *Celia* • Hale Hamilton *Andrew* ■ *Dir* George Fitzmaurice • *Scr* John Meehan, from the novel by Ursula Parrott • *Cinematographer* William H Daniels

Stranger's Meeting ★

Crime thriller 1957 · UK · BW · 63mins

Circus acrobat Peter Arne, convicted of killing his partner but innocent of the crime, escapes and sets out to clear his name and find the real culprit. Directed by Robert Day, this is an example of the British film industry at its worst. It's inconceivable that this pathetically feeble, clumsy and uninteresting film could have been made – even as a programme filler, which it is – as late as 1957. RK

Peter Arne *Harry Belair* • Delphi Lawrence *Margot Sanders* • Conrad Phillips *David Sanders* • Barbara Archer *Rosie Foster* • David Ritch *Giovanni* • David Lodge *Fred* ■ *Dir* Robert Day • *Scr* David Gordon

Strangers on a Train
★★★★★ PG

Classic thriller 1951 · US · BW · 96mins

This splendid thriller is testimony to Alfred Hitchcock's mastery of technique and his ability to transform even the most unpromising start into a gripping movie. After nearly a dozen writers had turned down the chance to adapt Patricia Highsmith's novel, Raymond Chandler stepped into the breach, only to disagree with Hitch on several key scenes and suffer the humiliation of having his dialogue polished by Czenzi Ormonde, a staff writer. Hitchcock was also underwhelmed by Farley Granger in a role he felt cried out for William Holden. Nevertheless, he turns the murderous proposal of eccentric playboy Robert Walker to tennis champ Granger into a veritable nail-biter, with the two fairground scenes outstanding. DP [video] DVD

Farley Granger *Guy Haines* • Ruth Roman *Anne Morton* • Robert Walker *Bruno Antony* • Leo G Carroll *Senator Morton* • Patricia Hitchcock *Barbara Morton* • Laura Elliot *Miriam* • Marion Lorne *Mrs Antony* • Jonathan Hale *Mr Antony* ■ *Dir* Alfred Hitchcock • *Scr* Raymond Chandler, Czenzi Ormonde, Whitfield Cook, from the novel by Patricia Highsmith

The Stranger's Return
★★ U

Drama 1933 · US · BW · 87mins

Having left her husband, Miriam Hopkins goes to live with her grandfather Lionel Barrymore on his farm in the Midwest, where she becomes passionately involved with married man and father Franchot Tone. Meanwhile, in between dispensing advice to Hopkins and expressing his disapproval of the affair, Barrymore, who is facing approaching death, has to fend off the grasping relatives who are trying to get their clutches on his land. King Vidor directed this dour drama which, despite its excellent cast, remains unappealing. RK

Lionel Barrymore *Grandpa Storr* • Miriam Hopkins *Louise Storr* • Franchot Tone *Guy Crane* • Stuart Erwin *Simon, farmhand* • Irene Hervey *Nettie Crane* • Beulah Bondi *Beatrice* ■ *Dir* King Vidor • *Scr* Brown Holmes, Phil Stong, from the novel by Phil Stong

Strangers When We Meet
★★★ 15

Romantic drama 1960 · US · Colour · 112mins

A sophisticated study of compulsive marital infidelity starring Kirk Douglas and Kim Novak, beautifully acted and glamorously photographed, this is marred only by a syrupy music score that undermines the bittersweet pathos of the events portrayed. Director Richard Quine's use of landscape and roadside assignations works well, and the supporting cast is exemplary. Despite censorship limitations at the time, Evan Hunter's adaptation of his own novel has the ring of truth to it and makes satisfying, though uncomfortable, viewing. TS [video]

Kirk Douglas *Larry Coe* • Kim Novak *Maggie Gault* • Ernie Kovacs *Roger Altar* • Barbara Rush *Eve Coe* • Walter Matthau *Felix Anders* • Virginia Bruce *Mrs Wagner* • Kent Smith *Stanley Baxter* ■ *Dir* Richard Quine • *Scr* Evan Hunter, from his novel

The Strangler
★★

Crime drama 1964 · US · BW · 88mins

Released to capitalise on the Boston Strangler frenzy of the time, this racy black-and-white thriller is better than most exploitation features. Young Boston nurses have been murdered, but the chief suspect, a solitary lab technician obsessed with dolls (played with relish by a creepy Victor Buono), seems to have an iron-clad alibi, which even a lie-detector test can't shake. Ellen Corby (Grandma Walton) plays his possessive and hated mother. JG

Victor Buono *Leon Kroll* • David McLean *Lt Benson* • Diane Sayer *Barbara* • Davey Davison *Tally* • Ellen Corby *Mrs Kroll* • Baynes Barron *Sgt Clyde* • Michael Ryan *Posner* ■ *Dir* Burt Topper • *Scr* Bill S Ballinger

Strapless
★★ 15

Romantic drama 1988 · UK · Colour · 95mins

A rather jarring and unconvincing look at romance from writer/director David Hare. Blair Brown is the 40-something doctor who re-evaluates her life when she is wooed by charming but unreliable Bruno Ganz. More believable is the relationship between Brown and her younger, freer – and pregnant – sister played by Bridget Fonda. This drama suffers from stilted dialogue and direction and an overall condescending attitude towards female independence. JB [video]

Blair Brown *Lillian Hempel* • Bridget Fonda *Amy Hempel* • Bruno Ganz *Raymond Forbes* • Alan Howard *Mr Cooper* • Michael Gough *Douglas Brodie* • Hugh Laurie *Colin* • Suzanne Burden *Romaine Salmon* • Rohan McCullough *Annie Rice* ■ *Dir/Scr* David Hare

Strass
★★★★

Satire 2001 · Bel · Colour · 91mins

The 20th Dogme outing is one of the sharpest to exploit the 1995 "Vow of Chastity", as it explores both the shifting line between life and performance and the viewer's complicity in establishing an agenda for Reality entertainment. Acting as his own interlocutor in this hand-held mockumentary, director Vincent Lannoo hones in on the controversial Open Door Theatre Method that is dividing a prestigious Belgian drama school as it readies its next productions. Pierre Lekeux and Lionel Bourguet excel as the feuding tutors, but everyone is so in the slot that it's often easy to forget you're watching a spoof. DP. In French with English subtitles.

Pierre Lekeux *Pierre Radowsky* • Carlo Ferrante *George Keller* • Lionel Bourguet *Lionel Desmevillier* • Gaëtan Bévernaege *Leopold* • Jérôme le Maire *Jérôme* • Hélène Ramet *Hélène* • Cédric Delplace *Cedric* ■ *Dir/Scr* Vincent Lannoo

Strategic Air Command
★★★ U

Drama 1955 · US · Colour · 113mins

In this unconvincing combination of domestic melodrama and high-flying flag-waving, James Stewart plays a baseball player-turned-bomber pilot, with June Allyson as his wife. Paramount's biggest money-spinner of 1955, the film is most effective during the thrilling aerial sequences. Director Anthony Mann seems more at home with the male-bonding between Stewart and his fellow trainee pilots, but Allyson still makes an impact in a role less saccharine than usual. DP

James Stewart *Lt Col Robert "Dutch" Holland* • June Allyson *Sally Holland* • Frank Lovejoy *General Ennis C Hawkes* • Barry Sullivan *Lt Col Rocky Samford* • Alex Nicol *Ike Knowland* • Bruce Bennett *General Espy* • Jay C Flippen *Doyle* ■ *Dir* Anthony Mann • *Scr* Valentine Davies, Beirne Lay Jr, from a story by Beirne Lay Jr • *Cinematographer* William Daniels [William H Daniels], Tom Tutwiler

The Stratford Adventure
★★★ U

Documentary 1954 · Can · Colour · 44mins

This Oscar-nominated documentary chronicles the sterling efforts of Stratford, Ontario, to stage an annual festival of Shakespeare. The local bigwigs get together, raise enough for a shoestring budget and persuade Tyrone Guthrie to produce the plays. Guthrie in turn persuades Alec Guinness to star in *All's Well That Ends Well* and *Richard III*, with a cast that also includes Irene Worth (who later starred with Guinness in *The Scapegoat*). Theatre fans won't want to miss this chance to see snatches of Guinness in these classic plays; they should also read his marvellous account of the festival in his 1985 memoir *Blessings in Disguise*. AT

Dir Morten Parker • *Scr* Gudrun Parker

The Stratton Story
★★★ U

Biographical sports drama
1949 · US · BW · 106mins

Douglas Morrow won a best original story Oscar for this biopic of Monty Stratton, the impoverished southern cotton picker who became a baseball star with the Chicago White Sox until a freak hunting accident threatened his career. James Stewart is typically affable in the lead, but he also does a good job of conveying Stratton's post-injury bitterness. In the first of a trio of collaborations with Stewart, June Allyson is just a tad too perfect. DP

James Stewart *Monty Stratton* • June Allyson *Ethel Stratton* • Frank Morgan *Barney Wile* • Agnes Moorehead *Ma Stratton* • Bill Williams *Eddie Dibson* • Bruce Cowling *Ted Lyons* • Cliff Clark *Josh Higgins* ■ *Dir* Sam Wood • *Scr* Douglas Morrow, Guy Trosper, from a story by Douglas Morrow

Straw Dogs
★★★★ 18

Thriller 1971 · UK · Colour · 116mins

Mild-mannered maths teacher Dustin Hoffman finds his manhood tested when, after he moves to a Cornish village, the local toughs viciously rape his wife Susan George and threaten his home. One of the key movies in the controversial 1970s debate about unacceptable screen violence, director Sam Peckinpah's cynical parable virtually states that all pacifists are cowardly thugs under their liberal exteriors. Reprehensible and disturbing in equal measure, this pitch black revenge drama remains potent and shocking, particularly the much-discussed and questionable rape scene. AJ [video] DVD

Dustin Hoffman *David Sumner* • Susan George *Amy Sumner* • Peter Vaughan *Tom Hedden* • TP McKenna *Major Scott* • Del Henney *Venner* • Ken Hutchison *Scutt* • Colin Welland *Reverend Hood* • Jim Norton *Cawsey* ■ *Dir* Sam Peckinpah • *Scr* David Zelag Goodman, Sam Peckinpah, from the novel *The Siege of Trencher's Farm* by Gordon M Williams

Strawberry and Chocolate
★★★ 18

Comedy 1993 · Cub · Colour · 105mins

Considering that America tries to prevent the worldwide distribution of Cuban films, it is remarkable that the island's first gay movie should have been nominated for the best foreign film Oscar. It was co-directed by Juan Carlos Tabio and Tomás Gutiérrez Alea, the latter perhaps the most gifted of all Cuban film-makers. What should have been a witty and subversive aside on Cuban socio-sexual politics has become, in fact, a showy, rather obvious film. DP. In Spanish with English subtitles. Contains sex scenes and nudity. [video]

Jorge Perugorria *Diego* • Mirta Ibarra *Nancy* • Francisco Gattorno *Miguel* • Joel Angelino *German* • Marilyn Solaya *Vivian* ■ *Dir* Tomás Gutiérrez Alea, Juan Carlos Tabio • *Scr* Senel Paz, from his story *El Lobo, El Bosque y el Hombre Nuevo*

The Strawberry Blonde
★★★★ U

Romantic comedy 1941 · US · BW · 94mins

Dentists don't often get to play romantic leads in the movies, but James Cagney does his bit by playing a struggling tooth-doctor. This is an agreeable comedy, set in turn-of-the-century New York, with the action flashing back to tell of Cagney's enduring passion for Rita Hayworth (in the title role). But his ultimate discovery is that, in nice, sweet Olivia de Havilland, he has married the right woman all along. PF [video]

James Cagney *Biff Grimes* • Olivia de Havilland *Amy Lind* • Rita Hayworth *Virginia Brush* • Alan Hale *Old Man Grimes* • Jack Carson *Hugo Barnstead* • George Tobias *Nicholas Pappalas* • Una O'Connor *Mrs Mulcahey* ■ *Dir* Raoul Walsh • *Scr* Julius J Epstein, Philip G Epstein, from the play *One Sunday Afternoon* by James Hogan

The Strawberry Statement
★★★

Political drama 1970 · US · Colour · 108mins

Easy Rider showed studio executives that there was a huge, untapped youth audience out there, running riot on the nation's campuses to protest against the Vietnam war. So Hollywood quickly came over all radical with movies such as this, in which student Bruce Davison is turned into a militant and free love advocate by fellow student Kim Darby. It all ends with a frenzied riot and a stand-off with the National Guard while John Lennon sings *Give Peace a Chance*. AT

Bruce Davison *Simon* • Kim Darby *Linda* • Bud Cort *Elliot, the coxswain* • Murray MacLeod *George* ■ *Dir* Stuart Hagmann • *Scr* Israel Horovitz, from the novel *The Strawberry Statement: Notes of a College Revolutionary* by James Simon Kunen

The Stray
★★

Thriller 1999 · US · Colour · 90mins

In this cod-Freudian thriller, Michael Madsen fails to generate the tension the action needs. This can partly be blamed on director Kevin Mock, but there's little chemistry between Madsen and Angie Everhart, who plays the restaurateur who takes him home after knocking him down in her car, only to realise that he bears an unnerving resemblance to her late father. DP

Michael Madsen *Ben* • Angie Everhart *Kate* • Stefan Lysenko *Gil* • Frank Zagarino *Carl* • Seidy Lopez *Tanya* ■ *Dir* Kevin Mock • *Scr* Terry Cunningham

Stray Dog
★★★ PG

Crime drama 1949 · Jpn · BW · 117mins

As is often the case with Akira Kurosawa, this is a film in which a quest results in self-discovery. Here, rookie detective Toshiro Mifune has his pistol stolen on a crowded bus and begins painstakingly tracking down the culprit as the gun is used in a series of crimes. Kurosawa gives the action an authentic feel by shooting in the more rundown areas of Tokyo, emphasising the sticky summer heat and Mifune's self-loathing. Aminor but compelling work. DP. In Japanese with English subtitles. [video] DVD

Toshiro Mifune *Murakami* • Takashi Shimura *Sato* • Ko Kimura [Isao Kimura] *Yuro* • Keiko Awaji *Harumi* • Reisaburo Yamamoto *Hondo* ■ *Dir* Akira Kurosawa • *Scr* Ryuzo Kikushima, Akira Kurosawa, from a novel by Akira Kurosawa

Streamers
★★★ 18

Drama 1983 · US · Colour · 113mins

Up close and personal animosity comes to the boil in the one-set locality of an army barracks dormitory.

S

Director Robert Altman developed the film from its original stage context, in much the same way as he did with his earlier offering, *Come Back to the Five and Dime, Jimmy Dean, Jimmy Dean.* The screenplay is an adaptation by David Rabe of his own Broadway venture and its claustrophobic tensions are expanded thanks to fine acting – especially from Matthew Modine and Michael Wright. TH

Matthew Modine *William "Billy" Wilson* • Michael Wright *Carlyle* • Mitchell Lichtenstein *Richard "Richie" Douglas* • David Alan Grier *Roger Hicks* • Guy Boyd *Sergeant Rooney* • George Dzundza *Sergeant Cokes* ■ *Dir* Robert Altman • *Scr* David Rabe, from his play

Streamline Express ★★

Drama 1935 · US · BW · 72mins

This train-bound melodrama provides berths for such accomplished character actors as Victor Jory and Sidney Blackmer, but it's let down by the simplicity of its plotlines and the mediocrity of its stars. Evelyn Venable lacks spark as the flaky actress who absconds before the opening of her new play and Ralph Forbes has a damp dishcloth quality as her devoted fiancé. Consequently, you wind up relying on subplots involving blackmail, twins and a ménâge à trois for amusement. DP

Evelyn Venable *Patricia Wells* • Victor Jory *Jimy Hart* • Esther Ralston *Elaine Vinson* • Ralph Forbes *Fred Arnold* • Sidney Blackmer *Gilbert Landon* • Erin O'Brien-Moore *Mrs Forbes* ■ *Dir* Leonard Fields • *Scr* Olive Cooper, Leonard Fields, Dave Silverstein

Street Angel ★★

Silent drama 1928 · US · BW · 102mins

At the first Academy Awards, Janet Gaynor was voted best actress Oscar-winner for three films: director Frank Borzage's *7th Heaven* and *Street Angel* and, best of all, FW Murnau's *Sunrise*. The least of these is *Street Angel*, a turgidly sentimental melodrama. It's the tale of a Neapolitan slum girl who resorts to illegal means to procure medicine for her sick mother. She temporarily avoids arrest by joining a circus, where artist Charles Farrell paints her as the Madonna. The film is now little more than a barely tolerable collector's item. Principally silent, it includes some sound sequences. RK

Janet Gaynor *Angela* • Charles Farrell *Gino* • Alberto Rabagliati *Policeman* • Gino Conti *Policeman* • Guido Trento *Neri, police sergeant* ■ *Dir* Frank Borzage • *Scr* Marion Orth, Katherine Hilliker (titles), HH Caldwell (titles), Philip Klein, Henry Roberts Symonds, from the novel *Cristilinda* by Monckton Hoffe

Street Angel ★★★★

Romance 1937 · Chi · BW · 100mins

Yuan Muzhi reaffirmed his left-wing credentials with this socially critical, yet warmly human drama, which proved to be his final feature. Both a tribute to the spirit of the poor and an indictment of Shanghai's post-colonial indifference, it is, essentially, a moving love story in which naive musician Zhao Dan attempts to rescue Manchurian exile Zhou Xuan from prostitution. However, with its frank discussion of contentious issues, its roots in traditional Chinese art and its stylistic debt to Hollywood and Soviet cinema, it merits its reputation as a proto-neorealist study. DP. In Mandarin with English subtitles.

Zhao Dan *Chen Shaoping* • Wei Heling *Wang, newspaper seller* • Zhou Xuan *Xiao Hong, little singer* • Zhao Huishen *Xiao Yun* ■ *Dir/Scr* Yuan Muzhi

The Street Fighter ★★★ 18

Martial arts action
1974 · Jpn · Colour and BW · 86mins

After more than a decade jobbing in Japanese B-movies, Sonny Chiba found international fame in this shameless Bruce Lee rip-off. Echoes of Akira Kurosawa's samurai masterpiece, *Yojimbo*, also abound as Chiba lets rip aboard an oil tanker after discovering that the yakuza who hired him to kidnap an heiress has reneged on the deal. The brutality of the fight sequences would recur in the sequels *Return of the Street Fighter* and *The Street Fighter's Last Revenge*. DP. In Japanese with English subtitles. Contains violence. DVD

Shinichi Chiba [Sonny Chiba] *Terry Tsuguri* • Waichi Yamada [Gerald Yamada] *Ratnose* • Yutaka Nakajima *Sarai* • Tony Cetera *Jadot* • Masashi Ishibashi *Junjou* ■ *Dir* Shigehiro Ozawa • *Scr* Koji Takada, Motohiro Torii

Street Fighter ★ 12

Action adventure 1994 · US · Colour · 97mins

Jean-Claude Van Damme and Kylie Minogue team up for a movie adaptation of the popular computer game. If that unlikely pairing isn't enough to put you off, the simple-minded plot will. It concerns an assignment to overthrow dictator Raul Julia (in his last role). Laughably bad. AJ. Contains violence, swearing. DVD

Jean-Claude Van Damme *Colonel William F Guile* • Raul Julia *Bison* • Wen Ming-Na [Ming-Na] *Chun-Li* • Damian Chapa *Ken* • Kylie Minogue *Cammy* • Simon Callow *AN official* • Roshan Seth *Dhalsim* • Wes Studi *Sagat* ■ *Dir/Scr* Steven E de Souza

Street of Crocodiles ★★★ PG

Animation
1986 · UK · Colour and BW · 20mins

A puppet warily explores the darkened rooms of a deserted lecture hall and finds other dolls acting in strange ways in a typical stop-motion animation production from the idiosyncratic Brothers Quay. This is gloomy, creepy and quite unsettling – Stephen and Timothy Quay tap into our worst childhood nightmares and the claustrophobic end result couldn't be further from the colourful fantasy of Ray Harryhausen. A relentlessly downbeat and unique nightmare, which continuously offers up one startling image after another. AJ

Dir Stephen Quay, Timothy Quay • *Scr* Brothers Quay [Stephen Quay, Timothy Quay], from the short story collection *Ulica Krokodyli* by Bruno Schulz

Street of No Return ★★ 18

Action crime thriller
1989 · Fr/Por · Colour · 88mins

Forty years after making his debut, Samuel Fuller wound up his directorial career with this disappointing adaptation. Here Keith Carradine plays a singer who falls foul of the underworld after he decides to take a sabbatical from stardom in the company of gangster's moll, Valentina Vargas. But once Carradine begins skulking round the backstreets seeking revenge on those who slit his throat, the action loses contact with its characters and descends into thick-ear violence. DP

Keith Carradine *Michael* • Valentina Vargas *Celia* • Bill Duke *Ltt Borel* • Andréa Ferréol *Rhoda* • Bernard Fresson *Morin* ■ *Dir* Samuel Fuller • *Scr* Samuel Fuller, Jacques Bral, from the novel by David Goodis

Street of Shadows ★★ PG

Thriller 1953 · UK · BW · 80mins

They used to churn out these pseudo *noir* thrillers by the van load in the early 1950s with varying degrees of success. This one moves along at a brisk trot, but basically there is little else to commend it, apart from a workmanlike performance by Cesar Romero as a casino owner madly in love with (the consistently under-rated) Kay Kendall. Kendall often had a strange luminescent quality on screen and this film shows it to moody advantage. SH

Cesar Romero *Luigi* • Kay Kendall *Barbara Gale* • Edward Underdown *Inspector Johnstone* • Victor Maddern *Limpy* • Simone Silva *Angele Abbe* • Liam Gaffney *Fred Roberts* • Robert Cawdron *Sergeant Hadley* • John Penrose *Captain Gerald Gale* • Bill Travers *Nigel Langley* ■ *Dir* Richard Vernon • *Scr* Richard Vernon, from the novel *The Creaking Chair* by Lawrence Meynall

Street of Shame ★★★★

Drama 1955 · Jpn · BW · 85mins

Set in Dreamland, in Tokyo's Yoshiwara red-light district, this study of oppressed womanhood was the final feature of Kenji Mizoguchi. Though denied the chance to shoot on location in docudramatic style, he exposes the exploitation and hypocrisy of bordello life with such power that the film was credited at the time with swaying the Diet during its debates on prostitution. The most impressive performance comes from Machiko Kyo as the flint-hearted hooker, who mercilessly denounces the father whose excesses have condemned her to unrelenting misery. Not the great director's most accomplished picture, but still a fitting swansong. DP. In Japanese with English subtitles.

Machiko Kyo *Mickey* • Ayako Wakao *Yasumi* • Aiko Mimasu *Yumeko* • Michiyo Kogure *Hanae* • Kumeko Urabe *Otane* • Yasuko Kawakami *Shizuko* • Hiroko Machida *Yorie* • Eitaro Shindo *Kurazo Taya, proprietor of Dreamland* ■ *Dir* Kenji Mizoguchi • *Scr* Masashige Narusawa, from the story *Susaki no Onna* by Yoshiko Shibaki

Street Scene ★★★★

Drama 1931 · US · BW · 80mins

Adapted by Elmer Rice from his play and directed by King Vidor, the film covers the events of a night and morning in the lives of tenement dwellers during a stifling Manhattan summer. It centres on young Sylvia Sidney and her unhappy mother's illicit affair, which leads to tragedy. Dated, and sometimes stagey, this is still riveting as an early attempt to capture a slice of tenement life and as an evocation of New York's melting pot of immigrants. It was a step on the way to stardom for Sidney, young, beautiful and demonstrating the poignant quality that became her trademark. RK

Sylvia Sidney *Rose Maurrant* • William Collier [William Collier Jr] *Sam Kaplan* • Estelle Taylor *Anna Maurrant* • Beulah Bondi *Emma Jones* • Max Montor *Abe Kaplan* • David Landau *Frank Maurrant* • Matt McHugh *Vincent Jones* ■ *Dir* King Vidor • *Scr* Elmer Rice, from his play

Street Smart ★★ 18

Thriller based on a true story
1987 · US · Colour · 92mins

Journalistic ethics come under rather fuzzy scrutiny in a tepid thriller based on a true story. Christopher Reeve plays a struggling magazine writer who finds his career taking off after the publication of his fictional exposé of Manhattan prostitution. Despite his success, Reeve soon discovers that his story has some very deadly consequences in a slow-moving melodrama sparked into sporadic life by Morgan Freeman's Oscar-nominated portrayal of a low-life pimp. AJ

Christopher Reeve *Jonathan Fisher* • Morgan Freeman *Fast Black* • Kathy Baker *Punchy* • Mimi Rogers *Alison Parker* • Jay Patterson *Leonard Pike* • Andre Gregory *Ted Avery* ■ *Dir* Jerry Schatzberg • *Scr* David Freeman

Street Song ★★

Musical 1935 · UK · BW · 64mins

British director Bernard Vorhaus who had his career ruined in the early 1950s by the evidence of his fellow film-makers during the Hollywood communist witch-hunt. There's a rather ominous ring, therefore, to the plotline of this creaky musical melodrama, directed and co-written by Vorhaus, in which singer John Garrick is sacked from his radio slot after being accused of a crime he didn't commit. DP

John Garrick *Tom Tucker* • René Ray *Lucy* • Lawrence Hanray *Tuttle* • Wally Patch *Wally* • Johnny Singer *Billy* ■ *Dir* Bernard Vorhaus • *Scr* Bernard Vorhaus, Paul Gangelin

A Street to Die ★★ PG

Drama 1985 · Aus · Colour · 92mins

A brave drama about the effect on humans of the defoliant Agent Orange used during the Vietnam War. When an Australian ex-soldier with leukaemia discovers many of his fellow veterans are also afflicted with the condition, he initiates a lawsuit against the authorities. Well made and well acted (particularly by Chris Haywood), it's a sympathetic demonstration of the hidden casualties of war. JG

Chris Haywood *Col Turner* • Jennifer Cluff *Lorraine Turner* • Peter Hehir *Peter Towney* • Arianthe Galani *Dr Walsea* • Peter Kowitz *Craig* ■ *Dir/Scr* Bill Bennett

The Street with No Name ★★★★

Crime thriller 1948 · US · BW · 90mins

When, in his screen debut in *Kiss of Death*, Richard Widmark giggled as he pushed an old lady in a wheelchair down the stairs, 20th Century-Fox knew it had a star on its books. This follow-up casts him as a psychotic hypochondriac, always snorting on an inhaler and beating his wife. Not many screen villains looked nastier than Widmark in those days, his thin-lipped mouth and bony face epitomising the look of a man with antisocial tendencies. FBI agent Mark Stevens is the nominal hero of this *noir*ish thriller, but he's no match for Widmark. AT

Mark Stevens *Cordell* • Richard Widmark *Alec Stiles* • Lloyd Nolan *Inspector Briggs* • Barbara Lawrence *Judy Stiles* • Ed Begley *Chief Harmatz* • Donald Buka *Shivvy* • Joseph Pevney *Matty* • John McIntire *Cy Gordon* ■ *Dir* William Keighley • *Scr* Harry Kleiner

A Streetcar Named Desire ★★★★★ 15

Classic drama 1951 · US · BW · 119mins

Marlon Brando is at the height of his powers here, reprising his acclaimed Broadway role as the brutal Stanley Kowalski in director Elia Kazan's classic adaptation of Tennessee Williams's play. Brando's bravura performance is matched by that of Vivien Leigh (as the neurotic southern belle Blanche DuBois) and their scenes together sizzle with sexual tension. The play's homosexual references were cut to comply with censorship rules of the day, though Blanche's implied violation and references to her sordid past remain. The film won four Oscars – awards for Leigh, Kim Hunter, Karl Malden and art director Richard Day – but Brando missed out to Humphrey Bogart for *The African Queen*. TH DVD

S

Vivien Leigh *Blanche DuBois* • Marlon Brando *Stanley Kowalski* • Kim Hunter *Stella Kowalski* • Karl Malden *Mitch* • Rudy Bond *Steve Hubbell* • Nick Dennis *Pablo Gonzales* • Peg Hillias *Eunice Hubbell* ■ *Dir* Elia Kazan • *Scr* Tennessee Williams, from his play, adapted by Oscar Saul • *Cinematographer* Harry Stradling • *Set Designer* George James Hopkins

Streets ★★★ 18

Thriller 1990 · US · Colour · 80mins

A gritty, often gripping drama about teen runaways in LA. Christina Applegate is Dawn, a 14-year-old junkie prostitute. David Mendenhall is a clean-cut suburban boy who arrives in LA with the vague idea of becoming a rock star and saves Applegate from a violent punter. The movie follows the couple as the psychotic punter tries to track them down. Neither tub-thumping nor slick, the movie says what it has to say without sentimentality or toning down the violence, with a great performance from Applegate. DA [video]

Christina Applegate *Dawn* • David Mendenhall *Sy* • Eb Lottimer *Lumley* • Patrick Richwood *Bob* • Kady Tran *Dawn's blonde roommate* • Mel Castelo *Elf* ■ *Dir* Katt Shea Ruben • *Scr* Katt Shea Ruben, Andy Ruben

Streets of Fire ★★★ 15

Action romance 1984 · US · Colour · 89mins

Director Walter Hill obviously had fun with this violent rock-fuelled fantasy shot in a sort of youth culture neverland. Viewers will have fun spotting the faces of future stars, although for Michael Paré, who plays the brooding loner hero, this was probably his career high spot. Paré arrives back in town just in time to gather up a posse of old friends and rescue his rock-star ex-girlfriend from the clutches of a merciless biker gang. Scored by the peerless Ry Cooder, the music also comes courtesy of retro-rockers the Blasters. JF [video] DVD

Michael Paré *Tom Cody* • Diane Lane *Ellen Aim* • Rick Moranis *Billy Fish* • Willem Dafoe *Raven* • Amy Madigan *McCoy* • Deborah Van Valkenburgh *Reva* • Bill Paxton *Clyde* • Lee Ving *Greer* • Robert Townsend *Lester* ■ *Dir* Walter Hill • *Scr* Walter Hill, Larry Gross

Streets of Gold ★★ 15

Sports drama 1986 · US · Colour · 89mins

Distinguished Austrian actor Klaus Maria Brandauer swaps meaningful European cinema for big American clichés in this boxing drama. He brings detail and a hint of depth to his role of Soviet champ turned dishwasher turned trainer, in a thrusting but dull outing. DP. Contains swearing. [video]

Klaus Maria Brandauer *Alek Neuman* • Wesley Snipes *Roland Jenkins* • Adrian Pasdar *Timmy Boyle* • Angela Molina *Elena Gitman* • Elya Baskin *Klebanov* ■ *Dir* Joe Roth • *Scr* Heywood Gould, Richard Price,Tim Cole, from a story by Dezso Magyar

Streets of Laredo ★★★ U

Western 1949 · US · Colour · 92mins

This is an inferior remake of King Vidor's splendid 1936 western *The Texas Rangers*, in which three outlaw pals go their separate ways, with two becoming lawmen and ending up chasing the third. Nevertheless, there is a fine star-making performance from a deceptively casual William Holden, whose burgeoning screen presence demands attention, especially when dull co-star Macdonald Carey is on screen. The stunning Technicolor photography is really what gives this western its distinction. TS

William Holden (2) *Jim Dawkins* • Macdonald Carey *Lorn Reming* • Mona Freeman *Rannie Carter* • William Bendix *Wahoo Jones* • Stanley Ridges *Major Bailey* • Alfonso Bedoya *Charley Calico* ■ *Dir* Leslie Fenton • *Scr* Charles Marquis Warren, from a story by Louis Stevens, Elizabeth Hill • *Cinematographer* Ray Rennahan

The Streetwalker ★★ 18

Erotic drama 1976 · Fr · Colour · 79mins

Master of stylised erotica Walerian Borowczyk may have had loftier ambitions with this tale of sexual obsession, but his "mistake" was to cast Sylvia Kristel and Joe Dallesandro in the leads, and then to get carried away with the lovemaking and lyrical imagery. The film was sold as soft porn and the critics turned against him. Dallesandro plays a happily married man titillated by the idea of sex with a cheap prostitute (Kristel). Stricken by remorse after a family tragedy, he is drawn deeper into her sordid world. DM. French dialogue dubbed into English. [video]

Sylvia Kristel *Diana* • Joe Dallesandro *Sigismond Pons* • Mireille Audibert *Sergine Pons* • Denis Manuel *Pimp* • André Falcon *Antonin Pons* • Louise Chevalier *Féline* ■ *Dir* Walerian Borowczyk • *Scr* Walerian Borowczyk, from the novel *La Marge* by André Pieyre de Mandiargues

Streetwise ★★★ 18

Documentary 1985 · US · Colour · 96mins

This Academy Award-nominated documentary examines the nightmare flip side of the American dream. Martin Bell's "shock doc" focuses on the teenagers who live rough on the streets of Seattle, where they earn what passes for a living as prostitutes, pimps, muggers and petty drug dealers. The film makes no judgements and offers no answers. This litany of lost souls is tough, sobering viewing. DA [video]

Dir Martin Bell • *Scr* from the article *Streets of the Lost* in *Life* magazine by Mary Ellen Mark, Cheryl McCall • *Editor* Nancy Baker • *Music* Tom Waits

Strictly Ballroom ★★★★★ PG

Romantic comedy drama
1992 · Aus · Colour · 90mins

Feel-good movies don't come any better than this Australian smash hit, which is an exuberant joy from sequined start to feathered finish. *Come Dancing* meets *Footloose* when rebel ballroom star Paul Mercurio hesitantly teams up with ugly duckling novice Tara Morice for an important contest. He wants to perform his own Latin routine, however, rather than the boring steps set by the conservative dancing federation. Will love be in the air? What do you think! As kitsch and as corny as anything, this hilariously heart-warming film is the ideal pick-me-up. Strictly fabulous. AJ. Contains swearing. [video] DVD

Paul Mercurio *Scott Hastings* • Tara Morice *Fran* • Bill Hunter *Barry Fife* • Pat Thomson *Shirley Hastings* • Gia Carides *Liz Holt* • Peter Whitford *Les Kendall* • Barry Otto *Doug Hastings* • John Hannan *Ken Railings* • Sonia Kruger *Tina Sparkle* ■ *Dir* Baz Luhrmann • *Scr* Baz Luhrmann, Craig Pearce, from a story by Baz Luhrmann, Andrew Bovell, from an original idea by Baz Luhrmann and the NIDA stage production

Strictly Sinatra ★★ 15

Romantic crime drama
2000 · UK · Colour · 92mins

Despite the efforts of actor/director Peter Capaldi in his feature debut and a strong cast, this takes us on yet another trip to turgid *Lock, Stock* territory. Ian Hart as the pseudo-Sinatra is sad, clad in shiny suits and sporting a dreadful perm. There's something inherently depressing about him as the film's focus; he sells out his pianist mentor Alun Armstrong and girlfriend Kelly Macdonald all too easily, and for a world that is so obviously full of hollow promises. Ironically the only great thing here is the Sinatra soundtrack. LH. Contains swearing and violence. [video] DVD

Ian Hart *Toni Cocozza* • Kelly Macdonald *Irene* • Brian Cox *Chisholm* • Alun Armstrong *Bill* • Tommy Flanagan *Michelangelo* • Iain Cuthbertson *Connolly* • Richard E Grant • Jimmy Tarbuck ■ *Dir/Scr* Peter Capaldi

Strike ★★★★ 12

Silent political drama
1924 · USSR · BW · 86mins

Sergei Eisenstein's debut feature was an electrifying testament to the dramatic and intellectual power of cinema. It chronicles the suppression of a 1912 factory uprising after one of the workers had committed suicide. The bold decision to focus on collective heroism invests the film with a scale and energy that is intensified by the brilliance of Eisenstein's rhythmic editing of Edouard Tissé's starkly realistic visuals. Juxtaposing images to give them satirical, metaphorical or emotional weight (the massacre being intercut with slaughterhouse scenes), Eisenstein transformed "kino-eye" footage into the "kino-fist" he hoped would inspire revolutionary endeavour. DP [video] DVD

Grigori Alexandrov *Factory foreman* • Aleksandr Antonov [Aleksander Antonov] *Member of strike committee* • Yduif Glizer *Queen of Thieves* • Mikhail Gomorov *Worker* • I Ivanov *Chief of police* ■ *Dir* Sergei Eisenstein • *Scr* Sergei Eisenstein, Grigori Alexandrov, V Pletniev, I Kravtchunovsky

Strike! ★★★ 12

Comedy drama
1998 · US/Can · Colour · 93mins

The girls of St Trinian's meet the *Dead Poets Society* in this sharp, witty tale of pupil power set in an exclusive American school in the early 1960s. Kirsten Dunst and Gaby Hoffmann are two of the students waging a campaign to prevent male pupils from being admitted to their beloved school. Rachael Leigh Cook and Lynn Redgrave are among the strong supporting cast. JF. Contains sexual references. [video]

Kirsten Dunst *Verena Von Stefan* • Gaby Hoffmann *Odette Sinclair* • Lynn Redgrave *Miss McVane* • Rachael Leigh Cook *Abby* • Tom Guiry *"Frosty" Frost* • Vincent Kartheiser *Snake* ■ *Dir/Scr* Sarah Kernochan

Strike Me Pink ★★★ U

Musical comedy 1936 · US · Colour · 95mins

The last, but by no means least, of the six films Eddie Cantor made for Samuel Goldwyn is a wacky comedy with songs that allegedly utilised many more writers than those credited. Cantor is a mild tailor who, inspired by a book called *Man or Mouse: What Are You?*, agrees to run an amusement park that gangsters have targeted for their slot-machine business. The farcical consequences become surreal at times – tough guy Edward Brophy breaks into a ballet routine in one priceless sequence. TV [video]

Eddie Cantor *Eddie Pink* • Ethel Merman *Joyce Lenox* • Sally Eilers *Claribel Hayes* • Parkyakarkus [Harry Einstein] *Harry Parke* • William Frawley *Copple* • Helen Lowell *Ma Carson* • Gordon Jones *Butch Carson* • Brian Donlevy *Vance* • Edward Brophy *Killer* ■ *Dir* Norman Taurog • *Scr* Frank Butler, Walter DeLeon, Francis Martin, Philip Rapp, from the novel *Dreamland* by Clarence Buddington Kelland • *Choreographer* Robert Alton

Strike Up the Band ★★★★ U

Musical 1940 · US · BW · 119mins

This is one of the great MGM Judy Garland/Mickey Rooney collaborations, a super Busby Berkeley-directed heartwarmer with a major bonus in a fine score. Very much of its period, from a time when band contests on radio were the peak of public entertainment and Paul Whiteman (here playing himself) was the "King of Jazz", this vehicle creates several marvellous moments for the two leads. The movie never palls during its long running time, and, despite the rubber-boned June Preisser, it's never unwatchable, avoiding the sentimentality that so often ruins these "let's put on a show" plots. TS

Mickey Rooney *Jimmy Connors* • Judy Garland *Mary Holden* • June Preisser *Barbara Frances Morgan* • William Tracy *Phillip Turner* • Ann Shoemaker *Mrs Connors* • Larry Nunn *Willie Brewster* • George Lessey *Mr Morgan* • Phil Silvers *Pitch man* ■ *Dir* Busby Berkeley • *Scr* John Monks [John Monks Jr], Fred F Finklehoffe, Herbert Fields (uncredited), Kay Van Riper (uncredited)

Striking Distance ★★★ 18

Crime thriller 1993 · US · Colour · 97mins

Bruce Willis plays his usual hard-nosed loner, who here finds himself relegated to the unfashionable water cops (and partnered with Sarah Jessica Parker) when he breaks ranks and testifies against a policeman. However, a serial killer with an unhealthy interest in Willis's life offers the chance of redemption. The aptly named Rowdy Herrington ensures the action roars along and that the set pieces are suitably big and brash. JF. Contains swearing, violence and a sex scene. [video] DVD

Bruce Willis *Tom Hardy* • Sarah Jessica Parker *Jo Christman* • Dennis Farina *Nick Detillo* • Tom Sizemore *Danny Detillo* • Brion James *Detective Eddie Eiler* • Robert Pastorelli *Jimmy Detillo* • Timothy Busfield *Tony Sacco* • John Mahoney *Vince Hardy* ■ *Dir* Rowdy Herrington • *Scr* Rowdy Herrington, Martin Kaplan

The Stringer ★★★

Romantic drama
1997 · Rus/UK · Colour · 88mins

Pawel Pawlikowski made his feature debut with this piercing insight into democratic Russia. The scene-setting sequences depicting the decay and potential for corruption and crime after decades of Communist misrule are both revealing and sobering. But the focus blurs once it falls on tele-news cameraman Sergei Bodrov Jr's relationships with British producer Anna Friel and Vladimir Ilyin's charismatic nationalist. The romantic subplot is pretty routine, while the thriller element that builds around a faked assassination attempt falters short of suspense. DP. In Russian and English with subtitles.

Anna Friel *Helen* • Sergei Bodrov Jr *Vadik Chernyshov* • Vladimir Ilyin *Yarvovsky* • Rob Knepper [Robert Knepper] *John* • Anna Kamenkova *Mother* ■ *Dir* Paul Pavlikovsky [Pawel Pawlikowski] • *Scr* Paul Pavlikovsky [Pawel Pawlikowski], Gennadi Ostrovsky

S

Strings ★★★★ PG

Puppet fantasy drama
2004 · Den/UK/Swe/Nor · Colour · 89mins

This puppet fantasy drama from Danish director Anders Ronnow Klarlund dazzles with its technical virtuosity, inventiveness and scope. The story follows Hal (voiced by James McAvoy), the prince of Hebalon who infiltrates the kingdom of his people's bitter enemies, the Zeriths, in an attempt to avenge the apparent murder of his father. There he falls for the mysterious Zita (Catherine McCormack), while at home his wicked Uncle Nezo (Derek Jacobi) tries to take control. The film's strength comes from the wholly credible universe it establishes for its characters. This is an impressive piece of work that dares to be political while remaining consistently imaginative. AJ

James McAvoy *Hal* • Catherine McCormack *Zita* • Julian Glover *Kahro* • Derek Jacobi *Nezo* • Ian Hart *Ghrak* • Claire Skinner *Jhinna* • David Harewood *Erito* • Samantha Bond *Eike* ■ *Dir* Anders Ronnow Klarlund • *Scr* Naja Maria Aidt, Anders Ronnow Klarlund

The Strip ★★★

Crime drama 1951 · US · BW · 85mins

Although *A Kiss to Build a Dream On* landed an Oscar nomination, turns by jazz greats such as Louis Armstrong and Vic Damone prove the highlight of this *noir*ish story with music. Mickey Rooney, playing the drummer at a nightclub owned by William Demarest, demonstrates a talent for downbeat drama when his passion for dancer and would-be actress Sally Forrest lands him in deep with ruthless bookie James Craig. Offering intriguing insights into the seedier side of showbiz, this unsung film merits more than its minor cult status. DP

Mickey Rooney *Stanley Maxton* • Sally Forrest *Jane Tafford* • William Demarest *Fluff* • James Craig *Delwyn "Sonny" Johnson* • Kay Brown *Edna* • Tommy Rettig *Artie* • Tom Powers *Detective Bonnabel* ■ *Dir* Leslie Kardos • *Scr* Allen Rivkin

Stripes ★★★ 15

Comedy 1981 · US · Colour · 101mins

This was the breakthrough film for Bill Murray, whose sleazy charisma helps disguise the formulaic "you're in the army now" plotting. Layabout Murray and chum Harold Ramis (also co-writer) are conned into joining up, and Murray's sparring with the obligatory hard-nosed NCO (Warren Oates, in one of his last film roles), is a constant delight. A surprise hit, this comedy also provided early high profile roles for Judge Reinhold, John Candy and Sean Young. JF [video]

Bill Murray *John* • Harold Ramis *Russell* • Warren Oates *Sergeant Hulka* • PJ Soles *Stella* • Sean Young *Louise* • John Candy *Ox* • John Larroquette *Captain Stillman* • Judge Reinhold *Elmo* ■ *Dir* Ivan Reitman • *Scr* Len Blum, Dan Goldberg, Harold Ramis

The Stripper ★★★

Melodrama 1963 · US · BW · 94mins

Politely retitled *Woman of Summer* in Britain, this is an atmospheric drama about a woman from small-town Kansas who, having failed as a movie actress, returns home as part of a sleazy dance troupe. There she gets involved with Claire Trevor's teenage son (Richard Beymer). Joanne Woodward is beautifully cast as the woman whose life resembles a never-ending car crash, though she's more self-reliant than wallowing in self-pity. The story is based on a play by William Inge and is fairly restrained compared to his other melodramas. AT

Joanne Woodward *Lila Green* • Richard Beymer *Kenny Baird* • Claire Trevor *Helen Baird* • Carol Lynley *Miriam Caswell* • Robert Webber *Ricky Powers* • Louis Nye *Ronnie Cavendish* • Gypsy Rose Lee *Madame Olga* ■ *Dir* Franklin J Schaffner • *Scr* Meade Roberts, from the play *A Loss of Roses* by William Inge

Stripper ★★★ 18

Documentary 1985 · US · Colour · 86mins

This documentary is a brave attempt to come up with a non-exploitative insight into the world of stripping. Against the backdrop of the first annual convention for the trade, Janette Boyd, Sara Costa and Kimberly Holcomb are among the dancers who speak frankly about the job, while director Jerome Gary keeps the actual scenes of stripping down to a minimum. The soundtrack is from ace composer Jack Nitzsche, who was responsible for the music for films such as *The Exorcist* and *One Flew over the Cuckoo's Nest*. JF. Contains swearing and nudity. [video]

Dir Jerome Gary

Stripshow ★★ 18

Erotic drama 1996 · US · Colour · 87mins

Tane McClure plays a veteran stripper who has just become a millionairess, courtesy of the fortune that a wealthy regular customer has left her in his will. She decides to fill her spare time by attempting to rekindle an affair with an ex-boyfriend and teaching young, would-be stripper Monique Parent the harsh realities of the profession. The acting is embarrassing, but there's also more emphasis on dialogue than in most films in the genre. RT [video]

Tane McClure *Raquel* • Steve Tietsort *Cowboy* • Monique Parent *Kara* • Bill Trillo *Indian* ■ *Dir/Scr* Gary Dean Orona

Striptease ★★ 15

Crime comedy drama 1996 · US · Colour · 112mins

When devoted mother Demi Moore loses custody of her daughter to her lowlife erstwhile husband Robert Patrick because she's unemployed, she finds work as a stripper in a Florida topless bar to earn money and get the child back. She becomes the object of oily, corrupt politician Burt Reynolds's lust, and finds herself involved in murder and blackmail. Andrew Bergman's direction makes this watchable, but his screenplay is a mess, pulling its punches on the sleaze, and combining tear-jerking sentimentality and inadequate humour with the drama. RK. Contains violence, swearing and nudity. [video] DVD

Demi Moore *Erin Grant* • Armand Assante *Al Garcia* • Ving Rhames *Shad* • Robert Patrick *Darrell Grant* • Burt Reynolds *Congressman Dilbeck* • Paul Guilfoyle (2) *Malcolm Moldovsky* • Jerry Grayson *Orly* • Rumer Willis *Angela Grant* ■ *Dir* Andrew Bergman • *Scr* Andrew Bergman, from the novel by Carl Hiaasen

Stroker Ace ★ PG

Comedy 1983 · US · Colour · 90mins

Burt Reynolds stars in a lame comedy about the larger-than-life exploits of racing car driver who is forced into loony promotional work (such as dressing up as a giant chicken) by his sponsor (Ned Beatty), who is the owner of a chain of fried chicken shops. The clash between the two loud personalities forms the core of the film. This one's the pits. DF [video]

Burt Reynolds *Stroker Ace* • Ned Beatty *Clyde Torkle* • Jim Nabors *Lugs* • Parker Stevenson *Aubrey James* • Loni Anderson *Pembrook Feeney* • Bubba Smith *Arnold* • John Byner *Doc Seegle* ■ *Dir* Hal Needham • *Scr* Hal Needham, Hugh Wilson, from the novel *Stand On It* by William Neely, Robert K Ottum

Stromboli ★★ PG

Drama 1950 · It/US · BW · 101mins

When Ingrid Bergman abandoned her husband (and Hollywood) for Italian director Roberto Rossellini, she found herself at the centre of the first major showbiz scandal of the postwar era. Denounced by religious groups, blacklisted by the studios and called "Hollywood's apostle of degradation" by a US senator, Bergman made this film with Rossellini (whom she soon married). Launched with a fanfare, it flopped noisily. Bergman is ill at ease as the refugee who marries an Italian fisherman, while the island of Stromboli's volcano simmers symbolically in the background. Part melodrama, part neorealist exercise, it never gels. AT [video]

Ingrid Bergman *Karin Bjiorsen* • Mario Vitale *Antonio* • Renzo Cesana *Priest* • Mario Sponza *Lighthouse keeper* ■ *Dir* Roberto Rossellini • *Scr* Roberto Rossellini, Art Cohn, Renzo Cesana, Sergio Amidei, CP Callegari

Strong Hands ★★★

Political thriller 1997 · It · Colour · 92mins

Linking the 1974 terrorist bombing of the Piazza del Loggia in Brescia with the Bosnian conflict, this conspiracy thriller makes intriguing, if laboured use of its factual foundation. Director Franco Bernini builds the suspense effectively enough, as he moves forward 20 years to the consultation between psychoanalyst Francesca Neri (who lost a sister in the atrocity) and war correspondent Claudio Amendola, who convinces her of government involvement in the blast. DP. An Italian language film.

Francesca Neri *Claudia* • Claudio Amendola *Tancredi* • Enzo De Caro *Giulio* • Toni Bertorelli *Judge Consoli* • Massimo De Francovich *Professor Sembriani* • Bruno Armando *Captain Landino* ■ *Dir* Franco Bernini • *Scr* Franco Bernini, Maura Nuccetelli

Strong Language ★ 18

Comedy drama 1998 · UK · Colour · 76mins

First-timer Simon Rumley is to be congratulated for his persistence in making this talking-heads scrapbook for a hard-earned £30,000. However, his portrait of 1990s London 20-somethings is as disappointingly contrived as its visual style is simple. In the mouths of a largely inexperienced cast, Rumley's ruminations sound self-conscious and too obviously scripted. DP [video] DVD

David Groves *Narrator* • Al Nedjari *Pete, unemployed* • Paul Tonkinson *Danny, lift attendant* • Julie Rice *Tatty, astrologer & tarot card reader* • Charlie De'Ath *Stuart, video director* • Kelly Marcel *Philippa, magazine production assistant* ■ *Dir/Scr* Simon Rumley

The Strong Man ★★★★ U

Silent comedy 1926 · US · BW · 73mins

Of the four great silent comedians, Harry Langdon is virtually forgotten – though, in popularity terms, he once stood beside Chaplin, Keaton and Harold Lloyd. The puny, sad-faced clown plays a Belgian immigrant who tours America with circus strong man Arthur Thalasso, while searching for his pen pal, who turns out to be a blind girl. It's not as sentimental as it sounds, and the sequences with Langdon being ravished by Gertrude Astor and labouring under the effects of a heavy cold are superb. As much a social drama about the immigrant experience as a comedy, this was probably Langdon's best movie and gave Frank Capra his first official directorial credit. AT [video]

Harry Langdon *Paul Bergot* • Priscilla Bonner *Mary Brown* • Gertrude Astor *"Gold Tooth"* • William V Mong *Parson Brown* • Robert McKim *Roy McDevitt* • Arthur Thalasso *Zandow the Great* ■ *Dir* Frank Capra • *Scr* Arthur Ripley, Frank Capra, Hal Conklin, Robert Eddy, Reed Heustis (titles), from the story by Arthur Ripley

The Strongest Man in the World ★★★ U

Comedy 1975 · US · Colour · 88mins

This was Kurt Russell's third outing as Disney's super-teen Dexter Riley (after *The Computer Wore Tennis Shoes* and *Now You See Him, Now You Don't*). This time his misadventures begin when he accidentally acquires phenomenal strength. Russell is amiable enough, but the real fun comes from the film's seasoned stars (Phil Silvers, Eve Arden, Cesar Romero), who wring smiles out of some pretty tired gags. DP [video]

Kurt Russell *Dexter Riley* • Joe Flynn *Dean Higgins* • Eve Arden *Aunt Harriet Crumply* • Cesar Romero *AJ Arno* • Phil Silvers *Kirwood Krinkle* • Dick Van Patten *Harry* • Harold Gould *Dietz* ■ *Dir* Vincent McEveety • *Scr* Herman Groves, Joseph L McEveety

Strongroom ★

Crime drama 1961 · UK · BW · 80mins

This low-budget thriller has all the mystery and tension of a shelved *Thunderbirds* episode. Two petty crooks discover their consciences after their accomplice dies in a hit-and-run accident, and they decide to break back into the bank they have just robbed, to prevent the manager and his secretary from suffocating in the safe. If the anxious expressions and banal utterances of the villains aren't bad enough, there are glutinous exchanges between the stuffy boss and his assistant. DP

Derren Nesbitt *Griff* • Colin Gordon *Mr Spencer* • Ann Lynn *Rose Taylor* • John Chappell *John Musgrove* • Keith Faulkner *Len* ■ *Dir* Vernon Sewell • *Scr* Max Marquis, Richard Harris, from an idea by Richard Harris

Stroszek ★★★ 15

Satirical drama 1977 · W Ger · Colour · 103mins

Tired of the degradation of Berlin, street singer Bruno S, prostitute Eva Mattes and the diminutive Clemens Scheitz head for freedom in Wisconsin. However, this being a Werner Herzog film, it proves to be anything but a land of opportunity and the troubled trio are forced apart after a bungled robbery. This is a sobering portrait of America as a desolate, unwelcoming wilderness (particularly the town of Railroad Flats) and while some of the culture clash jokes are rather obvious, there's still a visionary surrealism to the story that renders it a road movie like no other. DP. In German and English with subtitles. [video] DVD

Bruno S *Bruno Stroszek* • Eva Mattes *Eva* • Clemens Scheitz *Scheitz* • Clayton Szalpinski *Scheitz's nephew* • Ely Rodriguez *Ely* ■ *Dir/Scr* Werner Herzog

Struck by Lightning ★★★ 15

Comedy drama 1990 · Aus · Colour · 91mins

This Australian drama takes a refreshing and honest look at the subject of Down's syndrome. Director Jerzy Domaradzki refuses to wallow in sentimentality and draws lively performances from his Down's syndrome cast. There's also solid work from Garry McDonald and Brian Vriends, as the senior teachers at a special school who come into conflict. Compassionate but never corny, this is rewarding. DP. Contains swearing. [video]

Gary McDonald *Ollie Rennie* • Brian Vriends *Pat Cannizzaro* • Catherine McClements *Jill McHugh* • Jocelyn Betheras *Jody* • Dick Tomkins *Donald* • Roger Haddad *Peter* ■ *Dir* Jerzy Domaradzki • *Scr* Trevor Farrant

The Struggle ★★

Drama 1931 · US · BW · 77mins

Blaming his recent failures on a lack of independence, DW Griffith, the once-great director, decided to produce his final film quickly and cheaply himself. The title, which accurately reflects the last decade of Griffith's working life, refers to a millworker's struggle to give up the demon drink. Anita Loos and her husband John Emerson meant their screenplay, reminiscent of Emile Zola's *The Drunkard*, to be humorous, but Griffith turned it into a rather maudlin and naive morality tale. RB

Hal Skelly *Jimmie Wilson* • Zita Johann *Florrie Wilson* • Charlotte Wynters *Nina* • Evelyn Baldwin *Nan Wilson* • Jackson Halliday *Johnnie Marshall* ■ *Dir* DW Griffith • *Scr* Anita Loos, John Emerson

Strumpet ★★

Comedy drama 2001 · UK · Colour · 72mins

Shot on digital video by Danny Boyle, this verbose, pseudo-musical insight into the provincial proletariat couldn't be more different from screenwriter Jim Cartwright's previous variation on the same theme, *Little Voice*. There's an offbeat spark between scruffy street poet Christopher Eccleston and punkette Jenna Gee, as they're dragged by Stephen Walters from their squalid northern bedsit to London in search of fame. This is brisk and brash, but superficial. DP

Christopher Eccleston *Strayman* • Jenna Gee *Strumpet* • Stephen Walters *Knockoff* ■ *Dir* Danny Boyle • *Scr* Jim Cartwright

Stryker ★ 18

Science-fiction adventure
1983 · US · Colour · 80mins

What would the exploitation industry have done without *Mad Max*? Here's another quickie clone, directed by the all-too-prolific Filipino schlock merchant Cirio H Santiago. Cowboy-hatted Steve Sandor is the road warrior battling over water with various weirdly dressed tribes in this corny futuristic mess. A daft and poorly constructed apocalyptic fantasy failure. AJ. Contains violence, swearing and nudity. [video]

Steve Sandor *Stryker* • Andria Savio *Delha* • William Ostrander *Bandit* • Michael Lane [Mike Lane] *Kardis* • Julie Gray *Laurenz* ■ *Dir* Cirio H Santiago • *Scr* Howard R Cohen, from a story by Leonard Hermes

Stuart Little ★★★ U

Part-animated fantasy adventure
1999 · US · Colour · 81mins

Based on the much-loved novel by EB White, this half-digital, half-analogue charmer ought to be better. For while the animation is pixel-perfect, the narrative is short on inspiration and awash with sentiment. Both Stuart the orphan mouse and Snowbell, his feline nemesis, are expertly realised and superbly voiced by Michael J Fox and Nathan Lane respectively. But the human cast are awkward interlopers, with Geena Davis and Hugh Laurie overeager and Jonathan Lipnicki lacking his *Jerry Maguire* cuteness. Visually it's vibrant, inventive and inviting, but overall it's less adorable than *Babe*. DP [video] DVD

Michael J Fox *Stuart Little* • Geena Davis *Mrs Little* • Hugh Laurie *Mr Little* • Jonathan Lipnicki *George Little* • Nathan Lane *Snowbell* • Jennifer Tilly *Camille Stout* • Chazz Palminteri *Smokey* • Jeffrey Jones *Uncle Crenshaw* • Steve Zahn *Monty* ■ *Dir* Rob Minkoff • *Scr* M Night Shyamalan, Greg Brooker, from the novel by EB White

Stuart Little 2 ★★★ U

Part-animated fantasy adventure
2002 · US · Colour · 74mins

Despite lacking the wit that distinguished Stuart's first film outing, this amusing sequel will still appeal to those who were delighted by the original. Stuart (expertly voiced by Michael J Fox) falls for a flighty little bird, Margalo (Melanie Griffith), but doesn't realise that she's under the control of a villainous falcon (James Woods). Directed by Rob Minkoff, this blend of live action and animation is technically superb, but its real charm lies in the balance it maintains between enchantment and the everyday. TH [video] DVD

Michael J Fox *Stuart Little* • Geena Davis *Eleanor Little* • Hugh Laurie *Fredrick Little* • Nathan Lane *Snowbell* • Melanie Griffith *Margalo* • Jonathan Lipnicki *George Little* • James Woods *Falcon* • Steve Zahn *Monty* ■ *Dir* Rob Minkoff • *Scr* Bruce Joel Rubin, from a story by Bruce Joel Rubin, Douglas Wick, from characters created by EB White

Stuart Saves His Family ★★★ 12

Comedy 1995 · US · Colour · 93mins

This feature-length adaptation of Al Franken's Stuart Smalley sketches from TV's *Saturday Night Live* didn't deserve the critical and commercial panning it received on its release. The problem lies with the movie's attempt to combine serious drama with the mocking of neurotic TV host Stuart Smalley. Stuart's interactions with his equally neurotic friends on and off his self-help TV show are realistic, yet amusing all the same. The second half of the movie brings a change of pace, with Stuart rejoining his estranged and extremely dysfunctional family, prompting a number of heartbreaking confessions and outbursts. KB [video]

Al Franken *Stuart Smalley* • Laura San Giacomo *Julia* • Vincent D'Onofrio *Donnie* • Shirley Knight *Stuart's mom* • Harris Yulin *Stuart's dad* • Lesley Boone *Jodie* • John Link Graney *Kyle* ■ *Dir* Harold Ramis • *Scr* Al Franken, from his book

Stuck on You ★★★ 12

Comedy 2003 · US · Colour · 113mins

The Farrelly Brothers here shine their bad-taste spotlight on conjoined twins and deliver a slapstick tale that's full of fun. Matt Damon and Greg Kinnear play the brothers, a well-liked duo who quit their sleepy home town in favour of exploitative LA when amateur dramatics performer Kinnear decides he wants to become a serious actor. Despite the questionable subject matter, the film is not nearly as outrageous as it sounds. Where the movie excels is in the obvious sight gags afforded by the twins' condition, Damon and Kinnear's strong chemistry and a great send-up performance by Cher. SF [video] DVD

Matt Damon *Bo* • Greg Kinnear *Walt* • Eva Mendes *April* • Wen Yann Shih *May* • Pat Crawford Brown *Mimmy* • Ray "Rocket" Valliere *Rocket* • Tommy Songin *Tommy* • Cher ■ *Dir* Bobby Farrelly, Peter Farrelly • *Scr* Bobby Farrelly, Peter Farrelly, from a story by Bobby Farrelly, Peter Farrelly, Charles B Wessler, Bennett Yellin

The Stud ★★ 18

Sex drama 1978 · US · Colour · 91mins

The Jackie Collins novel about jet-set sex in swinging London was updated for this celebrated (for all the wrong reasons) example of disco and sexploitation, but it still looked coy and old-fashioned in 1978. Jackie's sister Joan revived her career as the rich bitch whose toy boy (Oliver Tobias) makes fruitless attempts to escape her clutches. The shallow plot and paper-thin characterisations matter little today, compared to the kitsch appeal of the Collins sisters and the dodgy disco milieu. It was one of the most successful of its ilk and spawned a sequel, *The Bitch*. DM [video] DVD

Joan Collins *Fontaine Khaled* • Oliver Tobias *Tony Blake* • Emma Jacobs *Alex Khaled* • Sue Lloyd *Vanessa* • Walter Gotell *Ben Khaled* ■ *Dir* Quentin Masters • *Scr* Jackie Collins, Humphries Dave, Christopher Stagg, from the novel by Jackie Collins

Student Bodies ★ 15

Horror spoof 1981 · US · Colour · 81mins

This has a masked killer cutting a swathe through his sassy classmates using an inventive array of sharp school supplies. The rare amusing moments include one victim being paper-clipped to death and the "producer" putting in an on-screen appearance to apologise for the lack of gore and then swearing to make up for it in ratings terms. AJ [video]

Kristen Riter *Toby* • Matthew Goldsby *Hardy* • Richard Brando *The Breather* • Joe Flood *Mr Dumpkin* • Joe Talarowski *Principal Peters* • Mimi Weddell *Miss Mumsley* • Carl Jacobs *Dr Sigmund* • Peggy Cooper *Ms Van Dyke* ■ *Dir/Scr* Mickey Rose

The Student Prince ★★★ U

Musical 1954 · US · Colour · 106mins

This was to have starred romantic tenor Mario Lanza as the prince who falls for a barmaid, only Lanza grew too obese to wear the period costumes, economically handed over from MGM's *The Prisoner of Zenda* remake. While his voice remains on the rousing soundtrack, he was replaced in the film by stiff Edmund Purdom. The film sounds magnificent and looks sumptuous, and the plot about the duties of royalty has resonances today. TS

Ann Blyth *Kathie* • Edmund Purdom *Prince Karl* • John Ericson *Count Von Asterburg* • Louis Calhern *King of Karlsburg* • Edmund Gwenn *Professor Juttner* • John Williams *Lutz* • SZ Sakall *Joseph Ruder* • Betta St John *Princess Johanna* • Mario Lanza *Prince Karl's singing voice* ■ *Dir* Richard Thorpe • *Scr* William Ludwig, Sonya Levien, from the operetta *The Student Prince* by Dorothy Donnelly, Sigmund Romberg and the play *Alt Heidelberg (Old Heidelberg)* by Wilhelm Meyer-Förster • *Music* Sigmund Romberg

The Student Prince in Old Heidelberg ★★★

Silent romantic comedy
1927 · US · BW · 102mins

This is a silent screen version of a play and a popular operetta about a Ruritanian prince, studying at Heidelberg university, who falls for the local innkeeper's pretty niece. Norma Shearer and "Latin lover" Ramon Novarro star in this early example of MGM in lavish mode. The absence of sound is well compensated for by the great Ernst Lubitsch's direction, with him stylishly extracting every ounce of charm and wistful romance from the piece and its stars. RK

Ramon Novarro *Prince Karl Heinrich* • Norma Shearer *Kathi* • Jean Hersholt *Dr Juttner* • Gustav von Seyffertitz *King Karl VII* • Philippe De Lacy *Heir apparent* ■ *Dir* Ernst Lubitsch • *Scr* Hans Kräly, Marian Ainslee (titles), Ruth Cummings (titles), from the operetta *The Student Prince* by Dorothy Donnelly, Sigmund Romberg and the play *Alt Heidelberg (Old Heidelberg)* by Wilhelm Meyer-Förster

Studs Lonigan ★★★

Period drama 1960 · US · BW · 95mins

Made on an inadequate budget, this ambitious and flawed study of restless teenagers in Chicago in the 1920s is highly imaginative visually (Haskell Wexler is credited as photographic adviser), with some inventive links between scenes courtesy of the editing experience of director Irving Lerner. But newcomer Christopher Knight makes a hash of the central character. Heavily cut before release and taking some liberties with James T Farrell's classic novel, this drama nevertheless views its young characters' foibles with sympathy and insight. AE

Christopher Knight (1) *Studs Lonigan* • Frank Gorshin *Kenny Killarney* • Venetia Stevenson *Lucy Scanlon* • Carolyn Craig *Catherine Banahan* • Jack Nicholson *Weary Reilly* • Robert Casper *Paulie Haggerty* • Dick Foran *Patrick Lonigan* ■ *Dir* Irving Lerner • *Scr* Philip Yordan, from the novel by James T Farrell

A Study in Terror ★★★ 15

Mystery 1965 · UK · Colour · 90mins

No fictional character has been portrayed more often on screen than Sherlock Holmes, but of the scores of actors to tackle the role, few deserved a second outing beneath the famous deerstalker more than John Neville. In this neatly plotted, at times gruesome, picture, he gives a stylish performance as Baker Street's most famous tenant – a portrayal that is all the more impressive for the lack of acting support he receives from Donald Houston as Watson. Director James Hill re-creates the Whitechapel of the Jack the Ripper era with relish, and the solution is a corker. DP [video] DVD

John Neville *Sherlock Holmes* • Donald Houston *Dr John Watson* • John Fraser *Lord Edward Carfax* • Anthony Quayle *Dr Murray* • Robert Morley *Mycroft Holmes* • Barbara Windsor *Annie Chapman* • Adrienne Corri *Angela* • Frank Finlay *Lestrade* • Judi Dench *Sally* ■ *Dir* James Hill • *Scr* Derek Ford, Donald Ford, from a novel by Ellery Queen [Frederic Dannay, Manfred Lee], from the characters created by Sir Arthur Conan Doyle

The Stuff ★★★ 15

Comedy horror 1985 · US · Colour · 82mins

Director Larry Cohen has one of the quirkiest minds in the fantasy genre and this gory junk-food horror satire is one of his best ever ideas. For here's a monster movie where the monster doesn't eat, you you eat it! "The Stuff" is a delicious new fast-food dessert that becomes a marketing sensation. But the bubbly goo turns out to be a living substance, a killer product that turns the nation into crazed, foaming addicts. A blackly comic attack on American consumerism, the military and the advertising world, this is a fun shocker chock full of spoof ingredients. AJ. Contains swearing. [video]

Michael Moriarty *David "Mo" Rutherford* • Andrea Marcovicci *Nicole* • Garrett Morris *"Chocolate Chip" Charlie* • Paul Sorvino *Colonel Spears* • Scott Bloom *Jason* • Danny Aiello *Vickers* • Patrick O'Neal *Fletcher* • James Dixon *Postman* ■ *Dir/Scr* Larry Cohen

The Stunt Man ★★★ 15

Drama 1980 · US · Colour · 125mins

Peter O'Toole soars off the overacting scale as a film director trying to make a war movie and hiring the fugitive Vietnam veteran who killed his chief stuntman. O'Toole later claimed that he based his character on the intimidating, ruthless perfectionist David Lean – and he got an Oscar nomination for it. If you can see through the smokescreen of O'Toole's performance, you'll find a slightly ramshackle satire about movies, illusion and politics. AT [video] DVD

Peter O'Toole *Eli Cross* • Barbara Hershey *Nina Franklin* • Steve Railsback *Cameron* • Sharon Farrell *Denise* • John Garwood *Gabe* • Allen Goorwitz [Allen Garfield] *Sam* • Alex Rocco *Jake* ■ *Dir* Richard Rush • *Scr* Lawrence B Marcus, Richard Rush (adaptation), from the novel by Paul Brodeur

Stunts ★★★

Action thriller 1977 · US · Colour · 83mins

This amiable film within a film cleverly exploits the public's fascination for stunts, while at the same time presenting an intriguing little murder mystery. Robert Forster is the man investigating the mysterious death of his stunt-man brother and discovering that there's a maniac stalking the film set. Mark L Lester provides slick direction in the bruising action scenes. One nice touch has the crew hands all sporting T-shirts saying "To hell with dialogue – let's wreck something". RS

Robert Forster *Glen Wilson* • Fiona Lewis *BJ Parswell* • Joanna Cassidy *Patti Johnson* • Darrell Fetty *Dave* • Bruce Glover *Chuck Johnson* • James Luisi *Blake* • Richard Lynch *Pete* ■ *Dir* Mark L Lester • *Scr* Dennis Johnson, Barney Cohen, from a story by Raymond Lofaro, from an idea by Robert Shaye, Michael Harpster

S

The Stupids ★★ PG

Comedy 1995 · US · Colour · 89mins

This misfiring comedy from director John Landis features Tom Arnold as the head of a family unable to cope with life in the 1990s. Thanks to the energetic efforts of the cast, this is not a total disaster, and there are even occasional moments of pleasing surrealism. But, for the most part, this is a loosely linked collection of crass slapstick gags. Bizarrely, several film-makers have cameo roles. DP

Tom Arnold *Stanley Stupid* • Jessica Lundy *Joan Stupid* • Bug Hall *Buster Stupid* • Alex McKenna *Petunia Stupid* • Scott Kraft *Policeman* • Christopher Lee *Evil Sender* • David Cronenberg *Postal supervisor* • Norman Jewison *TV director* • Costa-Gavras *Gas station guy* ■ *Dir* John Landis • *Scr* Brent Forrester, from the characters created by James Marshall, Harry Allard

Styx ★★ 18

Action thriller
2000 · S Afr/US · Colour · 89mins

The ingenious robbery enacted in the opening sequence holds out the hope that this could be a better than average crime thriller. Sadly, it's pretty much downhill after that as three of the original robbers – the reluctant Peter Weller, his debt-ridden brother Angus MacFayden and Bryan Brown, who everyone thought was dead – are reunited for one final job. Even in second gear, Brown and Weller are effortlessly watchable, but the rest of the cast isn't in the same class, and the action sequences are embarrassingly inept. JF DVD

Peter Weller *Nelson* • Bryan Brown *Art* • Angus MacFadyen *Mike* • Gerard Rudolph *Sloan* • Spencer Sykes *Ricky* ■ *Dir* Alex Wright • *Scr* George Ferris

The Subject Was Roses ★★★★

Drama 1968 · US · Colour · 108mins

Based on Frank D Gilroy's Pulitzer Prize-winning Broadway play about a young Second World War veteran's troubled relationship with his parents, this is famous as the movie comeback of Patricia Neal after a near-fatal stroke, and her Oscar-nominated performance is all the more affecting with this knowledge. Martin Sheen plays the returning serviceman in only his second film role. The action is a trifle enclosed and theatrical, but this actually enhances the emotional punch of the drama. It's a film that requires work, but if you can stay the course, it's hugely rewarding. SH

Patricia Neal *Nettie Cleary* • Jack Albertson *John Cleary* • Martin Sheen *Timmy Cleary* • Don Saxon *Nightclub master of ceremonies* • Elaine Williams *Woman* • Grant Gordon *Man in a restaurant* ■ *Dir* Ulu Grosbard • *Scr* Frank D Gilroy, from his play

S

Submarine Patrol ★★★

First World War action adventure
1938 · US · BW · 95mins

This is directed by the great John Ford, but it sure doesn't look like a John Ford movie. The director had been underwater before, for the submarine drama *Men without Women*, and this film about sub searchers contains several themes from the earlier tale. There is a love interest this time, with captain's daughter Nancy Kelly falling for playboy sailor Richard Greene. Before they set sail, there's a fair amount of those good-natured high jinks that tend to irritate Ford's detractors, but, once they cast off, suspense abounds and the well-handled climax is full of action. TS

Richard Greene *Perry Townsend III* • Nancy Kelly *Susan Leeds* • Preston Foster *Lieutenant John C Drake* • George Bancroft *Captain Leeds* • Slim Summerville *Ellsworth "Spotts" Ficketts* • Joan Valerie *Anne* • John Carradine *McAllison* • Ward Bond *Olaf Swanson* ■ *Dir* John Ford • *Scr* Rian James, Darrell Ware, Jack Yellen, from the novel *The Splinter Fleet* by John Milholland

Submarine Seahawk ★ U

Second World War drama
1959 · US · BW · 83mins

Spencer Gordon Bennet was a stuntman who acted in silent movies and became a prolific director of movie serials. Towards the end of his career, he made cheap B-features, which closely resembled the serial format, with shoddy sets, hackneyed plots and casts of unknowns and has-beens. Unfortunately, unlike Bennet's genuinely batty *Atomic Submarine*, which was filmed on the same sets – sorry, set – this has little to recommend it. TS

John Bentley *Paul Turner* • Brett Halsey *David Shore* • Wayne Heffley *Dean Stoker* • Steve Mitchell *Andy Flowers* • Henry McCann *Ellis* • Frank Gerstle *Captain Boardman* • Paul Maxwell *Bill Hallohan* ■ *Dir* Spencer Gordon Bennet • *Scr* Lou Rusoff, Owen Harris

Submarine X-1 ★★★ U

Second World War drama
1967 · UK · Colour · 89mins

One of the few cinema features made by prolific TV-movie director William Graham, this Second World War action film would never win any prizes for originality. But the story of a mini-sub raid on a German battleship is decently acted by James Caan and a supporting cast of British and American second-stringers. Graham brings an unexpected tension to the underwater finale, in spite of having to accommodate virtually every submarine cliché in the book. DP

James Caan *Lt Commander Bolton* • Rupert Davies *Vice-Admiral Redmayne* • Norman Bowler *Sub-Lt Pennington* • David Sumner *Lt Davies* • William Dysart *Lt Gogan* ■ *Dir* William Graham [William A Graham] • *Scr* Donald S Sanford, Guy Elmes, from a story by John C Champion, Edmund H North

Subspecies ★ 18

Horror 1991 · Rom/US · Colour · 80mins

Good vampire Michael Watson seeks to inherit a Transylvanian bloodstone's powers, but his evil brother Anders Hove wins the battle to put the bite on his former co-ed classmates from America who are visiting Romania. *Nosferatu* is shamelessly ripped-off by director Ted Nicolau in these relentlessly drab proceedings. Three equally feeble sequels (to date) followed. AJ DVD

Michael Watson *Stefan* • Michele McBride *Lillian* • Anders Hove *Radu* • Laura Tate *Michele* • Angus Scrimm *King Vlad* ■ *Dir* Ted Nicolaou • *Scr* Jackson Barr, David Pabian • *Special Effects* David Allen

The Substance of Fire ★★ 15

Drama 1996 · US · Colour · 97mins

Tony Goldwyn plays the gay son who coaxes his siblings – cancer patient Timothy Hutton and adulterous TV celebrity Sarah Jessica Parker – into thwarting their father's ambition to publish a worthy but commercially ruinous history of Nazi atrocities. Director Daniel G Sullivan is enslaved by the rigid characters and over-familiar themes, but Ron Rifkin, reprising his award-winning stage role, turns in a tour-de-force performance as the latter-day Lear, whose guilt at surviving the war has dictated his life. DP. Contains swearing.

Timothy Hutton *Martin Geldhart* • Sarah Jessica Parker *Sarah Geldhart* • Ron Rifkin *Isaac Geldhart* • Tony Goldwyn *Aaron Geldhart* • Lee Grant *Cora Cahn* • Eric Bogosian *Gene Byck* • Roger Rees *Max* • Gil Bellows *Val Chenard* ■ *Dir* Daniel G Sullivan • *Scr* Jon Robin Baitz, from his play

The Substitute ★★ 18

Action drama 1996 · US · Colour · 109mins

When his teacher girlfriend, Diane Venora, is savagely beaten up by one of her disgruntled students, ex-soldier of fortune Tom Berenger takes over her job at Columbus High School and uses mercenary tactics to exact revenge on the drug gang behind the attack. Director Robert Mandel's contemporary *Blackboard Jungle* meets *Rambo* nudges towards mindless camp far too often to be taken as anything but trashy exploitation. AJ. Contains violence, swearing and brief nudity.

Tom Berenger *Shale* • Ernie Hudson *Principal Claude Rolle* • Diane Venora *Jane Hetzko* • Glenn Plummer *Darryl Sherman* • Marc Anthony *Juan* • Raymond Cruz *Joey Six* • William Forsythe *Hollan* • Luis Guzman *Rem* ■ *Dir* Robert Mandel • *Scr* Alan Ormsby, Roy Frumkes, Rocco Simonelli

The Substitute 2: School's Out ★ 18

Action drama 1997 · US · Colour · 86mins

Aside from changing the hero and the motive, this pretty much plays like a rewrite of the original. Tom Berenger is gone in this made-for-video sequel, which asks us to believe that another mercenary (Treat Williams) also fakes his credentials and enters an inner-city school to find those responsible for hurting a loved one. This redundant retread has no redeeming features. Two more sequels followed. KB

Treat Williams *Thomasson* • BD Wong *Drummond* • Angel David *Joey Six* • Michael Michele *Kara* • Larry Gilliard Jr *Dontae* ■ *Dir* Steven Pearl • *Scr* Roy Frumkes, Rocco Simonelli, from their characters

Subterfuge ★★

Spy drama 1968 · US/UK · Colour · 91mins

This tortuous espionage "adventure" looks as though it dropped straight off the 1960s spy-drama conveyor belt. Gene Barry is as debonair (and bland) as ever as a CIA agent in London, who tangles with both his British and Eastern European counterparts, never knowing whom he can trust. Despite endless double-crossing and a kidnapping, this is low on excitement and lacks a strong villain. The presence of Joan Collins adds a bit of glamour. DM

Gene Barry *Donovan* • Joan Collins *Anne Langley* • Richard Todd *Col Victor Redmayne* • Tom Adams *Peter Langley* • Suzanna Leigh *Donetta* • Michael Rennie *Goldsmith* • Marius Goring *Shevik* ■ *Dir* Peter Graham Scott • *Scr* David Whitaker

The Subterraneans ★★

Drama 1960 · US · Colour · 88mins

A former graduate and sportsman abandons himself to looking for the meaning of life in San Francisco and takes up with acolytes of the Beat generation. He has an affair with a free-spirited member of the group and, when she becomes pregnant, they decide to rejoin conventional society. Starring George Peppard and Leslie Caron, this unsatisfying bowdlerisation of Jack Kerouac's novel entirely misses the point of Beat philosophy. It does at least offer an evocative atmosphere, along with a generous helping of jazz. RK

Leslie Caron *Mardou Fox* • George Peppard *Leo Percepied* • Janice Rule *Roxanne* • Roddy McDowall *Yuri Gligoric* • Anne Seymour *Charlotte Percepied* • Jim Hutton *Adam Moorad* • Ruth Storey *Analyst* ■ *Dir* Ranald MacDougall • *Scr* Robert Thom, from the novel by Jack Kerouac • *Cinematographer* Joseph Ruttenberg • *Music* André Previn

Suburban Commando ★★★ PG

Comedy adventure
1991 · US · Colour · 86mins

The appeal of Hulk Hogan may seem bewildering unless you enjoy seeing chaps pretending to throw each other around a wrestling ring, but at least he is well aware of his limitations when it comes to films. This is one of Hogan's more enjoyable efforts, in which he is the alien warrior who lands on Earth and struggles to blend in with Christopher Lloyd's puzzled family. Hogan makes Arnold Schwarzenegger look like an actor of great subtlety, but there are some nice one-liners and director Burt Kennedy ropes in a classy supporting cast. JF. Contains swearing and violence.

Hulk Hogan *Shep Ramsey* • Christopher Lloyd *Charlie Wilcox* • Shelley Duvall *Jenny Wilcox* • Larry Miller *Adrian Beltz* • William Ball *General Suitor* • JoAnn Dearing *Margie Tanen* • Jack Elam *Colonel Dustin "Dusty" McHowell* ■ *Dir* Burt Kennedy • *Scr* Frank Cappello

The Suburbans ★★ 15

Satirical comedy drama
1999 · US · Colour · 83mins

After a very promising start, director Donal Lardner Ward's pop music satire soon crashes and burns. That's a shame because the game cast injects a great deal of life into the obvious script. The Suburbans is the name of a rock group who acrimoniously disbanded after one mega-hit single. Now in boring jobs, they are given a second chance at stardom by hotshot record producer Jennifer Love Hewitt. Ward's flat direction and lack of dramatic smarts result in a morass of showbiz clichés. AJ

Jennifer Love Hewitt *Kate* • Craig Bierko *Mitch* • Amy Brenneman *Grace* • Will Ferrell *Gil* • Donal Lardner Ward *Danny* • Tony Guma *Rory* • Ben Stiller *Jay Rose* ■ *Dir* Donal Lardner Ward • *Scr* Donal Lardner Ward, Tony Guma

subUrbia ★★★ 15

Comedy drama 1996 · US · Colour · 95mins

Richard Linklater, king of the slacker movie, here brings a perfect slacker-type story to the screen. It's based on the stage play by Eric Bogosian and the story is inspired by his early life. Set in a parking lot during one long night, it's an ensemble piece about a group of aimless 20-somethings and their meeting with old friend Pony (Jayce Bartok) who's gone on to become a successful rock star. Dark and absorbing. DF. Contains swearing, sexual references, violence.

Giovanni Ribisi *Jeff* • Steve Zahn *Buff* • Amie Carey *Sooze* • Ajay Naidu *Nazeer* • Jayce Bartok *Pony* • Nicky Katt *Tim* • Parker Posey *Erica* ■ *Dir* Richard Linklater • *Scr* Eric Bogosian, from his play

Subway ★★★★ 15

Thriller 1985 · Fr · Colour · 97mins

Christopher Lambert goes underground in director Luc Besson's chic cult classic. He's a safe-cracker who falls in love with Isabelle Adjani while turning over her husband's strongbox and finds refuge from the authorities among the oddballs inhabiting the shady world of the Paris metro. Besson's darkly humorous script and spiky style, combined with the starkly depressing environment and weird subculture, give this New Wave suspense thriller a delightful edginess and unique look. AJ. In French with English subtitles. DVD

Isabelle Adjani *Helena* • Christopher Lambert *Fred* • Richard Bohringer *Florist* • Michel Galabru *Commisioner Gesberg* • Jean-Hugues Anglade *The Roller Skater* • Jean-Pierre Bacri *Batman* • Jean Reno *Drummer* ■ *Dir* Luc

Besson • *Scr* Luc Besson, Pierre Jolivet, Alain Le Henry, Marc Perrier, Sophie Schmit • *Art Director* Alexandre Trauner

Subway in the Sky ★★★

Crime drama 1958 · UK · BW · 86mins

Though not highly regarded on its release, thanks to its cast, subject matter and director, this crime drama bears re-evaluation today. It's set in postwar Germany and features two particularly watchable stars, both of whom have done better work. Ageing bobby-sox idol Van Johnson is a better actor than is generally acknowledged. Here he's hiding from the authorities in the flat of cabaret singer Hildegarde Neff. Director is Muriel Box was one of the few English women directors to have had a successful screen career, but she struggles to conceal the stage origins of the material. TS

Van Johnson *Major Baxter Grant* • Hildegarde Neff *Lilli Hoffman* • Albert Lieven *Carl von Schecht* • Cec Linder *Captain Carson* • Katherine Kath *Anna Grant* • Vivian Matalon *Stefan* • Carl Jaffe *Adler* ■ *Dir* Muriel Box • *Scr* Jack Andrews, from a play by Ian Main

Subway Stories: Tales from the Underground ★★★ 15

Portmanteau drama
1997 · US · Colour · 80mins

The result of a competition in which habitual users of the New York subway system were encouraged to submit their true-life experiences, this diverse portmanteau drama sees the ten most original entries interpreted by a host of stars and directors. Although the stories vary in quality, there are notable contributions from Denis Leary as a Vietnam veteran and Gregory Hines as a benevolent bystander. The overall result is a worthwhile, dramatically affecting TV movie. JF. Contains swearing.

Bill Irwin • Denis Leary *Guy in wheelchair* • Christine Lahti *Red shoes woman* • Steve Zahn *Tucker* • Jerry Stiller *Old man* • Bonnie Hunt *Fern McDermott* • Lili Taylor *Belinda* • Michael Rapaport *Jake* • Mercedes Ruehl *Leyla* • Sarita Choudhury *Humera* • Nicole Ari Parker *Sharon* • Kenny Garrett *Sax player* • Rosie Perez *Mystery girl* • Gretchen Mol *Wife* • Gregory Hines *Jack* • Anne Heche *Pregnant girl* ■ *Dir* Bob Balaban, Patricia Benoit, Julie Dash, Jonathan Demme, Ted Demme, Abel Ferrara, Alison Maclean, Craig McKay, Lucas Platt, Seth Zvi Rosenfeld • *Scr* Adam Brooks, Julie Dash, Lynn Grossman, John Guare, Marla Hanson, Angela Todd, Seth Zvi Rosenfeld, Albert Innaurato, Danny Hoch, Joe Viola

Success at Any Price ★★

Drama 1934 · US · BW · 74mins

Douglas Fairbanks Jr stars as an amoral and manipulative businessman, drunk on money and power, whose ruthlessness eventually becomes his undoing. Fairbanks is excellent in an otherwise mediocre film that should have been better than it is. The anti-capitalist message comes through loud and clear, reflecting the Marxist leanings of the playwright and co-screenwriter John Howard Lawson, who was jailed as one of the Hollywood Ten during the McCarthy era. RK

Douglas Fairbanks Jr *Joe Martin* • Genevieve Tobin *Agnes Carter* • Frank Morgan *Raymond Merritt* • Colleen Moore *Sarah Griswold* • Edward Everett Horton *Harry Fisher* • Nydia Westman *Dinah* ■ *Dir* J Walter Ruben • *Scr* John Howard Lawson, Howard J Green, from the play *Success Story* by John Howard Lawson

Success Is the Best Revenge ★★★ 15

Drama 1984 · UK/Fr · Colour · 89mins

Following *Moonlighting*, director Jerzy Skolimowski continued his theme of Polish exiles in London. Very much a family affair, in terms of the plot and the filming, it was shot at Skolimowski's Kensington home and co-written by his son, Michael Lyndon, who also appears in a main role. A Polish theatre director (Michael York) becomes totally absorbed with the play he is staging, to the point where his family feel alienated by his behaviour. The film suffers from being slightly unfocused, but cinematically there is much to admire. TH [video]

Michael York *Alex Rodak* • Joanna Szerzerbic *Wife* • Michael Lyndon *Adam* • Michel Piccoli *French official* • Anouk Aimée *Monique de Fontaine* • John Hurt *Dino Montecurva* ■ *Dir* Jerzy Skolimowski • *Scr* Michael Lyndon, Jerzy Skolimowski • *Cinematographer* Mike Fash

A Successful Calamity ★★★

Comedy 1932 · US · BW · 72mins

In his later years, British theatre actor George Arliss unexpectedly became a major Hollywood film star, usually playing an upper-class or royal role. Here he is a millionaire who returns home after a prolonged business trip in Europe to find his self-centered family are taking their money for granted. To teach them a lesson he feigns bankruptcy, sparking several amusing scenes. A deft morality tale which, while somewhat dated, still has much to recommend it. DF

George Arliss *Henry Wilton* • Mary Astor *Emmie Wilton* • Evalyn Knapp *Peggy Wilton* • Grant Mitchell *Connors* • David Torrence *Partington* • William Janney *Eddie Wilton* ■ *Dir* John G Adolfi • *Scr* Austin Parker, Maude Howell, Julien Josephson, from the play by Clare Kummer

Such a Long Journey ★★★ 15

Drama 1998 · Can/UK · Colour · 108mins

This allegorical study of India's socio-political problems in the early 1970s is held together by a performance of muddled idealism and dignified pride from Roshan Seth, as a Parsi bank clerk whose world begins to crumble after he agrees to do a favour for a friend in the secret service. This slowly simmering story is handled with care by director Sturla Gunnarsson, who exploits the contrasting colours and moods of Bombay to heighten the authenticity. DP. Contains swearing and sexual situations. [video]

Roshan Seth *Gustad Noble* • Om Puri *Ghulam* • Soni Razdan *Dilnavaz Noble* • Naseeruddin Shah *Jimmy Bilimoria* • Sam Dastor *Dinshawji* • Vrajesh Hirjee *Sohrab Noble* ■ *Dir* Sturla Gunnarsson • *Scr* Sooni Taraporevala, from the novel by Rohinton Mistry

Such Good Friends ★★★★

Black comedy 1971 · US · Colour · 101mins

This witty Otto Preminger film gives Dyan Cannon her best screen role to date. She's the wife of hospitalised New Yorker Laurence Luckinbill who discovers an awful lot about her hubby while he's in care. Sexy and clever by turns, the screenplay is by a pseudonymous Elaine May. The film contains one of the great telephone scenes, as Dyan prepares to "service" James Coco solicitously while he's engaged in conversation. Very funny and about as black as black comedies get – its ultra-sophisticated subtext bears repeated reviewings. TS

Dyan Cannon *Julie Messenger* • James Coco *Dr Timmy Spector* • Jennifer O'Neill *Miranda Graham* • Ken Howard *Cal Whiting* • Nina Foch *Mrs Wallman* • Laurence Luckinbill *Richard Messenger* • Burgess Meredith *Bernard Kalman* • Louise Lasser *Marcy Berns* ■ *Dir* Otto Preminger • *Scr* Esther Dale [Elaine May], David Shaber, from the novel by Lois Gould

Sudan ★★

Period romantic adventure
1945 · US · Colour · 76mins

This was the sixth and final teaming of the King and Queen of Technicolor. Yet, Jon Hall and Maria Montez weren't the romantic leads in this ancient Egyptian fantasy, as besieged queen Montez ultimately falls into the arms of rebel leader Turhan Bey. However, they share several scenes, as Hall and sidekick Andy Devine rescue Montez from the desert when she goes in search of those responsible for her father's assassination. Only the hissing villainy of George Zucco prevents the onset of tedium. DP

Maria Montez *Naila* • Jon Hall *Merah* • Turhan Bey *Herua* • Andy Devine *Nebka* • George Zucco *Horadef* ■ *Dir* John Rawlins • *Scr* Edmund L Hartmann

Sudden Death ★★★★ 18

Action thriller 1995 · US · Colour · 105mins

This is one of Jean-Claude Van Damme's best thrillers. As a fire officer at an ice hockey stadium, he is given the task of thwarting the deliciously menacing Powers Boothe, who plans to blow up the spectators – among them Van Damme's kids and the US vice president. Who can resist a movie in which the Muscles from Brussels has to fight an assassin dressed as a penguin? Although plausibility isn't its strongest suit, it moves at a rollicking pace and never takes itself too seriously. SR [video] DVD

Jean-Claude Van Damme *Darren McCord* • Powers Boothe *Joshua Foss* • Raymond J Barry *Vice-president* • Whittni Wright *Emily McCord* • Ross Malinger *Tyler McCord* • Dorian Harewood *Hallmark* • Jophery Brown *Wootton* ■ *Dir* Peter Hyams • *Scr* Gene Quintano, from a story by Karen Baldwin

Sudden Fear ★★★

Thriller 1952 · US · BW · 110mins

Joan Crawford has a splendid opportunity to suffer agonies in this contrived but lively thriller in which she accidentally discovers her husband is plotting to kill her. The woman's whirlwind passion for someone as sinister as Jack Palance does strain credulity, although her career as a playwright serves to explain why she devises her own scheme to trap Palance and his grasping girlfriend, Gloria Grahame. Dramatically photographed by Charles Lang Jr and forcefully acted, the film is always a visual treat. AE

Joan Crawford *Myra Hudson* • Jack Palance *Lester Blaine* • Gloria Grahame *Irene Neves* • Bruce Bennett *Steve Kearney* • Touch Connors [Mike Connors] *Junior Kearney* ■ *Dir* David Miller • *Scr* Lenore Coffee, Robert Smith, from the novel by Edna Sherry

Sudden Fury ★★ 15

Crime drama based on a true story
1993 · US · Colour · 88mins

Neil Patrick Harris attempts to ditch his nice kid *Doogie Howser, MD* image in this intense and unsettling TV-movie drama. He is surprisingly convincing as one of three adopted children who fall under suspicion when their parents are murdered. There's a solid supporting cast, but Craig R Baxley's direction is unspectacular. JF [video] DVD

Neil Patrick Harris *Brian Hannigan* • Johnny Galecki *Daniel Hannigan* • Linda Kelsey *Maureen Hannigan* • John M Jackson *Joe Hannigan* • Gregory Harrison *Tom Kelley* • Lisa Banes *Barbara Forester* ■ *Dir* Craig R Baxley • *Scr* Matthew Bombeck, from the book by Leslie Walker

Sudden Impact ★★★ 18

Crime thriller 1983 · US · Colour · 112mins

This fourth outing for Clint Eastwood's "Dirty" Harry Callahan has the big man with the big magnum hunting a woman who's systematically tracking down and terminating the sickos who raped her and her sister. Sondra Locke, Eastwood's partner at the time, plays the ladykiller. More down and dirty than previous *Harrys*, it won't disappoint series fans, even if the formula is starting to wear a little thin. Incidentally, this is the film in which Eastwood delivers his much quoted "Go ahead, make my day" quip. In 1988, *The Dead Pool* concluded Harry's run. DA. Contains violence, swearing, sex scenes and brief nudity. [video] DVD

Clint Eastwood *Inspector Harry Callahan* • Sondra Locke *Jennifer Spencer* • Pat Hingle *Chief Jannings* • Bradford Dillman *Captain Briggs* • Paul Drake *Mick* • Audrie J Neenan *Ray Parkins* ■ *Dir* Clint Eastwood • *Scr* Joseph C Stinson, from a story by Earl E Smith, Charles B Pierce, from characters created by Harry Julian Fink, RM Fink

Suddenly ★★★ PG

Thriller 1954 · US · BW · 72mins

Withdrawn from distribution for years because star Frank Sinatra found out Lee Harvey Oswald had watched it only days before assassinating President Kennedy, this is a must-see rarity, if for that reason alone. Ol' Blue Eyes is the killer who holds a family hostage in the hick town of Suddenly, California, as part of a plot to kill the President, who's passing through on a holiday. Sinatra plays this tension-laden thriller to the hilt, and he's given top-notch support by Sterling Hayden as the sheriff and James Gleason as the retired secret service agent whose house is taken over by the would-be assassin. AJ [video] DVD

Frank Sinatra *John Baron* • Sterling Hayden *Sheriff Tod Shaw* • James Gleason *Pop Benson* • Nancy Gates *Ellen Benson* • Kim Charney *Pidge Benson* • Paul Frees *Benny Conklin* • Christopher Dark *Bart Wheeler* ■ *Dir* Lewis Allen • *Scr* Richard Sale

Suddenly ★★★ 15

Comedy drama
2002 · Arg/Neth · BW · 88mins

Diego Lerman's stylish study of sexual awakening begins in sinister fashion, as country girl Tatiana Saphir is kidnapped outside the Buenos Aires lingerie shop where she works by lesbian ladettes Carla Crespo and Verónica Hassan. But the tone soon shifts as the trio head south to stay with Hassan's ageing aunt, Beatriz Thibaudín, whose tenants find the newcomers intriguing. Evocatively shot in black and white by Luciano Zito and Diego del Piano, this provides a seductive insight into life in a little-seen part of Argentina. DP. In Spanish with English subtitles. DVD

Tatiana Saphir *Marcia* • Carla Crespo *Mao* • Verónica Hassan *Lenin* • Beatriz Thibaudín *Blanca* • María Merlino *Delia* • Marcos Ferrante *Felipe* ■ *Dir* Diego Lerman • *Scr* Diego Lerman, María Meira, from the short film *La Prueba* by Diego Lerman, from the novel *La Prueba* by César Aira

Suddenly It's Spring ★★★

Romantic comedy 1947 · US · BW · 88mins

Paulette Goddard returns from the war as an officer to find that her lawyer husband, Fred MacMurray, has found someone else and wants a divorce, which she refuses. A woman's place is usually at the centre of director Mitchell Leisen's movies, and role-reversal is a constant theme. The gender switch is about the only novelty in this pleasantly familiar, lightweight comedy with two agreeable leads. RB

Paulette Goddard *WAC Captain Mary Morely/ "Captain Lonelyhearts"* • Fred MacMurray *Peter Morely* • MacDonald Carey [Macdonald Carey] *Jack Lindsay* • Arleen Whelan *Gloria Fay* • Lilian Fontaine *Mary's mother* • Frank

S

Faylen *Harold Michaels* ■ *Dir* Mitchell Leisen • *Scr* Claude Binyon, PJ Wolfson, from the story *Sentimental Journey* by PJ Wolfson

Suddenly, Last Summer ★★★★ 15

Drama 1959 · UK · BW · 109mins

This wonderfully overheated drama by Tennessee Williams, who wrote the screenplay with Gore Vidal, is animated by two ultra-powerful performances by Elizabeth Taylor and Katharine Hepburn. Taylor is the niece about to be committed to a mental instituton by southern matriarch Hepburn after witnessing the violent death of a homosexual cousin. Montgomery Clift is the neurosurgeon called in to assess the girl's sanity rating before a possible lobotomy. Director Joseph L Mankiewicz makes it a class act all round. TH DVD

Elizabeth Taylor *Catherine Holly* • Montgomery Clift *Dr John Cukrowicz* • Katharine Hepburn *Mrs Violet Venable* • Albert Dekker *Dr Hockstader* • Mercedes McCambridge *Mrs Holly* • Gary Raymond *George Holly* • Mavis Villiers *Mrs Foxhill* • Patricia Marmont *Nurse Benson* • Joan Young *Sister Felicity* ■ *Dir* Joseph L Mankiewicz • *Scr* Gore Vidal, Tennessee Williams, from the play by Tennessee Williams

Suez ★★★

Biographical drama
1938 · US · Sepia · 104mins

Twentieth Century-Fox was marvellously adept high-budget biopics. But one of the most unlikely candidates for Fox screen canonisation must surely have been 19th-century French engineer Ferdinand de Lesseps, who was the force behind the construction of the Suez Canal. Fox turned his story into a slice of romantic hokum for their contractee, popular matinée idol Tyrone Power, and the whole saga became a rattlingly entertaining melodrama under the expert direction of Allan Dwan and Otto Brower. TS

Tyrone Power *Ferdinand de Lesseps* • Loretta Young *Empress Eugenie* • Annabella *Toni* • J Edward Bromberg *Said* • Joseph Schildkraut *La Tour* • Henry Stephenson *Count de Lesseps* • Sidney Blackmer *du Brey* • Maurice Moscovich *Mohammed Ali* • Sig Rumann [Sig Ruman] *Sergeant Fellerin* ■ *Dir* Allan Dwan, Otto Brower • *Scr* Philip Dunne, Julien Josephson, from a story by Sam Duncan

Suffering Bastards ★★★

Comedy 1989 · US · Colour · 89mins

This is a provocative title for a well-crafted but chat-heavy comedy in which a guy regales a girl he meets in a bar with tall tales about his hard-luck past. Are they fact or fiction? And does it matter if they're just a weapon in his chat-up arsenal? Eric Bogosian and Gina Gershon star, with John C McGinley at the top of a talented support cast. McGinley also wrote the piece, which might have been better suited to the stage than the cinema screen. DA

Eric Bogosian *Mr Leech* • Gina Gershon *Sharnetta* • John C McGinley *Buddy Johnson* • David Warshofsky *Al Johnson* • Michael Wincott *Chazz* ■ *Dir* Bernard McWilliams • *Scr* John C McGinley

Sugar & Spice ★★★ 15

Black comedy 2001 · US · Colour · 77mins

The cast list – Mena Suvari, James Marsden, Rachel Blanchard – is an impressive roster of 20-something American actors, and they all look as if they had fun making this broad, if not always successful, comedy about a group of cheerleaders who turn to bank robbery when one of their number (Marley Shelton) gets pregnant and is disowned by her parents. Mildly amusing teen fare, with a grown-up cast that includes Sean Young and king of the annoying cameos, Jerry Springer. JB DVD

Marla Sokoloff *Lisa* • Marley Shelton *Diane* • Melissa George *Cleo* • Mena Suvari *Kansas* • Rachel Blanchard *Hannah* • Alexandra Holden *Fern* • Sara Marsh *Lucy* • James Marsden *Jack Barlett* • Sean Young *Mrs Hill* ■ *Dir* Francine McDougall • *Scr* Mandy Nelson

Sugar Hill ★★★ 15

Horror 1974 · US · Colour · 87mins

When her boyfriend is brutally murdered for standing up to a mafia syndicate, fashion photographer Marki Bey visits a voodoo queen who summons up evil baron Don Pedro Colley and his zombie hordes to take revenge. Mainly because first-time director Paul Maslansky learnt from producing such gruesome gems as *Death Line*, this blaxploitation horror is one of the best. The gore is leavened with a keen sense of genre ridiculousness that a knowing audience can share and a "right on" attitude is on show with the cobwebbed zombies all being former slaves. AJ DVD

Marki Bey *Diana "Sugar" Hill* • Robert Quarry *Morgan* • Don Pedro Colley *Baron Samedi* • Richard Lawson *Valentine* • Betty Anne Rees *Celeste* • Zara Culley *Mama Maitresse* ■ *Dir* Paul Maslansky • *Scr* Tim Kelley

Sugar Hill ★★★ 18

Crime thriller 1993 · US · Colour · 118mins

Director Leon Ichaso explores the difficulties involved in quitting the ghetto and starting over. As the dealer determined to leave behind the trade that has destroyed his family, Wesley Snipes is convincingly torn between a romance with well-heeled Theresa Randle and his loyalty to his brother (Michael Wright), who's in thrall to gangster Abe Vigoda. However, the wordiness of Barry Michael Cooper's script detracts from the film's authenticity. AT. Contains violence, swearing, drug abuse and nudity.

Wesley Snipes *Roemello Skuggs* • Michael Wright *Raynathan Skuggs* • Theresa Randle *Melissa* • Clarence Williams III *Ar Skuggs* • Abe Vigoda *Gus Molino* • Larry Joshua *Harry Molino* • Ernie Hudson *Lolly* ■ *Dir* Leon Ichaso • *Scr* Barry Michael Cooper

Sugar Town ★★ 18

Spoof music comedy
1999 · US/UK · Colour · 89mins

Allison Anders turns her attention to the downside of the music business in this eager, but over-familiar satire. Despite the presence of Duran Duran's John Taylor and Spandau Ballet's Martin Kemp, the music is neither intriguing nor good pastiche, while caricatures such as Ally Sheedy's neurotic New Age designer, Rosanna Arquette's ageing ingénue and Beverly D'Angelo's sugar mommy feel underwritten and overplayed. DP. Contains swearing and drug abuse.

Rosanna Arquette *Eva* • Ally Sheedy *Liz* • Jade Gordon *Gwen* • Lumi Cavazos *Rosio* • John Taylor (3) *Clive* • Michael Des Barres *Nick* • Beverly D'Angelo *Jane* • Martin Kemp *Jonesy* • John Doe *Carl* ■ *Dir* Allison Anders • *Scr* Kurt Voss, Allison Anders

Sugarbaby ★★★★ 15

Romantic comedy
1985 · W Ger · Colour · 85mins

Percy Adlon's unconventional romantic comedy was rightly hailed as a triumph for its star, Marianne Sägebrecht. She excels as the generously proportioned Munich mortuary assistant whose obsession with a married underground train driver (Eisi Gulp) inspires a scheme to seduce him. However, this is also a skilfully directed film, with the candified neon colour schemes suggesting a fairy-tale atmosphere that is reinforced by the wicked witch-like appearance of Gulp's wife, Manuela Denz. Remade as a TV movie in 1989, starring Ricki Lake. DP. In German with English subtitles.

Marianne Sägebrecht *Marianne* • Eisi Gulp *Eugen Huber* • Toni Berger *Funeral parlor boss* • Manuela Denz *Huber's wife* • Will Spindler *1st train driver* ■ *Dir* Percy Adlon • *Scr* Percy Adlon, Gwendolyn von Ambesser, from a story by Percy Adlon • *Cinematographer* Johanna Heer

Sugarfoot ★★ U

Western 1951 · US · Colour · 79mins

An undistinguished Warner Bros western, this pairs rugged Randolph Scott with suave Raymond Massey as his nemesis. It is better remembered today as one of the first western TV series based on a feature film. This is very average, and really only for fans of Scott, though the super 1950s Technicolor gives it a certain class. TS

Randolph Scott *Sugarfoot* • Adele Jergens *Reva Cairn* • Raymond Massey *Jacob Stint* • SZ Sakall *Don Miguel* • Robert Warwick *JC Crane* • Arthur Hunnicutt *Fly-up-the-Creek Jones* • Hugh Sanders *Asa Goodhue* ■ *Dir* Edwin L Marin • *Scr* Russell Hughes, from a novel by Clarence Budington

The Sugarland Express ★★★ PG

Action adventure based on a true story
1974 · US · Colour · 104mins

This is a marvellously constructed chase movie from a young Steven Spielberg, about a young couple heading for Sugarland, Texas, pursued by the police as they race across the state. As written, the couple are not particularly likeable, but as played by Goldie Hawn and William Atherton they're funny and sympathetic, even when they capture patrolman Michael Sacks and hold him hostage. The set pieces are beautifully handled and Ben Johnson is watchable as the head cop on their tail. Early proof of Spielberg's talent. TS. Contains violence, swearing. DVD

Goldie Hawn *Lou Jean Poplin* • Ben Johnson *Captain Tanner* • Michael Sacks *Officer Maxwell Slide* • William Atherton *Clovis Poplin* • Gregory Walcott *Officer Mashburn* • Steve Kanaly *Jessup* • Louise Latham *Mrs Looby* ■ *Dir* Steven Spielberg • *Scr* Hal Barwood, Matthew Robbins, from a story by Steven Spielberg, Hal Barwood, Matthew Robbins

Suicide Battalion ★★ U

Second World War adventure
1958 · US · BW · 78mins

This static action adventure is directed by Edward L Cahn, who churned out roughly ten similarly uninspired films a year during this period. This was drive-in fodder, made to support a horror or beach party flick and featuring actors who would appeal to the teenage market. Here, Michael Connors and John Ashley break into a captured American base to destroy some secret papers. TS

Michael Connors [Mike Connors] *Major Matt McCormack* • John Ashley *Tommy Novello* • Jewell Lian *Elizabeth Ann Mason* • Russ Bender *Harry Donovan* • Bing Russell *Lt Chet Hall* • Scott Peters *Wally Skilzowski* ■ *Dir* Edward L Cahn • *Scr* Lou Rusoff

Suicide Kings ★★★ 15

Comedy thriller 1997 · US · Colour · 102mins

Despite its tortuous plot, this black comedy provides a rewarding mix of amoral laughs and suspense. Christopher Walken stars as a Mob boss kidnapped by a group of youngsters who need to raise their own ransom to rescue one of their girlfriends. Henry Thomas, Jay Mohr and Sean Patrick Flanery more than hold their own with the experienced Walken, and there's also a nice turn from Denis Leary. A little too clever for its own good, this still holds the attention. JF. Contains swearing and violence.

Christopher Walken *Charles Barrett* • Denis Leary *Lono Vecchio* • Sean Patrick Flanery *Max Minot* • Johnny Galecki *Ira Reder* • Jay Mohr *Brett Campbell* • Jeremy Sisto *TK* ■ *Dir* Peter O'Fallon • *Scr* Josh McKinney, Wayne Rice, Gina Goldman, from the story *The Hostage* by Don Stanford

Suite 16 ★★★ 18

Erotic drama
1994 · UK/Bel/Neth · Colour · 106mins

A wealthy paraplegic offers sanctuary to a fleeing felon in return for his aiding him with his erotic fantasies. Pete Postlethwaite is the dirty old man, Antonie Kamerling his hunky helper, in an intriguing if somewhat pretentious piece that was badly mismarketed as soft-core porn by most of its distributors. Considering the presence of Postlethwaite and the co-scripting of *The Fast Show*'s Charlie Higson, it deserves a little more attention. DA. In English and French with subtitles. Contains swearing, sex scenes and violence. DVD

Pete Postlethwaite *Glover* • Antonie Kamerling *Chris* • Géraldine Pailhas *Helen* • Tom Jansen *Paul* • Bart Slegers *Rudy* ■ *Dir* Dominique Deruddere • *Scr* Charles Higson, Lise Mayer

Sujata ★★★ U

Melodrama 1959 · Ind · BW · 138mins

Ending the 1950s with a tale of family division to match the string of hits that had so illuminated the decade, Bimal Roy once more attacked the social prejudices that divided the subcontinent. Exploring both caste and class, this is the story of orphan Nutan, an untouchable (the name given to a member of the lowest class in India). Nutan is adopted and accepted by a wealthy family until she attracts the attentions of her adoptive sister's suitor. The tale has a Cinderella feel to it, even though Roy is at pains to emphasise the need for a more enlightened approach to the treatment of women. DP. In Hindi with English subtitles.

Nutan *Sujata* • Sunil Dutt *Adhir* • Tarun Bose *Upendranath Choudhury* • Soluchana *Charu* ■ *Dir* Bimal Roy • *Scr* Nabendu Ghosh

Sullivan's Travels ★★★★★ PG

Satirical comedy drama
1941 · US · BW · 86mins

A sparkling satire from writer/director Preston Sturges, this centres on the age-old Hollywood dilemma of art versus entertainment. Giving perhaps his best performance, Joel McCrea plays a hugely successful slapstick comedy director who yearns to make a serious movie. So he hits the road, disguised as a tramp, in a concerted attempt to find out what it means to suffer. With Veronica Lake in a star-making turn as McCrea's travelling companion, the plot veers from inspired insight to corny contrivance at such a rattling pace the sheer vigour of the action carries you along. This classic comedy should leave you in no doubt where Sturges thought a movie's first duty lay, yet it's also one of the few films that manages to strike a winning balance between the horns of its own dilemma. DP DVD

Joel McCrea *John L Sullivan* • Veronica Lake *The girl* • William Demarest *Mr Jones* • Robert Warwick *Mr Lebrand* • Franklin Pangborn *Mr Casalais* • Porter Hall *Mr Hadrian* • Robert Greig *Sullivan's butler* • Eric Blore *Sullivan's valet* • Arthur Hoyt *Preacher* • Preston Sturges *Man in film studio* ■ *Dir/Scr* Preston Sturges

The Sum of All Fears

★★★ 12

Thriller 2002 · US/Ger · Colour · 118mins

This absorbing adaptation of a typically intricate Tom Clancy novel takes a couple of big gambles. The first is replacing Harrison Ford as CIA analyst Jack Ryan with Ben Affleck, who's 30 years younger, and the story has been re-written to accommodate a less savvy, lower-ranking hero. The other is a shocking act of international terrorism that takes place around the halfway mark and transforms the film from a thinking person's thriller into a contemporary version of Sidney Lumet's doom-laden *Fail-Safe*. The appealing Affleck and director Phil Alden Robinson pull it off, thanks to a superior supporting cast, intelligent twists and taut pacing. JC [VIDEO] DVD

Ben Affleck *Jack Ryan* • Morgan Freeman *DCI William Cabot* • James Cromwell *President Fowler* • Liev Schreiber *John Clark* • Bridget Moynahan *Dr Cathy Muller* • Alan Bates *Richard Dressler* • Ciaran Hinds *President Nemerov* • Philip Baker Hall *Defense Secretary Becker* • Ron Rifkin *Secretary of State Owens* • Bruce McGill *National Security Advisor Revell* • Colm Feore *Olson* ■ *Dir* Phil Alden Robinson • *Scr* Paul Attanasio, Daniel Pyne, from the novel by Tom Clancy

The Sum of Us

★★★ 15

Comedy 1995 · Aus · Colour · 95mins

Although set against the familiar landmarks of Sydney, this well-meaning plea for sexual tolerance never quite escapes its theatrical origins. Too many stagey lines and matey nods to camera intrude upon widower Jack Thompson's eager efforts to make plumber son Russell Crowe feel at home with his homosexuality. Yet, such is the geniality of Thompson's one-man assault on Aussie macho culture that it's easy to forgive the contrivances. Warm and witty, but never as poignant or hilarious as it thinks. DP. Contains swearing. [VIDEO]

Jack Thompson *Harry Mitchell* • Russell Crowe *Jeff Mitchell* • John Polson *Greg* • Deborah Kennedy *Joyce Johnson* • Joss Morony *Young Jeff* • Mitch Mathews *Gran* • Julie Herbert *Mary* ■ *Dir* Kevin Dowling, Geoff Burton • *Scr* David Stevens, from his play

Summer and Smoke

★★

Drama 1961 · US · Colour · 118mins

Tennessee Williams's play, spanning several years in the life of the timid, sexually repressed and neurotic daughter of a minister in a small Southern town, won Geraldine Page plaudits and fame in the 1952 Broadway production. She repeated it on screen, with Laurence Harvey co-staring as the wild young doctor for whom Page harbours a passion, and Rita Moreno as the dance-hall girl who's much more his cup of tea. However, the material simply fails to ignite and is worth enduring only for Page's performance. RK

Geraldine Page *Alma Winemiller* • Laurence Harvey *John Buchanan* • Una Merkel *Mrs Winemiller* • Rita Moreno *Rosa Zacharias* • John McIntire *Dr Buchanan* ■ *Dir* Peter Glenville • *Scr* James Poe, Meade Roberts, from the play by Tennessee Williams • *Music* Elmer Bernstein

A Summer at Grandpa's

★★★★ PG

Drama 1984 · Tai · Colour · 97mins

Such is the mastery of Hou Hsiao-Hsien that he takes a situation ripe for sentimentalising and fills it with small moments of truth and insight into how kids relate to grown-ups. As Wang Qiguang and his younger sister witness the rivalry between their grandpa and uncle, it's the innocent immediacy of children's preoccupations that is most keenly observed. This rite-of-passage film offers no easy lessons and cosy resolutions, and is all the more charming and effective for it. DP. In Mandarin with English subtitles.

Wang Qiguang *Tung-Tung* • Gu Jun *Grandpa* • Mei Fang *Grandma* • Lin Xiuling *Pi-Yun* • Edward Yang ■ *Dir* Hou Hsiao-Hsien • *Scr* Zhu Tianwen, Hou Hsiao-Hsien

A Summer by the River

★★★

Period drama 1998 · Fin · Colour · 86mins

Evoking the popular adventures of the mid-1950s, Markku Polonen's period drama could easily have collapsed into mawkish nostalgia, as a widower rediscovers his self-esteem and grows closer to his 10-year-old son in the course of a single summer of tree felling. However, there's a touch of grit about his progress from mockable townie novice to respected logger; even his romance with a free-thinking blonde isn't all soft-centred. Making the most of his striking locations, Polonen achieves a genuine bond between Pertti Koivula and Imo Kontio. DP. A Finnish language film.

Imo Kontio *Topi* • Esko Nikkari *Hannes* • Anu Palevaara *Hilkka* • Peter Franzen *Kottarainen* • Pertti Koivula *Tenbo* ■ *Dir/Scr* Markku Polonen

Summer Catch

★★ 12

Sports comedy drama
2001 · US · Colour · 99mins

Not even a cast of fresh-faced acting hotshots can give flavour to this bland and undistinguished teen sporting romance. The film applies all the usual strength-through-adversity clichés, and wraps them up in a poor-boy-meets-rich-girl subplot. Freddie Prinze Jr is the quick-tempered lawn boy given a shot at major league baseball success, only to jeopardise his chances by falling for Jessica Biel, daughter of one of his rich clients. SF [VIDEO] DVD

Freddie Prinze Jr *Ryan Dunne* • Jessica Biel *Tenley Parrish* • Matthew Lillard *Billy Brubaker* • Brian Dennehy *John Schiffner* • Fred Ward *Sean Dunne* • Jason Gedrick *Mike Dunne* • Brittany Murphy *Dede Mulligan* • Bruce Davison *Rand Parrish* ■ *Dir* Mike Tollin • *Scr* Kevin Falls, John Gatins, from a story by Kevin Falls

Summer Holiday

★★★

Musical comedy
1948 · US · Colour and BW · 92mins

This musical version of Eugene O'Neill's play *Ah, Wilderness* (already filmed in 1935) is a spirited, if low-key, MGM production with little of lasting value, unless you warm to the brash Mickey Rooney in the lead. Co-star Gloria DeHaven is certainly mouthwatering, and the film does look superb and has the potential to be an acquired taste. TS

Mickey Rooney *Richard Miller* • Gloria DeHaven *Muriel McComber* • Walter Huston *Nat Miller* • Frank Morgan *Uncle Sid* • Jackie "Butch" Jenkins *Tommy Miller* • Marilyn Maxwell *Belle* • Agnes Moorehead *Cousin Lily* ■ *Dir* Rouben Mamoulian • *Scr* Frances Goodrich, Albert Hackett, Irving Brecher, Jean Holloway, from the play *Ah, Wilderness* by Eugene O'Neill

Summer Holiday

★★★ U

Musical comedy 1962 · UK · Colour · 103mins

Cliff Richard was still making hit records decades after this high-spirited romp. It's unlikely that his knighthood was awarded solely on the strength of this wholesome road movie (the less than august debut of director Peter Yates), in which four youths cross Europe in a London Transport double-decker bus. But there are plenty of fondly remembered songs, some splendid scenery and a willing supporting cast. DP [VIDEO] DVD

Cliff Richard *Don* • Lauri Peters *Barbara* • Melvyn Hayes *Cyril* • Una Stubbs *Sandy* • Teddy Green *Steve* • Pamela Hart (1) *Angie* • Jeremy Bulloch *Edwin* • Hank Marvin • Bruce Welch • Jet Harris • Tony Meehan ■ *Dir* Peter Yates • *Scr* Peter Myers, Ronald Cass

Summer Interlude

★★★★ PG

Drama 1950 · Swe · BW · 91mins

This is the picture that established Ingmar Bergman's international reputation. It contains the first intimations of the dramatic intensity and structural complexity that would characterise his more mature work. As the world-weary ballerina recalling her teenage affair with timid student Birger Malmsten, Maj-Britt Nilsson gives a performance of such sensitivity that one is at a loss to explain why Bergman dropped her from his stock company after *Secrets of Women* a couple of years later. Gunnar Fischer and Bengt Jarnmark's shimmering images of the sunny Swedish countryside further enhance this subtle, moving film. DP. In Swedish with English subtitles. [VIDEO] DVD

Maj-Britt Nilsson *Marie* • Birger Malmsten *Henrik* • Alf Kjellin *David Nystrom* • Georg Funkquist *Uncle Erland* • Mimi Pollak *Aunt Elizabeth* ■ *Dir* Ingmar Bergman • *Scr* Ingmar Bergman, Herbert Grevenius, from a story by Ingmar Bergman

Summer Lovers

★★ 18

Erotic comedy 1982 · US · Colour · 98mins

After 1980's *The Blue Lagoon*, director Randal Kleiser chose another, equally exotic, location for this slightly more grown-up tale of young romance. The setting this time is a sun-drenched Greek island, where poor old Peter Gallagher finds himself torn between Daryl Hannah and Valérie Quennessen. It looks great, but there's more depth in a teen magazine picture story than in this empty-headed nonsense. JF. Contains sex scenes and nudity. [VIDEO]

Peter Gallagher *Michael Papas* • Daryl Hannah *Cathy Featherest* • Valérie Quennessen *Lina* • Barbara Rush *Jean Featherest* • Carole Cook *Barbara Foster* • Hans Van Tongeren *Jan Tolin* ■ *Dir/Scr* Randal Kleiser

Summer Magic

★★★ U

Period comedy 1963 · US · Colour · 109mins

This cheerful remake of a 1938 film starring Anne Shirley was co-produced by Walt Disney and stars Hayley Mills. Mills is not at her effervescent best, but she's still suitably fresh-faced, as she finds time for a little innocent romance while helping widowed mother Dorothy McGuire raise her brothers. Director James Neilson lovingly re-creates the atmosphere of 1900s Maine, but the highlight is Burl Ives's rendition of *The Ugly Bug Ball*. DP [VIDEO]

Hayley Mills *Nancy Carey* • Burl Ives *Osh Popham* • Dorothy McGuire *Margaret Carey* • Deborah Walley *Julia Carey* • Una Merkel *Maria Popham* • Eddie Hodges *Gilly Carey* • Michael J Pollard *Digby Popham* ■ *Dir* James Neilson • *Scr* Sally Benson, from the novel *Mother Carey's Chickens* by Kate Douglas Wiggin

The Summer of Aviya

★★ PG

Drama 1988 · Is · Colour · 95mins

The Holocaust may have ended, but its effects linger on in this moving, semi-autobiographical tale from Israeli writer Eli Cohen. Set shortly after the end of the Second World War, Cohen's heart-tugging film tells of a disturbed and disturbing summer when the relationship between a young girl and her traumatised mother reaches a crisis point. Up close and personal. DA

Gila Almagor *Gila Almagor's mother* • Kaipo Cohen • Eli Cohen ■ *Dir* Eli Cohen • *Scr* Eli Cohen, Gila Almagor, Haim Buzaglo

The Summer of Ben Tyler

★★★★

Period drama 1996 · US · Colour · 134mins

Two-time Emmy-winner James Woods delivers a stirring performance as an ethical attorney who rocks a small southern town when he chooses to take in the teenage son of his recently deceased black housekeeper. Set during the Second World War, this highly emotional production eloquently illuminates the nature of racial prejudice and intolerance. It's poignant television drama with superb performances by Woods and a stunning supporting cast that includes Elizabeth McGovern and newcomer Charles Mattocks. A must-see, if only for Mattocks's sensitive portrayal and the provocative subject. MC

James Woods *Temple Rayburn* • Elizabeth McGovern *Celia Rayburn* • Charles Mattocks *Ben Tyler* • Len Cariou *Spencer Maitland* • Julia McIlvaine *Nell Rayburn* ■ *Dir* Arthur Allan Seidelman • *Scr* Robert Inman

Summer of '42

★★ 15

Wartime drama 1971 · US · Colour · 99mins

Robert Mulligan's surprisingly popular rite-of-passage picture is so shrouded in nostalgia that it arouses your suspicions. Home-front life in the year after America entered the Second World War simply couldn't have been this good. But there is something undeniably touching about 15-year-old Gary Grimes's relationship with war bride Jennifer O'Neill, which almost atones for the adolescent humour and the cosiness of the period detail. A sequel, *Class of '44*, was even less convincing. DP. Contains swearing, violence and sex scenes. [VIDEO]

Jennifer O'Neill *Dorothy* • Gary Grimes *Hermie* • Jerry Houser *Oscy* • Oliver Conant *Benjie* • Katherine Allentuck *Aggie* • Christopher Norris *Miriam* • Robert Mulligan *Narrator, older Hermie* ■ *Dir* Robert Mulligan • *Scr* Herman Raucher • *Music* Michel Legrand

Summer of My German Soldier

★★★★★

Second World War romantic drama
1978 · US · Colour · 98mins

A contender for the accolade as the best-ever TV movie, this moving work occasionally has sentimental moments but is never false in its emotions. The setting is Georgia, USA, where a group of German PoWs are interned to the dismay of the locals, apart from Jewish teenager Kristy McNichol. She befriends young soldier Bruce Davison, only to have her life turned upside down by bigotry and misunderstanding. Esther Rolle won an Emmy for her performance, but all the acting is memorable in a film of resonance, power and conviction. BB

Kristy McNichol *Patty Bergen* • Bruce Davison *Anton Reiker* • Esther Rolle *Ruth* • Michael Constantine *Harry Bergen* • Barbara Barrie *Mrs Bergen* • James Noble *Pierce* ■ *Dir* Michael Tuchner • *Scr* Jane-Howard Hammerstein, from the novel by Bette Greene

Summer of Sam

★★★ 18

Drama 1999 · US · Colour · 136mins

Full marks to Spike Lee for tackling a movie where all the main characters are white, in this case Italian-American. The year is 1977, and New York is being terrorised by David Berkowitz, the serial killer dubbed "Son of Sam". However, the focus here is on the troubled marriage of John Leguizamo and Mira Sorvino, and the rather seedy life of fledgeling punk rocker and part-time male hooker Adrien Brody. The scenes involving Berkowitz are disturbingly creepy, while Lee successfully evokes the seedy side of the late 1970s and captures the heat of the night brilliantly. JF DVD

John Leguizamo *Vinny* • Adrien Brody *Ritchie* • Mira Sorvino *Dionna* • Jennifer Esposito *Ruby* • Ben Gazarra *Luigi* • Michael Rispoli *Joey T* • Saverio Guerra *Woodstock* • Brian Tarantino *Bobby Del Fiore* • Al Palagonia *Anthony* • Spike Lee *John Jeffries* • John Turturro *Harvey the black dog* ■ *Dir* Spike Lee • *Scr* Victor Colicchio, Michael Imperioli, Spike Lee

Summer of the Colt ★★ U

Drama 1989 · Can/Arg · Colour · 96mins

André Melançon lost his way with this mediocre co-production. Though it stars two of Argentina's most respected stars, Héctor Alterio and China Zorrilla, they spend too much time in the wings during this sentimental story of three Buenos Aires kids who head for their grandfather's pampas farm for the holidays. The scenery and the horses are awesomely beautiful, however. DP. Spanish dialogue dubbed into English.

Héctor Alterio *Federico* • China Zorrilla *Ana* • Alexandra London-Thompson *Laura* • Juan de Benedictis *Daniel* • Santiago Gonzalez *Martin* • Mariano Bertolini *Felipe* • Gabriela Felperin *Manuela* ■ *Dir* André Melançon • *Scr* Geneviève Lefebvre, André Melançon, Rodolfo Otero, from a story by Rodolfo Otero

A Summer Place ★★★

Melodrama 1959 · US · Colour · 129mins

A lush assemblage of sexual matters dominates Delmer Daves's adaptation of Sloan Wilson's steamy bestseller about the middle-classes at play on the beaches of New England. This glossy affair was quite outspoken for its time and cleaned up at the box office. The youthful focus is on pretty-boy Troy Donahue's romance with Sandra Dee, while the adult coupling mainly involves married Dorothy McGuire and her lover Richard Egan. The soapy score and the hit title song, composed by Max Steiner, contribute greatly to this enjoyable trash. RK

Richard Egan *Ken Jorgenson* • Dorothy McGuire *Sylvia Hunter* • Sandra Dee *Molly Jorgenson* • Arthur Kennedy *Bart Hunter* • Troy Donahue *Johnny Hunter* • Constance Ford *Helen Jorgenson* ■ *Dir* Delmer Daves • *Scr* Delmer Daves, from the novel by Sloan Wilson

Summer Rental ★★ PG

Comedy 1985 · US · Colour · 83mins

Harassed and overworked air-traffic controller John Candy badly needs a vacation and takes his family away to holiday on a beach. But almost from the moment they arrive, things start to go wrong and the supposedly restful trip turns into a nightmare every bit as stressful as work. A thin comedy which, despite some good moments, fails to fully exploit its promising premise. JG

John Candy *Jack Chester* • Richard Crenna *Al Pellet* • Karen Austin *Sandy* • Rip Torn *Scully* • Kerri Green *Jennifer* • Joey Lawrence *Bobby* • John Larroquette *Don Moore* ■ *Dir* Carl Reiner • *Scr* Jeremy Stevens, Mark Reisman

Summer School ★★★ 15

Comedy 1987 · US · Colour · 92mins

A surprisingly genial teen comedy with Mark Harmon as the teacher who reluctantly agrees to cancel his vacation and teach English to a class of misfits over the summer holidays. It's a bit of a disappointment when you realise it was directed by Carl Reiner, but Harmon and co-star Kirstie Alley are funny and they are ably abetted by the teenage supporting cast. JB. Contains swearing and violence.

Mark Harmon *Freddy Shoop* • Kirstie Alley *Robin Bishop* • Robin Thomas *Phil Gills* • Dean Cameron *Francis "Chainsaw" Gremp* • Gary Riley *Dave Frazier* • Shawnee Smith *Rhonda Altobello* • Courtney Thorne-Smith *Pam House* ■ *Dir* Carl Reiner • *Scr* Jeff Franklin, from a story by Stuart Birnbaum, David Dashev, Jeff Franklin

Summer Stock ★★★★ U

Musical 1950 · US · Colour · 108mins

Also known in the UK as *If You Feel like Singing*, this was Judy Garland's last MGM feature and, despite rather obvious scene-by-scene weight fluctuations stemming from her attempts to withdraw from drug dependency, she managed to deliver another wonderful musical. Pure joy from beginning to end, this quintessential "let's put on a show in a barn" movie contains moments that are among the career highlights of the film's two stars. Gene Kelly's newspaper dance is a treat and Garland's *Get Happy* finale became an instant classic. There's a fabulous rapport between the two leads and the whole is wrapped up in that sumptuous MGM Technicolor. TS

Judy Garland *Jane Falbury* • Gene Kelly *Joe D Ross* • Eddie Bracken *Orville Wingait* • Gloria DeHaven *Abigail Falbury* • Marjorie Main *Esme* • Phil Silvers *Herb Blake* • Ray Collins *Jasper G Wingait* • Nita Bieber *Sarah Higgins* ■ *Dir* Charles Walters • *Scr* George Wells, Sy Gomberg, from a story by Sy Gomberg

Summer Storm ★★★

Period romantic drama
1944 · US · BW · 106mins

Based on Anton Chekhov's story *The Shooting Party*, this offering from director Douglas Sirk stars Linda Darnell as the wife of the manager of a country estate, whose affair with local judge George Sanders leads to murder and disintegration. Events take place both before and after the Russian Revolution in this interesting – if only partially successful – attempt to venture away from the Hollywood mainstream into character- and conversation-driven European-style drama. RK

George Sanders *Fedor Petroff* • Linda Darnell *Olga* • Anna Lee *Nadina* • Edward Everett Horton *Count Volsky* • Hugo Haas *Urbenin* • Lori Lahner *Clara* • John Philliber *Polycarp* • Sig Ruman *Kuzma* ■ *Dir* Douglas Sirk • *Scr* Rowland Leigh, Douglas Sirk, Robert Thoeren, from the story *The Shooting Party* by Anton Chekhov

A Summer Story ★★★★ 15

Period romantic drama
1987 · UK · Colour · 92mins

A beautifully filmed turn-of-the-century romance, based on John Galsworthy's tale *The Apple Tree*. James Wilby is the lawyer who falls for Devon country girl Imogen Stubbs while recuperating from an accident. When he has to leave, he promises to take her with him, but things don't go as planned. Wilby and Stubbs are ideally cast, and director Piers Haggard manages to keep the sentiment in check, so it never wanders into Mills and Boon territory. JB

Imogen Stubbs *Megan David* • James Wilby *Frank Ashton* • Kenneth Colley *Jim* • Sophie Ward *Stella Halliday* • Susannah York *Mrs Narracombe* • Jerome Flynn *Joe Narracombe* • Lee Billett *Nick Narracombe* • Oliver Perry *Rick Narracombe* ■ *Dir* Piers Haggard • *Scr* Penelope Mortimer, from the short story *The Apple Tree* by John Galsworthy • *Cinematographer* Kenneth MacMillan

Summer Things ★★★★ 15

Comedy 2002 · Fr/UK/It · Colour · 99mins

Shifting effortlessly between seaside farce and social satire, this touches on such serious topics as class, sexuality, envy, grief, rebellion and motherhood while remaining acerbically amusing. Director Michel Blanc revels in a cameo as Carole Bouquet's insanely jealous spouse, but it's Charlotte Rampling's delicious display of careless snobbery that dominates, as she interferes in impoverished friend Karin Viard's domestic travails while remaining blissfully unaware that her own privileged lifestyle is under threat from her reckless daughter and bisexual husband. The resolution is overly neat, but the ensemble's polished expertise ensures events remain irresistibly entertaining. DP. In French with English subtitles. Contains swearing and sex scenes. DVD

Charlotte Rampling *Elizabeth Lannier* • Jacques Dutronc *Bertrand Lannier* • Carole Bouquet *Lulu* • Michel Blanc *Jean-Pierre* • Karin Viard *Véronique* • Denis Podalydès *Jérôme* ■ *Dir* Michel Blanc • *Scr* Michel Blanc, from the novel by Joseph Connolly

Summer Vacation: 1999 ★★★★ 15

Drama 1988 · Jpn · Colour · 89mins

Following the Japanese stage tradition of *Takurazuka* in which girls play the story's teenaged boys, this is a dreamlike study of the adolescent agonies that arise from the pangs of first love. After one of their number seems to commit suicide on account of unrequited passion, three sexually awakening boarding school students are thrown into confusion by the arrival of another youth who bears an eerie resemblance to their friend. Both a gay ghost story and a hymn to lost innocence, Shusuke Kaneko's unique film combines disarmingly androgynous performances with lush visuals to hauntingly romantic effect. DP. In Japanese with English subtitles.

Eri Miyajima *Yu/Kaoru/Last new boy* • Tomoko Otakara *Kazuhiko* • Miyuki Nakano *Naoto* • Rie Mizuhara *Norio* ■ *Dir* Shusuke Kaneko • *Scr* Rio Kishida

Summer Wishes, Winter Dreams ★★

Drama 1973 · US · Colour · 88mins

When Joanne Woodward rails about her disappointing life to Martin Balsam, her patient, desperately dull husband and then concludes "I had no business inflicting all of this on you", audiences are likely to concur. This serious, well-intentioned drama is believably written, capably directed and beautifully acted (with Sylvia Sidney, making a comeback after 17 years, as Woodward's aged mother), but it fails to make these characters anything but tedious. Nevertheless, Woodward and Sidney received Oscar nominations for their performances. AE

Joanne Woodward *Rita Walden* • Martin Balsam *Harry Walden* • Sylvia Sidney *Mrs Pritchett, Rita's mother* • Dori Brenner *Anna* • Win Forman *Fred Goody* • Tresa Hughes *Betty Goody* ■ *Dir* Gilbert Cates • *Scr* Stewart Stern

Summer with Monika ★★★★★ PG

Romantic drama 1952 · Swe · BW · 91mins

The last of Ingmar Bergman's studies of young love and the alienating effects of city life, this is a masterpiece of contrasting images and emotions. The brilliant, sunlit scenes set on the isolated islands perfectly capture the joy and innocence of summer love, as sassy teenager Harriet Andersson and adoring Lars Ekborg splash in the dappled water and kiss beneath the stars. But Gunnar Fischer's stifling shots of Stockholm are perhaps more impressive, as he sets the visual tone for the gradual drift into desertion and disillusionment. DP. In Swedish with English subtitles. DVD

Harriet Andersson *Monika* • Lars Ekborg *Harry* • John Harryson *Lelle* • Georg Skarstedt *Harry's father* • Dagmar Ebbesen *Harry's aunt* ■ *Dir* Ingmar Bergman • *Scr* Per-Anders Fogelstrom, Ingmar Bergman

Summerfield ★★★

Mystery 1977 · Aus · Colour · 95mins

This thriller, which pays homage to many Hollywood movies of the genre, is an entertaining and atmospheric work. A new schoolteacher arrives in a small Australian town, following the disappearance of his predecessor and soon realises there is more to the place and the inhabitants than meets the eye. Ken Hannam successfully handles the suspense so that each new development is a surprise. JB

Nick Tate *Simon Robinson* • John Waters (3) *David Abbott* • Elizabeth Alexander *Jenny Abbott* • Michelle Jarman *Sally Abbott* • Charles Tingwell *Doctor Miller* • Geraldine Turner *Betty Tate* • Max Cullen *Jim Tate* ■ *Dir* Ken Hannam • *Scr* Cliff Green

A Summer's Tale ★★★★ U

Romantic comedy
1996 · Fr · Colour · 109mins

This is a sunny treatise on the agonies of holiday romance from director Eric Rohmer. Melvil Poupaud is torn between his love of music and his infatuations with girlfriend Aurélia Nolin, waitress Amanda Langlet and her friend Gwenaëlle Simon. His prevarications are as natural as they are frustrating, as comic as they are suspenseful. Displaying again Rohmer's gift for capturing the vernacular and behaviour of youth, this is a delight. DP. In French with English subtitles. DVD

Melvil Poupaud *Gaspard* • Amanda Langlet *Margot* • Aurélia Nolin *Léna* • Gwenaëlle Simon *Solène* ■ *Dir/Scr* Eric Rohmer

Summertime ★★★★ U

Romantic drama
1955 · US/UK · Colour · 100mins

This was the movie that whetted director David Lean's appetite for location filming with international stars. It's a touching take on Arthur Laurent's play about a lonely spinster enjoying a summer fling in Venice. In a piece of unlikely casting, Katharine Hepburn plays the sheltered secretary, with Rossano Brazzi as the married object of her affection. Hepburn turns out to be an inspired choice, her reserve melting under the liberating effect of the city and the charming Brazzi. Venice looks fabulous, thanks to cameraman Jack Hildyard, and the whole thing is perfect matinée fare. Originally released in the UK as *Summer Madness*. TS

Katharine Hepburn *Jane Hudson* • Rossano Brazzi *Renato Di Rossi* • Isa Miranda *Signora Fiorina* • Darren McGavin *Eddie Jaeger* • Mari Aldon *Phyl Jaeger* • Jane Rose *Mrs McIlhenny* • MacDonald Parke *Mr McIlhenny* • Gaitano Audiero *Mauro* ■ *Dir* David Lean • *Scr* David Lean, He Bates, from the play *The Time of the Cuckoo* by Arthur Laurents

Sumuru ★★★

Action spy drama 1967 · UK · Colour · 87mins

Producer and writer Harry Alan Towers, who made several films based on the exploits of Sax Rohmer's Fu Manchu, also made two featuring Rohmer's lesser-known female "evil genius" Su-Muru (Shirley Eaton). In this, the first, George Nader and Frankie Avalon, both looking ill at ease, discover that Eaton and her beautiful female warriors want nothing less than world domination. The stuff of a 1930s serial, spoofed 1960s-style and combining feeble humour with an international cast of shapely starlets, this may be too rich a mix for some – though others have spotted a cult in the making. The 1969 sequel, released under several titles including *Rio 70* and *Future Women*, is hard to find. DM

Frankie Avalon *Tommy Carter* • George Nader *Nick West* • Shirley Eaton *Su-Muru* • Wilfrid Hyde White *Colonel Baisbrook* • Klaus Kinski *President Boong* ■ *Dir* Lindsay Shonteff • *Scr* Kevin Kavanagh, from a story by Peter Welbeck [Harry Alan Towers], from the books by Sax Rohmer

The Sun Also Rises ★★★★

Drama 1957 · US · Colour · 130mins

An expansive version of Ernest Hemingway's great "lost generation" novel, this has a slightly too old Tyrone Power in the leading role of Jake Barnes, the impotent wartime flier adrift in Paris. Ava Gardner is Lady Brett Ashley, a dissolute sensualist roaming Europe, and Errol Flynn is simply magnificent as an alcoholic. Also particularly fine are Mel Ferrer and Eddie Albert as Power's cronies, and take note of the actor playing Gardner's bullfighter lover – Robert Evans, future producer of *Chinatown*. TS

Tyrone Power *Jake Barnes* • Ava Gardner *Lady Brett Ashley* • Mel Ferrer *Robert Cohn* • Errol Flynn *Mike Campbell* • Eddie Albert *Bill Gorton* • Gregory Ratoff *Count Mippipopolous* • Juliette Greco *Georgette* • Robert Evans *Pedro Romero* ■ *Dir* Henry King • *Scr* Peter Viertel, from the novel by Ernest Hemingway

The Sun Shines Bright ★★★ PG

Period drama 1953 · US · BW · 100mins

Charles Winninger inherits the role of Judge Priest from Will Rogers, who played him in Ford's 1934 movie *Judge Priest*. This time the benevolent judge is standing for re-election in Fairfield, Kentucky, in 1905, but he has some serious competition. There are comic and romantic strands to the story as well as serious subplots involving rape and racism – a mix that modern audiences may find naive or offensive, or both. Whatever the views of the critics or the public, Ford cited this as one of his personal favourites, and his feeling for the story and the period is easy to see. AT

Charles Winninger *Judge Priest* • Arleen Whelan *Lucy Lee Lake* • John Russell *Corwin* • Stepin Fetchit *Jeff Poindexter* • Russell Simpson *Dr Lewt Lake* • Ludwig Stossel *Herman Felsburg* • Francis Ford *Feeney* ■ *Dir* John Ford • *Scr* Laurence Stallings, from stories by Irvin S Cobb

The Sun, the Moon and the Stars ★★

Romantic comedy 1995 · Ire · Colour · 92mins

The heavenly bodies of the title are three tarot cards belonging to an occult-obsessed teenager who attempts to reunite her separated parents. After her mother walks out of her job, they go on a family vacation, where they meet eccentric Angie Dickinson and park keeper Jason Donovan. Not an Irish *Parent Trap*, but whimsical enough to be watchable. JG

Angie Dickinson *Abbie* • Jason Donovan *Pat* • Gina Moxley *Monica* • Elaine Cassidy *Shelley* ■ *Dir/Scr* Geraldine Creed

Sun Valley Serenade ★★★ U

Musical 1941 · US · BW · 82mins

Norwegian ice-skating champion Sonja Henie returned to the screen after a two-year absence for this smash hit. However the movie's success was doubtless helped by the presence of Glenn Miller in one of only two films he made, and the Mack Gordon/Harry Warren score. The characteristic candy-floss plot – Miller's star pianist (John Payne) is assigned to take care of refugee Henie – is only an excuse on which to hang the numbers, including a breathtaking finale that has Henie skating on black ice before she skis off into the sunset with Payne. RK

Sonja Henie *Karen Benson* • John Payne *Ted Scott* • Glenn Miller *Phil Carey* • Milton Berle *Nifty Allen* • Lynn Bari *Vivian Dawn* • Joan Davis *Miss Carstairs* • Dorothy Dandridge *Vocalist* ■ *Dir* H Bruce Humberstone • *Scr* Robert Ellis, Helen Logan, from a story by Art Arthur, Robert Harari • *Choreographer* Hermes Pan • *Cinematographer* Edward Cronjager • *Music Director* Emil Newman

Sunburn ★★

Detective comedy 1979 · US · Colour · 99mins

Those more inclined to swallow the idea of detective Charles Grodin and Farrah Fawcett (as the model he hires to pose as his wife) falling in love while investigating an insurance case in Mexico may enjoy this otherwise forgettable mystery romp. Fawcett is actually one of the better aspects of the movie, but she and the rest of the cast are unfortunately saddled with a story that has little mystery. KB

Farrah Fawcett-Majors [Farrah Fawcett] *Ellie Morgan* • Charles Grodin *Jake Dekker* • Art Carney *Al Marcus* • Joan Collins *Nera* • William Daniels *Crawford* • John Hillerman *Webb* • Eleanor Parker *Mrs Thoren* • Keenan Wynn *Mark Elmes* ■ *Dir* Richard C Sarafian • *Scr* John Daly, Stephen Oliver, James Booth, from the novel *The Bind* by Stanley Ellin

Sunchaser ★★ 15

Road movie 1996 · US · Colour · 117mins

Michael Cimino's over-egged pudding ambitiously seeks to mix elements of road and male-bonding movies, and to toss in some native American mysticism for good measure. Jon Seda is impressive as a teen hoodlum dying of cancer. After breaking out of prison, he takes a miscast Woody Harrelson hostage and forces him to drive to a mystical lake that, according to legend, has healing properties. Though well intentioned, it's somewhat pretentious. DA. Contains swearing and violence.

Woody Harrelson *Dr Michael Reynolds* • Jon Seda *Brandon "Blue" Monroe* • Anne Bancroft *Dr Renata Baumbauer* • Alexandra Tydings *Victoria Reynolds* • Matt Mulhern *Dr Chip Byrnes* • Talisa Soto *Navajo woman* ■ *Dir* Michael Cimino • *Scr* Charles Leavitt

Sunday ★★★

Drama 1997 · US · Colour · 93mins

Winner of the Grand Jury Prize at the Sundance Film Festival, this is a fascinating look at being lonely, and the lengths we'll go to to kid ourselves we're not. Spanning a single day, this quality character study stars David Suchet as a downsized executive, now homeless, who pretends to be a famous art-film director to woo washed-up actress Lisa Harrow. The pretence becomes an intrinsic part of their day's mating rituals. The film is a little arty and won't appeal to everyone, but there's much here to admire, not least the performances of the two leads. DA

David Suchet *Oliver/Matthew* • Lisa Harrow *Madeleine Vesey* • Jared Harris *Ray* • Larry Pine *Ben Vesey* • Joe Grifasi *Scottie Elster* • Arnold Barkus *Andy* • Bahman Soltani *Abram* ■ *Dir* Jonathan Nossiter • *Scr* James Lasdun, Jonathan Nossiter

Sunday, Bloody Sunday ★★★★ 15

Drama 1971 · UK · Colour · 105mins

Divorced Glenda Jackson shares bisexual Murray Head with gay Peter Finch in John Schlesinger's ground-breaking exploration of heterosexual and homosexual relationships. This 1970s moral tale caused shock waves thanks to Finch and Head sharing one of the first all-male on-screen kisses. Finch steals the acting honours with a sympathetic performance among the tangled web of verbalised angst about the real meaning of communication, sexual and otherwise, as symbolised by telephone wires linking the busy eternal triangle's lives together. AJ

Glenda Jackson *Alex Greville* • Peter Finch *Dr Daniel Hirsh* • Murray Head *Bob Elkin* • Peggy Ashcroft *Mrs Greville* • Maurice Denham *Mr Greville* • Vivian Pickles *Alva Hodson* • Frank Windsor *Bill Hodson* • Thomas Baptiste *Professor Johns* • Tony Britton *Mr Harding* ■ *Dir* John Schlesinger • *Scr* Penelope Gilliatt

Sunday Dinner for a Soldier ★★★ U

Romantic drama 1944 · US · BW · 86mins

Some find this whimsy charming, others glutinous, but in its day it chimed perfectly with popular taste, as lovely Anne Baxter yearned for just what it says – a GI to bring home for lunch on Sunday. Handsome John Hodiak turns up just in time. Expertly made schmaltz, this is one of those movies about impoverished people who don't actually suffer from being poor, but just get all philosophical with a foxy twinkle in their eye. TS

Anne Baxter *Tessa Osborne* • John Hodiak *Eric Moore* • Charles Winninger *Grandfather Osborne* • Anne Revere *Agatha* • Connie Marshall *Mary Osborne* • Chill Wills *Mr York* ■ *Dir* Lloyd Bacon • *Scr* Wanda Tuchock, Melvin Levy, from the story by Martha Cheavens

Sunday in August ★★★ U

Comedy drama 1949 · It · BW · 83mins

In his feature debut, Luciano Emmer captures the carefree spirit of this witty neorealist satire on middle-class morality, which numbers among its co-scenarists Cesare Zavattini and Sergio Amidei, who had collaborated on Vittorio De Sica's *Shoeshine* (1946). Prominent among the ensemble cast decamping for the day to the Roman resort of Ostia are two of Federico Fellini's protégés, Franco Interlenghi and Marcello Mastroianni. DP. In Italian with English subtitles.

Anna Baldini *Marcella* • Vera Carmi *Adriana* • Emilio Cigoli *Mantovani* • Andrea Compagnoni *Cesare Meloni* • Franco Interlenghi *Enrico* • Marcello Mastroianni *Ercole* ■ *Dir* Luciano Emmer • *Scr* Franco Brusati, Luciano Emmer, Giulio Macchi, Cesare Zavattini, from a story by Sergio Amidei

Sunday in New York ★★★

Comedy 1963 · US · Colour · 104mins

One of those early 1960s' capers in which provincial innocents, in this case a young Jane Fonda, head for the big city and fall madly in love with life in the fast lane. This is a delightfully skittish romp in the Big Apple, showing off Fonda's youthful charisma to best advantage and ably assisted by Peter Nero's memorable score. A film that harks back to those curiously winsome days when sex came tiptoeing out of the celluloid closet and everyone thought they were being daring. SH

Cliff Robertson *Adam Tyler* • Jane Fonda *Eileen Tyler* • Rod Taylor *Mike Mitchell* • Robert Culp *Russ Wilson* • Jo Morrow *Mona Harris* • Jim Backus *Flight dispatcher* • Peter Nero ■ *Dir* Peter Tewksbury • *Scr* Norman Krasna, from his play

Sunday in the Country ★★ 18

Crime thriller 1975 · Can · Colour · 87mins

Ernest Borgnine plays a farmer in the backwoods of America who takes the law into his own hands when three dangerous fugitives attempt to take him and his granddaughter hostage. John Trent's decidedly cruel and violent crime drama is distinguished by Borgnine's performance as the calm countryman who coolly exacts a terrible revenge against Michael J Pollard and his cronies. The whole premise is decidedly questionable. AJ

Ernest Borgnine *Adam Smith* • Michael J Pollard *Leroy* • Hollis McLaren *Lucy* • Louis Zorich *Dinelli* • Cec Linder *Ackerman* • Vladimir Valenta *Luke* • Al Waxman *Sergeant* ■ *Dir* John Trent • *Scr* Robert Maxwell, John Trent, from a story by David Main

Sunday in the Country ★★★★ U

Period drama 1984 · Fr · Colour · 90mins

This lyrical conversation piece deservedly won Bertrand Tavernier the best director award at Cannes. Beautifully evoking a balmy Sunday afternoon in the late summer of 1912, the film eavesdrops on the subtly charged encounters between ageing painter Louis Ducreux, his beloved but unreliable daughter Sabine Azéma and his married son Michel Aumont. All the performances are impeccable and Tavernier alights on such topics as Impressionism, family allegiances and the purpose of life with a light but restless touch. Bruno de Keyzer's gorgeous photography makes this serene drama quite irresistible. DP. In French with English subtitles.

Louis Ducreux *Monsieur Ladmiral* • Sabine Azéma *Irène* • Michel Aumont *"Gonzague" Edouard* • Geneviève Mnich *Marie-Thérèse* • Monique Chaumette *Mercédès* • Claude Winter *Madame Ladmiral* ■ *Dir* Bertrand Tavernier • *Scr* Bertrand Tavernier, Colo Tavernier, from the novella *Monsieur Ladmiral Va Bientôt Mourir* by Pierre Bost

Sunday Too Far Away ★★★★

Drama 1974 · Aus · Colour · 94mins

A real brawler set in the Australian outback. Life as a sheep-shearer can be rather monotonous, but hard man Jack Thompson has enough star power to keep us watching this tale of rivalry and hardship. He's chief shearer and troubleshooter, calling the men out on strike when the bosses try to introduce non-union labour. There's real integrity in Ken Hannam's direction, as he takes us right into the heart of a world very like that of the Wild West where rivalries are fuelled by booze and life is a real struggle. Men at work have rarely been so convincingly portrayed. TH. Contains some swearing.

Jack Thompson *Foley* • Phyllis Ophel *Ivy* • Peter Cummins *"Black" Arthur* • Reg Lye *Old Garth* • John Charman *Barman* • Gregory Apps *Michael Simpson* • Max Cullen *Tim King* ■ *Dir* Ken Hannam • *Scr* John Dingwall

Sundays and Cybèle ★★★

Drama 1962 · Fr · BW · 110mins

Debutant director Serge Bourguignon won the Oscar for best foreign language film with this self-promoting, arty affair. Hardy Kruger is the amnesiac German pilot who forges a friendship with pre-teen orphan Patricia Gozzi. There is an undeniable tenderness in their relationship, even though there's an inevitability about the consequences of their innocent Christmas sojourn in the woods. Cinematographer Henri Decaë's compositions, though elegant, strain too hard for lyrical effect. DP. A French language film.

Hardy Kruger *Pierre* • Nicole Courcel *Madeleine* • Patricia Gozzi *Françoise/Cybèle* • Daniel Ivernel *Carlos* • Michel de Re *Bernard* • André Oumansky *Nurse* ■ *Dir* Serge Bourguignon • *Scr* Antoine Tudal, Serge Bourguignon, Bernard Eschassériaux, from the novel *Les Dimanches de Ville D'Avray* by Bernard Eschassériaux

Sunday's Children ★★★★

Drama 1992 · Swe · Colour · 118mins

It's apt that this study of fathers and sons (the second part of the autobiographical trilogy scripted by Ingmar Bergman that began with *Best Intentions*) should be directed by Bergman's own son, Daniel. Recalling the summer of 1926, when the young Ingmar tried to become closer to his strict father (a chaplain to the Swedish royal family), this is such an assured film that it could easily have been directed by the master himself. The sunlit country picnics and cycle rides are joyous evocations of past times, but they also make the darker moments of doubt and the confrontations between Thommy Berggren and Henrik Linnros all the more powerful. *Private Confessions* (1996) completes the trilogy. DP. In Swedish with English subtitles.

Henrik Linnros *Pu* • Thommy Berggren *Pu's father* • Börje Ahlstedt *Uncle Carl* ■ *Dir* Daniel Bergman • *Scr* Ingmar Bergman, from his autobiography *The Magic Lantern*

Sundown ★★★

Wartime adventure 1941 · US · BW · 90mins

Gene Tierney's sultry looks are used to good effect in this Second World War yarn set in Africa, where a band of Nazis are supplying weapons to tribesmen in the hope that they will rise up against the British. Commissioner Bruce Cabot befriends the locals, while English major George Sanders wrestles with his distrust of Arabs. Tierney is the lynchpin, working undercover for the Allies but arousing Sanders's suspicions as she romances Cabot. The film is well photographed and rattles along efficiently enough. RT

Gene Tierney *Zia* • Bruce Cabot *Captain Bill Crawford* • George Sanders *Major Coombes* • Cedric Hardwicke *Bishop Coombes* • Harry Carey *Dewey* • Joseph Calleia *Pallini* • Reginald Gardiner *Lt Turner* • Dorothy Dandridge *Kipsang's bride* ■ *Dir* Henry Hathaway • *Scr* Barre Lyndon, Charles G Booth, from a story by Barre Lyndon • *Cinematographer* Charles Lang

The Sundowners ★★★ U

Western 1950 · US · Colour · 83mins

This agreeable western, filmed entirely on location in Texas, rests on the roguish charm of Robert Preston and the superb Technicolor photography by Winton Hoch. The film introduces John Barrymore Jr, who is unexceptional as the teenage kid idolising Preston as his bad outlaw brother. Leading western novelist Alan LeMay (*The Searchers*) produced and scripted this adaptation of one of his early pieces, as well as appearing uncredited as Preston's companion. AE DVD

Robert Preston *Kid Wichita* • Robert Sterling *Tom Cloud* • Chill Wills *Sam Beard* • John Litel *John Gaul* • Cathy Downs *Kathleen Boyce* • Jack Elam *Earl Boyce* • Don Haggerty *Elmer Gaul* • John Barrymore Jr [John Drew Barrymore] *Jeff Cloud* ■ *Dir* George Templeton • *Scr* Alan LeMay, from his story *Thunder in the Dust*

S

The Sundowners ★★★★ U

Adventure 1960 · US · Colour · 124mins

This marvellously authentic family epic from Warner Bros is set in Australia and contains superb performances (and moderately believable Australian accents) from Robert Mitchum and Deborah Kerr. Backing up the two leads in this sheep-shearing saga is a strong cast and excellent technical credits, notably the striking Technicolor photography from Jack Hildyard and an atmospheric Dimitri Tiomkin score. The film earned five Oscar nominations, a tribute to its director Fred Zinnemann, whose exquisite handling of the personal drama proves once again what a fine film-maker he was. TS

Deborah Kerr *Ida Carmody* • Robert Mitchum *Paddy Carmody* • Peter Ustinov *Venneker* • Michael Anderson Jr *Sean* • Glynis Johns *Mrs Firth* • Dina Merrill *Jean Halstead* • Ewen Solon *Bob Halstead* • Chips Rafferty *Quinlan* ■ *Dir* Fred Zinnemann • *Scr* Isobel Lennart, from the novel by Jon Cleary

Sunflower ★★ 15

Drama 1969 · It/Fr · Colour · 102mins

Co-screenwriter Cesare Zavattini and director Vittorio De Sica were two of the key figures in the neorealist movement that dominated Italian cinema in the postwar era. But there is little evidence of their celebrated humanism in this preposterous nonsense in which Sophia Loren goes to the USSR in search of missing husband Marcello Mastroianni only to find him married to Lyudmila Savelyeva and blissfully ignorant of her existence. If the leads are embarrassed, they don't let it show. DP. In Italian with English subtitles.

Sophia Loren *Giovanna* • Marcello Mastroianni *Antonio* • Lyudmila Savelyeva *Mascia* ■ *Dir* Vittorio De Sica • *Scr* Tonino Guerra, Cesare Zavattini, Gheorgi Mdivani

Sunny ★★

Musical comedy 1930 · US · BW · 78mins

A very early, creaky and mind-bendingly idiotic romantic comedy musical, this relies on low vaudeville gags for much of its dated humour. However, those who can survive the first 15 minutes will find that this tale of a circus bareback rider, who stows away on a New York-bound ship in order to follow her heart, does have a certain charm. More importantly, it's a rare opportunity to see the multi-talented all-singing, all-dancing Broadway legend Marilyn Miller in action. This was remade in 1941 with Anna Neagle. RK

Marilyn Miller *Sunny* • Lawrence Gray *Tom Warren* • Joe Donahue *Jim Deming* • Mackenzie Ward *Wendell-Wendell* ■ *Dir* William Seiter [William A Seiter] • *Scr* Humphrey Pearson, Henry McCarty, from the musical by Otto Harbach, Oscar Hammerstein II, Jerome Kern

Sunny ★★ PG

Romance 1941 · US · BW · 136mins

Producer/director Herbert Wilcox remade this hit Broadway musical for his wife, the oh-so-charming, restrained English actress Anna Neagle. Wilcox reworked the original book, cutting out most of the (admittedly silly) plot, and leaving a thin tale about a bareback-riding circus performer (Neagle) who marries New Orleans aristocrat John Carroll, despite his stiff-necked family's disapproval. RK

Anna Neagle *Sunny O'Sullivan* • Ray Bolger *Bunny Billings* • John Carroll *Larry Warren* • Edward Everett Horton *Henry Bates* • Grace Hartman *Juliet Runnymede* • Paul Hartman *Egghead* • Frieda Inescort *Elizabeth Warren* ■ *Dir* Herbert Wilcox • *Scr* Sid Herzig, from a play by Otto Harbach, Oscar Hammerstein II • *Music* Jerome Kern

Sunny Side Up ★★★

Musical comedy drama
1929 · US · BW and Colour · 80mins

A charming but creaky film from the early days of the talkies, this is a lightweight offering from 20th Century-Fox. It stars popular screen sweethearts Janet Gaynor and the lovable Charlie Farrell, and is almost a singing version of their standard tenement-girl-falls-for-Farrell plot. But who cares when the songs are such fabulous classics as *I'm a Dreamer (Aren't We All?)* and *If I Had a Talking Picture of You*. TS

Janet Gaynor *Molly Carr* • Charles Farrell *Jack Cromwell* • El Brendel *Eric Swenson* • Marjorie White *Bee Nichols* • Frank Richardson *Eddie Rafferty* • Sharon Lynn [Sharon Lynne] *Jane Worth* • Mary Forbes *Mrs Cromwell* • Joe Brown [Joe E Brown] *Joe Vitto* ■ *Dir* David Butler • *Scr* David Butler, Buddy De Sylva [BG De Sylva], Ray Henderson, Lew Brown, from a story by Buddy De Sylva [BG De Sylva], Ray Henderson, Lew Brown

Sunnyside ★★★

Silent satirical drama
1919 · US · BW · 41mins

In this pastoral fairy tale, Charlie Chaplin is a farm hand in love with Edna Purviance (again!). Chaplin said the production of *Sunnyside* was "like pulling teeth", and he must have appreciated the great ballet dancer Vaslav Nijinsky telling him that the dance with four nymphs was "pure delight". TH

Charlie Chaplin [Charles Chaplin] *Handyman* • Edna Purviance *Woman* • Tom Wilson *Boss* • Henry Bergman *Father* ■ *Dir* Charles Chaplin • *Scr* Charles Chaplin, from his story

Sunrise ★★★★★ U

Silent romantic drama
1927 · US · BW · 90mins

Janet Gaynor won the first ever best actress Oscar for her work in this exquisite silent feature, subtitled *A Song of Two Humans*. Emigré director FW Murnau has reduced a tale of threatened marriage to its bare essentials, as George O'Brien's farmer falls for visiting city girl Margaret Livingston. It is hard to convey briefly the wonder of imagery on display here, as Murnau both wittily and stylistically uses every aspect of visual storytelling, even making imaginative use of the back projection itself. Perspective design and stunning photography (by Charles Rosher and Karl Struss) help immeasurably. The tale is timeless, the setting nameless and the mood resolutely central European, though it was filmed in America. O'Brien brings a distinctively American presence to the romantically tortured hero, and Gaynor is perfection as his wife. TS DVD

George O'Brien *The Man* • Janet Gaynor *The Wife* • Bodil Rosing *Maid* • Margaret Livingston *Woman from the city* • J Farrell MacDonald *Photographer* ■ *Dir* FW Murnau • *Scr* Carl Mayer, from the novel *Die Reise nach Tilsit* by Hermann Sudermann • *Production Designer* Rochus Gliese

Sunrise at Campobello ★★★ U

Biographical drama
1960 · US · Colour · 143mins

This is a moving account of Franklin D Roosevelt's life during his battle with polio. Although the film at times betrays its theatrical origins, it remains enthralling, and it also leaves posterity a record of Ralph Bellamy's extraordinary stage performance, re-created here. Curiously, the Oscar nomination went to Greer Garson as Roosevelt's wife, Eleanor. The supporting cast is first class. RK

Ralph Bellamy *Franklin Delano Roosevelt* • Greer Garson *Eleanor Roosevelt* • Hume Cronyn *Louis Howe* • Jean Hagen *Missy Le Hand* • Ann Shoemaker *Sara Roosevelt* • Alan Bunce *Al Smith* • Tim Considine *James Roosevelt* ■ *Dir* Vincent J Donehue • *Scr* Dore Schary, from his play

Sunset ★★ 15

Comedy thriller 1988 · US · Colour · 102mins

As with many of Blake Edwards's films, the concept is great, but the execution disastrous. Set in silent-era Hollywood, this would-be comedy thriller finds the film industry's first western star Tom Mix (Bruce Willis) joining forces with the ageing Wyatt Earp (James Garner) to solve a murder involving corrupt studio chiefs. Edwards's clumsily fails to blend the comic and action elements, while Willis irritates in the lead role. Garner, though, easily rises above the substandard material. JF. Contains violence, swearing and nudity. DVD

Bruce Willis *Tom Mix* • James Garner *Wyatt Earp* • Malcolm McDowell *Alfie Alperin* • Mariel Hemingway *Cheryl King* • Kathleen Quinlan *Nancy Shoemaker* • Jennifer Edwards *Victoria Alperin* • Patricia Hodge *Christina Alperin* • Richard Bradford *Captain Blackworth* • M Emmet Walsh *Chief Dibner* • Joe Dallesandro *Dutch Kieffer* ■ *Dir* Blake Edwards • *Scr* Blake Edwards, from a story by Rod Amateau

Sunset Blvd ★★★★★ PG

Satirical drama 1950 · US · BW · 105mins

Even the title of this dark, deeply satisfying work of cinematic genius can be read as a metaphor for the Hollywood machine. Master director Billy Wilder's witty, brilliantly constructed Tinseltown satire is both canny and knowing about the film industry and those souls unfortunate, and yet willing, enough to be caught in its wheels. The stark story of former movie queen Norma Desmond, haunted by memories of her past greatness ("I am big. It's the pictures that got small"), is greatly aided by superb casting, notably of silent-movie siren Gloria Swanson, who brings a desperate, vampiric glamour to her role. William Holden, a last minute replacement for Montgomery Clift, is also excellent as the doomed writer who narrates the film in flashback from the scene of his death. Savage, dark and wholly original. TS DVD

William Holden (2) *Joe C Gillis* • Gloria Swanson *Norma Desmond* • Erich von Stroheim *Max Von Mayerling* • Nancy Olson *Betty Schaefer* • Fred Clark *Sheldrake* • Lloyd Gough *Morino* • Jack Webb *Artie Green* ■ *Dir* Billy Wilder • *Scr* Billy Wilder, Charles Brackett, DM Marshman Jr, from the story *A Can of Beans* by Charles Brackett, Billy Wilder • *Costume Designer* Edith Head • *Cinematographer* John F Seitz • *Music* Franz Waxman

Sunset Grill ★★ 18

Thriller 1992 · US · Colour · 99mins

A weary LA private detective gets more than he bargained for when he attempts to avenge the murder of his wife. For he uncovers a sinister conspiracy revolving around Mexicans being killed and sold for their body parts. Directed by former horror veteran Kevin Connor, this decidedly odd thriller is an equal mix of the bizarre and the mundane. *RoboCop*'s Peter Weller does bring some variety to his clichéd role as the drunken private eye, while Stacy Keach is suitably menacing as a sadistic tycoon. AJ. Contains swearing, violence, sex scenes and nudity.

Peter Weller *Ryder Hart* • Lori Singer *Loren Duquesne* • Stacy Keach *Harrison Shelgrove* • Michael Anderson Jr *Carruthers* • Alexandra Paul *Anita* • John Rhys-Davies *Stockton* • Pete Koch [Peter Koch] *Christian* ■ *Dir* Kevin Connor • *Scr* Marcus Wright, Faruque Ahmed

Sunset Heights ★★ 15

Science-fiction thriller
1996 · UK/Ire · Colour · 91mins

Set in the near future, this flawed but intriguing thriller presents a nightmare vision of life in Northern Ireland. Two gangs police their communities using fear and violence. Caught between them is Toby Stephens, whose child is believed to be latest victim of a serial killer known as The Preacher. The plotting is confused but there are strong performances from the cast, and director Colm Villa displays some stylish visual touches. JF. Contains violence. DVD

Toby Stephens *Luke* • Jim Norton *Sam Magee* • Patrick O'Kane *Friday Knight* • Joe Rea *Victor* • James Cosmo *MacDonald* ■ *Dir/Scr* Colm Villa

Sunset Park ★★ 15

Sports comedy drama
1996 · US · Colour · 94mins

A rare lead outing for Rhea Perlman, this is an uneasy amalgam of comedy and ghetto drama. The former *Cheers* star plays a basketball novice who reluctantly becomes the unlikely trainer to a struggling team from a deprived, inner city high school. Of course, it's not long before she is won over. It's a familiar enough tale, enthusiastically played, but the laughs are dampened by waves of sentimentality. JF

Rhea Perlman *Phyllis Saroka* • Fredro Starr *Shorty* • Carol Kane *Mona* • Terrence Dashon Howard [Terrence Howard] *Spaceman* • Camille Saviola *Barbara* • De'Aundre Bonds *Busy-Bee* • James Harris *Butter* ■ *Dir* Steve Gomer • *Scr* Seth Zvi Rosenfeld, Kathleen McGhee-Anderson

Sunset Strip ★ 15

Comedy drama 2000 · US · Colour · 86mins

This film about friends in 1970s LA desperately wants to be *American Graffiti* meets *Reality Bites*, but doesn't capture the nostalgia of one nor the humour, writing or skilled performances of either. Anna Friel is unconvincing as a fashion designer sleeping her way around LA's trendy people when her friend (played by Simon Baker) is the one everyone but her realises is the man for her. JB

Simon Baker *Michael Scott* • Anna Friel *Tammy Franklin* • Nick Stahl *"Zach" Zachary* • Rory Cochrane *Felix* • Adam Goldberg *Marty Shapiro* • Jared Leto *Glen Walker* ■ *Dir* Adam Collis • *Scr* Russell DeGrazier, Randall Jahnson, from a story by Randall Jahnson

Sunshine ★★★★ 15

Epic romantic drama
1999 · Hun/Ger/Can/Austria · Col · 172m

This sprawling epic is a glorious summation of the themes that have preoccupied István Szabó over the last 20 years. Ralph Fiennes essays a trio of flawed ancestors whose personal tragedies are enacted against the great events of the 20th century. Passing through Hungary's imperial, fascist and communist phases, the action chronicles the history of a Jewish family whose bid to belong is undermined by successive generations' susceptibility to passion, vanity and lust for power. Occasionally protracted, but always masterly. DP DVD

Ralph Fiennes *Ignatz Sonnenschein/Adam Sors/Ivan Sors* • Rosemary Harris *Valerie Sors* • Rachel Weisz *Greta Sors* • Jennifer Ehle *Valerie Sonnenschein* • Deborah Kara Unger *Major Carole Kovacs* • Molly Parker *Hannah Wippler* • James Frain *Gustave Sonnenschein* • David De Keyser *Emmanuel Sonnenschein* • William Hurt *Andor Knorr* ■ *Dir* István Szabó • *Scr* Istvan Szabo, Israel Horovitz, from a story by Istvan Szabo

The Sunshine Boys ★★★★ PG

Comedy 1975 · US · Colour · 106mins

George Burns, who died just a cigar length past his 100th birthday, made his big-screen comeback in this Neil Simon-scripted comedy about two ageing, rival vaudevillians. Burns stepped in when Jack Benny died and found himself co-starring with the best scene-stealer in the business, Walter Matthau. As with many of Simon's confections, it's a New York Jewish odd couple sort of story, overtly sentimental but played to perfection. Richard Benjamin also makes an impact as Matthau's nephew and agent, who tries to reconcile the two old boys. AT. Contains swearing.

Walter Matthau *Willy Clark* • George Burns *Al Lewis* • Richard Benjamin *Ben Clark* • Lee Meredith *Nurse in sketch* • Carol Arthur *Doris* • F Murray Abraham *Mechanic* • Howard Hesseman *Commercial director* ■ *Dir* Herbert Ross • *Scr* Neil Simon, from his play

The Sunshine Boys ★★★ U

Comedy 1997 · US · Colour · 85mins

The words Woody Allen and TV movie were once mutually exclusive, but here he's back as a jobbing actor in this update of Neil Simon's classic comedy. Allen takes on the role that won George Burns an Oscar, while Peter Falk steps into Walter Matthau's shoes as the struggling entertainer who calls on his now-detested partner to revive his fortunes. Simon's acerbic wit is as amusing as ever and he neatly turns nephew Richard Benjamin into niece Sarah Jessica Parker. It's a good try, but the original is unsurpassable. DP DVD

Woody Allen *Al Lewis* • Peter Falk *Willie Clark* • Sarah Jessica Parker *Nancy* • Michael McKean *Peter* • Liev Schreiber • Edie Falco ■ *Dir* John Erman • *Scr* Neil Simon, from his play

Sunshine State ★★★★★ 15

Drama 2002 · US · Colour · 134mins

This multilayered ensemble piece from writer/director/editor John Sayles takes as its notional theme the development of swampland for profit. In Florida's Delrona Beach, Edie Falco's motel owner sees the chance of escape from small-town drudgery with Timothy Hutton's visiting architect, who is paradoxically there to effectively run her out of town. Meanwhile, Angela Bassett returns to face her past, corruption rages from within the town council and a historical pageant is threatened by apathy. Too talky for a wide audience, it's intelligent, cool, questioning and humane – a small film that leaves a big impression. AC. Contains swearing. DVD

Edie Falco *Marly Temple* • Jane Alexander *Delia Temple* • Ralph Waite *Furman Temple* • Angela Bassett *Desiree Perry* • James McDaniel *Reggie Perry* • Mary Steenburgen *Francine Pickney* • Timothy Hutton *Jack Meadows* ■ *Dir/Scr* John Sayles

Sunstruck ★ U

Comedy drama
1972 · Aus/UK · Colour · 91mins

This star vehicle for singer and comedian Harry Secombe was made Down Under back in the days when the Welsh warbler used to summer there. Daft and dated, even at the time, the slight tale has Secombe playing a dimwit Welsh schoolteacher who emigrates to the Aussie outback. The simple-minded humour derives from his patent unsuitability for the new way of life. Thankfully, the sort of film they don't make any more. DA

Harry Secombe *Stanley Evans* • Maggie Fitzgibbon *Shirley Marshall* • John Meillon *Mick Cassidy* • Dawn Lake *Sal Cassidy* • Peter Whittle *Pete Marshall* • Dennis Jordan *Steve Cassidy* • Donald Houston ■ *Dir* James Gilbert • *Scr* James Grafton, Stan Mars

Supari ★★ 15

Crime drama 2003 · Ind · Colour · 142mins

Uday Chopra headlines this would-be *noir*ish tale of four bored friends whose cricket betting deposits them in the depths of the underworld. But, while he ably conveys the fecklessness of youth, Chopra lacks the range to convince as the drama intensifies. Consequently, it's Nandita Das's performance as a ruthless female gangster that most catches the eye, and Purab Kohli also impresses as he succumbs to a breakdown. But director Padam Kumar doesn't always avoid the crime genre clichés and indulges in sentimentality. DP. In Hindi with English subtitles. Contains violence and swearing. DVD

Nandita Das *Mamta Sekhri* • Uday Chopra *Ayran* • Rahul Dev *Papad* • Purab Kohli *Chicken* • Akash Saigal *Mushi* • Nauheed Cyrusi *Dilnawaz* • Ifran Khan *Baba* ■ *Dir* Padam Kumar • *Scr* Padam Kumar, Mushtaq Sheikh, Anuradha Tiwari

The Super ★★★ 15

Comedy 1991 · US · Colour · 85mins

Joe Pesci's Oscar for *GoodFellas* earned him the opportunity to become an unlikely leading man, but he enjoys mixed success here in his first such role. On paper it sounds great: Pesci plays a sleazy New York landlord who is taken to court and sentenced to living in one of his own rat-filled apartments. The star is fine, and there's good support from Rubén Blades and Vincent Gardenia, but director Rod Daniel indulges in too much soppy moralising, and the film veers uncomfortably between comedy and drama. JF. Contains swearing.

Joe Pesci *Louie Kritski* • Vincent Gardenia *Big Lou Kritski* • Madolyn Smith Osborne [Madolyn Smith] *Naomi Bensinger* • Rubén Blades *Marlon* • Stacey Travis *Heather* ■ *Dir* Rod Daniel • *Scr* Sam Simon

The Super Cops ★★★ 15

Detective comedy drama
1973 · US · Colour · 90mins

A fine telling of the true story of two cops, nicknamed "Batman and Robin", who used unconventional crime-busting techniques to stop drug dealing in the Bedford-Stuyvesant area of New York's Brooklyn. The film is fast, furious, and often very funny, and it benefits from using the actual locations where real-life events occurred. Ron Leibman and David Selby play the super cops, with the bona fide detectives popping up in bit parts. DA

Ron Leibman *David Greenberg* • David Selby *Robert Hantz* • Sheila Frazier *Sara* • Pat Hingle *Lieutenant Novick* • Dan Frazer *Krasna* • Joseph Sirola *Lieutenant O'Shaughnessy* • Arny Freeman *Judge Kellner* ■ *Dir* Gordon Parks • *Scr* Lorenzo Semple Jr, from the non-fiction book by LH Whittemore

Super 8 Stories ★★★★

Music documentary
2001 · Ger/It · BW and Colour · 90mins

Fronted by doctor Nele Karajlic and boasting film-maker Emir Kusturica on guitar, the No Smoking Orchestra has been entertaining and outraging Yugoslavia and its derivatives since 1980. Fusing rock, punk, jazz and traditional Romany folk, the band's musical style is as refreshing as its lyrics are irreverent. Yet, as this self-consciously grungy tour documentary reveals, the NSO – which comes across as Bosnia's raucous answer to the Leningrad Cowboys – is as committed to political comment as it is to crowd pleasing. Moreover, each of its ten members is a fully paid-up eccentric, whose opinions and backstage antics make for provocative and amusing viewing. DP. In German and Serbo-Croat with English subtitles.

Dir Emir Kusturica

Super Mario Bros ★★ PG

Fantasy adventure
1993 · US · Colour · 99mins

How do you turn a popular interactive video game into an equally engaging and exciting movie? Not like this, you don't! This awkward fantasy contains few trace elements from the "Super Mario Land" games themselves, thereby instantly betraying the very audience it was made for. Bob Hoskins and John Leguizamo try their best as the two plumbers adrift in a parallel dinosaur dimension, but it isn't super, amusing or thrilling by any stretch of the imagination. AJ. Contains swearing and violence.

Bob Hoskins *Mario Mario* • Dennis Hopper *King Koopa* • John Leguizamo *Luigi Mario* • Samantha Mathis *Daisy* • Fisher Stevens *Iggy* • Richard Edson *Spike* • Fiona Shaw *Lena* ■ *Dir* Rocky Morton, Annabel Jankel • *Scr* Parker Bennett, Terry Runté, Ed Solomon, from the characters created by Shigeru Miyamoto, Takashi Tezuka

Super Size Me ★★★★ 12

Documentary 2004 · US · Colour · 99mins

Describing himself as the "producer/director/guinea pig" of this, his first feature documentary, healthy 30-something Morgan Spurlock wondered what would happen if he ate nothing but McDonald's food for a month. With this headline-grabbing experiment at its core, *Super Size Me* looks more broadly at the hold fast food has over Americans in an age of ever-increasing obesity. An initially chipper host without a political axe to grind, Spurlock soon finds his strict new diet hard to stomach. After a few weeks, Spurlock's doctor tells him his "liver is like pâté" and the gross-out comedy takes a darker turn. Like Michael Moore, Spurlock presents his statistical material light-heartedly to make a serious point, but the success of his film depends on the likeability of his ubiquitous presence. AC DVD

Dir/Scr Morgan Spurlock

Super-Sleuth ★★★

Comedy mystery 1937 · US · BW · 65mins

Jack Oakie fans will enjoy his skilful clowning as an egotistical movie star in this brightly written comedy. Portraying a specialist in screen sleuthing, Oakie sets out to show up the LA police, represented by Edgar Kennedy, by catching a mysterious killer of celebrities. After receiving a death threat himself, along with a complaint over the quality of his last film, he seeks advice from Eduardo Ciannelli's amateur criminologist. Ann Sothern sparkles as the studio publicity head and there are entertaining glimpses of film-making on the RKO lot and on location. AE

Jack Oakie *Willard "Bill" Martin* • Ann Sothern *Mary Strand* • Eduardo Ciannelli *Professor Horman* • Alan Bruce *Larry Frank* • Edgar Kennedy *Lt Garrison* • Joan Woodbury *Doris Dunne* • Bradley Page *Ralph Waring* • Paul Guilfoyle (1) *Gibbons* ■ *Dir* Ben Stoloff • *Scr* Gertrude Purcell, Ernest Pagano, from a play by Harry Segall

S

Super Troopers ★ 15

Comedy 2001 · US · Colour · 95mins

This juvenile cop comedy resembles a cruder version of the *Police Academy* films. Written and performed by the five-man comedy group Broken Lizard – who are unknown on these shores and are likely to remain that way – this puerile affair concerns a bunch of idiotic Vermont State Troopers who enjoy nothing more than tormenting drivers with bizarre, unfunny pranks. There is a vague plot about the rivalry between the Troopers and the local police, but it's really just a series of sketches in which the lawmen behave like members of a particularly dim fraternity. JC DVD

Brian Cox *Capt John O'Hagan* • Daniel Von Bargen *Police Chief Grady* • Marisa Coughlan *Officer Ursula Hanson* • Lynda Carter *Governor Jessman* • Erik Stolhanske *Robert "Rabbit" Roto* • Steve Lemme *MacIntyre "Mac" Womack* • Paul Soter *Jeff Foster* • Jay Chandrasekhar *Arcot "Thorny" Ramathorn* ■ *Dir* Jay Chandrasekhar • *Scr* Jay Chandrasekhar, Kevin Heffernan, Steve Lemme, Paul Soter, Erik Stolhanske [Broken Lizard]

Superdad ★ U

Comedy 1974 · US · Colour · 91mins

Bob Crane is overprotective of his daughter Kathleen Cody. Cody then turns into an even bigger rebel, getting engaged to hippy artist and political agitator Joby Baker. When her former boyfriend Kurt Russell returns to the scene, her father is more than happy to embrace him as one of the family. Twee and sickly, with few redeeming factors. DF

Bob Crane *Charlie McCready* • Barbara Rush *Sue McCready* • Kurt Russell *Bart* • Joe Flynn *Cyrus Hershberger* • Kathleen Cody *Wendy McCready* • Bruno Kirby *Stanley* • Joby Baker *Klutch* • Dick Van Patten *Ira Hershaw* ■ *Dir* Vincent McEveety • *Scr* Joseph L McEveety, from a story by Harlan Ware

Superfly ★★★ 18

Cult blaxploitation
1972 · US · Colour · 88mins

By 1972 the conventions of the blaxploitation genre were well established and this notorious film exploited them to the hilt. The antihero, played by supercool martial artist Ron O'Neal, is a cocaine pusher who plans one last deal before retirement. The black men are little more than robots, the white men are crooked and the women (black and white) are sex objects. Today, its success is hard to understand; its cult status, however, makes it required viewing for fans of the crazy 70s. Two sequels followed. DM. Contains sex scenes, swearing, violence.

Ron O'Neal *Youngblood Priest* • Carl Lee *Eddie* • Sheila Frazier *Georgia* • Julius Harris *Scatter* • Charles McGregor *Fat Freddie* • Nate Adams *Dealer* • Polly Niles *Cynthia* ■ *Dir* Gordon Parks Jr • *Scr* Phillip Fenty

Supergirl ★★ PG

Fantasy adventure
1984 · UK · Colour · 111mins

A disastrous attempt to extend the *Superman* series by bringing the Man of Steel's comic book cousin (played here by Helen Slater) to Earth, to retrieve a vital power source that has fallen into the hands of the evil Faye Dunaway. The story is pretty daft, the special effects merely ordinary and Slater is a rather weak superheroine. Dunaway gets into the spirit of things with a wildly over-the-top performance, but Peter O'Toole and Peter Cook simply look embarrassed. JF

Helen Slater *Kara, Supergirl/Linda Lee* • Faye Dunaway *Selena* • Peter O'Toole *Zaltar* • Mia Farrow *Alura* • Brenda Vaccaro *Bianca* • Peter Cook *Nigel* • Simon Ward *Zor-El* ■ *Dir* Jeannot Szwarc • *Scr* David Odell

S

The Supergrass ★★ 15

Comedy 1985 · UK · Colour · 93mins

In a so-so comedy, a spin-off from *The Comic Strip* TV series, Ade Edmondson poses as a drug dealer to impress a girlfriend. However he finds that the pretence also fools the police, who pressure him into grassing on his nonexistent drugs ring. There's strong support from Dawn French, Jennifer Saunders and Peter Richardson, who also co-wrote and directed, but this is small-screen stuff that doesn't stand up to big-screen scrutiny. DA

Adrian Edmondson *Dennis* • Jennifer Saunders *Lesley* • Peter Richardson *Harvey Duncan* • Dawn French *Andrea* • Keith Allen *Wong* • Nigel Planer *Gunter* • Robbie Coltrane *Troy* ■ *Dir* Peter Richardson • *Scr* Pete Richens, Peter Richardson

Superman ★★★★★ PG

Fantasy adventure
1978 · US · Colour · 137mins

This big-budget, epic scale version of the Man of Steel legend is irresistible, fabulous entertainment. The elegiac opening – from the destruction of Krypton to Clark Kent's arrival at the *Daily Planet* in Metropolis – turns more traditional comic book when Clark falls for Lois Lane, before a bright and breezy confrontation with comedic criminal Lex Luthor. The deliberate clash of styles generates much excitement and, yes, you'll believe a man can fly. Christopher Reeve is perfectly cast and as a spectacle it's a masterful confection. AJ DVD

Christopher Reeve *Clark Kent/Superman* • Gene Hackman *Lex Luthor* • Margot Kidder *Lois Lane* • Marlon Brando *Jor-El* • Ned Beatty *Otis* • Jackie Cooper *Perry White* • Glenn Ford *Pa Kent* • Trevor Howard *First Elder* • Terence Stamp *General Zod* • Susannah York *Lara* • Larry Hagman *Major* ■ *Dir* Richard Donner • *Scr* Mario Puzo, David Newman, Leslie Newman, Robert Benton, from the story by Mario Puzo, from the comic strip by Jerry Siegel, Joe Shuster • *Cinematographer* Geoffrey Unsworth • *Music* John Williams • *Production Designer* John Barry (2)

Superman II ★★★★ PG

Fantasy adventure
1980 · UK/US · Colour · 127mins

Purists may not agree, but this is probably the best segment of the *Superman* saga in terms of plot, free from the occasionally po-faced seriousness of the first and the rampant silliness of the remaining two. Director Richard Lester delivers a knowing, knockabout cartoon with Superman (Christopher Reeve) finding out that he is no longer the toughest guy around when three baddies are exiled from his home planet and arrive on Earth. The effects are equal to the first film and there's a strong supporting cast, including an irascible Gene Hackman and the excellent Terence Stamp. JF DVD

Christopher Reeve *Clark Kent/Superman* • Gene Hackman *Lex Luthor* • Margot Kidder *Lois Lane* • Terence Stamp *General Zod* • Ned Beatty *Otis* • Sarah Douglas *Ursa* • Jack O'Halloran *Non* • Valerie Perrine *Eve Teschmacher* • Susannah York *Lara* • Jackie Cooper *Perry White* • EG Marshall *President* ■ *Dir* Richard Lester • *Scr* Mario Puzo, David Newman, Leslie Newman, from the story by Mario Puzo, from the characters created by Jerry Siegel, Joe Shuster

Superman III ★★ PG

Fantasy adventure
1983 · US · Colour · 119mins

Director Richard Lester injected a much needed irreverence into *Superman II*, but he lost his way badly with this third instalment of "the man from Krypton" saga. There are a few nice touches, such as when Christopher Reeve turns nasty, but this proved to be the beginning of the end for the series. Still, for die-hard fans of the superhero, this is adequate entertainment. JF

Christopher Reeve *Superman/Clark Kent* • Richard Pryor *Gus Gorman* • Robert Vaughn *Ross Webster* • Annette O'Toole *Lana Lang* • Annie Ross *Vera Webster* • Pamela Stephenson *Lorelei Ambrosia* • Margot Kidder *Lois Lane* • Jackie Cooper *Perry White* ■ *Dir* Richard Lester • *Scr* David Newman, Leslie Newman, from the characters created by Jerry Siegel, Joe Shuster

Superman IV: the Quest for Peace ★★ PG

Fantasy adventure
1987 · US · Colour · 92mins

Despite the return of Gene Hackman as the evil Lex Luthor, this creaky, tired third sequel sounded the final death knell for the *Superman* saga. In this one, Christopher Reeve's man in tights has finally brought about peace in our time, but soon finds himself up against Luthor (now a budding arms baron), his irritating nephew (Jon Cryer) and a powerful new foe called Nuclear Man. However, the enthusiastic hamming can't hide the clunking direction by Sidney J Furie and the poor special effects. JF

Christopher Reeve *Superman/Clark Kent* • Gene Hackman *Lex Luthor* • Jackie Cooper *Perry White* • Marc McClure *Jimmy Olsen* • Jon Cryer *Lenny* • Sam Wanamaker *David Warfield* • Mark Pillow *Nuclear Man* • Mariel Hemingway *Lacy Warfield* • Margot Kidder *Lois Lane* ■ *Dir* Sidney J Furie • *Scr* Lawrence Konner, Mark Rosenthal, from a story by Christopher Reeve, Lawrence Konner, Mark Rosenthal, from characters created by Jerry Siegel, Joe Shuster

Supernatural ★★

Mystery melodrama 1933 · US · BW · 65mins

Heiress Carole Lombard becomes involved with fake medium Alan Dinehart, who says he can put her in touch with her dead brother. Of course, he's only after her money. The extraordinarily convoluted plot then sees Lombard possessed by the spirit of a dead murderess as she threatens to exact revenge on the fraudulent Dinehart. This is a disappointing vehicle for the talents of the lovely Lombard, though it remains a collectable curiosity for her fans. RK

Carole Lombard *Roma Courtney* • Randolph Scott *Grant Wilson* • Vivienne Osborne *Ruth Rogen* • Alan Dinehart *Paul Bavian* • HB Warner *Dr Houston* • Beryl Mercer *Madame Gourjan* • William Farnum *Robert Hammond* ■ *Dir* Victor Halperin • *Scr* Harvey Thew, Brian Marlow, from the story by Garnett Weston

Supernova ★ 15

Science-fiction adventure
2000 · US · Colour · 90mins

Credited to a bogus name – Thomas Lee, the new century's Alan Smithee replacement – this relentlessly mediocre *Alien* rip-off at least looks good, as it shambles through the familiar conventions of the genre. A medical crew in deep space answer a distress call and take on board the only survivor of a mysterious mining accident. James Spader and Angela Bassett try in vain to soften the ridiculous impact of the clumsy theatrics, while the rest of the cast do little but disrobe. AJ DVD

James Spader *Nick Vanzant* • Angela Bassett *Kaela Evers* • Robert Forster *AJ Marley* • Lou Diamond Phillips *Yerzy Penalosa* • Peter Facinelli *Karl Larson* • Robin Tunney *Danika Lund* • Wilson Cruz *Benj Sotomejor* • Eddy Rice Jr *Flyboy* ■ *Dir* Thomas Lee [Walter Hill] • *Scr* David Campbell Wilson, from a story by William Malone

Superstar ★★ 15

Comedy 1999 · US · Colour · 78mins

Calling this particular *Saturday Night Live* spin-off a cut above their usual product isn't exactly a compliment. It does have its moments, but it sometimes has to go wildly out of its way to get to them. Molly Shannon's character is a nerdy Catholic high-school girl is determined not to let her dizzy nature or her snotty classmates stop her from becoming a star. The supporting characters are underused, and much of the action is generally lame. However, the non-stop attempts at humour do manage to induce a mild chuckle or two. KB DVD

Molly Shannon *Mary Katherine Gallagher* • Will Ferrell *Sky Corrigan/Jesus* • Elaine Hendrix *Evian* • Harland Williams *Slater* • Mark McKinney *Father Ritley* • Glynis Johns *Grandma* • Jason Blicker *Howard* • Gerry Bamman *Father John* ■ *Dir* Bruce McCulloch • *Scr* Steven Wayne Koren, from the character created by Molly Shannon

Superstar: the Karen Carpenter Story ★★★★

Experimental biographical fantasy
1987 · US · Colour · 43mins

Years before *Velvet Goldmine*, director Todd Haynes explored the opposite end of the musical spectrum with this notorious short about 1970s pop duo the Carpenters. Making unauthorised use of their music, Haynes presents a surreal re-enactment of the ill-fated life and career of singer Karen Carpenter and her brother Richard, using Barbie dolls instead of actors. Despite the superficially camp treatment, there's a serious message behind Haynes's portrayal of the doomed Karen, as she battles with overnight success, family pressures and the anorexia nervosa that would cause her death. Contemporary newsreel and TV-show footage provides the background to this bizarre yet moving examination of the dark side of 1970s pop culture. AJ

Gwen Kraus *Voice* • Bruce Tuthill *Voice* ■ *Dir* Todd Haynes • *Scr* Todd Haynes, Cynthia Schneider

Superstar: the Life and Times of Andy Warhol ★★★★

Documentary 1991 · US · Colour · 87mins

An absorbing documentary made three years after the death of pop artist and film-maker Warhol. Extremely well researched and well put together by Chuck Workman, it includes interviews with Warhol's relatives and famous friends, fascinating footage from the Warhol Factory, and clips from early films that many may not have seen. Paul Morrissey, who directed Warhol's biggest hits, is noticeably absent, and there is a tendency to eulogise rather than analyse, but anyone interested in the zeitgeist of the 1960s will not be disappointed. DM DVD

Dir/Scr Chuck Workman • *Cinematographer* Burleigh Wartes

Superstition ★★ 15

Supernatural horror
2001 · UK/Neth/Lux · Colour · 93mins

This uneven mixture of supernatural chiller and courtroom melodrama is based on the true story of a British au pair who was accused of arson and murder by her Italian employers after their baby died in extreme circumstances. The action lurches between stylised dream sequences and long passages of dialogue, primarily involving Sienna Guillory as the accused and Mark Strong as her put-upon lawyer. Alice Krige and Charlotte Rampling stand out in a strong supporting cast. DP DVD

Mark Strong *Antonio Gabrieli* • Sienna Guillory *Julie* • David Warner *Judge Padovani* • Charlotte Rampling *Frances Matteo* • Alice Krige *Mirella Cenci* • Frances Barber *Isabella Flores* ■ *Dir* Kenneth Hope • *Scr* Kate Dennis, Paul Hoffman, from a story by Stephen Volk

Supervixens ★★★★ 18

Satirical sex thriller
1975 · US · Colour · 104mins

Cult sexploiter Russ Meyer cranked up to overdrive his giddy formula of fast pacing, breathless editing and weird camera angles with this exaggerated cartoon romp, complete with a "That's all, folks!" ending. The convoluted plot, detailing the sexual misadventures of a man on the run for a murder he didn't commit, includes escaped Nazis and psycho cops alongside the usual bevy of well-proportioned fantasy females. A delightfully manic roller-coaster ride through the sexual mores of mid-1970s America, laced with outrageous comedy and extreme violence. AJ.

Contains violence, swearing, sex scenes and nudity. [video] DVD

Shari Eubank *Superangel/Supervixen* • Charles Pitts *Clint Ramsey* • Charles Napier *Harry Sledge* • Uschi Digard *Supersoul* • Henry Rowland *Martin Bormann* • Christy Hartburg *Superlorna* • Sharon Kelly *Supercherry* ■ *Dir/Scr* Russ Meyer

Support Your Local Gunfighter ★★★★ U

Comedy western 1971 · US · Colour · 88mins

Amiable James Garner polished up his TV *Maverick* persona for a wonderfully witty pair of cowboy satires directed by Burt Kennedy, who had secured his spurs by writing a cycle of Randolph Scott westerns. This isn't exactly a sequel to *Support Your Local Sheriff!*, except perhaps in tone, but is equally funny, as conman Garner passes himself off as a deadly gunman. Bumbling Jack Elam walks away with the movie as Garner's buddy and delivers one of the funniest last lines in American screen comedy. A side-splitting treat. TS [video] DVD

James Garner *Latigo Smith* • Suzanne Pleshette *Patience Barton* • Jack Elam *Jug May* • Joan Blondell *Jenny* • Harry Morgan *Taylor Barton* • Marie Windsor *Goldie* • Henry Jones *Ez* • Chuck Connors *Swifty Morgan* • Grady Sutton *Storekeeper* ■ *Dir* Burt Kennedy • *Scr* James Edward Grant

Support Your Local Sheriff! ★★★★ PG

Comedy western 1969 · US · Colour · 89mins

This is one of a pair of priceless comedy gems (*Support Your Local Gunfighter* followed in 1971) from director Burt Kennedy, which spoof the western genre with great affection and provide marvellous roles for James Garner. Here he utilises his easy-going, wry charm as a put-upon lawman. Western fans will enjoy the clever casting. Walter Brennan virtually reprises the role of Ike Clanton in *My Darling Clementine*, only this time for laughs, and there's Joan Hackett from *Will Penny*. Jack Elam and Bruce Dern are hysterically funny. TS [video] DVD

James Garner *Jason McCullough* • Joan Hackett *Prudy Perkins* • Walter Brennan *Pa Danby* • Harry Morgan *Mayor Olly Perkins* • Jack Elam *Jake* • Bruce Dern *Joe Danby* • Henry Jones *Preacher Henry Jackson* ■ *Dir* Burt Kennedy • *Scr* William Bowers

Suppose They Gave a War and Nobody Came? ★★★ 15

Satirical comedy drama
1970 · US · Colour · 112mins

A commander of a US army base in the American South hopes to foster good will with the nearby town by organising a dance. All seems well at first, but when army sergeant Tony Curtis is caught canoodling with local beauty Suzanne Pleshette, the resulting fracas leads to war breaking out between the town and the military. Sometimes farcical, sometimes satirical, it's a crazy sprawling mess of a comedy that manages to entertain, despite its many flaws. DF [video]

Brian Keith *Nace* • Tony Curtis *Shannon Gambroni* • Ernest Borgnine *Sheriff Harve* • Ivan Dixon *Sgt Jones* • Suzanne Pleshette *Ramona* • Tom Ewell *Billy Joe Davis* • Bradford Dillman *Capt Myerson* • Don Ameche *Col Flanders* ■ *Dir* Hy Averback • *Scr* Don McGuire, Hal Captain, from a story by Hal Captain

Supreme Sanction ★★ 18

Action thriller 1999 · US · Colour · 89mins

Michael Madsen sleepwalks through yet another ho-hum action thriller that offers little but some efficiently staged action pieces. He's the bad guy here, a hitman for a secret government-sponsored agency on the trail of old colleague Kristy Swanson, who has baulked at her latest assignment – the killing of journalist David Dukes. Even on autopilot, Madsen is alway watchable, while Swanson makes for a feisty heroine, but this is instantly forgettable. JF [video] DVD

Michael Madsen *Dalton* • Kristy Swanson *Jenna* • Holliston Coleman *Bailey* • David Dukes *Jordan McNamara* • Ron Perlman *The Director* • Tom "Tiny" Lister Jr *Lester* ■ *Dir/Scr* John Terlesky

El Sur ★★★★ U

Drama 1983 · Sp/Fr · Colour · 94mins

Victor Erice's first film in the decade since completing his masterpiece, *Spirit of the Beehive*, returns to the idea of cinema reflecting the hopes and misconceptions of an intense young girl. The poster advertising Alfred Hitchcock's *Shadow of a Doubt* suggests the notion of betrayal that is then confirmed by the film-within-the-film, *Flor en la Sombre*. But even more effective is the leisurely, lyrical manner in which Erice allows 1950s adolescent Iciar Bollain to realise the fragility of the dreams her younger self (Sonsoles Aranguren) has woven around her doting – and now mysteriously disappeared – father, Omero Antonutti. DP. In Spanish with English subtitles.

Omero Antonutti *Augustín* • Sonsoles Aranguren *Estrella, aged 8* • Iciar Bollain *Estrelle, teenager* • Lola Cardona *Julia* • Rafaela Aparicio *Milagros* • Aurore Clément *Irene Ríos* ■ *Dir* Victor Erice • *Scr* Victor Erice, from the novel by Adelaida García Morales

Sur ★★★★ 15

Drama 1987 · Arg/Fr · Colour · 118mins

Following his treatise on physical exile, *Tangos, Exilo de Gardel* (1985), Argentinian director Fernando E Solanas (himself heading home after a prolonged absence) explores the pain of the prisoner in this vibrant, lyrical, political and poignant study of national transition and individual turmoil. Consciously employing a theatrical style, he uses tango, poetry and song to counterpoint the jumble of emotions, memories, hopes and fears that beset newly released Miguel Angel Sola, as he returns to his Buenos Aires neighbourhood. However, his wife, Susu Pecoraro, also has to readjust, having turned to close friend Philippe Léotard for solace in her isolation. DP. A Spanish language film.

Susu Pecoraro *Rosi Echegoyen* • Miguel Angel Sola *Floreal Echegoyen* • Philippe Léotard *Roberto* • Lito Cruz *El Negro* • Ulises Dumont *Emilio* ■ *Dir/Scr* Fernando E Solanas

Sur ★★★ U

Musical drama 2002 · Ind · Colour · 137mins

After years of singing for others, playback vocalist Lucky Ali makes his screen debut in this Bollywood take on the Svengali story (with a smattering of *A Star Is Born* thrown in for good measure). Not content with being a musical superstar, he becomes obsessed with finding a student whom he can train to be his equal. But no sooner has the demure Gauri Karnik found fame than he becomes destructively jealous. Revelling in its melodramatic clichés, Tanuja Chandra's tearjerker is undemanding entertainment. DP. In Hindi with English subtitles. [video] DVD

Lucky Ali *Vikramaditya Singh* • Gauri Karnik *Tina Marie* ■ *Dir/Scr* Tanuja Chandra

Sure Fire ★★★

Drama 1990 · US · Colour · 83mins

Arrogant real-estate salesman Tom Blair embarks on a crooked scheme to sell vacation homes in Utah to wealthy Californians in micro-budget master Jon Jost's experimental 16mm gem. But as the scam collapses, so does Blair's family life, and he and his estranged wife start fighting for the loyalties of their teenage son. The resolution of this power struggle is tragic and haunting. Moody music, extended takes and innovative narrative mechanisms combine to lay bare a dark and disturbing portrait of warped politics and ethical values. AJ

Tom Blair *Wes* • Kristi Hager *Bobbi* • Robert Ernst *Larry* • Kate Dezina *Ellen* • Phillip R Brown *Phillip* • Dennis R Brown *Dennis* ■ *Dir/Scr* Jon Jost

The Sure Thing ★★★★ 15

Comedy 1985 · US · Colour · 90mins

This delightful comedy from director Rob Reiner should have made John Cusack a star. He's superb as a beer-guzzling, sex-obsessed freshman who travels from his eastern college to California during the holidays to meet up with a beautiful girl who's a "sure thing". However, during a series of misadventures he ends up on the road with clean-living Daphne Zuniga, and that's where the fun really begins. Both the leads are enjoyable to watch, and look out for a young Tim Robbins as the driver with whom no one should ever hitch a ride. JB. Contains some swearing. [video] DVD

John Cusack *Walter "Gib" Gibson* • Daphne Zuniga *Alison Bradbury* • Anthony Edwards *Lance* • Boyd Gaines *Jason* • Lisa Jane Persky *Mary Ann* • Viveca Lindfors *Professor Taub* • Nicollette Sheridan *The Sure Thing* • Tim Robbins *Gary* ■ *Dir* Rob Reiner • *Scr* Steven L Bloom, Jonathan Roberts

Surf Crazy ★★★

Documentary 1959 · US · Colour · 72mins

Hawaii had only just achieved statehood when Bruce Brown made his second surfing documentary there. So there's a sense of moment about the sequences filmed at the Waimea and Sunset beaches on Oahu. But this was a cross-continental odyssey, which sees Brown and his buddies push their Ford through 7,000 miles in search of breakers. The California sequences at Rincon and Cottons are spectacular. But the film's real interest lies in the Mexican segment, as it was still virgin surf territory, even around Acapulco. DP [video] DVD

Dir Bruce Brown

Surf Nazis Must Die ★ 18

Futuristic satire 1987 · US · Colour · 78mins

This is one of cinema's most notoriously titled movies and a typical release from Troma – the studio that gave us *Rabid Grannies* and *The Toxic Avenger* – featuring bad acting, a nonexistent budget and a ludicrous plotline. It's set in a future California, where a devastating earthquake has left millions homeless and the beaches have turned into battlegrounds, as rival surf gangs vie for control. Not as much fun as it could have been, and it takes itself way too seriously. RS [video] DVD

Barry Brenner *Adolf* • Gail Neely *Mama Washington* • Michael Sonye *Mengele* • Dawn Wildsmith *Eva* • Jon Ayre *Narrator* ■ *Dir* Peter George • *Scr* Jon Ayre

Surf Ninjas ★ PG

Comedy adventure
1993 · US · Colour · 83mins

Isn't it amazing that, in the midst of the 1990s ninja craze, with "kid ninja" movies being made every other year, not one of them had a decent martial arts sequence or a single line of decent dialogue? This one has the audacity to include both Rob Schneider and Leslie Nielsen for its odious comic relief. Polynesian brothers Ernie Reyes Jr and Nicholas Cowan discover that they are the royal heirs to an island nation, which was overthrown by evil warlord Nielsen. ST [video]

Ernie Reyes Sr *Zatch* • Ernie Reyes Jr *Johnny* • Nicholas Cowan *Adam* • John Karlen *Mac* • Rob Schneider *Iggy* • Leslie Nielsen *Colonel Chi* ■ *Dir* Neal Israel • *Scr* Dan Gordon

Suriyothai ★★★

Historical epic adventure
2001 · Thai · Colour · 185mins

Set in the early 16th century, when Thailand was divided into two kingdoms, the story of how Queen Suriyothai repelled the Burmese king is a national epic in every sense. The most expensive Thai movie ever made, it was directed by a royal prince, Chatrichalerm Yukol. There's a presumption that most viewers will have a working knowledge of Thai history, which makes things difficult for those who don't. Matters aren't helped by the emphasis on spectacle over character, but the climactic battle is stupendous and ML Piyapas Bhirombhakdi's performance is ravishingly regal. DP. In Thai with English subtitles.

ML Piyapas Bhirombhakdi *Somdet Phra Suriyothai* • Sarunyoo Wongkrachang *Somdet Phra Thienracha* • Chatchai Plengpanich *Khun Pirenthorathep* • Siriwimol Charoenpura *Tao Sri Sudachan* • Johnny Anfone *Panbut Srithep* • Pongpat Wachirabunjong *Somdet Phra Thienracha* • Sinjai Plengpanich *Tao Sri Chulalak* • Sorapong Chatri *Muen Ratchasaneha* ■ *Dir* Chatrichalerm Yukol • *Scr* Chatrichalerm Yukol, from a biography by Domingos de Seixas

Surprise Package ★★★ U

Comedy 1960 · UK · BW · 99mins

By now a major international star, Yul Brynner was given his first comic role as a mobster deported to a Greek island, where deposed king Noël Coward is already ensconced. Mitzi Gaynor is the surprise package, flown in for Brynner's delectation. The trio's nefarious adventures are fun, but not as funny as they should have been considering that the script is by Harry Kurnitz, writer of very polished comedies, and based on a novel by the great satirist Art Buchwald. DM

Yul Brynner *Nico March* • Bill Nagy *Johnny Stettina* • Mitzi Gaynor *Gabby Rogers* • Lionel Murton *US Marshall* • Barry Foster *US Marshall* • Eric Pohlmann *Stefan Miralis* • Noël Coward *King Pavel II* • George Coulouris *Dr Hugo Panzer* • Warren Mitchell *Klimatis* ■ *Dir* Stanley Donen • *Scr* Harry Kurnitz, from the novel *A Gift from the Boys* by Art Buchwald

Surrender ★★★ PG

Romantic comedy
1987 · US · Colour · 91mins

A light courtship comedy about a confused woman caught in two minds about the men in her life. Sally Field is Little Miss Muddle; Michael Caine and Steve Guttenberg are the twin objects of her affections. Though the film is trite and contrived at times, strong performances, in particular from the two male leads, just about carry it through. DA [video]

Sally Field *Daisy Morgan* • Michael Caine *Sean Stein* • Steve Guttenberg *Marty Caesar* • Peter Boyle *Jay Bass* • Julie Kavner *Ronnie* • Jackie Cooper *Ace Morgan* • Louise Lasser *Joyce* • Iman *Hedy* ■ *Dir/Scr* Jerry Belson

Survival Run ★ 18

Action crime drama
1979 · US · Colour · 93mins

Vincent Van Patten and five other teens get stranded in the middle of the desert, reacting to their situation by drinking beer, having sex, and singing badly around the campfire. Then they stumble onto the camp of drug dealers

S

Peter Graves and Ray Milland (looking very uncomfortable in the heat). There's never any sense of danger or tension and the limp fighting can barely be considered action sequences. KB. Contains swearing, sex scenes and violence.

Peter Graves (2) • Ray Milland • Vincent Van Patten • Pedro Armendáriz Jr • Susan Pratt O'Hanlon ■ *Dir* Larry Spiegel • *Scr* Larry Spiegel, GM Cahill, from a story by GM Cahill

Surviving ★★★★ 15

Drama 1985 · US · Colour · 137mins

An often fascinating and powerful TV movie about the devastating consequences of thwarted teenage romance. Zach Galligan and Molly Ringwald are the young lovers, driven to desperate measures when their parents oppose their relationship. A strong cast includes Ellen Burstyn and Marsha Mason as the mothers confronting this teenage angst and struggling to deal with their own feelings of guilt. JB

Ellen Burstyn *Tina Morgan* • Len Cariou *David Morgan* • Zach Galligan *Rick Morgan* • Marsha Mason *Lois Carlson* • Molly Ringwald *Lonnie Carlson* • Paul Sorvino *Harvey Carlson* • River Phoenix *Philip Morgan* • Heather O'Rourke *Sarah Morgan* ■ *Dir* Waris Hussein • *Scr* Joyce Eliason

Surviving Christmas ★ 12A

Seasonal comedy 2004 · US · Colour · 90mins

Ben Affleck plays a rich advertising executive who returns to his former home where he pays the blue-collar Valco family that now lives there to let him spend the holiday period with them as their son. Cue a mess of clichés, pratfalls and limp jokes. Even co-stars James Gandolfini and Catherine O'Hara as the Valco parents, who at least realise less is more, cannot rescue the movie. SF. Contains sexual references.

Ben Affleck *Drew Latham* • James Gandolfini *Tom Valco* • Christina Applegate *Alicia Valco* • Catherine O'Hara *Christine Valco* • Josh Zuckerman *Brian Valco* • Bill Macy *Doo-Dah* • Jennifer Morrison *Missy Vangilder* • Udo Kier *Heinrich* ■ *Dir* Mike Mitchell • *Scr* Deborah Kaplan, Harry Elfont, Jeffrey Ventimilia, Joshua Sternin, from a story by Deborah Kaplan, Harry Elfont

Surviving Picasso ★★★★ 15

Biographical drama
1996 · US · Colour · 120mins

James Ivory directs Anthony Hopkins in a vision of Picasso's life that argues his passion for women equalled his passion for painting. His objects of desire are all stunning – Natascha McElhone, Julianne Moore, Susannah Harker – but which of them will prove a match for him? Hopkins is excellent as the self-centred artist and McElhone makes a very impressive impact in her first major role. As ever Ivory directs with flair and aesthetic insight, but the subject matter may be too eclectic for many people's taste. LH. Contains swearing, violence and nudity.

Anthony Hopkins *Pablo Picasso* • Natascha McElhone *Françoise Gilot* • Julianne Moore *Dora Maar* • Joss Ackland *Henri Matisse* • Jane Lapotaire *Olga Koklova* • Joseph Maher *Kahnweiler* • Bob Peck *Françoise's father* • Diane Venora *Jacqueline Rocque* • Joan Plowright *Françoise's grandmother* • Susannah Harker *Marie-Thérèse* ■ *Dir* James Ivory • *Scr* Ruth Prawer Jhabvala, from the non-fiction book *Picasso: Creator and Destroyer* by Arianna Stassinopoulos Huffington

Surviving the Game ★★ 15

Action thriller 1994 · US · Colour · 92mins

Another variant on the shopworn manhunt premise, best exhibited back in the 1930s with *The Most Dangerous Game*. This time, rapper-cum-thespian Ice-T is a homeless derelict conned out of the city and into the wilderness to act as prey for a bunch of thrill-seeking high rollers including Gary Busey's ex-CIA agent, F Murray Abraham's Wall Street executive and Rutger Hauer. Former Spike Lee cinematographer Ernest R Dickerson brings technical bravado to the proceedings, but the whole premise of wealthy whites hunting homeless blacks is morally tasteless. RS DVD

Ice-T *Jack Mason* • Rutger Hauer *Burns* • Charles S Dutton *Cole* • Gary Busey *Hawkins* • F Murray Abraham *Wolf Sr* • John C McGinley *Griffin* • William McNamara *Wolf Jr* • Jeff Corey *Hank* ■ *Dir* Ernest R Dickerson • *Scr* Eric Bernt

The Survivor ★ 15

Thriller 1981 · Aus · Colour · 82mins

Robert Powell puts on that martyred look he keeps handy in lieu of acting as a pilot, the sole survivor of a crashed jet, who is prey to visions of dead passengers. Jenny Agutter simpers while Powell whimpers in this Australian oddity directed by David Hemmings, a would-be thriller that's sadly lacking in suspense. TH. Contains violence, swearing. DVD

Robert Powell *Keller* • Jenny Agutter *Hobbs* • Joseph Cotten *Priest* • Angela Punch McGregor *Beth Rogan* • Ralph Cotterill *Slater* • Peter Sumner *Tewson* ■ *Dir* David Hemmings • *Scr* David Ambrose, from the novel by James Herbert

The Survivors ★★ 15

Comedy 1983 · US · Colour · 98mins

What starts as a promising social satire soon descends into coarse slapstick and manic babble as Robin Williams and Walter Matthau come to terms with life after foiling a crime, but being identified by the miscreant. Williams is transformed from mild-mannered executive into gun-toting survivalist, while his fellow hero Matthau stays cynically calm. Director Michael Ritchie lets the picture and his stars run out of control. DP. Contains swearing and violence. DVD

Walter Matthau *Sonny Paluso* • Robin Williams *Donald Quinelle* • Jerry Reed *Jack Locke* • James Wainwright *Wes Huntley* • Kristen Vigard *Candice Paluso* • Annie McEnroe *Doreen* • Anne Pitoniak *Betty* ■ *Dir* Michael Ritchie • *Scr* Michael Leeson

Susan and God ★★★

Comedy drama 1940 · US · Colour · 115mins

Shallow and narcissistic society wife and mother Joan Crawford, whose disregard is alienating her husband Fredric March, returns from a European trip with a new fad – religion. Her verbal zealotry and pious interference in other people's lives causes havoc and drives her husband to drink. An unusual drama, it's directed by George Cukor, who draws a persuasive performance from Crawford. RK

Joan Crawford *Susan Trexel* • Fredric March *Barry Trexel* • Ruth Hussey *Charlotte* • John Carroll *Clyde Rochester* • Rita Hayworth *Leonora Stubbs* • Nigel Bruce *Hutchins Stubbs* • Bruce Cabot *Michael O'Hara* ■ *Dir* George Cukor • *Scr* Anita Loos, from a play by Rachel Crothers

Susan Lenox: Her Fall and Rise ★★★

Romantic melodrama
1931 · US · BW · 76mins

Based on the notorious novel by David Graham Phillips, the British film censor was having none of it, lopping out several key seconds and changing the title to *The Rise of Helga*. The whole steamy movie is tame today, save for the undeniable sexual magnetism between Greta Garbo and Clark Gable in their only screen pairing. She insisted on newcomer Gable as co-star, and their early country scenes make it easy to see why. Garbo is magic, and this movie is but a prologue to the greatness to come. TS

Greta Garbo *Susan Lenox* • Clark Gable *Rodney* • Jean Hersholt *Ohlin* • John Miljan *Burlingham* • Alan Hale *Mondstrum* • Hale Hamilton *Mike Kelly* • Hilda Vaughn *Astrid* • Russell Simpson *Doctor* ■ *Dir* Robert Z Leonard • *Scr* Wanda Tuchock, Zelda Sears, Leon Gordon, Edith Fitzgerald, from the novel by David Graham Phillips

Susan Slade ★

Melodrama 1961 · US · Colour · 116mins

The daughter of a respectable engineer falls pregnant by a mountaineer who is promptly killed in an accident. After hiding in South America, she returns to California with her illegitimate baby and has to deal with the consequences of her father's unexpected death. Turgid, unconvincing and boring. RK

Troy Donahue *Hoyt Brecker* • Connie Stevens *Susan Slade* • Dorothy McGuire *Leah Slade* • Lloyd Nolan *Roger Slade* • Brian Aherne *Stanton Corbett* • Grant Williams *Conn White* ■ *Dir* Delmer Daves • *Scr* Delmer Daves, from the novel *The Sin of Susan Slade* by Doris Hume • *Music* Max Steiner

Susan Slept Here ★★★

Comedy 1954 · US · Colour · 97mins

This super-sophisticated farce is as funny and risqué now as it was back in 1954, and Debbie Reynolds is simply terrific in one of her rare naughty-but-nice roles as a sexy teenage delinquent foisted on screenwriter Dick Powell. The Hollywood scene is well observed by director Frank Tashlin, and the humour is peppered with in-jokes. (The narrator is an Oscar statuette!) The Technicolor is particularly rich, and the Oscar-nominated theme song *Hold My Hand* went to number one in the charts. A film for 1950s freaks. TS

Dick Powell *Mark Christopher* • Debbie Reynolds *Susan* • Anne Francis *Isabella* • Glenda Farrell *Maude* • Alvy Moore *Virgil* • Horace McMahon *Maizel* ■ *Dir* Frank Tashlin • *Scr* Alex Gottlieb, from the play *Susan* by Alex Gottlieb, Steve Fisher

Susana ★★

Melodrama 1951 · Mex · BW · 82mins

Shot on a minuscule budget, Luis Buñuel considered this the low point of his career. While not one of his best efforts, it is still a stinging assault on Mexico's rich and religious, in particular their indolence and hypocrisy. Rosita Quintana tries hard in the title role, showing suitable humility as she begs God for a miraculous release from jail, yet revealing an irresistible sensuality as she seduces every man on Fernando Soler's ranch. DP. In Spanish with English subtitles.

Fernando Soler *Don Guadalupe* • Rosita Quintana *Susana* • Victor Manuel Mendoza *Jesus* • Matilde Palou *Carmen* ■ *Dir* Luis Buñuel • *Scr* Jaime Salvador, Luis Buñuel

Susannah of the Mounties ★★★ U

Adventure 1939 · US · BW · 79mins

Having survived a tribal massacre, little Shirley Temple is taken in by Mountie Randolph Scott and duly helps him get both his man (the truly villainous Victor Jory) and his woman (Margaret Lockwood, making her Hollywood debut). There's some toned-down action and a teeth-grinding sequence in which Scott is taught to tap dance, but it's mostly harmless. Avoid the colourised version. DP

Shirley Temple *Susannah Sheldon* • Randolph Scott *Inspector Angus "Monty" Montague* • Margaret Lockwood *Vicky Standing* • Martin Good Rider *Little Chief* • J Farrell MacDonald *Pat O'Hannegan* • Maurice Moscovich *Chief Big Eagle* • Victor Jory *Wolf Pelt* ■ *Dir* William A Seiter • *Scr* Robert Ellis, Helen Logan, from a story by Fidel La Barba, Walter Ferris, from the novel *Susannah, a Little Girl of the Mounties* by Muriel Denison

Susan's Plan ★★★ 18

Comedy 1998 · US · Colour · 84mins

A contrived, complex and intermittently hilarious comedy from John Landis, returning somewhat to form. Nastassja Kinski plays Susan, who's desperate to bump off her reprehensible ex-hubby for cash and hires a string of bumbling hitmen to do it. Routine stuff, elevated above the ordinary by a cracking cast. DA. Contains swearing, violence and nudity. DVD

Nastassja Kinski *Susan* • Billy Zane *Sam* • Michael Biehn *Bill* • Dan Aykroyd *Bob* • Lara Flynn Boyle *Betty* • Rob Schneider *Steve* • Adrian Paul *Paul* ■ *Dir/Scr* John Landis

The Suspect ★★★

Period thriller 1944 · US · BW · 85mins

Directed by German émigré Robert Siodmak, this Edwardian drama stars Charles Laughton in the kind of role in which he excelled. He plays a decent, ordinary shopkeeper whose life is made a misery by his deeply unpleasant wife Rosalind Ivan. Smitten with pretty stenographer Ella Raines, he beats his wife to death with a cane, but gets away with claiming she died in an accidental fall. He marries Raines and all is well until his blackmailing neighbour Henry Daniell begins to suspect the truth. Modest, suspenseful and absorbing. RK

Charles Laughton *Philip Marshall* • Ella Raines *Mary Gray* • Dean Harens *John Marshall* • Stanley C Ridges [Stanley Ridges] *Inspector Huxley* • Henry Daniell *Mr Gilbert Simmons* • Rosalind Ivan *Cora Marshall* • Molly Lamont *Mrs Edith Simmons* • Raymond Severn *Merridew* ■ *Dir* Robert Siodmak • *Scr* Bertram Millhauser, Arthur T Hormen, from the novel *This Way Out* by James Ronald

Suspect ★★

Spy drama 1960 · UK · BW · 80mins

This story of spies at a chemical research lab betrays its secret through casting. Nominal stars Tony Britton and Virginia Maskell are awful, and you soon wish splendid supports Peter Cushing, Donald Pleasence, Raymond Huntley and Ian Bannen had more to do. The Boulting brothers fail to create the claustrophobia that might have intensified the climate of suspicion, and the casting of Spike Milligan in an espionage drama is the only real talking point. DP

Tony Britton *Bob Marriott* • Virginia Maskell *Lucy Byrne* • Peter Cushing *Professor Sewall* • Ian Bannen *Alan Andrews* • Raymond Huntley *Sir George Gatling* • Thorley Walters *Mr Prince* • Donald Pleasence *Brown* • Spike Milligan *Arthur* ■ *Dir* Roy Boulting, John Boulting • *Scr* Nigel Balchin, Jeffrey Dell, Roy Boulting, from the novel *A Sort of Traitors* by Nigel Balchin

Suspect ★★★ 15

Courtroom thriller
1987 · US · Colour · 116mins

An early Hollywood role for Liam Neeson, playing a deaf-mute Vietnam veteran accused of murder. Cher is his lawyer and Dennis Quaid is the jury member who provides a glimmer of hope in a seemingly hopeless case. Director Peter Yates winds up the courtroom tension to some effect, but any sympathy for Neeson's plight soon gets lost as suspicion shifts to a higher legal authority and the plot becomes too far-fetched. TH. Contains violence and swearing. DVD

Cher *Kathleen Riley* • Dennis Quaid *Eddie Sanger* • Liam Neeson *Carl Wayne Anderson* • John Mahoney *Judge Matthew Helms* • Joe Mantegna *Charlie Stella* • Philip Bosco *Paul*

S

Gray • E Katherine Kerr *Grace Comisky* • Fred Melamed *Morty Rosenthal* ■ *Dir* Peter Yates • *Scr* Eric Roth

Suspect Zero ★★ 15

Crime thriller 2004 · US · Colour · 95mins

In this depressingly formulaic stab at the serial killer genre, Aaron Eckhart plays an FBI agent who finds a formidable new adversary in the shape of Ben Kingsley, a former agent with a unique insight into the minds of murderers who seems to be specialising in dispatching other serial killers. Despite the good cast and the glimmer of an intriguing idea in the plot, director E Elias Merhige generates little in the way of menace or tension. JF DVD

Aaron Eckhart *Thomas Mackelway* • Ben Kingsley *Benjamin O'Ryan* • Carrie-Anne Moss *Fran Kulok* • Harry J Lennix [Harry Lennix] *Rick Charleton* • Kevin Chamberlin *Harold Speck* • Julian Reyes *Highway patrolman* • Keith Campbell *Raymond Starkey* ■ *Dir* E Elias Merhige • *Scr* Zak Penn, Billy Ray, from a story by Zak Penn

Suspended Alibi ★★ U

Crime drama 1956 · UK · BW · 64mins

Innocuous British crime drama, only to be commended for its brevity. Patrick Holt is the newspaperman convicted of the murder of his best friend. Honor Blackman plays his loyal wife, Naomi Chance his mistress, Valentine Dyall the plodding police inspector and Andrew Keir the crime reporter who digs out the truth. The least ambitious feature made by film union ACT's production subsidiary. AE

Patrick Holt *Paul Pearson* • Honor Blackman *Lynn Pearson* • Valentine Dyall *Inspector Kayes* • Naomi Chance *Diana* • Lloyd Lamble *Waller* • Andrew Keir *Sandy Thorpe* ■ *Dir* Alfred Shaughnessy • *Scr* Kenneth R Hayles

Suspicion ★★★★ U

Psychological thriller
1941 · US · BW · 96mins

In this marvellous Hitchcock thriller, timid Joan Fontaine is in mortal fear of being bumped off by her husband, amoral Cary Grant. Fontaine won the best actress Oscar for her pouting female-in-trouble portrayal, though some believe it was to compensate her for not winning the award for *Rebecca* the previous year. It all begins well enough, with Grant's bounder a most unlikeable cad, but the film is hopelessly crippled by the censorship of the time, and is ultimately both predictable and implausible. But there's much to enjoy, not least a totally phoney Hollywood England and sterling support from British expatriates Nigel Bruce and Cedric Hardwicke. TS [video] DVD

Cary Grant *Johnnie Aysgarth* • Joan Fontaine *Lina McLaidlaw* • Cedric Hardwicke *General McLaidlaw* • Nigel Bruce *Gordon Cochran "Beaky" Thwaite* • Dame May Whitty *Mrs McLaidlaw* • Isabel Jeans *Mrs Newsham* ■ *Dir* Alfred Hitchcock • *Scr* Samson Raphaelson, Joan Harrison, Alma Reville, from the novel *Before the Fact* by Frances Iles [Anthony Berkeley Cox]

Suspicious River ★★ 18

Psychological drama
2000 · Can · Colour · 89mins

In this dark study of small-town sexuality, Molly Parker, as a married motel receptionist who prostitutes herself to guests, ably suggests the dazed fragility that delivers her into the clutches of brutal redneck Callum Keith Rennie. Lynne Stopkewich's direction chillingly reduces sex to its bestial basics, while her refusal to clarify whether young Mary Kate Welsh's brush with abuse is a parallel story or a flashback to Parker's own childhood adds tension. But her concern with shocking rather than intriguing the audience ultimately results in a feeling of disappointment. DP [video] DVD

Molly Parker *Leila Murray* • Callum Keith Rennie *Gary Jensen* • Mary Kate Welsh *Young girl* • Joel Bissonnette *Rick Schmidt* • Deanna Milligan *Millie* ■ *Dir* Lynne Stopkewich • *Scr* Lynne Stopkewich, from the novel by Laura Kasischke

Suspiria ★★★★ 18

Supernatural horror
1976 · It · Colour · 94mins

In this landmark horror fantasy from cult director Dario Argento – dubbed the Italian Hitchcock for his mastery of suspense – Jessica Harper plays a dancer at a German ballet school where witches prowl the corridors. The famous opening 20 minutes of this *Snow White* fairy tale (by way of Thomas De Quincey's hallucinatory *Confessions of an Opium Eater*) are an unforgettable experience, and the whole is a stunning combination of menacing *Grand Guignol* atmosphere, dazzling colours, gory violence, lush decor and pounding soundtrack. AJ. Contains violence. [video] DVD

Jessica Harper *Susy Bannion* • Joan Bennett *Madame Blanc* • Alida Valli *Miss Tanner* • Udo Kier *Frank* • Flavio Bucci *Daniel* • Stefania Casini *Sara* • Miguel Bose *Mark* • Rudolf Schündler *Professor Milius* ■ *Dir* Dario Argento • *Scr* Dario Argento, Dario Nicolodi

Suture ★★★ 15

Thriller 1993 · US · BW · 91mins

Great things were predicted for Scott McGehee and David Siegel after they debuted with this ultra-stylised *film noir*, a postmodern monochrome melodrama that delights in disorientating the viewer. At the centre of the confusion are half-brothers Dennis Haysbert and Michael Harris, whose racial and physical dissimilarity is turned into a mischievous lookalike gag on which depends the plot's dastardly game of interchangeable identities. It stumbles towards the end, but intrigues throughout. DP [video]

Dennis Haysbert *Clay Arlington* • Mel Harris *Dr Renée Descartes* • Sab Shimono *Dr Max Shinoda* • Dina Merrill *Alice Jameson* ■ *Dir/Scr* Scott McGehee, David Siegel

Suzhou River ★★★★ 12

Romantic drama
2000 · Chi/Ger/Neth/Jpn/Fr · Colour · 78mins

With an unseen videographer giving the action an intriguingly subjective viewpoint, Lou Ye's teasing treatise on perspective and identity irresistibly recalls Alfred Hitchcock's *Rear Window* and *Vertigo*. Hired by a vodka racketeer to chaperone his daughter Zhou Xun, motorcycle courier Jia Hongsheng connives at her kidnapping, only to be jailed for murder when she seems to commit suicide. On his release, Jia becomes besotted with an aquarium mermaid (Zhou again), with tragic consequences. With its world-weary narration, oppressive cityscapes and dangerous passions, this blend of *film noir* and psychological drama is as edgy as it's engrossing. DP. In Mandarin with English subtitles. Contains violence, swearing. [video] DVD

Zhou Xun *Meimei/Moudan* • Jia Hongshen *Mardar* • Yao Anlian *Boss* • Nai An *Mada* ■ *Dir/Scr* Lou Ye

Suzie Gold ★★ 15

Romantic comedy drama
2003 · UK · Colour · 89mins

This broad British comedy stars American actress Summer Phoenix as a north London Jewish "princess" defying her traditional folks for the love of a non-Jewish boy. First-time director Ric Cantor leaves no stereotype unturned in the telling of this cross-cultural romance and as much as one might wish the film occasionally to confound one's expectations, it never does. DA. Contains swearing, sex scenes and drug abuse. [video] DVD

Summer Phoenix *Suzie Gold* • Leo Gregory *Darren* • Stanley Townsend *Irving Gold* • Rebecca Front *Barbara Gold* • Frances Barber *Joy Spencer* • Iddo Goldberg *Anthony Silver* • Miriam Karlin *Nana* ■ *Dir* Ric Cantor • *Scr* Ric Cantor, Carry Franklin, Lisa Ratner, from a story by Rebecca Green

Suzy ★★★

Romantic melodrama
1936 · US · BW · 99mins

In London, penniless American chorus girl Jean Harlow marries Irish would-be inventor Franchot Tone but flees to a cabaret job in Paris after she believes him shot dead by a female spy. When the First World War breaks out, she marries French flying ace Cary Grant. Drama escalates when Tone, not dead after all, turns up in uniform. George Fitzmaurice directs this rather curious but effective and fast-moving piece that begins as romantic comedy and switches to espionage thriller. Harlow is ingenuous and charming, Tone is an attractive hero and Grant does well as a cad. RK

Jean Harlow *Suzy Trent* • Cary Grant *André Charville* • Franchot Tone *Terry Moore* • Benita Hume *Mme Diane Eyrelle* • Lewis Stone *Baron Charville* ■ *Dir* George Fitzmaurice • *Scr* Dorothy Parker, Alan Campbell, Horace Jackson, Lenore Coffee, from the novel by Herbert Gorman

Svengali ★★

Drama 1931 · US · BW · 76mins

George du Maurier's famous Victorian novel, *Trilby*, tells of a beautiful young girl whose singing teacher uses hypnotism to turn her into a great opera singer. This version shifts the novel's emphasis on to Svengali himself, played in his most uninhibited, histrionic style by John Barrymore, while Marian Marsh is the artist's model who falls under his spell. Apart from the Oscar-nominated cinematography and the historical interest of watching Barrymore in action, there's not much of interest in this melodrama. RK

John Barrymore *Svengali* • Marian Marsh *Trilby* • Bramwell Fletcher *Billee* • Donald Crisp *The Laird* • Lumsden Hare *Taffy* ■ *Dir* Archie Mayo • *Scr* J Grubb Alexander, from the novel *Trilby* by George du Maurier • *Cinematographer* Barry McGill

Svengali ★★

Drama 1954 · UK/US · Colour · 82mins

George du Maurier's novel *Trilby*, on which this film is based, was notorious in the late Victorian era for its overblown sexuality, telling the story of a manipulative music teacher/ hypnotist and an Irish artist's model who falls under his baleful spell. Set in Paris, it's a story of sexual jealousy that, in this version, conforms to censorship demands of the time and is less suggestive than the 1931 John Barrymore film (itself a remake of a 1915 silent). However, it's worth seeing for Donald Wolfit hamming away as the menacing Svengali. A miscast Jodie Foster starred in a 1983 TV movie remake. AT

Hildegarde Neff *Trilby O'Ferrall* • Donald Wolfit *Svengali* • Terence Morgan *Billy Bagot* • Derek Bond *The Laird* • Paul Rogers *Taffy* • David Kossoff *Gecko* • Alfie Bass *Carrell* • Harry Secombe *Barizel* ■ *Dir* Noel Langley • *Scr* Noel Langley, from the novel *Trilby* by George du Maurier

Swades ★★★ U

Drama 2004 · Ind · Colour · 194mins

Ashutosh Gowariker (*Lagaan*) here directs another patriotic and thoughtful epic. Shah Rukh Khan stars as an ambitious Nasa scientist who returns to his native India in search of his childhood nanny (Kishori Ballal). This nostalgic journey soon finds him in the heartland of rural India, where Khan encounters poverty, injustice and a young village girl (Gayatri Joshi) with whom he falls in love. Khan rises to the challenge of portraying a frustrated patriot, perturbed by the lack of progress in his homeland. OA. In Hindi with English subtitles.

Shah Rukh Khan *Mohan Bhargava* • Gayatri Joshi *Gita* • Kishori Ballal *Kaveriamma* • Master Smit Sheth *Chikku* • Farrukh Jaffar *Fatimabi* • Dayashankar Pandey *Mela Ram* ■ *Dir* Ashutosh Gowariker • *Scr* Ashutosh Gowariker, from his story

Swallows and Amazons ★★★ U

Adventure 1974 · UK · Colour · 88mins

Lovingly photographed by Denis Lewiston, this is an engaging if hardly enthralling adaptation of the Arthur Ransome novel. Director Claude Whatham clearly revels in the innocence of this 1920s summer, when the four swallows and two amazons embarked upon their adventures, and he makes the most of the beautiful Lake District scenery. But the story stubbornly refuses to come to life and, sadly, few modern youngsters will relate to such old-fashioned game-playing. DP [video] DVD

Virginia McKenna *Mrs Walker* • Ronald Fraser *Uncle Jim* • Brenda Bruce *Mrs Dixon* • Jack Woolgar *Old Billy* • John Franklyn-Robbins *Young Billy* • Simon West *John* • Zanna Hamilton *Susan* • Sophie Neville *Titty* ■ *Dir* Claude Whatham • *Scr* David Wood, from the novel by Arthur Ransome

Swamp Thing ★★ 15

Horror 1982 · US · Colour · 84mins

Wes Craven's terminally campy adaptation of the eco-friendly DC comic book character is a trivial pursuit into juvenile territory for the horror director. Ray Wise is transformed into the half-man/half-slime creature after an accident with a plant growth stimulant and battles evil genius Louis Jourdan, who sees the formula as a way to gain world domination. Adrienne Barbeau goes way beyond the call of duty as the vague heroine valiantly getting knocked around. Despite the tacky special effects, cheap budget and banal dialogue, this was successful enough for a sequel, *The Return of Swamp Thing*. AJ [video] DVD

Louis Jourdan *Arcane* • Adrienne Barbeau *Alice Cable* • Ray Wise *Dr Alec Holland* • David Hess *Ferret* • Nicholas Worth *Bruno* • Don Knight *Ritter* • Al Ruban *Charlie* • Dick Durock *Swamp Thing* ■ *Dir/Scr* Wes Craven

Swamp Water ★★

Thriller 1941 · US · BW · 89mins

Like other European émigrés, the gifted French director Jean Renoir went to Hollywood to escape the Nazi occupation. But this, the first of his American films, was a disappointment. He was plunged in at the deep end in the isolated setting of the Georgia swampland, where escaped convict Walter Brennan hides and befriends trapper Dana Andrews. It's a story that needs more explanation and a deeper understanding. TH

Walter Brennan *Tom Keefer* • Walter Huston *Thursday Ragan* • Anne Baxter *Julie* • Dana Andrews *Ben Ragan* • Virginia Gilmore *Mabel Mckenzie* • John Carradine *Jesse Wick* • Mary Howard *Hannah* • Eugene Pallette *Jeb McKane* ■ *Dir* Jean Renoir • *Scr* Dudley Nichols, from a story by Vereen Bell

S

The Swan ★★★ U

Romantic drama
1956 · US · Colour · 107mins

Best known today as Grace Kelly's final Hollywood production (it was released before *High Society*, though made after it), this features the star playing a very MGM version of a princess in a lavish adaptation of a hoary old play by Ferenc Molnar. The beautiful Kelly is in love with handsome tutor Louis Jourdan, but she's officially betrothed to prince Alec Guinness. Director Charles Vidor understands this glossy tosh and films it beautifully, but Guinness (in his first American film) is miscast. TS

Grace Kelly *Princess Alexandra* • Alec Guinness *Prince Albert* • Louis Jourdan *Dr Nicholas Agi* • Agnes Moorehead *Queen Maria Dominika* • Jessie Royce Landis *Princess Beatrix* • Brian Aherne *Father Hyacinth* • Leo G Carroll *Caesar* • Estelle Winwood *Symphorosa* ■ *Dir* Charles Vidor • *Scr* John Dighton, from the play by Ferenc Molnar

The Swan Princess ★★★ U

Animated musical fairy tale
1994 · US · Colour · 85mins

A brave bid to produce a Disneyesque feature on a fraction of the budget, this politically correct fairy tale is entertaining enough, but it lacks the sparkle of the films it's trying to emulate. Director Richard Rich and character designer Steve Gordon, both Disney old boys, know the formula, but some rather uninspired artwork and the feeble songs undercut the neat reworking of *Swan Lake*. Jack Palance makes a booming Rothbart, while John Cleese is great fun as a French frog. Odette is feisty, but Prince Derek is a bit of a drip. Two modest sequels followed. DP DVD

Jack Palance *Rothbart* • John Cleese *Jean-Bob* • Howard McGillin *Prince Derek* • Michelle Nicastro *Princess Odette* • Steven Wright *Speed* ■ *Dir* Richard Rich • *Scr* Brian Nissen, from a story by Richard Rich, Brian Nissen • *Animator* Steven E Gordon

Swanee River ★★ U

Musical biography
1939 · US · Colour · 86mins

Don Ameche plays composer Stephen Foster (*Beautiful Dreamer*) in 20th Century-Fox's unintentionally camp biopic, in which every cliché uttered becomes a cue for a song. Naturally enough, he wants to pen symphonies, but finds he can't stop drowning his sorrows. Andrea Leeds is his luckless spouse, but the surprise casting of the movie is the great Al Jolson himself as EP Christy, the forerunner of the black-faced minstrels. Unfortunately, Fox's garish Technicolor makes him look as though he's fallen into a tub of boot polish. Not high on taste. TS

Don Ameche *Stephen Foster* • Al Jolson *EP Christy* • Andrea Leeds *Jane* • Felix Bressart *Henry Kleber* • Chick Chandler *Bones* • Russell Hicks *Andrew McDowell* • George Reed *Old Joe* ■ *Dir* Sidney Lanfield • *Scr* John Taintor Foote, Philip Dunne

Swann ★★★★ 15

Drama 1996 · Can/UK · Colour · 91mins

An elegant, passionate meditation on feminism. Bestselling author Miranda Richardson arrives at a small Canadian town to prepare a biography of local poet, Mary Swann, murdered by her husband. Brenda Fricker was Mary's closest friend and the film examines Richardson's growing relationship with her as she unravels the secrets of Swann's tragic death. Adapted from a novel by Carol Shields and directed by Anna Benson Gyles, it's a small film of great impact. TH DVD

Miranda Richardson *Sarah Maloney* • Brenda Fricker *Rose Hindmarch* • Michael Ontkean *Stephen* • David Cubitt *Brownie* • John Neville *Cruzzi* • Sean McCann *Homer* • Sean Hewitt *Morton Jimroy* ■ *Dir* Anna Benson Gyles • *Scr* David Young, from the novel by Carol Shields

Swann in Love ★★ 18

Drama 1984 · Fr/W Ger · Colour · 105mins

Jeremy Irons makes a pig's ear out of Proust's novel *Un Amour de Swann*. As the French aristocrat, Irons scampers after working-class totty Ornella Muti through the scummy streets of Paris. His lust is fulfilled, but he remains lovelorn, troubled by the fact that he genuinely cares for her. Alain Delon is more charismatic as the gay, butch Baron and Muti is suitably smutty and sexy, but this is an awkward affair that lacks any true passion. LH. In French with English subtitles.

Jeremy Irons *Charles Swann* • Ornella Muti *Odette de Crecy* • Alain Delon *Baron de Charlus* • Fanny Ardant *Duchesse de Guermantes* • Marie-Christine Barrault *Mrs Vedurin* • Anne Bennent *Chloe* • Nathalie Juvent *Madame Cottard* ■ *Dir* Volker Schlöndorff • *Scr* Peter Brook, Jean-Claude Carrière, Marie-Hélène Estienne, Volker Schlöndorff, from the novel *Un Amour de Swann* by Marcel Proust

The Swarm ★ 12

Disaster movie 1978 · US · Colour · 148mins

African killer bees are moving west and threatening to engulf Houston, Texas. Quick, call on entomologist Michael Caine and a hive of Hollywood has-beens to out-ham each other while reciting terrible dialogue and getting stung by coloured Styrofoam pellets! AJ DVD

Michael Caine *Brad Crane* • Katharine Ross *Helena* • Richard Widmark *General Slater* • Richard Chamberlain *Dr Hubbard* • Olivia de Havilland *Maureen Schuster* • Ben Johnson *Felix* • Lee Grant *Anne MacGregor* • José Ferrer *Dr Andrews* • Patty Duke Astin [Patty Duke] *Rita Bard* • Fred MacMurray *Clarence* ■ *Dir* Irwin Allen • *Scr* Stirling Silliphant, from the novel by Arthur Herzog

Swashbuckler ★★★ PG

Swashbuckling adventure
1976 · US · Colour · 96mins

Unfairly dismissed at the time, this was a genuine attempt by Universal to re-create the kind of adventure film it used to deliver by the dozen: the good-natured pirate romp. Originally retitled *The Scarlet Buccaneer* for the UK, it evoked fond memories of its star's foray into similar territory on TV: a generation will recall a pre-*Jaws* Robert Shaw as swashbuckling Dan Tempest in the 1950s series *The Buccaneers*. Shaw does well here, romancing lovely Geneviève Bujold and swapping riddles with James Earl Jones, but there was no audience for this kind of derring-do in the 1970s. TS

Robert Shaw *Ned Lynch* • James Earl Jones *Nick Debrett* • Peter Boyle *Lord Durant* • Geneviève Bujold *Jane Barnet* • Beau Bridges *Major Folly* • Geoffrey Holder *Cudjo* • Avery Schreiber *Polonski* • Anjelica Huston *Woman of Dark Visage* ■ *Dir* James Goldstone • *Scr* Jeffrey Bloom, from a story by Paul Wheeler

SWAT ★★ 12

Police action thriller
2003 · US · Colour · 112mins

A billionaire international terrorist offers $100 million to the criminal who springs him from US custody. Then a SWAT (Special Weapons and Tactics) team has to escort him across LA while every hoodlum not locked up tries for the bounty. For the rest, this half-baked misfire follows Colin Farrell's interminable retraining as a SWAT officer. Farrell is bland, Samuel L Jackson appears to be aware he's slumming it and the result is leaden. AS DVD

Samuel L Jackson *Sgt Dan "Hondo" Harrelson* • Colin Farrell (2) *Jim Street* • Michelle Rodriguez *Chris Sanchez* • James Todd Smith [LL Cool J] *Deacon "Deke" Kaye* • Josh Charles *TJ McCabe* • Jeremy Renner *Brian Gamble* • Brian Van Holt *Michael Boxer* • Olivier Martinez *Alex Montel* ■ *Dir* Clark Johnson • *Scr* David Ayer, David McKenna, from a story by Ron Mita, Jim McClain, from characters created by Robert Hamner

Swearing Allegiance ★★ 15

Crime drama based on a true story
1997 · US · Colour · 89mins

The real-life case on which this TV movie is based made headline news all over the US, although British viewers may wonder what all the fuss is about. The story involves childhood sweethearts Diane Zamora and David Graham (played by Holly Marie Combs and David Lipper), who make a murderous pact after Graham confesses to sleeping with another girl. The performances can't be faulted, but director Richard A Colla's execution is nothing special. JF

Holly Marie Combs *Diane Zamora* • David Lipper *David Graham* • Cassidy Rae *Adrienne Jones* • Dee Wallace Stone *Linda Jones* ■ *Dir* Richard A Colla • *Scr* Steve Johnson

Swedenhielms ★★★

Drama 1935 · Swe · BW · 92mins

Directed by the great Gustav Molander, this was Ingrid Bergman's third film and, while she gives a wholehearted performance as an heiress hoping to marry into the family of a talented but poor scientist, the critics of the day considered her no more than "feelingful". The real star of the show, however, is Gösta Ekman as the scientist, while Karin Swanstrom also impresses as the sister-in-law who averts a scandal. DP. In Swedish with English subtitles.

Gösta Ekman (1) *Rolf Swedenhielm* • Karin Swanstrom *Marta Boman* • Bjorn Berglund *Rolf Swedenhielm Jr* • Håkan Westergren *Bo Swedenhielm* • Tutta Rolf *Julia Swedenhielm* • Ingrid Bergman *Astrid* ■ *Dir* Gustaf Molander • *Scr* Stina Bergman, Gustaf Molander, from the play by Hjalmar Bergman

Sweeney! ★★★ 18

Police drama 1976 · UK · Colour · 92mins

Not in the same manor as the legendary TV series, this spin-off is a reasonable reminder of what made John Thaw and Dennis Waterman the icons of 1970s law enforcement. Screenwriter Ranald Graham's unfamiliarity with the characters occasionally brings the action to a screeching halt. However, he cranks out a typically abrasive plot, which sees the boys investigating a suicide only to find themselves knee-deep in vice, blackmail and corruption. DP. Contains violence, swearing and nudity. DVD

John Thaw *Detective Inspector Regan* • Dennis Waterman *Detective Sergeant Carter* • Barry Foster *McQueen* • Ian Bannen *Baker* • Colin Welland *Chadwick* • Diane Keen *Bianca* • Brian Glover *Mac* • Lynda Bellingham *Janice* ■ *Dir* David Wickes • *Scr* Ranald Graham, from the TV series by Ian Kennedy Martin

Sweeney 2 ★★ 18

Police drama 1978 · UK · Colour · 103mins

In this second, dated-looking spin-off from the popular 1970s TV series, flying-squadders John Thaw and Dennis Waterman tackle upper-bracket bank robbers who fly in for each job to maintain their Mediterranean lifestyle. The leads struggle with material that would have barely filled a 50-minute television slot, let alone a full-length cinema feature. DA Contains violence. DVD

John Thaw *Detective Inspector Jack Regan* • Dennis Waterman *Detective Sergeant George Carter* • Denholm Elliott *Jupp* • David Casey *Goodyear* • Ken Hutchison *Hill* • Nigel Hawthorne *Dilke* • John Flanagan *Willard* • Derrick O'Connor *Llewellyn* ■ *Dir* Tom Clegg • *Scr* Troy Kennedy Martin, from the TV series by Ian Kennedy Martin

Sweeney Todd, the Demon Barber of Fleet Street ★★★

Horror 1936 · UK · BW · 66mins

Tod Slaughter was billed as "the Horror Man of Europe" for his forays into early chiller territory with titles such as *Murder in the Red Barn* and *Crimes at the Dark House*. As the legendary throat-slitting barber, the aptly-named Slaughter turns in what every genre historian agrees is a quintessential performance. He's at his highly theatrical, villainous best in this dainty slice of British horror and, if you can ignore the creaks, this film is melodramatic fun. AJ

Tod Slaughter *Sweeney Todd* • Eve Lister *Johanna* • Bruce Seton *Mack* • Davina Craig *Nan* • DJ Williams *Stephen Oakley* • Jerry Verno *Pearley* ■ *Dir* George King • *Scr* Frederick Hayward, HF Maltby, from the play by George Dibdin-Pitt

Sweepers ★★ 15

Action thriller 1999 · US · Colour · 92mins

In a standard action movie that has a veneer of political correctness, Dolph Lundgren plays a landmine clearance expert who disappears into the Angolan wilderness after his young son is killed. Lundgren is found by bomb squad boffin Clare Stansfield and recruited to track down the lethal new A6 super-mine that's in the hands of terrorists. Video favourite Bruce Payne offers solid support. JF DVD

Dolph Lundgren *Christian Erickson* • Claire Stansfield *Michelle Flynn* • Bruce Payne *Cecil Hopper* • Ian Roberts *Yager* • Fats Bookholane *Old Mo* • Sifiso Maphanga *Arthur* ■ *Dir* Darby Black [Keoni Waxman] • *Scr* Darby Black [Keoni Waxman], Kevin Bernhardt

Sweet Adeline ★★

Period musical 1935 · US · BW · 87mins

A sweet-as-honey Irene Dunne takes the title role in this period (late 19th-century) musical, set in Hoboken, New Jersey where Adeline is adored by all the men who frequent her father's lovely beer garden. Spoilt for choice, she finally settles for songwriter Donald Woods. Directed by Mervyn LeRoy with dances staged by Bobby Connolly, this otherwise unremarkable, overly winsome and dull movie is partly redeemed by the Jerome Kern-Oscar Hammerstein II songs. RK

Irene Dunne *Adeline Schmidt* • Donald Woods *Sid Barnett* • Hugh Herbert *Rupert Rockingham* • Ned Sparks *Dan Herziq* • Joseph Cawthorn *Oscar Schmidt* ■ *Dir* Mervyn LeRoy • *Scr* Irwin S Gelsey, from a musical by Jerome Kern, Oscar Hammerstein II

Sweet and Lowdown ★★

Musical romantic drama
1944 · US · BW · 76mins

Aspiring trombone player (James Cardwell) is given his chance by Benny Goodman and goes on the road with the orchestra. But his youthful arrogance and swollen head almost put him back where he started. A minor entry from Fox, this moral tale-cum-romance with a fairy-tale outcome, directed by journeyman Archie Mayo, is anodyne entertainment but with enough music to please fans of Goodman, who plays himself. RK

Linda Darnell *Trudy Wilson* • James Cardwell *Johnny Birch* • Lynn Bari *Pat Sterling* • Jack Oakie *Popsy* • Allyn Joslyn *Lester Barnes* • John Campbell *Dixie Zang* • Roy Benson *Skeets McCormick* • Dickie Moore *General Carmichael* • Benny Goodman ■ *Dir* Archie Mayo • *Scr* Richard English, from a story by Richard English, Edward Haldeman

S

Sweet and Lowdown

★★★★ PG

Period comedy drama
1999 · US · Colour · 91mins

After the disappointing *Celebrity*, Woody Allen returned to form with this sparkling comedy drama about a fictional 1930s jazzman whose life only makes sense when he's playing guitar. Sean Penn plays a kleptomaniac musical genius whose idea of a good time is to watch trains, shoot rats and seduce women. Happiness comes in a sweetly fulfilling relationship with mute innocent Samantha Morton, though the feckless Penn is soon up to his old tricks with society gal Uma Thurman. The costumes and production design are splendidly opulent, but it's Morton who steals the show. NS DVD

Sean Penn *Emmet Ray* • Samantha Morton *Hattie* • Uma Thurman *Blanche* • Brian Markinson *Bill Shields* • Anthony LaPaglia *Al Torrio* • Gretchen Mol *Ellie* • Vincent Guastaferro *Sid Bishop* • John Waters (2) *Mr Haynes* • Woody Allen ■ *Dir/Scr* Woody Allen • *Cinematographer* Zhao Fei • *Production Designer* Santo Loquasto

Sweet Angel Mine

★ 18

Psychological drama
1996 · UK/Can · Colour · 84mins

Shocking secrets are revealed when city teen Oliver Milburn goes to the bleak Canadian backwoods looking for his long-lost father. For barmy mother Alberta Watson kills any man lusting after her daughter Margaret Langrick and buries the victims in her "garden of dead roses". Director Curtis Radclyffe can't decide what sort of film he's making here – an exploitation horror movie complete with graphic gore, or a showy slice of art house surrealism taking an academic look at the taboo subjects of incest and child abuse. Pretentious. AJ

Oliver Milburn *Paul Davis* • Margaret Langrick *Rauchine* • Anna Massey *Mother* • Alberta Watson *Megan* • John Dunsworth *Billy Lee Davis* • Mike Crimp *Sergeant Taylor* ■ *Dir* Curtis Radclyffe • *Scr* Sam Maheu, Tim Willocks

Sweet Bird of Youth

★★★ 15

Melodrama 1962 · US · Colour · 115mins

The ingredients of Tennessee Williams's original stage play (racism, substance abuse, male prostitution, castration) are present, if muted in this bleak entertainment. The play, directed by Elia Kazan, starred Paul Newman and Geraldine Page. The movie, directed by Richard Brooks, retained the original leads and toned down the text for audiences in the conservative American Midwest. Despite obvious flaws, it's a polished production, with fine supporting performances from Rip Torn and Ed Begley, who won the best supporting actor Oscar. Elizabeth Taylor starred in a 1989 TV movie remake. AT

Paul Newman *Chance Wayne* • Geraldine Page *Alexandra Del Lago* • Ed Begley *"Boss" Finley* • Shirley Knight *Heavenly Finley* • Rip Torn *Thomas J Finley Jr* • Mildred Dunnock *Aunt Nonnie* • Madeleine Sherwood *Miss Lucy* • Philip Abbott *Dr George Scudder* ■ *Dir* Richard Brooks • *Scr* Richard Brooks, from the play by Tennessee Williams

Sweet Charity

★★★ PG

Musical comedy 1968 · US · Colour · 142mins

Dancer, theatre director and choreographic genius Bob Fosse made his film directing debut when he brought his Broadway hit to the screen. Based on Fellini's *Nights of Cabiria*, the musical was transposed to New York and chronicles the sad life of a dance-hall hostess whose sleazy experiences fail to dampen her belief in fairy-tale romance. Though it's jam-packed with stunning numbers, the film is brash, gaudy and overheated and lacks the sophisticated edge and sharp impact of the stage original, with Shirley MacLaine's turbine-powered Charity substituting energy for subtlety. However Sammy Davis Jr, Chita Rivera and Paula Kelly are as electrifying as Fosse's choreography. RK DVD

Shirley MacLaine *Charity Hope Valentine* • Sammy Davis Jr *Big Daddy* • Ricardo Montalban *Vittorio Vitale* • John McMartin *Oscar* • Chita Rivera *Nickie* • Paula Kelly *Helene* • Stubby Kaye *Herman* ■ *Dir* Bob Fosse • *Scr* Peter Stone, from the musical by Neil Simon, Cy Coleman, Dorothy Fields, from the film *Nights of Cabiria* by Federico Fellini, Ennio Flaiano, Tullio Pinelli

Sweet Dreams

★★★ 15

Biographical drama
1985 · US · Colour · 109mins

Having already produced the Loretta Lynn biopic *Coal Miner's Daughter*, Bernard Schwartz here turned his attention to her friendly rival for the Queen of Country title, Patsy Cline. The result is a film packed with fine acting and superb singing (provided, via record, by Cline herself). Unfortunately, the life story is pretty unremarkable, consequently, the sparks between Jessica Lange and Ed Harris ignite nothing but their scenes together, giving the action a disappointingly staccato rhythm. DP DVD

Jessica Lange *Patsy Cline* • Ed Harris *Charlie Dick* • Ann Wedgeworth *Hilda Hensley* • David Clennon *Randy Hughes* • James Staley *Gerald Cline* • Gary Basaraba *Woodhouse* • John Goodman *Otis* • PJ Soles *Wanda* ■ *Dir* Karel Reisz • *Scr* Robert Getchell

Sweet Emma Dear Böbe

★★★★ 18

Drama 1992 · Hun · Colour · 77mins

István Szabó demonstrates a sure grasp of contemporary reality in this despondent study of the newly liberated Hungary. Forced to abandon their careers as Russian teachers on the fall of Communism, Johanna Ter Steege and Enikő Börcsök personify the options open to a society emerging from decades of oppression. Reining in his fondness for stylistic flourish – yet barely suppressing his anger – Szabó struggles to find the light at the end of this dark passage of transition, as Ter Steege pursues a hopeless affair with her tyrannical headmaster and Börcsök flirts with rich foreign tourists. DP. A Hungarian language film.

Johanna Ter Steege *Emma* • Eniko Borcsok *Böbe* • Peter Andorai *Stefanics* • Eva Kerekes *Sleepy* ■ *Dir* István Szabó • *Scr* István Szabó, from an idea by Andrea Veszits

Sweet Hearts Dance

★★★ 15

Comedy drama 1988 · US · Colour · 96mins

Don Johnson and Susan Sarandon are high school sweethearts who've been married for 15 years and have three children. Then Johnson realises he doesn't love his wife any more, just as his best buddy, Jeff Daniels, gets himself a new girlfriend. Scripted by Ernest Thompson, writer of *On Golden Pond*, this is a slightly ponderous study of marital angst, often warm and witty but lacking real bite. There are good performances, though. AT. Contains swearing and nudity.

Don Johnson *Wiley Boon* • Susan Sarandon *Sandra Boon* • Jeff Daniels *Sam Manners* • Elizabeth Perkins *Adie Nims* • Kate Reid *Pearne Manners* • Justin Henry *Kyle Boon* • Holly Marie Combs *Debs Boon* • Heather Coleman *BJ Boon* ■ *Dir* Robert Greenwald • *Scr* Ernest Thompson

The Sweet Hereafter

★★★★ 15

Psychological drama
1997 · Can · Colour · 107mins

Atom Egoyan won the Grand Jury prize at Cannes and was also Oscar nominated for his direction and adaptation of Russell Banks's novel about the impact of a schoolbus crash (which kills 14 children) on a small Canadian community. Although the Pied Piper analogy is overemphasised, this is still an intricate and involving drama, in which the town's guilty secrets are slowly revealed as ambulance-chasing lawyer Ian Holm tries to persuade the bereaved to sue for damages. With Sarah Polley outstanding as a survivor paralysed by the accident, this is intense, atmospheric and deeply moving. DP. Contains swearing, nudity. DVD

Ian Holm *Mitchell Stephens* • Sarah Polley *Nicole Burnell* • Bruce Greenwood *Billy Ansell* • Tom McCamus *Sam Burnell* • Gabrielle Rose *Dolores Driscoll* • Arsinée Khanjian *Wanda Otto* • Alberta Watson *Risa Walker* • Maury Chaykin *Wendell Walker* ■ *Dir* Atom Egoyan • *Scr* Atom Egoyan, from the novel by Russell Banks

Sweet Home Alabama

★★ 12

Romantic comedy
2002 · US · Colour · 104mins

Reese Witherspoon stars here as a New York-residing, Alabama-raised fashion designer who needs a divorce from her childhood sweetheart so she can marry socialite Patrick Dempsey. She heads home, bristling with snobbish attitude, only to step into a corny Dixieland fantasy that opens her eyes sufficiently to blind her to the problems that caused her to abandon husband Josh Lucas in the first place. Negligible, but charming. DP DVD

Reese Witherspoon *Melanie Carmichael* • Josh Lucas *Jake Perry* • Patrick Dempsey *Andrew Hennings* • Candice Bergen *Kate* • Mary Kay Place *Pearl Smooter* • Fred Ward *Earl Smooter* • Jean Smart *Stella Kay* • Ethan Embry *Bobby Ray* ■ *Dir* Andy Tennant • *Scr* C Jay Cox, from a story by Douglas J Eboch

Sweet Hunters

★★★★

Drama 1969 · Pan · Colour · 100mins

This resolutely arty effort is about an American who lives with his wife and son on a private island. The arrival of the professor's sister-in-law starts to upset the already delicate balance of relationships. Then an escaped convict lands on the island. Some viewers may tire of this soul-searching drama after 20 minutes, but others will find it riveting, mainly due to Sterling Hayden's performance in which all of the actor's physical power and emotional weakness, as well as his troubled history, is laid open like a festering wound. AT

Sterling Hayden *Allan* • Maureen McNally *Clea* • Susan Strasberg *Lis* • Andrew Hayden *Bob* • Stuart Whitman *Prisoner* ■ *Dir* Ruy Guerra • *Scr* Ruy Guerra, Philippe Dumarçay, Gérard Zingg

Sweet Liberty

★★★ 15

Comedy 1986 · US · Colour · 101mins

Compared with *The Player*, this is little more than a mild nip at the movie world. However, there are still plenty of laughs to be had as small-town college professor Alan Alda (writer/director/star) gets sucked into the ego-ridden lives of a movie crew when they make a film based on his American War of Independence novel. Michael Caine steals the show as the womanising lead, but there is handsome support from Michelle Pfeiffer, Bob Hoskins and Saul Rubinek. Overall, though, the requisite bite is missing. JF. Contains some swearing and brief nudity.

Alan Alda *Michael Burgess* • Michael Caine *Elliott James* • Michelle Pfeiffer *Faith Healy* • Bob Hoskins *Stanley Gould* • Lise Hilboldt *Gretchen Carlsen* • Lillian Gish *Cecelia Burgess* • Saul Rubinek *Bo Hodges* • Lois Chiles *Leslie* ■ *Dir/Scr* Alan Alda

Sweet Nothing

★★ 18

Drama 1995 · US · Colour · 85mins

Mira Sorvino stars in this grim drama is about a white-collar worker who gets dragged into drug addiction. Three years after Michael Imperioli persuades his reluctant wife to agree to a three-month limited term of dealing crack in order to provide money for his family, they're both hooked: he to the drug, his wife to the money. His descent to rock bottom is portrayed without mercy to either the characters or the audience. FL. Contains swearing, violence.

Michael Imperioli *Angel* • Mira Sorvino *Monika* • Paul Calderon *Raymond* • Patrick Breen *Greg* • Richard Bright *Jack the Cop* • Billie Neal *Rio* ■ *Dir* Gary Winick • *Scr* Lee Drysdale

Sweet November

★★

Comedy drama 1968 · US · Colour · 112mins

Suffering from a chronic case of the cutes, Sandy Dennis and Anthony Newley star in an oddly effective, but eccentric tragicomedy. She's doing her best, as an amateur sex therapist, to take a lover a month to rid them of their inhibitions. Trouble is that November's lodger, tycoon Newley, wants to claim her permissive life all to himself. The idea works surprisingly well at first, but both stars seem to be in competition, trying to make irritating ad libs out of Herman Raucher's script. Exasperatingly coy. TH

Sandy Dennis *Sara Deever* • Anthony Newley *Charlie Blake* • Theodore Bikel *Alonzo* • Burr DeBenning *Clem Batchman* • Sandy Baron *Richard* • Marj Dusay *Carol* • Martin West *Gordon* ■ *Dir* Robert Ellis Miller • *Scr* Herman Raucher

Sweet November

★★ 12

Romantic drama
2001 · US · Colour · 115mins

Keanu Reeves takes the lead role of a narcissistic ad executive who gets too big for his Gucci slip-ons and ends up jobless. Vexed and confused, he encounters free-spirited Charlize Theron who out of the blue offers to be his November – she will commit herself to him for one month and in that time turn him into a nicer person. Love is in the air, but when Reeves wants to continue into December, he uncovers Theron's deep dark secret. The two leads are endearing, but this is too sickly sweet. LH DVD

Keanu Reeves *Nelson Moss* • Charlize Theron *Sara Deever* • Jason Isaacs *Chaz* • Frank Langella *Edgar Price* ■ *Dir* Pat O'Connor • *Scr* Kurt Voelker, from a story by Paul Yurick, Kurt Voelker, from the 1968 film

The Sweet Ride

★★

Drama 1967 · US · Colour · 109mins

Jacqueline Bisset fans covet this picture about the beach culture of southern California. It was Bisset's first major role in a Hollywood picture. Yes, one does miss Frankie Avalon, Fabian and Annette Funicello, but this is much more grown-up stuff that even alludes to the Vietnam War. Bisset plays a TV soap star who drops her producer for an affair with Michael Sarrazin, a tennis hustler. AT

Tony Franciosa [Anthony Franciosa] *Collie Ransom* • Michael Sarrazin *Denny McGuire* • Jacqueline Bisset *Vicki Cartwright, actress* • Bob Denver *Choo-Choo Burns, jazz pianist* • Michael Wilding *Mr Cartwright* • Michele Carey

S

Thumper • Norma Crane *Mrs Cartwright* ■ *Dir* Harvey Hart • *Scr* Tom Mankiewicz, from the novel by William Murray

Sweet Rosie O'Grady ★★★ U

Musical comedy 1943 · US · Colour · 75mins

An extremely entertaining 20th Century-Fox Technicolor musical and a vehicle for Betty Grable; for many that's recommendation enough. It's all about a burlesque queen and an inquisitive reporter (Robert Young). Set in late-19th century London, Adolphe Menjou is particularly watchable as the editor of the *Police Gazette*. TS

Betty Grable *Madeleine Marlowe* • Robert Young (1) *Sam MacKeever* • Adolphe Menjou *Morgan* • Reginald Gardiner *Duke Charles* • Virginia Grey *Edna Van Dyke* • Phil Regan *Composer* • Sig Rumann [Sig Ruman] *Joe Flugelman* • Alan Dinehart *Arthur Skinner* ■ *Dir* Irving Cummings • *Scr* Ken Englund, from a story by William R Lipman, Frederick Stephani, Edward Van Every

Sweet Sixteen ★★★★ 18

Drama
2002 · UK/Ger/Sp/Fr/It · Colour · 101mins

This grim, but moving slice of life is the fourth collaboration between Ken Loach and writer Paul Laverty. Liam, whose approaching birthday gives the film its title, is played with astonishing clarity and depth by non-professional actor Martin Compston. He is chasing the dream of a caravan for his currently imprisoned, ex-junkie mum and, paradoxically, it is through drug-dealing that he hopes to pay for it. In the process he crosses local gangsters and jeopardises relationships with his older sister and joyriding best pal, William Ruane. Hopes may be systematically dashed in this unforgiving world, but Loach and Laverty invest maximum humanity in the central character. AC. With English subtitles. Contains violence, swearing and drug abuse. DVD

Martin Compston *Liam* • William Ruane *Pinball* • Annmarie Fulton *Chantelle* • Michelle Abercromby *Suzanne* • Michelle Coulter *Jean* • Gary McCormack *Stan* • Tommy McKee *Rab* ■ *Dir* Ken Loach • *Scr* Paul Laverty

Sweet Smell of Success ★★★★★ PG

Satirical drama 1957 · US · BW · 92mins

Not a box-office success in its day, this mordant satire has rightly picked up admirers over the years, and is at long last recognised for the classic that it is. It contains key career highs for Burt Lancaster, as a vicious Broadway columnist, and Tony Curtis as the hustling press agent totally under his all-powerful thumb. Lancaster's relationship with his sister Susan Harrison is particularly perverse, and provides the plot thrust for the Faustian pact, which is still relevant in an era of dubious media ethics. Diamond-hard photography from the great James Wong Howe and a sizzling Clifford Odets screenplay contribute immeasurably to this film's brutal quality, and it remains a milestone tribute to its canny British director Alexander Mackendrick. TS DVD

Burt Lancaster *JJ Hunsecker* • Tony Curtis *Sidney Falco* • Susan Harrison *Susan Hunsecker* • Martin Milner *Steve Dallas* • Sam Levene *Frank D'Angelo* • Barbara Nichols *Rita* • Jeff Donnell *Sally* • Joseph Leon *Robard* ■ *Dir* Alexander Mackendrick • *Scr* Clifford Odets, Ernest Lehman, from the short story *Tell Me About It* by Ernest Lehman • *Music* Elmer Bernstein

Sweet Sweetback's Baad Asssss Song ★★★★ 18

Blaxploitation 1971 · US · Colour · 92mins

An important feature in the history of black film-making in the States, this is an angry riposte to the stereotypical characters that exist in both mainstream and blaxploitation pictures. Written, directed, edited and scored by its star, Melvin Van Peebles, it can be loosely labelled a road movie, yet the relentless stream of sex, violence and prejudice, described with a mixture of realism, artifice and grim humour, isn't supposed to entertain, but rather incite. Still astonishing 30 years after its controversial release. DP. Contains swearing and nudity.

Melvin Van Peebles *Sweetback* • Simon Chuckster *Beetle* • Hubert Scales *Mu-Mu* • John Dullaghan (1) *Commissioner* • Rhetta Hughes *Old girlfriend* ■ *Dir/Scr* Melvin Van Peebles

Sweet Torture ★★

Drama 1971 · Fr · Colour · 90mins

This could have been a sobering exposé of police brutality and corrupt detective practices. However, Edouard Molinaro overcooks the interrogation of Marc Porel, who is prepared to shop his partner (he killed a ticket clerk during a raid on a circus) in order to marry his loyal girlfriend, Caroline Cellier. But sadistic inspectors Philippe Noiret and Roger Hanin try to beat a self-incriminating confession out of him. For all the melodramatic fireworks, Molinaro doesn't seem interested in either theme or character. DP. French dialogue dubbed into English.

Philippe Noiret *Chief Inspector* • Roger Hanin *Insp Borelli* • Marc Porel *Dubreuilh* • Caroline Cellier *Catherine* ■ *Dir* Edouard Molinaro • *Scr* JF Hauduroy, Edouard Molinaro, from a play by Georges Arnaud

Sweet William ★★

Drama 1980 · UK · Colour · 91mins

A rather languid drama, adapted from her own novel by Beryl Bainbridge and directed by Claude Whatham. Sam Waterston plays a Scot with a bevy of ex-wives and girlfriends; Jenny Agutter falls for him and lives to regret it. Despite the presence of a decent cast, this portrait of a rather unpleasant cad lacks a real cutting edge. AT. Contains some swearing and nudity.

Sam Waterston *William McClusky* • Jenny Agutter *Ann Walton* • Anna Massey *Edna* • Geraldine James *Pamela* • Daphne Oxenford *Mrs Walton* • Rachel Bell *Mrs Kershaw* • David Wood *Vicar* • Tim Pigott-Smith *Gerald* ■ *Dir* Claude Whatham • *Scr* Beryl Bainbridge, from her novel

The Sweetest Thing ★★★ 15

Romantic comedy
2002 · US · Colour · 86mins

Director Roger Kumble gives crass humour a feminine edge in this bright and frothy take on the "chick flick". Essentially a straight romantic comedy clothed in Farrelly brothers-style laughs, it emphasises that women can be just as irreverent as their male counterparts. The end result is something akin to a celluloid hen night, as serial heart-breaker Cameron Diaz and her two brash best friends (the hilarious Selma Blair and Christina Applegate) encounter the highs and lows of commitment-free love. SF. Contains swearing, nudity. DVD

Cameron Diaz *Christina Walters* • Christina Applegate *Courtney Rockliffe* • Thomas Jane *Peter Donahue* • Selma Blair *Jane Burns* • Jason Bateman *Roger Donahue* • Parker Posey *Judy Webb* • Lillian Adams *Aunt Frida* ■ *Dir* Roger Kumble • *Scr* Nancy M Pimental

Sweetheart of the Campus ★

Musical 1941 · US · BW · 64mins

This small-scale clanger of a campus musical marked both the return to the screen after a three-year absence of Ruby Keeler and (with the exception of a forgotten cameo) her permanent exit remarriage and retirement. The one-note, boring plot has something to do with bandleader Ozzie Nelson and his troupe involved with attempts to encourage intake at a college where student enrolment has dropped. RK

Ruby Keeler *Betty Blake* • Ozzie Nelson *Ozzie Norton* • Harriet Hilliard [Harriet Nelson] *Harriet Hale* • Gordon Oliver *Terry Jones* • Don Beddoe *Sheriff Denby* • Charles Judels *Victor Demond* • Kathleen Howard *Mrs Minnie Sparr* • Alan Hale Jr *Football player* ■ *Dir* Edward Dmytryk • *Scr* Robert D Andrews, Edmund Hartmann [Edmund L Hartmann], from a story by Robert D Andrews

Sweethearts ★★★

Musical comedy 1938 · US · Colour · 120mins

As the first-ever MGM feature filmed wholly in three-strip Technicolor (*The Wizard of Oz* was part colour, part sepia), this musical comedy has historical significance, though that same process tends to overshadow the popular star team of Jeanette MacDonald and Nelson Eddy. They warble through the Victor Herbert score and struggle through a brand new Dorothy Parker–Alan Campbell screenplay, but much of their thunder is stolen by dance-whiz Ray Bolger. The Broadway to Hollywood plot was well worn even then, but the production value more than compensate. TS

Jeanette MacDonald *Gwen Marlowe* • Nelson Eddy *Ernest Lane* • Frank Morgan *Felix Lehman* • Ray Bolger *Hans the dancer* • Florence Rice *Kay Jordan* • Mischa Auer *Leo Kronk* • Fay Holden *Hannah the dresser* ■ *Dir* WS Van Dyke II [WS Van Dyke] • *Scr* Dorothy Parker, Alan Campbell, from the operetta by Harry B Smith, Fred DeGresac, Robert B Smith, Victor Herbert

Sweetie ★★★★ 15

Comedy drama 1989 · Aus · Colour · 95mins

Director Jane Campion's first film for the cinema, this is a quirky and original movie that quickly established her as one of the most interesting directors working today. Part comedy, part drama, it follows the lives of two eccentric sisters and their equally unstable lovers when they come together under one roof. Like David Lynch's *Blue Velvet*, the film shows us the surreal side of surburbia, where even the most ordinary person is not what he or she seems. Funny, affecting and wonderful. JB. Contains swearing and nudity.

Geneviève Lemon *Dawn, "Sweetie"* • Karen Colston *Kay* • Tom Lycos *Louis* • Jon Darling *Gordon* • Dorothy Barry *Flo* • Michael Lake *Bob* • André Pataczek *Clayton* ■ *Dir* Jane Campion • *Scr* Gerard Lee, Jane Campion, from an idea by Jane Campion

Swell Guy ★★

Melodrama 1946 · US · BW · 86mins

The ironic title refers to a war correspondent (Sonny Tufts) who returns home to his brother and sister-in-law in a small town where he is fêted as a celebrity. But he is in fact a manipulative, dishonest bad apple who wreaks havoc on his brother's marriage, dishonours a wealthy local girl (Ann Blyth) and cons the citizenry. The film as directed by Frank Tuttle is solid in all departments, but winds up as disappointingly aimless. RK

Sonny Tufts *Jim Duncan* • Ann Blyth *Marian Tyler* • Ruth Warrick *Ann Duncan* • William Gargan *Martin Duncan* • John Litel *Arthur Tyler* • Thomas Gomez *Dave Vinson* • Millard Mitchell *Steve* • Mary Nash *Sarah Duncan* ■ *Dir* Frank Tuttle • *Scr* Richard Brooks, from the play *The Hero* by Gilbert Emery

Swept Away ★ 15

Romantic comedy drama
2002 · UK/It · Colour · 85mins

Guy Ritchie's insipid vehicle for his wife, Madonna, went straight to video in the UK and it's obvious to see why. This romantic comedy is a lifeless and occasionally misogynistic bore. Madonna's role here as a spoilt socialite stranded on an island with one of her hired boat's crew only cements her less than distinguished reputation as an actress. Ritchie's direction and script are unimaginative, and only Adriano Giannini as the boat slave-turned-desert-island master has any spark. SF DVD

Madonna *Amber* • Adriano Giannini *Giuseppe* • Jeanne Tripplehorn *Marina* • Bruce Greenwood *Anthony* • Elizabeth Banks (2) *Debi* • David Thornton *Michael* • Michael Beattie *Todd* • Yorgo Voyagis *Captain* ■ *Dir* Guy Ritchie • *Scr* Guy Ritchie, from the film *Swept Away... by an Unusual Destiny in the Blue Sea of August* by Lina Wertmuller

Swept Away... by an Unusual Destiny in the Blue Sea of August ★★ 18

Romantic comedy drama
1974 · It · Colour · 114mins

Predictable sparks fly when dismissive Milanese socialite Mariangela Melato and communist sailor Giancarlo Giannini wash up on a desert island during a yachting trip. Forced back to nature, their class differences crumble, with Melato seemingly thrilled by Giannini's increasingly macho posturing. However, in defending her film against a feminist backlash, Lina Wertmuller claimed that everyone had got it wrong and that Melato symbolised bourgeois male arrogance rather than submissive womanhood. Nice try, but for all its lushness and actorly commitment, this lacks the ironic wit to be that incisive. DP. An Italian language film. DVD

Giancarlo Giannini *Gennarino Carunchio* • Mariangela Melato *Raffaella Lanzetti* • Riccardo Salvino *Raffaela's husband* ■ *Dir/Scr* Lina Wertmuller

Swimfan ★★★ 12

Thriller 2002 · US/UK · Colour · 81mins

A tautly paced and sharply executed thriller, this reworks the familiar psychotic cycle of female obsession and revenge. It's a cautionary tale, apparently unaware of its own clichés, as new-girl-in-town Erika Christensen unleashes her fury on handsome high-school swimming champ Jesse Bradford when she realises her affection for him is unrequited. Despite the obvious plot, what viewers won't anticipate is just how nasty Christensen gets – Glenn Close's Alex was a mere pussycat compared to this nightmare incarnate. Intelligent and non-patronising. SF DVD

Jesse Bradford *Ben Cronin* • Erika Christensen *Madison Bell* • Shiri Appleby *Amy* • Dan Hedaya *Coach Simkins* • Kate Burton *Carla Cronin* • Clayne Crawford *Josh* • Jason Ritter *Randy* • Kia Joy Goodwin *Rene* ■ *Dir* John Polson • *Scr* Charles Bohl, Phillip Schneider

The Swimmer ★★★★ PG

Drama 1968 · US · Colour · 90mins

Based on a short story by cult writer John Cheever, this stars Burt Lancaster as a washed-up suburban man who decides to swim home, using all the pools in his neighbourhood en route. This is not only healthy – and Lancaster looks terrific in his trunks – it's a metaphor for alienation from affluence, sexual desire, Vietnam – you

S

U = SUITABLE FOR ALL Uc = SUITABLE FOR ALL, ESPECIALLY FOR YOUNG CHILDREN (VIDEO ONLY) PG = PARENTAL GUIDANCE

name it, it's all at the bottom of the deep end. Not to everyone's taste, this weird picture now seems an oddly powerful companion piece to *The Graduate*. AT [VIDEO] DVD

Burt Lancaster *Ned Merrill* • Janet Landgard *Julie Hooper* • Janice Rule *Shirley Abbott* • Tony Bickley *Donald Westerhazy* • Marge Champion *Peggy Forsburgh* • Nancy Cushman *Mrs Halloran* • Bill Fiore *Howie Hunsacker* ■ *Dir* Frank Perry • *Scr* Eleanor Perry, from the short story by John Cheever

The Swimming Pool ★★

Drama 1968 · Fr/It · Colour · 119mins

A pool in St Tropez provides the setting for this sexual roundelay. The men are two of France's biggest stars – Alain Delon and Maurice Ronet – and the women are Romy Schneider and Jane Birkin, in her first major role. It's a case of he fancies her, she fancies him and round and round they go, until someone ends up in the deep end. A bit too long and the plot doesn't really get anywhere, but the glam trappings have a certain retro appeal. AT. French dialogue dubbed into English.

Alain Delon *Jean-Paul* • Romy Schneider *Marianne* • Maurice Ronet *Harry* • Jane Birkin *Penelope* • Paul Crauchet *Inspector Levêque* ■ *Dir* Jacques Deray • *Scr* Jean-Emmanuel Conil, Jean-Claude Carrière, Jacques Deray

Swimming Pool ★★★★ 15

Psychological mystery drama
2003 · Fr/UK · Colour · 98mins

François Ozon continues to pry into the psyche of the vulnerable in this teasingly ambiguous study of creative angst and sexual tension. Yorick Le Saux's cinematography is key to establishing the contrast between the drab frustration of London and the scorching temptation of the southern French hideaway of Luberon. This in turn serves to reinforce the differences between Charlotte Rampling's emotionally repressed crime writer and publisher Charles Dance's carefree daughter, Ludivine Sagnier. This knowing film compels right up to its mischievous conclusion. DP. In French and English with subtitles. [VIDEO] DVD

Charlotte Rampling *Sarah Morton* • Ludivine Sagnier *Julie* • Charles Dance *John Bosload* • Marc Fayolle *Marcel* • Jean-Marie Lamour *Franck* • Mireille Mossé *Marcel's daughter* ■ *Dir* François Ozon • *Scr* François Ozon, Emmanuèle Bernheim

Swimming to Cambodia ★★★ 18

Satirical monologue
1987 · US · Colour · 77mins

Spalding Gray described his experiences filming *The Killing Fields* in a one-man stage show, here condensed into a shorter film by director Jonathan Demme. Covering the same ground – the appalling conflict and atrocities which happened in Cambodia – Gray basically delivers a monologue to camera, explaining his experiences in the film from casting to finding out about the Khmer Rouge. Criticised for being a self-aggrandising attempt to capitalise on his small role in the film, Gray insisted that he was trying to show how his experiences as an actor helped him understand the nature of war. He succeeds in his objective, making the horror of war clearer to the audience, too. LH [VIDEO]

Spalding Gray • Sam Waterston *Sydney Schanberg* • Ira Wheeler *Ambassador Wade* ■ *Dir* Jonathan Demme • *Scr* Spalding Gray, from his play

Swimming Upstream ★★ 12A

Biographical sports drama
2003 · Aus · Colour · 97mins

This classy, if somewhat bloodless true story is based on the life of Australian swimming champion Anthony Fingleton. Set mainly in the 1950s and 60s, it focuses on the troubled relationship between Tony (Jesse Spencer) and his father and coach (Geoffrey Rush). The alcoholic Fingleton Senior prefers to lavish his attention on Tony's brother John (Tim Draxl), a successful swimmer in his own right, which leads to increasing tension within the family. As good as Rush is, Judy Davis steals the show as his long-suffering wife, but even they struggle to make this any more than a standard sporting biopic. JF

Geoffrey Rush *Harold Fingleton* • Judy Davis *Dora Fingleton* • Jesse Spencer *Tony Fingleton* • Tim Draxl *John Fingleton* • David Hoflin *Harold Fingleton Jr* • Craig Horner *Ronald Fingleton* • Brittany Byrnes *Diane Fingleton* • Deborah Kennedy *Billie* ■ *Dir* Russell Mulcahy • *Scr* Anthony Fingleton, from the memoirs by Anthony Fingleton, Diane Fingleton

Swimming with Sharks ★★★ 15

Comedy 1994 · US · Colour · 89mins

This savage Tinseltown satire from director George Huang is often hilarious in between its bouts of numbingly bleak cynicism. Unfolding its story in a series of flashbacks, it features Frank Whaley as the hapless assistant of heartless Hollywood mogul Kevin Spacey, who enjoys exercising his power right down to the brand of sweetener he wants in his coffee. Spacey's dazzling portrayal of the acid-tongued executive is the most memorable facet of this tar-black comedy, which is heavy on industry in-jokes and vicious put-downs. AJ. Contains swearing, violence. [VIDEO] DVD

Kevin Spacey *Buddy Ackerman* • Frank Whaley *Guy* • Michelle Forbes *Dawn Lockard* • Benicio Del Toro *Rex* • TE Russell *Foster Kane* • Roy Dotrice *Cyrus Miles* • Matthew Flynt *Manny* ■ *Dir/Scr* George Huang

The Swindle ★★★ 12

Crime drama 1955 · Fr/It · BW · 91mins

The fabled prospect of Federico Fellini directing Humphrey Bogart haunts this biting tragicomedy, although Broderick Crawford still makes a decent fist of playing alongside Richard Basehart and Franco Fabrizi as the provincial conmen out to fleece the desolate, the devout and the disabled. Having posed as priests and petty bureaucrats, the gang disperses, only for Crawford to hook up with new confrères and be undone by a fatal pang of conscience. Determined to bury his neorealist past, Fellini achieves a cynical authenticity here that even undermines the faint optimism of his ambiguous finale. DP. An Italian language film. DVD

Broderick Crawford *Augusto* • Richard Basehart *Picasso* • Franco Fabrizi *Roberto* • Giulietta Masina *Iris* • Lorella De Luca *Patrizia* ■ *Dir* Federico Fellini • *Scr* Federico Fellini, Ennio Flaiano, Tullio Pinelli, from a story by Federico Fellini, Ennio Flaiano

Swing ★★★★

Drama 1983 · W Ger · Colour · 130mins

Percy Adlon's warmly nostalgic, almost carelessly episodic study of an unconventional family's eccentric adventures, has a zest one rarely associates with costume dramas. The endless round of garden parties, recitals, balls, theatre visits and encounters with royalty and celebrity sweeps along the willing imagination and evokes a glorious sense of the *joie de vivre* of childhood that contrasts so mischievously with the stiffness of singing teacher Christine Kaufmann and court gardener Rolf Illig, the disapproving Prussian neighbours. DP. A German language film.

Anja Jaenicke *Mathias Lautenschlag* • Joachim Bernhard *Otto Lautenschlag* • Lena Stolze *Gervaise Lautenschlag* • Rolf Illig *Herr Lautenschlag* • Christine Kaufmann *Mme Lautenschlag* ■ *Dir* Percy Adlon • *Scr* Percy Adlon, from the novel *Die Schaukel* by Annette Kolb

Swing ★★ 15

Musical comedy drama
1998 · UK · Colour · 93mins

In a piece of uninspired casting, singer Lisa Stansfield plays a singer in this run-of-the-mill Liverpudlian romantic comedy. She's the ex-girlfriend of ex-con Hugo Speer, who joins his swing band against the wishes of her policeman husband Danny McCall. It's predictable but likeable fare, with a nice performance (and even better vocals) from Stansfield. JB. Contains swearing [VIDEO]

Hugo Speer *Martin Luxford* • Lisa Stansfield *Joan Woodcock* • Tom Bell *Sid Luxford* • Rita Tushingham *Mags Luxford* • Alexei Sayle *Mighty Mac* • Paul Usher *Liam Luxford* • Danny McCall *Andy* • Clarence Clemons *Jack* ■ *Dir* Nick Mead • *Scr* Nick Mead, from a story by Su Lim, Nick Mead

Swing Fever ★★

Musical sports comedy
1943 · US · BW · 80mins

Bespectacled, sophomoronic bandleader Kay Kyser, instead of remaining behind his baton where he belonged, was asked to carry it for this silly MGM second feature. As a hick composer who also knows how to hypnotise people, Kyser uses his skill on a boxer in order to fix a fight. On the plus side, Marilyn Maxwell plays a scheming blonde, and Lena Horne sings *You're So Indifferent*. RB

Kay Kyser *Lowell Blackford* • Marilyn Maxwell *Ginger Gray* • William Gargan *"Waltzy" Malone* • Nat Pendleton *"Killer" Kennedy* • Lena Horne • Ava Gardner *Receptionist* ■ *Dir* Tim Whelan • *Scr* Nat Perrin, Warren Wilson, from a story by Matt Brooks, Joseph Hoffman

Swing High, Swing Low ★★★

Drama 1937 · US · BW · 92mins

Here, comedy is effectively mixed in to the drama about a newly married showbiz couple who come unstuck when he, a trumpeter, gets a job in a New York nightclub and is seduced by the singer (Dorothy Lamour). Mitchell Leisen is in full command of this backstage drama. RK

Carole Lombard *Maggie King* • Fred MacMurray *Skid Johnson* • Charles Butterworth *Harry* • Jean Dixon *Ella* • Dorothy Lamour *Anita Alvarez* • Harvey Stephens *Harvey Howel* • Anthony Quinn *The Don* ■ *Dir* Mitchell Leisen • *Scr* Virginia Van Upp, Oscar Hammerstein Ii, from the play *Burlesque* by George Manker Watters, Arthur Hopkins

Swing Kids ★★ 15

Drama 1993 · US · Colour · 109mins

Set in Germany during the Nazi uprising, this film poses an interesting dilemma. A group of youngsters, led by Robert Sean Leonard and Christian Bale, are torn between the rise of Hitler Youth and the popularity of American Swing music and dance. The premise, however, is muted by a lack of directorial punch from Thomas Carter and though the actors are appealing, lack of period detail and overly long sequences of swing dull down a good idea. LH [VIDEO] DVD

Robert Sean Leonard *Peter* • Christian Bale *Thomas* • Frank Whaley *Arvid* • Barbara Hershey *Frau Muller* • Kenneth Branagh *SS official* • Tushka Bergen *Evey* • David Tom *Willi* • Julia Stemberger *Frau Linge* ■ *Dir* Thomas Carter • *Scr* Jonathan Marc Feldman

Swing Shift ★★★★ PG

Romantic drama 1984 · US · Colour · 95mins

Directed by Jonathan Demme, this is a small but often delightful romantic drama that went by largely unnoticed on its limited cinema release in Britain. Goldie Hawn is the unassuming housewife who goes to work in a factory during the Second World War while her husband Ed Harris is away fighting, and it is there that she meets free spirit Christine Lahti and cool trumpeter Kurt Russell. It was allegedly during filming that Hawn and Russell fell in love in real life, and they are certainly convincing as the two poles-apart lovers drawn together in a war-torn world. JB. Contains swearing. [VIDEO]

Goldie Hawn *Kay Walsh* • Kurt Russell *Lucky Lockhart* • Christine Lahti *Hazel Zanussi* • Fred Ward *Biscuits Toohey* • Ed Harris *Jack Walsh* • Holly Hunter *Jeannie Sherman* • Belinda Carlisle *Jamboree singer* ■ *Dir* Jonathan Demme • *Scr* Rob Morton

Swing Time ★★★★★ U

Classic musical comedy
1936 · US · BW · 103mins

Top Hat might have been more popular, but this is actually the finest of the Fred Astaire/Ginger Rogers movies. Working with a major director in George Stevens, Fred and Ginger achieve such heights that to single out a particular instance might seem invidious. But the climactic *Never Gonna Dance* seems to provide the perfect example of the effortless style Astaire conveyed, and the dialogue between the pair that precedes the dance is among their most poignant. The plot? Who cares. TS [VIDEO]

Fred Astaire *John "Lucky" Garnett* • Ginger Rogers *Penelope "Penny" Carrol* • Victor Moore *Dr Cardetti, "Pop"* • Helen Broderick *Mabel Anderson* • Eric Blore *Mr Gordon* • Betty Furness *Margaret Watson* • George Metaxa *Ricardo Romero* ■ *Dir* George Stevens • *Scr* Howard Lindsay, Allan Scott, from a story by Erwin Gelsey • *Music* Jerome Kern • *Choreographer* Hermes Pan

Swing Your Lady ★

Comedy 1937 · US · BW · 72mins

With five song-and-dance numbers appended to it, this really pitiful effort from Warner Bros qualifies as a musical of sorts. The plot concerns a wrestling promoter who, heading for financial ruin, decides to mount a match in which an Amazon of a lady blacksmith (Louise Fazenda) takes on a dim-witted hulk (Nat Pendleton). The big surprise is the appearance of an understandably uncomfortable-looking Humphrey Bogart as the promoter, while the supporting cast includes Ronald Reagan in a small part. RK

Humphrey Bogart *Ed* • Frank McHugh *Popeye* • Louise Fazenda *Sadie* • Nat Pendleton *Joe Skopapolous* • Penny Singleton *Cookie* • Allen Jenkins *Shiner* • Ronald Reagan *Jack Miller* ■ *Dir* Ray Enright • *Scr* Joseph Schrank, Maurice Leo, from the play by Kenyon Nicholson, Charles Robinson

The Swinger ★★

Romantic comedy
1966 · US · Colour · 80mins

This 1960s sex tale was designed to exploit the pneumatic charms of starlet Ann-Margret. Here she's a writer of love stories who is frustrated when saucy magazine *Girl-Lure* turns down her work for being too innocent. Determined to prove them wrong, she steals sleazy material from lurid paperbacks and passes it off as semi-autobiographical material, thus piquing the interest of editor Anthony Franciosa and his seedy boss Robert Coote. DF

Ann-Margret *Kelly Olsson* • Anthony Franciosa *Ric Colby* • Robert Coote *Sir Hubert Charles* • Yvonne Romain *Karen Charles* • Nydia Westman *Aunt Cora* • Craig Hill *Sammy*

Jenkins • Milton Frome *Mr Olsson* • Mary LaRoche *Mrs Olssen* ■ *Dir* George Sidney (2) • *Scr* Lawrence Roman

Swingers ★★★★ 15

Comedy drama 1996 · US · Colour · 92mins

This honest exploration of male friendship is based on lead actor Jon Favreau's autobiographical script about his first years in Hollywood. He and three other out-of-work buddies bar-hop around, bitch nonstop, try to pick up women and wait endlessly by the phone for that all important call. A highly original and entertaining delight using hilarious situations to illuminate male neuroses in an uncompromising way. This independent labour of love carries the solid ring of truth and superb performances by Vince Vaughn and Favreau. AJ. Contains swearing. DVD

Jon Favreau *Mike* • Vince Vaughn *Trent* • Ron Livingston *Rob* • Patrick Van Horn *Sue* • Alex Desert *Charles* • Heather Graham *Lorraine* • Deena Martin *Christy* ■ *Dir* Doug Liman • *Scr* Jon Favreau • *Cinematographer* Doug Liman

The Swiss Conspiracy ★ 15

Thriller 1975 · US/W Ger · Colour · 85mins

This dismal thriller features David Janssen, who is hired to protect high-class Swiss banking customers (at the same time proving you can still be a star with a face that completely lacks expression). At least John Ireland and Ray Milland display a few emotions, but they come across as too inhuman to elicit any sympathy. TH

David Janssen *David Christopher* • Senta Berger *Denise Abbott* • John Ireland *Dwight McGowan* • John Saxon *Robert Hayes* • Ray Milland *Johann Hurtil* • Elke Sommer *Rita Jensen* • Anton Diffring *Franz Benninger* ■ *Dir* Jack Arnold • *Scr* Norman Klenman, Philip Saltzman, Michael Stanley, from the novel by Michael Stanley

Swiss Family Robinson ★★★ U

Period adventure 1940 · US · BW · 93mins

A modest film version of Johann David Wyss's once popular novel about a family, shipwrecked during the Napoleonic wars, who set about building a house and a new life on a desert island. Four-square and agreeably old-fashioned "family" entertainment with a mild message about values, the film boasts the rich voice of Orson Welles as its narrator and a good cast headed by Thomas Mitchell as William Robinson and child star Freddie Bartholomew on loan from MGM. Inexplicably, the production was a box-office disaster for RKO. RK

Orson Welles *Narrator* • Thomas Mitchell *William Robinson* • Edna Best *Elizabeth Robinson* • Freddie Bartholomew *Jack Robinson* • Terry Kilburn *Ernest Robinson* • Tim Holt *Fritz Robinson* • Baby Bobby Quillan *Francis Robinson* ■ *Dir* Edward Ludwig • *Scr* Walter Ferris, Gene Towne, Graham Baker, from the novel by Johann David Wyss

Swiss Family Robinson ★★★★ U

Period adventure
1960 · US · Colour · 126mins

John Mills and Dorothy McGuire leading their family in a chorus of *Oh, Christmas Tree* (in an impossibly luxurious desert island tree house) is, for many, an abiding memory of childhood cinema-going. Viewed today, this lavish (if overlong) Disney version of Johann Wyss's novel has lost little of its appeal. British director Ken Annakin shot the film on the West Indian island of Tobago and keeps the action brisk. Compared to state-of-the-art sequences in modern action adventures, though, the shipwreck, the raft rescue and the pirate raid are perhaps not as thrilling as they once seemed. DP DVD

John Mills *Father Robinson* • Dorothy McGuire *Mother Robinson* • James MacArthur *Fritz Robinson* • Janet Munro *Roberta* • Sessue Hayakawa *Pirate chief* • Tommy Kirk *Ernst* • Kevin Corcoran *Francis* • Cecil Parker *Captain Moreland* ■ *Dir* Ken Annakin • *Scr* Lowell S Hawley, from the novel by Johann David Wyss

Swiss Miss ★★★ U

Comedy 1938 · US · BW · 64mins

Even the staunchest Laurel and Hardy fan won't eulogise this middling outing, in which their failed mousetrap salesmen become involved with a composer and his opera-singing wife. However, the film still contains a couple of classic sequences, most notably Stan's attempt to trick a St Bernard dog into letting him at its brandy keg and Ollie singing *Let Me Call You Sweetheart* to Stan's sousaphone accompaniment. DA

Stan Laurel *Stan* • Oliver Hardy *Ollie* • Della Lind *Anna Hoeful Albert* • Walter Woolf King *Victor Albert* • Eric Blore *Edward* ■ *Dir* John G Blystone • *Scr* James Parrott, Felix Adler, from a story by Jean Negulesco, Charles Rogers, Stan Laurel

Switch ★★ 15

Comedy 1991 · US · Colour · 98mins

A rather disappointing and decidedly lewd gender-swap tale from Blake Edwards. Perry King is the ladykiller, killed by ladies and reincarnated as Ellen Barkin. It's a story that has a lot going for it, but it cops out as soon as lesbianism rears its alternative head. Barkin has proved herself worthy of much better material than this, but here she made a grave mistake in putting her faith in Edwards's slapstick brand of humour. TH. Contains swearing and brief nudity.

Ellen Barkin *Amanda Brooks* • Jimmy Smits *Walter Stone* • JoBeth Williams *Margo Brofman* • Lorraine Bracco *Sheila Faxton* • Tony Roberts *Arnold Freidkin* • Perry King *Steve Brooks* • Bruce Martyn Payne [Bruce Payne] *Devil* • Lysette Anthony *Liz* ■ *Dir/Scr* Blake Edwards

The Switch ★★★★ PG

Drama based on a true story
1993 · US · Colour · 91mins

Presumably because of Tinseltown prejudice against the TV movie, there are perfectly decent actors who have practically no life beyond the small screen. Gary Cole and Craig T Nelson are a case in point. They have no trouble bringing an emotional and psychological authenticity to their roles as a seriously injured biker who wants to die and a DJ who is his political, and personal, opposite. Issues of life and death, responsibility and freedom are woven in with style. JM DVD

Gary Cole *Larry McAfee* • Craig T Nelson *Russ Fine* • Beverly D'Angelo *Dee Fine* • Kathleen Nolan *Amelia McAfee* • Chris Mulkey *Bill* • L Scott Caldwell *Mrs Linson* • Max Gail *Judge Johnson* ■ *Dir* Bobby Roth • *Scr* TS Cook, from a story by TS Cook, Ron Schultz

Switchback ★★★ 15

Action thriller 1997 · US · Colour · 113mins

This refreshingly different variation on the overused serial killer plot cuts between Dennis Quaid's miserable FBI man on the trail of the killer he believes has kidnapped his son, and travelling companions Danny Glover and Jared Leto, both of whom are just suspicious enough to be the culprit. Writer/director Jeb Stuart is confident enough to make the "suspects" more interesting than the hero, although his shaky plotting throws up its share of unlikely contrivances. JC. Contains violence, nudity and swearing.

Dennis Quaid *Agent Frank LaCrosse* • Danny Glover *Bob Goodall* • Jared Leto *Lane Dixon* • Ted Levine *Nate Booker* • R Lee Ermey *Sheriff Buck Olmstead* ■ *Dir/Scr* Jeb Stuart

Switchblade Romance ★★★★ 18

Horror thriller
2003 · Fr/Rom · Colour · 88mins

When French director and co-writer Alexandre Aja called this chiller *Haute Tension* (High Tension), he certainly picked the right title. Re-named less aptly for English audiences, it's still a nail-biter. Desperate student Cécile de France tries to rescue her best friend (Maïwenn) after she's kidnapped from a remote farmhouse by a psychopath who's slaughtered her entire family. Though relentlessly gruesome, the feature is more about atmosphere than gore. Every single frame is meticulously composed for maximum effect, while the ultra-glossy production values take it far beyond the realms of the traditional slasher flick. SF. In French with English subtitles. DVD

Cécile de France *Marie* • Maïwenn *Alex* • Philippe Nahon *Killer* • Franck Khalfoun *Jimmy* • Andrei Finti *Alex's father* • Oana Pellea *Alex's mother* • Marco Claudiu Pascu *Tom* • Jean-Claude de Goros *Police captain* ■ *Dir* Alexandre Aja • *Scr* Alexandre Aja, Grégory Levasseur

Switchblade Sisters ★★ 18

Crime action adventure
1975 · US · Colour · 86mins

Quentin Tarantino tried re-releasing this exploitation cheapie in 1999, though it still didn't really find an audience. Indeed, the movie has dated in a way that makes it more tacky than actually hilarious, and though a director known for campy exploitation movies was at the helm, the very low budget results in the characters providing more "attitude" and arguments than violence or sexual material. Still, this saga of the trials and battles of an all-girl gang does have its moments. KB. Contains violence and drug abuse.

Robbie Lee *Lace* • Joanne Nail *Maggie* • Monica Gayle *Patch* • Asher Brauner *Dominic* • Chase Newhart *Crabs* • Marlene Clark *Muff* • Kitty Bruce *Donut* • Janice Karman *Bunny* ■ *Dir* Jack Hill • *Scr* FX Maier, from a story by FX Maier, Jack Hill, John Prizer

Switching Channels ★★★ PG

Romantic comedy
1987 · US · Colour · 100mins

After three screen versions of *The Front Page* set in a newspaper office (including the best of them all, *His Girl Friday*), it was only a matter of time before someone brought the story into the TV age. Canadian director Ted Kotcheff never quite comes to grips with the pace of either the story or the humour, and his uncertain handling hampers his capable cast. Burt Reynolds keeps threatening to match two of his predecessors in the role, but Kathleen Turner and Christopher Reeve leave you longing for Rosalind Russell and Ralph Bellamy. DP. Contains swearing. DVD

Kathleen Turner *Christy Colleran* • Burt Reynolds *John L Sullivan IV* • Christopher Reeve *Blaine Bingham* • Ned Beatty *Roy Ridnitz* • Henry Gibson *Ike Roscoe* • George Newbern *Siegenthaler* • Al Waxman *Berger* ■ *Dir* Ted Kotcheff • *Scr* Jonathan Reynolds, from the play *The Front Page* by Ben Hecht, Charles MacArthur

Swoon ★★★ 18

Crime drama 1992 · US · BW · 93mins

Overly arty and surrealistic it might be, but writer/director Tom Kalin's take on the famous Leopold and Loeb murder case is still provocative, gripping and chilling, raising clever contemporary issues within its period confines. Using monochrome melodrama, archive footage and experimental narrative, Kalin starkly examines with haunting effectiveness the homophobia behind the conviction of the two wealthy gay Chicago college kids who killed a schoolboy for kicks in 1924. AJ. Contains swearing.

Daniel Schlachet *Richard Loeb* • Craig Chester *Nathan Leopold Jr* • Ron Vawter *State's Attorney Crowe* • Michael Kirby *Detective Savage* • Michael Stumm *Doctor Bowman* • Valda Z Drabla *Germaine Reinhardt* • Natalie Stanford *Susan Lurie* • Paul Connor *Bobby Franks* ■ *Dir/Scr* Tom Kalin

The Sword and the Cross ★★

Biblical drama 1958 · It · Colour · 93mins

The success of such films as MGM's *Quo Vadis* and *Ben-Hur* must have left a lot of props and costumes in the scene docks at Cinecittà studios in Rome. A whole sub-genre arose utilising existing materials with quasi-religious plots, invariably importing a Hollywood name to add international lustre. This one finds Yvonne De Carlo as Mary Magdalene in a fictional romance set during the last days of Christ. Not unwatchable, but don't expect taste. TS. Italian dialogue dubbed into English.

Yvonne De Carlo *Mary Magdalene* • Jorge Mistral *Caius Marcellus* • Rossana Podesta *Marthe* • Philippe Hersent *Pontius Pilate* • Mario Girotti [Terence Hill] *Lazarus* ■ *Dir* Carlo L Bragaglia [Carlo Ludovico Bragaglia]

The Sword and the Rose ★★ U

Historical drama 1952 · US · Colour · 87mins

In days of old when knights were bold and painted scenery was a cutting-edge special effect, this Disney costume drama would have had children in raptures. This corny romp has Michael Gough's pantomimically wicked lord standing between Glynis Johns's winsome Mary Tudor and true happiness. Gleefully dispensing with historical fact, it's all simply an excuse for Richard Todd to prance about in brightly coloured tights (again), while James Robertson-Justice demonstrates what a Scottish Henry VIII might have sounded like. DP

Richard Todd *Charles Brandon* • Glynis Johns *Princess Mary Tudor* • James Robertson-Justice *King Henry VIII* • Michael Gough *Duke of Buckingham* • Jane Barrett *Lady Margaret* • Peter Copley *Sir Edwin Caskoden* • Rosalie Crutchley *Queen Catherine of Aragon* ■ *Dir* Ken Annakin • *Scr* Lawrence E Watkin, from the novel *When Knighthood Was in Flower* by Charles Major

The Sword and the Sorcerer ★★ 18

Fantasy adventure
1982 · US · Colour · 95mins

This unexciting and overly bloody fantasy excursion was an attempt to jump on the sword-and-sorcery bandwagon that was kick-started by the success of Schwarzenegger's *Conan the Barbarian*. Much chewing of scenery is in evidence here as Errol Flynn-wannabe Lee Horsley and his merry band of mercenaries do battle with evil king Richard Lynch to rescue an enslaved kingdom. Directorial debutante Albert Pyun commits the three cardinal sins for a fantasy movie: being confusing, unimaginative and dull. RS. Contains violence.

Lee Horsley *Talon* • Kathleen Beller *Alana* • Simon MacCorkindale *Mikah* • George Maharis *Machelli* • Richard Lynch *Cromwell* • Richard Moll *Xusia* ■ *Dir* Albert Pyun • *Scr* Albert Pyun, John Stuckmeyer, Tom Karnowski

The Sword in the Stone
★★★ U

Animated adventure
1963 · US · Colour · 76mins

Disney's feature-length cartoon account of young King Arthur's magical misadventures may feature unmemorable songs by the Sherman brothers, but the film makes good use of its limited animation techniques (Disney was on a cost-cutting drive at the time) in relating the legend of Arthur, here nicknamed Wart, and the valuable life lessons taught to him by wizard Merlin. Memorable sequences include Wart's transformation into a fish to witness the wonders of the underwater world before pulling Excalibur from the stone and claiming his rightful inheritance. AJ [video] DVD

Rickie Sorensen *Wart* • Sebastian Cabot *Sir Ector* • Karl Swenson *Merlin, the magician* • Junius Matthews *Archimedes* • Norman Alden *Kay* • Martha Wentworth *Mad Madame Mim/ Granny Squirrel* • Alan Napier *Sir Pelinore* ■ *Dir* Wolfgang Reitherman • *Scr* Bill Peet, from the novel *The Once and Future King* by TH White

The Sword of Monte Cristo
★★ U

Period swashbuckling adventure
1951 · US · Colour · 79mins

Some vigorous swordplay, handsome settings and lavish costumes fail to make up for the convoluted plot and general shortcomings of this second-rate action adventure tale, very loosely inspired by Alexandre Dumas's classic novel. George Montgomery is merely adequate as the loyal French officer who helps save Napoleon III from the treachery of his tyrannical chief minister, and this sort of Gallic swashbuckler has been done far better many times before and since. PF

George Montgomery *Captain Renault* • Paula Corday [Rita Corday] *Lady Christiane* • Berry Kroeger *Minister Charles La Roche* • William Conrad *Major Nicolet* • Rhys Williams *Major of Varonne* • Steve Brodie *Sergeant* • Robert Warwick *Marquis de Montableau* • David Bond *Louis Napoleon III* ■ *Dir* Maurice Geraghty • *Scr* Maurice Geraghty, from the novel *The Count of Monte Cristo* by Alexandre Dumas

Sword of Sherwood Forest
★★ U

Adventure drama 1960 · UK · Colour · 76mins

To many, Richard Greene was the definitive Robin Hood, ushering in ITV in a cleverly cast (though cheaply made) television series with a remarkably catchy theme tune. This is the feature, co-produced by Greene for Hammer Films. Alan Wheatley makes way for Peter Cushing as the villainous Sheriff of Nottingham, and the film is directed by Cushing's Hammer colleague, Terence Fisher. Technicolor adds some scale, but this is really a cheap and cheerful affair. TS [video]

Richard Greene *Robin Hood* • Peter Cushing *Sheriff of Nottingham* • Niall MacGinnis *Friar Tuck* • Sarah Branch *Maid Marian Fitzwalter* • Richard Pasco *Earl of Newark* • Nigel Green *Little John* • Jack Gwillim *Archbishop of Canterbury, Hubert Walter* • Oliver Reed *Melton* ■ *Dir* Terence Fisher • *Scr* Alan Hackney

Sword of the Valiant
★ PG

Fantasy adventure
1984 · UK · Colour · 97mins

This is tantamount to a star-studded remake of Stephen Weeks's low-budget 1973 film *Gawain and the Green Knight*. He has made little improvement on his own original, however. Miles O'Keeffe is quite dreadful in the role of the squire Gawain, challenged by Sean Connery's Green Knight to answer a riddle within a year or risk having his head chopped off. Barely on screen, Trevor Howard and Peter Cushing are shamefully wasted, as are the locations. DP [video]

Miles O'Keeffe *Gawain* • Cyrielle Claire *Linet* • Leigh Lawson *Humphrey* • Sean Connery *Green Knight* • Trevor Howard *King Arthur* • Peter Cushing *Seneschal* • Ronald Lacey *Oswald* • Lila Kedrova *Lady of Lyonesse* ■ *Dir* Stephen Weeks • *Scr* Stephen Weeks, Philip M Breen, Howard C Pen

Sword of Vengeance
★★★ 18

Period martial arts adventure
1972 · Jpn · Colour · 83mins

This is the first of the original six *Lone Wolf and Cub* adventures produced by Toho studios. Incredibly, the series flopped commercially and remained forgotten until the character of samurai Ogami Itto was revived for television in the early 1980s. However, they rank among the most visceral movies in the warrior genre, with Tomisaburo Wakayama exuding Mifunesque indignation as the embittered widower, who wheels his infant son around the 17th-century countryside, righting wrongs and seeking vengeance on the Yagyu clan, which he'd served as executioner until he was framed for treason. Followed by *Baby Cart at the River Styx*. DP. In Japanese with English subtitles. [video] DVD

Tomisaburo Wakayama *Ogami Itto* • Akihiro Tomikawa *Daigoro* ■ *Dir* Kenji Misumi • *Scr* Kazuo Koike, from a story by Kazuo Koike, Goseki Kojima

Sword of Xanten
★★ 12A

Fantasy adventure
2004 · Ger/S Afr/UK/It · Colour · 132mins

German director Uli Edel delves into Nordic and Germanic mythology for this ambitious fantasy adventure that was originally made for television. Prince Siegfried (Benno Fürmann) is raised as a blacksmith's son and only discovers his true heritage after slaying a dragon. The beast is hoarding stolen gold that belongs to the ghostly Nibelungs, and when Siegfried claims it, he unleashes a terrible curse. An enthralling though badly acted story, the film is adequately executed, but can't escape its low-budget roots. SF. Contains violence.

Benno Fürmann *Siegfried* • Kristanna Loken *Brunhild* • Alicia Witt *Kriemhild* • Julian Sands *Hagen* • Samuel West *King Gunther* • Max von Sydow *Eyvind* • Robert Pattinson *Giselher* • Mavie Hörbiger *Lena* ■ *Dir* Uli Edel • *Scr* Diane Duane, Peter Morwood, Uli Edel

Swordfish
★★ 15

Action thriller 2001 · US · Colour · 95mins

This is a glossy, expensive computer-heist thriller that amounts to very little behind all the fireworks. If you've seen the trailer, you've seen the film, as it gives away the ending and shows part of a technically brilliant 360-degree view of an explosion that will act as director Dominic Sena's calling card. He's so proud of it, in fact, he gives it to us twice, such is the superficial nature of this film. The only saving grace is Hugh Jackman's performance as the cool super-hacker hired by counter-terrorist John Travolta to help steal $9.5 billion. AC. Contains nudity, violence, swearing. [video] DVD

John Travolta *Gabriel Shear* • Hugh Jackman *Stanley Jobson* • Halle Berry *Ginger* • Don Cheadle *Agent Roberts* • Vinnie Jones *Marco* • Sam Shepard *Senator Reisman* ■ *Dir* Dominic Sena • *Scr* Skip Woods

The Swordsman of Siena
★★ U

Swashbuckling adventure
1962 · Fr/It · Colour · 96mins

British actor Stewart Granger flails around with sabre and rapier in this Italian swashbuckler, set in the 16th century. Our hero plays a soldier of fortune who gets caught up in a struggle between a brutal nobleman and a rebel underground movement. He also gets to stretch his romantic muscles in dallying with Sylva Koscina and Tony Curtis's ex-wife, Christine Kaufmann. There's plenty of colourful costumes and swordfights, but the plot is as predictable as a calendar. TH. Italian dialogue dubbed into English.

Stewart Granger *Thomas Stanwood* • Sylva Koscina *Orietta Arconti* • Christine Kaufmann *Serenella Arconti* • Riccardo Garrone *Don Carlos* • Tullio Carminati *Father Giacomo* ■ *Dir* Etienne Périer, Baccio Bandini • *Scr* Michael Kanin, Fay Kanin, Alec Coppel, Sandro Continenza, Dominique Fabre, from a story by Anthony Marshall

Sylvester
★★★ PG

Drama 1985 · US · Colour · 99mins

Melissa Gilbert stars as the tomboy who rides her horse Sylvester to victory in the Olympics three-day event at Lexington, Kentucky. The plot superficially resembles *National Velvet*, but Hunter brings a darker touch to the proceedings by making Gilbert's character rather unlikeable. Veteran Richard Farnsworth gives a fine performance as Charlie's tipsy but tough mentor. DA [video]

Richard Farnsworth *Foster* • Melissa Gilbert *Charlie* • Michael Schoeffling *Matt* • Constance Towers *Muffy* • Pete Kowanko *Harris* ■ *Dir* Tim Hunter • *Scr* Carol Sobieski

Sylvia
★★★★

Drama 1964 · US · BW · 114mins

Hollywood's sex siren in residence – the one and only Carroll Baker – is about to marry a millionaire, so he hires a private detective to shed some light on her past. She's a champion rose grower and a published poet, so there shouldn't be too many surprises. But then comes the bad news: after being abused as a child, she became a prostitute and fell in with some very bad company indeed. As prurient and lurid as a mainstream Hollywood movie could be in 1965, this is superbly filmed and with a whole line of feeble, emasculated or disturbed men to trample over Baker's eventful life. AT

Carroll Baker *Sylvia West* • George Maharis *Alan Macklin* • Joanne Dru *Jane Philips* • Peter Lawford *Frederick Summers* • Viveca Lindfors *Irma Olanski* • Edmond O'Brien *Oscar Stewart* • Aldo Ray *Jonas Karoki* • Ann Sothern *Mrs Argona* ■ *Dir* Gordon Douglas • *Scr* Sydney Boehm, from the novel by EV Cunningham

Sylvia
★★★ PG

Drama 1984 · NZ · Colour · 94mins

Moving biopic from the fledgeling days of New Zealand cinema which recounts the early life of acclaimed novelist Sylvia Ashton-Warner, who, before finding fame as a writer, pioneered a radical new teaching programme to help Maori children. Eleanor David shines in the lead role, and there is sterling support from Tom Wilkinson and Nigel Terry. Director Michael Firth admirably evokes the conservatism and prejudices of post-Second World War New Zealand. JF [video]

Eleanor David *Sylvia Henderson* • Nigel Terry *Aden* • Tom Wilkinson *Keith Henderson* • Mary Regan *Opal* • Martyn Sanderson *Inspector Gulland* • Terence Cooper *Inspector Bletcher* • David Letch *Inspector Scragg* ■ *Dir* Michael Firth • *Scr* Michael Quill, F Fairfax, Michael Firth, from the books *Teacher* and *I Pass This Way* by Sylvia Ashton-Warner

Sylvia
★★★ 15

Biographical drama
2003 · UK/US · Colour · 109mins

Who was Sylvia Plath? According to this patchy, dislocated biopic, the American poet was a suicidal, husband-obsessed woman whose creative flame was prematurely extinguished when she took her own life in 1963. Relegating the people and events of the period to the background, the film centres on the love affair between Plath and her husband, future poet laureate Ted Hughes. What draws us in is the central performance of Gwyneth Paltrow – as steely as it is vulnerable – while Daniel Craig's turn as Hughes is also superbly conveyed. TH [video] DVD

Gwyneth Paltrow *Sylvia Plath* • Daniel Craig *Ted Hughes* • Jared Harris *Al Alvarez* • Amira Casar *Assia Wevill* • Andrew Havill *David Wevill* • Sam Troughton *Tom Hadley-Clarke* • Lucy Davenport *Doreen* • Antony Strachan *Michael Boddy* • Blythe Danner *Aurelia Plath* • Michael Gambon *Professor Thomas* ■ *Dir* Christine Jeffs • *Scr* John Brownlow

Sylvia Scarlett
★★ U

Comedy drama 1936 · US · BW · 86mins

Petty fraudster Edmund Gwenn and his daughter Katharine Hepburn (disguised as a boy to fool pursuing cops) join forces in England with cockney jewel thief Cary Grant. Their picaresque escapades and emotional entanglements defeat the script and George Cukor's direction. A bemused public gave the thumbs down to this sprawling and tedious adaptation hasn't improved with age. RK [video]

Katharine Hepburn *Sylvia Scarlett* • Cary Grant *Jimmy Monkley* • Brian Aherne *Michael Fane* • Edmund Gwenn *Henry Scarlett* • Natalie Paley *Lily Levetsky* • Dennie Moore *Maudie Tilt* ■ *Dir* George Cukor • *Scr* Gladys Unger, John Collier, Mortimer Offner, from the novel *The Early Life and Adventures of Sylvia Scarlett* by Compton Mackenzie

Sympathy for Mr Vengeance
★★★★ 18

Action thriller 2002 · S Kor · Colour · 120mins

Director Park Chan-wook examines the tensions inherent within South Korean society in this combustible tale of exploitation, despair and revenge. The opening section combines social critique, black comedy and domestic melodrama, as unemployed smelter Shin Ha-gyun decides to kidnap his ex-boss's daughter after he's cheated out of the savings intended for his sister's kidney transplant. The tone darkens after the plan backfires and the girl's father, Song Kang-ho, comes after them. Some may bridle at the violence, but Park's control over his bleak vision is impressive. DP. In Korean with English subtitles. [video] DVD

Song Kang-ho *Park Dong-jin* • Shin Ha-gyun *Ryu* • Bae Doo-na *Cha Yeong-mi* • Lim Ji-eun *Ryu's sister* • Han Bo-bae *Yu-sun* ■ *Dir* Park Chan-wook • *Scr* Lee Jae-sun, Lee Mu-yeong, Lee Yong-jong, Park Chan-wook

S

La Symphonie Pastorale
★★★★★

Drama 1946 · Fr · BW · 107mins

Blind orphan girl Michèle Morgan is brought up by pastor Pierre Blanchar and his wife in a small mountain village, where the pastor teaches his charge to understand the world as a place of beauty and serenity. However, he and his son Jean Desailly both fall in love with her, and the latter, hopeful of marriage, arranges an operation to restore her sight. Adapted from André Gide's painfully sad novella and filmed against a background of exquisite visuals, the film won the Grand Prix at Cannes in 1946, while Morgan's expressive performance saw her voted best actress. A French gem, redolent with beauty and despair. RK. In French with English subtitles.

Michèle Morgan *Gertrude* • Pierre Blanchar *Pastor Jean Martin* • Line Noro *Amélie Martin* • Jacques Louvigny *Casteran* • Jean Desailly *Jacques Martin* • Andrée Clément *Piette*

Casteran ■ *Dir* Jean Delannoy • *Scr* Pierre Bost, Jean Aurenche, Jean Delannoy, from the novel by André Gide

Symphony of Six Million ★★★

Drama 1932 · US · BW · 85mins

Directed by the efficient Gregory La Cava, this concerns Ricardo Cortez, a doctor of humble origins, who sells out his high ideals for money and status, only to fail in performing an operation on his father Gregory Ratoff. He redeems himself, however, by saving Irene Dunne, the woman he loves. Max Steiner's emotive score heightens the drama without disguising Cortez's wooden acting, but the film, complete with then rare scenes of surgical procedure, is a good wallow. RK

Ricardo Cortez *Dr Felix Klauber* • Irene Dunne *Jessica* • Anna Appel *Hannah Klauber* • Gregory Ratoff *Meyer "Lansman" Klauber* ■ *Dir* Gregory La Cava • *Scr* Bernard Schubert, J Walter Ruben, James Seymour, from a story by Fannie Hurst

Syncopation ★★ U

Period drama 1942 · US · BW · 88mins

Eleven musical numbers and the participation of Benny Goodman, Harry James, Gene Krupa, Charlie Barnet and Joe Venuti are the only possible reasons to sit through this dreary tale of a young trumpeter from Chicago (Jackie Cooper) and a New Orleans girl (Bonita Granville) who share an obsession with jazz and Walt Whitman. Top-billed Adolphe Menjou barely figures as Granville's father. RK

Adolphe Menjou *George Latimer* • Jackie Cooper *Johnnie* • Bonita Granville *Kit Latimer* • George Bancroft *Mr Porter* • Ted North *Paul Porter* • Todd Duncan *Rex Tearbone* • Connee Boswell *Café singer* ■ *Dir* William Dieterle • *Scr* Philip Yordan, Frank Cavett, from the story *The Band Played On* by Valentine Davies

The System ★★★

Romantic drama 1964 · UK · BW · 92mins

Once upon a time, teenage boys used to go to the unromantic English seaside to pick up their girls, before cheap air travel to the Costa Brava was introduced. This quaint period romp provides a mirror of those not-so-innocent times, elegantly photographed in black-and-white by cinematographer Nicolas Roeg and oozing early 1960s charm from Peter Draper's clever screenplay. The young, talented cast is headed by Oliver Reed, Jane Merrow, Barbara Ferris and Julia Foster, and watch closely for director Michael Winner in shot on the platform as the train arrives at Torquay. TS

Oliver Reed *Tinker* • Jane Merrow *Nicola* • Barbara Ferris *Suzy* • Julia Foster *Lorna* • Harry Andrews *Larsey* • Ann Lynn *Ella* • David Hemmings *David* • John Alderton *Nidge* ■ *Dir* Michael Winner • *Scr* Peter Draper

T

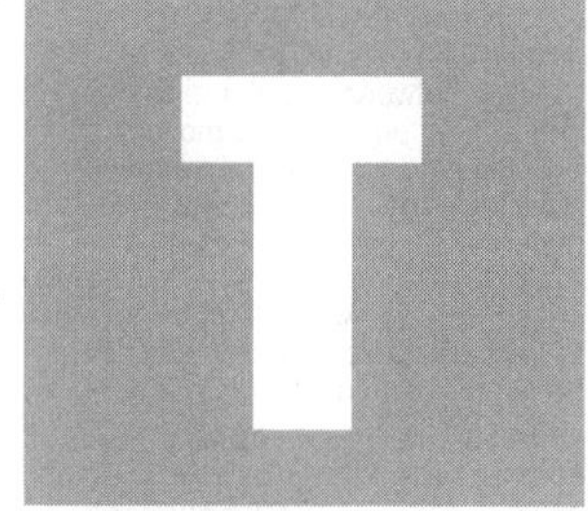

TC 2000 ★ 18

Science-fiction action thriller
1993 · US · Colour · 90mins

In the future, a depleted ozone layer has made living on the surface of the Earth almost impossible; the rich have retreated to an underground city. Billy Blanks plays one of the defenders of the city, soon finding himself on the surface and allying with Bolo Yeung when he stumbles onto the inevitable conspiracy. All the script gives them is a succession of not particularly exciting fight sequences. KB DVD

Billy Blanks *Jason Storm* • Bobbie Phillips *Zoey Kinsella* • Bolo Yeung *Sumai* • Jalal Merhi *Niki Picasso* • Matthias Hues *Bigalow* ■ *Dir* TJ Scott • *Scr* TJ Scott, from a story by J Stephen Maunder

T-Force ★ 18

Science-fiction action adventure
1995 · US · Colour · 89mins

The T-Force of the title is an anti-terrorist squad composed entirely of a form of android called cybernauts. This may excuse the lamentable acting by the main characters, but even the human characters are atrociously played. Long action sequences are broken up by half-brained ponderings on whether or not robots are sentient beings. ST DVD

Jack Scalia *Jack* • Erin Gray *Mayor Pendleton* • Vernon Wells *Samuel Washington* • Bobby Johnston *Cain* • Evan Lurie *Adam* ■ *Dir* Richard Pepin • *Scr* Jacobsen Hart

THX 1138 ★★★★ 15

Science-fiction drama
1971 · US · Colour · 82mins

The debut feature from *Star Wars* maestro George Lucas is a bleak, claustrophobic affair. The always excellent Robert Duvall takes the title role as a man quietly rebelling against a repressive world where everyone has to have Yul Brynner haircuts, and the police are as frighteningly bland as a McDonald's assistant. The obtuse script doesn't help, but it looks wonderful and Lucas conjures up a genuinely chilling air. JF DVD

Robert Duvall *THX 1138* • Donald Pleasence *SEN 5241* • Don Pedro Colley *SRT* • Maggie McOmie *LUH 3417* • Ian Wolfe *PTO* • Sid Haig *NCH* ■ *Dir* George Lucas • *Scr* George Lucas, Walter Murch, from a story by George Lucas

T-Men ★★★★

Film noir 1947 · US/UK · BW · 92mins

The "T" refers to Treasury Agents, as opposed to G-Men (FBI), and the picture is a real humdinger, one of director Anthony Mann's early works. It's a testament to the brilliance of cameraman John Alton, whose lighting can make a concrete wall as expressive as a Turner landscape. The story is hardly original – agents are assigned to smash a counterfeiting racket – but Mann's inventive telling belies the bargain-basement budget. Audiences at the time marvelled at Dennis O'Keefe's performance as one of the agents. AT

Dennis O'Keefe *Dennis O'Brien* • Alfred Ryder *Tony Genaro* • Mary Meade *Evangeline* • Wallace Ford *Schemer* • June Lockhart *Mary Genaro* • Charles McGraw *Moxie* • Jane Randolph *Diana* • Art Smith *Gregg* ■ *Dir* Anthony Mann • *Scr* John C Higgins, from a story by Virginia Kellogg

TR Baskin ★★

Comedy drama 1971 · US · Colour · 89mins

This handsome, but muddled, comedy-drama, was released in the UK as *A Date with a Lonely Girl*. As the titular country girl trying to make it as a typist in Chicago, Candice Bergen is simply too glamorous and assured to convince us she's a timid waif. However, director Herbert Ross's clumsy handling of the interminable flashbacks give her some sort of alibi. James Caan is a standout as a sympathetic admirer. DP

Candice Bergen *TR Baskin* • Peter Boyle *Jack Mitchell* • James Caan *Larry Moore* • Marcia Rodd *Dayle* • Erin O'Reilly *Kathy* • Howard Platt *Arthur* • William Wise *Gary* ■ *Dir* Herbert Ross • *Scr* Peter Hyams

Ta Dona ★★

Drama 1991 · Mali · Colour · 100mins

The clash between traditional rituals and the environmental realities of a changing world are explored in this slow-moving drama from Mali. Director/screenwriter Adama Drabo openly sides with the peasant farmers who are even exploited by corrupt government officials even in times of drought. Shot through with Bambara myths and superstitions, the film has few answers to the intractable questions it poses. DP. In French with English subtitles.

Balamoussa Keita [Balla Moussa Keita] • Diarrah Sanogo • Arouna Diarra ■ *Dir/Scr* Adama Drabo

Taal ★★★ U

Romantic musical melodrama
1999 · Ind · Colour · 178mins

This masala melodrama has the distinction of being the first Bollywood production to make it into the top 20 of the US box office. Director Subhash Ghai borrows liberally from recent blockbusters to fashion this star-crossed romance, which features Akshaye Khanna as a millionaire's son who teams up with his loyal friend Anil Kapoor to defy class prejudice and the ruthless materialism of modern society in order to win the heart of folk singer Aishwarya Rai. DP. In Hindi with English subtitles. DVD

Anil Kapoor *Vikrant Kapoor/Kapu* • Aishwarya Rai *Manasi* • Akshaye Khanna *Manav Mehta* • Alok Nath *Tara Babu* • Amrish Puri *Jagmohan* ■ *Dir/Scr* Subhash Ghai

Table for Five ★★★ PG

Drama 1983 · US · Colour · 116mins

Hankies at the ready for this sentimental heartstring-tugger. Jon Voight stars as the divorced dad who takes his kids on a Mediterranean holiday, only to learn while they are away that his ex-wife has died and her husband may want custody of the children. While gushy towards the finale, this is best enjoyed for the earlier scenes of Voight trying to get to know his children all over again. JB

Jon Voight *JP Tannen* • Richard Crenna *Mitchell* • Marie-Christine Barrault *Marie* • Millie Perkins *Kathleen* • Roxana Zal *Tilde* • Robby Kiger *Truman-Paul* ■ *Dir* Robert Lieberman • *Scr* David Seltzer

Tabu ★★★ U

Silent drama 1931 · US · BW · 81mins

After creative differences caused him to leave WS Van Dyke to complete *White Shadows in the South Seas* (1928), the father of the documentary film, Robert Flaherty, found the same thing happening to him with his collaborator on another Polynesian project, the great German expressionist, FW Murnau. Overruled in his bid to promote the ethnographical aspect above the film's melodramatic storyline, he left Murnau and Oscar-winning cameraman Floyd Crosby to tell the tale of forbidden love and tyrannical superstition, which they did with lyrical integrity. DP

Reri [Anna Chevalier] *The girl* • Matahi *The boy* • Robert J Flaherty [Robert Flaherty] *Narrator* ■ *Dir* FW Murnau • *Scr* from the story *Turia* by FW Murnau, Robert J Flaherty [Robert Flaherty]

Tactical Assault ★★ 15

Action thriller 1998 · US · Colour · 87mins

Rutger Hauer stars in this implausible revenge adventure. We learn through flashbacks that Rutger's USAF ace went a little battle crazy during the Gulf War and was only prevented from shooting down an Iraqi passenger jet by the quick thinking of fellow fighter pilot Robert Patrick. Hauer believes Patrick is out to sabotage his career and seeks revenge in the skies over Bosnia. The conflicts may be contemporary, but the flyboy action is dated. DP

Rutger Hauer *Captain John "Doc" Holiday* • Robert Patrick *Colonel Lee Banning* • Isabel Glasser *Jennifer Banning* • Ken Howard *General Horace White* • Dey Young *Doctor Baxter* ■ *Dir* Mark Griffiths • *Scr* David Golden

Tadpole ★★★ 15

Comedy 2002 · US · Colour · 75mins

This wry comedy is a variant on the theme of inter-generational lust; a low-budget, digital-video rendering of the obsession felt by 15-year-old Aaron Stanford for his 40-something stepmother (Sigourney Weaver) and the fallout from his unexpected liaison with her best friend (Bebe Neuwirth). The film's brevity means that the one-liners come thick and fast, but that very economy gives the movie an offhand attitude, despite the uniformly strong performances. Character and situation seem skimped on and the Voltaire-quoting Standford is far too self-confident for the audience to feel any sympathy for him. TH DVD

Sigourney Weaver *Eve Grubman* • Aaron Stanford *Oscar Grubman* • John Ritter *Stanley Grubman* • Bebe Neuwirth *Diane* • Robert Iler *Charlie* • Adam LeFevre *Phil* • Peter Appel *Jimmy* • Ron Rifkin *Professor Tisch* ■ *Dir* Gary Winick • *Scr* Heather McGowan, Niels Mueller

Taffin ★★ 18

Action thriller 1988 · US/UK · Colour · 92mins

Dull thriller, with Pierce Brosnan as a tough-guy debt collector confronting unscrupulous developers who want to build a chemical plant in a quiet Irish town. Brosnan's watchable, but displays little of the charisma that he'd bring years later to Bond. A rock-solid support cast includes Patrick Bergin, Alison Doody and Ray McAnally. DA

Pierce Brosnan *Mark Taffin* • Ray McAnally *O'Rourke* • Alison Doody *Charlotte* • Jeremy Child *Martin* • Dearbhla Molloy *Mrs Martin* • Jim Bartley *Conway* • Patrick Bergin *Mo Taffin* ■ *Dir* Francis Megahy • *Scr* David Ambrose, from a novel by Lyndon Mallett

Taggart ★★

Western 1964 · US · Colour · 84mins

Here, Dan Duryea holds sway as the hired gunslinger out to kill Tony Young for his part in a land feud, but Dick Foran as a miner and Elsa Cardenas as his opportunistic wife also show well. Undaunted by the amount of incident he has to pack into a modest running time, director RG Springsteen takes the action at a steady clip, and still finds time to flesh out his lowlife characters. DP

Tony Young *Kent Taggart* • Dan Duryea *Jason* • Dick Foran *Stark* • Elsa Cardenas *Consuela Stark* • Jean Hale *Miriam Stark* • David Carradine *Cal Dodge* ■ *Dir* RG Springsteen • *Scr* Robert Creighton Williams [Bob Williams], from the novel by Louis L'Amour

Tai-Pan ★★ 18

Period adventure drama
1986 · US · Colour · 121mins

Bryan Brown plays a 19th-century European trader who establishes his headquarters in Hong Kong, despite opposition from and frequent attacks by rivals, in this inept and lengthy adaptation of James Clavell's bestseller. Brown is the hero we're supposed to like but don't, while Joan Chen adds a touch of Oriental elegance to the sprawling plot over which director Daryl Duke seems to have no control. TH. Contains violence and nudity. [video] DVD

Bryan Brown *Dirk Struan/Tai-Pan* • John Stanton *Tyler Brock* • Joan Chen *May-May* • Tim Guinee *Culum* • Bill Leadbitter *Gorth* • Russell Wong *Gordon* • Kyra Sedgwick *Tess* ■ *Dir* Daryl Duke • *Scr* John Briley, Stanley Mann, from the novel by James Clavell

Tail of a Tiger ★★

Adventure fantasy drama
1984 · Aus · Colour · 84mins

Rolf De Heer keeps threatening to get this Sydney-based tale of individualism versus peer pressure off the ground, only to allow it to plummet back into old-fashioned mediocrity. The concept of ghostly airmen returning to repair a clapped out Tiger Moth is intriguing and original, but De Heer would rather concentrate on nerdy Grant Navin's rivalry with flashy flyboy Peter Feeley and his mawkish relationship with Gordon Poole, the plane's rejuvenated alcoholic owner. DP

Grant Navin *Orville Ryan* • Gordon Poole *Harry* • Caz Lederman *Lydia Ryan* • Gayle Kennedy *Beryl* ■ *Dir/Scr* Rolf De Heer

The Tailor of Panama ★★★ 15

Spy drama 2000 · US/Ire · Colour · 105mins

Although this movie is about a spy and stars Pierce Brosnan, don't expect Bond-style heroics from our man abroad. In fact, Brosnan's character is a rotter of a secret service agent, sent to Panama after one too many misadventures. Once there, he causes more problems by enlisting the information services of expatriate tailor Geoffrey Rush. Based on the John le Carré bestseller, this is one of those movies that you'll either love or detest with a vengeance, as Pierce looks handsome but devious, Rush bumbles and Jamie Lee Curtis is given very little to do as a clueless wife. JB. Contains swearing and sex scenes. [video] DVD

Pierce Brosnan *Andrew Osnard* • Geoffrey Rush *Harry Pendel* • Jamie Lee Curtis *Louisa Pendel* • Brendan Gleeson *Mickie Abraxas* • Catherine McCormack *Francesca* • Leonor Varela *Marta* • Martin Ferrero *Teddy* • Harold Pinter *Uncle Benny* ■ *Dir* John Boorman • *Scr* Andrew Davies, John le Carré, John Boorman, from a novel by John le Carré

Taipei Story ★★★★

Romantic drama
1984 · Tai · Colour · 110mins

Edward Yang confirmed his place in the vanguard of New Taiwanese Cinema with this episodic insight into the consumerist erosion of traditional values and the role of women in an increasingly emasculated patriarchal society. Cai Qin gradually comes to realise that she's being exploited by her reckless father and self-centred sister and has nothing in common with her fiancé Hou Hsiao-Hsien, as he subsists on nostalgia for his days as a baseball star and his relationship with a newly returned old flame. Played against harsh neon cityscapes, this is an uncompromising study of urban alienation and wasted lives. DP. In Mandarin with English subtitles.

Cai Qin *Chin* • Hou Xiaoxian [Hou Hsiao-Hsien] *Lon* • Ke Suyuan *Gwan* • Wu Hinnan *Chin's Father* • Lin Xiuling *Ling* • Wu Nianzhen *Kim* ■ *Dir* Edward Yang • *Scr* Edward Yang, Hou Xiaoxian, Zhu Tianwen

The Take ★★

Action crime drama
1974 · US · Colour · 91mins

A routine action pic, distinguished, if anything, by its eclectic cast. Billy Dee Williams stars as corrupt cop who plays a dangerous double-game with Mob boss Vic Morrow, taking bribes while at the same time trying to take him down in order to impress his superiors. DA

Billy Dee Williams *Sneed* • Eddie Albert *Chief Berrigan* • Frankie Avalon *Danny James* • Sorrell Booke *Oscar* • Tracy Reed *Nancy* • Albert Salmi *Dolek* • Vic Morrow *Manso* • A Martinez *Tallbear* ■ *Dir* Robert Hartford-Davis • *Scr* Del Reisman, Franklin Coen, from the novel *Sir, You Bastard* by GF Newman

Take a Giant Step ★★★

Drama 1959 · US · BW · 99mins

A black boy (Johnny Nash), sent to a white New England school in order to give him a better chance in life, has his adolescence complicated by the racial discrimination and hostility he encounters. He finds comfort with black maid Ruby Dee and wise counsel from his grandmother Estelle Hemsley. This modest film represents an earnest attempt to confront the race issue before it was fashionable to do so. It's very well played by Nash, but lacks both incisiveness of approach and depth of feeling. RK

Johnny Nash *Spencer Scott* • Ruby Dee *Christine the maid* • Estelle Hemsley *Grandma* • Frederick O'Neal *Lem Scott* • Ellen Holly *Carol* • Pauline Meyers *Violet* ■ *Dir* Philip Leacock • *Scr* Louis S Peterson, Julius J Epstein, from a play by Louis S Peterson

Take a Girl like You ★★ 15

Comedy drama 1970 · UK · Colour · 99mins

Kingsley Amis's novel about a northern girl who teaches in a London grammar school was published in 1960 and fed off the 1950s atmosphere of frugality and furtive sex. Filmed at the tail end of 1960s, it seemed dated on release, with Hayley Mills valiantly trying to remain virginal despite the best efforts of Labour councillor and landlord John Bird and art teacher Oliver Reed, who of course is a bit of a Bohemian. It's directed with an uncertain feeling by Jonathan Miller. AT [video]

Noel Harrison *Julian Ormerod* • Oliver Reed *Patrick Standish* • Hayley Mills *Jenny Bunn* • Sheila Hancock *Martha Thompson* • John Bird *Dick Thompson* • Aimi MacDonald *Wendy* • Ronald Lacey *Graham* • Geraldine Sherman *Anna* ■ *Dir* Jonathan Miller • *Scr* George Melly, from the novel by Kingsley Amis

Take a Hard Ride ★★

Western 1975 · US/It · Colour · 102mins

The spaghetti western meets blaxploitation industry in this violent example of genre crossbreeding. Cowboy Jim Brown on a mission to deliver $86,000 to his dying boss's wife and teaming up with gambler Fred Williamson. Unfortunately word gets around about the money and they become the target of bounty hunter Lee Van Cleef's ruthless posse. Williamson gives a nicely laconic performance in this Canary Islands shot shoot-em-up, where deft humour rides uncomfortable side-saddle with hosts of bloody corpses. AJ

Jim Brown *Pike* • Lee Van Cleef *Kiefer* • Fred Williamson *Tyree* • Catherine Spaak *Catherine* • Jim Kelly *Kashtok* • Barry Sullivan *Sheriff Kane* • Dana Andrews *Morgan* • Harry Carey Jr *Dumper* ■ *Dir* Anthony M Dawson [Antonio Margheriti] • *Scr* Eric Bercovici, Jerry Ludwig

Take a Letter, Darling ★★★

Comedy 1942 · US · BW · 93mins

Rosalind Russell replaced Claudette Colbert in this agreeable romantic comedy in which Russell portrays the sort of career woman with whom she became identified and brilliantly gets laughs from occasionally thin material. As a high-flying advertising executive, she hires Fred MacMurray as a private secretary and escort to keep wolves at bay, but what ensues is not as predictable as it may sound. Good fun, expertly played, with all the trappings – gorgeous costumes, lush settings – of Hollywood escapism. TV

Rosalind Russell *AM MacGregor* • Fred MacMurray *Tom Verney* • Macdonald Carey *Jonathan Caldwell* • Constance Moore *Ethel Caldwell* • Robert Benchley *GB Atwater* • Charles Arnt *Fud Newton* • Cecil Kellaway *Uncle George* • Kathleen Howard *Aunt Minnie* ■ *Dir* Mitchell Leisen • *Scr* Claude Binyon, from a story by George Beck

Take Care of My Cat ★★★ PG

Drama 2002 · S Kor · Colour · 111mins

Exploiting Inchon's industrial landscape and the false glamour of Seoul, this thoughtful drama delves deeply into the psyche of the single girl. Jeong Jae-eun's directorial debut succeeds in both exploring the ties that bind five former school friends and assessing the status of women in South Korean society. There's an occasional tendency to meander, as introverted artist Ok Ji-young becomes increasingly dependent on the unconventional Bae Doo-na, but Jeong is more interested in personality than story and, consequently, the ambitions and insecurities of this disparate group begin to exert a fascination that is both touching and intriguing. DP. In Korean with English subtitles.

Bae Doo-na *Tae-hee* • Lee Yo-won *Hae-joo* • Ok Ji-young *Ji-young* • Lee Eun-shil *Bi-ryu* • Lee Eun-joo *Ohn-jo* ■ *Dir/Scr* Jeong Jae-eun

Take Care of Your Scarf, Tatjana ★★★★

Comedy 1994 · Fin · BW · 65mins

Set in the early 1960s, this road movie is a brilliant study of sexual and cultural unease expressed almost exclusively in pregnant pauses and meaningful gestures, as a pair of morose music-loving Finns give a couple of Russian women a lift, against a soundtrack of suitably miserable rhythm-and-blues music. Aki Kaurismäki regulars Kati Outinen and Matti Pellonpaa give what amount to masterclasses in comic understatement. Sharp and hilarious. DP. In Finnish with English subtitles.

Kati Outinen *Tatjana* • Matti Pellonpaa *Reino* • Kirsi Tykkylainen *Klavdia* • Mato Valtonen *Valto* • Elina Salo *Hotel manageress* • Irma Junnilained *Valto's mother* • Veikko Lavi *Vepe* • Pertti Husu *Pepe* ■ *Dir* Aki Kaurismäki • *Scr* Aki Kaurismäki, Sakke Jarvenpaa

Take Down ★★★ PG

Sports drama 1978 · US · Colour · 106mins

English teacher Edward Herrmann grudgingly agrees to coach the wrestling team at his down-and-out high school and inspires the deadbeat students to greater glory in this warmly sentimental sports saga. The one major team hope is Lorenzo Lamas (in his first big movie role). But does the graduation no-hoper, also saddled with an alcoholic father, have the grit to succeed against all the odds? Medium range melodrama to be sure, yet Herrmann is highly engaging and Lamas impresses with a vulnerable and sensitive performance. AJ [video]

Edward Herrmann *Ed Branish* • Kathleen Lloyd *Jill Branish* • Lorenzo Lamas *Nick Kilvitus* • Maureen McCormick *Brooke Cooper* • Nicolas Beauvy *Jimmy Kier* • Stephen Furst *Randy Jensen* • Kevin Hooks *Jasper Macgruder* ■ *Dir* Kieth Merrill • *Scr* Kieth Merrill, Eric Hendershot

Take Her, She's Mine ★★★

Comedy 1963 · US · Colour · 97mins

James Stewart is the doting but conservative father who goes into panic mode when his teenage daughter Sandra Dee exhibits the traits of her generation by supporting ban the bomb and espousing the hippy ethos. The situation is aggravated when the girl goes to Paris to study art and gets involved with painter Philippe Forquet. A pleasing, if now dated, family comedy, which takes a light-hearted approach to the political and cultural upheavals of the 1960s. RK

James Stewart *Frank Michaelson* • Sandra Dee *Mollie Michaelson* • Audrey Meadows *Anne Michaelson* • Robert Morley *Pope-Jones* • Philippe Forquet *Henri Bonnet* • John McGiver *Hector G Ivor* ■ *Dir* Henry Koster • *Scr* Nunnally Johnson, from a play by Phoebe Ephron, Henry Ephron

Take It Easy ★★

Comedy 1971 · Fr · Colour · 90mins

The third of Alain Delon's nine outings under the direction of Jacques Deray lacks the class of their previous year's collaboration, *Borsalino*. Delon plays a priest who discovers that the wife he presumed long dead (real ex, Nathalie) is not only very much alive, but has also seen the light and plans to give up prostitution to enter a convent. Delon misjudges the film's comic tone, unlike Paul Meurisse, who steals the show as an irascible bishop. DP. French dialogue dubbed into English.

Alain Delon *Simon Médieu* • Paul Meurisse *Bishop* • Nathalie Delon *Rita* • Julien Guiomar *Francisco* • Paul Preboist *L'Abbé de Coeur* ■ *Dir* Jacques Deray • *Scr* Pascal Jardin

Take It like a Man, Ma'am ★★

Drama 1975 · Den · Colour · 96mins

This engaging Danish film has as its central character a middle-aged woman with adult children, who's married to a complacent and patronising husband. She dreams vividly of a world where gender roles are reversed and decides to take charge of her life, find a job and achieve fulfilment. Not particularly original, then, although the dream sequence where men assume so-called "negative" roles as sex objects has some delicious moments. A film very much of its time. BB. In Danish with English subtitles.

Tove Maes *Ellen Rasmussen* • Alf Lassen *Eric Rasmussen* • Berthe Quistgard *Karen* • Hans Kragh Jacobsen *Lars* ■ *Dir/Scr* Mette Knudsen, Elisabeth Rygaard, Li Vilstrup

Take Me High ★ U

Musical comedy 1973 · UK · Colour · 86mins

Cliff Richard plays a bank manager who recaptures his youth by helping a failing restaurant become the most talked-about eatery in the West Midlands. The songs are confined to the soundtrack, while the "comedy" plods along with all the zip of Spaghetti Junction at rush hour. DP [video]

Cliff Richard *Tim Matthews* • Debbie Watling *Sarah* • Hugh Griffith *Sir Harry Cunningham* • George Cole *Bert Jackson* • Anthony Andrews

T

Hugo Flaxman • Richard Wattis *Sir Charles Furness* • Madeline Smith *Vicki* ■ *Dir* David Askey • *Scr* Christopher Penfold

Take Me Home: the John Denver Story ★★ PG

Biographical drama
2000 · US · Colour · 86mins

Recalling the fanciful musical biopics of the studio era, this TV movie seeks out the domestic misery behind the public persona of one of the few folk singers to make an impact on the pop scene. The son of a hectoring USAF pilot, Henry John Deutchendorf only came into his own after he quit the Chad Mitchell Trio. In the 1970s, as John Denver, he scored a string of hits. Sincere but unpersuasive. DP DVD

Chad Lowe *John Denver* • Kristin Davis *Annie Denver* • Gerald McRaney *Dutch* • Brian Markinson *Hal Thau* ■ *Dir* Jerry London • *Scr* Stephen Harrigan, from the autobiography by John Denver, Arthur Tobier

Take Me Out to the Ball Game ★★★★ U

Musical 1949 · US · Colour · 89mins

This wonderful MGM musical has super songs, ravishing Technicolor and extraordinary talent both behind and in front of the camera. Star Gene Kelly and director Stanley Donen provide the original story, and take over both choreography and some directing chores from ailing veteran Busby Berkeley. The movie's enchanting, not just for Kelly's great all-stops-out Irish solo and the fabulous trio of Kelly, Frank Sinatra and the under-rated Jules Munshin, but also for a delightfully no-nonsense Esther Williams as the girl who inherits a baseball team. TS

Frank Sinatra *Dennis Ryan* • Esther Williams *KC Higgins* • Gene Kelly *Eddie O'Brien* • Betty Garrett *Shirley Delwyn* • Edward Arnold *Joe Lorgan* • Jules Munshin *Nat Goldberg* • Richard Lane *Michael Gilhuly* • Tom Dugan *Slappy Burke* ■ *Dir* Busby Berkeley • *Scr* Harry Tugend, George Wells, Harry Crane (uncredited), from a story by Gene Kelly, Stanley Donen

Take Me to Town ★★ U

Musical comedy adventure
1953 · US · Colour · 80mins

Ann Sheridan is a saloon singer with a past who takes refuge from the law in a remote lumber-jacking community where woodsman Sterling Hayden is also the local preacher. His three young sons decide that Sheridan would make them a perfect mom, but the locals are hostile. Needless to say, she wins them all over. Folksy, saccharine-coated gloop, directed by Douglas Sirk and hard to swallow. RK

Ann Sheridan *Vermilion O'Toole* • Sterling Hayden *Will Hall* • Philip Reed *Newton Cole* • Phyllis Stanley *Mrs Stoffer* • Larry Gates *Ed Daggett* • Lee Patrick *Rose* • Forrest Lewis *Ed Higgins* ■ *Dir* Douglas Sirk • *Scr* Richard Morris, from his story *Flame of the Timberline*

Take My Eyes ★★★★ 15

Drama 2003 · Sp · Colour · 102mins

This award-winning film from Iciar Bollain is a painful and unforgettable experience. Having walked out after suffering years of physical and mental humiliation, Laia Marull contemplates returning to her husband Luis Tosar when he claims to have finally controlled his violent temper. Marull's anguish is heart-rending; her portrayal of a broken spirit on the verge of repair too touching for words. Equally, Tosar's gruffly tender brute makes one understand why his wife wants their marriage to work. Bollain directs with deftness and an even-handed tone, building to a denouement of incredible power. AJ. In Spanish with English subtitles. Contains violence, swearing. DVD

Laia Marull *Pilar* • Luis Tosar *Antonio* • Candela Peña *Ana* • Rosa Maria Sarda *Aurora* • Kiti Manver *Rosa* • Sergi Calleja *Therapist* • Elisabet Gelabert *Lola* • Nicolás Fernández Luna *Juan* ■ *Dir* Iciar Bollain • *Scr* Iciar Bollain, Alicia Luna

Take My Life ★★★★ PG

Murder mystery 1947 · UK · BW · 75mins

This marks the impressive directorial debut from British cinematographer Ronald Neame. Hugh Williams is accused of murder and his opera singer wife Greta Gynt is determined to find out who really did it. This was the kind of intelligent thriller that Hollywood directors could churn out in their sleep and it is to Neame's credit that he makes it clever, convincing and, above, all stylish. TS

Hugh Williams *Nicholas Talbot* • Greta Gynt *Philippa Bentley* • Marius Goring *Sidney Flemming* • Francis L Sullivan *Prosecuting counsel* • Henry Edwards *Inspector Archer* • Rosalie Crutchley *Elizabeth Rusman* • Maurice Denham *Defending counsel* ■ *Dir* Ronald Neame • *Scr* Winston Graham, Valerie Taylor, Margaret Kennedy, from a story by Winston Graham, Valerie Taylor

Take the High Ground ★★

War drama 1953 · US · Colour · 101mins

Screenwriter Millard Kaufman was nominated for an Oscar for this insight into the realities of basic training for the Korean War. Carleton Carpenter seems suitably intimidated as the private singled out for especial ire by sergeant Richard Widmark, but the unit is comprised of stereotypical grunts. Much more convincing is the barely suppressed sadism with which Widmark barks out his orders. DP

Richard Widmark *Sergeant Thorne Ryan* • Karl Malden *Sergeant Laverne Holt* • Elaine Stewart *Julie Mollison* • Russ Tamblyn *Paul Jamison* • Carleton Carpenter *Merton Tolliver* • Steve Forrest *Lobo Naglaski* ■ *Dir* Richard Brooks • *Scr* Millard Kaufman

Take the Money and Run ★★★ PG

Comedy 1969 · US · Colour · 81mins

After years of writing for TV and doing his own stand-up routine, Woody Allen finally made his debut as co-writer, director and star with this ambitious cod documentary. Nicely joshing the "Voice of Doom" style of narration and such Hollywood movies as *The Defiant Ones*, the film gets off to a flying start, with public enemy Virgil Starkwell's childhood remaining among the funniest things Allen has ever done. The inspiration slowly ebbs away though, and the last ten minutes are something of a chore. DP DVD

Woody Allen *Virgil Starkwell* • Janet Margolin *Louise* • Marcel Hillaire *Fritz* • Jacquelyn Hyde *Miss Blaire* • Lonny Chapman *Jake* • Jan Merlin *Al* • James Anderson (2) *Chain gang warden* ■ *Dir* Woody Allen • *Scr* Woody Allen, Mickey Rose

Take This Job and Shove It ★★ PG

Comedy 1981 · US · Colour · 95mins

This big business comedy stars Robert Hays as a decent chap, who is sent by his firm back to his home town to increase the efficiency of the local brewery. His appointment is met with some hostility by the employees (many of whom he knows personally) but he soon proves his worth. Named after the hit song performed by Johnny Paycheck, this well-meaning comedy features an uneasy mix of sloppy slapstick and toothless satire. DF

Robert Hays *Frank Macklin* • Barbara Hershey *JM Halstead* • David Keith *Harry Meade* • Tim Thomerson *Ray Binkowski* • Eddie Albert *Samuel Ellison* • Penelope Milford *Lenore Meade* • Art Carney *Charlie Pickett* • Martin Mull *Dick Ebersol* • David Allan Coe *Mooney* ■ *Dir* Gus Trikonis • *Scr* Barry Schneider, from a story by Jeffrey Bernini, Barry Schneider, from a song by David Allen Coe

Taken ★★

Drama 1999 · Can · Colour · 98mins

Dabney Coleman plays an unpleasant housing tycoon who gets kidnapped in this mediocre thriller. And just about everyone either has a motive for wanting him dead or an urgent need for the $2 million ransom. Cheating wife Linda Smith, scheming partner Stewart Bick, corrupt accountant Michael Rudder and decadent stepson Brett Watson are all investigated by secretary-turned-sleuth Dorothée Berryman. Predictable. DP. Contains violence and sex scenes.

Dabney Coleman *Ethan Grover* • Stewart Bick *Alan Cross* • Dennis Boutsikaris *Bill McMurtrey* • Linda Smith *Judy Grover* • Michael Rudder *Syd Brooks* • Dorothée Berryman *Sandra Mathers* • Brett Watson *Alex* ■ *Dir* Max Fischer • *Scr* Pierre Lapointe

Taken Away ★★ 12

Drama based on a true story
1996 · US · Colour · 85mins

Since making their names in *LA Law*, real-life married couple Michael Tucker and Jill Eikenberry have regularly teamed up in TV movies. Here, Eikenberry plays a kidnap victim with a heart condition who has been left bound and gagged in her car; Tucker is her frantic husband who's desperately trying to locate her. The two leads turn in believable performances and, although it hardly taxes the brain, this is an intriguing enough time-passer. JF. Contains some swearing. DVD

Michael Tucker *Mark Hale* • Jill Eikenberry *Jan Hale* • James Marsden *Michael Galler* • Shane Meier *David Rattray* • Robert Wisden *Chief Ben Alpert* ■ *Dir* Jerry Jameson • *Scr* Ronald Parker

Taking Care of Business ★★ 15

Comedy 1990 · US · Colour · 107mins

This is a rather slight *Trading Places* rip-off with James Belushi as the prisoner on the run who finds wealthy Charles Grodin's Filofax and proceeds to steal his identity. The talented Belushi doesn't have enough good material here, while the usually excellent Grodin forfeits some of his substantial charm to the demands of the over-frenetic comedy. This is too uneven to be riproaring entertainment, but it's still harmless fun. Also known as *Filofax* in the UK. JB. Contains swearing. DVD

James Belushi *Jimmy Dworski* • Charles Grodin *Spencer Barnes* • Anne De Salvo *Debbie* • Loryn Locklin *Jewel* • Stephen Elliott *Walter Bentley* • Hector Elizondo *Warden* • Veronica Hamel *Elizabeth Barnes* ■ *Dir* Arthur Hiller • *Scr* Jill Mazursky, Jeffrey Abrams

Taking Lives ★★ 15

Psychological thriller
2004 · US/Aus · Colour · 98mins

Director DJ Caruso stumbles his way through the conventions of the psychological thriller in this dreary, by-the-numbers serial-killer film. Angelina Jolie plays a top FBI profiler, called in to help Canadian homicide detectives Jean-Hugues Anglade and Olivier Martinez catch a chameleon-like murderer who assumes his victims' identities. Ethan Hawke looks uncomfortable throughout, while the appearance of Kiefer Sutherland is lazy typecasting. SF. Contains swearing, violence and sex scenes. DVD

Angelina Jolie *Special Agent Illeana Scott* • Ethan Hawke *James Costa* • Kiefer Sutherland *Hart* • Olivier Martinez *Paquette* • Tcheky Karyo *Leclair* • Jean-Hugues Anglade *Duval* • Gena Rowlands *Mrs Asher* • Paul Dano *Young Asher* ■ *Dir* DJ Caruso • *Scr* Jon Bokenkamp, from a story by Jon Bokenkamp, from the novel by Michael Pye

The Taking of Beverly Hills ★★ 15

Action crime thriller
1991 · US · Colour · 90mins

Routine action film, in which crook Robert Davi fakes a toxic spill so that his men can loot the homes of LA's rich and famous during the evacuation. Predictably, die-hard hero Ken Wahl rumbles the ruse, and tosses several spanners in the works. It's a promising plot, indifferently handled by director Sidney J Furie. DA

Ken Wahl *Terry "Boomer" Hayes* • Harley Jane Kozak *Laura Sage* • Matt Frewer *Ed Kelvin* • Tony Ganios *EPA Man* • Robert Davi *Robert "Bat" Masterson* • Lee Ving James [Lee Ving] *Varney* • Branscombe Richmond *Benitez* ■ *Dir* Sidney J Furie • *Scr* Rick Natkin, David Fuller, David J Burke, from a story by Sidney J Furie, Rick Natkin, David Fuller

The Taking of Pelham One Two Three ★★★★ 15

Thriller 1974 · US · Colour · 102mins

Gerald Greenberg and Robert Q Lovett are the "stars" of this tough and compelling thriller about the hijacking of a New York subway train. They are the film editors whose superb sense of rhythm and pace brings real tension to the radio exchanges between villain Robert Shaw and transport cop Walter Matthau, who tries to prevent Shaw and his gang from killing hostages while waiting for the payment of a $1 million ransom. The motley collection of clichéd passengers doesn't deserve to be rescued, but director Joseph Sargent keeps the focus firmly on his leads. Shaw is admirably fanatical, and the world-weary, wisecracking Matthau is magnificent. DP. Contains violence, swearing. DVD

Walter Matthau *Lieutenant Garber* • Robert Shaw *Blue* • Martin Balsam *Green* • Hector Elizondo *Grey* • Earl Hindman *Brown* • James Broderick *Denny Doyle* • Dick O'Neill *Correll* • Lee Wallace *Mayor* • Jerry Stiller *Lieutenant Rico Patrone* ■ *Dir* Joseph Sargent • *Scr* Peter Stone, from the novel by John Godey

Taking Off ★★★★ 18

Comedy drama 1971 · US · Colour · 88mins

Director Milos Forman's (*Amadeus*, *One Flew over the Cuckoo's Nest*) first American movie is a comedy of manners. Like the Czech quasi-comedies that brought him international acclaim, it's charming, sexy, bittersweet, and, in truth, a trifle plotless, but, like them it contains gems of observation and a wondrous understanding of human nature. This deals with a dropout teenager's effect on her parents, with Buck Henry (who co-wrote *The Graduate*) playing the runaway's father, getting out of his depth in the permissive society. TS

Lynn Carlin *Lynn Tyne* • Buck Henry *Larry Tyne* • Linnea Heacock *Jeannie Tyne* • Georgia Engel *Margot* • Tony Harvey *Tony* • Audra Lindley *Ann Lockston* • Paul Benedict *Ben Lockston* • Ike Turner • Tina Turner • Carly Simon *Audition singer* ■ *Dir* Milos Forman • *Scr* Milos Forman, John Guare, Jean-Claude Carrière, John Klein

Taking Sides ★★★ 15

Second World War biographical drama
2001 · Ger/Fr/UK/Austria · Colour · 105mins

Hungarian director István Szabó returns to Central Europe in the mid-20th century for this intelligent adaptation. However, a resounding denunciation of America's current posturing as the world's policeman is also apparent in the way a defiantly uncultured war

T

crimes investigator (Harvey Keitel) attempts to impose his perceived moral superiority on an orchestra conductor accused of glorifying the Nazis. Keitel's blustering performance exaggerates the significance of this theme, whereas Stellan Skarsgård's nuanced depiction of the renowned Wilhelm Furtwängler explores the link between art and power. DP. Contains swearing. DVD

Harvey Keitel *Maj Steve Arnold* • Stellan Skarsgård *Dr Wilhelm Furtwängler* • Moritz Bleibtreu *Lt David Wills* • Birgit Minichmayr *Emmi Straube* • Oleg Tabakov *Col Dymshitz* • Ulrich Tukur *Helmuth Rode* • Hanns Zischler *Rudolf Werner* • Armin Rohde *Schlee* • R Lee Ermey *Gen Wallace* • August Zirner *Capt Ed Martin* • Frank LeBoeuf *Lt Simon* ■ *Dir* István Szabó • *Scr* Ronald Harwood, from his play

Tale of a Vampire ★★ 18

Horror 1992 · UK/Jpn · Colour · 97mins

Melancholic bloodsucker Julian Sands prowls suburban London searching for the double of his lost lover, in this arty postmodern Hammer homage. When Sands eventually finds her in the guise of librarian Suzanna Hamilton (giving a dreadful performance) he must battle occult historian Kenneth Cranham for her spirit. Depressingly ordinary, despite a few oriental flourishes, this Mills and Boon vampire romance is far too low-key. AJ

Julian Sands *Alex* • Suzanna Hamilton *Anne/Virginia* • Kenneth Cranham *Edgar* • Marian Diamond *Denise* • Michael Kenton *Magazine man* • Catherine Blake *Virginia, aged 5* ■ *Dir* Shimako Sato • *Scr* Shimako Sato, Jane Corbett, from a story by Shimako Sato, from the poem *Annabel Lee* by Edgar Allan Poe

A Tale of Springtime ★★★★ U

Romance 1989 · Fr · Colour · 102mins

Eric Rohmer's film shows keen intelligence, insight into the emotions of youth and an unrivalled genius for chamber drama. As ever in Rohmer's features, we feel we are eavesdropping on real people, with their behaviour, conversation and sheer unpredictability the very stuff of human nature. Deftly handled and effortlessly played, particularly by Anne Teyssèdre and Hugues Quester, this tale of matchmaking and friendship is utterly beguiling. DP. In French with English subtitles.

Anne Teyssèdre *Jeanne* • Hugues Quester *Igor* • Florence Darel *Natasha* • Eloise Bennett *Eve* • Sophie Robin *Gaelle* ■ *Dir/Scr* Eric Rohmer

The Tale of the Fox ★★★★

Satirical fantasy 1931 · Fr · BW · 65mins

Ladislaw Starewicz's only feature contains 100 different puppet characters and took a decade to prepare and 18 months to film. The story of the mischievous fox who is called to the court of the Lion King to explain his pranks works well as a children's film, thanks to the superbly judged blend of animal and human traits and the painstaking attention to natural detail. But it's also a subtle political satire that simmers with a deliciously naughty sexual tension. DP. A French language film.

Dir Ladislaw Starewicz, Irène Starewicz • *Scr* Wladyslaw Starewicz, Irène Starewicz, Roger Richebé, Jean Nohain, Antoinette Nordmann, from the story *Die Reineke Fuchs* by Johann Wolfgang von Goethe • *Animator* Ladislaw Starewicz, Irene Starewicz

A Tale of Two Cities ★★★★★ U

Period drama 1935 · US · BW · 120mins

Ronald Colman is convincingly noble as lawyer Sydney Carton, a victim of unrequited love, who finds purpose in an act of self-sacrifice during the ruthless period of the French Revolution. The other actors – Elizabeth Allan, Basil Rathbone and Edna May Oliver – are at the mercy of some massive crowd scenes, for which thousands of extras were recruited. The featured players survive very well through a magnificent storming of a rather flimsy Bastille, while the cut-off point of the final scene with Madame La Guillotine and Sydney Carton will bring tears to your eyes. It is a far, far better movie of the classic than they were to make thereafter with Dirk Bogarde. TH

Ronald Colman *Sydney Carton* • Elizabeth Allan *Lucie Manette* • Edna May Oliver *Miss Pross* • Blanche Yurka *Mme Defarge* • Reginald Owen *Stryver* • Basil Rathbone *Marquis St Evremonde* • Henry B Walthall *Dr Manette* • Donald Woods *Charles Darnay* ■ *Dir* Jack Conway • *Scr* WP Lipscomb, SN Behrman, from the novel by Charles Dickens

A Tale of Two Cities ★★★ U

Period drama 1957 · UK · BW · 112mins

Dirk Bogarde gives a good account of himself in this Rank remake of Dickens's French Revolution novel. TEB Clarke, who scripted many of the best Ealing comedies, was perhaps an odd choice for such a prestigious project and, in striving for dramatic weight, he is occasionally guilty of being both pompous and ponderous. But director Ralph Thomas brings the best out of his cast, with Dorothy Tutin making a fetching Lucie Manette and Christopher Lee a truly hissable Marquis St Evremonde. DP DVD

Dirk Bogarde *Sydney Carton* • Dorothy Tutin *Lucie Manette* • Cecil Parker *Jarvis Lorry* • Stephen Murray *Dr Manette* • Athene Seyler *Miss Pross* • Christopher Lee *Marquis St Evremonde* • Donald Pleasence *John Barsad* • Rosalie Crutchley *Madame Defarge* ■ *Dir* Ralph Thomas • *Scr* TEB Clarke, from the novel by Charles Dickens

A Tale of Two Cities ★★ U

Animated drama 1984 · Aus · Colour · 75mins

The best that makers of animated classics can hope for is that the film will not be denounced as a travesty that dishonours the original text. This Australian adaptation of Dickens's tale of selfless heroism set at the time of the French Revolution certainly has its faults, not least the atrocious accents. But the animation and the sense of fear generated by the Reign of Terror is rather well captured. As ever, the villains are better drawn than the goodies. DP

Dir Warwick Gilbert • *Scr* Russell Thornton, from the novel by Charles Dickens

A Tale of Two Sisters ★★★ 15

Gothic horror 2003 · S Kor · Colour · 109mins

South Korean film-maker Kim Ji-woon's atmospheric gothic horror may not be the most original tale, but with its sumptuous, colour-saturated visuals, it's certainly among the most beautiful. The feature is an eerie account of two sisters (Moon Geun-young and Im Soo-jung), who return home after a long psychiatric illness, only to grow increasingly fearful of their strange new stepmother. Yet for all its derivative elements, the meticulous direction and cinematography lend the picture a sense of freshness. SF. In Korean with English subtitles. DVD

Kim Kab-su *Mu-hyun* • Yeom Jeong-ah *Eun-joo* • Im Soo-jung *Su-mi* • Moon Geun-young *Su-yeon* ■ *Dir* Kim Ji-woon • *Scr* Kim Ji-woon, Lee Byung-woo

Talent for the Game ★★★ PG

Sports drama 1991 · US · Colour · 87mins

A modest but watchable entry in the baseball genre, this stars Edward James Olmos as a baseball scout who discovers a brilliant young pitcher in an Idaho backwater, but watches in dismay as he is ruthlessly exploited by his club. Olmos delivers a typically gutsy performance and, although the story is slight, director Robert M Young handles the proceedings commendably. JF. Contains some strong language. DVD

Edward James Olmos *Virgil Sweet* • Lorraine Bracco *Bobbie Henderson* • Jamey Sheridan *Tim Weaver* • Terry Kinney *Gil Lawrence* • Jeff Corbett *Sammy Bodeen* • Tom Bower *Reverend Bodeen* • Janet Carroll *Rachel Bodeen* ■ *Dir* Robert M Young • *Scr* David Himmelstein, Tom Donnelly [Thomas Michael Donnelly], Larry Ferguson

The Talented Mr Ripley ★★★★ 15

Crime thriller 1999 · US · Colour · 142mins

Director Anthony Minghella follows his award-winning *The English Patient* with this absorbing thriller, based on the novel by Patricia Highsmith. Matt Damon plays the eponymous Ripley, a young opportunist who seeks out Jude Law (Oscar-nominated), an American playboy living it up in Europe. Ripley becomes friends with Law, but gradually comes to covet the carefree lifestyle he shares with his glamorous girlfriend (Gwyneth Paltrow). Minghella's classy direction and the superior cast make this never less than compelling. LH. Contains swearing. DVD

Matt Damon *Tom Ripley* • Gwyneth Paltrow *Marge Sherwood* • Jude Law *Dickie Greenleaf* • Cate Blanchett *Meredith Logue* • Philip Seymour Hoffman *Freddie Miles* • Jack Davenport *Peter Smith-Kingsley* • James Rebhorn *Herbert Greenleaf* • Philip Baker Hall *Alvin MacCarron* ■ *Dir* Anthony Minghella • *Scr* Anthony Minghella, from the novel by Patricia Highsmith

Tales from a Hard City ★★★★

Documentary drama
1994 · UK/Fr · Colour · 80mins

The glorious British documentary tradition is alive and well and living in Sheffield. Director Kim Flitcroft spent a year with his subjects, and what a quartet they are: Glen the karaoke car thief; Paul the thespian boxer; Wayne the wannabe media mogul; and Sarah the star-in-the-making Wayne wants to promote. Fact repeatedly proves more bizarre than fiction throughout the film and, while the foursome are sometimes hard to live with, they are certainly never dull. DP

Dir Kim Flitcroft • *Scr* Geoffrey Beattie (story consultant)

Tales from the Crypt ★★★ 18

Horror 1972 · UK · Colour · 91mins

An excellent anthology of scares-with-a-smile stories drawn from EC horror comics, with Ralph Richardson as the crypt keeper revealing a quintet of fearsome futures to a veteran British cast of terror troupers. Peter Cushing returns from the grave, Patrick Magee is a victimised blind man, Joan Collins battles a psychotic Santa Claus, Richard Greene does a variation on *The Monkey's Paw* and Ian Hendry can't get used to being dead. Ace direction by genre favourite Freddie Francis adeptly leavens the vivid horror with seriocomic interludes. AJ

Ralph Richardson *Crypt keeper* • Geoffrey Bayldon *Guide* • Joan Collins *Joanne Clayton* • Ian Hendry *Carl Maitland* • Nigel Patrick *William Rogers* • Patrick Magee *George Carter* • Peter Cushing *Grimsdyke* • Richard Greene *Ralph Jason* • Roy Dotrice *Charles Gregory* ■ *Dir* Freddie Francis • *Scr* Milton Subotsky, from stories from the comic books *Tales from the Crypt* and *The Vault of Horror* by Al Feldstein, Johnny Craig, William Gaines

Tales from the Crypt: Demon Knight ★★ 18

Horror fantasy 1995 · US · Colour · 92mins

Not an anthology in the fondly remembered tradition of the original *Tales from the Crypt*, just one duff story ripped off from *Night of the Living Dead*. Billy Zane is the evil force who hounds an assortment of misfits trapped in a Texas motel in his search for an ancient talisman containing the blood of Jesus Christ. Crude sight gags and slimy schlock are accented over mordant humour. AJ. Contains swearing and violence.

Billy Zane *The Collector* • William Sadler *Brayker* • Jada Pinkett [Jada Pinkett Smith] *Jeryline* • Brenda Bakke *Cordelia* • CCH Pounder *Irene* • Dick Miller *Uncle Willy* ■ *Dir* Ernest R Dickerson • *Scr* Ethan Reiff, Cyrus Voris, Mark Bishop

Tales from the Crypt Presents: Bordello of Blood ★ 18

Horror comedy 1996 · US · Colour · 82mins

This B-movie gross-out is tedious, tawdry and tiresome. Stand-up comedian Dennis Miller is the detective hired by Erika Eleniak to find her wayward punk brother Corey Feldman, who has disappeared after patronising a brothel-cum-funeral home run by ancient vampire queen Angie Everhart. AJ. Contains swearing, violence, sex scenes and nudity.

John Kassir *Crypt Keeper* • Dennis Miller *Rafe Guttman* • Erika Eleniak *Katherine Verdoux* • Angie Everhart *Lilith* • Chris Sarandon *Reverend Current* • Corey Feldman *Caleb Verdoux* • Aubrey Morris *McCutcheon* ■ *Dir* Gilbert Adler • *Scr* Gilbert Adler, AL Katz, from a story by Bob Gale, Robert Zemeckis

Tales from the Darkside: the Movie ★★★ 18

Horror 1991 · US · Colour · 89mins

A 3,000-year-old mummy, a malignant moggy and a gruesome gargoyle take their monstrous turns in a taut, tight and fun trio of terror tales drawn from the work of authors Sir Arthur Conan Doyle and Stephen King. High on creepy atmosphere, low on boring exposition, this well-crafted movie version of its duff namesake TV series is an agreeably ambitious and solidly shocking outing. AJ. Contains violence and swearing. DVD

Deborah Harry *Betty* • David Forrester *Priest* • Matthew Lawrence *Timmy* • Christian Slater *Andy* • Steve Buscemi *Edward Bellingham* • Julianne Moore *Susan* • Micheal Deak *Mummy* • David Johansen *Halston* • William Hickey *Drogan* • James Remar *Preston* • Rae Dawn Chong *Carola* ■ *Dir* John Harrison • *Scr* Michael McDowell, George Romero, from the story *Lot 249* by Sir Arthur Conan Doyle, from the story *Cat from Hell* by Stephen King

T

Tales from the Hood ★★

Horror 1995 · US · Colour · 101mins

Spike Lee was the executive producer of this horror anthology that attempts to comment on an aspect of the African-American experience in each of its stories with uneven results. The first story (a rookie cop encounters brutal and bigoted colleagues) is flat and predictable, and the third story (a racist politician struck by an old slave curse) is derivative. Much better are the second story (a boy and the "monster" that appears in his room at night), and the fourth story, concerning the attempted reform of a gang member. An amusing Clarence Williams III plays the ghoulish mortician linking the four stories. KB

Clarence Williams III *Mr Simms* • Joe Torry *Stack* • Wings Hauser *Strom* • Anthony Griffith *Clarence* • Michael Massee *Newton* • Tom Wright *Martin Moorehouse* ■ *Dir* Rusty Cundieff • *Scr* Rusty Cundieff, Darin Scott

The Tales of Beatrix Potter ★★★ U

Dance fantasy 1971 · UK · Colour · 85mins

This big 1971 hit slips into ballet slippers to tell the lovely stories of Beatrix Potter, set in their original Lakeland landscape. Ballet maestro Frederick Ashton choreographs and makes an outstanding appearance as a fussy Mrs Tiggy-Winkle The *corps de ballet* comes with realistic-looking mouse heads, Mrs Puddleduck is a treat and there's a midnight *pas de deux* between two piglets. But the noteworthy costumes tend toward the bulky with a rather smothering effect, and though intended for children, its Peter Rabbit charm is too manipulative and humdrum to urge many balletomane stirrings. FL

Frederick Ashton *Mrs Tiggy-Winkle* • Alexander Grant *Pigling Bland/Peter Rabbit* • Julie Wood *Mrs Tittlemouse* • Keith Martin *Johnny Town Mouse* • Ann Howard *Jemina Puddle-Duck* • Robert Mead *Fox* • Wayne Sleep *Tom Thumb/ Squirrel Nutkin* ■ *Dir* Reginald Mills • *Scr* Richard Goodwin, Christine Edzard, from the stories by Beatrix Potter • *Costume Designer* Christine Edzard

The Tales of Hoffmann ★★★★ U

Opera 1951 · UK · Colour · 119mins

Three years after the success of *The Red Shoes*, Michael Powell and Emeric Pressburger returned to the world of ballet at the behest of Sir Thomas Beecham for this irresistible confection. With Moira Shearer and Frederick Ashton dancing superbly and Hein Heckroth's art design and costumes worthy of their Oscar nominations, this sumptuous adaptation of Offenbach's opera is a visual delight. With the Sadler's Wells Chorus backing singers of the calibre of Robert Rounseville and Ann Ayars, it sounds pretty good, too. Only the slightly muddled structure detracts from what is otherwise an audacious cinematic experiment. DP

Robert Rounseville *Hoffmann* • Moira Shearer *Stella/Olympia* • Robert Helpmann *Lindorff/ Coppelius/Dapertutto* • Pamela Brown *Nicklaus* • Frederick Ashton *Kleinzack/ Cochenille* • Léonide Massine *Spalanzani* • Ludmilla Tcherina *Giulietta* • Ann Ayars *Antonia* • John Ford *Nathaniel* ■ *Dir/Scr* Michael Powell, Emeric Pressburger

Tales of Manhattan ★★★

Portmanteau comedy
1942 · US · BW · 118mins

That title is really an awkward pun: the "tales" are those of a tail coat, and this charming all-star portmanteau comedy is a collection of playlets about the coat's adventures. Very much of its time and less than charming today, the episode involving the great Paul Robeson looks quite racist in its Uncle Remus sort of way, and one wonders why it wasn't deleted, instead of the notoriously missing WC Fields sequence. Edward G Robinson has a splendid moment, as does Charles Laughton at Carnegie Hall, and Rita Hayworth looks simply ravishing in the first story, but this movie is a curate's egg. TS

Charles Boyer *Paul Orman* • Rita Hayworth *Ethel Halloway* • Ginger Rogers *Diane* • Henry Fonda *George* • Cesar Romero *Harry Wilson* • Charles Laughton *Charles Smith* • Elsa Lanchester *Elsa Smith* • Edward G Robinson *Larry Browne* • George Sanders *Williams* • Paul Robeson *Luke* • Ethel Waters *Esther* ■ *Dir* Julien Duvivier • *Scr* Ben Hecht, Ferenc Molnar, Donald Ogden Stewart, Samuel Hoffenstein, Alan Campbell, Ladislas Fodor, Laszlo Vadnai, Laslo Gorog, Lamar Trotti, Henry Blankford, Ed Beloin, Bill Morrow

Tales of Ordinary Madness ★★ 18

Drama 1981 · It/Fr · Colour · 101mins

Italian director Marco Ferreri adapted this film from the autobiographical writings of the alcoholic Beat poet Charles Bukowski. Set mainly in Los Angeles, it stars Ben Gazzara as the disillusioned, womanising poet and he certainly gives a remarkable performance. But what might be wonderful pronouncements on paper certainly don't come across on screen and the effect is pretentious, tedious and very dated. BB. Contains violence, nudity, sex scenes, drug abuse and swearing.

Ben Gazzara *Charles Serking* • Ornella Muti *Cass* • Susan Tyrrell *Vera* • Tanya Lopert *Vicky* • Roy Brocksmith *Barman* ■ *Dir* Marco Ferreri • *Scr* Sergio Amidei, Marco Ferreri, Anthony Foutz, from the short story collection *Erections, Ejaculations, Exhibitions and General Tales of Ordinary Madness* by Charles Bukowski

Tales of Terror ★★★ 15

Horror 1962 · US · Colour · 84mins

One of cult director Roger Corman's classier productions, helped by ace genre writer Richard Matheson's skilled if loose adaptations of three Edgar Allan Poe stories. Ranging between macabre *Grand Guignol* and broad comedy, this cheerfully chilling collection is further boosted by the memorable teaming of Vincent Price and Peter Lorre, the latter in excellent scene-stealing form. AJ DVD

Vincent Price *Locke/Fortunato/Valdemar* • Maggie Pierce *Lenora* • Leona Gage *Morella* • Peter Lorre *Montresor* • Joyce Jameson *Annabel* • Basil Rathbone *Carmichael* • Debra Paget *Helene* ■ *Dir* Roger Corman • *Scr* Richard Matheson, from the stories *Morella*, *The Black Cat, The Facts in the Case of M Valdemar* and *The Cask of Amontillado* by Edgar Allan Poe

Tales of the Taira Clan ★★★ U

Historical drama
1955 · Jpn · Colour · 102mins

Set in a turbulent 12th-century Japan, when Buddhist monks, backed by the indolent nobility, took up arms against the rebellious samurai, the action is efficiently staged in the manner of John Ford. However, the rise of Raizo Ichikawa and his Taira kinsmen at the expense of the tyrannical Minamoto clan lacks the character complexity in which Kenji Mizoguchi revelled. His heart was clearly not in what was to be his penultimate picture. DP. In Japanese with English subtitles.

Raizo Ichikawa *Taira no Kiyomori* • Yoshiko Kuga *Tokiko* • Narutoshi Hayashi *Tokitada* • Michiyo Kogure *Yasuko* ■ *Dir* Kenji Mizoguchi • *Scr* Yoshikata Yoda, Masashige Narusawa, Hisakazu Miyagawa, from the novel by Eiji Yoshikawa

Tales That Witness Madness ★★ 18

Portmanteau horror
1973 · UK · Colour · 86mins

This portmanteau of four horror stories was mysteriously shelved for years, eventually turning up on TV in the 1980s. Director Freddie Francis had previously done better examples of the genre, notably *Torture Garden*. Here the most effective segments are the first (although derivative of Ray Bradbury's story *The Veldt*) and the last (quite gruesome). DM

Jack Hawkins *Nicholas* • Donald Pleasence *Dr Tremayne* • Russell Lewis *Paul* • Peter McEnery *Timothy* • Joan Collins *Bella* • Michael Jayston *Brian* • Kim Novak *Auriol* • Michael Petrovitch *Kimo* • Mary Tamm *Ginny* ■ *Dir* Freddie Francis • *Scr* Jennifer Jayne

Talk of Angels ★★ 12

Period romantic drama
1998 · US · Colour · 93mins

Though it's pretty to look at and finely acted, there is something missing from this rather insubstantial 1930s-set romantic tale. Polly Walker plays a young Irish woman who goes to Spain, which is on the brink of civil war. She is employed to look after the young daughters of a wealthy liberal doctor (Franco Nero), but her life becomes complicated when she catches the eye of his idealistic (and married) young son, Vincent Perez. JF. Contains violence.

Polly Walker *Mary Lavelle* • Vincent Perez *Francisco Areavaga* • Franco Nero *Dr Vicente Areavaga* • Marisa Paredes *Dona Consuelo* • Leire Berrocal *Milagros* • Penélope Cruz *Pilar* • Frances McDormand *Conlon* • Ruth McCabe *O'Toole* ■ *Dir* Nick Hamm • *Scr* Ann Guedes, Frank McGuinness, from the novel *Mary Lavelle* by Kate O'Brien

The Talk of the Town ★★★★ U

Comedy drama 1942 · US · BW · 113mins

The eternal triangle – two men besotted by the same woman who is attracted to both – is the central ingredient of this classy, intelligent and witty romantic comedy. However, skilfully interwoven into the mix is an examination of hypocrisy, the inequities of the law and a measure of suspense. Cary Grant, a politically reformist factory worker, is wrongfully accused of murder and hides out in Jean Arthur's house, where he becomes friends with Ronald Colman, a distinguished legal academic and Supreme Court judge lodging there. Ideas are exchanged and both fall for their hostess. Story, script and picture were Oscar-nominated, the stars deserved to be. RK DVD

Cary Grant *Leopold Dilg* • Jean Arthur *Nora Shelley* • Ronald Colman *Michael Lightcap* • Edgar Buchanan *Sam Yates* • Glenda Farrell *Regina Bush* • Charles Dingle *Andrew Holmes* ■ *Dir* George Stevens • *Scr* Irwin Shaw, Sidney Buchman, Dale Van Every, from a story by Sidney Harmon

Talk Radio ★★★★ 18

Drama 1988 · US · Colour · 104mins

This gripping picture dates from the time when director Oliver Stone made good films rather than sensational headlines, featuring a tour de force performance from Eric Bogosian. DJ Bogosian lets fly with a series of blistering diatribes against the callers to his late night radio show. The subplots rather get in the way of the monologues, which are delivered with such power and passion that one can only wonder why Bogosian's career has gone nowhere since. DP. Contains swearing and violence.

Eric Bogosian *Barry Champlain* • Alec Baldwin *Dan* • Ellen Greene *Ellen* • Leslie Hope *Laura* • John C McGinley *Stu* • John Pankow *Dietz* • Michael Wincott *Kent* • Linda Atkinson *Sheila Fleming* ■ *Dir* Oliver Stone • *Scr* Eric Bogosian, Oliver Stone, from the play by Eric Bogosian, Ted Savinar, from the non-fiction book *Talked to Death: the Life and Murder of Alan Berg* by Stephen Singular

Talk to Her ★★★★ 15

Romantic drama 2001 · Sp · Colour · 108mins

Pedro Almodóvar's genius as a creator of memorable images takes centre stage in this intriguing and sometimes controversial insight into survival, male bonding and the nature of love. The emotional core forms around the friendship forged between nurse Javier Cámara and travel writer Darío Grandinetti, as they wait, respectively, for ballerina Leonor Watling and bullfighter Rosario Flores to emerge from their comas. Amid the shifting timeframes and perspectives, it's the stylised set pieces rather than the unfolding story that really fire the imagination. DP. In Spanish with English subtitles. Contains violence, a sex scene, swearing, nudity. DVD

Javier Cámara *Benigno* • Darío Grandinetti *Marco* • Leonor Watling *Alicia* • Rosario Flores *Lydia* • Geraldine Chaplin *Katerina Bilova* • Mariola Fuentes *Nurse Rosa* • Pina Bausch ■ *Dir/Scr* Pedro Almodóvar

Talkin' Dirty after Dark ★★★ 18

Comedy 1991 · US · Colour · 86mins

This is set around John Witherspoon's LA comedy club where stand-up acts rub shoulders with the equally crazy staff of the late night cabaret venue. Amid the joke-telling there is a complex web of romantic entanglements and sexual liaisons. A good showcase for a bunch of young comedians, the film particularly highlights the amiable, fast-talking Martin Lawrence who wins over the crowd with blue routines about sex. This profane, undisciplined romp triumphs with some truly funny sequences. DF

Martin Lawrence *Terry* • John Witherspoon *Dukie* • Jedda Jones *Rubie Lin* • "Tiny" Lister Jr [Tom "Tiny" Lister Jr] *Bigg* • Phyllis Yvonne Stickney *Aretha* • Renee Jones *Kimmie* • Darryl Sivad *Percy* • Yolanda King *Mother* ■ *Dir/Scr* Topper Carew

The Tall Blond Man with One Black Shoe ★★★ PG

Spy comedy 1972 · Fr · Colour · 85mins

Physical French comedy, for those who like physical French comedies, and highly rated by those who do. This farce stars Pierre Richard as a bumbling innocent whose life becomes hectic when he is mistaken for a spy by rival groups of secret agents. Easy to watch, and surprisingly action-packed, with Richard showing himself to be a talented slapstick comic. The film spawned one French sequel, *The Return Of...*, two years later, and was oddly retitled *The Man With One Red Shoe* for the US remake. DA. A French language film.

Pierre Richard *François* • Bernard Blier *Milan* • Jean Rochefort *Toulouse* • Mireille Darc *Christine* • Jean Carmet *Maurice* • Colette Castel *Paulette* • Jean Obe *Botrel* ■ *Dir* Yves Robert • *Scr* Yves Robert, Francis Veber

Tall, Dark and Handsome ★★★

Crime comedy 1941 · US · BW · 78mins

Cesar Romero's genial gangster and nightclub owner pretends to be a banker and father to impress childminder and would-be singer Virginia Gilmore. The subterfuge seems quite unnecessary for a man of Romero's dashing good looks (the remake, *Love That Brute*, got it right by casting burly Paul Douglas) but, then, this is a hoodlum who's too softhearted to actually kill anyone. This Runyonesque tale lacks the requisite wit and lightness of touch except when Charlotte Greenwood's high-kicking housekeeper and Barnett Parker's gun-toting butler are around. AE

Cesar Romero *Shep Morrison* • Virginia Gilmore *Judy Miller* • Charlotte Greenwood *Winnie* • Milton Berle *Frosty Welch* • Sheldon Leonard *Pretty Willie* • Stanley Clements *Detroit Harry Jr* • Barnett Parker *Quentin* ■ *Dir* H Bruce Humberstone • *Scr* Karl Tunberg, Darrell Ware

The Tall Guy ★★★ 15

Romantic comedy
1989 · UK · Colour · 88mins

Now that she's regarded as one of Hollywood's leading thespians, it's unlikely that you'll ever see Emma Thompson like this again. So make the most of this often hilarious comedy directed by Mel Smith and written by Richard Curtis, particularly the brilliant knockabout love scene with the gangling Jeff Goldblum. They work well together throughout the film, with her deadpan approach and his neuroses perfectly matched. Rowan Atkinson's knowing send-up of his own image is both funny and generous. DP. Contains swearing, nudity. DVD

Jeff Goldblum *Dexter King* • Emma Thompson *Kate Lemon* • Rowan Atkinson *Ron Anderson* • Geraldine James *Carmen* • Emil Wolk *Cyprus Charlie* • Kim Thomson *Cheryl* • Harold Innocent *Timothy* • Anna Massey *Mary* ■ *Dir* Mel Smith • *Scr* Richard Curtis

Tall in the Saddle ★★★ U

Western 1944 · US · BW · 87mins

If ever there was a title made for Big John Wayne, this is it. However, the Duke barely gets a look-in, as in reality it's more of a vehicle for his tempestuous co-star Ella Raines, who goes gunning for the Duke in order to woo him. The complex plot has Wayne is framed for murder as he discovers Ward Bond's crooked plans to steal Audrey Long's ranch. Edwin L Marin's direction is fast-moving, and there are two terrific fist fights. TS

John Wayne *Rocklin* • Ella Raines *Arly Harolday* • Ward Bond *Robert Garvey* • George "Gabby" Hayes *Dave* • Audrey Long *Clara Cardell* • Elisabeth Risdon *Miss Elizabeth Martin* • Don Douglas *Harolday* • Paul Fix *Bob Clews* ■ *Dir* Edwin L Marin • *Scr* Michael Hogan, Paul Fix, from the novel by Gordon Ray Young

Tall Man Riding ★★ U

Western 1955 · US · Colour · 81mins

Randolph Scott returns to town to avenge a bullwhipping he received for daring to court a cattle baron's daughter some years earlier, and finds that she has married another. Her father, meanwhile, is now almost blind and about to lose his spread. With outlaws and landgrabbers stirring up trouble, Scott has his hands full. Dorothy Malone plays the girl he left behind, with Peggie Castle as the usual contrast, a saloon singer hooked up with the bad guys. AE

Randolph Scott *Larry Madden* • Dorothy Malone *Corinna Ordway* • Peggie Castle *Reva* • Bill Ching [William Ching] *Rex Willard* • John Baragrey *Cibo Pearlo* • Robert Barrat *Tucker "Tuck" Ordway* ■ *Dir* Lesley Selander • *Scr* Joseph Hoffman, from a novel by Norman A Fox

The Tall Men ★★★★ U

Western 1955 · US · Colour · 122mins

Clark Gable rarely ventured out West, but on the evidence of this impressive picture he should have done so more often. Few directors understood the man of action better than Raoul Walsh, who draws bristling performances from both Gable and Robert Ryan in a tough trail-driving tale. Jane Russell is also on top form, giving as good as she gets as the boys bid for her affections. Walsh stages the action sequences with typical bravado and handles the more intimate moments with great finesse. Superbly photographed by Leo Tover, this is one of the genre's most unjustly overlooked films. DP

Clark Gable *Ben Allison* • Jane Russell *Nella Turner* • Robert Ryan *Nathan Stark* • Cameron Mitchell *Clint Allison* • Juan Garcia *Luis* • Harry Shannon *Sam* • Emile Meyer *Chickasaw* ■ *Dir* Raoul Walsh • *Scr* Sydney Boehm, Frank Nugent, from a novel by Clay Fisher

Tall Stories ★★★

Drama 1990 · Por · Colour · 92mins

Shot in under 20 days, Joachim Pinto's rites of passage picture may be set alongside the sunlit Portuguese coast, but there are plenty of dark secrets lurking in the boarding house where most of the action takes place. Sent to stay with his aunt for the summer, impressionable 12-year-old Bruno Leite hero worships wastrel Manuel Lobao, who spends much of his time boasting of his sexual conquests. However, the truth about his proclivities emerges after doctor Luis Miguel Cintra checks in and the flighty maid seeks revenge for her wrongful dismissal. An assured investigation into adolescent angst. DP. A Portuguese language film.

Bruno Leite *Miguel* • Manuel Lobao *Joao* • Isabel De Castro *Dona Marta* • Luis Miguel Cintra *Dr Fernando* ■ *Dir/Scr* Joachim Pinto

The Tall Stranger ★★ PG

Western 1957 · US · Colour · 79mins

This very routine western is mainly of interest for reuniting the stars of Raoul Walsh's *Colorado Territory*, Joel McCrea and Virginia Mayo. Despite the spurious grandeur achieved by filming in CinemaScope, the two leads look too old and Thomas Carr's direction lacks focus. TS

Joel McCrea *Ned Bannon* • Virginia Mayo *Ellen* • Barry Kelley *Hardy Bishop* • Michael Ansara *Zarata* • Whit Bissell *Judson* • James Dobson *Dud* • George Neise [George N Neise] *Harper* ■ *Dir* Thomas Carr • *Scr* Christopher Knopf, from a story by Louis L'Amour

The Tall T ★★★★ U

Western 1957 · US · Colour · 76mins

Randolph Scott plays the very ordinary cowpoke who stumbles into the hands of kidnappers, carefully biding his time to turn the tables and free their captive, the rich man's wife played by Maureen O'Sullivan. The outlaws are finely etched in Burt Kennedy's screenplay as both ruthless and human, especially Richard Boone as their leader, a lonely, intelligent figure who cannot escape his nature. It is superbly filmed by director Budd Boetticher, and the vivid, desolate landscape enhances the drama. AE

Randolph Scott *Pat Brennan* • Richard Boone *Usher* • Maureen O'Sullivan *Doretta Mims* • Arthur Hunnicutt *Ed Rintoon* • Skip Homeier *Billy Jack* • Henry Silva *Chink* ■ *Dir* Budd Boetticher • *Scr* Burt Kennedy, from the story *The Captives* by Elmore Leonard • *Cinematographer* Charles Lawton Jr

Tall Tale ★★★ PG

Western adventure
1994 · US · Colour · 99mins

Jeremiah Chechik, who directed the disappointing movie version of *The Avengers*, also made this amiable western for Disney. Patrick Swayze has a lot of fun portraying the folk hero Pecos Bill who, with two companions, helps a family battle a greedy land agent (Scott Glenn in enjoyably pantomimic form). Chechik certainly seems at home on the range and children will lap up this updated version of good old-fashioned western action. JF DVD

Patrick Swayze *Pecos Bill* • Oliver Platt *Paul Bunyan* • Roger Aaron Brown *John Henry* • Nick Stahl *Daniel Hackett* • Scott Glenn *JP Stiles* • Stephen Lang *Jonas Hackett* • Jared Harris *Head Thug Pug* • Catherine O'Hara *Calamity Jane* ■ *Dir* Jeremiah Chechik • *Scr* Steven L Bloom, Robert Rodat

The Tall Target ★★★★ U

Period thriller 1951 · US · BW · 77mins

This ingeniously plotted, moody period thriller is a hidden nugget of gold among a great deal of early 1950s tosh. An exemplary Dick Powell plays Abraham Lincoln's bodyguard, a lone cop searching for an assassin as the newly elected president travels to Baltimore aboard a train in 1861. Director Anthony Mann's beautifully paced, atmospherically shot movie hums with intelligent intrigue and some neatly paced performances, particularly from Powell, who shines as the maverick with a mission. SH

Dick Powell *John Kennedy* • Paula Raymond *Ginny Beaufort* • Adolphe Menjou *Colonel Caleb Jeffers* • Marshall Thompson *Lance Beaufort* • Ruby Dee *Rachel* • Will Geer *Homer Crowley* • Richard Rober *Lieutenant Coulter* ■ *Dir* Anthony Mann • *Scr* Art Cohn, George Worthington Yates, from a story by George Worthington Yates, Geoffrey Homes [Daniel Mainwaring]

Talos the Mummy ★★★ 15

Horror adventure thriller
1997 · US/Lux · Colour · 114mins

A "me-too" Mummy quickie that cashed in on video while the Brendan Fraser blockbuster was cleaning up at the box office. The film is inventively cast, with martial arts star Jason Scott Lee popping up as a gun-toting detective and Louise Lombard providing the glamour. The strong pre-title sequence features horror great Christopher Lee. The story follows traditional bandaged lines as the remains of Talos, a very bad ancient Egyptian indeed, are disturbed by archaeologists, resulting in mayhem in modern-day London. JF

Jason Scott Lee *Riley* • Louise Lombard *Samantha Turkel* • Sean Pertwee *Bradley Cortese* • Lysette Anthony *Dr Claire Mulrooney* • Michael Lerner *Professor Marcus* • Jack Davenport *Detective Bartone* • Honor Blackman *Captain Shea* • Christopher Lee *Sir Richard Turkel* • Shelley Duvall *Edith Butros* ■ *Dir* Russell Mulcahy • *Scr* John Esposito, Russell Mulcahy, from a story by Keith Williams, Russell Mulcahy

Tamahine ★★

Comedy 1963 · UK · Colour · 95mins

Back in the 18th century, Captain Cook brought to England a Tahitian named Omai who caused considerable cultural uproar and became a sexual magnet for ladies of wealth and discrimination. Transposed to an English boys' public school in 1963 with Nancy Kwan playing a Tahitian, the cultural collision doesn't have quite the same impact. Even so, the demure Miss Kwan drives everyone into a lather, including art master Derek Nimmo, posh pupil James Fox and supercilious headmaster Dennis Price. AT

Nancy Kwan *Tamahine* • John Fraser *Richard* • Dennis Price *Poole* • Coral Browne *Madam Becque* • Dick Bentley *Storekeeper* • Derek Nimmo *Clove* • Justine Lord *Diana* • Michael Gough *Cartwright* • Allan Cuthbertson *Housemaster* • James Fox *Oliver* ■ *Dir* Philip Leacock • *Scr* Denis Cannan, from the novel by Thelma Nicklaus

Tamanna ★★★★ PG

Drama based on a true story
1997 · Ind · Colour · 124mins

This is the tale of a daughter who learns the horrifying truth about how she was left to die as a baby because of her gender. Boasting convincing performances from Pooja Bhatt as Tamanna and Paresh Rawal as her kindly adoptive father, this is a lively and intelligent film that moves on with tremendous pace and provides an effective and probing look at the controversial issue of infanticide. RT. In Hindi with English subtitles.

Paresh Rawal *Tikku* • Pooja Bhatt *Tamanna* ■ *Dir* Mahesh Bhatt • *Scr* Tanuja Chandra, Mahesh Bhatt, Yadar Rajt

The Tamarind Seed ★★ 15

Romantic thriller
1974 · UK · Colour · 119mins

"I am a man and I want you," Omar Sharif says to Julie Andrews. "I know we are dialectically opposed to each other, but we must keep materialist thinking out of it." Julie thinks for a minute, maybe of England, and then says, "Are you trying to enrol me in the KGB or are you really defecting?" Omar is the most gorgeous spy in the Soviet bloc and Julie is the prettiest foreign office employee, so why shouldn't the Iron Curtain melt? There are hints that Blake Edwards saw this as a satire on spy melodramas, but mostly it's tosh. AT DVD

Julie Andrews *Judith Farrow* • Omar Sharif *Feodor Sverdlov* • Anthony Quayle *Jack Loder* • Sylvia Syms *Margaret Stephenson* • Daniel O'Herlihy [Dan O'Herlihy] *Fergus Stephenson* • Oscar Homolka *Gen Golitsyn* ■ *Dir* Blake Edwards • *Scr* Blake Edwards, from the novel by Evelyn Anthony

The TAMI Show ★★★★★

Music concert documentary
1964 · US · BW · 113mins

This captures practically every significant chart act of the day at the height of their explosive performance powers. Filmed at the Santa Monica Civic Auditorium on 24 October 1964, the Teenage Awards Music International show begins with hosts Jan and Dean introducing Chuck Berry with Gerry and the Pacemakers and ends with the Rolling Stones whipping the crowd into an hysterical frenzy. In between, The Supremes and Lesley Gore boast huge hairdos, Billy J. Kramer sings Lennon and McCartney, The Beach Boys surf through their California Sound and James Brown struts his funky stuff. Fabulous talent in an amazingly witty and vivacious time capsule. AJ DVD

Dir Steve Binder

Taming Andrew ★★ PG

Drama based on a true story
2000 · US · Colour · 87mins

This TV movie explores similar territory to François Truffaut's *The Wild Child*. However, for all his sincerity, Artie Mandelberg isn't in the same league and his story lacks both cinematic imagination and emotional insight. Returning to his mother Park Overall after five years living on the hoof with the father who abducted him, Seth Adkins has none of the social or educational skills expected of a 10-year-old. DP DVD

Park Overall *Gail* • Seth Adkins *Andrew* • Jason Beghe *Eddie* • Shane Daly *Police officer* ■ *Dir* Artie Mandelberg • *Scr* Susan Rice

T

The Taming of the Shrew ★★

Comedy 1929 · US · BW · 63mins

Shakespeare's comedy has been much-filmed, perhaps most popularly in the musical version as *Kiss Me Kate*. This version co-stars the King and Queen of Hollywood, Douglas Fairbanks and Mary Pickford, paired for the first and last time. Unfortunately, working together revealed severe differences in temperament and approach – the battle between Shakespeare's lovers carried on and off the screen and ended their marriage. The Bard's verse takes second place to the stars' energetic mugging, and is done little service by their vocal deficiencies. RK

Mary Pickford *Katherine* • Douglas Fairbanks *Petruchio* • Edwin Maxwell *Baptista* • Joseph Cawthorn *Gremio* • Clyde Cook *Grumio* ■ *Dir* Sam Taylor • *Scr* Sam Taylor, from the play by William Shakespeare

The Taming of the Shrew

★★★★ U

Comedy 1967 · US/It · Colour · 116mins

Made at the height of one of their own violent love affairs, Richard Burton and Elizabeth Taylor breathe their own personal life into Shakespeare's not so politically correct tale of Petruchio subduing his shrewish wife. It's a lush version in which director Franco Zeffirelli opts for colourful action rather than well-wrought articulation. It's certainly a feast for the eye – ravishing photography, impressive sets and costumes – and benefits from the ebullient performances of one of film's greatest couples. TH [video] DVD

Richard Burton *Petruchio* • Elizabeth Taylor *Katharina* • Michael Hordern *Baptista* • Cyril Cusack *Grumio* • Michael York *Lucentio* • Alfred Lynch *Tranio* • Natasha Pyne *Bianca* • Alan Webb *Gremio* • Victor Spinetti *Hortensio* ■ *Dir* Franco Zeffirelli • *Scr* Paul Dehn, Suso Cecchi D'Amico, Franco Zeffirelli, from the play by William Shakespeare • *Cinematographer* Oswald Morris, Luciano Trasatti • *Costume Designer* Irene Sharaff, Danilo Donati

Tammy and the Bachelor

★★★ U

Comedy 1957 · US · Colour · 89mins

Something of a surprise smash hit in its day, this modest but utterly charming piece of whimsy started a series featuring the guileless heroine, who came from the backwoods to charm Louisiana society. Debbie Reynolds is endearingly energetic as the heroine with a talent for sorting out problems and wistfully sings the song *Tammy*, that was to top the Hit Parade in both the USA and UK. TV

Debbie Reynolds *Tammy Tyree* • Leslie Nielsen *Peter Brent* • Walter Brennan *Grandpa* • Mala Powers *Barbara* • Sidney Blackmer *Professor Brent* • Mildred Natwick *Aunt Renie* • Fay Wray *Mrs Brent* ■ *Dir* Joseph Pevney • *Scr* Oscar Brodney, from the novel *Tammy out of Time* by Cid Ricketts Sumner

Tammy and the Doctor

★★ U

Comedy 1963 · US · Colour · 88mins

Quintessential 1950s cutie Sandra Dee takes on the Debbie Reynolds mantle for the second time as the country girl among city folk, falling hook, line and sinker for handsome white-coated doctor Peter Fonda, here making his screen debut. This is truly a slight piece, but not without charm thanks to Universal's shrewd casting of a horde of veterans. TS

Sandra Dee *Tammy Tyree* • Peter Fonda *Dr Mark Cheswick* • Macdonald Carey *Dr Wayne Bentley* • Beulah Bondi *Mrs Call* • Margaret Lindsay *Rachel Coleman, Head Nurse* • Reginald Owen *Jason Tripp* • Adam West *Dr Eric Hassler* ■ *Dir* Harry Keller • *Scr* Oscar Brodney, from the character created by Cid Ricketts Sumner

T

Tammy Tell Me True

★★ U

Comedy 1961 · US · Colour · 96mins

Sandra Dee took over from Debbie Reynolds for the second of the three original movies featuring the character created by Cid Ricketts Sumner. She does a nice line in country cute as she sails down river to the college town where her errant boyfriend is studying. But she's quickly upstaged by Julia Meade, as the sniping niece who accuses Dee of doing away with her aunt, Virginia Grey. However, the acting honours undoubtedly go to the veteran trio of Beulah Bondi, Cecil Kellaway and Edgar Buchanan. DP

Sandra Dee *Tammy Tyree* • John Gavin *Tom Freeman* • Charles Drake *Buford Woodly* • Virginia Grey *Miss Jenks* • Julia Meade *Suzanne Rook* • Beulah Bondi *Mrs Call* • Cecil Kellaway *Captain Joe* • Edgar Buchanan *Judge Carver* ■ *Dir* Harry Keller • *Scr* Oscar Brodney, from the character created by Cid Ricketts Sumner

Tampopo

★★★★ 18

Satire 1986 · Jpn · Colour · 109mins

Juzo Itami's busy satire not only gives hungry viewers more than their fill of delicious food, but also satisfies the film gourmet. In addition to homages to *Shane*, *Seven Samurai* and *Death in Venice*, this story of a trucker (Tsutomu Yamazaki), who turns a roadside noodle bar owned by Nobuko Miyamoto (Itami's wife and regular star) into Tokyo's finest restaurant, is packed with parodies of westerns, samurai pictures and Japanese gangster and porn films. DP. In Japanese with English subtitles. [video]

Tsutomu Yamazaki *Goro* • Nobuko Miyamoto *Tampopo* • Koji Yakusho *Gangster* • Ken Watanabe *Gun* ■ *Dir/Scr* Juzo Itami

Tan-Badan

★★ 18

Melodrama 1986 · Ind · Colour · 123mins

The prodigal son is a staple theme in Bollywood and it's linked here to an exploration of wealth, duty and loyalty that is supposed to stand as a metaphor for the state of Indian society and the decline of her traditional industries. A rich man's son is more interested in the good life than running the family business. The story is pure melodrama, with the indolent man frittering away his inheritance while leaving to his devious manager and a diehard family friend the care of both his disabled millionaire father and the factory that made his fortune. DP. In Hindi with English subtitles. [video]

Govinda • Khushboo Jyoti Patel • Sharat Saxena • Satyen Kappu • Raj Mehra ■ *Dir* Anand

Tanganyika

★★ U

Adventure drama 1954 · US · Colour · 81mins

In East Africa around 1900, murderer Jeff Morrow is exerting an evil influence over the warlike Nakumbi natives, thus endangering the lives of white settlers in the colony. A safari, led by Van Heflin and including Morrow's decent brother Howard Duff, sets off on a manhunt to catch the renegade. A bizarre combination of jungle adventure and thriller, this is absolute piffle, but it's awful enough to be quite entertaining. RK

Van Heflin *John Gale* • Ruth Roman *Peggy Merion* • Howard Duff *Dan Harder* • Jeff Morrow *Abel McCracken* • Joe Comadore *Andolo* • Gregory Marshall *Andy Merion* • Noreen Corcoran *Sally Merion* ■ *Dir* Andre De Toth • *Scr* William Sackheim, Richard Alan Simmons, from a story by William R Cox

Tangier

★★

Thriller 1982 · UK · Colour · 82mins

When American Ronny Cox is arrested by UK customs, he is sent to North Africa to replace a British spy whom he resembles, in order to flush out an enemy bugging expert. This thriller has the gloss of a mini-series, but it also has the kind of plot twists, oddball characters and glib one-liners that were old hat in 1940s B-pictures, while the traitor is as unobtrusive as a camel in a kasbah. DP

Ronny Cox • Billie Whitelaw • Glynis Barber • Ronald Fraser ■ *Dir* Michael E Briant • *Scr* Michael Russell, from the novel by Nicholas Luard

Tango

★★ 15

Black comedy 1993 · Fr · Colour · 86mins

That it mocks its audience rather than satirises its characters is the main problem with this vulgar road movie about an unsavoury wife-murdering trio. Hopes were high for this freewheeling black comedy from Patrice Leconte, which he promised would rock the politically correct back on their self-righteous feet. But despite a quality cast, this lacks the restraint and wit that could have made it a minor masterpiece. DP. In French with English subtitles. [video] DVD

Philippe Noiret *The Elegant Man (L'Elégant)* • Richard Bohringer *Vincent* • Thierry Lhermitte *Paul* • Miou-Miou *Marie* • Judith Godrèche *Madeleine* • Michèle Laroque *Helene Baraduc* • Maxime Leroux *Mariano Escobar* • Jean Rochefort ■ *Dir* Patrice Leconte • *Scr* Patrice Leconte, Patrice Dewolf

Tango

★★ 12

Dance drama
1998 · Arg/Sp/Fr/Ger · Colour · 110mins

There's something about the tango that seems to bring out the arty and pretentious in film-makers. Here Carlos Saura's moody but monotonous tale of Miguel Angel Sola, an Argentinian theatre director, strives to give the tango some sort of social significance. His efforts at integrating rhythms and visuals gradually come to mirror Sola's midlife crisis, his troubles with women, even his feelings of political repression. DA. In Spanish with English subtitles. [video] DVD

Miguel Angel Sola *Mario Suarez* • Cecilia Narova *Laura Fuentes* • Mia Maestro *Elena Flores* • Juan Carlos Copes *Carlos Nebbia* • Carlos Rivarola *Ernesto Landi* ■ *Dir/Scr* Carlos Saura

Tango & Cash

★★★ 18

Action thriller 1989 · US · Colour · 101mins

Sylvester Stallone and Kurt Russell star in this hugely silly, hugely enjoyable action thriller. The main twist in this buddy caper is that Stallone is actually quite sophisticated, while Russell is the no-brain, all-brawn thug. The plot follows the bickering duo all the way to a brutal maximum security prison, where they're forced to become allies after being framed by evil drugs baron Jack Palance. Russian director Andrei Konchalovsky produces lots of big explosions and brainless fun. JF. Contains swearing, violence, drug abuse, sex scenes and nudity. [video] DVD

Sylvester Stallone *Ray Tango* • Kurt Russell *Gabe Cash* • Jack Palance *Yves Perret* • Teri Hatcher *Kiki* • Michael J Pollard *Owen* • Brion James *Requin* • Geoffrey Lewis *Police captain* • James Hong *Quan* • Robert Z'Dar *Face* ■ *Dir* Andrei Konchalovsky • *Scr* Randy Feldman

Tango Bar

★★★

Dance documentary drama
1988 · P Ric/Arg · Colour · 90mins

The tango is so inextricably woven into the fabric of Argentinian history that any socio-cultural overview is bound to have political implications. Thus, the live numbers performed by the Tango Argentino troupe and the film clips revealing how the dance has been depicted down the years are pregnant with a significance that is reinforced by the tense relationship between piano player Raul Julia, long-exiled bandoneonist Ruben Juarez and their mutual mistress, singer Valeria Lynch. Tango aficionados will revel in the performances, although film fans will be more intrigued by the juxtaposed classic clips. DP. In Spanish with English subtitles.

Raul Julia *Ricardo* • Valeria Lynch *Elena* • Ruben Juarez *Antonio* ■ *Dir* Marcos Zurinaga • *Scr* Marcos Zurinaga, Juan Carlos Codazzi, Jose Pablo Feinman

The Tango Lesson

★★ PG

Dance drama
1997 · UK/Fr · BW and Colour · 97mins

Writer/director Sally Potter plays herself, taking a break from writing her latest screenplay to attend a tango exhibition. So struck is she by the super-sexy rhythms, that she reshapes her film around the dance and the man who teaches it. This is the film about that film. The idea of dispensing with the distinction between life and art is interesting, if not exactly original. This film, also made with funding from Argentina, Japan and Germany, leaves you thinking of a certain emperor and his new clothes. DA. In English, French and Spanish with subtitles. [video]

Sally Potter *Sally* • Pablo Veron *Pablo* • Gustavo Naveira *Gustavo* • Fabian Salas *Fabian* • David Toole *Fashion designer* • Carolina Iotti *Pablo's partner* • Carlos Copello *Carlos* ■ *Dir/Scr* Sally Potter

Tangos, Exilo de Gardel

★★★

Drama 1985 · Arg/Fr · Colour · 119mins

One of the founders of Third Cinema, Argentinian director Fernando E Solanas explores the agony of exile in this politically charged variation on the "putting on a show" theme. Taking as his subject the life of tango star Carlos Gardel, who was killed in 1935, playwright Miguel Angel Sola smuggles the manuscript out of Buenos Aires to compatriots, who sacrifice both personal and national identities as they eke out their enforced absence in Paris. Very much a patchwork of emotions, events and ideas, the film leavens its melancholy with sublime moments of symbolic music. DP. In Spanish with English subtitles.

Marie Laforêt • Philippe Léotard • Miguel Angel Sola • Marina Vlady ■ *Dir/Scr* Fernando E Solanas

Tank

★★ PG

Comedy drama 1984 · US · Colour · 110mins

A Sherman tank is the unlikely vehicle of choice in this unusual road movie. Soon-to-retire sergeant major James Garner has spent years restoring an army tank. A clash with corrupt local lawman GD Spradlin results in the sheriff framing Garner's son and demanding money for his release from a prison camp. Garner is double-crossed and so takes his tank cross country to free his son. This leaden comedy is enlivened only by the consistent James Garner. DF

James Garner *Sergeant Major Zack Carey* • Shirley Jones *LaDonna Carey* • C Thomas Howell *Billy Carey* • Mark Herrier *Elliott* • Sandy Ward *General Hubik* • Jenilee Harrison *Sarah* • James Cromwell *Deputy Euclid* • GD Spradlin *Sheriff Buelton* ■ *Dir* Marvin J Chomsky • *Scr* Dan Gordon

Tank Girl

★★ 15

Science-fiction comedy
1995 · US · Colour · 99mins

This gets nowhere near the sassy black spark of the original comic strip, yet those unfamiliar with its source will find it goofy, undemanding fare. Lori Petty is the Tank Girl of the title, demonstrating an early manifestation of "girl power" as she takes on evil Malcolm McDowell in a water-starved post-apocalyptic world. Director Rachel Talalay never quite gets a handle on the mix of comedy and action, but Petty is credible in the lead and McDowell is suitably over the top as the villain. JF. Contains violence and swearing. [video] DVD

Lori Petty *Rebecca Buck/Tank Girl* • Ice T *[Ice-T] T-Saint* • Malcolm McDowell *Kesslee* • Naomi Watts *Jet Girl* • Don Harvey *Sergeant Small* • Jeff Kober *Booga* ■ *Dir* Rachel Talalay • *Scr* Tedi Sarafian, from the comic strip by Alan Martin, Jamie Hewlett

The Tao of Steve ★★★ 15

Romantic comedy
2000 · US · Colour · 83mins

Donal Logue impresses as a part-time kindergarten teacher whose success with the opposite sex can be attributed to his philosophy of cool. His Tao is based on a mythical Steve, who embodies the qualities of those cultural icons Steve McQueen, Steve McGarrett (*Hawaii Five-O*) and "Six Million Dollar Man" Steve Austin. Logue decides to avow the slacker lifestyle to pursue the equally excellent Greer Goodman, a set designer tired of dating silly boys. Jenniphr Goodman's directorial debut labours the point, but it's still a film of easy intelligence and insouciant charm. DP VIDEO DVD

Donal Logue *Dex* • Greer Goodman *Syd* • Kimo Wills *Dave* • Ayelet Kaznelson *Beth* • David Aaron Baker *Rick* • Nina Jaroslaw *Maggie* ■ *Dir* Jenniphr Goodman • *Scr* Jenniphr Goodman, Greer Goodman, Duncan North, from a story by Duncan North

Tap ★★ PG

Drama 1989 · US · Colour · 106mins

If the title had not already worked against this dull movie, then the improbable story certainly would have. Burglar Gregory Hines plays the nimble-footed son of a legendary dancer, who's released from prison faced with two options. He can either join mentor Sammy Davis Jr at his tap dancing club or regroup with his old partners in crime for one last job, a jewel heist. Tap dance fanatics may well adore the film but few will be engaged by its assembly of clichéd characters. BB VIDEO

Gregory Hines *Max Washington* • Suzzanne Douglas *Amy* • Sammy Davis Jr *Little Mo* • Savion Glover *Louis* • Joe Morton *Nicky* • Dick Anthony Williams *Francis* • Sandman Sims *Sandman* • Bunny Briggs *Bunny* ■ *Dir/Scr* Nick Castle

Tape ★★ 15

Drama 2001 · US · Colour · 83mins

Director Richard Linklater demonstrates why the physical restrictions of theatre commonly make stage-play adaptations big-screen mistakes. In filming the action of this unconventional reunion tale within a motel room in real time, without music, camera trickery or effects, Linklater tips his hat to the Dogme school of movie-making. But what begins as an interesting exercise in character-based drama – as three former friends reveal long-held resentments – soon turns into a self-indulgent bore. SF VIDEO DVD

Ethan Hawke *"Vin" Vince* • Robert Sean Leonard *"Jon" Johnny* • Uma Thurman *Amy Randall* ■ *Dir* Richard Linklater • *Scr* Stephen Belber, from his play

Tapeheads ★★ 15

Comedy 1988 · US · Colour · 87mins

John Cusack and Tim Robbins are a comedy combo in this lightweight offering from former video director Bill Fishman. The two play ex-security guards trying to make it as music video producers and setting their sights on becoming MTV's finest. Given that the film credits every bigwig in the music industry one expects more than this series of skits with Cusack and Robbins going from disaster to success. Surprisingly dated. LH VIDEO DVD

John Cusack *Ivan Alexeev* • Tim Robbins *Josh Tager* • Mary Crosby *Samantha Gregory* • Clu Gulager *Norman Mart* • Katy Boyer *Belinda Mart* • Jessica Walter *Kay Mart* • Sam Moore *Billy Diamond* • Junior Walker *Lester Diamond* • Doug McClure *Sid Tager* • Connie Stevens *June Tager* ■ *Dir* Bill Fishman • *Scr* Bill Fishman, Peter McCarthy, from a story by Ryan Rowe, Jim Herzfeld, Bill Fishman, Peter McCarthy

Taps ★★★ PG

Drama 1981 · US · Colour · 121mins

This marked Tom Cruise's first impact in the movies, Sean Penn's debut and Timothy Hutton's follow-up to his Oscar-winning role in *Ordinary People*. They play cadets who take over their military academy when it's threatened with redevelopment in Harold Becker's fascinating film. It sometimes gets hysterical and loses its narrative way, but the bright young stars and George C Scott as the commander see it through. RT VIDEO DVD

George C Scott *General Harlan Bache* • Timothy Hutton *Brian Moreland* • Ronny Cox *Colonel Kerby* • Sean Penn *Alex Dwyer* • Tom Cruise *David Shawn* • Brendan Ward *Charlie Auden* ■ *Dir* Harold Becker • *Scr* Darryl Ponicsan, Robert Mark Kamen, from the story *Father Sky* by Devery Freeman, James Lineberger

Tarana ★★★ PG

Drama 1951 · Ind · BW · 137mins

Although it's best known for its spectacular masala musicals, Bollywood also has a social conscience. Director Ram Daryani was renowned for the intelligence with which he tackled controversial issues, without ever losing sight of the central story. Here, he passes some pointed observations on arranged marriages, the class divide and the struggle between progress and tradition, but most eyes will be on regular co-stars Madhubala and Dilip Kumar as the star-crossed lovers whose path to happiness is strewn with prejudice. DP. In Hindi with English subtitles. VIDEO

Madhubala *Tarana* • Dilip Kumar • Kumar Shyama • Jeevan ■ *Dir* Ram Daryani

Tarang ★★★ 15

Drama 1983 · Ind · Colour · 163mins

This epic melodrama belongs to the tradition of social protest cinema made familiar to western audiences by the work of such directors as Satyajit Ray and Shyam Benegal. Kumar Shahani has neither Ray's humanity nor Benegal's political passion, but he packs his tale with plenty of incident and makes a number of telling points about India's industrial future. The family feuds might resemble *Dallas* at times, but the discussion of union activism and the acceptance of foreign investment gives the film a cutting edge. DP. A Hindi language film. VIDEO

Smita Patil • Amol Palekar ■ *Dir* Kumar Shahani • *Scr* Kumar Shahani, Roshan Shahani

Tarantula ★★★

Science-fiction horror
1955 · US · BW · 80mins

Director Jack Arnold's big bug shocker features excellent special effects and the potent use of haunting desert locations. Scientist Leo G Carroll is working in an isolated laboratory trying to solve world famine and injects a spider with special nutrients that cause it to grow to enormous size. The giant arachnid escapes, decimates cattle and then eats people. The stillness of the desert allows Arnold to mount the tension impeccably in between the compelling spectacle of a spider on the rampage. Look for Clint Eastwood has as a jet pilot. AJ

John Agar *Dr Matt Hastings* • Mara Corday *Stephanie Clayton* • Leo G Carroll *Prof Gerald Deemer* • Nestor Paiva *Sheriff Jack Andrews* • Ross Elliott *Joe Burch* • Edwin Rand *Lt John Nolan* • Clint Eastwood *First pilot* ■ *Dir* Jack Arnold • *Scr* Robert M Fresco, Martin Berkeley, from a story by Jack Arnold, Robert M Fresco • *Special Effects* Clifford Stine, David S Horsley

Taras Bulba ★★ U

Period epic 1962 · US · Colour · 123mins

This is real junk, but of a splendid, watchable awfulness that is absolutely compulsive. This would-be swashbuckling saga set in the Ukraine in the 16th century achieves some uniqueness for being filmed in Argentina. The locations are indeed impressive, as is the score by the distinguished Franz Waxman, but the casting is ludicrous and director J Lee Thompson fails to find the necessary scale. Of the leads Tony Curtis and Yul Brynner as Cossack son and father the less said the better. TS

Tony Curtis *Andrei Bulba* • Yul Brynner *Taras Bulba* • Christine Kaufmann *Natalia Dubrov* • Sam Wanamaker *Filipenko* • Brad Dexter *Shilo* • Guy Rolfe *Prince Grigory* • Perry Lopez *Ostap Bulba* • George Macready *Governor* ■ *Dir* J Lee Thompson • *Scr* Waldo Salt, Karl Tunberg, from the novel by Nikolai Gogol

Target ★★ 15

Spy thriller 1985 · US · Colour · 112mins

Arthur Penn has had an indifferent directorial career since the glories of the 1960s and 1970s. Here he directs Gene Hackman, starring as a seemingly ordinary American businessman who gets drawn into Cold War intrigue when his wife Gayle Hunnicutt is kidnapped in Paris. At the same time Hackman has to rebuild a relationship with his surly adolescent son Matt Dillon. Sadly, Penn never successfully marries the two conflicting elements. JF. Contains violence, swearing and nudity. VIDEO DVD

Gene Hackman *Walter Lloyd* • Matt Dillon *Chris Lloyd* • Gayle Hunnicutt *Donna Lloyd* • Victoria Fyodorova *Lise* • Ilona Grubel *Carla* • Herbert Berghof *Schroeder* • Josef Sommer *Barney Taber* • Guy Boyd *Clay* ■ *Dir* Arthur Penn • *Scr* Howard Berk, Don Petersen, from a story by Leonard Stern

Target Eagle ★★ PG

Action adventure
1982 · Sp/Mex · Colour · 94mins

Clever casting injects some life into a predictable action thriller centred around mercenaries hired to smash a smuggling ring. George Peppard, better known for his good guy TV roles in *Banacek* and *The A-Team*, relishes the chance to be the chief baddie, and Max von Sydow is also unusually cast as a police chief. NF VIDEO

George Rivero [Jorge Rivero] *David* • Maud Adams *Carmen* • George Peppard *Ronald McFadden* • Max von Sydow *Spanish police chief* • Chuck Connors *Sam Fisher* • Susana Dosamantes *Laura* ■ *Dir/Scr* J Anthony Loma

Target Unknown ★★ U

Second World War drama
1951 · US · BW · 89mins

The interrogation of an American aircrew by a Nazi intelligence unit is the intriguing premise of this wartime drama set in occupied France. There is some splendid aerial combat footage, but director George Sherman allows the plot to develop in a wholly predictable manner, as Mark Stevens and his crew play mind games with Robert Douglas's smug German colonel, who wants to uncover the target of the next USAF raid. The subplot involving quisling Malu Gatica and resistance fighter Suzanne Dalbert is no more inspired. DP

Mark Stevens *Captain Jerome Stevens* • Alex Nicol *Al Mitchell* • Robert Douglas *Colonel von Broeck* • Don Taylor *Lieutenant Webster* • Gig Young *Captain Reiner* • Suzanne Dalbert *Theresa* • Malu Gatica *French entertainer* ■ *Dir* George Sherman • *Scr* Harold Medford, from his story

Targets ★★★★ 15

Crime thriller 1968 · US · Colour · 86mins

The stunning feature debut of film critic-turned-writer/director Peter Bogdanovich is graced by a marvellous valedictory performance from Boris Karloff. Karloff plays Byron Orlok, an ageing horror star who finds himself in the gun sights of that scourge of contemporary America, a random sniper, chillingly portrayed by Tim O'Kelly. Based on the real-life killing spree of Charles Whitman in 1966, this is genuinely disturbing and immaculately crafted, with themes that are still relevant today. The cinematography, by debuting émigré Laszlo Kovacs, is superb. TS DVD

Boris Karloff *Byron Orlok* • Tim O'Kelly *Bobby Thompson* • Nancy Hsueh *Jenny* • James Brown (1) *Robert Thompson* • Sandy Baron *Kip Larkin* • Arthur Peterson *Ed Loughlin* • Mary Jackson *Charlotte Thompson* • Tanya Morgan *Ilene Thompson* • Monty Landis [Monte Landis] *Marshall Smith* • Peter Bogdanovich *Sammy Michaels* ■ *Dir* Peter Bogdanovich • *Scr* Peter Bogdanovich, from a story by Polly Platt, Peter Bogdanovich

Taris ★★★

Documentary 1931 · Fr · BW · 11mins

Although French swimming legend Jean Taris was notionally the subject of this avant-garde short, director Jean Vigo was far more interested in the shapes and rhythms he creates in the pool than his athletic prowess. The result is a cine-poem that captures the grace of classical ballet, as it uses dramatic lighting, slow-motion and Impressionist editing to give the underwater action an ethereal aura. Having already experimented with surrealism in *A Propos de Nice* (1930), Vigo employed it again to shock in *Zéro de Conduite* (1933) and enchant in *L'Atalante* (1934), which features a memorable subterranean sequence of its own. DP. In French with English subtitles.

Dir Jean Vigo

Tarka the Otter ★★★ PG

Adventure 1978 · UK · Colour · 87mins

Author Henry Williamson refused to allow Disney to film his much-loved wildlife novel. Instead, he entrusted the story of Tarka to director David Cobham, who co-wrote the script with Gerald Durrell. Cobham remains faithful to the original and, in collaboration with cameraman John McCallum, paints a glorious picture of the Devon countryside. Although the action is occasionally deflected by a nature ramble approach, Tarka's adventures are skilfully staged and vividly brought to life by Peter Ustinov's narration. DP VIDEO DVD

Peter Bennett *Master of the otter hounds* • Edward Underdown *Hibbert* • Brenda Cavendish *Lucy* • John Leeson *Hunt secretary* • Reg Lye *Farmer* • Peter Ustinov *Narrator* ■ *Dir* David Cobham • *Scr* Gerald Durrell, David Cobham, from the novel by Henry Williamson

Tarnation ★★★★ 15

Documentary
2004 · US · Colour and BW · 91mins

If there's one thing that's not in doubt about Jonathan Caouette's eccentric and ultimately moving documentary, it's that it is certainly one of the cheapest ever made. Assembled from material as diverse as Super-8 home movies, newspaper clippings and even answerphone messages, it was edited on his home computer for an original budget of $218. What emerges from the patchwork quilt of material is a picture of a troubled adolescent struggling to survive a childhood blighted not only by a mother whose mental stability was destroyed by electroshock treatment, but also his own abuse in various foster homes.

This is a film that's almost impossible to review in the normal sense, since any critique is necessarily a critique of Caouette's interpretation of his own life (he was 31 when he completed the movie) and is therefore redundant. But it's certainly stunningly original, and an affecting and honest an account of a deeply traumatic childhood. AS

Dir Jonathan Caouette

The Tarnished Angels

★★★★

Adventure drama 1957 · US · BW · 90mins

Journalist Rock Hudson joins ace barnstorming pilot Robert Stack and his sexy wife Dorothy Malone. Hudson's character is embarrassingly underwritten, but he manages to make his newshound eminently watchable, and the film never looks less than splendid in black-and-white CinemaScope. Shallow but well made, this melodrama fails to disguise the innate misanthropy of its literary source, though many have found much to admire in its sleazy bitterness. TS

Rock Hudson *Burke Devlin* • Robert Stack *Roger Shumann* • Dorothy Malone *Laverne Shumann* • Jack Carson *Jiggs* • Robert Middleton *Matt Ord* • Alan Reed *Colonel Fineman* • Alexander Lockwood *Sam Hagood* • Chris Olsen [Christopher Olsen] *Jack Shumann* • Robert J Wilke *Hank* • Troy Donahue *Frank Burnham* ■ *Dir* Douglas Sirk • *Scr* George Zuckerman, from the novel *Pylon* by William Faulkner

Tarnished Lady

★★

Drama 1931 · US · BW · 80mins

The film that marked the talkie debut of the already legendary, husky-voiced stage star Tallulah Bankhead, who returned to Hollywood after several years as the toast of London's West End stage. Sadly, Tallulah's exotic, erotic charms failed to make much impact on the camera. Despite glossy production, a Donald Ogden Stewart screenplay and direction by George Cukor, this tale of a Park Avenue girl who grows bored with marriage and leaves her husband (Clive Brook) to seek a more interesting life is no more than an efficient plod. RK

Tallulah Bankhead *Nancy Courtney* • Clive Brook *Norman Cravath* • Phoebe Foster *Germaine Prentiss* • Alexander Kirkland *DeWitt Taylor* • Osgood Perkins *Ben Sterner* • Eric Blore *Jewelry counter clerk* ■ *Dir* George Cukor • *Scr* Donald Ogden Stewart, from his story *New York Lady*

Tartuffe

★★★★★ U

Silent drama 1926 · Ger · BW · 63mins

Although his Nazi sympathies permanently tarnished his reputation, Emil Jannings remains one of the finest actors of the silent era and he delivers a performance of relishable roguery in this hilarious adaptation of Molière's scathing satire on religious hypocrisy. He's well supported by Lil Dagover as the wife willing to risk her honour in her determination to prevent gullible husband Werner Krauss from handing over his worldly goods. This sadly incomplete gem is also notable for Karl Freund's sombrely atmospheric cinematography. DP DVD

Emil Jannings *Tartuffe* • Lil Dagover *Elmire* • Werner Krauss *Orgon* • André Mattoni *Grandson* • Rosa Valetti *Housekeeper* • Lucy Höflich *Dorine* • Hermann Picha *Old councillor* ■ *Dir* FW Murnau • *Scr* Carl Mayer, from the play by Molière

Tarzan

★★ U

Animation 1999 · US · Colour · 84mins

Despite some visually arresting action scenes, the first ever cartoon based on the classic jungle hero falls short of Disney's recent output. With weak comic relief provided by assorted "Animalz N the Hood", this is a frenetic mix of *George of the Jungle* and *Gorillas in the Mist*, with constant bouts of animated mayhem to keep the kids amused. Laced with feeble background songs from Phil Collins (inexplicably awarded an Oscar), this is no jungle VIP. AJ DVD

Tony Goldwyn *Tarzan* • Minnie Driver *Jane* • Glenn Close *Kala* • Brian Blessed *Clayton* • Nigel Hawthorne *Professor Porter* • Lance Henriksen *Kerchak* ■ *Dir* Chris Buck, Kevin Lima • *Scr* Tab Murphy, Bob Tzudiker, Noni White, from characters created by Edgar Rice Burroughs

Tarzan and His Mate

★★★★★ U

Adventure 1934 · US · BW · 86mins

Generally regarded as the best of the Johnny Weissmuller MGM *Tarzans*, this is notable for being extremely raunchy, even by present-day standards, since it predates Hollywood's notorious censorship code. Cavorting semi-naked among the studio undergrowth is the lovely Maureen O'Sullivan as Jane. After this, the loincloths grew less revealing, but Weissmuller continued to cut a fine figure as the Lord of the Jungle. TS

Johnny Weissmuller *Tarzan* • Maureen O'Sullivan *Jane Parker* • Neil Hamilton *Harry Holt* • Paul Cavanagh *Martin Arlington* • Forrester Harvey *Beamish* • William Stack *Tom Pierce* • Desmond Roberts *Van Ness* ■ *Dir* Cedric Gibbons • *Scr* Howard Emmett Rogers, Leon Gordon, from a story by James Kevin McGuinness, from characters created by Edgar Rice Burroughs

Tarzan and the Amazons

★★ U

Adventure 1945 · US · BW · 75mins

It's not very good, and the Sol Lesser production values are decidedly cheesy, but any movie proffering tiny Maria Ouspenskaya as the queen of the Amazons has camp appeal – if little else. This reintroduced Jane, in the lacklustre person of Brenda Joyce, with Johnny Sheffield on hand as Boy, so it's down to a tired Johnny Weissmuller to make this tosh bearable. Fun of sorts, though, and certainly ecologically sound. TS

Johnny Weissmuller *Tarzan* • Johnny Sheffield *Boy* • Brenda Joyce *Jane* • Henry Stephenson *Henderson* • Maria Ouspenskaya *Amazon queen* • Barton MacLane *Ballister* ■ *Dir* Kurt Neumann, Sol Lesser • *Scr* Hans Jacoby, Marjorie L Pfaelzer, from characters created by Edgar Rice Burroughs

Tarzan and the Great River

★★ U

Adventure 1967 · US/Swi · Colour · 88mins

The Lord of the Jungle swings into action when an old zoo curator friend is murdered by a vicious cult of Leopard Men. Journeying up river towards the leader's hideout, accompanied by his trusty chimp and lion, Tarzan helps the local doctor to halt an epidemic. Not one of the best Tarzan adventures, but Mike Henry makes a decent job of the hero, and the Brazilian locations are watchable. JG

Mike Henry *Tarzan* • Jan Murray *Captain Sam Bishop* • Manuel Padilla Jr *Pepe* • Diana Millay *Dr Ann Phillips* ■ *Dir* Robert Day • *Scr* Bob Barbash, from a story by Bob Barbash, Lewis Reed, from characters created by Edgar Rice Burroughs

Tarzan and the Green Goddess

★★

Adventure 1938 · US · BW · 72mins

This feature is one of two culled from episodes of *The New Adventures of Tarzan*. It combines some previously unseen material with footage edited from the last ten reels of the 1935 serial. Its star was Herman Brix, but he changed his name to Bruce Bennett and enjoyed a long career, albeit not as the ape man. The story is as evergreen as the jungle, with Tarzan out to protect civilisation from evil men who want a secret explosive formula hidden in a Mayan idol. BB

Herman Brix [Bruce Bennett] *Tarzan* • Ula Holt *Ula Vale* • Frank Baker *Major Martling* • Don Castello *Raglan* ■ *Dir* Edward Kull • *Scr* Charles F Royal, from characters created by Edgar Rice Burroughs

Tarzan and the Huntress

★★ U

Adventure 1947 · US · BW · 72mins

The greatest Tarzan of them all, Johnny Weissmuller, was looking old and tired by this 11th film in his series. After *Tarzan and the Mermaids* the role of King of the Jungle passed to Lex Barker. Here, Brenda Joyce as Jane and Johnny Sheffield as Boy have more of a part to play than usual, as evil zoologist Patricia Morison plots to spirit animals into her private menagerie. All ecologically interesting, and certainly never boring. TS

Johnny Weissmuller *Tarzan* • Johnny Sheffield *Boy* • Brenda Joyce *Jane* • Patricia Morison *Tanya* • Barton MacLane *Weir* • John Warburton *Marley* • Wallace Scott *Smithers* • Charles Trowbridge *King Farrod* ■ *Dir* Kurt Neumann • *Scr* Jerry Gruskin, Rowland Leigh, from characters created by Edgar Rice Burroughs

Tarzan and the Jungle Boy

★★ U

Adventure 1968 · US/Swi · Colour · 90mins

Mike Henry made an engaging Tarzan, but he couldn't take the pace. Indeed, declining health while filming (including a chimp bite) prompted him to sue the producer. Tarzan is asked by a journalist to enter hostile territory to rescue a boy who has been lost for seven years. The area is dominated by an angry tribe whose dying chief is choosing which of his two sons – one bad, one good – should succeed him. Location photography means that the movie looks good. JG

Mike Henry *Tarzan* • Rafer Johnson *Nagambi* • Alizia Gur *Myrna Claudel* • Ed Johnson *Buhara* • Ronald Gans *Ken* • Steven Bond [Steve Bond] *Erik* ■ *Dir* Robert Gordon • *Scr* Stephen Lord, from characters created by Edgar Rice Burroughs

Tarzan and the Leopard Woman

★★ U

Adventure 1946 · US · BW · 72mins

Murder cults aren't a subject to be treated light-heartedly these days, but back in the mid-1940s they could still be wheeled out as a plot device. Here Tarzan, hindered and aided by Jane and Boy (Brenda Joyce and Johnny Sheffield), does what he can to destroy the titular villain, splendidly incarnated by Acquanetta. It's all jolly silly, but Johnny Weissmuller was getting a bit old for the role. TS

Johnny Weissmuller *Tarzan* • Johnny Sheffield *Boy* • Brenda Joyce *Jane* • Acquanetta *Lea* • Edgar Barrier *Lazar* • Tommy Cook *Kimba* ■ *Dir* Kurt Neumann • *Scr* Carroll Young, from characters created by Edgar Rice Burroughs

Tarzan and the Lost City

★★ PG

Action adventure
1998 · Aus/US · Colour · 80mins

Casper Van Dien dons the famous loincloth in this unambitious but enjoyable family adventure. Tarzan, now Lord Greystoke, has been fully integrated into British high society and is set to wed the beautiful Jane (Jane March). However, after experiencing a disturbing vision of the destruction of his childhood home, he's soon back swinging through the jungle. JF

Casper Van Dien *Tarzan* • Jane March *Jane* • Steven Waddington *Nigel Ravens* • Winston Ntshona *Mugambi* • Rapulana Seiphemo *Kaya* • Ian Roberts *Captain Dooley* ■ *Dir* Carl Schenkel • *Scr* Bayard Johnson, J Anderson Black, from characters created by Edgar Rice Burroughs

Tarzan and the Lost Safari

★★★ U

Adventure 1956 · UK · Colour · 81mins

One of the best 1950s episodes in the jungle saga brought a welcome mid-period lift to the series by being the first to venture into CinemaScope and Technicolor. Gordon Scott rescues the members of a safari team from the evil clutches of white hunter Robert Beatty. Thankfully, old stock footage was discarded and the movie was filmed on location in Africa, though studio scenes were shot in England. RK

Gordon Scott *Tarzan* • Robert Beatty *"Tusker" Hawkins* • Yolande Donlan *Gamage Dean* • Betta St John *Diana* • Wilfrid Hyde White *"Doodles" Fletcher* • George Coulouris *Carl Kraski* ■ *Dir* H Bruce Humberstone • *Scr* Montgomery Pittman, Lillie Hayward, from characters created by Edgar Rice Burroughs

Tarzan and the Mermaids

★★ U

Adventure 1948 · US · BW · 67mins

Filmed in Mexico (mainly Acapulco) with an ambitious music score by Dimitri Tiomkin, this is less of a jungle adventure than most Tarzan films, as water and swimming sequences dominate. The spectacular scenery is the film's main asset as the story is a slow-moving affair in which Tarzan helps Linda Christian from being forced into marriage to a phoney island god. During the shooting of the cliff diving sequence, Johnny Weissmuller's double, Angel Garcia, was killed. This was Weissmuller's 12th and last screen portrayal of Tarzan. TV

Johnny Weissmuller *Tarzan* • Brenda Joyce *Jane* • Linda Christian *Mara* • George Zucco *Palanth* • Andrea Palma *Luana* • Fernando Wagner *Varga* • Edward Ashley *Commissioner* ■ *Dir* Robert Florey • *Scr* Carroll Young, from characters created by Edgar Rice Burroughs

Tarzan and the She-Devil

★★ U

Adventure 1953 · US · BW · 75mins

Despite a great villain in Raymond Burr, this is a standard tale of ivory-seeking elephant hunters being stymied by the king of the jungle. Tarzan spends a good deal of the film in tied-up captivity, and director Kurt Neumann allows the pace to slacken too often before the climactic elephant stampede. This was the fifth and final Tarzan film for Lex Barker. TV

Lex Barker *Tarzan* • Joyce MacKenzie *Jane* • Raymond Burr *Vargo* • Monique Van Vooren *Lyra* • Tom Conway *Fidel* • Henry Brandon *M'Tara* • Michael Granger *Lavar* ■ *Dir* Kurt Neumann • *Scr* Karl Kamb, Carroll Young, from characters created by Edgar Rice Burroughs

Tarzan and the Slave Girl

★★ U

Adventure 1950 · US · BW · 74mins

The plotting of this adventure is exceptionally fanciful, as Jane is kidnapped by a tribe of lion worshippers who are being decimated by a strange malady and want to repopulate their civilisation. Tarzan finds himself fighting a native tribe called the Waddies, and fighting off the advances of a seductive nurse (Denise Darcel). Vanessa Brown is the first of several actresses to play Jane after the departure of Brenda Joyce. TV

Lex Barker *Tarzan* • Vanessa Brown *Jane* • Robert Alda *Neil* • Hurd Hatfield *Prince* • Arthur Shields *Dr Campbell* • Tony Caruso [Anthony Caruso] *Sengo* • Denise Darcel *Lola* ■ *Dir* Lee Sholem • *Scr* Hans Jacoby, Arnold Belgard, from characters created by Edgar Rice Burroughs

Tarzan and the Trappers ★

Adventure 1958 · US · BW · 70mins

The theme of white hunters searching for a lost city – said to be full of untold treasure – is so overworked that it needs the sort of production and cast that is totally missing in this compilation of three television episodes made for a series that failed to happen. Gordon Scott and Eve Brent are an acceptable Tarzan and Jane, but other elements on display are under par. A successful Tarzan television series was ultimately made in 1966, starring Ron Ely. TV

Gordon Scott *Tarzan* • Eve Brent *Jane* • Rickie Sorensen *Boy* ■ *Dir* Charles Haas, Sandy Howard • *Scr* Frederick Schlick, Robert Leach, from characters created by Edgar Rice Burroughs

Tarzan and the Valley of Gold ★★★ U

Adventure 1966 · US/Swi · Colour · 89mins

Mike Henry was poached from US pro football for this better than average jungle romp. A gold-obsessed archvillain, played with gusto by goateed David Opatoshu, kidnaps a boy, believing he holds the secret to a lost civilisation of gold. Enter a more gentlemanly Tarzan (by aircraft), who is persuaded to strip off his groovy suit, don a loincloth and re-enter the jungle to sort it all out. Those expecting a standard ape man adventure will be surprised by the sharp script and playful tone. JG

Mike Henry *Tarzan* • Nancy Kovack *Sophia Renault* • David Opatoshu *Vinaro* • Manuel Padilla Jr *Ramel* • Don Megowan *Mr Train* • Enrique Lucero *Perez* • Eduardo Noriega (1) *Talmadge* • John Kelly (3) *Voss* ■ *Dir* Robert Day • *Scr* Clair Huffaker, from characters created by Edgar Rice Burroughs

Tarzan Escapes ★★★

Adventure 1936 · US · BW · 95mins

The third entry in MGM's legendary jungle series was easily the most problematic, with a number of scenes being reshot from scratch. Much to the disgust of director Richard Thorpe, studio boss Louis B Mayer insisted that the more violent action be considerably toned down. Yet this is still a full-blooded adventure, as Johnny Weissmuller resists John Buckler's attempts to exhibit him as a freak of nature back in Britain. DP. An English/Swahili language film.

Johnny Weissmuller *Tarzan* • Maureen O'Sullivan *Jane Parker* • John Buckler *Captain Frye* • Benita Hume *Rita Parker* • William Henry *Eric Parker* • Herbert Mundin *Herbert Henry Rawlins* • EE Clive *Masters* ■ *Dir* Richard Thorpe • *Scr* Cyril Hume, Jack Cummings (uncredited), from characters created by Edgar Rice Burroughs

Tarzan Finds a Son! ★★★ U

Adventure 1939 · US · BW · 82mins

One of the splendid MGM Tarzans, starring the popular Johnny Weissmuller as the ape man and lovely Maureen O'Sullivan as Jane. Forbidden to produce children outside wedlock by the new film censorship code, the couple find a boy whose parents were killed in a plane crash, and begin a jungle version of a custody battle. It's a cleverly scripted and generally satisfying tale. TS

Johnny Weissmuller *Tarzan* • Maureen O'Sullivan *Jane* • John Sheffield [Johnny Sheffield] *Boy* • Ian Hunter *Austin Lancing* • Henry Stephenson *Sir Thomas Lancing* • Frieda Inescort *Mrs Lancing* • Henry Wilcoxon *Mr Sande* • Laraine Day *Mrs Richard Lancing* ■ *Dir* Richard Thorpe • *Scr* Cyril Hume, from characters created by Edgar Rice Burroughs

Tarzan Goes to India ★★★ U

Adventure 1962 · UK · Colour · 86mins

After playing a villain to Gordon Scott's King of the Jungle in *Tarzan the Magnificent*, former stunt man and western heavy Jock Mahoney took over the title role. This episode lifts the material out of its familiar rut by sending the hero to India for an elephant-rescuing operation, during which he encounters a company of Indians as well as Gajendra, King of the Elephants. RK

Jock Mahoney *Tarzan* • Mark Dana *O'Hara* • Jai *Jai the Elephant Boy* • Simi *Princess Kamara* • Leo Gordon *Bryce* ■ *Dir* John Guillermin • *Scr* Robert Hardy Andrews, John Guillermin, from characters created by Edgar Rice Burroughs

Tarzan of the Apes ★★★

Silent adventure 1918 · US · BW · 55mins

The first of the adventures of the jungle swinger, this has a rather wan Elmo Lincoln as the aristocrats' child reared by the apes. Years later, explorer Jane (Enid Markey) comes looking for the Greystoke heir, prompting some heroics from the smitten Tarzan. The series didn't really get going until Johnny Weissmuller donned the loincloth, but, as a curiosity, this is well worth seeing. Existing versions of the film run at less than half the length of the original 130 minute running time. TH

Elmo Lincoln *Tarzan* • Enid Markey *Jane Porter* • Gordon Griffith *Tarzan as a child* • True Boardman (1) *Lord Greystoke* • Kathleen Kirkham *Lady Greystoke* ■ *Dir* Scott Sidney • *Scr* William E Wing, from the novel by Edgar Rice Burroughs

Tarzan, the Ape Man ★★★★

Adventure 1932 · US · BW · 99mins

This is the first, and classiest, movie in the series starring Olympic swimming champion Johnny Weissmuller as the jungle swinger. Directed by WS Van Dyke with skill, the tale introduces the ape-reared boy to future partner Jane (Maureen O'Sullivan). Fighting a variety of big cats, armed with only a knife, may look unrealistic – as does some of the in-cut library material – but the fun at the expense of city dwellers on safari and the atmosphere of studio fantasy make it a living museum piece. TH

Johnny Weissmuller *Tarzan* • Maureen O'Sullivan *Jane Parker* • Neil Hamilton *Harry Holt* • C Aubrey Smith *James Parker* • Doris Lloyd *Mrs Cutten* • Forrester Harvey *Beamish* • Ivory Williams *Riano* ■ *Dir* WS Van Dyke • *Scr* Cyril Hume, Ivor Novello, from characters created by Edgar Rice Burroughs

Tarzan, the Ape Man ★ U

Adventure 1959 · US · Colour · 81mins

Twenty-seven years after MGM unveiled (literally) the now-legendary Johnny Weismuller in the film of the same title, the studio had the temerity to remake it with one of the most lacklustre of all Tarzans, Denny Miller, in his only outing in the role. Since the company owned the original they tinted some footage from that and, apparently, even earlier silent Tarzan films. Nothing helped. BB

Denny Miller *Tarzan* • Joanna Barnes *Jane Parker* • Cesare Danova *Holt* • Robert Douglas *Col Parker* • Thomas Yangha *Riano* ■ *Dir* Joseph M Newman • *Scr* Robert J Hill, from characters created by Edgar Rice Burroughs

Tarzan, the Ape Man ★ 15

Adventure 1981 · US · Colour · 107mins

A legendary turkey, with Bo Derek traipsing through the greenery looking for excuses to disrobe more often than Edgar Rice Burroughs's jungle king himself. Directed by Bo's husband, John Derek, this actionless soft-core spectacular is a demented vanity production on such an epic scale that all you can do is stare in disbelief. Wooden Miles O'Keeffe must be the worst screen Tarzan ever. AJ. Contains some swearing and nudity. [VIDEO]

Bo Derek *Jane Parker* • Richard Harris *James Parker* • John Phillip Law *Harry Holt* • Miles O'Keeffe *Tarzan* • Akushula Selayah *Nambia, "Africa"* • Steven Strong *Ivory King* • Maxime Philoe *Riano* • Leonard Bailey *Feathers* • Wilfrid Hyde White *Club member* ■ *Dir* John Derek • *Scr* Tom Rowe, Gary Goddard, from characters created by Edgar Rice Burroughs

Tarzan the Fearless ★★ U

Adventure 1933 · US · BW · 85mins

Made by independent producer Sol Lesser just after MGM had released its first Tarzan blockbuster with Johnny Weissmuller, this starred the equally muscular Buster Crabbe, and followed MGM's portrayal of Tarzan as a grunting ape man rather than the educated hero of the original stories. Made simultaneously as a serial, this feature version is episodic and crudely edited. Crabbe's athleticism is fine, but his acting consists mainly of showing his teeth in an inane smile. Jacqueline Wells is the heroine seeking her father in the jungle. TV [VIDEO]

Buster Crabbe [Larry "Buster" Crabbe] *Tarzan* • Jacqueline Wells [Julie Bishop] *Mary Brooks* • E Alyn Warren *Dr Brooks* • Edward Woods *Bob Hall* • Philo McCollough *Jeff Herbert* • Mischa Auer *High Priest* ■ *Dir* Robert F Hill • *Scr* Basil Dickey, George H Plympton, Ford Beebe, Walter Anthony, from characters created by Edgar Rice Burroughs

Tarzan the Magnificent ★★★ U

Adventure 1960 · UK · Colour · 86mins

This was the last of Gordon Scott's six outings as Edgar Rice Burroughs's jungle hero. His adversary here, Jock Mahoney, would succeed him two years later in *Tarzan Goes to India*. The real star of the show, however, is veteran John Carradine, who throws restraint to the wind as the head of Mahoney's clan intent on ambushing the ape man before he can turn him over for trial. DP

Gordon Scott *Tarzan* • Jock Mahoney *Coy Banton* • Betta St John *Fay Ames* • John Carradine *Abel Banton* • Lionel Jeffries *Ames* • Alexandra Stewart *Laurie* ■ *Dir* Robert Day • *Scr* Berne Giler, Robert Day, from characters created by Edgar Rice Burroughs

Tarzan Triumphs ★★★

Second World War adventure 1943 · US · BW · 76mins

The first of the RKO Tarzan movies, produced by Sol Lesser, pits our hero, still in the brawny form of Johnny Weissmuller, against a topical German foe. The plot this time has Nazi paratroopers landing in a lost city and, sadly, leaves no room for Jane. Instead there's a fabulous performance from Cheetah, who here gets a super coda as he does something quite ingenious with the Nazis' short-wave radio – so it's worth sitting tight until the very end. TS

Johnny Weissmuller *Tarzan* • Johnny Sheffield *Boy* • Frances Gifford *Zandra* • Stanley Ridges *Col Von Reichart* • Rex Williams *Schmidt* • Sig Ruman *Sergeant* • Pedro De Cordoba *Patriarch* ■ *Dir* William Thiele • *Scr* Carroll Young, Roy Chanslor, from a story by Carroll Young, from characters created by Edgar Rice Burroughs

Tarzan's Deadly Silence ★★ U

Adventure 1970 · US · Colour · 87mins

Routine outing for the loin-clothed ape man, cobbled together from two episodes of the *Tarzan* TV series. Ron Ely is the biggest swinger in town, here battling a crazed soldier whose private army is threatening an African village. The supporting cast includes a former Tarzan, Jock Mahoney. TV values, no real cinematic merit. Incidentally, do you know Tarzan's famous last words? "Who greased that viiiiiiiiiiiiiine?" DA

Ron Ely *Tarzan* • Jock Mahoney *The Colonel* • Manuel Padilla Jr *Jai* • Woody Strode *Marshak* • Rudolph Charles *Officer* • Nichelle Nichols *Ruana* ■ *Dir* Robert L Friend, Lawrence Dobkin • *Scr* Lee Erwin, Jack A Robinson, John Considine, Tim Considine, from characters created by Edgar Rice Burroughs

Tarzan's Desert Mystery ★★★ U

Spy adventure 1943 · US · BW · 69mins

Johnny Weissmuller's second jungle adventure for RKO is energetic hokum, a piece of lively wartime propaganda directed with zip by William Thiele. With Jane absent, the heroine is a chirpy showgirl (Nancy Kelly) with a secret message for a sheik, warning of foreign spies in his midst. The fast-moving action incorporates prehistoric monsters, man-eating plants and a totally unconvincing yet still gruesome giant spider which nearly devours Boy before turning its attention to the nasty Nazis. One of the most entertaining of the series. TV

Johnny Weissmuller *Tarzan* • Johnny Sheffield *Boy* • Nancy Kelly *Connie Bryce* • Otto Kruger *Paul Hendrix* • Joe Sawyer *Karl Straeder* • Lloyd Corrigan *Sheik Abdul El Khim* ■ *Dir* William Thiele • *Scr* Edward T Lowe, from a story by Carroll Young, from characters created by Edgar Rice Burroughs

Tarzan's Fight for Life ★★ U

Adventure 1958 · US · Colour · 86mins

In the third of six films in which he starred as Tarzan, former lifeguard Gordon Scott gets a new Jane, Eve Beck, and wrestles a live python in the film's best sequence. Otherwise it is business as usual when Tarzan's friendship with a doctor running a hospital in the jungle brings him into conflict with a tribal witch doctor and his superstitious followers. TV

Gordon Scott *Tarzan* • Eve Brent *Jane* • Rickie Sorensen *Tartu* • James Edwards *Futa* • Carl Benton Reid *Dr Sturdy* ■ *Dir* H Bruce Humberstone • *Scr* Thomas Hal Phillips, from characters created by Edgar Rice Burroughs

Tarzan's Greatest Adventure ★★★ U

Adventure 1959 · UK · Colour · 84mins

One of the best Tarzan movies, actually filmed on authentic African locations, with a fine plot and reliable direction from John Guillermin. Gordon Scott is Tarzan, with a greatly increased vocabulary compared with his predecessors, and the British co-stars are impressive. This is a splendid romp, beautifully photographed and edited, and it may even convert non-Tarzan fans. Watch out for Sean Connery as the diamond hunter. TS

Gordon Scott *Tarzan* • Anthony Quayle *Slade* • Sara Shane *Angie* • Niall MacGinnis *Kruger* • Sean Connery *O'Bannion* • Al Mulock *Dino* • Scilla Gabel *Toni* ■ *Dir* John Guillermin • *Scr* John Guillermin, Berne Giler, from a story by Les Crutchfield, from characters created by Edgar Rice Burroughs

Tarzan's Hidden Jungle ★★ U

Adventure 1955 · US · BW · 72mins

Gordon Scott – a former GI and fireman – makes his debut as Tarzan, opposing white hunters who are posing as United Nations photographers. Filmed in California with bought-in footage of African wildlife, this lacks wit and pace, but Scott went on to star in five more Tarzan adventures. He also married his co-star, Vera Miles, who plays a nurse he saves from restless natives. AT

Gordon Scott *Tarzan* • Vera Miles *Jill Hardy* • Peter Van Eyck *Dr Celliers* • Jack Elam *Burger* • Charles Fredericks *DeGroot* • Richard Reeves *Reeves* ■ *Dir* Harold Schuster • *Scr* William Lively, from characters created by Edgar Rice Burroughs

Tarzan's Magic Fountain ★★★ U

Adventure 1949 · US · BW · 72mins

The first film Lex Barker made as Tarzan is also his best. The narrative, dealing with an elixir of youth, is intriguing and gripping with a neat mixture of humour and suspense. Evelyn Ankers, one of the screen's great B-movie heroines, is an aviatrix who crashed in the jungle 20 years earlier and still looks youthful, and Albert Dekker is a convincingly duplicitous villain who sights a fortune in marketing the secret of eternal youth. Brenda Joyce, considered second only to Maureen O'Sullivan as an effective "Jane", retired from the screen after this movie. TV

Lex Barker *Tarzan* • Brenda Joyce *Jane* • Albert Dekker *Trask* • Evelyn Ankers *Gloria James* • Charles Drake *Dodd* • Alan Napier *Douglas Jessup* ■ *Dir* Lee Sholem • *Scr* Curt Siodmak, Harry Chandlee, from characters created by Edgar Rice Burroughs

Tarzan's New York Adventure ★★★ U

Adventure 1942 · US · BW · 70mins

One of the best-loved and best-remembered of all the MGM Johnny Weissmuller *Tarzans*, this might not seem quite so original today, and perhaps it owed more than a little to *King Kong* even then. Still, Tarzan's confrontation with interior plumbing is still mightily amusing, funny enough to make you forget the nastiness of the abduction plot, as Boy is snatched from his ersatz jungle "parents" by unscrupulous circus folk. Sadly, this was the last time the lovely Maureen O'Sullivan played Jane. TS

Johnny Weissmuller *Tarzan* • Maureen O'Sullivan *Jane* • Johnny Sheffield *Boy* • Chill Wills *Manchester Mountford* • Paul Kelly (1) *Jimmie Shields* • Charles Bickford *Buck Rand* • Virginia Grey *Connie Beach* • Cy Kendall *Colonel Ralph Sargent* ■ *Dir* Richard Thorpe • *Scr* William R Lipman, Myles Connolly, from a story by Myles Connolly, from characters created by Edgar Rice Burroughs

Tarzan's Peril ★★★ U

Adventure 1951 · US · BW · 78mins

Filmed largely in Africa, this is one of the better Tarzan films, with fascinating shots of wildlife and plenty of action in its tale of gun-runners attempting to start a war between tribes. Though Virginia Huston is ineffectual as Jane, there is a striking performance by Dorothy Dandridge, in a small role as a jungle queen who wants peace, and George Macready, one of the screen's most hissable villains, proves a worthy adversary for hero Tarzan. The film was also supposed to be the first of the series in colour, but after much of the colour footage was destroyed in an accident, it was decided to switch to black and white. TV

Lex Barker *Tarzan* • Virginia Huston *Jane* • George Macready *Radijek* • Douglas Fowley *Trask* • Glenn Anders *Andrews* • Dorothy Dandridge *Melmendi* ■ *Dir* Byron Haskin • *Scr* Samuel Newman, Francis Swann, John Cousins, from characters created by Edgar Rice Burroughs

Tarzan's Revenge ★

Adventure 1938 · US · BW · 70mins

This has the dubious distinction of being a contender for the worst Tarzan adventure ever made. Decathlon champion of the 1936 Olympics Glenn Morris co-stars with champion backstroke swimmer Eleanor Holm, but neither of them can act. The plot has Morris rescuing Holm from becoming part of a sultan's harem. Directed with no style whatsoever. TV

Glenn Morris *Tarzan* • Eleanor Holm *Eleanor* • George Barbier *Roger* • C Henry Gordon *Ben Alleu Bey* • Hedda Hopper *Penny* • George Meeker *Nevin* ■ *Dir* D Ross Lederman • *Scr* Robert Lee Johnson, Jay Vann, from characters created by Edgar Rice Burroughs

Tarzan's Savage Fury ★★ U

Adventure 1952 · US · BW · 80mins

This was the first movie to be directed by Cyril "Cy" Endfield in Britain, after he became one of the blacklisted Hollywood exiles. It was the beginning of a long career in Britain where his most famous film proved to be *Zulu*. Lex Barker becomes caught up in a typical adventure when his cousin, visiting him in Africa to obtain his help for Britain's military security, is killed. Plenty of action keeps the story bubbling along. BB

Lex Barker *Tarzan* • Dorothy Hart *Jane* • Patric Knowles *Edwards* • Charles Korvin *Rokov* • Tommy Carlton *Joey* ■ *Dir* Cyril Endfield [Cy Endfield] • *Scr* Cyril Hume, Hans Jacoby, Shirley White, from characters created by Edgar Rice Burroughs

Tarzan's Secret Treasure ★★ U

Adventure 1941 · US · BW · 81mins

High production values can't compensate for a ridiculous plot, but there is a certain perverse delight in watching Johnny Weissmuller's ape man and Maureen O'Sullivan's Jane cohabit in a tree house the like of which only the MGM art department could provide. There's a slew of dignified character players all looking worried, as well they might; after all, they 're trying to fool Tarzan into helping them find gold. He may be big, but he certainly ain't stupid. TS

Johnny Weissmuller *Tarzan* • Maureen O'Sullivan *Jane* • Johnny Sheffield *Boy* • Reginald Owen *Professor Elliot* • Barry Fitzgerald *O'Doul* • Tom Conway *Medford* • Philip Dorn *Vandermeer* ■ *Dir* Richard Thorpe • *Scr* Myles Connolly, Paul Gabeglin, from characters created by Edgar Rice Burroughs

Tarzan's Three Challenges ★★ U

Adventure 1963 · US · Colour · 92mins

The producers dropped some Tarzan staples, such as Jane and Cheetah, in this episode of the jungle-fresh franchise, added Far Eastern locations and spent some money – all to good effect. A wise Oriental ruler is near death, and Tarzan has to prove himself a worthy minder to take the shrewd boy successor safely to the throne. On location, Jock Mahoney, in his second outing as the ape man, lost lots of weight during several bouts of illness; his constantly changing body is one of this picture's incidental pleasures. JG

Jock Mahoney *Tarzan* • Woody Strode *Khan/Tarim* • Tsu Kobayashi *Cho San* • Earl Cameron *Mang* ■ *Dir* Robert Day • *Scr* Berne Giler, Robert Day, from characters created by Edgar Rice Burroughs

Task Force ★★ U

Action drama
1949 · US · BW and Colour · 116mins

This long-winded account of the struggle to persuade the American navy to develop aircraft carriers opens with Gary Cooper as the retiring admiral looking back on his days as an early advocate of their use, arguing with politicians, newspaper proprietors and stubborn navy bigwigs. Only as the film bursts into colour towards the end, to work in documentary footage from the Second World War and demonstrate the carriers' worth in the Battle of Okinawa, does Delmer Daves's picture achieve lift-off. AE

Gary Cooper *Jonathan L Scott* • Jane Wyatt *Mary Morgan Scott* • Wayne Morris *McKinney* • Walter Brennan *Pete Richard* • Julie London *Barbara McKinney* • Bruce Bennett *McCluskey* • Jack Holt *Reeves* ■ *Dir/Scr* Delmer Daves

A Taste of Cherry ★★★★ PG

Drama 1997 · Iran · Colour · 94mins

Sharing the Palme d'Or at Cannes with Shohei Imamura's *The Eel*, Abbas Kiarostami's unconventional road movie is as much about the filmic process as morality, mortality or modern Iran. World-weary, middle-aged Homayoon Irshadi cruises the suburbs of Tehran in search of someone willing to transgress Islamic law by burying him after his suicide. Each person he propositions has symbolic significance, including a Kurdistani soldier and an Afghan seminary student, before he finally finds a taxidermist, who accepts the reward to pay his son's medical bills. Endlessly fascinating, with the subtle shifts in landscape and palette quite masterly. DP. In Farsi with English subtitles. [video]

Homayoon Irshadi *Mr Badiei* • Abdol Hossain Bagheri *Mr Bagheri, taxidermist in Natural History Museum* • Afshin Khorshid Bakhtari *Worker* • Safar Ali Moradi *Soldier from Kurdistan* • Mir Hossain Nouri *Clergyman* ■ *Dir/Scr* Abbas Kiarostami

Taste of Fear ★★★★

Psychological thriller
1961 · UK · BW · 82mins

Hammer's first *Psycho*-inspired thriller, also known as *Scream of Fear*, is the best the House of Horror ever made. Squeezing maximum shocks from a clichéd story a plot to drive someone insane Seth Holt dazzles with his direction and gives Susan Strasberg her greatest role as the wheelchair-bound young woman haunted by her father's corpse at his French villa. Just when you think you know what's going on, the marvellous script takes another labyrinthine twist into the unknown. Shot in moody black and white, the creepy swimming pool scene is justifiably famous. AJ

Susan Strasberg *Penny Appleby* • Ronald Lewis *Bob, the chauffeur* • Ann Todd *Jane Appleby* • Christopher Lee *Dr Gerrard* • John Serret *Inspector Legrand* • Leonard Sachs *Spratt* ■ *Dir* Seth Holt • *Scr* Jimmy Sangster

A Taste of Honey ★★★★★ 15

Comedy drama 1961 · UK · BW · 96mins

A ground-breaking movie of its time, this features the mousy Rita Tushingham in her screen debut as the unwanted teenage daughter of Dora Bryan, a hilariously vulgar Salford lass who is being courted by a flash and pimpish Robert Stephens. Our Rita is saved from her living hell by two social exiles – a black sailor, who makes her pregnant, and a homosexual who makes her happy – until the poverty trap snaps shut around her. Set in dank bedsits amid the grimy smokestacks, polluted canals and the tacky prom at Blackpool, this movie – a romance of sorts, and a comedy – survives as a priceless barometer of England and English attitudes in 1961. AT [video] DVD

Rita Tushingham *Jo* • Dora Bryan *Helen* • Murray Melvin *Geoffrey* • Robert Stephens *Peter* • Paul Danquah *Jimmy* • David Boliver *Bert* • Moira Kaye *Doris* ■ *Dir* Tony Richardson • *Scr* Shelagh Delaney, Tony Richardson, from the play by Shelagh Delaney

Taste the Blood of Dracula ★★★ 15

Horror 1969 · UK · Colour · 87mins

Three Victorian gentlemen get more than they bargained for when they indulge in Satanism for fun with the assistance of Ralph Bates. They inadvertently resurrect Count Dracula (Christopher Lee), who sends their sons and daughters on a killing spree. Although Lee is given little to do apart from look suavely menacing, he does metamorphose into a caped hero battling the hypocrisy of Victorian family values in this flamboyantly romantic grim fairy tale. AJ [video] DVD

Christopher Lee *Dracula* • Geoffrey Keen *William Hargood* • Gwen Watford *Martha Hargood* • Linda Hayden *Alice Hargood* • Peter Sallis *Samuel Paxton* • Anthony Corlan [Anthony Higgins] *Paul Paxton* • Roy Kinnear *Weller* ■ *Dir* Peter Sasdy • *Scr* John Elder [Anthony Hinds], from the character created by Bram Stoker

Tatie Danielle ★★ 15

Black comedy 1990 · Fr · Colour · 107mins

Having mauled the middle-classes in *Life Is a Long Quiet River*, Etienne Chatiliez gives them an even more torrid time here at the hands of the auntie from hell, Tsilla Chelton. Relishing every little torture she inflicts upon Catherine Jacob and her dull, but decent family, Chelton gives a wonderfully malicious performance, but what began as a wicked satire ends up getting lost in the darkness of its own comedy, and we become increasingly drawn to the put-upon relatives. DP. In French with English subtitles. Contains swearing and nudity. [video] DVD

Tsilla Chelton *Auntie Danielle* • Catherine Jacob *Catherine Billard* • Isabelle Nanty *Sandrine* • Neige Dolsky *Odile* • Eric Pratt *Jean-Pierre Billard* • Laurence Février *Jeanne Billard* • Virginie Pradal *Madame Lafosse* • Mathieu Foulon *Jean-Marie Billard* ■ *Dir* Etienne Chatiliez • *Scr* Florence Quentin, Etienne Chatiliez

Tattoo ★ 18

Drama 1980 · US · Colour · 98mins

Bruce Dern kidnaps model Maud Adams in a sleazy psycho-drama. Written by Joyce Buñuel, daughter of Luis, it's supposed to be an insightful study of psychopathic behaviour; tattoo artist Dern's enforced needlework on Bond girl Adams is presented as a rape substitute. But, while it may have been Buñuel's intention to shower her controversial material in allegorical significance, former commercials director Bob Brooks isn't up to the job. AJ. Contains swearing and nudity. [video]

Bruce Dern *Karl Kinsky* • Maud Adams *Maddy* • Leonard Frey *Halsey* • Rikke Borge *Sandra* • John Getz *Buddy* • Peter Iacangelo *Dubin* • Alan Leach *Customer* • Cynthia Nixon *Cindy* ■ *Dir* Bob Brooks • *Scr* Joyce Buñuel, from a story by Bob Brooks

Tattoo ★★★ 18

Crime thriller
2002 · Fr/Ger · Colour · 108mins

Christian Redl and August Diehl spark as the maverick veteran and his rookie partner who are assigned to the case of a demented collector of tattoos, who is prepared to kill in order to possess a series of prized ornate Japanese designs. Director Robert Schwentke's thriller favours atmosphere over character and

T

incident, and the result is visually striking. DP. In German with English subtitles. Contains violence.

August Diehl *Marc Schrader* • Christian Redl *Detective Minks* • Nadeshda Brennicke *Maya Kroner* • Ilknur Bahadir *Meltem* • Jasmin Schwiers *Marie Minks* • Johan Leysen *Frank Schoubya* • Monica Bleibtreu *Snr Detective Roth* ■ *Dir/Scr* Robert Schwentke

Tawny Pipit ★★★ U

Comedy 1944 · UK · BW · 77mins

It was almost unthinkable in wartime that a British picture should criticise officialdom and poke fun at the eccentricities of national life. In Bernard Miles's independently produced feature, the only problem is that the satire is too gentle and the humour too whimsical. However, the story about rare birds that nest in a field outside a Cotswolds village is not without its charm, the excellent cast is a pleasure to watch and the photography is quite exquisite. DP

Bernard Miles *Colonel Barton-Barrington* • Rosamund John *Hazel Broome* • Niall MacGinnis *Jimmy Bancroft* • Jean Gillie *Nancy Forester* • Lucie Mannheim *Russian sniper* • Christopher Steele *Reverend Kingsley* ■ *Dir* Bernard Miles, Charles Saunders • *Scr* Bernard Miles, Charles Saunders, from a story by Bernard Miles • *Cinematographer* Eric Cross, Ray Sturgess

Taxi! ★★★

Crime drama 1932 · US · BW · 70mins

This is a fast-paced, tough-as-nails Warner Bros melodrama with crackling dialogue, starring the great James Cagney as the New York cabbie involved in some inter-taxi-company rivalry. The opening sequence is a real surprise, with Cagney speaking fluent Yiddish, learned during his East Side childhood. There's some early fancy footwork from George Raft, who, like Cagney, was better known as a screen gangster than for what was his real forte – hoofing. TS

James Cagney *Matt Nolan* • Loretta Young *Sue Riley* • George E Stone *Skeets* • Guy Kibbee *Pop Riley* • David Landau *Buck Gerard* • Ray Cooke *Danny Nolan* • Leila Bennett *Ruby* • Dorothy Burgess *Marie Costa* • Matt McHugh *Joe Silva* • George Raft *William "Willie" Kenny* ■ *Dir* Roy Del Ruth • *Scr* Kubec Glasmon, John Bright, from the play *The Blind Spot* by Kenyon Nicholson

Taxi ★★

Comedy drama 1953 · US · BW · 77mins

Directing his first movie in three years, Gregory Ratoff is deserted by the sure touch that persuaded 20th Century-Fox to entrust him with so many minor A features during the Second World War. Too many cooks were involved in concocting a script with little flavour of the New York streets. Dan Dailey plays a world-weary cabbie who has to shrug off the loan sharks on his tail to help Irish immigrant Constance Smith locate her husband. DP

Dan Dailey *Ed Nielson* • Constance Smith *Mary* • Neva Patterson *Miss Millard* • Blanche Yurka *Mrs Nielson* • Geraldine Page *Florence Albert* • Rex O'Malley *Butler* • John Cassavetes *Cab driver* ■ *Dir* Gregory Ratoff • *Scr* DM Marshman Jr, Daniel Fuchs, Alex Joffe, Jean Paul Le Chanois, from the story *Sans Laisser d'Adresse* by Hans Jacoby, Fred Brady

Taxi ★★ 15

Action comedy thriller
1998 · Fr · Colour · 86mins

The fancy automobile stunts are everything in this puerile, paper-thin comedy-thriller scripted by Luc Besson. Speed-freak taxi driver Samy Naceri and timid cop Frédéric Diefenthal team up to catch a slick bunch of bank robbers, leading to much squealing of tyres through the streets of Marseille. Director Gérard Pirès adds feeble *Carry On*-style stabs at slapstick humour as the couple screw up the case and the bumbling Diefenthal attempts to woo statuesque police officer Emma Sjöberg. JC. In French with English subtitles. Contains swearing, sex scenes and violence. DVD

Samy Naceri *Daniel* • Frédéric Diefenthal *Émilien* • Marion Cotillard *Lilly* • Emma Sjöberg *Petra* • Manuela Gourary *Camille* ■ *Dir* Gérard Pirès • *Scr* Luc Besson

Taxi ★★ 12

Action comedy
2004 · US/Fr · Colour · 93mins

This reworking of the 1998 French smash takes knockabout stupidity to new levels. Thrown together by fate, useless New York cop Jimmy Fallon and speed-demon taxi driver Queen Latifah try to nab a gang of female Brazilian bank robbers, headed by supermodel Gisele Bundchen. All screeching brakes and no real excitement, this buddy movie is just a series of car chases linked together by tragically unfunny comedy. Latifah's wannabe racing champion has an easy charm, but Fallon's dumb shtick is annoying and tired. SF. An English/ Portuguese language film. Contains swearing, sexual references. DVD

Queen Latifah *Belle Williams* • Jimmy Fallon *Andy Washburn* • Gisele Bundchen *Vanessa* • Jennifer Esposito *Lt Marta Robbins* • Ann-Margret *Washburn's mom* • Henry Simmons *Jesse* • Christian Kane *Agent Mullins* ■ *Dir* Tim Story • *Scr* Robert Ben Garant, Thomas Lennon, Jim Kouf, from the film by Luc Besson

Taxi 2 ★★★ 12

Action drama 2000 · Fr · Colour · 84mins

This harum scarum sequel reteams daredevil Marseille taxi driver Samy Naceri and laconic cop Frédéric Diefenthal. However, it benefits considerably from the snappier direction of Gérard Krawczyk, who not only keeps the plot ticking over, but also invests a Hollywood gusto into the action sequences. There's even some efficiently staged chop socky by way of variation, as a gang of ruthless ninjas kidnap a Japanese politician and Diefenthal's statuesque partner, Emma Sjöberg. DP. In French and Japanese with English subtitles. DVD

Samy Naceri *Daniel* • Frédéric Diefenthal *Emilien* • Marion Cotillard *Lilly* • Emma Sjöberg *Petra* • Bernard Farcy *Chief Inspector Gibert* ■ *Dir* Gérard Krawczyk • *Scr* Luc Besson

Taxi Blues ★★★

Drama 1990 · Fr/USSR · Colour · 110mins

Despite the visual excesses of a debutant, Pavel Lounguine won the best director prize at Cannes for this pioneering allegory on Russia at the crossroads. Alcoholic Jewish saxophonist Pyotr Nikolajevitch Mamonov epitomises the liberated intellectualism of the new era, while conservative Muscovite cabbie Piotr Zaitchenko represents the hard-pressed proletariat. The film can hardly be said to be subtle in its symbolism, especially once their unlikely camaraderie is soured by sudden wealth and romantic rivalry. DP. In Russian with English subtitles.

Pyotr Nikolajevitch Mamonov *Liocha* • Piotr Zaitchenko *Schlikov* • Vladimir Kachpour *Old Netchiporenko* • Natalia Koliakanova *Christina* • Hal Singer ■ *Dir/Scr* Pavel Lounguine

Taxi Driver ★★★★★ 18

Drama 1976 · US · Colour · 109mins

Robert De Niro is mesmerising as the Vietnam veteran trapped in one of director Martin Scorsese's most frightening circles of hell, as he seeks a twisted redemption by saving the soul of New York child prostitute Jodie Foster. This time the bustling helter-skelter of Scorsese's *Mean Streets* gives way to a measured, chilly calm, and cinematographer Michael Chapman ensures the Big Apple glistens with barely concealed menace. It's De Niro's show, but the supporting players (Foster, Harvey Keitel, Cybill Shepherd) are almost as good, and there's a genuinely scary cameo from Scorsese himself. This deeply disturbing modern masterpiece established Scorsese as a major figure in world cinema, and it has not lost any of its power to shock. JF. Contains violence and swearing. DVD

Robert De Niro *Travis Bickle* • Cybill Shepherd *Betsy* • Jodie Foster *Iris* • Peter Boyle *Wizard* • Leonard Harris *Charles Palantine* • Harvey Keitel *Sport* • Albert Brooks *Tom* • Martin Scorsese *Passenger* ■ *Dir* Martin Scorsese • *Scr* Paul Schrader

Taxi zum Klo ★★★★ 18

Erotic comedy 1980 · W Ger · Colour · 90mins

A distinctive progenitor of "queer cinema", Frank Ripploh's first, highly accomplished movie is a light-hearted, sometimes farcical, but always uncompromisingly honest depiction of his own life, in which he and his former lover Bernd Broaderup play themselves. Ripploh, a schoolteacher in Berlin, is torn between his reliable domesticity and the excitement of extracurricular sex. In 1981 it was startling but refreshing to see such material played as sexually uninhibited romantic comedy, with no political message. Now, post-Aids, the film is a museum piece, but none the less enjoyable. After an unsuccessful sequel, Ripploh faded from view. DM. In German with English subtitles.

Frank Ripploh *Frank* • Bernd Broaderup *Bernd* • Orpha Termin *Female neighbour* • Dieter Godde *Masseur* ■ *Dir/Scr* Frank Ripploh

A Taxing Woman ★★★★ 18

Comedy drama 1987 · Jpn · Colour · 127mins

The sharpest critic of Japanese mores in the 1980s, Juzo Itami focuses on the national obsession with all things material in this supremely controlled satire. His wife, Nobuko Miyamoto, is hilariously tenacious as the demure tax inspector whose slavish attention to detail is rewarded when she's given a pop at seedy motel mobster Tsutomu Yamazaki, whose flair for embezzlement matches her own devotion to duty. With an unlikely romance, this blend of yakuza comedy and procedural thriller is both socially revealing and slyly entertaining. DP. In Japanese with English subtitles.

Nobuko Miyamoto *Ryoko Itakura* • Tsutomu Yamazaki *Hideki Gondo* • Masahiko Tsugawa *Assistant Chief Inspector Hanamura* • Eitaro Ozawa *Tax accountant* ■ *Dir/Scr* Juzo Itami

Taxman ★★ 15

Crime action thriller
1998 · US · Colour · 96mins

Whether many people will be rooting for a heroic tax inspector remains to be seen, but this no-frills thriller at least provides a rare leading role for Joe Pantoliano, who makes the most of the opportunity. As a tough-talking investigator he sets out on a personal crusade to expose the murky dealings of the Russian Mob with the help of a young cop (the late Wade Dominguez). The two leads spark off each other nicely and there are strong straight turns from Michael Chiklis and Robert Townsend, both better known for their comic work . JF DVD

Joe Pantoliano *Al Benjamin* • Wade Dominguez *Joseph Romero* • Elizabeth Berkley *Nadia Rubakov* • Michael Chiklis *Andre Rubakov* • Robert Townsend *Peyton Cody* ■ *Dir* Avi Nesher • *Scr* Avi Nesher, Robert Berger

Taza, Son of Cochise ★★ U

Western 1954 · US · Colour · 79mins

A late entry in redressing the portrayal of native Americans started by *Broken Arrow*, this western starts with an uncredited Jeff Chandler making a third, brief appearance as the wise warrior chief Cochise, passing on the pipe of peaceful co-existence to his son, played rather stiffly by Rock Hudson. Unfortunately, a dissenting Geronimo and others stir up some predictable trouble. Shot entirely on location in Utah, it's vigorously staged by director Douglas Sirk whose main interest lay in exploring tribal lore. AE

Rock Hudson *Taza* • Barbara Rush *Oona* • Gregg Palmer *Captain Burnett* • Bart Roberts [Rex Reason] *Naiche* • Morris Ankrum *Gray Eagle* • Gene Iglesias [Eugene Iglesias] *Chato* ■ *Dir* Douglas Sirk • *Scr* George Zuckerman, Gerald Grayson Adams, from a story by Gerald Grayson Adams

Tea and Sympathy ★★★★

Drama 1956 · US · Colour · 121mins

"So the boy think's he's homosexual and the teacher's wife seduces him to prove he isn't, so what's the problem?", said a perplexed French producer to director, Vincente Minnelli. But in its day this was notorious, the play banned in the UK and the film "X" certificated. Re-creating their Broadway roles are Deborah Kerr, John Kerr (no relation) and Leif Erickson, who are all superbly cast, though the honesty of their performances is slightly threatened by the gloss in which MGM has almost drowned the tale. Forty years ago its dialogue was ground-breaking. TS

Deborah Kerr *Laura Reynolds* • John Kerr *Tom Robinson Lee* • Leif Erickson *Bill Reynolds* • Edward Andrews *Herb Lee* • Darryl Hickman *Al* • Norma Crane *Ellie Martin* • Dean Jones *Ollie* • Jacqueline de Wit *Lilly Sears* ■ *Dir* Vincente Minnelli • *Scr* Robert Anderson, from his play

Tea for Two ★★ U

Musical comedy 1950 · US · Colour · 93mins

Though popular enough in its day, this Technicolored Doris Day vehicle is not one of her better musicals, suffering greatly from lacklustre direction and an astoundingly stupid plotline. It's a loose remake of *No, No, Nanette*, in which the heroine has to reply "no" to every question asked of her in an otherwise uneventful weekend in order to fulfil a bet. A daft tale that's not even cute enough to be camp. TS

Doris Day *Nanette* • Gordon MacRae *Jimmy* • Gene Nelson *Tommy* • Eve Arden *Pauline* • Billy De Wolfe *Larry* • SZ Sakall *Max* • Patrice Wymore *Beatrice* ■ *Dir* David Butler • *Scr* Harry Clork, from the musical play *No, No, Nanette* by Frank Mandel, Otto Harbach, Vincent Youmans, Emil Nyitray

T

Tea with Mussolini ★★★ PG

Period comedy drama
1998 · It · Colour · 112mins

Franco Zeffirelli here turns his camera on to his own life as a young boy growing up in Mussolini's Italy of the 1930s. Following his mother's death, young Baird Wallace is rescued from the prospect of life in an orphanage by an eccentric group of expatriate women dubbed "Scorpioni". Through his eyes we see the corseted and costumed women: Judi Dench, Joan Plowright, Maggie Smith, Lily Tomlin and Cher, giving boisterously strong performances. An interesting anecdote rather than a rich character piece. JB. Contains swearing.

Cher *Elsa* • Judi Dench *Arabella* • Joan Plowright *Mary* • Maggie Smith *Lady Hester* • Lily Tomlin *Georgie* • Baird Wallace *Luca* ■ *Dir*

Franco Zeffirelli • *Scr* John Mortimer, Franco Zeffirelli, from an autobiography by Franco Zeffirelli

Teachers ★★ 15

Comedy 1984 · US · Colour · 102mins

Nick Nolte is a cynical teacher at the overcrowded and undisciplined John F Kennedy High School. When a graduating student is found to be illiterate, his family sue the school causing Vice Principal Judd Hirsch to rally the staff in defence of their teaching methods. The prosecuting lawyer, JoBeth Williams, turns out to have been a student at the school. A by-the-numbers story of a good teacher inspiring inspire the kids others ignore. Predictable, but enjoyable. DF

Nick Nolte *Alex* • JoBeth Williams *Lisa* • Judd Hirsch *Roger* • Ralph Macchio *Eddie* • Lee Grant *Dr Burke* • Richard Mulligan *Herbert* • Allen Garfield *Rosenberg* • Royal Dano *Ditto* • Laura Dern *Diane* • Crispin Glover *Danny* • Morgan Freeman *Lewis* ■ *Dir* Arthur Hiller • *Scr* WR McKinney

Teacher's Pet ★★★★ U

Comedy 1958 · US · BW · 119mins

A delightful comedy, with Clark Gable as a crusty, hard-bitten newspaper editor who, instead of lecturing to Doris Day's journalism class, decides to enrol as a pupil. And, of course, his initial disdain for reporters who learn from books is swayed by his attraction to the teacher. Fay and Michael Kanin's screenplay becomes thin by the end, but Gable and Day fill it out with boisterous enthusiasm, possibly realising what upstaging opposition they've got from the great Gig Young, who was Oscar-nominated for his performance as Doris's other beau. TH

Clark Gable *James Gannon* • Doris Day *Erica Stone* • Gig Young *Dr Hugo Pine* • Mamie Van Doren *Peggy DeFore* • Nick Adams *Barney Kovac* • Peter Baldwin *Harold Miller* • Charles Lane (2) *Roy* • Harry Antrim *Lloyd Crowley* ■ *Dir* George Seaton • *Scr* Fay Kanin, Michael Kanin

Teaching Mrs Tingle ★★ 15

Black comedy thriller
1999 · US · Colour · 90mins

Even a central performance by Helen Mirren and script packed with bitchy one-liners cannot rescue Kevin Williamson's directorial debut. In this bungled black comedy, Mirren is the mean-spirited teacher who stands in the way of student Katie Holmes and a scholarship. The tables are turned when Holmes and two friends hold their nemesis hostage after an incident with an exam paper. AC. Contains violence and drug abuse. DVD

Helen Mirren *Mrs Tingle* • Katie Holmes *Leigh Ann Watson* • Jeffrey Tambor *Coach Wenchell* • Barry Watson *Luke Churner* • Marisa Coughlan *Jo Lynn Jordan* • Liz Stauber *Trudie Tucker* • Michael McKean *Principal Potter* • Molly Ringwald *Miss Banks* ■ *Dir/Scr* Kevin Williamson

T

The Teahouse of the August Moon ★★★ U

Comedy 1956 · US · Colour · 122mins

Marlon Brando stars as the Japanese interpreter who comes into conflict with Glenn Ford, as the latter attempts to bring American democracy and materialism to the Japanese island of Okinawa. As a satire on the culture clash it has some teeth, though not quite as lethal-looking as those worn by Brando as part of his hilarious make-up. Brando made the film partly to raise money to make a documentary about the UN's role in Asia, but he disliked the result. AT

Marlon Brando *Sakini* • Glenn Ford *Captain Fisby* • Machiko Kyo *Lotus Blossom* • Eddie Albert *Captain McLean* • Paul Ford *Colonel Purdy* • Jun Negami *Mr Seiko* • Henry Morgan [Harry Morgan] *Sgt Gregovich* ■ *Dir* Daniel Mann • *Scr* John Patrick, from the play by John Patrick and the novel by Vern J Sneider

Team America: World Police ★★★ 15

Animated satirical comedy
2004 · US/Ger · Colour · 93mins

Trey Parker and Matt Stone here admirably live up to their reputation for scatological hijinks. The film, performed by Thunderbirds-style marionettes, follows the titular team as they battle terrorism across the world as well as tackling an enemy closer to home, the ultra-liberal Film Actors Guild (if you examine the acronym, you'll get an idea of the level of the film's humour). The running joke is that Team America invariably cause more damage battling terror than do the terrorists themselves. Sporadically very funny and astonishingly offensive. AS. Contains swearing, violence and sex scenes. DVD

Trey Parker *Gary/Joe/Kim Jong Il/Hans Blix* • Matt Stone *Chris* • Kristen Miller *Lisa* • Masasa *Sarah* • Daran Norris *Spottswoode* • Phil Hendrie *I.N.T.E.L.L.I.G.E.N.C.E.* • Maurice LaMarche *Alec Baldwin* ■ *Dir* Trey Parker • *Scr* Trey Parker, Matt Stone, Pam Brady

Tears of the Black Tiger ★★★ 18

Action melodrama
2000 · Thai · Colour · 97mins

The first Thai film ever to screen in competition at Cannes, Wisit Sasanatieng's directorial debut resembles a strikingly stylised hybrid of Bollywood masala movie and spaghetti western. But it's actually a pastiche of 1950s Thai films typified by the work of pioneer film-maker Ratana Pestonji. Using digital video techniques and computer manipulation to heighten the film's colour, Sasanatieng enhances the kitsch value of a routine story about childhood sweethearts, separated by class and now on opposite sides of the law. It's a pastel-shaded magpie of a movie, in which old-fashioned narrative devices rub shoulders with ham acting, eruptions of violence and obvious budget limitations. DP. In Thai with English subtitles. DVD

Chartchai Ngamsan *Seua Dum, "Black Tiger"* • Stella Malucchi *Rumpoey* • Suppakorn Kitsuwan *Mahesuan* • Arawat Ruangvuth *Police Captain Kumjorn* ■ *Dir/Scr* Wisit Sasanatieng

Tears of the Sun ★★ 15

War action thriller
2003 · US · Colour · 115mins

Bruce Willis is up to his neck in mud and bullets in this passable action thriller, playing the gruff, tough leader of an elite marine squad that's sent into civil war-torn Nigeria to extricate a mission worker (Monica Bellucci). But Willis's position is complicated by the fact that the mission medic wants to bring half the neighbourhood back with her. Cue two hours of bullets, blood and bombast. DA. Contains violence, swearing. DVD

Bruce Willis *Lt AK Waters* • Monica Bellucci *Dr Lena Kendricks* • Cole Hauser *James "Red" Atkins* • Eamonn Walker *Ellis "Zee" Pettigrew"* • Nick Chinlund *Michael "Slo" Slowenski* • Fionnula Flanagan *Sister Grace* • Malick Bowens *Col Idris Sadick* • Tom Skerritt *Capt Bill Rhodes* ■ *Dir* Antoine Fuqua • *Scr* Alex Lasker, Patrick Cirillo

Teaserama ★★ 15

Cult burlesque revue
1955 · US · Colour · 62mins

Tempest Storm was one of the last of the classic strippers of the burlesque era. In this poverty-row record of her revue, she's joined by other disrobing artists, dancing girls and comedians, including, in one legendary mistress/maid scenario, queen of the 1950s pin-ups, Betty Page. Shot (saying directed would give completely the wrong impression!) with a single, static camera, this "adults only" antique is so coy and innocent by today's standards it's hard to believe it was ever considered controversial or racy. AJ. Contains semi-nudity.

Tempest Storm • Betty Page • Honey Baer • Cherry Knight • Chris LaChris • Vicki Lynn • Joe E Ross • Dave Starr • Trudy Wayne • Twinnie Wallen ■ *Dir* Irving Klaw

The Teckman Mystery ★★ U

Thriller 1954 · UK · BW · 89mins

There's more than a hint of *The Third Man* in this passable thriller, co-written by Francis Durbridge from his own BBC serial. John Justin looks suitably bemused as an author who discovers that the dead air ace whose biography he's been commissioned to write may not have perished after all. Director Wendy Toye makes a reasonable fist at keeping the pace up and the clues hidden, but she's no Carol Reed. DP

Margaret Leighton *Helen Teckman* • John Justin *Philip Chance* • Roland Culver *Inspector Harris* • Michael Medwin *Martin Teckman* • George Coulouris *Garvin* • Duncan Lamont *Inspector Hilton* ■ *Dir* Wendy Toye • *Scr* Francis Durbridge, James Matthews, from the TV serial *The Teckman Biography* by Francis Durbridge

Ted & Venus ★★ 18

Romantic comedy drama
1991 · US · Colour · 95mins

An offbeat romance from Bud Cort, directing here but maybe better known as an actor in cult favourite *Harold and Maude*). Cort stars too, playing a poet whose obsession with dream-girl Kim Adams forces him to ever wilder efforts to attract her attention. Funny at times, but maybe it needed more of the endearing wackiness of Cort's most famous film to make it really work. Look for an early appearance by Woody Harrelson. DA

Bud Cort *Ted Whitley* • James Brolin *Max Waters* • Kim Adams *Linda Turner* • Carol Kane *Colette/Colette's twin sister* • Pamella D'Pella *Gloria* • Brian Thompson *Herb* • Rhea Perlman *Grace* • Woody Harrelson *Homeless Vietnam veteran* • Timothy Leary *Poetic judge* ■ *Dir* Bud Cort • *Scr* Paul Ciotti, Bud Cort, from a story by Paul Ciotti

Teen Agent ★★★ PG

Spy comedy 1991 · US · Colour · 84mins

Richard Grieco stars in a fun spy spoof laced with sly Ian Fleming references and 007-inspired gimmicks. He's mistaken for an undercover CIA agent when he flies to Paris for French lessons. Armed by MI5 with suction sneakers, X-ray specs and a tank-cum-sports car, he's sent to investigate Roger Rees, a megalomaniac in high camp *Goldfinger* mode. Although predictable every step of the way, this will leave you enjoyably shaken and pleasantly stirred. AJ. Contains swearing and violence.

Richard Grieco *Michael Corben* • Linda Hunt *Ilsa Grunt* • Roger Rees *Augustus Steranko* • Robin Bartlett *Mrs Grober* • Gabrielle Anwar *Mariska* • Geraldine James *Vendetta Galante* • Michael Siberry *Richardson* • Roger Daltrey *Blade* ■ *Dir* William Dear • *Scr* Darren Star, from a story by Fred Dekker

Teen Kanya ★★★ U

Comedy drama 1961 · Ind · BW · 114mins

Satyajit Ray filmed two of Tagore's stories on the centenary of the author's birth. Both are charming tales about the difficulties faced by young women in love. In *The Postmaster* an orphaned girl becomes attached to her employer, who repays her affection by helping with her education. A young man rejects an arranged marriage in *The Conclusion*, but finds that his own choice of bride resents being forced into matrimony. The film's success is due as much to the gifted playing and Ray's observant eye, as to Tagore's skills as a storyteller. DP. In Bengali with English subtitles.

Anil Chatterjee *Nandalal* • Chandana Bannerjee *Ratan* • Aparna Das Gupta *Mrinmoyee* • Soumitra Chatterjee *Amulya* ■ *Dir* Satyajit Ray • *Scr* Satyajit Ray, from the stories *The Postmaster* and *The Conclusion* by Rabindranath Tagore

Teen Witch ★★ PG

Fantasy comedy 1989 · US · Colour · 88mins

On learning she will become a witch on her 16th birthday, un-hip student Robin Lively uses her magic powers to become the most popular girl in school, get back at her uncaring teachers and snare a hunky boyfriend. Fortune teller Zelda Rubinstein guides her through the spell-casting until she discovers, the hard way, to be careful what she wishes for. Lightweight fare, with a few MTV-style musical dance numbers. AJ

Robyn Lively *Louise* • Dick Sargent *Frank* • Zelda Rubinstein *Serena* • Dan Gauthier *Brad* • Joshua Miller *Richie* • Shelley Berman *Mr Weaver* ■ *Dir* Dorian Walker • *Scr* Robin Menken, Vernon Zimmerman

Teen Wolf ★★★ PG

Comedy 1985 · US · Colour · 91mins

In this likeable, if lightweight, comedy, a teenager who longs to be a little less ordinary discovers a family curse that kicks in when the Moon is full. Beneath the facial fur, this is just another film about growing pains, although it does feature cinema's only werewolf slam dunk sports sequence. The ever engaging Michael J Fox is doing what he does best – turning a loser into a winner. Jason Bateman took over in the needless sequel *Teen Wolf Too*. JC DVD

Michael J Fox *Scott Howard* • James Hampton *Harold Howard* • Susan Ursitti *Lisa "Boof" Marconi* • Jerry Levine *Stiles* • Matt Adler *Lewis* • Lorie Griffin *Pamela* • Jim MacKrell [James MacKrell] *Mr Thorne* • Mark Arnold *Mick McAllister* • Jay Tarses *Coach Finstock* ■ *Dir* Rod Daniel • *Scr* Joseph Loeb III, Matthew Weisman

Teenage Caveman ★★ U

Fantasy adventure 1958 · US · BW · 65mins

Cult director Roger Corman's prehistoric *Rebel without a Cause* is justly famous for its catchpenny title, cheap dinosaurs (borrowed from *One Million BC*), the "stuffed deer" scene and lead actor Robert Vaughn in his pre-*Man from UNCLE* days. He's the titular boy who breaks tribal rules and ventures into the "forbidden land", where he learns his violent society is really a post-apocalyptic one. Vaughn calls this "one of the best-worst films of all time". AJ

Robert Vaughn *Boy* • Leslie Bradley *Symbol Maker* • Darrah Marshall *Maiden* • Frank De Kova *Villain* ■ *Dir* Roger Corman • *Scr* R Wright Campbell

Teenage Caveman ★★ 18

Science-fiction horror
2001 · US · Colour · 86mins

Larry Clark's re-imagining of the cult 1958 B-movie has moments of his trademark camp hedonism and near-the-knuckle voyeurism. Set in a post-apocalyptic dystopia, the action follows Andrew Keegan and friends, who escape into the wilderness after he's been left to die by his vengeful tribe. There are some droll asides on the primitivism underpinning our supposedly sophisticated lifestyles,

U = SUITABLE FOR ALL Uc = SUITABLE FOR ALL, ESPECIALLY FOR YOUNG CHILDREN (VIDEO ONLY) PG = PARENTAL GUIDANCE

when they are introduced to the retro luxury of sinister trendies Richard Hillman and Tiffany Limos. But it's just an excuse for some soft-core cavorting. DP. Contains violence, swearing and drug abuse. [video] DVD

Andrew Keegan *David* • Tara Subkoff *Sarah* • Richard Hillman *Neil* • Tiffany Limos *Judith* • Stephen Jasso *Vincent* • Crystal Grant *Elizabeth* • Shan Elliot *Joshua* ■ *Dir* Larry Clark • *Scr* Christos N Gage, from the 1958 film by R Wright Campbell

Teenage Gang Debs ★★

Crime drama 1966 · US · BW · 77mins

New York film-maker Sande N Johnsen explores the brutal world of street gangs in this uncompromising slice of inner-city exploitation. *West Side Story* it isn't, as Diana Conti persuades the leader of the Manhattan-based Golden Falcons into battle against the Brooklyn Rebels. The rumble involving the sadistic Aliens and the skin-carving finale are alarmingly authentic. There's also plenty of crucially unhip jive talk and one of the worst dance routines you are ever likely to see. DP

Diana Conti *Terry* • Linda Gale *Angel* • Eileen Scott *Ellie* • Sandra Kane *Annie* • Robin Nolan *Maria* • Linda Cambi *Shirley* • Sue McManus *Sally* • John Batis *Johnny* ■ *Dir* Sande N Johnsen • *Scr* Hy Cahl

Teenage Monster ★ PG

Science-fiction horror
1958 · US · BW · 62mins

This ho-hum science-fiction horror movie was titled *Meteor Monster* until the success of *I Was a Teenage Werewolf* caused every horror film to jump on the same bandwagon. In a plot that drags western clichés into its juvenile delinquent mix, teenager Gilbert Perkins is infected by rays from a weird meteor and slowly turns into a murderous hairy monster. AJ [video] DVD

Anne Gwynne *Ruth Cannon* • Gloria Castillo *Kathy North* • Stuart Wade *Sheriff Bob* • Gilbert Perkins *Charles Cannon* • Charles Courtney [Chuck Courtney] *Marv Howell* ■ *Dir* Jacques Marquette • *Scr* Ray Buffum

Teenage Mutant Ninja Turtles ★★ PG

Fantasy adventure
1990 · US · Colour · 87mins

Those kickboxing Teletubbies of yesteryear made their feature debut in this uneven comic-strip fantasy directed by pop-video whizzkid Steve Barron. In case you'd forgotten, the awesome foursome are pizza-munching, kung fu fighting, sewer-dwelling super-reptiles who, in this mindless adventure, help perky TV reporter Judith Hoag solve a Manhattan crime spree masterminded by the Shredder, a Darth Vader-voiced rogue ninja master. Elias Koteas scores as a mock turtle vigilante, but little else in this garish affair hits the target. AJ. [video] DVD

Judith Hoag *April O'Neil* • Elias Koteas *Casey Jones* • Josh Pais *Raphael* • Michelan Sisti *Michaelangelo* • Leif Tilden *Donatello* • David Forman *Leonardo* • Michael Turney *Danny Pennington* • Jay Patterson *Charles Pennington* ■ *Dir* Steve Barron • *Scr* Todd W Langen, Bobby Herbeck, from a story by Bobby Herbeck, from characters created by Kevin Eastman, Peter Laird

Teenage Mutant Ninja Turtles II: the Secret of the Ooze ★★ PG

Fantasy adventure
1991 · US · Colour · 84mins

This sequel is less abrasive than its predecessor and was considerably less successful at the box office. Seeking once more to stamp out the Foot clan, the turtles team up with reporter Paige Turco and gormless delivery boy Ernie Reyes Jr, but the human characters (even scientist David Warner) are pretty pointless. If you didn't know, Ooze is the nasty stuff that caused our heroes to live underground, shout "cowabunga" and gorge themselves on bizarre flavoured pizzas in the first place. DP [video] DVD

Paige Turco *April O'Neil* • David Warner *Professor Jordan Perry* • Michelan Sisti *Michaelangelo* • Leif Tilden *Donatello* • Kenn Troum *Raphael* • Mark Caso *Leonardo* • Kevin Clash *Splinter* • Ernie Reyes Jr *Keno* • François Chau *Shredder* • Toshishiro Obata *Tatsu* ■ *Dir* Michael Pressman • *Scr* Todd W Langen, from characters created by Kevin Eastman, Peter Laird

Teenage Mutant Ninja Turtles III ★★ PG

Fantasy adventure
1992 · US · Colour · 91mins

This second sequel was, by this stage, a largely irrelevant one, as the equally irritating Power Rangers had succeeded the Pizza-loving reptiles in the children's popularity stakes. Writer/director Stuart Gillard tries to inject some life into the project by including some tongue-in-cheek scenes in 17th-century Japan, but it quickly degenerates into half-hearted cartoonish action. JF. [video] DVD

Elias Koteas *Casey Jones/Whit Whitley* • Paige Turco *April O'Neil* • Stuart Wilson (1) *Captain Dirk Walker* • Sab Shimono *Lord Norinaga* • Vivian Wu *Princess Mitsu* • Mark Caso *Leonardo* • Matt Hill *Raphael* • Jim Raposa *Donatello* • David Fraser *Michaelangelo* • James Murray *Splinter* ■ *Dir* Stuart Gillard • *Scr* Stuart Gillard, from characters created by Kevin Eastman, Peter Laird

Teenage Rebel ★★

Comedy drama 1956 · US · BW · 94mins

A misleading title for a mediocre family picture about teenager Betty Lou Keim who, having lived with her father after her parents' divorce, is sent back to her mother Ginger Rogers when dad decides to remarry. Initially resentful of both maternal control and her stepfather Michael Rennie, she gradually warms to her surroundings. Entirely forgettable despite Oscar nominations for costume, art direction and set decoration. RK

Ginger Rogers *Nancy Fallon* • Michael Rennie *Jay Fallon* • Mildred Natwick *Grace Hewitt* • Betty Lou Keim *Dodie* • Warren Berlinger *Dick Hewitt* • Rusty Swope *Larry Fallon* ■ *Dir* Edmund Goulding • *Scr* Walter Reisch, Charles Brackett, from the play *A Roomful of Roses* by Edith Sommer

Teenagers from Outer Space ★★ PG

Science fiction 1959 · US · BW · 85mins

An all-time good bad classic featuring one of the most infamous special effects ever put on film – the shadow of a live lobster! When Earth is selected as a breeding ground for giant clawed cannibal Gargons by an intergalactic race, sensitive teen alien David Love arrives on the planet to warn mankind. Pursued by unearthly hit man Bryan Grant, Love falls for prom queen Dawn Anderson. A one-man-show by Tom Graeff, this is hilarious trash. AJ DVD

David Love *Derek* • Dawn Anderson [Dawn Bender] *Betty Morgan* • Harvey B Dunn *Grandpa Morgan* • Bryan Grant *Thor* • Tom Lockyear [Tom Graeff] *Joe Rogers* • King Moody *Captain* ■ *Dir/Scr* Tom Graeff

Teesri Kasam ★★★ U

Musical 1966 · Ind · BW · 148mins

Raj Kapoor reprises one of his most popular roles, as Hiraman, the bullock-cart driver. But this study of the oppression of women in general and the sexual exploitation of dancers in particular ultimately lacks the courage of its convictions. Director Basu Bhattacharya was making his feature debut, but he isn't helped by a script that can't decide whether its primary aim is to inform or to entertain. However, the songs and dance numbers are charming and effective. DP. In Hindi with English subtitles. [video]

Raj Kapoor *Hiraman* • Waheeda Rehman *Hirabai* ■ *Dir* Basu Bhattacharya • *Scr* Nabendu Ghosh

Tehzeeb ★★ PG

Drama 2003 · Ind · Colour · 145mins

This mother-daughter melodrama is lustrously photographed by Santosh Sivan and boasts six new songs by AR Rahman. But it's the performance of Shabana Azmi that dominates proceedings, despite a wealth of sensationalist subplots. As the Bollywood playback singer whose relationship with daughter Urmila Matondkar has been strained since she was acquitted of the murder of her husband many years earlier, Azmi knowingly portrays the craving for adulation of the fading star. DP. In Hindi with English subtitles. [video] DVD

Urmila Matondkar *Tehzeeb* • Arjun Rampal *Salim Mirza* • Dia Mirza [Diya Mirza] *Nazneen* • Shabana Azmi *Rukhsana Jamal* • Rishi Kapoor *Anwar Jamal* ■ *Dir/Scr* Khalid Mohamed

Telefon ★★★ PG

Spy thriller 1977 · US · Colour · 98mins

This is far from director Don Siegel's best work, but it's a more than acceptable thriller with a nifty plot and a couple of cracking performances. Charles Bronson is solid enough as a KGB troubleshooter sent to the USA to prevent "sleeping" agents from carrying out their missions, and Lee Remick is typically assured as his contact. But the film belongs to Donald Pleasence as a Stalinist spymaster and Tyne Daly as a CIA computer boffin. DP. Contains violence. [video]

Charles Bronson *Grigori Borzov* • Lee Remick *Barbara* • Donald Pleasence *Nicolai Dalchimsky* • Tyne Daly *Dorothy Putterman* • Alan Badel *Colonel Malchenko* • Patrick Magee *General Strelsky* • Sheree North *Marie Wills* • Frank Marth *Harley Sandburg* ■ *Dir* Don Siegel • *Scr* Peter Hyams, Stirling Silliphant, from the novel by Walter Wager

The Telegraph Trail ★★ U

Western 1933 · US · BW · 51mins

One of a short series of B-westerns that John Wayne shot for Warner Bros, this features him as an Indian-hating US army scout who routs hostile tribesmen after they've interrupted the construction of the telegraph wire across the plains. The impressive climax, with its shots of an Indian war dance, was lifted from a silent Ken Maynard western. The comic relief from Frank McHugh and Otis Harlan is a distinct minus. AE [video]

John Wayne *John Trent* • Marceline Day *Alice Ellis* • Frank McHugh *Sgt Tippy* • Otis Harlan *Zeke Keller* • Albert J Smith *Gus Lynch* • Yakima Canutt *"High Wolf"* ■ *Dir* Tenny Wright • *Scr* Kurt Kempler

The Telephone ★ 15

Comedy drama 1988 · US · Colour · 78mins

Poor Whoopi Goldberg has been involved in a number of dubious big screen projects in her time but this plumbs new depths. With a script by the unlikely pairing of musician Harry Nilsson and Terry Southern (co-writer of *Easy Rider*), and direction by dependable character actor Rip Torn, an intriguing project was on the cards, but it wasn't to be. This is virtually a one-woman show with Whoopi as a "resting" actress constantly ranting to her pet owl. DF [video]

Whoopi Goldberg *Vashti Blue* • Severn Darden *Max* • Elliott Gould *Rodney* • John Heard *Telephone man* • Amy Wright *Honey Boxe/Irate neighbor/Jennifer, answering machine voice* ■ *Dir* Rip Torn • *Scr* Terry Southern, Harry Nilsson

Tell It to the Judge ★★

Romantic comedy 1949 · US · BW · 85mins

Co-stars Rosalind Russell and Robert Cummings have to employ all their considerable skill as *farceurs* to keep this lightweight comedy afloat. The plot concerns the attempts of lawyer Cummings to get back with his ex-wife Russell, but the cause of their split – dumb blonde Marie McDonald – is the key witness in a case Cummings is working on. It's thin stuff, and Russell allows herself to be put through some undignified slapstick. TV

Rosalind Russell *Marsha Meredith* • Robert Cummings *Peter Webb* • Gig Young *Alexander Darvac* • Marie McDonald *Ginger Simmons* • Harry Davenport *Judge Meredith* • Fay Baker *Valerie Hobson* • Katharine Warren [Katherine Warren] *Kitty Lawton* • Douglass Dumbrille *George Ellerby* ■ *Dir* Norman Foster • *Scr* Nat Perrin, Roland Kibbee, from a story by Devery Freeman

Tell Me a Riddle ★★★

Drama 1980 · US · Colour · 90mins

Unaware that the illness from which she is suffering is terminal, elderly Lila Kedrova, who has been locked in mutually unsatisfying 40-year-marriage to Melvyn Douglas, visits her granddaughter Brooke Adams in San Francisco. There, she reflects on her unfulfilled life and, before her death, finds reconciliation with her husband. Marking the directorial debut of Oscar-winning actress Lee Grant (*Shampoo*), this is a truthful, perceptive and intelligent film, that is well-made and well-acted, but perhaps too sad and sombre to hold a broad appeal. RK

Melvyn Douglas *David* • Lila Kedrova *Eva* • Brooke Adams *Jeannie* • Lili Valenty *Mrs Mays* • Dolores Dorn *Vivi* • Bob Elross *Sammy* • Jon Harris *Mathew* • Zalman King *Paul* ■ *Dir* Lee Grant • *Scr* Joyce Eliason, Alev Lytle, from a novel by Tillie Olsen

Tell Me Lies ★★

Drama 1967 · UK · Colour and BW · 116mins

Following the disturbing film version of Peter Weiss's *Marat/Sade*, theatre director Peter Brook and Glenda Jackson reteamed for another all-out assault on the senses with this satirical swipe at the Vietnam War. This time, however, the chaotic structure (it's a mixture of sketches, music and news footage) fails to hold the attention and now seems self-indulgent rather than radical. Worth a look, if only for the eclectic cast. JF

Mark Jones (1) *Mark* • Pauline Munro *Pauline* • Robert Lloyd *Bob* • Kingsley Amis • Peggy Ashcroft • Glenda Jackson • Paul Scofield • Patrick Wymark • James Cameron • Ian Hogg ■ *Dir* Peter Brook • *Scr* Denis Cannan, Michael Kustow, Michael Scott, from the play *US* by Denis Cannan

Tell Me That You Love Me, Junie Moon ★★

Comedy drama 1970 · US · Colour · 112mins

One of Hollywood's most incisive, intelligent and provocative directors, Otto Preminger had seemingly lost his grip by the end of the 1960s, his judgement and objectivity replaced by trendy issues and glutinous sentimentality. A wildly over-emotional Liza Minnelli is Junie Moon while non-names Robert Moore and Ken Howard are her co-stars in this account of a facially disfigured young woman, a wheelchair-bound homosexual and an

T

epileptic drop-out. It should be inspiring, but it isn't. RK

Liza Minnelli *Junie Moon* • Ken Howard *Arthur* • Robert Moore *Warren* • James Coco *Mario* • Kay Thompson *Miss Gregory* • Ben Piazza *Jesse* ■ *Dir* Otto Preminger • *Scr* Marjorie Kellogg, from her novel

Tell No Tales ★★★

Crime drama 1939 · US · BW · 68mins

An excellent second-feature drama, utilising those familiar Hollywood companions, crime and newspapers, this stars Melvyn Douglas as the editor of a daily newspaper that is about to close. When Douglas gets a scoop on a kidnapping case, his troubles appear to be over, but then he finds his involvement plunging him into danger. Well characterised and tightly constructed for maximum tension, this is enhanced by the commanding presence of the star in a less suave man-about-town role than usual. RK

Melvyn Douglas *Michael Cassidy* • Louise Platt *Ellen Frazier* • Gene Lockhart *Arno* • Douglas Dumbrille [Douglass Dumbrille] *Matt Cooper* • Florence George *Lorna Travers* ■ *Dir* Leslie Fenton • *Scr* Lionel Houser, from a story by Pauline London, Alfred Taylor

The Tell-Tale Heart ★★

Horror 1934 · UK · BW · 49mins

This creaky adaptation of Edgar Allan Poe's macabre short story is a pretty terrible "quota quickie" with a few redeeming features. An amateur cast woodenly enacts the tale of a disturbed servant who kills his master, an act which tips him into madness. The dialogue is stilted and the pace ranges between dead slow and just nonexistent. But, in his first film, director Brian Desmond Hurst at least produces one or two surreal moments and, in the case of the old man's eye, some really chilling images. DM

Norman Dryden *Boy* • John Kelt *Old man* • Yolande Terrell *Girl* • Thomas Shenton *First investigator* • James Fleck *Second investigator* • Colonel Cameron *Doctor* ■ *Dir* Brian Desmond Hurst • *Scr* David Plunkett Greene, from the story by Edgar Allan Poe

Tell Them Willie Boy Is Here ★★★ 15

Western 1969 · US · Colour · 93mins

This sombre, allegorical western may seem too arty and introspective for today's tastes since the main thread of the story – a traditional pursuit across fine landscapes – is frequently broken for homilies on life and liberty. Even so, Robert Redford is excellent as the deputy sheriff chasing the Indian who's killed his prospective father-in-law. Robert Blake, as the fugitive, and Katharine Ross as his girlfriend, are less impressive. AT

Robert Redford *Christopher Cooper* • Katharine Ross *Lola Boniface* • Robert Blake *Willie Boy* • Susan Clark *Dr Elizabeth Arnold* • Barry Sullivan *Ray Calvert* • Charles McGraw *Frank Wilson* • John Vernon *Hacker* ■ *Dir* Abraham Polonsky • *Scr* Abraham Polonsky, from the book *Willie Boy* by Harry Lawton

T

Telling Lies in America ★★★★ 15

Drama 1997 · US · Colour · 97mins

This sweet and subtle coming-of-age story was written by Joe Eszterhas, who is more noted for steamy material like *Basic Instinct* and *Showgirls*. Partly autobiographical, the film tells of an immigrant Hungarian kid (Brad Renfro) who falls under the spell of Kevin Bacon's charismatic but ethic-free radio DJ. When Bacon is accused of taking record company backhanders, Renfro has to decide whether to jeopardise his father's citizenship assessment by lying for a friend. Terrific performances from Bacon and Renfro, and solid support from Maximilian Schell and *Ally McBeal's* Calista Flockhart. DA. Contains swearing and sexual references.

Kevin Bacon *Billy Magic* • Brad Renfro *Karchy Jonas* • Maximilian Schell *Dr Istvan Jonas* • Calista Flockhart *Diney Majeski* • Paul Dooley *Father Norton* • Luke Wilson *Henry* ■ *Dir* Guy Ferland • *Scr* Joe Eszterhas

Telling You ★ 15

Romantic comedy drama
1998 · US · Colour · 90mins

This debut indie written and directed by Robert DeFranco (who also features) has Jennifer Love Hewitt and Matthew Lillard to recommend it but very little else. Set in a pizzeria, this follows no-hopers Dash Mihok and Peter Facinelli as they return home from college and face a future of applying toppings to bases. When money goes missing from the restaurant, they scramble to replace it. LH DVD

Peter Facinelli *Phil Fazzulo* • Dash Mihok *Dennis Nolan* • Jennifer Love Hewitt *Deb Friedman* • Jennifer Jostyn *Beth Taylor* • Frank Medrano *Sal Lombardo* • Richard Libertini *Mr P* • Robert DeFranco *Steve Fagan* • Matthew Lillard *Adam Ginesberg* ■ *Dir* Robert DeFranco • *Scr* Robert DeFranco, Marc Palmieri, from a story by Marc Palmieri, from a story by Denis Flood

The Temp ★★ 15

Thriller 1993 · US · Colour · 92mins

After the nanny from hell (*The Hand That Rocks the Cradle*) and the lodger from hell (*Pacific Heights*), meet Satan's secretary. Lara Flynn Boyle is the shorthand expert wanting to make her way to the top no matter who stands in her way in this at times rather ludicrous thriller. Unfortunately, this film is neither as scary nor as funny as its predecessors, and serves only to embarrass a usually competent cast that includes Timothy Hutton and Faye Dunaway. JB. Contains swearing, sex scenes and violence.

Timothy Hutton *Peter Derns* • Lara Flynn Boyle *Kris Bolin* • Dwight Schultz *Roger Jasser* • Oliver Platt *Jack Hartsell* • Steven Weber *Brad Montroe* • Colleen Flynn *Sara Meinhold* • Faye Dunaway *Charlene Towne* • Scott Coffey *Lance* ■ *Dir* Tom Holland • *Scr* Kevin Falls, from a story by Kevin Falls, Tom Engelman

Tempest ★★

Drama 1959 · It/Yug/Fr · Colour · 120mins

Producer Dino de Laurentiis's attempt to do cinematically for Pushkin what his *War and Peace* did for Tolstoy. While the spectacle (Technicolor and Technirama photography by the great Aldo Tonti) certainly passes muster, the direction by former Italian neorealist Alberto Lattuada isn't up to the task. Some thought has gone into the retelling of the overthrow of Russia's Catherine the Great, and Viveca Lindfors makes a striking Empress, but the whole is undermined by a trashy, sexy subplot involving gauche Geoffrey Horne and an over-ripe Silvana Mangano. TS. Italian, Serbo-Croat and French dialogue dubbed into English.

Silvana Mangano *Masha* • Van Heflin *Pugacev* • Viveca Lindfors *Catherine II* • Geoffrey Horne *Peter Griniev* • Robert Keith (1) *Captain Mironov* • Agnes Moorehead *Vassilissa* • Oscar Homolka *Savelic* • Helmut Dantine *Svabrin* • Vittorio Gassman *Prosecutor* • Fulvia Franco *Palaska* • Finlay Currie *Count Griniev* ■ *Dir* Alberto Lattuada • *Scr* Alberto Lattuada, Ivo Perilli, from stories by Alexander Pushkin

The Tempest ★★★★ 15

Fantasy drama 1979 · UK · Colour · 87mins

Derek Jarman's experience as an art director is the key factor in this adaptation of Shakespeare's play, as his use of the Stoneleigh Abbey location is as inspired as his reworking of the material is audacious. Purists will bridle at the bowdlerisation of the action, but the shifting of emphasis to explore contemporary themes, the sensuality of Toyah Willcox's Miranda, the eccentricity of Heathcote Williams's Prospero and the carnality of Jack Birkett's Caliban make for provocative viewing. DP DVD

Heathcote Williams *Prospero* • Karl Johnson *Ariel* • Toyah Willcox *Miranda* • Peter Bull *Alonso* • Richard Warwick *Antonio* • Elisabeth Welch *Goddess* • Jack Birkett *Caliban* • Ken Campbell *Gonzalo* • Christopher Biggins *Stephano* • David Meyer *Ferdinand* • Neil Cunningham *Sebastian* ■ *Dir* Derek Jarman • *Scr* Derek Jarman, from the play by William Shakespeare

Tempest ★★ 15

Fantasy drama 1982 · US · Colour · 136mins

Director Paul Mazursky's transposition of Shakespeare's play into a modern setting is a lengthy, self-indulgent folly. As the architect who seeks solace on a Greek island, John Cassavetes introduces an unexpected conviction to an otherwise uninspired story, which, for all the beauty of Donald McAlpine's seascapes, is nothing more than another study in Manhattan angst. The Shakespearean links are clumsily forged, and the whole conceit is made faintly ridiculous by the zealous significance of the performances. DP. Contains swearing and nudity.

John Cassavetes *Phillip Dimitrious* • Gena Rowlands *Antonia Dimitrious* • Susan Sarandon *Aretha* • Vittorio Gassman *Alonzo* • Raul Julia *Kalibanos* • Molly Ringwald *Miranda* • Sam Robards *Freddy* ■ *Dir* Paul Mazursky • *Scr* Paul Mazursky, Leon Capetanos, from the play by William Shakespeare

Temptation ★★

Period melodrama 1946 · US · BW · 98mins

A striking Victorian beauty (strikingly beautiful Merle Oberon, fittingly gowned by Orry-Kelly) deserts her dreary husband (dreary George Brent) – an Egyptologist – for flashing-eyed Egyptian (an over-the-top Charles Korvin). A mistake – as was the film. Directed at sleepwalking pace by Irving Pichel, it's idiotic enough to be mildly enjoyable. RK

Merle Oberon *Ruby Chepstow Armine* • George Brent *Nigel Armine* • Charles Korvin *Mahmoud Baroudi* • Paul Lukas *Sir Meyer Isaacson* • Lenore Ulric *Marie* • Arnold Moss *Ahmed* • Robert Capa *Hamza* • Aubrey Mather *Dr Harding* ■ *Dir* Irving Pichel • *Scr* Robert Thoeron, from the novel *Bella Donna* by Robert Smythe Hichens, from the play *Bella Donna* by James Bernard Fagan

Tempted ★★★

Thriller 2001 · Fr/US/Aus · Colour · 95mins

Director Bill Bennett made his name with the unnerving, dislocated road movie *Kiss or Kill* and he brings some of the same edgy improvisational techniques to this. Burt Reynolds is the rich businessman who is the instigator of a dangerous *ménage à trois* when he hires a young carpenter (Peter Facinelli) to test the fidelity of his trophy wife Saffron Burrows. The three leads are excellent and Bennett avoids the usual tourist clichés in evoking the atmosphere of a sensuous New Orleans. JF

Burt Reynolds *Charlie Le Blanc* • Saffron Burrows *Lilly Le Blanc* • Peter Facinelli *Jimmy Mulate* • Mike Starr *Dot Collins* • George DiCenzo *Byron Blades* ■ *Dir/Scr* Bill Bennett

The Temptress ★★★

Silent drama 1926 · US · BW · 117mins

A Parisian aristocrat "sells" his wife Greta Garbo to a banker to secure himself a life of material luxury. She falls madly in love with Antonio Moreno, an Argentinian engineer who leaves her when he learns she is married. Following him to Argentina, Garbo inflames the passions of several men en route to a climactic fall-out. Begun under the direction of Garbo's Swedish mentor Mauritz Stiller, who was replaced by Fred Niblo, this raging inferno of lust, love and degeneracy was her second American film and it attracted ecstatic reviews. RK

Greta Garbo *Elena* • Antonio Moreno *Robledo* • Roy D'Arcy *Manos Duros* • Marc MacDermott *M Fontenoy* • Lionel Barrymore *Canterac* • Virginia Brown Faire *Celinda* ■ *Dir* Fred Niblo • *Scr* Dorothy Farnum, Mauritz Stiller, Marian Ainslee, from the novel *La Tierra de Todos* by Vicente Blasco-Ibañez, Leo Ongley (translation)

Temptress ★★ 18

Erotic thriller 1995 · US · Colour · 89mins

This lavishly produced erotic chiller is a class above the usual soft-core fare. Kim Delaney is transformed into the bad girl of the title after being possessed by the goddess Kali on a trip to India. There are sound supporting turns, and director Lawrence Lanoff brings at least a hint of style to the usual genre clichés. JF. Contains sex scenes and nudity.

Kim Delaney *Karin Swann* • Chris Sarandon *Matthew Christianson* • Corbin Bernsen *Nick* • Dee Wallace Stone *Allison Mackie* • Ben Cross *Dr Samudaya* • Jessica Walter *Dr Phyllis Evergreen* ■ *Dir* Lawrence Lanoff • *Scr* Melissa Mitchell

Temptress Moon ★★★ 15

Romantic period drama
1996 · HK/Chi · Colour · 115mins

Following its indifferent reception at Cannes, Chen Kaige's visually stunning period piece suffered substantial cuts and the imposition of gutsier subtitles. But this remains an overwrought melodrama, complete with operatic emotions, two-dimensional performances (even from Gong Li and Leslie Cheung) and fumbling attempts to depict passion. The tale of a country boy caught up in both the aftermath of the 1911 Revolution and the opium-induced decline of his Shanghai family is a tantalising disappointment. DP. In Mandarin with English subtitles. Contains swearing, sex scenes.

Leslie Cheung *Yu Zhongliang* • Gong Li *Pang Ruyi* • Kevin Lin *Pang Duanwu* • He Caifei *Yu Xiuyi, Zhongliang's sister* • Zhang Shi *Li Niangjui* • Lin Lianqun *Pang An* • Ge Xiangting *Elder Qi* ■ *Dir* Chen Kaige • *Scr* Shu Kei, from a story by Chen Kaige, Wang Anyi

10 ★★★★ 18

Comedy 1979 · US · Colour · 122mins

If George Segal hadn't walked off the set of this Blake Edwards film, would Dudley Moore have become a movie star? Desperately sexist in hindsight, this acerbic look at Los Angeles is still relentlessly funny, mixing satire and observation together with some really rude gags. Ravel's *Bolero* will never be the same after you see what our Dud and Bo Derek get up to during its strains. As dated as Derek's hair plaits, but still very perceptive, occasionally vulgar and a lot of fun. TS. Contains swearing, sex scenes and nudity. DVD

Dudley Moore *George* • Julie Andrews *Sam* • Bo Derek *Jenny* • Robert Webber *Hugh* • Dee Wallace [Dee Wallace Stone] *Mary Lewis* • Sam Jones *David* • Brian Dennehy *Bartender* ■ *Dir/Scr* Blake Edwards

Ten ★★★★ 12

Drama 2002 · Fr/Iran · Colour · 89mins

Taking a technical gamble by filming only the interior of a car from a camera fixed to the windscreen, Abbas Kiarostami provides a compelling insight into the current status of Iranian women in the light of recent liberalisation. As the divorcee ferrying her petulant eight-year-old son Amin Maher around town, Mania Akbari succeeds in moving between chic assurance and disconsolate fortitude as she encounters a variety of women, including a prostitute, a widow and a discarded bride, whose problems far outweigh her own. The issues raised are already momentous, but the simple immediacy of Kiarostami's approach makes them all the more poignant. DP. In Farsi with English subtitles. DVD

Mania Akbari *Driver* • Amin Maher *Amin* ■ *Dir/Scr* Abbas Kiarostami

The Ten Commandments ★★★★

Silent biblical epic
1923 · US · BW and Colour · 146mins

Cecil B DeMille's first silent version marked his emergence as an epic showman. Despite its odd combination of two unconnected tales, ancient and modern, the film is a "must see" combination of interesting curiosity, historical document, lavish spectacle and entertaining melodrama. The first section covers Old Testament episodes. The modern story is a parable of two brothers, bad Rod La Rocque and good Richard Dix. It's all done with full-blooded conviction and panache. RK

Theodore Roberts *Moses* • Charles De Roche *Rameses* • Estelle Taylor *Miriam* • Julia Faye *Pharaoh's wife* • Terrence Moore *Pharaoh's son* • James Neill *Aaron* • Lawson Butt *Dathan* • Edythe Chapman *Mrs Martha McTavish* • Richard Dix *John McTavish* • Rod La Rocque *Dan McTavish* • Leatrice Joy *Mary Leigh* ■ *Dir* Cecil B DeMille • *Scr* Jeanie Macpherson

The Ten Commandments ★★★★ U

Biblical epic 1956 · US · Colour · 219mins

This masterpiece of heroic vulgarity represents the Hollywood epic at the peak of its all-American powers. Cecil B DeMille's remake of his 1923 silent movie, about the life of Moses and his leadership of the Israelites in their exodus from Egypt, adds over an hour to his first telling of the story, but, with untypical restraint, sticks to the original ten commandments. It's a movie to savour, less for the sparkle of its dialogue or the complexity of its characterisations, than for the sheer magnificence of its set pieces and its casual deployment of 25,000 extras at the drop of a tablet. PF [video] DVD

Charlton Heston *Moses* • Yul Brynner *Rameses* • Anne Baxter *Nefretiti* • Edward G Robinson *Dathan* • Yvonne De Carlo *Sephora* • Debra Paget *Lilia* • John Derek *Joshua* • Nina Foch *Bithiah* • John Carradine *Aaron* • Vincent Price *Baka* • Cedric Hardwicke *Sethi* ■ *Dir* Cecil B DeMille • *Scr* Aeneas MacKenzie, Jesse L Lasky Jr [Jesse Lasky Jr], Jack Gariss, Fredric M Frank, from the novel *The Prince of Egypt* by Dorothy Clarke Wilson, from the novel *Pillar of Fire* by Rev JH Ingraham, from the novel *On Eagle's Wings* by Rev GE Southon

Ten Days in Paris ★★

Mystery spy drama 1939 · UK · BW · 81mins

This is a modest little programme filler with a lot to be modest about. It finds amnesiac crash victim Rex Harrison waking up in Paris to be told he's a spy. As an example of gentlemanly espionage, it has no suspense, and even the charismatic Harrison exhibits little of his usual flair. TH

Rex Harrison *Robert Stevens* • Karen Verne [Kaaren Verne] *Diane De Guermantes* • CV France *General De Guermantes* • Leo Genn *Lanson* • Joan Marion *Denise* ■ *Dir* Tim Whelan • *Scr* James Curtis, John Meehan Jr, from the novel *The Disappearance of Roger Tremayne* by Bruce Graeme

Ten Days' Wonder ★★★

Mystery drama 1971 · Fr · Colour · 108mins

Orson Welles plays Theo Van Horn, representing God no less, in Claude Chabrol's portentous and enigmatic theological thriller, in which the ten days of the action represent each of the Ten Commandments. In a magnificent private estate in Alsace, old patriarch Welles dictates to his child bride Marlène Jobert and adopted son (Anthony Perkins). The film was shot in a virtuoso, high-gothic style, while Perkins gives a typically nervous, agitated performance which the restless camera mirrors. RB. French dialogue dubbed into English.

Orson Welles *Theo Van Horn* • Marlène Jobert *Helene Van Horn* • Michel Piccoli *Paul Regis* • Anthony Perkins *Charles Van Horn* • Guido Alberti *Ludovic* ■ *Dir* Claude Chabrol • *Scr* Paul Gardner, Paul Gégauff, Eugene Archer, from a novel by Ellery Queen [Frederic Dannay, Manfred B Lee]

Ten Gentlemen from West Point ★★ U

Drama 1942 · US · BW · 103mins

Not quite the *Top Gun* of its day, though very gung ho, this propagandist frolic charts the founding in 1802 of West Point military academy. Directed by action maestro Henry Hathaway, it stars George Montgomery as one of the cadets and Maureen O'Hara, who appears for no other reason than to provide some romance and respite from all the scenes of men training. Episodic and contrived. AT

George Montgomery *Dawson* • Maureen O'Hara *Carolyn Bainbridge* • John Sutton *Howard Shelton* • Laird Cregar *Major Sam Carter* • John Shepperd [Shepperd Strudwick] *Henry Clay* • Victor Francen *Florimond Massey* • Harry Davenport *Bane* • Ward Bond *Scully* • Douglass Dumbrille *General William Henry Harrison* ■ *Dir* Henry Hathaway • *Scr* Richard Maibaum, George Seaton, from a story by Malvin Ward

Ten Little Indians ★★ 15

Thriller 1965 · UK · BW · 95mins

This is the second film version of Agatha Christie's ever-popular whodunnit (after 1945's *And Then There Were None*), complete with a hugely irritating "guess-the-killer" break. It's hard to think of Dame Agatha as the originator of the serial killer thriller, but that's essentially what this ingenious mystery is. The cast of fading British stars doesn't seem particularly enthralled, while director George Pollock might have injected the film with a little more enthusiasm. DP [video]

Hugh O'Brian *Hugh Lombard* • Shirley Eaton *Ann Clyde* • Fabian *Mike Raven* • Leo Genn *General Mandrake* • Stanley Holloway *William Blore* • Wilfrid Hyde White *Judge Cannon* • Daliah Lavi *Ilona Bergen* • Dennis Price *Dr Armstrong* ■ *Dir* George Pollock • *Scr* Peter Yeldham, Dudley Nichols, Peter Welbeck [Harry Alan Towers], from the novel and play *Ten Little Niggers* by Agatha Christie

Ten Minutes Older: the Cello ★★ 15

Portmanteau drama
2002 · Ger/UK/US · BW and Colour · 105mins

One Moment, Jirí Menzel's affectionate montage tribute to Czech actor Rudolf Hrusinsky, is the pick of this largely self-indulgent collection of musings on memory, fate and time. Bernardo Bertolucci's *Histoire d'Eaux* and István Szabó's *Ten Minutes After* are shrewd "cinecdotes", told with economy and wit. But the intriguing ideas in Claire Denis's *Vers Nancy* and Volker Schlöndorff's *The Enlightenment* are diluted respectively by inert visuals and trite melodramatics. Jean-Luc Godard revisits the iconic imagery of his past in *Dans le Noir du Temps*, while Mike Figgis recalls *Timecode* by quartering the screen for the negligible *About Time 2*. However, the nadir of this disappointingly inconsistent collection is Michael Radford's interminable sci-fi parable, *Addicted to the Stars*. DP

Valéria Bruni-Tedeschi *Marcellina* • Amit Arroz *Narada* • Mark Long *Man* • Alexandra Staden *Young woman* • Dominic West *Young man* • Ildiko Bansagi • Gabor Mate • Jean-Luc Nancy *The philosopher* • Ana Samardzija *The student* • Bibiana Beglau *Girl* • Irm Herrmann [Irm Hermann] *Mother* • Mario Irrek *Brother* • Daniel Craig *Cecil Thomas* • Charles Simon *Martin* ■ *Dir* Bernardo Bertolucci, Mike Figgis, Jirí Menzel, István Szabó, Claire Denis, Volker Schlöndorff, Michael Radford, Jean-Luc Godard • *Scr* Bernardo Bertolucci, Mike Figgis, Jirí Menzel, István Szabó, Claire Denis, Max E Frye from the religious text *Confessions* by Augustinus, Michael Radford, Anne-Marie Miéville

Ten Minutes Older: the Trumpet ★★★ 15

Portmanteau
2002 · Ger/UK/US · BW and Colour · 92mins

Seven directors took up the challenge of interpreting Marcus Aurelius's maxim that time is as relentless as a river. Aki Kaurismäki's wry romance *Dogs Have No Hell* and Chen Kaige's whimsical *1000 Flowers Hidden Deep* make effective bookmarks, but Jim Jarmusch's on-set snapshot *Int.Trailer.Night* and Wim Wenders's gimmicky road movie *Twelve Miles to Trona* are deeply disappointing. So, too, is Werner Herzog's well-meaning, but rather trivial eco-documentary, *Ten Thousand Years Older*. Much better is *We Wuz Robbed*, Spike Lee's typically pointed take on the 2000 US Presidential election. But easily outshining the rest is Victor Erice's superbly constructed, monochrome mini-masterpiece, *Lifeline*. DP. In English, German, Mandarin, Spanish, Portuguese and Finnish with subtitles.

Kati Outinen *Woman* • Markku Peltola *Man* • Ana Sofia Liano *Young mother* • Celia Poo *Midwife* • Chloë Sevigny *Actress* • Charles Esten *Bill* • Amber Tamblyn *Kate* • Feng Yuanzheng *Mr Feng* ■ *Dir* Aki Kaurismäki, Victor Erice, Werner Herzog, Jim Jarmusch, Wim Wenders, Spike Lee, Chen Kaige • *Scr* Aki Kaurismäki, Victor Erice, Werner Herzog, Jim Jarmusch, Wim Wenders, Zhang Tan

Ten North Frederick ★★★★

Drama 1958 · US · BW · 101mins

One of those fabulous extended soapy dramas based on the kind of bestselling doorstop novel that 20th Century-Fox seemed to specialise in during the early CinemaScope period. Gary Cooper stars as a successful lawyer, shoved into the political big time by grasping wife Geraldine Fitzgerald, who finds brief solace in the arms of ex-model Suzy Parker. Sit back and enjoy a good wallow. TS

Gary Cooper *Joe Chapin* • Diane Varsi *Ann Chapin* • Suzy Parker *Kate Drummond* • Geraldine Fitzgerald *Edith Chapin* • Tom Tully *Slattery* • Ray Stricklyn *Joby* • Philip Ober *Lloyd Williams* • John Emery *Paul Donaldson* • Stuart Whitman *Charley Bongiorno* ■ *Dir* Philip Dunne • *Scr* Philip Dunne, from the novel by John O'Hara

10 Rillington Place ★★★★★ 15

Biographical crime drama
1970 · UK · Colour · 106mins

Three years after Timothy Evans went to the gallows for the murder of his daughter Geraldine, John Reginald Christie, the family's landlord and a wartime special constable, was convicted at the Old Bailey of murdering his wife and was also shown to be responsible for the deaths of five other women, and, by his own admission, for the death of Mrs Evans. Although Christie denied killing the infant, Evans was found not to have killed his child in a subsequent inquiry. Richard Fleischer's film is not as visually audacious as his *Boston Strangler*, but it does contain an acting tour de force from Richard Attenborough as the seedy killer. Superbly re-creating the atmosphere of late-1940s London, this is a chilling study of an evil mind. DP. Contains swearing. [video] DVD

Richard Attenborough *John Reginald Christie* • Judy Geeson *Beryl Evans* • John Hurt *Timothy John Evans* • Pat Heywood *Mrs Ethel Christie* • Isobel Black *Alice* • Miss Riley *Baby Geraldine* • Phyllis McMahon *Muriel Eady* ■ *Dir* Richard Fleischer • *Scr* Clive Exton, from the book by Ludovic Kennedy

Ten Seconds to Hell ★★

Drama 1959 · US · BW · 93mins

A typically catchpenny title for a typically brash Robert Aldrich movie about German bomb-disposal experts in postwar Berlin coming to explosive blows over Martine Carol, a French sex symbol in the 1950s. Jack Palance and Jeff Chandler rant eloquently enough, but it's too stridently contrived for any credibility. A dampish squib. TH

Jeff Chandler *Karl Wirtz* • Jack Palance *Eric Koertner* • Martine Carol *Margot Hofer* • Robert Cornthwaite *Loeffler* • Dave Willock *Tillig* • Wesley Addy *Sulke* • Jimmy Goodwin *Globke* • Virginia Baker *Frau Bauer* • Richard Wattis *Major Haven* ■ *Dir* Robert Aldrich • *Scr* Robert Aldrich, Teddi Sherman, from the novel *The Phoenix* by Lawrence P Bachmann

Ten Tall Men ★★★ U

Comedy adventure
1951 · US · Colour · 96mins

Dr Kildare's veteran writer/director Willis Goldbeck fashioned a more-than-passable film from this robust tale of the Foreign Legion, but *Beau Geste* it isn't. Nevertheless, with Burt Lancaster at the peak of his teeth-and-glory years in the lead, and tough hombres Gilbert Roland and Kieron Moore in support, this comedy adventure is well worth catching, especially since it's in sharp 1950s Technicolor. TS

Burt Lancaster *Sergeant Mike Kincaid* • Jody Lawrance *Mahla* • Gilbert Roland *Corporal Luis Delgado* • Kieron Moore *Corporal Pierre Molier* • George Tobias *Londos* • John Dehner *Jardine* • Nick Dennis *Mouse* • Mike Mazurki *Roshko* ■ *Dir* Willis Goldbeck • *Scr* Roland Kibbee, Frank Davis, from a story by James Warner Bellah, Willis Goldbeck

10 Things I Hate about You ★★★★ 12

Romantic comedy
1999 · US · Colour · 97mins

Shakespeare's *The Taming of the Shrew* gets updated *Clueless*-style to high-school America for this engaging romantic comedy from debut director Gil Junger. Julia Stiles is the sulky teen who doesn't like anybody. This causes a problem for her hormonally-charged younger sister Larisa Oleynik, who has been told by their dad that she can't date until Stiles does. Newcomer Heath Ledger plays the unfortunate lad picked to introduce Stiles to the dating scene, while the rest of the cast is peppered with equally good-looking youngsters. Smartly paced, fun and funny. JB. Contains some sexual references. [video] DVD

Heath Ledger *Patrick Verona* • Julia Stiles *Katarina Stratford* • Joseph Gordon-Levitt *Cameron James* • Larisa Oleynik *Bianca Stratford* • David Krumholtz *Michael Eckman* • Andrew Keegan *Joey Donner* • Susan May Pratt *Mandella* ■ *Dir* Gil Junger • *Scr* Karen McCullah Lutz, Kirsten Smith

10:30 PM Summer ★

Drama 1966 · US/Sp · Colour · 84mins

French novelist Marguerite Duras and director Jules Dassin adapted the

T

former's novel as a vehicle for the latter's wife, Melina Mercouri. She brings her strident Greek passion to the role of a wife, holidaying in Spain with her husband Peter Finch and best friend Romy Schneider. While troubled with erotic and alarming dreams about hubby and friend getting together, she wanders the streets and meets Julian Mateos who has killed his wife and her lover. Intensely irritating drivel. RK

Melina Mercouri *Maria* • Romy Schneider *Claire* • Peter Finch *Paul* • Julian Mateos *Rodrigo Palestra* • Isabel Maria Perez *Judith* • Beatriz Savon *Rodrigo's wife* ■ *Dir* Jules Dassin • *Scr* Jules Dassin, Marguerite Duras, from a novel by Marguerite Duras

Ten Thousand Bedrooms ★★ U

Musical comedy 1957 · US · Colour · 114mins

Millionaire hotel owner Dean Martin visits Rome to check out his latest acquisition and becomes romantically entangled with four Italian sisters, particularly the eldest, Eva Bartok. Anna Maria Alberghetti, Lisa Montell, and Lisa Gaye are the other girls in a large cast, which also includes Walter Slezak as the girls' Italian papa. A witless and interminable romantic comedy, this was Martin's first film without Jerry Lewis. RK

Dean Martin *Ray Hunter* • Anna Maria Alberghetti *Nina Martelli* • Eva Bartok *Maria Martelli* • Dewey Martin *Mike Clark* • Walter Slezak *Papa Vittorio Martelli* • Paul Henreid *Anton* • Lisa Montell *Diana Martelli* • Lisa Gaye *Anna Martelli* ■ *Dir* Richard Thorpe • *Scr* Laslo Vadnay, Art Cohn, William Ludwig, Leonard Spigelgass

10 to Midnight ★★ 18

Thriller 1983 · UK · Colour · 95mins

Selecting the worst Charles Bronson film of the 1980s provides an embarrassment of riches. Not only are all of them pretty awful, but the plots are often strikingly similar. This nasty thriller, for example, could just have easily been an entry in the *Death Wish* series. This time Bronson plays a cop tracking down a serial killer of women. When orthodox methods fail, he's reduced to planting evidence and then stalking the murderer himself. JF

Charles Bronson *Leo Kessler* • Lisa Eilbacher *Laurie Kessler* • Andrew Stevens *Paul McAnn* • Gene Davis *Warren Stacey* • Geoffrey Lewis *Dave Dante* • Wilford Brimley *Captain Malone* • Robert F Lyons *Nathan Zager* • Bert Williams *Mr Johnson* ■ *Dir* J Lee Thompson • *Scr* William Roberts

Ten Who Dared ★★ PG

Historical adventure
1960 · US · Colour · 92mins

Set in the 19th century, this Disney production is based on the real-life diary chronicling the adventures of Major John Wesley Powell, an explorer/geologist/botanist who lost his arm in the Civil War but undaunted traversed nearly a thousand miles of the American west. The film features John Beal as Powell and Brian Keith as William Dunn negotiating uncharted territories. Opting for an episodic approach, veteran director William Beaudine fails to translate a scientific expedition into entertainment. TH

Brian Keith *William Dunn* • John Beal *Major John Wesley Powell* • James Drury *Walter Powell* • RG Armstrong *Oramel Howland* • Ben Johnson *George Bradley* • LQ Jones *Billy Hawkins* ■ *Dir* William Beaudine • *Scr* Lawrence Edward Watkin, from the journal of Major John Wesley Powell

The Tenant ★★★ 18

Psychological thriller
1976 · Fr · Colour · 119mins

Roman Polanski directs a male take on the themes of paranoia and delusion that he explored from a female perspective in *Repulsion* ten years earlier. Polanski also stars, playing an expatriate Pole in Paris who comes to believe that the tenants of his apartment block are devilishly conspiring to drive him to suicide. Melvyn Douglas and Shelley Winters co-star in a puzzling and absorbing thriller. DA DVD

Roman Polanski *Trelkovsky* • Isabelle Adjani *Stella* • Melvyn Douglas *Mr Zy* • Jo Van Fleet *Madame Dioz* • Bernard Fresson *Scope* • Lila Kedrova *Madame Gaderian* • Shelley Winters *Concierge* ■ *Dir* Roman Polanski • *Scr* Roman Polanski, Gerard Brach, from the novel *Le Locataire Chimérique* by Roland Topor

Tender Comrade ★★★ U

Second World War drama
1943 · US · BW · 102mins

On the surface, a harmless enough tale about women living together while their menfolk are off at war, but this slight drama had serious repercussions. Ginger Rogers's mother objected to her daughter uttering the sentiment "Share and share alike" in the film, and four years later writer Dalton Trumbo and director Edward Dmytryk were hauled before the House Un-American Activities Committee and imprisoned as "unfriendly" witnesses and alleged communists all because the women lived and worked communally in the movie! TS

Ginger Rogers *Jo Jones* • Robert Ryan *Chris Jones* • Ruth Hussey *Barbara* • Patricia Collinge *Helen Stacey* • Mady Christians *Manya* • Kim Hunter *Doris* • Jane Darwell *Mrs Henderson* • Mary Forbes *Jo's mother* • Richard Martin (1) *Mike* ■ *Dir* Edward Dmytryk • *Scr* Dalton Trumbo, from his story

Tender Hooks ★★★

Drama 1988 · Aus · Colour · 95mins

Talk about life in the raw. This is the remarkable feature debut of the Australian film-maker Mary Callaghan and it packs more squalor, indolence and misfortune into its running time than you would believe possible. Yet the characters who inhabit this part of Sydney's Kings Cross district are bursting with life, even though that life consists of botched robberies, prostitution, drug addiction and prison. Jo Kennedy is hugely impressive as the hairdresser whose world is turned upside down by her encounter with waster Nique Needles. DP

Jo Kennedy *Mitch* • Nique Needles *Rex Reeson* • Anna Phillips *Gaye* • Robert Menzies *Yawn* • John Polson *Tony* • Ian Mortimer *Vic* ■ *Dir/Scr* Mary Callaghan

Tender Is the Night ★★

Drama 1961 · US · Colour · 146mins

This adaptation of Scott Fitzgerald's semi-autobiographical novel fails to achieve a coherent film from the complex, opaque material. Jason Robards and Jennifer Jones are Dick and Nicole Diver, the "beautiful people" of the 1920s, squandering their lives on a hedonistic existence among the Jazz Age jet set on the French Riviera. Robards and a too-old Jones make a good stab at their roles and the enormous cast includes Joan Fontaine, Tom Ewell and Jill St John in the major supporting parts. There is some vicarious entertainment to be had from watching the unstable, amoral, idle rich playing and disintegrating, but to date the book remains unfilmable. RK

Jason Robards Jr [Jason Robards] *Dick Diver* • Jennifer Jones *Nicole Diver* • Joan Fontaine *Baby Warren* • Jill St John *Rosemary Hoyt* • Tom Ewell *Abe North* • Cesare Danova *Tommy Barban* • Paul Lukas *Dr Dohmler* • Carole Mathews *Mrs Hoyt* ■ *Dir* Henry King • *Scr* Ivan Moffat, from the novel by F Scott Fitzgerald

Tender Mercies ★★★★ PG

Drama 1982 · US · Colour · 87mins

A spare, lean performance from spare, lean Robert Duvall won him an Oscar. Duvall wakes up, after a drunken binge, in a Texan motel owned by religious widow Tess Harper and her young son Allan Hubbard. Having failed once in both his life and career as a country singer he hesitatingly tries again with Harper. Australian director Bruce Beresford shows a sympathetic connection to the hot dusty Texan locations for his first Hollywood film and screenwriter Horton Foote (who also won an Oscar) provides a realistic pace. A poignant portrayal of redemption. FL

Robert Duvall *Mac Sledge* • Tess Harper *Rosa Lee* • Allan Hubbard *Sonny* • Betty Buckley *Dixie* • Ellen Barkin *Sue Anne* • Wilford Brimley *Harry* • Michael Crabtree *Lewis Menefee* • Lenny Von Dohlen *Robert Dennis* ■ *Dir* Bruce Beresford • *Scr* Horton Foote

A Tender Place ★★★★

Drama 2001 · Jpn · Colour · 201mins

This stately blend of mystery and melodrama explores such weighty themes as recrimination and regret while also maintaining a high level of suspense, as Yuki Amami conducts a four-year search for the daughter who disappeared while she was engaged in a moment of illicit passion. Making evocative use of his Hokkaido locations, director Shunichi Nagasaki brings immediacy to proceedings through his digital video imagery, achieving a deeply moving intensity while allowing Amami the space to develop her relationship with Tomokazu Miura, a terminally ill retired cop who devotes his last days to her cause. DP. In Japanese with English subtitles.

Yuki Amami *Kasumi Moriwaki* • Tomokazu Miura *Yohei Ishiyama* • Shunsuke Matsuoka *Junichi Utsumi* ■ *Dir* Shunichi Nagasaki • *Scr* Shunichi Nagasaki, from a novel by Natsuo Kirino

The Tender Trap ★★★★

Romantic comedy
1955 · US · Colour · 110mins

A single swinger – the perfectly cast Frank Sinatra – falls into marriage (that's the "trap" of the title), but it's the wit and style of the ensemble playing that gives the film such charm. Debbie Reynolds co-stars, and Celeste Holm and David Wayne are the other principals, with Wayne's morning-after scene a particular joy to watch. TS

Frank Sinatra *Charlie Y Reader* • Debbie Reynolds *Julie Gillis* • David Wayne *Joe McCall* • Celeste Holm *Sylvia Crewes* • Jarma Lewis *Jessica Collins* • Lola Albright *Poppy Matson* • Carolyn Jones *Helen* • Howard St John *Sam Sayers* ■ *Dir* Charles Walters • *Scr* Julius J Epstein, from the play by Max Shulman, Robert Paul Smith

The Tender Years ★★ U

Period drama 1947 · US · BW · 79mins

In a rural American community around 1870, young Richard Lyon tries to save a local dog from his abusive owner, who also stages canine duels inside his barn. As the religious minister seeking to outlaw dog-fighting in response to his small son's love for an errant pooch, wide-mouthed comedian Joe E Brown takes it all very seriously. A determinedly schmaltzy movie that wears its heart all too obviously on its platitudinous sleeve. TH

Joe E Brown *Rev Will Norris* • Richard Lyon *Ted Norris* • Noreen Nash *Linda* • Charles Drake *Bob Wilson* • Josephine Hutchinson *Emily Norris* • James Millican *Kit Barton* • Griff Barnett *Senator Cooper* • Jeanne Gail *Jeanie* ■ *Dir* Harold Schuster • *Scr* Jack Jungmeyer Jr, Arnold Belgard, Abel Finkel, from a story by Jack Jungmeyer Jr

Tenebrae ★★★ 18

Horror thriller 1982 · It · Colour · 96mins

One of the best psycho-thrillers from Dario Argento, the Italian Hitchcock, full of stylish camerawork, kinky flashbacks, impressive gore and an ace electronic soundtrack. Novelist Anthony Franciosa visits Rome to promote his latest bestseller, only to find a murderer is copying the killings in his book. It's enormous fun sifting out the red herrings in this ultra-violent Agatha Christie-style whodunnit, and the twist ending really is twisted. AJ. Italian dialogue dubbed into English. Contains violence, sex scenes and some swearing. DVD

John Saxon *Bullmer* • Anthony Franciosa *Peter Neal* • Christian Borromeo *Gianni* • Mirella D'Angelo *Tilde* • Veronica Lario *Jane* • Ania Pieroni *Elsa* ■ *Dir/Scr* Dario Argento

Tennessee Champ ★★ U

Sports drama 1954 · US · Colour · 72mins

Dewey Martin, a religious young Southern boxer, gets his break when he is taken up by fight manager Keenan Wynn, but is horrified to learn that Wynn is fixing a match. Preaching his own message about morality and God, he eventually gets a clean fight with Charles Buchinsky. This sentimental minor entry from MGM doesn't exactly compel one's attention. Buchinsky, of course, would do rather more as Charles Bronson. RK

Shelley Winters *Sarah Wurble* • Keenan Wynn *Willy Wurble* • Dewey Martin *Daniel Norson* • Earl Holliman *Happy Jackfield* • Dave O'Brien *Luke MacWade* • Charles Buchinsky [Charles Bronson] *Sixty Jubel* ■ *Dir* Fred M Wilcox • *Scr* Art Cohn, from the story *The Lord in His Corner, and other stories by Eustace Cockrell*

Tennessee Johnson ★★★ U

Biographical drama 1942 · US · BW · 103mins

Directed by experienced old hand at the genre William Dieterle, this above-average biopic of Andrew Johnson, who became president following Lincoln's assassination, stars Van Heflin in the title role. Johnson's rise from illiterate backwoods boy to holder of the highest office in the land, until politically conservative enemies led by Senator Stevens (Lionel Barrymore) determine to get rid of him by impeachment, is carefully detailed, with an appreciation of the moral issues as well as the intrigues involved in the tale. RK

Van Heflin *Andrew Johnson* • Lionel Barrymore *Thaddeus Stevens* • Ruth Hussey *Eliza McCardle* • Marjorie Main *Mrs Fisher* • Regis Toomey *Blackstone McDaniel* • J Edward Bromberg *Coke* • Grant Withers *Mordecai Milligan* ■ *Dir* William Dieterle • *Scr* John L Balderston, Wells Root, from a story by Milton Gunzberg, Alvin Meyers

Tennessee's Partner ★★

Western 1955 · US · Colour · 85mins

Routine western with John Payne as a gambler, Rhonda Fleming running a gold rush saloon and cowboy Ronald Reagan arriving to marry his sweetheart Coleen Gray who turns out to be a "loose woman". More of a melodrama than a shoot-'em-up, the picture was made by RKO in Superscope to rival Fox's new CinemaScope process. However, it's clumsily shot, with a hand-me-down look. Disappointing. AT

John Payne *Tennessee* • Ronald Reagan *Cowpoke* • Rhonda Fleming *Duchess* • Coleen Gray *Goldie* • Anthony Caruso *Turner* • Morris Ankrum *Judge* • Leo Gordon *Sheriff* ■ *Dir* Allan Dwan • *Scr* Milton Krims, DD Beauchamp, Graham Baker, Teddi Sherman, from a story by Bret Harte

Tension ★★★

Crime drama 1949 · US · BW · 90mins

A title to take seriously, as in this case the film does pile on the suspense. Cyd Charisse is out of her ballet shoes for a low-budgeter, in which she plays the girl who falls for troubled Richard Basehart while he is trying to establish a new identity after plotting the murder of his wife's lover. Director John Berry was one of the best of the period's B-picture craftsmen until he was "named" as a communist and blacklisted. TH

Richard Basehart *Warren Quimby* • Audrey Totter *Claire Quimby* • Cyd Charisse *Mary Chanler* • Barry Sullivan *Lieutenant Collier Bonnabel* • Lloyd Gough *Barney Deager* • Tom D'Andrea *Freddie* • William Conrad *Lieutenant Edgar Gonsales* ■ *Dir* John Berry • *Scr* Allen Rivkin, from a story by John Klorer

Tension at Table Rock ★★★ U

Western 1956 · US · Colour · 93mins

Charles Marquis Warren was the creative force behind such great TV western shows as *Gunsmoke*, *Rawhide* and *The Virginian* and here directs a tale of smoking guns and smouldering passions. In an era when action men were second-class citizens in Hollywood, Richard Egan never quite made the big time, but here he gives a sterling and convincing performance alongside Dorothy Malone and lawman Cameron Mitchell. DP

Richard Egan *Wes Tancred* • Dorothy Malone *Lorna Miller* • Billy Chapin *Jody Barrows* • Cameron Mitchell *Sheriff Miller* • Joe De Santis *Ed Barrows* • Royal Dano *Jameson* • Edward Andrews *Kirk* • DeForest Kelley *Breck* • Angie Dickinson *Cathy Murdock* ■ *Dir* Charles Marquis Warren • *Scr* Winston Miller, from the novel *Bitter Sage* by Frank Gruber

Tentacles ★★

Horror 1977 · It · Colour · 101mins

A giant octopus goes on a murderous rampage during a resort's annual yacht race. John Huston is the reporter trying to get to the bottom of why the scary squid is acting so nasty. Shelley Winters is Huston's sister whose son nearly goes missing during one attack. A lively enough rip-off featuring direct lifts from the Spielberg shock handbook all wrapped up in a gorgeous Euro-pop score by Stelvio Cipriani. AJ. Some dialogue dubbed into English.

John Huston *Ned Turner* • Shelley Winters *Tillie Turner* • Bo Hopkins *Will Gleason* • Henry Fonda *Mr Whitehead* • Delia Boccardo *Vicky Gleason* • Cesare Danova *John Corey* • Claude Akins *Captain Robards* ■ *Dir* Ovidio G Assonitis • *Scr* Jerome Max, Tito Carpi, Steve Carabatsos, Sonia Molteni

The Tenth Victim ★★★

Science-fiction thriller
1965 · It · Colour · 92mins

Famous now as one of the inspirations for *Austin Powers* (Ursula Andress wore the first bullet-firing bra as sported by the "fembots"), this erratically engrossing science-fiction thriller has a fabulous 1960s pop art look. In the 21st century, war has been replaced with a legalised game in which the participants are licensed-to-kill assassins, and anyone reaching the score of ten victims hits the financial jackpot. Andress is assigned to kill a cropped blond Marcello Mastroianni, but he falls in love with his huntress in this convincing futuristic satire. AJ. Italian dialogue dubbed into English.

Ursula Andress *Caroline Meredith* • Marcello Mastroianni *Marcello Polletti* • Elsa Martinelli *Olga* • Salvo Randone *Professor* • Massimo Serato *Lawyer* • Evi Rigano *Victim* ■ *Dir* Elio Petri • *Scr* Elio Petri, Tonino Guerra, Giorgio Salvioni, Ennio Flaiano, from the novel *The Seventh Victim* by Robert Sheckley

Tenue de Soirée ★★★ 18

Comedy 1986 · Fr · Colour · 84mins

Although this scurrilous comedy reunited Bertrand Blier with the co-stars of *Les Valseuses*, Miou-Miou and Gérard Depardieu, it was the newcomer, Michel Blanc, who stole the picture and won himself the best actor prize at Cannes. Smugly iconoclastic, gleefully picaresque, hopelessly misogynistic and outrageously funny are all descriptions that could aptly be applied to the menage that develops between Depardieu's larger-than-life bisexual crook, Blanc's timid husband and Miou-Miou's opportunistic wife. DP. In French with English subtitles.

Gérard Depardieu *Bob* • Michel Blanc *Antoine* • Miou-Miou *Monique* • Bruno Cremer *Art collector* • Jean-Pierre Marielle *Depressed man* • Caroline Sihol *Depressed woman* ■ *Dir/Scr* Bertrand Blier

Tequila Sunrise ★★★ 15

Thriller 1988 · US · Colour · 110mins

Kurt Russell and Mel Gibson star as the former schoolfriends who have gone their separate ways, Russell into the police force and Gibson into drug dealing. When Gibson plans a final trade-off, Russell tries to persuade his old chum against the deal. Michelle Pfeiffer becomes romantically involved with both men. Writer/director Robert Towne occasionally allows his wordiness to get between the viewer and the characters, but the fine cast and Conrad Hall's Oscar-nominated cinematography provide compensation. TH. Contains swearing, drug abuse and nudity. [video] DVD

Mel Gibson *Dale McKussic* • Michelle Pfeiffer *Jo Ann Vallenari* • Kurt Russell *Lieutenant Nick Frescia* • Raul Julia *Carlos/ Commandante Escalante* • JT Walsh *Maguire* • Arliss Howard *Gregg Lindroff* • Ann Magnuson *Shaleen* ■ *Dir/Scr* Robert Towne

Tere Ghar Ke Saamne ★★★

Romantic musical drama
1963 · Ind · BW · 149mins

One of the finest songwriters in Bollywood history is in fine form in this breezy comedy romance. SD Burman enjoyed successful collaborations with Guru Dutt and Bimal Roy, but only truly flourished in partnership with Dev Anand. Anand stars with Nutan in this *Romeo and Juliet* tale; in the director's chair, Anand's younger brother, Vijay, incorporates plot and songs smoothly and, from dance numbers at Delhi landmarks to the miniaturising of Nutan for a duet from the bottom of a whisky glass, the movie remains both light and engaging. DP. In Hindi with English subtitles.

Dev Anand *Rakesh* • Nutan *Sulekha* • Harindranath Chattopadhyay *Seth Karamchand* • Om Prakash *Lala Jagannath* ■ *Dir/Scr* Vijay Anand

The Terence Davies Trilogy ★★★ 15

Drama 1984 · UK · BW · 91mins

Made over a seven-year period, these three short films from the writer/ director of *Distant Voices, Still Lives* record a man's singularly bleak life. In *Children* (1976), the young Robert Tucker is bullied at home and school. In *Madonna and Child* (1980), the middle-aged Robert appears to lead a nondescript life, but secretly haunts gay bars. In *Death and Transfiguration* (1983), the elderly Robert remembers. Made before, during and after Terence Davies's time at film school, these are clearly the work of a major visual artist; but his complex and austere material makes great demands on the viewer. The most touching episode is the first; thereafter the gloom is unrealistically relentless, and some may find the misery, tears and deaths almost ludicrous. DM [video]

Phillip Mawdsley *Robert Tucker, boy* • Terry O'Sullivan *Robert Tucker, middle age* • Wilfrid Brambell *Robert Tucker, old age* ■ *Dir/Scr* Terence Davies

Teresa ★★★

Romantic drama 1951 · US · BW · 101mins

Director Fred Zinnemann's tale of an imported GI bride was a courageously topical subject, and indicative of a now-forgotten trend at MGM to confront burning contemporary issues. Lovely Italian actress Pier Angeli brings great honesty and truth to the title role, and there are echoes of her own real-life plight in the plot, as she encounters small-town bigotry in the role of GI John Ericson's girl. As her psychiatrist, young Rod Steiger makes an impressive movie debut. Zinnemann's documentary-style treatment is winning, and the Stewart Stern script doesn't shirk the issues. TS

Pier Angeli *Teresa* • John Ericson *Philip Quas* • Patricia Collinge *Philip's mother* • Richard Bishop *Philip's father* • Peggy Ann Garner *Susan* • Ralph Meeker *Sergeant Dobbs* • Rod Steiger *Frank* ■ *Dir* Fred Zinnemann • *Scr* Stewart Stern, from the story by Stewart Stern, Alfred Hayes

Term of Trial ★★★★

Drama 1962 · UK · BW · 138mins

Made at the height of the "kitchen sink" boom in British cinema, this rather neglected drama boasts one of Laurence Olivier's most uncharacteristic and under-rated performances. As the teacher at an inner-city school who is looked down upon by everyone from his blowsy wife Simone Signoret to class bully Terence Stamp, he conveys a sense of both seedy decency and wounded resignation that makes his prosecution for molestation and persecution by Signoret all the more painful to endure. In her screen debut, Sarah Miles is superb as the scorned teenager and Thora Hird bristles with indignation as her grasping mother. DP

Laurence Olivier *Graham Weir* • Simone Signoret *Anna Weir* • Sarah Miles *Shirley Taylor* • Hugh Griffith *O'Hara* • Terence Stamp *Mitchell* • Roland Culver *Trowman* • Thora Hird *Mrs Taylor* ■ *Dir* Peter Glenville • *Scr* Peter Glenville, from the novel by James Barlow

The Terminal ★★★ 12

Comedy drama 2004 · US · Colour · 123mins

Tom Hanks is superb as the Eastern European who becomes trapped in visa hell after a military coup in his native Krakozhia means his country is no longer recognised by the US government. Stranded indefinitely at JFK airport, he learns English from TV, eats leftover fast food, finds work renovating the building, falls for ditzy flight attendant Catherine Zeta-Jones and is harassed by Stanley Tucci's power-hungry official. While the performances are appealing, director Steven Spielberg relies too heavily on the airport-terminal-as-microcosm-of-society angle and the saccharine sentimentality gets piled on as the credibility decreases. AJ. Contains swearing. [video] DVD

Tom Hanks *Viktor Navorski* • Catherine Zeta-Jones *Amelia Warren* • Stanley Tucci *Frank Dixon* • Chi McBride *Joe Mulroy* • Diego Luna *Enrique Cruz* • Barry Shabaka Henley [Barry "Shabaka" Henley] *Ray Thurman* • Kumar Pallana *Gupta Rajan* • Zoë Saldana *Dolores Torres* ■ *Dir* Steven Spielberg • *Scr* Jeff Nathanson, Sacha Gervasi, from a story by Andrew Niccol, Sacha Gervasi

Terminal Bliss ★ 18

Drama 1990 · US · Colour · 87mins

A sluggish, downbeat story of whiney, party-going rich kids who get stoned a lot and indulge themselves excessively on consumer goodies. But angst is the order of their day as they pop pills, shaft pals, swap gals, and generally OD on bourgeois ennui. It is hard to feel sympathy for such unpleasant, over-privileged under-achievers. DA [video]

Luke Perry *John Hunter* • Timothy Owen *Alex Golden* • Estee Chandler *Stevie Bradley* • Sonia Curtis *Kirsten Davis* • Micah Grant *Bucky O'Connell* • Alexis Arquette *Craig Murphy* • Brian Cox *Dream Surgeon* ■ *Dir/Scr* Jordan Alan

Terminal Choice ★★★ 18

Medical thriller 1983 · Can · Colour · 94mins

A suspenseful little chiller about a hospital that plays it less by the book than by the bookie. The staff lay wagers as to when patients will pop their clogs, and aren't above manipulating the odds in their favour. Rather bloodier than it needs to be, the film still manages to generate surprising tension, partly because of taut and economic direction, and partly because it's played dead straight by its high-calibre cast. DA [video]

Joe Spano *Dr Frank Holt* • Diane Venora *Anna Lang* • David McCallum *Dr Dodson* • Robert Joy *Dr Harvey Rimmer* • Don Francks *Chauncey Rand* • Nicholas Campbell *Henderson* • Ellen Barkin *Mary O'Connor* ■ *Dir* Sheldon Larry • *Scr* Neal Bell, from a story by Peter Lawrence

Terminal Entry ★★ 15

Thriller 1988 · US · Colour · 93mins

Competent and mildly exciting variant on the *WarGames* theme, with three kids hacking into what they think is a hot new video game. But the game is no game: it's a genuine computer programme, part of the US's hi-tech defence system. And the kids, unknowingly, are playing key roles in a real-life US anti-terrorist strike. The still-topical subject matter should appeal to kids. DA [video]

Edward Albert *Capt Danny Jackson* • Kabir Bedi *Terrorist commander* • Yaphet Kotto *Styles* • Heidi Helmer *Chris* • Patrick Labyorteaux *Bob* • Tracy Brooks Swope *Dominique* ■ *Dir* John Kincade • *Scr* David Mickey Evans, Mark Sobel, from a story by Mark Sobel

Terminal Island ★

Futuristic prison drama
1973 · US · Colour · 87mins

A crummy exploitation pic – terminal in all departments – about a future offshore prison colony where California's killers are sent because the death penalty has been abolished. The arrival of women prisoners results in their being treated as sex slaves. The sole point of interest is an early screen appearance by Tom Selleck. DA

Phyllis Davis *Joy Lang* • Don Marshall *AJ Thomas* • Ena Hartman *Carmen Sims* • Marta Kristen *Lee Phillips* • Tom Selleck *Dr Milford* ■ *Dir* Stephanie Rothman • *Scr* Jim Barnett, Charles S Swartz, Stephanie Rothman

The Terminal Man ★★★★ 15

Science-fiction thriller
1974 · US · Colour · 99mins

An intense performance from the usually laid-back George Segal nicely matches the desolation of this futuristic thriller, in which a scientist has a computer implant connected to his brain and becomes addicted to its killer vibes. Mike Hodges brilliantly creates a hi-tech parable in which meddling scientists get a moral comeuppance. The film was only patchily shown in cinemas on its original release, but deserved better;

T

its implications are as thought-provoking as they are scary. TH. Contains violence, swearing and brief nudity.

George Segal *Harry Benson* • Joan Hackett *Dr Janet Ross* • Richard A Dysart [Richard Dysart] *Dr John Ellis* • Jill Clayburgh *Angela Black* • Donald Moffat *Dr Arthur Mcpherson* • Matt Clark *Gerhard* • Michael C Gwynne *Dr Robert Morris* • Normann Burton [Norman Burton] *Detective Captain Anders* • William Hansen *Dr Ezra Manon* ■ *Dir* Mike Hodges • *Scr* Mike Hodges, from the novel by Michael Crichton

Terminal Velocity ★★ 15

Action thriller 1994 · US · Colour · 97mins

Terminal stupidity, more like it. The second in a brief Hollywood flirtation with skydiving movies – *Drop Zone* came out in the same year – this is a big, dumb action thriller that exhilarates when airborne, but drags dangerously when on solid ground. Charlie Sheen is the dogged parachuting instructor investigating the death of a pupil, who gets mixed up with Russian gangsters. JF. Contains violence, swearing, nudity. DVD

Charlie Sheen *Ditch Brodie* • Nastassja Kinski *Chris Morrow* • James Gandolfini *Ben Pinkwater* • Christopher McDonald *Kerr* • Gary Bullock *Lex* • Hans R Howes [Hans Howes] *Sam* • Melvin Van Peebles *Noble* • Suli McCullough *Robocam* • Cathryn De Prume *Karen* • Richard Sarafian Jr *Dominic* ■ *Dir* Deran Sarafian • *Scr* David N Twohy [David Twohy]

The Terminator ★★★★★ 18

Science-fiction action thriller
1984 · US · Colour · 102mins

Arnold Schwarzenegger said "I'll be back," and he was, seven years later. But the success of the sequel should not undermine the powerhouse strengths of James Cameron's original hi-tech nightmare, with violent cyborg Arnie time-warped from the future to alter the nuclear war-torn course of history. Generating maximum excitement from the first frame, the dynamic thrills are maintained right up to the nerve-jangling climax. Wittily written with a nice eye for sharp detail, it's hard sci-fi action all the way, and Linda Hamilton shines as the bewildered waitress who unwittingly becomes the saviour of the human race. AJ. Contains swearing, violence, a sex scene and nudity. DVD

Arnold Schwarzenegger *The Terminator* • Michael Biehn *Kyle Reese* • Linda Hamilton *Sarah Connor* • Paul Winfield *Traxler* • Lance Henriksen *Vukovich* • Rick Rossovich *Matt* • Bess Motta *Ginger* • Earl Boen *Silberman* • Dick Miller *Pawn shop clerk* • Shawn Schepps *Nancy* ■ *Dir* James Cameron • *Scr* James Cameron, Gale Anne Hurd, William Wisher Jr

Terminator 2: Judgment Day ★★★★★ 15

Science-fiction action thriller
1991 · US · Colour · 145mins

Director James Cameron piles on the hard-edged humour and rollercoaster action in a worthy sequel to his own 1984 horror fantasy classic. Adrenalin junkies get epic value for money, as cyborg Arnold Schwarzenegger comes back from the future to save our world from the T-1000 model, whose liquid metal shape-changing abilities set a new cinematic standard for stunning computer graphic special effects. Linda Hamilton turns in another marvellous performance as the fiercely committed heroine who puts a necessary human face on Cameron's high-decibel mayhem and pyrotechnical bravura. AJ. Contains swearing, violence. DVD

Arnold Schwarzenegger *The Terminator* • Linda Hamilton *Sarah Connor* • Edward Furlong *John Connor* • Robert Patrick *T-1000* • Earl Boen *Dr Silberman* • Joe Morton *Miles Dyson* • S Epatha Merkerson *Tarissa Dyson* • Castulo Guerra *Enrique Salceda* • Michael Biehn *Kyle Reese* ■ *Dir* James Cameron • *Scr* James Cameron, William Wisher

Terminator 3: Rise of the Machines ★★★ 12

Science-fiction action thriller
2003 · US/Ger · Colour · 104mins

With a reported $170 million budget, this buys its way into public affection. Accordingly, the latest addition to the saga is bigger, louder and darker. Arnie's T-101 cyborg arrives in the present to protect future saviour of the human race John Connor (an unprepossessing Nick Stahl); the twist here is that the TX killing machine sent to kill Connor takes telepathic female form (a poised performance from former model Kristanna Loken). Other than that it's more of the same – the thrills are expensive, the chase highly charged and Arnie's one-liners suitably wry. AC DVD

Arnold Schwarzenegger *Terminator* • Nick Stahl *John Connor* • Claire Danes *Kate Brewster* • Kristanna Loken *TX* • David Andrews *Robert Brewster* • Mark Famiglietti *Scott Petersen* • Earl Boen *Dr Silberman* ■ *Dir* Jonathan Mostow • *Scr* John Brancato, Michael Ferris, from a story by John Brancato, Michael Ferris, Tedi Sarafian

Terms of Endearment ★★★★ 15

Drama 1983 · US · Colour · 126mins

Showered with Oscars (it won five, and was nominated for a further seven), this is American mainstream movie-making at its best. Director James L Brooks succeeds in keeping sticky sentiment largely at bay in this story of the often strained mother-daughter relationship between Shirley MacLaine and Debra Winger. Jack Nicholson delivers one of his effortless scene-stealing supporting roles, and other familiar faces include Danny DeVito, Jeff Daniels and John Lithgow. MacLaine and Nicholson returned for the sequel, *Evening Star* (1996). JF. Contains swearing. DVD

Shirley MacLaine *Aurora Greenway* • Debra Winger *Emma Horton* • Jack Nicholson *Garrett Breedlove* • Danny DeVito *Vernon Dahlart* • Jeff Daniels *Flap Horton* • John Lithgow *Sam Burns* • Lisa Hart Carroll *Patsy Clark* • Betty R King *Rosie Dunlop* • Huckleberry Fox *Teddy Horton* • Troy Bishop *Tommy Horton* ■ *Dir* James L Brooks • *Scr* James L Brooks, from the novel by Larry McMurtry

La Terra Trema ★★★★ U

Drama 1947 · It · BW · 153mins

Intended as the first instalment of a trilogy on the exploitation of Sicilian labour (the other parts were to have focused on farmers and miners), this is much more of a neorealist document than Luchino Visconti's previous picture, *Ossessione*. Shooting without a script and using only non-professionals, he explores the trials of the fishermen of Aci Trezza as they are fleeced by worldly wholesalers and middlemen. Yet, despite the fact that the film was partially funded by the Communist Party, it still has an operatic realism, thanks to Visconti's editing of Graziati Aldo's meticulously composed vistas. DP. In Italian with English subtitles. DVD

Luchino Visconti *Narrator* • Antonio Pietrangeli *Narrator* • Antonio Arcidiacono *Narrator* ■ *Dir* Luchino Visconti • *Scr* Luchino Visconti, from the novel *I Malavoglia* by Giovanni Verga

A Terrible Beauty ★★ U

Second World War drama
1960 · UK · BW · 90mins

Stressing dramatic cliché, racial stereotyping and local colour over any kind of political analysis, this is a typical Hollywood yarn. Robert Mitchum is a reluctant recruit to the IRA, who finds leaving rather more difficult after the discovery that his new colleagues are collaborating with the Nazis to defeat the British. Made in Dublin, mainly on a studio set, with Mitchum well cast and ably supported by Richard Harris in an early role. AT

Robert Mitchum *Dermot O'Neill* • Anne Heywood *Neeve Donnelly* • Dan O'Herlihy *Don McGinnis* • Cyril Cusack *Jimmy Hannafin* • Richard Harris *Sean Reilly* • Marianne Benet *Bella O'Neill* • Niall MacGinnis *Ned O'Neill* ■ *Dir* Tay Garnett • *Scr* Robert Wright Campbell, from the novel by Arthur Roth

The Terror ★★ 15

Horror 1963 · US · Colour · 72mins

More famous for being made in three days with leftover actors and sets from *The Raven* than anything else, Roger Corman's impromptu ghost story is incomprehensible. Lost Napoleonic soldier Jack Nicholson follows spectral Sandra Knight (Nicholson's wife at the time) to a cliff-top mansion owned by the demented Boris Karloff where mysterious things are going on – so mysterious in fact, neither the film-makers nor the audience can work out what's happening! Although Corman took the overall credit, scenes were also directed by Francis Ford Coppola, Monte Hellman, Jack Hill, Dennis Jacob and Nicholson (all uncredited). A legendary mess. AJ DVD

Boris Karloff *Baron von Leppe* • Jack Nicholson *Lt André Duvalier* • Sandra Knight *Hélène* • Richard Miller [Dick Miller] *Stefan* • Dorothy Neumann *Old woman* ■ *Dir* Roger Corman • *Scr* Leo V Gordon, Jack Hill

Terror ★★ 18

Horror 1979 · UK · Colour · 79mins

In this efficient if rather nonsensical horror, a witch's curse is reactivated when surviving members of the family that persecuted her (including Carolyn Courage and John Nolan) base a horror film on the hex. *Inseminoid* director Norman J Warren piles on the gleefully gory chills, sleazy thrills and showbiz send-ups (courtesy of David McGillivray's endearingly wonky script), and the plot detours just about manage to belie the movie's micro-budget. AJ. Contains swearing, violence and nudity. DVD

John Nolan *James Garrick* • Carolyn Courage *Ann Garrick* • James Aubrey *Phillip* • Sarah Keller *Suzy* • Trishia Walsh *Viv* • Glynis Barber *Carol Tucker* • Michael Craze *Gary* • Patti Love *Hannah* ■ *Dir* Norman J Warren • *Scr* David McGillivray, from a story by Les Young, Moira Young

Terror by Night ★★★ U

Mystery 1946 · US · BW · 60mins

This Sherlock Holmes thriller moves fast enough to skim over the potholes in the plot. Basil Rathbone and Nigel Bruce are hired to safeguard a gem called the "Star of Rhodesia". Three murders later, the air-gun killer is revealed, and Dennis Hoey has overdone his comic act as Inspector Lestrade to an irritating degree. Years before, Alan Mowbray had appeared in the Clive Brook and Reginald Owen movies about Holmes, but he wrote that Rathbone's version of the sleuth was the best. TH DVD

Basil Rathbone *Sherlock Holmes* • Nigel Bruce *Dr John H Watson* • Alan Mowbray *Major Duncan Bleek* • Dennis Hoey *Inspector Lestrade* • Renee Godfrey *Vivian Vedder* • Skelton Knaggs *Sands* ■ *Dir* Roy William Neill • *Scr* Frank Gruber, from a story by Sir Arthur Conan Doyle

Terror Firmer ★★★

Comedy horror 1999 · US · Colour · 98mins

Taking postmodernism to new depths, this is a hilarious exercise in self-reflection and bad taste from Lloyd Kaufman, co-founder of schlock-horror film company Troma. Based on his knowing memoir, *All I Need to Know about Film-making I Learned from the Toxic Avenger*, the action centres on Kaufman's blind director, as he tries to make a slasher movie in spite of the fact that someone is butchering his cast and crew. The humour is often gross, but should keep fans amused. DP

Will Keenan *Casey* • Alyce LaTourelle *Jennifer* • Lloyd Kaufman *Larry Benjamin* • Trent Haaga *Jerry* ■ *Dir* Lloyd Kaufman • *Scr* Douglas Buck, Patrick Cassidy, Lloyd Kaufman

Terror from the Year 5,000 ★

Science-fiction horror
1958 · US · Colour · 66mins

Actually, it's a terror from the year 1958! This unbelievable claptrap features a hideously deformed sex kitten who materialises through a time machine to mate and save the future of mankind. The mutant cat with four eyes is a laugh, but not much else. More famous to horror film buffs these days because part of the soundtrack was later used in the classic *Night of the Living Dead*. AJ

Ward Costello *Robert Hedges* • Joyce Holden *Claire Erling* • John Stratton *Victor* • Frederic Downs *Professor Erling* • Fred Herrick *Angelo* • Beatrice Furdeaux *Miss Blake* • Salome Jens *AD 5000 woman* ■ *Dir/Scr* Robert J Gurney Jr

Terror in a Texas Town ★★★ PG

Western 1958 · US · BW · 77mins

This B-western has attracted a cult following over the years. It's directed by Joseph H Lewis, and is an extraordinary work, featuring harpoon-wielding hero Sterling Hayden facing up to black-clad gunman Ned Young. Many hardened western admirers consider the contrivances of this movie and its elegiac camera style phoney and theatrical, but there's no denying this film's originality, given the obvious constraints of plot and budget. TS

Sterling Hayden *George Hansen* • Sebastian Cabot *Ed McNeil* • Carol Kelly *Molly* • Eugene Martin *Pepe Mirada* • Ned Young [Nedrick Young] *Johnny Crale* • Victor Millan *José Mirada* ■ *Dir* Joseph H Lewis • *Scr* Ben L Perry

Terror in the City ★★

Drama 1963 · US · BW · 86mins

Indie director Allen Baron doesn't so much pay homage to his French New Wave heroes, as slavishly imitate them. The story focuses on a child who runs away to Manhattan, where he falls in with tribes of street urchins, petty criminals, ethnic gangs and a prostitute played by Lee Grant. Made for less than $200,000 and released under the title *Pie in the Sky*, it was shot entirely on location in the Times Square area of New York using the hand-held, semi-documentary techniques that brought Godard and Truffaut international acclaim. AT

Lee Grant *Suzy* • Richard Bray *Brill* • Michael Higgins *Carl* • Roberto Marsach *Paco* • Robert Allen *Brill's father* ■ *Dir/Scr* Allen Baron

Terror in the Wax Museum ★★

Horror 1973 · US · Colour · 93mins

Exhibits apparently come to life and commit murder in a very ordinary variation on the wax museum theme, with a mundane explanation for all the creepy goings-on. Poor scripting and direction doom the pedestrian plot further, although the cast – studded with an amazing array of intrepid old-timers – is enough of an attraction in itself to make this tired *House of Wax* retread worth watching. AJ

Ray Milland *Harry Flexner* • Broderick Crawford *Amos Burns* • Elsa Lanchester *Julia Hawthorn* • Maurice Evans *Inspector Daniels* • Shani Wallis *Laurie Mell* • John Carradine *Claude Dupree* ■ *Dir* Georg Fenady • *Scr* Jameson Brewer, from a story by Andrew Fenady

The Terror Inside ★★ 15

Psychological thriller
1996 · US · Colour · 90mins

This psychological TV thriller provides Heather Locklear with the opportunity to show that she's capable of rather more than just looking glamorous. Locklear plays a woman suffering from the effect of her multiple personalities, convincingly veering from feisty hooker and abrasive teen to vulnerable child and suicidal victim. But Thomas Baum's script is so confused that the schizophrenic manifestations exist in something of a vacuum. DP VIDEO DVD

Heather Locklear *Suzy Mitchell* • Brett Cullen *Sean* • Kevin Dunn *Eric Silver* • Caroline Kava *Martha Tremayne* ■ *Dir* Stephen Gyllenhaal • *Scr* Thomas Baum

Terror Is a Man ★★

Horror 1959 · US/Phil · BW · 76mins

This commendable rehash of *Island of Lost Souls* (1932) was shot in the Philippines on a low budget that could only extend to one "manimal" mutant instead of the usual pack. Francis Lederer is the mad doctor conducting experiments on a remote island, enabling him to turn a jungle cat into something resembling a human. His horrified wife Greta Thyssen confides in shipwreck victim Richard Derr. Originally an on-screen buzzer was the warning signal for the faint-hearted to look away from the gruesome operation footage. AJ

Francis Lederer *Dr Charles Girard* • Greta Thyssen *Frances Girard* • Richard Derr *William Fitzgerald* • Peyton Keesee *Tiago* • Oscar Keesee *Walter* • Flory Carlos *Beast-Man* ■ *Dir* Gerry DeLeon • *Scr* Harry Paul Harber

Terror of Mechagodzilla ★★★ 15

Monster horror 1975 · Jpn · Colour · 79mins

Practically all of Godzilla's enemies from Ghidorah to Rodan are assembled in this 20th anniversary production. So what else could alien powers do in yet another world domination scheme, except build a nasty robot version of the lovable T-Rex? But the old fire-snorter hits back and bangs his tail in suitable disdain at this outrageous ploy to upstage him with a pile of shiny junk. Talking of piles of shiny junk, veteran Godzilla creator Inoshiro Honda directs this monster mishmash with a lurid comic-strip style replete with engagingly daffy visual spectacle. AJ. Japanese dialogue dubbed into English. VIDEO

Tomoko Ai • Akihiko Hirata ■ *Dir* Inoshiro Honda • *Scr* Katsuhiko Sasaki

The Terror of Tiny Town ★ U

Western 1938 · US · BW · 57mins

Some "turkeys", like *Plan 9 from Outer Space*, are so bad they're fun. But this western with an all-midget cast is just boring. The dull story (bad guy causes trouble, good guy sees him off) doesn't exploit the individuality of the cast and would have suited average-sized players. Some confusion is also evident in the way that the actors ride Shetland ponies and yet walk underneath the standard-height hitching posts. Poor performances from the mostly amateur cast make this one strictly for lovers of novelty films. DM

Billy Curtis *The hero/Buck Lawson* • Yvonne Moray *The girl/Nancy* • Little Billy *The villain/Pat Haines* • Bill Platt *The rich uncle/Jim "Tex" Preston* • John Bambury *The ranch owner* • Joseph Herbst *The sheriff* ■ *Dir* Sam Newfield • *Scr* Fred Myton, Clarence Marks

Terror on a Train ★★ U

Thriller 1953 · UK · BW · 72mins

There are few more effective situations for building up tension than the race to defuse a ticking bomb. Glenn Ford plays a Canadian engineer searching for a bomb placed on a freight train. Meanwhile, the police hunt the saboteur. The direction is by former cameraman Ted Tetzlaff and he does an effective job visually, but the details of everyday British life sometimes ring false and the story is somewhat padded out. AE

Glenn Ford *Peter Lyncourt* • Anne Vernon *Janine Lyncourt* • Maurice Denham *Jim Warrilow* • Harcourt Williams *Vicar* • Victor Maddern *Saboteur* ■ *Dir* Ted Tetzlaff • *Scr* Kem Bennett, from his novel *Death at Attention*

Terror Train ★★★ 18

Horror 1980 · Can · Colour · 92mins

Several years after participating in a cruel fraternity initiation that backfired and traumatised the victim, scream queen Jamie Lee Curtis and her college buddies rent a train for a party, with conductor Ben Johnson and young magician David Copperfield along for the ride. It doesn't take long for one of the many masked party-goers on board to start bumping people off. Director Roger Spottiswoode generates a noticeable amount of atmosphere, making the most of the superior production values (including some excellent night photography) and the talented cast. KB VIDEO DVD

Ben Johnson *Carne* • Jamie Lee Curtis *Alana* • Hart Bochner *Doc Manley* • David Copperfield *Magician* • Derek MacKinnon *Kenny Hampson* • Sandee Currie *Mitchy* ■ *Dir* Roger Spottiswoode • *Scr* TY Drake

The Terror Within ★ 18

Science-fiction horror
1988 · US · Colour · 84mins

One of producer Roger Corman's countless imitations of *Alien*. The futuristic setting is not a spaceship, but an underground lab, where Andrew Stevens and George Kennedy are among the few survivors of a holocaust that has left the planet virtually uninhabitable. Trouble arrives when a pregnant woman gives birth to a monster. The rubber-suited mutant is an embarrassment to watch. A sequel followed in 1990. KB VIDEO

George Kennedy *Hal* • Andrew Stevens *David* • Starr Andreeff *Sue* • Terri Treas *Linda* • John Lafayette *Andre* • Tommy Hinchley *Neil* ■ *Dir* Thierry Notz • *Scr* Thomas M Cleaver

The Terroriser ★★★ 15

Drama 1986 · Tai · Colour · 108mins

Edward Yang was one of the driving forces of Taiwanese cinema's New Wave in the late 1980s and early 1990s. Here, he demonstrates a complete mastery of theme, narrative and technique as he weaves together episodes from the lives of characters bound together by mischievous phone calls. Exploring the nature of truth in fiction, film and photography, this complex picture demands your full attention: the stylish visuals and committed performances, notably from Cora Miao as a novelist suffering from writer's block and Wang An as the telephone terror, are the reward. DP. In Mandarin with English subtitles.

Cora Miao *Zhou Yufen [miu Qianren]* • Li Liqun *Li Lizhong* • Jin Shijie *Ah Shen* • Gu Baoming *Lao Gu* ■ *Dir* Edward Yang • *Scr* Li Yuan [Ye Xiao], Yang Dechang [Edward Yang]

The Terrorist ★★★★ 12

Political drama
1998 · Ind/US · Colour · 95mins

Bollywood cinematographer Santosh Sivan proves himself a natural film-maker with this powerful study of the human aspect of political extremism. He makes audacious use of close-ups to register the bewildering range of emotions passing through the mind of teenage terrorist Ayesha Dharkar, as a combination of simple charity and an unexpected pregnancy cause her to doubt the value of her suicide bombing mission. But perhaps the film would have been more provocative without the 11th-hour optimism. DP. In Hindi with English subtitles. Contains scenes of violence. VIDEO DVD

Ayesha Dharkar *Milla* • Vishnu Vardhan *Thyagu* • Bhanu Prakash *Perumal* • K Krishna *Lover* • Sonu Sisupal *Leader* ■ *Dir* Santosh Sivan • *Scr* Santosh Sivan, Ravi Deshpande, Vijay Deveshwar, from a story by Santosh Sivan

TerrorVision ★ 15

Science-fiction comedy
1986 · US · Colour · 81mins

This supposed satire on the media-obsessed, suburban middle classes is in fact a toe-curlingly embarrassing *Poltergeist* rip-off featuring a cartoonishly dysfunctional family. A new satellite dish accidentally beams an alien into the Putterman's living room. Writer/director Ted Nicolaou intentionally parodies those Z-grade monster movies of the 1950s, but has produced something of which Ed Wood would be proud. RS VIDEO

Diane Franklin *Suzy Putterman* • Gerrit Graham *Stanley Putterman* • Mary Woronov *Raquel Putterman* • Chad Allen *Sherman Putterman* • Jonathan Gries *O D* • Jennifer Richards *Medusa* • Alejandro Rey *Spiro* • Bert Remsen *Grampa* ■ *Dir/Scr* Ted Nicolaou

Tesis ★★★ 18

Thriller 1996 · Sp · Colour · 118mins

How is it possible to condemn our morbid fascination with violence without delivering the very imagery under scrutiny? It's a problem that Spanish director Alejandro Amenábar fails to solve in this otherwise compelling thriller. Yet, he can't be faulted for the way in which the story twists and turns, as post-graduate student Ana Torrent teams up with geek Fele Martínez to trace the origins of a snuff movie in a university's film vault. There may be only a handful of suspects, but even the most acute armchair detective will remain baffled. The suspense in the tunnel sequence is taken to almost sadistic levels. DP. In Spanish with English subtitles. Contains swearing, violence and sex scenes. VIDEO DVD

Ana Torrent *Angela* • Fele Martínez *Chema* • Eduardo Noriega (2) *Bosco* • Nieves Harranz *Sena* • Rosa Campillo *Yolanda* ■ *Dir/Scr* Alejandro Amenábar

Tess ★★★★ PG

Period drama 1979 · Fr/UK · Colour · 165mins

Roman Polanski's now classic adaptation of Hardy's black and ironic tragedy is not as good as the novel, but still has much to recommend it, not least the evocative Oscar-winning photography. Nastassja Kinski rocketed to stardom after her starring role as the country girl, whose disastrous sexual encounters with her rakish cousin come back to haunt her when she finally finds love in the arms of Peter Firth. Devastating and powerful, Polanski's film achieves the requisite pathos and the director shoots a stunning denouement against the backdrop of Stonehenge. The movie also won Oscars for costumes and art direction. LH VIDEO DVD

Nastassia Kinski [Nastassja Kinski] *Tess* • Leigh Lawson *Alec d'Urberville* • Peter Firth *Angel Clare* • John Collin *John Durbeyfield* • David Markham *Rev Mr Clare* • Rosemary Martin *Mrs Durbeyfield* • Richard Pearson *Vicar of Marlott* • Carolyn Pickles *Marian* ■ *Dir* Roman Polanski • *Scr* Roman Polanski, Gerard Brach, John Brownjohn, from the novel by Thomas Hardy • *Cinematographer* Geoffrey Unsworth, Ghislain Cloquet • *Music* Philippe Sarde • *Production Designer* Pierre Guffroy • *Costume Designer* Anthony Powell

Tess of the Storm Country ★★

Silent melodrama 1922 · US · BW · 137mins

This second adaptation of Grace Miller White's novel stars Mary Pickford – who'd starred in the 1914 original – as a fisherman's daughter who comes to the rescue of a woman about to be ostracised for her illegitimate baby. Pickford claims the baby as her own, admirably deflecting scorn away from the other woman. Naturally, it all comes right in the end. Pickford, a screen veteran at 21, acquired her top star status in the earlier version for Famous Players. RK

Mary Pickford *Tessibel Skinner* • Lloyd Hughes *Frederick Graves* • Gloria Hope *Teola Graves* • David Torrence *Elias Graves* • Forrest Robinson *Daddy Skinner* • Jean Hersholt *Ben Letts* ■ *Dir* John S Robertson • *Scr* Elmer Harris, from the novel by Grace Miller White

Tess of the Storm Country ★

Melodrama 1932 · US · BW · 75mins

The appealing and talented Janet Gaynor is the heroine in this remake of a melodrama, popularised twice in the silent era by Mary Pickford. Gaynor was teamed with her frequent co-star, Charles Farrell, for maximum box-office potential, but this lachrymose tale of the gutsy, self-sacrificing daughter of an old seafarer was already past its sell-by date in 1932. RK

Janet Gaynor *Tess Howland* • Charles Farrell *Frederick Garfield Jr* • Dudley Digges *Captain Howland* • June Clyde *Teola Garfield* • Claude Gillingwater *Frederick Garfield Sr* • George Meeker *Dan Taylor* ■ *Dir* Alfred Santell • *Scr* SN Behrmann, Sonya Levien, from the novel by Grace Miller White

Tess of the Storm Country ★★ U

Melodrama 1960 · US · Colour · 84mins

Amazingly, the fourth screen version of the popular Grace Miller White family novel about a Scottish girl growing up among the Pennsylvania Dutch. Beautifully shot on location in CinemaScope by 20th Century-Fox as a vehicle for Diane Baker, who became a successful producer and in-demand character actress. Trouble is, time hasn't been kind to this sentimental tale, and, although it worked twice for Mary Pickford (in 1914 and again in 1922), the 1960s found this good-looking opus reduced to being released as a supporting feature. TS

Diane Baker *Tess Maclean* • Jack Ging *Peter Graves* • Lee Philips *Eric Thorson* • Archie Duncan *Hamish Maclean* • Nancy Valentine *Teola Graves* • Bert Remsen *Mike Foley* • Wallace Ford *Fred Thorson* ■ *Dir* Paul Guilfoyle (1) • *Scr* Charles Lang, Rupert Hughes, from the novel by Grace Miller White

Test Pilot ★★★★

Romantic drama 1938 · US · BW · 118mins

Clark Gable stars in this top-notch MGM vehicle that teams him with ace director Victor Fleming. This is one of those flying movies based on the work of pioneering pilot-turned-writer Frank "Spig" Wead whose own courageous story was filmed in *The Wings of Eagles* and, like many such films, it rings true in the skies, but less so on the ground. Still, Gable's belle is sparky Myrna Loy and his mechanic pal is Spencer Tracy, so whatever the weaknesses in the action, it's certainly watchable. Acting honours, though, are stolen by crusty Lionel Barrymore as an aeronautic tycoon. TS

Clark Gable *Jim Lane* • Myrna Loy *Ann Barton* • Spencer Tracy *Gunner Sloane* • Lionel Barrymore *Howard B Drake* • Samuel S Hinds *General Ross* • Arthur Aylesworth *Frank Barton* • Claudia Coleman *Mrs Barton* ■ *Dir* Victor Fleming • *Scr* Vincent Lawrence, Waldemar Young, Howard Hawks (uncredited), from a story by Frank Wead.

Testament ★★★★★ PG

Disaster drama 1983 · US · Colour · 85mins

This sobering and moving movie details with chilling accuracy how a typical family copes after an unspecified nuclear attack devastates America. There are no fancy special effects, just a shocking interruption during *Sesame Street*, followed by a blinding flash. In the aftermath, Jane Alexander (giving a stunning performance) must cope with situations she has always dreaded – mourning her missing husband, burying her children and coming to terms with the stark reality that she too will eventually die of radiation sickness. Director Lynne Littman accomplishes so much without hammering home the points or preaching. This is one of the best movies ever made about the futility of nuclear war. AJ.

Jane Alexander *Carol Wetherly* • William Devane *Tom Wetherly* • Ross Harris [Rossie Harris] *Brad Wetherly* • Roxana Zal *Mary Liz Wetherly* • Lukas Haas *Scottie Wetherly* • Philip Anglim *Hollis* • Lilia Skala *Fania* • Leon Ames *Henry Abhart* • Rebecca De Mornay *Cathy Pitkin* • Kevin Costner *Phil Pitkin* ■ *Dir* Lynne Littman • *Scr* John Sacret Young, from the story *The Last Testament* by Carol Amen

Testament ★★ PG

Drama 1988 · UK · Colour · 79mins

TV journalist Tania Rogers returns to her Ghanaian homeland in search of Werner Herzog on the set of *Cobra Verde*. Working under the auspices of the Black Audio Film Collective, writer/director John Akomfrah demonstrates admirable control in leaking fragments of information that enable us to piece together the horrifying experience that scarred Rogers during the fall of the Nkrumah regime. But, in order to achieve this "War Zone of Memories", Akomfrah is occasionally obscure and inconsequential. DP

Tania Rogers *Abena* • Evans Hunter *Rashid* • Emma Francis Wilson *Danso* • Frank Parkes *Mr Parkes* ■ *Dir/Scr* John Akomfrah

Le Testament d'Orphée ★★★★ PG

Experimental drama 1960 · Fr · BW · 76mins

Testament to Jean Cocteau's influence on the New Wave, his final feature (a sequel to 1950's *Orphée*) was partly financed and produced by François Truffaut. But, while he exhorts the younger generation to bear his legacy, Cocteau is more interested here in looking back, with a potent mix of nostalgia and disillusionment, to the worlds and characters he created. No wonder this ragbag of references to his gloriously diverse artistic output is subtitled "Don't Ask Me Why". Anyone coming to this poetic sojourn seeking revelation is going to be disappointed, as it's strictly for aficianados. DP. In French with English subtitles.

Jean Cocteau *Jean Cocteau, the Poet* • Jean-Pierre Léaud *The Schoolboy* • Edouard Dermithe *Cegeste* • Henri Cremieux *The Professor* • Françoise Christophe *The Nurse* • Maria Casarès *The Princess* • Jean Marais *Oedipus* • Pablo Picasso • Charles Aznavour • Roger Vadim • Brigitte Bardot • Yul Brynner ■ *Dir/Scr* Jean Cocteau

The Testament of Dr Cordelier ★★★★

Horror drama 1959 · Fr · BW · 72mins

Jean Renoir was one of the first great directors to make a film using television methods. The shooting of this updated free adaptation of Robert Louis Stevenson's *Dr Jekyll and Mr Hyde* took around ten days at the Radio-Télévision Française studios. The use of multiple cameras gives the film the fluid, rough-edged spontaneous appeal of a live TV play. The switch between the cheap-looking studio interiors and the streets of Paris produces an appropriate sense of displacement and schism. Jean-Louis Barrault is extraordinary as the shaggy, bestial Monsieur Opale, the evil alter ego of the silver-haired, dignified Dr Cordelier. The film had to wait at least two years for a release. RB. In French with English subtitles.

Jean-Louis Barrault *Dr Cordelier/Opale* • Teddy Bilis *Maître Joly* • Michel Vitold *Dr Severin* • Jean Topart *Désiré* • Micheline Gary *Marguerite* • Jean Renoir *Narrator* ■ *Dir* Jean Renoir • *Scr* Jean Renoir, from the novel *Dr Jekyll and Mr Hyde* by Robert Louis Stevenson • *Cinematographer* Georges Leclerc

The Testament of Dr Mabuse ★★★★ 12

Classic horror 1932 · Ger · BW · 115mins

Fritz Lang always liked to boast that the second part of his celebrated crime trilogy (after 1922's *Dr Mabuse, the Gambler*) was such a calculated insult to the Nazis that he feared for his life. Always one to embroider his own legend, Lang was nevertheless correct in claiming that the depiction of a master criminal who hypnotised people into doing his evil bidding was a bit near the knuckle for Goebbels, who had the film banned. Yet Lang's wife and co-scenarist, Thea von Harbou, was a committed Nazi who refused to follow her husband into French exile. This is a dark tale, told with atmospheric panache. Lang's final film was 1960's *The Thousand Eyes of Dr Mabuse*. DP. In German with English subtitles. DVD

Rudolf Klein-Rogge *Dr Mabuse* • Otto Wernicke *Insp Karl Lohmann* • Oskar Beregi *Professor Baum* • Gustav Diessl *Thomas Kent* • Wera Liessem *Lilli* ■ *Dir* Fritz Lang • *Scr* Thea von Harbou, Fritz Lang, from characters created by Norbert Jacques

Testimony ★★ PG

Biographical drama
1987 · UK · BW and Colour · 150mins

This heavy and long-winded biopic of the Russian composer Dmitri Shostakovich, was directed by one of the *enfants terribles* of 1980s UK cinema and television, Tony Palmer. Ben Kingsley brings his customary excellence to the leading role, but he can't quite compensate for a dull narrative, and for the film's ponderous overemphasis on Shostakovich's clashes with the Soviet authorities. A plus though, is the excellent photography, mainly black and white but with bursts of colour. DA

Ben Kingsley *Dmitri Shostakovich* • Sherry Baines *Nina Shostakovich* • Magdalen Asquith *Galya* • Mark Asquith *Maxim* • Terence Rigby *Stalin* • Ronald Pickup *Tukhachevksy* • John Shrapnel *Zhdanov* • Frank Carson *Carnival fat man* • Chris Barrie *Carnival thin man* ■ *Dir* Tony Palmer • *Scr* David Rudkin, Tony Palmer, from the memoirs *The Memoirs of Dmitri Shostakovich* by Dmitri Shostakovich • *Cinematographer* Nicholas D Knowland

Tetsuo: the Iron Man ★★ 18

Science-fiction horror
1989 · Jpn · BW · 64mins

A Japanese businessman, apparently involved in a road accident, suddenly finds himself turning into a metallic mutant monster, providing an excuse for cult Japanese director Shinya Tsukamoto to bombard the viewer with surreal and nightmarish images. Employing grainy black-and-white photography, minimal dialogue and a pounding techno soundtrack this will either be seen as pretentious rubbish or a classy art movie. RS. In Japanese with English subtitles. DVD

Tomoroh Taguchi *Salaryman* • Kei Fujiwara *Salaryman's girlfriend* • Nobu Kanaoka *Woman in glasses* • Shinya Tsukamoto *Young metals fetishist* ■ *Dir/Scr* Shinya Tsukamoto

Tetsuo II: Body Hammer ★★★ 18

Science-fiction horror
1991 · Jpn · Colour · 78mins

Not so much a sequel to Shinya Tsukamoto's cult movie *Tetsuo*, as a radical reworking of that "body horror" study in mutant machine madness. Don't try and make sense of the story bizarre experiments turn people into weapons just savour the shiny images as Tsukamoto highlights "the beauty in destruction", in retina-scorching metallic hues. The central body-machine melding a frenzy of postmodern *Alien* and David Lynch industrial design is well worth waiting for in this homo- and sado-erotic avant-garde abstraction. AJ. In Japanese with English subtitles. DVD

Tomoroh Taguchi *Taniguchi Tomo* • Nobu Kanaoka *Kana* • Shinya Tsukamoto *Yatsu, "The Guy"* • Keinosuke Tomioka *Minori* ■ *Dir/Scr* Shinya Tsukamoto

Tex ★★★★ PG

Drama 1982 · US · Colour · 98mins

Early roles for Matt Dillon, Meg Tilly and Emilio Estevez in a terrific coming-of-age yarn, based on a book by S E Hinton, who also wrote *The Outsiders*. It focuses on the trials and tribulations of teenager Dillon and his elder brother, growing up footloose and parent-free in Oklahoma. Director Tim Hunter seemed to have the knack of drawing great performances from relatively inexperienced kids. Five years later, he'd do it again with the even more highly-rated *River's Edge*. DA

Matt Dillon *Tex McCormick* • Jim Metzler *Mason McCormick* • Meg Tilly *Jamie Collins* • Bill McKinney *Pop McCormick* • Frances Lee McCain *Mrs Johnson* • Ben Johnson *Cole Collins* • Emilio Estevez *Johnny Collins* ■ *Dir* Tim Hunter • *Scr* Charlie Haas, Tim Hunter, from a novel by SE Hinton

Tex and the Lord of the Deep ★★★

Western 1985 · It · Colour

Duccio Tessari plundered the Tex Willer comic strips for this refreshing western. What starts off as a routine outlaw tale, as Giuliano Gemma's Tex is called in to investigate an attack on an army convoy, turns into a far more sinister case when he is confronted by Riccardo Petrazzi's vicious Lord of the Deep. Die-hard comic fans will recognise Giovanni Luigi Bonelli (who created the strip in 1948) as the witch doctor. DP. Italian dialogue dubbed into English.

Giuliano Gemma *Tex Willer* • Carlo Mucari *Tiger Jack* • William Berger *Kit Carson* • Isabel Russinova *Tulac* • Flavio Bucci *Kanas* • Riccardo Petrazzi *Lord of the Deep* • Giovanni Luigi Bonelli *Witch doctor* ■ *Dir* Duccio Tessari • *Scr* Gianfranco Clerici, from the character created by Giovanni Luigi Bonelli

The Texan ★★

Western 1930 · US · BW · 72mins

One of Gary Cooper's first starring vehicles, this Paramount western presents him as a cocky bandit who is persuaded to impersonate the missing son of wealthy aristocrat Emma Dunn. Predictably, his innate good nature rebels at the deception, especially when he falls for one of the family, the lovely Fay Wray. Directed by John Cromwell from an O Henry's story, it has one of the celebrated storyteller's twists – a mild one – at the end. AE

Gary Cooper *Enrique "Quico", The Llano Kid* • Fay Wray *Consuelo* • Emma Dunn *Señora Ibarra* • Oscar Apfel *Thacker* • James A Marcus *John Brown* • Donald Reed *Nick Ibarra* ■ *Dir* John Cromwell • *Scr* Daniel N Rubin, Oliver HP Garrett, from the story *The Double-Dyed Deceiver* by O Henry

The Texans ★★★

Western 1938 · US · BW · 92mins

There's nothing really special here, but this would-be epic from Paramount is still interesting to watch for its period setting and a fine cast. It tells the tale of the opening up of the West, including the formation of the Ku Klux Klan and the first cattle drive along the Chisholm Trail. Randolph Scott is the trail boss, but he's second-billed to Joan Bennett (in her only western), who gives the impression that she would rather be somewhere else. TS

Joan Bennett *Ivy Preston* • Randolph Scott *Kirk Jordan* • May Robson *Granna* • Walter Brennan *Chuckawalla* • Robert Cummings *Captain Alan Sanford* • Raymond Hatton *Cal Tuttle* • Robert Barrat *Isaiah Middlebrack* ■ *Dir* James Hogan • *Scr* Bertrand Millhauser, Paul Sloane, William Wister Haines, from the story *North of '36* by Emerson H Hough

Texas ★★★ PG

Western 1941 · US · BW · 89mins

Here's a classy western from Columbia, teaming two matinée idols (and drinking buddies) William Holden and Glenn Ford, competing for the love of *Stagecoach's* Claire Trevor. To be appreciated today it really needs colour, but it stems from the period when you didn't waste your budget if you had stars who would attract an audience nevertheless. George Marshall directs like a man who knows his territory, and turns out a satisfying and well-crafted movie. TS

William Holden (2) *Dan Thomas* • Glenn Ford *Tod Ramsey* • Claire Trevor *"Mike" King* • George Bancroft *Windy Miller* • Edgar Buchanan *Doc Thorpe* • Don Beddoe *Sheriff* ■ *Dir* George Marshall • *Scr* Horace McCoy, Lewis Meltzer, from his story Lewis Meltzer

Texas across the River ★★★ PG

Comedy western 1966 · US · Colour · 96mins

Pairing likeable Dean Martin with French heart-throb Alain Delon, this was the first of a series of interesting, but failed attempts to turn Delon into a Hollywood star. There are simplistic pleasures to be had here, though not if you're a die-hard western fan. Others will delight in the performance of Rat Pack member Joey Bishop as a deadpan Indian, and there's super cinematography by the great Russell Metty. Amiable. TS

Dean Martin *Sam Hollis* • Alain Delon *Don Andrea Baldasar* • Rosemary Forsyth *Phoebe Ann Taylor* • Joey Bishop *Kronk* • Tina Marquand *Lonetta* • Peter Graves (2) *Captain Stimpson* ■ *Dir* Michael Gordon • *Scr* Wells Root, Harold Greene, Ben Star

Texas Adios ★★★ 15

Spaghetti western
1966 · US · Colour · 88mins

This lacks the stylisation and darkly comic touches that characterised the

U = SUITABLE FOR ALL Uc = SUITABLE FOR ALL, ESPECIALLY FOR YOUNG CHILDREN (VIDEO ONLY) PG = PARENTAL GUIDANCE

films of Italian western supremos Sergio Leone and Sergio Corbucci, with whom Franco Nero, the hero of this film, would team later in the same year for the cult classic *Django*. Nero plays a dutiful son who sets about avenging his father's death, but director Ferdinando Baldi's script lacks an innovative set piece that might have enlivened the all-too-familiar plotline. DP. Italian dialogue dubbed into English. [video] DVD

Franco Nero *Burt Sullivan* • Cole Kitosch *Jim* • José Suarez *Cisco Delgado* • Elisa Montés *Girl* ■ *Dir* Ferdinando Baldi • *Scr* Ferdinando Baldi, Franco Rossette

Texas Carnival ★★ U

Musical comedy 1951 · US · Colour · 76mins

Supposedly a vehicle for Esther Williams, much of this musical appears to have landed on the cutting-room floor, since Williams – playing a carnival performer who is immersed in a barrel of water when customers hit the target in a ball-and-target game – barely swims at all. Ann Miller's part is downsized to one dance number (a highlight) and Howard Keel is similarly underemployed. At the centre of the unengaging plot is comedian Red Skelton, playing a carnival barker who is mistaken for a Texan oil baron. RK

Esther Williams *Debbie Telford* • Red Skelton *Cornie Quinell* • Howard Keel *Slim Shelby* • Ann Miller *Sunshine Jackson* • Paula Raymond *Marilla Sabinas* • Keenan Wynn *Dan Sabinas* ■ *Dir* Charles Walters • *Scr* Dorothy Kingsley, from a story by Dorothy Kingsley, George Wells

The Texas Chain Saw Massacre ★★★★★ 18

Horror 1974 · US · Colour · 79mins

Time has not dimmed the shock value of this seminal classic from director Tobe Hooper that's based on the same real-life case that inspired *Psycho*. This scream-filled chiller, which was finally granted a certificate from the British Board of Film Classification for its 25th anniversary re-release, tells the story of five Texas teenagers who come across a demented family of murderous cannibals. Hooper masterfully uses a documentary-style realism, coupled with the horror of anticipation and suggestion, to take the terror factor into stunning and disturbing areas. Low on gore (the three sequels aren't) and made on a micro-budget that adds to the harsh tone, this razor-sharp nightmare is a must-see for fans of the genre. AJ. Contains violence, swearing. [video] DVD

Marilyn Burns *Sally* • Allen Danziger *Jerry* • Paul A Partain *Franklin* • William Vail *Kirk* • Teri McMinn *Pam* • Edwin Neal *Hitch-hiker* • Jim Siedow *Old man* • Gunnar Hansen *Leatherface* ■ *Dir* Tobe Hooper • *Scr* Kim Henkel, Tobe Hooper, from their story

The Texas Chainsaw Massacre ★★★ 18

Horror 2003 · US · Colour · 94mins

The raw terror of the 1974 original isn't replicated here, but director Marcus Nispel provides some great shocks in his gorgeous-looking update of Tobe Hooper's horror classic. Here, once again, five young people fight for their lives against the deranged Hewitts and their disfigured son, Leatherface. With just a hint of cannibalism, a leering upgrade in sexual content and more gore than the relatively bloodless original, this refit still manages to retain a grungy, unsavoury atmosphere as Scott Kosar's effective screenplay filters the now *déjà-vu* plot through seen-it-all slasher imagery and *Blair Witch* docu-realism. AJ [video] DVD

Jessica Biel *Erin* • Jonathan Tucker *Morgan* • Erica Leerhsen *Pepper* • Mike Vogel *Andy* • Eric Balfour *Kemper* • David Dorfman *Jedidiah* • R Lee Ermey *Sheriff Hoyt* • Andrew Bryniarski *Thomas Hewitt/Leatherface* ■ *Dir* Marcus Nispel • *Scr* Scott Kosar, from the film by Kim Henkel, Tobe Hooper

The Texas Chainsaw Massacre Part 2 ★★★★ 18

Horror 1986 · US · Colour · 96mins

Evangelical ex-Texas Ranger Dennis Hopper is determined to bring the demented cannibal family to justice after the disappearance of his nephew (the wheelchair victim in the original). He's helped by DJ Caroline Williams who's taped one of their atrocities during a live phone-in. With its power to shock, outrage and disturb still intact, Tobe Hooper's masterful sequel is a rich slice of unrelenting American Gothic. Jeff Burr took over as director for the second sequel, *Leatherface: the Texas Chainsaw Massacre III*. AJ. Contains violence and swearing. [video] DVD

Dennis Hopper *Lieutenant "Lefty" Enright* • Caroline Williams *Vanita "Stretch" Block* • Jim Siedow *Drayton "Cook" Sawyer* • Bill Moseley *Chop-Top* • Bill Johnson *Leatherface* • Ken Evert *Grandpa* ■ *Dir* Tobe Hooper • *Scr* LM Kit Carson, from characters created by Kim Henkel, Tobe Hooper

Texas Chainsaw Massacre: the Next Generation ★★★ 18

Horror 1994 · US · Colour · 83mins

Written and directed by Kim Henkel – the co-scripter of Tobe Hooper's original – this third sequel still shocks and horrifies. An unofficial remake of the first film, which rings weird changes on the whole demented, ultra-sadistic atmosphere, this has four senior Prom revellers taking a wrong turning down a dark Texas road and coming into contact with the cannibal clan. Featuring early appearances by Renee Zellweger and Matthew McConaughey, this makes completely explicit what the original only hinted at. AJ [video] DVD

Renee Zellweger *Jenny* • Matthew McConaughey *Vilmer* • Robert Jacks *Leatherface* • Tonie Perenski *Darla* • Joe Stevens *W E* • Lisa Newmyer *Heather* • John Harrison *Sean* • Tyler Cone *Barry* ■ *Dir* Kim Henkel • *Scr* Kim Henkel, from characters created by Kim Henkel, Tobe Hooper

Texas Lady ★★ U

Western 1955 · US · Colour · 81mins

This routine western is made mesmerisingly watchable by the sheer force of its star, Claudette Colbert, playing a crusading journalist in town to take over her father's newspaper against all odds. She looks splendid, and is well supported by goodies Barry Sullivan and John Litel, and baddies Ray Collins and Walter Sande. The Technicolor's nice, but then the cinematographer was *Gone with the Wind's* Ray Rennahan, one of Hollywood's finest. TS [video]

Claudette Colbert *Prudence Webb* • Barry Sullivan *Chris Mooney* • Gregory Walcott *Jess Foley* • Ray Collins *Ralston* • Walter Sande *Sturdy* • James Bell *Cass Gower* ■ *Dir* Tim Whelan • *Scr* Horace McCoy

The Texas Rangers ★★★★

Western 1936 · US · BW · 75mins

Released to coincide with the Lone Star state's centennial celebrations, this roistering good-natured adventure had the commercial effect of bringing the western back into public favour, rescuing it from poverty row B-movie obscurity. Allegedly based on official Texas Rangers records, this is a loosely woven tale about three buddies; Fred MacMurray, Jack Oakie and baddie Lloyd Nolan, who fall out. Director King Vidor has a firm grasp on the action sequences, and this offering is as satisfying a western as you're likely to see. TS

Fred MacMurray *Jim Hawkins* • Jack Oakie *Wahoo Jones* • Jean Parker *Amanda Bailey* • Lloyd Nolan *Sam Mcgee* • Edward Ellis *Major Bailey* • Bennie Bartlett *David* • Frank Shannon *Captain Stafford* ■ *Dir* King Vidor • *Scr* Louis Stevens, from a story by King Vidor, Elizabeth Hill Vidor, from the book by Walter Prescott Webb

Texas Rangers Ride Again ★★ U

Western 1940 · US · BW · 68mins

A misfiring sequel to director King Vidor's rollicking *Texas Rangers*, with a dull John Howard and a ludicrously over-the-top Akim Tamiroff. Still, Ellen Drew as the feisty heroine, Robert Ryan (early in his career) and May Robson (near the end of hers) make this worth a look, despite the contemporary setting and James Hogan's routine direction. TS

Ellen Drew *Ellen "Slats" Dangerfield* • John Howard (1) *Jim Kingston* • Akim Tamiroff *Mio Pio* • May Robson *Cecilia Dangerfield* • Broderick Crawford *Mace Townsley* • Charley Grapewin *Ben Caldwalder* • Anthony Quinn *Joe Yuma* ■ *Dir* James Hogan • *Scr* William R Lipman, Horace McCoy

Texas Terror ★★ U

Western 1935 · US · BW · 50mins

In the mid-1930s, John Wayne was busy releasing a string of movies, many of them B westerns that were made for producer Paul Malvern at Monogram Pictures, a poverty row outfit known for such westerns and the *Bowery Boys* series. Wayne was their workhorse and *Texas Terror* sticks to the formula, with Lucile Brown, plus his regular collaborator in these movies, famed stuntman Yakima Canutt. AT [video] DVD

John Wayne *John Higgins* • Lucile Brown *Beth Matthews* • LeRoy Mason *Joe Dickson* • George Hayes [George "Gabby" Hayes] *Sheriff Williams* • Buffalo Bill Jr *Blackie* ■ *Dir/Scr* Robert N Bradbury

Texasville ★ 15

Comedy drama 1990 · US · Colour · 120mins

The Last Picture Show was one of the iconic movies of early 1970s America, and its director Peter Bogdanovich was inevitably going to be drawn to novelist Larry McMurtry's 1987 sequel. The book was disappointing, but no one could have envisaged that the film version was going to be so mind-numbingly bad. The out-of-form Bogdanovich simply tries too hard, spending the first part of the picture debunking the original and longing despairingly for past glories in the cloying closing stages. DP [video] DVD

Jeff Bridges *Duane Jackson* • Cybill Shepherd *Jacy Farrow d'Olonne* • Annie Potts *Karla Jackson* • Cloris Leachman *Ruth Popper* • Timothy Bottoms *Sonny Crawford* • Eileen Brennan *Genevieve* • Randy Quaid *Lester Marlow* • William McNamara *Dickie Jackson* ■ *Dir* Peter Bogdanovich • *Scr* Peter Bogdanovich, from the novel by Larry McMurtry

Thank God He Met Lizzie ★★★ 15

Romantic comedy 1997 · Aus · Colour · 86mins

This quirky Australian comedy, starring a pre-*Elizabeth* Cate Blanchett, is no skeleton in the closet. Instead, it's a charming, amusingly eccentric affair, which tracks the romantic dilemmas of loner Richard Roxburgh (who co-starred with Blanchett in *Oscar and Lucinda*), who has reservations on the day of his wedding to Blanchett. JF [video]

Richard Roxburgh *Guy Jamieson* • Cate Blanchett *Lizzie O'Hara* • Frances O'Connor *Jenny Follett* • Linden Wilkinson *Poppy O'Hara* • John Gaden *Dr O'Hara* • Genevieve Mooy *Mrs Jamieson* • Michael Ross *Mr Jamieson* ■ *Dir* Cherie Nowlan • *Scr* Alexandra Long

Thank God It's Friday ★★★ 15

Musical 1978 · US · Colour · 85mins

Here's what disco was really like circa 1978. The flipside of *Saturday Night Fever*, director Robert Klane's exploitative movie doesn't carry any message as it focuses on different people assembling at the Zoo disco in Hollywood for that pop movie staple – a dance contest. Using a non-stop soundtrack of disco hits, it expertly communicates the exciting, buzzy and hip atmosphere of 1970s clubland. More fun than it pretends to be, Jeff Goldblum and Debra Winger make early movie appearances as disco queen Donna Summer belts out the Oscar-winning song *Last Dance*. AJ. Contains swearing. [video]

Donna Summer *Nicole Sims* • Valerie Landsburg *Frannie* • Terri Nunn *Jeannie* • Chick Vennera *Marv Gomez* • Ray Vitte *Bobby Speed* • Mark Lonow *Dave* • Andrea Howard *Sue* • Jeff Goldblum *Tony* • Robin Menken *Maddy* • Debra Winger *Jennifer* ■ *Dir* Robert Klane • *Scr* Barry Armyan Bernstein

Thank You and Good Night! ★★★

Documentary 1991 · US · Colour · 85mins

A moving documentary about the physical decline and ultimate death of film-maker Jan Oxenberg's Jewish grandmother, Mae Joffe. This isn't just a conventional documentary though, as Oxenberg experiments freely with various styles and techniques, from using cut-out characters to home movie and outright fantasy sequences. Apart from the loss of a grandparent, there's a wider message here about family relationships and dealing with illness and bereavement. But the various elements combine beautifully in an offbeat movie, that's also tenderhearted and touching. DA

Dir/Scr Jan Oxenberg

Thank You, Jeeves ★★

Comedy 1936 · UK · BW · 57mins

Jeeves and Wooster have been firm favourites with readers and TV audiences for many years, but their antics have yet to be brought to the big screen with any degree of success. There is only the faintest echo of the Wodehouse wit and brio in this silly story about industrial espionage and gunrunning. The excellent Arthur Treacher is the fish-eating valet for whom no crisis is insurmountable, but David Niven (in his first Hollywood starring role) is far too suave and knowing to convince as Bertie Wooster. Jeeves only appeared in the 1937 follow-up, *Step Lively, Jeeves*. DP

David Niven *Bertie Wooster* • Arthur Treacher *Jeeves* • Virginia Field *Marjorie Lowman* • Lester Matthews *Elliott Manville* • Colin Tapley *Tom Brock* ■ *Dir* Arthur Greville Collins • *Scr* Joseph Hoffman, Stephen Gross, from the story by PG Wodehouse

Thank You, Mr Moto ★★★

Crime mystery 1937 · US · BW · 66mins

The second series entry (after *Think Fast, Mr Moto*) featuring Peter Lorre as John P Marquand's Japanese sleuth, is perhaps the least tangled and most enjoyable, although the atmosphere is surprisingly sinister for a B-movie. The picture opens with Moto, disguised as a Gobi nomad, trying to infiltrate a gang preying on the desert's ancient treasure troves. The clues bring him into contact with a Chinese prince, his overprotective mother and some ruthless gangsters. Lorre bustles

T

around to good effect, and John Carradine is excellent as a shady antiques dealer. DP

Peter Lorre *Mr Moto* • Thomas Beck *Tom Nelson* • Pauline Frederick *Madame Chung* • Jayne Regan *Eleanor Joyce* • Sidney Blackmer *Eric Koerger* • Sig Rumann [Sig Ruman] *Colonel Tchernov* • John Carradine *Pereira* ■ *Dir* Norman Foster • *Scr* Norman Foster, Willis Cooper, from a story by John P Marquand

Thank Your Lucky Stars ★★★★ U

Musical 1943 · US · BW · 122mins

One of the most enjoyable of Hollywood's patriotic, star-studded wartime concoctions, this Warner Bros extravaganza is a joy from start to finish, as Eddie Cantor takes us on a magic carpet ride through show-biz land. Here are unlikely and delightful songbirds Errol Flynn and Bette Davis singing, respectively, *That's What You Jolly Well Get* and *They're Either Too Young or Too Old*; and there's also a particularly fine production number involving Hattie McDaniel. Watch also for tough palookas John Garfield and Humphrey Bogart sending themselves up. TS

Eddie Cantor *Joe Sampson/Himself* • Joan Leslie *Pat Dixon* • Dennis Morgan *Tommy Randolph* • Dinah Shore • SZ Sakall *Dr Schlenna* • Edward Everett Horton *Farnsworth* • Humphrey Bogart • John Garfield ■ *Dir* David Butler • *Scr* Norman Panama, Melvin Frank, James V Kern, from a story by Everett Freeman, from a story by Arthur Schwartz

Thanks a Million ★★

Musical comedy 1935 · US · BW · 85mins

A minor, but nevertheless enjoyable, musical comedy from 20th Century-Fox, effectively a star vehicle for crooner Dick Powell, with some interesting, but now dated sideswipes at political chicanery. Radio comedian Fred Allen has some moments as the troubled wisecracking manager pushing Powell for governor, and there's splendid period music from Paul Whiteman and his band and the Yacht Club Boys. TS

Dick Powell *Eric Land* • Ann Dvorak *Sally Mason* • Fred Allen *Ned Lyman* • Patsy Kelly *Phoebe Mason* • Raymond Walburn *Judge Culliman* • David Rubinoff *Orchestra Leader* • Benny Baker *Tammany* ■ *Dir* Roy Del Ruth • *Scr* Nunnally Johnson, from a story by Melville Crossman [Darryl F Zanuck]

Thanks for Everything ★★★

Comedy 1938 · US · BW · 70mins

Jack Haley is an unexceptional chap who wins a radio competition to find "Mr Average American". Unscrupulous advertising men Adolphe Menjou and Jack Oakie seize the opportunity to exploit Smith using his very averageness to sell any number of items. This fast paced satire on the advertising world benefits from the strong playing. DF

Adolphe Menjou *JB Harcourt* • Jack Oakie *Brady* • Jack Haley *Henry Smith* • Arleen Whelan *Madge Raines* • Binnie Barnes *Kay Swift* ■ *Dir* William A Seiter • *Scr* Harry Tugend, Curtis Kenyon, Art Arthur, from a story by Gilbert Wright

T

That Certain Age ★★★ U

Musical comedy 1938 · US · BW · 96mins

In her fourth feature, 17-year-old Deanna Durbin was allowed a boyfriend (Jackie Cooper, who was the same age), but no kiss yet. This amiable comedy has Durbin neglecting Cooper while developing a crush on her parents' houseguest, man-of-the-world journalist Melvyn Douglas. She also finds time to warble six songs. Former silent film star Irene Rich plays Deanna's mother. RB DVD

Deanna Durbin *Alice Fullerton* • Melvyn Douglas *Vincent Bullitt* • Jackie Cooper *Ken* • Irene Rich *Mrs Fullerton* • Nancy Carroll *Grace Bristow* • John Halliday *Mr Fullerton* • Jackie Searl [Jackie Searle] *Tony* • Charles Coleman *Stephens* • Peggy Stewart *Mary Lee* ■ *Dir* Edward Ludwig • *Scr* Bruce Manning, Billy Wilder, Charles Brackett, from a story by F Hugh Herbert

That Certain Feeling ★★

Comedy 1956 · US · Colour · 102mins

A romantic comedy that is neither romantic nor funny, this does at least offer the bizarre combination of George Sanders and Bob Hope competing for the favours of Sanders' fiancée, Eva Marie Saint, who happens to be Hope's ex-wife. The complications ensue when top cartoonist Sanders loses his touch and hires bumbling artist Hope to "ghost" his strip. Also involved in this inferior offering is the splendid Pearl Bailey as Sanders' maid and Hope's ally. RK

Bob Hope *Francis X Dignan* • Eva Marie Saint *Dunreath Henry* • George Sanders *Larry Larkin* • Pearl Bailey *Gussie* • David Lewis (1) *Joe Wickes* • Al Capp • Jerry Mathers *Norman Taylor* ■ *Dir* Norman Panama, Melvin Frank • *Scr* Norman Panama, Melvin Frank, IAL Diamond, William Altman

That Certain Woman ★★★

Melodrama 1937 · US · BW · 91mins

An example of a movie remade by its original director, this is a new version of the 1929 Gloria Swanson early talkie *The Trespasser*, with a simmering Bette Davis as the gangster's widow trying to go straight. Director Edmund Goulding has less luck with Bette than he did with Gloria in this overblown melodrama, though a young and gauche Henry Fonda does impress as a playboy, vying with lawyer Ian Hunter for Davis's affections. TS

Bette Davis *Mary Donnell* • Henry Fonda *Jack Merrick* • Ian Hunter *Lloyd Rogers* • Anita Louise *Flip* • Donald Crisp *Mr Merrick Sr* • Hugh O'Connell *Virgil Whitaker* • Katherine Alexander *Mrs Rogers* ■ *Dir* Edmund Goulding • *Scr* Edmund Goulding, from his film *The Trespasser*

That Championship Season ★★★ 15

Drama 1982 · US · Colour · 104mins

Jason Miller is probably best known for his role as Father Karras in *The Exorcist* and for being the father of Jason Patric. But Miller was really a playwright who dabbled in acting, and this movie marked his sole effort as a director, adapting his own Pulitzer Prize-winning play which also won a Tony Award and the New York Drama Critics' Award in 1972. It's the story of four former basketball players and their coach, who have a reunion and engage in the sort of bonding dialogue and down home wisdom, beloved of American playwrights. Some may find it smug and a bit too wordy. AT

Bruce Dern *George Sitkowski* • Stacy Keach *James Daley* • Robert Mitchum *Coach Delaney* • Martin Sheen *Tom Daley* • Paul Sorvino *Phil Romano* • Arthur Franz *Macken* • Michael Bernosky *Jacks* • Joseph Kelly *Malley* ■ *Dir* Jason Miller • *Scr* Jason Miller, from his play

That Cold Day in the Park ★★★

Psychological drama 1969 · US/Can · Colour · 113mins

This early Robert Altman film features the brilliant Sandy Dennis as an emotionally disturbed spinster who becomes infatuated with a young man she meets in the park, and takes him home to live with her. But her possessive jealousy soon renders him more prisoner than partner. The main theme of this rather disturbing film is repressed sexuality, but there are also odd hints of things darker and more taboo. Altman directs with aplomb. DA

Sandy Dennis *Frances Austen* • Michael Burns *Boy* • Susanne Benton *Nina* • Luana Anders *Sylvie* • John Garfield Jr *Nick* ■ *Dir* Robert Altman • *Scr* Gillian Freeman, from a novel by Richard Miles

That Dangerous Age ★★

Romantic drama 1949 · UK · BW · 100mins

Eminent barrister Roger Livesey in Capri with his wife Myrna Loy and daughter Peggy Cummins to recover from a nervous breakdown, is visited by young barrister Richard Greene with whom Loy has an illicit affair. Produced and directed by the Russian-born Gregory Ratoff – imported from Hollywood along with Loy – for Alexander Korda's London Films, this part-fraught, part sentimental melodrama is too old-fashioned to convince, despite decent production values and the best efforts of its polished leads. RK

Myrna Loy *Lady Cathy Brooke* • Roger Livesey *Sir Brian Brooke, KC* • Peggy Cummins *Monica Brooke* • Richard Greene *Michael Barclaigh* • Elizabeth Allan *Lady Sybil* • Gerard Heinz *Dr Thorvald* ■ *Dir* Gregory Ratoff • *Scr* Gene Markey, from the play *Autumn* by Margaret Kennedy, Ilya Surgutchoff

That Darn Cat! ★★ U

Comedy 1965 · US · Colour · 111mins

All the pieces slot together with ease in this lively, if overlong, Disney caper. Yet, while it makes efficient entertainment, the film is not as much fun as it should be, bearing in mind its exceptional cast. The cat steals the show by a whisker from nosey neighbours William Demarest and Elsa Lanchester. Hayley Mills is perky enough as the cat's owner, but all roles are dull compared to those of Dean Jones as the FBI agent with a cat allergy and Roddy McDowall as a drip whose ducks are the frisky feline's favourite playmates. DP

Hayley Mills *Patti Randall* • Dean Jones *Zeke Kelso* • Roddy McDowall *Gregory Benson* • Dorothy Provine *Ingrid Randall* • Neville Brand *Dan* • Elsa Lanchester *Mrs MacDougall* • William Demarest *Mr MacDougall* ■ *Dir* Robert Stevenson • *Scr* Gordon Gordon, Mildred Gordon, Bill Walsh, from the novel *Undercover Cat* by Gordon Gordon, Mildred Gordon

That Darn Cat ★★ U

Comedy 1997 · US · Colour · 85mins

This watchable enough remake of the lively 1965 comedy stars Christina Ricci in the role originally played by Hayley Mills. The story is much the same as Ricci and rookie FBI agent Doug E Doug team up with a talented moggy to pursue a gang of kidnappers. But there's nothing new or any improvement from the unexceptional original, which makes one wonder why Disney bothered making an almost exact copy. DA DVD

Christina Ricci *Patti* • Doug E Doug *Zeke Kelso* • Dean Jones *Mr Flint* • George Dzundza *Boetticher* • Peter Boyle *Pa* • Michael McKean *Peter Randall* • Bess Armstrong *Judy Randall* • Dyan Cannon *Mrs Flint* • John Ratzenberger *Dusty* • Estelle Parsons *Old Lady McCracken* ■ *Dir* Bob Spiers • *Scr* LA Karaszewski [Larry Karaszewski], SM Alexander [Scott Alexander], from the 1965 film, from the novel *Undercover Cat* by Mildred Gordon, Gordon Gordon

That Eye, the Sky ★★★

Fantasy drama 1994 · Aus · Colour · 105mins

A far cry from the black comedy of *Death in Brunswick*, John Ruane's second feature is a mystical melodrama Peter Coyote gives a memorable performance as the mysterious wandering evangelist who comes to the aid of a crisis-stricken farming family, though never quite assuaging the doubts of teenager Amanda Douge. With Lisa Harrow also impressive as the tether's-end wife taken by the stranger's charm and Jamie Croft suitably wide-eyed as her impressionable son, this is a film that will either enchant or infuriate. DP

Peter Coyote *Henry Warburton* • Lisa Harrow *Alice Flack* • Amanda Douge *Tegwyn Flack* • Jamie Croft *Ort* • Paul Sonkkila *Mr Cherry* • Louise Silversen *Mrs Cherry* ■ *Dir* John Ruane • *Scr* Jim Barton, John Ruane, from the novel by Tim Winton

That Funny Feeling ★★

Romantic comedy 1965 · US · Colour · 93mins

One of those familiar romantic comedies in which the leads continually cross each other's path before they get together. This time, pleasant performances from Bobby Darin and his then wife Sandra Dee distract attention from the coincidences. Dee is an aspiring actress who entertains rich publisher Darin in an apartment that she doesn't own, but works in as a maid. Unbeknown to her, it's his apartment. Daft, but you've seen worse. JG

Sandra Dee *Joan Howell* • Bobby Darin *Tom Milford* • Donald O'Connor *Harvey Granson* • Nita Talbot *Audrey* • Larry Storch *Luther* • James Westerfield *Officer Brokaw* • Leo G Carroll *O'Shea* ■ *Dir* Richard Thorpe • *Scr* David R Schwartz, from a story by Norman Barasch, Carroll Moore

That Gang of Mine ★★★

Sports comedy 1940 · US · BW · 62mins

Another trip out with the East Side Kids, which evolved from the Bowery Boys, which was a hangover from the far more serious Dead End Kids. This time Leo Gorcey is trying to be a jockey, though what distinction it does have comes from being directed by Joseph H Lewis – a cult film-maker who revs up the action a treat. TH

Bobby Jordan *Danny Dolan* • Leo Gorcey *Muggs Maloney* • Clarence Muse *Ben* • Dave O'Brien *Knuckles Dolan* • Joyce Bryant *Louise* • Donald Haines *Skinny* • David Gorcey *Peewee* • Sammy Morrison ["Sunshine Sammy" Morrison] *Scruno* ■ *Dir* Joseph H Lewis • *Scr* William Lively, from a story by Alan Whitman

That Hamilton Woman ★★★ PG

Historical drama 1941 · UK · BW · 124mins

"You cannot make peace with dictators," says Laurence Olivier as Lord Nelson, "You have to destroy them, wipe them out!" Audiences being bombed in London in 1941 caught the drift immediately and it was rumoured that Churchill not only urged Alexander Korda to make the film, but that he also wrote Nelson's maiden speech in the House of Lords. As propaganda, the picture is as single-minded as Olivier's later *Henry V*. But this is mainly a turgid love story, with Vivien Leigh as Lady Hamilton, whose adulterous affair with the naval hero was just as newsworthy as Napoleon's campaigns. AT

Vivien Leigh *Emma Hart Hamilton* • Laurence Olivier *Lord Horatio Nelson* • Alan Mowbray *Sir William Hamilton* • Sara Allgood *Mrs Cadogan-Lyon* • Gladys Cooper *Lady Nelson* • Henry Wilcoxon *Captain Hardy* ■ *Dir* Alexander Korda • *Scr* Walter Reisch, RC Sherriff • *Set Designer* Vincent Korda, Julia Heron

That Kind of Woman ★★

Romantic drama 1959 · US · Colour · 94mins

Sophia Loren, the mistress of millionaire George Sanders, meets a group of GIs during a train trip and ends up spending the night with Tab Hunter. To her, it's a one-night stand, but for him it's love eternal: he proposes marriage, thus presenting her with the conflict of choice between a fresh new life and her old one. Directed by Sidney Lumet, the movie can hardly fail to be competently made, but is actually an embarrassingly miscast and unconvincing bucketful of soap. RK

Sophia Loren *Kay* • Tab Hunter *Red* • George Sanders *The Man* • Barbara Nichols *Jane* • Jack Warden *Kelly* ■ *Dir* Sidney Lumet • *Scr* Walter Bernstein

That Lady ★★

Historical drama
1955 · UK · Colour · 100mins

Once mooted as a comeback vehicle for the great Garbo, it fell to an ill-cast Olivia de Havilland to portray the lusty one-eyed Princess of Eboli in this would-be spectacular 16th-century Spanish epic. Gilbert Roland is splendid, though, as de Havilland's lover, and King Philip II is played with intelligence by Paul Scofield, making his movie debut. The novelty of the CinemaScope process reduces director Terence Young to providing little more than a series of tableaux. TS

Olivia de Havilland *Ana De Mendoza, Princess of Eboli* • Gilbert Roland *Antonio Perez* • Paul Scofield *Philip II* • Françoise Rosay *Bernadina* • Dennis Price *Mateo Vasquez* • Robert Harris *Cardinal* • Christopher Lee *Captain* ■ *Dir* Terence Young • *Scr* Anthony Veiller, Sy Bartlett, from a novel by Kate O'Brien

That Lady in Ermine ★★★ U

Musical 1948 · US · Colour · 89mins

This richly Technicolored Betty Grable fantasy musical with a genuinely mythic sense to it is remembered more today for the fact that it was, sadly, the last movie of the great Ernst Lubitsch. The director famed for the stylish wit of his "Lubitsch Touch" died after only eight days shooting and was replaced by another notable European exile, Otto Preminger. The original wafer-thin material revolves around a 19th-century European army officer billeting his men in a castle with a past. The result is very entertaining, if not particularly memorable. TS

Betty Grable *Francesca/Angelina* • Douglas Fairbanks Jr *Colonel Teglash/The Duke* • Cesar Romero *Mario* • Walter Abel *Major Horvath/benvenuto* • Reginald Gardiner *Alberto* • Harry Davenport *Luigi* ■ *Dir* Ernst Lubitsch, Otto Preminger • *Scr* Samson Raphaelson, from an operetta by Rudolph Schanzer, Ernest Welisch

That Lucky Touch ★★★ PG

Romantic comedy
1975 · UK · Colour · 89mins

The setting is Brussels and a NATO war games event, with Roger Moore as an arms dealer and Susannah York a leftie *Washington Post* journalist. It breezes along nicely, has some barbed comments about American imperialism and a federal Europe, and Moore and York are attractive and relaxed. In his final screen role, Lee J Cobb adds some much-needed class playing an American general married to Shelley Winters, who sets everyone's teeth on edge. AT [video]

Roger Moore *Michael Scott* • Susannah York *Julia Richardson* • Shelley Winters *Diana Steedeman* • Lee J Cobb *General Steedeman* • Jean-Pierre Cassel *Leo* • Raf Vallone *General Peruzzi* • Sydne Rome *Sophie* • Donald Sinden *General Armstrong* ■ *Dir* Christopher Miles • *Scr* John Briley, from an idea by Moss Hart

That Man Bolt ★★ 18

Blaxploitation martial arts drama
1973 · US · Colour · 98mins

This violent action movie stars Fred Williamson as a martial arts specialist who agrees to deliver one million dollars of syndicate money, only to find himself involved in a catalogue of attempts on his life. Car chases, girls and acupuncture torture all figure in the escapist plot, which also weaves in Teresa Graves singing a rendition of Tom Jones's *She's a Lady*. An unwieldy chop-socky story that required two directors. TH [video]

Fred Williamson *Jefferson Bolt* • Byron Webster *Griffiths* • Miko Mayama *Dominique* • Teresa Graves *Samantha Nightingale* • Satoshi Nakamura *Kumada* • John Orchard *Carter* ■ *Dir* Henry Levin, David Lowell Rich • *Scr* Quentin Werty, Charles Johnson

That Man from Rio ★★★★ U

Crime comedy adventure
1964 · Fr/It · Colour · 112mins

How many other James Bond spoofs received an Oscar nomination for their screenplay? Moreover, how many could call upon Jean-Paul Belmondo in this kind of form – as a French air force pilot who spends his eight-day leave traversing the Atlantic and the Brazilian mainland, in a frantic bid to rescue feisty girlfriend Françoise Dorléac from the Amazon natives intent on finding a horde of lost jungle treasure. With Philippe de Broca roaring through the set pieces (which just get gleefully more preposterous) and exploiting every one of his exotic locations, this is hectic, hilarious and more than a match for Indiana Jones. DP. In French with English subtitles.

Jean-Paul Belmondo *Adrien Dufourquet* • Françoise Dorléac *Agnes* • Jean Servais *Professor Catalan* • Simone Renant *Lola* • Milton Ribeiro *Tupac* • Ubiracy De Oliveira *Sir Winston* • Adolfo Celi *Senor De Castro* ■ *Dir* Philippe de Broca • *Scr* Philippe de Broca, Jean-Paul Rappeneau, Ariane Mnouchkine, Daniel Boulanger

That Man George ★★

Crime adventure
1965 · Fr/It/Sp · Colour · 91mins

This is the type of colourful thriller that kept international audiences entertained throughout the 1960s, but generally didn't play too well in English-speaking territories owing to wholesale dubbing of the bulk of the cast. American lead George Hamilton lets his tan do the acting as he romances Claudine Auger and combats assorted other villains as he takes a shipment of gold bullion across Morocco. Mindless and uninvolving, although there's a nice twist at the end. TS. French dialogue dubbed into English.

George Hamilton *George* • Claudine Auger *Lila* • Alberto de Mendoza *Travis* • Daniel Ivernel *Vibert* • Tiberio Murgia *Jose* ■ *Dir* Jacques Deray • *Scr* Henri Lanoë, Jose Giovanni, Suzanne Arduini, Jacques Deray, from the novel *The Heisters* by Robert Page Jones

That Midnight Kiss ★★★ U

Romantic musical
1949 · US · Colour · 97mins

Not the best of MGM's musicals, but noteworthy as the feature debut of Mario Lanza, the star who brought opera to the movies and became the first tenor since Caruso to achieve massive popularity. This is virtually his biography, as Philadelphia opera patroness Ethel Barrymore has problems with the male lead of daughter Kathryn Grayson's stage debut, then Grayson discovers that local truck driver Lanza can more than hold his own with an aria. TS

Kathryn Grayson *Prudence Budell* • José Iturbi • Ethel Barrymore *Abigail Budell* • Mario Lanza *Johnny Donnetti* • Keenan Wynn *Artie Glenson* • J Carrol Naish *Papa Donnetti* • Jules Munshin *Michael Pemberton* • Thomas Gomez *Guido Betelli* ■ *Dir* Norman Taurog • *Scr* Bruce Manning, Tamara Hovey

That Night ★★★

Drama 1957 · US · BW · 87mins

There's an unpretentiousness and honesty to this work that makes for compelling viewing, even if the story sounds off-putting. John Beal suffers a heart attack and finds, in middle age, that it is his family that pulls him through the ordeal, rather than less than adequate medical care. Beal, an accomplished actor from the 1930s, and Augusta Dabney, as his supportive wife, give fine performances in a modest movie that is more of a docudrama than fiction. BB

John Beal *Chris Bowden* • Augusta Dabney *Maggie Bowden* • Malcolm Brodrick *Tommy Bowden* • Dennis Kohler *Chrissie Bowden* • Beverly Lunsford *Betsy Bowden* • Shepperd Strudwick *Dr Bernard Fischer* ■ *Dir* John Newland • *Scr* Jack Rowles, Robert Wallace, from the story/TV drama *The Long Way Home* by Jack Rowles, Robert Wallace

That Night ★★★ 12

Drama
1992 · US/Jpn/Ger/Fr · Colour · 85mins

An affectionate portrait of adolescent nostalgia from first-time director Craig Bolotin. The setting is the uneventful Long Island suburbia of the early 1960s, where impressionable youngster Eliza Dushku becomes the fascinated witness to a generation-gap battle between her neighbours – daughter Juliette Lewis and mum Helen Shaver. The story is very slight, but the young Dushku is a revelation, and Lewis and C Thomas Howell, Lewis's unsuitable beau, also deliver convincing performances. JF. Contains swearing and sexual references. [video]

C Thomas Howell *Rick* • Juliette Lewis *Sheryl* • Helen Shaver *Ann* • Eliza Dushku *Alice Bloom* • John Dossett *Larry Bloom* • J Smith-Cameron *Carol Bloom* • Katherine Heigl *Kathryn* ■ *Dir* Craig Bolotin • *Scr* Craig Bolotin, Alice McDermott

That Night in Rio ★★★

Musical comedy 1941 · US · Colour · 90mins

"I-yi-yi-yi-yi I like you vairy much" sings Carmen Miranda in, arguably, her greatest screen musical. This remake of *Folies Bergère*, later itself remade as *On the Riviera* (20th Century-Fox was renowned for recycling it's plots) is really a vehicle for Don Ameche, in a dual role, and Alice Faye. But, from the opening, it's Miranda who runs away with the film. By the way, if you're lusting for Rio, this movie never leaves the back lot. TS

Alice Faye *Baroness Cecilia Duarte* • Don Ameche *Larry Martin/Baron Duarte* • Carmen Miranda *Carmen* • SZ Sakall *Arthur Penna* • J Carrol Naish *Machado* • Curt Bois *Felicio Salles* • Leonid Kinskey *Pierre Dufont* • Frank Puglia *Pedro, the valet* • Maria Montez *Inez* ■ *Dir* Irving Cummings • *Scr* George Seaton, Bess Meredyth, Hal Long, Samuel Hoffenstein, Jessie Ernst, from a play by Rudolph Lothar, Hans Adler

That Obscure Object of Desire ★★★★★ 15

Drama 1977 · Fr/Sp · Colour · 99mins

Luis Buñuel's final film, is a fitting end to a dazzling career. A witty, ironic and barbed morality tale, it follows the increasingly desperate attempts of wealthy businessman Fernando Rey to seduce his maid, unaware that his world is collapsing around his ears. Buñuel only hit upon the intriguing idea of casting two actresses in the role of Conchita after Maria Schneider walked off the set, but it proved to be a creative masterstroke, as the switches between Carole Bouquet and Angela Molina teasingly suggest the indecision in Rey's mind as he searches for the elusive woman of his dreams. DP. In French with English subtitles. [video]

Fernando Rey *Mathieu* • Carole Bouquet *Conchita* • Angela Molina *Conchita* • Julien Bertheau *Edouard/d'Oleargues* • André Weber *Martin* • Piéral [Pierre Piéral] *Psychology professor* • Bernard Musson *Police inspector* ■ *Dir* Luis Buñuel • *Scr* Luis Buñuel, Jean-Claude Carrière, from the novel *La Femme et le Pantin* by Pierre Loüys

That Old Feeling ★★ 12

Romantic comedy
1997 · US · Colour · 100mins

More schmaltz than the average person can stomach. Bette Midler and Dennis Farina play feuding divorcees, meeting up at their daughter's wedding to a politician who trades on his squeaky clean image. It's not too long before they realise they still fancy each other. Alhough there's a nice quick-fire repartee between Midler and Farina, they aren't exactly in the Astaire and Rogers class when it comes to bickering. LH. Contains sexual references and swearing. [video]

Bette Midler *Lilly Leonard* • Dennis Farina *Dan De Mora* • Paula Marshall *Molly De Mora* • Gail O'Grady *Rowena* • David Rasche *Alan* • Jamie Denton *Keith Marks* • Danny Nucci *Joey Donna* ■ *Dir* Carl Reiner • *Scr* Leslie Dixon

That Riviera Touch ★★ PG

Comedy 1966 · UK · Colour · 93mins

Morecambe and Wise head for the south of France in what starts out looking like a customised remake of the old Laurel and Hardy comedy *Saps at Sea*. But Eric and Ernie's regular writers, Sid Green and Dick Hills, quickly run into the problem that blighted all three of their movies; the pair's relaxed, intimate style might have been perfect for the sketch format of their TV show, but it was totally wrong for sustaining narratives. Few laughs. DP [video] DVD

Eric Morecambe *Eric* • Ernie Wise *Ernie* • Suzanne Lloyd *Claudette* • Paul Stassino *Le Pirate* • Armand Mestral *Inspector Duval* ■ *Dir* Cliff Owen • *Scr* Sidney C Green [SC Green], Richard M Hills [RM Hills], Peter Blackmore

That Sinking Feeling ★★★ PG

Crime caper 1979 · UK · Colour · 85mins

Bill Forsyth made his directorial debut with this thin, but still enjoyable, comedy. This established the Forsyth style: underplayed humour and seemingly irrelevant gags, with a subtle pay-off and the quirky use of the local idiom. The theft of a consignment of sinks is planned with the intricacy of a *Rififi*-like heist but, as in so many caper movies, it just couldn't go smoothly. DP [video]

Robert Buchanan *Ronnie* • John Hughes *Vic* • Billy Greenlees *Wal* • Douglas Sannachan *Simmy* • Alan Love *Alec* • Danny Benson *Policeman* • Eddie Burt *Van Driver* • Tom Mannion *Doctor* • Eric Joseph *The Wee Man* • Gordon John Sinclair [John Gordon-Sinclair] *Andy* ■ *Dir/Scr* Bill Forsyth

T

That Summer of White Roses ★★ 15

Drama 1989 · UK/Yug · Colour · 98mins

Set in 1944 in a Yugoslavian backwater miraculously untouched by the ravages of the Second World War, Rajko Grlic's drama rapidly becomes muddled and unfocused as simple-minded lifeguard Tom Conti marries widow Susan George to shield her from the Nazis. This touches the heart, even if it doesn't engage the mind. TH. Contains swearing. [video]

Tom Conti *Andrija Gavrilovic* • Susan George *Ana* • Rod Steiger *Martin* • Nitzan Sharron *Danny* • Alun Armstrong *Zemba* • John Gill *Doctor* • John Sharp *Mayor* ■ *Dir* Rajko Grlic • *Scr* Borislav Pekic, Kajko Grlic, Simon MacCorkindale, from the novel *Defense and the Last Days* by Borislav Pekic

That Thing You Do!
★★★★ PG

Musical comedy 1996 · US · Colour · 103mins

Tom Hanks's directorial debut is an immensely likeable pop fable about the meteoric rise and fall of the mythical Wonders, an all-American small-town rock 'n' roll band. Set in a period-perfect 1964, and featuring a marvellously evocative soundtrack of cod-Golden Oldies, it deliberately emphasises the *Forrest Gump*-style feel-good nostalgia, rather than making any hard-hitting statement about the price of fame. Hanks also plays the group's opportunistic manager, but it's sweet-natured Tom Everett Scott who registers strongest as the drumming driving force behind the aspiring Beatles, with Liv Tyler equally affecting as the band mascot. AJ DVD

Tom Everett Scott *Guy Patterson* • Liv Tyler *Faye* • Johnathon Schaech *Jimmy* • Steve Zahn *Lenny* • Ethan Embry *The Bass Player* • Tom Hanks *Mr White* • Charlize Theron *Tina* • Chris Isaak *Uncle Bob* • Kevin Pollak *Boss Vic Koss* ■ *Dir/Scr* Tom Hanks

That Touch of Mink
★★★ U

Romantic comedy
1962 · US · Colour · 94mins

A very popular Doris Day vehicle, in which she co-stars with Cary Grant. The movie only works if you accept that Day won't sleep with Grant, which might have made sense back in 1962 but hardly makes any sense at all now: after all, these are two of the best-looking and most sophisticated people in the world. But that's the plot – will she or won't she, and we know she won't. This is quintessential Day fluff, complete with quite unnecessary heavily-gauzed close-ups, and Grant can barely disguise the fact that he's getting a little too long in the tooth for such foolishness. TS DVD

Cary Grant *Philip Shayne* • Doris Day *Cathy Timberlake* • Gig Young *Roger* • Audrey Meadows *Connie* • Alan Hewitt *Dr Gruber* • John Astin *Beasley* • John McKee *Collins, chauffeur* ■ *Dir* Delbert Mann • *Scr* Stanley Shapiro, Nate Monaster

That Uncertain Feeling
★★★

Romantic comedy 1941 · US · BW · 81mins

Ernst Lubitsch directed this remake of *Kiss Me Again* (1925), one of his best silent pictures, with that uncertain touch. Something was lost when sound was added, although the screenplay crackles wittily for the first quarter of the picture afterwards it becomes ever sillier and more desperate. Merle Oberon gets recurring hiccups after six years of marriage to insurance salesman Melvyn Douglas, and her psychiatrist diagnoses marriage trouble. She then has a brief flirtation with Burgess Meredith, who has the best zany moments in the film. RB

Merle Oberon *Jill Baker* • Melvyn Douglas *Larry Baker* • Burgess Meredith *Alexander Sebastian* • Alan Mowbray *Dr Vengard* • Olive Blakeney *Margie* • Harry Davenport *Jones* • Eve Arden *Sally Aikens* ■ *Dir* Ernst Lubitsch • *Scr* Donald Ogden Stewart, Walter Reisch, from the play *Divorçons* by Victorien Sardou, Emile de Najac

That Was Then... This Is Now
★★★ 15

Drama 1985 · US · Colour · 97mins

Emilio Estevez's directorial career has been largely undistinguished, but when he scripted this respectful adaptation of the SE Hinton novel, it seemed he might well have a career behind as well as in front of the camera. He and Craig Sheffer take the roles of two troubled adolescents whose friendship is threatened when romance rears its head. Although it is a little downbeat, this remains a moving drama about the traumas of growing up. JF. Contains swearing and violence.

Emilio Estevez *Mark Jennings* • Craig Sheffer *Bryon Douglas* • Kim Delaney *Cathy Carlson* • Jill Schoelen *Angela Shepard* • Barbara Babcock *Mrs Douglas* • Frank Howard *"M & M" Carlson* • Frank McCarthy *Mr Carlson* • Larry B Scott *Terry Jones* • Morgan Freeman *Charlie Woods* ■ *Dir* Christopher Cain • *Scr* Emilio Estevez, from the novel

That Woman Opposite
★★

Murder mystery 1957 · UK · BW · 83mins

Don't expect too much of this modest film, and you'll be agreeably entertained by an efficiently directed work graced by many recognisable faces. The setting is a small French town where an English antique dealer is found murdered. An inconsequential plot of intrigue and romance follows, as private detective Dan O'Herlihy attempts to solve the mystery. BB

Phyllis Kirk *Eve* • Dan O'Herlihy *Dermot Kinross* • Wilfrid Hyde White *Sir Maurice Lawes* • Petula Clark *Janice* • Jack Watling *Toby* • William Franklyn *Ned* ■ *Dir* Compton Bennett • *Scr* Compton Bennett, from the novel *The Emperor's Snuffbox* by John Dickson Carr

That Wonderful Urge
★★★

Comedy 1948 · US · BW · 81mins

Tyrone Power is a cocky and insistent reporter who ridicules heiress Gene Tierney. To get her own back, she declares to the world that he has married her for money. The plot was familiar to those who remembered the earlier version called *Love Is News* (1937). Suitably witty and slick, this film shows off Tierney's talent for light comedy. RB

Tyrone Power *Thomas Jefferson Tyler* • Gene Tierney *Sara Farley* • Reginald Gardiner *Count Andre de Guyon* • Arleen Whelan *Jessica Woods* • Lucile Watson *Aunt Cornelia* • Gene Lockhart *Judge* • Lloyd Gough *Duffy* • Porter Hall *Attorney Ketchell* ■ *Dir* Robert B Sinclair • *Scr* Jay Dratler, from the story *Love Is News* by William R Lipman, Frederick Stephani

That'll Be the Day
★★★ 15

Musical drama 1973 · UK · Colour · 87mins

Some critics consider this dose of rock 'n' roll to be a nostalgic delight, while others think it's a glam sham, viewing the 1950s through glitter-tinted spectacles. No matter where your sympathies lie, it's hard to avoid the fact that the film is beginning to show its age, but David Essex brings a certain swagger to the character of Jim MacLaine, while Ringo Starr and Billy Fury score in key cameos. Essex returned for the following year's sequel, *Stardust*. DP. Contains swearing. DVD

David Essex *Jim MacLaine* • Ringo Starr *Mike* • Rosemary Leach *Mrs MacLaine* • James Booth *Mr MacLaine* • Billy Fury *Stormy Tempest* • Keith Moon *JD Clover* • Rosalind Ayres *Jeanette* • Robert Lindsay *Terry Sutcliffe* ■ *Dir* Claude Whatham • *Scr* Ray Connolly

That's Carry On
★★★ PG

Comedy compilation
1977 · UK · Colour and BW · 91mins

You can almost guarantee that your favourite *Carry On* clip will be missing from this compilation, which sticks to all the obvious moments that had already been aired on the TV "best of" series. Kenneth Williams and Barbara Windsor shot a few linking scenes that contain some of the biggest laughs, but there's more than a ring of truth in Williams's contention that the later films scripted by Talbot Rothwell were overly dependent on smut and lacked the sharpness of his earlier efforts. With a little more imagination and discrimination, this could have been a cracking collection, but it's still well worth a watch. DP DVD

Kenneth Williams • Barbara Windsor ■ *Dir* Gerald Thomas • *Scr* Tony Church

That's Dancing!
★★★★ U

Dance compilation
1985 · US · Colour and BW · 100mins

Top-of-the-range tappers are featured in this all-dancing spectacular from Jack Haley Jr, who also made the *That's Entertainment!* films. And exhilarating fun it is, too, featuring not just tap-dancing, but many other forms of dance, from early Busby Berkeley extravaganzas to Michael Jackson, via ballet and acrobatics. Like those earlier compilation films, the movie is the best bits of numerous musicals, but within the limitations of the format, it's highly enjoyable. SG

Dir/Scr Jack Haley Jr

That's Entertainment!
★★★★★ U

Compilation
1974 · US · BW and Colour · 122mins

Here, lovingly assembled, is MGM's compilation of its greatest triumphs in a field that it had made its own: the musical. Wittily discussed and cleverly edited are some of the Crown Jewels of Hollywood, linked by a superb cast of comperes, including Frank Sinatra, Elizabeth Taylor and Liza Minnelli, whose tribute to her mother Judy Garland is both exquisite and moving. This is entertainment on a grand scale, the snippets making you ache to see the originals. Two sequels followed, but this was the great forerunner, and a big box-office hit. TS

Dir Jack Haley Jr

That's Entertainment, Part II
★★★★ U

Compilation
1976 · US · Colour and BW · 123mins

The first film was a hard act to follow, but director Gene Kelly's sequel is satisfying and includes a memorable sequence of new material featuring the ageing Kelly dancing again with the great Fred Astaire. There's also a witty Saul Bass title sequence: watch how the graphics mirror the artists' names. Although this MGM compilation is not as powerful as its unique predecessor, it's still a chance to recapture the lovely golden glow that watching an MGM musical can bring. TS

Gene Kelly • Fred Astaire ■ *Dir* Gene Kelly

That's Entertainment! III
★★★★ U

Compilation
1994 · US · Colour and BW · 108mins

There may be the suspicion that MGM was scraping the barrel for this third compilation from its vaults, but it's a gold plated barrel! It also provides an answer for all those who thought the 1946 musical comedy *The Harvey Girls* lacked a third act number – it's here, as Judy Garland belts out *March of the Dogies*, in a restored and remixed version. Another highlight is Garland performing Irving Berlin's *Mr Monotony*, which was cut from 1948's *Easter Parade*. Beautifully assembled and immaculately edited. TS

Dir Bud Friedgen, Michael J Sheridan

That's Life
★★★ 15

Comedy drama 1986 · US · Colour · 101mins

Failing to realise that smug, affluent Californians are of interest mainly to themselves, Blake Edwards invites us to share in their every tiny worry, their every waking moment. Stepping into the shoes of another midlife neurotic, Jack Lemmon succeeds in making him both sympathetic and irksome. Meanwhile his introspection has blinded him to the more pressing needs of his wife (Julie Andrews). Shot in the Malibu home of director Edwards and his real-life wife Andrews, the cast includes members of their family as well as appearances from Lemmon's wife Felicia Farr and son Chris. JM

Jack Lemmon *Harvey Fairchild* • Julie Andrews *Gillian Fairchild* • Sally Kellerman *Holly Parrish* • Robert Loggia *Father Baragone* • Jennifer Edwards *Megan Fairchild Bartlet* • Chris Lemmon *Josh Fairchild* • Felicia Farr *Madame Carrie* ■ *Dir* Blake Edwards • *Scr* Milton Wexler, Blake Edwards

That's My Boy
★★ U

Comedy 1951 · US · BW · 98mins

This is a college football caper redesigned as a vehicle for Dean Martin and Jerry Lewis. Lewis is the son of a wealthy college alumnus father, who wants his unathletic student son to play for his own old football team, and hires fellow-student and pigskin star Martin to train him. The movie, sparse on laughs, is even less amusing to those with no understanding of the intricacies of American football. RK

Dean Martin *Bill Baker* • Jerry Lewis *"Junior" Jackson* • Ruth Hussey *Ann Jackson* • Eddie Mayehoff *"Jarring Jack" Jackson* • Marion Marshall *Terry Howard* • Polly Bergen *Betty Hunter* • Hugh Sanders *Coach Wheeler* • John McIntire *Benjamin Green* ■ *Dir* Hal Walker • *Scr* Cy Howard, from his story

That's My Man
★★

Comedy 1947 · US · BW · 101mins

A compulsive gambler neglects his wife and baby in favour of the racetrack and card table, leading, inevitably, to a decline in his fortunes and marital break-up. Tear-master Frank Borzage, with no ace up his sleeve, employs every possible sentimental cliché on the slow journey to the predictable resolution. Don Ameche is the star, bravely battling with the script and direction. RK

Don Ameche *Joe Grange* • Catherine McLeod *Ronnie* • Roscoe Karns *Toby Gleeton* • Joe Frisco *Willie Wagonstatter* ■ *Dir* Frank Borzage • *Scr* Steve Fisher, Bradley King, from their story

That's Right – You're Wrong
★★★ U

Musical comedy 1939 · US · Colour · 94mins

The first – and best – of an increasingly inane series of comedy musicals starring popular radio bandleader Kay Kyser. Here, Kyser makes his screen debut with his musicians and his nonsensical "Kollege of Musical Knowledge" quiz. The plot involves a reluctant Kyser being lured to Hollywood, where producer Adolphe Menjou is under orders to star him in a hit. Chaos and confusion ensue when the scriptwriters are unable to come up with a plot. Directed by David Butler, this is a mix of childish rubbish with a nice spoof on Hollywood studio methods. RK

Kay Kyser *Kay* • Adolphe Menjou *Delmore* • Lucille Ball *Sandra Sand* • May Robson *Grandma* • Dennis O'Keefe *Chuck Deems* • Edward Everett Horton *Village* ■ *Dir* David Butler • *Scr* William Conselmann, James V Kern, from a story by David Butler, William Conselmann

That's Your Funeral
★

Comedy 1972 · UK · Colour · 81mins

In all its long years, the Hammer House of Horror never churned out anything as gruesome as this abysmal comedy. The original TV sitcom only ran for one six-part series, so why anyone thought it was worth making a feature version is beyond comprehension. Bill Fraser

T

sledgehammers his way through gags that should have been allowed to rest in peace years ago, while even the usually reliable Raymond Huntley struggles to raise a smile. DP. Contains swearing and drug abuse.

Bill Fraser *Basil Bulstrode* • Raymond Huntley *Emanuel Holroyd* • David Battley *Percy* • John Ronane *Mr Smallbody* • Sue Lloyd *Miss Peach* • Dennis Price *Mr Soul* • Roy Kinnear *Mr Purvis* ■ *Dir* John Robins • *Scr* Peter Lewis

Theatre of Blood ★★★★ 18

Horror 1973 · UK · Colour · 99mins

The magnum opus of Vincent Price's film career, this stylish, witty comedy horror boasts an irresistible premise, an inspired ensemble cast, fabulous music and first-rate production values. Price is classically trained actor Edward Lionheart, who murders theatre critics using famous death scenes from Shakespeare's plays as payback for being dismissive of his talents. Aided by his faithful daughter Edwina (Diana Rigg) and a group of tramps, Lionheart plans each killing with elaborate inventiveness and cunning disguise. Price does a superior job portraying an inferior actor and mines every nuance of tragedy and comedy with triumphant brilliance and delicious gusto. AJ. Contains violence. [VIDEO] DVD

Vincent Price *Edward Lionheart* • Diana Rigg *Edwina Lionheart* • Ian Hendry *Peregrine Devlin* • Harry Andrews *Trevor Dickman* • Coral Browne *Chloe Moon* • Robert Coote *Oliver Larding* • Jack Hawkins *Solomon Psaltery* • Michael Hordern *George Maxwell* • Arthur Lowe *Horace Sprout* • Robert Morley *Meredith Merridrew* • Dennis Price *Hector Snipe* ■ *Dir* Douglas Hickox • *Scr* Anthony Greville-Bell

Theatre of Death ★★★ 15

Horror 1966 · UK · Colour · 89mins

Is Christopher Lee, the obsessive director of a *Grand Guignol* theatre, responsible for a series of vampire-like killings terrorising Paris? It's fearful fun finding out in this odd horror whodunnit, played out against a neatly realised backdrop of fake gore, backstage seediness and macabre motives. Long revered by Lee cultists as a showcase for one of the actor's best performances, this baroque, moody, murder mystery also features a rare screen role for 1930s musical comedy star Evelyn Laye, and is impressively photographed by Gilbert Taylor. AJ [VIDEO] DVD

Christopher Lee *Philippe Darvas* • Lelia Goldoni *Dani Cirreaux* • Julian Glover *Charles Marquis* • Evelyn Laye *Madame Angele* • Jenny Till *Nicole Chapel* ■ *Dir* Samuel Gallu • *Scr* Ellis Kadison, Roger Marshall, from a story by Ellis Kadison

The Theft of the Mona Lisa ★★ PG

Romantic comedy
1965 · Fr/It · Colour · 94mins

This is a humdrum period caper movie that has none of the ingenuity or intensity of *Rififi* and even less of the bravura. However, it does have the advantage of being based on a true story, as Leonardo's masterpiece was lifted from the Louvre in 1911 and not returned for two years. DP. French dialogue dubbed into English. DVD

George Chakiris *Vincent* • Marina Vlady *Nicole* • Jean Lefebvre *Guard* • Margaret Lee *Titina* • Paul Frankeur *Boss* ■ *Dir* Michel Deville • *Scr* Nina Companéez, Michel Deville, Ottavio Poggi

Their First Mistake ★★★★ U

Comedy 1932 · US · BW · 20mins

A brilliant Laurel and Hardy short, featuring a non-stop array of gags around the subject of the boys and a baby. Ollie's wife is angry that he spends so little time with her and so much time with Stan. The boys come to the conclusion that if she had a baby, she wouldn't have time to harangue Ollie. So they adopt a child, only to find, when they return home, that the wife has left, leaving the lads holding the baby. DF [VIDEO] DVD

Stan Laurel *Stan* • Oliver Hardy *Ollie* • Mae Busch *Mrs Arabella Hardy* • Billy Gilbert *Process server* • George Marshall *Neighbour* ■ *Dir/Scr* George Marshall

Thelma & Louise ★★★★★ 15

Road movie 1991 · US · Colour · 129mins

In this hugely entertaining and controversial road movie, Geena Davis and Susan Sarandon star as the two friends whose weekend spree to escape the boredom of their small-town routines is curtailed when Louise (Sarandon) kills a man who's trying to rape Thelma (Davis). They flee, and thus begins their voyage of self-discovery. Ridley Scott's film sparked a row at the time over whether the sight of gals with guns was a symbol of liberated equality or depressing defeminisation. Whatever your viewpoint, films have a duty to provoke as well as entertain, and it's impossible to watch the plight of Thelma and Louise without feeling indignation. DP. Contains swearing, violence and a sex scene. [VIDEO] DVD

Susan Sarandon *Louise Sawyer* • Geena Davis *Thelma Dickinson* • Harvey Keitel *Hal Slocombe* • Michael Madsen *Jimmy* • Christopher McDonald *Darryl* • Stephen Tobolowsky *Max* • Brad Pitt *J D* • Timothy Carhart *Harlan* • Lucinda Jenney *Lena, Waitress* • Jason Beghe *State Trooper* • Sonny Carl Davis *Albert* • Ken Swofford *Major* ■ *Dir* Ridley Scott • *Scr* Callie Khouri

Thelonious Monk: Straight No Chaser ★★★ PG

Music documentary
1988 · US · BW and Colour · 89mins

Jazz buff Clint Eastwood acted as executive producer on this documentary about the great jazz pianist and composer of standards such as *Round Midnight*. Director Charlotte Zwerin uses concert footage of Monk on tour in the late 1960s, shot by Christian Blackwood with new interviews and biographical material about Monk, who died in 1982. Eastwood's own homage to Charlie Parker, *Bird*, was released in 1988. TH

Samuel E Wright *Narration* ■ *Dir* Charlotte Zwerin • *Cinematographer* Christian Blackwood

Them! ★★★★★ PG

Science fiction 1954 · US · BW · 88mins

The best of the giant bug movies of the 1950s is a science-fiction classic. Spawned by atomic radiation, mutant ants arrive in Los Angeles from the New Mexico desert and infest the sewer system in a taut, atmospheric and totally convincing shocker laden with clever visual and verbal puns. Terrific special effects, noble humanitarian sentiments, involving performances and a first-class script make for monster thrills. AJ [VIDEO] DVD

James Whitmore *Sgt Ben Peterson* • Edmund Gwenn *Dr Harold Medford* • Joan Weldon *Dr Patricia Medford* • James Arness *Robert Graham* • Onslow Stevens *Brig Gen O'Brien* • Leonard Nimoy *Sergeant* ■ *Dir* Gordon Douglas • *Scr* Ted Sherdeman, Russell Hughes, from a story by George Worthing Yates

Them Thar Hills! ★★★★ U

Comedy 1934 · US · BW · 18mins

Stan Laurel believed that he and Ollie should have "stayed in the short film category" and watching gems like this one can understand his reluctance to milk a comic situation beyond a perfectly realised twenty minutes. Oliver has been told to take it easy, so the duo head for the hills and a caravan site. Disaster follows when bootleggers fill the nearby well with moonshine whisky. A camper's wife joins the boys and by the time her husband arrives the trio are plastered. The inevitable destructive tit-for-tat routine follows. A lesser sequel with the same couple followed the next year, called *Tit-for-Tat*. BB [VIDEO] DVD

Stan Laurel *Stan* • Oliver Hardy *Ollie* • Billy Gilbert *Doctor* • Charlie Hall *Motorist who runs out of gas* • Mae Busch *Motorist's wife* ■ *Dir* Charles Rogers • *Scr* Stan Laurel, HM Walker

The Theme ★★★★

Drama 1979 · USSR · Colour · 99mins

This was among the first films to benefit from the thawing of Soviet cinema in the Gorbachev era. Michael Ulyanov stars as a pulp novelist whose subservience to the Party line has led to his advancement in Moscow's literary circles. Seeking inspiration, he travels to the country where he becomes infatuated with Inna Churikova, a suppressed artist who shames him for his compromises. The winner of the Golden Bear at the 1987 Berlin Film Festival, Gleb Panfilov's searching study of artistic integrity and freedom of movement is not an easy watch, but it rewards the effort. DP. In Russian with English subtitles.

Mikhail Ulyanov *Esenin* • Inna Churikova *Sasa Nikolaeva* ■ *Dir* Gleb Panfilov • *Scr* Gleb Panfilov, Aleksander Cervinski

Theodora Goes Wild ★★★★

Screwball comedy 1936 · US · BW · 94mins

A onderful, madcap comedy from the genre's golden period, with Irene Dunne utterly enchanting in her first comic starring role as an author who hits the big city and falls for debonair Melvyn Douglas. They make a delightful couple, for a while, and that's the main theme of Sidney Buchman's clever, twist-laden screenplay. Stanislavsky-trained émigré director Richard Boleslawski has the good sense to sit back and let the cast get on with it. TS

Irene Dunne *Theodora Lynn* • Melvyn Douglas *Michael Grant* • Thomas Mitchell *Jed Waterbury* • Thurston Hall *Arthur Stevenson* • Rosalind Keith *Adelaide Perry* • Spring Byington *Rebecca Perry* • Elisabeth Risdon *Aunt Mary* • Margaret McWade *Aunt Elsie* ■ *Dir* Richard Boleslawski • *Scr* Sidney Buchman, from a story by Mary E McCarthy

Theodore Rex ★ PG

Comedy fantasy 1995 · US · Colour · 87mins

Only the threat of litigation kept Whoopi Goldberg on board this turkey and it is to her credit that she does her best to make it fly. But she clearly didn't regard being teamed with a doltish detective (who just happens to be a tyrannosaurus) as one of the highlights of her career. Writer/director Jonathan Betuel needs someone more menacing than mad scientist Armin Mueller-Stahl to distract us from the woeful special effects. DP. Contains violence, and swearing. [VIDEO]

Whoopi Goldberg *Katie Coltrane* • Armin Mueller-Stahl *Dr Edgar Kane* • Juliet Landau *Dr Shade* • Bud Cort *Spinner* • Stephen McHattie *Edge* • Richard Roundtree *Commissioner Lynch* • Peter Mackenzie *Alex Summers* • Peter Kwong *Toymaker* • George Newbern *Theodore Rex* • Carol Kane *Molly Rex* ■ *Dir/Scr* Jonathan Betuel

Theorem ★★★★ 15

Drama 1968 · It · Colour · 94mins

Pier Paolo Pasolini found himself on an obscenity charge for this adaptation of his own novel, in which a handsome stranger seduces every member of a wealthy household before departing abruptly. Oblivious to whether Terence Stamp's intruder was messiah or demon, the Italian government banned the film, recognising that in its blend of Marxism and religion, Pasolini had created a scathing indictment of the sexually repressed bourgeoisie. Laura Betti won the best actress prize at Venice for her performance as the skittish maid, but it's Stamp's ethereal presence that dominates. DP. In Italian with English subtitles. [VIDEO]

Terence Stamp *Visitor* • Silvana Mangano *Mother* • Massimo Girotti *Father* • Anne Wiazemsky *Daughter* • Laura Betti *Maid* • Andrés José Cruz *Son* ■ *Dir* Pier Paolo Pasolini • *Scr* Pier Paolo Pasolini, from his novel

The Theory of Flight ★★★★ 15

Romantic drama
1998 · UK/US · Colour · 101mins

Depicting human fallibility – both mental and physical – this very tender and honest romantic drama was originally made as a BBC film for television and later reconsidered for theatrical release. Kenneth Branagh plays a man re-inventing the aeroplane as a futile expression of his lack of emotional freedom. After an attempted flight off a public building lands him on probation, he is assigned to take care of Helena Bonham Carter who, though terminally ill, is determined to lose her virginity before she dies. Together they pursue their dreams of literal and sexual flight; handled with sensitivity, this is very touching. LH. Contains swearing and sexual references.

Kenneth Branagh *Richard* • Helena Bonham Carter *Jane Hatchard* • Gemma Jones *Anne* • Holly Aird *Julie* • Ray Stevenson *Gigolo* ■ *Dir* Paul Greengrass • *Scr* Richard Hawkins

There Goes My Baby ★★★

Drama 1994 · US · Colour · 98mins

If imitation is the sincerest form of flattery, *American Graffiti* must be feeling very flattered indeed. This is one of the many attempts to recapture its teen angst, and it's better than some. Set in 1965, the film focuses on a clichéd bunch of senior high school students as they prepare to enter the real world. The characters are stereotypes, but the quality of the film's ensemble cast just about brings them to life. DA

Dermot Mulroney *Pirate* • Rick Schroder *Stick* • Kelli Williams *Sunshine* • Noah Wyle *Finnegan* • Jill Schoelen *Babette* • Kristin Minter *Tracy* • Lucy Deakins *Mary Beth* • Kenny Ransom [Kenneth Ransom] *Calvin* ■ *Dir/Scr* Floyd Mutrux

There Goes My Heart ★★

Romantic comedy 1938 · US · BW · 81mins

Fredric March stars as a newspaperman trying to interview heiress Virginia Bruce, in this comedy directed by Norman Z McLeod. Unfortunately she's escaped the control of her department store-owner grandfather and decamped to New York. Clearly lost for inspiration, the unbelievably convoluted plot sees Bruce adopting an alias, rooming with salesgirl Patsy Kelly and ending up as one herself in grandpa's department store, before March discovers her true identity. Well done, but predictable. RK

Fredric March *Bill Spencer* • Virginia Bruce *Joan Butterfield/Joan Baker* • Patsy Kelly *Peggy O'Brien* • Alan Mowbray *Pennypepper E Pennypepper* • Nancy Carroll *Dorothy Moore* ■ *Dir* Norman Z McLeod • *Scr* Eddie Moran, Jack Jevne, from a story by Ed Sullivan

There Goes the Bride ★ PG

Farce 1979 · UK · Colour · 86mins

On the day of his daughter's wedding in Florida, an advertising executive takes a couple of accidental bumps on

T

the head – each of which, in the time-honoured tradition of this sort of thing, causes embarrassing and supposedly hilarious hallucinations. An unamusing Ray Cooney farce with a curious melange of British and US actors. Contains poor jokes. JG

Tom Smothers *Timothy Westerby* • Twiggy *Polly Perkins* • Sylvia Syms *Ursula Westerby* • Michael Witney *Bill Shorter* • Martin Balsam *Elmer Babcock* • Phil Silvers *Psychiatrist* ■ *Dir* Terence Marcel [Terry Marcel] • *Scr* Ray Cooney, Terence Marcel, John Chapman, from a play by Ray Cooney

There Goes the Groom ★★

Comedy 1937 · US · BW · 64mins

This marginally screwball romantic comedy features a family with financial problems, hoping to solve them by hooking a wealthy son-in-law for their elder daughter Louise Henry. Enter her old high-school sweetheart Burgess Meredith, back from a successful foray in the Alaskan goldfields, but directing his attention to the younger daughter Ann Sothern. The cast keeps this good-natured but unmemorable movie just about intact in the face of its paper-thin plot. RK

Ann Sothern *Bettina "Betty" Russell* • Burgess Meredith *Derek "Dick" Mathews* • Mary Boland *Mrs Genevieve Pearson Russell* • Onslow Stevens *Dr Joel Becker* • William Brisbane *Potter Russell* • Louise Henry *Janet Russell* ■ *Dir* Joseph Santley • *Scr* SK Lauren, Dorothy Yost, Harold Kusell, from the short story *Let Freedom Swing* by David Garth

There Is Another Sun ★★★

Crime thriller 1951 · UK · BW · 97mins

This seedy tale of greed and betrayal among funfair folk focuses on a stunt rider and a boxer, who put aside their rivalries to steal the boss's life savings. There's nothing new in the story and the performances of Maxwell Reed and Laurence Harvey have little to commend them. But director Lewis Gilbert's thoroughly nasty atmosphere conjured up in a place dedicated to enjoyment makes this unusually effective movie worth watching. DP

Maxwell Reed *Racer* • Susan Shaw *Lillian* • Laurence Harvey *Maguire* • Hermione Baddeley *Gypsy Sarah* • Meredith Edwards *Bratcher* • Robert Adair *Sarno* • Leslie Dwyer *Foley* ■ *Dir* Lewis Gilbert • *Scr* Guy Morgan, from a story by James Raisin

There Was a Crooked Man ★★★★ U

Comedy 1960 · UK · BW · 106mins

Even some of those generally left cold by clown Norman Wisdom admit that this is one of his best films. This comedy allowed him to show more versatility, although he holds fast to his "poor but honest" persona, inspired by Chaplin. Released from jail, Wisdom teams up with crooks to outwit the venal mayor of a northern town. Alfred Marks as the gang boss and Andrew Cruickshank as the mayor are excellent foils. DM

Norman Wisdom *Davy Cooper* • Alfred Marks *Adolf Carter* • Andrew Cruickshank *McKillup* • Reginald Beckwith *Station master* • Susannah York *Ellen* • Jean Clarke *Freda* • Timothy Bateson *Flash Dan* ■ *Dir* Stuart Burge • *Scr* Reuben Ship, from the play *The Odd Legend of Schultz* by James Bridie

There Was a Crooked Man... ★★ 15

Western 1970 · US · Colour · 118mins

Kirk Douglas and Henry Fonda – actors as different in style and persona as could be – are pitted against each other in this period crime movie with a western flavour. Douglas is a tough outlaw who escapes from jail and goes in search of his hidden booty; Fonda is the gentle sheriff-turned-prison warden who pursues Douglas in the hope of rehabilitating him. The movie promises much, but delivers little. RK

Kirk Douglas *Paris Pitman Jr* • Henry Fonda *Woodward Lopeman* • Hume Cronyn *Dudley Whinner* • Warren Oates *Floyd Moon* • Burgess Meredith *The Missouri Kid* • John Randolph *Cyrus McNutt* • Arthur O'Connell *Mr Lomax* ■ *Dir* Joseph L Mankiewicz • *Scr* David Newman, Robert Benton, from the story *Prison Story* by David Newman, Robert Benton

There Was a Father ★★★★

Drama 1942 · Jpn · BW · 94mins

Filmed in accordance with wartime strictures and reminiscent of his earlier drama, *The Only Son*, this remains among Yasujiro Ozu's most unusual pictures, with its broad narrative span and diversity of setting standing in contrast to his more typically intense insularity. Its essential themes are patriarchy and patriotism. But the story of widowed Chishu Ryu's self-sacrificing devotion to his son also contains an element of Buddhist passivity, as each endures the pain of separation to make the best of their limited opportunities. Making symbolic use of train journeys and fishing trips, Ozu brings a human touch to the prescribed topic of tradition. DP. In Japanese with English subtitles.

Chishu Ryu *Shuhei Horikawa* • Shuji Sano *Ryohei, Horikawa's son* • Mitsuko Mito *Fumiko* • Takeshi Sakamoto *Makota Hirata* • Shin Saburi *Yasutaro Kurokawa* ■ *Dir* Yasujiro Ozu • *Scr* Tadao Ikeda, Takao Yanai

There Was Once a Cop ★★★

Comedy thriller 1969 · Fr · Colour · 95mins

The enduring partnership of director Georges Lautner and the dazzling Mireille Darc dashed off another slick comedy thriller with this often hilarious tale of the bachelor cop who takes on a fake family to help nail Nice's biggest drugs-ring. But what are gangsters, corrupt cops, the CIA and the Mafia when there's a little horror like Hervé Hillien to contend with? He is brattishly brilliant as Darc's lawless son and his exchanges with Michel Constantin are astutely scripted and briskly played. DP. French dialogue dubbed into English.

Michel Constantin *Inspector* • Mireille Darc *"Wife"* • Hervé Hillien *"Son"* • Michel Lonsdale ■ *Dir* Georges Lautner • *Scr* Georges Lautner, Francis Veber, from a book by Richard Caron

Theremin: an Electronic Odyssey ★★★★

Music documentary
1993 · US · Colour · 78mins

An informative and absorbing documentary, charting the life of Russian emigré Leon Theremin – inventor of the musical instrument used to make the eerie noises on such films as *The Day the Earth Stood Still*, *Spellbound* and *It Came from Outer Space* – and how he influenced the course of popular culture. Beach Boy Brian Wilson talks about the creation of the pop hit *Good Vibrations*, Robert Moog (inventor of the Moog synthesizer) credits him with launching the era of electronic music in 1920, and virtuoso player Clara Rockmore (Theremin's protégée) demonstrates the range of the instrument in performance. Director Steven M Martin hits the right notes of whimsy and dramatic insight, revealing political secrets from Theremin's life and the profound impact his other inventions had on society. AJ

Dir/Scr Steven M Martin

There's a Girl in My Soup ★★ 15

Comedy 1970 · UK · Colour · 91mins

This very tame sex comedy ran and ran on both sides of the Atlantic. Roy Boulting directs without much enthusiasm for his tale of womanising TV celebrity Peter Sellers, who is knocked off his stride by a chance encounter with dippy waif Goldie Hawn. Content to cruise through his meagre helping of wisecracks, the miscast Sellers still teams well with Hawn, who also has some funny scenes with ditched boyfriend Nicky Henson. DP. Contains swearing. DVD

Peter Sellers *Robert Danvers* • Goldie Hawn *Marion* • Tony Britton *Andrew Hunter* • Nicky Henson *Jimmy* • John Comer *John* • Diana Dors *John's wife* • Gabrielle Drake *Julia Halforde-Smythe* • Geraldine Sherman *Caroline* • Judy Campbell *Lady Heather* • Nicola Pagett *Clare* ■ *Dir* Roy Boulting • *Scr* Terence Frisby, Peter Kortner, from a play by Terence Frisby

There's Always a Woman ★★★

Detective crime comedy
1938 · US · BW · 82mins

Private eye Melvyn Douglas is hired by Mary Astor for a routine investigation that soon escalates into a murder case. His wife, Joan Blondell, an enthusiastic and charmingly meddlesome amateur sleuth, involves herself and beats her husband to the solution. Directed by Alexander Hall from a zany script, with Blondell the standout in an excellent cast. RK

Joan Blondell *Sally Reardon* • Melvyn Douglas *William Reardon* • Mary Astor *Lola Fraser* • Frances Drake *Anne Calhoun* • Jerome Cowan *Nick Shane* • Rita Hayworth *Ketterling's secretary* ■ *Dir* Alexander Hall • *Scr* Gladys Lehman, Joel Sayre, Philip Rapp, Morrie Ryskind, from a short story by Wilson Collison

There's Always Tomorrow ★★

Melodrama 1956 · US · BW · 84mins

Fred MacMurray is the model husband who feels that he is taken for granted by his family. The reappearance of old flame Barbara Stanwyck revitalises him and he dreams of starting a new life with her. His wife Joan Bennett remains blissfully unaware of the situation, but it's not long before his children sense that something is going on. Douglas Sirk directs and Stanwyck is terrific, but the soap opera fails to ignite due to a dull screenplay. RK

Barbara Stanwyck *Norma Miller* • Fred MacMurray *Clifford Groves* • Joan Bennett *Marion Groves* • Pat Crowley *Ann* • William Reynolds *Vinnie Groves* • Gigi Perreau *Ellen Groves* • Judy Nugent *Frankie Groves* ■ *Dir* Douglas Sirk • *Scr* Bernard C Schoenfeld, from a story by Ursula Parrott

There's No Business like Show Business ★★★★ U

Musical 1954 · US · Colour · 112mins

The title was so long it filled the CinemaScope screen and that was exactly what 20th Century-Fox intended, to show off its new (and then virtually exclusive) letterbox screen process. Fox also crammed this musical with as many stars as possible, adding zest to its hokey old "Broadway family" plot. The story rarely matters in this kind of film, though this does take a dive when "Prince of Wails" Johnnie Ray, shows a serious inclination towards the priesthood. Marilyn Marilyn hangs out with Donald O'Connor, while Ethel Merman, Dan Dailey and Mitzi Gaynor are all in good voice. TS DVD

Ethel Merman *Molly Donahue* • Donald O'Connor *Tim Donahue* • Marilyn Monroe *Vicky* • Dan Dailey *Terrance Donahue* • Johnnie Ray *Steve Donahue* • Mitzi Gaynor *Katy Donahue* • Richard Eastham *Lew Harris* • Hugh O'Brian *Charles Gibbs* ■ *Dir* Walter Lang • *Scr* Phoebe Ephron, Henry Ephron, from a story by Lamar Trotti

There's One Born Every Minute ★★ U

Comedy 1942 · US · BW · 59mins

Veteran comic actors Hugh Herbert, Guy Kibbee and Edgar Kennedy get what mileage they can from a plot which has Herbert as a small-town pudding manufacturer whose secret ingredient, Vitamin Z, puts "Zumph" into his product and gets him elected mayor. The Universal production's one claim to cinematic fame is that it was the screen debut of ten-year-old Elizabeth Taylor. The studio dropped Taylor shortly afterwards and its casting director spent the rest of his life living down his verdict on the young star: "The kid has nothing." TV

Hugh Herbert *Lemuel P Twine/Ghost of Abner Twine/Ghost of Claudius Twine* • Peggy Moran *Helen Barbara Twine* • Tom Brown *Jimmie Hanagan* • Guy Kibbee *Lester Cadwalader Sr* • Catharine Doucet [Catherine Doucet] *Minerva Twine* • Elizabeth Taylor *Gloria Ann Twine* • Carl "Alfalfa" Switzer *Junior Twine* ■ *Dir* Harold Young • *Scr* Robert B Hunt, Brenda Weisberg, from the story *Man or Mouse* by Robert B Hunt

There's Only One Jimmy Grimble ★★★ 12

Sports drama 2000 · UK/Fr · Colour · 101mins

In this feel-good fantasy football yarn, Lewis McKenzie plays Manchester teen Jimmy, a budding George Best, but only in the privacy of practice. Play him in a game and he's tackled by lack of confidence. Then an old crone gifts him a pair of "magic" football boots, and McKenzie is soon inspiring his school to the finals of the inter-school championships. With big guns Robert Carlyle (as his sports teacher) and Ray Winstone (as an ardent suitor in a subplot involving Jimmy's single mum), this has moments that are corny, clunky and crass, but it's still hard to dislike. DA DVD

Robert Carlyle *Eric Wirral* • Ray Winstone *Harry* • Gina McKee *Donna* • Lewis McKenzie *Jimmy Grimble* • Jane Lapotaire *Alice Brewer* ■ *Dir* John Hay • *Scr* Simon Mayle, John Hay, Rik Carmichael, from a story by Simon Mayle

There's Something about Mary ★★★★ 15

Romantic comedy
1998 · US · Colour · 114mins

Those kings of bad taste Peter and Bobby Farrelly (*Dumb and Dumber*, *Kingpin*) surpassed themselves with this defiantly non-PC but wickedly funny Hollywood smash. Ben Stiller plays a writer who, 13 years later, is still obsessed by his prom date, Cameron Diaz, even though the occasion ended in disaster. The problem is that a queue of fellow misfits have also fallen under her spell, including British comic Lee Evans and the seedy private eye (Matt Dillon) Stiller hired to find her. With gags about the mentally and physically disabled, dead dogs and serial killers, not to mention the now infamous "hair gel" scene, this is unwholesome entertainment for older members of the family. JF. Contains swearing, sexual references. DVD

Cameron Diaz *Mary Jenson* • Matt Dillon *Pat Healy* • Ben Stiller *Ted Stroehmann* • Lin Shaye *Magda* • Lee Evans *Tucker* • Chris Elliott *Dom* • Jonathan Richman *Jonathan* • Jeffrey Tambor *Sully* • Markie Post *Mary's mom* ■ *Dir* Peter Farrelly, Bobby Farrelly • *Scr* Peter Farrelly, Bobby Farrelly, Ed Decter, John J Strauss, from a story by Ed Decter, John J Strauss

Thérèse ★★★★ PG

Drama 1986 · Fr · Colour · 91mins

Taking a leaf out of Robert Bresson's stark book, director Alain Cavalier has created a film that has the purity and simplicity of its subject – the devout life of Thérèse Martin spent as a Carmelite nun in the convent at Lisieux. Thérèse, who was canonised in 1924, is serenely played by stage actress Catherine Mouchet from the age of 15 until her death of TB, aged 24, in 1897. Cavalier presents the story in a series of tableaux that recount, with little dialogue and action, the everyday existence of the nuns, without preaching or religiosity. RB. A French language film.

Catherine Mouchet *Thérèse Martin* • Aurore Prieto *Celine* • Sylvia Habault *Pauline* • Ghislaine Mona *Marie* • Hélène Alexandridis *Lucie* ■ *Dir* Alain Cavalier • *Scr* Alain Cavalier, Camille de Casabianca

Thérèse Desqueyroux ★★★★

Drama 1962 · Fr · BW · 107mins

Emmanuelle Riva won the Best Actress prize at Venice for her controlled portrayal of a bored provincial poisoner in this faithful adaptation of François Mauriac's novel. Director Georges Franju was attacked by contemporary critics for adhering so closely to the text, yet with its stately pace, flashback structure, steely detachment, enigmatic characterisation and minimalist performances, this is an unnerving Bressonian study in both the ennui that sets Riva against her husband, Philippe Noiret, and the unquestioning charity that prompts his family to forgive her. DP. In French with English subtitles.

Emmanuelle Riva *Thérèse Desqueyroux* • Philippe Noiret *Bernard Desqueyroux* • Edith Scob *Anne de la Trave* • Sami Frey *Jean Azevedo* • Renée Devillers *Mme de la Trave* • Richard Saint-Bris *Hector de la Trave* • Lucien Nat *Jérôme Larroque* ■ *Dir* Georges Franju • *Scr* Georges Franju, Claude Mauriac, François Mauriac, from his novel

Thérèse Raquin ★★★★

Crime drama 1953 · Fr · BW · 100mins

Marcel Carné updates the action of Emile Zola's dark psychological novel and relocates it to the backstreets of Lyons. However, all the naturalistic intensity of the original has been retained, as frustrated housewife Simone Signoret and trucker Raf Vallone suffer much more than pangs of conscience after they murder her husband. The deterioration of their relationship is charted with a lyrical realism that often approaches vintage Carné. Sylvie is superb as the mute mother-in-law, watching their torment with malicious satisfaction. DP. In French with English subtitles.

Simone Signoret *Thérèse Raquin* • Raf Vallone *Laurent* • Jacques Duby *Camille Raquin* • Roland Lesaffre *The sailor* • Sylvie *Mme Raquin* ■ *Dir* Marcel Carné • *Scr* Charles Spaak, Marcel Carné, from the novel by Emile Zola

These Foolish Things ★★★★ PG

Drama 1990 · Fr · Colour · 102mins

A nicely underplayed domestic drama from top French director Bertrand Tavernier. Jane Birkin plays a screenwriter who returns home to re-establish her interrupted relationship with her dying dad Dirk Bogarde. The film follows them as they work out their differences, reminisce about times past, and restore mutual respect and understanding. Smashing stuff, very moving, with terrific performances from the two leads. DA. A French language film. [VIDEO]

Dirk Bogarde *Daddy* • Jane Birkin *Caroline* • Odette Laure *Miche* • Emmanuelle Bataille *Juliette* • Charlotte Kady *Barbara* ■ *Dir* Bertrand Tavernier • *Scr* Colo Tavernier

These Old Broads ★★

Comedy 2001 · US · Colour · 100mins

The producers must have thought they were on to a winner when they succeeded in assembling the superstellar cast for this TV-movie comedy. But the harder the veteran quartet tries, the more their schtick begins to grate. As the ageing starlets forced to reunite after the reissue of their 1960s movie becomes a hit, Shirley MacLaine, Debbie Reynolds and Joan Collins sportingly throw themselves into the bitching and hoofing. But Elizabeth Taylor merely settles for hamming it up as the bickering trio's conniving agent. DP

Shirley MacLaine *Kate Westbourne* • Joan Collins *Addie Holden* • Debbie Reynolds *Piper Grayson* • Elizabeth Taylor *Beryl Mason* • Jonathan Silverman *Wesley Westbourne* • Peter Graves (2) *Bill* • Gene Barry *Mr Stern* ■ *Dir* Matthew Diamond • *Scr* Carrie Fisher, Elaine Pope

These Thousand Hills ★★

Western 1959 · US · Colour · 95mins

This is a solid 20th Century-Fox western featuring a long list of contract players, having been made toward the end of the studio contract system. It's a long-winded saga about a cowboy's loyalties and responsibilities, but talented director Richard Fleischer seems at a loss as to how to present the story with any degree of dynamism. TS

Don Murray *Lat Evans* • Richard Egan *Jehu* • Lee Remick *Callie* • Patricia Owens *Joyce* • Stuart Whitman *Tom Ping* • Albert Dekker *Conrad* • Harold J Stone *Ram Butler* ■ *Dir* Richard Fleischer • *Scr* Alfred Hayes, from the novel by AB Guthrie Jr

These Three ★★★ U

Drama 1936 · US · BW · 88mins

Time hasn't been kind to this fine adaptation of Lillian Hellman's play *The Children's Hour*. Deprived of its original sinister title, and with all references to lesbianism removed by the censors of the day, this still offers a stronger impact than the 1961 remake with Audrey Hepburn and Shirley MacLaine, which was also directed by William Wyler. What keeps this tale riveting is the superbly skilled portrayal by child actress Bonita Granville as the little horror who spreads the initial lie, and the well-matched teaming of Merle Oberon and Miriam Hopkins as the schoolteachers involved. TS [VIDEO]

Miriam Hopkins *Martha Dobie* • Merle Oberon *Karen Wright* • Joel McCrea *Dr Joseph Cardin* • Catherine Doucet *Mrs Lily Mortar* • Alma Kruger *Mrs Tilford* • Bonita Granville *Mary Tilford* ■ *Dir* William Wyler • *Scr* Lillian Hellman, from her play *The Children's Hour*

These Wilder Years ★★

Drama 1956 · US · BW · 90mins

It's a shame that two such powerful performers as Barbara Stanwyck and James Cagney met so late in their careers on such a mushy little picture. Directed with dull restraint, this old-fashioned weepie has unmarried millionaire Cagney trying to persuade Stanwyck, the head of a children's home, to reveal the whereabouts of the illegitimate son he handed over for adoption years before. AE

James Cagney *Steve Bradford* • Barbara Stanwyck *Ann Dempster* • Walter Pidgeon *James Rayburn* • Betty Lou Keim *Suzie* • Don Dubbins *Mark* • Edward Andrews *Mr Spottsford* • Basil Ruysdael *Judge* • Dean Jones *Hardware clerk* • Tom Laughlin *Football player* ■ *Dir* Roy Rowland • *Scr* Frank Fenton, from a story by Ralph Wheelwright

They ★★★ 15

Psychological horror thriller
2002 · US · Colour · 85mins

Director Robert Harmon returns to form with this nervy horror that makes up for a lack of originality with its dream-like style and tense atmosphere. Revolving around the monster-in-the-closet nightmares of childhood, it follows ambitious student Laura Regan and her pals as they're terrorised by inhuman creatures that materialise when the lights go out. Harmon harnesses the power of imagination, creating fear by suggestion with creepy sound effects and shadowy visuals. The end result is basic and manipulative, but also ruthlessly effective. SF [VIDEO] DVD

Laura Regan *Julia Lund* • Marc Blucas *Paul* • Ethan Embry *Sam* • Dagmara Dominczyk *Terry* • Jon Abrahams *Billy* • Wanda Cannon *Mrs Levin* • Desiree Zurowski *Mary Parks* ■ *Dir* Robert Harmon • *Scr* Brendan William Hood

They All Kissed the Bride ★★ U

Romantic comedy 1942 · US · BW · 87mins

An unexceptional and rather long-winded Joan Crawford comedy in which she spends much of the time arguing with, and ultimately romancing, reporter Melvyn Douglas. Crawford copes well enough with her bossy-boots role, but her character isn't likeable, and as a result the film isn't very watchable, despite sterling support from the likes of Roland Young and Billie Burke. Director Alexander Hall does what he can, but this is no *Philadelphia Story*, to which it rather obviously aspires. TS

Joan Crawford *Margaret J "Maggie" Drew* • Melvyn Douglas *Michael Holmes* • Roland Young *Marsh* • Billie Burke *Mrs Drew* • Allen Jenkins *Johnny Johnson* • Andrew Tombes *Crane* ■ *Dir* Alexander Hall • *Scr* PJ Wolfson, Andrew P Solt, Henry Altimus, from a story by Gina Kaus, Andrew P Solt

They All Laughed ★★★★

Comedy 1981 · US · Colour · 115mins

A stylish and splendidly wacky comedy about detectives who can't help getting involved with the women they are tailing. It's important as a late Audrey Hepburn entry, and she looks as lovely as ever, co-starring here with Ben Gazzara on wonderfully evocative New York locations. Director Peter Bogdanovich, seriously under-rated these days, pulls it all together with great élan, aided by a quirky cast. There's a morbid interest in watching murdered centrefold Dorothy Stratten, directed by lover Bogdanovich. She died before the film came out. TS

Audrey Hepburn *Angela Niotes* • Ben Gazzara *John Russo* • John Ritter *Charles Rutledge* • Colleen Camp *Christy Miller* • Patti Hansen *Deborah "Sam" Wilson* • Dorothy Stratten *Dolores Martin* ■ *Dir/Scr* Peter Bogdanovich

They Call Me Bruce ★★★ 15

Martial arts action comedy
1982 · US · Colour · 89mins

A naive Chinese cook in Los Angeles is unaware that the restaurant in which he works is run by the local Mafia. Modelling himself on his hero Bruce Lee, for whom he is often mistaken, the lad enrols in a local kung fu school and makes headlines when he defeats a gang of thieves in a fight. Noting his prowess, his gangster bosses dupe him into becoming a drug courier. This is a likeable martial arts/ganster movie spoof, with Johnny Yune excellent as Bruce. An equally smart sequel followed in 1987. DF [VIDEO]

Johnny Yune *Bruce* • Bill Capizzi *Lil Pete* • Martin Azarow *Big Al* • Tony Brande *Boss of Bosses* • Ralph Mauro *Freddy* • Pam Huntington *Anita* • John Fujioka *Master* • Margaux Hemingway *Karmen* • Bill Kirchenbauer *Polish Killer* ■ *Dir* Elliott Hong • *Scr* Johnny Yune, Elliott Hong, Tim Clawson, David Randolph

They Call Me Mister Tibbs! ★★★ 15

Police thriller 1970 · US · Colour · 105mins

With the emphasis on the Mister, it's Sidney Poitier, back again as the black detective after his love-hate relationship with sheriff Rod Steiger worked so well in *In the Heat of the Night*. This time he's investigating the killing of a hooker who was close to his friend Martin Landau, and the usual clichés about a cop's fraught domestic life form a counterpoint to the main action. Poitier is impressive in his ruthless integrity, but the film misses the character contrast of the original. TH. Contains violence and swearing. [VIDEO] DVD

Sidney Poitier *Virgil Tibbs* • Martin Landau *Reverend Logan Sharpe* • Barbara McNair *Valerie Tibbs* • Anthony Zerbe *Rice Weedon* • Jeff Corey *Captain Marden* • David Sheiner *Herbert Kenner* • Juano Hernandez *Mealie* • Norma Crane *Marge Garfield* • Edward Asner *Woody Garfield* ■ *Dir* Gordon Douglas • *Scr* Alan R Trustman, James R Webb, from a story by Alan R Trustman, from the character created by John Ball

They Call Me Trinity ★★★ PG

Spaghetti western comedy
1970 · It · Colour · 105mins

This successful spaghetti western made international superstars out of B-movie Italian actors Carlo Pedersoli (Bud Spencer) and Mario Girotti (Terence Hill). They play trouble-making brothers leading a group of Mormans against an outlaw band in journeyman director Enzo Barboni's easy-going cowboy comedy geared around slapstick saloon brawls, romantic farce and pratfall stunts. Lightweight, unpretentious and amiable fun. Followed by a number of sequels, including *Trinity Is Still My Name*. AJ. Italian dialogue dubbed into English. [VIDEO] DVD

Terence Hill *Trinity* • Bud Spencer *Bambino* • Farley Granger *Major Harriman* • Remo Capitani *Mezcal* • Elena Pedemonte *Judith* ■ *Dir/Scr* EB Clucher [Enzo Barboni]

They Came from beyond Space ★★

Science-fiction thriller
1967 · UK · Colour · 85mins

A pallid attempt by Hammer rivals Amicus to rehash some of the thematic lines from the *Quatermass* series. Astral invaders take over a Cornish factory to enslave Earthlings so they'll repair a spaceship that has crashed on the moon. Fortunately, astrophysicist Robert Hutton has a metal plate in his head, which makes him immune from alien control, and he single-handedly combats the evil extraterrestrials, led by stalwart genre icon Michael Gough. AJ

Robert Hutton *Dr Curtis Temple* • Jennifer Jayne *Lee Mason* • Michael Gough *Monj* • Zia Mohyeddin *Dr Farge* • Geoffrey Wallace *Alan Mullane* • Bernard Kay *Richard Arden* ■ *Dir* Freddie Francis • *Scr* Milton Subotsky, from the novel *The Gods Hate Kansas* by Joseph Millard

They Came to Cordura ★★★★ PG

Period drama 1959 · US · Colour · 118mins

This grim but satisfying drama stars a gaunt Gary Cooper as an army major accused of cowardice during an expedition against Pancho Villa in 1916 Mexico. Cooper can only avoid

T

disgrace if he recommends five men from his regiment who are worthy of receiving the Congressional Medal of Honor. There's a magnificent line-up of co-stars, including Rita Hayworth, but none of the characters they portray emerges with much credit as director Robert Rossen examines issues of bravery and cowardice. The location photography is stunning and the overall effect richly rewarding. TS DVD

Gary Cooper *Major Thomas Thorn* • Rita Hayworth *Adelaide Geary* • Van Heflin *Sergeant John Chawk* • Tab Hunter *Lieutenant William Fowler* • Richard Conte *Corporal Milo Trubee* • Michael Callan *Private Andrew Hetherington* ■ *Dir* Robert Rossen • *Scr* Ivan Moffat, Robert Rossen, from the novel by Glendon F Swarthout • *Cinematographer* Burnett Guffey

They Came to Rob Las Vegas ★★

Action thriller
1968 · It/Sp/ Fr/W Ger · Colour · 99mins

After his brother is killed during a Las Vegas heist, Gary Lockwood plans to do the job right. With a little help from Elke Sommer, he robs a heavily armoured truck, but agent Jack Palance is soon on his trail. Although let down slightly by some stiff dialogue, the film boasts a rock-solid cast and is a slick and ingenious computer-age thriller with a suggestion of humanity versus technology. JG

Gary Lockwood *Tony* • Elke Sommer *Anne* • Lee J Cobb *Skorsky* • Jack Palance *Douglas* • Jean Servais *Gino* • Roger Hanin *Boss* • Georges Geret *Leroy* ■ *Dir* Antonio Isasi • *Scr* Antonio Isasi, J Eisinger, L Comeron, J Illa

They Can't Hang Me ★★

Spy drama 1955 · UK · BW · 66mins

The themes of atomic secrets and double agents may have lost some of their resonance, but director Val Guest puts a neat spin on events by having condemned killer André Morell strike a death row deal with cop Terence Morgan to deliver a treacherous scientist in return for leniency. The back-up cast is as solid as a rock, with Guest's wife Yolande Donlan putting in an effective appearance. DP

Terence Morgan *Inspector Brown* • Yolande Donlan *Jill* • André Morell *Robert Pitt* • Ursula Howells *Antonia Pitt* • Anthony Oliver *Newcome* • Reginald Beckwith *Harold* ■ *Dir* Val Guest • *Scr* Val Guest, Val Valentine, from a novel by Leonard Mosley

They Crawl ★★ 15

Horror 2001 · US · Colour · 89mins

Convinced his wacko student brother's fireball death isn't an accident (the missing internal organs being something of a giveaway), Daniel Cosgrove teams with detective Tamara Davies to investigate. Cue army of genetically modified cockroaches developed for the US military. Director John Allardice sets up the insect attacks with mechanical proficiency, but this is worth seeing only for Mickey Rourke's eccentric turn – and that's not a recommendation. DP DVD

Daniel Cosgrove *Ted Cage* • Tamara Davies *Gina O'Bannon* • Dennis Boutsikaris *Professor* • Grace Zabriskie *Ted's mother* • Mickey Rourke *Tiny* • Tim Thomerson *Exterminator* • Tone Loc *Clarence* ■ *Dir* John Allardice • *Scr* Joseph Curtis, David Mason

They Dare Not Love ★★ U

Second World War romantic drama
1941 · US · BW · 75mins

This wartime propaganda movie was a disappointing swansong for director James Whale (he later directed a segment of the unreleased portmanteau film *Hello Out There*). A clichéd romantic drama, it stars George Brent as an Austrian playboy prince and Martha Scott as a Viennese girl, both fleeing the Nazis. They fall in love on board the ship taking them to America, but her father forbids marriage and they go their separate ways. Later they meet again. RK

George Brent *Prince Kurt von Rotenburg* • Martha Scott *Marta Keller* • Paul Lukas *Baron von Helsing* • Egon Brecher *Professor Keller* • Roman Bohnen *Baron Shafter* • Edgar Barrier *Captain Wilhelm Ehrhardt* • Lloyd Bridges *Blonde officer* ■ *Dir* James Whale, Charles Vidor • *Scr* Charles Bennett, Ernest Vajda, from a story by James Edward Grant

They Died with Their Boots On ★★★★ U

Biographical western
1941 · US · BW · 134mins

Errol Flynn stars in this rip-roaring biopic as General George Armstrong Custer, who works his way up the ranks and dies heroically at the Battle of the Little Bighorn. History is cast to the wind as Flynn's hero becomes sympathetic to the Indian cause, while Mrs Custer (Olivia de Havilland) fusses about trying to get her husband to settle down. Cast as Custer's chief adversary Crazy Horse is Anthony Quinn, who said of his director, Raoul Walsh, "He was the least technical director I knew, but he relished the process with such a fire that I could almost taste it with him." AT

Errol Flynn *George Armstrong Custer* • Olivia de Havilland *Elizabeth Libby Bacon* • Arthur Kennedy *Ned Sharp* • Charley Grapewin *California Joe* • Gene Lockhart *Samuel Bacon, Esq* • Anthony Quinn *Crazy Horse* • Stanley Ridges *Major Romulus Taipe* • John Litel *General Phil Sheridan* • Walter Hampden *William Sharp* • Sydney Greenstreet *Lt Gen Winfield Scott* • Regis Toomey *Fitzhugh Lee* • Hattie McDaniel *Callie* ■ *Dir* Raoul Walsh • *Scr* Wally Klein, Aeneas MacKenzie

They Drive by Night ★★★★ PG

Drama 1940 · US · BW · 91mins

A knockout cast stars in a "love and glory" saga of life among long-distance truck drivers on the Frisco Road. The movie neatly snaps into two thematically linked halves: the first a tale of perils on the road, the second a virtual reworking of Warner Bros' earlier *Bordertown*, with George Raft and Ida Lupino in the old Paul Muni/ Bette Davis roles. Co-stars Humphrey Bogart and sizzling Ann Sheridan also draw the attention in a crackingly directed film from Raoul Walsh. Lupino is superb, and the dialogue as crisp as it comes. TS DVD

George Raft *Joe Fabrini* • Ann Sheridan *Cassie Hartley* • Ida Lupino *Lana Carlsen* • Humphrey Bogart *Paul Fabrini* • Gale Page *Pearl Fabrini* • Alan Hale *Ed J Carlsen* • Roscoe Karns *"Irish" McGurn* ■ *Dir* Raoul Walsh • *Scr* Jerry Wald, Richard Macaulay, from the novel *The Long Haul* by Al Bezzerides

They Flew Alone ★★ U

Biographical drama 1941 · UK · BW · 107mins

This is producer/director Herbert Wilcox's version of the life of pioneer female flier Amy Johnson. Anna Neagle plays Johnson with vim and vigour, while her playboy husband is portrayed by Robert Newton as little more than an alcoholic co-pilot. Johnson perished in a plane crash in the Thames Estuary in 1941, and Wilcox's device of having the character return from beyond the grave to deliver a patriotic wartime sermon now seems mawkish. TS

Anna Neagle *Amy Johnson* • Robert Newton *Jim Mollison* • Edward Chapman *Mr Johnson* • Joan Kemp-Welch *Mrs Johnson* • Nora Swinburne *ATA commandant* ■ *Dir* Herbert Wilcox • *Scr* Miles Malleson, from the story by Lord Castlerosse

They Gave Him a Gun ★★★

Drama 1937 · US · BW · 93mins

Young First World War recruit Franchot Tone is so sickened by the idea of killing a man wants to go AWOL. But, propped up by his friend Spencer Tracy, he turns into a gun-happy hero. Later he carries the weaponry and new attitude into civilian life to become a mobster. WS Van Dyke directs this interesting melodrama with a pacifist and anti-crime message, and a love story that involves both men committed to the same girl (Gladys George). Quite absorbing, despite a few credibility gaps. RK

Spencer Tracy *Fred Willis* • Gladys George *Rose Duffy* • Franchot Tone *Jimmy Davis* • Edgar Dearing *Sgt Meadowlark* • Mary Lou Treen [Mary Treen] *Saxe* • Cliff Edwards *Laro* ■ *Dir* WS Van Dyke II [WS Van Dyke] • *Scr* Cyril Hume, Richard Maibaum, Maurice Rapf, from the novel by William Joyce

They Got Me Covered ★★★ U

Second World War comedy
1943 · US · BW · 89mins

Only Bing Crosby was missing from this wartime flag-waver that might otherwise have been called *The Road to Victory*. Bob Hope zings his way through a generous ration of wisecracks, as he and Dorothy Lamour root out Otto Preminger and his fellow Nazis. Screenwriter Harry Kurnitz, who was something of a dab hand at both comedies and thrillers, adeptly judges the mix of suspense and silliness, leaving director David Butler with little to do but keep up the tempo and show off the lavish sets. DP

Bob Hope *Robert "Kit" Kittredge* • Dorothy Lamour *Christina Hill* • Lenore Aubert *Mrs Vanescu, assumed name of Olga* • Otto Preminger *Otto Fauscheim* • Edward Ciannelli [Eduardo Ciannelli] *Baldanacco* • Marion Martin *Gloria, The "Glow Girl"* • Donald Meek *Little old man* • Phyllis Ruth *Sally Branch* ■ *Dir* David Butler • *Scr* Harry Kurnitz, Arthur Kober, Frank Fenton, Lynn Root, Don Hartman (uncredited), from a story by Leonard Q Ross, Leonard Spigelgass

They Had to See Paris ★★★

Comedy 1929 · US · BW · 96mins

When simple Oklahoma family man Will Rogers unexpectedly strikes oil and comes into a great deal of money, his wife Irene Rich develops delusions of grandeur. She drags the family to Paris, buys a chateau, tries to marry off her daughter Marguerite Churchill to a title, and battles to transform her husband from hick to gentleman. Rogers, America's favourite homespun philosopher and wit, entered talkies in this comedy, with director Frank Borzage pressing the laughter buttons as well as he does the tear ducts. RK

Will Rogers *Pike Peters* • Irene Rich *Mrs Peters* • Owen Davis Jr *Ross Peters* • Marguerite Churchill *Opal Peters* • Fifi D'Orsay *Claudine* ■ *Dir* Frank Borzage • *Scr* Sonya Levien, from a novel by Homer Croy

They Knew Mr Knight ★★

Drama 1945 · UK · BW · 101mins

Insurance clerk Mervyn Johns is content to struggle along until he's persuaded to invest in a sure-fire speculation by financier Alfred Drayton. His unexpected wealth goes to the family's head and, when the deal proves to have been a swindle, Drayton commits suicide and Johns is jailed for deception. Director Norman Walker rather wallows in this glum middle-class morality tale. But he prudently cashes in on Johns's fretful features and the solid support provided by Nora Swinburne and Joan Greenwood, as his wife and self-sacrificing daughter. DP

Mervyn Johns *Thomas* • Nora Swinburne *Celia* • Joyce Howard *Freda* • Joan Greenwood *Ruth* • Peter Hammond *Douglas* • Marie Ault *Grandma* • Alfred Drayton *Mr Knight* ■ *Dir* Norman Walker • *Scr* Victor MacLure, Norman Walker, from the novel *They Knew Mr Knight* by Dorothy Whipple

They Knew What They Wanted ★★

Drama 1940 · US · BW · 88mins

Charles Laughton stars as an Italian-American winemaker who cons pen pal waitress Carole Lombard into marriage by sending her a picture not of himself, but of his beefcake employee, William Gargan. The plan backfires when Lombard falls in love with Gargan. It's like a French farce transplanted to the Napa Valley, but it isn't played for laughs. AT

Carole Lombard *Amy Peters* • Charles Laughton *Tony Patucci* • William Gargan *Joe* • Harry Carey *Doctor* • Frank Fay *Father McKee* • Joe Bernard [Joseph Bernard] *RFD* • Janet Fox *Mildred* • Lee Tung-Foo *Ah Gee* • Karl Malden *Red* ■ *Dir* Garson Kanin • *Scr* Robert Ardrey, from the play by Sidney Howard

They Live ★★★ 18

Science-fiction thriller
1988 · US · Colour · 93mins

A return to his B-movie roots for John Carpenter, this is a knockabout salute to the alien invasion movies of the 1950s. Wrestler-turned-actor Roddy Piper is the working-class hero who, on finding a special pair of sunglasses, discovers that alien-like creatures appear to have taken over Los Angeles and are controlling the remaining human residents with subliminal advertising. There's a nicely relaxed feel to Carpenter's direction and he keeps the action roaring along, stopping only to take a few satirical swipes at yuppie life. JF. Contains violence, swearing. DVD

Roddy Piper *Nada* • Keith David *Frank* • Meg Foster *Holly Thompson* • George "Buck" Flower *Drifter* • Peter Jason *Gilbert* • Raymond St Jacques *Street preacher* • Jason Robards III *Family man* ■ *Dir* John Carpenter • *Scr* Frank Armitage [John Carpenter], from the short story *Eight O'Clock in the Morning* by Ray Nelson

They Live by Night ★★★★

Film noir romance 1948 · US · BW · 95mins

Nicholas Ray made his directorial debut with this Depression-era drama of young lovers on the run from the law, who find themselves staring into the abyss. Cathy O'Donnell and Farley Granger play the misfits who meet in the aftermath of a prison break-out. They fall in love and marry, but Granger is unable to shake off his criminal associations, leaving little prospect of a happy ending. This is a poignant story of idealism and romanticism betrayed by corruption, and a stunning debut from a future cult director. PF

Farley Granger *Bowie* • Cathy O'Donnell *Keechie* • Howard Da Silva *Chickamaw* • Jay C Flippen *T- Dub* • Helen Craig *Mattie* • Will Wright *Mobley* • Marie Bryant *Singer* • Ian Wolfe *Hawkins* ■ *Dir* Nicholas Ray • *Scr* Charles Schnee, Nicholas Ray, from the novel *Thieves Like Us* by Edward Anderson

They Made Me a Criminal ★★★ PG

Drama 1939 · US · BW · 87mins

John Garfield stars as a hard-boiled boxing champion on the run from what he believes is a murder rap in this rollicking tale that goes at breakneck pace and contains strong, well-played performances from the likes of Gloria Dickson, May Robson, Claude Rains and Ann Sheridan. Essentially, it's an ensemble piece, with everyone getting a stab at the limelight. Not to everyone's taste, but admirable for its impudent tone. SH

John Garfield *Johnny Bradfield/"Jack Dorney"* • Gloria Dickson *Peggy* • Claude Rains *Detective Monty Phelan* • Ann Sheridan *Goldie* • May Robson *Gramma* • Billy Halop *Tommy* • Bobby Jordan *Angel* • Leo Gorcey *Spit* • Huntz Hall *Dippy* ■ *Dir* Busby Berkeley • *Scr* Sid Herzig, from the book by Bertram Millhauser, Beulah Marie Dix

They Made Me a Fugitive ★★★

Crime thriller 1947 · UK · BW · 99mins

Alberto Cavalcanti was a Brazilian-born, Swiss-educated architect and lawyer, who went on to direct a number of praised British films, while also turning out this grim, but largely absorbing example of British *film noir*. Trevor Howard leads a strong cast in the story of an ex-RAF pilot for whom things go from bad to worse. PF

Trevor Howard *Clem Morgan* • Sally Gray *Sally* • Griffith Jones *Narcey* • René Ray *Cora* • Mary Merrall *Aggie* • Vida Hope *Mrs Fenshawe* ■ *Dir* Alberto Cavalcanti • *Scr* Noel Langley, from the novel *A Convict Has Escaped* by Jackson Budd

They Met in Bombay ★★★ U

Comedy adventure 1941 · US · BW · 91mins

Rosalind Russell and Clark Gable are rival thieves, both after a priceless necklace belonging to an English duchess in a movie that combines comedy with wartime flag-waving. They work well together in the first half of the film. The second half isn't so good, with Gable going all heroic and winning the Victoria Cross after impersonating a British army officer. AT

Clark Gable *Gerald Meldrick* • Rosalind Russell *Anya Von Duren* • Peter Lorre *Captain Chang* • Jessie Ralph *Duchess Of Beltravers* • Reginald Owen *General* • Matthew Boulton *Inspector Cressney* ■ *Dir* Clarence Brown • *Scr* Edwin Justus Mayer, Anita Loos, Leon Gordon, from a story by John Kafka

They Met in the Dark ★★ U

Mystery spy thriller 1943 · UK · BW · 91mins

Framed by Nazi agents, navy commander James Mason loses his job for accidentally revealing secret information. Determined to clear his name, he goes in search of the woman who set him up, only to find her dead. Joining forces with visiting Canadian Joyce Howard, they set out to unmask theatrical agent Tom Walls whose business is a front for Nazi spies. An old-fashioned, run-of-the-mill and unlikely espionage thriller, topical during the Second World War years, but rather unrewarding now. RK

James Mason *Comdr Richard Heritage* • Joyce Howard *Laura Verity* • Tom Walls *Christopher Child* • Phyllis Stanley *Lily Bernard* • Edward Rigby *Mansel* • Ronald Ward *Carter* • Ian Fleming ■ *Dir* Karel Lamac • *Scr* Anatole de Grunwald, Miles Malleson, Basil Bartlett, Victor McClure, James Seymour, from the novel *The Vanished Corpse* by Anthony Gilbert

They Might Be Giants ★★★ U

Mystery drama 1971 · US · Colour · 85mins

This curio features George C Scott as a New Yorker who thinks he's Sherlock Holmes. Donning the deerstalker, puffing on the pipe and adopting a quizzical look, Scott encounters a psychiatrist, Dr Watson, who declares him to be suffering from classic paranoia. And since this Dr Watson is played by Joanne Woodward, the tale also gains a weird romantic angle. Some may find this silly and sentimental, others a captivating romantic fantasy. Studio cuts certainly don't help matters, but it remains a rarity of some distinction. AT

George C Scott *Justin Playfair* • Joanne Woodward *Dr Mildred Watson* • Jack Gilford *Peabody* • Lester Rawlins *Blevins Playfair* • Rue McClanahan *Daisy* ■ *Dir* Anthony Harvey • *Scr* James Goldman

They Only Kill Their Masters ★★★

Crime mystery 1972 · US · Colour · 97mins

Police chief James Garner has a tough case on his hands: the death of a local divorcee and a suspect who's a dog, a doberman called Murphy. Despite the presence of the amiable Garner and the dog, however, this isn't a cutesy Disney movie, but a rather clever thriller about the sexual shenanigans that go on in a tightly knit coastal community. What's more, it has a cast that is guaranteed to make older film fans happy. AT

James Garner *Police Chief Abel Marsh* • Katharine Ross *Kate* • Hal Holbrook *Watkins* • Harry Guardino *Capt Streeter, sheriff* • June Allyson *Mrs Watkins* • Christopher Connelly *John, cop* • Tom Ewell *Walter, cop* • Peter Lawford *Campbell* • Ann Rutherford *Gloria* ■ *Dir* James Goldstone • *Scr* Lane Slate

They Passed This Way ★★ U

Western 1948 · US · BW · 89mins

A surprisingly low-key western from the short-lived independent Liberty production unit, releasing through Eagle-Lion, co-starring the bland (and married) star couple Joel McCrea and Frances Dee. Veteran Charles Bickford steals the acting honours as the lawman searching for McCrea, but Alfred E Green's direction seems in no hurry to advance the plot. This is almost a "western *noir*" in style. TS

Joel McCrea *Ross McEwen* • Frances Dee *Fay Hollister* • Charles Bickford *Pat Garrett* • Joseph Calleia *Monte Maqrquez* • William Conrad *Sheriff Egan* • Martin Garralaga *Florencio* ■ *Dir* Alfred E Green • *Scr* Graham Baker, Teddi Sherman, from the novel *Paso Por Aqui* by Eugene Manlove Rhodes, adapted by William Brent, Milarde Brent

They Rode West ★★★ U

Western 1954 · US · Colour · 84mins

This exciting western reunites the popular lovers from *The Caine Mutiny*, handsome Robert Francis and lovely May Wynn. The story deals with medical ethics, as medical officer Francis uses his skill to help the Kiowa Indians, to the disgust of the soldiers at his fort. It's directed with skill by Phil Karson, and also stars Donna Reed. Francis, a contemporary of James Dean, was tragically killed at the age of 25 in a plane crash soon after this film was released. TS

Robert Francis *Doctor Allen Seward* • Donna Reed *Laurie MacKaye* • May Wynn *Manyi-ten* • Phil Carey [Philip Carey] *Captain Peter Blake* • Onslow Stevens *Colonel Ethan Waters* ■ *Dir* Phil Karlson • *Scr* DeVallon Scott, Frank Nugent, from a story by Leo Katcher

They Shall Have Music ★★★ U

Musical drama 1939 · US · BW · 97mins

Producer Samuel Goldwyn fought a long, losing battle to make classical music popular on the big screen, but it certainly wasn't through lack of trying. Here, Archie Mayo directs a tale that finds room for top-billed virtuoso Jascha Heifetz to play no less than five violin pieces. In the story, tough youngster Gene Reynolds takes up the violin after hearing Heifetz perform, enrolling in music classes as a way out of the slums. TS

Jascha Heifetz • Joel McCrea *Peter McCarthy* • Walter Brennan *Professor Lawson* • Andrea Leeds *Ann Lawson* • Gene Reynolds *Frankie* • Terry Kilburn *Dominick* • Tommy Kelly *Willie* • Dolly Loehr [Diana Lynn] ■ *Dir* Archie Mayo • *Scr* Irmgard von Cube, John Howard Lawson, Robert Presnell and Anthony Veiller, from the novel by Charles L Clifford

They Shoot Horses, Don't They? ★★★ 15

Drama 1969 · US · Colour · 119mins

Portraying the dance-marathon craze that swept America during the Depression in the 1930s, director Sydney Pollack gives us plenty of cause for compassion in this hard-hitting adaptation of Horace McCoy's novel. Jane Fonda and Michael Sarrazin are among the partners wearily dragging themselves beyond the end of their tethers, spurred on by the monstrous master of ceremonies (an Oscar-winning Gig Young). It's too tunnel-visioned to work as the intended microcosm of America and the flash-forward narrative is peculiar, but the photography is suitably sickly hued and the performances are wittily authentic. TH. Contains violence, swearing and sex scenes. DVD

Jane Fonda *Gloria Beatty* • Michael Sarrazin *Robert Syverton* • Susannah York *Alice* • Gig Young *Rocky* • Red Buttons *Sailor* • Bonnie Bedelia *Ruby* • Michael Conrad *Rollo* • Bruce Dern *James* • Al Lewis *Turkey* ■ *Dir* Sydney Pollack • *Scr* James Poe, Robert E Thompson, from the novel by Horace McCoy

They Were Expendable ★★★★ U

Second World War drama
1945 · US · BW · 129mins

During the war, John Ford served in the navy and made several documentaries, including the classic *The Battle of Midway*. When the war looked like being won, he enlisted with MGM to make *They Were Expendable*, a drama about buying time for the navy after the disaster of Pearl Harbor. It is an epic – long, reflective, bursting with incident – and contains fine performances from Robert Montgomery, John Wayne, Donna Reed and members of Ford's stock company. AT

Robert Montgomery *Lt John Brickley* • John Wayne *Lt RG "Rusty" Ryan* • Donna Reed *Lt Sandy Davyss* • Jack Holt *General Martin* • Ward Bond *"Boats" Mulcahey* • Marshall Thompson *Ensign Snake Gardner* • Paul Langton *Ensign Andy Andrews* ■ *Dir* John Ford • *Scr* Frank W Wead, from the book by William L White

They Were Not Divided ★★

Second World War drama
1950 · UK · BW · 101mins

There's not much evidence in this stiff-upper-lipped Second World War drama to suggest that Terence Young would go on to direct three of the best Bond movies in the early 1960s. The action is almost totally reliant on the sort of gung-ho camaraderie that was characteristic of the recruiting propaganda that filled British screens in the first days of the conflict. Edward Underdown's Guards officer and Ralph Clanton's have-a-go Yank are nothing more than caricatures, but contemporary audiences queued round the block to see their exploits as they drove the Nazis back to Berlin. DP

Edward Underdown *Philip* • Ralph Clanton *David* • Helen Cherry *Wilhelmina* • Stella Andrews *Jane* • Michael Brennan *Smoke O'Connor* • Michael Trubshawe *Major Bushy Noble* • John Wynn *45 Jones* ■ *Dir/Scr* Terence Young

They Were Sisters ★★★ U

Drama 1945 · UK · BW · 109mins

A quintessential Gainsborough melodrama following the marriages of three sisters, whose husbands, it turns out, range from the tolerant to the tyrannical. The sisters are played by three splendid actresses whose looks (and diction) epitomise a long-gone era: Phyllis Calvert, Dulcie Gray and Anne Crawford. Today, though, the main interest is a young James Mason, giving a performance every bit as vicious as his work in *The Seventh Veil* and *The Man in Grey*. TS

Phyllis Calvert *Lucy* • James Mason *Geoffrey* • Hugh Sinclair *Terry* • Anne Crawford *Vera* • Peter Murray Hill *William* • Dulcie Gray *Charlotte* • Barrie Livesey *Brian* ■ *Dir* Arthur Crabtree • *Scr* Roland Pertwee, Katherine Strueby, from the novel by Dorothy Whipple

They Who Dare ★★★ U

Second World War drama
1953 · UK · Colour · 103mins

Considering director Lewis Milestone was responsible for those combat classics *All Quiet on the Western Front* and *A Walk in the Sun*, this is a very disappointing account of an Allied commando raid on Rhodes. Ordered to knock out a couple of airfields, Dirk Bogarde and Denholm Elliott spend as much time squabbling as they do confronting the enemy. The dialogue (much of which was improvised) is sloppy, but the action sequences are convincing. DP DVD

Dirk Bogarde *Lieutenant Graham* • Denholm Elliott *Sergeant Corcoran* • Akim Tamiroff *Captain George One* • Gérard Oury *Captain George Two* • Eric Pohlmann *Captain Papadopoulos* • Alec Mango *Patroklis* • Kay Callard *Nightclub singer* ■ *Dir* Lewis Milestone • *Scr* Robert Westerby

They Won't Believe Me ★★★

Crime drama 1947 · US · BW · 95mins

Robert Young sheds his good guy image to play a heel on trial for murder. He's cheated on his wealthy wife Rita Johnson, been involved with young writer Jane Greer and then with gold-digging secretary Susan Hayward. One has died in a car accident, one has committed suicide, but can Young persuade the jury that he didn't kill anybody? Told as a long flashback, this is slick and artificial but still engrossing. AE

Robert Young (1) *Larry Ballentine* • Susan Hayward *Verna Carlson* • Jane Greer *Janice Bell* • Rita Johnson *Gretta Ballentine* • Tom Powers *Trenton* • George Tyne *Lt Carr* ■ *Dir* Irving Pichel • *Scr* Jonathan Latimer, from a story by Gordon McDonell

They Won't Forget ★★★

Courtroom drama 1937 · US · BW · 95mins

Starring Claude Rains as a Deep South DA, the story spins on the murder of a student (Lana Turner) and the suspicion that falls on a black janitor and a college lecturer. When the politically ambitious Rains clears the janitor and condemns the lecturer, a smart-aleck lawyer arrives to defend him, leading us into a courtroom drama in which the real defendant is bigotry. Featuring strong performances and a deal of moralising. AT

Claude Rains *Andrew J Griffin* • Gloria Dickson *Sybil Hale* • Edward Norris *Robert Perry Hale* • Otto Kruger *Michael Gleason* • Allyn Joslyn *William P Brock* • Lana Turner *Mary Clay* • Linda Perry *Imogene Mayfield* • Elisha Cook Jr *Joe Turner* ■ *Dir* Mervyn LeRoy • *Scr* Robert Rossen, Aben Kandel, from the novel *Death in the Deep South* by Ward Greene

They're a Weird Mob ★ U

Romantic comedy
1966 · Aus · Colour · 112mins

This is a dire, and rightly neglected, Michael Powell/Emeric Pressburger collaboration. The lacklustre would-be comedy derives most of its laughs from Italian immigrant Walter Chiari battling with the Aussie dialect, while trying to locate his female cousin. All performances, with the honourable

T

exception of Australian veteran Chips Rafferty, are deplorable. TS

Walter Chiari *Nino Culotta* • Clare Dunne *Kay Kelly* • Chips Rafferty *Harry Kelly* • Alida Chelli *Giuliana* • Ed Devereaux *Joe* ■ *Dir* Michael Powell • *Scr* Richard Imrie [Emeric Pressburger], from the novel by Nino Culotta

They're Playing With Fire ★

Crime horror 1984 · US · Colour · 96mins

Sexy professor Sybil Danning seduces student Eric Brown and begs him to help her carry out a money-making murder scheme. Meanwhile, a masked maniac is on the loose, killing people with an axe. A preposterous thriller which rapidly descends into slasher territory and doesn't convince in either area. AJ. Contains nudity.

Sybil Danning *Diane Stevens* • Eric Brown *Jay Richards* • Andrew Prine *Michael Stevens* • Paul Clemens *Martin "Bird" Johnson* • KT Stevens *Lillian Stevens* ■ *Dir* Howard Avedis • *Scr* Howard Avedis, Marlene Schmidt

The Thick-Walled Room ★★★

Drama 1953 · Jpn · BW · 110mins

Convinced that films should focus on emotion not theory, the Sochiku company decided to withhold for three years Masaki Kobayashi's drama, which used the case of a soldier who killed an innocent Indonesian civilian to raise the issue of war guilt. The characters are underdeveloped and few answers are provided, but novelist Kobo Abe's debut screenplay provocatively suggests that Japan's real warmongers had escaped punishment by drawing on the diaries of war criminals. DP. A Japanese language film.

Ko Mishima • Torahiko Hamada • Keiko Kishi • Toshiko Kobayashi • Eitaro Ozawa ■ *Dir* Masaki Kobayashi • *Scr* Kobo Abe

Thicker than Blood ★★ PG

Drama based on a true story
1993 · US · Colour · 89mins

This TV movie explores the agony of a father who is not only torn from his son when his girlfriend leaves him, but also has to face up to the fact that the boy he has come to adore may not be his own. Peter Strauss produces a credible blend of anger, affection and determination as he battles for custody of the child. DP [video] DVD

Peter Strauss *Larry McLinden* • Rachel Ticotin *Diane Middleton* • Bob Dishy *Glen Schwartz* • Brenda Bazinet *Mary* • Lynn Whitfield *Bobbie Mallory* ■ *Dir* Michael Dinner • *Scr* Judson Klinger

Thicker than Blood ★★ 12

Drama 1998 · US · Colour · 92mins

This TV film features Hollywood bad boy Mickey Rourke in an uncharacteristic turn as a priest and mentor to former student Dan Futterman, who returns to teach at Rourke's inner-city mission school. The two come into conflict over Futterman's devotion to one particularly promising student. It's a story with emotional appeal, strengthened by a good cast and steady direction by Richard Pearce. There is not a lot of action, but it is surprisingly palatable. MC. Contains swearing, violence. [video] DVD

Mickey Rourke *Father Frank Larkin* • Dan Futterman *Griffin Byrne* • Carlo Alban *Lee Cortez* • Lauren Velez *Camilla Lopez* • Josh Mostel *Burke Kendall* • Peter Maloney *Mitch James* ■ *Dir* Richard Pearce • *Scr* Bill Cain, from his play *Stand-Up Tragedy*

Thicker than Water ★★★ U

Comedy 1935 · US · BW · 20mins

The last ever Laurel and Hardy short, in which the pair squander their family savings on a grandfather clock. Though not as brilliant as some of their earlier shorts, this still has some rib-tickling moments. After 1935, the duo concentrated on feature-length movies, although they did make a cameo appearance in the Charley Chase short, *On the Wrong Trek*. DF [video] DVD

Stan Laurel *Stan* • Oliver Hardy *Ollie* • Daphne Pollard *Mrs Daphne Hardy* • James Finlayson *Auction operator* • Harry Bowen *Auctioneer* • Charlie Hall *Bank teller* ■ *Dir* James W Horne • *Scr* from a story by Stan Laurel, HM Walker, Charles Rogers

The Thief ★★★

Spy drama 1952 · US · BW · 86mins

If you've ever cringed at the ridiculous dialogue in many Hollywood movies, this one may provide some relief. Ray Milland stars in a spy drama that features no dialogue at all, relying instead on narration, sound effects, creating the right ambience and the intelligence of the audience. Milland is a nuclear physicist who turns traitor for the Russians, but then finds himself under investigation by the FBI and forced to go into hiding. The gimmick isn't entirely successful as it leaves Milland's motivation unclear. RT

Ray Milland *Allan Fields* • Martin Gabel *Mr Bleek* • Rita Gam *The girl* • Harry Bronson *Harris* • John McKutcheon *Dr Linstrum* • Rita Vale *Miss Philips* ■ *Dir* Russell Rouse • *Scr* Clarence Greene, Russell Rouse

Thief ★★★★ 18

Crime drama 1981 · US · Colour · 119mins

Director Michael Mann's auspicious feature debut pins its story of a professional jewel thief (James Caan) to a near-abstract idea about the criminal's urge to self-destruct, despite the meticulous way he plans his life. The terrific opening sequence involving a diamond robbery set to the music of Tangerine Dream establishes the mood and style for a crime drama that's almost too intellectual for its own genre. TH. Contains swearing, violence and brief nudity. [video] DVD

James Caan *Frank* • Tuesday Weld *Jessie* • Willie Nelson *Okla* • James Belushi *Barry* • Robert Prosky *Leo* • Tom Signorelli *Attaglia* • Dennis Farina *Carl* ■ *Dir* Michael Mann • *Scr* Michael Mann, from the book *The Home Invaders* by Frank Hohimer

The Thief ★★★★ 15

Drama 1997 · Rus/Fr · Colour · 93mins

Echoing his father Grigori's socialist realist masterpiece, *Ballad of a Soldier* (1960), Pavel Chukrai's Oscar-nominated drama, chronicles the crimes of a very different type of trooper. Seen through the eyes of her six year-old son, Misha Filipchuk, Ekaterina Rednikova's abrupt romance with Vladimir Mashkov is both intimidating and bewildering, as the threesome flits between provincial towns exploiting Mashkov's Red Army respectability. Contrasting the conditions of postwar austerity with the post-Communist present, this allegory on Yeltsin's Russia is stylishly composed and superbly acted. DP. In Russian with English subtitles. Contains sex, swearing, violence. [video]

Vladimir Mashkov *Tolian* • Ekaterina Rednikova *Katia* • Misha Filipchuk *Sania, aged six* • Amaliia Mordvinova *Doctor's wife* • Dima Chigarev *Sania, aged 12* ■ *Dir/Scr* Pavel Chukhrai

The Thief of Bagdad ★★★★ U

Silent fantasy adventure
1924 · US · BW · 210mins

A grinning, bare-chested Douglas Fairbanks shimmies up a rope and enters a room in the palace, intending to steal a casket of baubles. Instead, his eyes fall on Princess Julanne Johnston, and he swears there and then to be worthy of her and take her for a ride on a magic carpet. Of such things movie myths are made, effortlessly embodied by Fairbanks in one of his most famous roles. Maybe it dawdles in some sections and some performances are distinctly wobbly, but even those, like the special effects, have a charm all their own. William Cameron Menzies, who later designed *Things to Come* and *Gone With the Wind*, provided the memorable sets, a clever combination of real structures and shots which utilised painted pieces of glass placed right next to the camera lens. AT [video] DVD

Douglas Fairbanks *The Thief of Bagdad* • Snitz Edwards *His evil associate* • Charles Belcher *The holy man* • Julanne Johnston *The princess* • Anna May Wong *The Mongol slave* • Winter Blossom *The slave of the lute* • Etta Lee *The slave of the sand board* • Brandon Hurst *The caliph* ■ *Dir* Raoul Walsh • *Scr* Lotta Woods, from a story by Elton Thomas [Douglas Fairbanks] • *Cinematographer* Arthur Edeson

The Thief of Bagdad ★★★★★ U

Fantasy adventure
1940 · UK · Colour · 101mins

A wonderfully atmospheric *Arabian Nights* adventure for children of all ages, particularly young lads who can identify with Sabu singing "I want to be a bandit, can't you understand it?" – part of a marvellous score by Miklos Rozsa, which, incidentally, was the first ever to be committed to record. Producer and co-director Alexander Korda spared no expense to bring the magic to the screen, undeterred by the outbreak of war which necessitated decamping from England to Hollywood. Oscar-winning Technicolor photography and sumptuous art direction make this the definitive movie of this particular tale. With a giant genie, flying carpets, magical mechanical horses, a beautiful princess, Sabu himself, and a wickedly wicked grand vizier in the person of Conrad Veidt, what more could any adventure-seeker ask for? TS [video]

Conrad Veidt *Jaffar* • Sabu *Abu* • June Duprez *Princess* • John Justin *Ahmad* • Rex Ingram *(2) Djinni* • Miles Malleson *Sultan* • Morton Selten *King* • Mary Morris *Halima* • Hay Petrie *Astrologer* ■ *Dir* Ludwig Berger, Michael Powell, Tim Whelan, Zoltan Korda, William Cameron Menzies, Alexander Korda • *Scr* Lajos Biró, Miles Malleson • *Cinematographer* Georges Périnal, Osmond Borradaile • *Art Director* Vincent Korda

The Thief of Baghdad ★ U

Fantasy adventure
1978 · UK/Fr · Colour · 96mins

This version of the *Arabian Nights* fantasy was filmed in France and uses the Zoptic system that also featured in *Superman* for the flying scenes. Otherwise, the effects are not special at all, and the whole enterprise has a listless air. Enjoyment depends on one's tolerance of Peter Ustinov's ad-libbing sprees and Roddy McDowall's tendency to camp everything up. Former ballerina Marina Vlady behaves like a zombie. AT [video]

Roddy McDowall *Hasan* • Peter Ustinov *Caliph* • Kabir Bedi *Prince Taj* • Terence Stamp *Wazir Jaudur* • Frank Finlay *Abu Bakar* • Marina Vlady *Perizadah* • Pavla Ustinov *Princess Yasmine* • Ian Holm *Gatekeeper* ■ *Dir* Clive Donner • *Scr* AJ Carothers

Thief of Damascus ★★★ U

Adventure 1952 · US · Colour · 78mins

This light-hearted *Arabian Nights* cock-up features Paul Henreid, Robert Clary and Lon Chaney Jr as Abu Andar, Aladdin and Sinbad. The band members pool their magical talents in order to rescue Princess Elena Verdugo from the nasty likes of desert mogul John Sutton. Despite its hotch-potch pantomime, it's likeable. TH

Paul Henreid *Abu Andar* • John Sutton *Khalid* • Jeff Donnell *Sheherazade* • Lon Chaney Jr *Sinbad* • Elena Verdugo *Neela* • Robert Clary *Aladdin* • Edward Colmans *Sultan Raudah* • Nelson Leigh *Ben Jammal* • Philip Van Zandt *Ali Baba* ■ *Dir* Will Jason • *Scr* Robert E Kent

Thief of Hearts ★★★ 18

Thriller 1984 · US · Colour · 96mins

A slick and sensual psychological drama, with Steven Bauer as a burglar who breaks into a married woman's home and steals a diary detailing her innermost sexual fantasies. He then uses them to woo the woman, who hasn't the faintest idea that he's acting on inside information. Sounds sleazy, and up to a point it is. But it's well-made with strong performances from Bauer and Barbara Williams, and fairly subtle use of its sex scenes. Spicier ones were reportedly added for the film's video release. DA [video] DVD

Steven Bauer *Scott Muller* • Barbara Williams (2) *Mickey Davis* • John Getz *Ray Davis* • David Caruso *Buddy Calamara* • Christine Ebersole *Janie Pointer* • George Wendt *Marty Morrison* ■ *Dir/Scr* Douglas Day Stewart

The Thief of Paris ★★★★

Period comedy drama
1967 · Fr/It · Colour · 120mins

A melancholy, even pessimistic, work from the fine French director, Louis Malle, set in and around 1900. Jean-Paul Belmondo stars as a wealthy young Parisian whose uncle squanders his fortune, then marries off the cousin he loves to a rich neighbour. Belmondo steals the jewels of the neighbour's family and, obsessed by the notion of revenge against bourgeois society and its hypocrisies, embarks on a life of crime as a master thief. Enriched by warm colour photography and a marvellous sense of period. BB. A French language film.

Jean-Paul Belmondo *Georges Randal* • Geneviève Bujold *Charlotte* • Marie Dubois *Geneviève* • Françoise Fabian *Ida* • Julien Guiomar *Lamargelle* • Paul Le Person *Roger La Honte* ■ *Dir* Louis Malle • *Scr* Louis Malle, Jean-Claude Carrière, Daniel Boulanger, from a story by Georges Darien • *Cinematographer* Henri Decaë

The Thief Who Came to Dinner ★★★ 15

Crime comedy drama
1973 · US · Colour · 100mins

Written by Walter Hill, this has moments of originality, but is otherwise a tepid, episodic comedy thriller. Ryan O'Neal plays the computer analyst-turned-jewel thief, with Jacqueline Bisset as his girl. But it's support actors Warren Oates, playing a bemused insurance investigator, and Austin Pendleton, as an exasperated editor, who make the most of the predictable plot. TH [video]

Ryan O'Neal *Webster Mcgee* • Jacqueline Bisset *Laura Keaton* • Warren Oates *Dave Reilly* • Jill Clayburgh *Jackie* • Charles Cioffi *Henderling* • Ned Beatty *Deams* • Austin Pendleton *Zukovsky* • George Morfogen *Rivera* • Gregory Sierra *Dynamite* • Michael Murphy *Ted* ■ *Dir* Bud Yorkin • *Scr* Walter Hill, from the novel by Terence Lore Smith

Thieves ★★ PG

Romantic comedy
1977 · US · Colour · 90mins

Herb Gardner's Broadway play was transferred virtually line-for-line to the screen, retaining the play's lead actress, Marlo Thomas, who co-stars with Charles Grodin, director of the original stage production. Relating the problems faced by married New York teachers Thomas and Grodin, it was roasted by the critics at the time – "Dull, dated, downbeat," said *Variety*

– but throaty Mercedes McCambridge and seedy Hector Elizondo do perk it up a bit. AT [video]

Charles Grodin *Martin Cramer* • Marlo Thomas *Sally Cramer* • Irwin Corey *Joe Kaminsky* • Hector Elizondo *Man below* • Mercedes McCambridge *Street lady* • John McMartin *Gordon* • Gary Merrill *Street man* • Bob Fosse *Mr Day* ■ *Dir* John Berry, Al Viola • *Scr* Herb Gardner, from his play

Thieves' Highway ★★★★

Thriller 1949 · US · BW · 92mins

This is a superb 20th Century-Fox melodrama from a great *film noir* period, about a tough soldier out to get the racketeer who ruined his dad while he was away fighting in the Second World War. Jules Dassin directs this committed socialist work, and his fine cast includes Lee J Cobb and the great Morris Carnovsky. This is American cinema at its most exciting: absorbing European influences and spitting them out in a tough, uniquely American way. TS

Richard Conte *Nick Garcos* • Valentina Cortesa [Valentina Cortese] *Rica* • Lee J Cobb *Mike Figlia* • Barbara Lawrence *Polly Faber* • Jack Oakie *Slob* • Millard Mitchell *Ed* • Joseph Pevney *Pete* • Morris Carnovsky *Yanko Garcos* ■ *Dir* Jules Dassin • *Scr* Ai Bezzerides, from the novel *Thieves' Market* by Al Bezzerides

Thieves' Holiday ★★★

Crime biography 1946 · US · BW · 99mins

This diversion utilises the suave persona and polished style of George Sanders in the unusual guise of an 18th-century Parisian. Drawing its story from the memoirs of Eugene Vidocq, a thief who mended his ways to become Prefect of Police and first chief of the Sûreté, the movie concerns his relationship with cabaret entertainer Carole Landis for whom he steals a bejewelled garter, his imprisonment, and his reformation under the influence of Signe Hasso. A light mix of drama and romantic comedy directed by Douglas Sirk and easy to digest. RK

George Sanders *Eugene-François Vidocq* • Signe Hasso *Thérèse* • Carole Landis *Loretta* • Akim Tamiroff *Emile Vernet* • Gene Lockhart *Chief of Police Richet* • Jo Ann Marlowe *Mimi* ■ *Dir* Douglas Sirk • *Scr* Ellis St Joseph, from a memoir by François Eugene Vidocq

Thieves like Us ★★★★ 15

Period crime drama
1974 · US · Colour · 117mins

Robert Altman's remake of Nicholas Ray's doom-laden *film noir They Live by Night*, has Shelley Duvall and Keith Carradine convincing and touching as the young lovers adrift in the poverty-stricken Deep South. Set in the 1930s and shot in Mississippi, the picture is classically made, lacking the "innovations" that were Altman's trademarks. Louise Fletcher appears in her screen debut. AT. Contains nudity. [video] DVD

Keith Carradine *Bowie* • Shelley Duvall *Keechie* • John Schuck *Chicamaw* • Bert Remsen *T-dub* • Louise Fletcher *Mattie* • Ann Latham *Lula* • Tom Skerritt *Dee Mobley* ■ *Dir* Robert Altman • *Scr* Calder Willingham, Joan Tewkesbury, Robert Altman, from the novel by Edward Anderson

The Thin Blue Line ★★★★★ 15

Documentary 1988 · US · Colour · 97mins

In 1976 a Dallas policeman, Robert Wood, routinely stopped a car and was shot dead. Later, a known delinquent, 16-year-old David Harris, was arrested after boasting about the murder. Under questioning, Harris protested his innocence and blamed a hitch-hiker he had picked up, Randall Adams. Adams was tried and sentenced to death, later commuted to life imprisonment. Twelve years after the crime, documentary film-maker Errol Morris re-opened the case and produced this stunning film, an unsurpassed blend of interviews and reconstruction. Our journey into the case is also Morris's, as he slowly uncovers a symphony of doubt and a miscarriage of justice. The sense of unease, heightened by an enthralling collection of witnesses, accumulates so that a random murder in Dallas puts all of America under the microscope. The picture earned its ultimate prize – not an Oscar but a retrial and, in the end, Adams's release. AT. Contains swearing. [video]

Dir/Scr Errol Morris • *Music* Philip Glass

Thin Ice ★★

Romantic musical comedy
1937 · US · BW · 78mins

This lightweight trifle stretches Norwegian skating star Sonja Henie's acting ability more than a little, as she plays an ice-skating coach who falls in love with a prince (Tyrone Power). His sly, knowing performance suggests that the plot is not exactly coincidental in the heady days of the romance between Edward VIII and Mrs Simpson. To follow Henie's movements on the ice, 20th Century-Fox constructed a special camera rig. TS

Sonja Henie *Lili Heiser* • Tyrone Power *Prince Rudolph* • Arthur Treacher *Nottingham* • Raymond Walburn *Uncle Dornic* • Joan Davis *Orchestra Leader* ■ *Dir* Sidney Lanfield • *Scr* Boris Ingster, Milton Sperling, from the play *Der Komet* by Attila Obok

Thin Ice ★ 15

Drama 1994 · UK · Colour · 85mins

Scarcely believable on any level, director Fiona Cunningham Reid's hopelessly naive, same-gender romance feels like it has come from another dim and distant era. Every cliché is stumbled into as a white heterosexual ice skater teams up with a black lesbian partner and enters the Gay Games in New York. Skating on thin ice in more ways than one. AJ [video]

Charlotte Avery *Natalie* • Sabra Williams *Steffi* • James Dreyfus *Greg* • Clare Higgins *Fiona* • Ian McKellen • Guy Williams *Charles* • Barbara New *Felicity* • Martha Freud *Cosima* ■ *Dir* Fiona Cunningham Reid • *Scr* Fiona Cunningham Reid, Geraldine Sherman

A Thin Line between Love and Hate ★ 18

Comedy thriller 1996 · US · Colour · 103mins

A feeble *Fatal Attraction* clone from comedian Martin Lawrence, who has no one else to blame considering he's the executive producer, director, co-writer and star. He plays a vulgar Casanova with limited ambitions, who gets his comeuppance after romancing glamorous real estate tycoon Lynn Whitfield and dumping her for his true love, Regina King. This unfunny, uncouth comedy thriller toes a thin line between bad and awful before stumbling into the latter. AJ [video]

Martin Lawrence *Darnell* • Lynn Whitfield *Brandi* • Regina King *Mia* • Bobby Brown *Tee* • Della Reese *Ma Wright* • Malinda Williams *Erica* • Daryl Mitchell *Earl* • Roger E Mosley *Smitty* ■ *Dir* Martin Lawrence • *Scr* Martin Lawrence, Bentley Kyle Evans, Kenny Buford, Kim Bass, from a story by Martin Lawrence

The Thin Man ★★★★

Classic detective comedy
1934 · US · BW · 93mins

The first in a popular series, based on Dashiell Hammett's characters, with William Powell and Myrna Loy amateur sleuths and the epitome of 1930s style and sophistication. Hammett had written a thriller, but MGM turned it into a screwball comedy, with Powell and Loy making a sizzling couple. Their excessive drinking and other shocking habits (the characters are based on Hammett and Lillian Hellman) delighted audiences at the time and still do now, even if the pacing now seems rather slow. Five more films followed, beginning with 1936's *After the Thin Man*. AT

William Powell *Nick Charles* • Myrna Loy *Nora Charles* • Maureen O'Sullivan *Dorothy Wynant* • Nat Pendleton *Lieutenant John Guild* • Minna Gombell *Mimi Wynant* • Porter Hall *MacCauley* • Henry Wadsworth *Tommy* ■ *Dir* WS Van Dyke • *Scr* Albert Hackett, Frances Goodrich, from the novel by Dashiell Hammett

The Thin Man Goes Home ★★★

Detective comedy drama
1944 · US · BW · 100mins

Fifth in the Dashiell Hammett-inspired series that began with *The Thin Man* in 1934. William Powell plays Nick Charles, a man aided by a sharp mind, several dry martinis and a glamorous wife Nora – usually in that order. In this film he's on a visit to his home town and as usual, the amateur sleuths and Asta the dog are up to their elegant necks in solving a murder mystery. The series concluded with *Song of the Thin Man*. BB

William Powell *Nick Charles* • Myrna Loy *Nora Charles* • Lucile Watson *Mrs Charles* • Gloria De Haven [Gloria DeHaven] *Laura Ronson* • Anne Revere *Crazy Mary* • Helen Vinson *Helena Draque* • Harry Davenport *Dr Bertram Charles* • Leon Ames *Edgar Draque* ■ *Dir* Richard Thorpe • *Scr* Robert Riskin, Dwight Taylor, from a story by Robert Riskin, from a story by Harry Kurnitz, from characters created by Dashiell Hammett

The Thin Red Line ★★★ 12

Second World War drama
1964 · US · BW · 86mins

Admirers of Terrence Malick's excellent 1998 version of James Jones' epic Second World War novel may find this disappointing. But this well-acted picture takes a more conventional approach, focusing on the spiky relationship between veteran first sergeant Jack Warden and raw private Keir Dullea. In the bitter conflict in Guadalcanal in the Pacific, the two men's loathing for each other develops into mutual respect. The combat sequences are first class. JG [video]

Keir Dullea *Private Doll* • Jack Warden *1st Sgt Welsh* • James Philbrook *Colonel Tall* • Ray Daley *Captain Stone* ■ *Dir* Andrew Marton • *Scr* Bernard Gordon, from the novel by James Jones

The Thin Red Line ★★★★★ 15

Second World War drama
1998 · US · Colour · 163mins

After 20 years in the film-making wilderness, Terrence Malick released this belated third feature – a magnificent account of the Second World War battle for Guadalcanal island in the South Pacific. It's a long, discursive and deeply philosophical evocation of war, beautifully shot by John Toll. The film boasts an all-star cast, with Sean Penn as a cynical sergeant and Nick Nolte as an uncompromising lieutenant colonel making deep impressions. The principal role, however, goes to the little known Jim Caviezel as the non-conformist and idealist who seems completely at one with the tropical surroundings, while British actor Ben Chaplin gives a convincing performance as the ordinary Joe who dreams of his wife back home. Malick's extraordinary direction is the real star turn, however. A modern masterpiece. AT. Contains swearing, violence. [video] DVD

Sean Penn *First Sgt Welsh* • Jim Caviezel *Private Witt* • John Cusack *Captain Gaff* • Ben Chaplin *Private Bell* • Nick Nolte *Lt Col Tall* • Woody Harrelson *Keck* • Elias Koteas *Captain "Bugger" Staros* • John Travolta *Qintard* • George Clooney *Bosche* ■ *Dir* Terrence Malick • *Scr* Terrence Malick, from the novel by James Jones

The Thing ★★★★ 18

Science-fiction horror
1982 · US · Colour · 103mins

John Carpenter's remake of Howard Hawks and Christian Nyby's influential 1951 creature feature *The Thing from Another World*, is a special-effects extravaganza of the highest order. In fact, the updated screenplay by Bill Lancaster (son of Burt) has the occupants of a polar research station menaced by an alien with the ability to change its shape and impersonate its enemies. Carpenter stresses the slimy ET at the expense of characterisation and mood, yet it's precisely this one grisly facet that makes it so compelling. AJ. Contains violence, swearing. [video] DVD

Kurt Russell *MacReady* • Wilford Brimley *Blair* • TK Carter *Nauls* • David Clennon *Palmer* • Keith David *Childs* • Richard Dysart *Dr Cooper* • Charles Hallahan *Norris* • Peter Maloney *Bennings* • Richard Masur *Clark* ■ *Dir* John Carpenter • *Scr* Bill Lancaster, from the story *Who Goes There?* by John Wood Campbell Jr

The Thing Called Love ★★ 15

Drama 1993 · US · Colour · 109mins

Peter Bogdanovich directs River Phoenix in one of his final roles, in a run-of-the-mill drama about love and fame among a group of aspiring country singers. Phoenix is fine as the young singer trying to make a name for himself in Nashville, and he's backed up by a competent young cast as well as a handful of bona fide country singers. But despite the authenticity of the music and winning performances, it never really kicks into gear and ends up as a brief footnote to Phoenix's promising career. JB [video]

River Phoenix *James Wright* • Samantha Mathis *Miranda Presley* • Dermot Mulroney *Kyle Davidson* • Sandra Bullock *Linda Lue Linden* • KT Oslin *Lucy* • Anthony Clark *Billy* • Webb Wilder *Ned* ■ *Dir* Peter Bogdanovich • *Scr* Carol Heikkinen

The Thing from Another World ★★★★ 12

Science-fiction horror
1951 · US · BW · 82mins

This pioneering science-fiction outing emphasises suspense and atmosphere, rather than the shock special effects of John Carpenter's 1982 remake *The Thing*, in a tense story of arctic scientists trying to cope with the first of Hollywood's Cold War aliens. Howard Hawks is only credited as producer, but the film is suspiciously full of his signature flourishes (camaraderie in the face of ambush, for instance) and director Christian Nyby never made anything half as good again. AJ [video]

Kenneth Tobey *Captain Patrick Hendry* • Margaret Sheridan *Nikki* • Robert Cornthwaite *Dr Carrington* • Douglas Spencer *Scotty* • James Young *Lt Eddie Dykes* • Dewey Martin *Crew Chief* • James Arness *The "Thing"* ■ *Dir* Christian Nyby • *Scr* Charles Lederer, from the story *Who Goes There?* by Don A Stuart [John Wood Campbell Jr]

The Thing with Two Heads ★★

Blaxploitation horror
1972 · US · Colour · 87mins

Probably the most lunatic blaxploitation horror film ever made, and also the genre's biggest missed opportunity to say something profound. Bigoted brain surgeon Ray Milland learns he's dying of cancer, so needs to transplant his head on to a healthy body. Unfortunately, racist Milland wakes to find his head next to that of

T

condemned black killer Rosey Grier, who is intent on clearing his name. With each head trying to seek control of Grier's body, the jokes should have been funnier, the racist allegory more up-front and the pacing more breakneck to cover the absolute idiocy of the premise. AJ

Ray Milland *Dr Maxwell Kirshner* • Rosey Grier *Jack Moss* • Don Marshall *Dr Fred Williams* • Roger Perry *Dr Philip Desmond* • Chelsea Brown *Lila* • Kathy Baumann [Katherine Baumann] *Patricia* • John Dullaghan (1) *Thomas* • John Bliss *Donald* ■ *Dir* Lee Frost • *Scr* Lee Frost, James Gordon White, Wes Bishop

Things Are Tough All Over ★★ 15

Comedy 1982 · US · Colour · 86mins

Double act "Cheech" Marin and Tommy Chong became (in)famous for their drug-related comedy routines that seemed perfectly suited to the American youth subculture of the 1970s. Here, the duo eschew the pharmaceutical theme for a more-or-less straight farce about the adventures of two musicians employed by some Arabs to drive a limousine full of money from Chicago to Vegas. The boys try hard but to little avail. DF

Richard "Cheech" Marin *Richard "Cheech" Marin/Mr Slyman* • Tommy Chong *Tommy Chong/Prince Habib* • Shelby Fiddis *1st French Girl* • Rikki Marin *2nd French Girl* • Evelyn Guerrero *Donna* • John Steadman *Oldtimer* • Rip Taylor ■ *Dir* Thomas K Avildsen • *Scr* Richard "Cheech" Marin, Thomas Chong [Tommy Chong]

Things Change ★★★★ PG

Crime comedy 1988 · US · Colour · 96mins

Hollywood veteran Don Ameche stars as an ageing shoeshine man who's persuaded to take the rap for a Mafia murder in return for the fulfilment of his lifelong dream in director David Mamet's charming follow-up to *House of Games*. Mamet regular Joe Mantegna co-stars as the well-meaning minder assigned to take care of Ameche, who decides to allow his charge one final fling. Ameche and Mantegna shared the best actor prize at Venice for their roles in this beautifully crafted film. DA

Don Ameche *Gino* • Joe Mantegna *Jerry* • Robert Prosky *Joseph Vincent* • JJ Johnston *Frankie* • Ricky Jay *Mr Silver* • Mike Nussbaum *Mr Green* ■ *Dir* David Mamet • *Scr* David Mamet, Shel Silverstein

The Things of Life ★★★

Drama 1969 · Fr/It/Swi · Colour · 89mins

An opening car crash, spectacularly filmed, sends this glossy marital drama into flashback mode, in which Michel Piccoli vacillates between estranged wife Lea Massari and mistress Romy Schneider. A movie of shifting moods and shifting allegiances rather than substance, well acted by the three leads although Piccoli is too rough-edged to be a sympathetic hero. It was a huge hit in France and was remade in 1994 as *Intersection* with Sharon Stone and Richard Gere. AT. French dialogue dubbed into English.

Michel Piccoli *Pierre Berard* • Romy Schneider *Hélène* • Lea Massari *Catherine Berard* • Gérard Lartigau *Bertrand Berard* • Jean Bouise *François* • Hervé Sand *Truck driver* ■ *Dir* Claude Sautet • *Scr* Paul Guimard, Jean-Loup Dabadie, Claude Sautet, from the novel *Les Choses de la Vie* by Paul Guimard

Things to Come ★★★★ PG

Science fiction 1936 · UK · BW · 89mins

Although a classic slice of British sci-fi, Alexander Korda's elaborate production of HG Wells's prophetic novel is weakened by a prevailing air of over-theatricality and naivety. Spanning almost 100 years from 1940 to 2036, it begins during a world war and goes through plague and a technological revolution, ending with everyone living in an enormous Art Deco underground city run by Raymond Massey. Awesome sets and magnificent design make this hugely ambitious antique vision of the future Britain's answer to *Metropolis*. Amazingly, Wells actually visited the studio while it was being made. AJ

Raymond Massey *John Cabal/Oswald Cabal* • Edward Chapman *Pippa Passworthy/Raymond Passworthy* • Ralph Richardson *The Boss* • Margaretta Scott *Roxana/Rowena* • Cedric Hardwicke *Theotocopulos* • Maurice Braddell *Dr Harding* • Sophie Stewart *Mrs Cabal* • Derrick de Marney *Richard Gordon* • Ann Todd *Mary Gordon* • George Sanders *Pilot* ■ *Dir* William Cameron Menzies • *Scr* HG Wells, Lajos Biró, from the book *The Shape of Things to Come* by HG Wells • *Cinematographer* Georges Périnal • *Production Designer* Vincent Korda

Things to Do in Denver When You're Dead ★★★★ 18

Crime drama 1995 · US · Colour · 110mins

The comparisons to Quentin Tarantino's work are inevitable, but Gary Fleder's witty, hip take on the gangster movie marked him out as an individual talent to watch. Andy Garcia plays a retired mobster who is called in by his ailing former boss, Christopher Walken, to carry out one more job. When it goes badly wrong, Garcia and his associates find themselves on the hit list. The vivid splashes of violence are ably handled by Fleder, but he also delights in the rich dialogue of his oddball collection of characters, warmly brought to life by an eclectic cast. JF. Contains violence, swearing and sex scenes. DVD

Andy Garcia *Jimmy "the Saint" Tosnia* • Christopher Lloyd *Pieces* • William Forsythe *Franchise* • Bill Nunn *Easy Wind* • Treat Williams *Critical Bill Dooley* • Jack Warden *Joe Heff* • Steve Buscemi *Mr Shhh* • Fairuza Balk *Lucinda* • Gabrielle Anwar *Dagney* • Christopher Walken *The Man with the Plan* ■ *Dir* Gary Fleder • *Scr* Scott Rosenberg

Things You Can Tell Just by Looking at Her ★★★★ 12

Romantic comedy
2000 · US · Colour · 109mins

Former cinematographer Rodrigo Garcia's feature debut is a set of five loosely overlapping stories that concentrates exclusively on the female characters. However, though blessed with a fine cast of performers, this film didn't get a cinematic release in the United States and only goes to show that distributors underestimate their audience and their ability to see A-list actresses in a new light. So what if Glenn Close is a lonely doctor, tending a senile mother? So what if Holly Hunter is an adulteress with an unwanted pregnancy? Yes, Calista Flockhart is a lesbian nursing her dying lover and Cameron Diaz is a blind bitch undermining her seeing sister's confidence. But that's what makes this original, interesting and honest. LH

Glenn Close *Dr Elaine Keener* • Holly Hunter *Rebecca* • Gregory Hines *Robert* • Miguel Sandoval *Sam* • Kathy Baker *Rose* • Calista Flockhart *Christine Taylor* • Valeria Golino *Lilly* • Cameron Diaz *Carol* • Amy Brenneman *Kathy* ■ *Dir/Scr* Rodrigo Garcia

Think Big ★ PG

Action comedy 1990 · US · Colour · 86mins

What is to be said about a movie where Richard Kiel ("Jaws" from the Bond films) manages to be boring as a villain? Only that his lacklustre performance seems to come from a realisation of the stupidity of the storyline, in which two dumb truck drivers (twins David and Peter Paul) are caught in a conspiracy to transport toxic waste. KB

Peter Paul *Vic* • David Paul *Rafe* • Martin Mull *Dr Bruekner* • David Carradine *John Sweeney* • Richard Kiel *Irving* • Claudia Christian *Dr Irene Marsh* ■ *Dir* Jon Turteltaub • *Scr* Edward Kovach, Jon Turteltaub, David Tausik, from a story by Jim Wynorski, RJ Robertson

Think Fast, Mr Moto ★★★

Crime mystery 1937 · US · BW · 66mins

The first in the eight-strong series featuring Peter Lorre as Mr Moto, the master of blindingly obvious disguises. Here, the Japanese sleuth is on the track of diamond smugglers operating out of San Francisco. Starting with the discovery of a body in an antique shop during Chinese New Year and transporting us, via a murderous ocean cruise, to the gambling joints of Shanghai, the story rapidly becomes impenetrable, with virtually every character acting shiftily. But, thanks to director Norman Foster and a wholehearted cast, the film has an irresistible momentum. DP

Peter Lorre *Mr Moto* • Virginia Field *Gloria Danton* • Thomas Beck *Bob Hitchings* • Sig Rumann [Sig Ruman] *Nicholas Marloff* • Murray Kinnell *Mr Joseph Wilkie* • Lotus Long *Lela Liu* • John Rogers *Carson* • George Cooper *Muggs Blake* ■ *Dir* Norman Foster • *Scr* Norman Foster, Howard Ellis Smith, from the novel by John P Marquand

The Third Alibi ★

Thriller 1961 · UK · BW · 68mins

This is the kind of shoddy crime thriller that gives even low-budget features a bad name. The action never for a second escapes its stage origins as composer Laurence Payne and his pregnant mistress Jane Griffiths plot to murder Payne's wife Patricia Dainton. Blame playwrights Pip and Jane Baker for the elaborate murder games, but even they are betrayed by a cast incapable of holding its own in an amateur theatrical. DP

Laurence Payne *Norman Martell* • Patricia Dainton *Helen Martell* • Jane Griffiths *Peggy Hill* • Edward Underdown *Dr Murdoch* • John Arnatt *Supt Ross* • Humphrey Lestocq *Theatre producer* • Lucy Griffiths *Miss Potter* • Cleo Laine *Singer* ■ *Dir* Montgomery Tully • *Scr* Maurice J Wilson, from the play *Moment of Blindness* by Pip Baker, Jane Baker

The Third Day ★★★

Drama 1965 · US · Colour · 102mins

Despite some lapses in the screenplay, this amnesia thriller works well as a psychodrama. There are convincing leading performances from George Peppard and Elizabeth Ashley, whose real-life marriage was heading for the rocks at the time, and an eclectic cast that includes Roddy McDowall, Mona Washbourne and Herbert Marshall. TS

George Peppard *Steve Mallory* • Elizabeth Ashley *Alexandria Mallory* • Roddy McDowall *Oliver Parsons* • Arthur O'Connell *Dr Wheeler* • Mona Washbourne *Catherine Parsons* • Herbert Marshall *Austin Parsons* ■ *Dir* Jack Smight • *Scr* Burton Wohl, Robert Presnell Jr, from the novel by Joseph Hayes

Third Finger, Left Hand ★★ U

Comedy 1940 · US · BW · 96mins

A perky Myrna Loy vehicle with a bogglingly unbelievable plot, this is pleasant, but undemanding. Here, as Melvyn Douglas's reluctant fiancée, Loy shines with her usual panache. But the script is thin and what starts out as a moderately pleasing soufflé, falls flat well before the final reel. SH

Myrna Loy *Margot Sherwood Merrick* • Melvyn Douglas *Jeff Thompson* • Raymond Walburn *Mr Sherwood* • Lee Bowman *Philip Booth* • Bonita Granville *Vicky Sherwood* • Felix Bressart *August Winkel* ■ *Dir* Robert Z Leonard • *Scr* Lionel Houser

The Third Generation ★★★

Black comedy
1979 · W Ger · Colour · 105mins

Not one of Rainer Werner Fassbinder's best films, but still an interesting depiction of middle-class urban radicals, dealing with a group of Berlin terrorists whose conflicts are gradually eating away at their nucleus. The director, who constantly ran out of money during the film's making, called it "a comedy in six parts", and it is played as political farce. It provoked violent controversy in Germany, where it was attacked by the left and right – the latter for glorifying terrorists and the former for betraying the heirs of the Baader-Meinhof Gang. RB. In German with English subtitles.

Volker Spengler *August Brem* • Bulle Ogier *Hilde Krieger* • Hanna Schygulla *Susanne Gast* • Harry Baer *Rudolf Mann* • Vitus Zeplichal *Bernhard von Stein* • Udo Kier *Edgar Gast* • Margit Carstensen *Petra Vielhaber* • Günther Kaufmann *Franz Walsch* • Eddie Constantine *Peter Lurz* ■ *Dir/Scr* Rainer Werner Fassbinder

The Third Man ★★★★★ PG

Classic thriller 1949 · UK · BW · 99mins

Developed by Graham Greene from an idea jotted down on the flap of an envelope, this virtually flawless feature is one of the best British films of all time. Set in postwar occupied Vienna, the plot is a corker, littered with memorable moments and played to perfection by an unforgettable cast, led with distinction by Orson Welles and Joseph Cotten. A master of place, angle and shade, director Carol Reed (helped by his Oscar-winning cinematographer Robert Krasker) fashions a city in which menace lurks around every corner, while Anton Karas's jaunty zither music echoes the wit and drama of this dark, yet daringly playful, picture. DP DVD

Joseph Cotten *Holly Martins* • Valli [Alida Valli] *Anna Schmidt* • Orson Welles *Harry Lime* • Trevor Howard *Major Calloway* • Bernard Lee *Sergeant Paine* • Paul Hoerbiger [Paul Hörbiger] *Harry's porter* • Ernst Deutsch *"Baron" Kurtz* • Siegfried Breuer *Popescu* • Erich Ponto *Dr Winkel* • Wilfrid Hyde-White [Wilfrid Hyde White] *Crabbin* • Hedwig Bleibtreu *Anna's "old woman"* ■ *Dir* Carol Reed • *Scr* Graham Greene, from his story

Third Man on the Mountain ★★★ U

Adventure 1959 · US · Colour · 100mins

A well-made and enjoyable Disney adventure, with youngster James MacArthur determined to scale the Alpine peak that claimed his father's life. However, when an early attempt ends in embarrassment, MacArthur is forced to seek training, transforming from callow youth to responsible adolescent along the way. MacArthur is a convincing lead, and this is life-affirming stuff with a clear moral purpose, and the location footage of the Swiss Alps is breathtaking. RT

Michael Rennie *Captain John Winter* • James MacArthur *Rudi Matt* • Janet Munro *Lizbeth Hempel* • James Donald *Franz Lerner* • Herbert Lom *Emil Saxo* • Laurence Naismith *Teo Zurbriggen* ■ *Dir* Ken Annakin • *Scr* Eleanore Griffin, from the book *Banner in the Sky* by James Ramsey Ullman

The Third Secret ★★★

Psychological thriller
1964 · UK · BW · 105mins

A psychiatrist is found shot dead. Did he kill himself or is something sinister going on? Directed by Charles Crichton, this is never as clever as it thinks it is, though the cast is outstanding, with the star of the show, as one of the dead shrink's patients trying to establish the truth, being Stephen Boyd, an Irish actor who, notwithstanding a riveting performance as Messala in *Ben-Hur*, never quite made it to the top. AT

Stephen Boyd *Alex Stedman* • Jack Hawkins *Sir Frederick Belline* • Richard Attenborough *Alfred Price-Gorham* • Diane Cilento *Anne Tanner* • Pamela Franklin *Catherine Whitset* • Paul Rogers *Dr Milton Gillen* • Alan Webb *Alden Hoving* • Rachel Kempson *Mildred Hoving* • Peter Sallis *Lawrence Jacks* • Judi Dench *Miss Humphries* • Nigel Davenport *Lew Harding* ■ *Dir* Charles Crichton • *Scr* Robert L Joseph

Third Time Lucky ★★

Drama 1949 · UK · BW · 90mins

A gambler doesn't realise that he loves his lucky mascot until the chips are down. Dermot Walsh and Glynis Johns just don't set the screen alight and similarly, Gordon Parry (in fairness, directing only his second feature) fails to capture the seedy world of gambling dens and backstreet drinking joints. Corny and moralising. DP

Glynis Johns *Joan* • Dermot Walsh *Lucky* • Charles Goldner *Flash* • Harcourt Williams *Doc* • Yvonne Owen *Peggy* • Helen Haye *Old Lady* ■ *Dir* Gordon Parry • *Scr* Gerald Butler, from his novel *They Cracked Her Glass Slipper*

The Third Voice ★★★★

Thriller 1960 · US · BW · 78mins

Extraordinarily stylish thriller by writer/director Hubert Cornfield, from Charles Williams's novel, *All the Way*, in which a woman kills her wealthy lover and an accomplice impersonates him through some financial processes. Edmond O'Brien, Laraine Day and Julie London form a suspenser-à-trois which lends credibility to an artificial situation. TH

Edmond O'Brien *The Voice* • Laraine Day *Marian Forbes* • Julie London *Corey Scott* • Ralph Brooks *Harris Chapman* • Roque Ybarra *Fisherman* • Ruben Moreno *Fisherman* ■ *Dir* Hubert Cornfield • *Scr* Hubert Cornfield, from the novel *All the Way* by Charles Williams

Third World Cop ★★★ 15

Crime drama 1999 · Jam · Colour · 98mins

Dirty Harry, Jamaican style. A rogue cop with a big gun and a disdain for police procedure is withdrawn from rural duties and transferred to Kingston, the island's front line of crime. There his maverick approach to policing brings him into conflict with a former best buddy who's now right-hand man to a vicious gunrunner. Filmed in the flashy fashion of a Hong Kong martial arts movie, this is neatly directed and solidly acted. DA. With subtitles. [VIDEO] DVD

Paul Campbell *Capone* • Mark Danvers *Ratty* • Carl Bradshaw *Wonie* • Audrey Reid *Rita* ■ *Dir* Chris Browne • *Scr* Suzanne Fenn, Chris Browne, Chris Salewicz

Thirst ★★ 18

Horror 1979 · Aus · Colour · 90mins

This intriguing modern-day vampire parable is set in a hospital in Australia's outback, where the hapless patients are "milked" for their blood by a secret society that believes its consumption bestows upon them great power. Sadly, Rod Hardy plays the whole thing totally deadpan, as if he's directing Chekhov. More ironic humour might have made the outrageous premise more effective. RS [VIDEO] DVD

Chantal Contouri *Kate Davis* • David Hemmings *Dr Fraser* • Henry Silva *Dr Gauss* • Max Phipps *Hodge* • Shirley Cameron *Mrs Barker* • Rod Mullinar *Derek* • Robert Thompson *Sean* • Walter Pym *Dichter* ■ *Dir* Rod Hardy • *Scr* John Pinkney

Thirst ★★★

Disaster movie 1998 · US · Colour · 120mins

During a withering heat wave, deadly parasites infect a town's water supply and water filtration engineer Adam Arkin struggles to a find a way to kill the pernicious microbe before everyone dies of dehydration. Mirroring actual events in the American Midwest, this TV movie is kept believable by John Mandel's purposeful script and Bill L Norton's taut direction. MC

Adam Arkin *Bob Miller* • Joely Fisher *Susan Miller* • Giancarlo Esposito *Dr Carver* • Ken Jenkins *Lou Wolford* • Phyllis Lyons *Allison* • Michael Cudlitz *Andy* ■ *Dir* Bill L Norton • *Scr* John Mandel, Paul A Kaufman

Thirteen ★★★ 18

Drama 2003 · US/UK · Colour · 95mins

Based on the adolescent experiences of 13-year-old Nikki Reed (who co-scripted and plays the vivacious "It Girl" Evie), this emotionally intense drama stars Evan Rachel Wood as a model daughter who goes off the rails. Director Catherine Hardwicke's spiky character study has low-budget, hand-held panache. Yet its spark comes principally from the bewitching young leads and a powerhouse turn from Holly Hunter as Wood's single mother. To its detriment, the film at times seems to be deliberately courting controversy and repetition creeps into the confrontation-heavy second half. JC. Contains violence, swearing, a sex scene and drug abuse. [VIDEO] DVD

Holly Hunter *Melanie* • Evan Rachel Wood *Tracy* • Nikki Reed *Evie Zamora* • Jeremy Sisto *Brady* • Brady Corbet *Mason* • Deborah Kara Unger *Brooke* • Kip Pardue *Luke* • Sarah Clarke *Birdie* • DW Moffett *Travis* ■ *Dir* Catherine Hardwicke • *Scr* Catherine Hardwicke, Nikki Reed

Thirteen at Dinner ★★★ U

Murder mystery 1985 · US · Colour · 90mins

Peter Ustinov gives another performance as Hercule Poirot, troubled by the murder of a peer. It's glossy, efficient entertainment, with a highly contrived denouement, but Ustinov is fine and Faye Dunaway holds back nothing as the suspected widow. DP [VIDEO]

Peter Ustinov *Hercule Poirot* • Faye Dunaway *Jane Wilkinson/Carlotta Adams* • David Suchet *Inspector Japp* • Jonathan Cecil *Arthur Hastings* • Bill Nighy *Ronald Marsh* • Diane Keen *Jenny Driver* • John Stride *Film director* • Benedict Taylor *Donald Ross* ■ *Dir* Lou Antonio • *Scr* Rod Browning, from the novel *Lord Edgware Dies* by Agatha Christie

13 Conversations about One Thing ★★★ 15

Drama 2001 · US · Colour · 103mins

The lives of disparate New Yorkers intertwine to poignant effect in this gentle, low-budget drama from Jill Sprecher. Loosely themed around the topic of happiness, the unhurried film is composed of a series of dialogue-driven vignettes about four key characters linked together by fate. Matthew McConaughey and Alan Arkin elicit deep empathy in their respective roles as a cocksure attorney who falls foul of the law and a bitter office middleman. Less successful are the strands concerning cleaner Clea DuVall and mooching physics professor John Turturro. Yet, though these weaker segments drag slightly, the mostly well-written script and subtle acting shine through. SF. Contains swearing.

Matthew McConaughey *Troy* • John Turturro *Walker* • Alan Arkin *Gene* • Clea DuVall *Beatrice* • Amy Irving *Patricia* • Barbara Sukowa *Helen* • Tia Texada *Dorrie* • Frankie Faison *Dick Lacey* • Shawn Elliott *Mickey Wheeler* • William Wise *Wade Bowman* ■ *Dir* Jill Sprecher • *Scr* Karen Sprecher, Jill Sprecher

Thirteen Days ★★★★ 12

Historical drama
2000 · US · Colour · 139mins

The Cuban Missile Crisis – a key event in the Kennedy presidency – is brought to life in this fascinating drama starring Kevin Costner and directed by Roger Donaldson. In October 1962, President John F Kennedy (a mesmerising performance by Canadian actor Bruce Greenwood) was faced with the prospect of a nuclear showdown, following the discovery of Soviet missile bases in Cuba. Costner is superb as Kenny O'Donnell, a real-life adviser to the President. Part history lesson and part political drama, Donaldson's film is gripping and powerful, despite the essentially static nature of the story. JB [VIDEO] DVD

Kevin Costner *Kenny O'Donnell* • Bruce Greenwood *John F Kennedy* • Steven Culp *Robert F Kennedy* • Dylan Baker *Robert McNamara* • Michael Fairman *Adlai Stevenson* • Henry Strozier *Dean Rusk* • Frank Wood *McGeorge Bundy* • Len Cariou *Dean Acheson* ■ *Dir* Roger Donaldson • *Scr* David Self, from the book *The Kennedy Tapes – Inside the White House During the Cuban Missile Crisis* by Ernest R May, Philip D Zelikow

13 East Street ★

Crime thriller 1952 · UK · BW · 70mins

Quota-quickie expert John Gilling scripted this tiresome affair, in which cop Patrick Holt poses as a jewel thief on the run in order to infiltrate a gang of warehouse breakers. Although moll Sandra Dorne convinces the boss to trust him, it's only a matter of time before he's exposed. Dora Bryan is good value as a nosey neighbour, but that's little compensation. DP

Patrick Holt *Detective Fraser/Gerald Blake* • Sandra Dorne *Judy* • Robert Ayres *Larry Conn* • Sonia Holm *Joan* • Dora Bryan *Valerie* • Michael Balfour *Joey Long* • Michael Brennan *George Mack* ■ *Dir* Robert S Baker • *Scr* John Gilling, from a story by Robert S Baker

13 Ghosts ★★★ PG

Horror 1959 · US · Colour and BW · 78mins

Forget the soulless 2001 remake and stick with gimmick king William Castle's campy and still spookily entertaining original. Donald Woods inherits a haunted mansion from an eccentric uncle under strict instructions from his last will to move his family in. Unaware that a vast fortune lies hidden in the house, the family is terrified they will soon join the poltergeist inmates, especially when somebody else is out to kill them and get the treasure. Originally filmed in Illusion-O, a 3-D variant allowing the viewer to see the ghosts (or not depending on their nervousness), Castle's sweetly juvenile shocker is one of his most endearing fright romps. AJ [VIDEO]

Charles Herbert *Buck Zorba* • Jo Morrow *Medea Zorba* • Martin Milner *Ben Rush* • Rosemary DeCamp *Hilda Zorba* • Donald Woods *Cyrus Zorba* • Margaret Hamilton *Elaine Zacharides* ■ *Dir* William Castle • *Scr* Robb White

Thir13en Ghosts ★★ 15

Horror thriller 2001 · US · Colour · 90mins

All fabulous production design and nothing else, this fails to capture the frightening fun of William Castle's 1959 original. Recently widowed Tony Shalhoub inherits the spectacular house of his late uncle F Murray Abraham, and learns that the 12 ghosts of the Black Zodiac are imprisoned there as part of uncle's plan to unlock the gateway to hell. Saddled with predictable twists and a plodding pace, this is just another dreaded remake. AJ. Contains violence, swearing, nudity. [VIDEO] DVD

Tony Shalhoub *Arthur Kriticos* • Embeth Davidtz *Kalina* • Matthew Lillard *Dennis Rafkin* • Shannon Elizabeth *Kathy Kriticos* • Alec Roberts *Bobby Kriticos* • JR Bourne *Ben Moss* • F Murray Abraham *Cyrus Kriticos* ■ *Dir* Steve Beck • *Scr* Neal Marshall Stevens [Neal Stevens], Richard D'Ovidio, from a story by Robb White

13 Going on 30 ★★★ 12

Romantic comedy fantasy
2004 · US · Colour · 93mins

Cute and frothy, this body-swap comedy is an ultra-girlie, wish-fulfilment fantasy that plays like a teen magazine come to life. In it, a nerdy 13-year-old's dreams become reality when she's miraculously transformed into gorgeous and successful 30-year-old Jennifer Garner. Though the events that follow are unrealistic fancy, Garner's delightful and authentic turn helps paper over many of the plot holes. Her adolescent take on the adult world is completely charming, infusing the film with a scatty innocence. SF. Contains sexual references. [VIDEO] DVD

Jennifer Garner *Jenna Rink* • Mark Ruffalo *Matt Flamhaff* • Judy Greer *Lucy Wyman* • Andy Serkis *Richard Kneeland* • Kathy Baker *Bev Rink* • Phil Reeves *Wayne Rink* • Samuel Ball *Alex Carlson* ■ *Dir* Gary Winick • *Scr* Josh Goldsmith, Cathy Yuspa

13 Rue Madeleine ★★ U

Second World War spy drama
1946 · US · BW · 95mins

This is one of several documentary-style dramas, produced by Louis de Rochemont and adopting the stentorian style of the *March of Time* newsreels he co-created. A narrator intones, the images look snatched from real-life... and a Hollywood star gives the game away. In this case it's James Cagney, slightly miscast as an American agent training spies for service in occupied Europe. Directed by that notorious on-set bully Henry Hathaway, the picture was shot in New England and Quebec, which was, as far as Hollywood was concerned, halfway to France. AT [VIDEO] DVD

James Cagney *Robert Sharkey* • Annabella *Suzanne de Beaumont* • Richard Conte *Bill O'Connell/Wilhelm Kuncel* • Frank Latimore *Jeff Lassiter* • Walter Abel *Charles Stevenson Gibson* • Melville Cooper *Pappy Simpson* • Sam Jaffe *Mayor Galimard* ■ *Dir* Henry Hathaway • *Scr* John Monks Jr, Sy Bartlett

13 West Street ★★

Drama 1962 · US · BW · 79mins

Alan Ladd makes his penultimate screen appearance in this early example of a *Death Wish* movie, a cynical attempt to tap into the burgeoning youth market. With a touch more thought, it could have offered an intriguing insight into the reasons why well-heeled kids become involved in violence just like their counterparts across the tracks. While Ladd conducts his vendetta against Michael Callan's gang with typically repressed rage, his performance lacks the conviction of Rod Steiger's as the cop who fails to bring the gang to book. DP

Alan Ladd *Walt Sherill* • Rod Steiger *Det Sgt Koleski* • Michael Callan *Chuck Landry* • Dolores Dorn *Tracey Sherill* • Kenneth MacKenna *Paul Logan* • Margaret Hayes *Mrs Landry* ■ *Dir* Philip Leacock • *Scr* Bernard Schoenfeld, Robert Presnell Jr, from the novel *The Tiger among Us* by Leigh Brackett

The Thirteenth Floor ★★★ 15

Science-fiction mystery thriller
1999 · US · Colour · 96mins

Computer technician Craig Bierko finds himself the main suspect when his boss – the mastermind behind a computer simulation of 1937 Los Angeles populated with programmed inhabitants who are oblivious to their

T

actual origin – is found murdered. Though Bierko's subsequent investigation uncovers plenty of twists and turns, this unravels predictably but still retains interest. The computer simulation of the 1930s world perfectly re-creates the era, the performances are acceptable, and the script is intelligent and plausible. KB. Contains violence and swearing. DVD

Craig Bierko *Douglas Hall* • Armin Mueller-Stahl *Hannon Fuller* • Gretchen Mol *Jane Fuller* • Vincent D'Onofrio *Whitney/Ashton* • Dennis Haysbert *Detective Larry McBain* • Steven Schub *Zev Bernstein* • Jeremy Roberts *Tom* ■ *Dir* Josef Rusnak • *Scr* Josef Rusnak, Ravel Centeno-Rodriguez, from the novel *Simulacron 3* by Daniel Galouye

The Thirteenth Guest ★★

Murder mystery comedy
1932 · US · BW · 69mins

In this low-budget ensemble mystery story from the tiny Monogram studio, 13 guests – who were all present 13 years earlier at a dinner that saw the sudden death of their host – reassemble, and find themselves under collective threat from a mysterious, hooded killer. Ginger Rogers is the leading lady of this old-fashioned but quite entertaining comedy thriller. RK

Ginger Rogers *Marie Morgan/Lela* • Lyle Talbot *Phil Winston* • J Farrell MacDonald *Capt Ryan* • James C Eagles *Harold "Bud" Morgan* • Eddie Phillips *Thor Jensen* • Erville Alderson *John Adams* • Robert Klein *John Barksdale* • Crauford Kent *Dr Sherwood* ■ *Dir* Albert Ray • *Scr* Frances Hyland, Arthur Hoerl, Armitage Trail, from the novel by Armitage Trail

The 13th Letter ★★★

Film noir mystery drama
1950 · US · BW · 85mins

Using a mixed French and American cast (along with Englishman Michael Rennie), producer/director Otto Preminger turned to Henri-George Clouzot's masterly French thriller, *The Raven*, for this tale about a series of poison-pen letters that cause havoc in a provincial French-Canadian town. Charles Boyer as a doctor, Constance Smith as his wife, Rennie – the object of Smith's unwelcome attentions – and Linda Darnell, as a woman whose beauty is marred by a club foot, all convince in the central roles. A little melodramatic, this is still suspenseful entertainment. RK

Linda Darnell *Denise* • Charles Boyer *Dr Laurent* • Michael Rennie *Dr Pearson* • Constance Smith *Cora Laurent* • Françoise Rosay *Mrs Sims* • Judith Evelyn *Sister Marie* • Guy Sorel *Robert Helier* ■ *Dir* Otto Preminger • *Scr* Howard Koch, from the story *Le Corbeau* by Louis Chavance

The 13th Warrior ★★★ 15

Period action adventure
1999 · US · Colour · 102mins

Director John McTiernan's old-fashioned horror adventure stars Antonio Banderas (looking decidedly uncomfortable) as a a tenth-century Arab emissary abducted by Norsemen to fight the barbaric cannibals who are terrorising their countrymen. How Banderas adapts to a totally alien culture and uncovers the secrets of the feared "spirits in the mist" makes for a visually arresting, if half-baked, saga. The film is never boring, but it's not really that exciting either. Jerry Goldsmith's marvellously stirring soundtrack is a major plus, however. AJ. Contains violence. DVD

Antonio Banderas *Ahmed Ibn Fahdlan* • Diane Venora *Queen Weilew* • Dennis Storhoi *Herger/Joyous* • Vladimir Kulich *Buliwyf* • Omar Sharif *Melchisidek* • Anders T Andersen *Wigliff, King's son* • Richard Bremmer *Skeld/Superstitious* • Tony Curran *Weath, musician* ■ *Dir* John McTiernan • *Scr* William Wisher, Warren Lewis, from the novel *Eaters of the Dead* by Michael Crichton

-30- ★★★ U

Drama
1959 · US · BW · 96mins

Jack Webb brought the deadpan *Dragnet* style to a select number of cinema features as producer, director and star. This one provides a documentary-like treatment of the few hours before a Los Angeles newspaper reaches its deadline. (The American title refers to the traditional sign for the end of a reporter's copy – in Britain, the film was retitled *Deadline Midnight*.) A story is breaking: a three-year-old girl and her dog have disappeared. It turns out she is lost down a storm drain and a massive search is launched. Webb (as the night editor) and a cast of little-known actors bring the characters vividly to life. AE

Jack Webb *Sam Gatlin* • William Conrad *Jim Bathgate* • David Nelson *Earl Collins* • Whitney Blake *Peggy Gatlin* • Louise Lorimer *Bernice Valentine* • James Bell *Ben Quinn* • Nancy Valentine *Jan Price* ■ *Dir* Jack Webb • *Scr* William Bowers

Thirty-Day Princess ★★★

Romantic comedy
1934 · US · BW · 73mins

Sylvia Sidney stars in a dual role here. She's a foreign princess, in New York for a series of public appearances to raise money, and a down-on-her-luck actress and lookalike, hired to impersonate the royal visitor when the latter gets mumps. Cary Grant is an upper-crust newspaper publisher and the romantic interest, Edward Arnold the banker behind the deception. This small-scale romantic comedy overcomes its well-worn plot, thanks to the performances, the Paramount house-style and a charming script. RK

Sylvia Sidney *Nancy Lane/Princess "Zizzi" Catterina* • Cary Grant *Porter Madison III* • Edward Arnold *Richard Gresham* • Henry Stephenson *King Anatole XII* ■ *Dir* Marion Gering • *Scr* Sam Hellman, Edwin Justus Mayer, Preston Sturges, Frank Partos, from the story by Clarence Budington Kelland

30 Is a Dangerous Age, Cynthia ★★★

Romantic comedy
1968 · US · Colour · 84mins

One of those 1960s oddities, with everyone rushing around being breezily neurotic as nightclub musician Dudley Moore panics at the thought of imminently turning 30. Moore basically plays himself, even fronting his real-life jazz trio, and it works enjoyably enough, with Suzy Kendall suitably kooky and charming as the girl he chases. Not a movie that has aged with any dignity, but there are considerably worse examples of "swinging" celluloid than this. SH

Dudley Moore *Rupert Street* • Eddie Foy Jr *Oscar* • Suzy Kendall *Louise Hammond* • John Bird *Herbert Greenslade* • Duncan Macrae *Jock McCue* • Patricia Routledge *Mrs Woolley* • Peter Bayliss *Victor* • John Wells *Hon Gavin Hopton* ■ *Dir* Joseph McGrath • *Scr* Dudley Moore, Joseph McGrath, John Wells

The 39 Steps ★★★★★ U

Classic spy thriller
1935 · UK · BW · 82mins

Alfred Hitchcock brings John Buchan's novel to the screen with characteristic wit and verve, a style forged during the 1930s. This has all the ingredients of classic Hitch, not least the innocent man on the run, in this case visiting Canadian Richard Hannay (a winning Robert Donat), who gets dragged into an espionage plot after a night at the London music hall and ends up in Scotland handcuffed to a blonde (Madeleine Carroll) he met on the train. Playing "spot the recurring Hitchcock motif" is almost as thrilling as the chase itself. The chemistry between Donat and Carroll is a rare treat – when they are forced to share a room (quite shocking in 1935) we are in very dark Whitehall farce territory. AC DVD

Robert Donat *Richard Hannay* • Madeleine Carroll *Pamela* • Lucie Mannheim *Miss Smith* • Godfrey Tearle *Professor Jordan* • Peggy Ashcroft *Crofter's wife* • John Laurie *Crofter* • Helen Haye *Mrs Jordan* • Frank Cellier *Sheriff Watson* • Wylie Watson *Mr Memory* ■ *Dir* Alfred Hitchcock • *Scr* Charles Bennett, Alma Reville, Ian Hay, from the novel by John Buchan

The Thirty-Nine Steps ★★ U

Spy thriller
1959 · UK · Colour · 90mins

Alfred Hitchcock cast a long and large shadow, leaving many a director in debt to a master film-maker. But this remake of his 1935 classic thriller is totally overwhelmed by the original. Kenneth More battles bravely to take on the role of Richard Hannay that Robert Donat made so very suavely his own, but succumbs to a bout of overplayed bravado. TH DVD

Kenneth More *Richard Hannay* • Taina Elg *Fisher* • Brenda de Banzie *Nellie Lumsden* • Barry Jones *Professor Logan* • Reginald Beckwith *Lumsden* • Faith Brook *Nannie* • Michael Goodliffe *Brown* • James Hayter *Mr Memory* ■ *Dir* Ralph Thomas • *Scr* Frank Harvey, from the novel by John Buchan

The Thirty-Nine Steps ★★★ PG

Spy thriller
1978 · UK · Colour · 98mins

The third film of John Buchan's novel goes back to the story's original era (the eve of the First World War), but lays on a little too much period colour along the way. Robert Powell has the bearing but not the charm as hero Richard Hannay, on the run in the Scottish Highlands from foreign agents. The sinister mystery at the beginning and the famous climax are good, exciting fun in the best daredevil tradition. Unfortunately, the middle sags. DM DVD

Robert Powell *Richard Hannay* • David Warner *Appleton* • Eric Porter *Chief Supt Lomas* • Karen Dotrice *Alex Mackenzie* • John Mills *Scudder* • George Baker *Sir Walter Bullivant* • Ronald Pickup *Bayliss* • Donald Pickering *Marshall* • Timothy West *Porton* ■ *Dir* Don Sharp • *Scr* Michael Robson, from the novel by John Buchan

Thirty Seconds over Tokyo ★★★ U

Second World War drama
1944 · US · BW · 132mins

This overlong but impressively-staged war drama depicts America's first secret bombing raid over Tokyo, just four months after Pearl Harbor. Apart from the inevitable "woman's angle" – scenes with Van Johnson's wife back home – the first part of the film concentrates on military planning, led by Spencer Tracy as the real-life Lt Col James Doolittle. The script, by future blacklistee Dalton Trumbo, is full of heroic speeches, and the special effects won an Oscar. AT

Spencer Tracy *Lt Col James H Doolittle* • Van Johnson *Capt Ted W Lawson* • Robert Walker *David Thatcher* • Phyllis Thaxter *Ellen Jones Lawson* • Tim Murdock *Dean Davenport* • Scott McKay *Davey Jones* • Robert Mitchum *Bob Gray* ■ *Dir* Mervyn LeRoy • *Scr* Dalton Trumbo, from the novel by Capt Ted W Lawson, Robert Considine

36 Chowringhee Lane ★★★

Drama
1982 · Ind · Colour · 112mins

Produced by Bollywood superstar Shashi Kapoor, Aparna Sen's directorial debut has the chintzy feel of an early Merchant Ivory picture. Yet it also contains several elements that go against the general atmosphere of post-colonial purdah and regret, notably a surreal dream sequence and some extravagant editing. Jennifer Kendal is magnificent as the sixty-something teacher who seizes upon the presence of writer Dhritiman Chatterjee and his lover, Debashree Roy, in her Calcutta apartment as a release from a life tinged with sadness and disappointment. Melancholic and melodramatic, yet quite affecting. DP

Jennifer Kendal *Miss Violet Stoneham* • Dhritiman Chatterjee *Samaresh Moitra* • Geoffrey Kendal *Eddie Stoneham* ■ *Dir/Scr* Aparna Sen

36 Hours ★★★★

Second World War spy thriller
1964 · US · BW · 114mins

An American intelligence officer is kidnapped by Nazi agents who want him to reveal the D-day invasion plans in this ingeniously scripted film that was a substantial hit in the UK. It's often remembered more for its plot than its title – there can't be many movie buffs around who haven't at one time or another been asked: "What was the name of that film where James Garner is captured by the Germans and told that he's spent the last six years in an amnesiac state?" Well, it's this one, in all its black-and-white splendour, a cleverly-mounted opus with a particularly persuasive Rod Taylor as a Nazi major. TS

James Garner *Major Jefferson Pike* • Rod Taylor *Major Walter Gerber* • Eva Marie Saint *Anna Hedler* • Werner Peters *Otto Schack* • Alan Napier *Colonel Peter MacLean* • Celia Lovsky *Elsa* ■ *Dir* George Seaton • *Scr* George Seaton, from a story by Carl K Hittleman, Luis H Vance and the story *Beware of the Dog* by Roald Dahl in *Harper's*

36 Hours to Die ★★ 18

Crime thriller
1999 · US/Can · Colour · 90mins

Recuperating from a heart attack, brewery owner Treat Williams learns that his brother has managed to embroil them in a deadly, Mob-run extortion scheme. His family and business are suddenly threatened, and he finds he has only 36 hours to fend off the gangsters. While the ending of this TV movie is never much in doubt, the script by Robert Rodat contains enough twists and idiosyncrasies to make it seem fresh. MC DVD

Treat Williams *Noah Stone* • Kim Cattrall *Kim Stone* • Saul Rubinek *Morano* • Carroll O'Connor *Uncle Jack O'Malley* • Alain Goulem *Frank Stone* • Barbara Eve Harris *Barbara Woods* • Stewart Bick *Sam* ■ *Dir* Yves Simoneau • *Scr* Robert Rodat

Thirty Two Short Films about Glenn Gould ★★★★★ U

Biographical drama
1993 · Can · Colour · 93mins

It's too close to say which is the better pianist biopic: this exceptional Canadian film inspired by Bach's *Goldberg Variations* or *Shine*, Scott Hicks's outstanding feature on the life of Australian David Helfgott. The key to François Girard's picture is that he leaves Gould an enigma, allowing us to draw our own conclusions from the 32 vignettes that range from childhood to his sudden decision to quit the concert hall and concentrate on recording. Colm Feore's performance is remarkable, while Girard's use of sound is as masterly as his visual ingenuity and his sense that the minor episode is often as revealing as a major turning point. DP

Colm Feore *Glenn Gould* • Derek Keurvorst *Gould's father* • Katya Ladan *Gould's mother* • Devon Anderson *Glenn aged 3* • Joshua Greenblatt *Glenn aged 8* • Sean Ryan *Glenn*

T

aged 12 • Kate Hennig *Chambermaid* ■ *Dir* François Girard • *Scr* François Girard, Don McKellar, Nick McKinney

This above All ★★★

Second World War drama
1942 · US · BW · 109mins

A soapy wartime drama, produced by 20th Century-Fox with all the patriotic stops out and starring Tyrone Power as an unlikely working-class British soldier, who romances upper-class WAAF Joan Fontaine while struggling with pacifist urges. There's a marvellous supporting cast of British expats, and director Anatole Litvak does so well by RC Sherriff's script that even the most cynical might be reaching for the tissues. TS

Tyrone Power *Clive Briggs* • Joan Fontaine *Prudence Cathaway* • Thomas Mitchell *Monty* • Henry Stephenson *General Cathaway* • Nigel Bruce *Ramsbottom* • Gladys Cooper *Iris* • Philip Merivale *Dr Roger Cathaway* • Alexander Knox *Rector* ■ *Dir* Anatole Litvak • *Scr* RC Sherriff, from the novel by Eric Knight

This Angry Age ★★★

Drama 1957 · It/US · Colour · 111mins

Shot by French director René Clement on an island off Thailand with a cast that included Italians Silvana Mangano and Alida Valli and Americans Jo Van Fleet and Anthony Perkins playing French colonials in Indochina, the film sufferes from its hybrid parentage and over-melodramatic moments. But it caught the rich hues of the tropics in Technirama, and is an absorbing enough study of a colonial family. RB

Anthony Perkins *Joseph Dufresne* • Silvana Mangano *Suzanne Dufresne* • Richard Conte *Michael* • Jo Van Fleet *Madame Dufresne* • Nehemiah Persoff *Albert* • Alida Valli *Claude* ■ *Dir* René Clément • *Scr* Irwin Shaw, Rene Clement, from the novel *Un Barrage contre le Pacifique (Sea Wall)* by Marguerite Duras

This Boy's Life ★★★★ 15

Biographical drama
1993 · US · Colour · 110mins

Anyone who doubts Leonardo DiCaprio's acting abilities should check out this moving coming-of-age drama. In this troubling tale set in Seattle in the 1950s, he plays the rebellious teenage son of struggling mum Ellen Barkin who finds himself locked in a battle of wills with bullying stepfather Robert De Niro. After the lightweight antics of his first American movie, *Doc Hollywood*, British director Michael Caton-Jones relishes the opportunity to try out meatier material and makes the most of Robert Getchell's largely unsentimental adaptation of Tobias Wolff's acclaimed autobiography. JF. Contains violence, swearing and sex scenes. [VIDEO] DVD

Robert De Niro *Dwight Hansen* • Ellen Barkin *Caroline Wolff* • Leonardo DiCaprio *Toby* • Jonah Blechman *Arthur Gayle* • Eliza Dushku *Pearl* • Chris Cooper *Roy* • Carla Gugino *Norma* • Tobey Maguire *Chuck Bolger* ■ *Dir* Michael Caton-Jones • *Scr* Robert Getchell, from the autobiography by Tobias Wolff

This Could Be the Night ★★★ U

Romantic comedy 1957 · US · BW · 104mins

Virginal New England college graduate Jean Simmons takes a night job as secretary to a Manhattan club owner with underworld connections (Paul Douglas). She clashes with his aggressive partner Anthony Franciosa and affects the lives of everybody connected with the establishment. Simmons is excellent and Douglas is terrific as the gentlemanly rough diamond who takes her to his heart. A lively case of wishful thinking. RK

Jean Simmons *Anne Leeds* • Paul Douglas *Rocco* • Anthony Franciosa *Tony Armotti* • Julie Wilson *Ivy Corlane* • Neile Adams *Patsy St Clair* • Joan Blondell *Crystal St Clair* ■ *Dir* Robert Wise • *Scr* Isobel Lennart, from stories by Cordelia Baird Gross

This Day and Age ★

Crime drama 1933 · US · BW · 82mins

Cecil B DeMille offers an extreme right-wing solution to the problem of the American gangster. When the law can't convict a known killer (Charles Bickford), a group of decent high school kids, led by Richard Cromwell, steps in to kidnap him and extract a confession by dangling him over a pit full of rats. The gangster is so broken by the experience that he signs a confession before the authorities. A hysterical and dangerous film. AE

Charles Bickford *Louis Garrett* • Richard Cromwell *Steve Smith* • Judith Allen *Gay Merrick* • Harry Green *Herman* • Bradley Page *Toledo* • Eddie Nugent [Edward Nugent] *Don Merrick* ■ *Dir* Cecil B DeMille • *Scr* Bartlett Cormack

This Earth Is Mine ★★★

Drama 1959 · US · Colour · 123mins

A melodrama on an epic scale, this enjoyable tosh provides ideal, undemanding matinée fare. Rock Hudson and Jean Simmons barely flex their acting muscles but look superb. The real acting comes from Dorothy McGuire and Claude Rains, who virtually steal this Prohibition-era saga of uproar in the Napa Valley vineyards from their co-stars. Although his eye for landscape never falters, veteran director Henry King has problems pulling together the sprawling script. TS

Rock Hudson *John Rambeau* • Jean Simmons *Elizabeth* • Dorothy McGuire *Martha* • Claude Rains *Philippe Rambeau* • Kent Smith *Francis Fairon* ■ *Dir* Henry King • *Scr* Casey Robinson, from the novel *The Cup and the Sword* by Alice Tisdale Hobart

This Filthy Earth ★★ 15

Drama 2001 · UK · Colour · 106mins

As a celebration of the soil, Andrew Kötting's highly individual adaptation of Emile Zola's novel is a laudable attempt at capturing the essence of its literary source. But the combination of naturalism and stylisation that so effectively informs the visuals proves the undoing of this film as a drama. Set in a remote rural community, it's a stormy tale of two sisters working the family farm until their relationships with men threaten to destroy their livelihood. Much of the dialogue is so exceedingly fruity that experienced actors and non-professionals alike are lured into overplaying the already fraught situations. DP

Rebecca Palmer *Francine* • Shane Attwooll *Buto* • Demelza Randall *Kath* • Xavier Tchili *Lek* • Dudley Sutton *Papa* ■ *Dir* Andrew Kötting • *Scr* Andrew Kötting, Sean Lock, from the novel *La Terre* by Emile Zola

This Gun for Hire ★★★

Crime drama 1942 · US · BW · 80mins

This is a tale involving ruthless fifth columnists, the cold-blooded hitman they hire and then try to dispose of, and the cabaret entertainer who gets caught up in the ensuing mess. The movie rocketed the unknown Alan Ladd to stardom on the strength of his performance as the loner-killer. It also began his popular teaming with Veronica Lake, whose combination of blonde cool and touching vulnerability clicked into box-office chemistry with the laconic and charismatic actor. RK

Veronica Lake *Ellen Graham* • Robert Preston *Michael Crane* • Laird Cregar *Willard Gates* • Alan Ladd *Philip Raven* • Tully Marshall *Alvin Brewster* ■ *Dir* Frank Tuttle • *Scr* Albert Maltz, WR Burnett, from the novel *A Gun For Sale* by Graham Greene

This Happy Breed ★★★★★ U

Drama 1944 · UK · Colour · 105mins

The second of David Lean's four collaborations with Noël Coward provides a fascinating picture of the way we were. The action is largely confined to an unremarkable but lovingly re-created Clapham home, but such is the ebb and flow of events (both domestic and historical) that the two hours it takes to cover the 20 inter-war years seem to fly by. Celia Johnson is superb as the sensible suburban housewife, while Kay Walsh gives a spirited performance as her mouthy daughter. But the best scenes belong to neighbours Robert Newton and Stanley Holloway, as a couple of very British chroniclers of their times. DP [VIDEO] DVD

Robert Newton *Frank Gibbons* • Celia Johnson *Ethel Gibbons* • John Mills *Billy Mitchell* • Kay Walsh *Queenie Gibbons* • Stanley Holloway *Bob Mitchell* • Amy Veness *Mrs Flint* • Alison Leggatt *Aunt Sylvia* • Laurence Olivier *Narrator* ■ *Dir* David Lean • *Scr* David Lean, Ronald Neame, Anthony Havelock-Allan, Noël Coward (uncredited), from the play by Noël Coward

This Happy Feeling ★★ U

Romantic comedy
1958 · US · Colour · 92mins

Hoping to repeat the success of the previous year's *Tammy and the Bachelor*, producer Ross Hunter put Debbie Reynolds in the path of another unsuspecting swain in this over-eager comedy, written and directed by Blake Edwards. But we're never quite caught up in the fun as Debbie tilts her cap at retired film star Curt Jurgens. Nor are we convinced by the arch quirkiness of such supporting characters as Estelle Winwood's tipsy cook. DP

Debbie Reynolds *Janet Blake* • Curt Jurgens *Preston Mitchell* • John Saxon *Bill Tremaine* • Alexis Smith *Nita Hollaway* • Mary Astor *Mrs Tremaine* ■ *Dir* Blake Edwards • *Scr* Blake Edwards, from the play *For Love or Money* by F Hugh Herbert

This Is a Hijack ★ 18

Crime thriller 1973 · US · Colour · 85mins

Along with "Fasten your safety belt and put your head between your knees", the title's statement is the scariest an airline passenger can hear. A pity, then, that this low-budget story of air-piracy is grounded by inadequacy of direction and blatant overacting, as Adam Roarke demands ransom money to pay off gambling debts. TH [VIDEO]

Adam Roarke *Mike Christie* • Neville Brand *Dominic Petrie* • Jay Robinson *Simon Scott* • Lynn Borden *Diane* • Milt Kamen *Arnold Phillips* • Dub Taylor *Sheriff Gordon* ■ *Dir* Barry Pollack

This Is Elvis ★★ PG

Biographical documentary drama
1981 · US · Colour and BW · 143mins

Not in the same league as John Carpenter's faithful biopic starring Kurt Russell (*Elvis – the Movie*), but an engaging failure, nevertheless. Writers/ directors Malcolm Leo and Andrew Solt blend in real footage with the staged scenes but, for all their efforts, do little more than scratch the surface of the myth behind the king of rock 'n' roll. JF. Contains swearing. [VIDEO]

David Scott *Elvis, aged 18* • Paul Boensch III *Elvis, aged ten* • Johnny Harra *Elvis, aged 42* • Lawrence Koller *Vernon Presley* • Rhonda Lyn *Priscilla Presley* • Dana Mackay *Elvis, aged 35* ■ *Dir/Scr* Malcolm Leo, Andrew Solt

This Is My Affair ★★★

Crime drama 1937 · US · BW · 99mins

This is a cracking crime story, set in the early 20th century. The "affair" turns out to be Robert Taylor's mission: he's been sent to the Midwest by President McKinley to root out bank robbers. Barbara Stanwyck is absolutely wonderful in an atypical role as a saloon singer, and it's easy to see how Taylor fell for her. They married for real two years later. TS

Robert Taylor (1) *Lieutenant Richard L Perry* • Barbara Stanwyck *Lil Duryea* • Victor McLaglen *Jock Ramsey* • Brian Donlevy *Batiste Duryea* • Sidney Blackmer *President Theodore Roosevelt* • John Carradine *Ed* • Alan Dinehart *Doc Keller* ■ *Dir* William A Seiter • *Scr* Allen Rivkin, Lamar Trotti, from the novel *The McKinley Case* by Melville Crossman

This Is My Father ★★★ 15

Romantic drama
1999 · Can/ Ire · Colour · 114mins

Compelling drama, with teacher James Caan learning a life lesson when a photo from his mother's past causes him to wonder about the identity of his father. This search for truth takes him to Ireland, where details of an unsuspected past romance emerge. Written and directed by Paul Quinn, and starring brother Aidan, James Caan, Stephen Rea, John Cusack and a who's who of Irish supporting actors. DA [VIDEO] DVD

Aidan Quinn *Kieran O'Day* • Moya Farrelly *Fiona Flynn* • Stephen Rea *Father Quinn* • John Cusack *Eddie Sharp, the pilot* • James Caan *Kieran Johnson* • Jacob Tierney *Jack, Kieran Johnson's nephew* • Colm Meaney *Seamus* ■ *Dir/Scr* Paul Quinn

This Is My Life ★★★ 15

Comedy drama 1992 · US · Colour · 89mins

The formidable Nora Ephron made her directorial debut with this tale of single mum Julie Kavner trying to pursue a career in the world of stand-up comedy. Her daughters (Gaby Hoffmann and Samantha Mathis) soon find that their increasingly absentee mother is using their experiences as material for her act. The cast is certainly a treat, while Ephron's writing is at her sharpest. Quite why the whole fails to gel is a great mystery, but there is definitely too much slack around the middle. SH [VIDEO]

Julie Kavner *Dottie Ingels* • Samantha Mathis *Erica Ingels* • Gaby Hoffmann *Opal Ingels* • Carrie Fisher *Claudia Curtis* • Dan Aykroyd *Arnold Moss* • Bob Nelson *Ed* • Marita Geraghty *Mia Jablon* ■ *Dir* Nora Ephron • *Scr* Nora Ephron, Delia Ephron, from the novel *This Is Your Life* by Meg Wolitzer

This Is My Love ★★

Drama 1954 · US · Colour · 90mins

Linda Darnell moves in to help her sister Faith Domergue and her brother-in-law Dan Duryea, who is confined to a wheelchair after an accident. Into this sad household comes dishy Rick Jason, with whom Darnell is desperately in love, but it is Domergue who captures his fancy. This is a high-octane mix of sexual frustration and passion, jealousy, deception and murder to be relished – but definitely not taken seriously – by fans of overheated melodrama. RK

Linda Darnell *Vida* • Rick Jason *Glenn* • Dan Duryea *Murray* • Faith Domergue *Evelyn* • Hal Baylor *Eddie* • Connie Russell ■ *Dir* Stuart Heisler • *Scr* Hugh Brooke, Hagar Wilde, from the story *Fear Has Black Wings* by Hugh Brooke

This Is My Street ★★

Drama 1963 · UK · BW · 102mins

The street of the title is a rather grim one in London's Battersea, before the place became gentrified, wherein a womanising lodger (Ian Hendry) seduces overburdened mother (June Ritchie). She becomes infatuated with him, but he dumps her for her sister. A well-written, nicely shot squalor fest. Fascinating fact: Mike Pratt and Annette Andre later starred together in

T

the original TV series, *Randall and Hopkirk (Deceased)*. JG

Ian Hendry *Harry King* • June Ritchie *Margery Graham* • John Hurt *Charlie* • Avice Landone *Lily* • Meredith Edwards *Steve* • Madge Ryan *Kitty* • Annette Andre *Jinny* • Mike Pratt *Sid* ■ *Dir* Sidney Hayers • *Scr* Bill MacIlwraith, from the novel by Nan Maynard

This Is Not a Love Song ★★ 18

Crime thriller 2002 · UK · Colour · 91mins

Following their lacklustre teaming on *The Darkest Light*, screenwriter Simon Beaufoy and director Bille Eltringham reunite for this equally sombre story about a couple of lower-rung townies who are forced to fend for themselves in the inhospitable wilderness following the accidental death of a farmer's daughter. The plot is clumsily contrived, the direction self-consciously rough 'n' ready and the workshop origins of the performances are always apparent. DP. Contains swearing, violence and drug abuse.

Michael Colgan *Spike* • Kenny Glenaan [Kenneth Glenaan] *Heaton* • David Bradley (3) *Mr Bellamy* • John Henshaw *Arthur* • Adam Pepper *William* • Keri Arnold *Gerry* • Chris Middleton *Policeman* ■ *Dir* Bille Eltringham • *Scr* Simon Beaufoy

This Is Spinal Tap ★★★★★ 15

Spoof documentary
1984 · US · Colour · 79mins

This brilliantly crafted and completely on-target satire of the rock 'n' roll industry is filmed in mock documentary style, with every rock-music cliché savagely lampooned for maximum hilarity, as director Rob Reiner follows a fictitious British heavy metal band on tour. The Stonehenge-inspired production number is a showstopping highlight, but there's also immense pleasure to be had in the details, particularly the unbelievably crass song lyrics. Christopher Guest and Michael McKean are perfect as the group's incredibly stupid lead guitarist and singer, and Reiner's unsurpassed spoof never hits a false note. A cult classic and a pop send-up landmark. AJ. Contains swearing. DVD

Christopher Guest *Nigel Tufnel (lead guitar)* • Michael McKean *David St Hubbins (lead guitar)* • Harry Shearer *Derek Smalls (bass)* • RJ Parnell *Mick Shrimpton (drums)* • David Kaff *Viv Savage (keyboards)* • Rob Reiner *Marti DiBergi* • Bruno Kirby *Tommy Pischedda* • Anjelica Huston *Designer* • Billy Crystal *Mime artist* • Patrick Macnee *Sir Denis Eaton-Hogg* ■ *Dir* Rob Reiner • *Scr* Christopher Guest, Michael McKean, Harry Shearer, Rob Reiner

T

This Is the Army ★★★ U

Musical revue 1943 · US · Colour · 116mins

Mainly of historical interest, this filmed record of Irving Berlin's patriotic 1940s stage revue is performed partly by amateur military personnel supported by a flock of Warner Brothers contract players, including hoofer and future Republican senator George Murphy, bizarrely playing the father of actor and future US president Ronald Reagan (Murphy was nine years Reagan's senior). Also in the cast is world heavyweight champion Joe Louis, and Berlin himself singing *Oh, How I Hate To Get Up In The Morning*. RB

Irving Berlin • George Murphy *Jerry Jones* • Joan Leslie *Eileen Dibble* • George Tobias *Maxie Twardofsky* • Alan Hale *Sgt McGee* • Charles Butterworth *Eddie Dibble* • Rosemary DeCamp *Ethel* • Kate Smith • Ronald Reagan *Johnny Jones* • Joe Louis ■ *Dir* Michael Curtiz • *Scr* Casey Robinson, Capt Claude Binyon, Philip G Epstein, Julius G Epstein, from the play by Irving Berlin

This Is the Night ★★★

Romantic comedy 1932 · US · BW · 78mins

Fifth-billed Cary Grant plays his first featured role at Paramount as an Olympic javelin champion and husband of Thelma Todd, who arrives at her Paris hotel with her lover Roland Young in tow, to find Grant unexpectedly there. The three of them, plus Young's pal Charlie Ruggles and Lily Damita, an actress hired to pose as Young's nonexistent wife, go to Venice where the male trio are captivated by Damita. Directed with brio by Frank Tuttle, it's mildly risqué, sophisticated and entertaining. RK

Lili Damita *Germaine* • Charlie Ruggles [Charles Ruggles] *Bunny West* • Roland Young *Gerald Gray* • Thelma Todd *Claire* • Cary Grant *Stephen* ■ *Dir* Frank Tuttle • *Scr* Benjamin Glazer, George Marion, from the play *Pouche* by René Peter, Henri Falk and the English-language adaptation, *Naughty Cinderella* by Avery Hopwood

This Is the Sea ★★ 15

Drama 1996 · Ire/UK/US · Colour · 103mins

It's hard on well-intentioned films with good moments to condemn them with faint praise, but that's the case with this *Romeo and Juliet* story set in Ireland just after the 1994 ceasefire. The film's chief merit is in the young performers. Samantha Morton plays a protestant much sheltered by her mother. When she goes to Belfast she meets Ross McDade, a Catholic with ties to the IRA. Honest and non-partisan. BB. Contains swearing.

Richard Harris *Old Man Jacobs* • Gabriel Byrne *Rohan* • John Lynch *Padhar McAliskey* • Dearbhla Molloy *Ma Stokes* • Ian McIlhinney *Da Stokes* • Samantha Morton *Hazel Stokes* • Ross McDade *Malachy McAliskey* • Rick Leaf *Pastor Lamthorn* ■ *Dir/Scr* Mary McGuckian

This Island Earth ★★★★ PG

Science-fiction adventure
1955 · US · Colour · 82mins

This intelligent slice of 1950s sci-fi ranks among the best and most cleverly conceived of the genre. Really it's a film of two parts. A talky earthbound section finds brainy boffins being recruited by the otherworldly Jeff Morrow to save his distant homeland from destruction by interplanetary warfare. That's followed by a full-blooded space opera featuring astounding surrealistic landscapes on the planet Metaluna and fearsome insect-like mutations with huge bulbous craniums. RS

Jeff Morrow *Exeter* • Faith Domergue *Dr Ruth Adams* • Rex Reason *Dr Cal Meacham* • Lance Fuller *Brack* • Russell Johnson *Steve Carlson* • Richard Nichols *Joe Wilson* • Karl Lindt *Engelborg* • Douglas Spencer *Monitor* ■ *Dir* Joseph M Newman • *Scr* Franklin Coen, Edward G O'Callaghan, from the novel *The Alien Machine* by Raymond F Jones

This Land Is Mine ★★

Second World War drama
1943 · US · BW · 103mins

Throughout the Second World War, Hollywood failed to capture the fear and suspicion that pervaded occupied Europe. This tale of a cowardly schoolteacher, played by Charles Laughton, who is inspired to heroism by his love for a Resistance fighter, Maureen O'Hara, is no exception. Jean Renoir's inability to re-create the atmosphere of Vichy France is partly excused by the fact that he had been living in exile from his homeland since 1940, after the Nazis placed him on a death list for his socialist sympathies. This bland picture is directed with virtually no enthusiasm for its clichéd villagers and hysterical Nazis. DP

Charles Laughton *Albert Lory* • Maureen O'Hara *Louise Martin* • George Sanders *George Lambert* • Walter Slezak *Major Erich von Keller* • Kent Smith *Paul Martin* ■ *Dir* Jean Renoir • *Scr* Dudley Nichols

This Love of Ours ★★

Melodrama 1945 · US · BW · 90mins

Merle Oberon and Charles Korvin star in this banal melodrama about a jealous husband who unjustly deserts his wife. Years later, he discovers her in a Chicago nightclub, assisting Claude Rains in his act, and begs her forgiveness. Director William Dieterle, given a budget of $2 million, expertly attempts to extract every ounce of drama he can from his low-voltage cast and the pitiful script, recycled in 1955 as *Never Say Goodbye* with Rock Hudson and Cornell Borchers. RK

Merle Oberon *Karin Touzac/Florence Hale* • Charles Korvin *Michel Touzac* • Claude Rains *Dr Joseph Targel* • Carl Esmond *Uncle Robert* • Sue England *Susette Touzac* • Jess Barker *Chadwick* • Harry Davenport *Dr Jerry Wilkerson* ■ *Dir* William Dieterle • *Scr* Bruce Manning, John Klorer, Leonard Lee, from the play *Come Prima Meglio de Prima* by Luigi Pirandello

This Man Can't Die ★★

Spaghetti western 1967 · It · Colour · 90mins

Director Giancarlo Baldanello reheats the familiar recipe in this violent, no-surprises spaghetti western which isn't a patch on the ones that Sergio Leone used to make. Set during the American Civil War, it's a tired tale of revenge, with Guy Madison as the soldier of fortune determined to mete out his own kind of justice to the affluent town boss who had his parents killed. DP. Italian dialogue dubbed into English.

Guy Madison *Martin Benson* • Peter Martell *Tony Guy* • Rik Battaglia *Vic Graham* • Lucienne Bridou *Susy Benson* • Steve Merrick *Daniel Benson* • Rosalba Neri *Jenny Benson* • John Bartha *Melin* ■ *Dir* Giancarlo Baldanello • *Scr* Luigi Emmanuele, Gino Mangini, from a story by Luigi Emmanuele

This Man Is Mine ★★

Drama 1934 · US · BW · 75mins

RKO and director John Cromwell surrounded the lovely Irene Dunne with all the elegant accoutrements – sets, clothes and a Max Steiner score – that her fans would expect, but neglected to give her a convincing script or a sufficiently attractive leading man. The plot has Dunne battling to keep the affections of her philandering husband (Ralph Bellamy) when he falls into the seductive clutches of Constance Cummings. Wafer-thin and disappointingly dull, but it's all over swiftly. RK

Irene Dunne *Tony Dunlap* • Ralph Bellamy *Jim Dunlap* • Constance Cummings *Francesca "Fran" Harper* • Kay Johnson *Bee McCrea* • Charles Starrett *Jud McCrea* • Sidney Blackmer *Mort Holmes* ■ *Dir* John Cromwell • *Scr* Jane Murfin, from the play *Love Flies in the Window* by Anne Morrison Chapin

This Man's Navy ★★ U

Second World War comedy drama
1945 · US · BW · 99mins

The appeal of Wallace Beery can be hard to fathom now, but he was one of MGM's most reliable draws for nearly 20 years. In this piece of sentimental twaddle, he's the airship pilot who boasts of a nonexistent son, then finds young Tom Drake to play the part. After the boy also becomes a flyer, the two have their differences but are reunited behind Japanese lines during the Second World War. A flyer himself, director William A Wellman must have been attracted by the location shooting at naval dirigible bases. AE

Wallace Beery *Ned Trumpet* • Tom Drake *Jess Weaver* • James Gleason *Jimmy Shannon* • Jan Clayton *Cathey Cortland* • Selena Royle *Maude Weaver* • Noah Beery Sr [Noah Beery] *Joe Hodum* ■ *Dir* William A Wellman • *Scr* Borden Chase, Allen Rivkin, from a story by Borden Chase, from an idea by Comdr Herman E Halland

This Modern Age ★★

Romantic drama 1931 · US · BW · 68mins

Joan Crawford arrives in Paris to seek Pauline Frederick, the mother who left when she was a child. The reunion is a success until Crawford's association with drunkard Monroe Owsley breaks up her engagement to the whiter-than-white knight Neil Hamilton. His discovery that her mother is the kept mistress of a wealthy married man sends the girl hurtling into bitter debauchery. Unconvincing, even by the standards of the genre, but this dated melodrama is an absolute must for collectors of early Crawford, here uncharacteristically innocent, arch and winsome, and blonde! RK

Joan Crawford *Valentine Winters* • Pauline Frederick *Diane Winters* • Neil Hamilton *Bob Blake* • Monroe Owsley *Tony* • Hobart Bosworth *Mr Blake* • Emma Dunn *Mrs Blake* ■ *Dir* Nicholas Grindé [Nick Grinde] • *Scr* Sylvia Thalberg, Frank Butler, John Meehan, from the short story *Girls Together* by Mildred Cram

This Other Eden ★★ U

Comedy 1959 · UK · BW · 80mins

This is an overwrought tale about the emotions that erupt when the statue of a long-dead IRA hero is blown up in the square of a sleepy Irish village. Leslie Phillips is fine as the son of the Black and Tan who shot the gunman, and who is blamed for the explosion. He is adequately supported by Audrey Dalton as his lover and Norman Rodway as the terrorist's seminarian son, but the film lacks power. DP

Audrey Dalton *Maire McRoarty* • Leslie Phillips *Crispin Brown* • Niall MacGinnis *Devereaux* • Geoffrey Golden *McRoarty* • Norman Rodway *Conor Heaphy* • Milo O'Shea *Pat Tweedy* ■ *Dir* Muriel Box • *Scr* Patrick Kirwan, Blanaid Irvine, from the play by Louis d'Alton

This Property Is Condemned ★★★ 15

Drama 1966 · US · Colour · 105mins

Francis Ford Coppola was one of the screenwriters, but though his name appears on the credits he had little to do with the film that was eventually made. The setting is a boarding house during the Depression where landlady Kate Reid exploits her daughter Natalie Wood's charms to attract custom, but Wood has her eye on nice Robert Redford. The beautiful camerawork of James Wong Howe, the fresh performances and Sydney Pollack's assured direction keep this impressive film from overheating. AT DVD

Natalie Wood *Alva Starr* • Robert Redford *Owen Legate* • Charles Bronson *JJ Nichols* • Kate Reid *Hazel Starr* • Mary Badham *Willie Starr* • Alan Baxter *Knopke* • Robert Blake *Sidney* • John Harding *Johnson* • Dabney Coleman *Salesman* ■ *Dir* Sydney Pollack • *Scr* Francis Ford Coppola, Fred Coe, Edith Sommer, from the play by Tennessee Williams

This Rebel Breed ★

Crime drama 1960 · US · BW · 92mins

Rita Moreno is the best thing about this crude and exploitative story of racial strife among teenage gangs of black, white and Latin Americans. A brief lecture at the end by a police officer hardly overcomes the relish with which the final riot is staged or the general air of sensationalism. AE

Rita Moreno *Lola* • Mark Damon *Frank* • Gerald Mohr *Lt Brooks* • Jay Novello *Papa* • Eugene Martin *Rudy* • Tom Gilson *Muscles* • Diane Cannon [Dyan Cannon] *Wiggles* ■ *Dir* Richard L Bare • *Scr* Morris Lee Green, from the story *All God's Children* by William Rowland, Irma Berk

This Reckless Age ★★★

Comedy 1932 · US · BW · 63mins

Charles "Buddy" Rogers and Frances Dee), whose parents have sacrificed themselves to a life of hardship to give them every advantage, turn out ungratefully self-absorbed and shallow. They rather unconvincingly come good over the course of a film that otherwise successfully treads a fine line between seriousness and humour, and demonstrates that the "generation gap" is nothing new. RK

Charles "Buddy" Rogers *Bradley Ingals* • Richard Bennett *Donald Ingals* • Peggy Shannon *Mary Burke* • Charles Ruggles *Goliath Whitney* • Frances Dee *Lois Ingals* • Frances Starr *Eunice Ingals* ■ *Dir* Frank Tuttle • *Scr* Joseph L Mankiewicz, from the play *The Goose Hangs High* by Lewis Beach

This Side of Heaven ★★

Comedy drama 1934 · US · BW · 76mins

A misleading title for what is essentially a heartwarming, albeit drama-filled, domestic tale. Lionel Barrymore and Fay Bainter star as a businessman and his wife who are parents to three grown-up children. When their eldest daughter's accountant fiancé uncovers an irregularity in the books of Barrymore's company, a series of crises and upheavals is unleashed, almost leading to tragedy. RK

Lionel Barrymore *Martin Turner* • Fay Bainter *Francene Turner* • Mae Clarke *Jane Turner* • Tom Brown *Seth Turner* • Una Merkel *Birdie* • Mary Carlisle *Peggy Turner* ■ *Dir* William K Howard • *Scr* Edgar Allan Woolf, Florence Ryerson, Zelda Sears, Eve Greene, from the novel *It Happened One Day* by Marjorie Bartholomew Paradis

This Sporting Life ★★★★★ 15

Drama 1963 · UK · BW · 128mins

Director Lindsay Anderson's first feature film is his best, giving Richard Harris and Rachel Roberts the roles of their lives. Harris is the miner turned ruthless professional rugby player; Roberts is the repressed, widowed landlady with whom he can only communicate through violence. There are some remarkable confrontation sequences – one particular quarrel between the two is painfully honest – and the northern town where it all takes place is as clearly defined. This numbers among the early ripples of the British New Wave. TH [VIDEO] DVD

Richard Harris *Frank Machin* • Rachel Roberts (1) *Mrs Hammond* • Alan Badel *Weaver* • William Hartnell *Johnson* • Colin Blakely *Maurice Braithwaite* • Vanda Godsell *Mrs Weaver* • Arthur Lowe *Slomer* • Anne Cunningham *Judith* • Jack Watson *Len Miller* ■ *Dir* Lindsay Anderson • *Scr* David Storey, from his novel

This Thing Called Love ★★★

Romantic comedy 1940 · US · BW · 94mins

This film not only acknowledges the existence of sex as a component of love and marriage, but actually builds its jokes on that fact of life. As a result, the Legion of Decency banned this otherwise innocuous offering. The story concerns Rosalind Russell's belief that marriages are best cemented on a celibate start, and she decides to keep her groom, Melvyn Douglas, waiting three months for her favours. This bright romantic farce is elegantly played. RK

Rosalind Russell *Ann Winters* • Melvyn Douglas *Tice Collins* • Binnie Barnes *Charlotte Campbell* • Allyn Joslyn *Harry Bertrand* • Gloria Dickson *Florence Bertrand* • Lee J Cobb *Julio Diestro* • Gloria Holden *Genevieve Hooper* ■ *Dir* Alexander Hall • *Scr* George Seaton, Ken Englund, PJ Wolfson, from the play by Edwin Burke

This Time for Keeps ★★ U

Musical 1947 · US · Colour · 104mins

Everything from Wagnerian tenor Lauritz Melchior belting a couple of popular opera arias, through Jimmy Durante delivering his deathless *Inka Dinka Doo* to Xavier Cugat and his orchestra letting rip is thrown into the mix in an attempt to liven up a desperately unoriginal and feeble vehicle for Esther Williams. The famous aquatic star plays a famous aquatic star, caught in an on-again, off-again, on-again romance with Johnnie Johnson. A lavish time-waster. RK

Esther Williams *Leonora "Nora" Cambaretti* • Jimmy Durante *Ferdi Farro* • Lauritz Melchior *Richard Herald* • Johnnie Johnson *Dick Johnson* ■ *Dir* Richard Thorpe • *Scr* Gladys Lehman, from a story by Erwin Gelsey, Lorraine Fielding

This Was a Woman ★★★

Film noir drama 1947 · UK · BW · 103mins

This barnstorming British melodrama allows Sonia Dresdel to indulge in some of the matriarchal tyrannising usually associated with Bette Davis and Joan Crawford. Not content with undermining daughter Barbara White's marriage, she also slowly poisons long-suffering husband, Walter Fitzgerald. However, one of the rules of movie soaps in this period was that crime never pays and Dresdel's ambitions are thwarted by her brain specialist son, Emrys Jones. It's novelettish fare, but Tim Whelan directs steadily and the ending's satisfyingly macabre. DP

Sonia Dresdel *Sylvia Russell* • Barbara White *Fenella Russell* • Walter Fitzgerald *Arthur Russell* • Cyril Raymond *Austin Penrose* • Marjorie Rhodes *Mrs Holmes* • Emrys Jones *Terry Russell* • Celia Lipton *Effie* • Julian Dallas [Scott Forbes] *Dr Valentine Christie* • Joan Hickson *Miss Johnson* ■ *Dir* Tim Whelan • *Scr* Val Valentine, from the play by Joan Morgan

This Woman Is Dangerous ★★

Melodrama 1952 · US · BW · 97mins

Not here she isn't, as ageing movie queen Joan Crawford nears the end of her glory days at Warner Bros. This was her last movie for the studio, and she's always watchable, but this vehicle strains credibility as the star assists at operations, cares for the daughter of widower doctor Dennis Morgan and tries to free herself from the clutches of gangster boyfriend David Brian. The kind of movie that gives Hollywood a bad name. TS

Joan Crawford *Beth Austin* • Dennis Morgan *Dr Ben Halleck* • David Brian *Matt Jackson* • Richard Webb *Franklin* • Mari Aldon *Ann Jackson* • Philip Carey *Will Jackson* • Ian MacDonald *Joe Grossland* ■ *Dir* Felix Feist • *Scr* Geoffrey Holmes, George W Yates, from the story *Stab of Pain* by Bernard Girard

This World, Then the Fireworks ★★★ 18

Crime drama 1996 · US · Colour · 95mins

This is a contrived but decent stab at contemporary *film noir*, with Billy Zane as an investigative reporter forced to hide out at the home of his sister Gina Gershon. Following a childhood trauma, Zane and his sibling enjoy a relationship that extends beyond the warm and loving. Soon they embark on a scam aimed at conning a pretty local policewoman out of her beach-front home. This may not produce true fireworks, but it's no damp squib either. DA. Contains swearing, violence and sex scenes. [VIDEO]

Billy Zane *Marty Lakewood* • Gina Gershon *Carol Lakewood-Wharton* • Sheryl Lee *Patrolwoman Lois Archer* • Rue McClanahan *Mom Lakewood* • Seymour Cassel *Detective Harris* • William Hootkins *Jake Krutz, private investigator* • Will Patton *Police Lt Morgan* ■ *Dir* Michael Oblowitz • *Scr* Larry Gross, from the story by Jim Thompson

This Year's Love ★★★ 18

Romantic comedy
1999 · UK · Colour · 104mins

Writer/director David Kane tries hard to tap into the "Cool Britannia" zeitgeist with this breezy romantic comedy, set in and around funky Camden Lock and charting three years in the lives of six London dropouts. However, while Catherine McCormack, Douglas Henshall and Dougray Scott deliver spunky, dynamic performances, the episodic script gives them little to work with. Sadly, the schematic plotting soon becomes yawningly predictable. NS. Contains drug abuse, swearing and sex scenes. [VIDEO] DVD

Ian Hart *Liam* • Kathy Burke *Marey* • Jennifer Ehle *Sophie* • Douglas Henshall *Danny* • Catherine McCormack *Hannah* • Dougray Scott *Cameron* • Emily Woof *Alice* • Sophie Okonedo *Denise* ■ *Dir/Scr* David Kane

Thomas and the Magic Railroad ★ U

Adventure 2000 · UK/US · Colour · 82mins

Writer/director Britt Allcroft may have translated the magic of the Rev W Awdry's books to the small screen, but this feature adaptation is crass, impenetrable and, frankly, embarrassing. Clumsily Americanised, the story has Mara Wilson and her grandfather Peter Fonda help a marginalised Thomas and miniature conductor Alec Baldwin confound Diesel 10's dastardly plan to eradicate steam trains by destroying a pink tank engine named Lady. A shameful betrayal of a national institution (and the songs are ghastly). DP [VIDEO] DVD

Alec Baldwin *Mr Conductor* • Peter Fonda *Burnett Stone* • Mara Wilson *Lily* • Russell Means *Billy Two-Feathers* • Didi Conn *Stacy* ■ *Dir* Britt Allcroft • *Scr* Britt Allcroft, from the books by Rev W Awdry

The Thomas Crown Affair ★★★ PG

Romantic crime caper
1968 · US · Colour · 97mins

Wound up by its Oscar-winning song, *The Windmills of Your Mind*, this is a work of clockwork precision by director Norman Jewison and cameraman Haskell Wexler, who give what is essentially a caper movie an reverent sheen. Steve McQueen is the businessman organising a bank heist out of boredom, while Faye Dunaway is the insurance investigator who falls for the bad guy. You can take or leave the story, but the style is something else. TH. Contains some violence. [VIDEO] DVD

Steve McQueen *Thomas Crown* • Faye Dunaway *Vicky Anderson* • Paul Burke *Eddy Malone* • Jack Weston *Erwin Weaver* • Biff McGuire *Sandy* • Yaphet Kotto *Carl* • Todd Martin *Benjy* • Sam Melville *Dave* ■ *Dir* Norman Jewison • *Scr* Alan R Trustman • *Music* Michel Legrand

The Thomas Crown Affair ★★★ 15

Romantic crime caper
1999 · US/Ire · Colour · 108mins

This loose remake of the 1968 caper has Pierce Brosnan as the millionaire who steals art in his spare time, and Rene Russo as the sultry insurance investigator with an unusually close interest in his extracurricular activities. It's considerably steamier than the original, and it's stylishly done by *Die Hard* director John McTiernan. But though Brosnan and Russo are a sexy and believable match, this cat-and-mouse thriller lacks the 1960s cool of the original. JB. Contains swearing, a sex scene and nudity. [VIDEO] DVD

Pierce Brosnan *Thomas Crown* • Rene Russo *Catherine Banning* • Denis Leary *Detective Michael McCann* • Ben Gazzara *Andrew Wallace* • Frankie Faison *Detective Paretti* • Fritz Weaver *John Reynolds* • Charles Keating *Golchan* • Faye Dunaway *Psychiatrist* ■ *Dir* John McTiernan • *Scr* Leslie Dixon, Kurt Wimmer, from a story by Alan R Trustman

Thomas Graal's Best Film ★★★★

Silent comedy 1917 · Swe · BW · 60mins

The kingpins of silent Swedish cinema collaborated for the eighth time on this pioneering lampoon of their craft. Victor Sjöström stars as a frustrated writer who fashions a screenplay around his infatuation with unyielding assistant Karin Molander. His romantic imaginings and speculative insights into Molander's fraught past, as well as glimpses of the film-making process, are diverting enough. But it's director Mauritz Stiller's control of facts, flashbacks and fantasies that gives the picture its sophistication and wit. He would repeat the formula in *Thomas Graal's First Child* (1918). DP

Victor Sjöström *Thomas Graal, writer* • Karin Molander *Bessie* • Albin Lavén *Alexander Douglas, Bessie's papa* • Jenny Tschernichin-Larsson *Clotilde Douglas, Bessie's mama* • Axel Nilsson *Johan, loyal servant* ■ *Dir* Mauritz Stiller • *Scr* Harlad B Harald [Gustaf Molander]

Thomas the Imposter ★★★★

First World War fantasy
1964 · Fr · BW · 94mins

Partly inspired by his own experiences with an ambulance unit during the First World War, Jean Cocteau's 1923 novel explored both the horrors of war and the creation of a personal myth. Drawing comparisons between combat and theatre, Georges Franju plays heavily on the notion of illusion, both in his baroque visuals (notably in the fantasy dream sequences) and in presenting teenager Fabrice Rouleau's deceptions as a morally inspired sleight of hand when he poses as a famous general's nephew to help princess Emmanuelle Riva's ambulance service return to Paris. DP. In French with English subtitles.

Emmanuelle Riva *Princess de Bormes* • Jean Servais *Pesquel-Duport* • Fabrice Rouleau *Guillaume Thomas* • Sophie Darès *Henriette* • Michel Vitold *Dr Vernes* • Rosy Varte *Mme Valiche* • Bernard Lavalette *Dr Gentil* ■ *Dir* Georges Franju • *Scr* Jean Cocteau, Georges Franju, Michel Worms, Raphael Cluzel, from the novel by Jean Cocteau

Thoroughbreds Don't Cry ★★

Sports comedy drama
1937 · US · BW · 80mins

Young jockey Mickey Rooney is hired to ride a dead cert for visiting English aristocrat C Aubrey Smith, but he is forced by his no-good father to lose the race. Directed by Alfred E Green for MGM, this undistinguished little racetrack tale is remembered for the first joint appearance of Rooney and Judy Garland, the latter as his friend and niece of Sophie Tucker (who runs the boarding house where Rooney lodges). RK

Judy Garland *Cricket West* • Mickey Rooney *Tim Donahue* • Sophie Tucker *Mother Ralph* • C Aubrey Smith *Sir Peter Calverton* • Ronald Sinclair *Roger Calverton* • Forrester Harvey *Wilkins* ■ *Dir* Alfred E Green • *Scr* Lawrence Hazard, from a story by Eleanore Griffin, J Walter Ruben

T

Thoroughly Modern Millie ★★★ PG

Musical 1967 · US · Colour · 138mins

This popular but overlong vehicle for Julie Andrews succeeds despite a confusing plot and a screenplay that never seems to know when to say "enough". But there's still much to enjoy, not least the bizarre appearances by Broadway divas Beatrice Lillie and Carol Channing, of whom a little goes an awfully long way. The real delight is co-star James Fox, dancing and romancing as if to the musical born, plus Mary Tyler Moore, whose natural good-naturedness proves a fine counterpoint to Andrews's studied brittleness. Sumptuous, but dated. TS DVD

Julie Andrews *Millie Dillmount* • Mary Tyler Moore *Dorothy Brown* • Beatrice Lillie *Mrs Meers* • James Fox *Jimmy Smith* • John Gavin *Trevor Graydon* • Carol Channing *Muzzy Van Hossmere* ■ *Dir* George Roy Hill • *Scr* Richard Morris • *Music* Elmer Bernstein

Those Calloways ★★★ PG

Drama 1964 · US · Colour · 125mins

Trapper Brian Keith spends his savings on some land by a lake in Maine to establish a sanctuary and protect the geese, and moves there with his wife Vera Miles and 19-year-old son Brandon de Wilde. The family's idealistic ambitions are beset with problems and danger, and Keith has to fend off the attentions of a fake conservationist who wants to develop the land for goose-hunters. This family film from Disney suffers from too many plot strands, but is sensitively made, well-acted and entertaining. RK

Brian Keith *Cam Calloway* • Vera Miles *Liddy Calloway* • Brandon de Wilde *Bucky Calloway* • Walter Brennan *Alf Simes* • Ed Wynn *Ed Parker* • Linda Evans *Bridie Mellot* • Philip Abbott *Dell Fraser* • John Larkin *Jim Mellot* • Tom Skerritt *Whit Turner* ■ *Dir* Norman Tokar • *Scr* Louis Pelletier, from the novel *Swiftwater* by Paul Annixter

Those Endearing Young Charms ★★★

Romance 1945 · US · BW · 82mins

Many wartime romances have a certain endearing, if not enduring charm, and this is no exception. Shop assistant Laraine Day has to choose between army officer Robert Young, who is a bit of a heel, and nice but dull Bill Williams (in his film debut) from back home. There is no doubt who is the more attractive for her, despite the warnings of her sensible mother, played beautifully by Ann Harding. RB

Robert Young (1) *Hank* • Laraine Day *Helen* • Ann Harding *Mrs Brandt* • Marc Cramer *Capt Larry Stowe* • Anne Jeffreys *Suzanne* ■ *Dir* Lewis Allen • *Scr* Jerome Chodorov, from a play by Edward Chodorov

Those Glory, Glory Days ★★★ PG

Biographical drama
1983 · UK · Colour · 90mins

Written by *The Observer's* football correspondent, Julie Welch, this amusing slice of pre-Swinging Sixties nostalgia was originally shown on Channel 4's *First Love* series. It enjoyed a brief theatrical run, following some glowing reviews by the nation's TV critics. Zoe Nathenson gives a wholehearted performance as the teenager obsessed with Tottenham Hotspur and their Northern Irish skipper, Danny Blanchflower (who crops up in a cameo). Some of the freshness might have worn off, but this is still unusual and enjoyable. DP

Zoe Nathenson *Julia, "Danny"* • Sara Sugarman *Toni* • Cathy Murphy *Tub* • Liz Campion *Jailbird* • Amelia Dipple *Petrina* • Elizabeth Spriggs *School mistress* • Julia McKenzie *Mrs Herrick* • Peter Tilbury *Mr Herrick* ■ *Dir* Philip Saville • *Scr* Julie Welch

Those Lips, Those Eyes ★★★★

Romantic comedy drama
1980 · US · Colour · 107mins

Michael Pressman directs this cute little movie about the lessons young student Tom Hulce learns when he spends one summer in the 1950s working for a theatre company. There's love, of course, with the older leading lady Glynnis O'Connor, but the best lines and performance come from Frank Langella as the troupe's ageing leading man. JB

Frank Langella *Harry Crystal* • Glynnis O'Connor *Ramona* • Tom Hulce *Artie Shoemaker* • George Morfogen *Sherman Spratt* • Jerry Stiller *Mr Shoemaker* • Rose Arrick *Mrs Shoemaker* • Herbert Berghof *Dr Julius Fuldauer* ■ *Dir* Michael Pressman • *Scr* David Shaber

Those Magnificent Men in Their Flying Machines ★★★★ U

Comedy 1965 · UK · Colour · 126mins

A host of international comedians don period garb, climb aboard wondrously ramshackle aircraft and dominate the screen over top-billed stars Stuart Whitman and Sarah Miles in this very entertaining comedy. Co-writer and director Ken Annakin keeps the action rattling along at a rate of knots, never slowing the pace for the romance, and allocates equal screen time to the different nationalities competing in the race. Wonderfully wacky and gloriously photographed. *Monte Carlo or Bust* is the 1969 sequel. TS

Sarah Miles *Patricia Rawnsley* • James Fox *Richard Mays* • Stuart Whitman *Orvil Newton* • Alberto Sordi *Count Emilio Ponticelli* • Robert Morley *Lord Rawnsley* • Gert Frobe [Gert Fröbe] *Colonel Manfred Von Holstein* • Jean-Pierre Cassel *Pierre Dubois* • Eric Sykes *Courtney* • Terry-Thomas *Sir Percival Ware-Armitage* • Tony Hancock *Harry Popperwell* • Benny Hill *Fire Chief Perkins* • Flora Robson *Mother Superior* ■ *Dir* Ken Annakin • *Scr* Jack Davies, Ken Annakin • *Cinematographer* Christopher Challis

Those Were the Days ★★★ U

Comedy 1934 · UK · BW · 80mins

Will Hay plays a Victorian magistrate in this enjoyable adaptation of Arthur Wing Pinero's brisk stage farce. Making his feature debut, Hay doesn't look totally at ease, having not yet mastered playing down for the camera. But no one could do pompous bemusement quite like him and his scenes with stepson John Mills are good value. DP

Will Hay *Brutus Poskett* • Iris Hoey *Agatha Poskett* • Angela Baddeley *Charlotte* • Claud Allister *Captain Horace Vale* • George Graves *Colonel Alexander Lukyn* • John Mills *Bobby* • Jane Carr (1) *Minnie Taylor* ■ *Dir* Thomas Bentley • *Scr* Fred Thompson, Frank Miller, Frank Launder, Jack Jordan, from the play *The Magistrate* by Arthur Wing Pinero

Those Who Love Me Can Take the Train ★★★★ 15

Drama 1998 · Fr · Colour · 116mins

Patrice Chéreau explores the dysfunctional dynamic between the members of a crumbling family and its immediate entourage. Shooting initially with handheld cameras on a Limoges-bound train, he bewilders with the sheer number of people heading for a once-great artist's funeral and the complexity of their relationships. But the skeletons and revelations soon fall into place as marriages, pregnancies, addictions, gay affairs, sex changes and all manner of ambitions and delusions are dragged into the open. What follows is soap opera of a sophistication even Douglas Sirk would have envied. DP. In French with English subtitles. DVD

Pascal Greggory *François* • Jean-Louis Trintignant *Lucien* • Valéria Bruni-Tedeschi *Claire* • Charles Berling *Jean-Marie* • Bruno Todeschini *Louis* • Sylvain Jacques *Bruno* • Vincent Perez *Viviane* ■ *Dir* Patrice Chéreau • *Scr* Danièle Thompson, Patrice Chéreau, Pierre Trividic

Thou Shalt Not Kill ★★

Period courtroom drama
1961 · Fr/It/Yug · BW · 128mins

Set in 1949, this follows the trial of both a French conscientious objector and a German priest who, under orders, has killed a member of the Resistance. The young Frenchman is condemned for "evading" his duty, while the priest is condemned for "doing" his duty. Sadly the execution of this sturdy, overlong movie is less compelling than the narrative suggests. BB. In French with English subtitles.

Laurent Terzieff *Jean-François Cordier* • Horst Frank *Adler* • Suzanne Flon *Mme Cordier* ■ *Dir* Claude Autant-Lara • *Scr* Claude Autant-Lara, Jean Aurenche, Pierre Bost, from a story by Jean Aurenche

A Thousand Acres ★★★ 15

Drama 1997 · US · Colour · 100mins

This modern reworking of *King Lear*, based on Jane Smiley's Pulitzer Prize-winning novel, is an anti-men melodrama given weight and class by its three female leads – Michelle Pfeiffer, Jessica Lange and Jennifer Jason Leigh. They play the sisters who fall out over some family land that is to be divided up by their gruff father Jason Robards. Their conflict, and their relationships with the men in their lives, form the centre of the film. While downbeat thanks to Jocelyn Moorhouse's pedestrian direction, this is nonetheless a rare showcase for three of Hollywood's best actresses. JB. Contains some swearing, sexual references and violence.

Michelle Pfeiffer *Rose Cook Lewis* • Jessica Lange *Ginny Cook Smith* • Jason Robards *Larry Cook* • Jennifer Jason Leigh *Caroline Cook* • Colin Firth *Jess Clark* • Keith Carradine *Ty Smith* • Kevin Anderson *Peter Lewis* • Pat Hingle *Harold Clark* ■ *Dir* Jocelyn Moorhouse • *Scr* Laura Jones, from the novel by Jane Smiley

A Thousand and One Nights ★★★ U

Fantasy comedy adventure
1945 · US · Colour · 89mins

This high-spirited Columbia comedy pokes gentle fun at the *Arabian Nights* genre, with a singing Cornel Wilde quite dashing as Aladdin. Wilde is well supported by a genial Phil Silvers and canny genie Evelyn Keyes. Much of this is genuinely spectacular, while director Alfred E Green proves *The Jolson Story* was no fluke. Rex Ingram, the "real" genie from the immortal 1940 movie *The Thief of Bagdad*, makes a knowing guest appearance. Fun for all ages. TS

Cornel Wilde *Aladdin* • Evelyn Keyes *Genie* • Phil Silvers *Abdullah* • Adele Jergens *Princess Armina* • Dusty Anderson *Novira* • Dennis Hoey *Sultan Kamar Al-Kir/Prince Hadji* • Philip Van Zandt *Grand Wazir Abu-Hassan* • Rex Ingram (2) *Giant* • Shelley Winter [Shelley Winters] *Handmaiden* ■ *Dir* Alfred E Green • *Scr* Wilfred H Pettitt, Richard English, Jack Henley, from a story by Wilfred H Pettitt

A Thousand Clowns ★★★ U

Comedy drama 1965 · US · BW · 115mins

Jason Robards, a free-spirited writer, quits his job on a kid's television series, mainly due to a personality clash with the show's star, Gene Saks. Robards is guardian to his precocious 12-year-old nephew Barry Gordon, but this arrangement is threatened by his unemployed status. This thoughtful and intriguing comedy was nominated for four Oscars, with Martin Balsam winning as best supporting actor for his role as Robard's brother. DF

Jason Robards Jr [Jason Robards] *Murray Burns* • Barbara Harris *Sandra* • Martin Balsam *Arnold Burns* • Barry Gordon *Nick* • Gene Saks *Leo* • William Daniels *Albert* ■ *Dir* Fred Coe • *Scr* Herb Gardner, from his play

Thousand Eyes ★★

Drama 1984 · W Ger · Colour · 85mins

This rather unsavoury offering has Barbara Rudnik as a respectable marine biologist who lives with her parents in a cosy part of Hamburg. However, when she's not listening to taped messages from her lover in Australia, she's on display at a peep show trying to earn the money for her ticket Down Under. Hans-Christoph Blumenberg directs with such earnestness that it seems closer to a bleeding heart TV movie than a provocative piece of cinema. DP. German dialogue dubbed into English.

Barbara Rudnik *Gabriele* • Armin Mueller-Stahl *Arnold* • Karin Baal *Vera* • Peter Kraus *Schirmer* • Vera Tschechowa *Victoria* ■ *Dir/Scr* Hans-Christoph Blumenberg

The Thousand Eyes of Dr Mabuse ★★★

Crime drama
1960 · W Ger/It/Fr · BW · 103mins

Fritz Lang returned to the criminal underworld for his swansong feature. The narrative owes much to the serials of yesteryear; the imagery is shot through with expressionist leitmotifs and the gadgetry is high kitsch rather than hi-tech. But the emphasis was very much on the extent to which the Nazi ethos, symbolised by Wolfgang Preiss's sinister mastermind, still pervaded contemporary Berlin. Critics detested it, but there are enough flashes of mastery to engross. DP. In German with English subtitles.

Dawn Addams *Marion Menil* • Peter Van Eyck *Henry B Travers* • Wolfgang Preiss *Dr Jordan* • Gert Fröbe *Inspector Krass* • Werner Peters *Hieronymous P Mistelzweig* • Andrea Checchi *Inspector Berg* • Howard Vernon *"No 12"* ■ *Dir* Fritz Lang • *Scr* Heinz Oskar Wuttig, Fritz Lang, from an idea by Jan Fethke, from characters created by Norbert Jacques • *Cinematographer* Karl Löb

A Thousand Months ★★★ 12A

Drama 2003 · Fr/Bel/Mor · Colour · 119mins

Moroccan Faouzi Bensaïdi makes his directorial debut with this engaging, episodic study of a young boy's initiation into the realities of village life. Unaware that his father is in jail for his political views, Fouad Labied is more devoted to the mayor's rebellious daughter than the mother and grandfather who sacrifice everything for his welfare. Cinematographer Antoine Heberle captures a landscape populated with schemers, survivors and eccentrics. DP. In Arabic with English subtitles. DVD

Fouad Labied *Mehdi* • Nezha Rahile *Amina* • Mohamed Majd *Grandfather* • Abdelati Lambarki *Caïd* • Mohamed Bastaoui *Caïd's brother* ■ *Dir* Faouzi Bensaïdi • *Scr* Faouzi Bensaïdi, Emmanuelle Sardou

Thousand Pieces of Gold ★★★

Period drama
1990 · US · Colour and BW · 105mins

Imposing modern attitudes on a period piece can sometimes corrupt the authenticity of the material, and that's pretty much the case with this adaptation of Ruthanne Lum McCunn's fact-based book. From the moment she is sold by her Manchurian father to an American marriage broker, Rosalind Chao is driven by fierce self-esteem (not feminist idealism) to resist the evils of prostitution, slavery and racial prejudice. Director Nancy Kelly re-creates the hardships of frontier life without resorting to western clichés and draws superior performances from Chao and Chris Cooper, the one man to show her charity. DP

Rosalind Chao *Lalu Nathoy* • Dennis Dun *Jim Chao* • Michael Paul Chan *Hong King* • Chris Cooper *American gambler* ■ *Dir* Nancy Kelly • *Scr* Anne Makepeace, from the novel by Ruthanne Lum McCunn

The 1,000 Plane Raid ★★ U

Second World War adventure
1969 · US · Colour · 93mins

Christopher George delivers a thick ear of a performance in this thoroughly routine war movie. As the abrasive USAF colonel who is convinced that his unit of B-17 bombers can knock out a key German aeroplane factory, despite the huge risks, he picks a fight with just about everyone he encounters. Even his girlfriend, Laraine Stephens, has to suffer his macho ire. The flying footage is fine, but repetitive. DP

Christopher George *Col Greg Brandon* • Laraine Stephens *Lt Gabrielle Ames* • JD Cannon *General Cotten Palmer* • Gary Marshall *Wing Commander Trafton Howard* • Michael Evans (1) *British Group Commander Leslie Hardwicke* • Ben Murphy *Lt Archer* • James Gammon *Major Varga* • Gavin Macleod *Sgt Kruger* ■ *Dir* Boris Sagal • *Scr* Donald S Sanford, from a story by Robert Vincent Wright, from a novel by Ralph Barker

Thousands Cheer ★★★ U

Second World War musical
1943 · US · Colour · 125mins

Pianist/conductor José Iturbi made his film debut in this blockbusting wartime musical romance, whose witless script is the excuse for a grand finale ostensibly staged for the boys at an army camp, compèred by Mickey Rooney and parading a host of MGM stars in songs, dances and sketches. The nominal stars are Kathryn Grayson and Gene Kelly. She's a singer who, while visiting her colonel father, organises the show, falls for private Kelly, a circus aerialist, and tries to bring her long-separated parents (John Boles, Mary Astor) together again. RK

Kathryn Grayson *Kathryn Jones* • Gene Kelly *Eddie Marsh* • Mary Astor *Hyllary Jones* • José Iturbi • John Boles *Col Bill Jones* • Dick Simmons *Captain Fred Avery* ■ *Dir* George Sidney (2) • *Scr* Paul Jarrico, Richard Collins

Thrashin' ★ 15

Action drama romance
1986 · US · Colour · 88mins

Josh Brolin (son of James) stars in yet another *Romeo and Juliet* retread – this time on skateboards. Brolin falls for Pamela Gidley, little sister of rival skater gang leader Robert Rusler. The acting is terrible, the story is worse, and the film is only notable for the appearance of rock group the Red Hot Chili Peppers. ST [video]

Josh Brolin *Corey Webster* • Robert Rusler *Tommy Hook* • Pamela Gidley *Chrissy* • Brooke McCarter *Tyler* • Brett Marx *Bozo* • Josh Richman *Radley* • David Wagner *Little Stevie* • Sherilyn Fenn *Velvet* ■ *Dir* David Winters • *Scr* Paul Brown, Alan Sacks

Three ★★★★

Portmanteau war drama
1965 · Yug · BW · 79mins

Aleksandar Petrovic emerged as the inspiration behind "Novi Film" with this ethically challenging, subtly symbolic yet grimly realistic portmanteau. In the first segment, young Velimir Bata Zivojinovic watches helplessly as an innocent man is summarily executed at the urging of a crowd of compatriots. He has joined the Partisans by the second episode, in which he is powerless to prevent a sadistic death of a fellow guerrilla. Finally, Zivojinovic is an army officer supervising the postwar execution of collaborators and Chetniks. DP. A Serbo-Croat language film.

Velimir Bata Zivojinovic [Bata Zivojinovic] *Milos* ■ *Dir* Aleksandar Petrovic • *Scr* Antonije Isakovic, Aleksandar Petrovic, from the book *Paprat i Vatra* by Antonije Isakovic

Three ★★★

Drama 1969 · UK · Colour · 104mins

A modish but offbeat adult drama about two American guys on a European tour who find their friendship strained when they become attracted to sexy Charlotte Rampling, who joins them on their trip. The story could easily have strayed into soap opera, but a mature script keeps the cast's heads above water. JG

Charlotte Rampling *Marty* • Robie Porter *Bert* • Sam Waterston *Taylor* • Pascale Roberts *Claude* • Edina Ronay *Liz* ■ *Dir* James Salter • *Scr* James Salter, from the story *Then There Were Three* by Irwin Shaw

The Three Ages ★★★★

Silent comedy 1923 · US · BW · 55mins

Buster Keaton's delightful parody of DW Griffith's epic *Intolerance* tells the same story intercut between different time periods, with Buster as the hero, Wallace Beery as the villain and Margaret Leahy as the girl. In the Stone Age, there's a mortal combat for love; in Roman times it is a battle to the death in the arena; while the Present Day sees a play off on the football field. The first of three full-length features for Metro, it was an investment they never regretted. TH

Buster Keaton *The hero* • Margaret Leahy *The girl* • Joe Roberts *Her father* • Lillian Lawrence *Her mother* • Wallace Beery *Rival* • Oliver Hardy *Rival's Roman helper* • Horace "Cupid" Morgan [Horace Morgan] *Emperor* • Blanche Payson *Amazon cavewoman* • Lionel Belmore ■ *Dir* Buster Keaton, Eddie Cline [Edward Cline] • *Scr* Clyde Bruckman, Jean Havez, Joseph Mitchell

Three Amigos! ★★★ PG

Comedy western
1986 · US · Colour · 103mins

This enjoyably indulgent comedy features Chevy Chase, Steve Martin and Martin Short. The leads play stars of silent westerns who end up in Mexico on what they think is a publicity tour, only to discover that they are expected to defend a village from an evil group of bandits. It's nowhere near as funny as it should have been, but the chemistry between the stars and the gentle digs at the western genre make for a diverting enough entertainment. JF. Contains swearing. [video] DVD

Chevy Chase *Dusty Bottoms* • Steve Martin *Lucky Day* • Martin Short *Ned Nederlander* • Patrice Martinez *Carmen* • Philip Gordon *Rodrigo* • Michael Wren *Cowboy* • Fred Asparagus *Bartender* ■ *Dir* John Landis • *Scr* Steve Martin, Lorne Michaels, Randy Newman

[Three] Après la Vie ★★★★ 15

Melodrama 2002 · Fr/Bel · Colour · 119mins

Although Lucas Belvaux's Grenoble trilogy can be watched in any order, this harrowing drama – the concluding instalment after *[One] Cavale* and *[Two] Un Couple Epatant*– makes the most impact, as it audaciously focuses on a peripheral character from the previous episodes and transforms our perceptions of her. Instead of being the timid victim of a flirtatious husband, Dominique Blanc emerges as a desperate junkie whose calculating manipulation of cop Gilbert Melki stands in stark contrast to the selfless risks he takes to keep her addiction both secret and satisfied. Moreover, her duplicity enables Belvaux to complete his shrewd and assured exposé of middle-class hypocrisy and superficiality on a note of both pity and disdain. DP. In French with English subtitles. Contains swearing, drug abuse and violence. DVD

Dominique Blanc *Agnès Manise* • Gilbert Melki *Pascal Manise* • Ornella Muti *Cécile Costes* • Catherine Frot *Jeanne Rivet* • Lucas Belvaux *Bruno Le Roux* • François Morel *Alain Costes* • Valérie Mairesse *Claire* • Patrick Descamps *Jaquillat* ■ *Dir/Scr* Lucas Belvaux

3 Bad Men ★★★★

Silent western 1926 · US · BW · 92mins

The second of John Ford's epic silent westerns – after *The Iron Horse* (1924) – had its contemporary appeal dented by the director's insistence on giving the prominent outlaw roles to grizzled character actors – J Farrell MacDonald, Tom Santschi and Frank Campeau. He did have the popular but bland George O'Brien as the young settler and Olive Borden as his sweetheart, both of whom are protected by the wanted threesome from a crooked sheriff and his gang. Ford shot much of the film on remote locations but re-created the spectacular Cherokee Strip land rush near Los Angeles, where the memorable shot of a baby being snatched to safety was done with a real infant. AE

George O'Brien *Dan O'Malley* • Olive Borden *Lee Carlton* • Lou Tellegen *Layne Hunter* • J Farrell MacDonald *Mike Costigan* • Tom Santschi *Bull Stanley* • Frank Campeau *Spade Allen* • George Harris (1) *Joe Minsk* ■ *Dir* John Ford • *Scr* John Stone, Ralph Spence (titles), Malcolm Stuart Boylan (titles)

Three Bites of the Apple ★★

Comedy 1967 · US · Colour · 98mins

David McCallum stars in this travelogue comedy set on the Italian Riviera, as an English travel courier whose life is changed one night when he goes to a casino in search of an American who has strayed from his tour. Cajoled into gambling, McCallum hits a winning streak and makes a small fortune. He is observed by the sexy Sylva Koscina, who contrives to meet him and then connives with her ex-husband, Domenico Modugno, to fleece the Englishman of his winnings. Good scenery, but lacklustre. DF

David McCallum *Stanley Thrumm* • Sylva Koscina *Carla Moretti* • Tammy Grimes *Angela Sparrow* • Harvey Korman *Harvey Tomlinson* • Domenico Modugno *Remo Romano* • Avril Angers *Gladys Tomlinson* ■ *Dir* Alvin Ganzer • *Scr* George Wells

Three Blind Mice ★★★

Romantic comedy 1938 · US · BW · 75mins

Fed up with running their Kansas chicken farm, three sisters take off to a fashionable Californian resort in search of rich husbands. There, the eldest and most determined (Loretta Young) masquerades as a wealthy socialite, while the other two pose as her maid and secretary. Situations go from mad to worse as events involving David Niven and Joel McCrea take several unexpected turns. Despite some limp moments, it's enjoyable romantic comedy nonsense, remade as *Moon over Miami* (1941) and *Three Little Girls in Blue* (1946). RK

Loretta Young *Pamela Charters* • Joel McCrea *Van Dam Smith* • David Niven *Steve Harrington* • Stuart Erwin *Mike Brophy* • Marjorie Weaver *Moira Charters* • Pauline Moore *Elizabeth Charters* • Binnie Barnes *Miriam Harrington* ■ *Dir* William A Seiter • *Scr* Brown Holmes, Lynn Starling, from the play by Stephen Powys

Three Brave Men ★★

Drama 1956 · US · BW · 88mins

This drama is a curious relic of the Cold War, showing how a civilian employee of the US Navy is suspended and investigated for being a security risk. As the unfortunate sap, Ernest Borgnine has the requisite physical presence and wide-eyed innocence. What this story needs, though, is a savage twist or surprise; instead it's just an exercise in righteousness and a veiled attack on McCarthyism. AT

Ray Milland *Joe DiMarco* • Ernest Borgnine *Bernie Goldsmith* • Frank Lovejoy *Captain Winfield* • Nina Foch *Lieutenant McCoy* • Dean Jagger *Rogers* • Virginia Christine *Helen Goldsmith* • Edward Andrews *Major Jensen* ■ *Dir* Philip Dunne • *Scr* Philip Dunne, from articles by Anthony Lewis

Three Brothers ★★★

Drama 1980 · It/Fr · Colour · 111mins

Returning to their hilltop village for the funeral of their mother, Roman judge Philippe Noiret, teacher of underprivileged Neapolitan children Vittorio Mezzogiorno and Turin mechanic with marital problems Michele Placido end up discussing how they've drifted apart and try to renew ties with their ageing father Charles Vanel. This is a laboured, if unexpectedly lyrical allegory on the social, cultural and political antagonisms that divide modern Italy. DP. In Italian with English subtitles.

Philippe Noiret *Raffaele Giuranna* • Michele Placido *Nicola Giuranna* • Vittorio Mezzogiorno *Rocco Giuranna/Young Donato* • Charles Vanel *Donato Giuranna* • Andréa Ferréol *Raffael's wife* ■ *Dir* Francesco Rosi • *Scr* Tonino Guerra, Francesco Rosi, from the story *The Third Son* by A Platonov

Three Brothers ★★★

Drama 2000 · Kaz · Colour · 77mins

An affecting blend of lyrical nostalgia and harsh reality informs Kazakh director Serik Aprymov's rites-of-passage picture. Related in flashback by a jet pilot based near his childhood home, the story centres on a gang of teenagers who become obsessed with the tales spun by an elderly concentration camp survivor about a group of beautiful but expensive courtesans. The elliptical structure makes some developments difficult to follow, while the pivotal decision to ambush a military payroll strains credibility, yet this tale still exudes an enticing charm. DP. In Russian and Kazakh with English subtitles.

Kasim Schakibajev *Klein* • Shakir Viliamov *Chibut* • Bolat Mazagulov *Tera* • Bakhtjar Kuatbaev *Kazanbas* • Jura Dankov *Jurka* • Baurschan Seitbaev *Baur* ■ *Dir/Scr* Serik Aprymov

The Three Caballeros ★★★ U

Part-animated fantasy
1944 · US · Colour · 84mins

This wonderful slice of richly-Technicolored magic from Walt Disney was a follow-up to the short *Saludos Amigos*, a product of the US "Good Neighbour" policy towards Latin America. Combining live-action and animation, it stars Joe Carioca, his friend Panchito and Donald Duck himself, enjoying a musical spree which gives vent to a marvellously creative burst of cartoon energy. There's more wizardry as Donald gets tied up with the soundtrack and falls in love with Carmen Miranda's sister Aurora. Bear with the coy opening scenes; this is a treat. TS [video] DVD

Dir Norman Ferguson, Clyde Geronimi, Jack Kinney, Bill Roberts, Harold Young • *Scr* Homer Brightman, Ernest Terrazzas, Ted Sears, Bill Peet, Ralph Wright, Elmer Plymmer, Roy Williams, William Cottrell, Del Connell, James Bodrero

Three Came Home ★★★★ 12

Second World War drama
1950 · US · BW · 105mins

Intensely moving and superbly acted adaptation of a true story, with magnificent performances from Claudette Colbert and Sessue Hayakawa as a Second World War internee and a cultured Japanese officer respectively. Generally underrated, this is a particularly fine example of postwar cinema, dealing with moral issues raised by the war itself. Although the Borneo setting is clearly a Hollywood soundstage, director Jean Negulesco creates a totally believable environment, and Hayakawa's performance prompted David Lean to cast him in *The Bridge on the River Kwai*. TS DVD

Claudette Colbert *Agnes Newton Keith* • Patric Knowles *Harry Keith* • Florence Desmond *Betty Sommers* • Sessue Hayakawa *Colonel Suga* • Sylvia Andrew *Henrietta* • Mark Keuning *George* • Phyllis Morris *Sister Rose* ■ *Dir* Jean Negulesco • *Scr* Nunnally Johnson, from the autobiography by Agnes Newton Keith

Three Cases of Murder ★★★

Portmanteau murder mystery
1953 · UK · BW · 88mins

This compendium of three tales of the not-entirely-unexpected variety is notable mainly for a typically larger-than-life performance from Orson Welles. He plays an aristocratic politician who undergoes a disturbing penance for a wrong-doing he perpetuated on a colleague. The other stories feature able performances from a reliable British cast. JF

Alan Badel *Mr X/Harry/Owen* • Hugh Pryse *Jarvis* • John Salew *Mr Rooke* • Emrys Jones *George Wheeler* • John Gregson *Edgar Curtain* • Elizabeth Sellars *Elizabeth* • Orson Welles *Lord Mountdrago* • Helen Cherry *Lady Mountdrago* ■ *Dir* Wendy Toye, David Eady, George More O'Ferrall • *Scr* Donald Wilson, Sidney Carroll, Ian Dalrymple, from stories by Roderick Wilkinson, Brett Halliday, W Somerset Maugham

Three Coins in the Fountain ★★★★ U

Romantic comedy
1954 · US · Colour · 97mins

Twentieth Century-Fox's stand-by plot was the one involving three assorted girls in any location, and here they're in Rome, throwing money for wishes into the Fountain of Trevi. Their wishes are granted, of course, by Clifton Webb, Louis Jourdan and Rossano Brazzi. Milton Krasner's cinematography won an Oscar, as did the (uncredited) Frank Sinatra title song. In its day, the movie's dialogue was considered quite risqué, and the clothes and performances were the epitome of sophisticated chic. Jean Negulesco remade his movie ten years later as *The Pleasure Seekers*. TS

Clifton Webb *Shadwell* • Dorothy McGuire *Miss Francis* • Jean Peters *Anita* • Louis Jourdan *Prince Dino Di Cessi* • Maggie McNamara *Maria* • Rossano Brazzi *Georgio* • Howard St John *Burgoyne* • Kathryn Givney *Mrs Burgoyne* • Cathleen Nesbitt *Principessa* ■ *Dir* Jean Negulesco • *Scr* John Patrick, from the novel by John H Secondari • *Music* Victor Young

Three Colours Blue ★★★★★ 15

Drama 1993 · Fr/Swi/Pol · Colour · 93mins

Polish director Krzysztof Kieslowski already had the sublime and unsurpassable *Dekalog* series to his credit when he embarked upon this trilogy, named after the colours of the French flag and derived from the Revolutionary principles of liberty, equality and fraternity. Juliette Binoche gives an intense yet sensitive performance as the survivor of a crash which killed her family, who discovers that, no matter how great her pain, she doesn't have the freedom to give up life. The process by which she deals with her grief is minutely observed, yet Kieslowski's direction is never intrusive, and his use of Zbigniew Preisner's score is inspired. DP. In French with English subtitles. Contains some nudity. DVD

Juliette Binoche *Julie* • Benoît Régent *Olivier* • Florence Pernel *Sandrine* • Charlotte Véry *Lucille* • Hélène Vincent *Journalist* • Philippe Volter *Estate agent* • Claude Duneton *Doctor* ■ *Dir* Krzysztof Kieslowski • *Scr* Krzysztof Piesiewicz, Krzysztof Kieslowski

Three Colours Red ★★★★★ 15

Drama 1994 · Fr/Swi/Pol · Colour · 99mins

Earning Krzysztof Kieslowski Oscar nominations for both script (co-written by Krzysztof Piesiewicz) and direction, the concluding part of his tricolour trilogy has much in common with his earlier *The Double Life of Véronique*. Not only does it reunite him with Irène Jacob, but it also explores the theme that people are bound together by fraternal ties that they can never fully understand. Gloriously shot on location in Geneva by Oscar-nominated cinematographer Piotr Sobocinski, the film's use of colour and sound is unparalleled in 1990s cinema, while the intricate plot linking model Jacob with snooping judge Jean-Louis Trintignant is spellbinding. DP. In French with English subtitles. Contains sex scenes and nudity. DVD

Irène Jacob *Valentine Dussaut* • Jean-Louis Trintignant *Judge Joseph Kern* • Frédérique Feder *Karin* • Jean-Pierre Lorit *Auguste Bruner* • Samuel Le Bihan *Photographer* • Marion Stalens *Veterinary surgeon* • Teco Celio *Barman* ■ *Dir* Krzysztof Kieslowski • *Scr* Krzysztof Kieslowski, Krzysztof Piesiewicz

Three Colours White ★★★★ 15

Comedy drama
1993 · Fr/Swi/Pol · Colour · 91mins

The second film in Krzysztof Kieslowski's trilogy is the slightest of the series, yet there is still much to admire in a movie intended as a tribute to Charlie Chaplin. Although a comedy, *White* is an examination of the aftermath of the Communist regime in Poland under which everyone was supposed to be equal. The picture painted of democratic Warsaw, with its shady deals and run-down streets, is both unflattering and affectionate, providing an animated backdrop to this droll story of love on the rocks. Zbigniew Zamachowski excels as the jilted hairdresser determined never to feel inferior again. DP. In Polish and French with English subtitles. Contains violence and nudity. DVD

Zbigniew Zamachowski *Karol Karol* • Julie Delpy *Dominique* • Janusz Gajos *Mikolaj* • Jerzy Stuhr *Jurek* • Grzegorz Warchol *Elegant man* • Jerzy Nowak *Old farmer* ■ *Dir* Krzysztof Kieslowski • *Scr* Krzysztof Piesiewicz, Krzysztof Kieslowski

Three Comrades ★★★

Drama 1938 · US · BW · 100mins

Three Germans who fought in the First World War run a repair shop and all are in love with the same girl – Margaret Sullavan – who just happens to have terminal tuberculosis. This overblown melodrama was intended to make American audiences cry buckets yet, at the same time, comprehend Hitler's Reich, though the word "Nazi" was *verboten*. F Scott Fitzgerald received credit for the script, though it was extensively rewritten by Joseph L Mankiewicz after Sullavan protested that Fitzgerald's dialogue was unplayable. AT

Robert Taylor (1) *Erich Lohkamp* • Margaret Sullavan *Pat Hollmann* • Franchot Tone *Otto Koster* • Robert Young (1) *Gottfried Lenz* • Guy Kibbee *Alfons* • Lionel Atwill *Franz Breuer* • Henry Hull *Dr Heinrich Becker* • George Zucco *Dr Plauten* ■ *Dir* Frank Borzage • *Scr* F Scott Fitzgerald, Edward Paramore [Edward E Paramore Jr], from the novel by Erich Maria Remarque

Three Daring Daughters ★★★ U

Musical comedy 1948 · US · Colour · 113mins

This schmaltzy, formula MGM musical is typical of the Joe Pasternak stable from which it came. Jeanette MacDonald stars as the divorced mother of three daughters (Jane Powell among them) who do not take kindly to mother's romance with a pianist (José Iturbi). Delightfully predictable, this is crammed with musical numbers both classical and popular and showcases Iturbi's dazzling pyrotechnics. Old-fashioned and fun. RK

Jeanette MacDonald *Louise Rayton Morgan* • José Iturbi *José Iturbi* • Jane Powell *Tess Morgan* • Edward Arnold *Robert Nelson* • Harry Davenport *Dr Cannon* • Mary Eleanor Donahue *Alix Morgan* • Ann E Todd *Ilka Morgan* ■ *Dir* Fred M Wilcox • *Scr* Albert Mannheimer, Frederick Kohner, Sonya Levien, John Meehan, from the play *The Birds and the Flowers* by Frederick Kohner, Albert Mannheimer

Three Days and a Child ★★★

Drama 1967 · Is · BW · 90mins

Uri Zohar's drama pries into the psychological state of Oded Kotler's Jerusalem-based botany lecturer, as he ruminates on his relationship with Judith Soleh, his one-time kibbutz lover whose three-year-old son he agrees to baby-sit while she takes an exam. Tormented by notions of potential paternity and envy of Soleh's new husband, Kotler exposes the toddler to various dangers as he wrestles with self-doubts and disappointments that partly reflect Israel's own pre-Six Day War situation. Kotler won the best actor prize at Cannes for this ambitious adaptation. DP. In Hebrew with English subtitles.

Oded Kotler *Eli* • Shuy Osherov *Shuy* • Judith Soleh *Noa* • Misha Asherov *Shuy's father* • Illy Gorlitzky *Zvi* ■ *Dir* Uri Zohar • *Scr* Uri Zohar, Amatsia Hiuni, David Gurfunkel, Dan Ben-Amotz, from a novella by AB Yehoshua

Three Days of the Condor ★★★★

Thriller 1975 · US · Colour · 116mins

Conspiracy theories abounded in Hollywood in the 1970s, as film-makers began to explore the nation's dark underside in the wake of Vietnam and Watergate. Directed by Sydney Pollack and starring Robert Redford, this tense thriller is a polished piece of work, as Redford holds photographer Faye Dunaway hostage while he tries to ascertain Max von Sydow's role in the murder of his undercover colleagues. The excellent cast makes up for Pollack's occasional lapses in pacing. DP. Contains violence and some swearing.

Robert Redford *Turner* • Faye Dunaway *Kathy Hale* • Cliff Robertson *Higgins* • Max von Sydow *Joubert* • John Houseman *Mr Wabash* • Addison Powell *Atwood* • Walter McGinn *Sam Barber* • Tina Chen *Janice* ■ *Dir* Sydney Pollack • *Scr* Lorenzo Semple Jr, David Rayfiel, from the novel *Six Days of the Condor* by James Grady

The Three Faces of Eve ★★★ PG

Psychological drama 1957 · US · BW · 87mins

An Oscar-winning performance from Joanne Woodward is the highlight of writer/director Nunnally Johnson's uneven film. Woodward is a young wife and mother who has three split personalities – insecure housewife, irresponsible floozy and educated woman. Her husband David Warner is sceptical, but psychiatrist Lee J Cobb soon sees all three personalities and takes on the task of trying to merge them into one again. Alistair Cooke adds some weight as the narrator, but despite the fact that it's based on a real case history, the movie falters when Woodward interacts with anyone except her doctor. JB

Joanne Woodward *Eve* • David Wayne *Ralph White* • Lee J Cobb *Dr Luther* • Edwin Jerome *Dr Day* • Alena Murray *Secretary* • Nancy Kulp *Mrs Black* • Douglas Spencer *Mr Black* • Terry Ann Ross *Bonnie* • Alistair Cooke *Narrator* ■ *Dir* Nunnally Johnson • *Scr* Nunnally Johnson, from a book by Corbett H Thigpen, Hervey M Cleckley

Three Faces West ★★ U

Drama 1940 · US · BW · 75mins

This modern western attempted to cash in on John Ford's *The Grapes of Wrath* by featuring the plight of Dust Bowl farmers as well as being a story of refugees from Nazi Germany settling in America. John Wayne arranges for Charles Coburn's eminent Viennese surgeon and his daughter, played by Norwegian actress Sigrid Gurie, to move away from the doomed farming area and settle in Oregon. Preaching self-help and optimism, the film shows no sign of a left-wing viewpoint, though the director, Bernard Vorhaus, and one of the writers, Samuel Ornitz, were later blacklisted. AE

John Wayne *John* • Sigrid Gurie *Leni* • Charles Coburn *Dr Braun* • Spencer Charters *Nunk* • Helen MacKellar *Mrs Welles* • Roland Varno *Eric* • Sonny Bupp *Billy Welles* ■ *Dir* Bernard Vorhaus • *Scr* Frederick Hugh Herbert [F Hugh Herbert], Samuel Ornitz, Doris Anderson, Joseph Moncure March

3:15 ★★ 18

Action drama 1986 · US · Colour · 80mins

Larry Gross, who co-wrote *48 HRS* and has enjoyed a successful screenwriting career since, directs this action drama. However, the chief point of interest in this derivative teen-gang thriller is looking out for upcoming stars in early outings. The lead role goes to Adam Baldwin, as a reformed gang thug who is dragged back into that violent world when his girlfriend is attacked. JF

Adam Baldwin *Jeff Hannah* • Deborah Foreman *Sherry Havilland* • René Auberjonois *Principal Horner* • Ed Lauter *Moran* • Scott McGinnis *Chris* • Danny De La Paz *Cinco* • Mario Van Peebles *Whisperer* • Gina Gershon *Cobrette* ■ *Dir* Larry Gross • *Scr* Sam Bernard, Michael Jacobs

Three for the Road ★★ 15

Drama 1987 · US · Colour · 87mins

Even after *Platoon*, Charlie Sheen was demonstrating his unerring ability to pick turkeys, and this would-be road movie was never released in cinemas over here. Sheen and the under-rated

Alan Ruck bite off more than they can chew when they are asked to escort the rebellious daughter of a politician to a reform school. JF

Charlie Sheen *Paul Tracy* • Kerri Green *Robin Kitteridge* • Alan Ruck *Tommy, "TS"* • Sally Kellerman *Blanche* • Blair Tefkin *Missy* • Raymond J Barry *Senator Kitteridge* • Alexa Hamilton *Virginia* • Bert Remsen *Stu* ■ *Dir* BWL Norton [Bill L Norton] • *Scr* Richard Martini, Tim Metcalfe, Miguel Tejada-Flores, from a story by Richard Martini

Three for the Show ★★★

Musical 1955 · US · Colour · 91mins

This is the one about the girl who, believing her husband dead, has remarried only for him to reappear and confront her with a dilemma. It was a successful romantic comedy as *Too Many Husbands* in 1940, and would resurface in reverse – James Garner playing a husband with two wives – as *Move Over, Darling* in 1963. Here, showgirl Betty Grable is caught between returning Jack Lemmon and incumbent Gower Champion in a lively musical version of the tale. RK

Betty Grable *Julie* • Marge Champion *Gwen Howard* • Gower Champion *Vernon Lowndes* • Jack Lemmon *Marty Stewart* • Myron McCormick *Mike Hudson* • Paul Harvey *Colonel Wharton* • Robert Bice *Sergeant O'Hallihan* ■ *Dir* HC Potter • *Scr* Edward Hope, Leonard Stern [Leonard B Stern], from the play *Too Many Husbands* by W Somerset Maugham

Three Fugitives ★★★ 15

Crime comedy 1989 · US · Colour · 92mins

French director Francis Veber made his Hollywood debut with this enjoyable remake of his own 1986 French odd-couple farce, *Les Fugitifs*. Nick Nolte does well enough as the armed robber out on parole, while Martin Short gets plenty of slapstick laughs as the incompetent bank robber who drags the unwilling Nolte into his bungled caper. The action gets off to a good start and, despite sentimental moments, keeps up a fair pace, with a healthy ration of amusement. PF. Contains violence, swearing. DVD

Nick Nolte *Daniel Lucas* • Martin Short *Ned Perry* • Sarah Rowland Doroff *Meg Perry* • James Earl Jones *Detective Dugan* • Alan Ruck *Tener* • Kenneth McMillan *Horvath* ■ *Dir/Scr* Francis Veber

Three Godfathers ★★★ U

Western 1948 · US · Colour · 102mins

The first half-hour of this western ranks among the very best of ace director John Ford's work. But then the plot starts, and the film turns out to be a western precursor of *Three Men and a Baby*, only here the trio is on the run from sheriff Ward Bond. Excellent though the three leads are, they only just manage to keep their embarrassment at bay, despite the sheer daftness of the whole exercise with its bizarre religious and allegorical connotations. TS DVD

John Wayne *Robert Hightower* • Pedro Armendáriz *Pete* • Harry Carey Jr *Kid* • Ward Bond *"Buck" Perley Sweet* • Mae Marsh *Mrs Perley Sweet* • Mildred Natwick *Mother* • Jane Darwell *Miss Florie* • Guy Kibbee *Judge* ■ *Dir* John Ford • *Scr* Laurence Stallings, Frank S Nugent, from the story by Peter B Kyne

Three Guns for Texas ★★ U

Western 1968 · US · Colour · 98mins

Three episodes of the hit TV western *Laredo* are shoehorned into this theatrical release, but the result leaves a lot to be desired. Shelley Morrison's native American outlaw features – even going to the trouble of kidnapping Texas Ranger William Smith as a prospective groom. But plotlines involving pompous lawman Philip Carey and Neville Brand's paranoid pal Albert Salmi are bland. DP

Neville Brand *Reese Bennett* • Peter Brown *Chad Cooper* • William Smith *Joe Riley* • Martin Milner *MacMillan* • Philip Carey *Captain Parmalee* • Albert Salmi *Cleetus Grogan* ■ *Dir* David Lowell Rich, Paul Stanley, Earl Bellamy • *Scr* John DF Black

Three Hats for Lisa ★★ U

Musical 1965 · UK · Colour · 95mins

Joe Brown stars in this trite tosh about a docker, a cabbie and a foreign film star. Not even the presence of the great Sidney James can elevate this story of Sophie Hardy's search for three typically English hats. The script, co-written by *Carry On* regular Talbot Rothwell, raises a few smiles, but the songs signified a new low in screen pop. DP

Joe Brown (2) *Johnny Howjego* • Sophie Hardy *Lisa Milan* • Sidney James *Sid Marks* • Una Stubbs *Flora* • Peter Bowles *Sammy* • Seymour Green *Signor Molfino* • Josephine Blake *Miss Penny* ■ *Dir* Sidney Hayers • *Scr* Leslie Bricusse, Talbot Rothwell, from a story by Leslie Bricusse

Three Hours to Kill ★★

Western 1954 · US · Colour · 76mins

A strange little western, one of dozens influenced by *High Noon's* emphasis on ticking clocks, in which Dana Andrews has three hours to find the man who killed his fiancée's brother. Having escaped a lynch mob and finding, three years later, that his lady love Dianne Foster is unhappily married to a former friend, Andrews is in a hurry to clear his name and give us a happy ending. The story rattles along in B-movie fashion, with an agreeable lack of pretension. AT

Dana Andrews *Jim Guthrie* • Donna Reed *Laurie Mastin* • Dianne Foster *Chris Plumber* • Stephen Elliott *Ben East* • Richard Coogan *Niles Hendricks* • Laurence Hugo *Marty Lasswell* • James Westerfield *Sam Minor* ■ *Dir* Alfred Werker • *Scr* Richard Alan Simmons, Roy Huggins, Maxwell Shane, from a story by Alex Gottlieb

The 300 Spartans ★★★ PG

Historical adventure
1962 · US · Colour · 113mins

At a time when the "sword and sandal" epic was flourishing in Italy, 20th Century-Fox went to Greece to shoot this antiquarian adventure about the stalwart defence of Thermopylae in 480 BC. The production looks a little threadbare, but the locations are intelligently used by director Rudolph Maté, who also manages to stage the battle sequences on a reasonably convincing scale. Less authentic, however, is the dialogue, which defeats an actor of the calibre of Ralph Richardson, and gives an animated statue like Richard Egan no chance at all. DP DVD

Richard Egan *King Leonidas of Sparta* • Ralph Richardson *Themistocles of Athens* • Diane Baker *Ellas* • Barry Coe *Phylon* • David Farrar *Xerxes* • Donald Houston *Hydarnes* ■ *Dir* Rudolph Maté • *Scr* George St George, based on the original story material by Ugo Liberatore, Remigio Del Grosso, Giovanni D'Eramo, Gian Paolo Callegari

Three in the Attic ★

Sex comedy drama
1968 · US · Colour · 90mins

Considering this film was made by a veteran director who had worked on Orson Welles's early classics and who made the cracking *Al Capone* (1959), this Swinging Sixties wish-fulfilment fantasy may come as something of a letdown. When three women discover they have been seeing the same man, they decide to take revenge. Tying him up in the attic, they try to kill him with constant sex. What a way to go! JG

Christopher Jones *Paxton Quigley* • Yvette Mimieux *Tobey Clinton* • Judy Pace *Eulice* • Maggie Thrett *Jan* • Nan Martin *Dean Nazarin* ■ *Dir* Richard Wilson • *Scr* Stephen H Yafa

Three into Two Won't Go ★★★

Sex drama 1969 · UK · Colour · 93mins

This seminal 1960s sex drama has Rod Steiger as a salesman who picks up sexy hitch-hiker Judy Geeson, has a fling with her, and then finds his marriage to Claire Bloom under threat when the girl brazenly moves in with them. Directed by Peter Hall, this has obvious class, but passing time and changing moral values have done it no favours. Considered quite shocking in its day, it's now hard to see what all the fuss was about. DA

Rod Steiger *Steve Howard* • Claire Bloom *Frances Howard* • Judy Geeson *Ella Patterson* • Peggy Ashcroft *Belle* • Paul Rogers *Jack Roberts* • Lynn Farleigh *Janet* • Elizabeth Spriggs *Marcia* ■ *Dir* Peter Hall • *Scr* Edna O'Brien, from a novel by Andrea Newman

3-iron ★★★★ 15

Romantic drama
2004 · S Kor/Jpn · Colour · 87mins

Korean director Kim Ki-Duk's captivating Zen romance combines the calm gentility of his *Spring, Summer, Autumn, Winter ... and Spring* with the wincing violence of *The Isle* to ethereally fascinating effect. Jae Hee illegally occupies vacant homes for as long as the real tenants are away, until in one dwelling he finds battered wife Lee Seung-yeon who joins his hand-to-mouth existence. It's when they find a dead man in another house, get accused of murder, and Lee is returned to her abusive husband (Kwon Hyuk-ho) that the mystical elements come to the fore. Insightful and moving. AJ. In Korean with English subtitles. Contains sex scenes and violence.

Lee Seung-yeon *Sun-hwa* • Jae Hee *Tae-suk* • Kwon Hyuk-ho *Min-kyu* • Choi Jeong-ho *Jailor* • Lee Joo-suk *Son of old man* • Lee Mi-sook *Daughter-in-law of old man* • Moon Sung-hyuk *Sung-hyuk* • Joo Jin-mo *Detective* ■ *Dir/Scr* Kim Ki-Duk

Three Kings ★★★★ 15

Wartime action adventure
1999 · US · Colour · 110mins

A superb – though very violent – mix of comedy, drama and action, set at the end of the Gulf War. Hearing a rumour that Saddam Hussein has stashed stolen gold in bunkers, US soldiers George Clooney, Ice Cube and Mark Wahlberg embark on a secret field trip. It seems simple enough: grab the bullion and be rich for the rest of their lives. However, when they encounter villagers being tortured by Saddam's men, the guys reluctantly agree to help them. This boasts terrific performances, while taking some well-aimed stabs at the late 20th-century phenomenon of war waged on television. JB. Contains swearing, violence and sex scenes. DVD

George Clooney *Major Archie Gates* • Mark Wahlberg *Sergeant Troy Barlow* • Ice Cube *Staff Sergeant Chief Elgin* • Spike Jonze *Private Conrad Vig* • Nora Dunn *Adriana Cruz* • Jamie Kennedy *Walter Wogaman* • Mykelti Williamson *Colonel Horn* • Cliff Curtis *Amir Abdulah* ■ *Dir* David O Russell • *Scr* David O Russell, from a story by John Ridley

Three Little Girls in Blue ★★★ U

Musical 1946 · US · Colour · 90mins

This is a light and chirpy musical remake of 1938's *Three Blind Mice* (the plot was later rehashed for *How to Marry a Millionaire* in 1953). Take three girls, bored with life down on the chicken farm, and each wanting to find a rich husband. Cut to the big city, add a handful of musical numbers, some frisky hoofing and lavish period art direction. Stir gently and end up with an agreeable movie that is unmomentous but entertaining. PF

June Haver *Pam Charters* • George Montgomery *Van Damm Smith* • Vivian Blaine *Liz Charters* • Celeste Holm *Miriam Harrington* • Vera-Ellen *Myra Charters* • Frank Latimore *Steve Harrinton* • Charles Smith *Mike Bailey* • Charles Halton *Hoskins* ■ *Dir* H Bruce Humberstone • *Scr* Valentine Davis, Brown Holmes, Lynn Starling, Robert Ellis, Helen Logan, from the play by Stephen Powys

The Three Little Pigs ★★★★★ U

Animated musical comedy
1933 · US · Colour · 8mins

This Oscar-winning short cartoon – one of the most popular in film history – was significant for a number of reasons. Within the animation industry it introduced, through Fred Moore's animation of the title characters' introductory sequence, the concept of "squash and stretch", the technique by which a character retains believability by maintaining a constant volume as its body distorts. Additionally, it was the first true example of "personality animation" – although the three pigs looked identical, they behaved differently. To the public, who may or may not have unconsciously responded to these innovations, the most obviously popular feature was Frank Churchill and Ann Ronell's theme song *Who's Afraid of the Big Bad Wolf?* To Depression-era audiences, this cheerful ditty of defiance was symbolically encouraging. CLP

Mary Moder *Fiddler Pig* • Dorothy Compton *Fife Pig* • Pinto Colvig *Practical Pig* • Billy Bletcher *Zeke Wolf* ■ *Dir* Burt Gillett

Three Little Words ★★★★ U

Musical biography
1950 · US · Colour · 102mins

This is another fanciful Hollywood biopic of popular composers used as an excuse for a string of good numbers, but it has more plot than usual. Bert Kalmar and Harry Ruby bear as much resemblance to Fred Astaire and Red Skelton as the story bears to their lives. But with Astaire in three dances, two with Vera-Ellen and Skelton (funny but more restrained than usual), it cannot miss as light entertainment. Debbie Reynolds has a cameo as Helen Kane, the "Boop-Boop-a-Doop" girl in *I Wanna Be Loved By You*. RB

Fred Astaire *Bert Kalmar, "Kendall the Great"* • Red Skelton *Harry Ruby* • Vera-Ellen *Jessie Brown Kalmar* • Arlene Dahl *Eileen Percy* • Keenan Wynn *Charlie Kope* • Gale Robbins *Terry Lordel* • Gloria DeHaven *Mrs Carter DeHaven* • Debbie Reynolds *Helen Kane* ■ *Dir* Richard Thorpe • *Scr* George Wells, from an autobiography by Bert Kalmar, Harry Ruby

Three Lives and Only One Death ★★★★

Fantasy comedy drama
1996 · Fr · Colour · 124mins

The genius of Marcello Mastroianni illuminates this amusing diversion from Raúl Ruiz. He plays four different roles in a seemingly disconnected quartet of stories: a travelling salesman who surprises his ex-wife and her new husband; a Sorbonne professor who takes up with a similarly detached prostitute; a sinister butler trying to poison his employers; and a tycoon with a tendency to panic in a crisis. The aim of this delicious mêlée of running gags and visual puns is to question the validity of a single

T

European culture. DP. In French with English subtitles.

Marcello Mastroianni *Mateo Strano/Georges Vickers/Butler/Luc Allamand* • Anna Galiena *Tania* • Marisa Paredes *Maria* • Melvil Poupaud *Martin* • Chiara Mastroianni *Cecile* • Arielle Dombasle *Helene* • Feodor Atkine *André* • Jean-Yves Gautier *Mario* ■ *Dir* Raúl Ruiz • *Scr* Raúl Ruiz, Pascal Bonitzer

The Three Lives of Thomasina ★★★ U

Period fantasy
1963 · US/UK · Colour · 94mins

Patrick McGoohan is superb in this British-made Disney fantasy about a veterinary surgeon whose decision to put down his daughter's ailing cat leads to magical encounters with a mysterious stranger. McGoohan is nicely supported by Susan Hampshire and Finlay Currie, but the adult leads are no match for the delightful Karen Dotrice as McGoohan's daughter and a very scene-stealing feline. TS

Patrick McGoohan *Andrew MacDhui* • Susan Hampshire *Lori MacGregor* • Karen Dotrice *Mary MacDhui* • Laurence Naismith *Reverend Angus Peddie* • Jean Anderson *Mrs MacKenzie* • Finlay Currie *Grandpa Stirling* ■ *Dir* Don Chaffey • *Scr* Robert Westerby, from the novel *Thomasina, the Cat Who Thought She Was God* by Paul Gallico

Three Loves ★★★

Silent romantic thriller 1929 · Ger · BW

In this strange, dreamlike, threatening and romantic story, young Frenchman Uno Henning, who has married for money rather than love, then meets the intriguing Marlene Dietrich on his honeymoon. He falls in love with her, and she begs him to save her from sinister Fritz Kortner. Directed by Kurt (later Curtis) Bernhardt, this is the film that first gained American attention for Dietrich, with *Variety* drawing comparisons to Garbo and pronouncing the German star "a strong contender for international honours". RK

Marlene Dietrich *Stascha* • Fritz Kortner *Dr Karoff* • Frida Richard *Frau Leblanc* • Oskar Sima *Charles Leblanc* • Uno Henning *Henry Leblanc* ■ *Dir* Kurt Bernhardt [Curtis Bernhardt] • *Scr* Ladislaus Vajda, from the novel *Die Frau, nach der Man sich Sehnt* by Max Brod

Three Loves Has Nancy ★

Romantic comedy 1938 · US · BW · 69mins

Janet Gaynor, a naive and irritating girl from a hick town down South, comes to New York to look for her missing fiancé, and seeks refuge with novelist Robert Montgomery whom she'd met earlier. Her presence, cooking and homespun simplicity cause general mayhem for Montgomery and his drunken friend and neighbour Franchot Tone. An absurd and unconvincing attempt at screwball comedy. RK

Janet Gaynor *Nancy Briggs* • Robert Montgomery *Malcolm Niles* • Franchot Tone *Robert Hansen* • Guy Kibbee *Pa Briggs* • Claire Dodd *Vivian Herford* • Reginald Owen *Valet* • Cora Witherspoon *Mrs Herford* ■ *Dir* Richard Thorpe • *Scr* Bella Spewack, Sam Spewack, George Oppenheimer, David Hertz, from a story by Lee Loeb, Mort Braus

The Three Marias ★★★ 15

Western drama
2002 · Bra/It/Neth · Colour · 88mins

Director Aluizio Abranches reworks many of the conventions of Brazilian revenge dramas in this wry blend of naturalism and surrealism. The most significant departure is that the task of avenging the family honour falls to Marieta Severo's daughters – Julia Lemmertz, Maria Luisa Mendonca and Luiza Mariani – each of whom must locate a specialist assassin. Their encounters all have their own distinctive tone that adds to the atmosphere of tension and intrigue. DP. In Portuguese with English subtitles. Contains violence.

Marieta Severo *Filomena Capadocio* • Julia Lemmertz *Maria Francisca* • Maria Luisa Mendonca *Maria Rosa* • Luiza Mariani *Maria Pia* • Carlos Vereza *Firmino Santos Guerra* • Enrique Diaz *Ze das Cobras* • Tuca Andrada *Chief Tenorio* • Wagner Moura *Jesuino Cruz* ■ *Dir* Aluizio Abranches • *Scr* Heitor Dhalia, Wilson Freire

Three Men and a Baby ★★★★ PG

Comedy 1987 · US · Colour · 98mins

The title says it all – bachelors Ted Danson, Steve Guttenberg and Tom Selleck are left holding the baby abandoned on their doorstep, and it's not long before they are knee-deep in bottles, nappies and gooey moments. The three leads look suitably harassed as they adapt to changing, feeding and burping duties, and director Leonard Nimoy (Mr Spock himself) keeps the comedy and entertainment coming thick and fast. Based on the French film *3 Men and a Cradle*, this is thoroughly enjoyable family fare. JB. Contains swearing. DVD

Tom Selleck *Peter Mitchell* • Steve Guttenberg *Michael Kellam* • Ted Danson *Jack Holden* • Nancy Travis *Sylvia* • Margaret Colin *Rebecca* • Celeste Holm *Jack's mother* • Philip Bosco *Det Melkowitz* ■ *Dir* Leonard Nimoy • *Scr* James Orr, Jim Cruickshank, from the film *3 Men and a Cradle/Trois Hommes et un Couffin* by Coline Serreau

3 Men and a Cradle ★★★★ PG

Comedy 1985 · Fr · Colour · 101mins

Former actress Coline Serreau hit the jackpot as a writer/director with this box-office smash about three die-hard bachelors who have to look after a freshly hatched baby girl. The plot centres around the allegation that one of the men is the baby's father. There's also a stash of drugs hidden in the cradle that attracts the attentions of the underworld and the cops. Smartly paced and engagingly acted by the relatively unknown cast, it's a sweet little satire about the demolition of the male ego in the era of feminism. Hollywood snapped up the remake rights and made the monster hit *Three Men and a Baby*. Belatedly followed by a disappointing sequel, *18 Years Later*. AT. French dialogue dubbed into English.

Roland Giraud *Pierre* • Michel Boujenah *Michel* • André Dussollier *Jacques* • Philippine Leroy-Beaulieu *Sylvia* • Gwendoline Mourlet *First Marie* • Jennifer Moret *Second Marie* • Dominique Lavanant *Madame Rapons* ■ *Dir/Scr* Coline Serreau

Three Men and a Little Lady ★★ PG

Comedy 1990 · US · Colour · 99mins

In this decidedly lacklustre comedy sequel to *Three Men and a Baby*, Tom Selleck, Steve Guttenberg and Ted Danson travel to London to try to prevent their adopted daughter from being sent to – horrors! – boarding school. As an insult to Britain it would have been more effective if it had been better made, but it wasn't. In addition, casting British actors to perform as if they are the befuddled eccentrics of an imaginary England of the 1950s seems almost contemptuous. TH DVD

Tom Selleck *Peter Mitchell* • Steve Guttenberg *Michael Kellam* • Ted Danson *Jack Holden* • Nancy Travis *Sylvia Bennington* • Robin Weisman *Mary Bennington* • Christopher Cazenove *Edward* • Sheila Hancock *Vera* • Fiona Shaw *Miss Lomax* • John Boswall *Barrow* ■ *Dir* Emile Ardolino • *Scr* Charlie Peters, from a story by Sara Parriott, Josann McGibbon

Three Men in a Boat ★★★★ U

Comedy 1956 · UK · Colour · 87mins

The nostalgic appeal of Jerome K Jerome's Victorian trio is undimmed – and perhaps even enhanced – by a rather childish approach to their messing about on the Thames with a scene-stealing dog. Despite a pretend feud between Jimmy Edwards and Laurence Harvey, kept up throughout filming for publicity purposes, the ensemble, including David Tomlinson, is amiability itself, while the parasol-toting girls are as radiant as the golden days of yesteryear. TH DVD

Laurence Harvey *George* • Jimmy Edwards *Harris* • David Tomlinson *J* • Shirley Eaton *Sophie Clutterbuck* • Jill Ireland *Bluebell Porterhouse* • Lisa Gastoni *Primrose Porterhouse* • Martita Hunt *Mrs Willis* • Campbell Cotts *Ambrose Porterhouse* • Joan Haythorne *Mrs Porterhouse* ■ *Dir* Ken Annakin • *Scr* Hubert Gregg, Vernon Harris, from the novel by Jerome K Jerome

Three Men in White ★★ U

Medical drama 1944 · US · BW · 84mins

The 1942 departure of its title star, Lew Ayres, ended the popular series of *Dr Kildare* films. However, with Lionel Barrymore still on hand, MGM segued into the *Dr Gillespie* series, focusing on the crusty old wheelchair-bound physician for six increasingly feeble movies, which finally put paid to Blair Hospital in 1947. This one has Gillespie seeking a new assistant and having to choose between Van Johnson and Keye Luke. RK

Lionel Barrymore *Dr Leonard Gillespie* • Van Johnson *Dr Randall Adams* • Marilyn Maxwell *Ruth Edley* • Keye Luke *Dr Lee Wong How* • Ava Gardner *Jean Brown* • Alma Kruger *Molly Byrd* ■ *Dir* Willis Goldbeck • *Scr* Martin Berkeley, Harry Ruskin, from the characters created by Max Brand

Three Men on a Horse ★★

Comedy 1936 · US · BW · 88mins

Frank McHugh is the timid author of greetings card verses who has an uncanny knack for picking winning horses, which leads to him falling into the bad company of racetrack touts. In making this mildly enjoyable film version of a Broadway smash hit, Warners and director Mervyn LeRoy commendably avoided using big stars so that it remains a character piece played by character actors. AE

Frank McHugh *Erwin Trowbridge* • Joan Blondell *Mabel* • Carol Hughes *Audrey Trowbridge* • Allen Jenkins *Charley* • Guy Kibbee *Mr Carver* • Sam Levene *Patsy* • Teddy Hart *Frankie* • Edgar Kennedy *Harry* • Eddie "Rochester" Anderson *Moses* ■ *Dir* Mervyn LeRoy • *Scr* Laird Doyle, from the play by John Cecil Holm, George Abbott

Three Men to Destroy ★★★

Crime thriller 1980 · Fr · Colour · 90mins

Stopping to help an accident victim, Alain Delon finds himself caught up in a bungled underworld hit and becomes the target of mobster Pierre Dux. However, when he turns himself into an efficient killing machine, the pursuit takes on a very different nature. This is a dark, almost Darwinian treatise on our potential for violence. Edgily directed, it's played with plenty of steel by Delon. DP. French dialogue dubbed into English.

Alain Delon *Michel Gerfaut* • Dalila DiLazzaro *Bea* • Pierre Dux *Emmerich* • Michel Auclair *Leprince* ■ *Dir* Jacques Deray • *Scr* Jacques Deray, Christopher Franck, from the novel by Jean-Patrick Manchette

The Three Musketeers ★★★★ U

Silent swashbuckling adventure
1921 · US · BW · 131mins

This was the first major screen version of Alexandre Dumas's literary romp, though it had been filmed several times since 1911. Douglas Fairbanks had himself dipped a toe in the Dumasian sea in 1917 with *A Modern Musketeer*, in which he played D'Artagnan of Kansas. But in 1921 it was all stops out, with lavish sets, slavish attention to detail and knavish behaviour on the screen. Producer/star Fairbanks and director Fred Niblo were fresh from *The Mark of Zorro* and they made this swordfest just as exuberantly entertaining. It was a smash hit everywhere and remained the definitive version until Richard Lester's two-parter of 1973. AT

Douglas Fairbanks *D'Artagnan* • Leon Barry *Athos* • George Siegmann *Porthos* • Eugene Pallette *Aramis* • Boyd Irwin *De Rochefort* • Thomas Holding *George Villiers, Duke of Buckingham* • Sidney Franklin *Bonacieux* • Charles Stevens *Planchet, D'Artagnan's lackey* • Nigel de Brulier *Cardinal Richelieu* • Willis Robards *Capt de Treville* • Adolphe Menjou *Louis XIII, King of France* ■ *Dir* Fred Niblo • *Scr* Edward Knoblock, Lotta Woods, from the novel by Alexandre Dumas

The Three Musketeers ★

Swashbuckling adventure
1935 · US · BW · 90mins

The first talkie version of the Dumas classic was slated at the time and remains a catastrophe, due mainly to the unappealing cast. The hangdog Walter Abel, who was imported from Broadway with much fanfare to play D'Artagnan, seems hopelessly lost, as do his uncharismatic co-stars. AT

Walter Abel *D'Artagnan* • Paul Lukas *Athos* • Margot Grahame *Milady de Winter* • Heather Angel *Constance* • Ian Keith *De Rochefort* • Moroni Olsen *Porthos* • Onslow Stevens *Aramis* • Rosamond Pinchot *Queen Anne* • Nigel de Brulier *Cardinal Richelieu* ■ *Dir* Rowland V Lee • *Scr* Dudley Nichols, Rowland V Lee, from the novel by Alexandre Dumas

The Three Musketeers ★★ U

Swashbuckling comedy
1939 · US · BW · 73mins

This 1939 effort does almost count as a musical (it was retitled *The Singing Musketeer* in Britain), though Dumas's story remains essentially unchanged. Don Ameche stars as D'Artagnan, Binnie Barnes is Milady and the Ritz Brothers (Fox's answer to the Marxes) are three slapstick lackeys. Songs include *My Lady*, *Song of the Musketeers* and *Viola*. Veteran director Allan Dwan also directed the 1917 Douglas Fairbanks picture *A Modern Musketeer*. AT

Don Ameche *D'Artagnan* • The Ritz Brothers [Al Ritz] *Lackey* • The Ritz Brothers [Jimmy Ritz] *Lackey* • The Ritz Brothers [Harry Ritz] *Lackey* • Binnie Barnes *Milady de Winter* • Lionel Atwill *De Rochefort* • Gloria Stuart *Queen* • Pauline Moore *Lady Constance* • Joseph Schildkraut *King* • John Carradine *Naveau* • Miles Mander *Cardinal Richelieu* • Douglass Dumbrille *Athos* ■ *Dir* Allan Dwan • *Scr* MM Musselman, William A Drake, Sam Hellman, Sid Kuller, Ray Golden, from the novel by Alexandre Dumas

The Three Musketeers ★★★ U

Swashbuckling adventure
1948 · US · Colour · 120mins

Directed in glorious Technicolor by under-rated maestro George Sidney, this has a marvellously athletic Gene Kelly as D'Artagnan. The long screen fencing sequences are the highlight of what is a rather overlong and relentlessly Americanised version of the classic tale. In order not to offend American Catholics, Richelieu (endearingly overacted by Vincent Price) is no longer a cardinal and all internecine court wrangling is played down. Nevertheless, Lana Turner is a ravishingly beautiful Countess de Winter. TS

Lana Turner *Milady, Countess Charlotte de Winter* • Gene Kelly *D'Artagnan* • June Allyson *Constance Bonacieux* • Van Heflin *Athos* • Angela Lansbury *Queen Anne* • Frank Morgan *King Louis XIII* • Vincent Price *Richelieu* ■ *Dir* George Sidney (2) • *Scr* Robert Ardrey, from the novel by Alexandre Dumas

The Three Musketeers ★★★★ U

Swashbuckling comedy adventure
1973 · Pan · Colour · 102mins

This is a sparkling version of the famous duel between the all-for-one quartet and Cardinal Richelieu and his scheming accomplice, Milady. Michael York gives D'Artagnan a clever twist of yokel to contrast him with his more worldly companions, played with wit and charm by Oliver Reed, Richard Chamberlain and Frank Finlay. The action has all the pace and unpredictability one has come to expect from director Richard Lester. The first sequel, *The Four Musketeers*, was filmed at the same time, while fans had to wait a further 15 years for the second sequel, *The Return of the Musketeers*. DP DVD

Michael York *D'Artagnan* • Raquel Welch *Constance Bonancieux* • Oliver Reed *Athos* • Richard Chamberlain *Aramis* • Frank Finlay *Porthos* • Charlton Heston *Cardinal Richelieu* • Faye Dunaway *Milady de Winter* • Christopher Lee *Rochefort* • Spike Milligan *M Bonancieux* • Roy Kinnear *Planchet* ■ *Dir* Richard Lester • *Scr* George MacDonald Fraser, from the novel by Alexandre Dumas

The Three Musketeers ★★ PG

Swashbuckling comedy adventure
1993 · US · Colour · 101mins

Richard Lester's knockabout, anarchic 1973 take on Alexandre Dumas's classic is unlikely to be surpassed, and this version for the grown-up Brat Pack is misconceived from start to finish. Kiefer Sutherland, Charlie Sheen and Oliver Platt are the swashbuckling trio, Chris O'Donnell is the idealistic D'Artagnan who joins their cause and Rebecca De Mornay the sinister The Americanisations constantly jar and the action set pieces are clumsily handled. JF DVD

Charlie Sheen *Aramis* • Kiefer Sutherland *Athos* • Chris O'Donnell *D'Artagnan* • Oliver Platt *Porthos* • Tim Curry *Cardinal Richelieu* • Rebecca De Mornay *Milady* • Gabrielle Anwar *Queen Anne* • Michael Wincott *Rochefort* • Paul McGann *Girad/Jussac* • Julie Delpy *Constance* • Hugh O'Conor *King Louis* ■ *Dir* Stephen Herek • *Scr* David Loughery, from the novel by Alexandre Dumas

3 Ninjas ★★★ PG

Martial arts adventure
1992 · US/S Kor · Colour · 84mins

This was the first of a series of four films featuring Victor Wong's high-kicking grandchildren and youngsters will probably revel in the pre-teen chop-socky adventure. As anyone who's seen *Home Alone* knows, the last thing villains should do is take on resourceful youngsters, especially when their dad is an FBI agent and grandpa is a martial arts master. But that's what the henchmen of an evil arms dealer do here – so they really were asking for trouble. DP

Victor Wong (2) *Grandpa* • Michael Treanor *Rocky* • Max Elliott Slade *Colt* • Chad Power *Tum Tum* • Rand Kingsley *Snyder* • Alan McRae *Sam Douglas* ■ *Dir* Jon Turteltaub • *Scr* Edward Emanuel, from the story *Three Ninja Kids* by Kenny Kim

3 Ninjas: High Noon at Mega Mountain ★★ PG

Martial arts adventure
1998 · US · Colour · 86mins

The fourth *3 Ninjas* adventure is almost indistinguishable from its predecessors, as a trio of crime-fighting youngsters take their Japanese grandfather's martial arts training on to the streets. The storyline has all the complexity of a *Scooby-Doo* cartoon, as incompetent supercrooks Loni Anderson and Jim Varney decide to extort a theme park on the very day that our heroes show up. Add martial arts expert Hulk Hogan into the mix and you have an utterly undemanding movie. DP DVD

Hulk Hogan *Dave Dragon* • Loni Anderson *Medusa* • Jim Varney *Lothar Zogg* • Mathew Botuchis *Rocky Douglas* • Michael J O'Laskey II *Colt Douglas* • James Paul Roeske II *Tum Tum Douglas* • Victor Wong (2) *Grandpa Mori* • Chelsea Earlywine *Amanda Morgan-Green* ■ *Dir* Sean McNamara • *Scr* Sean McNamara, Jeff Phillips

3 Ninjas Kick Back ★★ U

Martial arts adventure
1994 · US/Jpn · Colour · 88mins

The second film in the series about three children with formidable martial arts skills finds the boys faced with a conundrum. Should they go to Japan with grandpa Victor Wong, or play in the little league baseball championships? There wouldn't be much of a story if they didn't go to Japan, where they become embroiled in a standard *Goonies*-style hunt for hidden treasure. ST DVD

Victor Wong (2) *Grandpa* • Max Elliott Slade *Colt* • Sean Fox *Rocky* • Evan Bonifant [J Evan Bonifant] *Tum Tum* • Caroline Junko King *Miyo* • Dustin Nguyen *Glam* • Alan McRae *Sam* ■ *Dir* Charles T Kanganis • *Scr* Mark Saltzman, from a screenplay (unproduced) by Simon Sheen

3 Ninjas Knuckle Up ★ PG

Martial arts adventure
1995 · US · Colour · 82mins

In this, their third film, the three diminutive ninjas and their grandpa (Victor Wong) end up on an American Indian reservation, which is under siege by a polluting corporation and a gang of bikers. The fights seem to get longer and less inspired in each film, and the dust bowl setting smacks of a shrinking budget. This is sub-par children's entertainment. ST DVD

Victor Wong (2) *Grandpa* • Charles Napier *Jack* • Michael Treanor *Rocky* • Max Elliott Slade *Colt* • Chad Power *Tum Tum* • Crystle Lightning *Jo* • Patrick Kilpatrick *JJ* • Donald L Shanks [Don Shanks] *Charlie* ■ *Dir* Sang Okk Sheen • *Scr* Alex Sangok Kim

Three O'Clock High ★★ 15

Comedy
1987 · US · Colour · 85mins

Director Phil Joanou here turns his hand to a teen comedy, which is effectively a rip-off of *High Noon* but in a familiar high school setting. Casey Siemaszko is student, facing up to a showdown with a fearsome teen rival in this lightweight fare, which is only slightly redeemed by the sterling performances of the cast. JB

Casey Siemaszko *Jerry Mitchell* • Anne Ryan *Franny Perrins* • Richard Tyson *Buddy Revell* • Stacey Glick *Brei Mitchell* • Jonathan Wise *Vincent Costello* • Jeffrey Tambor *Mr Rice* • Philip Baker Hall *Detective Mulvahill* • John P Ryan *Mr O'Rourke* ■ *Dir* Phil Joanou • *Scr* Richard Christian Matheson, Thomas Szollosi

Three of Hearts ★★ 18

Romantic comedy drama
1992 · US · Colour · 105mins

A romantic tale with a twist. Kelly Lynch and Sherilyn Fenn play a gay couple who contrive to split up by the end of the opening credits. A devastated Lynch then hires stud and gigolo William Baldwin to escort her to a wedding. Baldwin suggests a plan to win Fenn back that involves him wooing her and then breaking her heart. Original and feisty initially, the film descends into more conventional territory when Baldwin falls for Fenn. Watchable, but average. LH DVD

William Baldwin *Joe Casella* • Kelly Lynch *Connie* • Sherilyn Fenn *Ellen* • Joe Pantoliano *Mickey* • Gail Strickland *Yvonne* • Cec Verrell *Allison* • Claire Callaway *Isabella* • Marek Johnson *Gail* ■ *Dir* Yurek Bogayevicz • *Scr* Adam Greenman, Mitch Glazer, from a story by Adam Greenman

Three on a Couch ★★★ U

Comedy 1966 · US · Colour · 108mins

In an art competition, Jerry Lewis wins prize money and a commission to paint a prestigious mural in Paris. His fiancée, psychiatrist Janet Leigh, is reluctant to go with him, however, as she is the middle of delicate therapy with three women who have suffered at the hands of thoughtless men. Lewis takes the drastic step of trying to cure the women himself. The idiosyncratic Jerry Lewis is more restrained than normal in this clumsy comedy that still contains moments of genius. DF

Jerry Lewis *Christopher Pride/Warren/Ringo/Rutherford/Heather* • Janet Leigh *Dr Elizabeth Acord* • Mary Ann Mobley *Susan Manning* • Gila Golan *Anna Jacque* • Leslie Parrish *Mary Lou Mauve* • James Best *Dr Ben Mizer* • Kathleen Freeman *Murphy* • Buddy Lester *Drunk* • Scatman Crothers ■ *Dir* Jerry Lewis • *Scr* Bob Ross, Samuel A Taylor, from a story by Arne Sultan, Marvin Worth

Three on a Match ★★★

Drama 1932 · US · BW · 63mins

The bizarre title of this tale hides an intelligent little movie about friendships and new rivalries. A suspenseful atmosphere pervades throughout and director Mervyn LeRoy makes good use of external locations to develop the theme of encroaching tragedy. Watch out for Humphrey Bogart, not yet a superstar, in a cast that plays a well honed script to the hilt. Not a masterpiece, but worth the effort. SH

Joan Blondell *Mary Keaton* • Warren William *Henry Kirkwood* • Ann Dvorak *Vivian Revere* • Bette Davis *Ruth Westcott* • Lyle Talbot *Mike Loftus* • Humphrey Bogart *Harve the Mug* • Patricia Ellis *Linda* ■ *Dir* Mervyn LeRoy • *Scr* Lucien Hubbard, Kubec Glasmon, John Bright, from the story by Kubec Glasmon, John Bright

Three on a Spree ★ U

Farce 1961 · UK · BW · 89mins

First made as a silent by Oscar Apfel and Cecil B De Mille in 1914, *Brewster's Millions* underwent another reworking in this shoddy British offering. The story lumbers around London as Jack Watling attempts to spend a small fortune in a bid to land a whopping inheritance. Carole Lesley comes along for the ride, without bring much to the picnic. Sidney J Furie's contribution is much better – his leaden, laugh-free direction saps the morale of a willing, but woefully wasted supporting cast. DP

Jack Watling *Michael Brewster* • Carole Lesley *Susan* • Renee Houston *Mrs Gray* • John Slater *Sid Johnson* • Colin Gordon *Mitchell* • John Salew *Mr Monkton* ■ *Dir* Sidney J Furie • *Scr* Siegfried Herzig, Charles Rogers, Wilkie Mahoney, James Kelly, Peter Miller, from the play *Brewster's Millions: a Comedy in Four Acts* by Winchell Smith, Byron Ongley, from the novel *Brewster's Millions* by George Barr McCutcheon

Three Ring Circus ★★

Drama 1954 · US · Colour · 103mins

Just what Dean Martin and Jerry Lewis saw in each other is beside the point, it's what audiences at the time saw in them. This film is typical of their routine mix of slapstick and schmaltz, with the pair playing discharged servicemen joining a circus. It's not to everyone's taste, but it was certainly popular with the public in the 1950s, with Martin's role as cynical smoothie more appealing to some than Lewis's rather less sophisticated interpretation of his character. TH

Dean Martin *Pete Nelson* • Jerry Lewis *Jerry Hotchkiss* • Joanne Dru *Jill Brent* • Zsa Zsa Gabor *Saadia* • Wallace Ford *Sam Morley* • Sig Ruman *Fritz Schlitz* • Gene Sheldon *Puffo* • Elsa Lanchester *Bearded lady* ■ *Dir* Joseph Pevney • *Scr* Don McGuire

Three Sailors and a Girl ★★ U

Musical 1953 · US · Colour · 95mins

This Warner Bros romp is, amazingly, based on a stage play by Pulitzer Prize-winning author George S Kaufman. There's little trace of its source as likeable Gordon MacRae, hoofer Gene Nelson and winsome Jane Powell get involved in one of those staple musical plots about raising the money to put on a show. Predictable stuff, pleasant but not inspiring. TS

Jane Powell *Penny Weston* • Gordon MacRae *Choir Boy Jones* • Gene Nelson *Twitch* • Sam Levene *Joe Woods* • George Givot *Rossi* • Veda Ann Borg *Faye Foss* • Archer MacDonald *Webster* • Raymond Greenleaf *Morrow* ■ *Dir* Roy Del Ruth • *Scr* Roland Kibbee, Devery Freeman, from the play *The Butter and Egg Man* by George S Kaufman

Three Seasons ★★★ 12

Drama 1999 · US/Viet · Colour · 108mins

Striking in its imagery but disappointingly cosy in its themes, Tony Bui's feature debut is the first American film to be made in Vietnam since the war. There's an element of bridge-building here, particularly in the plot strand concerning ex-GI Harvey Keitel's search for the daughter he's never seen. Other threads follow a young woman (Nguyen Ngoc Hiep) who learns to balance tradition and progress while picking flowers in a lotus garden and cyclo driver Don Duong, whose love for prostitute Zoë Bui is an object lesson in forgiving and forgetting the past. DP. In Vietnamese and English with subtitles. Contains sexual references, nudity. DVD

Don Duong *Hai* • Nguyen Ngoc Hiep *Kien An* • Tran Manh Cuong *Teacher Dao* • Harvey Keitel *James Hager* • Zoe Bui *Lan* • Nguyen Huu Duoc *Woody* • Minh Ngoc *Truck driver* ■ *Dir* Tony Bui • *Scr* Tony Bui, Timothy Linh Bui

Three Secrets ★★★

Drama 1950 · US · BW · 97mins

With a less talented director and actresses, this weepie could have drowned in its own tears. But Robert Wise keeps the drama on course and Eleanor Parker, Patricia Neal and Ruth Roman are splendid as the three mothers who wait together in a mountain cabin for news after a plane crash. Considerable emotion is derived from an admittedly contrived situation in which a five-year-old boy is the sole survivor of the crash. The news that the crash happened on his birthday and that he was given up for adoption unites the women, each of whom made a sacrifice years previously and believe the child may be theirs. BB

Eleanor Parker *Susan Chase* • Patricia Neal *Phyllis Horn* • Ruth Roman *Ann Lawrence* • Frank Lovejoy *Bob Duffy* • Leif Erickson *Bill Chase* • Ted De Corsia *Del Prince* • Larry Keating *Mark Harrison* ■ *Dir* Robert Wise • *Scr* Martin Rackin, Gina Kaus, from their story *Rock Bottom*

T

The Three Sisters ★★

Period drama 1966 · US · BW · 166mins

A filmed version of Lee Strasberg's Actors Studio production that ran comfortably on Broadway during the mid-1960s, this version of Chekhov's turn-of-the-century play doesn't quite come off, but it's certainly different. Three unhappy women for whom city life in Moscow is the centre of their universe search for a meaningful life in a Russian village. Though it may be interesting for students of the Method and/or fans of offbeat experiments with the classics, this transcription may irritate others. JG

Gerald Hiken *Andrei* • Shelley Winters *Natalya* • Geraldine Page *Olga* • Kim Stanley *Masha* • Sandy Dennis *Irina* • Albert Paulsen *Kulygin* • Kevin McCarthy *Vershinin* • James Olson *Baron Tuzenbach* • Robert Loggia *Solyony* • Luther Adler *Chebutikin* ■ *Dir* Paul Bogart • *Scr* from the play by Anton Chekhov

Three Sisters ★★ U

Period drama 1970 · UK · Colour · 155mins

Though of value to biographers and theatre historians, this record of Laurence Olivier's National Theatre production is a negligible cinematic experience. Apart from two added sequences, there is no attempt to make this a "movie". Olivier is simply content to have Geoffrey Unsworth's camera rooted to its tripod as it records some admittedly fine performances from the actors portraying the three sisters who grow bored with provincial life and yearn for the glamour of Tsarist Moscow. AT DVD

Jeanne Watts *Olga* • Joan Plowright *Masha* • Louise Purnell *Irina* • Derek Jacobi *Andrei* • Alan Bates *Colonel Vershinin* • Kenneth Mackintosh *Kulighin* • Sheila Reid *Natasha* • Laurence Olivier *Chebutikin* • Ronald Pickup *Tusenbach* ■ *Dir* Laurence Olivier, John Sichel • *Scr* Moura Budberg, from the play by Anton Chekhov

Three Sisters ★★★ 12

Drama 1988 · It/Fr/W Ger · Colour · 112mins

This reworking of Chekhov's play sees the action transported from Russia to the chilly Italian town of Pavia. The story has been updated, with Greta Scacchi unhappily married to a TV comic and the threat of the arms race hanging over the proceedings. Director Margarethe von Trotta has retained the subtle complexities of the original play, and, in a dual role, Scacchi acquits herself well. But the achingly beautiful visuals can't quite atone for the over-deliberate pacing. DP. In Italian, French and German with English subtitles.

Fanny Ardant *Velia* • Greta Scacchi *Maria/Maria's mother* • Valeria Golino *Sandra* • Peter Simonischek *Massimo* • Sergio Castellitto *Roberto* • Agnes Soral *Sabrina* • Paolo Hendel *Federico* • Jan-Paul Biczycki *Cecchini* ■ *Dir* Margarethe von Trotta • *Scr* Dacia Maraini, Margarethe von Trotta

T

Three Smart Girls ★★★ U

Romantic musical comedy
1937 · US · BW · 80mins

Three young daughters (Nan Grey, Barbara Read and Deanna Durbin) of divorced parents determine to stop the remarriage of their mega-rich Wall Street financier father Charles Winninger to young gold-digger Binnie Barnes, and reunite their parents. The driving force is the youngest sister, a precocious and irrepressible hoyden with an opera singer's voice. This is the comedy that made Durbin a huge star and established the formula for her subsequent clutch of moneymakers. It's complete nonsense from start to finish and, as played by a splendid cast, is thoroughly delightful. RK DVD

Deanna Durbin *Penny Craig* • Binnie Barnes *Donna Lyons* • Alice Brady *Mrs Lyons* • Ray Milland *Lord Michael Stuart* • Charles Winninger *Judson Craig* • Mischa Auer *Count Arisztid* • Nan Grey *Joan Craig* • Barbara Read *Kay Craig* • Franklin Pangborn *Jeweler* ■ *Dir* Henry Koster • *Scr* Adele Comandini, Austin Parker, from a story by Adele Comandini

Three Smart Girls Grow Up ★★★

Comedy drama 1939 · US · BW · 87mins

Teenage diva Deanna Durbin repeats her role as the youngest of three sisters in her debut feature, *Three Smart Girls*. This time, Deanna devotes her precocious energies to marrying off her two older sisters, in between which she exercises her bright soprano voice on *Because*, which became one of the major hits of her career. It's everything one would expect of a Durbin film. A second sequel, *Hers to Hold*, followed in 1943. RK

Deanna Durbin *Penelope "Penny" Craig* • Nan Grey *Joan Craig* • Helen Parrish *Katherine "Kay" Craig* • Charles Winninger *Judson Craig* • Nella Walker *Mrs Craig* • Robert Cummings *Harry Loren* • William Lundigan *Richard Watkins* ■ *Dir* Henry Koster • *Scr* Bruce Manning, Felix Jackson

The Three Stooges ★★★

Biographical drama
2000 · US · BW and Colour · 88mins

This is a fond, TV-movie memoir of the slapstick trio that hurled itself into countless Columbia shorts for little tangible reward. Paul Ben-Victor plays Moe Howard, whose flashbacked recollections chart how he rose through vaudeville to minor Hollywood celebrity in the pratfalling company of his brothers Curly (Michael Chiklis) and Shemp (John Kassir). The studio politics sequences involving monstrous mogul Harry Cohn rarely ring true. But director James Frawley efficiently explores the physical toll that the Stooges' routines took, as well as their comic legacy. DP

Paul Ben-Victor *Moe Howard* • Evan Handler *Larry Fine* • John Kassir *Shemp Howard* • Michael Chiklis *Jerome "Curly" Howard* • Rachael Blake *Helen Howard* • Anna-Lise Phillips *Mabel Fine* • Jeanette Cronin *Gertrude Howard* ■ *Dir* James Frawley • *Scr* Kirk Ellis, Janet Roach, from the book *From Amalgamated Morons to American Icons: The Three Stooges* by Michael Fleming

The Three Stooges Go around the World in a Daze ★★ U

Adventure farce 1963 · US · BW · 93mins

As the epitome of crazed and meaningless slapstick comedy, the Three Stooges are not to everyone's taste. However, this relentlessly silly homage to *Around the World in 80 Days* is chucklesome in spots. Phileas Fogg's great-grandson is challenged by a dastardly conman to re-create his ancestor's famous journey. Alas, he decides to take his servants, the Stooges, along for the ride. JG

Moe Howard • Larry Fine • Joe De Rita • Jay Sheffield *Phileas Fogg III* • Joan Freeman *Amelia* • Walter Burke *Lory Filch* • Peter Forster *Vickers Cavendish* • Maurice Dallimore *Crotchet* ■ *Dir* Norman Maurer • *Scr* Elwood Ullman, from a story by Norman Maurer, loosely based on the novel *Le Tour du Monde en Quatre-vingt Jours* by Jules Verne

The Three Stooges in Orbit ★★ U

Science-fiction comedy
1962 · US · BW · 87mins

After many years of tweaking, thumping, poking and brawling, the Stooges were moving into weirder areas. Here they're battling a pair of Martian invaders Ogg (George N Neise) and Zogg (Rayford Barnes) who are plotting to steal the secret plans of a super-vehicle invented by the eccentric professor Emil Sitka. Not one of the boys' best efforts, but there's plenty of the usual flesh-slapping antics once so beloved of small boys. DF

Moe Howard • Larry Fine • Joe De Rita • Carol Christensen *Carol* • Edson Stroll *Capt Tom Andrews* • Emil Sitka *Prof Danforth* • George N Neise *Ogg* • Rayford Barnes *Zogg* ■ *Dir* Edward Bernds • *Scr* Elwood Ullman, from a story by Norman Maurer

The Three Stooges Meet Hercules ★★ U

Comedy 1962 · US · BW · 88mins

After creating the expected havoc with the soda fountain, drug store clerks Moe, Larry, and "Curly" Joe are accidentally transported back to ancient Greece with their wimpy scientist friend when his new time machine malfunctions. When they meet Hercules (who is a villain here), the Stooges decide to get their friend to stand up for himself and become more of a man. Those who are familiar with the Stooges's brand of humour will pretty much know right away whether they will enjoy the movie. KB

Moe Howard • Larry Fine • Joe De Rita • Vicki Trickett *Diane Quigley* • Quinn Redeker *Schuyler Davis* • Samson Burke *Hercules* ■ *Dir* Edward Bernds • *Scr* Elwood Ullman, from a story by Norman Maurer

Three Strange Loves ★★★ 15

Drama 1949 · Swe · BW · 80mins

The most commercially successful of Ingmar Bergman's early films is also something of an artistic watershed, as it weaves flashbacks, dreams and subplots into an engaging dramatic whole, which places a new emphasis on the female perspective. Travelling in a train compartment that symbolises her confinement in a non-communicative marriage, former ballerina Eva Henning recalls the affair that left her unable to conceive. Juxtaposed with this is the sequence of events that drove art historian Birger Malmsten's first wife, Birgit Tengroth, to suicide. (Tengroth also wrote the source stories.) DP. In Swedish with English subtitles. DVD

Eva Henning *Rut* • Birger Malmsten *Bertil* • Birgit Tengroth *Viola* • Hasse Ekman *Dr Rosengren* • Mimi Nelson *Valborg* • Bengt Eklund *Raoul* ■ *Dir* Ingmar Bergman • *Scr* Herbert Grevenius, from short stories by Birgit Tengroth

Three Strangers ★★★

Drama 1946 · US · BW · 92mins

A New Year's Eve pact between three strangers culminates in each signing a sweepstake ticket that they hope will bring a change in their fortunes. Instead a combination of embezzlement, adultery and murder brings misery to all three. This story was dreamed up by John Huston who subsequently worked on the screenplay, but Jean Negulesco eventually took over the project. Sydney Greenstreet is his usual imperious self, Peter Lorre is bug-eyed and shifty and the third member of the triumvirate is Geraldine Fitzgerald. AT

Sydney Greenstreet *Arbutney* • Peter Lorre *Johnny West* • Geraldine Fitzgerald *Crystal* • Joan Lorring *Icy* • Robert Shayne *Fallon* • Marjorie Riordan *Janet* • Arthur Shields *Prosecutor* ■ *Dir* Jean Negulesco • *Scr* John Huston, Howard Koch, from the story *Three Men and a Girl* by John Huston

3 Strikes ★ 15

Crime comedy 2000 · US · Colour · 78mins

Hip-hop legend DJ Pooh comes seriously unstuck with this, his directorial debut. Pitching two-time loser Brian Hooks into an *After Hours* scenario after he becomes innocently involved in a police shoot-out, the film revels in lowbrow humour and witless misanthropy when some astute social satire might have been in order. An untidy, unfunny and mean-spirited mess. DP

Brian Hooks *Rob* • N'Bushe Wright *Juanita* • David Alan Grier *Jenkins* • Faizon Love *Tone* • George Wallace *Pops* ■ *Dir/Scr* DJ Pooh

3:10 to Yuma ★★★★★ PG

Western 1957 · US · BW · 88mins

Unquestionably one of the finest westerns ever made, this is a gripping and truly suspenseful tale. It features consummate performances from Glenn Ford, as the cocksure baddie, and Van Heflin, as the farmer pledged to hold Ford in check until the titular train arrives. Director Delmer Daves makes superior use of camera cranes and bleak horizons, and the screenplay (based on an Elmore Leonard original) is an object lesson in scripting for the screen. The scenes between Ford and bargirl Felicia Farr are exceptionally well crafted and the superb whole is boosted by a marvellous Frankie Laine theme song. TS DVD

Glenn Ford *Ben Wade* • Van Heflin *Dan Evans* • Felicia Farr *Emmy* • Leora Dana *Alice Evans* • Henry Jones *Alex Potter* • Richard Jaeckel *Charlie Prince* • Robert Emhardt *Mr Butterfield* ■ *Dir* Delmer Daves • *Scr* Halsted Welles, from the story by Elmore Leonard

Three Texas Steers ★★ U

Western 1939 · US · BW · 55mins

Any time the girl in a Hollywood B-movie inherits a circus, you can be sure of a swarm of villains plotting to take it away from her. But "The Three Mesquiteers" (John Wayne, Ray Corrigan, Max Terhune) are on hand to help her get back on her feet, after the bad guys have caused a series of accidents and reduced her circus to one cage and a trailer. Playing the heiress is the talented Carole Landis at the start of her brief career. AE

John Wayne *Stony Brooke* • Ray "Crash" Corrigan *Tucson Smith* • Max Terhune *Lullaby Joslin* • Carole Landis *Nancy Evans* • Ralph Graves *George Ward* • Roscoe Ates *Sheriff Brown* ■ *Dir* George Sherman • *Scr* Betty Burbridge, Stanley Roberts, from the characters created by William Colt MacDonald

Three the Hard Way ★★★

Blaxploitation action adventure
1974 · US · Colour · 90mins

This above-average blaxploitation flick teams a triumvirate of black action stars – Jim Brown, Fred Williamson and ex-karate champion Jim Kelly. The preposterous plot involves a bunch of neo-Nazis attempting to infect the water supply of several US cities with a serum that kills only black people. Director Gordon Parks Jr just about keeps a straight face amid the numerous shoot-outs and bouts of kung fu fighting. RS

Jim Brown *Jimmy Lait* • Fred Williamson *Jagger Daniels* • Jim Kelly *Mister Keyes* • Sheila Frazier *Wendy Kane* • Jay Robinson *Monroe Feather* • Charles McGregor *Charley* • Howard Platt *Keep* • Richard Angarola *Dr Fortrero* ■ *Dir* Gordon Parks Jr • *Scr* Eric Bercovici, Jerry Ludwig

3000 Miles to Graceland ★★ 18

Crime comedy thriller
2000 · US · Colour · 120mins

In this tired caper, Demian Lichtenstein over-indulges in the camera pyrotechnics that characterised his time as a director of commercials and pop videos. Kurt Russell gets to wear Elvis gear once more, as the leader of a gang planning a raid on a Las Vegas casino, while Kevin Costner attempts to kickstart his flagging career by playing against type as a foul-mouthed sociopath. Crass and excessive. DP. Contains swearing, violence and sex scenes. 📼 DVD

Kurt Russell *Michael Zane* • Kevin Costner *Murphy* • Courteney Cox Arquette [Courteney Cox] *Cybil Waingrow* • Christian Slater *Hanson* • Kevin Pollak *Federal Marshal Damitry* • David Arquette *Gus* • Jon Lovitz *Jay Peterson* • Howie Long *Jack* • Thomas Haden Church *Federal Marshal Quigley* ■ *Dir* Demian Lichtenstein • *Scr* Richard Recco, Demian Lichtenstein

Three to Tango ★★★ 12

Romantic comedy
1999 · US · Colour · 94mins

This sweet, if somewhat politically incorrect, romantic comedy is worth seeking out for a nice performance from Matthew Perry and a hilarious one from Oliver Platt. The plot is simple. Big businessman Dylan McDermott thinks Perry is gay, so he asks him to watch over his mistress Neve Campbell, little realising that Perry is falling for her. Cute rather than uproariously funny. JB 📼 DVD

Matthew Perry *Oscar Novak* • Neve Campbell *Amy Post* • Dylan McDermott *Charles Newman* • Oliver Platt *Peter Steinberg* • Cylk Cozart *Kevin Cartwright* • John C McGinley *Strauss* • Bob Balaban *Decker* • Deborah Rush *Lenore* ■ *Dir* Damon Santostefano • *Scr* Rodney Vaccaro, Aline Brosh McKenna, from a story by Rodney Vaccaro

Three Tough Guys ★★

Action crime drama
1974 · US/It · Colour · 91mins

This unusual Italian buddy movie features a two-fisted renegade ex-con priest, who's in Chicago to investigate a bank robbery. (Give it its due: bet you haven't seen that before). The cleric teams up with Isaac Hayes who, besides turning in a well-judged performance, supplies a pretty listenable soundtrack. The dubbing detracts somewhat from the dialogue, but it's fast moving and efficient. JG. Italian dialogue dubbed into English. Contains some violence.

Lino Ventura *Father Charlie* • Isaac Hayes *Lee Stevens* • Fred Williamson *Joe Snake* • Paula Kelly *Fay Collins* • William Berger *Captain Ryan* • Luciano Salce *Bishop* ■ *Dir* Duccio Tessari • *Scr* Luciano Vincenzoni, Nicola Badalucco

Three Violent People ★★

Western 1956 · US · Colour · 99mins

"They've got a saying in Texas – the Rio Grande changes its course, the Saunders don't." Charlton Heston is the inflexible Colt Saunders, the rancher who marries Anne Baxter's Southern woman on an impulse and throws her out on when he learns about her unsavoury past. Tom Tryon is the one-armed Cinch Saunders who falls out with his brother Colt. And then there's the post-Civil War adminstration making iniquitous tax demands. It ought to add up to highly combustible entertainment but the characters are one-dimensional. AE

Charlton Heston *Colt Saunders* • Anne Baxter *Lorna Hunter Saunders* • Gilbert Roland *Innocencio* • Tom Tryon *Cinch Saunders* • Forrest Tucker *Cable* • Bruce Bennett *Harrison* • Elaine Stritch *Ruby LaSalle* • Barton MacLane *Yates* ■ *Dir* Rudolph Maté • *Scr* James Edward Grant, from a story by Leonard Praskins, Barney Slater

The Three Weird Sisters ★★

Thriller 1948 · UK · BW · 83mins

One of two melodramas co-written by Dylan Thomas and directed by Daniel Birt (the other being *No Room at the Inn*), this is set in a Welsh village, where three elderly sisters in need of money plot to murder their wealthy brother. When he changes his will in favour of his secretary Nova Pilbeam, the old maids decide to kill her, too. This boasts a good cast (notably Nancy Price as the dominant sister) and some theatrically sinister moments. BB

Nancy Price *Gertrude Morgan-Vaughan* • Mary Clare *Maude Morgan-Vaughan* • Mary Merrall *Isobel Morgan-Vaughan* • Nova Pilbeam *Claire Prentiss* • Anthony Hulme *David Davies* • Raymond Lovell *Owen Morgan-Vaughan* ■ *Dir* Daniel Birt • *Scr* Louise Birt, David Evans, Dylan Thomas, from the novel *The Case of the Three Weird Sisters* by Charlotte Armstrong

Three Wise Girls ★★

Drama 1932 · US · BW · 66mins

Three girls (Mae Clarke, Jean Harlow, and Marie Prevost) leave their one-horse town for jobs, excitement and romance in the Big Apple. One, not so wisely, becomes a kept Park Avenue mistress; another settles happily for an agreeable chauffeur; and a third becomes a store mannequin. The last is Harlow who has to deal with the fact her lover is married – should she go or should she stay? Routine. RK

Jean Harlow *Cassie Barnes* • Mae Clarke *Gladys Kane* • Walter Byron *Jerry Dexter* • Marie Prevost *Dot* • Andy Devine *Chauffeur* • Natalie Moorhead *Ruth* • Jameson Thomas *Arthur Phelps* ■ *Dir* William Beaudine • *Scr* Agnes Christine Johnston, Robert Riskin, from the story *Blonde Baby* by Wilson Collison

Three Wishes ★★ PG

Fantasy drama 1995 · US · Colour · 110mins

Patrick Swayze stars as the stranger who comes into the family fold and changes everyone's life. A tramp with a dog on a string, he may be an angel sent to help them cope with the potential loss of their father, reported missing in action in the Korean War, and with one son's cancer. Clumsily structured as a flashback to the 1950s, the story is both daft and sentimental. LH 📼

Patrick Swayze *Jack McCloud* • Mary Elizabeth Mastrantonio *Jeanne Holman* • Joseph Mazzello *Tom Holman* • Seth Mumy *Gunny Holman* • David Marshall Grant *Phil* • Jay O Sanders *Coach Schramka* • Michael O'Keefe *Adult Tom* • John Diehl *Leland's dad* ■ *Dir* Martha Coolidge • *Scr* Elizabeth Anderson, from a story by Ellen Green, Clifford Green

3 Women ★★★★

Drama 1977 · US · Colour · 123mins

This very personal Robert Altman movie based on a dream is as enthralling as it is entertaining, with keen insights into feminine psychology. An enigmatic chamberwork, as opposed to the orchestrations of the original *MASH* or his masterpiece, *Nashville*, this is about the transference of personality. Shelley Duvall is vapidly splendid as the gossipy therapist into whose flat moves the adoring Sissy Spacek, while tongue-tied Janice Rule is the painter formulating fears of male aggression into mythic murals. TH

Shelley Duvall *Millie Lammoreaux* • Sissy Spacek *Pinky Rose* • Janice Rule *Willie Hart* • Robert Fortier *Edgar Hart* • Ruth Nelson *Mrs Rose* • John Cromwell *Mr Rose* • Sierra Pecheur *Mr Bunweill* ■ *Dir/Scr* Robert Altman

Three Women in Love ★★★ 18

Comedy drama
1988 · W Ger · Colour · 83mins

Littered with classical allusions, Rudolf Thome's metaphysical satire provides a sharp insight into the arrogance of even the most unworldly males in setting their expectations of women so low. Totally wrapped up in the minor success of his book on Heraclitus, academic Johannes Herrschmann is vain enough to believe that shopgirls Adriana Altaras, Friederike Tiefenbacher and Claudia Matschulla are adoring acolytes content to minister to his every need, instead of semi-divine agents of time using him as a messenger for their more ethereal pensées. DP. In German with English subtitles.

Johannes Herrschmann *Georg Hermes* • Adriana Altaras *Franziska* • Friederike Tiefenbacher *Beate* • Claudia Matschulla *Martha* • Jürgen Wink *Franziska's lover* • Werner Gerber *Martha's lover* • Anton Rey *Beate's lover* ■ *Dir/Scr* Rudolf Thome

The Three Worlds of Gulliver ★★★ U

Fantasy adventure
1959 · UK · Colour · 94mins

In spite of the title, Kerwin Mathews spends most of his time among the giants of Brobdingnag and the little people of Lilliput in this loose adaptation of Jonathan Swift's timeless classic novel. Playing down the satire in favour of family adventure, director Jack Sher benefits from the expertise of his supporting cast, but it's the Superdynamation work of effects maestro Ray Harryhausen that gives the action its fantastical feel. Equally impressive is Bernard Herrmann's soundtrack. DP 📼 DVD

Kerwin Mathews *Dr Lemuel Gulliver* • Jo Morrow *Gwendolyn* • June Thorburn *Elizabeth* • Lee Patterson *Reldresal* • Grégoire Aslan *King Brobdingnag* • Basil Sydney *Emperor of Lilliput* • Charles Lloyd Pack *Makovan* ■ *Dir* Jack Sher • *Scr* Arthur Ross, Jack Sher, from the novel *Gulliver's Travels* by Jonathan Swift

The Threepenny Opera ★★★★ PG

Musical black comedy
1931 · Ger/US · BW · 104mins

That master of early German cinema, GW Pabst, seemed the ideal choice for this reworking of Bertolt Brecht's play, but Brecht was furious with the film's toning down of his play's anti-capitalist content and sued the German production company. Several of Brecht and Kurt Weill's original songs are missing, but Weill's wife, Lotte Lenya, mesmerisingly re-creates her legendary stage role, and Rudolf Forster makes a roguish Mackie Messer. What's more, the film is a triumph of visual stylisation, thanks to Andre Andreiev's evocative sets and Fritz Arno Wagner's superb photography. DP. In German with English subtitles. 📼 DVD

Rudolf Forster *Mackie Messer* • Carola Neher *Polly Peachum* • Reinhold Schünzel *Tiger Brown* • Fritz Rasp *Peachum* • Valeska Gert *Mrs Peachum* • Lotte Lenya *Jenny* • Hermann Thimig *Vicar* ■ *Dir* GW Pabst • *Scr* Leo Lania, Ladislaus Vadja, Béla Balász, from the play by Bertolt Brecht, from the play *The Beggar's Opera* by John Gay

Threesome ★★★ 18

Romantic comedy
1994 · US · Colour · 89mins

A clerical error puts student Lara Flynn Boyle in the same digs as jock Stephen Baldwin and sensitive Josh Charles in Andrew Fleming's appealing, if contrived, look at teenage sexual identity. The romantic triangle that develops between the three is sometimes handled intelligently, but the writing lacks reality and conviction. This remains a prime example of Hollywood being just too tasteful with "controversial" material, and the end result is mawkish rather than truthful. AJ. Contains swearing, drug abuse, sex scenes, nudity. 📼 DVD

Lara Flynn Boyle *Alex* • Stephen Baldwin *Stuart* • Josh Charles *Eddy* • Alexis Arquette *Dick* • Martha Gehman *Renay* • Mark Arnold *Larry* • Michele Matheson *Kristen* ■ *Dir/Scr* Andrew Fleming

Threshold ★★★ PG

Drama 1981 · Can · Colour · 92mins

American distributors ignored this dramatically persuasive fictional story of the world's first artificial-heart transplant for two years – until speculative fiction became headline fact. This is a surprisingly low-key account of the effect on people of such revolutionary surgery. It's a pity that some strong performances – Donald Sutherland as the surgeon, Jeff Goldblum as the artificial heart's inventor and Mare Winningham as the worried recipient – were left in the dark for so long. TH 📼

Donald Sutherland *Dr Thomas Vrain* • Jeff Goldblum *Dr Aldo Gehring* • Allan Nicholls *Dr Basil Rents* • Sharon Acker *Tilla Vrain* • Jessica Steen *Tracy Vrain* • Michael Lerner *Henry De Vici* • John Marley *Edgar Fine* • Mare Winningham *Carol Severance* ■ *Dir* Richard Pearce • *Scr* James Salter

Thrill of a Romance ★★

Musical 1945 · US · Colour · 103mins

Another of the trite, vacuous musical romances dreamed up for MGM's human mermaid, Esther Williams. This one has romance blossoming in a mountain resort between Esther, who swims, and soldier on leave Van Johnson, who sings. The numbers include hits *I Should Care* and *Please Don't Say No, Say Maybe*, the latter memorable for being belted out by famous Wagnerian opera tenor Lauritz Melchior, making his film debut in the first of several such frivolities. RK

Esther Williams *Cynthia Glenn* • Van Johnson *Major Thomas Milvaine* • Frances Gifford *Maude Bancroft* • Henry Travers *Hobart Glenn* • Spring Byington *Nona Glenn* • Lauritz Melchior *Nils Knudsen* ■ *Dir* Richard Thorpe • *Scr* Richard Connell, Gladys Lehman

The Thrill of It All ★★★ U

Romantic comedy
1963 · US · Colour · 107mins

An enjoyably wacky satire on the world of advertising, this pairied Doris Day with the immensely likeable James Garner for the first time. It's the one in which Day becomes a star of soap commercials, much to the annoyance of her gynaecologist husband Garner. There's lots to chuckle over in the clever Carl Reiner screenplay, not least the super cameo he wrote in for himself. It may seem a bit dated now, but back in the 1960s this irreverent and glossy comedy was considered strong, anarchic stuff. TS 📼 DVD

Doris Day *Beverly Boyer* • James Garner *Dr Gerald Boyer* • Arlene Francis *Mrs Fraleigh* • Edward Andrews *Gardiner Fraleigh* • Reginald Owen *Old Tom Fraleigh* • ZaSu Pitts *Olivia* • Elliott Reid *Mike Palmer* • Carl Reiner ■ *Dir* Norman Jewison • *Scr* Carl Reiner, from a story by Carl Reiner, Larry Gelbart

T

Throne of Blood ★★★★★ PG

Drama 1957 · Jpn · BW · 104mins

TS Eliot considered this the finest film ever made, though several critics have attacked this loose adaptation of Shakespeare's *Macbeth* for the one-dimensionality of the characters. Whatever faults there may be in the dramatic structure, there's no denying the power of the atmosphere director Akira Kurosawa builds up through his majestic use of camera movement and the eerie sets that earned the film its alternative title, *Cobweb Castle*. At the centre of these Noh tableaux stands Toshiro Mifune, as the villain so much at the mercy of fate and the elements that all you can feel at his death is pity. DP. In Japanese with English subtitles. Contains violence. 📼 DVD

Toshiro Mifune *Taketoki Washizu* • Isuzu Yamada *Asaji* • Takashi Shimura *Noriyasu Odagura* • Minoru Chiaki *Yoshiaki Miki* ■ *Dir* Akira Kurosawa • *Scr* Hideo Oguni, Shinobu Hashimoto, Ryuzo Kikushima, Akira Kurosawa, from the play *Macbeth* by William Shakespeare

Through a Glass Darkly ★★★★ 15

Drama 1961 · Swe · BW · 85mins

Ingmar Bergman's unrelenting drama took the Oscar for best foreign film of 1961. Set on a remote Baltic island, it charts the descent into madness of Harriet Andersson (outstanding), while her father Gunnar Björnstrand and husband Max von Sydow look on with a mix of morbid curiosity and utter helplessness. Gone are the optimistic symbols Bergman usually associates with summer and in their place come some of the bleakest and most searching images of his career. One of the films that earned Bergman his reputation as a harbinger of doom, it is gripping nonetheless. DP. In Swedish with English subtitles. DVD

Harriet Andersson *Karin* • Gunnar Björnstrand *David* • Max von Sydow *Martin* • Lars Passgård *Minus* ■ *Dir/Scr* Ingmar Bergman • *Cinematographer* Sven Nykvist

Through the Olive Trees ★★★★ U

Romantic drama
1994 · Iran/Fr · Colour · 99mins

The final part of Abbas Kiarostami's "friendship" trilogy centres on the production of the second episode, *And Life Goes On...*, which was itself a revisitation of the first film, *Where Is My Friend's House?* Blurring the lines between life and art, Kiarostami pokes fun at the filming process, as his *cinéma vérité* project turns into an off-screen melodrama, after orphan student Tahereh Ladanian stops speaking to her leading man, stonemason Hossein Rezai, because she considers his marriage proposal insulting. But besides the self-reflection, this is also a tribute to the hardy inhabitants of Iran's earthquake-ravaged northlands. DP. In Farsi with English subtitles.

Hossein Rezai *Hossein* • Tahereh Ladanian *Tahereh* • Mohammad Ali Keshavarz *Film Director* • Zarifeh Shiva *Mrs Shiva* • Farhad Kheradmand *Farhad* • Mahbanou Darabi ■ *Dir/Scr* Abbas Kiarostami

Throw Momma from the Train ★★★★ 15

Comedy 1987 · US · Colour · 87mins

Danny DeVito made an assured directorial debut with this zany comedy, in which he also stars as the henpecked son of monstrous mother Anne Ramsey. Asked by his writing teacher Billy Crystal to view Hitchcock's *Strangers on a Train*, DeVito is inspired by the murder-swap idea. Chaos and spiky black comedy ensue as DeVito the director focuses on the vitality of his characters and the wonderfully creative dialogue, rather than overheating the barminess of the central situation. DeVito and Crystal give accomplished performances, but both are overshadowed by the marvellous Ramsey. JM DVD

Danny DeVito *Owen Lift* • Billy Crystal *Larry Donner* • Anne Ramsey *Momma* • Kim Greist *Beth* • Kate Mulgrew *Margaret* • Branford Marsalis *Lester* • Rob Reiner *Joel* • Bruce Kirby *Detective DeBenedetto* • Oprah Winfrey ■ *Dir* Danny DeVito • *Scr* Stu Silver

Thumb Tripping ★ 18

Road movie 1972 · US · Colour · 90mins

A strained counterculture road movie that nobody, not even the *Easy Rider* hippies is was aimed at, went to see. That's because its a jangling mess, with Meg Foster and Michael Burns hitching their way to California and coming into contact with various unhinged characters: switchblade-wielding Bruce Dern, lust-crazed trucker Mike Conrad and nymphomaniac housewife Mariana Hill. AJ

Michael Burns *Gary* • Meg Foster *Chay* • Mariana Hill [Marianna Hill] *Lynn* • Burke Burns *Jack* • Mike Conrad *Diesel* • Bruce Dern *Smitty* • Larry Hankin *Simp* • Joyce Van Patten *Mother* ■ *Dir* Quentin Masters • *Scr* Don Mitchell, from his novel

Thumbelina ★★ U

Animated adventure
1994 · US/Ire · Colour · 63mins

This is Don Bluth's cartoon version of Hans Christian Andersen's tale about the tiniest of tots who is parted from her fairy prince to suffer the attentions of Berkeley Beetle, a troupe of toads and an elderly, unsuitable mole. The song *Follow Your Heart*, co-written by Barry Manilow, adds more sweetener to an already saccharine story, while the animation is rather lifeless. TH DVD

Jodi Benson *Thumbelina* • Gino Conforti *Jacquimo* • Barbara Cook *Mother* • Will Ryan *Hero/Reverend Rat* • June Foray *Queen Tabitha* • Kenneth Mars *King Colbert* • Gary Imhoff *Prince Cornelius* • Joe Lynch *Grundel* ■ *Dir* Don Bluth, Gary Goldman • *Scr* Don Bluth, from the fairy tale by Hans Christian Anderson

Thunder Afloat ★★ U

War drama 1939 · US · BW · 94mins

This was intended as a straightforward First World War yarn, with Wallace Beery as a hard-nosed tugboat skipper joining the US Navy to get revenge on the German submarines that sank his ship. However the advent of the Second World War lent the film unexpected topicality, as Hitler once more pressed the dreaded U-boats into service in the Atlantic. Action adventures such as this one seem incredibly creaky by today's standards, but this rattles along efficiently. RT

Wallace Beery *Jon Thorson* • Chester Morris *"Rocky" Blake* • Virginia Grey *Susan Thorson* • Douglass Dumbrille *District commander* • Carl Esmond *U-boat Captain* • Clem Bevans *"Cap" Finch* • John Qualen *Milt* • Regis Toomey *Ives* ■ *Dir* George B Seitz • *Scr* Wells Root, Harvey Haislip, from a story by Ralph Wheelwright, Harvey Haislip

Thunder Alley ★★ 15

Sports drama 1967 · US · Colour · 96mins

This uninspired drama has one-time heart-throb Fabian as a former driver who joins a low-rent stock-car circus after a blackout destroys his racing career. Tension builds when he get the chance to run a 500-mile race, as his protégé and partner Warren Berlinger tries to take the lead against orders. Car aficionados might enjoy the stock footage of crashes, which pepper the picture. Love interest and songs are provided by Annette Funicello, another fondly remembered teen idol. JG

Annette Funicello *Francie Madsen* • Fabian *Tommy Callahan* • Diane McBain *Annie Blaine* • Warren Berlinger *Eddie Sands* • Jan Murray *Pete Madsen* • Stanley Adams *Mac Lunsford* • Maureen Arthur *Babe* ■ *Dir* Richard Rush • *Scr* Sy Salkowitz

Thunder and Lightning ★★ 15

Adventure 1977 · US · Colour · 94mins

This is a so-so action film about amiable moonshiners keeping one car chase ahead of the law. David Carradine and Kate Jackson play the spirited leads, and they're an attractive pairing. In terms of originality of plot, though, the film is anything but 100 per cent proof. OK if your idea of action is a neat car pursuit followed by a pile-up. DA

David Carradine *Harley Thomas* • Kate Jackson *Nancy Sue Hunnicutt* • Roger C Carmel *Ralph Junior Hunnicutt* • Sterling Holloway *Hobe Carpenter* ■ *Dir* Corey Allen • *Scr* William Hjortsberg

Thunder Bay ★★ U

Adventure drama
1953 · US · Colour · 102mins

James Stewart and partner Dan Duryea drill for oil off the Louisiana coast and threaten the local shrimp industry in a disappointing Universal adventure. It's the sort of movie that's made by numbers: a bit of action, a bit of romance, a bit of capitalist conflict and the weather turns bad. AT

James Stewart *Steve Martin* • Joanne Dru *Stella Rigaud* • Dan Duryea *Johnny Gambi* • Gilbert Roland *Teche Bossier* • Marcia Henderson *Francesca Rigaud* • Robert Monet *Phillipe Bayard* • Jay C Flippen *Kermit MacDonald* ■ *Dir* Anthony Mann • *Scr* Gil Doud, John Michael Hayes, from a story by John Michael Hayes, from an idea by George W George, George F Slavin

Thunder in the City ★★★

Satirical comedy drama
1937 · UK · BW · 76mins

Seeing Edward G Robinson and Ralph Richardson acting their respective socks off is the juicy prospect offered by this enjoyable comedy proving the old adage of America and England being two countries separated by a common language. Robinson is the Yank who arrives in London aiming to raise a million dollars to finance a mine in Africa; Richardson is the rather staid establishment banker he must win over. Nigel Bruce is Robinson's guide through the minefields of British class and etiquette. AT

Edward G Robinson *Dan Armstrong* • Luli Deste *Lady Patricia* • Nigel Bruce *The Duke of Glenavon* • Constance Collier *The Duchess of Glenavon* • Ralph Richardson *Henry Graham Manningdale* • Annie Esmond *Lady Challoner* • Arthur Wontner *Sir Peter Challoner* • Elizabeth Inglis *Dolly* ■ *Dir* Marion Gering • *Scr* Akos Tolnay, Aben Kandel, Robert E Sherwood, Walter Hackett, from a story by Robert E Sherwood, Aben Kandel

Thunder in the East ★

Period adventure 1953 · US · BW · 97mins

During the upheavals following India's independence in 1947, American arms trafficker Alan Ladd turns up in Kandahar to sell arms to pacifist leader Charles Boyer, who doesn't want them. In between times, Ladd falls for Deborah Kerr, the blind daughter of a lovable English missionary. Lavish production values and a grade-A cast are powerless to rescue a mind-numbingly wordy script that drains the film of any possible excitement or real drama. RK

Alan Ladd *Steve Gibbs* • Deborah Kerr *Joan Willoughby* • Charles Boyer *Singh* • Corinne Calvet *Lizette Damon* • Cecil Kellaway *Dr Willoughby* • Marc Cavell *Moti Lal* ■ *Dir* Charles Vidor • *Scr* Frederick Hazlitt Brennan, Jo Swerling, George Tabori, Lewis Meltzer, from the novel *Rage of the Vulture* by Alan Moorehead

Thunder in the Sun ★★ U

Western 1959 · US · Colour · 80mins

Susan Hayward falls for handsome wagon-train scout Jeff Chandler in a movie that can't make up its mind whether it's a western or the true story of the beginning of California's Napa Valley wine industry. Not that anybody cares – the pace is too sluggish, the plot is totally mind-numbing and Hayward is saddled with a ridiculous and almost incomprehensible fake accent as the wife of a Basque leader. Basically this film is an insult to Basques and everyone else. TS

Susan Hayward *Gabrielle Dauphin* • Jeff Chandler *Lon Bennett* • Jacques Bergerac *Pepe Dauphin* • Blanche Yurka *Louise Dauphin* • Carl Esmond *Andre Dauphin* • Fortunio Bonanova *Fernando Christophe* • Bertrand Castelli *Edmond Duquette* • Veda Ann Borg *Marie* ■ *Dir* Russell Rouse • *Scr* Russell Rouse, Stewart Stern, from a story by Guy Trosper, James Hill

Thunder Island ★★ U

Thriller 1963 · US · BW · 64mins

This fast-moving thriller finds professional assassin Gene Nelson forcing an American couple to help him murder a dictator exiled on a Latin American island. The job proves more difficult that the hitman intended, leading to an exciting chase in Puerto Rico's El Morro castle. An efficient and occasionally gripping movie, this has Jack Nicholson credited as co-screenwriter. JG

Gene Nelson *Billy Poole* • Fay Spain *Helen Dodge* • Brian Kelly (1) *Vincent Dodge* • Miriam Colon *Anita Chavez* • Art Bedard *Ramon Alou* • Evelyn Kaufman *Jo Dodge* • Antonio Torres Martino *Col Cepeda* • Stephanie Rifkinson *Linda Perez* ■ *Dir* Jack Leewood • *Scr* Don Devlin, Jack Nicholson

Thunder Mountain ★ PG

Western 1947 · US · BW · 60mins

This was the first of a new series of B westerns in which Tim Holt starred for RKO after four years of service in the Second World War. Since he was also in demand for such top-drawer pictures as *My Darling Clementine* and *The Treasure of the Sierra Madre*, it is a shame that the talented star preferred the security of churning out undistinguished formula westerns, such as this unacknowledged re-working of Zane Grey's *To the Last Man* with its background of feuding families. AE DVD

Tim Holt *Marvin Hayden* • Martha Hyer *Ellen Jorth* • Richard Martin (1) *Chito Rafferty* • Steve Brodie *Chick Jorth* • Virginia Owen *Ginger Kelly* • Harry Woods *Trimble Carson* • Jason Robards [Jason Robards Sr] *James Gardner* • Richard Powers [Tom Keene] *Johnny Blue* ■ *Dir* Lew Landers • *Scr* Norman Houston, from the novel *To the Last Man* by Zane Grey

A Thunder of Drums ★★★

Western 1961 · US · Colour · 96mins

This well-made western stars Richard Boone, fresh from his TV series *Have Gun Will Travel*, as a growling fort commander, and the dashing George Hamilton as a conscience-stricken lieutenant. *The Big Circus* director Joseph M Newman is clever enough to know how to get the most out of this familiar stuff. TS

Richard Boone *Capt Stephen Maddocks* • George Hamilton *Lt Curtis McQuade* • Luana Patten *Tracey Hamilton* • Arthur O'Connell *Sgt Rodermill* • Charles Bronson *Trooper Hanna* • Richard Chamberlain *Lt Porter* • Duane Eddy *Trooper Eddy* • James Douglas *Lt Gresham* • Slim Pickens *Trooper Erschick* ■ *Dir* Joseph M Newman • *Scr* James Warner Bellah

Thunder on the Hill ★★

Mystery melodrama 1951 · US · BW · 84mins

Claudette Colbert, one of Hollywood's most sparkling queens of sophisticated comedy, dons a nun's habit in this dramatic thriller, set in a convent presided over by Mother Superior Gladys Cooper. When, during a flood, a distraught Ann Blyth – who's accused of murder and under guard – arrives to take refuge from the storm, Sister Claudette sets out to prove she's innocent by unearthing the real killer. Director Douglas Sirk maintains a sense of atmosphere, but it's uneventful. RK

Claudette Colbert *Sister Mary Bonaventure* • Ann Blyth *Valerie Carns* • Robert Douglas *Dr Jeffreys* • Anne Crawford *Isabel Jeffreys* • Philip Friend *Sidney Kingham* • Gladys Cooper *Mother Superior* ■ *Dir* Douglas Sirk • *Scr* Oscar Saul, Andrew Solt, from the play *Bonaventure* by Charlotte Hastings

Thunder over Arizona ★★ U

Western 1956 · US · Colour · 74mins

George Macready is the town tyrant who evokes the arcane Apex Rule whereby, if a mineral vein runs through his land, the owners of the territory containing the head of the vein have to surrender their rights. Of course, he's not going to get away with that. Unfortunately, he fails to recognise that his hired gun, Skip Homeier, isn't actually the killer he thinks he is. A pacey, colourful B-western from Republic, this is shot in their cheap widescreen process, Naturama. TS

Skip Homeier *Tim Mallory* • Kristine Miller *Fay Warren* • George Macready *Ervin Plummer* • Wallace Ford *Hal Styles* • Jack Elam *Slats* • Nacho Galindo *Pancho* • Gregory Walcott *Mark* • George Keymas *"Shotgun" Kelly* ■ *Dir* Joe Kane [Joseph Kane] • *Scr* Sloan Nibley

Thunder over the Plains ★★ U

Western 1953 · US · Colour · 82mins

It's Texas just after the Civil War, as the state comes under the exploitative influence of northern carpetbaggers. Randolph Scott is the native Texan who, as a captain in the Union army of occupation, has the tricky job of enforcing law and order despite his sympathy for Charles McGraw's defiant band of vigilantes. Andre De Toth's direction keeps the complicated story on the move but he can't create any real tension. AE

Randolph Scott *Captain David Porter* • Lex Barker *Captain Bill Hodges* • Phyllis Kirk *Norah* • Charles McGraw *Ben Westman* • Henry Hull *Lt Col Chandler* • Elisha Cook Jr *Standish* • Fess Parker *Kirby* ■ *Dir* Andre De Toth • *Scr* Russell Hughes

Thunder Pass ★★ U

Western 1954 · US · BW · 78mins

Don't expect *Stagecoach* – despite the presence of two of that film's cast members, Andy Devine and John Carradine – as this is just another plodding Indian wars outing. It's directed without flourish by Frank McDonald, who spins a standard tale of pioneer settlers menaced by wily tribesmen. RT

Dane Clark *Storm* • Dorothy Patrick *Murdock* • Andy Devine *Injun* • Raymond Burr *Tulsa* • John Carradine *Bergstrom* • Mary Ellen Kay *Charity* • Raymond Hatton *Ancient* ■ *Dir* Frank McDonald • *Scr* Tom Hubbard, Fred Eggers, from a story by George Van Marter

Thunder Road ★★★ U

Crime drama 1958 · US · BW · 88mins

Robert Mitchum made the plunge into independent production with this pioneering drama of moonshiners brewing illicit whisky. He researched the subject, provided the story, put his son James into a key supporting role, and hired an obscure director with a penchant for surrealism, Arthur Ripley. He even wrote song lyrics for the movie. A cult favourite in Deep South drive-ins, this has obvious technical problems and some inept acting, but it perfectly reflects Mitchum's relaxed outlook and is very much one of a kind. AE DVD

Robert Mitchum *Lucas Doolin* • Gene Barry *Troy Barrett* • Jacques Aubuchon *Carl Kogan* • Keely Smith *Francie Wymore* • Trevor Bardette *Vernon Doolin* • James Mitchum *Robin Doolin* ■ *Dir* Arthur Ripley • *Scr* Robert Mitchum, James Atlee Phillips, Walter Wise, from a story by Robert Mitchum

Thunder Rock ★★★★ PG

Supernatural drama
1942 · UK · BW · 106mins

Without ever breaking entirely free from its theatrical origins, this propagandist allegory succeeds in creating an atmosphere that is at once haunting, mournful and inspiring. As the writer disillusioned by the world's complacent response to fascism, Michael Redgrave gives one of his most complex and tormented performances. He regains his crusading spirit as a result of his encounters with the victims of a shipwreck that occurred years before on the rocks near the lighthouse he now tends. With a bullish contribution from James Mason and truly touching support from Lilli Palmer, this is one of the Boulting brothers' finest achievements. DP DVD

Michael Redgrave *David Charleston* • Barbara Mullen *Ellen Kirby* • James Mason *Streeter* • Lilli Palmer *Melanie Kurtz* • Finlay Currie *Captain Joshua* • Frederick Valk *Dr Kurtz* • Frederick Cooper *Ted Briggs* ■ *Dir* Roy Boulting • *Scr* Jeffrey Dell, Bernard Miles, from the play by Robert Ardrey

Thunder Run ★ 15

Action thriller 1986 · US · Colour · 86mins

A shameless and inferior *Mad Max* rip-off, this amounts to little more than one long and largely unthrilling chase sequence across the Nevada and Arizona deserts, as a veteran trucker battles to bring a cargo of plutonium through in the face of fiendish opposition. The film is chiefly of interest as the last feature made by Forrest Tucker. PF. Contains swearing, nudity. [video]

Forrest Tucker *Charlie Morrison* • John Ireland *George Adams* • John Shepherd *Chris* • Jill Whitlow *Kim* • Wally Ward *Paul* • Cheryl M Lynn *Jilly* ■ *Dir* Gary Hudson • *Scr* Charles Davis, Carol Heyer, from a story by Carol Lynn, Clifford Wenger Sr

Thunderball ★★★ PG

Spy adventure 1965 · UK · Colour · 125mins

The Bond series went well and truly comic strip with this gadget-filled extravaganza that too often cuts plotline corners to squeeze in all the hi-tech hardware. Playing 007 for the fourth time, Sean Connery is still getting a kick out of the part, but he's less the suave spy and more the man of action than in previous outings. Adolfo Celi makes a worthy opponent, but Claudine Auger is one of the least memorable of the Bond girls. Director Terence Young never quite solves the pacing problems posed by filming underwater, but John Stears's Oscar-winning special effects more than compensate. DP [video] DVD

Sean Connery *James Bond* • Claudine Auger *Domino Derval* • Adolfo Celi *Emilio Largo* • Luciana Paluzzi *Fiona Volpe* • Rik Van Nutter *Felix Leiter* • Bernard Lee *"M"* • Martine Beswick *Paula Caplan* • Guy Doleman *Count Lippe* • Molly Peters *Patricia Fearing* • Desmond Llewelyn *"Q"* • Lois Maxwell *Moneypenny* ■ *Dir* Terence Young • *Scr* Richard Maibaum, John Hopkins, from the story by Kevin McClory, Jack Whittingham, Ian Fleming, from characters created by Ian Fleming

Thunderbird 6 ★★ U

Science-fiction adventure
1968 · UK/US · Colour · 85mins

The second and last big-screen outing (after 1966's *Thunderbirds Are Go!*) for the International Rescue crew is a step down from its predecessor but still diverting entertainment for children and fans of the series. This time Lady Penelope and chauffeur Parker take centre stage as they embark on the round-the-world maiden voyage of *Skyship One*, a new luxury aircraft. A bunch of puppets aren't enough to hold the viewer's attention for 85 minutes, and it turned out to be yet another box office dud. RS [video] DVD

Peter Dyneley *Jeff Tracy* • Shane Rimmer *Scott Tracy* • Sylvia Anderson *Lady Penelope* • Jeremy Wilkin *Virgil Tracy/Hogarth* • Matt Zimmerman *Alan Tracy/Carter* • David Graham *Gordon Tracy/Brains/Parker* • Christine Finn *Tin-Tin/Indian fortune teller* • Keith Alexander *John Tracy* ■ *Dir* David Lane • *Scr* Gerry Anderson, Sylvia Anderson

Thunderbirds ★★

Second World War drama
1952 · US · BW · 98mins

The late John Derek will always be remembered for his beautiful wives – Ursula Andress and Bo Derek in particular – and it's easy to forget that he was once famous in his own right as a handsome, if slightly wooden, leading man. This routine Second World War drama is spiced up by the square-jawed heroics of Derek and John Drew Barrymore (father of Drew) as raw recruits becoming men on the battlefields of Europe. RT

John Derek *Gil Hackett* • John Barrymore Jr [John Drew Barrymore] *Tom McCreery* • Mona Freeman *Lt Ellen Henderson* • Gene Evans *Mike Braggart* • Eileen Christy *Mary Caldwell* • Ward Bond *Sgt Logan* • Barton MacLane *Sgt Durkee* ■ *Dir* John H Auer • *Scr* Mary C McCall Jr, from a story by Kenneth Gamet

Thunderbirds ★★ PG

Science-fiction adventure
2004 · UK/US/Fr · Colour · 90mins

Fans of the original 1960s TV series may well feel short-changed by this pedestrian live action adventure. Here the focus is on sulky adolescent Brady Corbet, who resents studying at boarding school while his dad (Bill Paxton) and brothers are saving the world. He and his two cutesy pals are left to defeat The Hood (Ben Kingsley) after the dastardly villain deploys the International Rescue team on a fake mission and takes over Tracy Island. The retro-futuristic design and scenery look great, but style alone can't save a weak script. SF [video] DVD

Bill Paxton *Jeff Tracy* • Anthony Edwards *Hiram "Brains" Hackenbacker* • Sophia Myles *Lady Penelope Creighton-Ward* • Ben Kingsley *The Hood* • Brady Corbet *Alan Tracy* • Soren Fulton *Fermat Hackenbacker* • Vanessa Anne Hudgens *Tin-Tin* • Ron Cook *Parker* • Philip Winchester *Scott Tracy* • Lex Shrapnel *John Tracy* • Dominic Colenso *Virgil Tracy* • Ben Torgersen *Gordon Tracy* ■ *Dir* Jonathan Frakes • *Scr* William Osborne, Michael McCullers, from a story by Peter Hewitt, William Osborne, from the TV series by Gerry Anderson, Sylvia Anderson

Thunderbirds Are Go! ★★★ U

Science-fiction adventure
1966 · UK/US · Colour · 89mins

The first big-screen spin-off from Gerry Anderson's hugely popular TV series is directed with efficient briskness by David Lane. International Rescue is requested to oversee the launch of Zero X, a manned mission to Mars, but saboteur and arch nemesis the Hood (yes, the bald guy with the glowing eyes) is waiting in the wings. As ever the effects and model work are superb, but while the TV stories just about held one's interest for the full hour the novelty ultimately wears thin here. RS [video] DVD

Peter Dyneley *Jeff Tracy* • Shane Rimmer *Scott Tracy* • Sylvia Anderson *Lady Penelope* • Jeremy Wilkin *Virgil Tracy* • Matt Zimmerman *Alan Tracy* • David Graham *Gordon Tracy/Brains/Parker* • Ray Barrett *John Tracy/The Hood* • Bob Monkhouse *Brad Newman, the Swinging Star compère* ■ *Dir* David Lane • *Scr* Gerry Anderson, Sylvia Anderson

Thunderbolt ★★★★

Crime drama 1929 · US · BW · 91mins

Before Josef von Sternberg made Marlene Dietrich into a star, the very different George Bancroft was his favourite actor. In the fourth and last of his films with Sternberg, Bancroft, in the title role, plays a gangster. While on death row he plots to kill his moll's lover, falsely imprisoned in the same jail. Although the quality of the sound recording is primitive – it was Sternberg's first talkie – the director uses it as atmospherically as he does the camera. RB

George Bancroft *Thunderbolt Jim Lang* • Fay Wray *"Ritzy"* • Richard Arlen *Bob Morgan* • Tully Marshall *Warden* • Eugenie Besserer *Mrs Morgan* • James Spottswood *Snapper O'Shea* ■ *Dir* Josef von Sternberg • *Scr* Jules Furthman, Herman J Mankiewicz, from a story by Jules Furthman, Charles Furthman • *Cinematographer* Henry Gerrard

Thunderbolt ★★

Action adventure
1995 · HK · Colour · 110mins

Gordon Chan is credited as the director of this misfiring auto adventure, but just how much control he exercised is debatable – Sammo Hung, Frankie Chan and Jackie Chan himself are credited as the choreographers of the action, racing and fight sequences, respectively. The ever-affable Jackie plays a top-class driver who is forced to race against a Teutonic villain to secure the release of his kidnapped sisters. A disappointing vehicle of uninspired action. DP. In Cantonese with English subtitles.

Jackie Chan • Anita Yuen *Amy Yip* • Michael Wong *Steve Cannon* • Thorsten Nickel *Cougar* ■ *Dir* Gordon Chan • *Scr* Gordon Chan, Chan Hing Ka, Kwok Wai Chung

Thunderbolt and Lightfoot ★★★★ 18

Crime drama 1974 · US · Colour · 109mins

This marvellous crime drama marked the directing debut of Michael Cimino, who later distinguished himself with *The Deer Hunter*. Clint Eastwood plays the crook who teams up with drifter Jeff Bridges, and, with George Kennedy and Geoffrey Lewis in pursuit, goes on a quest for hidden loot. Eastwood takes a bit of a back seat, letting the other three walk away with the acting honours. Bridges is terrific, but it's the manic Lewis you will remember. The scenery is handsome and, if you can ignore its rather tasteless sense of humour, this is enormously enjoyable. TS. Contains violence, swearing, nudity. [video] DVD

Clint Eastwood *John "Thunderbolt" Doherty* • Jeff Bridges *"Lightfoot"* • George Kennedy *Red Leary* • Geoffrey Lewis *Goody* • Catherine Bach *Melody* • Garey Busey [Gary Busey] *Curly* • Burton Gilliam *Welder* ■ *Dir/Scr* Michael Cimino

T

Thundercrack! ★★★

Sex melodrama 1975 · US · BW · 158mins

Underground film-maker George Kuchar – lover of Hollywood melodrama, especially *film noir* – had many acolytes, the best-known of which was Curt McDowell, the director of this insane parody of *The Old Dark House*. It sounds and looks like Kuchar's work because Kuchar wrote it (indulgently) and lit it (often strikingly). He's also the actor inside the gorilla suit. Strangers seeking shelter from a nasty storm stumble upon an isolated house. The characters lounge and talk (and talk) and eventually get around to (unsimulated) sex. While the mock soap-opera dialogue is banal and the shock of the outlandish sex scenes is insufficient for the running time, this is genuinely a one-off. DM

Marion Eaton *Mrs Gert Hammond* • George Kuchar *Bing* • Melinda McDowell *Sash* • Mookie Blodgett *Chandler* • Moira Benson *Roo* • Rick Johnson (1) *Toydy* • Ken Scudder *Bond* • Maggie Pyle *Willene* ■ *Dir* Curt McDowell • *Scr* George Kuchar, from a story by Mark Ellinger, Curt McDowell

Thunderhead – Son of Flicka ★★★ U

Drama 1945 · US · Colour · 76mins

Roddy McDowall, Preston Foster and Rita Johnson return for this eventful sequel to *My Friend Flicka*. Once again the horses are shown in all their glory as Thunderhead overcomes the injury that forced him to quit racing, in order to drive away his own father, a rogue stallion that is troubling the herds of neighbouring ranchers. Pacier and more action-packed than the original, the film's highlight is undoubtedly the ferocious fight sequence. DP

Roddy McDowall *Ken McLaughlin* • Preston Foster *Rob McLaughlin* • Rita Johnson *Nelle* • James Bell *Gus* • Diana Hale *Hildy* • Carleton Young *Major Harris* • Ralph Sanford *Mr Sargent* • Robert Filmer *Tim* ■ *Dir* Louis King • *Scr* Dwight Cummins, Dorothy Yost, from a novel by Mary O'Hara

Thunderheart ★★★★ 15

Thriller 1992 · US · Colour · 114mins

In this intelligent, gripping thriller, set in the 1970s and loosely based on real events, Val Kilmer plays an FBI agent who, having long ago denied his native American heritage, is sent to investigate a murder on a reservation. Director Michael Apted treats the subject matter with some sensitivity and there are powerful supporting turns. This was one of the first projects undertaken by Robert De Niro's production house. JF. Contains violence and swearing. DVD

Val Kilmer *Ray Levoi* • Sam Shepard *Frank Coutelle* • Graham Greene (2) *Walter Crow Horse* • Fred Ward *Jack Milton* • Fred Dalton Thompson *William Dawes* • Sheila Tousey *Maggie Eagle Bear* • Chief Ted Thin Elk *Grandpa Sam Reaches* ■ *Dir* Michael Apted • *Scr* John Fusco

Thunderpants ★ PG

Fantasy adventure
2002 · UK/Ger · Colour · 83mins

This excruciatingly vulgar comedy fantasy is an absolute stinker. Ten-year-old Bruce Cook was born with two stomachs, which cause him to break wind continuously. When his boffin pal Rupert Grint designs a pair of Heath Robinson-like trousers allowing flatulence storage, his power-farting attracts the attention of the US Space Center. AJ DVD

Simon Callow *Sir John Osgood* • Stephen Fry *Sir Anthony Silk QC* • Celia Imrie *Miss Rapier* • Paul Giamatti *Johnson J Johnson* • Ned Beatty *Ed Sheppard* • Bruce Cook *Patrick Smash* • Rupert Grint *Alan A Allen* • Leslie Phillips *Judge* ■ *Dir* Pete Hewitt [Peter Hewitt] • *Scr* Phil Hughes, from a story by Pete Hewitt [Peter Hewitt]

Thursday ★★★★ 18

Comedy crime drama
1998 · US · Colour · 84mins

This Tarantino-esque movie relates the blackly comic tale of ex-criminal Thomas Jane, who has now taken the path of respectability, with all its suburban trappings. Cue 24 hours of hell on his doorstep. A relatively short film, but densely packed, this combines action (often culminating in murder), with luscious dialogue and a first-rate cast. Jane and old buddy Aaron Eckhart are fine, but both are overshadowed by Paulina Porizkova, as the slinkiest, sexiest heroine in years. Sick and sadistic, but in a fun way. JC. Contains swearing and violence.

Thomas Jane *Casey Wells* • Aaron Eckhart *Nick* • Paulina Porizkova *Dallas* • James LeGros *Billy Hilly* • Paula Marshall *Christine Wells* • Michael Jeter *Doctor Jarvis* • Glenn Plummer *Rasta Man* • Mickey Rourke *Kasarov* ■ *Dir/Scr* Skip Woods

Tiara Tahiti ★★ PG

Comedy drama 1962 · UK · Colour · 96mins

Director Ted Kotcheff's feature debut is an adequate showcase for the talents of James Mason and John Mills. Nobody can smarm like Mason and he breezes through the picture, as a cultured crook who sees Mills's arrival on Tahiti to negotiate a hotel deal as the chance to pay him back for his being cashiered at the end of the war. Mills occasionally struggles to convince in the more difficult role, not always managing to keep the lid on his histrionics. DP

James Mason *Captain Brett Aimsley* • John Mills *Lt Colonel Clifford Southey* • Claude Dauphin *Henri Farengue* • Herbert Lom *Chong Sing* • Rosenda Monteros *Belle Annie* • Jacques Marin *Marcel Desmoulins* • Libby Morris *Adele Franklin* • Madge Ryan *Millie Brooks* • Roy Kinnear *Captain Tom Enderby* ■ *Dir* William T Kotcheff [Ted Kotcheff] • *Scr* Geoffrey Cotterell, Ivan Foxwell, Mordecai Richler, from the novel by Geoffrey Cotterell • *Cinematographer* Otto Heller

The Tic Code ★★

Drama 1998 · US · Colour · 91mins

Polly Draper makes her screenwriting debut with this candid, but highly contrived drama. She also stars, as a single mother whose young son (Christopher George Marquette) with Tourette's Syndrome is helped in his ambition to become a jazz musician by saxophonist Gregory Hines, who shares the boy's affliction. But, when the adults embark on a hesitant romance, Marquette has to learn to stand alone and Hines is forced to confront emotions he's spent his life avoiding. Sincere. DP

Gregory Hines *Tyrone* • Polly Draper *Laura* • Christopher George Marquette *Miles* • Desmond Robertson *Todd* • Carlos McKinney *Chester* • Dick Berk *Dick* ■ *Dir* Gary Winick • *Scr* Polly Draper

The Tichborne Claimant ★★ PG

Period drama based on a true story
1998 · UK · Colour · 94mins

Based on a true tale of Victorian fortune-hunting, this period piece is more televisual than filmic, and sadly lacking in originality. Manservant John Kani takes to the seas in search of lost aristocrat and heir Sir Roger Tichborne. He returns to Blighty with a coarse alcoholic in Tichborne's place and it all becomes rather ridiculous. The presence of Stephen Fry, Robert Hardy and Sir John Gielgud adds class, but that isn't enough to make this good cinema. LH.

John Kani *Andrew Bogle* • Robert Pugh *The claimant* • John Gielgud *Cockburn* • Stephen Fry *Hawkins* • Robert Hardy *Lord Rivers* • Rachael Dowling *Mary Anne* • Paola Dionisotti *Dowager* • Charles Gray *Arundell* ■ *Dir* David Yates • *Scr* Joe Fisher

tick... tick... tick... ★★★

Drama 1969 · US · Colour · 96mins

Subtlety was never a hallmark of Ralph Nelson's movies, although occasionally – as here – there are qualities that transcend the bludgeoning. This has the unlikely premise of the black Jim Brown elected to replace white sheriff George Kennedy in a town in the American South during the 1950s. The election turns the formerly peaceful community into the time bomb alluded to in the film's title. What redeems this movie is the sense of atmosphere and the good performances, especially from Fredric March,as the town's irascible mayor. BB

Jim Brown *Jimmy Price* • George Kennedy *John Little* • Fredric March *Mayor Jeff Parks* • Lynn Carlin *Julia Little* • Don Stroud *Bengy Springer* • Janet MacLachlan *Mary Price* ■ *Dir* Ralph Nelson • *Scr* James Lee Barrett

Ticker ★★ 15

Action drama 2001 · US · Colour · 88mins

When it comes to knuckleheaded violence, few can match Albert Pyun's pyrotechnic proficiency. Of course, it always helps to have Dennis Hopper as your deranged bomber, detonating random devices all over San Francisco simply because girlfriend Jaime Pressly has been arrested. It does no harm, either, to have Tom Sizemore as the grizzled cop on the case. But Steven Seagal's best days are way behind him and his cameo as a Zen explosives expert introduces an unintentional comic element that raises more laughs than one of Hopper's trademark rants. DP DVD

Tom Sizemore *Chris Astoyan* • Nas *Art "Fuzzy" Rice* • Steven Seagal *Glass* • Dennis Hopper *Swann* • Jaime Pressly *Claire* ■ *Dir* Albert Pyun • *Scr* Paul B Margolis

The Ticket of Leave Man ★★

Crime melodrama 1937 · UK · BW · 71mins

Villainous Victorians were Tod Slaughter's stock in trade, and this film is no exception. Based on a 1918 silent, it's the story of a murderer who tries to drag criminals even further into a life of crime. Even in the 1930s, Slaughter's films were seen as old-fashioned melodrama, hysterically overacted. Now they're cherished as collector's items in the "so bad, they're good" category. The cast always seems to be having great fun hamming it up but, of course, we're laughing at the film, not with it. SG

Tod Slaughter *Tiger Dalton* • Marjorie Taylor *May Edwards* • John Warwick *Bob Brierly* • Robert Adair *Hawkshaw* • Frank Cochran *Melter Moss* • Peter Gawthorne *Joshua Gibson* ■ *Dir* George King • *Scr* HF Maltby, AR Rawlinson, from a play by Tom Taylor

Ticket to Heaven ★★★ 15

Drama 1981 · Can · Colour · 102mins

Nick Mancuso is on top form as a man on the rebound from a bad relationship, who's brainwashed into becoming a "heavenly child" by a fanatical sect. There's a top-notch supporting cast, but the most memorable performance comes from the obscure RH Thomson as a pragmatic cult deprogrammer. It's no barrel of laughs, but there are flashes of humour to lighten the load. DA

Nick Mancuso *David* • Saul Rubinek *Larry* • Meg Foster *Ingrid* • Kim Cattrall *Ruthie* • RH Thomson *Linc Strunk* • Jennifer Dale *Lisa* • Guy Boyd *Eric* ■ *Dir* Ralph L Thomas • *Scr* Ralph L Thomas, Anne Cameron, from the novel *Moonwebs* by Josh Freed

A Ticket to Tomahawk ★★★ U

Comedy western 1950 · US · Colour · 90mins

Western spoofs were rare in the earnest early 1950s, but this colourful 20th Century-Fox romp sends up the old "stagecoach versus incoming railroad" plot to grand effect. It's helped by a witty screenplay by director Richard Sale and his then wife, the novelist and playwright Mary Loos, and superb Technicolor photography from Harry Jackson. Amiable Dan Dailey is the travelling salesman who teams up with sharp-shootin' Anne Baxter, while slimy Rory Calhoun uses every means he can to stop the railroad from gettin' through to Colorado, including Indians, bandits and dancers. Look closely at the actress on Dan Dailey's right-hand side in the big production number: that's Marilyn Monroe. TS

Dan Dailey *Johnny Behind-the-Deuces* • Anne Baxter *Kit Dodge Jr* • Rory Calhoun *Dakota* • Walter Brennan *Terence Sweeney* • Charles Kemper *Chuckity* • Connie Gilchrist *Madame Adelaide* • Arthur Hunnicutt *Sad Eyes* • Will Wright *US Marshal Dodge* • Marilyn Monroe *Clara* ■ *Dir* Richard Sale • *Scr* Mary Loos, Richard Sale

Tickets for the Zoo ★★★

Drama 1991 · UK · Colour · 90mins

This was director Brian Crumlish's first feature. His background in documentaries and experience of working with the homeless are clearly evident in this hard-hitting portrait of teen alienation and despair in 1990s Edinburgh. Alice Bree and Mickey MacPherson are utterly convincing as the brother and sister forced to fend for themselves after they outgrow their orphanage. This stark story, based on workshops with kids from city squats and hostels, has a gritty character all of its own. DP

Alice Bree *Carol Forbes* • Tom Smith *George* • Mickey MacPherson *Pogo* ■ *Dir* Brian Crumlish • *Scr* Christeen Winford

Tickle Me ★ U

Musical comedy 1965 · US · Colour · 86mins

Judging by the improbable situation and silly set pieces, it is unsurprising to discover that a pair of ex-Three Stooges writers scripted this unengaging Elvis Presley vehicle. An ex-rodeo rider falls in love when he gets a job in a health spa (for women only, of course), and becomes involved in a hunt for hidden treasure. Elvis is watchable (just), but it's one for fans of the King only. JG

Elvis Presley *Lonnie Beale* • Jocelyn Lane *Pam Merritt* • Julie Adams *Vera Radford* • Jack Mullaney *Stanley Potter* • Merry Anders *Estelle Penfield* • Connie Gilchrist *Hilda* • Edward Faulkner *Brad Bentley* • Bill Williams *Deputy Sturdivant* ■ *Dir* Norman Taurog • *Scr* Elwood Ullman, Edward Bernds

A Ticklish Affair ★★ U

Romantic comedy
1963 · US · Colour · 87mins

This pleasant if unadventurous comedy concerns US naval commander Gig Young, who investigates a false alarm set off by a child, and falls in love with the boy's widowed mother Shirley Jones. Initially, she's unwilling to remarry. One of her kids (Billy Mumy, who played Will Robinson in TV's *Lost in Space*) saves the day. JG

Shirley Jones *Amy Martin* • Gig Young *Cmdr Key Weedon* • Red Buttons *Flight Officer Simon Shelley* • Carolyn Jones *Tandy Martin* • Edgar Buchanan *Gramps Martin* • Peter Robbins *Grover Martin* • Billy Mumy [Bill Mumy] *Alex Martin* • Bryan Russell *Luke Martin* ■ *Dir* George Sidney (2) • *Scr* Ruth Brooks Flippen, from the story *Moon Walk* by Barbara Luther

Ticks ★★ 18

Horror 1993 · US · Colour · 81mins

This affectionate homage to the big monster movies of the 1950s spoofs the typical moments of the genre while adding gore and dark humour for the 1990s audience. A marijuana farmer in a mountain village concocts a special fertiliser for his plants, but his leaky machine spills it on to some tick eggs, causing massive mutation and mayhem. Several plot holes and narrative gaps later, the level of gore is so extreme that it becomes comical instead of disgusting. KB. Contains violence and swearing. DVD

Peter Scolari *Charles Danson* • Rosalind Allen *Holly Lambert* • Ami Dolenz *Dee Dee Davenport* • Alfonso Ribeiro *Darrel "Panic" Lumley* • Ray Oriel *Rome Hernandez* • Seth Green *Tyler Burns* • Virginya Keehne *Melissa Danson* ■ *Dir* Tony Randel • *Scr* Brent V Friedman

Tie Me Up! Tie Me Down! ★★ 18

Black comedy drama
1990 · Sp · Colour · 97mins

In Pedro Almodóvar's unfocused and lurid tale of kinky sex and bondage, actress and former porn star Victoria Abril is kidnapped by Antonio Banderas, who's recently been released from psychiatric care. He hopes that she'll eventually fall in love with him and start the family he's always wanted. The fact that Abril does indeed fall for her captor makes this darkly orgiastic comedy of terrors and errors one of the more controversial entries in the Spanish wunderkind's cult camp canon. It's distressingly superficial and the knotty romance fails to convince. AJ. In Spanish with English subtitles. [video] DVD

Victoria Abril *Marina* • Antonio Banderas *Ricky* • Francisco Rabal *Maximo Espejo* • Loles Leon *Lola* • Julieta Serrano *Alma* ■ *Dir/Scr* Pedro Almodóvar

The Tie That Binds ★★★ 18

Thriller 1995 · US · Colour · 94mins

Debut director Wesley Strick delivers a double whammy of emotional manipulation in this tug-of-love movie. Julia Devin is abandoned by criminal couple Daryl Hannah and Keith Carradine, and adopted by yuppies Vincent Spano and Moira Kelly. When her parents returns to claim her, the traumatised child is caught between the two families. A gulp-in-the-throat tear-jerker. TH. Contains swearing and violence. [video]

Daryl Hannah *Leann Netherwood* • Keith Carradine *John Netherwood* • Moira Kelly *Dana Clifton* • Vincent Spano *Russell Clifton* • Julia Devin *Janie* • Ray Reinhardt *Sam Bennett* • Barbara Tarbuck *Jean Bennett* ■ *Dir* Wesley Strick • *Scr* Michael Auerbach

Tierra ★★★ 18

Romantic drama 1995 · Sp · Colour · 117mins

It all seems so simple. A stranger named Angel arrives to delouse a vineyard and falls for a free-spirited local girl. But he also has eyes for a farmer's put-upon wife. Julio Medem delights in dazzling and disorientating the viewer and the camera is his co-conspirator, constantly shifting its perspective as it roams across the dusty landscape, prowls through bedrooms and even peers deep down into the soil. There is tremendous satisfaction to be gained from rising to the picture's not inconsiderable challenges. DP. In Spanish with English subtitles. Contains sex scenes and swearing. [video]

Carmelo Gomez *Angel Bengoelxeo* • Emma Suarez *Angela* • Karra Elejalde *Patricio* • Silke Klein *Mari* • Nancho Novo *Alberto* • Txema Blasco *Tomas* ■ *Dir/Scr* Julio Medem

Tiffany Jones ★ 18

Comedy 1973 · UK · Colour · 86mins

Made in the days of dolly birds and psychedelia, this pathetic attempt to produce an *Avengers* clone, but with more nudity, is adapted from a newspaper's comic strip and has Anouska Hempel helping a denim-clad prince regain his throne from a wicked dictator. At least Ray Brooks has the talent to seem embarrassed, but nothing can faze director Pete Walker. TH. Contains swearing and nudity. [video]

Anouska Hempel *Tiffany Jones* • Ray Brooks *Guy* • Susan Sheers *Jo* • Damien Thomas *Salvador* • Eric Pohlmann *President Jabal* • Richard Marner *Vorjak* • Ivor Salter *Karatik* • Lynda Baron *Anna Karekin* ■ *Dir* Pete Walker • *Scr* Alfred Shaughnessy, from the comic strip by Pat Tourret, Jenny Butterworth

The Tiger and the Pussycat ★★

Comedy drama
1967 · US/It · Colour · 108mins

This US/Italian co-production makes almost nothing of either country's qualities, though it's filmed in Rome. Vittorio Gassman is a 45-year-old engineer and family man experiencing an early midlife crisis. Approaching American art student Ann-Margret to blame her for his spurned son's suicide attempt, he finds himself attracted to her. The film wastes several opportunities, though it has a certain box-office gloss. TH

Vittorio Gassman *Francesco Vincenzini* • Ann-Margret *Carolina* • Eleanor Parker *Esperia* • Caterina Boratto *Delia* • Eleonora Brown *Luisella* • Antonella Steni *Pinella* ■ *Dir* Dino Risi • *Scr* Agenore Incrocci, Furio Scarpelli, from a story by Agenore Incrocci, Furio Scarpelli, Dino Risi

Tiger Bay ★★★ PG

Thriller 1959 · UK · BW · 102mins

Hayley Mills gives an astonishing performance in her film debut, playing a young girl who befriends murderous sailor Horst Buchholz and hinders detective John Mills's investigation at every turn. The "kid and the killer" plot cropped up regularly during the 1950s and this variation has nothing new to say, but J Lee Thompson surrounds 12-year-old Hayley with credible characters and faithfully captures the sights and sounds of Cardiff's docklands. DP [video] DVD

John Mills *Superintendent Graham* • Horst Buchholz *Korchinsky* • Hayley Mills *Gillie* • Yvonne Mitchell *Anya* • Megs Jenkins *Mrs Phillips* • Anthony Dawson *Barclay* • George Selway *Det Sgt Harvey* ■ *Dir* J Lee Thompson • *Scr* John Hawkesworth, Shelley Smith from the novel *Rodolphe et le Revolver* by Noël Calef

Tiger by the Tail ★

Thriller 1955 · UK · BW · 82mins

Another trudge through the lowest depths of British movie-making, in the company of quota quickie specialist John Gilling. Larry Parks stars in this, one of his British movies, made after he was driven out of Hollywood at the height of his career during the McCarthy witch-hunts of the 1950s. He plods through a tatty little tale about a journalist threatened by hoodlums. DP

Larry Parks *John Desmond* • Constance Smith *Jane Claymore* • Lisa Daniely *Anna Ray* • Cyril Chamberlain *Foster* • Ronan O'Casey *Nick* • Donald Stewart (1) *Macaulay* ■ *Dir* John Gilling • *Scr* John Gilling, Willis Goldbeck, from the novel by John Mair

Tiger by the Tail ★★★

Mystery melodrama
1970 · US · Colour · 99mins

This is one of the first melodramas to use the aftermath of Vietnam as a context for its thrills. When veteran Christopher George is wrongly accused of killing his brother, his socialite girlfriend (Tippi Hedren) seeks to help him out. It's a neat little film, which director RG Springsteen contrives to make quite watchable. TH

Christopher George *Steve Michaelis* • Tippi Hedren *Rita Armstrong* • Dean Jagger *Top Polk* • John Dehner *Sheriff Chancey Jones* • Charo *Darlita* • Lloyd Bochner *Del Ware* • Glenda Farrell *Sarah Harvey* • Alan Hale [Alan Hale Jr] *Billy Jack Whitehorn* ■ *Dir* RG Springsteen • *Scr* Charles A Wallace

Tiger in the Smoke ★★★

Crime drama 1956 · UK · BW · 92mins

Margery Allingham's source novel provides a distinctly offbeat, metaphysical edge to this thriller, in which male lead Donald Sinden spends most of his time gagged and bound. Meanwhile Tony Wright's personification of evil terrorises his fiancée (Muriel Pavlow) and her clergyman father (Laurence Naismith) in his search for a treasure that proves to be worth more than he could ever have imagined. From its opening image of street musicians in the London fog, the film builds up a compelling atmosphere of strangeness. AE

Donald Sinden *Geoffrey Levett* • Muriel Pavlow *Meg Elgin* • Tony Wright *Jack Havoc* • Bernard Miles *Tiddy Doll* • Alec Clunes *Asst Commissioner Oates* • Laurence Naismith *Canon Avril* • Christopher Rhodes *Chief Inspector Luke* ■ *Dir* Roy Baker [Roy Ward Baker] • *Scr* Anthony Pelissier, from the novel by Margery Allingham • *Cinematographer* Geoffrey Unsworth

The Tiger Makes Out ★★

Comedy 1967 · US · Colour · 94mins

Mailman Eli Wallach is full of the brooding resentment that seems to infect many of those working for the US Mail. He decides to exact revenge for his crummy life by "freeing the tiger" within himself. Wallach plots to make a dramatic and symbolic gesture by kidnapping a pretty girl, but in error he snatches the wrong party. His victim Ann Jackson is a surburban housewife with as many frustrations as Wallach himself. Adapted from a play, the film obscures the finer points of the original. Watch out for a young Dustin Hoffman. DF

Eli Wallach *Ben Harris* • Anne Jackson *Gloria Fiske* • Bob Dishy *Jerry Fiske* • John Harkins *Leo* • Ruth White *Mrs Kelly* • Roland Wood *Mr Kelly* • Dustin Hoffman ■ *Dir* Arthur Hiller • *Scr* Murray Schisgal, from his play *The Tiger*

The Tiger of Eschnapur ★★★

Adventure drama
1959 · W Ger/Fr/It · Colour · 101mins

With his career nearing its end, Fritz Lang returned from Hollywood to Germany and to a script that he had written over 30 years earlier for an adventure directed by Joe May. The first of a two-part story (completed by *The Indian Tomb*, 1959) it uses many real Indian locations and creates a world that is both fabulous and authentic. The story of persecuted lovers fleeing a jealous maharajah has a comic-strip nature, and the acting is rather stilted, but Lang's use of colour and decor provides some pleasure. Both features were brutally re-edited for release as a single 95-minute film in the USA and the UK as *Journey to the Lost City*. RB. In German with English subtitles.

Debra Paget *Seeta* • Walter Reyer *Chandra* • Paul Hubschmid *Harald Berger* • Claus Holm *Dr Walter Rhode* • Sabine Bethmann *Irene Rhode* • Valery Inkijinoff *Yama* • René Deltgen *Prince Ramigani* • Jochen Brockmann *Padhu* ■ *Dir* Fritz Lang • *Scr* Fritz Lang, Werner Jörg Lüddecke, from an idea by Thea von Harbou, from a novel by Richard Eichberg

Tiger of the Seven Seas ★★ U

Action adventure 1962 · It · Colour · 89mins

Gianna Maria Canale returns as the feisty sea dog's daughter in this so-so sequel to *Queen of the Pirates*. Here she takes command of her father's ship and later has to uncover the identity of his murderer and clear her lover Anthony Steel of the crime. Italian film-makers have always had a penchant for costume pictures, and director Luigi Capuano manages to convey period atmosphere without ever persuading us we are anywhere but in a film studio and he stages the action sequences with gusto. DP. Italian dialogue dubbed into English.

Gianna Maria Canale *Consuelo* • Anthony Steel *William* • Grazia Maria Spina *Anna Da Cordoba* • Ernesto Calindri *Inigo Da Cordoba* • Andrea Aureli *Laura* ■ *Dir* Luigi Capuano • *Scr* Arpad De Riso, Luigi Capuano, Ottavio Poggi, from a story by Nino Battiferri

Tiger Shark ★★★

Drama 1932 · US · BW · 80mins

Rumoured to be an inspiration for *Jaws* and pre-dating that blockbuster by a few decades, this efficient little melodrama features Edward G Robinson as a tuna-fishing Captain Hook – he lost a hand to the sharks – who is involved in a vicious triangle with wife Zita Johann and Richard Arlen. An early film by Howard Hawks, it is, for all its tabloid theatricality, typically well crafted. TH

Edward G Robinson *Mike Mascarena* • Richard Arlen *Pipes Boley* • Zita Johann *Quita Silva* • Leila Bennett *Muggsey* • Vince Barnett *Engineer* • J Carrol Naish *Tony* • William Ricciardi *Manuel Silva* • Edwin Maxwell *Doctor* ■ *Dir* Howard Hawks • *Scr* Wells Root, from the story *Tuna* by Houston Branch

A Tiger Walks ★★ U

Drama 1964 · US · Colour · 84mins

A couple of years after making *The Lion* on location in Africa, child actor Pamela Franklin has a go at something similar for Disney, only this time it's an escaped tiger that's loose in small-town America. The tone is unusually downbeat for Disney, with the film's sense of provincial politics owing more to Ibsen than Burbank. The cast also includes one-time "Elephant Boy" Sabu in his last movie role. TS [video]

Brian Keith *Sheriff Pete Williams* • Vera Miles *Dorothy Williams* • Pamela Franklin *Julie Williams* • Sabu *Ram Singh* • Edward Andrews *Governor* • Peter Brown *Vern Goodman* • Kevin Corcoran *Tom Hadley* ■ *Dir* Norman Tokar • *Scr* Lowell S Hawley, from the novel by Ian Niall

Tiger Warsaw ★ 15

Drama 1988 · US · Colour · 88mins

Fifteen years after he shot and wounded his father during a violent argument, Patrick Swayze returns to his home town to try to make peace with his family. He finds it a long and slow struggle, as will anyone watching this movie, which is filled with both pointless scenes and no explanation of key details. KB [video]

Patrick Swayze *Chuck "Tiger" Warsaw* • Lee Richardson *Mitchell Warsaw* • Piper Laurie *Frances Warsaw* • Mary McDonnell *Paula Warsaw* • Barbara Williams (2) *Karen* • Bobby DiCicco *Tony* • Jenny Chrisinger *Val* • James Patrick Gillis *Roger* ■ *Dir* Amin Q Chaudhri • *Scr* Roy London

T

Tigerland ★★★ 18

Wartime drama
2000 · US/Ger · Colour · 96mins

Joel Schumacher is obviously revelling in going back to basics with this tale of infantry conscripts undergoing jungle combat training before being shipped out to Vietnam. Rising star Colin Farrell plays the charismatic lead. He's a disruptive dissenter who wants out of the army, and who'll do anything to get his wish. Determinedly low budget and filmed sometimes confusingly in an in-your-face, almost documentary style, this is potent screen drama with a genuinely real feel about it. DA. Contains violence, swearing, drug abuse and a sex scene. [video] DVD

Colin Farrell (2) *Roland Bozz* • Matthew Davis *Paxton* • Clifton Collins Jr *Miter* • Thomas

Guiry [Tom Guiry] *Cantwell* • Shea Whigham *Wilson* ■ *Dir* Joel Schumacher • *Scr* Ross Klavan, Michael McGruther

Tigers in Lipstick ★

Erotic comedy 1979 · It · Colour · 83mins

Four continental sex symbols gamely strut their stuff in this limp throwback to the fluffy Italian sex comedies that were popular in the 1960s. The seven-segment anthology revolves around women being the more assertive sex and begins with a half-dressed Ursula Andress walking down the street and causing car crashes, because of her deal with a repair garage. Laura Antonelli, Monica Vitti and Sylvia Kristel also feature. The tame material is blandly directed, the dubbing is atrocious, and fans of the leading ladies will be disappointed. AJ. Italian dialogue dubbed into English.

Ursula Andress • Laura Antonelli • Sylvia Kristel • Monica Vitti • Orazio Orlando • Michele Placido • Roberto Benigni • Roberto Benigni ■ *Dir* Luigi Zampa • *Scr* Tonino Guerra, Giorgio Salvioni

A Tiger's Tale ★★ 15

Romantic comedy
1987 · US · Colour · 93mins

Another of Kirk Douglas's sons, Peter, made his directorial debut with this self-penned effort, which tries to be too many things at once and ends up being very little at all. The age-gap romance between C Thomas Howell and his girlfriend's mother Ann-Margret, is vaguely credible, especially once she becomes pregnant. But too many other aspects smack of contrivance and the humour is tastelessly patronising. DP

Ann-Margret *Rose Butts* • C Thomas Howell *Bubber Drumm* • Charles Durning *Charlie Drumm* • Kelly Preston *Shirley Butts* • Ann Wedgeworth *Claudine* • William Zabka *Randy* ■ *Dir* Peter Vincent Douglas [Peter Douglas] • *Scr* Peter Vincent Douglas [Peter Douglas], from the novel *Love and Other Natural Disasters* by Allen Hannay III

The Tigger Movie ★★ U

Animated adventure
2000 · US · Colour · 73mins

Winnie the Pooh's striped sidekick takes centre stage for the first *Pooh* picture to hit cinemas in nearly two decades. The voice artists have changed, but otherwise it's the same formula as before, with a down-in-the-dumps Tigger bouncing off in search of his family and his pals mounting a rescue mission when he fails to return. This Disney offering is pitched at pre-school, nursery and younger kids. Accompanying adults, however, may yawn at the sluggish pace and simplistic moralising. DA DVD

Jim Cummings *Tigger/Winnie the Pooh* • Nikita Hopkins *Roo* • Ken Sansom *Rabbit* • John Fiedler *Piglet* • Peter Cullen *Eeyore* • Andre Stojka *Owl* • Kath Soucie *Kanga* • Tom Attenborough *Christopher Robin* • John Hurt *Narrator* ■ *Dir* Jun Falkenstein • *Scr* Jun Falkenstein, from a story by Eddie Guzelian, from the characters created by AA Milne

Tight Spot ★★★ PG

Film noir 1955 · US · BW · 92mins

Ginger Rogers stars as the wisecracking moll who's afraid to give evidence against big-time gangster Lorne Greene. Edward G Robinson co-stars as the attorney seeking her co-operation and Brian Keith is the cop in charge of her safety. This highly capable cast has the benefit of a well worked-out script and of tight direction that makes the most of the confined setting of a hotel room. The result is a gripping thriller, quite the best of Rogers's later films. AE

Ginger Rogers *Sherry Conley* • Edward G Robinson *Lloyd Hallett* • Brian Keith *Vince Striker* • Lorne Greene *Benjamin Costain* • Katherine Anderson *Mrs Willoughby* • Allen Nourse *Marvin Rickles* • Peter Leeds *Fred Packer* • Doye O'Dell *Mississippi Mac* ■ *Dir* Phil Karlson • *Scr* William Bowers, from the play *Dead Pigeon* by Lenard Kantor

Tightrope ★★★★ 18

Thriller 1984 · US · Colour · 109mins

One of Clint Eastwood's greatest strengths is that he has been willing to explore the darker side of his film persona. In this under-rated thriller, he portrays a flawed and at times disturbing extension of his Dirty Harry character. Once again he is the maverick detective on the trail of a serial killer, only this time he is worried that both he and the man he is hunting share the same sexual tastes. Writer/director Richard Tuggle is either unwilling or unable to develop the theme fully, but he does make good use of the New Orleans settings and secures a powerful performance from Geneviève Bujold as a rape counsellor. JF. Contains violence, swearing, sex scenes and nudity.

Clint Eastwood *Wes Block* • Geneviève Bujold *Beryl Thibodeaux* • Dan Hedaya *Detective Molinari* • Alison Eastwood *Amanda Block* • Jennifer Beck *Penny Block* • Marco St John *Leander Rolfe* • Rebecca Perle *Becky Jacklin* ■ *Dir/Scr* Richard Tuggle

Tigrero: a Film That Was Never Made ★★★

Documentary
1994 · Fin/Bra/Ger · Colour · 75mins

Hollywood history is littered with failed projects, but the dirt on them rarely sees the light of day – which makes Mika Kaurismäki's documentary all the more revelatory and valuable. Set in Brazil's Mato Grosso, *Tigrero* was a jungle adventure that was slated to star John Wayne, Tyrone Power and Ava Gardner, before 20th Century-Fox mogul Darryl F Zanuck wrote it off as an insurance risk. Escorted by Jim Jarmusch, director Sam Fuller returns to the jungle village of Karaja for the first time since he scouted locations back in the 1950s, offering his attentive protégé a colourful version of the truth as well as plentiful insights into his larger-than-life personality. DP

Dir/Scr Mika Kaurismäki • *Cinematographer* Jacques Cheuiche

'Til Death ★★★

Crime drama 1993 · Mex · Colour · 90mins

This is a surprisingly assured feature debut by Mexican director Fernando Sarinana. The film follows the attempts of two friends to raise the money they need to open a dog training school in the USA. In addition to presenting a disturbing picture of city life, the director explores the hardships facing the *cholos* (the border people). Although he can't resist the odd stylistic flourish, Sarinana convincingly combines violence, romance and humour, while also drawing fine performances from his young cast. DP. In Spanish with English subtitles.

Demian Bichir *Mauricio* • Juan Manuel Bernal *El Boy* • Veronica Merchant *Victoria* • Dolores Beristain *Chenta* ■ *Dir* Fernando Sarinana • *Scr* Marcela Fuentes Berain

'Til There Was You ★★ 12

Romantic comedy
1997 · US · Colour · 109mins

The woeful miscasting of Jeanne Tripplehorn sabotages this romantic comedy, as two people who are destined to meet contrive to keep missing each other. Tripplehorn fumbles all her attempts at comedy. Dylan McDermott fares better as the man she will one day meet and fall for, and at least director Scott Winant handles this with a refreshing lack of sentimentality. JB. Contains some swearing. DVD

Jeanne Tripplehorn *Gwen Moss* • Dylan McDermott *Nick Dawkan* • Sarah Jessica Parker *Francesca Lanfield* • Jennifer Aniston *Debbie* • Craig Bierko *Jon* ■ *Dir* Scott Winant • *Scr* Winnie Holzman

'Til We Meet Again ★★★

Romance 1940 · US · BW · 99mins

One of the greatest of all shipboard romances, this was definitively filmed in 1932 as *One Way Passage* with Kay Francis and William Powell as the doomed lovers. The remake isn't at all bad, but George Brent's savoir-faire always seemed assumed, and it's awfully hard to care whether Merle Oberon actually succumbs to her fatal disease or not. Nevertheless, the setting is superb and director Edmund Goulding certainly knows how to keep the romance simmering. TS

Merle Oberon *Joan Ames* • George Brent *Dan Hardesty* • Pat O'Brien *Steve Burke* • Geraldine Fitzgerald *Bonny Coburn* • Binnie Barnes *Countess Liz de Bresac* • Frank McHugh *Rockingham T Rockingham* • Eric Blore *Sir Harold Pinckard* ■ *Dir* Edmund Goulding • *Scr* Warren Duff, from a story by Robert Lord • *Cinematographer* Tony Gaudio

Tilaï ★★★★ PG

Drama
1990 · Burkina Faso/Swi/Fr · Colour · 78mins

Set in an isolated village in the scrublands of Burkina Faso, this is a compelling tale of filial disobedience and fraternal loyalty from Idrissa Ouedraogo. Deftly handling the complexities of the plot and making expert use of the colours and vistas of the landscape, Ouedraogo courageously questions an array of tribal customs, including the *tilaï*, the ancient law that insists that incest is punishable by death. The stately pace (so typical of much sub-Saharan cinema) and the glowing photography enhance the power of the drama. DP. In More with English subtitles.

Rasmane Ouedraogo *Saga* • Ina Cisse *Nogma* • Roukietou Barry *Kuilga* • Assane Ouedraogo *Kougri* • Sibidou Sidibe *Poko* • Moumouni Ouedraogo *Tenga* • Mariam Barry *Bore* ■ *Dir/Scr* Idrissa Ouedraogo

Till Death Us Do Part ★★ PG

Comedy 1968 · UK · Colour · 95mins

One of the great strengths of the original TV series of *Till Death Us Do Part* was the loose, discursive nature of each episode and the topicality of many of the Alf Garnett character's diatribes about politics, race, religion and royalty. Obviously, the feature format precluded the use of a similar structure and writer Johnny Speight's decision to opt for a *Millions like Us* account of family fortunes from the 1930s to contemporary times only partly comes off. DP

Warren Mitchell *Alf Garnett* • Dandy Nichols *Else Garnett* • Anthony Booth *Mike* • Una Stubbs *Rita Garnett* • Liam Redmond *Mike's father* • Bill Maynard *Bert* • Brian Blessed *Sergeant* ■ *Dir* Norman Cohen • *Scr* Johnny Speight, from his TV series

Till the Clouds Roll By ★★★★ U

Musical biography
1946 · US · Colour · 135mins

MGM's lush tribute to Jerome Kern was intended as a straightforward biography, but Kern's death in 1945 turned this biopic into a most moving celebration, as the studio's full roster of stars perform the composer's greatest numbers, climaxing with Frank Sinatra crooning *Ol' Man River*. The film has some marvellous highlights, including a sequence featuring Judy Garland as Broadway star Marilyn Miller. The dramatic stuff, though, is heavily handled by former actor Richard Whorf, and Robert Walker is not ideally cast as Kern. Watch this for the MGM talent on display, and the dazzling array of production numbers. TS DVD

Robert Walker *Jerome Kern* • Van Heflin *James I Hessler* • Judy Garland *Marilyn Miller* • Lucille Bremer *Sally* • Joan Wells *Sally as a girl* • Paul Langton *Oscar Hammerstein II* • Dorothy Patrick *Mrs Jerome Kern* • Mary Nash *Mrs Muller* • Dinah Shore *Julie Sanderson* • Frank Sinatra ■ *Dir* Richard Whorf • *Scr* Myles Connolly, Jean Holloway, George Wells (adaptation), from a story by Guy Bolton

Till the End of Time ★★★

Romantic drama 1946 · US · BW · 105mins

This melodrama about three returning Second World War veterans was a successful vehicle for heart-throb Guy Madison. Dorothy McGuire is sympathetic as a war widow, a role that could have become cloying in other hands, and Robert Mitchum provides a tough contrast to Madison's lightweight leading man. The theme song, adapted from Chopin's *Polonaise in A Flat Major*, was a massive hit in its day for Perry Como. TS

Dorothy McGuire *Pat Ruscomb* • Guy Madison *Cliff Harper* • Robert Mitchum *William Tabeshaw* • Bill Williams *Perry Kincheloe* • Tom Tully *CW Harper* • William Gargan *Sgt Gunny Watrous* • Jean Porter *Helen Ingersoll* • Johnny Sands *Tommy* ■ *Dir* Edward Dmytryk • *Scr* Allen Rivkin, from the novel *They Dream of Home* by Niven Busch

Till There Was You ★ PG

Romantic thriller 1990 · Aus · Colour · 90mins

A plotless, pointless mystery film, the sole purpose of which seems to be to promote tourism to Vanuatu, the South Seas island paradise on which it's set. Charisma-free Mark Harmon plays a saxophonist who visits the island at his brother's behest, only to find his sibling has been murdered. He bungee jumps with the natives, romances Deborah Unger and tootles a few bluesy tunes on his horn. DA

Mark Harmon *Frank Flynn* • Jeroen Krabbé *Viv* • Deborah Unger [Deborah Kara Unger] *Anna* • Shane Briant *Rex* ■ *Dir* John Seale • *Scr* Michael Thomas

Till We Meet Again ★★★

First World War romantic thriller
1936 · US · BW · 71mins

A largely forgotten, if beautifully made, First World War spy romance, with distinguished Herbert Marshall (who himself lost a leg during the 1914-18 conflict) quite brilliant as an actor from England who falls in love with German actress Gertrude Michael, only to lose contact with her when war breaks out. Marshall's clever underplaying is extremely moving, with Michael also excellent. A vintage Paramount picture, luminously photographed by the great Victor Milner, it's very touching. TS

Herbert Marshall *Alan Barclay* • Gertrude Michael *Elsa Durany* • Lionel Atwill *Ludwig* • Rod La Rocque *Carl Schrottle* • Guy Bates Post *Captain Minton* • Vallejo Gantner *Vogel* • Torben Meyer *Kraus* ■ *Dir* Robert Florey • *Scr* Edwin Justus Meyer, Brian Marlow, Alfred Davis, Morton Barteaux, from the play *The Last Curtain* by Alfred Davis

Till We Meet Again ★★

Second World War drama
1944 · US · BW · 88mins

Director Frank Borzage has a reputation for being one of the great romantic movie storytellers, but his actual output is rather patchy, ranging from sublime Janet Gaynor silents such as *Seventh Heaven* to sentimental tosh such as this routine wartime drama. B-movie regular

Barbara Britton is the French nun who flier Ray Milland get back behind Allied lines. Sadly, this isn't very good, but Milland is worth watching. TS

Ray Milland *John* • Barbara Britton *Sister Clothilde* • Walter Slezak *Mayor Vitrey* • Lucile Watson *Mother Superior* • Konstantin Shayne *Major Krupp* • Vladimir Sokoloff *Cabeau* • Marguerite D'Alvarez [Margarita D'Alvarez] *Madame Sarroux* • Mona Freeman *Elise* ■ *Dir* Frank Borzage • *Scr* Lenore Coffee, from the play by Alfred Maury

Tillie and Gus ★★

Comedy 1933 · US · BW · 58mins

The first of four films that infant Baby LeRoy (who retired from the screen aged four) made with on-screen child-hater WC Fields. This rather haphazard comedy, directed by Francis Martin, has Fields as a card-sharp married to a landlady from Alaska (the then 70-year-old Alison Skipworth), who helps to foil a conman who is fleecing Skipworth's niece and her husband. Fields has strong competition from his very funny leading lady, but the laughs occur in the context of a somewhat hazy plot. RK

WC Fields *Augustus Q Winterbottom* • Alison Skipworth *Tillie Winterbottom* • Baby LeRoy *The "King" Sheridan* • Jacqueline Wells [Julie Bishop] *Mary Blake Sheridan* • Clifford Jones [Philip Trent] *Tom Sheridan* • Clarence Wilson *Phineas Pratt* • George Barbier *Capt Fogg* • Barton MacLane *Commissioner McLennan* ■ *Dir* Francis Martin • *Scr* Walter DeLeon, Francis Martin, from a story by Rupert Hughes

Tillie's Punctured Romance ★★★ U

Silent comedy 1914 · US · BW · 74mins

America's first feature-length comedy (six reels) had Charles Chaplin in its cast, but Marie Dressler was the lead because she was the star of the stage musical comedy *Tillie's Nightmare*. Dressler is believed to be a recent heiress by Chaplin and Mabel Normand, and he rushes her into marriage. However, she realises love's deception and she and Normand soon regard themselves as victims of male treachery. Directed by Mack Sennett, it now appears crude and clumsy, but it was a ground-breaker for its time, and it made Chaplin a star. TH [video] DVD

Marie Dressler *Tillie Banks, country girl* • Charles Chaplin *Charlie, city slicker* • Mabel Normand *Mabel, his girl friend* • Charles Bennett *Douglas Banks, Tillie's millionaire uncle* • Mack Swain *John Banks, Tillie's father* • Chester Conklin *Mr Whoozis, friend of John Banks* ■ *Dir* Mack Sennett • *Scr* Hampton Del Ruth, from the play *Tillie's Nightmare* by Edgar Smith

Tilt ★★ 15

Drama 1978 · US · Colour · 106mins

Pinball player Brooke Shields teams up with budding rock star Ken Marshall, and their freewheeling adventures lead to a showdown with pinball ace Charles Durning. The camerawork from inside the machines brings tension to the long-running contest; but this isn't the pinball equivalent of *The Hustler*. Donald Cammell continued his disappointing career post-*Performance* by co-writing the screenplay. TH [video]

Brooke Shields *Tilt* • Ken Marshall *Neil Gallagher* • Charles Durning *The Whale* • John Crawford *Mickey* • Harvey Lewis *Henry Bertolino* • Robert Brian Berger *Replay* ■ *Dir* Rudy Durand • *Scr* Rudy Durand, Donald Cammell, from a story by Rudy Durand

Tim ★★★ PG

Romantic drama
1979 · Aus · Colour · 103mins

Mel Gibson starred in this low-profile weepie in between the first two *Mad Max* movies. It couldn't be further from the murder and mayhem of those action favourites. Gibson plays a trusting simpleton who tumbles into a relationship with the wary older woman (Piper Laurie) who is teaching him to read. The sexual tensions between this odd couple keep sentiment at bay, and Gibson's performance as the wide-eyed innocent alerted audiences to the fact that there was more to the man than just action movies. RT [video] DVD

Piper Laurie *Mary Horton* • Mel Gibson *Tim Melville* • Alwyn Kurts *Ron Melville* • Pat Evison *Emily Melville* • Peter Gwynne *Tom Ainsley* • Deborah Kennedy *Dawn Melville* • David Foster *Mick Harrington* • Margo Lee *Mrs Harrington* • James Condon *John Harrington* ■ *Dir* Michael Pate • *Scr* Michael Pate, from the novel by Colleen McCullough

Timberjack ★★ U

Western 1955 · US · Colour · 92mins

In this average western drama, Sterling Hayden seeks revenge for the murder of his father and pits the family timber business against powerful competitor David Brian, who's also his rival for Vera Ralston's saloon keeper. Some fresh scenery and details count for little against routine plotting and brawling, and, while veteran Adolphe Menjou revels in his flowery dialogue, the songs by a dubbed Ralston and Hoagy Carmichael are dreary. AE

Sterling Hayden *Tim Chipman* • Vera Ralston *Lynne Tilton* • David Brian *Croft Brunner* • Adolphe Menjou *Swiftwater Tilton* • Hoagy Carmichael *Jingles* • Chill Wills *Steve Riika* • Jim Davis *Poole* ■ *Dir* Joseph Kane • *Scr* Allen Rivkin, from the novel by Dan Cushman

Timbuktu ★★ U

Wartime adventure 1959 · US · BW · 91mins

These days anyone can fly to Timbuktu in central Mali, but the word still has a mythological ping that evokes a mystical place, somewhere at the very end of the earth. Victor Mature is the sort of beefcake actor who feels at home in Timbuktu – and in rubbishy action movies like this one. He's a trader and adventurer who sides with the French Foreign Legion over their skirmishes with the local Tuareg raiders. Mature also fancies the French commander's wife, Yvonne De Carlo, who just melts in his arms. AT

Victor Mature *Mike Conway* • Yvonne De Carlo *Natalie Dufort* • George Dolenz *Colonel Dufort* • John Dehner *Emir* • Marcia Henderson *Jeanne Marat* • James Foxx *Lieutenant Marst* • Leonard Mudie *Mohamet Adani* • Paul Wexler *Suleyman* ■ *Dir* Jacques Tourneur • *Scr* Anthony Veiller, Paul Dudley

Time after Time ★★★★ 15

Science-fiction crime thriller
1979 · US · Colour · 107mins

In Nicholas Meyer's splendid literary conceit, the novelist HG Wells (Malcolm McDowell) follows Jack the Ripper (David Warner) from Victorian London to contemporary San Francisco in his time machine. It's a sometimes gruesome experience, but it's wittily aware of anachronisms, as the blood-steeped Ripper, warped in nature as well as time, becomes gratefully aware that the present day has many more killing devices. TH. Contains violence and swearing. [video]

Malcolm McDowell *Herbert G Wells* • David Warner *Dr John Lesley Stevenson* • Mary Steenburgen *Amy Robbins* • Charles Cioffi *Lieutenant Mitchell* • Laurie Main *Inspector Gregson* • Andonia Katsaros *Mrs Turner* • Patti D'Arbanville *Shirley* ■ *Dir* Nicholas Meyer • *Scr* Nicholas Meyer, from a story by Karl Alexander, Steve Hayes

Time and Tide ★★★★ 18

Action crime thriller
2000 · HK · Colour · 108mins

Tsui Hark's kinetic, hyper-stylised thriller offers both high-velocity action and well-developed characters, as a hitman and a bodyguard are connected via both their work conflicts and impending fatherhood. This touches upon similar themes to many of John Woo's Hong Kong movies and Tsui's visual orchestration is no less impressive, with wild angles, incredible stunt work and audacious editing techniques that give the fast-paced story a dynamic edge. JC. In Cantonese, English, Hokkien, Mandarin and Spanish with subtitles. [video] DVD

Nicholas Tse *Tyler* • Wu Bai *Jack* • Candy Lo *Ah Hui* • Anthony Wong (1) *Uncle Ji* ■ *Dir* Tsui Hark • *Scr* Hui Koan, Tsui Hark

Time Bandits ★★★★ PG

Fantasy comedy 1981 · UK · Colour · 111mins

Before Terry Gilliam found success in the US with *The Fisher King* and *Twelve Monkeys*, he made a series of wondrously inventive fantasies, of which this was one of the best. Its story of a schoolboy accompanying a group of outlaw dwarves on a jolting trip through time has some astonishing sequences, while the marvellous cast includes John Cleese as Robin Hood, Sean Connery as a Greek warrior king and Ralph Richardson as God. Ex-Python Gilliam is one of the great conjurers of cinema, and this film is proof of his talent. TH. Contains some violence and swearing. [video] DVD

John Cleese *Robin Hood* • Sean Connery *King Agamemnon* • Craig Warnock *Kevin* • Shelley Duvall *Pansy* • Katherine Helmond *Mrs Ogre* • Ian Holm *Napoleon* • Michael Palin *Vincent* • Ralph Richardson *Supreme Being* • Kenny Baker (2) *Fidget* ■ *Dir* Terry Gilliam • *Scr* Michael Palin, Terry Gilliam

Time Bomb ★★

Action crime thriller
1991 · US · Colour · 96mins

Michael Biehn plays a bookish watch repairer who experiences strange and violent flashbacks, and who is repeatedly attacked by mysterious people trying to kill him. He hires psychiatrist Patsy Kensit to unlock his mind. After this intriguing setup, Biehn's character quickly becomes grating and unlikeable, and the unfolding mystery becomes progressively sillier. Good action sequences keep this watchable. KB

Michael Biehn *Eddie Kay* • Patsy Kensit *Dr Anna Nolmar* • Richard Jordan *Colonel Taylor* • Tracy Scoggins *Ms Blue* • Billy Blanks *Mr Brown* • Jim Maniaci *Mr Grey* • Steven J Oliver *Mr Redd* • Ray "Boom Boom" Mancini [Ray Mancini] *Mr Black* ■ *Dir/Scr* Avi Nesher

Time Flies ★★★ U

Fantasy comedy 1944 · UK · BW · 84mins

ITMA radio series star Tommy Handley takes a trip to Elizabethan England. Handley's regular radio writer Ted Kavanagh is part of the team serving up a generous portion of period gags, such as Handley pipping Sir Walter Raleigh to tobacco and a spot of cloak laying, and George Moon singing a music-hall song at the Globe. Some of the jokes have travelled less well and it falls flat in places, but it's an entertaining romp. DP [video]

Tommy Handley *Tommy* • Evelyn Dall *Susie Barton* • George Moon *Bill Barton* • Felix Aylmer *Professor* • Moore Marriott *Soothsayer* • Graham Moffatt *Nephew* • John Salew *William Shakespeare* • Leslie Bradley *Walter Raleigh* • Olga Lindo *Queen Elizabeth* ■ *Dir* Walter Forde • *Scr* Howard Irving Young, JOC Orton, Ted Kavanagh

A Time for Drunken Horses ★★★★ PG

Drama 2000 · Fr/Iran · Colour · 75mins

Refusing to flinch from the harshest of realities about the life of dispossessed Kurds on the Iran–Iraq border, writer/director Bahman Ghobadi focuses on the selfless determination of a couple of orphans to fund an operation for their severely handicapped brother. His juxtaposition of insistent close-ups and forbidding vistas highlights the reckless courage of the contraband smugglers, who resort to dosing their horses with alcohol to get them through the blizzard-blasted mountain passes. DP. In Farsi with English subtitles. [video] DVD

Ayoub Ahmadi *Ayoub* • Nezhad Ekhtiar-Dini • Mehdi Ekhtiar-Dini *Madi* • Amaneh Ekhtiar-Dini *Amaneh* • Rojin Younessi *Rojin* ■ *Dir/Scr* Bahman Ghobadi

A Time for Dying ★★ PG

Western 1971 · US · Colour · 69mins

This was the final film of director Budd Boetticher and actor/producer Audie Murphy, who reprises the role of Jesse James from 1950's *Kansas Raiders*. Boetticher's cult status was founded on the westerns he made with Randolph Scott but, sadly, this just isn't in the same league. It's a blend of western and youth movie as teenager Richard Lapp becomes a bounty hunter known for his love of animals, the ladies and quick-draw gunfights. Cheap-looking and was clearly made in a hurry. AT [video]

Richard Lapp *Cass* • Anne Randall *Nellie Winters* • Audie Murphy *Jesse James* • Victor Jory *Judge Roy Bean* • Beatrice Kay *Mamie* ■ *Dir/Scr* Budd Boetticher

A Time for Killing ★★★ 15

Western 1967 · US · Colour · 80mins

Confederate soldier George Hamilton escapes from a Union prison and is pursued by Captain Glenn Ford whose fiancée, Inger Stevens, has been taken hostage and is then raped by Hamilton as revenge for the South's defeat. Sadly, a weak performance from Hamilton and a bland one from Ford diminish the story, which otherwise has a startling realism and toughness in its evocation of America in the aftermath of the Civil War. Released on video in the UK as *The Long Ride Home*. AT [video]

Glenn Ford *Major Walcott* • George Hamilton *Capt Bentley* • Inger Stevens *Emily Biddle* • Paul Peterson *Blue Lake* • Max Baer Jr *Sgt Luther Liskell* • Todd Armstrong *Lt Prudessing* • Timothy Carey *Billy Cat* • Harrison Ford *Lt Shaffer* ■ *Dir* Phil Karlson • *Scr* Halsted Welles, from the novel *The Southern Blade* by Nelson Wolford, Shirley Wolford

A Time for Loving ★★

Portmanteau romantic drama
1971 · UK · Colour · 103mins

This British-made portmanteau film echoes the structure of the same year's *Plaza Suite* by setting a series of romantic episodes in the same Parisian apartment. Directed by Christopher Miles from a script by French playwright Jean Anouilh and with theme music by Michael Legrand, it features an international cast. Unfortunately, without Neil Simon's comic gifts or a sufficiently skilled or attractive cast, the intended soufflé falls flat more often than it rises. RK

Mel Ferrer *Dr Harrison* • Joanna Shimkus *Joan* • Britt Ekland *Josette* • Philippe Noiret *Marcel* • Susan Hampshire *Patricia* • Mark Burns *Geoff* • Lila Kedrova *Madame Dubillard* • Robert Dhéry *Leonard* ■ *Dir* Christopher Miles • *Scr* Jean Anouilh

Time Gentlemen Please! ★★ U

Comedy 1952 · UK · BW · 85mins

One of the few pictures produced by the ill-fated low-budget Group 3 company, this feeble film attempts to reproduce the whimsy of the Ealing comedies and succeeds only in being snobbish, predictable and dull. Eddie Byrne overplays his hand as the rascal

T

who is the blot on a village's 100-per cent employment record and threatens to ruin its chances of national publicity. Sid James scores as the pub landlord, but the plot is contrived and inconsequential. DP

Eddie Byrne *Dan Dance* • Hermione Baddeley *Emma Stebbins* • Raymond Lovell *Sir Digby Montague* • Jane Barrett *Sally* • Dora Bryan *Peggy Stebbins* • Robert Brown *Bill Jordan* • Thora Hird *Alice Crouch* • Sidney James *Eric Hace* ■ *Dir* Lewis Gilbert • *Scr* Peter Blackmore, Val Guest, from the novel *Nothing to Lose* by RJ Minney

The Time Guardian ★★★ PG

Science-fiction action adventure
1987 · Aus · Colour · 83mins

This reasonably exciting fantasy set in Australia has a quite complicated plot beginning in the year 4039. Earth has been destroyed by a cyborg master race called the Jen-Diki. Escaping ruler Dean Stockwell sends warriors Carrie Fisher and Tom Burlinson back in time to 1988 to engineer another future battle with the killer robots before they become too strong. In the outback, the two culture-clash soldiers meet loner Nikki Coghill, who helps them fight the corrupt Aussie police. Good special effects and a quick pace disguise plot holes you could fly a spaceship through. AJ

Tom Burlinson *Ballard/The Time Guardian* • Nikki Coghill *Annie* • Dean Stockwell *Boss* • Carrie Fisher *Petra* • Peter Merrill *Zuryk* • Tim Robertson *Sergeant McCarthy* • John Clark (2) • Jimmy James ■ *Dir* Brian Hannant • *Scr* Brian Hannant, John Baxter

Time in the Sun ★★★

Documentary drama
1939 · US/Mex · BW · 60mins

In 1931, Sergei Eisenstein spent some months in Mexico shooting his semi-documentary *Que Viva Mexico!*. After fighting bureaucracy and trying to obtain money to keep the film going, the great Russian director had to return to the USSR. However, his producer, the American novelist Upton Sinclair, never sent him the reels to edit. Instead he sold them to producer Sol Lesser, who assembled some of the raw material into a crude film called *Thunder over Mexico* (1933). Later Eisenstein's first biographer Marie Seton edited the reels to make this version, a superior travelogue with banal narration. Though not quite as Eisenstein envisaged, it still retains much of his bizarre humour and homoeroticism, and its magnificent photography. RB

Charles Frederick Lindsley *Narrator* • William Royal *Narrator* • Ponce Espino *Narrator* • Carlos Tarin *Narrator* ■ *Dir* Sergei Eisenstein • *Scr* Grigori Alexandrov, Marie Seton, Paul Burnford, Anita Breener, Franz Blom, Samuel A Datlowe

T

Time Lapse ★★ 15

Thriller 2001 · US · Colour · 84mins

Nowadays, Roy Scheider is often cast as the villain in mediocre genre movies – rather like this one, in which he slips agent William McNamara a dose of amnesia serum and then arranges a nuclear transaction with a Middle Eastern spy. There's a hint of *Memento* about the way in which McNamara pieces together his past, although he's helped by the loyal support of ex-wife Dina Meyer, who seems to buy his story of a major memory lapse a touch too willingly for an ace reporter. DP DVD

Roy Scheider *Agent La Nova* • Dina Meyer *Kate* • William McNamara *Clayton Pierce* • Henry Rollins *Gaines* • Cassandra Hitti *Soozy Li* • Gabriella Bern *Anna* ■ *Dir* David Worth • *Scr* David Keith Miller, Karen Kelly

Time Limit ★★★

Wartime courtroom drama
1957 · US · BW · 96mins

An engrossing, if stagey court-martial drama, this is the only film to have been directed by actor Karl Malden. It's set during the Korean War and deals with an American major (Richard Baseheart) charged with collaboration with the enemy during his time as a PoW. Baseheart pleads guilty but the investigating officer digs deeper and discovers a terrible secret. The cast, led by Richard Widmark, is uniformly excellent, especially the undervalued Baseheart. AT

Richard Widmark *Colonel William Edwards* • Richard Basehart *Major Harry Cargill* • Dolores Michaels *Corporal Jean Evans* • June Lockhart *Mrs Cargill* • Carl Benton Reid *General Connors* • Martin Balsam *Sergeant Baker* • Rip Torn *Lieutenant George Miller* • Alan Dexter *Mike* ■ *Dir* Karl Malden • *Scr* Henry Denker, from the play by Ralph Berkey, Henry Denker

Time Lock ★★★

Drama 1957 · UK · BW · 72mins

Shot on a shoestring at the old Beaconsfield Studios but set in Canada, this nail-biting thriller was based on a TV play by Arthur Hailey, who went on to find huge success as the writer of blockbuster novels such as *Airport* and *Hotel*. It's a race against time to free a small boy from a bank vault before he suffocates. Director Gerald Thomas builds the tension adroitly enough and gets a fine performance out of young Vincent Winter. It provided Sean Connery with his first speaking role, as a welder. DP

Robert Beatty *Peter Dawson* • Betty McDowall *Lucille Walker* • Vincent Winter *Steven Walker* • Lee Patterson *Colin Walker* • Sandra Francis *Evelyn Webb* • Alan Gifford *George Foster* • Robert Ayres *Inspector Andrews* • Victor Wood *Howard Zeeder* • Sean Connery *Welder* ■ *Dir* Gerald Thomas • *Scr* Peter Rogers, from a TV play by Arthur Hailey

The Time Machine ★★★★ PG

Science-fiction fantasy adventure
1960 · UK/US · Colour · 98mins

HG Wells's marvellous novel is superbly brought to life in this charming and stylish adaptation by *The War of the Worlds* producer George Pal. Leaving his comfortable Victorian life behind, inventor Rod Taylor hops aboard his ingenious time contraption to explore the horrors of the future. He speeds through two World Wars and atomic destruction (in 1966!) towards the eventual enslavement of the human race by subterranean cannibals. This richly speculative science-fiction classic both stimulates and entertains, and deservedly won an Oscar for special effects. AJ DVD

Rod Taylor *George* • Alan Young *David Filby/James Filby* • Yvette Mimieux *Weena* • Sebastian Cabot *Dr Philip Hillyer* • Tom Helmore *Anthony Bridewell* • Whit Bissell *Walter Kemp* • Doris Lloyd *Mrs Watchett* ■ *Dir* George Pal • *Scr* David Duncan, from the novel by HG Wells • *Special Effects* Gene Warren, Tim Baer, Wah Chang

The Time Machine ★★ PG

Science-fiction fantasy adventure
2002 · US · Colour · 91mins

What will this dull, philosophically fudged and digitally dependent remake say about the early 21st-century when seen in the future? Chiefly, that we can't tell a tried and tested yarn – Victorian inventor travels 800,000 years forward in time and finds that a post-apocalyptic civilisation has divided into a two-tier caste system – without recourse to standard action-movie heroics. Guy Pearce tries hard to inhabit the character of the driven professor, but a more experienced director than Simon Wells (the great-grandson of the esteemed author) was needed. AC DVD

Guy Pearce *Professor Alexander Hartdegen* • Samantha Mumba *Mara* • Jeremy Irons *Uber-Morlock* • Orlando Jones *Vox* • Mark Addy *Dr David Philby* • Sienna Guillory *Emma* • Phyllida Law *Mrs Watchit* ■ *Dir* Simon Wells • *Scr* John Logan, from the 1960 film, from the novel by HG Wells

A Time of Destiny ★ 15

Second World War drama
1988 · US · Colour · 112mins

The significant talents of William Hurt and Timothy Hutton are diminished by the pseudo-operatic approach in this overblown melodrama. Hurt is the revenge-driven son determined to kill Hutton, whom he believes caused the death of his Basque father. The two become best buddies during the Second World War and find themselves in mortal danger before Hurt hits the vengeance trail again. TH. Contains swearing and violence.

William Hurt *Martin* • Timothy Hutton *Jack* • Melissa Leo *Josie* • Francisco Rabal *Jorge* • Concha Hidalgo *Sebastiana* • Stockard Channing *Margaret* ■ *Dir* Gregory Nava • *Scr* Gregory Nava, Anna Thomas

Time of Favor ★★★ 12

Political drama 2000 · Is · Colour · 102mins

Joseph Cedar's directorial debut provides a commendably balanced insight into the intransigence sustaining the violent tensions that dominate life in Jerusalem and the West Bank. Although the military aspect of the story strains credibility, there's much to ponder in the relationship between Assi Dayan, a rabbi who advocates the reclamation of the Temple Mount, and his daughter, Tinkerbell, who resents his attempts to impose favoured student Edan Alterman as her husband when she has designs on his army buddy, Aki Avni. Undeniably melodramatic, but also provocative and emotive. DP. In Hebrew with English subtitles.

Aki Avni *Menachem* • Tinkerbell *Michal Meltzer* • Edan Alterman *Pini* • Assi Dayan *Rabbi Meltzer* • Micha Selektar *Itamar* • Amnon Volf *Mookie* ■ *Dir/Scr* Joseph Cedar

The Time of His Life ★★★ U

Comedy 1955 · UK · BW · 73mins

Richard Hearne's enduring creation Mr Pastry delighted audiences for over 25 years. The youthful Hearne's impersonation of an incident-prone old man was popular not just in the UK and the US, but all across Europe. The character made a record number of appearances on *The Ed Sullivan Show* and was a favourite of comedy superstar Buster Keaton. In this film, Mr Pastry is an ex-con paying an unwanted visit to his daughter, who has moved up in society. Not a patch on the TV shows, but still a nostalgic treat. DF

Richard Hearne *Charles Pastry* • Ellen Pollock *Lady Florence* • Richard Wattis *Edgar* • Robert Moreton *Humphrey* • Frederick Leister *Sir John* • Peter Sinclair *Kane* • John Downing *Simon* • Anne Smith *Penelope* ■ *Dir* Leslie Hiscott • *Scr* Leslie Hiscott, Richard Hearne, from the story by Leslie Hiscott, Brock Williams

Time of Indifference ★★

Period drama 1964 · Fr/It · BW · 84mins

Adapted from a novel by Alberto Moravia, this 1920s-set drama is dominated by director Francesco Maselli's communist contempt for the bourgeois family paralysed by financial problems and indecision. The dysfunctional group hope for salvation, but their "saviour" turns out to be a conman. Glum stuff, it boasts a trio of formidable American imports, each suffering a dip in their careers. BB

Rod Steiger *Leo* • Claudia Cardinale *Carla Ardengo* • Shelley Winters *Lisa* • Paulette Goddard *Maria Grazia Ardengo* • Tomas Milian *Michele Ardengo* ■ *Dir* Francesco Maselli • *Scr* Suso Cecchi D'Amico, Francesco Maselli, from the novel *Gli Indifferenti* by Alberto Moravia

Time of Miracles ★★★

Drama 1990 · Yug · Colour · 98mins

Clumsy in its symbolism, but still possessing the power to provoke, Goran Paskaljevic's historical allegory caused a storm of protest when it was released in a Yugoslavia on the brink of civil implosion, even though the swift passage of events somewhat undermined its political relevance. Set during the immediate aftermath of the Second World War, when the nation was similarly divided, the story concerns the appearance of a mysterious messianic figure who not only frustrates the mayor's attempts to put a small-town church to a more utilitarian use, but also resurrects a much-loved schoolteacher after his suspicious death. DP. In Serbo-Croat with English subtitles.

Predrag Miki Manojlovic [Miki Manojlovic] *Nicodemus* • Dragan Maksimovic *Lazarus* ■ *Dir* Goran Paskaljevic • *Scr* Goran Paskaljevic, Borislav Pekik, from a novel by Borislav Pekik

Time of the Gypsies ★★★★★ 15

Fantasy drama 1988 · Yug · Colour · 136mins

This astonishing fantasy drama, inspired by true events, is a blend of romance, realism and raw humour that won the best director prize at Cannes in 1989 for Sarajevo-born Emir Kusturica. Using both trained and non-professional performers, he reveals the divisions, deprivations and dreams of the Romany people, with Milan and the breathtaking but severe countryside of the former Yugoslavia as a backdrop. Davor Dujmovic gives a remarkable performance as the young gypsy with telekinetic powers who is prepared to sacrifice everything to win the hand of his beloved. At once epic and intimate, this is the work of a master film-maker. DP. In Romany and Serbo-Croat with English subtitles. Contains violence and nudity.

Davor Dujmovic *Perhan* • Bora Todorovic *Ahmed Dzida* • Ljubica Adzovic *Grandmother* • Husnija Hasmovic *Uncle Merdzan* • Elvira Sali *Daca* ■ *Dir* Emir Kusturica • *Scr* Emir Kusturica, Gordan Mihic

Time of the Wolf ★★★ 15

Drama
2003 · Fr/Austria/Ger · Colour · 108mins

Set against the bleak backdrop of an unexplained apocalypse, Michael Haneke's feature may despair of society's bestial excesses, but he's clearly not lost faith in humanity. Haneke pitches Isabelle Huppert and her children Lucas Biscombe and Anaïs Demoustier into a nightmare that begins with the murder of her husband and deepens on their arrival at a railway depot, presided over by Olivier Gourmet. Jürgen Jürges's nocturnal photography is outstanding and the performances painfully intense, but Haneke's dystopian vision won't persuade everyone. DP. In French with English subtitles. Contains violence and swearing. DVD

Isabelle Huppert *Anne Laurent* • Anaïs Demoustier *Eva Laurent* • Lucas Biscombe *Ben Laurent* • Patrice Chéreau *Thomas Brandt* • Béatrice Dalle *Lise Brandt* • Maurice Bénichou *Monsieur Azoulay* • Daniel Duval *Georges Laurent* • Olivier Gourmet *Koslowski* ■ *Dir/Scr* Michael Haneke

The Time of Their Lives ★★ PG

Period comedy fantasy
1946 · US · BW · 78mins

Between 1941 and the early 1950s, the comedy duo of Abbott and Costello were a national institution and earned around $800,0000 a year – a fantastic sum for actors in black-and-white B-movies. But in 1945, they temporarily fell out over a domestic matter and did not speak for months. Reunited, they made this "thriller" in which they did not work as a team but as individual characters. The plot involved two revolutionary ghosts haunting a country house – a phenomenon investigated with predictably comic results. BB

Bud Abbott *Ralph Greenways/Cuthbert Greenways* • Lou Costello *Horatio Prim* • Marjorie Reynolds *Melody Allen* • Binnie Barnes *Mildred "Millie" Dean* • John Shelton *Sheldon " Shelly" Gage* • Jess Barker *Tom Danbury* • Gale Sondergaard *Emily* ■ *Dir* Charles Barton • *Scr* Val Burton, Walter DeLeon, Bradford Ropes, John Grant

The Time of Your Life ★★★★ U

Comedy drama 1948 · US · BW · 100mins

Produced by William Cagney for Cagney Productions and starring brother James, this faithful rendering of William Saroyan's play, for which the author won, but refused, the 1940 Pulitzer Prize, is set entirely in a San Francisco waterfront bar run by gruff but kindly William Bendix. Here, a bunch of eccentrics, failures and wannabes live on dreams, acutely and understandingly observed by a mysterious Cagney, part tough guy, part altruist. Although leisurely, talky, too long and characterised by sentimental philosophising, it's extremely well acted and well directed, with some terrific tap-dancing from Paul Draper. RK DVD

James Cagney *Joe* • William Bendix *Nick* • Wayne Morris *Tom* • Jeanne Cagney *Kitty Duval* • Broderick Crawford *Krupp, a bewildered cop* • Ward Bond *McCarthy* • Paul Draper *Harry* ■ *Dir* HC Potter • *Scr* Nathaniel Curtis, from the play by William Saroyan

Time Out ★★★ PG

Drama 2001 · Fr · Colour · 128mins

Staged with meticulous care, this solemnly fascinating drama is loosely based on the case of Jean-Claude Romand, the seemingly successful businessman who wove a web of deception to prevent his family discovering he'd lost his job. Choosing not to follow the Romand case to its violent conclusion – Romand eventually murdered his family – director Laurent Cantet here re-creates the routines that occupied the man's empty days and the scams by which he sought to raise funds. DP. In French with English subtitles. DVD

Aurélien Recoing *Vincent* • Karin Viard *Muriel* • Serge Livrozet *Jean-Michel* • Jean-Pierre Mangeot *Vincent's father* • Nicolas Kalsch *Julien* • Marie Cantet *Alice* ■ *Dir* Laurent Cantet • *Scr* Robin Campillo, Laurent Cantet

Time Out for Rhythm ★ U

Comedy drama 1941 · US · BW · 74mins

Columbia produced this forgettable and forgotten effort about a couple of theatrical agents locked into an ongoing vendetta. Although jam-packed with speciality acts, orchestras, rhumba bands, crooner Rudy Vallee and the Three Stooges, the only moments able to surmount the dreary plot and pathetic screenplay are those featuring the great Ann Miller. RK

Ann Miller *Kitty Brown* • Rudy Vallee *Daniel Collins* • Rosemary Lane *Frances Lewis* • Allen Jenkins *Off-Beat "One Note" Davis* • Moe Howard • Larry Fine • Curly Howard ■ *Dir* Sidney Salkow • *Scr* Edmund Hartmann [Edmund L Hartmann], Bert Lawrence, from a story by Bert Granet, from the play *Show Business* by Alex Ruben

Time Out of Mind ★★

Period drama 1947 · US · BW · 88mins

Britain's ladylike Phyllis Calvert, unsuitably cast, made an undistinguished Hollywood debut in this tale of Robert Hutton whose aspirations to become a composer fall foul of his dictatorial seafaring father Leo G Carroll. Hutton seeks refuge in an unhappy marriage and the bottle, but is rescued and returned to music by the unstinting encouragement of housekeeper's daughter Calvert and by his sister Ella Raines. A dull effort. RK

Phyllis Calvert *Kate Fernald* • Robert Hutton *Christopher Fortune* • Ella Raines *Clarissa "Rissa" Fortune* • Eddie Albert *Jack Bullard* • Leo G Carroll *Captain Fortune* • Helena Carter *Dora Drake* ■ *Dir* Robert Siodmak • *Scr* Abem Finkel, Arnold Phillips, from the novel by Rachel Field

Time Regained ★★★★ 18

Drama 1999 · Fr/It/Por · Colour · 155mins

As time elapses from the optimistic 1880s to the depressed 1920s, Chilean director Raúl Ruiz calls on all manner of technical strategies to blend narrative, memory, emotion and dream into a sublime cinematic experience. Surrounded by such luminaries as Catherine Deneuve and John Malkovich, Marcello Mazzarella proves pivotal as Marcel, the writer whose life among the aristocracy becomes his art. Handsomely staged and acutely scripted, this is a triumph of technique and intellect. DP. In French with English subtitles. DVD

Catherine Deneuve *Odette* • Emmanuelle Béart *Gilberte* • Vincent Perez *Morel* • Pascal Greggory *Saint-Loup* • Marcello Mazzarella *Marcel Proust* • Chiara Mastroianni *Albertine* • Marie-France Pisier *Madame Verdurin* • John Malkovich *Baron de Charlus* ■ *Dir* Raúl Ruiz • *Scr* Raul Ruiz, Gilles Taurand, from the novel *Le Temps Retrouvé* by Marcel Proust

Time Runner ★ 15

Science-fiction action adventure
1993 · Can · Colour · 92mins

How far he has fallen since *Star Wars*. Mark Hamill's 21st-century character travels back to 1992 in order to warn Earth of a future alien invasion, but the invaders are already secretly in place and are out to stop him. Appallingly cheap and dull, with a time-jumping script and dim-witted characters, this makes no sense. KB

Mark Hamill *Michael Raynor* • Rae Dawn Chong *Karen* • Brion James *Neila* • Marc Baur *Colonel Freeman* • Gordon Tipple *Arnie* ■ *Dir* Michael Mazo • *Scr* Greg Derochie, Ron Tarrant, Ian Bray, Christopher Hyde, Michael Mazo, from a story by John A Curtis

Time to Die ★★★

Western 1985 · Col/Cuba · Colour · 98mins

Gabriel Garcia Marquez originally wrote the screenplay for *Time to Die* in 1965, when it was filmed as a western by Mexican Arturo Ripstein. Having already overseen a TV-movie remake in 1984, Czech-trained Columbian director Jorge Ali Triana fluently reworked it for the big screen. Exploring the juggernaut nature of fate and the futility of macho honour codes, the action follows Gustavo Angarita as he returns home 18 years after he killed a man, knowing that local custom dictates he must die at the hands of his victim's sons. DP. In Spanish with English subtitles.

Gustavo Angarita *Juan Sayago* • Sebastian Ospina *Julian Moscote* • Jorge Emilio Salazar *Pedro Moscote* • Maria Eugenia Davila *Mariana* • Lina Botero *Sonia* ■ *Dir* Jorge Ali Triana • *Scr* Gabriel Garcia Marquez

A Time to Die ★ 18

Crime drama 1991 · US · Colour · 89mins

Former porn star Traci Lords has hampered her attempt to become a serious actress by appearing in too many sleazy B-movies. She is completely miscast here as an unfairly convicted photographer, doing community service. She soon finds herself in danger when she photographs a murder by the cop who had arrested her earlier. Slow-moving and unbelievable. KB DVD

Traci Lords *Jackie Swanson* • Jeff Conaway *Frank* • Robert Miano *Eddie* • Jesse Thomas *Kevin* • Nitchie Barrett *Sheila* • Richard Roundtree *Captain Ralph Phipps* ■ *Dir/Scr* Charles T Kanganis

A Time to Kill ★★★★ 15

Thriller 1996 · US · Colour · 143mins

This dramatisation of John Grisham's first novel cleaned up at the box office and propelled the then unknown Matthew McConaughey to the front rank of Hollywood stars. McConaughey plays an inexperienced southern lawyer defending a working-class black man (Samuel L Jackson) who publicly murdered the white trash who abducted and raped his ten-year-old daughter. Sandra Bullock is the enthusiastic law student who offers to help McConaughey. In the redneck corner is politically ambitious district attorney Kevin Spacey and most of the small town of Clanton, Mississippi. McConaughey makes a pretty good fist of the lead role, but, as with most Grisham adaptations, the real strength is in the supporting turns. JF. Contains violence and swearing. DVD

Matthew McConaughey *Jack Brigance* • Sandra Bullock *Ellen Roark* • Samuel L Jackson *Carl Lee Hailey* • Kevin Spacey *Rufus Buckley* • Oliver Platt *Harry Rex Vonner* • Charles S Dutton *Sheriff Ozzie Walls* • Brenda Fricker *Ethel Twitty* • Donald Sutherland *Lucien Wilbanks* • Kiefer Sutherland *Freddie Cobb* ■ *Dir* Joel Schumacher • *Scr* Akiva Goldsman, from the novel by John Grisham

The Time to Live and the Time to Die ★★★★ PG

Period drama 1985 · Tai · Colour · 136mins

A fond evocation of life in Taiwan after the mainland revolution offering a shrewd insight into the pain of fumbling towards adolescent understanding, this is Hou Hsiao-Hsien's most autobiographical film. Passing from trusting youth to wannabe delinquent, more interested in acquiring teen-gang street-cred than filial duty, You Anshun gives a fine performance. Hou reinforces the allegorical aspects of the story, which sees the siblings rally round to survive the familial and financial crisis attending the death of their father. Steadily directed, it features typical flashes of gentle wit and deep humanity. DP. In Mandarin and Hokkien with English subtitles.

You Anshun • Tian Feng • Tang Ruyun • Xiao Ai ■ *Dir* Hou Hsiao-Hsien • *Scr* Zhu Tianwen

A Time to Love and a Time to Die ★★

Second World War romance
1958 · US · Colour · 132mins

Adapted from the novel by Erich Maria Remarque, this is set during the Second World War, essentially the tale of young German soldier John Gavin who marries Lilo Pulver during his leave, but still returns to the Russian front. The film fails to convince, with Gavin and his fellow soldiers so strongly American it's impossible to relate to them as Germans. RK

John Gavin *Ernst Graeber* • Lilo Pulver [Liselotte Pulver] *Elizabeth Kruse* • Jock Mahoney *Immerman* • Don DeFore *Boettcher* • Keenan Wynn *Reuter* • Erich Maria Remarque *Professor Pohlmann* • Dieter Borsche *Captain Rahe* • Thayer David *Oscar Binding* • Klaus Kinski *Gestapo Lieutenant* ■ *Dir* Douglas Sirk • *Scr* Orin Jannings, from the novel by Erich Maria Remarque

Time Trackers ★★ U

Science-fiction adventure
1989 · US · Colour · 81mins

In 2033, evil scientist Lee Bergere commandeers a time tunnel and uses the device to go back in history so he can claim the credit for inventing it. Unfortunately, he ends up in medieval England where a Robin Hood-type hero is the nemesis of villains everywhere. Produced on the cheap by Roger Corman, this sci-fi adventure is most successful on the humour front, thanks to Ned Beatty's sparkling turn as the cop in hot pursuit of Bergere through the centuries. AJ

Ned Beatty *Harry* • Wil Shriner *Charles* • Kathleen Beller *RJ* • Bridget Hoffman *Madeline* • Alex Hyde-White *Edgar* • Lee Bergere *Zandor* ■ *Dir/Scr* Howard R Cohen

The Time Travelers ★★★ PG

Science-fiction drama
1964 · US · Colour · 80mins

Conceived by director Ib Melchior as a sequel of sorts to *The Time Machine*, this is popcorn entertainment in the old-fashioned sense. A group of scientists led by Preston Foster hurtle 107 years into Earth's future, only to discover it in post-nuclear ruins and its human android survivors living underground and hiding from mutants who roam the surface. Given its modest budget, the film's ambition must be admired, though tarnished by stilted dialogue. RS

Preston Foster *Dr Erik von Steiner* • Philip Carey *Steve Connors* • Merry Anders *Carol White* • John Hoyt *Varno* • Forrest J Ackerman *Technician* ■ *Dir* Ib Melchior • *Scr* Ib Melchior, from a story by Ib Melchior, David L Hewitt • *Cinematographer* William Zsigmond [Vilmos Zsigmond]

Time Will Tell ★★★ 15

Documentary
1992 · UK · BW and Colour · 85mins

Bob Marley died of cancer at the age of 36 in 1981, and this documentary restricts itself largely to what proved to be the Jamaican's final tour. Reggae fans will revel in the footage of concert and rehearsal renditions of such classics as "Could You Be Loved" and "Coming in from the Cold". But Declan Lowney studiously avoids presenting a rounded portrait of the man who did more than most to bring Rastafarianism to a global audience. Indeed, Marley's pronouncements here tend towards proselytising, but the less laudable aspects of his life are ignored. DP DVD

Dir Declan Lowney

Time without Pity ★★★

Crime drama 1957 · UK · BW · 89mins

After years of dodging the Hollywood blacklist by releasing films under pseudonyms or crediting them to other film-makers, Joseph Losey was able to put his own name to this adaptation of Emlyn Williams's stage play. Although the story of a father trying to save his son from the gallows is supposed to be a thriller, Losey places so much emphasis on the capital punishment angle that the social theme too often swamps the suspense. Michael Redgrave is solid, however, as the alcoholic dad fighting against time. DP

Michael Redgrave *David Graham* • Ann Todd *Honor Stanford* • Leo McKern *Robert Stanford* • Peter Cushing *Jeremy Clayton* • Alec McCowen *Alec Graham* • Renee Houston *Mrs Harker* • Paul Daneman *Brian Stanford* • Lois

T

Maxwell *Vicky Harker* ■ *Dir* Joseph Losey • *Scr* Ben Barzman, from the play *Someone Waiting* by Emlyn Williams

Timecode ★★★★ 15

Experimental drama
1999 · US · Colour · 89mins

Shot on cutting-edge digital video, this quirky and innovative comedy thriller from Mike Figgis is a technical tour de force. It offers four separate but intertwined takes on the same series of events, shown simultaneously on a single, quartered screen. Emphasis on one or more of the four soundtracks provides guidance as to what to watch when, while the familiar faces help catch the eye. The sequences, which all feature characters directly or indirectly involved with a Los Angeles film-production company, play out in real time, and were filmed that way, too, in continuous takes with no edits. An intriguing and cleverly realised idea. DA DVD

Salma Hayek *Rose* • Jeanne Tripplehorn *Lauren Hathaway* • Saffron Burrows *Emma* • Kyle MacLachlan *Bunny Drysdale* • Stellan Skarsgård *Alex Green* • Holly Hunter *Executive* • Julian Sands *Quentin* • Glenne Headly *Therapist* ■ *Dir/Scr* Mike Figgis

Timecop ★★★ 18

Science-fiction adventure
1994 · US · Colour · 98mins

The Muscles from Brussels encounters his younger self when he's sent back in time to catch a sinister senator who is trying to change the past for his own monetary ends. If you can follow the time-travel logic, then director Peter Hyams's gleaming comic-strip action adventure is dumb fun. Most sci-fi fans, however, will find it desperately outdated. A sequel featuring Jason Scott Lee was released in 2003. AJ. Contains swearing, violence, sex scenes and nudity. DVD

Jean-Claude Van Damme *Max Walker* • Mia Sara *Melissa* • Ron Silver *McComb* • Bruce McGill *Matuzak* • Gloria Reuben *Fielding* • Scott Bellis *Ricky* • Jason Schombing *Atwood* ■ *Dir* Peter Hyams • *Scr* Mark Verheiden, from a story by Mark Verheiden, Mark Richardson, from their comic book series

Timeline ★★ 12

Science-fiction adventure fantasy
2003 · US · Colour · 110mins

In this time-travelling fantasy, director Richard Donner presses too heavily on the significance of events in Michael Crichton's source novel, leaving the absurdities to take over. When Billy Connolly, the professor leading an archaeological dig in the Dordogne valley, gets thrust back in time by the shady corporation sponsoring the dig, his son (Paul Walker) and fellow students follow to rescue him and find themselves in a 14th-century war. Featuring clunky dialogue and outrageous situations. TH. In English and French with subtitles. DVD

Paul Walker *Chris Johnston* • Frances O'Connor *Kate Ericson* • Gerard Butler *Andre Marek* • Billy Connolly *Professor Edward Johnston* • Anna Friel *Lady Claire* • Neal McDonough *Frank Gordon* • Ethan Embry *Josh Stern* • David Thewlis *Robert Doniger* • Matt Craven *Steven Kramer* • Michael Sheen *Lord Oliver* ■ *Dir* Richard Donner • *Scr* Jeff Maguire, George Nolfi, from the novel by Michael Crichton

The Times of Harvey Milk ★★★★ 15

Documentary 1983 · US · Colour · 34mins

Using TV news footage and a host of fascinating interviews, this absorbing Oscar-winning documentary outlines the brief political career of the charismatic Harvey Milk, America's first openly gay politician. Elected as a San Francisco Supervisor in 1977, Milk was assassinated the following year alongside Mayor George Moscone. The murders provoked storms of protest, especially when the killer, an ex-policeman, was given a light sentence (he pleaded temporary insanity induced by junk food!), and a very moving candle-lit vigil. Eloquent, insightful, and narrated by *Torch Song Trilogy*'s Harvey Fierstein. AJ. Contains swearing.

Harvey Fierstein *Narrator* ■ *Dir* Robert Epstein [Rob Epstein]

Times Square ★ 15

Comedy drama 1980 · US · Colour · 106mins

This overblown and laughable attempt by Hollywood to do for punk what *Saturday Night Fever* did for disco came at least three years too late. Poor little rich girl Trini Alvarado runs away to Manhattan. There she meets punkette Robin Johnson, who first inducts her into the New Wave scene and then turns them both into the cult singing sensations The Sleaze Sisters. Fatuous, glossy rubbish. AJ

Tim Curry *Johnny Laguardia* • Trini Alvarado *Pamela Pearl* • Robin Johnson *Nicky Marotta* • Peter Coffield *David Pearl* • Herbert Berghof *Dr Huber* • David Margulies *Dr Zymabsky* • Anna Maria Horsford *Rosie Washington* ■ *Dir* Allan Moyle • *Scr* Jacob Brackman, from a story by Allan Moyle, Leanne Unger

Timeslip ★★

Science-fiction thriller
1955 · UK · BW · 93mins

In this quaint British sci-fi oddity, a radiation overdose propels an atomic scientist seven seconds into the future. Numerous muddled plotlines intertwine, with gangsters and spies trying to exploit his reaction to events before they happen, but nothing too interesting is done with the nifty premise. AJ

Gene Nelson *Mike Delaney* • Faith Domergue *Jill Friday* • Joseph Tomelty *Inspector Cleary* • Donald Gray *Maitland* • Vic Perry *Vasquo* • Peter Arne *Stephen Maitland* • Launce Maraschal *Editor* • Charles Hawtrey *Scruffy* ■ *Dir* Ken Hughes • *Scr* Charles Eric Maine, Ken Hughes, from the novel *The Isotope Man* by Charles Eric Maine

Timetable ★★

Crime drama 1956 · US · BW · 80mins

First there's the ingenious robbery on a train, then there's the investigation by insurance man Mark Stevens and cop King Calder. A twist 25 minutes into the picture puts a new complexion on the case. As producer, director and star, Stevens tries to create an intelligent, out-of-the-rut thriller – but too many events happen off screen before the standard chase and final shoot-out in Mexico. The staging is unexceptional and Stevens's own performance is dull. AE

Mark Stevens *Charlie* • King Calder *Joe* • Felicia Farr *Linda* • Marianne Stewart *Wife* • Wesley Addy *Brucker* • Alan Reed *Wolfe* • Jack Klugman *Frankie* ■ *Dir* Mark Stevens • *Scr* Aben Kandel, from a story by Robert Angus

Tin Cup ★★★ 15

Romantic sports comedy
1996 · US · Colour · 129mins

This likeable film reunited Kevin Costner with his *Bull Durham* director Ron Shelton. Costner plays a drunken, down-at-heel pro of a driving range in the back of beyond. When Rene Russo, the girlfriend of his long-standing rival, Don Johnson, drops by for golf lessons, Costner is smitten, and since she turns out to be a therapist, she can help rid him of his inner demons. The scene is set for a suspenseful finale at the US Open. Accomplished, and you don't need to be a golfer to enjoy it. AT. Contains swearing, nudity. DVD

Kevin Costner *Roy McAvoy* • Rene Russo *Dr Molly Griswold* • Don Johnson *David Simms* • Cheech Marin [Richard "Cheech" Marin] *Romeo Posar* • Linda Hart *Doreen* • Dennis Burkley *Earl* • Rex Linn *Dewey* ■ *Dir* Ron Shelton • *Scr* Ron Shelton, John Norville

The Tin Drum ★★★★ 15

Wartime drama
1979 · W Ger/Fr/Yug/Pol · Colour · 135mins

The winner of the Palme d'Or at Cannes and an Oscar for best foreign film, Volker Schlöndorff's adaptation of Günter Grass's allegorical novel compensates for diminishing the original's thematic complexity with some supreme visual bravado. Even more laudable is the performance of David Bennent, who decides at the age of three to stop growing and express his disgust at the folly of the adults, so casually treading the path to Nazism, by emitting glass-shattering screams and thumping his beloved tin drum. Although occasionally over-reliant on expressionist excess, it's a film that still manages to be both powerful and memorable. DP. In German with English subtitles. DVD

David Bennent *Oskar* • Mario Adorf *Alfred Matzerath* • Angela Winkler *Agnes Matzerath* • Daniel Obrychski *Jan Bronski* • Katharina Thalbach *Maria Matzerath* • Charles Aznavour *Sigismund Markus* ■ *Dir* Volker Schlöndorff • *Scr* Jean-Claude Carrière, Franz Seitz, Volker Schlöndorff, from the novel by Günter Grass

Tin Men ★★★★ 15

Comedy drama 1987 · US · Colour · 107mins

Director Barry Levinson is much sought after in Hollywood, but his smaller personal projects remain the most fun. This, along with *Diner*, is one of his best. Danny DeVito and Richard Dreyfuss are the rival aluminium cladding salesmen who fall out after a car accident and become locked in an ever-escalating feud. The 1960s settings are lovingly re-created and Levinson wonderfully captures the hustling banter of the reps. In spite of the laughs, there's a bittersweet undercurrent running throughout. JF. Contains swearing. DVD

Richard Dreyfuss *Bill "BB" Babowsky* • Danny DeVito *Ernest Tilley* • Barbara Hershey *Nora Tilly* • John Mahoney *Moe* • Jackie Gayle *Sam* • Stanley Brock *Gil* • Seymour Cassel *Cheese* • Bruno Kirby *Mouse* • JT Walsh *Wing* ■ *Dir/Scr* Barry Levinson

Tin Pan Alley ★★★ U

Musical 1940 · US · BW · 94mins

One of the most attractive and popular of all the vehicles Alice Faye made for 20th Century-Fox. She's cast here with upcoming starlet Betty Grable, dynamic Jack Oakie and handsome but boring John Payne, in one of those stand-by plots about struggling songwriters. There are still plenty of highlights to enjoy, but despite Alfred Newman's Oscar-winning soundtrack, this movie's mainly for nostalgia lovers. TS

Alice Faye *Katie Blane* • Betty Grable *Lily Blane* • Jack Oakie *Harry Calhoun* • John Payne *Skeets Harrigan* • Allen Jenkins *Sergeant Casey* • Esther Ralston *Nora Bayes* • Ben Carter *Boy* • John Loder *Reggie Carstair* ■ *Dir* Walter Lang • *Scr* Robert Ellis, Helen Logan, from a story by Pamela Harris

The Tin Star ★★★★★ U

Western 1957 · US · BW · 92mins

Here's a *real* western. It's a sturdy, finely wrought work from masters of the genre in their prime, with lawman turned bounty hunter Henry Fonda helping young sheriff Anthony Perkins to hold down his job in a town ravaged by outlaws. Written by Dudley Nichols (*Stagecoach*) and Oscar-nominated for best story and screenplay, it's directed by maestro Anthony Mann, who takes a linear, classic and deliberately under-emphatic approach, allowing the setting and characters to tell the story. Mann eschews false *High Noon* ethics and really understands the essence of heroism. This is an under-rated must-see experience. TS

Henry Fonda *Morg Hickman* • Anthony Perkins *Sheriff Ben Owens* • Betsy Palmer *Nona Mayfield* • Michel Ray *Kip Mayfield* • Neville Brand *Bart Bogardus* • John McIntire *Dr McCord* • Mary Webster *Millie Parker* • Lee Van Cleef *Ed McGaffey* ■ *Dir* Anthony Mann • *Scr* Dudley Nichols, from the story *The Tin Badge* by Barney Slater, Joel Kane

Tina: What's Love Got to Do with It ★★★★ 18

Biographical drama
1993 · US · Colour · 112mins

As you would expect of a film based on the autobiography *I, Tina* and on which Tina Turner herself acted as on-set adviser, this is hardly the most objective showbiz biopic of all time. While Angela Bassett should be applauded for her beautifully observed portrait of the singing superstar, perhaps greater credit should be given to Laurence Fishburne for his warts-and-all performance as Ike, the man who, for all his faults, did put Tina in the spotlight. Both stars deserved their Oscar nominations for virtually carrying a picture that looks and sounds great, but is a little oversimplified. DP. Contains violence, swearing. DVD

Angela Bassett *Tina Turner* • Laurence Fishburne *Ike Turner* • Vanessa Bell Calloway *Jackie* • Jenifer Lewis *Zelma Bullock* • Phyllis Yvonne Stickney *Alline Bullock* • Khandi Alexander *Darlene* ■ *Dir* Brian Gibson • *Scr* Kate Lanier, from the autobiography *I, Tina* by Tina Turner, Kurt Loder

The Tingler ★★★★ 15

Horror 1959 · US · BW · 78mins

One of the best examples of the work of the great horror producer/director William Castle, the king of gimmick cinema, whose shockers always shouted "Boo!" with lurid style. Here, doctor Vincent Price discovers that fear creates a parasite, which grows on the spine unless the victim screams. Price isolates one of the large insect-like creatures and it escapes. Immensely enjoyable hokum, it was originally shown with the legendary stunt "Percepto" – selected cinema seats wired to administer mild electric shocks. This mini-classic abounds with bizarre chills and goofy psychedelic imagery. AJ DVD

Vincent Price *Dr William Chapin* • Judith Evelyn *Mrs Higgins* • Darryl Hickman *David Morris* • Patricia Cutts *Isabel Chapin* • Pamela Lincoln *Lucy Stevens* • Philip Coolidge *Ollie Higgins* ■ *Dir* William Castle • *Scr* Robb White

Tinpis Run ★★★

Drama
1991 · Bel/Fr/Papua New Guinea · Col · 90m

Directed by Pengau Nengo, the first indigenous feature produced in Papua New Guinea is a freewheeling combination of road movie, anthropological treatise, political satire and family melodrama. The action centres around Gerard Gabud, a village chief who divides his time between running a taxi service and coping with the caprices of his rebellious daughter, Rhoda Selan. It's an ill-disciplined rattlebag of incidents and ideas, but the energy is infectious. DP

Gerard Gabud *Village chief* • Leo Konga • Rhoda Selan *Chief's daughter* ■ *Dir* Pengau Nengo • *Scr* John Barre, Séverin Blanchet, Martin Maden, Pengau Nengo

Tinseltown ★

Black comedy 1997 · US · Colour · 91mins

This is a lamentably unfunny satire on the lengths some people will go to

T

make it in the movies. Arye Gross and Tom Wood are so keen to become screenwriters that they agree to churn out a script about a serial killer for shyster producer Joe Pantoliano. The cast busts a gut to suggest starstruck desperation and to raise the odd laugh, but fails miserably. DP

Tom Wood *Tiger* • Joe Pantoliano *Arnie* • Arye Gross *Max* • Ron Perlman *Cliff* • Kristy Swanson *Nikki* • Rebecca Gray *Artist's model* • John Considine *Wolfie* • David Dukes *Jake* ■ *Dir* Tony Spiridakis • *Scr* Tony Spiridakis, Shem Bitterman, from their play *Self Storage*

Tintin and the Lake of Sharks ★★★ U

Animated adventure
1972 · Bel/Fr · Colour · 76mins

After numerous books and several TV serials, Tintin finally graduated to feature-length films, including this rousing encounter with his arch-enemy, Rastapopoulos. Die-hard fans of Hergé's blond-quiffed troubleshooter may not be bowled over by this animated adventure, but the action rattles along nicely, as Tintin, Snowy, Captain Haddock and the inimitable Thomson and Thompson investigate skulduggery in Syldavia. DP [video]

Dir Raymond Le Blanc

Tintorera ★

Adventure drama
1977 · UK/Mex · Colour · 88mins

This is one of several international rip-offs rushed out following the success of Spielberg's *Jaws*. Several naked starlets (among them Susan George, who must have signed the contract purely for the Mexican holiday) frolic on board a yacht and in the sea and, almost incidentally, are menaced by a tiger shark. The views are pretty, but the direction is atrocious. DM

Susan George *Gabriella* • Hugo Stiglitz *Esteban* • Andres Garcia *Miguel* ■ *Dir* Rene Cardona Jr • *Scr* Ramon Bravo

Tip on a Dead Jockey ★★

Crime drama 1957 · US · BW · 98mins

A tepid piece based on a magazine story by Irwin Shaw, in which Robert Taylor's war-weary pilot mopes around Madrid, having lost his nerve for flying and all interest in his wife Dorothy Malone. She eventually stirs him up enough for him to take a smuggling job and then the film sputters briefly to life, as Taylor takes a moral stand on the difference between moving currency and moving drugs. AE

Robert Taylor (1) *Lloyd Tredman* • Dorothy Malone *Phyllis Tredman* • Gia Scala *Paquita Heldon* • Martin Gabel *Bert Smith* • Marcel Dalio *Toto del Aro* • Jack Lord *Jimmy Heldon* ■ *Dir* Richard Thorpe • *Scr* Charles Lederer, from a story by Irwin Shaw

The Tit and the Moon ★★ 18

Comedy drama 1994 · Sp/Fr · Colour · 86mins

Having set up his central relationships, Bigas Luna becomes so besotted with both Mathilda May's body and his own symbolic imagery that the film becomes as tedious as it is unfathomable. The young Biel Duan is appealing enough, while Gérard Darmon makes the impotent *pétomane* (professional farter) surprisingly sympathetic. Prurient nonsense. DP. In Catalan, Spanish and French with English subtitles. Contains nudity. [video]

Biel Duan *Tete* • Mathilda May *Estrellita "La Gabacha"* • Gérard Darmon *Maurice "El Gabacho"* • Miguel Poveda *Miquel "El Charmego"* • Abel Folk *Father* • Genis Sanchez *Stallone* • Laura Mañá *Mother* • Victoria Lepori *She of the Breasts* ■ *Dir* Bigas Luna • *Scr* Cuca Canals, Bigas Luna • *Cinematographer* José Luis Alcaine

Tit for Tat ★★★★ U

Comedy 1934 · US · BW · 19mins

In *Them Thar Hills* (1934) a health trip turned into an escalating battle, as Laurel and Hardy clashed with irascible Charlie Hall over a misunderstanding involving the latter's wife (Mae Busch) and a well full of bootlegged liquor. In this Oscar-nominated sequel, the two factions revive their feud when they find themselves as neighbouring shopkeepers – a situation that gives them plenty of painful props with which to abuse one another. A classic and hilarious example of the team's peculiar brand of patient, methodical aggression. TH [video] DVD

Stan Laurel *Stanley* • Oliver Hardy *Oliver* • Mae Busch *Grocer's wife* • Charlie Hall *Grocer* • James C Morton *Policeman* ■ *Dir* Charles Rogers • *Scr* Stan Laurel

Titan AE ★★★★ PG

Animated science-fiction adventure
2000 · US · Colour · 91mins

Talk about starting with a bang. Don Bluth kicks off this animated spectacular with nothing less than the blowing-up of the Earth, forcing survivors Cale (voiced by Matt Damon) and Akima (Drew Barrymore) to put one over on the offending aliens by reactivating a hidden supercraft, The Titan. Three parts *Star Wars* to one part *Star Trek III*, *Titan AE* (After Earth, in case you're wondering), the film imaginatively blends top-quality cel and digital animation, resulting in something well beyond mere eye candy for kids. DA [video] DVD

Matt Damon *Cale* • Drew Barrymore *Akima* • Bill Pullman *Korso* • John Leguizamo *Gune* • Nathan Lane *Preed* • Janeane Garofalo *Stith* • Ron Perlman *Prof Sam Tucker* • Alex D Linz *Young Cale* ■ *Dir* Don Bluth, Gary Goldman • *Scr* Ben Edlund, John August, Joss Whedon, from a story by Hans Bauer, Randall McCormick • *Animation Director* Len Simon

Titanic ★★★ PG

Drama 1953 · US · BW · 97mins

An impressively staged, all-star 20th Century-Fox account of the great 1912 luxury liner disaster. It's well mounted and well played, despite being markedly inferior to its 1997 namesake – the writers of this movie did pick up their own Oscar – and to a superb British version made five years later, Rank's *A Night to Remember*. Barbara Stanwyck and Clifton Webb are top-billed as a couple trapped in a doomed marriage, and a young Robert Wagner romances the couple's daughter, Audrey Dalton. TS [video]

Clifton Webb *Richard Sturges* • Barbara Stanwyck *Julia Sturges* • Robert Wagner *Giff Rogers* • Audrey Dalton *Annette Sturges* • Thelma Ritter *Mrs Maude Young* • Brian Aherne *Captain EJ Smith* ■ *Dir* Jean Negulesco • *Scr* Charles Brackett, Walter Reisch, Richard Breen [Richard L Breen]

Titanic ★★★★ 12

Epic romantic drama
1997 · US · Colour · 186mins

There are two love stories here: one is between James Cameron and a ship; the other is between society girl Kate Winslet and third-class passenger Leonardo DiCaprio. Cameron's script wouldn't have sustained Clark Gable and Vivien Leigh for 80 minutes, but, somehow, he and his magical cast revive that old-style studio gloss for three riveting hours. *Titanic* is a sumptuous assault on the emotions, with a final hour that captures the horror and the freezing, paralysing fear of the moment. At a cost of over $200 million, it's the most expensive movie ever made. It grossed nearly two billion dollars at the box office – a record. Winning 11 Oscars, it also shares – with *Ben-Hur* and *The Lord of the Rings: The Return of the King* – the record haul of Academy Awards. AT. Contains swearing and brief nudity. [video] DVD

Leonardo DiCaprio *Jack Dawson* • Kate Winslet *Rose DeWitt Bukater* • Billy Zane *Cal Hockley* • Kathy Bates *Molly Brown* • Frances Fisher *Ruth DeWitt Bukater* • Gloria Stuart *Old Rose* • Bill Paxton *Brock Lovett* • Bernard Hill *Captain EJ Smith* ■ *Dir/Scr* James Cameron • *Cinematographer* Russell Carpenter • *Music* James Horner • *Editor* Conrad Buff, James Cameron, Richard A Harris

Titanic Town ★★★ 15

Comedy drama
1998 · UK/Ger/Fr · Colour · 97mins

Based on a semi-autobiographical novel by Mary Costello, this woman's view of Belfast at the height of the Troubles in 1972 contains broad – sometimes slapstick – humour that is somewhat at odds with its subject matter. Nevertheless, fans of Julie Walters will not be disappointed by her barnstorming performance as Catholic housewife Bernie McPhelimy, who adopts a grassroots approach to bringing peace to the region. Others may still be intrigued by this little-known film made by Roger Michell, who went on to direct *Notting Hill*. DM. Contains swearing. [video]

Julie Walters *Bernie McPhelimy* • Ciaran Hinds *Aidan McPhelimy* • Ciaran McMenamin *Dino/ Owen* • Nuala O'Neill *Annie McPhelimy* • Lorcan Cranitch *Tony* • Oliver Ford Davies *George Whittington* ■ *Dir* Roger Michell • *Scr* Anne Devlin, from a novel by Mary Costello

The Titfield Thunderbolt ★★★ U

Comedy 1952 · UK · Colour · 79mins

Although it gives off an undeniably warm glow, this tale of the rescue of a much-loved branch line clearly shows that the Ealing comedy express was beginning to run out of steam. Only in this rather too cosy world could social protest be undertaken on behalf of the forelock-tugging lower classes by squires, bishops, vicars, bumbling town clerks and amiable drunks. Despite a patronising tone and writer TEB Clarke's failure to realise the full potential of the satire, this is still an entertaining piece, thanks to director Charles Crichton's formidable talent and the highly polished playing of a practised cast. DP [video] DVD

Stanley Holloway *Valentine* • George Relph *Reverend Weech* • Naunton Wayne *Blakeworth* • John Gregson *Gordon* • Godfrey Tearle *Bishop* • Hugh Griffith *Dan* • Gabrielle Brune *Joan* • Sidney James *Hawkins* ■ *Dir* Charles Crichton • *Scr* TEB Clarke

Titicut Follies ★★★★

Documentary 1967 · US · BW · 84mins

Banned for almost 25 years, Frederick Wiseman's uncompromising account of life inside the Bridgewater state hospital in Massachusetts remains the only film to be censored in America on grounds other than obscenity. The graphic presentation of the brutal cruelty meted out by guards, social workers and psychiatrists is disturbing enough. But what makes the treatment of the criminally insane inmates all the more shocking is what it reveals about a nation that would tolerate such inhumanity while claiming to be the global champion of social justice. Unbearable to watch, but impossible to forget, this is a landmark in documentary film-making. DP

Dir Frederick Wiseman • *Editor* Frederick Wiseman • *Cinematographer* John Marshall

Title Shot ★ 15

Crime drama 1979 · Can · Colour · 84mins

There have been several classic boxing movies, but this is not one of them. In fact, it's a contender for the title of worst pug pic ever made. Weighing in at well over his matinée idol poundage, Tony Curtis is beaten before he starts with this story of a crooked fight manager whose boxer is too dumb to take a dive. DP [video]

Tony Curtis *Frank Renzetti* • Richard Gabourie *Blake* • Susan Hogan *Sylvia* • Allan Royal *Dunlop* • Robert Delbert *Rufus Taylor* • Natsuko Ohama *Terry* ■ *Dir* Les Rose • *Scr* John Saxton, from a story by Richard Gabourie

Tito and Me ★★★★

Comedy drama
1992 · Yug/Fr · Colour · 105mins

With its blend of proletarian comedy and political allegory, could any film have been more fitting to be the last bearer of the imprint "Made in Yugoslavia" than this one? Exploding the cult of personality and poking fun at the socialist realist style that dominated Eastern Bloc cinema, Goran Markovic's semi-autobiographical rite-of-passage picture is set in 1954 and chronicles ten-year-old foodaholic Dimitrie Vojnov's bid to win the heart of classmate Milena Vukosav. DP. A Serbo-Croat language film.

Dimitrie Vojnov *Zoran* • Lazar Ristovski *Raja* • Anica Dobra *Mother* • Pedrag Manojlovic [Miki Manojlovic] *Father* • Ljiljana Dragutinovic *Aunt* • Milena Vukosav *Jasna* • Vojislav Brajovic *Marshall Tito* ■ *Dir/Scr* Goran Markovic

Titus ★★★ 18

Tragedy 1999 · US/UK · Colour · 155mins

Julie Taymor wowed Broadway with her musical version of Disney's *The Lion King* and this epic retelling of Shakespeare's gory tragedy, based on another stage production, has a similar knockout impact. A shame the same attention lavished on the visual elements wasn't afforded to the performances, which range from the gruff (Anthony Hopkins's wronged Roman general) and the camp (Alan Cumming's Hitler-esque emperor) to the downright bizarre (Jessica Lange's Amazonian warrior queen). Still, there are enough jaw-dropping scenes to entertain. NS [video] DVD

Anthony Hopkins *Titus Andronicus* • Jessica Lange *Tamora* • Alan Cumming *Saturninus* • Harry J Lennix [Harry Lennix] *Aaron* • Colm Feore *Marcus* • Angus MacFadyen *Lucius* • Jonathan Rhys Meyers *Chiron* • Matthew Rhys *Demetrius* • Laura Fraser *Lavinia* ■ *Dir* Julie Taymor • *Scr* Julie Taymor, from the play *Titus Andronicus* by William Shakespeare

Tizoc ★★★

Romantic drama
1956 · Mex · Colour · 110mins

Having started out singing *rancheras* on Mexican radio, Pedro Infante enjoyed a decade of screen stardom before he was killed in a plane crash. This was his penultimate appearance and it landed him the best actor prize at the Berlin Film Festival. While Infante's liaison with Maria Felix may be doomed from the start, they generate an electricity that ensured both the film's commercial success and national mourning at Infante's untimely demise. DP. In Spanish with English subtitles.

Maria Felix *Maria* • Pedro Infante *Tizoc* • Eduardo Fajardo *Arturo* • Julio Aldama *Nicuil* • Alicia del Lago *Machinza* ■ *Dir* Ismael Rodriguez • *Scr* Ismael Rodriguez, Manuel R Ojeda, Ricardo Parada Leon, Carlos Orellana

To Be or Not to Be ★★★★★ U

Second World War satire
1942 · US · BW · 94mins

"So they call me Concentration Camp Ehrhardt?". There's good taste, and there's this fabulously funny and original wartime comedy from director Ernst Lubitsch, which transcends taste.

T

Witty and cleverly satirical by turns, this movie avoids giving offence by its magnificent casting, with Jack Benny as "that great, great actor Joseph Tura" and the wonderful comedian Carole Lombard, in her final film. There's poignancy, too, and a terrific running joke involving Lombard's admirer, played by the young Robert Stack. Mel Brooks starred in an audacious remake of this story, but the immutable style of this classic proved impossible to re-create. TS

Carole Lombard *Maria Tura* • Jack Benny *Joseph Tura* • Robert Stack *Lt Stanislav Sobinski* • Felix Bressart *Greenberg* • Lionel Atwill *Rawitch* • Stanley Ridges *Professor Siletsky* • Sig Rumann [Sig Ruman] *Colonel Ehrhardt* • Tom Dugan *Bronski* ■ *Dir* Ernst Lubitsch • *Scr* Edwin Justus Mayer, from a story by Ernst Lubitsch (uncredited), Melchior Lengyel

To Be or Not to Be ★★★ PG

Second World War satire
1983 · US · Colour · 102mins

The coarse-grained humour makes one long for the sublime Ernst Lubitsch 1942 original, but this update is still a cracking comedy. Director Alan Johnson does remarkably well to keep the ebullient Mel Brooks in check, as the hammy head of a theatrical troupe who becomes involved in the Polish resistance's fight against the Nazis. Co-starring with husband Brooks for the first time, Anne Bancroft is tremendous fun, but what was the Academy thinking of when it nominated Charles Durning for his shocking performance as "Concentration Camp Erhardt"? DP

Mel Brooks *Frederick Bronski* • Anne Bancroft *Anna Bronski* • Tim Matheson *Lieutenant Andre Sobinski* • Charles Durning *Colonel Erhardt* • José Ferrer *Professor Siletski* • Christopher Lloyd *Captain Schultz* ■ *Dir* Alan Johnson • *Scr* Thomas Meehan, Ronny Graham, from the film *To Be or Not to Be* by Edwin Justus Mayer, from a story by Ernst Lubitsch, Melchior Lengyel

To Catch a Thief ★★★ PG

Romantic mystery
1955 · US · Colour · 102mins

Time has not been kind to this Alfred Hitchcock film, which seems to be no more than a hasty vehicle cobbled together to team his blonde obsession at the time, Grace Kelly, with his old favourite, Cary Grant. Often overlooked, it follows a retired jewel thief's attempts to catch a copycat criminal. Grant and Kelly are on sparkling form, but the real star here is the French Riviera, which is beautifully captured by the Oscar-winning cinematography of Robert Burks. RK. An English/French language film. DVD

Cary Grant *John Robie* • Grace Kelly *Frances Stevens* • Jessie Royce Landis *Mrs Stevens* • John Williams *HH Hughson* • Charles Vanel *Bertani* • Brigitte Auber *Danielle* • Jean Martinelli *Foussard* ■ *Dir* Alfred Hitchcock • *Scr* John Michael Hayes, from the novel by David Dodge • *Costume Designer* Edith Head • *Cinematographer* Robert Burks

To Die For ★★ 15

Fantasy comedy 1994 · UK · Colour · 96mins

The ghost of a drag queen, who has died from an Aids-related illness, returns to haunt his promiscuous boyfriend and to force him to mourn properly. It's a ponderously well-meaning, lightweight, fantasy comedy with a cast of British television personalities including Jean Boht and Tony Slattery. It's heart is in the right place, but nothing else really is. AJ

Thomas Arklie *Simon* • Ian Williams *Mark* • Tony Slattery *Terry* • Dillie Keane *Siobhan* • Jean Boht *Mrs Downs* • John Altman *Dogger* • Caroline Munro *Mrs Pignon* • Gordon Milne *Drop Dead Gorgeous* • Nicholas Harrison *Siobhan's first lover* • Ian McKellen *Quilt documentary narrator* • Sinitta *Quilt documentary narrator* ■ *Dir* Peter Mackenzie Litten • *Scr* Johnny Byrne, from a story by Paul McEnvoy, Pater Litten

To Die For ★★★★★ 15

Satirical crime drama
1995 · US · Colour · 102mins

Nicole Kidman gives a great performance in director Gus Van Sant's brilliantly acerbic satire on fame and the American Dream. She plays a shallow, suburban princess, whose entire life has been devoted to becoming a television celebrity. Trouble is, husband Matt Dillon keeps getting in the way of her grandiose plans, so he has to be eliminated. Sharply scripted by Buck Henry from Joyce Maynard's bestselling novel, which was inspired by true events, this frighteningly funny, razor-sharp anecdote is one of Van Sant's most accessible movies. The director simply allows the riveting story to shine through above any extraneous style. Kidman, all pretty in pink lipstick and poisonous plans, is a revelation. AJ. Contains violence, swearing, sex scenes and drug abuse. DVD

Nicole Kidman *Suzanne Stone* • Matt Dillon *Larry Maretto* • Joaquin Phoenix *Jimmy Emmett* • Casey Affleck *Russell Hines* • Illeana Douglas *Janice Maretto* • Alison Folland *Lydia Mertz* • Dan Hedaya *Joe Maretto* • Wayne Knight *Ed Grant* • David Cronenberg *Man at lake* ■ *Dir* Gus Van Sant • *Scr* Buck Henry, from the novel by Joyce Maynard

To Die in Madrid ★★★

Documentary 1963 · Fr · BW · 85mins

This is an impassioned account of the triumph of fascism in 1930s Spain. Frédéric Rossif makes little attempt to disguise his left-wing sympathies as he champions the cause of the International Brigade over the Condor Legion, with its Italo-German hardware and the remorseless backing of the nobility and the church. Gleaned from contemporary newsreels, the footage reveals the pitiless nature of the conflict and the growing hopelessness of Republican resistance. Complete with a melancholic score by Maurice Jarre, this is may not be an impartial record, but it's a powerful one. DP. In English and French with subtitles.

John Gielgud *Narration* • Irene Worth *Narration* ■ *Dir* Frédéric Rossif

To Dorothy, a Son ★★ U

Comedy 1954 · UK · BW · 88mins

Having made her name as both a playwright and screenwriter, Muriel Box turned director in 1952, and she struggles to make something of a story short on credibility and atmosphere. Shelley Winters stars as a vengeful divorcee trying to keep her mitts on a fortune by preventing her successor from producing a male heir. Co-stars John Gregson and Peggy Cummins have more trouble coping with Winters's overplaying. DP

Shelley Winters *Myrtle La Mar* • John Gregson *Tony Rapallo* • Peggy Cummins *Dorothy Rapallo* • Wilfrid Hyde White *Mr Starke* • Mona Washbourne *Nurse Appleby* • Hal Osmond *Livingstone Potts* • Hartley Power *Cy Daniel* ■ *Dir* Muriel Box • *Scr* Peter Rogers, from the play by Roger MacDougall

To Each His Own ★★★★

Melodrama 1946 · US · BW · 123mins

After two years' absence from the screen, while she conducted – and won – a court case against Warners Bros' draconian contractual regulations, Olivia de Havilland returned to star for Paramount in this example of a "woman's picture" at its best, and won the best actress Oscar. Impeccably directed by Mitchell Leisen, the movie has de Havilland as an unmarried mother haunted by regrets at having given up her baby for adoption during the First World War. A very satisfying contribution to a long and honourable tradition. RK

Olivia de Havilland *Jody Norris* • John Lund *Capt Cosgrove/Gregory Piersen* • Mary Anderson *Corinna Sturges Piersen* • Roland Culver *Lord Desham* • Phillip Terry *Alex Piersen* • Bill Goodwin *Mac Tilton* • Virginia Welles *Liz Lorimer* ■ *Dir* Mitchell Leisen • *Scr* Charles Brackett, Jacques Thery, from a story by Charles Brackett

To Each His Own Hell ★★★

Thriller 1977 · Fr · Colour · 100mins

As the cop whose daughter is kidnapped, Annie Girardot is distressingly credible, both as she consoles her husband and son before delivering the ransom and, then, as she seeks the perpetrator with a stern tenacity. With its unflinching attention to detail and a shocking conclusion, this is grimly realistic and a relentlessly harrowing affair from director André Cayatte. DP. French dialogue dubbed into English.

Annie Girardot *Madeleine* • Bernard Fresson *Bernard* • Hardy Kruger *Inspector* • Fernand Ledoux *Grandad* ■ *Dir* André Cayatte • *Scr* Jean Curtelin and André Cayatte

To End All Wars ★★ 15

Wartime drama based on a true story
2001 · UK/US/Thai · Colour · 118mins

This is a well-intentioned but leaden adaptation of Ernest Gordon's memoir about the building of the Burma railroad. Allied soldiers Ciaran McMenamin, Robert Carlyle and Kiefer Sutherland are among the PoWs forced to lay the infamous track. The subplots involving Sutherland's illicit still and Mark Strong's bush university only reinforce the aura of stereotype and cliché. DP. Contains swearing, violence. DVD

Robert Carlyle *Maj Ian Campbell* • Kiefer Sutherland *Lt Jim Reardon* • Ciaran McMenamin *Capt Ernest Gordon* • Mark Strong *Dusty Miller* • James Cosmo *Lt Col Stuart McLean* • Masayuki Yui *Capt Noguchi* • Sakae Kimura *Ito* • Shu Nakajima *Lt Col Nagatomo* • John Gregg *Dr Coates* ■ *Dir* David L Cunningham • *Scr* Brian Godawa, from the memoir *Miracle on the River Kwai* by Ernest Gordon

To Gillian on Her 37th Birthday ★★★ 15

Romantic drama 1996 · US · Colour · 88mins

Peter Gallagher as a widower still haunted not just by the memory of his dead wife, but by apparitions of her. *Ally McBeal* creator David E Kelley wrote the screenplay and co-produced, while the deceased Gillian is played by his wife, Michelle Pfeiffer. Claire Danes is the daughter Gallagher emotionally neglects, and Kathy Baker and Bruce Altman try to bring him to his senses during a celebration to mark what would have been his Gillian's 37th birthday. Sentimental tosh, but it will no doubt appeal to those who enjoy Kelley's unique insights into the female psyche. DA. Contains swearing and sexual references.

Peter Gallagher *David Lewis* • Michelle Pfeiffer *Gillian Lewis* • Claire Danes *Rachel Lewis* • Laurie Fortier *Cindy Bayles* • Wendy Crewson *Kevin Dollof* • Bruce Altman *Paul Wheeler* • Kathy Baker *Esther Wheeler* ■ *Dir* Michael Pressman, Michael Pressman • *Scr* David E Kelley, from the play by Michael Brady

To Have and Have Not ★★★★★ PG

Second World War romantic drama
1944 · US · BW · 96mins

When producer/director Howard Hawks accepted the drunken challenge of filming Ernest Hemingway's "unfilmable" novel, neither of the two reprobates could have foreseen this as the outcome. One of Hollywood's most satisfying romantic melodramas, this features Humphrey Bogart in one of his best roles, as a reluctant patriot who falls for sultry Lauren Bacall (in her movie debut), and the two leads created an on-screen chemistry that resulted in a lifetime's love affair: "If you want me, just whistle. You know how to whistle, don't you Steve?". This is a gloriously witty, wonderfully enjoyable movie. TS DVD

Humphrey Bogart *Harry Morgan* • Walter Brennan *Eddie* • Lauren Bacall *Marie Browning "Slim"* • Dolores Moran *Helene De Bursac* • Hoagy Carmichael *Crickett* • Walter Molnar *Paul De Bursac* • Sheldon Leonard *Lieutenant Coyo* ■ *Dir* Howard Hawks • *Scr* Jules Furthman, William Faulkner, from the novel by Ernest Hemingway

To Have and to Hold ★★

Drama 1951 · UK · BW · 66mins

A British programme-filler about Patrick Barr who, crippled in a riding accident and discovering that he has only a short time left to live, devotes himself to ensuring the security and happiness of his wife and daughter (Avis Scott, Eunice Gayson). His concern becomes obsessive to the point where he encourages his wife's so-far only friendly and affectionate relationship with another man. A non-starry but well-played little drama. RK

Avis Scott *June De Winter* • Patrick Barr *Brian Harding* • Robert Ayres *Max* • Eunice Gayson *Peggy Harding* • Ellen Pollock *Roberta* • Richard Warner *Cyril* • Harry Fine *Robert* ■ *Dir* Godfrey Grayson • *Scr* Reginald Long from a play by Lionel Brown

To Have & to Hold ★ 18

Romantic thriller 1996 · Aus · Colour · 95mins

The second feature film from Australian award-winner John Hillcoat is an uninteresting and unpleasant yarn about the destructive obsession of lovers Tcheky Karyo and Rachel Griffiths in the Papua New Guinea jungle. Great photography can't disguise a feeble plot, in which Karyo's ongoing obsession with his dead wife (Anni Finsterer) threatens his sanity and Griffiths's life. AJ. Contains swearing, sex scenes, violence.

Tcheky Karyo *Jack* • Rachel Griffiths *Kate Henley* • Steve Jacobs *Sal* • Anni Finsterer *Rose* • David Field *Stevie* ■ *Dir* John Hillcoat • *Scr* Gene Conkie, from a story by John Hillcoat, Gene Conkie

To Hell and Back ★★★ PG

Biographical war drama
1955 · US · Colour · 101mins

Cowboy star Audie Murphy was America's most celebrated hero in the Second World War, and this is the movie version of his life, based on his autobiography. This was a relatively big movie for Murphy and Universal, filmed in early CinemaScope with authentically re-created battle scenes. Murphy is a likeable lead, so it's regrettable that his subsequent career was confined almost solely to westerns. After years fighting insomnia and depression that led to an addiction to sleeping pills, Murphy died in an air crash at the age of 47. TS

Audie Murphy • Marshall Thompson *Johnson* • Charles Drake *Brandon* • Gregg Palmer *Lt Manning* • Jack Kelly *Kerrigan* • Paul Picerni *Valentino* • Susan Kohner *Maria* ■ *Dir* Jesse Hibbs • *Scr* Gil Doud, from Audie Murphy's autobiography

To Joy ★★★ PG

Drama 1950 · Swe · BW · 94mins

Only a minor entry in the Ingmar Bergman canon, but no film by him is without interest. Several themes that were to recur throughout his career are touched upon, notably the fragility of marital bliss and the conflict between artistic creativity and personal contentment. Gunnar Fischer's subtle cinematography reinforces the claustrophobia of the chamber drama, which is played with an occasionally overcooked intensity by Stig Olin and Maj-Britt Nilsson, as the musicians whose sterile marriage is torn apart by his affair. Legendary director Victor Sjöström impresses in a cameo as an orchestra conductor. DP. In Swedish with English subtitles. DVD

Stig Olin *Stig Ericsson* • Maj-Britt Nilsson *Martha* • Berit Holmström *Child* • Björn Montin *Child* • Victor Sjöström *Sönderby* • John Ekman *Mikael Bro* • Margit Carlqvist *Nelly Bro* • Georg Skarstedt *Anker* ■ *Dir/Scr* Ingmar Bergman

To Kill a Clown ★★

Drama 1972 · US · Colour · 83mins

This unremarkable effort is a strange mix of domestic drama and psycho-thriller. A couple whose marriage is on the rocks spends their make-or-break time together on a remote New England island, but then find themselves trapped and at the mercy of a crackpot Vietnam vet played by a pre-*MASH* Alan Alda. Gwyneth Paltrow's mum, Blythe Danner, co-stars with Alda and they ensure one or two quality acting moments. DA

Alan Alda *Major Ritchie* • Blythe Danner *Lily Frischer* • Heath Lamberts *Timothy Frischer* • Eric Clavering *Stanley* ■ *Dir* George Bloomfield • *Scr* George Bloomfield, IC Rapoport, from the story *Master of the Hounds* by Algis Budrys

To Kill a King ★★★ 12

Historical drama
2003 · UK/Ger · Colour · 98mins

Director Mike Barker's historical drama begins as the English Civil War ends, focusing on the relationship between the Parliamentarians' military commander Thomas Fairfax (Dougray Scott), and his deputy, Oliver Cromwell (Tim Roth). The Fairfax finds himself torn between Cromwell and his wife (Olivia Williams). The former seems determined to accept nothing less than the head of King Charles I, the latter refuses to abandon old friends and standards. Despite stilted dialogue, this is a fascinating, if controversial history lesson. BP. Contains violence. [video] DVD

Tim Roth *Oliver Cromwell* • Dougray Scott *Thomas Fairfax* • Rupert Everett *King Charles I* • Olivia Williams *Lady Anne Fairfax* • James Bolam *Denzil Holles, Speaker of the House* • Corin Redgrave *Lord De Vere, Lady Anne's father* • Patricia Kerrigan *Mrs Cromwell* ■ *Dir* Mike Barker • *Scr* Jenny Mayhew

To Kill a Mockingbird ★★★★ PG

Classic drama 1962 · US · BW · 123mins

This is a beautifully crafted and faithful screen adaptation (by playwright Horton Foote, who won an Oscar) of the now-classic Harper Lee novel about a lawyer in the Deep South and the effect of a rape trial on his children. Gregory Peck won the best actor Oscar as Atticus Finch, while Robert Duvall, making his screen debut as the disturbed Boo Radley, is excellent, as are the well-cast children. Robert Mulligan's direction is quietly impressive (even if the film's a shade overlong). TS [video] DVD

Gregory Peck *Atticus Finch* • Mary Badham *Scout Finch* • Phillip Alford *Jem Finch* • John Megna *Dill Harris* • Frank Overton *Sheriff Heck Tate* • Rosemary Murphy *Miss Maudie Atkinson* • Brock Peters *Tom Robinson* • Estelle Evans *Calpurnia* • Ruth White *Mrs Dubose* • Robert Duvall *Boo Radley* ■ *Dir* Robert Mulligan • *Scr* Horton Foote, from the novel by Harper Lee

To Kill a Priest ★★ 18

Biographical drama
1988 · Fr/US · Colour · 112mins

Chrisopher Lambert heads a strong cast in this biographical film about a radical priest in Poland in the early 1980s. Ed Harris is the militia man charged with finding and eliminating Solidarity supporter Father Alek (Lambert), before his fervent opposition to the government spreads any further. The film moves from convoluted scene to convoluted scene, and Lambert is bland and miscast, so Harris as his would-be killer becomes (wrongly) more sympathetic. LH [video]

Christopher Lambert *Father Alek* • Ed Harris *Stefan* • Joanne Whalley *Anna* • Joss Ackland *Colonel* • David Suchet *Bishop* • Tim Roth *Feliks* • Pete Postlethwaite *Joseph* • Timothy Spall *Igor* • Cherie Lunghi *Halina* • Gregor Fisher *Father Irek* • Brian Glover *Minister* ■ *Dir* Agnieszka Holland • *Scr* Agnieszka Holland, Jean-Yves Pitoun, from a story by Agnieszka Holland

To Kill a Rat ★★★

Crime thriller 1977 · Fr · Colour · 118mins

Essaying another laconic loner, Alain Delon becomes the target of a cabal of corrupt politicians after his friend (Maurice Ronet) tips him off to the whereabouts of an incriminating notebook. With seemingly everyone having something to hide, the suspense never lets up for a second, as Delon and Ronet's girlfriend, Ornella Muti, try to separate the devious from the deadly. DP. A French language film.

Alain Delon *Xavier "Xav" Maréchal* • Ornella Muti *Valérie* • Stéphane Audran *Christiane Dubaye* • Mireille Darc *Francoise* • Maurice Ronet *Philippe Dubaye* • Klaus Kinski *Nicolas Tomsky* • Michel Aumont *Morot* ■ *Dir* Georges Lautner • *Scr* Georges Lautner, Michel Audiard, from a novel by Raf Vallet

To Live ★★★★ 12

Epic drama 1994 · Chi · Colour · 126mins

While it might lack the visual splendour of *Red Sorghum* or the dramatic intensity of *Raise the Red Lantern*, this is still a superbly realised piece of work, combining the historical sweep of an epic with the finely etched characterisations of a chamber drama. Although it incurred the wrath of the authorities, the film isn't a condemnation of the errors of Mao, but a tribute to the spirit of the Chinese people who survived them. Gong Li seems to be incapable of giving a bad performance, but she's more than matched by Ge You, who won the best actor award at Cannes. DP. In Mandarin with English subtitles. Contains violence. [video]

Ge You *Xu Fugui* • Gong Li *Jiazhen* • Niu Ben *Town Chief Niu* • Guo Tao *Chunsheng* • Wu Jiang *Wan Erxi* ■ *Dir* Zhang Yimou • *Scr* Lu Wei, from the novel *Lifetimes* by Yu Hua

To Live and Die in LA ★★★ 18

Crime thriller 1985 · US · Colour · 110mins

Director William Friedkin's cult hi-tech thriller features excitingly kinetic car chases through the City of Angels and high-energy gun battles choreographed to a pounding uptempo rock score. Treasury agents William Petersen and John Pankow go to extraordinary lengths by bending their Federal rule book to crack the operation of sadistic counterfeiter Willem Dafoe. Dafoe is a suitably slimy adversary in the maverick director's exercise in nihilistic *noir*. AJ. Contains violence, swearing and nudity. [video] DVD

William L Petersen *Richard Chance* • Willem Dafoe *Eric Masters* • John Pankow *John Vukovich* • Debra Feuer *Bianca Torres* • John Turturro *Carl Cody* • Darlanne Fluegel *Ruth Lanier* • Dean Stockwell *Bob Grimes* • Steve James (1) *Jeff Rice* • Robert Downey Sr *Thomas Bateman* • Michael Greene *Jim Hart* ■ *Dir* William Friedkin • *Scr* William Friedkin, Gerald Petievich, from the novel by Gerald Petievich

To Live and Die in Tsimshatsui ★★★ 18

Action thriller 1994 · HK · Colour · 96mins

Aware of the large number of Hong Kong residents involved with the Triads, director Lau Wai Keung here sets out to show that many of them were drawn into crime because of their dire circumstances, rather than inveterate evil. Indeed, the crooks get the best press in this high-octane drama, as cop Jacky Cheung goes undercover and discovers his adversaries are, in many ways, more human than his superiors. This is a provocative study of the difference between social and legal justice. DP. In Cantonese with English subtitles. Contains violence, swearing. [video]

Jacky Cheung *Ah Lik* • Roy Cheung *Hung Tai* • Wu Chien-lien • Leung Ka-fai [Tony Leung (1)] ■ *Dir* Lau Wai Keung [Andrew Lau]

To Our Loves ★★★★ 15

Drama 1984 · Fr · Colour · 99mins

Three years after shocking audiences with Isabelle Huppert's adulterous pursuit of the boorish Gérard Depardieu in *Loulou*, Maurice Pialat explored the theme of teenage promiscuity in this equally controversial picture. Pialat draws a disturbingly authentic performance from Sandrine Bonnaire, whose confused relationship with her absentee father (Pialat) prompts her to adopt an increasingly reckless attitude towards sex. The violent slanging matches with her brother are grimly arresting, but less revealing than the still naive 15-year-old's excruciating encounters with the father whose love she craves. DP. In French with English subtitles.

Sandrine Bonnaire *Suzanne* • Dominique Besnéhard *Robert* • Maurice Pialat *The father* • Evelyne Ker *The mother* ■ *Dir* Maurice Pialat • *Scr* Maurice Pialat, Arlette Langmann

To Paris with Love ★★★

Romantic comedy
1954 · UK · Colour · 78mins

An amiable, light-hearted exercise in postwar "naughtiness", with Alec Guinness and Vernon Gray as father and son, each planning amorous adventures for the other. The ensuing complications are enlivened by Guinness's engaging performance. Both the leading lady, Odile Versois, and Paris itself are delightful in mid-1950s' Technicolor, and this movie is often shamefully under-rated. TS

Alec Guinness *Colonel Sir Edgar Fraser* • Odile Versois *Lisette Marconnet* • Vernon Gray *Jon Fraser* • Jacques François *Victor de Colville* • Elina Labourdette *Sylvia Gilbert* • Austin Trevor *Léon de Colville* ■ *Dir* Robert Hamer • *Scr* Robert Buckner

To Please a Lady ★★★ U

Romantic sports drama
1950 · US · BW · 91mins

Clark Gable and Barbara Stanwyck star for veteran MGM director Clarence Brown in an efficient, straightforward movie that combines motor-racing action with drama and romance. Gable is a champion midget-car driver, hated by the crowds after the death of another driver in an accident for which he is held responsible. Journalist Stanwyck tries to get his side of the story, but he won't talk. Needless to say, neither the action nor their relationship stops there. RK

Clark Gable *Mike Brannan* • Barbara Stanwyck *Regina Forbes* • Adolphe Menjou *Gregg* • Will Geer *Jack Mackay* • Roland Winters *Dwight Barrington* • William C McGaw *Joie Chitwood* ■ *Dir* Clarence Brown • *Scr* Barré Lyndon, Marge Decker, from their story

To Protect and Serve ★★ 18

Thriller 1992 · Swi · Colour · 88mins

An intriguing spin on the "bent coppers" scenario, this focuses on an investigation into why corrupt lawmen are turning up dead. The evidence points inexplicably to a young policeman (C Thomas Howell) but is he being set up? Although Howell struggles to carry off his leading role, the film does benefit from a strong supporting cast. JF. Contains swearing, violence, sex scenes, drug abuse. [video]

C Thomas Howell *Egan* • Lezlie Deane *Harriet* • Richard Romanus *Captain Maloul* • Joe Cortese *Kazinsky* • Steve Ganon *Lieutenant Burton* • Jessie Lawrence Ferguson *Becker* ■ *Dir* Eric Weston • *Scr* Darren Dalton, Kent Perkins, Eric Weston, Freeman King

To See Such Fun ★★★★ U

Comedy compilation
1977 · UK · Colour and BW · 90mins

This compilation contains some of the funniest and most memorable sequences from over a score of British film comedies. Originally intended for theatrical release, this loving exercise in comic nostalgia immediately ran into all sorts of copyright problems, which may explain why its first appearance was as a Christmas day special on British television (LWT) in 1977. However, it has always been trimmed for TV transmissions and is best seen in its video release form. This cornucopia of comical clips was compiled by writer/performer Dick Vosburgh and hosted by comedy aficionado Frank Muir. DF [video]

Frank Muir *Host* ■ *Dir* Jon Scoffield

To Sir, with Love ★★★ PG

Drama 1967 · UK · Colour · 100mins

Sidney Poitier plays a new teacher in London's East End motivating less surly pupils to be responsible citizens. Director James Clavell's adaptation of ER Braithwaite's novel is a soft-centred affair, though Poitier does punch Christian Roberts just to prove he's boss. Lulu sings the title song, while Judy Geeson develops a credible and poignant crush on her teacher. Naive it may have been, but it became one of the year's top box-office hits. In 1996, Peter Bogdanovich directed a belated made-for-TV sequel. TH. Contains swearing. [video] DVD

Sidney Poitier *Mark Thackeray* • Christian Roberts *Denham* • Judy Geeson *Pamela Dare* • Suzy Kendall *Gillian Blanchard* • Lulu *Barbara Pegg* • Faith Brook *Mrs Evans* • Geoffrey Bayldon *Weston* • Edward Burnham *Florian* • Gareth Robinson *Tich* • Grahame Charles *Fernman* • Roger Shepherd *Buckley* • Patricia Routledge *Clinty* ■ *Dir* James Clavell • *Scr* James Clavell, from the novel by ER Braithwaite

To Sleep with Anger ★★★★ 12

Drama 1990 · US · Colour · 97mins

Charles Burnett's story of a black family settled in Los Angeles from the South is an engrossing study of conflicts in black America. Danny Glover has never been better, playing a seductive charmer from the past whose storytelling moves from the comic to the sinister, a domestic demagogue who stirs up nightmare tensions in the family. TH. Contains swearing. [video] DVD

Danny Glover *Harry Mention* • Paul Butler *Gideon* • Mary Alice *Suzie* • Carl Lumbly *Junior* • Vonetta McGee *Pat* • Richard Brooks *Babe Brother* ■ *Dir/Scr* Charles Burnett

T

To the Devil a Daughter ★★ 18

Horror 1976 · UK/W Ger · Colour · 88mins

This Hammer film is a muddled mixture of post-*Exorcist* shock and the more traditional House of Horror style. Based on Dennis Wheatley's occult bestseller (he hated it), the plot has satanist Christopher Lee coercing nubile nun Nastassja Kinski into having the Devil's offspring, while Richard Widmark, a writer specialising in the supernatural, tries to foil his plan. Peter Sykes directs with a firm tendency towards a trendy fragmented narrative and explicit exploitation. AJ. Contains violence, swearing and nudity. DVD

Richard Widmark *John Verney* • Christopher Lee *Father Michael Raynor* • Honor Blackman *Anna Fountain* • Denholm Elliott *Henry Beddows* • Michael Goodliffe *George de Grass* • Nastassia Kinski [Nastassja Kinski] *Catherine Beddows* • Anthony Valentine *David* ■ *Dir* Peter Sykes • *Scr* Chris Wicking, from the novel by Dennis Wheatley

To the Ends of the Earth ★★★

Crime drama 1948 · US · BW · 108mins

The title refers to the many continents crossed by government agent Dick Powell in his quest for a gang of opium smugglers with fanatical ambitions for world domination. The plot, though complicated, is comprehensible and it's well handled by director Sidney Buchman, ensuring maximum tension and entertainment value. Swedish import Signe Hasso contributes the girl glamour; as almost always, crooner-turned-tough-guy Powell convinces as the sober-minded action hero. RK

Dick Powell *Mike Barrows* • Signe Hasso *Ann Grant* • Maylia *Shu Pan Wu* • Ludwig Donath *Nicolas Sokim* • Vladimir Sokoloff *Lum Chi Chow* • Edgar Barrier *Grieg* • John Hoyt *Bennett* ■ *Dir* Robert Stevenson, Sidney Buchman • *Scr* Jay Richard Kennedy, from his story

To the Shores of Tripoli ★★ U

Second World War drama
1942 · US · Colour · 85mins

A salute to the Marines, the title coming from the military song. There isn't much of a plot – merely the training of the blokes, their patriotism, the tough sergeant, the girl back home, winsome nurse – you know the drill. Much of it was shot at the Marines' major Pacific base in San Diego, in full Technicolor, a rarity for 1942 since most Second World War movies were in black-and-white, only changing to colour in 1944 when victory was assured. AT

John Payne *Chris Winters* • Maureen O'Hara *Mary Carter* • Randolph Scott *Sgt Dixie Smith* • Nancy Kelly *Helene Hunt* • William Tracy *Johnny Dent* • Maxie Rosenbloom *Okay Jones* • Henry Morgan [Harry Morgan] *Mouthy* ■ *Dir* Bruce Humberstone [H Bruce Humberstone] • *Scr* Lamar Trotti, from a story by Steve Fisher

T

To the Starry Island ★★★★

Drama 1994 · S Kor · Colour · 99mins

A poet returns to his island to discover that the locals are unwilling to bury his friend's father because of past events. Revisiting familiar places, he recalls the characters that inhabited his childhood and the moment when the Korean War turned everybody into strangers. Demonstrating a mastery of flashback and a keen insight into human interaction, Park Kwang-Su excels himself in the scene where the locals betray each other to invading troops. An affecting and superbly observed study of the impact of war on village life. DP. In Korean with English subtitles.

Moon Sung-Keun *Moon Duk-bae/Moon Chae-ku* • Ahn Sung-kee *Kim Senior/Kim Shul* ■ *Dir* Park Kwang-Su • *Scr* Park Kwang-Su, Lee Chang-Dong, Im Chulwoo

To Trap a Spy ★★★

Spy adventure 1966 · US · Colour · 92mins

The first movie spin-off from the highly successful TV spy show *The Man from UNCLE* also stands as one of the best. Comprising footage from the pilot episode, it contains additional new scenes which focused on turning Napoleon Solo, played with devilish charm by Robert Vaughn, into a playboy about town. Poor old David McCallum as sidekick Illya Kuryakin hardly gets a look in. The *femme fatale* quota was also enhanced to spice up the box office. Never mind the thin plot – UNCLE agents must protect a visiting African diplomat from assassination – just feel the nostalgia. RS. Contains violence.

Robert Vaughn *Napoleon Solo* • David McCallum *Illya Kuryakin* • Patricia Crowley [Pat Crowley] *Elaine May Donaldson* • Fritz Weaver *Vulcan* • Luciana Paluzzi *Angela* • William Marshall (2) *Ashumen* • Will Kuluva *Mr Allison* ■ *Dir* Don Medford • *Scr* Sam Rolfe

To Walk with Lions ★★★★ 12

Biographical drama
1999 · Can/UK/Ken · Colour · 105mins

Grittier and less sentimental than the original, this fine follow-up to *Born Free* stars Richard Harris as an ageing George Adamson, long separated from wife Joy, but still enjoying life with the lions despite the predations of poachers and the grudging tolerance of the Kenyan government. The story is seen through the eyes of an English backpacker (John Michie), who chronicles Adamson's life up to his brutal killing by poachers in 1989. The leonine-looking Harris delivers a towering lead performance. DA. Contains swearing, violence and a sex scene. DVD

Richard Harris *George Adamson* • John Michie *Tony Fitzjohn* • Ian Bannen *Terence Adamson* • Kerry Fox *Lucy Jackson* • Hugh Quarshie *Maxwell* • Honor Blackman *Joy Adamson* • Geraldine Chaplin *Victoria Andrecelli* ■ *Dir* Carl Schultz • *Scr* Sharon Buckingham, Keith Ross Leckie

To Wong Foo, Thanks for Everything, Julie Newmar ★★★ PG

Comedy 1995 · US · Colour · 103mins

America's riposte to *The Adventures of Priscilla, Queen of the Desert* is a good concept in search of a plot. The concept? Dress macho movie stars Patrick Swayze and Wesley Snipes in evening gowns, sit back, and watch the camp laughs roll in. And sometimes they do. The plot? Three New York drag queens on the road to Hollywood get stuck in small-town America. Although sentimentally shallow, Beeban Kidron's frock opera is diverting enough. AJ. Contains violence and swearing. DVD

Wesley Snipes *Noxeema Jackson* • Patrick Swayze *Vida Boheme* • John Leguizamo *Chi Chi Rodriguez* • Stockard Channing *Carol Ann* • Blythe Danner *Beatrice* • Arliss Howard *Virgil* • Jason London *Bobby Ray* • Chris Penn *Sheriff Dollard* • Melinda Dillon *Merna* • Beth Grant *Loretta* ■ *Dir* Beeban Kidron • *Scr* Douglas Carter

The Toast of New Orleans ★★★ U

Musical drama 1950 · US · Colour · 96mins

Tenor Mario Lanza's second starring role (the first was in the previous year's *That Midnight Kiss*) again teams him with glamorous co-star Kathryn Grayson. This was the film that helped him become a household name, belting out the momentous *Be My Love* at every possible opportunity, as he portrays a singing fisherman discovered by suave impresario David Niven. Lanza's next film was the smash hit *The Great Caruso*, and the seeds of both his stardom and his self-destruction were duly sown. TS

Kathryn Grayson *Suzette Micheline* • Mario Lanza *Pepe Abellard Duvalle* • David Niven *Jacques Riboudeaux* • J Carrol Naish *Nicky Duvalle* • James Mitchell *Pierre* • Richard Hageman *Maestro P Trellini* ■ *Dir* Norman Taurog • *Scr* Sy Gomberg, George Wells

The Toast of New York ★★★ U

Biographical drama 1937 · US · BW · 104mins

Rotund character actor Edward Arnold makes a strong fist of the leading role of the American 19th-century entrepreneur John Fisk, but the thunder (and there's quite a lot of that!) is stolen from Arnold by juvenile leads Cary Grant and Frances Farmer. Grant glides through the role of Fisk's partner, revealing that graceful quality that would serve him well, but he seems far too contemporary for this biopic, which, as Hollywood has a tendency to do, plays fast and loose with the known facts. TS

Edward Arnold *Jim Fisk* • Cary Grant *Nick Boyd* • Frances Farmer *Josie Mansfield* • Jack Oakie *Luke* • Donald Meek *Daniel Drew* • Thelma Leeds *Fleurique* • Clarence Kolb *Cornelius Vanderbilt* ■ *Dir* Rowland V Lee • *Scr* Dudley Nichols, John Twist, Joel Sayre, from the book *Book of Daniel Drew* by Bouck White, from the story *Robber Barons* by Matthew Josephson

Tobacco Road ★★★

Drama 1941 · US · BW · 84mins

Erskine Caldwell's novel was a solid sensation in its day, uncovering the (literal) dirt on a Georgia backwoods community, and went on to become an amazingly long-running Broadway success. When 20th Century-Fox filmed the piece, it wisely retained Charley Grapewin to repeat his role as the head of a clan beset by financial woes and seemingly incapable of sorting out its problems. He's terrific, but the studio settings look uncomfortably phony today, and Fox's resident beauty Gene Tierney looks strained and out of place. Darkly comic. TS

Charley Grapewin *Jeeter Lester* • Marjorie Rambeau *Sister Bessie* • Gene Tierney *Ellie May Lester* • William Tracy *Duke Lester* • Elizabeth Patterson *Ada Lester* • Dana Andrews *Dr Tim* ■ *Dir* John Ford • *Scr* Nunnally Johnson, from the play by Jack Kirkland, from the novel by Erskine Caldwell

Tobruk ★★★ PG

Second World War adventure
1966 · US · Colour · 104mins

Rock Hudson is in a decidedly Hollywood backlot North Africa, surrounded by assorted British war-film veterans, having a go at blowing up Rommel's fuel lines. While director Arthur Hiller makes it heavy going, it's watchable, thanks to the interesting screenplay by actor Leo V Gordon (who also appears in the film). The action scenes were used again in the Richard Burton action adventure *Raid on Rommel*. TS

Rock Hudson *Major Donald Craig* • George Peppard *Capt Kurt Bergman* • Nigel Green *Colonel John Harker* • Guy Stockwell *Lt Max Mohnfeld* • Jack Watson *Sgt Major Tyne* • Norman Rossington *Alfie* • Percy Herbert *Dolan* • Leo Gordon *Sgt Krug* ■ *Dir* Arthur Hiller • *Scr* Leo V Gordon

Toby Tyler, or Ten Weeks with a Circus ★★ Uc

Adventure 1960 · US · Colour · 90mins

Disney regular Kevin Corcoran is the young lad who succeeds in doing what most children dream of: swap life at home for the excitement of the circus. It's an easy-going if dated adventure, but the performances are pleasing and the youngsters will lap it up. JF

Kevin Corcoran *Toby Tyler* • Henry Calvin *Ben Cotter* • Gene Sheldon *Sam Treat* • Bob Sweeney *Harry Tupper* • Richard Eastham *Colonel Sam Castle* • James Drury *Jim Weaver* • Barbara Beaird *Mademoiselle Jeanette* ■ *Dir* Charles Barton • *Scr* Bill Walsh, Lillie Hayward, from the novel by James Otis Kaler

Today It's Me... Tomorrow You! ★★★ 15

Spaghetti western 1968 · It · Colour · 90mins

Although better known as one of the masters of "yellow" (*giallo*) horror, Dario Argento was no mug when it came to spaghetti westerns. Here, with director Tonino Cervi, he has concocted a rattling tale of revenge, deception and greed, that looks superb. Brett Halsey stars as an ex-jailbird who hires a gunslinging quartet to hunt the man who framed him. But he is outshone by Bud Spencer, who represses most of his comic instincts to give a performance of polished villainy. DP. Italian dialogue dubbed into English.

Montgomery Ford [Brett Halsey] *Bill Kiowa* • Bud Spencer *O'Bannion* • William Berger *Colt Moran* • Tatsuya Nakadai *Elfrego* • Wayde Preston *Jeff Milton* ■ *Dir* Tonino Cervi • *Scr* Dario Argento, Tonino Cervi

Today We Live ★★★

First World War romance
1933 · US · BW · 110mins

A First World War drama in which Joan Crawford, deeply attached to her brother Franchot Tone and engaged to her childhood sweetheart Robert Young, falls in love with Gary Cooper. All four end up on active service in France where, between air battles and tragedy, the complicated emotional triangle is played out. Co-scripted by William Faulkner and directed by Howard Hawks, this is surely one of the weirdest films ever made. The plot defies credibility at almost every turn, and the intimate scenes of high drama between the protagonists are written and spoken in a curiously clipped, semi-poetical shorthand. This is a real oddity, but an interesting one. RK

Joan Crawford *Diana Boyce-Smith* • Gary Cooper *Richard Bogard* • Robert Young (1) *Claude* • Franchot Tone *Ronnie Boyce-Smith* • Roscoe Karns *McGinnis* • Louise Closser Hale *Applegate* • Rollo Lloyd *Major* • Hilda Vaughn *Eleanor* ■ *Dir* Howard Hawks • *Scr* Edith Fitzgerald, Dwight Taylor, William Faulkner, from the story *Turn About* by William Faulkner

The Todd Killings ★★

Crime drama 1971 · US · Colour · 90mins

Director Barry Shear followed the satirical *Wild in the Streets* with this provocative study of another sort of teen "idol". Here, it's a young man in a small American town, adored by the girls, who despises the world that he sees and becomes a serial killer. Robert F Lyons plays this unremorseful character as coolly (or blandly) as possible while Shear's direction is thrustingly energetic. AE

Robert F Lyons *Skipper Todd* • Richard Thomas *Billy Roy* • Belinda J Montgomery *Roberta* • Barbara Bel Geddes *Mrs Todd* • Sherry Miles *Amata* • Joyce Ames *Haddie* • Holly Near *Norma* • James Broderick *Sam* • Gloria Grahame *Mrs Roy* • Fay Spain *Mrs Mack* • Edward Asner *Fred Reardon* ■ *Dir* Barry Shear • *Scr* Dennis Murphy, Joel Oliansky, from a story by Mann Rubin

Together ★★★ 15

Comedy drama
2000 · Swe/Den/It · Colour · 101mins

Life on a commune in the mid-1970s may seem like a soft target, but Swedish director Lukas Moodysson isn't interested in the obvious. There's plenty of *laissez-faire* liberalism in the attitudes of the chunky sweatered leader and his kaftan-wearing acolytes. Yet, amid all the dope-smoking and free-loving permissiveness, there's a real sense of socio-political conflict as human nature intrudes upon the idyll. Exploring the group's self-satisfied moral rectitude and their blithe disregard for how this alternative lifestyle will impact on their children, Moodysson provides a shrewd and sympathetic insight into the era. DP. In Swedish with English subtitles. VIDEO DVD

Lisa Lindgren *Elisabeth* • Michael Nyqvist *Rolf* • Gustav Hammarsten *Göran* • Anja Lundqvist *Lena* • Jessica Liedberg *Anna* • Ola Norell *Lasse* ■ *Dir/Scr* Lukas Moodysson

Together Again ★★★

Romantic comedy 1944 · US · BW · 99mins

The title unashamedly refers to the reteaming of Irene Dunne and Charles Boyer, the hit duo of *Love Affair* and *When Tomorrow Comes*, but this time eschewing the tempestuous storms of romantic melodrama for the shenanigans of romantic comedy. She plays the widowed mayoress of a New England town; he is a New York sculptor commissioned, at the suggestion of Dunne's cupid-playing father-in-law Charles Coburn, to cast a new statue of her late husband, the former mayor. Featherweight fun. RK

Irene Dunne *Anne Crandall* • Charles Boyer *George Corday* • Charles Coburn *Jonathan Crandall Sr* • Mona Freeman *Diana Crandall* • Jerome Courtland *Gilbert Parker* • Elizabeth Patterson *Jessie* • Charles Dingle *Morton Buchman* • Walter Baldwin *Witherspoon* ■ *Dir* Charles Vidor • *Scr* Virginia Van Upp, F Hugh Herbert, from a story by Stanley Russell, Herbert J Biberman

Together with You ★★★ PG

Drama 2002 · Chi · Colour · 113mins

Music has been an important feature of Chen Kaige's films since *Life on a String*. Yet, despite this Beijing melodrama turning around a provincial peasant who sacrifices all so that his son can study the violin, the unforced sincerity and acute insight of his early work continues to elude a director caught between China's dramatic socio-economic transformation and his own international art house celebrity. However, Liu Peiqi and Tang Yun are charmingly credible as proud father and teenage prodigy, while Wang Zhiwen and Chen Hong provide genial support as an eccentric genius and a good-time girl with a conscience. DP. In Mandarin with English subtitles. DVD

Liu Peiqi *Liu Cheng* • Tang Yun *Liu Xiaochun* • Chen Hong *Lili* • Wang Zhiwen *Professor Jiang* • Chen Kaige *Professor Yu Shifeng* • Cheng Qian *Hui, Lili's lover* ■ *Dir* Chen Kaige • *Scr* Chen Kaige, Xue Xiaolu

Tokyo Chorus ★★★★

Silent comedy drama
1931 · Jpn · BW · 91mins

Yasujiro Ozu was in his 20s and still refining his style when he directed this, so there is slightly more camera movement and overtly "cinematic" technique than in his later, greater sound works. Still, it's recognisably Ozu in its concern with family life – here given an extra dimension since the story tells of a man (Tokihiko Okada) who is sacked when he supports an unfairly treated fellow worker. He's forced to look for work in Depression-tainted Tokyo, so the film, which begins light heartedly, gradually darkens into a characteristically humane study of a lower middle-class victim of society. BB

Tokihiko Okada *Shinji Okajima* • Emiko Yagumo *Sugao, Okajima's wife* • Hideo Sugawara *Okajima's son* • Hideko Takamine *Miyoko, Okajima's daughter* • Tatsuo Saito *Omura, Okajima's old teacher* • Choko Iida *Omura's wife* ■ *Dir* Yasujiro Ozu • *Scr* Kogo Noda, from the novel *Tokyo no Gassho* by Komatsu Kitamura

Tokyo Cowboy ★★★

Comedy 1994 · Can · Colour and BW · 94mins

A festival favourite in its native Canada, this charming tale of movie mania and cross-cultural confusion sees Hiromoto Ida as the Japanese fast-food employee who quits his dead-end existence, for a chance to emulate his cowboy heroes in the backwoods home of his Canadian penpal. Neatly played, this warm, funny film owes its greatest debt to director Kathy Garneau and photographer Kenneth Hewlett, who stage Ida's black-and-white western daydreams with considerable skill. DP

Hiromoto Ida *No Ogawa* • Christianne Hirt *Kate Beatty* • Janne Mortil *Shelly* • Alec Willow *Postman* • Anna Ferguson *Kate's mother* ■ *Dir* Kathy Garneau • *Scr* Caroline Anderson

Tokyo Decadence ★★★ 18

Drama 1992 · Jpn · Colour · 84mins

The fourth film directed by Japanese novelist Ryu Murakami recalls *In the Realm of the Senses* in its graphic depiction of sex as a symbol for the nation's decay. Its exposé of a prostitute's relentless degradation (linked only by empty ritual to the romanticised image of the geisha) is made all the more powerful by the clinically unerotic sadomasochism in which timid graduate Miho Nikaido participates with yakuza and businessmen alike. Nikaido's performance is undeniably courageous, but the fragmentary detachment of Murakami's direction precludes involvement. DP. In Japanese with English subtitles. VIDEO DVD

Miho Nikaido *Ai* • Sayoko Amano *Saki* • Masahiko Shimada *Mr Ishioka* ■ *Dir* Ryu Murakami • *Scr* Ryu Murakami, from his novel novel *Topaz*

Tokyo Drifter ★★★★ 12

Cult action thriller
1966 · Jpn · Colour and BW · 80mins

This deliriously contrived yakuza flick earned director Seijun Suzuki a cult following outside a less receptive Japan. Combining elements from hard-boiled pulp, the spaghetti western and the Hollywood musical, this cartoon-like parody of the gangster movie also makes spectacular use of colour, stylised decor and an ambiguous narrative. At the centre of the often surreal mayhem is Tetsuya Watari, whose ambition to quit the rackets is frustrated by his inability to shake either his dark past or the attentions of hitman Hideaki Nitani. DP. In Japanese with English subtitles. VIDEO DVD

Tetsuya Watari *Tetsuya "Phoenix, Tetsu" Hondo* • Chieko Matsubara *Chiharu* • Hideaki Nitani *Kenji Aizawa* • Ryuji Kita *Kurata* • Tsuyoshi Yoshida *Keiichi* • Hideaki Esumi *Otsuka* ■ *Dir* Seijun Suzuki • *Scr* Yasunori Kawauchi, from his novel

Tokyo Fist ★★★★ 18

Action horror drama
1995 · Jpn · Colour · 83mins

This extraordinarily oppressive, raw and gore-drenched tale charts the mental and physical transformation of a wimpy insurance salesman (director Shinya Tsukamoto, who also produced, wrote, shot and edited), his disturbed girlfriend and an old school friend turned rival, a professional boxer. Shot with a darting hand-held camera, Tsukamoto demonstrates mesmerising mastery of light, colour and sound as the trio conflict outside and inside the fight ring in some of the most punishing, bloody fight scenes since *Raging Bull*. JC. In Japanese with English subtitles. Contains sex scenes, swearing, violence. VIDEO DVD

Kahori Fujii *Hizuru* • Kohji Tsukamoto *Kojima Takuji* • Shinya Tsukamoto *Tsuda Yoshiharu* • Naoto Takenaka *Ohizumi, trainer* ■ *Dir* Shinya Tsukamoto • *Scr* Shinya Tsukamoto, from a story by Hisashi Saito, Shinya Tsukamoto

Tokyo Joe ★★★

Melodrama 1949 · US · BW · 88mins

Humphrey Bogart is running a bar in an exotic location and trying to win back his ex-wife Florence Marly, who's gone off and married dull Alexander Knox. It's as uninvolving as it sounds, and dates from that awkward period in Bogart's career between his public recantation that he had no communist tendancies, and his public and industry return to favour with *The African Queen*. The main weakness is the casting of Marly, a totally uncharismatic Franco-Czech actress, but Bogie is, as ever, compulsively watchable. TS

Humphrey Bogart *Joe Barrett* • Alexander Knox *Mark Landis* • Florence Marly *Trina* • Sessue Hayakawa *Baron Kimura* • Jerome Courtland *Danny* • Gordon Jones *Idaho* • Teru Shimada *Ito* ■ *Dir* Stuart Heisler • *Scr* Cyril Hume, Bertram Millhauser, Walter Doniger, from a story by Steve Fisher

Tokyo Olympiad ★★★★

Documentary 1965 · Jpn · Colour · 154mins

The Tokyo Games of 1964 were preserved as a tribute to human athleticism and endurance in this lyrical documentary. Employing 164 camera units, many of which were equipped with especially-devised telephoto and night-vision lenses, Kon Ichikawa was only interested in winners and losers, if they exemplified the spirit of competition. Consequently, he focused on the last-minute preparations of sprinters, the watering techniques of marathon runners and the progress of the Olympic torch. Inspirational stuff. DP VIDEO

Dir Kon Ichikawa • *Scr* Kon Ichikawa, Natto Wada, Yoshio Shiraska, Shuntaro Tanikawa

Tokyo Pop ★★★ 18

Comedy drama 1988 · US · Colour · 98mins

An engaging teen romance that takes some very gentle pot-shots at the differences between East and West. Carrie Hamilton (daughter of actress Carol Burnett), is the impulsive budding singer who swaps New York for Tokyo and finds romance with band leader Yutaka Tadokoro. Fran Rubel Kuzui breathes fresh life into the clichéd story line and directs the proceedings with style, while the two leads turn in winning performances. JF

Carrie Hamilton *Wendy Reed* • Yutaka Tadokoro *Hiro Yamaguchi* • Taiji Tonoyama *Grandfather* • Tetsuro Tanba [Tetsuro Tamba] *Dota* • Masumi Harukawa *Mother* • Toki Shiozawa *Mama-san* • Hiroshi Mikami *Seki* ■ *Dir* Fran Rubel Kuzui • *Scr* Fran Rubel Kuzui, Lynn Grossman, from a story by Fran Rubel Kuzui

Tokyo Raiders ★★ 12

Martial arts action drama
2000 · HK · Colour · 96mins

Set in Japan, this tortuously plotted tale finds jilted bride Kelly Chen travelling to Tokyo to find her fiancé and discovering that he is mixed up with both the Japanese Mob and the CIA. Also along for for the ride are ace private eye Tony Leung and interior decorator Ekin Cheng. There's plenty of inventive martial arts, even if director Jingle Ma does overdo the slow motion a tad. The script, however, is cringe worthy. JF. In Cantonese and Japanese with English subtitles. VIDEO DVD

Tony Leung (2) *Lam* • Ekin Cheng *Yung* • Kelly Chen *Macy* • Cecilia Cheung *Saori* • Toru Nakamura *Takahashi* ■ *Dir* Jingle Ma • *Scr* Susan Chan, Felix Chong

Tokyo Story ★★★★★ U

Drama 1953 · Jpn · BW · 129mins

A moving story, simply and beautifully told. Yasujiro Ozu was a master film-maker who specialised in the kind of middle-class family melodrama known in Japanese as *shomin-geki*, and this one of his finest achievements. Chishu Ryu and Chieko Higashiyama give performances of great dignity as the parents who are rejected by their thankless children. Setsuko Hara, playing the widow of their favourite son, is the epitome of gentleness as the only relative to show them any kindness. Ryu and Hara were regular members of Ozu's acting troupe, and Hara retired from films when the director died in 1963. DP. In Japanese with English subtitles. VIDEO DVD

Chishu Ryu *Shukishi Hirayama* • Chieko Higashiyama *Tomi Hirayama* • Setsuko Hara *Noriko* • So Yamamura *Koichi* • Haruko Sugimura *Shige Kaneko* • Kuniko Miyake *Koichi's wife, Fumiko* ■ *Dir* Yasujiro Ozu • *Scr* Kogo Noda, Yasujiro Ozu

Tokyo Twilight ★★★★★

Drama 1957 · Jpn · BW · 139mins

Yasujiro Ozu's sublime, unassuming genius concerns itself with lower middle-class family life, as a microcosm of society. Stories may smack of melodrama or "soap", but there is no heightened drama or artificiality, simply snatches of conversation stemming from characters and reflections of the sometimes violent aspects of family relationships. In this intense, naturalistic work, he presents a portrait of two daughters living with their father – one in exile from an abusive husband, the other involved in an unhelpful relationship that has lead to pregnancy. The narrative is complicated by the unanticipated return of the family's mother, who had eloped with another man, resulting in distress and decline. BB. In Japanese with English subtitles.

Setsuko Hara *Takako Numata* • Isuzu Yamada *Kisako Soma* • Ineko Arima *Akiko Sugiyama* • Chishu Ryu *Shukichi Sugiyama* • Masami Taura *Kenji Kimura* ■ *Dir* Yasujiro Ozu • *Scr* Yasujiro Ozu, Kogo Noda

T

Tol'able David ★★★★

Silent melodrama 1921 · US · BW · 118mins

One of the best of Henry King's simple, nostalgic evocations of rural and small town America, the film gave 26-year-old Richard Barthelmess his finest role. He plays a gentle mailman living happily in Greenstream Valley until his idyll is disturbed by a family of fugitives from justice. He defends the community, becomes a hero and wins the girl. Beautifully shot on location in the Virginia mountains. RB

Richard Barthelmess *David Kinemon* • Gladys Hulette *Esther Hatburn* • Walter P Lewis *Iscah Hatburn* • Ernest Torrence *Luke Hatburn* • Ralph Yearsley *Luke's brother* • Forrest Robinson *Grandpa Hatburn* ■ *Dir* Henry King • *Scr* Edmund Goulding, Henry King, from the short story by Joseph Hergesheimer • *Cinematographer* Henry Cronjager

Tol'able David ★★

Melodrama 1930 · US · BW · 65mins

What worked through the inspired casting and eloquent direction of the 1921 silent masterpiece fails to make a similar impression in this fairly close talkie re-make. Adding spoken dialogue to the dramatic story of feuding families in rural America only makes it seem more old-fashioned and obvious. Richard Cromwell has the earnestness, but not the expressive qualities of Richard Barthelmess as he takes over the role of the boy who is branded a coward. AE

Richard Cromwell *David Kinemon* • Noah Beery Sr [Noah Beery] *Luke* • Joan Peers *Esther Hatburn* • Henry B Walthall *Amos Hatburn* • George Duryea [Tom Keene] *Tom Keene* • Alan Kinemon *Edmund Breese* • Barbara Bedford *Rose Kinemon* • Helen Ware *Mrs Kinemon* ■ *Dir* John Blystone [John G Blystone] • *Scr* Benjamin Glazer, from a story by Joseph Hergesheimer

Tollbooth ★★★★

Comedy drama 1994 · US · Colour · 108mins

A bona-fide "sleeper" of a movie, which all but disappeared after making quite a splash at Cannes 1994. In this dark, comic fable of Florida roadside life, Fairuza Balk is Doris, who has been waiting 20 years for her father, a cab driver, to return home. Her mother, Louise Fletcher, also awaits his return, though it transpires he was quite an unsavoury character. Balk's boyfriend, Lenny Von Dohlen, is a tollbooth attendant who takes snapshots of every cab to pass through the booth, determined to locate her father. The story, however, is secondary to the quirky style of the piece and director Salome Breziner serves up a sizzling slice of dysfunctional life. DF

Fairuza Balk *Doris* • Lenny Von Dohlen *Jack* • Will Patton *Dash* • Louise Fletcher *Lillian* • Seymour Cassel *Larry/Leon* • James Wilder *Vic* • William Katt *Waggy* • Roberta Hanley *Twyla* ■ *Dir/Scr* Salome Breziner

Tom and Huck ★★★ PG

Adventure 1995 · US · Colour · 88mins

Yet another adaptation of Mark Twain's classic story of the Missouri scamps who witness a graveyard killing and get caught up in the subsequent wrongful arrest and court case. Brad Renfro is a suitably mischievous Huck, but it's Jonathan Taylor Thomas who makes the better impression as the more responsible Tom Sawyer. Disney take typical care with the trappings, but Norman Taurog's 1938 version (*The Adventures of Tom Sawyer*) remains the best one to date. DP

Jonathan Taylor Thomas *Tom Sawyer* • Brad Renfro *Huck Finn* • Eric Schweig *Injun Joe* • Charles Rocket *Judge Thatcher* • Amy Wright *Aunt Polly* • Micheal McShane *Muff Potter* • Marian Seldes *Widow Douglas* • Rachael Leigh Cook *Becky Thatcher* ■ *Dir* Peter Hewitt • *Scr* Stephen Sommers, David Loughery, from the novel *The Adventures of Tom Sawyer* by Mark Twain

Tom and Jerry: the Movie ★★ U

Animation 1992 · US · Colour · 80mins

Having starred in 161 cartoons, won numerous Oscars and danced with Gene Kelly and Esther Williams, surely Tom and Jerry deserved more respect than this. Director Phil Roman and writer Dennis Marks should have Spike the bulldog set upon them for making the now-talking duo become friends in adversity. The whole point of those marvellous shorts was the comic mayhem, not the tacky bonhomie. Children who are not familiar with the original cartoons may find some enjoyment here – if they can get past the ghastly songs. DP

Richard Kind *Tom* • Dana Hill *Jerry* • Anndi Lynn McAfee [Anndi McAfee] *Robyn Starling* • Charlotte Rae *Aunt Figg* • Tony Jay *Lickboot* • Henry Gibson *Dr Applecheek* ■ *Dir* Phil Roman • *Scr* Dennis Marks, from characters created by William Hanna, Joseph Barbera

Tom & Viv ★★★ 15

Biographical drama
1994 · US/UK · Colour · 119mins

Willem Dafoe stars as Tom, otherwise known as the poet TS Eliot, and Miranda Richardson plays Viv, the society girl who marries him and ends up in a lunatic asylum. While she lets rip with a suitable display of madness, Dafoe behaves quietly and poetically, before locking her up and getting out his pen. Well done, although it often looks and sounds like a play, which it was. AT. Contains swearing.

Miranda Richardson *Vivienne Haigh-Wood* • Willem Dafoe *TS "Tom" Eliot* • Tim Dutton *Maurice Haigh-Wood* • Nickolas Grace *Bertrand Russell* • Clare Holman *Louise Purdon* • Rosemary Harris *Rose Haigh-Wood* • Philip Locke *Charles Haigh-Wood* • Joanna McCallum *Virginia Woolfe* ■ *Dir* Brian Gilbert • *Scr* Michael Hastings, Adrian Hodges, from the play by Michael Hastings

Tom Brown's Schooldays ★★ U

Drama 1940 · US · BW · 81mins

Rugby School relocates to the Bowery for this RKO adaptation of Thomas Hughes's novel. This is more about taming street urchins than reforming the iniquities of 19th-century public schooling, a fact confirmed by the presence of Dead End Kid Billy Halop as Flashman. Oozing with liberal sentimentality, the script emphasises the saintly deeds of Cedric Hardwicke's Dr Arnold, rather than the suffering of our hero. Of the boys, Freddie Bartholomew is less Fauntleroyish than usual, while Jimmy Lydon is out of his depth as Tom. DP

Cedric Hardwicke *Dr Thomas Arnold* • Freddie Bartholomew *East* • Jimmy Lydon [James Lydon] *Tom Brown* • Josephine Hutchinson *Mrs Arnold* • Billy Halop *Flashman* ■ *Dir* Robert Stevenson • *Scr* Walter Ferris, Frank Cavett, Gene Towne, Graham Baker, Robert Stevenson, from the novel by Thomas Hughes

Tom Brown's Schooldays ★★★ U

Drama 1951 · UK · BW · 94mins

Shot on location at Rugby School, this is a reverential, if rather lacklustre, rendition of Thomas Hughes's famous portrait of public school life. Robert Newton gives a performance of almost saintly sincerity as the headmaster intent on ridding his school of class prejudice and bullying. John Howard Davies does a nice line in smiling through the tears as Tom Brown, but the film belongs squarely to John Forrest, who, as Flashman, is the epitome of vicious snobbery. DP

John Howard Davies *Tom Brown* • Robert Newton *Doctor Arnold* • Diana Wynyard *Mrs Arnold* • Hermione Baddeley *Sally Harrowell* • Kathleen Byron *Mrs Brown* • James Hayter *Old Thomas* • John Charlesworth *East* • John Forrest *Flashman* • Michael Hordern *Wilkes* • Max Bygraves *Coach guard* ■ *Dir* Gordon Parry • *Scr* Noel Langley, from the novel by Thomas Hughes

Tom, Dick and Harry ★★★ U

Comedy 1941 · US · BW · 82mins

Here, Ginger Rogers is choosing between the three characters of the title, but her character's rather mercenary nature makes her ultimately hard to like. Will she marry for love or money or both. In fact, the bloke we end up rooting for is Phil Silvers's obnoxious ice-cream man, a clear precursor of Sergeant Bilko. With hindsight, perhaps writer Paul Jarrico, was trying to make some pertinent points about capitalism (he was later blacklisted), but director Garson Kanin just keeps the pace fast and the laughter flowing. Remade in 1957 as *The Girl Most Likely*. TS

Ginger Rogers *Janie* • George Murphy *Tom* • Alan Marshal *Dick Hamilton* • Burgess Meredith *Harry* • Joe Cunningham *Pop* • Jane Seymour (1) *Ma* • Leonore Lonergan *Babs* • Vicki Lester *Paula* • Phil Silvers *Ice Cream Man* ■ *Dir* Garson Kanin • *Scr* Paul Jarrico

Tom Horn ★★★ 15

Biographical western
1980 · US · Colour · 93mins

When Steve McQueen knew that his cancer was terminal, he swiftly made two features (the other was *The Hunter*) after a long period of chosen inactivity. This western is a good deal better than it deserves to be, given that McQueen fell out with the credited, relatively inexperienced director William Wiard, and the shoot was ramshackle, with pages of the script discarded daily. Nevertheless, this is extremely well photographed (by John Alonzo), with stunning landscapes, and McQueen captures the grim, realistic mood perfectly. TS. Contains swearing.

Steve McQueen *Tom Horn* • Linda Evans *Glendolene Kimmel* • Richard Farnsworth *John Coble* • Billy Green Bush *Joe Belle* • Slim Pickens *Sam Creedmore* ■ *Dir* William Wiard • *Scr* Thomas McGuane, Bud Shrake

Tom Jones ★★★★ PG

Period comedy adventure
1963 · UK · Colour · 116mins

This massively popular period romp carted off four Oscars, including best picture and best director. It was always arch, overlong and uncertain of tone, but nevertheless very funny and extraordinarily bawdy, especially in the notorious eating scene between Albert Finney (as Tom) and Joyce Redman. Technically, the film was massively influential and the desaturated colour, speeded-up action and lewd narration characterised the 1960s "Swinging England" cinema, and attracted all of the Hollywood majors to come and make movies here. TS DVD

Albert Finney *Tom Jones* • Susannah York *Sophie Western* • Hugh Griffith *Squire Western* • Edith Evans *Miss Western* • Diane Cilento *Molly Seagrim* • George Devine *Squire Allworthy* • David Warner *Blifil* • Lynn Redgrave *Susan* ■ *Dir* Tony Richardson • *Scr* John Osborne, from the novel *The History of Tom Jones, a Foundling* by Henry Fielding

Tom Sawyer ★★★

Adventure 1930 · US · BW · 85mins

The first of several sound versions of Mark Twain's novel – it was filmed as a silent in 1917 with Mary Pickford's brother, Jack, in the title role. In this version, Jackie Coogan plays Tom and at the age of only 16 it marked his screen comeback, for he had not made a film for three years. Huck Finn is played by Junior Durkin and both lads starred in the sequel, *Huckleberry Finn*, the following year. Off the set they were firm friends, but tragedy struck in 1935 when Durkin was killed in a car crash and Coogan was the only survivor. AT

Jackie Coogan *Tom Sawyer* • Junior Durkin *Huckleberry Finn* • Mitzi Green *Becky Thatcher* • Lucien Littlefield *Teacher* • Tully Marshall *Muff Potter* • Clara Blandick *Aunt Polly* • Mary Jane Irving *Mary* • Ethel Wales *Mrs Harper* • Jane Darwell *Widow Douglass* ■ *Dir* John Cromwell • *Scr* Sam Mintz, Grover Jones, William Slavens McNutt, from the novel *The Adventures of Tom Sawyer* by Mark Twain

Tom Sawyer ★★★★ U

Musical period adventure
1973 · US · Colour · 102mins

Co-financed by *Reader's Digest*, this is a simply marvellous children's version of Mark Twain's oft-filmed classic about two orphaned chillun – Tom and his pal, Huckleberry Finn – and life on the Mississippi riverbanks. All the famous scenes – like Tom's painting of the picket fence and the nocturnal body-snatching – are filmed just as they are described in the book. There are some dispensable songs, but what counts is the beautifully evocative photography, two nicely modulated juvenile performances and Warren Oates enjoying himself as the local drunkard. *Reader's Digest* also produced *Huckleberry Finn*, released the following year. AT

Johnny Whitaker *Tom Sawyer* • Celeste Holm *Aunt Polly* • Warren Oates *Muff Potter* • Jeff East *Huckleberry Finn* • Jodie Foster *Becky Thatcher* • Kunu Hank *Injun Joe* • Lucille Benson *Widder Douglas* • Henry Jones *Mr Dobbins* ■ *Dir* Don Taylor • *Scr* Robert B Sherman, Richard M Sherman, from the novel *The Adventures of Tom Sawyer* by Mark Twain • *Cinematographer* Frank Stanley

tom thumb ★★★★ U

Fantasy musical
1958 · US/UK · Colour · 95mins

The endearing and enduring MGM musical fantasy version of the Brothers Grimm fairy tale, made by Puppetoon king and special effects wizard George Pal, and partly shot at MGM's British studios. Technically this is a treat, with wonderfully acrobatic dancer Russ Tamblyn perfectly cast as the minuscule hero who brings joy to his elderly parents (Bernard Miles and Jessie Matthews). The production sequences are splendid entertainment for children of all ages, and Peter Sellers and Terry-Thomas make a very hissable pair of pantomime villains. The effects won an Oscar. TS

Russ Tamblyn *Tom Thumb* • Alan Young *Woody the piper* • Terry-Thomas *Ivan* • Peter Sellers *Tony* • Jessie Matthews *Anna* • June Thorburn *Forest Queen* • Bernard Miles *Jonathan* • Ian Wallace *Cobbler* • Peter Butterworth *Kapellmeister* ■ *Dir* George Pal • *Scr* Ladislas Foder, from the story by the Brothers Grimm

Tomahawk ★★★

Western 1951 · US · Colour · 82mins

Following the critical acclaim for 1950's *Broken Arrow*, Hollywood sought to present the native American in a more positive light. But, as this tale of betrayal and slaughter shows, old habits die hard and, even though director George Sherman emphasises the treachery of various soldiers, traders and politicians, the Sioux are once again depicted as savage warriors. Peace-loving scout Van Heflin reveals a more liberal attitude, but even he is more interested in the firepower of the new breach-loading rifle than race relations. DP

Van Heflin *Jim Bridger* • Yvonne De Carlo *Julie Madden* • Preston Foster *Col Carrington* • Jack Oakie *Sol Beckworth* • Alex Nicol *Lt Rob Dancy* • Tom Tully *Dan Costello* • Ann Doran *Mrs Carrington* • Rock Hudson *Burt Hanna* • Susan Cabot *Monahseetah* ■ *Dir* George Sherman • *Scr* Silvia Richards, Maurice Geraghty, from a story by Daniel Jarrett

The Tomb of Ligeia ★★★★

Horror 1964 · UK · Colour · 81mins

Stunningly photographed by Arthur Grant at an ancient Norfolk abbey, the last in Roger Corman's celebrated Edgar Allan Poe cycle is unquestionably one of the best. Set in England in the 1820s, the film departs somewhat from Poe's original tale, but there's a distinct chill in the air as Vincent Price

T

believes his new bride has been possessed by the evil spirit of his late first wife (both played by Elizabeth Shepherd). With more than a nod in the direction of Hitchcock's *Vertigo* (both in terms of theme and denouement), this stylish picture also marked Corman's temporary retirement as a horror director until *Frankenstein Unbound* in 1990. DP

Vincent Price *Verden Fell* • Elizabeth Shepherd *Lady Ligeia Fell/Lady Rowena Trevanion* • John Westbrook *Christopher Gough* • Oliver Johnston *Kenrick* • Derek Francis *Lord Trevanion* • Richard Vernon *Dr Vivian* ■ *Dir* Roger Corman • *Scr* Robert Towne, from the story *Ligeia* by Edgar Allan Poe

Tomboy ★ 15

Drama 1985 · US · Colour · 90mins

A dire *Flashdance*-style drama without the hit soundtrack, this is the tale of a female garage mechanic who finds her feminine side when she falls in love, but displays her macho tendencies when she decides to compete in the Daytona 500 in a car of her own design. Eric Douglas (son of Kirk, brother of Michael), is the villain of the piece, proving he has inherited none of his family's talent for acting. JB. Contains swearing and nudity. [Video]

Betsy Russell *Tommy Boyd* • Jerry Dinome *Randy Starr* • Kristi Somers *Seville Ritz* • Richard Erdman *Chester* • Eric Douglas *Ernie Leeds Jr* ■ *Dir* Herb Freed • *Scr* Ben Zelig, from an idea by Mark Tenser

Tomboy and the Champ ★★ U

Comedy drama 1961 · US · Colour · 76mins

Candy Moore turns in a willing performance as the 13-year-old Texan girl who befriends a calf while recovering from polio on uncle Ben Johnson's farm. However, there are also a few hard facts of country life to be learned after their victory at the Chicago International Exposition attracts the wrong kind of attention. Directed with shameless sentimentality. DP

Candy Moore *Tommy Jo* • Ben Johnson *Uncle Jim* • Jesse White *Windy Skiles* • Jess Kirkpatrick *Model T Parson* • Christine Smith *Aunt Sarah* • Paul Bernath *Jaspar Stockton* • Norman Sherry *Fowler Stockton* ■ *Dir* Francis D Lyon • *Scr* Virginia M Cooke, from a story by Tommy Reynolds, William Lightfoot

Tombstone ★★★★ 15

Western
1993 · US · Colour and BW · 124mins

Right from the dazzling opening of Robert Mitchum narrating over silent, black-and-white western footage accompanied by Bruce Broughton's expectant score, before the screen explodes into colour, this take on the Wyatt Earp legend never shifts out of top gear. This is very much a traditional western and far preferable to the rather self-important and overlong Kevin Costner version, *Wyatt Earp*, released later the same year. Kurt Russell makes a satisfyingly equivocal hero, while Val Kilmer has a field day in the showier role as the consumptive Doc Holliday. The film was sharply scripted by Kevin Jarre, who was abruptly sacked as director and replaced by George Pan Cosmatos. AT. Contains swearing and violence. [Video] DVD

Kurt Russell *Wyatt Earp* • Val Kilmer *Doc Holliday* • Sam Elliott *Virgil Earp* • Bill Paxton *Morgan Earp* • Powers Boothe *Curly Bill Brocius* • Michael Biehn *Johnny Ringo* • Charlton Heston *Henry Hooker* • Jason Priestley *Deputy Sheriff Billy Breckenridge* • Robert Mitchum *Narrator* ■ *Dir* George Pan Cosmatos • *Scr* Kevin Jarre

Tomcats ★★ 15

Comedy 2000 · US · Colour · 90mins

This crude, obnoxious comedy piles on gross-out humour, but mostly leaves a sour taste in the mouth. Heavily in debt to a Las Vegas gangster, Jerry O'Connell resorts to nefarious means to pocket the cash prize that will be awarded to the last single man among his friends. There's lots of surreal, cartoonish slapstick moments and no sick stone is left unturned. However, even with a game cast and a parade of fantasy women, there are far more misses than hits. JC [Video] DVD

Jerry O'Connell *Michael Delaney* • Shannon Elizabeth *Natalie Parker* • Jake Busey *Kyle Brenner* • Horatio Hanz *Steve* • Jaime Pressly *Tricia* • Bill Maher *Carlos* • David Ogden Stiers *Dr Crawford* ■ *Dir/Scr* Gregory Poirier

Tommy ★★★ 15

Musical 1975 · UK · Colour · 106mins

The Who's rock opera, about "a deaf, dumb and blind kid" who becomes an exploited "pinball wizard", gets the inimitable Ken Russell treatment, which is no more than it deserves. For, while eye-popping excess – what's done to Ann-Margret is unforgivable – keeps us watching, the story is as absurd as the grotesque nature of its telling. Stridency, both vocal and visual, is all, and Roger Daltrey's Tommy is flattened by the weight of celebrity. Elton John has the best of it, thumping away on a piano as though trying to prove something, rather like Ken Russell himself. TH [Video] DVD

Roger Daltrey *Tommy Walker* • Oliver Reed *Frank Hobbs* • Ann-Margret *Nora Walker Hobbs* • Elton John *Pinball Wizard* • Eric Clapton *Preacher* • Keith Moon *Uncle Ernie* • Jack Nicholson *Specialist* • Robert Powell *Group Captain Walker* • Paul Nicholas *Cousin Kevin* • Tina Turner *Acid Queen* ■ *Dir* Ken Russell • *Scr* Ken Russell, from the rock opera by Pete Townsend and The Who • *Cinematographer* Dick Bush, Ronnie Taylor

Tommy Boy ★★★ 12

Comedy 1995 · US · Colour · 93mins

Chris Farley's tragic career closely mirrored that of John Belushi's: fame on *Saturday Night Live*, an aversion to healthy pursuits and a young death at the age of 33. But he never had the *Blues Brothers* or *Animal House*-style success of his more famous contemporary, and most of his films disappeared quickly from view. This is about the best of the bunch: a big, dumb comedy about Farley's attempts to save the family business from gold-digger Bo Derek. Subtle it ain't, but there are enough gross moments to raise a few laughs. JF [Video] DVD

Chris Farley *Tommy* • David Spade *Richard* • Brian Dennehy *Big Tom* • Bo Derek *Beverly* • Dan Aykroyd *Zalinsky* • Julie Warner *Michelle* • Rob Lowe *Paul* ■ *Dir* Peter Segal • *Scr* Bonnie Turner, Terry Turner, Fred Wolf

The Tommy Steele Story ★★ U

Musical biography
1957 · UK · Colour · 77mins

Who else would have been able to carry the life story (such as it was after 21 years) of Britain's first rock'n'roll star, Tommy Steele, but the Bermondsey boy himself? Following young Tommy Hicks from his humble beginnings, through his days at sea to the contract with Decca and that breakthrough single *Rock with the Caveman*, this is an unremarkable meteoric rise story, not made any easier to swallow by Steele's swaggering performance. DP [Video]

Tommy Steele *Tommy* • Patrick Westwood *Brushes* • Hilda Fenemore *Tommy's mother* • Charles Lamb *Tommy's father* • Peter Lewiston *John Kennedy* ■ *Dir* Gerard Bryant • *Scr* Norman Hudis

Tommy the Toreador ★★★ U

Musical comedy 1959 · UK · Colour · 83mins

Perky pop star Tommy Steele, a former seaman himself, plays the part of a sailor in this lively and likeable musical comedy. The film concerns Steele's adventures after he saves the life of a bullfighter while on leave in Spain. Comic consequences include Tommy having to take the toreador's place and confronting a bull in the ring. A nice variety of songs intersperse the amusing events. TV [Video]

Tommy Steele *Tommy* • Janet Munro *Amanda* • Sidney James *Cadena* • Bernard Cribbins *Paco* • Kenneth Williams *Vice Consul* • Eric Sykes *Martin* • Warren Mitchell *Waiter* • Charles Gray *Gomez* ■ *Dir* John Paddy Carstairs • *Scr* Nicholas Phipps, Sid Colin, Talbot Rothwell, from a story by George H Brown, Patrick Kirwan

Tommy Tricker and the Stamp Traveller ★ U

Fantasy 1988 · Can · Colour · 101mins

After classmate Tommy Tricker swindles him into trading his father's rare stamp, a boy sets off on a magical journey halfway around the world to find a replacement using a magic spell that enables him to travel on stamps. More than half of this excruciatingly slow movie goes by before the journey actually starts, and the on-location shooting in China and Australia is remarkably uninspired. Even for such a young cast, the acting is remarkably poor. KB

Lucas Evans *Ralph* • Anthony Rogers *Tommy* • Jill Stanley *Nancy* • Andrew Whitehead *Albert* ■ *Dir/Scr* Michael Rubbo

Tomorrow ★★★★

Drama 1972 · US · BW · 103mins

Has Robert Duvall ever made a truly bad film? If so, this isn't it. Instead, it's Duvall firing on all cylinders in a fine adaptation of a lesser-known William Faulkner story. He plays a handyman who falls for a pregnant woman who mysteriously turns up at his place of work. The girl is played equally brilliantly by Olga Bellin, who seems to have since vanished without trace. Like her, the film is rarely seen, but worth seeking out. DA

Robert Duvall *Jackson Fentry* • Olga Bellin *Sarah Eubanks* • Sudie Bond *Mrs Hulie* • Richard McConnell *Isham Russell* • Peter Masterson *Lawyer* • William Hawley *Papa Fentry* ■ *Dir* Joseph Anthony • *Scr* Horton Foote, from a story by William Faulkner

Tomorrow at Ten ★★★

Crime drama 1962 · UK · BW · 80mins

A modest little thriller that managed to secure a grade A cast, but was still released as a B feature. Rank regular John Gregson is the cop sorting out a nasty child kidnapping case involving a psychotic bomber. The bad guy is *Jaws's* Robert Shaw (before he became an international star), while theatre actor Alec (father of Martin) Clunes plays the father of the kidnap victim. Veteran British director Lance Comfort expertly translates the workmanlike script, and the support cast contains many familiar faces. TS

John Gregson *Inspector Parnell* • Robert Shaw *Marlow* • Alec Clunes *Anthony Chester* • Alan Wheatley *Bewley* • Kenneth Cope *Sergeant Grey* • Ernest Clark *Doctor Towers* • Piers Bishop *Jonathan* • Helen Cherry *Robbie* • William Hartnell *Freddy* ■ *Dir* Lance Comfort • *Scr* Peter Millar, James Kelly

Tomorrow Is Forever ★★

Drama 1945 · US · BW · 103mins

This hackneyed melodrama, directed at a deadly tempo by Irving Pichel, stars Claudette Colbert as a Baltimore chemist who, after her husband Orson Welles is reported killed in the First World War, is taken in by her boss George Brent, whom she eventually marries. Many years later, when Brent imports a limping, heavily-bearded scientist from Austria to work for him, guess who he turns out to be? The most interesting aspect of this below average "woman's picture" is the early appearance of six-year-old Natalie Wood as Colbert's daughter. RK

Claudette Colbert *Elizabeth MacDonald Hamilton* • Orson Welles *John MacDonald/Erich Kessler* • George Brent *Larry Hamilton* • Lucile Watson *Aunt Jessie Hamilton* • Richard Long *John Andrew "Drew" Hamilton* • Natalie Wood *Margaret* ■ *Dir* Irving Pichel • *Scr* Lenore Coffee, from a novel by Gwen Bristow

Tomorrow Never Comes ★★★ 15

Crime drama
1977 · Can/UK · Colour · 86mins

A violent thriller, in which Stephen McHattie discovers his former girlfriend Susan George is seeing another man and takes her hostage. Oliver Reed is the police lieutenant given the job of breaking the siege. Peter Collinson directs with a sharp eye for the unsavoury detail, while Pinewood writing stalwarts Sydney Banks, David Pursall and Jack Seddon plumb the depths of seediness rather than character. TH [Video] DVD

Oliver Reed *Jim Wilson* • Susan George *Janie* • Raymond Burr *Burke* • John Ireland *Captain* • Stephen McHattie *Frank* • Donald Pleasence *Dr Todd* • Paul Koslo *Willy* • John Osborne *Lyne* ■ *Dir* Peter Collinson • *Scr* David Pursall, Jack Seddon, Sydney Banks

Tomorrow Never Dies ★★★★ 12

Spy adventure
1997 · US/UK · Colour · 114mins

For the first hour or so, this 18th Bond movie is up there with the best of them: it has terrific pace, Pierce Brosnan has romantic and rough-house appeal, Teri Hatcher is a match for him, and the post-Cold War story has grip and even plausibility. Sadly, the second half doesn't quite sustain the momentum: the story moves from Europe to Asia and Jonathan Pryce's media mogul is an unthreatening villain whose motto is "There's no news like bad news". Flaws aside, this is still one of the best Bond movies since the days of Sean Connery. AT. Contains violence, swearing and sex. [Video] DVD

Pierce Brosnan *James Bond* • Jonathan Pryce *Elliot Carver* • Michelle Yeoh *Wai Lin* • Teri Hatcher *Paris Carver* • Ricky Jay *Henry Gupta* • Götz Otto [Gotz Otto] *Stamper* • Joe Don Baker *Jack Wade* • Vincent Schiavelli *Dr Kaufman* • Judi Dench *"M"* • Desmond Llewelyn *"Q"* • Samantha Bond *Miss Moneypenny* • Colin Salmon *Robinson – Chief of Staff* • Geoffrey Palmer *Admiral Roebuck* ■ *Dir* Roger Spottiswoode • *Scr* Bruce Feirstein, from characters created by Ian Fleming

Tomorrow the World! ★★★

Drama 1944 · US · BW · 85mins

This eerily prefigures Maxwell Anderson's *The Bad Seed* in its portrayal of a nightmarish youngster on the loose in picket-fence America. Fresh from his stage success, 14-year-old Skippy Homeier reprises his role as the orphaned Hitler Youth member, sent to live with his liberal uncle (Frederic March) in the States. He soon begins spreading hatred and seeking recruits to his cause. Director Leslie Fenton doesn't do enough to open out the source material, but the central idea still retains its power to disturb. RT

Fredric March *Mike Frame* • Betty Field *Leona Richards* • Agnes Moorehead *Jessie Frame* • Skippy Homeier [Skip Homeier] *Emil Bruckner* • Joan Carroll *Pat Frame* • Edit Angold *Frieda* • Rudy Wissler *Stan* • Boots Brown *Ray* ■ *Dir*

Leslie Fenton • *Scr* Ring Lardner Jr, Leopold Atlas, from the play by James Gow, Arnaud D'Usseau

Tomorrow We Live ★★★ U

Spy melodrama 1942 · UK · BW · 87mins

In the darkest days of the Second World War, dashing John Clements gets mixed up with French freedom fighters, and two women: Greta Gynt, seemingly pro-Nazi, and waitress Judy Kelly, who actually is hustling for the occupying forces. *Casablanca* this isn't: it is, however, packed with action, and Clements is excellent in what today seems like a rather obvious piece of propaganda – unsurprising, really, since it was produced by British Aviation Films. TS

John Clements *Jean Batiste* • Godfrey Tearle *The Mayor* • Hugh Sinclair *Major Von Kleist* • Greta Gynt *Marie Duschen* • Judy Kelly *Germaine* • Yvonne Arnaud *Madame Labouche* • Karel Stepanek *Seitz* • Herbert Lom ■ *Dir* George King • *Scr* Anatole de Grunwald, from a story by Dorothy Hope

Tom's Midnight Garden ★★ U

Fantasy adventure
1998 · US/UK/Jpn · Colour · 102mins

This fantasy is unlikely to sustain the interests of children, while adults are unlikely to see it as anything other than a twee fable. Singer Anthony Way stars as a teenager who, during a summer stay with his childless aunt and uncle, discovers that at midnight, the ugly area around the building turns into a magical garden inhabited by a lonely orphan from the previous century. Sadly the scenes between the children are unengaging, while the adults add no lustre to an overlong effort. BB DVD

Greta Scacchi *Aunt Gwen* • James Wilby *Uncle Alan Kitson* • Joan Plowright *Mrs Bartholomew* • Anthony Way *Tom* • David Bradley (3) *Abel* • Penelope Wilton *Aunt Melbourne* • Nigel Le Vaillant *Tom Long, as adult* • Liz Smith *Mrs Willows* • Florence Hoath *Hatty at 12* ■ *Dir* Willard Carroll • *Scr* Willard Carroll, from the novel by Philippa Pearce

Tongues Untied ★★★

Documentary 1989 · US · Colour · 55mins

"If in America, a black is the lowest of the low, what is a gay black?" asks one of the characters in Marlon T Riggs's personal, positive and impassioned plea for an end to homophobia and racism. Combining poetry, testimony, mime, rap, voiceovers and archival footage in a manner that's simultaneously abrasive, compassionate, inelegant and articulate, Riggs makes his case for increased tolerance and "brother to brother" unity with wit and autobiographical frankness. It's poetic, chaotic, controversial and a fitting tribute to a film-maker who died from Aids in 1994, aged 37. DP

Marlon T Riggs ■ *Dir* Marlon T Riggs • *Scr* Joseph Bream, Craig Harris, Essex Hemphill, Reginald Jackson, Steve Langley, Alan Miller, Donald Woods

Toni ★★★★

Romantic crime drama
1935 · Fr · BW · 90mins

Jean Renoir's fact-based tale of marital angst was a key influence on neorealism, via the impact it made on one of his young assistants, Luchino Visconti. Shooting fluently and exclusively on location in the Midi, with a predominantly non-professional cast, Renoir succeeds in marrying character and environment in a way that not only emphasises their human nature and the authenticity of everyday existence, but also defuses the potentially melodramatic aspects of the plot – Italian quarry worker Charles Blavette takes the blame for his beloved's crime of passion. Simple, sensual and undervalued. DP. A French language film.

Charles Blavette *Antonio "Toni" Canova* • Célia Montalvan *Josepha* • Jenny Hélia *Marie* • Max Dalban *Albert* • Edouard Delmont *Fernand* ■ *Dir* Jean Renoir • *Scr* Jean Renoir, Carl Einstein, from an incident documented by Jacques Levert [Jacques Mortier]

Tonight and Every Night ★★★ U

Wartime romance
1945 · US · Colour · 88mins

This is a tribute to Soho's Windmill theatre (called the Music Box here), which claimed it never closed during the Blitz. Actually, it was more famous for its nude revues, although here the showgirls, including Rita Hayworth, keep well covered. Hayworth falls for pilot Lee Bowman and Janet Blair for dancer Marc Platt (a weak actor but a good dancer). The title number uses a trick of having the performers walking out of a film onto the stage. RB

Rita Hayworth *Rosalind "Roz" Bruce* • Lee Bowman *Paul Lundy* • Janet Blair *Judy Kane* • Marc Platt *Tommy Lawson* • Leslie Brooks *Angela* • Shelley Winters *Bubbles* ■ *Dir* Victor Saville • *Scr* Lesser Samuels, Abem Finkel, from the play *Heart of the City* by Lesley Storm

Tonight for Sure! 

Erotic comedy western
1961 · US · Colour · 69mins

Francis Ford Coppola's first movie – made while he was studying at UCLA – is a piece of audacity forgivable because of his youth. Don Kenney spies on women and Karl Schanzer imagines nude women everywhere. Not much evidence of Coppola's later talents, but interesting because of what is to come. TH

Don Kenney • Karl Schanzer • Virginia Gordon • Marli Renfro ■ *Dir/Scr* Francis Coppola [Francis Ford Coppola]

Tonight We Sing ★★ U

Musical biography
1953 · US · Colour · 109mins

Sol Hurok used his exceptional appreciation of musical talent to become the most famously dedicated, ambitious and successful of the American impresarios. What possessed 20th Century-Fox to cast the bloodless David Wayne as Hurok in this biopic, though, is something only the studio's late chiefs must know. The script, cobbled together from bits and pieces of Hurok's memoirs, is a similarly feeble affair, and Mitchell Leisen's direction is leaden. Fortunately, however, the film remains a feast of music. RK

David Wayne *Sol Hurok* • Ezio Pinza *Feodor Chaliapin* • Roberta Peters *Elsa Valdine* • Tamara Toumanova *Anna Pavlova* • Anne Bancroft *Emma Hurok* • Isaac Stern *Eugene Ysaye* ■ *Dir* Mitchell Leisen • *Scr* Harry Kurnitz, George Oppenheimer, from a book by Sol Hurok, Ruth Goode

Tonite Let's All Make Love in London ★★★

Documentary
1967 · UK · BW and Colour · 69mins

Director Peter Whitehead turns his camera on Swinging London – the era when Carnaby Street was the centre of the universe and even *Time* magazine featured it on the front cover. This documentary features some fascinating interviews with 1960s trendsetters like Mick Jagger, Julie Christie, Michael Caine and David Hockney. No real conclusions are drawn, apart from Caine's prediction: "All this dolly-bird stuff won't matter a damn in ten years' time. It's on the way out already." TH

Dir/Scr Peter Whitehead

Tonka ★★★ U

Period adventure 1958 · US · Colour · 92mins

This adventure set against the Sioux War arrived at a time when Hollywood was trying to make amends for its various injustices. Here Disney reverses a tendency towards negative portrayals of native American Indians, by casting Sal Mineo as a young Sioux tribesman who tames a wild, white horse he calls Tonka, only then for it to be taken away from him and sold to the cavalry, where it is renamed Comanche. After a series of attempts to win the horse back, the pair are reunited. TH

Sal Mineo *White Bull* • Philip Carey *Captain Miles Keogh* • Jerome Courtland *Lieutenant Henry Nowlan* • Rafael Campos *Strong Bear* • HM Wynant *Yellow Bull* • Joy Page *Prairie Flower* • Britt Lomond *General George Armstrong Custer* ■ *Dir* Lewis R Foster • *Scr* Lewis R Foster, Lillie Hayward, from the novel *Comanche* by David Appel

Tony Draws a Horse ★★

Comedy 1950 · UK · BW · 90mins

When their son draws a sexually explicit horse, his parents are divided over the right way to deal with the situation. The resulting fall out sees psychiatrist Anne Crawford leaving her doctor husband Cecil Parker and returning to the bosom of her family. Once there she takes off to France with her sister's fiancé, kick-starting a chain of farcical events. Prolific comedy director John Paddy Carstairs turns in a workmanlike, but nevertheless likeable, adaptation. DF

Cecil Parker *Dr Howard Fleming* • Anne Crawford *Clare Fleming* • Derek Bond *Tim Shields* • Barbara Murray *Joan Parsons* • Mervyn Johns *Alfred Parsons* • Barbara Everest *Mrs Parsons* • Edward Rigby *Grandpa* • Anthony Lang *Tony Fleming* ■ *Dir* John Paddy Carstairs • *Scr* Brock Williams, from the play by Lesley Storm

Tony Rome ★★★

Detective thriller
1967 · US · Colour · 109mins

Frank Sinatra always wanted to be Bogart, and here he successfully takes on his mantle of hard-boiled private eye à la Philip Marlowe or Sam Spade. This tough and nasty Miami-set thriller is a classy act, with searing dialogue, a fine Billy May score and top-notch support from the likes of Richard Conte and Gena Rowlands. Director Gordon Douglas cleverly masks the fact that the plot is no great shakes, though it does bear comparison with *The Big Sleep*. Sinatra returned as Tony Rome in *Lady in Cement*. TS

Frank Sinatra *Tony Rome* • Jill St John *Ann Archer* • Richard Conte *Lt Santini* • Gena Rowlands *Rita Kosterman* • Simon Oakland *Rudolph Kosterman* • Jeffrey Lynn *Adam Boyd* • Lloyd Bochner *Vic Rood* • Robert J Wilke *Ralph Turpin* • Rocky Graziano *Packy* ■ *Dir* Gordon Douglas • *Scr* Richard L Breen, from the novel *Miami Mayhem* by Anthony Rome [Marvin H Albert]

Too Bad She's Bad ★★

Comedy 1955 · It · BW · 103mins

Vittorio De Sica is a pickpocket who cajoles his beautiful daughter Sophia Loren into acting as his assistant. Complications arise when Loren, acting as a honey trap for a couple of crooks out to rob an honest cabbie, finds her own feelings start to stir when the taxi driver, Marcello Mastroianni, falls for her. A modest romantic comedy at best, it's notable as the first-time pairing of Loren and Mastroianni, and as the film where Loren first showed a penchant for comedy. DF. Italian dialogue dubbed into English.

Sophia Loren *Lina* • Vittorio De Sica *Stroppiani* • Marcello Mastroianni *Paolo* • Umberto Melnati *Man whose wallet is stolen* • Margherita Bagni *His wife* ■ *Dir* Alessandro Blasetti • *Scr* Suso Cecchi D'Amico, Ennio Flaiano, Alessandro Continenza, from a story by Alberto Moravia

Too Hard to Die ★★ 18

Crime thriller 1998 · US · Colour · 88mins

In the low-budget world of TV movies, you don't get much more of an A-list cast than this. Jeff Fahey, Michael Madsen and Gary Busey are the stars, and they're given fine support by Tim Thomerson and James Russo. The material itself is pretty standard stuff, concerning a plan to rob a Mob boss that goes badly wrong, but the direction from the less famous Travolta, John's brother Joey, is proficient enough, and the actors can do crime thrillers in their sleep. RT

Jeff Fahey *Danny Devlin* • Michael Madsen *Burl Rogers* • Gary Busey *Mo Ginsburg* • James Russo *Ziggy Rotella* • Tim Thomerson *Mel Kiner* ■ *Dir* Joey Travolta • *Scr* Raymond Martino, William Stroum

Too Hot to Handle ★★★★

Comedy adventure 1938 · US · BW · 105mins

This is a hugely enjoyable three-hander from Clark Gable, Myrna Loy and Walter Pidgeon, in which Gable and Pidgeon play devil-may-care newsreel photographers vying for the attentions of feisty aviatrix Loy. Gable is in his element – charming, wry, raffish and risk-taking – and his spoof bombing raid into China is the film's *pièce de résistance*. Everything gels in this movie: the stars, the action scenes and a stylish, witty script. SH

Clark Gable *Chris Hunter* • Myrna Loy *Alma Harding* • Walter Pidgeon *Bill Dennis* • Walter Connolly *Gabby MacArthur* • Leo Carrillo *Joselito* • Virginia Weidler *Hulda Harding* • Henry Kolker *Pearly Todd* • Marjorie Main *Miss Wayne* ■ *Dir* Jack Conway • *Scr* Laurence Stallings, John Lee Mahin, from a story by Len Hammond

Too Hot to Handle ★★ 12

Crime thriller 1960 · UK · Colour · 87mins

In 1960, British censors would tolerate a film about the new striptease sensation in London's Soho only if it depicted this world as thoroughly sordid. Consequently, in Terence Young's melodramatic thriller, the men are all corrupt, the women jaded or pathetic. Club owner Leo Genn knowingly fixes up underage stripper Barbara Windsor with a slimy patron. What busty blonde Jayne Mansfield is doing here is anyone's guess. This is wholly incredible – though often astonishing – nonsense. DM

Jayne Mansfield *Midnight Franklin* • Leo Genn *Johnny Solo* • Karlheinz Böhm *Robert Jouvel* • Danik Patisson *Lilliane Decker* • Christopher Lee *Novak* • Barbara Windsor *Pony Tail* ■ *Dir* Terence Young • *Scr* Herbert Kretzmer, from a story by Harry Lee

Too Hot to Handle ★★ 15

Comedy drama 1991 · US · Colour · 111mins

Originally released as *The Marrying Man*, this Kim Basinger/Alec Baldwin comedy is a clunker under any name. The rumours of on-set battles between the leads and the producers were far more interesting than the story itself, which follows the on-off love affair in the 1940s between nightclub singer/gangster's moll Basinger and millionaire playboy Baldwin. Unfortunately, neither lead is a deft hand at comedy, and the humour in the script is not that strong either. JB. Contains violence and swearing. DVD

Kim Basinger *Vicki Anderson* • Alec Baldwin *Charley Pearl* • Robert Loggia *Lew Horner* • Elisabeth Shue *Adele Horner* • Armand Assante *Bugsy Siegel* • Paul Reiser *Phil* • Fisher Stevens *Sammy* • Peter Dobson *Tony Madden* ■ *Dir* Jerry Rees • *Scr* Neil Simon

Too Late Blues ★★★

Musical drama 1961 · US · BW · 103mins

Director John Cassavetes, who had struck creative gold with the improvisational *Shadows*, tries to shoehorn his energy into a more conventional, plot-driven film. In this story about jazz pianist John "Ghost" Wakefield (Bobby Darin), notions about artistic commitment aren't fully explored. However, in the muso's brittle relationship with a neurotic aspiring singer (Stella Stevens) and his deteriorating relations with his band, the essential Cassavetes comes fully alive. The music, blasted out by the likes of Benny Carter and Red Mitchell, is a five-star treat. JM

Bobby Darin *John "Ghost" Wakefield* • Stella Stevens *Jess Polanski* • Cliff Carnell *Charlie* • Seymour Cassel *Red* • Bill Stafford *Shelly* • Richard Chambers *Pete* • Nick Dennis *Nick* ■ *Dir* John Cassavetes • *Scr* John Cassavetes, Richard Carr

Too Late the Hero ★★★ 15

Second World War drama
1970 · US · Colour · 133mins

This Second World War tale about male bonding is typical mid-career fare from director Robert Aldrich – exciting and violent, but rather too long – as soldiers Michael Caine and Cliff Robertson are dispatched on a suicide mission in the Pacific arena. This is entertaining, but with a bit of judicious pruning it could have been even more so. TS. Contains violence and swearing. [VIDEO] DVD

Michael Caine *Private Tosh Hearne* • Cliff Robertson *Lieutenant Lawson* • Ian Bannen *Thornton* • Harry Andrews *Lt Col Thompson* • Denholm Elliott *Captain Hornsby* • Ronald Fraser *Campbell* • Lance Percival *Corporal Mclean* • Percy Herbert *Johnstone* • Henry Fonda *Captain Nolan* • Ken Takakura *Major Yamaguchi* ■ *Dir* Robert Aldrich • *Scr* Robert Aldrich, Lukas Heller, from the story by Robert Aldrich, Robert Sherman

Too Many Crooks ★★★ U

Comedy 1958 · UK · BW · 81mins

The cast is a who's who of British comedy and the script is by Michael Pertwee, but this picture never lives up to its billing, largely owing to the cack-handed direction of Mario Zampi. Terry-Thomas gives a priceless performance as the wheeler-dealer unconcerned whether he sees abducted wife Brenda de Banzie ever again, but George Cole, Sid James and the gang overdo the "cor blimey" criminality. DP [VIDEO] DVD

Terry-Thomas *Billy Gordon* • George Cole *Fingers* • Brenda de Banzie *Lucy* • Bernard Bresslaw *Snowdrop* • Sidney James *Sid* • Joe Melia *Whisper* • Vera Day *Charmaine* • Delphi Lawrence *Beryl, secretary* • John Le Mesurier *Magistrate* • Nicholas Parsons *Tommy* ■ *Dir* Mario Zampi • *Scr* Michael Pertwee, from the story by Jean Nery, Christiane Rochefort

Too Many Girls ★★★ U

Musical comedy 1940 · US · BW · 84mins

This entertaining version of the hit show retains many of the original cast and is directed for the screen by the grand old man of Broadway himself, George Abbott. It's geared as a vehicle for Lucille Ball, who met future husband and business partner Desi Arnaz on set. Also having fun with what's left of the Rodgers and Hart score are Frances Langford and Ann Miller, and the movie also marks the debuts of stars-to-be Van Johnson and Eddie Bracken. The songs aren't vintage, but there's no denying the sheer verve of the piece. TS

Lucille Ball *Connie Casey* • Richard Carlson *Clint Kelly* • Ann Miller *Pepe* • Eddie Bracken *Jojo Jordan* • Frances Langford *Eileen Eilers* • Desi Arnaz *Manuelito* • Van Johnson *Chorus boy* ■ *Dir* George Abbott • *Scr* John Twist, from the stage musical by George Marion Jr, Richard Rodgers, Lorenz Hart

Too Many Husbands ★★★

Screwball comedy 1940 · US · BW · 81mins

Mistakenly believed to have drowned in a shipwreck, Fred MacMurray finds his way home to discover that his wife (Jean Arthur) is now remarried. The two men vie for the right to "their" wife, who encourages and relishes their attentions, until the matter of where she belongs must be decided in court. Slight but neat romantic comedy, tailor-made for its star trio and directed with his habitual flair by Wesley Ruggles. Remade as a musical, *Three for the Show*, with Betty Grable in 1955. RK

Jean Arthur *Vicky Lowndes* • Fred MacMurray *Bill Cardew* • Melvyn Douglas *Henry Lowndes* • Harry Davenport *George* • Dorothy Peterson *Gertrude Houlihan* • Melville Cooper *Peter* • Edgar Buchanan *McDermott* ■ *Dir* Wesley Ruggles • *Scr* Claude Binyon, from the play by W Somerset Maugham

Too Many Lovers ★★

Romantic comedy 1957 · Fr · Colour

Club singer Zizi Jeanmaire is saddled with so many losers: a rich slob, a punch-drunk boxer, an argumentative thief and a married man whose wife refuses to divorce him. Amid all this mediocrity, a mystery man keeps sending her flowers. With the exception of Gert Fröbe as the wealthy wolf, the suitors are all bores and Jeanmaire is hardly a ball of fire herself. DP. French dialogue dubbed into English.

Zizi Jeanmaire *Lulu* • Daniel Gélin *Alain* • Henri Vidal *Jo* • Gil Vidal *Max* • François Périer *Robert* • Marie Daems *Germaine* • Gert Fröbe *Edmond* ■ *Dir* Henri Decoin • *Scr* Charles Spaak

Too Much ★ U

Comedy 1987 · US · Colour · 85mins

Lonely little Bridgette Andersen lives in Japan, where she is given a prototype robot to befriend. When the evil professor Char Fontana and his stupid henchmen try and steal the experimental cyborg, the duo go on the run and have uninvolving misadventures. Banal and syrupy. AJ [VIDEO]

Bridgette Andersen *Suzy* • Masato Fukazama *Too Much* • Hiroyuki Watanabe *Tetsuro* • Char Fontana *Professor Finkel* • Uganda *Bernie* ■ *Dir/Scr* Eric Rochat

Too Much Sun ★ 18

Comedy 1990 · US · Colour · 93mins

Robert Downey Sr directs Junior in a totally tasteless farce about a multimillionaire, whose offspring must compete to produce an heir and inherit his fortune. The hitch is that the brother and sister are gay – cue much tasteless humour. This is laugh-an-hour stuff despite the best efforts of a cast which, in addition to Downey Jr, also features Ralph Macchio and Hollywood veteran Howard Duff. DA [VIDEO]

Robert Downey Jr *Reed Richmond* • Eric Idle *Sonny Rivers* • Andrea Martin *Bitsy Rivers* • Jim Haynie *Father Seamus Kelly* • Laura Ernst *Susan Connor* • Leo Rossi *George Bianco* • Ralph Macchio *Frank Della Rocca Jr* • Howard Duff *OM Rivers* ■ *Dir* Robert Downey Sr • *Scr* Robert Downey, Laura Ernst, Al Schwartz

Too Much, Too Soon ★★

Biographical drama 1958 · US · BW · 101mins

The Barrymores were known as the Royal Family of Broadway, but the second generation did much to tarnish the reputation as this lacklustre biopic of Diana Barrymore reveals. Dorothy Malone is suitably downbeat as the daughter destroyed by the drinking of her famous father John, who is played with disturbing authenticity by Errol Flynn. Flynn makes the most of a disappointing script, but it was a sad farewell to Warners Bros, the studio where he had once been the king of the swashbucklers. DP

Dorothy Malone *Diana Barrymore* • Errol Flynn *John Barrymore* • Efrem Zimbalist Jr *Vincent Bryant* • Ray Danton *John Howard* • Neva Patterson *Michael Strange* • Murray Hamilton *Charlie Snow* • Martin Milner *Lincoln Forrester* ■ *Dir* Art Napoleon • *Scr* Art Napoleon, Jo Napoleon, from the autobiography by Diana Barrymore, Gerold Frank

Too Outrageous! ★

Comedy drama 1987 · Can · Colour · 100mins

The very disappointing sequel to *Outrageous* (1977) picks up the story of female impersonator Robin Turner (played with camp aplomb once more by Craig Russell), now a smash on the New York drag queen circuit, who must decide between mainstream success or remaining true to his art. Where director Richard Benner's first movie was fresh, smart and funny, his follow-up is a hackneyed and boring affair with few laughs. AJ

Craig Russell *Robin Turner* • Hollis McLaren *Liza Connors* • David McIlwraith *Bob* • Ron White *Luke* • Lynne Cormack *Betty Treisman* • Michael J Reynolds *Lee Sturges* • Timothy Jenkins *Rothchild* ■ *Dir/Scr* Richard Benner

Too Scared to Scream ★★ 18

Psychological thriller
1982 · US · Colour · 94mins

Actor-turned-director Tony LoBianco's first-time slasher thriller has New York cops Mike Connors and Anne Archer investigate murders in a high-rise apartment block. Prime suspect is doorman Ian McShane, a bitter ex-actor eager to recite Shakespeare at the drop of a knife, who lives with his invalid mother Maureen O'Sullivan. Obvious red herrings defy the slow-building suspense but the cast brings a much needed zing to events. AJ [VIDEO]

Mike Connors *Lieutenant Dinardo* • Anne Archer *Kate* • Leon Isaac Kennedy *Frank* • Ian McShane *Hardwick* • Ruth Ford *Irma* • John Heard *Lab technician* • Carrie Nye *Graziella* • Maureen O'Sullivan *Mother* ■ *Dir* Tony LoBianco • *Scr* Glenn Leopold, Neal Barbera

Too Soon to Love ★★★

Drama 1960 · US · BW · 89mins

The first film directed by Richard Rush – one of a group of independent film-makers who formed an American version of the *Nouvelle Vague* – this tale of two teenage sweethearts driven by uncomprehending parents into a saga of unwanted pregnancy, abortion, robbery and attempted suicide, is better than it sounds and a social document of its time. Stars Jennifer West and Richard Evans had less than sparkling careers, but playing the hero's buddy is Jack Nicholson. TV

Jennifer West *Cathy Taylor* • Richard Evans *Jim Mills* • Warren Parker *Mr Taylor* • Ralph Manza *Hughie Wineman* • Jack Nicholson *Buddy* • Jacqueline Schwab *Irene* • Billie Bird *Mrs Jefferson* ■ *Dir* Richard Rush • *Scr* Laszlo Gorog, Richard Rush

The Toolbox Murders ★★ 18

Horror 1978 · US · Colour · 91mins

This deranged "video nasty" gore classic is TV director Dennis Donnelly's only feature film. Cameron Mitchell chews the scenery as a homicidal landlord killing helpless female tenants with an imaginative array of power tools, screwdrivers and hammers. Brutal, prurient stuff, yet still remarkably dull, this is notorious for the sleazy sequence in which adult movie star Marianne Walter gets nail-gunned to death. AJ. Contains violence, nudity. [VIDEO] DVD

Cameron Mitchell *Kingsley* • Pamelyn Ferdin *Laurie Ballard* • Wesley Eure *Kent* • Nicolas Beauvy *Joey Ballard* • Aneta Corsaut [Aneta Corseaut] *JoAnn Ballard* • Tim Donnelly *Detective Jamison* • Marianne Walter *Dee Ann* ■ *Dir* Dennis Donnelly • *Scr* Robert Easter, Neva Friedenn, Ann N Kindberg [Ann N Kindberg]

Toolbox Murders ★★ 15

Horror 2003 · US/UK · Colour · 95mins

Old-school exploitation gets an old-school reworking in this grimy chiller from director Tobe Hooper. Based on a 1970s slasher flick and one-time "video nasty", the film plays like a grindhouse sleaze-fest, with none of the precision or skill of Hooper's seminal classic *The Texas Chain Saw Massacre*. There's plenty of gore but very little else, as a ruthless psychopath picks off the residents of a decaying Hollywood apartment block with the contents of his toolbox (hence the title). SF. Contains swearing and violence. [VIDEO] DVD

Angela Bettis *Nell Barrows* • Juliet Landau *Julia Cunningham* • Brent Roam *Steven Barrows* • Rance Howard *Chas "Jazz" Rooker* • Marco Rodriguez *Luis Saucedo* • Adam Gierasch *Ned Lundy* ■ *Dir* Tobe Hooper • *Scr* Jace Anderson, Adam Gierasch

Toomorrow ★★

Science-fiction musical
1970 · UK · Colour · 93mins

Anthropologist Roy Dotrice is really an Alphoid alien in disguise whose Earth mission is to track down a "tonaliser" causing good vibrations on his planet. The instrument is the invention of Vic Cooper who, with fellow Chelsea art students Benny Thomas, Karl Chambers and Olivia Newton-John, has set up the pop group Toomorrow to earn money for college expenses. The group are whisked to his home planet to add soul to their out-of-tune computerised music. A lightweight musical fantasy, the contrived plot is sweetened enormously by some sophisticated humour, extravagant production design and expert direction by genre doyen Val Guest. AJ

Olivia Newton-John *Olivia* • Benny Thomas [Ben Thomas] *Benny* • Vic Cooper *Vic* • Karl Chambers *Karl* • Roy Dotrice *John Williams* • Roy Marsden *Alpha* ■ *Dir/Scr* Val Guest

Toot, Whistle, Plunk and Boom ★★★★★

Animated comedy documentary
1953 · US · Colour · 10mins

Having initially led the animation industry with such innovations as synchronised sound, full colour and feature-length cartoons, the Disney studio began adopting the ideas of its rivals in the 1940s, starting with the imitation of Warner Brothers' fast-paced, anarchic humour. The trend continued into the next decade with the use of United Production of America's highly stylised graphics, evident here in what is still recognisably Disney, with its broadly educational theme of the invention of musical instruments, each of which we are told originated with the four primitive sounds of the film's title. To further the studio's tradition of pioneering technical formats, Disney presented the film in CinemaScope, a striking departure that captured the imagination of all and won Disney its 11th short-cartoon Oscar, its first for more than ten years. CLP

T

Bill Thompson *Owl* ■ *Dir* Ward Kimball, C August Nichols [Charles A Nichols] • *Scr* Dick Huemer

Tooth ★ U

Fantasy adventure
2003 · UK · Colour · 87mins

This dreadful adventure about a modern-day tooth fairy is amateurish and old-fashioned, reliant on weak humour and bumbling performances from a host of minor British stars. Tooth fairy Yasmin Paige teams up with two human children to restore the lost magic to Fairytopia. The paper-thin script and sloppy direction only compound the mess. SF DVD

Yasmin Paige *Tooth* • Harry Enfield *Plug* • Sally Phillips *Mom* • Tim Dutton *Dad* • Phyllida Law *Mrs Claus* • Jim Broadbent *Rabbit* • Vinnie Jones *The Extractor* • Stephen Fry *Pedro* • Richard E Grant *Jarvis Jarvis* • Jerry Hall *Bon Bon* ■ *Dir/Scr* Edouard Nammour

Tootsie ★★★★ 15

Comedy 1982 · US · Colour · 111mins

One of the highlights of Dustin Hoffman's illustrious career, this cross-dressing comedy drama avoids all the obvious pitfalls and manages to make some pertinent comments on the role of women within both showbiz and society. Hoffman's Dorothy Michaels is a wonderfully realised creation and testament to the actor's painstaking preparation for a part. Director Sydney Pollack judges the shifts of tone to perfection, but special mention should be made of his clever pastiche of daytime soaps. Nominated for ten Oscars, the film landed only one – a best supporting statuette for Jessica Lange. DP DVD

Dustin Hoffman *Michael Dorsey/Dorothy Michaels* • Jessica Lange *Julie* • Teri Garr *Sandy* • Dabney Coleman *Ron* • Charles Durning *Les* • Bill Murray *Jeff* • Sydney Pollack *George Fields* • George Gaynes *John Van Horn* • Geena Davis *April* ■ *Dir* Sydney Pollack • *Scr* Larry Gelbart, Murray Schisgal, Elaine May (uncredited), from a story by Don McGuire, Larry Gelbart

Top Banana ★★★

Musical comedy 1953 · US · Colour · 103mins

The immortal Phil Silvers (Sgt Bilko), enjoyed a distinguished career before his small screen triumph. Undoubtably his biggest pre-Bilko success was in the Tony Award-winning Broadway musical comedy *Top Banana*. Silvers is brilliant as fast-talking TV comic Jerry Biffle, the "Top Banana" of the title (ie headlining comedian of a show) and his performance, along with the authentic burlesque routines on offer, make this rewarding viewing. Originally made in 3-D, a gimmick which was undergoing a boom at the time. DF

Phil Silvers *Jerry Biffle* • Rose Marie *Betty Dillon* • Danny Scholl *Cliff Lane* • Judy Lynn *Sally Peters* • Jack Albertson *Vic Davis* • Johnny Coy *Tommy Phelps* • Joey Faye *Pinky* • Herbie Faye *Moe* ■ *Dir* Alfred E Green • *Scr* Gene Towne, from the musical by Hy Kraft, Johnny Mercer

Top Dog ★★ 12

Action comedy 1995 · US · Colour · 89mins

Chuck Norris stars as a tough cop who teams up with the San Diego police force's most cavalier canine to solve the murder of the dog's former partner. Someone should tell Norris not to play alongside actors who are more dynamic than he is – the mutt is superior in every way. Parents should note that there is some violence and innuendo here, although children may love the dog's antics. ST DVD

Chuck Norris *Jake Wilder* • Clyde Kusatsu *Captain Callahan* • Michele Lamar Richards *Savannah Boyette* • Peter Savard Moore *Karl Koller* • Erik Von Detten *Matthew Swanson* • Carmine Caridi *Lou Swanson* ■ *Dir* Aaron Norris • *Scr* Ron Swanson, from a story by Aaron Norris, Tim Grayem

Top Gun ★★★ 15

Action drama 1986 · US · Colour · 105mins

Quentin Tarantino's vigorous assertion in *Sleep with Me* that this is the ultimate gay fantasy movie rather pulls the carpet from under the feet of those attempting to appraise this slavish tribute to flash fly boys and their hi-tech toys. There is no denying the quality and entertainment value of the flying sequences, which blend mile-high footage with state-of-the-art modelwork, but the rivalry between Tom Cruise and Val Kilmer, and Cruise's tempestuous affair with Kelly McGillis are pure bunk. Director Tony Scott takes the credit for preventing this mindless macho daydream from nose-diving. DP. Contains a sex scene, swearing. DVD

Tom Cruise *Pete "Maverick" Mitchell* • Kelly McGillis *Charlotte "Charlie" Blackwood* • Val Kilmer *Tom "Iceman" Kazansky* • Anthony Edwards *Nick "Goose" Bradshaw* • Tom Skerritt *Commander Mike Metcalf, "Viper"* • Michael Ironside *Dick "Jester" Wetherly* • John Stockwell *Bill "Cougar" Cortell* • Barry Tubb *Henry "Wolfman" Ruth* • Rick Rossovich *Ron "Slider" Kerner* • Tim Robbins *Sam "Merlin" Wills* • Meg Ryan *Carole* ■ *Dir* Tony Scott • *Scr* Jim Cash, Jack Epps Jr

Top Hat ★★★★★ U

Classic musical comedy
1935 · US · BW · 93mins

The quintessential Fred Astaire–Ginger Rogers movie; *Swing Time* may be more sophisticated, but there's no question that this fabulous production was more popular. The mistaken identity plot actually works, and the casting is simply flawless. Astaire consolidates his image with the title number *Top Hat, White Tie and Tails* and the Irving Berlin score is a constant delight. Good-natured, warm-hearted and very witty (especially the hansom cab scene), this is a movie to treasure for its sumptuous Art-Deco design and the pairing of its principal players. TS

Fred Astaire *Jerry Travers* • Ginger Rogers *Dale Tremont* • Edward Everett Horton *Horace Hardwick* • Erik Rhodes *Alberto Beddini* • Eric Blore *Bates* • Helen Broderick *Madge Hardwick* • Donald Meek *Curate* • Florence Roberts *Curate's wife* ■ *Dir* Mark Sandrich • *Scr* Dwight Taylor, Allan Scott, Karl Noti, from the play *The Girl Who Dared* by Alexander Farago, Aladar Laszlo

Top of the Form ★★ U

Crime comedy 1953 · UK · BW · 75mins

The Will Hay classic *Good Morning, Boys* is the inspiration for this misfiring Ronald Shiner vehicle. Shiner is a racing tipster mistakenly appointed head of a boys' school who discovers his charges have a natural proclivity for gambling, which comes in handy when he escorts them on a cultural trip to Paris. However, they're soon distracted from the tables when they uncover a plot to steal the Mona Lisa. This efficient but underwhelming caper is all too typical of its director. DP

Ronald Shiner *Ronnie Fortescue* • Harold Fowler *Albert* • Alfie Bass *Artie Jones* • Jacqueline Pierreux *Yvette* • Anthony Newley *Percy* • Mary Jerrold *Mrs Bagshott* • Richard Wattis *Willoughby-Gore* • Ronnie Corbett *Student* ■ *Dir* John Paddy Carstairs • *Scr* Leslie Arliss, John Paddy Carstairs, Marriott Edgar, Val Guest, Patrick Kirwan, Ted Willis, from a story by Anthony Kimmins

Top of the World ★ 18

Thriller 1997 · US · Colour · 94mins

This bottom-of-the-barrel cop thriller wastes a good cast in a weak heist plot and surrounds them with botched action and bad special effects. Ex-cop Peter Weller leaves prison after serving time for a pension fund scam only to find himself in the centre of a Las Vegas casino robbery planned by stereotypical baddie Dennis Hopper. So sloppy in places it defies belief, this gives new meaning to the word lacklustre. AJ. Contains swearing and violence. DVD

Peter Weller *Ray Mercer* • Dennis Hopper *Charles Atlas* • Tia Carrere *Rebecca Mercer* • David Alan Grier *Detective Augustus* • Cary-Hiroyuki Tagawa *Captain Hefter* • Joe Pantoliano *Vince Castor* ■ *Dir* Sidney J Furie • *Scr* Bart Madison

Top Secret! ★★★ 15

Spy spoof 1984 · US · Colour · 86mins

The *Airplane!* team is a touch off-form with this Cold War spoof that has an Elvis Presley-style musical grafted on. Part of the problem is the absence of Leslie Nielsen; instead, Val Kilmer makes his feature debut, playing a rock star who becomes involved in a plot to reunite Germany when he plays a gig in East Germany. Not as funny as it should be, but entertaining enough. AT. Contains swearing.

Val Kilmer *Nick Rivers* • Omar Sharif *Cedric* • Jeremy Kemp *General Streck* • Warren Clarke *Colonel von Horst* • Lucy Gutteridge *Hillary Flammond* • Michael Gough *Dr Flammond* • Tristram Jellinek *Major Crumpler* • Peter Cushing *Bookstore proprietor* ■ *Dir* Jim Abrahams, David Zucker, Jerry Zucker • *Scr* Jim Abrahams, David Zucker, Jerry Abrahams, Martyn Burke

Top Secret Affair ★★★ U

Comedy 1957 · US · BW · 99mins

The chemistry is missing between stars Kirk Douglas and Susan Hayward in this rather heavy-handed frolic, maybe because they were old buddies in real life who went to school together back in New York before Hollywood beckoned. Comedy was never really Douglas's forte, and his dimpled grimacing doesn't help this adaptation of John P Marquand's satire. Hayward, however, positively sizzles as the publisher who's trying to discredit newly-appointed diplomat Douglas. TS

Kirk Douglas *Maj Gen Melville Goodwin* • Susan Hayward *Dottie Peale* • Paul Stewart *Bentley* • Jim Backus *Colonel Gooch* • John Cromwell *General Grimshaw* • Michael Fox *Lotzie* • Frank Gerstle *Sergeant Kruger* ■ *Dir* HC Potter • *Scr* Roland Kibbee, Allan Scott, from the novel *Melville Goodwin, USA* by John P Marquand

Topaz ★★ PG

Spy thriller 1969 · US · Colour · 120mins

Leon Uris adapted his own bestseller for this lacklustre spy story. Alfred Hitchcock, who had no real enthusiasm for the project, eventually asked for a rewrite by Samuel Taylor (*Vertigo*), but there was still far too much plot, too many explanations, and not enough character depth to bring this Cold War thriller to life. The action centres on a Cuban revolutionary and double agents in the French secret service. DP DVD

John Forsythe *Michael Nordstrom* • Frederick Stafford *André Devereaux* • Dany Robin *Nicole Devereaux* • John Vernon *Rico Parra* • Karin Dor *Juanita de Cordoba* • Michel Piccoli *Jacques Granville* • Philippe Noiret *Henri Jarre* • Claude Jade *Michele Picard* • Michel Subor *François Picard* • Roscoe Lee Browne *Philippe Dubois* ■ *Dir* Alfred Hitchcock • *Scr* Samuel Taylor, from the novel by Leon Uris

Topaze ★★★★

Comedy drama 1933 · US · BW · 78mins

John Barrymore's wonderfully timed and sympathetic study as the honest but hugely naive schoolmaster lights up this Ben Hecht version of Marcel Pagnol's play. After losing his job in a private school, Barrymore is inveigled into a scheme to sell designer mineral water, organised by crooked baron Reginald Mason. Myrna Loy plays Mason's lover, who is attracted by Barrymore's transformation from dupe into man of substance. The story was later re-made by Peter Sellers as *Mr Topaze* (1961). TH

John Barrymore *Auguste Topaze* • Myrna Loy *Coco* • Albert Conti *Henri* • Luis Alberni *Dr Bomb* • Reginald Mason *Baron de Latour-Latour* • Jobyna Howland *Baroness de Latour-Latour* • Jackie Searle *Charlemagne de Latour-Latour* • Frank Reicher *Dr Stegg* ■ *Dir* Harry d'Abbadie D'Arrast • *Scr* Ben Hecht, Benn W Levy, from the play by Marcel Pagnol

Topaze ★★★

Satire 1951 · Fr · BW · 136mins

Proving that behind every cynic there's a lapsed idealist, Fernandel is superb as the bashful schoolmaster unable to declare his feelings for headmaster's daughter Jacqueline Pagnol. However, he is much less convincing as the fast-learning political dupe who outwits his corrupt master, Jacques Morel. Marcel Pagnol directs this version of his own play. DP. A French language film.

Fernandel *Topaze* • Hélène Perdrière *Suzy Courtois* • Jacqueline Pagnol *Ernestine Muche* • Pierre Larquey *Tamise* • Jacques Morel *Régis Castel-Vergnac* • Marcel Vallée *Muche* • Milly Mathis *Baroness Pitar-Vergnolles* • Yvette Etiévant *Secretary* ■ *Dir* Marcel Pagnol • *Scr* Marcel Pagnol, from his play

Topkapi ★★★★ U

Comedy crime caper
1964 · US · Colour · 114mins

In spoofing his own intricate heist classic, *Rififi*, Jules Dassin pioneered one of the most popular sub-genres of the 1960s, the comic crime caper. Deliciously scripted by one-time Ealing alumnus Monja Danischewsky, it combines sparkling dialogue with moments of unbearable tension, most notably during the prolonged heist on an Istanbul museum in a bid to purloin a priceless dagger. The band of misfits hired by Melina Mercouri and Maximilian Schell are effectively played, but it was the showy performance of Peter Ustinov that caught the eye and earned him a best supporting actor Oscar. DP DVD

Melina Mercouri *Elizabeth Lipp* • Peter Ustinov *Arthur Simon Simpson* • Maximilian Schell *Walter Harper* • Robert Morley *Cedric Page* • Akim Tamiroff *Geven* • Gilles Ségal *Giulio* • Jess Hahn *Hans Fischer* • Titos Wandis [Titos Vandis] *Harback* • Ege Ernart *Major Tufan* ■ *Dir* Jules Dassin • *Scr* Monja Danischewsky, from the novel *The Light of Day* by Eric Ambler

El Topo ★★★ 18

Surreal spaghetti western
1971 · Mex · Colour · 119mins

There's plenty to offend everyone here. Shot in Mexico by the Chilean-born actor/writer/director Alexandro Jodorowsky, *El Topo* which translates as *The Mole* is the cult film fan's cult film. A brief description would do scant justice to the bewildering array of images – some witty, some bleak and some so obscure that only Jodorowsky himself can have the foggiest idea what they actually mean. But, given the knowledge that the references range from Fellini and Buñuel to Marcel Marceau and the Bible, you will get a better idea of just how eclectic this western (yes, western!) really is. DP. In Spanish with English subtitles. Contains violence and sex scenes.

Alexandro Jodorowsky *El Topo* • Brontis Jodorowsky *Brontis (as a child)* • Mara Lorenzio *Mara* • David Silva *Colonel* • Paula Romo *Woman in black* ■ *Dir/Scr* Alexandro Jodorowsky

T

Topper ★★★★

Fantasy screwball comedy
1937 · US · BW · 98mins

This excellent whimsical comedy stars Cary Grant and Constance Bennett as the rich couple who drive their streamlined automobile into a tree. Surviving as ghosts, they harass Mr Topper (Roland Young), their starchy, hen-pecked bank manager, who has regarded them as irresponsible and trivial, which is exactly what they are. The movie aims for a soft subversiveness and was a huge hit, with two sequels following. AT

Cary Grant *George Kerby* • Constance Bennett *Marion Kerby* • Roland Young *Cosmo Topper* • Billie Burke *Mrs Topper* • Alan Mowbray *Wilkins* • Eugene Pallette *Casey* • Arthur Lake *Elevator boy* • Hedda Hopper *Mrs Stuyvesant* ■ *Dir* Norman Z McLeod • *Scr* Jack Jevne, Eric Hatch, Eddie Moran, from the novel *The Jovial Ghosts* by Thorne Smith

Topper Returns ★★★

Fantasy screwball comedy
1941 · US · BW · 88mins

The spooky slapstick series of three Topper pictures ended with this old dark house spoof. All the ingredients are here, including wall panels, hidden passages and disappearing bodies. The film begins with the killing of Joan Blondell, who then returns in phantom form to solve her own murder. There are quite a few laughs, but the movie is but a ghost of *Topper* (1937) and *Topper Takes a Trip* (1939), although Roland Young was his wonderfully bemused self again in the title role. RB

Roland Young *Cosmo Topper* • Joan Blondell *Gail Richards* • Carole Landis *Ann Carrington* • Billie Burke *Mrs Topper* • Dennis O'Keefe *Bob* • Patsy Kelly *Maid* • HB Warner *Henry Carrington/Walter Harberg* ■ *Dir* Roy Del Ruth • *Scr* Jonathan Latimer, Gordon Douglas, from characters created by Thorne Smith

Topper Takes a Trip ★★★ U

Fantasy screwball comedy
1939 · US · BW · 80mins

The sequel to the original *Topper* (1937), with Roland Young again playing hen-pecked banker Cosmo Topper, now being sued for divorce by Billie Burke. For no real reason, the action shifts to Europe where the spectral Constance Bennett – the reason for the divorce proceedings – works to save the marriage when Burke eyes a Riviera fancy boy. Cary Grant appears only a flashback to the first film but his role as Constance's constant companion is taken by a yapping dog. It's all very silly, but oddly sophisticated, too. AT

Constance Bennett *Marion Kerby* • Roland Young *Mr Cosmo Topper* • Billie Burke *Mrs Clara Topper* • Alan Mowbray *Wilkins* • Verree Teasdale *Mrs Parkhurst* • Franklin Pangborn *Louis, hotel manager* • Alexander D'Arcy [Alex D'Arcy] *Baron de Rossi* • Paul Hurst *Bartender* • Cary Grant *George Kerby* ■ *Dir* Norman Z McLeod • *Scr* Eddie Moran, Jack Jevne, Corey Ford, from the novel *Topper Takes a Trip* by Thorne Smith

Topsy-Turvy ★★★★★ 12

Biographical comedy drama
1999 · UK/US · Colour · 153mins

After Laurel and Hardy, the most notable odd couple in showbusiness is probably British operetta writers Gilbert and Sullivan. Director Mike Leigh here celebrates their collaborative genius, using the construction of *The Mikado* to show that their casual virtuosity was really painstaking craft. The newly-knighted Arthur Sullivan (Allan Corduner), a musician, lecher and dandy, met his literary match in William Schwenck Gilbert (Jim Broadbent), whose taste for the absurd extended to his librettos. Leigh skilfully convinces us that their separate talents spoke with one voice. TH. Contains one nude scene. [VIDEO] DVD

Jim Broadbent *William Schwenck Gilbert* • Allan Corduner *Arthur Sullivan* • Timothy Spall *Richard Temple* • Lesley Manville *Lucy "Kitty" Gilbert* • Ron Cook *Richard D'Oyly Carte* • Wendy Nottingham *Helen Lenoir* • Kevin McKidd *Durward Lely* • Shirley Henderson *Leonora Braham* • Alison Steadman *Madame Leon* ■ *Dir/Scr* Mike Leigh

Tora! Tora! Tora! ★★★ U

Second World War drama
1970 · US/Jpn · Colour · 136mins

This is a meticulous account of the preparations for and execution of the Japanese attack on the US naval base at Pearl Harbor on 7 December 1941. With Richard Fleischer staging the American segments and Toshio Masuda and Kinji Fukasaku directing events from the Japanese perspective, the film bends over backwards to show that patriotism, courage and commitment were present on both sides, and therein lies its weakness. The battle sequences are magnificent, but the production's even-handedness makes it impossible to judge the true impact of the happenings on either nation. DP. In Japanese and English with subtitles. [VIDEO] DVD

Martin Balsam *Admiral Husband E Kimmel* • Soh Yamamura [So Yamamura] *Admiral Isoroku Yamamoto* • Jason Robards Jr [Jason Robards] *General Walter C Short* • Joseph Cotten *Henry L Stimson* • Tatsuya Mihashi *Commander Minoru Genda* • EG Marshall *Lt Col Rufus S Bratton* • Takahiro Tamura *Lt Com Fuchida* • James Whitmore *Admiral William F Halsey* ■ *Dir* Richard Fleischer, Toshio Masuda, Kinji Fukasaku • *Scr* Larry Forrester, Hideo Oguni, Ryuzo Kikushima, from the book by Gordon W Prange and the book *The Broken Seal* by Ladislas Farago

Torch Singer ★★

Musical melodrama 1933 · US · BW · 70mins

Claudette Colbert, who seldom put a foot wrong in her long and prolific career, is the saving grace of this damp piece of soap that refuses to foam. She plays an unmarried entertainer who gives her baby away, regrets it and transforms herself from torch singer to children's radio show host while searching for the child. Feeble and unconvincing, but Colbert bravely battles against odds that include a dreary, wooden performance by Ricardo Cortez. RK

Claudette Colbert *Sally Trent/Mimi Benton* • Ricardo Cortez *Tony Cummings* • David Manners *Michael Gardner* • Lyda Roberti *Dora Nichols* • Charley Grapewin *Judson* ■ *Dir* Alexander Hall, George Somnes • *Scr* Lenore Coffee, Lynn Starling, from the short story *Mike* in *Liberty* magazine

Torch Song ★★

Romantic drama 1953 · US · Colour · 90mins

There's camp, and there's *Torch Song*. Joan Crawford (far too old) is an unhappy Broadway star, and Michael Wilding is a blind pianist who falls in love with her and nearly ruins his Hollywood career. Fortunately, his character can't see Crawford perform *Two-Faced Woman* in blackface, but, alas, we can. Charles Walters, appearing as Crawford's dancing partner in the opening number, directs this cliché-upon-cliché farrago. TS

Joan Crawford *Jenny Stewart* • Michael Wilding *Tye Graham* • Gig Young *Cliff Willard* • Marjorie Rambeau *Mrs Stewart* • Henry Morgan [Harry Morgan] *Joe Denner* • Dorothy Patrick *Martha* • James Todd *Philip Norton* ■ *Dir* Charles Walters • *Scr* John Michael Hayes, Jan Lustig, from the story *Why Should I Cry?* by IAR Wylie

Torch Song Trilogy ★★★★ 15

Drama 1988 · US · Colour · 114mins

The driving force behind this splendid gay romantic comedy drama is Harvey Fierstein, who repeats his Tony award-winning stage performance in this screen version of his own hit play. Although it occasionally lapses into soppiness, the script is a finely judged mix of sass and schmaltz. Gravel-voiced, camp and desperately vulnerable, Fierstein is tremendous, while Anne Bancroft does the best of her string of Jewish mama routines. The surprise is Matthew Broderick, who is perfect, playing against type, as Harvey's lover. DP [VIDEO]

Harvey Fierstein *Arnold Becker* • Anne Bancroft *Ma* • Matthew Broderick *Alan* • Brian Kerwin *Ed* • Karen Young *Laurel* • Eddie Castrodad *David* • Ken Page *Murray* • Charles Pierce *Bertha Venation* ■ *Dir* Paul Bogart • *Scr* Harvey Fierstein, from his play

Torchlight ★★ 18

Drama 1984 · US · Colour · 88mins

This "holier than thou" take on the dangers of cocaine addiction fails to be anything other than black and white. Artist Pamela Sue Martin meets construction boss Steve Railsback and, after a whirlwind romance, they marry. Their domestic bliss is shattered by the arrival of cocaine dealer Ian McShane. Director Tom Wright's morality tale may be a useful deterrent for teenagers, but adult audiences are likely to be unimpressed. LH [VIDEO] DVD

Pamela Sue Martin *Lillian Gregory* • Steve Railsback *Jake Gregory* • Ian McShane *Sidney* • Al Corley *Al* • Rita Taggart *Rita* • Arnie Moore *Richard* ■ *Dir* Tom Wright [Thomas J Wright] • *Scr* Eliza Moorman, Pamela Sue Martin

Torment ★★★ 12

Drama 1944 · Swe · BW · 96mins

This sombre work was the first big international Swedish success for more than two decades. It was rightly acclaimed at the time for its marvellous performances, especially from Mai Zetterling, and the clever sustained direction of Alf Sjöberg. Today, however, this study of schoolboy Alf Kjellin's affair with Zetterling, the mistress of his despised, despotic teacher (Stig Jarrel), is mainly of interest because its screenplay is by Ingmar Bergman, who would go on to become a giant of world cinema. TS. In Swedish with English subtitles. [VIDEO] DVD

Alf Kjellin *Jan-Erik* • Mai Zetterling *Bertha* • Stig Järrel *Caligula* • Olof Winnerstrand *School principal* • Gosta Cederlund *Pippi* ■ *Dir* Alf Sjöberg • *Scr* Ingmar Bergman

Torn Apart ★★

Romantic drama 1990 · US · Colour · 95mins

So much care has been taken not to offend anyone, that this adaptation of Chayym Zeldis's Romeo and Juliet novel offers few worthwhile insights into the extent to which the Middle East conflict affects everyday life. It also doesn't help casting a couple of photogenic Americans in the key roles of the Israeli soldier and his Arab girlfriend, even though both Adrian Pasdar and Cecilia Peck turn in creditable performances. DP

Adrian Pasdar *Ben Arnon* • Cecilia Peck *Laila Malek* • Barry Primus *Arie Arnon* • Machram Huri *Mahmoud Malek* • Arnon Zadok *Professor Mansour* • Margrit Polak *Ilana Arnon* ■ *Dir* Jack Fisher • *Scr* Marc Kristal, from the novel *A Forbidden Love* by Chayym Zeldis

Torn between Two Lovers ★★ PG

Romantic drama 1979 · US · Colour · 95mins

Lee Remick is torn between husband Joseph Bologna and George Peppard, the divorced architect she meets at an airport and has an affair with. The talented Remick is wasted in this stereotypical role, and viewers may not find her choice between Bologna and Peppard particularly enviable either. Director Delbert Mann – who won an Oscar for his first film, *Marty*, in 1955 – keeps a thin layer of crustiness over the slush. The movie was inspired by a a treacly 1970s ballad. AT [VIDEO]

Lee Remick *Diane Conti* • George Peppard *Paul Rassmussen* • Joseph Bologna *Ted Conti* • Derrick Jones *Andy Conti* • Murphy Cross *Nina Dworski* • Molly Cheek *Sherry Sanders* ■ *Dir* Delbert Mann • *Scr* Doris Silverton, from a story by Doris Silverton, Rita Lakin

Torn Curtain ★★★ 15

Spy thriller 1966 · US · Colour · 122mins

What looked in its day to be a failure and a disappointment to fans of Alfred Hitchcock does, at least, contain one of the maestro's most compelling sequences. "I wanted to show how difficult it is to kill someone," Hitch said, and in a prolonged scene involving Paul Newman played without dialogue he certainly does. It's the high spot in a remarkably ridiculous Cold War thriller, very much of its period, with phoney locations, phonier (although admittedly deliberate) back projection, and, phoniest of all, the casting of Newman and Julie Andrews as an alleged American defector and his fiancée. If there was any chemistry between the stars, it certainly doesn't show on the screen. TS [VIDEO] DVD

Paul Newman *Professor Michael Armstrong* • Julie Andrews *Sarah Sherman* • Lila Kedrova *Countess Kuchinska* • Hansjoerg Felmy [Hansjörg Felmy] *Heinrich Gerhard* • Tamara Toumanova *Ballerina* • Ludwig Donath *Professor Gustav Lindt* • Wolfgang Kieling *Hermann Gromek* • Günter Strack *Professor Karl Manfred* ■ *Dir* Alfred Hitchcock • *Scr* Brian Moore, from his story

Tornado! ★★ PG

Action adventure 1996 · US · Colour · 83mins

Ernie Hudson is the scientist looking to perfect a machine that can detect lethal tornados, while Bruce Campbell is his dashing, risk-taking chum. Shannon Sturges provides the love interest as the grumpy accountant who finally succumbs to Campbell's charms. The action breezes along, but this TV movie lacks the budget for any extraordinary visual effects. JF. Contains swearing. [VIDEO] DVD

Bruce Campbell *Jake Thorne* • Shannon Sturges *Sam Callen* • Ernie Hudson *Dr Branson* ■ *Dir* Noel Nosseck • *Scr* John Logan

Torpedo Run ★★★ U

Second World War drama
1958 · US · Colour · 95mins

Claustrophobically made in CinemaScope, this boasts a tense plot as commander Glenn Ford accidentally blows up a Japanese prison ship with his own family on board. The chase is then on to find the enemy aircraft carrier which used the ship as a shield. This is from the most successful period in Ford's career, and his nervy, tense performance is mesmerising. Director Joseph Pevney had made the enjoyable war drama *Away All Boats*, but here the pacing is a shade too slow. TS

Glenn Ford *Lt Cmdr Barney Doyle* • Ernest Borgnine *Lt Archer Sloan* • Diane Brewster *Jane Doyle* • Dean Jones *Lt Jake "Fuzz" Foley* • LQ Jones *"Hash" Benson* • Philip Ober *Admiral Samuel Setton* • Richard Carlyle *Cmdr*

T

Don Adams ■ *Dir* Joseph Pevney • *Scr* Richard Sale, William Wister Haines, from stories by Richard Sale

Torque ★★★ 15

Action thriller
2003 · US/Aus · Colour · 80mins

Tongue-in-cheek trash with flash doesn't get much more enjoyable than the feature debut of music video director Joseph Kahn. This pokes as much fun at the "choppers and chicks" genre as it does its high-gear self. The improbable tale has ace biker Martin Henderson returning from Thailand to clear his name of drug-smuggling charges, only to be framed for murder. The script is dumb and the acting dumber, but it doesn't matter. Kahn knows his audience wants to see mega-octane thrills and he doesn't disappoint. AJ. Contains swearing and violence. DVD

Martin Henderson *Cary Ford* • Ice Cube *Trey* • Monet Mazur *Shane* • Adam Scott *McPherson* • Matt Schulze *Henry* • Jaime Pressly *China* • Jay Hernandez *Dalton* • Will Yun Lee *Val* ■ *Dir* Joseph Kahn • *Scr* Matt Johnson

Torremolinos 73 ★★★ 15

Comedy
2003 · Sp/Den · Colour and BW · 91mins

This debut feature from Spanish director Pablo Berger gently pokes fun at the porn industry, art house movies and General Franco. In early 1970s Madrid, mild-mannered Javier Cámara is a struggling door-to-door salesman. When his employers decide to try their luck with sex education films for the Scandinavian market, Cámara begins making and appearing in them along with his wife (Candela Peña). Their efforts bring them success and wealth, but she wants a baby, while he aspires to become a serious director. Though it lacks the bite of a classic social satire, this small-scale production remains consistently funny. BP. In Spanish and Danish with English subtitles. Contains sex scenes and swearing.

Javier Cámara *Alfredo Alfredo López* • Candela Peña *Carmen* • Juan Diego *Don Carlos* • Malena Alterio *Vanessa* • Fernando Tejero *Juan Luis* • Mads Mikkelsen *Magnus* • Ramón Barea *José Carlos Romerales* • Thomas Bo Larsen *Dennis* ■ *Dir/Scr* Pablo Berger

The Torrent ★★★★

Silent romantic drama
1926 · US · BW · 68mins

Vicente Blasco-Ibañez was one of the most adapted novelists of the silent era, and it was one of his potboilers that provided Greta Garbo with her Hollywood entrance. Starring opposite MGM's very own Latin lover, Ricardo Cortez, she was somewhat improbably cast as a provincial Spanish girl, who recovers from their parting by becoming a famous Parisian diva. Even at the age of 20, Garbo's genius is apparent in the small, slow, seductive movements that reveal the psychological intensity that would become her trademark. DP

Ricardo Cortez *Don Rafael Brull* • Greta Garbo *Leonora* • Gertrude Olmsted *Remedios* • Edward Connelly *Pedro Moreno* ■ *Dir* Monta Bell • *Scr* Katherine Hilliker (titles), HH Caldwell (titles), from the novel *Entre Naranjos (Among the Orange Trees)* by Vicente Blasco-Ibañez, adapted by Dorothy Farnum

Torrents of Spring ★★ PG

Period romantic drama
1989 · Fr/It · Colour · 97mins

Jerzy Skolimowski has badly misjudged the tone of Ivan Turgenev's novel and turned a stifling chamber drama into a dreamily sunlit travelogue. Instead of being driven to distraction by his love for German baker's daughter Valeria Golino and his passion for married noblewoman Nastassja Kinski, Timothy Hutton merely looks alternately moon-faced and peevish. DP

Timothy Hutton *Dimitri Sanin* • Nastassja Kinski *Maria Nikolaevna Polozov* • Valeria Golino *Gemma Rosselli* • Francesca De Sapio *Signora Rosselli – Gemma's mother* • William Forsythe *Polozov* • Urbano Barberini *Von Doenhof* • Jacques Herlin *Pantaleone* ■ *Dir* Jerzy Skolimowski • *Scr* Jerzy Skolimowski, Arcangelo Bonaccorso, from the novel *Spring Torrents* by Ivan Turgenev

Torrid Zone ★★★

Adventure 1940 · US · BW · 93mins

The combustible James Cagney here sports a pencil-thin moustache and a sneer. Pat O'Brien, Cagney's boss, runs an export business in Central America and saloon singer Ann Sheridan, then known as the "Oomph Girl", competes with Helen Vinson for Cagney's attention. This sweaty piece of tropical torpor was never that torrid, but is still enjoyable. AT

James Cagney *Nick Butler* • Pat O'Brien *Steve Case* • Ann Sheridan *Lee Donley* • Andy Devine *Wally Davis* • Helen Vinson *Gloria Anderson* • George Tobias *Rosario* • Jerome Cowan *Bob Anderson* ■ *Dir* William Keighley • *Scr* Richard Macaulay, Jerry Wald

Tortilla Flat ★★★ U

Drama 1942 · US · Sepia · 105mins

Off-screen machinations marked the transition from page to screen of John Steinbeck's novel. John Garfield was keen to star as the newly wealthy Danny, but MGM had to pull out all the stops in their efforts to persuade Warner Bros to release him. Spencer Tracy and Akim Tamiroff have plum roles as a couple of freeloaders talking Garfield into letting them have one of the houses he's inherited. Hedy Lamarr had the best part of her career as the strong-minded object of Garfield's affections in this amiable drama that was a bigger hit with critics than public on its initial release. TH

Spencer Tracy *Pilon* • Hedy Lamarr *Dolores "Sweets" Ramirez* • John Garfield *Danny* • Akim Tamiroff *Pablo* • Frank Morgan *Pirate* • Sheldon Leonard *Tito Ralph* • John Qualen *Jose Maria Corcoran* • Donald Meek *Paul D Cummings* ■ *Dir* Victor Fleming • *Scr* John Lee Mahin, Benjamin Glaser, from the novel by John Steinbeck

Tortilla Soup ★★★ PG

Comedy drama 2001 · US · Colour · 99mins

The showboating of a miscast Raquel Welch and an over-abundance of feelgood elements are the only ingredients to sour this flavoursome remake of Ang Lee's *Eat Drink Man Woman*. Transposing the scene to a Los Angeles restaurant, the action turns around Hector Elizondo, a chef with failing taste buds. He has a trio of daughters: sanctimonious teacher Elizabeth Peña, firebrand foodie Jacqueline Obradors and dreamer Tamara Mello. Director Maria Ripoll could have added a pinch more social spice to the scenes of sibling bonding, but the performances are splendid. DP. Contains swearing. DVD

Hector Elizondo *Martin Naranjo* • Jacqueline Obradors *Carmen Naranjo* • Elizabeth Peña *Leticia Naranjo* • Tamara Mello *Maribel Naranjo* • Nikolai Kinski *Andy* • Paul Rodriguez *Orlando* • Raquel Welch *Hortensia* • Constance Marie *Yolanda* ■ *Dir* Maria Ripoll • *Scr* Tom Musca, Ramon Menendez, Vera Blasi, from the film *Eat Drink Man Woman* by Ang Lee, James Schamus, Hui-Ling Wang

The Tortoise and the Hare ★★★★★

Animated comedy 1935 · US · Colour · 8mins

One of the Disney studio's many landmark cartoons of the 1930s, this Oscar-winning retelling of Aesop's fable marked the first successful animation of speed. Whereas previous cartoons carefully delineated every stage of a character's movement, rendering it potentially graceful but sluggish, the movements of Max Hare in this film are often reduced to a mixture of extreme start-and-finish movements and intermediate blurs, some lasting for only a few frames. Meanwhile, the athletic accuracy of Max's movements lends credibility to his impossible speed as well as the far-fetched comedy that results. This film had a profound influence on the cartoon industry, especially at Warner Bros where speed became essential to Looney Tunes humour, reaching its apex in those Bugs Bunny shorts. CLP

Dir Wilfred Jackson

Torture Garden ★★★ 15

Horror 1967 · UK · Colour · 96mins

A group of fairground visitors are shown their futures by the strange Dr Diabolo (Burgess Meredith) in one of the better compendium chillers from Amicus, Hammer's main British horror rival. Robert (*Psycho*) Bloch's skilful script, which includes cannibal cats, haunted pianos, eternal Hollywood life and the reincarnation of Edgar Allan Poe, gives director Freddie Francis imaginative opportunities to indulge in stylish camerawork for maximum gothic effect. AJ

Jack Palance *Ronald Wyatt* • Beverly Adams *Carla Haynes* • Burgess Meredith *Dr Diabolo* • Peter Cushing *Lancelot Canning* • Michael Bryant *Colin Williams* • Maurice Denham *Colin's uncle* • John Standing *Leo* • Robert Hutton *Paul* ■ *Dir* Freddie Francis • *Scr* Robert Bloch, from his stories *Enoch*, *Terror Over Hollywood, Mr Steinway, The Man Who Collected Poe*

Tosca ★★ PG

Opera 2001 · Fr/It/Ger/UK · Col/BW · 124m

Less a record of a performance than the performance of a record, Benoît Jacquot's rarefied adaptation of Puccini's opera divides its time between lustrous monochrome footage of the cast's studio sessions with the orchestra and chorus of the Royal Opera House, and fragmented scenes meticulously staged on a deliciously artificial set. Ruggero Raimondi impresses as the machiavellian police chief who tricks singer Angela Gheorghiu into betraying artist Roberto Alagna's sheltering of a fugitive. However, the inconsistent lip-synching proves as distracting from the music as the utterly superfluous video inserts. DP. In Italian with English subtitles.

Angela Gheorghiu *Tosca* • Roberto Alagna *Mario Cavaradossi* • Ruggero Raimondi *Scarpia* • David Cangelosi *Spoletta* • Sorin Coliban *Sciarrone* • Enrico Fissore *Sacristan* • Maurizio Muraro *Angelotti* ■ *Dir* Benoît Jacquot • *Scr* Benoît Jacquot, from the opera by Giacomo Puccini, Luigi Illica, Giuseppe Giacosa, from the play by Victorien Sardou

The Total Balalaika Show ★★★★

Concert documentary
1994 · Fin · Colour · 56mins

The Leningrad Cowboys and the Red Army Choir might not sound like the perfect combination, but as Aki Kaurismäki's joyous concert movie proves, they are a match made in musical heaven. Considering they were once the self-proclaimed worst band in the world, the Cowboys belt out terrific versions of the Turtles's *Happy Together* and ZZ Top's *Gimme All Your Lovin'*, while the Army renditions of *Volga Boatmen, Kalinka* (complete with Cossack-dancing Cowboys) and *Dark Eyes* are sublime. Totally capturing the euphoric atmosphere of the event, this is quite an experience. DP. An English/Russian language film.

Dir Aki Kaurismäki

Total Eclipse ★★ 18

Biographical drama
1995 · UK/Fr/Bel · Colour · 106mins

Female *Titanic* fanatics will probably want to catch this film because it features teen heart-throb Leonardo DiCaprio in the buff, but apart from that they are likely to be disappointed. Director Agnieszka Holland and writer Christopher Hampton have produced a stodgy biopic that focuses on the more lurid aspects of the (sadomasochistic) relationship between 19th-century poets Verlaine (David Thewlis) and Rimbaud (DiCaprio). JB DVD

Leonardo DiCaprio *Arthur Rimbaud* • David Thewlis *Paul Verlaine* • Romane Bohringer *Mathilde Verlaine* • Dominique Blanc *Isabelle Rimbaud* • Nita Klein *Rimbaud's mother* • Christopher Hampton *The judge* ■ *Dir* Agnieszka Holland • *Scr* Christopher Hampton

Total Recall ★★★★ 18

Science-fiction thriller
1990 · US · Colour · 108mins

Director Paul Verhoeven, armed with a smart script loosely based on a short story by cult novelist Philip K Dick, cuts loose with a gloriously over-the-top mix of black humour, ultra-violence and spectacular effects. Arnold Schwarzenegger stars as the dull construction worker who is drawn into a conspiracy on the planet Mars when a virtual reality holiday awakens long-dormant memories. However, the real find turned out to be Sharon Stone, whose performance led to her ground-breaking role in Verhoeven's next movie, *Basic Instinct*. JF. Contains violence, swearing, nudity. DVD

Arnold Schwarzenegger *Douglas Quaid* • Rachel Ticotin *Melina* • Sharon Stone *Lori Quaid* • Ronny Cox *Cohaagen* • Michael Ironside *Richter* • Marshall Bell *George/Kuato* • Mel Johnson Jr *Benny* • Michael Champion *Helm* • Roy Brocksmith *Dr Edgemar* ■ *Dir* Paul Verhoeven • *Scr* Ronald Shusett, Dan O'Bannon, Gary Goldman, from a story by Ronald Shusett, Dan O'Bannon, Jon Povill, from the short story *We Can Remember It for You Wholesale* by Philip K Dick

Totally F***ed Up ★★★ 18

Comedy drama 1993 · US · Colour · 75mins

In 15 numbered chapters, six gay and lesbian LA teenagers divulge every minute detail about how screwed up their disenfranchised lives are. There's the slacker, the would-be film-maker, his artist boyfriend, the skateboarder, and two lesbians who dream of having a baby. Edgy, moody, humorous and containing some immensely powerful moments, this is a penetrating look at what it means to be young, gay and terminally bored. AJ

James Duval *Andy* • Roko Belic *Tommy* • Susan Behshid *Michele* • Jenee Gill *Patricia* • Gilbert Luna *Steven* • Lance May *Deric* • Alan Boyce *Ian* • Craig Gilmore *Brendan* ■ *Dir/Scr* Gregg Araki

Toto Le Héros ★★★★ 15

Drama 1991 · Bel/Fr/ Ger · Colour · 87mins

Jaco Van Dormael made an outstanding start to his directorial career with this remarkable film that is both a beguiling portrait of childhood and a touching treatise on unrealised dreams. Slipping between past and present through a sequence of stylish flashbacks, Van Dormael traces the lifelong resentment of Thomas, who has waited 60 years to avenge himself on Alfred, a business tycoon, with whom Thomas believes he was switched shortly after birth. The three actors who play Toto are all superb, but it's the dark humour, atmosphere and narrative complexity that make this

T

so enthralling. DP. In French with English subtitles. Contains violence, nudity. [video]

Michel Bouquet *Old Thomas* • Jo de Backer *Adult Thomas* • Thomas Godet *Young Thomas* • Gisela Uhlen *Old Evelyne* • Mireille Perrier *Adult Evelyne* • Sandrine Blancke *Alice* • Peter Böhlke *Old Alfred* • Didier Ferney *Adult Alfred* ■ *Dir/Scr* Jaco Van Dormael

The Touch ★★★ 15

Drama 1971 · US/Swe · Colour · 107mins

On the surface, this appears to be one of Ingmar Bergman's lesser chamber dramas. In the Swedish master's first English-language film, Elliott Gould appears uncomfortable playing the Jewish archaeologist who embarks on an affair with Bibi Andersson. The film takes on deeper meaning when we realise it is a meditation on the troubled marriage of Bergman's parents, with the photograph Andersson shows Gould of her mother actually depicting Karin Bergman. DP [video]

Bibi Andersson *Karin Vergerus* • Elliott Gould *David Kovac* • Max von Sydow *Andreas Vergerus* • Sheila Reid *Sara* • Staffan Hallerstram *Anders Vergerus* • Maria Nolgard *Agnes Vergerus* ■ *Dir/Scr* Ingmar Bergman

Touch ★★★ 15

Comedy drama
1996 · US/Fr · Colour · 93mins

Director Paul Schrader's first feature after a long lay-off is a quizzical adaptation of bestselling author Elmore Leonard's atypical novel. Deftly skirting supernatural satire, this uncommonly sophisticated and amusing comic fable focuses on Skeet Ulrich, an ex-monk with curative abilities, whose gift is seen by opportunist Christopher Walken as media gold. Loaded with fine performances and acute observations on media manipulation and right wing religious extremists, Schrader's deliciously oddball movie is wonderfully eccentric. AJ [video] DVD

Bridget Fonda *Lynn Faulkner* • Christopher Walken *Bill Hill* • Skeet Ulrich *Juvenal* • Gina Gershon *Debra Lusanne* • Tom Arnold *August Murray* • Paul Mazursky *Artie* • Janeane Garofalo *Kathy Worthington* • LL Cool J ■ *Dir* Paul Schrader • *Scr* Paul Schrader, from the novel by Elmore Leonard

Touch and Go ★ U

Comedy 1955 · UK · Colour · 81mins

A depressing wallow in the sort of whimsy that Ealing foisted upon the world as British Realism. This clumsy clash of ancient and modern revolves around the furniture designer Jack Hawkins's decision to emigrate to Australia when his latest efforts are deemed too futuristic by his stick-in-the-mud employer. DP [video]

Jack Hawkins *Jim Fletcher* • Margaret Johnston *Helen Fletcher* • June Thorburn *Peggy Fletcher* • John Fraser *Richard Kenyon* • Roland Culver *Reg Fairbright* • Alison Leggatt *Alice Fairbright* ■ *Dir* Michael Truman • *Scr* William Rose, from a story by Tania Rose, William Rose

Touch and Go ★ 15

Romantic comedy drama
1986 · US · Colour · 97mins

Comedian Michael Keaton tries flexing his dramatic muscle for the first time in a formula romance that, despite its violent conclusion, remains grounded in sentiment. He plays a Chicago hockey star who becomes involved with single mother Maria Conchita Alonso after her son has tried to mug him. The usual relationship problems ensue, which never hit any note of truth and stick essentially to sitcom parameters. AJ [video] DVD

Michael Keaton *Bobby Barbato* • Maria Conchita Alonso *Denise DeLeon* • Ajay Naidu *Louis DeLeon* • John Reilly *Jerry Pepper* • Maria Tucci *Dee Dee* ■ *Dir* Robert Mandel • *Scr* Alan Ormsby, Bob Sand, Harry Colomby

Touch Me ★★★

Romantic drama
1997 · US · Colour · 104mins

Although several films have been made about Aids from the gay perspective, few have explored the prevalence of the condition among heterosexuals. Striving to avoid the preachiness with which Hollywood invests so many of its message movies, this drama has its share of turmoils and betrayals. Amanda Peet may be playing struggling actress, but her reaction to discovering that she is HIV-positive is both human and understandable. Equally admirable is the emphasis placed on courage and hope rather than recrimination and self-pity. DP. Contains swearing, sex scenes and nudity.

Amanda Peet *Bridgette* • Michael Vartan *Adam* • Peter Facinelli *Bail* • Kari Wuhrer *Margot* • Erica Gimpel *Kareen* ■ *Dir* H Gordon Boos • *Scr* H Gordon Boos, from a story by H Gordon Boos, Greg H Sims

A Touch of Adultery ★ 15

Romantic comedy 1991 · It · Colour · 98mins

The teaming of perennial *Mary Poppins* virgin Julie Andrews with Italian heart-throb Marcello Mastroianni must have looked good on paper. But both stars are ill-served by a vacuous script about two recently divorced strangers finding solace and companionship with each other. Leaden direction by Gene Saks doesn't help. AJ [video]

Julie Andrews *Pamela Picquet* • Marcello Mastroianni *Cesareo Gramaldi* • Ian Fitzgibbon *Bobby Picquet* • Jean-Pierre Castaldi *Marcel* • Jean-Jacques Dulon *Dr Noiret* • Maria Marchado *Miss Knudson* ■ *Dir* Gene Saks • *Scr* Ronald Harwood, from the play *Tchin Tchin* by François Billetdoux

A Touch of Class ★★★★★

Romantic comedy
1973 · UK · Colour · 105mins

This is classy stuff, indeed, as married American George Segal becomes an emotional prisoner of Glenda Jackson, a divorcee designer whose British barbs sink home painfully as Segal attempts a series of romantic passes. Co-writer/director Melvin Frank hones the script to a cutting edge to ensure that sentimentality does not oversweeten the romance, and succeeds in keeping the piece ironically humorous rather than schmaltzily corny, which it so easily could have become. Jackson won an Oscar for this one, though Segal's harassed stud should have received an award for unbuttoned bewilderment. TH. Contains swearing.

George Segal *Steve Blackburn* • Glenda Jackson *Vicki Allessio* • Paul Sorvino *Walter Menkes* • Hildegard Neil *Gloria Blackburn* • Cec Linder *Wendell Thompson* • K Callan *Patty Menkes* • Mary Barclay *Martha Thompson* ■ *Dir* Melvin Frank • *Scr* Melvin Frank, Jack Rose

Touch of Evil ★★★★★ 12

Classic crime drama
1958 · US · BW · 104mins

It was star Charlton Heston (improbably cast as a Mexican) who persuaded Universal to hire Orson Welles to direct this crime thriller. In so doing, he secured not only Welles's most magnificent late character creation (as corrupt corpulent cop Hank Quinlan), but also the film that virtually capped a style the great Welles himself had helped create. It's a byzantine and brilliant melodrama that rivets an audience from its now justly-famed opening title sequence to its grisly finale. In composition, in dialogue and character, and in sheer style, this is what cinema can and should be capable of, and it took the genius of Orson Welles to turn the cheap novel *Badge of Evil* into this terrifically entertaining study in depravity. TS [video] DVD

Charlton Heston *Ramon Miguel "Mike" Vargas* • Janet Leigh *Susan Vargas* • Orson Welles *Hank Quinlan* • Joseph Calleia *Pete Menzies* • Akim Tamiroff *"Uncle" Joe Grandi* • Joanna Moore *Marcia Linnekar* • Ray Collins *Adair* • Dennis Weaver *The night man* • Valentin de Vargas *Pancho* • Marlene Dietrich *Tanya* • Zsa Zsa Gabor *Strip club owner* • Joseph Cotten *Coroner* • Mercedes McCambridge *Gang leader* • Keenan Wynn ■ *Dir* Orson Welles • *Scr* Orson Welles, from the novel *Badge of Evil* by Whit Masterson • *Cinematographer* Russell Metty

A Touch of Larceny ★★★ U

Comedy 1959 · UK · BW · 94mins

James Mason was never anything less than a suave and sophisticated performer. However, comedy was not really his forte, even when it was as gentle as in this urbane tale of treachery and libel. The film benefits from the polished presence of that other silky screen smoothie, George Sanders, and willing support from Vera Miles. DP

James Mason *Commander Max Easton* • George Sanders *Sir Charles Holland* • Vera Miles *Virginia Killain* • Oliver Johnston *Minister* • Robert Flemyng *Larkin* ■ *Dir* Guy Hamilton • *Scr* Roger MacDougall, Paul Winterton, Ivan Foxwell, Guy Hamilton, from the novel *The Megstone Plot* by Andrew Garve

A Touch of Love ★★★ 15

Drama 1969 · UK · Colour · 102mins

Margaret Drabble adapted her novel, *The Millstone*, for this capable and well-made social drama. An unwed student (Sandy Dennis, in one of her most effective performances) loses her virginity and becomes pregnant. The rest of the cast is also strong, including Ian McKellen's sharp television announcer, the unwitting father of the child. JG [video]

Sandy Dennis *Rosamund Stacey* • Ian McKellen *George* • Eleanor Bron *Lydia* • John Standing *Roger* • Michael Coles *Joe* • Rachel Kempson *Sister Harvey* • Margaret Tyzack *Sister Bennett* ■ *Dir* Waris Hussein • *Scr* Margaret Drabble, from her novel *The Millstone*

A Touch of the Sun ★★ U

Comedy 1956 · UK · BW · 77mins

Try as he might, Frankie Howerd just couldn't crack movies. This was his fifth feature after he made his name on radio's *Variety Bandbox*, but the harder he mugged, the less amusing he became. He stars here as a bellboy who uses an unexpected inheritance to buy the hotel where he once worked. He then installs his workmates as satisfied guests in a bid to dupe a cabal of avaricious snobs. DP [video]

Frankie Howerd *William Darling* • Ruby Murray *Ruby* • Dennis Price *Hatchard* • Dorothy Bromiley *Rose* • Katherine Kath *Lucienne* • Gordon Harker *Sid* • Reginald Beckwith *Hardcastle* ■ *Dir* Gordon Parry • *Scr* Alfred Shaughnessy

A Touch of the Sun ★

Comedy 1979 · UK/US · Colour · 93mins

This would-be comedy stars Oliver Reed as a bumbling US Army officer and Peter Cushing as a British commissioner who attempt to recover an American spaceship that's being held for ransom by an African emperor. The humour is so strained as to be sieved of all fun. TH. Contains violence and swearing.

Oliver Reed *Captain Nelson* • Sylvaine Charlet *Natasha* • Peter Cushing *Commissioner Potts* • Keenan Wynn *General Spelvin* • Edwin Manda *Emperor Sumumba* • Fred Carter *President P Nutts* • Hilary Pritchard *Miss Funnypenny* • Wilfrid Hyde White *M1* ■ *Dir* Peter Curran • *Scr* Alfred Shaughnessy

A Touch of Zen ★★★★ 12

Martial arts action drama
1969 · Tai · Colour · 169mins

Hu King was one of the masters of the *wu xia* or swordplay film, yet this labyrinthine epic is much more than a simple action flick. This is at the same time a study of rural life, a ghost story, a discussion of philosophical ideas and a thrilling fight film, with each element being handled with rare skill by Hu, a director whose love of Chinese opera and classical art is clearly evident in every frame. DP. In Mandarin with English subtitles. [video] DVD

Hsu Feng *Yang* • Chun Shih *Ku* • Pai Ying *Shih* • Tien Peng *Ou-Yang* • Hsueh Han *Lu* ■ *Dir/Scr* Hu King

The Touchables ★★★

Sex comedy 1968 · UK · Colour · 93mins

Nearly 30 years before the Spice Girls introduced us to Girl Power, there was this unashamedly trivial romp in which four young women kidnap a male pop star for their own pleasure. Disliked at the time, because of its shallowness, it now appears to be both ahead of and a true mirror of its time – the height of the Swinging Sixties. A weak script by Ian La Frenais without Dick Clement, suggests that the boys work better together. But debut director Robert Freeman, who photographed several Beatles album covers, creates some pretty pictures, and the credits feature many surprising names. DM

Judy Huxtable *Sadie* • Esther Anderson *Melanie* • Marilyn Rickard *Busbee* • Kathy Simmonds *Samson* • David Anthony (1) *Christian* • Ricki Starr *Ricki* ■ *Dir* Robert Freeman • *Scr* Ian La Frenais, from a script by David Cammell, Donald Cammell, from an idea by Robert Freeman

Touchdown ★★ 15

Drama 1981 · US · Colour · 86mins

Co-director Silvio Narizzano made *Georgy Girl* in 1966, so he can be forgiven for foisting this preachy slice of high-school angst on an unsuspecting public. A boy, crazy about football and music, goes into an emotional tailspin after being diagnosed as partially deaf, falling in with a bad lot who rampage through the school. The film was released on video five years later, for those who wanted to see Demi Moore making her movie debut. FL [video]

Paul Carafotes *John Carluccio* • Victor French *Gary Carluccio* • Lelia Goldoni *Jean Carluccio* • Val Avery *Coach Rizo* • Dennis Patrick *Dr Bowers* • Demi Moore *Corri* ■ *Dir* Silvio Narizzano, Rami Alon • *Scr* Rami Alon

Touched by Love ★★★ U

Drama based on a true story
1979 · US · Colour · 93mins

Also known as *To Elvis, with Love* (a title which tends to give away the plot), this moving if somewhat sentimental drama is based on a true story. It's a tale of a child with cerebral palsy who becomes more open and communicative after a nursing trainee (Deborah Raffin) encourages her to write a letter to Elvis Presley. Raffin gives a competent performance as Lena Canada (she received a Golden Globe nomination) but it is a young Diane Lane who steals the film. JB [video]

Deborah Raffin *Lena Canada* • Diane Lane *Karen* • Michael Learned *Dr Bell* • John Amos *Tony* • Cristina Raines *Amy* • Mary Wickes *Margaret* • Clu Gulager *Don Fielder* ■ *Dir* Gus Trikonis • *Scr* Hesper Anderson, from the book *To Elvis, with Love* by Lena Canada

T

Touching the Void ★★★★ 15

Documentary drama
2003 · UK/US · Colour · 101mins

This vivid survival docudrama recounts the harrowing story of British climbing buddies Joe Simpson and Simon Yates. When his own life is threatened, Yates is forced to abandon his partner, leaving him for dead high in the Peruvian Andes. But, remarkably, Simpson survives and despite a shattered leg manages to crawl painfully back to base camp. It's impossible not to wince as he makes the incredible journey. The film combines interviews with the climbers with terrific reconstructions of their ordeals, both physical and psychological. Directed by Kevin Macdonald, who made the equally impressive *One Day in September*, about the terrorist attack on the 1972 Munich Olympic Games, this is dramatised documentary-making at its peak. DA. Contains swearing. DVD

Brendan Mackey *Joe Simpson* • Nicholas Aaron *Simon Yates* • Ollie Ryall *Richard Hawking* ■ *Dir* Kevin Macdonald • *Scr* from the non-fiction book by Joe Simpson • *Cinematographer* Mike Eley

Tough Enough ★ 15

Sports drama 1982 · US · Colour · 101mins

This is a forgettable attempt by Richard Fleischer to explore the ugly world of the "Tough Man" fighting circuit in America. Dennis Quaid struggles as the failing singer turned fighter and the storyline is barely worthy of lasting the first round, let alone going the distance. NF

Dennis Quaid *Art Long* • Carlene Watkins *Caroline Long* • Warren Oates *James Neese* • Stan Shaw *PT Coolidge* • Pam Grier *Myra* • Bruce McGill *Tony Fallon* • Wilford Brimley *Bill Long* • Fran Ryan *Gert Long* ■ *Dir* Richard O Fleischer [Richard Fleischer] • *Scr* John Leone

Tough Guys ★★★ 15

Comedy 1986 · US · Colour · 99mins

To watch Kirk Douglas and Burt Lancaster use their combined star power to rescue a ropey script is to witness celebrity at its most intense and endearing. As the perpetrators of America's last train robbery, they are released from prison, elderly and bewildered, into an ageist world, so they mount their own grey offensive. Douglas's athletic and sexual prowess is a show-off embarrassment, but Lancaster retains a dignity and poise which confronts the dilemma of age with enormous poignancy. Both, though, spark an on-screen magic. TH. Contains violence, swearing. DVD

Burt Lancaster *Harry Doyle* • Kirk Douglas *Archie Long* • Charles Durning *Deke Yablonski* • Alexis Smith *Belle* • Dana Carvey *Richie Evans* • Darlanne Fluegel *Skye Foster* • Eli Wallach *Leon B Little* • Monty Ash *Vince* ■ *Dir* Jeff Kanew • *Scr* James Orr, Jim Cruickshank

Tough Guys Don't Dance ★★ 18

Black comedy 1987 · US · Colour · 104mins

This bizarre black comedy with *film noir* flourishes was written and directed by Norman Mailer as an exercise in experimental movie-making. Ryan O'Neal plays a downtrodden would-be writer who may have committed a murder – but can't quite remember. Yes, it's that sort of film, with lots of weird people running around, saying weird things. The movie seeks to send up Raymond Chandler, but only works intermittently. DA

Ryan O'Neal *Tim Madden* • Isabella Rossellini *Madeline* • Debra Sandlund *Patty Lareine* • Wings Hauser *Regency* • John Bedford Lloyd *Wardley Meeks III* • Clarence Williams III *Bolo* • Lawrence Tierney *Dougy Madden* ■ *Dir/Scr* Norman Mailer

Tourist Trap ★ 15

Horror 1979 · US · Colour · 89mins

Suspense is a rare commodity in this low-budget horror flick that focuses on a group of teens who get marooned in the desert when their jeep breaks down. Unluckily for them it's near a museum housing a collection of wax models controlled by nutty Chuck Connors. It's tempting to say that the dummies give the best performances. RS

Chuck Connors *Slausen* • Jon Van Ness *Jerry* • Jocelyn Jones *Molly* • Robin Sherwood *Eileen* • Tanya Roberts *Becky* • Keith McDermott *Woody* ■ *Dir* David Schmoeller • *Scr* David Schmoeller, J Larry Carroll

Tous les Matins du Monde ★★★★ 15

Historical drama 1991 · Fr · Colour · 109mins

The winner of seven Césars (the French equivalent to the Oscars), this majestic historical costume drama is a delight for both eyes and ears. Jean-Pierre Marielle is outstanding as 17th-century composer Sainte Colombe, while on his debut Guillaume Depardieu is splendidly dashing as his sole pupil, Marin Marais. Guillaume's father Gérard Depardieu has a choice cameo as the older Marais, who becomes Louis XIV's musical director, looking back with regret on his reckless youth, when he betrayed Sainte Colombe's daughter and only half learned the lessons of the master. Director Alain Corneau captures the period perfectly and the baroque viola da gamba music is magnificent. DP. In French with English subtitles. Contains sex scenes and nudity.

Jean-Pierre Marielle *Monsieur de Sainte Colombe* • Gérard Depardieu *Marin Marais* • Anne Brochet *Madeleine* • Guillaume Depardieu *Young Marin Marais* • Caroline Sihol *Mme de Sainte Colombe* • Carole Richert *Toinette* • Michel Bouquet *Baugin* ■ *Dir* Alain Corneau • *Scr* Pascal Quignard, Alain Corneau, from the novel by Pascal Quignard

Tout Va Bien ★★★ 18

Experimental political drama
1972 · Fr/It · Colour · 91mins

After four years of making 16mm and video movies, Marxist co-directors Jean-Luc Godard and Jean-Pierre Gorin returned to "commercial" film-making by casting Jane Fonda and Yves Montand in the leading roles. But audiences didn't exactly flock to see this depiction of workers occupying their factory and holding their bosses prisoner. Fonda plays an American journalist and Montand – her lover – a former New Wave director now forced to make TV ads for a living, as Godard himself had done. There is a lot of serious talk, a splendid composite set and a few jokes. RB. In French with English subtitles.

Jane Fonda *Susan* • Yves Montand *Jacques* • Vittorio Caprioli *Factory manager* • Pierre Oudrey *Frédéric* • Jean Pignol *CGT delegate* • Elizabeth Chauvin *Geneviève* ■ *Dir/Scr* Jean-Luc Godard, Jean-Pierre Gorin

Tovarich ★★★

Comedy 1937 · US · BW · 92mins

Claudette Colbert and Charles Boyer, anticipating the Russian Revolution, are the aristocrats who escape to Paris, where they deposit the tsar's billions in a Paris bank and, unwilling to spend the cash, set themselves up as a maid and butler in a grand French home. Inevitably, they are found out, leading to a farcical comedy of disguise. While not nearly as entertaining or as politically astute as the later *Ninotchka*, Colbert and Boyer make a suave and witty couple, ably supported by an imperious Basil Rathbone. AT

Claudette Colbert *The Grand Duchess Tatiana Petrovna/Tina Dubrovsky* • Charles Boyer *Prince Mikail Alexandrovitch Ouratieff/Michel* • Basil Rathbone *Gorotchenko* • Anita Louise *Helen Dupont* • Melville Cooper *Charles Dupont* • Isabel Jeans *Fernande Dupont* • Maurice Murphy *Georges Dupont* ■ *Dir* Anatole Litvak • *Scr* Casey Robinson, Robert E Sherwood, from the play by Jacques Deval

Toward the Unknown ★★ U

Drama 1956 · US · Colour · 114mins

Stressed pilot William Holden tries to regain the respect of his men in this dour, unexciting film. The flight sequences here probably looked spectacular at the time, but the action grinds to a halt when the planes are on the ground. James Garner makes his film debut. TS

William Holden (2) *Major Lincoln Bond* • Lloyd Nolan *Brig Gen Bill Banner* • Virginia Leith *Connie Mitchell* • Charles McGraw *Colonel "Mickey" McKee* • Murray Hamilton *Major "Bromo" Lee* • Paul Fix *Maj Gen Bryan Shelby* • LQ Jones *Lieutenant Sweeney* • James Garner *Major Joe Craven* ■ *Dir* Mervyn LeRoy • *Scr* Beirne Lay Jr

Towed in a Hole ★★★★ U

Comedy 1932 · US · BW · 20mins

The best Stan and Ollie movie is the one you are watching, although some masterpieces are so ingenious in their destructive comedy that they linger in the mind. The springboard here is Stanley's suggestion that they should not just sell fish, but catch it as well – thus doubling their income. A boat is found and its refit becomes an orgy of misfortune. Memorable jokes include Stanley, confined below, getting his head stuck behind the mast. Oliver is up a ladder painting it. Stanley finds a saw... Anticipation is more than half the pleasure with this duo – the most endearing and inventive comedians in cinema history. BB DVD

Stan Laurel *Stan* • Oliver Hardy *Ollie* • Billy Gilbert *Joe, junkyard owner* ■ *Dir* George Marshall • *Scr* HM Walker, Stan Laurel

Tower of Evil ★★ 18

Horror 1972 · UK · Colour · 89mins

A series of killings and some buried treasure lure detective Bryant Halliday and a group of unusually attractive, pot-smoking, sex-starved archaeologists to the archetypal accursed isle. It isn't long before further frenzied murders start to reduce their number. Terrible dialogue and not much suspense, but the nudity, violence and Robin Askwith are very 1970s, and this has found a new generation of fans. DM

Bryant Halliday *Det Brent* • Jill Haworth *Rose* • Anthony Valentine *Dr Simpson* • Anna Palk *Nora* • Jack Watson *Hamp Gurney* • Mark Edwards *Adam* • Derek Fowlds *Dan* • Robin Askwith *Des* ■ *Dir* Jim O'Connolly • *Scr* Jim O'Connolly, from a story by George Baxt

Tower of London ★★★

Historical drama 1939 · US · BW · 92mins

Universal, having hit pay dirt with their fictitious monsters, here turned their attentions to British history, producing a highly fanciful account of the Duke of Gloucester's machinations to seize the throne as Richard III. The Duke of Clarence is drowned in a wine barrel, but most of the rest, involving Gloucester and royal executioner Mord dispatching all and sundry, is fabrication, grim but too often plodding. The chief appeal is the fruity performances. DM

Basil Rathbone *Richard, Duke of Gloucester* • Boris Karloff *Mord* • Barbara O'Neil *Queen Elizabeth* • Ian Hunter *King Edward IV* • Vincent Price *Duke of Clarence* • Nan Grey *Lady Alice Barton* • John Sutton *John Wyatt* • Leo G Carroll *Hastings* ■ *Dir* Rowland V Lee • *Scr* Robert N Lee

Tower of London ★★

Horror 1962 · US · BW · 79mins

Roger Corman's film about Richard III keeps the basic structure of the better 1939 film of the same title, as the Duke of Gloucester murders everyone who blocks his path to the throne. This is more of a spook film, as Gloucester is troubled, like Macbeth, by the ghosts of his victims. Vincent Price, who played the Duke of Clarence in the earlier film, makes a formidable if camp Gloucester, and the script is unusually intelligent, but the action is grim without being chilling. DM

Vincent Price *Richard of Gloucester* • Michael Pate *Sir Ratcliffe* • Joan Freeman *Lady Margaret* • Robert Brown *Sir Justin* • Justice Watson *Edward IV* • Sarah Selby *Queen Elizabeth* • Richard McCauly *Clarence* • Eugene Martin *Edward V* ■ *Dir* Roger Corman • *Scr* Leo V Gordon, F Amos Powell, James B Gordon, from a story by Leo V Gordon, F Amos Powell • *Dialogue Director* Francis Ford Coppola

The Towering Inferno ★★★★ 15

Disaster movie 1974 · US · Colour · 158mins

It took two major studios – Fox and Warner Bros, pooling resources – and two similar novels – *The Tower* and *The Glass Inferno* – to make this triple-Oscar-winning disaster movie. The fun comes from guessing which superstars will get fried to a crisp in the burning San Francisco skyscraper, ignited during the opening ceremony, and who will be saved by daring fire chief Steve McQueen. The big-name cast plays second fiddle to the blazing special effects, but the mounting suspense and outlandish rescue attempts fan the consistently entertaining flames. AJ. Contains swearing. DVD

Steve McQueen *Fire Chief Michael O'Hallorhan* • Paul Newman *Doug Roberts* • William Holden (2) *Jim Duncan* • Faye Dunaway *Susan Franklin* • Fred Astaire *Harlee Claiborne* • Susan Blakely *Patty Simmons* • Richard Chamberlain *Roger Simmons* • Jennifer Jones *Lisolette Mueller* • OJ Simpson *Security Chief Jernigan* • Robert Vaughn *Senator Gary Parker* • Robert Wagner *Dan Bigelow* ■ *Dir* John Guillermin, Irwin Allen • *Scr* Stirling Silliphant, from the novels *The Tower* by Richard Martin Stern and *The Glass Inferno* by Thomas N Scortia, Frank M Robinson

Town & Country ★★★ 15

Comedy 2001 · US · Colour · 100mins

The tittle-tattle about on-set feuds and last-minute recuts has helped ensure that this ensemble farce became one of the biggest money losers of all time. But its only real crimes – a dated sense of humour and a lack of directorial acuity – mean that Peter Chelsom has turned out a movie that feels more Blake Edwards than Woody Allen. The marital shenanigans involving Warren Beatty and Diane Keaton and their buddies Garry Shandling and Goldie Hawn may be midlife and bourgeois, but the acting is always polished. DP DVD

Warren Beatty *Porter Stoddard* • Diane Keaton *Ellie Stoddard* • Goldie Hawn *Mona* • Garry Shandling *Griffin* • Andie MacDowell *Eugenie Claybourne* • Charlton Heston *Mr Claybourne* • Marian Seldes *Mrs Claybourne* • Josh Hartnett *Tom Stoddard* • Jenna Elfman *Auburn* • Nastassja Kinski *Alex* • Buck Henry *Suttler* ■ *Dir* Peter Chelsom • *Scr* Michael Laughlin, Buck Henry

A Town Called Hell ★★ 15

Spaghetti western
1971 · UK/Sp · Colour · 97mins

This brutal western, also known as *A Town Called Bastard*, is one of the few British ventures into the genre. Set in 1895 in Mexico (but shot in Spain), it follows Stella Stevens as she seeks out those who killed her husband a decade earlier, while Martin Landau threatens to reveal that his brother, Robert Shaw, is not a priest but a ruthless bandit. The interesting cast nearly compensates for a slackness in direction, as the film lurches from tightly shot moments of brooding tension to frantic outbursts of stylised violence. DP [VIDEO] DVD

Robert Shaw *Priest* • Telly Savalas *Don Carlos* • Stella Stevens *Alvira* • Michael Craig *Paco* • Martin Landau *Colonel* • Dudley Sutton *Spectre* • Fernando Rey *Old blind farmer* ■ *Dir* Robert Parrish • *Scr* Richard Aubrey

A Town like Alice ★★★ PG

War drama 1956 · UK · BW · 111mins

This is an earnest adaptation of Nevil Shute's celebrated wartime novel about a group of women route-marched across Malaya by the invading Japanese. While director Jack Lee has little difficulty setting his scene, he struggles to prevent some episodes contained in the rather underwhelming script from lapsing into overwrought melodrama. Sympathetic guard Tagaki, Jean Anderson – later one of the stars of the BBC PoW drama *Tenko* – and Renee Houston offer stout support to Virginia McKenna, whose romantic interludes with Peter Finch provide some charming relief from the trials of the trek. DP [VIDEO] DVD

Virginia McKenna *Jean Paget* • Peter Finch *Joe Harman* • Takagi *Japanese sergeant* • Tran Van Khe *Captain Sugaya* • Jean Anderson *Miss Horsefall* • Marie Lohr *Mrs Dudley Frost* • Maureen Swanson *Ellen* • Renee Houston *Ebbey* ■ *Dir* Jack Lee • *Scr* WP Lipscomb, Richard Mason, from the novel by Nevil Shute

Town on Trial ★★

Murder mystery 1956 · UK · BW · 96mins

In this very British whodunnit, John Mills stars as a Scotland Yard detective who's called in to investigate unsavoury goings-on in an English town. A woman with a dubious reputation has been found dead on club property and there's no shortage of suspects for Mills to grill, all of whom seem to have a dodgy past. It's a modest mystery in the Agatha Christie tradition, and it offers a modicum of tension. AT

John Mills *Supt Mike Halloran* • Charles Coburn *Dr John Fenner* • Barbara Bates *Elizabeth Fenner* • Derek Farr *Mark Roper* • Alec McCowen *Peter Crowley* • Elizabeth Seal *Fiona Dixon* ■ *Dir* John Guillermin • *Scr* Robert Westerby, Ken Hughes

Town Rat, Country Rat ★★★★

Silent animation 1923 · Fr · Tinted · 13mins

Ladislaw Starewicz demonstrates his cinematic ingenuity and a fondness for slapstick, as well as his genius for puppetry, in this spicily satirical retelling of the familiar fable of the country rat overwhelmed by city life. Starting with a mischievous use of back projection, as the town rat motors out of Paris, the film also includes iconic cartoon dialogue, a segment combining live-action and animation (as a curious kitten chases the rodentine revellers at a cabaret soirée) and an intricate superimposition flashback, as the country rat recalls the wine and the women that enlivened his adventure. DP

Dir Ladislaw Starewicz • *Scr* Ladislaw Starewicz, from a fable by Jean de La Fontaine

Town without Pity ★★ 15

Courtroom drama
1961 · US/W Ger/Swi · BW · 99mins

Kirk Douglas has often been drawn to roles in which he can express self-disgust. Here he stars as an army officer defending four American servicemen on a charge of raping a young girl in Germany (played by Christine Kaufmann). As the case progresses, Douglas reluctantly sullies the girl's reputation to save the men from a death sentence. Filmed in Germany, this is crude, revelling in its sensational aspects. AE [VIDEO]

Kirk Douglas *Maj Steve Garrett* • EG Marshall *Maj Jerome Pakenham* • Christine Kaufmann *Karin Steinhof* • Robert Blake *Jim* • Richard Jaeckel *Bidie* • Frank Sutton *Chuck* ■ *Dir* Gottfried Reinhardt • *Scr* Silvia Reinhardt, Georg Hurdalek, Jan Lustig, from the novel *Das Urteil* by Manfred Gregor

The Toxic Avenger ★★★ 18

Spoof horror 1985 · US · Colour · 75mins

After years of churning out teen comedies that weren't very funny, Troma Films hit the big time with this outrageously tacky superhero spoof. Weedy janitor Mark Torgl is transformed into good-guy monster the Toxic Avenger (Mitchell Cohen) after being dumped into a barrel of toxic goo by a gang of thugs. Toxie (as he's known to his friends) is very nice to his blind girlfriend but metes out violent punishment to local criminals. Loaded with infantile slapstick, amateurish acting, teen-orientated erotica and extreme gore (trimmed considerably in this country) this is B-movie making at its crudest and purest. RS [VIDEO] DVD

Andree Maranda *Sara* • Mitchell Cohen *Toxic Avenger* • Jennifer Baptist *Wanda* • Cindy Manion *Julie* • Robert Prichard *Slug* • Gary Schneider *Bozo* • Mark Torgl *Melvin* • Marisa Tomei *Health club girl* ■ *Dir* Michael Herz, Samuel Weil • *Scr* Joe Ritter, Lloyd Kaufman, Gay Partington Terry, Stuart Strutin

The Toxic Avenger, Part II ★ 18

Spoof horror 1988 · US · Colour · 90mins

Fans of Troma Films' most celebrated creation had to wait three years for the inevitable follow-up. In the meantime their hero had achieved near iconic status, but even his most die-hard fans will have trouble finding anything to enjoy in this wholesale debacle which sees Toxie travelling to Japan to save the planet's ecosystem from an evil industrial conglomerate. Shot back-to-back with the even more lamentable *Part III*, and followed in 2000 by a fourth instalment. RS [VIDEO] DVD

Ron Fazio *The Toxic Avenger* • John Altamura *The Toxic Avenger* • Phoebe Legere *Claire* • Rick Collins *Apocalypse Inc Chairman* • Rikiya Yasuoka *Big Mac* ■ *Dir* Lloyd Kaufman, Michael Herz • *Scr* Gay Partington Terry, from a story by Lloyd Kaufman

The Toy ★★ PG

Comedy 1982 · US · Colour · 97mins

Richard Pryor, a journalist fallen on hard times, is working as a janitor at the Bates department store. His slapstick incompetence at dealing with an inflatable toy is watched by nine-year-old Scott Schwartz, the spoiled heir to the Bates empire. Schwartz is allowed to visit his father (Jackie Gleason) at work once every year and to have anything he chooses for that week. He chooses to have Pryor as a human "toy". This has some fine moments (especially at the start) but soon degenerates into a mawkish message movie. DF [VIDEO]

Richard Pryor *Jack Brown* • Jackie Gleason *US Bates* • Ned Beatty *Morehouse* • Scott Schwartz *Eric Bates* • Teresa Ganzel *Fancy Bates* • Wilfrid Hyde White *Barkley* ■ *Dir* Richard Donner • *Scr* Carol Sobieski, from the film *Le Jouet* by Francis Veber

Toy Soldiers ★★ 15

Action thriller 1991 · US · Colour · 107mins

This dopey movie blends *Animal House* antics with Rambo-ish heroics to risible effect. Sean Astin and Wil Wheaton are the teenage pranksters who lead their classmates in a fight back when nasty South American mobsters take over their school. Louis Gossett Jr and Denholm Elliott provide a few memorable moments, but the sheer silliness of the concept doomed this project right from the start. JF. Contains violence. [VIDEO]

Sean Astin *Billy Tepper* • Wil Wheaton *Joey Trotta* • Keith Coogan *Snuffy Bradberry* • Andrew Divoff *Luis Cali* • R Lee Ermey *General Kramer* • Mason Adams *Deputy Director Brown* • Denholm Elliott *Headmaster* • Louis Gossett Jr *Dean Parker* ■ *Dir* Daniel Petrie Jr • *Scr* Daniel Petrie Jr, David Koepp, from the novel by William P Kennedy

Toy Story ★★★★★ PG

Animated comedy adventure
1995 · US · Colour · 88mins

The first completely computer-generated animation feature is a masterpiece from director John Lasseter, with voice-overs by Tom Hanks, Tim Allen, Don Rickles and others rounding out convincing characterisations. Woody, an old-fashioned pullstring cowboy, is his owner Andy's favourite toy, and lords it benevolently over Mr Potato Head, Bo-Peep and Rex the Dinosaur. Until, that is, the arrival of newcomer Buzz Lightyear, a hi-tech space-ranger. It's a great adventure story that will not only entertain children but can also be enjoyed as a jokey parable by adults. Mention should also be made of Randy Newman's masterly score, which was Oscar nominated along with his song *You've Got a Friend*. TH [VIDEO] DVD

Tom Hanks *Woody* • Tim Allen *Buzz Lightyear* • Don Rickles *Mr Potato Head* • Jim Varney *Slinky Dog* • Wallace Shawn *Rex* • John Ratzenberger *Hamm* • Annie Potts *Bo Peep* ■ *Dir* John Lasseter • *Scr* Joss Whedon, Andrew Stanton, Joel Cohen, Alec Sokolow, from a story by John Lasseter, Pete Docter, Andrew Stanton, Joe Ranft • *Animator* Pete Docter, Rich Quade, Ash Brannon

Toy Story 2 ★★★★★ U

Animated comedy adventure
1999 · US · Colour · 88mins

Originally intended as a 60-minute, straight-to-video project, this was a work in progress right up to its release – complete with last-minute additions to the cast. Yet who can be wholly cynical about a film that not only manages to surpass its predecessor, but also restores credibility to that much-debased term, "family entertainment"? Buzz Lightyear's bid to rescue Woody the cowboy from the clutches of a sleazy toy collector will keep the youngsters on the edge of their seats. However, it's the little touches that will delight the grown-ups, most notably the in-jokes and the charming re-creation of a 1950s TV puppet show. A straight-to-video spin-off, *Buzz Lightyear of Star Command*, led to a TV series. DP [VIDEO] DVD

Tom Hanks *Woody* • Tim Allen *Buzz Lightyear* • Joan Cusack *Jessie* • Kelsey Grammer *Prospector* • Don Rickles *Mr Potato Head* • Jim Varney *Slinky Dog* • Wallace Shawn *Rex* • John Ratzenberger *Hamm* • Annie Potts *Bo Peep* • John Morris *Andy* • Laurie Metcalf *Andy's mom* • R Lee Ermey *Sarge* • Jonathan Harris *Cleaner* ■ *Dir* John Lasseter, Lee Unkrich, Ash Brannon • *Scr* Andrew Stanton, Rita Hsiao, Doug Chamberlin, Chris Webb, from a story by John Lasseter, Pete Docter, Ash Brannon, Andrew Stanton

The Toy Wife ★★ U

Period romantic drama
1938 · US · BW · 93mins

Returned from Europe to the family seat in Louisiana, Luise Rainer throws off her beau Robert Young and steals her sister's fiancé, Melvyn Douglas. They marry and have a child, but she proves incapable of meeting the demands of her position. This overheated period melodrama was considered old-fashioned in its day, and now has little to offer other than high-class sets and costumes. RK

Luise Rainer *Gilberta "Frou Frou" Brigard* • Melvyn Douglas *Georges Sartoris* • Robert Young (1) *André Vallaire* • Barbara O'Neil *Louise Brigard* • HB Warner *Victor Brigard* • Alma Kruger *Mme Vallaire* • Libby Taylor *Suzanne* ■ *Dir* Richard Thorpe • *Scr* Zoë Akins [Zoe Akins], from the play *Frou-frou* by Henri Meilhac, Ludovic Halévy, and the play *Frou Frou* by Augustin Daly

Toys ★★ PG

Comedy fantasy 1992 · US · Colour · 116mins

War-addicted Michael Gambon inherits a toy factory, turning it into an assembly line for destructive toys. You'll gasp in sheer amazement at the magnificent sets and decor, which alone make this vainglorious slice of whimsy worth a look – just try to ignore the rather naive and self-indulgent plot. Robin Williams, playing the nephew who tries to stop Gambon manufacturing only war games, tanks and guns, is surprisingly low-key. A cult flop. AJ. Contains violence. [VIDEO] DVD

Robin Williams *Leslie Zevo* • Michael Gambon *The General* • Joan Cusack *Alsatia Zevo* • Robin Wright [Robin Wright Penn] *Gwen* • LL Cool J *Patrick* • Donald O'Connor *Kenneth Zevo* • Arthur Malet *Owens Owens* • Jack Warden *Zevo Sr* ■ *Dir* Barry Levinson • *Scr* Valerie Curtin, Barry Levinson

Toys in the Attic ★★★

Melodrama 1963 · US · BW · 90mins

Lillian Hellman's play is the basis for this steamy though softened drama about bizarre goings-on in a fading New Orleans family. Dean Martin is good as the ne'er-do-well who brings his young bride home to visit his poverty-stricken spinster sisters (Wendy Hiller and Geraldine Page), while hiding his ill-gotten riches. Not quite Tennessee Williams, but still engrossing. JG

Dean Martin *Julian Berniers* • Geraldine Page *Carrie Berniers* • Yvette Mimieux *Lily Prine Berniers* • Wendy Hiller *Anna Berniers* • Gene Tierney *Albertine Prine* • Nan Martin *Charlotte Warkins* • Larry Gates *Cyrus Warkins* ■ *Dir* George Roy Hill • *Scr* James Poe, from the play by Lillian Hellman

Traces of a Dragon: Jackie Chan & His Lost Family ★★★

Documentary 2003 · HK · Colour · 96mins

Interweaving newsreel footage, interviews and clips from nine Jackie Chan movies, this is a fascinating documentary portrait of Chan's parents' extended family in China. The Hong Kong chop socky star only recently discovered the connection, and director Mabel Cheung wisely focuses on Jackie's octogenarian father, Chan Chi-Long, who relates his past life as a Nationalist spy, Shanghai mobster and embassy handyman with vigour. Yet his wife Lily's experiences as an opium smuggler and glamorous gambler are equally compelling, as are the recollections of the couple's children from previous marriages – Lily's devoted daughters and Chi-Long's sons, a pig farmer and a

T

postman. DP. In Cantonese and Mandarin with English subtitles.

Dir Mabel Cheung • *Cinematographer* Arthur Wong • *Music* Henry Lai

Traces of Red ★★ 15

Erotic thriller 1992 · US · Colour · 100mins

It's shades of *Sunset Boulevard*, as the newly-killed corpse of cop James Belushi narrates the story of a serial killer with a penchant for Yves Saint Laurent lipstick and bad poetry. Unfortunately the similarity ends there, as the convoluted and implausible plot is interspersed with the standard mixture of soft-core porn and violence. A fair-quality cast includes a sexually ravenous Lorraine Bracco. DA

James Belushi *Jack Dobson* • Lorraine Bracco *Ellen Schofield* • Tony Goldwyn *Steve Frayn* • William Russ *Michael Dobson* • Faye Grant *Beth Frayn* • Michelle Joyner *Morgan Cassidy* ■ *Dir* Andy Wolk • *Scr* Jim Piddock

Track of the Cat ★★★

Western drama 1954 · US · Colour · 102mins

This strange and brooding western melodrama is distinguished by its unique sense of design. While filmed in CinemaScope and colour, the whole film is art directed, costumed, and lit for black-and-white – only occasional flashes of colour breaking up the wintery landscape. Although rather ponderous, there are fine performances from lead Robert Mitchum and from Beulah Bondi as the family matriarch. TS

Robert Mitchum *Curt Bridges* • Teresa Wright *Grace Bridges* • Diana Lynn *Gwen Williams* • Tab Hunter *Harold "Hal" Bridges* • Beulah Bondi *Ma Bridges* • Philip Tonge *Pa Bridges* • William Hopper *Arthur* • Carl "Alfalfa" Switzer *Joe Sam* ■ *Dir* William A Wellman • *Scr* Al Bezzerides, from a novel by Walter Van Tilburg Clark

Track 29 ★★★ 18

Fantasy melodrama
1988 · UK · Colour · 86mins

Surrealist director Nicolas Roeg joins arcane writer Dennis Potter for a well constructed Freudian psychodrama about cloaking sexual unfulfilment behind easy nostalgia. Taking its title from the song *Chattanooga Choo-Choo*, housewife Theresa Russell finds her erotic fantasies triggered by stranger Gary Oldman, while her dowdy husband plays with his model railway in the attic. However, Oldman's multiple-identity crisis means he could also be her adopted son. Shockingly original, amusingly chilling and occasionally inaccessible. AJ. Contains swearing, violence and nudity.

Theresa Russell *Linda Henry* • Gary Oldman *Martin* • Christopher Lloyd *Dr Henry Henry* • Sandra Bernhard *Nurse Stein* • Colleen Camp *Arlanda* • Seymour Cassel *Dr Bernard Fairmont* • Leon Rippy *Trucker* ■ *Dir* Nicolas Roeg • *Scr* Dennis Potter

Trackdown ★★ 18

Thriller 1976 · US · Colour · 93mins

Montana cowboy James Mitchum (son of Robert) goes to Los Angeles in pursuit of his sister, Karen Lamm, who has drifted into high class prostitution after being gang-raped and sold to Beverly Hills pimp Vince Cannon. Director Richard T Heffron choreographs the mayhem well in this little-seen vigilante thriller, but this is sleazy and violent. AJ

Jim Mitchum [James Mitchum] *Jim Calhoun* • Karen Lamm *Betsy Calhoun* • Anne Archer *Barbara* • Erik Estrada *Chucho* • Cathy Lee Crosby *Lynn* • Vince Cannon *Johnny Dee* ■ *Dir* Richard T Heffron • *Scr* Paul Edwards, from a story by Ivan Nagy

Tracks ★

Drama 1977 · US · Colour · 91mins

This is an unwatchable mess from Hollywood's most pretentious independent director, Henry Jaglom. Dennis Hopper plays a Vietnam veteran with problems, principally the dead body of a buddy he's transporting across the US for burial. Jaglom's slick symbolism and Hopper's "Hey man, like, real heavy" dialogue puts this into a time capsule that should be buried real deep, man. AT. Contains swearing, sex scenes and nudity.

Dennis Hopper *Sergeant Jack Falen* • Taryn Power *Stephanie* • Dean Stockwell *Mark* • Topo Swope *Chloe* • Michael Emil *Emile* ■ *Dir/Scr* Henry Jaglom

Trade Winds ★★

Detective comedy drama
1938 · US · BW · 93mins

Director Tay Garnett justified a tax-deductible sailing trip around the world by taking a cinematographer to record the sights and writing a story en route. The footage provided the backdrop for this lightweight tale of detective Fredric March's pursuit of high-class murder suspect Joan Bennett. The stars never had to leave the studio, as the film used a record amount of back projection. Predictably, this contributed to an air of tedium. AE

Fredric March *Sam Wye* • Joan Bennett *Kay Kerrigan* • Ralph Bellamy *Ben Blodgett* • Ann Sothern *Jean Livingstone* • Sidney Blackmer *Thomas Bruhme II* • Thomas Mitchell *Commissioner Blackton* • Robert Elliott *Capt George Faulkiner* ■ *Dir* Tay Garnett • *Scr* Dorothy Parker, Alan Campbell, Frank R Adams, from a story by Tay Garnett

Trader Horn ★★★★

Adventure 1931 · US · BW · 123mins

The first film to be made on location in Africa, the troubles that beset the production almost outweighed the life-and-death struggle of the title character (Harry Carey) and his young companion (Duncan Renaldo) as they venture among dangerous animals, and even more dangerous tribes, engaged in a search for the white daughter of missionaries abducted 20 years earlier. They find her, of course, in the beautiful, blonde guise of Edwina Booth. The film was almost abandoned when the studio saw the rag-bag of footage assembled by director WS Van Dyke, but another year's work in Hollywood and Mexico eventually earned it a best picture Oscar nomination. The actual filming (especially of animal behaviour) is impressive by any standards, especially those of 1931. RK

Harry Carey *Aloysius "Trader" Horn* • Edwina Booth *Nina Trent* • Duncan Renaldo *Peru* • Mutia Omoolu *Renchero* • Olive Golden *Edith Trent* • C Aubrey Smith *Trader* ■ *Dir* WS Van Dyke II [WS Van Dyke] • *Scr* Richard Schayer, Cyril Hume, Dale Van Every, John Thomas Neville, from the novel by Alfred Aloysius Horn, Ethelreda Lewis • *Cinematographer* Clyde De Vinna

Trading Hearts ★★★

Period romantic comedy
1988 · US · Colour · 88mins

Raul Julia is the dumped baseball player who hooks up with singer Beverly D'Angelo in this 1950s drama that flits between a light-hearted romance and a legal battle when D'Angelo is threatened with court action by her ex-husband who wants custody of their child. It's well played with some nice period details, but it's not exactly original. JB. Contains swearing.

Raul Julia *Vinnie* • Beverly D'Angelo *Donna* • Jenny Lewis *Yvonne* • Parris Buckner *Robert* • Robert Gwaltney *Ducky* ■ *Dir* Neil Leifer • *Scr* Frank Deford

Trading Places ★★★★ 15

Comedy 1983 · US · Colour · 111mins

This unacknowledged reworking of *The Prince and the Pauper* is a rattling comedy showcase for the unique talents of Eddie Murphy and Dan Aykroyd, who have never recaptured the form shown here. However, there is no question that the acting honours go to the veterans Don Ameche and Ralph Bellamy, as the mischievous business bigwigs whose wager brings about the respective rise and fall of the stars. Director John Landis tends to pull his satirical punches against yuppiedom, and it's a shame he settles for a brash slapstick finale after so many fresh, immaculately timed comic situations. DP. Contains swearing and nudity. DVD

Eddie Murphy *Billy Ray Valentine* • Dan Aykroyd *Louis Winthorpe III* • Jamie Lee Curtis *Ophelia* • Ralph Bellamy *Randolph Duke* • Don Ameche *Mortimer Duke* • Denholm Elliott *Coleman* • Paul Gleason *Beeks* • Bo Diddley *Pawnbroker* • Jim Belushi [James Belushi] *King Kong* ■ *Dir* John Landis • *Scr* Timothy Harris, Herschel Weingrod

Traffic ★★★★

Comedy 1970 · US · Colour · 100mins

Any number of things could go wrong as Monsieur Hulot takes the vehicle of the future to an Amsterdam motor show. The fact that not many did bothered the critics, who wanted something more spectacular than some loosely linked observations on motoring and modernity. But Jacques Tati's final feature is filled with astute musings about, for example, the way owners resemble their cars or have windscreen wipers in tune with their personalities. The nose-picking sequence and the grotesque ballet of the pile-up reinforce his thesis that life is increasingly lived in isolation and that progress is a highly relative term. DP. In French with English subtitles.

Jacques Tati *Monsieur Hulot* • Maria Kimberly *Maria* • Marcel Fravel *Truck driver* ■ *Dir* Jacques Tati • *Scr* Jacques Tati, Jacques Lagrange

Traffic ★★★★ 18

Crime drama 2000 · US · Colour · 140mins

Director Steven Soderbergh's brilliantly realised high-tone thriller is shot in scintillating docudrama style, using a broad but involving multi-strand story canvas to give a powerful overview of the complex chain supplying North America's drug culture. On the one hand, there's newly appointed drugs tsar Michael Douglas who is unaware that his teenage daughter has a serious drug habit. On the other is wealthy drug kingpin Steven Bauer whom DEA agents Don Cheadle and Luis Guzman are desperately trying to nail. Wonderfully acted by an amazing cast, the standout performances come from a magnetic Benicio Del Toro, playing a Mexican cop torn between morality and temptation, and Catherine Zeta-Jones as Bauer's shell-shocked pregnant wife. AJ. In English and Spanish with subtitles. Contains drug abuse, violence, swearing. DVD

Michael Douglas *Robert Wakefield* • Don Cheadle *Montel Gordon* • Benicio Del Toro *Javier Rodriguez* • Catherine Zeta-Jones *Helena Ayala* • Dennis Quaid *Arnie Metzger* • Steven Bauer *Carlos Ayala* • Luis Guzman *Ray Castro* • Erika Christensen *Caroline Wakefield* • Clifton Collins Jr *Francisco Flores* • Miguel Ferrer *Eduardo Ruiz* • Amy Irving *Barbara Wakefield* • Albert Finney *Chief of Staff* • James Brolin *General Ralph Landry* ■ *Dir* Steven Soderbergh • *Scr* Stephen Gaghan, from the TV series *Traffik* by Simon Moore • *Editor* Stephen Mirrione

Traffic in Souls ★★★★

Silent drama 1913 · US · BW · 74mins

A landmark in the history of the American cinema, miraculously preserved for posterity, this was remarkable in its time for both its subject matter and its length. Focusing on the white slave traffic that was obsessing America and its moral reformers, the plot sets a lily-white heroic cop (Matt Moore) against a corrupt organisation of traffickers led by publicly respectable "pillar" of New York society (William Welsh), who kidnap Moore's fiancée's sister (Ethel Grandin) for purposes of prostitution. With its histrionic style, the film raises the occasional giggle, but it's acted with commitment, photographed with wonderful depths of texture and edited for maximum suspense. RK

Jane Gail *Mary Barton* • Ethel Grandin *Lorna Barton* • William Turner (1) *Isaac Barton* • Matt Moore *Officer Larry Burke* • William Welsh *William Trubus* • Mrs Hudson Lyston *Mrs Trubus* • Irene Wallace *Alice Trubus* • William Cavanaugh *Bill Bradshaw* ■ *Dir* George Loane Tucker • *Scr* Walter MacNamara, George Loane Tucker

The Tragedy of a Ridiculous Man ★★★

Drama 1981 · It · Colour · 116mins

Ugo Tognazzi plays a rich cheese manufacturer who has to decide whether to sell everything to raise a ransom for his kidnapped son. The twist is that his offspring may be one of the gang, radicals dedicated to the overthrow of capitalism. It works as both a thriller and a black comedy, tuning in to then-current topics of kidnapping and Red Brigade terrorism. Interesting rather than exciting, this lacks the stylistic flourishes one expects of its director. AT. In Italian with English subtitles.

Ugo Tognazzi *Primo* • Anouk Aimée *Barbara* • Laura Morante *Laura* • Victor Cavallo *Adelfo* • Olimpia Carlisi *Chiromant* • Vittorio Caprioli *Marshal* ■ *Dir/Scr* Bernardo Bertolucci

The Trail Beyond ★★ U

Western 1934 · US · BW · 54mins

With a bigger budget than John Wayne was used to at his home-from-home, Monogram Studios, this Lone Star western was the first talkie version of popular cowboy novel *The Wolf Hunters*. The extra cash gave the Duke the benefit of both Noah Beery Sr and Noah Beery Jr in support, plus more location shooting, but the screenplay by future western producer Lindsley Parsons errs seriously on the side of melodrama. TS DVD

John Wayne *Rod Drew* • Noah Beery Sr [Noah Beery] *George Newsome* • Noah Beery Jr *Wabi* • Verna Hillie *Felice Newsome* • Iris Lancaster *Marie* • Robert Frazer *Jules Larocque* • Earl Dwire *Benoit* • Eddie Parker *Ryan, the Mountie* ■ *Dir* Robert N Bradbury • *Scr* Lindsley Parsons, from the novel *The Wolf Hunters* by James Oliver Curwood • *Cinematographer* Archie Stout

The Trail of '98 ★★★

Silent drama 1929 · US · BW · 87mins

Filmed mostly on arduous locations near Denver, this MGM epic was assigned to director Clarence Brown, who gathered 2,000 extras to trudge up a mountain pass in a powerful reconstruction of the Klondike gold rush. Snowfalls and rapids claimed the lives of several crew members. The film looks real enough, but is handicapped by a weak plot about the assorted fortunes of various gold seekers. Dolores Del Rio and Ralph Forbes make effective leads. The film was made as a silent, but also released with a music and effects soundtrack. AE

U = SUITABLE FOR ALL Uc = SUITABLE FOR ALL, ESPECIALLY FOR YOUNG CHILDREN (VIDEO ONLY) PG = PARENTAL GUIDANCE

Dolores Del Rio *Berna* • Ralph Forbes *Larry* • Karl Dane *Lars Petersen* • Harry Carey *Jack Locasto* • Tully Marshall *Salvation Jim* • George Cooper *Samuel Foote, the Worm* ■ *Dir* Clarence Brown • *Scr* Benjamin Glazer, Waldemar Young, Joe Farnham [Joseph Farnham] (titles), from the novel by Robert William Service

Trail of Robin Hood ★★ U

Western 1950 · US · Colour · 66mins

Jack Holt is cast as the retired western star intent on supplying Christmas trees to poor kids at a price they can afford, but a wicked commercial outfit obstructs his efforts. Rogers arranges for Holt to receive a helping hand from other western stars – cue guest appearances by the likes of Rex Allen, Allan "Rocky" Lane and William Farnum, plus regular villain George Chesebro, who wants to be on the other side for a change. There are the usual songs and this one has the dubious bonus of Trucolor. AE

Roy Rogers • Penny Edwards *Toby Aldridge* • Gordon Jones *Splinters McGonigle* • Rex Allen *Rex Allen the Arizona Cowboy* • Allan "Rocky" Lane [Allan Lane] *Allan "Rocky" Lane* • Monte Hale • William Farnum • Tom Tyler • Tom Keene • Jack Holt • George Chesebro ■ *Dir* William Witney • *Scr* Gerald Geraghty

The Trail of the Lonesome Pine ★★★

Drama 1936 · US · Colour · 102mins

Becky Sharp may have been first but it was this drama that really sold 1930s audiences on the new three-strip Technicolor process through the beauty of outdoor settings filmed on Californian locations by cameraman W Howard Greene. The tale of a long-running feud between two mountain clans was an old favourite, filmed twice before, but a young director and youthful stars give it a fresh look. Henry Fonda's performance is supposed to have been the inspiration for Al Capp's *Li'l Abner*. AE

Sylvia Sidney *June Tolliver* • Fred MacMurray *Jack Hale* • Henry Fonda *Dave Tolliver* • Fred Stone *Judd Tolliver* • Nigel Bruce *Mr Thurber* • Beulah Bondi *Melissa* • Robert Barrat *Buck Falin* ■ *Dir* Henry Hathaway • *Scr* Grover Jones, Harvey Thew, Horace McCoy, from the novel by John Fox Jr

Trail of the Pink Panther ★ PG

Comedy 1982 · US · Colour · 92mins

This purported tribute to the genius of Peter Sellers is exploitation at its most shameless. Released two years after Sellers's death, the film is a crudely assembled compilation of unremarkable out-takes and dismally unfunny new footage involving TV reporter Joanna Lumley descending on Clouseau's friends and foes to piece together a picture (if you will) of the Inspector after he vanishes on a case. Director Blake Edwards proceeded to direct two more *Pink Panther* movies (*The Curse of the Pink Panther* and *Son of the Pink Panther*), which hit new lows of taste and quality. DP [video] DVD

Peter Sellers *Inspector Clouseau* • David Niven *Sir Charles Litton* • Herbert Lom *Dreyfus* • Richard Mulligan *Clouseau Sr* • Joanna Lumley *Marie Jouvet* • Capucine *Lady Litton* • Robert Loggia *Bruno* • Harvey Korman *Professor Balls* • Burt Kwouk *Cato* • Graham Stark *Hercule* ■ *Dir* Blake Edwards • *Scr* Frank Waldman, Tom Waldman, Blake Edwards, Geoffrey Edwards, from a story by Blake Edwards

Trail of the Vigilantes ★★ U

Comedy western 1940 · US · BW · 74mins

A harmless enough western with one of those "undercover man infiltrates outlaws" plots, given some novelty by the casting of urbane Franchot Tone as the easterner out west. Classy Warren William is the gang leader, and Broderick Crawford and Andy Devine are good value as his henchmen. Veteran director Allan Dwan keeps the action moving, resulting in a brisk, bright, comedy western. TS

Franchot Tone *"Kansas" Tim Mason* • Warren William *Mark Dawson* • Broderick Crawford *Swanee* • Andy Devine *Meadows* • Mischa Auer *Dmitri Bolo* • Porter Hall *Sheriff Corley* • Peggy Moran *Barbara Thornton* ■ *Dir* Allan Dwan • *Scr* Harold Shumate

Trail Street ★★ U

Western 1947 · US · BW · 84mins

This bustling western has a nicely belated entry by star Randolph Scott as legendary lawman "Bat" Masterson, summoned to a Kansas town to stop the cattlemen from trampling wheat farmers underfoot. Though briskly directed by Ray Enright, it's over-stuffed with familiar ingredients, including the saloon singer played by Anne Jeffreys and the contrasting nice girl played by Madge Meredith, but its subplot of discovering a heat-resistant strain of wheat is based on fact. AE

Randolph Scott *"Bat" Masterson* • Robert Ryan *Allen Harper* • Anne Jeffreys *Ruby Stone* • George "Gabby" Hayes *Billy* • Madge Meredith *Susan Pritchett* • Steve Brodie *Logan Maury* • Billy House *Carmody* • Virginia Sale *Hannah* • Jason Robards [Jason Robards Sr] *Jason* ■ *Dir* Ray Enright • *Scr* Gene Lewis, from the novel *Golden Horizon* by William Corcoran

The Train ★★★★ PG

Second World War drama
1964 · Fr/It/US · BW · 127mins

Burt Lancaster is superb as the railwayman attempting to stop demented Nazi officer Paul Scofield from pillaging art treasures from France in the dying days of the Second World War. The technically flawless direction is by John Frankenheimer, who took over at short notice from Arthur Penn, and the sheer excitement of using real trains is palpable. The French locations are exceptionally well used, and Jeanne Moreau and the great Michel Simon contribute tellingly authentic portrayals. TS [video] DVD

Burt Lancaster *Labiche* • Paul Scofield *Colonel von Waldheim* • Jeanne Moreau *Christine* • Michel Simon *Papa Boule* • Suzanne Flon *Miss Villard* • Wolfgang Preiss *Herren* • Richard Münch *Von Lubitz* ■ *Dir* John Frankenheimer • *Scr* Franklin Coen, Frank Davis, Walter Bernstein, from a story by Franklin Coen, Frank Davis, derived from *Le Front de l'Art; Défense des Collections Françaises 1939-1945* by Rose Valland

Train of Dreams ★★★★

Documentary drama
1987 · Can · Colour · 89mins

A gritty, powerful docudrama about a wayward 17-year-old Montreal hoodlum and his descent into a life of professional crime and violence. He ends up in a correctional facility where a teacher attempts to bring poetry and music into his life. This is a thought-provoking movie which packs a tremendous emotional punch. There is a realistic feel to the piece which makes its no-holds-barred impact all the more startling. SH. Contains swearing, substance abuse and nudity.

Jason St Amour *Tony Abruzzi* • Marcella Santa Maria *Mrs Abruzzi* • Fred Ward *Teacher* • Christopher Neil *Nicky Abruzzi* • David Linesky *Tony's lawyer* • Milton Hartman *Crown attorney* ■ *Dir* John N Smith • *Scr* John N Smith, Sally Bochner, Sam Grana

Train of Events ★★★ PG

Portmanteau drama 1949 · UK · BW · 85mins

As the night express from Euston to Liverpool is about to career off the rails, the movie also lurches into flashback, showing why various passengers were making the fated journey. There's the engine driver; a philandering orchestra conductor; an actor who's killed his wife; and a girl in love with an escaped German PoW. This portmanteau effort is inevitably uneven, though the cast of stalwarts is worth watching. AT [video]

Jack Warner *Jim Hardcastle* • Gladys Henson *Mrs Hardcastle* • Susan Shaw *Doris Hardcastle* • Joan Dowling *Ella* • Laurence Payne *Richard* • Olga Lindo *Mrs Bailey* • Valerie Hobson *Stella* • John Clements *Raymond Hillary* • Irina Baronova *Irina* • Peter Finch *Phillip* • Mary Morris *Louise* • Laurence Naismith *Joe Hunt* ■ *Dir* Sidney Cole, Basil Dearden, Charles Crichton • *Scr* Basil Dearden, TEB Clarke, Ronald Millar, Angus MacPhail

Train of Life ★★★ 12

Second World War comedy adventure
1999 · Fr/Bel/Neth/Rom · Colour · 102mins

Following *Life Is Beautiful*, this raucous co-production attempts to cast comic light over the nightmare experienced by Europe's Jews during the Second World War. The central premise is inventive, but having the inhabitants of an isolated village pose as a trainload of prisoners and their escorts in a bid to reach Palestine leaves Radu Mihaileanu's film wide open to questions of taste. Whether celebrating the Yiddish spirit or caricaturing the Nazi threat, the action just manages to retain its equilibrium. DP. A French language film.

Lionel Abelanski *Schlomo* • Rufus *Mordechai* • Clément Harari *Le Rabbi* • Michel Muller *Yossi* • Bruno Abraham-Kremer *Yankele* • Agathe de la Fontaine *Esther* ■ *Dir/Scr* Radu Mihaileanu

The Train Robbers ★★★ U

Western 1973 · US · Colour · 88mins

This rather overlooked western is a typical example of director Burt Kennedy's rumbustious view of frontier life. John Wayne stars as a no-nonsense old-timer hired by grieving widow Ann-Margret to retrieve the gold stolen by her late husband. Wayne still cuts an imposing figure during the action sequences and shows again that he was a better actor than even he gave himself credit for. DP [video]

John Wayne *Lane* • Ann-Margret *Mrs Lowe* • Rod Taylor *Grady* • Ben Johnson *Wil Jesse* • Christopher George *Calhoun* • Bobby Vinton *Ben Young* • Jerry Gatlin *Sam Turner* • Ricardo Montalban *Pinkerton man* ■ *Dir/Scr* Burt Kennedy

Train to Pakistan ★★★

Period drama
1997 · Ind/UK · Colour · 108mins

This thought-provoking drama is set in the period immediately after the partition of India. The emphasis is on the tensions that arose between the subcontinent's various ethnic groups, with writer/director Pamela Rooks concentrating on the events that spark gang warfare between the dominant Sikhs and the Muslim minority in the small Punjabi town of Mano Majra. The politics aren't always easy to follow, but the cast members, led by Mohan Agashe, turn in committed performances. DP. In Hindi and Punjabi with English subtitles.

Mohan Agashe *Hukum Chand* • Nirmal Pandey *Jagga* • Rajit Kapur *Jailor* • Smriti Mishra *Nimmo* ■ *Dir* Pamela Rooks • *Scr* Pamela Rooks, from the novel by Khushwant Singh

Training Day ★★★★ 18

Police drama
2001 · US/Aus · Colour · 117mins

Arguably the edgiest and most pessimistic release from a major Hollywood studio since *Fight Club*, this is a powerful anti-buddy movie set on the mean streets of LA. Looking to join an elite narcotics squad, rookie cop Ethan Hawke is teamed with the unit's swaggering, street-wise commander Denzel Washington for an educational 24 hours during which he will be expected to prove his mettle. Directed with style and snap by Antoine Fuqua and anchored by highly credible characterisations from its two stars, this striking thriller paints a dark hued portrait of LA law enforcement. JC. Contains violence, swearing, drug abuse and brief nudity. [video] DVD

Denzel Washington *Alonzo Harris* • Ethan Hawke *Jake Hoyt* • Scott Glenn *Roger* • Tom Berenger *Stan Gursky* • Harris Yulin *Doug Rosselli* • Raymond J Barry *Lou Jacobs* • Dr Dre *Paul* • Snoop Dogg *Blue* ■ *Dir* Antoine Fuqua • *Scr* David Ayer

Trainspotting ★★★★★ 18

Drama 1995 · UK · Colour · 89mins

Irvine Welsh's controversial bestseller is brought to the screen as a dazzling assault on the senses, thanks to director Danny Boyle's cinematic imagination and invention. A fiercely original and provocative shocker, this focuses on the disintegrating friendship of four Edinburgh lads as they embark on an endless drugs and petty-crime bender heading seemingly towards self-destruction. The harrowing and bleak subject matter is presented as a hilariously funny walk on the wild side, with no moral stance taken or punches pulled. Ewan McGregor is absolutely brilliant as the smart-aleck junkie Renton, with high praise, too, for Robert Carlyle, who gives a stunning performance as the violent Begbie. A savagely sophisticated work and a landmark British classic. AJ. Contains violence, swearing, sex scenes, drug abuse, nudity. [video] DVD

Ewan McGregor *Mark Renton* • Ewen Bremner *Daniel "Spud"* • Jonny Lee Miller *Simon "Sick Boy"* • Kevin McKidd *Tommy* • Robert Carlyle *Begbie* • Kelly Macdonald *Diane* • Peter Mullan *Swanney* • James Cosmo *Mr Renton* • Eileen Nicholas *Mrs Renton* • Susan Vidler *Allison* • Irvine Welsh *Mikey* ■ *Dir* Danny Boyle • *Scr* John Hodge, from the novel by Irvine Welsh

The Traitor ★★

Spy drama 1957 · UK · BW · 87mins

Nuance was not Donald Wolfit's strong suit, but he had presence and power in spades. He totally dominates this story with a bluster and conviction that keeps an uninspiring tale of the hunt for a Second World War traitor from falling flat on its face. Writer/director Michael McCarthy had a splendid sense of place, but no talent whatsoever for generating and sustaining suspense. DP

Donald Wolfit *Colonel Price* • Robert Bray *Major Shane* • Jane Griffiths *Vicki Toller* • Carl Jaffe *Professor Toller* • Anton Diffring *Joseph Brezzini* • Oscar Quitak *Thomas Rilke* • Rupert Davies *Clinton* • John Van Eyssen *Lt Grant* • Christopher Lee ■ *Dir/Scr* Michael McCarthy

The Tramp ★★★★ U

Silent comedy 1915 · US · BW · 19mins

Having saved Edna Purviance from larcenous hobos, Charlie Chaplin is rewarded with a job on her farm. However, any romantic aspirations he has are frustrated by the arrival of her fiancé. Almost halfway through his Essanay contract, Chaplin here began to refine the "Little Fellow" who remains the most recognisable figure of the silent era. The pugnacious approach to bullies, the gentility around women and the balletic feuding with inanimate objects are all present and correct. So, unfortunately, is the pathos that many feel undermines his comic genius, manifesting itself in the first appearance of that trademark sashay down a dusty road. DP [video]

T

Charles Chaplin *Tramp* • Edna Purviance *Farmer's daughter* • Bud Jamison *Tramp* • Leo White *Tramp* • Lloyd Bacon *Lover* ■ *Dir/Scr* Charles Chaplin

Tramp, Tramp, Tramp ★★★★ U

Silent comedy 1926 · US · BW · 64mins

Whey-faced clown Harry Langdon, known as "The Wonderful Baby", made a number of shorts for Mack Sennett before his first feature, co-written by Frank Capra, who developed Langdon's innocent film persona. Although some of the gags are reminiscent of those performed by Buster Keaton and Harold Lloyd, there are many that belong to Langdon alone – watch how he throws rocks at a cyclone to persuade it to go away. The film is a series of amusing exploits he has while competing in a cross-country walk in order to win the heart of Joan Crawford. RB

Harry Langdon *Harry* • Joan Crawford *Betty Burton* • Edwards Davis *John Burton* • Carlton Griffin *Roger Caldwell* ■ *Dir* Harry Edwards • *Scr* Frank Capra, Tim Whelan, Hal Conklin, J Frank Holliday, Gerald Duffy, Murray Roth

Trancers ★★★ 15

Science-fiction fantasy thriller
1985 · US · Colour · 73mins

Tim Thomerson is a 23rd-century cop who goes back in time to capture his arch-nemesis who is planning to change the past in order to control the future with his zombie henchmen ("trancers"). Thomerson gives a wonderfully high-flying Dirty Harry-goes-cyber-punk portrayal and Helen Hunt makes an early appearance as his innocent sidekick in present day LA. A nail-biting quickie from minor cult director Charles Band. AJ DVD

Tim Thomerson *Jack Deth/Philip Dethon* • Helen Hunt *Leena* • Michael Stefani *Martin Whistler/Lt Wiesling* • Art LaFleur *McNulty* • Telma Hopkins *Engineer Raines* • Richard Herd *Chairman Spencer* • Anne Seymour *Chairman Ashe* ■ *Dir* Charles Band • *Scr* Danny Bilson, Paul De Meo

Trancers II: The Return of Jack Deth ★★ 15

Science-fiction action
1991 · US · Colour · 84mins

Tim Thomerson returns as the no-nonsense Jack Deth, a cop from the future stuck in modern-day Los Angeles, in Charles Band's belated sequel to his own mid-1980s cult hit. Once again pitted against zombie-like creatures (trancers), Thomerson's engagingly laconic Deth also has to deal with a convoluted love life – two wives in different centuries. Not nearly as much fun as its predecessor, but that didn't stop the makers from churning out four more more sequels (to date). RS DVD

Tim Thomerson *Jack Deth* • Helen Hunt *Lena Deth* • Megan Ward *Alice Stillwell* • Biff Manard *Hap Ashby* • Martine Beswick *Nurse Trotter* • Jeffrey Combs *Doctor Pyle* • Alyson Croft *McNulty* • Telma Hopkins *Raines* ■ *Dir* Charles Band • *Scr* Jackson Barr, from a story by Charles Band, Jackson Barr

Trans ★★★★

Road movie 1998 · US · Colour · 80mins

This indie movie marked the debuts of both director Julian Goldberger and his 16-year-old star, Ryan Daugherty. As the dead-end teenager who goes searching for his uncaring mother after escaping from a Florida reformatory, Daugherty manages to charm without compromising his authenticity. It was something of a risk to allow such an inexperienced actor the latitude to improvise. But this is a film of gambles – from the occasionally cockeyed cutting to the cut-price lyricism of the 16mm footage – and most of them pay off, thanks to Goldberger's courage and honesty. DP

Ryan Daugherty *Ryan Kazinski* • Justin Lakes *Justin Mallenkoff* • Michael Gulnac *Mike Gonzales* • Jon Daugherty *Little Brother* • Charles Walker *Inmate/Party rapper* • Elijah Smith *Inmate/Party rapper* ■ *Dir* Julian Goldberger • *Scr* Julian Goldberger, from a story by Michael Robinson, Martin Garner, Julian Goldberger

Trans-Europ-Express ★★★

Experimental drama 1966 · Fr · BW · 105mins

The audacious intellectualism of French musicians, novelists and film-makers in the 1950s and 1960s seems self-conscious today, thanks to our relentless trivialisation of the arts. But to anyone wanting to see what the fuss was about, Alain Robbe-Grillet's exhilarating – and irritating – journey on the express train from Paris to Antwerp remains essential viewing. He's cast himself as a movie-maker, writing a story about a sadistic drug dealer (Jean-Louis Trintignant). It's a self-referential parody of the New Wave, a treatise on reality (or what passes for it) with in-jokes and humour that may seem a little arch. But the cool star and the constant provocation make for intriguing viewing. BB. In French with English subtitles.

Jean-Louis Trintignant *Elias/Jean-Louis Trintignant* • Marie-France Pisier *Eva* • Charles Millot *Franck* • Christian Barbier *Lorentz* • Nadine Verdier *Hotel maid* • Alain Robbe-Grillet *Jean, the director* • Catherine Robbe-Grillet *Lucette* ■ *Dir/Scr* Alain Robbe-Grillet

Transformers – The Movie ★ U

Animated adventure
1986 · US · Colour · 84mins

The feature-length version of the cartoon TV series is based on the toys that mutate into hi-tech weaponry and vehicles. The fighting cyborgs must save the universe from the planet Unicron – voiced by Orson Welles – and its intergalactic army led by the evil Megatron. The mind-numbing blitz of cheap graphics, marginally vulgar dialogue and nasty violence means parents with impressionable children should take heed. AJ DVD

Leonard Nimoy *Galvatron* • Robert Stack *Ultra Magnus* • Eric Idle *Wreck Gar* • Judd Nelson *Hot Rod/Rodimus Prime* • Lionel Stander *Kup* • John Moschitta *Blurr* • Orson Welles *Planet Unicron* ■ *Dir* Nelson Shin • *Scr* Ron Friedman

The Transporter ★★ 15

Action drama 2002 · Fr/US · Colour · 88mins

Jason Statham plays second fiddle to a battery of special effects in this brainless high voltage action thriller. He plays the cool criminal driver who's paid to transport cargo with no questions asked. When he violates his code by looking in one of the "packages" and discovers a Chinese girl (Qi Shu), he's forced to go on the run. Much posturing macho extravagance follows. RT. Contains violence and swearing. DVD

Jason Statham *Frank Martin* • Qi Shu *Lai* • François Berléand *Tarconi* • Matt Schulze *Wall Street* • Ric Young *Mr Kwai* ■ *Dir* Corey Yuen • *Scr* Luc Besson, Robert Mark Kamen

Transylvania 6-5000 ★ PG

Comedy horror 1985 · US · Colour · 94mins

Jeff Goldblum and Ed Begley Jr are cringingly unfunny as journalists sent to Transylvania, where they encounter a werewolf, a mummy and other classic movie monsters. With a cast of comic notables, you would expect a fair quota of laughs, but the actors tiresomely overplay a surfeit of unoriginal gags. Geena Davis surely won't want reminding of her role as a nymphomaniac vampire. DM

Jeff Goldblum *Jack Harrison* • Joseph Bologna *Dr Malavaqua* • Ed Begley Jr *Gil Turner* • Carol Kane *Lupi* • Jeffrey Jones *Lepscu* • John Byner *Radu* • Geena Davis *Odette* • Michael Richards *Fejos* ■ *Dir/Scr* Rudy DeLuca

Transylvania Twist ★★★ 15

Horror parody 1989 · US · Colour · 78mins

Think *Carry On Screaming* meets *Airplane* and you'll have a pretty good idea of the merits of this better-than-average horror spoof. Terminally silly for sure, but enough of the gags hit their target to keep you watching as youngsters search for a fabled book with the power to raise evil spirits, hidden in a spooky castle. Director Jim Wynorski lampoons genre clichés, institutions such as *The Exorcist* and fright icons Jason and Leatherface. An undiscovered minor treat for horror buffs that's worth catching. RS

Robert Vaughn *Lord Byron Orlock* • Teri Copley *Marissa Orlock* • Steve Altman *Dexter Ward* • Ace Mask *Van Helsing* • Angus Scrimm *Stefan* • Monique Gabrielle *Patricia* ■ *Dir* Jim Wynorski • *Scr* RJ Robertson

The Trap ★

Mystery 1947 · US · BW · 68mins

After nine years and 22 films in the role, Sidney Toler was to bow out of the increasingly bankrupt series Charlie Chan series. Better known for his work on William Boyd's Hopalong Cassidy pictures, Howard Bretherton directs with little sense of the genre and resorts to such horror clichés as creeping around in the dark, as Charlie and "Number Two Son" Victor Sen Yung head for Malibu Beach to expose the killer in an acting troupe. DP

Sidney Toler *Charlie Chan* • Mantan Moreland *Birmingham* • Victor Sen Yung *Jimmy Chan* • Tanis Chandler *Adelaide* • Larry Blake [Larry J Blake] *Rick Daniels* • Kirk Alyn *Sgt Reynolds* ■ *Dir* Howard Bretherton • *Scr* Miriam Kissinger, from a character created by Earl Derr Biggers

The Trap ★★★★ 15

Romantic adventure
1966 · UK/Can · Colour · 101mins

Made at the height of the Swinging Sixties, this surprisingly moving drama was a distinct change of pace for stars Oliver Reed and Rita Tushingham. Set in Canada in the 1880s, it traces the relationship of fur trapper Reed and the waif-like Tushingham, a mute he purchases at a wife auction. Acting almost solely with her enormous eyes, Tushingham gives a genuinely affecting performance and, as impatience turns to understanding and ultimately affection, Reed also demonstrates a mellow side that he too rarely allows us to see. Director Sidney Hayers makes their bloodcurdling adventures wholly believable. DP

Rita Tushingham *Eve* • Oliver Reed *Jean La Bête* • Rex Sevenoaks *Trader* • Barbara Chilcott *Trader's wife* • Linda Goranson *Trader's daughter* • Blain Fairman *Clerk* ■ *Dir* Sidney Hayers • *Scr* David Osborn, from his story • *Cinematographer* Robert Krasker • *Music* Ron Goodwin

The Trap ★★★ 18

Thriller 1975 · Fr · Colour · 96mins

Positively bristling with malice, this unrelentingly nasty thriller from Pierre Granier-Deferre makes *The War of the Roses* look like an advertisement for marriage guidance counselling. Ingrid Thulin and Lino Ventura are equally despicable; in revenge for his casting her aside for a younger woman, she incarcerates him. Armed with the tricks she picked up from translating detective novels, the once downtrodden Thulin is more than a match for the ruthless Ventura, and the resolution of this sordid game of cat and mouse is always in doubt. DP. In French with English subtitles.

Lino Ventura *Julien* • Ingrid Thulin *Helene* • Sophie *Secretary* • William Sabatier • Dominique Zardi *Postman* ■ *Dir* Pierre Granier-Deferre • *Scr* Pascal Jardin, Pierre Granier-Deferre, from the play *La Cage* by Jack Jacquine

Trapeze ★★★ U

Drama 1956 · US · Colour · 101mins

Shot at the Cirque d'Hiver in Paris, this simmering melodrama was something of a departure for director Carol Reed after two decades of typically British themes and central European thrillers. However, Reed always knew where to place his camera and he achieves some of the finest ever big-top shots thanks to the high-flying work of cinematographer Robert Krasker. Burt Lancaster, an acrobat before he entered films, is perfectly cast as the only person to have completed the triple somersault, while Tony Curtis gives a good account of himself as both Lancaster's pupil and his rival for the affections of tumbler Gina Lollobrigida. DP DVD

Burt Lancaster *Mike Ribble* • Tony Curtis *Tino Orsini* • Gina Lollobrigida *Lola* • Katy Jurado *Rosa* • Thomas Gomez *Bouglione* • Johnny Puleo *Max the dwarf* • Minor Watson *John Ringling North* • Gérard Landry *Chikki* • Sidney James *Snake charmer* ■ *Dir* Carol Reed • *Scr* James R Webb, Liam O'Brien, from the novel *The Killing Frost* by Max Catto

Trapped ★★ 15

Crime thriller
2002 · US/Ger · Colour · 101mins

This begins with a terrifying jolt as the six-year-old daughter of yuppie parents Stuart Townsend and Charlize Theron is snatched by husband-and-wife extortionists, Kevin Bacon and Courtney Love. At this point, the tension is practically palpable and is given an extra edge by Bacon's superbly reptilian performance. Unfortunately, this soon descends into jaw-dropping stupidity as events become far-fetched. SF DVD

Charlize Theron *Karen Jennings* • Courtney Love *Cheryl Hickey* • Stuart Townsend *Will Jennings* • Kevin Bacon *Joe Hickey* • Pruitt Taylor Vince *Marvin* • Dakota Fanning *Abby Jennings* • Colleen Camp *Joan Evans* ■ *Dir* Luis Mandoki • *Scr* Greg Iles, from his novel *24 Hours*

Trapped in Paradise ★★★ PG

Seasonal comedy
1994 · US · Colour · 106mins

One from the days before Nicolas Cage reinvented himself as an action star, this is a slight, but engaging festive offering. Cage is the hapless good guy who is roped into a yuletide robbery by his brothers (Dana Carvey and Jon Lovitz), when they find themselves trapped by the weather in possibly the nicest small town in America. Carvey and Lovitz grab the best lines, but Cage is a commendable straight man. Writer/director George Gallo keeps the story moving in amiable fashion. JF. Contains swearing.

Nicolas Cage *Bill Firpo* • Dana Carvey *Alvin Firpo* • Jon Lovitz *Dave Firpo* • Mädchen Amick *Sarah Collins* • Vic Mazzucci *Vic Manni* • Florence Stanley *Ma Firpo* • Richard Jenkins *Shaddus Peyser* • Donald Moffat *Clifford Anderson* • Angela Patton *Hattie Anderson* ■ *Dir/Scr* George Gallo

Traps ★★★

Period drama 1994 · Aus · Colour · 98mins

Set in Vietnam in the 1950s, this film makes the disturbances in the nation become a metaphor for the disintegrating marriage of visiting photographer Saskia Reeves and her journalist husband Robert Reynolds. He refuses to see the country's unrest, but Reeves picks up on the volatile political situation, as communist guerrillas protest against French occupation. Their complicated relationship with plantation owner Sami Frey and his daughter brings matters to head. Reeves is excellent, though the film loses its way at the end. LH

Saskia Reeves *Louise Duffield* • Robert Reynolds *Michael Duffield* • Sami Frey *Daniel Renouard* • Jacqueline McKenzie *Viola Renouard* • Kiet Lam *Tuan* ■ *Dir* Pauline Chan • *Scr* Pauline Chan, Robert Carter, from the novel *Dreamhouse* by Kate Grenville

Trash ★★★ 18

Comedy drama 1970 · US · Colour · 103mins

This was arguably the first product from the Warhol studio to resemble a mainstream film. It has a conventional narrative, with actors playing parts as opposed to themselves, and it is "properly" edited. The story of a heroin addict rendered impotent carries a clear anti-drugs message, but this did not impress the British censor, who originally cut a shooting up scene. As the junkie, Joe Dallesandro enjoyed his finest hour, although he and others still stumble over their lines and have trouble sustaining their characters. Transvestite Holly Woodlawn, playing Dallesandro's roommate, has the funniest scenes. Too long, but too startling to be boring. DM [video] DVD

Joe Dallesandro *Joe* • Holly Woodlawn *Holly* • Jane Forth *Jane* • Michael Sklar *Welfare investigator* • Geri Miller *Go-go dancer* • Andrea Feldman *Rich girl* • Johnny Putnum *Boy from Yonkers* • Bruce Pecheur *Jane's husband* • Bob Dallesandro *Boy on street* ■ *Dir/Scr* Paul Morrissey • *Producer* Andy Warhol

Trauma ★

Horror 1962 · US · BW · 93mins

Lorrie Richards here makes the reluctant return to a musty mansion, in an attempt to recall the traumatic events that have ruined her life. Robert M Young, at the start of an undistinguished career, shuns the tongue-in-cheek approach that might have enlivened proceedings, while Richards has clearly forgotten how to act (if she ever knew how). DP

John Conte *Warren Clyner* • Lynn Bari *Helen Garrison* • Lorrie Richards *Emmaline Garrison* • David Garner *Craig Schoonover* • Warren Kemmerling *Luther* ■ *Dir* Robert Malcolm Young [Robert M Young] • *Scr* Robert Malcolm Young [Robert M Young], from his story

Trauma ★★ 18

Horror thriller 1993 · US/It · Colour · 101mins

Even fans of horror director Dario Argento are likely to find this boring. Asia Argento (Dario's daughter) plays a troubled young woman who may have the key to a killer's identity, but her semi-romantic involvement with a journalist slows the movie down. It's still an Argento film, what with the psycho on the loose who shows a fondness for decapitating his victims with an electric saw, but this features less of the fluid camerawork and over-the-top gore effects one expects from his best work. ST. Contains swearing, violence, nudity, drug abuse. [video] DVD

Christopher Rydell *David* • Asia Argento *Aura Petrescu* • Laura Johnson *Grace* • James Russo *Captain Travis* • Brad Dourif *Dr Lloyd* • Frederic Forrest *Dr Judd* • Piper Laurie *Adriana Petrescu* ■ *Dir* Dario Argento • *Scr* Dario Argento, TED Klein, from a story by Franco Ferrini, from a story by Giovanni Romoli, from a story by Dario Argento

Trauma ★ 15

Psychological thriller
2004 · UK/Ire/US · Colour · 90mins

Colin Firth awakens from a coma to restart his shattered life after the car crash death of his wife. Haunted by ghostly visions, his grip on reality is further eroded when police also blame him for a famous pop diva's murder. Slow, confusing and ultimately ridiculous, Marc Evans's film is done no favours by a fragmented screenplay over-loaded with enigmatic dialogue. Tiresome and timid. AJ. Contains violence and swearing. [video] DVD

Colin Firth *Ben* • Mena Suvari *Charlotte* • Naomie Harris *Elisa* • Tommy Flanagan *Tommy* • Sean Harris *Roland* • Brenda Fricker *Petra* • Kenneth Cranham *Inspector Jackson* ■ *Dir* Marc Evans • *Scr* Richard Smith

The Traveling Executioner ★★ 18

Period black comedy
1970 · US · Colour · 90mins

This is the strange tale of an ex-carnival man who, in 1918, travels around America with his portable electric chair, executing convicted criminals for $100. Events take a shocking turn in Alabama, when he falls for the surviving half of death-sentenced siblings. The story intrigues on paper, but falls flat, the result of rather dull direction. Played as some sort of fable, it also suffers from some corny acting. DA [video]

Stacy Keach *Jonas Candide* • Marianna Hill *Gundred Herzallerliebst* • Bud Cort *Jimmy* • Graham Jarvis *Doc Prittle* • James J Sloyan [James Sloyan] *Piquant* • M Emmet Walsh *Warden Brodski* ■ *Dir* Jack Smight • *Scr* Garrie Bateson

The Traveller ★★★★

Drama 1974 · Iran · BW · 75mins

Abbas Kiarostami made his feature film debut with this bittersweet story that demonstrates the enduring legacy of neorealism. Footie-mad Hassan Darabi is the epitome of rapscallion innocence, as he wheels, deals and steals his way to the money that buys him a ticket to Teheran for a big World Cup game. But it's the way Kiarostami sees through the boy's wide eyes each petty frustration and perceived injustice, as well as the awe-inspiring city sites, that makes this traveller's tale so shrewd, amusing and, ultimately, heartbreaking. DP. In Farsi with English subtitles.

Hassan Darabi *Ghassem Joulai* ■ *Dir* Abbas Kiarostami • *Scr* Abbas Kiarostami, from a short story by Hassan Rafi'ie

Traveller ★★★ 18

Drama 1997 · US · Colour · 96mins

A highly watchable buddy movie, set against the backdrop of the US's nomadic Irish-American community, with its rigid rules, intense distrust of outsiders, and almost Mob-style hierarchy. Bill Paxton plays a veteran traveller and scamster. Mark Wahlberg is the young semi-outsider who teams up with him to learn the ropes. The plot switches from character-driven to action-driven when Paxton cons cash from a crook to pay Julianna Margulies's medical bills. Boasting strong performances and a solid plot, this also looks terrific, courtesy of first-time director Jack Green's former incarnation as cinematographer. DA. Contains swearing, violence. [video]

Bill Paxton *Bokky* • Mark Wahlberg *Pat* • Julianna Margulies *Jean* • James Gammon *Double D* • Luke Askew *Boss Jack* • Nikki Deloach *Kate* • Danielle Wiener *Shane* ■ *Dir* Jack Green [Jack N Green] • *Scr* Jim McGlynn

Traveller's Joy ★★

Comedy 1949 · UK · BW · 86mins

Married in real life, John McCallum and Googie Withers star as a couple who, having divorced, both find themselves stranded and penniless in Sweden. Joining forces in order to obtain funds the pair are reconciled and their wild schemes cause local havoc. An adaptation of a popular British play, the film seems to have lost much of its comedy in the transfer. The usually excellent stars are frenzied rather than funny, leaving only the mildest of amusements. RK

Googie Withers *Bumble Pelham* • John McCallum *Reggie Pelham* • Yolande Donlan *Lil Fowler* • Maurice Denham *Fowler* • Colin Gordon *Tony Wright* • Gerard Heinz *Helstrom* • Geoffrey Sumner *Lord Tilbrook* • Dora Bryan *Eva* ■ *Dir* Ralph Thomas • *Scr* Allan Mackinnon, Bernard Quayle, from the play by Arthur Macrae

Travelling North ★★★★ 15

Comedy drama 1986 · Aus · Colour · 93mins

Film-makers have rarely been able to refrain from revealing the soft centres of grumpy old men. However, David Williamson's splendid adaptation of his stage hit resists the temptation and, by keeping Leo McKern's retired engineer cantankerous to the last, he presents us with a totally believable human being. In his first film in his native Australia, McKern gives an outstanding performance as a short-tempered know-all trying the patience of his new neighbours, and Julia Blake is equally impressive as the middle-aged divorcee who shares his new life. Carl Schultz imaginatively opens out the play and keeps the sentiment in check. DP. Contains swearing. [video]

Leo McKern *Frank* • Julia Blake *Frances* • Graham Kennedy *Freddie* • Henri Szeps *Saul* • Michele Fawdon *Helen* • Diane Craig *Sophie* ■ *Dir* Carl Schultz • *Scr* David Williamson, from his play

The Travelling Players ★★★★

Epic political drama
1975 · Gr · Colour · 230mins

This epic exploration of post-Civil War Greece (which won international acclaim and a number of awards) was partially made in secret during the military junta of 1967–74. Sprawling to nearly four hours, it makes extensive use of lingering long takes as a troupe of itinerant players and their (constantly interrupted) interpretation of a rustic idyll entitled *Golfo the Shepherdess* traverse 12 years of political turmoil from 1939 to 1952. With its stately pace and obscure references to mythology and contemporary events, the film requires patience, but its power and intelligence more than repay the effort. DP. In Greek with English subtitles.

Eva Kotamanidou *Electra* • Aliki Georgoulis *Mother* • Stratos Pachis *Agamemnon* • Maris Vassiliou *Clytemnestra* • Vaneglis Kazan *Aegisthos* • Grigoris Evangelatos *Poet* ■ *Dir/Scr* Theodoros Angelopoulos [Theo Angelopoulos]

Travels with Anita ★★

Romantic comedy
1978 · It · Colour · 125mins

Fresh from *Foul Play* and with *Private Benjamin* in the pipeline, this dark Italian comedy seems an odd role for Goldie Hawn, as the script is third-rate and the dubbing process robs her of that trademark ditziness. The story line is also unremarkable, as Goldie's American tourist hooks up with banker Giancarlo Giannini en-route to his father's funeral. DP. Italian dialogue dubbed into English.

Goldie Hawn *Anita* • Giancarlo Giannini *Guido* • Claudine Auger *Elisa* • Aurore Clément *Cora* • Renzo Montagnani *Omero* ■ *Dir* Mario Monicelli • *Scr* Leo Benvenuti, Piero De Bernardi, Tullio Pinelli, Paul Zimmerman, Mario Monicelli

Travels with My Aunt ★★★

Comedy 1972 · US · Colour · 109mins

This adaptation of Graham Greene's novel had a lot going for it – an Oscar-nominated turn from Maggie Smith, strong support from the likes of Alec McCowen and Robert Stephens, and direction from Hollywood veteran George Cukor. McCowen plays timid bank manager Henry Pulling, who meets his "aunt" (Smith) at his mother's cremation and is persuaded to accompany her on some freewheeling travels. Smith overdoes the eccentricity a bit and the plot obviously strains credibility, but it's colourful fun and one of the lighter and more entertaining screen versions of Greene's work. TH

Maggie Smith *Aunt Augusta* • Alec McCowen *Henry Pulling* • Louis Gossett Jr *Wordsworth* • Robert Stephens *Visconti* • Cindy Williams *Tooley* • Valerie White *Madame Dambreuse* ■ *Dir* George Cukor • *Scr* Jay Presson Allen, from the novel by Graham Greene

La Traversée de Paris ★★★

Second World War comedy drama
1956 · Fr/It · BW · 82mins

Jean Gabin, wonderfully cast as a well-off painter, and Bourvil, playing a grasping taxi driver, share the acting honours in a box-office hit that shed new light on life during the Occupation. The duo is traversing Paris with suitcases full of black-market pork, with Germans, collaborators and four-legged creatures making life tiresome. Thanks to fine acting, the talent of director Claude Autant-Lara and a sharp script, the film delivers neat observations on the less heroic aspects of Paris under the Nazis. BB. In French with English subtitles.

Jean Gabin *Grandgil* • Bourvil *Marcel Martin* • Jeanette Batti *Mariette* • Louis De Funès *Jambier* • Georgette Anys *La Patronne du Café Belotte* ■ *Dir* Claude Autant-Lara • *Scr* Jean Aurenche, Pierre Bost, from a novel by Marcel Aymé

La Traviata ★★★★ U

Opera 1982 · It · Colour · 105mins

Director Franco Zeffirelli's version of the classic opera with vocal heavyweights Placido Domingo and Teresa Stratas is entirely successful. Unlike most translations, this version of the Verdi opera hammers home the tragedy of the consumptive courtesan Violetta and her doomed love for Alfredo. Sumptuous, indulgent and cinematic, even an opera-resistant audience will find this accessible, and it is one of the few truly great filmed operas. LH. In Italian with English subtitles. [video]

Teresa Stratas *Violetta* • Placido Domingo *Alfredo* • Cornell MacNeil *Germont* • Alan Monk *Baron* • Axelle Gall *Flora* ■ *Dir* Franco Zeffirelli

T

Tread Softly ★

Musical murder mystery comedy
1952 · UK · BW · 70mins

An awesomely bad musical comedy thriller, offering only the melancholy spectacle of a once great star on her uppers. American Frances Day, a bubbly singer/comedian in Britain from the 1920s, was fading fast by the time she made this senseless feature about a company of actors trying to stage a revue in a haunted theatre. DM

Frances Day *Madeleine Peters* • Patricia Dainton *Tangye Ward* • John Bentley *Keith Gilbert* • John Laurie *Angus Mcdonald* • Olaf Olsen *Philip Defoe* • Nora Nicholson *Isobel Mayne* ■ *Dir* David MacDonald • *Scr* Gerald Verner, from his radio serial *The Show Must Go On*

Tread Softly Stranger ★ PG

Crime drama 1958 · UK · BW · 91mins

The big question here is, what on earth were Diana Dors, Terence Morgan and George Baker doing in such a dreary little film? Director Gordon Parry was capable of making involving pictures, but here he insists on his cast delivering each line as if it had the dramatic weight of a Russian novel, which is more than a little preposterous for a petty melodrama about criminal brothers falling for the same girl. DP

Diana Dors *Calico* • George Baker *Johnny Mansell* • Terence Morgan *Dave Mansell* • Patrick Allen *Paddy Ryan* • Jane Griffiths *Sylvia* • Maureen Delaney *Mrs Finnegan* • Betty Warren *Flo* ■ *Dir* Gordon Parry • *Scr* George Minter, Denis O'Dell, from the play *Blind Alley* by Jack Popplewell

Treasure Hunt ★★★ U

Comedy 1952 · UK · Colour · 82mins

Artist/novelist/screenwriter John Paddy Carstairs adapts MJ Farrell and John Perry's hit stage play, managing to capture much of the eccentric charm of the piece. An extended Irish family has mislaid its fortune and takes in lodgers to make ends meet. Wild chaos ensues. A first class cast is headed by Jimmy Edwards, here turning in another larger than life performance in a dual role. DF

Jimmy Edwards *Hercules Ryall/Sir Roderick* • Martita Hunt *Aunt Anna Rose* • Naunton Wayne *Eustace Mills* • Athene Seyler *Consuelo Howard* • June Clyde *Mrs Cleghorn-Thomas* • Miles Malleson *Mr Walsh* • Susan Stephen *Mary O'Leary* ■ *Dir* John Paddy Carstairs • *Scr* Anatole de Grunwald, from a play by MJ Farrell, from a play by John Perry

Treasure Island ★★★ U

Adventure 1934 · US · BW · 98mins

The first sound version of Robert Louis Stevenson's ripping yarn is directed by Victor Fleming who later made *Gone with the Wind*. Wallace Beery is well cast as Long John Silver (though not, perhaps, as memorably as Robert Newton in 1950), Lionel Barrymore is Billy Bones and young Jackie Cooper plays "Aaargh, Jim lad". More than 60 years on, a certain amount of woodworm has infested the foremasts, so what was always a rather ponderous adventure may seem even more so today. AT

Wallace Beery *Long John Silver* • Jackie Cooper *Jim Hawkins* • Lionel Barrymore *Billy Bones* • Otto Kruger *Dr Livesey* • Lewis Stone *Capt Alexander Smollett* • Nigel Bruce *Squire Trelawney* • Charles "Chic" Sale *Ben Gunn* • William V Mong *Pew* • Charles McNaughton *Black Dog* ■ *Dir* Victor Fleming • *Scr* John Lee Mahin, Leonard Praskins, John Howard Lawson, from the novel by Robert Louis Stevenson

T

Treasure Island ★★★ U

Adventure 1950 · UK · Colour · 95mins

This live-action Disney adventure owes its reputation to just one thing: Robert Newton's performance as Long John Silver. Here is the original, the one and only "Aargh, Jim lad," croaked by the extraordinary Newton whose body lurches drunkenly and whose piglet eyes have the twinkle of gin. Newton did not have to act this way; he was pickled much of the time. Apart from some pretty camerawork by Freddie Young, the rest of this production isn't much to shout about, and as Jim Hawkins, Bobby Driscoll is the worst sort of precocious American child star who, in real life, was headed for a very un-Disney future of drug addiction, poverty and an early death. Newton reprised his role in the sequel, *Long John Silver* (1954). AT DVD

Bobby Driscoll *Jim Hawkins* • Robert Newton *Long John Silver* • Basil Sydney *Capt Smollett* • Walter Fitzgerald *Squire Trelawney* • Denis O'Dea *Dr Livesey* • Ralph Truman *George Merry* • Finlay Currie *Billy Bones* • John Laurie *Blind Pew* ■ *Dir* Byron Haskin • *Scr* Lawrence E Watkin, from the novel by Robert Louis Stevenson

Treasure Island ★★★ PG

Adventure
1972 · UK/Sp/Fr/W Ger · Colour · 84mins

This reasonably entertaining canter through the oft-filmed pages of Robert Louis Stevenson has Orson Welles delivering a monstrously fat and fruity performance as Long John Silver. Although Welles gets a co-writer's credit, he actually initiated this project in 1966. He wrote the screenplay and started directing it back-to-back with his Shakespearian rumination, *Chimes at Midnight*. But the usual Welles gremlins and health problems forced him to abandon *Treasure Island* until his Spanish producer brought in another director, John Hough, to take over the reins. AT DVD

Orson Welles *Long John Silver* • Kim Burfield *Jim Hawkins* • Walter Slezak *Squire Trelawney* • Lionel Stander *Billy Bones* • Paul Muller *Blind Pew* • Maria Rohm *Mrs Hawkins* • Angel Del Pozo *Dr Livesey* • Michel Garland *Merry* ■ *Dir* John Hough • *Scr* Wolf Mankowitz, Orson Welles, from the novel by Robert Louis Stevenson

Treasure Island ★

Adventure 1986 · Fr/US · Colour · 115mins

Experimental, expatriate Chilean director Raúl Ruiz is far too clever to make your everyday adaptation; he has to make a film about a film *about Treasure Island*. This egg-head non-version, with its in-jokes, allusions and analysis of Stevenson's classic, sometimes looks and sounds like a Godard anti-movie. AT

Vic Tayback *Silver* • Melvil Poupaud *Jonathan* • Martin Landau *Old Captain* • Lou Castel *Doctor/Father* • Jeffrey Kime *Timothy* • Anna Karina *Mother* • Jean-Pierre Léaud *Midas* ■ *Dir* Raúl Ruiz • *Scr* Raúl Ruiz, from the novel by Robert Louis Stevenson

Treasure Island ★★★ PG

Adventure 1990 · US · Colour · 126mins

Robert Louis Stevenson's classic adventure gets the lavish telemovie treatment under Fraser C Heston's direction. His father Charlton is Long John Silver and *Empire of the Sun* star Christian Bale is Jim Hawkins. Shot on the same ship used for *Mutiny on the Bounty* (1962), the lush Caribbean locations make the familiar thrills easy on the eye. AJ

Charlton Heston *Long John Silver* • Christian Bale *Jim Hawkins* • Oliver Reed *Capt Billy Bones* • Christopher Lee *Blind Pew* • Richard Johnson *Squire Trelawney* • Julian Glover *Doctor Livesey* • Michael Thoma (2) *Hunter* ■ *Dir* Fraser C Heston • *Scr* Fraser C Heston, from the novel Robert Louis Stevenson

Treasure Island ★★ 12

Adventure 1998 · UK/Can · Colour · 91mins

Operating on a modest budget, director Peter Rowe has gone for a highly traditional approach and he's unable to set pulses racing, despite a willing cast and some splendid locations. Kevin Zegers is particularly anaemic as Jim Hawkins, while Jack Palance is given too much to do as Long John Silver. It's careful and reverential, but more than a mite dull. DP DVD

Jack Palance *Long John Silver* • Patrick Bergin *Billy Bones* • Kevin Zegers *Jim Hawkins* • Walter Sparrow *Ben Gunn* • David Robb *Doctor Livesey* • Christopher Benjamin *Squire Trelawney* ■ *Dir* Peter Rowe • *Scr* Peter Rowe, from the novel by Robert Louis Stevenson

Treasure of Lost Canyon ★★ U

Adventure 1952 · US · Colour · 81mins

After being conned out of his inheritance by a dubious San Francisco attorney, orphaned Tommy Ivo is given a home by kindly small-town doctor William Powell who helps him track down a treasure chest. Directed by former cameraman Ted Tetzlaff and loosely based on a story by Robert Louis Stevenson, this is a mediocre adventure movie for children. RK

William Powell *Doc Brown* • Tommy Ivo *David* • Rosemary DeCamp *Samuella* • Henry Hull *Lucius* • Julia Adams [Julie Adams] *Myra Wade* • Charles Drake *Jim Anderson* • Chubby Johnson *Baltimore Dan* ■ *Dir* Ted Tetzlaff • *Scr* Brainerd Dullfield, Emerson Crocker, from the story *The Treasure of Franchard* by Robert Louis Stevenson

Treasure of Matecumbe ★★ U

Adventure 1976 · US · Colour · 110mins

This movie is a typical example of a well-intentioned Disney family crowd-pleaser. An overlong, simplistic tale about two boys looking for treasure, helped by a useless batch of character actors. Location shooting on the Florida Keys is a plus, but the whole interminable mess looks no better than a TV pilot. DP

Peter Ustinov *Dr Snodgrass* • Robert Foxworth *Jim* • Joan Hackett *Lauriette* • Vic Morrow *Spangler* • Johnny Doran *Davie* • Billy Attmore *Thad* • Jane Wyatt *Aunt Effie* ■ *Dir* Vincent McEveety • *Scr* Don Tait, from the novel *A Journey to Matecumbe* by Robert Lewis Taylor

The Treasure of Monte Cristo ★★★

Period adventure 1960 · UK · Colour · 79mins

An interesting adventure involving buried treasure on the famous island, with Hollywood exile Rory Calhoun providing the muscle and Italy's Gianna Maria Canale the glamour. This is really only double-bill material, though there's plenty of action and thrills, plus a certain low-budget style that's rather endearing. The British contingent headed by genteel Patricia Bredin and slimy Peter Arne does what is required efficiently enough. TS

Rory Calhoun *Captain Adam Corbett* • Patricia Bredin *Pauline Jackson* • John Gregson *Renato* • Gianna Maria Canale *Lucetta* • Peter Arne *Count Boldini* • Sam Kydd *Albert* ■ *Dir* Monty Berman, Robert S Baker • *Scr* Leon Griffiths

The Treasure of Pancho Villa ★★ U

Western 1955 · US · Colour · 95mins

Although this western set during the Mexican Revolution of the early 20th century is rather lethargic, it has an interesting premise – cynical mercenary Rory Calhoun clashes with idealists Gilbert Roland and Shelley Winters en route to deliver a shipment of gold to legendary rebel leader Villa. But director George Sherman struggles under the gravitas of his theme and falters, thanks to the war of words. RT

Rory Calhoun *Tom Bryan* • Shelley Winters *Ruth Harris* • Gilbert Roland *Juan Castro* • Joseph Calleia *Pablo Morales* • Carlos Mosquiz *Commandant* ■ *Dir* George Sherman • *Scr* Niven Busch, from a story by J Robert Bren, Gladys Atwater

The Treasure of San Teresa ★★★

Drama 1959 · UK/W Ger · BW · 81mins

One of those "hunt for the wartime treasure" movies, cheerfully put together with an attractive international cast, headed by Eddie Constantine at his most rugged and Dawn Addams at her most gorgeous. The eclectic supporting cast includes double-dealing Marius Goring, Christopher Lee, Nadine Tallier and Clive Dunn, no less. Despite the diversity of nationalities, director Alvin Rakoff manages to hold all the accents together (not to mention the complexities of the plot). Co-feature fodder, but fun. TS

Eddie Constantine *Larry Brennan* • Dawn Addams *Hedi von Hartmann* • Gaylord Cavallaro *Mike Jones* • Marius Goring *Rudi Siebert* • Nadine Tallier *Zizi* • Willie White *General von Hartmann* • Walter Gotell *Inspector* • Christopher Lee *Jaeger* ■ *Dir* Alvin Rakoff • *Scr* Jack Andrews, from a story by Jeffrey Dell

Treasure of the Golden Condor ★★★ U

Adventure 1953 · US · Colour · 92mins

This has Cornel Wilde seeking his fortune in Central America, with a plot reminiscent of Tyrone Power's *Son of Fury*. To movie fans, the female members of the cast are the most interesting: although the lead is lacklustre Constance Smith, there's also *King Kong's* Fay Wray and a very young Anne Bancroft on the way up. TS

Cornel Wilde *Jean-Paul* • Constance Smith *Clara* • Finlay Currie *MacDougal* • Walter Hampden *Pierre* • Anne Bancroft *Marie* • George Macready *Marquis* • Fay Wray *Marquise* • Leo G Carroll *Dondel* ■ *Dir* Delmer Daves • *Scr* Delmer Daves, from the novel *Benjamin Blake* by Edison Marshall

The Treasure of the Sierra Madre ★★★★★ PG

Western adventure 1948 · US · BW · 125mins

As three losers try to find a crock of gold in bandit-infested Mexico, Humphrey Bogart turns in a memorable performance as drifter Fred C Dobbs who, along with Tim Holt's young idealist, latches onto gnarled old Klondike prospector Walter Huston (playing *sans* false teeth). Pitched as an updated biblical fable about greed and human despair, and partly shot in the Mojave Desert, the movie has a superb opening, some portentous passages and a thunderous score by Max Steiner. Much imitated – not least the ending – it proved a historic success for writer/director John Huston, who won Oscars for his direction and screenplay, while his father Walter won as best supporting actor. AT DVD

Humphrey Bogart *Dobbs* • Walter Huston *Howard* • Tim Holt *Curtin* • Bruce Bennett *Cody* • Barton MacLane *McCormick* • Alfonso Bedoya *"Gold Hat"* • A Soto Rangel *Presidente* • Manuel Donde *El Jefe* • José Torvay *Pablo* • John Huston *"White Suit"* ■ *Dir* John Huston • *Scr* John Huston, from the novel by B Traven • *Cinematographer* Ted McCord

Treasure of the Yankee Zephyr ★★ PG

Adventure 1981 · Aus/NZ · Colour · 93mins

Actor David Hemmings (*Blow Up*) directed this muddled and messy adventure with Donald Pleasence and Ken Wahl competing with George Peppard to recover a fortune from a Second World War plane wreck. It's not just the map to the treasure that gets lost, but also the plot. Lesley Ann Warren is the only guiding star. TH

Donald Pleasence *Gibbie* • George Peppard *Theo Brown* • Ken Wahl *Barney* • Lesley Ann Warren *Sally* • Bruno Lawrence *Barker* • Grant Tilly *Collector* ■ *Dir* David Hemmings • *Scr* Everett de Roche

Treasure Planet ★★ U

Animated science-fiction adventure
2002 · US · Colour · 91mins

Disney continues its literary plundering with an animated take on Robert Louis

Stevenson's classic novel. Slickly revamped for today's more sophisticated youngsters, the swashbuckling pirate adventure now unfolds in space. This allows for creative imaginations to run wild, as teen tearaway Jim Hawkins joins the crew of a space galleon to cross the universe in search of a fabled treasure trove, but while such artistic abandon does result in some stunning intergalactic landscapes, it also leads to a hotch-potch of flat alien characters. SF [video] DVD

Joseph Gordon-Levitt *Jim Hawkins* • Brian Murray *John Silver* • David Hyde Pierce *Doctor Doppler* • Emma Thompson *Captain Amelia* • Michael Wincott *Scroop* • Martin Short *BEN* • Laurie Metcalf *Sarah* • Patrick McGoohan *Billy Bones* ■ *Dir* John Musker, Ron Clements • *Scr* Ron Clements, John Musker, Rob Edwards, from a story by Ron Clements, John Musker, Ted Elliott, Terry Rossio, from the novel *Treasure Island* by Robert Louis Stevenson

The Treasure Seekers ★★ U

Adventure 1977 · US · Colour · 96mins

Rod Taylor wrote this story about the search for pirate Henry Morgan's sunken treasure as his own vehicle. That was the first mistake. The second was to have it made so turgidly with co-star Stuart Whitman. Despite the elfin femininity of Elke Sommer, it never succeeds in being anything other than a clone of so many movies about searchers for illusory riches. TH [video]

Rod Taylor *Marian Casey* • Stuart Whitman *Stack Baker* • Jeremy Kemp *Reginald Landers* • Elke Sommer *Ursula* • Keenan Wynn *"Meat Cleaver" Stewart* • Jennie Sherman *Debbie* • Bob Phillips *Joe* • Keith Foote *Lincoln* ■ *Dir* Henry Levin • *Scr* Rod Taylor

A Tree Grows in Brooklyn ★★★★ U

Period drama 1945 · US · BW · 123mins

The debut feature of celebrated director Elia Kazan is set in the early 1900s and is a tale of New York tenement life. Dorothy McGuire is excellent as the stoic Ma Nolan, whose efforts to keep her family together are hampered by an alcoholic husband (James Dunn) and the arrival of a third baby. Peggy Ann Garner received a special Academy Award for her role as the daughter, who dreams of a better life, free from grinding poverty, and for whom the titular tree is a symbol of hope. Stick with this one for the initial dull 30 minutes – it will reward your patience. SH DVD

Dorothy McGuire *Katie* • Joan Blondell *Aunt Sissy* • James Dunn *Johnny Nolan* • Lloyd Nolan *McShane* • Peggy Ann Garner *Francie Nolan* • Ted Donaldson *Neeley Nolan* • James Gleason *McGarrity* • Ruth Nelson *Miss McDonough* ■ *Dir* Elia Kazan • *Scr* Tess Slesinger, Frank Davis, from the novel by Betty Smith

Tree of Hands ★★ 18

Thriller 1988 · UK · Colour · 85mins

Novelist Ruth Rendell's psychological thriller is turned into a rather messy and underwhelming movie, with Helen Shaver as the woman whose own child dies and who then takes on a child kidnapped by her mother, played by Lauren Bacall. The parents of the kidnapped child bring one set of problems, while Shaver herself is being blackmailed. Lacklustre direction and a schlock script are the major weaknesses. AT [video]

Helen Shaver *Benet Archdale* • Lauren Bacall *Marsha Archdale* • Malcolm Stoddard *Dr Ian Raeburn* • Peter Firth *Terence* • Paul McGann *Barry* • Kate Hardie *Carol* • Tony Haygarth *Kostas* • Phyllida Law *Julia* • David Schofield *Detective Inspector* ■ *Dir* Giles Foster • *Scr* Gordon Williams, from the novel by Ruth Rendell

The Tree of Wooden Clogs ★★★★ 12

Drama 1978 · It · Colour · 178mins

Ermanno Olmi's sprawling study of peasant life in Lombardy at the end of the 19th century, is one of the last great neorealist films. Shot on 16mm and using only non-professional players, this pseudo-documentary epic finds drama in the changing of the seasons and the everyday tasks of the farm. Acting as his own cameraman, Olmi opts for muted colours that suggest both the period and the simplicity of the lifestyle. However, he is somewhat less subtle in emphasising the Marxist message, which he neatly conveys by means of religious, as well as traditional, rural imagery. DP. In Italian with English subtitles. [video] DVD

Luigi Ornaghi *Batisti* • Francesca Moriggi *Batistina* • Omar Brignoli *Minek* • Antonio Ferrari *Tuni* ■ *Dir/Scr* Ermanno Olmi

Trees Lounge ★★★★ 15

Comedy drama 1996 · US · Colour · 91mins

This is indie film-making à la John Cassavetes rather than Quentin Tarantino, with the humour being understated, the drama credible, the dialogue having an everyday ring and the performances ideally suited to a world of regrets and whiskey chasers. If the camerawork is occasionally prone to showiness, the atmosphere of both the neighbourhood Steve Buscemi prowls in his ice-cream van and the Trees Lounge itself is totally authentic. DP. Contains drug abuse, swearing and violence. [video] DVD

Steve Buscemi *Tommy* • Carol Kane *Connie* • Mark Boone Junior *Mike* • Chloë Sevigny *Debbie* • Bronson Dudley *Bill* • Anthony LaPaglia *Rob* • Michael Buscemi *Raymond* • Elizabeth Bracco *Theresa* ■ *Dir/Scr* Steve Buscemi

Trembling before G-d ★★ 15

Documentary
2000 · US/Is/Fr · Colour · 84mins

A heart-rending dilemma confronts the gay and lesbian subjects of Sandi Simcha DuBowski's documentary: their faith considers their sexuality to be an "abomination". Consequently, the majority are shown in shadow for fear of outing themselves and being ostracised by their Hasidic or Orthodox Jewish communities. The discussion of rigorous prayer regimes and aversion therapies is as disturbing as the testimony of those who admit to having lived their entire lives as a lie. However, DuBowski has such limited room for manoeuvre, as the delicate situation of nearly all the interviewees precludes both contact with estranged family members and the chance to locate their experiences in a wider context. DP. In English and Hebrew with subtitles.

Dir Sandi Simcha DuBowski

Tremors ★★★★★ 15

Comedy horror 1989 · US · Colour · 91mins

The spirit of the "Killer Bs" is gloriously resurrected in this, the ultimate story of the worm that turned. Kevin Bacon and Fred Ward are a sort of "Simple and Simpler", an endearingly goofy pair of handymen who discover that huge underground worms have broken through the earth's surface and are now swallowing up everything in their path. Director Ron Underwood keeps both the action and laughs roaring along at a tremendous pace and there's a string of entertaining cameos, most notably from Michael Gross and country star Reba McEntire as an unlikely pair of survivalists. Add to that a refreshingly tough and intelligent female lead (Finn Carter) and the result is the sharpest, funniest monster movie in years. JF. Contains swearing. [video] DVD

Kevin Bacon *Valentine McKee* • Fred Ward *Earl Bassett* • Finn Carter *Rhonda LeBeck* • Michael Gross *Burt Gummer* • Reba McEntire *Heather Gummer* • Bobby Jacoby *Melvin Plug* • Charlotte Stewart *Nancy* • Tony Genaro *Miguel* • Ariana Richards *Mindy* • Richard Marcus *Nestor* ■ *Dir* Ron Underwood • *Scr* SS Wilson, Brent Maddock, from a story by SS Wilson, Brent Maddock, Ron Underwood

Tremors II: Aftershocks ★★★ 12

Comedy horror 1995 · US · Colour · 95mins

Surprisingly entertaining made-for-video sequel to Ron Underwood's monster movie classic. The giant worms are munching in Mexico, so Fred Ward is called in along with Christopher Gartin. Sharply written and engagingly performed, this stays true to the jokey spirit of the original, while adding a new breed of overground "graboids" to literally chew the scenery. Although it lacks the frantic pace and sprightly camera work of the original, it's smarter and more fun than many cinema follow-ups. JC. Contains swearing and violence. [video] DVD

Fred Ward *Earl Bassett* • Michael Gross *Burt Gummer* • Helen Shaver *Kate* • Marcelo Tubert *Senor Ortega* • Christopher Gartin *Grady Hoover* ■ *Dir* SS Wilson • *Scr* SS Wilson, Brent Maddock

Tremors 3: Back to Perfection ★★ PG

Horror comedy 2001 · US · Colour · 99mins

First came the Graboids, then the Shriekers. Now, amid the theme park razzmatazz that has grown up around the town of Perfection, Nevada, come the Ass Blasters – giant critters that can both fly and detect targets by sensing body heat. Worm-waster Michael Gross is just one of the citizens returning to protect their burgh from the new generation of mutant man-eaters and director Brent Maddock slips in the old faces with almost parodic glee. Passable, if a little over-familiar. A further sequel, and a TV series, followed. DP [video] DVD

Michael Gross *Burt Gummer* • Shawn Christian *Desert Jack Sawyer* • Susan Chuang *Jodi Chang* • Charlotte Stewart *Nancy Sterngood* • Ariana Richards *Mindy Sterngood* • Tony Genaro *Miguel* ■ *Dir* Brent Maddock • *Scr* John Whelpley, from a story by SS Wilson, Brent Maddock

The Trench ★★ 15

First World War drama
1999 · UK/Fr · Colour · 94mins

William Boyd's directorial debut is a sincere, but stagey attempt to explore the psychological pressures weighing on diverse tommies awaiting their first day on the Somme. Although the camera restlessly suggests the cramped, primitive conditions, Tony Pierce-Roberts's glassy photography too often highlights the atmospheric shortcomings of the sets. Similarly, the cast rallies to the colours, but their commitment can't disguise the fact that the script is populated solely by stock combat characters. DP. Contains swearing and violence. [video] DVD

Paul Nicholls *Billy MacFarlane* • Daniel Craig *Sgt Telford Winter* • Julian Rhind-Tutt *Ellis Harte* • Danny Dyer *Victor Dell* • James D'Arcy *Colin Daventry* • Tam Williams *Eddie MacFarlane* • Antony Strachan *Horace Beckwith* ■ *Dir/Scr* William Boyd (2)

Trenchcoat ★★ PG

Comedy mystery 1983 · US · Colour · 87mins

A chirpy adventure in which an aspiring author finds herself drawn into a convoluted plot that seems to have leapt from the pages of her favourite fiction. Although the Maltese locations are easy on the eye and the conspiracy storyline scurries along without making too many demands on the imagination, the chief interest lies in the willing performances of Margot Kidder and Robert Hays. DP [video]

Margot Kidder *Mickey Raymond* • Robert Hays *Terry Leonard* • David Suchet *Inspector Stagnos* • Gila Von Weitershausen *Eva Werner* • Daniel Faraldo *Nino Tenucci* • Ronald Lacey *Princess Aida* ■ *Dir* Michael Tuchner • *Scr* Jeffrey Price, Peter S Seaman

Trent's Last Case ★★★ U

Crime mystery 1952 · UK · BW · 86mins

EC Bentley's diverting detective story was the prototype for the modern whodunnit. Michael Wilding stars as the shrewd sleuth of the title investigating the suspicious death of tycoon Orson Welles, who, in just a few flashbacks, masterfully creates a victim who was simply begging to be bumped off. Herbert Wilcox sprinkles the clues and red herrings with a steady hand, while John McCallum and Margaret Lockwood stand out among the suspects. DP [video]

Margaret Lockwood *Margaret Manderson* • Michael Wilding *Philip Trent* • Orson Welles *Sigsbee Manderson* • John McCallum *John Marlowe* • Miles Malleson *Burton Cupples* • Hugh McDermott *Calvin C Bunner* • Sam Kydd *Inspector Murch* • Jack McNaughton *Martin* ■ *Dir* Herbert Wilcox • *Scr* Pamela Bower, from the novel by EC Bentley

Trespass ★★ 18

Thriller 1992 · US · Colour · 96mins

Here, an unlikely premise (two firemen discover a map that points to a cache of gold in a disused factory) is buoyed up by a merely efficient set of thrills, which are sometimes funny, but veer towards the hysterical as the film approaches its tough finale. JM. Contains violence, swearing. [video]

Bill Paxton *Vince* • Ice T [Ice-T] *King James* • William Sadler *Don* • Ice Cube *Savon* • Art Evans *Bradlee* • De'Voreaux White *Lucky* • Bruce A Young *Raymond* • Glenn Plummer *Luther* • Stoney Jackson *Wickey* • TE Russell *Video* • Tiny Lister [Tom "Tiny" Lister Jr] *Cletus* ■ *Dir* Walter Hill • *Scr* Bob Gale, Robert Zemeckis

The Trespasser ★★★

Drama 1929 · US · BW · 91mins

Silent-screen drama queen Gloria Swanson produced, took a hand in the screenplay, and starred in this, her first talkie, making herself a million at the box office. She plays a secretary whose marriage to Robert Ames, the son of a multi-millionaire, is destroyed by Ames' father. A romantic melodrama on the familiar theme of mother love and self-sacrifice, the movie would not hold much interest now if it were not for the always mesmerising presence of la Swanson, who earned the film an Oscar nomination. Director/screenwriter Edmund Goulding rewrote and redirected it in 1937 as *That Certain Woman* with Bette Davis. RK

Gloria Swanson *Marion Donnell* • Robert Ames *Jack Merrick* • Purnell Pratt *Hector Ferguson* • Henry B Walthall *Fuller* • Wally Albright Jr [Wally Albright] *Jackie* • William Holden (1) *John Merrick Sr* • Blanche Frederici *Miss Potter* • Kay Hammond *Catherine "Flip" Merrick* ■ *Dir/Scr* Edmund Goulding

The Trespasser ★★ 18

Thriller 2001 · Bra · Colour · 96mins

In this disappointing thriller, a promising premise is undermined by director Beto Brant's inability to resist imposing his own visual signature. He's also distracted by the socio-sexual ramifications of the affair between Sao Paolo construction

T

heiress Mariana Ximenes and hitman Paolo Miklos. Miklos displays sinister malevolence, as he insinuates his way into unsuspecting lives, but the pacing is sluggish and the rap soundtrack cacophonous. DP. In Portuguese with English subtitles. Contains swearing, sex scenes and drug abuse.

Marco Ricca *Ivan* • Alexandre Borges *Gilberto, "Giba"* • Paulo Miklos *Anisio* • Mariana Ximenes *Marina* • Malu Mader *Claudia/ Fernanda* • Chris Couto *Cecilia, Ivan's wife* • George Freire *Estevao* • Tanah Correa *Dr Araujo* ■ *Dir* Beto Brant • *Scr* Beto Brant, Marçal Aquino, Renato Ciasca, from the novel *O Invasor* by Marçal Aquino

Trial ★★★★

Drama 1955 · US · BW · 108mins

Scripted by Don Mankiewicz from his own novel, this is a powerful study of courtroom justice, and one of the few movies to deal with the influence of Communism on US politics. Here, it's in open discussion as it impinges on the case of a Mexican youth (*Blackboard Jungle's* Rafael Campos) on trial for murder. The film is also the first to feature an African-American judge, played by Juano Hernandez. The Oscar-nominated Arthur Kennedy and the under-rated Dorothy McGuire provide excellent support, but this is Glenn Ford's movie, and what a screen presence he is – a rare combination of movie star and actor. TS

Glenn Ford *David* • Dorothy McGuire *Abbe* • Arthur Kennedy *Barney* • John Hodiak *John J. Armstrong* • Katy Jurado *Mrs Chavez* • Rafael Campos *Angel Chavez* • Juano Hernandez *Judge Theodore Motley* • Robert Middleton *AS "Fats" Sanders* ■ *Dir* Mark Robson • *Scr* Don Mankiewicz, from his novel

The Trial ★★★★ PG

Drama 1962 · Fr/It/W Ger · BW · 113mins

Orson Welles's film of Franz Kafka's novel is everything one expects: audacious, weird and impish, filled with references to Welles's own life as well as to *Citizen Kane*. Anthony Perkins is another citizen K, Joseph K, who is arrested and put on trial for no obvious reason in some strange autocratic state. Welles's use of locations (notably the Gare D'Orsay in Paris) is spellbinding, creating a dark labyrinth with the slenderest of resources. While Perkins is brilliantly paranoid, Jeanne Moreau and Romy Schneider are mysteriously exotic. Welles himself plays the Advocate, the ringmaster of this nightmare comedy. AT DVD

Orson Welles *The Advocate* • Anthony Perkins *Joseph K* • Jeanne Moreau *Miss Burstner* • Romy Schneider *Leni* • Elsa Martinelli *Hilda* • Akim Tamiroff *Bloch* • Arnoldo Foà *Inspector A* • William Kearns *First Asst Inspector* • Jess Hahn *Second Asst Inspector* • Suzanne Flon *Miss Pittl* • Michael Lonsdale [Michel Lonsdale] *Priest* ■ *Dir* Orson Welles • *Scr* Orson Welles, from the novel by Franz Kafka

The Trial ★★ 15

Drama 1993 · UK/It · Colour · 115mins

Kyle MacLachlan and Anthony Hopkins star in director David Jones's version of Kafka's classic novel about an innocent man accused. Unlike Orson Welles's 1963 version – and despite this version's scripting from Harold Pinter – this is seriously lacking the necessary dramatic darkness. MacLachlan is bland as Josef K, arrested and struggling to uncover the reason why, and Hopkins manages to steal the film completely with his very brief appearance as the priest who helps Josef. LH DVD

Kyle MacLachlan *Josef K* • Anthony Hopkins *The Priest* • Jason Robards Jr [Jason Robards] *Dr Huld* • Jean Stapleton *Landlady* • Juliet Stevenson *Fraulein Burstner* • Polly Walker *Leni* • Alfred Molina *Titorelli* ■ *Dir* David Jones (3) • *Scr* Harold Pinter, from the novel by Franz Kafka

Trial and Error ★★★ U

Comedy 1962 · UK · BW · 75mins

Also known as *The Dock Brief*, this neat little comedy was adapted from a radio play by John Mortimer (of *Rumpole* fame). The amusing storyline pits failed barrister Peter Sellers against Richard Attenborough's henpecked husband, who confounds all Sellers's ploys to have him acquitted on a charge of murdering his wife. Sellers does a nice line in comic despair, but this is not one of his most memorable characterisations and he is easily outflanked by Attenborough, who has a marvellous time playing the role of an unrepentant killer. DP DVD

Peter Sellers *Morgenhall/Doctor* • Richard Attenborough *Fowle/Judge/Jury foreman/ Member of public/Character witness* • Beryl Reid *Doris* • David Lodge *Bateson* • Frank Pettingell *Tuppy Morgan* • Eric Woodburn *Judge Banter* ■ *Dir* James Hill • *Scr* Pierre Rouve, from the radio play by John Mortimer

Trial and Error ★★ 12

Comedy 1997 · US · Colour · 94mins

Michael Richards provides a few laughs in this misfiring comedy as the pal of lawyer Jeff Daniels, who agrees to impersonate him in court when Daniels is indisposed, but hilarity is at a premium. Director Jonathan Lynn has shown a deft hand at comedy, but he's let down here by a lumpen script. It's a shame when he has a talented cast that includes Charlize Theron and Rip Torn. JB. Contains swearing.

Michael Richards *Richard "Ricky" Rietti* • Jeff Daniels *Charles "Charlie" Tuttle* • Charlize Theron *Billie Tyler* • Jessica Steen *Elizabeth Gardner* • Austin Pendleton *Judge Paul Z Graff* • Rip Torn *Benny Gibbs* ■ *Dir* Jonathan Lynn • *Scr* Sara Bernstein, Gregory Bernstein, from a story by Cliff Gardner, Sara Bernstein, Gregory Bernstein

Trial by Combat ★★

Comedy 1976 · UK · Colour · 89mins

Initially released as *Choice of Arms*, this is an idiotic fantasy about a secret society calling itself the Knights of Avalon, whose members dress up in medieval armour and act as a lynch mob, murdering dangerous criminals to make up for what they believe is an ineffective justice system. It has some nice touches, though it's not funny, stylish or subversive. AT. Contains violence and swearing.

John Mills *Bertie Cook* • Donald Pleasence *Sir Giles Marley* • Barbara Hershey *Marion Evans* • Margaret Leighton *Ma Gore* • Brian Glover *Sidney Gore* • David Birney *Sir John Gifford* • Peter Cushing *Sir Edward Gifford* ■ *Dir* Kevin Connor • *Scr* Julian Bond, Steve Rossen, Mitchell Smith, from a story by Fred Weintraub, Paul Heller

Trial by Jury ★★ 15

Thriller 1994 · US · Colour · 102mins

Joanne Whalley-Kilmer stars as the woman who stands up against mobster Armand Assante, who wants to ensure his court case goes his way. Director Heywood Gould does his best, but the plotting gets sillier by the minute and the performances from the starry cast are erratic. Assante is wildly over the top, William Hurt low key and sleazy as a bent ex-cop. JF. Contains sexual references, swearing, violence.

Joanne Whalley-Kilmer [Joanne Whalley] *Valerie Aston* • Armand Assante *Rusty Pirone* • Gabriel Byrne *Daniel Graham* • William Hurt *Tommy Vesey* • Kathleen Quinlan *Wanda* • Margaret Whitton *Jane Lyle* • Ed Lauter *John Boyle* • Richard Portnow *Leo Greco* ■ *Dir* Heywood Gould • *Scr* Jordan Katz, Heywood Gould

The Trial of Billy Jack ★

Drama 1974 · US · Colour · 170mins

The cult mixed ex-Green Beret is on trial for murder while fighting corrupt White House officials and the usual unappreciative rednecks, in this third entry in the hippy-dippy *Billy Jack* series which began in 1967 with *The Born Losers*. This is a stunningly pretentious and overlong vanity production from all-round auteur Tom Laughlin. Billy Jack finally came to rest in 1977's *Billy Jack Goes to Washington*. AJ

Tom Laughlin *Billy Jack* • Delores Taylor *Jean Roberts* • Victor Izay *Doc* • Teresa Laughlin *Carol* • William Wellman Jr *National Guardsman* ■ *Dir* Tom Laughlin • *Scr* Tom Laughlin, Delores Taylor, Teresa Christina

The Trial of Mary Dugan ★★

Crime melodrama 1941 · US · BW · 89mins

It started as a sensational Broadway courtroom melodrama of 1927, about a woman who lived in sin to help her brother through law college and is defended by him when she murders her lover. This is a dull and sanitised version has new star Laraine Day making little impression as a dull but decent stenographer and Robert Young playing a mere boyfriend, rather than her sibling. AE

Laraine Day *Mary Dugan* • Robert Young (1) *Jimmy Blake* • Tom Conway *Edgar Wayne* • Frieda Inescort *Mrs Wayne* • Henry O'Neill *Galway* • John Litel *Mr West* • Marsha Hunt *Agatha Hall* ■ *Dir* Norman Z McLeod • *Scr* Bayard Veiller, from his play

The Trial of the Incredible Hulk ★★ PG

Science-fiction adventure
1989 · US · Colour · 95mins

Surely after three TV movies and a four-year series, the Hulk would have vented all his anger and stopped going through his supply of shirts so rapidly? Well, no. Bill Bixby steps behind the camera to bring yet another instalment of the comic-book hero's adventures to the screen, with all the hallmarks of an idea that has run out of steam. Bixby went on to direct yet another helping of this tame action fare. NF DVD

Bill Bixby *Dr David Banner* • Lou Ferrigno *The Hulk* • Rex Smith *Matt Murdoch/Daredevil* • John Rhys-Davies *Wilson Fisk* • Marta DuBois *Ellie Mendez* • Nancy Everhard *Christa Klein* • Nicholas Hormann *Edgar* • Joseph Mascolo *Tendelli* • Richard Cummings Jr *Al Pettiman* ■ *Dir* Bill Bixby • *Scr* Gerald DiPego, from characters created by Stan Lee, Jack Kirby

Trial on the Road ★★★

Drama 1971 · USSR · BW · 97mins

Evocatively shot in lustrous widescreen monochrome, Alexei German's directorial debut was banned in the USSR for 15 years, primarily because the character played by Vladimir Zamansky is a Red Army deserter returning to the fold after collaborating with the Nazis. However, German is equally audacious in his presentation of Anatoli Solonitsyn's stiffly sadistic major (a chillingly pragmatic Stalinist) and Rolan Bykov's partisan commander, who operates according to instinct and humanity rather than dogma. DP. A Russian language film.

Rolan Bykov • Anatoli Solonitsyn • Vladimir Zamansky • Oleg Borisov ■ *Dir* Alexei German • *Scr* Eduard Volodarsky, from the book by Yuri German

The Trials of Henry Kissinger ★★★★

Documentary
2002 · US/UK/Den/Fr/Can/Aus · Col · 80m

No punches are pulled in this trenchant documentary assault on the reputation of Nobel Peace Prize Laureate Henry Kissinger. Opening with a satirical portrait that is both comic and vicious, director Eugene Jarecki then explores the charges made in Christopher Hitchens's source book. Drawing on a wealth of newly released evidence and making striking use of archive material, Jarecki examines the role of President Nixon's Secretary of State in Cambodia, Indonesia and Chile, and his involvement in the sabotaging of the 1969 Paris peace talks. This is pure political polemic, but it's persuasive and powerful. DP

Brian Cox *Narrator* ■ *Dir* Eugene Jarecki • *Scr* Alex Gibney, from the non-fiction book *The Trial of Henry Kissinger* by Christopher Hitchens

The Trials of Oscar Wilde ★★★★

Historical drama
1960 · UK · Colour · 123mins

This is a moving account of the fall from grace of the finest playwright of the Victorian era. Although Peter Finch looks nothing like Wilde, he gives an assured, poignant and Bafta-winning performance, excelling particularly during his courtroom jousts with James Mason. John Fraser makes an admirably self-centred Lord Alfred Douglas, while Lionel Jeffries plays impressively against type as the irascible Marquis of Queensberry, who first publicly accused Wilde of homosexuality. Gregory Ratoff's black-and-white picture, *Oscar Wilde* starring Robert Morley, was released almost simultaneously. DP

Peter Finch *Oscar Wilde* • James Mason *Sir Edward Carson* • Yvonne Mitchell *Constance Wilde* • Nigel Patrick *Sir Edward Clarke* • John Fraser *Lord Alfred Douglas* • Lionel Jeffries *Marquis of Queensberry* • Maxine Audley *Ada Leverson* • James Booth *Alfred Wood* ■ *Dir* Ken Hughes • *Scr* Ken Hughes, from the play *The Stringed Lute* by John Furnell and the book by Montgomery Hyde

Tribute ★★

Drama 1980 · Can · Colour · 125mins

Having enjoyed a Broadway triumph with this over-ripe and tragicomic role in the original play, it was inevitable that Jack Lemmon would be invited to immortalise his character on screen. It comes across as talkative and maudlin with Lemmon – as a glib theatrical press agent – encouraged to give a very mannered performance. Better acting comes from Lee Remick as his estranged wife and Robby Benson as the son who returns to discover his father has a fatal illness. BB

Jack Lemmon *Scottie Templeton* • Robby Benson *Jud Templeton* • Lee Remick *Maggie Stratton* • Colleen Dewhurst *Gladys Petrelli* • John Marley *Lou Daniels* • Kim Cattrall *Sally Haines* • Gale Garnett *Hilary* • Teri Keane *Evelyn* ■ *Dir* Bob Clark • *Scr* Bernard Slade, from his play

Tribute to a Bad Man ★★★★ PG

Western 1956 · US · Colour · 91mins

Well directed by Robert Wise and beautifully shot by the great cinematographer Robert Surtees, this fine MGM western has a genuine feel for life on the frontier. It's dominated by a larger-than-life performance from James Cagney as a ruthless cattle baron. Co-star Irene Papas's relationship with gruff Cagney forms the tough centre of the movie. The two leads are backed up by a knockout cast of western faces, including Lee Van Cleef and Royal Dano. TS

James Cagney *Jeremy Rodock* • Don Dubbins *Steve Miller* • Irene Papas *Jocasta Constantine* • Stephen McNally *McNulty* • Vic Morrow *Lars Peterson* • James Griffith *Barjack*

• Lee Van Cleef *Fat Jones* ■ *Dir* Robert Wise • *Scr* Michael Blankfort, from a short story by Jack Schaefer

Les Tricheurs ★★★

Melodrama 1958 · Fr/It · BW · 107mins

Marcel Carné's beatnik melodrama has been wrongly dismissed as a fogey's bid to get with the in-crowd. It actually explores the fascination of faddism with a dispassion that ensures the focus remains on the rebellious lovers whose brief encounter ends in tragedy. Pascale Petit and Jacques Charrier's romance is less significant than the attitudes they strike and the ideas they espouse, with Claude Renoir's moody monochrome cinematography helping to capture the atmosphere of Paris's jazz scene. Its sheen has faded, but this remains a valuable snapshot of pre-rock, pre-New Wave culture. DP. A French language film.

Jacques Charrier *Bob Letellier* • Pascale Petit *Mic* • Andréa Parisy *Clo* • Laurent Terzieff *Alain* • Roland Lesaffre *Roger* ■ *Dir* Marcel Carné • *Scr* Marcel Carné, Jacques Sigurd, from an idea by Charles Spaak

Trick ★★★ 15

Romantic comedy
1999 · US · Colour · 85mins

Jim Fall's unassuming gay romantic comedy pokes gentle fun at such stereotypes as the bitchy drag queen and the disco stud. Christian Campbell could hardly be more cherubic as the struggling musical composer whose chance to make it with a hunky stripper, JP Pitoc, is frustrated by a lack of privacy and a wealth of conflicting advice. Yet it's the much-maligned Tori Spelling's animated performance as a motor-mouthed off-Broadway wannabe that leaves the deepest impression. DP [VIDEO] DVD

Christian Campbell *Gabriel* • JP Pitoc *Mark Miranda* • Tori Spelling *Katherine Lambert* • Lorri Bagley *Judy* • Brad Beyer *Rich* • Steve Hayes *Perry* ■ *Dir* Jim Fall • *Scr* Jason Schafer

Trick or Treat ★★ 18

Comedy horror 1986 · US · Colour · 93mins

Evil Kiss-type rock star Tony Fields returns from the dead when one of his biggest fans, Marc Price, plays his last unreleased album backwards. At first Price caters to every murderous whim the spirit demands, until he realises he's being duped by the Devil. A tedious and adolescent heavy metal comedy-horror it features head-bangers Ozzie Osbourne and Gene Simmons in cameo roles and is perfunctorily directed by Charles Martin Smith. Featuring a killer toilet. AJ [VIDEO] DVD

Tony Fields *Sammi Curr* • Marc Price *Eddie Weinbauer* • Lisa Orgolini *Leslie Graham* • Doug Savant *Tim Hainey* • Elaine Joyce *Angie Weinbauer* • Ozzy Osbourne *Reverend Aaron Gilstrom* • Gene Simmons *Nuke* ■ *Dir* Charles Martin Smith • *Scr* Rhet Topham, Michael S Murphey, Joel Soisson, from a story by Rhet Topham

Trick or Treats ★★

Horror 1982 · US · Colour · 91mins

No-budget horror rip-off, about a girl who agrees to baby-sit a spoiled brat on Halloween. Jackelyn Giroux looks a bit too old to play the terrorised sitter, but there's solid support from Carrie Snodgress and David Carradine, and director Paul Bartel appears as a wino. Otherwise there's little to recommend this film, though movie buffs may like to note that director Gary Graver was the cameraman on some of Orson Welles's later films. DA

Jackelyn Giroux *Linda* • Peter Jason *Malcolm* • Chris Graver *Christopher* • David Carradine *Richard* • Carrie Snodgress *Joan* • Jillian Kesner *Andrea* • Paul Bartel *Wino* ■ *Dir/Scr* Gary Graver

The Trigger Effect ★★★ 15

Thriller 1996 · US · Colour · 90mins

A massive power failure causes panic among the inhabitants of a well-to-do US suburb. There's a parallel with *Lord of the Flies* in this stark reminder of the thin veneer that disguises our more savage instincts. Director David Koepp handles the chaos with some aplomb, despite his reduction of most characters to disaster-movie stereotypes. He's helped by a high calibre cast. DA. Contains swearing, sexual references, violence. [VIDEO]

Kyle MacLachlan *Matthew* • Elisabeth Shue *Annie* • Dermot Mulroney *Joe* • Richard T Jones *Raymond* • Bill Smitrovich *Steph* • Michael Rooker *Gary* ■ *Dir/Scr* David Koepp

Trigger Happy ★★★★ 15

Crime comedy 1996 · US · Colour · 92mins

Originally known as *Mad Dog Time*, this is a quirky gangster comedy featuring hilarious turns from an impressive all-star cast. Richard Dreyfuss is Vic, the Mob boss in a mental institution. Meanwhile, his associates and rivals battle over who takes control of his business and his girlfriend. Jeff Goldblum, Ellen Barkin, Diane Lane, Gabriel Byrne, Kyle MacLachlan and Gregory Hines are just some of the mobsters and their molls scattering the odd little film written and directed by Larry Bishop, which will delight those with a skewed sense of humour. JB [VIDEO]

Larry Bishop *Nick* • Richard Dreyfuss *Vic* • Gabriel Byrne *Ben London* • Ellen Barkin *Rita Everly* • Jeff Goldblum *Mickey Holliday* • Diane Lane *Grace Everly* • Gregory Hines *Jules Flamingo* • Kyle MacLachlan *Jake Parker* • Burt Reynolds *"Wacky" Jacky Jackson* ■ *Dir/Scr* Larry Bishop

Triggermen ★ 15

Crime comedy
2002 · Can/US · Colour · 92mins

This ghastly so-called comedy finds chancers Neil Morrissey and Adrian Dunbar getting mistaken for hitmen by Chicago mobsters keen to rub out rival gangster Pete Postlethwaite. Much allegedly comic mayhem ensues when the real hitmen turn up, and one of them falls for Postlethwaite's daughter, Claire Forlani. Duff material, indifferent direction. DA [VIDEO] DVD

Neil Morrissey *Pete Maynard* • Donnie Wahlberg *Terry Malloy* • Adrian Dunbar *Andy Jarrett* • Claire Forlani *Emma Cutler* • Amanda Plummer *Penny Archer* • Michael Rapaport *Tommy O'Brian* • Saul Rubinek *Jazzer* • Pete Postlethwaite *Ben Cutler* ■ *Dir* John Bradshaw • *Scr* Tony Johnston

Trilogy ★★★

Portmanteau drama
1969 · US · Colour · 110mins

Truman Capote enjoyed a fruitful relationship with the screen via adaptations of his original works – as here – and contributions to classics such as *The Innocents*. This trio of stories is directed , with delicacy and wit by Frank Perry. *Miriam*, based on his first published work, and *Among the Paths to Eden* are effective thanks to the fine acting that characterises the project. The longer *A Christmas Memory*, distinctively narrated by Capote, is the standout. Page is mesmerising as she ritually collects the ingredients and prepares the seasonal cake in this unsentimental evocation of a bygone era. BB

Mildred Natwick *Miss Miller* • Susan Dunfee *Miriam* • Carol Gustafson *Miss Lake* • Robin Ponterio *Emily* • Beverly Ballard *Nina* • Maureen Stapleton *Mary O'Meaghan* • Martin Balsam *Ivor Belli* • Geraldine Page *Woman* • Truman Capote *Narrator* ■ *Dir* Frank Perry • *Scr* Truman Capote, Eleanor Perry, from the Truman Capote stories *Miriam* and *A Christmas Memory* in *Mademoiselle* and *Among the Paths to Eden* in *Esquire*

Trilogy: the Weeping Meadow ★★★ PG

Romantic drama
2004 · Gr/Fr/It/Ger · Colour · 169mins

Despite its surfeit of glorious images, the first part of Theo Angelopoulos's projected "Greek exile" trilogy is too superficial to wholly engross. Following Alexandra Aidini, a Greek refugee from Russia who has been orphaned by the Bolshevik revolution, this spans 30 tumultuous years of history. While the plight of the interwar refugee is ably explored, this is swamped by momentous historical events that pass before their significance can be fully understood. DP. In Greek with English subtitles.

Alexandra Aidini *Eleni* • Nikos Poursanidis *Spyros's son* • Yorgos Armenis *Nikos, the fiddler* • Vasilis Kolovos *Spyros* • Eva Kotamanidou *Cassandra* • Toula Stathopoulou *Woman in coffee house* • Mihalis Yannatos *Zissis, the clarinetist* • Thalia Argyriou *Danae* ■ *Dir* Theo Angelopoulos • *Scr* Theo Angelopoulos, Tonino Guerra, Petros Markaris, Giorgio Silvagni

Trio ★★★

Portmanteau drama
1950 · UK/US · BW · 91mins

Sandwiched between *Quartet* and *Encore*, this is the second of Gainsborough's Somerset Maugham portmanteau pictures. Considering the writing talent involved and the quality of the performances, it seems slightly strange that the only Oscar-nomination the picture received was for best sound. Ken Annakin directs the first two stories, *The Verger*, with James Hayter and Kathleen Harrison on sparkling form, and *Mr Knowall*, with cheeky chappy supreme Nigel Patrick. The final half of the film contains Harold French's sentimental *Sanatorium*, starring Jean Simmons and Michael Rennie. DP

James Hayter *Albert Foreman* • Kathleen Harrison *Emma Brown* • Felix Aylmer *Bank manager* • Michael Hordern *Vicar* • Nigel Patrick *Max Kelada "Mr Know-All"* • Anne Crawford *Mrs Ramsay* • Wilfrid Hyde White *Mr Gray* • Jean Simmons *Evie Bishop* • Roland Culver *Ashenden* • Michael Rennie *George Templeton* ■ *Dir* Ken Annakin, Harold French • *Scr* W Somerset Maugham, RC Sherriff, Noel Langley, from the short stories by W Somerset Maugham • *Sound* Gordon McCallum, CC Stevens, J Mitchell

The Trip ★★★ 18

Drama 1967 · US · Colour · 75mins

"Feel Purple, Taste Green" screamed the posters for cult director Roger Corman's highly controversial drugs epic in which hippy Bruce Dern guides confused commercials director Peter Fonda through his first LSD acid trip. After scoring from Dennis Hopper (who else?) it's back to a luxury LA pad where Fonda digs an orange's aura, experiences good and bad vibes, has psychedelic visions of sex, death and dancing girls. Part exploitation flick, part non-preachy message picture, this fractured love-in, scripted by Jack Nicholson and told almost entirely through rapid-fire visuals, is a fascinating period piece. AJ [VIDEO] DVD

Peter Fonda *Paul Groves* • Susan Strasberg *Sally Groves* • Bruce Dern *John* • Dennis Hopper *Max* • Salli Sachse *Glenn* • Katherine Walsh *Lulu* • Barboura Morris *Flo* • Caren Bernsen *Alexandra* • Dick Miller *Cash* ■ *Dir* Roger Corman • *Scr* Jack Nicholson • *Cinematographer* Arch R Dalzell

The Trip to Bountiful ★★★★ U

Drama 1985 · US · Colour · 103mins

Geraldine Page's superb, Oscar-winning performance is the showpiece of this classy, intelligent, affecting and enjoyable drama, adapted with much skill by Horton Foote from his own stage and TV play. John Heard and Carlin Glynn give fine support as the son and peevish daughter-in-law of an elderly Texan woman (Page), who sets off from Houston on a journey of escape and returns to the small town of Bountiful where she was born. A far from conventional road movie, but one not to be missed. PF [VIDEO] DVD

Geraldine Page *Carrie Watts* • John Heard *Ludie Watts* • Carlin Glynn *Jessie Mae* • Richard Bradford *Sheriff* • Rebecca De Mornay *Thelma* • Kevin Cooney *Roy* ■ *Dir* Peter Masterson • *Scr* Horton Foote, from his TV play

Triple Agent ★★★★ U

Period thriller
2003 · Fr/It/Sp/Gr/Rus · Colour · 110mins

Inspired by fact, Eric Rohmer's period morality tale explores the notion of cause over country that has a subtle contemporary resonance. Set in Paris in 1936, the story concerns White Russian exile Serge Renko, who is prepared to conspire with democrats and fascists alike to undermine the Communist regime back home. But his duplicitous diplomacy comes to feel like a form of infidelity to his Greek artist wife Katerina Didaskalou. As ever with Rohmer, the literate dialogue is paramount, although he frequently resorts to newsreel footage to put the story into the context of unfolding world events. DP. In French, Greek and Russian with English subtitles. DVD

Katerina Didaskalou *Arsinoé Vorodin* • Serge Renko *Fiodor Vorodin* • Cyrielle Clair [Cyrielle Claire] *Maguy* • Grigori Manoukov [Grigori Manukov] *Boris* • Dimitri Rafalsky *General Dobrinsky* • Nathalia Krougly *General Dobrinsky's wife* • Amanda Langlet *Janine* • Jeanne Rambur *Dany* ■ *Dir/Scr* Eric Rohmer

Triple Bogey on a Par Five Hole ★★★★

Comedy 1991 · US · BW · 88mins

The Levys, a pair of married crooks who specialise in robbing people on golf courses, are both shot dead by one of their would-be victims. Thirteen years later screenwriter Remy Gravelle (played by underground film maker Eric Mitchell) is hired to research the story of the their three children who endlessly circle Manhattan on a luxury yacht ironically called the *Triple Bogey*. When he meets the Levy children, Mitchell tries to remain dispassionate, but gradually gets drawn in to their complex world. Fascinating, mesmerising and haunting. DF

Eric Mitchell *Remy Gravelle* • Daisy Hall *Amanda Levy* • Angela Goethals *Bree Levy* • Jesse McBride *Satch Levy* • Alba Clemente *Nina Baccardi* • Robbie Coltrane *Steffano Baccardi* • Philip Seymour Hoffman *Klutch* ■ *Dir/Scr* Amos Poe

Triple Cross ★★ PG

Biographical Second World War drama
1966 · Fr/UK · Colour · 120mins

Stuffed with plot and counterplot, this unexceptional drama is based on the allegedly true exploits of Eddie Chapman. Christopher Plummer plays Chapman, in jail on Jersey when the Nazis invade. He promptly secures a job in the Intelligence Service, leaving viewers to wonder if he's a traitor. Plummer makes the most of his enigmatic character and he's joined by heavyweights such as Yul Brynner, Trevor Howard and Romy Schneider. AT [VIDEO] DVD

T

Christopher Plummer *Eddie Chapman* • Romy Schneider *The Countess* • Trevor Howard *Distinguished civilian* • Gert Fröbe *Col Steinhager* • Yul Brynner *Baron von Grunen* • Claudine Auger *Paulette* • Georges Lycan *Leo* ■ *Dir* Terence Young • *Scr* René Hardy, William Marchant, from the autobiography *The Eddie Chapman Story* by Eddie Chapman, Frank Owen

The Triple Echo ★★★

Wartime drama 1972 · UK · Colour · 94mins

Adapted from a novel by HE Bates and set on a remote farm in 1942, this unlikely drama might have provoked a few unintentional smirks if it hadn't been so sensitively played by Glenda Jackson and Brian Deacon. Michael Apted's careful direction makes the ruse of disguising deserter Deacon as Jackson's sister seem almost credible, while his re-creation of the tranquil wartime countryside makes the abrupt intrusion of vulgar sergeant Oliver Reed all the more foreboding. DP. Contains swearing and violence.

Glenda Jackson *Alice Charlesworth* • Oliver Reed *Sergeant* • Brian Deacon *Barton* • Anthony May *Subaltern* • Gavin Richards *Stan* • Jenny Lee Wright *Christine* • Ken Colley [Kenneth Colley] *Corporal* • Daphne Heard *Shopkeeper* ■ *Dir* Michael Apted • *Scr* Robin Chapman, from the novel by HE Bates

Trippin' ★★

Comedy 1999 · US · Colour · 94mins

High school student Deon Richmond is faced with a number of problems. He has no date and no money for the prom, he hasn't even started applying for college, and is too shy to approach the prettiest girl in school. Instead of confronting his problems, he constantly daydreams about how he'd like his life to be. The movie never finds a constant tone, sometimes offering a refreshingly believable look at African-American life, sometimes immature, preachy and violent. Some funny moments and the likeability of Richmond's character make it tolerable. KB

Deon Richmond *Gregory Reed* • Donald Adeosun Faison *June* • Guy Torry *Fish* • Maia Campbell *Cinny Hawkins* • Aloma Wright *Louise Reed* • Harold Sylvester *Willie Reed* • Cleavon McClendon *Jamal* • Bill Henderson *Gramps* ■ *Dir* David Raynr [David Hubbard] • *Scr* Gary Hardwick

Tristana ★★★★★ PG

Period drama
1970 · Sp/It/Fr · Colour · 94mins

The last film that Luis Buñuel shot in his native Spain is not only a searing indictment of the Franco regime, but also an attack on the Spanish people as a whole for allowing their country to be consumed by corruption and decay. Set in Toledo in the late 1920s, the film explores the relationship between a depraved nobleman and his ward, who is determined to avenge the seduction that ruined her life. Revelling in his sins, Fernando Rey is superb as the pitiless Don Lope, while Catherine Deneuve is at her chilling best as the victim turned tormentor. It's bitter, biting and brilliant. DP. In Spanish with English subtitles. DVD

Catherine Deneuve *Tristana* • Fernando Rey *Don Lope* • Franco Nero *Horacio* • Lola Gaos *Saturna* • Antonio Casas *Don Cosme* • Jesus Fernandez *Saturno* • Vicente Soler *Don Ambrosio* ■ *Dir* Luis Buñuel • *Scr* Luis Buñuel, Julio Alejandro, from the novel by Benito Perez Galdos

The Triumph of Love ★★★ PG

Period comedy
2001 · It/UK/Ger · Colour · 111mins

Produced by her husband Bernardo Bertolucci, director Clare Peploe's unashamedly theatrical adaptation of Marivaux's 18th-century comedy of manners explores timeless themes of sexual and political power. Mira Sorvino gives a bravura performance as the cross-dressing princess who seeks to seduce usurped prince Jay Rodan in order to restore him to his rightful throne. However, Sorvino is more than matched by philosopher Ben Kingsley and his scientist sister Fiona Shaw, whose guardianship of Rodan is characterised by the bitter suspicion of romantic love. DP

Mira Sorvino *The Princess/Phocion/Aspasie* • Ben Kingsley *Hermocrates* • Fiona Shaw *Leontine* • Jay Rodan *Agis* • Ignazio Oliva *Harlequin* • Rachael Stirling *Hermidas/Corine* • Luis Molteni *Dimas* ■ *Dir* Clare Peploe • *Scr* Clare Peploe, Marilyn Goldin, Bernardo Bertolucci, from the play *Le Triomphe de l'Amour* by Pierre Marivaux, translated by Martin Crimp

Triumph of the Spirit ★★★ 15

Second World War drama
1989 · US · Colour · 115mins

In this powerful fact-based Holocaust drama filmed on location at the Auschwitz-Birkenau death camp, Willem Dafoe portrays a Jewish boxer who's forced, literally, to fight for his life, and for the lives of his family. It's a work of some restraint, preferring to forgo the familiar shock-horror Holocaust imagery, and opting instead to mirror the monstrosities in people's reactions to them. Dafoe, incidentally, shed 20 pounds to play the part, and looks suitably skeletal. Grimly hard-hitting in both senses of the phrase. DA

Willem Dafoe *Salamo Arouch* • Wendy Gazelle *Allegra* • Robert Loggia *Father Arouch* • Edward James Olmos *The Gypsy* • Kelly Wolf *Elena* • Costas Mandylor *Avram Arouch* • Kario Salem *Jacko Levy* ■ *Dir* Robert M Young • *Scr* Laurence Heath, Andrzej Krakowski, Robert M Young, Arthur Coburn, Millard Lampell, Shimon Arama, Zion Haen

Triumph of the Will ★★★★

Classic propaganda
1935 · Ger · BW · 120mins

Personally selected by Hitler, Leni Riefenstahl was given unlimited financial resources, the full co-operation of the Nazi hierarchy and a crew of more than a hundred to make a record of the 1934 Nuremberg Party rally. Special ramps, elevators, tracks and platforms were constructed so that every detail of Albert Speer's meticulously choreographed spectacle could be captured and used to convey the might and universality of Nazism and the messianic aura of the Führer. Taking eight months to edit, this remains one of the most potent pieces of propaganda ever produced, with Riefenstahl's mastery of her medium ensuring the total success of a pernicious project. DP. In German with English subtitles. DVD

Dir Leni Riefenstahl • *Scr* Walter Ruttmann (subtitles) • *Editor* Leni Riefenstahl • *Cinematographer* Sepp Allgeier, Karl Attenberger, Werner Bohne • *Music* Herbert Windt

Triumphs of a Man Called Horse ★ 15

Adventure 1983 · US/Mex · Colour · 85mins

Fans of the previous two *Horse* films (*A Man Called Horse* and *The Return of a Man Called Horse*) and will be disappointed by the relatively brief appearance of Richard Harris as the ageing Sioux leader. This lame sequel finds him joining with son Michael Beck and army captain Vaughn Armstrong to protect the tribe against settlers drawn by the gold rush. AT

Richard Harris *Man Called Horse* • Michael Beck *Koda* • Ana De Sade *Redwing* • Vaughn Armstrong *Capt Cummings* • Anne Seymour *Elk woman* • Buck Taylor *Sgt Bridges* • Simon Andreu *Gance* • Lautaro Murua *Perkins* ■ *Dir* John Hough • *Scr* Ken Blackwell, Carlos Aured, from a story by Jack DeWitt, from characters created by Dorothy M Johnson

Trixie ★★ 15

Comedy 2000 · US · Colour · 110mins

Ill-disciplined and over-written, this comedic sledgehammer nevertheless has a certain kooky charm, thanks to the gallant efforts of Emily Watson as a malapropping Chicago security guard with a yen to be a detective. Clearly director Alan Rudolph envisaged creating a screwball *noir*. Yet he never comes to terms with either the mystery – senator Nick Nolte's role in the disappearance of gangster's moll Lesley Ann Warren – or with the tone of the humour, which combines slapstick and wordplay with careless abandon. DP DVD

Emily Watson *Trixie Zurbo* • Dermot Mulroney *Dex Lang* • Nick Nolte *Senator Drummond Avery* • Nathan Lane *Kirk Stans* • Brittany Murphy *Ruby Pearli* • Lesley Ann Warren *Dawn Sloane* • Will Patton *RedRafferty* • Stephen Lang *Jacob Slotnick* ■ *Dir* Alan Rudolph • *Scr* Alan Rudolph, from a story by Alan Rudolph, John Binder

Trog ★ 15

Science-fiction horror
1970 · UK · Colour · 87mins

This indescribable nonsense sees anthropologist Joan Crawford battling Michael Gough over the fate of a recently discovered prehistoric caveman. Will Crawford teach the Missing Link all about life in the 20th century before Gough calls in the army to destroy him? This painful dud has intercut footage from *The Animal World* serving as Trog's memories in Crawford's last feature film. AJ

Joan Crawford *Dr Brockton* • Michael Gough *Sam Murdock* • Bernard Kay *Inspector Greenham* • Kim Braden *Anne* • David Griffin *Malcolm* • John Hamill *Cliff* • Thorley Walters *Magistrate* • Jack May *Dr Selbourne* ■ *Dir* Freddie Francis • *Scr* Aben Kandel, from a story by Peter Bryan, John Gilling

Trois Chambres à Manhattan ★★★

Drama 1965 · Fr/It · BW · 112mins

Marcel Carné specialised in claustrophobic melodramas featuring couples pondering the fate of their tortuous affair. But there's none of that oppressive melancholy in this adaptation of Georges Simenon's novel. Certainly the New York romance between French actor Maurice Ronet and diplomat's wife Annie Girardot (who won best actress at Venice) rarely runs smoothly, but there's a sustainable optimism about their reunion, which reinforces Carné's quaintly old-fashioned belief in the importance of love. DP. In French with English subtitles.

Annie Girardot *Kay Larsi* • Roland Lesaffre *Pierre* • OE Hasse *Hourvitch* • Maurice Ronet *François Comte* • Gabriele Ferzetti *Count Larsi* • Geneviève Page [Genevieve Page] *Yolande Combes* • Robert De Niro ■ *Dir* Marcel Carné • *Scr* Jacques Sigurd, Marcel Carné, from the novel by Georges Simenon

Trojan Eddie ★★★ 15

Drama 1996 · Ire/UK · Colour · 99mins

The totally different styles of bully-boy Richard Harris and hangdog Stephen Rea mesh to advantage in this slow-moving Irish fable. Rea is a loser, a peddler forced by circumstances to fetch and carry for Harris, godfather to the local travellers. The Irish landscape looks beautiful and there's plenty of time to observe it, but the depiction of the mentality of the people is as idiotic as it is idealistic. TH. Contains violence, swearing. DVD

Richard Harris *John Power* • Stephen Rea *Trojan Eddie* • Brendan Gleeson *Ginger Power* • Sean McGinley *Raymie* • Angeline Ball *Shirley* • Brid Brennan *Betty* • Stuart Townsend *Dermot* ■ *Dir* Gillies MacKinnon • *Scr* Billy Roche

The Trojan War ★★ U

Period action adventure
1961 · Fr/It · Colour · 103mins

In this routine, but watchable sword-and-sandal epic set a decade into the eponymous conflict, Trojan ruler Paris becomes jealous of people's champion Aeneas (Steve Reeves) and denounces him. Meanwhile, the Greeks plan their wooden horse trick. Very spectacular and the action moves along excitingly enough. JG. An Italian language film.

Steve Reeves *Aeneas* • John Drew Barrymore *Ulysses* • Warner Bentivegna *Paris* • Juliette Mayniel *Creusa* • Lidia Alfonsi *Cassandra* • Arturo Dominici *Achilles* ■ *Dir* Giorgio Ferroni • *Scr* Giorgio Stegani, Ugo Liberatore, Federico Zardi

Trojan War ★★ 12

Comedy 1997 · US · Colour · 79mins

Will Friedle plays a high-school student who gets the chance to bed the girl of his dreams, though he must first find a condom. What starts out as a five-minute trip quickly turns into a kind of *After Hours* experience, as the hapless hero encounters one disaster after another in his pursuit of a prophylactic. If the direction and editing had been less frenzied, chances are it would have been funnier. KB. Contains swearing, sexual references.

Will Friedle *Brad* • Jennifer Love Hewitt *Leah* • Marley Shelton *Brooke* • Jason Marsden *Josh* • Danny Masterson *Seth* • David Patrick Kelly *The Bagman* ■ *Dir* George Huang • *Scr* Andy Burg, Scott Myers

The Trojan Women ★

Drama 1971 · Gr/US · Colour · 111mins

This is as dull as counting sheep in a fog, despite the presence of such luminaries as Katharine Hepburn, Vanessa Redgrave and Irene Papas. Directed by Michael Cacoyannis, it's the story of Helen, Hecuba and that sassy seer Cassandra. Brian Blessed seems to be competing in the Anthony Quinn "River of Life" contest, but loses out to Patrick Magee who seems on the verge of imploding. AT

Katharine Hepburn *Hecuba* • Geneviève Bujold *Cassandra* • Vanessa Redgrave *Andromache* • Irene Papas *Helen* • Brian Blessed *Talthybius* • Patrick Magee *Menelaus* ■ *Dir* Michael Cacoyannis • *Scr* Michael Cacoyannis, from the play by Euripides

Troll ★ 15

Fantasy horror 1986 · US · Colour · 79mins

Michael Moriarty and Shelley Hack move into a new apartment building, and a mysterious troll possesses their little girl. The troll in his new guise then starts mutating the building's residents into creatures, or into forests as is the case with resident Sonny Bono. Whatever his actions are, the common factor is cheesiness. A dire, completely unrelated "sequel" followed in 1992. KB DVD

Noah Hathaway *Harry Potter Jr* • Michael Moriarty *Harry Potter Sr* • Shelley Hack *Anne Potter* • Jennifer Beck *Wendy Potter* • Sonny Bono *Peter Dickinson* • Phil Fondacaro *Malcolm Malory/Torok* • Julia Louis-Dreyfus *Jeanette Cooper* ■ *Dir* John Carl Buechler • *Scr* Ed Naha

The Trollenberg Terror ★★

Horror 1958 · UK · BW · 82mins

A Swiss ski resort is terrorised by tentacled monsters from outer space in an efficiently suspenseful British cheapie marred by awful special effects. Two bits of cotton wool stuck on a mountain photo make do for the cloudy snowscapes in veteran Hammer scriptwriter Jimmy Sangster's screen version of the BBC TV series. Forrest Tucker is miscast as the hero, but Janet Munro is affecting as the telepathic heroine the aliens seize as their mouthpiece. AJ

Forrest Tucker *Alan Brooks* • Laurence Payne *Philip Truscott* • Janet Munro *Anne Pilgrim* • Jennifer Jayne *Sarah Pilgrim* • Warren Mitchell *Professor Crevett* • Frederick Schiller *Klein* ■ *Dir* Quentin Lawrence • *Scr* Jimmy Sangster, from the BBC TV series by Peter Key

Tromeo & Juliet ★ 18

Erotic spoof 1996 · US · Colour · 102mins

The Troma team's take on *Romeo and Juliet* is unremittingly awful. With Motörhead's Lemmy as narrator, this mainly serves as an excuse to string together a series of loathsome and resolutely unfunny set-pieces. Quite appalling. JF. Contains swearing, sex scenes, violence. [video]

Jane Jensen *Juliet Capulet* • Will Keenan *Tromeo Que* • Valentine Miele *Murray Martini* • Maximillian Shaun *Cappy Capulet* • Steve Gibbons *London Arbuckle* • Sean Gunn *Sammy Capulet* • Lemmy *Narrator* ■ *Dir* Lloyd Kaufman • *Scr* James Gunn, Lloyd Kaufman

Tron ★★★ PG

Science-fiction adventure
1982 · US · Colour · 92mins

Disney's journey to *Toy Story* began with this dazzling electronic fantasy. Once computer genius Jeff Bridges entered cyberspace to prove himself the rightful inventor of stolen game patents, director Steven Lisberger broke cinematic territory by using, and inventing, state-of-the-art digital graphics to depict a bizarre video netherworld. The "light cycle" race – where machines create solid walls of colour behind them as they speed around a grid – is the highlight of a complex, but lighthearted, adventure. It's dated already, but video-game enthusiasts will love it. AJ [video] DVD

Jeff Bridges *Kevin Flynn/Clu* • David Warner *Ed Dillinger/Sark* • Bruce Boxleitner *Alan Bradley/Tron* • Cindy Morgan *Lora/Yori* • Barnard Hughes *Dr Walter Gibbs/Dumont* • Dan Shor *Ram* • Peter Jurasik *Crom* ■ *Dir* Steven Lisberger • *Scr* Steven Lisberger, from a story by Steven Lisberger, Bonnie MacBird

Troop Beverly Hills ★★ PG

Comedy 1989 · US · Colour · 101mins

In this airy comedy, a bunch of moneyed little misses strive to be hits as Wilderness Girls (a Girl Guide-type group), but a resentful area troop leader resolves to make them fail. Neatly made and hard to hate, stars Shelley Long and Craig T Nelson bring their customary professionalism to the movie. DA [video]

Shelley Long *Phyllis Nefler* • Craig T Nelson *Freddy Nefler* • Betty Thomas *Velda Plendor* • Mary Gross *Annie Herman* • Stephanie Beacham *Vicki Sprantz* • Audra Lindley *Frances Temple* • Edd Byrnes *Ross Coleman* • Ami Foster *Claire Sprantz* ■ *Dir* Jeff Kanew • *Scr* Pamela Norris, Margaret Grieco Oberman, from a story by Ava Ostern Fries

Trooper Hook ★★

Western 1957 · US · BW · 82mins

Barbara Stanwyck gives an intelligent performance as the rescued captive of the Apaches who won't give up the son she had by an Indian chief, but Joel McCrea is not quite tough enough as the cavalry sergeant who escorts her back to her rancher husband. There's a fatal lack of subtlety in the supporting characters, while the direction of Charles Marquis Warren is often clumsy, and Tex Ritter's title song soon becomes tiresome. AE

Joel McCrea *Sgt Hook* • Barbara Stanwyck *Cora Sutliff* • Earl Holliman *Jeff Bennett* • Edward Andrews *Charlie Travers* • John Dehner *Fred Sutliff* • Susan Kohner *Consuela* • Royal Dano *Trude* • Terry Lawrence *Quito* ■ *Dir* Charles Marquis Warren • *Scr* Charles Marquis Warren, David Victor, Herbert Little Jr, from a story by Jack Schaefer

Trop Belle pour Toi ★★★★ 18

Comedy 1989 · Fr · Colour · 87mins

Director Bertrand Blier was accused of sexism in many quarters for this tale of a successful car dealer who abandons his statuesque wife for a plain, older secretary. Yet, thanks to the wholehearted performances of Gérard Depardieu and Josiane Balasko, this is a genuinely touching love story. Blier can't resist mocking the sexual repression and social hypocrisy of the middle classes in a manner that recalls the later satires of Luis Buñuel. A touch short of stamina, but the blend of earthy drama and surrealist fantasy is thrilling. DP. In French with English subtitles. Contains swearing, nudity. [video] DVD

Gérard Depardieu *Bernard Barthélémy* • Josiane Balasko *Colette Chevassu* • Carole Bouquet *Florence Barthélémy/colette's Neighbour* • Roland Blanche *Marcello* • François Cluzet *Pascal Chevassu* • Didier Benureau *Léonce* • Philippe Loffredo *Tanguy* • Sylvie Orcier *Marie-Catherine* ■ *Dir/Scr* Bertrand Blier

Tropical Malady ★★★ 12A

Romantic fantasy drama
2004 · Fr/Thai/It/Ger · Colour · 118mins

Thai director Apichatpong Weerasethakul takes his predilection for experimentalism too far in this self-indulgent, if occasionally intriguing, anti-drama. The film is initially concerned with soldier Banlop Lomnoi's obsession with country boy Sakda Kaewbuadee, but then veers away from this tentative romance to follow Lomnoi's meandering pursuit of a shaman who has the power to transform into a tiger. The tale is atmospherically, but most people's patience will be tested by the avant-garde approach. DP. In Thai with English subtitles.

Banlop Lomnoi *Keng* • Sakda Kaewbuadee *Tong* • Udom Promma *Ekarat* ■ *Dir/Scr* Apichatpong Weerasethakul • *Cinematographer* Vichit Tanapanitch, Jarin Pengpanitch, Jean-Louis Vialard

Trottie True ★★ U

Romantic comedy
1949 · UK · Colour · 92mins

This could have been a nostalgic romp through an age when every stage-door johnny was a milord, waiting to sweep a chorus girl off to a life of luxury. However, in the hands of perpetual underachiever Brian Desmond Hurst, it becomes a cheap exercise in gold-digging set against backdrops that, in spite of the rich Technicolor, look second-hand rather than antique. Yet Jean Kent is plucky enough as she falls for trouper Bill Owen, balloonist Andrew Crawford and aristocrat James Donald. DP [video]

Jean Kent *Trottie True* • James Donald *Lord Digby Landon* • Hugh Sinclair *Maurice Beckenham* • Lana Morris *Bouncie Barrington* • Andrew Crawford *Sid Skinner* • Bill Owen *Joe Jugg* • Harcourt Williams *Duke of Wellwater* • Michael Medwin *Marquis Monty* • Hattie Jacques *Daisy Delaware* ■ *Dir* Brian Desmond Hurst • *Scr* C Denis Freeman, from the play by Caryl Brahms, SJ Simon

Le Trou ★★★★

Prison drama 1959 · Fr/It · BW · 123mins

Jacques Becker's final feature marks a significant stylistic departure from his previous pictures. Shot with an austerity that reinforces the grimly claustrophobic story of an attempted prison break, and made with a non-professional cast, it has inevitably been compared to Robert Bresson's *A Man Escaped*. But, the influence of Jean Renoir and John Huston ensures that this is more a study in psychology than spirituality, and there's also a painstaking attention to the finger-numbing mechanics of digging a tunnel with makeshift tools. Emotionally searing, yet deeply humanistic. DP. A French language film.

Michel Constantin *Geo* • Philippe Leroy *Manu* • Marc Michel *Gaspard* • Raymond Meunier *Monseigneur* • Jean Keraudy *Oldtimer* ■ *Dir* Jacques Becker • *Scr* Jacques Becker, Jean Aurel, José Giovanni

Trouble along the Way ★★★ U

Comedy drama 1953 · US · BW · 105mins

John Wayne stars in this uncharacteristically mawkish vehicle as a divorcee trying to retain custody of his daughter Sherry Jackson. Directed by Michael Curtiz, there's a lot of religiosity on hand, which some may find hard to take, and a school football team makes an uncomfortable metaphor for teamwork at home. Still, Donna Reed shines, and the whole is, if not entirely entertaining, at least quite fascinating. TS [video]

John Wayne *Steve Aloysius Williams* • Donna Reed *Alice Singleton* • Charles Coburn *Father Burke* • Tom Tully *Father Malone* • Sherry Jackson *Carole Williams* • Marie Windsor *Anne McCormick* • Tom Helmore *Harold McCormick* ■ *Dir* Michael Curtiz • *Scr* Melville Shavelson, Jack Rose, from the story *It Figures* by Douglas Morrow, Robert H Andrews

Trouble at Midnight ★★

Western 1937 · US · BW · 68mins

Universal turned out a series of features starring likeable Noah Beery Jr, but in truth audiences didn't warm to him as a leading man. Here, he plays a rancher in a daft mystery about rustling that can't seem to make up its mind whether it's a gangster flick, a western or a comedy. Ironically, Beery himself became a rancher when his career didn't pan out as planned. TS

Noah Beery Jr *Kirk Cameron* • Catherine Hughes *Catherine Benson* • Larry J Blake *Tony Michaels* • Bernadene Hayes *Marion* • Louis Mason *Elmer* ■ *Dir* Ford Beebe • *Scr* Ford Beebe, Maurice Geraghty, from the story *Night Patrol* by Kimball Herrick, from the story *Midnight Raiders* by Maurice Geraghty

Trouble Bound ★★★ 18

Action crime comedy
1993 · US · Colour · 85mins

Under-rated Michael Madsen plays an out-of-luck gambler who sets off across country with a dead body in the boot of a car he's just won. But it quickly proves the least of his problems as he then hooks up with winsome waitress Patricia Arquette, who's out to avenge the murder of her Mafia grandfather. Of course, this curious couple end up being pursued. This is tongue-in-cheek, if violent, entertainment. DA. Contains violence, swearing, nudity. [video] DVD

Michael Madsen *Harry Talbot* • Patricia Arquette *Kit Califano* • Florence Stanley *Granny* • Seymour Cassel *Santino* • Sal Jenco *Danny* • Paul Ben-Victor *Zand* • Darren Epton *Raphael* • Billy Bob Thornton *Coldface* ■ *Dir* Jeffrey Reiner • *Scr* Darrell Fetty, Francis Delia

Trouble Brewing ★★★ U

Comedy 1939 · UK · BW · 86mins

George Formby is a printer with a detective fixation, intent on capturing a gang of counterfeiters to impress fellow journo Googie Withers. It hardly takes Sherlock Holmes to figure out who is the master criminal, but the red herrings that pad out the story are amusing. Anthony Kimmins keeps the action brisk, but like all Formby directors he makes a stilted hash of the saucy songs. DP

George Formby *George Gullip* • Googie Withers *Mary Brown* • Gus McNaughton *Bill Pike* • Garry Marsh *AG Brady* • Joss Ambler *Lord Redhill* • Martita Hunt *Madame Berdi* ■ *Dir* Anthony Kimmins • *Scr* Anthony Kimmins, Angus MacPhail, Michael Hogan

Trouble Every Day ★★ 18

Horror 2000 · Fr/Ger/Jpn · Colour · 96mins

Claire Denis gets out of her depth with this tenebrous horror outing. The opening segments are enacted with scarcely any dialogue, as honeymooners Vincent Gallo and Tricia Vessey arrive in Paris just as doctor Alex Descas imprisons the carnivorous Béatrice Dalle in his mansion. Unfortunately, any sense of foreboding is rapidly frittered away once the characters begin justifying their actions and behaving in an increasingly bizarre manner. DP. In French and English with subtitles. Contains violence, nudity. [video] DVD

Vincent Gallo *Shane Brown* • Tricia Vessey *June* • Béatrice Dalle *Coré* • Alex Descas *Léo* • Florence Loiret-Caille *Christelle* • Nicolas Duvauchelle *Erwan* ■ *Dir* Claire Denis • *Scr* Claire Denis, Jean-Pol Fargeau

Trouble for Two ★★★

Comedy thriller 1936 · US · BW · 75mins

You'd never guess from the title, but this is MGM's version of Robert Louis Stevenson's "Suicide Club" stories. It's an expertly made, glossily produced oddity, pairing the excellent Robert Montgomery, playing an unlikely 19th-century prince, with an unusually mysterious Rosalind Russell. The theme is interesting: members of an anarchic London club set Montgomery a series of life-threatening tasks before he can marry his beloved, Russell. A wayward, off-the-wall product of the studio system that deserved greater recognition. TS

Robert Montgomery *Prince Florizel* • Rosalind Russell *Miss Vandeleur* • Frank Morgan *Colonel Geraldine* • Reginald Owen *Dr Franz Noel* • Louis Hayward *Young man with cream tarts* • EE Clive *King* • Walter Kingsford *Malthus* • Ivan Simpson *Collins* ■ *Dir* J Walter Ruben • *Scr* Manuel Seff, Edward E Paramore Jr, from the *Suicide Club,stories by Robert Louis Stevenson*

Trouble in Mind ★★★★ 15

Futuristic crime thriller
1985 · US · Colour · 107mins

This is an intelligent yet not wholly successful attempt by Alan Rudolph to re-create the kind of futuristic *film noir* pioneered by Jean-Luc Godard in *Alphaville*. Kris Kristofferson stars as an ex-cop just out of jail for murder, whose hopes for a fresh start with diner owner Geneviève Bujold are sidetracked by his involvement with Lori Singer and her violent partner, Keith Carradine, a petty crook whose behaviour and appearance grow increasingly bizarre and violent as he becomes entangled with Rain City crime boss, Divine. It's engrossing stuff and if the romance falls flat, the use of comedy to map Carradine's decline is inspired. DP [video] DVD

Kris Kristofferson *John Hawkins* • Keith Carradine *Coop* • Lori Singer *Georgia* • Geneviève Bujold *Wanda* • Joe Morton *Solo* • Divine *Hilly Blue* • George Kirby *Lieutenant Gunther* • John Considine *Nate Nathanson* ■ *Dir/Scr* Alan Rudolph

Trouble in Paradise ★★★★★

Romantic comedy 1932 · US · BW · 81mins

Two expert European thieves (Miriam Hopkins and Herbert Marshall) masquerading as aristocrats meet in

T

Venice, fall in love and team up professionally. Their elaborate plans almost come unstuck when, in the guise of secretaries, they infiltrate the household of a wealthy and glamorous Parisienne (Kay Francis) whose charms extend beyond her jewellery collection. Made by Ernst Lubitsch, whose famous "touch" is everywhere evident, this is arguably the most highly sophisticated romantic comedy ever to emerge from Hollywood. Brilliantly scripted, flawlessly stylish and faultlessly acted, it's a masterpiece, as well as being wonderfully good fun. RK. An English/ Italian language film.

Miriam Hopkins *Lily Vautier* • Kay Francis *Mariette Colet* • Herbert Marshall *Gaston Monescu, "LuValle"* • Charlie Ruggles [Charles Ruggles] *Major* • Edward Everett Horton *François Filiba* • C Aubrey Smith *Giron* ■ *Dir* Ernst Lubitsch • *Scr* Grover Jones, Samson Raphaelson, from the play *A Becsuletes Megtalalo (The Honest Finder)* by Aladar Laszlo • *Cinematographer* Victor Milner

Trouble in Store ★★★ U

Comedy 1953 · UK · BW · 82mins

This was Norman Wisdom's film debut and, according to some, it was all downhill from here. It's certainly one of his best outings, largely because the sentimentality that became almost unbearable in his later films is rigorously kept in check here by director John Paddy Carstairs. Wisdom is as willing and as hopeless as ever, but he still manages to take time off from his hectic schedule of driving store boss Jerry Desmonde to the brink of distraction to find romance with Lana Morris. DP [video] DVD

Norman Wisdom *Norman* • Margaret Rutherford *Miss Bacon* • Moira Lister *Peggy* • Derek Bond *Gerald* • Lana Morris *Sally* • Jerry Desmonde *Freeman* • Megs Jenkins *Miss Gibson* • Joan Sims *Edna* ■ *Dir* John Paddy Carstairs • *Scr* John Paddy Carstairs, Maurice Cowan, Ted Willis

Trouble in Texas ★★

Western drama 1937 · US · BW · 97mins

This was one of the first westerns to star singer Tex Ritter and one of the last in which a young Rita Cansino appeared before changing her name to Rita Hayworth. Ritter is the rodeo star and Hayworth the federal agent working undercover as a saloon singer to solve a series of robberies. The stars provide some compensation for the lame plot and obvious insertion of stock rodeo footage. AE

Tex Ritter *Tex Masters* • Rita Cansino [Rita Hayworth] *Carmen* • Earl Dwire *Barker* • Yakima Canutt *Squint* • Dick Palmer *Duke* ■ *Dir* RN Bradbury [Robert N Bradbury] • *Scr* Robert Tansey, from a story by Lindsley Parsons

T

Trouble in the Glen ★ U

Comedy 1954 · UK · Colour · 91mins

Margaret Lockwood enjoyed great success as an ingénue, then as Britain's leading actress during much of the 1940s, but films such as this contributed to her virtual retirement from the screen when barely 40. Co-star Orson Welles helps turn it into something nearer tragicomedy with his dodgy wig and even dodgier South American accent. Shot in a terrible process called Trucolor. BB

Margaret Lockwood *Marissa* • Orson Welles *Sanin Mengues/Sandy Menzies* • Forrest Tucker *Jim "Lance" Lancing* • Victor McLaglen *Parlan* • John McCallum *Malcolm* • Eddie Byrne *Dinny Sullivan* • Archie Duncan *Nolly Dukes* • Ann Gudrun *Dandy Dinmont* ■ *Dir* Herbert Wilcox • *Scr* Frank S Nugent, from a story by Maurice Walsh

Trouble Man ★

Blaxploitation crime thriller
1972 · US · Colour · 99mins

This crude and violent underworld melodrama hoped to reproduce the success of *Shaft's*. In a one-note role as Mr T, a supercool LA private eye drawn into a gangland feud, Robert Hooks is out-acted by Paul Winfield (as a double-crossing racketeer) and Julius Harris (as a rival hood). AE

Robert Hooks *Mr T* • Paul Winfield *Chalky* • Ralph Waite *Pete* • William Smithers *Captain Joe Marks* • Paula Kelly *Cleo* • Julius Harris *Big* • Bill Henderson *Jimmy* ■ *Dir* Ivan Dixon • *Scr* John DF Black

The Trouble with Angels ★★★ U

Comedy drama 1966 · US · Colour · 110mins

Best known for her acting in hard-bitten melodramas, Ida Lupino may seem a curious choice to direct this convent comedy. Yet she brings a much-needed hint of steel to what might otherwise have become another predictable journey down the road from rebellion to reformation. Hayley Mills is naughtier than in her Disney days, but much of her thunder is stolen by the debuting June Harding as her mousey friend, while Mother Superior Rosalind Russell walks away with every scene she's in. The sequel *Where Angels Go...Trouble Follows* hit the screen two years later. DP

Rosalind Russell *Mother Superior* • Hayley Mills *Mary Clancy* • June Harding *Rachel Devery* • Binnie Barnes *Sister Celestine* • Camilla Sparv *Sister Constance* • Gypsy Rose Lee *Mrs Phipps* ■ *Dir* Ida Lupino • *Scr* Blanche Hanalis, from the novel *Life with Mother Superior* by Jane Trahey

Trouble with Eve ★ U

Comedy 1959 · UK · BW · 66mins

The idea that a cosy country tearoom could become a den of vice is pretty hard to swallow at the best of times, but here it's as indigestible as a week-old rock cake in this dismal comedy from director Francis Searle. Hy Hazell is the proprietor whose activities are called into question when the local inspector is caught with his pants down. Unfunny from start to finish. DP

Robert Urquhart *Brian Maitland* • Hy Hazell *Louise Kingston* • Garry Marsh *Roland Axbridge* • Vera Day *Daisy* • Sally Smith *Eve* • Tony Quinn *Bellchambers* • Denis Shaw *George* ■ *Dir* Francis Searle • *Scr* Brock Williams, from the play *Widows Are Dangerous* by June Garland

The Trouble with Girls ★ U

Period comedy drama
1969 · US · Colour · 95mins

It's 1927, and Elvis Presley brings his mobile "chautauqua" show (an entertainment born out of the popular adult educational movement of the previous century), to Iowa, where he battles with Marilyn Mason as she tries to organise a performers' union. This love-hate scenario is disrupted when the local chemist is found dead. This is a joyless vehicle, providing only a handful of numbers for its star. JG [video] DVD

Elvis Presley *Walter Hale* • Marilyn Mason *Charlene* • Nicole Jaffe *Betty* • Sheree North *Nita Bix* • Edward Andrews *Johnny* • John Carradine *Mr Drewcolt* • Anissa Jones *Carol* • Vincent Price *Mr Morality* ■ *Dir* Peter Tewksbury • *Scr* Arnold Peyser, Lois Peyser, from a story by Mauri Grashin

The Trouble with Harry ★★★★★ PG

Black comedy 1954 · US · Colour · 94mins

This delicious black comedy flopped at the box office, but director Alfred Hitchcock always named it among his personal favourites. There's the odd suspenseful moment, but this is primarily a masterpiece of wry humour and dramatic understatement, as John Forsythe, Shirley MacLaine, Edmund Gwenn and Mildred Natwick decide in the most matter-of-fact way what to do with the body of a man three of them think they might have killed. The acting is perfection, with MacLaine (in her debut) quite wonderful. DP [video] DVD

Edmund Gwenn *Captain Albert Wiles* • John Forsythe *Sam Marlowe* • Shirley MacLaine *Jennifer Rogers* • Mildred Natwick *Miss Graveley* • Mildred Dunnock *Mrs Wiggs* • Jerry Mathers *Arnie Rogers* • Royal Dano *Calvin Wiggs* • Parker Fennelly *Millionaire* ■ *Dir* Alfred Hitchcock • *Scr* John Michael Hayes, from the novel by Jack Trevor Story

The Trouble with Spies ★★ PG

Spy spoof 1987 · US · Colour · 85mins

In this cheerful but anorexic spy spoof, Donald Sutherland plays a bumbling agent whose missions are so secret, everyone knows about them. He's sent to Ibiza to obtain the secret recipe for a truth serum but spends the time avoiding numerous attempts on his life. Fortunately for Sutherland, he has a cast of noted actors to support him. Unfortunately, the direction by Burt Kennedy is just inept. TH [video]

Donald Sutherland *Appleton Porter* • Ned Beatty *Harry Lewis* • Ruth Gordon *Mrs Arkwright* • Lucy Gutteridge *Mona Smith* • Michael Hordern *Jason Lock* • Robert Morley *Angus Watkins* • Gregory Sierra *Captain Sanchez* ■ *Dir* Burt Kennedy • *Scr* Burt Kennedy, Marc Lovell

The Troublemaker ★★

Crime comedy 1964 · US · BW · 81mins

This is a dated and very tame comedy about the adventures of a yokel (Tom Aldredge) at large in New York. It's made no better by being improvised by a group called "The Premise", which included the director Theodore J Flicker and source writer Buck Henry, presumably there to guard the few words he had written. TH

Tom Aldredge *Jack Armstrong* • Joan Darling *Denver James* • Theodore J Flicker *Crime Commissioner* • James Frawley *Sol/Sal/Judge Kelly* • Buck Henry *Tr Kingston* ■ *Dir* Theodore J Flicker • *Scr* Theodore J Flicker, Buck Henry, from a story by Buck Henry

Troy ★★★ 15

Epic period adventure
2004 · UK/US/Malta · Colour · 156mins

This attempts to retell the first half of Homer's *The Iliad* in gory *Gladiator* style and, for the most part, succeeds. Helen, Queen of Sparta (played by Diane Kruger) is seduced away from her much older husband Menelaus (Brendan Gleeson) by the impulsive Paris, Prince of Troy (Orlando Bloom). The aggrieved Greek forces demanding her return are lead by Brian Cox's Agamemnon, who numbers Achilles (a rather uncomfortable-looking Brad Pitt) among his allies. Director Wolfgang Petersen shows tremendous command of the wide-open spaces and the battle scenes are stupendous. Sadly, the dialogue is more Hollywood corn than Greek tragedy and the performances are uneven. TH. Contains violence. [video] DVD

Brad Pitt *Achilles* • Eric Bana *Hector* • Orlando Bloom *Paris* • Diane Kruger *Helen* • Brendan Gleeson *Menelaus* • Brian Cox *Agamemnon* • Peter O'Toole *Priam* • Sean Bean *Odysseus* • Rose Byrne *Briseis* • Saffron Burrows *Andromache* • Julie Christie *Thetis* ■ *Dir* Wolfgang Petersen • *Scr* David Benioff, from the poem *The Iliad* by Homer

The Truce ★★★

Biographical drama
1997 · It/Fr/Swi/Ger · Colour · 117mins

A prize-winning director, known initially for his uncompromising social realism, Francesco Rosi gained a reputation in his later career for literary adaptations. This faithful account of Primo Levi's postwar journey from Auschwitz back to Italy still has the power to provoke and move. But John Turturro's need to push through the chaos prevents us from fully empathising with either his tortured memories or his response to freedom. DP. In Italian with English subtitles. Contains swearing.

John Turturro *Primo* • Massimo Ghini *Cesare* • Rade Serbedzija *The Greek* • Stefano Dionisi *Daniele* • Teco Celio *Colonel Rovi* ■ *Dir* Francesco Rosi • *Scr* Francesco Rosi, Stefano Rulli, Sandro Petraglia, Tonino Guerra, from the novel by Primo Levi

Truck Stop Women ★★★

Action 1974 · US · Colour · 87mins

Here's a cult movie that really delivers in terms of raucous exploitation. Lieux Dressler plays the boss of a robbery and prostitution ring who has to fight off efforts by the Mob to take over her operation, based in a highway truck stop. Director Mark L Lester slams everything at us in terms of action – road crashes, sexual shenanigans, the denting of macho morale – while Dressler, *Playboy* playmate Claudia Jennings and Gene Drew could be in a Russ Meyer movie. TH

Claudia Jennings *Rose* • Lieux Dressler *Anna* • John Martino *Smith* • Dennis Fimple *Curly* • Dolores Dorn *Trish* • Gene Drew *Mac* ■ *Dir* Mark L Lester • *Scr* Mark L Lester, Paul Deason, from a story by Paul Deason

Truck Turner ★★ 18

Blaxploitation 1974 · US · Colour · 87mins

Apart from providing the voice for *South Park's* Chef, soul brother Isaac Hayes is probably better known for his Oscar-winning *Shaft* theme than for his acting. Here he makes a credible hero in a typical 1970s blaxploitation action movie. Hayes plays the title character, a ruthless bounty hunter whose targets are pimps and pushers. Director Jonathan Kaplan provides the no-frills, in-your-face action, while also eliciting an outrageous performance from *Star Trek's* Nichelle Nichols. RS [video] DVD

Isaac Hayes *Truck Turner* • Yaphet Kotto *Harvard Blue* • Alan Weeks *Jerry* • Annazette Chase *Annie* • Paul Harris *Gator* • Nichelle Nichols *Dorinda* • Sam Laws *Nate* ■ *Dir* Jonathan Kaplan • *Scr* Leigh Chapman, Oscar Williams, Michael Allin, from a story by Jerry Wilkes

Trucks ★★ 18

Science-fiction thriller
1997 · US/Can · Colour · 94mins

Killer trucks terrorise a small community. Sounds familiar? Sure enough, this is an unnecessary remake of horrormeister Stephen King's only directorial effort to date, *Maximum Overdrive*, itself no masterpiece. This time, Timothy Busfield heads the lacklustre cast of human victims. There are a few thrills. DM. Contains violence, swearing, sex scenes. [video]

Timothy Busfield *Ray* • Brenda Bakke *Hope* • Aidan Devine *Trucker Bob* • Jay Brazeau *Jack* • Brendan Fletcher *Logan* ■ *Dir* Chris Thomson • *Scr* Brian Taggert, from a short story by Stephen King

True as a Turtle ★ U

Comedy 1956 · UK · Colour · 92mins

This tiresome cross-Channel version of *Genevieve* has John Gregson and June Thorburn falling out over juvenile jealousies and petty pomposities while honeymooning on board Cecil Parker's yacht. Their bliss is further blighted by

U = SUITABLE FOR ALL Uc = SUITABLE FOR ALL, ESPECIALLY FOR YOUNG CHILDREN (VIDEO ONLY) PG = PARENTAL GUIDANCE

the discovery that they have become involved with a counterfeit gaming chip racket centred in a French casino. Crass. DP

John Gregson *Tony Hudson* • June Thorburn *Jane Hudson* • Cecil Parker *Dudley* • Keith Michell *Harry Bell* • Elvi Hale *Anne* • Avice Landone *Valerie* ■ *Dir* Wendy Toye • *Scr* Jack Davies, John Coates, Nicholas Phipps, from the novel by John Coates

True Believer ★★★ 15

Courtroom drama
1989 · US · Colour · 103mins

This under-rated courtroom thriller gives James Woods a rare good-guy role as a one-time radical lawyer who now scrapes a living defending drug dealers under dubious constitutional arguments. He rediscovers his idealism when he takes up the case of a young Korean, who claims he has been framed for a gangland murder. Woods turns in a edgy, passionate performance and is ably supported by Robert Downey Jr as his assistant. JF. Contains violence, swearing and drug abuse.

James Woods *Eddie Dodd* • Robert Downey Jr *Roger Baron* • Margaret Colin *Kitty Greer* • Yuji Okumoto *Shu Kai Kim* • Kurtwood Smith *Distric Attorney Robert Reynard* • Tom Bower *Cecil Skell* ■ *Dir* Joseph Ruben • *Scr* Wesley Strick

True Blue ★★ 15

Sports drama based on a true story
1996 · UK · Colour · 110mins

There's an intriguing story of macho rivalries and treacheries trying to get out of this account of events leading up to the 1987 Boat Race, when experienced American oarsmen were drafted into the Oxford team. But the potentially fascinating tale of modern sporting endeavour fights a losing battle with director Ferdinand Fairfax's laborious scene-setting and Brian Tufano's painterly photography, while talented young actors get caught in a backwash of bathos. TH. Contains swearing and brief nudity. DVD

Johan Leysen *Daniel Topolski* • Dominic West *Donald Macdonald* • Dylan Baker *Michael Suarez* • Geraldine Somerville *Ruth Macdonald* • Josh Lucas *Dan Warren* • Brian McGovern *Rick Ross* • Ryan Bollman *Morrison Black* ■ *Dir* Ferdinand Fairfax • *Scr* Rupert Walters, from the non-fiction book by Daniel Topolski, Patrick Robinson

True Colors ★★ 15

Drama 1991 · US · Colour · 105mins

It's perfectly clear from the outset of this by-the-numbers drama what will happen when two law students graduate and go their own ways, one to the Justice Department where spotless behaviour is seemingly the norm, the other into the moral sewer of politics. Fine actors John Cusack and James Spader are defeated by the all-too-obvious plot, yet both leads bring enough energy and detail to their roles. JM. Contains swearing.

John Cusack *Peter Burton* • James Spader *Tim Garrity* • Imogen Stubbs *Diana Stiles* • Mandy Patinkin *John Palmeri* • Richard Widmark *Senator James B Stiles* • Dina Merrill *Joan Stiles* • Philip Bosco *Senator Steubens* • Paul Guilfoyle (2) *John Lawry* ■ *Dir* Herbert Ross • *Scr* Kevin Wade

True Confession ★★★

Screwball comedy mystery
1937 · US · BW · 84mins

Fred MacMurray and Carole Lombard co-star as a highly moral attorney and his wife, a compulsive liar. When she's had up for murdering her boss, her husband gets her off on grounds of self-defence. A romantic screwball farce, directed by Wesley Ruggles and played with sufficient expertise to disguise some of the weaker aspects of the script, which declines to explain why Lombard is incapable of telling the truth. The movie spirals from mad to madder and is extremely funny. RK

Carole Lombard *Helen Bartlett* • Fred MacMurray *Kenneth Bartlett* • John Barrymore *Charley Jasper* • Una Merkel *Daisy McClure* • Porter Hall *Prosecutor* • Edgar Kennedy *Darsey* • Hattie McDaniel *Ella* ■ *Dir* Wesley Ruggles • *Scr* Claude Binyon, from the play *Mon Crime* by Louis Verneuil, Georges Berr

True Confessions ★★ 15

Crime drama 1981 · US · Colour · 105mins

Set in the 1940s, this crime drama, though entertaining enough, has ideas above its station. Robert Duvall plays a Los Angeles cop who suspects that his brother, a priest played by Robert De Niro, is linked with the murder of a prostitute. These two great actors, either of whom could emote ethical dilemmas in their sleep, can only furrow their brows when assailed by the predictable *film noir* plotting. Arid and generally uninspired. AT. Contains violence and swearing. DVD

Robert De Niro *Des Spellacy* • Robert Duvall *Tom Spellacy* • Charles Durning *Jack Amsterdam* • Kenneth McMillan *Frank Crotty* • Ed Flanders *Dan T Campion* • Burgess Meredith *Seamus Fargo* • Cyril Cusack *Cardinal Danaher* ■ *Dir* Ulu Grosbard • *Scr* John Gregory Dunne, Joan Didion, from the novel by John Gregory Dunne

True Crime ★★ 18

Thriller 1995 · US · Colour · 89mins

Alicia Silverstone plays a Catholic school girl who is a bit of a Nancy Drew. Addicted to detective novels, she naturally decides to do her own snooping when some teenage girls are murdered. Kevin Dillon has the thankless job of playing the cop she teams up with and loses her virginity to. This, of course, means he puts himself in danger when the killer decides to make Alicia his next target. JB. Contains violence. DVD

Alicia Silverstone *Mary Giordano* • Kevin Dillon *Tony Campbell* • Bill Nunn *Jerry* • Michael Bowen *Earl Parkins* • Ann Devaney *Sherry Tarnley* • Joshua Schaefer *John Giordano* • Marla Sokoloff *Vicki Giordano* ■ *Dir/Scr* Pat Verducci

True Crime ★★★ 18

Crime thriller 1999 · US · Colour · 127mins

Clint Eastwood directs and stars as a grizzled journalist with 12 hours to prove a prisoner on San Quentin's death row is innocent. Alternately tautly gripping and ridiculously facile, this suspense thriller at times resembles a big-budget episode of *Murder, She Wrote*, yet retains its "beat the clock" shape mainly because the superstar director accents character and detail above the mechanics of the whodunnit material. AJ. Contains swearing. DVD

Clint Eastwood *Steve "Ev" Everett* • Isaiah Washington *Frank Louis Beachum* • Lisa Gay Hamilton *Bonnie Beachum* • James Woods *Alan Mann* • Denis Leary *Bob Findley* • Bernard Hill *Warden Luther Plunkitt* • Diane Venora *Barbara Everett* • Michael McKean *Reverend Shillerman* ■ *Dir* Clint Eastwood • *Scr* Stephen Schiff, Paul Brickman, Larry Gross, from the novel by Andrew Klavan

True Grit ★★★★ PG

Western 1969 · US · Colour · 127mins

Big John Wayne finally won peer group recognition, taking the best actor Oscar for his portrayal of a cantankerous, one-eyed, drunken old reprobate hired by Kim Darby to avenge her father's death at the hands of thoroughly nasty Jeff Corey. This movie has acquired a reputation for being a rollicking fun western, but actually it is extraordinarily violent for its era and is not really suitable for family viewing, despite its strong moral theme. Glen Campbell is ineffective as a Texas Ranger (a role first offered to Elvis Presley, to whom Wayne wouldn't take second billing). A film of many memorable moments. TS DVD

John Wayne *Reuben J "Rooster" Cogburn* • Glen Campbell *La Boeuf* • Kim Darby *Mattie Ross* • Jeff Corey *Tom Chaney* • Robert Duvall *Ned Pepper* • Jeremy Slate *Emmett Quincy* • Dennis Hopper *Moon* ■ *Dir* Henry Hathaway • *Scr* Marguerite Roberts, from the novel by Charles Portis

True Identity ★★★ 15

Comedy thriller 1991 · US · Colour · 89mins

Comic Lenny Henry stars as a struggling actor who crosses the path of mobster Frank Langella, and decides he has to take a different identity so he can't be found. Naturally, Lenny's make-up artist pal turns our hero into a white man so he can avoid the wrath of the Mob. The script doesn't do justice to the star's talent, but the transformation is impressive, and Henry does a good job of turning every duff line and situation into a rib-tickling one. JB. Contains violence, swearing. DVD

Lenny Henry *Miles Pope* • Frank Langella *Frank Luchino/Leland Carver* • Charles Lane (3) *Duane* • JT Walsh *Craig Houston* • Anne-Marie Johnson *Kristi Reeves* • Andreas Katsulas *Anthony* • Michael McKean *Harvey Cooper* ■ *Dir* Charles Lane (3) • *Scr* Andy Breckman, Will Osborne, Will Davies, from a sketch by Andy Breckman

True Lies ★★★★ 15

Action comedy 1994 · US · Colour · 134mins

Arnold Schwarzenegger is the unshaken, unstirred secret agent, always saving the world in time to get home for dinner with his wife and kids, who are blissfully unaware of his dangerous job. Aside from the truly spectacular action, there's exceptional comedy support from Tom Arnold and a winning performance from Jamie Lee Curtis, who transforms from timid housewife to confident heroine. It may be wildly implausible and a trifle misogynistic, but, on the pure excitement level, James Cameron's blockbuster is unbeatable entertainment. AJ. Contains swearing and violence. DVD

Arnold Schwarzenegger *Harry Tasker* • Jamie Lee Curtis *Helen Tasker* • Tom Arnold *Gib* • Bill Paxton *Simon* • Tia Carrere *Juno* • Art Malik *Aziz* • Eliza Dushku *Dana* • Charlton Heston *Spencer Trilby* ■ *Dir* James Cameron • *Scr* James Cameron, from a screenplay (unproduced) by Claude Zidi, Simon Michael, Didier Kaminka

True Love ★★★★ 15

Comedy drama 1989 · US · Colour · 100mins

All imminent newlyweds should avoid this like the plague, because this is a film about the kind of doubts that can bring that thundering juggernaut known as your wedding day to a screeching halt. Directed with admirable insight by the debuting Nancy Savoca, this is comedy so close to the bone that it's often wincingly painful to watch. Annabella Sciorra is perfectly cast as the Italian-American who suddenly discovers dipsomanic Ron Eldard isn't the man of her dreams. A witty throwback to the days when Hollywood could do this kind of thing blindfold. DP. Contains swearing.

Annabella Sciorra *Donna* • Ron Eldard *Michael* • Star Jasper *JC* • Aida Turturro *Grace* • Roger Rignack *Dom* • Michael J Wolfe *Brian* • Kelly Cinnante *Yvonne* ■ *Dir* Nancy Savoca • *Scr* Nancy Savoca, Richard Guay

True Romance ★★★★ 18

Black comedy thriller
1993 · US · Colour · 116mins

Movie-obsessed comic-store worker Christian Slater meets hooker Patricia Arquette and, after getting married then accidentally stealing a fortune in cocaine from her pimp Gary Oldman, they hit the rocky road to possible oblivion. Scriptwriter Quentin Tarantino blends Hong Kong gangster movie clichés, *film noir* revisionism, slick but ultra-heavy violence and a host of great star cameos to create an acid cocktail. Director Tony Scott's superb visual style is the icing on the cake. AJ. Contains swearing, drug abuse, nudity, sex scenes and violence. DVD

Christian Slater *Clarence Worley* • Patricia Arquette *Alabama Whitman* • Dennis Hopper *Clifford Worley* • Val Kilmer *Mentor* • Gary Oldman *Drexl Spivey* • Brad Pitt *Floyd* • Christopher Walken *Vincenzo Coccotti* • Bronson Pinchot *Elliot Blitzer* • Samuel L Jackson *Big Don* • Michael Rapaport *Dick Ritchie* • Saul Rubinek *Lee Donowitz* • James Gandolfini *Virgil* • Chris Penn *Nicky Dimes* • Tom Sizemore *Cody Nicholson* • Conchata Ferrell *Mary Louise Ravencroft* ■ *Dir* Tony Scott • *Scr* Quentin Tarantino, Roger Avary (uncredited)

True Stories ★★★ PG

Comedy 1986 · US · Colour · 85mins

Not so much a movie as a feature-length rock video held together by a kooky storyline, with former Talking Head David Byrne strolling through the eccentric lives of the common, but secretly colourful, folk of the fictional community of Virgil, Texas, as they prepare for their annual "Celebration of Specialness". Alternately intriguing and condescending, Byrne's ironic detachment ultimately wears out its welcome, though the soundtrack, as you would expect, is consistently entertaining, and the ensemble cast is brilliant. AJ

David Byrne *Narrator* • John Goodman *Louis Fyne* • Swoosie Kurtz *Miss Rollings, the laziest woman in the world* • Spalding Gray *Earl Culver* • Alix Elias *Cute woman* • Annie McEnroe *Kay Culver* ■ *Dir* David Byrne • *Scr* David Byrne, Beth Henley, Stephen Tobolowsky

The True Story of Jesse James ★★ U

Western 1957 · US · Colour · 91mins

This is anything but the "true story" of the notorious outlaw. Bolstered by a fine score from the neglected Leigh Harline, the movie is seriously undermined by an unnecessary flashback structure and by the crippling use of contemporary Fox contractees. While attractive to watch, juvenile stars Robert Wagner and Jeffrey Hunter are wholly inadequate as Jesse and Frank James. Director Nicholas Ray here quite fails to grasp the tale's potential, and in his own words made "a very ordinary movie". TS

Robert Wagner *Jesse James* • Jeffrey Hunter *Frank James* • Hope Lange *Zee* • Agnes Moorehead *Mrs Samuel* • Alan Hale Jr *Cole Younger* • Alan Baxter *Remington* • John Carradine *Reverend Jethro Bailey* ■ *Dir* Nicholas Ray • *Scr* Walter Newman, from the film *Jesse James* by Nunnally Johnson

The True Story of Lynn Stuart ★★★

Crime thriller 1957 · US · BW · 76mins

In this gritty crime drama, dope smugglers are brought to book by a resourceful housewife. Although a minor production, Betsy Palmer gives an intelligent performance as the woman who cuddles up to Jack Lord's hoodlum in order to avenge the death of her dope-addicted nephew. It may sound far-fetched, but it's actually based on real-life events. Burnett

T

Guffey's photography, largely done on location, adds a touch of class to Lewis Seiler's competent direction. AE

Betsy Palmer *Phyllis Carter* • Jack Lord *Willie Down* • Barry Atwater *Hagan* • Kim Spalding *Ralph Carter* • Karl Lukas *Hal Bruck* • Casey Walters *Eddie Dine* • Harry Jackson *Husband Officer* ■ *Dir* Lewis Seiler • *Scr* John H Kneubuhl, from articles by Pat Michaels

True to Life ★★★ U

Comedy 1943 · US · BW · 93mins

This is an engaging comedy in which Dick Powell plays a radio writer who looks for a "typical" American family from which he can obtain material for his soap opera, but instead finds a household full of eccentrics. Although these include the irritating comic actor Victor Moore, Mary Martin, in one of her few straight roles, is charming. RB

Mary Martin *Bonnie Porter* • Franchot Tone *Fletcher Marvin* • Dick Powell *Link Ferris* • Victor Moore *Pop Porter* • Mabel Paige *Mom Porter* • William Demarest *Jake* • Clarence Kolb *Mr Huggins* • Yvonne De Carlo *Girl* ■ *Dir* George Marshall • *Scr* Don Hartman, Harry Tugend, from a story by Ben Barzman, Bess Taffel, Sol Barzman

Truly Madly Deeply ★★★★ PG

Romantic drama
1990 · UK · Colour · 102mins

It was dubbed the British *Ghost*, but this is a far more witty and incisive affair. It's distinguished by the glorious performances of Alan Rickman as the dearly departed who returns and Juliet Stevenson as his grief-stricken partner struggling to come to terms with her loss. But the strengths of this movie are numerous, most notably an emotional integrity that shines through in every scene and director Anthony Minghella's ability to inject the pathos with well-aimed humour. SH. Contains swearing. DVD

Juliet Stevenson *Nina* • Alan Rickman *Jamie* • Bill Paterson *Sandy* • Michael Maloney *Mark* • Deborah Findlay *Claire* • Christopher Rozycki *Titus* • David Ryall *George* • Jenny Howe *Burge* ■ *Dir/Scr* Anthony Minghella

Truman ★★★★ PG

Biographical drama
1995 · US · Colour · 133mins

This outstanding Emmy winner, based on the Pulitzer Prize-winning biography by David McCullough, features a tour-de-force performance from the incomparable Gary Sinise as Harry S Truman, the 33rd President of the United States. Insightful direction by Frank Pierson enlivens the intelligent script by Tom Rickman (*Coal Miner's Daughter*), while the authentic re-creation of the period adds class to the production. Diana Scarwid and Richard Dysart are standouts in the effective supporting cast. This captivating TV biopic is not just for history buffs, but for all those who enjoy fine film-making. MC DVD

Gary Sinise *Harry S Truman* • Diana Scarwid *Bess Wallace Truman* • Richard Dysart *Henry L Stimson* • Colm Feore *Charlie Ross* • James Gammon *Sam Rayburn* • Tony Goldwyn *Clark Clifford* • Pat Hingle *Thomas Joseph Pendergast* ■ *Dir* Frank Pierson • *Scr* Tom Rickman, from the biography by David McCullough

T

The Truman Show ★★★★★ PG

Satirical comedy drama
1998 · US · Colour · 98mins

From audacious start to poignant finale,this ingenious film is both dazzling and sophisticated. Truman Burbank (Jim Carrey) is the star of the world's most popular television show, only he doesn't know it. Although he thinks he lives in the idyllic island community of Seahaven, it's just an elaborate set housed in a vast studio, and all his family and friends are really actors. How that realisation slowly dawns and spurs him on to find out what's real and what's fake in his emotionally confused universe is the stuff of ambitious cinematic brilliance. With superlative support from Ed Harris (as the programme's creator Christof) and Laura Linney (as Truman's "wife", Meryl), Carrey reveals his dramatic range in this compelling fable about media omnipotence. AJ. Contains some swearing. DVD

Jim Carrey *Truman Burbank* • Ed Harris *Christof* • Laura Linney *Meryl* • Noah Emmerich *Marlon* • Natascha McElhone *Lauren/Sylvia* • Holland Taylor *Truman's mother* • Brian Delate *Truman's father* ■ *Dir* Peter Weir • *Scr* Andrew Niccol

Trust ★★★ 15

Drama 1990 · UK/US · Colour · 101mins

Dangerous things happen in this tragicomedy from independent film-maker Hal Hartley. Teenager Adrienne Shelly breaks the news of her pregnancy to her parents, causing dad to suffer a heart attack. Elsewhere, a baby is abducted and the antihero (Martin Donovan) carries a hand grenade around in case of emergency. This was Hartley's second feature (after 1989's *The Unbelievable Truth*), but such is the deadpan approach that you're never totally involved. TH

Adrienne Shelly *Maria Coughlin* • Martin Donovan (2) *Matthew Slaughter* • Merritt Nelson *Jean Coughlin* • John MacKay *Jim Slaughter* • Edie Falco *Peg Coughlin* • Gary Sauer *Anthony* ■ *Dir/Scr* Hal Hartley

Trust Me ★★ 15

Comedy thriller 1989 · US · Colour · 85mins

Adam Ant has never managed to shake off his Prince Charming/Dandy Highwayman pop image. Here he stars as an art gallery owner in debt who decides the only way out is to promote a respected artist and then kill him so the work increases in value. A daft idea, and the acting isn't much better as the star moves through each scene looking as if he's in search of a pop interlude. JB. Contains swearing.

Adam Ant *James Callendar* • David Packer *Sam Brown* • Talia Balsam *Catherine Walker* • William Deacutis *Billy Brawthwaite* • Joyce Van Patten *Nettie Brown* • Barbara Bain *Mary Casal* ■ *Dir* Bobby Houston • *Scr* Bobby Houston, Gary Rigdon

The Truth about Cats and Dogs ★★★★ 15

Romantic comedy
1996 · US · Colour · 96mins

This adorable and very funny romantic comedy stars a scene-stealing Janeane Garofalo as the radio talk show veterinary surgeon whom listener Ben Chaplin falls for. Garofalo is convinced Chaplin will be disappointed when he actually meets her, so she sends lovely but dim Uma Thurman in her place. Numerous romantic complications ensue as both women fall for the lucky fellow. It all zips along merrily, with Garofalo once again proving her skill as a comedian, while Thurman shows a previously unseen talent for comedy herself. A return to form for director Michael Lehmann. JB. Contains swearing and sexual references. DVD

Uma Thurman *Noelle* • Janeane Garofalo *Abby* • Ben Chaplin *Brian* • Jamie Foxx *Ed* • James McCaffrey *Roy* • Richard Coca *Eric* • Stanley DeSantis *Mario* ■ *Dir* Michael Lehmann • *Scr* Audrey Wells

The Truth about Charlie ★ 12

Romantic comedy thriller
2002 · US · Colour · 99mins

Expectations are automatically lowered for remakes of Hollywood classics – in this case, the classic is Stanley Donen's effervescent Hitchcock-homage *Charade* – but this is far worse than imagined. Director Jonathan Demme at least stays fairly close to the original's Paris-set story about the pursuit of a dead man's hidden fortune. But there isn't a single scene or performance (the pairing of Mark Wahlberg and Thandie Newton is spark free) that doesn't feel awkward or misjudged. JC DVD

Mark Wahlberg *Joshua Peters* • Thandie Newton *Regina Lambert* • Tim Robbins *Mr Bartholomew* • Park Joong-Hoon *Il-Sang Lee* • Ted Levine *Emil Zatapec* • Lisa Gay Hamilton *Lola Jansco* • Christine Boisson *Commandant Dominique* • Stephen Dillane *Charles Lambert* ■ *Dir* Jonathan Demme • *Scr* Jonathan Demme, Steve Schmidt, Jessica Bendinger, Peter Joshua [Peter Stone], from the film *Charade* by Peter Stone

The Truth about Demons ★★★ 18

Horror 2000 · NZ · Colour · 86mins

With a neo-punk visual edge, this glossy shocker features wonderfully elliptical CGI devils, heart-grabbing gore and numerous plot surprises. Karl Urban is the professor of esoteric cults and mysticism whose life becomes a paranoid nightmare when he becomes the sacrificial target for a Satanic cult. With only reformed black magician Katie Wolfe to help him over the hurdles of disbelief, he must fulfil an ancient prophecy to end the sect's reign of terror. Glenn Standring's creditable chiller consistently fires on all creepy cylinders. AJ DVD

Karl Urban *Harry* • Katie Wolfe *Benny* • Sally Stockwell *Celia* • Jonathon Hendry *Le Valliant* • Tony MacIver *Johnny* ■ *Dir/Scr* Glenn Standring • *Cinematographer* Simon Baumfield

The Truth about Spring ★★ U

Adventure 1964 · UK · Colour · 102mins

John Mills teams with daughter Hayley for the third time in this fanciful adventure that might well have passed for children's entertainment in the mid-1960s, but probably won't appeal to today's more sophisticated youngsters. Sir John hams it up as a crusty sea captain whose brush with smugglers lands tomboy Hayley in the arms of a young James MacArthur. Richard Thorpe directs at a fair clip, but too little stirs the imagination. DP

Hayley Mills *Spring Tyler* • John Mills *Tommy Tyler* • James MacArthur *William Ashton* • Lionel Jeffries *Cark* • Harry Andrews *Sellers* • Niall MacGinnis *Cleary* • Lionel Murton *Simmons* • David Tomlinson *Skelton* ■ *Dir* Richard Thorpe • *Scr* James Lee Barrett, from the story *Satan: a Romance of the Bahamas* by Henry de Vere Stacpoole

The Truth about Women ★★

Comedy 1958 · UK · Colour · 106mins

A bizarre charade in which Laurence Harvey plays a sort of Don Juan character, recalling his amorous, exotic adventures in Arabia, Paris, London, New York, the First World War and beyond. The moral is that one's first love is the only love that matters – aaah! – but the problem here is that Harvey is also something of a cold fish, not overly furnished with charm. The women make the most of their extended cameos, and pose in their Cecil Beaton costumes. AT

Laurence Harvey *Sir Humphrey Tavistock* • Julie Harris *Helen Cooper* • Diane Cilento *Ambrosine Viney* • Mai Zetterling *Julie* • Eva Gabor *Louise* • Michael Denison *Rollo* • Derek Farr *Anthony* • Elina Labourdette *Comtesse* ■ *Dir* Muriel Box • *Scr* Sydney Box, Muriel Box

The Truth Game ★★ 18

Drama 2000 · UK · Colour · 75mins

Every bit as verbose but less visually or thematically interesting than *Strong Language*, Simon Rumley's second feature is a claustrophobic character study that suffers from an over-reliance on improvisation and too many unnecessary camera movements. Three unsympathetic couples clash over dinner, but the cast's inexperience means they're always consciously acting, rather than role-playing. DP DVD

Paul Blackthorne *Dan* • Tania Emery *Charlotte* • Thomas Fisher *Alan* • Selina Giles *Lilly* • Stuart Laing *Eddy* • Wendy Wason *Kate* • Jennifer White *Alex* ■ *Dir/Scr* Simon Rumley

Truth or Consequences, NM ★★★ 18

Crime thriller 1997 · US · Colour · 102mins

For his feature directing debut Kiefer Sutherland might have chosen something just a little bit more original than the routine heist-goes-wrong scenario. Vincent Gallo is the ex-con setting up one last robbery with former cell-mate Sutherland, a trigger-happy sociopath. Naturally things don't go to plan and the gang end up taking hostages and falling foul of Rod Steiger's Las Vegas mobster and fruitcake Martin Sheen. Violently played out among the scenic mountains and deserts of Utah, this is expertly played by a solid cast, while Sutherland proves a safe pair of hands behind the lens. RS DVD

Kiefer Sutherland *Curtis Freley* • Vincent Gallo *Raymond Lembecke* • Mykelti Williamson *Marcus Weans* • Kevin Pollak *Gordon Jacobson* • Kim Dickens *Addy Monroe* • Grace Phillips *Donna Moreland* • Martin Sheen *Sir* • Rod Steiger *Tony Vago* ■ *Dir* Kiefer Sutherland • *Scr* Brad Mirman

The Trygon Factor ★★ 15

Crime drama 1967 · UK · Colour · 83mins

Fake nuns set up a million-dollar heist in this farcical British crime drama. Stewart Granger is the Scotland Yard detective called in to investigate a convent situated on the grounds of Cathleen Nesbitt's stately home; Susan Hampshire is her photographer daughter. Blackly comic at best, the film boasts a cast of British stalwarts, but they just end up milling around in the hope of being directed by Cyril Frankel. TH

Stewart Granger *Supt Cooper-Smith* • Susan Hampshire *Trudy Emberday* • Robert Morley *Hubert Hamlyn* • Cathleen Nesbitt *Livia Emberday* • Brigitte Horney *Sister General/Mrs Hamlyn* • Sophie Hardy *Sophie* • James Robertson-Justice *Sir John* ■ *Dir* Cyril Frankel • *Scr* Derry Quinn, Stanley Munro, from a story by Derry Quinn

Tuck Everlasting ★★★★

Animated fantasy
1980 · US · Colour · 114mins

In an utterly beguiling fable, a woods-dwelling family who are impervious to pain, ageing and death are stumbled upon by an inquisitive 12-year-old girl. Based on Natalie Babbit's award-winning novel, this independently-produced animation is almost as well-kept a secret as the family's immortality. But hunt it out: family entertainment doesn't come much better than this. DA

Fred A Keller *Angus Tuck* • James McGuire *Man in yellow suit* • Paul Flessa *Jesse Tuck* • Margaret Chamberlain *Winnie* • Sonia Raimi *Mary Tuck* • Bruce D'Auria *Miles Tuck* ■ *Dir* Frederick King Keller • *Scr* Stratton Rawson, Fred A Keller, Frederick King Keller, from the novel by Natalie Babbitt

Tuck Everlasting ★★★ PG

Period fantasy drama
2002 · US · Colour · 86mins

This Disney adaptation of Natalie Babbit's intelligent children's story is beautifully shot and without the rose-tinted glasses that might alienate older audiences. In upstate New York at the beginning of the 20th century, teenager Alexis Bledel runs away from her restrictive parents, discovering a woodland fountain of youth and the Tuck family. The innocent romance between her and Jonathan Jackson is well handled, and the supporting cast is strong. Tinged with both humour and melancholy, this holds a captivating affection for its period, characters and story. JC [video] DVD

Alexis Bledel *Winnie Foster* • William Hurt *Angus Tuck* • Sissy Spacek *Mae Tuck* • Jonathan Jackson *Jesse Tuck* • Scott Bairstow *Miles Tuck* • Ben Kingsley *Man in the Yellow Suit* • Amy Irving *Mother Foster* • Victor Garber *Robert Foster* • Elisabeth Shue *Narrator* ■ *Dir* Jay Russell • *Scr* Jeffrey Lieber, James V Hart, from the novel by Natalie Babbitt

Tucker: the Man and His Dream ★★ PG

Biographical drama
1988 · US · Colour · 105mins

Under the directorial auspices of Francis Ford Coppola, Jeff Bridges stars as Preston Tucker, a real-life innovative car designer whose career was gunned down by his big business competitors. Also a loyal family man, the portrayal of his home life with wife Joan Allen just plays like a bad sitcom. Beautiful to look at, though, thanks to the scintillating work of master cameraman Vittorio Storaro. LH [video]

Jeff Bridges *Preston Tucker* • Joan Allen *Vera Tucker* • Martin Landau *Abe Karatz* • Frederic Forrest *Eddie Dean* • Mako *Jimmy Sakuyama* • Dean Stockwell *Howard Hughes* • Lloyd Bridges *Senator Homer Ferguson* • Elias Koteas *Alex Tremulis* • Christian Slater *Junior* ■ *Dir* Francis Ford Coppola • *Scr* Arnold Schulman, David Seidler • *Executive Producer* George Lucas

Tudor Rose ★★★

Historical drama 1936 · UK · BW · 80mins

The short life and even shorter reign of Lady Jane Grey is given some poignancy by Nova Pilbeam, and heraldic significance and atmosphere by director Robert Stevenson. This is a Tudor story in which Elizabeth scarcely makes an appearance, but a mainly British cast make the "prithees" sound convincing. The American title, *Nine Days a Queen*, was an adequate description of the film's storyline. TH

John Mills *Lord Guildford Dudley* • Sir Cedric Hardwicke [Cedric Hardwicke] *Earl of Warwick* • Felix Aylmer *Edward Seymour* • Leslie Perrins *Thomas Seymour* • Frank Cellier *Henry VIII* • Desmond Tester *Edward VI* • Sybil Thorndike *Ellen* ■ *Dir* Robert Stevenson • *Scr* Robert Stevenson, Miles Malleson

Tuesdays with Morrie ★★★★ PG

Drama based on a true story
1999 · US · Colour · 89mins

Mitch Albom's memoir of his afternoons spent chewing the fat with his old college professor became a fixture on the US bestseller lists. It's not an easy book to adapt and there are moments in this TV movie when the fortune-cookie philosophy threatens to take over. But thanks to Mick Jackson's sensitive handling and Theo van de Sande's nostalgically shot Boston vistas, this is an old-fashioned, heart-warming delight. Hank Azaria impresses as the workaholic sports writer who regains a sense of perspective through his mentor's bon mots. But this is Jack Lemmon's show, as he dexterously portrays both Morrie Schwartz's physical decline and his zest for life. DP [video] DVD

Jack Lemmon *Morrie Schwartz* • Hank Azaria *Mitch Albom* • Wendy Moniz *Janine* • Caroline Aaron *Connie* • Bonnie Bartlett *Charlotte* ■ *Dir* Mick Jackson • *Scr* Tom Rickman, from the non-fiction book *Tuesdays with Morrie* by Mitch Albom

Tuff Turf ★★ 18

Drama 1984 · US · Colour · 106mins

This unremarkable teen drama has new kid in town James Spader falling for streetwise local girl Kim Richards. Trouble looms in the shape of her hot-tempered lover (Paul Mones), who doesn't take too kindly to Spader muscling in on his turf. Despite vague undertones of *West Side Story*, this is worth watching solely for Spader and for a brief, early appearance by Robert Downey Jr. DA [video]

James Spader *Morgan Hiller* • Kim Richards *Frankie Croyden* • Paul Mones *Nick Hauser* • Robert Downey Jr *Jimmy Parker* • Matt Clark *Stuart Hiller* • Claudette Nevins *Page Hiller* • Olivia Barash *Ronnie* ■ *Dir* Fritz Kiersch • *Scr* Jette Rinck, from a story by Greg Collins O'Neill, Murray Michaels

Tugboat Annie ★★★

Comedy drama 1933 · US · BW · 87mins

A ramshackle vehicle (in all senses of the word) reuniting the popular star team of the 1930 hit *Min and Bill*, lovable Marie Dressler and gruff Wallace Beery. It was based on Norman Reilly Raine's *Saturday Evening Post* stories about Annie Brennan and her no-good hubby Terry, who never hit Annie "'cept in self-defence". When this was made, Oscar-winner Dressler was number one at the box office; a year later she was dead from cancer. TS

Marie Dressler *Annie Brennan* • Wallace Beery *Terry Brennan* • Robert Young (1) *Alec Brennan* • Maureen O'Sullivan *Pat Severn* • Willard Robertson *Red Severn* • Tammany Young *Shif'less* ■ *Dir* Mervyn LeRoy • *Scr* Zelda Sears, Eve Green, Norman Reilly Raine, from stories by Norma Reilly Raine

Tulsa ★★ U

Drama 1949 · US · Colour · 87mins

Leading lady Susan Hayward is building an empire based on oil, the black gold, with the help of Robert Preston's geologist, but enters into an unholy partnership with oil baron Lloyd Gough. Producer Walter Wanger throws a conservation angle into this otherwise formula-bound entertainment as oil pollutes the traditional grazing lands of her native American friend, Pedro Armendáriz. AE [video] DVD

Susan Hayward *Cherokee "Cherry" Lansing* • Robert Preston *Brad "Bronco" Brady* • Pedro Armendáriz *Jim Redbird* • Chill Wills *Pinky Jimpson* • Harry Shannon *Nelse Lansing* • Ed Begley *"Crude" Johnny Brady* • Jimmy Conlin *Homer Triplette* ■ *Dir* Stuart Heisler • *Scr* Frank Nugent, Curtis Kenyon, from a story by Richard Wormser

Tumbleweed ★★ U

Western 1953 · US · Colour · 78mins

This very average Universal western stars its resident cowboy, Audie Murphy, who this time out is accused of deserting a wagon train during an Indian raid. There are lots of familiar western faces on hand, including Chill Wills and Lee Van Cleef, but perhaps it's worth mentioning that the title role goes to a horse. TS.

Audie Murphy *Jim Harvey* • Lori Nelson *Laura* • Chill Wills *Sheriff Murchoree* • Roy Roberts *Nick Buckley* • Russell Johnson *Lam* • KT Stevens *Louella Buckley* • Lee Van Cleef *Marv* ■ *Dir* Nathan Juran • *Scr* John Meredyth Lucas, from the novel *Three Were Renegades* by Kenneth Perkins

Tumbleweeds ★★★

Silent western epic 1925 · US · BW · 82mins

The first real cowboy star – just a gallop ahead of Tom Mix – and a major influence on the development of the western during the silent era, William S Hart made his final appearance in what is probably the best-known of his films. The plot has Hart vanquishing the lawless with the aid of his sharpshooting and playing protector to pioneer settler Barbara Bedford. Simple, formula stuff to be sure, but with an authentic flavour of the Old West and a famous land-rush action sequence. In 1939, the star reissued *Tumbleweeds* with sound effects and a prologue, spoken by himself, about how the West had changed. RK

William S Hart *Don Carver* • Barbara Bedford *Molly Lassiter* • Lucien Littlefield *Kentucky Rose* • J Gordon Russell *Noll Lassiter* • Richard R Neill *Bill Freel* • Jack Murphy *Bart Lassiter* ■ *Dir* King Baggot • *Scr* C Gardner Sullivan, from a story by Hal G Evarts

Tumbleweeds ★★★ 12

Drama 1999 · US · Colour · 98mins

Janet McTeer gives an Oscar-nominated performance as a free spirit who drags her 12-year-old daughter (newcomer Kimberley J Brown) out west in search of a better life. This funny, tender and predictably tear-stained slice of life echoes other parent-and-child road movies, yet it has a sassy charm all its own. McTeer's unselfconscious sexuality provides a vivid contrast to Brown's unaffected innocence. Writer/director Gavin O'Connor (whose ex-wife Angela Shelton based the story on her own mother) also appears as McTeer's truck-driving lover. AME [video] DVD

Janet McTeer *Mary Jo Walker* • Kimberly J Brown *Ava Walker* • Jay O Sanders *Dan* • Gavin O'Connor *Jack Ranson* • Michael J Pollard *Mr Cummings* • Laurel Holloman *Laurie Pendleton* ■ *Dir* Gavin O'Connor • *Scr* Gavin O'Connor, Angela Shelton

Tuna Clipper ★★ U

Adventure drama 1949 · US · BW · 77mins

William Beaudine directs this no-nonsense, serviceable melodrama, in which Roddy McDowall (who also co-produced) postpones his ambition to become a lawyer to ship out with a tuna crew in order to pay a friends's debt. The scenes involving McDowall's snobby Scottish family and girlfriend Elena Verdugo are somewhat stuffy, but once Beaudine gets on to the ocean, the action takes on a rugged authenticity. DP

Roddy McDowall *Alec* • Elena Verdugo *Bianca* • Roland Winters *Ransome* • Rick Vallin *Silvestre* • Dickie Moore *Frankie* • Russell Simpson *Fergus* • Doris Kemper *Mrs McLennan* ■ *Dir* William Beaudine • *Scr* W Scott Darling [Scott Darling]

The Tune ★★★ PG

Animated musical comedy
1992 · US · Colour · 66mins

Bill Plympton's feature debut pays homage to the collages of image and rhythm from the 1930s avant-garde, as a failed songwriter tries his hand at a variety of musical styles in order to relaunch his career. The action occasionally becomes a little mushy, as the inhabitants of the fantasy world of Flooby Nooby try to teach their guest to write from the heart, but there is undoubted beauty in the 30,000 pencil-and-watercolour drawings that comprise this entertaining film. DP [video]

Daniel Nieden *Del* • Maureen McElheron *Didi* • Marty Nelson *Mayor/Mr Mega/Mrs Mega* • Emily Bindiger *Dot* ■ *Dir* Bill Plympton • *Scr* Bill Plympton, Maureen McElheron, PC Vey

Tunes of Glory ★★★★ PG

Drama 1960 · UK · Colour · 106mins

John Mills won best actor at the Venice film festival for his priggish performance in this stiff-upper-lipped military drama, but few critics would have had any complaints had he shared the prize with his co-star Alec Guinness. Mills is the blue-blooded Pacific veteran who's determined to make his new regiment fit for the demands of peacetime, while Guinness is the time-serving Alamein hero who remains stubbornly obsessed with past glories. James Kennaway's rather bombastic script, and, if Ronald Neame's direction is occasionally stodgy, the conflict between Mills and Guinness remains as compelling as its resolution is shocking. DP [video]

Alec Guinness *Lt Col Jock Sinclair* • John Mills *Lt Col Basil Barrow* • Dennis Price *Major Charlie Scott* • Susannah York *Morag Sinclair* • John Fraser *Corporal Piper Fraser* • Allan Cuthbertson *Captain Eric Simpson* • Kay Walsh *Mary* • John MacKenzie *Pony Major* • Gordon Jackson *Captain Jimmy Cairns* ■ *Dir* Ronald Neame • *Scr* James Kennaway, from his novel

The Tunnel ★★ U

Science-fiction drama
1935 · UK · BW · 88mins

This remake of a German film was heavily geared towards the American market, with Hollywood stars including Richard Dix as the engineering genius behind the scheme for a railway tunnel under the Atlantic, Walter Huston (seen only briefly) as the US President, and Madge Evans as Dix's anxious wife. Leslie Banks leads the British contingent, while George Arliss matches Huston as Britain's prime minister. The massive drilling operations which bring the team into explosive contact with volcanic lava are far more impressive than the human story. AE [video]

Richard Dix *McAllan* • Leslie Banks *Robbie* • Madge Evans *Ruth McAllan* • Helen Vinson *Varlia* • C Aubrey Smith *Lloyd* • Basil Sydney *Mostyn* • Henry Oscar *Grellier* • Walter Huston *President of the United States* • George Arliss *Prime Minister* ■ *Dir* Maurice Elvey • *Scr* L Du Garde Peach, Kurt Siodmak [Curt Siodmak], from the novel by Bernhard Kellermann

The Tunnel of Love ★★

Comedy 1958 · US · BW · 98mins

This film marked the first time Gene Kelly had directed a picture which he was not in, and though he makes an efficient job of transcribing a Broadway comedy, it comes out as one of those plays that convulsed theatre audiences in New York and London but seems only mildly amusing on screen. Doris Day and Richard Widmark (the latter in a rare comedy role) play a married couple forced to battle through all sorts of bureaucratic formalities in order to adopt a child. Shot in only three weeks on virtually one set, the film still lost money. TV

Doris Day *Isolde Poole* • Richard Widmark *Augie Poole* • Gig Young *Dick Pepper* • Gia Scala *Estelle Novick* • Elisabeth Fraser *Alice Pepper* • Elizabeth Wilson *Miss MacCracken* • Vikki Dougan *Actress* ■ *Dir* Gene Kelly • *Scr* Joseph Fields, Jerome Chodorov (uncredited), Peter De Vries, from their play

Tunnel Vision ★★ 18

Thriller 1994 · Aus · Colour · 90mins

Patsy Kensit and Robert Reynolds play two detectives on the trail of an artistically minded serial killer. To complicate things further, Reynolds finds himself a suspect in a separate case when the man he suspects of sleeping with his wife turns up dead. The leads are no more than competent, but at least Kensit doesn't make any wince-inducing attempts at

T

an accent, and there are some nifty twists in the plot. JF. Contains swearing and nudity. DVD

Patsy Kensit *Kelly Wheatstone* • Robert Reynolds *Frank Yanovitch* • Rebecca Rigg *Helena Martelli* • Gary Day *Steve Docherty* • Shane Briant *Kevin Bosey* ■ *Dir/Scr* Clive Fleury

Tunnelvision ★★

Comedy 1976 · US · Colour · 67mins

There are more misses than hits in this satire on what television, allegedly, would deliver in the future with a series of themed sketches not unlike the similiarly anarchic *Kentucky Fried Movie*, but not nearly as clever or as funny. This is one of those collectors-only items that is of less interest for what's actually on the screen than for who shows up in the relentlessly unfunny and crass sketches. TS

Philip Proctor *Christian A Broder* • Howard Hesseman *Senator McMannus* • Ernie Anderson *Quant O'Neil* • Edwina Anderson *Melanie Edwards* • Chevy Chase • Laraine Newman *Sonja* • Rick Hurst *Father Phaser Gun* ■ *Dir* Brad Swirnoff, Neal Israel • *Scr* Neal Israel, Michael Mislove

Tupac: Resurrection ★★★★ 15

Documentary
2003 · US · Colour and BW · 108mins

This powerful documentary charts the life and sudden death of the rap superstar. Told in Tupac's own words, it's a compelling story of "ambition, violence, redemption and love". The film's strength lies in its wealth of archival material and Tupac's voiceover – culled from interviews – which is used to good effect. Unsurprisingly the soundtrack is packed with excellent tunes, but these are sometimes used a little too literally to illustrate key points. Tupac himself comes across as a charismatic yet deeply conflicted man, and it's this constant battle between the public *Thug Life* version of himself and the private, intelligent, politically savvy man that gives the film depth. It's a little overlong and highly subjective, but as a reverential portrait of an influential figure in American popular culture, it's hard to beat. GM DVD

Dir Lauren Lazin • *Cinematographer* Jon Else

Turbo: a Power Rangers Adventure ★ PG

Science-fiction adventure
1997 · US · Colour · 95mins

Viewers who have never seen the *Mighty Morphin Power Rangers* TV show will be absolutely lost in this second big-screen adaptation. Painfully bad dialogue and technical incompetence rule here as the Power Rangers face a new alien menace, Divatox. At least the previous movie had some ambition to entertain beyond being a toy commercial. KB DVD

Nakia Burrise *Tanya* • Jason David Frank *Tommy* • Catherine Sutherland *Kat* • Johnny Yong Bosch *Adam* • Blake Foster *Justin* • Paul Schrier *Bulk* • Jason Narvy *Skull* • Richard Genelle *Ernie* • Hilary Shepard Turner [Hilary Shepard] *Divatox* ■ *Dir* David Winning, Shuki Levy • *Scr* Shuki Levy, Shell Danielson

Turbulence ★★★ 18

Action thriller 1997 · US · Colour · 96mins

Ray Liotta stars as a psycho who hijacks a Christmas Eve flight transporting him to prison. Lauren Holly plays the plucky flight attendant who has to beat off Liotta's advances and attempt to land the aircraft safely. This is far from sophisticated adult entertainment, but it's so ludicrously overblown that it's hard not to be entertained by the sheer enthusiasm and abandonment of logic and credibility. Two sequels followed. JC. Contains swearing, violence. DVD

Ray Liotta *Ryan Weaver* • Lauren Holly *Teri Halloran* • Brendan Gleeson *Stubbs* • Hector Elizondo *Detective Aldo Hines* • Rachel Ticotin *Rachel Taper* • Jeffrey DeMunn *Brooks* • John Finn *Sinclair* • Ben Cross *Captain Bowen* ■ *Dir* Robert Butler • *Scr* Jonathan Brett

Turk 182! ★★ 15

Drama 1985 · US · Colour · 92mins

Timothy Hutton plays a New York graffiti artist who uses his talent to shame mayor Robert Culp after the city fathers fail to compensate his fireman brother, injured in an off-duty rescue. Hutton is seriously miscast as the spray-can vigilante, while Peter Boyle, Darren McGavin and Paul Sorvino are wasted in minor roles. The presence of Robert Urich as Hutton's brother and Kim Cattrall as his girlfriend tips us off that this is B-movie fare. DP

Timothy Hutton *Jimmy Lynch* • Robert Urich *Terry Lynch* • Kim Cattrall *Danny Boudreau* • Robert Culp *Mayor Tyler* • Darren McGavin *Detective Kowalski* • Steven Keats *Jockamo* • Paul Sorvino • Peter Boyle *Detective Ryan* ■ *Dir* Bob Clark • *Scr* James Gregory Kingston, Denis Hamill, John Hamill, from a story by James Gregory Kingston

Turkey Shoot ★★★ 18

Futuristic action thriller
1981 · Aus · Colour · 83mins

Set in the Australian outback of the future, where social deviants (freedom fighter Steve Railsback, shoplifter Olivia Hussey, prostitutes et al) are sent to barbaric concentration camps, supposedly for re-education. But in reality it's to provide human prey for warden Michael Craig to indulge his sadistic predilection for extreme blood sports. Convincingly mounted and violent, this cynical political allegory may be exploitation, but it does deliver a high shock quotient. AJ

Steve Railsback *Paul Anders* • Olivia Hussey *Chris Walters* • Michael Craig *Charles Thatcher* • Carmen Duncan *Jennifer* • Noel Ferrier *Mallory* • Lynda Stoner *Rita Daniels* • Roger Ward *Ritter* • Michael Petrovitch *Tito* • Gus Mercurio *Red* ■ *Dir* Brian Trenchard-Smith • *Scr* Jon George, Neill Hicks, from a story by George Schenck, Robert Williams, David Lawrence

Turkish Delight ★★★★ 18

Erotic drama 1973 · Neth · Colour · 101mins

Dutch director Paul Verhoeven burst onto the international film scene with this truly bizarre and shocking romance featuring unprecedented amounts of frontal nudity, graphic sex and scatological behaviour. It also shot star Rutger Hauer to fame. He plays a sex-obsessed artist/sculptor whose exhibitionism is fuelled by an intense relationship with suburban Monique van de Ven. But whereas his carnal conduct is more about affronting respectable society with revolutionary values, hers has a darker base in mental imbalance due to a brain tumour. A surprisingly tender and touching tale. AJ. Dutch dialogue dubbed into English. DVD

Monique van de Ven *Olga* • Rutger Hauer *Eric* • Tonny Huurdeman *Mother* • Dolf de Vries *Paul* ■ *Dir* Paul Verhoeven • *Scr* Gerard Soeteman, from the novel *Turks Fruit* by Jan Wolkers

Turn Back the Clock ★

Drama 1933 · US · BW · 80mins

Cigar store owner Lee Tracy is run over by a car and dreaming how he might have lived a better life, been nicer to his wife, fought better in the First World War and warned President Woodrow Wilson about European policy. In 1933, when the Depression was ripping through lives like a tornado, this sugary sort of thing was what audiences wanted. A dreadful cringe-athon. AT

Lee Tracy *Joe Gimlet* • Mae Clarke *Mary Gimlet* • Otto Kruger *Ted Wright* • George Barbier *Pete Evans* • Peggy Shannon *Elvina Wright* • C Henry Gordon *Mr Holmes* • Clara Blandick *Mrs Gimlet* ■ *Dir* Edgar Selwyn • *Scr* Edgar Selwyn, Ben Hecht

The Turn of the Screw ★ 18

Supernatural horror
1992 · UK/US/Fr · Colour · 91mins

Yet another adaptation of Henry James's classic horror novel, and yet another adaptation which falls short of the original 1961 film version *The Innocents*. Director Rusty Lemorande has gone at the material and stripped it of all subtlety, which includes adding superfluous narration from Marianne Faithful and updating the context to 1960s England. Patsy Kensit is also sadly inadequate as the young governess whose charges appear possessed by their former manservant and governess. LH

Patsy Kensit *Jenny* • Julian Sands *Mr Cooper* • Stéphane Audran *Mrs Grose* • Clare Szekeres *Flore* • Olivier Debray *Quint* • Joseph England *Miles* • Bryony Brind *Miss Jessel* • Marianne Faithfull *Narrator* ■ *Dir* Rusty Lemorande • *Scr* Rusty Lemorande, from the novella by Henry James

Turn the Key Softly ★★

Drama 1953 · UK · BW · 81mins

Worthy intentions are still discernible beneath this superficial social melodrama essaying 24 hours in the lives of three women (played by Yvonne Mitchell, Joan Collins and Kathleen Harrison) released from Holloway prison. In her first starring role, Mitchell makes a silk purse out of a sow's ear, but the rest of the cast go with the caricatures they're given. Extensive location work shows London in the grip of postwar austerity. DM

Joan Collins *Stella Jarvis* • Yvonne Mitchell *Monica Marsden* • Kathleen Harrison *Mrs Quilliam* • Terence Morgan *David* • Thora Hird *Landlady* • Dorothy Alison *Joan* • Glyn Houston *Bob* • Geoffrey Keen *Gregory* ■ *Dir* Jack Lee • *Scr* Maurice Cowan, Jack Lee, John Brophy, from a novel by John Brophy

Turnabout ★★

Comedy 1940 · US · Colour · 83mins

Producer Hal Roach directed few films and we can see why with this one. Adapted from a sex fantasy by Thorne Smith (who also wrote *Topper*), this tells of the marital role-reversal of businessman John Hubbard and housewife Carole Landis through the magical powers of an Indian statue. Whatever satirical sting the idea might might have had is withdrawn by the cuteness and the inadequacy of the direction. TH

Adolphe Menjou *Phil Manning* • Carole Landis *Sally Willows* • John Hubbard *Tim Willows* • William Gargan *Joel Clare* • Verree Teasdale *Laura Bannister* • Mary Astor *Marion Manning* ■ *Dir* Hal Roach • *Scr* Mickell Novack, Berne Giler, John McClain, Rian James, from a novel by Thorne Smith

Turner & Hooch ★★★ PG

Comedy 1989 · US · Colour · 95mins

In this enjoyable comedy, Tom Hanks stars as a dapper California detective who teams up with slob-dog Hooch to solve a drug-related murder. While the script is sometimes short on laughs, British director Roger Spottiswoode keeps the action jogging along, giving Hanks room to display the kind of comic timing that established his Hollywood reputation. Hanks is well-served by his canine co-star, but Mare Winningham is sadly wasted. DP. Contains swearing, violence. DVD

Tom Hanks *Scott Turner* • Mare Winningham *Emily Carson* • Craig T Nelson *Police Chief Hyde* • Reginald VelJohnson *Detective David Sutton* • Scott Paulin *Zack Gregory* • JC Quinn *Walter Boyett* • John McIntire *Amos Reed* ■ *Dir* Roger Spottiswoode • *Scr* Dennis Shryack, Michael Blodgett, Daniel Petrie Jr, Jim Cash, Jack Epps Jr, from a story by Dennis Shryack, Michael Blodgett, Daniel Petrie Jr

The Turning ★ 18

Drama 1992 · US · Colour · 87mins

A 20-year old skinhead returns to his rural home town to torment his parents, who have recently decided to divorce. In an attempt to reconcile the family, he takes his dad's new girlfriend hostage. This movie, based on a stage play, would have deservedly languished in total obscurity if not for the fact that Gillian Anderson of *The X Files* fame made her motion picture debut here. Other than that, there's no reason to watch. ST

Karen Allen *Glory* • Raymond J Barry *Mark Harnish* • Michael Dolan *Cliff Harnish* • Tess Harper *Martha Harnish* • Gillian Anderson *April Cavanaugh* ■ *Dir* Lou Puopolo • *Scr* Lou Puopolo, from the play *Home Fires Burning* by Chris Ceraso

The Turning Point ★★★

Crime 1952 · US · BW · 85mins

This powerful, well-cast Hollywood crime drama was one of several suggested by the Kefauver hearings on organised crime in the early 1950s. It builds considerable tension as Edmond O'Brien's crimebusting lawyer heads an investigation into a city's racketeering and is slowly exposed to the depth of corruption and villainy involved. William Holden is astutely cast as the cynical reporter who finds himself helping O'Brien. Director William Dieterle creates a visual style to convey a dark world in which a villain will burn down an occupied tenement block to cover his tracks. AE

William Holden (2) *Jerry McKibbon* • Edmond O'Brien *John Conroy* • Alexis Smith *Amanda Waycross* • Tom Tully *Matt Conroy* • Ed Begley *Eichelberger* • Dan Dayton *Ackerman* ■ *Dir* William Dieterle • *Scr* Warren Duff, from the story *Storm in the City* by Horace McCoy

The Turning Point ★★★ PG

Drama 1977 · US · Colour · 114mins

This woman's movie was nominated for 11 Oscars but astonishingly won none. The American Ballet Theatre stops off in Oklahoma reuniting two former colleagues: Anne Bancroft, now prima ballerina in the company, and Shirley MacLaine, who opted for marriage and children. In the course of the movie both wonder whether they made the right decision, finally coming to terms with their lives and futures through the fate of MacLaine's daughter Leslie Browne. The dancing is relegated to second place behind the drama, but is still splendid and intoxicating, featuring many of the stars of the day. FL

Shirley MacLaine *Deedee Rodgers* • Anne Bancroft *Emma Jacklin* • Mikhail Baryshnikov *Kopeikine* • Leslie Browne *Emilia* • Tom Skerritt *Wayne* • Martha Scott *Adelaide* • Antoinette Sibley *Sevilla* • Alexandra Danilova *Dahkarova* • Starr Danias *Carolyn* ■ *Dir* Herbert Ross • *Scr* Arthur Laurents

Turtle Beach ★ 15

Political drama 1992 · US · Colour · 84mins

A strong subject – the plight of the Vietnamese boat people – is squandered by this movie in which everything except the scenery looks shoddy. Greta Scacchi plays an Australian journalist who heads for Malaysia to cover events as the locals hack the refugees to pieces. Preview responses were so bad that the film was drastically shortened, though it still bombed everywhere. AT. Contains violence and sex scenes.

Greta Scacchi *Judith Wilkes* • Joan Chen *Lady Minou Hobday* • Jack Thompson *Ralph Hamilton* • Art Malik *Kanan* • Norman Kaye *Sir Adrian Hobday* • Victoria Longley *Sancha Hamilton* • Martin Jacobs *Richard* ■ *Dir* Stephen Wallace • *Scr* Ann Turner, from the novel by Blanche d'Alpuget

Turtle Diary ★★★ PG

Comedy drama 1985 · UK · Colour · 91mins

An odd two-hander from Glenda Jackson and Ben Kingsley as a pair of lonely liberals desperate to liberate the turtles in a zoo from what they see as their cruel plight. As you would expect, the acting is subtle and intelligent, with John Irvin's direction giving the film a stately but oversimplified pace. The movie's main problem is that it fails to bring out the great insights on Britain and the Brits which distinguish Russell Hoban's insightful novel from other stabs at the genre. SH

Glenda Jackson *Neaera Duncan* • Ben Kingsley *William Snow* • Richard Johnson *Mr Johnson* • Michael Gambon *George Fairbairn* • Rosemary Leach *Mrs Inchcliff* • Eleanor Bron *Miss Neap* • Harriet Walter *Harriet* • Jeroen Krabbé *Sandor* • Nigel Hawthorne *Publisher* ■ *Dir* John Irvin • *Scr* Harold Pinter, Bill Darrid, from the novel by Russell Hoban

Turtles Can Fly ★★★★ 15

Black comedy drama

2004 · Iraq/Iran · Colour · 97mins

Set in a camp on the Iraqi-Turkish border shortly before coalition forces launched their attack on Saddam Hussein, Bahman Ghobadi's hellish drama makes an unlikely vehicle for absurdist comedy. But it's impossible not to be amused by Kurdish teenager Soran Ebrahim's wheeler-dealing or his liberal translations for various US satellite news broadcasts. Similarly, the plight of the countless orphans who survive by collecting landmines and the despair of demure refugee Avaz Latif bring home the reality of childhoods shattered by tyranny and conflict. DP. In Kurdish with English subtitles.

Soran Ebrahim *Kak Satellite* • Hiresh Feyssal Rahman *Henkov* • Avaz Latif *Agrin* • Saddam Hossein Feysal *Pasheo* • Abdol Rahman Karim *Riga* ■ *Dir/Scr* Bahman Ghobadi

The Tuskegee Airmen ★★★★ PG

Wartime drama based on a true story

1995 · US · Colour · 101mins

In the tradition of *Glory*, this TV movie recalls the exploits of the first black aerial combat unit sent into action during the Second World War. Billeted at the Tuskegee air base, the "Fighting 99th" was formed to boost the civil rights cause, although the recruits were subjected to racial abuse from the top brass down. While the emphasis is on Hannibal Lee (played with distinction by Laurence Fishburne), this is very much an ensemble piece. DP.

Laurence Fishburne *Hannibal Lee* • Cuba Gooding Jr *Billy Roberts* • Allen Payne *Walter Peoples* • Malcolm-Jamal Warner *Leroy Cappy* • Courtney B Vance *Lieutenant Jeffrey Glenn* • André Braugher *Lt Col Benjamin O Davis* • John Lithgow *Senator Conyers* ■ *Dir* Robert Markowitz • *Scr* Paris H Qualles, Ron Hutchinson, Trey Ellis, from a story by Robert Williams, TS Cook

The Tuttles of Tahiti ★★★ U

Comedy 1942 · US · BW · 91mins

This South Sea island comedy starring Charles Laughton is based on a novel by the authors of *Mutiny on the Bounty*. Laughton's performance here is far removed from his memorable Captain Bligh, but he has fun as the idler who engages in a verbal battle with the formidable Florence Bates, while Bates's daughter Peggy Drake makes eyes at Laughton's son Jon Hall. Mindless nonsense, but skilfully handled by director Charles Vidor, and the literate screenplay makes this eminently watchable. TS

Charles Laughton *Jonas* • Jon Hall *Chester* • Peggy Drake *Tamara* • Victor Francen *Dr Blondin* • Florence Bates *Emily* • Gene Reynolds *Ru* • Curt Bois *Jensen* • Adeline De Walt Reynolds *Mama Ruau* ■ *Dir* Charles Vidor • *Scr* S Lewis Meltzer, Robert Carson, James Hilton, from the novel *No More Gas* by Charles Nordhoff, James Norman Hall

The Tuxedo ★★ 12

Action comedy 2002 · US · Colour · 94mins

Jackie Chan stars as the chauffeur to millionaire super-spy Jason Isaacs, whose hospitalisation leads Chan to try on his boss's hi-tech dinner jacket. Our hero finds it imbues him with acrobatic powers that confusingly lead to his involvement in an international espionage plot. Sadly, the mechanical gadgets are given precedence over his physical talent, leaving the martial arts maestro with little to do. Jennifer Love Hewitt, as an inept CIA agent, provides the best comedy moments. TH. Contains swearing, violence. DVD

Jackie Chan *Jimmy Tong* • Jennifer Love Hewitt *Delilah "Del" Blaine* • Jason Isaacs *Clark Devlin* • Debi Mazar *Steena* • Ritchie Coster *Diedrich Banning* • Peter Stormare *Dr Simms* • Mia Cottet *Cheryl* ■ *Dir* Kevin Donovan • *Scr* Michael J Wilson, Michael Leeson, from a story by Phil Hay, Matt Manfredi, Michael J Wilson

Tweety's High Flying Adventure ★★ U

Animated comedy adventure

2000 · US · Colour · 68mins

No one watched the Sylvester and Tweety Pie cartoons for the canary. So why did Warner Bros deem him worthy of a solo feature? There are dozens of puddy tats in this slapdash reworking of *Around the World in 80 Days*, but only Sylvester is the cat's miaow. Seriously missing the vocal subtlety of the great Mel Blanc, this musical misfire fails primarily because Tweety has become too smart and too cynical for his own good. DP

Joe Alaskey *Tweety/Sylvester* • June Foray *Granny* ■ *Dir* James T Walker, Karl Toerge, Charles Visser • *Scr* Tom Minton, Tim Cahill, Julie McNally

Twelfth Night ★★★ U

Comedy 1996 · UK/US · Colour · 128mins

Beautifully designed in a pre-Raphaelite sort of way by Sophie Becher and with rich autumnal photography by Clive Tickner, this is a handsome version of Shakespeare's cruellest comedy. The film skirts around virtually all of the social and sexual themes raised by the various misunderstandings and alliances that follow the storm-tossed arrival of Imogen Stubbs and brother Steven Mackintosh on the shores of Illyria. Notwithstanding the conservative direction, the performances, are highly polished. DP DVD

Helena Bonham Carter *Olivia* • Imogen Stubbs *Viola* • Nigel Hawthorne *Malvolio* • Richard E Grant *Sir Andrew Aguecheek* • Ben Kingsley *Feste* • Mel Smith *Sir Toby Belch* • Imelda Staunton *Maria* • Toby Stephens *Orsino* • Steven Mackintosh *Sebastian* • Nicholas Farrell *Antonio* ■ *Dir* Trevor Nunn • *Scr* Trevor Nunn, from the play by William Shakespeare

12 Angry Men ★★★★★ U

Classic courtroom drama

1957 · US · BW · 92mins

Based on a television play by Reginald Rose about a lone juror holding out for a not guilty verdict with the remaining 11 ready to convict, this marvellous movie has become part of life's currency. Henry Fonda stars as juror eight (no characters have names), and he also co-produced the movie. Although acclaimed as an instant classic, the film made no money on release, and Fonda wasn't able to pay himself his deferred acting fee. His integrity illuminates the film, which benefits immeasurably from debut director Sidney Lumet's masterly sense of cinema: the action takes place on a single claustrophobic set (an actual New York jury room), yet Lumet finds an infinite variety of visual set-ups and angles within the confines. Genuinely brilliant. TS DVD

Henry Fonda *Juror eight* • Lee J Cobb *Juror three* • Ed Begley *Juror ten* • EG Marshall *Juror four* • Jack Warden *Juror seven* • Martin Balsam *Juror one* • John Fiedler *Juror two* • Jack Klugman *Juror five* • Edward Binns *Juror six* • Joseph Sweeney *Juror nine* • George Voskovec *Juror eleven* • Robert Webber *Juror twelve* ■ *Dir* Sidney Lumet • *Scr* Reginald Rose, from his TV play

12 Angry Men ★★★★ 12

Courtroom drama

1997 · US · Colour · 112mins

Writer Reginald Rose updated his original 1954 Emmy-winning TV play and 1957 feature screenplay for this classy made-for-cable remake. An all-star cast including George C Scott and Jack Lemmon headlines this absorbing drama that centres around 12 jurors who, having been charged by the judge to deliver a verdict, retire to the jury room to deliberate. It seems to be an open-and-shut case of an inner-city boy accused of murdering his father, but one juror (Lemmon) believes the youth is innocent on grounds of "reasonable doubt". Under William Friedkin's skilful direction, Lemmon gives a brilliant performance, as does the distinguished supporting cast. MC

Jack Lemmon *Juror No 8* • Courtney B Vance *Juror No 1* • Ossie Davis *Juror No 2* • George C Scott *Juror No 3* • Armin Mueller-Stahl *Juror No 4* • Dorian Harewood *Juror No 5* • James Gandolfini *Juror No 6* • Tony Danza *Juror No 7* • Hume Cronyn *Juror No 9* • Mykelti Williamson *Juror No 10* • Edward James Olmos *Juror No 11* • William L Petersen *Juror No 12* ■ *Dir* William Friedkin • *Scr* Reginald Rose, from his TV play

The Twelve Chairs ★★★ U

Black comedy 1970 · US · Colour · 89mins

Russian bureaucrat Ron Moody learns that his mother is dying and races home, only to be told that she has hidden the family fortune in one of 12 dining chairs left in their ancestral home. He hurries home, only to find the chairs have gone to the Ministry of Housing to be relocated. Moody teams up with young conman Frank Langella and the pair go off in search of the chairs. Mel Brooks's second feature is a sustained laugh-fest with a much more disciplined plot than his later works. DF

Ron Moody *Ippolit Vorobyaninov* • Frank Langella *Ostap Bender* • Dom DeLuise *Father Fyodor* • Mel Brooks *Tikon* • Bridget Brice *Young woman* • Robert Bernal *Curator* • David Lander *Engineer Bruns* • Diana Coupland *Madame Bruns* ■ *Dir* Mel Brooks • *Scr* Mel Brooks, from the play by Ilya Ilf, Yevgeny Petrov

Twelve Monkeys ★★★★ 15

Science-fiction thriller

1995 · US/UK/Ger/Jpn/Fr · Colour · 124mins

Inspired by Chris Marker's acclaimed 1962 short film, *La Jetée*, this labyrinthine sci-fi thriller was penned by the co-writer of *Blade Runner*, David Webb Peoples, and his wife, Janet. Yet it's very much the work of Monty Python alumnus Terry Gilliam, who imposes his own pseudo-poetic vision onto a world that is doomed to viral annihilation unless time traveller Bruce Willis can prevent the disaster. Although it was Brad Pitt who landed the Oscar nomination for his twitchy performance as the leader of the Army of the Twelve Monkeys, it is Willis's anguished introvert who holds this gripping, hauntingly atmospheric film together. DP. Contains swearing, violence and nudity. DVD

Bruce Willis *James Cole* • Madeleine Stowe *Dr Kathryn Railly* • Brad Pitt *Jeffrey Goines* • Christopher Plummer *Dr Goines* • Joseph Melito *Young Cole* • Jon Seda *Jose* • David Morse *Dr Peters* • Frank Gorshin *Dr Fletcher* ■ *Dir* Terry Gilliam • *Scr* David Peoples, Janet Peoples, from the film *La Jetée* by Chris Marker • *Cinematographer* Roger Pratt

12:01 ★★★★ 15

Science-fiction thriller

1993 · US · Colour · 90mins

Whereas *Groundhog Day* used the idea of living the same day over and over again for laughs, director Jack Sholder takes the same premise (from Richard Lupoff's 1973 novella) and goes for dynamic action to craft a clever thriller. Engaging Jonathan Silverman is the clerk caught in a time-loop involving an associate's murder, who tries to prevent the killing from taking place by changing incidental details each time the same day dawns. A neatly cut and highly polished gem, the tale is never contrived, continuously engrossing and has a gut-wrenching climax. AJ

Jonathan Silverman *Barry Thomas* • Helen Slater *Lisa Fredericks* • Martin Landau *Dr Thadius Moxley* • Jeremy Piven *Howard Richter* • Robin Bartlett *Ann Jackson* • Nicholas Surovy [Nicolas Surovy] *Robert Denk* ■ *Dir* Jack Sholder • *Scr* Philip Morton, from a short film by Jonathan Heap, Hillary Ripps, from the novella *12:01 PM* by Richard Lupoff

Twelve O'Clock High ★★★★ U

Second World War drama

1949 · US · BW · 126mins

To watch Gregory Peck crack under the strain of high command (he's in charge of a pressure-cooked American bomber unit based in England during the Second World War) is as alarming as the collapse of the Statue of Liberty: he's such a monument to liberal integrity. However, although he was nominated for an Oscar for his performance here, it was Dean Jagger who won the award for best supporting actor. It's all a wonderful example of ensemble acting, so any trophies are a bit redundant, though no doubt they were gratefully received. TH DVD

Gregory Peck *General Frank Savage* • Hugh Marlowe *Lt Col Ben Gately* • Gary Merrill *Colonel Keith Davenport* • Dean Jagger *Major Harvey Stovall* • Millard Mitchell *General Pritchard* • Robert Arthur *Sergeant McIllhenny* • Paul Stewart *Captain "Doc" Kaiser* • John Kellogg *Major Cobb* ■ *Dir* Henry King • *Scr* Sy Bartlett, Beirne Lay Jr, from their novel

Twelve plus One ★★

Comedy 1969 · It/Fr · Colour · 95mins

There are 13 salon chairs, one of which contains a hidden fortune in jewels. Mel Brooks made a movie out of this Russian story in the same year. This version is watchable due to the chocolate-box assortment of stars on show, including the positively sofa-like Orson Welles, ageing Italian heart-throb Vittorio Gassman and eccentric Englishman Terry-Thomas. Hollywood starlet Sharon Tate makes her final appearance before her murder. AT

Vittorio Gassman *Mike* • Orson Welles *Markau* • Mylène Demongeot *Judy* • Sharon Tate *Pat* • Terry-Thomas *Albert* • Tim Brooke-Taylor *Jackie* • Vittorio De Sica *Di Seta* ■ *Dir* Luciano Lucignani • *Scr* Nicolas Gessner, Marc Benham, from a story by Ilya Ilf, Yevgeny Petrov

T

The 12 Tasks of Asterix ★★★★ U

Animated adventure
1975 · Fr · Colour · 78mins

Written especially for the screen by René Goscinny and Albert Uderzo, this is the best of the Asterix cartoons, if only because something of the wit and ingenuity of the original books shines through. Determined to rid himself of the indomitable Gauls once and for all, Caesar sets Asterix and Obelix a Herculean quota of seemingly impossible tasks. But crocodiles, ghosts, Greek sprinters, German wrestlers, Egyptian sorcerers and even Rome's bureaucrats prove no match for our intrepid heroes. Graphically it's on the conservative side, but otherwise this is brisk, slick and hugely entertaining. This also comes in a French language version. DP

Dir René Goscinny, Albert Uderzo • *Scr* René Goscinny, Albert Uderzo

Twentieth Century ★★★★★ U

Screwball comedy 1934 · US · BW · 88mins

The title refers to the express train that ran between New York and Chicago, where movie producers and stars changed for the connection to Los Angeles. Aboard this deliriously enjoyable trip is a Broadway impresario (John Barrymore) and a recalcitrant Hollywood star (Carole Lombard). She is his protégé, but after several flops he's trying to lure her back to Broadway. Directed at supersonic speed by Howard Hawks, this is a stream of acidic barbs, offering the stars ample scope for grandiose caricature. In fact, the arch theatricality of the piece functions as a comment on movie-making and the edgy relationship between Hollywood and Broadway in the early years of the talkies. First class all the way. AT

John Barrymore *Oscar Jaffe* • Carole Lombard *Lily Garland* • Walter Connolly *Webb* • Roscoe Karns *O'Malley* • Charles Levison [Charles Lane (2)] *Jacobs* • Etienne Girardot *Clark* • Dale Fuller *Sadie* ■ *Dir* Howard Hawks • *Scr* Charles Macarthur, Ben Hecht, from their play, from the play *Napoleon on Broadway* by Charles Bruce Millholland

Twenty Bucks ★★★ 15

Comedy drama 1993 · US · Colour · 87mins

This erratic but pleasing ensemble piece follows the fortunes of a $20 note as it changes hands. This simple premise allows director Keva Rosenfeld to tell a bundle of stories – some funny, some downbeat – involving an eclectic cast. Amazingly, despite the sprawling concept, Rosenfeld maintains a narrative thread for most of the film. Originated in 1935 by writer/producer Endre Bohem (who died in 1990), it was brought up to date by his son Leslie. JF. Contains swearing, violence and nudity.

Linda Hunt *Angeline* • Brendan Fraser *Sam* • Melora Walters *Stripper* • Gladys Knight *Mrs McCormac* • Elisabeth Shue *Emily Adams* • Steve Buscemi *Frank* • Christopher Lloyd *Jimmy* • William H Macy *Property Clerk* ■ *Dir* Keva Rosenfeld • *Scr* Endre Bohem, Leslie Bohem

20 Dates ★★ 15

Comedy documentary
1998 · US · Colour · 84mins

Although it finds itself up the odd dead-end, this is a mildly amusing mockumentary, in which Myles Berkowitz attempts to film his search for true love. Working on a $60,000 budget, he is forced to endure all manner of humiliations from both the women he meets and his cynical friends. Some of the dates are very funny, but the pace drops once Berkowitz encounters shopgirl Elisabeth Wagner. Film buffs, however, will relish his session with screenwriting guru Robert McKee, whose dissection of *Sleepless in Seattle* is priceless. DP. Contains swearing.

Myles Berkowitz *Myles* • Elisabeth Wagner *Elisabeth* • Richard Arlook *The Agent* • Tia Carrere • Robert McKee ■ *Dir/Scr* Myles Berkowitz

28 Days ★★ 15

Drama 2000 · US · Colour · 99mins

Sandra Bullock is the Manhattan wild child forced into rehab after hijacking a limo at her sister's wedding and driving it into a house. Refusing to admit she has a drink problem, Bullock comes to terms with her addiction with help from tough-but-fair guidance counsellor Steve Buscemi and the usual round of kooky Hollywood misfits. This is the kind of sentimental hogwash that's more likely to drive people to drink than keep them off it. NS. Contains violence, swearing, sex scenes, drug abuse and nudity. DVD

Sandra Bullock *Gwen Cummings* • Viggo Mortensen *Eddie Boone* • Dominic West *Jasper* • Diane Ladd *Bobbie Jean* • Elizabeth Perkins *Lily* • Steve Buscemi *Cornell* • Alan Tudyk *Gerhardt* • Michael O'Malley [Mike O'Malley] *Oliver* • Marianne Jean-Baptiste *Roshanda* ■ *Dir* Betty Thomas • *Scr* Susannah Grant

28 Days Later... ★★★★ 18

Science-fiction horror
2002 · UK/US/Neth · Colour · 108mins

This Dogme-driven apocalyptic nightmare from director Danny Boyle is a tense, exciting and terrifying zombie horror. As a highly contagious virus spreads across the country, locking its victims into a permanent state of homicidal rampage, four individuals who have so far escaped infection have to fight off the deranged hordes. This triumphantly executed piece of contemporary horror (written by *The Beach*'s Alex Garland) generates genuine shocks with its down-and-dirty violence and disturbing authenticity. Shot on digital video for a documentary feel, Garland's compelling story grips on every level. AJ. Contains violence, swearing and sex scenes. DVD

Cillian Murphy *Jim* • Naomie Harris *Selena* • Christopher Eccleston *Major Henry West* • Megan Burns *Hannah* • Brendan Gleeson *Frank* • Noah Huntley *Mark* ■ *Dir* Danny Boyle • *Scr* Alex Garland

The 25th Hour ★★

Second World War drama
1967 · Fr/It/Yug · Colour · 118mins

A lavishly made, episodic war epic with Anthony Quinn as a Romanian peasant who is accused of being Jewish and condemned to slave labour. Shunned by the Jewish prisoners he becomes essentially stateless and thus a walking, talking metaphor. He changes sides and becomes a German soldier, all the time searching for his wife, Virna Lisi. AT. A French language film.

Anthony Quinn *Johann Moritz* • Virna Lisi *Suzanna Moritz* • Grégoire Aslan *Nicolai Dobresco* • Michael Redgrave *Defense counsel* • Serge Reggiani *Trajan Koruga* • Marcel Dalio *Strul* • Marius Goring *Col Müller* • Alexander Knox *Prosecutor* • John Le Mesurier *Magistrate* ■ *Dir* Henri Verneuil • *Scr* Henri Verneuil, François Boyer, Wolf Mankowitz, from the novel *La Vingt-Cinquieme Heure* by Constantin Virgil Gheorghiu

25th Hour ★★★ 15

Drama 2002 · US · Colour · 129mins

Fine ensemble acting and the frisson of this being the first film to use post-11 September Manhattan as a bleak character mirror make this edgy version of David Benioff's novel one of director Spike Lee's better dramas. Due to begin a seven-year prison sentence, drug dealer Edward Norton spends his last day of freedom hanging out with his friends, his father and girlfriend, taking stock of his life and weighing up his choices: should he give in gracefully, flee or commit suicide? Despite Lee's pace being a little too leisurely at times, the sense of human aimlessness and desolation is powerfully conveyed. AJ. Contains violence, swearing, sex scenes, drug abuse and nudity. DVD

Edward Norton *Monty Brogan* • Philip Seymour Hoffman *Jacob Elinsky* • Barry Pepper *Francis Xavier Slaughtery* • Rosario Dawson *Naturelle Rivera* • Anna Paquin *Mary D'Annunzio* • Brian Cox *James Brogan* • Tony Siragusa *Kostya Novotny* ■ *Dir* Spike Lee • *Scr* David Benioff, from his novel

20 Fingers ★★★

Romantic drama 2004 · Iran · Colour · 72mins

Having excelled in Abbas Kiarostami's masterly *Ten*, actress Mania Akbari borrows several of its themes and staging ideas for her directorial debut, which focuses on the battle of the sexes raging in contemporary Iran. Set against a backdrop of symbolic journeys, the verbose and often heated exchanges between a succession of urban couples, all played by Akbari and producer Bijan Daneshmand, touch on everything from traditional views of male hegemony to a woman's right to explore her sexuality. Daneshmand is invariably exposed as an unregenerate chauvinist, but Akbari tries to balance the debate by occasionally coming across as spoilt and irrational. DP. In Farsi with English subtitles.

Mania Akbari *The Wife/The Woman* • Bijan Daneshmand *The Husband/The Man* ■ *Dir/Scr* Mania Akbari • *Cinematographer* Turaj Aslani

24 Hour Party People ★★★★ 18

Comedy drama based on a true story
2001 · UK · Colour · 117mins

Prolific director Michael Winterbottom is unafraid of mythologising a slice of recent musical/cultural history in this comedy drama, which tells the story of the rise and fall of Manchester's Factory Records and the world-famous Hacienda nightclub. Tony Wilson, played with relish by Steve Coogan, is in real life a self-publicist of gigantic proportions, so when he compares shambolic Happy Mondays singer Shaun Ryder (an uncanny impersonation by Danny Cunningham) to WB Yeats, you take it with a pinch of salt but buy into it anyway. This is a well-cast blend of evocative energy, fine vintage music and irreverent humour. AC. Contains swearing, drug abuse and nudity. DVD

Steve Coogan *Tony Wilson* • Lennie James *Alan Erasmus* • Shirley Henderson *Lindsay Wilson* • Paddy Considine *Rob Gretton* • Andy Serkis *Martin Hannett* • Sean Harris *Ian Curtis* • Danny Cunningham *Shaun Ryder* ■ *Dir* Michael Winterbottom • *Scr* Frank Cottrell Boyce

The 24 Hour Woman ★★

Comedy drama 1999 · US · Colour · 93mins

There are shades of the Diane Keaton vehicle *Baby Boom* in this comedy about a morning television show producer (Rosie Perez) who attempts to juggle career and baby. While the film does have some funny moments, it's mainly due to a bitchy supporting turn from Patti LuPone (as Perez's calculating boss) rather than Perez's screechy performance or the script from director Nancy Savoca. A disappointment. JB

Marianne Jean-Baptiste *Madeline Labelle* • Rosie Perez *Grace Santos* • Patti LuPone *Joan Marshall* • Margo Lynn *Karen Duffy* • Diego Serrano *Eddie Diaz* • Wendell Pierce *Roy Labelle* ■ *Dir* Nancy Savoca • *Scr* Nancy Savoca, Richard Guay

24 Hours in London ★★ 18

Futuristic crime thriller
1999 · UK · Colour · 86mins

It's apt that the illegal trade in body parts rips the heart out of *The Long Good Friday* and attempts to transplant it into a stubbornly lifeless cadaver. It's not the sight of Gary Olsen as an opera-loving, sword-wielding Mr Big that takes the most swallowing, but the indigestible blend of Hong Kong "heroic bloodshed", laddish comedy and *Lock, Stock* swagger. There are plenty of twists in writer/director Alexander Finbow's verbose screenplay, but they're all clearly signposted by the arch playing of an unconvincing cast. DP. Contains swearing, violence and drug abuse.

Gary Olsen *Christian* • Anjela Lauren Smith *Martha* • Sara Stockbridge *Simone* • John Benfield *Inspector Duggan* • Amita Dhiri *Helen Lucas* • Tony London *Leon* ■ *Dir/Scr* Alexander Finbow

TwentyFourSeven ★★★ 15

Comedy drama 1997 · UK · BW · 92mins

The first full-length feature from British director Shane Meadows provides the often under-used Bob Hoskins with his best role in years. Hoskins plays an amiable former boxer who sets up a council-estate fight club as a focus for the unharnessed energies of local youth. The performances, many of them from first-time actors, pack a punch, and Meadows brings a gritty feel to proceedings through his decision to shoot it all in black and white. DA. Contains violence, swearing and drug abuse. DVD

Bob Hoskins *Alan Darcy* • Danny Nussbaum *Tim* • Justin Brady *Gadget* • James Hooton *Knighty* • Darren Campbell *Daz* • Karl Collins *Stuart* ■ *Dir* Shane Meadows • *Scr* Shane Meadows, Paul Fraser

20 Million Miles to Earth ★★★ PG

Science-fiction horror
1957 · US · BW · 79mins

A spaceship returning from an expedition to Venus crashes near Sicily, releasing a fast-growing reptilian beast that rampages through Rome in one of animation master Ray Harryhausen's best fantasy films, and his own personal favourite. The snake-tailed giant Ymir monster is also one of Harryhausen's finest creations: it has a well-defined personality and evokes sympathy for its plight. The Ymir's fight with an elephant and the Roman locations add unique touches to this minor classic. AJ DVD

William Hopper *Calder* • Joan Taylor *Marisa* • Frank Puglia *Dr Leonardo* • John Zaremba *Dr Judson Uhl* • Thomas B Henry [Thomas Browne Henry] *General AD McIntosh* • Tito Vuolo *Police commissioner* ■ *Dir* Nathan Juran • *Scr* Bob Williams, Christopher Knopf, from a story by Charlott Knight, Ray Harryhausen

29 Acacia Avenue ★★★

Comedy 1945 · UK · BW · 84mins

The film version of the West End success about a couple who return home unexpectedly after a holiday and surprise their teenage offspring fails to fully disguise its theatrical origins. It nevertheless makes for pleasant period entertainment, with particularly likeable performances from British veterans Gordon Harker and Betty Balfour as the parents. Today, though, the problems encountered seem relatively trivial, but it's nice to see stars Jimmy Hanley and Dinah Sheridan (once husband and wife) in their youth. TS

Gordon Harker *Mr Robinson* • Betty Balfour *Mrs Robinson* • Jimmy Hanley *Peter* • Carla Lehmann *Fay* • Hubert Gregg *Michael* • Jill Evans *Joan* • Henry Kendall *Mr Wilson* • Dinah Sheridan *Pepper* ■ *Dir* Henry Cass • *Scr* Muriel and Sydney Box, from the play by Denis Constanduros, Mabel Constanduros

29 Palms ★★ 15

Crime thriller 2002 · US · Colour · 89mins

When a Native American Indian casino boss (Russell Means) hires hitman Chris O'Donnell to kill an alleged undercover agent (Jeremy Davies), he sparks off a frantic chase across the desert revolving around a bag stuffed with cash. This unremarkable straight-to-video fodder mistakenly thinks violence and hysteria equal black humour. There are precious few laughs in the script or wit in the direction, and the talented cast is reduced to mugging. JF. Contains violence, sex scenes, swearing, drug abuse. DVD

Chris O'Donnell *Hitman* • Jeremy Davies *Drifter* • Rachael Leigh Cook *Waitress* • Michael Rapaport *Cop* • Michael Lerner *Judge* • Jon Polito *Security guard* • Russell Means *Chief* ■ *Dir* Leonardo Ricagni • *Scr* Tino Lucente

29th Street ★★★ 15

Comedy drama based on a true story 1991 · US · Colour · 97mins

Frank Pesce Jr is a remarkable character. Cursed with a lucky streak that constantly seems to work against him, the garrulous New Yorker crops up in a cameo and also had a hand in the writing of this breezy comedy based on his win on the state lottery that ended up being more trouble than it was worth. Speaking Brooklynese like a native, Australian-born Anthony LaPaglia gives a spirited performance as Pesce, while Danny Aiello makes a splendid sparring partner as his opinionated father. But it's Lainie Kazan as Pesce's dotty mother who steals the show. DP [video] DVD

Danny Aiello *Frank Pesce Sr* • Lainie Kazan *Mrs Pesce* • Anthony LaPaglia *Frank Pesce Jr* • Robert Forster *Sergeant Tartaglia* • Frank Pesce *Vito Pesce* • Donna Magnani *Madeline Pesce* • Ron Karabatsos *Philly the Nap* ■ *Dir* George Gallo • *Scr* George Gallo, from a story by Frank Pesce Jr, James Franciscus

Twenty-One ★★★ 15

Drama 1991 · UK · Colour · 97mins

Patsy Kensit has a long list of movies to her name, but it must to be said that most were forgettable. This, though, is one of her more commendable efforts: a brave, breezy 20-something comedy drama, with Kensit discovering the dating game is not all that it is cracked up to be. With her straight-to-camera observations, Kensit has a lot of weight to carry, but generally convinces as a sparky, independent young woman. JF. Contains swearing, sex scenes, drug abuse and nudity. [video]

Patsy Kensit *Katie* • Jack Shepherd *Kenneth* • Patrick Ryecart *Jack* • Maynard Eziashi *Baldie* • Rufus Sewell *Bobby* • Sophie Thompson *Francesca* • Susan Wooldridge *Janet* ■ *Dir* Don Boyd • *Scr* Don Boyd, Zoe Heller, from a story by Don Boyd

21 Days ★★★ PG

Melodrama 1937 · UK · BW · 71mins

Here's a classy pedigree: Graham Greene co-wrote the screenplay of this Alexander Korda production based on a John Galsworthy West End hit. The story, about two lovers who spend precious time together before the man is tried for murder, features a well-cast Laurence Olivier making a dashing leading man, but it's his later real-life wife, the top-billed Vivien Leigh, who positively sparkles. Rather wordy, but still worthy. TS [video]

Vivien Leigh *Wanda* • Laurence Olivier *Larry Durrant* • Leslie Banks *Keith Durrant* • Francis L Sullivan *Mander* • Hay Petrie *John Aloysius Evans* • Esme Percy *Henry Walenn* • Robert Newton *Tolly* • Victor Rietti *Antonio* ■ *Dir* Basil Dean • *Scr* Graham Greene, Basil Dean, from the play *The First and the Last* by John Galsworthy

21 Grams ★★★★ 15

Drama 2003 · US/Ger · Colour · 119mins

Showcasing some of the finest screen acting, Mexican director Alejandro González Iñárritu has created an astonishing account of faith and redemption. As with Iñárritu's first film, the acclaimed *Amores Perros*, an auto accident links three disparate lives: Naomi Watts's husband and two daughters have been killed by Benicio Del Toro's drunk-turned-Jesus freak; Sean Penn's professor receives the husband's heart and is drawn into an affair with his widow. Iñárritu again uses a non-linear, mosaic narrative technique to lure us into a maze of contradictions that eventually lead to revelation. An extraordinary vision. TH. Contains swearing, violence, sex scenes and drug abuse. [video] DVD

Sean Penn *Paul Rivers* • Benicio Del Toro *Jack Jordan* • Naomi Watts *Cristina Peck* • Charlotte Gainsbourg *Mary Rivers* • Melissa Leo *Marianne Jordan* • Eddie Marsan *Rev John* • Clea DuVall *Claudia* • Danny Huston *Michael* • Paul Calderon *Brown* ■ *Dir* Alejandro González Iñárritu • *Scr* Guillermo Arriaga, from a story by Guillermo Arriaga, Alejandro González Iñárritu

The 27th Day ★★★ U

Science fiction 1957 · US · BW · 75mins

This quite extraordinary anti-communist tract masquerades as naive science fiction. An alien gives five people from five different countries a box of capsules capable of destroying life on their continent if opened. The capsules become harmless after 27 days or on the owner's death. Suicide or destruction is the choice until the Russian emissary is ordered to annihilate the western world. A real Cold War curio with an equally bizarre pay-off despite pedestrian direction. AJ

Gene Barry *Jonathan Clark* • Valerie French *Eve Wingate* • George Voskovec *Professor Klaus Bechner* • Arnold Moss *The Alien* • Stefan Schnabel *Leader* • Ralph Clanton *Mr Ingram* • Friedrich Ledebur *Dr Karl Neuhaus* • Paul Birch *Admiral* ■ *Dir* William Asher • *Scr* John Mantley, from his novel

23rd March 1931: Shaheed ★★★ 12

Historical drama 2002 · Ind · Colour · 187mins

This is another biopic of the Lahore revolutionary who was hanged by the Raj authorities for his part in the bombing of the National Assembly. Guddu Dhanoa's portrait strives to justify Bhagat's resort to violence by stressing the impact of British atrocities and his growing disillusion with Gandhi's policy of passive resistance. But while Bobby Deol is earnest during the apprenticeship scenes with mentor Chandrashekar Azad (Sunny Deol), he mistakes dashing heroism for patriotic zeal once battle is enjoined. DP. In Hindi with English subtitles.

Bobby Deol *Bhagat Singh* • Sunny Deol *Chandrashekhar Azad* • Amrita Singh *Bhagat Singh's mother* • Rahul Dev *Sukhdev* • Vicky Ahuja *Rajguru* • Aishwariya Rai ■ *Dir* Guddu Dhanoa

20,000 Leagues under the Sea ★★★ U

Silent adventure 1916 · US · BW · 94mins

Captain Nemo (Allan Holubar) and his crew of the submarine *Nautilus* journey through the ocean depths to a tropical island to rescue Nemo's daughter, encountering challenges such as a fight with an octopus. Written and directed by Stuart Paton, this is an impressive achievement for so early a film. The pioneering Williamson brothers built an underwater camera for the production, which cost Universal founder Carl Laemmle such a fortune that even the film's popularity was unable to yield a profit. RK [video]

Allan Holubar *Captain Nemo/Prince Daaker* • Jane Gail *A child of nature/Princess Daaker* • Dan Hanlon *Professor Aronnax* • Edna Pendleton *Aronnax's daughter* • Curtis Benton *Ned Land* • Matt Moore *Lt Bond* ■ *Dir* Stuart Paton • *Scr* Stuart Paton, from the novel by Jules Verne

20,000 Leagues under the Sea ★★★★ U

Adventure 1954 · US · Colour · 121mins

James Mason is marvellous as submariner Captain Nemo in this beautifully designed (Oscars for art direction and special effects) and fabulously cast cinema retelling of Jules Verne's fantasy saga. Also on board the *Nautilus* is Kirk Douglas, who gives a bravura performance as harpoonist Ned Land, even using his own voice for the song *A Whale of a Tale*. Peter Lorre adds comic relief, while Paul Lukas and the under-rated Robert J Wilke bring dignity to the proceedings. Director Richard Fleischer makes the most of the action sequences, notably a sensational battle with a giant squid. TS [video] DVD

Kirk Douglas *Ned Land* • James Mason *Captain Nemo* • Paul Lukas *Professor Aronnax* • Peter Lorre *Conseil* • Robert J Wilke *Mate on the Nautilus* • Carleton Young *John Howard* • Ted De Corsia *Captain Farragut* ■ *Dir* Richard Fleischer • *Scr* Earl Felton, from the novel by Jules Verne

20,000 Years in Sing Sing ★★★

Prison drama 1933 · US · Colour · 81mins

One of Warners' torrid crime melodramas, allegedly "torn from today's headlines", filmed in a quasi-documentary style and providing gutsy entertainment in the guise of moral enlightenment. Spencer Tracy is a jailed gangster taking on the prison authorities, and Bette Davis is his moll. The movie wears its social conscience on its sleeve, but it also remains solid enough, with good performances from the two stars and sleek direction from Hollywood's finest workhorse, Michael Curtiz. AT

Spencer Tracy *Tom Connors* • Bette Davis *Fay* • Lyle Talbot *Bud* • Arthur Byron *Warden Long* • Grant Mitchell *Dr Ames* • Warren Hymer *Hype* • Louis Calhern *Joe Finn* ■ *Dir* Michael Curtiz • *Scr* Courtney Terrett, Robert Lord, Wilson Mizner, Brown Holmes, from the book by Warden Lewis E Lawes

23 Paces to Baker Street ★★★★ U

Thriller 1956 · US · Colour · 102mins

Former musical star Van Johnson confirms his acting versatility in this cracking London-set thriller, starring as a blind playwright who overhears dastardly doings. Londoners will enjoy seeing director Henry Hathaway's skewwhiff city geography, and there's a fair amount of on-screen fog. However, despite the clichés, the suspense is kept taut, the English support cast is faultless, and American import Vera Miles is notably sympathetic. TS

Van Johnson *Phillip Hannon* • Vera Miles *Jean Lennox* • Cecil Parker *Bob Matthews* • Patricia Laffan *Miss Alice MacDonald* • Maurice Denham *Inspector Grovening* • Estelle Winwood *Barmaid* • Liam Redmond *Mr Murch/Joe* ■ *Dir* Henry Hathaway • *Scr* Nigel Balchin, from the novel *A Warrant for X* by Philip MacDonald

Twice Dead ★★ 18

Thriller 1988 · US · Colour · 83mins

When a family moves into a creaky old mansion, the ghost of a long-dead movie star is disturbed by their skirmishes with a gang of local thugs. This is a strictly by-the-numbers offering and adds nothing new to the mothballed haunted house genre. Nevertheless, there are a few effective mood swings as light relief suddenly gives way to violent death. RS [video]

Tom Breznahan *Scott* • Jill Whitlow *Robin/Myrna* • Jonathan Chapin *Crip/Tyler* • Christopher Burgard *Silk* • Sam Melville *Harry* • Brooke Bundy *Sylvia* • Joleen Lutz *Candy* • Todd Bridges *Petie* ■ *Dir* Bert L Dragin • *Scr* Bert L Dragin, Robert McDonnell

Twice in a Lifetime ★★★★ 15

Drama 1985 · US · Colour · 106mins

The cast and production team use their considerable experience to good effect in this fine drama. Colin Welland, who won an Oscar for his *Chariots of Fire* screenplay, was responsible for the script, which tells an all-too-common story of a family being torn apart when the husband strays, in this case with a local barmaid on the eve of his 50th birthday. The well-judged performances by Gene Hackman as the blue-collar husband, Ellen Burstyn as his quietly despairing wife and Ann-Margret as the other woman help make Bud Yorkin's film a moving, and at times riveting, experience. NF [video]

Gene Hackman *Harry Mackenzie* • Ann-Margret *Audrey Minnelli* • Ellen Burstyn *Kate Mackenzie* • Amy Madigan *Sunny* • Ally Sheedy *Helen Mackenzie* • Stephen Lang *Keith* • Darrell Larson *Jerry Mackenzie* ■ *Dir* Bud Yorkin • *Scr* Colin Welland

Twice round the Daffodils ★★ PG

Comedy 1962 · UK · BW · 85mins

This is a watered-down *Carry On Nurse* set (tastefully) in a male tuberculosis ward, with nurse Juliet Mills running the show. The *Carry On* producer/director team of Peter Rogers and Gerald Thomas would occasionally make these forays away from their popular series, but would invariably use a similar cast. Here's Joan Sims and Kenneth Williams again, plus Donalds Sinden and Houston, chasing nurses Jill Ireland and Nanette Newman. This obsession with nurses continued in *Nurse on Wheels* (also with Mills and the excellent Ronald Lewis). TS [video]

Juliet Mills *Catty* • Donald Sinden *Ian Richards* • Donald Houston *John Rhodes* • Kenneth Williams *Harry Halfpenny* • Ronald Lewis *Bob White* • Joan Sims *Harriet Halfpenny* • Andrew Ray *Chris Walker* • Lance Percival *George Logg* • Jill Ireland *Janet* • Sheila Hancock *Dora* • Nanette Newman *Joyce* ■ *Dir* Gerald Thomas • *Scr* Norman Hudis, from the play *Ring for Catty* by Patrick Cargill, Jack Beale

Twice Told Tales ★★

Horror 1963 · US · Colour · 119mins

This crudely creepy anthology failed to give horror writer Nathaniel Hawthorne the same box-office cred already achieved by Edgar Allan Poe. Given the sparse production values and varying degrees of horror and atmosphere, it's not difficult to see why, despite the fine source material. Vincent Price discovers the elixir of eternal youth, tragically injects his beloved offspring with a potion that makes her lethal to the touch and tangles with warlocks and ancestral karma, in three different

T

tales. The film still offers enough lush photography and great acting to make it a chocolate box fantasy horror that works more often than not. AJ

Vincent Price *Alex Medbourne/Dr Rappaccini/Gerald Pyncheon* • Sebastian Cabot *Dr Carl Heidegger* • Mari Blanchard *Sylvia Ward* • Brett Halsey *Giovanni Guastconti* • Abraham Sofaer *Prof Pietro Baglioni* • Joyce Taylor *Beatrice Rappaccini* • Beverly Garland *Alice Pyncheon* • Richard Denning *Jonathan Maulle* • Jacqueline de Wit *Hannah* ■ *Dir* Sidney Salkow • *Scr* Robert E Kent, from stories by Nathaniel Hawthorne

Twice Two ★★★ U

Comedy 1933 · US · BW · 20mins

Laurel and Hardy reached their creative peak in the 1930s with films that ranged from the sublime (*The Music Box*) to the ordinary. This oddity falls in between and revives a gimmick from *Brats* (1930), where they played their own sons. That film used elaborate sets and trick photography, but here they tackle four roles utilising clever editing. Stanley and Oliver have each married the other's twin sisters. They share a house and the "boys" work together. The nub of the story is a dinner during which the "girls" chaotically fall out. BB DVD

Stan Laurel *Stan/Mrs Hardy* • Oliver Hardy *Ollie/Mrs Laurel* • Baldwin Cooke *Soda jerk* • Charlie Hall *Delivery boy* • Ham Kinsey *Passer-by outside store* • Carol Tevis *Mrs Hardy* • Mae Wallace *Mrs Laurel* ■ *Dir* James Parrott • *Scr* Stanley Laurel

Twice upon a Time ★★★ U

Animated fantasy adventure
1983 · US · Colour · 75mins

This little-seen and neglected animation was executive produced by George Lucas, and uses the old-fashioned Lumage technique of photographing miniature cut-outs through glass. Ralph the All-Purpose Animal and his sidekick Mum (who only speaks in noises) heroically fight Synonamess Botch, the tyrannical ruler of the Murkworks Nightmare Factory, when he uses his maniacal powers to invade the sweet dreams of the gentle Rushers of Din with horrific and scary images. The unusual animation and sophisticated humour make director John Korty and Charles Swenson's unique flight of fancy a treat. AJ

Lorenzo Music *Ralph* • Judith Kaham Kampmann *Fairy Godmother* • Marshall Efron *Synonamess Botch* • James Cranna *Rod Rescueman Scuzzbopper* • Julie Payne *Flora Fauna* • Hamilton Camp *Greensleeves* ■ *Dir* John Korty, Charles Swenson • *Scr* John Korty, Charles Swenson, Suella Kennedy, Bill Couturie, from a story by John Korty, Suella Kennedy, Bill Couturie

T

Twilight ★★★ 15

Detective drama 1998 · US · Colour · 90mins

Gene Hackman, Susan Sarandon and Paul Newman star in this low-key detective drama that harks back to the heyday of *film noir*. Newman stars as a private eye who lives with cancer-stricken actor Hackman and his wife Sarandon. Asked to deliver blackmail money, Newman finds himself resurrecting a 20-year-old murder case involving Sarandon's ex-husband. Newman as a 70-something is still convincing in both action and love scenes, but the overall pace of the film tends towards the sluggish and reflective. LH. Contains swearing, violence and sex scenes. DVD

Paul Newman *Harry Ross* • Susan Sarandon *Catherine Ames* • Gene Hackman *Jack Ames* • Stockard Channing *Verna* • Reese Witherspoon *Mel Ames* • Giancarlo Esposito *Reuben* • James Garner *Raymond Hope* • Liev Schreiber *Jeff Willis* ■ *Dir* Robert Benton • *Scr* Robert Benton, Richard Russo

Twilight Avengers ★★

Spaghetti western 1970 · It · Colour

Director Adalberto Albertini was shrewd enough to realise that several masters of the spaghetti western appended English pseudonyms to their films. The fact that Albertini chose to call himself Al Albert is symptomatic of the creative poverty that blights this tame tale. Set against the backdrop of the great Californian gold rush, it grimly follows the tried and trusted formula, and not even the pitting of a troupe of travelling players against the desperadoes peps it up. DP. Italian dialogue dubbed into English.

Tony Kendall • Helen Parker • Peter Thorrys • Robert Widmark ■ *Dir* Al Albert [Adalberto Albertini]

Twilight for the Gods ★★

Drama 1958 · US · Colour · 118mins

A love story between Rock Hudson and the *Cannibal*, a sailing ship that's rotten to the timbers and threatens to sink with the usual assortment of passengers – a call girl, suicidal businessman and refugees from communism. Filmed in and around Hawaii, it gave Hudson a well-earned break from his romantic melodramas and the chance to play a disgraced, drunken wreck not unlike Humphrey Bogart in *The Caine Mutiny*. AT

Rock Hudson *Captain David Bell* • Cyd Charisse *Charlotte King* • Arthur Kennedy *Ramsay* • Leif Erickson *Hutton* • Charles McGraw *Yancy* • Ernest Truex *Butterfield* • Richard Haydn *Wiggins* ■ *Dir* Joseph Pevney • *Scr* Ernest K Gann, from his novel

Twilight in the Sierras ★★

Western 1950 · US · Colour · 66mins

One of the few varying elements in Roy Rogers's series of westerns was the type of criminal activity he thwarted. Here he's up against counterfeiting when a gang kidnap a paroled practitioner of the art and force him to create plates for printing gold certificates. There's a shocking moment when Roy's steed, Trigger, takes a bullet in the neck. To fill out the running time, the film has a subplot about a mountain lion on the rampage, in addition to the usual handful of songs. AE

Dale Evans *Deputy Patricia Callahan* • Estelita Rodriguez *Lola Chavez* • Pat Brady *Dr Sparrow Biffle* • Russ Vincent *Ricardo Chavez* • George Meeker *Matt Brunner* ■ *Dir* William Witney • *Scr* Sloan Nibley

Twilight of Honor ★★★

Drama 1963 · US · BW · 104mins

This is something of a *déjà vu* melodrama. Richard Chamberlain – on sabbatical from *Dr Kildare* – plays a small-town, small-time lawyer who takes on the defence of a young hooligan (Oscar nominee Nick Adams) aided by the sage advice of veteran attorney Claude Rains. Not exactly a star-making turn for Chamberlain but it's directed with some style. TH

Richard Chamberlain *David Mitchell* • Joey Heatherton *Laura Mae Brown* • Nick Adams *Ben Brown* • Claude Rains *Art Harper* • Joan Blackman *Susan Harper* • James Gregory *Norris Bixby* • Pat Buttram *Cole Clinton* • Jeanette Nolan *Amy Clinton* ■ *Dir* Boris Sagal • *Scr* Henry Denker, from the novel by Al Dewlen

The Twilight of the Ice Nymphs ★★★

Drama 1997 · Can · Colour · 91mins

Cult Canadian director Guy Maddin is one of the most idiosyncratic talents of contemporary cinema, but his work is something of an acquired taste. Maddin here fashions another opaque exercise in eccentric melodrama and obscure film references. He's helped by a cast of notables, all of whom seem in tune with their director's weirdness. However, the film's leading man, Nigel Whitmey, had his name removed from the credits after Maddin redubbed his dialogue. RT

Pascale Bussières *Juliana Kossel* • Shelley Duvall *Amelia Glahn* • Frank Gorshin *Cain Ball* • Alice Krige *Zephyr Eccles* • RH Thomson *Dr Issac Solti* • Ross McMillan *Matthew Eccles* ■ *Dir* Guy Maddin • *Scr* George Toles

Twilight on the Prairie ★★ U

Musical western 1944 · US · BW · 61mins

This enjoyable musical features Johnny Downs and Vivian Austin, but is distinguished by the presence of both Australian-born comic Leon Errol and the great Jack Teagarden and his Orchestra. While tis is very pleasant for fans of obscure 1940s musical westerns, others should give it a miss by a mile! TS

Johnny Downs *Bucky Williams* • Vivian Austin *Sally Barton* • Leon Errol *Cactus Barton* • Connie Haines *Ginger Lee* • Eddie Quillan *Phil Travers* ■ *Dir* Jean Yarbrough • *Scr* Clyde Bruckman, from a story by Warren Wilson

Twilight People ★★ 15

Horror 1973 · Phil · Colour · 75mins

This film from Filipino fright-master Eddie Romero has John Ashley is transported to a remote South Pacific island where a crazed doctor is creating the usual half human/half animal rebellious menagerie. The nice line in crude monsters includes a flying bat man, an antelope man and blaxploitation icon Pam Grier as the Panther woman. A silly yet quite gory exploiter. AJ

John Ashley *Matt Farrell* • Pat Woodell *Neva Gordon* • Pam Grier *Panther woman* ■ *Dir* Eddie Romero • *Scr* Eddie Romero, Jerome Small • *Executive Producer* Roger Corman

The Twilight Samurai ★★★★ 12

Period drama 2002 · Jpn · Colour · 129mins

Director Yoji Yamada is known in Japan for his domestic melodramas and for this much-lauded film, his first period drama, he adds a touch of family circumstance to ratchet up the tension. There is a class-conscious desperation about the samurai hero, Hiroyuki Sanada, which makes the setting of the 19th century even more credible. Sanada holds a lowly position within his clan, and he's nicknamed Twilight Samurai (Tasogore Seibei) because he doesn't join them for after-work drinks, but heads home to look after his motherless daughters and their elderly grandmother. Then Rie Miyazawa, a battered wife, finds shelter in their home, brightening up their poverty-stricken existence. Yamada's film looks into the hearts of the men wielding the lethal weapons, and so achieves an inspirational quality. TH. In Japanese with English subtitles. DVD

Hiroyuki Sanada *Iguchi Seibei* • Rie Miyazawa *Tomoe* • Ren Osugi *Kouda Toyotarou* • Mitsuru Fukikoshi *Michinojo Iinuma* • Min Tanaka *Yogo Zenemon* ■ *Dir* Yoji Yamada • *Scr* Yoji Yamada, Yoshitaka Asama, from novels by Shuhei Fujisawa

Twilight Zone: the Movie ★★★ 15

Portmanteau supernatural drama
1983 · US · Colour · 96mins

Despite the involvement of Hollywood major league directors Steven Spielberg, John Landis and Joe Dante, it was Australian George Miller, responsible for cult hit *Mad Max* and its sequels, who produced the one truly scary section of this feature-length stab at Rod Serling's classic TV series. In Miller's tale, paranoid passenger John Lithgow is the only person on a plane who can see a creature gnawing away at the wings. The rest of the stories are a mixed bag. Landis's contribution remains overshadowed by the controversial death of star Vic Morrow during filming. JF. Contains violence, swearing.

Burgess Meredith *Narrator* • Dan Aykroyd *Passenger* • Albert Brooks *Driver* • Vic Morrow *Bill* • Doug McGrath *Larry* • Charles Hallahan *Ray* • Bill Quinn *Conroy* ■ *Dir* John Landis, Steven Spielberg, Joe Dante, George Miller (2) • *Scr* John Landis, George Clayton Johnson, Josh Rogan, Richard Matheson

Twilight's Last Gleaming ★★★★★ 15

Political thriller
1977 · US/W Ger · Colour · 137mins

If Colonel Kurtz from *Apocalypse Now* had survived, he might have ended up like Burt Lancaster in this absolutely riveting thriller. Lancaster, a brilliant, medal-heavy war hero, decides to force the US government to come clean about why it fought in Vietnam. He does this by hijacking a nuclear missile silo and periodically raises the temperature by pushing the right buttons. While President Charles Durning sweats, Richard Widmark and the army gathers outside Lancaster's underground bunker. This is a clever, plausible and subversive movie that capitalised on President Carter's avowed policy of open government. AT. Contains swearing, violence.

Burt Lancaster *Lawrence Dell* • Richard Widmark *Martin MacKenzie* • Charles Durning *President Stevens* • Melvyn Douglas *Zachariah Guthrie* • Paul Winfield *Willis Powell* • Burt Young *Augie Garvas* • Joseph Cotten *Arthur Renfrew* ■ *Dir* Robert Aldrich • *Scr* Ronald M Cohen, Edward Huebsch, from the novel *Viper Three* by Walter Wager

Twin Beds ★★★ U

Comedy 1942 · US · Colour · 83mins

This fast, furious and often funny bedroom farce has George Brent and Joan Bennett as newlyweds who never seem able to be alone together because their apartment keeps being invaded by two other couples. When they all decide to move away from each other, they find they have all moved to the same apartment block. As the two other women are played by the delightful Una Merkel and Glenda Farrell, we can only be pleased. RB

George Brent *Mike Abbott* • Joan Bennett *Julie Abbott* • Mischa Auer *Nicolai Cherupin* • Una Merkel *Lydia* • Glenda Farrell *Sonya Cherupin* • Ernest Truex *Larky* • Margaret Hamilton *Norah* ■ *Dir* Tim Whelan • *Scr* Curtis Kenyon, Kenneth Earl, E Edwin Moran, from a play by Margaret Mayo, Salisbury Field

Twin Dragons ★★★ PG

Action comedy 1992 · HK · Colour · 99mins

This sprightly chopsocky comedy once again has Jackie Chan combining the styles of Bruce Lee and Charlie Chaplin to entertaining effect. As twins separated at birth, Chan keeps both girlfriends Maggie Cheung and Nina Chi Li and a gangster's gormless henchmen guessing through a series of slick set pieces. Such is the pace of the action that it's impossible to detect the seams between the scenes handled by co-directors Tsui Hark and Ringo Lam. DP. Cantonese dialogue dubbed into English. DVD

Jackie Chan *Boomer/John Ma* • Cheung Man-Yuk [Maggie Cheung] *Barbara* • Nina Chi Li *Tammy* • Anthony Chan *Hotel staffer* • Philip Chan *Hotel manager* • John Wu [John Woo] *Priest* ■ *Dir* Lam Ling-Tung [Ringo Lam], Tsui Hark • *Scr* Barry Wong, Tsui Hark, Cheung Tung Jo, Yik Wong, Val Kuklowsky, Rod Dean

Twin Falls Idaho ★★ 15

Drama 1999 · US · Colour · 110mins

Screenwriters and real-life brothers Mark and Michael Polish take a page from David Lynch in this bizarre movie. They also play the parts of Siamese twins holed up in a seedy hotel who are eventually befriended by hooker Michele Hicks. It starts off well, promising to be darkly funny, tragic and a fascinating look at the nature of twins. After Hicks's initially shocked character takes an active interest in the two, the movie's momentum comes to a dead halt and doesn't revive until the last 20 minutes. KB

Michele Hicks *Penny* • Teresa Hill *Sissy* • Robert Beecher *D'Walt* • Michael Polish *Francis Falls* • Mark Polish *Blake Falls* • Patrick Bauchau *Miles* • Lesley Ann Warren *Francine* ■ *Dir* Michael Polish • *Scr* Michael Polish, Mark Polish

Twin Peaks: Fire Walk with Me ★★★★ 18

Cult drama 1992 · US · Colour · 134mins

The exploding TV set at the beginning is the tip-off that David Lynch's deeply disturbing descent into Laura Palmer's private hell, which begins seven days before she's found wrapped in plastic, will pursue dark introspective themes that his landmark pseudo-psychic series dared only hint at. Undervalued on cinema release, the Sultan of Strange's Rubik cube glorification of the terror-filled magic of life is a spaced-out odyssey of extraordinary obsession and power. As one hypnotic sequence follows another, Lynch's startling contemplation on our unfair universe is a must for *Twin Peaks* freaks. AJ. Contains drug abuse, swearing, nudity. [VIDEO] DVD

Sheryl Lee *Laura Palmer* • Ray Wise *Leland Palmer* • Moira Kelly *Donna Hayward* • David Bowie *Phillip Jeffries* • Chris Isaak *Special agent Chester Desmond* • Harry Dean Stanton *Carl Rodd* • Kyle MacLachlan *Special agent Dale Cooper* • Mädchen Amick *Shelly Johnson* ■ *Dir* David Lynch • *Scr* David Lynch, Robert Engels • *Cinematographer* Ronald Victor Garcia • *Music* Angelo Badalamenti

Twin Sisters ★★★ 12A

Period drama
2002 · Neth/Lux · Colour · 137mins

The cruel separation of adoring six-year-old twins has a lifetime of tragic repercussions in this atmospheric feature from Dutch director Ben Sombogaart. Orphaned siblings Anna and Lotte are individually farmed off to relatives, and their subsequent upbringings and experiences – Anna in poverty in Germany and Lotte in luxury in the Netherlands – are so disparate that when they reunite in the periods before and after the Second World War, painful misunderstandings drive them apart until old age. Never judgemental – to the point of being perhaps excessively even-handed – this is a rich drama that affects both the head and the heart. SF. In Dutch, German and English with subtitles. Contains violence and sex scenes.

Ellen Vogel *Old Lotte Bamberg* • Thekla Reuten *Young Lotte Bamberg* • Gudrun Okras *Old Anna Bamberg* • Nadja Uhl *Young Anna Bamberg* • Julia Koopmans *Lotte Bamberg as a child* • Sina Richardt *Anna Bamberg as a child* • Betty Schuurman *Henriette Rockanje* • Jaap Spijkers *Ferdinand Rockanje* ■ *Dir* Ben Sombogaart • *Scr* Marieke van der Pol, from the novel by Tessa de Loo

Twin Sisters of Kyoto ★★★★

Melodrama 1963 · Jpn · Colour · 107mins

This Oscar-nominated class drama concerns sisters who were abandoned at birth because twins were reputed to bring bad luck. Now the daughter of a wealthy merchant, Chieko goes in search of her sibling, only for their contentment to be short-lived as she becomes convinced Naeko is attempting to steal her beau. Appearing in over 100 films, Shima Iwashita worked many times with Yasujiro Ozu and her husband, Masahiro Shinoda. But nothing surpasses her dual performance in this affecting study of identity and self-image which is handled with tact and insight by Noboru Nakamura. DP. In Japanese with English subtitles.

Shima Iwashita *Chieko/Naeko* • Seiji Miyaguchi *Takichiro Sada* • Teruo Yoshida *Ryusuke Mizuki* • Tamotsu Hayakawa *Shinichi Mizuki* ■ *Dir* Noboru Nakamura • *Scr* Toshihide Gondo, from the novel *Koto* by Yasunari Kawabata

Twin Town ★★ 18

Black comedy 1997 · UK · Colour · 95mins

Described by some as a Welsh *Trainspotting*, this muddled, Swansea-set black comedy does share some superficial similarities, but has none of the style, energy or invention of that movie. Real-life brothers Llyr Evans and Rhys Ifans (*Notting Hill*) are manic, moral-free young criminals who exact revenge when their builder father is refused compensation for an accident at work. There's no shortage of candid sex, drugs and rock 'n' roll, but the fun soon drains away and the tone turns really nasty. JC. Contains sex scenes and drug abuse. [VIDEO] DVD

Llyr Evans *Julian Lewis* • Rhys Ifans *Jeremy Lewis* • Dorien Thomas *Greyo* • Dougray Scott *Terry Walsh* • Biddug Williams *Mrs Mort* • Ronnie Williams *Mr Mort* ■ *Dir* Kevin Allen • *Scr* Kevin Allen, Paul Durden

Twin Warriors ★★ 15

Martial arts action drama
1993 · HK · Colour · 89mins

The first and as of yet only pairing of two of the biggest names in Hong Kong film, Jet Li and Michelle Yeoh, this boasts enough astonishing martial arts action to allow you to overlook the clumsy storyline. Friends Li and Chin Siu-hou are monks and martial arts experts who part ways after a clash with their temple's leaders. Faced with an oppressive ruler the ambitious Chin is quickly won over to the dark side, leaving Li and new love Yeoh to lead a small group of rebels to a climactic showdown. JF. Cantonese dialogue dubbed into English. [VIDEO] DVD

Jet Li *Zhang Junbao* • Michelle Yeoh *Siu Lin* • Chin Siu-hou *Chin Bo* • Fennie Yuen *Miss Li* • Yuen Chueng-Yan *Rev Ling* ■ *Dir* Yuen Woo-Ping • *Scr* Kwong Kim Yip

The Twinkle in God's Eye ★★ U

Western 1955 · US · BW · 72mins

In this personally produced project, Mickey Rooney plays a former wild boy who turns over a new leaf to become a parson and brings religion to a frontier mining town. Rooney was so keen on the project he also wrote the title song (but refrains from singing it). In actual fact, Rooney's self-assurance suits the part and he converts the toughest of hombres as well as the dancing girls in the saloon. Coleen Gray co-stars as one of the floozies with Hugh O'Brian as the gambling hall proprietor. AE

Mickey Rooney *Reverend Macklin* • Coleen Gray *Laura* • Hugh O'Brian *Marty* • Joey Forman *Ted* • Don "Red" Barry [Donald Barry] *Dawson* • Touch Connors [Mike Connors] *Lou* • Jill Jarmyn *Millie* • Kem Dibbs *Johnny* ■ *Dir* George Blair • *Scr* PJ Wolfson

Twinky ★ 15

Romantic drama
1969 · UK/It · Colour · 94mins

Director Richard Donner helms this abysmal relic from Swinging London that not even its distinguished supporting cast can salvage. Twinky is Susan George, a 16-year-old schoolgirl who elopes with an American novelist played by Charles Bronson. Both sets of parents, on both sides of the Atlantic, are appalled and most viewers will be, too. AT [VIDEO]

Charles Bronson *Scott Wardman* • Susan George *Lola Twinky Londonderry* • Trevor Howard *Grandfather* • Honor Blackman *Mrs Londonderry* • Michael Craig *Mr Londonderry* • Robert Morley *Judge Roxburgh* • Jack Hawkins *Judge Millington-Draper* • Lionel Jeffries *Mr Creighton* • Orson Bean *Hal* ■ *Dir* Richard Donner • *Scr* Norman Thaddeus Vane

Twins ★★★★ PG

Comedy 1988 · US · Colour · 102mins

One of those rare things: a one-joke comedy that actually works. Danny DeVito is the dim-witted scuzzball who discovers naive, intelligent Arnold Schwarzenegger is his genetically engineered brother. Comic moments abound as the odd couple team up to find their long-lost mom, including Arnie's first awkward attempts at romance with Kelly Preston. DeVito is on form and Schwarzenegger shows he can handle comedy. JB. Contains swearing. [VIDEO] DVD

Arnold Schwarzenegger *Julius Benedict* • Danny DeVito *Vincent Benedict* • Kelly Preston *Marnie Mason* • Chloe Webb *Linda Mason* • Bonnie Bartlett *Mary Ann Benedict* • Marshall Bell *Webster* • Trey Wilson *Beetroot McKinley* • David Caruso *Al Greco* ■ *Dir* Ivan Reitman • *Scr* William Davies, William Osborne, Timothy Harris, Herschel Weingrod

Twins of Evil ★★★ 15

Horror 1971 · UK · Colour · 83mins

Hammer ransacked J Sheridan Le Fanu's classic terror tale *Carmilla* for the last time in this completion of its trilogy following *The Vampire Lovers* and *Lust for a Vampire*. Mary and Madelaine Collinson, *Playboy* magazine's first twin centrefolds, play "which one's the vampire?" in a streamlined, if predictable, period piece laced with the usual quota of heaving bosoms, blood-red lipstick, lesbianism and gory decapitations. Touches of ethereal Gothic atmosphere and a neat funereal flamboyancy lift this slick shock package. AJ [VIDEO] DVD

Peter Cushing *Gustav Weil* • Kathleen Byron *Katy Weil* • Dennis Price *Dietrich* • Madelaine Collinson *Frieda Gellhorn* • Mary Collinson *Maria Gellhorn* • Damien Thomas *Count Karnstein* • David Warbeck *Anton Hoffer* • Isobel Black *Ingrid Hoffer* ■ *Dir* John Hough • *Scr* Tudor Gates, from the story *Carmilla* by J Sheridan Le Fanu

The Twist ★★

Comedy 1976 · Fr · Colour · 105mins

When he's good he's exceptional, but when he's off form even the most devoted fan is hard pressed to explain the appeal of Claude Chabrol. Although at his best with thrillers, he has produced a number of incisive character studies, but he struggles to separate the poignant from the pretentious in this languid study of the infidelities and prejudices of diverse bourgeois couples. Shamefully throwing away a top-drawer Franco-American cast, this will appeal only to the most ardent Chabrol devotees. DP

Bruce Dern *William Brandeis* • Stéphane Audran *Claire Brandeis* • Sydne Rome *Nathalie* • Jean-Pierre Cassel *Jacques Lalovet* • Ann-Margret *Charlie Minerva* • Curd Jürgens [Curt Jurgens] *Jeweller* • Charles Aznavour *Dr Lartigue* ■ *Dir* Claude Chabrol • *Scr* Claude Chabrol, Norman Enfield, Ennio De Concini, Maria Pafusto, from a novel by Licie Faure

Twist ★★★

Documentary 1992 · Can · Colour · 78mins

Whatever happened to dance crazes? There was a time when anybody not knowing the steps to the charleston or the carioca was squarer than square. This entertaining documentary charts the ups and downs of the twist, which had hips swinging across the world in the early 1960s. Revealing that the song itself was a forgotten B-side written and recorded by Hank Ballard before Chubby Checker re-recorded it, the film shows that it was far more than a dance-hall phenomenon, catching on when other dances like the watusi sank without trace. DP

Dir Ron Mann

Twist and Shout ★★★

Drama 1985 · Den · Colour · 100mins

Adam Tonsberg's Beatle-mad drummer has to repay a debt to old flame Ulrikke Juul Bondo after getting Camilla Soeberg pregnant, while Lars Simonsen tries to prevent his abusive father from committing his depressive mother to an asylum. Refusing to rely on easy nostalgia, Bille August captures the energy of Copenhagen in the just-Swinging Sixties, but also highlights the realities attendant on this new-found freedom. DP. A Danish language film.

Adam Tonsberg *Bjorn* • Lars Simonsen *Erik* • Ulrikke Juul Bondo *Kirsten* • Camilla Soeberg *Anna* ■ *Dir* Bille August • *Scr* Bille August, Bjarne Reuter, from a novel by Bjarne Reuter

Twist of Fate ★★★

Crime thriller 1997 · US · Colour · 95mins

This is a surprisingly suspenseful B-thriller from director Max Fischer, with Mädchen Amick as a young attorney who loses a seemingly straightforward case against a serial murderer. Amick is forced to seek advice from the killer – and set herself up as a target – in order to prevent a more sinister crime. It's reminiscent of *The Silence of the Lambs*, though the acting isn't of the same standard. DP. Contains violence and swearing.

Mädchen Amick *Rachel Dwyer* • Chris Mulkey *Lennox* • Don Jordan *Krasko* • Bruce Dinsmore *Carmichael* • Lynne Adams *Laura Carmichael* ■ *Dir* Max Fischer • *Scr* William Lee, Cameron Kent

A Twist of Sand ★★ U

Adventure 1967 · UK · Colour · 91mins

Dubious opportunist Jeremy Kemp persuades Second World War submarine skipper Richard Johnson to make for the Skeleton Coast of Africa to retrieve some hidden diamonds in this lacklustre aquatic adventure. This sort of B-movie plotline was long past its sell-by date by 1967, and director Don Chaffey rather goes through the motions as his cast encounters some decidedly unspectacular storms and the usual underwater dangers. Honor Blackman just looks bored. DP

Richard Johnson *Geoffrey Peace* • Honor Blackman *Julie Chambois* • Jeremy Kemp *Harry Riker* • Peter Vaughan *Johann* • Roy Dotrice *David Carland* • Guy Doleman *Patrol boat commander* ■ *Dir* Don Chaffey • *Scr* Marvin H Albert, from the novel by Geoffrey Jenkins

Twisted ★★ 15

Crime thriller 2003 · US · Colour · 92mins

Ashley Judd stars in this monotonous thriller from *Quills* director Philip Kaufman. Joined by Andy Garcia as her cop partner, she plays a newly-promoted police inspector hunting for a serial killer who's murdering her casual lovers. There are so many red herrings and so little real action that it all becomes tiresome, especially when

Judd's contribution is a repeated cycle of drinking, passing out and waking up to find another corpse. SF. Contains swearing and violence. DVD

Ashley Judd *Jessica Shepard* • Samuel L Jackson *John Mills* • Andy Garcia *Mike Delmarco* • David Strathairn *Dr Melvin Frank* • Russell Wong *Lieutenant Tong* • Camryn Manheim *Lisa* • Mark Pellegrino *Jimmy Schmidt* • Titus Welliver *Dale Becker* • DW Moffett *Ray Porter* • Richard T Jones *Wilson Jefferson* ■ *Dir* Philip Kaufman • *Scr* Sarah Thorp

Twisted Nerve ★★★ 18

Thriller 1968 · UK · Colour · 112mins

In its day, this was a highly controversial and, to some, tasteless thriller. One would expect nothing less from Leo Marks, writer of *Peeping Tom*. But this time round, the story of a seemingly nice young man, who is in fact a homicidal maniac, went too far by implying a link between Down's syndrome and psychosis. Film-makers the Boulting Brothers had to add a disclaimer to the front of the film. Hayley Mills and Hywel Bennett are ludicrously miscast, and suspense is not comedy director Roy Boulting's forte, but the bizarre story is still gripping, and the murders, though a long time coming, provide a suitably ghastly climax. DM

Hayley Mills *Susan Harper* • Hywel Bennett *Martin Durnley/Georgie Clifford* • Billie Whitelaw *Joan Harper* • Phyllis Calvert *Enid Durnley* • Frank Finlay *Henry Durnley* • Barry Foster *Gerry Henderson* • Timothy West *Superintendent Dakin* ■ *Dir* Roy Boulting • *Scr* Leo Marks, Roy Boulting, from a story by Roger Marshall, from an idea by Roger Marshall, Jeremy Scott

Twister ★★ 15

Drama 1989 · US · Colour · 89mins

This is an irritating "crazy gang" comedy about a bunch of batty siblings who find themselves trapped with their dotty old dad in the family mansion during a freak weather storm. Harry Dean Stanton plays the dad, while Suzy Amis and the genuinely odd Crispin Glover (*River's Edge*) are among the offspring in a film that sorely mistakes being way-out for being remotely interesting. DA

Harry Dean Stanton *Eugene Cleveland* • Suzy Amis *Maureen Cleveland* • Crispin Glover *Howdy Cleveland* • Dylan McDermott *Chris* • Jenny Wright *Stephanie* ■ *Dir* Michael Almereyda • *Scr* Michael Almereyda, from the novel *Oh!* by Mary Robison

Twister ★★★ PG

Action adventure
1996 · US · Colour · 108mins

Speed director Jan De Bont takes destruction to new levels in this daft but breathtaking adventure, a salute to the daredevil meteorologists who chase the tornados that plague America's Midwest. Here, Bill Paxton stars as a TV weatherman who is drawn back to his dangerous former profession as a storm chaser to help estranged wife Helen Hunt place a tornado-measuring invention in the eye of a storm. Don't worry about the laboured storyline or the lack of chemistry between the leads; just enjoy the wondrous effects. JF. Contains swearing. DVD

Bill Paxton *Bill Harding* • Helen Hunt *Jo Harding* • Jami Gertz *Melissa* • Cary Elwes *Dr. Jonas Miller* • Lois Smith *Aunt Meg* • Alan Ruck *Dusty* • Philip Seymour Hoffman *Rabbit* ■ *Dir* Jan De Bont • *Scr* Michael Crichton, Anne-Marie Martin

Two a Penny ★★★

Drama 1968 · UK · Colour · 99mins

In 1966, while searching for a new direction, Cliff Richard found God via evangelist Billy Graham and this film followed shortly after. It is surprisingly well balanced – offering both pro and con viewpoints – and contains some fine performances from Dora Bryan, Avril Angers and other well-known character actors of the time. The obstacle is Cliff himself, who was already a popular family entertainer but is awkwardly miscast as a hoodlum who would rather push drugs than marry his Bible-thumping girlfriend. Today, of course, the film has considerable curiosity value. DM

Cliff Richard *Jamie Hopkins* • Dora Bryan *Ruby Hopkins* • Avril Angers *Mrs Burry* • Ann Holloway *Carol Turner* • Geoffrey Bayldon *Alec Fitch* • Peter Barkworth *Vicar* ■ *Dir* James F Collier • *Scr* Stella Linden

Two against the Law ★★★★

Crime drama 1973 · Fr/It · Colour · 100mins

Trying to go straight after serving ten years for robbery, Alain Delon falls back on the support of Jean Gabin's social worker when his wife is killed in a car crash. However, a new romance with bank clerk Mimsy Farmer coincides with the escape of his former buddy, Victor Lanoux, and suspicious cop Michel Bouquet begins to turn up the heat. With its unforgettable final scene, the third and last collaboration between the iconic Gabin and young pretender Delon not only makes for a fascinating contrast between their acting styles, but also provides some penetrating insights into the problems facing released prisoners. DP. French and Italian dialogue dubbed into English.

Alain Delon *Gino* • Mimsy Farmer *Lucy* • Michel Bouquet *Goitreau* • Victor Lanoux *Mariel* • Ilaria Occhini *Sophie* • Jean Gabin *Germain* ■ *Dir/Scr* José Giovanni

Two and Two Make Six ★★ U

Romantic comedy 1961 · UK · BW · 50mins

Ace cinematographer Freddie Francis made his directorial debut with this trifle about a US Air Force deserter who rides off on his motorbike and falls in love with his pillion passenger. George Chakiris takes a leading film role for the first time and Janette Scott co-stars. Francis seemed happier with later horror fare and eventually went back behind the camera for such movies as *The Elephant Man*. TS

George Chakiris *Larry Curado* • Janette Scott *Irene* • Alfred Lynch *Tom* • Jackie Lane [Jocelyn Lane] *Julie* • Athene Seyler *Aunt Phoebe* • Bernard Braden *Sgt Sokolow* • Malcolm Keen *Harry Stoneham* • Ambrosine Philpotts *Lady Smith-Adams* ■ *Dir* Freddie Francis • *Scr* Monja Danischewsky

Two Arabian Knights ★★★

Silent romantic comedy
1927 · US · BW · 92mins

Relative newcomer Lewis Milestone won an Oscar for best comedy direction (the only time this award was given) at the first Academy Awards ceremony. It tells of the rivalry between a tough sergeant (Louis Wolheim) and a smart private (William Boyd, the future Hopalong Cassidy) who seem to hate each other more than the enemy. But when they are captured by the Germans, they make their escape disguised as Arabs, and rescue a maiden (Mary Astor) from an evil bey. This profitable and amusing farce was only the second production of the 22-year-old Howard Hughes. RB

William Boyd (1) *Pte W Daingerfield Phelps* • Mary Astor *Anis Bin Adham* • Louis Wolheim *Sgt Peter McGaffney* • Michael Vavitch *Emir of Jaffa* • Boris Karloff *Purser* ■ *Dir* Lewis Milestone • *Scr* James T O'Donohue, Wallace Smith, George Marion Jr (titles)

Two Bits ★★★ 12

Period drama 1995 · US · Colour · 80mins

Displaying ingenuity in adversity, a Depression-era kid concocts all manner of schemes to make the money he needs to attend the opening of a new movie theatre. Newcomer Jerry Barone is terrific as the tyke. Al Pacino is as excellent as ever as the kid's inspirational but dying grandad, and there's good support from Mary Elizabeth Mastrantonio as Barone's mum. With a crack cast and crew, this is solid entertainment. DA DVD

Mary Elizabeth Mastrantonio *Luisa* • Al Pacino *Grandpa* • Jerry Barone *Gennaro* • Patrick Borriello *Tullio* • Andy Romano *Dr Bruna* • Donna Mitchell *Mrs Bruna* ■ *Dir* James Foley • *Scr* Joseph Stefano

Two-Bits and Pepper ★★

Comedy 1995 · US · Colour · 90mins

This is a rather dire, though quirky, *Home Alone* rip-off, with Joe Piscopo starring in a dual role as a pair of burglars who kidnap a couple of girls and decide to hold them for ransom. It gets decidedly weird when the girls outwit their captors with the help of two Mr Ed-like talking horses. While funny in places, this is too uneven and downright silly to work for its entire running time, despite the presence of deft comedian Piscopo. JB

Joe Piscopo *Spider/Zike* • Lauren Eckstrom *Tyler* • Rachel Crane *Katie* • Perry Stephens *Roger* • Kathrin Lautner *Carla* • Dennis Weaver *Sheriff Pratt* • Shannon Gallant *Monica* • Ethan Erickson *Boyfriend* ■ *Dir/Scr* Corey Michael Eubanks

Two Brothers ★★★ U

Adventure drama
2004 · Fr/UK · Colour · 100mins

As he proved with *The Bear* (1988), Jean-Jacques Annaud has always had a way with animals, and the tigers Kumal and Sangha are the undoubted stars of this uneven melodrama set in French Indochina during the 1920s. The opening sequences in which the parents mate and the cubs find their feet are enchanting. But once big-game hunter Guy Pearce stumbles across the family and captures the adorably clumsy Kumal, the action is hijacked by the humans, who are nowhere near as engaging. DP DVD

Guy Pearce *Aidan McRory* • Jean-Claude Dreyfus *Eugène Normandin* • Philippine Leroy-Beaulieu *Mathilde Normandin* • Freddie Highmore *Young Raoul* • Vincent Scarito *Zerbino* • Stéphanie Lagarde *Miss Paulette* • Le Mai Anh *Nai-Rea* • Moussa Maaskri *Saladin* • Oanh Nguyen *Prince* ■ *Dir* Jean-Jacques Annaud • *Scr* Jean-Jacques Annaud, Alain Godard, from an idea by Jean-Jacques Annaud

2by4 ★★★

Drama 1998 · US · Colour · 90mins

With a rough edge to shame even the rawest indie movie, Jimmy Smallhorne's scowling investigation into the lingering effects of child abuse has an authenticity and immediacy that makes for deeply uncomfortable, if utterly compelling viewing. Also taking the part of the Bronx-Irish construction worker whose laddish lifestyle is increasingly disturbed by harrowing nightmares, Smallhorne admirably conveys the sexual confusion that alienates his girlfriend, Kimberly Topper, and draws him ever closer to Aussie street hustler, Bradley Fitts. Chris O'Neill is also impressive as the uncle with the darkest of secrets. DP

Jimmy Smallhorne *Johnnie Maher* • Chris O'Neill *Uncle Trump* • Bradley Fitts *Christian* • Joe Holyoake *Joe* • Terrence McGoff *Billy* • Ronan Carr *Brains* • Leo Hamill *Paddy* ■ *Dir* Jimmy Smallhorne • *Scr* Jimmy Smallhorne, Terry McGoff, Fergus Tighe, from a screenplay (unproduced) by Jimmy Smallhorne, Terry McGoff

Two Came Back ★★★ PG

Thriller 1997 · US · Colour · 84mins

The title is a bit of a giveaway, but this TV movie is still an admirably grim story of survival on the high seas. Jonathan Brandis and Melissa Joan Hart play a couple of young sailors who are brought together with three others to deliver a yacht to its owners. When a storm hits, the youngsters find themselves in a desperate battle for survival. There are plucky performances from the cast and TV-movie veteran Dick Lowry keeps the direction on an even keel. JF DVD

Melissa Joan Hart *Susan Clarkson* • Jonathan Brandis *Jason O'Donnel* • David Gail *Matt* • Jon Pennell *Rick* • Susan Walters *Stacy* • Susan Sullivan *Patrica Clarkson* ■ *Dir* Dick Lowry • *Scr* Raymond Hartung, from the book *Albatross* by Deborah Scaling-Kiley, Meg Noonan

Two Can Play That Game ★★★ 15

Romantic comedy
2001 · US · Colour · 87mins

Mark Brown makes a sharply observed directorial debut with this likeable and intelligent movie about relationships. It's as perky and attractive as its female protagonists – a group of sassy African-Americans who turn to their best friend Shanté (a delightful Vivica A Fox) whenever man trouble dampens their spirits. However, when Fox's boyfriend Morris Chestnut is caught with her arch rival, it's time for the love guru to follow her own "Ten Day Plan" to get him back in line. Spiked with astute observations, this is a well acted and funny battle of the sexes. SF. Contains swearing. DVD

Vivica A Fox *Shanté Smith* • Morris Chestnut *Keith Fenton* • Anthony Anderson *Tony* • Gabrielle Union *Conny* • Wendy Raquel Robinson *Karen* • Tamala Jones *Tracye Edwards* • Mo'Nique *Diedre* • Ray Wise *Bill Parker* ■ *Dir/Scr* Mark Brown

2 Days in the Valley ★★★ 18

Comedy crime thriller
1996 · US · Colour · 104mins

This interestingly quirky and occasionally steamy comedy tips its hat at Tarantino's *Pulp Fiction* and Robert Altman's *Short Cuts*. Danny Aiello, James Spader, Teri Hatcher, Jeff Daniels and then-unknown Charlize Theron play just some of the unusual characters who inhabit the strange environs of LA in this amoral and often bizarre tale. Writer/director John Herzfeld is better known for less hip fare, including a number of TV movies. JB. Contains swearing, violence and sex scenes. DVD

Danny Aiello *Dosmo Pizzo* • Greg Cruttwell *Allan Hopper* • Jeff Daniels *Alvin Strayer* • Teri Hatcher *Becky Foxx* • Glenne Headly *Susan Parish* • Peter Horton *Roy Foxx* • Marsha Mason *Audrey Hopper* • Paul Mazursky *Teddy Peppers* • Charlize Theron *Helga Svelgen* • James Spader *Lee Woods* ■ *Dir/Scr* John Herzfeld

two days, nine lives ★ 18

Drama 2000 · UK · Colour · 93mins

"Cracking up or checking out – the choice is theirs" reads the tagline for Simon Monjack's rehab clinic drama. Cringing with embarrassment or roaring with laughter is the likely choice facing those who can bear to sit through this farrago. Given dialogue culled from a novice writer's workshop, the cast struggles hopelessly with a plot that seeks to explore psychological problems ranging from drug-induced paranoia to murderous rage. DP

U = SUITABLE FOR ALL Uc = SUITABLE FOR ALL, ESPECIALLY FOR YOUNG CHILDREN (VIDEO ONLY) PG = PARENTAL GUIDANCE

Luke Goss *Saul* • Georgia Reece *Joanna* • Sienna Guillory *Katie* • Jonathan Bruun *Danny* • Sabrina Van Tassel *Star* • Glenn Carter *Jesus* ■ *Dir* Simon Monjack • *Scr* Nick McDowell, Simon Monjack, Jessica Wells

Two Deaths ★★★ 18

Drama 1994 · UK · Colour · 98mins

Director Nicolas Roeg and screenwriter Allan Scott have shifted the scene from Chile to Romania for this adaptation of Stephen Dobyns's novel. This set-bound drama could be situated anywhere, however, and it would still have the same resonance. There's no escaping the theatricality of the piece, but the story that unfolds over dinner is both compelling and disturbing. Michael Gambon effortlessly conveys pride and regret as he reveals how he has mistreated his housekeeper, Sonia Braga, whose statuesque dignity masks a burning desire for revenge. Far from Roeg's best, but still solid. DP. Contains violence, a sex scene and nudity. [VIDEO]

Michael Gambon *Daniel Pavenic* • Sonia Braga *Ana Puscasu* • Patrick Malahide *George Buscan* • Ion Caramitru *Carl Dalakis* • Nickolas Grace *Marius Vernescu* • Lisa Orgolini *Young Ana* • Niall Refoy *Young Pavenic* ■ *Dir* Nicolas Roeg • *Scr* Allan Scott, from the novel *The Two Deaths of Senora Puccini* by Stephen Dobyns

Two Evil Eyes ★★★ 18

Horror 1990 · It/US · Colour · 114mins

Masters of horror George A Romero and Dario Argento joined forces to create this double bill based on a pair of Edgar Allan Poe stories. Romero's contribution is *The Facts in the Case of M Valdemar*, in which a man is mesmerised at the moment of death but with awful consequences. Poe's slim story is stretched to no avail, and the new material is handled in a conventional TV style. Argento's version of *The Black Cat* is more successful. The adaptation, a radical update involving Harvey Keitel as a photographer who goes mad and murders his girlfriend, is again overlong but builds to a mad and bloody climax. DM [VIDEO] DVD

Adrienne Barbeau *Jessica Valdemar* • EG Marshall *Steven Pike* • Bingo O'Malley *Ernest Valdemar* • Harvey Keitel *Rod Usher* • Madeleine Potter *Annabel* • John Amos *Legrand* • Sally Kirkland *Eleonora* • Martin Balsam *Mr Pym* • Kim Hunter *Mrs Pym* ■ *Dir* George A Romero, Dario Argento • *Scr* George A Romero, Dario Argento, Franco Ferrini, from the stories *The Facts in the Case of M Valdemar* and *The Black Cat* by Edgar Allan Poe • *Music* Pino Donaggio

Two-Faced Woman ★★★

Screwball comedy 1941 · US · BW · 93mins

Greta Garbo's last movie is nowhere near as bad as contemporary reviews would have you believe, and certainly didn't warrant the most fabulous female screen face of all opting for a retirement that would last until her death almost 50 years later. There's much to enjoy in this sophisticated comedy, especially Garbo dancing the "Chica-Chocka". The risqué material led to the Catholic League of Decency condemning the movie, and it was actually banned in Australia. Today we can appreciate it for what it is: a very well-performed piece of froth. TS

Greta Garbo *Karin Borg Blake/Katherine Borg* • Melvyn Douglas *Larry Blake* • Constance Bennett *Griselda Vaughn* • Roland Young *OO Miller* • Robert Sterling *Dick Williams* • Ruth Gordon *Miss Ellis* ■ *Dir* George Cukor • *Scr* SH Behrman, Salka Viertel, George Oppenheimer, from the play by Ludwig Fulda

The Two Faces of Dr Jekyll ★★

Erotic horror 1960 · UK · Colour · 88mins

Hammer's flop version of the overworked Robert Louis Stevenson classic grafts on Oscar Wilde's *The Picture of Dorian Gray* for extra literacy amid the tired Gothic chills. This time the old and weak Jekyll (Paul Massie) transforms into a dashing and virile playboy with an eye for London's cancan girls. Christopher Lee lends his usual excellent support as the lecherous best friend. AJ

Paul Massie *Dr Henry Jekyll/Mr Edward Hyde* • Dawn Addams *Kitty Jekyll* • Christopher Lee *Paul Allen* • David Kossoff *Ernest Litauer* • Francis De Wolff *Inspector* • Norma Marla *Maria* • Joy Webster *Sphinx girl* • Magda Miller *Sphinx girl* • Oliver Reed *Bouncer* ■ *Dir* Terence Fisher • *Scr* Wolf Mankowitz, from the novel by Robert Louis Stevenson

2 Fast 2 Furious ★★★ 12

Action thriller
2003 · US/Ger · Colour · 102mins

Model-turned-actor Tyrese is no substitute for Vin Diesel, and the crude story is lower-octane than its predecessor *The Fast and the Furious*, but director John Singleton's splashily shallow sequel provides enough revved-up cheap thrills to make the grade as loud dumb fun. Paul Walker is back – and blanker than ever – as the discredited cop here forced to go undercover to infiltrate the evil empire of Miami drug baron Cole Hauser. Entertaining, if pretty standard-issue stuff – a souped-up B-movie. AJ. Contains violence and swearing. [VIDEO] DVD

Paul Walker *Brian O'Conner* • Tyrese [Tyrese Gibson] *Roman Pearce* • Eva Mendes *Monica Fuentes* • Cole Hauser *Carter Verone* • Chris "Ludacris" Bridges *Tej* • James Remar *Agent Markham* • Thom Barry *Agent Bilkins* • Michael Ealy *Slap Jack* • Mark Boone Junior *Detective Whitworth* ■ *Dir* John Singleton • *Scr* Michael Brandt, Derek Haas, from a story by Michael Brandt, Derek Haas, Gary Scott Thompson, from the characters created by Gary Scott Thompson

Two Flags West ★★★ U

Wartime western 1950 · US · BW · 91mins

It took a lot of nerve for anyone but John Ford to make cavalry westerns, but writer/producer Casey Robinson and director Robert Wise gave it a good try with this dramatic story built on the fact that Confederate prisoners were allowed to serve in Union army posts out west during the Civil War. Jeff Chandler makes a strong impression as an embittered commanding officer; Joseph Cotten is the Confederate leader plotting to escape. There's more talk and less action than in most westerns, but director Wise brings the fort setting to life and stages the final Indian attack with considerable vigour. AE

Joseph Cotten *Col Clay Tucker* • Linda Darnell *Elena Kenniston* • Jeff Chandler *Maj Henry Kenniston* • Cornel Wilde *Capt Mark Bradford* • Dale Robertson *Lem* • Jay C Flippen *Sgt Terrance Duffy* • Noah Beery [Noah Beery Jr] *Cy Davis* • Harry Von Zell *Ephraim Strong* ■ *Dir* Robert Wise • *Scr* Casey Robinson, from a story by Frank S Nugent, Curtis Kenyon

Two for Texas ★★★ 15

Western 1998 · US · Colour · 92mins

Going over familiar historical territory, this made-for-cable western is a high quality, pacy retelling of the war between the fledgeling United States and Mexico over who gets to own Texas. This time around, though, the valiant last stand of Davy Crockett and company at the Alamo is only one part of the story, with director Rod Hardy opting to look at the aftermath as well. The story itself is seen from the perspective of two escaped convicts, Kris Kristofferson and Scott Bairstow, who inadvertently find themselves caught up in the making of history. JF. Contains violence. [VIDEO]

Kris Kristofferson *Hugh Allison* • Scott Bairstow *Son Holland* • Tom Skerritt *Sam Houston* • Peter Coyote *Jim Bowie* • Irene Bedard *Sana* • Victor Rivers *Emile Landry* ■ *Dir* Rod Hardy • *Scr* Larry Brothers, from the novel by James Lee Burke

Two for the Road ★★★★ PG

Comedy drama
1967 · UK/US · Colour · 110mins

The relationship of Audrey Hepburn and Albert Finney, from the youthful idyll of their love affair and early years of marriage through the stages of disillusion to the brink of collapse, is told in a series of sometimes confusing flashbacks and flash-forwards. Directed by Stanley Donen with his customary flair, the comedy drama is played out in glossy French locations as the couple make a series of road trips across the country over a period of 12 years. Frederic Raphael's Oscar-nominated screenplay is a quintessentially Swinging Sixties piece, reflecting both the strengths and weakness of the period. Hepburn evinces a range of emotions with controlled subtlety, while Finney is also excellent. RK [VIDEO] DVD

Audrey Hepburn *Joanna Wallace* • Albert Finney *Mark Wallace* • Eleanor Bron *Cathy Manchester* • William Daniels *Howard Manchester* • Claude Dauphin *Maurice Dalbret* • Nadia Gray *Françoise Dalbret* ■ *Dir* Stanley Donen • *Scr* Frederic Raphael

Two for the Seesaw ★★ PG

Romantic comedy drama
1962 · US · BW · 114mins

Jewish dancer Shirley MacLaine befriends Robert Mitchum, a sultry out-of-towner who arrives in New York after his marriage breaks up. Based on a 1950s Broadway play, it's really an extended conversation piece about the moral climate of the time, with the camera anchored to the spot while the stars wade through the reams of dialogue. It looks tame today, but the British censor thought all this "adult" talk worthy of an X-rating. AT DVD

Robert Mitchum *Jerry Ryan* • Shirley MacLaine *Gittel Mosca* • Edmon Ryan *Taubman* • Elisabeth Fraser *Sophie* • Eddie Firestone *Oscar* • Billy Gray *Mr Jacoby* ■ *Dir* Robert Wise • *Scr* Isobel Lennart, from the play by William Gibson

Two Gentlemen Sharing ★★

Drama 1969 · UK · Colour · 106mins

One of the many daring, if trendy attacks on racial prejudice and class barriers that 1960s television and cinema specialised in. Ted Kotcheff's film focuses on the love lives of a white, aristocratic advertising executive and a black Jamaican lawyer – both Oxford graduates – sharing a flat in London. There are few surprises on offer, but the film is competently acted, particularly by flatmates Robin Philips and Hal Frederick and love interest Judy Geeson. JG

Robin Phillips *Roddy* • Judy Geeson *Jane* • Hal Frederick *Andrew* • Esther Anderson *Caroline* • Norman Rossington *Phil* • Hilary Dwyer *Ethne* • Rachel Kempson *Mrs Ashby-Kydd* ■ *Dir* Ted Kotcheff • *Scr* Evan Jones, from the novel by David Stuart Leslie

Two Girls and a Guy ★★★★ 18

Comedy drama 1997 · US · Colour · 82mins

Robert Downey Jr gives a superb performance as the egotistical struggling actor who is confronted by his two girlfriends – neither of whom knew the other existed – when he returns to his New York home following a trip. The film takes place almost entirely in the apartment, as Heather Graham and Natasha Gregson Wagner battle it out for the man both believed was perfect but whom they've discovered is anything but. More like a riveting performance piece than a narrative film, writer/director James Toback's darkly comic story of infidelity is every actor's dream and a fascinating experiment. JB. Contains swearing and a sex scene. [VIDEO]

Robert Downey Jr *Blake Allen* • Natasha Gregson Wagner *Lou* • Heather Graham *Carla* • Angel David *Tommy* • Frederique Van Der Wal *Carol* ■ *Dir/Scr* James Toback

Two Girls and a Sailor ★★★ U

Musical 1944 · US · Colour · 124mins

This overlong MGM extravaganza is rewarding if you feel inclined to stick with it. Highlights include Jimmy Durante in his bizarre prime and Lena Horne singing *Paper Doll*. As for the two girls of the title, who are a wartime nightclub song-and-dance act, June Allyson seems too knowing, but the always under-rated Gloria DeHaven charms, while Van Johnson gives a delightful, easy-going performance of great charisma. Look for a very young Ava Gardner in support. TS

June Allyson *Patsy Deyo* • Gloria DeHaven *Jean Deyo* • Van Johnson *John "Johnny" Dyckman Brown III* • Tom Drake *Sgt Frank Miller* • Henry Stephenson *John Dyckman Brown I* • Henry O'Neill *John Dyckman Brown II* • Jimmy Durante *Billy Kipp/"Junior" Kipp* • Ava Gardner *Canteen dancer* ■ *Dir* Richard Thorpe • *Scr* Richard Connell, Gladys Lehman

Two Guys from Milwaukee ★★★

Comedy 1946 · US · BW · 90mins

Dennis Morgan is a young Balkan prince travelling incognito and making friends with talkative cab driver Jack Carson in this Warner Bros programme filler. Joan Leslie is the girl who catches the prince's eye and IAL Diamond, who went on to great things with Billy Wilder, co-wrote the script. Of its kind, a diverting entertainment; look out for cameos from Humphrey Bogart and Lauren Bacall. TH

Dennis Morgan *Prince Henry* • Joan Leslie *Connie Read* • Jack Carson *Buzz Williams* • Janis Paige *Polly* • SZ Sakall *Count Oswald* • Patti Brady *Peggy Evans* • Rosemary DeCamp *Nan Evans* • Lauren Bacall • Humphrey Bogart ■ *Dir* David Butler • *Scr* Charles Hoffman, IAL Diamond

Two Hands ★★★ 15

Crime comedy 1999 · Aus · Colour · 99mins

Heath Ledger and Bryan Brown star in this stylish, slyly scripted urban crime caper, with a neat twist that makes amends for some failed gambits. The decision to have the proceedings narrated by Ledger's dead brother is unfortunate, as is a contrivance involving a street urchin. Moreover, the storyline, in which a routine courier job on behalf of Mob boss Brown goes wrong, is doggedly predictable. Yet, the bank raid sequence has a pleasing knockabout quality and Ledger's attempt to seduce country girl Rose Byrne is winningly awkward. DP. Contains violence. [VIDEO] DVD

Heath Ledger *Jimmy* • Bryan Brown *Pando* • David Field *Acko* • Rose Byrne *Alex* • Susie Porter *Dierdre* • Steven Vidler *Michael/The Man* ■ *Dir/Scr* Gregor Jordan

The Two-Headed Spy ★★★ U

Second World War spy drama
1958 · UK · BW · 93mins

This taut little wartime spy saga, directed by the one-eyed Andre De

T

Toth, stars Jack Hawkins as the Englishman who has been planted by British intelligence in Germany since the end of the First World War. By the time the Second World War breaks out, Hawkins has a senior admin job in Berlin and passes information to his contact, a clockmaker, and then to a singer played by Gia Scala. The emphasis is on Hawkins's character and his refusal to become romantically involved with anyone and therefore vulnerable. Meanwhile, a young Michael Caine exhibits his flair for foreign accents playing a Gestapo agent. RT

Jack Hawkins *Gen Alex Schottland* • Gia Scala *Lili Geyr* • Erik Schumann *Lt Reinisch* • Alexander Knox *Gestapo leader Mueller* • Felix Aylmer *Cornaz* • Walter Hudd *Adm Canaris* • Kenneth Griffith *Adolf Hitler* • Michael Caine *2nd Gestapo agent* • Donald Pleasence *Gen Hardt* ■ *Dir* Andre De Toth • *Scr* James O'Donnell, from a story by J Alvin Kugelmass

200 Cigarettes ★★ 15

Romantic comedy
1999 · US · Colour · 97mins

What looks very promising – a 20-something comedy starring top Hollywood young guns – is almost immediately disappointing. Ben Affleck and brother Casey, Courtney Love, Jay Mohr and Christina Ricci are all angst-ridden young adults trying to get their lives in gear on New Year's Eve, 1981. But we've seen these relationship and insecurity problems played out ad infinitum and sadly this has a feel of a sitcom not worthy of the silver screen. LH. Contains swearing, sex scenes.

Ben Affleck *Bartender* • Casey Affleck *Tom* • Angela Featherstone *Caitlyn* • Janeane Garofalo *Ellie* • Kate Hudson *Cindy* • Courtney Love *Lucy* • Jay Mohr *Jack* • Martha Plimpton *Monica* • Christina Ricci *Val* • Paul Rudd *Kevin* ■ *Dir* Risa Bramon Garcia • *Scr* Shana Larsen

200 Motels ★★★

Music documentary
1971 · US · Colour · 98mins

Taking a leaf out of the cute anarchy of *A Hard Day's Night*, directors Frank Zappa and Tony Palmer invest Zappa's own music (performed by the Mothers of Invention) with animation, sketches and jokes, much of it skewed towards a comic critique of touring, rock-band style. As with Zappa's own brand of guitar hysteria, many of the interludes are imaginative, funny or mad and depend on the viewer having some knowledge of the fab world of pop. His libretto was declared obscene, and so what was conceived as a live show became this film instead. JM. Contains swearing.

Ringo Starr *Larry the dwarf* • Frank Zappa • Theodore Bikel *Rance Muhammitz* • Don Preston *Bif Debris* • Jimmy Carl Black *Cowboy Burtram* • Keith Moon *Hot Nun* ■ *Dir* Frank Zappa, Tony Palmer • *Scr* Frank Zappa, Tony Palmer, from a story by Frank Zappa

T

The Two Jakes ★★★ 15

Detective thriller
1990 · US · Colour · 131mins

If Robert Towne and Roman Polanski fell out over *Chinatown*, worse happened during this sequel. With Towne directing, shooting was cancelled after the first day when Robert Evans – the producer of the first film – was fired in the role of the villain, the other Jake. Shooting resumed four years later with Jack Nicholson as director/star and Harvey Keitel as his co-star, and Towne and Nicholson haven't spoken since. The second in Towne's planned trilogy about land deals in Los Angeles in the late 1940s, it evokes eerie echoes of the first story, but is muddled. AT. Contains violence, swearing. DVD

Jack Nicholson *Jake Gittes* • Harvey Keitel *Jake Berman* • Meg Tilly *Kitty Berman* • Madeleine Stowe *Lillian Bodine* • Eli Wallach *Cotton Weinberger* • Rubén Blades *Mickey Nice* • Frederic Forrest *Chuck Newty* • David Keith *Loach* • Richard Farnsworth *Earl Rawley* ■ *Dir* Jack Nicholson • *Scr* Robert Towne

Two-Lane Blacktop ★★★

Road movie drama
1971 · US · Colour · 102mins

This existential road movie takes its cue from *Easy Rider* and features Beach Boys' drummer Dennis Wilson and 1970s singer/songwriter James Taylor in their first straight leading roles. They play drifters cruising the American Southwest in their souped-up 1955 Chevrolet, who challenge old-timer Warren Oates (a career-best performance) and his GTO Pontiac to a cross-country race with car ownership as the prize. Monte Hellman's intense direction and quirky charm compensate for a low-key script, and there are nice supporting turns from Laurie Bird and Harry Dean Stanton as hitch-hikers. RS

Warren Oates *GTO* • James Taylor *Driver* • Dennis Wilson *Mechanic* • Laurie Bird *Girl* • HD Stanton [Harry Dean Stanton] *Oklahoma hitchhiker* • David Drake *Needles station attendant* • Richard Ruth *Needles station mechanic* • Jaclyn Hellman *Driver's girl* ■ *Dir* Monte Hellman • *Scr* Rudy Wurlitzer, Will Corry, from a story by Will Corry

Two Left Feet ★★★ 15

Comedy
1963 · UK · BW · 89mins

In this adult comedy about adolescent sexual complications, Michael Crawford is an unworldly 19-year-old who goes out on a date to a jazz club with older waitress Nyree Dawn Porter. At the club Porter ignores him, instead flirting with two other guys. Crawford in turn meets Julia Foster with whom he seems far happier. A stark look at 1960s sexual mores with fine performances, especially from Crawford and Porter. DF

Michael Crawford *Alan Crabbe* • Nyree Dawn Porter *Eileen* • Julia Foster *Beth Crowley* • Michael Craze *Ronnie* • David Hemmings *Brian* • Dilys Watling *Mavis* • David Lodge *Bill* • Bernard Lee *Mr Crabbe* ■ *Dir* Roy Baker [Roy Ward Baker] • *Scr* Roy Baker [Roy Ward Baker], John Hopkins, from the novel *In My Solitude* by David Stuart Leslie

The Two Little Bears ★★ U

Fantasy drama
1961 · US · BW · 84mins

When two young brothers receive instructions from a gypsy on how to transform themselves into bears, they perform the trick for their school principal father (Eddie Albert), whose sanity is called into serious question by the local education board when he attempts to spread word of the miracle. His wife doesn't believe him either, but then neither would Goldilocks. An ursine caper of very little consequence. TH

Eddie Albert *Harry Davis* • Jane Wyatt *Anne Davis* • Brenda Lee *Tina Davis* • Soupy Sales *Officer Pat McGovern* • Donnie Carter *Timmy Davis* • Butch Patrick *Billy Davis* • Jimmy Boyd *Tina's boyfriend* • Nancy Kulp *Miss Wilkins* ■ *Dir* Randall F Hood • *Scr* George W George, from a story by Judy George

Two Living, One Dead ★★ U

Psychological crime drama
1961 · UK/Swe · BW · 101mins

One postal clerk dies in an armed robbery, another resists and is acclaimed as a hero, the third hands over the cash and is branded a coward. This study of small town attitudes is based on a Swedish novel and filmed on location there by director Anthony Asquith with a strong British cast. It becomes an awkward hybrid, abandoning social critique for a melodramatic conclusion and never finding the right tone. AE

Virginia McKenna *Helen Berger* • Bill Travers *Anderson* • Patrick McGoohan *Berger* • Dorothy Alison *Esther Kester* • Alf Kjellin *Rogers* • Noel Willman *Inspector Johnson* • Pauline Jameson *Miss Larsen* ■ *Dir* Anthony Asquith • *Scr* Lindsay Galloway, from the novel *Två Levande och en Död* by Sigurd Wesley Christiansen

Two Loves ★

Drama
1961 · US · Colour · 99mins

This bizarre melodrama stars Shirley MacLaine as a teacher in New Zealand who drinks brandy for breakfast, burns on a short fuse and is probably bonkers. Her pupils love her. So does teaching colleague Laurence Harvey, a bit mad himself, but his amorous attentions are snubbed. MGM bungles everything about this hotbed of emotion in prim, middle-class New Zealand and makes it laughable in quite the wrong way. AT

Shirley MacLaine *Anna Vorontosov* • Laurence Harvey *Paul Lathrope* • Jack Hawkins *WWJ Abercrombie* • Nobu McCarthy *Whareparita* • Ronald Long *Headmaster Reardon* • Norah Howard *Mrs Cutter* • Juano Hernandez *Rauhuia* • Edmund Vargas *Matawhero* ■ *Dir* Charles Walters • *Scr* Ben Maddow, from the novel *Spinster* by Sylvia Ashton-Warner

Two Men in Manhattan ★★★

Crime
1959 · Fr · BW · 100mins

Having been forced to abandon two projects following *Bob Le Flambeur*, Jean-Pierre Melville somewhat understandably took a hands-on approach to this study in journalistic ethics. In addition to scripting, directing and starring, he also shot a good deal of the New York location footage himself, capturing the seedy underside of the city, while still giving it an irresistible allure. Melville's reporter teams with scoop-chasing photographer Pierre Grasset to track down a missing UN diplomat, only to fall out when they discover his corpse. A hard-nosed, cynical film with an unexpectedly poetic heart. DP. In English and French with subtitles.

Jean-Pierre Melville *Moreau* • Pierre Grasset *Delmas* • Michèle Bailly • Jean Darcante ■ *Dir/Scr* Jean-Pierre Melville

Two Men Went to War ★★★ PG

Second World War comedy drama
2002 · UK · Colour · 104mins

Had it been made 50 years ago, with Roger Livesey as the Great War veteran and the Ian Carmichael as his young charge, setting off together for occupied France with a knapsack of grenades, hellbent on taking a pop at Hitler, this fact-based story would have evolved into a much-loved tribute to British eccentricity. Even now, with Kenneth Cranham and Leo Bill as the ill-matched duo who go AWOL from the dental corps, it has considerable period feel and comic charm. But, as with *Dad's Army*, the humour also belies a shrewd social analysis that gives the combat finale that vital ring of authenticity. DP DVD

Kenneth Cranham *Sergeant Peter King* • Leo Bill *Private Leslie Cuthbertson* • Rosanna Lavelle *Emma Fraser* • Derek Jacobi *Major Merton* • Phyllida Law *Faith* • James Fleet *Major Bates* • Julian Glover *Colonel Hatchard* • Anthony Valentine *Sergeant Major Dudley* ■ *Dir* John Henderson • *Scr* Richard Everett, Christopher Villiers

Two-Minute Warning ★★

Thriller
1976 · US · Colour · 115mins

The recipient of an Oscar nomination for its editing, this interminable drama has all the character sophistication of a disaster movie. In a cast littered with guest stars, everyone is a loser of sorts, unlike the sniper at the NFL play-off and his police pursuer, who are both psychopaths. While the acting styles of John Cassavetes and Charlton Heston clash like cymbals, director Larry Peerce preoccupies himself with grandstanding camerawork that does little to heighten tension. DP. Contains violence and swearing.

Charlton Heston *Captain Peter Holly* • John Cassavetes *Sergeant Chris Button* • Martin Balsam *Sam McKeever* • Beau Bridges *Mike Ramsay* • Marilyn Hassett *Lucy* • David Janssen *Steve* • Jack Klugman *Stu Sandman* • Gena Rowlands *Janet* • Walter Pidgeon *Pickpocket* ■ *Dir* Larry Peerce • *Scr* Edward Hume, from the novel by George La Fountaine • *Editor* Walter Hanneman, Eve Newman

Two Moon Junction ★★ 18

Erotic drama
1988 · US · Colour · 100mins

Another soft porn flick from the stable of director Zalman King, with a poor plot forming an excuse for various pornographic encounters, but it's naff fun nevertheless. Sherilyn Fenn rejects her educated past to run off with hunk Richard Tyson. The couple are chased by her family and local law enforcers intent on stopping their adventures. Watch out for supermodel and future *Joan of Arc* star Milla Jovovich in one of her first acting attempts. A sequel, *Return to Two Moon Junction*, followed six years later. LH DVD

Sherilyn Fenn *April Delongpre* • Kristy McNichol *Patti-Jean* • Richard Tyson *Perry* • Louise Fletcher *Belle* • Burl Ives *Sheriff Earl Hawkins* • Martin Hewitt *Chad Douglas Fairchild* • Millie Perkins *Mrs Delongpre* • Don Galloway *Senator Delongpre* ■ *Dir* Zalman King • *Scr* Zalman King, from a story by Zalman King, MacGregor Douglas

The Two Mrs Carrolls ★★★ PG

Crime drama
1945 · US · BW · 94mins

The only teaming of two great movie icons, Humphrey Bogart and Barbara Stanwyck, this sordid tale about a wife-killer leaves much to be desired. Today, this nasty old tosh is resolutely entertaining, though you can still understand why Warners kept it on the shelf for a couple of years after it was filmed in 1945. Bogie is seriously miscast as the psychopathic artist murderer, Stanwyck is equally under-used as his intended victim, and the whole betrays its stage origins. TS

Humphrey Bogart *Geoffrey Carroll* • Barbara Stanwyck *Sally Morton Carroll* • Alexis Smith *Cecily Latham* • Nigel Bruce *Dr Tuttle* • Isobel Elsom *Mrs Latham* • Pat O'Moore [Patrick O'Moore] *Charles Fennington* ■ *Dir* Peter Godfrey • *Scr* Thomas Job, from the play by Martin Vale

Two Much ★ PG

Romantic comedy
1995 · Sp/US · Colour · 113mins

Making a good screwball comedy is an exact science, but unfortunately director Fernando Treuba fumbles with every aspect of this one, ultimately producing a stupid movie which most of the cast members are sure to omit from their CVs. Antonio Banderas comes off worst as the art dealer who romances socialite Melanie Griffith but then falls for her sister Daryl Hannah, causing him to pretend he actually has an identical twin. Cue lots of ridiculous situations and Banderas looking increasingly ill-at-ease. JB

Antonio Banderas *Art Dodge* • Melanie Griffith *Betty Kerner* • Daryl Hannah *Liz Kerner* • Danny Aiello *Gene Paletto* • Joan Cusack *Gloria* • Eli Wallach *Sheldon* • Gabino Diego *Manny* ■ *Dir* Fernando Trueba • *Scr* Fernando Trueba, David Trueba, from the novel by Donald E Westlake

Two Much Trouble ★★

Comedy 1995 · US · Colour · 88mins

Beverly D'Angelo plays an ex-con who babysits the spoilt kids of wealthy Ed Begley Jr and Carol Kane in this lacklustre, occasionally saccharine retread of that favourite Hollywood theme: little brats running rings around uncaring adults. The relentlessly juvenile script defeats the combined talents of the eclectic cast, and even children may find it is a little beneath them. JF. Contains swearing.

Beverly D'Angelo *Edie* • Brady Bluhm *Jason Van Arsdale* • Rachel Duncan *Bea Van Arsdale* • Ed Begley Jr *Paul Van Arsdale* • Carol Kane *Treva Van Arsdale* • Lisa Kudrow ■ *Dir/Scr* Michael James McDonald

Two Mules for Sister Sara ★★★★ 15

Western 1970 · US · Colour · 100mins

Clint Eastwood plays a quizzical, slightly bemused cowboy in this immensely enjoyable Don Siegel caper, saving nun Shirley MacLaine from a fate worse than death in the Mexican desert. The two leads are perfectly paired, and MacLaine in particular turns in a great comic performance as her ill-fitting habit begins to slip. Siegel keeps the tension and pace roaring along as he pitches them into the middle of the Mexican Revolution, though some may find the final, gory battle scene out of kilter with the light-hearted tone of the rest of the movie. SH [video] DVD

Clint Eastwood *Hogan* • Shirley MacLaine *Sister Sara* • Manolo Fabregas *Colonel Beltran* • Alberto Morin *General LeClaire* • Armando Silvestre *1st American* • John Kelly (3) *2nd American* • Enrique Lucero *3rd American* • David Estuardo *Juan* ■ *Dir* Don Siegel • *Scr* Albert Maltz, from a story by Budd Boetticher

Two O'Clock Courage ★

Murder mystery 1945 · US · BW · 66mins

It starts promisingly, with a bloodied Tom Conway staggering forward to lean on a signpost at a deserted city crossroads. But it goes downhill rapidly and stays there after Ann Rutherford's wisecracking cabbie picks him up and improbably decides to help Conway solve his case of amnesia. Anthony Mann's alert staging tries to bring some life to the verbose story, but it's beyond resuscitation. Jane Greer makes her screen debut as a drunken cutie, billed as Bettejane Greer. AE

Tom Conway *Man* • Ann Rutherford *Patty Mitchell* • Richard Lane *Haley* • Lester Matthews *Mark Evans* • Roland Drew *Steve Maitland* • Emory Parnell *Inspector Bill Brenner* • Bettejane Greer [Jane Greer] *Helen Carter* ■ *Dir* Anthony Mann • *Scr* Robert E Kent, from a novel by Gelett Burgess

Two of a Kind ★★ PG

Fantasy romantic comedy
1983 · US · Colour · 83mins

Five years on from *Grease*, John Travolta and Olivia Newton-John re-teamed for a fantasy romance about a couple used as guinea pigs by God in an experiment to prove that not all mortals are irredeemably corrupt. Played as a screwball comedy, it has its stupid moments, and its endearing ones, but not enough of them. True fans of the stars will probably quite like it. DA [video] DVD

John Travolta *Zach Melon* • Olivia Newton-John *Debbie Wylder* • Charles Durning *Charlie* • Oliver Reed *Beazley* • Beatrice Straight *Ruth* • Scatman Crothers *Earl* • Richard Bright *Stuart* ■ *Dir/Scr* John Herzfeld

The Two of Us ★★★★ U

Second World War comedy drama
1967 · Fr · BW · 86mins

Michel Simon won the best actor prize at Berlin for his work in Claude Berri's autobiographical tale about a Catholic, Pétain-supporting anti-Semite who unknowingly forms a close friendship with a young Jewish refugee. This is a superlative performance, as Simon humanises the fascist who never lets up for a second in his attempt to indoctrinate the boy with his hideous views. It's also a courageous and selfless piece of acting, as he allows young Alain Cohen to steal scene after scene as the irrepressible eight year-old who delights in deflating his host. DP. In French with English subtitles.

Michel Simon *Pépé* • Alain Cohen *Claude* • Luce Fabiole *Granny Mémé* • Roger Carel *Victor* • Paul Preboist *Maxime* ■ *Dir* Claude Berri • *Scr* Claude Berri, Gérard Brach, Michel Rivelin

Two on a Guillotine ★★

Mystery 1964 · US · BW · 107mins

To claim her magician father's estate, Connie Stevens (who also plays her deceased mother) has to spend a week in his scary mansion. A quintessential haunted house picture, produced and directed by TV's *Cannon* William Conrad. Cesar Romero has a lot of camp fun with better than average material. JG

Connie Stevens *Melinda Duquesne/Cassie Duquesne* • Dean Jones *Val Henderson* • Cesar Romero *John "Duke" Duquesne* • Parley Baer *"Buzz" Sheridan* • Virginia Gregg *Dolly Bast* • Connie Gilchrist *Ramona Ryerdon* ■ *Dir* William Conrad • *Scr* Henry Slesar, John Kneubuhl, from a story by Henry Slesar

Two or Three Things I Know about Her ★★★★ 15

Experimental drama
1966 · Fr · Colour · 83mins

Inspired by an article on high-rise prostitution and shot simultaneously with *Made in USA*, this is, according to Jean-Luc Godard, "a sociological essay in the form of a novel, written not with words, but with notes of music". Marina Vlady stars as the housewife hooker who turns tricks to survive in an increasingly consumerist society. But the real "Her" of the title is Paris, which cinematographer Raoul Coutard captures with a symphonic energy that matches Godard's audacious combination of ideas, images and sounds. A tad dated, but still daring, dazzling and dynamic. DP. In French with English subtitles. [video] DVD

Marina Vlady *Juliette Janson* • Anny Duperey *Marianne* • Roger Montsoret *Robert Janson* • Jean Narboni *Roger* • Christophe Bourseiller *Christophe* • Marie Bourseiller *Solange* • Raoul Lévy *The American* • Jean-Luc Godard *Narrator* ■ *Dir* Jean-Luc Godard • *Scr* Jean-Luc Godard, suggested by the article *Les Etoiles Filantes* by Catherine Vimenet in *Le Nouvel Observateur*

Two Pennyworth of Hope ★★★

Romantic comedy drama
1952 · It · BW · 102mins

Having established himself as perhaps the finest exponent of "calligraphism" or the literary period picture, Renato Castellani proved he was capable of tackling contemporary concerns with his rose-tinted trilogy of young love. This Neapolitan melodrama shared first prize at Cannes with Orson Welles's *Othello*. Set on the slopes of Vesuvius, the shamelessly optimistic story, in which Maria Fiore determines to persuade her parents that the hapless Vincenzo Musolino is worthy of her affection, stands in cosy contrast to the fading gloom of the neorealist era. DP. In Italian with English subtitles.

Vincenzo Musolino *Antonio* • Maria Fiore *Carmela* • Filomeno Russo *Antonio's mother* • Luigi Astarita *Carmela's father* • Luigi Barone *Priest* ■ *Dir* Renato Castellani • *Scr* Renato Castellani, Titina de Filippo, from a story by Renato Castellani, M Margadonna [Ettore Maria Margadonna]

Two People ★

Romance 1973 · US · Colour · 100mins

Robert Wise unwisely dives into the "youth market" with this romance between guilt-ridden draft dodger Peter Fonda and unhappy fashion model Lindsay Wagner. There's far too much "hey man" soul-searching and a rush of domestic crises that would occupy a TV soap for months. Wise's direction also seems to have been influenced by the worst excesses of the French New Wave and the intellectualism of Michelangelo Antonioni. AT

Peter Fonda *Evan Bonner* • Lindsay Wagner *Deirdre McCluskey* • Estelle Parsons *Barbara Newman* • Alan Fudge *Fitzgerald* • Philippe March *Gilles* • Frances Sternhagen *Mrs McCluskey* • Brian Lima *Marcus McCluskey* ■ *Dir* Robert Wise • *Scr* Richard DeRoy

Two Rode Together ★★ PG

Western 1961 · US · Colour · 104mins

This rather slow moving late John Ford western stars James Stewart and Richard Widmark, who both seem slightly ill at ease in underwritten roles as a cynical sheriff and a gallant cavalry officer out to rescue victims of Comanche raids. The Stewart character has most of the dialogue but none of the answers, and neither, one suspects, has director Ford. TS [video]

James Stewart *Guthrie McCabe* • Richard Widmark *Lt Jim Gary* • Shirley Jones *Marty Purcell* • Linda Cristal *Elena de la Madriaga* • Andy Devine *Sgt Darius P Posey* • John McIntire *Major Frazer* • Paul Birch *Edward Purcell* ■ *Dir* John Ford • *Scr* Frank Nugent, from the novel *Comanche Captives* by Will Cook

Two Seconds ★★★

Crime drama 1932 · US · BW · 68mins

The greatest decade for Warner Bros, the 1930s, was characterised by realist dramas and gangster movies, showing particular sympathy for blue-collar workers and the oppressed. Mervyn Le Roy's brisk and powerful adaptation stars Edward G Robinson as one such victim – a construction worker whose life during the Depression flashes before him in the seconds prior to his dying by execution. A sap tricked into marriage by a "taxi-dancer" who then betrays him, he accidentally kills his best friend and later shoots his wife. But he is shown accepting the consequences of a life at once pathetic yet decent in its simple humanity. BB

Edward G Robinson *John Allen* • Vivienne Osborne *Shirley Day* • Guy Kibbee *Bookie* • Preston Foster *Bud Clark* • J Carrol Naish *Tony* ■ *Dir* Mervyn LeRoy • *Scr* Harvey Thew, from the play by Elliott Lester

2 Seconds ★★★ 15

Romantic comedy drama
1998 · Can · Colour · 97mins

Charlotte Laurier plays a mountain-bike champion who finds it difficult to adjust to the pace of life after she becomes a courier in Montreal. However, her outlook is radically altered by her friendship with ex-racing repairman Dino Tavarone, whose tale of thwarted love convinces her never to let another opportunity slip by. Despite their age difference, Laurier and Tavarone have a sparkling chemistry, as well as an identical taste in women. Winning, if occasionally winsome, Manon Briand's comedy has an infectious charm. DP. In French with English subtitles. [video]

Charlotte Laurier *Laurie* • Dino Tavarone *Lorenzo* • Pascal Auclair *Leblond* • Yves Pelletier *Steff* • André Brassard *Gasket* ■ *Dir/Scr* Manon Briand

Two Sisters from Boston ★★★

Musical romantic comedy
1946 · US · BW · 112mins

Boston blue-blood Kathryn Grayson works as the belle of a Bowery nightspot to finance her opera studies. She conceals the fact from her family with the help of her initially outraged younger sister June Allyson and her boss Jimmy Durante, and achieves her ambitions. Sometimes very funny, and with some cute touches – along with famous tenor Lauritz Melchior strutting his stuff, and a very young and pretty Peter Lawford contributing to the romance – it's a charming dose of heavenly nonsense. RK

Kathryn Grayson *Abigail Chandler* • June Allyson *Martha Canford Chandler* • Lauritz Melchior *Olstrom* • Jimmy Durante *"Spike"* • Peter Lawford *Lawrence Patterson Jr* • Ben Blue *Wrigley* • Isobel Elsom *Aunt Jennifer* • Harry Hayden *Uncle Jonathan* ■ *Dir* Henry Koster • *Scr* Myles Connolly, James O'Hanlon, Harry Crane, Charles Previn, William Wymetal

Two Small Bodies ★

Crime drama 1993 · Ger · Colour · 85mins

There are some movies that you can tell instantly were made from stage plays. This unpleasant film only has two actors, Fred Ward and Suzy Amis. Amis plays a hostess in a strip joint whose two small children have disappeared, and Ward is the cop who conducts his interviews at her home. It's not really a mystery (the fate of the kids is discovered off camera), as the emphasis is on the psychosexual relationship that develops between the two characters. ST

Suzy Amis *Eileen Mahoney* • Fred Ward *Lieutenant Brann* ■ *Dir* Beth B • *Scr* Beth B, from the play by Neal Bell

Two Stage Sisters ★★★★★

Period melodrama
1964 · Chi · Colour · 114mins

Denounced for a formalism that supposedly undermined its political value, Xie Jin's period musical drama is one of the glories of pre-Cultural Revolution cinema. Rarely have colour, camera movement and composition been so harmoniously combined for what is, essentially, a backstage melodrama. Showgirls Xie Fang and Cao Yindi drift apart in wartime Shanghai, with the latter marrying in pursuit of material comfort, while the former begins to see the political light. Feminist tract, political thesis and nationalist paean it may be, but this is also an impeccably realised film that succeeds equally as art, propaganda and entertainment. DP. A Mandarin language film.

Xie Fang *Chunhua* • Cao Yindi *Yuehong* • Feng Ji *Xing* • Gao Yuansheng *Jiang Bo* • Shen Fengjuan *Xiao Xiang* ■ *Dir* Xie Jin • *Scr* Lin Gu, Xu Jin, Xie Jin

The Two Tars ★★★★★ U

Silent comedy 1928 · US · BW · 21mins

As an example of what Stan called "reciprocal destruction", this is one of the greatest of Laurel and Hardy's early silents. It features them as two sailors on leave from the USS *Oregon*, doing the kind of comic damage only they are capable of – from wrecking a gum machine to causing a traffic jam of mutilated cars. The girls they pick up on the way – Thelma Hill and Ruby Blaine – are only too happy to get a lift in the rented Model T, but they sneak off quickly when things get tough and bad-tempered characters such as

T

Edgar Kennedy appear. This has the classic final shot in which Stan and Ollie's tin lizzie has an argument with a train and slims down considerably. "Everybody follow them sailors," shouts an irate traffic cop. For years audiences have delighted in following that order. TH

Stan Laurel *Stan* • Oliver Hardy *Ollie* • Thelma Hill *Brunette coquette* • Ruby Blaine *Blonde coquette* • Charley Rogers *Man whose fenders are ripped back* • Edgar Kennedy *Family motorist* ■ *Dir* James Parrott • *Scr* Leo MacCarey, HM Walker (titles)

2001: a Space Odyssey ★★★★★ U

Science-fiction epic
1968 · UK/US · Colour · 135mins

Stanley Kubrick's seminal sci-fi work is now considered by many to be less a supreme piece of cinema than an interesting, innovative product of the 1960s. But the memorable celluloid images still strongly resonate, like the giant, vulnerable foetus floating through space and the tribe of apes painfully putting two and two together. It is Kubrick's haunting, stylised combination of music and visuals that gives *2001* its eerie, mesmerising quality, but even its most devoted disciples are hard pressed to tell you what it's actually about, and, as a slice of philosophy on how we all got started and where we ultimately go, the movie has little credence. Still, it's a must-see. SH

Keir Dullea *David "Dave" Bowman* • Gary Lockwood *Frank Poole* • William Sylvester *Dr Heywood Floyd* • Daniel Richter *Moonwatcher* • Leonard Rossiter *Smyslov* • Margaret Tyzack *Elena* • Robert Beatty *Halvorsen* • Sean Sullivan *Michaels* • Douglas Rain *HAL 9000* ■ *Dir* Stanley Kubrick • *Scr* Stanley Kubrick, Arthur C Clarke, from the short story *The Sentinel* by Arthur C Clarke in *Ten Story Fantasy*

2010 ★★★ PG

Science fiction 1984 · US · Colour · 111mins

Some spectacular special effects (the space walk transference) are the highlights of this unnecessary sequel to the monumental *2001: a Space Odyssey*, which quickly runs out of rocket fuel after a bright start. Based on the novel by Arthur C Clarke, writer/director Peter Hyams's earnest script unites Soviets and Americans to discover why astronaut Bowman vanished. The Black Monolith is back, but there is little of Stanley Kubrick's epic sense or masterfully ambiguous myths and mysteries. Instead, director Peter Hyams replaces them with banal over-explicitness. AJ

Roy Scheider *Heywood Floyd* • John Lithgow *Walter Curnow* • Helen Mirren *Tanya Kirbuk* • Bob Balaban *R Chandra* • Keir Dullea *Dave Bowman* • Douglas Rain *Voice of Hal 9000* • Madolyn Smith *Caroline Floyd* • Dana Elcar *Dimitri Moisevitch* ■ *Dir* Peter Hyams • *Scr* Peter Hyams, from the novel *2010: Odyssey Two* by Arthur C Clarke

2046 ★★ 12

Romantic science-fiction drama
2004 · HK/Fr/It/Chi · Colour · 123mins

Tony Leung once again stars as a writer living in a seedy Hong Kong hotel in the 1960s in this disappointing quasi-sequel to *In the Mood for Love*. Still obsessed with his earlier unconsummated love for married woman Maggie Cheung, his dreamy dalliances with three other women (Zhang Ziyi, Carina Lau, Gong Li) who move into room 2046 next door inspire him to write sci-fi stories that, although set in the year 2046, detail his desire to recapture past memories. Pretentious. AJ. In Cantonese with English subtitles. Contains sex scenes.

Tony Leung Chiu-Wai [Tony Leung (2)] *Chow Mo-Wan* • Gong Li *Su Lizhen* • Zhang Ziyi *Bai Ling* • Maggie Cheung *slz 1960* • Takuya Kimura *Tak* • Faye Wong *Wang Jingwen/wjw 1967* • Carina Lau *Lulu/Mimi cc 1966* • Wang Sum *Mr Wang/Train captain* ■ *Dir/Scr* Wong Kar-Wai

Two Thousand Maniacs! ★★ 18

Horror 1964 · US · Colour · 87mins

Just outside the southern town of Pleasant Valley, whose citizens were massacred by Union troops during the Civil War, the dead villagers reappear to wreak horrific revenge on six northern tourists. While as badly acted and technically inept as any Herschell G Lewis drive-in exploiter, the cheaply graphic effects still carry a potent charge and this was the nearest the agony auteur ever got to a crossover success. AJ

Connie Mason *Terry Adams* • Thomas Wood [William Kerwin] *Tom White* • Jeffrey Allen *Mayor Buckman* • Ben Moore *Lester* • Shelby Livingston *Bea Miller* ■ *Dir* Herschell G Lewis [Herschell Gordon Lewis] • *Scr* Herschell G Lewis [Herschell Gordon Lewis], from his story

Two Thousand Women ★★★ PG

Second World War drama
1944 · UK · BW · 92mins

This is an effective piece of propaganda, with an uplifting plot (co-written by Launder and Sidney Gilliat), a celebration of British pluck, a healthy spot of Nazi bashing and a dash of gallows humour. However, while this was just what Churchill ordered in 1944, it weighs a little heavily today. Fortunately, among the two thousand of the title are some of the finest actresses of the time, whose appeal remains undiminished. DP

Phyllis Calvert *Freda Thompson* • Flora Robson *Miss Manningford* • Patricia Roc *Rosemary Brown* • Renee Houston *Maud Wright* • Anne Crawford *Margaret Long* • Jean Kent *Bridie Johnson* • Reginald Purdell *Alec Harvey* ■ *Dir* Frank Launder • *Scr* Frank Launder, Sidney Gilliat, from a story by Frank Launder, Michael Pertwee

Two Tickets to Broadway ★★★ U

Musical comedy 1951 · US · Colour · 106mins

There's a super cast and a nice line in satire in this immensely likeable Technicolor musical that sends up the then-new medium of television. Bob Crosby gives a superb mickey-take of his famous brother Bing, the girls are particularly scintillating and the Busby Berkeley-choreographed routines are all you'd expect. Tony Martin is a bit of a pudding in the lead, but amiable sidekick Eddie Bracken more than compensates. Lawyer-turned-director James V Kern wisely stands back and lets the musical numbers and comedy skits work for themselves. TS

Tony Martin *Dan Carter* • Janet Leigh *Nancy Peterson* • Gloria DeHaven *Hannah Holbrook* • Eddie Bracken *Lew Conway* • Ann Miller *Joyce Campbell* • Barbara Lawrence *"Foxy" Rogers* • Bob Crosby • Joe Smith *Harry* • Charles Dale *Leo* ■ *Dir* James V Kern • *Scr* Sid Silvers, Hal Kanter, from a story by Sammy Cahn

[Two] Un Couple Epatant ★★★ PG

Romantic comedy
2002 · Fr/Bel · Colour · 93mins

This French farce is an abrupt shift in tone from the *noirish* pessimism of the first part of Lucas Belvaux's trilogy (*[One] Cavale*). But while it serves as pleasing comic relief between its two weightier companions, their intensity only emphasises this tale's triviality and over-reliance on unlikely contrivance. That said, Ornella Muti revels in the role of the suspicious bourgeoise whose conviction that husband François Morel is sleeping with his secretary and/or her teaching colleague (Dominique Blanc), prompts her to hire smitten cop Gilbert Melki to tail him. Followed by *[Three] Après la Vie*. DP. In French with English subtitles. Contains swearing and violence.

Ornella Muti *Cécile Costes* • François Morel *Alain Costes* • Dominique Blanc *Agnès Manise* • Gilbert Melki *Pascal Manise* • Valérie Mairesse *Claire* • Catherine Frot *Jeanne Rivet* • Lucas Belvaux *Pierre* ■ *Dir/Scr* Lucas Belvaux

Two Way Stretch ★★★★ U

Prison comedy 1960 · UK · BW · 83mins

Fans of Peter Sellers rate this British venture, made before he started to believe his own publicity, as one of the best things he did. It's a prison comedy with a snarling stand-off between cocky convict Sellers, his cellmates Bernard Cribbins and David Lodge, and paranoid warden Lionel Jeffries. The plot – about a group of prisoners trying to break back into jail after a heist – is wonderfully developed and there are delightful cameos along the way. TH

Peter Sellers *Dodger Lane* • Wilfrid Hyde White *Reverend Basil "Soapy" Fowler* • David Lodge *Jelly Knight* • Bernard Cribbins *Lennie Price* • Maurice Denham *Cmdr Horatio Bennet, the prison governor* • Lionel Jeffries *Sidney Crout* • Irene Handl *Mrs Price* • Liz Fraser *Ethel* • Beryl Reid *Miss Pringle* ■ *Dir* Robert Day • *Scr* John Warren, Len Heath, Alan Hackney, from the story by John Warren

Two Weeks in Another Town ★★★★

Melodrama 1962 · US · Colour · 106mins

If you think film-makers are unstable, this overwrought but convincing fable about Hollywood has-beens will confirm it. Kirk Douglas is the on-the-skids actor in Rome for a small part in a low-budget movie directed by the equally struggling Edward G Robinson, but he's hampered by ex-wife Cyd Charisse and jet-set corruption. This examines the soul-destroying insecurity that goes with celebrity, and it's extraordinarily well acted, with the tricksy style suiting the devious characters. TH

Kirk Douglas *Jack Andrus* • Edward G Robinson *Maurice Kruger* • Cyd Charisse *Carlotta* • George Hamilton *Davie Drew* • Dahlia Lavi *Veronica* • Claire Trevor *Clara Kruger* • James Gregory *Brad Byrd* • Rosanna Schiaffino *Barzelli* • Joanna Roos *Janet Bark* ■ *Dir* Vincente Minnelli • *Scr* Charles Schnee, from the novel by Irwin Shaw

Two Weeks Notice ★★ 12

Romantic comedy
2002 · US/Aus · Colour · 96mins

Sandra Bullock plays a liberal lawyer who fights for environmental causes; Hugh Grant is a real estate tycoon who plans to knock down her local community centre in Coney Island to build condominiums. She agrees to work for him if he doesn't go ahead with the demolitionBullock ends up running the hapless tycoon's life until she gets fed up, hands in her (two weeks) notice and quits. The formulaic plot is not the main problem here: it's Bullock and Grant. They're just trying too hard and with little result. StH

Sandra Bullock *Lucy Kelson* • Hugh Grant *George Wade* • Alicia Witt *June Carter* • Dana Ivey *Ruth Kelson* • Robert Klein *Larry Kelson* • Heather Burns *Meryl* • David Haig *Howard Wade* ■ *Dir/Scr* Marc Lawrence (2)

Two Women ★★★ 15

Second World War drama
1960 · It/Fr · BW · 99mins

Two Women marked the graduation of Sophia Loren from pouting sex-kitten to major league actress as she and her daughter experience the ravages of war, the desolation of being refugees and the horror of rape following the Allied bombing of Rome. Filmed in the neorealist style of De Sica's earlier classic, *Bicycle Thieves*, the picture earned Loren an Oscar – the first ever awarded to a non-American actor or actress performing in a foreign language. It was a feat not repeated until Roberto Benigni won in 1999 for *Life is Beautiful*. AT. In Italian with English subtitles. Contains violence and some swearing.

Sophia Loren *Cesira* • Jean-Paul Belmondo *Michele* • Raf Vallone *Giovanni* • Eleanora Brown *Rosetta* • Renato Salvatori *Florindo* • Carlo Ninchi *Michele's father* • Andrea Checchi *Fascist* ■ *Dir* Vittorio De Sica • *Scr* Cesare Zavattini, Vittorio De Sica, Alberto Moravia

Two Years before the Mast ★★★

Drama 1946 · US · BW · 97mins

They say worse things happen at sea, and they don't come any worse than serving under Howard Da Silva's martinet of a captain in this grim saga of 19th-century seafaring based on a classic book which aimed at reforming sailors' working conditions. Alan Ladd is the shipowner's son, shanghaied into serving under Da Silva and soon stripped to the waist for a flogging. Director John Farrow had a real-life passion for the sea and this lavishly staged and strongly cast production (with William Bendix, Barry Fitzgerald and Brian Donlevy as members of the crew) is the best of his several maritime adventures. AE

Alan Ladd *Charles Stewart* • Brian Donlevy *Richard Henry Dana* • William Bendix *Amazeen* • Howard Da Silva *Captain Francis Thompson* • Barry Fitzgerald *Dooley* • Esther Fernandez *Maria Dominguez* • Albert Dekker *Brown* ■ *Dir* John Farrow • *Scr* Seton I Miller, George Bruce, from the novel by Richard Henry Dana Jr

Twogether ★★ 18

Drama 1994 · US · Colour · 117mins

This wry look at modern love is not quite as trite as the title suggests. It's a twist on the old "morning after the night before" story, as artist Nick Cassavetes and environmental activist Brenda Bakke get drunk, get married, conceive and get divorced – although not necessarily in that order. Poking none-too-subtle fun at 1990s hedonism, this could have done with less lust and more laughs. DP

Nick Cassavetes *John Madler* • Brenda Bakke *Allison McKenzie* • Jeremy Piven *Arnie* • Jim Beaver *Oscar* • Tom Dugan *Paul* • Damian London *Mark Saffron* ■ *Dir/Scr* Andrew Chiaramonte

Tycoon ★★★ U

Drama 1947 · US · Colour · 123mins

John Wayne may seem unlikely casting as a railroad engineer in this epic saga, but he's actually very good at conveying steely determination required of his character. It's certainly entertaining enough, though a stronger director than Richard Wallace may well have got more out of the romance between the Duke and mine-owner's daughter Laraine Day. Nevertheless, there's a very distinguished supporting cast and it's shot in exceptionally fine Technicolor. TS

John Wayne *Johnny Munroe* • Laraine Day *Maura Alexander* • Cedric Hardwicke *Frederick Alexander* • Judith Anderson *Miss Braithwaite*

T

• James Gleason *Pop Mathews* • Anthony Quinn *Ricky* • Grant Withers *Fog Harris* ■ *Dir* Richard Wallace • *Scr* Borden Chase, John Twist, from a novel by CE Scoggins

Typhoon ★★

Romantic adventure
1940 · US · Colour · 70mins

After Sam Goldwyn borrowed Dorothy Lamour and had a huge hit with *The Hurricane*, the star's contract studio, Paramount, tried to go one better with *Typhoon*, photographing their famous "Sarong Girl" in glorious Technicolor. It's set on an island in the Pacific and the irretrievably silly plot has Lamour as a castaway since childhood who's discovered by a couple of sailors. The rest of the action involves the stock ingredients of a South Seas romantic adventure, with Robert Preston as Lamour's amour. RK

Dorothy Lamour *Dea* • Robert Preston *Johnny Potter* • Lynne Overman *Skipper Joe* • J Carrol Naish *Mekaike* ■ *Dir* Louis King • *Scr* Allen Rivkin, from a story by Steve Fisher

UFO ★★★ 18

Science-fiction comedy
1993 · UK · Colour · 75mins

Ultra-blue comedian Roy "Chubby" Brown made his screen debut in this raucous, very British sci-fi comedy. (Not since Sid Field had a comic gone direct from stage to film without doing TV in between). When Brown is being his cheekily offensive self, it is often hard to suppress a smile. But when he is abducted by female extraterrestrials, who punish him for his sexism, the plot goes to pieces, entire scenes make no sense and the laughs are few. A pity that a live act of undoubted talent was not better coached for films. ("Contains swearing" is putting it mildly.) DM [video]

Roy "Chubby" Brown • Sara Stockbridge *Zoe* • Amanda Symonds *Ava* • Roger Lloyd Pack *Solo* • Shirley Anne Field *Supreme commander* • Sue Lloyd *Judge* • Kiran Shah *Genghis Khan* • Kenny Baker (2) *Casanova* ■ *Dir* Tony Dow • *Scr* Richard Hall, Simon Wright, Roy "Chubby" Brown

U-571 ★★★ 12

Second World War action thriller
2000 · US · Colour · 111mins

This rip-roaring throwback to the wartime adventures of old finds Matthew McConaughey as a rookie submarine skipper in charge of a crippled U-boat after a secret plot to steal an Enigma code machine from the Nazis goes pear-shaped in the middle of the Atlantic. Since it was British sailors who got hold of the Enigma, it's a tad galling to see the likes of Bill Paxton, Harvey Keitel and Jon Bon Jovi take the credit. Not a patch on Wolfgang Petersen's seminal *Das Boot*, Jonathan Mostow's film does at least deliver its fair share of undemanding popcorn entertainment. NS. Contains swearing. [video] DVD

Matthew McConaughey *Lt Andrew Tyler* • Bill Paxton *Lt Commander Mike Dahlgren* • Harvey Keitel *Chief Klough* • Jon Bon Jovi *Lt Peter Emmett* • David Keith *Marine Major Coonan* ■ *Dir* Jonathan Mostow • *Scr* Jonathan Mostow, Sam Montgomery, David Ayer, from a story by Jonathan Mostow

UHF ★★ PG

Comedy
1989 · US · Colour · 92mins

Comic musician "Weird Al" Yankovic (who co-wrote the script) plays a slacker who takes over the management of a failing TV station, and is soon producing bizarre yet top-rated shows, raising the ire of rival TV station manager Kevin McCarthy. Michael Richards gives a side-splittingly funny performance as a simple-minded janitor, and the occasional laughs found in the samples of the TV programming make this fun for those willing to put their brain in neutral. KB [video] DVD

"Weird Al" Yankovic *George Newman* • Victoria Jackson *Teri* • Kevin McCarthy *RJ Fletcher* • Michael Richards *Stanley Spadowski* • David Bowe *Bob* • Stanley Brock *Uncle Harvey* • Anthony Geary *Philo* • Trinidad Silva *Raul Hernandez* ■ *Dir* Jay Levey • *Scr* Al Yankovic ["Weird Al" Yankovic], Jay Levey

US Marshals ★★ 15

Action thriller 1998 · US · Colour · 125mins

This is not so much a belated sequel to *The Fugitive* as a rehash, with Tommy Lee Jones reprising his Oscar-winning role. In place of Harrison Ford we have Wesley Snipes, and in place of a murdered wife we have a corkscrew plot about the CIA. Former editor Stuart Baird keeps the action rolling along in a rather monotonous manner and characterisation is limited to the odd one-liner before the next big bang. AT. Contains violence and swearing. [video] DVD

Tommy Lee Jones *Chief Deputy Marshal Samuel Gerard* • Wesley Snipes *Mark Sheridan* • Robert Downey Jr *John Royce* • Joe Pantoliano *Deputy Marshal Cosmo Renfro* • Daniel Roebuck *Deputy Marshal Biggs* • Tom Wood *Deputy Marshal Newman* • LaTanya Richardson *Deputy Marshal Cooper* • Irène Jacob *Marie* • Kate Nelligan *US Marshal Walsh* ■ *Dir* Stuart Baird • *Scr* John Pogue, from the characters created by Roy Huggins

U Turn ★★★★ 18

Black comedy thriller
1997 · US/Fr · Colour · 119mins

After the information overload of *Nixon* and the controversy of *Natural Born Killers*, Oliver Stone directed this low-budget, compact thriller. It's a rarity from the normally serious director – a surreal black comedy, starring Sean Penn as the mysterious drifter who arrives in Superior, Arizona, and becomes involved in a small-town conspiracy involving local flirt Jennifer Lopez and her husband Nick Nolte. As a sustained mood piece, the movie is a triumph. AT. Contains swearing, violence and sex scenes. [video] DVD

Sean Penn *Bobby Cooper* • Jennifer Lopez *Grace McKenna* • Nick Nolte *Jake McKenna* • Powers Boothe *Sheriff Potter* • Claire Danes *Jenny* • Joaquin Phoenix *Toby N Tucker* • Billy Bob Thornton *Darrell* • Jon Voight *Blind man* • Julie Hagerty *Flo* • Bo Hopkins *Ed* • Liv Tyler *Girl in bus station* ■ *Dir* Oliver Stone • *Scr* John Ridley, from his novel *Stray Dogs*

U2 Rattle and Hum ★★★ 15

Concert documentary
1988 · US · Colour and BW · 94mins

After the very wonderful *This Is Spinal Tap*, it's hard to take any "rockumentary" seriously these days, particularly one about the ever sincere U2. In fact, the Irish band even make a very moving visit to Gracelands during their 1987–88 North American tour. That said, this is stylishly shot in a mixture of grainy black and white and colour by Phil Joanou, there's a scene-stealing performance from blues legend BB King and the concert footage is stunning. JF [video]

Dir Phil Joanou • *Cinematographer* Robert Brinkmann, Jordan Cronenweth

UFOria ★★★ PG

Science-fiction comedy
1980 · US · Colour · 89mins

Grocery store cashier and born-again Christian Cindy Williams awaits the appearance of a flying saucer, which she believes will bring salvation. Her boyfriend Fred Ward works for phoney evangelist Harry Dean Stanton who intends to exploit the "God is an astronaut" phenomenon for all that it's worth. Made in 1980 but shelved until the mid-1980s, this is an amiable, oddball movie that, on its eventual release, picked up quite a few admirers. The acting is fine and the piece, while undisciplined in places, has charm. DF [video]

Cindy Williams *Arlene* • Harry Dean Stanton *Brother Bud* • Fred Ward *Sheldon* • Robert Gray *Emile* • Darrell Larson *Toby* • Harry Carey Jr *George Martin* • Hank Worden *Colonel* ■ *Dir/Scr* John Binder

Ugetsu Monogatari ★★★★★ PG

Period melodrama 1953 · Jpn · BW · 92mins

Drawing on two stories by Akinari Ueda and one by Guy de Maupassant, this ethereal *jidai-geki* (Japanese period drama) won a top prize at Venice and confirmed Kenji Mizoguchi's reputation in the west. Set during the 16th-century civil wars, the story concerns two peasants whose weakness spells disaster for their wives. Farmer Sakae Ozawa's dream of becoming a samurai precipitates the rape of Mitsuko Mito, while potter Masayuki Mori's obsession with the ghostly Machiko Kyo results in the death of Kinuyo Tanaka. In exploring the transience of happiness and the injustice of patriarchal society, Mizoguchi makes lyrical use of gliding long takes that reinforce his material and mystical themes. It's a work of sheer genius. DP. A Japanese language film. [video]

Machiko Kyo *Lady Wakasa* • Masayuki Mori *Genjuro* • Kinuyo Tanaka *Miyagi* • Sakae Ozawa [Eitaro Ozawa] *Tobei* • Mitsuko Mito *Ohama* ■ *Dir* Kenji Mizoguchi • *Scr* Matsutaro Kawaguchi, Yoshikata Yoda, from the stories *Asaji Ga Yado* and *Jasei No In* from *Ugetsu Monogatari* by Akinari Ueda and from the story *Décoré!* by Guy de Maupassant • *Cinematographer* Kazuo Miyagawa

The Ugly ★★ 18

Horror 1996 · NZ · Colour · 89mins

Kiwi Scott Reynolds's first feature revolves around a male psycho being interviewed by a female shrink and was cheekily dubbed by one wag "The Silence of the New Zealand Lambs". It's all style (for some reason the colour scheme is almost entirely blue and red) and not enough content. The complex flashback structure is deliberately disorienting; this and lots of gory bloodletting make for a disturbing, but rarely pulse-pounding, experience. DM. Contains swearing, violence. [video]

Paolo Rotondo *Simon Cartwright* • Rebecca Hobbs *Dr Karen Shumaker* • Roy Ward *Dr Marlowe* • Vanessa Byrnes *Julie, aged 25* • Sam Wallace *Simon, aged 13* • Paul Glover *Phillip* ■ *Dir/Scr* Scott Reynolds

The Ugly American ★★★ PG

Political drama 1963 · US · Colour · 115mins

Marlon Brando stars in one of his least known roles, as the American ambassador to Sarkhan, an Asian state divided between north and south, capitalist and communist. Brando intended this as a hard-hitting critique of American foreign policy and a movie that supported the work of the UN – he even cast his sister, Jocelyn, as a UN aid worker. But as usual with Brando, things got rather muddled, the studio interfered and no one could make a decision about anything – least of all the director, who shot it in Thailand. But despite its obvious flaws and bungled scenes, it's eerily prophetic about the Vietnam war. TS [video]

Marlon Brando *Harrison Carter MacWhite* • Eiji Okada *Deong* • Sandra Church *Marion MacWhite* • Pat Hingle *Homer Atkins* • Arthur Hill *Grainger* • Jocelyn Brando *Emma Atkins* • Kukrit Pramoj *Prime Minister Kwen Sai* ■ *Dir* George Englund • *Scr* Stewart Stern, from the novel by William J Lederer, Eugene Burdick

The Ugly Dachshund ★★★ U

Comedy 1966 · US · Colour · 89mins

Ideal entertainment for dog lovers everywhere, this Disney story is about a Great Dane called Brutus who's brought up with dachshunds and thinks he's one of them – however tall he gets. Dean Jones and Suzanne Pleshette are the human stars having to face up to the havoc caused in this charming family fare. Barking mad, maybe, but delightfully so. TH [video]

U

Dean Jones *Mark Garrison* • Suzanne Pleshette *Fran Garrison* • Charlie Ruggles [Charles Ruggles] *Dr Pruitt* • Kelly Thordsen *Officer Carmody* • Parley Baer *Mel Chadwick* • Robert Kino *Mr Toyama* • Mako *Kenji* • Charles Lane (2) *Judge* ■ *Dir* Norman Tokar • *Scr* Albert Aley, from the book *Dogs in an Omnibus* by Gladys Bronwyn Stern

Ulee's Gold ★★★★ 15

Drama 1997 · US · Colour · 112mins

The winner of a Golden Globe (though denied a best actor Oscar), Peter Fonda returned from years in the cinematic wilderness to give the best performance of his career in this slow-burning southern drama. Fonda meticulously builds up the character of the Florida beekeeper and Vietnam veteran who has to interrupt his strict routine to rescue his estranged daughter-in-law and tackle the villains double-crossed by his jailed son. Wisely, director Victor Nunez lets the pace roll as languorously as Tupelo honey dripping off a comb. With so much empty entertainment around, this is a rare treat. DP. Contains some swearing, sexual references and violence. DVD

Peter Fonda *Ulysses "Ulee" Jackson* • Patricia Richardson *Connie Hope* • Jessica Biel *Casey Jackson* • J Kenneth Campbell *Sheriff Bill Floyd* • Christine Dunford *Helen Jackson* • Steven Flynn *Eddie Flowers* • Dewey Weber *Ferris Dooley* ■ *Dir/Scr* Victor Nunez

Ultimate Betrayal ★★★ 15

Drama based on a true story
1994 · US · Colour · 93mins

Donald Wrye's film is a well-acted, thoughtful and harrowing tale about the abuse lurking beneath the surface of a seemingly stable American family, when the youngest daughter (Ally Sheedy) sues her father (Henry Czerny) who, she alleges, molested his children when they were young. However, not all the siblings are keen to see their past raked over in public. There are moving performances and Wrye's direction is level-headed, even though this TV movie does occasionally tip into melodrama. SH DVD

Marlo Thomas *Sharon Rodgers* • Mel Harris *Susan Rodgers* • Ally Sheedy *Mary Rodgers* • Kathryn Dowling *Beth Rodgers* • Eileen Heckart *Sarah McNeil* ■ *Dir* Donald Wrye • *Scr* Gregory Goodell

The Ultimate Warrior ★★★★ 15

Science-fiction thriller
1975 · US · Colour · 89mins

Ecological catastrophes have left New York in ruins and under Max von Sydow's ruthless leadership. Yul Brynner is the "street fighter" who guides his own posse of survivors to a better life away from such post-Armageddon tyranny. This is exciting, intelligent stuff from Robert Clouse, with loads of ingenious details and chilling moments. The final chase is a model of gripping suspense. AJ. Contains swearing. DVD

Yul Brynner *Carson* • Max von Sydow *The Baron* • Joanna Miles *Melinda* • William Smith *Carrot* • Richard Kelton *Cal* • Stephen McHattie *Robert* • Darrell Zwerling *Silas* ■ *Dir/Scr* Robert Clouse

Ulysses ★★★ U

Adventure 1954 · It · Colour · 99mins

Several Italians plus classy Hollywood hacks Ben Hecht and Irwin Shaw laboured on this film of Homer's *Odyssey*, but whenever the actors open their mouths the movie loses its credibility (and the dubbing doesn't help). However, Kirk Douglas has tremendous presence – even barefoot and in a mini-skirt – on the long commute home from the Trojan wars and going in to battle with the Cyclops, sultry Sirens and Anthony Quinn. The special effects are cheap and wonky but the movie has an élan that makes it hard to resist. AT. Italian dialogue dubbed into English.

Kirk Douglas *Ulysses* • Silvana Mangano *Penelope/Circe* • Anthony Quinn *Antinous* • Rossana Podesta *Nausicaa* • Sylvie *Euriclea* • Daniel Ivernel *Euriloco* • Jacques Dumesnil *Alicinous* ■ *Dir* Mario Camerini • *Scr* Franco Brusati, Mario Camerini, Ennio De Concini, Hugh Gray, Ben Hecht, Ivo Perilli, Irwin Shaw, from the poem *The Odyssey* by Homer

Ulysses ★★★ 15

Fantasy drama
1967 · US/UK · Colour · 126mins

If ever a great novel was unfilmable, this is it – James Joyce's sublime chronicle of Dublin Jew Leopold Bloom's long night's journey into day. Milo O'Shea is poignant as everyman Bloom and Barbara Jefford is superb as his rancid, randy wife Molly, but the enthusiasm of producer/director/co-writer Joseph Strick just isn't enough to lift Joyce's classic work from the pages and bring it to life. A flawed enterprise, the film is partly salvaged by the use of genuine Dublin locations and the marvellous performances of the mainly Irish cast. TH DVD

Barbara Jefford *Molly Bloom* • Milo O'Shea *Leopold Bloom* • Maurice Roëves *Stephen Dedalus* • TP McKenna *Buck Mulligan* • Martin Dempsey *Simon Dedalus* • Sheila O'Sullivan *May Goulding Dedalus* ■ *Dir* Joseph Strick • *Scr* Joseph Strick, Fred Haines, from the novel by James Joyce

Ulysses' Gaze ★★★★ PG

Epic drama 1995 · Gr/Fr/It · Colour · 169mins

Harvey Keitel stars as a Greek film-maker who goes in search of his Balkan roots in director Theodorus Angelopoulos's lengthy and haunting political fable. Clearly based on Angelopoulos's own experiences, the film slips between past and present, with both classical and personal allusions, until, by the end of a bleak odyssey of self-discovery, the film-maker has learned more than he ever wanted to know about his former home. This gently unfolding epic drama has an assurance that's matched by its audacious courage. AJ. In English and Greek with subtitles.

Harvey Keitel *A* • Maia Morgenstern *Woman* • Erland Josephson *Preserver* • Thanassis Vengos *Chauffeur* • Yorgos Michalakopoulos *Correspondent* • Dora Volonaki *Old woman (Athens)* ■ *Dir* Theodoros Angelopoulos [Theo Angelopoulos] • *Scr* Theodoros Angelopoulos, Tonino Guerra, Petro Markaris

Ulzana's Raid ★★★★ 18

Western 1972 · US · Colour · 96mins

This was attacked by some for being a reactionary return to the depiction of native Americans as bloodthirsty savages and mocked by others for its attempts to combine violent action with diatribes about racial prejudice. Yet Robert Aldrich's powerful 1970s western also has many champions, who see it as both a bold Vietnam allegory and an attempt to restore a semblance of historical accuracy to events coloured by decades of horse-opera exploitation and liberal revisionism. Burt Lancaster is superb as the scout saddened by conflict, while Alan Sharp's script and Joseph Biroc's cinematography are first class. AT. Contains violence, some swearing and brief nudity. DVD

Burt Lancaster *McIntosh* • Bruce Davison *Lt Garnett DeBuin* • Jorge Luke *Ke-Ni-Tay* • Richard Jaeckel *Sergeant* • Joaquin Martinez *Ulzana* • Lloyd Bochner *Captain Gates* • Karl Swenson *Rukeyser* ■ *Dir* Robert Aldrich • *Scr* Alan Sharp

Umberto D ★★★★★ PG

Drama 1952 · It · BW · 85mins

The ideal film," wrote Cesare Zavattini, the theoretical father of neorealism, "would be 90 minutes in the life of a man to whom nothing happens." Shot on location, with a non-professional cast and an attention to detail that allows the viewer to discover the emotional or dramatic content of a scene, Vittorio De Sica's poignant study of an ageing civil servant, ostracised by the society he'd so faithfully served, comes close to fulfilling that vision. Fighting despair with dignity, Carlo Battisti is outstanding, whether coddling his devoted dog, Flike, or relishing his chats with pregnant maid, Maria-Pia Casilio. A sublime piece of humanist, observational cinema. DP. In Italian with English subtitles.. DVD

Carlo Battisti *Umberto Domenico Ferrari* • Maria-Pia Casilio *Maria* • Lina Gennari *Landlady* • Alberto Albani Barbieri *Fiancé* • Elena Rea *Sister* • Ileana Simova *Surprised woman in the bedroom* • Memmo Carotenuto *Voice of light for Umberto in hospital* ■ *Dir* Vittorio De Sica • *Scr* Cesare Zavattini, Vittorio De Sica, from a story by Cesare Zavattini

The Umbrellas of Cherbourg ★★★★★ U

Musical 1964 · Fr/W Ger · Colour · 86mins

Everything is sung – even the most mundane dialogue – in director Jacques Demy's enchanting French throwback to the Hollywood musicals of the late 1920s. The stunning design (Cherbourg citizens allowed their buildings to be painted pink and red) and Catherine Deneuve's ethereal performance add to the fairy-tale qualities of the haunting love story between a shop girl and a garage attendant. It's when he leaves her pregnant to fight in the Algerian War that Demy's tuneful heartbreaker reaches the dizzy romantic heights. Michel Legrand's gorgeous score includes the standard *I Will Wait for You* and *Watch What Happens*. Absolutely beguiling. AJ. In French with English subtitles. DVD

Catherine Deneuve *Geneviève Emery* • Nino Castelnuovo *Guy Foucher* • Anne Vernon *Madame Emery* • Ellen Farner *Madeleine* • Marc Michel *Roland Cassard* • Mireille Perrey *Aunt Elise* • Jean Champion *Aubin* • Harald Wolff *Dubourg* ■ *Dir/Scr* Jacques Demy

The Unbearable Lightness of Being ★★★ 18

Romantic political drama
1988 · US · Colour · 165mins

The problem of coming to terms with reality is the simplest explanation for this blatant, European-style art film directed by American Philip Kaufman. Lengthily elaborated from Milan Kundera's bestseller, it concerns a womanising surgeon (Daniel Day-Lewis) whose main loves are sacred (Juliette Binoche) and profane (Lena Olin), and how their involvement collides with the communist authorities in Czechoslovakia. Some wonderful atmospherics of a besieged culture don't make up for the fact that, at nearly three hours, it runs out of important things to say. TH. Contains swearing and sex scenes. DVD

Daniel Day-Lewis *Tomas* • Juliette Binoche *Tereza* • Lena Olin *Sabina* • Derek De Lint *Franz* • Erland Josephson *The Ambassador* • Pavel Landowsky *Pavel* • Donald Moffat *Chief Surgeon* ■ *Dir* Philip Kaufman • *Scr* Philip Kaufman, Jean-Claude Carrière, from the novel by Milan Kundera

The Unbelievable Truth ★★★ 15

Drama 1989 · US · Colour · 86mins

Hal Hartley's feature debut (shot in just 11 days) is the closest thing yet to a suburban western – a sort of *Shane* on Long Island. Robert Burke is terse and mysterious as the man in black who gives discontented Adrienne Shelly something more to think about than parental suffocation, nuclear holocaust and teenage romance. Full of quirky conversations and eccentric characters, but with occasionally overintrusive direction. DP. Contains swearing. DVD

Adrienne Shelly *Audry Hugo* • Robert John Burke [Robert Burke] *Josh Hutton* • Christopher Cooke [Chris Cooke] *Vic Hugo* • Julia McNeal *Pearl* • Katherine Mayfield *Liz Hugo* • Gary Sauer *Emmet* • Mark Bailey *Mike* • David Healy *Todd Whitbread* • Edie Falco *Jane, a waitress* ■ *Dir/Scr* Hal Hartley

The Unborn ★★ 18

Horror 1991 · US · Colour · 80mins

This schlocky film has a young wife convinced that her doctor has inseminated her with mutant sperm. She's proved right when the offspring avoids abortion and goes on the rampage. The film earns a second star simply for the earnestness of some of the actors, who must have realised what twaddle they were in, but put a brave face on things anyway. Aptly, the film gave birth to a sequel three years later. DA

Brooke Adams *Virginia Marshall* • Jeff Hayenga *Brad Marshall* • James Karen *Dr Richard Meyerling* • K Callan *Martha* • Jane Cameron *Beth* • Lisa Kudrow *Louisa* ■ *Dir* Rodman Flender • *Scr* Henry Dominic

Unbreakable ★★★★ 12

Fantasy drama 2000 · US · Colour · 106mins

Director M Night Shyamalan's follow-up to *The Sixth Sense* also stars Bruce Willis and deals with a paranormal phenomenon. While not quite as good, it does have much going for it, moving the supernatural genre to a thought-provoking and surreal new level. After becoming the sole survivor of a train crash, security guard Willis is told by brittle-boned comic-art gallery owner Samuel L Jackson that he's an invincible superhero in disguise. What's more, Jackson believes that comic books are the only way this ancient heroic history has been kept alive for contemporary mass consumption. An enthralling and subtle fantasy. AJ DVD

Bruce Willis *David Dunn* • Samuel L Jackson *Elijah Price* • Robin Wright Penn *Audrey Dunn* • Spencer Treat Clark *Joseph Dunn* • Charlayne Woodard *Elijah's mother* ■ *Dir/Scr* M Night Shyamalan

The Uncanny ★ 15

Portmanteau horror
1977 · Can/UK · Colour · 84mins

Petrified Peter Cushing has written a book proving that cats are planning world domination and tries to persuade Ray Milland to publish it on the strength of a trio of creepy tales. In the first, Simon Williams and Susan Penhaligon try to cheat Joan Greenwood's cats out of their inheritance, while in the second an orphan shrinks her evil cousin and uses her as a cat toy. But Donald Pleasence and Samantha Eggar put some vim into their *Pit and the Pendulum* pastiche. Overall, however, this dismal picture induces more cringes than chills. DP

Peter Cushing *Wilbur Gray* • Ray Milland *Frank Richards* • Susan Penhaligon *Janet* • Joan Greenwood *Miss Malkin* • Alexandra Stewart

U

Mrs Joan Blake • Donald Pleasence *Valentine De'Ath* • Samantha Eggar *Edina Hamilton* ■ *Dir* Denis Héroux • *Scr* Michel Parry

Uncensored ★★ U

Second World War drama
1942 · UK · BW · 106mins

The problem with this wartime movie is that it's too polite. There's no sense of menace or danger in the Belgian setting, where the Nazis are in occupation. That's partly the fault of the screenplay and of director Anthony Asquith, who hadn't the temperament for such a story. Eric Portman, an entertainer, and Phyllis Calvert revive a patriotic underground newspaper, *La Libre Belgique*, only to be betrayed. BB

Eric Portman *Andre Delange* • Phyllis Calvert *Julie Lanvin* • Griffith Jones *Father de Gruyte* • Raymond Lovell *Von Koerner* • Peter Glenville *Charles Neels* • Frederick Culley *Victor Lanvin* • Irene Handl *Frau von Koerner* ■ *Dir* Anthony Asquith • *Scr* Wolfgang Wilhelm, Terence Rattigan, Rodney Ackland

Uncertain Glory ★★★ U

Second World War drama
1944 · US · BW · 97mins

Only too obviously typecast, Errol Flynn plays a philandering criminal in Second World War-ravaged Europe who gives his life, hoping to redeem himself. Though rather talky for a Raoul Walsh-directed movie, it features fine performances by Flynn, Paul Lukas and Jean Sullivan. TH [video]

Errol Flynn *Jean Picard* • Paul Lukas *Marcel Bonet* • Jean Sullivan *Marianne* • Lucile Watson *Mme Maret* • Faye Emerson *Louise* • James Flavin *Captain of the Guard Mobile* • Douglas Dumbrille [Douglass Dumbrille] *Police commissioner* ■ *Dir* Raoul Walsh • *Scr* Laszlo Vadnay, Max Brand, from a story by Joe May, Laszlo Vadnay

Unchained ★★ U

Prison drama 1955 · US · BW · 75mins

This well-intentioned, serious study of an actual experiment in penal reform is a little dull compared with the average Hollywood prison picture. It was filmed at an actual prison without bars, with veteran star Chester Morris playing the real-life originator of the scheme and blond football star Elroy "Crazylegs" Hirsch in the lead role of an inmate who is tempted to escape. AE

Elroy "Crazylegs" Hirsch *Steve Davitt* • Barbara Hale *Mary Davitt* • Chester Morris *Kenyon J Scudder* • Todd Duncan *Bill Howard* • Johnny Johnston *Eddie Garrity* • Peggy Knudsen *Elaine* • Jerry Paris *Joe Ravens* • John Qualen *Leonard Haskins* ■ *Dir* Hall Bartlett • *Scr* Hall Bartlett, from the book *Prisoners Are People* by Kenyon J Scudder

The Uncle ★★★★

Drama 1964 · UK · BW · 89mins

This little charmer caused controversy by being denied a release for two years, during which time the film was slightly re-edited against its director's wishes. But *The Uncle* is one of the cinema's most inventive and perceptive portraits of childhood. It's about a seven-year-old boy (Robert Duncan) who becomes an uncle rather suddenly. The shock of the birth catapults him into an emotional crisis, leading to isolation from his family and school friends. Filmed in and around Plymouth, it's a touching story, and beautifully performed. AT

Rupert Davies *David* • Brenda Bruce *Addie* • Robert Duncan *Gus* • William Marlowe *Wayne* • Ann Lynn *Sally* • Barbara Leake *Emma* • Helen Fraser *Mary* ■ *Dir* Desmond Davis • *Scr* Desmond Davis, Margaret Abrams, from a novel by Margaret Abrams

Uncle Benjamin ★★★

Swashbuckling comedy
1969 · Fr · Colour · 91mins

The name of Edouard Molinaro will forever be associated with *La Cage aux Folles*. All the good taste and restraint that made that picture an Oscar winner for best foreign language film is gleefully absent in this rollicking piece of costume bawdiness, which comes over as a cross between a Henry Fielding novel and a Hollywood swashbuckler. Jacques Brel is solid enough as the 18th-century country doctor of the title, but veteran actor Bernard Blier steals the picture as a coarse, cruel aristocrat. DP. French dialogue dubbed into English.

Jacques Brel *Benjamin Rathery* • Claude Jade *Manette* • Rosy Varte *Bettine* • Robert Dalban *Aubergiste* • Bernard Blier *Cambyse* • Armand Mestral *Machecourt* ■ *Dir* Edouard Molinaro • *Scr* André Couteaux, Jean-François Hauduroy, from a story by Claude Tillier

Uncle Buck ★★★ 15

Comedy 1989 · US · Colour · 99mins

This movie marked writer/director John Hughes's move away from adolescence, after films such as *The Breakfast Club* and *Ferris Bueller's Day Off*, and return to childhood. Despite the fact that this was also the film that unleashed Macaulay Culkin on to the world at large, there is still much to enjoy. John Candy makes the most of his starring role as the lovable slob who is pressed into looking after his brother's children and Hughes stages some neat comic set pieces. Only the sentimental moralising strikes a false note. JF. Contains swearing. [video] DVD

John Candy *Buck Russell* • Macaulay Culkin *Miles Russell* • Jean Louisa Kelly *Tia Russell* • Gaby Hoffman [Gaby Hoffmann] *Maizy Russell* • Amy Madigan *Chanice Kobolowski* • Elaine Bromka *Cindy Russell* • Garrett M Brown *Bob Russell* • Laurie Metcalf *Marcie Dahlgren-Frost* • Jay Underwood *Bug* ■ *Dir/Scr* John Hughes

Uncle Silas ★★★

Thriller 1947 · UK · BW · 102mins

Though dated, this melodrama is distinguished by a glowing performance from the lovely Jean Simmons as the teenage ward sent to live with creepy old Uncle Silas (Derrick de Marney) in his ramshackle mansion. Atmospherics abound, with the nightmarish feel superbly sustained by the cinematography of Robert Krasker and Nigel Huke, and helped by the over-the-top performances of de Marney and Greek actress Katina Paxinou. TS

Jean Simmons *Caroline Ruthyn* • Katina Paxinou *Madame de la Rougierre* • Derrick de Marney *Uncle Silas* • Derek Bond *Lord Richard Ilbury* • Sophie Stewart *Lady Monica Waring* • Manning Whiley *Dudley Ruthyn* • Esmond Knight *Dr Bryerly* • Reginald Tate *Austin Ruthyn* ■ *Dir* Charles Frank • *Scr* Ben Travers, from the novel by Sheridan Le Fanu

Uncommon Valor ★★★ 15

Action drama 1983 · US · Colour · 100mins

Gene Hackman brings an unusual psychological depth to the part of an embittered father leading a hand-picked platoon into Laos to find his son, reported missing in action ten years before in Vietnam. Joe Gayton's script would win no prizes for originality or political correctness, and the direction of Ted Kotcheff only just passes muster. However, co-producer John Milius knows how to put on a show. DP. Contains violence and swearing. [video] DVD

Gene Hackman *Colonel Rhodes* • Robert Stack *MacGregor* • Fred Ward *Wilkes* • Reb Brown *Blaster* • Randall "Tex" Cobb *Sailor* • Patrick Swayze *Scott* • Harold Sylvester *Johnson* • Tim Thomerson *Charts* ■ *Dir* Ted Kotcheff • *Scr* Joe Gayton

Unconditional Love ★★ 15

Comedy mystery
2001 · US · Colour · 116mins

Alternating between laugh-out-loud hilarious and cringingly bad, this contrived comedy is both wildly unconventional and totally traditional. Kathy Bates is an obsessed American housewife who treks off to Britain for the funeral of her favourite crooner (Jonathan Pryce), only to become embroiled in a hunt for his murderer with the star's lover, Rupert Everett. Though this odd-couple pairing has charm, it's the sharp tongue of Bates's dwarf daughter-in-law, Meredith Eaton, that's the real delight. SF. Contains swearing, violence. [video] DVD

Kathy Bates *Grace Beasley* • Rupert Everett *Dirk Simpson* • Meredith Eaton *Maudey* • Peter Sarsgaard *Window washer* • Lynn Redgrave *Nola Fox* • Stephanie Beacham *Harriet Fox-Smith* • Richard Briers *Barry Moore* • Marcia Warren *Lynette Fox-Moore* • Jake Noseworthy *Andrew* • Jonathan Pryce *Victor Fox* ■ *Dir* PJ Hogan • *Scr* Jocelyn Moorhouse, PJ Hogan

Unconquered ★★★

Period adventure
1947 · US · Colour · 146mins

Cecil B DeMille's vast western epic stars Paulette Goddard as a cockney murderess transported to slavery in colonial America, where Gary Cooper saves her from the clutches of fur trapper Howard Da Silva. As if that weren't enough, there's savage tribesmen, shooting the rapids and being burned at the stake to contend with, too. Fortunately, DeMille keeps the moralising to a minimum and just seems anxious to pack as much passion, drama, and colour into it as the budget will allow. AT

Paulette Goddard *Abby Hale* • Gary Cooper *Capt Chris Holden* • Howard Da Silva *Martin Garth* • Boris Karloff *Guyasuta* • Cecil Kellaway *Jeremy Love* • Ward Bond *John Fraser* • Katherine DeMille *Hannah* • Henry Wilcoxon *Capt Steele* • C Aubrey Smith *Lord Chief Justice* ■ *Dir* Cecil B DeMille • *Scr* Charles Bennett, Frederic M Frank, Jesse Lasky Jr, from the novel *The Judas Tree* by Neil H Swanson

Unconquered ★★★★ PG

Drama based on a true story
1989 · US · Colour · 113mins

This TV movie combines an uplifting true story of individual sporting success against the odds with an illuminating study of racial hatred in the American South at the time of Martin Luther King. The worthy cast is headed by Peter Coyote as a progressive senator and Dermot Mulroney as his athlete son, coping with both the prejudice against his father and his own physical disabilities. The result is an above-average effort that could be described as *Chariots of Fire* with a social conscience. PF [video]

Peter Coyote *Richmond Flowers Sr* • Dermot Mulroney *Richmond Flowers Jr* • Tess Harper *Mary Flowers* • Jenny Robertson *Cindy Shiver* • Frank Whaley *Arnie Woods* • Bob Gunton *George Wallace* • Larry Riley *Martin Luther King* • RD Call *Floyd Petrie* • Noble Willingham *Bear Bryant* ■ *Dir* Dick Lowry • *Scr* Pat Conroy, from a story by Martin Chitwood

Uncovered: the War on Iraq ★★★★ PG

Documentary 2004 · US · Colour · 83mins

Robert Greenwald's authoritative documentary is an uncompromising assessment of George W Bush's "war on terror". More considered and less self-congratulatory than *Fahrenheit 9/11*, this nevertheless shares Michael Moore's incredulity that the president was able to use the September 11 terrorist attacks to justify the invasion of Iraq. Intelligence and diplomatic experts, including former chief weapons inspector Dr David Kay, analyse and pour scorn over the arguments for going to war, backing up their revelations with damning evidence. It's impossible to watch this clinical exposé without harbouring grave misgivings about the way the modern world is run. DP

Dir Robert Greenwald

The Undead ★★★ 15

Horror 1957 · US · BW · 71mins

Cult director Roger Corman's first "real" horror movie – albeit one with sci-fi overtones – was this quickie reincarnation tale that cashed in on the "previous existence" craze of the 1950s. Filmed in a derelict supermarket (hence the strangely effective, claustrophobic atmosphere), the film has Pamela Duncan as a hapless hooker who, hypnotised by her psychiatrist, returns to medieval times where she's condemned as a witch. Textbook Corman. AJ [video] DVD

Pamela Duncan *Helene/Diana* • Richard Garland *Pendragon* • Allison Hayes *Livia* • Val Dufour *Quintus* • Mel Welles *Smolkin* • Dorothy Neuman *Meg Maud* • Billy Barty *The Imp* ■ *Dir* Roger Corman • *Scr* Charles Griffith, Mark Hanna

Undead ★★ 15

Horror 2002 · Aus · Colour · 104mins

Every gory moment of note from the past four decades of zombie horror ends up present and politically incorrect in this low-budget feature debut from twins Peter and Michael Spierig. Set in rural Queensland, it begins with a meteor shower that soon has the effect of turning the population of a small fishing village into brain-munching zombies. A badly paced mess, this becomes increasingly repetitive and incomprehensible as it meanders on. AJ DVD

Felicity Mason *Rene* • Mungo McKay *Marion* • Rob Jenkins *Wayne* • Lisa Cunningham *Sallyanne* • Dirk Hunter *Harrison* • Emma Randall *Molly* • Steve Grieg *Agent* • Noel Sheridan *Chip* ■ *Dir/Scr* Michael Spierig, Peter Spierig

The Undeclared War ★★★★

Documentary 1992 · Fr · Colour · 240mins

Gleaned from 50-odd hours of interviews with 28 conscripted veterans of the battle for Algeria (1954–62), Bertrand Tavernier's documentary broke a silence that had existed since a divided France ceded what to many was less a colony than an integral part of *La Patrie*. Employing personal photos and establishing shots of the north African desert and the city of Grenoble (home to the interviewees and site of one of the most ferocious antiwar demonstrations), Tavernier allows the men to explore their own memories and emotions. While some deliver impenitent diatribes, others simply break down. Harrowing and revelatory. DP. In French with English subtitles.

Dir Bertrand Tavernier

The Undefeated ★★ PG

Western 1969 · US · Colour · 113mins

This western is undistinguished but beautifully photographed by veteran cameraman William Clothier. A toupeed, paunchy John Wayne is the Union colonel on his way to Mexico, who confronts mustachioed Confederate colonel Rock Hudson. The theme of post-Civil War reconciliation ensures that no sparks fly between the two main characters, nor is there any real chemistry between the stars. Director Andrew V McLaglen seems to

U

have had problems establishing the right tone for this tale. TS

John Wayne *Colonel John Henry Thomas* • Rock Hudson *Colonel James Langdon* • Tony Aguilar *General Rojas* • Roman Gabriel *Blue Boy* • Marian McCargo *Ann Langdon* • Lee Meriwether *Margaret Langdon* • Michael Vincent [Jan-Michael Vincent] *Bubba Wilkes* • Ben Johnson *Short Grub* • Harry Carey Jr *Webster* ■ *Dir* Andrew V McLaglen • *Scr* James Lee Barrett, from a story by Stanley L Hough

Under a Texas Moon ★★

Western comedy 1930 · US · Colour · 82mins

Its entertainment value is minor but this recently restored picture gains some historical interest as the first outdoors talkie to be filmed completely in two-strip Technicolor. Smoothly made by ace director Michael Curtiz, who includes his signature shadow shot, it was Warner Bros' answer to Fox's *Cisco Kid* adventures with a similar twist in the tale as a dashing caballero (competently played by the now obscure Frank Fay) dallies with young women (including future star Myrna Loy) when he might be out rounding up rustlers. AE

Frank Fay *Don Carlos* • Raquel Torres *Raquella* • Myrna Loy *Lolita Romero* • Armida *Dolores* • Noah Beery Sr [Noah Beery] *Jed Parker* ■ *Dir* Michael Curtiz • *Scr* Gordon Rigby, from a story by Steward Edward White

Under California Stars ★★ U

Western 1948 · US · Colour · 69mins

In this minor late entry in the career of self-styled "king of the cowboys" Roy Rogers, much of the pleasure is provided by B-musical star Jane Frazee, a former radio singer. She provides a watchable alternative to Trigger, as Rogers once again manages to avoid damage to his cowboy outfits, despite fisticuffs and some hard riding. TS

Roy Rogers *Roy Rogers* • Jane Frazee *Caroline Maynard* • Andy Devine *Cookie Bullfincher* • George H Lloyd [George Lloyd] *Jonas "Pop" Jordan* • Wade Crosby *Lye McFarland* • Michael Chapin *Ted Conover* • House Peters Jr *Ed* ■ *Dir* William Witney • *Scr* Sloan Nibley, Paul Gangelin, from a story by Paul Gangelin

Under Capricorn ★★★ PG

Period melodrama
1949 · UK · Colour · 112mins

Although this is one of Alfred Hitchcock's oddest movies, the master's hand is firmly in evidence. It's a melodrama set in 19th-century Australia, starring Ingrid Bergman as a rich woman coming to terms with her marriage to stablehand and transported convict Joseph Cotten. The production was troubled by the start of Bergman's infamous love affair with Roberto Rossellini and by Hitchcock's eagerness to finish the film quickly to avoid paying British taxes. You may notice some shots that run for more than five minutes without a cut, contributing to the film's heady, half-baked romanticism. AT

Ingrid Bergman *Lady Henrietta Flusky* • Joseph Cotten *Sam Flusky* • Michael Wilding *Charles Adare* • Margaret Leighton *Milly* • Cecil Parker *Governor* • Denis O'Dea *Corrigan* • Jack Watling *Winter* ■ *Dir* Alfred Hitchcock • *Scr* James Bridie, Hume Cronyn, from the play by John Colton, Margaret Linden and from the novel by Helen Simpson

Under Fire ★★★★ 15

Political drama 1983 · US · Colour · 122mins

This exceptional political thriller, part morality tale and part action adventure, has three journalists (Nick Nolte, Gene Hackman and Joanna Cassidy) covering the Nicaraguan revolution and becoming involved in the violent struggle. Director Roger Spottiswoode has brilliantly realised the electric atmosphere generated by rubble-strewn streets, above which snipers lurk and in which people die just because they get in the way. The three stars stand out and Jean-Louis Trintignant is credibly creepy as a double agent. TH. Contains swearing. DVD

Nick Nolte *Russell Price* • Ed Harris *Oates* • Gene Hackman *Alex Grazier* • Joanna Cassidy *Claire Stryder* • Alma Martinez *Isela* • Holly Palance *Journalist* • Jean-Louis Trintignant *Marcel Jazy* ■ *Dir* Roger Spottiswoode • *Scr* Ron Shelton, Clayton Frohman, from a story by Clayton Frohman

Under Milk Wood ★★★ 15

Drama 1971 · UK · Colour · 87mins

Dylan Thomas's celebrated 1954 radio play was a complex blend of dream, reality and poetry, which dealt with life, love and liquid refreshment in the mythical Welsh fishing village of Llareggub. Richard Burton, who plays "First Voice" – the narrator – knew Thomas well and had performed the play on radio. He's joined here by his then-wife Elizabeth Taylor as the childhood sweetheart of Captain Cat, the blind seafarer played by Peter O'Toole. There's a fascinating cast and Thomas's dialogue remains exceptionally vivid – especially with Burton's voice driving much of it. Andrew Sinclair's direction sensibly avoids any fireworks. AT DVD

Richard Burton *First Voice* • Elizabeth Taylor *Rosie Probert* • Peter O'Toole *Captain Cat* • Glynis Johns *Myfanwy Price* • Vivien Merchant *Mrs Pugh* • Sian Phillips *Mrs Ogmore-Pritchard* • Victor Spinetti *Mog Edwards* ■ *Dir* Andrew Sinclair • *Scr* Andrew Sinclair, from the radio play by Dylan Thomas

Under Pressure ★★★ 15

Thriller 1997 · US · Colour · 84mins

Charlie Sheen – here billed as Charles – plays a fireman who wins a bravery medal. But because his wife leaves him he turns into the neighbour from hell, menacing little kids, killing repair men and generally behaving badly. Sheen gives a fine performance, the direction is too mild-mannered to make this TV thriller as chilling as it should have been. AT DVD

Charles Sheen [Charlie Sheen] *Lyle Wilder* • Mare Winningham *Catherine Braverton* • David Andrews *Reese Braverton* • Noah Fleiss *Zach Braverton* • Chelsea Russo *Marcie Braverton* • John Ratzenberger *Al Calavito* • Dawnn Lewis *Sandy Tierra* ■ *Dir* Craig R Baxley • *Scr* Betsy Giffen Nowrasteh

Under Siege ★★★★ 15

Action adventure 1992 · US · Colour · 98mins

Steven Seagal struck gold with this slick nautical spin on the *Die Hard* concept. Portraying possibly the unlikeliest cook in the history of cinema, Seagal is the US Navy's only hope when a crack squad of terrorists, led by Tommy Lee Jones, hijacks his ship. Seagal lacks natural charisma, but a flamboyant performance from Jones, plus some sterling work from fellow baddies Gary Busey and Colm Meaney, more than compensate for his deficiencies. Director Andrew Davis never misses a beat and stages some awesome set pieces. JF. Contains violence, swearing, nudity. DVD

Steven Seagal *Casey Ryback* • Tommy Lee Jones *William Strannix* • Gary Busey *Commander Krill* • Erika Eleniak *Jordan Tate* • Patrick O'Neal *Captain Adams* • Damian Chapa *Tackman* • Troy Evans *Granger* • David McKnight *Flicker* • Colm Meaney *Daumer* ■ *Dir* Andrew Davis • *Scr* JF Lawton

Under Siege 2 ★★ 18

Action thriller 1995 · US · Colour · 93mins

The original *Under Siege* was a hugely entertaining affair, thanks mainly to the sheer scale of the destruction and its top-drawer cast of cartoon villains. This sequel sadly falls down in both departments. Basically, it's the same story – this time set on a train. Steven Seagal is a chef who finds himself up against another gang of international terrorists, led by the faintly ludicrous mad professor Eric Bogosian. JF. Contains swearing, violence. DVD

Steven Seagal *Casey Ryback* • Eric Bogosian *Travis Dane* • Katherine Heigl *Sarah Ryback* • Morris Chestnut *Bobby Zachs* • Everett McGill *Penn* • Kurtwood Smith *General Stanley Cooper* • Nick Mancuso *Tom Breaker* • Andy Romano *Admiral Bates* ■ *Dir* Geoff Murphy • *Scr* Richard Hatem, Matt Reeves, from the characters created by JF Lawton

Under Suspicion ★★★ 18

Thriller 1991 · US/UK · Colour · 95mins

An intriguing if not entirely successful attempt to create a home-grown *noir* thriller, this stars Liam Neeson as a cynical private eye caught up in a tortuous murder plot involving *femme fatale* Laura San Giacomo. The 1950s Brighton setting is suitably seedy and, as with other films of its ilk, there's plenty of twists and turns. However the story is a little far-fetched and Neeson never really convinces as the hard-boiled private detective. JF

Liam Neeson *Tony Aaron* • Laura San Giacomo *Angeline* • Kenneth Cranham *Frank* • Maggie O'Neill *Hazel* • Alan Talbot *Powers* • Malcolm Storry *Waterston* • Martin Grace *Colin* • Kevin Moore *Barrister* ■ *Dir/Scr* Simon Moore

Under Suspicion ★★★ 15

Murder mystery thriller
2000 · US/Fr · Colour · 110mins

Gene Hackman and Morgan Freeman star in director Stephen Hopkins's absorbing remake of the 1981 French thriller *Garde à Vue*, now relocated to Puerto Rico. Following the rape and murder of two young girls, police captain Freeman questions lawyer Hackman, who discovered one of the bodies. What starts as a friendly chat escalates into a thought-provoking battle as Freeman's suspicions are fuelled by inconsistencies in Hackman's story. LH. Contains swearing and sex scenes. DVD

Morgan Freeman *Capt Victor Benezet* • Gene Hackman *Henry Hearst* • Thomas Jane *Detective Felix Owens* • Monica Bellucci *Chantal Hearst* • Nydia Caro *Isabella* • Miguel Angel Suarez *Superintendent* ■ *Dir* Stephen Hopkins • *Scr* Tom Provost, W Peter Iliff, from the film *Garde à Vue* by Claude Miller, Jean Herman, from the novel *Brainwash* by John Wainwright

Under Ten Flags ★★ U

Second World War drama
1960 · US/It · BW · 113mins

Produced in Italy by Dino De Laurentiis with an Italian director and crew, this stars Charles Laughton as a British bulldog admiral and Van Heflin as a German skipper, playing cat and mouse with each other. While Van Heflin is not your usual card-carrying Nazi, just a clever tactician, Laughton goes for the full Churchillian effect. A derisory love story with French import Mylène Demongeot is thrown in but just slows things down. AT

Van Heflin *Reger* • Charles Laughton *Adm Russell* • Mylène Demongeot *Zizi* • John Ericson *Krueger* • Liam Redmond *Windsor* • Alex Nicol *Knoche* • Grégoire Aslan *Master of Abdullah* • Cecil Parker *Col Howard* ■ *Dir* Duilio Coletti • *Scr* Vittoriano Petrilli, Duilio Coletti, Ulrich Mohr, Leonardo Bercovici (uncredited), William Douglas Home, from the diaries of Bernhard Rogge

Under the Boardwalk ★ 15

Comedy 1988 · US · Colour · 98mins

This update of Shakespeare's *Romeo and Juliet* is set on the beaches of California. Here members of rival surf teams fall in love during a weekend of fierce competition at an annual surf-off. Weirdly, this teen romance is narrated by a character from the future, but even this oddity fails to add spark to what is a lucklustre story hampered by cheap production values. DF

Keith Coogan *Andy* • Danielle Von Zerneck *Allie* • Richard Joseph Paul *Nick Rainwood* • Steve Monarque *Reef* • Roxana Zal *Gitch* • Brian Avery (2) *Hap Jordan* • Hunter Von Leer *Midas* ■ *Dir* Fritz Kiersch • *Scr* Robert King, from a story by Matthew Irmas, King Robert

Under the Cherry Moon ★ 15

Musical romance 1986 · US · BW · 100mins

Even ardent fans of the "artist formerly known as Prince" will scoff at this monumentally pretentious ego trip, in which His Purpleness plays a piano-playing gigolo on the French Riviera, wooing rich Kristin Scott Thomas against her father's wishes. In a gob-smacking black-and-white exercise in narcissistic posturing, Prince endlessly compares wardrobes with Jerome Benton, makes love on a bed of rose petals, and finally dies (thank goodness!). Not even worth watching for kitsch value. AJ. Contains some violence and swearing.

Prince *Christopher Tracy* • Jerome Benton *Tricky* • Kristin Scott Thomas *Mary Sharon* • Steven Berkoff *Mr Sharon* • Francesca Annis *Mrs Wellington* • Emmanuelle Sallet *Katy* • Alexandra Stewart *Mrs Sharon* ■ *Dir* Prince • *Scr* Becky Johnston

Under the Doctor ★ 18

Comedy 1976 · UK · Colour · 81mins

Such was the state of British screen comedy in the 1970s that even its stalwarts were reduced to accepting roles as nudie cuties. Indeed, Liz Fraser did nothing but peek-a-boo fluff in the middle of the decade, managing to retain her dignity while all else were losing their clothes. She's joined here by Barry Evans, who gets to play four different roles, the most significant being an amorous psychiatrist coping with a clientele made up exclusively of sexually frustrated females. DP

Barry Evans *Colin/Dr Boyd/Mr Johnson/Lt Cranshaw* • Liz Fraser *Sandra* • Hilary Pritchard *Lady Victoria* • Penny Spencer *Marion* • Jonathan Cecil *Rodney Harrington-Harrington/Lord Woodbridge* ■ *Dir* Gerry Poulson • *Scr* Ron Bareham

Under the Hula Moon ★★★

Comedy thriller 1995 · US · Colour · 96mins

This is an eccentric film about a trailer-park couple who have only their dream of moving to Hawaii to sustain them. Their dream is put on the backburner when the husband's convict brother escapes from prison and comes a-calling. Stephen Baldwin and Chris Penn play the male leads, but any British interest resides in the film's leading lady, the watchable Emily Lloyd. DA. Contains violence, swearing.

Stephen Baldwin *Buzz* • Emily Lloyd *Betty* • Chris Penn *Turk* • Musetta Vander *Maya Gundinger* • Pruitt Taylor Vince *Bob* ■ *Dir* Jeff Celentano • *Scr* Jeff Celentano, Gregory Webb

Under the Piano ★★★ 15

Drama based on a true story
1995 · Can · Colour · 87mins

One of the world's leading opera stars takes centre stage in this heart-rending melodrama. As the faded diva who is too wrapped up in her own woes to recognise the talent of her autistic savant daughter, Teresa Stratas sweeps through every scene with imperious disdain. Strong performances from Megan Follows and Amanda Plummer maintain the balance, however, with Follows particularly impressive as she battles her domineering mother to fulfil her

U

musical potential. Based on the true story of sisters Dolly and Henrietta Giardini, this TV movie is thoughtful and powerfully played. DP [video] DVD

Amanda Plummer *Franny* • Megan Follows *Rosetta* • Teresa Stratas *Regina* • James Carroll *Nick* • John Juliani *Frank* • Jackie Richardson *Mrs Syms* • Richard Blackburn *Dr Banman* • Dan Lett *Dr Harkness* ■ *Dir* Stefan Scaini • *Scr* Blair Ferguson

Under the Rainbow ★ PG

Comedy 1981 · US · Colour · 93mins

Despite the presence of the great Eve Arden, a former Ziegfeld girl and put-down queen of screwball comedies, this strange attempt at a comedy set in Hollywood's golden era is a grotesque misfire. Chevy Chase and Carrie Fisher are a talent scout and FBI agent respectively who uncover a Nazi plot in a hotel over-run with scores of oddball eccentrics from the cast of *The Wizard of Oz*. A yellow brick road to nowhere – and certainly not to any form of entertainment. TH [video]

Chevy Chase *Bruce Thorpe* • Carrie Fisher *Annie Clark* • Billy Barty *Otto Kriegling* • Eve Arden *Duchess* • Joseph Maher *Duke* • Robert Donner *Assassin* • Mako *Nakamuri* • Cork Hubbert *Rollo Sweet* ■ *Dir* Steve Rash • *Scr* Pat McCormick, Harry Hurwitz, Martin Smith, Pat Bradley, Fred Bauer, from a story by Pat Bradley, Fred Bauer

Under the Red Robe ★★

Swashbuckling drama
1937 · UK · BW · 80mins

Victor Sjöström was the director of many silent classics in his native Sweden and, most famously, *The Wind*, made in Hollywood, and *The Divine Woman*, the sole Garbo film lost to history. Also a fine actor, he retired from directing in 1930, then returned to the megaphone for this final movie, made for Alexander Korda. It's set in 17th-century France, with Conrad Veidt as a gambler condemned to be executed, who's then given a deadly mission by Cardinal Richelieu (Raymond Massey). It has the odd moment, but was not to be the crowning glory of Sjöström's career. AT

Conrad Veidt *Gil de Berault* • Annabella *Lady Marguerite* • Raymond Massey *Cardinal Richelieu* • Romney Brent *Marius* • Sophie Stewart *Elise, Duchess of Foix* • Wyndham Goldie *Edmond, Duke of Foix* • Lawrence Grant *Father Joseph* ■ *Dir* Victor Seastrom [Victor Sjöström] • *Scr* Lajos Biró, Philip Lindsay, JL Hodson, Arthur Wimperis, from the play by Edward E Rose and the novel by Stanley J Weyman

Under the Sand ★★★★ 15

Drama 2000 · Fr/Jpn · Colour · 92mins

Charlotte Rampling turns in the finest performance of her career in this sensitively relentless study of melancholic delusion. Convinced she still sees him every day, a sophisticated Parisienne teacher (Rampling) simply refuses to accept that her husband (Bruno Cremer) drowned on their seaside holiday and treats her liaison with Jacques Nolot as a deliciously reckless adultery. Reducing dialogue to essentials and making exemplary use of cool, reflective surfaces, François Ozon finds poetry and optimism in the depths of grief. DP. In French with English subtitles. Contains swearing and sex scenes. [video] DVD

Charlotte Rampling *Marie Drillon* • Bruno Cremer *Jean Drillon* • Jacques Nolot *Vincent* • Alexandra Stewart *Amanda* • Pierre Vernier *Gérard* ■ *Dir* François Ozon • *Scr* Ozon François, Emmanuèle Bernheim, Marina de Van, Marcia Romano

Under the Skin ★★★★ 18

Drama 1997 · UK · Colour · 79mins

When their mother (Rita Tushingham) dies, two Liverpool sisters react differently to the bereavement. Claire Rushbrook, who is pregnant, cries a lot but gets on with her life, whereas the younger, wilder Samantha Morton starts a downward moral spiral of sordid sex and alcohol binges. This quest for emotional fulfilment in tragic times may lack overall polish, but with its *cinéma vérité* style, this is wrenching, thanks to Morton's raw and riveting portrayal. AJ. Contains swearing and sex scenes. [video] DVD

Samantha Morton *Iris Kelley* • Claire Rushbrook *Rose* • Rita Tushingham *Mum* • Christine Tremarco *Veronica/"Vron"* • Stuart Townsend *Tom* • Matthew Delamere *Gary* • Mark Womack *Frank* • Clare Francis *Elana* ■ *Dir/Scr* Carine Adler

Under the Sun ★★★

Period drama 1998 · Swe · Colour · 118mins

The theme of mistrust within a close-knit community that informed director Colin Nutley's acclaimed *House of Angels* is also evident in this Oscar-nominated adaptation. Nutley's wife, Helena Bergström, is once again the star, on this occasion playing the housekeeper who arrives at Rolf Lassgård's isolated farm and immediately drives a wedge between the middle-aged illiterate oaf and his scheming buddy, Johan Widerberg. Nutley directs with a focused, but unforced maturity that not only captures the gentler pace of 1950s life, but also the tension underpinning this enthralling battle of wits. DP. In Swedish with English subtitles.

Rolf Lassgård *Olof* • Helena Bergström *Ellen* • Johan Widerberg *Erik* • Gunilla Röör *Newspaper receptionist* • Jonas Falk *Preacher* ■ *Dir* Colin Nutley • *Scr* Johanna Hald, David Neal, Colin Nutley, from the short story *The Little Farm* by HE Bates

Under the Tuscan Sun ★ 12

Romantic comedy drama
2003 · US · Colour · 108mins

Diane Lane stars in this corny, old-fashioned slushfest as a successful writer who journeys to Italy after a messy divorce and impulsively buys a broken-down villa in Tuscany. It's the cue for encounters with every kind of local stereotype, from cutely rustic repairmen to lusty Latin lotharios. Lane looks ravishing. So does the scenery. But the whole thing has the depth of a puddle. DA [video] DVD

Diane Lane *Frances* • Sandra Oh *Patti* • Lindsay Duncan *Katherine* • Raoul Bova *Marcello* • Vincent Riotta [Vincenzo Ricotta] *Martini* • Giulia Steigerwalt *Chiara* • Pawel Szajda *Pawel* • Mario Monicelli *Old man with flowers* ■ *Dir* Audrey Wells • *Scr* Audrey Wells, from a story by Audrey Wells, from the memoirs by Frances Mayes

Under the Volcano ★★★ 15

Drama 1984 · UK · Colour · 107mins

Malcolm Lowry's 1947 novel is a cult classic about an alcoholic British consul adrift in Mexico with his unfaithful ex-wife and his half-brother, a journalist just back from the Spanish Civil War. John Huston long cherished a movie version and – as with *Moby Dick* – it proved to be a daunting task, since the novel is a stream of consciousness, a river of booze and a mountain of poetic symbolism. Albert Finney gives the drunk act to end all drunk acts and rather overshadows the beautiful Jacqueline Bisset. AT [video]

Albert Finney *Geoffrey Firmin* • Jacqueline Bisset *Yvonne Firmin* • Anthony Andrews *Hugh Firmin* • Ignacio Lopez Tarso *Dr Vigil* • Katy Jurado *Señora Gregoria* • James Villiers *Brit* • Dawson Bray *Quincey* ■ *Dir* John Huston • *Scr* Guy Gallo, from the novel by Malcolm Lowry • *Cinematographer* Gabriel Figueroa

Under the Yum Yum Tree ★★

Comedy 1963 · US · Colour · 109mins

With *The Apartment*, Jack Lemmon defined the urbanised, neurotic, sexually insecure American male. Thus typecast, Lemmon drifted through a series of movies including this "sex comedy". Lemmon plays a lecherous landlord who starts to lust after one of his tenants, Carol Lynley, who is living with her boyfriend Dean Jones. Lemmon always has his precious moments and those make this comedy of frustration worth watching – just. AT

Jack Lemmon *Hogan* • Carol Lynley *Robin* • Dean Jones *David* • Edie Adams *Irene* • Imogene Coca *Dorkus* • Paul Lynde *Murphy* • Robert Lansing *Charles* ■ *Dir* David Swift • *Scr* Lawrence Roman, David Swift, from the play by Lawrence Roman

Under Two Flags ★★★

Action adventure 1936 · US · BW · 110mins

This Foreign Legion saga, already filmed twice in the silent era, stars Ronald Colman and Victor McLaglen,as the desert-based soldiers, and Claudette Colbert and Rosalind Russell as zee women in zee kasbah. Frank Lloyd directed the talkie bits, Otto Brower the battles, which look like afterthoughts since the real battle is between the sexes and between two Oxford graduates, Colman and Arab chieftain Onslow Stevens. It's *Boys' Own* stuff, with Colman often caught posing for the camera and Colbert tossing aside her usual chic and letting her hair down. AT

Ronald Colman *Corporal Victor* • Claudette Colbert *Cigarette* • Victor McLaglen *Major Doyle* • Rosalind Russell *Lady Venetia* • J Edward Bromberg *Colonel Ferol* • Nigel Bruce *Captain Menzies* • Herbert Mundin *Rake* • Gregory Ratoff *Ivan* ■ *Dir* Frank Lloyd, Otto Brower • *Scr* WP Lipscomb, Walter Ferris, from the novel by Ouida

Under Western Skies ★★ U

Musical western 1945 · US · BW · 56mins

A programme filler about a vaudeville singer, played by Martha O'Driscoll, who fetches up in an Arizona town and gets involved in all sorts of trouble. There are some funny moments, but this is very slight indeed, though the songs are pleasant enough. TS

Martha O'Driscoll *Katie* • Noah Beery Jr *Tod* • Leo Carrillo *King Randall* • Leon Errol *Willie* • Irving Bacon *Sheriff* • Ian Keith *Prof Moffet* • Jennifer Holt *Charity* ■ *Dir* Jean Yarbrough • *Scr* Stanley Roberts, Clyde Bruckman, from a story by Stanley Roberts

Under Your Hat ★ U

Musical comedy 1940 · UK · BW · 79mins

You really needed to have been there at the time to appreciate the humour in this woeful comedy of errors. Wartime audiences were so grateful to see just about anything that they were willing to forgive even the most dismal movies – particularly morale-boosting flagwavers. The lowest of many dips below zero is the scene in which Cicely Courtneidge poses as French maid to catch hubby Jack Hulbert with Leonora Corbett, unaware they are spies. DP

Jack Hulbert *Jack Millett* • Cicely Courtneidge *Kay Millett* • Austin Trevor *Boris Vladimir* • Leonora Corbett *Carole Markoff* • Cecil Parker *Sir Geoffrey Arlington* • Tony Hayes *George* • Charles Oliver *Carl* • HF Maltby *Colonel Sheepshanks* ■ *Dir* Maurice Elvey • *Scr* Rodney Ackland, Anthony Kimmins, L Green, Jack Hulbert, from the play by Jack Hulbert, Archie Menzies, Geoffrey Kerr, Arthur Macrae

Undercover ★

Second World War drama
1943 · UK · BW · 88mins

This Ealing Resistance drama aims for a docudramatic feel, but realism was outside the range of such starchy actors as John Clements, Michael Wilding and Tom Walls. The result is, frankly, embarrassing. DP

John Clements *Milosh Petrovitch* • Tom Walls *Kossan Petrovitch* • Mary Morris *Anna Petrovitch* • Godfrey Tearle *General Von Staengel* • Michael Wilding *Constantine* • Niall MacGinnis *Dr Jordan* • Robert Harris *Colonel Von Brock* • Rachel Thomas *Maria Petrovitch* ■ *Dir* Sergei Nolbandov • *Scr* John Dighton, Monja Danischewsky, Sergei Nolbandov, Milos Sokulich, from a story by George Slocombe

Undercover ★★

Period comedy drama
1983 · Aus · Colour · 87mins

Launched in the 1920s after extensive research, the House of Burley 's range of underwear became one of the first Australian products to corner an international market. Unfortunately, Stevens allows himself to be distracted from his fascinating story and spends too much time wondering whether country girl Genevieve Picot will plump for old-fashioned salesman Peter Phelps or his go-ahead American rival, Michael Paré. An uneasy mix of fact and whimsy. DP. Contains swearing.

Genevieve Picot *Libby McKenzie* • John Walton *Fred Burley* • Michael Paré *Max Wylde* • Sandy Gore *Nina* • Peter Phelps *Theo Finch* • Barry Otto *Professor Henckel* ■ *Dir* David Stevens • *Scr* Miranda Downes

Undercover Blues ★★★ 15

Comedy thriller 1993 · US · Colour · 86mins

Dennis Quaid and Kathleen Turner are super spies on leave in New Orleans with their infant, who are called back into service to help foil a plot to sell off top secret weapons. Quaid and Turner make charismatic leads and are surrounded by a talented support cast. Herbert Ross's direction is suitably light and, while it isn't as funny as it should be, it's still undemanding fun. JF. Contains some swearing. [video] DVD

Kathleen Turner *Jane Blue* • Dennis Quaid *Jeff Blue* • Fiona Shaw *Novacek* • Stanley Tucci *Muerte* • Larry Miller *Detective Sergeant Halsey* • Tom Arnold *Vern Newman* ■ *Dir* Herbert Ross • *Scr* Ian Abrams

Undercover Brother ★★ 12

Blaxploitation spoof
2002 · US · Colour · 82mins

The first major feature film to be adapted from an internet cartoon, this satire-cum-spoof stars comedian Eddie Griffin as a leather-clad, afro-sporting secret agent who's recruited by an organisation called The Brotherhood. His arch-enemy is The Man, a white racist megalomaniac. This attempts to poke fun at white perceptions of black culture while celebrating the glories of blaxploitation movies and 1970s fashions and music, but many of the jokes are just too stale to work. BP [video] DVD

Eddie Griffin *Undercover Brother* • Chris Kattan *Mr Feather* • Denise Richards *White She Devil* • Aunjanue Ellis *Sistah Girl* • Dave Chappelle *Conspiracy Brother* • Chi McBride *Chief* • Neil Patrick Harris *Lance* • Billy Dee Williams *General Boutwell* ■ *Dir* Malcolm D Lee • *Scr* John Ridley, Michael McCullers, from a story by John Ridley, from characters created by John Ridley

Undercover Girl ★★★

Crime 1950 · US · BW · 82mins

Policewoman Alexis Smith joins forces with plain-clothes policeman Scott Brady and is sent undercover to pose as a drug buyer in order to nail a

U

narcotics ring. This is a routine 1950s programme filler, but no less entertaining for that, and it's refreshing to have a glamorous woman at the centre of the rough stuff. RK

Alexis Smith *Christine Miller/"Sal Willis"* • Scott Brady *Lt Mike Trent* • Richard Egan *Jess Taylor* • Gladys George *Liz Crow* • Edmon Ryan *Doc Holmes* • Gerald Mohr *Reed Menig* • Royal Dano *Moocher* ■ *Dir* Joseph Pevney • *Scr* Harry Essex, from a story by Robert Hardy Andrews, Francis Rosenwald

Undercover Girl ★★

Crime drama 1957 · UK · BW · 76mins

This cheap British B-movie has the regulation "glamour" leading lady and the obligatory American (in this case Canadian) leading man. Former band crooner Paul Carpenter is an amiable star of sorts and co-star Kay Callard has a passable second-string leading lady quality – though a few acting lessons wouldn't have gone amiss. The real interest lies in the appearance in an "acting" role of Jackie Collins, now better known for writing raunchy novels. TS

Paul Carpenter *Johnny Carter* • Kay Callard *Joan Foster* • Monica Grey *Evelyn King* • Bruce Seton *Ted Austin* • Jackie Collins *Peggy Foster* • Maya Koumani *Miss Brazil* ■ *Dir* Francis Searle • *Scr* Bernard Lewis, Bill Luckwell, from a story by Bernard Lewis

The Undercover Man ★★★

Crime thriller 1949 · US · BW · 84mins

This is an entertaining co-feature from cult director Joseph H Lewis, best known for his remarkable thriller *Gun Crazy*. It's based on the real-life entrapment of gangster Al Capone for tax evasion, a tale beloved of Hollywood scriptwriters. The story is economically filmed and driven at a fine pace, and there are terrific performances by leads Glenn Ford, Nina Foch and James Whitmore, making his screen debut. The crisp images of *Bonnie and Clyde* cinematographer Burnett Guffey are also a major plus. TS

Glenn Ford *Frank Warren* • Nina Foch *Judith Warren* • James Whitmore *George Pappas* • Barry Kelley *Edward O'Rourke* • David Wolfe *Stanley Weinburg* • Frank Tweddell *Inspector Herzog* • Howard St John *Joseph S Horan* • Leo Penn *Sidney Gordon* ■ *Dir* Joseph H Lewis • *Scr* Sydney Boehm, Malvin Wald, Jerry Rubin, from the article *Undercover Man: He Trapped Capone* by Frank J Wilson

Undercurrent ★★★ 15

Spy drama 1946 · US · BW · 115mins

With a knockout cast (Katharine Hepburn, Robert Taylor, Robert Mitchum), a director (Vincente Minelli) hitting his creative stride and MGM (the Rolls-Royce of studios near its prime), how can you go wrong? Easy. By having a moth-eaten cardboard script, obvious studio interiors, a cast that doesn't care and a director plagued by domestic problems. It's over-written, overwrought and overlong, but sheer star power saves the day, and the three principals make this mesmerisingly watchable. TS

Katharine Hepburn *Ann Hamilton* • Robert Taylor (1) *Alan Garroway* • Robert Mitchum *Michael Garroway* • Edmund Gwenn *Prof Dink Hamilton* ■ *Dir* Vincente Minnelli • *Scr* Edward Chodorov, Marguerite Roberts, George Oppenheimer, from the novel *You Were There* by Thelma Strabel

Underground ★★

Second World War drama adventure
1941 · US · BW · 94mins

This anti-Nazi propaganda piece still retains some of its didactic power thanks to its unconventional staging within the realms of the Third Reich. Jeffrey Lynn and Philip Dorn play two German brothers, the former immersed in Hitler's doctrine, the latter struggling to resist his homeland's ill-fated trajectory. Unsurprisingly, it's Dorn's viewpoint that triumphs, and the wayward Lynn manages to see the error of his ways in time for the melodramatic denouement. Functional rather than inspired. RT

Jeffrey Lynn *Kurt Franken* • Philip Dorn *Eric Franken* • Kaaren Verne *Sylvia Helmuth* • Mona Maris *Fräulein Gessner* • Peter Whitney *Alex* ■ *Dir* Vincent Sherman • *Scr* Charles Grayson, from a story by Oliver HP Garrett, Edwin Justus Mayer

Underground ★★★ 15

Epic Second World War comedy
1995 · Fr/Ger/Hun · Colour · 163mins

Although it won Emir Kusturica a second Palme d'Or at Cannes, this bittersweet dramatisation of the decline of Yugoslavia so angered critics in his native Bosnia (for failing to condemn Serbian aggression) that he threatened to abandon cinema altogether. Beneath the black farce – Second World War partisans take refuge in a cellar, which becomes their home for decades – there are traces of nostalgia for the illusory union of Tito's Yugoslavia. With much of the action taken at a frantic pace, to the accompaniment of brass or gypsy bands, this is as breathless as it is perplexing. DP. In Serbian and German with English subtitles.

Miki Manojlovic *Marko* • Lazar Ristovski *Petar "Blacky" Popara* • Mirjana Jokovic *Natalija* • Slavko Stimac *Ivan* • Ernst Stotzner *Franz* • Srdjan Todorovic *Jovan* • Mirjana Karanovic *Vera* ■ *Dir* Emir Kusturica • *Scr* Emir Kusturica, from a story by Dusan Kovacevic

Underground ★★★★ 18

Crime thriller 1998 · UK · Colour · 93mins

This gritty, ultra low-budget, British thriller is about teen drug-dealer Billy Smith, who makes deliveries around the clock. When he wanders into another supplier's patch, the film follows him as he spends a long night of hide and seek. Writer/director Paul Spurrier (who also performed just about every technical role) does an exceptional job. The naturalistic performances are good and the music soundtrack is comparable to most major releases. Amazingly, it was shot in a fortnight and the climactic car chase was filmed entirely without permission or stunt drivers. JC. Contains swearing. DVD

Billy Smith *Rat* • Zoe Smale *Skye* • Ian Dury *Rat's dad* • Chrissie Cotterill *Rat's mum* • Nick Sutton *Raymond* • Alison Lintott *Debbie* ■ *Dir/Scr* Paul Spurrier

The Underground Orchestra ★★★

Documentary 1998 · Neth · Colour · 108mins

Heddy Honigmann's documentary about the multinational band of buskers who perform on the streets and trains of the French capital not only provides a diverse musical education, but also a sobering insight into the penury and humiliation they're forced to endure. This is despite her rather naive and intrusive insistence on trying to make political capital out of both her subjects and the supposedly sophisticated Parisians who either watch or ignore them. Drawn from trouble spots around the world, these latter-day troubadours have long ceased to play for pleasure, but their artistry and integrity still shine through. DP. A Dutch language film.

Dir Heddy Honigmann • *Scr* Heddy Honigmann, Nosh van der Lely • *Cinematographer* Eric Guichard

The Underneath ★★★ 15

Crime thriller 1995 · US · Colour · 94mins

In director Steven Soderbergh's intriguing remake of the 1949 *film noir Criss Cross*, Peter Gallagher takes on the Burt Lancaster role of the black sheep who returns to his Texas home town for his mother's wedding and gets caught up with former lover Alison Elliott and her crooked husband, William Fichtner. Soderbergh mixes erotic duplicity, sibling rivalry and sizzling suspense into an increasingly corkscrew plot with a surprise pay-off. A few style inconsistencies and a rather slow build-up aside, this is a tautly constructed thriller that makes pertinent points about sexual jealousy and cynical manipulation. AJ. Contains swearing and violence.

Peter Gallagher *Michael Chambers* • Alison Elliott (2) *Rachel* • William Fichtner *Tommy Dundee* • Adam Trese *David Chambers* • Joe Don Baker *Clay Hinkle* • Paul Dooley *Ed Dutton* • Elisabeth Shue *Susan* ■ *Dir* Steven Soderbergh • *Scr* Sam Lowry, Daniel Fuchs, from the film *Criss Cross* by Daniel Fuchs, from the novel *Criss Cross* by Don Tracy

Undertow ★★

Crime drama 1949 · US · BW · 71mins

Although he's better known for gimmicky horror movies, William Castle makes the most of this muted B feature crime drama, which marked the second screen appearance of one Rock Hudson. Star Scott Brady plays a war hero with a criminal past, whose hopes of opening a ski lodge seem dashed when he's framed for the murder of a mobster while stopping off in Chicago to collect girlfriend Dorothy Hart. A passable diversion. DP

Scott Brady *Tony Reagan* • John Russell *Danny Morgan* • Dorothy Hart *Sally Lee* • Peggy Dow *Ann McKnight* • Charles Sherlock *Cooper* • Rock Hudson *Detective* ■ *Dir* William Castle • *Scr* Lee Loeb, Arthur T Horman, from the story *The Big Frame* by Arthur T Horman

Undertow ★★★ 15

Crime drama 2004 · US · Colour · 107mins

Jamie Bell's first American film has the *Billy Elliot* boy pursued by a psychopathic uncle (Josh Lucas) who's after the gold coins that he and his younger brother have fled with after the killing of their father (Dermot Mulroney). Set among the backwater hamlets of Georgia, it's a strange and quirky chase thriller that chronicles the offbeat characters and situations the brothers encounter while running for their lives. This warped fairy tale's concerns are as much symbolic as they are realistic. An impressive international calling card for Bell, whose "Americanisation" is wholly convincing. DA. Contains violence.

Jamie Bell *Chris Munn* • Josh Lucas *Deel Munn* • Devon Alan *Tim Munn* • Dermot Mulroney *John Munn* • Shiri Appleby *Violet* • Pat Healy *Grant the mechanic* • Bill McKinney *Grandfather* ■ *Dir* David Gordon Green • *Scr* David Gordon Green, Joe Conway, from a story by Lingard Jervey

Underwater! ★★★ U

Adventure 1955 · US · Colour · 94mins

The most remarkable thing about this Jane Russell movie was not that it was the first film in Superscope, nor that it was started by cult director Nicholas Ray, but that its world premiere was held underwater in a headline-grabbing stunt organised by ace publicist Russell Birdwell (the man who once engineered the search for Scarlett O'Hara). The film itself is interesting enough. John Sturges eventually took over the directorial reins, but not even he could do much with the routine plot. TS

Jane Russell *Theresa* • Richard Egan *Johnny* • Gilbert Roland *Dominic* • Lori Nelson *Gloria* • Robert Keith (1) *Father Cannon* • Joseph Calleia *Rico* • Eugene Iglesias *Miguel* ■ *Dir* John Sturges • *Scr* Walter Newman, from the story *The Big Rainbow* by Hugh King, Robert B Bailey

Underworld ★★★★

Silent crime melodrama
1927 · US · BW · 75mins

Considered by some critics to be the first gangster picture, the model for a prolific genre, this silent film was based on an original story by Ben Hecht who, as a reporter, had witnessed several of the elements incorporated into the film. However, Hecht wanted his name taken off the credits because he felt that director Josef von Sternberg had distorted his intentions – though that didn't prevent him picking up his Oscar. It was only Sternberg's third solo feature and already his strong visual sense and eye for detail was evident. The plot involves a racketeer (George Bancroft), his moll (Evelyn Brent) and an alcoholic lawyer (Clive Brook), but it's less important than the atmosphere. RB

George Bancroft *"Bull" Weed* • Clive Brook *"Rolls Royce"* • Evelyn Brent *"Feathers"* • Larry Semon *"Slippy" Lewis* • Fred Kohler *"Buck" Mulligan* • Helen Lynch *Mulligan's girl* ■ *Dir* Josef von Sternberg • *Scr* Robert N Lee, Charles Furthman, from a story by Ben Hecht, George Marion Jr • *Cinematographer* Bert Glennon • *Set Designer* Hans Dreier

Underworld ★★★ 18

Comedy crime thriller
1996 · US · Colour · 95mins

Comedian-cum-actor Denis Leary stars in this violent gangster thriller as an ex-con who has to confront his past before looking to his future. That means killing the men who put his dad in a coma. Rooted in the idea of revenge as therapy, the film is solidly directed by Roger Christian, and evidently owes something to both *Pulp Fiction* and *The Usual Suspects*. However, spirited acting prevents familiarity breeding too much contempt. DA. Contains violence, swearing and sex scenes.

Denis Leary *Johnny Crown/Johnny Alt* • Joe Mantegna *Frank Gavilan/Richard Essex* • Annabella Sciorra *Dr Leah* • Larry Bishop *Ned Lynch* • Abe Vigoda *Will Cassady* • Robert Costanzo *Stan* • Traci Lords *Anna* • Jimmie F Skaggs *Smilin' Phil Fox/Todd Streeb* ■ *Dir* Roger Christian • *Scr* Larry Bishop

Underworld ★★ 15

Horror
2003 · US/Ger/Hun/ UK · Colour · 116mins

Debut director Len Wiseman has crafted the most stylistically derivative and monotonously plotted horror film possible. The casting is equally defective, with Kate Beckinsale unconvincing as a sullen vampire and Michael Sheen lacking stature as her werewolf enemy. Set against a hackneyed melancholy gothic backdrop, the story piles on scene after scene of portentous, humourless exposition. The film's final battle is faintly enjoyable, but only Bill Nighy makes any sort of real impression. JC. Contains swearing, violence. DVD

Kate Beckinsale *Selene* • Scott Speedman *Michael Corvin* • Michael Sheen *Lucian* • Bill Nighy *Viktor* • Shane Brolly *Kraven* • Erwin Leder *Singe* • Sophia Myles *Erika* • Robbie Gee *Kahn* ■ *Dir* Len Wiseman • *Scr* Danny McBride, from a story by Kevin Grevioux, Len Wiseman, Danny McBride

The Underworld Story ★★★

Crime drama 1950 · US · BW · 90mins

This tough-as-nails crime drama from director Cy Endfield was made before he fell foul of the Hollywood blacklist and moved to Britain. A co-feature

U

about a crusading reporter who uncovers small-town corruption, it's given muscle by rugged Dan Duryea as the hero and suave Herbert Marshall as the villain, while Gale Storm is intriguingly cast as a *femme fatale*. TS

Dan Duryea *Mike Reese* • Herbert Marshall *Stanton* • Gale Storm *Cathy* • Howard Da Silva *Durham* • Michael O'Shea *Munsey* • Mary Anderson *Molly* • Gar Moore *Clark* • Melville Cooper *Major Radford* ■ *Dir* Cy Endfield • *Scr* Henry Blankfort, Cy Endfield, from a story by Craig Rice

Underworld USA ★★★★

Crime drama 1961 · US · BW · 98mins

What sets this apart from other revenge movies is Cliff Robertson's brooding, stricken presence as a man seeking vengeance upon the four gangsters who, when he was young, killed his father. Sam Fuller's writing and direction substantiate the authenticity of the theme of sin without salvation and – unusually for a Fuller movie – women get a look in in this macho world. Dolores Dorn is a sympathetic girlfriend and Beatrice Kay a pillar of compassion. TH

Cliff Robertson *Tolly Devlin* • Dolores Dorn *Cuddles* • Beatrice Kay *Sandy* • Paul Dubov *Gela* • Robert Emhardt *Conners* • Larry Gates *Driscoll* • Richard Rust *Gus* ■ *Dir* Samuel Fuller • *Scr* Samuel Fuller, from articles in the *The Saturday Evening Post* by Joseph F Dinneen

Undisputed ★★★ 15

Prison sports drama
2002 · US · Colour · 89mins

Walter Hill's boxing drama exemplifies the director's predilection for studies of no-nonsense tough guys taking care of business. He rattles through the preamble, which witnesses both the sentencing of heavyweight champion Ving Rhames for rape and lifer Wesley Snipes attracting the attention of wily mobster Peter Falk after whupping a white supremacist in Sweetwater Prison's "combat cage". A rumble is inevitable and when it comes, it's unrivalled in its brutality. Rhames excels as the cocky champ. DP. Contains violence, swearing. [VIDEO] DVD

Wesley Snipes *Monroe Hutchens* • Ving Rhames *Iceman Chambers* • Peter Falk *Mendy Ripstein* • Michael Rooker *AJ Mercker* • Jon Seda *Jesus "Chuy" Campos* • Wes Studi *Mingo Pace* • Fisher Stevens *Ratbag Dolan* ■ *Dir* Walter Hill • *Scr* David Giler, Walter Hill

The Undying Monster ★★★

Monster horror 1942 · US · BW · 62mins

This Holmesian affair about a cursed English family places the emphasis on brooding atmosphere rather than horrific effects. Director John Brahm made his name with shadowy costume melodramas such as *Hangover Square*, and this thoughtful, if stolid, outing is one of his best – particularly for the brilliant striking-clock opening, which sets the gloomy tone. AJ

James Ellison *Bob Curtis* • Heather Angel *Helga Hammond* • John Howard (1) *Oliver Hammond* • Bramwell Fletcher *Dr Geoffrey Covert* • Heather Thatcher *Christy* • Aubrey Mather *Inspector Craig* ■ *Dir* John Brahm • *Scr* Lillie Hayward, Michael Jacoby, from the play by Jessie Douglas Kerruish

The Unearthly ★

Horror 1957 · US · BW · 68mins

Mad scientist John Carradine and his assistant Marilyn Buferd discover a new gland containing the secret of youth and, in their crazed efforts to achieve immortality, end up with a cellar full of grotesque monsters. Poorly scripted, crudely directed and overacted by Carradine to a distracting degree, this is cheap fear fodder. AJ

John Carradine *Professor Charles Conway* • Allison Hayes *Grace Thomas* • Myron Healey *Mark Houston* • Sally Todd *Natalie* • Marilyn Buferd *Dr Sharon Gilchrist* • Arthur Batanides *Danny Green* • Tor Johnson *Lobo* • Harry Fleer *Harry Jedrow* ■ *Dir* Brook L Peters • *Scr* Geoffrey Dennis [John DF Black], Jane Mann, from a story by Jane Mann

Unearthly Stranger ★★★

Science-fiction thriller
1963 · UK · Colour · 78mins

This under-rated sci-fi chiller stars John Neville stars as a scientist working on a secret space project, who discovers his wife (Gabriella Licudi) is an alien – after all, she does sleep with her eyes open and lift hot dishes out of the oven with her bare hands! John Krish directs with the kind of pace and imagination that's sadly lacking in so many of today's blockbusters, and the film includes the unforgettable image of the Licudi's tears burning marks down her face like acid. There's sterling support work, too, from Jean Marsh and Warren Mitchell. RS

John Neville *Dr Mark Davidson* • Gabriella Licudi *Julie Davidson* • Philip Stone *Professor John Lancaster* • Patrick Newell *Major Clarke* • Jean Marsh *Miss Ballard* • Warren Mitchell *Munro* ■ *Dir* John Krish • *Scr* Rex Carlton, from a story by Jeffrey Stone

The Unexpected Mrs Pollifax ★★★

Spy drama 1999 · US · Colour · 90mins

Venerable stage and screen actress Angela Lansbury gives a plucky performance as the silver-haired secret agent Emily Pollifax, who, recently widowed, pursues her lifelong ambition to become a spy. In a case of mistaken identity, she is hired by the CIA and sent to Morocco to pick up a book containing an encrypted message. Filmed on location in Ireland, Paris and Morocco, this diverting TV movie is fast-paced and fun. MC

Angela Lansbury *Mrs Pollifax* • Thomas Ian Griffith *Farrell* • Ed Bishop *Carstairs* • Joseph Long *Alekseiyagoda* • Paul Birchard *Bishop* ■ *Dir* Anthony Pullen Shaw • *Scr* Robert T Megginson, from the novel *A Palm for Mrs Pollifax* by Dorothy Gilman

The Unfaithful ★★★

Melodrama 1947 · US · BW · 108mins

Seven years after Bette Davis and Herbert Marshall starred so effectively in an adaptation of Somerset Maugham's *The Letter* for Warner Bros, the studio returned to the material, rearranging it, but retaining the central plot. Ann Sheridan is the woman who, having been unfaithful to her husband (Zachary Scott) during his absence on war duty, suffers genuine remorse over her infidelity and finds herself implicated in the murder of her erstwhile lover. Director Vincent Sherman, well in control, elicits a strong central performance from Sheridan and delivers an altogether respectable remake of a classic of stage and screen. RK

Ann Sheridan *Chris Hunter* • Lew Ayres *Larry Hannaford* • Zachary Scott *Bob Hunter* • Eve Arden *Paula* • Jerome Cowan *Prosecuting attorney* • Steven Geray *Martin Barrow* • John Hoyt *Detective-Lt Reynolds* • Peggy Knudsen *Claire* ■ *Dir* Vincent Sherman • *Scr* David Goodis, James Gunn, from the play *The Letter* by W Somerset Maugham (uncredited)

Unfaithful ★★ 15

Erotic thriller 2002 · US · Colour · 118mins

Director Adrian Lyne made a big impact in the 1980s with slick but enjoyable erotic dramas and he returns to familiar territory with this tale of adultery and its violent aftermath. Diane Lane is flung into the path of French super stud Olivier Martinez and embarks on a steamy affair that jeopardises her happy marriage to Richard Gere. Gere smells a rat and hires a private detective. It's stylishly executed, but is let down by an ambiguous ending. LH [VIDEO] DVD

Richard Gere *Edward Sumner* • Diane Lane *Constance "Connie" Sumner* • Olivier Martinez *Paul Martel* • Chad Lowe *Bill Stone* • Kate Burton *Tracy* • Margaret Colin *Sally* ■ *Dir* Adrian Lyne • *Scr* Alvin Sargent, William Broyles Jr, from the film *La Femme Infidèle* by Claude Chabrol

Unfaithfully Yours ★★★★ PG

Screwball comedy 1948 · US · BW · 100mins

In this highly amusing look at suspicion and revenge, Rex Harrison plays a celebrated conductor who believes his wife, Linda Darnell, is having an affair. Laced with director Preston Sturges's customary acidic humour, it has great wit and flair, and the scenes in which Harrison attempts to humiliate Darnell add a dash of strychnine in the mix. Darnell is sublime and the dramatic swathes of Rossini, Tchaikovsky and Wagner add to the dark atmosphere. This beautifully crafted black comedy was in no danger of being overshadowed by the 1984 remake. SH [VIDEO] DVD

Rex Harrison *Sir Alfred de Carter* • Linda Darnell *Daphne de Carter* • Rudy Vallee *August Henschler* • Barbara Lawrence *Barbara Henschler* • Kurt Kreuger *Anthony Windborn* • Lionel Stander *Hugo Standoff* • Edgar Kennedy *Detective Sweeney* ■ *Dir/Scr* Preston Sturges

Unfaithfully Yours ★★★ 15

Comedy 1983 · US · Colour · 92mins

Dudley Moore gives one of his better performances in this gently diverting and broadly satisfactory remake of the 1948 Preston Sturges comedy about a symphony orchestra conductor who suspects his young wife of making beautiful music with a handsome violinist. Indeed, as both a comedian and musician, Moore could hardly have better credentials for the role of a jealous conductor, originally played by Rex Harrison, while Nastassja Kinski is coquettish as his flirting spouse. A slighter film than the original, this is also a pacier one. PF [VIDEO]

Dudley Moore *Claude Eastman* • Nastassja Kinski *Daniella Eastman* • Armand Assante *Maximillian Stein* • Albert Brooks *Norman Robbins* • Cassie Yates *Carla Robbins* • Richard Libertini *Giuseppe* • Richard B Shull *Jess Keller* ■ *Dir* Howard Zieff • *Scr* Valerie Curtin, Barry Levinson, Robert Klane, from the 1948 film by Preston Sturges

Unfinished Business ★★★ U

Romantic comedy drama
1941 · US · BW · 95mins

En route to the big city, small-town girl Irene Dunne enjoys a trainboard romance with Preston Foster, but is later taken up by his brother, Robert Montgomery, whom she marries. The path of matrimony fails to run smoothly and Dunne runs off and joins the chorus of an opera house. This vapid romantic comedy, neither particularly romantic nor especially amusing, is elevated by the 18-carat direction of Gregory La Cava and the stylish performances of Dunne and Montgomery. RK

Irene Dunne *Nancy Andrews Duncan* • Robert Montgomery *Tommy Duncan* • Preston Foster *Steve Duncan* • Eugene Pallette *Elmer* • Esther Dale *Aunt Mathilda* • Dick Foran *Frank* ■ *Dir* Gregory La Cava • *Scr* Eugene Thackrey, Vicki Baum, from a story by Gregory La Cava

Unfinished Business ★★★

Drama 1983 · Can · Colour · 99mins

In *Nobody Waved Goodbye* (1964), Don Owen introduced us to Peter (Peter Kastner), an impulsive adolescent who ran away from his overbearing bourgeois parents and descended into petty crime before marrying Julie Biggs. Now, some 20 years later, they are divorced and struggling to maintain control over their own teenage daughter (Isabelle Mejias). Here was a golden opportunity to explore the way in which the flower-power generation handled the concerns of the kids of the nuclear age. But, instead, Owen concentrates on heredity and allows himself to be sidetracked by domestic melodrama. DP

Isabelle Mejias *Izzy Marks* • Peter Spence *Jesse* • Leslie Toth *Matthew* • Peter Kastner *Peter Marks* • Julie Biggs *Julie Marks* • Chuck Shamata *Carl* ■ *Dir/Scr* Don Owen

Unfinished Business ★★★

Comedy drama 1985 · Aus · Colour · 78mins

Bob Ellis made his directorial debut with this acerbic comedy of sexual manners, but while his screenplay contains the odd insight and some choice banter, his pacing and shot selection leave much to be desired. John Clayton and Michele Fawdon do, however, rise to the occasion as the old flames who embark on a clandestine relationship to provide her childless marriage with issue. DP

John Clayton *Geoff* • Michele Fawdon *Maureen* • Norman Kaye *George* • Bob Ellis *Geoff's Flatmate* • Andrew Lesnie *Telegraph Boy* ■ *Dir/Scr* Bob Ellis

Unfinished Business... ★★

Drama 1987 · US · Colour · 65mins

Great things were predicted for Swedish actress Viveca Lindfors when she first arrived in Hollywood in 1946. Though she married director Don Siegel, things didn't work out and she returned to Europe. In 78 films she never really found a role to showcase her talents and so she wrote one for herself. Based on her relationship with the playwright George Tabori (with whom she had a son, actor Kristoffer Tabori), the story concerns an actress deliberating whether to renew an affair with the Hungarian lover who hurt her so badly 15 years earlier. DP

Viveca Lindfors *Helena* • Peter Donat *Ferenzy* • Gina Hecht *Vickie* • James Morrison *Jonathan* • Anna Deavere Smith *Anna* • Hayley Taylor-Block *Kristina* ■ *Dir/Scr* Viveca Lindfors

The Unfinished Dance ★★

Dance drama 1947 · US · Colour · 100mins

Keen to break with her goodie image, Margaret O'Brien is superficially petulant as the trainee ballerina who sabotages Karin Booth's career to protect her idol Cyd Charisse. But she mugs less fiercely than comedian Danny Thomas, who is clearly out to make an impact in his film debut. The musical interludes are largely intrusive, but David Lichine's *Holiday for Strings* ballet will please dance fans. DP

Margaret O'Brien *Margaret "Meg" Merlin* • Cyd Charisse *Mlle Ariane Bouchet* • Karin Booth *Anna La Darina* • Danny Thomas *Mr Paneros* • Esther Dale *Olga* • Thurston Hall *Mr Ronsell* ■ *Dir* Henry Koster • *Scr* Myles Connolly, from the novel *La Mort du Cygne* by Paul Morand

U

An Unfinished Piece for Mechanical Piano ★★★★ U

Period romantic drama
1976 · USSR · Colour · 97mins

The cryptic title refers to Anton Chekhov's early unfinished play *Platanov*, which director Nikita Mikhalkov, who also plays the drunken doctor, has skilfully adapted for the screen. Set in 1910 and at times a tragic farce, the film beautifully captures the atmosphere of the lazy summer's day at widow Antonina Shuranova's country estate. The leisurely pace reflects the lethargy of the characters, who are superbly portrayed by the ensemble cast. RB. A Russian language film.

Aleksandr Kalyagin *Platonov* • Elena Solovei *Sophia* • Evgenia Glushenko *Sasha* • Antonina Shuranova *Anna Petrovna* • Yuri Bogatyrev *Sergei* ■ *Dir* Nikita Mikhalkov • *Scr* Nikita Mikhalkov, Aleksander Adabashyan, from the play *Platonov* by Anton Chekhov

The Unfinished Symphony ★★★

Musical biographical drama
1934 · Austria/UK · BW · 83mins

Hans Jaray plays Franz Schubert in a lush account of the composer's life and the story behind his failure to finish his most famous work. Filmed in Vienna and given a production rich in romantic atmosphere, the film benefits greatly from the Vienna Philharmonic Orchestra playing the composer's great works, with the chorus of the State Opera providing a stirring rendition of the *Ave Maria*. Heroine Marta Eggerth was an operetta star in Germany and Austriain the 1930s before a brief Hollywood career. TV

Helen Chandler *Emmie Passenter* • Marta Eggerth *Caroline Esterhazy* • Hans Jaray *Franz Schubert* • Ronald Squire *Count Esterhazy* • Beryl Laverick *Mary* • Hermine Sterler *Princess Kinsky* • Cecil Humphreys *Salieri* ■ *Dir* Willy Forst, Anthony Asquith • *Scr* Benn W Levy, from a story by Walter Reisch

Unforgettable ★★ 15

Thriller 1996 · US · Colour · 112mins

In order to find his wife's killer, police medical examiner Ray Liotta injects himself with the secret memory-transfer formula of researcher Linda Fiorentino, together with the brain fluid of his wife, in order to "see" her last memories. Amazingly, this outrageous premise never comes across as the least bit goofy, but that's where the problem lies. The film is so solemn and serious that it never gets a chance to be exciting and mysterious. KB. Contains swearing.

Ray Liotta *Dr David Krane* • Linda Fiorentino *Dr Martha Briggs* • Peter Coyote *Don Bresler* • Christopher McDonald *Stewart Gleick* • David Paymer *Curtis Avery* • Duncan Fraser *Michael Stratton* • Caroline Elliott *Cara Krane* ■ *Dir* John Dahl • *Scr* Bill Geddie

An Unforgettable Summer ★★★★

Period political drama
1994 · Fr/Rom · Colour · 80mins

Directed with the unflinching honesty that has characterised Lucian Pintilie's canon, this adaptation may be set in the mid-1920s, but it packs a powerful contemporary punch. Dispatched to an isolated garrison on Romania's border with Bulgaria, Claudiu Bleont is ordered to shoot local Bulgarian-speaking peasants as a reprisal for an ambush by Macedonian bandits. However, his judgement is clouded by the compassion of his wife, Kristin Scott Thomas. Exposing the racial hatred that blights this tinder-box region, Pintilie's impeccably performed picture is not so much a plea for tolerance as an anguished cry to stop the insanity. DP. In Romanian, French and English with subtitles.

Kristin Scott Thomas *Marie-Therese Von Debretsy* • Claudiu Bleont *Captain Dumitriu* • Olga Tudorache *Mme Vorvoreanu* • George Constantin *General Tchilibia* • Ion Pavlescu *Serban Lascari* ■ *Dir* Lucian Pintilie • *Scr* Lucian Pintilie, from the short story *La Salade* by Petru Dumitriu

U

Unforgivable ★★ 15

Drama based on a true story
1995 · US · Colour · 87mins

Based on a true story, this TV movie centres on a compulsive wife-beater's attempts to save his marriage by undergoing counselling. John Ritter is perhaps not everyone's idea of an abusive thug, but he nevertheless turns in a creditable performance, and he's neatly supported by Harley Jane Kozak. But this slice of sensationalism dressed as sincerity will fool no one. DP. Contains violence. DVD

John Ritter *Paul Hegstrom* • Harley Jane Kozak *Judy Hegstrom* • Kevin Dunn *Milt Steiner* • Susan Gibney *Beth* • Gina Phillips [Gina Philips] *Tammy Hegstrom* ■ *Dir* Graeme Campbell • *Scr* Dan Levine, AR Simoun, from a story by AR Simoun

The Unforgiven ★★★★ PG

Western 1960 · US · Colour · 116mins

This handsome Texas-set western from director John Huston is based on a novel by Alan LeMay, whose more famous *The Searchers* tells the flipside of this tale. Huston is particularly well served by Burt Lancaster and an interesting support cast. Only Audrey Hepburn, unusually, lacks credibility. Superbly photographed on location by Franz Planer, with a fine Dimitri Tiomkin score, this film deserves to be better known. The racial issues it deals with are no less comfortable now than they were at both the time of the historical events and when the movie was made. TS DVD

Burt Lancaster *Ben Zachary* • Audrey Hepburn *Rachel Zachary* • Audie Murphy *Cash Zachary* • John Saxon *Johnny Portugal* • Charles Bickford *Zeb Rawlins* • Lillian Gish *Mattilda Zachary* • Albert Salmi *Charlie Rawlins* ■ *Dir* John Huston • *Scr* Ben Maddow, from the novel by Alan LeMay

Unforgiven ★★★★★ 15

Western 1992 · US · Colour · 125mins

Winner of four Oscars, including best picture and best director, Clint Eastwood's western is one of the finest films made in the genre. Exploring the harsh realities of frontier life, he depicts the west as an unforgiving place. It's clear from the fevered manner in which Saul Rubinek's dime novelist gathers his Wild West stories that an era is about to pass into legend. Eastwood's own world-weary performance as the retired gunslinger, forced to strap on the six-shooters one last time to feed his children, is exemplary. The support playing of Morgan Freeman as his former partner, Richard Harris as a vain killer and Oscar-winning Gene Hackman as the vicious sheriff is unsurpassable. DP. Contains violence and swearing. DVD

Clint Eastwood *William Munny* • Gene Hackman *Sheriff "Little Bill" Daggett* • Morgan Freeman *Ned Logan* • Richard Harris *English Bob* • Jaimz Woolvett *"Schofield Kid"* • Saul Rubinek *WW Beauchamp* • Frances Fisher *Strawberry Alice* • Anna Thomson [Anna Levine] *Delilah Fitzgerald* ■ *Dir* Clint Eastwood • *Scr* David Webb Peoples

The Unholy ★ 18

Horror 1988 · US · Colour · 97mins

In a misguided and ultimately tedious attempt at a theologically-themed horror movie, Ben Cross is the priest who, after surviving a drop from a five-storey building, becomes the "Chosen One" and is assigned to rid a church of a demonic presence that's seducing and killing clergymen. Good location work in New Orleans, but Camilo Vila's slow-paced direction kills this stone dead. RS DVD

Ben Cross *Father Michael* • Ned Beatty *Lieutenant Stern* • William Russ *Luke* • Jill Carroll *Millie* • Hal Holbrook *Archbishop Mosley* • Trevor Howard *Father Silva* • Peter Frechette *Claude* ■ *Dir* Camilo Vila • *Scr* Philip Yordan, Fernando Fonseca

The Unholy Garden ★★ U

Crime drama 1931 · US · BW · 71mins

This decidedly creaky Samuel Goldwyn production stars Ronald Colman and Fay Wray in a tale of desert intrigue. It was the first original screenplay written for Hollywood by the New York theatre team of Ben Hecht and Charles MacArthur, who quickly devised the plot (a den of thieves, a beautiful girl, etc) in return for an astronomical $25,000 and a slice of the profits. Slightly unfairly trashed by the critics and ended up losing $200,000. AT

Ronald Colman *Barrington Hunt* • Fay Wray *Camille de Jonghe* • Estelle Taylor *Eliza Mowbray* • Tully Marshall *Baron de Jonghe* • Ulrich Haupt [Ullrich Haupt] *Colonel Von Axt* • Henry Armetta *Nick the Goose* • Lawrence Grant *Dr Shayne* ■ *Dir* George Fitzmaurice • *Scr* Ben Hecht, Charles MacArthur

Unholy Partners ★★

Crime drama 1941 · US · BW · 94mins

Edward G Robinson and Mervyn LeRoy made one of the first of the crusading newspaper movies, *Five Star Final*, in 1931. But this similarly themed story, set just after the First World War, isn't in the same league – though Robinson is incapable of delivering a boring performance. He plays an idealistic editor whose paper is bankrolled by racketeer Edward Arnold. The story of their feud features too many ridiculous contrivances and melodramatics. AT

Edward G Robinson *Bruce Corey* • Edward Arnold *Merrill Lambert* • Laraine Day *Miss Cronin* • Marsha Hunt *Gail Fenton* • William T Orr *Tommy Jarvis* • Don Beddoe *Michael Z Reynolds* • Walter Kingsford *Managing editor* • Charles Dingle *Clyde Fenton* ■ *Dir* Mervyn LeRoy • *Scr* Earl Baldwin, Bartlett Cormack, Lesser Samuels

The Unholy Rollers ★★★

Sports action drama
1972 · US · Colour · 88mins

A funky and very funny cult classic from the Roger Corman production line, this stars the wonderful Claudia Jennings, the *Playboy* model-turned-action heroine. She hits the *Rocky* road to fame as a single-minded factory worker desperate for glory in the roller-derby ring. How she overcomes the usual slew of obstacles – vicious rivals, bitchy opponents and domestic problems – is brilliantly marshalled with zip, zing and charm by director Vernon Zimmerman. AJ

Claudia Jennings *Karen* • Louis Quinn *Stern* • Betty Anne Rees *Mickey* • Roberta Collins *Jennifer* • Alan Vint *Greg* • Candice Roman *Donna* ■ *Dir* Vernon Zimmerman • *Scr* Howard R Cohen, from a story by Vernon Zimmerman, Howard R Cohen

The Unholy Three ★★★★

Silent crime drama 1925 · US · BW · 86mins

A midget who masquerades as a baby, a giant strongman and a cross-dressing ventriloquist (Lon Chaney) become a crime syndicate in miniature in director Tod Browning's strangely affecting silent melodrama. This is a serious and imaginative presentation of diabolical deeds, cruel vindictiveness and ghoulish humour. Genre creator Browning fashions unique thrills from the sheer novelty value of the freak-show outlaw story and highlights the twisted scenario with a wealth of deft cinematic touches. This sensational shocker is one of his, and Chaney's, finest achievements. AJ

Lon Chaney *Professor Echo/Granny O'Grady* • Harry Earles *Tweedledee* • Victor McLaglen *Hercules* • Mae Busch *Rosie O'Grady* • Matt Moore *Hector McDonald* • Matthew Betz *Regan* • William Humphreys *Defense attorney* ■ *Dir* Tod Browning • *Scr* Waldemar Young, from the story *The Terrible Three* by Clarence Aaron "Tod" Robbins

The Unholy Three ★★

Crime drama 1930 · US · BW · 75mins

The success of the 1925 version of Clarence Aaron "Tod" Robbins's story about a triumvirate of circus exiles becoming master criminals led to this remake, cashing in on the novelty of sound. It's Lon Chaney's first talkie and his last picture ever as he died from throat cancer shortly afterwards. Director Jack Conway is clearly not in the same class as *auteur* Tod Browning and his quick refit is far inferior to the original. AJ

Lon Chaney *Prof Echo* • Lila Lee *Rosie O'Grady* • Elliott Nugent *Hector McDonald* • Harry Earles *Midget* • John Miljan *Prosecuting attorney* • Ivan Linow *Hercules* • Clarence Burton *Regan* • Crauford Kent *Defense attorney* ■ *Dir* Jack Conway • *Scr* JC Nugent, Elliott Nugent, from the story *The Terrible Three* by Clarence Aaron "Tod" Robbins

The Unholy Wife ★★

Crime drama 1957 · US · Colour · 94mins

Diana Dors's Hollywood sojourn yielded two RKO programme fillers, this crime melodrama and the dreadful *I Married a Woman*. Unfortunately for Dors, there were just too many starlets in the studio system, and she couldn't compete with the likes of Marilyn Monroe and Jayne Mansfield. Rod Steiger manages to chew less scenery than usual in his role as Dors's cuckolded husband, but overall this has few memorable moments. TS

Rod Steiger *Paul Hochen* • Diana Dors *Phyllis Hochen* • Tom Tryon *San* • Beulah Bondi *Emma Hochen* • Marie Windsor *Gwen* • Arthur Franz *Reverend Stephen Hochen* • Luis Van Rooten *Ezra Benton* • Joe De Santis *Gino Verdugo* ■ *Dir* John Farrow • *Scr* Jonathan Latimer, from a story by William Durkee

Unhook the Stars ★★★ 15

Comedy drama 1996 · Fr · Colour · 100mins

Nick Cassavetes (son of actor/director John) directs his mother Gena Rowlands in this comedy drama. Marisa Tomei gives a nice performance as the young mother who disrupts the life of neighbour Rowlands while looking for a babysitter for her son. However, Rowlands unsurprisingly steals the film from not only Tomei, but also male co-star Gérard Depardieu, who seems slightly ill at ease throughout. Nonetheless, it's an interesting and character-driven film which once again confirms what a superb acting treasure America has in Rowlands. JB. Contains swearing and sexual references.

Gena Rowlands *Mildred* • Marisa Tomei *Monica* • Gérard Depardieu *Big Tommy* • Jake Lloyd *JJ* • Moira Kelly *Ann Mary Margaret* • David Sherrill *Ethan* ■ *Dir* Nick Cassavetes • *Scr* Nick Cassavetes, Helen Caldwell

The Uninvited ★★★★★

Horror 1944 · US · BW · 98mins

The *Casablanca* of horror, this is a programme filler in which all the elements came together to produce a classic of the genre. Brother and sister Ray Milland and Ruth Hussey buy a house in Cornwall and find it haunted. Though containing what are now narrative clichés (a mysterious room, sinister housekeeper) and strained humour, this is an ingenious ghost story. Aided by Charles Lang's photography and Victor Young's score, it still sends shivers up the spine. This was the first film by Lewis Allen who failed to re-create the formula in his follow-up, *The Unseen*. DM

Ray Milland *Roderick "Rick" Fitzgerald* • Ruth Hussey *Pamela Fitzgerald* • Donald Crisp *Commander Beech* • Cornelia Otis Skinner *Miss Holloway* • Dorothy Stickney *Miss Bird* • Barbara Everest *Lizzie Flynn* • Alan Napier *Dr Scott* • Gail Russell *Stella Meredith* ■ *Dir* Lewis Allen • *Scr* Dodie Smith, Frank Partos, from the novel *Uneasy Freehold* by Dorothy Macardle

Union City ★★ 15

Drama 1980 · US · Colour · 81mins

Blondie singer Debbie Harry plays the plain, frustrated wife of a meek businessman (Dennis Lipscomb) whose obsession with catching a petty thief leads to murder. Director Mark Reichert plays it too offbeat, arty and tricksy for it to emerge as another classic from Cornell Woolrich's work. Most of the opportunities for smart black comedy are blown by the relentlessly downbeat tone and Reichert's fudged aim for Fassbinder-esque European irony. AJ [video]

Dennis Lipscomb *Harlan* • Deborah Harry *Lillian* • Irina Maleeva *Mrs Gofka – the Contessa* • Everett McGill *Larry Longacre* • Sam McMurray *Young vagrant* • Terina Lewis *Evelyn – secretary* • Pat Benatar *Jeanette* ■ *Dir* Mark Reichert • *Scr* Mark Reichert, from the story *The Corpse Next Door* by Cornell Woolrich

Union Depot ★★★

Comedy drama 1932 · US · BW · 75mins

Completely overshadowed by MGM's *Grand Hotel* to which it is often compared, this modest offering from First National, set amid the bustle of a major train station, is a snappy and appealing entertainment. Douglas Fairbanks Jr stars as a young hobo who finds some money, decks himself out as a gentleman, and falls for a broke dancer (Joan Blondell) who needs $64 to get to Salt Lake City. Quite silly, but the stars are charming and attractive and the supporting players excellent. RK

Douglas Fairbanks Jr *Chic Miller* • Joan Blondell *Ruth* • Guy Kibbee *Scrap Iron* • Alan Hale *Baron* • Frank McHugh *Drunk* • George Rosener *Bernardi* • Dickie Moore *Little Boy* ■ *Dir* Alfred E Green • *Scr* Kenyon Nicholson, Walter DeLeon, John Bright, Kubec Glasmon, from the play by Gene Fowler, Douglas Durkin, Joe Laurie

Union Pacific ★★★ U

Western 1939 · US · BW · 134mins

This epic about the construction of the first transcontinental railroad was a smash hit in 1939. It stars Joel McCrea as the overseer for Union Pacific, fighting local tribesman and saboteurs on the way to linking up with the Central Pacific line. Barbara Stanwyck is a tomboy postmistress and Robert Preston (in his first big role) impresses as a likeable gambler. As usual, producer/director Cecil B DeMille stages too many scenes in the comfort of a sound stage, relying on obvious back projection, and it is the outdoor footage, including the raid on the train, that provides the film's most memorable moments. AE

Barbara Stanwyck *Mollie Monahan* • Joel McCrea *Jeff Butler* • Akim Tamiroff *Fiesta* • Robert Preston *Dick Allen* • Lynne Overman *Leach Overmile* • Brian Donlevy *Sid Campeau* • Lon Chaney Jr *Dollarhide* ■ *Dir* Cecil B DeMille • *Scr* Walter DeLeon, C Gardner Sullivan, Jesse Lasky Jr, Jack Cunningham, from the novel *Trouble Shooters* by Ernest Haycox

Union Station ★★★

Crime thriller 1950 · US · BW · 80mins

Considered a real nailbiter in its day, this competent police thriller benefits from the real location of the concourse, platforms and threatening bowels of a bustling Art Deco station. Here, a millionaire is instructed to deliver the ransom for his kidnapped blind daughter. William Holden, tight-jawed and efficient, is in charge of the on-the-spot manhunt, Barry Fitzgerald is the kindly police chief and Nancy Olson the necessary feminine interest. Ace cinematographer-turned-director Rudolph Maté extracts maximum mileage from the settings, and wrings tension from the simple plot. RK

William Holden (2) *Lt William Calhoun* • Nancy Olson *Joyce Willecombe* • Barry Fitzgerald *Insp Donnelly* • Lyle Bettger *Joe Beacom* • Jan Sterling *Marge Wrighter* • Allene Roberts *Lorna Murcall* • Herbert Heyes *Henry Murcall* • Don Dunning *Gus Hadder* ■ *Dir* Rudolph Maté • *Scr* Sydney Boehm, from the story *Nightmare in Manhattan* by Thomas Walsh

The United States of Leland ★★★ 15

Crime drama 2002 · US · Colour · 104mins

When moody but intelligent teenager Ryan Gosling murders a learning disabled youngster, juvenile detention teacher Don Cheadle is determined to discover what provoked such a senseless, shocking act. However, like most of the characters in this thoughtful indie drama, he also has an ulterior motive. While it's a little contrived at times, writer/director Matthew Ryan Hoge's impressive debut feature offers an unsettling portrait of alienated youth and explores how the lines between good and evil have become increasingly blurred. JF DVD

Ryan Gosling *Leland P Fitzgerald* • Don Cheadle *Pearl Madison* • Chris Klein *Allen Harris* • Jena Malone *Becky Pollard* • Lena Olin *Marybeth Fitzgerald* • Kevin Spacey *Albert T Fitzgerald* • Michelle Williams *Julie Pollard* • Martin Donovan (2) *Harry Pollard* ■ *Dir/Scr* Matthew Ryan Hoge

Universal Horror ★★★★ PG

Documentary
1998 · UK · Colour and BW · 95mins

Kevin Brownlow ranks alongside Henri Langlois as one of cinema's most significant archivists, and here he has compiled a fascinating insight into the working methods of the production unit that made Universal the biggest name in horror. Recalling the achievements of such craftsmen as Karl Freund, James Whale and Jack Pierce (who created the now legendary bolt-necked Frankenstein make-up), this documentary explores the German Expressionist influence on 1930s Hollywood horror and the debt owed to such European actors as Boris Karloff and Bela Lugosi. Combining clips, archive interviews and the reminiscences of stalwarts such as Fay Wray, it is both hugely informative and highly entertaining. DP [video]

Kenneth Branagh *Narrator* ■ *Dir* Kevin Brownlow

Universal Soldier ★★★ 18

Futuristic action thriller
1992 · US · Colour · 99mins

This sci-fi potboiler from director Roland Emmerich is a by-the-numbers affair, with dialogue you'd swear appears in comic balloons. But as no one takes the ultimate warrior premise seriously, the unpretentious pandering to the action-plus brigade is a likeable strength, not a jarring weakness. The Muscles from Brussels (Jean-Claude Van Damme) has the edge over the Swedish Meatball (Dolph Lundgren) in every respect, from his showcase kick boxing to his send-up nude scene, in this OTT jeopardy jackpot. AJ. Contains violence and swearing [video] DVD

Jean-Claude Van Damme *Luc Devreux* • Dolph Lundgren *Andrew Scott* • Ally Walker *Veronica Roberts* • Ed O'Ross *Colonel Perry* • Jerry Orbach *Dr Gregor* • Leon Rippy *Woodward* • Tico Wells *Garth* • Ralph Moeller *GR76* ■ *Dir* Roland Emmerich • *Scr* Richard Rothstein, Christopher Leitch, Dean Devlin

Universal Soldier 2: Brothers in Arms ★★ 18

Futuristic action thriller
1998 · Can · Colour · 89mins

Although Jean-Claude Van Damme eventually returned for a big-screen follow-up to *Universal Soldier*, this is the official sequel, even though it's a TV movie with a totally different cast. Having been starved of funds to develop his army of undead warriors, UnSol supremo Gary Busey sets out to teach Washington a lesson. However, he hasn't counted on journalist Chandra West and her combat-hardened boyfriend, Matt Battaglia. Undemanding. DP. Contains violence, swearing and nudity. [video]

Matt Battaglia *Luc Devreaux* • Jeff Wincott *Eric* • Chandra West *Veronica Roberts* • Gary Busey *Mazur* • Burt Reynolds *Mentor* ■ *Dir* Jeff Woolnough • *Scr* Peter M Lenkov

Universal Soldier 3: Unfinished Business ★★ 18

Futuristic action thriller
1998 · US · Colour · 91mins

Having been less than enthralled with the results of reconstructing an army from the dead in part two, those fiendish UnSol boffins set out to create test-tube troopers in this follow-up TV movie. Although it starts tiresomely with a lengthy resumé of previous events, the new adventure eventually kicks in, with Matt Battaglia and reporter sidekick Chandra West being challenged with halting the dangerous research. DP [video]

Matt Battaglia *Luc Devreaux* • Jeff Wincott *Eric* • Chandra West *Veronica Roberts* • Gary Busey *Mazur* • Burt Reynolds *Mentor* ■ *Dir* Jeff Woolnough • *Scr* Peter M Lenkov

Universal Soldier – the Return ★ 18

Futuristic action thriller
1999 · US · Colour · 83mins

This is an insultingly awful big-screen follow-up to the 1992 Jean-Claude Van Damme hit. His nice guy terminator is now a technical adviser on the secret government project that turns dead soldiers into killing machines. Thinly plotted and painfully clichéd even by genre standards, this is a moronic mess. JC. Contains violence, swearing and nudity. [video] DVD

Jean-Claude Van Damme *Luc Devreaux* • Michael Jai White *SETH* • Heidi Schanz *Erin* • Xander Berkeley *Dylan Cotner* • Justin Lazard *Captain Blackburn* • Kiana Tom *Maggie* • Daniel Von Bargen *General Radford* • James Black *Sergeant Morrow* ■ *Dir* Mic Rodgers • *Scr* William Malone, John Fasano, from the characters created by Richard Rothstein, Christopher Leitch, Dean Devlin

The Unkissed Bride ★

Comedy 1966 · US · Colour · 82mins

The term "unkissed" is a rather polite euphemism: the person struggling here to fulfil his wedding night sexual obligations with Anne Helm is former Disney juvenile lead Tommy Kirk. To cure his condition, Kirk has LSD sprayed on him while he sleeps, so his dreamy fairy-tale fantasies become real, and that's why this mindless opus never passed the British censor. TS. Contains drug abuse.

Tom Kirk [Tommy Kirk] *Ted* • Anne Helm *Margie* • Jacques Bergerac *Jacques Phillipe* • Danica d'Hondt *Doctor Marilyn Richards* ■ *Dir/Scr* Jack H Harris

The Unknown ★★★★ PG

Silent drama 1927 · US · BW · 49mins

Single-minded in its brutality, perversity and odd shock value, Tod Browning's Freudian nightmare is the most accomplished and morbid melodrama the Master of Silent Macabre ever directed. Lon Chaney straps his arms down with a painful harness as Alonzo the Armless Wonder, a circus performer who throws knives with his feet. It's when he falls in love with Joan Crawford who has a fear of being touched that murder, amputation and obsession come under the dark carnival spotlight. A fascinating silent classic, it still appals because of its sadomasochistic and devious tone. AJ. Contains violence DVD

Lon Chaney *Alonzo* • Norman Kerry *Malabor* • Joan Crawford *Estrellita* • Nick De Ruiz *Zanzi* • John George *Cojo* • Frank Lanning *Costra* ■ *Dir* Tod Browning • *Scr* Waldemar Young, from a story by Tod Browning

The Unknown Guest ★★ U

Mystery drama 1943 · US · BW · 64mins

A script by Philip Yordan and a score by Dmitri Tiomkin (although hardly their best work) add to the unnerving atmosphere of this curious country chiller in which the arrival of renegade Victor Jory coincides with the disappearance of his aged aunt and uncle from their hotel. Director Kurt Neumann puts an interesting slant on small-town life. DP

Victor Jory *Chuck Williams* • Pamela Blake *Julie* • Veda Ann Borg *Helen* • Harry Hayden *Nadroy* • Nora Cecil *Martha Williams* • Lee White [Lee "Lasses" White] *Joe Williams* • Paul Fix *Fats* ■ *Dir* Kurt Neumann • *Scr* Philip Yordan, from a story by Maurice Franklin

Unknown Pleasures ★★★ 12

Comedy drama
2002 · Chi/Jpn/Fr/S Kor · Colour · 107mins

Shooting on digital video in the rundown industrial town of Datong, director Jia Zhang Ke offers a wry look at the flip side of China's much-vaunted consumer boom. Wu Qiong and Zhao Wei Wei are persuasively indolent as the unemployed teenagers latching on to anything to occupy their time, with Wu's obsession with Zhao Tao (a self-deluded dancer with a brewery road show) providing much of the comic incident. But it's his fellow slacker's more considered approach to the future that proves more poignant, especially once he's diagnosed with hepatitis. DP. In Mandarin with English subtitles. [video] DVD

Zhao Tao *Qiao Qiao* • Zhao Wei Wei *Bin Bin* • Wu Qiong *Xiao Ji* • Zhou Qing Feng *Yuan Yuan* • Wang Hong Wei *Xiao Wu* ■ *Dir/Scr* Jia Zhang Ke

The Unknown Soldier ★★★★ 15

War drama 1983 · Fin · Colour · 149mins

Having lost land to the USSR in the "Winter War" of 1939–40, Finland briefly allied with Hitler during the so-called "Continuation War" of 1941–44, when 80,000 men were lost in a counterattack for which the Finnish forces were singularly unprepared. The implications of that alliance were still a source of shame, but Rauni Mollberg's epic is more concerned with the emotions of the teenage conscripts who were sent on what amounted to a suicide mission. DP. A Finnish language film. Contains some swearing, sexual references and violence. [video]

Risto Tuorila *Koskela* • Pirkka-Pekka Petelius *Hietanen* • Paavo Liski *Rokka* • Mika Makela *Rahikainen* • Pertti Koivula *Lahtinen* ■ *Dir* Rauni Mollberg • *Scr* Rauni Mollberg, Veikko Aaltonen, from a novel by Väinö Linna

U

Unknown World ★ U

Science-fiction adventure
1951 · US · BW · 74mins

Scientists bore into the Earth aboard a half tank/half submarine mole ship, dubbed a "cyclotram", to find a subterranean safe haven from atomic war. Unfortunately, the peaceful centre proves harmful to human reproduction in a highly moral sci-fi quickie containing a wordy script, plodding direction, dinky special effects and not even an occasional thrill. AJ

Victor Kilian *Dr Jeremiah Morley* • Bruce Kellogg *Wright Thompson* • Otto Waldis *Dr Max A Bauer* • Marilyn Nash *Joan Lindsey* • Jim Bannon *Andy Ostengaard* ■ *Dir* Terrell O Morse [Terry Morse] • *Scr* Millard Kaufman

Unlawful Entry ★★★ 18

Thriller 1992 · US · Colour · 106mins

Meet the psychotic cop – so unbalanced that you see him unravelling before your eyes. He's portrayed with credibility by Ray Liotta, who never reduces his character to caricature. As he targets innocent couple Kurt Russell and Madeleine Stowe, his insecurities become unnervingly mixed in with his charm. Sadly, there are yawning gaps in the plot, and the climax is overcooked you can't help but laugh. JM. Contains violence, swearing, nudity. DVD

Kurt Russell *Michael Carr* • Ray Liotta *Officer Pete Davis* • Madeleine Stowe *Karen Carr* • Roger E Mosley *Officer Roy Cole* • Ken Lerner *Roger Graham* • Deborah Offner *Penny* • Carmen Argenziano *Jerome Lurie* ■ *Dir* Jonathan Kaplan • *Scr* Lewis Colick, from a story by George D Putnam, John Katchner, Lewis Colick

Unlawful Passage ★★

Drama 1994 · US · Colour · 125mins

Lee Horsley and his soap-star wife Felicity Waterman are totally out of their depth as the stylish couple whose luxury yacht is commandeered by drug smugglers. Waterman has her moments, using her charms to befuddle her kidnappers, but Horsley is less than convincing as the architect-turned-action hero in this ocean-going thriller. DP. Contains violence, swearing, sex scenes and nudity.

Lee Horsley *Peter Browning* • Felicity Waterman *Gale Browning* • William Zabka *Howie* • Leslie Ming *Patrick* ■ *Dir* Camilo Vila • *Scr* Peter L Dixon

Unleashed ★★★ 18

Action thriller
2005 · Fr/US/UK · Colour · 101mins

Martial arts star Jet Li plays a sort of human Rotweiller, raised and kept caged like an animal, who is only unleashed when gangster Bob Hoskins needs some fighting done. Set in Glasgow, this sees Li rediscovering his humanity, courtesy of the relationship he builds with blind piano tuner Morgan Freeman. The fight scenes are fast, brutal and with a feel of the real about them, but this is also Li's most interesting non-Hong Kong work to date. DA. Contains violence, swearing and nudity.

Jet Li *Danny* • Morgan Freeman *Sam* • Bob Hoskins *Bart* • Kerry Condon *Victoria* • Michael Jenn *Wyeth* ■ *Dir* Louis Leterrier • *Scr* Luc Besson

Unman, Wittering and Zigo ★★★★

Mystery 1971 · UK · BW · 101mins

No surprise that this creepy script by Giles Cooper moved from medium to medium (a radio play in 1957, then a TV play in 1965, and then this 1971 film) as it is a truly nightmarish scenario. Teacher David Hemmings is informed by his pupils at a boys' public school that they murdered his predecessor and will bump him off as well if he doesn't follow orders. Hemmings conveys very well the terror of being at the mercy of a class of delinquents, and the suspense is marred only by occasionally fussy camerawork. DM

David Hemmings *John Ebony* • Douglas Wilmer *Headmaster* • Anthony Haygarth [Tony Haygarth] *Cary Farthingale* • Carolyn Seymour *Silvia Ebony* • Hamilton Dyce *Mr Winstanley* • Barbara Lott *Mrs Winstanley* • Michael Cashman *Terhew* ■ *Dir* John Mackenzie • *Scr* Simon Raven, from the play by Giles Cooper

An Unmarried Woman ★★★★ 18

Romantic comedy
1978 · US · Colour · 119mins

Jill Clayburgh produces an assured and sensitive portrayal of wounded Big Apple womanhood when her privileged Manhattan lifestyle is undermined by her husband leaving her. Director Paul Mazursky has a sharp eye for New York detail – lots of vacuous parties, sweaty aerobics and a perceptive parade of Clayburgh's self-obsessed beaus. As her character inches towards feminism, Clayburgh truly comes into her own as the movie's second half gains neat pace and momentum. It doesn't matter that it all looks a little dated at times. SH

Jill Clayburgh *Erica* • Alan Bates *Saul* • Michael Murphy *Martin* • Cliff Gorman *Charlie* • Pat Quinn [Patricia Quinn] *Sue* • Kelly Bishop *Elaine* • Lisa Lucas *Patti* • Linda Miller *Jeannette* • Andrew Duncan *Bob* ■ *Dir/Scr* Paul Mazursky

The Unnamable ★ 18

Horror 1988 · US · Colour · 83mins

This tedious haunted house tale ransacks the ingeniously twisted work of HP Lovecraft to little horrific effect. A demon pursues four university students through an old mansion sealed years before by a priest. Lots of annoying false scares, fake tree monsters and bloody decapitations lead to a daft climax. Unwatchable. JF. Contains violence. DVD

Charles King (3) *Howard Damon* • Mark Kinsey Stephenson *Randolph Carter* • Alexandra Durrell *Tanya Heller* • Katrin Alexandre *The Creature* • Laura Albert *Wendy Barnes* • Delbert Spain *Joshua Winthrop* ■ *Dir* Jean-Paul Ouellette • *Scr* Jean-Paul Ouellette, from the story by HP Lovecraft

The Unnamable Returns ★ 18

Horror 1992 · US · Colour · 99mins

...but whatever for? Literally picking up the story on exactly the same night the uninspired original ended, this sequel features Maria Ford as an ancient monster's beautiful alter ego who can't stop her beastly half gorily killing off more Arkham County inhabitants. While marginally better than its predecessor (this one actually has a budget), this is not only unnamable, but unnecessary. AJ. Contains swearing. DVD

Mark Kinsey Stephenson *Randolph Carter* • Charles Klausmeyer *Eliot Damon Howard* • Maria Ford *Alyda Winthrop* • John Rhys-Davies *Professor Harley Warren* • David Warner *Chancellor Thayer* • Richard Domeier *Officer Malcolm Bainbridge* • Siobhan McCafferty *Officer Debbie Lesh* ■ *Dir* Jean-Paul Ouellette • *Scr* Jean-Paul Ouellette, from the stories *The Statement of Randolph Carter* and *The Unnamable* by HP Lovecraft

Unpublished Story ★★

Second World War drama
1942 · UK · BW · 91mins

Richard Greene was seconded from the Army to star in this flag-waver, which bears a passing resemblance to *Foreign Correspondent*. As in Hitchcock's picture, a peace organisation is at the centre of some disreputable dealings until it's exposed by a reporter. Greene is captured by Nazi spies using their privileged position to snoop with impunity. Luckily, plucky Valerie Hobson is on hand to bail him out – though this requires plenty of noble sacrifice. Diverting rather than involving. DP

Richard Greene *Bob Randall* • Valerie Hobson *Carol Bennett* • Basil Radford *Lamb* • Roland Culver *Stannard* • Brefni O'Rorke *Denton* • Miles Malleson *Farmfield* ■ *Dir* Harold French • *Scr* Anatole de Grunwald, Patrick Kirwan, Sidney Gilliat, Lesley Storm, from a story by Anthony Havelock-Allan, from a story by Allan MacKinnon

An Unremarkable Life ★★

Drama 1989 · US · Colour · 98mins

A melodramatic talk-fest about two elderly cohabiting sisters who fall out when one decides to start dating, thus upsetting the duo's finely balanced equilibrium. This is a cue for much bickering and even more reminiscing. There are quality performances from Hollywood veterans Patricia Neal and Shelley Winters, but their efforts are wasted on a script that needed to be sharper and wittier. DA

Patricia Neal *Frances McEllany* • Shelley Winters *Evelyn McEllany* • Mako *Max Chin* ■ *Dir* Amin Q Chaudhri • *Scr* Marcia Dinneen

Les Uns et les Autres ★★★

Historical drama 1981 · Fr · Colour · 185mins

As a bloated, all-stops-out melodrama this effort from Claude Lelouch takes some beating, though an hour may be enough for the majority of viewers. Starting in 1936, it chronicles the lives of four couples (played by actors in multiple roles) – American, Russian, French and German – and takes them through the obstacle race and marathon that is that thing called life. The music links everyone together in a sort of hey-ho, let's-go medley. Exhausting yet somehow amazing. AT. In French with English subtitles.

James Caan *Glenn Sr/Glenn Jr* • Robert Hossein *Simon Meyer/Robert Prat* • Nicole Garcia *Anne* • Geraldine Chaplin *Suzan/Sarah Glenn* • Daniel Olbrychski *Karl* • Jacques Villeret *Jacques* ■ *Dir/Scr* Claude Lelouch

The Unseen ★★★

Murder mystery 1945 · US · BW · 81mins

Although co-scripted by Raymond Chandler, this has none of the sawn-off dialogue for which he was famous. Nevertheless, it's full of an atmosphere of foreboding as governess Gail Russell starts to believe that dark deeds were done in a neighbouring house and Joel McCrea's children had something to do with them. There is a mood of authentic creepiness that was obviously meant to follow in the same shuddery footfalls as the previous year's *The Uninvited*, which was also directed by Lewis Allen. TH

Joel McCrea *David Fielding* • Gail Russell *Elizabeth Howard* • Herbert Marshall *Dr Charles Evans* • Richard Lyon *Barnaby Fielding* • Nona Griffith *Ellen Fielding* • Phyllis Brooks *Maxine* • Isobel Elsom *Marian Tygarth* • Norman Lloyd *Jasper Goodwin* ■ *Dir* Lewis Allen • *Scr* Raymond Chandler, Hagar Wilde, Ken Englund, from the novel *Her Heart in Her Throat* by Ethel Lina White

The Unsinkable Molly Brown ★★★★ U

Musical 1964 · US · Colour · 123mins

This has much to recommend it, particularly the leading performance of the Oscar-nominated Debbie Reynolds. Despite marrying well, the once-impoverished Molly Brown (Reynolds) still craves acceptance by Denver's high society. Director Charles Walters does what he can with a substandard score by *The Music Man's* Meredith Willson, but is helped by a sparkling cast, especially Jack Kruschen and *grande dame* Martita Hunt, revelling in their roles. The Colorado scenery (filmed on location) is splendid, as is leading man Harve Presnell. TS

Debbie Reynolds *Molly Brown* • Harve Presnell *Johnny Brown* • Ed Begley *Shamus Tobin* • Jack Kruschen *Christmas Morgan* • Hermione Baddeley *Mrs Grogan* • Vassili Lambrinos *Prince Louis de Laniere* • Fred Essler *Baron Karl Ludwig von Ettenburg* • Martita Hunt *Grand Duchess Elise Lupovinova* • Harvey Lembeck *Polak* ■ *Dir* Charles Walters • *Scr* Helen Deutsch, from the musical by Meredith Willson, Richard Morris

The Unspoken Truth ★★ 15

Drama based on a true story
1995 · US · Colour · 87mins

This TV movie stars Lea Thompson as a wife who is so loyal to her abusive husband (James Marshall) that she agrees to share the blame for a murder he has committed. The drama then switches to her bid to retain custody of her daughter and her sister's determination to leak a dark family secret to secure her release. Full of unlikely events and resistible characters. DP. Contains violence. DVD

Lea Thompson *Brianne Hawkins* • Patricia Kalember *Margaret Trainor* • James Marshall *Clay Hawkins* • Dick O'Neill *Thomas Cleary* • Karis Paige Bryant *Lily Hawkins* ■ *Dir* Peter Werner • *Scr* JA Mitty

Unstrung Heroes ★★★★ PG

Comedy drama based on a true story
1995 · US · Colour · 89mins

This is a charming film from actress/director Diane Keaton (who remains behind the camera for this one). Nathan Watt plays the little boy who grows up under the influence of his quirky father John Turturro (superb) and his even wackier uncles (Maury Chaykin and Michael Richards) when his mother Andie MacDowell (in her best performance to date) becomes seriously ill. Keaton capably handles the mix of humour and sadness, delivering a superbly performed, moving and very funny tale about growing up and the weirdness of families. JB DVD

Andie MacDowell *Selma Lidz* • John Turturro *Sid Lidz* • Michael Richards *Danny Lidz* • Maury Chaykin *Arthur Lidz* • Nathan Watt *Steven/Franz Lidz* • Kendra Krull *Sandy Lidz* ■ *Dir* Diane Keaton • *Scr* Richard LaGravenese, from the book by Franz Lidz

An Unsuitable Job for a Woman ★★★ 15

Mystery 1981 · UK · Colour · 90mins

This is the original film adaptation of PD James's bestseller, later made into a TV series starring Helen Baxendale. Pippa Guard is quietly efficient as Cordelia Gray, who takes over a detective agency after her partner commits suicide. There's certainly nothing straightforward about her first case: she's hired to investigate the "suicide" of a businessman's son in a picturesque cottage. Director Christopher Petit casts a moody pall over traditional whodunnit country and scatters clues with skill. DP

Billie Whitelaw *Elizabeth Leaming* • Pippa Guard *Cordelia Gray* • Paul Freeman *James Callender* • Dominic Guard *Andrew Lunn* • Elizabeth Spriggs *Miss Markland* • David Horovitch *Sergeant Maskell* • Dawn Archibald *Isobel* • James Gilbey *Boy* ■ *Dir* Christopher Petit • *Scr* Elizabeth McKay, Brian Scobie, Christopher Petit, from the novel by PD James

The Unsuspected ★★★★

Crime drama 1947 · US · BW · 102mins

This virtually unknown but highly under-rated suspense thriller is impeccably

U

directed by the great Michael Curtiz and features the urbane Claude Rains as a radio star performer specialising in spine-shivering broadcasts. This was actually intended as a starring vehicle for one Michael North, a Curtiz discovery who didn't work out, and the subsequent revoicing of North and the minimising of his role creates a truly unsettling feeling throughout the film. The period insights into the workings of radio are deftly done, as are the action sequences, but the clever scripting is the real bonus. TS

Claude Rains *Victor Grandison* • Joan Caulfield *Matilda Frazier* • Audrey Totter *Althea Keane* • Constance Bennett *Jane Moynihan* • Hurd Hatfield *Oliver Keane* • Michael North [Ted North] *Steven Francis Howard* • Fred Clark *Richard Donovan* • Jack Lambert *Mr Press* ■ *Dir* Michael Curtiz • *Scr* Ranald MacDougall, Bess Meredyth, from a novel by Charlotte Armstrong

Untamed ★★★

Romantic adventure
1955 · US · Colour · 108mins

This is a splendid early CinemaScope melodrama, with the then-new widescreen process deployed effectively in a South Africa-located tale of a trek across the veldt. Passions flare and Zulus attack the wagon train in this lusty adaptation of a bodice-ripper of a novel. Featuring two of 20th Century-Fox's finest (handsome Tyrone Power and fiery redhead Susan Hayward), this is one of the last examples of this type of imperialist tosh. There's some fine support, but the real star here is the stunning photography. TS

Tyrone Power *Paul Van Riebeck* • Susan Hayward *Katie O'Neill* • Richard Egan *Kurt Hout* • John Justin *Shawn Kildare* • Agnes Moorehead *Aggie* • Rita Moreno *Julia* • Hope Emerson *Maria De Groot* ■ *Dir* Henry King • *Scr* Talbot Jennings, Frank Fenton, William A Bacher, Michael Blankfort, from the novel by Helga Moray • *Cinematographer* Leo Tover

Untamed Frontier ★★

Western 1952 · US · Colour · 75mins

This is a routine range war western, despite talented Argentine director Hugo Fregonese's attempts to make something more of the territorial theme. Joseph Cotten and Shelley Winters star, but there's certainly nothing in the script worthy of attention. As much of a chore to watch as the cast and crew obviously felt it was to make. TS

Joseph Cotten *Kirk Denbow* • Shelley Winters *Jane Stevens* • Scott Brady *Glenn Denbow* • Suzan Ball *Lottie* • Minor Watson *Matt Denbow* • Katherine Emery *Camilla Denbow* • Lee Van Cleef *Dave Chittun* ■ *Dir* Hugo Fregonese • *Scr* Gerald Drayson Adams, John Bagni, Polly James, Gwen Bagni, from a story by Houston Branch, Eugenia Night

Untamed Heart ★★★ 15

Romantic drama 1993 · US · Colour · 97mins

Marisa Tomei and Christian Slater both work hard to wring every ounce of emotion from director Tony Bill's well-meaning, if slightly contrived, romance. Slater is the shy kitchen guy with a congenital heart defect who saves waitress Tomei from some thugs, an event that leads the bruised souls to embark on a hesitant relationship. Everyone says it can't last, especially delicious Rosie Perez in another of her trademark sassy, wisecracking roles but, although the outcome is fairly predictable, there's enough here to engage. AJ. Contains violence, swearing, nudity. [VIDEO] DVD

Christian Slater *Adam* • Marisa Tomei *Caroline* • Rosie Perez *Cindy* • Kyle Secor *Howard* • Willie Garson *Patsy* • Claudia Wilkens *Mother Camilla* ■ *Dir* Tony Bill • *Scr* Tom Sierchio

Untamed Love ★★★ 12

Drama based on a true story
1994 · US · Colour · 91mins

An affecting and compassionate look at child abuse through the true story of a six-year-old girl and her special education teacher. The Americans do this kind of TV movie in two ways, as either embarrassingly mawkish or thoughtful and mature. *Untamed Love* is in the latter category, with good performances from Cathy Lee Crosby and Ashlee Lauren as the determined teacher and her hapless pupil respectively. SH [VIDEO] DVD

Cathy Lee Crosby *Maggie Bernard* • John Getz *Chad* • Gary Frank *Mr Eldridge* • Ashlee Lauren *Caitlin Eldridge* • Jaime P Gomez [Jaime Gomez] *Miguel* • Mel Winkler *Sam Powers* ■ *Dir* Paul Aaron • *Scr* Peter Nelson, from the book *One Child* by Torey Hayden

Untamed Youth ★

Musical prison drama
1957 · US · BW · 77mins

Mamie Van Doren and Lori Nelson star as hitch-hiking chanteuses, who are forced to work on John Russell's Californian plantation by his corrupt paramour, judge Lurene Tuttle. However, their scantily-clad exploitation is exposed by Tuttle's hunk son, Don Burnett, although not before Van Doren has belted out a quartet of woeful ditties that leave room for only one tune from rocker Eddie Cochran. Unintentionally hilarious. DP

Mamie Van Doren *Penny* • Lori Nelson *Janey* • John Russell *Tropp* • Don Burnett *Bob* • Eddie Cochran *Bong* • Lurene Tuttle *Mrs Steele* • Yvonne Lime *Baby* ■ *Dir* Howard W Koch • *Scr* John C Higgins, from a story by Stephen Longstreet

Until September ★★ 15

Romantic drama 1984 · US · Colour · 92mins

Richard Marquand directs this ill-conceived romantic drama. Karen Allen is the Yank visiting France who misses her flight home and then falls for dashing Thierry Lhermitte (*Le Cop*). The international cast does its best, but no-one's heart really seems to be in it. JF. Contains swearing and nudity. [VIDEO]

Karen Allen *Mo Alexander* • Thierry Lhermitte *Xavier de la Perouse* • Christopher Cazenove *Philip* • Marie Catherine Conti *Isabelle* • Hutton Cobb *Andrew* • Michael Mellinger *Colonel Viola* ■ *Dir* Richard Marquand • *Scr* Janice Lee Graham

Until the End of the World ★★ 15

Science-fiction road movie
1991 · Ger/Fr/Aus · Colour · 151mins

This misbegotten epic shows how an art house director can blow $23 million and still emerge with a three-hour film that's less than perfect. Thus Wim Wenders took William Hurt, Max von Sydow, Sam Neill and others to eight countries without a script, assuming that sheer genius was enough. All they had was an idea about a nuclear satellite crashing to Earth in 1999 and a cluster of unrelated subplots. Nicely shot, though. AT. Contains violence, swearing and nudity. [VIDEO]

William Hurt *Trevor McPhee/Sam Farber* • Solveig Dommartin *Claire Tourneur* • Sam Neill *Eugene Fitzpatrick* • Max von Sydow *Henry Farber* • Rüdiger Vogler *Philip Winter* • Ernie Dingo *Burt* • Jeanne Moreau *Edith Farber* ■ *Dir* Wim Wenders • *Scr* Wim Wenders, Peter Carey, from the story by Wim Wenders, Solveig Dommartin

Until They Sail ★★★

Second World War drama
1957 · US · BW · 94mins

A marvellously overwrought war drama, brought to the screen with a superb cast: Joan Fontaine, Jean Simmons, Piper Laurie and Sandra Dee as sisters, getting emotionally wrapped up with American servicemen, with murder and melodrama as the result. Superbly directed by ace craftsman Robert Wise, this also features a handsome Paul Newman and the excellent pre-Disney Dean Jones. No great shakes, but a jolly good matinée weepie. TS

Jean Simmons *Barbara Leslie Forbes* • Joan Fontaine *Anne Leslie* • Paul Newman *Captain Jack Harding* • Piper Laurie *Delia Leslie* • Charles Drake *Captain Richard Bates* • Sandra Dee *Evelyn Leslie* • Wally Cassell *"Shiner" Phil Friskett* • Alan Napier *Prosecution* • Dean Jones ■ *Dir* Robert Wise • *Scr* Robert Anderson, from a story by James A Michener

Untold Scandal ★★★★ 18

Period drama 2003 · S Kor · Colour · 124mins

By translating the action of Choderlos de Laclos's novel *Les Liaisons Dangereuses* to 18th-century Korea, director E J-Yong breathes new life into the story of an unscrupulous noblewoman (Lee Mi-Sook) who challenges her predatory would-be lover (Bae Yong-Jun) to seduce a famously chaste widow (Jun Do-Youn). The vicious games of power and seduction that ensue are given an extra intensity as the forces of Confucianism and Catholicism (the widow is Catholic) clash with the conservatism of the Chosun dynasty. A majestic film, impeccably played, handsomely designed and gloriously photographed. DP. In Korean with English subtitles. Contains sex scenes.

Bae Yong-Jun *Cho-won* • Lee Mi-Sook *Lady Cho* • Jun Do-Youn *Lady Sook* • Cho Hyun-Jae *Kwon In-ho* • Lee So-Yeon *Lee So-ok* ■ *Dir* E J-Yong • *Scr* Kim Deh-Woo, Kim Hyun-Jung, E J-Yong, from the novel *Les Liaisons Dangereuses* by Choderlos de Laclos • *Cinematographer* Kim Byung-Il

The Untouchables ★★★★★ 15

Crime drama 1987 · US · Colour · 114mins

In Brian De Palma's riveting take on the old TV show, Kevin Costner gives a star-making performance as Eliot Ness, the quiet Treasury agent and family man who picks up a pump-action rifle in order to rid Chicago of bootlegger Al Capone. Always a showman, De Palma lets loose with a barrage of bloody set pieces, notably the climax at the railway station – a nod to the famous Odessa steps sequence in *The Battleship Potemkin*. David Mamet's dialogue crackles, Ennio Morricone's music soars and the production design sparkles. Andy Garcia joins the team, and a plumped-up Robert De Niro plays Capone, yet for many the main attraction is Sean Connery's Oscar-winning performance as the veteran cop who shows Costner the ropes. AT. Contains violence, swearing. [VIDEO] DVD

Kevin Costner *Eliot Ness* • Sean Connery *Jim Malone* • Andy Garcia *George Stone* • Robert De Niro *Al Capone* • Charles Martin Smith *Oscar Wallace* • Richard Bradford *Mike* • Jack Kehoe *Payne* • Brad Sullivan *George* • Billy Drago *Frank Nitti* ■ *Dir* Brian De Palma • *Scr* David Mamet, suggested by the TV series and from the works of Oscar Fraley, with Eliot Ness, Paul Robsky • *Cinematographer* Stephen H Burum • *Production Designer* Patrizia von Brandenstein

Unzipped ★★★★ 15

Documentary
1995 · US · Colour and BW · 73mins

This hugely enjoyable documentary follows New York fashion designer Isaac Mizrahi as he plans his 1994 show around an "Eskimo" look inspired by another documentary, 1922's *Nanook of the North*. Mizrahi performs very amusingly for the camera, and his supermodels (Naomi Campbell, Cindy Crawford, Kate Moss et al) also seem to know exactly how to behave for maximum effect; and yet, despite the artifice, this is a far truer portrait of the world of haute couture than Altman's farcical *Pret-a-Porter*. Not surprisingly, director Douglas Keeve is a fashion photographer, and his mostly black-and-white footage contrasts strikingly with colour for the clothes sequences. DM

Dir Douglas Keeve

Up ★★★ 18

Sex comedy 1976 · US · Colour · 78mins

The penultimate movie from the notorious Russ Meyer stars the inexplicably named Raven De La Croix as a woman who revenges herself against the man who raped her. It's one of his best and most outrageous, typically overflowing with outsize bosoms, cartoon violence and Bible-thumbing morality that ensures wrongdoers get their just deserts. The Meyer sense of humour is also intact, one shot takes place inside a man's trousers as his flies are unzipped. From a story co-written by celebrated US film critic Roger Ebert, this is likely to offend most fragile sensibilities, feminists especially. RS. Contains strong sex scenes and violence. [VIDEO]

Robert McLane *Paul* • Edward Schaaf *Adolph Schwartz* • Mary Gavin *Headsperson* • Elaine Collins *Ethiopian chief* • Su Ling *Limehouse* • Linda Sue Ragsdale *Gwendolyn* • Janet Wood *Sweet Li'l Alice* • Raven De La Croix *Margo Winchester* ■ *Dir* Russ Meyer • *Scr* B Callum [Russ Meyer], from a story by Russ Meyer, Reinhold Timme [Roger Ebert], Jim Ryan

Up at the Villa ★★★★ 12

Period romantic thriller
1998 · US · Colour · 110mins

The dark forces of fascism intrude upon idyllic Tuscany in this stylishly shot 1930s drama. Kristin Scott Thomas, a penniless aristocrat on the verges of colonial society, is befriended by countess Anne Bancroft and pursued by a stalwart Edward Fox. In a matter of hours her world is turned upside down by two chance encounters: one with a refugee that results in murder, the other with a rakish Sean Penn whose appearance sparks mutual passion. The chemistry between the two leads is tangible, while Philip Haas directs with an energy that makes his film very compelling indeed. LH. [VIDEO]

Kristin Scott Thomas *Mary Panton* • Sean Penn *Rowley Flint* • Anne Bancroft *Princess San Ferdinando* • James Fox *Sir Edgar Swift* • Jeremy Davies *Karl Richter* • Derek Jacobi *Lucky Leadbetter* • Dudley Sutton *Harold Atkinson* ■ *Dir* Philip Haas • *Scr* Belinda Haas, from a novella by W Somerset Maugham

Up Close & Personal ★★★ 15

Romantic drama
1996 · US · Colour · 119mins

Robert Redford and Michelle Pfeiffer star in this romantic drama set in a Miami television newsroom. Redford plays the veteran former White House correspondent who takes small-town girl Pfeiffer under his wing, helping her overcome stage fright and seeing her career as a television journalist take off as his idles. It's all tosh, of course, but its *Star Is Born* theme of male self-sacrifice is finely manipulated by director Jon Avnet so, as a three-hankie movie, it's not to be sniffed at. TH. Contains swearing, violence and sexual references. [VIDEO] DVD

Robert Redford *Warren Justice* • Michelle Pfeiffer *Tally "Sallyanne" Atwater* • Stockard Channing *Marcia McGrath* • Joe Mantegna *Bucky Terranova* • Kate Nelligan *Joanna Kennelly* • Glenn Plummer *Ned Jackson* • James Rebhorn *John Merino* • Scott Bryce *Rob Sullivan* • Dedee Pfeiffer *Luanne Atwater* ■ *Dir* Jon Avnet • *Scr* Joan Didion, John Gregory Dunne, from the book *Golden Girl* by Alanna Nash

U

Up from the Beach ★★★ U

Second World War drama
1965 · US · BW · 98mins

Cliff Robertson gives his usual distinguished performance as an American army sergeant who becomes involved with Resistance civilians after the D-Day landings. Slow-moving, but it has its gripping moments, especially with Françoise Rosay playing an elderly peasant-woman whom you just don't know whether to trust or not. Director Robert Parrish controls the action, but takes it all at too steady a pace. TH

Cliff Robertson *Sgt Edward Baxter* • Red Buttons *Pfc Harry Devine* • Irina Demick *Lili Rolland* • Marius Goring *German Commandant* • Slim Pickens *Artillery Colonel* • James Robertson-Justice *British Beachmaster* • Broderick Crawford *US MP Major* • Françoise Rosay *Lili's grandmother* ■ *Dir* Robert Parrish • *Scr* Stanley Mann, Claude Brulé, Howard Clewes, from the novel *Epitaph For an Enemy* by George Barr

Up in Arms ★★★ U

Musical comedy 1944 · US · Colour · 105mins

A remake of the 1930 Eddie Cantor vehicle *Whoopee!*, this first starring vehicle for Danny Kaye has dated badly, its wartime theme about a hypochondriac who's drafted into the army seeming faintly distasteful today, and the obvious studio settings aren't enhanced by the garish 1940s Technicolor. Nevertheless, former Broadway comedian Kaye proves to be far superior to his surroundings, aided by some wonderful material. Dinah Shore and Constance Dowling both look ravishing in 1940s get-up. TS

Danny Kaye *Danny Weems* • Constance Dowling *Mary Morgan* • Dinah Shore *Virginia Merrill* • Dana Andrews *Joe Nelson* • Louis Calhern *Colonel Ashley* • George Mathews *Blackie* • Benny Baker *Butterball* • Elisha Cook Jr *Info Jones* ■ *Dir* Elliott Nugent • *Scr* Don Hartman, Allen Boretz, Robert Pirosh, from the play *The Nervous Wreck* by Owen Davis

Up in Central Park ★★★

Musical comedy 1948 · US · BW · 86mins

This is a disappointing adaptation of the Broadway success, dealing with the unlikely subject of city hall corruption, revolving around New York's notoriously crooked statesman Boss Tweed, played effectively by Vincent Price. Turned here into a vehicle for Deanna Durbin, the film loses most of the original Sigmund Romberg score, though Dick Haymes makes a likeable enough leading man. The film needed a more expensive production, but Durbin fans will cherish this, her penultimate movie before her retirement. TS

Deanna Durbin *Rosie Moore* • Dick Haymes *John Matthews* • Vincent Price *Boss Tweed* • Albert Sharpe *Timothy Moore* • Tom Powers *Regan* • Hobart Cavanaugh *Mayor Oakley* • Thurston Hall *Governor Motley* ■ *Dir* William A Seiter • *Scr* Karl Tunberg, from the play by Dorothy Fields, Herbert Fields, Sigmund Romberg

U

Up in Mabel's Room ★★

Farce 1944 · US · BW · 76mins

The marital bliss of newly married Dennis O'Keefe and Marjorie Reynolds is shattered when O'Keefe's friendship with glamorous Gail Patrick, the fiancée of his business partner Lee Bowman, is misinterpreted. A standard bedroom farce, it's directed by Allan Dwan, it's good-natured but uninterestingly tame. RK

Dennis O'Keefe *Gary Ainsworth* • Marjorie Reynolds *Geraldine Ainsworth* • Gail Patrick *Mabel Essington* • Mischa Auer *Boris* • Charlotte Greenwood *Martha* • Lee Bowman *Arthur Weldon* • John Hubbard *Jimmy Larchmont* • Binnie Barnes *Alicia Larchmont* ■ *Dir* Allan Dwan • *Scr* Tom Reed, Isobel Dawn, from a play by Wilson Collison, Otto Harbach, from the story *Oh Chemise* by Wilson Collison

Up in the Cellar ★★★★

Comedy 1970 · US · Colour · 93mins

Wes Stern is a hapless student whose life is turned upside down when his poetry scholarship is annulled by a rogue computer. He finds himself a puppet in a battle between David Arkin, a wealthy student with ideas of revolution, and the monstrous college president Larry Hagman. Using sex as a weapon, Stern tries to get at Hagman through the women in his life. Director Theodore J Flicker's follow-up to his magnificent satire *The President's Analyst* is another effervescent comedy overflowing with great ideas and cunning twists. DF

Wes Stern *Colin Slade* • Joan Collins *Pat Camber* • Larry Hagman *Maurice Camber* • Nira Barab *Tracy Camber* • Judy Pace *Harlene Jones* • David Arkin *Hugo* ■ *Dir* Theodore J Flicker • *Scr* Theodore J Flicker, from the novel *The Late Wonder Boy* by Angus Hall

Up in the World ★★ U

Comedy 1956 · UK · BW · 86mins

This tacky comedy gave notice that Norman Wisdom's winning formula was beginning to wear thin. The slapstick centres around ladders and broken windows, as window cleaner Wisdom becomes friends with a lonely boy millionaire (Michael Caridia), much to the annoyance of sniffy guardian Jerry Desmonde. The scenes involving Caridia and a hamster called Harold are bathed in sentiment, but the worst aspect of this maudlin mishmash is that Wisdom gets to warble so often. DP DVD

Norman Wisdom *Norman* • Maureen Swanson *Jeannie* • Jerry Desmonde *Major Willoughby* • Ambrosine Philpotts *Lady Banderville* • Colin Gordon *Fletcher Hetherington* • Michael Caridia *Sir Reginald Banderville* ■ *Dir* John Paddy Carstairs • *Scr* Jack Davies, Henry E Blyth, Peter Blackmore

Up 'n' Under ★★ 12

Sports comedy 1997 · UK · Colour · 98mins

A top line-up of British sitcom stars takes to the rugby field in a mildly diverting by-the-numbers sports comedy. Gary Olsen bets his house on a ridiculous wager with smug rival Tony Slattery. Naturally, Olsen's team is the least enthusiastic and skilful in the land. Very, very predictable fare, but it pushes some of the right buttons. JC. Contains swearing.

Gary Olsen *Arthur Hoyle* • Neil Morrissey *Steve* • Samantha Janus *Hazel Scott* • Richard Ridings *Frank* • Ralph Brown *Phil* • Adrian Hood *Tommy* • David MacCreedy *Tony* • Tony Slattery *Reg Welch* • Griff Rhys Jones *Ray Mason* ■ *Dir* John Godber • *Scr* John Godber, from his play

Up on the Roof ★★ 15

Musical drama 1997 · UK · Colour · 95mins

It's difficult to identify with the dreams and disappointments of a group of Hull University buddies, despite the best efforts of a bullish cast of British newcomers. The trouble is that Adrian Lester's pop wannabe, Daniel Ryan's garden-centre boss, Clare Cathcart's singing waitress and Billy Carter's children's television star have been designed to fit their slots in the storyline. They don't click as people, whether as 1970s students or their older selves reuniting for Amy Robbins's wedding and for a 15-year-anniversary of their graduation. DP. Contains a sex scene, swearing.

Billy Carter *Tim* • Clare Cathcart *Angela* • Adrian Lester *Scott* • Amy Robbins *Bryony* • Daniel Ryan *Keith* • Lavinia Bertram *Bryony's mother* • Robin Herford *Gavin* ■ *Dir* Simon Moore • *Scr* Simon Moore, Jane Prowse

Up Periscope ★★★ U

Second World War drama
1959 · US · Colour · 99mins

Warner Bros knew the box-office value of a good submarine flick, having produced *Destination Tokyo*. Here the ever-economic studio reworked the sets from the previous year's Alan Ladd vehicle *The Deep Six* to showcase its new star, TV's *Maverick* James Garner, in a nail-biting Second World War drama. This also benefits from the skill of veteran director Gordon Douglas, and from stalwart Edmond O'Brien in support. TS

James Garner *Ken Braden* • Edmond O'Brien *Stevenson* • Andra Martin *Sally* • Alan Hale Jr *Malone* • Carleton Carpenter *Carney* • Frank Gifford *Mount* • William Leslie *Doherty* ■ *Dir* Gordon Douglas • *Scr* Richard Landau, from the novel by Robb White

Up Pompeii ★★ 15

Comedy 1971 · UK · Colour · 86mins

Frankie Howerd dons a toga for a film version of his TV series based on the life of Roman slave Lurcio. Unfortunately, the blatantly obvious *Carry On*-style formula (the cast even features *Carry On* regular Bernard Bresslaw) only works sporadically. There's more interest in trying to put names to the plethora of familiar British faces in the cast, among them Patrick Cargill as the Emperor Nero and Michael Hordern as the unfortunate Ludicrus Sextus. NF. Contains nudity. DVD

Frankie Howerd *Lurcio* • Patrick Cargill *Nero* • Michael Hordern *Ludicrus* • Barbara Murray *Ammonia* • Lance Percival *Bilius* • Bill Fraser *Prosperus* • Adrienne Posta *Scrubba* • Julie Ege *Voluptua* • Bernard Bresslaw *Gorgo* • Roy Hudd *MC* ■ *Dir* Bob Kellett • *Scr* Sid Colin, from an idea by Talbot Rothwell

Up the Academy ★★ 15

Comedy 1980 · US · Colour · 83mins

Trying to emulate the success of *National Lampoon*, *Mad* magazine got into the movie business with this irreverent, bad-taste saga of high jinks at a military academy. Star Ron succeeded in getting his name taken off the credits and later even *Mad* magazine itself, disowned the movie. Despite all this, the film does have a crude energy. DF

Ron Leibman *Major* • Wendell Brown *Ike* • Tom Citera *Hash* • J Hutchinson *Oliver* • Ralph Macchio *Chooch* • Harry Teinowitz *Ververgaert* • Tom Poston *Sisson* • Ian Wolfe *Commandant Caseway* ■ *Dir* Robert Downey Sr • *Scr* Tom Patchett, Jay Tarses

Up the Chastity Belt ★★ PG

Period comedy 1971 · UK · Colour · 89mins

A glance at the credits – produced by Ned Sherrin, script by Sid Colin, Ray Galton and Alan Simpson, score by Carl Davis – raises one's hopes for this medieval incarnation of Frankie Howerd's TV hit *Up Pompeii*. But, sadly, expectations are soon dashed as it becomes clear that Lurkalot is a pale imitation of his ancient ancestor Lurcio. Howerd looks very ordinary beside the infinitely more versatile supporting cast of top character comics. DP DVD

Frankie Howerd *Lurkalot/King Richard The Lionheart* • Graham Crowden *Sir Coward de Custard* • Bill Fraser *Sir Braggart de Bombast* • Roy Hudd *Nick the Pick* • Hugh Paddick *Robin Hood* • Anna Quayle *Lady Ashfodel* • Lance Percival *Reporter* • Godfrey Winn *Archbishop of all England* • Eartha Kitt *Scheherazade* ■ *Dir* Bob Kellett • *Scr* Sid Colin, Ray Galton, Alan Simpson

Up the Creek ★★★ U

Comedy 1958 · UK · BW · 79mins

Veteran writer/director Val Guest and an experienced cast of *farceurs* enliven this British naval farce with its timeworn story of an incompetent officer pitted against the wily lower ranks. Silly, accident-prone David Tomlinson is given the command of an ancient destroyer, where Peter Sellers controls the rackets. The chaos when admiral Wilfrid Hyde White arrives for an inspection is extremely funny. The film's success inspired a sequel, *Further up the Creek*. DM DVD

David Tomlinson *Lt Humphrey Fairweather* • Peter Sellers *Bosun Docherty* • Wilfrid Hyde White *Admiral Foley* • Vera Day *Lily* • Liliane Sottane *Susanne* • Tom Gill *Flag Lieutenant* • Michael Goodliffe *Nelson* • Reginald Beckwith *Publican* ■ *Dir* Val Guest • *Scr* Val Guest, Len Heath, John Warren

Up the Down Staircase ★★

Drama 1967 · US · Colour · 123mins

Sandy Dennis plays a young, novice teacher who has her ideals severely tested in an underfunded, bureaucratic inner-city school. Much of the movie is shot on location but, even though the kids perform well, the adult characters are a little too pat for the film to be totally convincing. JG

Sandy Dennis *Sylvia Barrett* • Patrick Bedford *Paul Barringer* • Eileen Heckart *Henrietta Pastorfield* • Ruth White *Beatrice Schracter* • Jean Stapleton *Sadie Finch* • Sorrell Booke *Dr Bester* ■ *Dir* Robert Mulligan • *Scr* Tad Mosel, from the novel by Bel Kaufman

Up the Front ★ PG

Comedy 1972 · UK · Colour · 84mins

The final film to be spun off from TV's *Up Pompeii* leaves Frankie Howerd stranded in the middle of no man's land with nothing more than a tattoo to cover his blushes. Not even Morecambe and Wise's regular writer Eddie Braben could do anything to pep up Sid Colin's desperate script, while the lacklustre performances really merit reproach. DP

Frankie Howerd *Lurk* • Zsa Zsa Gabor *Mata Hari* • Bill Fraser *Groping* • Lance Percival *Von Gutz* • Stanley Holloway *Vincento* • Madeline Smith *Fanny* • Hermione Baddeley *Monique* • William Mervyn *Lord Twithampton* • Dora Bryan *Cora Crumpington* • Bob Hoskins *Recruiting sergeant* ■ *Dir* Bob Kellett • *Scr* Sid Colin, Eddie Braben

Up the Junction ★★

Drama 1967 · UK · Colour · 118mins

When Ken Loach adapted Nell Dunn's provocative novel *Up the Junction* for TV in the 1960s, it shocked the nation. Director Peter Collinson's big screen version was more polished, and therein lay his undoing. Loach's semi-documentary style gave Battersea the suitably bleak look that made the central character's decision to move there from Chelsea seem both politically significant and socially courageous. Collinson, however, offers a working-class wonderland and has Suzy Kendall play the girl as a cross between a 1960s supermodel and a melodramatic sob sister. DP

Suzy Kendall *Polly* • Dennis Waterman *Peter* • Adrienne Posta *Rube* • Maureen Lipman *Sylvie* • Michael Gothard *Terry* • Liz Fraser *Mrs McCarthy* • Hylda Baker *Winny* • Alfie Bass *Charlie* ■ *Dir* Peter Collinson • *Scr* Roger Smith, from the novel by Nell Dunn

Up the River ★★

Prison comedy 1930 · US · BW · 92mins

A major movie for collectors of screen debuts since no lesser personages than Spencer Tracy and Humphrey Bogart made their start in features right here. It started out as a prison drama but when MGM's *The Big House* cornered that market it was quickly transformed into a comedy. Bogart plays an upper-class convict who is in love with fellow jailbird, Claire Luce. Tracy is an escaped con who voluntarily returns to help his prison win a crucial ball game. Director John Ford called it "a piece of junk", but you can't deny the novelty of two of Hollywood's finest beginning their careers in such an offbeat comedy. AT

Spencer Tracy *St Louis* • Warren Hymer *Dannemora Dan* • Humphrey Bogart *Steve* • Claire Luce *Judy* • William Collier Sr *Pop* • Joan Lawes *Jean* • Sharon Lynn [Sharon Lynne] *Edith La Verne* ■ *Dir* John Ford • *Scr* Maurine Watkins, John Ford, William Collier Sr

Up the Sandbox ★★★ 15

Comedy 1972 · US · Colour · 93mins

A genuinely charming performance by Barbra Streisand redeems this awkward yet fitfully touching theatrical account of being alone in a crowded and thoughtless New York. Streisand has any number of fantasies – including one that involves being seduced by Fidel Castro! – and director Irvin Kershner cleverly manages to integrate them into the main narrative. Not a success at the time, this now has more than a little period appeal. TS. Contains some violence, swearing, nudity and a sex scene. [video] DVD

Barbra Streisand *Margaret Reynolds* • David Selby *Paul Reynolds* • Jane Hoffman *Mrs Yussim* • John C Becher *Mr Yussim* • Jacobo Morales *Fidel Castro* • Ariane Heller *Elizabeth* ■ *Dir* Irvin Kershner • *Scr* Paul Zindel, from the novel by Anne Richardson Roiphe

Up to His Ears ★★★ U

Comedy adventure
1965 · Fr/It · Colour · 96mins

An updated version of a Jules Verne novel, this is one of several comic adventure movies Philippe de Broca made with the energetic Jean-Paul Belmondo in a daredevil role. Belmondo is a millionaire, bored with life, who hires a hitman to assassinate him, but changes his mind after meeting the statuesque Ursula Andress, who is as easy on the eye as the Far Eastern locations. But, filmed at a frenzied pace, it loses much of its initial humour and impetus along the way. RB. A French language film.

Jean-Paul Belmondo *Arthur Lempereur* • Ursula Andress *Alexandrine* • Maria Pacôme *Suzy* • Valérie Lagrange *Alice Ponchabert* • Valery Inkijinoff *M Goh* • Jean Rochefort *Léon* ■ *Dir* Philippe de Broca • *Scr* Philippe de Broca, Daniel Boulanger, from the novel *Les Tribulations d'un Chinois en Chine* by Jules Verne

Up to His Neck ★★ U

Comedy 1954 · UK · BW · 90mins

Detailed to guard naval supplies, Ronald Shiner is abandoned on a South Sea island, only to be installed as king. However, his whereabouts are discovered and he's ordered to train a fighting force to help recover a stolen submarie. Naturally, the mission is botched – but not as badly as the comedy. Shiner's wisecracking finagling passes muster, but the patronising depiction of the islanders most certainly does not. DP

Ronald Shiner *Jack Carter* • Laya Raki *Lao Win Tan* • Harry Fowler *Smudge* • Brian Rix *Wiggy* • Colin Gordon *Lt Cmdr Sterning* • Michael Brennan *CPO Brazier* ■ *Dir* John Paddy Carstairs • *Scr* Patrick Kirwan, Ted Willis, John Paddy Carstairs

Uphill All the Way ★ PG

Western comedy adventure
1985 · US · Colour · 82mins

It might have seemed a good idea at the time to team country music stars Roy Clark and Mel Tillis in a *Smokey and the Bandit*-style chase movie, but it's a cryin' shame nobody bothered to find out if they could act. They can't, and this unintentional farce is a total non-starter. TS [video]

Roy Clark *Ben Hooker* • Mel Tillis *Booger Skaggs* • Glen Campbell *Captain Hazleton* • Trish Van Devere *Widow Quinn* • Richard Paul *Dillman* • Burt Reynolds *Poker player* • Elaine Joyce *Miss Jesse* • Jacque Lynn Colton *Lucinda* • Burl Ives *Sheriff John Catledge* • Frank Gorshin *Pike* ■ *Dir/Scr* Frank Q Dobbs

Upkaar ★★ 15

Melodrama 1967 · Ind · Colour · 161mins

A decade after making his acting bow, Manoj Kumar turned director with a film he described as "a 16,000-foot-long celluloid flag of India". He's not kidding, either, as this musical melodrama is so strident an affirmation of patriotic fervour as often to be embarrassing to watch. Kumar also stars as a hard-working farmer, who sacrifices everything to put brother Prem Chopra through college. Imposing, but its overt nationalism borders on the fanatical. DP. A Hindi language film. [video]

Asha Parekh • Manoj Kumar • Pran • Kamini Kaushal • Prem Chopra • Madan Puri ■ *Dir/Scr* Manoj Kumar

Upper World ★★★

Crime drama 1934 · US · BW · 72mins

This fine Warner Bros melodrama is based on a Ben Hecht story, about a romance across the tracks between dancer Ginger Rogers and married businessman Warren William, whose socialite ("upper world") wife is impeccably played by Mary Astor. When the burlesque girl is found dead, the cops are loathe to incriminate William, and thereby hangs a terrific tale, unhindered in its day by the new censorship code that movies like this one encouraged. Look out for a very young Mickey Rooney. TS

Warren William *Alexander Stream* • Mary Astor *Hettie Stream* • Ginger Rogers *Lilly Linder* • Theodore Newton *Rocklen* • Andy Devine *Oscar, the Chauffeur* • Dickie Moore *Tommy Stream* • J Carrol Naish *Lou Colima* • Robert Barrat *Commissioner Clark* • Mickey Rooney *Jerry* ■ *Dir* Roy Del Ruth • *Scr* Ben Markson, from a story by Ben Hecht

Ups and Downs of a Handyman ★★ 18

Sex comedy 1975 · UK · Colour · 85mins

Barry Stokes brings a certain cheeky charm to the title role, but what little comedy there is comes from Benny Hill stalwart Bob Todd, as the local magistrate, and Chic Murray, as a harassed bobby. Derrick Slater's script is one long smutty gag, while the direction is perfunctory at best. DP. Contains nudity. [video]

Barry Stokes *Bob* • Gay Soper *Maisie* • Sue Lloyd *The blonde* • Bob Todd *Squire Bullsworthy* • Chic Murray *PC Knowles* • Robert Dorning *Newsagent* • Valerie Leon *Redhead* • Penny Meredith *Margaretta* ■ *Dir* John Sealey • *Scr* Derrick Slater

Upstairs and Downstairs ★★★

Comedy 1959 · UK · Colour · 100mins

It must have been very frustrating for the cast of accomplished British comedy performers, let alone for international stars Claudia Cardinale and Mylène Demongeot, to have watched all their efforts being frittered away by such dull leads as Michael Craig and Anne Heywood. As the newlyweds searching for the perfect servant, they are the weak link in every scene. But you can still enjoy seeing Cardinale as a man-mad maid, Joan Hickson as a secret tippler, Joan Sims as a timid Welsh nanny, Sid James as a put-upon bobby and Demongeot as a Pollyanna-like au pair. DP

Michael Craig *Richard Barry* • Anne Heywood *Kate Barry* • Mylène Demongeot *Ingrid Gunnar* • James Robertson-Justice *Mansfield* • Claudia Cardinale *Maria* • Sidney James *PC Edwards* • Joan Hickson *Rosemary* • Joan Sims *Blodwen* • Joseph Tomelty *Arthur Farringdon* • Nora Nicholson *Mrs Edith Farringdon* • Daniel Massey *Wesley Cotes* ■ *Dir* Ralph Thomas • *Scr* Frank Harvey, from the novel by Ronald Scott Thorne

Uptight ★★★

Drama 1968 · US · Colour · 104mins

Although it misfires on many levels, this is still an ambitious attempt to rework John Ford's 1935 Oscar-winning drama, *The Informer*. In shifting the scene away from Dublin in the 1920s to Cleveland in the aftermath of Martin Luther King's assassination, director Jules Dassin attempts to explore both the impact the event had on the African-American community and on the divisions that existed within its ranks. The performances now seem strained, but the power of the film's messages is undimmed. DP

Raymond St Jacques *BG* • Ruby Dee *Laurie* • Frank Silvera *Kyle* • Roscoe Lee Browne *Clarence* • Julian Mayfield *Tank* • Janet MacLachlan *Jeannie* ■ *Dir* Jules Dassin • *Scr* Jules Dassin, Ruby Dee, Julian Mayfield, from the novel *The Informer* by Liam O'Flaherty

Uptown Girls ★★ 12

Comedy 2003 · US · Colour · 88mins

Newly broke "It Girl" Brittany Murphy takes a job as nanny to precocious youngster Dakota Fanning in this predictable comedy. A frothy tale of trust and responsibility, it buries the strong performances of its leads under a nauseating script and an embarrassing romantic subplot. Fanning is remarkably sophisticated as an uptight eight-year-old, while the always quirky Murphy fits the bill perfectly as a dead rock star's immature daughter. SF. Contains some swearing. [video] DVD

Brittany Murphy *Molly Gunn* • Dakota Fanning *Ray Schleine* • Marley Shelton *Ingrid* • Donald Faison [Donald Adeosun Faison] *Huey* • Jesse Spencer *Neal* • Austin Pendleton *Mr McConkey* • Heather Locklear *Roma Schleine* ■ *Dir* Boaz Yakin • *Scr* Julia Dahl, Mo Ogrodnik, Lisa Davidowitz, from a story by Allison Jacobs

Uptown Saturday Night ★★★ PG

Comedy 1974 · US · Colour · 99mins

Sidney Poitier directs and stars in this comedy about a pair of buddies (Poitier and Bill Cosby) who become involved with the criminal underworld when they try to retrieve a stolen winning lottery ticket. There's a very funny Harry Belafonte as a black godfather – Brando-style – and such comic talents as Richard Pryor and Flip Wilson. Sociologists might argue that these amiable romps did nothing to advance African-American cinema, but audiences at the time didn't care. The film generated two sequels: *Let's Do It Again* and *A Piece of the Action*. TS. Contains swearing. [video]

Sidney Poitier *Steve Jackson* • Bill Cosby *Wardell Franklin* • Harry Belafonte *Geechie Dan Beauford* • Flip Wilson *The Reverend* • Richard Pryor *Sharp Eye Washington* • Rosalind Cash *Sarah Jackson* • Roscoe Lee Browne *Congressman Lincoln* ■ *Dir* Sidney Poitier • *Scr* Richard Wesley

The Upturned Glass ★★★

Crime 1947 · UK · BW · 86mins

In his last British film before taking off for Hollywood, James Mason returned to the kind of brooding figure that female audiences had adored in *The Seventh Veil* and *Odd Man Out*. He's the brain surgeon who concocts an elaborate revenge on the shrewish figure responsible for the death of the married woman he loved. Pamela Kellino (Mason's wife, who co-scripted) plays the murderess. Heavily contrived, but Mason's performance and Lawrence Huntington's directorial flair keep you hooked. AE

James Mason *Michael Joyce* • Rosamund John *Emma Wright* • Pamela Kellino *Kate Howard* • Ann Stephens *Ann Wright* • Morland Graham *Clay* ■ *Dir* Lawrence Huntington • *Scr* John P Monaghan, Pamela Kellino, from a story by John P Monaghan

Upworld ★★ PG

Comedy thriller 1992 · US · Colour · 87mins

Another variation on the mismatched cops scenario sees a detective paired with a leftover from *The Lord of the Rings*. Detective Anthony Michael Hall discovers that the only witness to an undercover assignment that goes wrong is a furry little creature from the depths of the Earth who has been sent to the surface to recharge a magical stone that provides power for his subterranean world. Kids would love the Ewok-style capers; most parents will probably marvel at the sheer stupidity of the concept. JF [video]

Anthony Michael Hall *Casey Gallagher* • Claudia Christian *Samantha Kennedy* • Jerry Orbach *Stan Walton* • Mark Harelik *Derek Kaminsky* • Eli Danker *Zadar* • Robert Z'Dar *Reggie* • Joseph R Sicari *Lou Ferril* ■ *Dir* Stan Winston • *Scr* Pen Densham, John Watson, from a story by Pen Densham

Uranus ★★ 15

Historical drama 1990 · Fr · Colour · 99mins

Cinema has rarely explored the tumult of recrimination that seized postwar France. So this adaptation, with its scrupulously balanced refusal to reopen old wounds, has to be considered something of a missed opportunity. It also has to be ranked as high melodrama. For while the topic of political expediency is as compelling as it is troubling, the shading in Claude Berri's dour reconstruction of a bitter period is a bit too black and white. DP. A French language film.

Philippe Noiret *Watrin* • Gérard Depardieu *Léopold* • Jean-Pierre Marielle *Archambaud* • Michel Blanc *Gaigneux* • Michel Galabru *Monglat* • Gérard Desarthe *Maxime Loin* • Fabrice Luchini *Jourdan* • Daniel Prévost *Rochard* ■ *Dir* Claude Berri • *Scr* Claude Berri, Arlette Langmann, from the novel by Marcel Aymé

Urban Cowboy ★★★ 15

Drama 1980 · US · Colour · 128mins

A steamy romance between Texas oil worker John Travolta and strong-willed Debra Winger is played out against the backdrop of honky-tonk dancing and mechanical rodeos in an uneven country-and-western soap opera. Packed with music from the likes of the Eagles, the Charlie Daniels Band and Linda Ronstadt, director James Bridges's overlong portrait of American manhood in the early 1980s was an effort to re-promote Travolta as the nightclub macho man. AJ. Contains some violence and swearing. [video] DVD

John Travolta *Bud Davis* • Debra Winger *Sissy Davis* • Scott Glenn *Wes Hightower* • Madolyn Smith *Pam* • Barry Corbin *Uncle Bob* • Brooke Alderson *Aunt Corene* • Cooper Huckabee *Marshall* ■ *Dir* James Bridges • *Scr* James Bridges, Aaron Latham, from a story by Aaron Latham

Urban Ghost Story ★★★ 15

Supernatural horror
1998 · UK · Colour · 84mins

This low-budget – yes – urban ghost story has a 12-year-old girl (newcomer Heather Ann Foster) in a Glasgow tenement, who starts to detect supernatural rumblings while recovering from an ecstasy-linked near-death experience. Jason Connery plays against type as a tabloid reporter seeking to exploit the story, as ghostbusters and spiritualists descend on the council flat. Original and naturalistic film-makers, Genevieve Jolliffe and Chris Jones certainly have the promise to back up their vision and ultimately the constraints of a £220,000 budget prove the mother of invention. AC DVD

Jason Connery *John Fox* • Stephanie Buttle *Kate Fisher* • Heather Ann Foster *Lizzie Fisher* • Nicola Stapleton *Kerrie* • James Cosmo *Minister* ■ *Dir* Genevieve Jolliffe • *Scr* Chris Jones, Genevieve Jolliffe

Urban Legend ★★ 18

Horror thriller 1998 · US/Fr · Colour · 95mins

One of the weaker examples of the late 1990s resurgence in stalk 'n' slash movies, this shows attractive teenagers being dispatched in the form of – you've guessed it – urban legends. The gimmicky murders are the film's sole stab at innovation, although some of the later "legends" seem made up for the purposes of the plot. The pedestrian direction, bland cast and a ludicrous final unmasking don't add up to much. JC. Contains violence and swearing. DVD

Alicia Witt *Natalie* • Jared Leto *Paul* • Rebecca Gayheart *Brenda* • Michael Rosenbaum *Parker* • Loretta Devine *Reese* • Joshua Jackson *Damon* • Robert Englund *Professor Wexler* • Brad Dourif *Gas station attendant* ■ *Dir* Jamie Blanks • *Scr* Silvio Horta

Urban Legends: Final Cut ★★ 15

Horror thriller 2000 · US/Fr · Colour · 94mins

As with the original, this sequel doesn't deliver the promise of its premise. The first film maintained the storyline about a serial killer murdering in the style of notorious folk-myths until about the half-way mark: here it's ditched after the first few minutes. Then it turns into son-of-*Scream*, complete with movie in-jokes, as the serial slayer dices his way through the students at a film school. Adequately performed, this under-achieves in the scare department. DA DVD

Jennifer Morrison *Amy Mayfield* • Matthew Davis *Travis/Trevor* • Hart Bochner *Professor Solomon* • Loretta Devine *Reese* • Joseph Lawrence *Graham Manning* • Anson Mount *Toby* ■ *Dir* John Ottman • *Scr* John Harris Boardman, Scott Derrickson, from characters created by Silvio Horta

Urga ★★★★ PG

Drama 1990 · Fr/USSR · Colour · 114mins

The winner of the Golden Lion at the Venice Film Festival, this is a visually stunning parable on the dubious benefits of progress. Alternating between the rolling expanses of the steppe and the homely clutter of a shepherd's tent, director Nikita Mikhalkov manages to make both the traditional lifestyle of the Mongolian family and the trappings of consumerism seem attractive, while at the same time pointing out their pitfalls. Vladimir Gostukhin is superb as the coarse Russian truck driver, while Badema and Bayaertu are quietly impressive as the couple who give him shelter. DP. In Russian and Mongolian with English subtitles.

Badema *Pagma* • Bayaertu *Gombo* • Vladimir Gostukhin *Sergei* • Babushka *Grandma* • Larissa Kuznetsova *Marina* • Jon Bochinski *Stanislas* ■ *Dir* Nikita Mikhalkov • *Scr* Roustam Ibraguimbekov, from a short story by Roustam Ibraguimbekov, Nikita Mikhalkov

Urotsukidoji: Legend of the Overfiend ★★★ 18

Animated fantasy horror
1987 · Jpn · Colour · 102mins

This was one of the first Japanese *animé* to gain widespread attention in the UK, no doubt due to the novelty value of the insane levels of splattery violence and extremely graphic sexual content. The story (something about a search for a super fiend who can unite the three worlds of humans, beasts and demons) isn't easy to follow. Although the animation is simplistic compared to modern standards, the story barely pauses for breath and provides some genuinely disturbing imagery. What's more, the English dubbing is first-rate. The story continued in *Legend of the Demon Womb*. JC. Japanese dialogue dubbed into English. DVD

Christopher Courage *Amano* • Rebel Joy *Akemi* • Danny Bush *Nagumo* • Lucy Morales *Megumi* ■ *Dir* Hideki Takayama • *Scr* Noboru Aikawa, Michael Lawrence, from the comic strip by Toshio Maeda

Used Cars ★★★★ 15

Comedy 1980 · US · Colour · 107mins

Tasteless, risqué, outrageous and amoral, this early offering from director Robert Zemeckis is all these things and more. But it's also one of the funniest ruminations on American values, as the car showroom becomes a warped microcosm of society. Revealing Kurt Russell's under-utilised talent as a first-rate comedian, it's a good-natured, if highly eccentric, wisecracker, finding untold amounts of amusement in the misfortunes and embarrassment of others. AJ. Contains swearing. DVD

Kurt Russell *Rudy Russo* • Jack Warden *Roy L Fuchs/Luke Fuchs* • Gerrit Graham *Jeff* • Frank McRae *Jim the Mechanic* • Deborah Harmon *Barbara Fuchs* • Joseph P Flaherty *Sam Slaton* • David L Lander *Freddie Paris* • Michael McKean *Eddie Winslow* ■ *Dir* Robert Zemeckis • *Scr* Robert Zemeckis, Bob Gale

Used People ★★★ 15

Comedy drama 1992 · US · Colour · 111mins

One of those huge "feel good" ensemble pieces where the sheer size and quality of the cast help disguise the lack of substance. The fact that this was Italian star Marcello Mastroianni's first true Hollywood movie was the main talking point on the film's release, and he delivers a typically charming performance as he courts the recently widowed Shirley MacLaine. British director Beeban Kidron, also making her Hollywood debut, orchestrates the proceedings with confidence. JF. Contains sex scenes and swearing.

Shirley MacLaine *Pearl Berman* • Marcello Mastroianni *Joe Meledandri* • Kathy Bates *Bibby* • Jessica Tandy *Frieda* • Sylvia Sidney *Becky* • Marcia Gay Harden *Norma* • Bob Dishy *Jack Berman* ■ *Dir* Beeban Kidron • *Scr* Todd Graff, from his play *The Grandma Plays*

The Usual Suspects ★★★★★ 18

Crime thriller 1995 · US · Colour · 101mins

What made this audacious but unheralded thriller the must-see film of 1995? Maybe it was the intricacy of the flashback-packed script and the deft sleights of hand executed by its fledgeling director. Perhaps everyone admired the outstanding ensemble acting. Yes, Kevin Spacey stole the show and fully merited the best supporting actor Oscar for his mesmerising performance, but everyone in that rogues' gallery played their part to perfection, not to mention the mysterious Pete Postlethwaite and confused cops Dan Hedaya and Chazz Palminteri. Or was it simply that noticeboard that kept coming back to haunt everyone? Whatever the reason, this is a film that demands to be watched repeatedly – a good old-fashioned pulp fiction told in the slickest 1990s style. DP. Contains violence and swearing. DVD

Gabriel Byrne *Dean Keaton* • Kevin Spacey *Roger "Verbal" Kint* • Chazz Palminteri *Dave Kujan* • Benicio Del Toro *Fred Fenster* • Stephen Baldwin *Michael McManus* • Kevin Pollak *Todd Hockney* • Pete Postlethwaite *Kobayashi* • Suzy Amis *Edie Finneran* • Giancarlo Esposito *Jack Baer* • Dan Hedaya *Sergeant Jeff Rabin* • Paul Bartel *Smuggler* ■ *Dir* Bryan Singer • *Scr* Christopher McQuarrie

Utilities ★★ 15

Romantic comedy
1981 · Can · Colour · 89mins

Robert Hays stars as a well-meaning social worker, who, fed up with their business practices and profiteering, rallies against the phone, gas and electric companies. Brooke Adams plays the cop with divided loyalties – determined to curb Hays's activities on the one hand, but at the same time harbouring romantic feelings towards him. Some nice scenes and some unexpected crude humour, but a case of wasted potential. DF

Robert Hays *Bob Hunt* • Brooke Adams *Marion Edwards* • John Marley *Roy Blue* • James Blendick *Kenneth Knight* ■ *Dir* Harvey Hart • *Scr* David Greenwalt, M James Kouf Jr [Jim Kouf], from a story by Carl Manning

Utopia ★★ U

Comedy 1950 · Fr/It · BW · 82mins

Sadly, Laurel and Hardy's last film, unavailable for many years, is as mediocre as we had been led to believe – not badly made, just ill-conceived and dull. The boys are shipwrecked on an atoll while en route to a desert island, after which most of the action focuses on Suzy Delair, who is fleeing a jealous boyfriend. Stan and Ollie become supporting players in an increasingly bizarre tale involving the discovery of uranium. Also known as *Atoll K*. DM. French dialogue dubbed into English. DVD

Stan Laurel *Stanley* • Oliver Hardy *Oliver* • Suzy Delair *Cherie Lamour* • M Elloy [Max Elloy] *Antoine* • M Dalmatoff *Alecto* ■ *Dir* Leo Joannon [Léo Joannon], John Berry • *Scr* Monty Collins [Monte Collins], Piero Tellini, R Wheeler, from an idea by Léo Joannon

Utu ★★★ 15

Action drama 1983 · NZ · Colour · 99mins

This is a powerful drama which plays like a New Zealand western. A Maori serving with the colonial British Army finds his family massacred by some of its rogue elements and vows *utu*, Maori for "retribution". He then raises a rebel army and goes in for a spot of payback. Action-packed yet poignant, the film was made by Geoff Murphy, director of the equally competent *The Quiet Earth*. DA

Anzac Wallace *Te Wheke* • Bruno Lawrence *Williamson* • Wi Kuki Kaa *Wiremu* • Tim Elliott *Colonel Elliott* • Ilona Rodgers *Emily Williamson* • Tania Bristowe *Kura* • Maerata Mita *Matu* ■ *Dir* Geoff Murphy • *Scr* Geoff Murphy, Keith Aberdein

Utz ★★★ 12

Mystery drama
1992 · UK /Ger/It · Colour · 93mins

With an award-winning performance from Armin Mueller-Stahl, this is a complex character study of an obsessive Czech collector of fine porcelain figures who's understandably distraught when the country's then-communist government decrees his collection actually belongs to the State. A top-notch cast features in a film that's as fine and detailed as the figures Utz collects, though it may be too dry for some tastes. DA

Armin Mueller-Stahl *Baron Kaspar Joachim von Utz* • Brenda Fricker *Marta* • Peter Riegert *Marius Fischer* • Paul Scofield *Doctor Vaclav Orlik* • Miriam Karlin *Grandmother Utz* ■ *Dir* George Sluizer • *Scr* Hugh Whitemore, from the novel by Bruce Chatwin

Uzak ★★★★ 15

Drama 2003 · Tur/Neth · Colour · 106mins

Mehmet Emin Toprak and Muzaffer Ozdemir shared the best actor prize at Cannes for their work in Nuri Bilge Ceylan's meticulous insight into the disintegration of traditional ties and the crisis of masculinity in modern Turkey. Making evocative use of snow, Ceylan conveys both the isolation and the alienation of Ozdemir's disillusioned Istanbul photographer and Toprak's optimistically indolent country cousin. Indeed, his emphasis on their inability to communicate is reinforced by his studied pacing and mastery of environment. Not an easy film, but a deeply moving one. DP. In Turkish with English subtitles. Contains swearing and nudity. DVD

Muzaffer Ozdemir *Mahmut* • Mehmet Emin Toprak *Yusuf* • Zuhal Gencer Erkaya *Nazan* • Nazan Kirilmis *Lover* • Feridun Koc *Janitor* • Fatma Ceylan *Mother* • Ebru Ceylan *Young girl* ■ *Dir/Scr* Nuri Bilge Ceylan

U

The VIPs ★★

Drama 1963 · UK · Colour · 119mins

Made principally to cash in on the Richard Burton/Elizabeth Taylor romance, this is glossy, but as tedious as the delay at Heathrow that the story depicts. Only Margaret Rutherford's deliriously dotty, Oscar-winning duchess and Orson Welles's movie mogul fleeing the taxman breathe life into the bottomless pit of clichés. AT

Elizabeth Taylor *Frances Andros* • Richard Burton *Paul Andros* • Louis Jourdan *Marc Champselle* • Elsa Martinelli *Gloria Gritti* • Margaret Rutherford *Duchess of Brighton* • Maggie Smith *Miss Mead* • Rod Taylor *Les Mangrum* • Linda Christian *Miriam Marshall* • Orson Welles *Max Buda* • Dennis Price *Commander Millbank* ■ *Dir* Anthony Asquith • *Scr* Terence Rattigan

VI Warshawski ★★ 15

Crime mystery 1991 · US · Colour · 85mins

A rasping, sassy Kathleen Turner stars as the spiky, difficult, liberal-feminist private eye VI "Vic" Warshawski. But here the investigator becomes a man-fearing, baseball-obsessed pain in the rear, in a film that's sunk by its plot – a lame piece of fluff about a 13-year-old and a dodgy inheritance. Only worth watching for Turner, who desperately attempts to inject some grit into the proceedings. SH. Contains violence and swearing. DVD

Kathleen Turner *Victoria I Warshawski* • Jay O Sanders *Murray Ryerson* • Charles Durning *Lieutenant Mallory* • Angela Goethals *Kat Grafalk* • Nancy Paul *Paige Grafalk* • Frederick Coffin *Horton Grafalk* • Charles McCaughan *Trumble Grafalk* ■ *Dir* Jeff Kanew • *Scr* Edward Taylor, David Aaron Cohen, Nick Thiel, from a story by Edward Taylor, from novels by Sara Paretsky

Va Savoir ★★★★ PG

Romantic comedy drama
2001 · Fr/Ger/It · Colour · 147mins

Jacques Rivette again demonstrates his skills as a director of nuance and pace in this gratifyingly literate charade. Set in present-day Paris, the old French master here explores the complicated love affairs that emerge between three men and three women during a theatrical troupe's production of Pirandello's *As You Desire Me*. No one puts a foot wrong in an exemplary ensemble cast that is headed by Jeanne Balibar and Sergio Castellitto. Rivette's exploration of the relationship between art and life is so precisely staged and performed, it seems almost effortless. DP. In French and Italian with English subtitles. DVD

Jeanne Balibar *Camille Renard* • Sergio Castellitto *Ugo Bassani* • Jacques Bonnaffé *Pierre Mauduit* • Marianne Basler *Sonia* • Hélène de Fougerolles *Dominique "Do" Desprez* • Bruno Todeschini *Arthur Delamarche* ■ *Dir* Jacques Rivette • *Scr* Pascal Bonitzer, Christine Laurent, Jacques Rivette

Vacas ★★★ 15

Historical drama 1991 · Sp · Colour · 92mins

Described as a "negative comedy", Julio Medem's directorial debut is a difficult film to like. Yet the standard of its imaginative camerawork, its playful shifts from reality to fantasy and the assuredness with which the narrative strands have been woven together have to be admired. Following the fortunes of two Basque families between the civil wars of 1875 and 1936, the four stories have something of a fairy-tale quality and are interesting enough, but the lack of character depth prevents total involvement. DP. In Spanish with English subtitles. Contains violence. DVD

Emma Suarez *Cristina* • Carmelo Gomez *Manuel/Ignacio/Peru* • Ana Torrent *Catalina* • Karra Elejalde *Ilegorri/Lucas* • Klara Badiola *Madalen* • Txema Blasco *Manuel* • Kandido Uranga *Carmelo/Juan* • Pilar Bardem *Paulina* ■ *Dir* Julio Medem • *Scr* Julio Medem, Michel Gaztambide, from a story by Julio Medem

Vacuuming Completely Nude in Paradise ★★★★

Comedy drama 2001 · UK · Colour · 75mins

Meet a vacuum-cleaner huckster from the *Glengarry Glen Ross* school of salesmanship. Timothy Spall gives a rip-roaring performance as the door-to-door dervish who lives for the thrill of the demonstration and the scratch of biro on the dotted line. But his new apprentice Michael Begley would rather be mixing pop records, in spite of the fact his stripper-gram girlfriend has imposed a sexual embargo until he makes good. Written with a rapier insight into hard-sell mentality and directed with zest by Danny Boyle, this is brisk, brash and brilliant. DP

Timothy Spall *Tommy Rag* • Michael Begley *Pete* • David Crellin *Mr Ron* • Katy Cavanagh *Sheila* • Sandra Gough *Spaniard* ■ *Dir* Danny Boyle • *Scr* Jim Cartwright

The Vagabond ★★★ U

Silent comedy drama
1916 · US · BW · 21mins

This short fully confirmed Charlie Chaplin as the Little Tramp – with tarnished bowler hat, holey baggy pants and jaunty cane. He plays a fiddling busker who rescues Edna Purviance from the clutches of the ever-villainous and even-more-mountainous Eric Campbell. Shameless sentiment in a timeless world, this effort prefers straight drama to belly laughs, but that's not to say it doesn't entertain. TH DVD

Charles Chaplin *Street musician* • Edna Purviance *Girl stolen by gypsies* • Eric Campbell *Gypsy chieftain* • Leo White *Old Jew/Gypsy woman* ■ *Dir* Charles Chaplin • *Scr* Charles Chaplin, Vincent Bryan

Vagabond ★★★★ 15

Mystery drama 1985 · Fr · Colour · 101mins

Opening with the discovery of Sandrine Bonnaire's body, this is less an investigation into the personality and problems of the teenage drifter than a penetrating examination of the society that was culpable for her demise. Combining eyewitness testimonies with reconstructions of Bonnaire's peripatetic final days, director Agnès Varda reveals a cold, alienated individual who reflects the prejudices and fears of those she encounters, including liberal academic Macha Méril, who finds herself uncomfortably fascinated by her. Shot with spartan poetry and solemnly played by a largely non-professional cast, this is a cheerless study of displacement, waste and collective responsibility. DP. In French with English subtitles.

Sandrine Bonnaire *Mona Bergeron* • Macha Méril *Madame Landier* • Yolande Moreau *Yolande* • Stéphane Freiss *Jean-Pierre* • Marthe Jarnais *Aunt Lydie* • Joël Fosse *Paulo* ■ *Dir/Scr* Agnès Varda

The Vagabond King ★★★ U

Musical 1956 · US · Colour · 87mins

Maltese baritone Oreste "Kirkop" stars as the beggar-rogue poet François Villon in this screen outing of Rudolf Friml's operetta. Sadly, though a pleasant personality and singer, both the star's name and voice have been forgotten, as this was his only movie. It was also the last film appearance of soprano Kathryn Grayson. Familiar and old-fashioned, it has some good songs such as *Love Me Tonight*, as well as new ones composed by Friml. RB

Kathryn Grayson *Catherine de Vaucelles* • Oreste "Kirkop" *Francois Villon* • Rita Moreno *Huguette* • Sir Cedric Hardwicke [Cedric Hardwicke] *Tristan* • Walter Hampden *King Louis XI* • Leslie Nielsen *Thibault* • William Prince *Rene* • Jack Lord *Ferrebone* ■ *Dir* Michael Curtiz • *Scr* Ken Englund, Noel Langley, from the musical by Rudolf Friml, Brian Hooker, William H Post, from the play *If I Were King* by Justin Huntly McCarthy, from a novel by RH Russell

The Vagrant ★★ 18

Comedy horror 1992 · US/Fr · Colour · 87mins

Bill Paxton, unwisely cast against type, is the ordinary middle-class professional who finds himself the target for homeless derelict Marshall Bell, who proceeds to make his life a living hell. Chris Walas directs with flamboyance and the cast, including Michael Ironside as an investigating police officer, certainly hams it up enthusiastically. However, the film is undone by a script lacking in depth and bite. JF. Contains swearing, violence and sex scenes.

Bill Paxton *Graham Krakowski* • Michael Ironside *Lieutenant Ralf Barfuss* • Marshall Bell *The vagrant* • Mitzi Kapture *Edie Roberts* • Colleen Camp *Judy Dansig* • Patrika Darbo *Doatti* • Marc McClure *Chuck* ■ *Dir* Chris Walas • *Scr* Richard Jeffries

The Valachi Papers ★★ 18

Crime drama 1972 · It/Fr · Colour · 119mins

Based on the true story of famed Mob informant Joe Valachi, and with Charles Bronson playing Valachi, this study of early 20th-century gangster life should have had more of an impact. Instead, it views Valachi's rise and fall, and the intricacies of rules and roles in the Mafia in a rather casual fashion. The almost European look of the movie also dilutes the gritty feel the movie tries to generate. The 50-year-old Bronson is good, but isn't convincing in the flashback scenes of his character as a young man. KB

Charles Bronson *Joseph Valachi* • Lino Ventura *Vito Genovese* • Jill Ireland *Maria Valachi* • Walter Chiari *Dominic "The Gap" Petrilli* • Joseph Wiseman *Salvatore Maranzano* • Gerald S O'Loughlin *Ryan* • Amedeo Nazzari *Gaetano Reina* • Fausto Tozzi *Albert Anastasia* ■ *Dir* Terence Young • *Scr* A Maiuri [Dino Maiuri], Massimo De Rita, Stephen Geller, from the book by Peter Maas

The Valdez Horses ★★★ 15

Western 1973 · It/Sp/Fr · Colour · 92mins

Charles Bronson gives one of his best performances in this little-known European western. He stars as a mixed-race cowboy who takes in young runaway Vincent Van Patten on his small ranch. Bronson's character is more complex than the typical western loner; he's not always sympathetic and handles the local racists in an atypical way for both the genre and for the star. KB DVD

Charles Bronson *Chino Valdez* • Jill Ireland *Louise* • Vincent Van Patten *Jamie Wagner* • Marcel Bozzuffi *Maral* • Melissa Chimenti *Indian Girl* • Fausto Tozzi *Cruz* ■ *Dir* John Sturges • *Scr* Dino Maiuri, Massimo De Rita, Clair Haffaker, from the novel by Lee Hoffman

Valdez Is Coming ★★

Western 1971 · US · Colour · 90mins

This western is notable only for a performance of immense dignity from the great Burt Lancaster as a Mexican-American lawman bent on justice. An unlikely debut for Broadway theatre director Edwin Sherin, who fails to get the most out of the material and quite clearly has no cinema technique. The film is crucially under-cast, with a far stronger screen presence than Jon Cypher required as Lancaster's nemesis. TS. Contains violence, swearing and sex scenes.

Burt Lancaster *Bob Valdez* • Susan Clark *Gay Erin* • Jon Cypher *Frank Tanner* • Barton Heyman *El Segundo* • Richard Jordan *RI Davis* • Frank Silvera *Diego* • Hector Elizondo *Mexican rider* • Phil Brown *Malson* ■ *Dir* Edwin Sherin • *Scr* Ronald Kibbee, David Rayfiel, from the novel by Elmore Leonard

Valentín ★★★ PG

Drama
2002 · Arg/Neth/Fr/Sp · Colour · 79mins

Argentinian director Alejandro Agresti draws on his own childhood memories for this delightful tale of a eight-year-old outsider discovering his place in a world that consistently bemuses him. Occasionally, the nuggets of insight contained in young Rodrigo Noya's narration don't chime with his presentation as a space-obsessed innocent who mooches round the backstreets of 1960s Buenos Aires torn between affection for the mother who abandoned him and loyalty towards his violent father (Agresti). But Noya's rapport with his grumbling grandmother (played by Carmen Maura) gives the film a genuine charm. DP. In Spanish with English subtitles. DVD

Carmen Maura *Grandmother* • Rodrigo Noya *Valentín* • Julieta Cardinali *Leticia* • Jean Pierre Noher *Uncle Chiche* • Alejandro Agresti *Vicente, Valentín's father* ■ *Dir/Scr* Alejandro Agresti

Valentina ★★★

Romantic wartime drama
1982 · Sp · Colour · 85mins

This appealing account of the making of a hero is told from a French prison camp at the end of the Spanish Civil War by a defeated Republican volunteer. Set in a small north-eastern Spanish town in 1911, it follows eight-year-old Jorge Sanz, as he is inspired in his pursuit of his pretty neighbour, Paloma Gomez, by the local priest's tales of the champions, saints and poets of days past. Drawing fine performances from both his young cast and Hollywood veteran Anthony Quinn, writer/director Antonio J Betancor bathes the action in an uplifting nostalgic glow. Betancor continued the story in *1919* (1983). DP. Spanish dialogue dubbed into English.

Anthony Quinn *Mosen Joaquin* • Jorge Sanz *Jose Garces (boy)* • Paloma Gomez *Valentina* • Saturno Cerra *Don Jose* • Conchita Leza *Dona Luisa* • Alfredo Lucchetti *Don Arturo* ■ *Dir* Antonio J Betancor [Antonio Jose Betancor] • *Scr* Antonio J Betancor, Carlos Escobedo, Antonio José, Javier Moro, Lautano Murua, from the novel *Days of Dawn* by Ramon J Sender

V

Valentine ★ 15

Horror 2001 · US/Aus · Colour · 92mins

A handful of girls who were spiteful to a schoolboy when they were young find themselves the target of a brutal killer 13 years later. This lame chiller contains all the horror clichés and dumb moves (girls wandering off on their own while a killer is on the loose) you can fit into an hour and a half, plus a handful of inexcusable plot holes. JB. Contains violence and swearing. DVD

David Boreanaz *Adam Carr* • Denise Richards *Paige Prescott* • Marley Shelton *Kate Davies* • Katherine Heigl *Shelley* • Jessica Capshaw *Dorothy Wheeler* • Jessica Cauffiel *Lily* ■ *Dir* Jamie Blanks • *Scr* Donna Powers, Wayne Powers, Gretchen J Berg, Aaron Harberts, from a novel by Tom Savage

Valentino ★★

Romantic drama
1951 · US · Colour · 104mins

It probably seemed a good idea to film the life of Hollywood's most famous Latin lover, but unfortunately the tale proved impossible to cast. Newcomer Anthony Dexter was unveiled in a welter of publicity, hair brilliantined and duly parted in the middle, but unfortunately he had no personal charisma whatsoever. Despite being paired with ravishing redhead Eleanor Parker, the screen stubbornly refused to ignite. TS

Anthony Dexter *Rudolph Valentino* • Eleanor Parker *Joan Carlisle* • Richard Carlson *William King* • Patricia Medina *Lila Reyes* • Joseph Calleia *Luigi Verducci* • Dona Drake *Maria Torres* • Otto Kruger *Mark Towers* ■ *Dir* Lewis Allen • *Scr* George Bruce

Valentino ★★★ 18

Biographical drama
1977 · UK · Colour · 122mins

Director Ken Russell seems to have approached the life story of Rudolph Valentino with no particular aim, and structures it simply as a series of flashbacks spinning out of the silent star's funeral. Much of what is depicted is probably far from the truth. Valentino's conflicts with power-crazy moguls and totally crazy actresses are irresistibly entertaining. There is also the endless fascination of watching Rudolf Nureyev (in his screen acting debut) attempt the role of the Great Lover. DM [video] DVD

Rudolf Nureyev *Rudolph Valentino* • Leslie Caron *Alla Nazimova* • Michelle Phillips *Natasha Rambova* • Carol Kane *"Fatty"'s girl* • Felicity Kendal *June Mathis* • Seymour Cassel *George Ullman* • Peter Vaughan *Rory O'Neil* • Huntz Hall *Jesse Lasky* • Ken Russell *Rex Ingram* ■ *Dir* Ken Russell • *Scr* Ken Russell, Mardik Martin, from the book *Valentino: An Intimate Exposé of the Sheik* by Brad Steiger, Chaw Mank

Valentino Returns ★★★ 15

Period romantic drama
1987 · US · Colour · 91mins

No, Rudy hasn't risen from his grave. Instead, "Valentino Returns" turns out to be the pet name for the pink Cadillac purchased by small-town boy Barry Tubb, who hopes it will prove a big girl-puller, like the real Rudy was. The film has a nice feeling for its time and place – 1950s California – but it lacks focus, meandering along too many backroads when it should have stuck to life's highways. Good performances, though. DA [video]

Barry Tubb *Wayne Gibbs* • Frederic Forrest *Sonny Gibbs* • Veronica Cartwright *Pat Gibbs* • Jenny Wright *Sylvia Fuller* • Macon McCalman *Leroy Fuller* • Seth Isler *Harry Ames* ■ *Dir* Peter Hoffman • *Scr* Leonard Gardner, from his story

Valerie ★★★

Western courtroom drama
1957 · US · BW · 82mins

With the ghost of *Rashomon* hovering over its approach, this mix of western and courtroom drama, although manoeuvred in and out of flashback skilfully enough by director Gerd Oswald, inevitably suffers by comparison. Sterling Hayden, a former Civil War hero and now a respected member of a ranching community, is on trial for murdering wife Anita Ekberg's parents and violently assaulting her. A curious little drama with a melodramatic and unconvincing climax, but not without interest. RK

Sterling Hayden *John Garth* • Anita Ekberg *Valerie* • Anthony Steel *Reverend Blake* • Peter Walker (1) *Herb Garth* • John Wengraf *Louis Horvat* • Iphigenie Castiglioni *Mrs Horvat* • Jerry Barclay *Mingo* ■ *Dir* Gerd Oswald • *Scr* Leonard Heideman, Emmett Murphy

The Valiant ★★★

Crime drama 1929 · US · BW · 66mins

Paul Muni earned an Oscar nomination on debut for his work in this adaptation a celebrated one-act play. The problems inherent in filming in the early sound era largely explain director William K Howard's stilted staging. But Muni surpasses these limitations in his sensitive portrayal of the drifter who conceals his true identity to avoid bringing shame on his well-to-do family after he's sentenced to death for the accidental killing of a police witness. The sequence in which he convinces mother Edith Yorke and sister Marguerite Churchill that he is a stranger is particularly affecting. DP

Paul Muni *James Dyke* • John Mack Brown [Johnny Mack Brown] *Robert Ward* • Edith Yorke *Mrs Douglas* • Richard Carlyle *Chaplain* • Marguerite Churchill *Mary Douglas* • DeWitt Jennings *Warden* • Henry Kolker *Judge* ■ *Dir* William K Howard • *Scr* Tom Barry, John Hunter Booth, from the play by Robert Middlemass, Holworthy Hall

Valiant ★★ U

Animated comedy adventure
2005 · UK/US · Colour · 75mins

This old-fashioned CGI adventure draws on historical fact about the crucial role played by homing pigeons during the Second World War. Valiant (voiced by Ewan McGregor) is a country wood pigeon who follows his dream to join the Royal Homing Pigeon Service, despite his small stature. When Nazi falcon General Von Talon (Tim Curry) captures a number of his comrades, Valiant's courage is put to the test. Nothing more than technically adequate, the film never really takes off due to its clichéd, stiff-upper-lip story and lack of visual invention. AJ

Ewan McGregor *Valiant* • Ricky Gervais *Bugsy* • Tim Curry *General Von Talon* • John Cleese *Mercury* • John Hurt *Felix* • Jim Broadbent *Sergeant* • Hugh Laurie *Gutsy* • Rik Mayall *Cufflingk* • Olivia Williams *Victoria* • Pip Torrens *Lofty* ■ *Dir* Gary Chapman • *Scr* Jordan Katz, George Melrod, George Webster, from a story by George Webster

Valiant Is the Word for Carrie ★★★

Melodrama 1936 · US · BW · 109mins

The undervalued actress Gladys George was nominated for a best actress Oscar for her performance in this uninhibited melodrama, a quintessential four-handkerchief weepie. As the town trollop who selflessly devotes herself to caring for two orphans, George suffers with style and was unlucky to lose the Oscar to Luise Rainer for *The Great Ziegfeld*. TV

Gladys George *Carrie Snyder* • Arline Judge *Lady* • John Howard (1) *Paul Darnley* • Dudley Digges *Dennis Ringrose* • Harry Carey *Phil Yonne* • Isabel Jewell *Lili Eipper* ■ *Dir* Wesley Ruggles • *Scr* Claude Binyon, from the novel by Barry Benefield

The Valley ★★★

Erotic road movie
1972 · Fr · Colour · 114mins

The second movie by Barbet Schroeder to use the music of Pink Floyd (the first was *More*), this hippy epic has dropout Bulle Ogier and friends travelling through New Guinea looking for a mythical Eden-like valley where they can freely indulge their alternative lifestyles. The professional actors interact with the primitive tribesman, and even join in with their stripped-down rituals to fascinating and hyper-exotic effect, highlighted by the trance-like Floyd score. Strangely compelling. AJ. In French with English subtitles.

Jean-Pierre Kalfon *Gaetan* • Bulle Ogier *Viviane* • Michael Gothard *Olivier* • Valérie Lagrange *Hermine* • Jerome Beauvarlet *Yann* ■ *Dir/Scr* Barbet Schroeder

Valley Girl ★★★★ 15

Romantic comedy
1983 · US · Colour · 98mins

This bright and breezy teen film features the barrier-crossing romance between an upscale San Fernando Valley suburbanite (Deborah Foreman) and an out-there Hollywood punk (the out-there Nicolas Cage). Funny, sexy and almost impossible to dislike, *Valley Girl* is widely rated as one of the top teen romances. Director Martha Coolidge brings some much-needed class to the normally male-made genre. DA

Nicolas Cage *Randy* • Deborah Foreman *Julie* • Elizabeth Daily *Loryn* • Michael Bowen *Tommy* • Cameron Dye *Fred* • Heidi Holicker *Stacey* • Michelle Meyrink *Suzie* ■ *Dir* Martha Coolidge • *Scr* Wayne Crawford, Andrew Lane

The Valley of Decision ★★★

Period drama 1945 · US · BW · 118mins

Greer Garson is the daughter of Irish steel worker Lionel Barrymore in Pittsburgh, who goes to work as a maid in the household of mill owner Donald Crisp and becomes indispensable to his family. Although loved by one of the mill owner's sons (Gregory Peck), the possibility of their marriage is thwarted by industrial strife between Barrymore and Crisp that ends in tragedy. The winning warmth of Garson won the actress her fifth consecutive Oscar nomination and Peck climbed higher in the star stakes, while the film grossed nearly $6 million on its first release. RK

Gregory Peck *Paul Scott* • Greer Garson *Mary Rafferty* • Donald Crisp *William Scott* • Lionel Barrymore *Pat Rafferty* • Preston Foster *Jim Brennan* • Gladys Cooper *Clarissa Scott* • Marsha Hunt *Constance Scott* • Reginald Owen *McCready* ■ *Dir* Tay Garnett • *Scr* John Meehan, Sonya Levien, from the novel by Marcia Davenport

Valley of Eagles ★★ U

Crime drama 1951 · UK · BW · 85mins

There are really three films here: a wildlife adventure, a Cold War thriller and a standard issue cop yarn complete with Jack Warner. The story concerns a boffin's wife who absconds to Lapland with her husband's invention and his assistant, played by Anthony Dawson. The husband, the policeman and two children set off in pursuit and, after being attacked by bears en route, meet the Laplanders who hunt with eagles. Ambitious for what is really a B-movie. AT

Jack Warner *Inspector Petersen* • John McCallum *Dr Nils Ahlen* • Nadia Gray *Kara Niemann* • Anthony Dawson *Sven Nystrom* • Mary Laura Wood *Helga Ahlen* • Christopher Lee *First Detective* ■ *Dir/Scr* Terence Young

Valley of Fire ★★ U

Western 1951 · US · BW · 62mins

A minor Gene Autry programme filler, featuring the singing cowboy star in the kind of B-flick guaranteed to satisfy fans and the occasional Saturday children's matinée audience, but which really offers very little to anyone else. Not, of course, that Autry cared: he knew his audience well, and shrewd manipulation of his career and investments made him one of Hollywood's richest men. TS

Gene Autry • Pat Buttram *Breezie Larrabee* • Gail Davis *Laurie* • Russell Hayden *Steve Guilford* • Christine Larson *Bee Laverne* • Harry Lauter *Tod Rawlings* • Terry Frost *Grady McKean* ■ *Dir* John English • *Scr* Gerald Geraghty, from a story by Earle Snell

The Valley of Gwangi ★★ 12

Fantasy adventure
1969 · US · Colour · 91mins

An unsuccessful touring circus encounters a forbidden valley full of prehistoric animals, and captures its massive allosaurus leader. Guess what? It escapes to terrorise the cast. A very watchable fantasy adventure, though as with other films Ray Harryhausen had a hand in, the stop-motion special effects put the flat characters and routine plot in the shade. JG [video] DVD

James Franciscus *Tuck Kirby* • Gila Golan *TJ Breckenridge* • Richard Carlson *Champ Connors* • Laurence Naismith *Prof Horace Bromley* • Freda Jackson *Tia Zorina* ■ *Dir* James O'Connolly [Jim O'Connolly] • *Scr* William E Bast, Julian More, from the story by William E Bast

Valley of Mystery ★

Adventure 1967 · US · Colour · 93mins

This lacklustre effort contains a bunch of second division film stars trying to salvage what's left of their careers by appearing in a plane-crash drama originally made for television. Ending up in the South American jungle, the survivors are made up of familiar screen characters – has-been comedian, escaped killer, famous singer, novelist on a quest. Like the plane after the crash, it's a pile of junk though it still managed to get a cinema release. JA

Richard Egan *Wade Cochran* • Peter Graves (2) *Ben Barstow* • Joby Baker *Pete Patton* • Lois Nettleton *Rita Brown* • Harry Guardino *Danny O'Neill* • Julie Adams *Joan Simon* • Fernando Lamas *Francisco Rivera* ■ *Dir* Joseph Leytes • *Scr* Richard Neal, Lowell Barrington, from a story by Lawrence B Marcus, Richard Neal

Valley of Song ★★ U

Comedy 1953 · UK · BW · 74mins

War breaks out among a bickering group of Welsh choristers preparing for a major concert in this engaging little comedy, scripted by Phil Park and Cliff Gordon from the latter's radio play. There's no Harry Secombe but look out for Rachel Roberts and Kenneth Williams in early screen roles. JF

Mervyn Johns *Minister Griffiths* • Clifford Evans *Geraint Llewellyn* • Maureen Swanson *Olwen Davies* • John Fraser *Cliff Lloyd* • Rachel Thomas *Mrs Lloyd* • Betty Cooper *Mrs Davies* • Rachel Roberts (1) *Bessie Lewis* • Hugh Pryse *Lloyd, the undertaker* • Edward Evans *Davies, the shopkeeper* • Kenneth Williams *Lloyd, the haulage man* ■ *Dir* Gilbert Gunn • *Scr* Cliff Gordon, Phil Park, from the radio play *Choir Practice* by Cliff Gordon

Valley of the Dolls ★★★★ 15

Melodrama 1967 · US · Colour · 118mins

Based on Jacqueline Susann's landmark mega-best-seller, this rags-to-bitches exposé of how Broadway singer Patty Duke, sex starlet Sharon Tate and demure model Barbara Parkins claw their way to Hollywood success on the boozy, pill-popping fame express heading for inevitable derailment is one of the all-time great, and most beloved, trash movies. Every backstabbing line is a classic and every glitzy showbiz second is an over-the-top hyper-cliché in director Mark Robson's fabulously camp extravaganza. AJ [video] DVD

Barbara Parkins *Anne Welles* • Patty Duke *Neely O'Hara* • Sharon Tate *Jennifer North* • Paul Burke *Lyon Burke* • Tony Scotti *Tony Polar* • Martin Milner *Mel Anderson* • Charles Drake *Kevin Gilmore* • Alexander Davion *Ted*

Casablanca • Lee Grant *Miriam* • Susan Hayward *Helen Lawson* • Jacqueline Susann *Reporter* ■ *Dir* Mark Robson • *Scr* Helen Deutsch, Dorothy Kingsley, from the novel by Jacqueline Susann

Valley of the Kings ★★ U

Romantic adventure
1954 · US · Colour · 85mins

Apart from the majestic musical score by Miklos Rozsa, there's not much to recommend this archaeological adventure. Set in 1900, Robert Taylor is the rough, tough treasure hunter who's persuaded by old flame Eleanor Parker to go on an expedition to the ancient tombs of Egypt. Of course, feelings are rekindled but Parker is now married to Carlos Thompson. Into this romantic mix can be added a band of tomb robbers and some attractive locations but that's all there is to this tomb with a view. TH

Robert Taylor (1) *Mark Brandon* • Eleanor Parker *Ann Mercedes* • Carlos Thompson *Philip Mercedes* • Kurt Kasznar *Hamed Bachkour* • Victor Jory *Taureg chief* • Leon Askin *Valentine Arko* ■ *Dir* Robert Pirosh • *Scr* Robert Pirosh, Karl Tunberg, from the book *Gods, Graves and Scholars* by CW Ceram

Valley of the Sun ★★ U

Western 1942 · US · BW · 78mins

Director George Marshall, who had made a great job of combining the conventions of comedy with those of the western in *Destry Rides Again*, was hauled in to repeat the trick here but clearly mislaid his magic wand. The nub of the story concerns rivalry and conflict between army scout James Craig and nasty Indian agent Dean Jagger, both after Lucille Ball. The former also objects to the latter's treatment of the Indians. Violent action and imbecilic farce fail to mix here. RK

Lucille Ball *Christine Larson* • James Craig *Jonathan Ware* • Sir Cedric Hardwicke [Cedric Hardwicke] *Warrick* • Dean Jagger *Jim Sawyer* • Tom Tyler *Geronimo* • Antonio Moreno *Chief Cochise* ■ *Dir* George Marshall • *Scr* Horace McCoy, from a story by Clarence Budington Kelland

Valmont ★★★★ 15

Period drama 1989 · Fr/UK · Colour · 136mins

Coming hot on the heels of *Dangerous Liaisons*, this opulent reworking of the notorious Choderlos de Laclos novel plays on the emotions in the same way that Stephen Frears's film teased the intellect. Director Milos Forman is more concerned with the perils of pursuing your desires than in the machinations of the indolent and, consequently, the characters take as much pleasure in the act of seduction as in its art. It's impossible to resist comparing the two productions, but while Frears's is truer to the calculating spirit of the book and boasts the showier cast, Forman's has greater human interest and the more heartfelt performances. DP

Colin Firth *Vicomte de Valmont* • Annette Bening *Marquise de Merteuil* • Meg Tilly *Madame de Tourvel* • Fairuza Balk *Cécile de Volanges* • Sian Phillips *Madame de Volanges* • Jeffrey Jones *Gercourt* • Henry Thomas *Danceny* • Fabia Drake *Madame de Rosemonde* • TP McKenna *Baron* • Isla Blair *Baroness* ■ *Dir* Milos Forman • *Scr* Jean-Claude Carrière, from the novel *Les Liaisons Dangereuses* by Choderlos de Laclos

Les Valseuses ★★★★ 18

Drama 1974 · Fr · Colour · 112mins

Bertrand Blier's often shocking film was named after the French slang word for "testicles". As the grotesque, joy-riding delinquents who tend to think with that part of their anatomy, Gérard Depardieu and Patrick Dewaere are the personification of ignorance, indulgence and insensitivity. Their sexual encounters with newly sprung jailbird Jeanne Moreau and drifting thrill-seeker Miou-Miou manage to be both repellent and compelling. But the film loses its bite after Depardieu and Dewaere go on the run, although the sequence with a young Isabelle Huppert has a dark fascination. DP. In French with English subtitles. [VIDEO]

Gérard Depardieu *Jean-Claude* • Patrick Dewaere *Pierrot* • Miou-Miou *Marie-Ange* • Jeanne Moreau *Jeanne* • Jacques Chailleux *Jacques* • Michel Peyrelon *Surgeon* • Brigitte Fossey *Young mother* • Isabelle Huppert *Jacqueline* ■ *Dir* Bertrand Blier • *Scr* Bertrand Blier, Philippe Dumarcay, from the novel by Bertrand Blier

Value for Money ★★

Comedy 1955 · UK · Colour · 93mins

Take one bluff, penny-wise Yorkshireman and a blowsy, blonde showgirl, exaggerate every regional characteristic and then whisk them together into a romantic froth. Season with a couple of quaint cameos and you have this. The on-screen antics of John Gregson and Diana Dors (neither of whom are on form) are mediocre in this featherweight comedy. DP

John Gregson *Chayley Broadbent* • Diana Dors *Ruthine West* • Susan Stephen *Ethel* • Derek Farr *Duke Popplewell* • Frank Pettingell *Higgins* • Jill Adams *Joy* • Charles Victor *Lumm* • James Gregson *Oldroyd* • Ernest Thesiger *Lord Dewsbury* • Donald Pleasence *Limpy* ■ *Dir* Ken Annakin • *Scr* RF Delderfield, William Fairchild, from the novel by Derrick Boothroyd

Vamp ★★ 18

Horror comedy 1986 · US · Colour · 89mins

Grace Jones oozes animal sexuality and danger as the sensual vampire of the title, but even she can't save this botched attempt to mix *Animal House* laughs with kinky horror. Chris Makepeace and Robert Rusler are the college students who stumble upon a den of strippers with serious dental problems, but the one good gag is lifted directly from the far superior *An American Werewolf in London*. JF [VIDEO]

Grace Jones *Katrina* • Chris Makepeace *Keith* • Robert Rusler *AJ* • Sandy Baron *Vic* • Dedee Pfeiffer *Amaretto* • Gedde Watanabe *Duncan* ■ *Dir* Richard Wenk • *Scr* Richard Wenk, from a story by Donald P Borchers, Richard Wenk

Vampira ★★ 15

Comedy horror 1975 · UK · Colour · 84mins

David Niven dons the cloak of Dracula in this long-in-the-tooth vampire comedy well past its Swinging Sixties sell-by-date. The Count, who has turned his castle into a Playboy-style tourist resort, is searching for a rare blood type donor to revive his wife Vampira. The stale gag is that she's eventually reincarnated as black babe Teresa Graves. Niven adds a touch of class to the ridiculously old-fashioned proceedings and is the only reason for watching this dire farce from director Clive Donner. AJ [VIDEO]

David Niven *Count Dracula* • Teresa Graves *Countess Vampira* • Peter Bayliss *Maltravers* • Jennie Linden *Angela* • Nicky Henson *Marc* • Linda Hayden *Helga* ■ *Dir* Clive Donner • *Scr* Jeremy Lloyd

The Vampire ★★★ PG

Horror 1957 · Mex · BW · 83mins

While Hollywood subjected 1950s audiences to A-bombs, insect mutations and alien invaders, Mexico got busy cloning classic American horror movies such as *Dracula* for export. This South of the Border shocker is one of the best and stars the impressive German Robles as Count Lavud, who leaves an undead trail of destruction. Also featuring top terror hero Abel Salazar, the story may be familiar, but the odd atmosphere and funereal lyricism make for some deft surprises. It was so successful in Latin countries, it spawned an instant sequel, *The Vampire's Coffin*. AJ. In Spanish with English subtitles. DVD

Abel Salazar *Dr Enrique* • Ariadna Welter *Marta* • German Robles *Count Duval/Lavud* • Carmen Montejo *Eloisa* ■ *Dir* Fernando Mendez • *Scr* Ramon Obon, from his story

The Vampire Bat ★ PG

Horror 1933 · US · BW · 60mins

A series of small-town murders turn out to be the work of scientist Lionel Atwill who drains his victims of blood in order to nourish a flesh parasite he has created. A standard-issue mad doctor tale, it was evidently made to cash-in on the success of Universal's *Dracula* with frightened Fay Wray and hero Melvyn Douglas lending limp support to the hopelessly outdated proceedings. AJ [VIDEO]

Lionel Atwill *Dr Otto von Niemann* • Fay Wray *Ruth Bertin* • Melvyn Douglas *Karl Brettschneider* • Maude Eburne *Gussie Schnappmann* • George E Stone *Kringen* • Dwight Frye *Herman Gleib* ■ *Dir* Frank R Strayer • *Scr* Edward T Lowe

Vampire Circus ★★★ 18

Horror 1971 · UK · Colour · 88mins

This isn't the freak show its title might suggest, but a fast-moving, imaginative Hammer vampire tale of punishment and revenge. It's set in an isolated plague-ridden town in 19th-century central Europe that welcomes the arrival of a circus, until the vampire count's revenge becomes clear. Adrienne Corri's intense beauty shines like a beacon in the murky atmosphere, but the delicacy of mood collapses into blood-spurting horrifics towards the end. TH [VIDEO] DVD

Adrienne Corri *Gypsy woman* • Laurence Payne *Professor Mueller* • Thorley Walters *Burgermeister* • John Moulder-Brown *Anton Kersh* • Lynne Frederick *Dora Mueller* ■ *Dir* Robert William Young [Robert Young (2)] • *Scr* Judson Kinberg, from a story by George Baxt, Wilbur Stark

Vampire Hunter D ★★★ 15

Animated science-fiction horror
1985 · Jpn · Colour · 80mins

An adventurous *manga* animation melange of JRR Tolkien, Sergio Leone, Hammer horror and mainstream sci-fi. Far off in the 13th millennium, D is hired by village beauty Doris to save her from Count Magnus Lee's clutches. Having sampled her jugular, the ancient giant now wants Doris for his bride and D must infiltrate his mountain fortress in order to halt his plans. Director Toyoo Ashida uses a wildly eclectic palate of styles and astonishing depth to achieve his helter-skelter imagery in one of the best Japanese cartoons in the *Akira* tradition. AJ. Japanese dialogue dubbed into English. [VIDEO] DVD

Dir Toyoo Ashida, Carl Macek • *Scr* Yasuhi Hirano

Vampire in Brooklyn ★★★ 15

Horror 1995 · US · Colour · 97mins

Eddie Murphy's streetwise persona is often at odds here with director Wes Craven's more explicit, doom-laden beastliness, and the intended comedy becomes lost in the horror. Murphy stars as suave Caribbean vampire Maximillian, a master of disguise, who comes to America to find his soulmate – NYPD cop Angela Bassett, who is unaware that she is Murphy's bride-to-be. There are some good moments, but too often Craven puts on the frighteners so heavily that the chuckles get squeezed out. TH [VIDEO] DVD

Eddie Murphy *Maximillian/Preacher Pauley/Guido* • Angela Bassett *Rita* • Allen Payne *Justice* • Kadeem Hardison *Julius* • John Witherspoon *Silas* • Zakes Mokae *Dr Zeko* • Joanna Cassidy *Dewey* • Simbi Khali *Nikki* ■ *Dir* Wes Craven • *Scr* Charles Murphy, Christopher Parker, Michael Lucker, from a story by Charles Murphy, Eddie Murphy, Vernon Lynch Jr

Vampire in Venice ★★ 18

Horror 1987 · It · Colour · 89mins

Returning to the role of Dracula, Klaus Kinski is here confronted with vampire hunter Christopher Plummer as he wearily inducts a princess and her eager sister into the ranks of the undead. Kinski gives a demonstration of melancholic malevolence that is every bit as impressive as his performance in Werner Herzog's *Nosferatu*. But, Augusto Caminito relies too much on Venetian splendour and close-ups of Kinski's eyes to conjure up atmosphere and the result is languor, not horror. DP. Italian dialogue dubbed into English. Contains violence and sexual content. [VIDEO]

Klaus Kinski *Nosferatu* • Barbara De Rossi *Helietta Canins* • Christopher Plummer *Paris Catalano* • Yorgo Voyagis *Giuseppe Barnabo* • Clara Colosimo *Medium* • Maria C Cumani *Matilde Canins* • Donald Pleasence *Don Alvise* ■ *Dir* Augusto Caminito • *Scr* Augusto Caminito, Leandro Lucchetti, from a story by Alberto Alfieri

The Vampire Lovers ★★ 15

Horror 1970 · UK · Colour · 90mins

The first of Hammer's three Karnstein chillers (based on Sheridan LeFanu's *Carmilla*) is an atmospheric and erotic undead tale detailing the life of lesbian vampire Mircalla, voluptuously played by Ingrid Pitt. Peter Cushing lends a greater credibility to the sensuality-heavy production than the repetitious script would normally warrant. Inventive direction by Roy Ward Baker conspires to make this brazenly exploitative horror hokum better than it deserves to be. *Lust for a Vampire* and *Twins of Evil* followed. AJ [VIDEO] DVD

Ingrid Pitt *Mircalla/Marcilla/Carmilla Karnstein* • Peter Cushing *General Spielsdorf* • Madeline Smith *Emma* • Jon Finch *Carl* • Pippa Steele *Laura Spielsdorf* • George Cole *Morton* • Dawn Addams *Countess* • Douglas Wilmer *Baron Hartog* • Kate O'Mara *Mme Perrodot* • Ferdy Mayne *Doctor* ■ *Dir* Roy Ward Baker • *Scr* Tudor Gates, from the story *Carmilla* by J Sheridan Le Fanu, adapted by Harry Fine, Michael Style

Vampires ★★★ 18

Horror 1998 · US · Colour · 107mins

James Woods gives a wonderfully laconic performance as a vampire slayer on the Vatican payroll in director John Carpenter's rip-roaring western horror flick. Woods is out to destroy a 600-year-old bloodsucker before the evil creature gets his hands on an ancient relic that will enable him to appear during daylight hours. Carpenter laces the suspense and splatter with agreeable humour and arty special effects, and there's smart support from Sheryl Lee as the psychic link to the undead leader. Followed in 2001 by a sequel, *Vampires: los Muertos*. AJ. Horror from director John Carpenter. Contains violence and sex scenes. [VIDEO] DVD

James Woods *Jack Crow* • Daniel Baldwin *Montoya* • Sheryl Lee *Katrina* • Thomas Ian Griffith *Valek* • Maximilian Schell *Cardinal Alba* • Tim Guinee *Father Adam Guiteau* • Mark Boone Junior *Catlin* • Gregory Sierra *Father Giovanni* ■ *Dir* John Carpenter • *Scr* Don Jakoby, from the novel by John Steakley • *Cinematographer* Gary B Kibbe

Vampires in Havana ★★

Animated horror comedy
1985 · Cub · Colour · 80mins

Vampirism is equated to the Mafia in a delightfully stylised, if sometimes crudely drawn, Cuban cartoon feature combining Hammer horror, gangster movies, James Bond and Latin American history. Professor Von Dracula and his nephew Joseph Amadeus become the focus of a war between the undead of Chicago and Düsseldorf, thanks to Vampisol, a sun-block drug that allows vampires to walk around in daylight. Light-hearted fun with little political comment. AJ. In Spanish with English subtitles.

Dir/Scr Juan Padron

Vampire's Kiss ★ 18

Horror comedy 1988 · US · Colour · 99mins

Yuppie Nicolas Cage gets bitten by sexy vampire Jennifer Beals, but when he doesn't turn into a vampire, he fakes it and becomes a mixed-up psycho wearing plastic fangs and prowling discos for victims. Falling between horror comedy and a serious study of mental illness, director Robert Bierman's farrago is hideously unfunny, witless and offensively stupid. AJ. Contains violence. DVD

Nicolas Cage *Peter Loew* • Maria Conchita Alonso *Alva Restrepo* • Jennifer Beals *Rachel* • Elizabeth Ashley *Dr Glaser* • Kasi Lemmons *Jackie* • Bob Lujan *Emilio* • Jessica Lundy *Sharon* • John Walker *Donald* ■ *Dir* Robert Bierman • *Scr* Joseph Minion

Vampyr ★★★★★ PG

Horror 1932 · Fr/Ger · BW · 62mins

Based on *Carmilla*, Carl Th Dreyer's hypnotic psychological chiller also borrows from other stories contained in J Sheridan Le Fanu's collection, *In a Glass Darkly*. The film's visual ethereality was an accident caused by the fogging of a lens, but the dreamlike structure (with its shifting perspectives, unexpected juxtapositions and defiance of logic) was a conscious attempt to keep the viewer disorientated. Shot on location in France, this was Dreyer's first talkie, although dialogue was subordinate to the way his eerily poetic, almost erotic, imagery probes the links between good and evil, imagination and reality, faith and the supernatural. A singular masterwork. DP. In German with English subtitles.

Julian West *David Gray* • Maurice Schutz *Lord of the Manor* • Rena Mandel *Gisèle* • Sybille Schmitz *Léone* • Jan Hieronimko *Village doctor* • Henriette Gérard *Marguerite Chopin* • Albert Bras *Old servant* ■ *Dir* Carl Th Dreyer • *Scr* Carl Th Dreyer, Christen Jul, from the story *Carmilla* by J Sheridan Le Fanu • *Cinematographer* Rudolph Maté, Louis Née

Vampyros Lesbos ★ 18

Cult erotic horror
1970 · Sp/W Ger · Colour · 85mins

Maverick Spanish film-maker Jesus Franco strikes out again with this abysmal erotic horror very loosely based on the Bram Stoker short story *Dracula's Guest*. The count's descendant Soledad Miranda entices women via striptease dreams to her isolated Mediterranean island so she can suck their blood and live for ever. To Franco lovers, this one's a surreal melancholic poem about vampire loneliness. It will strike everyone else as nothing more than a slow, trivial and irritating slice of sleazy "Horrotica" that barely even qualifies as a home movie. AJ. In German with English subtitles. DVD

Soledad Miranda *Countess Nadine Carody* • Dennis Price *Dr Alwin Seward* • Paul Muller *Dr Steiner* • Ewa Stromberg *Linda Westinghouse* ■ *Dir* Franco Manera [Jesus Franco] • *Scr* Jesus Franco, Jaime Chavarri, from their story

The Van ★★ 15

Comedy drama
1996 · Ire/UK · Colour · 95mins

It's been a case of diminishing returns as far as the cinematic adaptations of Roddy Doyle's Barrytown trilogy are concerned. Following the soulful success of Alan Parker's *The Commitments*, Stephen Frears struggled to bring much bite to *The Snapper*, and in this concluding episode he never gets out of first gear. The flashes of the Republic of Ireland's achievements at the 1990 World Cup are wonderfully evocative, but the tale of unemployed scalliwags Colm Meaney and Donal O'Kelly feels forced. DP. Contains swearing.

Colm Meaney *Larry* • Donal O'Kelly *Bimbo* • Ger Ryan *Maggie* • Caroline Rothwell *Mary* • Neili Conroy *Diane* • Ruaidhri Conroy *Kevin* • Brendan O'Carroll *Weslie* • Stuart Dunne *Sam* ■ *Dir* Stephen Frears • *Scr* Roddy Doyle, from his novel

Van Gogh ★★★★ 15

Biographical drama
1991 · Fr · Colour · 151mins

Maurice Pialat's superbly photographed account of Van Gogh's last few months is by far the most compelling of the films about the tortured artist. Creating the atmosphere of Auvers-sur-Oise with great care, he builds up his portrait through a wealth of tiny details. Gaunt, withdrawn and acting on impulses that are terrifying in their suddenness and ferocity, Jacques Dutronc is magnificent in the title role, whether ranting against his brother Theo, seeking consolation in women or drink, or simply painting in the fields. DP. In French with English subtitles.

Jacques Dutronc *Vincent van Gogh* • Alexandra London *Marguerite Gachet* • Gérard Séty *Doctor Gachet* • Bernard Le Coq *Theo van Gogh* • Corinne Bourdon *Jo* • Elsa Zylberstein *Cathy* ■ *Dir/Scr* Maurice Pialat • *Cinematographer* Gilles Henry, Emmanuel Machuel

Van Helsing ★★★ 12

Action fantasy horror
2004 · US · Colour · 126mins

Writer/director Stephen Sommers delivers an exciting, effects-driven romp that combines the pulling power of Dracula, the Wolf Man and Frankenstein's Monster. Gabriel Van Helsing (Hugh Jackman) is dispatched by a secret, Vatican-based organisation to 19th-century Transylvania where he comes to the aid of Anna Valerious (Kate Beckinsale) in her long-running battle against the vampire Count and his evil allies. The CGI could have been better – as could the dialogue – but viewed solely as escapism, this is an exhilarating ride. SF. Contains violence. DVD

Hugh Jackman *Gabriel Van Helsing* • Kate Beckinsale *Anna Valerious* • Richard Roxburgh *Count Dracula* • David Wenham *Carl* • Shuler Hensley *Frankenstein's Monster* • Elena Anaya *Aleera* • Kevin J O'Connor *Igor* • Will Kemp *Velkan Valerious* • Alun Armstrong *Cardinal Jinette* • Samuel West *Dr Victor Frankenstein* ■ *Dir/Scr* Stephen Sommers

Van Nuys Blvd ★★

Comedy drama 1979 · US · Colour · 93mins

This raunchy late 1970s B-movie about drag racing has Bill Adler as the country boy who heads for the Californian town of Van Nuys in search of the fast-lane. He's rapidly inducted into a ludicrously drawn subculture of cheeseburgers, chicks and cars, cars, cars, pushing himself and his beloved automobile to the limit, before opting for the charms of former *Playboy* Playmate Cynthia Wood. A meaningless exercise in male wish-fulfilment, it's tacky but kind of enjoyable, too. RT

Bill Adler *Bobby* • Cynthia Wood *Moon* • Dennis Bowen *Greg* • Melissa Prophet *Camille* • David Hayward *Chooch* • Tara Strohmeier *Wanda* • Dana Gladstone *Al Zass* ■ *Dir/Scr* William Sachs

Van Wilder: Party Liaison ★ 15

Comedy 2002 · US/Ger · Colour · 88mins

The *National Lampoon* franchise continues its nosedive into mediocrity with this lacklustre teen comedy. A spiritless melting pot of fratboy high jinks and syrupy sentimentality, director Walt Becker's first film doesn't seem to know whether it's a cheeky romance or a moralistic farce.This tale of world-shy student Van Wilder (Ryan Reynolds), who will do anything to maintain his indefinite college stay, is a pitiful failure. SF DVD

Ryan Reynolds *Van Wilder* • Tara Reid *Gwen Pearson* • Tim Matheson *Vance Wilder Sr* • Kal Penn *Taj Mahal Badalandabad* • Teck Holmes *Hutch* • Daniel Cosgrove *Richard Bagg* ■ *Dir* Walt Becker • *Scr* Brent Goldberg, David T Wagner

Vanessa, Her Love Story ★

Melodrama 1935 · US · BW · 74mins

Unaware that her husband is suffering from inherited insanity, unhappily married Helen Hayes takes a lover (Robert Montgomery), who later loses an arm while on military duty with the British army in Egypt. Although the film features a quality supporting cast, this is a really deathly soap opera that belongs on the bottom of the heap. RK

Helen Hayes *Vanessa* • Robert Montgomery *Benjie* • Otto Kruger *Ellis* • May Robson *Judith* • Lewis Stone *Adam* • Henry Stephenson *Barney* • Violet Kemble-Cooper *Lady Herries* ■ *Dir* William K Howard • *Scr* Lenore Coffee, Hugh Walpole, from the novel by Hugh Walpole

Vanilla Sky ★★ 15

Romantic fantasy thriller
2001 · US · Colour · 130mins

Writer/director Cameron's Crowe's disappointing remake of Alejandro Amenábar's off-kilter Spanish thriller *Open Your Eyes* makes the fatal error of jettisoning the original's potent psychological suspense. Crowe has turned a disquieting and disorientating murder mystery into a superficial showcase for star Tom Cruise. There's no chemistry between Cruise and Penélope Cruz (reprising her role from the original), and both look uncomfortable. JC. Contains violence, swearing, sex scenes, nudity. DVD

Tom Cruise *David Aames* • Penélope Cruz *Sofia Serrano* • Cameron Diaz *Julie Gianni* • Kurt Russell *McCabe* • Jason Lee *Brian Shelby* • Noah Taylor *Edmund Ventura* • Timothy Spall *Thomas Tipp* • Tilda Swinton *Rebecca Dearborn* • Alicia Witt *Libby* ■ *Dir* Cameron Crowe • *Scr* Cameron Crowe, from the film *Abre los ojos (Open Your Eyes)* by Alejandro Amenábar, Mateo Gil

Vanished without a Trace ★★★ PG

Drama based on a true story
1993 · US · Colour · 89mins

When it comes to TV movies based on true stories, Hollywood relishes the chance to exploit the unsettling and horrid goings-on in the trim gardens of small-town America. Here, a rather imaginative kidnapping involving 26 children, their bus driver and three rich-kid criminals causes ructions in the setting of Chowchilla, California. The suspense is ably sustained by director Vern Gillum, and Karl Malden, as the driver, enlivens the proceedings with his trademark mix of doggedness and decency. JM DVD

Karl Malden *Edward Ray* • Tim Ransom *Fred Woods IV* • Travis Fine *Rick Schoenfeld* • Tom Hodges *Jim Schoenfeld* • Julie Harris *Odessa Ray* • Bobby Zameroski *Tim Pearson* ■ *Dir* Vern Gillum • *Scr* David Eyre Jr, from the book *Why Have They Taken Our Children* by Jack W Baugh, Jefferson Morgan

The Vanishing ★★★★ 15

Psychological thriller
1988 · Neth/Fr · Colour · 101mins

George Sluizer's chilling tale of premeditation, abduction and obsession stars Bernard-Pierre Donnadieu as the unassuming family man infatuated with the perfect kidnap. He emerges as one of the screen's most chilling, calculating and conceited psychotics, and the quiet satisfaction with which he explains his technique to the victim's boyfriend, Gene Bervoets, is unnerving in the extreme. From the moment we realise Johanna Ter Steege is in danger to the final shocking twist, Sluizer inexorably, expertly draws us deeper into the mystery, exposing our own morbid curiosity in the process. DP. In Dutch and French with English subtitles. Contains violence. DVD

Bernard-Pierre Donnadieu *Raymond Lemorne* • Gene Bervoets *Rex Hofman* • Johanna Ter Steege *Saskia Wagter* • Gwen Eckhaus *Lienexe* • Bernadette Le Saché *Simone Lemorne* • Tania Latarjet *Denise* ■ *Dir* George Sluizer • *Scr* Tim Krabbé, George Sluizer (adaptation), from the novel *The Golden Egg* by Tim Krabbé

The Vanishing ★★ 15

Thriller 1993 · US · Colour · 105mins

George Sluizer directs this Hollywood remake of his outstanding original European version. Kiefer Sutherland is the troubled holidaymaker whose girlfriend vanishes without a trace at a service station. His obsessive search for her leads him to eccentric teacher Jeff Bridges. Sluizer fails to sustain the icy air of menace of the first film, and the movie is further unhinged by a bizarre, over-the-top performance from the normally reliable Bridges. JF. Contains swearing, violence. DVD

Jeff Bridges *Barney Cousins* • Kiefer Sutherland *Jeff Harriman* • Nancy Travis *Rita Baker* • Sandra Bullock *Diane Shaver* • Park Overall *Lynn* • Maggie Linderman *Denise Cousins* • Lisa Eichhorn *Helene* • George Hearn *Arthur Bernard* ■ *Dir* George Sluizer • *Scr* Todd Graff, from the novel *The Golden Egg* by Tim Krabbé

The Vanishing Corporal ★★★★

Second World War comedy drama
1962 · Fr · BW · 106mins

Jean-Pierre Cassel is the vanishing corporal, a prisoner of war who dedicates himself to escape, but all his attempts fail and he is sent to detention camps for punishment. Finally, he and his buddy (Claude Brasseur) get back to Paris where they vow to join the Resistance. Set in a German PoW camp, like his masterpiece *La Grande Illusion*, though this time in the Second World War, Jean Renoir approaches the subject as comedy but he manages to suggest the grimmer reality beneath the surface. RB. A French language film.

Jean-Pierre Cassel *The Corporal* • Claude Brasseur *Dad* • Claude Rich *Ballochet* • Jean Carmet *Emile* • Jacques Jouanneau *Penche à gauche* • Conny Froboess [Cornelia Froboess] *Erika* ■ *Dir* Jean Renoir • *Scr* Jean Renoir, Guy Lefranc, from the novel *Le Caporal Epinglé* by Jacques Perret

Vanishing Frontier ★★

Western 1932 · US · BW · 65mins

Former American football hero Johnny Mack Brown made a major impact in the title role of 1930's *Billy the Kid*, but an alleged affair with William Randolph Hearst's mistress Marion Davies cost him true stardom. This romp was one of his last major movies, though he continued to headline in popular programme-fillers throughout the next three decades. Here he has a half-decent role, playing a Robin Hood of the west. TS

Johnny Mack Brown *Kirby Tornell* • Evalyn Knapp *Carol Winfield* • ZaSu Pitts *Aunt Sylvia* • Raymond Hatton *Waco* • J Farrell MacDonald *Hornet* • Wallace MacDonald *Capt Kearney* ■ *Dir* Phil Rosen • *Scr* Stuart Anthony

Vanishing Point ★★★ 18

Cult road movie 1971 · US · Colour · 94mins

Car delivery boy Barry Newman takes a bet that he can't drive a Dodge Challenger from Denver to San Francisco in 15 hours in this gritty cult road move. Newman switches on the ignition, puts his foot down and, stopping only for fuel (petrol for the Dodge, amphetamines for him), follows in the wake of *Easy Rider* and sets out to be a similar essay in alienation, but has little of that film's low-budget magic. AT [VIDEO] DVD

Barry Newman *Kowalski* • Cleavon Little *Super Soul* • Dean Jagger *Prospector* • Victoria Medlin *Vera* • Paul Koslo *Young cop* • Robert Donner *Older cop* ■ *Dir* Richard C Sarafian • *Scr* Guillermo Cain, from a story outline by Malcolm Hart

The Vanishing Virginian ★★★ U

Biographical comedy drama
1941 · US · BW · 96mins

Life in the happy and comfortably off family of dedicated public prosecutor, husband and father of five Robert Yancey (Frank Morgan), as lived down South between 1918 and 1929 is the subject of this affectionate drama. Fewer spoonfuls of sugar would have helped this somewhat rambling exercise in nostalgia, but it's a good-hearted, well-characterised and enjoyable excursion into an era when the mere idea of votes for women was enough to cause consternation. Newcomer Kathryn Grayson gets to exercise her vocal chords with a handful of songs. RK

Frank Morgan *Robert "Cap'n Bob" Yancey* • Kathryn Grayson *Rebecca Yancey* • Spring Byington *Rosa Yancey* • Natalie Thompson *Margaret Yancey* • Douglass Newland *Jim Shirley* • Mark Daniels *Jack Holden* • Louise Beavers *Aunt Emmeline Preston* ■ *Dir* Frank Borzage • *Scr* Jan Fortune, from the biography by Rebecca Yancey Williams

Vanity Fair ★★★ PG

Period comedy drama
2004 · US/UK · Colour · 135mins

It can't have been easy condensing William Makepeace Thackeray's sprawling, dense novel into a movie. Small wonder, then, that Mira Nair's film is a little lacking in linear plot, being more a series of bitty scenes than a coherent narrative. But there's still much to admire in this nicely written and handsomely mounted adaptation. Reese Witherspoon is good as Becky Sharp, Thackeray's calculating, ambitious heroine. James Purefoy, as the gambler she marries during her no-holds-barred bid for a better life, stands out in a starry supporting cast. DA DVD

Reese Witherspoon *Becky Sharp* • Eileen Atkins *Miss Matilda Crawley* • Jim Broadbent *Mr Osborne* • Gabriel Byrne *The Marquess of Steyne* • Romola Garai *Amelia Sedley* • Bob Hoskins *Sir Pitt Crawley* • Rhys Ifans *William Dobbin* • Geraldine McEwan *Lady Southdown* • James Purefoy *Rawdon Crawley* • Jonathan Rhys Meyers *George Osborne* ■ *Dir* Mira Nair • *Scr* Matthew Faulk, Mark Skeet, Julian Fellowes, from the novel by William Makepeace Thackeray

The Vanquished ★★★ U

Portmanteau drama 1953 · It · BW · 86mins

This collection of stories explores the moral turpitude of postwar Europe. In the opening episode, French pupils kill a classmate for cash; an Italian college student becomes involved with the black market in the second, while an English poet seeks to profit from the death of an apparently respectable woman in the third. Censorship problems dogged the picture, but Michelangelo Antonioni's genius for linking the inner self and environment is well established. DP. An Italian language film.

Jean-Pierre Mocky *Pierre* • Etchika Choureau *Simone* • Franco Interlenghi *Claudio* • Anna-Maria Ferrero *Marina* • Evi Maltagliati *Claudio's Mother* • Eduardo Ciannelli *Claudio's Father* • Peter Reynolds *Aubrey* • Fay Compton *Mrs Pinkerton* • Patrick Barr *Kent Watton* ■ *Dir* Michelangelo Antonioni • *Scr* Michelangelo Antonioni, Suso Cecchi D'Amico, Giorgio Bassani, Diego Fabbri, Turi Vasile, Roger Nimier

Vanya on 42nd Street ★★★ U

Drama 1994 · US · Colour · 115mins

Three directors on different continents took on Anton Chekhov's *Uncle Vanya* within the space of two years. Michael Blakemore staged his version of the play *Country Life* in the Australian outback, while Anthony Hopkins located his interpretation called *August* in North Wales. But only Louis Malle could have thought of setting the play in a dilapidated New York theatre, with the action being performed by a rehearsing cast sitting around a table in their day clothes. Wallace Shawn is excellent in the title role, but, while Malle's approach allows us to concentrate on the text and offers an insight into the acting process, his final film marks a slightly disappointing end to an exceptional career. DP [VIDEO]

Wallace Shawn *Vanya* • Julianne Moore *Yelena* • Andre Gregory • George Gaynes *Serebryakov* • Brooke Smith *Sonya* • Larry Pine *Dr Astrov* • Phoebe Brand *Nanny* • Lynn Cohen *Maman* • Jerry Mayer *Waffles* • Madhur Jaffrey *Mrs Chao* ■ *Dir* Louis Malle • *Scr* David Mamet, from the play *Uncle Vanya* by Anton Chekhov

Varian's War ★★★

Wartime drama based on a true story
2000 · Can/US/UK · Colour · 122mins

This is an earnest, if unquestioning made-for-TV tribute to a selfless individual who risked all to counter the effects of the Holocaust. Having failed to alert Americans to the imminent plight of European Jews, journalist Varian Fry returned to France during the early days of the war with the aim of rescuing some of the continent's leading intellectuals. William Hurt and Julia Ormond perform admirably. DP

William Hurt *Varian Fry* • Julia Ormond *Miriam* • Matt Craven *Beamish* • Maury Chaykin *Marcello* • Alan Arkin *Freier* • Lynn Redgrave *Alma Werfel-Mahler* ■ *Dir/Scr* Lionel Chetwynd

Variety Girl ★★ U

Comedy musical
1947 · US · BW and Colour · 86mins

This is yet another entry in the seemingly interminable string of studio star cavalcades of which Paramount seemed to be particularly fond. The characteristic non-plot has two hopefuls (Mary Hatcher, Olga San Juan) arriving at the studio in search of a future. Here, they encounter a starry roster of names. RK

Mary Hatcher *Catherine Brown Variety Sheridan* • Olga San Juan *Amber La Vonne* • DeForest Kelley *Bob Kirby* • Bing Crosby • Bob Hope • Gary Cooper • Ray Milland • Alan Ladd • Barbara Stanwyck • Paulette Goddard • Dorothy Lamour • Sonny Tufts • William Holden (2) ■ *Dir* George Marshall • *Scr* Edmund Hartmann [Edmund L Hartmann], Frank Tashlin, Robert Welch, Monte Brice

Variety Jubilee ★★★ U

Musical 1942 · UK · BW · 92mins

This simple, nostalgic tribute to the British music hall tradition begins with two former variety artists who become partners in running a vaudeville venue at the dawn of the 20th century. One of their sons is then killed in the First World War, before a grandson takes over the family enterprise and makes it a success again. The film consists largely of musical variety acts performed by numerous forgotten old-timers of a bygone era. Wonderful! RK

Reginald Purdell *Joe Swan* • Ellis Irving *Kit Burns* • Lesley Brook *Evelyn Vincent* • Marie Lloyd Jr *Marie Lloyd* • Tom E Finglass *Eugene Stratton* • John Rorke *Gus Elen* • Betty Warren *Florrie Forde* • Charles Coborn ■ *Dir* Maclean Rogers • *Scr* Kathleen Butler, from a story by Mabel Constanduros

Variety Time ★★★ U

Compilation 1948 · US · BW · 58mins

Long before *That's Entertainment!*, studios would assemble clips from past productions into compilations. RKO made this, shooting new footage of Jack Paar as MC to link the songs, sketches and two comedy shorts (both very funny) that comprised the bill. As several of the song-and-dance numbers are from B-movies which are hard to see nowadays, musical fans will find a look worthwhile. TV

Jack Paar *MC* ■ *Dir* Hal Yates

Varsity Blues ★★★ 15

Comedy drama 1999 · US · Colour · 104mins

James Van Der Beek is the high-school football player who challenges the authority of his control-freak coach Jon Voight (giving another hilariously over-the-top performance) when he becomes the team's star quarterback. This teenage drama is basically a 1990s throwback to 1980s sports movies such as *Youngblood* and *All the Right Moves* with the usual mix of sports action, drinking and girls and the odd moral tale thrown in. Predictable stuff. JB. Contains swearing and nudity. [VIDEO]

James Van Der Beek *Jonathan "Mox" Moxon* • Jon Voight *Coach Bud Kilmer* • Paul Walker *Lance Harbor* • Ron Lester *Billy Bob* • Scott Caan *Tweeter* • Richard Lineback *Joe Harbor* • Tiffany C Love *Collette Harbor* ■ *Dir* Brian Robbins • *Scr* W Peter Iliff

Vassa ★★★★ PG

Drama 1983 · USSR · Colour · 136mins

Gleb Panfilov directed Maxim Gorky's play as a vehicle for his wife Inna Churikova, and depicts her as the last bastion of strength in a morass of corruption, indolence and perversion. Her husband is charged with child molestation, her drunken brother is accused of impregnating the maid, her daughters are insane and nymphomaniac, and then her detested daughter-in-law arrives with news of her son's terminal illness. It's soap operatic, but the pre-Revolutionary trappings are sumptuous. DP. In Russian with English subtitles.

Inna Churikova *Vassa Zheleznova* • Vadim Medvedev *Sergei* • Nikolai Skorobogatov *Prokhor, Vassa's brother* • Valentina Telichkina *Anna, Vassa's secretary* • Valentina Yakunina *Rachel* ■ *Dir* Gleb Panfilov • *Scr* Gleb Panfilov, from the play *Vassa Zheleznova* by Maxim Gorky

Vatel ★★

Period comedy drama
2000 · Fr/US · Colour · 117mins

All the ingredients seem right – a screenplay co-written by Tom Stoppard, an Ennio Morricone score and Gérard Depardieu as François Vatel, the backstreet urchin whose culinary expertise and genius for baroque entertainments enchanted the court of Louis XIV. But under Roland Joffé's undistinguished direction, what emerges is a disappointing romp, where sexual and political intrigue intersperse with misfiring spectacle and inconsequential banter. DP

Gérard Depardieu *François Vatel* • Uma Thurman *Anne de Montausier* • Tim Roth *Marquis de Lauzun* • Julian Glover *Prince de Conde* • Julian Sands *King Louis XIV* • Timothy Spall *Gourville* ■ *Dir* Roland Joffé • *Scr* Jeanne Labrune, Tom Stoppard (English adaptation)

Vaudeville ★★★★

Silent melodrama 1925 · Ger · BW · 57mins

EA Dupont was handed this assignment after producer Erich Pommer felt FW Murnau was approaching it with too little enthusiasm. However, the dazzling display of visual artistry that transformed this otherwise humdrum showbiz melodrama was fashioned not by the director, but by his cinematographer Karl Freund. His bravura use of chiaroscuro lighting, subjective camera, overlapping dissolves and expressionist montage is quite masterly and demonstrates the pictorial sublimity of silent cinema. The story of the trapeze artist who murders his rival in love was much butchered for its US release to remove its moral ambiguities, although both versions have their merits. DP

Emil Jannings *Boss Huller* • Lya de Putti *Bertha-Marie* • Warwick Ward *Artinelli* • Charles Lincoln *Actor* ■ *Dir* EA Dupont • *Scr* EA Dupont, Leo Birinksi, from the novel *Der Eid des Stephan Huller* by Felix Holländer

Vault of Horror ★★ 15

Horror 1973 · UK · Colour · 82mins

Five men trapped in a mysterious basement room following a journey in an elevator, tell each other their recurring nightmares in this formulaic horror movie. The film was adapted from William Gaines's terror comics, which would account for such bizarre section titles as *Midnight Mess* and *This Trick'll Kill You*. This was the sixth horror compendium made by Amicus, for a time Hammer's most formidable rival. British actors such as Terry-Thomas and Daniel Massey bring a touch of class to an otherwise pedestrian production. TH [VIDEO] DVD

Daniel Massey *Rogers* • Anna Massey *Donna* • Michael Craig *Maitland* • Edward Judd *Alex* • Curt Jurgens *Sebastian* • Dawn Addams *Inez* • Terry-Thomas *Critchit* • Glynis Johns *Eleanor* • Marianne Stone *Jane* • Tom Baker *Alex Moore* • Denholm Elliott *Diltant* ■ *Dir* Roy Ward Baker • *Scr* Milton Subotsky, from the comic magazines *The Vault of Horror* and *Tales from the Crypt* by Al Feldstein, William Gaines

V

Veer-Zaara ★★★★ U

Epic romantic drama
2004 · Ind · Colour · 192mins

Yash Chopra's politically hard-hitting romantic drama stars Bollywood's alternative to Tom Cruise, Shahrukh Khan. It's a big, stylish and deeply enjoyable melodrama that uses an unlikely romance to tackle the continuing cross-border conflict between India and Pakistan. Khan plays a principled rescue pilot with the Indian air force who becomes obsessed with Preity Zinta, a provincial Pakistani girl he befriends after a bus accident strands her in India. Khan is suitably heroic, while Zinta gives a persuasive portrayal of a complex woman tested by recent events. OA. In Urdu and Hindi with English subtitles.

Shahrukh Khan [Shah Rukh Khan] *Veer Pratap Singh* • Preity Zinta *Zaara Hayaat Khan* • Rani Mukerji [Rani Mukherji] *Saamiya Siddiqui* • Amitabh Bachchan *Mr Singh* ■ *Dir* Yash Chopra • *Scr* Aditya Chopra

Vegas Vacation ★★ PG

Comedy 1997 · US · Colour · 90mins

The hapless Chevy Chase and long-suffering wife Beverly D'Angelo head for Las Vegas and get mixed up in a series of unamusing misadventures, in yet another *National Lampoon* venture. Randy Quaid, as Chase's trailer trash cousin, fares the best, but laughs are pretty much thin on the ground. Not even a talented supporting cast (Wallace Shawn, Sid Caesar) can do much to rescue this. JF

Chevy Chase *Clark W Griswold* • Beverly D'Angelo *Ellen Griswold* • Randy Quaid *Cousin Eddie* • Ethan Embry *Rusty Griswold* • Marisol Nichols *Audrey Griswold* • Wayne Newton ■ *Dir* Stephen Kessler • *Scr* Elisa Bell, from a story by Bob Ducsay

The Velocity of Gary ★★ 15

Drama 1998 · US · Colour · 96mins

Exploring the critical issue of sexual responsibility in the Aids era, James Still's play is translated to the screen with calculating theatricality by director Dan Ireland. The set-up itself is highly contrived, as country boy Thomas Jane arrives in the big city and intrudes upon bisexual porn star Vincent D'Onofrio's on-off relationship with mouthy doughnut waitress Salma Hayek. The melodramatics are enacted at such a furious pitch, particularly by a near-hysterical Hayek, that the story has already passed several emotional peaks before the real revelations begin. DP DVD

Vincent D'Onofrio *Valentino* • Salma Hayek *Mary Carmen* • Thomas Jane *Gary* • Olivia D'Abo *Veronica* • Chad Lindberg *Kid Joey* • Lucky Luciano *The King* ■ *Dir* Dan Ireland • *Scr* James Still, from his play *The Velocity of Gary (Not His Real Name)*

Velocity Trap ★★ 15

Science-fiction action adventure
1997 · US · Colour · 86mins

It's 2150 and Earth is over-run with computer crime, which means a return to hard cash and more work for the likes of security guard Olivier Gruner. He has to escort millions of dollars through space with pirates aboard, the crew in rebellion and a giant asteroid on a collision course. Essentially, it's an interstellar western, with the spaceship standing in for the wagon train. Negligible, but efficiently done. DP. Contains violence, swearing.

Olivier Gruner *Raymond Stokes* • Alicia Coppola *Beth Sheffield* • Ken Olandt *Nick* • Bruce Weitz *Captain Fenner* • Jorja Fox *Pallas* ■ *Dir* Phillip J Roth

V

Velvet Goldmine ★★ 15

Drama 1998 · UK/US · Colour · 118mins

Todd Haynes is an imaginative and original director, and he employs both these qualities here but, sadly, they fail to make this mish-mash of a movie work. Ewan McGregor and Jonathan Rhys Meyers star as a couple of cultish singers over-indulging on sex, drugs and rock'n'roll, and failing to make their lives function. It looks great and has tons of atmosphere, but this is a soulless, unstructured piece of film-making. LH. Contains swearing, nudity, sex scenes and violence. DVD

Ewan McGregor *Curt Wild* • Jonathan Rhys Meyers *Brian Slade* • Toni Collette *Mandy Slade* • Christian Bale *Arthur Stuart* • Eddie Izzard *Jerry Devine* • Emily Woof *Shannon* • Janet McTeer *Female narrator* ■ *Dir* Todd Haynes • *Scr* Todd Haynes, from a story by James Lyons, Todd Haynes

The Velvet Touch ★★

Crime drama 1948 · US · BW · 97mins

Rosalind Russell and her husband, producer Frederick Brisson played safe with this mechanical and lifeless melodrama, for which she specially hired top cinematographer Joseph Walker to ensure she looked her best in dresses by Travis Banton. She plays the Broadway star who kills her former lover in an argument and lets another actress, take the blame. AE

Rosalind Russell *Valerie Stanton* • Leo Genn *Michael Morrell* • Claire Trevor *Marion Webster* • Sydney Greenstreet *Captain Danbury* • Leon Ames *Gordon Dunning* • Frank McHugh *Ernie Boyle* • Walter Kingsford *Peter Gunther* • Dan Tobin *Jeff Trent* • Lex Barker *Paul Banton* ■ *Dir* John Gage • *Scr* Leo Rosten, Walter Reilly, from a story by William Mercer, from a story by Annabel Ross

The Velvet Vampire ★★★

Erotic horror 1971 · US · Colour · 79mins

This strange vampire tale is given an interesting feminist slant by Stephanie Rothman, one of the few female directors to work in the genre. After their dune buggy breaks down, Michael Blodgett and Sherry Miles accept an invitation to spend the weekend at Celeste Yarnall's Mojave desert ranch, unaware that she is an undead descendant of *Carmilla* author Sheridan Le Fanu. But Yarnall, who wears protective clothing in daylight, is more interested in Miles than her husband. An offbeat and comedy-laced psychedelic shocker. AJ

Michael Blodgett *Lee Ritter* • Sherry Miles *Susan Ritter* • Celeste Yarnall *Diane LeFanu* • Paul Prokop *Cliff* • Gene Shane *Carl Stoker* • Jerry Daniels *Juan* • Sandy Ward *Amos* ■ *Dir* Stephanie Rothman • *Scr* Maurice Jules, Charles S Swartz, Stephanie Rothman

Vendredi Soir ★★★★ 15

Drama 2002 · Fr · Colour · 85mins

Both an unconventional love story and a piercing study of urban dislocation, this chance encounter on a chilly Parisian night says a good deal about modern society with the minimum of dialogue. Whether in the snarled traffic that compounds Valérie Lemercier's doubts about committing to her partner or the spartan hotel room where her tentative relationship with hitcher Vincent Lindon develops into liberating passion, director Claire Denis and cinematographer Agnès Godard capture character and emotion with the utmost discretion. But it's the impressionistic use of hazy lights and jumbled sounds to re-create the trappings and pitfalls of city life that most impresses. DP. In French with English subtitles. Contains swearing and sex scenes. DVD

Valérie Lemercier *Laure* • Vincent Lindon *Jean* • Hélène de Saint Père *Marie* • Hélène Fillières *Woman in pizzeria* • Florence Loiret Caille *Girl playing pinball* • Grégoire Colin *Passer-by in parka* ■ *Dir* Claire Denis • *Scr* Emmanuèle Bernheim, Claire Denis, from the novel by Emmanuèle Bernheim

The Venetian Affair ★★

Spy thriller 1966 · US · Colour · 92mins

Evidently made by MGM to cash in on the popularity of Robert Vaughn in *The Man from UNCLE*, this thriller is a gritty exploration of the murky world of espionage. Vaughn is an ex-agent who's brought in from the cold to investigate the death of a diplomat at a Venetian peace conference. The involvement of Elke Sommer – his ex-wife and the reason he was sacked in the first place – only complicates matters further. An unremarkable affair apart from a welcome bit of menace from Boris Karloff. TH

Robert Vaughn *Bill Fenner* • Elke Sommer *Sandra Fane* • Felicia Farr *Claire Connor* • Karlheinz Böhm *Robert Wahl* • Luciana Paluzzi *Giulia Almeranti* • Boris Karloff *Dr Pierre Vaugiroud* • Roger C Carmel *Mike Ballard* • Edward Asner *Frank Rosenfeld* ■ *Dir* Jerry Thorpe • *Scr* E Jack Neuman, from the novel by Helen MacInnes

Venetian Bird ★★

Crime drama 1952 · UK · BW · 95mins

Borrowing liberally from *The Third Man*, this is a tolerable time-passer, although a little lightweight in the suspense department. Director Ralph Thomas offers some pretty postcard views of Venice, but he only fully exploits his fascinating location during the ingenious final chase sequence, which culminates in a Hitchcockian use of a famous landmark. Richard Todd is below par as the detective dispatched to uncover information about an air-raid victim who might be a war hero, a master criminal or both. DP

Richard Todd *Edward Mercer* • Eva Bartok *Adriana* • John Gregson *Cassana* • George Coulouris *Spadoni* • Margot Grahame *Rosa Melitus* • Walter Rilla *Count Boria* • Sidney James *Bernardo* ■ *Dir* Ralph Thomas • *Scr* Victor Canning, from his novel

Vengeance ★ 15

Spaghetti western
1968 · It/W Ger · Colour · 96mins

Years after Clint Eastwood had hung up his holsters and ridden back to his home turf, the Italians were still cranking out spaghetti westerns and this is the usual mix of bad dubbing, stylish visuals and violence. Director Antonio Margheriti (here working under the name Anthony Dawson) has since cashed in on all the big movie trends: when the westerns dried up, he concentrated on horror. JF. Italian dialogue dubbed into English.

Richard Harrison *Joko* • Claudio Camaso *Mendoza* • Werner Pochath *Riky* • Paolo Gozlino *Domingo* • Guido Lollobrigida *Lee Burton* ■ *Dir* Anthony Dawson [Antonio Margheriti] • *Scr* Antonio Margheriti, Renato Savino

Vengeance Is Mine ★★★

Biographical crime drama
1979 · Jpn · Colour · 128mins

A constant feeling of uneasiness is to be found in this telling of the true story of Iwao Enokizu (played here by Ken Ogata), a Japanese serial killer who went on a murder and robbery spree. Shohei Imamura simply shows his life and actions. Yet this simple presentation works, as it encourages the viewer to find some answer somewhere to his motivation. KB. In Japanese with English subtitles.

Ken Ogata *Iwao Enokizu* • Rentaro Mikuni *Shizuo Enokizu* • Chocho Mikayo *Kayo Enokizu* • Mitsuko Baisho *Kazuko Enokizu* ■ *Dir* Shohei Imamura • *Scr* Masaru Baba, from a book by Ryuzo Saki

The Vengeance of Fu Manchu ★★ PG

Crime drama
1967 · UK/W Ger/HK/Ire · Colour · 87mins

The inscrutable Oriental arch villain forces a surgeon to create a killer clone of his Scotland Yard nemesis, Nayland Smith, in the third Fu Manchu tale starring Christopher Lee. Don Sharp's light direction in the original *The Face of Fu Manchu* is sorely missed here, and director Jeremy Summers half-heartedly trys to patch a lacklustre affair together out of plodding material. AJ DVD

Christopher Lee *Fu Manchu* • Tony Ferrer *Inspector Ramos* • Tsai Chin *Lin Tang* • Douglas Wilmer *Nayland Smith* • Wolfgang Kieling *Dr Lieberson* • Suzanne Roquette *Maria Lieberson* • Howard Marion-Crawford *Dr Petrie* ■ *Dir* Jeremy Summers • *Scr* Peter Welbeck [Harry Alan Towers], from characters created by Sax Rohmer

The Vengeance of She ★★ PG

Fantasy adventure
1968 · UK · Colour · 97mins

Czechoslovakian beauty Olinka Berova is taken for the reincarnation of novelist H Rider Haggard's Ayesha (as immortalised by Ursula Andress) in this mediocre sequel to *She* (1965). Director Cliff Owen piles on the close-ups of Berova in a Lost City fantasy adventure with reliable Hammer production values and colourful exotica. AJ DVD

John Richardson *King Killikrates* • Olinka Berova [Olga Schoberova] *Carol* • Edward Judd *Philip Smith* • Colin Blakely *George Carter* • Derek Godfrey *Men-Hari* • Jill Melford *Sheila Carter* • George Sewell *Harry Walker* ■ *Dir* Cliff Owen • *Scr* Peter O'Donnell, from characters created by H Rider Haggard

Vengeance Valley ★★★ PG

Western 1951 · US · Colour · 82mins

In this decent psychological western, Burt Lancaster plays a rancher's adopted son who always takes the rap for his foster-brother, played by snivelling, sneering Robert Walker. A woman comes between them – gets pregnant – and we're into Eugene O'Neill territory or a Wild West spin on Cain and Abel, nicely shot in the Rocky Mountains. AT DVD

Burt Lancaster *Owen Daybright* • Robert Walker *Lee Strobie* • Joanne Dru *Jen Strobie* • Ray Collins *Arch Strobie* • Sally Forrest *Lily Fasken* • John Ireland *Hub Fasken* • Hugh O'Brian *Dick Fasken* • Carleton Carpenter *Hewie* ■ *Dir* Richard Thorpe • *Scr* Irving Ravetch, from the novel by Luke Short

Venice/Venice ★

Comedy drama 1992 · US · Colour · 108mins

This is an exasperating and self-indulgent exercise from director Henry Jaglom. After taking his latest movie to Venice, Italy, for the annual film festival and baring his soul to journalists (while being annoyingly ignored by John Landis, his friend on the critics' jury), it's back to Venice, California, for some embarrassing sexual guru posturing. Nothing more than an elaborate home movie and, despite some scathing showbiz truths and a neat turn by David Duchovny (as the star of Jaglom's festival offering), just as intolerable to watch. AJ

Nelly Alard *Jeanne* • Henry Jaglom *Dean* • Suzanne Bertish *Carlotta* • Daphna Kastner *Eve* • David Duchovny *Dylan* • Suzanne Lanza *Dylan's girlfriend* • Vernon Dobtcheff *Alexander* • John Landis ■ *Dir/Scr* Henry Jaglom

Venom ★★★ 15

Thriller 1981 · UK · Colour · 88mins

This ridiculously enjoyable thriller looks as though it was dreamed up during an extremely drunken weekend. Kidnappers plus child (with asthma) are holed up in a house, together with (for reasons not worth going into) a deadly black mamba snake. The script may be weak in places, but be prepared to shriek when the serpent slithers up wicked Oliver Reed's trouser leg. DM. Contains violence and swearing. DVD

Klaus Kinski *Jacmel* • Oliver Reed *Dave* • Nicol Williamson *Commander William Bulloch* • Sarah Miles *Dr Marion Stowe* • Sterling Hayden *Howard Anderson* • Cornelia Sharpe *Ruth Hopkins* • Lance Holcomb *Philip Hopkins* • Susan George *Louise* ■ *Dir* Piers Haggard • *Scr* Robert Carrington, from the novel by Alan Scholefield

Vent d'Est ★★★

Political documentary drama
1969 · Fr/It/ W Ger · Colour · 92mins

Hailed as the first Marxist western, this is the fourth of the six anti-movies that Jean-Luc Godard made under the auspices of the Dziga-Vertov Group. He sought to bring down what he considered to be the crumbling edifice of traditional filmic language by constructing a political argument out of pure sounds and images. However, as this resolutely non-narrative essay reveals, the very act of articulating a statement or creating an impression is impossible without betraying a degree of subjectivity. DP. In French with English subtitles.

Gian Maria Volonté *Soldier* • Anne Wiazemsky *Whore* ■ *Dir* Jean-Luc Godard • *Scr* Jean-Luc Godard, Daniel Cohn-Bendit

Le Vent de la Nuit ★★★

Romantic drama 1999 · Fr · Colour · 95mins

Desire, doubt and disillusion dominate this intense character study from the under-rated Philippe Garrel. Art student Xavier Beauvois vacillates between an unsatisfactory liaison with a possessive housewife and a dream job with a celebrated architect Daniel Duval. Catherine Deneuve gives a brittle performance as the mistress racked by fears that Beauvois is only interested in her money. However, she is matched all the way by Duval's blend of ruthless professionalism and personal pain, as he remains haunted by both his wife's suicide and the electroshock therapy he endured after his participation in the 1968 Paris riots. DP. In French with English subtitles.

Catherine Deneuve *Hélène* • Daniel Duval *Serge* • Xavier Beauvois *Paul* • Jacques Lasalle *Hélène's husband* ■ *Dir* Philippe Garrel • *Scr* Xavier Beauvois, Marc Cholodenko, Arlette Lagmann

Venus Beauty Institute ★★★ 15

Comedy drama 1998 · Fr · Colour · 106mins

Nathalie Baye is a beautician who seeks casual sex to numb the sense of loneliness she feels when not working at prudish Bulle Ogier's Paris salon. But, while Baye's brittle performance holds the film together, the eccentric collection of clients and co-workers adds intrigue to Tonie Marshall's disarmingly frank study of modern woman and what she'll do to remain true to her self-image. DP. In French with English subtitles. Contains swearing, sex scenes. [VIDEO]

Nathalie Baye *Angèle Piana* • Bulle Ogier *Nadine* • Samuel LeBihan [Samuel Le Bihan] *Antoine Dumont* • Jacques Bonnaffé *Jacques* ■ *Dir* Tonie Marshall • *Scr* Tonie Marshall, Jacques Audiard, Marion Vernoux

Venus Peter ★★ 12

Drama 1989 · UK · Colour · 92mins

After many fine performances, Ray McAnally deserved a more distinguished swan song than this muddled piece of mysticism and malarkey. This view of Orkneys' life in the late 1940s brims o'er with eccentric characters and meaningless dialogue. Debuting director Ian Sellar throws in some haunting seascapes, but little of interest happens to disturb the flow of words. DP. Contains nudity.

Ray McAnally *Grandfather* • David Hayman *Kinnear* • Sinead Cusack *Miss Balsilbie* • Gordon R Strachan *Peter* • Sam Hayman *Baby Peter* • Caroline Paterson *Mother* • Alex McAvoy *Beadle* ■ *Dir* Ian Sellar • *Scr* Ian Sellar, Christopher Rush, from the book *A Twelvemonth and a Day* by Christopher Rush

Vera Cruz ★★★★ PG

Western 1954 · US · Colour · 89mins

Gary Cooper headlines but co-star Burt Lancaster is the man to watch in this terrific Mexico-set western in which a former Confederate soldier and an outlaw join forces to escort a shipment of gold. Produced by Lancaster's own company, it's directed by Robert Aldrich, who would collaborate out west once more with Lancaster in *Ulzana's Raid*. The movie has a rattling pace (thanks to editor Alan Crosland Jr) and a fine sense of style that's hard to top, plus a supporting cast that includes Ernest Borgnine and Charles Bronson, well before they teamed up with Aldrich again for *The Dirty Dozen*. TS [VIDEO] DVD

Gary Cooper *Benjamin Trane* • Burt Lancaster *Joe Erin* • Denise Darcel *Countess Marie Duvarre* • Cesar Romero *Marquis de Labordere* • Sarita Montiel *Nina* • George Macready *Emperor Maximilian* • Ernest Borgnine *Donnegan* • Morris Ankrum *General Aguilar* • Henry Brandon *Danette* • Charles Buchinsky [Charles Bronson] *Pittsburgh* ■ *Dir* Robert Aldrich • *Scr* Roland Kibbee, James R Webb, from the story by Borden Chase

Vera Drake ★★★★ 12

Period drama 2004 · UK/Fr · Colour · 119mins

Set in the repressed and repressive Britain of 1950, director Mike Leigh's drama hinges on a stunning lead performance from Imelda Staunton. She plays an altruistic but naive cleaning lady who secretly helps out unfortunate girls by performing backstreet abortions. But when her actions are discovered, the law reprimands her severely. Staunton is nothing less than superb; equally fine are the support performances, plus Leigh's impeccable re-creation of both place and period. If there's one small criticism to be made of the film, it's perhaps a touch too relentlessly dark and dour. Otherwise, this is as good, if as grim, as it gets. DA [VIDEO] DVD

Imelda Staunton *Vera Drake* • Phil Davis [Philip Davis] *Stan Drake* • Peter Wight *Det Inspector Webster* • Adrian Scarborough *Frank* • Heather Craney *Joyce* • Daniel Mays *Sid Drake* • Alex Kelly *Ethel Drake* • Sally Hawkins *Susan Wells* • Eddie Marsan *Reg* • Ruth Sheen *Lily* • Helen Coker *WPC Best* ■ *Dir/Scr* Mike Leigh

Verboten! ★★ PG

Thriller 1959 · US · BW · 86mins

This high-flown melodrama is much beloved by fans of maverick director Samuel Fuller, though other viewers may think it's hardly worth passing the time of day with. James Best brings dignity to a rare leading role as the GI uncovering a neo-Nazi conspiracy in postwar Germany, but Susan Cummings is woefully inadequate as his romantic interest. There's a naive subtext that's either quite disturbing, or enjoyable, depending on your point of view. TS [VIDEO]

James Best *Sgt David Brent* • Susan Cummings *Helga Schiller* • Tom Pittman *Bruno Eckart* • Paul Dubov *Capt Harvey* • Harold Daye *Franz Schiller* • Dick Kallman *Helmuth* ■ *Dir/Scr* Samuel Fuller

The Verdict ★★★

Crime mystery 1946 · US · BW · 86mins

Dirty Harry director Don Siegel's first feature marked the last reteaming of Sydney Greenstreet and Peter Lorre, the dynamic duo from *The Maltese Falcon*, where Scotland Yard superintendent Greenstreet is forced to resign, only to become embroiled in another murder case. A little dusty maybe, but still enjoyable. AJ

Sydney Greenstreet *George Edward Grodman* • Peter Lorre *Victor Emmric* • Joan Lorring *Lottie* • George Coulouris *Superintendent Buckley* • Rosalind Ivan *Mrs Benson* • Paul Cavanagh *Clive Russell* • Arthur Shields *Reverend Holbrook* • Morton Lowry *Arthur Kendall* ■ *Dir* Don Siegel • *Scr* Peter Milne, from the novel *The Big Bow Mystery* by Israel Zangwill

Verdict ★★★

Courtroom thriller
1974 · Fr/It · Colour · 97mins

In his penultimate picture, the great Jean Gabin gives a typically gutsy performance as a judge whose diabetic wife is abducted by a besotted mother, determined to have her student son acquitted when he's charged with rape and murder. Less sure-footed is Sophia Loren, who overdoes the eye-rolling as the kidnapper, and director André Cayatte also betrays his limitations in the scenes outside the courtroom. DP. In French with English subtitles. Contains violence.

Sophia Loren *Térésa Léoni* • Jean Gabin *Président Leguen* • Henri Garcin *Maître Lannelonge* • Julien Bertheau *Advocate General Verlac* • Michel Albertini *André Léoni* • Gisèle Casadesus *Nicole Leguen* • Muriel Catala *Annie Chartier* ■ *Dir* André Cayatte • *Scr* André Cayatte, Henri Coupon, Pierre Dumayet, Paul Andreota

The Verdict ★★★ 15

Courtroom drama
1982 · US · Colour · 123mins

This is a return to court for Sidney Lumet, director of the masterly *12 Angry Men*. Paul Newman was widely (and wrongly) tipped to win his first Oscar for his portrayal of an alcoholic lawyer on the skids, who fights to redeem himself when a medical malpractice case pits him against the power of the Catholic Church. Scripted by David Mamet, it's a compelling, if wordy, piece, rooted in liberalism and stubbornly refusing to deliver the promised fireworks. Charlotte Rampling and James Mason are in the fine supporting cast. AT. Contains swearing. [VIDEO] DVD

Paul Newman *Frank Galvin* • Charlotte Rampling *Laura Fischer* • Jack Warden *Mickey Morrissey* • James Mason *Ed Concannon* • Milo O'Shea *Judge Hoyle* • Lindsay Crouse *Kaitlin Costello Price* • Edward Binns *Bishop Brophy* ■ *Dir* Sidney Lumet • *Scr* David Mamet, from the novel by Barry Reed

La Vérité ★★★

Thriller 1960 · Fr/It · BW · 125mins

Henri-Georges Clouzot had a reputation as one of the darkest French film-makers, but here he strays into the courtroom territory usually associated with André Cayatte and rather loses his way in a maze of flashbacks. Brigitte Bardot digs deep into her acting resources as the young girl accused of murdering her sister's trendy boyfriend, but, although she breezes through certain scenes, it's hard to escape the suspicion that the role is beyond her talents. DP. In French with English subtitles.

Brigitte Bardot *Dominique Marceau* • Charles Vanel *Maître Guerin, defence attorney* • Paul Meurisse *Eparvier, prosecuting attorney* • Sami Frey *Gilbert Tellier* • Marie-José Nat *Annie Marceau* • Louis Seigner *President of the Court* ■ *Dir* Henri-Georges Clouzot • *Scr* Henri-Georges Clouzot, Simone Drieu, Michèle Perrein, Jérôme Géronimi, Christiane Rochefort, Simone Marescat, Vera Clouzot

Veronica Guerin ★★★★ 18

Biographical drama
2003 · US/UK/Ire · Colour · 94mins

The age of the newspaper reporter as crusading hero is given an excellent treatment in this real-life drama. Veronica Guerin (emphatically played by Cate Blanchett) was assassinated after writing a series of revelatory stories exposing the drug overlords who battled for control of Dublin in the mid-1990s. Her courageous story has already provided the inspiration for the 2000 film *When the Sky Falls*, but director Joel Schumacher's retelling is a superior affair, thanks to Blanchett's star appeal. Colin Farrell also offers a sly portrait of a druggie informer and Brenda Fricker a poignant cameo as Veronica's mother. TH. Contains violence, swearing, drug abuse, sex scenes and nudity. [VIDEO] DVD

Cate Blanchett *Veronica Guerin* • Gerard McSorley *John Gilligan* • Ciaran Hinds *John Traynor* • Brenda Fricker *Bernadette Guerin* • Barry Barnes *Graham Turley* • Joe Hanley *Holland* • David Murray *Bowden* • David Herlihy *Peter "Fatso" Mitchell* • Colin Farrell (2) *Spanky McSpank* ■ *Dir* Joel Schumacher • *Scr* Carol Doyle, Mary Agnes Donoghue, from a story by Carol Doyle

Véronico Cruz ★★★ PG

Drama 1987 · Arg/UK · Colour · 99mins

This is a well-intentioned attempt to understand the divisions in Argentinian society in the period between the 1976 military coup and the invasion of the Falkland Islands. But debutant director Miguel Pereira never quite comes to terms with the political realities explored in Fortunato Ramos's novel, with the result that he winds up producing a sentimental human melodrama instead of a perceptive neorealist tract. Yet there remains a touching connection between shepherd boy Gonzalos Morales and Juan José Camero, the city schoolteacher coming to terms with the expectations and beliefs of his new neighbours. DP. In Spanish with English subtitles.

Juan José Camero *Teacher* • Gonzalo Morales *Véronico Cruz* • Juanita Cáceres *Juanita* • René Olaguivel *Beamter* • Anna Maria Gonzáles *Grandmother* • Guillermo Delgado *Policeman* ■ *Dir* Miguel Pereira • *Scr* Eduardo Leiva Muller, Miguel Pereira, from the novel by Fortunato Ramos

Veronika Voss ★★★ 12

Drama 1982 · W Ger · BW · 100mins

Rainer Werner Fassbinder's film is inspired by the tragic life of Sybille Schmitz, "the German Garbo", whose death eerily presages the director's own, later in the year. As ever, exploiting the conventions of Hollywood melodrama, he draws parallels between the worlds promised by politicians and film-makers alike, as he sets sports writer Hilmar Thate the impossible task of saving faded Nazi star Rosel Zech from herself and her coterie. The piercing monochrome conveys both the period and a *noirish* sense of doom. DP. A German language film. [VIDEO]

Rosel Zech *Veronika Voss* • Hilmar Thate *Robert Krohn* • Cornelia Froboess *Henriette* • Annemarie Düringer *Dr Marianne Katz* • Doris Schade *Josefa* • Erik Schumann *Dr Edel* ■ *Dir* Rainer Werner Fassbinder • *Scr* Rainer Werner Fassbinder, Peter Marthesheimer, Pea Fröhlich

Versus ★★ 18

Martial arts action horror
2000 · US/Jpn · Colour · 120mins

An exaggerated mix of martial arts, gunplay and gore, this hyperactive slice of extreme Asian cinema features zombie yakuzas battling to avenge their deaths in the appropriately named Forest of Resurrection. Co-writer/director Ryuhei Kitamura goes all out to entertain, and though there's consequently more style than substance, his grisly set pieces and almost balletic confrontations are both darkly comic and exciting. With judicious pruning, this overlong tale could have been a corker. SF. In Japanese with English subtitles. Contains swearing, violence. [VIDEO] DVD

Tak Sakaguchi *Prisoner KSC2-303* • Hideo Sakaki *The Man* • Chieko Misaka *The Girl* • Kenji Matsuda *Yakuza leader with butterfly knife* • Yuichiro Arai *Motorcycle-riding yakuza with revolver* • Minoru Matsumoto *Crazy yakuza with amulet* ■ *Dir* Ryuhei Kitamura • *Scr* Ryuhei Kitamura, Yudai Yamaguchi

Vertical Limit ★★ 12

Action adventure thriller
2000 · US/Ger · Colour · 119mins

Snapped ropes, dislodged boulders and crumbling ledges are just some of the perils facing mountaineer Chris O'Donnell in this predictable but watchable adventure. Now working as a photographer, O'Donnell is still haunted by memories of the harrowing climb that ended in his father's death. O'Donnell is an uncharismatic hero, but some enjoyable action sequences almost make up for the clichéd characterisations. DA. Contains swearing, violence. DVD

Chris O'Donnell *Peter Garrett* • Bill Paxton *Elliot Vaughn* • Robin Tunney *Annie Garrett* • Scott Glenn *Montgomery Wick* • Izabella Scorupco *Monique Aubertina* ■ *Dir* Martin Campbell • *Scr* Robert King, Terry Hayes, from a story by Robert King

Vertigo ★★★★★ PG

Classic psychological thriller
1958 · US · Colour · 122mins

In one of the truly great later Hitchcocks, James Stewart plays the retired cop with a terror of heights who's hired by Tom Helmore to follow his suicidal wife, Kim Novak. Stewart falls in love with the enigmatic blonde but can't prevent her falling to her death. Some months later he spots a woman (also played by Novak) who bears an uncanny resemblance to the dead woman, and is drawn into a complex web of deceit. Novak gives her greatest performance, while the darker side of Stewart shatters his all-American Mr Nice Guy persona. A hallucinatory movie, of dreamlike revelations in its glistening San Francisco locations, it remains one of the most painful depictions of romantic fatalism in all of cinema. TH DVD

James Stewart *John "Scottie" Ferguson* • Kim Novak *Madeleine/Judy* • Barbara Bel Geddes *Midge* • Tom Helmore *Gavin Elster* • Henry Jones *Coroner* • Raymond Bailey *Doctor* • Ellen Corby *Manageress* • Konstantin Shayne *Pop Leibel* • Paul Bryar *Captain Hansen* ■ *Dir* Alfred Hitchcock • *Scr* Alex Coppel, Samuel Taylor, from the novel *D'entre les Morts* by Pierre Boileau, Thomas Narcejac • *Cinematographer* Robert Burks

Very Annie-Mary ★★★ 15

Musical comedy
2000 · UK/Fr · Colour · 99mins

Rhyl-born Sara Sugarman's film – a quirky tragicomedy about the healing powers of song – seeks to meet the clichés about Wales head on. The village of Ogw is determined to win the prize money in a Cardiff talent contest so that a local, terminally ill girl can go to Disneyland. Can gangling Rachel Griffiths find her voice in time? That's the simple plot, but it's told with a Dylan Thomas-like attention to local colour, made more authentic through the use of non-actors. AC DVD

Rachel Griffiths *Annie-Mary* • Jonathan Pryce *Father* • Ruth Madoc *Mrs Ifans* • Matthew Rhys *Nob* • Ioan Gruffudd *Hob* ■ *Dir/Scr* Sara Sugarman

V

Very Bad Things ★★★★ 18

Black comedy 1998 · US · Colour · 100mins

This very black comedy, which marked the directorial debut of actor/writer Peter Berg, is certainly not for the easily offended. Berg brings together a cool cast for a twisted and hilarious tale of mayhem that begins when bridegroom Jon Favreau and his pals embark on a stag weekend in Las Vegas, before his marriage to the beautiful but ruthless Cameron Diaz. Their booze and drug-fuelled party goes awry, however, when an unfortunate accident leaves them with a dead stripper on their hands. This gruesome tale is propelled by a sharp script and top-notch performances. JB

Christian Slater *Robert Boyd* • Cameron Diaz *Laura Garrety* • Daniel Stern *Adam Berkow* • Jeanne Tripplehorn *Lois Berkow* • Jon Favreau *Kyle Fisher* • Jeremy Piven *Michael Berkow* • Leland Orser *Charles Moore* • Lawrence Pressman *Mr Fisher* ■ *Dir/Scr* Peter Berg

A Very Brady Sequel ★★★ 12

Comedy 1996 · US · Colour · 86mins

One of the rare occasions when a sequel works better than the original, this follow-up to the big-screen adaptation of TV's *The Brady Bunch* not only pokes more fun at the Bradys, but mocks them more savagely. Yet the movie still has great affection for the characters, who are wonderfully played by the cast, especially Shelley Long and Gary Cole as parents Carol and Mike Brady. Still stuck in a 1970s time warp in the 1990s, the Bradys are stunned by the appearance of a man claiming to be Carol's former husband, who was previously believed to have been dead. KB DVD

Shelley Long *Carol Brady* • Gary Cole *Mike Brady* • Christopher Daniel Barnes *Greg Brady* • Christine Taylor *Marcia Brady* • Paul Sutera *Peter Brady* • Jennifer Elise Cox *Jan Brady* • Jesse Lee *Bobby Brady* • Olivia Hack *Cindy Brady* • Henriette Mantel *Alice* ■ *Dir* Arlene Sanford • *Scr* Harry Elfont, Deborah Kaplan, James Berg, Stan Zimmerman, from a story by Harry Elfont, Deborah Kaplan, from the characters created by Sherwood Schwartz

The Very Edge ★

Drama 1962 · UK · Colour · 89mins

This is another British cheapie that hoped to lure audiences into auditoriums with the sort of sensationalist story found in their Sunday papers. Here, we have sexual pervert Jeremy Brett's obsession with pregnant Anne Heywood passing from harassment to assault, with the result that she loses her baby. Husband Richard Todd takes the law into his own hands, basing his dispirited perfomance in his stock quality of stuffy indignance. DP

Anne Heywood *Tracey Lawrence* • Richard Todd *Geoffrey Lawrence* • Jack Hedley *McInnes* • Nicole Maurey *Helen* • Jeremy Brett *Mullen* • Barbara Mullen *Dr Shaw* • Maurice Denham *Crawford* ■ *Dir* Cyril Frankel • *Scr* Elizabeth Jane Howard, from a story by Vivian Cox, Leslie Bricusse, Raymond Stross

Very Important Person ★★★ U

Comedy 1961 · UK · BW · 93mins

The key to this winning comedy is a witty script by Jack Davies and Henry Blyth, which cleverly lampoons many of the conventions and stereotypes of the prisoner-of-war pictures that had been a staple of the British film industry for over a decade. Stanley Baxter gives one of his best film performances as a PoW posing as a high-ranking Nazi in a bid to spring scientist James Robertson-Justice, while the deft comic support from Leslie Phillips, Eric Sykes and the deadpan Richard Wattis is of a high order. DP DVD

James Robertson-Justice *Sir Ernest Pease* • Leslie Phillips *Jimmy Cooper* • Stanley Baxter *Everett/Major Stampfel* • Eric Sykes *Willoughby* • Richard Wattis *Woodcock* ■ *Dir* Ken Annakin • *Scr* Jack Davies, Henry Blyth

A Very Long Engagement ★★★★ 15

Period romantic drama
2004 · Fr/USA · Colour · 127mins

Jean-Pierre Jeunet's lyrical treat for the eye and heart is grittier in tone than his international hit *Amélie*, containing unflinching scenes of battlefield carnage, but still has whimsical charm to spare. The gorgeously gamine Audrey Tautou stars as the fiancée of a First World War soldier who was abandoned to face an ignominious death in no-man's land as punishment for a self-inflicted wound. Tatou refuses to believe he has been killed and begins an investigation into her lover's fate. This sweeping saga is fabulous looking, beautifully performed and, though overlong, remains an engaging, utterly involving portrait of unswerving devotion. AJ. In French with English subtitles. Contains violence and sex scenes. DVD

Audrey Tautou *Mathilde* • Gaspard Ulliel *Manech* • Jean-Pierre Becker *Lieutenant Esperanza* • Dominique Bettenfeld *Ange Bassignano* • Clovis Cornillac *Benoît Notre Dame* • Marion Cotillard *Tina Lombardi* • Jean-Pierre Daroussin *Benjamin Gordes* • Jodie Foster *Elodie Gordes* • Jean-Claude Dreyfus *Commandant Lavrouye* • Ticky Holgado *Germain Pire* • Tcheky Karyo *Captain Favourier* ■ *Dir* Jean-Pierre Jeunet • *Scr* Jean-Pierre Jeunet, Guillaume Laurant, from the novel *Un Long Dimanche de Fiançailles* by Sébastien Japrisot

A Very Private Affair ★★★

Drama 1962 · Fr/It · Colour · 93mins

Brigitte Bardot plays a movie star, an idolised sex symbol, suffering from the pressures of stardom and seeking love. She finds it in Marcello Mastroianni, an intellectual theatre director. There is some fascination in seeing Bardot playing a role that is modelled on herself, but both she and Mastroianni cannot overcome the shallowness of the screenplay. One of Louis Malle's least distinguished movies, it does have some superb camerawork by Henri Decaë. RB. In French with English subtitles.

Brigitte Bardot *Jill* • Marcello Mastroianni *Fabio* • Gregor von Rezzori *Gricha* • Eléonore Hirt *Cecile* ■ *Dir* Louis Malle • *Scr* Louis Malle, Jean-Paul Rappeneau, Jean Ferry

A Very Special Favor ★★

Comedy 1965 · US · Colour · 104mins

In the mid-1960s, Rock Hudson made a whole string of farces in which he was coupled with the most seductive actresses Europe had to offer. The aim was to titillate mildly, then vacillate, with Hudson playing his own secret games of sexual deception. In this effort, Hudson is an oil zillionaire, with an eye only for a balance sheet who starts to romance lawyer Charles Boyer's daughter, a psychiatrist played by Leslie Caron. Very dated in its general tone. AT

Rock Hudson *Paul Chadwick* • Leslie Caron *Lauren Boullard* • Charles Boyer *Michel Boullard* • Walter Slezak *Etienne, proprietor* • Dick Shawn *Arnold Plum* • Larry Storch *Harry, taxi driver* ■ *Dir* Michael Gordon • *Scr* Stanley Shapiro, Nate Monaster

The Very Thought of You ★★

Drama 1944 · US · BW · 98mins

Very much of its period, not just in title but also in wartime content, this tale of romance and marriage falls flat due to bland Dennis Morgan. He is seriously undercast as the male lead opposite volatile (and ever under-rated) Eleanor Parker, whose hairstyle alone makes this worth watching. Skilled director Delmer Daves, almost as well-known for his melodramas as he was for his westerns, doesn't seem to bring too much to the table here. TS

Dennis Morgan *Sgt Dave Stewart* • Eleanor Parker *Janet Wheeler* • Dane Clark *"Fixit"* • Faye Emerson *Cora* • Beulah Bondi *Mrs Wheeler* ■ *Dir* Delmer Daves • *Scr* Alvah Bessie, Delmer Daves, from a story by Lionel Wiggam

Vessel of Wrath ★★★★

Comedy drama 1938 · UK · BW · 86mins

The story (by Somerset Maugham) of a spinster missionary and her attempts to reform a drunken beach bum, has obvious similarities to *The African Queen*, and happily this is nearly in the same league as that classic. Elsa Lanchester and Charles Laughton are delightful as the mismatched pair, the quirky Lanchester having her largest (and favourite) screen role. The only film directed by the legendary European producer Erich Pommer, it was a box-office failure, but is a real gem. Robert Newton, who has a supporting role in this version, starred with Glynis Johns in a fair remake titled *The Beachcomber* in 1954. TV

Charles Laughton *Ginger Ted* • Elsa Lanchester *Martha Jones* • Tyrone Guthrie *Owen Jones, M D* • Robert Newton *Controleur* • Dolly Mollinger *Lia* • Rosita Garcia *Kati* ■ *Dir* Erich Pommer, Bartlett Cormack • *Scr* Bartlett Cormack, B Van Thal, from the short story by W Somerset Maugham

La Veuve de Saint-Pierre ★★★ 15

Period romantic drama
2000 · Fr/Can · Colour · 107mins

Set in 1850, Patrice Leconte's sombre tragedy unfolds against the austere backdrop of Saint-Pierre, a small French island off the Canadian coast. A drunken drifter (played by Yugoslavian film director Emir Kusturica) is found guilty of murder and is sentenced to death. There being neither guillotine nor executioner on the isle, the condemned man is placed in the custody of captain Daniel Auteuil and his wife, Juliette Binoche, who become attached to their prisoner and plot his escape. It's an unusual story, told with empathy and precision, while Binoche and Auteuil are well-matched as the couple who risk all in an act of compassion. NS. In French with English subtitles. DVD

Juliette Binoche *Madame La* • Daniel Auteuil *The Captain* • Emir Kusturica *Neel Auguste* • Michel Duchaussoy *The Governor* • Philippe Magnan *President Venot* ■ *Dir* Patrice Leconte • *Scr* Claude Faraldo

Via Dolorosa ★★★

Drama 2000 · US · Colour · 99mins

Apart from the energetic use of four cameras, few attempts have been made to disguise the stage origins of this impassioned one-man show, delivered as a monologue by playwright David Hare. Acclaimed on both sides of the Atlantic, Hare's enthusiastic, but rarely rose-tinted consideration of the customs and causes that shaped the state of Israel is a combination of anecdotes and opinions that will infuriate as many as it intrigues. DP

David Hare ■ *Dir* John Bailey • *Scr* David Hare • *Music* Christopher Klatman

Vibes ★ PG

Adventure comedy
1988 · US · Colour · 95mins

This attempt to launch an acting career for singer Cyndi Lauper, of *Girls Just Want to Have Fun* fame, was a disaster. Lauper and Jeff Goldblum play rent-a-psychics hired by Peter Falk to find a legendary lost city of gold. Goldblum survived the debacle. Lauper made *Life with Mikey* and *Off and Running*, but has rarely been seen on screen since. The only vibes you'll get from this fiasco are bad ones. DA

Cyndi Lauper *Sylvia Pickel* • Jeff Goldblum *Nick Deezy* • Julian Sands *Dr Harrison Steele* • Googy Gress *Ingo Swedlin* • Peter Falk *Harry Buscafusco* • Michael Lerner *Burt Wilder* • Ramon Bieri *Eli Diamond* • Elizabeth Peña

Consuela ■ *Dir* Ken Kwapis • *Scr* Lowell Ganz, Babaloo Mandel, from a story by Babaloo Mandel, Deborah Blum, Lowell Ganz

The Vicar of Bray ★★

Period drama 1937 · UK · BW · 66mins

Making extravagantly expansive gestures and projecting to hit the rear of the music hall stalls, Stanley Holloway shows why it took so long for him to establish himself as a screen performer. Here he plays the Irish clergyman who is hired to tutor the future Charles II and finds himself matchmaking in an English Civil War version of *Romeo and Juliet*. The songs are ghastly and the period trappings cheap and inaccurate, but Felix Aylmer and Garry Marsh go some way to atoning. DP

Stanley Holloway *Bray* • Hugh Miller *King Charles I* • K Hamilton Price *Prince Charles Stuart* • Felix Aylmer *Earl of Brendon* • Margaret Vines *Lady Norah Brendon* • Garry Marsh *Sir Richard Melross* • Esmond Knight *Dennis Melross* • Martin Walker *Sir Patrick Condon* • Eve Gray *Meg Clancy* • Kitty Kirwan *Molly* ■ *Dir* Henry Edwards • *Scr* H Fowler Mear, from the story by Anson Dyer

Vice Squad ★★

Crime drama 1953 · US · BW · 88mins

A day in the life of a Los Angeles cop, played by Edward G Robinson, and co-starring Paulette Goddard as the owner of an escort agency. Semi-documentary in style, it lurches from one murder to the next. It's serious and slightly dull, and Robinson and Goddard have few opportunities to display their talents. Spaghetti western fans should watch for Lee Van Cleef as a heavy. AT

Edward G Robinson *Captain Barnaby* • Paulette Goddard *Mona* • KT Stevens *Ginny* • Porter Hall *Jack Hartrampf* • Adam Williams *Marty Kusalich* • Edward Binns *Al Barkis* • Lee Van Cleef *Pete* ■ *Dir* Arnold Laven • *Scr* Lawrence Roman, from the novel *Harness Bull* by Leslie T White

Vice Squad ★★★ 18

Crime thriller 1982 · US · Colour · 86mins

This is the movie that made Wings Hauser a star, deservedly bringing him critical raves as a psychotic pimp who brutally murders one of his prostitutes when she tries to walk out on him. When hooker Season Hubley is forced by police into taking part in a sting operation that results in Hauser's arrest, he plans to kill her when he escapes custody. It's unusual that an exploitation movie set in the world of prostitution has no nudity or real sex, with more chitchat than action in or out of the bedroom. KB [VIDEO]

Season Hubley *Princess* • Gary Swanson *Tom Walsh* • Wings Hauser *Ramrod* • Pepe Serna *Pete Mendez* • Beverly Todd *Louise Williams* • Joseph DiGiroloma *Kowalski* • Maurice Emmanuel *Edwards* ■ *Dir* Gary A Sherman [Gary Sherman] • *Scr* Sandy Howard, Robert Vincent O'Neil, Kenneth Peters

Vice Versa ★★★ U

Comedy 1947 · UK · BW · 111mins

This is quite a treat, even funnier now than when it first came out and better than its 1988 Judge Reinhold remake. Under Peter Ustinov's nimble direction, father and son Roger Livesey and Anthony Newley swap places, and succeed in outraging all and sundry. There are some lovely supporting performances, especially from a bemused, schoolmasterly James Robertson-Justice. TS

Roger Livesey *Paul Bultitude* • Kay Walsh *Mrs Verlayne* • David Hutcheson *Marmaduke Paradine* • Anthony Newley *Dick Bultitude* • James Robertson-Justice *Dr Grimstone* • Petula Clark *Dulcie Grimstone* • Patricia Raine *Alice* • Joan Young *Mrs Grimstone* • Vida Hope *First nanny* ■ *Dir* Peter Ustinov • *Scr* Peter Ustinov, from the novel by F Anstey

Vice Versa ★★★ PG

Comedy 1988 · US · Colour · 94mins

Although it lacks the charm of the 1947 British film of the same name, this is a better-than-average body-swap movie. Most of it is down to the inspired playing of Judge Reinhold and Fred Savage, who learn that their respective lives are not quite as enjoyable as they imagine when they switch bodies. The two leads are fresh and convincing in both their personae, and, although sentimentality occasionally raises its head, director Brian Gilbert keeps the action flowing at a pleasing rate. JF. Contains swearing. [VIDEO] DVD

Judge Reinhold *Marshall Seymour* • Fred Savage *Charlie Seymour* • Corinne Bohrer *Sam* • Swoosie Kurtz *Tina* • David Proval *Turk* • Jane Kaczmarek *Robyn* • Gloria Gifford *Marcie* • William Prince *Avery* • Beverly Archer *Mrs Luttrell* • James Hong *Kwo* ■ *Dir* Brian Gilbert • *Scr* Dick Clement, Ian La Frenais

The Vicious Circle ★★ U

Crime drama 1957 · UK · BW · 84mins

Adapting his own serial, *My Friend Charles*, Francis Durbridge was evidently over-attached to his material as there is simply too much plot. John Mills has a fair stab at the Hitchcockian "wrong man", playing a respectable London doctor desperate to discover who is trying to frame him for the murder of an actress whose body has fetched up in his flat. *Carry On* stalwart Gerald Thomas directs with an affinity for the whodunnit. DP

John Mills *Dr Howard Latimer* • Derek Farr *Ken Palmer* • Noelle Middleton *Laura James* • Wilfrid Hyde White *Robert Brady* • Roland Culver *Inspector Dane* • Mervyn Johns *Dr George Kimber* • René Ray *Mrs Ambler* • Lionel Jeffries *Geoffrey Windsor* ■ *Dir* Gerald Thomas • *Scr* Francis Durbridge, from his TV series *My Friend Charles*

Victim ★★★ 15

Drama 1961 · UK · BW · 95mins

A ground-breaker in its depiction of homosexuality, this film marks Dirk Bogarde's brave bid to break free of his matinée idol image. He plays a homosexual barrister whose former lover commits suicide after he's arrested to protect Bogarde's name. Bogarde can either say nothing or "come out", putting a strain on his marriage to Sylvia Syms and possibly ending his career. By today's standards the film is tame, and director Basil Dearden insisted that homosexuals should be called "inverts". However, the movie refuses to glamorise its subject. AT. Contains swearing. [VIDEO] DVD

Dirk Bogarde *Melville Farr* • Sylvia Syms *Laura Farr* • Dennis Price *Calloway* • Anthony Nicholls *Lord Fullbrook* • Peter Copley *Paul Mandrake* • Norman Bird *Harold Doe* • Peter McEnery *Jack Barrett* • Donald Churchill *Eddy Stone* ■ *Dir* Basil Dearden • *Scr* Janet Green, John McCormick

Victim of Beauty ★★★ 15

Thriller based on a true story
1991 · US · Colour · 86mins

This above average TV-movie thriller tells the real-life story of a bold attempt to rescue a diabetic teenager being held hostage by a serial killer in South Carolina. The film is held together by a solid performance from William Devane as the local sheriff forced into using the hostage's beauty-queen sister (Jeri Lynn Ryan) as bait, and by Roger Young's steady direction, which keeps sensationalism at bay. DP. Contains violence and nudity. [VIDEO]

William Devane *Sheriff Jim Metts* • Jeri Lynn Ryan [Jeri Ryan] *Dawn Smith* • Michele Abrams *Shari Smith* • Butch Slade *Larry Gene Bell* • Linda Pierce *Hilda Smith* ■ *Dir* Roger Young • *Scr* John Robert Bensink

Victim of Love ★★★ 15

Thriller 1991 · US · Colour · 88mins

A pre-007 Pierce Brosnan stars in a role that's far removed from that of the suave and sophisticated secret agent. He plays a British professor who, following the recent death of his wife, charms his way into the life of psychologist JoBeth Williams, who is unaware that he has a rather sinister side. This TV movie has a fair quota of tense moments, and Brosnan is perfect as the villian. JB. Contains swearing and nudity. [VIDEO] DVD

Pierce Brosnan *Paul Tomlinson* • JoBeth Williams *Tess Palmer* • Virginia Madsen *Carla Simmons* • Georgia Brown *Emma Walters* • Murphy Cross *Roz Fleisher* ■ *Dir* Jerry London • *Scr* James J Desmarais, Alison Rosenfeld Desmarais

Victim of Rage ★★ 18

Drama based on a true story
1994 · US · Colour · 90mins

This made-for-TV movie is based on the true story of a Los Angeles woman for whom a blind date is the start of a nightmare. Jaclyn Smith suffers glamorously, while Brad Johnson chews the scenery as the husband whose body-building pills turn him into a maniac. Yet more proof that the truth doesn't always make great drama. DP. Contains violence. [VIDEO] DVD

Jaclyn Smith *Donna Yaklich* • Brad Johnson *Dennis Yaklich* • David Lascher *Denny Yaklich* • Hilary Swank *Patty* ■ *Dir* Armand Mastroianni • *Scr* Christopher Canaan

Victor Frankenstein ★★

Horror 1977 · Ire/Swe · Colour · 92mins

This elegantly photographed, but dull co-production of Mary Shelley's classic tale of terror was promoted as being the most faithful version ever committed to film. Too melodramatic and psychologically straightforward to qualify as authentic, Per Oscarsson plays The Creature as a juvenile delinquent, brutally railing against his experimental creator, Leon Vitali, and society in general. This pretentious reading was a festival favourite, but not an audience one. AJ

Leon Vitali *Victor Frankenstein* • Per Oscarsson *Monster* • Nicholas Clay *Henry* • Stacy Dorning *Elisabeth* • Jan Ohlsson *William* • Olof Bergström *Father* ■ *Dir* Calvin Floyd • *Scr* Calvin Floyd, Yvonne Floyd, from the novel *Frankenstein* by Mary Shelley • *Cinematographer* Tony Forsberg

Victor/Victoria ★★★ 15

Screwball comedy
1982 · UK · Colour · 128mins

Julie Andrews as a bloke? Although this decision earns it an honourable mention in the hall of fame for monumental pieces of miscasting, this typically crude Blake Edwards comedy remains quite a hoot. Andrews is the struggling singer who leaps to fame and fortune in 1930s Paris when she decides to impersonate a man impersonating a woman. James Garner is the very heterosexual American troubled by his attraction to him/her. There are a few songs to keep Andrews fans happy, plus an outrageously camp turn from Robert Preston. JF [VIDEO] DVD

Julie Andrews *Victor/Victoria* • James Garner *King Marchan* • Robert Preston *Carroll "Toddy" Todd* • Lesley Ann Warren *Norma* • Alex Karras *Squash* • John Rhys-Davies *André Cassell* • Graham Stark *Waiter* ■ *Dir* Blake Edwards • *Scr* Blake Edwards, from the play *Viktor und Viktoria* by Reinhold Schünzel • *Music* Henry Mancini

Victoria the Great ★★★ U

Historical biographical drama
1937 · UK · BW and Colour · 105mins

Laurence Housman's play *Victoria Regina* was banned by the Lord Chamberlain as, in 1935, the royal family could not be shown on the British stage. But the play was a hit on Broadway and such was the enthusiasm of King Edward VIII, he commissioned producer and director Herbert Wilcox to make it into a film to commemorate the centenary of Victoria's accession to the throne. Anna Neagle takes Victoria from girlhood to old age, and the drama concentrates on her relationship with Prince Albert (Anton Walbrook). Her sympathy for the monarch shines through, and the final reel, which bursts into glorious Technicolor for the Diamond Jubilee, is a delightful piece of patriotic pomp. RT [VIDEO]

Anna Neagle *Queen Victoria* • Anton Walbrook *Prince Albert* • Walter Rilla *Prince Ernest* • Mary Morris *Duchess of Kent* • HB Warner *Lord Melbourne* • Grete Wegener *Baroness Lehzen* • CV France *Archbishop of Canterbury* ■ *Dir* Herbert Wilcox • *Scr* Miles Malleson, Charles de Grandcourt, from the play *Victoria Regina* by Laurence Housman

The Victors ★★★

War epic 1963 · US/UK · BW · 186mins

Carl Foreman's film is one of the most ambitious war movies ever made, shot in black and white with an all-star cast and designed to show how war degrades people on all sides. A shot of victors and vanquished – both exhausted and looking like vagrants – rams home the point. Subtlety was never on Foreman's agenda and three hours of episodic hectoring and ironic twists of fate do get a bit wearisome. However, there are some stunning sequences. AT

George Hamilton *Cpl Trower* • George Peppard *Cpl Chase* • Jeanne Moreau *Frenchwoman* • Romy Schneider *Regine* • Melina Mercouri *Magda* • Eli Wallach *Sgt Craig* • Vincent Edwards [Vince Edwards] *Baker* • Rosanna Schiaffino *Maria* • Maurice Ronet *French Lt Cohn* • Peter Fonda *Weaver* • Senta Berger *Trudi* • Elke Sommer *Helga* • Albert Finney *Russian soldier* ■ *Dir* Carl Foreman • *Scr* Carl Foreman, from the novel *The Human Kind: a Sequence* by Alexander Baron

Victory ★★

Drama 1940 · US · BW · 78mins

Fredric March is the perpetual exile who lives on an island in the Malay archipelago, contentedly detached from life until he rescues an English girl and has to cope with three rogues sent by local strongman Sig Ruman. Time and time again, Joseph Conrad's deeply metaphysical dramas prove tough nuts to crack, though in this case the studio-imposed restriction on length doomed everyone to failure before the cameras started rolling. AT

Fredric March *Hendrik Heyst* • Betty Field *Alma* • Sir Cedric Hardwicke [Cedric Hardwicke] *Mr Jones* • Jerome Cowan *Martin Ricardo* • Sig Rumann [Sig Ruman] *Mr Schomberg* • Margaret Wycherly *Mrs Schomberg* ■ *Dir* John Cromwell • *Scr* John L Balderston, from the novel by Joseph Conrad

Victory ★★ 15

Period romance
1995 · UK/Fr/Ger · Colour · 94mins

This sluggish screen version of the Joseph Conrad novel focuses on a Dutch East Indies recluse who rescues a woman from bothersome baddies and offers her refuge on his remote island. Unfortunately, the island obviously isn't remote enough, and their troubles soon come looking for them. The attractive cast is given little to get their teeth into by a film that's long on steamy languor, but short on characterisation. DA. Contains violence and nudity.

Willem Dafoe *Axel Heyst* • Sam Neill *Mr Jones* • Irène Jacob *Alma* • Rufus Sewell *Martin Ricardo* • Jean Yanne *Schomberg* • Ho Yi *Wang* • Bill Paterson *Captain Davidson* ■ *Dir* Mark Peploe • *Scr* Mark Peploe, from the novel by Joseph Conrad

Victory at Entebbe ★★

Drama based on a true story
1976 · US · Colour · 118mins

In June 1976, Palestinian and German terrorists hijacked an Air France airbus and flew to Idi Amin's Uganda. After six days, an Israeli commando unit stormed the airport at Entebbe to free the hostages. Within five months two lousy movies had been made – *Raid on Entebbe* and this one, both for American TV, but released in cinemas elsewhere. The movie reduces everything to the level of a soap opera, but with an all-star cast. AT

Kirk Douglas *Hershel Vilnofsky* • Burt Lancaster *Shimon Peres* • Elizabeth Taylor *Edra Vilnofsky* • Anthony Hopkins *Yitzhak Rabin* • Richard Dreyfuss *Colonel Yonatan "Yonni" Netanyahu* • Helen Hayes *Mrs Wise* • Theodore Bikel *Yakov Shlomo* • Julius Harris *President Idi Amin* • Linda Blair *Chana Vilnofsky* • Harris Yulin *General Dan Shomron* • Helmut Berger *German terrorist* ■ *Dir* Marvin J Chomsky • *Scr* Ernest Kinoy

The Victory of Women ★★★

Drama 1946 · Jpn · Colour · 80mins

Returning to the director's chair for the first time after the Second World War, Kenji Mizoguchi's innate sympathy for the plight of women in Japanese society again came to the fore in this indictment of the prejudicial legal system and the sinister legacy of old-style militarism. Kinuyo Tanaka gives a typically feisty performance as the lawyer defending a poverty-stricken mother who killed her baby in a desperate fit of grief following the death of her husband. DP. In Japanese with English subtitles.

Kinuyo Tanaka *Hiroko Hosokawa* • Michiko Kuwano *Michiko* • Mitsuko Miura *Moto Asakura* • Shin Tokudaiji *Keita Yamaoka* • Toyoko Takahashi *Mother* • Yoshihira Matsumoto [Katsuhira Matsumoto] *Prosecutor Kono* ■ *Dir* Kenji Mizoguchi • *Scr* Kogo Noda, Kaneto Shindo

Victory through Air Power ★★★ U

Part-animated wartime documentary
1943 · US · Colour · 65mins

This is one of the best known of the many propaganda and training films produced by the Disney studio during the Second World War. Although it begins with a comic history of aviation, the real purpose of the picture was to convince the top brass of the viability of Major Alexander de Seversky's theories on strategic long-range bombing and how it could disrupt enemy weapons production and supply lines, as well as demoralise the civilian population. The mix of live action, knockabout cartooning and serious graphics worked on wartime audiences and remains powerful today. DP

Dir Clyde Geronimi, Jack Kinney, James Algar • *Scr* Perce Pearce, from the non-fiction book by Major Alexander de Seversky

Videodrome ★★★★ 18

Horror thriller 1982 · Can · Colour · 84mins

With its subject matter of screen violence, this remains one of David Cronenberg's most personal, complex and disturbing films, even if it doesn't always make a lot of sense. James Woods is the amoral cable programmer who gets drawn to a sickening sadomasochistic channel called "Videodrome", which turns out to have a much more sinister purpose. Cronenberg uses this framework to explore his favourite themes (new technology fusing with the human body, voyeurism, the links between sex and violence) and, although the plot begins to unravel, the startling imagery and Woods's fierce performance make for a deeply unsettling experience. JF. Contains violence, swearing and nudity. DVD

James Woods *Max Renn* • Sonja Smits *Bianca O'Blivion* • Deborah Harry *Nicki Brand* • Peter Dvorsky *Harlan* • Les Carlson *Barry Convex* • Jack Creley *Brian O'Blivion* • Lynne Gorman *Masha* ■ *Dir/Scr* David Cronenberg

Vidheyan ★★★

Drama 1993 · Ind · Colour · 112mins

Novelist Zachariah objected to this adaptation of his story, but it remains a powerful indictment of political indolence. Mammooty gives a towering performance as the tyrannical village landlord, who not only enslaves the timid Gopha Kumar (a Christian immigrant from Kerala), but also compels him to participate in the murder of his kindly wife, Tanvi Azmi, and the prostitution of Kumar's own bride, Sabita Anand. This is stirring good versus evil melodrama. DP. A Malayalam language film.

Mammooty *Bhaska Patelar* • Gopha Kumar *Thommie* • Tanvi Azmi *Sarojakka* • Sabita Anand *Omana* ■ *Dir* Adoor Gopalakrishnan • *Scr* Adoor Gopalakrishnan, from a story by Zachariah

Vidocq ★★

Period detective thriller
2001 · Fr · Colour · 98mins

The adventures of the eponymous 19th-century Parisian detective were first screened in the silent era. However, they've never received such a shock-tactic makeover as in this eye-popping thriller, which was the first theatrical feature to be shot entirely in high-resolution digital video. Opening with the hero's death, the action then flashes back through Vidocq's various battles with arch nemesis, The Alchemist. Special effects maestro Pitof's directorial debut is a fussy, flashy, furiously edited farrago, which is sustained solely by the hulkingly assured presence of Gérard Depardieu. DP. In French with English subtitles.

Gérard Depardieu *Vidocq* • Guillaume Canet *Etienne Boisset* • Inés Sastre *Préah* • André Dussollier *Lautrennes* • Edith Scob *Sylvia* • Moussa Maaskri *Nimier* ■ *Dir* Pitof • *Scr* Jean-Christophe Grange, Pitof

La Vie de Château ★★★★ U

Wartime comedy drama
1965 · Fr · BW · 89mins

This gripping and extremely evocative comedy drama about the French Resistance is set in the crumbling Normandy manor house owned by the staid Philippe Noiret and his beautiful wife Catherine Deneuve. Into their midst arrives a Free French agent on a mission from England to prepare for D-Day. Deneuve falls in love with him and things are further complicated by the Germans who suddenly take over the château. Part wartime thriller, part marital drama, it's about the bravery and heroism that lies dormant in everyone. AT. In French with English subtitles. DVD

Catherine Deneuve *Marie* • Philippe Noiret *Jérôme* • Pierre Brasseur *Dimanche* • Mary Marquet *Charlotte* • Henri Garcin *Julien* • Carlos Thompson *Klopstock* ■ *Dir* Jean-Paul Rappeneau • *Scr* Jean-Paul Rappeneau, Alain Cavalier, Claude Sautet, Daniel Boulanger

La Vie de Jésus ★★★

Drama 1996 · Fr · Colour · 96mins

This pseudo-Bressonian study of teenage ennui by debuting director Bruno Dumont is based on his time as a teacher of disaffected small-town kids. Despite looking older, David Douche is the skinheaded 19-year-old leader of a scooter gang in Bailleul, northern France. His relationship with cashier Marjorie Cottreel is based on perfunctory sex and he responds to her interest in Arab teenager Kader Chaatouf with a violence that's both proprietorial and racist. As surly a study of spiritual humanism as cinema has seen. DP. In French with English subtitles. Contains violence.

David Douche *Freddy* • Marjorie Cottreel *Marie* • Kader Chaatouf *Kader* • Sébastien Delbaere *Gégé* • Samuel Boidin *Michou* • Steve Smagghe *Robert* • Sébastien Bailleul *Quinquin* • Geneviève Cottreel *Yvette, Freddy's mother* ■ *Dir/Scr* Bruno Dumont

La Vie Est à Nous ★★★

Propaganda 1936 · Fr · BW · 62mins

Although Jean Renoir was never a member of the French Communist Party, he was asked by them to supervise this propaganda film of sketches, newsreels and political speeches. Despite the fact that there were eight directors on the project, including the great still photographer Henri Cartier-Bresson, with the styles ranging from French naturalism to Russian Socialist Realism, the collaborative effort has the stamp of Renoir on it. An interesting and uneven document of the day, it glows with enthusiasm and optimism (the Popular Front had just won a victory in the Spanish election). Banned soon after, it resurfaced after May 1968. RB. In French with English subtitles.

Julien Bertheau *Unemployed worker* • Marcel Duhamel *Garage owner* • O'Brady [Frédéric O'Brady] *Washer* • Jean Dasté *Schoolteacher* • Emile Drain *Worker* • Jean Renoir *Bistro owner* ■ *Dir* Jean Renoir, Jean-Paul Le Chanois, Jacques Becker, André Zwobada, Pierre Unik, Henri Cartier-Bresson, P Vaillant-Couturier, Jacques Brunius • *Scr* Jean Renoir, Jean-Paul Le Chanois, Jacques Becker, André Zwobada, Pierre Unik, P Vaillant-Couturier, Henri Cartier-Bresson, Jacques Brunius

La Vie Est Belle ★★★ PG

Comedy musical
1987 · Bel/Fr/Zaire · Colour · 82mins

Papa Wemba leaves his village for Kinshasa to pursue his ambition to become a recording star, only to have to work as a houseboy. He falls in love with Bibi Krubwa, but her mother forces an end to the relationship until a witch doctor intervenes. Co-written and co-directed by Belgian-born Benoît Lamy and Zaire's Ngangura Mweze, this is an interesting insight into an unfamiliar culture. It's charming, cheerful and well-played, particularly by Wemba, a Paris-based international pop star. RK. In French with English subtitles.

Papa Wemba *Kourou* • Bibi Krubwa *Kabibi* • Landu Nzunzimbu Matshia *Mamou* • Kanku Kasongo *Nvouandou* • Lokinda Mengi Feza *Nzazi* • Kalimazi Lombume *Mongali* ■ *Dir* Benoît Lamy, Ngangura Mweze • *Scr* Benoît Lamy, Maryse Léon, Ngangura Mweze

The View from Pompey's Head ★★

Drama 1955 · US · Colour · 96mins

Writer/producer/director Philip Dunne brought in little-known British actress Dana Wynter and promoted action player Richard Egan to the male lead for this adaptation. Wynter is highly proficient as a Southern belle but lacks that extra something. Egan is monotonous as the successful lawyer returning to his home town and his old love. Their rekindled passion proves less interesting than the revelation of a deep secret in the past of Sidney Blackmer's elderly novelist. AE

Richard Egan *Anson Page* • Dana Wynter *Dinah* • Cameron Mitchell *Mickey Higgins* • Sidney Blackmer *Garvin Wales* • Marjorie Rambeau *Lucy Wales* • Rosemarie Bowe *Kit* ■ *Dir* Philip Dunne • *Scr* Philip Dunne, from a novel by Hamilton Basso

View from the Top ★ PG

Romantic comedy
2003 · US · Colour · 83mins

Even an over-used and under-funny Mike Myers can't salvage this flight-attendant comedy that never leaves the terminal, let alone gets off the ground. It's hard to see what first attracted Myers and top-billed Gwyneth Paltrow to this mediocre tale of a small-town stewardess who wants to fly high with a major airline. DA DVD

Gwyneth Paltrow *Donna Jensen* • Christina Applegate *Christine Montgomery* • Mark Ruffalo *Ted Stewart* • Candice Bergen *Sally Weston* • Kelly Preston *Sherry* • Rob Lowe *Pilot Steve Bench* • Mike Myers *John Whitney* • Josh Malina [Joshua Malina] *Randy Jones* ■ *Dir* Bruno Barreto • *Scr* Eric Wald

A View to a Kill ★★ PG

Spy adventure 1985 · UK · Colour · 125mins

This below-average Bond movie has Roger Moore as 007 for the seventh and final time. His smoothness is now a bit tired, but there's still some action and excitement to be had. The baddies are headed by Christopher Walken and his accomplice, girlfriend Grace Jones, and, while both can look pretty scary, you don't get the impression that they're particularly evil. Tanya Roberts does what Bond girls do pretty well, but the plot doesn't really convince. AT. Contains violence. DVD

Roger Moore *James Bond* • Christopher Walken *Max Zorin* • Tanya Roberts *Stacey Sutton* • Grace Jones *May Day* • Patrick Macnee *Tibbett* • David Yip *Chuck Lee* • Fiona Fullerton *Pola Ivanova* • Desmond Llewelyn *"Q"* • Robert Brown *"M"* • Lois Maxwell *Miss Moneypenny* • Walter Gotell *General Gogol* ■ *Dir* John Glen • *Scr* Richard Maibaum, Michael G Wilson, from characters created by Ian Fleming

Vigil ★★★ 15

Drama 1984 · NZ · Colour · 86mins

This is an early film from Vincent Ward, director of the excellent *The Navigator – a Medieval Odyssey* and *Map of the Human Heart*, and the ghastly *What Dreams May Come*. Ward is noted for his visual style, and there's plenty on which to feast the eyes in this attractive tale of a New Zealand farm girl struggling to adapt when a young drifter fills the family place vacated by her recently dead dad. Absorbing viewing. DA

Penelope Stewart *Elizabeth Peers* • Frank Whitten *Ethan Ruir* • Fiona Kay *Lisa Peers, "Toss"* • Bill Kerr *Birdie* • Gordon Shields *Justin Peers* ■ *Dir* Vincent Ward • *Scr* Vincent Ward, Graeme Tetley

Vigil in the Night ★★★

Medical melodrama 1940 · US · BW · 95mins

This exciting melodrama features the marvellous Carole Lombard as a committed nurse who takes the blame for a fatal mistake made by her sister Anne Shirley. The RKO studio's re-creation of England is, unusually for a Hollywood film of this period, remarkably convincing, and the British support cast headed by handsome doctor Brian Aherne is also excellent. (Watch out for a very young Peter Cushing.) Director George Stevens's straightforward, no-nonsense cinematic style makes this very satisfying. TS

V

Carole Lombard *Anne Lee* • Anne Shirley *Lucy Lee* • Brian Aherne *Dr Prescott* • Julien Mitchell *Matthew Bowley* • Robert Coote *Dr Caley* • Rita Page *Glennie* • Peter Cushing *Joe Shand* ■ *Dir* George Stevens • *Scr* Fred Guiol, PJ Wolfson, Rowland Leigh, from the novel by AJ Cronin

Vigilante Force ★★ 18

Action drama 1975 · US · Colour · 85mins

Kris Kristofferson is the Vietnam vet brought in by his brother (Jan-Michael Vincent) to fight off lawless oil workers in a booming California town in this awkward combination of western and war genres from director George Armitage. Highlighting male bonding and nasty violence above a cohesive story, at heart it's a self-conscious retelling of the Cain and Abel saga. But Kristofferson acquits himself well, as does Bernadette Peters in a barnstorming portrayal as a down-at-heel cabaret artist. AJ. Contains violence and swearing.

Kris Kristofferson *Aaron Arnold* • Jan-Michael Vincent *Ben Arnold* • Victoria Principal *Linda Christopher* • Bernadette Peters *Little Dee* • Brad Dexter *Mayor Bradford* • Judson Pratt *Harry Lee* ■ *Dir/Scr* George Armitage

The Vigilantes Return ★★ U

Western 1947 · US · Colour · 66mins

This is a pretty average western, with marshal Jon Hall hiding his true identity to trap villain Robert Wilcox, whose saloon is the front for an outlaw lair. Nothing special, but efficiently done. Watch for terrific baddie Jack Lambert in one of his earliest roles. TS

Jon Hall *Johnnie Taggart* • Margaret Lindsay *Kitty* • Paula Drew *Louise Holden* • Andy Devine *Andy* • Robert Wilcox *Clay Curtwright* • Jonathan Hale *Judge Holden* • Arthur Hohl *Sheriff* ■ *Dir* Ray Taylor • *Scr* Roy Chanslor

Vigo: Passion for Life ★★ 15

Biographical drama
1997 · UK/Jpn/Fr/Sp/Ger · Colour · 98mins

Sadly, this filmic essay on the tragic life of 1930s French film director Jean Vigo fails to improve on director Julien Temple's earlier efforts. Though imaginatively shot, this is ultimately a depressing, dragging tale of Vigo and his wife Lydu's terminal tuberculosis and how the couple live under feelings of acute mortality. Though lifted by earnest and endearing performances from leads James Frain and Romane Bohringer, the film fails to convey the revolutionary legacy Vigo left behind him; he died at 29, having already made classics *Zéro de Conduite* and *L'Atalante*. LH. Contains swearing and sex scenes.

Romane Bohringer *Lydu Lozinska* • James Frain *Jean Vigo* • Diana Quick *Emily* • William Scott-Masson *Marcel* • James Faulkner *Dr Gerard* • Jim Carter *Bonaventure* • Paola Dionisotti *Marie* • Lee Ross *Oscar Levy* ■ *Dir* Julien Temple • *Scr* Peter Ettedgui, Anne Devlin, Julien Temple, from the play *Love's a Revolution* by Chris Ward, from the biography *Jean Vigo* by Paulo Emilio Salles Gomes

The Viking Queen ★

Period adventure 1967 · UK · Colour · 91mins

There's only one reason for catching this risible offering from Hammer and that's the chance to spot the Viking wearing a wristwatch! Otherwise, there's little pleasure to be gained from watching seasoned performers making fools of themselves in a story that would struggle to get a pass grade in GCSE English. DP

Don Murray *Justinian* • Carita *Salina* • Donald Houston *Maelgan* • Andrew Keir *Octavian* • Adrienne Corri *Beatrice* • Niall MacGinnis *Tiberion* • Wilfrid Lawson *King Priam* • Nicola Pagett *Talia* • Patrick Troughton *Tristram* ■ *Dir* Don Chaffey • *Scr* Clarke Reynolds, from a story by John Temple-Smith

The Viking Sagas ★★★ 15

Period adventure
1995 · Ice/US · Colour · 79mins

An entertaining mix of utter tosh and surprising historical accuracy, this opens with an explicit death sequence that has to be seen to be disbelieved. A warrior prince vows vengeance when his father is murdered and his people are run off their land. The action scenes are exciting, but the performances are dreary in comparison and the pacing is rather pedestrian. It looks good, however, perhaps because director Michael Chapman was cinematographer on such Martin Scorsese films as *Taxi Driver* and *Raging Bull*. DA

Ralph Moeller *Kjartan* • Sven-Ole Thorsen *Gunnar* • Ingibjorg Stefansdottir *Gudrun* • Thorir Waagfjord *Bolli* ■ *Dir* Michael Chapman • *Scr* Paul R Gurian, Dale Herd

Viking Women and the Sea Serpent ★ PG

Period adventure 1957 · US · BW · 65mins

This is an attempt to set a standard escape story in a distinct historical time period. Unfortunately the paltry budget meant all Norse fact had finally to be ignored and enough cheap fantasy tossed in to please the horror crowd. Hence the last minute appearance of the cheesy sea monster. Badly lit and ultra-phoney (the cast members all wear blond wigs), this is a seldom-seen Roger Corman quickie. You'll soon realise why. AJ DVD

Abby Dalton *Desir* • Susan Cabot *Enger* • Brad Jackson *Vedric* • June Kenney *Asmild* • Richard Devon *Stark* ■ *Dir* Roger Corman • *Scr* Lawrence Goldman, from a story by Irving Block

The Vikings ★★★★★ PG

Period adventure
1958 · US · Colour · 110mins

This tremendously exciting, if gory, adventure epic was a huge hit for independent producer/star Kirk Douglas, who generously changed the title of Edison Marshall's novel *The Viking* in order to include his friends Tony Curtis, Janet Leigh and Ernest Borgnine. Jack Cardiff's location photography is superb, and Harper Goff's splendid art direction gives a remarkably authentic sense of period. There is a fine feel of lusty enjoyment pervading this movie, and it's hard to see how it could have been made any better. The uncredited title narration is by Orson Welles. TS. Contains violence. DVD

Tony Curtis *Eric* • Kirk Douglas *Einar* • Ernest Borgnine *Ragnar* • Janet Leigh *Morgana* • James Donald *Egbert* • Alexander Knox *Father Godwin* • Frank Thring *Aella* ■ *Dir* Richard Fleischer • *Scr* Calder Willingham, Dale Wasserman, from the novel *The Viking* by Edison Marshall

Viktor und Viktoria ★★★

Period comedy musical
1933 · Ger · BW · 100mins

This delightful German original (filmed concurrently in French as *Georges et Georgette*) went on to inspire the 1936 British remake *First a Girl* and, more famously, *Victor/Victoria* in 1982. It's the story of struggling female impersonator Renate Müller who is persuaded to pretend she's a man cross-dressing as a woman. Müller then becomes the talk of the town, but complications soon arise from the merry-go-round of gender swapping. Light-hearted and atmospheric. BB. In German with English subtitles.

Renate Müller *Susanne Lohr* • Hermann Thimig *Viktor Hempel* • Hilde Hildebrand *Ellinor* • Friedel Pisetta *Lilian* • Adolf Wohlbruck [Anton Walbrook] *Robert* ■ *Dir* Reinhold Schünzel • *Scr* Reinhold Schünzel, from the play by Reinhold Schünzel

Villa! ★★

Western 1958 · US · Colour · 71mins

A rattling, far-from-accurate account of Pancho Villa's conversion to the Mexican revolutionary cause. As played by Rodolfo Hoyos, Villa is more of a rogue than a rebel, chasing money and women in equal measure; but the focus here is on gun-runner Brian Keith, moved by the suffering of the peasants around him to take sides with Hoyos against the oppressive regime. James B Clark keeps the action moving, but this is run-of-the-mill fare. RT

Brian Keith *Bill Harmon* • Cesar Romero *Fierro Lopez* • Margia Dean *Julie North* • Rodolfo Hoyos *Pancho Villa* • Rosenda Monteros *Mariana* • Carlos Muzquiz *Cabo* • Elisa Loti *Manuela* • Enrique Lucero *Tenorio* ■ *Dir* James B Clark • *Scr* Louis Vittes

Villa des Roses ★★ 12

Period romantic drama
2002 · Bel/UK/Neth/Lux · Colour · 114mins

Despite looking suitably gaunt, Julie Delpy fails to convey the emotional fragility of the provincial widow who accepts work as a maid in Harriet Walter and Timothy West's crumbling Parisian guest house, only to fall under the spell of a shiftless German artist (Shaun Dingwall). Director Frank Van Passel makes moody use of the dingy interiors, but his use of anachronistic camera effects proves intrusive, while he leaves intriguing minor characters in the shadows. DP DVD

Julie Delpy *Louise Créteur* • Shaun Dingwall *Richard Grünewald* • Shirley Henderson *Ella* • Harriet Walter *Olive Burrell* • Timothy West *Hugh Burrell* • Frank Vercruyssen *Aasgaard* ■ *Dir* Frank Van Passel • *Scr* Christophe Dirickx, from the novel by Willem Elsschot

Villa Rides ★★ 15

Western 1968 · US · Colour · 116mins

Yul Brynner wears a wig and a sadistic sneer as the Mexican folk hero. The original script was written by Sam Peckinpah, who hoped to direct it; but Brynner objected to Peckinpah's story. Buzz Kulik was brought in and Robert Towne who later wrote *Chinatown* gave the script a makeover. The result is a botched job, watchable only for a few rousing action scenes and for Robert Mitchum's sleepy-eyed gun-runner. AT. Contains violence and swearing.

Yul Brynner *Pancho Villa* • Robert Mitchum *Lee Arnold* • Maria Buccella [Maria Grazia Buccella] *Fina Gonzalez* • Charles Bronson *Fierro* • Robert Viharo *Urbina* • Frank Wolff *Captain Francisco Ramirez* • Herbert Lom *General Huerta* • Alexander Knox *President Francisco Madero* • Fernando Rey *Colonel Fuentes* ■ *Dir* Buzz Kulik • *Scr* Robert Towne, Sam Peckinpah, from the book *Pancho Villa* by William Douglas Lansford

The Village ★★★ 12

Horror thriller 2004 · US · Colour · 103mins

Set in an unspecified time and place, this beautifully photographed tale concerns an isolated rural community that seems idyllic, except for the mysterious creatures that inhabit the surrounding woods. The villagers respect the territory of these rarely seen beings, but the uneasy truce is challenged when Joaquin Phoenix steps across the boundary line. Director M Night Shyamalan uses just about every trick in the book to create a sense of unease and his cast performs admirably, particularly newcomer Bryce Dallas Howard (daughter of director Ron Howard). However, Shyamalan piles on the twists till the story buckles. BP. Contains violence. DVD

Joaquin Phoenix *Lucius Hunt* • Bryce Dallas Howard *Ivy Walker* • Adrien Brody *Noah Percy* • William Hurt *Edward Walker* • Sigourney Weaver *Alice Hunt* • Brendan Gleeson *August Nicholson* • Cherry Jones *Mrs Clack* • Jayne Atkinson *Mrs Walker* • Judy Greer *Kitty Walker* ■ *Dir/Scr* M Night Shyamalan • *Cinematographer* Roger Deakins

Village in the Mist ★★★

Drama 1983 · S Kor · Colour · 90mins

Im Kwon-taek had already directed more than 70 films by the time he made this startlingly graphic commercial success, which many critics have cited as a South Korean take on *Straw Dogs*. Dark secrets lurk beneath the surface calm of the remote village to which Chong Yun-hee is dispatched as a supply teacher, but they begin to emerge after she's raped by a sinister outsider, Ahn Sung-kee. As ever Im's preoccupation is with the way in which tradition and culture impact upon modern society, although the main focus of this technically dazzling film is on the status of women within the Confucian morality system. DP. In Korean with English subtitles.

Ahn Sung-kee *Sinister outsider* • Chong Yun-hee *Teacher* ■ *Dir* Im Kwon-taek • *Scr* Song Kil-han, from the book *Island without a Name* by I Mun-yol

Village of Daughters ★★ U

Comedy 1961 · UK · BW · 90mins

Eric Sykes rarely landed leading roles and he struggles to make an impact in this slight Sicilian farce. Travelling saleman Sykes arrives in a village that's so short of eligible men that a letter from London requesting a bride for an exile's son is a cause for commotion. He is invited by local priest John Le Mesurier to select the most suitable candidate. However, he's soon abusing his position. Corrupt mayor Grégoire Aslan has his moments, but, essentially, this is a mediocre one-gag film. DP

Eric Sykes *Herbert Harris* • Scilla Gabel *Angelina Vimercati* • Yvonne Romain *Annunziata Gastoni* • Jill Carson *Lucia Puccelli* • Talitha Pol *Gioia Spartaco* • Bettine Le Beau *Alisa Marcio* • Carol White *Natasha Passoti* • Grégoire Aslan *Gastoni* • John Le Mesurier *Don Calogero* ■ *Dir* George Pollock • *Scr* David Pursall, Jack Seddon

Village of the Damned ★★★★

Science-fiction horror
1960 · UK · BW · 77mins

Twelve women give birth to blond alien offspring after a strange force puts their community into a 24-hour trance, in this remarkably faithful adaptation of John Wyndham's novel *The Midwich Cuckoos*. In a film that is compelling, creepy and often unbearably tense, an icy George Sanders becomes their teacher and then tries to halt their world domination plans. Superbly acted, with the human/family side of the horror unusually explored more than the fantasy elements, this British near-classic is a sci-fi treat and remains so. A less satisfying sequel, *Children of the Damned*, followed in 1964. AJ. Contains violence.

George Sanders *Gordon Zellaby* • Barbara Shelley *Anthea Zellaby* • Martin Stephens *David* • Michael Gwynn *Major Alan Bernard* • Laurence Naismith *Dr Willers* • Richard Warner *Harrington* • Jenny Laird *Mrs Harrington* • Sarah Long *Evelyn Harrington* ■ *Dir* Wolf Rilla • *Scr* Wolf Rilla, Stirling Silliphant, George Barclay [Ronald Kinnoch], from the novel *The Midwich Cuckoos* by John Wyndham

V

Village of the Damned ★★ 15

Science-fiction horror
1995 · US · Colour · 93mins

Those blond alien youngsters return to wreak havoc in a small town in cult director John Carpenter's update of the 1960 British sci-fi near-classic. Despite the setting being transferred to California, superior special effects heightening the nastiness and Christopher Reeve giving a nicely heroic performance, the end result forgoes the touches and stylish atmosphere you might expect from Carpenter for a bland TV movie-style sheen. AJ. Contains violence. DVD

Christopher Reeve *Alan Chaffee* • Kirstie Alley *Dr Susan Verner* • Linda Kozlowski *Jill McGowan* • Michael Paré *Frank McGowan* • Meredith Salenger *Melanie Roberts* • Mark Hamill *Reverend George* • Pippa Pearthree *Mrs Sarah Miller* ■ *Dir* John Carpenter • *Scr* David Himmelstein, from the 1960 film, from the novel *The Midwich Cuckoos* by John Wyndham

Village of the Giants ★★ PG

Science-fiction comedy drama
1965 · US · Colour · 77mins

Producer Bert I Gordon was a master of crude productions with gimmicky titles, and this improbable but fun tale about a boy genius (Ron Howard) who invents a food that causes growth to gigantic proportions is down to his usual standard. However, it's enjoyable hokum, supposedly based on an HG Wells original, which gets by on pure brio. JG

Tommy Kirk *Mike* • Johnny Crawford *Horsey* • Beau Bridges *Fred* • Ronny Howard [Ron Howard] *Genius* • Joy Harmon *Merrie* • Bob Random *Rick* • Tisha Sterling *Jean* ■ *Dir* Bert I Gordon • *Scr* Alan Caillou, by Bert I Gordon, from the novel *The Food of the Gods* by HG Wells

Village Tale ★★★

Drama 1935 · US · BW · 80mins

The dark side of human nature is to the fore in this tale of bitter rivalry between wealthy Randolph Scott and local landowning nonentity Arthur Hohl for the affections of Hohl's wife, Kay Johnson. The simmering feud, in a small rural community, becomes the focus for the collected pettiness and malice of the townspeople. A somewhat static drama, steeped in unpleasantness, but interesting and well acted, particularly by the supporting players. RK

Randolph Scott *TN "Slaughter" Somerville* • Kay Johnson *Janet Stevenson* • Arthur Hohl *Elmer Stevenson* • Robert Barrat *Drury Stevenson* • Janet Beecher *Amy Somerville* • Edward Ellis *Old Ike* • Dorothy Burgess *Lulu Stevenson* • Donald Meek *Charlie* • Guinn Williams [Guinn "Big Boy" Williams] *Ben Roberts* ■ *Dir* John Cromwell • *Scr* Allan Scott, from the novel *Village Tale* by Phil Stong

V

Villain ★★★ 18

Crime drama 1971 · UK · Colour · 93mins

Richard Burton stars as a vicious East End gangster, who rules by fear and the cut-throat razor. Clearly inspired, if that's the word, by the career of the Kray twins, the picture is one of unrelieved ugliness, from the run-down locations to the run-down bulk of Burton himself: overweight, shabby, self-loathing. Adored by his mother, he's a homosexual with a toy-boy lover, and a Labour voter who worries about OAPs. Wavering uneasily between horror, black comedy and sentimentality, it's held together by Burton's performance. AT. Contains violence and swearing.

Richard Burton *Vic Dakin* • Ian McShane *Wolfe Lissner* • Nigel Davenport *Bob Matthews* • Donald Sinden *Gerald Draycott* • Fiona Lewis *Venetia* • TP McKenna *Frank Fletcher* • Joss Ackland *Edgar Lowis* ■ *Dir* Michael Tuchner • *Scr* Dick Clement, Ian La Frenais, Al Lettieri, from the novel *The Burden of Proof* by James Barlow

The Villain Still Pursued Her ★★

Comedy 1940 · US · BW · 65mins

Ham abounds in this spoof on old-time melodrama, directed by Edward Cline, former creative aide to Buster Keaton and other silent clowns. Keaton makes a guest appearance in this tale of villainous landlord Alan Mowbray, who terrorises the sweet-natured Margaret Hamilton and her attractive daughter Anita Louise. Boos and hisses are encouraged but it doesn't work as it should and audiences generally sit silent and baffled. TH

Hugh Herbert *Frederick Healy* • Anita Louise *Mary Wilson* • Alan Mowbray *Cribbs* • Buster Keaton *William Dalton* • Joyce Compton *Hazel Dalton* • Richard Cromwell *Edward Middleton* • Billy Gilbert *Announcer* • Margaret Hamilton *Mrs Wilson* ■ *Dir* Edward F Cline [Edward Cline] • *Scr* Elbert Franklin, from the play *The Fallen Saved*

La Ville Est Tranquille ★★★★ 18

Drama 2000 · Fr · Colour · 127mins

Robert Guédiguian directs this multilayered portrait of everyday life among the lower-class denizens of Marseille. As ever, he receives excellent service from his trusted ensemble cast in their depiction of numerous interlocking stories. Jean-Pierre Darroussin exhibits genuine pain as the lonely cab driver whose good intentions towards part-time prostitute Ariane Ascaride and her drug-addled daughter fail to alleviate an increasingly desperate situation. Awash with drugs, vice, violence, poverty and racial tension, Guédiguian's beloved Marseille is very much a city on a knife edge, yet he commends the spirit of her inhabitants as they battle on against insurmountable odds. DP. In French with English subtitles. DVD

Ariane Ascaride *Michèle* • Jean-Pierre Darroussin *Paul* • Gérard Meylan *Gérard* • Jacques Boudet *Paul's father* • Pascale Roberts *Paul's mother* • Christine Brücher *Viviane Froment* • Jacques Pieiller *Yves Froment* ■ *Dir* Robert Guédiguian • *Scr* Robert Guédiguian, Jean-Louis Milesi

Vincent and Theo ★★★ 15

Biographical drama
1990 · UK/Fr/US · Colour · 134mins

Outlining the last years of painter Vincent van Gogh (Tim Roth), as seen through the eyes of his brother Theodore (Paul Rhys), this is a haunting study in loneliness, obsession and the tough quest for validation in the blinkered art world. Unusual direction by Robert Altman and an intense performance by Roth as the tortured genius make this a thought-provoking look at the nature of the creative impulse as it impacts on family life. AJ DVD

Tim Roth *Vincent van Gogh* • Paul Rhys *Theodore van Gogh* • Bernadette Giraud *Marguerite Gachet* • Adrian Brine *Uncle Cent* • Jip Wijngaarden *Sien Hoornik* • Wladimir Yordanoff *Paul Gauguin* ■ *Dir* Robert Altman • *Scr* Julian Mitchell

Vincent, François, Paul and the Others ★★★

Comedy drama 1974 · It/Fr · Colour · 118mins

The lives, loves and midlife crises of a group of middle-class Parisians, principally a doctor, a writer and a factory owner who are all 50-somethings and looking for something better. Surrounding them are the "others" – friends, wives, mistresses – and they all interact with ingenious timing and often witty results. As in all authentically French movies, coffee is sipped, cigarettes smoked and philosophy explored, but Claude Sautet's film is really just an extremely glossy soap opera made eminently watchable by its heavyweight cast. AT. A French language film.

Yves Montand *Vincent* • Michel Piccoli *Francois* • Serge Reggiani *Paul* • Gérard Depardieu *Jean* • Stéphane Audran *Catherine* • Marie Dubois *Lucie* • Antonella Lualdi *Julia* ■ *Dir* Claude Sautet • *Scr* Jean-Loup Dabadie, Claude Néron, Claude Sautet, from the novel *La Grande Marrade* by Claude Néron

Vincent: the Life and Death of Vincent Van Gogh ★★★ PG

Biographical documentary
1987 · Austria · Colour · 95mins

This is a film closer in spirit to documentary than Vincente Minnelli's *Lust for Life* or Robert Altman's *Vincent and Theo.* Paul Cox's essay uses the artist's letters (sensitively read by John Hurt) to both examine the sources of his creative inspiration and reassess his mental state during those tormented final years, when he not only painted at a furious rate, but also suffered an anguish that finally crushed his ferocious resolve to remain sane. The film also traces the development of Van Gogh's style from the earliest line drawings to the powerfully emotive canvases of his Arles period. Enthralling. DP

John Hurt *Reader* ■ *Dir* Paul Cox • *Scr* Paul Cox, from the letters of Vincent Van Gogh

Vintage Wine ★★

Comedy 1935 · UK · BW · 81mins

Despite his grand age, Seymour Hicks, head of a wine dynasty, refuses to slow down and maintains a boisterous life with his new young wife, Claire Luce. Scandalised by his behaviour, the other members of his family descend on his home allowing his wife to discover that he is actually 20 years older than he led her to believe. This flowery farce stars the great British stage actor Sir Seymour Hicks, a reliable purveyor of such comedy. DF

Seymour Hicks *Charles Popinot* • Claire Luce *Nina Popinot* • Eva Moore *Josephine Popinot* • Judy Gunn *Blanche Popinot* • Miles Malleson *Henri Popinot* • Kynaston Reeves *Benedict Popinot* ■ *Dir* Henry Edwards • *Scr* Seymour Hicks, Ashley Dukes, H Fowler Mear, from the play *Der Ewige Jungeling (The Eternal Youth)* by Alexander Engel

Vinyl ★★

Satire 1965 · US · BW · 70mins

One of several films Andy Warhol made with playwright Ronald Tavel during 1965. The quasi-script, reputedly based on Anthony Burgess's novel *A Clockwork Orange*, focuses on sado-masochism and features a lot of bondage and torture. The dialogue in the second reel is inaudible because there are records playing in another part of the studio. Finally the cast get stoned on amyl nitrate, and an orgy begins. Dedicated cineastes may retain a modicum of interest. DM

Gerard Malanga *Victor* • Edie Sedgwick *Woman on trunk* • John MacDermott *Detective* • Ondine ■ *Dir* Andy Warhol • *Scr* Ronald Tavel, from the novel *A Clockwork Orange* by Anthony Burgess

Violent City ★★

Action crime drama
1970 · Fr/It · Colour · 99mins

Following his compelling appearance as a stone-faced mystery man in *Once upon a Time in the West,* Charles Bronson then moved on to this thriller and played a stone-faced hitman. Bronson is out to avenge the double-cross by Telly Savalas that put him in prison. To make matters worse, Savalas is now with the ex-con's girlfriend (Jill Ireland). The body count is high. It's a pity the same can't be said for the tension. TH

Charles Bronson *Jeff* • Jill Ireland *Vanessa* • Umberto Orsini *Steve* • Telly Savalas *Weber* • Michel Constantin *Killian* • George Savalas *Shapiro* ■ *Dir* Sergio Sollima • *Scr* Sauro Scavolini, Gianfranco Calligarich, Lina Wertmuller

Violent Cop ★★★★ 18

Thriller 1989 · Jpn · Colour · 98mins

Although he was already a massive star in Japan, this brooding thriller made actor/first-time director Takeshi "Beat" Kitano the hip name to drop in film circles over here. The plot itself could have come from any mainstream blockbuster: a tough, unconventional cop (Kitano) and his new, inexperienced partner find themselves up against their fellow officers when investigating a drugs case. However, the usual Hollywood clichés are turned on their head by Kitano's highly stylised direction, the splashes of quirky black humour and sudden jolts of extreme violence. On the screen, Kitano's charismatic performance is riveting. JF. In Japanese with English subtitles. DVD

"Beat" Takeshi [Takeshi Kitano] *Detective Azuma* • Maiko Kawakami *Akari* • Haku Ryu *Kiyohiro, hit man* • Makoto Ashikawa *Kikuchi, rookie* • Shiro Sano *Police Chief Yoshinari* • Shigeru Hiraizumi *Detective Iwaki* ■ *Dir* Takeshi Kitano • *Scr* Hisashi Nozawa

The Violent Enemy ★★ U

Political thriller 1969 · UK · Colour · 93mins

This downbeat thriller stars Tom Bell as an IRA man on the run, who is reluctantly recruited to blow up a British-owned power station. It's efficiently made, if unsurprising, and familiar American actor Ed Begley is worth watching as the fanatical Irish mastermind behind the scheme. JG

Tom Bell *Sean Rogan* • Susan Hampshire *Hannah Costello* • Ed Begley *Colum O'More* • Jon Laurimore *Austin* • Michael Standing *Fletcher* • Noel Purcell *John Michael Leary* ■ *Dir* Don Sharp • *Scr* Edmund Ward, from the novel *A Candle For The Dead* by Hugh Marlowe [Jack Higgins]

The Violent Men ★★★ PG

Western 1955 · US · Colour · 91mins

This well-cast but under-scripted western has Edward G Robinson as a disabled land baron, who discovers that his venal wife Barbara Stanwyck is in love with his own brother, played by the ever-excellent Brian Keith. Into this positively seething morass of emotion walks rancher Glenn Ford, intent on pacifying the townsfolk who've turned against the unscrupulous empire-building Robinson. There's real star power on display here, and Ford is superb, but the whole isn't quite as good as the sum of its parts. TS

Glenn Ford *John Parrish* • Barbara Stanwyck *Martha Wilkison* • Edward G Robinson *Lew Wilkison* • Dianne Foster *Judith Wilkison* • Brian Keith *Cole Wilkison* • May Wynn *Caroline Vail* • Warner Anderson *Jim McCloud* ■ *Dir* Rudolph Maté • *Scr* Harry Kleiner, from the novel *Rough Company* by Donald Hamilton

The Violent Ones ★★★

Crime drama 1967 · US · Colour · 87mins

Actor Fernando Lamas directed himself stylishly in this grim drama about three Anglo-American strangers implicated in the rape and murder of a girl in a small Mexican town. Lamas plays the sheriff who has to protect the Mexican-hating suspects from a lynch mob spurred on by the dead girl's father. Not particularly original in its examination of prejudice, the movie nevertheless does all it needs to convince and contains an exciting desert-chase climax. TH

Fernando Lamas *Manuel Vega* • Aldo Ray *Joe Vorzyck* • Tommy Sands *Mike Marain* • David Carradine *Lucas Barnes* • Lisa Gaye *Dolores* • Melinda Marx *Juanita* ■ *Dir* Fernando Lamas • *Scr* Doug Wilson, Charles Davis, from a story by Fred Freiberger, Herman Miller

Violent Playground ★★

Crime drama 1958 · UK · BW · 107mins

From the producing/directing team of Michael Relph and Basil Dearden, a drearily predictable but well-handled slice of dour British realism, set in Liverpool. Stanley Baker is a policeman who, after unsuccessfully investigating an outbreak of arson, is transferred to the job of juvenile liaison officer in a depressed area. He falls in love with Anne Heywood, only to discover that her young brother David McCallum is the arsonist. RK

Stanley Baker *Sgt Truman* • Anne Heywood *Cathie Murphy* • David McCallum *Johnny Murphy* • Peter Cushing *Priest* • John Slater *Sgt Walker* • Clifford Evans *Heaven Evans* • Moultrie Kelsall *Superintendent* • George A Cooper *Chief Inspector* ■ *Dir* Basil Dearden • *Scr* James Kennaway, from his novel

Violent Road ★★ U

Drama 1958 · US · BW · 77mins

This ordinary Hollywood picture shows three pairs of drivers taking trucks full of dangerous rocket fuel along a rough mountain road. The journey is full of contrived incidents and, naturally, not everyone makes it – but it's hard to care one way or the other. AE

Brian Keith *Mitch* • Dick Foran *Sarge* • Efrem Zimbalist Jr *George Lawrence* • Merry Anders *Carrie* • Sean Garrison *Ken Farley* • Joanna Barnes *Peg Lawrence* • Perry Lopez *Manuelo* • Ann Doran *Edith* ■ *Dir* Howard W Koch • *Scr* Richard Landau, from a story by Don Martin

Violent Saturday ★★★★

Crime drama 1955 · US · Colour · 89mins

A well-made, tense and exciting study of the preparations for a bloody and daring bank raid in a small Arizona town, this was filmed on actual locations in early CinemaScope, a process favoured by talented director Richard Fleischer. The assembled cast is impressive: a pre-stardom Lee Marvin, Stephen McNally and J Carrol Naish are the baddies, and there's back-up from the likes of Victor Mature and Ernest Borgnine. But the real star of the film is its superb climax, as the gripping robbery unfolds. TS

Victor Mature *Shelley Martin* • Richard Egan *Boyd Fairchild* • Stephen McNally *Harper* • Virginia Leith *Linda* • Tommy Noonan *Harry Reeves* • Lee Marvin *Dill* • Margaret Hayes *Emily* • J Carrol Naish *Chapman* • Sylvia Sidney *Elsie* • Ernest Borgnine *Stadt* ■ *Dir* Richard Fleischer • *Scr* Sydney Boehm, from the novel by William L Heath

Violent Summer ★★

Thriller 1961 · Fr · BW · 84mins

Mysterious and sinister events that befall author Henri-Jacques Huet while a house guest of wealthy widow Martine Carol on the Riviera, where she lives with her doctor lover Jean Desailly and two children. Sex, murder, a strong atmosphere and a proficient cast promise a good thriller, but the screenplay appears to run out of ideas halfway through, leaving the film to limp to a weak and unsatisfying conclusion. RK. A French language film.

Martine Carol *Georgina* • Jean Desailly *Francis* • Daliah Lavi *Marie* • Geneviève Grad *Sylvie* • Henri-Jacques Huet *Michel* ■ *Dir* Michel Boisrond • *Scr* Annette Wademant

Violets Are Blue ★★★ PG

Romantic drama 1986 · US · Colour · 82mins

There are some great performances in this strong film, with Kevin Kline and Sissy Spacek leading the way playing former high-school sweethearts. Since graduation Kline has settled down and become a family man and Spacek is now a world famous photographer. When she returns to her home town and encounters him, he welcomes her into his family fold. This is a subtle and sophisticated handling of difficult choices that avoids being trite and schmaltzy. The result makes for compelling and mature viewing. LH [video]

Sissy Spacek *Gussie Sawyer* • Kevin Kline *Henry Squires* • Bonnie Bedelia *Ruth Squires* • John Kellogg *Ralph Sawyer* • Jim Standiford *Addy Squires* • Augusta Dabney *Ethel Sawyer* ■ *Dir* Jack Fisk • *Scr* Naomi Foner

Violette Nozière ★★★

Historical crime drama
1977 · Fr · Colour · 123mins

Based on a sensational 1930s murder case, this film is every bit as mixed-up as its heroine; for while Claude Chabrol teases us with extravagant ellipses, he actually tells the story of the Parisienne who murdered her father in a highly traditional, typically sub-Hitchcockian manner. Isabelle Huppert won the best actress prize at Cannes for her work as the demure teenager whose wild nights in the Latin Quarter result in syphilis and the opportunity to poison Jean Carmet and the more durable Stéphane Audran. DP. A French language film.

Isabelle Huppert *Violette Noziere* • Stéphane Audran *Germaine Noziere* • Jean Carmet *Baptiste Noziere* ■ *Dir* Claude Chabrol • *Scr* Odile Barski, Herve Bromberger, Frederic Grendel, from a non-fiction book by Jean-Marie Fitere

Virasat ★★★ 15

Drama 1997 · Ind · Colour · 160mins

Anil Kapoor impresses as the British-educated son whose plan to open a chain of fast-food restaurants is dashed when he realises that his true calling lies in ending the feud that has riven his community. But more significant is the performance of Amrish Puri, whose liberal modernity breaks with the caricatured depiction of tyrannical fatherhood. The musical interludes are a touch intrusive, but they provide the perfect showcase for Tabu and newcomer Pooja Batra. DP. In Hindi with English subtitles. [video]

Anil Kapoor *Shakti* • Tabu *Gehna* • Pooja Batra *Anita* • Milind Gunaji *Balli Thakur* • Govind Namdeo *Birju Thakur* • Amrish Puri *Raja Thakur* ■ *Dir* Priyadarshan • *Scr* Vinay Shukla, from a story by Kamala Hassan

Virgil Bliss ★★★ 15

Drama 2001 · US · Colour · 93mins

Writer/director Joe Maggio strives to emulate the improvisational style of John Cassavetes, Mike Leigh and Ken Loach throughout his feature debut, which makes it all the more disappointing that he settles for so melodramatic a finale. Shot on grainy digital video and set in New York's less salubrious neighbourhoods, it follows the tortuous relationship between paroled crook Clint Jordan and crack-addicted hooker Kirsten Russell. This has some shaky moments dramatically, but also a certain rough charm. DP

Clint Jordan *Virgil Bliss* • Kirsten Russell *Ruby* • Anthony Gorman *Manny* • Marc Romeo *Devo* • Greg Amici *Gillette* • Tom Brangle *Captain* • Rich Bierman *Prison guard* ■ *Dir/Scr* Joe Maggio

The Virgin and the Gypsy ★★★

Period drama 1970 · UK · Colour · 95mins

Published posthumously, DH Lawrence's novella explored many of the sexual and social themes that recurred so often in his work. In this film version, Joanna Shimkus plays the curious innocent, whose strict upbringing drives her to sample the forbidden temptations offered by traveller Franco Nero. Both give decent performances, while the supporting cast is accomplished. Director Christopher Miles captures the period well, but the film smoulders when it should catch fire. DP. Contains nudity.

Joanna Shimkus *Yvette Saywell* • Franco Nero *Gypsy* • Honor Blackman *Mrs Fawcett* • Mark Burns *Major Eastwood* • Maurice Denham *Rector* • Fay Compton *Grandma* • Kay Walsh *Aunt Cissie* • Harriet Harper *Lucille Saywell* ■ *Dir* Christopher Miles • *Scr* Alan Plater, from the novella by DH Lawrence

Virgin Island ★★ U

Romantic drama 1958 · UK · Colour · 98mins

Perfect English rose Virginia Maskell is cruising the Virgin Islands when archaeologist John Cassavetes sweeps her off her feet. Within a few days they are married, and they subsequently have a baby and become tediously contented. Even Maskell's mum, Isabel Dean, seems happy, despite the fact that Cassavetes, an inwardly seething method actor, is hardly romantic leading man material. Nothing more than a travelogue with silly dialogue, it's bland and pleasant. AT

John Cassavetes *Evan* • Virginia Maskell *Tina* • Sidney Poitier *Marcus* • Isabel Dean *Mrs Lomax* • Colin Gordon *The Commissioner* • Howard Marion-Crawford *Prescott* • Edric Connor *Captain Jason* ■ *Dir* Pat Jackson • *Scr* Philip Rush, Pat Jackson, from the novel *Our Virgin Island* by Robb White

Virgin Machine ★★★

Satirical drama 1988 · W Ger · BW · 85mins

Updating the medieval quest for courtly love to the California of sex lines, S&M and lipstick lesbians, Monika Treut has created a picaresque satire that not only explores the nature of gender orientation, but also modern morality and the cultural gulf between Europe and America. Quitting Hamburg to go in search of her mother, Ina Blum soon forgets her book on romance as she encounters a number of women prepared to give her a practical insight into her sexual identity. Elfi Mikesch's sensuous monochrome photography conveys the atmosphere of her contrasting environments. DP. In German with English subtitles.

Ina Blum *Dorothee Müller* • Marcelo Uriona *Bruno* • Gad Klein *Heinz* • Peter Kern *Hormone specialist* • Dominique Gaspar *Dominique* • Susie Bright *Susie Sexpert* ■ *Dir/Scr* Monika Treut

The Virgin Queen ★★ U

Historical drama 1955 · US · Colour · 87mins

Bette Davis stars as the last Tudor in this colourful but rather tepid melodrama. She gets to chew a little scenery as she realises that Richard Todd's Walter Raleigh is in love with lady-in-waiting Joan Collins, but the history lesson script keeps her on a short leash. Todd comes across as a sulky boy who isn't allowed to play in the Americas rather than an ambitious man of action, and his romance with the demure Collins is soggier than a cloak over a puddle. DP [video]

Bette Davis *Queen Elizabeth I* • Richard Todd *Sir Walter Raleigh* • Joan Collins *Beth Throgmorton* • Jay Robinson *Chadwick* • Herbert Marshall *Lord Leicester* • Dan O'Herlihy *Lord Derry* ■ *Dir* Henry Koster • *Scr* Harry Brown, Mindret Lord

The Virgin Soldiers ★★★ 15

War comedy drama
1969 · UK · Colour · 90mins

Leslie Thomas's first novel went straight to the top of the bestseller charts in 1966 and this movie version quickly tried to capitalise on its success. Thomas wrote about his national service experiences in Singapore, where manhood was discovered through "sex" and military action during the Malayan Emergency. In one sense the movie is just *Private's Progress* with a touch of *Carry On Sergeant*, but the vivid action scenes and the probability of getting shot give it a blacker dramatic edge. A follow-up film, *Stand Up Virgin Soldiers*, arrived eight years later. AT [video]

Hywel Bennett *Private Brigg* • Lynn Redgrave *Phillipa Raskin* • Nigel Davenport *Sergeant Driscoll* • Nigel Patrick *Regimental Sergeant Major Raskin* • Rachel Kempson *Mrs Raskin* • Jack Shepherd *Sergeant Wellbeloved* • Tsai Chin *Juicy Lucy* • Christopher Timothy *Corporal Brook* ■ *Dir* John Dexter • *Scr* John Hopkins, John McGrath, Ian La Frenais, from the novel by Leslie Thomas

The Virgin Spring ★★★★ 15

Period drama 1960 · Swe · BW · 85mins

Winner of the 1960 Oscar for best foreign film, Ingmar Bergman's stark study of the cruelty and superstition of the Middle Ages positively drips with symbolism. However, it also works as a powerful revenge tragedy, as Max von Sydow encounters the men who raped and murdered his daughter after she'd been cursed by her half-sister. Often considered one of Bergman's bleakest films, the story has a miraculous ending that dispels his doubts about the presence of God. The acting has a rare intensity and the photography of Sven Nykvist (working with Bergman for the first time) is a joy to behold. DP. In Swedish with English subtitles. Contains violence. [video] DVD

Max von Sydow *Herr Tore* • Birgitta Valberg *Mareta Tore* • Gunnel Lindblom *Ingeri* • Birgitta Pettersson *Karin Tore* • Axel Duberg *Thin herdsman* • Tor Isedal *Mute herdsman* ■ *Dir* Ingmar Bergman • *Scr* Ulla Isaksson, from the 14th-century ballad *Tores Dotter I Vange*

The Virgin Suicides ★★★★ 15

Drama 1999 · US · Colour · 92mins

Sofia Coppola's directorial debut confirmed real talent behind the camera. Based on the 1970s-set Jeffrey Eugenides novel about five sisters in an affluent Michigan suburb who obsess the local adolescent males and eventually kill themselves, Coppola (who also wrote the screenplay) captures a melancholic truth about the awkwardness of blooming adolescent sexuality without jeopardising an otherworldly, backlit lyricism. Kirsten Dunst, as the eldest sister, and Josh Harnett, as the cocky stud, are exceptional, as is the music by French duo Air. But the secret of the film lies in the quiet symbolism and the evocative, sun-bleached splendour. AC [video] DVD

James Woods *Mr Lisbon* • Kathleen Turner *Mrs Lisbon* • Kirsten Dunst *Lux Lisbon* • Josh Hartnett *Trip Fontaine* • Hanna Hall *Cecilia Lisbon* • Chelse Swain *Bonnie Lisbon* • AJ Cook *Mary Lisbon* • Leslie Hayman *Therese Lisbon* • Danny DeVito *Dr Hornicker* ■ *Dir* Sofia Coppola • *Scr* Sofia Coppola, from the novel by Jeffrey Eugenides

Virginia City ★★★ U

Western 1940 · US · Sepia · 120mins

A badly miscast Warner Bros western, set during the American Civil War, this features Humphrey Bogart, on the cusp of stardom, playing the most unlikely snarling Mexican bandit you'll ever see. It's hard to believe in prissy Miriam Hopkins, not a hair out of place, as a Confederate spy posing as a dance-hall girl. Nevertheless, the scale is lavish, the camerawork is professional, and Errol Flynn and Randolph Scott are very watchable. TS

Errol Flynn *Kerry Bradford* • Miriam Hopkins *Julia Hayne* • Randolph Scott *Vance Irby* • Humphrey Bogart *John Murrell* • Frank McHugh *Mr Upjohn* • Alan Hale *Olaf "Moose" Swenson* • Guinn "Big Boy" Williams *"Marblehead"* • John Litel *Marshal* ■ *Dir* Michael Curtiz • *Scr* Robert Henry Buckner [Robert Buckner], Norman Reilly Raine (uncredited), Howard Koch (uncredited)

The Virginian ★★★★

Western 1929 · US · BW · 92mins

This early talkie (with clear recording) retains its bite even though so many of its details have since become clichés. Gary Cooper is splendid as the Virginian, a ranch foreman forced into a romantic rivalry with his weak friend Richard Arlen. The object of their affection is Mary Brian's priggish schoolmarm who tries to restrain Cooper from shooting it out with Walter Huston's rustler villain. Besides its celebrated line, "If you want to call me that... smile!", there's also the first voicing of "This town ain't big enough for the both of us". Victor Fleming's direction is assured and at times imaginative. AE

Gary Cooper *The Virginian* • Walter Huston *Trampas* • Richard Arlen *Steve* • Mary Brian *Molly Wood* • Chester Conklin *Uncle Hughey* • Eugene Pallette *Honey Wiggin* • EH Calvert *Judge Henry* • Helen Ware *Ma Taylor* • Victor Potel *Nebraskey* ■ *Dir* Victor Fleming • *Scr* Howard Estabrook, Edward E Paramore Jr, Grover Jones, Keene Thompson, Joseph L Mankiewicz, from the play by Owen Wister, Kirk La Shelle, from the novel by Owen Wister

The Virginian ★★ U

Western 1946 · US · Colour · 83mins

This version of Owen Wister's classic western has poker-faced Joel McCrea warning off Brian Donlevy as the villainous Trampas. The Technicolor helps the aged tale, but overall there's nothing particularly special about the story any more, and the direction (by former editor Stuart Gilmore) is quite unremarkable. TS DVD

Joel McCrea *The Virginian* • Brian Donlevy *Trampas* • Sonny Tufts *Steve Andrews* • Barbara Britton *Molly Wood* • Fay Bainter *Mrs Taylor* • Henry O'Neill *Mr Taylor* • Bill Edwards *Sam Bennett* ■ *Dir* Stuart Gilmore • *Scr* Frances Goodrich, Albert Hackett, Edward E Paramore Jr, Howard Estabrook, from the play by Owen Wister, Kirk La Shelle, from the novel by Owen Wister

Viridiana ★★★★★ 15

Satirical drama 1961 · Mex/Sp · BW · 86mins

Luis Buñuel's most scathing attack on the Catholic Church and the depravity of the modern world was filmed with the uncomprehending approval of Franco's fascist cinema supremos. Later they unsuccessfully tried to withdraw the picture after nominating it as Spain's official entry at Cannes. *Viridiana* traces the moral decline of a saintly girl who inadvertently drives her lascivious uncle to suicide and is then brutally exploited by the outcasts she shelters on his estate. The apex of Buñuel's satire is a mocking pastiche of Leonardo da Vinci's *Last Supper*. The Vatican censured the film as "an insult to Christianity" but it still won the Cannes Golden Palm. DP. In Spanish with English subtitles.

Silvia Pinal *Viridiana* • Francisco Rabal *Jorge* • Fernando Rey *Don Jaime* • Margarita Lozano *Ramona* • Victoria Zinny *Lucia* • Teresa Rabal *Rita* ■ *Dir* Luis Buñuel • *Scr* Luis Buñuel, Julio Alajandro, from a story by Luis Buñuel

Virtual Girl ★ 18

Erotic science-fiction thriller
1998 · US · Colour · 83mins

A daft erotic thriller about a computer programmer who creates the eponymous girl (the alluring Charlie Curtis), while developing a new game. Director Richard Gabai (who also stars) made *Assault of the Party Nerds*, *Virgin High* and many more of this ilk, which gives you a good indication of how awful this is. Followed by a sequel, but exclusively for collectors of straight-to-video trash. DM DVD

Charlie Curtis *Virtuality/Cynthia Lee* • Richard Gabai *Fred Renfield* • Max Dixon *John Lewis* • Warren Draper *Charlie R Poppy* ■ *Dir* Richard Gabai • *Scr* Richard Gabai, LA Maddox

Virtual Nightmare ★★ 12

Science-fiction action fantasy
2000 · Aus · Colour · 85mins

There are shades of *The Matrix* in this modest but rewarding sci-fi thriller, which, like the latter, was shot in Australia. Michael Muhney is the ad man who starts losing his grip on reality when he discovers that he may have been living in a virtual world all along. There are no big names in the cast but the performances are solid and director Michael Pattinson works well with a limited budget. JF

Michael Muhney *Dale Hunter* • Tasma Walton *Wendy* • Jennifer Congram *Natalie* • Paul Gleeson *Sanford* • John Noble *Dad* ■ *Dir* Michael Pattinson • *Scr* Dan Mazur, David Tausik

Virtual Sexuality ★★★ 15

Fantasy comedy 1999 · UK · Colour · 89mins

Laura Fraser is the lovelorn teenage girl who accidentally creates her ideal man in this *Weird Science*-style British comedy scripted by former agony uncle Nick Fisher. Smartly written and aimed firmly at young girls, this has an attractive cast and zips along merrily to a fun conclusion. Possibly a bit slight for anyone over the age of 18, but perfect low-budget fun for *Just Seventeen* readers. JB DVD

Laura Fraser *Justine* • Rupert Penry-Jones *Jake* • Luke de Lacey *Chas* • Kieran O'Brien *Alex* • Marcelle Duprey *Fran* • Natasha Bell *Hoover* • Steve John Shepherd *Jason* ■ *Dir* Nick Hurran • *Scr* Nick Fisher

Virtuosity ★★★ 15

Science-fiction thriller
1995 · US · Colour · 101mins

If disgraced cop-turned-convict Denzel Washington can eliminate the computer-generated serial killer SID 6.7, he'll be gratefully pardoned in director Brett Leonard's spasmodically entertaining hi-tech fantasy adventure. Problem is, SID 6.7 (played by Russell Crowe) has 183 separate homicidal tendencies – including those of Hitler and Charles Manson – to his personality. Cyberspace wizardry covers the yawning gaps in this soulless thriller and the loose ends mount up faster than the body count, despite expert performances by the two commanding leads. AJ DVD

Denzel Washington *Parker Barnes* • Kelly Lynch *Madison Carter* • Russell Crowe *Sid 6.7* • Stephen Spinella *Lindenmeyer* • William Forsythe *William Cochran* • Louise Fletcher *Elizabeth Deane* ■ *Dir* Brett Leonard • *Scr* Eric Bernt

The Virtuous Sin ★★

Romantic drama 1930 · US · BW · 80mins

This drawn-out drama revolves around the efforts of Kay Francis in 1917 Russia to save her bacteriologist husband Kenneth MacKenna, a military misfit, from having to go to war by seducing his commanding officer Walter Huston. Matters are complicated when she falls in love with the officer. The Russian setting and characters are of no visible benefit to this forgotten offering from Paramount, which marked George Cukor's second directing effort, shared with Louis Gasnier and giving no indication of his future prominence. RK

Walter Huston *Gen Gregori Platoff* • Kay Francis *Marya Ivanovna* • Kenneth MacKenna *Lt Victor Sablin* ■ *Dir* George Cukor, Louis Gasnier • *Scr* Martin Brown, Louise Long, from the novel *A Tábornok (The General)* by Lajos Zilahy

Virus ★★ PG

Disaster fantasy
1980 · Jpn · Colour · 102mins

It seems more of the cash went to the all-star cast than on the special effects in this big-budget movie. Not content to focus on the few survivors of a worldwide plague, it also packs in forced prostitution and nuclear holocaust. The results don't completely make sense, especially in prints that cut about an hour from the running time. Some striking visuals and badly cast stars provide the main curiosity value. KB

Sonny Chiba *Dr Yamauchi* • Chuck Connors *Captain MacCloud* • Stephanie Faulkner *Sarah Baker* • Glenn Ford *Richardson* • Stuart Gillard *Dr Mayer* • Olivia Hussey *Marit* • George Kennedy *Admiral Conway* • Ken Ogata *Professor Tsuchiya* • Edward James Olmos *Captain Lopez* • Henry Silva *Garland* ■ *Dir* Kinji Fukasaku • *Scr* Koji Takada, Gregory Knapp, Kinji Fukasaku, from a novel by Sakyo Komatsu

Virus ★★ 18

Science-fiction horror
1998 · US · Colour · 95mins

A sinking tugboat crew takes refuge on a deserted Russian science vessel during a typhoon only to find it harbouring an alien energy force. John Bruno's hybrid mass of genre clichés barely entertains on a schlock level, with Jamie Lee Curtis, William Baldwin and Donald Sutherland giving undistinguished performances. AJ. Contains violence, swearing. DVD

Jamie Lee Curtis *Kit Foster* • William Baldwin *Steve Baker* • Donald Sutherland *Captain Everton* • Joanna Pacula *Nadia* • Marshall Bell *JW Woods Jr* • Julio Oscar Mechoso *Squeaky* • Sherman Augustus *Richie* • Cliff Curtis *Hiko* ■ *Dir* John Bruno • *Scr* Chuck Pfarrer, Dennis Feldman, from the comic books by Chuck Pfarrer

Vision Quest ★★ 15

Sports drama 1985 · US · Colour · 107mins

Matthew Modine stars as an overly thin high school wrestling champ, whose obsession with his sport is confused by a growing infatuation with his father's lodger Linda Fiorentino. Wrestling is a strange sport and, as a subject, makes for an even stranger movie. Fiorentino is as strong as ever and Modine just about holds his own, given the risible storyline. LH

Matthew Modine *Louden Swain* • Linda Fiorentino *Carla* • Michael Schoeffling *Kuch* • Ronny Cox *Loudon's father* • Harold Sylvester *Tanneran* • Charles Hallahan *Coach* • JC Quinn *Elmo* • Daphne Zuniga *Margie Epstein* • Forest Whitaker *Bulldozer* ■ *Dir* Harold Becker • *Scr* Darryl Ponicsan, from a novel by Terry Davis

Visions of Eight ★★

Sports documentary
1973 · US · Colour · 105mins

It was hoped that having eight directors from different nationalities working on the official film of the 1972 Munich Olympics would be symbolic of the internationalism of the sportsmen and women themselves. However, the result was a spoiled broth that gave neither statistics nor expressed any of the excitement of the events. Instead we are given a series of arty, tricksy and often spectacular moments created in a vacuum. The killing of eleven members of the Israeli team by Palestinian guerrillas is touched upon only with the memorial service. RB

Dir Yuri Ozerov, Mai Zetterling, Arthur Penn, Michael Pfleghar, Kon Ichikawa, Claude Lelouch, Milos Forman, John Schlesinger • *Scr* Deliara Ozerova, David Hughes, Arthur Penn, Michael Pfleghar, Shuntaro Tanikawa, Claude Lelouch, John Schlesinger

Visions of Light ★★★★ PG

Documentary
1992 · US/Jpn · Colour and BW · 90mins

This fascinating documentary pays handsome tribute to the forgotten artists of film, the cinematographers. Passing with regrettable speed over silent geniuses like Billy Bitzer, who truly sculpted with light, the film sings the praises of black-and-white photography and reveals how some of the most memorable images ever shot in Hollywood were achieved. The work of such master craftsmen as George Barnes, Gregg Toland, William Daniels and John Alton is illustrated with well-chosen clips and heartfelt praise from the leading lighting cameramen of today. If you've ever marvelled at an image and wondered how they did it, this is for you. DP

Todd McCarthy *Narrator* ■ *Dir* Arnold Glassman, Todd McCarthy, Stuart Samuels • *Scr* Todd McCarthy

The Visit ★★

Drama 1964 · W Ger/Fr/It/US · BW · 100mins

Ingrid Bergman is the richest woman in the world who returns to her impoverished home village. On arriving she promises the peasants riches but only if they execute Anthony Quinn – her former lover and the father of her dead child who, to save his own skin, forced her into exile and prostitution. This is a good dramatic story that might have made a western, though the original play was set in Switzerland, as is this movie version. Even Bergman can't quite bring this stodgy Euro-pudding to life. AT

Ingrid Bergman *Karla Zachanassian* • Anthony Quinn *Serge Miller* • Irina Demick *Anya* • Paolo Stoppa *Doctor* • Hans Christian Blech *Capt Dobrick* • Romolo Valli *Town painter* • Valentina Cortese *Mathilda Miller* ■ *Dir* Bernhard Wicki • *Scr* Ben Barzman, from the play by Maurice Valency, from the play *Der Besuch der alten Dame* by Friedrich Dürrenmatt

Visit to a Small Planet ★★ U

Fantasy comedy 1960 · US · BW · 85mins

Jerry Lewis is an unemotional alien visitor who comes to a small Virginian town and encounters the all too emotional inhabitants – including Joan Blackman who manages to capture Lewis's heart. Based on Gore Vidal's satirical stage play, this was another failed attempt to capture the genius of Jerry Lewis on screen. Vidal despised the movie and contemporary critics were less than enthusiastic; time has added a certain period charm, though it's still pretty wide of the mark. DF

Jerry Lewis *Kreton* • Joan Blackman *Ellen Spelding* • Earl Holliman *Conrad* • Fred Clark

Major Roger Putnam Spelding • Lee Patrick *Rheba Spelding* • Gale Gordon *Bob Mayberry* • Ellen Corby *Mrs Mayberry* ■ *Dir* Norman Taurog • *Scr* Edmund Beloin, Henry Garson, from the play by Gore Vidal

Les Visiteurs ★★★★ 15

Fantasy comedy 1993 · Fr · Colour · 102mins

A bawdy riposte to French cinema's propensity for intellectual navel-gazing, this time-travelling farce smashed box-office records on its original release. The slapstick adventures of a medieval nobleman and his squire who wind up in 1990s France will strike many as a sort of *Carry On Blackadder*. But there's also a mischievous social subtext here, as Jean Reno and Christian Clavier's search for a book of spells brings them into contact with various bourgeois caricatures. A sequel, plus a disappointing Hollywood remake, *Just Visiting* (2001), followed. DP. In French with English subtitles. Contains swearing. [VIDEO] DVD

Christian Clavier *Jacquouille La Fripouille/ Jacquart* • Jean Reno *Godefroy de Montmirail* • Valérie Lemercier *Frénégonde de Pouille/ Béatrice* • Marie-Anne Chazel *Ginette la clocharde* ■ *Dir* Jean-Marie Poiré • *Scr* Jean-Marie Poiré, Christian Clavier

Les Visiteurs 2: Les Couloirs du Temps ★★★

Fantasy comedy 1998 · Fr · Colour · 116mins

The French have never been particularly prone to sequelitis, but Jean-Marie Poiré succumbed on this occasion and made a pretty fair job of re-creating both the madcap comedy and commercial success of the original. Opening with a neat illuminated manuscript reprise, the action darts back and forth through time, as 12th-century knight Jean Reno returns to the future to avert a curse on his forthcoming marriage. Patchy, but energetically played and anarchic. DP. A French language film.

Jean Reno *Godefroy de Montmirail* • Christian Clavier *Jacquouille/Jacquart* • Muriel Robin *Béatrice/Frénégonde* • Marie-Anne Chazel *Ginette* • Christian Bujeau *Jean-Pierre* ■ *Dir* Jean-Marie Poiré • *Scr* Jean-Marie Poiré, Christian Clavier

Les Visiteurs du Soir ★★★★

Romantic fantasy 1942 · Fr · BW · 122mins

Forced by the German Occupation to make "escapist" films, the team of Marcel Carné and Jacques Prévert went back to the 15th century for this rather stilted and whimsical fairy tale. Alain Cuny and Arletty play servants of the Devil disguised as minstrels. They arrive at a wedding of a baron's daughter with the intention of causing mischief. It was seen by many of the French audiences at the time as an allegory of their situation with the Devil as Hitler (Jules Berry). Today we can enjoy the performances and the superb art design and photography. RB. In French with English subtitles.

Arletty *Dominique* • Alain Cuny *Gilles* • Jules Berry *The Devil* • Marie Déa *Anne* • Fernand Ledoux *Baron Hughes* • Marcel Herrand *Renaud* • Simone Signoret • Alain Resnais ■ *Dir* Marcel Carné • *Scr* Jacques Prévert, Pierre Laroche • *Art Director* Alexandre Trauner, Georges Wakhevitch • *Cinematographer* Roger Hubert

Visiting Hours ★★ 18

Horror thriller 1982 · Can · Colour · 99mins

A scalpel-wielding psycho stalks the wards and hallways of a major metropolitan hospital. *Star Trek*'s William Shatner, who should have beamed himself up from this one, stars along with Michael Ironside and Lee Grant in a solid, if sick, slasher movie that lingers a little too lovingly on its dirty deeds. DA [VIDEO]

Michael Ironside *Colt Hawker* • Lee Grant *Deborah Ballin* • Linda Purl *Sheila Munroe* • William Shatner *Gary Baylor* • Lenore Zann *Lisa* • Harvey Atkin *Vinnie Bradshaw* • Helen Hughes *Louise Shepherd* ■ *Dir* Jean-Claude Lord • *Scr* Brian Taggert

The Visitor ★ 18

Horror 1980 · It/US · Colour · 97mins

From opportunist producer Ovidio G Assonitis comes the Italian *Omen*, souped up with reheated sci-fi and horror leftovers from every success in the genre. A rich occultist tries to father a devil child in this incoherent mess, complete with odd special effects, weird camera angles and religious mumbo jumbo. Directors Sam Peckinpah and John Huston also appear in baffling cameo roles in this triumph of bad taste. AJ [VIDEO]

Mel Ferrer *Dr Walker* • John Huston *Jersey Colsowitz, the visitor* • Glenn Ford *Jake* • Lance Henriksen *Raymond* • Paige Conner *Katie Collins* • Joanne Nail *Barbara Collins* • Shelley Winters *Jane Phillips* • Sam Peckinpah *Sam* ■ *Dir* Michael J Paradise [Giulio Paradisi] • *Scr* Lou Comici, Robert Mundi, from a story by Michael J Paradise [Giulio Paradisi], Ovidio G Assonitis

The Visitors ★★★ 15

Drama 1972 · US · Colour · 102mins

Elia Kazan self-financed this drama on a shoestring, shooting it in and around his own New England home from a script by his son, Chris. It deals with Vietnam, showing how a GI accuses two of his confrères of raping and murdering a Vietnamese girl. After the war, the two ex-GIs show up looking for vengeance. Barely released anywhere – it had a controversial screening at Cannes, mainly because jury president Joseph Losey had a long-standing feud with Kazan over the McCarthy witch-hunts – it has many flaws, but should be seen for its treatment of a complex theme and for the feature-film debut of James Woods. AT [VIDEO]

Patrick McVey *Harry Wayne* • Patricia Joyce *Martha Wayne* • James Woods *Bill Schmidt* • Chico Martinez *Tony Rodriguez* • Steve Railsback *Mike Nickerson* ■ *Dir* Elia Kazan • *Scr* Chris Kazan

Visitors of the Night ★★ 12

Science-fiction drama
1995 · US · Colour · 90mins

Did Markie Post's daughter get abducted by aliens when she disappeared for a few hours one night? Post believes the same thing happened to her when she was a girl, so is history repeating itself? A lightweight addition to the *Communion* school of science fiction. AJ. Contains some violence, swearing. [VIDEO] DVD

Markie Post *Judith* • Candace Cameron *Katie* • Dale Midkiff *Sheriff Marcus Ashley* • Stephen McHattie *Bryan English* • Pam Hyatt *Judith's mother* • Susan Hogan *Dr Dillard* • Allan Royal *Dr Geary* ■ *Dir* Jorge Montesi • *Scr* Michael J Murray

Vital Signs ★★ 15

Drama 1990 · US · Colour · 98mins

A bunch of third-year med students live and love their way through training. Packed with all the usual medical clichés, from ward emergencies to quickies in the linen cupboard, the film is flattered by a cast that includes Adrian Pasdar, Diane Lane and Laura San Giacomo. A pre-*NYPD Blues* Jimmy Smits is especially good as the instructing surgeon, but this is routine and unmemorable. DA [VIDEO]

Adrian Pasdar *Michael Chatham* • Diane Lane *Gina Wyler* • Jack Gwaltney *Kenny Rose* • Laura San Giacomo *Lauren Rose* • Jane Adams (2) *Suzanne Maloney* • Jimmy Smits *Dr David Redding* • Tim Ransom *Bobby Hayes* ■ *Dir* Marisa Silver • *Scr* Larry Ketron, Jeb Stuart, from a story by Larry Ketron

I Vitelloni ★★★★ PG

Drama 1953 · It/Fr · BW · 103mins

Federico Fellini was trying to greenlight *La Strada* when he devised this portrait of the reckless *vitelloni* (literally "overgrown calves") he'd known during his youth in Rimini. Sketched with satirical insight, this tale focuses on five boys who are gradually forced to confront their bleak futures. At the centre of the action is a carnival, in which the buddies' costumes, masks and grotesque pranks are symbolically linked to the alienation and sexual frustration rife in early 1950s Italy. DP. In Italian with English subtitles. [VIDEO]

Franco Interlenghi *Moraldo* • Franco Fabrizi *Fausto* • Alberto Sordi *Alberto* • Leopoldo Trieste *Leopoldo* • Riccardo Fellini *Riccardo* • Elenora Ruffo *Sandra* ■ *Dir* Federico Fellini • *Scr* Federico Fellini, Ennio Flaiano, Tullio Pinelli, from a story by Federico Fellini, Ennio Flaiano, Tullio Pinelli

Viva Italia! ★★★

Portmanteau black comedy
1978 · It · Colour · 115mins

A portmanteau black comedy, made up of nine episodes designed to show that the typical Italian male is a monster. Some segments run less than five minutes while others last nearly 15, linked by a surprise ending. Three of Italy's biggest stars – Vittorio Gassman, Alberto Sordi and Ugo Tognazzi – seize their chances, either tossing food all over the kitchen, giving a lift to a crime victim in a Rolls-Royce and then chucking him out after he bleeds over the leather, or breaking a wife's legs to try to revive her fading singing career. AT. In Italian with English subtitles.

Ugo Tognazzi *The Husband* • Vittorio Gassman *The Cardinal* • Ornella Muti *The Hitchhiker* • Orietta Berti *The Singer* ■ *Dir* Mario Monicelli, Dino Risi, Ettore Scola • *Scr* Agenore Incrocci, Ruggero Maccari, Giuseppe Moccia, Ettore Scola, Bernardino Zapponi

Viva Knievel! ★★ PG

Action thriller 1977 · US · Colour · 99mins

This amazingly kitsch one-off stars the man himself – Evel Knievel, a non-actor if ever there was one – in a movie so absurd it simply has to be seen to be believed. Directed by veteran Gordon Douglas, this is vanity cinema with a vengeance: the opening sequence involving Knievel and a group of orphans is truly amazing. However, there is a real and perverse pleasure to be gained from watching the work of true professionals such as Douglas and Gene Kelly, as they manage to save this from becoming a complete laughing stock. TS [VIDEO]

Evel Knievel • Gene Kelly *Will Atkins* • Lauren Hutton *Kate Morgan* • Red Buttons *Ben Andrews* • Leslie Nielsen *Stanley Millard* • Frank Gifford • Sheila Allen *Sister Charity* • Cameron Mitchell *Barton* ■ *Dir* Gordon Douglas • *Scr* Antonio Santillan, Norman Katkov, from a story by Santillan

Viva Las Vegas ★★★★ U

Musical 1964 · US · Colour · 81mins

This is one of the last great MGM musicals, in which, for once, the fabulous Elvis Presley found himself in the hands of a good director, *Kiss Me Kate's* George Sidney, and teamed with a worthy co-star, the vivacious Ann-Margret. Choreography is by *West Side Story's* David Winters, there's wonderful Panavision cinematography by Joseph Biroc (who was camera operator on all the Astaire/Rogers musicals) and the whole glossy package is Elvis's best post-*Blue Hawaii* movie. TS [VIDEO] DVD

Elvis Presley *Lucky Jackson* • Ann-Margret *Rusty Martin* • Cesare Danova *Count Elmo Mancini* • William Demarest *Mr Martin* • Nicky Blair *Shorty Farnsworth* • Robert B Williams *Swanson* • Bob Nash *Big Gus Olson* ■ *Dir* George Sidney (2) • *Scr* Sally Benson

Viva Maria! ★★★

Comedy 1965 · Fr/It · Colour · 120mins

The pairing of Brigitte Bardot and Jeanne Moreau created enough excitement in 1965 for this to be an art house blockbuster. Bardot was France's reigning sex symbol and so was Moreau, but in artier movies, here they're singers who tussle with a typically disorganised Mexican revolution. Both actresses seem to be enjoying the occasion, as does a perfectly cast George Hamilton. Georges Delerue's songs are pleasing, and the photography is ravishingly beautiful, but the picture's length has it running out of steam. AT. In French and German with English subtitles.

Brigitte Bardot *Maria II* • Jeanne Moreau *Maria I* • George Hamilton *Florès* • Gregor von Rezzori *Diogène* • Paulette Dubost *Mme Diogène* • Carlos Lopez Moctezuma *Rodriguez* ■ *Dir* Louis Malle • *Scr* Louis Malle, Jean-Claude Carrière

Viva Max! ★★★ U

Comedy 1969 · US · Colour · 92mins

It's impossible to ignore Peter Ustinov, but try to let your eye drift away from the master scene-stealer and on to John Astin (Gomez in TV's *The Addams Family*), who gives an understated comic performance as his doltish sidekick. His twitchy idiocy stands in stark contrast to Ustinov's heavily-accented showboating as the Mexican general who leads a ramshackle band across the border in a bid to retake the Alamo. Buoyantly played, but sloppily directed. DP

Peter Ustinov *General Maximilian Rodrigues de Santos* • Pamela Tiffin *Paula Whitland* • Jonathan Winters *General Billy Joe Hallson* • John Astin *Sgt Valdez* • Keenan Wynn *General Barney LaComber* • Harry Morgan *Chief of Police George Sylvester* • Alice Ghostley *Hattie Longstreet Daniel* • Kenneth Mars *Dr Sam Gillison* ■ *Dir* Jerry Paris • *Scr* Elliot Baker, from a novel by James Lehrer

Viva Villa! ★★★

Biographical drama 1934 · US · BW · 115mins

An intelligently crafted, David O Selznick-produced MGM adventure epic, credited to director Jack Conway, but actually started by Howard Hawks. Some obvious studio-bound sequences mar enjoyment, and the whole thing is a tad overlong, but with some excellent supporting performances. Beery plays Villa, the Mexican revolutionary, as scripted by Ben Hecht, warts and all. The crowd scenes are particularly well handled (the assistant director, John Waters, received an Oscar) and the scale is undeniably epic. TS

Wallace Beery *Pancho Villa* • Fay Wray *Teresa* • Stuart Erwin *Johnny Sykes* • Leo Carillo *Sierra* • Donald Cook *Don Felipe* • George E Stone *Chavito* • Joseph Schildkraut *General Pascal* ■ *Dir* Jack Conway • *Scr* Ben Hecht, from the book by Edgcumb Pinchon, OB Stade

Viva Zapata! ★★★ PG

Biographical drama 1952 · US · BW · 108mins

Marlon Brando stars as Mexican revolutionary leader Emiliano Zapata in director Elia Kazan's celebrated drama. When the movie was first planned, producer Darryl Zanuck wanted Tyrone Power for the lead, but Kazan, who had just made *A Streetcar Named Desire*, persuaded him to go with Brando. This is a strong, exciting and heavily politicised picture, the script (by John Steinbeck) won Anthony Quinn an Oscar, playing Brando's brother and revolutionary colleague. AT. Contains violence. DVD

Marlon Brando *Emiliano Zapata* • Jean Peters *Josefa Espejo* • Anthony Quinn *Eufemio Zapata* • Joseph Wiseman *Fernando Aguirre* • Arnold Moss *Don Nacio* • Alan Reed *Pancho Villa* • Margo *La Soldadera* • Harold Gordon *Don Francisco Madero* ■ *Dir* Elia Kazan • *Scr* John Steinbeck, from the novel *Zapata the Unconquered* by Edgcumb Pichon

Vivacious Lady ★★★ U

Screwball comedy 1938 · US · BW · 90mins

Professor James Stewart tries to tell his conservative dad, the wonderfully irascible Charles Coburn, that he has married showgirl Ginger Rogers in this sparkling screwball comedy, directed by the great George Stevens. It's a funny idea, and you don't really notice that it's a one-joke movie. Super support actors include Beulah Bondi, playing slightly against type as Stewart's mum, and lovable Hattie McDaniel. TS

Ginger Rogers *Frances Brent* • James Stewart *Peter Morgan* • James Ellison *Keith Beston* • Charles Coburn *Doctor Morgan* • Beulah Bondi *Mrs Morgan* • Frances Mercer *Helen* • Phyllis Kennedy *Jenny* • Alec Craig *Joseph* • Franklin Pangborn *Apartment manager* • Grady Sutton *Culpepper* • Hattie McDaniel *Hattie, the maid* • Jack Carson *Charlie, the waiter captain* ■ *Dir* George Stevens • *Scr* PJ Wolfson, Ernest Pagano, by I AR Wylie

Vive L'Amour ★★★★ 15

Drama 1994 · Tai · Colour · 117mins

Virtually silent, yet saying more about urban alienation than the most eloquent of screenplays, this is a saturnine study of life in modern Taipei. Exploring the socio-economic ironies of a city with a surplus of accommodation and a shortage of graves, Tsai Ming-liang notes how easily people lose the ability to communicate once ambition is turned to despair. He's admirably served by a sensitive cast, led by Yang Kuei-Mei as the estate agent who begins a passionless relationship with street vendor Chen Chao-jung, unaware that they are being observed by Lee Kang-sheng, a gay suicidal cemetery salesman squatting in one of Yang's properties. DP. In Mandarin with English subtitles.

Yang Kuei-Mei *May* • Chen Chao-jung *Ah-jung* • Lee Kang-sheng *Hsiao-kang* ■ *Dir* Tsai Ming-liang • *Scr* Tsai Ming-liang, Tsai Yi-chun, Yang Pi-ying

The Vivero Letter ★★ 18

Action adventure 1998 · US · Colour · 92mins

After travelling to Costa Rica to deliver a prized Mayan plate to his brother, insurance assessor Robert Patrick finds himself assailed from all sides, not to mention being unsure whether to trust either of his companions – Italian academic Chiara Caselli or American bounty hunter Fred Ward. This action adventure has all the hallmarks of a straight-to-video production: flabby direction, haphazard editing and decidedly amateur supporting performances. DP

Robert Patrick *James Wheeler* • Fred Ward *Andrew Fallon* • Chiara Caselli *Caterina Cararra* ■ *Dir* H Gordon Boos • *Scr* Denne Bart Petitclerc, Arthur Sellers, from the novel by Desmond Bagley

Vivre pour Vivre ★

Romantic drama 1967 · Fr · Colour · 130mins

Despite the talents of Yves Montand and Candice Bergen, this sun-saturated, overstylised and poorly scripted film couldn't be worse. Montand plays a TV reporter who is married to Annie Girardot, but is unable to resist the charms of super-glamorous model Bergen. Cue an all too familiar love triangle with lashings of sex and tears, accompanied by a terrible soundtrack. LH. In French with English subtitles.

Yves Montand *Robert Colomb* • Candice Bergen *Candice* • Annie Girardot *Catherine Colomb* • Irène Tunc *Mireille* • Anouk Ferjac *Jacqueline* ■ *Dir* Claude Lelouch • *Scr* Claude Lelouch, Pierre Uytterhoeven

Vivre Sa Vie ★★★★★ 15

Drama 1962 · Fr · BW · 83mins

Jean-Luc Godard's New Wave masterpiece concerns a prostitute who maintains a sort of spiritual integrity before falling victim to gangsters. Abandoning conventional narrative, Godard offers the story as 12 chapters and names his heroine Nana, after Zola's heroine; he also has her go to the cinema to see Carl Theodor Dreyer's legendary silent classic about another martyr, Joan of Arc. The then frank depiction of sex earned the film a certain notoriety, not to mention the application of the British censor's scissors. Now, though, what's most noticeable is Godard's technique and the luminous filming of Anna Karina, who had just become the director's wife and here gives a marvellous performance. AT. In French with English subtitles. DVD

Anna Karina *Nana Kleinfrankenheim* • Sady Rebbot *Raoul* • André S Labarthe *Paul* • Guylaine Schlumberger *Yvette* • Jean-Luc Godard *Voice* ■ *Dir* Jean-Luc Godard • *Scr* Jean-Luc Godard, with additional narrative from *Où en Est la Prostitution* by Judge Marcel Sacotte and from the short story *The Oval Portrait* by Edgar Allen Poe

Vixen! ★★★★ 18

Cult sex satire 1968 · US · Colour · 72mins

The one genuinely erotic movie made by cult director Russ Meyer. A huge box-office hit, it led him to mainstream Hollywood and his stunning trash satire *Beyond the Valley of the Dolls*. Pneumatic Erica Gavin is the Canadian nymphomaniac of the title, a pun on the then popular lesbian drama *The Fox*. Meyer got his explosive sexual cocktail past the censors of the day (not in Britain, though!) by cleverly incorporating the hot contemporary issues of racism, communism and Vietnam into his histrionic mix. Gavin rises to the occasion with a truthful abandon and conviction rarely seen in the soft-core genre. AJ. Contains swearing, sex scenes. DVD

Erica Gavin *Vixen Palmer* • Harrison Page *Niles* • Garth Pillsbury *Tom Palmer* • Michael Donovan O'Donnell *O'Bannion* • Vincene Wallace *Janet King* • Jon Evans *Jud* • Robert Aitken *Dave King* ■ *Dir* Russ Meyer • *Scr* Robert Rudelson, from a story by Russ Meyer, Anthony James Ryan

Vizontele ★★★ 15

Comedy 2001 · Tur · Colour · 110mins

A huge hit in its native Turkey, this is a genial, but slyly barbed social comedy, set in a tightly knit community divided by the intrusion of the outside world. The bone of contention is the first TV set to arrive in a small southern village in 1974. The mayor, Altan Erkekli, sees it as a symbol of progress, but outdoor cinema owner Cezmi Baskin considers it a threat to his perilous business and tries to convince patrons the "vision-tele" is an affront to Islam. DP. In Turkish with English subtitles. Contains swearing.

Yilmaz Erdogan *Deli Emin* • Demet Akbag *Siti Ana* • Altan Erkekli *Nazmi* • Cem Yilmaz *Sitki* • Cezmi Baskin *Latif* ■ *Dir* Yilmaz Erdogan, Omer Faruk Sorak • *Scr* Yilmaz Erdogan

Vizontele Tuuba ★★★ 12A

Comedy 2003 · Tur · Colour · 110mins

This sequel was an even bigger hit at the Turkish box office than its predecessor. Yet, there's also a darker tone to the satire, as Yilmaz Erdogan explores the combustible political situation that existed in the summer of 1980. As before, the citizens of the isolated mountain town are divided, this time into two political parties whose policies are an irrelevance. But equally contentious are the fate of the new library (which has no books) and the beautiful daughter of a civil servant. DP. In Turkish with English subtitles. Contains swearing.

Yilmaz Erdogan *Crazy Emin* • Demet Akbag *Siti Ana* • Altan Erkekli *Mayor Nazmi* • Tarik Akan *Guner Semikli* • Tuba Unsal *Tuuba Semikli* • Tolga Cevik *Nafiz* ■ *Dir/Scr* Yilmaz Erdogan

Vladimir et Rosa ★★★

Experimental political drama
1970 · Fr/W Ger/US · Colour · 103mins

Ostensibly, this one of Jean-Luc Godard and Jean-Pierre Gorin's Dziga-Vertov experiments, is a reconstruction of the Chicago Seven conspiracy trial. But Godard's main purpose is to explore the film-making process, from the technical and artistic choices involved to the compromises that inevitably have to be made. Comprising peeks at the off-stage lives of the characters and tactical discussions between the directors, the film alights on everything from the Black Panthers to radical feminism. DP. In French with English subtitles.

Jean-Luc Godard *Jean-Luc Godard/Vladimir Lenin* • Jean-Pierre Gorin *Jean-Pierre Gorin/Karl Rosa (after Rosa Luxemburg)* • Anne Wiazemsky *Ann, women's liberation militant* • Juliet Berto *Juliet/Weatherwoman/Hippie* • Yves Alfonso *Yves, revolutionary student from Berkeley* ■ *Dir/Scr* Jean-Luc Godard, Jean-Pierre Gorin

Vodka Lemon ★★★★ PG

Comedy drama
2003 · Fr/It/Swi/Arm · Colour · 86mins

Kurdish director Hiner Saleem evokes the wry observational humour of Otar Iosseliani in this gentle take on life in post-Soviet Armenia. The story of elderly Romen Avinian's cemetery encounters with widow Lala Sarkissian is consistently charming and proves more engaging than sub-plots involving Avinian's sons and his granddaughter's wedding. But it's the community that Saleem assembles around the reticent couple – including such eccentrics as a bed-ridden flautist, a singing bus driver and a galloping horseman – that gives the comedy its satirical edge and keeps despair at bay. DP. In Armenian with English subtitles. DVD

Romen Avinian *Hamo* • Lala Sarkissian *Nina* • Ivan Franek *Dilovan* • Armen Marouthian *Romik* • Astrik Avaguian *Avin* ■ *Dir* Hiner Saleem • *Scr* Hiner Saleem, Lei Dinety, Pauline Gouzenne

Vogues of 1938 ★★★

Musical comedy 1937 · US · Colour · 108mins

A breathtaking and, unusually, blonde Joan Bennett stars as an impoverished debutante who ditches hateful millionaire Alan Mowbray at the altar and goes to work as a model at New York's top fashion house, only to fall for its owner, Warner Baxter. However, the plot – involving dirty tricks from rival designer Mischa Auer and romantic complications – is totally unimportant to a film whose *raison d'être* is high fashion. And what fashion it is – an extravaganza of magnificent clothes donned by America's top models of the time, plus a pageant of outrageous costumes worn by Park Avenue matrons at the Seven Arts Ball. RK

Warner Baxter *George Curson* • Joan Bennett *Wendy Van Klettering* • Helen Vinson *Mary Curson* • Mischa Auer *Prince Muratorv* • Alan Mowbray *Henry Morgan* • Jerome Cowan *Mr Brockton* • Alma Kruger *Sophie Miller* • Marjorie Gateson *Mrs Lemke* • Hedda Hopper *Mrs Van Klettering* ■ *Dir* Irving Cummings • *Scr* Bella Spewack, Samuel Spewack • *Costume Designer* Helen Taylor

Voice in the Mirror ★★★

Drama 1958 · US · BW · 102mins

This second cousin to the screen's classic study of alcoholism, *The Lost Weekend* (1945), charts the decline of successful LA commercial artist Richard Egan who, after his daughter dies, takes refuge in the bottle, despite the support and sympathy of his wife Julie London and his doctor Walter Matthau. Rather wafty and sentimental, but this modest and non-starry movie does fine in the wake of its hard-hitting predecessor. RK

Richard Egan *Jim Burton* • Julie London *Ellen Burton* • Walter Matthau *Dr Leon Karnes* • Arthur O'Connell *William Tobin* • Ann Doran *Mrs Devlin* • Bart Bradley *Gene Devlin* • Hugh Sanders *Mr Hornsby* ■ *Dir* Harry Keller • *Scr* Larry Marcus

Voice of Merrill ★★

Mystery 1952 · UK · BW · 81mins

This complex and rather dull suspenser has Valerie Hobson and James Robertson-Justice as a husband and wife under suspicion for murdering a blackmailer. A talent much stronger than John Gilling's (who both wrote and directed this tosh) was needed to bring off this tale of murder among the plummy voices, but these days there's pleasure to be gained just from watching the elegant cast go through their preposterous paces. TS

Valerie Hobson *Alycia Roach* • Edward Underdown *Hugh Allen* • James Robertson-Justice *Jonathan Roach* • Henry Kendall *Ronald Parker* ■ *Dir* John Gilling • *Scr* John Gilling, from a story by Gerald Landeau, Terence Austin

Voice of the Turtle ★★★

Comedy drama 1947 · US · BW · 102mins

During the Second World War, a lonely soldier on leave in New York meets an actress suffering from a broken love affair and falls for her. The synopsis belies a tender, sophisticated, witty Broadway romantic comedy hit, which was still running when the movie opened. Ronald Reagan, in one of his more distinguished outings, is excellent, although outshone by his co-stars Eleanor Parker and the brilliantly acerbic, wisecracking Eve Arden as her friend. The original three-handed play was opened out slightly and some characters added for the movie. RK

Ronald Reagan *Sgt Bill Page* • Eleanor Parker *Sally Middleton* • Eve Arden *Olive Lashbrooke* • Wayne Morris *Cmdr Ned Burling* • Kent Smith *Kenneth Bartlett* ■ *Dir* Irving Rapper • *Scr* John Van Druten, Charles Hoffman, from the play by John Van Druten

Voices ★★ 15

Drama 1979 · US · Colour · 101mins

This rock-singer story has an idea so far-fetched it has jet lag. Michael Ontkean is the wannabe rocker who falls in love with deaf Amy Irving who – perhaps because of her deafness – falls in love with him. A story as silly as this requires more careful direction than it gets from Robert Markowitz. TH

Michael Ontkean *Drew Rothman* • Amy Irving *Rosemarie Lemon* • Alex Rocco *Frank Rothman* • Barry Miller *Raymond Rothman* ■ *Dir* Robert Markowitz • *Scr* John Herzfeld

V

Volcano ★★

Drama 1950 · It · BW · 106mins

In the early 1950s William Dieterle was tainted – but never officially blacklisted – by the McCarthy witch-hunts, so he fled to Europe and made this drama in the neorealist style of *Stromboli*, which it closely resembles as it was shot in the same location. Anna Magnani stars as a Naples prostitute, sentenced by the courts to return to her village on a volcanic island where life is as harsh as a prison sentence. Rossano Brazzi, a man with a past and not much of a future, arrives and upsets the apple cart. AT. An Italian language film.

Anna Magnani *Maddalena Natoli* • Rossano Brazzi *Donato* • Geraldine Brooks *Maria* • Eduardo Ciannelli *Giulio* ■ *Dir* William Dieterle • *Scr* Piero Tellini, Victor Stoloff, Erskine Caldwell, from a story by Renzo Avanzo

Volcano ★★★ 12

Disaster thriller 1997 · US · Colour · 99mins

Emergency chief Tommy Lee Jones has to save Los Angeles from being covered by molten lava in this taut, effects-laden disaster movie. Director Mick Jackson uses the simple suspense device of cross-cutting, as the cast members go about their daily activities with magma bubbling menacingly just under LA's threatened streets. The digital special effects come into their own when the city is awash with rivers of fire and the urban destruction goes into overdrive. Gripping and spectacular. AJ. Contains swearing and violence. DVD

Tommy Lee Jones *Mike Roark* • Anne Heche *Dr Amy Barnes* • Gaby Hoffman [Gaby Hoffmann] *Kelly Roark* • Don Cheadle *Emmit Reese* • Jacqueline Kim *Dr Jaye Calder* • Keith David *Lieutenant Ed Fox* • John Corbett *Norman Calder* • Michael Rispoli *Gator Harris* ■ *Dir* Mick Jackson • *Scr* Jerome Armstrong, from a story by Billy Ray

Volere, Volare ★★★★ 15

Part-animated romantic fantasy
1991 · It · Colour · 91mins

Even though Maurizio Nichetti and Guido Manuli ingeniously combine live-action and animated footage in this endlessly inventive comedy, it's the noises that linger in the memory. As the exacting sound editor who begins to turn into a cartoon on encountering kinky hooker Angela Finocchiaro, Nichetti combines slapstick and psychological humour to great effect. Things get off to a sluggish start, but once animated animals and Nichetti's pornographer brother start interfering in his love life, the action becomes increasingly amusing and audacious. DP. In Italian with English subtitles. Contains nudity.

Angela Finocchiaro *Martina* • Maurizio Nichetti *Maurizio* • Mariella Valentini *Loredana* • Patrizio Roversi *Patrizio* • Remo Remotti *Professor Bambino* ■ *Dir* Maurizio Nichetti, Guido Manuli, Walter Cavazutti • *Scr* Maurizio Nichetti, Guido Manuli

Les Voleurs ★★ 18

Thriller 1996 · Fr · Colour · 111mins

By shuffling perspectives and alternating time frames, André Téchiné makes a bold assault here on the structure of the traditional police drama. But in seeking to show that truth is often fragmentary, he concentrates too much on technique, with too little emotion expended on his characters. The action centres primarily on the relationship between tomboy shoplifter Laurence Côte, Daniel Auteuil (a cop in a family of thieves) and lesbian philosophy teacher Catherine Deneuve. DP. In French with English subtitles. Contains sex scenes, swearing, violence.

Catherine Deneuve *Marie* • Daniel Auteuil *Alex* • Laurence Côte *Juliette* • Benoît Magimel *Jimmy* • Fabienne Babe *Mireille* • Didier Bezace *Ivan* • Julien Rivière *Justin* ■ *Dir* André Téchiné • *Scr* André Téchiné, Gilles Taurand, Michel Alexandre, Pascal Bonitzer

Volpone ★★★

Comedy 1941 · Fr · BW · 94mins

Made before the outbreak of war, this handsome version of Ben Jonson's classic comedy was released during the occupation of France. It starred the great French actor Harry Baur in the title role, who had a Jewish wife and had played Jewish roles since the silent days. In 1943 after the film was shown, he was arrested, strenuously tortured by the Gestapo and died a few days later. Directed by Maurice Tourneur, the film altered the central characterisation but otherwise acknowledged its origins with stylish visuals and memorable performances. BB. In French with English subtitles.

Harry Baur *Volpone* • Louis Jouvet *Mosca* • Fernand Ledoux *Corvino* • Marion Dorian *Canina* • Jean Temerson *Voltore* • Alexandre Rignault *Leone* ■ *Dir* Maurice Tourneur • *Scr* Jules Romains, from the play by Ben Jonson

Volunteers ★★ 15

Comedy 1985 · US · Colour · 102mins

Tom Hanks is reunited with his *Splash* co-star John Candy for this clumsy, but occasionally amusing outing. Hanks plays the arrogant heir running away from his gambling debts who joins the Peace Corps in the early 1960s and gets caught up with Asian warlords, communist guerrillas and the CIA. Candy steals the show playing an earnest patriot brainwashed into becoming a Maoist revolutionary, but director Nicholas Meyer plays down the satirical opportunities of the plot in the search for easy laughs. JF. Contains violence, swearing.

Tom Hanks *Lawrence Bourne III* • John Candy *Tom Tuttle From Tacoma* • Rita Wilson *Beth Wexler* • Tim Thomerson *John Reynolds* • Gedde Watanabe *At Toon* • George Plimpton *Lawrence Bourne Jr* • Ernest Harada *Chung Mee* ■ *Dir* Nicholas Meyer • *Scr* Ken Levine, David Isaacs, from a story by Keith Critchlow

Von Richthofen and Brown ★★ PG

War action drama
1971 · US · Colour · 92mins

Also known as *The Red Baron*, this epic was released in the slipstream of *The Blue Max* and though it's often cheap and tawdry, it also looks more like an A movie than anything else made by B-movie supremo Roger Corman. The legendary German flying ace von Richthofen is played by John Phillip Law and his Canadian rival, Roy Brown, is played by Don Stroud. One has a phony German accent, the other doesn't and both are conceived as *Boys' Own* cardboard cut-outs. AT

John Phillip Law *Baron von Richthofen* • Don Stroud *Roy Brown* • Barry Primus *Hermann Goering* • Karen Huston *Ilse* • Corin Redgrave *Hawker* • Hurd Hatfield *Fokker* • George Armitage *Wolff* • Stephen McHattie *Voss* ■ *Dir* Roger Corman • *Scr* John William Corrington, Joyce Hooper Corrington

Von Ryan's Express ★★★ PG

Second World War drama
1965 · US · Colour · 111mins

This rattlingly exciting Second World War escape adventure has a well cast Frank Sinatra as a tough PoW who seizes a German train delivering Allied prisoners. Sinatra's character is unusually uncompromising, even for him, and the star delivers one of his best performances. Director Mark Robson uses his camera skilfully, and the support cast, including Trevor Howard, is exceptionally well chosen. The film was a major commercial success in its day. TS. In English and German with subtitles. DVD

Frank Sinatra *Col Joseph L Ryan* • Trevor Howard *Major Eric Fincham* • James Brolin *Private Ames* • Raffaela Carra *Gabriella* • Brad Dexter *Sergeant Bostick* • Sergio Fantoni *Captain Oriani* • John Leyton *Orde* • Edward Mulhare *Costanzo* • Wolfgang Preiss *Major von Klemment* ■ *Dir* Mark Robson • *Scr* Wendell Mayes, Joseph Landon, from a novel by David Westheimer

Voodoo Man ★

Horror 1944 · US · BW · 62mins

Bela Lugosi continued his downward career trend in this Monogram mediocrity as mad Dr Marlowe, the lunatic occultist who kidnaps women to transfer their souls into his comatose wife, who has been in a permanent trance for over 20 years. Viewing this chronic schlock ordeal would make anyone equally catatonic. AJ

Bela Lugosi *Dr Richard Marlowe* • John Carradine *Toby* • George Zucco *Nicolas* • Michael Ames [Tod Andrews] *Ralph Dawson* • Wanda McKay *Betty Benton* • Ellen Hall *Mrs Evelyn Marlowe* ■ *Dir* William Beaudine • *Scr* Robert Charles

Voodoo Woman ★ PG

Horror 1957 · US · BW · 67mins

A mad professor carries out horrible experiments on a young (and beautiful, of course) woman. The stilted acting and dialogue may raise a laugh for some fans of this sort of cult nonsense, but one thing is for sure, no one will be remotely frightened by it. JF DVD

Marla English *Marilyn Blanchard* • Tom Conway *Dr Roland Gerard* • Touch Connors [Mike Connors] *Ted Bronson* • Lance Fuller *Rick/Harry* • Mary Ellen Kaye *Susan* • Paul Dubov *Marcel the Innkeeper* ■ *Dir* Edward L Cahn • *Scr* Russell Bender, VI Voss

Vote for Huggett ★★ U

Comedy 1948 · UK · BW · 81mins

The endearing Huggett family first appeared as characters in *Holiday Camp*. After *Here Come the Huggetts*, this was the second of three films following their progress. Later a long-running radio series ensured their popularity. Here, Joe is standing for election as a councillor but runs into trouble when he proposes a war memorial site on land part-owned by his wife. Jack Warner and Kathleen Harrison are wonderful as mum and dad and young Diana Dors plays the troublesome niece. BB

Jack Warner *Joe Huggett* • Kathleen Harrison *Ethel Huggett* • Susan Shaw *Susan Huggett* • Petula Clark *Pet Huggett* • David Tomlinson *Harold Hinchley* • Diana Dors *Diana* • Peter Hammond *Peter Hawtrey* • Amy Veness *Grandma* ■ *Dir* Ken Annakin • *Scr* Mabel Constanduros, Denis Constanduros, Allan Mackinnon, from characters created by Godfrey Winn

The Voyage ★★

Drama 1974 · It · Colour · 101mins

This dreary and ill-cast commercial disaster is based upon Pirandello's tale of two lovers – not allowed to marry – who find themselves destroyed by fate. Neither Sophia Loren nor Richard Burton seem comfortable here, and it's depressing to discover that it was directed by the once-great neorealist genius Vittorio De Sica. There's effective support from Ian Bannen, but the dubbing of the Italian supports leaves much to be desired. TS. Italian dialogue dubbed into English.

Sophia Loren *Adriana* • Richard Burton *Cesar* • Ian Bannen *Antonio* • Renato Pinciroli *Doctor* • Daniele Pitani *Notary* • Barbara Pilavin *Mother* • Sergio Bruni *Armando Gill* ■ *Dir* Vittorio De Sica • *Scr* Diego Fabbri, Massimo Franciosa, Luisa Montagnana, from a play by Luigi Pirandello

The Voyage ★★★ 15

Political satire
1991 · Arg/Fr · Colour · 133mins

This pessimistic odyssey through Latin America laments not only the lingering legacy of oppression and neglect, but also the intrusive and exploitative presence of the United States. Travelling by bicycle from the world's southernmost city, Ushaia, in search of his anthropologist father, Walter Quiroz responds to such sights as flooded valleys, remote villages, rickety gold mines and jungle outposts with a mix of awe and disillusion. But, for all its arresting imagery, the film lacks thematic focus. DP. In Spanish with English subtitles.

Walter Quiroz *Martin* • Soledad Alfaro *Vidala* • Ricardo Bartis *Monitor* • Cristina Becerra *Violeta* • Marc Berman *Nicolás* • Chiquinho Brandao *Paizinho* • Franklin Caicedo *Rower* ■ *Dir/Scr* Fernando E Solanas

Voyage ★★ 15

Drama 1993 · US · Colour · 85mins

Rutger Hauer sleepwalks his way through this routine straight-to-video thriller, which unsuccessfully attempts to cash in on the success of *Dead Calm*. Hauer and Karen Allen play a couple who rather unwisely decide to repair their marriage by taking a sea cruise with charming, but psychotic Eric Roberts and his girlfriend, Connie Nielsen. Despite the quality cast, there's little in the way of suspense. JF. Contains violence, sex scenes and swearing.

Rutger Hauer *Morgan Norvell* • Eric Roberts *Gil Freeland* • Karen Allen *Catherine "Kit" Norvell* • Connie Nielsen *Ronnie Freeland* ■ *Dir* John Mackenzie • *Scr* Mark Montgomery, from a story by Mark Montgomery, Khris Baxter

Le Voyage dans la Lune ★★★★★

Silent science-fiction 1902 · Fr · BW · 14mins

A cornerstone of narrative cinema – and probably celluloid's first foray into science fiction – Georges Méliès's beautifully designed space adventure about an exploratory trip to the moon comprises 31 scenes – each one a *tableau vivant* shot front on from a stationary camera – whose most famous shot depicts a rocket landing in the Man in the Moon's eye. Drawing from the writings of Jules Verne and HG Wells, this early treasure offers much more in the way of a league of swimsuited beauties waving off the intrepid (and rather aged) members of the Astronomic Club followed by a lunar encounter with the hostile Selenites. An inspired masterwork from a true visionary of early cinema. DP

Georges Méliès *Professor Barbenfouillis* • Bleuette Bernon *La lune* ■ *Dir* Georges Méliès • *Scr* Georges Méliès, from the works of Jules Vernes, HG Wells • *Cinematographer* Lucien Tainguy, Michaut

Voyage into Prehistory ★★★★

Part-animated fantasy
1955 · Cz · BW · 87mins

This was the first feature to boast full-colour stop-motion animation. Unfortunately, much of Karel Zeman's achievement was corrupted by William Clayton's 1966 US reissue, which incorporated thumbnail palentological information to bring an unnecessary educational dimension to the time-travelling adventures of four boys in a cave beneath New York's Central Park. What remains unimpeachable, however, is the scope of Zeman's imagination, the beauty of his stylised backdrops and the ingenuity of his combination of live/animatronic and animated footage. Ranging from woolly rhinos to a battling stegosaurus, the prehistoric menagerie includes more than the predictably rampaging carnivores to truly suggest a lost world. DP. A Czech language film.

Vladimir Bejval *Jirka* • Petr Hermann *Tonik/Tony* • Zdenek Hustak *Jenda* • Josef Lukas *Petr* • James Lucas *Doc (US sequences)* • Victor Betral *Joe/"Jo-Jo" (US sequences)* • Charles Goldsmith *Ben (US sequences)* ■ *Dir* Karel Zeman • *Scr* JA Novotny, Karel Zeman, William Cayton (US sequences), Fred Ladd (US sequences)

Voyage of the Damned ★★ PG

Drama based on a true story
1976 · UK · Colour · 174mins

This drama from director Stuart Rosenberg is based on the real-life voyage of the SS *St Louis*, which set sail for Cuba in 1939 with 937 Jewish refugees on board, only to be forced back to Europe when it was refused a berth. As the ship's captain, Max von Sydow brings some much needed gravitas to the proceedings, but the script is desperate and the direction unbearably ponderous. The odds against so many star names giving such bad performances in the same film are incalculable. A miserable memorial to a tragic event. DP

Faye Dunaway *Denise Kreisler* • Max von Sydow *Captain Gustav Schroeder* • Oskar Werner *Dr Egon Kreisler* • Malcolm McDowell *Max* • James Mason *Dr Juan Remos* • Orson Welles *Jose Estedes* • Katharine Ross *Mira Hauser* • Ben Gazzara *Morris Troper* • Lee Grant *Lili Rosen* • Sam Wanamaker *Carl Rosen* • Lynne Frederick *Anna Rosen* • Julie Harris *Alice Feinchild* ■ *Dir* Stuart Rosenberg • *Scr* Steve Shagan, David Butler, from the book by Max Morgan-Witts, Gordon Thomas

Voyage to Cythera ★★★★

Drama 1984 · Gr · Colour · 120mins

Returning home after 32 years exiled in the Soviet Union, Manos Katrakis refuses to discuss his past regrets or hopes for the future. But rather than settle into *ennui*, he follows the example of Odysseus in pre-Homeric legend and makes for Cythera, the island of dreams and domain of Aphrodite, to continue his lifelong pursuit of happiness. Dispirited by the depoliticisation of Greek society – what he called "the silence of history" – Theo Angelopoulos sets out to contrast the truths inherent in myth and reality in this complex, but always fascinating drama that makes densely symbolic use of the evocative landscape. DP. In Greek with English subtitles.

Manos Katrakis *Old man* • Mary Chronopoulou *Voula* • Dora Volanaki *Old woman* • Giulio Brogi *Alexandros* ■ *Dir* Theo Angelopoulos • *Scr* Theo Angelopoulos, Thanassis Valtinos, Tonino Guerra

Voyage to the Bottom of the Sea ★★★ U

Science-fiction adventure
1961 · US · Colour · 100mins

Walter Pidgeon and Joan Fontaine are top billed in this entertaining sci-fi outing, but the real star is the submarine *Seaview*. Accounting for $400,000 of the picture's budget, the glass-fronted nuclear sub went on to star in its own TV series following its exploits here, as admiral Pidgeon fires its missiles into the Van Allen radiation belt and saves Earth from meltdown. Fontaine is totally out of her depth, but Peter Lorre and the rest of the cast are splendid. Co-writer/producer/director Irwin Allen went on to become the king of the disaster movie in the early 1970s. DP DVD

Walter Pidgeon *Admiral Harriman Nelson* • Joan Fontaine *Dr Susan Hiller* • Barbara Eden *Cathy Connors* • Peter Lorre *Commodore Lucius Emery* • Robert Sterling *Capt Lee Crane* • Michael Ansara *Miguel Alvarez* • Frankie Avalon *Chip Romano* • Regis Toomey *Dr Jamieson* ■ *Dir* Irwin Allen • *Scr* Irwin Allen, Charles Bennett, from a story by Allen

Voyage to the Planet of Prehistoric Women ★

Science-fiction fantasy
1966 · US · Colour · 78mins

Following *Voyage to the Prehistoric Planet*, this also recycles special effects highlights from the 1962 Russian science-fiction spectacle *Planeta Burg*. A disorientating dog's dinner of a movie with new footage shot by Peter Bogdanovich, it features 1950s' sex bomb Mamie Van Doren as the leader of a tribe of bikini-clad alien maidens. None of the new scenes really match in this tortuously repackaged exploiter. AJ

Mamie Van Doren *Moana* • Mary Mark • Paige Lee ■ *Dir* Derek Thomas [Peter Bogdanovich] • *Scr* Henry Ney

Voyage to the Prehistoric Planet ★

Fantasy 1965 · US · Colour · 80mins

Roger Corman used cannibalised footage from the 1962 Russian space epic *Planeta Burg* and incorporated new material shot by director Curtis Harrington. A spaceship crew crash-land on a planet and relay their encounters with robot men and dinosaurs to a space platform orbiting above them. As was often the case with Corman quickies of the 1960s, the story behind the movie is more interesting than the movie itself. AJ

Basil Rathbone *Professor Hartman* • Faith Domergue *Marcia* ■ *Dir/Scr* John Sebastian [Curtis Harrington]

Voyager ★★★ 15

Drama
1991 · Ger/Fr/Gr · Colour and BW · 108mins

A complex drama with the always impressive Sam Shepard as a Unesco worker and compulsive traveller who drifts through Europe and across the Atlantic on an ocean liner in search of love and the meaning of life. He's haunted by an affair from his past and a new romance with a young woman only takes him further back in time. Director Volker Schlöndorff cleverly conveys the mood of postwar Europe, and, even though the locations veer far and wide, the main aim of the story is to journey inside Shepard's head. AT. Contains sex scenes.

Sam Shepard *Walter Faber* • Julie Delpy *Sabeth* • Barbara Sukowa *Hannah* • Dieter Kirchlechner *Herbert Hencke* • Deborra-Lee Furness *Ivy* • Traci Lind *Charlene* • August Zirner *Joachim* ■ *Dir* Volker Schlöndorff • *Scr* Rudy Wurlitzer, from the novel *Homo Faber* by Max Frisch

Voyages ★★★

Drama 1999 · Fr/Pol · Colour · 115mins

This emotive, if airless, drama centres on three elderly female Holocaust survivors. Israeli Shulamit Adar suffers a breakdown while revisiting Auschwitz and the Warsaw Ghetto. Meanwhile Russian emigré Esther Gorintin searches Tel Aviv for her long-lost cousin, while Parisian Liliane Rovère receives a call from a man claiming to be the father she thought had perished in the camps 50 years before. Emmanuel Finkiel directs with studied reverence, yet this does a disservice to the doughty dignity of his non-professional leads. DP. In French and Yiddish with English subtitles.

Shulamit Adar *Rivka* • Liliane Rovère *Régine* • Esther Gorintin *Vera* • Moscu Alcalay *Shimon* • Maurice Chevit *Mendlebaum* • Natan Cogan *Graneck* ■ *Dir/Scr* Emmanuel Finkiel

Vroom ★★ 15

Road movie drama
1988 · UK · Colour · 84mins

David Thewlis and Clive Owen hope to fulfil their dreams by hitting the open road in a classic American car they have lovingly restored. Unfortunately, they also take along a sultry divorcee, and soon the libidos and tensions begin to rise. Although nothing more than a formulaic road movie with a few quirky twists, the acting from the leads makes it worthwhile. AJ

Clive Owen *Jake* • David Thewlis *Ringe* • Diana Quick *Susan* • Jim Broadbent *Donald* • Philip Tan *Shane* ■ *Dir* Beeban Kidron • *Scr* Jim Cartwright

The Vulture ★★

Horror 1966 · US/Can/UK · Colour · 90mins

This horror film about a giant bird (loose in a Cornwall largely populated by Americans) is ludicrous, tortuous and about as horrific as the average episode of *Doctor Who*. The shots of big claws landing on victims' shoulders are fun, but to get to them you have to wade through a truly astonishing amount of walking in and out of rooms, and getting in and out of cars. The acting is mostly grim although Akim Tamiroff, as the inevitable mysterious professor, is rather grand. Released to cinemas in black and white, this can now be seen in its original colour version. DM

Robert Hutton *Eric Lutyens* • Akim Tamiroff *Professor Koniglich* • Broderick Crawford *Brian Stroud* • Diane Clare *Trudy Lutyens* • Philip Friend *Vicar* • Patrick Holt *Jarvis* ■ *Dir/Scr* Lawrence Huntington

W ★★ 15

Thriller 1974 · US · Colour · 91mins

This humdrum thriller is something of a comedown for director Richard Quine. Former fashion model Twiggy plays an amnesiac recovering from an abusive first marriage, but then her new marriage is disrupted when she is pursued by a mysterious attacker. Naturally, her first husband (Dirk Benedict) is the prime suspect. If only Twiggy could have acted, this might have been plausible. TH

Twiggy *Katie Lewis* • Michael Witney *Ben Lewis* • Eugene Roche *Charles Jasper* • Dirk Benedict *William Caulder* • John Vernon *Arnie Felson* • Michael Conrad *Lt Whitfield* ■ *Dir* Richard Quine • *Scr* Gerald Di Pego, James Kelly, from the story *Chance for a Killing* by Ronald Shusett

WC Fields and Me ★★★

Biographical drama
1976 · US · Colour · 111mins

Lambasted on release for taking liberties with the truth, Arthur Hiller's biopic of famed tippler comedian WC Fields (Rod Steiger) is still impressive. Covering the life of the vaudevillian-turned-film-star from the perspective of his lover Carlotta Monti, there's a feel of the real in its re-creation of the Hollywood of long ago. Like Fields, Steiger never lets you forget he's the star, but there are sterling support performances from Valerie Perrine and Bernadette Peters among others. DA

Rod Steiger *WC Fields* • Valerie Perrine *Carlotta Monti* • John Marley *Studio Head Bannerman* • Jack Cassidy *John Barrymore* • Bernadette Peters *Melody* • Dana Elcar *Agent Dockstedter* • Paul Stewart *Florenz Ziegfeld* • Billy Barty *Ludwig* ■ *Dir* Arthur Hiller • *Scr* Bob Merrill, from the book by Carlotta Monti, Cy Rice • *Music* Henry Mancini

WR – Mysteries of the Organism ★★★ 18

Experimental documentary drama
1971 · Yug · Colour · 79mins

The WR of the title is Wilhelm Reich, the Austrian-born sexologist whose theories on the correlation between erogenous satisfaction and political freedom inspired this anarchic, almost stream-of-imagery dissertation from Dusan Makavejev. Achieving cult status on its release, the film is beginning to betray its age, although the clips of Stalin in the 1946 propaganda feature, *The Vow*, remain as amusing as the footage from the Nazi documentary advocating euthanasia is horrifying. But Makavejev's allegorical fiction involving the romance between a Yugoslav girl and an inhibited Russian skater is clumsy. DP. In Serbian and English with subtitles. Contains sex scenes and swearing.

Milena Dravic *Milena* • Jagoda Kaloper *Jagoda* • Zoran Radmilovic *Radmilovic* • Ivica Vidovic *Vladimir Ilyich* ■ *Dir/Scr* Dusan Makavejev

WUSA ★★★★

Drama 1970 · US · Colour · 114mins

A clutch of famous faces – Paul Newman, Joanne Woodward, Laurence Harvey – are upstaged by Anthony Perkins in this dark drama. Newman stars as a cynical disc jockey at a right-wing New Orleans radio station; Perkins is the liberal conscience whose confrontations with the station are so raw and relevant they sideline the brittle affair between Woodward and Newman. Despite such dramatic imbalance, there are enough insights here to make this one of the more important movies about the state of America in the 1970s. TH

Paul Newman *Rheinhardt* • Joanne Woodward *Geraldine* • Anthony Perkins *Rainey* • Laurence Harvey *Farley* • Pat Hingle *Bingamon* • Cloris Leachman *Philomene* • Don Gordon *Bogdanovich* ■ *Dir* Stuart Rosenberg • *Scr* Robert Stone, from his novel *A Hall of Mirrors*

WW and the Dixie Dancekings ★★★

Comedy 1975 · US · Colour · 90mins

This amiable redneck dirt-kickin' romp comes from the days when genial Burt Reynolds could do no wrong, and when John G Avildsen was a director of promise. The "Dixie Dancekings" of the title are a hokey country-and-western outfit fronted by genuine country star Jerry Reed. Reynolds's attempts to propel the band onwards and upwards are amusing and the easy charm that became his trademark makes this pleasant viewing. SH. Contains violence and swearing.

Burt Reynolds *WW Bright* • Conny Van Dyke *Dixie* • Jerry Reed *Wayne* • Ned Beatty *Country Bull* • James Hampton *Junior* • Don Williams *Leroy* • Richard D Hurst *Butterball* • Art Carney *Deacon Gore* ■ *Dir* John G Avildsen • *Scr* Thomas Rickman [Tom Rickman]

Waati ★★

Political drama 1995 · Fr · Colour · 140mins

Souleymane Cissé, Mali's best-known film-maker, turns his focus on apartheid, telling the story of a young South African girl who flees to the Ivory Coast after she kills a policeman in revenge for the murder of her family – shot for walking on a "whites only" beach. Four cinematographers worked on this sprawling drama to give each location a fresh feel, but even those impressed by the film's power and intensity will find it a little hard going at times. DP. In Zulu, Sotho, Afrikaans, French and English with subtitles. Contains violence, swearing.

Lineo Tsolo • Sidi Yaya • Mary Twala • Eric Meyeni ■ *Dir/Scr* Souleymane Cissé

Wabash Avenue ★★★

Musical 1950 · US · Colour · 92mins

One of Betty Grable's most popular and well-remembered musical vehicles, this Technicolor frolic is the one where she sings *I Wish I Could Shimmy like My Sister Kate*, among the 26 song standards propping up the soundtrack, and where hunk Victor Mature and casino owner Phil Harris vie for her favours in 1890s Chicago. Director Henry Koster injects pace and overall brightness into a likeable and quaintly vulgar venture. TS

Betty Grable *Ruby Summers* • Victor Mature *Andy Clark* • Phil Harris *Uncle Mike* • Reginald Gardiner *English Eddie* • James Barton *Hogan* • Barry Kelley *Bouncer* • Margaret Hamilton *Tillie Hutch* ■ *Dir* Henry Koster • *Scr* Harry Tugend, Charles Lederer

The Wackiest Ship in the Army ★★ U

Comedy 1961 · US · Colour · 95mins

A broken-down boat is used as a decoy in the Second World War, but the tone is uncertain: is it meant to be funny, or isn't it? As a screenwriter, Richard Murphy worked on some interesting films, but here, he proves not to be the ideal director of his own material, despite a cast headed by the genial Jack Lemmon and teen idol Ricky Nelson, for whom underplaying is no real substitute for acting ability. Even though it later spawned a TV series, the film simply doesn't work. TS [video]

Jack Lemmon *Lt Rip Crandall* • Ricky Nelson *Ensign Tommy Hanson* • John Lund *Commander Vandewater* • Chips Rafferty *Patterson* • Tom Tully *Capt McClung* • Joby Baker *Josh Davidson* • Warren Berlinger *Sparks* • Patricia Driscoll *Maggie* ■ *Dir* Richard Murphy (1) • *Scr* Richard Murphy, Herbert Margolis, William Raynor, from a story by Herbert Carlson

Wacko ★★★

Spoof horror 1981 · US · Colour · 80mins

This is a sloppy but lively and funny *Airplane!*-style spoof of *Halloween* and other famous horror movies. Whoever had the idea of casting Joe Don Baker as the world's sloppiest and most dirty-minded cop deserves a medal for his brilliance. His policeman character is in pursuit of the "Lawnmower Killer", who has left signs that he'll strike again 13 years to the day from when he first appeared. The best gags involve the skewering of the countless clichés found in slasher movies. KB

Joe Don Baker *Dick Harbinger* • Stella Stevens *Marg Graves* • George Kennedy *Dr Graves* • Julia Duffy *Mary Graves* • Scott McGinnis *Norman Bates* • Andrew Clay [Andrew Dice Clay] *Tony* • Elizabeth Daily *Bambi* • Michele Tobin *Rosie* • Anthony James *Zeke* ■ *Dir* Greydon Clark • *Scr* Dana Olsen, Michael Spound, M James Kauf Jr, David Greenwalt

Waco ★★

Western 1966 · US · Colour · 71mins

While the local citizenry is being terrorised by a gang of lawless thugs, Howard Keel – a gunslinger with a hot reputation – is cooling his heels behind bars until somebody has the bright idea that he is the man to drive out the desperados. Released for the purpose, he does what's expected of him, with glamorous Jane Russell on hand for encouragement. A run-of-the-mill, second-rung western. RK

Howard Keel *Waco* • Jane Russell *Jill Stone* • Brian Donlevy *Ace Ross* • Wendell Corey *Preacher Sam Stone* • Terry Moore *Dolly* • John Smith *Joe Gore* • John Agar *George Gates* • Gene Evans *Deputy Sheriff O'Neill* • DeForest Kelley *Bill Rile* ■ *Dir* RG Springsteen • *Scr* Steve Fisher, from the novel *Emporia* by Harry Sanford, Max Lamb

Wadi 1981–1991 ★★★

Documentary 1991 · Is · Colour · 97mins

In 1981, Amos Gitai explored the daily reality of the Arab-Israeli conflict in *Wadi*, a revealing talking-head documentary. Returning to the scrubland of Wadi Rushmia, near Haifa, Gitai discovers that much has changed in the decade since his original documentary about the difficulties of co-existence in Israel's disputed territories. The main focus this time is on a couple of Russian immigrants, one of whom has fallen in love with a Galilean woman, while the other lives in isolation with his animals, having been shunned by this tinderbox of a community. DP

Dir/Scr Amos Gitai

Wag the Dog ★★★★ 15

Satirical comedy 1997 · US · Colour · 92mins

Shot by Barry Levinson in a mere 29 days, this satire on the media and politics is a joy from start to finish. Just before an election, the US President is accused of molesting a teenage girl in the Oval Office. To divert interest away from the scandal, he orders his spin doctors to come up with something quickly. In consultation with a Hollywood producer, they invent a war against Albania. Robert De Niro is creepily effective as the spin doctor hired by White House PR woman Anne Heche, but best of all is Dustin Hoffman, who gives a hilarious performance as a Hollywood mogul. AT. Contains swearing. [video] DVD

Dustin Hoffman *Stanley Motss* • Robert De Niro *Conrad Brean* • Anne Heche *Winifred Ames* • Denis Leary *Fad King* • Willie Nelson *Johnny Green* • Andrea Martin *Liz Butsky* • Kirsten Dunst *Tracy Lime* • William H Macy *Mr Young* • Craig T Nelson *Senator Neal* • Woody Harrelson *Sergeant William Schumann* • Jim Belushi [James Belushi] ■ *Dir* Barry Levinson • *Scr* David Mamet, Hilary Henkin, from the novel *American Hero* by Larry Beinhart

The Wages of Fear ★★★★★ PG

Adventure thriller 1953 · Fr · BW · 147mins

The tension is unbearable as two trucks full of nitroglycerin are driven over 300 miles of inhospitable Latin American terrain in order to help extinguish an oilfield fire. But, for all it says about courage and endurance, this is also a grindingly cynical study of human nature, with each member of the quartet willing to sacrifice the others for a bigger pay-off. In bringing Georges Arnaud's novel to the screen, Henri-Georges Clouzot wisely spends time shading in the background detail that intensifies the excitement of the action by drenching it in a sweaty spirit of rivalry. This is cinema's most suspenseful condemnation of capitalism. DP. In English and French with subtitles. [video] DVD

Yves Montand *Mario* • Charles Vanel *Jo* • Vera Clouzot *Linda* • Folco Lulli *Luigi* • Peter Van Eyck *Bimba* • William Tubbs *O'Brien* • Dario Moreno *Hernandez* ■ *Dir* Henri-Georges Clouzot • *Scr* Henri-Georges Clouzot, Jérome Géronimi, from the novel *Le Salaire de la Peur* by Georges Arnaud

Wagner ★★ 15

Epic biographical drama
1983 · UK/Hun/Austria · Colour · 488mins

This biopic of the composer was conceived by maverick director Tony Palmer on a very grand scale indeed. It was shot in six countries with Richard Burton in the title role; Olivier, Gielgud and Richardson on screen together; and a supporting cast of thousands. Wagner's music is played by three orchestras, conducted by Georg Solti. The first cut, nine hours long, premiered in London in 1983 to mixed reviews. Wagnerians hoping for new insight into the obsessions of a highly complex mind will find instead an epic folly of the old school. DM [video]

Richard Burton *Richard Wagner* • Vanessa Redgrave *Cosima* • Gemma Craven *Minna Wagner* • Laszlo Galffi *Ludwig II* • John Gielgud *Pfistermeister* • Ralph Richardson *Pfordten* • Laurence Olivier *Pfeufer* • Ekkehard Schall *Franz Liszt* ■ *Dir* Tony Palmer • *Scr* Charles Wood • *Cinematographer* Vittorio Storaro

Wagonmaster ★★★★ PG

Western 1950 · US · BW · 85mins

One of the most warmly human of the series of westerns made by the master of the genre, John Ford, with a simple plot about two young itinerant cowboys who help lead a Mormon wagon train to Utah. As youths, Harry Carey Jr and Ben Johnson reveal a callow expectancy of what life has in store, and are profoundly moving as they play off each other when deciding to "fall in 'hind the wagon train". Many sequences are beautifully filmed, and it is interesting to see Ward Bond, who would later play the lead in *Wagon Train*, the TV series inspired by the movie. TS [video]

Ben Johnson *Travis* • Ward Bond *Wiggs* • Joanne Dru *Denver* • Harry Carey Jr *Sandy* • Charles Kemper *Uncle Shiloh* • Alan Mowbray *Dr Locksley Hall* • Jane Darwell *Sister Ledeyard* • James Arness *Floyd Clegg* ■ *Dir* John Ford • *Scr* Frank S Nugent [Frank Nugent], Patrick Ford, from a story by John Ford • *Cinematographer* Bert Glennon

Wagons East! ★ PG

Comedy western
1994 · US · Colour · 102mins

It's always a shame when a star dies young, but it seems doubly unfair that someone as likeable and talented as John Candy should have bowed out part-way through the production of this stinker. The idea of having a bunch of lily-livered pioneers quit the Wild West and head home is essentially a good one. Yet director Peter Markle buries it in a quagmire of comic incompetence and dismal slapstick. Quite dreadful. DP. Contains swearing. [video] DVD

John Candy *James Harlow* • Richard Lewis *Phil Taylor* • John C McGinley *Julian* • Ellen Greene *Belle* • Robert Picardo *Ben Wheeler* • Ed Lauter *John Slade* • William Sanderson *Zeke* • Rodney A Grant *Little Feather* ■ *Dir* Peter Markle • *Scr* Matthew Carlson, from a story by Jerry Abrahamson

The Wagons Roll at Night ★★

Crime drama 1941 · US · BW · 83mins

Humphrey Bogart is the owner of a seedy carnival, intent on protecting his convent-educated young sister, Joan Leslie, from his rough life. Meanwhile, when a lion escapes, he fires his tamer (Sig Ruman) and takes on Eddie Albert instead, who proceeds to fall for Leslie. A melodramatic farrago that ill-befits its star. RK

Humphrey Bogart *Nick Coster* • Sylvia Sidney *Flo Lorraine* • Eddie Albert *Matt Varney* • Joan Leslie *Mary Coster* • Sig Rumann [Sig Ruman] *Hoffman the Great* • Cliff Clark *Doc* ■ *Dir* Ray Enright • *Scr* Fred Niblo Jr, Barry Trivers, from the novel *Kid Galahad* by Francis Wallace

Waikiki Wedding ★★★

Musical comedy 1937 · US · BW · 88mins

This good-natured sun-drenched musical, characteristic of the period, is set in a Paramount studio version of Hawaii. Here, amid the grass skirts and exotic scenery, pineapple growers' PR man Bing Crosby is masterminding a Miss Pineapple beauty contest. Bing, of course, falls for the winner, Shirley Ross, and croons his way through several "South Seas" numbers, including Oscar-winning mega-hit *Sweet Leilani*, while his sidekick Bob Burns tangles with motor-mouthed Martha Raye to supply the comedy. RK

Bing Crosby *Tony Marvin* • Bob Burns *Shad Buggle* • Martha Raye *Myrtle Finch* • Shirley Ross *Georgia Smith* • George Barbier *JP Todhunter* • Leif Erickson *Dr Victor Quimby* • Anthony Quinn *Kimo* ■ *Dir* Frank Tuttle • *Scr* Frank Butler, Don Hartman, Walter DeLeon, Frances Martin, from a story by Frank Butler, Don Hartman • *Choreographer* LeRoy Prinz

Wait 'til the Sun Shines, Nellie ★★★ U

Drama 1952 · US · Colour · 107mins

Produced by vaudeville legend George Jessel, this is a polished and thoroughly professional piece of period melodrama that demonstrates the virtue of that old-fashioned concept – a story with a beginning, a middle and an end. David Wayne gives his finest screen performance as the homely small-town barber who accepts the joys and trials of life with equal grace. Directed by Henry King with a sure grasp of bygone America, this is finely crafted entertainment. DP

David Wayne *Ben Halper* • Jean Peters *Nellie* • Hugh Marlowe *Ed Jordan* • Albert Dekker *Lloyd Slocum* • Helene Stanley *Eadie Jordan* • Tommy Morton [Tom Morton] *Ben Halper Jr, aged 20* • Joyce MacKenzie *Bessie Jordan* •

W

Alan Hale Jr *George Oliphant* ■ *Dir* Henry King • *Scr* Allan Scott, Maxwell Shane, from the novel *I Heard Them Sing* by Ferdinand Reyher

Wait until Dark ★★★★

Thriller 1967 · US · Colour · 108mins

A powerful piece of theatre can often seem very flat on film because the screen distances the viewer from the immediacy and intimacy of the stage performance. Terence Young's version of Frederick Knott's Broadway hit is a magnificent exception. Oscar-nominated Audrey Hepburn is quite superb as the blind woman who keeps her wits about her when drug dealers break into her apartment to recover a doll full of heroin. Alan Arkin pulls out all the psychotic stops as the leader of the gang, and Young never lets the suspense drop. DP. Contains violence.

Audrey Hepburn *Susy Hendrix* • Alan Arkin *Roat* • Richard Crenna *Mike Talman* • Efrem Zimbalist Jr *Sam Hendrix* • Jack Weston *Carlino* • Samantha Jones *Lisa* • Julie Herrod *Gloria* • Frank O'Brien *Shatner* ■ *Dir* Terence Young • *Scr* Robert Carrington, Jane-Howard Carrington, from the play by Frederick Knott • *Cinematographer* Charles Lang

Wait until Spring, Bandini ★★

Period drama 1989 · Bel/Fr/It/US · Colour · 100mins

Too little is asked of a fine cast in this handsome, but uninspiring adaptation of John Fante's autobiographical novel. Belgian director Dominique Deruddere brings a keen outsider's eye to the Colorado setting, but his grasp of the 1920s atmosphere is less assured. Joe Mantegna offers a typically bullish performance, as the unemployed bricklayer with a penchant for gambling and a deep-seated loathing of his mother-in-law, Renata Vanni. But neither Ornella Muti, as his put-upon wife, nor Faye Dunaway, as a seductive neighbour make much of an impact. DP

Joe Mantegna *Svevo Bandini* • Ornella Muti *Maria Bandini* • Faye Dunaway *Mrs Effie Hildegarde* • Burt Young *Rocco Saccone* • Michael Bacall *Arturo Bandini* • Renata Vanni *Donna Toscana, Maria's mother* ■ *Dir* Dominique Deruddere • *Scr* Dominique Deruddere, from the novel by John Fante

Waiting ★★★ 15

Drama 1990 · Aus · Colour · 93mins

An artist agrees to be a surrogate mum to a childless couple's baby. This domestic drama follows the girl and her friends through the pregnancy, with events taking a dramatic turn when she starts having second thoughts about giving the baby up. Noni Hazlehurst plays the lady who waits while her co-stars include Deborra-Lee Furness, the bike-riding avenger in cult Aussie movie *Shame*. DA

Noni Hazlehurst *Clare* • Deborra-Lee Furness *Diane* • Frank Whitten *Michael* • Helen Jones *Sandy* • Denis Moore *Bill* • Fiona Press *Therese* • Ray Barrett *Frank* • Noga Bernstein *Rosie* ■ *Dir/Scr* Jackie McKimmie

Waiting for Guffman ★★★ 15

Satire 1996 · US · Colour · 80mins

This straight-faced "mockumentary" sends up am-dram pretentiousness and middle American values in equal measure. Directed by and starring Christopher Guest (*Spinal Tap*), the film's spot-on spoofery focuses on a small-town "auteur" and his ambitious plan to stage a musical review to mark the town's 150th anniversary. The results are far funnier than the film's inability to secure UK distribution might suggest, and there's a strong supporting cast. DA

Christopher Guest *Corky St Clair* • Eugene Levy *Dr Allan Pearl* • Fred Willard *Ron Albertson* • Catherine O'Hara *Sheila Albertson* • Parker Posey *Libby Mae Brown* • Bob Balaban *Lloyd Miller* • Lewis Arquette *Clifford Wooley* ■ *Dir* Christopher Guest • *Scr* Christopher Guest, Eugene Levy • *Music/lyrics* Michael McKean, Harry Shearer, Christopher Guest

Waiting for Happiness ★★★★ U

Drama 2002 · Fr/Swi/Neth/Cz · Colour · 91mins

The clash between tradition and progress is a familiar theme in African cinema. But rarely has it been explored with such poignancy as in this collection of characters from Mauritanian director Abderrahmane Sissako. The coastal town of Nouadhibou serves as a microcosm for a continent whose menfolk are leaving in their droves in search of work, whose women have few rights and many responsibilities, and whose children are increasingly exposed to cultures the elderly regard with disdain. The largely improvised performances of the non-professional cast convey the contrasting moods and attitudes with conviction. DP. In Hassianya and French with English subtitles. DVD

Khatra Ould Abdel Kader *Khatra* • Maata Ould Mohamed Abeid *Maata* • Mohamed Mahmoud Ould Mohamed *Abdallah* • Fatimetou Mint Ahmeda *Soukeyna* • Nana Diakite *Nana* • Makanfing Dabo *Makan* ■ *Dir/Scr* Abderrahmane Sissako

Waiting for Michelangelo ★★

Romantic comedy drama 1995 · Can/Swi · Colour · 93mins

Typical! You wait ages for a bloke and then two come along at once. That's the situation in which single mother and TV journalist Renée Coleman finds herself in this amiable romantic comedy. The two men who match her identikit ideal are a Swiss gallery owner and a successful writer, but which one is as perfect as Michelangelo's David? Coleman holds things together nicely, although the story is a little too familiar and the characters a touch too contrived. DP

Renée Coleman *Kelly Hildon* • Roy Dupuis *Thomas Schumacher* • Rick Roberts *Jonathan* • Jeremy Chance *Peter* • Michael Adam *Austin Hildon* ■ *Dir* Curt Truninger • *Scr* Margrit Ritzmann, Curt Truninger

Waiting for the Light ★★★ PG

Comedy drama 1989 · US · Colour · 90mins

In her later years Shirley MacLaine has specialised in portrayals of eccentric ladies of a certain age. This is one of her best – a former circus performer, now children's entertainer, whose behaviour brings trouble to her niece Teri Garr, who has taken on a diner in a small town in Washington State. It's pleasant enough, but director Chris Monger's debut feature has little rhyme or reason. MacLaine gives a polished performance and the surface sheen makes for enjoyable viewing. TH. Contains some swearing.

Shirley MacLaine *Aunt Zena* • Teri Garr *Kay Harris* • Colin Baumgartner *Eddie Harris* • Hillary Wolf *Emily Harris* • Clancy Brown *Joe* • Vincent Schiavelli *Mullins* • John Bedford Lloyd *Reverend Stevens* • Jeff McCracken *Charlie* ■ *Dir/Scr* Christopher Monger

Waiting for the Moon ★★

Biographical drama 1987 · US · Colour · 88mins

Linda Bassett and Linda Hunt play one of the 20th century's most interesting couples, author Gertrude Stein and cookery writer Alice B Toklas. The infamous pair lived together in Paris for more than 20 years and played host to artists from Hemingway to Picasso. Sadly, this great story is still waiting to be told well as Jill Godmilow's film only skims the surface. There is no depth to the relationship between the women despite the talent of the two actresses. LH

Linda Hunt *Alice B Toklas* • Linda Bassett *Gertrude Stein* • Andrew McCarthy *Henry Hopper* • Bernadette Lafont *Fernande Olivier* • Bruce McGill *Ernest Hemingway* • Jacques Boudet *Guillaume Apollinaire* ■ *Dir* Jill Godmilow • *Scr* Mark Magill, from a story by Jill Godmilow, Mark Magill

Waiting to Exhale ★★★ 15

Drama 1995 · US · Colour · 118mins

No matter what problems confront the female quartet in this crowd-pleasing melodrama, the most pressing concern always seems to be the shortage of good men. Like that woman's picture extraordinaire *Thelma & Louise*, it's directed by a man – marking the directorial debut of Forest Whitaker. There's a patronising tone of indulgence pervading the film that manifests itself in the smart one-liners, the minor triumphs designed to elicit high-fives among the audience and the tear-jerking feel-good of the finale. Expertly acted, this owes little to life and a bit too much to glossy magazine aspirations. DP

Whitney Houston *Savannah* • Angela Bassett *Bernadine* • Loretta Devine *Gloria* • Lela Rochon *Robin* • Gregory Hines *Marvin* • Dennis Haysbert *Kenneth* • Mykelti Williamson *Troy* • Michael Beach *John Sr* ■ *Dir* Forest Whitaker • *Scr* Terry McMillan, Ronald Bass, from the novel by Terry McMillan

Waiting Women ★★★ 12

Comedy 1952 · Swe · BW · 103mins

This episodic drama from Ingmar Bergman continued his fascination with exploring the battle of the sexes from the female perspective. Waiting for their partners to join them for the summer, three sisters-in-law describe key moments in their relationships. Anita Björk talks about an extramarital affair and the effect it had on her husband; Maj-Britt Nilsson recalls the pregnancy that led her to marry painter Birger Malmsten; and Eva Dahlbeck alights on a night stuck in a lift with her pompous spouse, Gunnar Björnstrand. It's a patchy anthology, but the comic finale is splendid. DP. In Swedish with English subtitles. DVD

Anita Björk *Rakel* • Eva Dahlbeck *Karin* • Maj-Britt Nilsson *Marta* • Karl Arne Holmsten *Eugen* • Jarl Kulle *Kaj* • Birger Malmsten *Martin* • Gunnar Björnstrand *Fredrik* ■ *Dir/Scr* Ingmar Bergman

Wake Island ★★★★

Second World War drama 1942 · US · BW · 87mins

Director John Farrow achieves an almost documentary-style realism, even though the film is relentlessly Hollywood in style and features that well-known studio platoon consisting entirely of stereotypes. News of the heroic December 1941 defence of Wake, a Pacific island lost to the Japanese, was barely off the presses when filming began, and a grim gung-ho mood is apparent throughout the feature. It received four Oscar nominations, including best picture, best director and best supporting actor for William Bendix, who, along with Brian Donlevy, gives a particularly fine performance. The ending is very moving and extraordinarily patriotic. TS

Brian Donlevy *Major Geoffrey Caton* • Macdonald Carey *Lieutenant Cameron* • Robert Preston *Joe Doyle* • William Bendix *Smacksie Randall* • Albert Dekker *Shad McClosky* • Walter Abel *Commander Roberts* • Mikhail Rasumny *Probenzky* • Don Castle *Private Cunkel* ■ *Dir* John Farrow • *Scr* WR Burnett, Frank Butler

Wake Me When It's Over ★★ U

Comedy 1960 · US · Colour · 125mins

Dick Shawn cashes in on the clerical error that drafted him into the military by setting up a luxury hotel on an isolated Japanese island. There's a good chemistry between Shawn and Ernie Kovacs, the platoon captain whose men are the joint's most dedicated patrons, but the dialogue could do with a little more snap, especially in the court-martial sequences. DP

Ernie Kovacs *Captain Stark* • Margo Moore *Lt Nora McKay* • Jack Warden *Doc Farrington* • Nobu McCarthy *Ume* • Dick Shawn *Gus Brubaker* • Don Knotts *Sgt Warren* ■ *Dir* Mervyn LeRoy • *Scr* Richard L Breen, from a novel by Howard Singer • *Cinematographer* Leon Shamroy

Wake of the Red Witch ★★★ PG

Adventure 1949 · US · BW · 102mins

This John Wayne seafaring action adventure would have benefited from colour, but still provides reasonable entertainment. Gail Russell is the girl Wayne and rival ship owner Luther Adler are fighting over, and the South Seas setting is very studio-bound. The *Red Witch* herself was used again in 1953's *Fair Wind to Java*, and now resides in the Hollywood Wax Museum on Hollywood Boulevard. Incidentally, Wayne named his film production company, Batjac, after the fictional shipping line in this movie. TS

John Wayne *Captain Ralls* • Gail Russell *Angelique Desaix* • Gig Young *Sam Rosen* • Luther Adler *Mayrant Ruysdaal Sidneye* • Adele Mara *Teleia Van Schreeven* • Paul Fix *Antonio "Ripper" Arrezo* • Eduard Franz *Harmenszoon Van Schreeven* ■ *Dir* Edward Ludwig • *Scr* Harry Brown, Kenneth Gamet, from the novel by Garland Roark

Wake Up and Live ★★★

Musical comedy 1937 · US · BW · 91mins

Alice Faye's beautiful rendition here of *There's a Lull in My Life* should be more than enough for most of her fans. But this Faye vehicle (one of four she made the same year) also has a plot involving a feud between band leader Ben Bernie and arch-columnist and broadcaster Walter Winchell, no less. There's some nice clowning, too, from Jack Haley as a performer with a phobia about microphones. Former jazz musician Sidney Lanfield provides the pacy direction for this fine example of Hollywood taking revenge on its then-current rival, radio. TS

Walter Winchell • Ben Bernie • Alice Faye *Alice Huntley* • Patsy Kelly *Patsy Kane* • Ned Sparks *Steve Cluskey* • Jack Haley *Eddie Kane* • Grace Bradley *Jean Roberts* ■ *Dir* Sidney Lanfield • *Scr* Harry Tugend, Jack Yellen, from a story by Curtis Kenyon, from the book by Dorothea Brande

Waking Life ★★★ 15

Animated drama 2001 · US · Colour · 96mins

Intellectually acute viewers may occasionally be alienated by the sophomoric posturings in director Richard Linklater's dazzlingly innovative attempt to provoke audience introspection, as an array of characters voice their philosophies of life to Wiley Wiggins's latter-day Candide during a series of dreamlike perambulations. It's impossible not to be impressed by Linklater's inspired imagery. Created by a 31-strong animation team, the hybrid visuals consist of live-action digital video footage that has been "painted" over, frame by frame, using software developed by art director Bob Sabiston. This provides a striking graphic diversity that perfectly complements the conflicting philosophical reflections. DP [VIDEO] DVD

Wiley Wiggins *Main Character* • Ethan Hawke *Jesse* • Julie Delpy *Celine* • Steven Soderbergh ■ *Dir/Scr* Richard Linklater

Waking Ned ★★★ PG

Comedy 1998 · UK/Fr · Colour · 87mins

This charming film from first-time director Kirk Jones was a surprise hit Stateside thanks to an imaginative marketing effort. Set on a tiny Irish island, two old men become hysterical when they discover an anonymous local has won the lottery. Their attempts to uncover the lucky so-and-so involve bribery and much false nicety until success results in them orchestrating a complex lie which involves the entire community. Ian Bannen stars with David Kelly as the avaricious OAPs in a tale that is both laugh-out-loud funny and touching. LH. Contains nudity. [VIDEO] DVD

Ian Bannen *Jackie O'Shea* • David Kelly *Michael O'Sullivan* • Fionnula Flanagan *Annie O'Shea* • Susan Lynch *Maggie* • James Nesbitt *Pig Finn* • Maura O'Malley *Mrs Kennedy* • Robert Hickey *Maurice* • Paddy Ward *Brendy* ■ *Dir/Scr* Kirk Jones

Waking the Dead ★★ 15

Romantic mystery drama
2000 · US · Colour · 100mins

A fine supporting cast props up this sometimes uncomfortable combination of *The Way We Were* and *The Sixth Sense*. Achieving little of the intrigue generated by *Mother Night*, director Keith Gordon pulls together an ambiguous plotline, but it's hard to believe in the passion between budding politician Billy Crudup and radical activist Jennifer Connolly, which seems to survive her death a decade earlier in a car bombing. DP [VIDEO] DVD

Billy Crudup *Fielding Pierce* • Jennifer Connelly *Sarah Williams* • Janet McTeer *Caroline Pierce* • Molly Parker *Juliet Beck* • Sandra Oh *Kim* • Hal Holbrook *Isaac Green* • Ed Harris *Jerry Carmichael* ■ *Dir* Keith Gordon • *Scr* Robert Dillons, from the novel by Scott Spencer

Waking Up Horton ★★

Fantasy adventure
1997 · US · Colour · 92mins

This recent effort from British horror director Harry Bromley Davenport is a fantasy adventure in which Ashley Peldon is helped in her quest for buried treasure by an incompetent Indian spirit guide, Raoul Trujillo. Two former TV stars, Dirk Benedict and Barbara Carrera add nostalgia value to an otherwise unimpressive tale. DM

Dirk Benedict *Tyler* • Barbara Carrera *Isadora* • Ashley Peldon *Amelia* • Zachary Browne *Mark* • Raoul Trujillo *Horton Laughing Feather* • Billy Maddox *Holliman* ■ *Dir* Harry Bromley Davenport • *Scr* Elke Petersen Rudman, Sonia Zyvatkauskas

Walk a Crooked Mile ★★

Spy drama 1948 · US · BW · 90mins

Dennis O'Keefe of the FBI and Louis Hayward of Scotland Yard join forces to investigate a trail of murders concealing a plot to smuggle atom bomb plans from America to London. One of the original Cold War spy yarns, the urgent documentary style of this thriller reflects the political climate of the time, with the communists cast as stage villains and respectful nods to the postwar "special relationship" between America and Britain. AT

Louis Hayward *Philip Grayson* • Dennis O'Keefe *Daniel O'Hara* • Louise Allbritton *Dr Toni Neva* • Carl Esmond *Dr Ritter Van Stolb* • Onslow Stevens *Igor Braun* • Raymond Burr *Krebs* • Art Baker *Dr Frederick Townsend* ■ *Dir* Gordon Douglas • *Scr* George Bruce, from a story by Bertram Millhauser

Walk a Crooked Path ★★★

Drama 1969 · UK · Colour · 85mins

Tenniel Evans is an embittered boarding school housemaster who, passed over for promotion, plans to murder his rich, alcoholic wife Faith Brook and live with his mistress Patricia Haynes. Bizarrely, he does this by paying student Clive Endersby to claim that he was homosexually abused by Evans, thus humiliating Brook so badly that she commits suicide. The plot is quite clever, revealed in flashbacks and sudden twists and revelling in the rather risqué elements. AT

Tenniel Evans *John Hemming* • Faith Brook *Elizabeth Hemming* • Christopher Coll *Bill Colman* • Patricia Haines *Nancy Colman* • Clive Endersby *Philip Dreaper* • Georgina Simpson *Elaine* • Georgina Cookson *Imogen Dreaper* ■ *Dir* John Brason • *Scr* Barry Perowne

Walk, Don't Run ★★★ U

Romantic comedy
1966 · US · Colour · 113mins

Cary Grant is as magically urbane as ever playing a British industrialist in this, his final movie, but sadly leaves the romance to the youngsters in a so-so comedy set during the 1964 Tokyo Olympic Games. Samantha Eggar is the embassy secretary with whom Grant lodges and Jim Hutton the member of the American Olympic squad he introduces into her life. A remake of the 1943 film *The More the Merrier*, it's lower on laughs but notable for Grant's sleek charm. TH

Cary Grant *Sir William Rutland* • Samantha Eggar *Christine Easton* • Jim Hutton *Steve Davis* • John Standing *Julius P Haversack* • Miiko Taka *Aiko Kurawa* • Ted Hartley *Yuri Andreyovitch* • Ben Astar *Dimitri* • George Takei *Police captain* ■ *Dir* Charles Walters • *Scr* Sol Saks, from the film *The More the Merrier* by Robert Russell, Frank Ross, Richard Flournoy, Lewis R Foster • *Cinematographer* Harry Stradling

Walk East on Beacon ★ U

Spy thriller 1952 · US · BW · 97mins

Totally inept "red scare" thriller, with George Murphy trailing communist agents across a paranoid free world. The script is based on a *Reader's Digest* article written by the then head of the FBI, J Edgar Hoover. The whole picture (and many others of its ilk) seems to be bankrolled by the FBI as both a recruitment advertisement and a dire warning to ordinary Americans about the dangers of communism. AT

George Murphy *Inspector Belden* • Finlay Currie *Professor Kafer* • Virginia Gilmore *Millie* • Karel Stepanek *Alex* • Louisa Horton *Elaine* • Peter Capell *Gino* • Bruno Wick *Danzig* ■ *Dir* Alfred Werker • *Scr* Leo Rosten, Virginia Shaler, Emmett Murphy, Leonard Heidemann, from the magazine article *The Crime of the Century* by J Edgar Hoover

A Walk in the Clouds ★★ PG

Period romantic drama
1995 · US · Colour · 98mins

Keanu Reeves stars in this cliché-ridden, 1940s-set romantic drama – the American debut of Mexican director Alfonso Arau. Returning from the Second World War to be reunited with his unfaithful wife, travelling salesman Reeves meets a pregnant girl during a business trip and agrees to pose as her husband to protect her from the wrath of her strict, vineyard-owning family in California. Grandpa Anthony Quinn overacts as if only he can make up for Reeves's wooden performance. TH. Contains violence, nudity. [VIDEO] DVD

Keanu Reeves *Paul Sutton* • Aitana Sanchez-Gijon *Victoria Aragon* • Anthony Quinn *Don Pedro Aragon* • Giancarlo Giannini *Alberto Aragon* • Angélica Aragón *Marie Jose Aragon* • Evangelina Elizondo *Guadelupe Aragon* • Freddy Rodriguez *Pedro Aragon Jr* • Debra Messing *Betty Sutton* ■ *Dir* Alfonso Arau • *Scr* Robert Mark Kamen, Mark Miller, Harvey Weitzman, from the 1942 film *Four Steps in the Clouds* by Piero Tellini, Guiseppe Amato, Cesare Zavattini, Vittorio De Benedetti

A Walk in the Spring Rain ★

Romantic melodrama
1970 · US · Colour · 98mins

The bored, middle-aged wife (Ingrid Bergman) of a bored, middle-aged college professor (Fritz Weaver), while vacationing in Tennessee mountain country, meets a local farmer (Anthony Quinn) who is the polar opposite of her husband. One of far too many films which marked the nadir of Bergman's post-Rossellini career, this is turgid rubbish, whose stars make a frankly incredible duo. RK

Anthony Quinn *Will Cade* • Ingrid Bergman *Libby Meredith* • Fritz Weaver *Roger Meredith* • Katherine Crawford *Ellen Meredith* • Tom Fielding *Boy Cade* • Virginia Gregg *Ann Cade* • Mitchell Silberman *Bucky* ■ *Dir* Guy Green • *Scr* Stirling Silliphant, from the novella by Rachel Maddux

A Walk in the Sun ★★★★

Second World War drama
1945 · US · BW · 117mins

The story is simple: a ragbag of foot-slogging GIs are part of the invasion force in Italy and chase the Germans north to eventual defeat. The excellent but unstarry cast means no John Wayne or Clark Gable-style heroics, but they all "talk the talk" in a way that seems completely authentic and most of the time they are just coping with boredom, exhaustion and the probability of sudden death. There are mercifully no overt "war is hell" messages in this prototype platoon picture directed by Lewis Milestone. AT

Dana Andrews *Sgt Tyne* • Richard Conte *Rivera* • John Ireland *Windy* • George Tyne *Friedman* • Lloyd Bridges *Sgt Ward* • Sterling Holloway *McWilliams* • Herbert Rudley *Sgt Porter* • Norman Lloyd *Archimbeau* • Steve Brodie *Judson* • Huntz Hall *Carraway* ■ *Dir* Lewis Milestone • *Scr* Robert Rossen, from a story by Harry Brown

Walk like a Dragon ★★

Western 1960 · US · BW · 94mins

James Clavell was known primarily as a writer but also produced and directed a couple of his screenplays including this well-intentioned western drama with a central theme of racial conflict. Jack Lord (later of *Hawaii Five-O* fame) plays an American who rescues a young Chinese woman (Nobu McCarthy) from slavery and the prospect of enforced prostitution. When he takes her to his home in San Francisco, he is faced by prejudice. BB

Jack Lord *Line Bartlett* • Nobu McCarthy *Kim Sung* • James Shigeta *Cheng Lu* • Mel Tormé *The Deacon* • Josephine Hutchinson *Ma Bartlett* ■ *Dir* James Clavell • *Scr* James Clavell, Daniel Mainwaring

Walk like a Man ★ PG

Comedy 1987 · US · Colour · 82mins

Howie Mandel has never quite made the transition to the big screen, and this one-joke comedy is a good example why. He plays a man raised by wolves who returns to civilisation just in time to make life extremely difficult for his brother, Christopher Lloyd. Most of the jokes revolve around slobbering and other social faux pas, and it's painful to watch. JB [VIDEO]

Howie Mandel *Bobo Shand* • Christopher Lloyd *Reggie Henry* • Cloris Leachman *Margaret Shand* • Colleen Camp *Rhonda Shand* • Amy Steel *Penny* • Stephen Elliott *Walter Welmont* • George DiCenzo *Bub Downs* • John McLiam *HP Truman* ■ *Dir* Melvin Frank • *Scr* Robert Klane

A Walk on the Moon ★★ 15

Drama 1999 · US · Colour · 107mins

Woodstock and "one giant leap for mankind" form a life-changing backdrop to this run-of-the-mill holiday of discovery. Diane Lane and Anna Paquin are on great form, as an unfulfilled wife succumbing to a campsite affair and her confused teenage daughter respectively. The script is very mundane, though, and is hampered by predictable plotting and meagre dramatic moments that never really catch fire. JC. Contains swearing and sex scenes. [VIDEO]

Diane Lane *Pearl Kantrowitz* • Viggo Mortensen *Walker Jerome* • Liev Schreiber *Marty Kantrowitz* • Anna Paquin *Alison Kantrowitz* • Tovah Feldshuh *Lilian Kantrowitz* • Bobby Boriello *Daniel Kantrowitz* • Stewart Bick *Neil Leiberman* • Jess Platt *Herb Fogler* ■ *Dir* Tony Goldwyn • *Scr* Pamela Gray

Walk on the Wild Side ★★★ 15

Melodrama 1962 · US · BW · 109mins

Although purporting to be a frank exploration of prostitution and lesbianism, Edward Dmytryk's adaptation of Nelson Algren's racy novel pulls its punches in virtually every scene. Too much time is spent in the company of dull Texan Laurence Harvey as he searches for his runaway lover, Capucine, and helps Anne Baxter and Jane Fonda to see the error of their ways. Far more interesting is madame Barbara Stanwyck's obsession with Capucine, but both script and direction keep the action at a gentle simmer rather than pressing on to boiling point. Saul Bass's title credits are rightly renowned as classic examples of the art. DP [VIDEO]

Laurence Harvey *Dove Linkhorn* • Capucine *Hallie* • Jane Fonda *Kitty Twist* • Anne Baxter *Teresina Vidaverri* • Barbara Stanwyck *Jo Courtney* • Joanna Moore *Miss Precious* • Richard Rust *Oliver* • Karl Swenson *Schmidt* • Donald Barry *Dockery* • Juanita Moore *Mama* ■ *Dir* Edward Dmytryk • *Scr* John Fante, Edmund Morris, from the novel by Nelson Algren

Walk on Water ★★★ 15

Thriller 2004 · Is/Swe · Colour · 103mins

This Israeli political thriller grabs the attention and only rarely relaxes its grip. It tells the story of Mossad hitman Lior Ashkenazi, who is tailing a German brother and sister whose grandfather was a high-ranking Nazi. Spending time with the siblings (Knut Berger and Caroline Peters) exposes the Arab-hating, homophobic assassin to their liberal views, and Ashkenazi soon begins to lose interest in his real mission – to find and kill the old man. Deftly spelling out what it feels like to live in modern-day Israel, the story is a surprisingly enlightening experience. KK. In Hebrew with English subtitles.

Lior Ashkenazi *Eyal* • Knut Berger *Axel Himmelman* • Caroline Peters *Pia Himmelman* • Gidon Shemer *Menachem* • Carola Regnier *Axel's mother* • Hanns Zischler *Axel's father* • Ernest Lenart *Alfred Himmelman* • Eyal Rozales *Jello* ■ *Dir* Eytan Fox • *Scr* Gal Uchovsky

W

Walk Proud ★★ 15

Drama 1979 · US · Colour · 93mins

Robby Benson is a Chicano who falls for a white girl. The relationship is put to the test when Benson's gang buddies disapprove of him dating outside his race, and he has to choose between following his heart and following his friends. Like Benson's character, the film proves to have its heart in the right place, if perhaps not its art. The whole thing lacks pace and punch, but Benson gives a good performance. DA

Robby Benson *Emilio* • Sarah Holcomb *Sarah* • Henry Darrow *Mike* • Pepe Serna *Cesar* • Trinidad Silva *Dagger* ■ *Dir* Robert Collins • *Scr* Evan Hunter

Walk Softly, Stranger ★★

Drama 1949 · US · BW · 81mins

Filmed before Joseph Cotten and Alida Valli teamed up for *The Third Man*, but released afterwards, this marked the end of RKO's collaboration with David O Selznick's Vanguard Films. It proved the studio's biggest flop of the year, losing $775,000. The fault lies less with Robert Stevenson's unimaginative direction than with Frank Fenton's melodramatic screenplay, in which Cotten's charming fugitive hides out in a Midwestern backwater where he falls for Valli's disabled heiress. DP

Joseph Cotten *Chris Hale* • Alida Valli *Elaine Corelli* • Spring Byington *Mrs Brentman* • Frank Puglia *AJ Corelli* • Paul Stewart *Whitey* • Jeff Donnell *Gwen* • Howard Petrie *Bowen* • Jack Paar *Ray Healey* ■ *Dir* Robert Stevenson • *Scr* Frank Fenton, from a story by Manuel Seff, Paul Yawitz

Walk the Proud Land ★★ U

Biographical western
1956 · US · Colour · 84mins

Baby-faced war hero Audie Murphy stars as John Philip Clum, the Indian agent who was responsible for liaising with the captured Apache warrior Geronimo. This potentially powerful story of conflict is rather spoiled by the emphasis on Clum's domestic troubles, which nullifies the original premise. Nevertheless, Murphy is convincing, and both Pat Crowley and Anne Bancroft are excellent in supporting roles. TS

Audie Murphy *John P Clum* • Anne Bancroft *Tianay* • Pat Crowley *Mary Dennison* • Charles Drake *Tom Sweeney* • Tommy Rall *Taglito* • Robert Warwick *Eskiminzin* • Jay Silverheels *Geronimo* ■ *Dir* Jesse Hibbs • *Scr* Gil Doud, Jack Sher, from the biography *Apache Agent* by Woodworth Clum

A Walk to Remember ★★ PG

Romantic drama 2002 · US · Colour · 97mins

Based on Nicholas Sparks's bestseller and featuring MTV pop singer Mandy Moore in her first leading movie role, this type of love story might have worked back in the 1970s, but it's far too cloying and contrived to seduce today's teenagers. Peter Coyote and Daryl Hannah cope well in their atypical roles as a preacher and a single mother. However, Moore barely convinces as the ultra-demure daughter of a small-town Baptist minister who falls for rebellious Shane West. Few will buy the mawkish approach to a tragic turn of events. DP DVD

Shane West *Landon Carter* • Mandy Moore *Jamie Sullivan* • Peter Coyote *Reverend Sullivan* • Daryl Hannah *Cynthia Carter* • Lauren German *Belinda* • Clayne Crawford *Dean* • Al Thompson *Eric* • Paz de la Huerta *Tracie* ■ *Dir* Adam Shankman • *Scr* Karen Janszen, from the novel by Nicholas Sparks

W

A Walk with Love and Death ★

Period drama 1969 · US · Colour · 90mins

John Huston got the worst notices of his long career for this fiasco and he was vilified for casting his own daughter, Anjelica, in the leading role of the nobleman's daughter caught up in the Hundred Years' War. As her suitor, Huston rejected actors and cast Assaf Dayan, the son of Moshe Dayan, the defence minister of Israel. It was a crazy project from the start, born of nepotism, egotism and the flower-power movement of the 1960s. AT

Anjelica Huston *Lady Claudia* • Assaf Dayan [Assi Dayan] *Heron of Foix* • Anthony Corlan [Anthony Higgins] *Robert* • John Hallam *Sir Meles of Bohemia* • Eileen Murphy *Gypsy girl* • Anthony Nicholls *Father Superior* ■ *Dir* John Huston • *Scr* Dale Wasserman, from the novel by Hans Koningsberger • *Music* Georges Delerue

Walkabout ★★★★★ 12

Drama 1970 · Aus · Colour · 96mins

Nicolas Roeg's second film as director is an atmospheric masterpiece of sexual tension, with Jenny Agutter and Lucien John as the children stranded in the Australian outback when their father commits suicide. As the youngsters are guided by young Aborigine David Gulpilil, who teaches them to live off the seemingly arid land, the film examines the relationship between the youth and the girl – one that has to span a chasm of misunderstandings caused by cultural differences and the innocence of childhood. Roeg conjures up a tale as dazzling as the shimmering landscape against which it is set. TH. Contains nudity. DVD

Jenny Agutter *Girl* • Lucien John [Luc Roeg] *Brother* • David Gulpilil *Aborigine* • John Meillon *Father* • Peter Carver *No-hoper* • John Illingsworth *Husband* ■ *Dir* Nicolas Roeg • *Scr* Edward Bond, from the novel *The Children* by James Vance Marshall • *Music* John Barry (1)

Walker ★★ 18

Period biographical drama
1987 · US · Colour · 90mins

Made only three years after *Repo Man*, this highly stylised film from director Alex Cox shows him as only a shadow of his former self, with the stiffly told story of American mercenary William Walker who, backed by a tycoon, took over as President of Nicaragua in the mid-19th century. Ed Harris is bombastically charismatic, though the anti-American rant, which may have been justified, proves too one-sided for real drama. TH. Contains some swearing. DVD

Ed Harris *William Walker* • Peter Boyle *Cornelius Vanderbilt* • Richard Masur *Ephraim Squier* • René Auberjonois *Major Siegfried Henningson* • Marlee Matlin *Ellen Martin* • Sy Richardson *Captain Hornsby* ■ *Dir* Alex Cox • *Scr* Rudy Wurlitzer

Walking across Egypt ★★★ 12

Drama 1999 · US · Colour · 96mins

This is yet another eloquent showcase for the talents of Ellen Burstyn. Abandoned by her grown-up children, Judge Reinhold and Gail O'Grady, the small-town God-fearing busybody sets out to reform dogcatcher Mark Hamill and his delinquent orphan nephew, Jonathan Taylor Thomas. This could easily have lapsed into liberal sentimentality, but quadruple Emmy-winning director Arthur Allan Seidelman brings a shabby Deep Southern charm to proceedings that are brimful of gently comic set pieces and wry wisdom. DP DVD

Ellen Burstyn *Mattie Rigsbee* • Jonathan Taylor Thomas *Wesley Benfield* • Mark Hamill *Lamar* • Edward Herrmann *Reverend Vernon* • Judge Reinhold *Robert Rigsbee* • Gail O'Grady *Elaine Rigsbee* • Dana Ivey *Beatrice Vernon* ■ *Dir* Arthur Allan Seidelman • *Scr* Paul Tamasy, from the novel by Clyde Edgerton

Walking and Talking ★★★ 15

Comedy drama
1996 · UK/US · Colour · 82mins

Writer/director Nicole Holofcener makes an impressive debut with this New York-based tale of fantasy, angst and desire, which had her somewhat cynically dismissed as a young Woody Allen. Sharply scripted and smartly cast, this comedy of discontent is inhabited by credible characters who have something approximating real conversations. As the longtime friends whose lives begin to unravel when marriage rears its head, Catherine Keener and Anne Heche are both fresh and funny. However, they do have nearly all the best lines, as the chaps are less well defined although Kevin Corrigan's geeky video clerk is hilarious. DP. Contains swearing.

Catherine Keener *Amelia* • Anne Heche *Laura* • Todd Field *Frank* • Liev Schreiber *Andrew* • Kevin Corrigan *Bill* • Randall Batinkoff *Peter* ■ *Dir/Scr* Nicole Holofcener

The Walking Dead ★★★

Horror 1936 · US · BW · 66mins

Boris Karloff is framed for murder and sent to the electric chair. A mad doctor electronically revives him, however, to wreak vengeance on the gangsters responsible for his fate, in a moving and macabre variation on the *Frankenstein* theme. Benefiting enormously from Karloff's first-rate turn as the hollow-eyed zombie with a penchant for the piano, director Michael Curtiz keeps predictability at bay with a slick style and some marvellously expressionistic lighting. AJ

Boris Karloff *John Ellman* • Ricardo Cortez *Nolan* • Warren Hull *Jimmy* • Robert Strange *Merritt* • Joseph King (1) *Judge Shaw* • Edmund Gwenn *Dr Evan Beaumont* • Marguerite Churchill *Nancy* • Barton MacLane *Loder* • Henry O'Neill *Warner* • Paul Harvey *Blackstone* ■ *Dir* Michael Curtiz • *Scr* Ewart Adamson, Peter Milne, Robert Andrews, Lillie Hayward, from a story by Ewart Adamson, Joseph Fields

The Walking Dead ★★★

War drama 1995 · US · Colour · 89mins

This ambitious project has an excellent cast, especially the under-used Joe Morton as the leader of a group of black soldiers in Vietnam on what, unbeknown to them, is a suicide mission. When the impossible nature of their mission becomes apparent, the soldiers go through fluctuations in their loyalty to Morton, who harbours a dark secret in his own past. Good direction and convincing set pieces can't save the script, which is a bit too contrived and predictable. ST

Allen Payne *Pfc Cole Evans* • Eddie Griffin *Pte Hoover Blanche* • Joe Morton *Sgt Barkley* • Vonte Sweet *Pfc Joe Brooks* • Roger Floyd *Cpl Pippins* • Ion Overman *Shirley Evans* ■ *Dir/Scr* Preston A Whitmore II

The Walking Hills ★★★

Western 1949 · US · BW · 78mins

Nine men and one woman look for buried treasure in the desert. Partly filmed in Death Valley, it's an old story with the usual assortment of incompatible characters but cleverly written by western novelist Alan LeMay, smartly directed by a young John Sturges, and ably cast. The setting is made to count and there's a memorable sandstorm in which a fight with shovels occurs. AE

Randolph Scott *Jim Carey* • Ella Raines *Chris Jackson* • William Bishop *Shep* • Edgar Buchanan *Old Willy* • Arthur Kennedy *Chalk* • John Ireland *Frazee* ■ *Dir* John Sturges • *Scr* Alan LeMay, Virginia Roddick

The Walking Stick ★★★★

Drama 1970 · UK · Colour · 101mins

This bittersweet romance, charmingly played by David Hemmings and Samantha Eggar and set in lovely Hampstead, develops unexpectedly. Disabled businesswoman Eggar is courted by mysterious artist Hemmings, but is quite inhibited. However the love story (old-fashioned for its time with bedroom scenes dissolving to the next morning) switches gear into another genre with surprising ease. Director Eric Till has a fine eye for detail, and the supporting cast is distinguished. DM

David Hemmings *Leigh Hartley* • Samantha Eggar *Deborah Dainton* • Emlyn Williams *Jack Foil* • Phyllis Calvert *Erica Dainton* • Ferdy Mayne *Douglas Dainton* • Francesca Annis *Arabella Dainton* • Bridget Turner *Sarah Dainton* ■ *Dir* Eric Till • *Scr* George Bluestone, from the novel by Winston Graham

Walking Tall ★★ 18

Crime drama based on a true story
1973 · US · Colour · 119mins

The influence of *Dirty Harry* can be felt in every stride of Tennessee county sheriff Buford Pusser, as he declares war on the various low-lifes who pollute his jurisdiction. During the course of his campaign, he's widowed and nearly bludgeoned to death. Based on the story of a real-life character, the picture muddles any moral argument and instead piles on the skull-crushing violence and crude stereotypes on both sides. Joe Don Baker wisely opted out of the two sequels (*Part 2 Walking Tall* and *Final Chapter – Walking Tall*). AT. Contains violence.

Joe Don Baker *Buford Pusser* • Elizabeth Hartman *Pauline Pusser* • Gene Evans *Sheriff Thurman* • Noah Beery Jr *Grandpa Pusser* • Brenda Benet *Luan* • John Brascia *Prentiss* • Bruce Glover *Grady Coker* • Arch Johnson *Buel Jaggers* ■ *Dir* Phil Karlson • *Scr* Mort Briskin

Walking Tall ★★ 15

Action drama 2004 · US · Colour · 82mins

Former wrestling star The Rock takes on an ambitious role in a film that requires him to flex his acting muscles. Like the 1973 movie of the same name, this is inspired by the story of Tennessee sheriff Buford Pusser. The Rock returns to his home town after years in the US Special Forces to discover it changed for the worse. The town's lumber mill has been closed by villain Neal McDonough, who's opened a casino. The star becomes sheriff and with the help of best friend Johnny Knoxville and a large hunk of wood batters small-town values into the corrupted citizens. TH. DVD

The Rock *Chris Vaughn* • Johnny Knoxville *Ray Templeton* • Neal McDonough *Jay Hamilton Jr* • Kristen Wilson *Michelle Vaughn* • Ashley Scott *Deni* • Khleo Thomas *Pete Vaughn* • John Beasley *Chris Vaughn Sr* • Barbara Tarbuck *Connie Vaughn* • Michael Bowen *Sheriff Stan Watkins* • Kevin Durand *Booth* ■ *Dir* Kevin Bray • *Scr* David Klass, Channing Gibson, David Levien, Brian Koppelman, from the 1973 film by Mort Briskin

Wall ★★★★ 12A

Documentary
2004 · Fr/Is/US · Colour · 100mins

The tragic folly of the construction of a barrier between Israel and the Palestinian territories is exposed in this mournfully laconic documentary by Moroccan-born Jewish director, Simone Bitton. The genius of her approach is that it's never obviously apparent on which side of the wall she's filming, nor which cause is being espoused by the faceless voices on the soundtrack. Contradictions abound everywhere, as impoverished Palestinians take jobs building the wall, while Israelis find irony in the comparisons to the European ghettos of the past. But hardline attitudes are also displayed by the unrepentant settlers and the youths prepared to martyr themselves for freedom. Courageous, revealing and dispiriting. DP. In Hebrew and Arabic with English subtitles.

Dir/Scr Simone Bitton

U = SUITABLE FOR ALL Uc = SUITABLE FOR ALL, ESPECIALLY FOR YOUNG CHILDREN (VIDEO ONLY) PG = PARENTAL GUIDANCE

Wall of Silence ★★★

Drama 1993 · Arg · Colour · 106mins

Set seven years after the collapse of the junta, Lita Stantic's poised study of the scars tearing apart the newly democratic Argentina would have been more effective had it focused on why the survivors preferred to forget the military tyranny they endured. Instead it explores the problems faced by a film-maker whose project is foundering because of their reticence. Nevertheless, Ofelia Medina gives a subtle performance as the widow who slowly comes to suspect that her activist husband is alive after all. Vanessa Redgrave is more mannered as the visiting documentarist. DP. In English and Spanish with subtitles.

Vanessa Redgrave *Kate Benson* • Ofelia Medina *Silvia Cassini* ■ *Dir* Lita Stantic • *Scr* Graciela Maglie, Lita Stantic, Gabriela Massuh

Wall Street ★★★★ 15

Drama 1987 · US · Colour · 125mins

Oliver Stone co-wrote and directed this stylish morality tale about insider trading – a topical subject at the time. Charlie Sheen gives a believable performance as the gullible broker who's prepared to break the law in pursuit of riches, and he's matched by his father Martin (also playing his screen father) as the blue-collar union representative who takes a dim view of his son's wheeler-dealing. Stealing the show, however, is Oscar-winner Michael Douglas, who is memorable as ruthless corporate raider Gordon Gekko. JM [video] DVD

Michael Douglas *Gordon Gekko* • Charlie Sheen *Bud Fox* • Daryl Hannah *Darien Taylor* • Martin Sheen *Carl Fox* • Terence Stamp *Sir Larry Wildman* • Hal Holbrook *Lou Mannheim* • Sean Young *Kate Gekko* • James Spader *Roger Barnes* • Sylvia Miles *Sylvie Drimmer* • Saul Rubinek *Harold Salt* ■ *Dir* Oliver Stone • *Scr* Oliver Stone, Stanley Weiser

Waller's Last Walk ★★★

Drama 1989 · W Ger · Colour · 100mins

Three years in the making and mournfully played by Rolf Illig, Christian Wagner's film is set in the director's childhood home of Allgäu in Bavaria. The story centres on an old railway inspector, as he makes his final journey down the condemned track that has been his life. Cleverly littering this steady progress with flashbacks to fond recollections, much-missed friends and events best forgot (most notably the line's usage during the Second World War), Wagner also shows the track becoming increasingly overgrown and dilapidated, as time catches up with memory. DP. In German with English subtitles.

Rolf Illig *Waller* • Sibylle Canonica *Rosina* • Franz Boehm *Stumpf* • Volker Prechtel *Karg* • Herbert Knaup *Waller as a young man* • Crescentia Dünsser *Angelika Heindl* ■ *Dir* Christian Wagner • *Scr* Christian Wagner, from the novel *Die Strecke* by Gerhard Kopf

Walls ★★★ 18

Drama based on a true story
1984 · Can · Colour · 84mins

Based on a true story, this is a solidly mounted account of the kidnap of a Canadian prison officer-cum-reformer and her colleagues by a killer driven to breaking point by a prolonged stretch in solitary confinement. A liberal lawyer attempts to bring to wider attention the fact that a prison regime is as much responsible for a prisoner's actions as his so-called criminal mentality. This modest, sometimes violent, atmospheric production still leaves you with plenty to think about. DP [video]

Andrée Pelletier *Joan Tremblay* • Winston Rekert *Danny Baker* • Alan Scarfe *Ron Simmons* • John Wright *Curt Willis* • John Lord *Louis Martin* ■ *Dir* Thomas Shandell • *Scr* Christian Bruyere, from his play

Walls of Glass ★★★ 15

Drama 1985 · US · Colour · 82mins

As odd as its title, this likeable independent one-off gives the opportunity of a lifetime to character actor Philip Bosco, a face you'll certainly recognise even if the name doesn't ring any bells. He plays a Shakespeare-spouting New York cabbie, but this quirky drama failed to turn Bosco into a star, and, despite a distinguished cast, the public didn't respond to this winning tale. TS. Contains swearing. [video]

Philip Bosco *James Flanagan* • Geraldine Page *Mama* • Linda Thorson *Andrea* • William Hickey *Papa* • Olympia Dukakis *Mary* • Brian Bloom *Danny* • Steven Weber *Sean* ■ *Dir* Scott Goldstein [Scott D Goldstein] • *Scr* Edmond Collins, Scott Goldstein

Walnut Creek ★★

Erotic thriller 1996 · US · Colour · 95mins

The setting may be rustic, but there is very little fresh air in this erotic thriller from director Edward Holzman. Kate Rodger plays the new farm manager at David Christensen's ranch, who starts to drive a wedge between him and his wife Rochelle Swanson and daughter Renee Weldon. Rodger vamps it up for all she's worth, but Swanson wears the look of someone who's used to better things. DP

Kate Rodger *Tonya Peters* • Rochelle Swanson *Laura Styles* • David Christensen *Preston Styles* • Renee Weldon *Lacy Styles* • Greg Collins *Anthony DePrince* ■ *Dir/Scr* Edward Holzman

Walpurgis Night ★★★★

Drama 1935 · Swe · BW · 82mins

Hailed on its release as one of the best films ever made in Sweden, this sensationalist melodrama packed a powerful social punch of the kind that few pictures made anywhere else in the world could match. Tackling both adultery and abortion, Gustaf Edgren's film focuses on the unhappy marriage between Lars Hanson and his vain wife Karin Kavli. While both give earnest performances, the film belongs to Ingrid Bergman as Hanson's devoted lover and to Victor Sjöström as her father, a crusading editor leading a campaign to boost the birth rate. DP. In Swedish with English subtitles.

Lars Hanson *Johan Borg* • Karin Kavli *Clary Borg* • Victor Seastrom [Victor Sjöström] *Fredrik Bergstrom* • Ingrid Bergman *Lena* • Erik Berglund *Gustav Palm* • Sture Lagerwall *Svenson* ■ *Dir* Gustaf Edgren • *Scr* Oscar Rydqvist, Gustaf Edgren

Waltz of the Toreadors ★★★★ 15

Comedy 1962 · UK · Colour · 100mins

In one of his most impressive performances, Peter Sellers plays a retired general, unhappily married to Margaret Leighton and given a second chance at fulfilment with old flame Dany Robin. French playwright Jean Anouilh, from whose comedy the movie is derived, made despair glossily fashionable in the 1960s and director John Guillermin and writer Wolf Mankowitz transform bleak emotional undercurrents into a seductively bittersweet proposition. TH [video] DVD

Peter Sellers *General Leo Fitzjohn* • Dany Robin *Ghislaine* • Margaret Leighton *Emily Fitzjohn* • John Fraser *Robert* • Cyril Cusack *Doctor Grogan* • Prunella Scales *Estella* • Denise Coffey *Sidonia* • Jean Anderson *Agnes* • John Le Mesurier *Vicar* ■ *Dir* John Guillermin • *Scr* Wolf Mankowitz, from the play *La Valse des Toréadors* by Jean Anouilh

Waltzes from Vienna ★

Musical drama 1933 · UK · BW · 80mins

There's discord in the Strauss household as composer Johann senior (Edmund Gwenn) resents the competition from his son. Johann junior (Esmond Knight) gets his big break with a commission from a wealthy countess (Fay Compton) and, hey presto, comes up with *The Blue Danube* waltz. This tedious period drama, laced with the Waltz King's music, was an unsuitable and uncharacteristic assignment for Alfred Hitchcock and is completely devoid of his signature trademarks. RK

Jessie Matthews *Rasi* • Esmond Knight *"Shani", Johann Strauss the Younger* • Frank Vosper *The Prince* • Fay Compton *Countess Von Stahl* • Edmund Gwenn *Johann Strauss the Elder* • Robert Hale *Ebezeder* ■ *Dir* Alfred Hitchcock • *Scr* Guy Bolton, Alma Reville, from a play by Guy Bolton

Waltzing Regitze ★★★

Drama 1989 · Den · Colour · 85mins

This is a superbly acted chronicle of a durable, if often tempestuous marriage. Alternating between a celebratory garden party and events long passed, Kaspar Rostrup brings warmth to the story of the wartime lovers, who defy convention by not only living together unmarried, but also refusing to baptise their son. Rikke Bendsen and Ghita Norby excel playing the free-spirited wife, a woman as likely to invite a tramp to Christmas dinner as set upon the local headmaster, while Mikael and Frits Helmuth look on with bemusement and pride. DP. A Danish language film.

Frits Helmuth *Karl Age* • Mikael Helmuth *Karl Age, as a young man* • Ghita Norby *Regitze* • Rikke Bendsen *Regitze, as a young woman* • Henning Moritzen *Borge* • Michael Moritzen *Borge, as a young man* ■ *Dir* Kaspar Rostrup • *Scr* Kaspar Rostrup, from a novel by Martha Christensen

Wanda ★★★★ 15

Crime drama 1971 · US · Colour · 97mins

The winner of the International Critics' Prize at Venice, Barbara Loden's charming film also earned her the distinction of being the first woman director to have her debut feature awarded a cinema release since Ida Lupino's *Not Wanted* in 1949. Based on a true story and shot in 16mm, it is an unsentimental hard luck tale, in which Loden also stars as an outsider who agrees to act as a getaway driver for her neurotic lover, Michael Higgins. Loden, who was married to Elia Kazan, is totally believable. DP [video]

Barbara Loden *Wanda* • Michael Higgins *Mr Dennis* • Charles Dosinan *Dennis's father* • Frank Jourdano *Soldier* • Valerie Manches *Girl in roadhouse* ■ *Dir/Scr* Barbara Loden

Wanda Nevada ★★

Western 1979 · US · Colour · 105mins

Notable solely for being the only film to feature father and son Henry and Peter Fonda together, this western, set in the 1950s, has Fonda Jr as a poker-faced poker player who wins orphaned Brooke Shields as his jackpot and takes her gold prospecting in the Grand Canyon. The whimsicality of the piece is sometimes hard to take and Shields, then aged 14, lacks the quirkiness of, say, Tatum O'Neal in *Paper Moon*. Fonda Sr appears late in the picture as a prospector. AT

Peter Fonda *Beaudray Demerille* • Brooke Shields *Wanda Nevada* • Fiona Lewis *Dorothy Deerfield* • Luke Askew *Ruby Muldoon* • Ted Markland *Strap Pangburn* • Severn Darden *Merlin Bitterstix* • Paul Fix *Texas Curly* • Henry Fonda *Old Prospector* • Fred Ashley *Barber* ■ *Dir* Peter Fonda • *Scr* Dennis Hackin

The Wanderer ★★

Period romantic drama
1967 · Fr · Colour · 103mins

One of the great delights of Alain Fournier's 1913 novel, *Le Grand Meaulnes*, is that the rational world and the realm of childlike dreams seem able to co-exist without straining credibility. Unfortunately, director Jean-Gabriel Albicocco was unable to reproduce that delicate balance, even though his screenplay was co-written by the novelist's sister, Isabelle Rivière. Instead, this adaptation is shot through with false poetry and a visual flamboyance that owes little either to the book or life in rural France in the 1890s. DP. In French with English subtitles.

Jean Blaise *Augustin Meaulnes* • Brigitte Fossey *Yvonne de Galais* • Alain Libolt *François Seurel* • Alain Noury *Frantz de Galais* • Juliette Villard *Valentine Blondeau* • Christian de Tilière *Ganache* • Marcel Cuvelier *M Seurel* ■ *Dir* Jean-Gabriel Albicocco • *Scr* Jean-Gabriel Albicocco, Isabelle Rivière, from the novel *Le Grand Meaulnes* by Alain Fournier

The Wanderers ★★★ 18

Drama 1979 · US/Neth · Colour · 112mins

Though less lauded than the broadly similar *American Graffiti*, and more variable in its tone and quality (it's a bit episodic), this tale of the high-school life of a bunch of Italian-American kids in New York's Bronx in the early 1960s remains thoroughly entertaining. Indeed, in some quarters it has become something of a retro cult fave. AT [video] DVD

Ken Wahl *Richie* • John Friedrich *Joey* • Karen Allen *Nina* • Toni Kalem *Despie Galasso* • Alan Rosenberg *"Turkey"* • Jim Youngs *Buddy* • Tony Ganios *Perry* • Linda Manz *"Peewee"* ■ *Dir* Philip Kaufman • *Scr* Rose Kaufman, Philip Kaufman, from the novel by Richard Price • *Cinematographer* Michael Chapman

The Wandering Jew ★★

Fantasy drama 1933 · UK · BW · 111mins

Between 1913 and 1957, Maurice Elvey directed some 300 features, including many comedies and two versions of this work – the first a silent treatment in 1923. Ten years later this starry version of E Temple Thurston's once famous play emerged to mixed reviews and a bemused public. It stars the mesmeric Conrad Veidt as the eponymous figure who demands the release of Barabbas at the Crucifixion and is thereafter condemned to everlasting life. BB

Conrad Veidt *Matathias/The Unknown Knight/Matteos Battadios/Dr Matteos Battadios* • Marie Ney *Judith* • Cicely Oates *Rachel* • Basil Gill *Pontius Pilate* • Anne Grey *Joanne de Beaudricourt/* • Bertram Wallis *Boemund, Prince of Tarentum* • Jack Livesey *Godfrey, Duke of Normandy* • Hay Petrie *Merchant* • Peggy Ashcroft *Olalla Quintana* ■ *Dir* Maurice Elvey • *Scr* H Fowler Mear, from the play by E Temple Thurston

Wanted Dead or Alive ★★ 18

Action adventure
1986 · US · Colour · 101mins

Rutger Hauer stars as a former CIA agent turned bounty hunter – referred to as the grandson of Steve McQueen's character from the identically named 1950s TV show – with a reputation for hauling in the toughest criminals. However he has his hands full when Arab terrorists, led by Kiss frontman Gene Simmons, start a bombing campaign in downtown LA. Hauer excels as an action man, but the daft plot and excessive violence do him no favours. RS [video] DVD

Rutger Hauer *Nick Randall* • Robert Guillaume *Philmore Walker* • Gene Simmons *Malak Al Rahim* • Mel Harris *Terry* • William Russ *Danny Quintz* • Susan MacDonald *Louise*

W

Quintz • Jerry Hardin *John Lipton* ■ *Dir* Gary Sherman • *Scr* Michael Patrick Goodman, Brian Taggert, Gary Sherman

Wanted for Murder ★★★

Crime thriller 1946 · UK · BW · 102mins

Eric Portman is on fine form in this chilling thriller as the descendant of a public hangman who strangles young women in London's open spaces, creating a tragic figure of a man who can't help his inherited impulses. Roland Culver is a skilful adversary as the Scotland Yard inspector who slowly and patiently closes in on his man. This makes superb use of London backgrounds and has a memorable climax near the Serpentine in Hyde Park, which has the cold grip of nightmare about it. AE

Eric Portman *Victor Colebrooke* • Dulcie Gray *Anne Fielding* • Derek Farr *Jack Williams* • Roland Culver *Inspector Conway* • Stanley Holloway *Sgt Sullivan* • Barbara Everest *Mrs Colebrooke* • Kathleen Harrison *Florrie* • Bonar Colleano *Corporal Mappolo* ■ *Dir* Lawrence Huntington • *Scr* Emeric Pressburger, Rodney Ackland, Maurice Cowan, from the play by Percy Robinson, Terence de Marney

Waqt ★★★★ 15

Drama 1965 · Ind · Colour · 163mins

A major box-office success, this lavish melodrama is so full of plot that there is scarcely room for the songs, many of which went on to become popular hits. Beginning with an earthquake and a family tragedy, the film ends with a nail-biting courtroom sequence, when a lawyer has to defend his thief brother, who has been framed for murder. Superstar Sunil Dutt is splendid as the lawyer and there is sterling support from Raaj Kumar and Sadhana as the girl for whose affections they both vie. Director Yash Chopra juggles drama, comedy and spectacle with great aplomb. DP. In Hindi with English subtitles. DVD

Sunil Dutt • Raaj Kumar • Sadhana • Sharmila Tagore • Shashi Kapoor ■ *Dir* Yash Chopra • *Scr* Akhtar-ul-Iman

WAQT: the Race Against Time ★★★ PG

Drama 2005 · Ind · Colour · 152mins

In this intense family saga, Akshay Kumar plays the layabout son who refuses to shoulder his responsibilities and persistently tries the patience of his wealthy tycoon father (Amitabh Bachchan, giving another powerhouse performance). The storyline is awash with sentiment and emotion and it is matched perfectly by Kumar's unflinching performance. The melodrama is occasionally overwhelming but, for the most part, this is neatly polished and skilfully assembled. OA. In Hindi with English subtitles.

Amitabh Bachchan *Ishwar* • Akshay Kumar *Aditya* • Shefali Shah [Shefali Shetty] *Sumi* • Priyanka Chopra *Pooja* ■ *Dir* Vipul Amrutlal Shah • *Scr* Aatish Kapadia, from a story by Aatish Kapadia

The War ★★ 12

Drama 1994 · US · Colour · 119mins

Had this slender tale of childhood in the 1970s simply focused on the feud between neighbourhood kids from different sides of the tracks, it would have engrossed viewers of all ages. But no one bought the heavy-handed pacifism and the *Pollyanna* morality that Jon Avnet felt were essential. With both Kevin Costner and Mare Winningham on the wrong side of earnestness, it's left to Elijah Wood and the rest of the junior cast to provide the dramatic impetus. DP

Elijah Wood *Stu* • Kevin Costner *Stephen* • Mare Winningham *Lois* • Lexi Randall *Lidia* • LaToya Chisholm *Elvadine* • Christopher Fennell *Billy* • Donald Sellers *Arliss* • Leon Sills *Leo* • Will West *Lester Lucket* ■ *Dir* Jon Avnet • *Scr* Kathy McWorter

War ★★ 15

Action drama 2002 · Rus · Colour · 119mins

Sergei Bodrov Jr's cynical captain helps British actor Ian Kelly deliver Danish fiancée Ingeborga Dapkunaite from the clutches of Chechen warlord Georgi Gurgulia. Yet it also has some suitably acerbic comments to make on the opportunism of the media (with Channel 4 stumping up part of the ransom money in return for Kelly's video diary). However, its scarcely concealed racism renders this an unworthy swansong for Bodrov, who was killed on location shortly afterwards. DP. In Russian, English and Chechen with subtitles. DVD

Alexei Chadov *Ivan Yermakov* • Ian Kelly *John* • Sergei Bodrov Jr *Captain Medvedev* • Ingeborga Dapkunaite *Margaret* ■ *Dir/Scr* Alexei Balabanov

The War against Mrs Hadley ★★★ U

Second World War drama
1942 · US · BW · 85mins

When the Second World War comes to America with the bombing of Pearl Harbor, the spoiled, wealthy, snobbish and stubborn Fay Bainter, widow of a Washington newspaper magnate, regards it as a personal affront that her needs are ignored, and learns a lot of hard lessons about life and herself. This is a cunning mix of family drama, psychological study, moral fable and patriotic wartime propaganda. RK

Edward Arnold *Elliott Fulton* • Fay Bainter *Stella Hadley* • Richard Ney *Theodore Hadley* • Jean Rogers *Patricia Hadley* • Sara Allgood *Mrs Michael Kirkpatrick* • Spring Byington *Cecilia Talbot* • Van Johnson *Michael Fitzpatrick* ■ *Dir* Harold S Bucquet • *Scr* George Oppenheimer

War and Peace ★★★ U

Historical epic
1956 · It/US · Colour · 199mins

No less than four versions of Tolstoy's epic novel were planned by Hollywood in the mid-1950s, but producer Dino De Laurentiis moved faster than anyone else: he hired King Vidor to direct, he hired the Italian army and, crucially, he hired Audrey Hepburn. As a spectacle, it's still impressively humane, though not particularly Russian, and the casting is decidedly odd: Henry Fonda as Pierre, Mel Ferrer (Hepburn's then husband) as Prince Andrei, plus John Mills, Herbert Lom and the amazing Anita Ekberg. The vast battle scenes were later dwarfed by the six-hour Soviet version. AT

Audrey Hepburn *Natasha Rostov* • Henry Fonda *Pierre Bezukhov* • Mel Ferrer *Prince Andrei Bolkonsky* • Vittorio Gassman *Anatole Kuragin* • John Mills *Platon Karatayev* • Herbert Lom *Napoleon* • Oscar Homolka *General Mikhail Kutuzov* • Anita Ekberg *Helene* • Helmut Dantine *Dolokhov* ■ *Dir* King Vidor • *Scr* Bridget Boland, Robert Westerby, King Vidor, Mario Camerini, Ennio De Concini, Ivo Perilli, Irwin Shaw, from the novel by Leo Tolstoy • *Cinematographer* Jack Cardiff

War and Peace ★★★★ PG

Historical epic
1966 · USSR · Colour · 399mins

All the resources of the Soviet film industry and the Red Army were put at Sergei Bondarchuk's disposal to make what was intended to be an expression of Soviet pride – designed to be premiered in instalments at international film festivals – and to dwarf anything turned out by capitalist Hollywood. The sumptuous ballroom scenes match those in Visconti's *The Leopard* while the battle scenes are awesome in their scope and filmed with overhead cameras which glide over thousands of extras as they fight Napoleon's army at Austerlitz and Borodino. Just how Sergei Bondarchuk directed all this while also playing the major role of Pierre is anyone's guess. Avoid the edited English-dubbed version; the original version, though patchy, is masterly and fascinating to watch. AT. A Russian language film.

Lyudmila Savelyeva *Natasha Rostov* • Sergei Bondarchuk *Pierre Bezuhov* • Vyacheslav Tikhonov *Prince Andrei Bolkonsky* • Viktor Stanitsyn *Ilya Andrevevich Rostov* • Kira Golovko *Countess Rostova* • Oleg Tabakov *Nikolay Rostov* • Norman Rose *Narrator* ■ *Dir* Sergei Bondarchuk • *Scr* Sergei Bondarchuk, Vasily Solovyov, from the novel by Leo Tolstoy

War Arrow ★★ U

Western 1953 · US · Colour · 78mins

Jeff Chandler and Maureen O'Hara make a spirited pair in this innocuous western. He's the cavalry major who over-rides the opposition of fort commander John McIntire and recruits friendly native American Seminoles to help defeat hostile Kiowas, while O'Hara plays the feisty wife of a missing captain. Handsomely photographed in Technicolor and adequately directed by George Sherman, it's assembly line stuff. AE

Maureen O'Hara *Elaine Corwin* • Jeff Chandler *Major Howell Brady* • Suzan Ball *Avis* • John McIntire *Colonel Jackson Meade* • Charles Drake *Luke Schermerhorn* • Dennis Weaver *Pino* • Noah Beery Jr *Augustus Wilks* • Henry Brandon *Maygro* ■ *Dir* George Sherman • *Scr* John Michael Hayes

The War at Home ★★ 18

Drama 1996 · US · Colour · 118mins

Emilio Estevez directs and stars in this leaden tale of a young Vietnam vet finding it impossible to readjust to family life. Its trump cards are the always brilliant Kathy Bates and real-life dad Martin Sheen, but James Duff's script is long on clichés, short on characterisation and becomes less plausible as it goes along. Estevez's embittered, one-note performance is less than believable and his direction never more than workmanlike. JC. Contains swearing, violence.

Emilio Estevez *Jeremy Collier* • Kathy Bates *Maurine Collier* • Martin Sheen *Bob Collier* • Kimberly Williams *Karen Collier* • Corin Nemec *Donald* • Ann Hearn *Music teacher* • Carla Gugino *Melissa* ■ *Dir* Emilio Estevez • *Scr* James Duff, from his play *Homefront*

The War between Men and Women ★★★

Comedy drama 1972 · US · Colour · 105mins

Based on the cartoons of James Thurber, this sounds like a comedy but it's more of a mawkish drama with funny bits about cynical cartoonist Jack Lemmon who is going blind and the divorced mother of three (Barbara Harris) whom he marries. Then her ex-husband shows up – the excellent Jason Robards as a war photographer. Lemmon does his usual neurotic schtick but Harris matches him scene for scene. However, the real embodiment of Thurber's sense of the ridiculous is their pregnant dog which all but steals the show. AT

Jack Lemmon *Peter Wilson* • Barbara Harris *Terry Kozlenko* • Jason Robards *Stephen Kozlenko* • Herb Edelman *Howard Mann* • Lisa Gerritsen *Linda Kozlenko* • Moosie Drier *David Kozlenko* ■ *Dir* Melville Shavelson • *Scr* Melville Shavelson, Danny Arnold, from writings and drawings by James Thurber

The War between Us ★★★

Drama 1995 · Can · Colour · 93mins

Surprisingly few films have been made about the experiences of Japanese people in North America during the Second World War. Rather than exploring the subject in any great depth, this film from Canadian director Anne Wheeler uses it as the backdrop for the friendship that develops between a Japanese woman who has to leave behind everything she has worked for in the city and a housewife who knows little of life beyond her mining town in the wastes of British Columbia. Sensibly directed and uncloyingly played. DP.

Shannon Lawson *Peg Parnham* • Mieko Ouchi *Aya Kawashima* • Robert Wisden *Ed Parnham* • Ian Tracey *Jig Parnham* • Juno Ruddell *Marg Parnham* • Edmond Kato *Masaru Kawashima* • Robert Ito *Mr Kawashima* ■ *Dir* Anne Wheeler • *Scr* Sharon Gibbon

The War Bride ★★ PG

Second World War romantic drama
2001 · UK/Can · Colour · 103mins

Anna Friel has problems nailing good movies and this doesn't change her run of duff luck. Ringing of TV rather than film, this details the experiences of two London lasses who marry Canadian soldiers during the Blitz. Friel and her daughter are then shipped over to Canada to live with husband Aden Young's family until his return. Disparate performances and a lightweight plot make this wash over you. LH DVD

Anna Friel *Lily* • Molly Parker *Sylvia* • Brenda Fricker *Betty* • Loren Dean *Joe* • Julie Cox *Sophie* • Aden Young *Charlie Travis* ■ *Dir* Lyndon Chubbuck • *Scr* Angela Workman

The War Game ★★★★ 12

Documentary drama 1965 · UK · BW · 46mins

Such was the power of this documentary drama that the BBC, which produced it, refused to transmit Peter Watkins's film, leaving it to sit on the shelf, gathering dust and notoriety, before a cinema release in 1966. Watkins uses documentary-style techniques to create an image of England in the moments before a nuclear attack. It's a nightmarish blend of Ealing comedy, *Dad's Army* and wartime Ministry of Information. View it in the context of 1965 when the Cold War was at its hottest and when the youth of the world awoke each day thinking they would be vaporised at any minute. AT DVD

Michael Aspel *Commentator* • Dick Graham *Commentator* ■ *Dir/Scr* Peter Watkins • *Cinematographer* Peter Bartlett

War Hunt ★★

War drama 1962 · US · BW · 82mins

One of the most enduring actor-director partnerships has been that of Robert Redford and Sydney Pollack. This is where they first met, both making their screen debuts as actors in this low-budget, rapidly shot platoon drama set in the Korean War. Redford is a private and Pollack a sergeant and they are both disturbed by the psychotic behaviour of John Saxon, a knife-wielding private who has an adoring, orphaned Korean boy as some sort of mascot. All rather pretentious. AT

John Saxon *Pte Raymond Endore* • Robert Redford *Pte Roy Loomis* • Charles Aidman *Capt Wallace Pratt* • Sydney Pollack *Sgt Van Horn* • Gavin Macleod *Pte Crotty* • Tommy Matsuda *Charlie* • Tom Skerritt *Corporal Showalter* ■ *Dir* Denis Sanders • *Scr* Stanford Whitmore

War Italian Style ★★

Second World War comedy
1966 · It · Colour · 74mins

This feeble Italian Second World War satire features comedy double-act Franco Franchi and Ciccio Ingrassia. The Italian comics play a pair of incompetent spies in a piece that would be forgettable if it wasn't for the fact that it features one of Buster Keaton's last screen roles. The genius of silent comedy died later in the year. Sadly there's little to recommend in this film, miles away in quality from his golden age comedies and the later good work on US television. DF. An English/Italian language film.

Buster Keaton *General Von Kassler* • Franco Franchi *Frank* • Ciccio Ingrassia *Joe* • Martha Hyer *Lieut Inge Schultze* ■ *Dir* Luigi Scattini • *Scr* Franco Castellano, Pipolo, from an idea by Fulvio Lucisano

The War Lord ★★★★

Period epic 1965 · US · Colour · 122mins

In this sombre, beautifully photographed historical epic, Charlton Heston plays a feudal warlord who exerts his *droit du seigneur* – the knight's right to spend the night with any new wife-to-be he chooses. He selects blushing bride Rosemary Forsyth but Heston only takes her reluctantly since he's delirious from a wound and – against all reason – he seems influenced by pagan tradition and the druid fertility symbols that litter the landscape of 11th-century Normandy. This fascinating, literate and rather disturbing. AT

Charlton Heston *Chrysagon* • Richard Boone *Bors* • Rosemary Forsyth *Bronwyn* • Maurice Evans *Priest* • Guy Stockwell *Draco* • Niall MacGinnis *Odins* • James Farentino *Marc* ■ *Dir* Franklin Schaffner [Franklin J Schaffner] • *Scr* John Collier, Millard Kaufman, from the play *The Lovers* by Leslie Stevens • *Cinematographer* Russell Metty

The War Lover ★★★ PG

War drama 1962 · US/UK · BW · 101mins

Steve McQueen stars as a US bomber pilot based in East Anglia whose recklessness in the air over Germany is mirrored by his disregard for the feelings of the women who share his bed. But it's McQueen's sensitive friend, Robert Wagner, who wins Shirley Anne Field's heart and their love affair is set beside McQueen's love for war. Philip Leacock easily twists McQueen's charisma to bring out the psychopathic qualities of his character, for whom war is a convenience and not a crime. AT [VIDEO] DVD

Steve McQueen *Buzz Rickson* • Robert Wagner *Ed Bolland* • Shirley Ann Field [Shirley Anne Field] *Daphne Caldwell* • Gary Cockrell *Lynch* • Michael Crawford *Junior Sailen* • Billy Edwards [Bill Edwards] *Brindt* • Chuck Julian *Lamb* ■ *Dir* Philip Leacock • *Scr* Howard Koch, from the novel by John Hersey

A War of Children ★★★★

Political drama
1972 · US/UK · Colour · 87mins

George Schaefer, a former stage and occasional film director, was at his best with television drama, usually dealing with intimate, serious topics and this made-for-TV movie about the conflict in Northern Ireland is typical of his best work. Set contemporaneously to its production, this docudrama was – and sadly remains – timely in its story of two families, the Catholic Tomeltys and the Protestant McCullums trying to remain friends against all the odds. When Jenny Agutter, the young daughter of the Tomelty family, falls in love with Anthony Andrews, a British soldier, an already tense situation leads to inevitable heartache. BB

Jenny Agutter *Maureen Tomelty* • Vivien Merchant *Nora Tomelty* • John Ronane *Frank Tomelty* • Danny Figgis *Donal Tomelty* • Anthony Andrews *Reg Hogg* • Aideen O'Kelly *Meg McCullum* • David G Meredith *Robbie McCullum* ■ *Dir* George Schaefer • *Scr* James Costigan

War of the Buttons ★★★

Comedy drama 1962 · Fr · BW · 93mins

Louis Pergaud's novel is brought to the screen with an irresistible mix of nostalgia, satire and adolescent high jinks. But there's a pronounced sentimental streak undermining Yves Robert's account of the rivalry between two gangs of French schoolboys which results in their leaders, André Treton and Michel Isella, being sent to a reformatory. The most famous sequence is undoubtedly the nude attack made by Treton's gang to prevent their buttons and belts being captured as war trophies. DP. In French with English subtitles.

Martin Lartigue *Tigibus* • André Treton *Lebrac* • Michel Isella *Aztec* • Jacques Dufilho *Aztec's father* • Pierre Trabaud *Teacher* ■ *Dir* Yves Robert • *Scr* François Boyer, Yves Robert, from the novel *La Guerre des Boutons* by Louis Pergaud

War of the Buttons ★★ PG

Comedy drama
1993 · UK/Fr · Colour · 90mins

Producer David Puttnam and writer Colin Welland, both Oscar winners for *Chariots of Fire*, teamed up again for this remake of the 1962 French movie in which gangs of boys from rival villages stalk the forests and steal each other's buttons, forcing them to fight stark naked. Transplanted to Ireland, the story retains its whimsy as well as its hints at allegory. Sadly, energetic performances from the kids and well paced direction from debutant John Roberts didn't prevent a box-office disaster. AT [VIDEO]

Gregg Fitzgerald *Fergus* • Gerard Kearney *Big Con* • Daragh Naughton *Boffin* • Brenda McNamara *Tim* • Kevin O'Malley *Fishy* • John Cleere *Peter* • John Coffey *Geronimo* • Colm Meaney *Geronimo's dad* ■ *Dir* John Roberts • *Scr* Colin Welland, from the novel *La Guerre des Boutons* by Louis Pergaud

War of the Colossal Beast ★ PG

Cult science-fiction
1958 · US · BW and Colour · 68mins

The Amazing Colossal Man didn't die! He turned up in Mexico with a disfigured face and a gigantic appetite in a "what have we done to deserve this" sequel from trash-master supremo, Bert I Gordon. The producer/director's initials are the only thing that is BIG about this fourth division dud, though. AJ [VIDEO] DVD

Sally Fraser *Joyce Manning* • Dean Parkin [Dean Parkin] *Colonel Glenn Manning* • Roger Pace *Major Baird* • Russ Bender *Dr Carmichael* • Charles Stewart *Captain Harris* • George Becwar *Swanson* ■ *Dir* Bert I Gordon • *Scr* George Worthing Yates, from a story by Bert I Gordon

War of the Gargantuas ★★

Science-fiction monster horror
1970 · Jpn/US · Colour · 92mins

Intended as the sequel to *Frankenstein Conquers the World*, the American re-edited version of director Inoshiro Honda's wackily conceived continuation obscures all reference to the original only to emerge as one of the funniest monster extravaganzas ever. No point trying to make sense of the deconstructed plot – scientist Russ Tamblyn blaming himself for an epic battle between a furry brown giant monster and his evil green-hued twin which destroys Tokyo – just thrill along to the spectacular effects. AJ

Russ Tamblyn *Dr Paul Stewart* • Kumi Mizuno *His assistant* • Kipp Hamilton *Singer* • Yu Fujiki *Army commander* ■ *Dir* Inoshiro Honda • *Scr* Inoshiro Honda, Kaoru Mabuchi

The War of the Roses ★★★★ 15

Black comedy 1989 · US · Colour · 111mins

This blistering black comedy from Danny DeVito is less an assault on marriage than on the acquisitiveness of Reaganite America. Suggesting that hell is not other people, but other people's possessions, the film rapidly escalates into a frenzy of comic viciousness. Michael Douglas and Kathleen Turner hurl themselves into their parts, tainting expressions of vengeful glee with real bile. The scene in which Douglas seasons the fish stew is a standout among several wickedly excessive incidents that raise laughs as well as hackles thanks to DeVito's bravura direction. DP. Contains violence, swearing. [VIDEO] DVD

Michael Douglas *Oliver Rose* • Kathleen Turner *Barbara Rose* • Danny DeVito *Gavin D'Amato* • Marianne Sägebrecht *Susan* • Peter Donat *Larrabee* • Sean Astin *Josh, aged 17* • Heather Fairfield *Carolyn, aged 17* • GD Spradlin *Harry Thurmont* ■ *Dir* Danny DeVito • *Scr* Michael Leeson, from the novel by Warren Adler

War of the Satellites ★ U

Science fiction 1958 · US · BW · 66mins

Within months of the first Russian Sputnik being launched into space, cult director Roger Corman had this cash-in released in cinemas. Aliens threaten the destruction of Earth unless the planet's space programme is terminated. Scientist Richard Devon's dead body is taken over by the aliens to sabotage further intergalactic explorations in this excruciatingly dull exploiter. AJ

Dick Miller *Dave Royer* • Susan Cabot *Sybil Carrington* • Richard Devon *Dr Van Pander* • Eric Sinclair *Dr Lazar* • Michael Fox *Akad* • Roger Corman *Ground control* ■ *Dir* Roger Corman • *Scr* Lawrence Louis Goldman, from the story by Irving Block, Jack Rabin • *Special Effects* Jack Rabin, Irving Block, Louis DeWitt

War of the Wildcats ★★ U

Western 1943 · US · BW · 97mins

John Wayne drills for oil and tries to win the hand of Martha Scott from rival Albert Dekker. Political matters enter the fray when Wayne starts fighting for the rights of American Indians – the "little fellers" as he calls them. Reputedly, this caused consternation in Washington where it was thought the implication that native Americans had been treated badly by the government could be exploited by the Nazis. Republic made the changes asked of them and made a box-office hit, too. AT [VIDEO]

John Wayne *Daniel Somers* • Martha Scott *Catherine Allen* • Albert Dekker *James E Gardner* • George "Gabby" Hayes *Desprit Dean* • Marjorie Rambeau *Bessie Baxter* • Dale Evans *Cuddles Walker* • Grant Withers *Richardson* • Sidney Blackmer *Teddy Roosevelt* ■ *Dir* Albert S Rogell • *Scr* Ethel Hill, Eleanor Griffin, from a story by Thomson Burtis

The War of the Worlds ★★★★ PG

Science-fiction adventure
1953 · US · Colour · 81mins

Although it never comes close to reproducing the panic generated by Orson Welles's famous 1938 radio broadcast, this is a splendid version of HG Wells's sci-fi classic. When the "meteor" that lands in southern California turns out to be the mothership of a Martian invasion, the governments of the world unleash their most potent weapons in an attempt to stem the tide of destruction. Director Byron Haskin enhances the impact of the Oscar-winning special effects by ensuring that his extras convey a genuine sense of terror as civilisation collapses around them. DP. Contains violence. [VIDEO] DVD

Gene Barry *Dr Clayton Forrester* • Ann Robinson *Sylvia Van Buren* • Les Tremayne *General Mann* • Robert Cornthwaite *Doctor Pryor* • Sandro Giglio *Doctor Bilderbeck* • Lewis Martin *Pastor Collins* • William Phipps *Wash Perry* • Paul Birch *Alonzo Hogue* • Cedric Hardwicke *Narrator* ■ *Dir* Byron Haskin • *Scr* Barré Lyndon, from the novel by HG Wells • *Cinematographer* George Barnes • *Special Effects* Gordon Jennings

War of the Worlds ★★★★ 12A

Science-fiction thriller
2005 · US · Colour · 116mins

Steven Spielberg's mega-upgrade of the science-fiction landmark is a spectacular disaster epic of two halves. The first (and much the superior) hour is a masterclass in escalating tension, with grandiose and brilliantly executed sequences following in rapid succession. Unusually for a special-effects blockbuster, the human drama (though admittedly clichéd in construction) is transfixing, as divorced dockworker Tom Cruise flees the invasion with his two estranged children (played by Justin Chatwin and Dakota Fanning). It's in the second hour that the story begins to wilt, petering out until a rather abrupt ending in which Hollywood schmaltz wins the day. AJ

Tom Cruise *Ray Ferrier* • Dakota Fanning *Rachel Ferrier* • Miranda Otto *Mary Ann Ferrier* • Justin Chatwin *Robbie Ferrier* • Tim Robbins *Ogilvy* • David Alan Basche *Tim* • Yul Vazquez *Julio* ■ *Dir* Steven Spielberg • *Scr* David Koepp, from the novel by HG Wells

War Paint ★★★

Western 1953 · US · Colour · 89mins

Boasting a strong leading performance by Robert Stack, a tense and involving plot, and stark desert locations in Death Valley, this is a notch above average among cavalry and Indian westerns. The grim drama centres on the efforts of Stack's lieutenant to deliver an urgent peace treaty to an Indian chief. He finds himself up against sabotage within his patrol, lack of water, and a rebellion over gold. The steady pace is disrupted only by a campfire song interlude. AE

Robert Stack *Lt Billings* • Joan Taylor *Wanima* • Charles McGraw *Sgt Clarke* • Keith Larsen *Taslik* • Peter Graves (2) *Tolson* ■ *Dir* Lesley Selander • *Scr* Martin Berkeley, Richard Alan Simmons, from a story by Fred Freiberger, William Tunberg

War Party ★★★ 18

Action drama 1988 · US · Colour · 93mins

An alternative take on the western, with modern-day white folk and native Americans taking opposite sides for a town's centennial re-creation of an old cowboy/Indian fight. But old wounds are reopened, and old prejudices reignited, when someone starts using live ammunition. A potentially intriguing idea, but it's exhausted in the first 20 minutes; the film then becomes just a variant on the traditional western. There are good performances, though. DA [VIDEO]

Billy Wirth *Sonny Crowkiller* • Kevin Dillon *Skitty Harris* • Tim Sampson *Warren Cutfoot* • Jimmy Ray Weeks [Jimmie Ray Weeks] *Jay Stivic* • Kevyn Major Howard *Calvin Morrisey* ■ *Dir* Franc Roddam • *Scr* Spencer Eastman

W

War Requiem ★★★★ PG

Experimental documentary drama
1988 · UK · BW and Colour · 88mins

Benjamin Britten's *War Requiem*, written in 1962 for the dedication of the new Coventry Cathedral, is visualised as an elongated music video by director Derek Jarman. Laurence Olivier, in his last work on film before his death, plays a disabled veteran Second World War soldier whose memories and reflections accompany the highly acclaimed Britten opus. Newsreel footage of the Great War and atomic explosions are intercut with sequences featuring Owen Teale (as the Unknown Soldier) and Tilda Swinton (a battlefield nurse) looking powerlessly on at all the devastation and wasted lives. Jarman's ultimately inspiring, negative statement on war matches the intense emotions of Britten's music to perfection. AJ

Nathaniel Parker *Wilfred Owen* • Tilda Swinton *Nurse* • Laurence Olivier *Old Soldier* • Patricia Hayes *Mother* • Rohan McCullough *Enemy Mother* • Nigel Terry *Abraham* • Owen Teale *Unknown Soldier* • Sean Bean *German Soldier* ■ *Dir* Derek Jarman • *Scr* Derek Jarman, from the original music to oratorio *War Requiem* by Benjamin Britten and the original libretto to oratorio *War Requiem* by Wilfred Owen • *Music* Benjamin Britten • *Cinematographer* Richard Greatrex

The War Room ★★★★

Political documentary
1993 · US · Colour · 90mins

DA Pennebaker hit the campaign trial in this Oscar-nominated account of the 1992 election. The focus is less on Bill Clinton than the contrasting temperaments of his chief spin-doctors – plain-speaking campaign boss James Carville and suave press spokesman George Stephanopoulos – as they seek to counter allegations of adultery, dope-smoking and draft-dodging. There are also fascinating insights into the in-fighting within the Democratic camp and the romantic liaison between Carville and George Bush's senior aide, Mary Matalin. DP

Dir DA Pennebaker, Chris Hegedus • *Cinematographer* Nick Doob, DA Pennebaker, Kevin Rafferty

The War Wagon ★★★ U

Western 1967 · US · Colour · 96mins

Westerns starring John Wayne and Kirk Douglas approached the genre from very different directions. It's not surprising, therefore, that there's an uneasy tension behind the pair's bonhomie in this rugged comedy adventure. Yet nobody was better at directing this kind of romp than Burt Kennedy, who not only exploits the rivalry between his stars, but also gets superior supporting performances the supporting cast. The action might have been a little more robust, but the wagon itself (with its swivelling turret and machine gun) is a real scene-stealer. DP DVD

John Wayne *Taw Jackson* • Kirk Douglas *Lomax* • Howard Keel *Levi Walking Bear* • Robert Walker [Robert Walker Jr] *Billy Hyatt* • Keenan Wynn *Wes Catlin* • Bruce Cabot *Frank Pierce* • Valora Noland *Kate Catlin* • Joanna Barnes *Lola* • Bruce Dern *Hammond* • Gene Evans *Hoag* ■ *Dir* Burt Kennedy • *Scr* Clair Huffaker, from his novel *Badman*

The War Zone ★★★★ 18

Drama 1999 · UK/It · Colour · 98mins

Actor Tim Roth makes a stunning directorial debut with a distressingly believable story of incest within a close-knit family. Adapted by Alexander Stuart from his acclaimed novel, this bleak drama elicits supremely natural performances from young newcomers Freddie Cunliffe and Lara Belmont, while Ray Winstone portrays their abusive father as no *Nil by Mouth* monster, but as a loving parent. Roth also makes inspired, emotive use of the stark, jagged Devon landscapes, whose grey-hued coldness seems to mirror Belmont's pain and turns an already uncomfortable experience into a devastating one. JC. Contains swearing and nudity. DVD

Ray Winstone *Dad* • Lara Belmont *Jessie* • Freddie Cunliffe *Tom* • Tilda Swinton *Mum* • Annabelle Apsion *Nurse* • Kate Ashfield *Lucy* • Colin J Farrell [Colin Farrell (2)] *Nick* ■ *Dir* Tim Roth • *Scr* Alexander Stuart, from his novel

WarGames ★★★★ PG

Thriller 1983 · US · Colour · 108mins

Whizzkid Matthew Broderick accidentally hacks into a Pentagon computer and starts playing what he thinks is a game called Global Thermonuclear War, only to discover he's pushing the world toward destruction for real. This is an inventive nail-biter that's consistently entertaining and worryingly thought-provoking, laced by director John Badham with just the right amount of invigorating humour. Great edge-of-the-seat suspense is generated as defence specialist Dabney Coleman desperately tries to avert the impending holocaust, while preachy sentiment is kept to a minimum. AJ. Contains swearing. DVD

Matthew Broderick *David Lightman* • Dabney Coleman *John McKittrick* • John Wood *Professor Falken* • Ally Sheedy *Jennifer Mack* • Barry Corbin *General Beringer* • Juanin Clay *Pat Healy* • Dennis Lipscomb *Lyle Watson* ■ *Dir* John Badham • *Scr* Lawrence Lasker, Walter F Parkes

Warlock ★★★★ U

Western 1959 · US · Colour · 116mins

This impressive psychological western has Henry Fonda on magnificent form as a former gunfighter, aching with regret for a passing age and a wasted life, whose success as a lawman means that his corrupt regime is tolerated by the locals. The gradual disintegration of Fonda's friendship with gambler Anthony Quinn is deftly handled by director Edward Dmytryk, allowing the stars' contrasting acting styles to define their characters. This deserves to be better known. DP DVD

Richard Widmark *Johnny Gannon* • Henry Fonda *Clay Blaisdell* • Anthony Quinn *Tom Morgan* • Dorothy Malone *Lilly Dollar* • Dolores Michaels *Jessie Marlow* • Wallace Ford *Judge Holloway* • Tom Drake *Abe McQuown* • Richard Arlen *Bacon* • DeForest Kelley *Curley Burne* • Regis Toomey *Skinner* ■ *Dir* Edward Dmytryk • *Scr* Robert Alan Aurthur, from the novel by Oakley Hall

Warlock ★★★ 15

Horror 1989 · US · Colour · 97mins

Richard E Grant's great central performance as a witchfinder elevates this gory "bell, book and candle" tale to convincing heights. He's hunting warlock Julian Sands who, having escaped through a 1691 time portal to present-day LA, is looking for a Satanic bible to help him destroy the world. Slasher veteran Steve Miner's assured direction keeps everything exciting while unusual plot twists maintain a level of constant surprise. It spawned a couple of lame sequels. AJ

Richard E Grant *Giles Redferne* • Julian Sands *The Warlock* • Lori Singer *Kassandra* • Kevin O'Brien *Chas* • Mary Woronov *Channeller* • Richard Kuss *Mennonite* ■ *Dir* Steve Miner • *Scr* David Twohy • *Music* Jerry Goldsmith

Warlock: the Armageddon ★★ 18

Horror 1993 · US · Colour · 94mins

Julian Sands returns for the second time as the titular warlock, emerging fully grown, if you please, from a woman recently impregnated. He's on a quest to track down six magical stones that hold the power to herald the second coming of his satanic master, or dad as he likes to call him. Horror veteran Anthony Hickox knows it's a load of old tosh so directs with total disregard for the boundaries of taste or style. RS. Contains violence and swearing. DVD

Julian Sands *The Warlock* • Chris Young *Kenny Travis* • Paula Marshall *Samantha Ellison* • Joanna Pacula *Paula Dare* • Steve Kahan *Will Travis* • RG Armstrong *Franks* • Charles Hallahan *Ethan Larson* • Bruce Glover *Ted Ellison* ■ *Dir* Anthony Hickox • *Scr* Kevin Rock, Sam Bernard

Warlock III: the End of Innocence ★★ 18

Horror 1999 · US · Colour · 90mins

Better than the first sequel, but not a patch on the original black magic frightener, director Eric Freiser's effort generates a fair amount of atmosphere and chills thanks to its unpretentious story that embroiders on haunted house conventions. Art student Ashley Laurence takes possession of a family home she never knew existed and, with several of her school friends, takes up residence to stop it being demolished. Enter architect Bruce Payne (slicing the theatrical ham thickly) who is really the Devil's disciple and wants Laurence for satanic sacrifice. AJ DVD

Ashley Laurence *Kris Miller* • Bruce Payne *Warlock/Philip Covington* • Paul Francis *Michael* • Jan Schweiterman *Jerry* • Boti Ann Bliss *Robin* ■ *Dir* Eric Freiser • *Scr* Eric Freiser, Bruce David Eisen

Warlords of Atlantis ★★★ PG

Action adventure 1978 · UK · Colour · 92mins

It may be small beer compared with the monster movies of the computer age, but this is still a decent romp from director Kevin Connor. Doug McClure is the clean-cut Hollywood hero (and about as Victorian as skateboards) who discovers the fabled city (ruled, would you believe, by Cyd Charisse and Daniel Massey) and its monstrous menagerie of sundry sea beasties – including a giant octopus. The sets and the creatures are as wobbly as the script and the performances, but that's just part of the charm. AT DVD

Doug McClure *Greg Collinson* • Peter Gilmore *Charles Aitken* • Shane Rimmer *Captain Daniels* • Lea Brodie *Delphine Briggs* • Michael Gothard *Atmir* • Hal Galili *Grogan* • John Ratzenberger *Fenn* • Cyd Charisse *Atsil* • Daniel Massey *Atraxon* ■ *Dir* Kevin Connor • *Scr* Brian Hayles

A Warm December ★★

Romantic drama
1973 · UK · Colour · 100mins

This mawkish affair begins as a thriller and ends up as a romance. Sidney Poitier (making his second film as director) stars as an American widower, a doctor who falls for the supposedly hounded niece (Esther Anderson) of an African diplomat, only to discover that the people who are following her are doing it for her own good. Tough all round, especially for audiences. TH

Sidney Poitier *Doctor Matt Younger* • Esther Anderson *Catherine* • Yvette Curtis *Stefanie Younger* • George Baker *Henry Barlow* • Earl Cameron *Ambassador George Oswandu* • Johnny Sekka *Myomo* ■ *Dir* Sidney Poitier • *Scr* Lawrence Roman

Warm Nights on a Slow Moving Train ★★★ 18

Drama 1986 · Aus · Colour · 87mins

This intriguing Australian tale of dual personality was withheld from release after its completion in 1986. However, director Bob Ellis's simmering thriller deserves a wider showing. As the mousey Catholic school art teacher who works as a train-board prostitute by night to help her morphine-addicted, paraplegic brother, Wendy Hughes gives a performance that is as subtle and sensitive as it is dark and disturbing. Colin Friels also does well as the client who draws her into a dangerous liaison. DP

Wendy Hughes *Girl* • Colin Friels *Man* • Norman Kaye *Salesman* • John Clayton *Football coach* • Lewis Fitz-Gerald *Girl's brother* • Rod Zuanic *Soldier* • Steve J Spears *Singer* • Grant Tilly *Politician* ■ *Dir* Bob Ellis • *Scr* Bob Ellis, Denny Lawrence

Warm Water under a Red Bridge ★★★ 15

Comedy 2001 · Jpn/ Fr · Colour · 114mins

Shohei Imamura's adaptation of Henmi Yo's fantastical novel – about a young woman who expels torrents of water during sex – seems more like an over-elaborate anecdote than a profound meditation on female sensuality. Hisao Inagaki's designs are exquisite, and are captured in all their glory by cinematographer Shigeru Komatsubara, but the film lacks the philosophical depth to complement its gleeful physicality. DP. In Japanese with English subtitles. DVD

Koji Yakusho *Yosuke Sasano* • Misa Shimizu *Saeko Aizawa* • Mitsuko Baisho *Mitsu Aizawa* • Kazuo Kitamura *Taro* • Mansaku Fuwa *Gen* ■ *Dir* Shohei Imamura • *Scr* Shohei Imamura, Motofumi Tomikawa, Daisuke Tengan, from a novel by Henmi Yo

Warming Up ★★★

Comedy 1983 · Aus · Colour · 94mins

Without ever quite striking the right balance between the satirical and the downright silly, this is, nevertheless, an entertaining comedy, in which the worlds of ballet and Australian Rules football meet head on. Barbara Stephens is hugely impressive as the no-nonsense dance instructor whose refusal to accept the "men only" regime in the backwater town of Wilgunyah prompts her to train the Wombats football team behind the back of their coach and her nemesis, cop Henri Szeps. Director Bruce Best stages the training sequences very well, but the matches themselves are less convincing. DP

Barbara Stephens *Juliet Cavanagh-Forbes* • Henri Szeps *Peter Sullivan* • Queenie Ashton *Mrs Marsh* • Adam Fernance *Randolph Cavanagh-Forbes* • Lloyd Morris *Ox* • Tim Grogan *Snoopy* • Ron Blanchard *Lennie* ■ *Dir* Bruce Best • *Scr* James Davern

Warning Shot ★★★

Crime thriller 1967 · US · Colour · 99mins

David Janssen was at the height of his fame from playing the title role in TV's long-running series *The Fugitive* when he starred in this pacey and entertaining thriller about a policeman's bid to clear his name – not unlike the Fugitive himself – of killing an apparently unarmed and upstanding medic. In the process, he encounters plenty of drama, excitement and an all-star cast. PF

David Janssen *Sergeant Tom Valens* • Ed Begley *Captain Roy Klodin* • Keenan Wynn *Sergeant Ed Musso* • Sam Wanamaker *Frank Sanderman* • Lillian Gish *Alice Willows* • Stefanie Powers *Liz Thayer* • Eleanor Parker *Mrs Doris Ruston* • George Grizzard *Walt Cody* • George Sanders *Calvin York* • Steve Allen *Perry Knowland* • Carroll O'Connor *Paul Jerez* •

W

Joan Collins *Joanie Valens* • Walter Pidgeon *Orville Ames* ■ *Dir* Buzz Kulik • *Scr* Mann Rubin, from the novel *711 – Officer Needs Help* by Whit Masterson

Warning Sign ★★★ 15

Science-fiction thriller
1985 · US · Colour · 94mins

Although derivative of a dozen other mind-melt movies, Hal Barwood's thriller is engrossing action all the way with its bacterial twists and brain-damaged turns. The excellent acting lifts it way above the norm, although mouth-foaming maniac Richard Dysart delivers some stupidly inspired dialogue about rage being beautiful. You'll be sorry when the curtain falls on this exciting tale. AJ [video]

Sam Waterston *Cal Morse* • Kathleen Quinlan *Joanie Morse* • Yaphet Kotto *Major Connolly* • Jeffrey DeMunn *Dan Fairchild* • Richard Dysart *Dr Nielsen* • GW Bailey *Tom Schmidt* • Jerry Hardin *Vic Flint* ■ *Dir* Hal Barwood • *Scr* Hal Barwood, Matthew Robbins

Warpath ★★ U

Western 1951 · US · Colour · 95mins

A sobering pre-revisionist western, a reminder of a Hollywood where Red Indians were treated like dirt, this Paramount caper is actually dedicated to the Seventh Cavalry. Using events leading up to the Battle of Little Bighorn as a background for a stark revenge plot, Edmond O'Brien (too chubby for a western hero) rides out to avenge his slaughtered fiancée. In the hands of director Byron Haskin, it's a perfectly functional time-passer. TS

Edmond O'Brien *John Vickers* • Dean Jagger *Sam Quade* • Charles Stevens *Courier* • Forrest Tucker *Sergeant O'Hara* • Harry Carey Jr *Captain Gregson* • Polly Bergen *Molly Quade* • James Millican *General Custer* • Wallace Ford *Private Potts* • Paul Fix *Private Fiore* ■ *Dir* Byron Haskin • *Scr* Frank Gruber • *Cinematographer* Ray Rennahan

Warrendale ★★★

Documentary 1967 · Can · BW · 102mins

A *cause célèbre* after it was rejected by the Canadian Broadcasting Corporation on account of its four-letter content, Allan King's "Direct Cinema" documentary still makes for disconcerting viewing. Priding itself on allowing its residents as much latitude as possible, Warrendale was a hostel for emotionally disturbed adolescents run by Dr John Brown on the outskirts of Toronto. Observing the kids at leisure, in therapy and (most tellingly) in shock after the death of their beloved cook, King provides no commentary and presents a graphic and frequently shocking picture of a generation with little self-respect and even less hope. DP

Dir Allan King

The Warrior ★★★ 12

Drama
2001 · UK/Fr/Ger/Ind · Colour · 82mins

Writer/director Asif Kapadia draws on both eastern and western cultural and cinematic influences for his inspiration for this languorous odyssey. But while this retains its visual splendour, the story quickly loses its focus, as Irfan renounces violence and quits his life as head of a warlord's private army, only to be pursued through the Himalayan foothills by his master's enforcer, Sheikh Annuddin. Dealing in types not characters, and situations rather than psychology, Kapadia's debut feature is auspicious, but aloof. DP. In Hindi with English subtitles. Contains violence. [video] DVD

Irfan Khan *Lafcadia, the warrior* • Puru Chhibber *Katiba, Lafcadia's son* • Sheikh Annuddin *Biswas* ■ *Dir* Asif Kapadia • *Scr* Asif Kapadia, Tim Miller

The Warrior and the Sorceress ★★ 18

Martial arts action adventure
1983 · US · Colour · 74mins

Part samurai movie, part western and part fantasy, in the end this fumbling affair comes across as nothing more than a blatant rip-off of Akira Kurosawa's *Yojimbo*. David Carradine plays a holy warrior, in all but name his television *Kung Fu* character, who arrives in an impoverished village where two rival gangs vie for control over a water well. Exotic Maria Socas, cast as the sorceress, spends the entire movie topless. Maybe the budget was so small they could only afford half her costume! RS [video] DVD

David Carradine *Kain* • Luke Askew *Zeg* • Maria Socas *Naja* • Anthony De Longis *Kief* • Harry Townes *Bludge* ■ *Dir* John C Broderick • *Scr* John C Broderick, from a story by William Stout, John C Broderick

Warrior Queen ★ 18

Period sex drama 1986 · US · Colour · 67mins

Silliness, thy name is *Warrior Queen*. Sybil Danning stars as the titular Queen Berenice, an attractive but deadly woman who arrives in Pompeii for a festival and to negotiate with the city's ruler, Clodius. Donald Pleasence leaves no bit of scenery unchewed as the self-indulgent mayor, so it's no wonder his wife wants to hook up with an attractive young gladiator. ST [video]

Sybil Danning *Berenice* • Donald Pleasence *Clodius* • Richard Hill *Marcus* • Josephine Jacqueline Jones *Chloe* • Tally Chanel *Vespa* • Stasia Micula [Samantha Fox] *Philomena/Augusta* • Suzanna Smith *Veneria* ■ *Dir* Chuck Vincent • *Scr* Rick Marx, from a story by Harry Alan Towers

The Warriors ★★★★ 18

Action drama 1979 · US · Colour · 88mins

This vivid and violent gangland thriller from director Walter Hill is, essentially, an urban western. It centres on a New York gang whose members battle their way back to home turf following the murder of a rival gang leader during a ceasefire meeting. Despite the gritty storyline and locations, there's a doomed, romantic feel to the film and a poetic quality to the exhilarating fight scenes. Hill sketches the characters with some sympathy and is rewarded with excellent performances from the largely unknown cast. JF. Contains swearing and drug abuse. [video] DVD

Michael Beck *Swan* • James Remar *Ajax* • Thomas Waites [Thomas G Waites] *Fox* • Dorsey Wright *Cleon* • Brian Tyler (2) *Snow* • David Harris *Cochise* • Tom McKitterick *Cowboy* • Mercedes Ruehl *Policewoman* ■ *Dir* Walter Hill • *Scr* Walter Hill, David Shaber, from the novel by Sol Yurick • *Cinematographer* Andrew Laszlo

Warriors of Virtue ★★ PG

Fantasy action adventure
1996 · US/Chi · Colour · 98mins

The warriors are plentiful, but there's very little virtue in this children's fantasy about a boy who's sucked down a kind of intergalactic plughole to a planet where the kangaroo-style natives are battling an evil overlord. While youngsters may appreciate the imaginative sets and director Ronny Yu's well staged fight scenes, the feebleness of the acting, the thin characterisation and the cod new-age treatment make this a sub-standard effort. An equally weak sequel followed. DA [video]

Angus MacFadyen *Komodo* • Mario Yedidia *Ryan Jeffers* • Marley Shelton *Elysia* • Chi Chao-Li *Master Chung* • Tom Towles *General Grillo* ■ *Dir* Ronny Yu • *Scr* Michael Vickerman, Hugh Kelley, from characters created by Dennis Law, Ronald Law, Christopher Law, Jeremy Law

The Wash ★★ 15

Comedy 2001 · US · Colour · 92mins

Rappers Snoop Dogg and Dr Dre head the cast in this shipshod comedy as a couple of losers who briefly sideline their fixation with getting high and pursuing foxy females in order to rescue car-wash boss George Washington from a gang of incompetent kidnappers. Utterly reliant on the kind of African-American stereotypes and clichés that writer/director Robert Townsend lamented in *Hollywood Shuffle*, this is a lazy film that trades cynically on supposedly subversive chic and the notoriety of its leads. DP [video] DVD

Dr Dre *Sean* • Snoop Dogg *Dee Loc* • George Wallace *Mr Washington* • Angell Conwell *Antoinette* • Tommy "Tiny" Lister Jr [Tom "Tiny" Lister Jr] *Bear* • Bruce Bruce *DeWayne* ■ *Dir/Scr* DJ Pooh

Washington Merry-Go-Round ★★

Political melodrama 1932 · US · BW · 78mins

Lee Tracy finds himself on the trail of corruption in high places in this creaky ode to the American way. Although it touches on many of the points later raised in *Mr Smith Goes to Washington*, James Cruze's half-hearted picture lacks the sharpness of the Frank Capra classic, and Tracy (more at home in his familiar role as a fast-talking reporter) is no James Stewart. The enthusiastic Constance Cummings is given too little to do as Tracy's Girl Friday. DP

Lee Tracy *Button Gwinnett Brown* • Constance Cummings *Alice Wylie* • Alan Dinehart *Norton* • Walter Connolly *Senator Wylie* • Clarence Muse *Clarence, the Valet* • Arthur Vinton *Beef Brannigan* • Frank Sheridan *Kelleher* ■ *Dir* James Cruze • *Scr* Jo Swerling, from a story by Maxwell Anderson

Washington Square ★★★ PG

Romantic drama
1997 · US · Colour · 111mins

Jennifer Jason Leigh is the dowdy spinster in 19th century America, whose chance of marriage is cruelly denied her by her domineering father Albert Finney. It starts promisingly as director Agnieszka Holland sets the scene with a breathtaking camera swoop from above the treetops to a bedroom where a beautiful woman has just died, bloodily, in childbirth. From then on, however, Holland is less assured and this Henry James adaptation ultimately fails to live up to its early promise. TH [video]

Jennifer Jason Leigh *Catherine Sloper* • Albert Finney *Dr Austin Sloper* • Ben Chaplin *Morris Townsend* • Maggie Smith *Aunt Lavinia Penniman* • Judith Ivey *Aunt Elizabeth Almond* • Betsy Brantley *Mrs Montgomery* • Jennifer Garner *Marian Almond* • Peter Maloney *Jacob Webber/Notary* • Robert Stanton *Arthur Townsend* • Arthur Laupus *Mr Almond* ■ *Dir* Agnieszka Holland • *Scr* Carol Doyle, from the novel by Henry James

Washington Story ★★ U

Political drama 1952 · US · BW · 81mins

MGM was given access to the Washington's major landmarks to add a touch of authenticity to the story of congressman Van Johnson, who becomes the subject of a smear campaign. This is calculatingly noble fare, with Patricia Neal dewey-eyed as the journalist who betrays muck-raking boss Philip Ober to defend liberal do-gooder Johnson. DP

Van Johnson *Joseph T Gresham* • Patricia Neal *Alice Kingsly* • Louis Calhern *Charles W Birch* • Sidney Blackmer *Philip Emery* • Philip Ober *Gilbert Nunnally* • Patricia Collinge *Miss Galbreth* • Moroni Olsen *Speaker* • Elizabeth Patterson *Miss Dee* ■ *Dir/Scr* Robert Pirosh

The Wasp Woman ★★ PG

Science-fiction horror
1959 · US · BW · 72mins

Cosmetics boss Susan Cabot uses wasp enzymes for a rejuvenation formula and turns into a blood-lusting bug-eyed monster in cult director Roger Corman's ironic rip-off of *The Fly*. It's pretty slow, and more ridiculous than frightening, but Cabot's coolly professional performance makes up for the cheapness of the production (the first to be made by Corman's own company, Filmgroup) and helps paper over the weak scripting. AJ DVD

Susan Cabot *Janice Starlin* • Fred Eisley [Anthony Eisley] *Bill Lane* • Barboura Morris *Mary Dennison* • Michael Mark *Dr Eric Zinthrop* • Frank Gerstle *Hellman* ■ *Dir* Roger Corman • *Scr* Leo Gordon

Watch It, Sailor! ★★ U

Comedy 1961 · UK · BW · 83mins

The path of true love never runs smooth, which is handy for makers of romantic comedies. Here it's the courtship between naval lieutenant Dennis Price and his bride-to-be Liz Fraser which is in danger of running aground when Price is served with a paternity suit. A host of familiar British comedy talent fill out the cast of this unexceptional comedy. DF

Miriam Karlin *Mrs Lack* • Dennis Price *Lt Cmdr Hardcastle* • Liz Fraser *Daphne* • Irene Handl *Edie Hornett* • Graham Stark *Carnoustie Bligh* • Vera Day *Shirley Hornett* • Marjorie Rhodes *Emma Hornett* • Cyril Smith *Mr Hornett* • John Meillon *Albert Tufnell* • Frankie Howerd *Organist* ■ *Dir* Wolf Rilla • *Scr* Falkand Cary, Philip King, from their play

Watch on the Rhine ★★★★★ U

Drama 1943 · US · BW · 107mins

Lillian Hellman's hit 1941 play came to the screen directed by Herman Shumlin, responsible for the Broadway production, and retained much of its original stage cast. One of the most powerful and impassioned pleas for resistance to fascism in modern drama, the action takes place before the outbreak of the Second World War and involves German Paul Lukas, his American wife Bette Davis and their children, who, while staying with Davis's mother Lucille Watson, encounter dispossessed Romanian count George Coulouris. The count discovers Lukas's true identity as an anti-Nazi resistance worker and prepares to sell the information to the Germans. The film combines politics, heroism, poignancy, suspense and sophisticated wit to gripping effect. Lukas won the best actor Oscar, with picture, screenplay and Watson nominated. RK [video]

Bette Davis *Sara Muller* • Paul Lukas *Kurt Muller* • Geraldine Fitzgerald *Marthe de Brancovis* • Lucile Watson *Fanny Farrelly* • Beulah Bondi *Anise* • George Coulouris *Teck de Brancovis* • Donald Woods *David Farrelly* ■ *Dir* Herman Shumlin • *Scr* Dashiell Hammett, Lillian Hellman, from the play by Lillian Hellman • *Music* Max Steiner • *Cinematographer* Hal Mohr

Watch the Birdie ★★ U

Comedy 1950 · US · BW · 70mins

Although red-haired comic Red Skelton was one of MGM's top comedians, the studio executives never quite knew what to do with him, as this dreary remake of Buster Keaton's *The Cameraman* (1928) shows. In it, photographer Skelton inadvertently films a private conversation revealing a crooked scam and saves rich girl Arlene Dahl from financial ruin. Skelton insisted on also playing the roles of his father and grandfather, which was not a good idea. TH

W

Red Skelton *Rusty Cammeron/Pop Cammeron/Grandpop Cammeron* • Arlene Dahl *Lucia Corlane* • Ann Miller *Miss Lucky Vista* • Leon Ames *Grantland D Farns* • Pam Britton [Pamela Britton] *Mrs Shanway* • Richard Rober *Mr Shanway* ■ *Dir* Jack Donohue • *Scr* Ivan Tors, Devery Freeman, Harry Ruskin, from a story by Marshall Neilan Jr

Watch Your Stern ★★ PG

Comedy 1960 · UK · BW · 84mins

Gerald Thomas's nautical comedy may be full of *Carry On* names on both sides of the camera, but it's a disappointing affair. There aren't actually all that many laughs as twitchy tar Connor assumes a range of disguises to cover up a blunder over torpedo plans. But the by-play between the characters is slick and there is some amusing slapstick. DP DVD

Kenneth Connor *Ordinary Seaman Blissworth* • Eric Barker *Captain David Foster* • Leslie Phillips *Lieutenant Commander Fanshawe* • Joan Sims *Ann Foster* • Hattie Jacques *Agatha Potter* • Spike Milligan *Dockyard mate* • Eric Sykes *Dockyard mate* • Sidney James *Chief Petty Officer Mundy* • Ed Devereaux *Commander Phillips* • David Lodge *Security sergeant* ■ *Dir* Gerald Thomas • *Scr* Alan Hackney, Vivian A Cox, from the play *Something about a Sailor* by Earle Couttie

Watched ★★★ 15

Psychological drama
1974 · US · Colour · 92mins

The old chestnut of a government agent going underground is given some spark by the acting of Stacy Keach as a man who stalked dope addicts. Mentally unstable, he's now at odds with Harris Yulin, head of the narcotics department. Some social relevancies put a tighter spin on the usual procedures than is customary. TH

Stacy Keach *Mike Mandell/Sonny* • Harris Yulin *Gordon Pankey* • Bridget Pole *Informer* • Turid Aarsted *Blonde* • Valeri Parker *Hitchhiker* ■ *Dir/Scr* John Parsons

The Watcher ★★ 15

Psychological thriller
2000 · US · Colour · 92mins

In this dismal thriller, Keanu Reeves portrays an FBI-taunting serial killer. Reeves plays the strangler who's relocated to Chicago to continue his game of psychological warfare with James Spader's troubled agent. There are a few creepy sequences, but pop video-maker and first-time director Joe Charbanic never manages to sustain a credible air of menace. JF. Contains violence and swearing. DVD

James Spader *Joel Campbell* • Marisa Tomei *Polly* • Keanu Reeves *David Allen Griffin* • Ernie Hudson *Ibby* • Chris Ellis *Hollis* ■ *Dir* Joe Charbanic • *Scr* David Elliot, Clay Ayers, from a story by Darcy Meyers, David Elliot

The Watcher in the Woods ★★ PG

Supernatural horror
1982 · US/UK · Colour · 79mins

Disney attempted to shake its popcorn image with this tale of a composer's family moving into a mysterious cottage owned by sinister Bette Davis. But the psychic alien time-warp plot is too silly for adults and not daft enough to make it a proper children's treat. Director John Hough knows how to use atmosphere, though, and sustains it quite well, despite ex-ice skater Lynn-Holly Johnson's bland central performance. Disney changed the climax after a disastrous test screening. AJ DVD

Bette Davis *Mrs Aylwood* • Carroll Baker *Helen Curtis* • David McCallum *Paul Curtis* • Lynn-Holly Johnson *Jan Curtis* • Kyle Richards *Ellie Curtis* • Ian Bannen *John Keller* • Richard Pasco *Tom Colley* ■ *Dir* John Hough, Vincent McEveety • *Scr* Brian Clemens, Harry Spalding, Rosemary Anne Sisson, from the novel by Florence Engel Randall

Watchers ★ 18

Science-fiction horror
1988 · Can · Colour · 86mins

Horror novelist Dean R Koontz was extremely unhappy with this adaptation of his work, though he had plenty of warning with bargain-basement producers Roger Corman and Damian Lee attaching themselves to the project. Corey Haim is cast as the teen hero who finds an extremely intelligent dog, not knowing that it is the result of a government experiment. Once again Michael Ironside gives a stereotyped and poorly written character some menace and personality. KB

Corey Haim *Travis* • Barbara Williams (2) *Nora* • Michael Ironside *Lem* • Lala Sloatman *Tracey* • Duncan Fraser *Sheriff Gaines* ■ *Dir* Jon Hess • *Scr* Bill Freed, Damian Lee, from the novel by Dean R Koontz

The Watchmaker of St Paul ★★★★ PG

Crime drama 1973 · Fr · Colour · 100mins

Bertrand Tavernier made his feature debut with this reworking of Georges Simenon's US-set novella. The fact that it was co-scripted by veterans Jean Aurenche and Pierre Bost betrays Tavernier's desire to produce a literate picture in the "Tradition of Quality" mode. But there's no studio-bound realism here, as Tavernier captures the authentic Lyonnais atmosphere and uses his own birthplace as the setting for several key scenes. Philippe Noiret is superb as the watchmaker questioning both his bourgeois beliefs and his paternal value on learning of his son's involvement in a political killing. Equally impressive is Jean Rochefort's quietly dignified cop. DP. In French with English subtitles.

Philippe Noiret *Michel Descombes* • Jean Rochefort *Inspector Guiboud* • Jacques Denis *Antoine* • Yves Afonso *Inspector Bricard* • Sylvain Rougerie *Bernard* • Christine Pascal *Liliane Torrini* ■ *Dir* Bertrand Tavernier • *Scr* Bertrand Tavernier, Jean Aurenche, Pierre Bost, from the novel *L'Horloger d'Everton* by Georges Simenon

Water ★ 15

Comedy 1985 · UK · Colour · 93mins

One of the disasters that sank HandMade Films, this stars Michael Caine as a British diplomat on a West Indian island awash with Communist insurrection and Americans dredging mineral water. Intended as a satire on the Falklands and Grenada, it falls flat in all departments. AT. Contains swearing.

Michael Caine *Baxter Thwaites* • Valerie Perrine *Pamela* • Brenda Vaccaro *Dolores* • Leonard Rossiter *Sir Malcolm Leveridge* • Billy Connolly *Delgado* • Dennis Duggan *Rob* • Fulton Mackay *Eric* • Jimmie Walker *Jay Jay* • Dick Shawn *Deke Halliday* • Fred Gwynne *Spender* • Maureen Lipman *Prime minister* • Ruby Wax *Spenco executive* ■ *Dir* Dick Clement • *Scr* Dick Clement, Ian La Frenais, Bill Persky, from a story by Bill Persky

The Water Babies ★ U

Part-animated fantasy adventure
1978 · UK/Pol · Colour · 81mins

Combining cartoon and live action, this is a ghastly adaptation of the Charles Kingsley classic. Admittedly, director Lionel Jeffries had to revert to animation to tell the tale of a young chimney sweep who rescues a group of underwater children from a tyrannical shark. But the cartooning is bland, the voicing of the sea creatures and the water babies too cute and the songs are a disgrace. DP DVD

James Mason *Grimes* • Billie Whitelaw *Mrs Doasyouwouldbedoneby* • Tommy Pender *Tom* • Bernard Cribbins *Masterman* • Joan Greenwood *Lady Harriet* • David Tomlinson *Sir John* • Samantha Gates *Ellie* • Paul Luty *Sladd* ■ *Dir* Lionel Jeffries • *Scr* Michael Robson, from the novel by Charles Kingsley

Water Drops on Burning Rocks ★★★ 18

Drama 1999 · Fr/Jpn · Colour · 85mins

Written when he was 19 yet unperformed in his lifetime, Rainer Werner Fassbinder's first full-length play is here artfully translated to the screen by iconoclastic director François Ozon. The highly charged action chronicles bisexual Bernard Girardeau's relationships with a callow youth, the youth's naive girlfriend and his own transsexual ex-wife. The film is made notable by Ozon's fidelity to Fassbinder's cinematic style, particularly in his use of glass and reflective surfaces, and in his treatment of the characters as marionettes at the mercy of the story's twists and turns. DP. In French and German with English subtitles. Contains swearing. DVD

Bernard Giraudeau *Léopold Blum* • Malik Zidi *Franz Meister* • Ludivine Sagnier *Anna* • Anna Thomson [Anna Levine] *Véra* ■ *Dir* François Ozon • *Scr* François Ozon, from the play *Tropfen auf Heisse Steine* by Rainer Werner Fassbinder

The Waterboy ★★★ 12

Sports comedy 1998 · US · Colour · 86mins

Incredibly dumb but equally infectious, this stars Adam Sandler as a lowly, put-upon dispenser of water to sweaty college footballers. One day, their abuse (this time about his beloved Cajun mum, Kathy Bates) is just too much and he strikes back by charging one of the players, so impressing the coach that he ends up on the team. Featuring great performances from Bates and Henry Winkler, this popular hit allows Sandler to put his modest comedic talent to good use. JB. Contains swearing, nudity. DVD

Adam Sandler *Bobby Boucher* • Kathy Bates *Mama Boucher* • Henry Winkler *Coach Klein* • Fairuza Balk *Vicki Vallencourt* • Jerry Reed *Red Beaulieu* • Larry Gilliard Jr *Derek Wallace* • Blake Clark *Farmer Fran* • Peter Dante *Gee Grenouille* ■ *Dir* Frank Coraci • *Scr* Tim Herlihy, Adam Sandler

The Waterdance ★★★ 15

Drama 1991 · US · Colour · 102mins

This gritty, syrup-free movie is about a disparate group of young men attempting to come to terms with the fact that they will be paralysed for the rest of their lives. As a young novelist who has an accident on a hiking holiday and slowly puts his life back together, Eric Stoltz is excellent in the lead, with Wesley Snipes and William Forsythe equally good as two fellow paraplegics. A well-acted, moving and often witty tour through a variety of fears and neuroses. JF. Contains violence, swearing and nudity.

Eric Stoltz *Joel Garcia* • Wesley Snipes *Raymond Hill* • William Forsythe *Bloss* • Helen Hunt *Anna* • Elizabeth Peña *Rosa* • William Allen Young *Les* • Henry Harris *Mr Gibson* ■ *Dir* Neal Jimenez, Michael Steinberg • *Scr* Neal Jimenez

Waterfront ★★★

Drama 1950 · UK · BW · 80mins

Having co-directed *Private Angelo*, Michael Anderson went solo with this sobering portrait of Liverpool in the Depression. The film is undeniably melodramatic, yet it has a surprisingly raw naturalism that suggests the influence of both Italian neorealism and the proud British documentary tradition. As the seaman whose drunken binges mean misery for his family and trouble for his shipmates, Robert Newton reins in his tendency for excess, and he receives solid support from the ever-dependable Kathleen Harrison and a young Richard Burton, in his third feature. DP

Robert Newton *Peter McCabe* • Kathleen Harrison *Mrs McCabe* • Richard Burton *Ben Satterthwaite* • Avis Scott *Nora McCabe* • Susan Shaw *Connie McCabe* • Robin Netscher *George Alexander* • Kenneth Griffith *Maurice Bruno* ■ *Dir* Michael Anderson • *Scr* John Brophy, Paul Soskin, from the novel by John Brophy

Waterhole #3 ★★★ 15

Comedy western 1967 · US · Colour · 91mins

Where else would you expect a western about deception, ambition and naked greed to be set but Integrity, Arizona? James Coburn becomes the hero of this comedy tale by dint of the fact that he is marginally less repellent than his rivals, all scouring this particular desert watering hole for the proceeds of a gold robbery. The ever-vivacious Joan Blondell is on sparkling form as an avaricious madam, while Carroll O'Connor hams up a storm as a sheriff with some highly personal views on upholding the law. DP

James Coburn *Lewton Cole* • Carroll O'Connor *Sheriff John Copperud* • Margaret Blye [Maggie Blye] *Billee Copperud* • Claude Akins *Sgt Henry Foggers* • Timothy Carey *Hilb* • Joan Blondell *Lavinia* • Robert Cornthwaite *George* • Bruce Dern *Deputy Sheriff* • James Whitmore *Captain Shipley* ■ *Dir* William Graham [William A Graham] • *Scr* Joseph T Steck, Robert R Young

Waterland ★★ 15

Drama 1992 · UK · Colour · 90mins

Based on Graham Swift's Booker Prize-winning novel, this was very much a pet project of Jeremy Irons who stars with his wife Sinead Cusack. The story charts the emotional collapse of a teacher and his wife who grew up on the flat marshlands of the East Anglian fens. This landscape, superbly captured, serves to underline the characters as they flash back and forward through the bleak wreckage of their lives, all for the benefit of Irons's American students. Earnest, unpleasant and tedious. AT. Contains swearing and nudity.

Jeremy Irons *Tom Crick* • Sinead Cusack *Mary Crick* • Ethan Hawke *Mathew Price* • Grant Warnock *Young Tom* • Lena Headey *Young Mary* • David Morrissey *Dick Crick* • John Heard *Lewis Scott* • Callum Dixon *Freddie Parr* ■ *Dir* Stephen Gyllenhaal • *Scr* Peter Prince, from the novel by Graham Swift

Waterloo ★★★★ U

Historical epic
1970 · It/USSR · Colour · 126mins

Rod Steiger gives a magnificent performance as Napoleon – all hot rages and cool calculation – as he heads for his destiny in Belgium in Ukrainian director Sergei Bondarchuk's epic history lesson. Steiger even manages to upstage the thousands of Soviet soldiers recruited as extras for the battle scenes, yet he's nearly outshone by Christopher Plummer as the Duke of Wellington, whose arrogance shows his contempt for cannon-fodder. Bondarchuk filmed in Italy and the Ukraine, and the result is a mightily credible reconstruction of a crunch-point that changed the course of history. TH DVD

Rod Steiger *Napoleon Bonaparte* • Orson Welles *Louis XVIII* • Virginia McKenna *Duchess of Richmond* • Michael Wilding *Sir William Ponsonby* • Donal Donnelly *Private O'Connor* • Christopher Plummer *Duke of Wellington* • Jack Hawkins *General Thomas Picton* • Dan O'Herlihy *Marshal Michel Ney* • Terence Alexander *Lord Uxbridge* ■ *Dir* Sergei Bondarchuk • *Scr* HAL Craig, Sergei Bondarchuk, Vittorio Bonicelli

Waterloo Bridge ★★

Romantic war melodrama
1931 · US · BW · 72mins

The first screen version of Robert Sherwood's play about the doomed love affair between an army officer and a young woman of questionable morals sits respectably in the canon of early 1930s woman's weepie melodramas, but it isn't a patch on the truly heartrending MGM remake nine years later. It does, however, feature a strong performance from Mae Clarke as the tragic heroine, and a very early role for Bette Davis. RK

Mae Clarke *Myra Deauville* • Kent Douglass [Douglass Montgomery] *Roy Cronin* • Doris Lloyd *Kitty* • Frederick Kerr *Major Wetherby* • Enid Bennett *Mrs Wetherby* • Bette Davis *Janet Cronin* • Ethel Griffies *Mrs Hobley* ■ *Dir* James Whale • *Scr* Tom Reed, from the play by Robert E Sherwood

Waterloo Bridge ★★★★ PG

Romantic war melodrama
1940 · US · BW · 104mins

This was the second version of Robert E Sherwood's celebrated stage play of star-crossed lovers to make it to the screen, and MGM director Mervyn LeRoy went for an unashamedly tear-jerking approach, even though the Hollywood prudishness of the day forced him to draw some of the sting from the story. Vivien Leigh gives a heartbreaking performance as the ballerina who falls in love with army captain Robert Taylor during a First World War air raid, only to be driven on to the streets after she is misinformed of his death. Taylor was never more handsome, and there's sterling support from Hollywood's British colony. DP [VIDEO]

Vivien Leigh *Myra Lester* • Robert Taylor (1) *Captain Roy Cronin* • Lucile Watson *Lady Margaret Cronin* • Virginia Field *Kitty* • Maria Ouspenskaya *Madame Olga Kirowa* • C Aubrey Smith *Duke* • Janet Shaw *Maureen* • Janet Waldo *Elsa* ■ *Dir* Mervyn LeRoy • *Scr* SN Behrman, Hans Rameau, George Froeschel, from the play by Robert E Sherwood

Waterloo Road ★★

Wartime drama 1944 · UK · BW · 75mins

This is best remembered today as the wartime movie with a terrific fist-fighting climax as tiny John Mills beats up his wife's lover, six-foot-plus spiv Stewart Granger. If you believe that, you'll probably believe in the rest of this atypically stodgy Sidney Gilliat production. Told in a rather woolly flashback structure by Alastair Sim's kindly philosophising doctor, the plot is extremely realistic for its day, but Arthur Crabtree's stark photography fails to disguise the cramped studio interiors used for much of the film. TS

John Mills *Jim Colter* • Stewart Granger *Ted Purvis* • Alastair Sim *Dr Montgomery* • Joy Shelton *Tillie Colter* • Beatrice Varley *Mrs Colter* • Alison Leggatt *Ruby* • Leslie Bradley *Mike Duggan* ■ *Dir* Sidney Gilliat • *Scr* Val Valentine, from a story by Sidney Gilliat

Watermelon Man ★★★

Comedy drama 1970 · US · Colour · 99mins

Bigoted white insurance salesman Godfrey Cambridge wakes up one morning to find he has turned black overnight. The transformation, which baffles doctors, sees Cambridge being ostracised by his friends and family, and having to seek a new life in the black community. Melvin Van Peebles's savage satire may have dated but its message (hammered home in Herman Raucher's script) is still potent. Comedian Godfrey Cambridge is marvellous in the lead. DF

Godfrey Cambridge *Jeff Gerber* • Estelle Parsons *Althea Gerber* • Howard Caine *Mr Townsend* • D'Urville Martin *Bus driver* • Mantan Moreland *Counterman* • Kay Kimberly *Erica* • Kay E Kuter *Dr Wainwright* • Scott Garrett *Burton Gerber* • Erin Moran *Janice Gerber* ■ *Dir* Melvin Van Peebles • *Scr* Herman Raucher • *Music* Melvin Van Peebles

The Watermelon Woman ★★ 15

Comedy drama 1996 · US · Colour · 80mins

It might have won the Teddy Bear for the best gay film at the 1996 Berlin festival, but Cheryl Dunye's fictional documentary is too inward-looking for its own good. Hollywood's denial of opportunity to black (let alone gay and lesbian) performers in the 1930s and 1940s is certainly a topic worthy of discussion. But Dunye's pursuit of the "watermelon woman", a character actress she keeps spotting in old movies, gets tangled up too often in her relationships with her closest friend and a new white lover. DP [VIDEO] DVD

Cheryl Dunye *Cheryl* • Guinevere Turner *Diana* • Valerie Walker *Tamara* • Lisa Marie Bronson *Fae "The Watermelon Woman" Richards* • Irene Dunye • Brian Freeman *Lee Edwards* • Ira Jeffries *Shirley Hamilton* • Camille Paglia ■ *Dir/Scr* Cheryl Dunye

Watership Down ★★★ U

Animation 1978 · UK · Colour · 87mins

Martin Rosen inherited this adaptation of Richard Adams's cult novel – about the adventures of a diverse group of rabbits – after John Hubley, who helped animate many Disney classics of the 1940s, had departed owing to "creative differences". The visual and vocal characterisations are of variable quality, but it's hard to see what Hubley could have done to improve on Rosen's version of what is a very difficult book to translate to the screen. This isn't your average cuddly bunny movie, and some scenes may be disturbing for children. DP [VIDEO] DVD

John Hurt *Hazel* • Richard Briers *Fiver* • Michael Graham-Cox *Bigwig* • John Bennett *Captain Holly* • Ralph Richardson *Chief Rabbit* • Simon Cadell *Blackberry* • Terence Rigby *Silver* • Roy Kinnear *Pipkin* • Hannah Gordon *Hyzenthlay* • Zero Mostel *Kehaar* • Michael Hordern *Frith* ■ *Dir* Martin Rosen • *Scr* Martin Rosen, from the novel by Richard Adams

Waterworld ★★★★ 12

Futuristic adventure
1995 · US · Colour · 129mins

Declared dead in the water owing to escalating costs, nightmarish production problems and clashing egos, Kevin Reynolds's lavish *Mad Max* on jet-skis emerged as a spectacular and thrilling sci-fi fantasy. In the far future, the polar icecaps have melted, covering the entire planet in water and making dirt the most valuable commodity. Only the enigmatic loner Kevin Costner offers a ray of hope to Jeanne Tripplehorn and Tina Majorino. He battles bandits led by Dennis Hopper and continues his search to find the one piece of mythical Dryland. Costner gives one of his finest performances as the half man/half amphibian whose steely character holds the whole full-blooded epic adventure together. AJ. Contains violence, swearing, nudity. [VIDEO] DVD

Kevin Costner *Mariner* • Dennis Hopper *Deacon* • Jeanne Tripplehorn *Helen* • Tina Majorino *Enola* • Michael Jeter *Gregor* • Gerard Murphy *Nord* • RD Call *Enforcer* ■ *Dir* Kevin Reynolds • *Scr* Peter Rader, David Twohy, Joss Whedon (uncredited) • *Cinematographer* Dean Semler

Wattstax ★★★

Documentary 1972 · US · Colour · 101mins

This is a filmed record of the 1972 benefit concert held at the Los Angeles Coliseum to raise money for the Watts community on the seventh anniversary of the violent riots. Amusingly emceed by Richard Pryor, the impressive roster of black soul and R&B acts includes the Dramatics, the Staple Singers, Carla Thomas, William Bell, Kim Weston and the Bar-Kays. The highlights are Isaac Hayes belting out *Shaft*, Rufus Thomas doing the *Funky Chicken* and the Reverend Jesse Jackson singing *I Am Somebody*. AJ

Dir Mel Stuart

Wavelength ★★★★

Experimental 1967 · Can · Colour · 45mins

A key film in the evolution of Structuralist cinema, Michael Snow's masterpiece explores the camera's ability to represent and redefine space and, thus, challenges the viewer's perception of its illusion. Utilising different film stocks and lighting designs, the action comprises a 45-minute slow zoom towards the windows on the distant wall of a New York loft. The entrance of three people with a bookshelf, the death of a man and the telephone reporting of his demise are all incidental to the play of light, shape and depth. This remains an astonishing work. DP

Hollis Frampton *Man who dies* • Joyce Wieland *Woman with bookcase/Woman listening to radio* • Amy Taubin *Woman on telephone/Woman listening to radio* ■ *Dir/Scr* Michael Snow

Wavelength ★★ 15

Science-fiction thriller
1983 · US · Colour · 83mins

The title comes from psychic Cherie Currie being able to mentally "hear" the cries of aliens who were shot down and then imprisoned by the government in a secret desert facility. She enlists the aid of singer Robert Carradine and prospector Keenan Wynn to help her break the visitors out before they're put under the knife. The three actors are very likeable in their roles, and the excellently creepy score by Tangerine Dream generates a decent amount of atmosphere. Somewhat slow, but the main problem is its low budget. KB [VIDEO]

Robert Carradine *Bobby Sinclaire* • Cherie Currie *Iris Longacre* • Keenan Wynn *Dan* • Cal Bowman *General Milton Ward* • James Hess *Colonel James MacGruder* ■ *Dir/Scr* Mike Gray • *Music* Tangerine Dream

Wax Mask ★★ 18

Horror 1997 · It · Colour · 94mins

A nostalgic salute to vintage Hammer horror by way of *House of Wax* and souped up with extra gore and kinky sex, this car-boot-sale chiller is a luridly engaging if shoddy shocker. Robert Hossein is the Roman wax museum owner hiding dark secrets and a scarred face behind masks that allow him to masquerade as every other cast member in the convoluted whodunnit plot. AJ. An Italian language film. Contains violence, sex scenes and swearing. [VIDEO] DVD

Robert Hossein *Boris* • Romina Mondello *Sonia* • Riccardo Serventi Longhi *Andrea* • Gabriella Giogelli *Francesca* • Umberto Balli *Alex* ■ *Dir* Sergio Stivaletti • *Scr* Lucio Fulci, Daniele Stroppa, from a story by Dario Argento, from the novel *The Wax Museum* by Gaston Leroux

Waxwork ★★ 18

Horror 1988 · US · Colour and BW · 92mins

When a mysterious waxworks museum appears overnight in a small town, its sinister owner invites a group of teens to a special midnight showing. The youngsters are then sucked into the wax tableaux to meet a grisly doom. Director Anthony Hickox certainly has tongue firmly in cheek, but his pastiches of old-time movie monsters such as Dracula and the Mummy lack wit and soon become repetitive. RS [VIDEO] DVD

Zach Galligan *Mark* • Deborah Foreman *Sarah* • Michelle Johnson *China* • Dana Ashbrook *Tony* • Miles O'Keeffe *Count Dracula* • Patrick Macnee *Sir Wilfred* • David Warner *Mr Lincoln* • John Rhys-Davies *Anton Weber* ■ *Dir/Scr* Anthony Hickox

Waxwork II: Lost in Time ★★

Horror 1992 · US · Colour and BW · 104mins

This dull and dumber sequel reunites the star and director of an original which wasn't all that great. This picks up directly where the first one left off with Zach Galligan surviving the apocalyptic end of the deadly waxwork museum only to be propelled into various time periods – all recognisable horror settings – to defeat evil. This ploy enables Anthony Hickox to once again prove his uninspired talent for spoofing various genre movies. RS

Zach Galligan *Mark Loftmore* • Sophie Ward *Eleanore Pratt* • Patrick Macnee *Sir Wilfred* • Alexander Godunov *Scarabus* • Martin Kemp *Baron Frankenstein* • Monika Schnarre *Sarah* • Bruce Campbell *John Wright* • David Carradine *Beggar* • Marina Sirtis *Gloria* • John Ireland *King Arthur* • Drew Barrymore *Vampire victim* ■ *Dir/Scr* Anthony Hickox

Waxworks ★★★★

Silent gothic horror 1924 · Ger · BW · 93mins

Paul Leni's last film in Germany before continuing on his chilly way to America is also one of his best, and gives us a chance to see four of Germany's finest actors in their earlier days. Wilhelm Dieterle, who was to become a renowned Hollywood director, plays a young poet who tells three stories behind three exhibits in a wax museum: Haroun-al-Raschid (Emil Jannings), Ivan the Terrible (Conrad Veidt) and Jack the Ripper (Werner Krauss). The expressionist lighting and designs are symbolic of character and plot, creating a haunting atmosphere. RB

Wilhelm Dieterle [William Dieterle] *Young poet/Assad/Groom* • Emil Jannings *Haroun-al-Raschid* • Conrad Veidt *Ivan the Terrible* • Werner Krauss *Jack the Ripper, "Spring Heeled Jack"* • Olga Belajeff *Showman's daughter/Zarah/Bride* • John Gottowt *Showman* ■ *Dir* Paul Leni • *Scr* Henrik Galeen • *Cinematographer* Helmar Lerski • *Art Director* Paul Leni, Fritz Maurischat

The Way Ahead ★★★★ U

Second World War drama
1944 · UK · BW · 109mins

This is one of the finest flagwavers produced in Britain during the Second World War. From Eric Ambler and Peter Ustinov's script, director Carol Reed, who had earned a reputation for social realism in the mid-1930s and had spent part of the war making army documentaries, creates a totally believable world in which a squad of raw recruits becomes an integral part of the local community as they go through basic training. David Niven is top-billed, but he enters into the ensemble spirit that makes this beautifully observed drama as uplifting today as it was in 1944. DP [VIDEO] DVD

David Niven *Lieutenant Jim Perry* • Raymond Huntley *Davenport* • Billy Hartnell [William Hartnell] *Sergeant Fletcher* • Stanley Holloway *Brewer* • James Donald *Lloyd* • John Laurie *Luke* • Leslie Dwyer *Beck* • Hugh Burden *Parsons* • Jimmy Hanley *Stainer* • Renee Ascherson [Renée Asherson] *Marjorie Gillingham* ■ *Dir* Carol Reed • *Scr* Eric Ambler, Peter Ustinov, from a story by Eric Ambler

W

Way Down East ★★★★★ U

Silent melodrama
1920 · US · BW Tinted · 144mins

Lillian Gish, at her most lovely and moving, is the innocent and trusting young country girl tricked into a fake marriage by wealthy, womanising wastrel Lowell Sherman, who leaves her pregnant. The baby dies and the destitute girl finds employment with fanatically religious farmer Burr McIntosh, whose son Richard Barthelmess falls in love with Gish. DW Griffith's film is a miracle of visual composition, brilliantly acted, with Gish giving one of the most eloquent performances of the silent screen. Justly celebrated for the climactic sequence where Gish, drifting unconscious on a raft of ice in a storm, is rescued by Barthelmess, the film offers many moments just as memorable. RK DVD

Lillian Gish *Anna Moore* • Richard Barthelmess *David Bartlett* • Mrs David Landau *Anna's mother* • Lowell Sherman *Lennox Sanderson* • Burr McIntosh *Squire Bartlett* • Josephine Bernard *Mrs Tremont* • Norma Shearer *Barn dancer* ■ *Dir* DW Griffith • *Scr* Anthony Paul Kelly, from the play *Annie Laurie* by Lottie Blair Parker • *Cinematographer* GW Bitzer [Billy Bitzer], Hendrik Sartov, Paul H Allen

Way Down East ★★

Melodrama 1935 · US · BW · 84mins

Fifteen years after the silent collaboration of DW Griffith and Lillian Gish, Fox handed a sound version to Henry King and Rochelle Hudson, with Henry Fonda in the Richard Barthelmess role. King's work is all right, especially his re-creation of the ice-river climax, but Hudson is no match for Gish, leaving the honours to Fonda in a much smaller role. The major problem though, is the material, which, by the mid-1930s, played as outmoded melodrama. RK

Rochelle Hudson *Anna Moore* • Henry Fonda *David Bartlett* • Slim Summerville *Constable Seth Holcomb* • Edward Trevor *Lennox Sanderson* • Margaret Hamilton *Martha Perkins* • Russell Simpson *Squire Bartlett* • Spring Byington *Mrs Bartlett* ■ *Dir* Henry King • *Scr* Howard Estabrook, William Hurlbut, from the 1920 film by Anthony Paul Kelly

Way of a Gaucho ★★★ U

Western 1952 · US · Colour · 90mins

Director Jacques Tourneur was a dab hand at many styles of film-making. Out West, he responded to the landscape with a natural eye, turning out this clever but forgotten Argentinian-set western. Although not ideally cast, Rory Calhoun does well as the disaffected gaucho of the title, who greets the arrival of civilisation on the pampas by organising outlaw resistance. It's an interesting concept, and Tourneur's direction is striking. TS

Rory Calhoun *Martin* • Gene Tierney *Teresa* • Richard Boone *Salinas* • Hugh Marlowe *Miguel* • Everett Sloane *Falcon* ■ *Dir* Jacques Tourneur • *Scr* Philip Dunne, from the novel by Herbert Childs

The Way of All Flesh ★★★★

Silent melodrama 1927 · US · BW · 90mins

The great German actor Emil Jannings, in his first American film, stars as a respectable bank clerk – a model husband and father of six – who, en route to delivering a package of bonds in Chicago, is conned by a girl and her criminal boyfriend. The latter is killed by a passing train. Jannings changes places with the dead man and then disappears, an act which leads to his steady descent into the gutter. Jannings won the first ever Oscar jointly for his full-blooded performances in this and *The Last Command*. Directed by Victor Fleming, it was also nominated for best picture. RK

Emil Jannings *August Schiller* • Belle Bennett *Mrs Schiller* • Phyllis Haver *Mayme* • Donald Keith *August Jr* • Fred Kohler *The Tough* ■ *Dir* Victor Fleming • *Scr* Jules Furthman, Lajos Biró, Julian Johnson (titles)

The Way of All Flesh ★★

Melodrama 1940 · US · BW · 85mins

Louis King directs and Akim Tamiroff stars in this pointless remake of the 1927 film. Stripped of the more awesomely melodramatic aspects that proved effective in the silent version, this tale of a respectable bank cashier who goes to the dogs in the big city, leaving his wife (the wonderful Gladys George) and family to nurse their memories, is competent, but dated and all-too predictable. RK

Akim Tamiroff *Paul Kriza Sr* • Gladys George *Anna Kriza* • William Henry *Paul Jr* • John Hartley *Victor Kriza* • Marilyn Knowlden *Julie Kriza* • Betty McLaughlin *Mitzi Kriza* ■ *Dir* Louis King • *Scr* Lenore Coffee, from the 1927 film by Jules Furthman, Lajos Biró

A Way of Life ★★★ 15

Drama 2004 · UK · Colour · 87mins

This is a relentlessly dispiriting portrait of life among the underprivileged in Britain from debuting director Amma Asante. Newcomer Stephanie James delivers a blistering performance as the teenage single mum on a South Wales estate who blames everyone for her destitution while refusing to accept responsibility for any of her actions. By stressing the desperation and irrationality of James's crimes, Asante draws attention to the creeping resentment that is fuelling racism in so many deprived environments in 21st-century Britain. DP. Contains swearing, violence and sex scenes. DVD

Brenda Blethyn *Annette* • Stephanie James *Leigh-Anne Williams* • Nathan Jones (2) *Gavin Williams* • Gary Sheppeard *Robbie Matthews* • Dean Wong *Stephen Rajan* • Sara Gregory *Julie Osman* • Oliver Haden *Hassan Osman* ■ *Dir/Scr* Amma Asante

The Way of the Dragon ★★★ 18

Martial arts adventure
1973 · HK · Colour · 94mins

This was the only film martial arts icon Bruce Lee had complete control over, being director, writer and fight choreographer. Maybe he should have had help in some areas, for it's a desperately thin tale of about a country bumpkin, played by Lee, who arrives in Rome to help out at a Chinese restaurant that's at the mercy of local gangsters. It's typical of its genre; the dubbing is lousy, the characters are mere ciphers, and there are too many clumsy comedy routines that play well in Hong Kong but look merely amateurish to us. However, the action more than compensates: Lee's face-off with Chuck Norris inside the Colosseum is one of the best two-man scraps in movie history. RS. A Cantonese language film. Contains violence. DVD

Bruce Lee *Tang Lung* • Nora Miao *Chen Ching Hua* • Chuck Norris *Colt* • Wang Chung Hsin *Uncle Wang* • Tong Liu *Tony* • Ti Chin *Ah K'ung* • Jon T Benn *Boss* • Robert Wall *Robert, Colt's pupil* ■ *Dir/Scr* Bruce Lee

The Way of the Gun ★★★ 18

Crime drama 2000 · US · Colour · 114mins

Outrageous, unrelenting and blood-soaked, the directorial debut of Christopher McQuarrie – the Oscar-winning screenwriter of *The Usual Suspects* – is a quirky crime thriller. McQuarrie's visceral ode to contemporary cowboys is an edgy and smartly cynical treat for those who like raw action and provocative themes. Small-time villains Ryan Phillippe and Benicio Del Toro abduct flaky surrogate mother Juliette Lewis in order to hold the wealthy parents-to-be to ransom. Unfortunately for the crooked duo, the expectant father has underworld connections. AJ DVD

Ryan Phillippe *Parker* • Benicio Del Toro *Longbaugh* • Juliette Lewis *Robin* • James Caan *Sarno* • Taye Diggs *Jeffers* • Nicky Katt *Obecks* • Scott Wilson *Hale Chidduck* ■ *Dir/Scr* Christopher McQuarrie

Way Out West ★★★★★ U

Classic comedy western
1937 · US · BW · 63mins

Stan Laurel and Oliver Hardy get to sing their hit song *Trail of the Lonesome Pine* as they go west to deliver a mine-deed inheritance to prospector's daughter Rosina Lawrence. However they are waylaid by crooked saloon owner James Finlayson and his moll, Sharon Lynne. This inspired western parody contains some of the duo's most memorable routines, making it one of those films you can watch umpteen times and still come back for more. DP DVD

Stan Laurel *Stan* • Oliver Hardy *Ollie* • James Finlayson *Mickey Finn* • Sharon Lynne *Lola Marcel* • Rosina Lawrence *Mary Roberts* • Stanley Fields *Sheriff* ■ *Dir* James W Horne • *Scr* Charles Rogers, Felix Adler, James Parrott, from a story by Jack Jevne, Charles Rogers

The Way to the Gold ★★ U

Adventure drama 1957 · US · BW · 94mins

Ex-con Jeffrey Hunter sets out to uncover loot buried 30 years before by a now-deceased villain, only to discover the treasure site covered by an artificial lake. Barry Sullivan, Walter Brennan and Neville Brand feature as the rivals on his trail, but act like self-pitying automata. Only Sheree North, as Hunter's girlfriend, seems to bring a touch of life to her role. TH

Jeffrey Hunter *Joe Mundy* • Sheree North *Hank Clifford* • Barry Sullivan *Marshal Hannibal* • Walter Brennan *Uncle George* • Neville Brand *Little Brother Williams* • Jacques Aubuchon *Clem Williams* • Ruth Donnelly *Mrs Williams* ■ *Dir* Robert D Webb • *Scr* Wendell Mayes, from the novel by Wilbur Daniel Steele

The Way to the Stars ★★★★ U

Second World War drama
1945 · UK · BW · 104mins

This well-judged Second World War drama concerns the stiff-upper-lipped antics of an RAF squadron and its members' relationships with their loved-ones and the flashy flyboys who have recently arrived from America. The first joint project of director Anthony Asquith, producer Anatole de Grunwald and writer Terence Rattigan, this perfectly captures the spirit of Britain at a moment when loss was perhaps even more agonising, simply because victory was so close at hand. Michael Redgrave and Rosamund John are straight out of the Noël Coward school of British bourgeoisie, but John Mills and Renée Asherson are closer to reality as the couple dallying over a wartime wedding. DP DVD

Michael Redgrave *David Archdale* • John Mills *Peter Penrose* • Rosamund John *Miss Toddy Todd* • Douglass Montgomery *Johnny Hollis* • Stanley Holloway *Mr Palmer* • Trevor Howard *Squadron Leader Carter* • Renée Asherson *Iris Winterton* • Felix Aylmer *Rev Charles Moss* ■ *Dir* Anthony Asquith • *Scr* Terence Rattigan, Anatole de Grunwald, from a story by Terence Rattigan, from a story by Richard Sherman

Way... Way Out ★★

Comedy 1966 · US · Colour · 104mins

When Russian astronomer Anita Ekberg claims she was attacked by a US astronaut on a jointly run moonbase, US Lunar Division chief Robert Morley decrees that in future all US moonbase personnel will be married couples. Consequently Jerry Lewis, next in line to man the station, has to arrange a hasty wedding to fellow worker Connie Stevens in order to fulfil his mission. Another uncomfortable vehicle for Lewis. DF

Jerry Lewis *Peter* • Connie Stevens *Eileen* • Robert Morley *Quonset* • Dennis Weaver *Hoffman* • Howard Morris *Schmidlap* • Brian Keith *General Hallenby* • Dick Shawn *Igor* • Anita Ekberg *Anna* ■ *Dir* Gordon Douglas • *Scr* William Bowers, Laslo Vadnay

The Way We Were ★★★★ PG

Romantic drama
1973 · US · Colour · 113mins

Barbra Streisand and Robert Redford play the ideal odd couple – she's poor, jittery, Jewish and a radical, and he's rich, self-assured, Gentile and conservative. Set against the backdrop of a changing America, including the McCarthy-era witch-hunts, every scene seems dreamed up by a dating-agency computer, though the sheer professionalism of the picture and the performances can't fail to touch you. Redford, as a character seemingly hewn from the pages of F Scott Fitzgerald, is perfectly cast and Streisand is simply Streisand. AT. Contains swearing. DVD

Barbra Streisand *Katie Morosky* • Robert Redford *Hubbell Gardiner* • Bradford Dillman *JJ* • Lois Chiles *Carol Ann* • Patrick O'Neal *George Bissinger* • Viveca Lindfors *Paula Reisner* • Allyn Ann McLerie *Rhea Edwards* • Murray Hamilton *Brooks Carpenter* • Herb Edelman *Bill Verso* • Diana Ewing *Vicki Bissinger* • James Woods *Frankie McVeigh* ■ *Dir* Sydney Pollack • *Scr* Arthur Laurents, from his novel

The Way West ★★★★

Western 1967 · US · Colour · 122mins

Directed by Andrew V McLaglen from the Pulitzer Prize-winning novel by AB Guthrie Jr, this spectacular western boasts a magnificent leading trio of Kirk Douglas, Robert Mitchum and Richard Widmark in roles they were born to play. The scale is impressive as politician Douglas leads a wagon train west along the hazardous Oregon trail to California. Mitchum is remarkably good as a trail scout and watch out for a young Sally Field in her movie debut. Bronislau Kaper's outstanding score is a splendid accompaniment to the action and deserves to be better known. TS

Kirk Douglas *Senator William J Tadlock* • Robert Mitchum *Dick Summers* • Richard Widmark *Lije Evans* • Lola Albright *Rebecca Evans* • Michael Witney *Johnnie Mack* • Michael McGreevey *Brownie Evans* • Sally Field *Mercy McBee* • Katherine Justice *Amanda Mack* • Stubby Kaye *Sam Fairman* • Jack Elam *Preacher Wetherby* ■ *Dir* Andrew V McLaglen • *Scr* Ben Maddow, Mitch Lindemann, from the novel by AB Guthrie Jr

waydowntown ★★★★

Comedy 2000 · Can · Colour · 87mins

Set in the Canadian city of Calgary, where a central commercial complex has been linked together by a series of glass tunnels, this is a compelling investigation into the modern tendency to cocoon ourselves, whether by architecture, technology or apathy. Taking sly pot shots at office politics and mall culture, Gary Burns's cracklingly tense comedy centres on a bet between four colleagues to see who can stay indoors the longest. But while the increasingly desperate competition enthrals, it's Burns's use of space, place and colour that creates the sinisterly satirical atmosphere. DP

Fab Filippo *Tom* • Don McKellar *Brad* • Marya Delver *Sandra West* • Gordon Currie *Curt*

Schwin • Jennifer Clement *Vicki* • Tobias Godson *Randy* ■ *Dir* Gary Burns • *Scr* Gary Burns, James Martin

Wayne's World ★★★★ PG

Comedy 1992 · US · Colour · 90mins

This spin-off from the TV show *Saturday Night Live* brought "teen speak" to a new level. Mike Myers and Dana Carvey are Wayne and Garth, whose low-budget public access cable show is transformed into a national TV phenomenon by sleazy producer Rob Lowe. Along the way, Myers falls in love with rock chick Tia Carrere and, along with Carvey, gets to meet their idol Alice Cooper. Aiming for the unashamedly moronic, director Penelope Spheeris still sneaks in some sly satiric jibes and it benefits from inspired casting. JF. Contains swearing and sex scenes. DVD

Mike Myers *Wayne Campbell* • Dana Carvey *Garth Algar* • Rob Lowe *Benjamin Oliver* • Tia Carrere *Cassandra* • Brian Doyle-Murray *Noah Vanderhoff* • Lara Flynn Boyle *Stacy* • Michael DeLuise *Alan* ■ *Dir* Penelope Spheeris • *Scr* Mike Myers, Bonnie Turner, Terry Turner, from characters created by Mike Myers

Wayne's World 2 ★★★ PG

Comedy 1993 · US · Colour · 90mins

Wayne and Garth return for another goofy pop culture delve into suburban Americana. This time Mike Myers's cleverly conceived alter ego is searching for meaning in his life and decides to mount a "Waynestock" rock concert. The gleeful party atmosphere conjured up by the first and funnier movie continues here with silly gags, daft catch phrases and hip in-jokes. But it's a sloppy hit-and-miss affair despite the odd hysterical highlight. AJ. Contains some swearing. DVD

Mike Myers *Wayne Campbell* • Dana Carvey *Garth Algar* • Tia Carrere *Cassandra* • Christopher Walken *Bobby Cahn* • Ralph Brown *Del Preston* • Olivia D'Abo *Betty Jo* • Kim Basinger *Honey Hornée* • James Hong *Mr Wong* • Heather Locklear ■ *Dir* Stephen Surjik • *Scr* Mike Myers, Terry Turner, Bonnie Turner, from characters created by Mike Myers

The Wayward Bus ★★

Drama 1957 · US · BW · 88mins

A *Grand Hotel* type story from a novel by John Steinbeck about a group of people whose lives are changed on a bus trip in California, this is a patchy affair with an interesting cast that deserved a better script. Jayne Mansfield gives a touching performance as a stripper who wants to become a "real actress", and there are good performances by Dan Dailey as a travelling salesman and Joan Collins as the driver's tipsy wife, but the characterisation is superficial and situations pat. TV

Joan Collins *Alice* • Jayne Mansfield *Camille* • Dan Dailey *Ernest Horton* • Rick Jason *Johnny Chicoy* • Betty Lou Keim *Norma* • Dolores Michaels *Mildred Pritchard* • Larry Keating *Pritchard* ■ *Dir* Victor Vicas • *Scr* Ivan Moffat, from the novel by John Steinbeck

We All Loved Each Other So Much ★★★★

Romantic drama
1974 · It · BW and Colour · 136mins

With guest appearances by Vittorio De Sica and Federico Fellini, a wealth of clips from the likes of Rossellini, Visconti and Antonioni, and impudent pastiches of some classic scenes, this cinematic rattlebag will prove an endless delight for fans of postwar Italian film. However, the casual viewer is also catered for, as Ettore Scola chronicles the 30-year friendship between political activist Nino Manfredi, radical cinéaste Stefano Satta Flores and self-made bourgeois, Vittorio Gassman, who not only share a common history, but also a mutual passion for the ravishing Stefania Sandrelli. Alternately broad and sentimental, inspired and contrived, but always sympathetic and amusing. DP. An Italian language film.

Nino Manfredi *Antonio* • Vittorio Gassman *Gianni* • Stefania Sandrelli *Luciana* • Stefano Satta Flores *Nicola* • Vittorio De Sica • Federico Fellini • Giovanna Ralli *Elide* ■ *Dir* Ettore Scola • *Scr* Age [Agenore Incrocci], Furio Scarpelli, Ettore Scola

We Are Not Alone ★★

Drama 1939 · US · BW · 105mins

This Hollywood melodrama is set in one of those quiet English villages where dark passions flow just as strongly as the Earl Grey. Paul Muni is the local doctor, Flora Robson is his fearsome wife and Jane Bryan the dancer with whom he falls in love. The story seldom rises above Mills and Boon levels of cliché and predictability, but the setting at the outbreak of the First World War, with Britain close to panic meant much to audiences in 1939. AT

Paul Muni *Dr David Newcome* • Jane Bryan *Leni-Krafft* • Flora Robson *Jessica Newcome* • Raymond Severn *Gerald Newcome* • Una O'Connor *Susan* • Alan Napier *Archdeacon* • James Stephenson *Sir William Clintock* • Montagu Love *Major Millman* • Henry Daniell *Sir Ronald Dawson* ■ *Dir* Edmund Goulding • *Scr* James Hilton, Milton Krims, from the novel by James Hilton

We Dive at Dawn ★★★ U

Second World War drama
1943 · UK · BW · 92mins

This tense British study of submarine warfare, directed by Anthony Asquith, is packed with incident (as a determined crew pursues a Nazi battleship across the Baltic) and credible characters, played by the likes of John Mills and Eric Portman, who remain human for all their quiet heroism. DP DVD

Eric Portman *James Hobson* • John Mills *Lt Freddie Taylor* • Reginald Purdell *CPO Dicky Dabbs* • Niall MacGinnis *PO Mike Corrigan* • Joan Hopkins *Ethel Dabbs* • Josephine Wilson *Alice Hobson* ■ *Dir* Anthony Asquith • *Scr* JP Williams, Frank Launder, Val Valentine

We Don't Live Here Anymore ★★★★ 15

Drama 2003 · US/Can · Colour · 98mins

In this autumnal chamber piece, the four libidinous characters are motivated less by pleasure or love than by loneliness and revenge. Rumpled academic Mark Ruffalo is married to alcoholic Laura Dern but having an affair with elegant Naomi Watts who's married to his best friend Peter Krause, a teacher who sleeps mostly with his students. Painfully poignant at times, the misery quotient is cut by stabs of much-needed humour, while the superb acting nails through looks and gestures what the characters can't actually say in words. LF. Contains swearing and sex scenes.

Mark Ruffalo *Jack Linden* • Laura Dern *Terry Linden* • Peter Krause *Hank Evans* • Naomi Watts *Edith Evans* • Sam Charles *Sean Linden* • Haili Page *Natasha Linden* • Jennifer Bishop (2) *Sharon Evans* ■ *Dir* John Curran • *Scr* Larry Gross, from the short stories *We Don't Live Here Anymore* and *Adultery* by Andre Dubus

We Don't Want to Talk about It ★★★★ PG

Drama 1993 · Arg/It · Colour · 93mins

This is essentially a touching parable on the blindness of love, though some will find the romance between an ageing Casanova and a fabulously cultured dwarf rather hard to take. Yet the only dubious character in this intriguing flashback to an imaginary Latin American town in the 1930s is scheming widow Luisina Brando, whose motives for pairing Marcello Mastroianni with her daughter, Alejandra Podesta, are not exactly selfless. Flirting occasionally with lapses in taste and the lazy deceits of magic realism, this is kept on track by the excellence of the performances. DP. In Spanish with English subtitles. Contains nudity.

Marcello Mastroianni *Ludovico D'Andrea* • Luisina Brando *Leonor* • Alejandra Podesta *Charlotte* • Betiana Blum *Madama* • Roberto Carnaghi *Padre Aurelio* • Alberto Segado *Dr Blanes* • Jorge Luz *Alcalde* ■ *Dir* Maria Luisa Bemberg • *Scr* Maria Luisa Bemberg, Jorge Goldenberg, from a short story by Julio Llinas

We Joined the Navy ★★ U

Comedy 1962 · UK · Colour · 109mins

Kenneth More stars as a blithering idiot ordered to train navy cadets at Dartmouth College. Making a hash of that billet, More is transferred to the American fleet in the Med, thus allowing Hollywood hero Lloyd Nolan to help the film at the box-office in America. It's really little more than *Doctor in the House* in uniform, but is modestly amusing. AT

Kenneth More *Lt Cmdr "Bodger" Badger* • Lloyd Nolan *Admiral Ryan* • Joan O'Brien *Carol Blair* • Mischa Auer *Colonel/President* • Jeremy Lloyd *Dewberry* • Dinsdale Landen *Bowles* • Derek Fowlds *Carson* • Denise Warren *Collette* • John Le Mesurier *Dewberry Senior* • Lally Bowers *Mrs Dewberry* • Laurence Naismith *Admiral Blake* • Andrew Cruickshank *Admiral Filmer* • Brian Wilde *Petty Officer Gibbons* • Esma Cannon *Consul's Wife* • Dirk Bogarde *Dr Simon Sparrow* • Michael Bentine *Psychologist* • Sidney James *Dancing instructor* ■ *Dir* Wendy Toye • *Scr* Arthur Dales [Howard Dimsdale], from a novel by John Winton

We Live Again ★★★ PG

Melodrama 1934 · US · BW · 78mins

The Russian answer to the Swedish Garbo, Anna Sten was exceptionally well cast opposite dashing Fredric March in this uncredited adaptation of Tolstoy's *Resurrection*, but the public never really warmed to her. Today, this movie is an impressive work, beautifully photographed by Gregg Toland and impressively condensed into 80-odd minutes, in part by newcomer Preston Sturges. Director Rouben Mamoulian's sense of scale is awesome, from the opening scenes on the steppes, and including a detailed Russian Orthodox Easter Mass. TS

Fredric March *Prince Dmitri* • Anna Sten *Katusha Maslova* • Jane Baxter *Missy Kortchagin* • C Aubrey Smith *Prince Kortchagin* • Sam Jaffe *Gregory Simonson* • Ethel Griffies *Aunt Maria* • Gwendolyn Logan *Aunt Sophia* • Mary Forbes *Mrs Kortchagin* ■ *Dir* Rouben Mamoulian • *Scr* Maxwell Anderson, Leonard Praskins, Preston Sturges, from the novel *Resurrection* by Leo Tolstoy

We of the Never Never ★★★ U

Adventure drama
1982 · Aus · Colour · 127mins

This is an influential Aussie drama, one of the first to really register in the UK, and based on a true story. Angela Punch McGregor packs her middle name as a gutsy high-society girl who marries a cattle-station manager, and leaves for an outback life among macho men who regard women as a liability. Handsomely mounted and impeccably played. DA

Angela Punch McGregor *Jeannie Gunn* • Arthur Dignam *Aeneas Gunn* • Tony Barry *Mac* • Tommy Lewis *Jackeroo* • Lewis Fitz-Gerald *Jack* • Martin Vaughan *Dan* • John Jarratt *Dandy* ■ *Dir* Igor Auzins • *Scr* Peter Schreck, from an autobiography by Jane Taylor Gunn

We Still Kill the Old Way ★★★

Crime drama 1967 · It · Colour · 99mins

This is perhaps the least effective of director Elio Petri's collaborations with screenwriter Ugo Pirro. Less ferocious than *Investigation of a Citizen Under Suspicion*, the film uses a murder mystery to comment on contemporary Italian society from a distinctly left-wing perspective. Gian Maria Volonté gives a typically steady performance as the teacher convinced that two friends have fallen foul of a poison pen campaign. But Irene Papas overplays the widow for whom he falls. DP. An Italian language film.

Gian Maria Volonté *Paolo Laurana* • Irene Papas *Luisa Roscio* • Gabriele Ferzetti *Rosello* • Salvo Randone *Professor Roscio* • Luigi Pistilli *Arturo Manno* • Mario Scaccia *Priest* • Laura Nucci *Paulo's mother* ■ *Dir* Elio Petri • *Scr* Elio Petri, Ugo Pirro, from the novel *A ciascuno il suo* by Leonardo Sciascia

We the Living ★★★★

Political drama 1942 · It · BW · 270mins

Director Goffredo Alessandrini's splendid film version of Ayn (*The Fountainhead*) Rand's novel stars Alida Valli and Rossano Brazzi, both first-class and at the peak of their youthful beauty, as a student in love with an anti-Communist aristocrat in 1920s Russia. To help Brazzi, who is suffering from TB but being denied medical treatment, Valli engages in an affair with an influential member of the secret police (Fosco Giachetti), setting the rest of the action in motion. After a successful run in Italy, the film was withdrawn on political grounds by the Mussolini-era authorities and disappeared until 1986, when Rand's legal advisers tracked down a copy and restored it. RK. In Italian with English subtitles, when re-released in 1986.

Alida Valli *Kira Argounova* • Rossano Brazzi *Leo Kovalensky* • Fosco Giachetti *Andrei Taganov* • Giovanni Grasso *Tishenko* • Emilio Cigoli *Pavel Syerov* • Cesrina Gheraldi *Comrade Sonia* ■ *Dir* Goffredo Alessandrini • *Scr* Anton Giulio Majano, from the novel by Ayn Rand, adapted by Corrado Alvaro, Orio Vergani

We Think the World of You ★★★ PG

Comedy drama 1988 · UK · Colour · 94mins

Tackling homosexual prejudice in 1950s Britain, Alan Bates is a civil servant with an ongoing passion for bad boy Gary Oldman. In return, Oldman plays Bates for his money and when he is sent to prison, Oldman's wife continues the scrounging. Aware he is being taken for a ride but helpless in his unrequited passion, Bates projects all his feelings about the younger man onto Oldman's Alsatian dog. Not an easy film, this is masterfully intelligent and understated with spot on performances from Oldman and Bates. LH

Alan Bates *Frank Meadows* • Gary Oldman *Johnny Burney* • Frances Barber *Megan* • Liz Smith *Millie Burney* • Max Wall *Tom Burney* • Kerry Wise *Rita* • Ivor Roberts *Harry* ■ *Dir* Colin Gregg • *Scr* Hugh Stoddart, from a novel by Joseph R Ackerley

W

We Were Soldiers ★★ 15

War drama based on a true story
2002 · US · Colour · 132mins

This is an overlong account of how Lt General Harold G Moore's men stood their ground against overwhelming numbers of North Vietnamese soldiers in the first major confrontation of the Vietnam War in November 1965. The film earnestly treads familiar ground as director Randall Wallace manipulates the audience between violent action, sentimental pep talks and scenes from the homefront. Devoid of political comment and historical background, with no real characterisation. AJ DVD

Mel Gibson *Lt Col Harold G Moore* • Madeleine Stowe *Julie Moore* • Greg Kinnear *Maj Bruce Crandall* • Sam Elliott *Sgt Maj Basil Plumley* • Chris Klein *Second Lt Jack Geoghegan* • Keri Russell *Barbara Geoghegan* • Barry Pepper *Joseph L Galloway* ■ *Dir* Randall Wallace • *Scr* Randall Wallace, from the non-fiction book *We Were Soldiers Once... and Young* by Lt Gen Harold G Moore Moore, Joseph L Galloway

We Were Strangers ★★★

Adventure drama 1949 · US · BW · 105mins

The charismatic John Garfield, nearing the end of a career destroyed by the McCarthy blacklist, stars in this sombre political drama set in the early 1930s and well directed by John Huston. Garfield plays a Cuban-born American who returns to the country of his birth to help with a revolutionary group's elaborate plan to assassinate some government ministers. There's also time for an obligatory romance (with Jennifer Jones). Even though it dissipates its serious political theme with too much mechanical detail, the film is still tense and atmospheric. RK

Jennifer Jones *China Valdes* • John Garfield *Tony Fenner* • Pedro Armendáriz *Armando Ariete* • Gilbert Roland *Guillermo Mantilla* • Ramon Novarro *Chief* • Wally Cassell *Miguel* ■ *Dir* John Huston • *Scr* Peter Viertel, John Huston, from the episode *China Valdez* in the novel *Rough Sketch* by Robert Sylvester

The Weak and the Wicked ★★★ PG

Prison drama 1953 · UK · BW · 83mins

This is one of those riveting women's prison pictures full of sneering warders and snarling, sulky inmates that alternates alarmingly between enlightening social comment and overloaded melodrama. A robust cast that contains all the usual suspects (there's a fine performance from Diana Dors) acts out the story, which provides a meaty glimpse behind the clanging doors. SH

Glynis Johns *Jean Raymond* • Diana Dors *Betty* • John Gregson *Michael* • Jane Hylton *Babs* • Sidney James *Sid Baden* • AE Matthews *Harry Wicks* • Anthony Nicholls *Chaplain* ■ *Dir* J Lee Thompson • *Scr* J Lee Thompson, Anne Burnaby, Joan Henry, from the book *Who Lie in Gaol* by Joan Henry

Weak at Denise ★ 18

Black comedy 2000 · UK · Colour · 83mins

Harking back to the unlamented days of the British sex comedy, this cataclysm of a movie marks the directorial debut of Julian Nott. Nott assaults mild-mannered Bill Thomas with a domineering mum, a gold-digging wife, a lesbian punk stepdaughter and a plot to bump him off for his money. Outdated and unfunny. DP DVD

Bill Thomas *Colin* • Chrissie Cotterill *Denise* • Craig Fairbrass *Roy* • Tilly Blackwood *Wendy* • Claudine Spiteri *Sharon* • Edna Doré *Iris* ■ *Dir* Julian Nott • *Scr* Graham Williams, Julian Nott, from a novel by Graham Williams

W

The Weaker Sex ★★ U

Second World War drama
1948 · UK · BW · 84mins

A marvellous British cast plays out this nostalgic and very human story of the latter war years, leading up to D-Day. Ursula Jeans adds to her housewife duties with stints as a canteen worker and fire watcher. Her son is away fighting and her two daughters are Wrens living at home. With two navy men billeted at the house, Jeans's life is full as she waits for the war's end and a family reunion. Based on a successful play, *No Medals*, this gentle film was given a nicely ironic title for the sentimental screen version. BB

Ursula Jeans *Martha Dacre* • Cecil Parker *Geoffrey Radcliffe* • Joan Hopkins *Helen Dacre* • Derek Bond *Nigel* • Lana Morris *Lolly Dacre* • John Stone (1) *Roddy* • Thora Hird *Mrs Gaye* ■ *Dir* Roy Baker [Roy Ward Baker] • *Scr* Esther McCracken, Paul Soskin, from the play *No Medals* by Esther McCracken

Weather Woman ★★★

Satire 1995 · Jpn · Colour · 84mins

Based on a cult *manga* comic, this dark Japanese comedy will feel vaguely familiar to anyone who's seen Gus Van Sant's *To Die For*, as a gorgeous eccentric (this one can fly!) employs the most nefarious tactics to fulfil her goal of appearing on television. However, Tomoaki Hosoyama's film is much nearer the knuckle, with the ruthlessly driven Kei Mizutani not only introducing a peek-a-boo sexual element to her nightly forecasts, but also going through a peculiar sadomasochistic routine to prepare for her battle with Yasuyo Shiroshima, the snobbish daughter of the station owner who has meteorological ambitions of her own. A sequel followed in 1996. DP. In Japanese with English subtitles.

Kei Mizutani *Keiko Nakadai* • Eisei Amamoto *Chairman Shimamori* • Kunihiko Iida *Masao Yanabe* • Yasuyo Shiroshima *Kaori Shimamori* ■ *Dir/Scr* Tomoaki Hosoyama

The Web ★★★

Film noir thriller 1947 · US · BW · 87mins

In an exceptionally well-scripted thriller, Vincent Price stands out as the wealthy New York businessman who twice uses Edmond O'Brien's young bodyguard to dispose of his adversaries and almost gets away with it. Ella Raines makes a spirited secretary who helps O'Brien clear himself while William Bendix is the police lieutenant who's not as dumb as he looks. AE

Ella Raines *Noel Faraday* • Edmond O'Brien *Bob Regan* • William Bendix *Lt Damico* • Vincent Price *Andrew Colby* • Maria Palmer *Martha Kroner* • John Abbott *Murdock, Charles* • Fritz Leiber *Leopold Kroner* • Howland Chamberlin *James Nolan* ■ *Dir* Michael Gordon • *Scr* William Bowers, Bertram Milhauser, from a story by Harry Kurnitz

Web of Lies ★★

Thriller 1999 · US · Colour · 90mins

Seth Green plays a computer geek student who teams up with country boy Brad Rowe to dupe a crime boss out of a small fortune. Director Byron W Thompson occasionally overplays his hand as he toys with our expectations and the resolution is something of a disappointment, but this is still watchable. DP. Contains violence.

Brad Rowe *Erik* • Seth Green *Cornelius* • Stanley Kamel *Alex Tali* • William Mesnik *Franklin* • Raymond Dooley *Rosewood* ■ *Dir* Byron W Thompson • *Scr* Steven Robert Morris

Web of Passion ★★★

Mystery drama 1959 · Fr · Colour · 108mins

This adaptation of Stanley Ellin's novel marked Claude Chabrol's entry into the full-colour, big-budget mainstream. Yet the detachment that would undermine several future projects is already in evidence, as he prioritises technique over dialogue and character. However, the influence of Hitchcock and Lang is also felt in this astute blend of thriller and social drama, in which Chabrol takes savage delight in dissecting Jacques Dacqmine's dysfunctional bourgeois household. Madeleine Robinson won the best actress prize at Venice as Dacqmine's shrewish wife, but it's Jean-Paul Belmondo's coarse Hungarian catalyst who catches the eye. DP. A French language film.

Madeleine Robinson *Thérèse Marcoux* • Jacques Dacqmine *Henri Marcoux* • Jean-Paul Belmondo *Laszlo Kovacs* • Bernadette Lafont *Julie* • Antonella Lualdi *Léda* ■ *Dir* Claude Chabrol • *Scr* Paul Gégauff, from the novel *The Key to Nicholas Street* by Stanley Ellin

A Wedding ★★★★ 15

Comedy drama 1978 · US · Colour · 119mins

Not so much a nuptial mass as a marital massacre, as Robert Altman sets his sights on a high-society wedding with his scattershot technique, as two families collide, booze floats Sunday-best appearances out of the window, and skeletons rattle out of cupboards. The performers are marvellous enough in isolation, but Altman's splintering style slides them into a mosaic as comic as it is dramatic as it is poignant. TH. Contains swearing.

Carol Burnett *Tulip Brenner, mother of the bride* • Paul Dooley *Snooks Brenner, father of the bride* • Amy Stryker *Muffin Brenner, the bride* • Mia Farrow *Buffy Brenner, the bride's sister* • Dennis Christopher *Hughie Brenner, the bride's brother* • Lillian Gish *Nettie Sloan, the groom's grandmother* • Geraldine Chaplin *Rita Billingsley, wedding co-ordinator* • Desi Arnaz Jr *Dino Corelli, the groom* • Nina Van Pallandt *Regina Corelli, the groom's mother* • Vittorio Gassman *Luigi Corelli, the groom's father* ■ *Dir* Robert Altman • *Scr* John Considine, Patricia Resnick, Allan Nicholls, Robert Altman, from a story by John Considine, Robert Altman

The Wedding Banquet ★★★★ 15

Comedy 1993 · Tai/US · Colour · 103mins

The clash between eastern and western cultures is adeptly wrung for marvellously rich comedy and pathos in Ang Lee's refreshing look at the marriage-go-round that occurs when gay Winston Chao decides to wed for convenience. Unfortunately, his thrilled parents decide to hop over from Taiwan for the ceremony and that's when the hilarious complications really start in the absorbing efforts to hide his real sexuality, nonconformist lifestyle and boyfriend. Sharply observed and never once striking a false note, this sweet-and-sour rib-tickler is a real treat. AJ. In English and Mandarin with subtitles. Contains sex scenes and nudity.

Winston Chao *Gao Wai-Tung* • May Chin *Wei-Wei* • Gua Ah-Leh *Mrs Gao* • Lung Sihung *Mr Gao* • Mitchell Lichtenstein *Simon* • Neal Huff *Steve* • Ang Lee *Wedding guest* ■ *Dir* Ang Lee • *Scr* Ang Lee, Neil Peng, James Schamus

Wedding Bell Blues ★★★

Comedy 1996 · US · Colour · 111mins

Three single women go to Las Vegas in order to get sham marriages so their families will get off their backs. The concept may sound like a bad sitcom, but the film scores points thanks to a cast that includes Illeana Douglas, Paulina Porizkova, and Julie Warner. Most of the stereotypical Las Vegas elements show up, such as Elvis impersonators and a cameo by a casino lounge star (Debbie Reynolds in this case), but this makes you take an interest in the fates of the main characters. ST

Illeana Douglas *Jasmine* • Paulina Porizkova *Tanya* • Julie Warner *Micki* • John Corbett *Cary* • Jonathan Penner *Matt* • Charles Martin Smith *Oliver* • Stephanie Beacham *Tanya's mother* • Debbie Reynolds ■ *Dir* Dana Lustig • *Scr* Annette Goliti Gutierrez, from a story by Dana Lustig, Annette Goliti Gutierrez

Wedding Crashers ★★ 15

Romantic comedy
2005 · US · Colour · 118mins

Paired in this low-brow comedy as buddies who spend their free time gate-crashing weddings to pick up women, Owen Wilson and Vince Vaughn enjoy an easy chemistry that's difficult to dislike. There are some hilarious moments as their season-end event is a weekend with Christopher Walken and his dysfunctional family, after Wilson falls for engaged daughter Rachel McAdams. Sadly, the leads can't sustain the humour, and struggle with an over-stretched storyline and stale, contrived material. SF. Contains swearing and sex scenes.

Owen Wilson *John Beckwith* • Vince Vaughn *Jeremy Grey* • Christopher Walken *William Cleary* • Rachel McAdams *Claire Cleary* • Jane Seymour (2) *Kathleen Cleary* • Isla Fisher *Gloria Cleary* ■ *Dir* David Dobkin • *Scr* Steve Faber, Bob Fisher

The Wedding Date ★★ 12A

Romantic comedy
2004 · US · Colour · 88mins

Tying the knot proves a messy business here, but it's British director Clare Kilner who winds up in a tangle. *Will & Grace* star Debra Messing is left to coast on charm alone as a lonely New York-based singleton who employs professional escort Dermot Mulroney to hang off her arm at her sister's posh English wedding. Matters are complicated by the fact that her former fiancé (Jeremy Sheffield) is the best man. Both leads struggle with the thin script. SP. Contains swearing, sexual references.

Debra Messing *Kat Ellis* • Dermot Mulroney *Nick Mercer* • Amy Adams *Amy* • Jack Davenport *Edward Fletcher-Wooten* • Sarah Parish *TJ* • Jeremy Sheffield *Jeffrey* • Peter Egan *Victor Ellis* • Holland Taylor *Bunny* • Jolyon James *Woody* ■ *Dir* Clare Kilner • *Scr* Dana Fox, from the novel *Asking for Trouble* by Elizabeth Young

Wedding in Galilee ★★★ 12

Drama 1987 · Bel/Fr · Colour · 111mins

Set in the occupied West Bank at a time of martial law, Palestinian director Michel Khleifi's debut feature is an impassioned, if naive, plea for tolerance. An elder is intent on giving his son a traditional Arab wedding, and must enlist the help of the local Israeli governor. Maintaining a documentarist's distance, Khleifi concentrates on the human interaction of these implacable foes. Performed by a largely non-professional cast, the film successfully contrasts political tension with the undeniable sexual *frisson* between the guests. DP. An Arabic/Hebrew/Turkish language film. Contains some nudity.

Ali Mohammed El Akili *The Mukhtar* • Nazih Akleh *The Groom* • Bushra Karaman *The mother* • Anna Achdian *Bride* ■ *Dir/Scr* Michel Khleifi

The Wedding March ★★★★★

Silent melodrama
1928 · US · BW and Colour · 113mins

A silent masterpiece by the great Erich von Stroheim, who also stars as a dissolute Viennese aristocrat falling in love with a peasant girl. The complex combination of cynicism, irony and genuine romanticism elevates this work to great cinematic art, and it contains many truly startling sequences, not least of which is the astounding scene in which Stroheim's mother virtually seduces her own son into marrying for money, or the one where the respective fathers seal the wedding pact in a brothel. There is a remarkable pageant scene in early Technicolor, replete with robust reds, and the whole is enhanced by a new score by Carl Davis. But the real glory is in the casting – to watch Stroheim and the lovely Fay Wray flirt and fall in love is transcendental. An uncredited Josef von Sternberg edited the film. TS

Erich von Stroheim *Prince Nicki* • Fay Wray *Mitzi Schrammell* • Matthew Betz *Schani Eberle* • ZaSu Pitts *Cecelia Schweisser* • Hughie Mack *Anton Eberle, Schani's father* • George Fawcett *Prince Ottokar von Wildeliebe-Rauffenburg* • Maude George *Princess Maria von Wildeliebe-Rauffenburg* • George Nichols *Fortunat Schweisser* • Dale Fuller *Katerina Schrammell* • Cesare Gravina *Martin Schrammel* ■ *Dir* Erich von Stroheim • *Scr* Erich von Stroheim, Harry Carr • *Cinematographer* Hal Mohr, B Sorenson, Ben Reynolds • *Set Designer* Richard Day, Erich von Stroheim

The Wedding Night ★★ PG

Drama 1935 · US · BW · 79mins

The third, and last, of producer Samuel Goldwyn's attempts to turn his Russian protégée Anna Sten into a new Garbo. Although charismatic in her European films, Sten seemed hard and unlikeable in English. Here, she's well cast as a Polish tobacco-grower's daughter in an interesting and original story, and supported by an endearing Gary Cooper performance, but the public didn't take to her at all. The moody photography by Gregg Toland is first-rate, though. TS [video]

Gary Cooper *Tony Barrett* • Anna Sten *Manya Novak* • Ralph Bellamy *Fredrik* • Helen Vinson *Dora Barrett* • Siegfried Rumann [Sig Ruman] *Jan Novak* • Esther Dale *Mrs Kaise Novak* • Walter Brennan *Bill Jenkins* ■ *Dir* King Vidor • *Scr* Edith Fitzgerald, from a story by Edwin Knopf

The Wedding Party ★★

Comedy 1966 · US · BW · 90mins

Brian De Palma's directorial first was actually shot in 1964, completed in 1966 and released, even then only briefly, in 1969. It's a comedy drama about an impending wedding, with the groom getting cold feet once he discovers what boors his fiancée and her family are. Made wholly in collaboration with a teacher and fellow student from De Palma's college days, the film is a curiosity for its debutante appearances by both Jill Clayburgh and Robert De Niro. DA

Jill Clayburgh *Josephine Fish* • Charles Pfluger *Charlie* • Valda Setterfield *Mrs Fish* • Jennifer Salt *Phoebe* • Raymond McNally *Mr Fish* • John Braswell *Reverend Oldfield* • Judy Thomas *Celeste, organist* • Robert DeNero [Robert De Niro] *Cecil* ■ *Dir/Scr* Cynthia Munroe, Brian De Palma, Wilford Leach

The Wedding Planner ★★ PG

Romantic comedy
2001 · US/UK/Ger · Colour · 99mins

Jennifer Lopez strays into Julia Roberts territory with another romantic comedy that explores the rocky road to matrimony and true love. Lopez plays a wedding organiser who spends her free time playing Scrabble. Charged with arranging the nuptials for Bridgette Wilson-Sampras, Lopez commits the sin of falling for the groom-to-be, Matthew McConaughey. The star makes a slightly implausible spinster, but McConaughey is far more believable. LH [video] DVD

Jennifer Lopez *Mary Fiore* • Matthew McConaughey *Steve Edison* • Bridgette Wilson-Sampras [Bridgette Wilson] *Fran Donolly* • Justin Chambers *Massimo* • Judy Greer *Penny* ■ *Dir* Adam Shankman • *Scr* Pamela Falk, Michael Ellis

Wedding Present ★★★

Screwball comedy 1936 · US · BW · 80mins

Two attractive, devil-may-care newspaper reporters fall in love with each other, only to have their romance turn sour when he is promoted to editor and she decides to marry a more conventionally reliable man. That, of course, is not the end of the story which, though it starts promisingly, degenerates into somewhat heavy-handed farce in an attempt to pep up rather thin formula fair. Three stars though, for the pleasure of keeping company with top-leaguers Cary Grant and Joan Bennett. RK

Joan Bennett *Monica "Rusty" Fleming* • Cary Grant *Charlie Mason* • George Bancroft *Pete Stagg* • Conrad Nagel *Roger Dodacker* • Gene Lockhart *Archduke Gustav Ernest* • William Demarest *"Smiles" Benson* ■ *Dir* Richard Wallace • *Scr* Joseph Anthony, from the short story by Paul Gallico in *The Saturday Evening Post*

Wedding Rehearsal ★★ U

Comedy 1932 · UK · BW · 75mins

Grandmother Kate Cutler is going to curtail bachelor marquis Roland Young's allowance if he doesn't marry one of her chosen wedding candidates, but he falls for his mother's secretary, who believe it or not turns out to be beautiful without her glasses. Unsurprising, since she's lovely Merle Oberon. Unfortunately, no one in this creaky comedy, except for leading man Young, seems able to act their way out of a paper bag. As a period piece, though, this is fascinating. TS [video]

Roland Young *Reggie, Marquis of Buckminster* • George Grossmith *Lord Stokeshire* • John Loder *"Bimbo"* • Maurice Evans *"Tootles"* • Wendy Barrie *Lady Mary Rose Wroxbury* • Joan Gardner *Lady Rosemary Wroxbury* • Merle Oberon *Miss Hutchinson* • Lady Tree *Lady Stokeshire* ■ *Dir* Alexander Korda • *Scr* Arthur Wimperis, Helen Gordon, from a story by Lajos Biró, George Grossmith

The Wedding Singer ★★★★ 12

Romantic comedy
1998 · US · Colour · 92mins

Adam Sandler is pitch-perfect in his role here as hopelessly romantic cabaret wedding singer Robbie Hart, who falls in love with a waitress (Drew Barrymore) at a nuptial function only to discover that she's engaged to someone else. The chemistry between the two stars works like a charm and director Frank Coraci has enormous fun with the music, fashions and fads of the mid-1980s setting. This good-natured romp has a knowing sense of the ridiculous and a great pop soundtrack. AJ. Contains sexual references and swearing. [video] DVD

Adam Sandler *Robbie Hart* • Drew Barrymore *Julia* • Christine Taylor *Holly* • Allen Covert *Sammy* • Matthew Glave *Glenn* • Ellen Albertini Dow *Rosie* • Angela Featherstone *Linda* • Alexis Arquette *George* ■ *Dir* Frank Coraci • *Scr* Tim Herlihy

The Wedding Tackle ★★ 15

Comedy 2000 · UK · Colour · 89mins

Take a comedy of errors, toss in some soap-opera crises and lace with innuendo, and the result is this glorified British sitcom. The ensemble cast gives it everything, but their characters feel like dismally uncool outcasts from *This Life*, with each infantile, groin-motivated male trying to squirm out of (or wriggle into) the affections of their marginally more mature female counterparts. Skeletons fall out of the stag-night cupboard with alarming regularity, and Rami Dvir's film is difficult to warm to. DP. Contains swearing. [video] DVD

Adrian Dunbar *Mr Mac* • James Purefoy *Hal* • Tony Slattery *Little Ted* • Neil Stuke *Salty* • Leslie Grantham *George* • Victoria Smurfit *Clodagh* • Susan Vidler *Vinni* • Amanda Redman *Petula* • Sara Stockbridge *Felicity* ■ *Dir* Rami Dvir • *Scr* Nigel Horne

Wee Willie Winkie ★★★

Comedy drama 1937 · US · Sepia · 103mins

Shirley Temple stars as yet another cute moppet in this sickly sweet reworking of Rudyard Kipling's vigorous tale of military life during the Raj. It is prevented from lapsing into unbearable sentimentality by the firm but sympathetic hand of western maestro John Ford, the polished reserve of C Aubrey Smith as Temple's malleable grandpa and the gruff good nature of sergeant Victor McLaglen. DP

Shirley Temple *Priscilla Williams* • Victor McLaglen *Sergeant MacDuff* • C Aubrey Smith *Colonel Williams* • June Lang *Joyce Williams* • Michael Whalen *Lieutenant "Coppy" Brandes* • Cesar Romero *Khoda Khan* ■ *Dir* John Ford • *Scr* Ernest Pascal, Julien Josephson, from the story by Rudyard Kipling

Weeds ★★ 18

Drama 1987 · US · Colour · 113mins

Nick Nolte is the prisoner at San Quentin who forms a theatre group with his fellow convicts in this drama, loosely based on a true story. While Nolte and his worthy co-stars (William Forsythe, Joe Mantegna) give strong performances, they are bogged down by a script that can't decide whether to be light-hearted or deadly serious. JB. Contains violence and swearing. [video]

Nick Nolte *Lee Umstetter* • Lane Smith *Claude* • William Forsythe *Burt the Booster* • John Toles-Bey *Navarro* • Joe Mantegna *Carmine* • Ernie Hudson *Bagdad* • Rita Taggart *Lillian Bingington, newspaper critic* ■ *Dir* John Hancock • *Scr* Dorothy Tristan, John Hancock

Week-End at the Waldorf ★★★

Portmanteau comedy drama
1945 · US · BW · 129mins

Borrowing the idea from its more famous *Grand Hotel*, MGM came up with this star-studded portmanteau movie covering nefarious goings-on and various romances during a weekend at Manhattan's glitzy Waldorf Astoria. Robert Benchley provides a narrative link between the stories, which feature Edward Arnold, Lana Turner, Van Johnson, Keenan Wynn and, centrally, the romantic comedy entanglement between Ginger Rogers as a famous movie star and Walter Pidgeon as a famous war correspondent. Diverting, but slightly heavy-handed. RK

Ginger Rogers *Irene Malvern, the actress* • Lana Turner *Bunny Smith, the stenographer* • Walter Pidgeon *Chip Collyer, the war correspondent* • Van Johnson *Capt James Hollis, the flyer* • Edward Arnold *Martin X Edley, the promoter* • Keenan Wynn *Oliver Webson, the cub reporter* • Robert Benchley *Randy Morton, the columnist* • Phyllis Thaxter *Cynthia Drew* ■ *Dir* Robert Z Leonard • *Scr* Sam Spewack, Bella Spewack, Guy Bolton (adaptation, from the play *Menschen im Hotel (Grand Hotel)* by Vicki Baum

Weekend ★★★★★ 18

Drama 1967 · Fr · Colour · 98mins

Jean-Luc Godard's nightmare vision of the collapse of western capitalism has lost none of its blistering power. Hurling traditional narrative methods to the winds, Godard sends Mireille Darc and Jean Yanne on a journey to her mother's during the course of which they encounter such diverse characters as Emily Brontë dressed as Alice in Wonderland, the French Revolutionary Saint-Just and a cell of Maoist cannibals who persuade Darc to join them. The most audacious moment in this film of ceaseless invention is the lengthy traffic jam tracking shot, in which increasingly disturbing images are recorded with an unchanging lack of passion. DP. In French with English subtitles. [video] DVD

Mireille Darc *Corinne* • Jean Yanne *Roland* • Jean-Pierre Kalfon *Leader of the FLSO* • Valérie Lagrange *His moll* • Jean-Pierre Léaud *Saint-Just/Young man in phone booth* • Yves Beneyton *Member of FLSO* • Paul Gégauff *Pianist* ■ *Dir/Scr* Jean-Luc Godard

Weekend at Bernie's ★★★ 15

Comedy 1989 · US · Colour · 94mins

OK, it's a one-joke movie and, yes, the gags are largely moronic, but this is still pretty good fun. Andrew McCarthy and Jonathan Silverman are the two junior executives who are forced to pretend their crooked boss (Terry Kiser) is still alive over a weekend in which he is to host a swinging party at the beach. It's a lot more tasteless than you would expect, and Kiser makes it all worthwhile in a scene-stealing performance as the much put-upon corpse. JF [video] DVD

Andrew McCarthy *Larry Wilson* • Jonathan Silverman *Richard Parker* • Catherine Mary Stewart *Gwen Saunders* • Terry Kiser *Bernie Lomax* • Don Calfa *Paulie, the "Iceman"* • Catherine Parks *Tina* • Eloise Broady *Tawny* ■ *Dir* Ted Kotcheff • *Scr* Robert Klane

Weekend at Bernie's II ★ PG

Comedy 1992 · US · Colour · 85mins

The central idea – 101 uses for a corpse – was barely substantial enough to sustain the first movie, but, unbelievably, most of the original team were talked into this foolish sequel. The now jobless McCarthy and Silverman use the hapless Bernie (Terry Kiser), who's been turned into a walking zombie through voodoo, in a bid to locate the money he stole from their old company. JF [video]

Andrew McCarthy *Larry Wilson* • Jonathan Silverman *Richard Parker* • Terry Kiser *Bernie Lomax* • Troy Beyer *Claudia* • Barry Bostwick *Hummel* • Tom Wright *Charles* • Steve James (1) *Henry* ■ *Dir/Scr* Robert Klane

Weekend in Havana ★★★

Comedy musical 1941 · US · Colour · 80mins

This characteristic entry in the series of anodyne, colourful Fox musicals of the period packs Alice Faye off to Havana as a department store assistant who goes on a trip to the Cuban hot spot and falls in love with John Payne. As in all these movies, Carmen Miranda is on hand as a nightclub entertainer, showcasing her outrageously ebullient Latin-American flavoured dance routines and camp, exotic headgear. Agreeable nonsense. RK

Alice Faye *Nan Spencer* • Carmen Miranda *Rosita Rivas* • John Payne *Jay Williams* • Cesar Romero *Monte Blanca* • Cobina Wright Jr *Terry McCracken* • George Barbier *Walter McCracken* • Sheldon Leonard *Boris* • Leonid Kinskey *Rafael* • Billy Gilbert *Arbolado* ■ *Dir* Walter Lang • *Scr* Karl Tunberg, Darrell Ware

Weekend of Shadows ★★★

Action drama 1978 · Aus · Colour · 94mins

John Waters, star of this action drama set in pre-war Australia, has appeared in some of the landmark films of Australian cinema, including *Breaker Morant* and *The Getting of Wisdom*. This film is not up to their standard, but still allows Waters to give another convincing performance as a member of a posse chasing a Polish immigrant suspected of murder. PF

John Waters (3) *Rabbit* • Melissa Jaffer *Vi* • Wyn Roberts *Sergeant Caxton* • Barbara West *Helen Caxton* • Graham Rouse *Ab Nolan* • Graeme Blundell *Bernie Collins* • Bill Hunter *Bosun* • Keith Lee *David Wayne* ■ *Dir* Tom Jeffrey • *Scr* Peter Yeldham, from the novel *The Reckoning* by Hugh Atkinson

W

Weekend Pass ★ 18

Comedy 1984 · US · Colour · 85mins

In this inane sex comedy, four navy men fresh out of boot camp go wild on leave in Los Angeles. There they have the usual drunken brawls and meet a bevy of strippers. Their weekend comes to an end sooner for them than this mild exploitation picture does for the viewer. AJ

DW Brown *Paul Fricker* • Peter Ellenstein *Lester Gidley* • Patrick Hauser *Webster Adams* • Chip McAllister *Bunker Hill* ■ *Dir* Lawrence Bassoff • *Scr* Lawrence Bassoff, from a story by Mark Tenser

Weekend Warriors ★★

Comedy 1986 · US · Colour · 85mins

In 1961, a group of Hollywood wannabe actors and singers join the National Guard to avoid the draft. Initially the ruse works and they have an easy time of it but the plan backfires when some top brass descend on the camp and threaten to send them away on active service. The boys decide to stage a show to prove that they would be more use as entertainers than fighters. This strained comedy stars Chris Lemmon (Jack's son) and Lloyd Bridges (father of Jeff and Beau). DF

Chris Lemmon *Vince Tucker* • Lloyd Bridges *Colonel Archer* • Vic Tayback *Sergeant Burge* • Graham Jarvis *Congressman Balljoy* • Daniel Greene *Phil McCracken* ■ *Dir* Bert Convy • *Scr* Bruce Belland, Roy M Rogosin

Weekend with Father ★★★

Romantic comedy 1951 · US · BW · 83mins

Van Heflin and Patricia Neal, usually unsmiling in downbeat dramas, manage to display a lighter touch in this modest family comedy-romance directed by Douglas Sirk, before he gained his reputation for rich and ripe Technicolor melodramas. Heflin plays a widower with two daughters, and Neal is a widow with two sons. They meet while taking their respective children to summer camp, and naturally fall in love. Predictable and cosy it may be, but it's harmless and amusing. RB

Van Heflin *Brad Stubbs* • Patricia Neal *Jean Bowen* • Gigi Perreau *Anne Stubbs* • Virginia Field *Phyllis Reynolds* • Richard Denning *Don Adams* • Jimmy Hunt *Gary Bowen* • Janine Perreau *Patty Stubbs* • Tommy Rettig *David Bowen* ■ *Dir* Douglas Sirk • *Scr* Joseph Hoffman, from a story by George F Slavin, George W George

The Weight of Water ★★ 15

Thriller 2000 · Fr/US/Can · Colour · 109mins

Kathryn Bigelow's downbeat, character-driven drama bypassed British cinemas and went straight to video. It's better than it sounds, despite its mild delusions of grandeur and confused and confusing ending. The split-level plotline involves a grisly murder 100 years earlier of two young girls that has a resonance and ramifications for two couples on a present-day yacht trip. Sean Penn, Catherine McCormack and Sarah Polley head a quality cast. DA. Contains violence, swearing, sex scenes and nudity. DVD

Catherine McCormack *Jean Janes* • Sarah Polley *Maren Hontvedt* • Sean Penn *Thomas Janes* • Josh Lucas *Rich Janes* • Elizabeth Hurley *Adaline Gunne* • Ciaran Hinds *Louis Wagner* • Ulrich Thomsen *John Hontvedt* • Anders W Berthelsen *Evan Christenson* • Katrin Cartlidge *Karen Christenson* ■ *Dir* Kathryn Bigelow • *Scr* Alice Arlen, Christopher Kyle, from the novel *The Weight of Water* by Anita Shreve

Weird Science ★★ 15

Comedy fantasy 1985 · US · Colour · 89mins

This is the worst of John Hughes's early comedies, but still a cut above most teen fodder of the time. Hughes regular Anthony Michael Hall and Ilan Mitchell-Smith are the sex-obsessed hi-tech anoraks who summon up the computer-generated woman of their dreams (Kelly LeBrock). Hughes remains a sharp observer of teenage woes but this time around there is a crassness to much of the humour and far too much time is spent leering. The best performance comes from Bill Paxton as Mitchell-Smith's fascist brother, and look out, too, for an early role for Robert Downey Jr. JF. Contains swearing and brief nudity.

Anthony Michael Hall *Gary* • Ilan Mitchell-Smith *Wyatt* • Kelly LeBrock *Lisa* • Bill Paxton *Chet* • Suzanne Snyder *Deb* • Judie Aronson *Hilly* • Robert Downey Jr *Ian* • Robert Rusler *Max* ■ *Dir/Scr* John Hughes

Weird Woman ★★

Horror 1944 · US · BW · 63mins

This *Inner Sanctum* series entry was adapted from Fritz Leiber Jr's novel *Conjure Wife*, also the inspiration for *Night of the Eagle* and *Witches' Brew*. Although Lon Chaney Jr was the series mainstay, this film firmly belongs to scream queen Evelyn Ankers, who becomes deliriously jealous when Chaney's college professor returns from an exotic holiday with new bride Anne Gwynne. In dealing with her rival, whose past is steeped in voodoo mystery, Ankers resorts to poisonous insinuation and murder. DP

Lon Chaney [Lon Chaney Jr] *Prof Norman Reed* • Anne Gwynne *Paula Reed* • Evelyn Ankers *Ilona Carr* • Ralph Morgan *Prof Millard Sawtelle* • Elisabeth Risdon *Grace Gunnison* ■ *Dir* Reginald Le Borg • *Scr* Brenda Weisberg, W Scott Darling [Scott Darling], from the novel *Conjure Wife* by Fritz Leiber Jr

Welcome Home ★★★ 15

Drama 1989 · US · Colour · 88mins

Or not, as the case may be, when Kris Kristofferson, a Vietnam veteran, is shipped home after 17 years living contentedly with his Cambodian wife and children. His American wife, JoBeth Williams, is now remarried and cut the yellow ribbon years ago. This is a partially successful attempt to examine the consequences of rising from the dead, but it's exceptionally mushy stuff. Sam Waterston, as Williams's husband number two, gives a sterling portrayal of compassion. SH. Contains swearing, nudity. DVD

Kris Kristofferson *Jake* • JoBeth Williams *Sarah* • Sam Waterston *Woody* • Brian Keith *Harry* • Thomas Wilson Brown *Tyler* • Trey Wilson *Colonel Barnes* • Ken Pogue *Senator Camden* • Kieu Chinh *Leang* • Matthew Beckett *Kim* • Jessica Ramien *Siv* ■ *Dir* Franklin J Schaffner • *Scr* Maggie Kleinman

Welcome Home, Roxy Carmichael ★★★ 15

Comedy 1990 · US · Colour · 91mins

This subtle comedy starring Winona Ryder relies heavily on her performance and that of co-star Jeff Daniels. Ryder plays a 15-year-old misfit who is awaiting the return to the town of legendary local Roxy Carmichael, whom she believes is her real mother. Predictable in places, the plot surrounding Ryder hasn't been fully developed, but once again the young actress gives a winning performance. JB. Contains some nudity. DVD

Winona Ryder *Dinky Bossetti* • Jeff Daniels *Denton Webb* • Laila Robins *Elizabeth Zaks* • Thomas Wilson Brown *Gerald Howells* • Joan McMurtrey *Barbara Webb* • Graham Beckel *Leo Bossetti* • Frances Fisher *Rochelle Bossetti* • Robby Kiger *Beannie Billings* ■ *Dir* Jim Abrahams • *Scr* Leigh Hopkins

Welcome Home, Soldier Boys ★★

Drama 1971 · US · Colour · 90mins

This wildly over-the-top action film is rooted in the hoary old movie myth that all Vietnam veterans are damaged goods. The film centres on four former Green Berets who celebrate their return to "the world" by taking over and terrorising a town. Cue much nastiness and mayhem. Mindless tosh. DA

Joe Don Baker *Danny* • Paul Koslo *Shooter* • Alan Vint *Kid* • Elliott Street *Fatback* • Jennifer Billingsley *Broad* • Billy Green Bush *Sheriff* ■ *Dir* Richard Compton • *Scr* Guerdon Trueblood

Welcome Stranger ★★

Medical comedy drama 1947 · US · BW · 107mins

Paramount scored a massive box-office hit with *Going My Way* (1944), in which Barry Fitzgerald and Bing Crosby co-starred as a crusty old priest and a new young assistant. In this flagrant rerun of the formula, the pair are doctors, running a clinic and adored by their patients. Crosby bursts into song on several occasions, romances blonde schoolteacher Joan Caulfield, and saves curmudgeonly old Fitzgerald's life, much as he saved his church in the earlier film. RK

Bing Crosby *Dr Jim Pearson* • Joan Caulfield *Trudy Mason* • Barry Fitzgerald *Dr Joseph McRory* • Wanda Hendrix *Emily Walters* • Frank Faylen *Bill Walters* • Elizabeth Patterson *Mrs Gilley* ■ *Dir* Elliott Nugent • *Scr* Arthur Sheekman, Richard Nash [N Richard Nash], from a story by Frank Butler

Welcome to Arrow Beach ★ 18

Horror 1974 · US · Colour · 80mins

What on earth drew Laurence Harvey to such lurid material? This exploration of cannibalism was an all the more regrettable choice when it proved to be his swan song. Harvey directs and also stars as a Korean War veteran who developed a taste for human flesh when his bomber crashed on a deserted island and he was forced to live off his comrades. Now living with his sister (played by the neglected Joanna Pettet) his unusual table manners attract the attention of local cops. Inept and distasteful. RS

Laurence Harvey *Jason Henry* • Joanna Pettet *Grace Henry* • Stuart Whitman *Deputy Rakes* • John Ireland *Sheriff H "Duke" Bingham* • Gloria LeRoy *Ginger* • David Macklin *Alex Heath* ■ *Dir* Laurence Harvey • *Scr* Wallace C Bennett, Jack Gross Jr, from a story by Wallace C Bennett

Welcome to Blood City ★ 15

Science-fiction thriller 1977 · UK/Can · Colour · 91mins

This dull Anglo-Canadian production owes more than just a little to *Westworld*, as Samantha Eggar monitors kidnapped Keir Dullea's fight for survival against "immortal" sheriff Jack Palance in a Wild West town. It's listlessly directed by Peter Sasdy and so badly constructed that caring about Dullea's plight is the last thing on an audience's mind. TS

Jack Palance *Frendlander* • Keir Dullea *Lewis* • Samantha Eggar *Katherine* • Barry Morse *Supervisor* • Hollis McLaren *Martine* • Chris Wiggins *Gellor* • Henry Ramer *Chumley* • Allan Royale *Peter* ■ *Dir* Peter Sasdy • *Scr* Stephen Schneck, Michael Winder

Welcome to Collinwood ★★ 15

Crime caper 2002 · US/Ger · Colour · 82mins

Could film-maker siblings Joe and Anthony Russo be the new Coen brothers? Well, despite obvious cinematic verve and a keen eye for sleaze, this quite simply lacks their originality. Petty crook Luis Guzman is given details of the perfect crime or a "Bellini" – the script is at least full of enjoyable made-up slang – and a ragtag band of lowlifes is assembled for the job. Relying too heavily on the skills of its offbeat cast there is little suspense here and the promising individual elements never really add up to a significant whole. AC. Contains violence and swearing. DVD

Luis Guzman *Cosimo* • Michael Jeter *Toto* • Patricia Clarkson *Rosalind* • Andrew Davoli *Basil* • Isaiah Washington *Leon* • William H Macy *Riley* • Sam Rockwell *Pero* • Gabrielle Union *Michelle* • George Clooney *Jerzy* ■ *Dir* Anthony Russo, Joe Russo • *Scr* Anthony Russo, Joe Russo, from the film *Big Deal on Madonna Street* by Suso D'Amico Cecchi, Mario Monicelli, Agenore Incrocci, Furio Scarpelli

Welcome to Hard Times ★★

Western 1967 · US · Colour · 102mins

This hard-to-watch, grim and slow allegorical western is somewhat of a surprise coming from director Burt Kennedy, better known for his comedy westerns. Aldo Ray is a vicious killer, forced into confrontation with mayor Henry Fonda, and the supporting cast is marvellous, with great performances from western regulars Warren Oates, Edgar Buchanan and Elisha Cook Jr. But the whole leaves a very nasty taste in the mouth, and the symbolism doesn't really come off. TS

Henry Fonda *Will Blue* • Janice Rule *Molly Riordan* • Keenan Wynn *Zar* • Janis Page *Adah* • Aldo Ray *Man from Bodie* • John Anderson *Ezra/Isaac Maple* • Warren Oates *Jenks* • Fay Spain *Jessie* • Edgar Buchanan *Brown* • Denver Pyle *Alfie* ■ *Dir* Burt Kennedy • *Scr* Burt Kennedy, from the novel by EL Doctorow

Welcome to LA ★★★ 15

Drama 1976 · US · Colour · 89mins

Produced by Robert Altman, this early Alan Rudolph picture is clearly modelled after *Nashville* and centres on cynical songwriter Keith Carradine arriving in LA to work on an album and sleeping around with a number of women. Rudolph blends together sour social satire, musical numbers, improvisational scenes and jaundiced views on marriage for a compelling whole, sharply summing up Tinseltown attitudes. AJ

Keith Carradine *Carroll Barber* • Sally Kellerman *Ann Goode* • Geraldine Chaplin *Karen Hood* • Harvey Keitel *Ken Hood* • Lauren Hutton *Nona Bruce* • Viveca Lindfors *Susan Moore* • Sissy Spacek *Linda Murray* • Denver Pyle *Carl Barber* ■ *Dir/Scr* Alan Rudolph

Welcome to Mooseport ★★ PG

Comedy 2004 · US · Colour · 105mins

American TV star Ray Romano fails to transfer successfully to the big screen in this flaccid, by-the-numbers comedy. It's all about a mayoral race between an ex-president (played by the dependable Gene Hackman) and an average Joe (Romano) in small-town America. This is a toothless satire that relies on clichéd characterisation as it lurches from one predictable scene to another. GM DVD

Gene Hackman *Monroe Cole* • Ray Romano *Handy Harrison* • Marcia Gay Harden *Grace Sutherland* • Maura Tierney *Sally Mannis* • Christine Baranski *Charlotte Cole* • Fred Savage *Bullard* • Rip Torn *Bert Langdon* • June Squibb *Irma* ■ *Dir* Donald Petrie • *Scr* Tom Schulman, from a story by Doug Richardson

W

Welcome to Sarajevo
★★★ 15

Drama 1997 · UK/US · Colour · 97mins

This is a vigorously unsentimental treatment of love in a time of war – the Bosnian conflict – based on a true story in which TV reporter Michael Henderson (Stephen Dillane, based ITN's Michael Nicholson) decides to smuggle a young refugee girl out to Britain. The seedy hotel-based world of foreign correspondents is expertly evoked by director Michael Winterbottom, though Woody Harrelson's tough-talking American journalist manages to upstage even the conflict itself. TH. Contains violence and swearing. DVD

Stephen Dillane *Michael Henderson* • Woody Harrelson *Flynn* • Marisa Tomei *Nina* • Emira Nusevic *Emira* • Kerry Fox *Jane Carson* • Goran Visnjic *Risto* • James Nesbitt *Gregg* • Emily Lloyd *Annie McGee* ■ *Dir* Michael Winterbottom • *Scr* Frank Cottrell Boyce, from the book *Natasha's Story* by Michael Nicholson

Welcome to the Club
★★

Comedy 1971 · UK · Colour · 82mins

Brian Foley, morale officer for a unit of American troops stationed in Hiroshima, is appalled by the casual racism of virtually every man in the unit. The men believe that Foley's liberal ideas, which stem from his Quaker upbringing, will lead him into clashes with his superiors and this seems likely when he questions their attitude to a group of black entertainers visiting the camp. DF

Brian Foley *Andrew Oxblood* • Jack Warden *General Strapp* • Andrew Jarrell *Robert E Lee Fairfax* • Kevin O'Connor *Harrison W Morve* • Francisca Tu *Hogan* • David Toguri *Hideki Ikada* ■ *Dir* Walter Shenson • *Scr* Clement Biddle Wood, from his novel

Welcome to the Dollhouse
★★★★ 15

Comedy drama 1995 · US · Colour · 87mins

Before he made his name with the controversial *Happiness* (1998), Todd Solondz also raised a few eyebrows with this truthful look at the nightmares of growing up. Eleven-year-old New Jersey misfit Dawn Wiener (a superb performance from young Heather Matarazzo) has all the problems of an average school girl, and more: she has an unrequited crush on her brother's friend, is being threatened by the school tough guy and is overlooked by her mother in favour of her ballet-dancing younger sister. Thanks to Solondz's original ideas, no-holds-barred script and determination never to stray into sentimentality, plus an impressive young cast, this is a fascinating and ironic look at teenage life. JB

Heather Matarazzo *Dawn Wiener* • Victoria Davis *Lolita* • Christina Brucato *Cookie* • Christina Vidal *Cynthia* • Siri Howard *Chrissy* • Brendan Sexton Jr [Brendan Sexton III] *Brandon McCarthy* • Daria Kalinina *Missy Wiener* ■ *Dir/Scr* Todd Solondz

Welcome to the Jungle
★★★ 15

Action comedy adventure
2003 · US · Colour · 99mins

Former wrestler The Rock vies for the 21st-century action man crown in this energetic comedy adventure, in which he demonstrates acting prowess to match his physical strength. He plays a Mob "retrievals expert" who's eager to go straight and become a chef, but he's given the final job of recovering his boss's double-dealing son (the wisecracking Seann William Scott) from the Brazilian jungle. The frenetically paced film delivers exciting set pieces and quick-hit humour. SF. Contains violence. DVD

The Rock *Beck* • Seann William Scott *Travis* • Rosario Dawson *Mariana* • Christopher Walken *Hatcher* • Ewen Bremner *Declan* • Jon Gries [Jonathan Gries] *Harvey* • William Lucking *Walker* • Ernie Reyes Jr *Manito* ■ *Dir* Peter Berg • *Scr* RJ Stewart, James Vanderbilt, from a story by RJ Stewart

Welcome II the Terrordome
★★ 18

Science-fiction thriller
1994 · UK · Colour · 89mins

This semi-futuristic thriller certainly has more than its fair share of heavy-handed messages to the detriment of any discernible entertainment value. Its starting point, the hounding into the sea of black slaves in 17th-century North Carolina, is powerfully drawn and provides a thumpingly dramatic opening that director Ngozi Onwurah fails to build on. A bit of a yawn. SH. Contains violence.

Suzette Llewellyn *Angela McBride/African woman #1* • Saffron Burrows *Jodie* • Felix Joseph *Black Rad/African leader* • Valentine Nonyela *Spike/African Man #1* • Ben Wynter *Hector/African boy* • Sian Martin *Chrisele/African woman #2* • Jason Traynor *Jason/Assistant overseer* ■ *Dir/Scr* Ngozi Onwurah

Welcome to Woop Woop
★★ 18

Black comedy
1997 · UK/Aus · Colour · 92mins

Johnathon Schaech plays a New York conman who falls for earthy Aussie hitch-hiker Susie Porter, only to find himself abducted and taken to the freak-filled town of Woop Woop, ruled over by his psychopathic father-in-law Rod Taylor. It's not for the faint-hearted – the kangaroo abattoir scenes will upset Skippy fans – and clumsily plotted but it's certainly an original. JF. Contains swearing, sex scenes and some violence.

Johnathon Schaech *Teddy* • Rod Taylor *Daddy O* • Susie Porter *Angie* • Dee Smart *Krystal* • Barry Humphries *Blind Wally* • Richard Moir *Reggie* • Mark Wilson *Duffy* • Paul Mercurio *Midget* ■ *Dir* Stephan Elliott • *Scr* Michael Thomas, from the novel *The Dead Heart* by Douglas Kennedy

The Well
★★★

Drama 1951 · US · BW · 85mins

The disappearance of a young black girl leads to the wrongful arrest of a white man (Harry Morgan) on a kidnapping charge. When the girl is discovered to have fallen down a deep well, the arrested man is released and eventually helps with the digging operation to rescue her. Leo Popkin and Russell Rouse direct this suspenseful race relations drama from an Oscar-nominated screenplay by Rouse and Clarence Greene, drawing excellent performances from a non-star cast, and mining the rescue action for maximum tension. RK

Gwendolyn Laster *Carolyn Crawford* • Richard Rober *Sheriff Ben Kellogg* • Maidie Norman *Mrs Crawford* • George Hamilton *Grandfather* • Ernest Anderson *Mr Crawford* • Harry Morgan *Claude Packard* • Barry Kelley *Sam Packard* • Tom Powers *Mayor* ■ *Dir* Leo C Popkin, Russell Rouse • *Scr* Russell Rouse, Clarence Greene

The Well Groomed Bride
★★★ U

Romantic comedy 1946 · US · BW · 75mins

There's a severe champagne shortage in San Francisco. Naval officer Ray Milland needs some to launch a ship. Bride-to-be Olivia de Havilland has some, but insists on keeping it for her wedding to ex-footballer Sonny Tufts. Why only one bottle of the stuff is available remains a mystery in a plot so slight as to border on the invisible, but Milland's efforts to wrest the precious liquid from de Havilland bubble along merrily enough. RK

Olivia de Havilland *Margie* • Ray Milland *Lt Dudley Briggs* • Sonny Tufts *Torchy McNeil* • James Gleason *Capt Hornby* • Constance Dowling *Rita Sloane* • Percy Kilbride *Mr Dawson* ■ *Dir* Sidney Lanfield • *Scr* Claude Binyon, Robert Russell, from a story by Robert Russell

We'll Meet Again
★★★ PG

Musical 1942 · UK · BW · 343mins

No prizes for guessing who's the star of this British wartime flagwaver. Based on what remains to this day her signature tune, Vera Lynn shows in this sugary confection why you can count her film appearances on the fingers of one hand. However, nostalgia nuts will not be disappointed as she keeps smiling through even though her best pal, Patricia Roc, has clouded her blue skies by eloping with her soldier boyfriend. This is a pretty amateurish affair, but tune in for a sing-song with Dame Vera, and Geraldo and his orchestra. DP

Vera Lynn *Peggy Brown* • Geraldo *Gerry* • Patricia Roc *Ruth* • Ronald Ward *Frank* • Donald Gray *Bruce McIntosh* • Frederick Leister *Mr Hastropp* • Betty Jardine *Miss Bohne* ■ *Dir* Phil Brandon • *Scr* James Seymour, Howard Thomas, from a story by Derek Sheils

We'll Smile Again
★★★ U

Second World War musical comedy
1942 · UK · BW · 93mins

Unlike many stage, radio or television double acts who flounder when put on the big screen, Bud Flanagan and Chesney Allen fared rather well as movie stars, and this is a typical effort, combining bright comedy with songs and human interest. Flanagan (who had a hand in the script) plays a down-and-out hired by stage star Allen to be his dresser, but his actions are misunderstood when he tries to rout Nazi spies who are using Allen's act to send coded messages. Directed with no pretension by John Baxter, it is an engaging showcase for one of Britain's best-loved song-and-comedy teams. TV

Bud Flanagan *Bob Parker* • Chesney Allen *Gordon Maxwell* • Meinhart Maur *Herr Steiner* • Phyllis Stanley *Gina Cavendish* • Peggy Dexter *Googie* • Horace Kenney *George* • Gordon McLeod *MacNaughton* • Alexander Kardan *Holtzman* ■ *Dir* John Baxter • *Scr* Bud Flanagan, Austin Melford, Barbara K Emary

Wells Fargo
★★★

Western 1937 · US · BW · 115mins

Oscar-winning director Frank Lloyd is virtually forgotten today, his epic style and passionate narrative sense well out of fashion. This is the story of America's famous freight carrier, unfolding as we follow the screen marriage of leads Joel McCrea and Francis Dee (a married couple in real life). Regrettably, their tortuous relationship gets in the way of the truly epic saga of Wells Fargo itself. This was McCrea's first substantial leading role, and he stoically underplays in the style of the great silent western stars. Stirring entertainment. TS

Joel McCrea *Ramsay MacKay* • Bob Burns *Hank York* • Frances Dee *Justine* • Lloyd Nolan *Del Slade* • Porter Hall *James Oliver* • Ralph Morgan *Mr Pryor* • Mary Nash *Mrs Pryor* • Robert Cummings *Trimball* • Henry O'Neill *Henry Wells* ■ *Dir* Frank Lloyd • *Scr* Paul Schofield, Gerald Geraghty, Frederick Jackson, from a story by Stuart N Lake

Wendigo
★★ 15

Horror thriller 2001 · US · Colour · 88mins

Devoid of any sense of terror or even tension, this snail's pace horror tale barely features the ravenous, mythological spirit of its title. Instead, writer/director Larry Fessenden creates a kind of low budget *Deliverance*, in which a haughty New York couple and their overly sensitive son get on the wrong side of the redneck locals in the snowy Catskill Mountains. Fessenden relies on creaky doors and obscure camera angles to create much needed atmosphere. SF DVD

Patricia Clarkson *Kim* • Jake Weber *George* • Erik Per Sullivan *Miles* • John Speredakos *Otis* • Christopher Wynkoop *Sheriff* ■ *Dir/Scr* Larry Fessenden

Went the Day Well?
★★★★★ PG

Second World War drama
1942 · UK · BW · 88mins

Without question the finest Home Front picture made during the Second World War. Adapted from Graham Greene's short story, it depicts the seizure of a quiet English village by disguised Nazi soldiers in league with local quislings with such plausibility that it must have chilled contemporary audiences to the bone. Those watching today will be similarly struck by the steel beneath the quintessential Englishness of the villagers. What still makes this such compelling cinema is the realism and restraint with which director Alberto Cavalcanti tells his tale and the naturalistic playing of his splendid cast. DP DVD

Leslie Banks *Oliver Wilsford* • Elizabeth Allan *Peggy* • Frank Lawton *Tom Sturry* • Basil Sydney *Ortler* • Valerie Taylor *Nora Ashton* • Mervyn Johns *Sims* • Edward Rigby *Poacher* • Marie Lohr *Mrs Frazer* • CV France *Vicar* • David Farrar *Jung* • Muriel George *Mrs Collins* • Thora Hird *Land girl* • Harry Fowler *George Truscott* • Patricia Hayes *Daisy* ■ *Dir* Alberto Cavalcanti • *Scr* Angus MacPhail, Diana Morgan, John Dighton, from the short story *The Lieutenant Died Last* by Graham Greene

Werckmeister Harmonies
★★★★ 12

Drama
2000 · Hun/Fr/Ger/It/Swi · BW · 139mins

This confirms Bela Tarr's status as a director of extraordinary vision. Set in a town about to implode into anarchy, it's a terrifying study of the helplessness of the individual in the face of cowardly repression and mob rule. Yet there's a bleak beauty about the monochrome imagery (credited to cinematographer Gabor Medvigy, among others), whether it's capturing the growing tension on the windswept streets, the pathos of a stuffed whale exhibited in the main square or the brutality of the climactic assault on a hospital. Densely symbolic, yet never inaccessible, this is artistically unique and overwhelmingly powerful. DP. In Hungarian with English subtitles. DVD

Lars Rudolph *Janos Valuska* • Peter Fitz *Gyorgy Eszter* • Hanna Schygulla *Tunde Eszter* • Janos Derzsi *Man in broad-cloth coat* • Djoko Rossich *Man in western boots* • Tamas Wichmann *Man in the sailor cap* • Ferenc Kallai *Director* ■ *Dir* Bela Tarr • *Scr* Laszlo Krasznahorkai, Bela Tarr, from the novel *Melancholy of Resistance* by Laszlo Krasznahorkai

We're Back! A Dinosaur's Story
★★★ U

Animated fantasy 1993 · US · Colour · 67mins

This animated tale wasn't widely shown in the UK – a shame since it's a jolly enough affair, well designed and featuring a literate script from Oscar-winning writer John Patrick Shanley. The story revolves around four dinosaurs who travel through time to New York and get mixed up in a series of adventures. Children will adore the dino-antics while adults will recognise some familiar voices. JF DVD

John Goodman *Rex* • Blaze Berdahl *Buster* • Rhea Perlman *Mother Bird* • Jay Leno *Vorb* • Rene Levant *Woo* • Felicity Kendal *Elsa* • Charles Fleischer *Dweeb* • Walter Cronkite *Captain Neweyes* • Julia Child *Doctor Bleeb* • Martin Short *Stubbs, the Clown* ■ *Dir* Dick Zondag, Ralph Zondag, Phil Nibbelink, Simon Wells • *Scr* John Patrick Shanley, from the book *We're Back* by Hudson Talbott

We're Going to Be Rich ★★

Musical drama 1938 · UK · BW · 80mins

Made for 20th Century-Fox, this attempt to launch Gracie Fields as an international star was a failure outside of England. This is hardly surprising, given the feebleness of the material which finds Gracie as a 19th-century singer married to feckless Victor McLaglen. They go to South Africa where he has invested their savings in a gold mine, and find they have lost the money. She sings in a saloon, becomes romantically involved with its owner Brian Donlevy and parts from hubby, but not irrevocably... RK

Gracie Fields *Kit Dobson* • Victor McLaglen *Dobbie Dobson* • Brian Donlevy *Yankee Gordon* • Coral Browne *Pearl* • Ted Smith *Tim Dobson* • Gus McNaughton *Broderick* • Charles Carson *Keeler* ■ *Dir* Monty Banks • *Scr* Sam Hellman, Rohama Siegel, from a story by James Edward Grant

We're No Angels ★★ U

Comedy 1955 · US · Colour · 105mins

Humphrey Bogart, Peter Ustinov and Aldo Ray are the three cons who escape from Devil's Island and intend to rip off French shopkeeper, Leo G Carroll, and his alluring wife, Joan Bennett, in this unruly caper. Reunited with the director of *Casablanca*, Bogart isn't well matched with his co-stars or best suited to this sort of farce. And when the script turns all moralistic and gooey (with Bogart dressing up as Santa Claus and singing carols) you start looking around for Bing Crosby. A misjudgement for all concerned. AT

Humphrey Bogart *Joseph* • Joan Bennett *Amelie Ducotel* • Peter Ustinov *Jules* • Aldo Ray *Albert* • Leo G Carroll *Felix Ducotel* • Basil Rathbone *André Trochard* • Gloria Talbott *Isabelle Ducotel* ■ *Dir* Michael Curtiz • *Scr* Ranald MacDougall, from the play *La Cuisine des Anges* by Albert Husson

We're No Angels ★★ 15

Comedy thriller 1989 · US · Colour · 101mins

Neil Jordan's film, while not that bad, is a disappointing waste of an impressive array of talent. The script is by David Mamet, and the cast includes Robert De Niro, Sean Penn and Demi Moore. Yet the result is a leaden, only fitfully funny farce in which escaped cons De Niro (over the top) and Penn pose as priests as they attempt to cross the border to Canada. Moore's role is mainly decorative and the best performances come from a wily support cast. JF. Contains violence, swearing and brief nudity.

Robert De Niro *Ned* • Sean Penn *Jim* • Demi Moore *Molly* • Hoyt Axton *Father Levesque* • Bruno Kirby *Deputy* • Ray McAnally *Warden* • James Russo *Bobby* • Wallace Shawn *Translator* • Jay Brazeau *Sheriff* • Elizabeth Lawrence *Mrs Blair* ■ *Dir* Neil Jordan • *Scr* David Mamet, from the play *La Cuisine des Anges* by Albert Husson

W

We're Not Dressing ★★★

Musical comedy 1934 · US · BW · 74mins

Culled without credit from JM Barrie's *The Admirable Crichton*, this gives the plum role to Bing Crosby and, accordingly, supplies a handful of songs for him to croon. Crosby is the deck hand on millionairess Carole Lombard's luxury yacht, cruising with a bunch of disparate, sometimes eccentric, friends and her pet bear in the South Seas. Shipwrecked on a desert island, none are able to cope except Crosby, who takes charge of the situation – and of spoiled heiress Lombard. Inconsequential, but madcap and enjoyable. RK

Bing Crosby *Stephen Jones* • Carole Lombard *Doris Worthington* • George Burns *George* • Gracie Allen *Gracie* • Ethel Merman *Edith* • Leon Errol *Hubert* • Raymond Milland [Ray Milland] *Prince Michael* ■ *Dir* Norman Taurog • *Scr* Horace Jackson, Francis Martin, George Marion Jr, from a story by Benjamin Glazer • *Music/lyrics* Mack Gordon, Harry Revel

We're Not Married ★★★ U

Portmanteau comedy
1952 · US · BW · 82mins

This portmanteau movie is delightful froth, all about five couples who discover they're not legally married in a clever, censor-circumventing series of tales. The major attraction for today's audience, however, is not in the witty Nunnally Johnson/Dwight Taylor screenplay, but in the fourth-billed presence of Marilyn Monroe, beginning her ascendancy at 20th Century-Fox. And don't blink or you'll miss an uncredited Lee Marvin. TS DVD

Ginger Rogers *Ramona* • Fred Allen *Steve Gladwyn* • Victor Moore *Justice of the Peace* • Marilyn Monroe *Annabel Norris* • David Wayne *Jeff Norris* • Eve Arden *Katie Woodruff* • Paul Douglas *Hector Woodruff* • Eddie Bracken *Willie Fisher* • Mitzi Gaynor *Patsy Fisher* • Louis Calhern *Freddie Melrose* • Zsa Zsa Gabor *Eve Melrose* • Lee Marvin ■ *Dir* Edmund Goulding • *Scr* Nunnally Johnson, Dwight Taylor, from a story by Gina Kaus, Jay Dratler

The Werewolf ★★

Horror 1956 · US · BW · 79mins

Scientists S John Launer and George Lynn experiment on tormented family man Steven Ritch to find a cure for radiation poisoning and turn him into a werewolf in the process. A competent and timely marriage of horror with science fiction just as the latter form was going out of favour in the 1950s. Clever trick photography and Ritch's sympathetic performance make this up a few notches from routine. AJ

Steven Ritch *Duncan Masch/The Werewolf* • Don Megowan *Jack Haines* • Joyce Holden *Amy Standish* • Eleanore Tanin *Helen Marsh* • Harry Lauter *Clovey* • Ken Christy *Dr Gilchrist* • S John Launer *Dr Emery Forrest* • George Lynn *Dr Morgan Chambers* ■ *Dir* Fred F Sears • *Scr* Robert E Kent, James B Gordon

Wes Craven's Don't Look Down ★★ 12

Horror thriller 1998 · US · Colour · 86mins

Despite the presence of *Scream* director Wes Craven as co-executive producer, this TV movie struggles to make an impression. After her sister falls off a cliff in a freak accident, Megan Ward joins a controversial support group to overcome her fear of heights. When the members of the group start getting killed one by one, the weak terror begins. Not so much a classy *Vertigo* riff as a throwback to such 1960s Hammer whodunnits as *Nightmare* and *Paranoiac*. AJ DVD

Megan Ward *Carla Engel* • Billy Burke *Mark Engel* • Terry Kinney *Dr Paul Sadowski* • Angela Moore *Jocelyn* • William MacDonald *Ben* • Kate Robbins (1) *Hallie* • Aaron Smolinski *Zak* ■ *Dir* Larry Shaw • *Scr* Gregory Goodell

Wes Craven's Mind Ripper ★★ 18

Science-fiction horror
1995 · US · Colour · 91mins

This mutant 1950s-style B-movie is directed with a refreshing disregard for style or cohesion by Joe Gayton. Lance Henriksen mugs valiantly as he investigates a commotion in the desert, but he's in more danger from the risible dialogue than from the brain-slurping super-soldier he's been ordered to wipe out. DP. Contains swearing, violence. DVD

Lance Henriksen *James Stockton* • Claire Stansfield *Joanne* • Natasha Gregson Wagner *Wendy* ■ *Dir* Joe Gayton • *Scr* Jonathan Craven, Phil Mittleman

Wes Craven's New Nightmare ★★★ 18

Horror 1994 · US · Colour · 107mins

Before director Wes Craven came back big time with *Scream*, he took a stab at the intellectual horror film, adding this semi-documentary style sequel to the *Nightmare on Elm Street* series. The terrorised teen from the original, Heather Langenkamp, plays herself, an actress troubled by (a real?) Freddy Krueger. There's a healthy dose of shocks, a look behind the scenes of the horror flick, and, although the project occasionally reeks of self-indulgence, you have to credit Craven (who also appears as himself) with trying something new. AJ. Contains violence, swearing. DVD

Robert Englund *Freddy Krueger/Robert Englund* • Heather Langenkamp • Miko Hughes *Dylan* • David Newsom *Chase Porter* • Jeffrey John Davis *Freddy's hand double* • Matt Winston *Chuck* • Rob LaBelle *Terry* • Wes Craven • Marianne Maddalena ■ *Dir* Wes Craven • *Scr* Wes Craven, from his characters

West Beirut ★★★★ 15

Drama
1998 · Fr/Leb/Bel/Nor · Colour · 105mins

Having served as assistant cameraman on Quentin Tarantino's first three features, Ziad Doueiri makes his directorial debut with this autobiographical account of growing up in war-torn Lebanon in the 1970s. Capturing the exuberance of youth and the vicarious thrill of the situation without ever losing sight of the seriousness of the conflict, Doueiri draws an outstanding performance from his younger brother, Rami, as the rebellious Muslim teenager whose passion for movies prompts him to travel across the barricaded city in search of adventure. A real eye-opener. DP. In French and Arabic with English subtitles. Contains swearing.

Rami Doueiri *Tarek* • Mohamad Chamas *Omar* • Rola Al Amin *May* • Carmen Lebbos *Hala* • Joseph Bou Nassar *Riad* ■ *Dir/Scr* Ziad Doueiri

West 11 ★★

Crime drama 1963 · UK · BW · 94mins

Michael Winner's skirmish with British social realism shows what life was like in the bedsits of Notting Hill, years before Julia Roberts showed up. Among the cast are Alfred Lynch as a drifter, Eric Portman as a cashiered officer and Diana Dors as a lonely heart. The script is mostly a series of loosely connected sketches, though the film's sole virtue nowadays is the location camerawork of Otto Heller that captures the then peeling and shabbily converted Regency houses that were riddled with dry rot and Rachmanism, which exchanged squalor for extortionate rents. AT

Alfred Lynch *Joe Beckett* • Kathleen Breck *Ilsa Barnes* • Eric Portman *Richard Dyce* • Diana Dors *Georgia* • Kathleen Harrison *Mrs Beckett* • Finlay Currie *Mr Cash* • Patrick Wymark *Father Hogan* • Freda Jackson *Mrs Hartley* ■ *Dir* Michael Winner • *Scr* Keith Waterhouse, Willis Hall, from the novel *The Furnished Room* by Laura del Rivo

West of the Divide ★★★ U

Western 1934 · US · BW · 52mins

Monogram studio fans insist that this is the best of John Wayne's "Lone Star" series; it melds two familiar western plots, the revenge for the death of the hero's father and the cowboy masquerading as an outlaw to avenge the said death, and Wayne proves himself at ease with such material. TS DVD

John Wayne *Ted Hayden* • Virginia Brown Faire *Fay Winters* • Lloyd Whitlock *Gentry* • George Hayes [George "Gabby" Hayes] *Dusty Rhodes* • Yakima Canutt *Hank* • Billy O'Brien *Spud* ■ *Dir/Scr* Robert N Bradbury

West of Zanzibar ★★★

Silent melodrama 1928 · US · BW · 63mins

Lon Chaney gives his most twisted performance in silent genius Tod Browning's bitterly grim morality fable that proved to be another bizarre and amazing signpost in the evolution of modern horror. Paralysed in an altercation with his wife's lover, sadistic magician "Dead Legs" Flint (Chaney) takes their offspring to Africa, leaves her in a whorehouse and plots a terrible ritual revenge after becoming the wheelchaired god to the local natives. The ultimate Browning/Chaney freak show is an extreme depiction of parent-child alienation and as sordid a slice of atrocity exotica as 1920s censors would allow. AJ

Lon Chaney *Flint* • Lionel Barrymore *Crane* • Warner Baxter *Doc* • Mary Nolan *Maizie* ■ *Dir* Tod Browning • *Scr* Elliott Clawson, Waldemar Young, Joe Farnham [Joseph Farnham] (titles), from a story by Chester De Vonde, Kilbourne Gordon • *Set Designer* Cedric Gibbons

West of Zanzibar ★★ U

Adventure 1954 · UK · Colour · 90mins

The sequel to *Where No Vultures Fly* again features Anthony Steel as African wildlife conservationist and game warden Bob Payton. Payton's wife is now played by Sheila Sim, replacing Dinah Sheridan but perfectly transferring the social graces of Tunbridge Wells to the African bush. The emphasis is on travelogue material and shots of animals, most of which were rehashed from the earlier film. Drama is trumped up by ivory poachers and the ravages of drought. It all seems simplistic and racist today, and it was banned by the Kenyan government, then in the grip of the Mau Mau uprising, who felt the film was patronising. AT

Anthony Steel *Bob Payton* • Sheila Sim *Mary Payton* • William Simons *Tim Payton* • Orlando Martins *M'Kwongwi* • Edric Connor *Chief Ushingo* • David Osieli *Ambrose* • Bethlehem Sketch *Bethlehem* • Martin Benson *Lawyer Dhofar* ■ *Dir* Harry Watt • *Scr* Max Catto, Jack Whittingham, from a story by Harry Watt

The West Point Story ★★ U

Musical comedy 1950 · US · BW · 106mins

James Cagney is in *Yankee Doodle Dandy* mode here, putting on a musical show for the cadets at West Point military academy. Cagney displays plenty of energy but struggles to shine, while co-stars Virginia Mayo, Doris Day and Gordon MacRae sing and strut their way through a roster of songs that badly needs a showstopper. Roy Del Ruth, a veteran of the *Broadway Melody* movies, could direct this sort of thing with his eyes closed, and probably did. AT

James Cagney *Elwin Bixby* • Virginia Mayo *Eve Dillon* • Doris Day *Jan Wilson* • Gordon MacRae *Tom Fletcher* • Gene Nelson *Hal Courtland* • Alan Hale Jr *Bull Gilbert* • Roland Winters *Harry Eberhart* • Raymond Roe *Bixby's "wife"* ■ *Dir* Roy Del Ruth • *Scr* John Monks Jr, Charles Hoffman, Irving Wallace, from the story *Classmates* by Irving Wallace

West Side Story ★★★★★ PG

Musical 1961 · US · Colour · 145mins

Ten well-deserved Oscars – plus a special award for Jerome Robbins's dynamic choreography – adorned this electrifying version of the magnificent Leonard Bernstein-Stephen Sondheim musical. It's an update of *Romeo and Juliet*, here turned into a New York gang parable set in the turbulent late 1950s. And surely the only Oscar ever given to an actor for merely looking good went to the elegant George Chakiris. Natalie Wood is touching as the tragic Maria and Richard Beymer – criticised at the time as Tony – now seems the very quintessence of 50s yearning. TS [video] DVD

Natalie Wood *Maria* • Richard Beymer *Tony* • Russ Tamblyn *Riff* • Rita Moreno *Anita* • George Chakiris *Bernardo* • Simon Oakland *Lieutenant Schrank* • Ned Glass *Doc* • Tucker Smith *Ice* • Tony Mordente *Action* • Jose De Vega *Chino* • Jay Norman *Pepe* ■ *Dir* Robert Wise, Jerome Robbins • *Scr* Ernest Lehman, from the stage play by Arthur Laurents, from an idea by Jerome Robbins, from Shakespeare's *Romeo and Juliet* • *Costume Designer* Irene Sharaff • *Cinematographer* Daniel L Fapp • *Editor* Thomas Stanford • *Art Director* Boris Leven

The West Side Waltz ★★★

Comedy drama 1995 · US · Colour · 90mins

Ernest Thompson, Oscar-winning screenplay writer of *On Golden Pond*, wrote and directed this starry, if slightly sudsy, TV-movie drama. Shirley MacLaine and Liza Minnelli play the grumpy older women whose lives are opened up when they encounter aspiring young actress Jennifer Grey. The two stars give sterling performances – Minnelli in particular is cast effectively against type – and they're well backed by classy supporting turns from the likes of Robert Pastorelli and Kathy Bates. RT

Shirley MacLaine *Margaret Mary Elderdice* • Liza Minnelli *Cara Varnum* • Jennifer Grey *Robin Ouiseau* • Kathy Bates *Mrs Goo* • Robert Pastorelli *Sookie Cerullo* • August Schellenberg *Serge* ■ *Dir/Scr* Ernest Thompson

Westbound ★★★ U

Western 1959 · US · Colour · 68mins

This decent Civil War western stars genre stalwart Randolph Scott as a Union officer transporting gold from California to finance the war effort and running into Confederate sympathisers and old flame Virginia Mayo along the way. While not breaking any new ground, this re-ploughs the old furrows with consummate professionalism, pacing and style. SH

Randolph Scott *John Hayes* • Virginia Mayo *Norma Putnam* • Karen Steele *Jeannie Miller* • Michael Dante *Rod Miller* • Andrew Duggan *Clay Putnam* • Michael Pate *Mace* ■ *Dir* Budd Boetticher • *Scr* Berne Giler, from the story *The Great Divide No 2* by Berne Giler, Albert Shelby LeVino

Westbound Limited ★★

Action drama 1937 · US · BW · 76mins

A hectic, low-budget Universal melodrama in which railroad agent Lyle Talbot tries to prove his innocence after he's wrongly blamed for a train crash. Director Ford Beebe, best known for such classic serials as *Flash Gordon's Trip to Mars* and *Buck Rogers*, also wrote the original story for this one, and keeps the action rattling along at a rate of knots. TS

Lyle Talbot *Dave Tolliver* • Polly Rowles *Janet Martin* • Henry Brandon *Joe Forbes* • Frank Reicher *Pop Martin* • Henry Hunter *Howard* ■ *Dir* Ford Beebe • *Scr* Maurice Geraghty, from a story by Ford Beebe

Western ★★ 15

Romantic comedy road movie
1997 · Fr · Colour · 128mins

Quirky French road movie which won the Grand Jury Prize at Cannes in 1997. Two rootless men, Sergi Lopez and Sacha Bourdo meet, fight and become firm friends, both falling on French female hospitality in their search of hearth, love and home made bread. With its thin story line and some very questionable moral commentary this treads a fine line between good and bad taste. LH. In French with English subtitles. Contains swearing and sex scenes. [video]

Sergi Lopez *Paco Cazale* • Sacha Bourdo *Nino* • Elisabeth Vitali *Marinette* • Marie Matheron *Nathalie* • Basile Siekoua *Baptiste* ■ *Dir* Manuel Poirier • *Scr* Manuel Poirier, Jean-François Goyet, from an idea by Manuel Poirier

Western Union ★★★ U

Western 1941 · US · Colour · 91mins

German émigré director Fritz Lang seemed comfortable out west, and this movie followed quickly on the heels of his *The Return of Frank James*. Today these films seem a little tame, and this tale of the building of the telegraph line between Omaha, Nebraska, and Salt Lake City, Utah, suffers from being undercast – there's a particularly uncharismatic lead in Robert Young, but the set pieces are done with bravura and the cinematography is ravishing. TS DVD

Robert Young (1) *Richard Blake* • Randolph Scott *Vance Shaw* • Dean Jagger *Edward Creighton* • Virginia Gilmore *Sue Creighton* • John Carradine *Doc Murdoch* • Chill Wills *Homer* • Barton MacLane *Jack Slade* ■ *Dir* Fritz Lang • *Scr* Robert Carson, from the novel by Zane Grey • *Cinematographer* Edward Cronjager, Allen M Davey

The Westerner ★★★★ U

Western 1940 · US · BW · 95mins

Director William Wyler cut his teeth on westerns, and here brings all his professional skills to bear in a fine example of the genre. In the lead is the star who always looked at home in the West, lanky Gary Cooper, in a tale based on the life of the notorious Judge Roy Bean, played by Walter Brennan, who won a third best supporting actor Oscar for his ferocious performance. The story itself may be fable, but Bean's celebrated obsession with Lillie Langtry was real enough, and the clever screenplay makes good use of it, particularly at the climax. TS [video]

Gary Cooper *Cole Hardin* • Walter Brennan *Judge Roy Bean* • Doris Davenport *Jane-Ellen Mathews* • Fred Stone *Caliphet Mathews* • Paul Hurst *Chickenfoot* • Chill Wills *Southeast* • Forrest Tucker *Wade Harper* ■ *Dir* William Wyler • *Scr* Jo Swerling, Niven Busch, from a story by Stuart N Lake • *Cinematographer* Gregg Toland

Westfront 1918 ★★★★

First World War drama
1930 · Ger · BW · 98mins

Released in the same year as Lewis Milestone's *All Quiet on the Western Front*, GW Pabst's film on the same subject, the Great War, caught the antiwar mood of the times. The film captures the horror of trench warfare, something audiences were only then becoming familiar with 12 years after the event. The story of how it effects four soldiers is rather simple, and the plea for universal brotherhood is expressed in a naive manner, but Pabst, using sound for the first time, and low tracking shots over the battleground, gives one of the most vivid impressions of what it was actually like on the spot. RB. A German language film.

Fritz Kampers *The Bavarian* • Gustav Diessl *Karl* • Hans Joachim Moebis *The Student* • Claus Clausen *The Lieutenant* ■ *Dir* GW Pabst • *Scr* Ladislaus Vajda, Peter Martin Lampel, from the novel *Vier von der Infanterie* by Ernst Johannsen

Westward Ho ★★

Western 1935 · US · BW · 61mins

This is a B-western with John Wayne before he was worth watching. It does rate a footnote in film history as the first release of Republic, a newly-formed amalgamation of several small outfits, though there is little difference between this effort and those he was making beforehand. Wayne plays the vigilante leader hunting badmen with a vengeance. Be warned that the Duke warbles a love song (dubbed, of course!) to the girl in the moonlight. AE

John Wayne *John Wyatt* • Sheila Mannors [Sheila Bromley] *Mary Gordon* • Frank McGlynn Jr *Jim Wyatt* • James Farley *Lafe Gordon* • Jack Curtis (1) *Walt Ballard* • Yakima Canutt *Red* ■ *Dir* RN Bradbury [Robert N Bradbury] • *Scr* Lindsley Parsons, Robert Emmett [Robert Emmett Tansey]

Westward Ho the Wagons! ★★ U

Western 1956 · US · Colour · 90mins

After making Fess Parker a star as Davy Crockett, Walt Disney quickly came up with other westerns for him. This one's visually handsome, overly episodic, undemanding family entertainment with Parker as the wagon-train scout whose hobbies are singing ballads to his own guitar accompaniment and studying medicine. Kids can identify with the boy who's captured by Indians and with the small girl they want to adopt as a princess. The lengthy battle with Pawnees is the work of the famous stunt specialist and second unit director Yakima Canutt. AE [video]

Fess Parker *John "Doc" Grayson* • Kathleen Crowley *Laura Thompson* • Jeff York *Hank Breckenridge* • David Stollery *Dan Thompson* • Sebastian Cabot *Bissonette* • George Reeves *James Stephen* • Doreen Tracey *Bobo Stephen* • Barbara Woodell *Mrs Stephen* ■ *Dir* William Beaudine • *Scr* Tom Blackburn, from the novel by Mary Jane Carr

Westward Passage ★★

Romantic comedy 1932 · US · BW · 72mins

Laurence Olivier is the vain but blocked writer who believes his wife, Ann Harding, is responsible. They bicker all day long, get divorced and she marries Irving Pichel until realising it's Olivier she loves truly, madly, deeply. The tone is decidedly Shaftesbury Avenue rather than Hollywood because Olivier, under contract to RKO, was being touted as the toast of the London stage. The title promised a western which is perhaps why it flopped. AT

Ann Harding *Olivia Van Tyne* • Laurence Olivier *Nick Allen* • ZaSu Pitts *Mrs Truedale* • Juliette Compton *Henriette* • Irving Pichel *Harry Lenman* • Irene Purcell *Diane Van Tyne* ■ *Dir* Robert Milton • *Scr* Bradley King, Humphrey Pearson, from the novel by Margaret Ayer Barnes

Westward the Women ★★

Western 1951 · US · BW · 116mins

Frank Capra had wanted to make this western but his story was purchased by MGM and assigned to director William A Wellman. Its novelty is that Robert Taylor recruits over a hundred women in Chicago to start a new life as the wives of men out west and they make up his wagon train – learning to shoot, fight hostile tribes and endure various hardships en route to their new life. It's something of an ensemble piece, with Denise Darcel as the standout. AE

Robert Taylor (1) *Buck Wyatt* • Denise Darcel *Fifi Danon* • Hope Emerson *Patience Hawley* • John McIntire *Roy Whitman* • Julie Bishop *Laurie Smith* • Beverly Dennis *Rose Meyers* • Marilyn Erskine *Jean Johnson* ■ *Dir* William A Wellman • *Scr* Charles Schnee, from a story by Frank Capra

Westworld ★★★★ 15

Futuristic thriller 1973 · US · Colour · 85mins

Writer/director Michael Crichton's futuristic suspense thriller about a holiday resort where people go to live out safely their fantasies. But Richard Benjamin and James Brolin's dream cowboy vacation turns into a nightmare when the android population malfunctions and robot gunslinger Yul Brynner pursues them relentlessly. This is a fun scare flick that puts its clever gimmicks to imaginative use, with the inspired casting of chilling Brynner, good special effects and an incisive message about the dark side of male fantasies adding extra resonance. The less successful *Futureworld* followed in 1976. AJ. Contains violence and swearing. [video]

Yul Brynner *Gunslinger* • Richard Benjamin *Peter Martin* • James Brolin *John Blane* • Norman Bartold *Medieval Knight* • Alan Oppenheimer *Chief Supervisor* • Victoria Shaw *Medieval Queen* • Dick Van Patten *Banker* ■ *Dir/Scr* Michael Crichton

The Wet Parade ★★

Period drama 1932 · US · BW · 118mins

This self-important MGM production is a real oddity that condemns demon drink while also criticising Prohibition, trying to be hard-hitting while not giving offence to any point of view. Despite fine production and a strong cast, it is heavy going. The first half depicts Southern patriarch Lewis Stone being destroyed by alcohol addiction, while the second half focuses on the thankless work of Prohibition agents. The casting of Jimmy Durante as a government agent is just one of the film's perverse qualities. TV

Dorothy Jordan *Maggie May Chilcote* • Lewis Stone *Roger Chilcote* • Neil Hamilton *Roger Chilcote Jr* • Emma Dunn *Mrs Sally Chilcote* • Frederick Burton *Judge Brandon* • Reginald Barlow *Major Randolph* • Robert Young (1) *Kip Tarleton* • Walter Huston *Pow Tarleton* • Jimmy Durante *Abe Shilling* • Wallace Ford *Jerry Tyler* • Myrna Loy *Eileen Pinchon* ■ *Dir* Victor Fleming • *Scr* John Lee Mahin, from the novel by Upton Sinclair

Wetherby ★★★★ 15

Drama 1985 · UK · Colour · 98mins

Written and directed by playwright David Hare, this a subtle, suddenly shocking, story set in Wetherby, a cold, bleak town in Yorkshire, where unmarried local teacher Vanessa Redgrave gives a small dinner party. The next day she is visited by one of the guests, Tim McInnerny, who suddenly takes out a gun and kills himself. The reasons are not at all explicable at first, but as they gradually emerge, the apparently innocuous party is seen again in a whole new light. An intriguing British movie, under-rated in its day. TH [video]

Vanessa Redgrave *Jean Travers* • Ian Holm *Stanley Pilborough* • Judi Dench *Marcia Pilborough* • Marjorie Yates *Verity Braithwaite* • Tom Wilkinson *Roger Braithwaite* • Tim McInnerny *John Morgan* • Suzanna Hamilton *Karen Creasy* • Joely Richardson *Young Jean* ■ *Dir/Scr* David Hare

Whale Music ★★★

Romance 1994 · Can · Colour · 110mins

Maury Chaykin won the best actor Genie (the Canadian equivalent of an Oscar) for his performance as a washed-up rock star in this touching but rather low-key drama. The song *Claire* also took an award, but the musical centrepiece is a symphony for whales that Chaykin hopes will be his lasting memorial. However, life seems to be conspiring against his completing the piece. Chaykin is convincing, as is Cyndy Preston as the teenage runaway who befriends him. DP. Contains swearing, sex scenes and nudity.

Maury Chaykin *Desmond Howl* • Cyndy Preston *Claire Lowe* • Jennifer Dale *Fay Ginzburg-Howl* • Kenneth Walsh *Kenneth Sexston* • Paul Gross *Daniel Howl* • Blu Mankuma *Mookie Saunders* • Alan Jordan *Sal Goneau* ■ *Dir* Richard J Lewis • *Scr* Paul Quarrington, Richard J Lewis, from the novel by Paul Quarrington

Whale Rider ★★★ PG

Drama 2002 · NZ/Ger · Colour · 97mins

If you want a family drama that takes in such weighty issues as spirituality, destiny and the role of women in Maori culture, then this unsentimental drama from director Niki Caro fits the bill. Can schoolgirl Paikea (Oscar-nominated Keisha Castle-Hughes) prove her ancestral worth and leadership qualities to her old-fashioned grandfather, a believer in upholding masculine tribal traditions? The stern character of the patriarchal Koro (Rawiri Paratene), the stunning scenery of the New Zealand coastline, the often sharply funny and well-observed script and the uniformly solid acting ensure any cloying worthiness is well disguised. AJ DVD

Keisha Castle-Hughes *Paikea* • Rawiri Paratene *Koro* • Vicky Haughton *Flowers* • Cliff Curtis *Porourangi* • Grant Roa *Uncle Rawiri* • Mana Taumaunu *Hemi* ■ *Dir* Niki Caro • *Scr* Niki Caro, from the novel by Witi Ihimaera

The Whales of August ★★★★ U

Drama 1987 · US · Colour · 90mins

While Lindsay Anderson is chiefly remembered for classic and explosive movies such as *if....*, he was also in love with the theatre and with stage actors, especially illustrious names such as John Gielgud and Ralph Richardson. So Anderson naturally jumped at the chance to make this autumnal showcase for Bette Davis and Lillian Gish. It's chiefly a battle of wits between two curmudgeonly stars. Gish, then aged 91, nurses her sister Davis who is blind. Gish – in her last film – is still the delicate actress from the silent days. Fans of Old Hollywood will adore it. AT

Lillian Gish *Sarah Webber* • Bette Davis *Libby Strong* • Vincent Price *Mr Nikolai Maranov* • Ann Sothern *Tisha Doughty* • Harry Carey Jr *Joshua Brackett* • Frank Grimes *Mr Beckwith* ■ *Dir* Lindsay Anderson • *Scr* David Berry, from his play

What? ★

Drama 1973 · It/Fr/W Ger · Colour · 112mins

Roman Polanski said this showed the absurdity and extravagance of the outgoing 1960s, dealing with an American flower child (Sydne Rome) who arrives at a Mediterranean villa, strips off and indulges in sex and power games with Marcello Mastroianni and non-acting jet-set types. A crass, self-indulgent mess. AT. Italian dialogue dubbed into English.

Marcello Mastroianni *Alex* • Sydne Rome *The Girl* • Romolo Valli *Administrator* • Hugh Griffith *Owner of Villa* • Guido Alberti *Priest* • Giancarlo Piacentini *Stud* • Carlo Delle Piane *The Boy* • Roman Polanski *Zanzara* ■ *Dir* Roman Polanski • *Scr* Roman Polanski, Gérard Brach

What a Carve Up! ★★★ U

Comedy 1961 · UK · BW · 84mins

An old dark house comedy, co-written by that master of the *double entendre*, Ray Cooney. *Carry On* regulars Sid James and Kenneth Connor are among those gathering at a musty mansion in the hope of inheriting a fortune, but, as anyone who has seen *The Cat and the Canary* can tell you, the chances of a will being read without blood being shed are pretty slim. The cast works wonders with a script that too often settles for a cheap laugh. DP

Kenneth Connor *Ernie Broughton* • Sidney James *Syd Butler* • Shirley Eaton *Linda Dickson* • Dennis Price *Guy Broughton* • Donald Pleasence *Mr Sloane, solicitor* • Michael Gough *Fisk, the butler* • Valerie Taylor *Janet Broughton* • Esma Cannon *Aunt Emily* ■ *Dir* Pat Jackson • *Scr* Ray Cooney, Tony Hilton, Leonard J Hines, from the novel and play *The Ghoul* by Dr Frank King, Leonard J Hines

What a Crazy World ★★

Musical drama 1963 · UK · BW · 90mins

With Tommy Steele and Cliff Richard making movies, it was only a matter of time before Joe Brown would have a go. The result is an amiable but outdated musical that is still worth catching to see Brown and the Bruvvers, Freddie and the Dreamers, Susan Maughan and Marty Wilde at the height of their powers. The longueurs between the musical numbers, which the more generous might call the plot, are dodgy. DP

Joe Brown (2) *Alf Hitchens* • Susan Maughan *Marilyn* • Marty Wilde *Herbie Shadbolt* • Harry H Corbett *Sam Hitchens* • Avis Bunnage *Mary Hitchens* • Michael Ripper *Common Man* • Grazina Frame *Doris Hitchens* ■ *Dir* Michael Carreras • *Scr* Alan Klein, Michael Carreras, from the play by Alan Klein

What a Girl Wants ★★ PG

Comedy 2003 · US · Colour · 100mins

Previously filmed as *The Reluctant Debutante* with Sandra Dee and Rex Harrison in 1958, this lightweight comedy stars Amanda Bynes as the love child of American Kelly Preston and titled Brit Colin Firth, who leaves her home in New York to go in search of her father in England. After the usual fish-out-of-water calamities, Firth and Bynes learn to like as well as love each other, as in all the best father-and-daughter fantasies. JA DVD

Amanda Bynes *Daphne Reynolds* • Colin Firth *Henry Dashwood* • Kelly Preston *Libby Reynolds* • Eileen Atkins *Jocelyn Dashwood* • Anna Chancellor *Glynnis Payne* • Jonathan Pryce *Alistair Payne* • Oliver James *Ian Wallace* • Sylvia Syms *Princess Charlotte* ■ *Dir* Dennie Gordon • *Scr* Jenny Bicks, Elizabeth Chandler, from the film *The Reluctant Debutante* by William Douglas Home, from the play by William Douglas Home

What a Way to Go! ★★★

Comedy 1964 · US · Colour · 110mins

This lavish, frantic comedy has Shirley MacLaine as a serial wife, marrying one of the best casts ever assembled: Dick Van Dyke's humble storekeeper turned zillionaire; Paul Newman's American artist in Paris; Robert Mitchum's Howard Hughes-type tycoon; and Gene Kelly's matinée idol. Occasionally the movie falls flat, but the script comes up with some clever demises for the husbands and mercilessly satirises the egotism of Gene Kelly. In 1964 the visual style was a knockout; today one might need to watch it through sunglasses. AT

Shirley MacLaine *Louisa* • Paul Newman *Larry Flint* • Robert Mitchum *Rod Anderson* • Dean Martin *Leonard Crawley* • Gene Kelly *Jerry Benson* • Bob Cummings [Robert Cummings] *Dr Stephanson* • Dick Van Dyke *Edgar Hopper* ■ *Dir* J Lee Thompson • *Scr* Betty Comden, Adolph Green, from a story by Gwen Davis • *Cinematographer* Leon Shamroy

What a Whopper! ★★ U

Comedy 1961 · UK · BW · 89mins

Adam Faith stars in this whimsical tale about a struggling writer who fakes photographs of the Loch Ness monster and then heads for the Highlands to convince the locals so that they'll back his book. Just about every comedy stalwart you can think of crops up in support, and even Spike Milligan has a cameo as a tramp, but the laughs are as elusive as Nessie. DP

Adam Faith *Tony Blake* • Sidney James *Harry* • Charles Hawtrey *Arnold* • Freddie Frinton *Gilbert Pinner* • Terry Scott *Sergeant* • Marie France *Marie* • Carole Lesley *Charlie* • Spike Milligan *Tramp* ■ *Dir* Gilbert Gunn • *Scr* Terry Nation, from a story by Trevor Peacock, Jeremy Lloyd

What a Widow! ★★

Romantic comedy 1930 · US · BW · 90mins

Gloria Swanson lives up to the exclamation mark as the wealthy widow who changes her men as often as the attractive costumes she wears. Among the many beaus to her string are a lawyer, a violinist, a Spanish baritone and a nightclub dancer. Allan Dwan directs swiftly, as if unwilling to dwell on the unfunny sequences, and Swanson sings a couple of songs. Its box-office failure caused a rift between Swanson and her patron Joseph P Kennedy, father of John F. RB

Gloria Swanson *Tamarind* • Owen Moore *Gerry* • Lew Cody *Victor* • Margaret Livingston *Valli* • William Holden (1) *Mr Lodge* ■ *Dir* Allan Dwan • *Scr* James Gleason, James Seymour, from a story by Josephine Lovett

What a Woman! ★★

Romantic comedy 1943 · US · BW · 93mins

Rosalind Russell stars as an all-powerful literary agent in this silly and plot-starved romantic comedy. While busily attempting to persuade author Willard Parker, whose novel she has just sold to Hollywood, that he should star in the film version, she is interviewed by journalist Brian Aherne, who gets caught up in the general mayhem. Despite its failings, the movie is kept bubbling along by Russell, a powerhouse of comedic accomplishment; Shelley Winters makes her debut in a bit part. RK

Rosalind Russell *Carol Ainsley* • Brian Aherne *Henry Pepper* • Willard Parker *Professor Michael Cobb aka Anthony Street* • Alan Dinehart *Pat O'Shea* • Edward Fielding *Senator Ainsley* • Ann Savage *Jane Hughes* • Shelley Winter [Shelley Winters] *Actress* ■ *Dir* Irving Cummings • *Scr* Therese Lewis, Barry Trivers, from a story by Erik Charell

What about Bob? ★★★★ PG

Comedy 1991 · US · Colour · 99mins

Richard Dreyfuss and Bill Murray make a dynamic comedy duo in this amiably manic satire on the therapy business directed by ex-Muppeteer Frank Oz. Murray is especially funny as the annoying multi-phobic patient who follows psychiatrist Dreyfuss on holiday and totally ruins his control-freak life. His carefree schizo slobbishness contrasts with Dreyfuss's Freudian posing, and the frenzied laughs come thick and fast without losing their welcome sharp edge or delightfully twisted compassion. AJ. Contains swearing. DVD

Bill Murray *Bob Wiley* • Richard Dreyfuss *Dr Leo Marvin* • Charlie Korsmo *Siggy Marvin* • Julie Hagerty *Fay Marvin* • Kathryn Erbe *Anna Marvin* • Tom Aldredge *Mr Guttman* • Susan Willis *Mrs Guttman* ■ *Dir* Frank Oz • *Scr* Tom Schulman, from a story by Alvin Sargent, Laura Ziskin

What Becomes of the Broken Hearted? ★★ 18

Drama 1999 · NZ/Aus · Colour · 98mins

Once Were Warriors was a frighteningly believable account of domestic violence and did a lot to overturn the cosy picture postcard view of modern New Zealand. It was a lot to live up to and sadly this belated sequel has to go down as a disappointment despite the return of star Temuera Morrison and writer Alan Duff. Morrison still spends his time drinking himself – and beating other people – senseless. However, when his son Julian Arahanga is killed in a gang shooting, he is forced to re-evaluate his life. Director Ian Mune is fine on detailing the despair of working class Maori, but focuses too much on the gang lifestyle. JF DVD

Temuera Morrison *Jake Heke* • Clint Eruera *Sonny Heke* • Nancy Brunning *Tania Rogers* • Pete Smith *Apeman* • Lawrence Makoare *Grunt* • Rawiri Paratene *Mulla Rota* • Julian Arahanga *Nig Heke* • Edna Stirling *Rita* ■ *Dir* Ian Mune • *Scr* Alan Duff, from his novel

What Changed Charley Farthing? ★

Comedy adventure
1974 · UK · Colour · 100mins

This British attempt at a featherweight frolic by regular writing partners Jack Seddon and David Pursall sinks with scarcely a ripple of loss. Toothsome Doug McClure tries to escape a Cuba-style republic, while Lionel Jeffries, Warren Mitchell and Hayley Mills attempt to make some impact on the resolutely flabby plot. That they do not succeed is partly their fault: they should have read the script before they agreed to take part. TH

Doug McClure *Charley Farthing* • Lionel Jeffries *Henry Houlihan* • Hayley Mills *Jenny* • Warren Mitchell *MacGregor* • Alberto de Mendoza *Jumbo De Santos* • Dilys Hamlett *Miss Parchment* ■ *Dir* Sidney Hayers • *Scr* David Pursall, Jack Seddon, from a novel by Mark Hebdon

What Did You Do in the War, Daddy? ★★

Second World War comedy
1966 · US · Colour · 115mins

You start wishing Peter Sellers had agreed to star in this silly Blake Edwards war comedy about a Sicilian village whose inhabitants will only surrender to the US Army if they can hold their annual soccer match and wine festival first. Edwards's *Pink Panther* collaborator might have breathed life into William Peter Blatty's ponderous script. As it is, James Coburn, Dick Shawn, Aldo Ray and Sergio Fantoni are just too heavy-handed for this kind of comedy. TH

James Coburn *Lieutenant Christian* • Dick Shawn *Captain Cash* • Sergio Fantoni *Captain Oppo* • Giovanna Ralli *Gina Romano* • Aldo Ray *Sergeant Rizzo* • Harry Morgan *Major Pott* • Carroll O'Connor *General Bolt* ■ *Dir* Blake Edwards • *Scr* William Peter Blatty, from a story by Blake Edwards, Maurice Richlin

What Dreams May Come ★★ 15

Fantasy romantic drama
1998 · US · Colour · 108mins

A ghastly love-after-death fantasy, with Annabella Sciorra as a suicide consigned to her own private hell, and Robin Williams as her dead hubby, a car-crash victim, consigned to his own painterly paradise, but forsaking it to be reunited with the love of his life – and death. Vincent Ward brings his usual visual style to this tosh and as a result the film looks wonderful. But that's all that is wonderful about it as, visuals aside, this is slow and

W

sentimental slush. DA. Contains swearing, violence, nudity. [Video] DVD

Robin Williams *Chris Nielsen* • Cuba Gooding Jr *Albert* • Annabella Sciorra *Annie Nielsen* • Max von Sydow *The Tracker* • Jessica Brooks Grant *Marie Nielsen* • Josh Paddock *Ian Nielsen* • Rosalind Chao *Leona* ■ *Dir* Vincent Ward • *Scr* Ron Bass [Ronald Bass], from the novel by Richard Matheson

What Ever Happened to Baby Jane? ★★★★★ 18

Gothic drama 1962 · US · BW · 127mins

This innovative and much imitated chiller set the trend for ageing Hollywood divas to revive their careers by playing unhinged maniacs – but no one beats Bette Davis or Joan Crawford in the snarl-and-shriek department. Here the former queens of Hollywood play actress sisters divided by age-old Tinseltown resentments, with Davis's grotesquely made-up former child star torturing her paralyzed sister (Crawford). The on-screen fireworks were reportedly fuelled by off-screen hatred, but the chemistry between the stars is hair-raising and upped the Gothic stakes to camp shock levels. On a more serious note, this deals with the frightening decay of illusions by cleverly incorporating both actresses' earlier work into the psychodrama. AJ [Video]

Bette Davis *Jane Hudson* • Joan Crawford *Blanche Hudson* • Victor Buono *Edwin Flagg* • Anna Lee *Mrs Bates* • Maidie Norman *Elvira Stitt* • Marjorie Bennett *Della Flagg* ■ *Dir* Robert Aldrich • *Scr* Lukas Heller, from the novel by Henry Farrell • *Costume Designer* Norma Koch • *Cinematographer* Ernest Haller

What Every Woman Knows ★★★

Political comedy drama
1934 · US · BW · 90mins

This charts the rise of a poverty-stricken but brilliant and ambitious young Scottish socialist (Brian Aherne) from humble beginnings to becoming a Member of Parliament. His success is made possible by financial help from the brothers of a mousy spinster (Helen Hayes) on condition that he will later marry her. Adapted from JM Barrie's sentimental play, the movie has a tedious first 25 minutes or so. It's worth persevering, though, for the poignant and charming tale that follows, for Aherne's performance. RK

Helen Hayes *Maggie Wylie* • Brian Aherne *John Shand* • Madge Evans *Lady Sybil Tenterden* • Lucile Watson *La Comtesse* • Dudley Digges *James Wylie* • Donald Crisp *David Wylie* • David Torrence *Alick Wylie* ■ *Dir* Gregory La Cava • *Scr* Monckton Hoffe, John Meehan, James K McGuinness, Marian Ainslee, from the play by JM Barrie

What Happened to Santiago ★★★

Romantic comedy
1989 · P Ric · Colour · 105mins

Forgetting the past and living for the present is the message of this affecting drama from director Jacobo Morales. Clinging to memories of his happy marriage, widower Tommy Muñiz has an accountant's liking for order, which is shaken both by his daughter's chaotic existence and the fact that his new lover, Gladys Rodriguez, refuses to reveal anything of her life before they met in a leafy city park. Part age-gap romance, study in dysfunction and political allegory, the action builds steadily to shocking revelations. DP. In Spanish with English subtitles.

Tommy Muñiz *Santiago Rodriguez* • Gladys Rodriguez *Angelina* • Jacobo Morales *Arístides Esquilín* • Johanna Rosaly *Nereida* • Roberto Vigoreaux *Geraldo* ■ *Dir/Scr* Jacobo Morales

What Happened Was... ★

Romantic comedy drama
1994 · US · Colour · 90mins

What happened was... not very much. We spend an evening with two very strange lonely hearts on their first date. Director Tom Noonan plays a paranoid, conspiracy theory-prone paralegal. Karen Sillas is Jackie, a legal assistant in the same firm who has invited him over to dinner. Together they discuss their insecurities and lack of success with the opposite sex without really getting anywhere. Depressing and difficult. LH

Tom Noonan *Michael* • Karen Sillas *Jackie* ■ *Dir/Scr* Tom Noonan

What Have I Done to Deserve This? ★★★ 18

Black comedy 1984 · Sp · Colour · 97mins

A typical "kitsch 'n' think" mixture of tragedy and comedy from Spanish director Pedro Almodóvar. Carmen Maura is the unhappy Madrid housewife who rebels against the pressures of modern life with drugs and manslaughter when her family's myriad problems drag her deeper into depression. Using the language of Italian neorealism, sexual taboos, fake commercials for bogus products and his skewed sense of autobiographical social conscience, Almodóvar mines this spiky black farce for all its allegorical worth. AJ. In Spanish with English subtitles. [Video] DVD

Carmen Maura *Gloria* • Luis Hostalot *Polo* • Angel De Andrés-López *Antonio* • Gonzalo Suarez *Lucas Villalba* • Verónica Forqué *Cristal* • Juan Martinez *Toni* • Chus Lampreave *Grandmother* ■ *Dir/Scr* Pedro Almodóvar

What Lies Beneath ★★★ 15

Supernatural thriller
2000 · US · Colour · 124mins

Harrison Ford and Michelle Pfeiffer star in this formulaic but highly enjoyable supernatural thriller from director Robert Zemeckis. Scientist Ford and his wife Pfeiffer have renovated their idyllic Vermont lakeside house, but their domestic bliss is disturbed when she starts seeing and hearing ghostly apparitions. A creaking cocktail of light suspense and implausible plotting that pushes every tried-and-tested scare button, this shocker is illuminated by Pfeiffer's believable performance as the traumatised wife. AJ. Contains violence, swearing. [Video] DVD

Harrison Ford *Norman Spencer* • Michelle Pfeiffer *Claire Spencer* • Diana Scarwid *Jody* • Joe Morton *Dr Drayton* • James Remar *Warren Feur* • Miranda Otto *Mary Feur* • Amber Valletta *Madison Elizabeth Frank* ■ *Dir* Robert Zemeckis • *Scr* Clark Gregg, from a story by Sarah Kernochan, Clark Gregg

What Love Sees ★★ PG

Drama based on a true story
1996 · US · Colour · 91mins

A fantastically syrupy TV movie about a romance between two blind people from different sides of the tracks in the 1930s. Annabeth Gish stars as a wealthy woman who finds true love with farmer Richard Thomas, much to the distress of her city-based family who worry that he won't be able to look after her out West. The performances from the two leads are pretty good, but the treacle's a little too thick. JF [Video]

Richard Thomas *Gordon Holly* • Annabeth Gish *Jean Treadway* • Edward Herrmann *Morton Treadway* • Kathleen Noone *Sarah Treadway* • August Schellenberg *Earl* • Romy Rosemont *Lucy Treadway* ■ *Dir* Michael Switzer • *Scr* Robert L Freedman, from the book by Susan Vreeland

What – No Beer? ★★

Comedy 1933 · US · BW · 65mins

Yoked together by MGM for several comedies, Buster Keaton and Jimmy Durante here play dopey friends who put their money into a run-down brewery in the hope that Prohibition will soon be lifted. It isn't and the duo find themselves in trouble with the police and gangsters. Little of the old Keaton magic is in evidence while the rasp-voiced Durante abrades the soundtrack with unsubtle gags. TH

Buster Keaton *Elmer J Butts* • Jimmy Durante *Jimmy Potts* • Rosco Ates [Roscoe Ates] *Schultz* • Phyllis Barry *Hortense* • John Miljan *Butch Lorado* • Henry Armetta *Tony* • Edward Brophy *Spike Moran* • Charles Dunbar *Mulligan* ■ *Dir* Edward Sedgwick • *Scr* Carey Wilson, Jack Cluett, from a story by Robert E Hopkins

What Planet Are You From? ★★ 15

Science-fiction comedy
2000 · US · Colour · 100mins

When is Greg Kinnear going to tire of playing smarmy love rats? He's at it again in Gary Shandling's hugely disappointing big screen debut, but at least he provides a welcome distraction from the film's only joke – a humming penis. Clearly uneasy with Shandling's screenplay, director Mike Nichols resorts to stuffing the action with cameos, but there's just no escaping Shandling's timid alien and his bid to seduce recovering alcoholic Annette Bening in order to repopulate his planet. DP. Contains swearing and sex scenes. [Video] DVD

Garry Shandling *Harold Anderson* • Annette Bening *Susan* • Greg Kinnear *Perry Gordon* • Ben Kingsley *Graydon* • Linda Fiorentino *Helen Gordon* • John Goodman *Roland Jones* ■ *Dir* Mike Nichols • *Scr* Garry Shandling, Michael Leeson, Ed Solomon, Peter Tolan, from a story by Garry Shandling, Michael Leeson

What Price Glory ★★★

Silent war comedy 1926 · US · BW · 122mins

Considered very daring in its day for its mix of pathos and jokes, director Raoul Walsh's depiction of the First World War as a slapstick farrago is still a feat of arms. Rivalling US Marines Captain Flagg and Sergeant Quirk (Victor McLaglen and Edmund Lowe) squabble over women (Dolores Del Rio in particular) on the front line. The film juxtaposes some very realistic battle scenes with boisterous comedy. Compelling for its unusual blend of realism and farce. The stars reprised their characters in 1929's *The Cock-Eyed World*. TH

Victor McLaglen *Captain Flagg* • Edmund Lowe *Sergeant Quirt* • Dolores Del Rio *Charmaine de la Cognac* • William V Mong *Cognac Pete* • Phyllis Haver *Hilda of China* ■ *Dir* Raoul Walsh • *Scr* James T O'Donohoe, Malcolm Stuart Boylan (titles), from the play by Laurence Stallings, Maxwell Anderson

What Price Glory? ★★★ U

First World War comedy
1952 · US · Colour · 109mins

This is a slightly misguided attempt to remake the 1926 silent hit. The garish Technicolor and Robert Wagner's brilliantined hairstyle are quite wrong for such a tale. Even so, director John Ford seems to regard the whole enterprise as a lark, with a past-his-prime James Cagney and a likeable Dan Dailey performing as though this were a musical without songs. Still enjoyable. TS [Video]

James Cagney *Captain Flagg* • Corinne Calvet *Charmaine* • Dan Dailey *Sergeant Quirt* • William Demarest *Corporal Kiper* • Craig Hill *Lieutenant Aldrich* • Robert Wagner *Lewisohn* ■ *Dir* John Ford • *Scr* Phoebe Ephron, Henry Ephron, from the play by Laurence Stallings, Maxwell Anderson

What Price Hollywood? ★★★★

Drama 1932 · US · BW · 88mins

George Cukor's sophisticated and still appealing Hollywood story with Constance Bennett as a waitress at the famous Brown Derby restaurant who becomes a star. Meanwhile, her discoverer and mentor, played by real-life director Lowell Sherman, slips into drunken obscurity. Sherman, it is said, modelled his alcoholism on observing his then brother-in-law, John Barrymore. The picture offers an atmospheric and authentic portrait of Hollywood at the time and gave producers a cast-iron storyline which they have recycled as *A Star Is Born* three times. AT

Constance Bennett *Mary Evans* • Lowell Sherman *Maximilian Carey* • Neil Hamilton *Lenny Borden* • Gregory Ratoff *Julius Saxe* • Brooks Benedict *Muto* • Louise Beavers *Bonita, the maid* • Eddie "Rochester" Anderson *James* ■ *Dir* George Cukor • *Scr* Jane Murfin, Ben Markson, Gene Fowler, Rowland Brown, from a story by Adela Rogers St John

What Rats Won't Do ★★

Romantic comedy
1998 · UK · Colour · 84mins

From the producers of *Four Weddings and a Funeral*, this movie crams in elements from that hit plus a sprinkling of *A Fish Called Wanda*. It's a romantic farce about two barristers falling in love while contesting a case. Natascha McElhone is fun and Charles Dance in a leopard-skin G-string could be considered a visual bonus. Don't let the ghastly title put you off, as there is an oddly Swinging Sixties charm here. AT

James Frain *Jack* • Natascha McElhone *Kate* • Charles Dance *Gerald* • Parker Posey *Mirella* • Samantha Bond *Jane* • Peter Capaldi *Tony* ■ *Dir* Alastair Reid • *Scr* Steve Coombes, Dave Robinson, William Osborne

What the Butler Saw ★ U

Comedy 1950 · UK · BW · 61mins

Elderly Edward Rigby heads a B-movie cast in this impoverished (one set), stiffly directed comedy, an early product from the Hammer studio. The plot, about a Polynesian princess who follows her lover, a butler, home to England and causes consternation in a country house, has a distinctly pre-war feel. DM

Edward Rigby *The Earl* • Henry Mollison *Bembridge* • Mercy Haystead *Lapis* • Michael Ward *Gerald* • Eleanor Hallam *Lady Mary* • Peter Burton *Bill Fenton* ■ *Dir* Godfrey Grayson • *Scr* AR Rawlinson, Edward J Mason, from a story by Roger Good, Donald Good

What the Deaf Man Heard ★★★

Period comedy drama
1997 · US · Colour · 98mins

This sly comedy stars Matthew Modine as the small-town handyman in whom everyone confides their secrets in the belief that he's a deaf mute. However, his silence is simply a ten-year-old's response to his mother's last instruction before they are accidentally parted forever at a bus depot. Wearing its charm lightly and with the excellent Modine being well supported by Claire Bloom, Tom Skerritt and James Earl Jones, this TV movie is an unassuming pleasure. DP

Matthew Modine *Sammy Ayers* • Claire Bloom *Mrs Tynan* • Judith Ivey *Lucille* • James Earl Jones *Archibald Thacker* • Jerry O'Connell *Rev Perry Ray Pruitt* • Bernadette Peters *Helen Ayers* • Tom Skerritt *Norm Jenkins* ■ *Dir* John Kent Harrison • *Scr* Robert W Lenski, from the novel *What the Deaf-Mute Heard* by GD Gearino

W

What the #$*! Do We Know!? ★★ 12A

Drama documentary
2004 · US · Colour · 108mins

This hybrid purports to unravel the mysteries of quantum physics, but actually serves as a facile recruiting advert for the Ramtha School of Enlightenment. The three film-makers are students of Ramtha, a 35,000-year-old philosopher from the lost continent of Atlantis, whose voice is "channelled" through former saleswoman JZ Knight. Exemplifying the hokey arguments about how each individual can create their own reality is a hearing-impaired photographer (played by Marlee Matlin), who's wondering what the "bleep" life's all about after enduring a messy divorce. According to the film-makers, she'll be happier once she realises that quantum physics has proved that man can walk on water. JR

Marlee Matlin *Amanda* • Elaine Hendrix *Jennifer* • Robert Bailey Jr *Reggie* • Armin Shimerman *Man in subway* • Barry Newman *Frank* • John Ross Bowie *Elliot* • Larry Brandenburg *Bruno* ■ *Dir* Mark Vicente, Betsy Chasse, William Arntz • *Scr* Betsy Chasse, William Arntz, Matthew Hoffman

What Time Is It There? ★★★★

Drama
2001 · Tai/Fr/It · Colour and BW · 116mins

Laden with filmic references, this is Tsai Ming-liang's most sardonic exploration of his perennial themes of impersonality and isolation in a teeming, urban world. Seemingly oblivious to the fact that his newly widowed mother is becoming increasingly distraught in her efforts to locate his father's reincarnated spirit, street vendor Li Kangsheng becomes so obsessed with Chen Shiang-chyi (a pretty stranger who bought his watch before heading for a miserably lonely sojourn in Paris) that he adjusts every chronometer he can find to share her time zone. Combining pathos, compassion and satire, this is a minimalist delight. DP. In Mandarin, English and French with subtitles.

Li Kangsheng *Hsiao Kang* • Chen Xiangqi *Shiang-chyi* • Lu Yi-Ching *Hsiao Kang's mother* • Miao Tien *Hsiao Kang's father* • Jean-Pierre Léaud *Man at the cemetery* • Cecilia Yip *Chinese woman in Paris* ■ *Dir* Tsai Ming-liang • *Scr* Tsai Ming-liang, Yang Pi-ying

What Women Want ★★★★ 12

Romantic comedy
2001 · US · Colour · 121mins

Mel Gibson stars as a chauvinistic advertising executive who accidentally suffers an electric shock, and suddenly finds himself able to hear women's thoughts. His unique gift sometimes proves to be a mixed blessing, but when bitchy rival Helen Hunt beats him to a top job, Gibson decides to play dirty. Gradually, his insights into how women think, and what they want, bring out his feminine side. Despite the daft premise, this is wittily written and sharply directed, with Gibson effortlessly running the gamut from sheer obnoxiousness to utter charm. Hunt is great, too, as his far-from-perfect love match. DA. Contains swearing. DVD

Mel Gibson *Nick Marshall* • Helen Hunt *Darcy Maguire* • Marisa Tomei *Lola* • Mark Feuerstein *Morgan Farwell* • Lauren Holly *Gigi* • Ashley Johnson *Alex Marshall* • Alan Alda *Dan Wanamaker* • Judy Greer *Erin* • Bette Midler *Therapist* ■ *Dir* Nancy Meyers • *Scr* Josh Goldsmith, Cathy Yuspa, from a story by Josh Goldsmith, Cathy Yuspa, Diane Drake

Whatever ★★ 15

Drama 1998 · US/Fr · Colour · 108mins

Debuting director Susan Skoog, who also wrote and produced this, presents a portrait of teenage disillusion in the early 1980s that never rings true. Dismissive of her gold-digging mother and odious brother, Liza Weil allows her passion for art to be diluted by her sexual curiosity and a self-destructive streak. The main focus is on those old adolescent chestnuts – conformity and rebellion – but Skoog's views are as predictable as her choices on the post-punk soundtrack. DP

Liza Weil *Anna Stockard* • Chad Morgan *Brenda Talbot* • Frederic Forrest *Mr Chaminsky* • Gary Wolf *Eddie* • Dan Montano *Zak* ■ *Dir/Scr* Susan Skoog

Whatever Happened to Aunt Alice? ★★★★ 15

Mystery thriller 1969 · US · Colour · 96mins

Produced by Robert Aldrich, who directed Bette Davis and Joan Crawford in the classic gothic drama *What Ever Happened to Baby Jane?*, this scary story isn't quite in the same class. Ruth Gordon poses as a housekeeper to Geraldine Page, who's got into the unpleasant habit of disposing of her domestic help. Director Lee H Katzin contrives a baleful bitches' brew of women at war with each other, and he maintains the suspense with considerable skill. TH DVD

Geraldine Page *Mrs Claire Marrable* • Ruth Gordon *Mrs Alice Dimmock* • Rosemary Forsyth *Harriet Vaughn* • Robert Fuller *Mike Darrah* • Mildred Dunnock *Miss Tinsley* • Joan Huntington *Julia Lawson* ■ *Dir* Lee H Katzin • *Scr* Theodore Apstein, from the novel *The Forbidden Garden* by Ursula Curtiss

Whatever Happened to Harold Smith? ★★★ 15

Comedy 1999 · UK · Colour · 92mins

Veteran British star Tom Courtenay makes a magnificent comeback as Harold Smith, whose magical powers stop three pacemakers at an old people's home in 1970s Sheffield. While his son Michael Legge dithers between punk and disco, Courtenay becomes a scandalous celebrity thanks to his occult powers. Peter Hewitt's comedy offers a quirky account of the times. This is a home-grown product that, like *The Full Monty*, proves regional ideas can have a powerful metropolitan impact. TH

Tom Courtenay *Harold Smith* • Michael Legge *Vince Smith* • Laura Fraser *Joanna Robinson* • Stephen Fry *Doctor Peter Robinson* • Charlotte Roberts *Lucy Robinson* • Amanda Root *Margaret Robinson* • Lulu *Irene Smith* • David Thewlis *Keith Nesbitt* ■ *Dir* Peter Hewitt • *Scr* Ben Steiner

Whatever It Takes ★ 12

Romantic comedy
2000 · US · Colour · 90mins

Shane West and Marla Sokoloff are high school neighbours, friends who don't fancy each other. But in order to start dating the school bimbo Jodi Lyn O'Keefe, West feels he must make his best mate woo Sokoloff to get her out of the way. Cue a crass Cyrano pastiche of West in the bushes whispering words of wonder to his dumb buddy. LH DVD

Jodi Lyn O'Keefe *Ashley "Ash" Grant* • Shane West *Ryan Woodman/Brian Ryan* • Marla Sokoloff *Maggie Carter* • Manu Intiraymi *Dunleavy* • Aaron Paul *Floyd* • Julia Sweeney *Kate Woodman* ■ *Dir* David Raynr • *Scr* Mark Schwahn

What's Cooking? ★★★ 12

Drama 2000 · US/UK · Colour · 109mins

Gurinder Chadha turns to the great melting pot society of the United States to see how an African-American, Hispanic, Vietnamese and Jewish family each celebrates Thanksgiving Day. As the narrative threads intertwine, secondary themes such as patriarchy, homophobia, adultery, delinquency, age-gap tension and class snobbery have their moment under the microscope. Yet while Chadha handles each storyline with creditable democracy, she overseasons with life/food metaphors and melodramatic revelations. However, the sizeable ensemble largely succeeds in avoiding caricature. DP. Contains some swearing and sexual references.

Joan Chen *Trinh Nguyen* • Julianna Margulies *Carla* • Mercedes Ruehl *Elizabeth Avila* • Kyra Sedgwick *Rachel Seelig* • Alfre Woodard *Audrey Williams* • Maury Chaykin *Herb Seelig* • Victor Rivers *Javier Avila* • Dennis Haysbert *Ronald Williams* ■ *Dir* Gurinder Chadha • *Scr* Gurinder Chadha, Paul Mayeda Berges

What's Eating Gilbert Grape ★★★ 12

Comedy drama 1993 · US · Colour · 112mins

Johnny Depp takes the title role in this gentle oddity, playing the sensitive but level-headed teenager who has his hands full coping with an obese mother (Darlene Cates), who won't leave the house, and a mentally disabled younger brother (Leonardo DiCaprio). The latter steals the show, but the entire cast turns in winning performances. Director Lasse Hallström lets sentiment creep in, but still demonstrates a sharp outsider's eye for the quirkiness of Americana. JF. Contains swearing and sex scenes. DVD

Johnny Depp *Gilbert Grape* • Juliette Lewis *Becky* • Mary Steenburgen *Betty Carver* • Leonardo DiCaprio *Arnie Grape* • John C Reilly *Tucker Van Dyke* • Darlene Cates *Bonnie Grape* • Laura Harrington *Amy Grape* • Mary Kate Schellhardt *Ellen Grape* • Crispin Glover *Bobby McBurney* • Kevin Tighe *Mr Carver* ■ *Dir* Lasse Hallström • *Scr* Peter Hedges, from his novel • *Cinematographer* Sven Nykvist

What's Good for the Goose ★ PG

Comedy 1969 · UK · Colour · 98mins

With a contrived title and a simply appalling script (co-written by Norman Wisdom himself), this is one of the biggest blots on the British movie copybook. Directed with no feel for Wisdom's unique brand of comedy, it is jam-packed with cringeworthy moments. Norman the sexy banker? No wonder he didn't make another film for three years. DP

Norman Wisdom *Timothy Bartlett* • Sally Geeson *Nikki* • Sarah Atkinson *Meg* • Terence Alexander *Frisby* • Sally Bazely *Margaret Bartlett* • Derek Francis *Harrington* • David Lodge *Hotel porter* ■ *Dir* Menahem Golan • *Scr* Norman Wisdom, Menahem Golan, Christopher Gilmore

What's New, Pussycat? ★★★ 15

Comedy 1965 · US/Fr · Colour · 104mins

Woody Allen has never had much time for this frantic farce, which marked his debut as both writer and performer. Originally planned as a low-key black-and-white affair, it snowballed into a freewheeling star vehicle over which director Clive Donner was not always in total control. Even though the film was a box-office smash, Allen complained that unchecked ad-libbing and a disinclination to excise the mediocre had swamped his material, with Peter Sellers particularly guilty as the psychiatrist jealous of patient Peter O'Toole's success with women. Glossy, exhilarating and often hilarious. DP DVD

Peter Sellers *Doctor Fritz Fassbender* • Peter O'Toole *Michael James* • Romy Schneider *Carol Werner* • Capucine *Renée Lefèbvre* • Paula Prentiss *Liz* • Woody Allen *Victor Shakapopolis* • Ursula Andress *Rita* • Richard Burton ■ *Dir* Clive Donner • *Scr* Woody Allen

What's Opera, Doc? ★★★★★ U

Animated classic 1957 · US · Colour · 6mins

In spite of the many excellent contributions from such directors as Friz Freleng and Bob Clampett, Chuck Jones remains Bugs Bunny's best-known director. This is partly due to his penchant for placing the star in rarified cultural circumstances, a passion which endeared him to those critics who might otherwise have dismissed Hollywood cartoons as mere programme-fillers. This justly-celebrated short marks the culmination of Jones's interest in classical music as a context for comedy, as the familar Bugs and Elmer rabbit hunt is played out as opera, with dialogue sung to music from Wagner's *Ring Cycle* and *Tannhäuser*. With over a hundred striking designs by Maurice Noble (nearly twice as many as the average cartoon), and the Warner studio orchestra's magnificent condensation of Wagner's epic, the result is a milestone in Hollywood animation. CLP

Mel Blanc *Bugs Bunny* • Arthur Q Bryan *Elmer Fudd* ■ *Dir* Chuck Jones • *Scr* Michael Maltese • *Layout* Maurice Noble • *Music Director* Milt Franklyn

What's So Bad About Feeling Good? ★★

Comedy 1968 · US · Colour · 93mins

A quintessential 1960s title about a toucan infected with a happiness virus that spreads the "disease" throughout Manhattan. Among the grouchy New Yorkers whose personalities are transformed are advertising executive turned artist George Peppard, his hippy girlfriend Mary Tyler Moore and guest star Thelma Ritter, whose acerbity is most welcome. The studio East Village backlot, period clothes and garish Universal-style Technicolor make it strangely watchable. TS

George Peppard *Pete* • Mary Tyler Moore *Liz* • Dom DeLuise *J Gardner Monroe* • John McMartin *The Mayor* • Nathaniel Frey *Conrad* • Charles Lane (2) *Dr Shapiro* • Jeanne Arnold *Gertrude* • George Furth *Murgatroyd* • Thelma Ritter *Mrs Schwartz* • Cleavon Little *Phil* ■ *Dir* George Seaton • *Scr* George Seaton, Robert Pirosh, from the novel *I Am Thinking of My Darling* by Vincent McHugh

What's the Matter with Helen? ★★★

Thriller 1971 · US · Colour · 100mins

Answer: nothing a good bout of killing wouldn't cure. Strong female stars pull this number though a hedge of campy production, set in the 1930s as Debbie Reynolds and Shelley Winters try to forget their sordid past by setting up a school for talented youngsters in Hollywood. Curtis Harrington directs with an acute feel for the period and personalities, which include Dennis Weaver and Agnes Moorehead. TH

Debbie Reynolds *Adelle Bruckner* • Shelley Winters *Helen Hill* • Dennis Weaver *Lincoln Palmer* • Agnes Moorehead *Sister Alma* • Michael MacLiammoir *Hamilton Starr* • Sammee Lee Jones *Winona Palmer* • Robbi Morgan *Rosalie Greenbaum* • Helene Winston *Mrs Greenbaum* ■ *Dir* Curtis Harrington • *Scr* Henry Farrell • *Cinematographer* Lucien Ballard

What's the Worst That Could Happen? ★ 15

Crime comedy 2001 · US · Colour · 94mins

Trite, unfunny and shockingly mediocre, one wonders what lead actors Danny DeVito and Martin Lawrence could have been thinking. Lawrence is a professional thief who

W

steals his way into the affections of sweet English actress, Carmen Ejogo. But her attempts to straighten him out go belly up when he robs crooked mogul DeVito and starts a vendetta, that puts each actor at the end of a very large ego bone. LH [video] DVD

Martin Lawrence *Kevin Caffery* • Danny DeVito *Max Fairbanks* • John Leguizamo *Berger* • Glenne Headly *Gloria* • Carmen Ejogo *Amber Belhaven* • Bernie Mac *Uncle Jack* • Larry Miller *Earl Radburn* ■ *Dir* Sam Weisman • *Scr* Matthew Chapman, from a novel by Donald E Westlake

What's Up, Doc? ★★★★★ U

Screwball comedy
1972 · US · Colour · 90mins

Barbra Streisand stars as the zany dropout with her eyes on absent-minded professor Ryan O'Neal in director Peter Bogdanovich's hilarious homage to the screwball comedies of the 1930s by Howard Hawks and Preston Sturges. The tone is set by the wacky title, a reference to the scene when Streisand meets O'Neal for the first time – she's chomping on a carrot à la Bugs Bunny. There's also brilliant support from Madeline Kahn as O'Neal's fiancée, and beautiful photography from Laszlo Kovacs. It's a shame that Bogdanovich has never again touched these heights of cartoonish wit. TH [video] DVD

Barbra Streisand *Judy Maxwell* • Ryan O'Neal *Professor Howard Bannister* • Madeline Kahn *Eunice Burns* • Kenneth Mars *Hugh Simon* • Austin Pendleton *Frederick Larrabee* • Michael Murphy *Mr Smith* • Phil Roth *Mr Jones* • Sorrell Booke *Harry* • Stefan Gierasch *Fritz* • Mabel Albertson *Mrs Van Hoskins* • Liam Dunn *Judge Maxwell* • Randall R "Randy" Quaid [Randy Quaid] *Professor Hosquith* ■ *Dir* Peter Bogdanovich • *Scr* Buck Henry, David Newman, from a story by Peter Bogdanovich

What's Up, Tiger Lily? ★★★ PG

Action farce 1966 · US/Jpn · Colour · 79mins

A year after the sex farce *What's New, Pussycat?* which Woody Allen both appeared in and wrote came this even more questionable comedy, in which he spoofs a Japanese James Bond-style thriller by re-dubbing it with English voices at variance to the action. It's a single-track joke, which soon runs out of steam, but some of the mismatched words work wonderfully well. TH. Contains some violence and swearing. [video] DVD

Woody Allen *Narrator/Host/Voice* • Tatsuya Mihashi *Phil Moscowitz* • Mie Hama *Terri Yaki* • Akiko Wakabayashi *Suki Yaki* • Tadao Nakamaru *Shepherd Wong* • Susumu Kurobe *Wing Fat* • China Lee • Frank Buxton • Len Maxwell • Louise Lasser ■ *Dir* Senkichi Taniguchi • *Scr* Woody Allen, Frank Buxton, Len Maxwell, Louise Lasser, Mickey Rose, Bryna Wilson, Julie Bennett, from a film by Kazuo Yamada

The Wheeler Dealers ★★★ U

Comedy caper 1963 · US · Colour · 104mins

James Garner goes to Wall Street. More than just a shrewd hick from the sticks, he's in his most likeable mode as a Texas tycoon showing New York businesswoman Lee Remick how to make a bundle from a non-existent product. There's a whole lot of chicanery going on, but director Arthur Hiller manoeuvres his comedy options with a shrewd hand. TH

James Garner *Henry Tyroon* • Lee Remick *Molly Thatcher* • Phil Harris *Ray Jay* • Chill Wills *Jay Ray* • Charles Watts *JR* • Jim Backus *Bullard Bear* • Patricia Crowley [Pat Crowley] *Eloise* • John Astin *Hector Vanson* ■ *Dir* Arthur Hiller • *Scr* George JW Goodman, Ira Wallach, from the novel by George JW Goodman

Wheels on Meals ★★★ 15

Martial arts comedy thriller
1984 · HK · Colour · 104mins

Swinging wildly from full-speed action to dozy interludes, this is an extremely strange mix of comedy, romance and kung fu. Jackie Chan plays one of two brothers who run a fast-food business in Spain. It reaches a witty high by spoofing *The Three Musketeers*, yet even during the longueurs there is a sense of the weird which keeps the film ticking. JM. Cantonese dialogue dubbed into English. Contains violence and some swearing. [video]

Jackie Chan *Thomas* • Sammo Hung *Moby* • Yuen Biao *David* • Lola Forner *Sylvia* • Susanna Sentis *Gloria* • Pepe Sancho *Mondale* ■ *Dir* Sammo Hung • *Scr* Edward Tang, Johnny Lee

When a Man Loves ★★★

Silent period romance
1926 · US · BW · 110mins

Following the success of *Don Juan*, Warners reteamed director Alan Crosland and the mercurial John Barrymore for its third feature to benefit from a synchronised Vitaphone soundtrack. But it wasn't the prospect of a score and some sound effects that prompted audiences to flock to this reworking of Abbé Prevost's classic novel. It was Barrymore's French aristocrat wielding his sword in defence of Dolores Costello, who'd been exploited as a courtesan by her wicked brother Warner Oland. DP

John Barrymore *Chevalier Favien des Grieux* • Dolores Costello *Manon Lescaut* • Warner Oland *André Lescaut* • Sam De Grasse *Comte Guillot de Morfontaine* • Holmes Herbert *Jean Tiberge* • Stuart Holmes *Louis XV, King of France* ■ *Dir* Alan Crosland • *Scr* Bess Meredyth, from the opera *Manon Lescaut* by Giacomo Puccini, from the novel *L'Histoire du Chevalier des Grieux et de Manon Lescaut* by Abbé Prévost

When a Man Loves a Woman ★★ 15

Drama 1994 · US · Colour · 131mins

In this sobering drama, Meg Ryan proves no more adept portraying a drunk than she was playing an action heroine in 1996's *Courage under Fire*. As a wife and mother attempting to face life without the consolation of a bottle, she's guilty of trying too hard to convince. Andy Garcia is hardly more impressive as her insensitive husband, while Ellen Burstyn is wasted in a brief appearance as Ryan's mother. DP. Contains swearing. [video] DVD

Andy Garcia *Michael Green* • Meg Ryan *Alice Green* • Ellen Burstyn *Emily* • Tina Majorino *Jess Green* • Mae Whitman *Casey Green* • Lauren Tom *Amy* • Philip Seymour Hoffman *Gary* ■ *Dir* Luis Mandoki • *Scr* Ronald Bass, Al Franken

When a Stranger Calls ★★ 15

Horror thriller 1979 · US · Colour · 93mins

Don't watch the opening of this suspense shocker alone. The build-up of claustrophobic tension is near-masterly, as a baby-sitter, alone in a dark house, is terrorised by a crank call from a homicidal maniac lurking in a room upstairs! But after that blistering beginning, Fred Walton's film stalls badly – with the killer escaping years later to wreak havoc upon the same woman – and only truly comes alive again in the last reel. RS [video]

Charles Durning *John Clifford* • Carol Kane *Jill Johnson* • Tony Beckley *Curt Duncan* • Colleen Dewhurst *Tracy* • Rachel Roberts (1) *Dr Monk* • Ron O'Neal *Lt Garber* • Bill Boyett *Sgt Sacker* • Kirsten Larkin *Nancy* ■ *Dir* Fred Walton • *Scr* Steve Feke, Fred Walton

When Brendan Met Trudy ★★★ 15

Romantic comedy
2000 · Ire/UK · Colour · 90mins

Roddy Doyle's first work written directly for the screen is a romantic comedy, with, unsurprisingly, a very Irish flavour. Flora Montgomery is a star in the making as the brash, foul-mouthed Dubliner who steamrolls her way into the life of timid teacher Peter McDonald. While their romance is very unlikely – he's a stay-at-home film buff and singer in the local choir – watching her completely obliterate his quiet life is often great fun, aided by Doyle's sparkling script. JB. Contains swearing, sex scenes and nudity. [video] DVD

Peter McDonald *Brendan* • Flora Montgomery *Trudy* • Marie Mullen *Mother* • Pauline McLynn *Nuala* • Don Wycherley *Niall* ■ *Dir* Kieron J Walsh • *Scr* Roddy Doyle

When Dinosaurs Ruled the Earth ★★★ PG

Prehistoric adventure
1969 · UK · Colour · 92mins

Hammer's sequel to *One Million Years BC* doesn't star Raquel Welch or Ray Harryhausen's marvellous special effects, but it's still pretty solid entertainment. *Playboy* playmate Victoria Vetri wears the fur bikini this time and American stop-motion animation expert Jim Danforth supplies the prehistoric monster battles. With no more than 27 words of dialogue between them, rival tribe members Vetri and Robin Hawdon fall in love, escape death and cope with the harsh elements. The sort of dotty, endearing and exotic fun that only Hammer in its heyday could possibly make. AJ [video]

Victoria Vetri *Sanna* • Robin Hawdon *Tara* • Patrick Allen *Kingsor* • Drewe Henley *Khaku* • Sean Caffrey *Kane* ■ *Dir* Val Guest • *Scr* Val Guest, from a treatment by JG Ballard

When Eight Bells Toll ★★★ 15

Adventure 1971 · UK · Colour · 93mins

Made at an early stage in Anthony Hopkins's film career, this Alistair MacLean adventure gave him one of his rare opportunities to play an action hero. In a story about piracy (adapted by MacLean himself), he plays his naval agent as a single-minded professional, intent on doing the job without falling for the high-life distractions that other spies are prone to. Consequently, he comes across as rather charmless and we find ourselves longing for more of Robert Morley's delicious turn as a spymaster. DP. Contains violence. [video] DVD

Anthony Hopkins *Philip Calvert* • Robert Morley *Sir Arthur Arnold-Jones* • Jack Hawkins *Sir Anthony Skouras* • Nathalie Delon *Charlotte Skouras* • Corin Redgrave *Hunslett* • Derek Bond *Lord Charnley* • Ferdy Mayne *Lavorski* • Maurice Roëves *Helicopter pilot* ■ *Dir* Etienne Périer • *Scr* Alistair MacLean, from his novel

When Father Was Away on Business ★★★★ 15

Drama 1985 · Yug · Colour · 130mins

Written by Bosnian poet Abdulah Sidran, this Oscar-nominated drama was the surprise winner of the Palme d'Or at Cannes. In 1950s Sarajevo, no one is safe from wagging tongues and spiteful vendettas and Miki Manojlovic is arrested by his own brother-in-law. Told from the half-comprehending perspective of his son, Moreno D'e Bartolli, this naturalistic insight into Tito's Yugoslavia in the last days of Stalinism compels thanks to Emir Kusturica's assured blend of satire, whimsy and harsh historical comment. The harrowing circumcision, whoring and rape scenes stand as startling metaphors for the corruption, brutality and treachery of the period. DP. A Serbo-Croat language film. [video]

Moreno D'e Bartolli *Malik* • Miki Manojlovic *Mesa* • Mirjana Karanovic *Senija* ■ *Dir* Emir Kusturica • *Scr* Abdulah Sidran

When Harry Met Sally... ★★★★★ 15

Romantic comedy
1989 · US · Colour · 91mins

This romantic comedy argues the question whether men and women can ever have friendship without sex. In truth, the movie, with its glitzy New York locations, offers a cutesy, superficial and glamorised excursion into Woody Allen territory, but triumphs nevertheless as expert and irresistible escapist entertainment. The teaming of Meg Ryan and Billy Crystal is perfect, while supporting stars Carrie Fisher and Bruno Kirby are outstanding and add a welcome suggestion of edge. The fake-orgasm-in-a-deli set piece propelled Ryan into stratospheric stardom, but there are numerous other pleasures to be found in Nora Ephron's Oscar-nominated screenplay and Rob Reiner's astute direction. RK. Contains swearing. [video] DVD

Billy Crystal *Harry Burns* • Meg Ryan *Sally Albright* • Carrie Fisher *Marie* • Bruno Kirby *Jess* • Steven Ford *Joe* • Lisa Jane Persky *Alice* ■ *Dir* Rob Reiner • *Scr* Nora Ephron

When Knights Were Bold ★★

Musical comedy 1936 · UK · BW · 57mins

Film version of a (then) famous West End play with Jack Buchanan teamed with Fay Wray. A satire on the British aristocracy, Buchanan plays a soldier in India who inherits a vast English estate and returns there and dreams he is the chain-mailed reincarnation of an ancestor, a medieval warlord who, being Buchanan, can also sing and tap dance. It's dated, of course. AT

Jack Buchanan *Sir Guy De Vere* • Fay Wray *Lady Rowena* • Garry Marsh *Brian Ballymote* • Kate Cutler *Aunt Agatha* • Martita Hunt *Aunt Esther* • Robert Horton *Cousin Bertie* • Aubrey Mather *Canon* ■ *Dir* Jack Raymond • *Scr* Austin Parker, Douglas Furber, from the play by Charles Marlowe

When Ladies Meet ★★★★

Romantic comedy drama
1933 · US · BW · 73mins

Successful lady novelist Myrna Loy falls desperately in love with her publisher, Frank Morgan, and spurns her devoted suitor, newspaper reporter Robert Montgomery. However, when she meets Morgan's wife, Ann Harding, without knowing who she is, matters come to a head. Adapted from a stage play and directed by Harry Beaumont, this is an intelligent, sophisticated romantic comedy drama of the highest level, exquisitely played – especially by the sublime and undeservedly forgotten Harding – marvellously designed and dressed. Robert Z Leonard, who would remake the film eight years later, directed the re-takes here. RK

Ann Harding *Claire Woodruf* • Robert Montgomery *Jimmy Lee* • Myrna Loy *Mary Howard* • Alice Brady *Bridget Drake* • Frank Morgan *Rogers Woodruf* • Martin Burton *Walter Manning* • Sterling Holloway *Jerome* ■ *Dir* Harry Beaumont • *Scr* John Meehan, Leon Gordon, from the play by Rachel Crothers • *Art Director* Cedric Gibbons • *Costume Designer* Adrian

When Ladies Meet ★★

Romantic comedy drama
1941 · US · BW · 105mins

Directed by Robert Z Leonard and sticking more or less to the original 1933 version, this updated remake of what was a stylish look at the consequences of a lady novelist's love for her married publisher coarsens the bitingly sharp original, even vulgarising the settings. Joan Crawford makes a decent fist of the leading character, Greer Garson is probably the best substitute for Ann Harding, and Robert Taylor is fine as the newsman who loves Crawford. Only the usually impeccable Herbert Marshall as the publisher lover fails to convince. RK

Joan Crawford *Mary Howard* • Robert Taylor (1) *Jimmy Lee* • Greer Garson *Claire Woodruff* • Herbert Marshall *Rogers Woodruff* • Spring Byington *Bridget Drake* • Rafael Storm *Walter Del Canto* • Max Willenz *Pierre* ■ *Dir* Robert Z Leonard • *Scr* SK Lauren, Anita Loos, from the play by Rachel Crothers

When London Sleeps ★★

Crime drama 1932 · UK · BW · 70mins

Well, it probably didn't take the city's residents long to nod off when they were watching this creaky old British thriller. Leslie Hiscott is often cited as the director who brought "quota quickies" into disrepute. The seventh of the ten films he churned out in 1932, this is a trashy tale in which only gambler Harold French can save wealthy heiress René Ray from the clutches of her villainous cousin, Francis L Sullivan. The action rattles along, but it's poor stuff. DP

Harold French *Tommy Blythe* • Francis L Sullivan *Rodney Haines* • René Ray *Mary* • A Bromley Davenport *Colonel Grahame* • Alexander Field *Sam* • Diana Beaumont *Hilda* • Ben Field *Lamberti* • Barbara Everest *Mme Lamberti* • Herbert Lomas *Pollard* ■ *Dir* Leslie Hiscott • *Scr* Bernard Merivale, H Fowler Mear, from a play by Charles Darrell

When Love Comes ★★ 18

Romantic drama 1998 · NZ · Colour · 91mins

Neither director Garth Maxwell nor his star Rena Owen comes remotely close to recapturing former glories in this dull diva drama. Tired of the US cabaret circuit, Owen's 1970s pop icon returns to Auckland to get her head together and draws strength from her gay buddy Simon Prast, whose own life is in crisis thanks to songwriter Dean O'Gorman's sexual confusion. Throw in a grungy girl band, an unexpected pregnancy and a crunch weekend at the beach and you have a melodrama packed with resistible characters and obsessed with its own trivialities. DP [subtitles] DVD

Rena Owen *Katie* • Dean O'Gorman *Mark* • Simon Prast *Stephen* • Nancy Brunning *Fig* ■ *Dir* Garth Maxwell • *Scr* Garth Maxwell, Rex Pilgrim, Peter Wells

When Magoo Flew ★★★★ U

Animated comedy 1955 · US · Colour · 6mins

Since the animation studio United Productions of America grew out of the ashes of the Disney strike of 1941, it was probably inevitable that it should sport a conscious attempt to break away from the traditional Disney approach to animation. The most obvious manifestation of this was in its use of stylised design and staccato animation, yet there were other departures, including the decision to abandon animal characters in favour of humans. This they achieved brilliantly with the creation of Mr Magoo, who quickly became a star and eventually won two Oscars, the first for this, UPA's first CinemaScope cartoon. The simple plot has the myopic, mood-swinging old man boarding an aeroplane in the belief that he's entering a cinema. When a potential hijack takes place, he thinks it's part of a film that's playing. CLP

Jim Backus *Mr Magoo* • Jerry Hausner *Waldo* ■ *Dir* Pete Burness • *Scr* Barbara Hammer, Tedd Pierce [Ted Pierce]

When My Baby Smiles at Me ★★★★

Musical 1948 · US · Colour · 97mins

Though largely forgotten nowadays, Dan Dailey was nominated as best actor at the 1948 Academy Awards for his performance in this film. He is magnificent in this remake of a hoary old Broadway play, and, while top-billed Betty Grable isn't Dailey's equal in the drama stakes, she tries hard. Director Walter Lang knows well enough when to sit back and let the actors get on with it. A very satisfying movie. TS

Betty Grable *Bonny* • Dan Dailey *Skid* • Jack Oakie *Bozo* • June Havoc *Gussie* • Richard Arlen *Harvey* • James Gleason *Lefty* • Vanita Wade *Bubbles* ■ *Dir* Walter Lang • *Scr* Elizabeth Reinhardt, Lamar Trotti, from the play *Burlesque* by George Manker Watters, Arthur Hopkins

When Night Is Falling ★★★ 18

Drama 1995 · Can · Colour · 89mins

A companion piece to *I've Heard the Mermaids Singing*, this is a less obviously comic and far more sensual study of lesbian awakening from Patricia Rozema. From its contrived beginning, the romance follows along overly familiar lines, but the performances of tempestuous circus artist Rachael Crawford and prissy Protestant academic Pascale Bussières give it a truth to match its rising passion. Henry Czerny is also impressive as Bussières's colleague and confused lover. Dreamily photographed but gushingly scripted and symbolically clumsy. DP [subtitles]

Pascale Bussières *Camille* • Rachael Crawford *Petra* • Henry Czerny *Martin* • David Fox *Reverend DeBoer* • Don McKellar *Timothy* • Tracy Wright *Tory* • Clare Coulter *Tillie* ■ *Dir/Scr* Patricia Rozema

When Saturday Comes ★★★ 15

Sports drama 1995 · UK · Colour · 94mins

Football and cinema have never been the best of bedfellows. However, anyone who can look back nostalgically at *Roy of the Rovers* will lap up this unashamedly clichéd rags-to-riches tale. Sean Bean obviously relishes every minute of his role here as the working-class lad who is plucked from obscurity by wise old talent scout Pete Postlethwaite to play in the big time. Along the way he wins and loses his mentor's niece (Emily Lloyd) and even gets the chance to indulge in some *Rocky*-style training. JF. Contains a sex scene, swearing, nudity. [subtitles] DVD

Sean Bean *Jimmy Muir* • Emily Lloyd *Annie Doherty* • Pete Postlethwaite *Ken Jackson* • Craig Kelly (2) *Russell Muir* • John McEnery *Joe Muir* • Ann Bell *Sarah Muir* • Melanie Hill *Mary Muir* • Chris Walker *Mac* ■ *Dir/Scr* Maria Giese

When the Bough Breaks ★★★

Drama 1947 · UK · BW · 80mins

Gainsborough turned from costume melodrama to contemporary problem picture with this story aimed firmly at female picturegoers. Patricia Roc is the working-class woman who allows her child to be adopted by middle-class Rosamund John and years later wants the boy back. Should he be plucked from his comfortable existence and promising future to live with his real mother in poverty? Either way, it's a tear-jerker, made on the cheap but forcefully acted and ably directed by Lawrence Huntington. AE

Patricia Roc *Lily Bates* • Rosamund John *Frances Norman* • Bill Owen *Bill* • Brenda Bruce *Ruby Chapman* • Patrick Holt *Robert Norman* • Cavan Malone *Jimmy* • Leslie Dwyer *George* ■ *Dir* Lawrence Huntington • *Scr* Peter Rogers, Muriel Box, Sydney Box, from a story by Moie Charles, Herbert Victor

When the Bough Breaks ★★★ 18

Thriller 1993 · US · Colour · 102mins

It's a stunning, shocking premise: after heavy rainfall, the drains in an American town throw up a gruesome find – a bag containing the severed hands of children. And although writer/director Michael Cohn doesn't quite manage to sustain the chilling horror of the opening scenes, this remains a gripping serial killer thriller, as psychological expert Ally Walker follows the murderer's trail to an autistic child who may hold the key to the case. Cohn draws out a fine central performance from Walker in this under-rated gem. JF [subtitles] DVD

Ally Walker *Audrey MacLeah* • Martin Sheen *Swaggert* • Ron Perlman *Dr Eben* • Tara Subkoff *Jordan/Jenny* • Robert Knepper *Creedmore* ■ *Dir/Scr* Michael Cohn

When the Bough Breaks 2: Perfect Prey ★★ 18

Thriller 1998 · US · Colour · 99mins

The original was a genuinely chilling affair. This sequel is not in the same league – none of the original cast is on hand, either – but it is still a creepy affair, with Kelly McGillis stepping into Ally Walker's shoes as the Texas Ranger tracking a serial killer who's preying on successful career women, torturing them and then dumping their suffocated bodies in a series of bizarre poses around the state. JF [subtitles] DVD

Kelly McGillis *Audrey MacLeah* • Bruce Dern *Captain Swaggert* • David Keith *Dwayne Alan Clay* • DW Moffett *Jimmy Cerullo* • Joely Fisher *Elizabeth Crane* ■ *Dir* Howard McCain • *Scr* Robert McDonnell

When the Boys Meet the Girls ★★ U

Comedy 1965 · US · Colour · 96mins

Escaping from a showgirl suing him for breach of promise, womanising playboy Harve Presnell travels out of harm's way to a college in the Nevada backwoods. Once there he meets Connie Francis and gets involved in the problems she and her father are having with the latter's gambling debts. This updated remake of the twice-filmed stage musical *Girl Crazy* is poor despite the five George and Ira Gershwin numbers that survive from the original, although Herman's Hermits, Louis Armstrong and Liberace provide some novelty value. DF

Connie Francis *Ginger* • Harve Presnell *Danny* • Sue Ane Langdon *Tess* • Fred Clark *Bill* • Frank Faylen *Phin* • Joby Baker *Sam* • Hortense Petra *Kate* • Stanley Adams *Lank* ■ *Dir* Alvin Ganzer • *Scr* Robert E Kent, from the musical *Girl Crazy* by Guy Bolton, John McGowan

When the Cat's Away... ★★★★ 15

Romantic comedy 1996 · Fr · Colour · 90mins

Cédric Klapisch's witty and stylish urban comedy is as much about the changing face of Paris as the romantic fortunes of make-up artist Garance Clavel. This is something of a wild cat chase in terms of plot, but the search for missing moggy Gris Gris serves as an excellent excuse for some character study and conversations that are refreshingly authentic. Providing a sparkling slant on the familiar theme of love in the city, Klapisch draws vibrant performances from his cast. DP. In French with English subtitles. Contains swearing, sex scenes. [subtitles]

Garance Clavel *Chloé* • Zinedine Soualem *Djamel* • Olivier Py *Michel* • Renée Lecalm *Madame Renée* • Simon Abkarian *Carlos* ■ *Dir/Scr* Cédric Klapisch

When the Daltons Rode ★★★

Biographical western 1940 · US · BW · 80mins

One of the classy big-budget westerns of its time, this rousing adventure pays little heed to historic truth as it re-creates the lives and times of the notorious Dalton gang, taking its leads, Randolph Scott and Brian Donlevy, from the previous year's big hit *Jesse James*. The elegant Kay Francis is stunning, and Scott is sturdy as the lawyer out to give the outlaws a fair trial, but the real treats in this movie are the superb stunts which have seldom, if ever, been equalled. TS

Randolph Scott *Tod Jackson* • Kay Francis *Julie King* • Brian Donlevy *Grat Dalton* • George Bancroft *Caleb Winters* • Broderick Crawford *Bob Dalton* • Stuart Erwin *Ben Dalton* • Andy Devine *Ozark* • Frank Albertson *Emmett Dalton* ■ *Dir* George Marshall • *Scr* Harold Schumate, Lester Cole, Stuart Anthony, from the non-fiction book by Emmett Dalton, Jack Jungmeyer Sr

When the Last Sword Is Drawn ★★★★ 15

Period martial arts drama 2003 · Jpn · Colour · 137mins

While exploring the same period as *The Last Samurai*, Yojiro Takita's *chambara* (Japanese swordplay film) is far less ostentatious in its assessment of the transition between the warrior tradition of the Tokugawa Shogunate and the firearmed might of the Meiji Restoration. Comprised of a series of flashbacks, the story charts Koichi Sato's relationship with Kiichi Nakai, a celebrated swordsman whose loyalty to both his clan and the cause earns him the enmity of those who once admired him. Takita stages several striking set pieces and allows some occasional comic relief, but his primary concern is the effect on individuals of the decline of the bushido code. DP. In Japanese with English subtitles. DVD

Kiichi Nakai *Kanichiro Yoshimura* • Koichi Sato *Hajime Saito* • Yui Natsukawa *Shizu* • Takehiro Murata *Chiaki Ono* • Miki Nakatani *Nui* • Yuji Miyake *Jiroemon Ono* ■ *Dir* Yojiro Takita • *Scr* Takehiro Nakajima, from a story by Jiro Asada

When the Legends Die ★★★★

Western drama 1972 · US · Colour · 105mins

One of those fly-blown modern westerns so full of atmosphere that you can almost smell the apple pie on the empty diner's counter. But this beautifully constructed piece is far more than mere effective staging and the central performances from Richard Widmark and Frederic Forrest are quite superb. Widmark's dissolute drunk stands out as a man riven by emotional pain, while Forrest's talented young Indian rodeo rider is the perfect foil. Director Stuart Millar proves that you don't have to take the easiest options to produce a popular western. SH

Richard Widmark *Red Dillon* • Frederic Forrest *Tom Black Bull* • Luana Anders *Mary* • Vito Scotti *Meo* • Herbert Nelson *Dr Wilson* • John War Eagle *Blue Elk* • John Gruber *Tex Walker* ■ *Dir* Stuart Millar • *Scr* Robert Dozier, from the novel by Hal Borland

When the Party's Over ★★ 15

Drama 1992 · US · Colour · 110mins

There's something here, but you have to wade through an awful lot of 20-something angst to find it. Three

W

women and a gay man share a house in LA, and through the various flashbacks to which we are subjected, it's established that none of them are very nice people. Sandra Bullock and Rae Dawn Chong lend some limited class to this tale of desperation and manipulation, but in the end it's too confusing, petty, and exploitative to maintain interest. ST

Elizabeth Berridge *Frankie* • Rae Dawn Chong *M J* • Sandra Bullock *Amanda* • Kris Kamm *Banks* • Brian McNamara *Taylor* • Fisher Stevens *Alexander* • Michael Landes *Willie* ■ *Dir* Matthew Irmas • *Scr* Ann Wycoff, from a story by Matthew Irmas, Ann Wycoff

When the Sky Falls ★★★ 18

Biographical drama
2000 · Ire/US · Colour · 102mins

This thinly disguised biography of Veronica Guerin, the crusading Irish journalist shot dead by the Dublin criminals she sought to expose, marks a return to form for director John Mackenzie (*The Long Good Friday*). Joan Allen stars as a wife and mother whose single-minded determination to bring the city's gangsters to justice becomes increasingly perilous for both herself and her family. Despite having an American lead, Mackenzie resists the temptation to Hollywood things up, while Allen brings conviction and depth to her performance. NS DVD

Joan Allen *Sinead Hamilton* • Patrick Bergin *Mackey* • Jimmy Smallhorne *Mickey O'Fagan* • Liam Cunningham *The Runner* • Kevin McNally *Tom Hamilton* • Pete Postlethwaite *Martin Shaughnessy* • Jason Barry *Dempsey* ■ *Dir* John Mackenzie • *Scr* Michael Sheridan, Ronan Gallagher, Colum McCann

When the Whales Came ★★★ U

Drama 1989 · UK · Colour · 95mins

In this modest but touching drama set in the Scilly Isles at the start of the First World War, Paul Scofield plays an elderly loner, hiding away from the world, who is befriended by two curious children. The story is slight, but it is attractively directed by Clive Rees, who draws refreshingly natural performances from young leads Helen Pearce and Max Rennie. A galaxy of familiar British faces lends solid support. JF

Paul Scofield *The Birdman* • Helen Mirren *Clemmie Jenkins* • Helen Pearce *Gracie Jenkins* • Max Rennie *Daniel Pender* • David Suchet *Will* • Kerra Spowart *Margaret Pender* • Barbara Ewing *Mary Pender* • John Hallam *Treve Pender* • Barbara Jefford *Auntie Mildred* • David Threlfall *Jack Jenkins* ■ *Dir* Clive Rees • *Scr* Michael Morpurgo, from his novel

When the Wind Blows ★★★★ PG

Animation 1986 · UK · Colour · 80mins

With the threat of Armageddon now, hopefully, behind us, this adaptation of Raymond Briggs's chilling cartoon book seems rather quaint. However, the fact that few of us know how to conduct ourselves should there be a nuclear winter is powerfully brought home in the superbly told story. Animator Jimmy T Murakami's decision to use flat figures against three-dimensional backgrounds hauntingly begs the question, "It can't happen here, can it?", while the disarmingly charming voiceovers of John Mills and Peggy Ashcroft, recalling more innocent conflicts, add poignancy to the proceedings. Clever, credible and, ultimately, heartbreaking. DP

Peggy Ashcroft *Hilda Bloggs* • John Mills *Jim Bloggs* • Robin Houston *Announcer* ■ *Dir* Jimmy T Murakami • *Scr* Raymond Briggs, from his comic book

When Time Ran Out ★ PG

Disaster adventure
1980 · US · Colour · 104mins

Irwin Allen, the producer of *The Poseidon Adventure* and *The Towering Inferno*, rehashed the disaster formula yet again with this clinker about a volcano that threatens to trash a luxury holiday resort. Paul Newman leads his co-stars and their associated subplots to possible safety, while William Holden is the tycoon who owns the hotel. The eruption, when it finally comes, is a wonderfully cheesy amalgam of wobbly back projection, bathtub tidal wave and scared expressions from the cast. AT

Paul Newman *Hank Anderson* • Jacqueline Bisset *Kay Kirby* • William Holden (2) *Shelby Gilmore* • Edward Albert *Brian* • Red Buttons *Francis Fendly* • Barbara Carrera *Iolani* • Burgess Meredith *Rene Valdez* • Ernest Borgnine *Tom Conti* • James Franciscus *Bob Spangler* ■ *Dir* James Goldstone • *Scr* Carl Foreman, Stirling Silliphant, from the novel *The Day the World Ended* by Gordon Thomas, Max Morgan Witts • *Music* Lalo Schifrin

When Tomorrow Comes ★★★

Romantic melodrama
1939 · US · BW · 91mins

Irene Dunne and Charles Boyer, after their phenomenal success in RKO's *Love Affair* earlier in the year, reunite for this tale of a waitress and a concert pianist who meet when she serves him in a restaurant. Friendship turns to love when they're stranded in a Long Island church during a hurricane. Boyer, however, turns out to have a wife (Barbara O'Neil) who has lost her mind. A clichéd weepie, but impeccably assembled and irresistible. Badly remade in 1957 as *Interlude*. RK

Irene Dunne *Helen* • Charles Boyer *Philip André Chagal* • Barbara O'Neil *Madeleine* • Onslow Stevens *Holden* • Nydia Westman *Lulu* • Nella Walker *Madame Dumont* ■ *Dir* John M Stahl • *Scr* Dwight Taylor, from a story by James M Cain

When Trumpets Fade ★★★★ 15

Second World War drama
1998 · US · Colour · 92mins

This made-for-cable film based on a true story plays like a fine art house feature, with some genuinely gripping and novel situations. During the winter of 1944, in western Germany, an emotionally and physically exhausted American private (Ron Eldard) is promoted against his will when he serendipitously survives as the rest of his comrades die around him. Whether or not he's a hero, coward or pure victim of circumstance is the point of this searingly affecting film, which dramatises one of the most senseless battles of the Second World War. Given both intelligence and power by the sure-handed direction of John Irvin, this is wise, affecting television that should not be missed. MC. Contains swearing, violence and brief nudity. DVD

Ron Eldard *Private David Manning* • Frank Whaley *Medic Chamberlain* • Zak Orth *Warren Sanderson* • Dylan Bruno *Sergeant Talbot* • Martin Donovan (2) *Captain Pritchett* • Dwight Yoakam *Lieutenant Colonel* ■ *Dir* John Irvin • *Scr* WW Vought

When We Were Kings ★★★★★ PG

Sports documentary
1996 · US · Colour · 83mins

The experts had Muhammad Ali out for the count even before he stepped into the ring against George Foreman in Zaire in 1974. But the "Rumble in the Jungle" turned out to be anything but a "Disaster in Kinshasa", as Ali fought his way to a remarkable victory. Leon Gast's Oscar-winning documentary not only focuses on Ali the athlete, but also examines his importance to the African-American community at large. With telling contributions from Norman Mailer, George Plimpton and Spike Lee, and footage from the soul concerts that accompanied the big bout, this exceptional film proves beyond any doubt that Ali was "The Greatest". DP DVD

Dir Leon Gast

When Willie Comes Marching Home ★★★

Comedy 1950 · US · BW · 82mins

John Ford may be remembered best for making westerns, but he also made dramas, war movies and, though it is sometimes forgotten, comedies, of which this is a prime example. It wasn't his most natural genre, but this is still a competent, likeable and even funny movie about the ups and downs of a small-town boy during the Second World War. Dan Dailey does well in the title role, while an intelligent screenplay by Mary Loos and Richard Sale has some thoughtful things to say about wartime patriotism. PF

Dan Dailey *Bill Kluggs* • Corinne Calvet *Yvonne* • Colleen Townsend *Marge Fettles* • William Demarest *Herman Kluggs* • James Lydon *Charles Fettles* • Lloyd Corrigan *Mayor Adams* • Evelyn Varden *Gertrude Kluggs* ■ *Dir* John Ford • *Scr* Mary Loos, Richard Sale, from the story *When Leo Comes Marching Home* by Sy Gomberg

When Worlds Collide ★★★ U

Science-fiction adventure
1951 · US · Colour · 78mins

From *War of the Worlds* producer George Pal, this paranoid parable about Earth's imminent collision with a runaway planet – the only hope of survival being a Noah's Ark expedition to a satellite moon – is a prime example of 1950s science fiction. Compensating for the bland script and uninspired cast are the Oscar-winning special effects and Rudolph Maté's arresting direction. AJ DVD

Richard Derr *David Randall* • Barbara Rush *Joyce Hendron* • Larry Keating *Dr Cole Hendron* • Peter Hanson *Dr Tony Drake* • John Hoyt *Sydney Stanton* • Stephen Chase (1) *Dean Frye* • Judith Ames *Julie Cummings* ■ *Dir* Rudolph Maté • *Scr* Sydney Boehm, Philip Wylie, from the novel *When Worlds Collide* by Edwin Balmer

When You Come Home ★ U

Comedy 1947 · UK · BW · 97mins

Director John Baxter, once Britain's most uncompromising disciple of social realism, hit his cinematic nadir with this desperate flashback comedy. Rarely able to project his popular music-hall persona into movies, Frank Randle comes across as a colossal bore in this nostalgic wallow as he regales his granddaughter with tall tales from his chequered past. Adding to the torment are the songs. For movie masochists only. DP

Frank Randle • Leslie Sarony *First songwriter* • Leslie Holmes *Second songwriter* • Diana Decker *Paula Ryngelbaum* • Fred Conyngham *Mike O'Flaherty* ■ *Dir* John Baxter • *Scr* David Evans, Geoffrey Orme, Frank Randle

When You Comin' Back, Red Ryder? ★

Drama 1979 · US · Colour · 91mins

Hopefully never, if this adaptation of Mark Medoff's Broadway play is anything to go by. Former child evangelist Marjoe Gortner plays the psychopath who, partnered by hippy girlfriend Candy Clark, menaces the patrons of a Texas diner for nearly two hours. Without giving any convincing motivation for Gortner's actions, the story's just unpleasant. TH

Candy Clark *Cheryl* • Marjoe Gortner *Teddy* • Stephanie Faracy *Angel Childress* • Dixie Harris *Grandma Childress* • Anne Ramsey *Rhea Childress* • Lee Grant *Clarisse Ethridge* • Hal Linden *Richard Ethridge* • Peter Firth *Stephen Ryder* ■ *Dir* Milton Katselas • *Scr* Mark Medoff, from his play

When You're in Love ★★★ U

Musical romantic comedy
1937 · US · BW · 98mins

Robert Riskin was Columbia's ace screenwriter, responsible for such Frank Capra hits as *It Happened One Night* and *Mr Deeds Goes to Town*, and Columbia boss Harry Cohn rewarded him with this opera star Grace Moore vehicle to direct, believing it to be director-proof. Cohn wasn't wrong. Grace Moore was an immensely likeable soprano, sexy and talented, and an ideal partner for screen "hubby" Cary Grant. Fun, in its period sort of way. TS

Grace Moore *Louise Fuller* • Cary Grant *Jimmy Hudson* • Aline MacMahon *Marianne Woods* • Henry Stephenson *Walter Mitchell* • Thomas Mitchell *Hank Miller* • Catherine Doucet *Jane Summers* • Luis Alberni *Luis Perugini* • Gerald Oliver Smith *Gerald Meeker* ■ *Dir* Robert Riskin • *Scr* Robert Riskin, from an idea by Ethel Hill, Cedric Worth

Where Angels Fear to Tread ★★★ PG

Drama 1991 · UK · Colour · 107mins

This adaptation of EM Forster's novel, brought to the screen by the team responsible for the *Brideshead Revisited* TV drama, is a classy story about earthy passion and xenophobia, with Helen Mirren as the strong-willed, widowed Englishwoman, who falls in love with Tuscany and acquires a young Italian lover. Back home, her frosty family sinks in shame and sends Rupert Graves to sort things out. The lashings of dappled Tuscan sunlight and some strong performances by the cast add up to the movie equivalent of high tea. AT DVD

Helena Bonham Carter *Caroline Abbott* • Judy Davis *Harriet Herriton* • Rupert Graves *Philip Herriton* • Helen Mirren *Lilia Herriton* • Giovanni Guidelli *Gino Carella* • Barbara Jefford *Mrs Herriton* • Thomas Wheatley *Mr Kingcroft* ■ *Dir* Charles Sturridge • *Scr* Tim Sullivan, Derek Granger, Charles Sturridge, from the novel by EM Forster

Where Angels Go...Trouble Follows ★★ U

Comedy 1968 · US · Colour · 93mins

Although nun films are generally neither funny nor clever, this sequel to *The Trouble with Angels* (1966) is a pleasant culture clash comedy with Rosalind Russell returning to her role as the Mother Superior, this time trying to keep her young rebellious charges on the straight and narrow on a convent school trip. Look out for Susan Saint James as one of the teenage tearaways. JG

Rosalind Russell *Mother Simplicia* • Stella Stevens *Sister George* • Binnie Barnes *Sister Celestine* • Mary Wickes *Sister Clarissa* • Dolores Sutton *Sister Rose Marie* • Susan Saint James *Rosabelle* • Milton Berle *Film director* • Van Johnson *Father Chase* • Robert Taylor (1) *Mr Farriday* ■ *Dir* James Neilson • *Scr* Blanche Hanalis, from characters created by Jane Trahey

Where Are the Children? ★

Thriller 1986 · US · Colour · 92mins

In this stupid and overly manipulative whodunnit, packed with daft red herrings, Jill Clayburgh's children are kidnapped by nasty Frederic Forrest and taken to an old dark house where

W

he intends to kill them. Clayburgh hardly stretches herself in a banal performance, but Forrest enlivens the monotony by getting under the skin of the abductor in this turgid mess. AJ

Jill Clayburgh *Nancy Eldridge* • Max Gail *Clay Eldridge* • Harley Cross *Michael Eldridge* • Elisabeth Harnois *Missy Eldridge* • Elizabeth Wilson *Dorothy Prentiss* • Barnard Hughes *Jonathan Knowles* • Frederic Forrest *Courtney Parrish* • James Purcell *Robin Legler* ■ *Dir* Bruce Malmuth • *Scr* Jack Sholder, from the novel by Mary Higgins Clark

Where Danger Lives ★★★

Film noir 1950 · US · BW · 80mins

A minor-league but effective *film noir*, directed by John Farrow and featuring his wife, Maureen O'Sullivan, as well as Robert Mitchum, Claude Rains and Faith Domergue. Mitchum is a doctor, Domergue is his mentally unstable temptress and the open road to Mexico is their refuge, until she thinks maybe she should kill him – after all, she's just done the same to her husband. This doomed romance is well worth watching, not least for the way that Mitchum's physical presence is constantly undermined by the plot. AT

Robert Mitchum *Jeff Cameron* • Faith Domergue *Margo Lannington* • Claude Rains *Frederick Lannington* • Maureen O'Sullivan *Julie* • Charles Kemper *Police chief* • Ralph Dumke *Klauber* • Billy House *Mr Bogardus* ■ *Dir* John Farrow • *Scr* Charles Bennett, from a story by Leo Rosten

Where Do We Go from Here? ★★★ U

Musical fantasy 1945 · US · Colour · 77mins

An unfairly forgotten musical fantasy that's very much of its time, its satirical barbs numbed by the aftermath of the Second World War. Nevertheless, sympathetically viewed today, it remains a genuinely engaging period piece, and features a clever and neglected score by composing greats Kurt Weill and Ira Gershwin. The main theme involving a genie sending Fred MacMurray back through time is quite affecting, and certainly original. MacMurray and the lovely June Haver (MacMurray's future wife) play sweetly together. The superb 1940s Technicolor is especially effective. TS

Fred MacMurray *Bill* • Joan Leslie *Sally* • June Haver *Lucilla* • Gene Sheldon *Ali* • Anthony Quinn *Indian Chief* • Carlos Ramírez *Benito* • Alan Mowbray *General George Washington* • Fortunio Bonanova *Christopher Columbus* • Otto Preminger *General Rahl* ■ *Dir* Gregory Ratoff • *Scr* Morrie Ryskind, from a story by Morrie Ryskind, Sig Herzig

Where Does It Hurt? ★

Black comedy 1971 · US · Colour · 87mins

Crooked administrator Peter Sellers runs his hospital stictly for profit, with the willing help of his motley, under-qualified staff. But patient Rick Lenz sees through the charade and is determined to bring Sellers down. A mess of a movie that, if it were a patient, would be on the critical list. DF

Peter Sellers *Albert T Hopfnagel* • Jo Ann Pflug *Alice Gilligan* • Rick Lenz *Lester Hammond* • Eve Bruce *Nurse Lamarr* • Harold Gould *Dr Zerny* • William Elliott *Oscar* • Norman Alden *Katzen* • Keith Allison *Hinkley* ■ *Dir* Rod Amateau • *Scr* Rod Amateau, Budd Robinson, from their novel *The Operator*

W

Where Eagles Dare ★★★★ PG

Second World War action thriller
1969 · UK · Colour · 148mins

Clint Eastwood called this wartime frolic "Where Doubles Dare", in view of the army of stuntmen who performed the acrobatics in the Austrian Alps. His co-star, Richard Burton, was paid a million dollars plus a big percentage of what turned out to be a hugely profitable picture. It's the usual espionage hokum, with Burton and Eastwood infiltrating a Nazi stronghold to discover a hornets' nest of spies. There are so many double- and triple-crosses that the plot is at times incomprehensible. But this is a picture about big bangs, James Bond-style fights on cable cars and body counts. It's hilarious and exciting, often at the same time. AT DVD

Richard Burton *Major John Smith* • Clint Eastwood *Lieutenant Morris Schaffer* • Mary Ure *Mary Ellison* • Michael Hordern *Vice Admiral Rolland* • Patrick Wymark *Colonel Wyatt Turner* • Robert Beatty *Cartwright Jones* • Anton Diffring *Colonel Kramer* • Donald Houston *Olaf Christiansen* ■ *Dir* Brian G Hutton • *Scr* Alistair MacLean, from his novel

Where Is My Friend's House? ★★★★

Drama 1987 · Iran · Colour · 83mins

The first part of the "friendship" trilogy (completed by *And Life Goes On...* and *Through the Olive Trees*) was made under the auspices of Iran's Institute for the Intellectual Development of Children and Young Adults and provides a deceptively simple account of conscientious schoolboy Babek Ahmed Poor's quest to the neighbouring village to spare a classmate from being expelled by returning a missing notebook. Abbas Kiarostami explores innocent notions of loyalty and everyday heroics with a mixture of realism, touching earnestness and gentle humour. DP. In Farsi with English subtitles.

Babek Ahmed Poor *Ahmed* • Ahmed Ahmed Poor *Mahamed Reda Nematzadeh* • Kheda Barech Defai *Teacher* • Iran Outari *Mother* • Ait Ansari *Father* ■ *Dir/Scr* Abbas Kiarostami

Where Is Parsifal? ★ 15

Comedy 1983 · UK · Colour · 86mins

Orson Welles plays a rich Romany who is interested in the laser skywriter patented by hypochondriac eccentric Tony Curtis. But he faces stiff competition from both millionaire Erik Estrada and Donald Pleasence, who is trying to gain access to Curtis's castle to seize goods equivalent to his debts. The chaotic approach overshoots madcap and crash-lands in a mess. DP

Tony Curtis *Parsifal Katzenellenbogen* • Erik Estrada *Henry Board II* • Peter Lawford *Montague Chippendale* • Orson Welles *Klingsor* • Berta Dominguez D *Elba* • Ron Moody *Beersbohm* • Donald Pleasence *Mackintosh* ■ *Dir* Henri Helman • *Scr* Berta Dominguez D

Where It's At ★★★

Comedy drama 1969 · US · Colour · 104mins

Belying its fashionable "1960s speak" title, this is actually a reasonably sharp portrait of a father and son in conflict. David Janssen is surprisingly convincing as a Vegas casino boss who decides it's time his laid-back offspring (played by Robert Drivas) learnt a little more about the real world. The young man gets a lesson in love courtesy of a showgirl arranged by Janssen and when it comes to the business side of things, Princeton-educated Drivas is more than a match for dad. The tale is crisply handled by writer/director Garson Kanin. RT

David Janssen *AC Smith* • Robert Drivas *Andy Smith* • Rosemary Forsyth *Diana Mayhew* • Brenda Vaccaro *Molly Hirsch* • Warrene Ott *Betty Avery* • Edy Williams *Phyllis Horrigan* • Vince Howard *Ralph* • Don Rickles *Willie* ■ *Dir/Scr* Garson Kanin

Where Love Has Gone ★★★

Melodrama 1964 · US · Colour · 114mins

The pot of venomous passions boils over in this lurid melodrama as mother and daughter Bette Davis and Susan Hayward act out their mutual hatred with all stops out. The temperature rises further when Hayward's own daughter (Joey Heatherton) kills Hayward's lover. Adapted from the bestselling novel by Harold Robbins, who drew on the Lana Turner-Cheryl Crane-Johnny Stompanato scandal for his material, the film was slaughtered by critics while audiences flocked. Fans of the genre are guaranteed a richly entertaining wallow watching these two great stars at their committed worst. RK

Susan Hayward *Valerie Hayden Miller* • Bette Davis *Mrs Gerald Hayden* • Michael Connors [Mike Connors] *Luke Miller* • Joey Heatherton *Danielle Valerie "Dani" Miller* • Jane Greer *Marian Spicer* • DeForest Kelley *Sam Corwin* • George Macready *Gordon Harris* • Anne Seymour *Dr Sally Jennings* ■ *Dir* Edward Dmytryk • *Scr* John Michael Hayes, from the novel by Harold Robbins

Where No Vultures Fly ★★★★ U

Adventure 1951 · UK · Colour · 103mins

Chosen for the Royal film performance of its year, this is a splendid semi-documentary shot on exotic African locations, with an ecological message still potently relevant today. Anthony Steel plays a game warden on the lookout for evil ivory hunters in the shadow of Mount Kilimanjaro. The suspense is exceptionally well maintained, with a stunning fight sequence between Steel and Harold Warrender, and the Technicolor matching of studio material and location footage is particularly clever. So successful was this film that it led to a sequel, the equally popular *West of Zanzibar*. TS

Anthony Steel *Robert Payton* • Dinah Sheridan *Mary Payton* • Harold Warrender *Mannering* • Meredith Edwards *Gwil Davies* • William Simons *Tim Payton* ■ *Dir* Harry Watt • *Scr* Ralph Smart, WP Lipscomb, from a story by Leslie Norman Watt • *Cinematographer* Geoffrey Unsworth

Where Sleeping Dogs Lie ★ 15

Psychological thriller
1991 · US · Colour · 87mins

A dreadful thriller in which Dylan McDermott plays a self-absorbed author who moves into a run-down house in which an entire family was once murdered. Tom Sizemore is his twitchy tenant, taking an active interest in the author's portrait of the killer with grisly consequences. Disjointed, predictable and leaden-paced, with surprisingly unconvincing performances from the decent cast. JC

Dylan McDermott *Bruce Simmons* • Tom Sizemore *Eddie Hale* • Sharon Stone *Serena Black* • Joan Chen *Sara* • Kristen Hocking *Marlee* ■ *Dir* Charles Finch • *Scr* Charles Finch, Yolande Turner

Where the Boys Are ★★★ PG

Romantic comedy
1960 · US · Colour · 95mins

The boys are at a Fort Lauderdale resort, invaded by college kids in search of romance during the Easter vacation. Against this background of youthful sun-seeking and partying, the action focuses on the contrasting relationships that develop between four girls and guys, of whom Paula Prentiss (her debut) and Jim Hutton are the most charming. Good-natured, nostalgic stuff with an interesting moral take on virginity. RK DVD

Dolores Hart *Merritt Andrews* • George Hamilton *Ryder Smith* • Yvette Mimieux *Melanie* • Jim Hutton *TV Thompson* • Barbara Nichols *Lola* • Paula Prentiss *Tuggle Carpenter* • Connie Francis *Angie* • Chill Wills *Police Captain* ■ *Dir* Henry Levin • *Scr* George Wells, from a story by Glendon Swarthout

Where the Buffalo Roam ★★★ 18

Comedy 1980 · US · Colour · 94mins

Through the eyes of the pioneer of "gonzo journalism", Hunter S Thompson, we see various facets of US political life in the late 1960s and early 1970s. The under-rated Bill Murray is Thompson while Peter Boyle plays his outrageous legal acquaintance, Lazlo. This movie was "based on the twisted legend of Hunter S Thompson" according to its title sequence. It was panned on release in the US but it's actually an interesting and savage little piece which deserved better. DF

Peter Boyle *Lazlo* • Bill Murray *Dr Hunter S Thompson* • Bruno Kirby *Marty Lewis* • René Auberjonois *Harris* • RG Armstrong *Judge Simpson* • Danny Goldman *Porter* • Rafael Campos *Rojas* • Leonard Frey *Desk clerk* ■ *Dir* Art Linson • *Scr* John Kaye, from writings by Hunter S Thompson • *Music* Neil Young

Where the Bullets Fly ★★★

Spy spoof 1966 · UK · Colour · 88mins

The British have the Spurium Apparatus, a small nuclear device for powering aircraft. The Russians want it and enlist the aid of Michael Ripper and his clandestine international crime organisation to steal it. To succeed he has to clash with super secret agent Charles Vine (Tom Adams), on his second outing following 1965's *Licensed to Kill*. One of a huge number of Bond spoofs about at the time, none of which seemed to realise that the 007 movies themselves were spoofs. A jaunty enough romp. A third and final segment *Somebody's Stolen Our Russian Spy* followed. DF

Tom Adams *Charles Vine* • Dawn Addams *Felicity "Fiz" Moonlight* • Sidney James *Mortuary attendant* • Wilfrid Brambell *Train guard* • Joe Baker *Minister* • Tim Barrett *Seraph* • Michael Ripper *Angel* • John Arnatt *Rockwell* • Ronald Leigh-Hunt *Thursby* ■ *Dir* John Gilling • *Scr* Michael Pittock

Where the Day Takes You ★★ 18

Drama 1992 · US · Colour · 98mins

This quasi-documentary looks at kids living rough on the mean streets of Los Angeles. There's a feel of the real in its depiction of the seamy underside, set against the glam and glitzy City of Angels. But the characters never really engage you, and the film's so relentlessly downbeat that you're soon numb to its nastiness. Literally slumming it is a crack cast of Hollywood's younger lions. DA DVD

Dermot Mulroney *King* • Lara Flynn Boyle *Heather* • Balthazar Getty *Little J* • Sean Astin *Greg* • James LeGros *Crasher* • Ricki Lake *Brenda* • Kyle MacLachlan *Ted* • Robert Knepper *Rock Singer* • Peter Dobson *Tommy* • Will Smith *Manny* • Adam Baldwin *Officer Black* • Christian Slater *Rocky* • Alyssa Milano *Kimmy* ■ *Dir* Marc Rocco • *Scr* Michael Hitchcock, Kurt Voss, Marc Rocco

Where the Green Ants Dream ★★★ 15

Drama 1984 · W Ger · Colour · 100mins

Imbued with the romanticism that has characterised Werner Herzog's film-making exploits around the globe, this study of the clash between tradition and progress in the Australian outback is one of his least memorable accomplishments. Jörg Schmidt-Reitwein's vistas are suitable evocative and the ethnographic and environmental messages are essentially sound. But, despite the eloquent championing of a wholly fictitious 40,000 year-old Aboriginal tradition that green ants will wreak havoc if their dreaming ground is disturbed by Bruce Spence's mining company, Herzog fails to sustain the dramatic tension, even during the pivotal court case. DP

Bruce Spence *Lance Hackett* • Wandjuk Marika *Miliritbi* • Roy Marika *Dayipu* • Ray Barrett *Cole* • Norman Kaye *Baldwin Ferguson* ■ *Dir/Scr* Werner Herzog

Where the Heart Is ★ 15

Comedy drama
1990 · US/Can · Colour · 102mins

Seeing that director John Boorman's prior effort was *Hope and Glory* one expected more of him than this dreadful comedy. Under the auspices of Disney, Boorman has produced an unfunny, unappealing movie about demolition expert Dabney Coleman who chucks his children (Uma Thurman, David Hewlett and Suzy Amis) into squalor in downtown Brooklyn. Written by Boorman and his daughter Telsche, this might have worked on the page but it sure is a Bernard Matthews on screen. LH [video] DVD

Dabney Coleman *Stewart McBain* • Uma Thurman *Daphne* • Christopher Plummer *Homeless gent* • Joanna Cassidy *Jean* • Suzy Amis *Chloe* • Crispin Glover *Lionel* • David Hewlett *Jimmy* ■ *Dir* John Boorman • *Scr* John Boorman, Telsche Boorman

Where the Heart Is ★★ 12

Comedy drama 2000 · US · Colour · 115mins

Natalie Portman here stars in what could be seen as a paean to product placement, playing a heavily pregnant teenager who's dumped by her no-good boyfriend outside a Wal-Mart convenience store in Oklahoma. Secretly setting up home inside, she gives birth to what the media immediately dub the "Wal-Mart Baby". The film lacks pace and purpose, and Portman is a little lightweight in her first leading role. But there are some memorable moments courtesy of her scene-stealing co-stars. DA [video] DVD

Natalie Portman *Novalee Nation* • Ashley Judd *Lexie Coop* • Stockard Channing *Sister Husband* • Joan Cusack *Ruth Meyers* • James Frain *Forney Hull* • Dylan Bruno *Willy Jack Pickens* • Keith David *Moses Whitecotten* • Sally Field *Mama Lil* ■ *Dir* Matt Williams • *Scr* Lowell Ganz, Babaloo Mandel, from a novel by Billie Letts

Where the Hot Wind Blows! ★★ 12

Drama 1959 · Fr/It · BW · 111mins

Adapted from the Prix Goncourt-winning novel by Roger Vailland, this is a classic case of a film being ruined through commercial interference. Jules Dassin was about to begin shooting (from what he considered the best script he'd ever written) when the backers insisted he cast Marcello Mastroianni and Gina Lollobrigida. Thus, an intense study of the misuse of power in a patriarchal southern Italian community is transformed into an imbalanced star vehicle. DP. An Italian language film. [video]

Gina Lollobrigida *Marietta* • Pierre Brasseur *Don Cesare* • Marcello Mastroianni *Engineer* • Melina Mercouri *Donna Lucrezia* • Yves Montand *Matteo Brigante* ■ *Dir* Jules Dassin • *Scr* Jules Dassin, Françoise Giroud, from the novel *La Loi* by Roger Vailland

Where the Lilies Bloom ★★★ U

Drama 1974 · US · Colour · 97mins

This is the old story of the loving kids who can't bear the thought of being parted and so hide the death of their parents from the authorities by putting on a show of business as usual. But don't give up on this movie as just another chunk of family values mush. Scriptwriter Earl Hamner Jr (*The Waltons*) has not only produced a sensitive and well-observed portrait of backwoods American life, but he has also come up with flesh-and-blood children who don't seem to have been born on Walton's Mountain. DP

Julie Gholson *Mary Call* • Jan Smithers *Devola* • Matthew Burrill *Romey* • Helen Harmon *Ima Dean* • Harry Dean Stanton *Kiser Pease* • Rance Howard *Roy Luther* ■ *Dir* William A Graham • *Scr* Earl Hamner Jr, from a novel by Vera Cleaver, Bill Cleaver

Where the Money Is ★★★ 15

Comedy crime thriller
2000 · Ger/US/UK · Colour · 84mins

Paul Newman proves his star quality hasn't dimmed in this lively crime caper. He plays a jailed bank robber who is transferred to a convalescent home after suffering a stroke that seemingly leaves him paralysed. One of the home's nurses, played by Linda Fiorentino, suspects Newman might be faking, and it's not long before she has seen through his very impressive act. In return for keeping his secret, she persuades him to help her and her husband (Dermot Mulroney) pull a robbery of their own. It's a witty adventure, made enjoyable by the three central performances. JB. Contains swearing. [video] DVD

Paul Newman *Henry Manning* • Linda Fiorentino *Carol* • Dermot Mulroney *Wayne* • Susan Barnes *Mrs Foster* • Anne Pitoniak *Mrs Tetlow* • Bruce MacVittie *Karl* ■ *Dir* Marek Kanievska • *Scr* E Max Frye, Topper Lilien, Carroll Cartwright, from a story by E Max Frye

Where the Red Fern Grows ★★★ U

Adventure 1974 · US · Colour · 96mins

In this entertaining family movie, a 12-year-old boy (Stewart Petersen) living in 1930s Oklahoma finds caring for his two hounds helps him overcome the trials and tribulations of the Depression era. Directed by children's adventure specialist Norman Tokar, it stars James Whitmore as the boy's grandfather and former Roger Corman ingénue Beverly Garland as his mother. This was successful enough to lead to a straight-to-video sequel nearly two decades later, 1992's *Where the Red Fern Grows II*. TH

James Whitmore *Grandpa* • Beverly Garland *Mother* • Jack Ging *Father* • Lonny Chapman *Sheriff* • Stewart Petersen *Billy* • Jill Clark *Alice* • Jeanne Wilson *Sara* ■ *Dir* Norman Tokar • *Scr* Douglas Day Stewart, Eleanor Lamb, from the novel by Wilson Rawls

Where the River Runs Black ★★ PG

Adventure 1986 · US · Colour · 96mins

This is a family pic about a boy in the Brazilian forest who is the result of a sudden union between a beautiful local girl and a priest who then dies for his sins. Thought to possess heavenly powers, the boy is raised with the help of river dolphins and is therefore naturally a whizz at swimming. In addition to all that, there's the ravaging of the rainforest by gold-miners and a portentous score by James Horner. AT [video]

Charles Durning *Father O'Reilly* • Peter Horton *Father Mahoney* • Alessandro Rabelo *Lazaro* • Ajay Naidu *Segundo* • Conchata Ferrell *Mother Marta* • Dana Delany *Sister Ana* • Chico Diaz *Raimundo* ■ *Dir* Christopher Cain • *Scr* Peter Silverman, Neal Jimenez, from the novel *Lazaro* by David Kendall

Where the Rivers Flow North ★★★ 15

Period drama 1993 · US · Colour · 106mins

In 1920s Vermont, a stubborn logger and landowner (a suitably ursine Rip Torn) is refusing to sell his property to the government-backed power company about to build a dam. It's not as dull as it sounds, as director Jay Craven concentrates on the relationship between Torn and his long-suffering native American housekeeper Tantoo Cardinal. The two central performances are both excellent and moving, elevating a dreary and overused premise and making this a very watchable film. LH [video]

Rip Torn *Noel Lord* • Tantoo Cardinal *Bangor* • Bill Raymond *Wayne Quinn* • Michael J Fox *Clayton Farnsworth* • Treat Williams *Champ's Manager* • Amy Wright *Loose Woman* ■ *Dir* Jay Craven • *Scr* Jay Craven, Don Bredes, from the novel *Where the Rivers Run North* by Howard Frank Mosher

Where the Sidewalk Ends ★★★★ 12

Film noir 1950 · US · BW · 92mins

A superb example of 20th Century-Fox *film noir* at its finest, this is a clearly plotted thriller, impeccably directed by the great Otto Preminger, which creates a nightmare world of guilt and corruption. Brutal cop Dana Andrews tries to hide the fact that, while searching for a murderer, he himself has killed Craig Stevens. The beautiful Gene Tierney is excellent in an enigmatic role as Stevens's estranged wife – a part that manages to keep her acting limitations well concealed – and watch for Neville Brand's chilling portrayal of a homosexual criminal in some censor-circumventing scenes well ahead of their time. TS [video] DVD

Dana Andrews *Mark Dixon* • Gene Tierney *Morgan Taylor* • Gary Merrill *Tommy Scalise* • Bert Freed *Paul Klein* • Tom Tully *Jiggs Taylor* • Karl Malden *Lieutenant Bill Thomas* • Ruth Donnelly *Martha* • Oleg Cassini ■ *Dir* Otto Preminger • *Scr* Ben Hecht, from a novel by William L Stuart, adapted by Frank P Rosenberg, Victor Trivas, Robert E Kent • *Cinematographer* Joseph LaShelle

Where the Spies Are ★★

Spy adventure 1965 · UK · Colour · 112mins

One of the many dozens of Bond send-ups and rip-offs, this spoofy affair is distinguished by a typically suave and disarming performance from David Niven, who in 1967 played Bond himself in *Casino Royale*. Niven is recruited by MI6 and sent to the Middle East to defend Britain's vital oil interests. The usual scrapes, escapes, explosions, lethal gadgets and bedroom seductions ensue, all treated in a rather obvious satirical style by co-writer/director Val Guest. AT

David Niven *Dr Jason Love* • Françoise Dorléac *Vikki* • John Le Mesurier *Col Douglas MacGillivray* • Cyril Cusack *Peter Rosser* • Eric Pohlman [Eric Pohlmann] *Farouk* • Richard Marner *Josef* • Paul Stassino *Simmias* • Noel Harrison *Jackson* • Geoffrey Bayldon *Lecturer* ■ *Dir* Val Guest • *Scr* Wolf Mankowitz, Val Guest, James Leasor

Where There's a Will ★★★ PG

Comedy 1936 · UK · BW · 76mins

Will Hay created wonderful comic characters, incompetent because they were masquerading in their work or were not up to the job. Here the latter is true, as he plays an unsuccessful solicitor whose office happens to be over a bank that a gang decides to rob. Hay is knocked out but later, as he sponges off wealthy relatives at a party, the same gang turn up for a repeat performance. Can the master of the supercilious sniff save the day? It's notable as the first collaboration between the devious Hay and his regular sidekick, Graham Moffatt, here playing an office boy. BB [video] DVD

Will Hay *Benjamin Stubbins* • Gina Malo *Goldie Kelly* • Hartley Power *Duke Wilson* • Graham Moffatt *Willie* • HF Maltby *Sir Roger Wimpleton* • Norma Varden *Lady Margaret Wimpleton* • Peggy Simpson *Barbara Stubbins* • Gibb McLaughlin *Martin* ■ *Dir* William Beaudine • *Scr* William Beaudine, Will Hay, Ralph Spence, Robert Edmunds, from a story by Leslie Arliss, Sidney Gilliat

Where There's a Will ★★ U

Comedy 1955 · UK · BW · 77mins

This sporadically charming fish-out-of-water comedy sees a family of cockneys moving to the Devon countryside when they inherit a run-down farm. Director Vernon Sewell manages a few sly touches, as local housekeeper Kathleen Harrison tries to whip the work-shy Londoners into shape. George Cole gives his rent-a-spiv character another airing, and there's a young Edward Woodward lurking among the bit players. RT

George Cole *Fred Slater* • Kathleen Harrison *Annie Yeo* • Leslie Dwyer *Alfred Brewer* • Ann Hanslip *June Hodge* • Michael Shepley *Mr Cogent* • Dandy Nichols *Maud Hodge* • Thelma Ruby *Amy Slater* • Edward Woodward *Ralph Stokes* ■ *Dir* Vernon Sewell • *Scr* RF Delderfield, from his play

Where There's Life ★★★★

Comedy 1947 · US · BW · 75mins

Bob Hope is a small-time New York DJ who discovers he is the heir to a mysterious European kingdom. He is then chased through New York by not only those wish to take him back to the country to take up the throne but also anti-royalists who are out to kill him. This is from the golden era of Hope's work, with the fast-talking comedy actor on top wisecracking form. Satisfaction is guaranteed with this combination and at the time there was no-one better than Hope at combining thrills and comedy. DF

Bob Hope *Michael Valentine* • Signe Hasso *Katrina Grimovitch* • William Bendix *Victor O'Brien* • George Coulouris *Premier Krivoc* • Vera Marshe *Hazel O'Brien* • George Zucco *Paul Stertorius* • Dennis Hoey *Minister of War Grubitch* • John Alexander *Mr Herbert Jones* ■ *Dir* Sidney Lanfield • *Scr* Allen Boretz, Melville Shavelson, Barney Dean, Frank Tashlin, from a story by Melville Shavelson

Where Were You When the Lights Went Out? ★★ PG

Comedy 1968 · US · Colour · 89mins

Doris Day's penultimate picture is notable only for the fact that she spent much of its production in traction, having pinched a nerve in her back, and for an excruciating in-joke that had her character starring in a play called *The Constant Virgin*. It's a contrived affair from start to finish, relying on blackouts, sleeping pills, embezzled funds and sexual jealousy to bring Doris and husband Patrick O'Neal to a happy ending. DP [video]

Doris Day *Margaret Garrison* • Robert Morse *Waldo Zane* • Terry-Thomas *Ladislau Walichek* • Patrick O'Neal *Peter Garrison* • Lola Albright *Roberta Lane* • Steve Allen *Radio announcer* • Jim Backus *Tru-Blue Lou* ■ *Dir* Hy Averback • *Scr* Everett Freeman, Karl Tunberg, from the play *Monsieur Masure* by Claude Magnier

Where's Firuze? ★★ 15

Musical comedy
2004 · Tur · Colour · 138mins

With its frantic pace, eccentric characters and camp colour schemes, this Turkish musical comedy feels like a Bollywood masala that's under the influence. Haluk Bilginer and Cem Ozen play seedy record producers who sign singer Ozcan Deniz in the hope of making the quick cash needed to pay off their Mob creditors. Director Ezel Akay starts in the middle and works backwards before plunging towards his sentimental finale. DP. In Turkish with English subtitles. Contains swearing, violence and drug abuse.

Haluk Bilginer *Hayri* • Ozcan Deniz *Ferhat* • Demet Akbag *Firuze* • Cem Ozer *Orhen* ■ *Dir* Ezel Akay • *Scr* Levent Kazak

Where's Jack? ★★ U

Period drama 1969 · UK · Colour · 119mins

The damaging flaw in this 18th-century account of highway skulduggery is the miscasting of pop-singer Tommy Steele as ruffian Jack Sheppard, who is pursued – and, to an extent, manipulated by – the venal Stanley Baker (who also co-produced). But director James Clavell, who would go on to write blockbuster novels such as *Shogun*, makes a brave attempt at re-creating the bawdy, squalid times. TH

Tommy Steele *Jack Sheppard* • Stanley Baker *Jonathan Wild* • Fiona Lewis *Edgworth Bess Lyon* • Alan Badel *The Lord Chancellor* • Dudley Foster *Blueskin* • Noel Purcell *Leatherchest* • William Marlowe *Tom Sheppard* • Sue Lloyd *Lady Darlington* • Michael Elphick *Hogarth* ■ *Dir* James Clavell • *Scr* David Newhouse, Rafe Newhouse

Where's Poppa? ★★★★

Black comedy 1970 · US · Colour · 83mins

Successful lawyer George Segal lives with his sometimes senile, widowed mother Ruth Gordon. Whenever he brings a girl home his mother undergoes a remarkable change, springing to life and scuppering his chances. When he falls for his mother's new nurse Trish Van Devere, Segal is driven to try to kill Gordon. A fast-paced, jet black comedy with fine performances all around. DF

George Segal *Gordon Hocheiser* • Ruth Gordon *Mrs Hocheiser* • Trish Van Devere *Louise Callan* • Ron Leibman *Sidney Hocheiser* • Rae Allen *Gladys Hocheiser* • Florence Tarlow *Miss Morgiani* • Paul Sorvino *Owner of "Gus and Grace's Home"* • Rob Reiner *Roger* • Vincent Gardenia *Coach Williams* ■ *Dir* Carl Reiner • *Scr* Robert Klane, from his novel

Where's That Fire? ★★★ U

Comedy 1939 · UK · BW · 73mins

In this comic gem, Will Hay creates another variant in his gallery of incompetents – this time he's a fireman in a small village. His regular sidekicks Graham Moffatt and Moore Marriott help form what was once described as "the holy trinity of the [British] studio system". They stumble across a gang of thieves, who reassure them that they are making an historical film, when in fact they are after the crown jewels. As usual, things turn out for the best in the slightly askew world created by these three wonderful comedians. BB

Will Hay *Capt Benjamin Viking* • Moore Marriott *Jerry Harbottle* • Graham Moffatt *Albert Brown* • Peter Gawthorne *Chief Officer* • Eric Clavering *Hank Sullivan* • Hugh McDermott *Jim Baker* • Charles Hawtrey *Youth* ■ *Dir* Marcel Varnel • *Scr* Marriott Edgar, Val Guest, JOC Orton, from a story by Maurice Braddell

Where's Willie? ★★ U

Fantasy drama 1977 · US · Colour · 89mins

Ten-year-old Marc Gilpin gives a good account of himself in this amusing fantasy drama, relishing every jape in his role as the mischievous whizzkid whose latest invention raises the hackles of his small-town neighbours. The fact that a "magic box" (which is, essentially, a primitive computer) could be regarded with such suspicion rather dates the picture and shows how drastically the tone of children's entertainment has changed. DP

Marc Gilpin *Willie* • Henry Darrow *Sheriff Charlie Wade* • Kate Woodville *Beth Wade* • Rock Montanio *Tracks* • Guy Madison ■ *Dir* John Florea • *Scr* Frank Koomen, Ann Koomen, Alan Cassidy, from a story by William H White

Which Way Is Up? ★★★

Comedy 1977 · US · Colour · 94mins

Richard Pryor is a simple migrant orange picker who is manipulated into management by the boss of the large agricultural concern that employs him. But this is just the start of his seduction. This US version of Lina Wertmüller's 1972 Italian comedy *The Seduction of Mimi* doesn't match the original despite some fine work from Pryor in a triple role. DF

Richard Pryor *Leroy Jones/Rufus Jones/ Reverend Thomas* • Lonette McKee *Vanetta* • Margaret Avery (2) *Annie Mae* • Morgan Woodward *Mr Mann* • Marilyn Coleman *Sister Sarah* ■ *Dir* Michael Schultz • *Scr* Carl Gottlieb, Cecil Brown, from the film *The Seduction of Mimi* by Lina Wertmüller

Which Way to the Front? ★ U

Comedy 1970 · US · Colour · 92mins

Few things in showbusiness are sadder to see than a comedian deserted by his muse. Jerry Lewis hits rock bottom with some untenable and tasteless material (a group of misfits deciding to wage their own war against Hitler), appallingly assembled and perfunctorily put together. Jerry himself mugs unwatchably, and John Wood and Jan Murray offer futile support. TS

Jerry Lewis *Brendan Byers III* • Jan Murray *Sid Hackle* • John Wood *Finkel* • Steve Franken *Peter Bland* • Willie Davis *Lincoln* • Dack Rambo *Terry Love* • Paul Winchell *Schroeder* • Sidney Miller *Adolf Hitler* • Robert Middleton *Colonico* ■ *Dir* Jerry Lewis • *Scr* Gerald Gardner, Dee Caruso, from a story by Gerald Gardner, Dee Caruso, Richard Miller

Whiffs ★ 15

Crime comedy 1975 · US · Colour · 88mins

Soldier Elliott Gould is pensioned out of the army due to the disabling effects of the toxins he has encountered on behalf of the military. He teams up with Harry Guardino and the two form a criminal partnership, using their knowledge of chemicals to rob banks. This is a tired caper comedy, which tries to capture the style of *MASH* but fails ignominiously, despite the presence of Gould. DP

Elliott Gould *Dudley Frapper* • Eddie Albert *Colonel Lockyer* • Harry Guardino *Chops* • Godfrey Cambridge *Dusty* • Jennifer O'Neill *Scottie* • Alan Manson *Sgt Poultry* ■ *Dir* Ted Post • *Scr* Malcolm Marmorstein

While I Live ★★

Drama 1947 · UK · BW · 84mins

Veteran moviegoers might just remember seeing this excitable melodrama under the title *The Dream of Olwen*, under which it was re-released to exploit the success of Charles Williams's theme tune. Sonia Dresdel dominates the proceedings with a Mrs Danvers-like display of neurotic malice, playing a Cornish spinster who becomes convinced that amnesiac Carol Raye is her reincarnated sister. DP

Sonia Dresdel *Julia Trevelyan* • Tom Walls *Nehemiah* • Clifford Evans *Peter* • Carol Raye *Sally Warwick* • Patricia Burke *Christine* • John Warwick *George Warwick* ■ *Dir* John Harlow • *Scr* John Harlow, Doreen Montgomery, from the play *This Same Garden* by Robert Bell

While the City Sleeps ★★★ PG

Thriller 1956 · US · BW · 95mins

This thriller about who gets to run a newspaper is quite intriguing, and boasts a starry cast as well as revered director Fritz Lang. With such a roster of familiar faces, it's compulsively watchable, even if Vincent Price and Ida Lupino, in particular, have little to do. Lang, making one of his final American movies, filmed this in Superscope, which means, if you watch it on TV, you'll see a lot of ceilings and floors. TS

Dana Andrews *Edward Mobley* • Rhonda Fleming *Dorothy Kyne* • Vincent Price *Walter Kyne Jr* • George Sanders *Mark Loving* • Thomas Mitchell *John Day Griffith* • Sally Forrest *Nancy* • Ida Lupino *Mildred* • Howard Duff *Lt Kaufman* • John Barrymore Jr [John Drew Barrymore] *Manners* ■ *Dir* Fritz Lang • *Scr* Casey Robinson, from the novel *The Bloody Spur* by Charles Einstein

While the Sun Shines ★★

Drama 1946 · UK · BW · 83mins

A boisterous American and a suave young Frenchman both pursue the daughter of an impoverished aristocrat. This causes some upheavals in her relationship with her wealthy and titled fiancé, who is serving in the navy as a humble sailor. This light romantic comedy, based on a play by Terence Rattigan, fails to translate adequately to the screen. The leads lack the necessary sparkle, being stalwart rather than starry, and it's left to a top-notch supporting cast of famous British character actors to flavour an otherwise bland concoction. RK

Barbara White *Lady Elisabeth Randall* • Ronald Squire *Duke of Ayr and Stirling* • Brenda Bruce *Mabel Crum* • Bonar Colleano *Joe Mulvaney* • Michael Allan *Colbert* • Ronald Howard *Earl of Harpenden* • Miles Malleson *Horton* • Margaret Rutherford *Dr Winifred Frye* • Joyce Grenfell *Daphne* • Wilfrid Hyde White *Male receptionist* ■ *Dir* Anthony Asquith • *Scr* Terence Rattigan, Anatole de Grunwald, from the play by Terence Rattigan

While You Were Sleeping ★★★★ PG

Romantic comedy 1995 · US · Colour · 99mins

This warmly engaging and winning romantic comedy has plenty of novel twists and witty turns. Sandra Bullock is nothing short of sensational as the lonely Chicago subway clerk, who poses as the fiancée of coma victim Peter Gallagher after saving his life, much to the thrilled amazement of his family and the yearning of his sceptical brother Bill Pullman. This smartly scripted Cinderella love story is crammed with charm and Jon Turteltaub's expert direction hits all the right emotional buttons. AJ. Contains some swearing. DVD

Sandra Bullock *Lucy Moderatz* • Bill Pullman *Jack Callaghan* • Peter Gallagher *Peter Callaghan* • Peter Boyle *Ox* • Jack Warden *Saul* • Glynis Johns *Elsie* • Michael Rispoli *Joe Jr* • Jason Bernard *Jerry* • Micole Mercurio *Midge* ■ *Dir* Jon Turteltaub • *Scr* Daniel G Sullivan, Fredric Lebow

The Whip Hand ★★★

Thriller 1951 · US · BW · 81mins

This taut thriller may lack star names, but it is masterfully directed and designed by William Cameron Menzies. Elliott Reid plays the photojournalist on vacation in Wisconsin who stumbles on a village of unfriendly inhabitants, a lake where the fish have vanished and a mysterious, heavily guarded lodge. The original ending involved Adolf Hitler plotting a comeback, but RKO studio boss Howard Hughes, who was virulently anti-communist, opted for a Red threat instead. AE

Elliott Reid *Matt Corbin* • Raymond Burr *Steve Loomis* • Carla Balenda *Janet Koller* • Edgar Barrier *Dr Edward Koller* • Otto Waldis *Dr Bucholtz* • Michael Steele *Chick* • Lurene Tuttle *Molly Loomis* ■ *Dir* William Cameron Menzies • *Scr* George Bricker, Frank L Moss, from a story by Roy Hamilton

Whipped ★ 18

Comedy 1999 · US · Colour · 78mins

Peter M Cohen clearly rates his directorial debut as a marvel of cutting-edge technique depicting a riotous lads' night out. It's stuffed with wiseacre dialogue and cocksure incorrectness, and there's nothing amusing about the way in which Brian Van Holt, Zorie Barber and Jonathan Abrahams stalk the supposedly enigmatic Amanda Peet. Coarse, crass and abysmally acted. DP DVD

Amanda Peet *Mia* • Brian Van Holt *Brad* • Jonathan Abrahams *Jonathan* • Zorie Barber *Zeke* ■ *Dir/Scr* Peter M Cohen

Whipsaw ★★★

Crime drama 1935 · US · BW · 78mins

A trio of crooks, one of whom is Myrna Loy, steals some valuable jewels in Europe. Back in New York, where the booty is lifted by rival thieves, G-man Spencer Tracy is assigned to find the gems. He courts Loy, who believes he is also a thief, and they fall in love before the truth is revealed. The felicitous pairing of Loy with Tracy (replacing the intended but unavailable William Powell) and Sam Wood's direction, which has enough pace and spirit to hide the holes in a basically unconvincing script, result in an entertaining romantic crime drama. RK

Myrna Loy *Vivian Palmer* • Spencer Tracy *Ross McBride* • Harvey Stephens *Ed Dexter* • William Harrigan *Doc Evans* • Clay Clement *Harry Ames* • Robert Gleckler *Steve Arnold* • Robert Warwick *Wadsworth* • Georges Renavent *Monetta* ■ *Dir* Sam Wood • *Scr* Howard Emmett Rogers, from the story by James Edward Grant

Whirlpool ★★★ PG

Crime drama 1949 · US · BW · 93mins

This is a chunk of pure 20th Century-Fox late 1940s *film noir*, a highly entertaining melodrama directed by one of the past masters, Otto Preminger. He even manages to make ace ham José Ferrer credible as a dubious hypnotist treating vivacious kleptomaniac Gene Tierney. The screenplay is by a group of left-wing intellectuals, including a blacklisted Ben Hecht using the pseudonym Lester Barstow. The subtext about mind control is, therefore, by no means accidental. TS DVD

Gene Tierney *Ann Sutton* • Richard Conte *Dr William Sutton* • José Ferrer *David Korvo* • Charles Bickford *Lieutenant Colton* • Barbara O'Neil *Theresa Randolph* • Eduard Franz *Martin Avery* • Constance Collier *Tina Cosgrove* • Fortunio Bonanova *Feruccio di Ravallo* • Ruth Lee *Miss Hall* ■ *Dir* Otto Preminger • *Scr* Lester Barstow [Ben Hecht], Andrew Solt, from the novel by Guy Endore • *Cinematographer* Arthur Miller

Whisky ★★★★

Romantic comedy drama 2004 · Urug/Arg/Sp/Ger · Colour · 99mins

Juan Pablo Rebella and Pablo Stoll put Uruguayan cinema on the map with this deliciously deadpan study of sibling envy, unrequited loyalty and late-life disappointment. The opening sequences at Andrés Pazos's Montevideo sock factory smack of Aki Kaurismäki. The film develops its own quirky charm, though, as the scene shifts to the coastal resort of Piriapolis, where dowdy assistant Mirella Pascual unexpectedly blossoms as she poses as Pazos's wife in order impress his younger, more successful

W

brother, Jorge Bolani. Full of small smiles and wise insights, this is a little gem. DP. In Spanish with English subtitles.

Andrés Pazos *Jacobo Koller* • Mirella Pascual *Marta Acuña* • Jorge Bolani *Herman Koller* ■ *Dir* Juan Pablo Rebella, Pablo Stoll • *Scr* Juan Pablo Rebella, Pablo Stoll, Gonzalo Delgado Galiana

Whisky Galore! ★★★★★ PG

Classic comedy 1949 · UK · BW · 79mins

Alexander Mackendrick's sublime film is one of the jewels in the Ealing crown. At the centre of this droll story of whisky smuggling in the Hebrides during the Second World War stands Basil Radford, who gives the performance of his career as the despised Sassenach commanding the local Home Guard. The Todday islanders are played to perfection by such accomplished players as Gordon Jackson, Wylie Watson and Joan Greenwood, while Catherine Lacey is a delight as Radford's wife, who greets his posturing and humiliation with equal detachment. *Rockets Galore* (1958) followed. DP [video] DVD

Basil Radford *Captain Paul Waggett* • Catherine Lacey *Mrs Waggett* • Bruce Seton *Sergeant Odd* • Joan Greenwood *Peggy Macroon* • Gordon Jackson *George Campbell* • Wylie Watson *Joseph Macroon* • Gabrielle Blunt *Catriona Macroon* • Jean Cadell *Mrs Campbell* • James Robertson-Justice *Dr MacLaren* ■ *Dir* Alexander MacKendrick • *Scr* Compton Mackenzie, Angus MacPhail, from the novel by Compton Mackenzie

The Whisperers ★★★★

Drama 1967 · UK · BW · 105mins

One of writer/director Bryan Forbes's most admired films, this is essentially an effective and moving study of loneliness, which has as its subject an old lady teetering on the edge of senility. One does feel a little sidetracked by the plot development involving the poor old dear being exploited by her criminal son (Ronald Fraser) and husband (Eric Portman), but there is still the constant pleasure of Dame Edith Evans at her finest, moving us to laughter and tears. DM

Edith Evans *Mrs Maggie Ross* • Eric Portman *Archie Ross* • Nanette Newman *Girl upstairs* • Gerald Sim *Mr Conrad* • Avis Bunnage *Mrs Noonan* • Ronald Fraser *Charlie Ross* • Leonard Rossiter *National Assistance official* • Kenneth Griffith *Mr Weaver* • Sarah Forbes *Mrs Ross as a child* ■ *Dir* Bryan Forbes • *Scr* Bryan Forbes, from the novel *Mrs Ross* by Robert Nicolson

Whispering Corridors ★★★

Supernatural horror
1998 · S Kor · Colour · 105mins

More an allegory on the rigidity of the Korean education system than a gory chiller, Park Ki-Hyung's debut feature is an assured amalgam of generic tropes and populist snipes. Its setting, in an all-girls' school briefly evokes Dario Argento's *Suspiria*. But as various sadistic teachers meet their grisly ends, it's clear that Park is more interested in the militarisation of youth than graphic displays of Gothic bloodletting. Lee Mi-Youn impresses as the resourceful heroine, although Kim Kyu-Li has more fun as the teen possessed by a suicide's malevolent spirit. DP. A Korean language film.

Lee Mi-Youn • Kim Kyu-Li • Park Yong-Su • Lee Yong-Nyuh • Kim Yu-Seok ■ *Dir* Park Ki-Hyung • *Scr* In Jung-Ok, Park Ki-Hyung

Whispering Ghosts ★

Comedy murder mystery
1942 · US · BW · 74mins

This feeble programme filler from Fox provides a showcase for the comic Milton Berle. He plays radio detective HH Van Buren, who solves crimes on the air and has to deal with the 10-year-old murder of a ship's captain. He visits the captain's old vessel in the search for clues and learns that it could be haunted. It's uninspired, with few opportunities for Berle to display his particular humorous persona, and, worst of all, plain boring. RK

Milton Berle *HH Van Buren* • Willie Best *Euclid White* • Brenda Joyce *Elizabeth Woods* • Abner Biberman *Mack Wolf* • John Carradine *Nobert/Long Jack* • Charles Halton *Gruber* ■ *Dir* Alfred Werker • *Scr* Lou Breslow, from a story by Philip McDonald

Whispering Pages ★★★

Experimental drama
1993 · Rus/Ger · BW and Colour · 80mins

Aleksandr Sokurov sets himself a near impossible task here in seeking to create a visual equivalent to the bleak spirit of 19th-century Russian literature. But, to his credit, he comes close to pulling it off by allowing wisps of colour to permeate the resolutely monochrome and virtually silent world inhabited by anti-hero Aleksandr Cherednik and his female companion, Elizaveta Korolyova. Indeed, such is the hallucinatory texture of the visuals that the lower depths experienced by the various beggars and lunatics (as described by the likes of Dostoyevsky, Gogol and Gorky) become manifest in the city's forbidding buildings and labyrinthine passageways. DP. In Russian with English subtitles.

Aleksandr Cherednik *Hero* • Sergei Barkovsky *Official* • Elizaveta Korolyova *Girl* • Galina Nikulina ■ *Dir/Scr* Aleksandr Sokurov

Whispering Smith ★★★

Western 1948 · US · Colour · 88mins

Alan Ladd hit his peak during the 1940s, mainly in thrillers, with his slightly glacial good looks suiting *noir* films. Towards the end of the decade he made this, his first starring western, which works more as a detective story with Ladd playing an undercover agent on the trail of train wreckers. It was his first film in colour, made just five years before he achieved immortality as Shane. The film is briskly handled by journeyman director Leslie Fenton, who brings the story to a rousing climax. BB

Alan Ladd *Luke "Whispering" Smith* • Robert Preston *Murray Sinclair* • Donald Crisp *Barney Rebstock* • Brenda Marshall *Marian Sinclair* • William Demarest *Bill Dansing* • Fay Holden *Emmy Dansing* • Murvyn Vye *Blake Barton* • Frank Faylen *Whitey Du Sang* ■ *Dir* Leslie Fenton • *Scr* Frank Butler, Karl Kamb, from the novel by Frank H Spearman

Whispers ★★ 18

Thriller 1990 · Can · Colour · 89mins

Based on a novel by Dean R Koontz, this Canadian-made thriller puts Victoria Tennant into a real jam – she thinks she has murdered her assailant, Jean Leclerc, until he inconveniently shows up at the police station. The unfortunate cop on duty is Chris Sarandon. Tennant sometimes tends to act as if English is not her first language. Here she just needs to look scared and guilty. AT [video]

Victoria Tennant *Hilary Thomas* • Jean LeClerc *Bruno* • Chris Sarandon *Sgt Clemenza* • Linda Sorenson *Kayla* • Peter MacNeill *Frank* ■ *Dir* Douglas Jackson • *Scr* Anita Doohan, from a novel by Dean R Koontz

Whispers: an Elephant's Tale ★★

Wildlife adventure
2000 · US · Colour · 72mins

This Disney real-life adventure merely highlights the difficulties of combining wildlife footage with an invented storyline. The film was shot over 18 months in Botswana, but the action doesn't gel with the screenplay, which feels like a rush job. There's no novelty in the story of a calf that gets separated from its mother, and the dialogue is undistinguished. DP

Angela Bassett *Groove* • Joanna Lumley *Half Tusk* • Anne Archer *Gentle Heart* • Debi Derryberry *Whispers* • Kevin Michael Richardson *Adult Whispers* • Alice Ghostley *Tuskless* • Betty White *Round* • Kat Cressida *Princess* • Joan Rivers *Spike* • Tone Loc *Macho Bull* ■ *Dir* Dereck Joubert • *Scr* Dereck Joubert, Jordan Moffet, Holly Goldberg Sloan

Whispers in the Dark ★★★ 18

Erotic thriller 1992 · US · Colour · 98mins

This pacey little thriller overextends a thin plot, but still grips agreeably from the start. Annabella Sciorra is convincing as the psychiatrist who's perturbed by her response to a female patient – and gets herself and everyone else into extremely hot water by not grasping the Freudian nettle firmly enough. The high spots are Alan Alda as Sciorra's psychiatrist guru and Anthony LaPaglia as a tough cop who will have no truck with all this "talkie feelie" stuff. SH. Contains swearing, sex scenes and nudity. [video]

Annabella Sciorra *Ann Hecker* • Jamey Sheridan *Doug McDowell* • Anthony LaPaglia *Morgenstern* • Jill Clayburgh *Sarah Green* • Alan Alda *Leo Green* • John Leguizamo *Johnny C* • Deborah Unger [Deborah Kara Unger] *Eve Abergray* ■ *Dir/Scr* Christopher Crowe

The Whistle Blower ★★★ PG

Spy thriller 1986 · UK · Colour · 99mins

In a low-key but satisfying thriller, Michael Caine investigates the mysterious death of his son, Nigel Havers, who worked as a Russian translator at GCHQ. Caine is tremendously convincing as the former Korean war veteran (which he was in real life) who now feels betrayed by his country. Eschewing the usual thrills, the picture creates a plausible and creepy world of whispers and a seemingly impenetrable wall of class privilege and secrecy. AT [video] DVD

Michael Caine *Frank Jones* • James Fox *Lord* • Nigel Havers *Robert Jones* • John Gielgud *Sir Adrian Chapple* • Felicity Dean *Cynthia Goodburn* • Barry Foster *Charles Greig* • Gordon Jackson *Bruce* • Kenneth Colley *Bill Pickett* ■ *Dir* Simon Langton • *Scr* Julian Bond, from the novel by John Hale

Whistle down the Wind ★★★★ PG

Drama 1961 · UK · BW · 94mins

In this daring allegory, Alan Bates plays a dishevelled murderer on the run who's confronted by three Lancashire children who think he's the persecuted Jesus Christ deserving of their protection. First-time director Bryan Forbes treats his material with heart-touching gravity and delicacy, and the symbolism only starts to come to pieces when the grown-up need for justice intrudes. Young Hayley Mills – her mother wrote the novel on which this film is based – is wonderfully wide-eyed, while Bates, as the ambiguous stranger, gives one of his most involving performances. TH [video] DVD

Hayley Mills *Kathy* • Alan Bates *The man* • Bernard Lee *Mr Bostock* • Norman Bird *Eddie* • Diane Holgate *Nan* • Alan Barnes *Charles* • Roy Holder *Jackie* • Barry Dean *Raymond* ■ *Dir* Bryan Forbes • *Scr* Keith Waterhouse, Willis Hall, from the novel by Mary Hayley Bell

Whistle Stop ★★

Crime melodrama 1946 · US · BW · 83mins

One of three American films made by the Paris-based Russian Léonide Moguy, this is a complicated crime farrago involving George Raft, Tom Conway, Victor McLaglen and – as the catalyst that sets cross and double-cross in motion – Ava Gardner. Having left gambler-lover Raft for the big city, Gardner returns and takes up with club owner Conway, whereupon McLaglen enlists Raft in a scheme to bump off Conway. Formula crime fodder. RK

George Raft *Kenny Veech* • Ava Gardner *Mary* • Victor McLaglen *Gitlo* • Tom Conway *Lew* • Jorja Curtright *Fran* ■ *Dir* Léonide Moguy • *Scr* Philip Yordan, from the novel by Maritta Wolff • *Music* Dimitri Tiomkin [Dmitri Tiomkin]

The Whistler ★★★

Mystery 1944 · US · BW · 60mins

This is the first instalment in Columbia's B-movie series, culled from a long-running radio show in which a whistling omniscient narrator introduced the weekly mystery. A doughty star of the silent era, Richard Dix eked out his twilight years in seven of the eight films (with Michael Duane taking over for the final entry). Here Dix hires killer Don Costello to finish him off after his wife drowns – only for the missus to turn up and the unreachable J Carrol Naish to inherit responsibility for the hit after Costello is killed. Director William Castle keeps the story rattling along. DP

Richard Dix *Earl Conrad* • J Carrol Naish *The killer* • Gloria Stuart *Alice Walker* • Alan Dinehart *Gorman* • Don Costello (1) *Lefty Vigran* • Joan Woodbury *Toni Vigran* • Otto Forrest *The Whistler* ■ *Dir* William Castle • *Scr* Eric Taylor, from a story by J Donald Wilson, from the radio series by J Donald Wilson

Whistling in Brooklyn ★★

Crime comedy 1943 · US · BW · 86mins

The third and last of a set of breezy comedies starring Red Skelton (following *Whistling in the Dark* and *Whistling in Dixie*), this features more escapades of Skelton's radio sleuth. He is suspected of being a mystery killer and is chased by both cops and villain. The comic highlights include his masquerade as a bearded baseball player during a Dodgers game and a scare sequence on top of a descending freight elevator. AE

Red Skelton *Wally Benton* • Ann Rutherford *Carol Lambert* • Jean Rogers *Jean Pringle* • "Rags" Ragland [Rags Ragland] *Chester* • Ray Collins *Grover Kendall* • Henry O'Neill *Inspector Holcomb* • William Frawley *Detective Ramsey* • Sam Levene *Creeper* ■ *Dir* S Sylvan Simon • *Scr* Nat Perrin, Wilkie Mahoney, Stanley Roberts (uncredited)

Whistling in Dixie ★★★ U

Crime comedy 1942 · US · BW · 73mins

The sequel to MGM's surprise 1941 hit *Whistling in the Dark* has Red Skelton returning as the radio detective known as "The Fox". This time he's off to marry fiancée Ann Rutherford but their sojourn in the south is interrupted by the search for some Confederate gold. While not up to the standard of the similar Bob Hope comedy thrillers, it still has some good moments. DF

Red Skelton *Wally Benton* • Ann Rutherford *Carol Lambert* • George Bancroft *Sheriff Claude Stagg* • Guy Kibbee *Judge George Lee* • Diana Lewis *Ellamae Downs* • Peter Whitney *Frank V Bailie* • "Rags" Ragland [Rags Ragland] *Chester Conway/Lester Conway* ■ *Dir* S Sylvan Simon • *Scr* Nat Perrin, Wilkie Mahoney, Lawrence Hazard (uncredited), Jonathan Latimer (uncredited)

Whistling in the Dark ★★★

Crime comedy 1941 · US · BW · 77mins

Red Skelton gets his first starring role playing a writer and star of a radio series in which his character, "The Fox", unravels seemingly unsolveable crimes. Skelton is kidnapped by an unscrupulous religious cult, headed by Conrad Veidt, and forced into

W

concocting a perfect murder for them so they can get their hands on a million-dollar inheritance. Gripping, clever and funny, the film was a surprise success for MGM and spawned two sequels. RT

Red Skelton *Wally Benton* • Conrad Veidt *Joseph Jones* • Ann Rutherford *Carol Lambert* • Virginia Grey *"Fran" Post* • Rags Ragland *Sylvester* • Henry O'Neill *Philip Post* • Eve Arden *"Buzz" Baker* ■ *Dir* S Sylvan Simon • *Scr* Robert MacGonigle, Harry Clork, Albert Mannheimer, from the play by Laurence Gross, Edward Childs Carpenter

The White Angel ★★★

Biographical drama 1936 · US · BW · 75mins

An old-fashioned, thoroughly workmanlike and somewhat sentimentally idealised biopic of Florence Nightingale, heroine of the Crimean War. The casting of beautiful, sophisticated Kay Francis, more at home in the drawing rooms of Park Avenue than the bloody field hospitals of Scutari, is an initial impediment to credibility, but the star makes a noble effort, and the distressing war scenes are powerfully effective. RK

Kay Francis *Florence Nightingale* • Ian Hunter *Fuller* • Donald Woods *Charles Cooper* • Nigel Bruce *Dr West* • Donald Crisp *Dr Hunt* • Henry O'Neill *Dr Scott* ■ *Dir* William Dieterle • *Scr* Mordaunt Shairp

White Angel ★★ 18

Thriller 1993 · UK · Colour · 95mins

This minor addition to the serial-killer cycle was made by Chris Jones and Genevieve Jolliffe, Britain's youngest film-makers in the early 1990s. The story concerns an American crime writer and her dentist lodger who both, as it transpires, have something to hide. Shot, all too obviously, on a shoestring, in and around a house in Ruislip Manor, the thriller offers very little psychological motivation, but at least it isn't stalk-and-slash. DM. Contains violence and swearing.

Harriet Robinson *Ellen Carter* • Peter Firth *Leslie Steckler* • Don Henderson *Inspector Taylor* • Anne Catherine Arton *Mik* • Harry Miller *Alan Smith* • Joe Collins *Graham* • Caroline Staunton *Steckler's wife* • Mark Stevens *Carter's husband* ■ *Dir* Chris Jones • *Scr* Chris Jones, Genevieve Jolliffe

The White Balloon ★★★★ U

Drama 1995 · Iran · Colour · 80mins

Scripted by Abbas Kiarostami, who shared the Palme d'Or at Cannes for *The Taste of Cherries* in 1997, this delightful picture from director Jafar Panahi won the Camera d'Or at the same festival in 1995 for the best newcomer. Told in real time, this is a journey of discovery. As the seven-year-old experiencing the mysteries of the bazaar for the first time, Aida Mohammadkhani gives a remarkable performance, but it's Panahi's ability to convey both what she sees and what she feels that makes this deceptively simple film so miraculous. DP. In Farsi with English subtitles.

Aida Mohammadkhani *Razieh* • Mohsen Kafili *Ali* • Fereshteh Sadr Orfani *Mother* • Anna Bourkowska *Old woman* ■ *Dir* Jafar Panahi • *Scr* Abbas Kiarostami

W

White Banners ★★★

Drama 1938 · US · BW · 88mins

This earnest morality tale seems less impressive today than it did to audiences on release, despite fine direction by Edmund Goulding and an Oscar-nominated star performance by Fay Bainter (who also won in the supporting category the same year for *Jezebel*). She plays a mystic figure who comes into the home of inventor Claude Rains and his family, and has a profound effect on their lives. TV

Claude Rains *Paul Ward* • Fay Bainter *Hannah Parmalee* • Jackie Cooper *Peter Trimble* • Bonita Granville *Sally Ward* • Henry O'Neill *Sam Trimble* • Kay Johnson *Marcia Ward* • James Stephenson *Thomas Bradford* • J Farrell MacDonald *Dr Thompson* ■ *Dir* Edmund Goulding • *Scr* Lenore Coffee, Cameron Rogers, Abem Finkel, from the novel by Lloyd C Douglas

The White Buffalo ★

Western 1977 · US · Colour · 97mins

This attempt at an allegorical western features Charles Bronson as Wild Bill Hickok, returning to the plains in search of the white buffalo that he dreams of every night. Deep, deep down there is the potential for a meditative and mythical western but almost everything about this doesn't work. A real clinker. AT

Charles Bronson *James Otis/Wild Bill Hickok* • Jack Warden *Charlie Zane* • Will Sampson *Chief Crazy Horse/"Worm"* • Kim Novak *Poker Jenny Schermerhorn* • Clint Walker *Whistling Jack Kileen* • Stuart Whitman *Winifred Coxy* • Slim Pickens *Abel Pickney* • John Carradine *Amos Briggs* ■ *Dir* J Lee Thompson • *Scr* Richard Sale, from his novel

White Cargo ★★

Drama 1942 · US · BW · 87mins

Walter Pidgeon runs a British government rubber plantation in the heart of the Congo, with only drink-sodden doctor Frank Morgan, disillusioned clergyman Henry O'Neill, and his newly-arrived assistant Richard Carlson for company. Emotions boil over when Carlson falls for Hedy Lamarr, a dangerously devious native sexpot. Although the atmosphere is strong and the film's early sequences are quite interesting, the descent into absurdity is total, making the result unintentionally hilarious. RK

Hedy Lamarr *Tondelayo* • Walter Pidgeon *Harry Witzel* • Frank Morgan *Doctor* • Richard Carlson *Langford* • Reginald Owen *Skipper* • Henry O'Neill *Rev Roberts* • Bramwell Fletcher *Wilbur Ashley* ■ *Dir* Richard Thorpe • *Scr* Leon Gordon, from his play, from the novel *Hell's Playground* by Ida Vera Simonton

White Cargo ★ 15

Comedy 1973 · UK · Colour · 73mins

A rare feature film appearance from TV star David Jason, this is a daft comedy in which a dithering civil servant becomes overinvolved in the plight of a Soho stripper. It's a lacklustre strike at "fish out of water" territory that soon descends into ludicrous farce. SH

David Jason *Albert Toddey* • Hugh Lloyd *Chumley* • Imogen Hassall *Stella* • Tim Barrett *Fosdyke* • Dave Prowse *Harry* • Raymond Cross *Dudley* • John Barber *Special agent* ■ *Dir* Ray Selfe • *Scr* Ray Selfe, David McGillivray, from a story by Ray Selfe

White Chicks ★ 15

Comedy 2004 · US · Colour · 110mins

In this terminally lowbrow comedy, real-life siblings Marlon and Shawn Wayans play FBI agents and brothers. To save their jobs after messing up a drugs bust, the dim-witted duo are forced to don latex masks, flesh-tight miniskirts and receive a full-body blanching in to impersonate and protect a pair of spoilt, brattish socialites. The central inter-racial, cross-dressing idea might have provided a clever engine for risk-taking humour, but this isn't even mildy amusing. LF DVD

Shawn Wayans *Kevin Copeland* • Marlon Wayans *Marcus Copeland* • Jaime King *Heather Vandergeld* • Frankie Faison *Section Chief Elliott Gordon* • Lochlyn Munro *Agent Jake Harper* • John Heard *Warren Vandergeld* • Busy Philipps *Karen* • Terry Crews *Latrell Spencer* • Brittany Daniel *Megan Vandergeld* ■ *Dir* Keenen Ivory Wayans • *Scr* Keenen Ivory Wayans, Marlon Wayans, Shawn Wayans, Andy McElfresh, Michael Anthony Snowden, Xavier Cook, from a story by Keenen Ivory Wayans, Marlon Wayans, Shawn Wayans

White Christmas ★★★★ U

Musical 1954 · US · Colour · 115mins

This partial remake of the 1942 film *Holiday Inn* – the Bing Crosby movie that gave the world the Irving Berlin song *White Christmas* – provided Paramount with an opportunity to introduce its new screen process Vistavision. Crosby's *Holiday Inn* partner Fred Astaire wasn't available, and Donald O'Connor pulled out, so Danny Kaye reluctantly agreed to second billing to co-star with Crosby, in what proved to be a fortuitous move. Kaye is superb, especially in his knockout dance routine with Vera-Ellen. Veteran Michael Curtiz directed, rightly embracing the sentiment rather than keeping it at bay. TS DVD

Bing Crosby *Bob Wallace* • Danny Kaye *Phil Davis* • Rosemary Clooney *Betty* • Vera-Ellen *Judy* • Dean Jagger *General Waverly* • Mary Wickes *Emma* • John Brascia *Joe* • Anne Whitfield *Susan* • Sig Rumann [Sig Ruman] *Landlord* ■ *Dir* Michael Curtiz • *Scr* Norman Krasna, Norman Panama, Melvin Frank

The White Cliffs of Dover ★★★ U

Wartime drama 1944 · US · BW · 124mins

This is a long, lavish, starry, and tear-jerkingly sentimental account of a woman's courage through the First World War, in which her husband is killed, and the Second World War, during which her dying soldier son (Peter Lawford) is brought in to the hospital where she works as a Red Cross nurse. One of several admiring, pro-British flag-wavers from MGM, the film stars Irene Dunne as the indestructible heroine. RK

Irene Dunne *Lady Susan Dunn Ashwood* • Alan Marshal *Sir John Ashwood* • Roddy McDowall *John Ashwood II, as a boy* • Frank Morgan *Hiram Porter Dunn* • Van Johnson *Sam Bennett* • C Aubrey Smith *Colonel Walter Forsythe* • Gladys Cooper *Lady Jean Ashwood* • Peter Lawford *John Ashwood II, as a young man* • Elizabeth Taylor *Betsy Kenney, aged 10* ■ *Dir* Clarence Brown • *Scr* Claudine West, Jan Lustig, George Froeschel, from the poem by Alice Duer Miller, with additional poetry by Robert Nathan

White Corridors ★★★ U

Medical drama 1951 · UK · BW · 101mins

This Midlands-set medical tale charts the various comings and goings of doctors and patients. The central plot involves doctor James Donald who, perfecting a serum for treating a blood disease, infects himself – thus requiring the intervention of the doctor who loves him (Googie Withers). While it may sound like a hokey soap opera, it is actually a well-made British A-feature, realistically played by a large and excellent cast that includes a number of well-known faces. RK

James Donald *Neil Marriner* • Googie Withers *Sophie Dean* • Godfrey Tearle *Groom Sr* • Jack Watling *Dick Groom* • Petula Clark *Joan Shepherd* • Moira Lister *Dolly Clark* • Barry Jones *Shoesmith* ■ *Dir* Pat Jackson • *Scr* Pat Jackson, Jan Read, from the novel *Yeoman's Hospital* by Helen Ashton

The White Dawn ★★★★

Period adventure drama
1974 · US · Colour and BW · 109mins

A group of whalers are shipwrecked and left stranded among an Inuit tribe in 1896. It's a study of cultural collision, done with an almost wordless script, and a paean to the beauties of the Arctic. Part Herman Melville, part Jack London and part "new-age" San Francisco, this stirring drama knocks spots off most other films of the genre. Never condescending and remarkably open-minded about the conflict between nature's and capitalism's hunters, it's superbly filmed on Frobisher Bay and well acted by a cast that must have endured a lot of discomfort. AT. In Inuktitut and English with subtitles.

Warren Oates *Billy* • Timothy Bottoms *Daggett* • Louis Gossett Jr *Portagee* • Simonie Kopapik *Sarkak* • Joanasie Salomonie *Kangiak* • Pilitak *Neevee* ■ *Dir* Philip Kaufman • *Scr* James Houston, Tom Rickman, Martin Ransohoff, from the novel by James Houston • *Cinematographer* Michael Chapman

White Dog ★★★★ 15

Drama 1981 · US · Colour · 85mins

In his first Hollywood movie in years, director Sam Fuller tackled the controversial subject of racism in a story about a German shepherd dog that has been trained to kill black people. Kristy McNichol plays an actress who adopts the ostensibly docile dog and uncovers its terrible history after it attacks a rapist in her home. This was never released theatrically in the US and eventually found its way on to cable in a watered down version. Fuller turned his back on Hollywood, taking the complete version to Europe where it was hailed as a masterpiece by some critics. TH. Contains violence and swearing.

Kristy McNichol *Julie Sawyer* • Paul Winfield *Keys* • Burl Ives *Carruthers* • Jameson Parker *Roland Gray* • Lynne Moody *Molly* • Marshall Thompson *Director* • Bob Minor *Joe* ■ *Dir* Samuel Fuller • *Scr* Samuel Fuller, Curtis Hanson, from the novella and *Life* magazine article by Romain Gary • *Cinematographer* Bruce Surtees • *Music* Ennio Morricone

White Fang ★★

Adventure 1936 · US · BW · 70mins

The novel *White Fang* was Jack London's sequel to his hugely popular *Call of the Wild,* filmed by Fox in 1935 with Clark Gable and Loretta Young. Writer Gene Fowler scripted both movies as outdoor adventures aimed at the family audience, though this second movie doesn't boast the same fine cast or the same primitive flair. Michael Whalen makes a pallid hero and Jean Muir is the love interest, her only rival the wolf of the title. AT

Michael Whalen *Gordon Scott/Scotty* • Jean Muir *Sylvia Burgess* • Slim Summerville *Slats Magee* • Charles Winninger *Doc McFane* • John Carradine *Beauty Smith* • Jane Darwell *Maud Mahoney* • Thomas Beck *Hal Burgess* • Joseph Herrick *Kobi* ■ *Dir* David Butler • *Scr* Gene Fowler, Hal Long, SG Duncan, from the novel by Jack London

White Fang ★★★ PG

Adventure 1991 · US · Colour · 104mins

Jack London's ferocious story about the half-wolf in the Klondike is tamed *Lassie*-style by Disney, with most of the savagery squeezed out. Ethan Hawke, with dubious partners Klaus Maria Brandauer and Seymour Cassel, is the young gold prospector who seeks to establish a prosperous claim. The film may be a bit of a letdown for previously Oscar-nominated Brandauer, but he turns a minor role into a major one. TH DVD

Klaus Maria Brandauer *Alex* • Ethan Hawke *Jack* • Seymour Cassel *Skunker* • Susan Hogan *Belinda* • James Remar *Beauty* • Bill Moseley *Luke* • Clint B Youngreen *Tinker* • Pius Savage *Grey Beaver* ■ *Dir* Randal Kleiser • *Scr* Jeanne Rosenberg, Nick Thiel, David Fallon, from the novel by Jack London

White Fang 2: Myth of the White Wolf ★★ U

Adventure 1994 · US · Colour · 101mins

Ethan Hawke puts in an uncredited appearance at the start of this handsome Disney adventure, which, unlike its predecessor, owes little or nothing to the much-loved novel by Jack London. Scott Bairstow steps into Hawke's shoes as he abandons the Alaskan gold fields and, along with his beautiful canine companion, searches for a herd of lost caribou for a tribe of starving Indians. The soppy romance won't do much for the majority of younger viewers, but they should find the tribal mythology and mysticism fascinating. DP

Scott Bairstow *Henry Casey* • Charmaine Craig *Lily Joseph* • Al Harrington *Moses Joseph* • Anthony Michael Ruivivar *Peter* • Victoria Racimo *Katrin* • Alfred Molina *Reverend Leland Drury* • Ethan Hawke *Jack* • Geoffrey Lewis *Heath* ■ *Dir* Ken Olin • *Scr* David Fallon

White Feather ★★ U

Western 1955 · US · Colour · 102mins

Gauche Robert Wagner is the government surveyor trying to persuade the Cheyenne that living on a reservation is their best option, but they find his resolutely 1950s' cool bravado as hard to take as we do. Jeffrey Hunter looks equally uncomfortable as a brave and cavalryman John Lund acts throughout as though he'd rather be somewhere else. Yet, despite the poor casting, Lucien Ballard's handsome CinemaScope photography gives this film all the dignity it needs. TS

Robert Wagner *Josh Tanner* • John Lund *Colonel Lindsay* • Debra Paget *Appearing Day* • Jeffrey Hunter *Little Dog* • Eduard Franz *Chief Broken Hand* • Noah Beery Jr *Lieutenant Ferguson* • Virginia Leith *Ann Magruder* • Emile Meyer *Magruder* ■ *Dir* Robert Webb [Robert D Webb] • *Scr* Delmer Daves, Leo Townsend, from a story by John Prebble

White Heat ★★★★★ 15

Classic crime drama
1949 · US · BW · 109mins

"Made it, Ma! Top of the world!" shrieks a demented James Cagney from the top of an oil tank before going out in a blaze of vainglory. Directed by Raoul Walsh, this is one of the greatest of all gangster pictures, a nightmarish excursion into the maladjusted mind of Arthur Cody Jarrett, a thug who sits on his mother's knee, steals and kills for pure pleasure, and probably sucks his thumb in private. All the major gangster heroes of the 1930s had their psychological problems, but here Cagney is a whole library of Freudian theory put through the blender, and the poor lad suffers from epilepsy to boot. Operatic, sinisterly funny and utterly compelling. AT DVD

James Cagney *Arthur Cody Jarrett* • Virginia Mayo *Verna Jarrett* • Edmond O'Brien *Hank Fallon/Vic Pardo* • Margaret Wycherly *Ma Jarrett* • Steve Cochran *"Big Ed" Somers* • John Archer *Philip Evans* • Wally Cassell *Giovanni "Cotton" Valetti* • Mickey Knox *Het Kohler* ■ *Dir* Raoul Walsh • *Scr* Ivan Goff, Ben Roberts, from a story by Virginia Kellogg • *Cinematographer* Sid Hickox

White Hunter, Black Heart ★★★★ PG

Adventure drama
1990 · US · Colour · 107mins

Clint Eastwood's ambitious film is a thinly veiled account of the making of John Huston's *The African Queen*, already well documented in books by Katharine Hepburn and screenwriter Peter Viertel. As "Huston", Eastwood is just marvellous – aristocratic, bombastic and so obsessed with hunting and killing an elephant that his movie-making is left on the back burner. Beautifully filmed on location in Zimbabwe, the movie has pace, drama, a genuine sense of adventure and an astutely critical eye for the dying vestiges of British imperialism. AT. Contains violence, swearing.

Clint Eastwood *John Wilson* • Jeff Fahey *Pete Verrill* • George Dzundza *Paul Landers* • Alun Armstrong *Ralph Lockhart* • Marisa Berenson *Kay Gibson* • Timothy Spall *Hodkins* • Catherine Neilson *Irene Saunders* • Norman Lumsden *Butler George* ■ *Dir* Clint Eastwood • *Scr* Peter Viertel, James Bridges, Burt Kennedy, from the novel by Peter Viertel • *Cinematographer* Jack N Green

White Lightning ★★★ 15

Action crime thriller
1973 · US · Colour · 97mins

One of the best of Burt Reynolds's good ol' boy movies, in which he's a moonshiner whose manufacture of illicit liquor puts him up against crooked sheriff Ned Beatty. As the corrupt lawman was responsible for the death of Burt's brother, revenge is also on the menu. Director Joseph Sargent makes good use of some interesting swampland locations and keeps the drama from being too formulaic. A sequel, *Gator*, followed in 1976. TH DVD

Burt Reynolds *Gator McKlusky* • Jennifer Billingsley *Lou* • Ned Beatty *Sheriff Connors* • Bo Hopkins *Roy Boone* • Matt Clark *Dude Watson* • Louise Latham *Martha Culpepper* • Diane Ladd *Maggie* • RG Armstrong *Big Bear* ■ *Dir* Joseph Sargent • *Scr* William Norton

White Line Fever ★★★ 15

Action drama 1975 · US · Colour · 85mins

Back on civvy street after a stint in the air force, Jan-Michael Vincent buys a truck, marries his sweetheart Kay Lenz and gets started in the hauling business, only to learn that it is run by racketeers and smugglers. Refusing to bow to the system, he endangers himself by fighting corruption. The movie, convincingly played by Vincent and the supporting cast, marked a step up for director Jonathan Kaplan who handles the material extremely well. RK

Jan-Michael Vincent *Carrol Jo Hummer* • Kay Lenz *Jerri Hummer* • Slim Pickens *Duane Haller* • LQ Jones *Buck Wessle* • Don Porter *Josh Cutler* • Sam Laws *Pops* • Johnny Ray McGhee *Carnell* ■ *Dir* Jonathan Kaplan • *Scr* Ken Friedman, Jonathan Kaplan

The White Lions ★★★

Adventure 1980 · US · Colour · 96mins

Directed by Mel Stuart (*Willy Wonka and the Chocolate Factory*), this location-shot safari movie in the *Born Free* mould stars Michael York as the naturalist who takes his wife and daughter with him when he goes out to Africa to study endangered wildlife. It's too twee for comfort, but children who love natural-history TV programmes should like it. TH

Michael York *Chris McBride* • Glynnis O'Connor *Mrs McBride* • Donald Moffat *Vreeland* • Lauri Lynn Myers *Laura McBride* ■ *Dir* Mel Stuart • *Scr* Corey Blechman, Peter Dixon

White Mane ★★★★

Adventure drama 1952 · Fr · BW · 47mins

Winner of the Prix Jean Vigo, Albert Lamorisse's third film may not be as well known as *The Red Balloon*, but it is still a charming study of the all-too-fleeting wonder of childhood. Young Alain Emery gives a spirited performance as the kid whose daily routine of fishing and poaching with his grandfather is interrupted by the appearance of a proud white stallion, which defies all attempts by the local ranchers to capture it. With the Camargue marshlands emphasising the wildness of both the horse and his boy, this is a poetic and truly inspiring tribute to the beauty of nature. DP. A French language film.

Alain Emery *Folco* • Pascal Lamorisse • Frank Silvera ■ *Dir/Scr* Albert Lamorisse

White Man's Burden ★★★ 15

Fantasy drama 1995 · US · Colour · 85mins

This reversed-reality drama is set in an alternate Los Angeles where blacks hold all the positions of power and influence, and where whites do all the menial work. John Travolta plays a blue-collar worker who, more by default than design, winds up kidnapping black boss Harry Belafonte when he calls at his mansion to protest at being unfairly fired. It's a neat idea, less fully realised than it might have been. There are good performances from the two stars, though. DA. Contains swearing and some violence.

John Travolta *Louis Pinnock* • Harry Belafonte *Thaddeus Thomas* • Kelly Lynch *Marsha Pinnock* • Margaret Avery (2) *Megan Thomas* • Tom Bower *Stanley* • Carrie Snodgress *Josine* ■ *Dir/Scr* Desmond Nakano

White Men Can't Jump ★★★★ 15

Sports comedy drama
1992 · US · Colour · 110mins

Writer/director Ron Shelton is that rare beast: someone who can make movies with wit, warmth and perception about American sports. This is a marvellous tale of two basketball players (Wesley Snipes and Woody Harrelson) who make their living hustling fellow street players around Los Angeles. The plot is fairly simplistic, but the pleasure comes from Shelton's fizzing foul-mouthed dialogue, the charismatic performances and the superbly choreographed basketball sequences. Rosie Perez, as Harrelson's girlfriend, stays on the right side of irritating. JF. Contains violence, swearing and nudity. DVD

Wesley Snipes *Sidney Deane* • Woody Harrelson *Billy Hoyle* • Rosie Perez *Gloria Clemente* • Tyra Ferrell *Rhonda Deane* • Cylk Cozart *Robert* • Kadeem Hardison *Junior* • Ernest Harden Jr *George* • John Marshall Jones *Walter* ■ *Dir/Scr* Ron Shelton

White Mischief ★★★ 18

Historical drama
1987 · UK · Colour · 103mins

The less-than-wholesome traits of Kenya's scandal-ridden "Happy Valley" crowd in the 1940s are nicely delineated, in all their dissolute, gin-swilling, expat glory, by director Michael Radford. Based on a true story about the murder of a promiscuous aristocrat who was servicing half of the valley's bored ladies, this rather over-egged drama has no one in who elicits any sympathy. Charles Dance makes a believable stud, however, and Greta Scacchi is gorgeous, even if Joss Ackland overacts as her cuckolded husband. SH. Contains violence, swearing, sex scenes, nudity.

Charles Dance *Josslyn Hay, Earl of Erroll* • Greta Scacchi *Diana* • Joss Ackland *Sir John "Jock" Delves Broughton* • Sarah Miles *Alice de Janze* • John Hurt *Gilbert Colvile* • Geraldine Chaplin *Nina Soames* • Ray McAnally *Morris* • Trevor Howard *Jack Soames* • Hugh Grant *Hugh* ■ *Dir* Michael Radford • *Scr* Michael Radford, Jonathan Gems, from the book by James Fox

White Nights ★★★ U

Drama 1957 · It/Fr · BW · 98mins

Based on a Dostoyevsky story, this touching fantasy concerns a meek and lonely clerk who falls deeply in love with a girl on a bridge – she goes there every night to meet her own lover, a sailor, who has promised to return but never does. This movie marked a radical departure for the arch neorealist and communist Luchino Visconti, who treats it rather like a Fellini film. It was staged on deliberately artificial sets – supposedly the canals of Livorno – and has the ambience of a dream. Marcello Mastroianni gives one of his best performances of the 1950s as the doomed clerk. AT. In Italian with English subtitles.

Maria Schell *Natalia* • Marcello Mastroianni *Mario* • Jean Marais *Lodger* • Clara Calamai *Prostitute* • Marcella Rovena *Housewife* • Maria Zanolli *Housekeeper* ■ *Dir* Luchino Visconti • *Scr* Luchino Visconti, Suso Cecchi D'Amico, from the story *Belye Nochi* by Fyodor Mikhailovich Dostoyevsky

White Nights ★★★ 15

Political thriller 1985 · US · Colour · 130mins

This entertaining blend of ballet and bullets stars dancer Mikhail Baryshnikov as a bolshy Bolshoi-er who finds himself back in the USSR when the plane he's defecting on is forced to make a (spectacular) crash-landing. Fellow hoofer Gregory Hines co-stars, as an expatriate tap-star who helps him to re-defect. Not the world's most credible plot, but Baryshnikov is good and there are stunning dance and action sequences. DA

Mikhail Baryshnikov *Nikolai "Kolya" Rodchenko* • Gregory Hines *Raymond Greenwood* • Jerzy Skolimowski *Colonel Chaiko* • Helen Mirren *Galina Ivanova* • Geraldine Page *Anne Wyatt* • Isabella Rossellini *Darya Greenwood* • John Glover *Wynn Scott* ■ *Dir* Taylor Hackford • *Scr* James Goldman, Eric Hughes, from a story by James Goldman

White Noise ★★ 15

Supernatural thriller
2004 · UK/Can/US · Colour · 93mins

Michael Keaton obsessively communicates with his deceased wife via paranormal messages in this slow-moving supernatural thriller. Captured as "white noise" on his TV and other electronic devices, the eerie snippets appear to be guiding him to save others from death. What unfolds is a dangerous race against time that is meant to be twisting and dramatic but is actually rather dull. SF DVD

Michael Keaton *Jonathan Rivers* • Deborah Kara Unger *Sarah Tate* • Chandra West *Anna Rivers* • Ian McNeice *Raymond Price* • Sarah Strange *Jane* • Nicholas Elia *Mike Rivers* • Mike Dopud *Detective Smits* ■ *Dir* Geoffrey Sax • *Scr* Niall Johnson

White of the Eye ★★★ 18

Psychological thriller
1986 · UK · Colour · 106mins

Donald Cammell ended a decade-long exile from the director's chair with this bizarre, yet decidedly disturbing thriller. The Indian mysticism is pretty half-baked, the symbolism is anything but subtle and the Steadicam work is overly intrusive. But Cammell creates an atmosphere of real menace as he delves beneath the surface calm of a sleepy former mining town in Arizona. He's well served by a cast that never quite made the front rank. DP. Contains violence and swearing.

David Keith *Paul White* • Cathy Moriarty *Joan White* • Art Evans *Detective Charles Mendoza* • Alan Rosenberg *Mike Desantos* • Alberta Watson *Ann Mason* • Michael Green *Phil Ross* • Danko Gurovich *Arnold White* • William G Schilling *Harold Gideon* • China Cammell [China Kong] *Ruby Hoy* ■ *Dir* Donald Cammell • *Scr* China Cammell [China Kong], Donald Cammell, from the novel *Mrs White* by Margaret Tracy

W

White Oleander ★★★ 12

Drama 2002 · US · Colour · 104mins

It would have been easy to rework Janet Fitch's bestseller – a teenager is fostered out after her artist mother is jailed for murdering her lover – as a stellar TV movie, but director Peter Kosminsky rejects the melodrama-by-numbers option and uses attention-grabbing imagery to convey much of the confusion Alison Lohman feels after Michelle Pfeiffer's arrest. His assured grasp of structure and pacing, and some accomplished acting, ensure that we only gradually come to appreciate the shifting nature of their relationship, as Lohman learns to think for herself while living with Robin Wright Penn's trailer-park Christian, Renée Zellweger's touchingly tragic actress and Svetlana Efremova's wily hustler. DP DVD

Alison Lohman *Astrid Magnussen* • Robin Wright Penn *Starr Thomas* • Michelle Pfeiffer *Ingrid Magnussen* • Renée Zellweger [Renee Zellweger] *Claire Richards* • Billy Connolly *Barry Kolker* • Svetlana Efremova *Rena Grushenka* • Patrick Fugit *Paul Trout* • Cole Hauser *Ray* • Noah Wyle *Mark Richards* ■ *Dir* Peter Kosminsky • *Scr* Mary Agnes Donoghue, from the novel by Janet Fitch

White Palace ★★★★ 18

Romantic drama 1990 · US · Colour · 98mins

James Spader plays a youngish middle-class ad man who falls for 40-something waitress Susan Sarandon, much to the dismay of his peers. Spader and Sarandon spark off each other superbly, making the most of a mature script that intelligently explores class and sexuality in modern America. Luis Mandoki's direction is admirably level-headed, and he successfully sidesteps the usual clichés and melodramatics. JF. Contains swearing and sex scenes. DVD

Susan Sarandon *Nora Baker* • James Spader *Max Baron* • Jason Alexander *Neil Horowitz* • Kathy Bates *Rosemary Powers* • Eileen Brennan *Judy* • Steven Hill *Sol Horowitz* • Corey Parker *Larry Klugman* ■ *Dir* Luis Mandoki • *Scr* Ted Tally, Alvin Sargent, from the novel by Glenn Savan

The White Parade ★★★

Medical drama 1934 · US · BW · 83mins

Set in a school for trainee nurses in the American Midwest, the focus is on Loretta Young, whose dedication to her calling is challenged by romantic involvement with wealthy Bostonian John Boles, who forces her to choose between him and her career. Young is excellent in a film that combines an almost documentary approach with old-fashioned romantic soap opera. Directed by Irving Cummings, it's entertaining enough and was a big box-office success on release, but its Oscar nomination as best picture is something of a surprise. RK

Loretta Young *June Arden* • John Boles *Ronald Hall III* • Dorothy Wilson *Zita Scofield* • Muriel Kirkland *Glenda Farley* • Astrid Allwyn *Gertrude Mack* • Frank Conroy *Doctor Thorne* • Jane Darwell *Sailor Roberts* ■ *Dir* Irving Cummings • *Scr* Sonya Levien, Ernest Pascal, from the novel by Rian James, adapted by Rian James, Jesse Lasky Jr

White Room ★★★

Drama 1990 · Can · Colour · 93mins

This bizarre suburban fairy tale is about a peeping tom who witnesses a singer's rape and murder, then becomes entangled with a strange woman he meets at the singer's funeral and who lives in a gingerbread house. Directed by Patricia Rozema, the film is crammed with colour codings and metaphors. The over-intellectualisation won't appeal to all tastes but is evidence of a mind at work. DA

Kate Nelligan *Jane* • Maurice Godin *Norm* • Margot Kidder *Madelaine X* • Sheila McCarthy *Zelda* • Barbara Gordon *Mrs Gentle* • Nicky Guadagni *Narrator* ■ *Dir/Scr* Patricia Rozema

White Sands ★★★ 15

Thriller 1992 · US · Colour · 97mins

Mega-black doings in New Mexico in a *film noir*, which takes to the hills when deputy sheriff Willem Dafoe finds half-a-million mysterious dollars in a suitcase belonging to a dead FBI agent. Roger Donaldson's direction loses focus when Dafoe meets up with arms dealer Mickey Rourke and his society girlfriend Mary Elizabeth Mastrantonio; while the plot's twists and turns become entangled, there's still enough intriguing action to keep us involved. AT. Contains swearing, violence. DVD

Willem Dafoe *Ray Dolezal* • Mary Elizabeth Mastrantonio *Lane Bodine* • Mickey Rourke *Gorman Lennox* • Sam Jackson [Samuel L Jackson] *Greg Meeker* • M Emmet Walsh *Bert Gibson* • Mimi Rogers *Molly Dolezal* ■ *Dir* Roger Donaldson • *Scr* Daniel Pyne

White Savage ★★★

Fantasy adventure
1943 · US · Colour · 75mins

Following the success of *Arabian Nights* (1942), Universal realised the appeal of undemanding Technicolor escapism to war-weary audiences and dispatched the reunited quartet of Jon Hall, Maria Montez, Sabu and Turhan Bey to a South Pacific island for this gloriously camp island adventure. A variety of insurmountable obstacles (including a showstopping earthquake) litter the path to true love, but no one really doubts that Sabu will eventually persuade princess Montez that villain Tomas Gomez is the rogue after the treasure in her temple pool and not Hall's rugged shark fisherman. DP

Jon Hall *Kaloe* • Maria Montez *Princess Tahia* • Sabu *Orano* • Don Terry *Gris* • Turhan Bey *Tamara* • Thomas Gomez *Sam Miller* • Sidney Toler *Wong* ■ *Dir* Arthur Lubin • *Scr* Richard Brooks, from a story by Peter Milne

White Shadows in the South Seas ★★★

Drama 1928 · US · BW · 88mins

MGM sent acclaimed documentary director Robert Flaherty and rising outdoor action director WS Van Dyke to shoot a South Seas adventure on location at a time when real exotic settings had huge box-office appeal. Flaherty resigned early on and Van Dyke made his reputation with this pictorially magnificent, sombre story of a white trader corrupting pagans, in which a small cast worked well with native performers. The studio then decided to launch the film as its first sound release, adding some crude dialogue, sound effects and music score, and these now have a quaint charm although criticised for their technical shortcomings at the time. AE

Monte Blue *Lloyd* • Raquel Torres *Faraway* • Robert Anderson (1) *Sebastian* ■ *Dir* WS Van Dyke • *Scr* Jack Cunningham, John Colton, Ray Doyle, from the novel by Frederick O'Brien • *Cinematographers* Clyde De Vinna • *Cinematographer* George Nagle, Bob Roberts

The White Sheik ★★★ U

Romantic comedy drama
1951 · It · BW · 83mins

Originally devised by Michelangelo Antonioni (who retained a story credit), Federico Fellini's first solo outing not only lampoons bourgeois sensibilities, but also the photo-romance magazines that did a roaring trade in the 1950s. Arriving in Rome for her honeymoon, Brunella Bovo ditches husband Leopoldo Trieste's carefully planned itinerary in order to meet both her favourite fumetti star, Alberto Sordi, and the Pope. Vital to this sympathetic study of shattered illusions is Fellini's mischievous sense of fantasy, but Sordi's performance as the dissolute, hen-pecked idol is also top drawer. A key cinematic stepping-stone. DP. In Italian with English subtitles.

Alberto Sordi *Fernando Rivoli, "The White Sheik"* • Brunella Bovo *Wanda Cavalli* • Leopoldo Trieste *Ivan Cavalli* • Giulietta Masina *Cabiria* ■ *Dir* Federico Fellini • *Scr* Federico Fellini, Tullio Pinelli, Ennio Flaiano, from a story by Federico Fellini, Tullio Pinelli, from an idea by Michelangelo Antonioni

The White Sister ★★★

Silent romantic drama
1923 · US · BW · 143mins

After the death of her father, Italian aristocrat Lillian Gish is thrown out of the ancestral home and cheated of her inheritance by her vindictive sister. Hearing that Italian army officer Ronald Colman, whom she loves, has been killed, she becomes a nun, only for Colman to reappear and attempt to prise her out of the convent. An impressive silent drama, unusual for its time in dealing with religion against a contemporary background, and well-directed by Henry King (with help from the Vatican) on location in Italy. RK

Lillian Gish *Angela Chiaromonte* • Ronald Colman *Capt Giovanni Severini* • Gail Kane *Marchesa di Mola* • J Barney Sherry *Monsignor Saracinesca* • Charles Lane (1) *Prince Chiaromonte* ■ *Dir* Henry King • *Scr* George V Hobart, Charles E Whittaker, Will M Ritchey, Don Bartlett, from the novel by F Marion Crawford

The White Sister ★★

Melodrama 1933 · US · BW · 105mins

Clark Gable and Helen Hayes play the lovelorn couple, he a soldier and she his beloved who believes he has been killed in combat. But Gable returns and is totally gutted to discover that Hayes has married someone else, namely God, for she has taken her vows as a nun. Because of its profoundly religious theme, this load of tosh is wisely located in Italy. The story had been a major success as a silent film ten years earlier. AT

Helen Hayes *Angela Chiaromonte* • Clark Gable *Lt Giovanni Severi* • Lewis Stone *Prince Guido Chiaromonte* • Louise Closser Hale *Mina* • May Robson *Mother Superior* • Edward Arnold *Father Saracinesca* • Alan Edwards *Ernesto Traversi* ■ *Dir* Victor Fleming • *Scr* Donald Ogden Stewart, from the play by F Marion Crawford, Walter Hackett, from the novel by F Marion Crawford

White Squall ★★★ 12

Adventure based on a true story
1996 · US · Colour · 123mins

Neither Jeff Bridges's quiet authority nor the "in-your-face" dramatics of a killer storm can lift director Ridley Scott's attempt to remake *Top Gun* (which was directed by brother Tony) at sea. School-ship skipper Bridges gathers a group of undisciplined students aboard the brigantine *Albatross* for a voyage of self-discovery to South America. Unfortunately, this undemanding but entertaining rites-of-passage adventure takes a sudden lurch into disaster with the arrival of the storm of the title. TH. Contains swearing, brief nudity. DVD

Jeff Bridges *"Skipper" Christopher Sheldon* • Caroline Goodall *Dr Alice Sheldon* • John Savage *McCrea* • Scott Wolf *Chuck Gieg* • Jeremy Sisto *Frank Beaumont* • Ryan Phillippe *Gil Martin* • David Lascher *Robert March* ■ *Dir* Ridley Scott • *Scr* Todd Robinson

The White Stripes: Under Blackpool Lights ★★★ 12A

Concert documentary
2004 · UK/US · Colour · 80mins

Despite playing two nights at the cavernous Alexandra Palace in London, Jack and Meg White ultimately decided to release the gig from Blackpool's Empress Ballroom as the official record of their 2004 tour since it was both more intimate and immediate. The musicianship is occasionally as shaky as Dick Carruthers's agitated, atmospherically grainy camerawork, but the sheer energy of the band burns through. Some will be disappointed that the 26-song set doesn't include *Fell in Love with a Girl*, but this still amounts to a rousing resumé for the garage rockers, with White Stripes originals jostling alongside Robert Johnson blues standards and treats such as Dolly Parton's *Jolene*. DP

Dir Dick Carruthers

The White Tower ★★★ U

Drama 1950 · US · Colour · 97mins

A mountaineering drama with Glenn Ford joining a climb in the Swiss Alps. A lot of emotional baggage is carried along with the mountaineers: Ford falls for fellow climber Alida Valli, whose father was killed on the same peak; Lloyd Bridges is an arrogant former Nazi army officer; Cedric Hardwicke is an ageing British botanist; Claude Rains is a self-destructive French writer who is drunk most of the time. Despite the predictability of the symbolism and some wooden performances, there is excellent location photography. AT

Glenn Ford *Martin Ordway* • Valli [Alida Valli] *Carla Alton* • Claude Rains *Paul Delambre* • Oscar Homolka *Andreas* • Cedric Hardwicke *Nicholas Radcliffe* • Lloyd Bridges *Mr Hein* ■ *Dir* Ted Tetzlaff • *Scr* Paul Jarrico, from the novel by James Ramsay Ullman

The White Warrior ★★★ U

Period adventure
1959 · It/Yug · Colour · 85mins

This rousing rendition of the classic 19th-century adventure is elegantly directed by Italian horror maestro Riccardo Freda and ravishingly photographed by future genre genius, Mario Bava. With muscleman Steve Reeves agreeably stretching his (albeit dubbed) acting ability more than his weightlifting prowess for a change, this somewhat stilted romp delivers some low-budget epic thrills. Reeves plays a rebel chief who clashes with the Tsar's army over Caucasian land rights. The full Italian print features scenes of sadistic erotica and torture, but deleted in the edited US version. A mini-*War and Peace*, spaghetti style. AJ. Italian dialogue dubbed into English.

Steve Reeves *Hadji Murad* • Georgia Moll [Giorgia Moll] *Sultanet* • Renato Baldini *Akmet Khan* • Scilla Gabel *Princess Maria* • Gerard Herter *Prince Sergei/General Vorontzov* ■ *Dir* Riccardo Freda • *Scr* Gino De Santis, Akos Tolnay, from the novel *Khadzhi-Murat* by Leo Tolstoy

White Water Summer ★★★ 15

Action adventure 1987 · US · Colour · 85mins

This superior coming-of-age story stars Kevin Bacon as a bullyboy wilderness guide and Sean Astin as one of four kids he hikes off into the middle of nowhere to make men of them. The plot kicks in when Bacon gets badly injured and finds his life dependent on Astin, previously the main butt of his bullying. Good plot, good performances and nice scenery. DA

Kevin Bacon *Vic* • Sean Astin *Alan* • Jonathan Ward *Mitch* • KC Martel *George* • Matt Adler *Chris* • Caroline McWilliams *Virginia Block* • Charles Siebert *Jerry Block* ■ *Dir* Jeff Bleckner • *Scr* Manya Starr, Ernest Kinoy

White Wilderness ★★★ U

Drama documentary
1958 · US · Colour · 72mins

One of Walt Disney's *True-Life Adventure* series, this view of life in the Arctic was shot by nine photographers over a period of three years, catching many unique sights including the migration of the caribous, plus intriguing footage of such residents as the polar bear, the snowshoe rabbit, the walrus and the white whale. A highlight is an extended sequence revealing the truth about the "mass suicide" of lemmings. Winston Hibler's narration and the film's music score are both overdone, but the visual material is fascinating. TV

Winston Hibler *Narrator* ■ *Dir/Scr* James Algar • *Cinematographer* James R Simon

White Witch Doctor ★★★ U

Romantic adventure
1953 · US · Colour · 93mins

Nurse Susan Hayward arrives in the Congo and is taken in hand by treasure hunter Robert Mitchum. Black water fever, tribal dancing, skirmishes with the Bakuba tribe and a man-eating lion persuade them to dedicate the rest of their lives to helping the Africans. This blend of old-fashioned adventure and post-Imperial politics has the advantage of two appealing stars, some striking location work and an evocative score by Bernard Herrmann. AT

Susan Hayward *Ellen Burton* • Robert Mitchum *Lonni Douglas* • Walter Slezak *Huysman* • Mashood Ajala *Jacques* • Joseph C Narcisse *Utembo* • Elzie Emanuel *Kapuka* • Timothy Carey *Jarrett* • Otis Greene *Bakuba boy* ■ *Dir* Henry Hathaway • *Scr* Ivan Goff, Ben Roberts, from the novel by Louise A Stinetorf • *Cinematographer* Leon Shamroy

White Woman ★★★

Romantic melodrama
1933 · US · BW · 73mins

A torrid melodrama, this steamy vehicle can only be enjoyed if approached in the right spirit. Carole Lombard is a penniless showgirl, stranded in Malaya, who marries plantation owner Charles Laughton to get out of her predicament and is soon seeking true love in younger arms while her husband takes it out on the natives. The men all sweat a lot and grow designer stubble while Lombard remains expertly gowned and coiffured in this totally artificial but irresistible slice of hokum. TV

Carole Lombard *Judith Denning* • Charles Laughton *Horace H Prin* • Charles Bickford *Ballister* • Kent Taylor *David von Elst* • Percy Kilbride *Jakey* • James Bell *Hambly* • Charles B Middleton [Charles Middleton] *Fenton* ■ *Dir* Stuart Walker • *Scr* Samuel Hoffenstein, Gladys Lehman, from the play *Hangman's Whip* by Norman Reilly Raine, Frank Butler

White Zombie ★★★ PG

Horror 1932 · US · BW · 64mins

The first feature about Haiti's undead, this was a bold attempt by director Victor Halperin to break away from the endless chat of the early talkies. The long wordless passages allow an eerie atmosphere to develop as the camera glides menacingly around the jungle to the unnerving accompaniment of distant wailing. And who could be more at home in such sinister surroundings than Bela Lugosi as the evil voodoo sorcerer. The zombie make-up is devised by Jack Pierce, who created Boris Karloff's Frankenstein's monster look. DP [video]

Bela Lugosi *"Murder" Legendre* • Madge Bellamy *Madeline Short* • John Harron *Neil Parker* • Joseph Cawthorn *Dr Bruner, Missionary* • Robert Frazer *Charles Beaumont* • Clarence Muse *Coach Driver* ■ *Dir* Victor Halperin • *Scr* Garnett Weston

Whiteboys ★★ 15

Comedy 1999 · US · Colour and BW · 84mins

Lacking the cultural empathy and social insight of *Slam*, Marc Levin's wannabe comedy is little more than a long-playing promo. Performance artist Danny Hoch headlines as the Iowa teen who's a rapper at heart and heads for Chicago with homies Dash Mihok and Trevor Webber to lay some tracks, score some blow and dig some chicks. In other words, it's a white boy's hip-hop daydream (complete with fantasy sequences featuring a bewildered Snoop Dogg). DP. Contains swearing and violence. [video]

Danny Hoch *Flip* • Dash Mihok *James* • Mark Webber *Trevor* • Piper Perabo *Sara* • Eugene Byrd *Khalid* • Bonz Malone *Darius* • Snoop Dogg *Snoop Dog* ■ *Dir* Marc Levin • *Scr* Garth Belcon, Danny Hoch, Marc Levin, Richard Stratton, from a story by Garth Belcon, Danny Hoch

Whity ★★★

Melodrama 1970 · W Ger · Colour · 95mins

Shot on a spaghetti western set in Spain by Rainer Werner Fassbinder, this Deep South plantation melodrama has all the laconic intensity of Sergio Leone, the narrative rigour of classical Hollywood and the thematic resonance of Fassbinder's literary bible, Theodor Fontane's *Effi Briest*. Handsomely photographed by Michael Ballhaus and played with deliberation, the story focuses on Günther Kaufmann, a slave who acquiesces in Ron Randell's tyranny until he learns of its murderous immorality from prostitute Hanna Schygulla. DP. In German with English subtitles.

Günther Kaufmann *Whity* • Hanna Schygulla *Hanna* • Ulli Lommel *Frank* • Harry Baer *Davy* • Katrin Schaake *Katherine* • Ron Randell *Mr Nicholson* • Rainer Werner Fassbinder *Guest in saloon* ■ *Dir/Scr* Rainer Werner Fassbinder

Who? ★★

Science-fiction thriller
1974 · UK/W Ger · Colour · 93mins

This intriguing but not wholly successful sci-fi thriller attempts to probe somewhat seriously into the nature of identity. The narrative isn't helped by being told in flashback, and Elliott Gould is perhaps a little too laid-back in the lead. There is a stunning performance, however, from third-billed actor Joseph Bova as the scientist Martino, whose face has been restructured following an alleged car crash in Russia, and he alone makes this curious mix of sci-fi and spy drama worth watching. TS. Contains some swearing and sex scenes.

Elliott Gould *Rogers* • Trevor Howard *Azarin* • Joseph Bova *Martino* • Ed Grover [Edward Grover] *Finchley* • John Lehne *Haller* • James Noble *Deptford* • Lyndon Brook *Barrister* ■ *Dir* Jack Gold • *Scr* John Gould, from the novel by Algis Budrys

Who Dares Wins ★★ 18

Action adventure
1982 · UK · Colour · 119mins

Lewis Collins, managing to look stern-faced throughout, lives up to his tough-guy image in a British action movie inspired by the 1980 storming of the Iranian Embassy in London by the SAS. This is not much more than a glamorised episode of *The Professionals*, which at least had some wit and spark provided by Gordon Jackson. NF. Contains violence and swearing. [video] DVD

Lewis Collins *Captain Peter Skellen* • Judy Davis *Frankie Leith* • Richard Widmark *Secretary of State Curry* • Edward Woodward *Commander Powell* • Robert Webber *General Ira Potter* • Tony Doyle *Colonel Hadley* • John Duttine *Rod* • Kenneth Griffith *Bishop Crick* ■ *Dir* Ian Sharp • *Scr* Reginald Rose

Who Done It? ★★ U

Comedy mystery 1942 · US · BW · 78mins

Part of the abiding success of Abbott and Costello was that there were few – if any – surprises in their films. Familiarity lent contentment and Lou was always going to be put upon (but emerge triumphant) and Bud was always going to be surly. Their characters are equally familiar as two not-very-bright soda jerks with ambitions to write for radio. When they go to the station with an idea for a mystery series, the duo find themselves mixed up in a real case. Cue action and mild comedy. BB [video]

Bud Abbott *Chick Larkin* • Lou Costello *Mervyn Milgrim* • Patric Knowles *Jimmy Turner* • Louise Allbritton *Jane Little* • Thomas Gomez *Col JR Andrews* • Mary Wickes *Juliet Collins* ■ *Dir* Erle C Kenton • *Scr* Stanley Roberts, Edmund Joseph, John Grant, from a story by Stanley Roberts

Who Done It? ★★ U

Comedy 1956 · UK · BW · 78mins

Considering he was then one of Britain's most important directors, Basil Dearden might have seemed a peculiar choice for TV comic Benny Hill's sole starring venture. But Dearden adeptly judges the slapstick content of this amiable caper, in which Hill's hapless gumshoe bungles along in pursuit of eastern bloc spies David Kossoff and George Margo. Belinda Lee shows to advantage as Benny's sidekick, but this was all a bit of a come down for TEB Clarke, who had penned some of Ealing's best-known comedies. DP [video]

Benny Hill *Hugo Dill* • Belinda Lee *Frankie Mayne* • David Kossoff *Zacco* • Garry Marsh *Inspector Hancock* • George Margo *Barakov* • Ernest Thesiger *Sir Walter Finch* • Denis Shaw *Otto Stumpf* • Irene Handl *Customer* • Charles Hawtrey *Disc jockey* ■ *Dir* Basil Dearden • *Scr* TEB Clarke

Who Fears the Devil? ★★★

Fantasy 1972 · US · Colour · 89mins

A rare example, along with *Daniel and the Devil*, of a film about the Devil as perceived in American folklore – in this case a book of legends from the Carolinas. Singer Hedges Capers (in his only screen role) battles with Old Nick, who takes on various forms, all over America. There is a lot of hillbilly-cum-rock music and many familiar faces in the cast. Judged too parochial for UK cinema release, this scores marks for its beautiful photography and odd charm. DM

Severn Darden *Mr Marduke* • Sharon Henesey *Lily* • Honor Hound • Sidney Clute *Charles* • Denver Pyle *Grandpappy John* • Hedges Capers *John* ■ *Dir* John Newland • *Scr* Melvin Levy, from the novel by Manly Wade Wellman

Who Framed Roger Rabbit ★★★★★ PG

Part-animated detective comedy
1988 · US · Colour · 99mins

This whizz-bang breakthrough in mixing live action with cartoon characters won a special achievement Oscar for animator Richard Williams. It follows the adventures of private eye Bob Hoskins, who ventures into Toontown – where the cartoon personalities live – to help animated superstar Roger Rabbit, who suspects his wife of adultery. Guest appearances by a wealth of cartoon favourites adorn the tale as Hoskins's investigation leads to villain Christopher Lloyd, who's planning to cleanse Toontown of its animated inhabitants. Highlights include Hoskins's encounter with Roger's wife Jessica (voiced by Kathleen Turner) and the fantastic opening sequence. TH [video] DVD

Bob Hoskins *Eddie Valiant* • Christopher Lloyd *Judge Doom* • Joanna Cassidy *Dolores* • Charles Fleischer *Roger Rabbit/Benny the Cab/Greasy/Psycho* • Kathleen Turner *Jessica* • Amy Irving *Jessica (singing voice)* • Stubby Kaye *Marvin Acme* • Alan Tilvern *RK Maroon* • Mel Blanc ■ *Dir* Robert Zemeckis • *Scr* Jeffrey Price, Peter S Seaman, from the novel *Who Censored Roger Rabbit?* by Gary K Wolf • *Cinematographer* Dean Cundey

Who Has Seen the Wind ★★

Drama 1977 · Can · Colour · 100mins

This fictional tale, based on a much-loved Canadian novel about two children growing up in Depression-hit Saskatchewan, is concerned with the psychology of juveniles but lacks the punch of director Allan King's earlier *Warrendale* (1967). However, there's a strong supporting cast, including Gordon Pinsent and José Ferrer, who gives a great performance as a silver-tongued bootlegger. Ultimately, though, it's rather dreary. TH

Brian Painchaud *Brian* • Douglas Junor *Young Ben* • Gordon Pinsent *Gerald O'Connal* • Chapelle Jaffe *Maggie* • José Ferrer *The Ben* ■ *Dir* Allan King • *Scr* Patricia Watson, from a novel by WO Mitchell

Who Is Harry Kellerman, and Why Is He Saying Those Terrible Things about Me? ★

Comedy drama 1971 · US · Colour · 107mins

This is one of those weird, vaguely experimental, sub-culture self-indulgences that got made into movies in the sixties and early 1970s. Dustin Hoffman plays a pop musician driven to despair by anonymous phone calls and by sessions with his shrink, Jack Warden. Woody Allen turned this sort of material into satirical gold but here it's just a dollop of American psychobabble about life, art, ageing and all that stuff. AT

Dustin Hoffman *Georgie Soloway* • Jack Warden *Dr Moses* • Barbara Harris *Allison* • David Burns *Leon Soloway* • Gabriel Dell *Sid* • Betty Walker *Margot Soloway* • Dom DeLuise *Irwin* ■ *Dir* Ulu Grosbard • *Scr* Herb Gardner, from his short story

Who Is Killing the Great Chefs of Europe? ★★

Murder mystery comedy
1978 · US/W Ger · Colour · 112mins

When food connoisseur Robert Morley publishes his list of the world's greatest chefs, he inadvertently sets in motion a stream of jealousy, anger and eventually murder. George Segal, ex-husband of Jacqueline Bisset, who's on the list, finds himself in the midst of the murder spree. It's a promising premise with a soupçon of good jokes, a sprinkle of bad puns and more than a dash of bad taste. But the recipe just doesn't gel resulting in a good looking dish that unfortunately leaves the nagging feeling that it could have been much tastier. DF

George Segal *Robby Ross* • Jacqueline Bisset *Natasha O'Brien* • Robert Morley *Max Vandervere* • Jean-Pierre Cassel *Louis Kohner* • Philippe Noiret *Jean-Claude Moulineau* ■ *Dir* Ted Kotcheff • *Scr* Peter Stone, from the novel *Someone Is Killing the Great Chefs of Europe* by Nan Lyons, Ivan Lyons

Who Killed Bambi? ★★

Thriller 2003 · Fr · Colour · 126mins

Charismatic doctor Laurent Lucas is predictably up to no good in director Gilles Marchand's daft psychological thriller. Trainee nurse Sophie Quinton suspects him when patients start waking up mid-surgery, but an inner ear disorder that causes her to collapse periodically (hence the nickname "Bambi") is just one of many distracting plot annoyances. The more this mundane and sterile suspense melodrama progresses, the more contrived the illogical actions become. Vague and unconvincing. AJ. In French with English subtitles.

Laurent Lucas *Dr Philipp* • Sophie Quinton *Isabelle, "Bambi"* • Catherine Jacob *Véronique* • Yasmine Belmadi *Sami* • Michèle Moretti *Mme Vachon* • Valérie Donzelli *Nathalie* ■ *Dir* Gilles Marchand • *Scr* Gilles Marchand, Vincent Dietschy

W

Who Killed Gail Preston? ★★

Mystery 1938 · US · BW · 60mins

The spotlight is on a very young Rita Hayworth in this Columbia B-feature, but only for the first 20 minutes as her nightclub singer (her voice mostly dubbed), dark-haired and voluptuously gowned, is shot dead in mid-number. It turns out she was not a nice person and there are many suspects until Don Terry's police inspector terrifies the killer into confessing. The nightclub has an amusing prison theme with the orchestra in striped outfits and cell-like cubicles for the patrons. AE

Don Terry *Inspector Kellogg* • Rita Hayworth *Gail Preston* • Robert Paige *Swing Traynor* • Wyn Cahoon *Ann Bishop* ■ *Dir* Leon Barsha • *Scr* Robert E Kent, Henry Taylor

Who Killed Mary Whats'ername? ★★★

Mystery 1971 · US · Colour · 89mins

The character set-up of this crime mystery is unusual, with Red Buttons as the diabetic former boxer seeking the killer of an anonymous prostitute about whom nobody cared. Directed by one-time animator Ernest Pintoff, it doesn't exactly carry conviction, but the idea is interesting for what amounts to a B-movie. TH

Red Buttons *Mickey* • Alice Playten *Della* • Sylvia Miles *Christine* • Sam Waterston *Alex* • Donald Marye *Leo* • Dick Williams [Dick Anthony Williams] *Malthus* ■ *Dir* Ernest Pintoff • *Scr* John O'Toole

Who Killed Teddy Bear? ★★

Mystery thriller 1965 · US · BW · 94mins

This sleazy thriller, with a needlessly strong cast and ample budget, seems to work in as many unpalatable situations as possible, including rape, stalking and pornography. New York discotheque hostess Juliet Prowse becomes the victim of an obscene phone caller and suspects over-enthusiastic detective Jan Murray of being the culprit. Bizarre and exploitative, but enjoyable if you're in the right mood. JG. Contains sexual situations and violence.

Sal Mineo *Lawrence* • Juliet Prowse *Norah* • Jan Murray *Bill Madden* • Elaine Stritch *Billie* • Dan Travanty [Daniel J Travanti] ■ *Dir* Joseph Cates • *Scr* Leon Tokatyan, Arnold Drake, from a story by Arnold Drake

Who Says I Can't Ride a Rainbow? ★★★

Adventure 1971 · US · Colour · 85mins

This is an offbeat children's adventure about a battle to preserve an urban zoo. It stars likeable Jack Klugman as a man who believes that children hold the key to the world's future. This movie also marked the feature debut of talented Morgan Freeman. TS

Jack Klugman *Barney Marcovitz* • Norma French *Mary Lee* • Ruben Figueroa [Reuben Figueroa] *Angel* • David Mann *David* • Kevin Riou *Kevin* • Morgan Freeman *Afro* ■ *Dir* Edward Mann • *Scr* Edward Mann, Daniel Hauer

W

Who Shot Patakango? ★★

Drama 1989 · US · Colour · 104mins

More serious, and thus more insightful, than the usual high-school romp, this peek at events at a Brooklyn school was a labour of love for director Robert Brooks. He not only scripted and edited the film along with his wife Halle (who produced), he even worked the camera. As the director homes in on a group of final-year pupils, he proves more skilled at documentary-style detail than at building sustained drama. Even though the film is knocked off course on more than one occasion, it does possess a convincing sense of time and place. JM. Contains swearing and violence.

David Knight *Bic Bickham* • Sandra Bullock *Devlin Moran* • Kevin Otto *Mark Bickham* • Aaron Ingram *Cougar* • Brad Randall *Patakango* ■ *Dir* Robert Brooks • *Scr* Robert Brooks, Halle Brooks

Who Slew Auntie Roo? ★★ 15

Satirical horror
1971 · US/UK · Colour · 87mins

This is an oddball update of the Hansel and Gretel fairy tale, with a frenetic Shelley Winters menacing two orphan children (Mark Lester and Chloe Franks). What begins as a well-intentioned fantasy becomes a crass nightmare of *Grand Guignol*, maybe because it's co-written by Jimmy Sangster, maestro of so many Hammer horrors. Definitely not for children. TH

Shelley Winters *Rosie Forrest* • Mark Lester (2) *Christopher* • Ralph Richardson *Mr Benton* • Lionel Jeffries *Inspector Willoughby* • Judy Cornwell *Clarine* • Michael Gothard *Albie* • Hugh Griffith *The Pigman/mr Harrison* • Chloe Franks *Katy* • Rosalie Crutchley *Miss Henley* ■ *Dir* Curtis Harrington • *Scr* Robert Blees, James [Jimmy] Sangster, Gavin Lambert, from a story by David Osborn

Who Was That Lady? ★★ U

Comedy 1960 · US · BW · 115mins

This is a strained romantic comedy that has already outstayed its welcome before it turns into a Cold War farce. Caught in flagrante with one of his students, professor Tony Curtis persuades his TV writer buddy, Dean Martin, to concoct an excuse to assuage his jealous wife, Janet Leigh (then Mrs Curtis off screen, too). However, their story about the FBI and a nest of Russian spies is closer to the truth than they suspect. It's polished enough, but there's more to screwball than just pace. DP

Tony Curtis *David Wilson* • Dean Martin *Michael Haney* • Janet Leigh *Ann Wilson* • James Whitmore *Harry Powell* • John McIntire *Bob Doyle* • Barbara Nichols *Gloria Coogle* • Larry Keating *Parker* • Larry Storch *Orenov* ■ *Dir* George Sidney (2) • *Scr* Norman Krasna, from his play *Who Was That Lady I Saw You With?* • *Music* André Previn

The Whole Nine Yards ★★ 15

Black comedy 2000 · US · Colour · 94mins

Friends star Matthew Perry makes another stab at big-screen stardom in this limp black comedy from British director Jonathan Lynn. Perry is the humble, hen-pecked dentist, none too chuffed to discover that Mafia iceman Bruce Willis has just bought a house in his dull Montreal neighbourhood. The farce is too forced, the humour too broad and the end result a far cry from such superior hitman comedies as *Prizzi's Honor* and *Grosse Pointe Blank*. NS. Contains violence, sex scenes, swearing, nudity. DVD

Bruce Willis *Jimmy "The Tulip" Tudeski* • Matthew Perry *"Oz" Oseransky* • Rosanna Arquette *Sophie* • Michael Clarke Duncan *Frankie Figs* • Natasha Henstridge *Cynthia* ■ *Dir* Jonathan Lynn • *Scr* Mitchell Kapner

The Whole Ten Yards ★★ 12

Crime comedy 2004 · US · Colour · 94mins

This sequel to *The Whole Nine Yards* reunites Matthew Perry and Bruce Willis, reprising their roles of nervy dentist and retired Mafia hitman respectively. Willis comes to the rescue when Perry's wife Natasha Henstridge is kidnapped by a Hungarian mob led by Kevin Pollack. Bruce Willis's usually reliable comic timing is nowhere to be seen and the actresses seem bored by the contrivances haphazardly put together by director Howard Deutch. The only real winner is Matthew Perry. TH DVD

Bruce Willis *Jimmy "The Tulip" Tudeski* • Matthew Perry *"Oz" Oseransky* • Amanda Peet *Jill* • Kevin Pollak *Laszlo* • Natasha Henstridge *Cynthia* • Frank Collison *Strabo* • Johnny Messner *Zevo* • Silas Weir Mitchell *Yermo* • Tallulah Belle Willis *Buttercup Scout* ■ *Dir* Howard Deutch • *Scr* George Gallo, from a story by Mitchell Kapner, from characters created by Mitchell Kapner

The Whole Town's Talking ★★★★

Crime comedy 1935 · US · BW · 92mins

There's a double helping of Edward G Robinson in this crime comedy as he plays the dual role of a gangster and a meek little clerk. The clerk is the spitting image of a notorious hoodlum and is mistakenly arrested. He's eventually released and issued with an identity card, so police won't confuse the two again – that is, until the real Mannion turns up and demands a loan of the card. This is a rare pure comedy effort from John Ford, but with a script co-written by Frank Capra favourite Robert Riskin, there's also a certain Capra-esque element to it. A hilarious comedy of mistaken identity. RB

Edward G Robinson *Arthur Ferguson Jones/ "Killer" Manion* • Jean Arthur *Wilhelmina "Bill" Clark* • Arthur Hohl *Det Sgt Mike Boyle* • Wallace Ford *Healy* • Arthur Byron *Spencer* • Donald Meek *Hoyt* ■ *Dir* John Ford • *Scr* Jo Swerling, Robert Riskin, from the story *Jail Breaker* by WR Burnett

The Whole Truth ★★★

Thriller 1958 · UK · BW · 84mins

A B-movie plot performed by an A-list cast; that is to say, stars who had had their day in Hollywood and were now looking to Britain for an honest bob. Thus, Stewart Granger plays a movie producer whose affair with an Italian starlet leads to him covering up her imagined murder and then being arrested when she's found dead for real. George Sanders makes a suitably creepy villain and Donna Reed appears as Granger's wife. The over-the-top performances and overwrought direction ensure it's never boring. AT

Stewart Granger *Max Paulton* • Donna Reed *Carol Paulton* • George Sanders *Carliss* • Gianna Maria Canale *Gina Bertini* • Michael Shillo *Inspector Simon* • Peter Dyneley *Willy Reichel* ■ *Dir* John Guillermin • *Scr* Jonathan Latimer, from the stage and TV play by Philip Mackie

The Whole Wide World ★★★

Biographical romantic drama
1996 · US · Colour · 111mins

In 1933, Novalyne Price (Renee Zellweger) began a stormy relationship with Robert E Howard (Vincent D'Onofrio), a morose author prone to sudden psychotic acts, who became a pulp fantasy icon as creator of *Conan the Barbarian*. This engrossing biopic reveals a tender portrait of the man she loved, who could never reciprocate her feelings, as well as a telling insight into his imaginative writing philosophy. Director Dan Ireland's poignant character study is greatly enhanced by the two wonderful central performances and is an affecting appreciation of the man and the myth that overtook him after he died of a self-inflicted gunshot wound. AJ

Vincent D'Onofrio *Robert E Howard* • Renee Zellweger *Novalyne Price* • Ann Wedgeworth *Mrs Howard* • Harve Presnell *Dr Howard* • Benjamin Mouton *Clyde Smith* • Helen Cates *Enid* ■ *Dir* Dan Ireland • *Scr* Michael Scott Myers, from the novel *One Who Walked Alone* by Novalyne Price Ellis

Who'll Stop the Rain? ★★★★ 18

Crime drama 1978 · US · Colour · 121mins

Nick Nolte stars as a disillusioned Vietnam veteran who is roped into a drug deal organised by traumatised former Vietnam journalist Michael Moriarty. Directed by Karel Reisz, it's a powerful study of alienation, a story about outsiders and a country that has turned its back on heroism and patriotism. It's bleak but gripping, with terrific performances from Nolte, Moriarty and Tuesday Weld as the latter's drug-addict wife. The film was a flop on release, but its reputation is growing all the time. AT. Contains swearing, drug abuse. DVD

Nick Nolte *Ray Hicks* • Tuesday Weld *Marge Converse* • Michael Moriarty *John Converse* • Anthony Zerbe *Antheil* • Richard Masur *Danskin* • Ray Sharkey *Smitty* • Gail Strickland *Charmian* • Charles Haid *Eddie Peace* ■ *Dir* Karel Reisz • *Scr* Judith Rascoe, Robert Stone, from the novel *Dog Soldiers* by Robert Stone

Wholly Moses! ★★ 15

Comedy 1980 · US · Colour · 99mins

Everything's coming up Moses in this sub-*Monty Python* frolic in which Dudley Moore – coming from his success in *10* – tries to establish himself as an Old Testament prophet instead of the upstart Moses. Directed by Gary Weis, it has some great guest cameos by Jack Gilford, Dom DeLuise and Richard Pryor, but comes across as fatuous rather than funny. TH

Dudley Moore *Harvey Orkin/Herschel* • Laraine Newman *Zoey/Zerelda* • James Coco *Hyssop* • Paul Sand *Angel of the Lord* • Jack Gilford *Tailor* • Dom DeLuise *Shadrach* • John Houseman *Archangel* • Madeline Kahn *Sorceress* • Richard Pryor *Pharoah* • John Ritter *Devil* • Tom Baker *Egyptian Captain* ■ *Dir* Gary Weis • *Scr* Guy Thomas

Whoopee! ★★★

Musical comedy 1930 · US · Colour · 94mins

It may look awfully stagebound now, but this inane early Eddie Cantor vehicle was a huge hit in its day, and was cinematically important for being one of the first movies in Technicolor, albeit only two-strip. The theme of a hypochondriac at large – reused in several later films, including the remake of this one, Danny Kaye's *Up in Arms* – is enhanced here by the sumptuous early Busby Berkeley-choreographed production numbers. Watch very closely; the lead chorus girl is a ridiculously young Betty Grable. TS

Eddie Cantor *Henry Williams* • Eleanor Hunt *Sally Morgan* • Paul Gregory *Wanenis* • John Rutherford *Sheriff Bob Wells* • Ethel Shutta *Mary Custer* • Spencer Charters *Jerome Underwood* ■ *Dir* Thornton Freeland • *Scr* William Conselman, from the musical by William Anthony McGuire, Walter Donaldson, Gus Kahn, from the play *The Nervous Wreck* by Owen Davis, from the story *The Wreck* by EJ Rath

The Whoopee Boys ★ 15

Comedy 1986 · US · Colour · 84mins

Paul Rodriguez teams up with Michael O'Keefe as a pair of wide boys who attempt to rub shoulders with society's elite in Palm Beach. Our gauche twosome stick out like sore thumbs. Stand-up star Rodriguez here spectacularly fails to follow in the footsteps of other stage comedians that have made the transition to the big screen. DF

Michael O'Keefe *Jake Bateman* • Paul Rodriguez *Barney* • Denholm Elliott *Colonel Hugh Phelps* • Carole Shelley *Henrietta Phelps* • Lucinda Jenney *Olivia Farragut* ■ *Dir* John Byrum • *Scr* Steve Zacharias, Jeff Buhai, David Obst

U = SUITABLE FOR ALL Uc = SUITABLE FOR ALL, ESPECIALLY FOR YOUNG CHILDREN (VIDEO ONLY) PG = PARENTAL GUIDANCE

Whoops Apocalypse ★★ 15

Comedy 1986 · UK · Colour · 87mins

The four-year gap between the often hilarious TV original and this inconsistent feature seems to have sapped the inspiration from writers Andrew Marshall and David Renwick. The need to introduce a degree of narrative logic precludes much of the wackiness that made the series so biting and fresh. Even though it dissects sombre subjects like the Cold War and a Falklands-style invasion, the satire has mostly been toned down, with only the swipes at the Royals, Peter Cook's performance as a doltish prime minister and a wonderful clown funeral hitting the mark. DP. Contains swearing and nudity. [VIDEO] DVD

Loretta Swit *Barbara Adams* • Peter Cook *Sir Mortimer Chris* • Michael Richards *Lacrobat* • Rik Mayall *Specialist Catering Commander* • Ian Richardson *Rear Admiral Bendish* • Alexei Sayle • Herbert Lom *General Mosquera* ■ *Dir* Tom Bussmann • *Scr* Andrew Marshall, David Renwick

Whore ★ 18

Drama 1991 · US · Colour · 81mins

Largely talking directly to camera, Theresa Russell is an inner city prostitute who tells of and acts out the humiliations of her job and the viciousness of her pimp, Benjamin Mouton. The movie offensively wallows in misogyny, exuding an excited air whenever Russell suffers abuse and giving the swaggering Mouton powerful centre stage, which at times borders on admiration. Ken Russell directs it all with a staggeringly inappropriate and jokey approach. SH. Contains violence, swearing, nudity. [VIDEO] DVD

Theresa Russell *Liz* • Benjamin Mouton *Blake* • Antonio Fargas *Rasta* • Sanjay *Indian* • Elizabeth Morehead *Katie* • Michael Crabtree *Man in car* • John Diehl *Derelict* ■ *Dir* Ken Russell • *Scr* Ken Russell, Deborah Dalton, from the play *Bondage* by David Hines

Who's Afraid of Red Yellow Blue? ★★★

Drama 1990 · W Ger · Colour · 115mins

The hegemony of the West over the East in the newly unified Germany is the underlying theme of Heiko Schier's slyly satirical drama, in which a painter of broad, vulgar canvases finds fame, while a talented miniaturist is overlooked by critics and dealers alike. However, beneath the allegorical veneer, this is also a perceptive study of the art world, with its pretensions and greed, as typified by the capitalist artist who pays a seeming eccentric to damage his pictures in the hope of boosting their prices through newsworthy notoriety. Not a subtle film, but intriguing nonetheless. DP. In German with English subtitles.

Stephanie Philipp • Max Tidof • Heino Ferch • Gunter Berger ■ *Dir/Scr* Heiko Schier

Who's Afraid of Virginia Woolf? ★★★★ 15

Drama 1966 · US · BW · 123mins

Should your front room be in need of redecoration, then Elizabeth Taylor's performance here is guaranteed to strip the paint off the walls with just one verbal volley. In tandem with her screen husband (played by then real-life husband Richard Burton), she spits malicious barbs across their abode, often hitting their dinner guests en route. The ebb and flow of the full-blown arguments are acutely judged by director Mike Nichols, who typically laces his film with juicy psychological and social pointers. He also ensures that Taylor and Burton never reduce their characters to caricature. This five Oscar-winner was regarded as punishingly honest in its day, though inevitably it seems a tad more muted now. JM. Contains swearing. [VIDEO]

Elizabeth Taylor *Martha* • Richard Burton *George* • George Segal *Nick* • Sandy Dennis *Honey* ■ *Dir* Mike Nichols • *Scr* Ernest Lehman, from the play by Edward Albee • *Costume Designer* Irene Sharaff • *Cinematographer* Haskell Wexler

Who's Been Sleeping in My Bed? ★★

Comedy 1963 · US · Colour · 103mins

Dean Martin plays a TV matinée idol who is a smoothie male sex symbol, but not slick enough to avoid amorous shenanigans with the wives of various friends. It's up to girlfriend Elizabeth Montgomery to persuade him to abandon his loose living and settle down with her. A nudge-nudge, wink-wink bedroom farce, superficially glossy, but largely boring except for a handful of laughs and Carol Burnett in the supporting cast. RK

Dean Martin *Jason Steel* • Elizabeth Montgomery *Melissa Morris* • Martin Balsam *Sanford Kaufman* • Jill St John *Toby Tobler* • Richard Conte *Leonard Ashley* • Macha Méril *Jacqueline Edwards* • Louis Nye *Harry Tobler* ■ *Dir* Daniel Mann • *Scr* Jack Rose

Who's Got the Action? ★★

Comedy 1962 · US · Colour · 94mins

Dean Martin and Lana Turner are a married couple in a comedy whose humour resides in a lot of stock but nonetheless quite amusing clichés about bookies and gamblers. Martin is a lawyer who also bets compulsively on the horses, to the increasing detriment of his bank balance and the despair of his wife. She finally takes matters into her own hands, colludes with a bookie in handling his bets and turns him into a winner. The supporting cast offers a standout performance from Walter Matthau as a Mr Big on the wrong side of the law. RK

Dean Martin *Steve Flood* • Lana Turner *Melanie Flood* • Eddie Albert *Clint Morgan* • Nita Talbot *Saturday Knight* • Walter Matthau *Tony Gagoots* • Paul Ford *Judge Boatwright* • Margo *Roza* ■ *Dir* Daniel Mann • *Scr* Jack Rose, from the novel *Four Horse-Players Are Missing* by Alexander Rose

Who's Harry Crumb? ★ PG

Comedy 1989 · US · Colour · 86mins

The question on most people's lips before this lacklustre comedy is over will be, "Who cares?" The late John Candy was quite funny when he allowed a director to control his unrestrained manic mugging. Unfortunately, here Paul Flaherty just lets him get away with farcical murder as a bungling private detective assigned to solve a kidnapping case. Heavy going with very little wit and a great deal of slapstick. AJ [VIDEO]

John Candy *Harry Crumb* • Jeffrey Jones *Eliot Draisen* • Annie Potts *Helen Downing* • Tim Thomerson *Vince Barnes* • Barry Corbin *PJ Downing* • Shawnee Smith *Nikki Downing* ■ *Dir* Paul Flaherty • *Scr* Robert Conte, Peter Martin Wortmann

Who's Minding the Mint? ★★★ U

Comedy 1967 · US · Colour · 96mins

This comedy has a superb cast and a truly daft premise, in which a group of crooks help US mint employee Jim Hutton replace money he has accidentally disposed of, with wonderfully funny results. This is an overlooked gem, shrewdly directed by Sid Caesar associate Howard Morris with a baleful eye for the absurd. The cast is uniformly excellent, but special praise should go to the pompously demented Victor Buono. Sadly, the production values are only average. TS

Jim Hutton *Harry Lucas* • Dorothy Provine *Verna Baxter* • Milton Berle *Luther Burton* • Walter Brennan *Pop Gillis* • Joey Bishop *Ralph Randazzo* • Bob Denver *Willie Owens* • Victor Buono *Captain* • Jamie Farr *Mario* ■ *Dir* Howard Morris • *Scr* RS Allen, Harry Bullock

Who's Minding the Store? ★★★ U

Comedy 1963 · US · Colour · 89mins

Jerry Lewis relaxes under the direction of one of Hollywood's cleverest and wittiest craftsmen, former cartoonist Frank Tashlin, whose Lewis movies resembled a series of manic sketches strung together, and this is one of the funniest. It's wildly inventive, and peppered with a gallery of fabulously eccentric character actors, used in the most simple of ideas – Lewis let loose in a department store. TS

Jerry Lewis *Raymond Phiffier* • Jill St John *Barbara Tuttle* • Agnes Moorehead *Phoebe Tuttle* • John McGiver *Mr Tuttle* • Ray Walston *Mr Quimby* • Francesca Bellini *Shirley* ■ *Dir* Frank Tashlin • *Scr* Frank Tashlin, Harry Tugend, from a story by Harry Tugend

Who's That Girl ★★ PG

Screwball comedy 1987 · US · Colour · 87mins

With Griffin Dunne hot off the back of his triumph in Martin Scorsese's *After Hours* and Madonna in dire need of a hit after the *Shanghai Surprise* fiasco, you would have thought the two stars would have plumped for something more substantial than this woeful attempt at screwball comedy. Slouching, chewing gum and mistiming wisecracks with the nonchalance of a rock star convinced her presence is a favour to the producer, Madonna is a shadow of the sassy star of *Desperately Seeking Susan*. DP [VIDEO]

Madonna *Nikki Finn* • Griffin Dunne *Loudon Trott* • Haviland Morris *Wendy Worthington* • John McMartin *Simon Worthington* • Bibi Besch *Mrs Worthington* • John Mills *Montgomery Bell* ■ *Dir* James Foley • *Scr* Andrew Smith, Ken Finkleman, from a story by Andrew Smith

Who's That Knocking at My Door ★★★ 15

Drama 1968 · US · BW · 86mins

The first film not just for director Martin Scorsese, but also actor Harvey Keitel (if you overlook his uncredited appearance in *Reflections in a Golden Eye* the previous year). Displaying early indications of all Scorsese's trademark concerns, this autobiographical film is crude but compelling, with Keitel as a strict but streetwise Catholic taking a guilt trip through his relationship with free-thinking Zina Bethune. It's essential viewing as an early example of two masters learning their respective crafts. DA DVD

Harvey Keitel *JR* • Zina Bethune *The girl* • Lennard Kuras *Joey* • Ann Colette *Girl in dream* • Michael Scala *Sally* • Wendy Russell *Sally's girl friend* • Philip Carlson *Mountain guide* • Robert Uricola *Gunman at stag party* ■ *Dir/Scr* Martin Scorsese

Who's the Man? ★★ 15

Comedy 1993 · US · Colour · 85mins

Ted Demme (nephew of famed director Jonathan Demme) brings his *Yo! MTV Raps* stars Ed Lover and Dr Dre to the big screen for this undistinguished hip-hop effort. The makers clearly wanted to say something pertinent about exploitative inner-city landlords, but a farce built around a couple of nitwit barbers who accidentally become cops is hardly the best way to go about it. The leads are amiable enough and the presence of Denis Leary and cameos by several rappers is most welcome, but they don't atone for the shortage of gags and the clumsiness of Demme's approach. DP. Contains violence and swearing. [VIDEO]

Dr Dre • Ed Lover • Jim Moody *Nick Crawford* • Badja Djola *Lionel Douglas* • Denis Leary *Sergeant Cooper* • Richard Bright *Demetrius* • Ice-T *Nighttrain/Chauncey* ■ *Dir* Ted Demme • *Scr* Seth Greenland, from a story by Seth Greenland, Dr Dre, Ed Lover

Whose Life Is It Anyway? ★★★ 15

Drama 1981 · US · Colour · 118mins

Brian Clark's award-winning play is well transposed to the screen by director John Badham and stars Richard Dreyfuss as the artist who is rendered immobile from the neck down after a terrible car accident. The crux of the narrative is his persistent demand to the hospital chief of staff (John Cassavetes) to be allowed the right to die. Meanwhile he's cared for and develops relationships with doctor Christine Lahti and nurse Kaki Hunter. Amazingly funny given the circumstances, this is both touching and relevant. LH [VIDEO]

Richard Dreyfuss *Ken Harrison* • John Cassavetes *Dr Michael Emerson* • Christine Lahti *Dr Clare Scott* • Bob Balaban *Carter Hill* • Kenneth McMillan *Judge Wyler* • Kaki Hunter *Mary Jo Sadler* • Thomas Carter *Orderly John* ■ *Dir* John Badham • *Scr* Brian Clark, Reginald Rose, from the play by Brian Clark

Why Change Your Wife? ★★★

Silent comedy 1920 · US · BW · 100mins

The name of director Cecil B DeMille has become synonymous with the historical and Biblical epic. However, this mighty Hollywood pioneer and starmaker was responsible for dozens of sparkling and successful bedroom farces during his long and infuential association with Paramount, of which this is just one. The soufflé plot, concerning the complications of extramarital flirtations, serves as an excuse the delightful cast going through their risqué paces, cleverly manipulated by DeMille. RK

Thomas Meighan *Robert Gordon* • Gloria Swanson *Beth Gordon* • Bebe Daniels *Sally Clark* • Theodore Kosloff *Radinoff* • Clarence Geldart *The doctor* • Sylvia Ashton *Aunt Kate* ■ *Dir* Cecil B DeMille • *Scr* Olga Printzlau, Sada Cowan, from a story by William C de Mille

Why Do Fools Fall in Love? ★★★ 15

Biographical musical drama
1998 · US · Colour · 111mins

This is a fun, if not exactly deeply probing, look at the short life of 1950s teenage singer Frankie Lymon (Larenz Tate) who left three wives (he never got around to divorcing any of them) behind when he died in 1968 at the age of 25. Because there are so many conflicting opinions about what Frankie was actually like, Tate isn't given a great deal to work with, but the wives are better drawn and well played by a cast of talented actresses. Ben Vereen and Little Richard add some history to the snappily directed proceedings. JB. Contains swearing and violence. [VIDEO]

Ben Vereen *Richard Barrett* • Larenz Tate *Frankie Lymon* • Halle Berry *Zola Taylor* • Lela Rochon *Emira Eagle* • Vivica A Fox *Elizabeth Waters* • Little Richard • Miguel A Nunez Jr *Young Little Richard* • Paul Mazursky *Morris Levy* ■ *Dir* Gregory Nava • *Scr* Tina Andrews

Why Does Herr R Run Amok? ★★★

Drama 1970 · W Ger · Colour · 88mins

This film is brutal in its story and in its unwillingness to come to conclusions, since the murderous Herr R of the title is not presented as a villain but as a victim of emotional exploitation, unhappy in his family and work. Director Rainer Werner Fassbinder takes no sides, but presents his central character, played by Kurt Raab, in his comfortable home, enjoying the fruits of a decent job. Why then does all this lead to shocking violence? This is a sombre work of undeniable power and pessimism. BB. In German with English subtitles.

Kurt Raab *Kurt Raab, "Herr R"* • Lilith Ungerer *Frau Raab* • Amadeus Fengler *Amadeus, their son* • Franz Maron *Boss* • Hanna Schygulla *Schoolfriend* • Peter Raben *Schoolfriend* ■ *Dir/Scr* Rainer Werner Fassbinder, Michael Fengler

Why Has Bhodi-Dharma Left for the East? ★★★

Drama 1989 · S Kor · Colour · 135mins

South Korean painter Bae Yong-Kyun devoted several years of his life to making this debut feature. His genius for a telling image is readily apparent, notably in a stunning silhouetted sequence framed against some gnarled trees and a glorious sunset. But the pacing of his story is also impeccable, reflecting the contrast between life in the town and the mountain hermitage in which a Zen master imparts his wisdom to a wavering acolyte and a mischievous orphan. This is an intellectually and artistically rewarding experience. DP. In Korean with English subtitles.

Yi Pan-Yong *Hyegok* • Sin Won-Sop *Kibong* • Huang Hae-Jin *Haejin* ■ *Dir/Scr* Bae Yong-Kyun

Why Me? ★ 15

Comedy 1990 · US · Colour · 87mins

Anyone who has seen Christopher Lambert act knows that he has absolutely no flair for comedy, but that didn't stop him from being cast in this excruciatingly unfunny caper movie. Lambert's jewel thief character unknowingly steals a very valuable ruby belonging to the Turkish government, and soon finds himself pursued by not only them, but also the police, the CIA and Armenian terrorists. So heavy-handed that not even Christopher Lloyd can generate a single laugh. KB

Christopher Lambert *Gus Cardinale* • Christopher Lloyd *Bruno* • Kim Greist *June Cardinale* • JT Walsh *Inspector Mahoney* • Michael J Pollard *Ralph* • Tony Plana *Benjy* • John Hancock *Tiny* ■ *Dir* Gene Quintano • *Scr* Donald E Westlake, Leonard Mass Jr [Leonard Mass], from the novel by Donald E Westlake

Why Shoot the Teacher ★★★ PG

Period drama 1976 · Can · Colour · 95mins

Canadian director Silvio Narizzano came to fame with *Georgy Girl*, but this altogether more attractive work found him back on home ground with an adaptation of a novel set in the mid-1930s. Bud Cort plays a young teacher whose only offer of a job is in the depressed prairie lands of Saskatchewan. He moves there but proves unpopular because of his youth and eastern manners. Not particularly original, but the central story of his progress to manhood is nicely set against a picturesque background. BB

Bud Cort *Max Brown* • Samantha Eggar *Alice Field* • Chris Wiggins *Lyle Bishop* • Gary Reineke *Harris Montgomery* • John Friesen *Dave McDougall* • Michael J Reynolds *Bert Field* ■ *Dir* Silvio Narizzano • *Scr* James DeFelice, from the novel by Max Braithwaite

Why Would I Lie? ★ 15

Comedy drama 1980 · US · Colour · 100mins

Treat Williams uses his considerable talent to try to save this film from being entirely awful. Unfortunately, the task is too great even for him and this comic tale of a lying social worker trying to reunite a hard-bitten woman with her ex-con mother should only be viewed as an example of how not to make a movie. Miscast, unfunny and unfortunate. JB

Treat Williams *Cletus Hayworth* • Lisa Eichhorn *Kay Lindsey* • Gabriel Swann *Jeorge* • Susan Heldfond *Amy* • Anne Byrne *Faith* ■ *Dir* Larry Peerce • *Scr* Peter Stone, from the novel *The Fabricator* by Hollis Hodges

Wichita ★★★ U

Western 1955 · US · Colour · 81mins

This is an excellent, intelligent and moving study of US marshal Wyatt Earp. As Earp, Joel McCrea is superbly cast, his rugged middle-aged features creating instant empathy for the troubled lawman. Jacques Tourneur's direction is exemplary, as ever, and if certain incidents seem to presage later westerns such as Sam Peckinpah's *The Wild Bunch*, perhaps that's because Peckinpah himself worked on this movie as dialogue director. TS

Joel McCrea *Wyatt Earp* • Vera Miles *Laurie* • Lloyd Bridges *Gyp* • Wallace Ford *Whiteside* • Edgar Buchanan *Doc Black* • Peter Graves (2) *Morgan Earp* • Keith Larsen *Bat Masterson* • Carl Benton Reid *Mayor* • John Smith *Jim Earp* ■ *Dir* Jacques Tourneur • *Scr* Daniel Ullman [Daniel B Ullman]

Wicked ★★ 15

Black comedy thriller
1998 · US · Colour · 85mins

Julia Stiles plays a mature teenager who tries to take the place of her murdered mother in this mediocre thriller. Director Michael Steinberg employs some expressive camerawork to try to pep things up, but fails to make the telegraphed twists feel anything more than second-hand, particularly in the climactic stages. However, Stiles still brings a reasonable air of menace to her role of shrewd manipulator. JC DVD

Julia Stiles *Ellie Christianson* • Chelsea Field *Karen Christianson* • Patrick Muldoon *Lawson Smith* • Vanessa Zima *Inger Christianson* • William R Moses *Ben Christianson* • Michael Parks *Detective Boland* ■ *Dir* Michael Steinberg • *Scr* Eric A Weiss

Wicked City ★★★ 18

Animated science-fiction adventure
1992 · Jpn · Colour · 80mins

This Japanese animated adaptation of Hideyuki Kikuchi's comic book is coherent enough to pass the typical hurdle of crunching down a *manga* story to 90 minutes. Some details remain murky, but they're almost forgotten because of the eye-catching images of the bizarre and grotesque. The story concerns Earth's centuries-old relationship with alternate universe the "Black World" and the renewal of a peace treaty. It's never dull, though the extreme violence and sexual material may be too much for even the most jaded viewer. KB Japanese dialogue dubbed into English.

Dir Yoshiaki Kawajiri, Carl Macek • *Scr* Kiseo Choo, from his story, from a comic book by Hideyuki Kikuchi

The Wicked Dreams of Paula Schultz ★★

Comedy 1968 · US · Colour · 112mins

Proving once again that TV stars seldom transfer well to the big screen, the stars of *Hogan's Heroes* (Bob Crane, John Banner and Werner Klemperer) belly-flopped with this corny Cold War comedy in which American black marketeer Crane helps East German athlete Elke Sommer with a novel plan to defect to the west. The actors do their best with weak material, indulgently overstretched, but inevitably they disappointed audiences probably led to expect something spicier by the title. DM

Elke Sommer *Paula Schultz* • Bob Crane *Bill Mason* • Werner Klemperer *Klaus* • Joey Forman *Herbert Sweeney* • John Banner *Weber* • Leon Askin *Oscar* • Maureen Arthur *Barbara Sweeney* ■ *Dir* George Marshall • *Scr* Burt Styler, Albert E Lewin, Nat Perrin, from a story by Ken Englund

The Wicked Lady ★★★★ PG

Period drama 1945 · UK · BW · 99mins

This period drama struck a resounding chord with the public and gave British cinema one of its most striking images: that of highway robber Margaret Lockwood's beauty-spotted bosom heaving as she sneered at some poor male victim. Despite its popularity at the time (it was the highest earning movie in England in 1946), this is a fairly predictable costume affair, with a large selection of B-movie regulars striding about in thigh-length boots. Yet, seen from the distance of time, it is wonderful entertainment, with James Mason catching the swaggering heart of the movie, and Ms Lockwood could give Glenn Close a run for her money in the villainess stakes. SH DVD

Margaret Lockwood *Barbara Worth/Lady Skelton* • James Mason *Captain Jackson* • Patricia Roc *Caroline* • Griffith Jones *Sir Ralph Skelton* • Enid Stamp-Taylor *Henrietta Kingsclere* • Michael Rennie *Kit Locksby* • Felix Aylmer *Hogarth* • David Horne *Martin Worth* • Martita Hunt *Cousin Agatha* ■ *Dir* Leslie Arliss • *Scr* Leslie Arliss, Aimee Stuart, Gordon Glennon, from the novel *The Life and Death of the Wicked Lady Skelton* by Magdalen King-Hall

The Wicked Lady ★★★ 18

Adventure 1983 · UK · Colour · 94mins

Michael Winner's Technicolor remake of the effective 1945 hokum that made Margaret Lockwood a star fields Faye Dunaway as the amoral "lady" who takes up with a highwayman. Winner's version is in dubious taste, frankly exploitative and trashy in its unashamed injection of sex and violence, and famously caused a furore with the censors over a scene in which Dunaway takes a whip to another woman, ripping her clothes to shreds. Questionable though it may be, however, the movie is enjoyable high camp and efficiently made. RK

Faye Dunaway *Lady Barbara Skelton* • Alan Bates *Captain Jerry Jackson* • John Gielgud *Hogarth* • Denholm Elliott *Sir Ralph Skelton* • Prunella Scales *Lady Henrietta Kingsclere* • Glynis Barber *Caroline* • Oliver Tobias *Kit Locksby* • Joan Hickson *Aunt Agatha Trimble* ■ *Dir* Michael Winner • *Scr* Leslie Arliss, Michael Winner, from the novel *The Life and Death of the Wicked Lady Skelton* by Magdalen King-Hall

Wicked Stepmother ★ PG

Comedy horror 1989 · US · Colour · 89mins

A catastrophic climax to Bette Davis's glittering career. The actress who took on the Hollywood studio system and won in the 1930s was equally prepared to fight her corner in what turned out to be her last movie. Her disgust with director Larry Cohen's work led to her walking out, and her part as the stepmother who uses her paranormal powers to torment her family was drastically reduced. One hopes her atrocious performance was a poisonous act of revenge. DP. Contains violence and swearing.

Bette Davis *Miranda* • Barbara Carrera *Priscilla* • Colleen Camp *Jenny* • David Rasche *Steve* • Lionel Stander *Sam* • Tom Bosley *Lieutenant MacIntosh* • Shawn Donahue *Mike* • Richard Moll *Nat* ■ *Dir/Scr* Larry Cohen

The Wicker Man ★★★★★ 18

Classic horror 1973 · UK · Colour · 84mins

Edward Woodward stars as the devoutly Christian policeman who finds his beliefs tested to the limit when he investigates the disappearance of a young girl on the pagan shores of Summerisle in this cult horror classic. With a literate script by *Sleuth* playwright Anthony Shaffer and a memorable Scottish folk score, director Robin Hardy's fascinating mixture of horror, eroticism and religion is a thoughtful, challenging and highly provocative experience. Christopher Lee, who plays the lord of the island, thinks it's the finest film he's ever made – and he's right. AJ. Contains violence, swearing, nudity. DVD

Edward Woodward *Sergeant Neil Howie* • Christopher Lee *Lord Summerisle* • Diane Cilento *Miss Rose* • Britt Ekland *Willow MacGregor* • Ingrid Pitt *Librarian/Clerk* • Lindsay Kemp *Alder MacGregor* • Russell Waters *Harbour master* • Aubrey Morris *Old gardener/Gravedigger* • Irene Sunters *May Morrison* ■ *Dir* Robin Hardy • *Scr* Anthony Shaffer • *Cinematographer* Harry Waxman

Wicker Park ★★★ 12

Romantic thriller
2004 · US · Colour · 110mins

On the eve of a business trip, Josh Hartnett catches a fleeting glimpse of old flame Diane Kruger, who mysteriously disappeared from his life a few years earlier. Postponing his trip and abandoning his fiancée, Hartnett determines to track her down, only to discover the woman he saw is really someone else (Rose Byrne). But this lady has her own agenda, and is on the point of starting a relationship with Hartnett's friend (played by a scene-stealing Matthew Lillard). The inventive visuals in this American take on Gilles Mimouni's *L'Appartement* keep you engrossed, and the film retains the Hitchcockian thrills of the original. BP. Contains swearing. DVD

Josh Hartnett *Matthew* • Rose Byrne *Alex* • Matthew Lillard *Luke* • Diane Kruger *Lisa* • Jessica Paré *Rebecca* ■ *Dir* Paul McGuigan • *Scr* Brandon Boyce, from the film *L'Appartement* by Gilles Mimouni

Wide Awake ★★★

Drama 1998 · US · Colour · 90mins

Prior to writing and directing the smash hit *The Sixth Sense*, M Night Shyamalan made this film about a Catholic schoolboy who starts to question his faith after his grandfather dies, and devotes a whole school year to reassuring himself that grandad is spending eternity in good hands. The film is intriguing enough, but is a little let down by a sugary script. DA

Denis Leary *Mr Beal* • Rosie O'Donnell *Sister Terry* • Dana Delany *Mrs Beal* • Robert Loggia *Grandpa Beal* • Joseph Cross *Joshua Beal* • Timothy Reifsnyder *Dave O'Hara* ■ *Dir/Scr* M Night Shyamalan

Wide Sargasso Sea ★ 18

Period drama 1992 · Aus · Colour · 94mins

This adaptation of the Jean Rhys novel explores the story behind *Jane Eyre* by telling the history of the future Mrs Rochester. Set in 19th-century Jamaica, Rochester (Nathaniel Parker) encounters the passionate and erotic Creole heiress Antoinette (Karina Lombard) and, after marrying her, discovers a family history of insanity. Unlike the novel, this is firstly pure melodrama and secondly poorly disguised erotica. What was an interesting literary tale is lost in a sea of sweaty sheets and bad acting. LH

Karina Lombard *Antoinette Cosway* • Nathaniel Parker *Rochester* • Rachel Ward *Annette Cosway* • Michael York *Paul Mason* • Martine Beswicke [Martine Beswick] *Aunt Cora*

■ *Dir* John Duigan • *Scr* Jan Sharp, Carole Angier, John Duigan, from the novel by Jean Rhys • *Music* Stewart Copeland

The Widow Couderc ★★★★

Romantic drama 1971 · Fr · Colour · 90mins

With such an idyllic canal-side setting and an overwhelming sense of well-being, Simone Signoret's rural idyll can only turn sour, as it so often does in the world of novelist Georges Simenon. Initially, the canker comes from her scheming in-laws seizing upon her relationship with fugitive Alain Delon as a pretext for reclaiming her late husband's farm. But just as sinister is the rise of fascism, which underpins the family's skulduggery. Pierre Granier-Deferre judges the tone to perfection, but it's the inspired pairing of Signoret and Delon that gives the film its heart. DP. French dialogue dubbed into English.

Alain Delon *Jean* • Simone Signoret *Widow Couderc* • Ottavia Piccolo *Félicie* • Jean Tissier *Henri* ■ *Dir* Pierre Granier-Deferre • *Scr* Pierre Granier-Deferre, Pascal Jardin, from a story by Georges Simenon

Widows' Peak ★★★ PG

Black comedy drama
1993 · UK · Colour · 97mins

The malicious, delicious old biddies of a picturesque Irish village declare war when their ranks are infiltrated by a wealthy and attractive new widow. It's tea-and-biscuits at 20 paces as hostilities prompt shameless behaviour, de-closeted skeletons and maybe even murder. Mia Farrow, Joan Plowright and Natasha Richardson play the black widows; Jim Broadbent and Adrian Dunbar are the menfolk desperate to avoid being eaten alive by them. DP. Contains violence. [video] DVD

Mia Farrow *Catherine O'Hare* • Joan Plowright *Mrs "DC" Doyle Counihan* • Natasha Richardson *Edwina Broome* • Adrian Dunbar *Godfrey* • Jim Broadbent *Clancy* • Anne Kent *Miss Grubb* • John Kavanagh *Canon* ■ *Dir* John Irvin • *Scr* Hugh Leonard, from his story

Wife, Doctor and Nurse ★★★

Comedy 1937 · US · BW · 85mins

Loretta Young made five movies for Fox in 1937, and this was the only one in which she didn't co-star with either Tyrone Power or Don Ameche. However, she did manage to change her wardrobe for virtually every scene; even the *New York Times* commented on her changes of outfit in their normally austere review. The plot's a wisp: Young is married to doctor Warner Baxter, who is also loved by his nurse, Virginia Bruce. The ending's daring, and Walter Lang directs with skill, helped by a cast that contains many well-loved faces. TS

Loretta Young *Ina* • Warner Baxter *Dr Judd Lewis* • Virginia Bruce *Steve, Lewis's nurse* • Jane Darwell *Mrs Krueger, the Housekeeper* • Sidney Blackmer *Dr Therberg* • Maurice Cass *Pomout* ■ *Dir* Walter Lang • *Scr* Kathryn Scola, Darrell Ware, Lamar Trotti

Wife, Husband and Friend ★★★

Musical comedy 1939 · US · BW · 75mins

Classy comedy from 20th Century-Fox, produced and written for the screen by that laconic southerner Nunnally Johnson, who would remake it to greater success ten years later as *Everybody Does It* with a more sophisticated cast. Loretta Young looks lovely, but never really convinces as the would-be singer whose husband really has the tuneful voice. Binnie Barnes as a prima donna and Helen Westley as Young's supportive mother get the most out of two splendidly written roles. TS

Loretta Young *Doris Blair Borland* • Warner Baxter *Leonard Borland/Logan Bennett* • Binnie Barnes *Cecil Carver* • Cesar Romero *Hugo* • George Barbier *Major Blair* • J Edward Bromberg *Rossi* • Eugene Pallette *Mike Craig* ■ *Dir* Gregory Ratoff • *Scr* Nunnally Johnson, from the novel *Career in C Major* by James M Cain in *American Magazine*

Wife vs Secretary ★★★★

Comedy drama 1936 · US · BW · 85mins

Clark Gable, Myrna Loy and Jean Harlow are the gold-plated stars in this snappy, intelligent comedy drama about marital misunderstanding. Harlow's personal secretary has a close, demanding but entirely innocent working relationship with Gable's magazine publisher; Loy is the wife who almost loses Gable through jealous suspicion of Harlow. The on-screen empathy of the familiar Gable-Harlow team, devoid of the usual sexual pull, is wonderful to watch. James Stewart, pre-leading man stardom, is Harlow's boyfriend. RK

Clark Gable *Van Stanhope/Jake* • Jean Harlow *Helen "Whitey" Wilson* • Myrna Loy *Linda Stanhope* • May Robson *Mimi Stanhope* • George Barbier *JD Underwood* • James Stewart *Dave* • Hobart Cavanaugh *Joe* • Tom Dugan *Finney* ■ *Dir* Clarence Brown • *Scr* Norman Krasna, John Lee Mahin, Alice Duer Miller, from the short story by Faith Baldwin

Wigstock: The Movie ★★

Documentary 1995 · US · Colour · 82mins

Each year since 1985, drag queen the Lady Bunny has staged Wigstock, a mainly transvestite festival in the gay sector of New York's Greenwich Village. This documentary combines footage from the 1993 and 1994 events. However, much of the show's fun does not come across, primarily because so many of the performers display such modest talents. Exceptions are the amusing Duelling Bankheads (two men dressed as husky-voiced star Tallulah), stylish singer Crystal Waters, and the eye-popping British performance artist Leigh Bowery who died soon after. DM

Dir Barry Shils • *Cinematographer* Wolfgang Held

Wilbur (Wants to Kill Himself) ★★★★ 15

Black comedy drama
2002 · Den/UK/Swe/Fr · Colour · 104mins

Danish director Lone Scherfig examines the unpredictability of love in her English-language debut. The consequences of single mother Shirley Henderson's encounter with second-hand bookshop owner Adrian Rawlins and his suicidal sibling James Sives are melodramatic. But the misfits' romantic triangle is so deftly underplayed that an unfussy realism seeps into proceedings, which are further authenticated by the Glaswegian mix of hard-knock compassion and deadpan humour. The supporting cast also catches the mood, with Julia Davis splendid as an insensitive nurse. DP [video] DVD

Jamie Sives *Wilbur North* • Adrian Rawlins *Harbour North* • Shirley Henderson *Alice* • Lisa McKinlay *Mary* • Mads Mikkelsen *Dr Horst* • Julia Davis *Moira* • Susan Vidler *Sophie* ■ *Dir* Lone Scherfig • *Scr* Anders Thomas Jensen, Lone Scherfig

The Wilby Conspiracy ★★★ 15

Political thriller 1975 · UK · Colour · 101mins

In this drama set at the height of apartheid in South Africa, Sidney Poitier plays a political activist who drags unwilling Michael Caine on a cross-country flight from law and order, represented by the bigoted figure of Nicol Williamson. Villainous Williamson bides his time in the hope that the two fugitives will lead him to a rebel leader. Although the South African milieu is significant, Ralph Nelson's apparent return to the anti-racist controversy of *Soldier Blue* is merely a chase thriller. Rutger Hauer appears in his first English language film. TH [video]

Sidney Poitier *Shack Twala* • Michael Caine *Keogh* • Nicol Williamson *Horn* • Prunella Gee *Rina Van Nierkirk* • Persis Khambatta *Dr Persis Ray* • Saeed Jaffrey *Dr Mukerjee* • Rutger Hauer *Blaine Van Niekirk* ■ *Dir* Ralph Nelson • *Scr* Rod Amateau, Harold Nebenzal, from the novel by Peter Driscoll

Wild about Harry ★★★★ 15

Romantic comedy
2000 · UK/Ger/Ire · Colour · 87mins

This is like *Regarding Henry* with heart, humour and no American schmaltz. Brendan Gleeson is the naffest of Irish TV chefs, whose serial womanising is tabloid news. In the midst of divorce proceedings from his long-suffering wife Amanda Donohoe, Gleeson slips into a coma. Awakening with amnesia he turns into a new man and gradually wins back the hearts of his wife and family. But old habits die hard and both booze and bad feeling resurface. *Father Ted* director Declan Lowney handles this emotional merry-go-round with a deft touch, and the performances are excellent. LH. Contains violence, swearing. [video] DVD

Brendan Gleeson *Harry McKee* • Amanda Donohoe *Ruth McKee* • James Nesbitt *Walter Adair* • Adrian Dunbar *JJ MacMahon* • Bronagh Gallagher *Miss Boyle* • George Wendt *Frankie* ■ *Dir* Declan Lowney • *Scr* Colin Bateman, Adrian Dunbar, George Wendt, James Nesbitt

The Wild Affair ★★★

Comedy drama 1963 · UK · BW · 88mins

Before her wedding, secretary Nancy Kwan decides to have a final fling, taking advantage of a the opportunities offered by an office party. Kwan was not the best choice for the lead and, this being the early 1960s, the affair is not as wild as it pretends to be. But after a slow start, the party atmosphere becomes infectious, mainly because of a wealth of comedy talent. Wonderful Terry-Thomas plays the boss and his staff includes giants of the British music-hall (Bud Flanagan, Jimmy Logan, Gladys Morgan) rarely seen on screen. DM

Nancy Kwan *Marjorie Lee* • Terry-Thomas *Godfrey Dean* • Jimmy Logan *Craig* • Bud Flanagan *Sergeant Bletch* • Gladys Morgan *Mrs Tovey* • Betty Marsden *Mavis Cook* • Paul Whitsun-Jones *Tiny Hearst* • Victor Spinetti *Quentin* • Frank Finlay *Drunk* ■ *Dir* John Krish • *Scr* John Krish, from the novel *The Last Hours of Sandra Lee* by William Sansom

Wild America ★★ PG

Adventure based on a true story
1997 · US · Colour · 101mins

Teen heart-throbs Devon Sawa and Jonathan Taylor Thomas star in this clunky eco-tale about a group of children who embark on a trans-American trek to photograph their country's fast-disappearing wildlife. This has its heart in the right place, but director William Dear relies a little too much on a series of staged encounters with animals. DA [video]

Jonathan Taylor Thomas *Marshall* • Devon Sawa *Mark* • Scott Bairstow *Marty* • Frances Fisher *Agnes* • Jamey Sheridan *Marty Senior* • Tracey Walter *Leon* ■ *Dir* William Dear • *Scr* David Michael Wieger

The Wild and the Innocent ★★

Comedy western 1959 · US · Colour · 84mins

Audie Murphy and Sandra Dee play a couple of innocents from the mountains who find themselves out of their depth in an unruly town. Also on hand are tough and sexy Joanne Dru, whose experience of character roles in John Ford and Howard Hawks westerns is put to good use here, and the always watchable Gilbert Roland. Not one of Murphy's best efforts, but not unwatchable and nicely shot in CinemaScope. TS

Audie Murphy *Yancey* • Joanne Dru *Marcy Howard* • Gilbert Roland *Sheriff Paul Bartell* • Jim Backus *Cecil Forbes* • Sandra Dee *Rosalie Stocker* • George Mitchell *Uncle Hawkes* ■ *Dir* Jack Sher • *Scr* Sy Gomberg, Jack Sher, from a story by Jack Sher

The Wild and the Willing ★★★

Drama 1962 · UK · BW · 113mins

An unsuccessful play is the source of this exposé of British student life. Once shocking, it has aged as badly as others of its ilk, but now has considerable curiosity value, not least because of early appearances by Ian McShane, Samantha Eggar, John Hurt and others. McShane shines as the scholarship boy who vents his wrath on privileged society by having a fling with a professor's wife. Relatively explicit bedroom scenes are disconcertingly combined with student japes. DM

Virginia Maskell *Virginia* • Paul Rogers *Professor Chown* • Ian McShane *Harry* • John Hurt *Phil* • Samantha Eggar *Josie* • Catherine Woodville *Sarah* • Jeremy Brett *Gilby* ■ *Dir* Ralph Thomas • *Scr* Nicholas Phipps, Mordecai Richler, from the play *The Tinker* by Laurence Dobie, Robert Sloman

Wild and Wonderful ★★ U

Comedy 1964 · US · Colour · 87mins

Tony Curtis and his then wife Christine Kaufmann team in this frippery that is more notable for the performance of a poodle called Monsieur Cognac than for the efforts of its human stars. Curtis plays yet another American in Paris, who allows his music to suffer once he hits the right note with movie star Kaufmann. The leads are clearly in love, but it gets in the way of their acting, which is as unconvincing as the fake Paris sets. DP

Tony Curtis *Terry Williams* • Christine Kaufmann *Giselle Ponchon* • Larry Storch *Rufus Gibbs* • Pierre Olaf *Jacquot* • Mary Ingels *Doc Bailey* • Jacques Aubuchon *Papa Ponchon* ■ *Dir* Michael Anderson • *Scr* Larry Markes, Michael Morris, Waldo Salt, from a treatment by Richard M Powell, Phillip Rapp, from a short story by Dorothy Crider

The Wild Angels ★★★★ 18

Action drama 1966 · US · Colour · 82mins

The first and most controversial Hell's Angel shocker from cult director Roger Corman kick-started a whole cycle of biker movies. None were better than this brutal tale of leather-clad punks taking drugs, gang-raping women, beating up priests and having a drunken orgy at the church funeral of chapter member Bruce Dern. Shot documentary-style for added realism, it's based on true incidents as related to Corman by Californian Angels. Super cool Peter Fonda heads a hip cast of B-movie stalwarts, anti-establishment icons and pop singers. Graphic violence and the final message "There's nowhere to go" caused Corman's counterculture portrait to be banned in many countries. AJ [video]

Peter Fonda *Heavenly Blues* • Nancy Sinatra *Mike* • Bruce Dern *Loser* • Lou Procopio *Joint* • Coby Denton *Bull Puckey* • Marc Cavell *Frankenstein* • Buck Taylor *Dear John* • Norman Alden *Medic* • Michael J Pollard *Pigmy* ■ *Dir* Roger Corman • *Scr* Charles Griffith

W

Wild at Heart ★★★★ 18

Drama 1990 · US · Colour · 119mins

Director David Lynch goes over the top, over people's heads and somewhere over the psychedelic rainbow in another ultra-violent and sleazily sexy pulp art attack. Forget the story; Lynch clearly has. Just follow convict and Elvis fan Nicolas Cage and his white trash girlfriend Laura Dern as they are pursued through the Deep South by her crazed mother's gumshoe lover. Stuffed with the Sultan of Strange's transfixing brand of deranged visuals, haunting weirdness and exuberant camp, it's another hypnotic ride through the twin peaks of pretentiousness and exhilaration. AJ. Contains violence, swearing, sex scenes and nudity. DVD

Nicolas Cage *Sailor Ripley* • Laura Dern *Lula Pace Fortune* • Diane Ladd *Marietta Pace* • Willem Dafoe *Bobby Peru* • Isabella Rossellini *Perdita Durango* • Harry Dean Stanton *Johnnie Farragut* • Crispin Glover *Dell* • Grace Zabriskie *Juana* ■ *Dir* David Lynch • *Scr* David Lynch, from the novel by Barry Gifford • *Music* Angelo Badalamenti

Wild Beauty ★★ U

Western 1946 · US · BW · 61mins

This desperately over-complicated Universal programme filler is ostensibly about an Indian boy and his horse called Wild Beauty, but also contains an unsavoury subplot about capturing mustangs and turning their hides into shoe leather. There's relief from the tedium in producer/director Wallace Fox's deathless combination of earnestness and cheapskate production values. TS

Don Porter *Dave Morrow* • Lois Collier *Linda Gibson* • Jacqueline de Wit *Sissy* • George Cleveland *Barney* • Robert Wilcox *Gordon Madison* ■ *Dir* Wallace W Fox [Wallace Fox] • *Scr* Adele Buffington

Wild Bill ★★★★ 15

Western 1995 · US · Colour · 93mins

This is a flawed but fascinating look at an American legend. Starring a superbly cast Jeff Bridges as William "Wild Bill" Hickok, the movie opens with the killing of a dozen or so men over the course of a decade, then focuses on the ageing gunslinger's quest for old flame Calamity Jane (Ellen Barkin) while setting up a confrontation with a vengeful youngster who may be Hickok's bastard son. Walter Hill paints a far from pretty picture of the West and of Hickok: he's a drug addict, a killer and a monster haunted by his past. It oozes period atmosphere and stands as an epic of disillusionment. AT DVD

Jeff Bridges *James Butler "Wild Bill" Hickok* • Ellen Barkin *Calamity Jane* • John Hurt *Charley Prince* • Diane Lane *Susannah Moore* • David Arquette *Jack McCall* • Keith Carradine *Buffalo Bill Cody* • Christina Applegate *Lurline* • Bruce Dern *Will Plummer* ■ *Dir* Walter Hill • *Scr* Walter Hill, from the play *Fathers and Sons* by Thomas Babe and the novel *Deadwood* by Pete Dexter

The Wild Bunch ★★★★★ 18

Classic western 1969 · US · Colour · 138mins

Arguably, one of the greatest westerns ever made. And argument is what Sam Peckinpah's masterpiece has always caused for its slow-motion spurting of blood, its surrealistically choreographed gunfights and its portrayal of Pike Bishop's amoral Texas outlaws as heroes. Yet William Holden's laconic Bishop, however violent, is of a truly romantic breed as he leads his bunch to their deaths. Lucien Ballard's photography gives a funereal hue to this elegy to the passing of a certain breed of chivalry. You can see why John Wayne is said to have hated the film; Peckinpah was practically reinventing a genre, with no place left for false nobility. TH. Contains violence, nudity. DVD

William Holden (2) *Pike Bishop* • Ernest Borgnine *Dutch Engstrom* • Robert Ryan *Deke Thornton* • Edmond O'Brien *Sykes* • Warren Oates *Lyle Gorch* • Jaime Sanchez *Angel* • Ben Johnson *Tector Gorch* • Emilio Fernandez *Mapache* ■ *Dir* Sam Peckinpah • *Scr* Walon Green, Sam Peckinpah, from a story by Walon Green, Roy N Sickner

The Wild Country ★★ U

Adventure 1971 · US · Colour · 88mins

Disney tames the wilderness yarn into suitable family fare, but in doing so creates a much dumbed-down adventure. Steve Forrest and Vera Miles take on a run-down Wyoming ranch and, incidentally, the local inhabitants, including wall-eyed Jack Elam. The characters are as two-dimensional as Disney cartoons, though Ron Howard, the *Happy Days* star and now blockbuster director, gives a creditable performance as the teenage son. TH

Steve Forrest *Jim Tanner* • Vera Miles *Kate Tanner* • Jack Elam *Thompson* • Ronny Howard [Ron Howard] *Virgil Tanner* • Frank De Kova *Two Dog* • Morgan Woodward *Ab Cross* • Clint Howard *Andrew Tanner* • Dub Taylor *Phil* ■ *Dir* Robert Totten • *Scr* Calvin Clements Jr [Cal Clements Jr], Paul Savage, from the novel *Little Britches* by Ralph Moody

The Wild Duck ★★★

Drama 1983 · Aus · Colour · 95mins

Henri Safran makes so little capital out of relocating Henrik Ibsen's play to turn-of-the-century Australia that one wonders why he bothered. Yet the structure and brooding atmosphere of this fiercely melodramatic story remain intact and, apart from name changes, so do the characters. Thus Arthur Dignam is wilfully pompous as he hauls family skeletons before the bemused Jeremy Irons, who can scarcely believe that his timid wife, Liv Ullmann, bore him another man's child. This highly symbolic piece ends on a note of shocking tragedy, which nowadays seems strangely grotesque. DP

Liv Ullmann *Gina Ackland* • Jeremy Irons *Harold* • Lucinda Jones *Henrietta Ackland* • John Meillon *Major Ackland* • Arthur Dignam *Gregory Wardle* • Michael Pate *George Wardle* • Colin Croft *Mollison* ■ *Dir* Henri Safran • *Scr* Peter Smalley, John Lind, Henri Safran, from the play by Henrik Ibsen

The Wild Geese ★★★ 15

Action adventure
1978 · UK · Colour · 128mins

Richards Burton and Harris, plus Roger Moore, are evidently enjoying themselves here as mercenaries hired by Stewart Granger to rescue a deposed African president and put him back in power, all for the sake of big-business interests. There's hardly a moment when a hand grenade isn't in the air and, as a firework display, the movie is often exciting. Politically, it's a dog's dinner of woolly liberalism and right-wing rhetoric – it was filmed in South Africa during the height of apartheid. AT DVD

Richard Burton *Col Allen Faulkner* • Roger Moore *Shawn Fynn* • Richard Harris *Rafer Janders* • Hardy Kruger *Pieter Coetzee* • Stewart Granger *Sir Edward Matherson* • Jack Watson *Sandy Young* • Winston Ntshona *President Julius Limbani* • Frank Finlay *Priest* ■ *Dir* Andrew V McLaglen • *Scr* Reginald Rose, from the novel by Daniel Carney

Wild Geese II ★ 18

Action adventure
1985 · UK · Colour · 119mins

This infantile follow-up to *The Wild Geese* hinges on a gang of mercenaries trying to get the ageing Rudoph Hess (Laurence Olivier in a positively embarrassing performance) out of Spandau Prison. It revamps the original in having a brutal and tedious training sequence before the actual mission. The film is cobbled together with leaden predictability and absolutely no narrative flow whatsoever. BB

Scott Glenn *John Haddad* • Barbara Carrera *Kathy Lukas* • Edward Fox *Alex Faulkner* • Laurence Olivier *Rudolf Hess* • Robert Webber *Robert McCann* • Robert Freitag *Stroebling* • Kenneth Haigh *Col Reed-Henry* • Stratford Johns *Mustapha El Ali* ■ *Dir* Peter Hunt • *Scr* Reginald Rose, from the novel *The Square Circle* by Daniel Carney

Wild Geese Calling ★★

Drama 1941 · US · BW · 78mins

Restless lumberjack Henry Fonda, in search of excitement, tracks down old pal and gambler Warren William in Seattle. There he meets and marries saloon dancer Joan Bennett who, unbeknown to him, is William's old flame and gets involved in William's dangerous dispute with big Barton MacLane. With a top-notch cast and enough plot to fill two movies, one could have expected more of this adventure drama. For all its incident, however, the script is not sharp enough, and is further flattened by John Brahm's laboured direction. RK

Henry Fonda *John Murdock* • Joan Bennett *Sally Murdock* • Warren William *Blackie Bedford* • Ona Munson *Clarabella* • Barton MacLane *Pirate Kelly* • Russell Simpson *Len Baker* • Iris Adrian *Mazie* • James C Morton *Mack* ■ *Dir* John Brahm • *Scr* Horace McCoy, Sam Hellman, Jack Andrews, Robert Carson, from the novel by Stewart Edward White

A Wild Hare ★★★★

Animated comedy 1940 · US · Colour · 8mins

Before he made his official debut in this cartoon, Bugs Bunny had been through many different stages of development. Two years earlier, Bob Clampett used Tex Avery's rejected Daffy Duck gags to create a similarly daffy rabbit. Later, animator Charles Thorson redesigned him and named him after director Bugs Hardaway while Chuck Jones subdued his crazy ways. It wasn't until Tex Avery combined these elements with his own revolutionary ideas that a rabbit recognisable as Bugs Bunny appeared. Mischievous but relaxed, Bugs is the antithesis of his zany origins, as well as his real-life counterparts, as he resists dopey Elmer Fudd's attempts to shoot him ("What's up, Doc" being his first line of dialogue). CLP

Mel Blanc *Bugs Bunny* • Arthur Q Bryan *Elmer Fudd* ■ *Dir* Fred Avery [Tex Avery] • *Scr* Rich Hogan

Wild Hearts Can't Be Broken ★★★ U

Romantic drama 1991 · US · Colour · 85mins

A lovingly re-created Depression-era America provides the setting for this beautifully mounted Disney drama about the life of legendary stunt diver Sonora Webster, who overcame personal tragedy to become a star attraction with her horse-diving act. Gabrielle Anwar gives a gutsy performance in the lead role, while veteran actor Cliff Robertson provides the necessary eccentricity as her cranky employer. SH

Gabrielle Anwar *Sonora Webster* • Cliff Robertson *Doctor Carver* • Dylan Kussman *Clifford* • Michael Schoeffling *Al Carver* • Kathleen York *Marie* • Frank Renzulli *Mr Slater* • Nancy Moore Atchison *Arnette* • Lisa Norman *Aunt Helen* ■ *Dir* Steve Miner • *Scr* Matt Williams, Oley Sassone

Wild Heritage ★★★ U

Western 1958 · US · Colour · 78mins

This absorbing saga made on the cheap involves a brace of pioneer families and their trials and tribulations, mainly associated with their teenage offspring. Appearing among the youngsters are such icons of the era as folksie composer Rod McKuen and teen idol Troy Donahue. Newly widowed Maureen O'Sullivan presides over the gunplay, and gnarly Will Rogers Jr makes a fair bid at his real-life father's style of homespun wisdom. But the film belongs to the teenagers, as they demonstrate the solidarity rule of the Old West by ganging together and blasting the baddies. TS

Will Rogers Jr *Judge Copeland* • Maureen O'Sullivan *Emma Breslin* • Rod McKuen *Dirk Breslin* • Casey Tibbs *Rusty* • Troy Donahue *Jesse Bascomb* • Judy Meredith [Judi Meredith] *Callie Bascomb* • Gigi Perreau *Missouri Breslin* • George "Foghorn" Winslow [George Winslow] *Talbot Breslin* ■ *Dir* Charles Haas • *Scr* Paul King, Joseph Stone, from a story by Steve Frazee

Wild in the Country ★★ PG

Musical drama 1961 · US · Colour · 109mins

This drama about a backwoods delinquent on parole, who ends up going to college to become a great writer, represents an attempt to unveil Elvis Presley as a straight dramatic actor. He makes a respectable attempt but is not quite good enough, and has no help from an unconvincing plot and script. Strangely, this unlikely piece is based on the true story of one Jesse Stuart, a Kentucky hillbilly who became a successful writer. RK DVD

Elvis Presley *Glenn Tyler* • Hope Lange *Irene Sperry* • Tuesday Weld *Noreen* • Millie Perkins *Betty Lee Parsons* • Rafer Johnson *Davis* • Christina Crawford *Monica George* • John Ireland *Phil Macy* • Gary Lockwood *Cliff Macy* • Jason Robards Jr [Jason Robards] *Judge Parker* ■ *Dir* Philip Dunne • *Scr* Clifford Odets, from the novel *The Lost Country* by JR Salamanca

Wild in the Streets ★★ 15

Drama 1968 · US · Colour · 92mins

Christopher Jones, a world-famous pop megastar with a mother complex, starts a political campaign buoyed by Barry Mann and Cynthia Weil protest songs. When several states lower the voting age, the door is open for the first teenager to win the presidency, and Jones helps the political process along by putting LSD in the Washington water supply. When this modish satire of teenage rebellion was released at the fag-end of the 1960s, it must have seemed a lot more cutting then. However, the film is well-made, lively and often funny. JG

Shelley Winters *Mrs Flatow* • Christopher Jones *Max Frost* • Diane Varsi *Sally LeRoy* • Ed Begley *Senator Allbright* • Millie Perkins *Mary Fergus* • Hal Holbrook *John Fergus* • Richard Pryor *Stanley X* ■ *Dir* Barry Shear • *Scr* Robert Thom, from his article *The Day It All Happened, Baby*

Wild Is the Wind ★★

Melodrama 1957 · US · BW · 114mins

This gloomy, po-faced melodrama features Anthony Quinn as a widowed Italian shepherd farming in Nevada. Needing a new wife, he imports his sister-in-law (Anna Magnani) from Italy and marries her. The sparks start to fly when she makes off with Quinn's adopted son, Anthony Franciosa. George Cukor came on board when John Sturges was diverted to *The Old Man and the Sea*. It was apparently a turbulent production thanks to an uncomfortable relationship with prima donna Magnani. AT

Anna Magnani *Gioia* • Anthony Quinn *Gino* • Anthony Franciosa *Bene* • Dolores Hart *Angie* • Joseph Calleia *Alberto* • Lili Valenty *Teresa* ■ *Dir* George Cukor • *Scr* Arnold Schulman, from the novel *Furia* by Vittorio Nino Novarese

The Wild Life ★ 18

Comedy 1984 · US · Colour · 90mins

Like *Fast Times at Ridgemont High*, this is a collection of vignettes concerning eccentric teenagers as they embark on entering the adult world. Not only does the movie frequently forget to be funny, it is executed without any energy or passion in front of or behind the camera; aside from the golden oldie/Eddie Van Halen soundtrack, the only thing wild about it is its title. KB

Chris Penn *Tom Drake* • Ilan Mitchell-Smith *Jim Conrad* • Eric Stoltz *Bill Conrad* • Jenny Wright *Eileen* • Lea Thompson *Anita* • Rick Moranis *Harry* • Randy Quaid *Charlie* ■ *Dir* Art Linson • *Scr* Cameron Crowe

Wild Man Blues ★★★★ 12

Music documentary
1997 · US · Colour · 100mins

Music is low on director Barbara Kopple's list of priorities in this account of Woody Allen's 1996 European tour with his jazz band. Instead, she tags along as he's hurtled from pillar to post by civic and cultural dignitaries to receive awards and greet the great and the good (with a priceless mix of embarrassment and irritation). But it's the private moments with his then girlfriend – now his wife – Soon-Yi Previn that make this compelling portrait of a highly complex man so intriguing. Completely at home in the limelight, she comes across as the guiding light of their relationship. Yet, if you think she's overbearing, wait until you see Allen's parents in action during a hilarious coda. DP. Contains swearing.

Dir Barbara Kopple

The Wild North ★★ U

Adventure 1952 · US · Colour · 97mins

A first-rate cast figures in this below-standard adventure in which Stewart Granger kills a man in self-defence and is forced to flee into the Canadian wilderness. Hotly following is Mountie Wendell Corey, but trapper Granger knows every inch of the harsh countryside and leads him on a perilous trail. Andrew Marton directs with some pace, but with Cyd Charisse also featuring, it's the stars who are of main interest here. TH

Stewart Granger *Jules Vincent* • Wendell Corey *Constable Pedley* • Cyd Charisse *Indian girl* • Morgan Farley *Father Simon* • JM Kerrigan *Callahan* • Howard Petrie *Brody* • Houseley Stevenson *Old man* • John War Eagle *Indian chief* ■ *Dir* Andrew Marton • *Scr* Frank Fenton

Wild on the Beach ★★

Musical comedy 1965 · US · BW · 77mins

Sherry Jackson and singer Frankie Randall (being hailed as a new Sinatra at the time) head the cast in this tale of a group of teenagers who take over a beach house when there is a housing shortage on their campus. Their wrangling and romantic entanglements take up most of the screen time, and the film would be totally forgettable were it not for the presence of Sonny and Cher. The couple had just become pop sensations, and the film marked Cher's screen debut. TV

Frankie Randall *Adam* • Sherry Jackson *Lee Sullivan* • Sonny Bono *Sonny Bono* • Cher ■ *Dir* Maury Dexter • *Scr* Harry Spalding, from a story by Hank Tani

The Wild One ★★★★ PG

Drama 1953 · US · BW · 75mins

"What are you rebelling against, Johnny?" asks waitress Mary Murphy. "What've you got?" snarls Marlon Brando, his leather-clad biker entering the iconography of the decade. Long-banned in Britain, this is the first, the best, the quintessential motorbike movie, actually based on a 1947 incident when a cycle gang terrorised the small town of Hollister, California one desperate Fourth of July. OK, the back projection is a joke, Lee Marvin's far too old and the direction's often inadequate (as is the budget), but Brando is simply brilliant and the film still retains its unique power to astound. TS DVD

Marlon Brando *Johnny* • Mary Murphy *Kathie* • Robert Keith (1) *Harry Bleeker* • Lee Marvin *Chino* • Jay C Flippen *Sheriff Singer* • Peggy Maley *Mildred* • Hugh Sanders *Charlie Thomas* • Ray Teal *Frank Bleeker* ■ *Dir* Laslo Benedek • *Scr* John Paxton, from a story by Frank Rooney • *Cinematographer* Hal Mohr

Wild Orchid ★ 18

Erotic drama 1990 · US · Colour · 106mins

A ghastly piece of soft-pore corn from trashmaster Zalman King. Carré Otis plays a lawyer who courts trouble when she falls for earring-wearing, super-bronzed Mickey Rourke during the carnival celebrations in Rio. Silly girl! It's the cue for much simulated sex, and precious little else. DA DVD

Mickey Rourke *James Wheeler* • Jacqueline Bisset *Claudia* • Carré Otis *Emily Reed* • Assumpta Serna *Hanna* • Bruce Greenwood *Jerome* ■ *Dir* Zalman King • *Scr* Zalman King, Patricia Louisianna Knop

Wild Orchid 2: Two Shades of Blue ★★ 18

Erotic drama 1992 · US · Colour · 103mins

Nina Siemaszko is the young girl who is lured into working for brothel madam Wendy Hughes, while mourning her jazz drifter dad Tom Skerritt. As usual with King productions, this looks terrific, but the plotting and dialogue are risible. Still, it's marginally better than the largely unconnected original. Followed by *The Red Shoe Diaries*, starring David Duchovny, which spawned a long-running series of its own. JF

Nina Siemaszko *Blue* • Tom Skerritt *Ham* • Robert Davi *Sully* • Brent Fraser *Josh* • Christopher McDonald *Senator Dixon* • Wendy Hughes *Elle* • Joe Dallesandro *Jules* ■ *Dir* Zalman King • *Scr* Zalman King, Patricia Louisiana Knop

Wild Orchids ★★★

Silent romantic drama
1929 · US · BW · 100mins

On a boat to Java, the beautiful young wife (Greta Garbo) of a middle-aged, unemotional business tycoon (Lewis Stone), twice her age, is lusted after by a foreign prince (Nils Asther) who invites them to stay at his opulent Javanese palace. There, the tension mounts and the situation reaches its climax during a tiger shoot. This little-known Garbo silent, lavishly mounted and directed with excellent judgement by Sidney Franklin, is out of the school of exotic, erotic, fantasy melodrama. Garbo is good, Asther is perfectly cast as the scheming lover, and Stone is superb as the seemingly impervious husband. RK

Greta Garbo *Lili Sterling* • Lewis Stone *John Sterling* • Nils Asther *Prince De Gace* ■ *Dir* Sidney Franklin • *Scr* Hans Kräly, Richard Schayer, Willis Goldbeck, Marian Ainslee, Ruth Cummings, from the story *Hunt* by John Colton

The Wild Pair ★★ 18

Action crime drama
1987 · US · Colour · 91mins

This thoroughly routine action movie outing features Beau Bridges and Bubba Smith as, respectively, a yuppie FBI agent and a streetwise cop who team up to track down a bunch of drug-dealing killers. Bridges directs, his first time for the big screen, while dad Lloyd Bridges makes it something of a family affair by taking one of the chunkier supporting roles. DA

Beau Bridges *Joe Jennings* • Bubba Smith *Benny Avalon* • Lloyd Bridges *Colonel Hester* • Raymond St Jacques *Ivory* • Gary Lockwood *Captain Kramer* • Danny De La Paz *Tucker* • Lela Rochon *Debby* ■ *Dir* Beau Bridges • *Scr* Joseph Gunn, from a story by John Crowther, Joseph Gunn

The Wild Party ★★★

Comedy drama 1929 · US · BW · 77mins

Clara Bow's first talking picture has the original "It Girl" as a larky student who develops a crush on her tutor, played by Fredric March. Gossip, pranks, insubordination and 1920s sophomore slang all play their part in a fascinating period piece that is hard to watch today due to its forgivable technical limitations, yet which retains enough of its original energy to be entertaining. Bow acquits herself well here, and it is more likely that scandal (including her elopement with screen cowboy Rex Bell) was the main reason for her subsequent obscurity rather than the advent of sound. RB

Clara Bow *Stella Ames* • Fredric March *Gil Gilmore* • Shirley O'Hara (1) *Helen Owens* • Marceline Day *Faith Morgan* • Joyce Compton *Eva Tutt* ■ *Dir* Dorothy Arzner • *Scr* E Lloyd Sheldon, John VA Weaver, from a story by Warner Fabian

The Wild Party ★★★

Drama 1975 · US · Colour · 100mins

In an impressive re-creation of silent-era Hollywood, James Coco plays a fading film funnyman whose hopes are pinned on a comeback movie hit. Raquel Welch plays the girlfriend who hosts a wild party for Tinseltown's moviebiz movers and shakers to promote it. It's a grim film that's based on the story of Fatty Arbuckle, the silent-era comic whose fan following vanished like mist when he was charged with killing a girl during a sex romp gone wrong. Welch is actually very good and it's directed by James Ivory with scarcely a cucumber sarnie to be seen. DA

James Coco *Jolly Grimm* • Raquel Welch *Queenie* • Perry King *Dale Sword* • Tiffany Bolling *Kate* • Royal Dano *Tex* • David Dukes *James* • Dena Dietrich *Mrs Murchison* ■ *Dir* James Ivory • *Scr* Walter Marks, from a poem by Joseph Moncure March • *Producer* Ismail Merchant • *Cinematographer* Walter Lassally

The Wild Racers ★★

Action drama 1968 · US · Colour · 83mins

Although he'd been script doctoring for several years and had already directed a couple of features, Francis Ford Coppola had to be content with a second-unit credit on this typically effusive exploitation offering from B feature maestro, Roger Corman. The story of an ambitious racing driver who jeopardises his chances by living in the fast lane is classic Corman, with its achingly unhip dialogue and surfeit of inserted stock footage. DP

Fabian *Jo-Jo Quillico* • Mimsy Farmer *Katherine* • Alan Haufrect *Virgil* • Judy Cornwell *Pippy* • David Landers *Manager* • Talia Coppola [Talia Shire] *First girlfriend* ■ *Dir* Daniel Haller • *Scr* Max House

The Wild Ride ★★ PG

Drama 1960 · US · BW · 59mins

In one of Jack Nicholson's earliest films, the future superstar plays a homicidal hot-rodder fed up with a former pal who's given up the wild life to settle down with girlfriend Georgianna Carter. Kidnapping the girl, he takes her on a high-speed rampage pursued by the local constabulary. It's a cheap quickie, but it has its own exploitative charm. AT DVD

Jack Nicholson *Johnny Varron* • Georgianna Carter *Nancy* • Robert Bean *Dave* ■ *Dir* Harvey Berman • *Scr* Ann Porter, Marion Rothman • *Editor* Monte Hellman

Wild River ★★★★ PG

Drama 1960 · US · Colour · 105mins

This was a commercial failure for Elia Kazan, one of the key directors of postwar American cinema. But today this study of an old woman's intransigence when faced by the Tennessee Valley Authority's need to sequester her property in order to build a dam proves to be an intelligent and moving film, graced by a superbly tender performance from Montgomery Clift in one of his last and most tortured roles. Lee Remick is touching as his confidante, and there's a sharply-etched portrait by Jo Van Fleet in the role of the old woman. Watch out too for Bruce Dern in his movie debut. TS DVD

Montgomery Clift *Chuck Glover* • Lee Remick *Carol Baldwin* • Jo Van Fleet *Ella Garth* • Albert Salmi *FJ Bailey* • Jay C Flippen *Hamilton Garth* • James Westerfield *Cal Garth* • Big Jeff Bess *Joe John Garth* • Bruce Dern *Jack Roper* ■ *Dir* Elia Kazan • *Scr* Paul Osborn, from the novels *Mud on the Stars* by William Bradford Huie and *Dunbar's Cove* by Borden Deal

Wild Rovers ★★★★ 15

Western 1971 · US · Colour · 125mins

This fine western stars William Holden, Ryan O'Neal and Karl Malden. It's very much a film made in the wake of *The Wild Bunch* (in which Holden also starred), telling the story of an ageing cowboy and his adoring younger partner who dream of getting rich by robbing a bank. Beautifully shot and with a fine Jerry Goldsmith score, this is an exciting and often touching study of honour, heroism and changing times. O'Neal is perfectly cast, for once, and Holden is as craggy and magnificent as the Rocky Mountains scenery. AT

William Holden (2) *Ross Bodine* • Ryan O'Neal *Frank Post* • Karl Malden *Walter Buckman* • Lynn Carlin *Sada Billings* • Tom Skerritt *John Buckman* • Joe Don Baker *Paul Buckman* • James Olson *Joe Billings* • Leora Dana *Nell Buckman* • Moses Gunn *Ben* • Victor French *Sheriff* ■ *Dir/Scr* Blake Edwards • *Cinematographer* Philip Lathrop

Wild Search ★★ 15

Crime thriller 1989 · UK · Colour · 94mins

One of Hong Kong star Chow Yun-Fat's more obscure films, this is a more than able crime thriller, expertly choreographed by director Ringo Lam. While this lacks the bravura of the best Hong Kong thrillers, it still bears comparison with most Hollywood fodder. JF. In Cantonese with English subtitles. Contains violence.

Chow Yun-Fat *Mickey Lau* • Cherie Chung *Cher* • Paul Chin *Mr Hung* • Chan Cheuk-yan *Ka-ka* • Lau Kong *Leung* • Tommy Wong *Lam* • Roy Cheung *Tiger* ■ *Dir* Ringo Lam • *Scr* Nam Yin

Wild Seed ★★

Road movie 1965 · US · BW · 98mins

One of the results of a Universal Studios policy in the mid-1960s to encourage inexperienced talent – and it shows. Celia Kaye, in search of her

W

birth parents, crosses America bound for LA. On the way she hooks up with ne'er-do-well Michael Parks. The set-up is of course a familiar one, but this highly visual film is watchable thanks to cinematographer Conrad Hall (whose first major studio film this is). JG

Michael Parks *Fargo* • Celia Kaye *Daphne, "Daffy"* • Ross Elliott *Mr Collinge* • Woodrow Chambliss *Mr Simms* • Rupert Crosse *Hobo* ■ *Dir* Brian G Hutton • *Scr* Les Pine, from a story by Ike Jones, Les Pine

Wild Side ★★★ 18

Erotic thriller 1995 · US · Colour · 110mins

Anne Heche stars as a banker who also works as a call girl to make ends meet. But an encounter with infamous money launderer Christopher Walken leads to an affair with his wife (Joan Chen) and involvement in an undercover FBI operation. The fourth and final film made by director Donald Cammell, this was re-cut without his permission and released on cable in a severely truncated form (Cammell was credited as Franklin Brauner). Cammell committed suicide shortly afterwards, and his widow China Kong and longtime editor Frank Mazzola have here reconstructed a seemingly improvised pulp thriller that's closer to the director's original vision. It won't be to everyone's taste – there's a brutal rape scene – yet it stands as a compelling piece of cinema from a sadly underused talent. JA DVD

Christopher Walken *Bruno Buckingham* • Anne Heche *Alex Lee* • Joan Chen *Virginia Chow* • Steven Bauer *Tony* • Allen Garfield *Dan Rackman* • Adam Novack *Lyle Litvak* ■ *Dir* Donald Cammell • *Scr* Donald Cammell, China Kong • *Music* Ryuichi Sakamoto

Wild Side ★★★ 18

Drama 2004 · Fr/Bel/UK · Colour · 94mins

This is a thoughtful treatise on individuality and the courage needed to make difficult choices. Having established the humiliation that transsexual prostitute Stéphanie (played by Stéphanie Michelini) endures in Paris, director Sébastien Lifshitz reveals the true extent of her vulnerability when she returns to her childhood home in northern France to nurse her dying mother (Josiane Stoleru). However, the arrival of Michelini's bisexual Russian lover (Edouard Nikitine) and an Arab hustler (Yasmine Belmadi) further complicates her attempt to reconcile herself to her past. DP. In French and Russian with English subtitles. Contains swearing and sex scenes.

Stéphanie Michelini *Stéphanie* • Edouard Nikitine *Mikhail* • Yasmine Belmadi *Djamel* • Josiane Stoleru *Mother* • Antony Hegarty *Café singer* ■ *Dir* Sébastien Lifshitz • *Scr* Sébastien Lifshitz, Stéphane Bouquet

Wild Strawberries ★★★★★ 15

Drama 1957 · Swe · BW · 87mins

Contrasting the innocent expectancy of youth with the bitter regret of old age, this is Ingmar Bergman's warmest and most accessible film. Sweden's greatest silent director, Victor Sjöström, gives a magisterial performance as the frosty, vain professor who seizes the chance for redemption offered to him in the dreams and nightmares he experiences while travelling to a degree ceremony with his daughter-in-law, Ingrid Thulin. The symbolism of the nightmares (including handless clocks and runaway hearses) is occasionally overpowering, but the memories of idyllic summers spent with cousin Bibi Andersson rank among the finest moments of the director's career. DP. In Swedish with English subtitles. DVD

Victor Sjöström *Professor Isak Borg* • Bibi Andersson *Sara* • Ingrid Thulin *Marianne Borg* • Gunnar Björnstrand *Evald Borg* ■ *Dir/Scr* Ingmar Bergman

Wild Style ★★★ 15

Documentary drama
1982 · US · Colour · 82mins

Ever wondered what hip-hop culture is all about? Look no further than director Charlie Ahearn's accurate representation of the scene, starring legendary New York graffiti artist Georges "Lee" Quinones. Forget the plot – how the "Next Big Thing" in the art world copes with the pressures of success and the strain it puts on his relationships – the reason why this movie is considered the *Saturday Night Fever* of the B-boy brigade is due to the documentary feel of the break dancing, the freestyle MC-ing, the Rocksteady Crew in performance, the basketball rapping and rare scratch-mixing footage of Grand Master Flash, a godfather of rap. A memorable movie that preserves the true essence of early hip-hop for all time. AJ DVD

"Lee" Georges Quinones *Raymond "Zoro"* • Sandra "Pink" Fabara *Rose "Lady Bug"* • Patti Astor *Virginia* • Frederick "Fab Five Freddy" Brathwaite [Fab Five Freddy] *Phade* • Grand Master Flash ■ *Dir/Scr* Charlie Ahearn

Wild Target ★★★★ 15

Comedy thriller 1993 · Fr · Colour · 84mins

Jean Rochefort, one of the finest character actors currently working in French cinema, has rarely been better than in this scorching debut from writer/director Pierre Salvadori. Rochefort is quite superb as a meticulous hitman whose ordered existence begins to disintegrate when he takes on impetuous accomplice Guillaume Depardieu – son of Gérard – and falls in love with his next hit, glamorous art forger and petty thief Marie Trintignant (daughter of Jean-Louis and Nadine). The scenes at the hotel and Rochefort's country house are executed with great flair and a delicious black wit. DP. In French with English subtitles.

Jean Rochefort *Victor Meynard* • Marie Trintignant *Renée* • Guillaume Depardieu *Antoine* • Patachou *Madame Meynard* • Charlie Nelson *Dremyan* • Wladimir Yordanoff *Casa Bianca* • Serge Riaboukine *Manu* • Philippe Girard *Tony* ■ *Dir/Scr* Pierre Salvadori

Wild Thing ★★ 15

Crime drama
1987 · US/Can · Colour · 88mins

Screenwriter John Sayles – a notable film-maker in his own right – has a solid track record in providing decent scripts for other people's movies. However, this is an anaemic affair concerning Robert Knepper, whose parents are murdered, forcing him to grow up wild in the city slums. Eventually he becomes a sort of feral cut-price Batman figure, vengefully protecting local inhabitants from nasty drug dealer Robert Davi. Even if Sayles's original script was any good on paper, the execution by director Max Reid does it no justice at all. TH

Rob Knepper [Robert Knepper] *Wild Thing* • Kathleen Quinlan *Jane* • Robert Davi *Chopper* • Maury Chaykin *Trask* • Betty Buckley *Leah* • Clark Johnson *Winston* • Sean Hewitt *Father Quinn* ■ *Dir* Max Reid • *Scr* John Sayles, from a story by John Sayles, Larry Stamper

Wild Things ★★★ 18

Thriller 1998 · US · Colour · 103mins

Things are certainly steamy in Florida in this eyebrow-raising thriller. Neve Campbell and Denise Richards star as high-school students who falsely accuse teacher Matt Dillon of rape in a preposterous tale that's more notable for its X-rated scenes than for its great acting or script. There are a few nice twists, however, and the handsome cast clearly enjoys vamping it up in what is essentially a sexed-up, feature-length MTV video. Popular enough to produce a sequel in 2004. JB. Contains swearing, sex scenes and some violence. DVD

Kevin Bacon *Ray Duquette* • Matt Dillon *Sam Lombardo* • Neve Campbell *Suzie Toller* • Theresa Russell *Sandra Van Ryan* • Denise Richards *Kelly Van Ryan* • Daphne Rubin-Vega *Gloria Perez* • Robert Wagner *Tom Baxter* • Bill Murray *Ken Bowden* ■ *Dir* John McNaughton • *Scr* Stephen Peters

The Wild Thornberrys Movie ★★ U

Animated comedy
2003 · US · Colour · 81mins

Bespectacled, brace-wearing Eliza Thornberry and her eccentric nature documentary-making family are given the feature-length treatment in Nickelodeon's small-screen spin-off. But while this is more than palatable in bite-sized servings, stretched over 85 minutes it rapidly loses its verve. There's not enough plot, or indeed action, to engage young minds for the movie's duration. SF DVD

Lacey Chabert *Eliza Thornberry* • Tom Kane *Darwin* • Tim Curry *Nigel Thornberry/Col Thornberry* • Lynn Redgrave *Cordelia Thornberry* • Jodi Carlisle *Marianne Thornberry* • Danielle Harris *Debbie Thornberry* • Flea *Donnie Thornberry* • Rupert Everett *Sloan Blackburn* • Marisa Tomei *Bree Blackburn* • Brenda Blethyn *Mrs Fairgood* ■ *Dir* Jeff McGrath, Cathy Malkasian • *Scr* Katie Boutilier, from characters created by Arlene Klasky, Gabor Csupo, Steve Pepoon, David Silverman, Stephen Sustarsic

Wild West ★★★ 15

Comedy 1992 · UK · Colour · 80mins

Rip-roaring tale of the old west (old west London, that is), with a bunch of country music-loving Pakistani "outlaws" from Southall who want to make music – but instead find themselves facing it when their band leader falls for an Asian girl who's unhappily wed to a villainous "gringo". Naveen Andrews and Sarita Choudhury star in an enjoyable romp that was one of the first films to portray multi-ethnic Britain accurately. DA

Naveen Andrews *Zaf Ayub* • Sarita Choudhury *Rifat* • Ronny Jhutti *Kay Ayub* • Ravi Kapoor *Ali Ayub* • Ameet Chana *Gurdeep* • Bhasker *Jagdeep* • Lalita Ahmed *Mrs Ayub* ■ *Dir* David Attwood • *Scr* Harwant Bains

Wild Wheels ★★★

Documentary 1992 · US · Colour · 64mins

This highly engaging, witty and touching documentary is all about unconventional car owners and the way they customise their vehicles to reflect their personalities or important moments in their lives. Written and directed by Harrod Blank, whose own Volkswagen is lovingly covered in plastic globes and sunflowers with a huge black fly on the hood, his tribute shows other cars decorated with buttons, beads, huge crucifixes, taps and even plastic flamingos. The drivers come from all walks of life and ethnic groups, and although Blank's focus is goofy eccentricity, there is frequently a meaningful motivation behind the decor. Unusual and quirky. AJ

Dir/Scr Harrod Blank • *Cinematographer* Harrod Blank, Paul Cope, Les Blank

The Wild, Wild Planet ★★★

Science fiction 1965 · It · Colour · 92mins

Shot back-to-back with *War of the Planets*, this cops-and-robbers-in-outer-space epic from cult Italian journeyman director Antonio Margheriti is a dazzling cocktail of groovy 1960s sci-fi, kitschy psychedelia and outrageous special effects. In the 21st century insane scientist Massimo Serato fabricates female androids in order to kidnap VIP space officials, who are miniaturised and transported in special attaché cases. Commander Tony Russel investigates the disappearances and pinpoints the planetoid Delphos, where Serato is experimenting to populate the Earth with perfect specimens. AJ. Italian dialogue dubbed into English.

Tony Russel *Cmdr Mike Halstead* • Lisa Gastoni *Connie Gomez* • Massimo Serato *Nels Nurmi* • Franco Nero *Jake* • Charles Justin [Carlo Giustini] *Ken* ■ *Dir* Anthony M Dawson [Antonio Margheriti] • *Scr* Ivan Reiner, Renato Moretti

Wild Wild West ★★ 12

Western adventure fantasy
1999 · US · Colour · 105mins

Superficial and predictable, with special effects bloated out of all proportion, director Barry Sonnenfeld's big screen adaptation of the cult 1960s TV series may have an invisible script, but it's still fun thanks to the charisma of Will Smith and some fabulous gadgetry. Smith and Kevin Kline star as mismatched US secret service agents using out-of-time contraptions and fancy disguises to stop mad genius Kenneth Branagh from assassinating President Grant (Kline again). The one-liners are below average. AJ. Contains violence and sexual references. DVD

Will Smith *James West* • Kevin Kline *Artemus Gordon/President Ulysses S Grant* • Kenneth Branagh *Dr Arliss Loveless* • Salma Hayek *Rita Escobar* • M Emmet Walsh *Coleman* • Ted Levine *General McGrath* • Frederique Van Der Wal *Amazonia* • Musetta Vander *Munitia* ■ *Dir* Barry Sonnenfeld • *Scr* SS Wilson, Brent Maddock, Jeffrey Price, Peter S Seaman, from a story by Jim Thomas, John Thomas • *Music* Elmer Bernstein

The Wild Women of Wongo ★ U

Fantasy comedy 1958 · US · Colour · 52mins

This is one of several films that were voted the worst ever made and consequently gained a new lease of life among camp followers in the 1980s. A prehistoric comedy, closer in spirit to a burlesque sketch than parody, it is about the romance between the Princess of Wongo, where the women are beautiful and the men are ugly, and the Prince of Goona, where it's vice versa. The unspeakable dialogue and risible performances are fun for a while, although the joke wears thin pretty quickly. DM

Jean Hawkshaw *Omoo* • John Walsh *Engor* • Mary Ann Webb *Mona* • Cande Gerrard *Ahtee* • Adrienne Bourbeau *Wana* • Ed Fury *Gahbo* ■ *Dir* James L Wolcott • *Scr* Cedric Rutherford

Wildcats ★★ 15

Comedy 1986 · US · Colour · 101mins

Most of the interest in this routine Goldie Hawn comedy is generated by the sight of some familiar faces in the supporting cast who were making their first steps on the way to stardom. Hawn is the fledgeling American football coach who sets about transforming a terrible college side, much to the disbelief of the macho team members, who include a young Wesley Snipes and Woody Harrelson. There are some amusing moments, and, as usual, Hawn's comic timing can't be faulted. In the end, however, it remains one for die-hard fans only. JF. Contains swearing and nudity.

Goldie Hawn *Molly McGrath* • Swoosie Kurtz *Verna* • Robyn Lively *Alice McGrath* • Brandy Gold *Marian McGrath* • James Keach *Frank McGrath* • Jan Hooks *Stephanie* • Nipsey Russell *Ben Edwards* • M Emmet Walsh *Coes*

• Wesley Snipes *Trumaine* • Woody Harrelson *Krushinski* ■ *Dir* Michael Ritchie • *Scr* Ezra Sacks

The Wildcats of St Trinian's ★

Comedy 1980 · UK · Colour · 91mins

In truth, there was only one genuinely funny entry – *The Belles of St Trinian's* – in this five-film series, with each instalment failing more dismally than the last to match the comic anarchy of the original movie. Why Frank Launder felt the need to return to the old place after a 14-year hiatus is hard to fathom, especially as he could only come up with this lame story about kidnapping and strikes, which is essentially an excuse for scantily clad sixth-formers and dodgy gags. DP

Sheila Hancock *Olga Vandemeer* • Michael Hordern *Sir Charles Hackforth* • Joe Melia *Flash Harry* • Thorley Walters *Hugo Culpepper-Brown* • Rodney Bewes *Peregrine Butters* • Deborah Norton *Miss Brenner* • Maureen Lipman *Katy Higgs* • Julia McKenzie *Dolly Dormancott* ■ *Dir* Frank Launder • *Scr* Frank Launder, from the drawings by Ronald Searle

Wilde ★★★★ 15

Biographical drama
1997 · UK · Colour · 111mins

Once you've seen Stephen Fry in the title role of Oscar Wilde it's difficult to imagine anyone better suited. Playing to the myth of the giant of wit, restraint and wisdom, Fry conveys the strain of a public figure tied to a false marriage (with Jennifer Ehle) while besieged by his love for another man (a bitingly excellent Jude Law as the rich and spoilt Lord Alfred Douglas). Assertive in its graphic exploration of male love, this may not suit all tastes, but nevertheless it is beautifully written with spot-on attention to period detail. LH. Contains swearing, sex scenes and nudity. DVD

Stephen Fry *Oscar Wilde* • Jude Law *Lord Alfred Douglas* • Vanessa Redgrave *Lady Speranza Wilde* • Jennifer Ehle *Constance Wilde* • Gemma Jones *Lady Queensberry* • Judy Parfitt *Lady Mount-Temple* • Michael Sheen *Robert Ross* • Zoë Wanamaker *Ada Leverson* • Tom Wilkinson *Marquess of Queensberry* • Ioan Gruffudd *John Gray* ■ *Dir* Brian Gilbert • *Scr* Julian Mitchell, from the biography *Oscar Wilde* by Richard Ellman

Wilder ★★★ 18

Detective thriller
2000 · Can · Colour · 88mins

This pairing of Pam Grier and straight-to-video specialist Rutger Hauer doesn't promise great things, yet this is a tough, amusing and eventfully plotted police thriller. Grier is a formidable presence as a spirited Chicago cop unravelling a deep big business conspiracy with amiable doctor Hauer, the prime suspect in a murder investigation. Although the opening section suggests routine police procedural clichés, this develops into an enjoyable, funky thriller, with pleasing chemistry between the stars and a commendable balance of brutal action and light comedy. JC DVD

Pam Grier *Det Della Wilder* • Rutger Hauer *Dr Sam Charney* • Luccio Romano Orzari *Det Harlan Lee* • John Dunn-Hill *Capt Jerry Crandall* • Eugene Clark *Attorney Marlowe King* • Richard Robitaille *Ricky Harwell* ■ *Dir* Rodney Gibbons • *Scr* Terry Abrahamson

Wilder Napalm ★ 15

Comedy 1993 · US · Colour · 104mins

Debra Winger stars in this lamentable comedy (to use the word in its loosest sense). She is caught up in the feud between brothers Dennis Quaid and Arliss Howard, who can't decide how best to exploit their fire-starting genius. It rapidly becomes almost unbearable to watch otherwise talented performers getting so badly burned. DP. Contains violence, swearing and sex scenes.

Debra Winger *Vida* • Dennis Quaid *Wallace Foudroyant* • Arliss Howard *Wilder Foudroyant* • M Emmet Walsh *Fire chief* • Jim Varney *Rex* • Mimi Lieber *Snake lady* • Marvin J McIntyre *Deputy Sheriff Spivey* ■ *Dir* Glenn Gordon Caron • *Scr* Vince Gilligan

Wildflower ★★★ 15

Period drama 1991 · US · Colour · 90mins

Directed by actress Diane Keaton, this moving TV drama is set in 1930s Georgia and follows the experiences of Patricia Arquette, a partially deaf epileptic imprisoned by her stepfather, who is convinced she is possessed by the Devil. Adapted by Sara Flanigan from her own book, this is subtly handled by Keaton, and her direction is complemented by involving performances. JB DVD

Patricia Arquette *Alice Guthrie* • Beau Bridges *Jack Perkins* • Susan Blakely *Ada Guthrie* • Reese Witherspoon *Ellie Perkins* • William McNamara *Sammy Perkins* ■ *Dir* Diane Keaton • *Scr* Sara Flanigan, from her non-fiction book *Alice*

Wildflower ★★ 18

Erotic thriller 1999 · US · Colour · 87mins

A regulation late-night erotic thriller, but with a moderately intriguing set-up. Travelling home to settle their late father's affairs, scheming siblings pick up a seemingly distressed hitch-hiker and more trouble than they bargained for. Thereafter, of course, it's just one steamy session after another. As the sexy *femme fatale* in a cast made up of complete unknowns, CC Costigan acts enthusiastically. DM DVD

CC Costigan *Nicole* • Kim Little *Audrey Hobbs* • Chris Hoffman *Dennis Hobbs* • Dean Stapleton *Ethan Hobbs* • Tamie Sheffield *Zoey* ■ *Dir* David Michael Latt • *Scr* Angel Orona

Wildly Available ★ 18

Erotic drama 1996 · US · Colour · 99mins

A cameo appearance by singer Lou Rawls is the only thing to recommend this tiresome softcore melodrama from writer/director Michael Nolin. He clearly thinks that he's pushing boundaries with the bondage sequences featuring married businessman Kristoffer Tabori and Jennifer Sommerfield, the exotic dancer with whom he begins a kinky affair. The cast wastes their talents on this wildly unappealing twaddle. DP

Kristoffer Tabori *Joe Goodman* • Jennifer Sommerfield *Wendy* • Jane Kaczmarek *Rita Goodman* • Lou Rawls *Jazz singer* • Rachel Crane *Samantha Goodman* • Megan Cole *Therapist* ■ *Dir/Scr* Michael Nolin

Will Any Gentleman...? ★★ U

Comedy 1953 · UK · Colour · 84mins

Michael Anderson directs this over-literal adaptation of Vernon Sylvaine's stage success. However, even laying aside the clumsiness of much of the comedy, a fair proportion of modern viewers won't be particularly well disposed towards a story in which a hypnotist turns a timid bank clerk into a swaggering lothario. As the entranced enchanter, George Cole makes the most of his awkward charm, but his enthusiasm too often gets the better of him. DP

George Cole *Henry Sterling* • Veronica Hurst *Mrs Sterling* • Jon Pertwee *Charlie Sterling* • James Hayter *Dr Smith* • Heather Thatcher *Mrs Whittle* • William Hartnell *Inspector Martin* • Sidney James *Mr Hobson* • Joan Sims *Beryl* ■ *Dir* Michael Anderson • *Scr* Vernon Sylvaine, from his play

Will It Snow for Christmas? ★★★ 12

Drama 1996 · Fr · Colour · 86mins

Sandrine Veysett won a César for this, her directorial debut. It's an oblique, slow-moving tribute to farm labour and a universal commentary on the nature of dysfunctional family. Dominique Reymond is a mother with seven illegitimate children who rents and works a farm. Her life is punctuated by the periodic visits of her wayward lover, Daniel Duval. Married with a family elsewhere, he continues returning to bed Reymond. However, when Duval makes advances on their eldest daughter, Reymond is forced into making a crucial decision about their lives. LH. In French with English subtitles.

Dominique Reymond *Mother* • Daniel Duval *Father* • Jessica Martinez *Jeanne* • Alexandre Roger *Bruno* • Xavier Colonna *Pierrot* • Fanny Rochetin *Marie* ■ *Dir/Scr* Sandrine Veysset

Will Penny ★★★★ 12

Western 1967 · US · Colour · 105mins

Charlton Heston gives a fine performance as the grizzled lone rider of the title, confronting the memorable Joan Hackett and uncertain of how to break the tough habits of a lifetime: "I'm a cowboy. I don't know nuthin' else." Director Tom Gries never hit these heights again: this is one of the great westerns, invariably overlooked, and marred only by the florid performance of an ill-cast Donald Pleasence. The photography by Lucien Ballard is particularly outstanding, as is the fine score from David Raksin. TS. Contains violence, swearing. DVD

Charlton Heston *Will Penny* • Joan Hackett *Catherine Allen* • Donald Pleasence *Preacher Quint* • Lee Majors *Blue* • Bruce Dern *Rafe Quint* • Ben Johnson *Alex* • Slim Pickens *Ike Wallerstein* ■ *Dir/Scr* Tom Gries

Will Success Spoil Rock Hunter? ★★★ U

Satirical drama 1957 · US · Colour · 94mins

Fresh from her Broadway success, Jayne Mansfield reprises her role as the pouting movie star with voluptuous glee in Frank Tashlin's film version of George Axelrod's hit play. However, it's Tony Randall, as the meek advertising agent who is forced to play the fame game to keep a prestigious lipstick account, who keeps this ambitious satire on track. Swiping at everything from media hype and public gullibility to sex and the morality of advertising, Tashlin was never going to land all his punches, but this glossy, rather hollow enterprise, while very much a hit-and-miss affair, has undeniable charm. DP

Tony Randall *Rockwell Hunter* • Jayne Mansfield *Rita Marlowe* • Betsy Drake *Jenny* • Joan Blondell *Violet* • John Williams *Le Salle Jr* • Henry Jones *Rufus* • Lili Gentle *April* • Mickey Hargitay *Bobo* • Groucho Marx *Surprise guest* ■ *Dir* Frank Tashlin • *Scr* Frank Tashlin, from the play by George Axelrod

Willard ★★★

Horror 1971 · US · Colour · 95mins

In this hugely successful story of violent vermin, oppressed office boy Bruce Davison turns the tables on his tormentors by training his two pet rats, Socrates and Ben, and their sewer pals, to attack on command. But when he neglects them after falling in love with Sondra Locke, hell hath no fury like rodents scorned! Solid direction by Daniel Mann and Davison's creepily introverted performance turned this horror revenge tale into a huge box-office hit. A sequel, *Ben*, followed. AJ

Bruce Davison *Willard Stiles* • Ernest Borgnine *Al Martin* • Elsa Lanchester *Henrietta Stiles* • Sondra Locke *Joan* • Michael Dante *Brandt* • Jody Gilbert *Charlotte Stassen* ■ *Dir* Daniel Mann • *Scr* Gilbert A Ralston, from the novel *Ratman's Notebooks* by Stephen Gilbert [Gilbert A Ralston]

Willard ★★★ 15

Horror 2003 · US · Colour · 96mins

Hollywood eccentric Crispin Glover is perfectly cast in this quirky reinterpretation of the 1971 horror classic. All tics and emotional insecurities, he shines as the down-trodden office boy who uses his two pet rats and their furry pals to wreak violent revenge on his tormentors. The film is more gothic fantasy fable than outright chiller and, despite a sinister core, its childlike imagination and visual strangeness make the barbed tale as weird and whimsical as it is creepy. SF DVD

Crispin Glover *Willard* • R Lee Ermey *Mr Martin* • Laura Elena Harring [Laura Harring] *Catherine* • Jackie Burroughs *Mrs Stiles* • Kimberly Patton [Kim McKamy] *Ms Leach* • William S Taylor *Mr Garter* ■ *Dir* Glen Morgan • *Scr* Glen Morgan, from the film by Gilbert A Ralston, from the novel *Ratman's Notebooks* by Stephen Gilbert [Gilbert A Ralston]

William at the Circus ★★ U

Comedy 1948 · UK · BW · 92mins

No devotee of Richmal Crompton's creation would be satisfied by a screen version of William. However, Val Guest captures a little of the exuberant antics of the original and William Graham is nicely cast as the ever questioning boy. His parents have promised him an outing to the circus – if he's good. Not the most likely of outcomes then, especially when he is campaigning for shorter school hours. BB

William Graham *William Brown* • Garry Marsh *Mr Brown* • Jane Welsh *Mrs Brown* • AE Matthews *Minister* • Muriel Aked *Emily* • Hugh Cross *Robert Brown* • Kathleen Stuart *Ethel Brown* • Brian Roper *Ginger* ■ *Dir* Val Guest • *Scr* Val Guest, from the stories by Richmal Crompton

William Shakespeare's Romeo + Juliet ★★★★ 12

Romantic tragedy
1996 · US/Aus/Can · Colour · 115mins

Baz Luhrmann's updated, richly visualised version of the Bard's chronicle of star-crossed young lovers made Leonardo DiCaprio an authentic teen idol. Claire Danes plays the Juliet yearning for DiCaprio's Romeo on Verona Beach, where family gang warfare explodes into violent attacks and biker battles. There's no doubting the quality of DiCaprio's performance, though Danes is too eye-flutteringly winsome for comfort. As a magnet to attract youngsters to Shakespeare, it couldn't be bettered. TH. Contains some violence. DVD

Leonardo DiCaprio *Romeo* • Claire Danes *Juliet* • Brian Dennehy *Ted Montague* • John Leguizamo *Tybalt* • Pete Postlethwaite *Father Laurence* • Paul Sorvino *Fulgencio Capulet* • Diane Venora *Gloria Capulet* • Harold Perrineau *Mercutio* • Paul Rudd *Dave Paris* • Jesse Bradford *Balthasar* • Dash Mihok *Benvolio* • Miriam Margolyes *Nurse* ■ *Dir* Baz Luhrmann • *Scr* Craig Pearce, Baz Luhrmann, from the play by William Shakespeare

William Shakespeare's The Merchant of Venice ★★★ PG

Period drama 2004 · UK/It · Colour · 126mins

Al Pacino stars in this sumptuous production of one of the Bard's more controversial plays, which is often regarded as being anti-Semitic. As Jewish moneylender Shylock, Pacino gives a subtle performance, but he's obviously having to work hard just to keep up with Jeremy Irons's quietly noble merchant Antonio, whose flesh Shylock demands as recompense for an unrepaid loan, and Lynn Collins's

W

hugely impressive Portia. Michael Radford's direction is straightforward and unflashy, while the film benefits from shooting scenes on location in Venice itself. DA DVD

Al Pacino *Shylock* • Jeremy Irons *Antonio* • Lynn Collins *Portia* • Joseph Fiennes *Bassanio* • Zuleikha Robinson *Jessica* • Kris Marshall *Gratiano* • Charlie Cox *Lorenzo* • John Sessions *Salerio* • Mackenzie Crook *Lancelot Gobbo* ■ *Dir* Michael Radford • *Scr* Michael Radford, from the play by William Shakespeare

Willie and Phil ★★★ 18

Drama 1980 · US · Colour · 111mins

Paul Mazursky was on a hiding to nothing when he embarked on this updating of François Truffaut's classic *Jules et Jim*. The *joie de vivre* that made the original so beguiling is clearly missing from this episodic drama that is more about Mazursky's perception of the 1970s than it is about the relationships between teacher Michael Ontkean, photographer Ray Sharkey and the girl they both love, Margot Kidder. The performances are fine considering the shallowness of all the characters, but the lifestyle satire has dated badly. DP. Contains swearing and nudity.

Michael Ontkean *Willie Kaufman* • Margot Kidder *Jeanette Sutherland* • Ray Sharkey *Phil D'Amico* • Jan Miner *Mrs Kaufman* • Tom Brennan *Mr Kaufman* • Julie Bovasso *Mrs D'Amico* • Louis Guss *Mr D'Amico* ■ *Dir/Scr* Paul Mazursky

Willow ★★ PG

Fantasy adventure
1988 · US · Colour · 120mins

This rare clunker from director Ron Howard takes too long mating the Saturday-morning-pictures wonderment of *Raiders* with the Tolkienesque elfin-twaddle of *Lord of the Rings*. Val Kilmer and Joanne Whalley look uncomfortable in this tale of a baby whose safekeeping will overthrow an evil empire. Forced, formulaic and sadly lacking in that sense of magic that's at the root of all successful fantasy. DA DVD

Val Kilmer *Madmartigan* • Joanne Whalley *Sorsha* • Warwick Davis *Willow Ufgood* • Jean Marsh *Queen Bavmorda* • Patricia Hayes *Fin Raziel* • Billy Barty *High Aldwin* • Pat Roach *General Kael* ■ *Dir* Ron Howard • *Scr* Bob Dolman, from a story by George Lucas

Willy/Milly ★★★ 15

Comedy 1986 · US · Colour · 83mins

Years before Hilary Swank produced her Oscar-winning cross-gender performance in *Boys Don't Cry*, Pamela Segall gave an equally sterling turn in *Willy/Milly*, albeit in a comedy. Segall is a girl who longs to be a boy and gets her wish (sort of) when she takes a magic potion during an eclipse. Overnight she develops an additional set of genitals. Segall then has to decide whether to spend her life as a girl or as a boy. Patty Duke Astin is good as the mother. DF

Pamela Segall *Milly/Willy* • Eric Gurry *Alfie* • Mary Tanner *Stephanie* • Patty Duke *Mrs Niceman* • John Glover *Mr Niceman* • Seth Green *Malcolm* • John David Cullum *Tom* • Jeb Ellis-Brown *Harry* ■ *Dir* Paul Schneider • *Scr* Walter Carbone, Carla Reuben, from the story by Alan Friedman

W

Willy Wonka and the Chocolate Factory ★★★ U

Fantasy 1971 · US · Colour · 95mins

Adults might view Roald Dahl's musical fantasy as a grim fairy tale, with wild-eyed candy-maker Gene Wilder ruthlessly sorting out the honest from the two-faced among the child winners of a tour of his sweetmeat depot. But a child's-eye view usually sees through the sadistic coating – Dahl adapted it from the even more cruel *Charlie and the Chocolate Factory* – to realise there's a happily soft centre to all this black magic. TH DVD

Gene Wilder *Willy Wonka* • Jack Albertson *Grandpa Joe* • Peter Ostrum *Charlie Bucket* • Michael Bollner *Augustus Gloop* • Ursula Reit *Mrs Gloop* • Denise Nickerson *Violet Beauregarde* • Leonard Stone *Mr Beauregarde* • Roy Kinnear *Mr Salt* ■ *Dir* Mel Stuart • *Scr* Roald Dahl, from his novel *Charlie and the Chocolate Factory* • *Music/lyrics* Anthony Newley, Leslie Bricusse

Wilson ★★ U

Biographical drama
1944 · US · Colour · 153mins

This was to be 20th Century-Fox chief Darryl F Zanuck's finest hour: he personally produced this lengthy biopic about Woodrow Wilson, America's 28th president, who founded the League of Nations. But, despite his idealism, the great man is a boring subject for a movie. Apart from winning five Oscars, the only thing really impressive about *Wilson* is that it was made at all. Alexander Knox is a resolutely uncharismatic lead, and, despite the award-winning Technicolor photography of Leon Shamroy, there's precious little to look at. TS

Alexander Knox *Woodrow Wilson* • Charles Coburn *Professor Henry Holmes* • Geraldine Fitzgerald *Edith Wilson* • Thomas Mitchell *Joseph Tumulty* • Ruth Nelson *Ellen Wilson* • Cedric Hardwicke *Henry Cabot Lodge* • Vincent Price *William G McAdoo* ■ *Dir* Henry King • *Scr* Lamar Trotti

Wilt ★★ 15

Comedy 1989 · UK · Colour · 88mins

Tom Sharpe's brilliantly comic novel is about a liberal studies lecturer (Griff Rhys Jones) pursued for the murder of his wife (Alison Steadman) by police inspector Mel Smith, a copper incompetent enough to make Clouseau seem like Sherlock Holmes. The story kicks in with a hint of lesbianism, a life-sized sex doll and the kind of smut-tinged humour you might have thought British comedies had grown out of. Steadman and Rhys Jones manage to make their characters as authentic as possible with an expertise sorely missing in the rest of the film. TH. Contains swearing, nudity. DVD

Griff Rhys Jones *Henry Wilt* • Mel Smith *Inspector Flint* • Alison Steadman *Eva Wilt* • Diana Quick *Sally* • Jeremy Clyde *Hugh* • Roger Allam *Dave* • David Ryall *Reverend Froude* • Roger Lloyd Pack *Dr Pittman* ■ *Dir* Michael Tuchner • *Scr* Andrew Marshall, David Renwick, from the novel by Tom Sharpe

Wimbledon ★★★ 12

Romantic sports comedy
2004 · US/UK/Fr · Colour · 93mins

Paul Bettany takes on the role of a fading British tennis player who's facing his last Wimbledon but gets fuel-injected when he falls for US tennis prodigy Kirsten Dunst. Richard Loncraine's movie is great on the loser mentality of British sport, and the actual matches are thrillingly souped-up by some decent CGI effects. However, away from tennis, this doesn't really nail either the comedic or romantic spots. It's amusing rather than hilarious, sweet as opposed to heartfelt; still, Bettany and Dunst have appealing charm. IF. Contains sexual references. DVD

Kirsten Dunst *Lizzie Bradbury* • Paul Bettany *Peter Colt* • Sam Neill *Dennis Bradbury* • Jon Favreau *Ron Roth* • Bernard Hill *Edward Colt* • Eleanor Bron *Augusta Colt* • Nikolaj Coster-Waldau *Dieter Prohl* • Austin Nichols *Jake Hammond* • Robert Lindsay *Ian Frazier* • James McAvoy *Carl Colt* • John McEnroe • Chris Evert ■ *Dir* Richard Loncraine • *Scr* Adam Brooks, Jennifer Flackett, Mark Levin

Win a Date with Tad Hamilton! ★★★ PG

Romantic comedy
2004 · US · Colour · 92mins

This pleasing romantic comedy may break no new ground, but it treads old territory with surprising sweetness. Kate Bosworth plays a small-town supermarket checkout girl who enters a competition to win a date with dreamboat Hollywood superstar Tad (Josh Duhamel. And, of course, she wins, much to the chagrin of her co-worker Pete, who's secretly in love with her. The star gradually finds himself falling head over heels for the girl's simple charms. Next thing you know, he's off to Hicksville to woo and win her. Nicely underplayed, with likeably credible leads. DA DVD

Kate Bosworth *Rosalee Futch* • Topher Grace *Pete Monash* • Josh Duhamel *Tad Hamilton* • Gary Cole *Henry Futch* • Ginnifer Goodwin *Cathy Feely* • Kathryn Hahn *Angelica* • Octavia Spencer *Janine* • Sean Hayes *Richard Levy the Shameless* • Nathan Lane *Richard Levy the Driven* • Amy Smart *Nurse* ■ *Dir* Robert Luketic • *Scr* Victor Levin

Winchester '73 ★★★★ U

Western 1950 · US · BW · 92mins

The first of a marvellous series of movies pairing star James Stewart and director Anthony Mann, this western doesn't really tell the tale of "the gun that won the West". Instead, it focuses on the legendary "one in a thousand" perfect Winchester, first seen here as a prize in a Dodge City shooting contest where Will Geer, as Wyatt Earp, presides over sharpshooters Stewart and a brilliantly sneering Stephen McNally. This is a fine, mature work, creating a laconic new persona for the admirable Stewart. The brilliant black-and-white camerawork is by Garbo's favourite, William Daniels, and director Mann's use of transition (dissolves, fades to black) is exemplary. TS DVD

James Stewart *Lin McAdam* • Shelley Winters *Lola Manners* • Dan Duryea *Waco Johnny Dean* • Stephen McNally *Dutch Henry Brown* • Millard Mitchell *Johnny "High Spade" Williams* • Charles Drake *Steve Miller* • John McIntire *Joe Lamont* • Will Geer *Wyatt Earp* • Jay C Flippen *Sergeant Wilkes* • Rock Hudson *Young Bull* • Steve Brodie *Wesley* • Anthony Curtis [Tony Curtis] *Doan* ■ *Dir* Anthony Mann • *Scr* Robert L Richards, Borden Chase, from the story by Stuart N Lake • *Cinematographer* William Daniels [William H Daniels]

The Wind ★★★★★

Silent drama 1928 · US · BW · 94mins

Swedish émigré Victor Sjöström made this stunning antidote to the western just prior to sound. In one of the greatest screen performances in history, Lillian Gish plays the fragile Virginian girl who heads for the Texas panhandle to share a wooden shack with her cousin and his family. Not only does she cause an emotional earthquake, the weather seems to conspire against her as well, resulting in a sandstorm of Biblical proportions. Filmed under the most arduous conditions in the Mojave Desert, the film is marred only by the unconvincing ending which was added when preview audiences found the original conclusion too bleak. AT

Lillian Gish *Letty* • Lars Hanson *Lige* • Montagu Love *Roddy Wirt* • Dorothy Cumming *Cora* • Edward Earle *Beverly* • William Orlamond *Sourdough* ■ *Dir* Victor Seastrom [Victor Sjöström] • *Scr* Frances Marion, from the novel by Dorothy Scarborough

Wind ★★ PG

Sports drama 1992 · US · Colour · 120mins

Carroll Ballard brings his usual visual flair to this tale of ocean racing; it's just a shame the story is so hackneyed. Matthew Modine is the sailor, haunted by a mistake that cost his country the America's Cup, who gets another shot at wresting the trophy back from the Australians. While the story remains on water, Ballard doesn't put a foot wrong and there is some breathtaking racing footage; however, on dry land the film flounders as trite sporting cliché. JF DVD

Matthew Modine *Will Parker* • Jennifer Grey *Kate Bass* • Cliff Robertson *Morgan Weld* • Jack Thompson *Jack Neville* • Stellan Skarsgård *Joe Heiser* • Rebecca Miller *Abigail Weld* • Ned Vaughn *Charley Moore* ■ *Dir* Carroll Ballard • *Scr* Rudy Wurlitzer, Mac Gudgeon, Larry Gross, from a story by Jeff Benjamin, Howard Chelsey, Kimball Livingston, Roger Vaughan

Wind across the Everglades ★★★

Period drama 1958 · US · Colour · 84mins

A strange eco-melodrama, scripted by Budd Schulberg of *On the Waterfront* fame, this is about an alcoholic game warden intent on chasing poachers out of the swamps in turn-of-the-century Florida. Cult director Nicholas Ray fails to control his eclectic scenery-chewing cast, headed by Burl Ives and Christopher Plummer. Watch out, however, for a promising screen debut from Peter Falk. Despite its many faults, there are memorable moments in this unusual effort. TS

Burl Ives *Cottonmouth* • Christopher Plummer *Walt Murdock* • Gypsy Rose Lee *Mrs Bradford* • George Voskovec *Aaron Nathanson* • Tony Galento *Beef* • Howard I Smith [Howard Smith] *George* • Emmett Kelly *Bigamy Bob* • Peter Falk *Writer* ■ *Dir* Nicholas Ray • *Scr* Budd Schulberg, from his story *Across the Everglades*

The Wind and the Lion ★★★★

Period adventure
1975 · US · Colour · 118mins

In this stunning desert adventure, Sean Connery stars as the Berber chieftain who kidnaps Candice Bergen (in a role intended for Katharine Hepburn) and incurs the wrath of US President Teddy Roosevelt, who sends the "big stick" into Morocco. This brilliant satire on colonialism, written and directed by John Milius, pays due tribute to such diverse movies as *Lawrence of Arabia* and the Samurai epics and is both funny and thrilling. Add to this a soaring Jerry Goldsmith score and some marvellous locations and you have one of the most enjoyable movies of the 1970s. AT

Sean Connery *Mulay El Raisuli* • Candice Bergen *Eden Pedecaris* • Brian Keith *Theodore Roosevelt* • John Huston *John Hay* • Geoffrey Lewis *Gummere* • Steve Kanaly *Captain Jerome* • Roy Jenson *Admiral Chadwick* • Vladek Sheybal *Bashaw* • Darrell Fetty *Dreighton* • Nadim Sawalha *Sherif of Wazan* ■ *Dir/Scr* John Milius

The Wind Cannot Read ★★ U

Second World War romantic drama
1958 · UK · Colour · 108mins

Dirk Bogarde's fifth film in just over a year, as the Rank Organisation relentlessly paraded its biggest box-office attraction before an adoring public. But the strain shows in his tired portrayal of an RAF officer who falls for Japanese teacher Yoko Tani. Ralph Thomas certainly knows how to make the most of his looks and charm, and wrings every drop of sentiment out of this four-hankie weepie, but neither plot nor performances really convince. DP

Dirk Bogarde *Flight Lt Michael Quinn* • Yoko Tani *"Sabby" Suzuki San* • Ronald Lewis *Squadron Leader Fenwick* • John Fraser *Flying Offficer Peter Munroe* • Anthony Bushell

Brigadier • Henry Okawa *Lt Nakamura* • Marne Maitland *Bahadur* ■ *Dir* Ralph Thomas • *Scr* Richard Mason, from his novel

Wind Dancer ★★

Drama based on a true story
1991 · US · Colour · 90mins

This sensitive drama delves deep into the subject of the healing forces of nature. The tale, based on a true story, has Raeanin Simpson as a young girl injured in a riding accident, coaxed back to good health with a course of equine therapy at a country ranch. It's sugar lumps all round for virtually the whole movie. JF

Brian Keith *Truman* • Raeanin Simpson *Paige* • Nicholas Guest *Raymond* • Don Shanks *Halfmoon* • Pamela Guest *Nicole* • Mel Harris *Susan* • Matt McCoy *Jim McDonald* ■ *Dir* Craig Clyde

The Wind in the Willows ★★ U

Adventure 1996 · UK · Colour · 83mins

This clumsy live-action version of Kenneth Grahame's timeless classic by writer/director Terry Jones has captured little of the magic of the book. Jones's rendition of Toad is suitably ebullient, while fellow Python Eric Idle and Steve Coogan are pleasing enough as Rat and Mole. However, the addition of a dog-meat factory subplot to supplement Toad's brushes with the law is a major misjudgement, as is the decision to pack the supporting cast with cameoing celebrities. Not as much fun as it should be. DP [video] DVD

Steve Coogan *Mole* • Eric Idle *Rat* • Terry Jones *Toad* • Antony Sher *Chief Weasel* • Nicol Williamson *Badger* • John Cleese *Mr Toad's lawyer* • Stephen Fry *Judge* • Bernard Hill *Engine driver* • Michael Palin *The Sun* • Nigel Planer *Car salesman* • Julia Sawalha *Jailer's daughter* • Victoria Wood *Tea lady* ■ *Dir* Terry Jones • *Scr* Terry Jones, from the novel by Kenneth Grahame

The Wind of Change ★★

Crime drama 1961 · UK · BW · 63mins

Vernon Sewell's attempt at depicting gang racial hatred and its effect on a family fails mainly because of its overly simplistic approach to a complex problem. Donald Pleasence appears in an unusual role as the father of a troubled gang teenager, who is played by none other than a young Johnny Briggs, who became better known as Mike Baldwin of *Coronation Street*. NF

Donald Pleasence *Pop* • Johnny Briggs *Frank* • Antonita Dias *Sylvia* • Ann Lynn *Josie* • Hilda Fenemore *Gladys* • Glyn Houston *Sgt Parker* • Norman Gunn *Ron* • Bunny May *Smithy* • David Hemmings *Ginger* ■ *Dir* Vernon Sewell • *Scr* Alexander Doré, John McLaren

Wind River ★★

Western drama based on a true story
1999 · US · Colour · 97mins

Apart from credible displays of native American nobility from A Martinez and Wes Studi, there's little to recommend in this sanitised, fact-based account of tribal life in 1850s Wyoming. Director Tom Shell rewrites the realities of the culture into which teenager Blake Heron tries to assimilate after he leaves behind his Utah farmstead. The occasional bouts of mysticism and the achingly nostalgic ballads don't help, either. DP. An English and Shoshone language film.

Blake Heron *Nick Wilson* • A Martinez *Moragoni* • Russell Means *Washakie* • Wes Studi *Pocatello* • Devon Gummersall *Sylvester* • Karen Allen *Martha* • Tom Shell *Pilgrim* ■ *Dir* Tom Shell • *Scr* Elizabeth Hansen

The Wind Will Carry Us ★★★★ U

Drama 1999 · Fr/Iran · Colour · 113mins

A stranger arrives in a Kurdish village on a mission he conducts with eccentric secrecy. The winner of the Golden Lion at Venice, Abbas Kiarostami's enigmatic anti-drama challenges the spectator to speculate about withheld information and, thus, play an active role in the action unfolding before a distant, largely static camera. Melding character and location, he maintains an emotional detachment in passing subtle social comment on the suppression of all things beautiful and the indolence of the intelligentsia. A masterly film from a cinematic original. DP. In Farsi with English subtitles. [video]

Behzad Dourani *Engineer* ■ *Dir* Abbas Kiarostami • *Scr* Abbas Kiarostami, from an idea by Mahmoud Ayedin • *Editor* Abbas Kiarostami

Wind with the Gone ★★★★

Surreal comedy drama
1998 · Sp/Fr/Arg/Neth · Colour · 91mins

Set in a small village in Patagonia, Alejandro Agresti's fable is filled with lovable eccentrics, from the scientist whose inventions already have patents, to the cinema projectionist who keeps showing films in the wrong order – which goes some way to explaining this isolated community's cockamamie worldview. However, everything changes with the arrival of two unsuspecting intruders, Buenos Aires cab-driver Vera Fogwill, and fading French movie-star, Jean Rochefort. Testament to the enduring power of cinema, this is deliciously eccentric, yet cuttingly acute. DP. In Spanish with English subtitles.

Vera Fogwill *Soledad* • Angela Molina *Dona Maria* • Fabian Vena *Pedro* • Jean Rochefort *Edgar Wexley* • Ulises Dumont *Antonio* • Carlos Roffe *Amalfi* ■ *Dir/Scr* Alejandro Agresti

Windbag the Sailor ★★★ U

Comedy 1936 · UK · BW · 81mins

Even though he had a hand in the script, Will Hay is a shade below par in this patchy comedy that is significant only for his first teaming with those much loved stooges Moore Marriott and Graham Moffatt. After a promising start, the film is all too quickly blown off course once we're at sea, before finally running aground. Yet Hay's always watchable and still raises a few chuckles as a blustering sea dog whose bluff is called by a crooked tycoon bent on scuttling his ship for the insurance. DP [video] DVD

Will Hay *Capt Ben Cutlet* • Moore Marriott *Jeremiah Harbottle* • Graham Moffatt *Albert* • Norma Varden *Olivia Potter-Porter* • Dennis Wyndham *Maryatt* ■ *Dir* William Beaudine • *Scr* Marriott Edgar, Will Hay, Stafford Dickens, Robert Edmunds, Val Guest, from a story by Robert Stevenson, Leslie Arliss

Windom's Way ★★★★ U

Drama 1957 · UK · Colour · 108mins

This neglected gem stars a charismatic Peter Finch at the height of his heart-throb powers. He plays Alec Windom, a doctor full of confident dedication, toiling away in a remote Malayan village and helping the locals to resist a rebellious takeover. It's a very powerful, tightly directed film with some stunning supporting performances. What could have been a cliché-ridden outing and a one-man demonstration of star ego emerges as a simply great movie. SH

Peter Finch *Dr Alec Windom* • Mary Ure *Lee Windom* • Michael Hordern *Patterson* • Natasha Parry *Anna* • John Cairney *Jan Vidal* • Robert Flemyng *George Hasbrook* ■ *Dir* Ronald Neame • *Scr* Jill Craigie, from the novel by James Ramsey Ullman

The Window ★★★★

Thriller 1949 · US · BW · 73mins

In this superior B-movie, based on Cornell Woolrich's short novel, a youngster (the excellent Bobby Driscoll) witnesses a killing but can't get anyone to take him seriously because he has a reputation for telling tales. Despite its age-old plot, this film made a huge impression on audiences of the day, and has since been relentlessly plundered, rehashed and remade. The adults are well cast, while Driscoll was awarded a special miniature Oscar for his performance. TS

Barbara Hale *Mrs Woodry* • Arthur Kennedy *Mr Woodry* • Bobby Driscoll *Tommy Woodry* • Paul Stewart *Mr Kellerton* • Ruth Roman *Mrs Kellerton* • Anthony Ross *Ross* ■ *Dir* Ted Tetzlaff • *Scr* Mel Dinelli, from the novelette *The Boy Cried Murder* by Cornell Woolrich

A Window in London ★★★

Thriller 1939 · UK · BW · 77mins

From the window of a train, Michael Redgrave sees what appears to be somebody strangling a woman in a house. He goes to the police, but the couple in question (Paul Lukas, Sally Gray) turn out to be an illusionist and his wife rehearsing their act. Some weeks later, Redgrave and his wife (Patricia Roc), again from a train, witness a repeat performance of the incident. A short, modest but intriguing British-made thriller which offers a good cast and supplies a satisfyingly neat twist. RK

Michael Redgrave *Peter Thompson* • Sally Gray *Vivienne* • Paul Lukas *Louis Zoltini* • Hartley Power *Max Preston* • Patricia Roc *Pat Thompson* • Glen Alyn *Andrea* ■ *Dir* Herbert Mason • *Scr* Ian Dalrymple, Brigid Cooper, from the story *Metropolitain* by Herbert Maret

Windprints ★★★ 15

Political crime drama
1989 · UK · Colour · 95mins

Set in Namibia during the apartheid regime, David Wicht's drama approaches this complexities of southern African politics from a white liberal, rather than a rebel, perspective. Sent to track down a notoriously elusive killer (played by Lesley Fong), Sean Bean's Afrikaner cameraman is caught between ethnic loyalty and professional ethics, as he comes to suspect that Fong is in league with Marius Weyers's supremacist landowner. Provocatively fair-minded. DP [video]

John Hurt *Charles Rutherford* • Sean Bean *Anton Van Heerden* • Marius Weyers *Henning* • Eric Nobbs *"Platvoet" Du Plessis* • Lesley Fong *Nhadiep* ■ *Dir/Scr* David Wicht

Windrider ★★★ 15

Romantic drama 1986 · Aus · Colour · 88mins

Buried beneath a mass of permed hair, Nicole Kidman is suitably perky as the pop singer pursued by beach bum Tom Burlinson, who needs her to tell his mates that she witnessed his perfect 360-degree surf turn. The usual round of squabbles and misunderstandings ensues, with former cinematographer Vincent Monton demonstrating a good grasp of soundbite storytelling. DP. Contains swearing, sex scenes. [video]

Tom Burlinson *PC Simpson* • Nicole Kidman *Jade* • Charles Tingwell *Simpson Sr* • Jill Perryman *Miss Dodge* ■ *Dir* Vincent Monton • *Scr* Everett de Roche, Bonnie Harris

The Winds of Jarrah ★★ PG

Romantic drama 1983 · Aus · Colour · 77mins

Ill winds from Australia that blow few people any good, except actors needing the work. It's soap opera frothed up not at all convincingly about a lover-pursued Susan Lyons who becomes teacher to the children of a bitter recluse. Two points in its favour: the lush Australian scenery and its breezy brevity. TH [video]

Terence Donovan *Timber Marlow* • Susan Lyons *Diana Venness* • Emil Minty *Andy Marlow* • Nikki Gemmel *Kathy Marlow* • Mark Kounnas *Peter Marlow* • Dorothy Alison *Mrs Sullivan* • Martin Vaughan *Ben* ■ *Dir* Mark Egerton • *Scr* by Bob Ellis, Anne Brooksbank

Winds of the Wasteland ★★ U

Western 1936 · US · Colour · 53mins

John Wayne stars in this pre-*Stagecoach* B western. He is a Pony Express rider put out of work by the arrival of the telegraph. Wayne competes for a new government mail-hauling contract against the dirty tricks of Douglas Cosgrove's stage line owner. Attractive scenery, a friendly skunk and a brief running time are in its favour. AE [video] DVD

John Wayne *John Blair* • Phyllis Fraser *Barbara Forsythe* • Douglas Cosgrove *Cal Drake* • Lane Chandler *Larry Adams* • Sam Flint *Dr William Forsythe* • Lew Kelly *Rocky O'Brien* ■ *Dir* Mack V Wright • *Scr* Joseph Poland

Windtalkers ★★ 15

Second World War action drama
2001 · US · Colour · 128mins

John Woo's booming and bloody drama had the potential for a fresh perspective on the war epic, chronicling the real-life contribution of native Americans, responsible for a military code that couldn't be cracked by the Japanese. Yet this is explored with the heaviest of hands, as the nicely performed relationship between genial Navajo Adam Beach and cynical sergeant Nicolas Cage is buried beneath a barrage of gargantuan explosions and melodramatic skirmishes. JC. Contains violence, swearing. [video] DVD

Nicolas Cage *Joe F Enders* • Adam Beach *Ben Yahzee* • Christian Slater *Pete "Ox" Anderson* • Peter Stormare *Gunnery Sergeant Hjelmstad* • Noah Emmerich *Chick* • Mark Ruffalo *Pappas* ■ *Dir* John Woo • *Scr* John Rice, Joe Batteer

Windwalker ★★★★

Western 1980 · US · Colour · 108mins

Trevor Howard is the only star in this ground-breaking independent movie by director Kieth Merrill. He plays a Cheyenne chief recounting his life story on his deathbed, including how his wife was killed and one of his twin sons kidnapped by enemy Crow Indians. Set before the forked-tongued white man took over, this stunningly shot drama uses English subtitles for the Crow and Cheyenne dialogue spoken by the amateur cast. TH. An English/Crow/Cheyenne language film.

Trevor Howard *Windwalker* • Nick Ramus *Narration* • James Remar *Windwalker, as a young man* • Serene Hedin *Tashina* • Dusty "Iron Wing" McCrea *Dancing Moon* • Silvana Gallardo *Little Feather* • Billy Drago *Crow Scout* • Rudy Diaz *Crow Eyes* ■ *Dir* Kieth Merrill • *Scr* Ray Goldrup, from a novel by Blaine M Yorgason

W

Windy City ★★★ 15

Romantic drama
1984 · US · Colour · 102mins

Yuppies are caught on the downbeat in a world where heartbreak and disillusion are happy bedfellows. John Shea, Kate Capshaw and Josh Mostel look back in regretful nostalgia as a marriage and illness threaten to alter their friendship. Director Armyan Bernstein makes it moody and melancholy and Shea gives a moving portrayal of a man about to lose everything. TH

John Shea *Danny Morgan* • Kate Capshaw *Emily Ruebens* • Josh Mostel *Sol* • Jim Borrelli *Mickey* • Jeffrey DeMunn *Bobby* • Eric Pierpoint *Pete* ■ *Dir/Scr* Armyan Bernstein

Wing and a Prayer ★★★ PG

Second World War drama
1944 · US · Colour · 93mins

Don Ameche is so familiar as the septuagenarian of *Cocoon*, it's hard to visualise his first incarnation as a versatile leading man in the 1930s and 1940s. Here he plays the sleek hero on a Pacific-bound aircraft carrier, leading Dana Andrews and fellow pilots into battle against the Japanese just prior to the Battle of Midway. Rousing stuff, directed with an eye for detail by Henry Hathaway. RT DVD

Don Ameche *Flight Commander Bingo Harper* • Dana Andrews *Squadron Commander Edward Moulton* • William Eythe *Oscar Scott* • Charles Bickford *Captain Waddell* • Cedric Hardwicke *Admiral* • Kevin O'Shea *Cookie Cunningham* • Richard Jaeckel *Beezy Bessemer* ■ *Dir* Henry Hathaway • *Scr* Jerome Cady, Mortimer Braus

Wing Commander ★ PG

Science-fiction action drama
1999 · US · Colour · 96mins

Based on a popular computer game, this movie plays like a pale rip-off of *Star Wars*. Most of the Gen-X actors playing pilots are atrocious and neither the game's space battles, nor its fun feline aliens – who have been drained of all their personality and now look like seals – are well transposed. ST. Contains swearing. DVD

Freddie Prinze Jr *Christopher "Maverick" Blair* • Matthew Lillard *Todd "Maniac" Marshall* • Saffron Burrows *Jeanette "Angel" Deveraux* • Jürgen Prochnow *Commander Gerald* • Tcheky Karyo *Commander James "Paladin" Taggart* • David Warner *Admiral Geoffrey Tolwyn* • David Suchet *Captain Sansky* • Ginny Holder *Rosie Forbes* ■ *Dir* Chris Roberts • *Scr* Kevin Droney, from characters created by Chris Roberts, from the computer game by Electronic Arts

Winged Migration ★★★★ U

Documentary
2001 · Fr/Ger/Sp/It/Swi · Colour · 85mins

The production statistics for Jacques Perrin's visually stunning avian documentary speak for themselves. Five film crews comprising 14 cinematographers and 17 aircraft pilots laboured for three years following dozens of species of birds as they made their lengthy seasonal journeys. What emerges is a breathtaking visual experience, with shot after seemingly impossible shot of birds in flight – to achieve this photography the crew raised some of the birds to be oblivious to aircraft noise. Sadly a pretentious, uninformative commentary and a truly noxious new-age soundtrack intrude on the exquisite images occasionally, but they only slightly spoil what is an otherwise astonishing piece of lyrical film-making. AS. An English/French language film. DVD

Jacques Perrin *Narrator* ■ *Dir* Jacques Perrin, Jacques Cluzaud, Michel Debats • *Scr* Stéphane Durand, Jacques Perrin, from an idea by Valentine Perrin

Winged Victory ★★ U

Second World War drama
1944 · US · BW · 130mins

George Cukor's contribution to the war effort, about the training of fighter pilots with a pathetic leading man (Lon McCallister), a pretty but vacuous heroine (Jeanne Crain) and an interesting supporting cast. With the full resources of the Army Air Force at his disposal, Cukor revelled in his power: "All I had to say was, it would be nice to have some movement in the background and next thing there were hundreds of men, planes landing and taking off. But the story was silly, full of patriotism and nothing else." AT

Lon McCallister *Frankie Davis* • Jeanne Crain *Helen* • Edmond O'Brien *Irving Miller* • Jane Ball *Jane Preston* • Judy Holliday *Ruth Miller* ■ *Dir* George Cukor • *Scr* Moss Hart, from his play

Wings ★★★

Silent war drama 1927 · US · BW · 139mins

Winner of the very first best picture Oscar, this silent epic about fighter pilots in the First World War is still exciting aloft but terribly sentimental and cliché-ridden on the ground. The director, William A "Wild Bill" Wellman, had himself been a highly decorated fighter pilot with the Lafayette Flying Corps, so he brought to the project much of his own experience, giving the thrilling action sequences their excitement and veracity. But the story – devised by former pilot John Monk Saunders – switches between a lame love affair and the friendship between two pilots who join up together. AT

Clara Bow *Mary Preston* • Charles "Buddy" Rogers *Jack Powell* • Richard Arlen *David Armstrong* • Jobyna Ralston *Sylvia Lewis* • Gary Cooper *Cadet White* • Arlette Marchal *Celeste* • El Brendel *Patrick O'Brien* • Hedda Hopper *Mrs Powell* ■ *Dir* William A Wellman • *Scr* Hope Loring, Louis D Lighton, from a story by John Monk Saunders

Wings in the Dark ★★★

Romantic drama 1935 · US · BW · 68mins

The wings are those of flier Cary Grant's plane, the dark is the fact that he has been blinded in an accident but nonetheless manages to pilot his aircraft to the rescue when his stunt-flier girlfriend gets into trouble during her Moscow to New York run. She, incredibly, is Myrna Loy, who was borrowed from MGM by Paramount for what one would expect to be a romantic comedy but is in fact a romantic drama. Bizarre casting and an unbelievable story line, but played with such conviction and polish by its two gleaming stars under the well-judged direction of James Flood that it's easy to suspend disbelief. RK

Myrna Loy *Sheila Mason* • Cary Grant *Ken Gordon* • Roscoe Karns *Nick Williams* • Hobart Cavanaugh *Mac* • Dean Jagger *Tops Harmon* • Russell Hopton *Jake Brashear* ■ *Dir* James Flood • *Scr* Jack Kirkland, Frank Partos, from the story *Eyes of the Eagle* by Nell Shipman, Philip D Hurn, adapted by Dale Van Every, EH Robinson

Wings of Danger ★ U

Crime drama 1952 · UK · BW · 74mins

Poor Zachary Scott. Dropped by Warner Bros, this forceful character actor was reduced to working for Hammer in its pre-horror days on a routine crime picture pre-sold for American release. He's miscast as the hero, a pilot who investigates the disappearance of a fellow flyer, played by Robert Beatty, and exposes a currency smuggling racket. Kay Kendall and Diane Cilento are among the supporting cast but nowhere near as interesting as they would later become, while Terence Fisher's direction is merely routine. AE

Zachary Scott *Van* • Robert Beatty *Nick Talbot* • Kay Kendall *Alexia* • Colin Tapley *Maxwell* • Naomi Chance *Avril* • Arthur Lane *Boyd Spencer* • Diane Cilento *Jeannette* • Harold Lang *Snell* ■ *Dir* Terence Fisher • *Scr* John Gilling, from the novel *Dead on Course* by Elleston Trevor

Wings of Desire ★★★ PG

Fantasy drama
1987 · W Ger · Colour and BW · 122mins

Mystic style matters more than emotional substance in this fable from Wim Wenders about two angels visiting present-day Berlin and encountering the past – and love. One angel (Bruno Ganz) decides he wants to be human because he's fallen for a circus performer (Solveig Dommartin) but passing through from the other side is more difficult than it seems. Peter Falk wanders into the action as aimlessly as the progress of the plot which, although it's magnificently photographed, never gets airborne as an idea about ongoing reality. Followed by a sequel, *Faraway, So Close* (1993), and a Hollywood remake, 1998's *City of Angels*. TH. In German with English subtitles. DVD

Bruno Ganz *Damiel* • Solveig Dommartin *Marion* • Otto Sander *Cassiel* • Curt Bois *Homer* • Peter Falk • Lajos Kovacs *Marion's coach* • Bruno Rosaz *Clown* ■ *Dir* Wim Wenders • *Scr* Wim Wenders, Peter Handke, Richard Reitinger

The Wings of Eagles ★★★ U

Biographical drama
1957 · US · Colour · 105mins

This is a ramshackle but nonetheless enjoyable biopic of tragic screenwriter/flying ace Frank "Spig" Wead. A strangely subdued John Wayne plays Wead, actually appearing in the later scenes without his characteristic toupee. Dan Dailey is fun as Wead's buddy, but Maureen O'Hara is wasted with little more than two good scenes as the navy wife. The film's greatest delight is Ward Bond as movie director "John Dodge", in other words John Ford (Ford's study was authentically duplicated here using real props, including his Oscars). But there's a smug and sentimental feel to the whole piece. TS

John Wayne *Frank W "Spig" Wead* • Maureen O'Hara *Minnie Wead* • Dan Dailey *"Jughead" Carson* • Ward Bond *John Dodge* • Ken Curtis *John Dale Price* • Edmund Lowe *Admiral Moffett* • Kenneth Tobey *Captain Herbert Allen Hazard* • James Todd *Jack Travis* ■ *Dir* John Ford • *Scr* Frank Fenton, Wiliam Wister Haines, from the life and writings of Commander Frank W Wead Usn and the biography *Wings of Men*

Wings of Fame ★★ 15

Fantasy 1990 · Neth · Colour · 109mins

A fantasy tale in which spirits of the dead end up at a huge offshore hotel, a sort of halfway house for the famous. Peter O'Toole is a movie star, murdered by writer Colin Firth, who himself has died in an accident. The pair meet at the hotel and talk about what happened and why. And, oh yes, Albert Einstein, the kidnapped Lindbergh child and even Lassie are there as well. It's Agatha Christie meets *Last Year in Marienbad*. The performances have some gusto, but it's weird – very weird indeed. AT. Contains swearing and nudity.

Peter O'Toole *Valentin* • Colin Firth *Smith* • Marie Trintignant *Bianca* • Andréa Ferréol *Theresa* • Maria Becker *Dr Frisch* • Gottfried John *Zlatogorski* ■ *Dir* Otakar Votocek • *Scr* Otakar Votocek, Herman Koch

The Wings of Honneamise ★★★★ PG

Animation 1987 · Jpn · Colour · 119mins

Made the year before *Akira* introduced western audiences to the *animé* movies based on Japanese *manga* comics, this was the most costly example made to date. Yet the budget has clearly been well spent, with a superb Ryuichi Sakamoto score, the feuding nations convincingly futuristic and the camera movements and lighting effects worthy of a Hollywood blockbuster. But, although our hero is a member of the Royal Space Force, his journey is more one of self-discovery than all-conquering bravado. For all his ingenuity, 23-year-old writer/director Hiroyuki Yamaga overdoes the religious symbolism, while revealing a political naivety akin to his hero's. Nevertheless, a classic of its kind. DP. In Japanese with English subtitles.

Dir/Scr Hiroyuki Yamaga • *Music* Ryuichi Sakamoto • *Art Director* Hiromasa Ogura

Wings of the Apache ★★ 15

Action drama 1990 · US · Colour · 82mins

Nicolas Cage's heart doesn't seem to be in his role of a maverick helicopter pilot, while Sean Young is even less convincing as a fellow flier/former girlfriend. In the end, it is left to the reliable Tommy Lee Jones to mop up the acting honours as the hard-nosed commander preparing his troops for the war against the drug dealers. Phil Collins is a possible attraction among those crooning away on the soundtrack, but this is really for lads who have never grown up. JF. Contains swearing, violence.

Nicolas Cage *Jake Preston* • Tommy Lee Jones *Brad Little* • Sean Young *Billie Lee Guthrie* • Bryan Kestner *Breaker* • Dale Dye *AK McNeil* • Mary Ellen Trainor *Janet Little* • JA Preston *General Olcott* • Peter Onorati *Rice* ■ *Dir* David Green • *Scr* Nick Thiel, Paul F Edwards, from a story by Step Tyner, John K Swensson, Dale Dye

The Wings of the Dove ★★★★ 15

Period romantic drama
1997 · US · Colour · 97mins

Newcomer Hossein Amini was Oscar nominated for his adaptation of one of Henry James's most difficult novels, and director Iain Softley also succeeds in doing James justice in this visually arresting, lyrical and dark film. Helena Bonham Carter gives her best performance to date as a modern miss who encourages her rough lover Linus Roache to fall for dying heiress Alison Elliott. The friendship that develops between the women and the genuine love that Elliott arouses in Roache complicate the callous scheme and threaten to destroy them all. LH. Contains sex scenes, nudity. DVD

Helena Bonham Carter *Kate Croy* • Linus Roache *Merton Densher* • Alison Elliott (2) *Millie Theale* • Charlotte Rampling *Aunt Maude* • Elizabeth McGovern *Susan Stringham* • Michael Gambon *Lionel Croy* • Alex Jennings *Lord Mark* ■ *Dir* Iain Softley • *Scr* Hossein Amini, from the novel by Henry James

Wings of the Morning ★★★

Romantic sports drama
1937 · UK · Colour · 87mins

Henry Fonda and Annabella co-star with beautiful soft-toned colour, lush Irish and English scenery and a racehorse in Britain's first Technicolor feature. A prologue set in the 1890s has Irish aristocrat Leslie Banks defying convention to marry beautiful Spanish gypsy Annabella. After his death in a riding accident, she goes back to Spain, returning many years later (and played by Irene Vanbrugh) with her granddaughter (who Annabella now plays) and a horse to train for the Derby. Initially disguised as a boy, Annabella meets Canadian race trainer Fonda and both fall in love... Gentle, charming and lovely to look at. RK

Annabella *Maria/Marie* • Henry Fonda *Kerry Gilfallen* • Stewart Rome *Sir Valentine MacFarland* • Irene Vanbrugh *Marie* • Harry Tate *Paddy* • Helen Haye *Jenepher* • Leslie Banks *Lord Clontarf* ■ *Dir* Harold D Schuster [Harold Schuster] • *Scr* Tom Geraghty, from short stories by Donn Byrne

The Winner ★★★ 15

Black comedy thriller
1996 · US/Aus · Colour · 85mins

One of the more coherent films from the maverick independent director Alex Cox, of *Sid and Nancy* fame. Vincent D'Onofrio plays a Las Vegas man who can't lose. Rebecca DeMornay, Billy Bob Thornton and Michael Madsen are among the losers who latch on to him, in the hope of grabbing a share of his pot. A strange little story, nicely played and compellingly told. DA. Contains swearing, violence.

Vincent D'Onofrio *Philip* • Richard Edson *Frankie* • Saverio Guerra *Paulie* • Delroy Lindo *Kingman* • Michael Madsen *Wolf* • Billy Bob Thornton *Jack* • Frank Whaley *Joey* • Alex Cox *Gaston* ■ *Dir* Alex Cox • *Scr* Wendy Riss, from her play *A Darker Purpose*

Winnie the Pooh's Most Grand Adventure ★★ U

Animated adventure
1997 · US · Colour · 72mins

As *The Tigger Movie* proved, searching is what the residents of the Hundred Acre Wood do best. The end of this quest is Christopher Robin, who doesn't have the heart to tell Pooh he is off to school, so leaves a note that the bear of little brain interprets as a plea for help. Devotees of the original Disney cartoons will probably mourn the absence of Kanga and Roo and will find the songs as trite as the story's theme of self-reliance. However, there is the compensation of hearing stalwarts John Fiedler and Paul Winchell reprise their vocalisations of Piglet and Tigger. DP DVD

Jim Cummings *Winnie the Pooh/Skullasaurus* • John Fiedler *Piglet* • Ken Sansom *Rabbit* • Andre Stojka *Owl* • Peter Cullen *Eeyore* • Brady Bluhm *Christopher Robin* • Paul Winchell *Tigger* • David Warner *Narrator* ■ *Dir* Karl Geurs • *Scr* Karl Geurs, Carter Crocker, from characters created by AA Milne

Winning ★★★ PG

Sports drama 1969 · US · Colour · 117mins

Paul Newman and Steve McQueen, the two biggest male stars of the 1960s, loved to race cars in their spare time and both made their own motor-racing movies. Newman's was *Winning*, followed two years later by McQueen's *Le Mans*. Both were flops because no one had figured out what to do with the cast during pit stops, but this is the better movie. Newman plays a driver who values racing more than his wife (Joanne Woodward) and stepson (callow Richard Thomas), and Robert Wagner is the rival racer who steps into the romantic breach. It's all very macho stuff, with predictably exciting racing sequences. AT

Paul Newman *Frank Capua* • Joanne Woodward *Elora* • Richard Thomas *Charley* • Robert Wagner *Luther Erding* • David Sheiner *Crawford* • Clu Gulager *Larry* • Barry Ford *Les Bottineau* ■ *Dir* James Goldstone • *Scr* Howard Rodman

Winning London ★★ U

Comedy adventure
2001 · US · Colour · 93mins

The American pre-teen marketing phenomenon that is the Olsen twins makes for Europe in this twee teenybop adventure. The result is more travelogue than drama, although it could also be mistaken for a feature-length exercise in product placement. Amid the landmarks and labels, Mary-Kate falls for charming Jesse Spencer, while Ashley gets cosy with Brandon Tyler, a fellow US member of the Model United Nations. DP DVD

Mary-Kate Olsen *Chloe Lawrence* • Ashley Olsen *Riley Lawrence* • Eric Jungmann *Dylan* • Brandon Tyler *Brian* • Rachel Roth *Rachel* • Paul Ridley *Lord Browning* • Jesse Spencer *James Browning* ■ *Dir* Craig Shapiro • *Scr* Karol Ann Hoeffner

The Winning of Barbara Worth ★★★★

Silent romantic western
1926 · US · BW · 83mins

After playing extras and bit parts in two-reelers, Gary Cooper was suddenly cast as a last minute replacement for one of the supporting players. Cooper plays a local Arizona boy and rival of eastern engineer Ronald Colman for the hand of Vilma Banky (the eponymous Barbara). Shot in the Nevada desert, the film, about the harnessing of the Colorado river, offers sandstorms, floods and romance. There is some fine camerawork by George Barnes and his 22-year-old assistant Gregg Toland, who 15 years later would shoot *Citizen Kane*. RB

Ronald Colman *Willard Holmes* • Vilma Banky *Barbara Worth* • Charles Lane (1) *Jefferson Worth* • Paul McAllister *The Seer* • EJ Ratcliffe *James Greenfield* • Gary Cooper *Abe Lee* ■ *Dir* Henry King • *Scr* Frances Marion, from the novel by Harold Bell Wright

Winning of the West ★★ U

Western 1953 · US · BW · 57mins

This unremarkable Gene Autry western will appeal only to fans of the chubby-cheeked singin' cowboy, his "Wonder Horse" Champion and his oafish sidekick Smiley Burnette. He has never made a really good movie, at least not for grown-ups, and these days his clean-cut cowboy code has little relevance to youngsters. The title's a gross misnomer. TS

Gene Autry • Gail Davis *Ann Randolph* • Richard Crane *Jack Austin* • Robert Livingston *Art Selby* • House Peters Jr *Marshal Hackett* • Gregg Barton *Clint Raybold* ■ *Dir* George Archainbaud • *Scr* Norman S Hall

The Winslow Boy ★★★★ U

Drama 1948 · UK · BW · 113mins

An object lesson in how to transfer stage to screen, this proves it *can* be done well. Terence Rattigan's tightly wound text is left largely untouched, but the scenes are broadened out to give the original play room to breathe. Robert Donat is wonderful as the celebrated barrister defending a naval cadet charged with theft, and Rattigan's insights into class and hypocrisy are sharpened by Anthony Asquith's assured direction. Primarily a cinematic experience, but the play is left unscarred. SH

Robert Donat *Sir Robert Morton* • Margaret Leighton *Catherine Winslow* • Cedric Hardwicke *Arthur Winslow* • Basil Radford *Esmond Curry* • Kathleen Harrison *Violet* • Francis L Sullivan *Attorney General* • Marie Lohr *Grace Winslow* • Jack Watling *Dickie Winslow* • Frank Lawton *John Watherstone* • Neil North *Ronnie Winslow* • Wilfrid Hyde White *Wilkinson* ■ *Dir* Anthony Asquith • *Scr* Terence Rattigan, Anatole de Grunwald, from the play by Terence Rattigan

The Winslow Boy ★★★★ U

Period drama 1999 · US · Colour · 100mins

David Mamet adapts and directs Terence Rattigan's play about about a father's unwavering and potentially destructive love for his son. When Guy Edwards is expelled from the Royal Naval Academy for theft, Nigel Hawthorne believes in the boy's virtue so much he nearly bankrupts his family trying to prove it. Suffragette daughter Rebecca Pidgeon falls for barrister Jeremy Northam, while mother Gemma Jones cannot understand her husband's obsessive pursuit of justice. Mamet and his remarkable cast reveal the truth behind the motives. TH DVD

Nigel Hawthorne *Arthur Winslow* • Jeremy Northam *Sir Robert Morton* • Rebecca Pidgeon *Catherine Winslow* • Gemma Jones *Grace Winslow* • Guy Edwards *Ronnie Winslow* • Matthew Pidgeon *Dickie Winslow* • Aden Gillett *John Watherstone* ■ *Dir* David Mamet • *Scr* David Mamet, from the play by Terence Rattigan

Winstanley ★★★★ PG

Historical drama 1975 · UK · BW · 91mins

Kevin Brownlow and Andrew Mollo's second film is set in Cromwellian England and deals with a disparate group of people, united in their disillusion, poverty and landlessness who create a commune and call themselves Diggers. Their leader is Gerrard Winstanley, a man with a utopian dream of social equality. Based on David Caute's novel *Comrade Jacob*, it fits into the world of a 1960s agitprop, riding the anti-everything, drop-out tide of student protest, but Brownlow and Mollo are not firebrand radicals, much less flower power hippies. They are, first and foremost, serious historians who shot the film for over a year, often in harsh conditions. As a period reconstruction it has few equals. AT

Miles Halliwell *Gerrard Winstanley* • Jerome Willis *General Lord Fairfax* • Terry Higgins *Tom Haydon* • Phil Oliver *Will Everard* • David Bramley *Parson John Platt* • Allison Halliwell *Mrs Platt* • Dawson France *Captain Gladman* ■ *Dir* Kevin Brownlow, Andrew Mollo • *Scr* Kevin Brownlow, Andrew Mollo, from the novel *Comrade Jacob* by David Caute

Winter Carnival ★★ U

Romantic drama 1939 · US · BW · 90mins

Although he's not credited, F Scott Fitzgerald had a hand in scripting this lacklustre comedy that co-scenarist Budd Schulberg (who was fired by producer Walter Wanger) used as the backdrop for his 1950 novel, *The Disenchanted*. Ann Sheridan takes the lead as a divorced countess returning to Dartmouth College for the annual ice fest to see if baby sister Helen Parrish can follow in her footsteps as carnival queen. However, she spends much of her time flirting with alumnus Richard Carlson who is now a penniless professor. DP

Ann Sheridan *Jill Baxter* • Richard Carlson *Professor John Weldon* • Helen Parrish *Ann Baxter* • James Corner *Mickey Allen* • Alan Baldwin *Don Reynolds* • Robert Armstrong *Tiger Reynolds* ■ *Dir* Charles F Reisner [Charles Reisner] • *Scr* Lester Cole, Bud Schulberg, Maurice Rapf, from a story by Bud Schulberg, Maurice Rapf, from the short story *Echoes That Old Refrain* by Corey Ford in *The Saturday Evening Post*

The Winter Guest ★★★ 15

Drama 1996 · US/UK · Colour · 104mins

Alan Rickman's directorial debut stars Emma Thompson as a mother grieving over the death of her husband, unable to support and nurture their son and also unable to see her own mother's ill health. As family events unfold, Rickman introduces other elements from the isolated Scottish village setting: two old dears get their kicks out of going to funerals and two small boys play on the always-blustery beach. It's a brave attempt to open up Sharman MacDonald's play, but overall the film never quite escapes from its theatrical roots. LH DVD

Emma Thompson *Frances* • Phyllida Law *Elspeth* • Sheila Reid *Lily* • Sandra Voe *Chloe* • Arlene Cockburn *Nita* • Gary Hollywood *Alex* • Sean Biggerstaff *Tom* • Douglas Murphy *Sam* ■ *Dir* Alan Rickman • *Scr* Alan Rickman, Sharman MacDonald, from the play by Sharman MacDonald

Winter Kills ★★★ 18

Political black comedy
1979 · US · Colour · 87mins

This genuine collector's item is based on the remarkable satirical novel about the Kennedys by Richard Condon, who also wrote *The Manchurian Candidate* and *Prizzi's Honor*. Jeff Bridges, playing the son of patriarch John Huston, tries to discover who was responsible for killing his brother, the US President. In the starry cast, the likes of Anthony Perkins, Sterling Hayden, Dorothy Malone and Toshiro Mifune make telling contributions, while Elizabeth Taylor appears in a cameo, and it's all held together by William Richert's assured direction. TS. Contains swearing and nudity. DVD

Jeff Bridges *Nick Kegan* • John Huston *Pa Kegan* • Anthony Perkins *John Ceruti* • Sterling Hayden *ZK Dawson* • Eli Wallach *Joe Diamond* • Dorothy Malone *Emma Kegan* • Tomas Milian *Frank Mayo* • Belinda Bauer *Yvette Malone* • Ralph Meeker *Gameboy Baker* • Toshiro Mifune *Keith* • Richard Boone *Keifitz* • Elizabeth Taylor *Lola Comante* ■ *Dir* William Richert • *Scr* William Richert, from the novel by Richard Condon

Winter Light ★★★ PG

Drama 1962 · Swe · BW · 77mins

Tormented by doubts about his own faith and tempted by an offer of marriage from schoolteacher Ingrid Thulin, pastor Gunnar Björnstrand is also aware of the duty he owes to parishioner Max von Sydow, who is contemplating suicide in the face of a nuclear crisis. Composed for the most part in close-ups, Ingmar Bergman's film is a powerful and pessimistic look at God's relationship with humanity, but, in spite of exceptional performances, it won't be for all tastes. DP. In Swedish with English subtitles. DVD

Ingrid Thulin *Marta Lundberg* • Gunnar Björnstrand *Tomas Ericsson* • Max von Sydow *Jonas Persson* • Gunnel Lindblom *Karin Persson* • Allan Edwall *Algot Frovik* ■ *Dir/Scr* Ingmar Bergman

Winter Meeting ★

Drama 1948 · US · BW · 104mins

Even Bette Davis, characteristically accomplished and uncharacteristically restrained, can't save audiences from the mind-numbing tedium of this bleak and ponderously verbose drama. Davis is a repressed spinster poetess who becomes involved with naval officer James Davis (no relation - and little talent) who really wants to become a Catholic priest. The movie is one of Bette's last duds before finally leaving Warner Bros to freelance. RK

Bette Davis *Susan Grieve* • Janis Paige *Peggy Markham* • James Davis [Jim Davis] *Lt Slick Novak* • John Hoyt *Stacy Grant* • Florence Bates *Mrs Castle* • Walter Baldwin *Mr Castle* • Ransom Sherman *Mr Moran* ■ *Dir* Bretaigne Windust • *Scr* Catherine Turney, from the novel by Ethel Vance

The Winter of Our Dreams ★★ 15

Drama 1981 · Aus · Colour · 84mins

Judy Davis stars as a deeply troubled prostitute who strikes up a relationship with married bookseller Bryan Brown while he's investigating an ex-girlfriend's suicide. The soapy plot and crude direction are nothing to shout about, but John Duigan has always had a reputation for extracting great performances from his actors and here Davis, in particular, is terrific. DA

Judy Davis *Lou* • Bryan Brown *Rob* • Cathy Downes *Gretel* • Baz Luhrmann *Pete* • Peter Mochrie *Tim* ■ *Dir/Scr* John Duigan

Winter People ★★ 15

Drama 1988 · US · Colour · 105mins

It's the backwoods of North Carolina in the 1930s, and Kurt Russell is deeply into his macho mode, sniffin' and snarlin' like a rampant grizzly bear and with one eye on the script and another on his personal trainer. Actually he's pretty silly here, and so's the picture, a lot of moonshine about clan rivalry that heats up when the widowed Russell comes across unmarried mother Kelly McGillis. Corny and clumsy. AT. Contains swearing.

Kurt Russell *Wayland Jackson* • Kelly McGillis *Collie Wright* • Lloyd Bridges *William Wright* • Mitchell Ryan *Drury Campbell* • Amelia Burnette *Paula Jackson* • Eileen Ryan *Annie Wright* • Lanny Flaherty *Gudger Wright* ■ *Dir* Ted Kotcheff • *Scr* Carol Sobieski, from the novel by John Ehle

The Winter's Tale ★★ U

Romantic comedy
1966 · UK · Colour · 150mins

Frank Dunlop's theatre production, which presumably wowed audiences at the 1966 Edinburgh Festival, transfers unconvincingly to celluloid, and the usual faults of cine-theatre, such as over-frequent close-ups, are here in all their vainglory. Nevertheless, the film has its moments. Laurence Harvey makes a competent Leontes, the king who for little apparent reason develops a jealous streak which threatens to destroy all around him. However, he's nearly upstaged by Jim Dale, who makes a fine Autolycus as well as composing the score. JG

Laurence Harvey *Leontes* • Jane Asher *Perdita* • Diana Churchill *Paulina* • Moira Redmond *Hermione* • Jim Dale *Autolycus* • Esmond Knight *Camillo* ■ *Dir* Frank Dunlop • *Scr* from the play by William Shakespeare

A Winter's Tale ★★★★ 15

Romantic drama 1992 · Fr · Colour · 109mins

Eric Rohmer is unique in his ability to fashion fully fleshed characters to persuade us to become utterly absorbed in the petty problems that beset lives that are every bit as ordinary as our own. Exploring the emotions, confusions and contradictions attendant on romance, this witty adult fairy tale, set in the heart of the callous city, is a joy to behold thanks to the naturalism of its performances and the sublime subtlety of its direction. DP. In French with English subtitles.

Charlotte Very *Félicie* • Frédéric Van Den Driessche *Charles* • Michel Voletti *Maxence* • Hervé Furic *Loïc* • Ava Loraschi *Elise* ■ *Dir/Scr* Eric Rohmer

Winterhawk ★★★

Western 1975 · US · Colour · 86mins

The whites are the baddies in this cowboys and Indians film. Michael Dante plays a Blackfoot brave who comes to a white settlement for a smallpox serum, only to be attacked. The Indian then takes revenge by abducting two white kids. It's good to see genre conventions being broken down, but the film is still clichéd, even if the clichés are inverted. It's watchable, though, and notable for a panoply of familiar "cowboy" faces. DA

Leif Erickson *Guthrie* • Woody Strode *Big Rude* • Denver Pyle *Arkansas* • LQ Jones *Gates* • Michael Dante *Winterhawk* • Elisha Cook Jr *Reverend Will Finley* ■ *Dir* Charles B Pierce • *Scr* Charles B Pierce, Earl E Smith

Winterset ★★★

Drama 1936 · US · BW · 75mins

Burgess Meredith, repeating his Broadway role, is the star of this adaptation of Maxwell Anderson's once-famous play, originally written in blank verse and inspired by the Sacco and Vanzetti case. Very much a prestige production in its day, hailed by the critics and the cognoscenti but ignored by the customers, this account of a man seeking to clear the name of his wrongfully executed, liberal father is stagey, talky, and now dated, but its passionate arguments against intolerance and mob hysteria have a powerful ring. RK

Burgess Meredith *Mio Romagna* • Margo *Miriamne Esdras* • Eduardo Ciannelli *Trock Estrella* • Maurice Moscovitch [Maurice Moscovich] *Esdras* • Paul Guilfoyle (1) *Garth Esdras* • Mischa Auer *Radical* • John Carradine *Bartolomeo Romagna* ■ *Dir* Alfred Santell • *Scr* Anthony Veiller, from the play by Maxwell Anderson

Wintersleepers ★★★ 15

Melodrama 1997 · Ger · Colour · 122mins

German director Tom Tykwer revives the long-dormant "mountain film" with this cool take on heroism and the formidability of nature. After a superbly controlled opening that culminates in a shocking road accident, the pace drops – a tad too deliberately – to allow the snowball of coincidence to gather momentum. Yet there's a ghoulish fascination in watching the links emerge between amnesiac projectionist Ulrich Matthes and the family of his victim. Tykwer doesn't always keep the lid on the more extreme emotions, but this is still tense and beautifully filmed. DP. In German with English subtitles. Contains sex scenes, swearing.

Ulrich Matthes *Rene* • Marie-Lou Sellem *Laura* • Floriane Daniel *Rebecca* • Heino Ferch *Marco* • Josef Bierbichler *Theo* • Laura Tonke *Nina* ■ *Dir* Tom Tykwer • *Scr* Tom Tykwer, Anne-Françoise Pyszora, from the novel *Expense of the Spirit* by Anne-Françoise Pyszora

Wintertime ★★ U

Musical comedy 1943 · US · BW · 82mins

Norwegian skating star Sonja Henie, in a triumph of scriptwriting imagination, plays a Norwegian skating star in this last of her Fox musicals. She turns up at the declining Canadian resort hotel owned by her dear old uncle, SZ "Cuddles" Sakall, where her mere presence puts the place back on the tourist map. And that, as well as her romance with Cornel Wilde, is it – aside from the skating, that is. RK

Sonja Henie *Nora* • Jack Oakie *Skip Hutton* • Cesar Romero *Brad Barton* • Carole Landis *Flossie Fouchere* • SZ Sakall *Hjalmar Ostgaard* • Cornel Wilde *Freddy Austin* ■ *Dir* John Brahm • *Scr* E Edwin Moran, Jack Jevne, Lynn Starling, from a story by Arthur Kober

Wired ★ 18

Biographical drama
1989 · US · Colour · 104mins

As if the death of comedian John Belushi wasn't tragic enough, this dreadful biopic purports to tell the truth about his career and the drugged-out events leading up to his fatal heroin and cocaine overdose in LA's Chateau Marmont hotel in 1982. Michael Chiklis fails to convince as the doomed Blues Brother, and this crude low-budget exploiter is a grotesque character assassination. JM. Contains swearing and drug abuse.

Michael Chiklis *John Belushi* • Ray Sharkey *Angel Velasquez* • JT Walsh *Bob Woodward* • Patti D'Arbanville *Cathy Smith* • Lucinda Jenney *Judy Belushi* • Gary Groomes *Dan Aykroyd* • Alex Rocco *Arnie Fromson* ■ *Dir* Larry Peerce • *Scr* Earl Mac Rauch, from the book *Wired: the short life and fast times of John Belushi* by Bob Woodward

Wisdom ★ 18

Crime drama 1986 · US · Colour · 104mins

If only director Emilio Estevez would demonstrate a little wisdom by quitting directing and sticking to acting. Here he directs himself for the first time as a high school dropout who turns into a local Robin Hood and, with girlfriend Demi Moore at his side, begins bombing banks to help his debt-ridden neighbours. There is nothing to recommend this except an exhilarating car chase but it's unlikely that you'll be awake long enough. LH

Emilio Estevez *John Wisdom* • Demi Moore *Karen Simmons* • Tom Skerritt *Lloyd Wisdom* • Veronica Cartwright *Samantha Wisdom* • William Allen Young *Williamson* • Richard Minchenberg *Cooper* • Bill Henderson *Theo* ■ *Dir/Scr* Emilio Estevez

The Wisdom of Crocodiles ★★★ 18

Horror romance 1998 · UK · Colour · 94mins

By day a medical researcher, by night a vampire, Jude Law stars as the undead preying on women in the hope of finding the true love that will bring about his redemption. Rescuing Kerry Fox from a suicide attempt, he then beds and bloods her. However, his subsequent encounter with the beautiful Elina Lowensohn becomes a complex love affair when he can't bring himself to bite her jugular. Over-stylised by director Po Chih Leong, realism is on hand in Timothy Spall's characterisation of the downbeat detective who soon gets on Law's case. LH. Contains violence, sex scenes, swearing.

Jude Law *Steven Grlscz* • Elina Lowensohn *Anne Levels* • Timothy Spall *Inspector Healey* • Kerry Fox *Maria Vaughan* • Jack Davenport *Sergeant Roche* • Colin Salmon *Martin* ■ *Dir* Po Chih Leong • *Scr* Paul Hoffman

Wise Blood ★★★ 15

Gothic drama
1979 · US/W Ger · Colour · 101mins

A greatly admired and critically acclaimed film in many quarters, this blood-and-salvation southern Gothic fantasy seems to cry out for a more outré approach than that of director John Huston, who clearly relished (since he also appears in) this virtually blasphemous and undeniably strange version of Flannery O'Connor's obsessive fable. Brad Dourif is mightily effective as the leader of "The Church of Truth without Jesus Christ" but, while the movie's taste becomes highly questionable, there's no denying its powerful appeal and extremely subversive humour. TS

Brad Dourif *Hazel Motes* • Harry Dean Stanton *Asa Hawks* • Ned Beatty *Hoover Shoates* • Daniel Shor [Dan Shor] *Enoch Emery* • Amy Wright *Sabbath Lily Hawks* • John Huston *Hazel's grandfather* • William Hickey *Preacher* ■ *Dir* John Huston • *Scr* Benedict Fitzgerald, Michael Fitzgerald, from the novel by Flannery O'Connor

Wise Guys ★ 15

Black comedy 1986 · US · Colour · 87mins

Comedy is not Brian De Palma's forte, as most people who saw his supposed satire *The Bonfire of the Vanities* will confirm. Conclusive evidence that De Palma can't tell a joke is provided by this woeful effort in which Danny DeVito plays a Mafia messenger boy and Harvey Keitel is a hotelier. The comedy is pitched so low you need a mechanical digger to find it. AT

Danny DeVito *Harry Valentini* • Joe Piscopo *Moe Dickstein* • Harvey Keitel *Bobby Dilea* • Ray Sharkey *Marco* • Dan Hedaya *Anthony Castelo* • Captain Lou Albano *Frank the Fixer* • Julie Bovasso *Lil Dickstein* • Patti LuPone *Wanda Valentini* ■ *Dir* Brian De Palma • *Scr* George Gallo

Wisecracks ★★★★

Documentary 1991 · Can · Colour · 91mins

Gail Singer's impressive documentary provides a valuable insight into the careers of some of comedy's most important female stars. It combines film footage of Mae West, Gracie Allen, Lucille Ball and the like with contemporary clips from and interviews with Whoopi Goldberg, Phyllis Diller, Jenny Lecoat and others. Liberal chunks of the participants' comedy routines ensure a high level of humour throughout this excellent production. Shorter versions turn up occasionally but the original 91-minute cut is the one to see. DF

Dir Gail Singer • *Cinematographer* Zoe Dirse, Bob Fresco • *Editor* Gordon McClellan

Wisegirls ★★★ 15

Crime thriller
2001 · US/UK/Can · Colour · 92mins

The gangster thriller gets a feminine twist in this well-executed feature from director David Anspaugh. Mira Sorvino stars as a woman trying to forget her past, who takes on a restaurant waitressing job, only to become embroiled with its Mafia clientele. Centred on a trio of strong performances, from Sorvino and her co-worker friends Mariah Carey and Melora Walters, it's a gripping tale of sisterhood that's as warm as it is brutal. Essentially a chick flick in mobster clothing, this benefits from an above average script and plenty of meaty drama. SF. Contains swearing, violence, drug abuse. DVD

Mira Sorvino *Meg Kennedy* • Mariah Carey *Raychel* • Melora Walters *Kate* • Arthur Nascarella *Mr Santalino* • Saul Stein *Umberto* • Joseph Siravo *Gio* • Christian Maelen *Frankie* • Anthony Alessandro *Lorenzo* ■ *Dir* David Anspaugh • *Scr* John Meadows

The Wiser Sex ★★

Crime drama 1932 · US · BW · 72mins

Berthold Viertel's penultimate Hollywood picture before he relocated to the UK is pretty racy for its day, with sophisticate Claudette Colbert posing as a woman of easy virtue to deliver her lawyer lover, Melvyn Douglas, from a murder rap. Sadly, there's not a shred of conviction about either her performance or the storyline, in which her dealings with mobster William "Stage" Boyd are complicated by his vengeful mistress, Lilyan Tashman DP

Claudette Colbert *Margaret Hughes/Ruby Kennedy* • Melvyn Douglas *District Attorney David Rolfe* • Lilyan Tashman *Claire Foster* • William "Stage" Boyd *Harry Evans* • Ross Alexander (1) *Jimmie O'Neill* • Franchot Tone *Phil Long* ■ *Dir* Berthold Viertel • *Scr* Harry Hervey, Caroline Francke, from the play *The Woman in the Case* by Clyde Fitch

Wish You Were Here ★★★★ 15

Comedy drama 1987 · UK · Colour · 88mins

Emily Lloyd's startling debut as a sexually defiant seaside teenager prevents writer/director David Leland's 1950s-set comedy drama from being just another rebellious youngster movie. Her vibrant performance as the 16-year-old intent on shocking everyone begs the question: why has her career since failed to make any impact? There's also strong support from Tom Bell in a decidedly unsympathetic role as a lecherous family friend. RT. Contains swearing, sex scenes and nudity. DVD

Emily Lloyd *Lynda* • Tom Bell *Eric* • Clare Clifford *Mrs Parfitt* • Barbara Durkin *Valerie* • Geoffrey Hutchings *Hubert* • Charlotte Barker *Gillian* • Chloe Leland *Margaret* • Jesse Birdsall *Dave* • Pat Heywood *Aunt Millie* ■ *Dir/Scr* David Leland

W

Wishful Thinking ★★ 15

Fantasy comedy 1990 · US · Colour · 90mins

One of the hit acts from the twisted talent series *The Gong Show* in the 1970s was a fast-talking gagster called the Unknown Comic who performed with a paper bag covering his head. The man beneath that bag was Murray Langston, the director, co-writer and star of this which tells the tale of a frustrated screenwriter who is given a (supposedly) magic writing pad by a gnome who says that whatever he writes in the pad will come true. Langston should have written that his film would become a huge hit movie – he didn't and it didn't. DF [video]

Michelle Johnson *Diane Jacobs* • Murray Langston *Michael Moore* • Ruth Buzzi *Jody Moore* • Ray "Boom Boom" Mancini [Ray Mancini] *Jake Malone* ■ *Dir* Murray Langston • *Scr* Steve Finly, Murray Langston

Wishful Thinking ★ 15

Romantic comedy drama
1997 · US · Colour and BW · 85mins

You will wishfully be thinking of anything else while watching this romantic comedy which succeeds as neither. Cinema projectionist and commitment-phobe James LeGros can't say "I do" to girlfriend Jennifer Beals and instead accuses her of infidelity. Meanwhile the cinema's overly quirky cashier Drew Barrymore harbours a hidden love for LeGros which she restricts to *Brief Encounter*-esque black-and-white daydreams. Told separately from these three characters' points of view, you care little for them or their fates. LH [video]

Drew Barrymore *Lena* • Jennifer Beals *Elizabeth* • James LeGros *Max* • Jon Stewart *Henry* • Mel Gorham *Lourdes* • Eric Thal *Jack* ■ *Dir/Scr* Adam Park

Wishman ★★★

Romantic fantasy 1991 · US · Colour · 90mins

Paul Le Mat delivers a typically astute performance as a Hollywood hustler whose talent for smooth talking fails him whenever he sees his heart's desire, Quin Kessler. But Le Mat is totally upstaged by a quirky turn from Geoffrey Lewis, as a two million-year-old genie who agrees to grant Le Mat's wishes providing he helps locate Lewis's stolen bottle. Paul Gleason and Brion James head a seasoned supporting cast that wisely stands aside and lets Lewis steal every scene. DP

Paul Le Mat *Basie* • Geoffrey Lewis *Hitchcock the genie* • Paul Gleason *Silverstein* • Quin Kessler *Lily Andon* • Nancy Parsons *Miss Crabbe* • Brion James *Staten Jack Rose* ■ *Dir/Scr* Mike Marvin

Wishmaster ★★★ 18

Horror 1997 · US · Colour · 86mins

This is an oddly comforting throwback to the early 1980s slasher glory days, directed by former special-effects genius Robert Kurtzman and executive produced by Wes Craven. Los Angeles gem specialist Tammy Lauren must stop the evil 12th-century Persian Djinn (genie), played by Andrew Divoff, wreaking havoc after he tries to trick her into making three wishes when she discovers him trapped in an enchanted opal. The one-jolt premise does get stretched out to vanishing point, yet the casting, plus all the exploding body parts, will be a nostalgic tonic for splatter addicts. Three listless straight-to-video sequels followed. AJ. Contains violence and swearing. [video] DVD

Tammy Lauren *Alexandra Amberson* • Andrew Divoff *The Djinn/Nathaniel Demerest* • Kane Hodder *Merritt's guard* • Tony Todd *Johnny Valentine* • Robert Englund *Raymond Beaumont* • Angus Scrimm *Narrator* • Ari Barak *Zoroaster* ■ *Dir* Robert Kurtzman • *Scr* Peter Atkins

Wit ★★★★

Drama 2001 · US · Colour · 98mins

In seeking suitably cinematic solutions to the considerable problems posed by Margaret Edson's Pulitzer Prize-winning play, director Mike Nichols places the greatest emphasis in this TV movie on the text, with its wealth of allusions, rhythms and insights. He's not intimidated by its intellectual discussion of the religious poetry of John Donne and the emotions experienced by scholar Emma Thompson, as she takes a leap of faith in battling ovarian cancer. Such is the intensity and honesty of Thompson's performance that the occasional contrivance can be forgiven. DP

Emma Thompson *Vivian Bearing* • Christopher Lloyd *Dr Harvey Kelekian* • Eileen Atkins *EM Ashford* • Audra McDonald *Susie Monahan* • Jonathan M Woodward *Dr Jason Posner* • Harold Pinter *Mr Bearing* ■ *Dir* Mike Nichols • *Scr* Emma Thompson, Mike Nichols, from the play by Margaret Edson

Witchboard ★ 15

Supernatural horror
1987 · US · Colour · 93mins

A group of young people play around with a Ouija board at a party, indirectly leading to an evil spirit possessing Tawny Kitaen. This is bad news for those around her as they get killed off one by one. Technically poor, with cameraman shadows clearly seen and special effects of the quality and scale found in high school productions, the worst part of the entire ordeal is that hardly anything (horrible or otherwise) happens. Two equally bad sequels followed. KB [video] DVD

Todd Allen *Jim Morar* • Tawny Kitaen *Linda Brewster* • Stephen Nichols *Brandon Sinclair* • Kathleen Wilhoite *Zarabeth* • Burke Byrnes *Lieutenant Dewhurst* ■ *Dir/Scr* Kevin S Tenney

Witchcraft ★★ 18

Horror 1988 · US · Colour · 85mins

New mother Anat Topol-Barzilai reluctantly moves in with her strange mother-in-law and starts having demonic visions of witch-burnings and decapitations. Slow-moving occult nonsense grafting the *Nightmare on Elm Street* dreams-within-false-dreams concept into a basic *Rosemary's Baby* scenario. Plenty of bogus scares and very little sense keep this half-hearted horror dud grounded. AJ [video] DVD

Anat Topol-Barzilai *Grace* • Gary Sloan *John* • Mary Shelley *Elizabeth* • Alexander Kirkwood *Priest* ■ *Dir* Robert Spera [Rob Spera] • *Scr* Jody Savin

Witchcraft ★ 18

Horror 1989 · It · Colour · 92mins

German actress Hildegarde Knef came out of retirement to play a witch holding demonic sway over a New England island in this nasty slice of Italian exploitation. Stranded visitors fall foul to *Omen*-style murders thanks to her black magic and suffer assorted fates including crucifixion, grotesque rape, mouth-stitching and being hung upside down in a fireplace. So much graphic unpleasantness and still so boring. AJ [video] DVD

Linda Blair *Jane Brooks* • David Hasselhoff *Gary* • Hildegarde Knef [Hildegarde Neff] *Lady in Black* • Annie Ross *Rose Brooks* • Catherine Hickland *Linda Sullivan* • Leslie Cummings *Leslie* ■ *Dir* Fabrizio Laurenti • *Scr* Danielle Stroppa

The Witches ★★★

Horror 1966 · UK · Colour · 89mins

Hollywood stars never faded, they simply made films in Britain. Joan Fontaine here reprises her "frightened lady" turn, first seen in *Rebecca*, as the cursed schoolmistress discovering devil worship in rural parts. It's a Hammer that never quite makes contact with your nerves, even though it's written by Nigel Kneale, who created *Quatermass*. At least director Cyril Frankel treats it as though it mattered, but for Fontaine it signalled her big screen career's end. TH

Joan Fontaine *Gwen Mayfield* • Kay Walsh *Stephanie Bax* • Alec McCowen *Alan Bax* • Ann Bell *Sally* • Ingrid Brett *Linda* • John Collin *Dowsett* • Michele Dotrice *Valerie* • Gwen Ffrangcon-Davies *Granny Rigg* • Duncan Lamont *Bob Curd* • Leonard Rossiter *Dr Wallis* ■ *Dir* Cyril Frankel • *Scr* Nigel Kneale, from the novel *The Devil's Own* by Peter Curtis

The Witches ★★★

Surreal portmanteau drama
1966 · Fr/It · Colour · 105mins

This portmanteau picture, featuring work by some of Italy's most celebrated directors, gave Clint Eastwood a rare opportunity to appear in a European art movie. He features in Vittorio De Sica's bookend segment as a banker being forced to compete with comic-book characters for the love of his bored wife Silvana Mangano. Mangano also stars in the other four stories: as a holidaying movie star in Luchino Visconti's opener; a woman driver whose dithering spells trouble for injured trucker Alberto Sordi; a spinster with a short-fused father in Franco Rossi and Luigi Magni's Sicilian comedy; and an imaginary maid in Pier Paolo Pasolini's silent gem. The movie is inconsistent, but the individual segments are intriguing. DP. Italian dialogue dubbed into English.

Silvana Mangano *Gloria/Lady/Giovanna* • Annie Girardot *Valeria* • Francisco Rabal *Valeria's husband* • Alberto Sordi *Truck driver* • Clint Eastwood *Husband* ■ *Dir* Luchino Visconti, Mauro Bolognini, Pier Paolo Pasolini, Franco Rossi, Vittorio De Sica • *Scr* Giuseppe Patroni Griffi, Cesare Zavattini, Agenore Incrocci, Furio Scarpelli, Bernardino Zapponi, Pier Paolo Pasolini, Franco Rossi, Luigi Magni, Fabio Carpi, Enzio Muzii

The Witches ★★★ PG

Fantasy adventure
1989 · UK · Colour · 87mins

Roald Dahl's story about a little boy on a seaside holiday who discovers a witches' convention plotting to annihilate children is brilliantly brought to life by director Nicolas Roeg. As chief witch, Anjelica Huston gets a gruesome Jim Henson's Creature Shop makeover, while Mai Zetterling is transformed into lavender and old lace as the boy's granny. Memorable sequences include the one in which the boy is turned into a mouse. Children should hold their parents' hands through some of it – grown-ups are notoriously nervous. TH [video]

Anjelica Huston *Miss Ernst/Grand High Witch* • Mai Zetterling *Helga* • Bill Paterson *Mr Jenkins* • Brenda Blethyn *Mrs Jenkins* • Rowan Atkinson *Mr Stringer* • Jasen Fisher *Luke* • Charlie Potter *Bruno Jenkins* • Jane Horrocks *Miss Irvine* ■ *Dir* Nicolas Roeg • *Scr* Allan Scott, from the novel by Roald Dahl

Witches' Brew ★★ 15

Fantasy comedy 1979 · US · Colour · 93mins

File under "Bad Weird Oddity One Ought to See". Originally made in 1978 as *Which Witch Is Which?*, but not released until 1985 with additional footage, this is an uncredited version of Fritz Leiber Jr's classic novel *Conjure Wife*. The story concerns Professor Richard Benjamin forcing his witch wife Teri Garr to forsake her spell-casting ways, thus allowing super-witch Lana Turner to meddle in their lives. Sadly neither the gags nor the special effects are up to much. AJ [video]

Richard Benjamin *Joshua Lightman* • Teri Garr *Margaret Lightman* • Lana Turner *Vivian Cross* • Kathryn Leigh Scott *Susan Carey* • James Winker *Linus Cross* • Bill Sorrels *Nick Carey* • Kelly Jean Peters *Linda Reynolds* • Jordan Charney *Charlie Reynolds* ■ *Dir* Richard Shorr • *Scr* Syd Dutton, Richard Shorr

The Witches of Eastwick ★★★★ 18

Comedy drama 1987 · US · Colour · 113mins

This raunchy metaphor for the battle between the sexes from *Mad Max* director George Miller soars with inspired lunacy as three romance-starved suburban women dabble in off-white magic for some offbeat chandelier swinging. While Jack Nicholson dominates this spellbinding adaptation of John Updike's ironic bestseller as the horny little devil, the luminous female talent (Cher, Susan Sarandon and Michelle Pfeiffer) almost matches him in a charming sensual fantasy that's slightly overloaded with needless special effects. AJ. Contains swearing and violence. [video] DVD

Jack Nicholson *Daryl Van Horne* • Cher *Alexandra Medford* • Susan Sarandon *Jane Spofford* • Michelle Pfeiffer *Sukie Ridgemont* • Veronica Cartwright *Felicia Alden* • Richard Jenkins *Clyde Alden* • Keith Jochim *Walter Neff* • Carel Struycken *Fidel* • Helen Biddie *Mrs Biddie* ■ *Dir* George Miller (2) • *Scr* Michael Cristofer, from the novel by John Updike

The Witches of Salem ★★★

Period drama 1957 · Fr/E Ger · BW · 147mins

Belgian actor-turned-director Raymond Rouleau proved an uninspired choice for this first screen version of Arthur Miller's compelling play, *The Crucible*. In spite of star performances from real-life husband and wife Yves Montand and Simone Signoret, playing the persecuted Proctors, the play's intense commitment and political conviction are weakened by Jean-Paul Sartre's stodgy adaptation and Rouleau's flat direction. Still, nothing could ruin the story of a young woman in 1692 Massachusetts, who vengefully accuses Signoret of witchcraft. BB. In French with English subtitles.

Yves Montand *John Proctor* • Simone Signoret *Elisabeth Proctor* • Mylène Demongeot *Abigail* • Jean Debucourt *Reverend Parris* • Raymond Rouleau *Danforth, the governor* • Françoise Lugagne *Mrs Putnam* ■ *Dir* Raymond Rouleau • *Scr* Jean-Paul Sartre, from the play *The Crucible* by Arthur Miller

Witchfinder General ★★★★★ 18

Horror 1968 · UK · Colour · 88mins

Condemned on first release as extremely bloody and sadistic, Michael Reeves's penetrating chronicle of the social evils at large during the English Civil War is now an acknowledged horror classic. Vincent Price plays it straight for once as the cynical religious maniac instigating torture and degradation for pleasure and profit in an intense study of pathological cruelty. With non-gratuitous violent imagery crucial to the brutal history lesson, Reeves's final work (he died of an overdose shortly after) is a thematically fascinating and gruesomely incisive look at the lust for and abuse of power. AJ [video] DVD

Vincent Price *Matthew Hopkins* • Ian Ogilvy *Richard Marshall* • Rupert Davies *John Lowes* • Hilary Dwyer *Sara* • Robert Russell *John Stearne* • Patrick Wymark *Oliver Cromwell* • Wilfrid Brambell *Master Coach* • Nicky Henson *Trooper Swallow* ■ *Dir* Michael Reeves • *Scr* Michael Reeves, Tom Baker, from the novel by Ronald Bassett

W

With a Song in My Heart
★★★★ U

Musical biographical drama
1952 · US · Colour · 116mins

Some of the finest song standards ever written turn up in this fine Technicolor wallow, purportedly the true, tragic (but inspiring) life story of singer Jane Froman who rose from radio commercials to universal acclaim in the 1930s, but was then badly injured in a wartime plane crash. It's Froman's voice on the soundtrack, and lip-synching the vocals with credible conviction is Susan Hayward, here displaying character-steel as only she can, earning a best actress Oscar nomination in the process. An Oscar did go to brilliant musical director Alfred Newman, and mention should also be made of the notable star-making performance from a very young Robert Wagner as a shell-shocked soldier. This is finely performed and intelligently crafted. TS

Susan Hayward *Jane Froman* • Rory Calhoun *John Burns* • David Wayne *Don Ross* • Thelma Ritter *Clancy* • Robert Wagner *GI Paratrooper* • Helen Westcott *Jennifer March* • Una Merkel *Sister Marie* ■ *Dir* Walter Lang • *Scr* Lamar Trotti

With Honors
★★ PG

Comedy drama 1994 · US · Colour · 96mins

This patchy campus comedy has homeless Joe Pesci trading the pages of student Brendan Fraser's dissertation for food. The problem here is predictability. We know Pesci can't just be any old tramp, and soon the wit and wisdom come tumbling out for the benefit of Fraser and his undeserving room-mates. Pesci trots out his familiar tricks and wipes the floor with his juvenile co-stars. DP

Joe Pesci *Simon Wilder* • Brendan Fraser *Monty Kessler* • Moira Kelly *Courtney Blumenthal* • Patrick Dempsey *Everett Calloway* • Josh Hamilton *Jeff Hawkes* • Gore Vidal *Professor Philip Hayes* ■ *Dir* Alek Keshishian • *Scr* William Mastrosimone

With or without You
★★★ 18

Romantic comedy drama
1999 · UK · Colour · 87mins

Originally titled *Old New Borrowed Blue*, this low-key, Belfast-based drama from director Michael Winterbottom has Dervla Kirwan and Christopher Eccleston as a young couple desperate to start a family. When an old French pen pal of hers (Yvan Attal) turns up out of the blue, the tension that has been building between them threatens to capsize their marriage. Writer John Forte does not shy away from Ulster's age-old sectarian divisions, but neither does he let them interfere with the refreshing seam of optimism that runs through this gentle gem. NS DVD

Christopher Eccleston *Vincent Boyd* • Dervla Kirwan *Rosie Boyd* • Yvan Attal *Benoit* • Julie Graham *Cathy* • Alun Armstrong *Sammy* • Lloyd Hutchinson *Neil* • Michael Liebman *Brian* • Doon Mackichan *Deidre* • Gordon Kennedy *Ormonde* • Fionnula Flanagan *Irene* ■ *Dir* Michael Winterbottom • *Scr* John Forte

With Six You Get Eggroll
★★ U

Comedy 1968 · US · Colour · 90mins

Doris Day's last movie is this amiable trifle, in which she plays a widow with three sons who marries convenient widower Brian Keith, father of teenage daughter Barbara Hershey, hence the arch title. The offspring naturally object to the relationship. There's a tired 1960s gloss to the whole thing, and it's easy to see why Doris called it a Day. TS DVD

Doris Day *Abby McClure* • Brian Keith *Jake Iverson* • Pat Carroll *Maxine Scott* • Barbara Hershey *Stacey Iverson* • George Carlin *Herbie Fleck* • Alice Ghostley *Housekeeper* • John Findlater *Flip McClure* • Jimmy Bracken *Mitch McClure* • Richard Steele *Jason McClure* ■ *Dir* Howard Morris • *Scr* Gwen Bagni, Paul Dubov, Harvey Bullock, RS Allen, from a story by Gwen Bagni, Paul Dubov

Withnail & I
★★★★ 15

Cult black comedy
1986 · UK · Colour · 107mins

Those born before 1950 will regard this cult classic about two dissolute 1960s hippies (Richard E Grant and Paul McGann) with unbridled horror. There are empty bottles and dirty underwear everywhere, along with half-finished joints and fag ends stubbed out in congealing boiled eggs. But this is in fact a glorious rites-of-passage movie, as the lads decamp to a cottage in the Lake District where they struggle to survive the weather and a lecherous Uncle Monty. Written and directed by Bruce Robinson, based on his own experiences in London's Camden Town. SH. Contains swearing and drug abuse. DVD

Richard E Grant *Withnail* • Paul McGann *...and I* • Richard Griffiths *Monty* • Ralph Brown *Danny* • Michael Elphick *Jake* • Daragh O'Malley *Irishman* • Michael Wardle *Isaac Parkin* • Una Brandon-Jones *Mrs Parkin* • Noel Johnson *General* ■ *Dir/Scr* Bruce Robinson

Without a Clue
★★★ PG

Comedy mystery
1988 · UK · Colour · 101mins

The real brains behind Sherlock Holmes belonged to Dr Watson, according to this hit-and-miss, hammy Baker Street farce; in fact, the shy doctor (Ben Kingsley) invented the fictitious sleuth as a front for his own brilliant crime detection skills. As Holmes captured the public's imagination, Kingsley is forced to hire actor Michael Caine to impersonate him. How they fare while investigating a plot to undermine the British Empire with forged five pound notes is the comedy basis for this mismatched buddy movie. Good fun despite the patchy laughs. AJ DVD

Michael Caine *Sherlock Holmes/Reginald Kincaid* • Ben Kingsley *Dr John Watson* • Jeffrey Jones *Inspector Lestrade* • Lysette Anthony *Leslie Giles* • Paul Freeman *Professor Moriarty* • Nigel Davenport *Lord Smithwick* • Pat Keen *Mrs Hudson* • Peter Cook *Greenhough* ■ *Dir* Thom Eberhardt • *Scr* Gary Murphy, Larry Strawther

Without a Paddle
★ 12

Comedy 2004 · US · Colour · 94mins

This truly awful buddy comedy features Matthew Lillard, Seth Green and Dax Shepard, who embark on a whitewater rafting adventure in memory of a recently deceased childhood friend, only to be pursued by insane backwoodsmen. The trio are a thoroughly unappealing and boorish lot and the asinine screenplay is irritating, tedious and tasteless. AS DVD

Seth Green *Dr Dan Mott* • Matthew Lillard *Jerry Conlaine* • Dax Shepard *Tom Marshall* • Ethan Suplee *Elwood* • Burt Reynolds *Del Knox* • Abraham Benrubi *Dennis* • Rachel Blanchard *Flower* • Christina Moore *Butterfly* ■ *Dir* Steven Brill • *Scr* Jay Leggett, Mitch Rouse, from a story by Fred Wolf, Harris Goldberg, Tom Nursall

Without a Trace
★★★ 15

Drama based on a true story
1983 · US · Colour · 115mins

This impressive drama sadly falls down thanks to a rather ludicrous conclusion. Kate Nelligan is the mother who continues to believe her six-year-old son will return after he vanishes, though everyone around her loses faith. Nelligan is very watchable as the overwrought mother, while Judd Hirsch and stage and screen actress Stockard Channing both match her scene for scene. JB

Kate Nelligan *Susan Selky* • Judd Hirsch *Al Menetti* • David Dukes *Graham Selky* • Stockard Channing *Jocelyn Norris* • Jacqueline Brookes *Margaret Mayo* • Keith McDermott *Phillippe* • Kathleen Widdoes *Ms Hauser* ■ *Dir* Stanley R Jaffe • *Scr* Beth Gutcheon, from her novel *Still Missing*

Without Apparent Motive
★★★

Crime thriller 1972 · Fr · Colour · 100mins

This downbeat *film noir* stages its dark tale of murder in the brilliant Riviera sunshine. Combining hangdog cynicism with intuition and tenacity, Jean-Louis Trintignant's police inspector is the epitome of hard-boiled world-weariness, as he conducts an investigation into a series of seemingly motiveless killings, to which the only clue is a diary detailing the first victim's love affairs. Director Philippe Labro reveals his hand with methodical thoroughness, but a touch of suspense might not have gone amiss. DP. In French with English subtitles.

Jean-Louis Trintignant *Carella* • Dominique Sanda *Sandra* • Carla Gravina *Jocelyne* • Paul Crauchet *Palombo* • Sacha Distel *Julien* • Gilles Ségal *Bozzo* • Laura Antonelli *Juliette* • Jean-Pierre Marielle *Perry Rupert-Foote* • Stéphane Audran *Hélène Vallee* ■ *Dir* Philippe Labro • *Scr* Philippe Labro, Jacques Lanzmann, from the novel *Ten Plus One* by Ed McBain [Evan Hunter]

Without Limits
★★★ 15

Sports biography
1998 · US · Colour · 118mins

Co-produced by Tom Cruise, this is the tragic tale of American runner Steve Prefontaine, who came close to winning gold at the 1972 Munich Olympics, only to die in a car crash three years later. The rather uninteresting Billy Crudup stars as Prefontaine, and it's Donald Sutherland who steals the show playing coach Bill Bowerman, known for the running shoes he designed for his team and as the man who invented Nike trainers. Monica Potter plays the underwritten love interest, and she, like everyone else, is upstaged by the lovingly filmed athletic scenes. JB. Contains some swearing.

Billy Crudup *Steve Prefontaine* • Donald Sutherland *Bill Bowerman* • Monica Potter *Mary Marckx* • Jeremy Sisto *Frank Shorter* • Matthew Lillard *Roscoe Devine* • Billy Burke *Kenny Moore* ■ *Dir* Robert Towne • *Scr* Robert Towne, Kenny Moore • *Producer* Paula Wagner, Tom Cruise

Without Love
★★★

Romantic comedy 1945 · US · BW · 110mins

Spencer Tracy and Katharine Hepburn survive the long arm of coincidence in Donald Ogden Stewart's screenplay, as well as the pedestrian direction of Harold S Bucquet, in this tale of a weary scientist who lodges himself and his work in the home of a woman who, under her cool exterior, longs for love. *Adam's Rib* it isn't, but the stars are on form, and there is added zest from Keenan Wynn and a wisecracking Lucille Ball. RK

Spencer Tracy *Pat Jamieson* • Katharine Hepburn *Jamie Rowan* • Lucille Ball *Kitty Trimble* • Keenan Wynn *Quentin Ladd* • Carl Esmond *Paul Carrell* • Patricia Morison *Edwina Collins* • Felix Bressart *Professor Grinza* • Emily Massey *Anna* • Gloria Grahame *Flower girl* ■ *Dir* Harold S Bucquet • *Scr* Donald Ogden Stewart, from the play by Philip Barry

Without Malice
★★

Thriller 2000 · US · Colour · 89mins

The only thing puzzling about this thriller is why such a competent cast was attracted to it. Perhaps the Canadian locations tempted Craig Sheffer and Corey Haim, who play prospective brothers-in-law whose "get-to-know-you" hunting trip turns sour when they accidentally shoot a forest ranger and cover up the deed. With Jennifer Beals taking so long to find out the truth and Gabrielle Anwar reduced to simpering support, this is a real patience-tester. DP

Craig Sheffer *Dr Paul Venters* • Jennifer Beals *Samantha Wilkes* • Gabrielle Anwar *Susan* • Corey Haim *Marty* • Ian Black *Nick* ■ *Dir* Rob King • *Scr* Peter Layton

Without Reservations
★★★ U

Comedy 1946 · US · BW · 102mins

This deft and under-rated Hollywood-on-Hollywood comedy has the irresistible Claudette Colbert as a wacky author searching for a leading man to play the screen hero in the movie of her book. She settles on marine flier John Wayne and won't let him out of her sight. Director Mervyn LeRoy knows this territory well and calls on some personal friends to prop up the story: Cary Grant's surprise appearance is very funny, and keep your eyes open, too, for guest star Jack Benny. Froth, but expertly done. TS DVD

Claudette Colbert *Christopher "Kit" Madden/Kit Klotch* • John Wayne *Captain Rusty Thomas* • Don DeFore *Lt Dink Watson* • Anne Triola *Consuela "Connie" Callaghan* • Phil Brown *Soldier* • Frank Puglia *Ortega* • Thurston Hall *Baldwin* • Dona Drake *Dolores Ortega* • Louella Parsons • Cary Grant • Jack Benny • Raymond Burr *Paul Gill* ■ *Dir* Mervyn LeRoy • *Scr* Andrew Solt, from the novel *Thanks, God, I'll Take It from Here* by Jane Allen, Mae Livingston

Without Warning
★★★

Thriller 1973 · Fr · Colour · 98mins

Bruno Gantillon has only made a handful of features and his second is generally regarded as the most accomplished. It's certainly based on an intriguing premise, beginning with Maurice Ronet being hounded out of the police for prosecuting the drug-trafficking son of a senior officer. But Ronet is anything but an innocent victim, as Bruno Cremer is convinced he served under him as a mercenary in Indochina. This is a dark thriller full of disturbing insights into the power-broking process. DP. French dialogue dubbed into English.

Maurice Ronet *Maury* • Mario Adorf *Capra* • Bruno Cremer *Donetti* • Anny Duperey *Cora* • Mario Pisu *Louvai* • Marina Malfatti *Isabelle* ■ *Dir/Scr* Bruno Gantillon

Without Warning
★

Horror 1980 · US · Colour · 96mins

This absolute turkey from the director of *Satan's Cheerleaders* is derailed by the outrageous ham acting from two of its all-tarnished-star cast, Jack Palance and Martin Landau. An alien lands in a remote rural area and starts flinging pizza-shaped, flesh-sucking parasites around in order to decorate his spaceship with human trophies gleaned from hapless campers and redneck locals. AJ

Jack Palance *Taylor* • Martin Landau *Fred* • Tarah Nutter *Sandy* • Christopher S Nelson *Greg* • Cameron Mitchell *Hunter* • Neville Brand *Leo* • Sue Ann Langdon [Sue Ane Langdon] *Aggie* ■ *Dir* Greydon Clark • *Scr* Lyn Freeman, Daniel Grodnik, Ben Nett, Steve Mathis

Without Warning: the James Brady Story
★★★★

Drama based on a true story
1991 · US · Colour · 85mins

James Brady was the Presidential press secretary shot in the head during John Hinckley's assassination attempt on Ronald Reagan in 1981. The film is

W

a deeply moving tribute to the way that Brady and his wife (Joan Allen) fought his disabilities and campaigned for tighter gun control – the so-called Brady Bill. Produced by David Puttnam for American cable TV, it is notable for a truly astonishing performance by Beau Bridges, and for its literate and insightful final script by Robert Bolt, who was himself disabled by a stroke in 1979. AT. Contains swearing.

Beau Bridges *James Brady* • Joan Allen *Sarah Brady* • David Strathairn *Dr Kobrine* • Christopher Bell *Scotty* • Christine Healy *Ruth* • Timothy Landfield *Bob* • Bryan Clark *Ronald Reagan* • Susan Brown *Nancy Reagan* • Steven Flynn *John W Hinckley Jr* ■ *Dir* Michael Toshiyuki Uno • *Scr* Robert Bolt, from the book *Thumbs Up: the Life and Courageous Comeback of White House Press Secretary Jim Brady* by Mollie Dickenson

Without You I'm Nothing ★★★ 15

Comedy 1990 · US · Colour · 89mins

This filmed record of bisexual comedian Sandra Bernhard's Off-Broadway show features her on full-throttle assault. As uncomfortably mean-spirited as she is funny, Bernhard makes mincemeat of such pop icons as Diana Ross, Barbra Streisand, Andy Warhol and Prince, and also explores Jewish envy, her attraction to black culture and decries the male gender. Director John Boskovich cuts from Bernhard's edgy routines to shocked audience members, conjuring up the sense of flirtatious danger that makes her brand of abrasive comedy work. Hilarious, offensive, ugly and true. AJ [VIDEO]

Sandra Bernhard • John Doe • Steve Antin • Lu Leonard *Sandra's manager* • Cynthia Bailey *Roxanne* • Denise Vlasis *Shoshanna* • Ken Foree *Emcee* ■ *Dir* John Boskovich • *Scr* Sandra Bernhard, John Boskovich

Witness ★★★★★ 15

Romantic thriller
1985 · US · Colour · 107mins

A murder at a city railway station is witnessed by a small boy, Lukas Haas, who is a member of the Amish community, a religious sect living in rural Pennsylvania that eschews as much of modern life – notably machinery – as they can. Pursued by the bad guys, the boy and his widowed mother (Kelly McGillis) are protected by cop Harrison Ford, who takes them back to their village and awaits the killers' arrival. Directed by Peter Weir, this is partly a love story and partly a thriller, but mainly a study of cultural collision. The performances are immaculate, yet it's Weir's delicacy of touch that impresses the most. He juggles the various elements of the story and makes the violence seem even more shocking when played out on the fields of Amish denial. JF. Contains swearing, nudity. [VIDEO] DVD

Harrison Ford *John Book* • Kelly McGillis *Rachel Lapp* • Josef Sommer *Deputy Commissioner Schaeffer* • Lukas Haas *Samuel Lapp* • Jan Rubes *Eli Lapp* • Alexander Godunov *Daniel Hochleitner* • Danny Glover *McFee* • Brent Jennings *Carter* • Patti LuPone *Elaine* • Viggo Mortensen *Moses Hochleitner* ■ *Dir* Peter Weir • *Scr* Earl W Wallace, William Kelley, from a story by Kelley, Earl W Wallace, Pamela Wallace • *Cinematographer* John Seale • *Music* Maurice Jarre • *Editor* Thom Noble

Witness for the Prosecution ★★★★★ U

Courtroom drama 1957 · US · BW · 111mins

Director Billy Wilder's gleefully enjoyable film version of Agatha Christie's play stars Tyrone Power (in his last completed role) as the husband on trial for murder and Marlene Dietrich as his wife testifying against him. The whole plot is an intricate, slightly leaky bag of tricks, with a trademark "surprise" ending. But to conceal the cracks, Wilder throws up a variety of smokescreens and provides the broadest stage imaginable for Charles Laughton's barrister – a performance of epic extravagance, invention and downright hamminess. Ralph Richardson, Deborah Kerr and Diana Rigg assumed the key parts for an enjoyable but less accomplished TV remake 25 years later. AT [VIDEO] DVD

Tyrone Power *Leonard Stephen Vole* • Marlene Dietrich *Christine Helm Vole* • Charles Laughton *Sir Wilfrid Robarts* • Elsa Lanchester *Miss Plimsoll* • John Williams *Brogan-Moore* • Henry Daniell *Mayhew* • Ian Wolfe *Carter* • Torin Thatcher *Mr Myers* • Norma Varden *Mrs Emily French* • Una O'Connor *Janet McKenzie* • Francis Compton *Judge* ■ *Dir* Billy Wilder • *Scr* Billy Wilder, Harry Kurnitz, Larry Marcus, from the play by Agatha Christie, from her short story • *Art Director* Alexandre Trauner

Witness in the Dark ★★ U

Crime 1959 · UK · BW · 62mins

This is one of Wolf Rilla's lesser efforts, but he conjures up a pleasing sense of menace as he subjects blind telephonist Patricia Dainton to the murderous machinations of a prowler. As so often in thrillers of this kind, much depends on contrivance and the script might have concealed its hand with a little more artfulness. Dainton's performance, however, is superior to that in the majority of British Bs. DP

Patricia Dainton *Jane Pringle* • Conrad Phillips *Inspector Coates* • Madge Ryan *Mrs Finch* • Nigel Green *Intruder* • Enid Lorimer *Mrs Temple* • Richard O'Sullivan *Don Theobold* ■ *Dir* Wolf Rilla • *Scr* Leigh Vance, John Lemont

Witness in the War Zone ★★★ 15

Political drama
1986 · UK/W Ger/Is · Colour · 95mins

This stars Christopher Walken as an American reporter covering the war in Lebanon. The excellent Walken can play a cynical newshound as well as anyone, but the plot starts to unravel when Walken falls for nurse Marita Marschall and finds himself making news instead of simply covering it. Tighter direction would have heightened the suspense. DP. Contains violence, swearing and nudity. [VIDEO]

Christopher Walken *Don Stevens* • Marita Marschall *Linda Larson* • Hywel Bennett *Mike Jessop* • Arnon Zadok *Hamdi Abu-Yussuf* • Amos Lavie *Yessin Abu-Riadd* • Etti Ankri *Samira* • Martin Umbach *Bernard* ■ *Dir* Nathaniel Gutman • *Scr* Hanan Peled

Witness Protection ★★★ 15

Crime drama 1999 · US · Colour · 96mins

The under-rated Tom Sizemore landed a Golden Globe nomination for his performance in this compelling, made-for-TV insight into life within the Federal Witness Protection Programme. Forced to abjure his wealth and power, Sizemore agrees to accept a new identity after his associates turn against him. However, the combined pressures of enduring high-security confinement and having to start again in a strange town soon begin to undermine his marriage to Mary Elizabeth Mastrantonio. Both tense and intense. DP [VIDEO] DVD

Tom Sizemore *Bobby Batton* • Mary Elizabeth Mastrantonio *Cindy Batton* • Forest Whitaker *Steven Beck* • Shawn Hatosy *Sean Batton* • Skye McCole Bartusiak *Suzie Batton* • William Sadler *Sharp* ■ *Dir* Richard Pearce • *Scr* Daniel Therriault, from a story by Daniel Therriault, Robert Sabbag, from the article *The Invisible Family* by Robert Sabbag

Witness to Murder ★★★

Crime thriller 1954 · US · BW · 81mins

Barbara Stanwyck is the unfortunate witness who sees George Sanders murdering a girl in the apartment across the way. But, since he cannily disposes of the corpse and all the evidence, detective Gary Merrill simply doesn't believe her. A run-of-the-mill script and a plot idea as old as the hills is turned into a gripping little thriller, thanks to the all-stops-out performances and direction by Roy Rowland. He milks the material for every possible element of nail-biting tension as silky ex-Nazi Sanders closes in on a terrified Stanwyck. RK

Barbara Stanwyck *Cheryl Draper* • George Sanders *Albert Richter* • Gary Merrill *Lawrence Mathews* • Jesse White *Eddie Vincent* • Harry Shannon *Captain Donnelly* • Claire Carleton *The Blonde* • Lewis Martin *Psychiatrist* ■ *Dir* Roy Rowland • *Scr* Chester Erskine

Wittgenstein ★★★ 15

Biographical drama
1993 · UK · Colour · 69mins

With his health and eyesight failing from Aids-related complications, avant-garde director Derek Jarman somehow managed to shoot this lucid and glowingly vibrant portrait of the tormented 20th-century gay philosopher Ludwig Wittgenstein on a minuscule budget in two weeks. Karl Johnson plays the man searching for intellectual self-development, while struggling with alienation because of his sexual preferences, in a starkly realised series of bleakly amusing and acid-coloured vignettes. One of Jarman's best, although still of a typically rarefied nature. AJ [VIDEO]

Karl Johnson *Ludwig Wittgenstein* • Tilda Swinton *Lady Morrell* • Michael Gough *Bertrand Russell* • John Quentin *John Maynard Keynes* • Clancy Chassay *Young Ludwig* • Kevin Collins *Johnny* • Jill Balcon *Leopoldine Wittgenstein* • Sally Dexter *Hermine Wittgenstein* • Nabil Shaban *Martian* ■ *Dir* Derek Jarman • *Scr* Derek Jarman, Terry Eagleton, Ken Butler

Wives and Lovers ★★

Comedy drama 1963 · US · BW · 103mins

This domestic comedy-drama about the pitfalls of the American dream is directed by John Rich, a graduate of the hit television comedy *The Dick Van Dyke Show*. There's also more than a touch of *The Seven Year Itch* to the tale about a struggling New York writer who suddenly hits the big time, moves to Connecticut and starts to mix with the rich and famous, leaving his marriage to crumble into pieces. There's an anaemic performance by Van Johnson and a scene-stealing one from Shelley Winters. AT

Janet Leigh *Bertie Austin* • Van Johnson *Bill Austin* • Shelley Winters *Fran Cabrell* • Martha Hyer *Lucinda Ford* • Ray Walston *Wylie Driberg* • Jeremy Slate *Gar Aldrich* • Claire Wilcox *Julie Austin* • Lee Patrick *Mrs Swanson* ■ *Dir* John Rich • *Scr* Edward Anhalt, from the play *The First Wife* by Jay Presson Allen

Wives under Suspicion ★★

Courtroom drama 1938 · US · BW · 68mins

Warren William stars as a tough-minded, morally upright and obsessively dedicated district attorney. In prosecuting a man who has murdered his faithless wife in a fit of jealousy, William comes to realise that the case is a mirror of his own life in which his neglected wife (Gail Patrick) is seeking solace with William Lundigan. A modest and mildly interesting drama, directed by James Whale who made a more stylish job of *The Kiss before the Mirror* in 1933, of which this is a remake. RK

Warren William *District Attorney Jim Stowell* • Gail Patrick *Lucy Stowell* • Constance Moore *Elizabeth* • William Lundigan *Phil* • Ralph Morgan *Professor Shaw MacAllen* • Cecil Cunningham *"Sharpy"* • Samuel S Hinds *David Marrow* ■ *Dir* James Whale • *Scr* Myles Connolly, from the play *The Kiss before the Mirror* by Ladislaus Fodor [Ladislas Fodor]

The Wiz ★★ U

Musical fantasy 1978 · US · Colour · 128mins

A 34-year-old Diana Ross plays Dorothy in this all-black version of *The Wizard of Oz*, which casts a pall over memories of the 1939 classic. It's easy to see why director Sidney Lumet's clunker ranks as one of the most expensive movie flops of all time. While the Tony Walton sets are fabulous, the famous plot is immersed in a dark inner-city impressionism, the quasi-rocker songs are lacklustre, and diva Ross is just ludicrous in the Judy Garland role. Michael Jackson is surprisingly good as the Scarecrow, though. AJ [VIDEO]

Diana Ross *Dorothy* • Michael Jackson (3) *Scarecrow* • Nipsey Russell *Tin Man* • Ted Ross *Lion* • Mabel King *Evillene* • Theresa Merritt *Aunt Em* • Thelma Carpenter *Miss One* • Lena Horne *Glinda the Good* • Richard Pryor *The Wiz* • Stanley Greene *Uncle Henry* ■ *Dir* Sidney Lumet • *Scr* Joel Schumacher, from the musical by William F Brown, Charlie Smalls, from the novel *The Wonderful Wizard of Oz* by L Frank Baum

The Wizard of Baghdad ★★ U

Fantasy comedy 1960 · US · Colour · 92mins

After all the cardboard cutout Oriental fantasies that have masqueraded as movies over the years, at last comes a parody of the genre, though it's of little consequence. Dick Shawn, playing a lazy genie threatened with being turned human for not completing any duties, gives a performance that ensures indolence will affect the amount of laughs as well. The special effects – including a rather frayed flying carpet – are as dodgy as the plot line which, of course, involves the uniting of a prince and princess in wedded bliss. TH

Dick Shawn *Ali Mahmud, Genie* • Diane Baker *Princess Yasmin* • Barry Coe *Prince Husan* • John Van Dreelen *Jullnar* • Robert F Simon *Shamadin* • Vaughn Taylor *Norodeen* ■ *Dir* George Sherman • *Scr* Jesse L Lasky Jr [Jesse Lasky Jr], Pat Silver, from a story by Samuel Newman

The Wizard of Gore ★★★ 18

Horror 1970 · US · Colour · 95mins

Slasher pioneer Herschell Gordon Lewis could never be accused of pretension or artifice in his unashamedly fuctional approach to slaughter. Taking his own nickname for its title, this hilarious offering is right out of the Roger Corman school of exploitation as it follows the demented Montag the Magician (Ray Sager) on a mesmeric killing spree. The eviscerations Montag performs before a mind-numbed audience are schlock of the most gloriously silly variety and Sager's performance is 5 per cent inspiration, 95 per cent ineptitude. DP [VIDEO] DVD

Ray Sager *Montag the Magnificent* • Judy Cler *Sherry Carson* • Wayne Ratay *Jack* • Phil Laurenson *Greg* • Jim Rau *Steve* ■ *Dir* Herschell Gordon Lewis • *Scr* Allen Kahn

W

The Wizard of Loneliness ★★★ 15

Drama 1988 · US · Colour · 106mins

Lukas Haas gives one of the best performances of his career to date in this rites-of-passage drama set in New England during the Second World War. This is an engaging tale in which Haas finds himself at the centre of a family crisis when the shady past of aunt Lea Thompson comes to light. Director

Jenny Bowen does a good job of creating the period atmosphere, but she might have tightened up the action in places. DP. Contains violence and swearing.

Lukas Haas *Wendall Olet* • Lea Thompson *Sybil* • Lance Guest *John T* • John Randolph *Doc* • Dylan Baker *Duffy* • Anne Pitoniak *Cornelia* • Jeremiah Warner *Tom* ■ *Dir* Jenny Bowen • *Scr* Nancy Larson, from the novel by John Nichols

The Wizard of Oz ★★★ U

Silent fantasy 1925 · US · BW · 85mins

It's fascinating to compare the classic movie we all love with this earlier version. It was created by comedian Larry Semon as a vehicle for himself – even Dorothy (played by Semon's real-life wife Dorothy Dwan) is a supporting character to Semon's Scarecrow. Dorothy gets blown to Oz in a tornado, but there are no witches and no Munchkins. Instead the people of Oz hail Dorothy as their ruler. The farm-hand who briefly becomes the Tin Man is a very young Oliver Hardy. The Lion is a substantial role for a young, black acrobat named G Howe Black, who is subjected to some awesomely racist humour. The ending is startlingly abrupt. DM DVD

Larry Semon *Scarecrow* • Bryant Washburn *Prince Kynde* • Dorothy Dwan *Dorothy* • Virginia Pearson *Countess Vishuss* • Charles Murray *Wizard* • Oliver Hardy *Tin Woodsman* • G Howe Black *Rastus* ■ *Dir* Larry Semon • *Scr* Larry Semon, L Frank Baum Jr, Leon Lee, from the novel *The Wonderful Wizard of Oz* by L Frank Baum

The Wizard of Oz ★★★★★ U

Classic musical fantasy
1939 · US · Colour and sepia · 97mins

One of Hollywood's quintessential productions, this musical adaptation of L Frank Baum's classic fable is probably the most beloved fantasy film of all time and the ultimate family picture. It has something for everyone: wonderfully strange lands, fun-scary moments, a dazzling assortment of fairy-tale characters, fabulous songs to take us all somewhere over the rainbow, a peerless Judy Garland performance, and meaningful messages in abundance. Continuously enthralling, this is one hardy perennial you can never tire of watching. Uncredited King Vidor directed some of the sequences. AJ DVD

Judy Garland *Dorothy Gale* • Ray Bolger *Scarecrow/"Hunk"* • Bert Lahr *Cowardly Lion/"Zeke"* • Jack Haley *Tin Man/"Hickory"* • Billie Burke *Glinda* • Margaret Hamilton *Wicked Witch of the West/Miss Almira Gulch* • Frank Morgan *Prof Marvel/Wizard of Oz/Doorkeeper of the Emerald City/Coachman/Wizard's doorkeeper* • Charley Grapewin *Uncle Henry* • Clara Blandick *Auntie Em* ■ *Dir* Victor Fleming • *Scr* Noel Langley, Florence Ryerson, Edgar Allan Woolf, from the novel *The Wonderful Wizard of Oz* by L Frank Baum • *Cinematographer* Harold Rosson • *Art Director* Cedric Gibbons, William A Horning • *Music/lyrics* Harold Arlen, EY Harburg

The Wizard of Speed and Time ★★ PG

Fantasy comedy 1988 · US · Colour · 94mins

A trippy, almost psychedelic effects extravaganza, entirely home-produced by one-man-band movie-maker Mike Jittlov. He also stars, as a freelance film effects whizz given the chance to make his own movie. Supremely self-indulgent, this labour of love nonetheless offers some interesting insights into the trials and tribulations of indie film-making. Jittlov was Hollywood flavour of the month for five minutes back in the late 1980s. He's barely been heard of since. DA

Mike Jittlov *Mike, the Wizard/Torch carrier* • Paige Moore *Cindy Lite/Dancer/Pretty hitchhiker* • Richard Kaye *Harvey Bookman/Voice over artist* • David Conrad *Brian Lucas/Photographer (Wizard Film)* • John Massari *Steve Shostakovich/Photographer (Wizard Film)* • Philip Michael Thomas *Policeman Mick Polanko* • Steve Brodie *Lucky Straeker* ■ *Dir/Scr* Mike Jittlov

Wizards ★★ PG

Animated fantasy adventure
1977 · US · Colour · 77mins

This ambitious animated tale from the director of *Fritz the Cat*, Ralph Bakshi, is set in Earth's far-flung future where nuclear holocaust has left the world in the hands (and claws) of elves, fairies, wizards and mutants. Out of this messy miasma come twin wizards – the good Avatar and the evil Blackwolf – who duke it out for survival. Uncertain whether it wants to appeal to children, grown-ups or both, it's something of a dull affair. DA

Bob Holt *Avatar* • Jesse Wells *Elinore* • Richard Romanus *Weehawk* • David Proval *Peace* • James Connell *President* • Mark Hamill *Sean* ■ *Dir/Scr* Ralph Bakshi

Wizards of the Lost Kingdom ★★★ PG

Fantasy adventure
1985 · US/Arg · Colour · 72mins

Things that go bump in the night abound in this fantasy adventure about mercenary swordsman Bo Svenson helping wizard's son Vidal Peterson whose father Edward Morrow has fallen foul of evil magician Thom Christopher. Ogres help out in the scuffles between good and evil, but it's not as dependent on special effects as it would be these days. Director Hector Olivera conjures up an alien atmosphere, while the sanitised events are well up to squeaky-clean Disney standards. A sequel followed three years later. TH

Bo Svenson *Kor* • Vidal Peterson *Simon* • Thom Christopher *Shurka* • Barbara Stock *Udea* • Maria Socas *Acrasia* • Dolores Michaels *Aura* • Edward Morrow *Wulfrick/Old Simon/Gulfax* • August Larreta *King Tylor* ■ *Dir* Hector Olivera • *Scr* Tom Edwards

Wolf ★★★ 15

Horror 1994 · US · Colour · 120mins

Everything is right about this film apart from the direction. Jack Nicholson and Michelle Pfeiffer are suitably stellar – he as the middle-aged book editor, she as his boss's daughter whose burgeoning romance is cursed by the fangs of a werewolf. Giuseppe Rotunno's glossy photography lends a sinister sophistication, Ennio Morricone's eerie score plays on our unease and make-up maestro Rick Baker's transformations combine ingenuity with a real sense of agony. But director Mike Nichols is so interested in the romantic entanglements that he forgets to make the horror horrific. DP. Contains sex scenes, violence, swearing. DVD

Jack Nicholson *Will Randall* • Michelle Pfeiffer *Laura Alden* • James Spader *Stewart Swinton* • Kate Nelligan *Charlotte Randall* • Richard Jenkins *Detective Bridger* • Christopher Plummer *Raymond Alden* • Eileen Atkins *Mary* • David Hyde Pierce *Roy* • Om Puri *Dr Vijay Alezias* • Ron Rifkin *Doctor* • Prunella Scales *Maude* ■ *Dir* Mike Nichols • *Scr* Jim Harrison, Wesley Strick

The Wolf at the Door ★★★ 18

Biographical drama
1986 · Fr/Den · Colour · 86mins

Danish director Henning Carlsen found an international audience with this biopic of the artist Paul Gauguin. In a far cry from Anthony Quinn's portrayal in *Lust for Life*, Donald Sutherland plays Gauguin as a man at the crossroads, caught between the need to support his mistresses and the desire to fulfil his artistic destiny. Intelligently scripted by Christopher Hampton and beautifully shot by Mikael Salomon, this is a laudable attempt to understand a complex personality. DP. Contains nudity.

Donald Sutherland *Paul Gauguin* • Valerie Morea *Annah-la-Javanaise* • Max von Sydow *August Strindberg* • Sofie Grabol *Judith Molard* • Merete Voldstedlund *Mette Gauguin* • Jørgen Reenberg *Edward Brandes* • Yves Barsack *Edgar Degas* ■ *Dir* Henning Carlsen • *Scr* Christopher Hampton, from a story by Henning Carlsen, Jean-Claude Carriere

Wolf Lake ★★ 18

Thriller 1979 · US · Colour · 83mins

Further evidence of Rod Steiger's declining fortunes was obvious in this depressing movie (also known as *Honor Guard*), laden with Vietnam overtones. When four ex-marines meet a deserter while staying in a Canadian hunting lodge, one of them decides to avenge his son's death in Vietnam. Steiger's usual heavyweight presence only adds to the grim nature of the story. However, if writer/director Burt Kennedy was trying to get a message about Vietnam across, he fails to make it clear here. NF

Rod Steiger *Charlie* • David Huffman *David* • Robin Mattson *Linda* • Jerry Hardin *Wilbur* • Richard Herd *George* • Paul Mantee *Sweeney* ■ *Dir/Scr* Burt Kennedy

Wolf Larsen ★★★

Action adventure 1958 · US · BW · 83mins

This robust screen adaptation of Jack London's novel *The Sea Wolf* stars Barry Sullivan as the eponymous sea captain and Peter Graves as the shipwreck victim with whom he spars. A rousing musical score sets the pace for this tale of cruelty, loyalty and, ultimately, mutiny. RT

Barry Sullivan *Wolf Larsen* • Peter Graves (2) *Van Weyden* • Gita Hall *Kristina* • Thayer David *Mugridge* • John Alderson *Johnson* ■ *Dir* Harmon Jones • *Scr* Jack DeWitt, Turnley Walker, from the novel *The Sea Wolf* by Jack London • *Music* Paul Dunlap

The Wolf Man ★★★★ PG

Classic horror 1941 · US · BW · 69mins

This Universal movie not only established Lon Chaney Jr as a horror star but it also instigated most of the cinematic werewolf lore concerning pentagrams, the Moon and the fatality of silver. Chaney returns home to Wales and, after being warned of life-threatening danger by gypsy Maria Ouspenskaya, is attacked by her werewolf son Bela Lugosi and cursed to transform into a wolf man himself whenever the moon is full. An intelligent, literate script, fine direction by George Waggner, convincing make-up by Jack Pierce and a sympathetic performance by Chaney put this chiller in the top rank. AJ DVD

Lon Chaney [Lon Chaney Jr] *Lawrence "Larry" Talbot/The Wolf Man* • Claude Rains *Sir John Talbot* • Evelyn Ankers *Gwen Conliffe* • Ralph Bellamy *Captain Paul Montford* • Warren William *Dr Lloyd* • Patric Knowles *Frank Andrews* • Maria Ouspenskaya *Maleva* • Bela Lugosi *Bela* ■ *Dir* George Waggner • *Scr* Curt Siodmak • *Makeup* Jack P Pierce [Jack Pierce] • *Cinematographer* Joseph Valentine

Wolfen ★★★ 18

Horror 1981 · US · Colour · 109mins

Michael Wadleigh directs this classy, thoughtful, gory, but not in the least bit scary horror movie about a mutant breed of killer wolf with super-intelligent tracking abilities running wild in the Bronx. New York cop Albert Finney investigates, and, in a typical Wadleigh eco addition to Whitley Strieber's so-so supernatural novel, links the plight of the American Indian to the wolves' brutally violent acts. Subjective camerawork, denoting the wolves' point of view, features extensive optical special effects so the prowling always makes for galvanising viewing, while Finney makes the most of his tart dialogue. AJ. Contains violence, swearing, nudity. DVD

Albert Finney *Dewey Wilson* • Diane Venora *Rebecca Neff* • Edward James Olmos *Eddie Holt* • Gregory Hines *Whittington* • Tom Noonan *Ferguson* • Dick O'Neill *Warren* ■ *Dir* Michael Wadleigh • *Scr* David Eyre, Michael Wadleigh, from the novel by Whitley Strieber

The Wolves ★★★ 15

Period crime drama
1971 · Jpn · Colour · 130mins

Set against the backdrop of the nascent Showa era, this is a bruising insight into the unforgiving underworld of 1920s Japan. Pardoned during an amnesty, Tatsuya Nakadai returns to discover his ambitious brother, Noboru Ando, has not only arranged a merger between their Enokiya gang and their deadly Kannon rivals, but has also planned a Manchurian railroad takeover that could spell disaster for his partners in crime. Although it ends with a ferocious moonlight swordfight, the emphasis in this stylish thriller is more on the bushido influence on yakuza culture, with its sense of clan loyalty and honour. DP. In Japanese with English subtitles. DVD

Tatsuya Nakadai *Iwahashi* • Noboru Ando *Ozeki* • Komaki Kurihara *Asakura* • Kyoko Enami *Oyu* ■ *Dir/Scr* Hideo Gosha

The Wolves of Willoughby Chase ★★★ PG

Adventure 1988 · UK · Colour · 88mins

Based on Joan Aiken's children's novel, this is a fun romp set in a snowy Yorkshire overrun by wolves, during the Industrial Revolution. Emily Hudson and Aleks Darowska are the two girls trying to foil a plot by their evil governess, who is played with bitchy glee by Stephanie Beacham. Grown-up viewers may find parts of the film tedious, but it is brightened up by the over-the-top performances from Mel Smith, Geraldine James and Richard O'Brien. JB

Stephanie Beacham *Letitia Slighcarp* • Mel Smith *Mr Grimshaw* • Geraldine James *Mrs Gertrude Brisket* • Richard O'Brien *James* • Emily Hudson *Bonnie Willoughby* • Aleks Darowska *Sylvia* • Jane Horrocks *Pattern* • Eleanor David *Lady Willoughby* • Jonathan Coy *Lord Willoughby* • Lynton Dearden *Simon* ■ *Dir* Stuart Orme • *Scr* William M Akers, from the novel by Joan Aiken

The Woman and the Hunter ★★

Drama 1957 · US · BW · 89mins

As a child actor, Paris-born George Breakston appeared in several high-profile pictures before taking on the recurring role of Beezy Anderson in MGM's Andy Hardy series. But his attention turned to directing after he launched his own production company in Kenya in the late 1940s. This is more a melodrama than an adventure, although it still contains plenty of local scenery. However, being torn between John Loder and David Farrar proved a disappointing swansong for one-time "Oomph Girl" Ann Sheridan. DP

Ann Sheridan *Laura Dodds* • David Farrar *David Kirby* • John Loder *Robert Gifford* ■ *Dir* George Breakston • *Scr* Maurice Conn, from his story

Woman Chases Man ★★★ U

Screwball comedy 1937 · US · BW · 66mins

A screwball comedy about money, booze and property that is fairly typical of its genre, and is played with ineffable skill by the sparkling trio of Miriam Hopkins, Charles Winninger and

W

a very young Joel McCrea. Unfortunately crippled by a screenplay that runs out of ideas about three-quarters of the way through, the film leaves its principal characters quite literally up a tree! Nevertheless, this is a class act from producer Samuel Goldwyn. TS

Miriam Hopkins *Virginia Travis* • Joel McCrea *Kenneth Nolan* • Charles Winninger *BJ Nolan* • Erik Rhodes *Henri Saffron* • Ella Logan *Judy Williams* • Leona Maricle *Nina Tennyson* • Broderick Crawford *Hunk Williams* • Charles Halton *Mr Judd* ■ *Dir* John Blystone [John G Blystone] • *Scr* Joseph Anthony, Mannie Seff, David Hertz, from the story *The Princess and the Pauper* by Lynn Root, Frank Fenton

The Woman Eater ★

Horror 1957 · UK · BW · 70mins

Fans of mad scientists and killer vegetables should on no account miss this little-known Z-grade affair, a British studio's successful attempt to match trash coming out of Hollywood in the late 1950s. Boffin George Coulouris propagates a tree that eats young women in the belief that the sap excreted will make him immortal. DM

George Coulouris *Dr James Moran* • Vera Day *Sally* • Joy Webster *Judy Ryan* • Peter Wayn *Jack Venner* • Jimmy Vaughan *Tanga* • Sara Leighton *Susan Curtis* ■ *Dir* Charles Saunders • *Scr* Brandon Fleming

The Woman for Joe ★★ U

Drama 1955 · UK · BW · 91mins

A slow and rather disappointing Rank production. The story is the old "hunchback of Notre Dame" chestnut, about fairground owner George Baker who hires a midget, only for him to turn into a Napoleon figure, lusting for power and lusting, too, for Diane Cilento, who's in love with Baker. It's pretty nasty, in fact, with none of the poetry of Victor Hugo's story, let alone Tod Browning's similarly themed masterpiece, *Freaks*. AT

Diane Cilento *Mary* • George Baker *Joe Harrap* • Jimmy Karoubi *George Wilson* • David Kossoff *Max* • Earl Cameron *Lemmie* • Sydney Tafler *Butch* • Violet Farebrother *Ma Gollatz* ■ *Dir* George More O'Ferrall • *Scr* Neil Paterson, from his story *And Delilah*

Woman from Rose Hill ★★

Drama 1989 · Swi/Fr · Colour · 95mins

Despite employing his traditionally detached, naturalist approach, Alain Tanner is unable to prevent this treatise on Swiss isolationism from descending into barnstorming melodrama. Arriving from an island in the Indian Ocean, Marie Gaydu is soon disillusioned with her pen-pal husband and embarks on an affair with Jean-Philippe Ecoffey, despite the opposition of his industrialist father. Tanner seems curiously drawn to the soap operatic excesses that he uses to resolve his tale. DP. In French with English subtitles.

Marie Gaydu *Julie* • Jean-Philippe Ecoffey *Jean* • Denise Peron *Jeanne* • Roger Jendly *Marcel* ■ *Dir/Scr* Alain Tanner

Woman Hater ★★ U

Romantic comedy 1948 · UK · BW · 96mins

A French film star, played by legendary French star and beauty Edwige Feuillère, retreats into seclusion in an English country house, claiming she has given up men and wants to be alone. Landed gentleman Stewart Granger, suspecting a publicity stunt, sets out to prove it by courting her. A creaky, tedious and witless romantic comedy that totally squanders the talents of an excellent cast. RK

Stewart Granger *Terence, Lord Datchett* • Edwige Feuillère *Colette Marly* • Jeanne de Casalis *Claire* • Ronald Squire *Jameson* • David Hutcheson *Robert* • Mary Jerrold *Dowager Lady Datchett* ■ *Dir* Terence Young • *Scr* Robert Westerby, Nicholas Phipps, from a story by Alec Coppel

A Woman, Her Men and Her Futon ★

Romantic drama 1992 · US · Colour · 90mins

Few things are worse than self-absorbed sex movies, but one of those things is a self-absorbed sex movie about Hollywood. Jennifer Rubin is a sexual castaway, drifting from one man to another in hopes of finding what she wants out of life. Along the way she becomes peripherally involved in the writing and production of a film that parallels events in this movie. Filled with senseless avant-garde dialogue and a few cheap thrills. ST

Jennifer Rubin *Helen* • Lance Edwards *Donald* • Grant Show *Randy* • Michael Cerveris *Paul* • Delaune Michel *Gail* • Robert Lipton *Max* ■ *Dir/Scr* Mussef Sibay

The Woman I Love ★★★

Wartime melodrama 1937 · US · BW · 85mins

European director Anatole Litvak was brought to RKO to make his Hollywood debut with this tale, set in France during the First World War. Paul Muni stars as a fighter pilot whose safety record is questionable until he is joined by new man Louis Hayward. They form a successful partnership in the air and close friendship on the ground, until Hayward falls in love with Miriam Hopkins, unaware that she is Muni's wife. This solid romantic melodrama features some good aerial action. RK

Paul Muni *Lt Claude Maury* • Miriam Hopkins *Denise LaValle/Hélène Maury* • Louis Hayward *Lt Jean Herbillion* • Colin Clive *Capt Thelis* • Minor Watson *Deschamps* • Elisabeth Risdon *Mme Herbillion* • Paul Guilfoyle (1) *Berthier* ■ *Dir* Anatole Litvak • *Scr* Ethel Borden, from the film *L'Equipage* by Joseph Kessel, Anatole Litvak, from the novel *L'Equipage* by Joseph Kessel

Woman in a Dressing Gown ★★★★

Drama 1957 · UK · BW · 94mins

This painfully honest drama, based on a play by Ted Willis, was light years ahead of its time in its treatment of women and their place in marriage, starring Yvonne Mitchell in a role that should have seen her showered in awards. Mitchell's portrayal of clinical depression is stunning in its depth and understanding, and director J Lee Thompson pulls no punches in his exploration of a partnership gone sour with the intrusion of a younger woman. In many ways this movie heralded a new dawn in gritty British film-making which culminated in the "kitchen sink" social dramas of the 1960s. SH

Yvonne Mitchell *Amy Preston* • Anthony Quayle *Jim Preston* • Sylvia Syms *Georgie Harlow* • Andrew Ray *Brian Preston* • Carole Lesley *Hilda* • Michael Pripper *Pawnbroker* • Nora Gordon *Mrs Williams* ■ *Dir* J Lee Thompson • *Scr* Ted Willis, from his play

The Woman in Green ★★★ PG

Mystery 1945 · US · BW · 66mins

This is one of the weirdest films in Universal's series of mysteries based on Sir Arthur Conan Doyle's characters. It pits Sherlock Holmes (Basil Rathbone) against the evil Professor Moriarty (Henry Daniell) and a beautiful hypnotist (Hillary Brooke) as he investigates the murders of women who are found with their right forefingers severed. The grindingly eerie music used to mesmerise the victims sounds a note of real unease, which not even the bumbling banalities of Nigel Bruce (as Dr Watson) can dispel. TH DVD

Basil Rathbone *Sherlock Holmes* • Nigel Bruce *Dr John H Watson* • Hillary Brooke *Lydia Marlow* • Henry Daniell *Professor Moriarty* • Paul Cavanagh *Sir George Fenwick* • Matthew Boulton *Inspector Gregson* • Eve Amber *Maude Fenwick* ■ *Dir* Roy William Neill • *Scr* Bertram Millhauser, from characters created by Sir Arthur Conan Doyle

The Woman in Question ★★★

Crime mystery 1950 · UK · BW · 99mins

One of Dirk Bogarde's earlier pictures, this inventive thriller is directed by Anthony Asquith and co-stars Jean Kent as a fortune teller whose death leads to a serious case of flashback syndrome during which we try to spot her killer. Kent has a juicy role here, since all her acquaintances have a different view of her ranging from kindly neighbour to drunken bitch. AT

Jean Kent *Madame Astra* • Dirk Bogarde *Bob Baker* • John McCallum *Murray* • Susan Shaw *Catherine* • Hermione Baddeley *Mrs Finch* • Charles Victor *Pollard* • Duncan Macrae *Superintendent Lodge* • Lana Morris *Lana* • Joe Linnane *Inspector Butler* ■ *Dir* Anthony Asquith • *Scr* John Cresswell

The Woman in Red ★★

Melodrama 1935 · US · BW · 68mins

Barbara Stanwyck struggles valiantly against an uninspired script and an irritating leading man in this thankfully short tale of a professional horsewoman who, to the ire of her mega-rich employer Genevieve Tobin, marries Gene Raymond, the man Tobin wants for herself. John Eldredge is good in support, but the only honours in this dreary little film go to Tobin, who plays with relish and polish. RK

Barbara Stanwyck *Shelby Barrett* • Gene Raymond *Johnny Wyatt* • Genevieve Tobin *Nicko Nicholas* • John Eldredge *Eugene Fairchild* • Russell Hicks *Clayton* • Philip Reed *Dan McCall* • Nella Walker *Aunt Bettina* • Dorothy Tree *Olga* ■ *Dir* Robert Florey • *Scr* Mary McCall Jr, Peter Milne, from the novel *North Shore* by Wallace Irwin

The Woman in Red ★★★ 15

Comedy 1984 · US · Colour · 82mins

One of the enduring cinema images of the 1980s is Kelly LeBrock dancing over an air vent in her flame-red dress *à la* Marilyn Monroe in *The Seven Year Itch*, hypnotising pink-cheeked Gene Wilder. The rest of this warm-hearted, bouncily amusing story of obsession and extramarital longings doesn't quite live up to this promising opening, but it's a movie that just about holds the attention. Wilder is at his frantic best, ably supported by the likes of real-life wife Gilda Radner and Charles Grodin. Stevie Wonder's hit single *I Just Called to Say I Love You* features on the soundtrack. SH. Contains violence, swearing and nudity. DVD

Gene Wilder *Theodore Pierce* • Kelly LeBrock *Charlotte* • Charles Grodin *Buddy* • Joseph Bologna *Joe* • Judith Ivey *Didi* • Michael Huddleston *Michael* • Gilda Radner *Ms Milner* ■ *Dir* Gene Wilder • *Scr* Gene Wilder, from the film *Pardon Mon Affaire* by Jean-Loup Dabadie, Yves Robert

The Woman in the Moon ★★★

Silent fantasy 1929 · Ger · BW · 107mins

One of the last silent films made in Germany, Fritz Lang's comic-strip fantasy concerns scientist Klaus Pohl who believes the moon is rich in gold and, with the help of rocket designer Willy Fritsch, organises the first flight there. However melodramatic and farcical the plot, the takeoff is portrayed using dramatic montage and camera angles, and there are a few sinister Langian touches. Despite the quaintness of the technology, the Nazis took the film out of distribution because they felt the rocket was too close to one they were creating on the V2 programme at the time. RB

Gerda Maurus *Friede Velten* • Willy Fritsch *Wolf Helius* • Fritz Rasp *Walter Turner* • Gustav von Wangenheim *Hans Windegger* • Klaus Pohl (1) *Prof Georg Manfeldt* ■ *Dir* Fritz Lang • *Scr* Thea von Harbou, Fritz Lang, from a story by Thea von Harbou

The Woman in the Window ★★★★ PG

Film noir 1945 · US · BW · 94mins

This clever melodrama, written and produced by Nunnally Johnson, is directed with just the right amount of moody atmosphere by expressionist master Fritz Lang. Edward G Robinson is marvellous as the academic who makes that fatal 1940s error of falling for the subject of a portrait and then finds himself swept up in a convoluted web of murder and deception. Joan Bennett is an ideal "ideal" in one of her four fine performances for Lang. The famous ending is still controversial, but whatever conclusion you come to there's no denying the power of this nightmare. TS

Edward G Robinson *Professor Richard Wanley* • Joan Bennett *Alice Reed* • Raymond Massey *Frank Lalor* • Edmond Breon [Edmund Breon] *Dr Michael Barkstone* • Dan Duryea *Heidt/Doorman* • Thomas E Jackson *Inspector Jackson* • Arthur Loft *Claude Mazard* ■ *Dir* Fritz Lang • *Scr* Nunnally Johnson, from the novel *Once Off Guard* by JH Wallis

The Woman in White ★★★

Period mystery drama
1948 · US · BW · 108mins

Based on the classic Victorian gothic thriller by Wilkie Collins, the film stars an effectively histrionic Sydney Greenstreet as the evil Count Fosco, plotting to get his hands on Eleanor Parker's fortune. He has her twin sister (also Parker) committed to an insane asylum from where she escapes, returning in the guise of a ghostly apparition to foil Greenstreet's plans. The descent of Agnes Moorehead, Greenstreet's already somewhat mad wife, into murderous insanity is one of the high points of a film which, though atmospheric, is hampered by over-respectful restraint and a dull Parker. RK

Alexis Smith *Marian Halcombe* • Eleanor Parker *Laura Fairlie/Ann Catherick* • Sydney Greenstreet *Count Alesandro Fosco* • Gig Young *Walter Hartright* • Agnes Moorehead *Countess Fosco* • John Abbott *Frederick Fairlie* • John Emery *Sir Percival Glyde* • Curt Bois *Louis* ■ *Dir* Peter Godfrey • *Scr* Stephen Morehouse Avery, from the novel by Wilkie Collins

The Woman Next Door ★★★ 15

Drama 1981 · Fr · Colour · 101mins

This study of provincial infidelity is both suspenseful and romantic thanks to François Truffaut's affinity for characters trapped in an obsession they're powerless to abandon. Contemporary critics weren't convinced by Fanny Ardant (who was Truffaut's lover), as the neighbour who rekindles a long-suppressed passion in contented Grenoble bourgeois Gérard Depardieu. But they both generate a *frisson* that explains their commitment to a relationship that each knows to be ruinous. DP. In French with English subtitles.

Gérard Depardieu *Bernard Coudray* • Fanny Ardant *Mathilde Bauchard* • Henri Garcin *Philippe Bauchard* • Michèle Baumgartner *Arlette Courdray* • Véronique Silver *Madame Jouve* ■ *Dir* François Truffaut • *Scr* Jean Aurel, Suzanne Schiffman, François Truffaut

W

Woman Obsessed ★★

Romantic adventure
1959 · US · Colour · 102mins

A star vehicle for tempestuous redhead Susan Hayward, and, alas, little else. Hayward's a "widder-woman" who marries rugged Stephen Boyd, and there's plenty of cussin' and feudin', but no real dramatic force. Star Hayward (always a pleasure to watch) and director Henry Hathaway fail to rise above the puerile material. TS

Susan Hayward *Mary Sharron* • Stephen Boyd *Fred Carter* • Barbara Nichols *Mayme Radzevitch* • Dennis Holmes *Robbie Sharron* • Theodore Bikel *Dr Gibbs* • Ken Scott *Sergeant Le Moyne* • Arthur Franz *Tom Sharron* ■ *Dir* Henry Hathaway • *Scr* Sydney Boehm, from the novel *The Snow Birch* by John Mantley

A Woman of Affairs ★★★

Silent melodrama 1928 · US · BW · 92mins

Prevented from marrying John Gilbert, whom she loves, rich and beautiful young English society woman Greta Garbo (with alcoholic brother Douglas Fairbanks Jr) finds her reputation tarnished by circumstance. She then goes from man to man in Europe, but meets her only love again with tragic consequences. This over-the-top romantic melodrama is absolute rubbish, but a characteristic silent Garbo vehicle with a starry cast. RK

Greta Garbo *Diana* • John Gilbert (1) *Neville* • Lewis Stone *Hugh* • John Mack Brown [Johnny Mack Brown] *David* • Douglas Fairbanks Jr *Jeffrey* ■ *Dir* Clarence Brown • *Scr* Bess Meredyth, Marian Ainslee (titles), Ruth Cummings (titles), from the novel *The Green Hat* by Michael Arlen

Woman of Desire ★★ 18

Erotic thriller 1994 · US · Colour · 98mins

Two macho men (Jeff Fahey and Steven Bauer) and one sexy woman (Bo Derek) head off in a yacht and, in a stunning turn of events, Derek takes her clothes off a lot. OK, the actual stunning turn of events is that only Derek and Fahey's characters come back. However she accuses him of murder and rape. Robert Mitchum does a turn here as the luckless Fahey's defence lawyer. ST

Bo Derek *Christina Ford* • Robert Mitchum *Walter Hill* • Jeff Fahey *Jack Lynch* • Steven Bauer *Jonathan Ashby* ■ *Dir/Scr* Robert Ginty

A Woman of Distinction ★★ U

Romantic comedy 1950 · US · BW · 84mins

With its focus on middle-aged protagonists, this idiotic romantic comedy is part farce and occasionally embarrassing but still manages to be quite entertaining. Rosalind Russell is the uptight college dean, who has devoted her mind and her life to higher things than love and marriage. When visiting professor Ray Milland is installed, a journalist on the local paper runs a story which, to Russell's horror and Milland's bewilderment, suggests they're having an affair. RK

Rosalind Russell *Susan Manning Middlecott* • Ray Milland *Alec Stevenson* • Edmund Gwenn *Mark Middlecott* • Janis Carter *Teddy Evans* • Mary Jane Saunders *Louisa Middlecott* • Francis Lederer *Paul Simone* • Jerome Courtland *Jerome* ■ *Dir* Edward Buzzell • *Scr* Charles Hoffman, Frank Tashlin, from a story by Ian McLellan Hunter, Hugo Butler

W

A Woman of Paris ★★★★ U

Silent drama 1923 · US · BW · 78mins

This silent rags-to-riches drama from Charles Chaplin marked a breakthrough in romantic realism in its day. Chaplin makes only a brief appearance as a railway porter and devotes most of his energies to directing his favoured actress, Edna Purviance. She plays a country girl who retains her illusions about love, despite being seduced by the big city and a suave Adolphe Menjou. The idea may be very dated, but it's Chaplin's near-Dickensian insights that make the tale as relevant today as ever, and this is enchanting and spellbinding. TH DVD

Edna Purviance *Marie St Clair* • Adolphe Menjou *Pierre Revel* • Carl Miller *Jean Millet* • Lydia Knott *Jean's mother* • Charles French [Charles K French] *Jean's father* • Clarence Geldert *Marie's stepfather* • Betty Morrissey *Fifi* • Malvina Polo *Paulette* • Charles Chaplin *Station Porter* ■ *Dir/Scr* Charles Chaplin

Woman of Straw ★★

Mystery thriller 1964 · UK · Colour · 121mins

Sean Connery stars in this set-bound thriller, which sets off at a lively pace, but gets bogged down once wheelchair-bound tyrant Ralph Richardson has been found dead and gold-digging nephew Connery finds himself among the murder suspects. Revelling in Richardson's wonderfully cantankerous performance, director Basil Dearden seems to lose interest after his demise, leaving Connery and Gina Lollobrigida, as the old devil's nurse, somewhat in the lurch. DP

Gina Lollobrigida *Maria* • Sean Connery *Anthony Richmond* • Ralph Richardson *Charles Richmond* • Alexander Knox *Lomer* • Johnny Sekka *Thomas* • Laurence Hardy *Baines* • Danny Daniels *Fenton* ■ *Dir* Basil Dearden • *Scr* Robert Muller, Stanley Mann, Michael Relph, from the novel *La Femme de Paille* by Catherine Arley

Woman of the Dunes ★★★★★ 15

Drama 1963 · Jpn · BW · 118mins

Adapted by Kobo Abe from his own novel, this stark human condition parable was denounced by some critics for its photographic neutrality. But director Hiroshi Teshigahara and cinematographer Hiroshi Segawa achieve a rich diversity of visual textures that adds to the sensual atmosphere of this intense drama, in which entomologist Eiji Okada finds himself trapped in the deep-dune home of social outcast, Kyoko Kishida. Even the editorial technique (shifting from languid dissolves to sharp cuts) reflects the environment and the state of the couple's relationship, which Teshigahara further explores through his use of symbolic imagery. DP. In Japanese with English subtitles.

Eiji Okada *Jumpei Niki* • Kyoko Kishida *Widow* • Koji Mitsui • Sen Yano • Hiroko Ito ■ *Dir* Hiroshi Teshigahara • *Scr* Kobo Abe, from his novel *Suna No Onna*

Woman of the River ★★★

Drama 1955 · Fr/It · Colour · 92mins

This is an uncomfortable blend of rose-tinted neorealism, bawdy comedy and high melodrama. Sophia Loren is the village temptress who spurns the coy advances of policeman Gérard Oury, only to be left pregnant by cigarette smuggler Rik Battaglia. There's a distinct air of *Carmen* about the proceedings, especially when Loren performs a dance number, but it lacks class and cohesion. DP. Italian dialogue dubbed into English.

Sophia Loren *Nives Mongolini* • Gérard Oury *Enzo Cinti* • Lise Bourdin *Tosca* • Rik Battaglia *Gino Lodi* • Enrico Olivieri *Oscar* ■ *Dir* Mario Soldati • *Scr* Basilio Franchina, Giorgio Bassani, Pier Paolo Pasolini, Florestano Vancini, Antonio Altoviti, Mario Soldati, Ben Zavin, from an idea by Ennio Flaiano, Alberto Moravia

Woman of the Year ★★★★ U

Romantic comedy 1942 · US · BW · 114mins

The first teaming of one of Hollywood's greatest couples: the inimitable Katharine Hepburn and laconic, rugged Spencer Tracy. They're beautifully matched, she a columnist wishing to ban baseball until the end of the Second World War, he a reporter defending the sport in print. They meet, wed and generally provide a high old time for audiences everywhere. This is close to the apex of sophisticated romantic comedy, today marred slightly by its wartime conventions and a subplot involving the adoption of a young refugee. Nevertheless, adroit director George Stevens doesn't let the fun get bogged down. TS DVD

Spencer Tracy *Sam Craig* • Katharine Hepburn *Tess Harding* • Minor Watson *William Harding* • Fay Bainter *Ellen Whitcomb* • Reginald Owen *Clayton* • William Bendix *Pinkie Peters* • Gladys Blake *Flo Peters* ■ *Dir* George Stevens • *Scr* Ring Lardner Jr, Michael Kanin

The Woman on Pier 13 ★★

Drama 1949 · US · BW · 72mins

When mogul Howard Hughes seized control of RKO, one of his credos was to use the studio and its product as an anti-communist tool, and this moody and suspenseful thriller was the first fruit of his labours. The film ostensibly concerns a shipyard boss being blackmailed over past affiliations, with, interestingly, real-life liberal Robert Ryan playing the "hero". The mercifully short movie was plagued by Hughes's predilection for constant reshoots, so don't blame director Robert Stevenson for what is, or isn't, on the screen. The film leaves a genuinely nasty taste in the mouth today, but is interesting as a social document of its time. TS

Laraine Day *Nan Collins* • Robert Ryan *Brad Collins* • John Agar *Don Lowry* • Thomas Gomez *Vanning* • Janis Carter *Christine* • Richard Rober *Jim Travis* • William Talman *Bailey* • Paul E Burns *Arnold* • Paul Guilfoyle (1) *Ralston* ■ *Dir* Robert Stevenson • *Scr* Charles Grayson, Robert Hardy Andrews, from a story by George W George, George F Slavin

The Woman on the Beach ★★★★

Drama 1947 · US · BW · 70mins

Jean Renoir regarded his seven-year sojourn in America as wasted time. Yet, in spite of the harmful cuts ordered by studio bosses at RKO, there is no denying the quality of his parting shot to Hollywood. Joan Bennett, in the title role, reinforced her reputation as one of *film noir*'s finest *femmes fatales*. By focusing on her highly charged interaction with blind husband Charles Bickford and shell-shocked lifeguard Robert Ryan, Renoir produced a smouldering melodrama that never relaxes its grip. DP

Joan Bennett *Peggy Butler* • Robert Ryan *Lt Scott Burnett* • Charles Bickford *Ted Butler* • Nan Leslie *Eve Geddes* • Jay Norris *Jimmy* • Walter Sande *Otto Wernecke* • Irene Ryan *Mrs Wernecke* ■ *Dir* Jean Renoir • *Scr* Frank Davis, Jean Renoir, Michael Hogan [JR Michael Hogan], from the novel *None So Blind* by Mitchell Wilson

Woman on Top ★★ 15

Romantic comedy
2000 · US · Colour · 87mins

Penélope Cruz is the young wife with a knack for creating hot, tasty dishes who flees from Brazil to San Francisco when she discovers husband Murilo Benicio has been cheating on her. Her talents in the kitchen are soon discovered and she ends up hosting a TV cookery show. There are a few insights into the the power of food and the sensuality of cooking before everyone ends up living happily ever after. Slight stuff. JB DVD

Penélope Cruz *Isabella Oliveira* • Murilo Benicio *Toninho Oliveira* • Harold Perrineau Jr [Harold Perrineau] *Monica Jones* • Mark Feuerstein *Cliff Lloyd* • John de Lancie *Alex Reeves* • Anne Ramsay *TV director* • Ana Gasteyer *Claudia Hunter* ■ *Dir* Fina Torres • *Scr* Vera Blasi

A Woman Rebels ★★

Historical drama 1936 · US · BW · 88mins

Katharine Hepburn, her popularity in decline after a series of misconceived failures, is perfectly cast as Pamela Thistlewaite, a non-conformist, asserting women's rights and her own independence in Victorian England. Her fight against the rigid constraints of society, embodied by her unbending father (Donald Crisp), makes for an interesting film, but it degenerates into soft-centred melodrama when she has an illegitimate child. RK

Katharine Hepburn *Pamela Thistlewaite* • Herbert Marshall *Thomas Lane* • Elizabeth Allan *Flora Thistlewaite* • Donald Crisp *Judge Thistlewaite* • Doris Dudley *Young Flora* • David Manners *Alan* • Van Heflin *Gerald* ■ *Dir* Mark Sandrich • *Scr* Anthony Veiller, Ernest Vajda, from the novel *Portrait of a Rebel* by Netta Syrett

The Woman They Almost Lynched ★★★ U

Western 1953 · US · BW · 90mins

Women take over the action in this delightfully ludicrous Republic western, set in an outlaw-ridden town trying to preserve neutrality during the Civil War. Joan Leslie and Audrey Totter strap on six-guns for a shoot-out on main street while Leslie, the good girl of the two, is almost strung up on the orders of lady mayor Nina Varela when she is thought to be a Confederate spy. Totter's worst crime is to attempt two song numbers. AE

John Lund *Lance Horton* • Brian Donlevy *William Quantrill* • Audrey Totter *Kate Quantrill* • Joan Leslie *Sally Maris* • Ben Cooper *Jesse James* • Nina Varela *Mayor Delilah Courtney* • James Brown (1) *Frank James* ■ *Dir* Allan Dwan • *Scr* Steve Fisher, from the story by Michael Fessier

Woman Times Seven ★★★ 15

Portmanteau comedy drama
1967 · US/Fr/It · Colour · 103mins

Shirley MacLaine stars in seven vignettes, paired with or pitted against seven different men, ranging from Peter Sellers to Rossano Brazzi to Michael Caine who appears in the final episode as a mysterious stranger who never says a word. As with all portmanteau movies, some segments work better than others and much depends on one's tolerance for MacLaine's mannerisms and trademark kookiness. AT

Shirley MacLaine *Paulette (Funeral Procession)/Maria Terese (Amateur Night)/Linda (Two Against One)/Edith (The Super-Simone)/Eve Minou (At the Opera)/Marie (The Suicides)/Jeanne (Snow)* • Alan Arkin *Fred* • Peter Sellers *Jean* • Rossano Brazzi *Giorgio* • Vittorio Gassman *Cenci* • Lex Barker *Rik* • Robert Morley *Dr Xavier* • Michael Caine *Handsome stranger* • Anita Ekberg *Claudie* • Philippe Noiret *Victor* ■ *Dir* Vittorio De Sica • *Scr* Cesare Zavattini

A Woman under the Influence ★★★ 15

Drama 1974 · US · Colour · 140mins

Gena Rowlands, wife of blue-collar worker Peter Falk and mother of three children, falls prey to increasingly erratic behaviour, slipping in and out of reality until her devoted but distressed family are forced to institutionalise her.

U = SUITABLE FOR ALL Uc = SUITABLE FOR ALL, ESPECIALLY FOR YOUNG CHILDREN (VIDEO ONLY) PG = PARENTAL GUIDANCE

Discharged some months later, not much has changed. Written and directed by John Cassavetes as a vehicle for his wife, the magnificent Rowlands, this was two years in the making, financed by friends and family. Despite a multifaceted and awesome tour de force from Rowlands, and sterling support, the film is badly disadvantaged by its running time. Nonetheless, it should be seen for its undeniably brilliant elements. RK [video]

Peter Falk *Nick Longhetti* • Gena Rowlands *Mabel Longhetti* • Matthew Cassel *Tony Longhetti* • Matthew Laborteaux *Angelo Longhetti* • Christina Grisantii *Maria Longhetti* • Katherine Cassavetes *Mama Longhetti* • Lady Rowlands *Martha Mortensen* ■ *Dir/Scr* John Cassavetes

Woman Wanted ★★

Crime drama 1935 · US · BW · 65mins

Desperately routine, seen-it-all-before mix of crime and romance in which good-hearted lawyer Joel McCrea gives refuge to Maureen Sullivan who is wanted on a murder charge. The bulk of the running time is taken up with McCrea's efforts to prove her innocence, which involves him in searching for the real culprit. RK

Maureen O'Sullivan *Ann Gray* • Joel McCrea *Tony Baxter* • Lewis Stone *District Attorney Martin* • Louis Calhern *Smiley* • Edgar Kennedy *Sweeney* • Adrienne Ames *Betty Randolph* ■ *Dir* George B Seitz • *Scr* Leonard Fields, Dave Silverstein, from the story or play *Get That Girl* by Wilson Collison

A Woman without Love ★★

Drama 1951 · Mex · BW · 90mins

Luis Buñuel considered this rudimentary and overblown melodrama the worst film he ever made – shot in just 30 days and edited in three. Paternal tyranny and sibling rivalry dominate the action, as inseparable half-brothers Tito Junco and Joaquin Cordero fall out over the inheritance of their respective fathers, a vulgar antique dealer and a kindly engineer. DP. In Spanish with English subtitles.

Rosario Granados *Rosario Jiménez de Montero* • Tito Junco *Julio Mistral* • Julio Villarreal *Don Carlos Montero* • Joaquin Cordero *Carlos, hijo* • Xavier Loyà *Miguel* • Elda Peralta *Luisa Asúnsolo* • Niño Jaime Calpe *Carlitos* ■ *Dir* Luis Buñuel • *Scr* Luis Buñuel, Jaime Salvador (adaptation), Rodolfo Usigli (dialogue), from the novel *Pierre et Jean* by Guy de Maupassant

A Woman's Face ★★★★

Melodrama 1938 · Swe · BW · 100mins

Grotesquely disfigured in an accident during childhood, Ingrid Bergman has grown into a hard and bitter woman, but her vengeful nature is transformed, along with her face, after an operation restores her beauty. However, further distress is just around the corner when she becomes involved in a murder plot. The young Bergman gives a brilliant performance in this high-toned melodrama, adapted from a French play and made in Sweden before Hollywood adopted her. RK. A Swedish language film.

Ingrid Bergman *Anna Holm* • Tore Svennberg *Magnus Barring* • Georg Rydeberg *Torsten Barring* • Goran Bernhard *Lars-Erik Barring* • Anders Henrikson *Dr Wegert* • Karin Kavli *Fru Vera Wegert* ■ *Dir* Gustaf Molander • *Scr* Gösta Stevens, Ragnhild Prim, Stina Bergman, from the play *Il Etait une Fois* by Francis de Croisset [François Wiener]

A Woman's Face ★★★★

Melodrama 1941 · US · BW · 106mins

This melodrama about a woman whose plastic surgery changes her looks but not, it would appear, her soul was a major MGM vehicle for Joan Crawford. Previously filmed in Sweden with Ingrid Bergman, this version is a stirring and exciting reminder of Crawford's heyday and still manages to hold an audience. Co-stars Melvyn Douglas as the surgeon and Conrad Veidt as the scheming love interest give consummate performances, and it's superbly directed by the great George Cukor, but this is Crawford's movie through and through. Her embittered and literally scarred blackmailer is one of her all-time great creations. TS

Joan Crawford *Anna Holm* • Melvyn Douglas *Dr Gustav Segert* • Conrad Veidt *Torsten Barring* • Osa Massen *Vera Segert* • Reginald Owen *Bernard Dalvik* • Albert Basserman *Consul Magnus Barring* • Marjorie Main *Emma Kristiansdotter* • Donald Meek *Herman Rundvik* • Connie Gilchrist *Christina Dalvik* ■ *Dir* George Cukor • *Scr* Donald Ogden Stewart, Elliott Paul, from the play *Il Etait une Fois* by Francis de Croisset [François Wiener]

A Woman's Secret ★★

Crime drama 1949 · US · BW · 84mins

Fans of Nicholas Ray will find little to satisfy them here. As one of the famed director's apprentice works, there's little indication of the glories to come, even for the most die-hard members of his cult following. This is a daft-as-a-brush, turgid melodrama, told in contrived and unnecessary flashback. Gloria Grahame, Ray's wife at the time, has her moments, as does suave Victor Jory, but the whole is a very minor piece. TS

Maureen O'Hara *Marian Washburn* • Melvyn Douglas *Luke Jordan* • Gloria Grahame *Susan Caldwell* • Bill Williams *Lee* • Victor Jory *Brook Matthews* • Jay C Flippen *Detective Fowler* • Mary Philips *Mrs Fowler* • Robert Warwick *Roberts* ■ *Dir* Nicholas Ray • *Scr* Herman J Mankiewicz, from the novel by Vicki Baum

A Woman's Tale ★★★

Drama 1991 · Aus · Colour · 93mins

Writer/director Paul Cox continues examining eccentric individuals with this touching tale of old age, independence and undying friendship. Sheila Florance takes centre stage as the terminally ill woman determined to die on her own terms, against the wishes of her uncomprehending son. Cox lays on the sentiment a bit thickly and offers few original insights, but it's still a pleasingly offbeat concoction. DP

Sheila Florance *Martha* • Gosia Dobrowolska *Anna* • Norman Kaye *Billy* • Chris Haywood *Johnathan* • Ernest Gray *Peter* ■ *Dir* Paul Cox • *Scr* Paul Cox, Barry Dickins

Woman's World ★★★ U

Drama 1954 · US · Colour · 94mins

This is a credible and entertaining look at how a giant corporation operated in the 1950s, with particular reference to the treatment of its executives' wives. Clifton Webb turns in a neat portrayal as a business tycoon and has some able support from the likes of June Allyson and Van Heflin. The problem is that a great opportunity is partially thrown away to concentrate on theatrical trifles. Pretty impressive in its day, but now dated. SH

Lauren Bacall *Elizabeth* • June Allyson *Katie* • Clifton Webb *Gifford* • Van Heflin *Jerry* • Fred MacMurray *Sid* • Arlene Dahl *Carol* • Cornel Wilde *Bill Baxter* ■ *Dir* Jean Negulesco • *Scr* Claude Binyon, Mary Loos, Howard Lindsay, Russel Crouse, Richard Sale, from a story by Mona Williams

Wombling Free ★ U

Comedy musical 1977 · UK · Colour · 92mins

The litter-gathering Wombles of Wimbledon Common turned into movie stars after first conquering television and having a number of Top 20 hits. But director Lionel Jeffries's silly and charmless musical confection came far too late to revive the careers of the adult-sized furry creations or make them as globally popular as the Muppets. Here the creatures, invisible to mankind unless they believe, lead a protest against pollution. AJ [video] DVD

David Tomlinson *Roland Frogmorton* • Frances de la Tour *Julia Frogmorton* • Bonnie Langford *Kim Frogmorton* • Bernard Spear *Arnold Takahashi* • Yasuko Nagazumi *Doris Takahashi* • Lionel Jeffries *Womble* • David Jason *Womble* • Jon Pertwee *Womble* ■ *Dir* Lionel Jeffries • *Scr* Lionel Jeffries, from characters created by Elisabeth Beresford

The Women ★★★★ U

Comedy 1939 · US · BW and Colour · 133mins

"There's a name for you ladies, but it's not used in high society outside of kennels." This enjoyable and witty MGM special is immaculately cast without any men, even down to the sex of the featured animals. The complicated plot, from Clare Boothe Luce's Broadway comedy, centres around divorce and infidelity, with star Norma Shearer upstaged by the magnificent Joan Crawford and the utterly superb Rosalind Russell. George Cukor was in his element with such material and such a cast, and there is a famous fashion sequence in Technicolor. The 1956 musical remake entitled *The Opposite Sex* introduced men and was markedly inferior. TS

Norma Shearer *Mary, Mrs Stephen Haines* • Joan Crawford *Crystal Allen* • Rosalind Russell *Sylvia, Mrs Howard Fowler* • Mary Boland *Flora, the Countess De Lave* • Paulette Goddard *Miriam Aarons* • Joan Fontaine *Peggy, Mrs John Day* • Lucile Watson *Mrs Moorehead* • Phyllis Povah *Edith, Mrs Phelps Potter* • Virginia Weidler *Little Mary Haines* • Marjorie Main *Lucy* • Hedda Hopper *Dolly DePuyster* ■ *Dir* George Cukor • *Scr* Anita Loos, Jane Murfin, from the play by Clare Boothe Luce • *Costume Designer* Adrian

Women in Cages ★★ 18

Prison drama 1972 · US · Colour · 74mins

This Roger Corman co-produced sexploitation movie ups the sadism quotient, lowers the humour and softens the political feminist stance prevalent in other examples of the chicks-in-chains genre from the same era. Black icon Pam Grier is the whip-cracking, lesbian warden of a Filipino women's prison who has it in for inmates Roberta Collins and Judy Brown. Little gore, copious topless nudity and lip-smacking direction give this a vile vitality. AJ [video]

Jennifer Gan *Jeff* • Judy Brown [Judith Brown] *Sandy* • Roberta Collins *Stoke* • Pam Grier *Alabama* ■ *Dir* Gerardo De Leon • *Scr* Jim Watkins

Women in Love ★★★★ 18

Drama 1969 · UK · Colour · 125mins

This is one of Ken Russell's most successful and, for its time, sensational forays into literature, and works so well because it is cohesively respectful of its source, besides allowing its stars acting leeway. Set in the mining community of Nottinghamshire, it stars Oliver Reed and Alan Bates who woo Glenda Jackson (an Oscar winner) and Jennie Linden, in the process bringing love and tragedy upon them all. The nude male wrestling scene makes unnecessary macho points that didn't need emphasis, but gave the film notoriety. TH. Contains sex scenes. [video] DVD

Alan Bates *Rupert Birkin* • Oliver Reed *Gerald Crich* • Glenda Jackson *Gudrun Brangwen* • Jennie Linden *Ursula Brangwen* • Eleanor Bron *Hermione Roddice* • Alan Webb *Thomas Crich* • Vladek Sheybal *Loerke* • Catherine Willmer *Mrs Crich* • Sarah Nicholls [Phoebe Nicholls] *Winifred Crich* • Michael Gough *Tom Brangwen* ■ *Dir* Ken Russell • *Scr* Larry Kramer, from the novel by DH Lawrence

Women in Revolt ★★★ 18

Comedy drama 1971 · US · Colour · 94mins

The last feature film from Andy Warhol's Factory may be the only one on which the artist genuinely collaborated with film-maker Paul Morrissey. (The early static films were created by Warhol alone, but after Morrissey arrived, his was the sole presence behind the camera). The result is a satire of women's liberation, in which the leading female roles are played by Warhol's transvestite superstars (Jackie Curtis, Candy Darling and Holly Woodlawn). On the one hand, it's a tiresomely sustained joke, pulled in different directions. On the other, it's strangely moving to see the performers strutting their stuff for the last time under the King of Pop Art's direct influence. DM [video]

Jackie Curtis *Jackie* • Candy Darling *Candy* • Holly Woodlawn *Holly* • Marty Kove [Martin Kove] *Marty* • Maurice Braddell *Candy's father* • Duncan MacKenzie *Duncan, Candy's brother* ■ *Dir/Scr* Paul Morrissey

Women of the Night ★★★

Drama 1948 · Jpn · BW · 75mins

War widow and mobster's mistress Kinuyo Tanaka joins her sister and sister-in-law in denouncing the evils of prostitution, only to be charged by their fellow hookers with betraying their class. This study of life in a bagnio (or legalised brothel) proved to be one of Kenji Mizoguchi's most difficult productions. Accused of being politically and cinematically obsolete, in need of funds to support his ailing sister and lambasted in the press for a phantom affair with Tanaka, it's a wonder the film is so coherent, moving and persuasive. DP. In Japanese with English subtitles.

Kinuyo Tanaka *Fusako Owada* • Sanae Takasugi *Natsuko* • Mitsuo Nagata *Kuiyama* • Tomie Tsunoda *Kumiko* ■ *Dir* Kenji Mizoguchi • *Scr* Yoshikata Yoda, from the novel *Joseimatsuri (Girl's Holiday)* by Eijiro Hisiata

Women of Twilight ★

Drama 1952 · UK · BW · 91mins

The worst aspect of this tawdry example of tabloid film-making is that it was penned by Anatole de Grunwald, who wrote and/or produced some of the most impressive features made in postwar Britain. The twilight women are single mothers who are lured to the boarding house run by Freda Jackson as a front for her baby-farming operation. Clichéd and tasteless. DP

Freda Jackson *Helen Allistair* • René Ray *Vivianne Bruce* • Lois Maxwell *Christine Ralston* • Joan Dowling *Rosie Gordon* • Dora Bryan *Olga Lambert* • Vida Hope *Jess Smithson* • Laurence Harvey *Jerry Nolan* ■ *Dir* Gordon Parry • *Scr* Anatole de Grunwald, from the play by Sylvia Rayman

Women on the Verge of a Nervous Breakdown

★★★★★ 15

Comedy 1988 · Sp · Colour · 85mins

A classic comedy of treachery, lust and drugged gazpacho, this is the glorious summation of the themes and visual devices of Pedro Almodóvar's early career. The pace is unrelenting, as actress Carmen Maura tries to cope with the emotional and human fallout after she is dumped by her married lover. Immaculately designed and edited, and deliciously filmed in a riot of colour by José Luis Alcaine, this is art house at its most accessible. It seems almost unfair to select key moments from such a bewilderingly busy and uproariously funny film, but the sight of Julieta Serrano speeding along on a motorbike will stay with you for ever. DP. In Spanish with English

W

subtitles. Contains swearing and sex scenes. DVD

Carmen Maura *Pepa* • Antonio Banderas *Carlos* • Fernando Guillen [Fernando Guillen-Cuervo] *Ivan* • Julieta Serrano *Lucia* • Maria Barranco *Candela* • Rossy de Palma *Marisa* • Kiti Manver *Paulina* ■ *Dir/Scr* Pedro Almodóvar • *Cinematographer* José Luis Alcaine

Women Talking Dirty ★★ 15

Comedy drama
1999 · UK/US · Colour · 93mins

Set in Edinburgh, this female buddy movie has Helena Bonham Carter and Gina McKee as friends who share everything. Drawn together by their bad experiences with the opposite sex (in particular the dastardly James Purefoy), they wail on each other's shoulder, paddle in the Scottish sea and relish their differences. Not surprisingly, a dark secret threatens their relationship – the problem is that you don't really care. The excellent McKee is criminally misused, and the direction is uneven. LH DVD

Helena Bonham Carter *Cora* • Gina McKee *Ellen* • James Purefoy *Daniel* • James Nesbitt *Stanley* • Richard Wilson *Ronald* • Kenneth Cranham *George* • Eileen Atkins *Emily Boyle* ■ *Dir* Coky Giedroyc • *Scr* Isla Dewar, from her novel

Women without Men ★★

Crime drama 1956 · UK · BW · 72mins

Beverly Michaels, imprisoned for injuring a man in self-defence, escapes over Christmas in order to meet her boyfriend, who discharges himself from hospital to keep the date. Second-feature British prison drama of no particular distinction, but deploying some humour and employing some interesting names which up the entertainment quotient. RK

Beverly Michaels *Angela Booth* • Jim Davis *Nick Randall* • Joan Rice *Cleo* • Richard Travis *Kent Foster* • Paul Cavanagh *Inspector Hedges* • Thora Hird *Granny* • Avril Angers *Bessie* • Gordon Jackson *Percy* ■ *Dir* Elmo Williams • *Scr* Richard Landau, Val Guest

Women's Prison ★★★

Drama 1955 · US · BW · 79mins

Yesterday's thick-ear melodrama becomes today's camp trash, as the enjoyable elements in this Columbia programme filler include Ida Lupino, described in the movie as a "borderline psychopath", supervisor in a jail full of 1950s blondes, including forger Jan Sterling, killer Phyllis Thaxter and a clever stripper played by the now-forgotten Vivian Marshall. The men don't get much of a look-in, and it disappoints overall because of its lack of surprises. The title says it all. TS

Ida Lupino *Amelia Van Zant* • Jan Sterling *Brenda Martin* • Cleo Moore *Mae* • Audrey Totter *Joan Burton* • Phyllis Thaxter *Helene Jensen* • Howard Duff *Dr Clark* • Warren Stevens *Glen Burton* ■ *Dir* Lewis Seiler • *Scr* Crane Wilbur, Jack DeWitt

Won Ton Ton, the Dog Who Saved Hollywood ★

Period parody 1976 · US · Colour · 91mins

In this dismal spoof of the Golden Age of Hollywood, Michael Winner mistakes fast for fun and excess for success, as he ploughs haphazardly through a Rin Tin Tin-type plot about a dog that becomes a movie star. Star-spotting remains the film's only abiding appeal. DA

Bruce Dern *Grayson Potchuck* • Madeline Kahn *Estie Del Ruth* • Art Carney *JJ Fromberg* • Ron Leibman *Rudy Montague* • Teri Garr *Fluffy Peters* ■ *Dir* Michael Winner • *Scr* Arnold Schulman, Cy Howard

Wonder Bar ★★★★

Musical romance 1934 · US · BW · 84mins

This "La Ronde" of romances serves as an excuse for Busby Berkeley's choreography, which notably includes a production showstopper done with mirrors and an embarrassing blackface number. Plotwise, nightclub owner Al Jolson and his band singer Dick Powell are both in love with dancer Dolores Del Rio, while she has her sights set on her dance partner Ricardo Cortez, who is also the choice of wealthy socialite Kay Francis. Dirty old man comedy native to the genre is provided by Guy Kibbee and Hugh Herbert, who play married men pursuing the chorus girls. Terrific entertainment. RK

Al Jolson *Al Wonder* • Kay Francis *Liane Renaud* • Dolores Del Rio *Ynez* • Ricardo Cortez *Harry* • Dick Powell *Tommy* • Guy Kibbee *Simpson* ■ *Dir* Lloyd Bacon • *Scr* Earl Baldwin, from the play *Die Wunderbar,, book by Geza Herczeg, Karl Farkas, music by Robert Katscher* • *Director (musical Numbers)* Busby Berkeley

Wonder Boys ★★★★ 15

Comedy drama
2000 · US/Ger/UK/Jpn · Colour · 111mins

Director Curtis Hanson followed the marvellous *LA Confidential* with this quirky, dark and unforgettable comedy drama. Michael Douglas is an ageing, pot-smoking college professor whose life is on shaky ground – his young third wife has left him, he's having an affair with the (married) college chancellor (Frances McDormand) and she's pregnant, he's struggling with the follow-up to his celebrated first novel, and he also has to deal with odd, but potentially talented, student Tobey Maguire. Hanson expertly weaves all of these threads into a mesmerising drama complete with fascinating characters and a wicked sense of humour. JB. Contains swearing and drug abuse. DVD

Michael Douglas *Grady Tripp* • Tobey Maguire *James Leer* • Frances McDormand *Sara Gaskell* • Robert Downey Jr *Terry Crabtree* • Katie Holmes *Hannah Green* • Richard Thomas *Walter Gaskell* • Rip Torn *Q* • Philip Bosco *Hank Winters* ■ *Dir* Curtis Hanson • *Scr* Steve Kloves, from the novel by Michael Chabon

Wonder Man ★★★ U

Musical comedy 1945 · US · Colour · 94mins

A splendidly Technicolored fantasy in which the talented Danny Kaye plays two roles, a mild-mannered academic and his brother, a nightclub performer bumped off by gangsters, enabling his spirit to enter his brother's body. Producer Samuel Goldwyn spared no expense in surrounding Kaye with good-looking co-stars and a fine supporting cast, and the whole enterprise ended up taking that year's Oscar for best special effects. Kaye's verve and genial madness keep this endeavour buoyantly afloat. TS

Danny Kaye *Buzzy Bellew/Edwin Dingle* • Virginia Mayo *Ellen Shanley* • Vera-Ellen *Midge Mallon* • Donald Woods *Monte Rossen* • SZ Sakall *Schmidt* • Allen Jenkins *Chimp* • Steve Cochran *Ten-Grand Jackson* • Otto Kruger *DA O'Brien* ■ *Dir* Bruce Humberstone [H Bruce Humberstone] • *Scr* Don Hartman, Melville Shavelson, Philip Rapp, Jack Jevne, Eddie Moran, from a story by Arthur Sheekman

The Wonderful Country ★★★★ U

Western 1959 · US · Colour · 97mins

Westerns usually offer positive leading men with a purpose, but here Robert Mitchum makes a very passive figure as the gunman for hire, an American who has adopted Mexican ways, slowly learning on which side of the Rio Grande he really belongs. Made by the star's own production company, this introspective journey of discovery has little conventional action (a broken leg sidelines Mitchum for quite a while) but presents an absorbing range of well-detailed characters that are far from the usual western stereotypes. Deftly scripted by Robert Ardrey from the novel by Tom Lea (who appears briefly as the barber), it is always superbly photographed, slow but ultimately most rewarding. AE

Robert Mitchum *Martin Brady* • Julie London *Ellen Colton* • Gary Merrill *Major Stark Colton* • Pedro Armendáriz *Governor Cipriano Castro* • Jack Oakie *Travis Hight* • Albert Dekker *Captain Rucker* • Victor Mendoza [Victor Manuel Mendoza] *General Castro* • Charles McGraw *Doc Stovall* ■ *Dir* Robert Parrish • *Scr* Robert Ardrey, from the novel by Tom Lea

The Wonderful, Horrible Life of Leni Riefenstahl ★★★★

Biographical documentary
1993 · Ger · Colour and BW · 186mins

How can you possibly hope to sustain a reputation as the finest female film-maker of all time when your sponsor was Adolf Hitler? No one can watch either *Triumph of the Will* or *Olympia* without being repulsed by their fascist overtones. But it's equally impossible to deny that Leni Riefenstahl had an unrivalled eye for a telling image and a supreme sense of visual rhythm. Celebrating her acting career and her post-Nazi achievements as a stills photographer, cultural anthropologist and underwater documentarist, Ray Muller attempts a rounded portrait that balances Riefenstahl's anti-propagandist claims with some pretty damning evidence. Riveting, revealing, but rarely irrefutable. DP. In English and German with subtitles. DVD

Leni Riefenstahl ■ *Dir/Scr* Ray Muller

The Wonderful Lie of Nina Petrovna ★★★★

Silent romantic melodrama
1929 · Ger · BW · 92mins

Originally screened with a lyrical orchestral score by Maurice Jaubert, Hanns Schwarz's silent melodrama was restored to something approaching its pristine glory in the late 1980s. Brigitte Helm revealed herself to be a sensitive and soulful actress with this affecting display of self-sacrificing love. Francis Lederer also impresses as the impoverished lieutenant in the Tsarist army who steals her heart, although he's made to look a little fey by Warwick Ward, as the jilted colonel, who suggests they play poker for her affections. Pure melodrama, but tinged with art. DP

Brigitte Helm *Nina Petrowna* • Franz Lederer [Francis Lederer] *Lt Michael Rostoff* • Warwick Ward *Colonel Beranoff* ■ *Dir* Hanns Schwarz • *Scr* Hans Székely

Wonderful Life ★★ U

Musical comedy 1964 · UK · Colour · 108mins

The happy-clappy pop musical had been dealt a fatal blow in 1964 by the release of the Beatles' endlessly innovative and iconoclastic *A Hard Day's Night*. Yet the winsome formula continued to rear its sweetly smiling head throughout the decade. Here, Cliff Richard and the Shadows rescue timid actress Susan Hampshire from tyrannical director Walter Slezak. DP DVD

Cliff Richard *Johnnie* • Susan Hampshire *Jenny* • Walter Slezak *Lloyd Davis* • Hank Marvin • Bruce Welch • Brian Bennett • John Rostill • Melvyn Hayes *Jerry* • Richard O'Sullivan *Edward* • Una Stubbs *Barbara* • Derek Bond *Douglas Leslie* ■ *Dir* Sidney J Furie • *Scr* Peter Myers, Ronald Cass

The Wonderful World of the Brothers Grimm ★★ U

Musical fantasy 1962 · US · Colour · 130mins

Fantasy producer George Pal followed up his *tom thumb* with another fairy-tale picture, only this time it was inflated for the giant screen Cinerama process, losing most of its potential lightness and charm. Two rather humourless actors, Laurence Harvey and Karlheinz Böhm, play the writer brothers in a framing story for three of their tales. Some excellent puppetry and animation are featured in the imaginary fables, while Mary Wills won an Oscar for her costumes. AE

Laurence Harvey *Wilhelm Grimm* • Karl Boehm [Karlheinz Böhm] *Jacob Grimm* • Claire Bloom *Dorothea Grimm* • Walter Slezak *Stossel* • Barbara Eden *Greta Heinrich* • Oscar Homolka *The Duke* • Arnold Stang *Rumpelstiltskin* • Yvette Mimieux *The Princess* • Russ Tamblyn *The Woodsman* • Jim Backus *The King* • Beulah Bondi *The Gypsy* • Terry-Thomas *Ludwig* • Martita Hunt *Story-teller* ■ *Dir* Henry Levin, George Pal • *Scr* David P Harmon, Charles Beaumont, William Roberts, from a story by David P Harmon, from the non-fiction book *Die Brüder Grimm* by Hermann Gerstner and from stories by Jacob Grimm, Wilhelm Grimm

Wonderland ★★★★ 15

Drama 1999 · UK · Colour · 104mins

Though the title may seem odd for a film depicting the harsh reality of London life, this celebrates the ordinary people who have found the capital isn't paved with the gold of opportunity. Chekhovian in form, Laurence Coriat's screenplay tells the intertwined stories of three sisters and their bickering parents (Kika Markham and Jack Shepherd). Lonely Gina McKee seeks love and sex via a dating agency; pregnant Molly Parker is having trouble with her husband John Simm; while good-time-girl Shirley Henderson neglects her 11-year-old son. The narrative seems to be in haphazard free fall, but the film resolves its issues in dramatic fashion. TH. Contains swearing, sex scenes and nudity.

Gina McKee *Nadia* • Molly Parker *Molly* • Shirley Henderson *Debbie* • Ian Hart *Dan* • Stuart Townsend *Tim* • John Simm *Eddie* • Jack Shepherd *Bill* • Kika Markham *Eileen* ■ *Dir* Michael Winterbottom • *Scr* Laurence Coriat

Wonderland ★★ 18

Crime drama based on a true story
2003 · US · Colour · 100mins

The life story of porn legend John Holmes has already been brought to the screen in fictionalised form in *Boogie Nights*, but this true-crime saga takes up where Paul Thomas Anderson's film left off. It charts the performer's descent into a drug-addled hell, during which he is implicated in a quadruple homicide. Val Kilmer's portrayal of Holmes as a doe-eyed dope leavens what could have been an intolerably sleazy tale, but James Cox's direction is distractingly bombastic. AS. Contains violence and drug abuse. DVD

Val Kilmer *John Holmes* • Kate Bosworth *Dawn Schiller* • Lisa Kudrow *Sharon Holmes* • Josh Lucas *Ron Launius* • Tim Blake Nelson *Billy Deverell* • Dylan McDermott *David Lind* • Christina Applegate *Susan Launius* • Eric Bogosian *Eddie Nash* • Carrie Fisher *Sally Hansen* • Franky G *Louis Cruz* • MC Gainey *Bill Ward* • Janeane Garofalo *Joy Miller* • Ted Levine *Sam Nico* • Faizon Love *Greg Diles* • Natasha Gregson Wagner *Barbara Richardson* ■ *Dir* James Cox • *Scr* James Cox, Captain Mauzner, Todd Samovitz, D Loriston Scott

Wonderwall ★★★ 15

Drama 1968 · UK · Colour · 74mins

This is one of the quintessential (and now forgotten) Swinging London films of the late 1960s. Eccentric professor Jack MacGowran peers through his hole in the wall at disturbed model Jane Birkin amid psychedelic butterfly effects and swirling sitars. Though Joe Massot is the movie's credited director, its real inspiration comes from its four superb collaborators: cameraman Harry Waxman, art director Assheton Gorton, editor Rusty Coppleman, and composer, Beatle George Harrison. TS. Contains sex scenes and drug abuse. [video]

Jack MacGowran *Oscar Collins* • Jane Birkin *Penny* • Irene Handl *Mrs Peurofoy* • Richard Wattis *Perkins* • Iain Quarrier *Young Man* • Beatrix Lehmann *Mother* ■ *Dir* Joe Massot • *Scr* Guillermo Cain, from a story by Gérard Brach

Wondrous Oblivion ★★ PG

Period comedy drama
2003 · UK/Ger · Colour · 101mins

The problem with this rite-of-passage tale is that writer/director Paul Morrison can't decide whether to focus on 11-year-old Sam Smith's desire to silence bullying schoolboys by improving his cricket batting skills or on his Jewish mother Emily Woof's crush on Caribbean neighbour Delroy Lindo. Moreover, instead of tackling racial prejudice in suburban London in the early 1960s, Morrison opts for a cosy feel-good approach that neither charms nor convinces. DP DVD

Delroy Lindo *Dennis Samuels* • Emily Woof *Ruth Wiseman* • Stanley Townsend *Victor Wiseman* • Angela Wynter *Grace Samuels* • Leonie Elliott *Judy Samuels* • Sam Smith *David Wiseman* • Naomi Simpson *Dorothy Samuels* ■ *Dir/Scr* Paul Morrison

Woo ★ 15

Romantic comedy
1998 · US · Colour · 81mins

Jada Pinkett Smith is the stuck-up girl who proves a nightmare for date Tommy Davidson in this unfunny and hugely irritating comedy that's slightly redeemed by a decent hip-hop soundtrack. Pinkett Smith overacts ridiculously, while the rest of the cast stands on the sidelines watching this disaster of a movie plod to its predictable conclusion. JB. Contains violence, swearing, drug abuse, sex scenes and nudity. [video]

Jada Pinkett Smith *Woo/Off the wall babe* • Tommy Davidson *Tim* • Duane Martin *Frankie* • Michael Ralph *Romaine* • Darrel M Heath *Hop* • Dave Chappelle *Lenny* • Paula Jai Parker *Claudette* • LL Cool J *Darryl* • Aida Turturro *Tookie* ■ *Dir* Daisy von Scherler Mayer • *Scr* David C Johnson

The Woo Woo Kid ★★ PG

Biographical romantic comedy
1987 · US · Colour · 94mins

This is a documentary-style nostalgia film about the shenanigans of 15-year-old Ellsworth "Sonny" Wisecarver, who was put on trial in 1944 for being utterly irresistible after two affairs with older women – one of whom he married. The film is simply an excuse for a lingering look at a Waltonesque life style with Patrick Dempsey playing the seducer, Talia Balsam as his love interest and the real Wisecarver putting in a cameo amid some fake newsreel footage. LH [video]

Patrick Dempsey *Ellsworth "Sonny" Wisecarver* • Talia Balsam *Judy Cusimano* • Beverly D'Angelo *Francine Glatt* • Michael Constantine *Mr Wisecarver* • Ellsworth "Sonny" Wisecarver *Mailman* ■ *Dir* Phil Alden Robinson • *Scr* Phil Alden Robinson, from a story by Bob Kosberg, David Simon, Robinson

The Wood ★★★ 15

Comedy 1999 · US · Colour · 102mins

A trio of middle-class African-Americans use one of their number's impending nuptials as an excuse to recall their early experiences in the LA suburb of Inglewood. Cue a series of extended flashbacks that show the friends dealing with school, bullies and girls. Wedding day jitters are a comedy staple, and Rick Famuyiwa's debut feature adds no new spins to the formula. What does impress is the way he steers clear of the usual gangsta/ghetto clichés while wittily revisiting the sights, sounds and outrageous fashions of the 1980s. NS [video] DVD

Taye Diggs *Roland* • Omar Epps *Mike* • Richard T Jones *Slim* • Sean Nelson *Young Mike* • Trent Cameron *Young Roland* • Duane Finley *Young Slim* • Malinda Williams *Young Alicia* • De'Aundre Bonds *Stacey* ■ *Dir* Rick Famuyiwa • *Scr* Rick Famuyiwa, from a story by Rick Famuyiwa, Todd Boyd

The Wooden Horse ★★★ U

Second World War drama
1950 · UK · BW · 98mins

This is one of the most famous escape stories of the Second World War in which PoWs use a vaulting horse to hide their tunnel. Scripted by Eric Williams (from his own bestseller) and directed by ex-documentary maker Jack Lee, it has a ring of authenticity that is reinforced by a splendid cast led by Leo Genn and David Tomlinson. However, the action only really becomes compelling outside Stalag Luft III as the escapees make for the coast. DP [video]

Leo Genn *Peter* • David Tomlinson *Phil* • Anthony Steel *John* • David Greene *Bennett* • Peter Burton *Nigel* • Patrick Waddington *Commanding Officer* • Michael Goodliffe *Robbie* • Anthony Dawson *Pomfret* ■ *Dir* Jack Lee • *Scr* Eric Williams, from his book *The Tunnel Escape*

The Woodlanders ★★ U

Drama 1997 · UK · Colour · 93mins

Phil Agland's feature debut is this Thomas Hardy tale of fickle passion and betrayed devotion. Yet, while Agland admirably captures the atmosphere of the woodlands, he struggles to bring the drama to life. Much of the problem stems from the length and pacing of the scenes, although a hesitant cast, cinematographer Ashley Rowe's gloomy interiors and George Fenton's glutinous score don't help. DP [video]

Emily Woof *Grace Melbury* • Rufus Sewell *Giles Winterbourne* • Cal MacAninch *Dr Fitzpiers* • Tony Haygarth *Melbury* • Jodhi May *Marty South* • Polly Walker *Mrs Charmond* • Walter Sparrow *Old Creedle* • Sheila Burrell *Grandma Oliver* ■ *Dir* Phil Agland • *Scr* David Rudkin, from the novel by Thomas Hardy

The Woodsman ★★★★ 15

Drama 2004 · US · Colour · 87mins

It's a brave actor who plays a paedophile and attempts to invest the role with some humanity. Kevin Bacon, long one of Hollywood's underappreciated talents, pulls it off magnificently in this sombre, disturbing tale of a convicted child molester trying to make a life for himself after parole. He finds himself living within sight of a primary school, being harassed by a local cop (rapper Mos Def) and falling in love with a co-worker (played by Bacon's wife Kyra Sedgwick) who's unaware of his past. It's never comfortable to watch, but it's also an intelligent and humane film. AS. Contains swearing. DVD

Kevin Bacon *Walter Rossworth* • Kyra Sedgwick *Vickie* • Eve *Mary-Kay* • Mos Def *Sgt Lucas* • David Alan Grier *Bob* • Benjamin Bratt *Carlos* • Michael Shannon *Rosen* • Hannah Pilkes *Robin* ■ *Dir* Nicole Kassell • *Scr* Nicole Kassell, Steven Fechter, from the play by Steven Fechter

Woodstock ★★★★★ 15

Music documentary
1970 · US · Colour · 177mins

Some three decades on, Woodstock the event is more ridiculed than revered. Yet, as Michael Wadleigh's vibrant documentary demonstrates, this concert in some muddy fields in upstate New York was much more than a simple moment in time – it was the end of an era. Wadleigh and assistant directors Thelma Schoonmaker and Martin Scorsese waded through untold miles of footage, using split-screen techniques to do justice to the goings-on both on stage and in the audience. Time may not have been kind to some of the views espoused here, but this is a dazzling piece of film-making and an invaluable insight into late-1960s youth. DP. Contains swearing, drug abuse, nudity. [video] DVD

Dir Michael Wadleigh • *Scr* Country Joe and the Fish

Words and Music ★★★ U

Musical biography
1948 · US · Colour · 121mins

An engaging MGM extravaganza that purports to tell the story of brilliant songsmiths Richard Rodgers and Lorenz Hart through their music – and, to a degree, it does. Trouble is, Tom Drake is such a colourless Rodgers and Mickey Rooney such a bumptious, unsympathetic Hart that you don't give two hoots for the men behind the songs. It's a major flaw, even allowing for the fact that in 1948 Hart's homosexuality and Rodgers's ice-cold business deals couldn't really be dealt with on film at all. Still, there are many pleasures to be had. TS

Mickey Rooney *Lorenz "Larry" Hart* • Tom Drake *Richard "Dick" Rodgers* • Marshall Thompson *Herbert Fields* • Janet Leigh *Dorothy Feiner* • Betty Garrett *Peggy Lorgan McNeil* • Ann Sothern *Joyce Harmon* • Perry Como *Eddie Lorrison Anders* • Judy Garland • Mel Tormé • Gene Kelly • Vera-Ellen ■ *Dir* Norman Taurog • *Scr* Fred Finklehoffe, Ben Feiner Jr, from a story by Guy Bolton, Jean Holloway

Work ★★★ U

Silent comedy drama
1915 · US · BW · 24mins

Usually screened with another two-reeler, *Police*, Charlie Chaplin's silent short is about a family that hires him to re-paper their home. Adapted from a music-hall sketch that was created during Chaplin's early days with Fred Karno, it has lost little of its slapstick hilarity and moves at a terrifically jocular pace. TH [video] DVD

Charles Chaplin *Paperhanger's assistant* • Charles Insley *Paperhanger* • Edna Purviance *Maid* • Billy Armstrong *Husband* • Marta Golden *Wife* • Leo White *Secret lover* ■ *Dir/Scr* Charles Chaplin

Work Is a Four Letter Word ★★

Comedy fantasy 1968 · UK · Colour · 93mins

In a near future dominated by automation, unemployed eccentric David Warner, under pressure from his fiancée, takes a job at the local power station. However, the hot and damp conditions of the plant are ideal for growing his hallucinogenic magic mushrooms which he proceeds to distribute as a protest against a machine-led society. This is one of those films that tells you more about its own decade than the projected futuristic era in which it is set. Still, it's interesting to see Cilla Black trying to be more than just a pop star. DF

David Warner *Val Brose* • Cilla Black *Betty Dorrick* • Elizabeth Spriggs *Mrs Murray* • Zia Mohyeddin *Dr Narayana* • Joe Gladwin *Pa Brose* • Julie May *Mrs Dorrick* ■ *Dir* Peter Hall • *Scr* Jeremy Brooks, from the play *Eh?* by Henry Livings

The Working Class Goes to Heaven ★★★

Drama 1971 · It · Colour · 126mins

The joint winner of the Palme d'Or at Cannes, Elio Petri's uncompromising study of politics in the workplace may seem a little strident at times. Factory worker Gian Maria Volonté's transformation from capitalist lackey to impassioned unionist might take some swallowing. But, viewed as a portrait of a man unable to temper his convictions, the story takes on a greater universal significance by virtue of the discomforting realism of Volonté's domestic disputes with girlfriend, Mariangela Melato. DP. In Italian with English subtitles.

Gian Maria Volonté *Ludovico Massa, "Lulu"* • Mariangela Melato *Lidia* • Mietta Albertini *Adalgisa* • Salvo Randone *Militina* • Gino Pernice *Union politician* ■ *Dir* Elio Petri • *Scr* Ugo Pirro, Elio Petri

Working Girl ★★★★ 15

Comedy 1988 · US · Colour · 108mins

This appealing executive-suite comedy shows feminism triumphing as Melanie Griffith climbs the corporate ladder to success by stepping on Sigourney Weaver's fingers, falling for Harrison Ford in the process. Griffith is the exploited and bossed-about secretary to Weaver, taking over from her in her absence and getting Ford as the main prize. This secretary's wish-fulfillment comedy is an easy-going treat for all in director Mike Nichols's assured hands. Carly Simon's Oscar-winning song, *Let the River Run*, makes the soundtrack one to treasure. TH. Contains swearing and nudity. [video]

Harrison Ford *Jack Trainer* • Sigourney Weaver *Katharine Parker* • Melanie Griffith *Tess McGill* • Alec Baldwin *Mick Dugan* • Joan Cusack *Cyn* • Oliver Platt *Lutz* • Kevin Spacey *Bob Speck* • Olympia Dukakis *Personnel Director* ■ *Dir* Mike Nichols • *Scr* Kevin Wade

Working Girls ★★★ 18

Drama 1986 · US · Colour · 89mins

Director Lizzie Borden has made a movie about prostitution that is interesting, empathic and intelligent. Set within a Manhattan brothel, the film depicts men as seeking individuality and reassurance by acting out their sexual fantasies. Not a great film by any means, it is nevertheless a refreshing take on an industry that is usually portrayed with cliché and prejudice. Here we have the nitty gritty from birth control to bondage and Borden is frank about both. LH [video]

Louise Smith *Molly* • Ellen McElduff *Lucy* • Amanda Goodwin *Dawn* • Marusia Zach *Gina* • Janne Peters *April* • Helen Nicholas *Mary* ■ *Dir* Lizzie Borden • *Scr* Lizzie Borden, Sandra Kay, from a story by Borden

The World According to Garp ★★★ 15

Drama 1982 · US · Colour · 130mins

This magical mystery tour of a New England writer's life – based on John Irving's sprawling and virtually unfilmable satirical novel – involves the mind but never engages the heart. Robin Williams stars as Garp, a writer married to Mary Beth Hurt, who's forever at the mercy of lethal modern contraptions and overshadowed by his domineering mum (brilliantly played by Glenn Close in her feature debut). Director George Roy Hill contrives some felicitous moments, but f doesn't resolve into clarity de good intentions. AT. Contains violence, swearing and nudity.

Robin Williams *TS Garp* • Mary Beth Hurt *Helen Holm* • Glenn Close *Jenny Fields* • John Lithgow *Roberta Muldoon* • Hume Cronyn *Mr Fields* • Jessica Tandy *Mrs Fields* • Swoosie Kurtz *Hooker* ■ *Dir* George Roy Hill • *Scr* Steve Tesich, from the novel by John Irving

A World Apart ★★★★ PG

Drama based on a true story
1987 · UK · Colour · 108mins

This very well received anti-apartheid drama is based on the true story of a white South African mother who was jailed for her support of the African National Congress. Barbara Hershey is excellent as the woman torn between the love of her family and her political beliefs, and the underused Jodhi May gives an unforgettable performance as the daughter through whose eyes the story unfolds. Stirring stuff from director Chris Menges, and a must see. LH

Jodhi May *Molly Roth* • Barbara Hershey *Diana Roth* • Jeroen Krabbé *Gus Roth* • David Suchet *Muller* • Paul Freeman *Kruger* • Tim Roth *Harold* • Linda Mvusi *Elsie* • Carolyn Clayton-Cragg *Miriam Roth* • Yvonne Bryceland *Bertha* ■ *Dir* Chris Menges • *Scr* Shawn Slovo

The World Changes ★★★★

Drama 1933 · US · BW · 90mins

This dynastic saga begins in uncharted 1850s Dakota and ends with the 1929 Wall Street crash, this stars Paul Muni as a farm lad who becomes Chicago's leading meat industry tycoon. He is forced to watch helplessly as his wealth corrupts the values of his wife (Mary Astor) and his children and grandchildren, bringing misery and destruction in its wake. At once a hymn to the American pioneering spirit, enterprise and progress, and a pointed morality tale, the film, directed by Mervyn LeRoy, brings a striking central performance from 38-year-old Muni, who ages from early 20s to late 70s. RK

Paul Muni *Orin Nordholm Jr* • Aline MacMahon *Anna Nordholm* • Mary Astor *Virginia* • Donald Cook *Richard Nordholm* • Patricia Ellis *Natalie* • Jean Muir *Selma Peterson* • Margaret Lindsay *Jennifer* • Guy Kibbee *Claflin* ■ *Dir* Mervyn LeRoy • *Scr* Edward Chodorov, from the story *America Kneels* by Sheridan Gibney

World for Ransom ★★★

Crime drama 1953 · US · BW · 81mins

Robert Aldrich's second feature was a standard private-eye outing but set in Singapore – the movie was shot in a Hollywood studio in 11 days. The private eye's trail leads at first to the underworld, then to Cold War intrigue and atomic meltdown while the lady in the case proves to be the biggest mystery of all. The script is by Hugo Butler, a blacklistee, so the credit went to "front" Lindsay Hardy. AT

Dan Duryea *Mike Callahan* • Gene Lockhart *Alexis Pederas* • Patric Knowles *Julian March* • Reginald Denny *Major Bone* • Nigel Bruce *Governor Coutts* • Marian Carr *Frennessey March* • Arthur Shields *Sean O'Connor* • Douglass Dumbrille *Inspector McCollum* ■ *Dir* Robert Aldrich • *Scr* Lindsay Hardy (front for Hugo Butler)

World Gone Wild ★★ 18

Science-fiction action adventure
1988 · US · Colour · 90mins

This undistinguished post-holocaust action adventure has a few imaginative riffs along the way to keep interest maintained. It's 2087, water is a precious commodity, and hippy clan leader Bruce Dern is looking for mercenaries to protect the Lost Wells oasis from an attack by power-mad Adam Ant. Guru Dern acts everybody else off the screen as this drifts into predictability. AJ

Bruce Dern *Ethan* • Adam Ant *Derek Abernathy* • Michael Paré *George Landon* • Catherine Mary Stewart *Angie* • Rick Podell *Exline* • Julius J Carry III *Nitro* • Alan Autry *Hank* • Anthony James *Ten Watt* ■ *Dir* Lee H Katzin • *Scr* Jorge Zamacona

The World in His Arms ★★★ U

Romantic adventure
1952 · US · Colour · 104mins

In a corny but enjoyable romantic adventure, Gregory Peck plays an illegal sealskin trader who sails into San Francisco from Alaska, falls for a Russian countess (Ann Blyth) and has to use his fists and his sailing savvy to keep her. Directed by action expert Raoul Walsh, it's macho stuff, professionally done, with the high point an exciting race on the high seas. And way down the cast list, before he abandoned his acting career, is writer/director Bryan Forbes, with sideburns and an American accent. AT

Gregory Peck *Captain Jonathan Clark* • Ann Blyth *Countess Marina Selanova* • Anthony Quinn *Portugee* • John McIntire *Deacon Greathouse* • Andrea King *Mamie* • Carl Esmond *Prince Semyon* • Eugenie Leontovich *Madame Selanova* • Sig Ruman *General Ivan Vorashilov* • Bryan Forbes *William Cleggett* ■ *Dir* Raoul Walsh • *Scr* Borden Chase, Horris McCoy, from the novel by Rex Beach

The World Is Full of Married Men ★★ 18

Melodrama 1979 · UK · Colour · 102mins

With a title like this, it comes as no surprise that this film is based on a sex 'n' shopping novel by Jackie Collins. Anthony Franciosa and Carroll Baker star in this tale of a faithful wife who reassesses her life when her husband begins an affair. This is typical British 1970s titillation (lots of make-up, jewellery and low-cut tops and that's just the men), with a cast of actors who would probably now choose to leave this opus off their CVs. JB. Contains swearing, nudity.

Anthony Franciosa *David Cooper* • Carroll Baker *Linda Cooper* • Sherrie Cronn *Claudia Parker* • Gareth Hunt *Jay Grossman* • Georgina Hale *Lori Grossman* • Paul Nicholas *Gem Gemini* • Anthony Steel *Conrad Lee* ■ *Dir* Robert William Young [Robert Young (2)] • *Scr* Jackie Collins, from her novel

The World Is Not Enough ★★★★ 12

Spy adventure
1999 · US/UK · Colour · 122mins

A welcome return to the gritty glamour of such early outings as *From Russia with Love*, the 19th James Bond adventure effortlessly juggles a hard-hitting story with all the expected "super spy" embellishments and keeps it in diamond-cut focus for maximum suspense and thrills. Thank director Michael Apted for the stirring, not shaky, blend of casino/ski slopes/submarine components, contained within a topical plot about the power struggle for global domination of pipelines from the oil-rich capital of Azerbaijan. Pierce Brosnan is clearly more comfortable as 007 and has more meaty drama to play besides the usual series of stunts. AJ. Contains violence and swearing. DVD

Pierce Brosnan *James Bond* • Sophie Marceau *Elektra* • Robert Carlyle *Renard* • Denise Richards *Christmas Jones* • Robbie Coltrane *Valentin Zukovsky* • Judi Dench *"M"* • Desmond Llewelyn *"Q"* • John Cleese *"R"* ■ *Dir* Michael Apted • *Scr* Neal Purvis, Robert Wade, Bruce Fierstein, from a story by Neal Purvis, Robert Wade, from characters created by Ian Fleming

The World Moves On ★★★

Period drama 1934 · US · BW · 104mins

The least-known of the three films John Ford directed in 1934 is a saga charting the fortunes of two New Orleans families from the 1800s to the 1920s. Along the way, it depicts the acquisition of their wealth across continents, the collapse of their commercial empires through war and the subsequent Depression, and the promise of renewal by a new generation. Ford directs this sometimes lumbering but ambitious film with impressive battlefront sequences, a strong pacifist message, and a solid cast. RK

Madeleine Carroll *Mary Warburton* • Franchot Tone *Richard Girard* • Reginald Denny *Erik von Gerhardt* • Siegfried Rumann [Sig Ruman] *Baron von Gerhardt* • Louise Dresser *Baroness von Gerhardt* • Raul Roulien *Carlos Girard/Henri Girard* • Lumsden Hare *Sir John Warburton* ■ *Dir* John Ford • *Scr* Reginald Berkeley, from his story

The World of Apu ★★★★★ U

Drama 1959 · Ind · BW · 100mins

Concluding the "Apu" trilogy that began with *Pather Panchali* and *Aparajito*, this confirmed Satyajit Ray as the natural heir to both Jean Renoir and the neorealist tradition. Adapted from Bibhutibhushan Bannerjee's semi-autobiographical novel, the unexpectedly linear narrative focuses on Soumitra Chatterjee's bid to become a writer and his struggle to accept Alok Chakravarty, the son whose birth caused the death of his beloved wife, Sharmila Tagore. Shooting on location in detail-packed long takes (pausing only for the delightfully comic father/son montage sequence), Ray coaxes heartfelt performances from his largely non-professional cast to ensure a fittingly humanist conclusion to this sublimely cinematic masterpiece. DP. In Bengali with English subtitles. DVD

Soumitra Chatterjee *Apurba Kumar Ray (Apu)* • Sharmila Tagore *Aparna* • Alok Chakravarty *Kajal* ■ *Dir* Satyajit Ray • *Scr* Satyajit Ray, from a novel by Bibhutibhushan Bannerjee

The World of Henry Orient ★★★★ U

Comedy 1964 · US · Colour · 104mins

This is a charming and neglected rite-of-passage comedy, centring on the obsession of two teenage girls with a womanising concert pianist. Although Peter Sellers and his mistress Paula Prentiss turn in broadly amusing performances, it's the fantasising innocents, Tippy Walker and Merrie Spaeth, who catch the eye. Nora and Nunnally Johnson's playful script (based on the former's novel) also provides showy supporting roles for Tom Bosley and Angela Lansbury as Walker's parents. If only someone had told director George Roy Hill to stop mucking about with the film speeds, this might have garnered the attention it deserves. DP DVD

Peter Sellers *Henry Orient* • Paula Prentiss *Stella* • Tippy Walker *Valerie Boyd* • Merrie Spaeth *Marion "Gil" Gilbert* • Angela Lansbury *Isabel Boyd* • Tom Bosley *Frank Boyd* • Phyllis Thaxter *Mrs Gilbert* ■ *Dir* George Roy Hill • *Scr* Nora Johnson, Nunnally Johnson, from the novel by Nora Johnson

The World of Suzie Wong ★★

Romantic drama
1960 · UK · Colour · 128mins

William Holden plays an American artist who becomes involved with a Hong Kong prostitute, played by Nancy Kwan. Unbeknown to Holden, Kwan has a baby son whom she hides in a slum. When Holden rejects her offer to become his "steady girlfriend", Kwan turns her attention to playboy Michael Wilding. Seriously hampered by censorship restrictions, Richard Quine treats it as a comic travelogue that exploits the heroine in its own way. AT

William Holden (2) *Robert Lomax* • Nancy Kwan *Suzie Wong* • Sylvia Syms *Kay O'Neill* • Michael Wilding *Ben* • Laurence Naismith *Mr O'Neill* • Jacqui Chan *Gwenny Lee* • Bernard Cribbins *Otis* ■ *Dir* Richard Quine • *Scr* John Patrick, from the play by Paul Osborn and the novel by Richard Mason

The World Ten Times Over ★★

Melodrama 1963 · UK · BW · 94mins

When it appeared, this gloomy stylised melodrama struck some as a failed British attempt to emulate the French *nouvelle vague* cinema of the likes of Godard and Truffaut. Nowadays, it seems more interesting for its offbeat central situation: two over-the-hill nightclub hostesses (Sylvia Syms and June Ritchie) live together happily as long as they keep men at bay. A depressing though intelligent movie. JG

Sylvia Syms *Billa* • Edward Judd *Bob* • June Ritchie *Ginnie* • William Hartnell *Dad* • Sarah Lawson *Elizabeth* • Francis De Wolff *Shelbourne* • Davy Kaye *Compere* • Linda Marlowe *Penny* ■ *Dir/Scr* Wolf Rilla

The World, the Flesh and the Devil ★★

Science-fiction drama
1959 · US · BW · 94mins

A passionate, earnest and totally daft post-holocaust racial allegory. Miner Harry Belafonte lives through an atomic attack and meets two other survivors – gorgeous Inger Stevens and bigoted Mel Ferrer – when he arrives in devastated New York City. Aside from a few impressively mounted sequences on the deserted Manhattan streets where the two men stalk each other, this eternal triangle plea for harmony is condescending and unbelievable. AJ

Harry Belafonte *Ralph Burton* • Inger Stevens *Sarah Crandall* • Mel Ferrer *Benson Thacker* ■ *Dir* Ranald MacDougall • *Scr* Ranald MacDougall, from the story *End of the Wall* by Ferdinand Reyher and the novel *The Purple Cloud* by Matthew Phipps Shiel

The World Was His Jury ★ U

Drama 1957 · US · BW · 81mins

Edmond O'Brien is the defence attorney who has never lost a case. Odd then that he takes the case of a ship's captain accused of criminal negligence resulting in numerous fatalities when there's not a shred of evidence in the man's favour. This is a drearily predictable production by Columbia's B team, producer Sam Katzman and director Fred F Sears. AE

Edmond O'Brien *David Carson* • Mona Freeman *Robin Carson* • Karin Booth *Polly Barrett* • Robert McQueeney *Captain Jerry Barrett* • Paul Birch *Martin Ranker* • John Berardino [John Beradino] *Tony Armand* • Richard H Cutting *DA Wendell* ■ *Dir* Fred F Sears • *Scr* Herbert Abbott Spiro

World without End ★★

Science fiction 1955 · US · Colour · 80mins

Returning from a Mars mission, an American spaceship enters a time warp and ends up on Earth in the 26th century. Unfortunately, it's after a nuclear war has left the planet's surface inhabited by mutant cavemen, giant spiders and a superior, if listless, race forced to live underground. This colourful and very loose unofficial adaptation of HG Wells's *The Time Machine* is tacky and fast-paced fun, if a little moralistic. The subterranean fairy-tale-style costumes were designed by famed pin-up artist Vargas. AJ

Hugh Marlowe *John Borden* • Nancy Gates *Garnet* • Rod Taylor *Herbert Ellis* • Nelson Leigh *Dr Galbraithe* • Christopher Dark *Henry Jaffe* ■ *Dir/Scr* Edward Bernds

A World without Pity ★★★ 15

Romantic drama 1989 · Fr · Colour · 84mins

Eric Rochant's directorial debut is a French equivalent of the American slacker movie. Rochant won the César (France's Oscar equivalent) for best first film, while Yvan Attal took the best newcomer prize for his performance. His co-star, Hippolyte Girardot, is the waster who comes to realise there might be more to life than scamming and partying after he falls for the ultra-respectable Mireille Perrier. Rochant hurries through the action with a restless energy that reflects the pace of the young Parisians' lifestyle. DP. In French with English subtitles. Contains swearing.

Hippolyte Girardot *Hippo* • Mireille Perrier *Nathalie* • Yvan Attal *Halpern* • Jean-Marie Rollin *Xavier* • Cécile Mazan *Francine* • Aline Still *Mother* ■ *Dir/Scr* Eric Rochant

World without Sun ★★★★

Documentary 1964 · Fr · Colour · 90mins

Eight years after he won the best documentary Oscar for *The Silent World*, which he co-directed with Louis Malle, Captain Jacques-Yves Cousteau landed a second statuette for this account of his mission to the bottom of the Red Sea. Living one thousand feet below the surface in a prefabricated house, Cousteau and his oceanauts conducted a thorough investigation into the region's highly diverse plant life and encountered all manner of friendly and potentially lethal creatures. DP. In French with English commentary.

Dir Jacques-Yves Cousteau • *Scr* James Dugan, Al Ramrus, Jim Schmerer

The World's Greatest Athlete ★★★ U

Comedy 1973 · US · Colour · 88mins

In this hugely enjoyable nonsense from Disney, beleaguered coaches John Amos and Tim Conway return from a trip to Africa with jungle dweller Jan-Michael Vincent and his pet tiger. Vincent does a nice line in bewilderment and athletic prowess, but the main fun comes when one of the coaches is shrunk by witch doctor Roscoe Lee Browne and stumbles around some giant props. DP

Jan-Michael Vincent *Nanu* • Tim Conway *Milo* • John Amos *Coach Sam Archer* • Roscoe Lee Browne *Gazenga* • Dayle Haddon *Jane Douglas* • Nancy Walker *Mrs Petersen* • Danny Goldman *Leopold Maxwell* ■ *Dir* Robert Scheerer • *Scr* Gerald Gardner, Dee Caruso • *Music* Marvin Hamlisch

The World's Greatest Lover ★★ 15

Period comedy 1977 · US · Colour · 89mins

In the 1920s, Gene Wilder travels to Hollywood to enter a contest run by Rainbow Studios to find a screen lover to rival Paramount's Rudolph Valentino. His wife Carol Kane comes along for the ride but once in town she soon falls under the spell of the real Valentino (Matt Collins). Gene Wilder's slapstick-laden romantic comedy looks handsome enough but is derailed by some lame plotting and indifferent acting. Wilder's direction is understandably similar to that of his mentor Mel Brooks, but he needed to write himself a better script. DF

Gene Wilder *Rudy Hickman/Rudy Valentine* • Carol Kane *Annie Hickman* • Dom DeLuise *Zitz* • Fritz Feld *Hotel Manager* • Cousin Buddy • Matt Collins *Rudolph Valentino* ■ *Dir/Scr* Gene Wilder

The Worst Woman in Paris? ★

Drama 1933 · US · BW · 75mins

In Paris, pretty American art student Benita Hume is dubbed the city's "worst woman" by gossips because of her association with wealthy shipping tycoon Adolphe Menjou. She leaves for home, becomes the heroine of a train crash in Kansas, and gets involved in various other situations before returning to Paris. A series of jarringly different events make for a most peculiar plot in an odd, under-characterised movie. RK

Benita Hume *Peggy Vane* • Adolphe Menjou *Adolphe Ballou* • Harvey Stephens *John Strong* • Helen Chandler *Mary Dunbar* • Margaret Seddon *Mrs Strong* ■ *Dir* Monta Bell • *Scr* Monta Bell, Marion Dix

Would I Lie to You? ★★ 15

Comedy 1997 · Fr · Colour · 100mins

Director Thomas Gilou explores the experience of Paris's Sephardic Jews in this patchy rag-trade satire. The brash caricatures – such as José Garcia's wheeler-dealer and Elie Kakou's eccentric designer – whom Richard Anconina encounters when he's mistaken for a Jew by fabric merchant Richard Bohringer, helped make this a huge hit at the French box office. The humour doesn't travel well, however, while Anconina's attempt to prise Bohringer's daughter, Amira Casar, away from the shifty Anthony Delon frequently feels somewhat far-fetched. DP. In French, Arabic and English with subtitles.

Richard Anconina *Eddie Vuibert* • Amira Casar *Sandra Benzakem* • Vincent Elbaz *Dov Mimran* • Elie Kakou *Rafi Stylmod* • José Garcia *Serge Benamou* • Richard Bohringer *Victor Benzakem* • Anthony Delon *Maurice Aflalo* • Gilbert Melki *Patrick Abitbol* ■ *Dir* Thomas Gilou • *Scr* Gérard Bitton, Michel Munz

Woyzeck ★★★★ 15

Drama 1978 · W Ger · Colour · 77mins

Georg Büchner's famous anti-militarist play has never been more perceptively staged than by Werner Herzog and his on-screen alter ego, Klaus Kinski. Revisiting the Expressionist tropes he had so recently employed on *Nosferatu, the Vampire*, Herzog conveys the mental and spiritual disintegration of Kinski's impoverished soldier, as he endures not only the dietary experiments of a local quack and the bullying of his commanding officers, but also the humiliation of being cuckolded by his wife Eva Mattes. The heavy stylisation also reinforces the sense of socio-political and sexual suppression. DP. A German language film. DVD

Klaus Kinski *Woyzeck* • Eva Mattes *Marie* • Wolfgang Reichmann *Captain* • Willy Semmelrogge *Doctor* ■ *Dir* Werner Herzog • *Scr* Werner Herzog, from the play *Woyzeck* by Georg Büchner

The Wraith ★ 18

Supernatural action horror
1986 · US · Colour · 88mins

Charlie Sheen stars as a leather-clad avenging angel who returns to wreak revenge upon a gang of car thieves responsible for his death. It's a plot boring enough to make you play spot the famous sibling in the cast, which should keep you busy for most of the picture. RS

Charlie Sheen *Jake Kesey/The Wraith* • Nick Cassavetes *Packard Walsh* • Sherilyn Fenn *Keri Johnson* • Randy Quaid *Loomis* • Matthew Barry *Billy Hankins* • Clint Howard *Rughead* • David Sherrill *Skank* • James Bozian *Gutterboy* • Griffin O'Neal *Oggie Fisher* ■ *Dir/Scr* Mike Marvin

The Wrath of God ★★

Satirical western
1972 · US · Colour · 111mins

A certain sadness hangs over this banana republic epic since it marked the final screen appearance of Rita Hayworth, one of Hollywood's legendary sex goddesses who had developed Alzheimer's disease. She plays the mother of Frank Langella, a warlord in Central America in the 1920s, while Robert Mitchum is cast as a defrocked priest who carries a gun in his Bible and ends up wired to a crucifix. It's hard to tell if the aim was to make a surrealist drama, a black comedy or merely a post-Peckinpah exercise in violence. AT

Robert Mitchum *Father Van Horne* • Frank Langella *Tomas De La Plata* • Rita Hayworth *Senora De La Plata* • John Colicos *Colonel Santilla* • Victor Buono *Jennings* • Ken Hutchison *Emmet* • Paula Pritchett *Chela* ■ *Dir* Ralph Nelson • *Scr* Ralph Nelson, from the novel by James Graham

The Wreck of the Mary Deare ★★★ U

Adventure drama
1959 · US · Colour · 104mins

In a richly entertaining mystery adventure, Gary Cooper stars as the only man left on a freighter drifting in the English Channel when it is boarded by Charlton Heston's salvage expert. This MGM picture has some spectacular scenes at sea and is lavishly staged with a strong supporting cast in the later scenes. Cooper gives his co-star Heston a lesson in underplaying, while Michael Anderson's unshowy direction helps make this a fine late example of a highly polished studio product. AE

Gary Cooper *Gideon Patch* • Charlton Heston *John Sands* • Michael Redgrave *Mr Nyland* • Emlyn Williams *Sir Wilfred Falcett* • Cecil Parker *Chairman* • Alexander Knox *Petrie* • Virginia McKenna *Janet Taggart* • Richard Harris *Higgins* ■ *Dir* Michael Anderson • *Scr* Eric Ambler, from the novel by Hammond Innes

The Wrecking Crew ★★★ PG

Action spy comedy
1969 · US · Colour · 100mins

For the fourth and last of the Matt Helm spy spoofs starring Dean Martin, Phil Karlson, director of the original movie (*The Silencers*), was dragooned back into service. Helm has to locate tons of hijacked American bullion before its theft leads to economic meltdown. Needless to say, Helm's investigation involves the seduction of several women (including Sharon Tate), a trek across Europe and a lot of gadgets. Fans of Austin Powers will lap up its sexism, groovy styling and general lack of subtlety. AT

Dean Martin *Matt Helm* • Elke Sommer *Linka Karensky* • Sharon Tate *Freya Carlson* • Nancy Kwan *Yu-Rang* • Nigel Green *Count Massimo Contini* • Tina Louise *Lola Medina* • John Larch *MacDonald* • Chuck Norris *Garth* ■ *Dir* Phil Karlson • *Scr* William P McGivern, from the novel by Donald Hamilton • *Karate Advisor* Bruce Lee

Wrestling Ernest Hemingway ★★★ 12

Drama 1993 · US · Colour · 117mins

The most startling fact about this good-natured study of growing old in Florida is that it was actually written by a 23-year-old! Young screenwriter Steve Conrad provides meaty roles that are seized on with relish by Robert Duvall, as a lonely Cuban barber, and the sublime Richard Harris, as a flamboyant old sea dog. Extra spice is provided by the excellent supporting cast, and only Shirley MacLaine grates, with a performance that merely goes through the motions. Overall, however, this is poignant and likeable. TS

Robert Duvall *Walt* • Richard Harris *Frank* • Shirley MacLaine *Helen* • Sandra Bullock *Elaine* • Micole Mercurio *Bernice* • Marty Belafsky *Ned Ryan* • Harold Bergman *Sleeper* • Piper Laurie *Georgia* ■ *Dir* Randa Haines • *Scr* Steve Conrad

Wrestling with Alligators ★★★

Romantic drama
1998 · US/UK · Colour · 95mins

Even though rock 'n' roll was breaking down barriers, it's sometimes easy to forget just how many taboos survived into the late 1950s. Writer/director Laurie Weltz perhaps tries to tackle too many of them in this small-town melodrama, but her insights into teenage first love, abortion, matrimonial breakdown and faded glory are thoughtful and unhurried. Aleksa Palladino holds things together, as the runaway who befriends abandoned French war bride Joely Richardson. However, the standout is Claire Bloom, as an embittered silent movie star reduced to running a boarding house for waifs and strays. DP

Aleksa Palladino *Maddy Hawkins* • Joely Richardson *Claire* • Claire Bloom *Lulu Fraker* • Sam Trammell *Will* • Jay O Sanders *Rick* • Adrienne Shelly *Mary* • Tom Guiry *Pete* ■ *Dir* Laurie Weltz • *Scr* Laurie Weltz, Scott Kraft

Written on the Wind ★★★★ PG

Melodrama 1956 · US · Colour · 99mins

For all its flaunting of wealth and power, Douglas Sirk's movie is a brutal indictment of the way the American dream plunges spiritual values down-market. Rock Hudson and Lauren Bacall are the "normals" sucked into the hysterical paranoia of a Texas oil millionaire's spoilt offspring – Robert Stack and Oscar-winning Dorothy Malone are outstanding in their portrayals of unleashed anger and arousal. It could have been trashy, but in Sirk's masterful hands this becomes a riveting case history. TH

Rock Hudson *Mitch Wayne* • Lauren Bacall *Lucy Moore* • Robert Stack *Kyle Hadley* • Dorothy Malone *Marylee Hadley* • Robert Keith (1) *Jasper Hadley* • Grant Williams *Biff Miley* • Harry Shannon *Hoak Wayne* • Robert J Wilke *Dan Willis* ■ *Dir* Douglas Sirk • *Scr* George Zuckerman, from the novel by Robert Wilder • *Cinematographer* Russell Metty

The Wrong Arm of the Law ★★★★ U

Crime comedy 1962 · UK · BW · 90mins

Peter Sellers is at his funniest as a cockney criminal mastermind who uses a West End dress salon as a front for the illegal activities of his inept gang. He's up against inspector Lionel Jeffries, whose bungling would give the future Inspector Clouseau a run for his money. Cliff Owen directs the marvellously inventive script with due care as Scotland Yard and Sellers decide to co-operate to apprehend a bunch of Australian crooks posing as policemen. TH DVD

Peter Sellers *Pearly Gates* • Lionel Jeffries *Inspector Parker* • Bernard Cribbins *Nervous O'Toole* • Davy Kaye *Trainer King* • Nanette Newman *Valerie* • Bill Kerr *Jack Coombes* • John Le Mesurier *Assistant Commissioner* • Michael Caine ■ *Dir* Cliff Owen • *Scr* John Warren, Len Heath, Ray Galton, Alan Simpson, John Antrobus, from a story by Ivor Jay, William Whistance Smith

W

The Wrong Box ★★★ U

Period comedy 1966 · UK · Colour · 101mins

Shambolic and slackly directed, Bryan Forbes's overlong period comedy was based on a Robert Louis Stevenson original about the Tontine lottery. Fortunately it preserves a veritable cornucopia of British comedy talent in a film that owes more to the freewheeling Swinging Sixties than to the Victorian era in which it is set. The daft plot involves John Mills trying to kill Ralph Richardson over some inheritance nonsense, and among all this vintage talent new boy Michael Caine more than holds his own. TS

John Mills *Masterman Finsbury* • Ralph Richardson *Joseph Finsbury* • Michael Caine *Michael Finsbury* • Peter Cook *Morris Finsbury* • Dudley Moore *John Finsbury* • Nanette Newman *Julia Finsbury* • Tony Hancock *Detective* • Peter Sellers *Dr Pratt* • Wilfrid Lawson *Peacock* ■ *Dir* Bryan Forbes • *Scr* Larry Gelbart, Burt Shevelove, from the novel by Robert Louis Stevenson

The Wrong Guy ★★

Comedy 1997 · Can/US · Colour · 87mins

Kids in the Hall star Dave Foley plays a man on the run in this far from subtle parody of *The Fugitive*. In *Carry On*-style, Foley flees to Mexico after discovering his detested boss has been murdered, but the laughs are in short supply when the real murderer, Colm Feore, shows up in the same hideaway with detective David Anthony Higgins on his tail. DP

Dave Foley *Nelson Hibbert* • David Anthony Higgins *Detective Arlen* • Jennifer Tilly *Lynn Holden* • Joe Flaherty *Fred Holden* • Colm Feore *The Killer* ■ *Dir* David Steinberg • *Scr* Dave Foley, David Anthony Higgins, Jay Kogen

The Wrong Man ★★★★ PG

Crime drama based on a true story
1956 · US · BW · 100mins

This murky and unpopular film in the Alfred Hitchcock canon sees the maestro of suspense opting for a grim and stark style, almost documentary in nature, as he relates the true story of New York musician Manny Balestrero, arrested for a crime he did not commit. Henry Fonda is superbly believable in the title role, suggesting genuine puzzlement and dismay, and Vera Miles is a revelation as the wife who can't handle the situation. Only distinguished English thespian Anthony Quayle seems out of place in a role that needed an American actor. A fine and disturbing work that deserves to be better known. TS DVD

Henry Fonda *Christopher Emmanuel "Manny" Balestrero* • Vera Miles *Rose Balestrero* • Anthony Quayle *Frank O'Connor* • Harold J Stone *Lieutenant Bowers* • Esther Minciotti *Mrs Balestrero* • Charles Cooper *Detective Matthews* • Nehemiah Persoff *Gene Conforti* • Laurinda Barrett *Constance Willis* ■ *Dir* Alfred Hitchcock • *Scr* Maxwell Anderson, Angus MacPhail, from the non-fiction book *The True Story of Christopher Emmanuel Balestrero* by Angus MacPhail • *Cinematographer* Robert Burks • *Music* Bernard Herrmann

Wrong Turn ★★★ 18

Horror 2003 · US/Ger/Can · Colour · 80mins

Director Rob Schmidt pays tribute to 1970s exploitation cinema with this simplistic but satisfying horror feature. Mutant hillbillies are turning the woods of West Virginia into their personal (human) hunting ground, but the grisly extent of their "sport" only becomes clear when five campers and a stranded doctor fall prey to their cannibalistic urges. While Desmond Harrington and Eliza Dushku deliver the heroics, it's producer Stan Winston's special effects that steal the show. Pretension-free, but derivative, this really packs a punch. SF DVD

Desmond Harrington *Chris Finn* • Eliza Dushku *Jessie Burlingame* • Emmanuelle Chriqui *Carly* • Jeremy Sisto *Scott* • Kevin Zegers *Evan* • Lindy Booth *Francine* • Julian Richings *Three Finger* • Garry Robbins *Saw-Tooth* • Ted Clark *One-Eye* ■ *Dir* Rob Schmidt • *Scr* Alan B McElroy

Wrongfully Accused ★ PG

Crime spoof 1998 · US/Ger · Colour · 82mins

A non-stop assault of lame verbal and visual gags fails to elevate this second-rate spoof. Leslie Nielsen spreads himself alarmingly thin playing a superstar classical violinist accused of murder and on the run to find the real culprit, a one-armed, one-legged, one-eyed man. Pat Proft's rough-and-ready hotch-potch misses practically every single target it tries so desperately to hit. AJ. Contains swearing and sexual references.

Leslie Nielsen *Ryan Harrison* • Kelly LeBrock *Lauren Goodhue* • Michael York *Hibbing Goodhue* • Richard Crenna *Marshal Fergus Falls* • Sandra Bernhard *Doctor Fridley* ■ *Dir/Scr* Pat Proft

Wuthering Heights ★★★★★ U

Classic romantic drama
1939 · US · BW · 99mins

Laurence Olivier's Heathcliff is even more handsome than the Yorkshire moors across which he howls his doomed love for Cathy (Merle Oberon) in this stirring melodrama of seething and brooding passion set in England in the 19th century. Produced by Sam Goldwyn, directed by William Wyler, and also starring David Niven, Geraldine Fitzgerald and Flora Robson, this is still the best by some way of the five big screen versions of Emily Brontë's novel (including Spanish and Egyptian productions). It garnered eight Oscar nominations, including best picture, but only won one, for Gregg Toland's black-and-white cinematography. Had there also been an Oscar for best smouldering, Olivier would have walked it. PF DVD

Merle Oberon *Cathy Linton* • Laurence Olivier *Heathcliff* • David Niven *Edgar Linton* • Donald Crisp *Dr Kenneth* • Flora Robson *Ellen Dean* • Geraldine Fitzgerald *Isabella Linton* • Hugh Williams *Hindley Earnshaw* • Leo G Carroll *Joseph* • Cecil Humphreys *Judge Linton* ■ *Dir* William Wyler • *Scr* Ben Hecht, Charles MacArthur, from the novel by Emily Brontë

Wuthering Heights ★★★

Romantic drama 1953 · Mex · BW · 91mins

Luis Buñuel first set out to film Emily Brontë's classic novel in 1934, but lost interest in the idea. The same diminution of enthusiam occurred in 1953, but this time he found he could not withdraw and shot the film with a script in which he had little confidence. The Mexican uplands could not be more different from the Yorkshire moors, but they still provide a suitable backdrop for this intense drama of bitterness and revenge. Notable for the ferocity of Jorge Mistral, Irasema Dilian's passion and the cruelty inflicted on animals, the film clearly captures the book's glowering mood. DP. A Spanish language film.

Irasema Dilian *Catalina* • Jorge Mistral *Alejandro* • Lilia Prado *Isabel* • Ernesto Alonso *Eduardo* • Luis Aceves Castañeda *Ricardo* ■ *Dir* Luis Buñuel • *Scr* Luis Buñuel, Dino Maiuri [Arduino Maiuri], Julio Alejandro, from the novel *Wuthering Heights* by Emily Brontë

Wuthering Heights ★★★ U

Romantic drama 1970 · UK · Colour · 80mins

In this atmospheric adaptation of Emily Brontë's famous novel Timothy Dalton smoulders to good effect as Heathcliff and Anna Calder-Marshall makes an appealing Cathy. Obviously aiming for a little cultural respectability, producers Samuel Z Arkoff and James H Nicholson (co-founders of B-movie factory AIP) were rewarded with some striking images from cinematographer John Coquillon and steady direction from Robert Fuest. DP DVD

Anna Calder-Marshall *Catherine Earnshaw* • Timothy Dalton *Heathcliff* • Harry Andrews *Mr Earnshaw* • Pamela Brown *Mrs Linton* • Judy Cornwell *Nellie* • James Cossins *Mr Linton* • Rosalie Crutchley *Mrs Earnshaw* • Hilary Dwyer *Isabella Linton* ■ *Dir* Robert Fuest • *Scr* Patrick Tilley, from the novel by Emily Brontë

Wuthering Heights ★ PG

Romantic drama
1992 · UK · Colour · 101mins

Why there was a need for another adaptation of the Emily Brontë novel is one question. And then why adapt it so badly is the other. Ralph Fiennes and Juliette Binoche are poorly directed in this tepid tale of Heathcliff, the wild child orphan, and his lover Cathy. Binoche struggles with her English while they both fail to raise any sexual chemistry. LH DVD

Juliette Binoche *Cathy/Catherine* • Ralph Fiennes *Heathcliff* • Janet McTeer *Ellen Dean* • Sinead O'Connor *Emily Brontë* • Sophie Ward *Isabella Linton* • Simon Shepherd *Edgar Linton* • Jeremy Northam *Hindley Earnshaw* • Jason Riddington *Hareton* ■ *Dir* Peter Kosminsky • *Scr* Anne Devlin, from the novel by Emily Brontë

Wyatt Earp ★★★★ 12

Western drama 1994 · US · Colour · 182mins

Director Lawrence Kasdan's epic journey to the notorious shoot-out at the OK Corral is a monumental western that works both as a serious history lesson and as a quietly understated drama. Beautifully filmed, it portrays the man not the legend, tracing Earp's move from boyhood innocence to knowing cynicism. Kevin Costner has seldom been better as the older Earp, yet he still leaves plenty of room for Dennis Quaid to steal the show as the tuberculosis-ridden dentist Doc Holliday. AJ. Contains violence, swearing. DVD

Kevin Costner *Wyatt Earp* • Dennis Quaid *John "Doc" Holliday* • Gene Hackman *Nicholas Earp* • David Andrews *James Earp* • Linden Ashby *Morgan Earp* • Jeff Fahey *Ike Clanton* • Joanna Going *Josie Marcus* • Mark Harmon *Sheriff Johnny Behan* • Michael Madsen *Virgil Earp* • Catherine O'Hara *Allie Earp* • Bill Pullman *Ed Masterson* • Isabella Rossellini *Big Nose Kate* ■ *Dir* Lawrence Kasdan • *Scr* Lawrence Kasdan, Dan Gordon • *Cinematographer* Owen Roizman

Wyoming Mail ★★ U

Western 1950 · US · Colour · 86mins

This routine Universal western is made more interesting today by the fact that the supporting cast became more famous than unremarkable stars Stephen McNally and Alexis Smith. Future leading man Richard Egan steals the scenes he's in, while James Arness, the bargain-basement John Wayne, makes a strong impression in his pre-Matt Dillon days. Dull as ditchwater, thanks to Reginald LeBorg's turgid direction. TS

Stephen McNally *Steve Davis* • Alexis Smith *Mary Williams* • Howard Da Silva *Cavanaugh* • Ed Begley *Haynes* • Dan Riss *George Armstrong* • Roy Roberts *Charles DeHaven* • Whit Bissell *Sam Wallace* • James Arness *Russell* ■ *Dir* Reginald LeBorg [Reginald Le Borg] • *Scr* Harry Essex, Leonard Lee, from a story by Robert Hardy Andrews

Wyoming Outlaw ★★ U

Western 1939 · US · BW · 57mins

This is a routine *Three Mesquiteers* B-western, which John Wayne made before Republic recognised that his loan-out for *Stagecoach* had turned him into a major star. He puts a professional face on having to team up with Ray Corrigan and Raymond Hatton in another trite story, about helping an outlaw expose a crooked politician. Playing the outlaw is future western lead Don Barry. Silent star Elmo Lincoln came out of retirement for the small role of a US marshal. AE

John Wayne *Stony Brooke* • Ray "Crash" Corrigan *Tucson Smith* • Raymond Hatton *Rusty Joslin* • Don Barry [Donald Barry] *Will Parker* • Adele Pearce [Pamela Blake] *Irene Parker* • LeRoy Mason *Balsinger* • Charles Middleton *Luke Parker* • Katherine Kenworthy *Mrs Parker* • Elmo Lincoln *US marshal* • Yakima Canutt *Ed Sims* ■ *Dir* George Sherman • *Scr* Betty Burbridge, Jack Natteford, from a story by Jack Natteford, from characters created by William Colt MacDonald

W

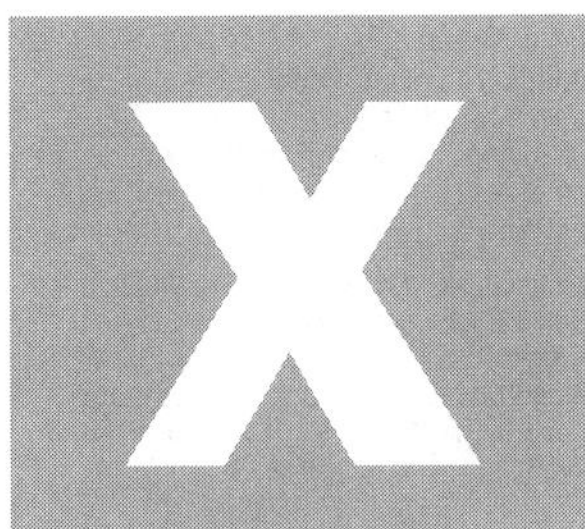

X-15 ★

Drama 1961 · US · Colour · 106mins

Charles Bronson climbs into X-15, a rocket that will take man into space. On the ground, meanwhile, various boffins and military types bombard us with technobabble. James Stewart's narration is intended to give this gravitas, but it nose-dived at the box office, though it did mark the debut of director Richard Donner. AT

David McLean *Matt Powell* • Charles Bronson *Lt Colonel Lee Brandon* • Ralph Taeger *Major Ernest Wilde* • Brad Dexter *Major Anthony Rinaldi* • Kenneth Tobey *Colonel Craig Brewster* • Mary Tyler Moore *Pamela Stewart* • James Stewart *Narrator* ■ *Dir* Richard Donner • *Scr* Tony Lazzarino, James Warner Bellah, from a story by Tony Lazzarino

The X-Files ★★★★ 15

Science-fiction thriller
1998 · US · Colour · 117mins

The TV phenomenon of the 1990s makes an effortless transition to the big screen, and, while the plot remains firmly grounded in the themes of the series, it plays equally well as a classy conspiracy thriller. Here, intrepid FBI duo Mulder and Scully (David Duchovny and Gillian Anderson) investigate an explosion at a federal building and stumble across the biggest alien cover-up in the world's history. Director Rob Bowman (who has also worked on the series) is faithful to the show's paranoiac roots, but gleefully opens the action out to stage some spectacular set pieces. JF. Contains violence, swearing. VIDEO DVD

David Duchovny *Special Agent Fox Mulder* • Gillian Anderson *Special Agent Dana Scully* • John Neville *Well-Manicured Man* • William B Davis *Cigarette-Smoking Man* • Martin Landau *Dr Alvin Kurtzweil* • Mitch Pileggi *FBI Assistant Director Walter Skinner* • Armin Mueller-Stahl *Strughold* ■ *Dir* Rob Bowman • *Scr* Chris Carter, from a story by Chris Carter, Frank Spotnitz

X-Men ★★★ 12

Fantasy action adventure
2000 · US · Colour · 104mins

Directed and co-written by Bryan Singer, this is set in the not-too-distant future and follows the power struggle between two factions of a new breed of humans with assorted strange powers – the good led by disabled professor Patrick Stewart and the bad led by Ian McKellen. The Marvel Comics characters are well realised and Singer mixes the classic values of good storytelling with liberal amounts of digital magic. On the down side, this plays a little too much like the beginning of a franchise and – with the exception of Stewart and McKellen – star quality is in rather short supply. AC. Contains violence. VIDEO DVD

Hugh Jackman *Logan/Wolverine* • Patrick Stewart *Professor Charles Xavier/Professor X* • Ian McKellen *Magneto/Erik Magnus Lehnsherr* • Famke Janssen *Jean Grey* • James Marsden *Scott Summers/Cyclops* • Halle Berry *Ororo Munroe/Storm* • Anna Paquin *Marie/Rogue* • Tyler Mane *Sabretooth* • Ray Park *Toad* • Rebecca Romijn-Stamos *Mystique* • Bruce Davison *Senator Robert Frank Kelly* ■ *Dir* Bryan Singer • *Scr* David Hayter, from a story by Tom DeSanto, Bryan Singer, from the characters created by Stan Lee, Jack Kirby

X2 ★★★★ 12

Fantasy action adventure
2003 · US · Colour · 128mins

This sequel to *X-Men* capitalises on the original's groundwork and pays the audience back in spades. This is what a mega-budget comic-book action movie should be and the pace never lets up. Former nemesis Magneto (played with relish by Ian McKellen) is now allied with the X-Men against Brian Cox's ruthless military scientist. Our Marvel heroes, again led by Hugh Jackman's cigar-chomping Wolverine and augmented by Alan Cumming's camp shape-shifter and a handsome new intake of students, are pleasingly human and a sharp script leavens the dark melancholy at the tale's core with soap-opera romance and comic one-liners. AC VIDEO DVD

Patrick Stewart *Professor Charles Xavier* • Hugh Jackman *Wolverine/Logan* • Ian McKellen *Magneto/Erik Magnus Lehnsherr* • Halle Berry *Storm/Ororo Munroe* • Famke Janssen *Dr Jean Grey* • James Marsden *Cyclops/Scott Summers* • Rebecca Romijn-Stamos *Mystique/Raven Darkholme* • Anna Paquin *Rogue/Marie D'Ancanto* • Alan Cumming *Nightcrawler/Kurt Wagner* • Brian Cox *General William Stryker* • Bruce Davison *Senator Robert Kelly* ■ *Dir* Bryan Singer • *Scr* Dan Harris [Daniel P Harris], Michael Dougherty, David Hayter, from a story by David Hayter, Bryan Singer, Zak Penn, from the graphic novel *God Lives, Man Kills* by Chris Claremont, Brent Anderson, from the characters created by Stan Lee, Jack Kirby

X the Unknown ★★ PG

Science-fiction horror
1956 · UK · BW · 75mins

In the wilds of Scotland there are some baffling deaths at an atomic research establishment. It could be bog-standard radiation leaks and poisoning but maybe something else is going on, some alien slime on the loose? A typical product of the Cold War, it's all jolly polite as British boffins are led by American import Dean Jagger. AT VIDEO DVD

Dean Jagger *Dr Adam Royston* • Edward Chapman *Elliott* • Leo McKern *McGill* • Marianne Brauns *Zena, nurse* • William Lucas *Peter Elliott* • John Harvey *Major Cartwright* • Peter Hammond *Lt Bannerman* ■ *Dir* Leslie Norman • *Scr* Jimmy Sangster

xXx ★★★ 12

Spy action thriller
2002 · US · Colour · 118mins

Vin Diesel cements his action-star status as "a new breed of secret agent", but, in every other respect, director Rob Cohen's film is just pure, turbo-driven exploitation. Diesel plays an extreme-sports hero who is coerced by US government agent Samuel L Jackson into infiltrating a Prague-based terrorist organisation. The movie lacks wit and consistency, but the stunts are overblown and outrageous enough to produce sheer adrenalin-pumping excitement. AJ. Contains violence, swearing. VIDEO DVD

Vin Diesel *Xander Cage, "X"* • Asia Argento *Yelena* • Marton Csokas *Yorgi* • Samuel L Jackson *Agent Augustus Gibbons* • Danny Trejo *El Jefe* • Michael Roof *Toby Lee Shavers* • Tom Everett *Senator Dick Hotchkiss* ■ *Dir* Rob Cohen • *Scr* Rich Wilkes

xXx: the Next Level ★★ 12A

Spy action thriller
2005 · US · Colour · 100mins

Ice Cube replaces Vin Diesel for this sequel, playing an imprisoned Special Ops soldier who's sprung by Samuel L Jackson's shadowy NSA agent to thwart Willem Dafoe's military coup against US President Peter Strauss. Not as good as the first film, it's entertaining enough for the videogame generation. DA. Contains violence and swearing.

Ice Cube *Darius Stone* • Willem Dafoe *George Deckert* • Samuel L Jackson *Augustus Gibbons* • Scott Speedman *Kyle Steele* • Xzibit *Zeke* • Peter Strauss *President Sanford* • Nona Gaye *Lola* • Sunny Mabrey *Charlie Mayweather* ■ *Dir* Lee Tamahori • *Scr* Simon Kinberg, from characters created by Rich Wilkes

XX/XY ★★ 15

Drama 2001 · US · Colour · 86mins

Superficially, Austin Chick's debut feature is a spicy slice of indie chic, but beneath the stylish veneer is an implausible world of narcissism and female immaturity. Fledgling animator Mark Ruffalo gets embroiled in a complicated three-way relationship with college girls Maya Stange and Kathleen Robertson. Ten years later a chance encounter sets the sexual sparks flying again. Only Ruffalo's vulnerable charm has any sort of appeal. Meandering and plodding. SF. Contains swearing, sex scenes and drug abuse. VIDEO DVD

Mark Ruffalo *Coles Burroughs* • Kathleen Robertson *Thea* • Maya Stange *Sam* • Petra Wright *Claire* • Kel O'Neill *Sid* • Joshua Spafford *Jonathon* • Zach Shaffer *Nick* • David Thornton *Miles* ■ *Dir/Scr* Austin Chick

Xala ★★★★ 12

Satirical comedy drama
1974 · Senegal · Colour · 117mins

This savage attack on the Senegal bourgeoisie and their eagerness to indulge in the vices of their former colonial masters is couched in terms of a hilarious sex comedy, in which Thierno Leye's political promotion coincides with his third marriage and the onset of impotence. His status and dignity crumble in the face of traditional curses and cures, and Leye becomes a symbol for outdated patriarchy. His wives, on the other hand, embrace diverse historical and contemporary influences, standing for the future. Ousmane Sembene confirmed his reputation as a key sub-Saharan film-maker. DP. In Senegalese and French with English subtitles. VIDEO

Thierno Leye *El Hadji Aboukader Beye* • Seune Samb *Adja Assatou* • Miriam Niang *Rama* ■ *Dir* Ousmane Sembene • *Scr* Ousmane Sembene, from his novel *Xala*

Xanadu ★ PG

Musical 1980 · US · Colour · 91mins

Olivia Newton-John stars as a muse, who's descended from her heavenly seat to inspire artist Michael Beck, in a veritable cult classic of camp and glitter, roller-skating dance numbers and Gene Kelly in his final feature film role. Unfortunately, it's also an excuse for dreadful song and dance numbers, a nonexistent plot and a dose of 1980s disco. Critically derided, it is a laugh if only for its mind-boggling awfulness. LH VIDEO DVD

Olivia Newton-John *Kira* • Gene Kelly *Danny McGuire* • Michael Beck *Sonny Malone* • James Sloyan *Simpson* • Dimitra Arliss *Helen* • Katie Hanley *Sandra* • Fred McCarren *Richie* ■ *Dir* Robert Greenwald • *Scr* Richard Christian Danus, Marc Reid Rubel, Michael Kane • *Music/lyrics* Jeff Lynne, John Farrar

XChange ★★★ 18

Futuristic action thriller
2000 · Can · Colour · 105mins

In this smart, swiftly paced futuristic thriller, a corporate executive is "floated" into another man's body to attend an important meeting (there wasn't time for air travel), then finds his own stand-in is a terrorist with a plan. More creative than the premise suggests, this is nicely performed by Kyle MacLachlan as the initial body swap and Stephen Baldwin as the short-life clone acquired as a means of escape. Although the action scenes are unremarkable, there's some clever ideas mined from the body-swap scenario, as well as a droll injection of black humour. JC VIDEO DVD

Stephen Baldwin *Clone No 1/Toffler 3* • Pascale Bussières *Madeleine Ranard* • Kim Coates *Toffler/Fisk 2* • Kyle MacLachlan *Fisk/Toffler 2* • Tom Rack *Mr Fineman* • Arnold Pinnock *Dickerson* ■ *Dir* Allan Moyle • *Scr* Christopher Pelham

Xiao Wu ★★★

Drama 1997 · Chi/HK · Colour · 113mins

Shot on 16mm and set in the provincial town of Fenyang, Jia Zhang Ke's directorial debut is a frank portrait of a society as much in the thrall of consumerism and the black market as rigid Beijing rhetoric. Non-professional Wang Hong Wei excels as the petty thief whose world falls apart because he has neither the resolve nor the resources to move with the times. With its ultra-naturalistic style, this is a blend of uncompromising social comment and sly wit. DP. In Mandarin with English subtitles.

Wang Hong Wei *Xiao Wu* ■ *Dir/Scr* Jia Zhang Ke

Xiu Xiu: The Sent Down Girl ★★★

Political drama
1999 · US/Tai/Chi · Colour · 110mins

Actress Joan Chen makes an accomplished directorial debut with this haunting tale of unconventional love in the dying days of the Chinese Cultural Revolution. Pretty tailor's daughter Lu Lu is "sent down" to the countryside to share her big city smarts with the peasantry. Though painfully slow in parts, Chen's powerful drama shows her to be a director of great promise. NS. In Mandarin with English subtitles.

Lu Lu *Xiu Xiu* • Qian Zheng *Li Chuanbei* • Gao Jie *Mother* • Lopsang *Lao Jin* ■ *Dir* Joan Chen • *Scr* Yan Geling, Joan Chen, from the story *Tian Yu* by Yan Geling

Xtro ★ 18

Science-fiction horror
1983 · UK · Colour · 82mins

British family man Philip Sayer is abducted by a UFO. Three years later, he returns to his family, claiming to remember nothing of what happened to him in the intervening years. Soon his wife and son begin to notice some odd behavior, like his penchant for eating snake eggs, and the string of horribly mutilated bodies he leaves in his wake. Released a year after *ET* with the tagline "Not all aliens are friendly", it's only memorable now for its incredibly graphic violence and for Maryam D'Abo's first film role (and her first nude scene). Surprising, this spawned two equally inferior sequels. ST VIDEO

Philip Sayer *Sam Phillips* • Bernice Stegers *Rachel Phillips* • Danny Brainin *Joe Daniels* • Simon Nash *Tony Phillips* • Maryam D'Abo *Analise* • David Cardy *Michael* ■ *Dir* Harry Bromley Davenport • *Scr* Robert Smith, Iain Cassie, Jo Ann Kaplan, from a screenplay (unproduced) by Harry Bromley Davenport, Michel Parry

Y Tu Mamá También ★★★ 18

Road movie comedy
2001 · Mex · Colour · 101mins

This road movie became the biggest home-grown box-office hit in Mexican history. There's more to it than sex as two high school graduates (played by Diego Luna and Gael García Bernal) borrow a car and head off for the mythical "Heaven's Mouth" beach with unhappily married older woman Maribel Verdú. Throughout the journey, director Alfonso Cuarón highlights the economic rift between Mexico's middle classes and poor with comments by a deadpan narrator. AC. In Spanish with English subtitles. Contains swearing, sex scenes, drug abuse and nudity. DVD

Maribel Verdú *Luisa Cortés* • Gael García Bernal *Julio Zapata* • Diego Luna *Tenoch Iturbide* • Marta Aura *Enriqueta "Queta" Allende* • Diana Bracho *Silvia Allende de Iturbide* ■ *Dir* Alfonso Cuarón • *Scr* Carlos Cuarón, Alfonso Cuarón

Yaaba ★★★ PG

Drama tragedy
1989 · Burkina Faso · Colour · 89mins

Inspired by the folk tales he heard as a child and played with finesse by a non-professional cast, Idrissa Ouedraogo's delicately paced, neorealist study of life in rural Burkina Faso returns to the familiar sub-Saharan themes of superstition, patriarchal arrogance and the need to strike a balance between tradition and progress. Young Noufou Ouedraogo is torn between personal feelings and communal responsibility as he tries to remain loyal to Fatima Sanga, a wizened yaaba, or grandmother, who has been ostracised by the village. DP. In Burkinabé with English subtitles.

Fatima Sanga *Yaaba* • Noufou Ouedraogo *Bila* • Roukietou Barry *Nopoko* • Adama Ouedraogo *Kougri* ■ *Dir/Scr* Idrissa Ouedraogo

Yaadein ★★★ PG

Romantic musical drama
2001 · Ind · Colour · 182mins

Hrithik Roshan is teamed for the first time with Kareena Kapoor in this sprawling melodrama from master showman Subhash Ghai. This explores the problems facing emigrant parents whose children don't see the relevance of traditional Indian values. The focus is on the young lovers, but Jackie Shroff and Anang Desai turn in nuanced performances as the restaurant owner and business tycoon, whose class rivalry stands in the way of true love. DP. In Hindi with English subtitles. DVD

Jackie Shroff *Raj Singh Puri* • Hrithik Roshan *Ronit Malhotra* • Kareena Kapoor *Isha Singh Puri* • Kiran Rathod *Monishka Rai* • Anang Desai *LK Mahotra* ■ *Dir/Scr* Subhash Ghai

Yahudi ★★★ U

Romantic melodrama
1958 · Ind · BW · 162mins

This is a classic Hindi film in Urdu about a Jewish woman and a Roman prince, Bimal Roy's movie is a version of the classic story, *The Jew's Daughter*. Set in Rome at a time of Jewish persecution, it portrays the tragic love affair between a couple separated by religion. The story offers both Shakespearian echoes and universal truths, but still has room for many popular songs. PF. In Urdu with English subtitles.

Dilip Kumar *Prince Marcus* • Sohrab Modi *Ezra, the Jew* • Meena Kumari *Hannah* ■ *Dir* Bimal Roy • *Scr* Nabendu Ghosh, from the play *The Jew's Daughter* by Agha Hashar

The Yakuza ★★★★ 15

Thriller 1975 · US/Jpn · Colour · 107mins

Robert Mitchum gives a brilliant performance as an ex-serviceman taking on the might of the Japanese underworld when the daughter of his best friend is kidnapped by gangsters. Writers Robert Towne (*Chinatown*) and Paul Schrader (*Taxi Driver*) working from a story by Schrader's brother Leonard, transform this simple idea into a complex and compelling thriller. Director Sydney Pollack sweeps the action along at a fast pace, allowing his cast plenty of room for manoeuvre and making the most of his Japanese locations. A must-see. TH. Contains violence and swearing.

Robert Mitchum *Harry Kilmer* • Ken Takakura *Ken Tanaka* • Brian Keith *George Tanner* • Herb Edelman *Oliver Wheat* • Richard Jordan *Dusty* • Keiko Kishi *Tanaka Eiko* • James Shigeta *Goro* ■ *Dir* Sydney Pollack • *Scr* Paul Schrader, Robert Towne, from a story by Leonard Schrader

The Yakuza Papers ★★★★ 18

Crime drama 1973 · Jpn · Colour · 98mins

The opening instalment of the crime series that forged Kinji Fukasaku's bloody reputation is a fearless indictment of the Japanese underworld and the descent of the bushido code into an excuse for pitiless brutality. The violence appalled contemporaries, yet there's no attempt to glorify the part played by Bunta Sugawara in Nobuo Kaneko's clan victory over Hiroshi Nawa. But he's accorded a shred of honour by the fact his fury is partly inspired by the death of his friend. DP. In Japanese with English subtitles. DVD

Bunta Sugawara *Hirono Shoz* • Hiroki Matsukata *Sakai Tetsuya* • Nobuo Kaneko • Tatsuo Umemiya *Wakasugi Hiroshi* • Hiroshi Nawa ■ *Dir* Kinji Fukasaku • *Scr* Kazuo Kasahara, from a story by Koichi Iiboshi

Yam Daabo ★★★

Drama 1986 · Burkina Faso · Colour · 80mins

This is a harrowing picture of the impact of drought and famine on Idrissa Ouedraogo's homeland, Burkina Faso. Just as the later *Yaaba* would rework the rites-of-passage picture, this is an sub-Saharan variation on the road movie, as a desperate family quits its parched farm and heads south in the hope of a fresh start. Some of the symbolism is heavy-handed, notably the hit-and-run death of the young son when they stop off in the city to sell their donkey, but the film concludes on a note of optimism. DP. In Burkinabé with English subtitles.

Auoa Guiraud *Mother* • Moussa Bologo *Bintou* • Assita Ouedraogo *Tipoko* ■ *Dir/Scr* Idrissa Ouedraogo

Yangtse Incident ★★★ PG

War drama based on a true story
1956 · UK · BW · 88mins

This adventure is a fact-based yarn about a British warship, HMS *Amethyst*, which sails up the Yangtse in 1949 intending to relieve the British embassy at Nanking. Instead, it comes under massive bombardment from Chinese communists, who blockade the river and trap the ship. Made less than ten years after Mao's revolution, one shouldn't expect an analysis of Chinese politics. What we get is standard British heroics from a crew commanded by Richard Todd, courtesy of an Eric Ambler script, efficiently handled by Michael Anderson. AT

Richard Todd *Lieutenant Commander Kerans* • William Hartnell *Leading Seaman Frank* • Akim Tamiroff *Colonel Peng* • Keye Luke *Captain Kuo Tai* • Donald Houston *Lieutenant Weston* • Robert Urquhart *Flight Lieutenant Fearnley* • Sophie Stewart *Charlotte Dunlap* ■ *Dir* Michael Anderson • *Scr* Eric Ambler, from the non-fiction book *Escape of the Amethyst* by Laurence Earl

A Yank at Eton ★★ U

Comedy drama 1942 · US · BW · 88mins

This is as much a wartime treatise on Anglo-American relations as an adolescent entertainment, yet it amuses, thanks to Mickey Rooney's well-honed blend of bluster and sentiment. Arriving in Blighty with a sizeable chip on his shoulder, following his mother's remarriage to horse-breeding landowner Ian Hunter, Rooney embarks on bucking the system, until he comes to appreciate its values and traditions. Pure corn. DP

Mickey Rooney *Timothy Dennis* • Edmund Gwenn *Justin* • Ian Hunter *Roger Carlton* • Freddie Bartholomew *Peter Carlton* • Marta Linden *Winifred Dennis Carlton* • Juanita Quigley *Jane "The Runt" Dennis* • Peter Lawford *Ronnie Kenvil* ■ *Dir* Norman Taurog • *Scr* George Oppenheimer, Lionel Houser, Thomas Phipps, from a story by George Oppenheimer

A Yank at Oxford ★★★

Comedy 1938 · US/UK · BW · 100mins

Designed to foster good relationships between Britain and America as Nazi stormclouds were gathering in Europe, this is the movie that marked the moment when Hollywood star factory MGM set up production in the heart of Ye Olde England. Robert Taylor plays a brash American student at Oxford who shines at athletics and gains the envy of his fellow students while Maureen O'Sullivan goes weak at the knees at the very sight of him. It's still good fun, especially for the Hollywood view of the way we were then. AT

Robert Taylor (1) *Lee Sheridan* • Lionel Barrymore *Dan Sheridan* • Maureen O'Sullivan *Molly Beaumont* • Vivien Leigh *Elsa Craddock* • Edmund Gwenn *Dean of Cardinal College* • Griffith Jones *Paul Beaumont* • CV France *Dean Snodgrass* • Edward Rigby *Scatters* ■ *Dir* Jack Conway • *Scr* Malcolm Stuart Boylan, Walter Ferris, George Oppenheimer, Roland Pertwee, F Scott Fitzgerald, Frank Wead, Angus MacPhail, from a story by Leon Gordon, Sidney Gilliat, Michael Hogan, from an idea by John Monk Saunders

A Yank in Ermine ★★ U

Comedy 1955 · UK · Colour · 84mins

As there had already been a Yank at Oxford and in the RAF, it was only a matter of time before one was elevated to the peerage. Unfortunately, he came in the shape of Peter Thompson, a particularly charmless specimen of American manhood. Admittedly, he's not helped by a damp squib of a script, adapted by John Paddy Carstairs from his own novel. DP

Peter M Thompson *Joe Turner* • Jon Pertwee *"Slowburn" Jenks* • Noelle Middleton *Angela* • Harold Lloyd Jr *"Butch" Halliday* • Diana Decker *Gloria* • Reginald Beckwith *Kimp* • Edward Chapman *Duke of Fontenham* • Richard Wattis *Boone* • Guy Middleton *Bertram Maltravers* • Harry Locke *Clayton* ■ *Dir* Gordon Parry • *Scr* John Paddy Carstairs, from his novel *Solid, Said the Earl*

A Yank in the RAF ★★ U

Second World War romance
1941 · US · BW · 93mins

The need for a patriotic lift was often enough to get audiences into the threepenny fleapits. Here, aside from Betty Grable giving it her all-singing, all-dancing all in a couple of numbers, this is a bit of a damp squib. The stars look good, however, with Tyrone Power as a cocky American pilot and Grable as the girlfriend. JM DVD

Tyrone Power *Tim Baker* • Betty Grable *Carol Brown* • John Sutton *Wing Commander Morley* • Reginald Gardiner *Roger Pillby* • Donald Stuart *Corporal Harry Baker* • John Wilde *Graves* • Richard Fraser *Thorndyke* • Morton Lowry *Squadron Leader* ■ *Dir* Henry King • *Scr* Darrell Ware, Karl Tunberg, from a story by Melville Crossman [Darryl F Zanuck]

Yankee Doodle Dandy ★★★★ U

Musical biography 1942 · US · BW · 125mins

Under director Michael Curtiz's wing, the great James Cagney gives the performance of his life as Broadway's George M Cohan. The film needs to be viewed in context today; it is fearsomely patriotic, overlong to a degree and extremely sentimental, but it was geared to serve a major purpose. It reminded Americans that there was a war going on in Europe and, in saluting the composer of *Over There*, Warner Bros fashioned a celluloid recruiting poster. So, if you find it heavy going, bear with it for Cagney's classic dance routines: if you only know him as a gangster, here's the reminder that he was a match for both Gene Kelly and Fred Astaire. TS

James Cagney *George M Cohan* • Joan Leslie *Mary* • Walter Huston *Jerry Cohan* • Richard Whorf *Sam Harris* • George Tobias *Dietz* • Irene Manning *Fay Templeton* • Rosemary DeCamp *Nellie Cohan* • Jeanne Cagney *Josie Cohan* • SZ Sakall *Schwab* ■ *Dir* Michael Curtiz • *Scr* Robert Buckner, Edmund Joseph, from a story by Buckner

Yankee Pasha ★★ U

Period romantic adventure
1954 · US · Colour · 83mins

Technicolored tosh set in the early 19th century, this features Rhonda Fleming as the New England gal captured by Barbary pirates and sold to a Moroccan sultan for his harem. Jeff Chandler is her rough-and-ready boyfriend who comes to the rescue. Mamie Van Doren, Universal's potential rival to Marilyn Monroe, is one of the harem slaves, while the others are Miss Universe beauty contestants. This covers a lot of territory without ever becoming interesting. AE

Jeff Chandler *Jason* • Rhonda Fleming *Roxana* • Mamie Van Doren *Lilith* • Bart Roberts [Rex Reason] *Omar-Id-Din* • Lee J Cobb *Sultan* ■ *Dir* Joseph Pevney • *Scr* Joseph Hoffman, from the novel by Edison Marshall

Yanks ★★★ 15

Second World War romantic drama
1979 · UK · Colour · 133mins

This pleasing effort from director John Schlesinger glows with a homely period charm, but never descends into sentimentality. Richard Gere stars in this story is about GIs stationed in Britain during the Second World War, and Schlesinger gives a nice touch to the juxtaposition of British working-class morality on a collision course with young adult hormones. The strong ensemble cast interplays well, and the scene where the lads march off for D-Day is moving. SH DVD

Richard Gere *Sergeant Matt Dyson* • Vanessa Redgrave *Helen* • William Devane *John* • Lisa Eichhorn *Jean Moreton* • Chick Vennera *Sergeant Danny Ruffelo* • Rachel Roberts (1) *Clarrie Moreton* • Tony Melody *Jim Moreton* • Wendy Morgan *Mollie* ■ *Dir* John Schlesinger • *Scr* Walter Bernstein, Colin Welland, from his story

The Yards ★★★ 15

Crime drama 2000 · US · Colour · 110mins

New York's mass transit train yards provide the backdrop for this brooding tale of murder and union corruption. The top-notch cast includes Mark Wahlberg as a newly sprung con, Joaquin Phoenix as his hair-trigger buddy and James Caan as his grafting uncle. But director James Gray wastes what could have been the film's greatest asset – the atmospheric marshalling yards – while the strong female contingent is underemployed. A tough, workmanlike drama, but lacking pace and personality. DP. Contains violence, swearing and brief nudity. [VIDEO] DVD

Mark Wahlberg *Leo Handler* • Joaquin Phoenix *Willie Gutierrez* • Charlize Theron *Erica Stoltz* • James Caan *Frank Olchin* • Ellen Burstyn *Val Handler* • Faye Dunaway *Kitty Olchin* • Steve Lawrence *Arthur Mydanick* ■ *Dir* James Gray • *Scr* James Gray, Matt Reeves

The Year My Voice Broke ★★★★ 15

Drama 1987 · Aus · Colour · 100mins

One of those rare movies about teenagers that doesn't treat them as an alien species, this neither patronises nor exploits. That's because writer/director John Duigan constructs his piece with understanding and insight, while the young actors in the lovesick triangle – Noah Taylor, Loene Carmen, Ben Mendelsohn – bring their characters to life with subtle authority. The story continues in the even better *Flirting* (1989). TH. Contains swearing. [VIDEO]

Noah Taylor *Danny Embling* • Loene Carmen *Freya Olson* • Ben Mendelsohn *Trevor* • Graeme Blundell *Nils Olson* • Lynette Curran *Anne Olson* • Malcolm Robertson *Bruce Embling* • Judi Farr *Sheila Embling* ■ *Dir/Scr* John Duigan

The Year of Living Dangerously ★★★★ PG

Political thriller
1982 · Aus/US · Colour · 109mins

This atmospheric thriller sees Aussie radio journalist Mel Gibson on assignment in Indonesia in the mid-1960s, where the dictatorship is shaky and Sigourney Weaver is working as an attaché at the British embassy. Peter Weir's film wanders at times, but also offers plenty of spectacle and colour, a steamy romance between Gibson and Weaver, and its share of excitement when Gibson discovers more than it is safe for him to know. But the highlight is Linda Hunt's performance as a male Chinese-Australian photographer, for which she won an Oscar. PF. Contains swearing. [VIDEO]

Mel Gibson *Guy Hamilton* • Sigourney Weaver *Jill Bryant* • Linda Hunt *Billy Kwan* • Bembol Roco *Kumar* • Domingo Landicho *Hortono* • Hermino De Guzman *Immigration officer* • Michael Murphy *Pete Curtis* • Noel Ferrier *Wally O'Sullivan* ■ *Dir* Peter Weir • *Scr* David Williamson, Peter Weir, CJ Koch, from the novel by CJ Koch

Year of the Comet ★★★ PG

Romantic comedy adventure
1992 · US · Colour · 86mins

This sardonic screwball adventure is set around the Scottish Highlands and the French Riviera. Wine merchant Penelope Ann Miller discovers a rare bottle of wine worth $1 million and plans to escort it to auction. But bon viveur villain Louis Jourdan wants it because written on the label is a formula for the elixir of life. Tim Daly is the suave action man hero who accidentally gets sucked into the *Boy's Own* adventure complete with offbeat action and sassy one-liners. An under-rated black comedy romp with many fun moments. AJ [VIDEO] DVD

Penelope Ann Miller *Maggie Harwood* • Timothy Daly *Oliver Plexico* • Louis Jourdan *Philippe* • Art Malik *Nico* • Ian Richardson *Sir Mason Harwood* • Ian McNeice *Ian* • Timothy Bentinck *Richard Harwood* • Julia McCarthy *Landlady* ■ *Dir* Peter Yates • *Scr* William Goldman

Year of the Dragon ★★ 18

Crime drama 1985 · US · Colour · 128mins

Michael Cimino's violent crime thriller is unexceptional in every respect, barring some accusations of inherent Asian racism. With a script co-written by Oliver Stone, this sour-tasting tale of highly decorated cop Mickey Rourke cleaning up corrupt Chinatown features some incredibly intense action and one of Rourke's more believable characterisations. Trouble is, there's not a likeable character in sight, the tone is absurdly melodramatic and it seems to go on forever. JC [VIDEO] DVD

Mickey Rourke *Stanley White* • John Lone *Joey Tai* • Ariane *Tracy Tzu* • Leonard Termo *Angelo Rizzo* • Raymond Barry [Raymond J Barry] *Louis Bukowski* • Caroline Kava *Connie White* • Eddie Jones *William McKenna* ■ *Dir* Michael Cimino • *Scr* Oliver Stone, Michael Cimino, from the novel by Robert Daley

Year of the Gun ★★★ 15

Political thriller 1991 · US · Colour · 107mins

Set in Rome in 1978, when the Red Brigades terrorist group was active, this reasonably gripping and intriguing thriller follows the fortunes of two journalists. Andrew McCarthy is writing a novel that features a fictitious terrorist mission; Sharon Stone is a photographer whose efforts to gatecrash McCarthy's project and his love life lead to mayhem. While Stone looks good and looks the part, too, the main problem is the bland McCarthy. AT. Contains violence, swearing, nudity. [VIDEO] DVD

Andrew McCarthy *David Raybourne* • Sharon Stone *Alison King* • Valeria Golino *Lia Spinelli* • John Pankow *Italo Bianchi* • George Murcell *Pierre Bernier* • Mattia Sbragia *Giovanni* • Roberto Posse *Lucio Spinelli* • Thomas Elliot *Marco Spinelli* ■ *Dir* John Frankenheimer • *Scr* David Ambrose, from the novel by Michael Mewshaw

The Year of the Horse ★ 15

Musical documentary
1997 · US · BW and Colour · 107mins

Even fans of folk rocker Neil Young and his band Crazy Horse will find this arch rockumentary tedious. Filmed in Europe and America during the group's 1996 tour, cult director Jim Jarmusch combines new concert footage with archive material of Young when he was at the height of his popularity. Jarmusch's minimalist style and the band's boring musings provide little insight into the Crazy Horse universe and many will be left wondering why they even bothered. AJ. Contains swearing and drug abuse.

Dir Jim Jarmusch • *Cinematographer* Jim Jarmusch, LA Johnson

A Year of the Quiet Sun ★★★★ 15

Romantic drama
1984 · Pol/US/W Ger · Colour · 108mins

The winner of the Golden Lion at Venice, Krzysztof Zanussi's gentle love story, involving an emotionally fractured GI and a fatalistic Polish widow, is set in 1946 against a backdrop of political transformation, war-crimes trials and lingering psychological trauma. Using the devastated landscape to contrast the inhumanity of war with the indomitability of the human spirit, Zanussi similarly sets the couple's communication difficulties against their tentative passion. Scott Wilson and Maja Komorowska excel, while Zanussi's direction has a keen sense of place and poetry. DP. In Polish and English with subtitles.

Maja Komorowska *Emilia* • Scott Wilson *Norman* • Hanna Skarzanka *Emilia's mother* • Ewa Dalkowska *Stella* • Vadiln Glowna *Niemiec* • Daniel Webb *David* ■ *Dir/Scr* Krzysztof Zanussi

The Yearling ★★★★ U

Drama 1946 · US · Colour · 122mins

This lovely story of a boy and his pet fawn, based on Marjorie Kinnan Rawlings's Pulitzer Prize-winning novel, takes its strength from an understatement of dramatic events and the underplaying of the actors (Gregory Peck and Jane Wyman as poor crop farmers; special Oscar-winning Claude Jarman Jr as their son). Director Clarence Brown shapes it into a tale that touches the heart while never patronising the mind. Sentiment without sentimentality. TH [VIDEO]

Gregory Peck *Pa Baxter* • Jane Wyman *Ma Baxter* • Claude Jarman Jr *Jody Baxter* • Chill Wills *Buck Forrester* • Clem Bevans *Pa Forrester* • Margaret Wycherly *Ma Forrester* • Henry Travers *Mr Boyles* • Forrest Tucker *Lem Forrester* • Donn Gift *Fodderwing* ■ *Dir* Clarence Brown • *Scr* Paul Osborn, from the novel by Marjorie Kinnan Rawlings

The Years Between ★★

Drama 1946 · UK · BW · 108mins

Marital harmony and political ambition are severely challenged when an MP, supposed killed in the war, turns up alive to find his wife has taken over his seat in parliament and is about to remarry. She gives him back his seat but determines to pursue her own career in politics. This poorly scripted adaptation verges on the unsuitably melodramatic, but the glamorous casting of Michael Redgrave and Valerie Hobson as the couple renders it watchable. RK

Michael Redgrave *Colonel Michael Wentworth* • Valerie Hobson *Diana Wentworth* • Flora Robson *Nanny* • James McKechnie *Richard Llewellyn* • Felix Aylmer *Sir Ernest Foster* • Dulcie Gray *Jill* ■ *Dir* Compton Bennett • *Scr* Muriel Box, Sydney Box, from the play by Daphne du Maurier

Yeelen ★★★★ PG

Fantasy 1987 · Mali · Colour · 104mins

The timeless significance of ancient custom to the Bambara peoples of Mali is explored in this haunting political fable from Souleymane Cissé. Having been threatened with death by his shaman father, Issiaka Kane goes into exile, where he learns the power and value of the magical gifts he will need to succeed in his Oedipal struggle. Although much of the symbolism is as obscure to non-Malian viewers as the story's historical background, there's no denying the simple poetry of the landscape or Cissé's technical mastery, as he explores in minute detail the secret Komo rituals that will ensure prosperity through self-sacrifice. DP. In Bambara with English subtitles.

Issiaka Kane *Nianankoro* • Aova Sangere *Attu* • Niamanto Sanogo *Soma* • Balla Moussa Keita *Peul King* ■ *Dir/Scr* Souleymane Cissé

The Yellow Balloon ★★

Crime drama 1952 · UK · BW · 79mins

This is typical of the many dour dramas churned out by postwar British cinema. Writer/director, J Lee Thompson would have done better to focus on the relationship between timid pre-teen Andrew Ray and fugitive killer William Sylvester, but he can't resist throwing in a social message and a family crisis that slows the action and dilutes the suspense. Kenneth More flops as the doting dad, but Kathleen Ryan makes a monstrously shrewish mother. DP

Andrew Ray *Frankie* • Kathleen Ryan *Em* • Kenneth More *Ted* • Bernard Lee *Constable Chapman* • Stephen Fenemore *Ron* • William Sylvester *Len* • Marjorie Rhodes *Mrs Stokes* • Peter Jones *Spiv* • Eliot Makeham *Pawnbroker* • Sidney James *Barrow boy* ■ *Dir* J Lee Thompson • *Scr* Anne Burnaby, J Lee Thompson, from the story by Anne Burnaby

The Yellow Cab Man ★★★ U

Comedy 1950 · US · BW · 84mins

Three years after he stole the show from Cary Grant and Loretta Young in *The Bishop's Wife*, that unsung character actor James Gleason was back behind the wheel of a cab for this knockabout Red Skelton vehicle. Indeed, it's the supporting cast that keeps this scatterbrained comedy on the road, as Skelton mugs along in typical fashion as an eccentric inventor who causes chaos wherever he goes. Walter Slezak is a standout as the unscrupulous villain desperate to get his hands on the secret of unbreakable glass. DP

Red Skelton *Augustus "Red" Pirdy* • Gloria DeHaven *Ellen Goodrich* • Walter Slezak *Doctor Byron Dokstedder* • Edward Arnold *Martin Creavy* • James Gleason *Mickey Corkins* ■ *Dir* Jack Donohue • *Scr* Devery Freeman, Albert Beich, from a story by Devery Freeman

Yellow Canary ★★ U

Second World War spy drama
1943 · UK · BW · 98mins

Anna Neagle stars as an improbable British spy, pretending to be a Nazi sympathiser in Canada. Director Herbert Wilcox hasn't a clue how to build the thrills inherent in this kind of material, and as Neagle and her intelligence shadow Richard Greene sabotage the Nazi plot to blow up a Nova Scotia harbour, the whole thing becomes gently risible. TS

Anna Neagle *Sally Maitland* • Richard Greene *Jim Garrick* • Margaret Rutherford *Mrs Towcester* • Nova Pilbeam *Betty Maitland* • Albert Lieven *Jan Orlock* • Lucie Mannheim *Madame Orlock* • Marjorie Fielding *Lady Maitland* ■ *Dir* Herbert Wilcox • *Scr* Miles Malleson, DeWitt Bodeen, from a story by Pamela Bower

The Yellow Canary ★★

Thriller 1963 · US · BW · 92mins

Pop star Pat Boone and his wife Barbara Eden are experiencing marriage difficulties. But their differences are forgotten when they return home one night to find their nursemaid murdered and their baby son missing. The kidnappers have left a note citing "canary" as a code word in future dealings and soon a $200,000 ransom demand is made. A by-numbers thriller with sadly few twists and turns en route. DF

Pat Boone *Andy Paxton* • Barbara Eden *Lissa* • Steve Forrest *Hub Wiley* • Jack Klugman *Lieutenant Bonner* • Jesse White *Ed Thornburg* ■ *Dir* Buzz Kulik • *Scr* Rod Serling, from the novel *Evil Come, Evil Go* by Whit Masterson

Yellow Earth ★★★★★ U

Period drama 1984 · Chi · Colour · 90mins

This adaptation of Ke Lan's novel was a key film in the evolution of Fifth Generation Chinese cinema. Set in 1939, the story concerns the hopes of emancipation raised in a peasant girl by a soldier on a mission to collect folk songs. Inspired by the compositional values of traditional art, debuting director Chen Kaige and cinematographer Zhang Yimou firmly root the characters in their desolate Shaanxi environment and use space, colour and nuance to suggest the contrast between Communist zeal and rural complacency. More philosophical than political, this is also a provocative treatise on the need for a balance between tradition and progress. DP

Xue Bai • Wang Xueqi • Tan Tuo • Liu Qiang ■ *Dir* Chen Kaige • *Scr* Zhang Ziliang from the novel by Ke Lan

Yellow Jack ★★★

Period drama 1938 · US · BW · 83mins

In Cuba at the end of the 19th century, an American medical research team led by a lifeless Lewis Stone battles to find the cause of yellow fever – or "yellow jack" as the American soldiers call it – that is decimating the country. Irish sergeant Robert Montgomery and four of his men eventually answer the call for volunteers for a life-threatening experiment. Although informative, intelligent, and even at times gripping, the uneven script periodically collapses into dull repetition. RK

Robert Montgomery *John O'Hara* • Virginia Bruce *Frances Blake* • Lewis Stone *Major Walter Reed* • Andy Devine *Charlie Spell* • Henry Hull *Dr Jesse Lazear* • Charles Coburn *Dr Finlay* • Buddy Ebsen *Jellybeans* ■ *Dir* George B Seitz • *Scr* Edward Chodorov, from the play by Sidney Howard, Paul de Kruif

The Yellow Mountain ★★

Western 1954 · US · Colour · 77mins

The "yellow" in the mountain is gold, of course, and it leads to some pretty unremarkable sparring between former Tarzan Lex Barker and former radio actor Howard Duff in a very average Universal western. Produced by Ross Hunter before he got into his stride as the purveyor of gloss 'n' froth. TS

Lex Barker *Andy Martin* • Mala Powers *Nevada Wray* • Howard Duff *Pete Menlo* • William Demarest *Jackpot Wray* • John McIntire *Bannon* • Leo Gordon *Drake* ■ *Dir* Jesse Hibbs • *Scr* George Zuckerman, Russell Hughes, Robert Blees, from a story by Harold Channing Wire

Yellow Pages ★★ 15

Spoof thriller 1984 · UK/US · Colour · 87mins

This uneven comedy was made in 1984, but for some odd reason (because it was a clunker, perhaps?) remained unseen for four years. Lea Thompson is the spoilt brat on a trip to Europe who is kept under surveillance by Chris Lemmon, a private eye so unskilled that she gets kidnapped right under his nose. Incredibly silly stuff, it's notable only for the supporting performances of Jean Simmons and Viveca Lindfors, who manage to rise above the otherwise poor material. JB

Chris Lemmon *Henry Brilliant* • Jean Simmons *Maxine De La Hunt* • Lea Thompson *Marigold De La Hunt* • Viveca Lindfors *Mrs Bellinger* • Mills Watson *Billy O'Shea* • Nancy Cartwright *Stephanie* ■ *Dir/Scr* James Kenelm Clarke

The Yellow Rolls-Royce ★★

Drama 1964 · UK · Colour · 121mins

A typically British trilogy of thin anecdotes about the owners of a Rolls-Royce Phantom II – four wheels, famous radiator, painted yellow, three careful owners. The writer and director have a similar pedigree, though Terence Rattigan and Anthony Asquith's readiness to recycle their previous excursion into jet-set gloss, *The VIPs*, seemed a foolish idea in the first place. The European locations match poorly with the kitsch sets and the whole thing seems all dressed up with nowhere to go. AT

Rex Harrison *Marquess of Frinton* • Jeanne Moreau *Marchioness of Frinton* • Edmund Purdom *John Fane* • Michael Hordern *Harmsworth* • Shirley MacLaine *Mae Jenkins* • George C Scott *Paolo Maltese* • Alain Delon *Stefano* • Art Carney *Joey* • Ingrid Bergman *Gerda Millett* • Omar Sharif *Davich* • Joyce Grenfell *Hortense Astor* • Wally Cox *Ferguson* ■ *Dir* Anthony Asquith • *Scr* Terence Rattigan

The Yellow Rose of Texas ★★ U

Western 1944 · US · BW · 69mins

There's a showboat setting for this otherwise routine Roy Rogers western in which Dale Evans plays opposite him: more than two dozen further co-starring roles and off-screen marriage would follow. Here Evans runs the showboat and gives Rogers a singing job on board, not knowing he's an insurance investigator after money supposedly stolen by her father. AE

Roy Rogers • Dale Evans *Betty Weston* • Grant Withers *Lukas* • Harry Shannon *Sam Weston* • George Cleveland *Captain Joe* ■ *Dir* Joseph Kane • *Scr* Jack Townley

Yellow Sky ★★★

Western 1948 · US · BW · 96mins

Highly regarded in many critical quarters, this bleak western owes much to superb location photography by Joe MacDonald, and to the confrontational leading roles played by two of 20th Century Fox's best stars – Gregory Peck and Richard Widmark – in their glorious early years. But the pace is often staggeringly slow and the story, which is clearly inspired by Shakespeare's *The Tempest*, sits awkwardly in its majestic Death Valley setting. TS

Gregory Peck *Stretch* • Anne Baxter *Mike* • Richard Widmark *Dude* • Robert Arthur *Bull Run* • John Russell *Lengthy* • Henry Morgan [Harry Morgan] *Half Pint* • James Barton *Grandpa* • Charles Kemper *Walrus* • Robert Adler *Jed* ■ *Dir* William A Wellman • *Scr* Lamar Trotti, from the novel by WR Burnett

Yellow Submarine ★★★★ U

Animated musical fantasy
1968 · UK · Colour · 86mins

The Beatles had little to do with this amazing animated feature (although they do crop up at the end). Directed by George Dunning and boasting *Love Story*'s Erich Segal among the screenwriters, this is an endlessly inventive picture that blends 1960s psychedelia with such diverse styles as pop art and Art Deco to create the fantastical world of Pepperland and its bizarre inhabitants. The mix of new songs and old favourites works a treat, but George Martin's superb score is also worth a listen. DP DVD

John Clive *John* • Geoffrey Hughes *Paul* • Peter Batten *George* • Paul Angelis *Ringo/ Chief Blue Meanie* • Dick Emery *Lord Mayor/ Nowhere Man/Max* • Lance Percival *Old Fred* ■ *Dir* George Dunning • *Scr* Lee Minoff, Al Brodax, Erich Segal, Jack Mendelsohn, from a story by Lee Minoff, from the song by John Lennon, Paul McCartney

The Yellow Tomahawk ★★

Western 1954 · US · Colour · 82mins

Feathers fly in a strongly pro-Indian western as Rory Calhoun's scout is forced to fight his good friend, Lee Van Cleef's Cheyenne warrior. The yellow tomahawk is sent as a declaration of war to Warner Anderson's arrogant army major who has massacred native American women and children and plans to build a fort in their territory. Peggie Castle has the female lead while Rita Moreno plays an Indian woman called Honey Bear. Veteran B-western director Lesley Selander puts pace before subtlety. AE

Rory Calhoun *Adam* • Peggie Castle *Katherine* • Noah Beery Jr *Tonio* • Warner Anderson *Major Ives* • Peter Graves (2) *Sawyer* • Lee Van Cleef *Fireknife* • Rita Moreno *Honey Bear* • Walter Reed *Keats* ■ *Dir* Lesley Selander • *Scr* Richard Alan Simmons, from a story by Harold Jack Bloom

Yellowbeard ★ 15

Comedy adventure
1983 · US · Colour · 92mins

What a way to go! Surely Marty Feldman deserved a better screen swan song than this diabolical comedy. Co-stars Graham Chapman and Peter Cook should have been made to walk the plank for their contributions to a sloppy script, and they can count themselves lucky that the cast was made up of old friends, otherwise they might have had a mutiny on their hands. Awful is charitable. DP. Contains violence, swearing and nudity.

Graham Chapman *Yellowbeard* • Peter Boyle *Moon* • Richard "Cheech" Marin *El Segundo* • Tommy Chong *El Nebuloso* • Peter Cook *Lord Lambourn* • Marty Feldman *Gilbert* • Michael Hordern *Dr Gilpin* • Eric Idle *Commander Clement* • James Mason *Captain Hughes* • John Cleese *Blind Pew* • Spike Milligan *Flunkie* • Susannah York *Lady Churchill* • Beryl Reid *Lady Lambourn* ■ *Dir* Mel Damski • *Scr* Graham Chapman, Peter Cook, Bernard McKenna

Yellowstone Kelly ★★★ U

Western 1959 · US · Colour · 92mins

Veteran Warner Bros director Gordon Douglas is in charge as buckskin-clad Clint Walker attempts to quell an "Injun" uprising, supported by other TV names of the time such as Edward Byrnes (*77 Sunset Strip*) and *The Lawman's* John Russell. The Technicolor exteriors are superb, but the monosyllabic Walker never cut it as a movie star, becoming a useful supporting player and occasional lead in programme fillers. TS

Clint Walker *"Yellowstone" Kelly* • Edward Byrnes [Edd Byrnes] *Anse* • John Russell *Gall* • Ray Danton *Sayapi* • Claude Akins *Sergeant* • Warren Oates *Corporal* ■ *Dir* Gordon Douglas • *Scr* Burt Kennedy, Clay Fisher

Yentl ★★ PG

Musical drama
1983 · UK/US · Colour · 127mins

Based on a story by Isaac Bashevis Singer and set in 1904 in central Europe, Barbra Streisand's first film as a director is about a Jewish girl who dresses as a boy to receive a religious education. Such complications suggest a kosher *Victor/Victoria* or *Tootsie*, but Streisand approaches it very seriously. Despite the obvious pains taken with the period setting (British studio interiors plus Czech location work), it rather lumbers along. The film won the Oscar for best original score and two of the songs were nominated. AT. Contains brief nudity. DVD

Barbra Streisand *Yentl* • Mandy Patinkin *Avigdor* • Amy Irving *Hadass* • Nehemiah Persoff *Reb Mendel* • Steven Hill *Reb Alter Vishkower* ■ *Dir* Barbra Streisand • *Scr* Jack Rosenthal, Barbra Streisand, from the short story *Yentl, the Yeshiva Boy* by Isaac Bashevis • *Music/Lyrics* Michel Legrand, Marilyn Bergman, Alan Bergman

Yes ★★★

Romantic drama
2004 · UK/US · Colour · 95mins

Joan Allen and Sam Neill are a long-married couple whose relationship is as cold and clean as their home. Their intimate life is exposed to their psychoanalysing cleaning lady (Shirley Henderson), who reads deeper meanings into stains and rubbish. At a formal dinner, Allen catches the eye of a Lebanese chef (Simon Abkarian) and so begins a torrid affair. The cadenced dialogue (the characters often begin speaking in rhyming couplets) brings a lyricism to their love affair. While this may not be for everyone, it is a beautiful, bold adventure into the psyche of modern life. KK

Joan Allen *She* • Simon Abkarian *He* • Sam Neill *Anthony* • Shirley Henderson *Cleaner* • Sheila Hancock *Aunt* • Samantha Bond *Kate* • Stephanie Leonidas *Grace* • Gary Lewis *Billy* ■ *Dir/Scr* Sally Potter

Yes, Giorgio ★ PG

Romantic musical
1982 · US · Colour · 106mins

Alp-sized tenor Luciano Pavarotti's film debut ended up as a contrived star vehicle, with the singing mountain playing an opera star (surprise, surprise) who falls for the woman throat specialist called in to cure him when his voice fails during a US tour. It's just about as bad as it sounds. But add an extra star to the rating if you're potty about Pav, and have to see anything he sings in. DA

Luciano Pavarotti *Giorgio Fini* • Kathryn Harrold *Dr Pamela Taylor* • Eddie Albert *Henry Pollack* • Paola Borboni *Sister Teresa* • James Hong *Kwan* • Beulah Quo *Mei Ling* ■ *Dir* Franklin J Schaffner • *Scr* Norman Steinberg, from the novel *Yes, Giorgio* by Anne Piper

The Yes Men ★★ 15

Documentary 2003 · US · Colour · 78mins

This documentary follows the mayhem caused by two antiglobalisation activists who passed themselves off as representatives of the World Trade Organisation. Andy Bichlbaum and Mike Bonnano created a spoof WTO website that was so convincing it led to invitations to speak at several prestigious trade events around the globe. The film follows the duo as they lecture bemused audiences on the benefits of vote-selling and "involuntary labour", as well as demonstrating their "Management Leisure Suit", complete with a phallic, inflatable communications console. But the "Yes Men" waste their unique access by settling for student-style skits that serve only to embarrass their victims, rather than challenge the spread of globalisation itself. DP. Contains swearing. DVD

Dir Dan Ollman, Sarah Price, Chris Smith

Yesterday Girl ★★★★

Drama 1966 · W Ger · BW · 92mins

Alexander Kluge was already a lawyer before he made his first feature, which is based on the case of a woman he encountered during his work. Played superbly by Alexandra Kluge, the director's sister, she is an anarchic East German woman who escapes to West Germany only to find herself at odds with a different but equally conservative society. Kluge, obviously influenced by the French New Wave, gives the film the feeling of a case history by using documentary-style interviews. The movie came as a breath of fresh air to the moribund German film industry. RB. In German with English subtitles.

Alexandra Kluge *Anita G* • Günther Mack *Pichota* • Eva Maria Meineke [Eva-Maria Meineke] *Frau Pichota* • Hans Korte *Judge* • Edith Kuntze-Pellogio *Parole board officer* • Peter Staimmer *Young man* ■ *Dir/Scr* Alexander Kluge

Yesterday, Today and Tomorrow ★★★ 15

Portmanteau comedy drama
1963 · Fr/It · Colour · 118mins

Notwithstanding its superstar backstage credentials, this Oscar-winning portmanteau only occasionally delivers on the screen. In spite of story credits for Alberto Moravia, screenwriting nods for playwright Eduardo De Filippo and neorealist guru Cesare Zavattini and the directorial elegance of Vittorio De Sica, only the first tale *Adelina*, about Neapolitan husband-and-wife smugglers who exploit a law forbidding the arrest of pregnant women, is consistently amusing. In *Mara*, a Roman prostitute ends a week-long vow of chastity with a striptease that was to garner all the film's headlines. DP. An Italian language film. [video] DVD

Sophia Loren *Adelina/Anna/Mara* • Marcello Mastroianni *Carmine/Renzo/Augusto Rusconi* • Tina Pica *Grandmother* ■ *Dir* Vittorio De Sica • *Scr* Eduardo DeFilippo, Isabella Quarantotti, Cesare Zavattini, Billa Billa Zanuso, from the story *Troppo Ricca* by Alberto Moravia

Yesterday's Enemy ★★★

Second World War drama
1959 · UK · BW · 95mins

This Val Guest-directed tough war movie was one of a group that introduced a note of cynicism and irony, replacing the slightly softer, almost nostalgic war films of the late 1940s. It's set in 1942 and tells of the unexpected consequences when a group of British soldiers take over a Burmese village. The absence of music and the widescreen black-and-white photography lend a gritty feel to this well acted film. BB

Stanley Baker *Capt Langford* • Guy Rolfe *Padre* • Leo McKern *Max* • Gordon Jackson *Sgt MacKenzie* • David Oxley *Doctor* • Richard Pasco *2nd Lt Hastings* • Russell Waters *Brigadier* ■ *Dir* Val Guest • *Scr* Peter R Newman, from a TV play by Peter R Newman

Yesterday's Hero ★

Sports drama 1979 · UK · Colour · 94mins

Ian McShane is the George Best-inspired footballer aiming for a comeback after beating a booze problem. Will he make it to the cup final? Paul Nicholas (playing an Elton John-type rock star chairman) and Adam Faith (as McShane's manager) help him achieve his goal. But the end result of this Jackie Collins-scripted effort is strictly fourth division. AJ

Ian McShane *Rod Turner* • Suzanne Somers *Cloudy Martin* • Adam Faith *Jake Marsh* • Paul Nicholas *Clint Simon* • Sandy Ratcliff *Rita* • Sam Kydd *Sam Turner* • Glynis Barber *Susan* ■ *Dir* Neil Leifer • *Scr* Jackie Collins

Yesterday's Tomorrow ★★

Drama 1978 · W Ger · Colour · 106mins

Pola Kinski – the half-sister of Nastassja – makes a rare appearance as a traumatised survivor of the Second World War who falls in love with a German-born American officer, played by Mel Ferrer. Tragedy looms all over this Occupation drama and the film doesn't surprise in this regard. In the end, the relationship isn't explored in any depth and despite the fine performances it's really just people talking in rooms while Chopin drones away on the soundtrack. AT. German dialogue dubbed into English.

Mel Ferrer *Colonel Henry Stone* • Pola Kinski *Anna Eichmayr* • Martin Luttge *Alfons* • Hannelore Schroth *Frau Almany* ■ *Dir* Wolfgang Staudte • *Scr* Dorothee Dhan

Yield to the Night ★★★ 15

Crime drama 1956 · UK · BW · 95mins

Directed with a grim sense of purpose by J Lee Thompson, this sincere plea for the abolition of capital punishment was based on the case of Ruth Ellis, the last woman in Britain to be hanged and whose story was retold some 30 years later with a good deal more style by Mike Newell in *Dance with a Stranger*. Diana Dors gives one of the best performances of her career as the murderess recalling the circumstances that drove her to kill while waiting to hear if she will be reprieved. DP [video]

Diana Dors *Mary Hilton* • Yvonne Mitchell *MacFarlane* • Michael Craig *Jim Lancaster* • Geoffrey Keen *Chaplain* • Olga Lindo *Hill* • Mary Mackenzie *Maxwell* • Joan Miller *Barker* ■ *Dir* J Lee Thompson • *Scr* Joan Henry, John Cresswell, from the novel by Joan Henry

Yojimbo ★★★★★ PG

Action drama 1961 · Jpn · BW · 105mins

Such was the influence of the Hollywood western on Akira Kurosawa's superb samurai action adventure that it seems only fair that it, in turn, inspired Sergio Leone's *A Fistful of Dollars*, the film that launched the Italian "spaghetti" western. Combining moments of comedy, intrigue and sudden, shocking violence, Kurosawa celebrates the samurai genre at the same time as he is subtly subverting it. Toshiro Mifune is tremendous as the wandering warrior who sells his sword skills to both sides in a divided village only to dupe them into mutual slaughter. He returned in the sequel, *Sanjuro*, the following year. DP. In Japanese with English subtitles. [video] DVD

Toshiro Mifune *Sanjuro Kuwabatake* • Eijiro Tono *Gonji* • Seizaburo Kawazu *Seibei* • Isuzu Yamada *Orin* • Hiroshi Tachikawa *Yoichiro* • Susumu Fujita *Homma* ■ *Dir* Akira Kurosawa • *Scr* Akira Kurosawa, Ryuzo Kikushima, Hideo Oguni, from the novel *Red Harvest* by Dashiell Hammett • *Music* Masaru Sato

Yol ★★★★★ 15

Drama 1982 · Tur · Colour · 109mins

Anger and sadness lie at the heart of this treatise on the perpetuation of the patriarchal prejudices underpinning Turkish society. The film was written by Yilmaz Guney, while in prison for so-called political offences, and directed from explicit instructions by his longtime assistant, Serif Gören. The negative was then smuggled to Switzerland, where Guney edited it following his escape. The winner of the Palme d'Or at Cannes, it testifies to the courage of Turkey's greatest-ever film-maker. But, perhaps more significantly, the story of the five parolees who must face up to personal calamity also highlights the tragedy of a nation whose future is so hidebound by its past. DP. In Turkish with English subtitles. [video]

Tarik Akan *Seyit Ali* • Halil Ergun *Mehmet Salih* • Necmettin Cobanoglu *Omer* • Serif Sezer *Ziné* ■ *Dir* Serif Goren • *Scr* Yilmaz Guney

Yolanda and the Thief ★★★ U

Romantic fantasy musical
1945 · US · Colour · 107mins

Fred Astaire, more balletic than usual, and Lucille Bremer, an expressionless red-haired dancer, play the title roles in an MGM musical that gave Vincente Minnelli ample scope to express his taste for decorative fantasy with some stunning dream sequences. These numbers, drenched in exotic colours, burst forth when Fred dreams himself into a surrealistic landscape and are the best parts of the film. Set in a mythical Latin American country, the mediocre yet whimsical story has Astaire as a confidence trickster, who pretends to be the guardian angel (literally) of the convent-educated heroine... and her millions. RB

Fred Astaire *Johnny Parkson Riggs* • Lucille Bremer *Yolanda Aquaviva* • Frank Morgan *Victor Budlow Trout* • Mildred Natwick *Aunt Amarilla* • Mary Nash *Duenna* • Leon Ames *Mr Candle* ■ *Dir* Vincente Minnelli • *Scr* Ludwig Bemelmans, Irving Brecher, from a short story by Jacques Thery, Ludwig Bemelmans

Yom Yom ★★★

Period drama
1998 · Fr/Is/It · Colour · 105mins

Amos Gitai directs this family comedy set in Haifa about the clash between personal destiny and national identity – one that is more prevalent than many outsiders would assume. Moshe Ivgi stars as the middle-aged mommy's boy, of mixed Arab-Jewish stock, who is forced to rethink his fatalistic approach to life, when his family bakery is threatened by plans for a shopping mall. Exposing the intransigence that makes compromise in the region a near impossibility, Gitai gently satirises the traditions that stand in the way of progress. DP. In Hebrew with English subtitles.

Moshe Ivgi *Moshe* • Hanna Maron *Hanna* • Juliano Merr *Jules* • Dalit Kahan *Didi* • Yussef Abu Warda *Yussef* • Nataly Atiya *Grisha* ■ *Dir* Amos Gitai • *Scr* Jacky Cukier, Amos Gitai

Yor, the Hunter from the Future ★ 15

Science-fiction adventure
1983 · It/Tur · Colour · 84mins

An inept, cheesy muscleman epic from Italian hack director Antonio Margheriti, who obviously thought mixing *Conan* with *Star Wars* was a stunningly original idea. Starring one-time Captain America Reb Brown (which says it all really), this absolute stinker features the blond-wigged hero fighting cardboard dinosaurs and robot hordes, accompanied by a tacky disco theme song. AJ [video]

Reb Brown *Yor* • Corinne Cléry *Ka-Laa* • John Steiner *Overlord* • Carole Andre *Ena* ■ *Dir* Anthony M Dawson [Antonio Margheriti] • *Scr* Robert Bailey, Anthony M Dawson [Antonio Margheriti], from the novel *Yor* by Juan Zanotto, Ray Collins

You and Me ★★★

Crime drama 1938 · US · BW · 90mins

In a department store whose humane owner employs ex-convicts on parole, a love affair blossoms, but goes horribly wrong because of a misguided deceit practised by one of the sweethearts. George Raft and Sylvia Sidney star in this very curious mixture of crime melodrama, moral message and feel-good love story, directed by Fritz Lang who injects some equally curious stylistic devices, as well as his characteristic gift for creating tension. Much reviled by serious critics at the time of its release, seen now it's actually very entertaining. RK

Sylvia Sidney *Helen* • George Raft *Joe Dennis* • Harry Carey *Mr Morris* • Barton MacLane *Mickey* • Warren Hymer *Gimpy* • Roscoe Karns *Cuffy* ■ *Dir* Fritz Lang • *Scr* Virginia Van Upp, from a story by Norman Krasna • *Music* Kurt Weill • *Lyrics* Sam Coslow

You Belong to Me ★★★

Romantic comedy 1941 · US · BW · 94mins

Barbara Stanwyck is a successful doctor married to wealthy Henry Fonda. He doesn't need to work so, with time on his hands, develops an obsessive jealousy of her male patients from which springs both the humorous situations and the more sober moments. The stars are a dream, superseding the otherwise one-dimensional material. RK

Barbara Stanwyck *Dr Helen Hunt* • Henry Fonda *Peter Kirk* • Edgar Buchanan *Billings* • Roger Clark *"Van" Vandemer* • Ruth Donnelly *Emma* • Melville Cooper *Moody* • Ralph Peters *Joseph* • Maude Eburne *Ella* ■ *Dir* Wesley Ruggles • *Scr* Claude Binyon, from the story *You Belong to Me* by Dalton Trumbo

You Better Watch Out ★★★ 18

Horror 1980 · US · Colour · 96mins

A taut and tense little suspense movie to put the gloom on any Christmas festival, this stars Brandon Maggart as the psycho who delivers death dressed as Santa Claus. Directed by Lewis Jackson, it was also released as *Christmas Evil* and *Terror in Toyland*. It lives up to those titles as well. TH [video]

Brandon Maggart *Harry Stadling* • Dianne Hull *Jackie Stadling* • Scott McKay *Fletcher* • Joe Jamrog *Frank Stoller* • Peter Friedman *Grosch* • Ray Barry [Raymond J Barry] *Gleason* • Bobby Lesser *Gottleib* • Sam Gray *Grilla* ■ *Dir/Scr* Lewis Jackson

You Can Count on Me ★★★★ 15

Drama 1999 · US · Colour · 106mins

Laura Linney deserved her Oscar nomination for a fine performance in this humour-tinged drama. She plays a strong-minded single mum who still lives in the small town where she and her brother (Mark Ruffalo) were orphaned as children. The return of her sibling – a drifter with a chequered past – initially suggests that Linney's character is the smart and stable one, and Ruffalo is the black sheep. But perceptions shift as she embarks on an ill-judged fling with her bank manager boss (Matthew Broderick), and Ruffalo tries to rebuild the relationship between her son (Rory Culkin) and his estranged dad. Writer/director Kenneth Lonergan delivers a sharp script, with acute observations. DA. Contains swearing, drug abuse and sex scenes. [video] DVD

Laura Linney *Sammy Prescott* • Mark Ruffalo *Terry Prescott* • Matthew Broderick *Brian* • Rory Culkin *Rudy* • Bob Tenney *Bob* • J Smith-Cameron *Mabel* ■ *Dir/Scr* Kenneth Lonergan

You Can Thank Me Later ★★★

Comedy drama 1998 · Can · Colour · 110mins

As the Cooperberg family anxiously waits in a hospital ward for news of their beloved patriarch, they each flash back to black-and-white confessionals outlining some of the more unsavoury moments in their lives. Jewish director Shimon Dotan takes the dysfunctional family concept to new theatrical heights in a melodramatic comedy rich in character if not in plot. The superlative ensemble cast revels in acting out the home truths and dark secrets of a family slowly losing its roots, values and morals. AJ

Geneviève Bujold *Joelle* • Ellen Burstyn *Shirley Cooperberg* • Amanda Plummer *Susan Cooperberg* • Ted Levine *Eli Cooperberg* • Mark Blum *Edward Cooperberg* ■ *Dir* Shimon Dotan • *Scr* Oren Safdie, from his play *Hyper-Allergenic*

You Can't Cheat an Honest Man ★★

Comedy 1939 · US · BW · 76mins

Devised by WC Fields, this comedy had a fraught production involving two directors besides the credited George Marshall. A double had to be used in some of Fields's scenes, thanks to on-set arguments and his penchant for drinking doubles. Although not one of his classics, the film allows Fields considerable rein as an impecunious circus owner whose daughter is prepared to marry a wealthy toff to help her father, even though she's in love with someone else. Some of the best moments come when Fields turns up at the proposed wedding. BB

WC Fields *Larson E Whipsnade* • Edgar Bergen *The Great Edgar* • Constance Moore *Victoria Whipsnade* • John Arledge *Phineas Whipsnade* • James Bush *Roger Bel-Goodie* ■ *Dir* George Marshall • *Scr* George Marion Jr, Richard Mack, Everett Freeman, Henry Johnson, Lew Lipton, from a story by Charles Bogle [WC Fields]

Y

You Can't Escape Forever ★

Crime drama 1942 · US · BW · 77mins

George Brent portrays the managing editor of a newspaper who's demoted to looking after the personal advice column. He stages a comeback by exposing racketeer Eduardo Ciannelli. Long-time Warner Bros dialogue coach Jo Graham occupies the director's chair with lacklustre results. AE

George Brent *Steve "Mitch" Mitchell* • Brenda Marshall *Laurie Abbott* • Gene Lockhart *Carl Robelink* • Edward Ciannelli [Eduardo Ciannelli] *Boss Greer* ■ *Dir* Jo Graham • *Scr* Fred Niblo Jr, Hector Chevigny, from the story *Hi Nellie!* by Roy Chanslor

You Can't Get Away with Murder ★★

Prison crime drama 1939 · US · BW · 75mins

The unwieldy but graphically accurate title of this movie says it all: a formula second-rung crime tale that demands the death of both protagonists. Humphrey Bogart recycles the standard gangster he played 11 times in four years, co-starring with Dead End Kid Billy Halop. Bogart is an irredeemable, conscience-free thug who seduces the youngster into a life of crime, with Halop's disillusion and repentance coming too late to save him. Ponderously directed and containing not a single original idea. RK

Humphrey Bogart *Frank Wilson* • Gale Page *Madge Stone* • Billy Halop *Johnnie Stone* • John Litel *Attorney Carey* • Henry Travers *Pop* • Harvey Stephens *Fred Burke* ■ *Dir* Lewis Seiler • *Scr* Robert Buckner, Don Ryan, Kenneth Gamet, from the play *Chalked Out* by Lewis E Lawes, Jonathan Finn

You Can't Have Everything ★★★

Musical comedy 1937 · US · BW · 89mins

Would you believe Alice Faye as the descendant of Edgar Allan Poe? And that she despises musical comedy? An unlikely peg on which to hang the appearance of a lot of vaudeville troupers, but this movie's got a cast-and-a-half for connoisseurs: the Ritz Brothers, Louis Prima, Tony Martin, and Tip, Tap and Toe. And watch out for featured Louise Hovick – better known as Gypsy Rose Lee. Faye is her usual self, and sings the title with style, but the plot eventually defeats her. It doesn't matter, though: it's all expertly done. TS

Alice Faye *Judith Poe Wells* • Harry Ritz • Al Ritz • Jimmy Ritz • Don Ameche *George Macrea* • Charles Winninger *Sam Gordon* • Louise Hovick [Gypsy Rose Lee] *Lulu Riley* • David Rubinoff • Tony Martin *Bobby Walker* • Arthur Treacher *Bevins* ■ *Dir* Norman Taurog • *Scr* Harry Tugend, Jack Yellen, Karl Tunberg, from a story by Gregory Ratoff

You Can't Hurry Love ★★ 18

Comedy 1988 · US · Colour · 88mins

This is a routine if well-acted story of a hick from the sticks who comes to stay with his trendy LA cousin and hits the swinging-singles scene by signing up to a video-dating service. His ensuing love life has thoroughly predictable ups (a few) and downs (a lot). This episodic comedy has its wry and amusing moments, but is generally flattered by its strong cast. DA

David Packer *Eddie* • Scott McGinnis *Skip* • Bridget Fonda *Peggy* • David Leisure *Newcomb* • Anthony Geary *Tony* • Frank Bonner *Chuck Hayes* • Sally Kellerman *Kelly Bones* • Charles Grodin *Mr Glerman* • Kristy McNichol *Rhonda* ■ *Dir* Richard Martini • *Scr* Richard Martini

You Can't Run Away from It ★★ U

Musical 1956 · US · Colour · 94mins

A remake of the Oscar-winning classic *It Happened One Night*, this has June Allyson as the runaway heiress and Jack Lemmon as the newsman she runs into on a Greyhound bus. Some sequences, including the famous "Walls of Jericho" and hitch-hiking sketches are transferred from 1934 almost shot-for-shot, but there are also some musical numbers, including a cringe-making song from Stubby Kaye on the bus. Allyson has a dance sequence that is a show stopper in quite the wrong way. AT

June Allyson *Ellie Andrews* • Jack Lemmon *Peter Warne* • Charles Bickford *AA Andrews* • Paul Gilbert *George Shapely* • Jim Backus *Danker* • Stubby Kaye *Fred Toten* ■ *Dir* Dick Powell • *Scr* Claude Binyon, from the film *It Happened One Night* by Robert Riskin, from the short story *Night Bus* by Samuel Hopkins Adams

You Can't Take It with You ★★★★★ U

Comedy 1938 · US · BW · 120mins

Frank Capra won a third, well-deserved Oscar in five years for this sparkling comedy (it also won best picture). Based on the George S Kaufman and Moss Hart play and scripted by Oscar-winner Robert Riskin, it's about the eccentric Vanderhof family, New Yorkers whose wealth belies a vast range of eccentricity and political opinion. It's also a fable about individualism and everyone's need to resist corporate or group control. The movie contains wonderful performances from a cast that includes bubbly Jean Arthur and James Stewart as her drawling fiancé, and, if it is a touch overlong, that is a minor fault considering the vast comic talent on display. AT DVD

Jean Arthur *Alice Sycamore* • Lionel Barrymore *Martin Vanderhof* • James Stewart *Tony Kirby* • Edward Arnold *Anthony P Kirby* • Mischa Auer *Kolenkhov* • Ann Miller *Essie Carmichael* • Spring Byington *Penny Sycamore* • Samuel S Hinds *Paul Sycamore* ■ *Dir* Frank Capra • *Scr* Robert Riskin, from the play by George S Kaufman, Moss Hart • *Cinematographer* Joseph Walker • *Music* Dimitri Tiomkin [Dmitri Tiomkin]

You Can't Win 'em All ★★★ PG

Adventure comedy
1970 · UK · Colour · 95mins

During the collapse of the Ottoman Empire in 1920s Turkey, former American soldiers Tony Curtis and Charles Bronson are hired to protect the Sultan's three daughters and a shipment of gold. Leo V Gordon's poor script is given vitality by Peter Collinson's zippy direction and the repartee of the stars. TH

Tony Curtis *Adam Dyer* • Charles Bronson *Josh Corey* • Michèle Mercier *Aila* • Grégoire Aslan *Osman Bey* • Fikret Hakan *Colonel Elci* • Salih Guney *Captain Enver* • Patrick Magee *General* • Tony Bonner *Reese* ■ *Dir* Peter Collinson • *Scr* Leo V Gordon

You Got Served ★★ PG

Dance drama 2004 · US · Colour · 90mins

This is a lively but formulaic teen drama, featuring members of top hip-hop groups. The story is a simple-minded one involving street-dance clashes between rival "crews", with two friends falling out over a girl but reconciling to whup their opponents. The dance sequences are dynamic, the acting serviceable and the production values decent enough. But there's little here to appeal beyond the film's young core audience, and even they might find film too safe and too predictable. DA DVD

Marques Houston *Elgin* • Omari Grandberry *David* • Jarell Houston *Rico* • DeMario Thornton *Vick* • Dreux Frederic *Rashaan* • Jennifer Freeman *Liyah* • Lil' Kim • Michael "Bear" Taliferro *Emerald* ■ *Dir/Scr* Christopher B Stokes

You Gotta Stay Happy ★★ U

Romantic comedy 1948 · US · BW · 100mins

Joan Fontaine stars in this attempt at screwball romantic comedy. She plays a runaway bride who persuades flyer James Stewart and his buddy Eddie Albert to spirit her off to California. The plane crashes in Oklahoma farmland en route, Stewart and Fontaine fall in love, and you can guess the rest. It's amiable enough and Stewart is a perfect fit for his role. RK

Joan Fontaine *Diana "Dee Dee" Dillwood Benson aka Dottie Blucher* • James Stewart *Marvin Payne* • Eddie Albert *Bullets Baker* • Roland Young *Ralph Tutwiler* • Willard Parker *Henry Benson* ■ *Dir* HC Potter • *Scr* Karl Tunberg, from the story by Robert Carson

You Know What Sailors Are ★★ U

Comedy 1954 · UK · Colour · 89mins

This is one of Ken Annakin's lesser outings, with too many cheap jibes, but there is some fun to be had as drunken sailor Donald Sinden plants a pawnbroker's sign and a pram on top of a ship and tries to pass it off as "Secret Weapon 998". Akim Tamiroff does what he can with one of his few leading roles, but the mediocre Cold War jokes eventually force him to surrender. DP

Donald Sinden *Lieutenant Sylvester Green* • Akim Tamiroff *President of Agraria* • Sarah Lawson *Betty* • Naunton Wayne *Captain Owbridge* • Bill Kerr *Lieutenant Smart* • Dora Bryan *Gladys* • Michael Hordern *Captain Hamilton* ■ *Dir* Ken Annakin • *Scr* Peter Rogers, from the novel *Sylvester* by Edward Hyams

You Light Up My Life ★ PG

Musical 1977 · US · Colour · 86mins

Having made such a good impression as Frenchy in *Grease*, Didi Conn looked set for stardom. But this schmaltzy showbiz melodrama virtually put paid to her movie prospects. Even though the title song won an Oscar (in a very slow year), Joseph Brooks's story of the comedian's daughter with ambitions to become a singer-actress creaks under the weight of its clichés. For tackaholics only. DP

Didi Conn *Laurie Robinson* • Joe Silver *Si Robinson* • Michael Zaslow *Chris Nolan* • Stephen Nathan *Ken Rothenberg* • Melanie Mayron *Annie Gerrard* • Jerry Keller *Conductor* ■ *Dir/Scr* Joseph Brooks

You Must Be Joking! ★★ U

Farce 1965 · UK · BW · 102mins

This scattershot comedy from Michael Winner has a sound premise: give five soldiers various unlikely tasks to assess their initiative. The trouble is, there are too many different tests and the slapstick solutions to them soon try the patience. Denholm Elliott and Lionel Jeffries go flat out for laughs, but with a little more gag selectivity on the part of Winner, they would not have had to work quite so hard. DP

Michael Callan *Lieutenant Tim Morton* • Lionel Jeffries *Sergeant Major McGregor* • Denholm Elliott *Captain Tabasco* • Wilfrid Hyde White *General Lockwood* • Bernard Cribbins *Sergeant Clegg* • James Robertson-Justice *Librarian* • Leslie Phillips *Young husband* • Terry-Thomas *Major Foskett* ■ *Dir* Michael Winner • *Scr* Alan Hackney, form a story by Michael Winner, Alan Hackney

You Only Live Once ★★★★★ 12

Classic crime drama 1937 · US · BW · 82mins

This ironic masterpiece set in the Depression era borrows from the real-life Bonnie and Clyde saga, as Sylvia Sidney and Henry Fonda play small-timers caught up in an escalation of violence. Fonda has never been better, while Sidney is just wonderful: tender, poignant, vulnerable, scared. Director Fritz Lang creates a bleak half-world of sheer greyness, and, apparently, during the 46-day shoot, forced his actors and production team to stay awake so they'd look and be suitably tired. It's a brilliant, stunning classic you'll remember for ever. TS DVD

Henry Fonda *Eddie Taylor* • Sylvia Sidney *Joan Graham* • Barton MacLane *Stephen Whitney* • Jean Dixon *Bonnie Graham* • William Gargan *Father Dolan* • Warren Hymer *Muggsy* • Charles "Chic" Sale *Ethan* • Margaret Hamilton *Hester* ■ *Dir* Fritz Lang • *Scr* Gene Towne, Graham Baker, from a story by Gene Towne • *Cinematographer* Leon Shamroy • *Music* Alfred Newman

You Only Live Twice ★★★★★ PG

Spy adventure 1967 · UK · Colour · 111mins

One of the very best of the Sean Connery Bonds, this dispatches 007 to Japan, where, having faked his own death, he goes native, "marries" a local girl and, in his quest to discover why spaceships keep going missing, unearths a volcano with a false crater. Donald Pleasence's scarred, cat-stroking Blofeld – although unseen for much of the film – proves one of the all-time great screen villains. Director Lewis Gilbert keeps the pace up, and the script (co-written by Roald Dahl) is suitably arch, but it is surely production designer Ken Adam's triumph: the secret base, where the film's explosive climax unfolds, remains definitive. AC DVD

Sean Connery *James Bond* • Donald Pleasence *Ernst Stavro Blofeld* • Akiko Wakabayashi *Aki* • Tetsuro Tamba *Tiger Tanaka* • Mie Hama *Kissy Suzuki* • Teru Shimada *Osato* • Karin Dor *Helga Brandt* • Lois Maxwell *Miss Moneypenny* • Desmond Llewelyn *"Q"* • Bernard Lee *"M"* ■ *Dir* Lewis Gilbert • *Scr* Roald Dahl, Harry Jack Bloom, from the novel by Ian Fleming • *Cinematographer* Freddie Young

You Pay Your Money ★ U

Crime drama 1957 · UK · BW · 66mins

The much maligned Butcher's Film Service mostly churned out dismal offerings such as this tale of kidnap and rare book smuggling, given only the merest modicum of respectability by the presence of Hugh McDermott and Honor Blackman. Maclean Rogers's screenplay is as flat as his direction. DP

Hugh McDermott *Bob Westlake* • Jane Hylton *Rosemary Delgardo* • Honor Blackman *Susie Westlake* • Hugh Moxey *Tom Cookson* • Ivan Samson *Steve Mordaunt* ■ *Dir* Maclean Rogers • *Scr* Maclean Rogers, from the novel *You Pay Your Money* by Michael Cronin

You Talkin' to Me? ★★★

Black comedy 1987 · US · Colour · 97mins

This is the tale of an obsessed Robert De Niro fan, specifically an unemployed actor who lives and breathes the Travis Bickle character from *Taxi Driver*. When he finds work in Hollywood through a rabidly racist TV producer, it's clear that this is a two-tier film which wants to make pithy observations about the image-making process and the danger of delusion. At times, however, it's all too cumbersome, but its star Jim Youngs certainly did not deserve to be panned by New York critics for not reproducing De Niro's class act to perfection. JM. Contains swearing.

Jim Youngs *Bronson Green* • James Noble *Peter Archer* • Mykel T Williamson [Mykelti Williamson] *Thatcher Marks* • Faith Ford *Dana Archer* • Bess Motta *Judith Margolis* • Rex Ryon *Kevin* • Brian Thompson *James* • Alan King ■ *Dir/Scr* Charles Winkler

Y

You Were Meant for Me ★★★

Musical 1948 · US · BW · 91mins

A good example of the kind of musical made to use up contracts of personable stars. Jeanne Crain and Dan Dailey play smoothly together as the nice girl and the bandleader she marries in America during the Depression years. Dailey's stock was rising, and the same year he was nominated for the best actor Oscar for *When My Baby Smiles at Me*. Not bad for a song-and-dance man. TS

Jeanne Crain *Peggy Mayhew* • Dan Dailey *Chuck Arnold* • Oscar Levant *Oscar Hoffman* • Barbara Lawrence *Louise Crane* • Selena Royle *Mrs Cora Mayhew* • Percy Kilbride *Mr Andrew Mayhew* ■ *Dir* Lloyd Bacon • *Scr* Elick Moll, Valentine Davies

You Were Never Lovelier ★★★ U

Musical 1942 · US · BW · 93mins

The second wartime pairing (after *You'll Never Get Rich*) of the marvellous Rita Hayworth and the ineffable Fred Astaire is a delight, as they dance to a superb Jerome Kern score with Johnny Mercer lyrics. The plot is silly and the budget skimpy, but the two stars are radiant, possibly owing to the fact that they were "an item" on this movie. They also happened to have known each other all their dancing lives, since Fred was half of Fred and Adele Astaire and the young Hayworth, as Margarita Carmen Cansino, was part of the Dancing Cansinos. TS [video] DVD

Fred Astaire *Robert Davis* • Rita Hayworth *Maria Acuna* • Adolphe Menjou *Eduardo Acuno* • Leslie Brooks *Cecy Acuna* • Adele Mara *Lita Acuna* • Isobel Elsom *Mrs Maria Castro* ■ *Dir* William A Seiter • *Scr* Michael Fessier, Ernest Pagano, Delmer Daves, from a story and • *Scr* (unproduced) by Carlos Olivari, Sixto Pondal Rios • *Costume Designer* Irene

You'll Find Out ★★

Horror spoof 1940 · US · BW · 96mins

Murderous plotters Boris Karloff, Bela Lugosi and Peter Lorre encounter band leader Kay Kyser (with his Kollege of Musical Knowledge) in an apparently haunted house. This odd slice of 1940s popular music history also showcased Dennis O'Keefe and musician Ish Kabibble. Advertised as "A Seance In Swing with the Ha-Ha Horror Boys", it's crammed with enough thriller devices (despite the terror trio being criminally wasted) and good clean fun to qualify as a lightweight nostalgia binge. AJ

Kay Kyser • Peter Lorre *Professor Fenninger* • Bela Lugosi *Prince Saliano* • Boris Karloff *Judge Mainwaring* • Dennis O'Keefe *Chuck Deems* • Helen Parrish *Janis Bellacrest* ■ *Dir* David Butler • *Scr* James V Kern, Monte Brice, Andrew Bennison, RTM Scott, from a story by James V Kern, David Butler

You'll Like My Mother ★★★

Thriller 1972 · US · Colour · 92mins

This refreshingly low-key psycho thriller eschews all the obvious horror trappings to deliver a nail-biting climax. Pregnant widow Patty Duke stumbles on some dark family secrets when she arrives at mother-in-law Rosemary Murphy's house for the first time to grieve over her husband's death in Vietnam. Murphy is not only keeping a mentally disabled girl locked in the attic, she's also hiding her rapist son in the cellar! Trapped in the house by a snowstorm, Duke gives birth and Murphy tells her the baby has died, which sets the scene for unnerving suspense. Despite a few lapses in logic and a certain sloppiness on director Lamont Johnson's part, this is scare show with finesse. AJ

Patty Duke *Francesca Kinsolving* • Rosemary Murphy *Mrs Kinsolving* • Richard Thomas *Kenny* • Sian Barbara Allen *Kathleen Kinsolving* • Dennis Rucker *Red Cooper* • James Neumann *Joey* • James Glazman *Breadman* ■ *Dir* Lamont Johnson • *Scr* Jo Heims, from the novel by Naomi A Hintze

You'll Never Get Rich ★★★ U

Musical comedy 1941 · US · BW · 88mins

The only co-star Fred Astaire became romantically involved with in real life was, allegedly, the lovely Rita Hayworth, herself a skilled and trained dancer. They made two movies together at Columbia (this was followed by *You Were Never Lovelier* in 1942) and their dancing together is simply exquisite: it's quite clear that there's something extra-special going on between these two extraordinary talents. Ignore the dumb wartime plot about Fred being caught in the draft, or the relentlessly pedestrian direction by Sidney Lanfield, and just revel in the Cole Porter songs. TS [video] DVD

Fred Astaire *Robert Curtis* • Rita Hayworth *Sheila Winthrop* • John Hubbard *Tom Barton* • Robert Benchley *Martin Cortland* • Osa Massen *Sonya* • Frieda Inescort *Mrs Cortland* • Guinn Williams [Guinn "Big Boy" Williams] *Kewpie Blain* ■ *Dir* Sidney Lanfield • *Scr* Michael Fessier, Ernest Pagano

Young Adam ★★★★ 18

Period drama 2003 · UK/Fr · Colour · 93mins

In 1950s Glasgow, rootless drifter Ewan McGregor becomes employed as a barge hand on the local canals. Haunted by his past after fishing a drowned woman out of the water, he's thrown into an existential crisis that leads to a series of unfulfilling sexual encounters. Combining *film noir* and kitchen-sink melodrama, director David Mackenzie's moody and intimate picture is a superbly crafted performance piece. The movie smoulders with sensuality and raw emotion, thanks in part to a brilliant McGregor's brooding masculinity, but it's Tilda Swinton who is most mesmerising, boldly baring all as his boss's intimacy-hungry wife. SF. Contains swearing, nudity and sex scenes. [video] DVD

Ewan McGregor *Joe Taylor* • Tilda Swinton *Ella Gault* • Peter Mullan *Les Gault* • Emily Mortimer *Cathie Dimly* • Jack McElhone *Jim Gault* • Therese Bradley *Gwen* • Ewan Stewart *Daniel Gordon* • Stuart McQuarrie *Bill* • Pauline Turner *Connie* • Alan Cooke (2) *Bob M'bussi* ■ *Dir* David Mackenzie • *Scr* David Mackenzie, from the novel by Alexander Trocchi

The Young Americans ★★★ 18

Thriller 1993 · UK · Colour · 98mins

Hard-bitten New York cop Harvey Keitel arrives in London to nail the drug racketeers terrorising the capital's hip night spots in this flashy movie, which landed newcomer Danny Cannon the job of directing 1995's big budget flop *Judge Dredd*. Visually impressive on all fronts, with designer violence being Cannon's forte, this glossily graphic drama at times plays as a tough documentary. AJ. Contains violence, swearing and drug abuse. [video]

Harvey Keitel *John Harris* • Iain Glen *Edward Foster* • Thandie Newton *Rachael Stevens* • Viggo Mortensen *Carl Fraser* • Craig Kelly (2) *Christian O'Neill* • Nigel Clauzel *Lionel Stevens* • James Duggan *Dermott O'Neill* • Keith Allen *Jack Doyle* ■ *Dir* Danny Cannon • *Scr* Danny Cannon, David Hilton

Young and Dangerous ★★ 18

Action 1996 · HK · Colour · 95mins

This violent Hong Kong crime thriller is about a bunch of inexperienced thugs climbing the ladder of the Hung Hing Society Triads. Based on a popular series of graphic novels, this has an unusually youthful cast, who are supposed to be intimidating, although it's hard to believe that this bunch of idiotic juveniles could provoke much fear. It certainly captures the brutality of the Triad gangs, but most of the major action scenes are wrecked by the misjudged use of a gimmicky blurring effect. In Hong Kong, this was released as two films: Parts 1 and 2, with essentially identical cast and crew. A host of sequels followed. JC. In Cantonese with English subtitles. [video] DVD

Cheng Yee-kin *Ho Nam* • Jordan Chan *Chicken* • Gigi Lai *Smartie* ■ *Dir* Andrew Lau • *Scr* Manfred Wong, Sharon Hui, from a story by Dickey Yau, Cow Man

Young and Innocent ★★★★ U

Murder mystery 1937 · UK · BW · 79mins

This may be a minor entry in the Hitchcock canon, but, as it boasts one of the most stunning sequences he ever executed – the audacious travelling shot to the murderer's twitching eye – this film still proves him to be the master of technique, as well as suspense. One of Hitch's many "wrong man" thrillers, it takes viewers on a breathless pursuit, pausing only for a nerve-jangling children's party and a mine-shaft cliffhanger, that will leave you as frayed and exhausted as the imperilled Derrick de Marney and Nova Pilbeam. DP [video] DVD

Derrick de Marney *Robert Tisdall* • Nova Pilbeam *Erica* • Percy Marmont *Colonel Burgoyne* • Edward Rigby *Old Will* • Mary Clare *Erica's aunt* • John Longden *Kent* • George Curzon *Guy* • Basil Radford *Uncle Basil* ■ *Dir* Alfred Hitchcock • *Scr* Charles Bennett, Alma Reville, from the novel *A Shilling for Candles* by Josephine Tey

Young and Willing ★★ U

Comedy drama 1942 · US · BW · 83mins

A bunch of penurious aspiring young actors share a small New York apartment, as well as their hopes, dreams, squabbles and romances, as they wait for the big break on Broadway. A forgettable, lightweight comedy, it whiles away the time pleasantly enough. It also showcases the youthful pre-stardom talents of William Holden, Susan Hayward, and Eddie Bracken, helped along by humorist, writer and actor Robert Benchley (grandfather of Peter, who wrote *Jaws*). RK

William Holden (2) *Norman Reese* • Eddie Bracken *George Bodell* • Robert Benchley *Arthur Kenny* • Susan Hayward *Kate Benson* • Martha O'Driscoll *Dottie Coburn* • Barbara Britton *Marge Benson* • Mabel Paige *Mrs Garnet* ■ *Dir* Edward H Griffith • *Scr* Virginia Van Upp, from the play *Out of the Frying Pan* by Francis Swann

Young at Heart ★★★ U

Romantic drama
1955 · US · Colour · 112mins

A well-crafted remake from Warner Bros of *Four Daughters*, this features a surly Frank Sinatra, finely cast in the role that made John Garfield a star in the original. Playing opposite Sinatra is Doris Day, who offers a performance of great warmth and sensitivity. Although not a musical (it's a drama with songs), the film still offers plenty of precious moments for the audience to savour. The supporting cast is exemplary, but the tacked-on ending is an unnecessary sop. TS [video] DVD

Frank Sinatra *Barney Sloan* • Doris Day *Laurie Tuttle* • Gig Young *Alex Burke* • Ethel Barrymore *Aunt Jessie* • Dorothy Malone *Fran Tuttle* • Robert Keith (1) *Gregory Tuttle* • Elisabeth Fraser *Amy Tuttle* • Alan Hale Jr *Robert Neary* ■ *Dir* Gordon Douglas • *Scr* Liam O'Brien, from the film *Four Daughters* by Julius J Epstein, Lenore Coffee, from the story *Sister Act* by Fannie Hurst

Young Bess ★★★ U

Historical drama
1953 · US · Colour · 111mins

Hollywood journeyman director George Sidney did an admirable job in preventing this historical drama from toppling over into an unintentional laugh fest. With characters endlessly explaining (in a welter of thous and dosts) who they are to people they've known all their lives, the story of Elizabeth I's relationship with Thomas Seymour is told with a disregard for fact that ultimately becomes endearing. Bygone age, indeed. DP

Jean Simmons *Young Bess* • Stewart Granger *Thomas Seymour* • Deborah Kerr *Catherine Parr* • Charles Laughton *King Henry VIII* • Kay Walsh *Mrs Ashley* • Guy Rolfe *Ned Seymour* • Kathleen Byron *Anne Seymour* ■ *Dir* George Sidney (2) • *Scr* Jan Lustig, Arthur Wimperis, from the novel by Margaret Irwin

Young Billy Young ★★★ PG

Western adventure
1969 · US · Colour · 85mins

Not Robert Mitchum's finest hour, but a serviceable western nonetheless. *Young Billy Young* has a convoluted plot enlivened by strong performances from Mitchum, Angie Dickinson and David Carradine as a nasty villain. The Billy Young of the title (Robert Walker Jr) is a murderer on the run, picked up by lawman Mitchum during the search for the killer of his son (played by Mitchum's own son, Chris). RT [video]

Robert Mitchum *Ben Kane* • Angie Dickinson *Lily Beloit* • Robert Walker Jr *Billy Young* • David Carradine *Jesse Boone* • Jack Kelly *John Behan* • John Anderson *Frank Boone* ■ *Dir* Burt Kennedy • *Scr* Burt Kennedy, from the novel *Who Rides with Wyatt?* by Will Henry

The Young Captives ★★

Drama 1958 · US · BW · 86mins

Steven Marlo plays a maladjusted youth – in fact a psychopath with one corpse to his credit – who hitches a ride with an eloping couple heading for Mexico. Awash with social comment, not to mention solemnity, it's a movie that wants its kicks but doesn't want to be regarded as irresponsible. Made on a dime budget, it has a real feel for the highway and is shot by tyro director Irvin Kershner who went on to make *The Empire Strikes Back*. AT

Steven Marlo *Jamie Forbes* • Tom Selden *Benje Whitney* • Luana Patten *Ann Howel* • Joan Granville *Mrs Howel* • Ed Nelson *Norm Britt* • Dan Sheridan *Dave* • James Chandler *Tony* ■ *Dir* Irvin Kershner • *Scr* Andrew J Fenady, from a story by Gordon Hunt, Al Burton

Young Cassidy ★★

Biographical drama
1965 · US/UK · Colour · 110mins

Rod Taylor plays Irish writer Sean O'Casey who for unfathomable reasons is called Johnny Cassidy in this screen treatment. John Ford directed barely 20 minutes of it before illness forced him to be replaced by Jack Cardiff. Taylor sees the prettified poverty and violence of Dublin and falls in and out of love – perfect preparation for his plays and poetry. The women in the cast make this just about worth watching, but Michael Redgrave is frankly unconvincing as WB Yeats. AT

Rod Taylor *John Cassidy* • Maggie Smith *Nora* • Julie Christie *Daisy Battles* • Flora Robson *Mrs Cassidy* • Sian Phillips *Ella* • Michael Redgrave *William Butler Yeats* • Edith Evans *Lady Gregory* ■ *Dir* Jack Cardiff, John Ford • *Scr* John Whiting, from the autobiography *Mirror in My House* by Sean O'Casey

Young Connecticut Yankee in King Arthur's Court ★★

Fantasy adventure
1995 · Can/Fr/UK · Colour · 95mins

Yet another in the long line of movies spun from Mark Twain's satirical fantasy, this time with a streetwise teen (Phillipe Ross) doing the time-travelling – itself a familiar device. It's the magicians who take centre stage here, with Michael York and Theresa Russell hamming it up for all they're worth as eternal adversaries Merlin and Morgan Le Fay. RT

Michael York *Merlin* • Theresa Russell *Morgan Le Fay* • Philippe Ross *Hank* • Nick Mancuso *King Arthur* • Polly Shannon *Alisande/ Alexandra* • Jack Langedijk *Ulrich* • Paul Hopkins *Sir Galahad* ■ *Dir* Ralph L Thomas • *Scr* Frank Encarnacao, Ralph L Thomas, from the novel *A Connecticut Yankee in King Arthur's Court* by Mark Twain

Young Dillinger ★

Crime drama 1965 · US · BW · 104mins

Not simply *Dillinger*, but *Young Dillinger*, in an attempt to lure the teen audience to a dime-budget gangster picture made principally for the drive-in theatres. More of a beach party than a gangster movie, it stops short of seeing our heroes die beneath a hail of FBI bullets because that happened when they were old. AT

Nick Adams *John Dillinger* • Robert Conrad *Pretty Boy Floyd* • John Ashley *Baby Face Nelson* • Dan Terranova *Homer Van Meter* • Victor Buono *Professor Hoffman* ■ *Dir* Terry Morse • *Scr* Arthur Hoerl, Don Zimbalist, from a story by Don Zimbalist

Young Dr Kildare ★★★

Medical drama 1938 · US · BW · 81mins

After the success of the Hardy Family series, MGM was looking for another series to equal it. They developed it from the hospital stories of Max Brand, immediately establishing the magic formula and cast. Lew Ayres as the idealistic young Kildare decides to reject a country practice with his father and takes up an offer from a big city hospital. Lionel Barrymore, playing his mentor Dr Gillespie, had recently found himself unable to walk because of a crippling hip disease, but continued his acting career in a wheelchair. The sparky relationship between the pair is one of the delights of the series. RB

Lew Ayres *Dr James Kildare* • Lionel Barrymore *Dr Leonard Gillespie* • Lynne Carver *Alice Raymond* • Nat Pendleton *Joe Wayman* • Jo Ann Sayers *Barbara Chanler* • Samuel S Hinds *Dr Stephen Kildare* • Emma Dunn *Mrs Martha Kildare* • Walter Kingsford *Dr Walter Carew* • Monty Woolley *Dr Lane Porteus* ■ *Dir* Harold S Bucquet • *Scr* Willis Goldbeck, Harry Ruskin, from a story by Max Brand

The Young Doctors ★★★

Drama 1961 · US · BW · 102mins

Some heavyweight actors lend their personalities and expertise to this standard hospital soap. There are no surprises as new young pathologist (Ben Gazzara) clashes with venerable Fredric March about correct procedure on a couple of cases, or in the romantic entanglements between medics and nurses. Eddie Albert is a senior doctor and George Segal makes his debut in a supporting role. RK

Fredric March *Dr Joseph Pearson* • Ben Gazzara *Dr David Coleman* • Dick Clark *Dr Alexander* • Ina Balin *Cathy Hunt* • Eddie Albert *Dr Charles Dornberger* • George Segal *Dr Howard* ■ *Dir* Phil Karlson • *Scr* Joseph Hayes, from the novel *The Final Diagnosis* by Arthur Hailey

Young Doctors in Love ★★★ 15

Comedy 1982 · US · Colour · 91mins

The first film from *Pretty Woman* director Garry Marshall is a wacky comedy that applies the *Airplane* approach to a laugh-a-minute look at the wilder side of life in a big-city hospital. As ever with such scattergun tactics, some jokes stick, and some don't. But even when they don't, there's a crack cast to keep you interested, including Sean Young, Harry Dean Stanton, Patrick Macnee and a young Demi Moore, who was then appearing in *General Hospital*, the sort of telly medico-soap that this film is sending up. Stupidly watchable. DA

Michael McKean *Dr Simon August* • Sean Young *Dr Stephanie Brody* • Harry Dean Stanton *Dr Oliver Ludwig* • Patrick Macnee *Dr Jacobs* • Hector Elizondo *Angelo/Angela Bonafetti* • Dabney Coleman *Dr Joseph Prang* • Demi Moore *New intern* ■ *Dir* Garry Marshall • *Scr* Michael Elias, Rich Eustis • *Music* Maurice Jarre

Young Einstein ★★★ PG

Comedy 1988 · Aus · Colour · 87mins

The deliciously named Yahoo Serious, the Australian one-man band who co-wrote, directed, co-produced and stars in this oddity, has more gifts as an actor than a director. Based on the notion that Einstein not only came from Tasmania, but also invented rock 'n' roll, the film is let down by Serious's flat direction and a frantic approach to gags. However, its sheer inventiveness grabs the attention, and its eccentricity and innocence are endearing. JM. Contains swearing.

Yahoo Serious *Albert Einstein* • Odile Le Clezio *Marie Curie* • John Howard (2) *Preston Preston* • Pee Wee Wilson *Mr Einstein* • Su Cruickshank *Mrs Einstein* • Basil Clarke *Charles Darwin* • Esben Storm *Wilbur Wright* ■ *Dir* Yahoo Serious • *Scr* David Roach, Yahoo Serious

Young Frankenstein ★★★★ 15

Horror spoof 1974 · US · BW · 105mins

This loopy send-up of classic chiller clichés from Universal's monster heyday is one of director Mel Brooks's best comedies and it's also one of the genre's most thorough and successful fright film parodies. Gene Wilder plays the infamous baron's grandson, who copies his ancestor's experiments only to create the singularly inane Peter Boyle. Filmed in sumptuous black and white, and shot on sets used in the 1931 original *Frankenstein*, Brooks's ingenious tribute is often hysterically funny and always a scream. Madeleine Kahn's "bride", Gene Hackman's blind hermit, Marty Feldman's hunchbacked Igor and the marvellous "Putting on the Ritz" musical number give this loving homage real staying power. AJ. Contains violence, swearing. DVD

Gene Wilder *Doctor Frederick Frankenstein* • Peter Boyle *Monster* • Marty Feldman *Igor* • Madeline Kahn *Elizabeth* • Cloris Leachman *Frau Blücher* • Teri Garr *Inga* • Kenneth Mars *Inspector Kemp* • Gene Hackman *Blindman* • Richard Haydn *Herr Falkstein* ■ *Dir* Mel Brooks • *Scr* Gene Wilder, Mel Brooks, from characters created by Mary Shelley

The Young Girls of Rochefort ★★★ PG

Musical comedy 1967 · Fr · Colour · 126mins

Jacques Demy failed to charm the critics with this fond tribute to the Hollywood musical. Not even Gene Kelly as an American in Rochefort could entrance in this fairy tale about the caprices of love and the showbiz ambitions of twin sisters, Catherine Deneuve and Françoise Dorléac (in the last film before her car-crash death). Michel Legrand's songs ingeniously propel the narrative, the performances are spirited and the atmosphere is all pastel shades and sunshine. But, apart from the opening number, the choreography is undistinguished. DP. In French with English subtitles.

Catherine Deneuve *Delphine Garnier* • Françoise Dorléac *Solange Garnier* • George Chakiris *Etienne* • Gene Kelly *Andy Miller* • Danielle Darrieux *Yvonne Garnier* ■ *Dir/Scr* Jacques Demy

The Young Guns ★★

Western 1956 · US · BW · 84mins

The juvenile delinquency cycle of the mid-1950s looks rather out of place transposed to the Old West in this story about the offspring of notorious outlaws being tempted to follow in their fathers' footsteps. Russ Tamblyn is too lightweight playing the victim of small-town prejudice, who becomes the leader of a gang but wavers over launching a criminal career. Too much debate, too little action. AE

Russ Tamblyn *Tully* • Gloria Talbott *Nora* • Scott Marlowe *Knox Cutler* • Wright King *Jonesy* ■ *Dir* Albert Band • *Scr* Louis Garfinkle

Young Guns ★★★ 18

Western 1988 · US · Colour · 102mins

Emilio Estevez plays Billy the Kid in this attempt to breath new life into the western. The movie's casual violence, breakneck pace and relentless hard rock score offended purists who chose to ignore the fact that, at 26, Estevez was closer in age to the real Billy (who died aged 22) than most previous actors. Estevez chooses to play him as a social bandit, a Robin Hood figure, in a film which also pays much attention to the look, broad racial mix and eccentric characters of the Old West. It's a western that shows both box-office calculation and respect for American history. AT. Contains swearing and violence. DVD

Emilio Estevez *"Billy the Kid"* • Kiefer Sutherland *Josiah "Doc" Scurlock* • Lou Diamond Phillips *Chavez* • Charlie Sheen *Dick Brewer* • Dermot Mulroney *"Dirty Steve" Stephens* • Casey Siemaszko *Charley Bowdre* • Terence Stamp *John Henry Tunstall* • Jack Palance *Lawrence G Murphy* ■ *Dir* Christopher Cain • *Scr* John Fusco

Young Guns II ★★ 15

Western 1990 · US · Colour · 99mins

More western romping with a modern spin in the company of Billy the Kid who, as played by Emilio Estevez with scene-stealing shamelessness, seems to have been little more than a violent show-off. Kiefer Sutherland and Lou Diamond Phillips also return from the first film, but this time round the tone is less certain, wavering uneasily between a serious appreciation of the western and an in-joke with the audience. JM. Contains violence, swearing and brief nudity. DVD

Emilio Estevez *William H Bonney/Bushey Bill Roberts* • Kiefer Sutherland *Doc Scurlock* • Lou Diamond Phillips *Chavez Y Chavez* • Christian Slater *Arkansas Dave Rudabaugh* • William L Petersen *Pat Garrett* • Alan Ruck *Hendry French* • RD Call *DA Ryerson* • James Coburn *John Chisum* • Balthazar Getty *Tom O'Folliard* • Jack Kehoe *Ashmun Upson* ■ *Dir* Geoff Murphy • *Scr* John Fusco

Young Guns of Texas ★★ U

Western 1962 · US · Colour · 77mins

Leads James Mitchum, Alana Ladd and Jody McCrea lack the charisma of their fathers, Robert, Alan and Joel. Still, this is an OK western, which opens with a fight involving McCrea and Gary Conway and soon has a quartet of youngsters on the run after a shooting. Nothing more than routine. BB

James Mitchum *Morgan Coe* • Alana Ladd *Lily Glendenning* • Jody McCrea *Jeff Shelby* • Chill Wills *Preacher Sam Shelby* • Gary Conway *Tyler Duane* ■ *Dir* Maury Dexter • *Scr* Henry Cross [Harry Spalding]

Young Husbands ★★★

Drama 1958 · It/Fr · BW · 101mins

Mauro Bolognini (and his co-writers which included Ennio Flaiano and Pier Paolo Pasolini) won the best screenplay prize at Cannes for this amusing but somewhat superficial study of male bonding and patriarchal notions of fidelity. The film explores how a group of married friends on a last unfettered blowout realise that their days of macho posturing and social irresponsibility are over. Played with spirit, but directed with detachment, this is and entertaining, but not particularly revealing, film. DP. An Italian language film.

Sylva Koscina *Mara* • Antonella Lualdi *Lucia* • Gérard Blain *Marcello* • Franco Interlenghi *Antonio* • Antonio Cifariello *Ettore* ■ *Dir* Mauro Bolognini • *Scr* Mauro Bolognini, Ennio Flaiano, Cureli, Pier Paolo Pasolini, Martino, from a story by Pasquale Festa Campanile, Massimo Franciosa

Young Ideas ★★ U

Comedy 1943 · US · BW · 76mins

Two student siblings (Susan Peters and Elliott Reid) try to thwart the new relationship of their widowed mother, played by Mary Astor. Featherweight stuff, this harmless MGM comedy has one or two touches of sophistication courtesy of director Jules Dassin, who would go on to make classic films such as *Naked City* and *Rififi*. Watch out for an uncredited appearance by a young Ava Gardner. RT

Susan Peters *Susan Evans* • Herbert Marshall *Michael Kingsley* • Elliott Reid *Jeff Evans* • Richard Carlson *Tom Farrell* • Allyn Joslyn *Adam Trent* • Dorothy Morris *Co-ed* • Frances Rafferty *Co-ed* • Ava Gardner ■ *Dir* Jules Dassin • *Scr* Ian McLellan Hunter, Bill Noble

The Young in Heart ★★★★

Comedy drama 1938 · US · BW · 90mins

A family of charming and scatty con tricksters is hounded out of the Riviera where the parents (Roland Young, Billie Burke), masquerading as aristocrats, have been trying to marry their offspring (warm and loving Janet Gaynor, and devil-may-care idler Douglas Fairbanks Jr) to rich spouses. En route to England and penniless, they befriend a lonely, very rich old lady (Minnie Dupree) who takes them in. Their intentions to fleece her and become her heirs slowly disappear as their affection for her grows and brings unexpected changes to their lives. A gloriously funny, original, sentimental, and thoroughly beguiling comedy. RK

Janet Gaynor *George-Anne* • Douglas Fairbanks Jr *Richard, her brother* • Paulette Goddard *Leslie Saunders* • Roland Young *"Sahib", their father* • Billie Burke *"Marmy", their mother* • Minnie Dupree *Miss Ellen Fortune* ■ *Dir* Richard Wallace • *Scr* Paul Osborn, Charles Bennett (adaptation), from the novel *The Gay Banditti* by IAR Wylie

Young Ivanhoe ★

Adventure
1994 · Can/Fr/UK · Colour · 95mins

There's far more talk than action in this account of Ivanhoe as a teenager, who, with a young Friar Tuck, battles not only King John but his evil henchman De Bourget in medieval England. If that sounds muddled, it's only typical of this confusing movie, which even at 95 minutes seems to be missing key scenes and lines of dialogue. Suggestive dialogue and some surprising violence make this questionable for younger viewers. KB

Y

U = SUITABLE FOR ALL Uc = SUITABLE FOR ALL, ESPECIALLY FOR YOUNG CHILDREN (VIDEO ONLY) PG = PARENTAL GUIDANCE

Kris Holdenried *Young Ivanhoe* • Stacy Keach *Pembrooke* • Margot Kidder *Lady Margarite* • Nick Mancuso *De Bourget* • Rachel Blanchard *Rowena* • Matthew Daniels *Tuck* ■ *Dir* Ralph L Thomas • *Scr* Frank Encarnacao, Ralph L Thomas

The Young Ladies of Wilko ★★★★

Drama 1979 · Pol/Fr · Colour · 115mins

Andrzej Wajda demonstrates an elegiac side with this melancholic adaptation, set in the late 1920s. The story follows Daniel Olbrychski on a convalescent return to the rural estate where he enjoyed an idyllic summer before the First World War, only to discover that the object of his youthful affection has died, while her five sisters (like himself disillusioned and jaded by the passage of time) have always adored him from afar. Superbly played and exquisitely bittersweet. DP. A Polish language film.

Daniel Olbrychski *Wiktor Ruben* • Anna Seniuk *Julia* • Christine Pascal *Tunia* • Maja Komorowska *Yola* ■ *Dir* Andrzej Wajda • *Scr* Zbigniew Kaminski, from the novella *Panny Z Wilka* by Jaroslav Iwaszkiewicz

Young Lady Chatterley ★★ 18

Erotic drama 1976 · US · Colour · 100mins

Not the prequel one might have expected, but rather a sequel to DH Lawrence's classic novel, in which Lady Chatterley's niece, Cynthia, inherits the family home where she romps with a lot more lovers than her auntie ever did. A "respectable" piece of soft porn inspired by the success of *Emmanuelle* and its ilk, the movie is at least elegantly turned out and passably erotic. The film was successful enough to produce a sequel, *Young Lady Chatterley II*, that was not seen in British cinemas. DM [video]

Harlee McBride *Lady Cynthia Chatterley* • Peter Ratray *Paul* • William Beckley *Philip Kensington* • Ann Michelle *Gwen* • Joi Staton *Mary* ■ *Dir* Alan Roberts • *Scr* Alan Roberts, from characters created by DH Lawrence

The Young Land ★★ U

Western 1959 · US · Colour · 88mins

A rare example of a minor sub-genre, the western courtroom drama, this attempts historical accuracy in its exploration of racial tension in 1840s California. When a young Anglo murders a Mexican, sheriff Patrick Wayne and judge Dan O'Herlihy must tread carefully while the largely Hispanic population watches to see if America's justice system is as unbiased as it claims. Unfortunately this is not the best made of films; its one saving grace is the charismatic Dennis Hopper as the villain. RT

Patrick Wayne *Jim Ellison* • Yvonne Craig *Elena de la Madrid* • Dennis Hopper *Hatfield Carnes* • Dan O'Herlihy *Judge Isham* • Roberto De La Madrid *Don Roberto* ■ *Dir* Ted Tetzlaff • *Scr* Norman Shannon Hall, from the story *Frontier Frenzy* by John Reese

The Young Lions ★★★ PG

Second World War drama
1958 · US · BW · 160mins

Adapted by Edward Anhalt from the doorstop novel by Irwin Shaw, this oozes self-importance in every scene. The action leapfrogs from Paris to America and from North Africa to Bavaria, taking nearly three hours to unravel. But, while the script is turgid, and Edward Dmytryk's direction often slows to a crawl, the picture succeeds for three reasons: Marlon Brando as a nice guy who becomes a Nazi and ends up a martyr, Montgomery Clift as a Jewish GI and Dean Martin as a cowardly Broadway star. AT [video]

Marlon Brando *Christian Diestl* • Montgomery Clift *Noah Ackerman* • Dean Martin *Michael Whiteacre* • Hope Lange *Hope Plowman* • Barbara Rush *Margaret Freemantle* • May Britt *Gretchen Hardenberg* • Maximilian Schell *Captain Hardenberg* • Lee Van Cleef *Sergeant Rickett* ■ *Dir* Edward Dmytryk • *Scr* Edward Anhalt, from the novel by Irwin Shaw

The Young Lovers ★★ U

Romantic drama 1954 · UK · BW · 92mins

For all his technical proficiency and fidelity to the written word, Anthony Asquith had a detached style that all too frequently diluted the dramatic impact of his pictures. With its soulless core and its slickly constructed chase finale, this Cold War tale of star-crossed lovers is a case in point, suffering as it does from that very style. The romance between an American Romeo (David Knight) and an Eastern European Juliet (Odile Versois) lacks both the passion and the sense of danger that might have raised the temperature. DP [video]

Odile Versois *Anna Szobeck* • David Knight *Ted Hutchens* • Joseph Tomelty *Moffatt* • Paul Carpenter *Gregg Pearson* • David Kossoff *Geza Szobeck* • Theodore Bikel *Joseph* • Jill Adams *Judy* • Betty Marsden *Mrs Forrester* • Joan Sims *Operator* ■ *Dir* Anthony Asquith • *Scr* Robin Estridge, George Tabori

The Young Lovers ★★

Melodrama 1964 · US · BW · 108mins

Art student Peter Fonda and trainee teacher Sharon Hugueny are enjoying a carefree affair until she becomes pregnant. Fonda, broke, feels unable to marry Hugueny, fearing it would harm his chances of getting a fellowship. She decides to forget him and have an abortion but finds she cannot go through with the treatment. A melodramatic morality tale that takes a long time to get going. DF

Peter Fonda *Eddie Slocum* • Sharon Hugueny *Pam Burns* • Nick Adams *Tarragoo* • Deborah Walley *Debbie* • Beatrice Straight *Mrs Burns* • Malachi Throne *Prof Schwartz* • Joseph Campanella *Prof Reese* ■ *Dir* Samuel Goldwyn Jr • *Scr* George Garrett, from the novel by Julian Halevy [Julian Zimet]

Young Man with a Horn ★★★ PG

Musical drama 1950 · US · BW · 107mins

When Isodore Demsky and Betty Perske dated in New York, they little dreamed they'd one day co-star in a movie biopic of their hero, jazz cornetist Bix Beiderbecke. But here they are on the Warner Bros lot, now rechristened Kirk Douglas and Lauren Bacall respectively, he dubbed by the great Harry James on trumpet, and she playing a daring-for-its-day society closet lesbian. Warners softened the source novel substantially, but enough of the sordid drama gets through, and this is a finely wrought melodrama of its time, with Douglas particularly outstanding as the self-absorbed horn player, leading vocalist and good girl Doris Day on some superbly staged standards. TS [video]

Kirk Douglas *Rick Martin* • Lauren Bacall *Amy North* • Doris Day *Jo Jordan* • Hoagy Carmichael *Smoke Willoughby* • Juano Hernandez *Art Hazzard* • Jerome Cowan *Phil Morrison* • Mary Beth Hughes *Margo Martin* ■ *Dir* Michael Curtiz • *Scr* Carl Foreman, Edmund H North, from the novel by Dorothy Baker

Young Man with Ideas ★★★ U

Comedy 1952 · US · BW · 84mins

Glenn Ford is the eponymous hero of this MGM production – a small-time lawyer from a small town, trying to break into the Los Angeles legal circuit, at the insistence of his ambitious wife Ruth Roman. Director Mitchell Leisen approaches what could be called camp in the treatment, but pulls it back securely to make it a likeable, if modest, comedy. TH

Glenn Ford *Maxwell Webster* • Ruth Roman *Julie Webster* • Denise Darcel *Dorianne Gray* • Nina Foch *Joyce Laramie* • Donna Corcoran *Caroline Webster* • Ray Collins *Edmund Jethrow* • Mary Wickes *Mrs Gilpin* ■ *Dir* Mitchell Leisen • *Scr* Arthur Sheekman

The Young Master ★★ 15

Martial arts comedy adventure
1979 · HK · Colour · 86mins

Jackie Chan embarked on his first film for the famous Golden Harvest studio without a completed script and there's an inescapable sense of muddle throughout this tale set in the Chinese city of Guangzhou in the early 1920s. Chan (who also co-wrote and directed the picture) plays a raw martial arts student who's forced to fight for the honour of his school. It's pretty standard stuff, but entertaining. DP. In Cantonese with English subtitles. [video] DVD

Jackie Chan *Ching Loong "Dragon"* • Wei Pai *Cheng Keung* • Lily Li ■ *Dir* Jackie Chan • *Scr* Jackie Chan, Lau Tin-Chee, Tun Lu, Tank Kin-Sang

Young Mr Lincoln ★★★★ U

Biographical drama 1939 · US · BW · 95mins

If ever a movie could be said to encapsulate the attitudes and ideals of its director, it is this study by John Ford of the early life of Abraham Lincoln, when the future president was a lawyer in Springfield, Illinois. A statesmanlike Henry Fonda is perfectly cast as Lincoln, portraying the man as a truly romantic and heroic figure despite being lumbered with a quite unnecessary false nose. Some may find this pure hagiography, but it is a mighty fine slice of Americana, and Ford keeps up the tension in the courtroom scenes. TS DVD

Henry Fonda *Abraham Lincoln* • Alice Brady *Abigail Clay* • Marjorie Weaver *Mary Todd* • Arleen Whelan *Hannah Clay* • Eddie Collins *Efe Turner* • Pauline Moore *Ann Rutledge* ■ *Dir* John Ford • *Scr* Lamar Trotti • *Cinematographer* Bert Glennon

The Young Mr Pitt ★★★★ U

Biographical drama 1942 · UK · BW · 118mins

This under-rated film was designed to show how Britain would always triumph over tyranny providing there was a born war leader at the helm. Yet director Carol Reed's account of how Pitt the Younger simultaneously resisted domestic disquiet and tamed Napoleon rises far above its flag-waving objectives. Reed handles the passing parade of political luminaries with an assurance that has rarely been surpassed. The period detail is nearly perfect and the parliamentary sequences are highly impressive. Leading a fine cast, Robert Donat is a model of embattled dignity, while Robert Morley is suitably flamboyant as Charles James Fox. DP

Robert Morley *Charles James Fox* • Robert Donat *William Pitt/Earl of Chatham* • Phyllis Calvert *Eleanor Eden* • Raymond Lovell *George III* • Max Adrian *Richard Brinsley Sheridan* • Felix Aylmer *Lord North* ■ *Dir* Carol Reed • *Scr* Frank Launder, Sidney Gilliat

The Young One ★★★

Drama 1960 · US/Mex · BW · 95mins

"This film was made with love, but American morality just couldn't accept it," said Luis Buñuel about this tale of racial hatred, corruption and seduction. The controversial subject concerns the rape of a 14-year-old orphan girl on an isolated island by her guardian. The Lolita-like girl is played rather amateurishly by Key Meersman, while Zachary Scott does his usual nasty bit. Rather turgid, but it does have a rough poetry, and even a gleam of hope. RB

Zachary Scott *Miller* • Key Meersman *Evalyn* • Bernie Hamilton *Traver* • Crahan Denton *Jackson* • Claudio Brook *Reverend Fleetwood* ■ *Dir* Luis Buñuel • *Scr* Luis Buñuel, HB Addis [Hugo Butler], from the story *Travellin' Man* in *Harper's* by Peter Matthiessen

The Young Ones ★★★ U

Musical comedy drama
1961 · UK · Colour · 103mins

This is the epitome of the "it's trad, dad" musical. The "putting on a show" format was as old as the talkies, but Sidney J Furie spruces it up with the help of a sprightly Cliff Richard, the Shadows and Robert Morley, on top form as the millionaire father who refuses to cough up the dough needed to save a youth club. The songs are a hit-and-miss bunch, but it's still amiable. DP [video] DVD

Cliff Richard *Nicky Black* • Robert Morley *Hamilton Black* • Carole Gray *Toni* • Richard O'Sullivan *Ernest* • Melvyn Hayes *Jimmy* • Teddy Green *Chris* • Hank Marvin • Bruce Welch • Jet Harris • Tony Meehan ■ *Dir* Sidney J Furie • *Scr* Ronald Cass, Peter Myers, from their story

Young People ★★ U

Musical drama 1940 · US · BW · 79mins

With her startlingly successful star career already on the downward slide at age 12, Shirley Temple's seven-year Fox contract ended here, and saw her playing second fiddle to Jack Oakie and Charlotte Greenwood. They are a pair of married vaudevillians who retire, briefly, to a farm; she's their adopted daughter. Standard cosy, innocent musical hokum, delivered with vigour, and fans will enjoy the briefly interpolated clips from some of Temple's early hits. RK

Shirley Temple *Wendy* • Jack Oakie *Joe Ballantine* • Charlotte Greenwood *Kit Ballantine* • Arleen Whelan *Judith* • George Montgomery *Mike Shea* • Kathleen Howard *Hester Appleby* ■ *Dir* Allan Dwan • *Scr* Edwin Blum, Don Ettlinger

The Young Philadelphians ★★★ PG

Melodrama 1959 · US · BW · 136mins

A polished example of the "poor boy who'll stop at nothing to succeed" melodrama – much in vogue in the late 1950s – gets a charisma boost from a devastatingly handsome Paul Newman. He plays a hungry young lawyer conniving his way to success. Barbara Rush is fine, too, as the society girl he craves, but it was Robert Vaughn who won an Oscar nomination for his performance as the army buddy on trial for murder for whom Newman risks everything to defend. AME [video]

Paul Newman *Tony Lawrence* • Barbara Rush *Joan Dickinson* • Alexis Smith *Carol Wharton* • Brian Keith *Mike Flanagan* • Diane Brewster *Kate Judson* • Billie Burke *Mrs J Arthur Allen* • Robert Vaughn *Chester "Chet" Gwynn* • Otto Kruger *John M Wharton* ■ *Dir* Vincent Sherman • *Scr* James Gunn, from the novel *The Philadelphian* by Richard Powell

The Young Poisoner's Handbook ★★★★ 15

Black comedy
1994 · UK/Ger · Colour · 95mins

Hugh O'Conor is frightfully wonderful in this controversial, fact-based crime drama as the teen chemist who poisons his family and co-workers as part of a warped series of experiments to satisfy his deviant curiosity. Director Benjamin Ross expertly balances black humour, morbidity and heightened reality, and along the creepy way perfectly captures the atmosphere of 1960s London suburbia. This witty

Y

delight is extraordinary if disturbing entertainment. AJ. Contains swearing.

Hugh O'Conor *Graham* • Antony Sher *Dr Zeigler* • Ruth Sheen *Molly* • Roger Lloyd Pack *Fred* • Charlotte Coleman *Winnie* • Paul Stacey *Dennis* • Samantha Edmonds *Sue* • Vilma Hollingberry *Aunt Panty* ■ *Dir* Benjamin Ross • *Scr* Jeff Rawle, Benjamin Ross

The Young Savages ★★★

Crime drama 1961 · US · BW · 103mins

A typical slice of New York liberal drama stars Burt Lancaster as the DA who prosecutes three delinquents accused of murdering a blind Puerto Rican youth. The story is spiced up by Lancaster's love life as well as his own background in the city slums – he sees in the three kids a mirror image of himself. It's taut, literate and forcefully directed by John Frankenheimer – his second feature. The eagle-eyed may spot Lee Grant in long shots – she walked off the picture and was replaced by Shelley Winters. AT

Burt Lancaster *Hank Bell* • Dina Merrill *Karin Bell* • Shelley Winters *Mary Di Pace* • Edward Andrews *Dan Cole* • Vivian Nathan *Mrs Escalante* • Larry Gates *Randolph* • Telly Savalas *Lt Richard Gunnison* • Pilar Seurat *Louisa Escalante* ■ *Dir* John Frankenheimer • *Scr* Edward Anhalt, JP Miller, from the novel *A Matter of Conviction* by Evan Hunter

Young Sherlock Holmes ★★★ PG

Mystery adventure
1985 · US · Colour · 104mins

Director Barry Levinson, working for Steven Spielberg's production company Amblin, gives a sensational, even supernatural, slant to this supposed biography of the young sleuth, which is hardly surprising considering the film's pedigree. As an account of the detective team's first meeting at school, it's quite commendable – Nicholas Rowe is a dashing Holmes, Alan Cox a solid Watson – but it's rather deficient in the proper atmosphere of hansom cabs and ugly deeds. TH DVD

Nicholas Rowe *Sherlock Holmes* • Alan Cox *John Watson* • Anthony Higgins *Rathe* • Freddie Jones *Chester Cragwitch* • Sophie Ward *Elizabeth* • Susan Fleetwood *Mrs Dribb* • Nigel Stock *Waxflatter* ■ *Dir* Barry Levinson • *Scr* Chris Columbus, from the characters created by Sir Arthur Conan Doyle

Young Soul Rebels ★ 18

Drama 1991 · UK · Colour · 100mins

There's no soul whatsoever in Isaac Julien's inept social drama set during the Queen's Silver Jubilee year of 1977. Heavily promoted as the first movie from a British-born gay black director, Julien throws everything into his unsubtle appraisal of how both minority groups blossomed during the punk era. Valentine Nonyela and Mo Sesay, as the two pirate radio disc jockeys out to solve the violent death of a gay friend, just don't have the presence to focus attention away from the embarrassment of glitches they're surrounded by. AJ. Contains swearing and drug abuse. DVD

Valentine Nonyela *Chris* • Mo Sesay *Caz* • Dorian Healy *Ken* • Frances Barber *Ann* • Sophie Okonedo *Tracy* • Jason Durr *Billibud* ■ *Dir* Isaac Julien • *Scr* Isaac Julien, Paul Hallam, Derrick Saldaan McClintock

The Young Stranger ★★★ U

Drama 1957 · US · BW · 84mins

James MacArthur is the young son whose film-executive father James Daly and mother Kim Hunter are too busy with their lives to support his. Resentful of this neglect, he eventually bursts out and assaults a cinema manager and a cop. Self-therapy of the worst kind. This was director John Frankenheimer's first movie after working in TV, a fact betrayed by the small-screen style of the segmented narrative, but the acting is true and touching, with MacArthur's performance – unlike his role – marvellously mature. TH

James MacArthur *Hal Ditmar* • Kim Hunter *Helen Ditmar* • James Daly *Tom Ditmar* • James Gregory *Sgt Shipley* • Whit Bissell *Grubbs, theatre manager* • Jeff Silver *Jerry* • Jack Mullaney *Confused boy* ■ *Dir* John Frankenheimer • *Scr* Robert Dozier, from his TV play *Deal a Blow*

Young Tom Edison ★★★ U

Biographical drama 1940 · US · BW · 85mins

MGM's attempt to make a genius seem like the kid next door, though Mickey Rooney acquits himself more than adequately as the American inventor in his early days as a small-town lad with brilliant thoughts. This was the first of a two-parter for MGM's best-known redheads, with Spencer Tracy following hot on Rooney's heels in *Edison, the Man*. TH

Mickey Rooney *Tom Edison* • Fay Bainter *Mrs Samuel Nancy Edison* • George Bancroft *Samuel Edison* • Virginia Weidler *Tannie Edison* • Eugene Pallette *Mr Nelson* • Victor Killian [Victor Kilian] *Mr Dingle* • Bobbie Jordan [Bobby Jordan] *Joe Dingle* • JM Kerrigan *Mr McCarney* ■ *Dir* Norman Taurog • *Scr* Bradbury Foote, Dore Schary, Jack Mintz, from material assembled by H Alan Dunn

Young Toscanini ★★

Biographical drama
1988 · Fr/It/Tur · Colour · 120mins

This is an all-too-easily overlooked period biopic from director Franco Zeffirelli. Facts are at a premium and soap operatic excess is very much to the fore in this handsome, sincere, but painfully overwrought melodrama, in which acting styles clash more loudly than the cymbals. C Thomas Howell is hopelessly miscast as the 18-year-old Arturo Toscanini, touring Latin America under the baton of John Rhys-Davies. But his over-exuberance pales beside the grande dame antics of Elizabeth Taylor, as the mistress of Brazilian emperor Philippe Noiret. DP

C Thomas Howell *Arturo Toscanini* • Elizabeth Taylor *Nadina Bulichoff* • Sophie Ward *Margherita* • John Rhys-Davies *Claudio Rossi* • Pat Heywood *Mother Allegri* • Philippe Noiret *Dom Pedro II* ■ *Dir* Franco Zeffirelli • *Scr* William Stadiem, Meno Menjes, from a story by Franco Zeffirelli, Ennio De Concini

The Young Warriors ★★

Second World War drama
1967 · US · Colour · 93mins

A standard Universal programme filler, made to break in a string of contract players, here the star is James Drury – who, at the time, was appearing in the popular TV series *The Virginian*. Nobody in the supporting cast is worthy of note, but what is somewhat surprising is that this compendium of clichés is scripted by the estimable Richard Matheson. TS

James Drury *Sergeant Cooley* • Steve Carlson (1) *Hacker* • Jonathan Daly *Guthrie* • Robert Pine *Foley* • Jeff Scott *Lippincott* • Michael Stanwood *Riley* ■ *Dir* John Peyser • *Scr* Richard Matheson, from his novel *The Beardless Warriors*

Young Warriors ★★ 18

Crime drama 1983 · US · Colour · 102mins

When his sister is raped and murdered, student James Van Patten won't wait for justice to take its course like his cop father, Ernest Borgnine, and rounds up some college friends to get revenge on the gang responsible. As the vigilante group roam the neighbourhood looking for the culprits, they viciously punish any other criminals they come across. The rule-of-law message of this brutal exploitation movie is swamped by the one-man-above-all action, making it all the more unpleasant. TH

Ernest Borgnine *Lieutenant Bob Carrigan* • Richard Roundtree *Sergeant John Austin* • Lynda Day George *Beverly Carrigan* • James Van Patten *Kevin Carrigan* • Anne Lockhart *Lucy* ■ *Dir* Lawrence D Foldes • *Scr* Lawrence D Foldes, Russell W Colgin

Young Winston ★★★ PG

Biographical drama
1972 · UK · Colour · 119mins

Richard Attenborough's account of Winston Churchill's early years, from school at Harrow to the Boer War to his first major parliamentary speech as MP for Oldham. Lavishly mounted but often lifeless, this is stodgily scripted by producer Carl Foreman. Robert Shaw and Anne Bancroft are excellent as Churchill's parents, and there's an impressive array of British talent in supporting roles, while young Simon Ward makes a fair stab at playing the budding British bulldog. AT

Simon Ward *Young Winston Churchill/Sir Winston Churchill's voice* • Robert Shaw *Lord Randolph Churchill* • Anne Bancroft *Lady Jennie Churchill* • John Mills *General Herbert Kitchener* • Ian Holm *George Buckle* • Anthony Hopkins *Lloyd George* ■ *Dir* Richard Attenborough • *Scr* Carl Foreman, from the autobiography *My Early Life: A Roving Commission* by Sir Winston Churchill

Young Wives' Tale ★★

Comedy 1951 · UK · BW · 78mins

This comedy of domestic chaos suffers from the problem that blights so many theatrical transfers – the inability to re-create the breathlessly contrived precision of a stage farce on the screen. To his credit, director Henry Cass keeps the action brisk, but the story of two respectable couples who share their house with a man-mad minx lacks the frantic danger that clearly made the live renditions so appealing. A young and flirtatious Audrey Hepburn steals every scene. DP

Joan Greenwood *Sabina Pennant* • Nigel Patrick *Rodney Pennant* • Derek Farr *Bruce Banning* • Guy Middleton *Victor Manifold* • Athene Seyler *Nanny Gallop* • Helen Cherry *Mary Banning* • Audrey Hepburn *Eve Lester* ■ *Dir* Henry Cass • *Scr* Ann Burnaby, from the play by Ronald Jeans

Youngblood ★★ 15

Sports drama 1986 · US · Colour · 105mins

A routine sports drama which features Rob Lowe as an up-and-coming hockey player who joins a small-town team, and falls for the daughter of its stereotypically tough-nut coach. The film toddles along, but never really gets its skates on. If you've seen any *Rocky* or *Karate Kid* films, then the "plot" will have a familiar ring, so to stay awake, try to spot Keanu Reeves. It's his feature debut. DA

Rob Lowe *Dean Youngblood* • Cynthia Gibb *Jessie Chadwick* • Patrick Swayze *Derek Sutton* • Ed Lauter *Coach Murray Chadwick* • Keanu Reeves *Heaver* ■ *Dir* Peter Markle • *Scr* Peter Markle, from a story by John Whitmore, Peter Markle

Youngblood Hawke ★★

Drama 1964 · US · BW · 136mins

James Franciscus may be the centre of attention as the Kentucky trucker who flirts with literary fame, but it's his female co-stars who contribute the more telling performances. Suzanne Pleshette is elegantly vulnerable as the editor he spurns, but she's given a lesson in scene-stealing from Mary Astor as a self-seeking actress and Genevieve Page as a man-mad socialite. Veteran director Delmer Daves does his best to imbue this potboiler with artistic significance. DP

James Franciscus *Youngblood Hawke* • Suzanne Pleshette *Jeanne Greene* • Genevieve Page *Frieda Winter* • Eva Gabor *Fannie Prince* • Mary Astor *Irene Perry* • Lee Bowman *Jason Prince* • Edward Andrews *Quentin Judd* ■ *Dir* Delmer Daves • *Scr* Delmer Daves, from the novel by Herman Wouk

Younger and Younger ★★ 15

Comedy 1993 · Ger/Fr/Can · Colour · 93mins

Another quirky story from German director Percy Adlon: a wife drops dead when she overhears her husband having his latest fling. But her image returns to haunt him and grows younger with every visit, ultimately resulting in him being aptly punished for his misdeeds. The film strives for an offbeat charm, but there's an air of desperation about it; the main interest resides in the strong cast. DA

Donald Sutherland *Jonathan Younger* • Lolita Davidovich *Penelope Younger* • Brendan Fraser *Winston Younger* • Sally Kellerman *Zig Zag Lilian* • Julie Delpy *Melodie* • Linda Hunt *Frances* • Nicholas Gunn *Benjamin* ■ *Dir* Percy Adlon • *Scr* Percy Adlon, Felix O Adlon

The Younger Brothers ★★ U

Western 1949 · US · Colour · 77mins

This utterly routine Technicolor western casts Wayne Morris, Bruce Bennett and James Brown as brothers and former outlaws hoping to make a fresh start as farmers. Only two weeks of parole are left before their pardon, but that's enough time for a revenge-seeking detective to try to involve them in a bank robbery. This is just about worth seeing for Janis Paige's enjoyable turn as the bandit out to lure the boys back to their old ways. AE

Wayne Morris *Cole Younger* • Janis Paige *Kate Shepherd* • Bruce Bennett *Jim Younger* • Geraldine Brooks *Mary Hathaway* • Robert Hutton *Johnny Younger* • Alan Hale *Sheriff Knudson* • James Brown (1) *Bob Younger* • Monte Blue *Joe* ■ *Dir* Edwin L Marin • *Scr* Edna Anhalt, from a story by Morton Grant

The Younger Generation ★★

Drama 1929 · US · BW · 75mins

An early sound entry, directed by Frank Capra, this melodrama concerns the emotional upheavals and moral conflicts that beset a poor New York Jewish family when their son makes a mint of money and leaves tradition behind for a Park Avenue life. Not without interest, and fielding a good cast headed by Jewish actors Jean Hersholt and the now-forgotten Rosa Rosanova, but it's woolly-minded, contrived, and over-sentimental. RK

Jean Hersholt *Julius Goldfish* • Lina Basquette *Birdie Goldfish* • Rosa Rosanova *Tildie Goldfish* • Ricardo Cortez *Morris* • Rex Lease *Eddie Lesser* • Martha Franklin *Mrs Lesser* ■ *Dir* Frank R Capra [Frank Capra] • *Scr* Sonya Levien, Howard J Green, from a story by Fannie Hurst

The Youngest Profession ★★★ U

Comedy 1943 · US · BW · 81mins

This innocent teens' frolic stars Virginia Weidler as the leader of an autograph collector's club at her girls' school, whose dedication gets her meetings with MGM stars Greer Garson, Walter Pidgeon and Robert Taylor. Parallel with her celebrity-seeking activities, Weidler acts as Little Miss Fixit at home, sorting out various misunderstandings involving her father and the governess. Bright and breezy, cute, and old-fashioned family entertainment. RK

Virginia Weidler *Joan Lyons* • Edward Arnold *Burton V Lyons* • John Carroll *Dr Hercules* • Ann Ayars *Susan Thayer* • Marta Linden *Edith*

U = SUITABLE FOR ALL Uc = SUITABLE FOR ALL, ESPECIALLY FOR YOUNG CHILDREN (VIDEO ONLY) PG = PARENTAL GUIDANCE

Lyons • Agnes Moorehead *Miss Featherstone* ■ *Dir* Edward Buzzell • *Scr* George Oppenheimer, Charles Lederer, Leonard Spigelgass, from the novel by Lillian Day

Your Beating Heart ★★★ 15

Romantic drama 1991 · Fr · Colour · 99mins

Making stylishly symbolic use of his Parisian locations, director François Dupeyron has succeeded in fashioning a Rohmeresque romance for 40-somethings. Unwilling to risk her marriage to an antique dealer, Dominique Faysse, nevertheless, can't resist Thierry Fortineau, the stranger who seduced her in a trance and now offers her a passion that is absent from her ordered houseboat existence. Faysse gives a marvellous display of disarranged dignity, which is given space to develop by Dupeyron's use of leisurely takes and gentle humour. DP. A French language film.

Dominique Faysse *Mado* • Thierry Fortineau *Yves* • Jean-Marie Winling *Jean* • Christophe Pichon *Stéphane* • Steve Kalfa *Luc* • Coralie Seyrig *Jeanne* ■ *Dir/Scr* François Dupeyron

Your Cheatin' Heart ★★★ U

Musical biography 1964 · US · BW · 98mins

George Hamilton turns in one of his most memorable performances as country singer Hank Williams, whose work is probably more famous in the hands of artists as diverse as The Carpenters (*Jambalaya*) and Ray Charles (*Your Cheatin' Heart*). Williams died young in 1953, after alcoholism put paid to a swift and packed career. His son, Hank Jr, who's a respected country star in his own right, provides the vocals. JG

George Hamilton *Hank Williams* • Susan Oliver *Audrey Williams* • Red Buttons *Shorty Younger* • Arthur O'Connell *Fred Rose* • Shary Marshall *Ann Younger* • Rex Ingram (2) *Teetot* • Chris Crosby *Sam Priddy* ■ *Dir* Gene Nelson • *Scr* Stanford Whitmore

Your Friends & Neighbours ★★★ 18

Black comedy drama
1998 · US · Colour · 95mins

Neil LaBute's follow-up to his stirring, nasty debut, *In the Company of Men*, is a slightly tamer affair that suffers somewhat from an imbalance of unlikeable characters. Jason Patric finds his niche in the role of an insensitive macho who has no problem bedding the wives and girlfriends of the men he hangs out with. Ben Stiller – unhappy in his domesticated relationship with Catherine Keener – lusts after pal Aaron Eckhart's missus (Amy Brenneman), while she has given up on having a fulfilling sex life with anyone. Troubling, twisted stuff. JB. Contains swearing, sex scenes and nudity. [video]

Amy Brenneman *Mary* • Aaron Eckhart *Barry* • Catherine Keener *Terri* • Nastassja Kinski *Cheri* • Jason Patric *Cary* • Ben Stiller *Jerry* ■ *Dir/Scr* Neil LaBute

Your Money or Your Wife ★

Comedy 1960 · UK · BW · 90mins

Nice title, shame about the movie. This is a farce in every sense of the word, as blissfully married Peggy Cummins and Donald Sinden have to divorce in order to come into an inheritance. Both screenwriter Ronald Jeans and director Anthony Simmons seemed to think that an abundance of slapstick, a little innuendo and bags of mugging would be enough to have the audience in convulsions. How wrong they were. DP

Donald Sinden *Pelham Butterworth* • Peggy Cummins *Gay Butterworth* • Richard Wattis *Hubert Fry* • Peter Reynolds *Theodore Malek* • Georgina Cookson *Thelma Cressingdon* ■ *Dir* Anthony Simmons • *Scr* Ronald Jeans

Your Three Minutes Are Up ★★

Comedy drama 1973 · US · Colour · 93mins

Beau Bridges and Ron Leibman star in this comedy about two wildly different friends and their relationship, Bridges being the straight arrow trying to come to terms with his wayward pal. Not as funny as you'd hope, this is still an interesting film thanks to the characterisations and the observations about America in the 1970s. JB

Beau Bridges *Charlie Reed* • Ron Leibman *Mike Robinson* • Janet Margolin *Betty* • Kathleen Freeman *Mrs Wilk* • David Ketchum *Mr Kellogg* • Stu Nisbet *Dr Claymore* ■ *Dir* Douglas N Schwartz [Douglas Schwartz] • *Scr* James Dixon

You're a Big Boy Now ★★★

Comedy drama 1966 · US · Colour · 97mins

This laid-back coming-of-age tale is probably most important nowadays as an example of the early work of director Francis Ford Coppola. As such, it is easy enough to overlook the quality cast, as teenager Peter Kastner, the pampered son of parents Geraldine Page and Rip Torn, discovers sex and drugs in the big wide world of New York when he falls for disco-dancer Elizabeth Hartman. Coppola's style and insight are already apparent in the range of characters and situations offered by this entertaining movie. And, as a bonus, there's music by the Lovin' Spoonful. TH

Elizabeth Hartman *Barbara Darling* • Geraldine Page *Margery Chanticleer* • Julie Harris *Miss Thing* • Rip Torn *IH Chanticleer* • Michael Dunn *Richard Mudd* • Karen Black *Amy* ■ *Dir* Francis Ford Coppola • *Scr* Francis Ford Coppola, from the novel by David Benedictus

You're a Sweetheart ★

Musical 1937 · US · BW · 96mins

The shenanigans of a publicity-hungry producer's attempts to get a new show onto Broadway constitute the main plot of an uninspired musical which, despite the star presence of 20th Century Fox's Alice Faye, did nothing for Universal Studios. Miss Faye and leading man George Murphy contribute a smooth and attractive dance routine to the title number, but that aside, it's a dull, rambling and silly contribution to the 1930s musical genre. RK

Alice Faye *Betty Bradley* • George Murphy *Hal Adams* • Ken Murray *Don King* • Charles Winninger *Cherokee Charlie* • Andy Devine *"Daisy" Day* • William Gargan *Fred Edwards* • Donald Meek *Conway Jeeters* ■ *Dir* David Butler • *Scr* Monte Brice, Charles Grayson, from a story by Warren Wilson, Maxwell Shane, William Thomas

You're Dead ★ 15

Crime comedy
1999 · US/Ger · Colour · 92mins

This is supposed to be a darkly surreal exploration of how civilised people can descend into savagery under pressure. Yet what emerges is a crass crime caper, in which a bungled bank raid goes nowhere near as badly wrong as the film itself. DP [video] DVD

John Hurt *Michael Maitland* • Rhys Ifans *Eddie Hayderhall* • Claire Skinner *Jo Simpson* • Barbara Flynn *Professor Corner* • John Benfield *Inspector Dick Badger* • David Schneider (1) *Ian Jeffries* ■ *Dir/Scr* Andy Hurst

You're In the Army Now ★ U

Comedy 1936 · UK · BW · 79mins

Surprisingly enough, this turgid slab of British melodrama was directed by the great Raoul Walsh. But this picture predates his glory years at Warner Bros and so it can be explained away as the kind of assignment a journeyman director was forced to accept in order to eat. Wallace Ford also made the trip across the Atlantic to give a dreadful performance as a New York gangster lying low in Blighty to avoid a murder rap. DP

Wallace Ford *Jim Tracey* • John Mills *Corporal Bert Dawson* • Anna Lee *Sally Bridges* • Grace Bradley *Jean Burdett* • Frank Cellier *Sergeant major Briggs* ■ *Dir* Raoul Walsh • *Scr* Bryan Edgar Wallace, Austin Melford, AR Rawlinson, from a story by Lesser Samuels, Ralph Gilbert Bettinson

You're in the Navy Now ★★ U

Comedy 1951 · US · BW · 92mins

The gag in this weary comedy is that the ship's running on steam (hence the original title *USS Teakettle*), but the tone is extremely uncertain, and the comedic intentions misfire as often as the ship's engine. Cooper has the good grace to look uncomfortable, but always in character. Watch very closely for a couple of major movie debuts: Lee Marvin and Charles Bronson (then known as Buchinsky) made their official screen bows in this film. TS

Gary Cooper *Lieutenant John Harkness* • Jane Greer *Ellie* • Millard Mitchell *Larrabee* • Eddie Albert *Lieutenant Bill Barron* • John McIntire *Commander Reynolds* • Ray Collins *Admiral Tennant* ■ *Dir* Henry Hathaway • *Scr* Richard Murphy, from a magazine article in the *New Yorker* by John W Hazard

You're My Everything ★★ U

Musical 1949 · US · Colour · 94mins

This rose-tinted slice of 20th Century-Fox nostalgia is set at the beginning of the talkie era, a time that producer George Jessel (who also wrote the original story) had more than a passing interest in, since he was once a star of early sound films. Hard-working Dan Dailey is in the lead, but the pace is leaden, the plotline cliché-ridden, and leading lady Anne Baxter inadequate. The unexpected bonus is the great Buster Keaton, in the re-creation of a silent movie, his stone face alone making this worth a look. TS

Dan Dailey *Timothy O'Connor* • Anne Baxter *Hannah Adams* • Anne Revere *Aunt Jane* • Stanley Ridges *Mr Mercer, producer* • Shari Robinson *Jane O'Connor* • Buster Keaton ■ *Dir* Walter Lang • *Scr* Lamar Trotti, Will H Hays Jr, from a story by George Jessel

You're My Hero ★★★ 15

Comedy drama 2003 · Sp · Colour · 102mins

Spanish director Antonio Cuadri uses his country's transition from fascist dictatorship to constitutional monarchy to mirror the confusion felt by teenager Manuel Lozano as he arrives at yet another new school. Cuadri cleverly coats the political subtext with nostalgia for the trappings of the mid-1970s, reinforced by the Europop soundtrack. Lozano's dealings with bully Alfonso Mena, tousled pretty boy Félix López and spiky Carmen Navarro are spiritedly enacted, but the contrast between liberal teacher Toni Cantó and martinet priest Juan Fernández, could have been more shaded and Lozano's heart-to-hearts with a fantasy comic-book native American feel forced. DP. In Spanish with English subtitles. Contains swearing.

Manuel Lozano *Ramón* • Toni Cantó *Mateo* • Félix López *David* • Antonio Dechent *Water cloud* • Carmen Navarro *Paloma* • Juan Fernández *Don Félix* • Alfonso Mena *Rafa* • Pablo Acosta *Ortega* ■ *Dir* Antonio Cuadri • *Scr* Antonio Cuadri, Miguel Angel Pérez, Carlos Asorey

You're Never Too Young ★★★ U

Comedy 1955 · US · Colour · 102mins

Dean Martin and Jerry Lewis were in their prime for this funny movie, though the personal cracks were starting to appear in their relationship after six years on screen together. If the plot seems a mite familiar, that's because it's a Sidney Sheldon reworking of Billy Wilder's directing debut *The Major and the Minor*, only this time with the great Lewis masquerading as the 12-year-old Ginger Rogers – don't ask! The film looks stunning in rich Technicolor and trivia buffs might care to note that Diana Lynn appeared in both film versions of this plot. TS

Dean Martin *Bob Miles* • Jerry Lewis *Wilbur Hoolick* • Diana Lynn *Nancy Collins* • Nina Foch *Gretchen Brendan* • Raymond Burr *Noonan* • Mitzi McCall *Skeets* • Veda Ann Borg *Mrs Noonan* ■ *Dir* Norman Taurog • *Scr* Sidney Sheldon, from the play *Sunny Goes Home* by Edward Childs Carpenter, from the story *Connie Goes Home* by Fannie Kilbourne • *Cinematographer* Daniel L Fapp

You're Only Young Once ★★

Comedy drama 1938 · US · BW · 77mins

The second of the Andy Hardy films, with Lewis Stone taking over the role of Mickey Rooney's dad from Lionel Barrymore who played him in the first film, *A Family Affair*. Adored by studio boss Louis B Mayer, a Jewish émigré who wished to extol the virtues of small-town American life and childhood, the films struck a chord with American audiences on the brink of war. If *A Family Affair* was a try-out, this was the full dress rehearsal for a series that spawned 14 more movies between 1938 and 1958. AT

Lewis Stone *Judge James K Hardy* • Cecilia Parker *Marian Hardy* • Mickey Rooney *Andy Hardy* • Fay Holden *Mrs Emily Hardy* • Frank Craven *Frank Redman* • Ann Rutherford *Polly Benedict* • Eleanor Lynn *"Jerry" Lane* ■ *Dir* George B Seitz • *Scr* Kay Van Riper, from characters created by Aurania Rouverol

You're Only Young Twice ★★ U

Comedy 1952 · UK · BW · 84mins

This theatrical comedy was shakily brought to the screen by an unlikely alliance of producers, including documentary pioneer John Grierson, then involved in a publicly funded outfit called Group 3, based at studios in Southall. Dealing with various shenanigans at a Scottish university, the story involves mistaken identity, Celtic poetry, horse racing and the rigging of Rectorial elections. AT

Duncan Macrae *Professor Hayman* • Joseph Tomelty *Dan McEntee* • Patrick Barr *Sir Archibald Asher* • Diane Hart *Ada Shore* • Charles Hawtrey *Adolphus Hayman* • Robert Urquhart *Sheltie* • Ronnie Corbett ■ *Dir* Terry Bishop • *Scr* Terry Bishop, Reginald Beckwith, Lindsay Galloway, from the play *What Say They* by James Bridie

You're Telling Me! ★★★

Comedy 1934 · US · BW · 67mins

This sound remake of his silent vehicle, *So's Your Old Man*, gave WC Fields the chance to trot out his legendary golf course sketch one last time. But there's plenty to enjoy before this classic finale, as Fields's failed small-town inventor receives some unexpected support from holidaying royal Adrienne Ames. The highlights are the demonstration of his puncture-proof car tyre and the merciless repartee he shares with his shrewish wife, Louise Carter, and snobbish daughter, Joan Marsh, whose boyfriend is played by a pre-*Flash Gordon* Larry "Buster" Crabbe. DP

WC Fields *Sam Bisbee* • Larry "Buster" Crabbe *Bob Murchison* • Joan Marsh *Pauline Bisbee* • Adrienne Ames *Princess Marie Lescaboura* • Louise Carter *Mrs Bessie Bisbee* • Kathleen Howard *Mrs Edward*

Quimby Murchison ■ *Dir* Erle C Kenton • *Scr* Walter DeLeon, Paul M Jones, JP Mcevoy, from the short story *Mr Bisbee's Princess* by Julian Leonard Street

Yours, Mine and Ours ★★★ PG

Comedy drama 1968 · US · Colour · 106mins

Widower Henry Fonda has ten children. When he starts dating nurse Lucille Ball he neglects to tell her of his huge family just as she doesn't tell him about her own eight children. Eventually they come clean, marry and amalgamate their offspring – but its then their troubles really start. Based on the story of a real-life household, this is a slick and professional bit of fluff. Some of Ball's wilder antics seem out of step with the rest of the film but it certainly works as an undemanding family comedy. DF

Lucille Ball *Helen North* • Henry Fonda *Frank Beardsley* • Van Johnson *Darrel Harrison* • Tom Bosley *Doctor* • Louise Troy *Frank's Date* • Ben Murphy *Larry* • Jennifer Leak *Colleen* ■ *Dir* Melville Shavelson • *Scr* Melville Shavelson, Mort Lachman, from the story *Who Gets the Drumstick?* by Madelyn Davis, Bob Carroll Jr

Youth Runs Wild ★

Second World War drama
1944 · US · BW · 66mins

The working class community of a town is changed by war. With parents working in the local munitions factory, kids are neglected, misunderstandings arise, and teenagers get into trouble. A misjudged programmer produced by RKO's horror specialist, Val Lewton, who intended a "social conscience" drama but ended up with an earnest, preachy, unfocused mess. All involved are hamstrung by a simplistic, cliché-ridden and heavy-handed script. RK

Bonita Granville *Toddy* • Kent Smith *Danny* • Jean Brooks *Mary* • Glenn Vernon *Frank* • Tessa Brind *Sarah Taylor* • Ben Bard *Mr Taylor* • Mary Servoss *Mrs Hauser* • Arthur Shields *Mr Dunlop* • Lawrence Tierney *Duncan* ■ *Dir* Mark Robson • *Scr* John Fante, Ardel Wray, from a story by John Fante, Herbert Klein

You've Got Mail ★★★ PG

Romantic comedy
1998 · US · Colour · 114mins

Reworking director Ernst Lubitsch's classic *The Shop around the Corner*, and billed as the screen's first internet love story, this frail but winsome comedy reunited Tom Hanks with his *Sleepless in Seattle* co-star Meg Ryan and its director Nora Ephron. Rarely as amusing as it should be, this is frustratingly unromantic, with the stars coming together more like merged files than infatuated lovers. However, this latter-day screwball tale is certainly slickly staged and played with consummate ease, and Ryan and her bookshop staff exude a pleasant feeling of cosiness. DP. Contains swearing. DVD

Meg Ryan *Kathleen Kelly* • Tom Hanks *Joe Fox* • Greg Kinnear *Frank Navasky* • Parker Posey *Patricia Eden* • Steve Zahn *George Pappas* • Dave Chappelle *Kevin Scanlon* • Dabney Coleman *Nelson Fox* ■ *Dir* Nora Ephron • *Scr* Nora Ephron, Delia Ephron, from the film *The Shop around the Corner* by Samson Raphaelson, from the play *Parfumerie* by Miklos Laszlo

Yoyo ★★★★

Silent comedy 1964 · Fr · BW · 92mins

Pierre Etaix assisted Jacques Tati on *Mon Oncle*, and, while it is not exactly true to say that if you love Tati you'll like Etaix, in his second feature film, the similarities were never more apparent. The picture is as much a tribute to the much-mourned visual delights of the silent cinema as it is a homage to mime and clowning. As director, Etaix makes superb use of the camera, while in the dual role of a millionaire and a circus clown he gives a performance worthy of Chaplin. DP

Pierre Etaix *Millionaire/Yoyo* • Philippe Dionnet *Yoyo, as a child* • Luce Klein *Equestrienne* • Claudine Auger *Isolina* ■ *Dir* Pierre Etaix • *Scr* Pierre Etaix, Jean-Claude Carrière

Yu-Gi-Oh! The Movie ★★ PG

Animated fantasy adventure
2004 · Jpn/US/S Kor · Colour · 86mins

Like *Pokémon* and *Digimon* before it, popular Japanese animation *Yu-Gi-Oh!* seems to exist solely in order to sell its tie-in merchandise. Hero Yugi, the master of a Top Trumps-style game called Duel Monsters, discovers that his hobby has a mysterious (and dangerous) past. Yugi has to battle an evil ancient Egyptian spirit called Anubis. Only fans of the TV series will be able to follow the largely incomprehensible plot and the bog-standard animation won't win it any new ones. LB. Japanese dialogue dubbed into English. DVD

Dan Green *Yugi Moto/Yami Yugi* • Amy Birnbaum *Tea Garnder* • Wayne Grayson *Joey Wheeler* • Eric Stuart *Seto Kaiba* ■ *Dir* Hatsuki Tsuji • *Scr* From a story by Junki Takegami, Masahiro Hikokubu, from a comic book by Kazuki Takahashi

Z ★★★★ 15

Political drama
1968 · Fr/Alg · Colour · 121mins

Two of Europe's finest actors – Yves Montand and Jean-Louis Trintignant – star in this Oscar-winning political thriller about corruption in high places. Though shot in Algeria and serving as a universal condemnation of totalitarianism, Costa-Gavras's film is in fact based on the murder of a prominent liberal opponent of the military regime in Greece in 1963. As the investigating magistrate, Trintignant uncovers a vicious betrayal surrounding the death of Montand and, as his inquiry progresses and links to the government are established, he is increasingly under pressure to discontinue his probe. This is a landmark, eye-opening movie for its depiction of government depravity; unsurprisingly, it was banned in Greece until the military government was overthrown in 1974. TH. In French with English subtitles.

Yves Montand *The Deputy* • Jean-Louis Trintignant *Examining Magistrate* • Irene Papas *Hélène* • Charles Denner *Manuel* • Georges Géret [Georges Geret] *Nick* • Jacques Perrin *Journalist* • François Périer *Attorney* • Pierre Dux *General* ■ *Dir* Costa-Gavras • *Scr* Costa-Gavras, Jorge Semprun, from the novel by Vassilis Vassilikos • *Cinematographer* Raoul Coutard • *Music* Mikis Theodorakis

ZPG: Zero Population Growth ★★

Science fiction 1971 · US · Colour · 96mins

With thought outlawed in *Nineteen Eighty-Four* and age prohibited in *Logan's Run*, it was only a matter of time before reproduction would find itself outside the law. In a smog-bound, overpopulated future a tyrannical regime has launched a line of robot-children and made birth a death penalty offence. Oliver Reed and Geraldine Chaplin play the parents in peril in this dreary hide-and-seek saga. DP. Contains violence.

Oliver Reed *Russ McNeil* • Geraldine Chaplin *Carole McNeil* • Don Gordon *George Borden* • Diane Cilento *Edna Borden* • David Markham *Dr Herrick* • Sheila Reed *Dr Mary Herrick* • Aubrey Woods *Dr Mallory* ■ *Dir* Michael Campus • *Scr* Max Ehrlich, Frank De Felitta

Zabriskie Point ★★★ 15

Drama 1970 · US · Colour · 106mins

Michelangelo Antonioni's US debut is a sprawling and often unconvincing examination of American decadence. Made when the radical activism of the 1960s had begun to wane, it has student Mark Frechette and pot-smoking secretary Daria Halprin throw themselves into a Death Valley love affair. The endless billboards, the carefree frolics in the sand and the psychedelic painting of Frechette's stolen plane all drip with significance, but you can't help feeling that Antonioni hadn't really got to grips with the States or modern youth. Cracking last shot, though. DP. Contains swearing and nudity.

Mark Frechette *Mark* • Daria Halprin *Daria* • Rod Taylor *Lee Allen* • Paul Fix *Cafe owner* • GD Spradlin *Lee Allen's associate* • Bill Garaway *Morty* • Kathleen Cleaver *Kathleen* ■ *Dir* Michelangelo Antonioni • *Scr* Michelangelo Antonioni, Fred Gardner, Sam Shepard, Tonino Guerra, Clare Peploe, from a story by Michelangelo Antonioni • *Cinematographer* Alfio Contini

Zachariah ★★ 15

Musical western 1970 · US · Colour · 92mins

An offbeat and satirical rock western about two young men embarking on a life of violent crime features Don Johnson in an early role. This boasts appearances by a whole host of contemporary musicians, including Country Joe and The Fish (of *Woodstock* fame), The James Gang, Elvin Jones and the New York Rock Ensemble. It's the sort of film for which the phrase "you'll either love it or loathe it" might have been specially coined. DA DVD

John Rubinstein *Zachariah* • Pat Quinn [Patricia Quinn] *Belle Starr* • Don Johnson *Matthew* • Elvin Jones *Job Cain* • Doug Kershaw *Fiddler* • Dick Van Patten *The Dude* ■ *Dir* George Englund • *Scr* Joe Massot, Philip Austin, Peter Bergman, David Ossman, Philip Proctor

Zandalee ★★ 18

Romantic thriller 1991 · US · Colour · 99mins

In sultry New Orleans, feisty Erika Anderson tires of her pre-occupied poet husband Judge Reinhold and starts an affair with his best friend, painter Nicolas Cage. Standard love-tangle stuff, which is notable mainly for its steamy sex scenes and daft dialogue ("I want to shake you naked and eat you alive"). AJ DVD

Nicolas Cage *Johnny Collins* • Judge Reinhold *Thierry Martin* • Erika Anderson *Zandalee Martin* • Joe Pantoliano *Gerri* • Viveca Lindfors *Tatta* • Aaron Neville *Jack* • Steve Buscemi *OPP Man* • Marisa Tomei *Remy* ■ *Dir* Sam Pillsbury • *Scr* Mari Kornhauser

Zandy's Bride ★★

Western 1974 · US · Colour · 115mins

Even though it's set in the Old West, don't expect stampedes and shoot-outs, for the only showdowns at high noon in what is actually a domestic drama are between a coarse rancher and his feisty mail-order bride. Swedish director Jan Troell is so preoccupied with scenery, mood and period detail that he has left his cast with precious little to do. In the circumstances, Gene Hackman and Liv Ullmann's over-the-top performances are excusable. DP

Gene Hackman *Zandy Allan* • Liv Ullmann *Hannah Lund* • Eileen Heckart *Ma Allan* • Harry Dean Stanton *Songer* • Joe Santos *Frank Gallo* • Frank Cady *Pa Allan* • Sam Bottoms *Mel Allan* ■ *Dir* Jan Troell • *Scr* Marc Norman, from the novel *The Stranger* by Lillian Bos Ross

Zapped! ★★★ 15

Comedy 1982 · US · Colour · 93mins

Scott Baio is a nerdy high-school kid who gets zapped in a chem-lab explosion, and finds he has the power to move objects by thought alone. Cue lots of teen high-jinks, such as telekinetically divesting the busty local girls of their blouses, and taking control of the ball during a school baseball game. Madcap, and surprisingly amusing. DA

Scott Baio *Barney Springboro* • Willie Aames *Peyton Nichols* • Robert Mandan *Walter Johnson* • Felice Schachter *Bernadette* • Scatman Crothers *Dexter Jones* ■ *Dir* Robert J Rosenthal • *Scr* Bruce Rubin, Robert J Rosenthal

Zar Gul ★★★

Action adventure
1997 · Pak/UK · Colour · 140mins

Achieving notoriety through its use of live ammunition in the action sequences, Salmaan Peerzada's controversial blockbuster is both a

Z

politically inspired adventure and a passionate love story. Imraan Peerzada stars as the philanthropic businessman who becomes a latterday Robin Hood, seeking to fight the injustices that oppress the masses. However, he is also bent on revenge against Jamil Malik, the gangster who enslaved him as a boy and is now seeking election to the National Assembly. This is epic, angry and thrilling. DP. In Pushtu, Urdu, Punjabi and English with subtitles.

Imraan Peerzada *Zar Gul* • Talat Hussain *Zahid* • Steve Masty *Jack* • Salmaan Alik *Salmaan* • Faryal Gohar *Yasmin* • Jamil Malik *Yar Badshah* ■ *Dir/Scr* Salmaan Peerzada

Zarak ★★

Adventure 1956 · UK · Colour · 88mins

Victor Mature, in full Afghan mode, leads his gang of cut-throats against the might of the British army, headed by Michael Wilding, in a trashy adventure yarn set in the halcyon days of Empire. Apart from a belly dance by Anita Ekberg – which should have earned the movie an X rating – it's notable only as one of producer "Cubby" Broccoli's pre-Bond collaborations with director Terence Young, writer Richard Maibaum and cameraman Ted Moore, all of whom went on to make *Dr No*. AT

Victor Mature *Zarak Khan* • Anita Ekberg *Salma* • Michael Wilding *Major Ingram* • Bonar Colleano *Biri* • Finlay Currie *The Mullah* • Bernard Miles *Hassu* • Frederick Valk *Haji Khan* • Eunice Gayson *Cathy Ingram* • Patrick McGoohan *Moor Larkin* ■ *Dir* Terence Young • *Scr* Richard Maibaum, from the novel *The Story Of Zarak Khan* by AJ Bevan

Zardoz ★★ 15

Science-fiction adventure
1973 · UK · Colour · 101mins

Poor Sean Connery – Burt Reynolds obviously knew what he was doing when he said no to this naive futuristic hokum. Yet, thanks to Geoffrey Unsworth's stunning photography, this patently silly story, set in 2293 and telling of a rebellion against sexless intellectualism and soulless technology, has become one of those "risible but unmissable" cult movies, whose main attraction now is the unintentional comedy. The title is a contraction of "Wizard of Oz". DP. Contains swearing, nudity. [VIDEO] DVD

Sean Connery *Zed* • Charlotte Rampling *Consuella* • Sara Kestelman *May* • Sally Anne Newton *Avalow* • John Alderton *Friend* • Niall Buggy *Zardoz/Arthur Frayn* • Bosco Hogan *George Saden* • Jessica Swift *Apathetic* • Bairbre Dowling *Star* • Christopher Casson *Old scientist* • Reginald Jarman *Death* ■ *Dir/Scr* John Boorman

Zatoichi ★★★

Action adventure 1962 · Jpn · Colour · 96mins

This is the first of the 26 features about an itinerant blind masseur with a samurai's instinctive sword skills that would star Shintaro Katsu, not to mention more than 100 television episodes. Setting the series' scene, much of the story is taken up with establishing Zatoichi's low social status, his penchant for gambling and the acuity of his remaining senses. Yet considerable emphasis is also placed on his respect for Shigeru Amachi, the ronin with whom he will eventually have to duel to settle a clan turf war It's B-movie-making at its most meticulous. No wonder a cult was born. DP. A Japanese language film.

Shintaro Katsu *Zatoichi* • Masayo Banri *Otane* • Ryuzu Shimada *Sasagawa boss* • Hajime Mitamura *Hanji of Matsugishi* • Shigeru Amachi *Hirate* • Chitose Maki *Yoshi* • Michio Minami *Tatekichi* ■ *Dir* Kenji Misumi • *Scr* Minoru Inuzuka, from a short story by Kan Shimozawa

Zatoichi ★★★★ 18

Period action adventure
2003 · Jpn · Colour · 110mins

Shintaro Katsu may have starred as Zatoichi the blind swordsman in 26 B-movie adventures, but none of those can match the cinematic panache of Takeshi Kitano's thrilling variation on the traditional themes of duty, honour and championing the cause of the oppressed. Kitano takes on the iconic role of the itinerant masseur/swordsman, but his inevitable showdown with the warring clans terrorising the residents of a small town in 19th-century Japan isn't simply a homage to a cult hero. It's a glorious visual scrapbook referencing the greats of Japanese film-making who have influenced Kitano's unique blend of pitiless violence, slapstick comedy and sensitive social detail. Superbly shot and scored, this is both riotous entertainment and exquisite art. DP. In Japanese with English subtitles. Contains violence. [VIDEO] DVD

"Beat" Takeshi [Takeshi Kitano] *Zatoichi* • Tadanobu Asano *Hattori, the bodyguard* • Michiyo Ogusu *Aunt O-Ume* • Yui Natsukawa *Hattori's wife* • Guadalcanal Taka *Shinkichi* • Daigoro Tachibana *O-Sei, the geisha* • Yuko Daike *O-Kinu, the geisha* ■ *Dir* Takeshi Kitano • *Scr* Takeshi Kitano, from a short story by Kan Shimozawa

Zatoichi Meets Yojimbo ★★★ 12

Action adventure
1970 · Jpn · Colour · 115mins

This is one of the more engaging entries in the Blind Swordsman series, largely because director Kihachi Okamoto is so clearly attempting to duplicate the tone of Akira Kurosawa's 1961 classic *Yojimbo*. Shintaro Katsu again headlines as the one-time masseur who returns to his favourite village and finds it in the thrall of a ruthless merchant. The merchant's feud with his son has prompted the arrival of a couple of sinister samurai, Toshiro Mifune – secretly on a mission to recover the shogun's stolen gold – and sword-for-hire Shin Kishida. There's some explosive action, but also plenty of cerebral strategising. DP. In Japanese with English subtitles. [VIDEO] DVD

Shintaro Katsu *Zatoichi* • Toshiro Mifune *Yojimbo* • Mori Kishida *Kuzuryu* • Kanjuro Arashi *Hyoroku* ■ *Dir* Kihachi Okamoto • *Scr* Tetsuro Yoshida, Kihachi Okamoto, from a story by Kan Shimozawa

Zaza ★

Drama 1939 · US · BW · 83mins

Claudette Colbert stars as a touring vaudeville singer in the French provinces who falls in love with classy, middle-aged Parisian businessman Herbert Marshall and temporarily abandons her career until she discovers that he is married. Marshall looks uncomfortable and Colbert substitutes stridency for vivacity. RK

Claudette Colbert *Zaza* • Herbert Marshall *Dufresne* • Bert Lahr *Cascart* • Helen Westley *Anais* • Constance Collier *Nathalie* • Genevieve Tobin *Florianne* • Walter Catlett *Malaidot* • Ann E Todd *Toto* ■ *Dir* George Cukor • *Scr* Zoë Akins [Zoe Akins], from the play *Zaza* by Pierre Breton, Charles Simon, adapted by David Belasco

Zazie dans le Métro ★★★ 15

Surreal comedy 1960 · Fr · Colour · 88mins

Although he is often spoken of in the same breath as Jean-Luc Godard and François Truffaut, Louis Malle was always on the periphery of the French New Wave rather than an integral part of it. Here, however, he employs all the paraphernalia of his more iconoclastic contemporaries – jump cuts, games with film speed, rapid editing and movie in-jokes – to fashion an exhilarating comic fantasy, which follows the adventures of a young girl and her female impersonator uncle. Demonstrating ridiculous precocity, Catherine Demongeot almost blows the brilliant Philippe Noiret and the whole city of Paris off the screen. DP. In French with English subtitles. [VIDEO]

Catherine Demongeot *Zazie* • Philippe Noiret *Uncle Gabriel* • Hubert Deschamps *Turnadot* • Antoine Roblot *Charles* • Annie Fratellini *Mado* • Carla Marlier *Albertine* ■ *Dir* Louis Malle • *Scr* Louis Malle, Jean-Paul Rappeneau, from the novel *Zazie dans le Métro* by Raymond Queneau • *Cinematographer* Henri Raichi

Zebrahead ★★ 15

Romantic drama 1992 · US · Colour · 97mins

Made with the backing of Robert Redford's Sundance Institute and executive produced by Oliver Stone, this inter-racial romance boldly attempts to tackle a number of controversial themes. But such is the uncertainty of debutant Anthony Drazan's direction that the action all-too-rapidly becomes entangled in the knot of loose ends. Somewhere in the middle of the protests against their relationship, Michael Rapaport and N'Bushe Wright turn in touchingly honest performances. DP [VIDEO]

Michael Rapaport *Zack Glass* • Kevin Corrigan *Dominic* • Lois Bendler *Dominic's mother* • Dan Ziskie *Mr Cimino* • DeShonn Castle *Dee Wimms* • N'Bushe Wright *Nikki* • Marsha Florence *Mrs Wilson* • Shula Van Buren *Michelle* • Ron Johnson *Nut* • Ray Sharkey *Richard Glass* ■ *Dir/Scr* Anthony Drazan

A Zed & Two Noughts ★★ 15

Surreal drama
1985 · UK/Neth · Colour · 111mins

British director Peter Greenaway is one of those cinematic luminaries who provoke extreme reactions in people. Some fervently regard his highly stylised, elliptical films as works of deep and majestic genius while others think Greenaway is a classic case of the Emperor's New Celluloid Clothes. This is a perfect example of the latter. Concerned with the behaviour of two zoologist brothers after the bizarre demise of their wives, it looks wonderful, but is so painfully slow and visually driven that this is merely a painting on a cinema screen. SH. Contains nudity. [VIDEO] DVD

Andréa Ferréol *Alba Bewick* • Brian Deacon *Oswald Deuce* • Eric Deacon *Oliver Deuce* • Frances Barber *Venus de Milo* • Joss Ackland *Van Hoyten* • Jim Davidson *Joshua Plate* • Agnes Brulet *Beta Bewick* • David Attenborough *Narrator of wild-life footage* ■ *Dir/Scr* Peter Greenaway • *Cinematographer* Sacha Vierny • *Music* Michael Nyman

Zee and Co ★★

Drama 1971 · UK · Colour · 110mins

They might have called this *Who's Afraid of Elizabeth Taylor?* Scripted by Edna O'Brien, this preposterous marital malarkey should raise a few smirks as Taylor, Michael Caine (as her husband), Susannah York (as his lover) and Margaret Leighton (as a society hostess) play it close to the edge. Taylor slashes her wrists, York's earlier affair with a nun comes to the surface and before long the pair are in bed together. Pity poor Mr Caine. But pity everyone except the costume designer who works wonders with see-through materials. AT. Contains swearing and nudity.

Elizabeth Taylor *Zee Blakeley* • Michael Caine *Robert Blakeley* • Susannah York *Stella* • Margaret Leighton *Gladys* • John Standing *Gordon* • Michael Cashman *Gavin* ■ *Dir* Brian G Hutton • *Scr* Edna O'Brien

Zelary ★★★

Second World War drama
2003 · Cz Rep/Slo/Austria · Colour · 150mins

There's little novelty in Ondrej Trojan's Oscar-nominated adaptation, but it's easy to admire the way in which the Czech director slips moments of moving intimacy into this wartime epic. Forced to flee Prague when her doctor lover is betrayed to the Gestapo, nurse Anna Geislerova takes refuge in the Moravian mountains with Gyorgy Cserhalmi, a dishevelled loner whose lowly standing in the nearby village arouses suspicion of their unlikely marriage. Their growing affection is as inevitable as Geislerova's journey of self-discovery and the tragic climax, but this handsome drama is spiritedly played and never less than involving. DP. In Czech with English subtitles.

Anna Geislerova *Eliska/Hana* • Gyorgy Cserhalmi *Joza* • Jaroslava Adamova *Lucka* • Miroslav Donutil *Priest* • Jaroslav Dusek *Teacher* • Iva Bittova *Zena* • Ivan Trojan *Richard* • Jan Hrusinsky *Slavek* ■ *Dir* Ondrej Trojan • *Scr* Petr Jarchovsky, from the novel *Jozova Hanule* by Kveta Legatova

Zelig ★★★★ PG

Spoof documentary
1983 · US · BW and Colour · 78mins

Shot as a mock 1930s documentary in scratchy black and white, this defiantly uncommercial film from Woody Allen is not just technically groundbreaking – inserting "human chameleon" Leonard Zelig (Allen) into newsreel footage of Hitler and archive photos of Jack Dempsey and President Coolidge – but laugh-out-loud funny, too. In assimilating the characteristics of those around him, whether physical, religious or ethnic, Zelig speaks of a human desire to fit in, and it is apt that the thrust of the documentary is one of doctors (including the sympathetic Mia Farrow) trying to "cure" him, while the media fêtes him. A poignant, melancholy, beautifully realised hymn to individualism. AC [VIDEO] DVD

Woody Allen *Leonard Zelig* • Mia Farrow *Dr Eudora Fletcher* • John Buckwalter *Dr Sindell* • Garrett Brown [Garrett M Brown] *Actor Zelig* • Stephanie Farrow *Sister Meryl* • Will Holt *Rally Chancellor* • Sol Lomita *Martin Geist* ■ *Dir/Scr* Woody Allen • *Cinematographer* Gordon Willis • *Editor* Susan E Morse • *Production Designer* Mel Bourne

Zelly and Me ★★★ 15

Drama 1988 · US · Colour · 88mins

This is a graceful film that deals with an ungraceful subject: psychological violence visited on the young. Alexandra Johnes is an orphaned eight-year-old who goes to live with her grandmother Glynis Johns, a lonely woman who jealously tries to keep Johnes for herself. The young girl is attached to her nanny Isabella Rossellini, but her grandmother tries to separate the two by banishing Rossellini for a jumped-up violation of trust. Johns is excellent at evincing selfish cruelty just as Tina Rathborne's fine direction adds that extra dimension to the turn of the screw. Watch out for Rossellini's then partner, film director David Lynch, in a supporting role. FL [VIDEO]

Isabella Rossellini *Zelly* • Glynis Johns *Co-Co* • Alexandra Johnes *Phoebe* • Kaiulani Lee *Nora* • David Lynch *Willie* • Joe Morton *Earl* ■ *Dir/Scr* Tina Rathborne

Zenobia ★★★ U

Comedy 1939 · US · BW · 69mins

Known in Britain as *Elephants Never Forget*, this gentle comedy would be forgettable except for the fact that Oliver Hardy starred without Stan Laurel (who was having contract difficulties with the Hal Roach Studios).

Z

So Ollie has it all his own way as a doctor in a small town who is given an elephant to look after by showman Harry Langdon. The pesky pachyderm then follows Ollie everywhere, even into court when his benefactor is put on trial. Amiable stuff. TH

Oliver Hardy *Dr Henry Tibbett* • Harry Langdon *Prof McCrackle* • Billie Burke *Mrs Bessie Tibbett* • Alice Brady *Mrs Carter* • James Ellison *Jeff Carter* • Jean Parker *Mary Tibbett* • Step'n Fetchit [Stepin Fetchit] *Zero* • Hattie McDaniel *Dehlia* ■ *Dir* Gordon Douglas • *Scr* Corey Ford, from a story by Walter DeLeon, Harold Belgard, from the short story *Zenobia's Infidelity* by Henry C Bunner

Zeppelin ★★ PG

First World War drama
1971 · UK · Colour · 97mins

Warner Bros threw money at this drama, but it simply failed to take off with audiences. Michael York admirably conveys the dilemma facing a Scottish-German soldier who's unsure where his true loyalties lie, but his spying mission for the Admiralty is hamstrung by an over-abundance of civilised chat and a lack of tension. However, the finale is breathtaking. DP. Contains swearing.

Michael York *Geoffrey Richter-Douglas* • Elke Sommer *Erika Altschul* • Marius Goring *Professor Christian Altschul* • Peter Carsten *Major Alfred Tauntler* • Anton Diffring *Colonel Johann Hirsch* • Andrew Keir *Lt Cmdr Horst von Gorian* • Rupert Davies *Captain Whitney* • Alexandra Stewart *Stephanie Ross* ■ *Dir* Etienne Périer • *Scr* Arthur Rowe, Donald Churchill, from a story by Owen Crump

Zéro de Conduite ★★★★★ PG

Classic comedy drama
1933 · Fr · BW · 41mins

Comical, lyrical, surreal and packed with references to animator Emile Cohl, Abel Gance and Charlie Chaplin, this savage satire on public school life was considered so inflammatory by the French authorities that it was banned until 1945. Reflecting the militancy of his anarchist father and a loathing of the institutions that blighted his sickly childhood, Jean Vigo abandoned traditional narrative and formal principles and experimented with angles, perspectives and space to convey the pschological state of the rebellious students. However, the film's elliptical poetry was something of an accident, as Vigo was forced to abbreviate the action to fit the agreed running time. DP. In French with English subtitles. DVD

Jean Dasté *Superintendent Huguet* • Robert Le Flon *Superintendent Parrain, "Pète-Sec"* • Delphin *Principal* • Blanchar *Superintendent Général aka "Bec de gaz"* • Larive [Léon Larive] *Chemistry professor* • Mme Emile *Madame Colin, "Mère Haricot"* • Louis de Gonzague-Frick *Le Préfet* ■ *Dir/Scr* Jean Vigo • *Cinematographer* Boris Kaufman

Zero Effect ★★★★ 15

Detective comedy thriller
1997 · US · Colour · 111mins

Bill Pullman is the world's greatest private detective, but he's also a recluse who only ventures out when on a case, relying the rest of the time on frontman Ben Stiller. The pair are hired by tycoon Ryan O'Neal to solve a quirky mystery, and we're taken on a *Moonlighting*-style ride of comedy, romance and sleuthing as the reclusive Pullman tangles with paramedic Kim Dickens, who seems to have found a way through his defences. Packed with wickedly wacky moments and a terrific performance from Pullman, this is decidedly offbeat, but also smart, witty and entertaining. JB. Contains swearing, violence, sex scenes.

Bill Pullman *Daryl Zero* • Ben Stiller *Steve Arlo* • Ryan O'Neal *Gregory Stark* • Kim Dickens *Gloria Sullivan* • Angela Featherstone *Jess* • Hugh Ross *Bill* • Sara Devincentis *Daisy* ■ *Dir/Scr* Jake Kasdan

Zero Hour! ★★★ U

Drama 1957 · US · BW · 81mins

Watching this 1950s airborne drama now, you can see what a wonderful template it was for the spoof *Airplane!* Passengers and crew on a jetplane suffer from food poisoning leaving stressed-out former pilot Dana Andrews as the man of the hour. He's forced to take over the controls – more than director Hall Bartlett does – much to the joy of wife Linda Darnell and the sneers of ground controller Sterling Hayden. Solid entertainment. TH

Dana Andrews *Ted Stryker* • Linda Darnell *Elena Stryker* • Sterling Hayden *Capt Treleaven* • Peggy King *Stewardess* • Raymond Ferrell *Joey Stryker* • Elroy "Crazylegs" Hirsch *Capt Wilson* • Jerry Paris *Tony Decker* • Geoffrey Toone *Dr Baird* ■ *Dir* Hall Bartlett • *Scr* Arthur Hailey, Hall Bartlett, John C Champion, from a story by Arthur Hailey, from his teleplay *Flight into Danger*

Zero Kelvin ★★★

Period adventure drama
1995 · Nor · Colour · 113mins

Set in 1925, this titanic battle of wills shuns an easy reliance on blockbuster-style heroics to concentrate on the complex interaction between the members of an expedition stranded in the frozen Arctic. Hans Petter Moland's intense adventure contains striking photography by Philip Øgaard. It's also simmeringly played by Gard B Eidsvold as the poet seeking inspiration for a book, Stellan Skarsgård as the trapper who incurs his ire and Bjorn Sundquist, as the scientist whose disappearance forces the rivals to reassess their relationship. DP. In Norwegian with English subtitles.

Gard B Eidsvold *Larsen* • Stellan Skarsgård *Randbaek* • Bjorn Sundquist *Holm* • Camilla Martens *Gertrude* ■ *Dir* Hans Petter Moland • *Scr* Hans Petter Moland, Lars Bill Lundheim, from the novel *Larsen* by Peter Tutein

Zero Patience ★★ 18

Musical 1993 · Can · Colour · 96mins

Out of the glut of Aids awareness movies, this stands alone for treating the subject in a light-hearted and irreverent manner. Normand Fauteux is the promiscuous airline steward supposedly responsible for introducing the virus into the Northern Hemisphere. Through his ghostly visitations to Victorian anthropologist Richard Burton (don't ask!), we're taken on an outrageous musical odyssey through aspects of gay life. Tasteless and trivial. AJ. Contains swearing and nudity. DVD

John Robinson (2) *Sir Richard Francis Burton* • Normand Fauteux *Patient Zero* • Dianne Heatherington *Mary* • Richardo Keens-Douglas *George* • Bernard Behrens *Doctor Placebo* ■ *Dir/Scr* John Greyson

Zero to Sixty ★★ 15

Comedy 1978 · Can · Colour · 97mins

This lively if raucous car-chase comedy involves a middle-aged man (Darren McGavin) and a teenage girl (Denise Nickerson) who fall foul of the Mafia when they repossess a car with a body in the boot. This is watchable enough, though it lacks depth. JG

Darren McGavin *Mike* • Denise Nickerson *Larry* • Joan Collins *Gloria* • Dick Martin *Attorney* • Sylvia Miles *Flo* ■ *Dir* Don Weis • *Scr* W Lyle Richardson, from a story by Peg Shirley, Judith Bustany

Zeta One ★ 18

Science fiction 1969 · UK · Colour · 82mins

Adapted from a short-lived comic strip, this British sexploitation comedy makes the Robin Askwith *Confession* films look like the works of Sergei Eisenstien. Told in flashback, Robin Hawdon plays the unlikely spy who foils an invasion of the Earth by a race of alien superwomen led by Dawn Addams. Michael Cort directs the yawn-inducing titillation and soft-core romping with all the style of a 1970s cinema commercial for a local curry house. RS

Robin Hawdon *James Word* • Yutte Stensgaard *Ann Olsen* • James Robertson-Justice *Major Bourdon* • Charles Hawtrey *Swyne* • Lionel Murton *"W"* • Anna Gael *Clotho* • Dawn Addams *Zeta* ■ *Dir* Michael Cort • *Scr* Michael Cort, Alastair McKenzie

Zeus and Roxanne ★★ U

Comedy adventure
1997 · US · Colour · 94mins

In this adequate family film, neighbouring kids play Cupid in a bid to bring their respective single parents together – the mother's a marine biologist, the father's a rock composer. Meanwhile, his pet dog strikes up a special relationship with her research dolphin, leading to much talk about inter-species communication, and even more about inter-human communication. DA

Steve Guttenberg *Terry* • Kathleen Quinlan *Mary Beth* • Arnold Vosloo *Claude Carver* • Dawn McMillan *Becky* ■ *Dir* George Miller (1) • *Scr* Tom Benedek

Ziegfeld Follies ★★★★ U

Musical 1944 · US · Colour · 104mins

In this completely plotless musical, William Powell is in heaven reprising his persona in the title role of 1936's *The Great Ziegfeld* and dreaming of the kind of show he could produce in the gloriously Technicolored 1940s. This potpourri of a music fest, started in 1944 but not properly released until 1946, contains some of the most brilliant examples of MGM's finest: here's *This Heart of Mine* with the inimitable Fred Astaire and Lucille Bremer in their heart-stopping pas de deux; here's the witty Judy Garland mercilessly imitating Greer Garson in a devastating lavender-hued parody; and here's a rarity: Astaire and Gene Kelly stepping out with each other for the first time on screen. A real one-off to treasure. TS

Fred Astaire • Lucille Ball • Lena Horne • Judy Garland • Fanny Brice • Cyd Charisse • Kathryn Grayson • Virginia O'Brien • Gene Kelly • Esther Williams • William Powell *Florenz Ziegfeld* ■ *Dir* Vincente Minnelli, George Sidney (2), Robert Lewis (1), Charles Walters, Roy Del Ruth, Lemuel Ayres, Norman Taurog • *Scr* Peter Barry, Harry Tugend, George White, Al Lewis, Robert Alton, David Freedman, Irving Brecher

Ziegfeld Girl ★★★

Musical 1941 · US · Sepia · 132mins

It looks lavish, it's fabulously cast, and it wears all the production hallmarks of an MGM classic, but closer inspection reveals that this high-octane melodrama is really an excuse to utilise those leftover stock shots from 1936's *The Great Ziegfeld*. But this is MGM, and the three Ziegfeld recruits couldn't be more glam: Hedy Lamarr and the young Lana Turner emote to the manner born, but it's Judy Garland who steals the show. TS

James Stewart *Gilbert Young* • Judy Garland *Susan Gallagher* • Hedy Lamarr *Sandra Kolter* • Lana Turner *Sheila Regan* • Tony Martin *Frank Merton* • Jackie Cooper *Jerry Regan* • Ian Hunter *Geoffrey Collis* • Charles Winninger *Pop Gallagher* • Edward Everett Horton *Noble Sage* • Eve Arden *Patsy Dixon* ■ *Dir* Robert Z Leonard • *Scr* Marguerite Roberts, Sonya Levien, from a story by William Anthony McGuire

Ziggy Stardust and the Spiders from Mars ★★★ PG

Concert movie 1982 · UK · Colour · 85mins

As the director of the Bob Dylan documentary *Don't Look Back* and the concert film *Monterey Pop*, DA Pennebaker was the ideal person to capture the Hammersmith Odeon gig that saw David Bowie bid farewell to his most famous alter ego. Released nearly a decade after the event, the sight of Bowie and his band in full glam regalia is likely to induce more chuckles than nostalgic longing, and Pennebaker's *cinéma-vérité* style is often too intrusive. But there are some cracking songs on offer, notably the glorious *All the Young Dudes*, the Bowie-penned anthem made famous by Mott the Hoople. DP

Dir DA Pennebaker

Zigzag ★★★ PG

Thriller 1970 · US · Colour · 99mins

Though he usually plays the heavy, George Kennedy here has a sympathetic starring role as a dying insurance investigator who confesses to a murder he didn't commit in order to ensure a hefty pay-off for his family. This intriguingly complex drama may seem far-fetched, but Kennedy makes it work by the sheer weight of his personality. Released on video as *False Witness*. TH

George Kennedy *Paul R Cameron* • Anne Jackson *Jean Cameron* • Eli Wallach *Mario Gambretti* • Steve Ihnat *Assistant District Attorney Gates* • William Marshall (2) *Morrie Bronson* • Joe Maross *Lt Max Hines* • Dana Elcar *Harold Tracey* • Walter Brooke *Adam Mercer* ■ *Dir* Richard A Colla • *Scr* John T Kelley, from a story by Robert Enders

Zina ★★★ 15

Biographical drama
1985 · UK · BW and Colour · 94mins

Skipping around from Berlin to Blackpool to Lanzarote, this intellectually static but emotionally volatile drama draws an analogy between the disturbed mind of Zina (Domiziana Giordano) and the gathering forces of Nazism and communism in the 1930s. It's a connection made more relevant because she's the daughter of Leon Trotsky, arch rival to Stalin. Psychiatrist Ian McKellen sees her divided nature as a symbol of a divided Europe; fatiguing, but intriguing. TH

Domiziana Giordano *Zina Bronstein* • Ian McKellen *Professor Kronfeld* • Philip Madoc *Trotsky* • Rom Anderson *Maria* • Micha Bergese *Molanov* • Gabrielle Dellal *Stenographer* • Paul Geoffrey *Lyova* • William Hootkins *Walter Adams* ■ *Dir* Ken McMullen • *Scr* Ken McMullen, Terry James

Zoltan... Hound of Dracula ★ 18

Horror 1977 · US · Colour · 83mins

Russian soldiers discover Dracula's crypt and unwittingly resurrect the Count's undead pet dog in this barking mad horror howler. It gets even worse when the fanged fido travels to the USA and finds his master's descendant on a lakeside holiday. José Ferrer slums it as the bargain basement Van Helsing-style investigator on the scent of zombie Zoltan, who is about as scary as Lassie! AJ DVD

Michael Pataki *Michael Drake/Count Dracula* • Jan Shutan *Marla Drake* • Libbie Chase *Linda Drake* • John Levin *Steve Drake* • Reggie Nalder *Veidt Smit* • José Ferrer *Inspector Branco* ■ *Dir* Albert Band • *Scr* Frank Ray Perilli, from characters created by Bram Stoker

Zombie Flesh Eaters

★★★ 18

Horror 1979 · It · Colour · 87mins

Voodoo causes an army of cannibal zombies to leave its tropical island paradise and head for New York in this ultra-gory rip-off of *Dawn of the Dead*, which put Italian director Lucio Fulci on the cult map. Although the movie is extremely silly (a crusty underwater zombie battling a shark) and extremely violent, with several watershed special effects, Fulci often creates a chilling atmosphere amid the hard-core splatter. Tisa Farrow (Mia's sister) had a mini career as a starlet in Italy and heads the cast here. AJ. Contains violence and nudity. [VIDEO] DVD

Tisa Farrow *Anne* • Ian McCulloch *Peter* • Richard Johnson *Dr Menard* • Al Cliver [Pier Luigi Conti] *Brian* • Auretta Gay *Susan* • Olga Karlatos *Mrs Menard* • Stefania D'Amario *Nurse* ■ *Dir* Lucio Fulci • *Scr* Elisa Briganti

Zombie High

★★ 15

Horror thriller 1987 · US · Colour · 86mins

When female students are admitted to a formerly all-male prep school for the first time, they discover their new classmates are walking zombies, the results of experiments carried out by teachers who crave immortal life. The title suggests a kind of camp teen horror flick, but what you get plays more like a masculine version of *The Stepford Wives* – albeit one that's alternately tedious and unintentionally hilarious. RS [VIDEO]

Virginia Madsen *Andrea* • Richard Cox *Philo* • James Wilder *Barry* • Sherilyn Fenn *Suzi* • Paul Feig *Emerson* • Kay E Kuter *Dean Eisner* ■ *Dir* Ron Link • *Scr* Elizabeth Passerelli, Tim Doyle, Aziz Ghazal

Zombie Holocaust

★★ 18

Horror 1979 · It · Colour · 80mins

Hack director Marino Girolami's legendary Italian exploitation item is a gory mess in more ways than one. Doctor Alexandra Delli Colli and scientist Ian McCullough go to a tiny Pacific island to investigate native rites involving human sacrifice and encounter mad surgeon Donald O'Brien who is experimenting with zombie transplants to extend human life. Combining the cannibal and living dead genres for extra shock value, Girolami then briskly piles on the gratuitous carnage and extreme splatter with little time for logic. AJ. Italian dialogue dubbed into English. [VIDEO] DVD

Ian McCulloch *Dr Peter Chandler* • Sherry Buchanan *Susan Kelly* • Alexandra Delli Colli *Lori Ridgway* • Peter O'Neal *George* ■ *Dir* Frank Martin [Marino Girolami] • *Scr* Romano Scandariato, Fabrizio De Angelis

Zoo

★★★★

Documentary 1993 · US · Colour · 130mins

The fact that there are some 2,000 crosscuts in this epic portrait of the Miami Metro Zoo emphasises the importance Frederick Wiseman places on the editorial process in the creation of his impressionistic documentaries. Shooting some 80 hours of footage during his six-week sojourn, Wiseman took a year to fashion scenes of fabulous creatures, diligent keepers, dedicated veterinarians and curious visitors into a compelling whole that is all the better for its lack of linear structure and intrusive narration. He also takes time to balance ethical and scientific concerns, as he explores every aspect of this institution's meticulous daily routine. DP

Dir Frederick Wiseman

Zoo in Budapest

★★★

Romantic drama 1933 · US · BW · 85mins

This must rank as one of the cinema's most romantic movies, thanks to the sublime technique of cinematographer Lee Garmes. Framed by the highly stylised zoo sets, his subtle, misty compositions enhance the natural beauty of lovely Loretta Young, creating a look unique to this over-whimsical film and making it a rare collector's item. Sadly, director Rowland V Lee fails to extract an acceptable performance from fey leading man Gene Raymond or convey the Hungarian atmosphere. Nevertheless, this is a real one-off. TS

Loretta Young *Eve* • Gene Raymond *Zani* • OP Heggie *Dr Grunbaum* • Wally Albright *Paul Vandor* • Paul Fix *Heine* • Murray Kinnell *Garbosh* • Ruth Warren *Katrina* • Roy Stewart *Karl* ■ *Dir* Rowland V Lee • *Scr* Dan Totheroh, Louise Long, Rowland V Lee, from a story by Melville Baker, John Kirkland

Zoolander

★★★★ 12

Satirical comedy
2001 · US/Ger/Aus · Colour · 85mins

Director/star Ben Stiller's rapier-sharp satire on the fashion industry balances hipness and endearing stupidity with expert precision. Stiller is the king of the male modelling world thanks to the "blue steel" stare that's been the key to his cover-boy fortune. However, when the hilariously self-absorbed oaf loses his title to new boy Owen Wilson and decides to retire, furtive fashion mogul Will Ferrell comes to his rescue, but only to brainwash the foolish fop into assassinating the Prime Minister of Malaysia. Brilliantly conceived and executed, this mercilessly exposes the shallow and bitchy world of haute couture, and is loaded with fun cameos. AJ [VIDEO] DVD

Ben Stiller *Derek Zoolander* • Owen Wilson *Hansel* • Will Ferrell *Mugatu* • Christine Taylor *Matilda Jeffries* • Milla Jovovich *Katinka* • Jerry Stiller *Maury Ballstein* • Jon Voight *Larry Zoolander* • David Duchovny *JP Prewitt* • Anne Meara *Protestor* ■ *Dir* Ben Stiller • *Scr* Drake Sather, Ben Stiller, John Hamburg, from a story by Drake Sather, Ben Stiller

Zoot Suit

★★

Musical drama 1981 · US · Colour · 103mins

Luis Valdez directed this film adaptation of his hit stage musical, which is loosely based on the 1940s Sleepy Lagoon murder trial that unfairly convicted several Mexican-American zoot suit gang members. Except for the spirited musical numbers and an arresting performance by Edward James Olmos, the movie largely fails to bring the impact it had on stage. KB

Daniel Valdez *Henry Reyna* • Edward James Olmos *El Pachuco* • Charles Aidman *George* • Tyne Daly *Alice* • John Anderson *Judge* • Abel Franco *Enrique* • Mike Gomez *Joey* ■ *Dir* Luis Valdez • *Scr* Luis Valdez, from his stage musical

Zorba the Greek

★★★★ PG

Drama 1964 · US/Gr · BW · 135mins

A marvellously emotive and perfectly cast film version of the novel about the salt-of-the-earth peasant who teaches an uptight Englishman the secret of life. As Zorba, Anthony Quinn plays the part of a lifetime, so much so that the role greatly impinged on the actor both in real life and in all his movies ever since. Also adding to the film's particular and unusual grace are wonderful Oscar-winning black-and-white photography by Walter Lassally, a haunting Mikis Theodorakis score and a glowingly warm portrayal (also Oscar-rewarded) by Lila Kedrova as an aged prostitute. It's a shade too long for its own good, though. TS [VIDEO] DVD

Anthony Quinn *Alexis Zorba* • Alan Bates *Basil* • Irene Papas *Widow* • Lila Kedrova *Madame Hortense* • George Foundas *Mavrandoni* • Eleni Anousaki *Lola* • Sotiris Moustakas *Mimithos* • Takis Emmanuel *Manolakas* ■ *Dir* Michael Cacoyannis • *Scr* Michael Cacoyannis, from the novel by Nikos Kazantzakis

Zorro

★★

Action adventure
1975 · Fr/It · Colour · 120mins

Dashing French star Alain Delon takes on the black cape and rapier of the legendary swordsman, although the province governed by Spanish hardman Stanley Baker is more banana republic than old California. Unfortunately, that isn't the only liberty taken with Johnston McCulley's immortal man in black. Pitched as a children's film, it's probably a bit too long and might well test youthful patience. AT. French and Italian dialogue dubbed into English.

Alain Delon *Diego/Zorro* • Stanley Baker *Colonel Huerta* • Ottavia Piccolo *Hortensia* • Giampiero Albertini *Brother Francisco* ■ *Dir* Duccio Tessari • *Scr* Giorgio Alorio, from characters created by Johnston McCulley

Zorro, the Gay Blade

★ PG

Swashbuckling spoof
1981 · US · Colour · 89mins

George Hamilton hams it up shamelessly playing the legendary Zorro's twin sons – one a dashing, macho swordfighter, the other a limp-wristed queen – in a witless swashbuckling parody. When villainous Ron Liebman threatens the peace of a Mexican village, both brothers swish into action and the cheap laughs come thin and slow. AJ [VIDEO]

George Hamilton *Don Diego Vega/Bunny Wigglesworth* • Lauren Hutton *Charlotte Taylor Wilson* • Brenda Vaccaro *Florinda* • Ron Leibman *Esteban* • Donovan Scott *Paco* • James Booth *Velasquez* • Helen Burns *Consuela* • Clive Revill *Garcia* ■ *Dir* Peter Medak • *Scr* Hal Dresner

Zotz

★★ U

Comedy 1962 · US · BW · 86mins

Professor Tom Poston discovers that an ancient coin found on an archaeological dig has magical powers that allow the owner to inflict pain from a distance, make things move in slow motion and even kill. Poston offers the coin to the Pentagon as a weapon, but it's Nikita Khrushchev and his Russian spies who are more interested. This fantasy comedy from schlock horror maestro William Castle isn't a classic but it's pleasingly weird. DF

Tom Poston *Prof Jonathan Jones* • Julia Meade *Prof Virginia Fenster* • Jim Backus *Horatio Kellgore* • Fred Clark *General Bulliver* • Cecil Kellaway *Dean Updike* • Zeme North *Cynthia Jones* • Margaret Dumont *Persephone Updike* ■ *Dir* William Castle • *Scr* Ray Russell, from a novel by Walter Karig

Zu Warriors

★★★★ PG

Fantasy 1983 · HK · Colour · 93mins

In the distant past all humanity is at war with itself. Evil beings from the netherworld see their opportunity to take over the Earth while its inhabitants are divided. A young warrior hiding out on a magical mountain embarks on a quest through a mythological realm to find the two swords that, when brought together, form the only weapon powerful enough to repel the evil hordes. A truly mind-blowing Hong Kong action fantasy, with director Tsui creating a state-of-the-art adventure. DF. In Cantonese with English subtitles. [VIDEO] DVD

Adam Cheng *Ting Ying* • Chung Yan Lau *Spellbinder* • Yuen Biao *Ti Ming-chi (virgin boy)* • Meng Hai *I-chen* • Brigitte Lin *Ice Countess* • Tsui Siu Keung *Heaven's Blade* • Judy Ongg *Li-chi* • Samo Hung [Sammo Hung] *Long Brows* ■ *Dir* Tsui Hark • *Scr* Hong Sze To Chuck

Zubeidaa

★★★ PG

Biographical romantic drama
2000 · Ind · Colour · 143mins

Zubeidaa was already a popular silent icon before she headlined the subcontinent's earliest talkie, *Alam Ara*. That 1931 melodrama co-starred Prithviraj Kapoor, whose great-granddaughter, Karishma Kapoor, takes the title role in this *Citizen Kane*-like study of the actress's turbulent private life. Whether resisting the dictates of her bullying father (Amrish Puri), enduring a loveless marriage or competing for the affections of a maharajah (Manoj Bajpai), Karishma balances glamour with realism, although she's outshone by Rekha as Bajpai's first wife. DP. In Hindi and Urdu with English subtitles. [VIDEO] DVD

Karishma Kapoor *Zubeidaa* • Rekha *Mandira* • Manoj Bajpai *Maharaja Vijayendra Singh* • Amrish Puri *Suleman Seth* • Rajit Kapoor *Riyaz* ■ *Dir* Shyam Benegal • *Scr* Khalid Mohamed

Zulu

★★★★ PG

Historical war drama
1964 · UK · Colour · 138mins

This superb re-creation of the 1879 battle of Rorke's Drift is a personal triumph for producer/director Cy Endfield and Welsh producer/star Stanley Baker. Baker heads a remarkable cast, including Michael Caine in a star-making performance, playing against type as a toffee-nosed lieutenant. Technically the movie is a revelation, with stunning Technirama photography, brilliant picture editing and a wonderfully evocative soundtrack – who could ever forget the approaching sound of the 4,000 Zulu warriors before we see them, while Richard Burton's narration is genuinely moving. TS [VIDEO] DVD

Stanley Baker *Lieutenant John Chard, RE* • Michael Caine *Lieutenant Gonville Bromhead* • Jack Hawkins *Reverend Otto Witt* • Ulla Jacobsson *Margareta Witt* • James Booth *Private Henry Hook* • Nigel Green *Colour-Sergeant Bourne* • Ivor Emmanuel *Private Owen* • Paul Daneman *Sergeant Maxfield* • Glynn Edwards *Corporal Allen* • Neil McCarthy *Private Thomas* • David Kernan *Private Hitch* ■ *Dir* Cy Endfield • *Scr* John Prebble, Cy Endfield, from an article by John Prebble • *Cinematographer* Stephen Dade • *Editor* John Jympson • *Music* John Barry (1)

Zulu Dawn

★★ PG

Historical drama
1979 · UK · Colour · 112mins

Zulu plonked us down in the heat of battle and didn't have the time to tell us why Britain and the Zulus were arguing so violently. But because the 1964 epic was such a big hit, star Stanley Baker and writer/director Cy Endfield conceived this prequel, although by the time it came out in 1979 Baker had died and Endfield was sidelined. There's spectacle in abundance here but little of the characterisation that made *Zulu* so memorable. AT [VIDEO] DVD

Burt Lancaster *Colonel Anthony Durnford* • Peter O'Toole *Lord Chelmsford* • Simon Ward *William Vereker* • John Mills *Sir Henry Bartle Frere* • Nigel Davenport *Colonel Hamilton-Brown* • Denholm Elliott *Lt Col Pulleine* • Freddie Jones *Bishop Colenso* • Bob Hoskins *Sgt Major Williams* ■ *Dir* Douglas Hickox • *Scr* Cy Endfield, Anthony Storey, from a story by Cy Endfield

Z

Directors

A

Aaron, Paul aka **Smithee, Alan** (1961–) *A Different Story* 1978; *A Force of One* 1979; *Deadly Force* 1983; *Maxie* 1985; *Home Front* 1987; *Untamed Love* 1994

Abashidze, Dodo (1924–1990) *The Legend of the Suram Fortress* 1984; *Ashik Kerib* 1988

Abbas *Baazigar* 1993; *Aitraaz* 2004

Abbott, George (1887–1995) *Manslaughter* 1930; *My Sin* 1931; *Too Many Girls* 1940; *The Pajama Game* 1957; *Damn Yankees* 1958

Abel, Robert (1937–2001) *Elvis on Tour* 1972; *Let the Good Times Roll* 1973

Abrahams, Jim (1944–) *Airplane!* 1980; *Top Secret!* 1984; *Ruthless People* 1986; *Big Business* 1988; *Welcome Home, Roxy Carmichael* 1990; *Hot Shots!* 1991; *Hot Shots! Part Deux* 1993; *First Do No Harm* 1997; *Jane Austen's Mafia* 1998

Ackerman, Robert Allan *David's Mother* 1994; *Safe Passage* 1994; *Double Platinum* 1999; *Forget Me Never* 1999

Adams, Marcus *Long Time Dead* 2001; *Octane* 2003

Adamson, Al (1929–1995) *Blood of Dracula's Castle* 1967; *The Female Bunch* 1969; *Dracula vs Frankenstein* 1970

Adamson, Andrew *Shrek* 2001; *Shrek 2* 2004

Adidge, Pierre (1939–1974) *Mad Dogs and Englishmen* 1971; *Elvis on Tour* 1972

Adler, Lou *Cheech & Chong's Up in Smoke* 1978; *Ladies and Gentlemen, the Fabulous Stains* 1981

Adlon, Percy (1935–) *Swing* 1983; *Sugarbaby* 1985; *Bagdad Café* 1987; *Rosalie Goes Shopping* 1989; *Salmonberries* 1991; *Younger and Younger* 1993

Adolfi, John G (1888–1933) *The Show of Shows* 1929; *The Man Who Played God* 1932; *A Successful Calamity* 1932; *The King's Vacation* 1933

Agresti, Alejandro (1961–) *Secret Wedding* 1989; *Wind with the Gone* 1998; *Valentín* 2002

Akerman, Chantal (1950–) *Je, Tu, Il, Elle* 1974; *Jeanne Dielman, 23 Quai du Commerce, 1080 Bruxelles* 1975; *Les Rendez-vous d'Anna* 1978; *Golden Eighties* 1986; *Night and Day* 1991; *The Captive* 2000

Akkad, Moustapha (1935–) *The Message* 1976; *Lion of the Desert* 1981

Alda, Alan (1936–) *The Four Seasons* 1981; *Sweet Liberty* 1986; *A New Life* 1988; *Betsy's Wedding* 1990

Aldrich, Robert (1918–1983) *Big League*r 1953; *World for Ransom* 1953; *Apache* 1954; *Vera Cruz* 1954; *The Big Knife* 1955; *Kiss Me Deadly* 1955; *Attack!* 1956; *Autumn Leaves* 1956; *The Angry Hills* 1959; *Ten Seconds to Hell* 1959; *The Last Sunset* 1961; *Sodom and Gomorrah* 1962; *What Ever Happened to Baby Jane?* 1962; *4 for Texas* 1963; *Hush… Hush, Sweet Charlotte* 1964; *The Flight of the Phoenix* 1965; *The Dirty Dozen* 1967; *The Killing of Sister George* 1968; *The Legend of Lylah Clare* 1968; *Too Late the Hero* 1970; *The Grissom Gang* 1971; *Ulzana's Raid* 1972; *Emperor of the North* 1973; *The Mean Machine* 1974; *Hustle* 1975; *The Choirboys* 1977; *Twilight's Last Gleaming* 1977; *The Frisco Kid* 1979; *The California Dolls* 1981

Alea, Tomás Gutiérrez (1928–1996) *Death of a Bureaucrat* 1966; *Memories of Underdevelopment* 1968; *The Last Supper* 1976; *Strawberry and Chocolate* 1993; *Guantanamera* 1995

Aleksandrov, Grigori V (1903–1984) *October* 1928; *The General Line* 1929

Algar, James (1912–1998) *Fantasia* 1940; *Victory through Air Power* 1943; *The Adventures of Ichabod and Mr Toad* 1949; *The Living Desert* 1953; *White Wilderness* 1958; *Jungle Cat* 1959; *Fantasia 2000* 1999

Algrant, Daniel aka **Algrant, Dan** *Naked in New York* 1994; *People I Know* 2002

Ali, Shaad aka **Ali Sehgal, Shaad** *Saathiya* 2002; *Bunty Aur Babli* 2005

Allégret, Marc (1900–1973) *Fanny* 1932; *Gribouille* 1937; *Blanche Fury* 1948; *The Loves of Three Queens* 1954

Allégret, Yves (1907–1987) *The Seven Deadly Sins* 1952; *The Proud Ones* 1953

Allen, Corey (1934–) *Thunder and Lightning* 1977; *Avalanche* 1978

Allen, Irwin (1916–1991) *The Story of Mankind* 1957; *The Lost World* 1960; *Voyage to the Bottom of the Sea* 1961; *Five Weeks in a Balloon* 1962; *City beneath the Sea* 1971; *The Towering Inferno* 1974; *The Swarm* 1978; *Beyond the Poseidon Adventure* 1979

Allen, Kevin (1962–) *Twin Town* 1997; *The Big Tease* 1999; *Agent Cody Banks 2: Destination London* 2003

Allen, Lewis (1905–2000) *The Uninvited* 1944; *Those Endearing Young Charms* 1945; *The Unseen* 1945; *Desert Fury* 1947; *The Imperfect Lady* 1947; *Appointment with Danger* 1950; *Sons of the Musketeers* 1951; *Valentino* 1951; *Suddenly* 1954; *A Bullet for Joey* 1955; *Illegal* 1955; *Another Time, Another Place* 1958

Allen, Woody (1935–) *Take the Money and Run* 1969; *Bananas* 1971; *Everything You Always Wanted to Know about Sex … but Were Afraid to Ask* 1972; *Sleeper* 1973; *Love and Death* 1975; *Annie Hall* 1977; *Interiors* 1978; *Manhattan* 1979; *Stardust Memories* 1980; *A Midsummer Night's Sex Comedy* 1982; *Zelig* 1983; *Broadway Danny Rose* 1984; *The Purple Rose of Cairo* 1985; *Hannah and Her Sisters* 1986; *Radio Days* 1987; *September* 1987; *Another Woman* 1988; *Crimes and Misdemeanors* 1989; *New York Stories* 1989; *Alice* 1990; *Shadows and Fog* 1991; *Husbands and Wives* 1992; *Manhattan Murder Mystery* 1993; *Bullets over Broadway* 1994; *Mighty Aphrodite* 1995; *Everyone Says I Love You* 1996; *Deconstructing Harry* 1997; *Celebrity* 1998; *Sweet and Lowdown* 1999; *Small Time Crooks* 2000; *The Curse of the Jade Scorpion* 2001; *Hollywood Ending* 2002; *Anything Else* 2003; *Melinda and Melinda* 2004

Allouache, Merzak (1944–) *Bab El-Oued City* 1994; *Salut Cousin!* 1996

Almereyda, Michael (1960–) *Twister* 1989; *Nadja* 1995; *The Eternal* 1998; *Hamlet* 2000

Almodóvar, Pedro (1951–) *Pepi, Luci, Bom…* 1980; *Labyrinth of Passion* 1982; *Dark Habits* 1983; *What Have I Done to Deserve This?* 1984; *Matador* 1986; *The Law of Desire* 1987; *Women on the Verge of a Nervous Breakdown* 1988; *Tie Me Up! Tie Me Down!* 1990; *High Heels* 1991; *Kika* 1993; *The Flower of My Secret* 1995; *Live Flesh* 1997; *All about My Mother* 1999; *Talk to Her* 2001; *Bad Education* 2004

Almond, Paul (1931–) *Act of the Heart* 1970; *Captive Hearts* 1988; *The Dance Goes On* 1990

Altman, Robert (1925–) *The Delinquents* 1957; *The James Dean Story* 1957; *Countdown* 1968; *Nightmare in Chicago* 1968; *MASH* 1969; *That Cold Day in the Park* 1969; *Brewster McCloud* 1970; *McCabe and Mrs Miller* 1971; *Images* 1972; *The Long Goodbye* 1973; *California Split* 1974; *Thieves like Us* 1974; *Nashville* 1975; *Buffalo Bill and the Indians, or Sitting Bull's History Lesson* 1976; *3 Women* 1977; *A Wedding* 1978; *A Perfect Couple* 1979; *Quintet* 1979; *HEALTH* 1980; *Popeye* 1980; *Come Back to the Five and Dime, Jimmy Dean, Jimmy Dean* 1982; *Streamers* 1983; *Secret Honor* 1984; *Fool for Love* 1985; *Aria* 1987; *Beyond Therapy* 1987; *OC and Stiggs* 1987; *Vincent and Theo* 1990; *The Player* 1992; *Short Cuts* 1993; *Pret-a-Porter* 1994; *Kansas City* 1995; *Robert Altman's Jazz '34: Remembrances of Kansas City Swing* 1996; *The Gingerbread Man* 1997; *Cookie's Fortune* 1999; *Dr T & the Women* 2000; *Gosford Park* 2001; *The Company* 2003

Amateau, Rod (1923–2003) *Where Does It Hurt?* 1971; *The Seniors* 1978; *The Garbage Pail Kids Movie* 1987

Amelio, Gianni (1945–) *Open Doors* 1990; *The Stolen Children* 1992; *Lamerica* 1994; *The Keys to the House* 2004

Amenábar, Alejandro (1972–) *Tesis* 1996; *Open Your Eyes* 1997; *The Others* 2001; *The Sea Inside* 2004

Amenta, Pino (1952–) *Boulevard of Broken Dreams* 1988; *Heaven Tonight* 1990

Amiel, Jon (1948–) *Queen of Hearts* 1989; *Aunt Julia and the Scriptwriter* 1990; *Sommersby* 1993; *Copycat* 1995; *The Man Who Knew Too Little* 1997; *Entrapment* 1999; *The Core* 2002

Amurri, Franco (1958–) *Flashback* 1990; *Monkey Trouble* 1994

Amyes, Julian (1917–1992) *A Hill in Korea* 1956; *Miracle in Soho* 1957

Anciano, Dominic *Final Cut* 1998; *Love, Honour and Obey* 2000

Anders, Allison (1954–) *Border Radio* 1987; *Gas, Food, Lodging* 1992; *Mi Vida Loca* 1993; *Four Rooms* 1995; *Grace of My Heart* 1996; *Sugar Town* 1999

Anderson, Brad (1964–) *Next Stop Wonderland* 1998; *Session 9* 2001; *The Machinist* 2003

Anderson, Jane (1954–) *If These Walls Could Talk 2* 2000; *Normal* 2002

Anderson, Lindsay (1923–1994) *This Sporting Life* 1963; *if…* 1968; *O Lucky Man!* 1973; *In Celebration* 1974; *Britannia Hospital* 1982; *The Whales of August* 1987

Anderson, Michael (1920–) *Waterfront* 1950; *Night Was Our Friend* 1951; *Will Any Gentleman…?* 1953; *The Dam Busters* 1954; *1984* 1955; *Around the World in 80 Days* 1956; *Yangtse Incident* 1956; *Chase a Crooked Shadow* 1957; *Shake Hands with the Devil* 1959; *The Wreck of the Mary Deare* 1959; *All the Fine Young Cannibals* 1960; *The Naked Edge* 1961; *Flight from Ashiya* 1964; *Wild and Wonderful* 1964; *Operation Crossbow* 1965; *The Quiller Memorandum* 1966; *The Shoes of the Fisherman* 1968; *Pope Joan* 1972; *Conduct Unbecoming* 1975; *Doc Savage: the Man of Bronze* 1975; *Logan's Run* 1976; *Orca … Killer Whale* 1977; *Dominique* 1978; *Murder by Phone* 1982; *Separate Vacations* 1986; *Millennium* 1989; *The New Adventures of Pinocchio* 1999

Anderson, Paul aka **Anderson, Paul W S** (1965–) *Shopping* 1993; *Mortal Kombat* 1995; *Event Horizon* 1997; *Soldier* 1998; *Resident Evil* 2002; *AVP: Alien vs Predator* 2004

Anderson, Paul Thomas (1970–) *Hard Eight* 1996; *Boogie Nights* 1997; *Magnolia* 1999; *Punch-Drunk Love* 2002

Anderson, Steve aka **Anderson, Stephen M** *South Central* 1992; *Dead Men Can't Dance* 1997

Anderson, Wes (1970–) *Bottle Rocket* 1996; *Rushmore* 1998; *The Royal Tenenbaums* 2001; *The Life Aquatic with Steve Zissou* 2004

Angelo, Robert *Forbidden Sins* 1998; *Dead Sexy* 2001; *Sexual Predator* 2001

Angelopoulos, Theo aka **Angelopoulos, Theodoros** (1936–) *The Travelling Players* 1975; *Voyage to Cythera* 1984; *The Bee Keeper* 1986; *Landscape in the Mist* 1988; *Ulysses' Gaze* 1995; *Eternity and a Day* 1998; *Trilogy: the Weeping Meadow* 2004

Anger, Kenneth (1927–) *Fireworks* 1947; *Eaux d'Artifice* 1953; *Inauguration of the Pleasure Dome* 1954; *Scorpio Rising* 1963; *Invocation of My Demon Brother* 1969; *Lucifer Rising* 1981

Annakin, Ken (1914–) *Holiday Camp* 1947; *Miranda* 1947; *Broken Journey* 1948; *Here Come the Huggetts* 1948; *Quartet* 1948; *Vote for Huggett* 1948; *The Huggetts Abroad* 1949; *Landfall* 1949; *Trio* 1950; *Hotel Sahara* 1951; *The Planter's Wife* 1952; *The Story of Robin Hood and His Merrie Men* 1952; *The Sword and the Rose* 1952; *The Seekers* 1954; *You Know What Sailors Are* 1954; *Value for Money* 1955; *Loser Takes All* 1956; *Three Men in a Boat* 1956; *Across the Bridge* 1957; *Nor the Moon by Night* 1958; *Third Man on the Mountain* 1959; *Swiss Family Robinson* 1960; *Very Important Person* 1961; *Crooks Anonymous* 1962; *The Longest Day* 1962; *The Fast Lady* 1963; *The Informers* 1963; *Battle of the Bulge* 1965; *Those Magnificent Men in Their Flying Machines* 1965; *The Long Duel* 1966; *The Biggest Bundle of Them All* 1968; *Monte Carlo or Bust* 1969; *Call of the Wild* 1972; *Paper Tiger* 1974; *The Fifth Musketeer* 1979; *The Pirate Movie* 1982; *The New Adventures of Pippi Longstocking* 1988

Annaud, Jean-Jacques (1943–) *Black and White in Color* 1976; *Quest for Fire* 1981; *The Name of the Rose* 1986; *The Bear* 1988; *The Lover* 1992; *Seven Years in Tibet* 1997; *Enemy at the Gates* 2001; *Two Brothers* 2004

Anspaugh, David (1946–) *Hoosiers* 1986; *Fresh Horses* 1988; *Rudy* 1993; *Moonlight and Valentino* 1995; *Wisegirls* 2001

Anthony, Joseph (1912–1993) *The Rainmaker* 1956; *The Matchmaker* 1958; *Career* 1959; *All in a Night's Work* 1960; *Captive City* 1962; *Tomorrow* 1972

Antonio, Lou (1934–) *Something for Joey* 1977; *Between Friends* 1983; *Thirteen at Dinner* 1985; *Pals* 1986

Antonioni, Michelangelo (1912–) *Chronicle of a Love* 1950; *Love in the City* 1953; *La Signora senza Camelie* 1953; *The Vanquished* 1953; *Le Amiche* 1955; *Il Grido* 1957; *L'Avventura* 1960; *La Notte* 1961; *The Eclipse* 1962; *The Red Desert* 1964; *Blowup* 1966; *Zabriskie Point* 1970; *The Passenger* 1975; *The Oberwald Mystery* 1980; *Identification of a Woman* 1982; *Beyond the Clouds* 1995

Apted, Michael (1941–) *The Triple Echo* 1972; *Stardust* 1974; *The Squeeze* 1977; *Agatha* 1978; *Coal Miner's Daughter* 1980; *Continental Divide* 1981; *P'Tang, Yang, Kipperbang* 1982; *Gorky Park* 1983; *Firstborn* 1984; *Bring On the Night* 1985; *Critical Condition* 1987; *Gorillas in the Mist* 1988; *Class Action* 1991; *Thunderheart* 1992; *Blink* 1994; *Nell* 1994; *Extreme Measures* 1996; *The World Is Not Enough* 1999; *Me & Isaac Newton* 2000; *Enigma* 2001; *Enough* 2002

Araki, Gregg (1963–) *The Living End* 1992; *Totally F***ed Up* 1993; *Doom Generation* 1995; *Nowhere* 1997; *Splendor* 1999; *Mysterious Skin* 2004

Aranda, Vicente (1926–) *Lovers* 1991; *Carmen* 2003

Arau, Alfonso (1932–) *Like Water for Chocolate* 1993; *A Walk in the Clouds* 1995; *Picking Up the Pieces* 2000

Arcady, Alexandre (1947–) *Le Grand Pardon* 1981; *Hold-Up* 1985; *Brothers in Arms* 1990; *Day of Atonement* 1992

Arcand, Denys (1941–) *The Decline of the American Empire* 1986; *Jesus of Montreal* 1989; *Love and Human Remains* 1993; *Stardom* 2000; *The Barbarian Invasions* 2003

Archainbaud, George (1890–1959) *The Lost Squadron* 1932; *The Penguin Pool Murder* 1932; *Murder on the Blackboard* 1934; *Some Like It Hot* 1939; *The Devil's Playground* 1946; *Fool's Gold* 1946; *The Marauders* 1947; *The Dead Don't Dream* 1948; *False Paradise* 1948; *Silent Conflict* 1948; *Blue Canadian Rockies* 1952; *Last of the Pony Riders* 1953; *On Top of Old Smoky* 1953; *Winning of the West* 1953

Archibugi, Francesca (1960–) *Mignon Has Left* 1988; *Shooting the Moon* 1998

Ardolino, Emile (1943–1993) *Dirty Dancing* 1987; *Chances Are* 1989; *Three Men and a Little Lady* 1990; *Sister Act* 1992; *George Balanchine's The Nutcracker* 1993; *Gypsy* 1993

Argento, Dario (1940–) *The Bird with the Crystal Plumage* 1969; *Cat o'Nine Tails* 1971; *Deep Red* 1975; *Suspiria* 1976; *Inferno* 1980; *Tenebrae* 1982; *Opera* 1987; *Two Evil Eyes* 1990; *Trauma* 1993; *The Stendhal Syndrome* 1996; *The Phantom of the Opera* 1998; *The Card Player* 2004

Argyle, John aka **Argyle, John F** (1911–1962) *Send for Paul Temple* 1946; *The Hills of Donegal* 1947

Aristarain, Adolfo (1943–) *The Stranger* 1987; *A Place in the World* 1992

Arkin, Alan (1934–) *Little Murders* 1971; *Fire Sale* 1977

Arkush, Allan (1948–) *Hollywood Boulevard* 1976; *Deathsport* 1978; *Rock 'n' Roll High School* 1979; *Heartbeeps* 1981; *Get Crazy* 1983; *Caddyshack II* 1988; *Shake, Rattle and Rock* 1994

Arliss, Leslie (1901–1987) *The Night Has Eyes* 1942; *The Man in Grey* 1943; *Love Story* 1944; *The Wicked Lady* 1945; *A Man about the House* 1947

Armitage, George *Hit Man* 1972; *Vigilante Force* 1975; *Miami Blues* 1990; *Grosse Pointe Blank* 1997; *The Big Bounce* 2004

Armstrong, Gillian (1950–) *My Brilliant Career* 1979; *Mrs Soffel* 1984; *High Tide* 1987; *Fires Within* 1991; *The Last Days of Chez Nous* 1992; *Little Women* 1994; *Oscar and Lucinda* 1997; *Charlotte Gray* 2001

Armstrong, Michael (1944–) *The Haunted House of Horror* 1969; *Mark of the Devil* 1970

Arnold, Jack (1916–1992) *The Glass Web* 1953; *It Came from Outer Space* 1953; *Creature from the Black Lagoon* 1954; *The Man from Bitter Ridge* 1955; *Revenge of the Creature* 1955; *Tarantula* 1955; *Red Sundown* 1956; *The Incredible Shrinking Man* 1957; *Man in the Shadow* 1957; *High School Confidential* 1958; *The Lady Takes a Flyer* 1958; *Monster on the Campus* 1958; *The Mouse That Roared* 1959; *No Name on the Bullet* 1959; *Bachelor in Paradise* 1961; *A Global Affair* 1964; *Hello Down There* 1969; *The Swiss Conspiracy* 1975

Aronofsky, Darren (1969–) *Pi* 1997; *Requiem for a Dream* 2000

Arteta, Miguel (1970–) *Star Maps* 1997; *Chuck & Buck* 2000; *The Good Girl* 2001

Arthur, Karen (1941–) *The Rape of Richard Beck* 1985; *Lady Beware* 1987

Arzner, Dorothy (1900–1979) *The Wild Party* 1929; *Anybody's Woman* 1930; *Paramount on Parade* 1930; *Sarah and Son* 1930; *Honor among Lovers* 1931; *Merrily We Go to Hell* 1932;

Christopher Strong 1933; *Nana* 1934; *Craig's Wife* 1936; *The Bride Wore Red* 1937; *Dance, Girl, Dance* 1940
Asbury, Kelly *Spirit: Stallion of the Cimarron* 2002; *Shrek 2* 2004
Ashby, Hal (1929–1988) *The Landlord* 1970; *Harold and Maude* 1972; *The Last Detail* 1973; *Shampoo* 1975; *Bound for Glory* 1976; *Coming Home* 1978; *Being There* 1979; *Let's Spend the Night Together* 1982; *Lookin' to Get Out* 1982; *The Slugger's Wife* 1985; *8 Million Ways to Die* 1986
Asher, Robert (1915–1979) *Follow a Star* 1959; *The Bulldog Breed* 1960; *Make Mine Mink* 1960; *She'll Have to Go* 1961; *On the Beat* 1962; *A Stitch in Time* 1963; *The Early Bird* 1965; *The Intelligence Men* 1965; *Press for Time* 1966
Asher, William (1919–) *The 27th Day* 1957; *Beach Party* 1963; *Johnny Cool* 1963; *Bikini Beach* 1964; *Muscle Beach Party* 1964; *Beach Blanket Bingo* 1965; *How to Fill a Wild Bikini* 1965; *Fireball 500* 1966; *Night Warning* 1981; *Movers and Shakers* 1985
Ashida, Toyoo *Vampire Hunter D* 1985; *Fist of the North Star* 1986
Asquith, Anthony (1902–1968) *The Unfinished Symphony* 1934; *Moscow Nights* 1935; *Pygmalion* 1938; *French without Tears* 1939; *Freedom Radio* 1940; *Quiet Wedding* 1940; *Cottage to Let* 1941; *Uncensored* 1942; *The Demi-Paradise* 1943; *We Dive at Dawn* 1943; *Fanny by Gaslight* 1944; *The Way to the Stars* 1945; *While the Sun Shines* 1946; *The Winslow Boy* 1948; *The Woman in Question* 1950; *The Browning Version* 1951; *The Importance of Being Earnest* 1952; *The Final Test* 1953; *The Net* 1953; *Carrington VC* 1954; *The Young Lovers* 1954; *The Doctor's Dilemma* 1958; *Orders to Kill* 1958; *Libel* 1959; *The Millionairess* 1960; *Two Living, One Dead* 1961; *Guns of Darkness* 1962; *The VIPs* 1963; *The Yellow Rolls-Royce* 1964
Assayas, Olivier (1955–) *L'Eau Froide* 1994; *Irma Vep* 1996; *Late August, Early September* 1998; *Les Destinées Sentimentales* 2000; *Demonlover* 2002; *Clean* 2004
Astruc, Alexandre (1923–) *The Crimson Curtain* 1952; *The Bad Liaisons* 1955
Attenborough, Richard (1923–) *Oh! What a Lovely War* 1969; *Young Winston* 1972; *A Bridge Too Far* 1977; *Magic* 1978; *Gandhi* 1982; *A Chorus Line* 1985; *Cry Freedom* 1987; *Chaplin* 1992; *Shadowlands* 1993; *In Love and War* 1996; *Grey Owl* 1999
Audiard, Jacques (1952–) *See How They Fall* 1993; *A Self-Made Hero* 1995; *Read My Lips* 2001
Audry, Jacqueline (1908–1977) *Olivia* 1950; *No Exit* 1954; *Mitsou* 1957
Auer, John H (1906–1975) *A Man Betrayed* 1941; *Music in Manhattan* 1944; *Pan-Americana* 1945; *Thunderbirds* 1952; *City That Never Sleeps* 1953; *Hell's Half Acre* 1954; *Johnny Trouble* 1957
August, Bille (1948–) *Buster's World* 1984; *Twist and Shout* 1985; *Pelle the Conqueror* 1987; *Best Intentions* 1992; *The House of the Spirits* 1993; *Jerusalem* 1996; *Smilla's Feeling for Snow* 1996; *Les Misérables* 1997
Auster, Paul (1947–) *Blue in the Face* 1995; *Lulu on the Bridge* 1998
Austin, Michael *Killing Dad* 1989; *Princess Caraboo* 1994
Autant-Lara, Claude (1903–2000) *Devil in the Flesh* 1947; *The Seven Deadly Sins* 1952; *The Ripening Seed* 1953; *Le Rouge et le Noir* 1954; *Marguerite de la Nuit* 1955; *La Traversée de Paris* 1956; *Thou Shalt Not Kill* 1961; *The Oldest Profession* 1967
Auzins, Igor (1949–) *We of the Never Never* 1982; *The Gold and Glory* 1984
Avakian, Aram (1926–1987) *End of the Road* 1970; *Cops and Robbers* 1973; *11 Harrowhouse* 1974
Avary, Roger (1965–) *Killing Zoe* 1993; *The Rules of Attraction* 2002
Avati, Pupi (1938–) *Noi Tre* 1984; *Christmas Present* 1986; *Fratelli e Sorelle* 1992; *The Best Man* 1998
Avedis, Howard *Scorchy* 1976; *The Fifth Floor* 1980; *Separate Ways* 1981; *They're Playing With Fire* 1984
Averback, Hy (1920–1997) *Chamber of Horrors* 1966; *I Love You, Alice B Toklas* 1968; *Where Were You When the Lights Went Out?* 1968; *The Great Bank Robbery* 1969; *Suppose They Gave a War and Nobody Came?* 1970
Avery, Tex aka **Avery, Fred** (1907–1980) *A Wild Hare* 1940; *King-Size Canary* 1947
Avildsen, John G aka **Mulroon, Danny** (1935–) *Joe* 1970; *Save the Tiger* 1973; *WW and the Dixie Dancekings* 1975; *Rocky* 1976; *Slow Dancing in the Big City* 1978; *The Formula* 1980; *Neighbors* 1981; *A Night in Heaven* 1983; *The Karate Kid* 1984; *The Karate Kid Part II* 1986; *For Keeps* 1987; *Happy New Year* 1987; *The Karate Kid III* 1989; *Lean on Me* 1989; *Rocky V* 1990; *The Power of One* 1991; *8 Seconds* 1994; *Desert Heat* 1999
Avnet, Jon (1949–) *Fried Green Tomatoes at the Whistle Stop Cafe* 1991; *The War* 1994; *Up Close & Personal* 1996; *Red Corner* 1997
Axel, Gabriel (1918–) *Babette's Feast* 1987; *Prince of Jutland* 1994
Axelrod, George (1922–2003) *Lord Love a Duck* 1966; *The Secret Life of an American Wife* 1968
Azzopardi, Mario (1950–) *Nowhere to Hide* 1987; *Bone Daddy* 1998

B

B, Beth (1955–) *Salvation! Have You Said Your Prayers Today?* 1987; *Two Small Bodies* 1993
Babenco, Hector (1946–) *Pixote* 1981; *Kiss of the Spider Woman* 1985; *Ironweed* 1987; *At Play in the Fields of the Lord* 1991; *Foolish Heart* 1998; *Carandiru* 2003
Bacon, Lloyd (1890–1955) *The Singing Fool* 1928; *Say It with Songs* 1929; *Moby Dick* 1930; *Kept Husbands* 1931; *Fireman Save My Child* 1932; *Footlight Parade* 1933; *42nd Street* 1933; *Picture Snatcher* 1933; *He Was Her Man* 1934; *Here Comes the Navy* 1934; *Wonder Bar* 1934; *Devil Dogs of the Air* 1935; *Frisco Kid* 1935; *In Caliente* 1935; *The Irish in Us* 1935; *Cain and Mabel* 1936; *Gold Diggers of 1937* 1936; *Marked Woman* 1937; *San Quentin* 1937; *Boy Meets Girl* 1938; *Racket Busters* 1938; *A Slight Case of Murder* 1938; *Indianapolis Speedway* 1939; *Invisible Stripes* 1939; *The Oklahoma Kid* 1939; *Brother Orchid* 1940; *Knute Rockne – All American* 1940; *Affectionately Yours* 1941; *Footsteps in the Dark* 1941; *Larceny, Inc* 1942; *Action in the North Atlantic* 1943; *The Fighting Sullivans* 1944; *Sunday Dinner for a Soldier* 1944; *Captain Eddie* 1945; *Home Sweet Homicide* 1946; *I Wonder Who's Kissing Her Now* 1947; *Give My Regards to Broadway* 1948; *You Were Meant for Me* 1948; *It Happens Every Spring* 1949; *Miss Grant Takes Richmond* 1949; *Mother Is a Freshman* 1949; *The Fuller Brush Girl* 1950; *Call Me Mister* 1951; *The Frogmen* 1951; *Golden Girl* 1951; *The I Don't Care Girl* 1952; *The Great Sioux Uprising* 1953; *Beautiful but Dangerous* 1954; *The French Line* 1954
Badger, Clarence (1880–1964) *Hands Up!* 1926; *It* 1927
Badham, John (1939–) *Isn't It Shocking?* 1973; *The Bingo Long Travelling All-Stars and Motor Kings* 1976; *Saturday Night Fever* 1977; *Dracula* 1979; *Whose Life Is It Anyway?* 1981; *Blue Thunder* 1983; *WarGames* 1983; *American Flyers* 1985; *Short Circuit* 1986; *Stakeout* 1987; *Bird on a Wire* 1990; *The Hard Way* 1991; *Another Stakeout* 1993; *The Assassin* 1993; *Point of No Return* 1993; *Drop Zone* 1994; *Nick of Time* 1995; *Incognito* 1997; *The Jack Bull* 1999; *The Last Debate* 2000
Baer Jr, Max (1937–) *Ode to Billy Joe* 1976; *Hometown USA* 1979
Bagdadi, Maroun (1950–1993) *Hors la Vie* 1991; *La Fille de l'Air* 1992
Bail, Chuck *Cleopatra Jones and the Casino of Gold* 1975; *The Gumball Rally* 1976; *On Dangerous Ground* 1986
Bailey, Fenton *The Eyes of Tammy Faye* 2000; *Party Monster* 2003; *Inside Deep Throat* 2005
Bailey, John (1914–1989) *The Search for Signs of Intelligent Life in the Universe* 1991; *China Moon* 1994; *Via Dolorosa* 2000
Baird, Stuart (1948–) *Executive Decision* 1996; *US Marshals* 1998; *Star Trek: Nemesis* 2002
Baker, Graham *Omen III: the Final Conflict* 1980; *Impulse* 1984; *Alien Nation* 1988; *Born to Ride* 1991
Baker, Robert S (1916–) *Blackout* 1950; *13 East Street* 1952; *The Steel Key* 1953; *Passport to Treason* 1956; *Jack the Ripper* 1958; *The Siege of Sidney Street* 1960; *The Treasure of Monte Cristo* 1960; *The Hellfire Club* 1961
Baker, Roy Ward aka **Baker, Roy** (1916–) *The October Man* 1947; *The Weaker Sex* 1948; *Highly Dangerous* 1950; *Morning Departure* 1950; *Don't Bother to Knock* 1952; *Inferno* 1953; *Passage Home* 1955; *Jacqueline* 1956; *Tiger in the Smoke* 1956; *The One That Got Away* 1957; *A Night to Remember* 1958; *The Singer Not the Song* 1960; *Flame in the Streets* 1961; *Two Left Feet* 1963; *Quatermass and the Pit* 1967; *The Anniversary* 1968; *Moon Zero Two* 1969; *The Scars of Dracula* 1970; *The Vampire Lovers* 1970; *Dr Jekyll and Sister Hyde* 1971; *Asylum* 1972; *And Now the Screaming Starts!* 1973; *Vault of Horror* 1973; *The Legend of the 7 Golden Vampires* 1974; *The Monster Club* 1980
Bakshi, Ralph (1938–) *Fritz the Cat* 1972; *Wizards* 1977; *The Lord of the Rings* 1978; *Fire and Ice* 1983; *Cool World* 1992
Balaban, Bob (1945–) *Parents* 1988; *My Boyfriend's Back* 1993; *The Last Good Time* 1994; *Subway Stories: Tales from the Underground* 1997
Balaban, Burt (1922–1965) *Stranger from Venus* 1954; *High Hell* 1957; *Murder, Inc* 1960; *Mad Dog Coll* 1961; *The Gentle Rain* 1966
Balabanov, Alexei (1959–) *Brother* 1997; *Of Freaks and Men* 1998; *War* 2002
Baldi, Ferdinando (1927–) *Duel of Champions* 1961; *Texas Adios* 1966; *Comin' at Ya* 1981
Ballard, Carroll (1937–) *The Black Stallion* 1979; *Never Cry Wolf* 1983; *Nutcracker* 1986; *Wind* 1992; *Fly Away Home* 1996; *Duma* 2005
Band, Albert (1924–2002) *The Young Guns* 1956; *Face of Fire* 1959; *Zoltan… Hound of Dracula* 1977; *Prehysteria!* 1993; *Robot Wars* 1993
Band, Charles (1951–) *Crash!* 1977; *The Alchemist* 1981; *Parasite* 1982; *Trancers* 1985; *Trancers II: The Return of Jack Deth* 1991; *Prehysteria!* 1993
Banks, Monty (1897–1950) *No Limit* 1935; *Keep Your Seats, Please* 1936; *We're Going to Be Rich* 1938; *Shipyard Sally* 1939; *Great Guns* 1941
Barba, Norberto (1963–) *Blue Tiger* 1994; *Solo* 1996
Barbash, Uri *Beyond the Walls* 1984; *One of Us* 1989
Barbato, Randy *The Eyes of Tammy Faye* 2000; *Party Monster* 2003; *Inside Deep Throat* 2005
Barbera, Joseph (1911–) *Mouse Trouble* 1944; *The Cat Concerto* 1947; *The Man Called Flintstone* 1966; *Jetsons: the Movie* 1990
Barboni, Enzo aka **Clucher, E B** (1922–) *They Call Me Trinity* 1970; *Renegade* 1987
Bardem, Juan Antonio (1922–2002) *Death of a Cyclist* 1955; *Calle Mayor* 1956
Bare, Richard L aka **Bare, Richard** (1925–) *Prisoners of the Casbah* 1953; *Shoot-Out at Medicine Bend* 1957; *Girl on the Run* 1958; *This Rebel Breed* 1960
Barker, Clive (1952–) *Hellraiser* 1987; *Nightbreed* 1990; *Lord of Illusions* 1995
Barker, Mike aka **Barker, Michael** (1966–) *The James Gang* 1997; *Best Laid Plans* 1999; *To Kill a King* 2003; *A Good Woman* 2004
Barker, Reginald (1886–1937) *Civilization* 1916; *The Moonstone* 1934
Barney, Matthew (1967–) *Cremaster 4* 1994; *Cremaster 1* 1995; *Cremaster 5* 1997; *Cremaster 2* 1999; *Cremaster 3* 2002
Barr, Douglas (1949–) *Dead Badge* 1995; *Mistaken Identity* 1999
Barreto, Bruno (1955–) *Dona Flor and Her Two Husbands* 1977; *Gabriela* 1983; *A Show of Force* 1990; *The Heart of Justice* 1992; *Acts of Love* 1995; *Four Days in September* 1997; *One Tough Cop* 1998; *View from the Top* 2003
Barron, Arthur *Jeremy* 1973; *Brothers* 1977
Barron, Steve (1956–) *Electric Dreams* 1984; *Teenage Mutant Ninja Turtles* 1990; *Coneheads* 1993; *The Adventures of Pinocchio* 1996; *Rat* 2000; *Mike Bassett: England Manager* 2001
Barron, Zelda *Secret Places* 1984; *Shag* 1988
Barry, Ian *The Chain Reaction* 1980; *Blackwater Trail* 1995
Barrymore, Lionel (1878–1954) *Madame X* 1929; *The Rogue Song* 1930
Bartel, Paul (1938–2000) *Death Race 2000* 1975; *Cannonball* 1976; *Eating Raoul* 1982; *Lust in the Dust* 1984; *Not for Publication* 1984; *The Longshot* 1986; *Scenes from the Class Struggle In Beverly Hills* 1989; *Shelf Life* 1993
Bartkowiak, Andrzej (1950–) *Romeo Must Die* 2000; *Exit Wounds* 2001; *Cradle 2 the Grave* 2003
Bartlett, Hall (1922–1993) *Unchained* 1955; *Drango* 1957; *Zero Hour!* 1957; *All the Young Men* 1960; *The Caretakers* 1963; *The Defiant* 1972; *Jonathan Livingston Seagull* 1973; *The Children of Sanchez* 1978
Bartlett, Richard (1922–1994) *Rock, Pretty Baby* 1956; *Money, Women and Guns* 1958
Barton, Charles aka **Barton, Charles T** (1902–1981) *The Last Outpost* 1935; *Hell Town* 1937; *Reveille with Beverly* 1943; *The Time of Their Lives* 1946; *Buck Privates Come Home* 1947; *Abbott and Costello Meet Frankenstein* 1948; *The Noose Hangs High* 1948; *Abbott and Costello Meet the Killer, Boris Karloff* 1949; *Africa Screams* 1949; *Double Crossbones* 1951; *Dance with Me Henry* 1956; *The Shaggy Dog* 1959; *Toby Tyler, or Ten Weeks with a Circus* 1960
Bass, Jules (1935–) *Mad Monster Party* 1966; *The Last Unicorn* 1980
Bassoff, Lawrence *Weekend Pass* 1984; *Hunk* 1987
Baumbach, Noah (1969–) *Kicking and Screaming* 1995; *Mr Jealousy* 1997
Bava, Mario aka **Lion, Mickey** (1914–1980) *The Mask of Satan* 1960; *Black Sabbath* 1963; *Blood and Black Lace* 1964; *Planet of the Vampires* 1965; *Dr Goldfoot and the Girl Bombs* 1966; *Danger: Diabolik* 1967; *Hatchet for the Honeymoon* 1969; *Bay of Blood* 1971; *Baron Blood* 1972; *Four Times That Night* 1972; *Lisa and the Devil* 1976
Baxley, Craig R *Action Jackson* 1988; *Dark Angel* 1989; *Stone Cold* 1991; *Sudden Fury* 1993; *Under Pressure* 1997
Baxter, John (1896–1975) *Doss House* 1933; *Song of the Road* 1937; *Crooks' Tour* 1940; *The Common Touch* 1941; *Love on the Dole* 1941; *We'll Smile Again* 1942; *Dreaming* 1944; *Here Comes the Sun* 1945; *When You Come Home* 1947; *Judgement Deferred* 1951
Bay, Michael (1965–) *Bad Boys* 1995; *The Rock* 1996; *Armageddon* 1998; *Pearl Harbor* 2001; *Bad Boys II* 2003
Beaird, David (1952–) *My Chauffeur* 1986; *Pass the Ammo* 1988; *Scorchers* 1991
Beatty, Warren (1937–) *Heaven Can Wait* 1978; *Reds* 1981; *Dick Tracy* 1990; *Bulworth* 1998
Beaudine, William (1892–1970) *Little Annie Rooney* 1925; *Sparrows* 1926; *Make Me a Star* 1932; *Three Wise Girls* 1932; *The Old-Fashioned Way* 1934; *Boys Will Be Boys* 1935; *Where There's a Will* 1936; *Windbag the Sailor* 1936; *Clancy Street Boys* 1943; *Ghosts in the Night* 1943; *Bowery Champs* 1944; *Follow the Leader* 1944; *Voodoo Man* 1944; *Come Out Fighting* 1945; *Kidnapped* 1948; *Tuna Clipper* 1949; *Bela Lugosi Meets a Brooklyn Gorilla* 1952; *Jalopy* 1953; *Pride of the Blue Grass* 1954; *Jail Busters* 1955; *Westward Ho the Wagons!* 1956; *Ten Who Dared* 1960; *Lassie's Great Adventure* 1963; *Billy the Kid vs Dracula* 1966; *Jesse James Meets Frankenstein's Daughter* 1966
Beaumont, Gabrielle (1942–) *The Godsend* 1980; *He's My Girl* 1987; *The Other Woman* 1994
Beaumont, Harry (1888–1966) *Our Dancing Daughters* 1928; *The Broadway Melody* 1929; *Dance, Fools, Dance* 1931; *Laughing Sinners* 1931; *Faithless* 1932; *When Ladies Meet* 1933
Beck, Steve *Thir13en Ghosts* 2001; *Ghost Ship* 2002
Becker, Harold (1950–) *The Ragman's Daughter* 1972; *The Onion Field* 1979; *The Black Marble* 1980; *Taps* 1981; *Vision Quest* 1985; *The Boost* 1988; *Sea of Love* 1989; *Malice* 1993; *City Hall* 1996; *Mercury Rising* 1998; *Domestic Disturbance* 2001
Becker, Jacques (1906–1960) *La Vie Est à Nous* 1936; *Casque d'Or* 1952; *Casque d'Or* 1952; *Honour among Thieves* 1954; *Montparnasse 19* 1958; *Le Trou* 1959
Becker, Jean (1938–) *One Deadly Summer* 1983; *Elisa* 1994; *The Children of the Marshland* 1998; *Strange Gardens* 2003
Becker, Walt (1968–) *Buying the Cow* 2000; *Van Wilder: Party Liaison* 2002
Becker, Wolfgang (1954–) *Life Is All You Get* 1998; *Good Bye Lenin!* 2003
Beebe, Ford (1888–1978) *Laughing at Life* 1933; *Trouble at Midnight* 1937; *Westbound Limited* 1937; *Fantasia* 1940; *The Reluctant Dragon* 1941; *Frontier Badmen* 1943; *Enter Arsene Lupin* 1944; *The Invisible Man's Revenge* 1944; *Challenge to Be Free* 1972
Beeman, Greg (1962–) *License to Drive* 1988; *Mom and Dad Save the World* 1992; *Bushwhacked* 1995; *A Ring of Endless Light* 2002

Beineix, Jean-Jacques (1946–) *Diva* 1981; *The Moon in the Gutter* 1983; *Betty Blue* 1986; *Roselyne and the Lions* 1989; *IP5* 1992
Bell, Martin *Streetwise* 1985; *American Heart* 1992
Bell, Monta (1891–1958) *The Torrent* 1926; *The Worst Woman in Paris?* 1933
Bellamy, Earl (1917–2003) *Stagecoach to Dancer's Rock* 1962; *Fluffy* 1965; *Gunpoint* 1966; *Incident at Phantom Hill* 1966; *Munster, Go Home!* 1966; *Three Guns for Texas* 1968; *Backtrack* 1969; *Seven Alone* 1974; *Against a Crooked Sky* 1975; *Part 2 Walking Tall* 1975; *Sidewinder One* 1977
Bellocchio, Marco (1939–) *Fists in the Pocket* 1965; *The Prince of Homburg* 1997; *Good Morning, Night* 2003
Belmont, Véra (1931–) *Rouge Baiser* 1985; *Milena* 1990; *Marquise* 1997
Belson, Jerry *Jekyll and Hyde... Together Again* 1982; *Surrender* 1987
Belvaux, Lucas (1961–) *Pour Rire!* 1996; *[One] Cavale* 2002; *[Three] Après la Vie* 2002; *[Two] Un Couple Epatant* 2002
Bemberg, Maria Luisa (1922–1995) *Camila* 1984; *Miss Mary* 1986; *I, the Worst of All* 1990; *We Don't Want to Talk about It* 1993
Bender, Jack *Child's Play 3* 1991; *The Face* 1996
Benedek, Laslo *aka* **Benedek, Laszlo** (1905–1992) *The Kissing Bandit* 1949; *Port of New York* 1949; *Death of a Salesman* 1951; *The Wild One* 1953; *Bengal Brigade* 1954; *Affair in Havana* 1957; *Moment of Danger* 1960; *Namu, the Killer Whale* 1966; *Daring Game* 1968; *The Night Visitor* 1970
Benegal, Dev (1960–) *English, August* 1994; *Split Wide Open* 1999
Benegal, Shyam (1934–) *Ankur* 1974; *Nishant* 1975; *Junoon* 1978; *Mandi* 1983; *The Making of the Mahatma* 1995; *Zubeidaa* 2000
Benigni, Roberto (1952–) *Johnny Stecchino* 1991; *Life Is Beautiful* 1997; *Pinocchio* 2002
Benjamin, Richard (1938–) *My Favorite Year* 1982; *City Heat* 1984; *Racing with the Moon* 1984; *The Money Pit* 1985; *Little Nikita* 1988; *My Stepmother Is an Alien* 1988; *Downtown* 1990; *Mermaids* 1990; *Made in America* 1993; *Milk Money* 1994; *Mrs Winterbourne* 1996; *The Pentagon Wars* 1998; *Laughter on the 23rd Floor* 2000; *The Shrink Is In* 2000; *Marci X* 2003
Benner, Richard (1943–1990) *Outrageous!* 1977; *Happy Birthday, Gemini* 1980; *Too Outrageous!* 1987
Bennet, Spencer Gordon *aka* **Bennet, Spencer G** (1893–1987) *Submarine Seahawk* 1959; *The Atomic Submarine* 1960; *The Bounty Killer* 1965
Bennett, Bill (1953–) *A Street to Die* 1985; *Backlash* 1986; *Malpractice* 1989; *Mortgage* 1989; *Spider & Rose* 1994; *Stolen Hearts* 1996; *Kiss or Kill* 1997; *Tempted* 2001; *The Nugget* 2002
Bennett, Compton (1900–1974) *The Seventh Veil* 1945; *Daybreak* 1946; *The Years Between* 1946; *The Forsyte Saga* 1949; *King Solomon's Mines* 1950; *The Gift Horse* 1951; *It Started in Paradise* 1952; *Desperate Moment* 1953; *The Flying Scot* 1957; *That Woman Opposite* 1957; *Beyond the Curtain* 1960
Bentley, Thomas (1880–1953) *Scotland Yard Mystery* 1933; *The Old Curiosity Shop* 1934; *Those Were the Days* 1934; *Music Hath Charms* 1935
Benton, Robert (1932–) *Bad Company* 1972; *The Late Show* 1977; *Kramer vs Kramer* 1979; *Still of the Night* 1982; *Places in the Heart* 1984; *Nadine* 1987; *Billy Bathgate* 1991; *Nobody's Fool* 1994; *Twilight* 1998; *The Human Stain* 2003
Bercovici, Luca (1957–) *Ghoulies* 1985; *Rockula* 1989; *Luck of the Draw* 2000
Beresford, Bruce (1940–) *The Adventures of Barry McKenzie* 1972; *Barry McKenzie Holds His Own* 1974; *Side by Side* 1975; *Don's Party* 1976; *The Getting of Wisdom* 1977; *Money Movers* 1978; *Breaker Morant* 1979; *The Club* 1980; *Puberty Blues* 1981; *Tender Mercies* 1982; *The Fringe Dwellers* 1985; *King David* 1985; *Crimes of the Heart* 1986; *Aria* 1987; *Driving Miss Daisy* 1989; *Her Alibi* 1989; *Black Robe* 1991; *Mister Johnson* 1991; *Rich in Love* 1992; *A Good Man in Africa* 1993; *Silent Fall* 1994; *Last Dance* 1996; *Paradise Road* 1997; *Double Jeopardy* 1999; *Bride of the Wind* 2001; *Evelyn* 2002
Berg, Peter (1964–) *Very Bad Things* 1998; *Welcome to the Jungle* 2003; *Friday Night Lights* 2004
Bergeron, Eric "Bibo" *The Road to El Dorado* 2000; *Shark Tale* 2004
Bergman, Andrew (1945–) *So Fine* 1981; *The Freshman* 1990; *Honeymoon in Vegas* 1992; *It Could Happen to You* 1994; *Striptease* 1996; *Isn't She Great* 1999
Bergman, Ingmar (1918–) *Crisis* 1945; *It Rains on Our Love* 1946; *A Ship to India* 1947; *Night Is My Future* 1948; *Port of Call* 1948; *The Devil's Wanton* 1949; *Three Strange Loves* 1949; *Summer Interlude* 1950; *To Joy* 1950; *Summer with Monika* 1952; *Waiting Women* 1952; *Sawdust and Tinsel* 1953; *Lesson in Love* 1954; *Dreams* 1955; *Smiles of a Summer Night* 1955; *The Seventh Seal* 1957; *So Close to Life* 1957; *Wild Strawberries* 1957; *The Magician* 1958; *The Devil's Eye* 1960; *The Virgin Spring* 1960; *Through a Glass Darkly* 1961; *Winter Light* 1962; *The Silence* 1963; *All These Women* 1964; *Persona* 1966; *The Hour of the Wolf* 1967; *Shame* 1968; *A Passion* 1969; *The Rite* 1969; *The Touch* 1971; *Cries and Whispers* 1972; *Scenes from a Marriage* 1973; *The Magic Flute* 1974; *Face to Face* 1976; *The Serpent's Egg* 1977; *Autumn Sonata* 1978; *From the Life of the Marionettes* 1980; *Fanny and Alexander* 1982; *After the Rehearsal* 1984; *Saraband* 2003
Berke, William *aka* **Berke, William A** (1903–1958) *The Falcon in Mexico* 1944; *Betrayal from the East* 1945; *Dick Tracy* 1945; *The Falcon's Adventure* 1946; *Jungle Jim* 1948
Berkeley, Busby (1895–1976) *Footlight Parade* 1933; *Gold Diggers of 1935* 1935; *Stage Struck* 1936; *Hollywood Hotel* 1937; *Garden of the Moon* 1938; *Babes in Arms* 1939; *Fast and Furious* 1939; *They Made Me a Criminal* 1939; *Strike Up the Band* 1940; *Babes on Broadway* 1941; *For Me and My Gal* 1942; *The Gang's All Here* 1943; *Cinderella Jones* 1946; *Take Me Out to the Ball Game* 1949
Berliner, Alain (1963–) *Ma Vie en Rose* 1997; *Passion of Mind* 2000
Berlinger, Joe (1961–) *Paradise Lost: the Child Murders at Robin Hood Hills* 1996; *Book of Shadows: Blair Witch 2* 2000; *Metallica: Some Kind of Monster* 2004
Berman, Monty (1913–) *Jack the Ripper* 1958; *The Siege of Sidney Street* 1960; *The Treasure of Monte Cristo* 1960; *The Hellfire Club* 1961
Berman, Ted (1919–2001) *The Fox and the Hound* 1981; *The Black Cauldron* 1985
Bernard, Raymond (1891–1977) *The Chess Player* 1927; *Les Misérables* 1934
Bernds, Edward (1905–2000) *The Bowery Boys Meet the Monsters* 1954; *Jungle Gents* 1954; *World without End* 1955; *Reform School Girl* 1957; *Quantrill's Raiders* 1958; *Queen of Outer Space* 1958; *Space Master X 7* 1958; *Return of the Fly* 1959; *The Three Stooges in Orbit* 1962; *The Three Stooges Meet Hercules* 1962
Bernhard, Jack (1913–) *Appointment with Murder* 1948; *Search for Danger* 1949
Bernhardt, Curtis *aka* **Bernhardt, Kurt** (1899–1981) *Three Loves* 1929; *Million Dollar Baby* 1941; *Happy Go Lucky* 1943; *Conflict* 1945; *Devotion* 1946; *My Reputation* 1946; *A Stolen Life* 1946; *High Wall* 1947; *Possessed* 1947; *The Doctor and the Girl* 1949; *The Blue Veil* 1951; *Payment on Demand* 1951; *Sirocco* 1951; *The Merry Widow* 1952; *Miss Sadie Thompson* 1953; *Beau Brummell* 1954; *Interrupted Melody* 1955; *Gaby* 1956; *Kisses for My President* 1964
Bernstein, Armyan *Windy City* 1984; *Cross My Heart* 1987
Berri, Claude (1934–) *The Two of Us* 1967; *Marry Me! Marry Me!* 1968; *Un Moment d'Egarement* 1977; *Je Vous Aime* 1980; *Le Maître d'Ecole* 1981; *Jean de Florette* 1986; *Manon des Sources* 1986; *Uranus* 1990; *Germinal* 1993; *Lucie Aubrac* 1997
Berry, John (1917–1999) *Miss Susie Slagle's* 1945; *From This Day Forward* 1946; *Casbah* 1948; *Tension* 1949; *Utopia* 1950; *He Ran All the Way* 1951; *Claudine* 1974; *Thieves* 1977; *The Bad News Bears Go to Japan* 1978; *A Captive in the Land* 1991; *Boesman & Lena* 2000
Berry, Tom *Something about Love* 1987; *The Amityville Curse* 1990
Bertolucci, Bernardo (1940–) *La Commare Secca* 1962; *Before the Revolution* 1964; *Partner* 1968; *The Conformist* 1969; *The Spider's Stratagem* 1970; *Last Tango in Paris* 1972; *1900* 1976; *La Luna* 1979; *The Tragedy of a Ridiculous Man* 1981; *The Last Emperor* 1987; *The Sheltering Sky* 1990; *Little Buddha* 1993; *Stealing Beauty* 1995; *Besieged* 1998; *Ten Minutes Older: the Cello* 2002; *The Dreamers* 2003
Bertucelli, Jean-Louis (1942–) *Ramparts of Clay* 1969; *Doctor Françoise Gailland* 1975
Besson, Luc (1959–) *The Last Battle* 1983; *Subway* 1985; *The Big Blue* 1988; *Nikita* 1990; *Atlantis* 1991; *Leon* 1994; *The Fifth Element* 1997; *Joan of Arc* 1999
Betancor, Antonio Jose *aka* **Betancor, Antonio J** (1944–) *Valentina* 1982; *1919* 1983
Betuel, Jonathan (1949–) *My Science Project* 1985; *Theodore Rex* 1995
Beyer, Troy (1965–) *Let's Talk about Sex* 1998; *Love Don't Cost a Thing* 2003
Bhansali, Sanjay Leela *Hum Dil De Chuke Sanam* 1999; *Devdas* 2002; *Black* 2004
Bharadwaj, Radha *Closet Land* 1991; *Basil* 1998
Bhatt, Vikram *Raaz* 2001; *Awara Paagal Deewana* 2002
Bianchi, Edward (1942–) *The Fan* 1981; *Off and Running* 1991
Biberman, Abner (1909–1977) *The Looters* 1955; *Running Wild* 1955; *Gun for a Coward* 1957; *The Night Runner* 1957
Biberman, Herbert J *aka* **Biberman, Herbert** (1900–1971) *Meet Nero Wolfe* 1936; *The Master Race* 1944; *Salt of the Earth* 1954; *Slaves* 1969
Bier, Susanne (1960–) *Open Hearts* 2002; *Brothers* 2004
Bierman, Robert *Vampire's Kiss* 1988; *Keep the Aspidistra Flying* 1997
Bigelow, Kathryn (1951–) *The Loveless* 1981; *Near Dark* 1987; *Blue Steel* 1990; *Point Break* 1991; *Strange Days* 1995; *The Weight of Water* 2000; *K-19: the Widowmaker* 2002
Bill, Tony (1940–) *My Bodyguard* 1980; *Six Weeks* 1982; *Five Corners* 1987; *Crazy People* 1990; *A Home of Our Own* 1993; *Untamed Heart* 1993; *Beyond the Call* 1996
Billington, Kevin (1934–) *Interlude* 1968; *The Rise and Rise of Michael Rimmer* 1970; *The Light at the Edge of the World* 1971
Bilson, Bruce (1928–) *Hill's Angels* 1979; *Chattanooga Choo Choo* 1984
Binder, Mike (1958–) *Indian Summer* 1993; *Blankman* 1994; *The Sex Monster* 1998; *Londinium* 1999; *The Search for John Gissing* 2001
Binder, Steve *The TAMI Show* 1964; *Give 'em Hell, Harry!* 1975
Bindley, William *Judicial Consent* 1995; *The Eighteenth Angel* 1997
Binyon, Claude (1905–1978) *The Saxon Charm* 1948; *Stella* 1950; *Dreamboat* 1952; *Here Come the Girls* 1953
Bird, Antonia (1959–) *Priest* 1994; *Mad Love* 1995; *Face* 1997; *Ravenous* 1999
Bird, Brad (1963–) *The Iron Giant* 1999; *The Incredibles* 2004
Birkin, Andrew (1945–) *Burning Secret* 1988; *The Cement Garden* 1992; *Salt on Our Skin* 1992
Birt, Daniel (1907–1955) *No Room at the Inn* 1948; *The Three Weird Sisters* 1948; *The Interrupted Journey* 1949; *Background* 1953
Bishop, Terry (1917–1981) *You're Only Young Twice* 1952; *Cover Girl Killer* 1959; *Life in Danger* 1959
Bixby, Bill (1934–1993) *The Trial of the Incredible Hulk* 1989; *The Death of the Incredible Hulk* 1990
Black, Noel (1937–) *Pretty Poison* 1968; *Jennifer on My Mind* 1971; *A Man, a Woman and a Bank* 1979; *Private School* 1983; *A Conspiracy of Love* 1987
Blair, Les (1941–) *Number One* 1984; *Bad Behaviour* 1992; *Jump the Gun* 1996
Blakeley, John E (1889–1958) *Somewhere on Leave* 1942; *Demobbed* 1944; *Home Sweet Home* 1945; *It's a Grand Life* 1953
Blakemore, Michael (1928–) *Privates on Parade* 1982; *Country Life* 1994
Blanc, Michel (1952–) *The Escort* 1999; *Summer Things* 2002
Blanks, Jamie (1971–) *Urban Legend* 1998; *Valentine* 2001
Blasetti, Alessandro (1900–1987) *1860* 1933; *Four Steps in the Clouds* 1942; *Lucky to Be a Woman* 1955; *Too Bad She's Bad* 1955
Blatt, Edward A (1903–1991) *Between Two Worlds* 1944; *Smart Woman* 1948
Blatty, William Peter (1928–) *The Ninth Configuration* 1979; *The Exorcist III* 1990
Bleckner, Jeff (1943–) *Do You Remember Love* 1985; *White Water Summer* 1987; *Rear Window* 1998
Blier, Bertrand (1939–) *Les Valseuses* 1974; *Get out Your Handkerchiefs* 1977; *Buffet Froid* 1979; *Tenue de Soirée* 1986; *Trop Belle pour Toi* 1989; *Merci la Vie* 1991; *Mon Homme* 1996
Bloom, Jason *Bio-Dome* 1996; *Overnight Delivery* 1997
Bloom, Jeffrey *Dogpound Shuffle* 1974; *Blood Beach* 1981; *Flowers in the Attic* 1987
Bloomfield, George (1930–) *Jenny* 1969; *To Kill a Clown* 1972; *Nothing Personal* 1980; *Jacob Two Two Meets the Hooded Fang* 1999
Blumenberg, Hans-Christoph (1947–) *Thousand Eyes* 1984; *Operation Madonna* 1987
Bluth, Don (1938–) *The Secret of NIMH* 1982; *An American Tail* 1986; *The Land before Time* 1988; *All Dogs Go to Heaven* 1989; *Rock-a-Doodle* 1990; *Stanley's Magic Garden* 1994; *Thumbelina* 1994; *The Pebble and the Penguin* 1995; *Anastasia* 1997; *Bartok the Magnificent* 1999; *Titan AE* 2000
Blystone, John G *aka* **Blystone, John** (1892–1938) *Our Hospitality* 1923; *Tol'able David* 1930; *Shanghai Madness* 1933; *Change of Heart* 1934; *Great Guy* 1936; *Woman Chases Man* 1937; *Blockheads* 1938; *Swiss Miss* 1938
Bochner, Hart (1956–) *PCU* 1994; *High School High* 1996
Bodrov, Sergei (1948–) *I Wanted to See Angels* 1992; *Prisoner of the Mountains* 1996; *Running Free* 1999
Boetticher, Budd (1916–2001) *The Bullfighter and the Lady* 1951; *The Cimarron Kid* 1951; *Bronco Buster* 1952; *Horizons West* 1952; *Red Ball Express* 1952; *City beneath the Sea* 1953; *East of Sumatra* 1953; *The Man from the Alamo* 1953; *Seminole* 1953; *The Magnificent Matador* 1955; *The Killer Is Loose* 1956; *Seven Men from Now* 1956; *Decision at Sundown* 1957; *The Tall T* 1957; *Buchanan Rides Alone* 1958; *Ride Lonesome* 1959; *Westbound* 1959; *Comanche Station* 1960; *The Rise and Fall of Legs Diamond* 1960; *A Time for Dying* 1971
Bogart, Paul (1919–) *The Three Sisters* 1966; *Marlowe* 1969; *Halls of Anger* 1970; *Skin Game* 1971; *Cancel My Reservation* 1972; *Class of '44* 1973; *Mr Ricco* 1975; *Oh, God! You Devil* 1984; *Torch Song Trilogy* 1988; *Broadway Bound* 1991
Bogayevicz, Yurek (1948–) *Anna* 1987; *Three of Hearts* 1992; *Exit in Red* 1996
Bogdanovich, Peter *aka* **Thomas, Derek** (1939–) *Voyage to the Planet of Prehistoric Women* 1966; *Targets* 1968; *The Last Picture Show* 1971; *What's Up, Doc?* 1972; *Paper Moon* 1973; *Daisy Miller* 1974; *At Long Last Love* 1975; *Nickelodeon* 1976; *Saint Jack* 1979; *They All Laughed* 1981; *Mask* 1985; *Illegally Yours* 1988; *Texasville* 1990; *Noises Off* 1992; *The Thing Called Love* 1993; *The Cat's Meow* 2001
Boisrond, Michel (1921–2002) *Une Parisienne* 1957; *Violent Summer* 1961
Boisset, Yves (1939–) *The Evil Trap* 1975; *The Purple Taxi* 1977; *The Lady Cop* 1979
Boleslawski, Richard *aka* **Boleslavsky, Richard** (1889–1937) *Rasputin and the Empress* 1932; *Hollywood Party* 1934; *Men in White* 1934; *Operator 13* 1934; *The Painted Veil* 1934; *Clive of India* 1935; *Les Misérables* 1935; *The Garden of Allah* 1936; *Theodora Goes Wild* 1936; *The Last of Mrs Cheyney* 1937
Boll, Uwe (1965–) *Sanctimony* 2000; *House of the Dead* 2003
Bolognini, Mauro (1922–2001) *Young Husbands* 1958; *Le Bambole* 1965; *The Witches* 1966; *Arabella* 1967; *The Oldest Profession* 1967; *The Inheritance* 1976
Bolotin, Craig *That Night* 1992; *Light It Up* 1999
Bondarchuk, Sergei (1920–1994) *Destiny of a Man* 1959; *War and Peace* 1966; *Waterloo* 1970
Bonitzer, Pascal (1946–) *Rien sur Robert* 1998; *Petites Coupures* 2002
Bonnard, Mario (1889–1965) *Aphrodite Goddess of Love* 1957; *The Last Days of Pompeii* 1960
Boorman, John (1933–) *Catch Us If You Can* 1965; *Point Blank* 1967; *Hell in the Pacific* 1968; *Leo the Last* 1970; *Deliverance* 1972; *Zardoz* 1973; *Exorcist II: The Heretic* 1977; *Excalibur* 1981; *The Emerald Forest* 1985; *Hope and Glory* 1987; *Where the Heart Is* 1990; *Beyond Rangoon* 1995; *The General* 1998; *The Tailor of Panama* 2000
Boos, H Gordon (1958–2004) *Red Surf* 1990; *Touch Me* 1997; *The Vivero Letter* 1998

Booth, Harry *On the Buses* 1971; *Go for a Take* 1972; *Mutiny on the Buses* 1972
Borden, Lizzie (1954–) *Born in Flames* 1983; *Working Girls* 1986; *Love Crimes* 1991; *Erotique* 1994
Boris, Robert (1945–) *Oxford Blues* 1984; *Buy & Cell* 1988; *Frank and Jesse* 1995
Bornedal, Ole (1959–) *Nightwatch* 1994; *Nightwatch* 1997
Borowczyk, Walerian (1923–) *Goto, l'Ile d'Amour* 1968; *Blanche* 1971; *Immoral Tales* 1974; *La Bête* 1975; *The Story of Sin* 1975; *The Streetwalker* 1976; *Behind Convent Walls* 1977; *Heroines of Evil* 1979; *The Art of Love* 1983
Borsos, Phillip (1953–1995) *The Grey Fox* 1982; *The Mean Season* 1985; *One Magic Christmas* 1985; *Bethune: the Making of a Hero* 1990; *Far from Home: the Adventures of Yellow Dog* 1994
Borthwick, Dave *The Secret Adventures of Tom Thumb* 1993; *The Magic Roundabout* 2005
Borzage, Frank (1893–1962) *7th Heaven* 1927; *Street Angel* 1928; *They Had to See Paris* 1929; *Song o' My Heart* 1930; *Bad Girl* 1931; *A Farewell to Arms* 1932; *Man's Castle* 1933; *Secrets* 1933; *Flirtation Walk* 1934; *Little Man, What Now?* 1934; *No Greater Glory* 1934; *Shipmates Forever* 1935; *Desire* 1936; *Big City* 1937; *Green Light* 1937; *History Is Made at Night* 1937; *Mannequin* 1937; *The Shining Hour* 1938; *Three Comrades* 1938; *Flight Command* 1940; *The Mortal Storm* 1940; *Strange Cargo* 1940; *Smilin' Through* 1941; *The Vanishing Virginian* 1941; *His Butler's Sister* 1943; *Stage Door Canteen* 1943; *Till We Meet Again* 1944; *The Spanish Main* 1945; *I've Always Loved You* 1946; *Magnificent Doll* 1946; *That's My Man* 1947; *Moonrise* 1948; *China Doll* 1958; *The Big Fisherman* 1959
Boulting, John (1913–1985) *Journey Together* 1944; *Brighton Rock* 1947; *Seven Days to Noon* 1950; *The Magic Box* 1951; *Seagulls over Sorrento* 1954; *Private's Progress* 1956; *Lucky Jim* 1957; *I'm All Right Jack* 1959; *Suspect* 1960; *Heavens Above!* 1963; *Rotten to the Core* 1965
Boulting, Roy (1913–2001) *Pastor Hall* 1940; *Thunder Rock* 1942; *Fame Is the Spur* 1947; *The Guinea Pig* 1948; *Seven Days to Noon* 1950; *Sailor of the King* 1953; *Seagulls over Sorrento* 1954; *Josephine and Men* 1955; *Brothers in Law* 1956; *Run for the Sun* 1956; *Happy Is the Bride* 1957; *Carlton-Browne of the FO* 1958; *A French Mistress* 1960; *Suspect* 1960; *The Family Way* 1966; *Twisted Nerve* 1968; *There's a Girl in My Soup* 1970; *Soft Beds, Hard Battles* 1973
Bourguignon, Serge (1928–) *Sundays and Cybèle* 1962; *The Reward* 1965; *The Picasso Summer* 1969
Bowen, Jenny *aka* **Riley, H Anne** *The Wizard of Loneliness* 1988; *Animal Behavior* 1989
Bowers, George *The Hearse* 1980; *Body and Soul* 1981; *My Tutor* 1983; *Private Resort* 1985
Bowman, Antony J *aka* **Bowman, Anthony** *Relatives* 1985; *Cappuccino* 1989; *Paperback Hero* 1998
Bowman, Rob (1960–) *Airborne* 1993; *The X-Files* 1998; *Reign of Fire* 2001; *Elektra* 2005
Bowser, Kenneth *In a Shallow Grave* 1988; *Easy Riders, Raging Bulls* 2003
Box, Muriel (1905–1991) *The Lost People* 1949; *The Happy Family* 1952; *The Beachcomber* 1954; *To Dorothy, a Son* 1954; *Simon and Laura* 1955; *Eyewitness* 1956; *The Passionate Stranger* 1957; *Subway in the Sky* 1958; *The Truth about Women* 1958; *This Other Eden* 1959; *The Piper's Tune* 1962; *Rattle of a Simple Man* 1964
Boyd, Don (1948–) *East of Elephant Rock* 1976; *Twenty-One* 1991; *Lucia* 1998; *My Kingdom* 2001; *Andrew & Jeremy Get Married* 2004
Boyle, Danny (1956–) *Shallow Grave* 1994; *Trainspotting* 1995; *A Life Less Ordinary* 1997; *The Beach* 2000; *Strumpet* 2001; *Vacuuming Completely Nude in Paradise* 2001; *28 Days Later...* 2002; *Millions* 2004
Brabin, Charles (1883–1957) *Sporting Blood* 1931; *The Beast of the City* 1932; *The Mask of Fu Manchu* 1932; *The Secret of Madame Blanche* 1933
Bradbury, Robert N *aka* **Bradbury, Robert North** *aka* **Bradbury, R N** (1886–1949) *Riders of Destiny* 1933; *Blue Steel* 1934; *The Lucky Texan* 1934; *The Man from Utah* 1934; *The Star Packer* 1934; *The Trail Beyond* 1934; *West of the Divide* 1934; *The Dawn Rider* 1935; *The Lawless Frontier* 1935; *Texas Terror* 1935; *Westward Ho* 1935; *Trouble in Texas* 1937
Bradshaw, John (1952–) *Lethal Tender* 1996; *Triggermen* 2002
Brahm, John (1893–1982) *Broken Blossoms* 1936; *Wild Geese Calling* 1941; *The Undying Monster* 1942; *Wintertime* 1943; *Guest in the House* 1944; *The Lodger* 1944; *Hangover Square* 1945; *The Locket* 1946; *Singapore* 1947; *Face to Face* 1952; *The Miracle of Our Lady of Fatima* 1952; *The Diamond Queen* 1953; *The Mad Magician* 1954; *Bengazi* 1955; *Special Delivery* 1955
Brambilla, Marco (1960–) *Demolition Man* 1993; *Excess Baggage* 1997
Branagh, Kenneth (1960–) *Henry V* 1989; *Dead Again* 1991; *Peter's Friends* 1992; *Much Ado about Nothing* 1993; *Mary Shelley's Frankenstein* 1994; *In the Bleak Midwinter* 1995; *Hamlet* 1996; *Love's Labour's Lost* 1999
Brandstrom, Charlotte (1959–) *Road to Ruin* 1992; *A Business Affair* 1993
Brass, Tinto *aka* **Tinto Brass, Giovanni** (1933–) *Salon Kitty* 1976; *Caligula* 1979
Breathnach, Paddy *Ailsa* 1994; *I Went Down* 1997; *Blow Dry* 2000
Brecher, Irving (1914–) *Somebody Loves Me* 1952; *Sail a Crooked Ship* 1961
Breillat, Catherine (1948–) *Romance* 1998; *A Ma Soeur!* 2001; *Sex Is Comedy* 2002; *Anatomy of Hell* 2003
Brenon, Herbert (1880–1958) *Beau Geste* 1926; *Laugh, Clown, Laugh* 1928; *Beau Ideal* 1931; *Someone at the Door* 1936; *Housemaster* 1938; *Black Eyes* 1939
Bresson, Robert (1907–1999) *Les Affaires Publiques* 1934; *Les Anges du Péché* 1943; *Les Dames du Bois de Boulogne* 1946; *Diary of a Country Priest* 1950; *A Man Escaped* 1956; *Pickpocket* 1959; *Le Procès de Jeanne d'Arc* 1962; *Au Hasard, Balthazar* 1966; *Mouchette* 1966; *A Gentle Creature* 1969; *Four Nights of a Dreamer* 1971; *Lancelot du Lac* 1974; *The Devil, Probably* 1977; *L'Argent* 1983
Brest, Martin (1951–) *Going in Style* 1979; *Beverly Hills Cop* 1984; *Midnight Run* 1988; *Scent of a Woman* 1992; *Meet Joe Black* 1998; *Gigli* 2003
Bretherton, Howard (1896–1969) *Hills of Kentucky* 1927; *Ladies They Talk About* 1933; *Hopalong Cassidy* 1935; *The Trap* 1947; *The Prince of Thieves* 1948
Brickman, Marshall (1941–) *Simon* 1980; *Lovesick* 1983; *The Deadly Game* 1986
Brickman, Paul (1949–) *Risky Business* 1983; *Men Don't Leave* 1990
Bridges, Alan (1927–) *Invasion* 1965; *The Hireling* 1973; *Brief Encounter* 1974; *Out of Season* 1975; *The Return of the Soldier* 1982; *The Shooting Party* 1984
Bridges, Beau (1941–) *The Wild Pair* 1987; *Seven Hours to Judgment* 1988
Bridges, James (1936–1993) *The Baby Maker* 1970; *The Paper Chase* 1973; *September 30, 1955* 1977; *The China Syndrome* 1979; *Urban Cowboy* 1980; *Mike's Murder* 1984; *Perfect* 1985; *Bright Lights, Big City* 1988
Bright, Matthew (1952–) *Freeway* 1996; *Confessions of a Trickbaby* 1999; *Bundy* 2002
Brill, Steven *Heavyweights* 1995; *Little Nicky* 2000; *Mr Deeds* 2002; *Without a Paddle* 2004
Brinckerhoff, Burt (1936–) *Acapulco Gold* 1976; *Dogs* 1976; *The Cracker Factory* 1979
Brisseau, Jean-Claude (1944–) *Noce Blanche* 1989; *Secret Things* 2002
Brizzi, Gaetan *Asterix vs Caesar* 1985; *Fantasia 2000* 1999
Brizzi, Paul *Asterix vs Caesar* 1985; *Fantasia 2000* 1999
Broderick, John C (1942–2001) *Sam's Song* 1969; *The Warrior and the Sorceress* 1983
Brodie, Kevin (1952–) *Delta Pi* 1985; *A Dog of Flanders* 1999
Bromley Davenport, Harry (1950–) *Xtro* 1983; *Waking Up Horton* 1997; *Erasable You* 1998
Brook, Peter (1925–) *The Beggar's Opera* 1953; *Lord of the Flies* 1963; *Marat/Sade* 1966; *Tell Me Lies* 1967; *King Lear* 1970; *Meetings with Remarkable Men* 1979
Brooks, Adam (1956–) *Almost You* 1984; *Red Riding Hood* 1987; *The Invisible Circus* 2000
Brooks, Albert (1947–) *Real Life* 1979; *Modern Romance* 1981; *Lost in America* 1985; *Defending Your Life* 1991; *Mother* 1996; *The Muse* 1999
Brooks, James L (1940–) *Terms of Endearment* 1983; *Broadcast News* 1987; *I'll Do Anything* 1994; *As Good as It Gets* 1997; *Spanglish* 2004
Brooks, Joseph (1938–) *You Light Up My Life* 1977; *Invitation to the Wedding* 1983
Brooks, Mel (1926–) *The Producers* 1968; *The Twelve Chairs* 1970; *Blazing Saddles* 1974; *Young Frankenstein* 1974; *Silent Movie* 1976; *High Anxiety* 1977; *History of the World Part 1* 1981; *Spaceballs* 1987; *Life Stinks* 1991; *Robin Hood: Men in Tights* 1993; *Dracula: Dead and Loving It* 1995
Brooks, Richard (1912–1992) *Crisis* 1950; *The Light Touch* 1951; *Deadline – USA* 1952; *Battle Circus* 1953; *Take the High Ground* 1953; *The Last Time I Saw Paris* 1954; *The Blackboard Jungle* 1955; *The Catered Affair* 1956; *The Last Hunt* 1956; *Something of Value* 1957; *The Brothers Karamazov* 1958; *Cat on a Hot Tin Roof* 1958; *Elmer Gantry* 1960; *Sweet Bird of Youth* 1962; *Lord Jim* 1965; *The Professionals* 1966; *In Cold Blood* 1967; *The Happy Ending* 1969; *Dollars* 1971; *Bite the Bullet* 1975; *Looking for Mr Goodbar* 1977; *The Man with the Deadly Lens* 1982; *Fever Pitch* 1985
Brooks, Sue (1953–) *Road to Nhill* 1997; *Japanese Story* 2003
Broomfield, Nick (1948–) *Chicken Ranch* 1983; *Diamond Skulls* 1989; *Monster in a Box* 1991; *Aileen Wuornos: the Selling of a Serial Killer* 1992; *Fetishes* 1996; *Kurt & Courtney* 1997; *Biggie & Tupac* 2001; *Aileen: Life and Death of a Serial Killer* 2003
Bross, Eric (1964–) *Restaurant* 1998; *Stranger than Fiction* 1999; *On the Line* 2001
Brower, Otto (1895–1946) *Paramount on Parade* 1930; *Fighting Caravans* 1931; *Under Two Flags* 1936; *Suez* 1938; *The Gay Caballero* 1940
Brown, Bruce (1937–) *Slippery When Wet* 1958; *Surf Crazy* 1959; *Barefoot Adventure* 1960; *The Endless Summer* 1964; *On Any Sunday* 1971; *The Endless Summer II* 1994
Brown, Clarence (1890–1987) *The Last of the Mohicans* 1920; *The Eagle* 1925; *The Goose Woman* 1925; *Flesh and the Devil* 1926; *A Woman of Affairs* 1928; *The Trail of '98* 1929; *Anna Christie* 1930; *Romance* 1930; *A Free Soul* 1931; *Inspiration* 1931; *Possessed* 1931; *Emma* 1932; *Night Flight* 1933; *Chained* 1934; *Sadie McKee* 1934; *Ah, Wilderness!* 1935; *Anna Karenina* 1935; *The Gorgeous Hussy* 1936; *Wife vs Secretary* 1936; *Conquest* 1937; *Of Human Hearts* 1938; *Idiot's Delight* 1939; *The Rains Came* 1939; *Edison, the Man* 1940; *Come Live with Me* 1941; *They Met in Bombay* 1941; *The Human Comedy* 1943; *National Velvet* 1944; *The White Cliffs of Dover* 1944; *The Yearling* 1946; *Song of Love* 1947; *Intruder in the Dust* 1949; *To Please a Lady* 1950; *Angels in the Outfield* 1951; *It's a Big Country* 1951; *Plymouth Adventure* 1952
Brown, Harry Joe (1890–1972) *Sitting Pretty* 1933; *Knickerbocker Holiday* 1944
Brown, Rowland (1897–1963) *Quick Millions* 1931; *Hell's Highway* 1932
Browning, Tod (1882–1962) *The Unholy Three* 1925; *The Black Bird* 1926; *The Road to Mandalay* 1926; *London after Midnight* 1927; *The Unknown* 1927; *West of Zanzibar* 1928; *Dracula* 1931; *The Iron Man* 1931; *Freaks* 1932; *Mark of the Vampire* 1935; *The Devil-Doll* 1936; *Miracles for Sale* 1939
Brownlow, Kevin (1938–) *It Happened Here* 1963; *Winstanley* 1975; *Universal Horror* 1998
Bruckman, Clyde (1894–1955) *The General* 1927; *Feet First* 1930; *Movie Crazy* 1932; *The Man on the Flying Trapeze* 1935
Brunel, Adrian (1892–1958) *The Constant Nymph* 1928; *An Old Spanish Custom* 1935; *The Lion Has Wings* 1939
Bucquet, Harold S *aka* **Bucquet, Harold** (1891–1946) *Young Dr Kildare* 1938; *Calling Dr Kildare* 1939; *The Secret of Dr Kildare* 1939; *Dr Kildare Goes Home* 1940; *Dr Kildare's Crisis* 1940; *Dr Kildare's Strange Case* 1940; *Dr Kildare's Wedding Day* 1941; *The Penalty* 1941; *The People vs Dr Kildare* 1941; *Calling Dr Gillespie* 1942; *The War against Mrs Hadley* 1942; *The Adventures of Tartu* 1943; *Dragon Seed* 1944; *Without Love* 1945
Buechler, John Carl *Troll* 1986; *Friday the 13th Part VII: the New Blood* 1988
Bugajski, Ryszard *aka* **Bugajski, Richard** (1943–) *Interrogation* 1982; *Clearcut* 1992
Buñuel, Luis (1900–1983) *Un Chien Andalou* 1928; *L'Age d'Or* 1930; *Land without Bread* 1933; *The Great Madcap* 1949; *Los Olvidados* 1950; *La Hija del Engaño* 1951; *Mexican Bus Ride* 1951; *Susana* 1951; *A Woman without Love* 1951; *The Adventures of Robinson Crusoe* 1952; *El Bruto* 1952; *El* 1953; *Wuthering Heights* 1953; *The River and Death* 1954; *The Criminal Life of Archibaldo de la Cruz* 1955; *Celà S'Appelle l'Aurore* 1956; *Death in the Garden* 1956; *Nazarín* 1958; *La Fièvre Monte à el Pao* 1959; *The Young One* 1960; *Viridiana* 1961; *The Exterminating Angel* 1962; *The Diary of a Chambermaid* 1964; *Simon of the Desert* 1965; *Belle de Jour* 1967; *The Milky Way* 1968; *Tristana* 1970; *The Discreet Charm of the Bourgeoisie* 1972; *Le Fantôme de la Liberté* 1974; *That Obscure Object of Desire* 1977
Burdis, Ray (1958–) *Final Cut* 1998; *Love, Honour and Obey* 2000
Burge, Stuart (1918–2002) *There Was a Crooked Man* 1960; *Othello* 1965; *Julius Caesar* 1970
Burke, Martyn *Power Play* 1978; *The Last Chase* 1981; *Avenging Angelo* 2002
Burnett, Charles (1944–) *To Sleep with Anger* 1990; *The Glass Shield* 1995; *Martin Scorsese Presents The Blues: Warming by the Devil's Fire* 2003
Burns, Edward (1968–) *The Brothers McMullen* 1995; *She's the One* 1996; *No Looking Back* 1998; *Sidewalks of New York* 2000; *Ash Wednesday* 2002
Burns, Ken (1953–) *Huey Long* 1985; *Frank Lloyd Wright* 1997
Burr, Jeff (1963–) *Stepfather II* 1989; *Leatherface: the Texas Chainsaw Massacre III* 1990; *The Revenge of Pumpkinhead – Blood Wings* 1994
Burrowes, Geoff (1945–) *Return to Snowy River* 1988; *Run* 1991
Burstall, Tim (1929–2004) *Alvin Purple* 1973; *Petersen* 1974; *Attack Force Z* 1981; *The Naked Country* 1985; *Kangaroo* 1986
Burton, David (1877–1963) *Fighting Caravans* 1931; *Lady by Choice* 1934; *Princess O'Hara* 1935; *The Man Who Wouldn't Talk* 1940
Burton, Tim (1960–) *Pee-wee's Big Adventure* 1985; *Beetle Juice* 1988; *Batman* 1989; *Edward Scissorhands* 1990; *Batman Returns* 1992; *Ed Wood* 1994; *Mars Attacks!* 1996; *Sleepy Hollow* 1999; *Planet of the Apes* 2001; *Big Fish* 2003
Buscemi, Steve (1957–) *Trees Lounge* 1996; *Animal Factory* 2000
Butler, David (1894–1979) *Fox Movietone Follies of 1929* 1929; *Sunny Side Up* 1929; *Just Imagine* 1930; *A Connecticut Yankee* 1931; *Delicious* 1931; *Bright Eyes* 1934; *The Little Colonel* 1935; *The Littlest Rebel* 1935; *Captain January* 1936; *Pigskin Parade* 1936; *White Fang* 1936; *You're a Sweetheart* 1937; *Kentucky* 1938; *Kentucky Moonshine* 1938; *East Side of Heaven* 1939; *That's Right – You're Wrong* 1939; *You'll Find Out* 1940; *Playmates* 1941; *Road to Morocco* 1942; *Thank Your Lucky Stars* 1943; *They Got Me Covered* 1943; *The Princess and the Pirate* 1944; *Shine On, Harvest Moon* 1944; *San Antonio* 1945; *Two Guys from Milwaukee* 1946; *My Wild Irish Rose* 1947; *It's a Great Feeling* 1949; *Look for the Silver Lining* 1949; *The Story of Seabiscuit* 1949; *The Daughter of Rosie O'Grady* 1950; *Tea for Two* 1950; *Lullaby of Broadway* 1951; *Painting the Clouds with Sunshine* 1951; *April in Paris* 1952; *By the Light of the Silvery Moon* 1953; *Calamity Jane* 1953; *The Command* 1954; *King Richard and the Crusaders* 1954; *The Girl He Left Behind* 1956
Butler, George *Pumping Iron* 1976; *Pumping Iron II: the Women* 1984; *The Endurance: Shackelton's Legendary Antarctic Expedition* 2000
Butler, Robert (1927–) *The Computer Wore Tennis Shoes* 1969; *Guns in the Heather* 1969; *The Barefoot Executive* 1971; *Scandalous John* 1971; *Now You See Him, Now You Don't* 1972; *The Blue Knight* 1973; *Dark Victory* 1976; *Hot Lead and Cold Feet* 1978; *Night of the Juggler* 1980; *Turbulence* 1997
Butoy, Hendel *The Rescuers Down Under* 1990; *Fantasia 2000* 1999
Butterworth, Jez (1969–) *Mojo* 1998; *Birthday Girl* 2001
Buzzell, Edward *aka* **Buzzell, Edward N** (1895–1985) *Fast Company* 1938; *Paradise for Three* 1938; *At the Circus* 1939; *Honolulu* 1939; *Go West* 1940; *Ship Ahoy* 1942; *Best Foot Forward* 1943; *The Youngest Profession* 1943; *Keep Your Powder Dry* 1945; *Easy to Wed* 1946; *Song of the Thin Man* 1947; *Neptune's Daughter* 1949; *A Woman of Distinction* 1950; *Confidentially Connie* 1953; *Ain't Misbehavin'* 1955
Bye, Ed *Kevin & Perry Go Large* 2000; *Fat Slags* 2004

Byrum, John (1947–) *Inserts* 1975; *Heart Beat* 1979; *The Razor's Edge* 1984; *The Whoopee Boys* 1986

Cabanne, Christy (1888–1950) *The Last Outlaw* 1936; *Criminal Lawyer* 1937; *The Mummy's Hand* 1940; *Scared to Death* 1947
Cacoyannis, Michael (1922–) *Stella* 1955; *A Matter of Dignity* 1957; *Elektra* 1962; *Zorba the Greek* 1964; *The Day the Fish Came Out* 1967; *The Trojan Women* 1971; *Iphigenia* 1976; *The Cherry Orchard* 1998
Cadiff, Andy *Leave It to Beaver* 1997; *Chasing Liberty* 2004
Caesar, David *Idiot Box* 1996; *Mullet* 2001; *Dirty Deeds* 2002
Caffrey, David (1969–) *Divorcing Jack* 1998; *Grand Theft Parsons* 2003
Cahn, Edward L (1899–1963) *Law and Order* 1932; *Confidential* 1935; *Destination Murder* 1950; *Creature with the Atom Brain* 1955; *Runaway Daughters* 1956; *The She-Creature* 1956; *Dragstrip Girl* 1957; *Invasion of the Saucer Men* 1957; *Motorcycle Gang* 1957; *Shake, Rattle and Rock!* 1957; *Voodoo Woman* 1957; *It! The Terror from beyond Space* 1958; *Jet Attack* 1958; *Suicide Battalion* 1958; *A Dog's Best Friend* 1960; *The Boy Who Caught a Crook* 1961; *Beauty and the Beast* 1962
Cain, Christopher aka **Cain, Chris** (1943–) *Grand Jury* 1976; *Sixth and Main* 1977; *The Stone Boy* 1984; *That Was Then... This Is Now* 1985; *Where the River Runs Black* 1986; *The Principal* 1987; *Young Guns* 1988; *Pure Country* 1992; *The Next Karate Kid* 1994; *The Amazing Panda Adventure* 1995; *Gone Fishin'* 1997; *A Father's Choice* 2000
Camerini, Mario (1895–1981) *Ulysses* 1954; *The Miller's Wife* 1955
Cameron, James (1954–) *Piranha II: the Spawning* 1981; *The Terminator* 1984; *Aliens* 1986; *The Abyss* 1989; *Terminator 2: Judgment Day* 1991; *True Lies* 1994; *Titanic* 1997
Cameron, Ken (1946–) *Monkey Grip* 1983; *The Good Wife* 1986; *Payback* 1997
Cammell, Donald (1934–1996) *Performance* 1970; *Demon Seed* 1977; *White of the Eye* 1986; *Wild Side* 1995
Camp, Joe (1939–) *Benji* 1974; *Hawmps* 1976; *For the Love of Benji* 1977; *The Double McGuffin* 1979; *Oh, Heavenly Dog!* 1980; *Benji the Hunted* 1987
Campanella, Juan José (1959–) *The Boy Who Cried Bitch* 1991; *Love Walked In* 1997; *Son of the Bride* 2001
Campanile, Pasquale Festa (1927–1986) *The Girl and the General* 1967; *On My Way to the Crusades, I Met a Girl Who...* 1967
Campbell, Graeme (1954–) *Unforgivable* 1995; *Nico the Unicorn* 1998
Campbell, Martin *Criminal Law* 1988; *Defenseless* 1991; *No Escape* 1994; *GoldenEye* 1995; *The Mask of Zorro* 1998; *Vertical Limit* 2000; *Beyond Borders* 2003
Campion, Jane (1955–) *Sweetie* 1989; *An Angel at My Table* 1990; *The Piano* 1993; *The Portrait of a Lady* 1996; *Holy Smoke* 1999; *In the Cut* 2003
Campus, Michael *ZPG: Zero Population Growth* 1971; *The Mack* 1973; *The Passover Plot* 1976
Camus, Mario (1935–) *Los Santos Inocentes* 1984; *The House of Bernarda Alba* 1987
Cannon, Danny (1968–) *The Young Americans* 1993; *Judge Dredd* 1995; *I Still Know What You Did Last Summer* 1998; *Phoenix* 1998
Cantet, Laurent (1961–) *Human Resources* 1999; *Time Out* 2001
Cappello, Frank *American Yakuza* 1994; *No Way Back* 1996
Capra, Frank aka **Capra, Frank R** (1897–1991) *The Strong Man* 1926; *For the Love of Mike* 1927; *Long Pants* 1927; *The Matinee Idol* 1928; *Flight* 1929; *The Younger Generation* 1929; *Ladies of Leisure* 1930; *Rain or Shine* 1930; *Dirigible* 1931; *The Miracle Woman* 1931; *Platinum Blonde* 1931; *American Madness* 1932; *Forbidden* 1932; *The Bitter Tea of General Yen* 1933; *Lady for a Day* 1933; *Broadway Bill* 1934; *It Happened One Night* 1934; *Mr Deeds Goes to Town* 1936; *Lost Horizon* 1937; *You Can't Take It with You* 1938; *Mr Smith Goes to Washington* 1939; *Meet John Doe* 1941; *The Battle of Russia* 1943; *Arsenic and Old Lace* 1944; *It's a Wonderful Life* 1946; *State of the Union* 1948; *Riding High* 1950; *Here Comes the Groom* 1951; *A Hole in the Head* 1959; *Pocketful of Miracles* 1961
Capuano, Luigi (1904–) *Tiger of the Seven Seas* 1962; *The Executioner of Venice* 1963; *Kidnapped to Mystery Island* 1964; *Sandokan against the Leopard of Sarawak* 1964; *Sandokan Fights Back* 1964
Carax, Léos (1960–) *The Night Is Young* 1986; *Les Amants du Pont-Neuf* 1990; *Pola X* 1999
Cardiff, Jack (1914–) *Intent to Kill* 1958; *Beyond This Place* 1959; *Scent of Mystery* 1960; *Sons and Lovers* 1960; *The Lion* 1962; *My Geisha* 1962; *The Long Ships* 1963; *Young Cassidy* 1965; *The Liquidator* 1966; *Dark of the Sun* 1967; *The Girl on a Motorcycle* 1968; *The Mutations* 1973; *Penny Gold* 1973
Cardinal, Roger *Malarek* 1989; *Dead Silent* 1999
Cardone, J S *Shadowzone* 1990; *A Row of Crows* 1991; *The Forsaken* 2001
Cardos, John "Bud" *The Female Bunch* 1969; *Kingdom of the Spiders* 1977; *The Dark* 1979; *The Day Time Ended* 1980; *Mutant* 1984; *Act of Piracy* 1990
Carlei, Carlo (1960–) *Flight of the Innocent* 1993; *Fluke* 1995
Carlino, Lewis John (1932–) *The Sailor Who Fell from Grace with the Sea* 1976; *The Great Santini* 1979; *Class* 1983
Carlsen, Henning (1927–) *Hunger* 1966; *The Wolf at the Door* 1986
Carlson, Richard (1912–1977) *Four Guns to the Border* 1954; *The Saga of Hemp Brown* 1958; *Kid Rodelo* 1966
Carnahan, Joe (1969–) *Blood, Guts, Bullets & Octane* 1997; *Narc* 2001
Carné, Marcel (1909–1996) *Le Grand Jeu* 1933; *Drôle de Drame* 1937; *Hôtel du Nord* 1938; *Le Quai des Brumes* 1938; *Le Jour Se Lève* 1939; *Les Visiteurs du Soir* 1942; *Les Enfants du Paradis* 1945; *Les Portes de la Nuit* 1946; *Thérèse Raquin* 1953; *Les Tricheurs* 1958; *Trois Chambres à Manhattan* 1965
Caro, Marc (1956–) *Delicatessen* 1990; *The City of Lost Children* 1995
Caron, Glenn Gordon (1954–) *Clean and Sober* 1988; *Wilder Napalm* 1993; *Love Affair* 1994; *Picture Perfect* 1997
Carpenter, John (1948–) *Dark Star* 1973; *Assault on Precinct 13* 1976; *Halloween* 1978; *Elvis – the Movie* 1979; *The Fog* 1980; *Escape from New York* 1981; *The Thing* 1982; *Christine* 1983; *Starman* 1984; *Big Trouble in Little China* 1986; *Prince of Darkness* 1987; *They Live* 1988; *Memoirs of an Invisible Man* 1992; *In the Mouth of Madness* 1994; *Village of the Damned* 1995; *Escape from LA* 1996; *Vampires* 1998; *John Carpenter's Ghosts of Mars* 2001
Carpenter, Stephen aka **Carpenter, Steve** *The Kindred* 1986; *Soul Survivors* 2001
Carr, Steve *Next Friday* 1999; *Dr Dolittle 2* 2001; *Daddy Day Care* 2003
Carr, Thomas (1907–1997) *Captain Scarlett* 1953; *Dino* 1957; *The Tall Stranger* 1957; *Cast a Long Shadow* 1959
Carreras, Michael (1927–1994) *The Steel Bayonet* 1957; *Maniac* 1962; *What a Crazy World* 1963; *The Curse of the Mummy's Tomb* 1964; *The Lost Continent* 1968; *Blood from the Mummy's Tomb* 1971; *Shatter* 1974
Carroll, Willard *The Runestone* 1991; *Playing by Heart* 1998; *Tom's Midnight Garden* 1998
Carstairs, John Paddy (1910–1970) *The Saint in London* 1939; *Spare a Copper* 1940; *Dancing with Crime* 1946; *Sleeping Car to Trieste* 1948; *The Chiltern Hundreds* 1949; *Fools Rush In* 1949; *Tony Draws a Horse* 1950; *Made in Heaven* 1952; *Treasure Hunt* 1952; *Top of the Form* 1953; *Trouble in Store* 1953; *One Good Turn* 1954; *Up to His Neck* 1954; *Jumping for Joy* 1955; *Man of the Moment* 1955; *The Big Money* 1956; *Up in the World* 1956; *Just My Luck* 1957; *The Square Peg* 1958; *Tommy the Toreador* 1959; *Sands of the Desert* 1960
Carter, Peter (1933–1982) *High-ballin'* 1978; *Highpoint* 1979
Carter, Thomas *Swing Kids* 1993; *Metro* 1997; *Save the Last Dance* 2000; *Coach Carter* 2005
Caruso, D J (1965–) *The Salton Sea* 2002; *Taking Lives* 2004
Carver, Steve (1945–) *Big Bad Mama* 1974; *Capone* 1975; *Drum* 1976; *Fast Charlie: the Moonbeam Rider* 1978; *Steel* 1980; *An Eye for an Eye* 1981; *Lone Wolf McQuade* 1983; *Jocks* 1986; *Bulletproof* 1987; *River of Death* 1989
Cass, Henry (1902–1989) *29 Acacia Avenue* 1945; *The Glass Mountain* 1949; *No Place for Jennifer* 1949; *Last Holiday* 1950; *Young Wives' Tale* 1951; *Father's Doing Fine* 1952; *No Smoking* 1954; *Booby Trap* 1957; *The Crooked Sky* 1957; *Blood of the Vampire* 1958
Cassavetes, John (1929–1989) *Shadows* 1959; *Too Late Blues* 1961; *A Child Is Waiting* 1962; *Faces* 1968; *Husbands* 1970; *Minnie and Moskowitz* 1971; *A Woman under the Influence* 1974; *The Killing of a Chinese Bookie* 1976; *Opening Night* 1977; *Gloria* 1980; *Love Streams* 1984; *Big Trouble* 1985
Cassavetes, Nick (1959–) *Unhook the Stars* 1996; *She's So Lovely* 1997; *John Q* 2001; *The Notebook* 2003
Castellani, Renato (1913–1985) *Two Pennyworth of Hope* 1952; *Romeo and Juliet* 1954; *Ghosts – Italian Style* 1967
Castellari, Enzo G (1938–) *Keoma* 1976; *The Loves and Times of Scaramouche* 1976; *Extralarge: Moving Target* 1990
Castle, Nick (1947–) *The Last Starfighter* 1984; *The Boy Who Could Fly* 1986; *Tap* 1989; *Dennis* 1993; *Mr Wrong* 1996
Castle, William (1914–1977) *Betrayed* 1944; *The Whistler* 1944; *Johnny Stool Pigeon* 1949; *Undertow* 1949; *Cave of Outlaws* 1951; *Serpent of the Nile* 1953; *Charge of the Lancers* 1954; *The Iron Glove* 1954; *The Americano* 1955; *House on Haunted Hill* 1958; *Macabre* 1958; *13 Ghosts* 1959; *The Tingler* 1959; *Homicidal* 1961; *Mr Sardonicus* 1961; *Zotz* 1962; *The Old Dark House* 1963; *Strait-Jacket* 1963; *The Night Walker* 1964; *I Saw What You Did* 1965; *The Busy Body* 1967; *Project X* 1968; *Shanks* 1974
Cates, Gilbert (1934–) *I Never Sang for My Father* 1969; *The Affair* 1973; *Summer Wishes, Winter Dreams* 1973; *One Summer Love* 1975; *Face of a Stranger* 1978; *The Last Married Couple in America* 1980; *Oh God! Book II* 1980; *Backfire* 1987
Cates, Joseph (1924–1998) *Girl of the Night* 1960; *Who Killed Teddy Bear?* 1965
Caton-Jones, Michael (1958–) *Scandal* 1988; *Memphis Belle* 1990; *Doc Hollywood* 1991; *This Boy's Life* 1993; *Rob Roy* 1995; *The Jackal* 1997; *City by the Sea* 2002
Cattaneo, Peter (1964–) *The Full Monty* 1997; *Lucky Break* 2001
Cavalcanti, Alberto (1897–1982) *Went the Day Well?* 1942; *Champagne Charlie* 1944; *Dead of Night* 1945; *Nicholas Nickleby* 1947; *They Made Me a Fugitive* 1947; *The Monster of Highgate Ponds* 1961
Cavalier, Alain (1931–) *Fire and Ice* 1962; *La Chamade* 1968; *Thérèse* 1986
Cavani, Liliana (1936–) *The Night Porter* 1973; *La Pelle* 1981; *Francesco* 1989; *Ripley's Game* 2002
Cayatte, André (1909–1989) *Nous Sommes Tous des Assassins* 1952; *Verdict* 1974; *To Each His Own Hell* 1977
Celentano, Jeff *Under the Hula Moon* 1995; *Primary Suspect* 2000
Cellan Jones, Simon *Some Voices* 2000; *The One and Only* 2001
Chabat, Alain (1958–) *Didier* 1997; *Asterix & Obelix: Mission Cleopatra* 2001
Chabrol, Claude (1930–) *Le Beau Serge* 1958; *Les Cousins* 1959; *Web of Passion* 1959; *Les Bonnes Femmes* 1960; *The Seven Deadly Sins* 1961; *Bluebeard* 1962; *Ophélia* 1962; *The Beautiful Swindlers* 1964; *Paris Vu Par...* 1965; *The Champagne Murders* 1966; *The Road to Corinth* 1967; *Les Biches* 1968; *La Femme Infidèle* 1968; *Le Boucher* 1969; *Que la Bête Meure* 1969; *La Rupture* 1970; *Juste avant la Nuit* 1971; *Ten Days' Wonder* 1971; *Les Noces Rouges* 1973; *Nada* 1974; *Une Partie de Plaisir* 1974; *Les Innocents aux Mains Sales* 1975; *The Twist* 1976; *Blood Relatives* 1977; *Violette Nozière* 1977; *Le Cheval d'Orgeuil* 1980; *The Blood of Others* 1984; *Cop au Vin* 1984; *Inspecteur Lavardin* 1986; *Le Cri du Hibou* 1987; *Masques* 1987; *Une Affaire de Femmes* 1988; *Dr M* 1989; *Madame Bovary* 1991; *L'Enfer* 1994; *La Cérémonie* 1995; *Rien Ne Va Plus* 1997; *The Colour of Lies* 1999; *Merci pour le Chocolat* 2000; *The Flower of Evil* 2002; *The Bridesmaid* 2004
Chadha, Gurinder *Bhaji on the Beach* 1993; *What's Cooking?* 2000; *Bend It like Beckham* 2001; *Bride & Prejudice* 2004
Chaffey, Don (1917–1990) *The Girl in the Picture* 1956; *The Flesh Is Weak* 1957; *Danger Within* 1958; *The Man Upstairs* 1958; *Dentist in the Chair* 1960; *Greyfriars Bobby* 1961; *A Matter of WHO* 1961; *Nearly a Nasty Accident* 1961; *The Prince and the Pauper* 1962; *Jason and the Argonauts* 1963; *The Three Lives of Thomasina* 1963; *The Crooked Road* 1964; *A Jolly Bad Fellow* 1964; *One Million Years BC* 1966; *A Twist of Sand* 1967; *The Viking Queen* 1967; *Creatures the World Forgot* 1971; *Persecution* 1974; *Ride a Wild Pony* 1976; *Pete's Dragon* 1977; *The Magic of Lassie* 1978; *CHOMPS* 1979
Chahine, Youssef (1926–) *Cairo Station* 1958; *Alexandria Why?* 1979; *Alexandria Encore* 1990; *Silence... We're Rolling* 2001; *11'09''01 – September 11* 2002
Champion, Gower (1919–1980) *My Six Loves* 1962; *Bank Shot* 1974
Champion, Gregg *Short Time* 1990; *The Cowboy Way* 1994; *The Simple Life of Noah Dearborn* 1999
Chan, Benny *Jackie Chan's Who Am I?* 1998; *Gen-X Cops* 1999
Chan, Gordon aka **Chan Ka-Seung, Gordon** (1960–) *Fist of Legend* 1994; *Thunderbolt* 1995; *Beast Cops* 1998; *The Medallion* 2003
Chan, Jackie (1954–) *The Young Master* 1979; *Project A* 1983; *Police Story* 1985; *The Armour of God* 1986; *Police Story 2* 1986; *Project A: Part II* 1987; *Operation Condor: the Armour of God II* 1990; *Jackie Chan's Who Am I?* 1998
Chandrasekhar, Jay *Super Troopers* 2001; *Broken Lizard's Club Dread* 2004
Chaplin, Charles aka **Chaplin, Charlie** (1889–1977) *His New Job* 1915; *The Tramp* 1915; *Work* 1915; *Behind the Screen* 1916; *The Floorwalker* 1916; *The Pawnshop* 1916; *The Rink* 1916; *The Vagabond* 1916; *The Cure* 1917; *The Immigrant* 1917; *Shoulder Arms* 1918; *A Day's Pleasure* 1919; *Sunnyside* 1919; *The Idle Class* 1921; *The Kid* 1921; *Pay Day* 1922; *The Pilgrim* 1923; *A Woman of Paris* 1923; *The Gold Rush* 1925; *The Circus* 1928; *City Lights* 1931; *Modern Times* 1936; *The Great Dictator* 1940; *Monsieur Verdoux* 1947; *Limelight* 1952; *A King in New York* 1957; *A Countess from Hong Kong* 1967
Chapman, Matthew (1950–) *Hussy* 1979; *Strangers Kiss* 1983; *Heart of Midnight* 1988
Chapman, Michael (1935–) *All the Right Moves* 1983; *The Clan of the Cave Bear* 1986; *The Viking Sagas* 1995
Chappelle, Joe *Halloween 6: the Curse of Michael Myers* 1995; *Phantoms* 1998; *Dark Prince – the Legend of Dracula* 2000
Charell, Erik (1895–1974) *Congress Dances* 1931; *Caravan* 1934
Chatiliez, Etienne (1952–) *Life Is a Long Quiet River* 1988; *Tatie Danielle* 1990; *Le Bonheur Est dans le Pré* 1995
Chaudhri, Amin Q *Tiger Warsaw* 1988; *An Unremarkable Life* 1989
Chechik, Jeremiah aka **Chechik, Jeremiah S** *National Lampoon's Christmas Vacation* 1989; *Benny and Joon* 1993; *Tall Tale* 1994; *Diabolique* 1996; *The Avengers* 1998
Chelsom, Peter (1956–) *Hear My Song* 1991; *Funny Bones* 1994; *The Mighty* 1998; *Serendipity* 2001; *Town & Country* 2001; *Shall We Dance* 2004
Chen, Joan (1961–) *Xiu Xiu: The Sent Down Girl* 1999; *Autumn in New York* 2000
Chen Kaige (1952–) *Yellow Earth* 1984; *The Big Parade* 1986; *King of the Children* 1987; *Life on a String* 1991; *Farewell My Concubine* 1993; *Temptress Moon* 1996; *The Emperor and the Assassin* 1999; *Killing Me Softly* 2001; *Ten Minutes Older: the Trumpet* 2002; *Together with You* 2002
Chenal, Pierre (1903–1990) *Crime and Punishment* 1935; *Clochemerle* 1948; *Native Son* 1951
Chéreau, Patrice (1944–) *The Flesh of the Orchid* 1974; *La Reine Margot* 1994; *Those Who Love Me Can Take the Train* 1998; *Intimacy* 2000; *Son Frère* 2003
Cherry III, John R aka **Cherry, John** *Ernest Goes to Camp* 1987; *Ernest Saves Christmas* 1988; *Ernest Goes to Jail* 1990; *Ernest Scared Stupid* 1991; *Ernest Rides Again* 1993; *Slam Dunk Ernest* 1995
Chetwynd, Lionel (1940–) *Hanoi Hilton* 1987; *Varian's War* 2000
Ching Siu-Tung (1953–) *A Chinese Ghost Story* 1987; *A Chinese Ghost Story II* 1990
Cholodenko, Lisa (1964–) *High Art* 1998; *Laurel Canyon* 2002
Chomsky, Marvin J (1929–) *Evel Knievel* 1971; *Live a Little, Steal a Lot* 1974; *Victory at Entebbe* 1976; *Good Luck, Miss Wyckoff* 1979; *Tank* 1984
Chong, Tommy aka **Chong, Thomas** (1938–) *Cheech and Chong's Next Movie* 1980; *Cheech and Chong's Nice Dreams* 1981; *Cheech & Chong's Still*

Smokin' 1983; Cheech & Chong's The Corsican Brothers 1984
Chopra, Aditya (1971–) *Dilwale Dulhania Le Jayenge* 1995; *Mohabbatein* 2000
Chopra, B R (1914–) *Ek Hi Rasta* 1956; *Naya Daur* 1957; *Sadhna* 1958; *Kanoon* 1960
Chopra, Joyce (1938–) *Smooth Talk* 1985; *The Lemon Sisters* 1989; *Murder in New Hampshire* 1991; *The Lady in Question* 1999; *Murder in a Small Town* 1999
Chopra, Yash (1932–) *Waqt* 1965; *Kabhi Kabhie* 1976; *Veer-Zaara* 2004
Chouikh, Mohamed (1943–) *The Citadel* 1989; *L'Arche du Désert* 1997
Chouraqui, Elie (1950–) *Love Songs* 1984; *Man on Fire* 1987; *Harrison's Flowers* 2000
Chow, Stephen (1962–) *Shaolin Soccer* 2001; *Kung Fu Hustle* 2004
Christian, Roger (1944–) *The Sender* 1982; *Lorca and the Outlaws* 1985; *Nostradamus* 1993; *The Final Cut* 1995; *Underworld* 1996; *Masterminds* 1997; *Battlefield Earth* 2000
Christian-Jaque (1904–1994) *Fanfan la Tulipe* 1951; *Madame du Barry* 1954; *Nana* 1955; *Madame* 1961; *The Black Tulip* 1963; *The Dirty Game* 1965; *Dead Run* 1967
Chubbuck, Lyndon *Naked Souls* 1995; *The War Bride* 2001
Chudnow, Byron Ross (1926–) *The Doberman Gang* 1972; *The Daring Dobermans* 1973; *The Amazing Dobermans* 1976
Ciccoritti, Jerry *aka* **Ciccoritti, Gerard** (1955–) *Graveyard Shift* 1986; *Paris France* 1993; *The Life before This* 1999
Cimber, Matt *aka* **Ottaviano, Matteo** *Single Room Furnished* 1968; *Butterfly* 1982
Cimino, Michael (1943–) *Thunderbolt and Lightfoot* 1974; *The Deer Hunter* 1978; *Heaven's Gate* 1980; *Year of the Dragon* 1985; *The Sicilian* 1987; *Desperate Hours* 1990; *Sunchaser* 1996
Cissé, Souleymane (1940–) *Yeelen* 1987; *Waati* 1995
Clair, René *aka* **Clair, Rene** (1898–1981) *Paris Qui Dort* 1923; *Entr'Acte* 1924; *An Italian Straw Hat* 1927; *Sous les Toits de Paris* 1930; *A Nous la Liberté* 1931; *Le Million* 1931; *The Ghost Goes West* 1935; *The Flame of New Orleans* 1941; *I Married a Witch* 1942; *Forever and a Day* 1943; *It Happened Tomorrow* 1944; *And Then There Were None* 1945; *Man about Town* 1947; *La Beauté du Diable* 1949; *Les Belles de Nuit* 1952; *Les Grandes Manoeuvres* 1955; *Gates of Paris* 1957
Clark, Bob (1941–) *Dead of Night* 1972; *Black Christmas* 1974; *Breaking Point* 1976; *Murder by Decree* 1978; *Tribute* 1980; *Porky's* 1981; *A Christmas Story* 1983; *Porky's II: The Next Day* 1983; *Rhinestone* 1984; *Turk 182!* 1985; *From the Hip* 1987; *Loose Cannons* 1990; *It Runs in the Family* 1994; *Baby Geniuses* 1999; *I'll Remember April* 1999
Clark, Duane *Shaking the Tree* 1990; *Bitter Harvest* 1993
Clark, Greydon (1943–) *Satan's Cheerleaders* 1977; *Without Warning* 1980; *Wacko* 1981; *Lambada! The Forbidden Dance* 1990
Clark, James B (1908–2000) *Sierra Baron* 1958; *Villa!* 1958; *A Dog of Flanders* 1959; *The Sad Horse* 1959; *One Foot in Hell* 1960; *The Big Show* 1961; *Flipper* 1963; *Island of the Blue Dolphins* 1964; *And Now Miguel* 1966; *My Side of the Mountain* 1969; *The Little Ark* 1971
Clark, Jim (1931–) *Every Home Should Have One* 1970; *Rentadick* 1972; *Madhouse* 1974
Clark, Larry (1943–) *kids* 1995; *Another Day in Paradise* 1998; *Bully* 2001; *Teenage Caveman* 2001; *Ken Park* 2002
Clarke, Alan (1935–1990) *Scum* 1979; *Rita, Sue and Bob Too* 1987
Clarke, James Kenelm (1941–) *Exposé* 1975; *Hardcore* 1977; *Let's Get Laid* 1977; *Yellow Pages* 1984
Clarke, Shirley (1925–1997) *The Connection* 1961; *The Cool World* 1963; *Portrait of Jason* 1967
Clavell, James (1925–1994) *Five Gates to Hell* 1959; *Walk like a Dragon* 1960; *To Sir, with Love* 1967; *Where's Jack?* 1969; *The Last Valley* 1971
Claxton, William F (1914–1996) *Desire in the Dust* 1960; *Night of the Lepus* 1972
Clayton, Jack (1921–1995) *The Bespoke Overcoat* 1955; *Room at the Top* 1958; *The Innocents* 1961; *The Pumpkin Eater* 1964; *Our Mother's House* 1967; *The Great Gatsby* 1974; *Something Wicked This Way Comes* 1983; *The Lonely Passion of Judith Hearne* 1987
Clegg, Tom *Sweeney 2* 1978; *McVicar* 1980; *The Inside Man* 1984; *Any Man's Death* 1990
Clemens, William (1905–1980) *The Case of the Velvet Claws* 1936; *The Case of the Stuttering Bishop* 1937; *Nancy Drew – Detective* 1938; *Devil's Island* 1940; *The Falcon and the Co-Eds* 1943; *The Falcon in Danger* 1943; *The Falcon Out West* 1944
Clement, Dick (1937–) *Otley* 1968; *A Severed Head* 1970; *Catch Me a Spy* 1971; *Porridge* 1979; *Bullshot* 1983; *Water* 1985
Clément, René (1913–1996) *La Bataille du Rail* 1946; *La Belle et la Bête* 1946; *Jeux Interdits* 1953; *Knave of Hearts* 1954; *Gervaise* 1956; *This Angry Age* 1957; *Plein Soleil* 1960; *The Love Cage* 1964; *Is Paris Burning?* 1966; *Rider on the Rain* 1970; *The Deadly Trap* 1971; *And Hope to Die* 1972
Clements, Ron (1953–) *Basil the Great Mouse Detective* 1986; *The Little Mermaid* 1989; *Aladdin* 1992; *Hercules* 1997; *Treasure Planet* 2002
Clifford, Graeme (1942–) *Frances* 1982; *Burke and Wills* 1985; *Gleaming the Cube* 1988; *Ruby Cairo* 1992
Cline, Edward *aka* **Cline, Eddie** *aka* **Cline, Edward F** (1892–1961) *Neighbors* 1920; *One Week* 1920; *The Scarecrow* 1920; *The Paleface* 1921; *Day Dreams* 1922; *The Three Ages* 1923; *Million Dollar Legs* 1932; *Go Chase Yourself* 1938; *The Bank Dick* 1940; *My Little Chickadee* 1940; *The Villain Still Pursued Her* 1940; *Never Give a Sucker an Even Break* 1941; *Private Buckaroo* 1942; *Ghost Catchers* 1944
Cloche, Maurice (1907–1990) *Monsieur Vincent* 1947; *Never Take No for an Answer* 1951
Clouse, Robert (1928–1997) *Darker than Amber* 1970; *Enter the Dragon* 1973; *Black Belt Jones* 1974; *Golden Needles* 1974; *The Ultimate Warrior* 1975; *The Pack* 1977; *The Amsterdam Kill* 1978; *Game of Death* 1978; *The Big Brawl* 1980; *Gymkata* 1985; *China O'Brien* 1988
Clouzot, Henri-Georges (1907–1977) *The Raven* 1943; *Quai des Orfèvres* 1947; *The Wages of Fear* 1953; *Les Diaboliques* 1954; *Le Mystère Picasso* 1956; *Les Espions* 1957; *La Vérité* 1960
Cochran, Stacy *My New Gun* 1992; *Boys* 1995
Cocteau, Jean (1889–1963) *The Blood of a Poet* 1930; *La Belle et la Bête* 1946; *The Eagle Has Two Heads* 1948; *Les Parents Terribles* 1948; *Orphée* 1950; *Le Testament d'Orphée* 1960
Coen, Joel (1955–) *Blood Simple* 1983; *Raising Arizona* 1987; *Miller's Crossing* 1990; *Barton Fink* 1991; *The Hudsucker Proxy* 1994; *Fargo* 1995; *The Big Lebowski* 1997; *O Brother, Where Art Thou?* 2000; *The Man Who Wasn't There* 2001; *Intolerable Cruelty* 2003; *The Ladykillers* 2004
Cohen, Howard R (1942–1999) *Saturday the 14th* 1981; *Space Raiders* 1983; *Saturday the 14th Strikes Back* 1988; *Time Trackers* 1989
Cohen, Larry (1938–) *Bone* 1972; *Black Caesar* 1973; *Hell Up in Harlem* 1973; *It's Alive* 1974; *God Told Me to* 1976; *The Private Files of J Edgar Hoover* 1977; *It Lives Again* 1978; *Full Moon High* 1982; *Q – the Winged Serpent* 1982; *Blind Alley* 1984; *The Stuff* 1985; *Deadly Illusion* 1987; *It's Alive III: Island of the Alive* 1987; *A Return to Salem's Lot* 1987; *Wicked Stepmother* 1989; *The Ambulance* 1990; *Original Gangstas* 1996
Cohen, Norman (1936–1983) *Till Death Us Do Part* 1968; *Dad's Army* 1971; *Adolf Hitler – My Part in His Downfall* 1972; *Confessions of a Pop Performer* 1975; *Confessions of a Driving Instructor* 1976; *Confessions from a Holiday Camp* 1977; *Stand Up Virgin Soldiers* 1977
Cohen, Rob (1949–) *A Small Circle of Friends* 1980; *Scandalous* 1983; *Dragon: the Bruce Lee Story* 1993; *Daylight* 1996; *DragonHeart* 1996; *The Rat Pack* 1998; *The Skulls* 2000; *The Fast and the Furious* 2001; *xXx* 2002
Cohn, Michael *When the Bough Breaks* 1993; *Snow White: a Tale of Terror* 1996
Cokliss, Harley (1945–) *Battletruck* 1982; *Black Moon Rising* 1985; *Malone* 1987; *Dream Demon* 1988
Cole, Nigel *Saving Grace* 2000; *Calendar Girls* 2003; *A Lot like Love* 2005
Coleman, Herbert (1907–2001) *Battle at Bloody Beach* 1961; *Posse from Hell* 1961
Colizzi, Giuseppe (1925–1978) *Ace High* 1968; *Boot Hill* 1969
Colla, Richard A (1918–) *Zigzag* 1970; *Fuzz* 1972; *Battlestar Galactica* 1978; *The Great Balloon Adventure* 1978; *Swearing Allegiance* 1997; *Blue Valley Songbird* 1999
Collector, Robert *aka* **Blake, T C** *Red Heat* 1985; *Nightflyers* 1987
Collier, James F (1929–1991) *Two a Penny* 1968; *The Hiding Place* 1975; *The Prodigal* 1983; *China Cry* 1990
Collins, Robert *Walk Proud* 1979; *Gideon's Trumpet* 1980; *Savage Harvest* 1981
Collinson, Peter (1936–1980) *The Penthouse* 1967; *Up the Junction* 1967; *The Long Day's Dying* 1968; *The Italian Job* 1969; *You Can't Win 'em All* 1970; *Fright* 1971; *Innocent Bystanders* 1972; *And Then There Were None* 1974; *Open Season* 1974; *The Sellout* 1975; *Tomorrow Never Comes* 1977; *The Earthling* 1980
Columbus, Chris (1958–) *A Night on the Town* 1987; *Heartbreak Hotel* 1988; *Home Alone* 1990; *Only the Lonely* 1991; *Home Alone 2: Lost in New York* 1992; *Mrs Doubtfire* 1993; *Nine Months* 1995; *Stepmom* 1998; *Bicentennial Man* 1999; *Harry Potter and the Philosopher's Stone* 2001; *Harry Potter and the Chamber of Secrets* 2002
Comencini, Luigi (1916–2005) *Bread, Love and Dreams* 1953; *Le Bambole* 1965; *Somewhere beyond Love* 1974
Comerford, Joe (1949–) *Reefer and the Model* 1988; *High Boot Benny* 1993
Comfort, Lance (1908–1966) *Hatter's Castle* 1941; *Great Day* 1944; *Hotel Reserve* 1944; *Bedelia* 1946; *Daughter of Darkness* 1948; *Silent Dust* 1948; *Portrait of Clare* 1950; *Eight O'Clock Walk* 1953; *Bang! You're Dead* 1954; *Man from Tangier* 1957; *The Man in the Road* 1957; *Make Mine a Million* 1959; *Rag Doll* 1960; *The Breaking Point* 1961; *The Painted Smile* 1961; *Pit of Darkness* 1961; *The Break* 1962; *Tomorrow at Ten* 1962; *Live It Up* 1963; *Devils of Darkness* 1964; *Be My Guest* 1965
Compton, Richard *Welcome Home, Soldier Boys* 1971; *Macon County Line* 1973; *Return to Macon County* 1975; *Maniac* 1977
Condon, Bill (1957–) *Candyman: Farewell to the Flesh* 1995; *Gods and Monsters* 1998; *Kinsey* 2004
Connor, Kevin (1937–) *From beyond the Grave* 1973; *The Land That Time Forgot* 1974; *At the Earth's Core* 1976; *Trial by Combat* 1976; *The People That Time Forgot* 1977; *Warlords of Atlantis* 1978; *Arabian Adventure* 1979; *Motel Hell* 1980; *The House Where Evil Dwells* 1982; *Sunset Grill* 1992; *Jack Reed: Badge of Honor* 1993
Conrad, William (1920–1994) *Two on a Guillotine* 1964; *Brainstorm* 1965; *My Blood Runs Cold* 1965
Conway, Jack (1887–1952) *Our Modern Maidens* 1929; *The Unholy Three* 1930; *Arsene Lupin* 1932; *Red-Headed Woman* 1932; *The Gay Bride* 1934; *The Girl from Missouri* 1934; *Viva Villa!* 1934; *A Tale of Two Cities* 1935; *Libeled Lady* 1936; *Saratoga* 1937; *Too Hot to Handle* 1938; *A Yank at Oxford* 1938; *Lady of the Tropics* 1939; *Boom Town* 1940; *Honky Tonk* 1941; *Love Crazy* 1941; *Crossroads* 1942; *Dragon Seed* 1944; *High Barbaree* 1947; *The Hucksters* 1947; *Julia Misbehaves* 1948
Conway, James L (1950–) *Hangar 18* 1980; *Earthbound* 1981
Conyers, Darcy (1919–1973) *The Night We Dropped a Clanger* 1959; *The Night We Got the Bird* 1960; *In the Doghouse* 1961
Cook, Fielder (1923–2003) *Patterns* 1956; *A Big Hand for a Little Lady* 1966; *How to Save a Marriage and Ruin Your Life* 1968; *Prudence and the Pill* 1968; *Eagle in a Cage* 1971; *The Hideaways* 1973
Coolidge, Martha (1946–) *Valley Girl* 1983; *The City Girl* 1984; *Joy of Sex* 1984; *Real Genius* 1985; *Plain Clothes* 1988; *Rambling Rose* 1991; *Crazy in Love* 1992; *Lost in Yonkers* 1993; *Angie* 1994; *Three Wishes* 1995; *Out to Sea* 1997; *Introducing Dorothy Dandridge* 1999; *If These Walls Could Talk 2* 2000; *The Prince & Me* 2004
Cooney, Ray (1932–) *Not Now Darling* 1972; *Not Now, Comrade* 1976
Cooper, George A (1894–1947) *The Black Abbot* 1934; *The Shadow* 1936
Cooper, Merian C *aka* **Cooper, Merian** (1893–1973) *Grass: a Nation's Battle for Life* 1925; *Chang* 1927; *The Four Feathers* 1929; *King Kong* 1933
Cooper, Stuart (1942–) *Little Malcolm and His Struggle Against the Eunuchs* 1974; *Overlord* 1975; *The Disappearance* 1977; *The Hunted* 1998
Coppola, Christopher (1962–) *Dracula's Widow* 1988; *Deadfall* 1993; *Palmer's Pick-Up* 1999; *G-Men from Hell* 2000
Coppola, Francis Ford *aka* **Coppola, Francis** (1939–) *Tonight for Sure!* 1961; *Dementia 13* 1963; *You're a Big Boy Now* 1966; *Finian's Rainbow* 1968; *The Rain People* 1969; *The Godfather* 1972; *The Conversation* 1974; *The Godfather, Part II* 1974; *Apocalypse Now* 1979; *One from the Heart* 1982; *The Outsiders* 1983; *Rumble Fish* 1983; *The Cotton Club* 1984; *Peggy Sue Got Married* 1986; *Gardens of Stone* 1987; *Tucker: the Man and His Dream* 1988; *New York Stories* 1989; *The Godfather Part III* 1990; *Bram Stoker's Dracula* 1992; *Jack* 1996; *John Grisham's The Rainmaker* 1997
Coppola, Sofia (1971–) *The Virgin Suicides* 1999; *Lost in Translation* 2003
Coraci, Frank (1965–) *The Waterboy* 1998; *The Wedding Singer* 1998; *Around the World in 80 Days* 2004
Corbiau, Gérard (1941–) *The Music Teacher* 1988; *Farinelli il Castrato* 1994; *Le Roi Danse* 2000
Corbucci, Sergio (1927–1990) *Duel of the Titans* 1961; *Django* 1966; *The Man Who Laughs* 1966; *Navajo Joe* 1966; *Ringo and His Golden Pistol* 1966; *The Great Silence* 1967; *A Professional Gun* 1968; *The Con Artists* 1976
Corcoran, Bill *Shattered Trust* 1993; *Mary Higgins Clark's Let Me Call You Sweetheart* 1997
Corley, David *aka* **Corley, David L** *Executive Power* 1998; *Angel's Dance* 1999
Corman, Roger (1926–) *Apache Woman* 1955; *Five Guns West* 1955; *The Day the World Ended* 1956; *The Gunslinger* 1956; *It Conquered the World* 1956; *Not of This Earth* 1956; *The Oklahoma Woman* 1956; *Attack of the Crab Monsters* 1957; *Rock All Night* 1957; *Sorority Girl* 1957; *The Undead* 1957; *Viking Women and the Sea Serpent* 1957; *Machine Gun Kelly* 1958; *The Mobster* 1958; *Teenage Caveman* 1958; *War of the Satellites* 1958; *A Bucket of Blood* 1959; *The Wasp Woman* 1959; *Atlas* 1960; *The Fall of the House of Usher* 1960; *The Last Woman on Earth* 1960; *The Little Shop of Horrors* 1960; *The Intruder* 1961; *The Pit and the Pendulum* 1961; *The Premature Burial* 1962; *Tales of Terror* 1962; *Tower of London* 1962; *The Haunted Palace* 1963; *The Man with the X-Ray Eyes* 1963; *The Raven* 1963; *The Terror* 1963; *The Masque of the Red Death* 1964; *The Secret Invasion* 1964; *The Tomb of Ligeia* 1964; *The Wild Angels* 1966; *The St Valentine's Day Massacre* 1967; *The Trip* 1967; *Bloody Mama* 1970; *Gas-s-s-s, or It Became Necessary to Destroy the World in Order to Save It* 1970; *Von Richthofen and Brown* 1971; *Frankenstein Unbound* 1990
Corneau, Alain (1943–) *Choice of Arms* 1981; *Fort Saganne* 1984; *Tous les Matins du Monde* 1991; *Les Enfants de Lumière* 1995; *Fear and Trembling* 2003
Cornelius, Henry (1913–1958) *Passport to Pimlico* 1949; *Genevieve* 1953; *I Am a Camera* 1955; *Next to No Time* 1958
Cornell, John (1941–) *"Crocodile" Dundee II* 1988; *Almost an Angel* 1990
Cornfield, Hubert (1929–) *Plunder Road* 1957; *The Third Voice* 1960; *Pressure Point* 1962; *The Night of the Following Day* 1968
Cornwell, Stephen *The Philadelphia Experiment 2* 1993; *Marshal Law* 1996
Correll, Charles (1944–2004) *In the Deep Woods* 1992; *Dead before Dawn* 1993
Corrente, Michael (1960–) *Federal Hill* 1994; *American Buffalo* 1995; *Outside Providence* 1999; *A Shot at Glory* 2000
Corrigan, Lloyd (1900–1969) *No One Man* 1932; *Murder on a Honeymoon* 1935
Coscarelli, Don (1954–) *Phantasm* 1978; *The Beastmaster* 1982; *Phantasm II* 1988; *Phantasm III – Lord of the Dead* 1994; *Bubba Ho-tep* 2002
Cosmatos, George Pan (1941–2005) *Sin* 1972; *Massacre in Rome* 1973; *The Cassandra Crossing* 1976; *Escape to Athena* 1979; *Of Unknown Origin* 1983; *Rambo: First Blood, Part II* 1985; *Cobra* 1986; *Leviathan* 1989; *Tombstone* 1993; *Shadow Conspiracy* 1996
Costa, Mario (1904–1995) *The Barber of Seville* 1946; *Pagliacci* 1948; *Queen of the Pirates* 1960; *Gordon the Black Pirate* 1961
Costa-Gavras *aka* **Costa-Gavras, Constantin** (1933–) *The Sleeping Car Murders* 1965; *Z* 1968; *The*

Confession 1970; *State of Siege* 1972; *Missing* 1981; *Betrayed* 1988; *Music Box* 1989; *Mad City* 1997; *Amen.* 2002

Costner, Kevin (1955–) *Dances with Wolves* 1990; *The Postman* 1997; *Open Range* 2003

Coto, Manny *Cover-Up* 1991; *Dr Giggles* 1992; *Star Kid* 1997

Couffer, Jack (1922–) *Ring of Bright Water* 1969; *The Darwin Adventure* 1972; *Living Free* 1972

Cousteau, Jacques-Yves (1910–1997) *Le Monde du Silence* 1956; *World without Sun* 1964

Couturie, Bill *Dear America: Letters Home from Vietnam* 1987; *Ed* 1996

Cox, Alex (1954–) *Repo Man* 1984; *Sid and Nancy* 1986; *Straight to Hell* 1987; *Walker* 1987; *Highway Patrolman* 1991; *The Winner* 1996; *Revengers Tragedy* 2002

Cox, Paul (1940–) *Lonely Hearts* 1981; *Man of Flowers* 1984; *My First Wife* 1984; *Cactus* 1986; *Vincent: the Life and Death of Vincent Van Gogh* 1987; *Island* 1989; *Golden Braid* 1991; *A Woman's Tale* 1991; *The Nun and the Bandit* 1992; *Erotic Tales* 1994; *Innocence* 2000

Cozzi, Luigi *aka* **Coates, Lewis** (1947–) *Hercules* 1983; *Hercules II* 1983

Crabtree, Arthur (1900–1975) *Madonna of the Seven Moons* 1944; *They Were Sisters* 1945; *Caravan* 1946; *Dear Murderer* 1947; *The Calendar* 1948; *Quartet* 1948; *Don't Ever Leave Me* 1949; *Hindle Wakes* 1952; *Fiend without a Face* 1957; *Horrors of the Black Museum* 1959

Craven, Wes (1939–) *Last House on the Left* 1972; *The Hills Have Eyes* 1977; *Deadly Blessing* 1981; *Swamp Thing* 1982; *A Nightmare on Elm Street* 1984; *Chiller* 1985; *The Hills Have Eyes Part II* 1985; *Deadly Friend* 1986; *The Serpent and the Rainbow* 1987; *Shocker* 1989; *The People under the Stairs* 1991; *Wes Craven's New Nightmare* 1994; *Vampire in Brooklyn* 1995; *Scream* 1996; *Scream 2* 1997; *Music of the Heart* 1999; *Scream 3* 1999; *Cursed* 2005

Crichton, Charles (1910–1999) *For Those in Peril* 1943; *Dead of Night* 1945; *Against the Wind* 1947; *Hue and Cry* 1947; *Another Shore* 1948; *Train of Events* 1949; *Dance Hall* 1950; *The Lavender Hill Mob* 1951; *Hunted* 1952; *The Titfield Thunderbolt* 1952; *The Love Lottery* 1953; *The Divided Heart* 1954; *The Man in the Sky* 1956; *Floods of Fear* 1958; *Law and Disorder* 1958; *The Battle of the Sexes* 1960; *The Boy Who Stole a Million* 1960; *The Third Secret* 1964; *He Who Rides a Tiger* 1965; *A Fish Called Wanda* 1988

Crichton, Michael (1942–) *Westworld* 1973; *Coma* 1977; *The First Great Train Robbery* 1978; *Looker* 1981; *Runaway* 1984; *Physical Evidence* 1988

Crisp, Donald (1880–1974) *The Navigator* 1924; *Don Q, Son of Zorro* 1925

Cristofer, Michael (1945–) *Gia* 1998; *Body Shots* 1999; *Original Sin* 2001

Croghan, Emma-Kate (1972–) *Love and Other Catastrophes* 1996; *Strange Planet* 1999

Crombie, Donald (1942–) *Caddie* 1976; *The Irishman* 1978; *Cathy's Child* 1979; *The Killing of Angel Street* 1981; *Kitty and the Bagman* 1982; *Rough Diamonds* 1994

Cromwell, John (1888–1979) *The Texan* 1930; *Tom Sawyer* 1930; *Ann Vickers* 1933; *The Silver Cord* 1933; *The Fountain* 1934; *Of Human Bondage* 1934; *Spitfire* 1934; *This Man Is Mine* 1934; *I Dream Too Much* 1935; *Village Tale* 1935; *Banjo on My Knee* 1936; *Little Lord Fauntleroy* 1936; *The Prisoner of Zenda* 1937; *Algiers* 1938; *In Name Only* 1939; *Made for Each Other* 1939; *Spirit of the People* 1940; *Victory* 1940; *So Ends Our Night* 1941; *Son of Fury* 1942; *Since You Went Away* 1944; *The Enchanted Cottage* 1945; *Anna and the King of Siam* 1946; *Dead Reckoning* 1947; *Night Song* 1947; *Caged* 1950; *The Company She Keeps* 1950; *The Racket* 1951; *The Goddess* 1958

Cronenberg, David (1943–) *Stereo* 1969; *Crimes of the Future* 1970; *Shivers* 1975; *Rabid* 1976; *The Brood* 1979; *Scanners* 1980; *Videodrome* 1982; *The Dead Zone* 1983; *The Fly* 1986; *Dead Ringers* 1988; *Naked Lunch* 1991; *M Butterfly* 1993; *Crash* 1996; *eXistenZ* 1999; *Spider* 2002; *A History of Violence* 2005

Crosland, Alan (1894–1936) *Don Juan* 1926; *When a Man Loves* 1926; *The Jazz Singer* 1927; *The Case of the Howling Dog* 1934

Crowe, Cameron (1957–) *Say Anything...* 1989; *Singles* 1992; *Jerry Maguire* 1996; *Almost Famous* 2000; *Vanilla Sky* 2001

Crowe, Christopher (1948–) *Saigon* 1988; *Whispers in the Dark* 1992

Cruze, James (1884–1942) *The Covered Wagon* 1923; *Hollywood* 1923; *Ruggles of Red Gap* 1923; *The Pony Express* 1925; *The Great Gabbo* 1929; *If I Had a Million* 1932; *Washington Merry-Go-Round* 1932; *I Cover the Waterfront* 1933

Crystal, Billy (1947–) *Mr Saturday Night* 1992; *Forget Paris* 1995; *61** 2001

Cuadri, Antonio *Living It Up* 2000; *You're My Hero* 2003

Cuarón, Alfonso (1961–) *A Little Princess* 1995; *Great Expectations* 1997; *Y Tu Mamá También* 2001; *Harry Potter and the Prisoner of Azkaban* 2004

Cukor, George (1899–1983) *Grumpy* 1930; *The Royal Family of Broadway* 1930; *The Virtuous Sin* 1930; *Girls about Town* 1931; *Tarnished Lady* 1931; *A Bill of Divorcement* 1932; *Rockabye* 1932; *What Price Hollywood?* 1932; *Dinner at Eight* 1933; *Little Women* 1933; *Our Betters* 1933; *David Copperfield* 1935; *Romeo and Juliet* 1936; *Sylvia Scarlett* 1936; *Camille* 1937; *Holiday* 1938; *The Women* 1939; *Zaza* 1939; *The Philadelphia Story* 1940; *Susan and God* 1940; *Two-Faced Woman* 1941; *A Woman's Face* 1941; *Her Cardboard Lover* 1942; *Keeper of the Flame* 1942; *Gaslight* 1944; *Winged Victory* 1944; *A Double Life* 1947; *Adam's Rib* 1949; *Edward, My Son* 1949; *Born Yesterday* 1950; *A Life of Her Own* 1950; *The Model and the Marriage Broker* 1951; *The Marrying Kind* 1952; *Pat and Mike* 1952; *The Actress* 1953; *It Should Happen to You* 1954; *A Star Is Born* 1954; *Bhowani Junction* 1956; *Les Girls* 1957; *Wild Is the Wind* 1957; *Heller in Pink Tights* 1960; *Let's Make Love* 1960; *Song without End* 1960; *The Chapman Report* 1962; *My Fair Lady* 1964; *Justine* 1969; *Travels with My Aunt* 1972; *Love among the Ruins* 1975; *The Blue Bird* 1976; *Rich and Famous* 1981

Cummings, Irving (1888–1959) *In Old Arizona* 1929; *The Cisco Kid* 1931; *The Mad Game* 1933; *The White Parade* 1934; *Curly Top* 1935; *Poor Little Rich Girl* 1936; *Vogues of 1938* 1937; *Just around the Corner* 1938; *Little Miss Broadway* 1938; *Hollywood Cavalcade* 1939; *The Story of Alexander Graham Bell* 1939; *Down Argentine Way* 1940; *Lillian Russell* 1940; *Belle Starr* 1941; *Louisiana Purchase* 1941; *That Night in Rio* 1941; *My Gal Sal* 1942; *Springtime in the Rockies* 1942; *Sweet Rosie O'Grady* 1943; *What a Woman!* 1943; *The Dolly Sisters* 1945; *Double Dynamite* 1951

Cundieff, Rusty (1965–) *Fear of a Black Hat* 1992; *Tales from the Hood* 1995

Cunningham, Sean S (1941–) *Kick!* 1979; *Friday the 13th* 1980; *DeepStar Six* 1989

Curtis, Dan (1928–) *House of Dark Shadows* 1970; *Night of Dark Shadows* 1971; *Dracula* 1974; *Burnt Offerings* 1976; *Me and the Kid* 1993

Curtis-Hall, Vondie (1956–) *Gridlock'd* 1996; *Glitter* 2001; *Redemption* 2004

Curtiz, Michael (1888–1962) *Noah's Ark* 1928; *Mammy* 1930; *Under a Texas Moon* 1930; *God's Gift to Women* 1931; *The Mad Genius* 1931; *Cabin in the Cotton* 1932; *Doctor X* 1932; *The Strange Love of Molly Louvain* 1932; *Female* 1933; *The Kennel Murder Case* 1933; *Mystery of the Wax Museum* 1933; *20,000 Years in Sing Sing* 1933; *British Agent* 1934; *Jimmy the Gent* 1934; *The Key* 1934; *Mandalay* 1934; *Black Fury* 1935; *Captain Blood* 1935; *Front Page Woman* 1935; *The Charge of the Light Brigade* 1936; *The Walking Dead* 1936; *Kid Galahad* 1937; *The Perfect Specimen* 1937; *The Adventures of Robin Hood* 1938; *Angels with Dirty Faces* 1938; *Four Daughters* 1938; *Four's a Crowd* 1938; *Gold Is Where You Find It* 1938; *Daughters Courageous* 1939; *Dodge City* 1939; *Four Wives* 1939; *The Private Lives of Elizabeth and Essex* 1939; *Santa Fe Trail* 1940; *The Sea Hawk* 1940; *Virginia City* 1940; *Dive Bomber* 1941; *The Sea Wolf* 1941; *Captains of the Clouds* 1942; *Casablanca* 1942; *Yankee Doodle Dandy* 1942; *Mission to Moscow* 1943; *This Is the Army* 1943; *Passage to Marseille* 1944; *Mildred Pierce* 1945; *Roughly Speaking* 1945; *Night and Day* 1946; *Life with Father* 1947; *The Unsuspected* 1947; *Romance on the High Seas* 1948; *Flamingo Road* 1949; *My Dream Is Yours* 1949; *The Breaking Point* 1950; *Bright Leaf* 1950; *Young Man with a Horn* 1950; *Force of Arms* 1951; *I'll See You in My Dreams* 1951; *The Jazz Singer* 1952; *Trouble along the Way* 1953; *The Boy from Oklahoma* 1954; *The Egyptian* 1954; *White Christmas* 1954; *We're No Angels* 1955; *The Best Things in Life Are Free* 1956; *The Vagabond King* 1956; *The Helen Morgan Story* 1957; *King Creole* 1958; *The Proud Rebel* 1958; *The Hangman* 1959; *The Man in the Net* 1959; *The Adventures of Huckleberry Finn* 1960; *A Breath of Scandal* 1960; *The Comancheros* 1961; *Francis of Assisi* 1961

Cutts, Graham (1885–1958) *Looking on the Bright Side* 1931; *The Sign of Four* 1932; *Car of Dreams* 1935; *Oh, Daddy!* 1935; *Over She Goes* 1937; *Just William* 1939

Czinner, Paul (1890–1972) *Ariane* 1931; *The Rise of Catherine the Great* 1934; *Escape Me Never* 1935; *As You Like It* 1936; *Stolen Life* 1939; *Romeo and Juliet* 1966

D

Da Costa, Morton (1914–1989) *Auntie Mame* 1958; *The Music Man* 1962; *Island of Love* 1963

Dahl, John (1956–) *Kill Me Again* 1989; *Red Rock West* 1992; *The Last Seduction* 1993; *Unforgettable* 1996; *Rounders* 1998; *Roadkill* 2001

Daldry, Stephen (1960–) *Billy Elliot* 2000; *The Hours* 2002

Dalen, Zale (1947–) *Skip Tracer* 1977; *Expect No Mercy* 1995

Dalrymple, Ian (1903–1989) *Storm in a Teacup* 1937; *Old Bill and Son* 1940; *Esther Waters* 1948

Damiani, Damiano (1922–) *The Empty Canvas* 1963; *A Bullet for the General* 1966; *Amityville II: the Possession* 1982

Damski, Mel (1946–) *Yellowbeard* 1983; *Mischief* 1985; *Everybody's Baby: the Rescue of Jessica McClure* 1989; *Happy Together* 1989

Daniel, Rod *Teen Wolf* 1985; *Like Father, like Son* 1987; *K-9* 1989; *The Super* 1991; *Beethoven's 2nd* 1993

Dante, Joe (1946–) *Hollywood Boulevard* 1976; *Piranha* 1978; *The Howling* 1981; *Twilight Zone: the Movie* 1983; *Gremlins* 1984; *Explorers* 1985; *Amazon Women on the Moon* 1987; *Innerspace* 1987; *The 'Burbs* 1989; *Gremlins 2: the New Batch* 1990; *Matinee* 1993; *The Second Civil War* 1997; *Small Soldiers* 1998; *Looney Tunes: Back in Action* 2004

Darabont, Frank (1959–) *Buried Alive* 1990; *The Shawshank Redemption* 1994; *The Green Mile* 1999; *The Majestic* 2001

Darby, Jonathan *The Enemy Within* 1994; *Hush* 1998

Dardenne, Jean-Pierre (1951–) *La Promesse* 1996; *Rosetta* 1999; *The Son* 2002

Dardenne, Luc (1954–) *La Promesse* 1996; *Rosetta* 1999; *The Son* 2002

Darling, Joan (1935–) *First Love* 1977; *The Check Is in the Mail* 1986

Darnell, Eric *Antz* 1998; *Madagascar* 2005

D'Arrast, Harry d'Abbadie (1893–1968) *Laughter* 1930; *Raffles* 1930; *Topaze* 1933

Dash, Julie (1952–) *Daughters of the Dust* 1991; *Subway Stories: Tales from the Underground* 1997

Dassin, Jules (1911–) *The Affairs of Martha* 1942; *Reunion in France* 1942; *Young Ideas* 1943; *The Canterville Ghost* 1944; *Brute Force* 1947; *The Naked City* 1948; *Thieves' Highway* 1949; *Night and the City* 1950; *Rififi* 1955; *Celui Qui Doit Mourir* 1957; *Where the Hot Wind Blows!* 1959; *Never on Sunday* 1960; *Phaedra* 1962; *Topkapi* 1964; *10:30 PM Summer* 1966; *Uptight* 1968; *A Dream of Passion* 1978; *Circle of Two* 1980

Daugherty, Herschel (1910–1993) *The Light in the Forest* 1958; *The Raiders* 1964

Daves, Delmer (1904–1977) *Destination Tokyo* 1943; *Hollywood Canteen* 1944; *The Very Thought of You* 1944; *Pride of the Marines* 1945; *Dark Passage* 1947; *The Red House* 1947; *A Kiss in the Dark* 1949; *Task Force* 1949; *Broken Arrow* 1950; *Bird of Paradise* 1951; *Never Let Me Go* 1953; *Treasure of the Golden Condor* 1953; *Demetrius and the Gladiators* 1954; *Drum Beat* 1954; *Jubal* 1956; *The Last Wagon* 1956; *3:10 to Yuma* 1957; *The Badlanders* 1958; *Cowboy* 1958; *Kings Go Forth* 1958; *The Hanging Tree* 1959; *A Summer Place* 1959; *Parrish* 1961; *Susan Slade* 1961; *Rome Adventure* 1962; *Spencer's Mountain* 1963; *Youngblood Hawke* 1964; *The Battle of the Villa Fiorita* 1965

David, Pierre *Scanner Cop* 1994; *Serial Killer* 1996

Davidson, Boaz (1943–) *Lemon Popsicle* 1978; *Salsa* 1988

Davidson, Martin (1939–) *The Lords of Flatbush* 1974; *Almost Summer* 1977; *Hero at Large* 1980; *Eddie and the Cruisers* 1983; *Heart of Dixie* 1989; *Hard Promises* 1991; *A Murderous Affair* 1992

Davies, Terence (1945–) *The Terence Davies Trilogy* 1984; *Distant Voices, Still Lives* 1988; *The Long Day Closes* 1992; *The Neon Bible* 1995; *The House of Mirth* 2000

Davis, Andrew (1946–) *Code of Silence* 1985; *Nico* 1988; *The Package* 1989; *Under Siege* 1992; *The Fugitive* 1993; *Steal Big, Steal Little* 1995; *Chain Reaction* 1996; *A Perfect Murder* 1998; *Collateral Damage* 2001; *Holes* 2003

Davis, Desmond (1927–) *Girl with Green Eyes* 1963; *The Uncle* 1964; *I Was Happy Here* 1966; *Smashing Time* 1967; *A Nice Girl like Me* 1969; *Clash of the Titans* 1981; *The Country Girls* 1983; *The Sign of Four* 1983; *Ordeal by Innocence* 1984

Davis, Eddie (1907–) *Panic in the City* 1968; *Color Me Dead* 1969

Davis (3), Michael (1961–) *Eight Days a Week* 1996; *Monster Man* 2003

Davis, Ossie (1917–2005) *Cotton Comes to Harlem* 1970; *Black Girl* 1972; *Gordon's War* 1973

Davis, Philip *aka* **Davis, Phil** (1953–) *ID* 1994; *Hold Back the Night* 1999

Davis, Robin (1943–) *The Police War* 1979; *Le Choc* 1982; *I Married a Dead Man* 1983

Davis, Tamra (1962–) *Guncrazy* 1992; *CB4* 1993; *Billy Madison* 1995; *Best Men* 1997; *Half-Baked* 1998; *Crossroads* 2002

Day, Robert (1922–) *The Green Man* 1956; *Stranger's Meeting* 1957; *First Man into Space* 1958; *Grip of the Strangler* 1958; *Bobbikins* 1959; *Life in Emergency Ward 10* 1959; *The Rebel* 1960; *Tarzan the Magnificent* 1960; *Two Way Stretch* 1960; *Corridors of Blood* 1962; *Operation Snatch* 1962; *Tarzan's Three Challenges* 1963; *She* 1965; *Tarzan and the Valley of Gold* 1966; *Tarzan and the Great River* 1967; *The Man with Bogart's Face* 1980

Dayton, Lyman *aka* **Dayton, Lyman D** *Baker's Hawk* 1976; *The Dream Machine* 1990

De Bont, Jan (1943–) *Speed* 1994; *Twister* 1996; *Speed 2: Cruise Control* 1997; *The Haunting* 1999; *Lara Croft Tomb Raider: the Cradle of Life* 2003

de Broca, Philippe (1933–2004) *Cartouche* 1961; *The Seven Deadly Sins* 1961; *That Man from Rio* 1964; *Up to His Ears* 1965; *King of Hearts* 1966; *The Oldest Profession* 1967; *Le Bossu* 1997

De Cordova, Frederick (1910–2001) *The Countess of Monte Cristo* 1948; *For the Love of Mary* 1948; *The Gal Who Took the West* 1949; *Bedtime for Bonzo* 1951; *Column South* 1953; *I'll Take Sweden* 1965; *Frankie & Johnny* 1966

de Courville, Albert (1887–1960) *Seven Sinners* 1936; *Crackerjack* 1938

De Filippo, Eduardo (1900–1984) *The Seven Deadly Sins* 1952; *Shout Loud, Louder... I Don't Understand* 1966

De Heer, Rolf (1951–) *Tail of a Tiger* 1984; *Encounter at Raven's Gate* 1988; *Dingo* 1991; *Bad Boy Bubby* 1993; *The Old Man Who Read Love Stories* 2000

De Jarnatt, Steve *Cherry 2000* 1988; *Miracle Mile* 1989

De Jong, Ate (1953–) *Drop Dead Fred* 1991; *Highway to Hell* 1992; *All Men Are Mortal* 1995; *Fogbound* 2002

de la Iglesia, Alex (1965–) *Acción Mutante* 1993; *The Day of the Beast* 1995; *Perdita Durango* 1997; *Dying of Laughter* 1999; *La Comunidad* 2000

de Lautour, Charles *The Limping Man* 1953; *Impulse* 1955; *Child in the House* 1956

De Martino, Alberto (1929–) *The Spartan Gladiators* 1964; *Operation Kid Brother* 1967; *Holocaust 2000* 1977

de Oliveira, Manoel (1908–) *Aniki-Bobó* 1942; *The Divine Comedy* 1992; *Abraham Valley* 1993; *The Convent* 1995; *Journey to the Beginning of the World* 1997; *I'm Going Home* 2001; *Un Filme Falado* 2003

De Palma, Brian (1941–) *The Wedding Party* 1966; *Greetings* 1968; *Murder à la Mod* 1968; *Dionysus in '69* 1970; *Hi, Mom!* 1970; *Get to Know Your Rabbit* 1972; *Sisters* 1973; *Phantom of the Paradise* 1974; *Carrie* 1976; *Obsession* 1976; *The Fury* 1978; *Home Movies* 1979; *Dressed to Kill* 1980; *Blow Out* 1981; *Scarface* 1983; *Body Double* 1984; *Wise Guys* 1986; *The Untouchables* 1987; *Casualties of*

War 1989; *The Bonfire of the Vanities* 1990; *Raising Cain* 1992; *Carlito's Way* 1993; *Mission: Impossible* 1996; *Snake Eyes* 1998; *Mission to Mars* 1999; *Femme Fatale* 2002

de Rycker, Piet *The Little Polar Bear* 2001; *Laura's Star* 2004

De Sica, Vittorio (1902–1974) *The Children Are Watching Us* 1943; *Shoeshine* 1946; *Bicycle Thieves* 1948; *Miracle in Milan* 1950; *Umberto D* 1952; *Gold of Naples* 1954; *Indiscretion of an American Wife* 1954; *Two Women* 1960; *Boccaccio '70* 1961; *The Condemned of Altona* 1962; *Yesterday, Today and Tomorrow* 1963; *Marriage – Italian Style* 1964; *After the Fox* 1966; *The Witches* 1966; *Woman Times Seven* 1967; *A Place for Lovers* 1968; *Sunflower* 1969; *The Garden of the Finzi-Continis* 1971; *The Voyage* 1974

de Souza, Steven E *Street Fighter* 1994; *Possessed* 2000

De Toth, Andre (1913–2002) *Dark Waters* 1944; *None Shall Escape* 1944; *The Other Love* 1947; *Ramrod* 1947; *Pitfall* 1948; *Slattery's Hurricane* 1949; *Man in the Saddle* 1951; *Carson City* 1952; *Last of the Comanches* 1952; *Springfield Rifle* 1952; *House of Wax* 1953; *The Stranger Wore a Gun* 1953; *Thunder over the Plains* 1953; *The Bounty Hunter* 1954; *The City Is Dark* 1954; *Riding Shotgun* 1954; *Tanganyika* 1954; *The Indian Fighter* 1955; *Hidden Fear* 1957; *The Two-Headed Spy* 1958; *Day of the Outlaw* 1959; *Morgan the Pirate* 1960; *The Mongols* 1961; *Gold for the Caesars* 1964; *Play Dirty* 1969

Dean, Basil (1888–1978) *Escape* 1930; *Looking on the Bright Side* 1931; *The Constant Nymph* 1933; *Lorna Doone* 1934; *Sing as We Go* 1934; *Look Up and Laugh* 1935; *The Show Goes On* 1937; *21 Days* 1937

Dear, William (1944–) *Bigfoot and the Hendersons* 1987; *Teen Agent* 1991; *Angels in the Outfield* 1994; *Wild America* 1997; *Santa Who?* 2000

Dearden, Basil (1911–1971) *The Black Sheep of Whitehall* 1941; *The Goose Steps Out* 1942; *The Bells Go Down* 1943; *The Halfway House* 1943; *My Learned Friend* 1943; *Dead of Night* 1945; *The Captive Heart* 1946; *Frieda* 1947; *Saraband for Dead Lovers* 1948; *The Blue Lamp* 1949; *Train of Events* 1949; *Cage of Gold* 1950; *Pool of London* 1950; *The Gentle Gunman* 1952; *I Believe in You* 1952; *The Square Ring* 1953; *Out of the Clouds* 1954; *The Ship That Died of Shame* 1955; *Who Done It?* 1956; *The Smallest Show on Earth* 1957; *The Rainbow Jacket* 1958; *Violent Playground* 1958; *Sapphire* 1959; *The League of Gentlemen* 1960; *Man in the Moon* 1960; *All Night Long* 1961; *The Secret Partner* 1961; *Victim* 1961; *Life for Ruth* 1962; *The Mind Benders* 1963; *A Place to Go* 1963; *Woman of Straw* 1964; *Masquerade* 1965; *Khartoum* 1966; *Only When I Larf* 1968; *The Assassination Bureau* 1969; *The Man Who Haunted Himself* 1970

Dearden, James (1949–) *Pascali's Island* 1988; *A Kiss before Dying* 1991; *Rogue Trader* 1998

DeBello, John *Attack of the Killer Tomatoes* 1978; *Return of the Killer Tomatoes* 1988

Decoin, Henri (1896–1969) *Secrets d'Alcove* 1954; *Razzia sur la Chnouf* 1955; *One Night at the Music Hall* 1956; *Too Many Lovers* 1957; *Le Masque de Fer* 1962

DeCoteau, David (1962–) *Creepozoids* 1987; *Skeletons* 1996; *I've Been Watching You* 2000

Dehlavi, Jamil *Born of Fire* 1987; *Immaculate Conception* 1991; *Jinnah* 1998

Dein, Edward (1907–1984) *Shack Out on 101* 1955; *Calypso Joe* 1957; *The Leech Woman* 1960

Deitch, Donna (1945–) *Desert Hearts* 1985; *The Devil's Arithmetic* 1999

Dekker, Fred *The Monster Squad* 1987; *RoboCop 3* 1993

Del Ruth, Roy (1895–1961) *The Desert Song* 1929; *Gold Diggers of Broadway* 1929; *Blonde Crazy* 1931; *Dangerous Female* 1931; *Blessed Event* 1932; *Taxi!* 1932; *Bureau of Missing Persons* 1933; *Employees' Entrance* 1933; *Lady Killer* 1933; *The Little Giant* 1933; *The Mind Reader* 1933; *Bulldog Drummond Strikes Back* 1934; *Kid Millions* 1934; *Upper World* 1934; *Broadway Melody of 1936* 1935; *Folies Bergère* 1935; *Thanks a Million* 1935; *Born to Dance* 1936; *Broadway Melody of 1938* 1937; *On the Avenue* 1937; *Happy Landing* 1938; *My Lucky Star* 1938; *The Star Maker* 1939; *The Chocolate Soldier* 1941; *Topper Returns* 1941; *DuBarry Was a Lady* 1943; *Barbary Coast Gent* 1944; *Broadway Rhythm* 1944; *Ziegfeld Follies* 1944; *It Happened on Fifth Avenue* 1947; *The Babe Ruth Story* 1948; *Always Leave Them Laughing* 1949; *Red Light* 1949; *The West Point Story* 1950; *On Moonlight Bay* 1951; *Stop, You're Killing Me* 1952; *Three Sailors and a Girl* 1953; *Phantom of the Rue Morgue* 1954; *The Alligator People* 1959

del Toro, Guillermo (1965–) *Cronos* 1992; *Mimic* 1997; *The Devil's Backbone* 2001; *Blade II* 2002; *Hellboy* 2004

Delannoy, Jean (1908–) *Eternal Love* 1943; *La Symphonie Pastorale* 1946; *Dieu A Besoin des Hommes* 1950; *Obsession* 1954; *Secrets d'Alcove* 1954; *The Hunchback of Notre Dame* 1956; *Marie Antoinette* 1956; *Maigret Sets a Trap* 1957; *Imperial Venus* 1963

Dell, Jeffrey (1904–1985) *Don't Take It to Heart* 1944; *It's Hard to Be Good* 1948; *Carlton-Browne of the FO* 1958

DeMille, Cecil B *aka* **De Mille, Cecil B** (1881–1959) *Carmen* 1915; *The Cheat* 1915; *A Romance of the Redwoods* 1917; *Male and Female* 1919; *Why Change Your Wife?* 1920; *The Ten Commandments* 1923; *The Road to Yesterday* 1925; *The King of Kings* 1927; *Dynamite* 1929; *Madam Satan* 1930; *The Squaw Man* 1931; *The Sign of the Cross* 1932; *This Day and Age* 1933; *Cleopatra* 1934; *Four Frightened People* 1934; *The Crusades* 1935; *The Plainsman* 1936; *The Buccaneer* 1938; *Union Pacific* 1939; *North West Mounted Police* 1940; *Reap the Wild Wind* 1942; *The Story of Dr Wassell* 1944; *Unconquered* 1947; *Samson and Delilah* 1949; *The Greatest Show on Earth* 1952; *The Ten Commandments* 1956

Demme, Jonathan (1944–) *Caged Heat* 1974; *Crazy Mama* 1975; *Fighting Mad* 1976; *Citizens Band* 1977; *Last Embrace* 1979; *Melvin and Howard* 1980; *Stop Making Sense* 1984; *Swing Shift* 1984; *Something Wild* 1986; *Swimming to Cambodia* 1987; *Married to the Mob* 1988; *The Silence of the Lambs* 1991; *Cousin Bobby* 1992; *Philadelphia* 1993; *Subway Stories: Tales from the Underground* 1997; *Beloved* 1998; *Storefront Hitchcock* 1998; *The Truth about Charlie* 2002; *The Agronomist* 2003; *The Manchurian Candidate* 2004

Demme, Ted (1964–2002) *Who's the Man?* 1993; *Hostile Hostages* 1994; *Beautiful Girls* 1996; *Noose* 1997; *Subway Stories: Tales from the Underground* 1997; *Life* 1999; *Blow* 2001; *A Decade under the Influence* 2003

Demy, Jacques (1931–1990) *Lola* 1960; *The Seven Deadly Sins* 1961; *Bay of the Angels* 1963; *The Umbrellas of Cherbourg* 1964; *The Young Girls of Rochefort* 1967; *Model Shop* 1969; *The Magic Donkey* 1970; *The Pied Piper* 1971

Denis, Claire (1948–) *Chocolat* 1988; *Beau Travail* 1999; *Trouble Every Day* 2000; *Ten Minutes Older: the Cello* 2002; *Vendredi Soir* 2002

Dennehy, Brian (1939–) *Jack Reed: a Search for Justice* 1994; *Jack Reed: One of Our Own* 1995; *Jack Reed: Death and Vengeance* 1996; *A Father's Betrayal* 1997

Densham, Pen *The Kiss* 1988; *Moll Flanders* 1995

Deodato, Ruggero (1939–) *Cannibal Holocaust* 1979; *Phantom of Death* 1988

Deray, Jacques (1929–2003) *That Man George* 1965; *The Swimming Pool* 1968; *Borsalino* 1970; *Take It Easy* 1971; *The Outside Man* 1973; *Borsalino and Co* 1974; *Police Story* 1975; *Three Men to Destroy* 1980; *The Outsider* 1983

Derek, John (1926–1998) *Once Before I Die* 1965; *Tarzan, the Ape Man* 1981; *Bolero* 1984; *Ghosts Can't Do It* 1990

Deruddere, Dominique (1957–) *Wait until Spring, Bandini* 1989; *Suite 16* 1994

Deschanel, Caleb (1941–) *The Escape Artist* 1982; *Crusoe* 1988

DeSimone, Tom *Hell Night* 1981; *The Concrete Jungle* 1982; *Reform School Girls* 1986

Desplechin, Arnaud (1960–) *Ma Vie Sexuelle* 1996; *Esther Kahn* 2000; *Kings & Queen* 2004

Detiege, David (1926–) *The Man from Button Willow* 1965; *Bugs Bunny 1001 Rabbit Tales* 1982

Deutch, Howard (1950–) *Pretty in Pink* 1986; *Some Kind of Wonderful* 1987; *The Great Outdoors* 1988; *Article 99* 1992; *Getting Even with Dad* 1994; *Grumpier Old Men* 1996; *The Odd Couple II* 1998; *The Replacements* 2000; *The Whole Ten Yards* 2004

Deville, Michel (1931–) *The Theft of the Mona Lisa* 1965; *Death in a French Garden* 1985; *Le Paltoquet* 1986; *La Lectrice* 1988; *Almost Peaceful* 2002

DeVito, Danny (1944–) *Throw Momma from the Train* 1987; *The War of the Roses* 1989; *Hoffa* 1992; *Matilda* 1996; *Death to Smoochy* 2002; *Our House* 2003

Dewolf, Patrick *Lapse of Memory* 1992; *Innocent Lies* 1995

Dexter, John (1925–1990) *The Virgin Soldiers* 1969; *The Sidelong Glances of a Pigeon Kicker* 1970; *I Want What I Want* 1971

Dexter, Maury (1927–) *Young Guns of Texas* 1962; *Wild on the Beach* 1965

Dey, Tom *Shanghai Noon* 2000; *Showtime* 2002

Dhanoa, Guddu *23rd March 1931: Shaheed* 2002; *Hawa* 2003

Dhawan, David *Chal Mere Bhai* 2000; *Ek Aur Ek Gyarah* 2003; *Mujhse Shaadi Karogi* 2004

DiCillo, Tom (1954–) *Johnny Suede* 1991; *Living in Oblivion* 1995; *Box of Moonlight* 1996; *The Real Blonde* 1997; *Double Whammy* 2001

Dick, Kirby *Sick: the Life and Death of Bob Flanagan, Supermasochist* 1997; *Derrida* 2001

Dick, Nigel (1953–) *Private Investigations* 1987; *Final Combination* 1993; *Seeing Double* 2003

Dickerson, Ernest R *aka* **Dickerson, Ernest** (1952–) *Juice* 1991; *Surviving the Game* 1994; *Tales from the Crypt: Demon Knight* 1995; *Bulletproof* 1996; *Futuresport* 1998; *Strange Justice* 1999; *Bones* 2001; *Never Die Alone* 2004

Dickinson, Thorold (1903–1984) *The Arsenal Stadium Mystery* 1939; *Gaslight* 1940; *The Prime Minister* 1940; *Next of Kin* 1942; *Men of Two Worlds* 1946; *The Queen of Spades* 1948; *The Secret People* 1951

Diegues, Carlos (1940–) *Bye Bye Brazil* 1979; *Quilombo* 1984

Dieterle, William *aka* **Dieterle, Wilhelm** *aka* **Dieterle, William S** (1893–1972) *Her Majesty Love* 1931; *The Last Flight* 1931; *Jewel Robbery* 1932; *Lawyer Man* 1932; *Scarlet Dawn* 1932; *The Devil's in Love* 1933; *Fashions of 1934* 1934; *Fog over Frisco* 1934; *Madame Du Barry* 1934; *The Secret Bride* 1934; *Dr Socrates* 1935; *A Midsummer Night's Dream* 1935; *Satan Met a Lady* 1936; *The Story of Louis Pasteur* 1936; *The White Angel* 1936; *Another Dawn* 1937; *The Great O'Malley* 1937; *The Life of Emile Zola* 1937; *Blockade* 1938; *The Hunchback of Notre Dame* 1939; *Juarez* 1939; *A Dispatch from Reuters* 1940; *Dr Ehrlich's Magic Bullet* 1940; *Daniel and the Devil* 1941; *Syncopation* 1942; *Tennessee Johnson* 1942; *I'll Be Seeing You* 1944; *Kismet* 1944; *Love Letters* 1945; *This Love of Ours* 1945; *The Searching Wind* 1946; *Portrait of Jennie* 1948; *The Accused* 1949; *Rope of Sand* 1949; *Dark City* 1950; *Paid in Full* 1950; *September Affair* 1950; *Volcano* 1950; *Boots Malone* 1951; *Peking Express* 1951; *Red Mountain* 1951; *The Turning Point* 1952; *Salome* 1953; *Elephant Walk* 1954; *Magic Fire* 1956; *Omar Khayyam* 1957; *Quick, Let's Get Married* 1964

Dindal, Mark *Cats Don't Dance* 1998; *The Emperor's New Groove* 2000

Dinner, Michael *Catholic Boys* 1985; *Off Beat* 1986; *Hot to Trot* 1988; *Thicker than Blood* 1993

Dmytryk, Edward (1908–1999) *The Devil Commands* 1941; *Sweetheart of the Campus* 1941; *Seven Miles from Alcatraz* 1942; *Behind the Rising Sun* 1943; *The Falcon Strikes Back* 1943; *Hitler's Children* 1943; *Tender Comrade* 1943; *Farewell My Lovely* 1944; *Back to Bataan* 1945; *Cornered* 1945; *Till the End of Time* 1946; *Crossfire* 1947; *So Well Remembered* 1947; *Obsession* 1948; *Give Us This Day* 1949; *Eight Iron Men* 1952; *Mutiny* 1952; *The Sniper* 1952; *The Juggler* 1953; *Broken Lance* 1954; *The Caine Mutiny* 1954; *The End of the Affair* 1954; *The Left Hand of God* 1955; *Soldier of Fortune* 1955; *The Mountain* 1956; *Raintree County* 1957; *The Young Lions* 1958; *The Blue Angel* 1959; *Warlock* 1959; *The Reluctant Saint* 1962; *Walk on the Wild Side* 1962; *The Carpetbaggers* 1964; *Where Love Has Gone* 1964; *Mirage* 1965; *Alvarez Kelly* 1966; *Anzio* 1968; *Shalako* 1968; *Bluebeard* 1972; *The Human Factor* 1975

Dobkin, David (1969–) *Clay Pigeons* 1998; *Shanghai Knights* 2002; *Wedding Crashers* 2005

Doillon, Jacques (1944–) *Le Jeune Werther* 1992; *Ponette* 1996

Domaradzki, Jerzy (1943–) *Legend of the White Horse* 1985; *Struck by Lightning* 1990

Donaldson, Roger (1945–) *Smash Palace* 1981; *The Bounty* 1984; *Marie: a True Story* 1985; *No Way Out* 1986; *Cocktail* 1988; *Cadillac Man* 1990; *White Sands* 1992; *The Getaway* 1994; *Species* 1995; *Dante's Peak* 1997; *Thirteen Days* 2000; *The Recruit* 2002

Done, Harris (1963–) *Storm* 1999; *Firetrap* 2001

Donehue, Vincent J (1915–1966) *Lonelyhearts* 1958; *Sunrise at Campobello* 1960

Donen, Stanley (1924–) *On the Town* 1949; *Love Is Better Than Ever* 1951; *Royal Wedding* 1951; *Singin' in the Rain* 1952; *Give a Girl a Break* 1953; *Deep in My Heart* 1954; *Seven Brides for Seven Brothers* 1954; *It's Always Fair Weather* 1955; *Funny Face* 1957; *Kiss Them for Me* 1957; *The Pajama Game* 1957; *Damn Yankees* 1958; *Indiscreet* 1958; *Once More, with Feeling* 1959; *The Grass Is Greener* 1960; *Surprise Package* 1960; *Charade* 1963; *Arabesque* 1966; *Bedazzled* 1967; *Two for the Road* 1967; *Staircase* 1969; *The Little Prince* 1974; *Lucky Lady* 1975; *Movie Movie* 1978; *Saturn 3* 1980; *Blame It on Rio* 1984

Doniger, Walter (1917–) *House of Women* 1962; *Safe at Home* 1962

Donner, Clive (1926–) *Some People* 1962; *The Caretaker* 1963; *Nothing but the Best* 1963; *What's New, Pussycat?* 1965; *Here We Go round the Mulberry Bush* 1967; *Luv* 1967; *Alfred the Great* 1969; *Vampira* 1975; *The Thief of Baghdad* 1978; *The Nude Bomb* 1980; *Charlie Chan and the Curse of the Dragon Queen* 1981; *Oliver Twist* 1982; *The Scarlet Pimpernel* 1982; *Dead Man's Folly* 1986; *Stealing Heaven* 1988

Donner, Richard (1939–) *X-15* 1961; *Salt & Pepper* 1968; *Twinky* 1969; *The Omen* 1976; *Superman* 1978; *Inside Moves: the Guys from Max's Bar* 1980; *The Toy* 1982; *The Goonies* 1985; *Ladyhawke* 1985; *Lethal Weapon* 1987; *Scrooged* 1988; *Lethal Weapon 2* 1989; *Lethal Weapon 3* 1992; *Radio Flyer* 1992; *Maverick* 1994; *Assassins* 1995; *Conspiracy Theory* 1997; *Lethal Weapon 4* 1998; *Timeline* 2003

Donohue, Jack (1908–1984) *Watch the Birdie* 1950; *The Yellow Cab Man* 1950; *Lucky Me* 1954; *Babes in Toyland* 1961; *Marriage on the Rocks* 1965; *Assault on a Queen* 1966

Donovan (1), Martin (1950–) *Apartment Zero* 1988; *Mad at the Moon* 1992

Donovan, Paul (1954–) *Def-Con 4* 1984; *George's Island* 1991

Dorfmann, Jacques *Shadow of the Wolf* 1992; *Druids* 2001

Dornhelm, Robert (1947–) *The Children of Theatre Street* 1977; *She Dances Alone* 1981; *Echo Park* 1985; *Cold Feet* 1989; *Requiem for Dominic* 1990; *A Further Gesture* 1996

Dörrie, Doris (1955–) *In the Belly of the Whale* 1984; *Men…* 1985

Dotan, Shimon (1949–) *The Finest Hour* 1991; *You Can Thank Me Later* 1998

Douglas, Bill (1934–1991) *My Childhood* 1972; *My Ain Folk* 1973; *My Way Home* 1978; *Comrades: a Lanternist's Account of the Tolpuddle Martyrs and What Became of Them* 1986

Douglas, Gordon *aka* **Douglas, Gordon M** (1907–1993) *General Spanky* 1936; *Zenobia* 1939; *Saps at Sea* 1940; *Broadway Limited* 1941; *Road Show* 1941; *The Falcon in Hollywood* 1944; *Girl Rush* 1944; *First Yank into Tokyo* 1945; *Dick Tracy vs Cueball* 1946; *San Quentin* 1946; *The Black Arrow* 1948; *If You Knew Susie* 1948; *Walk a Crooked Mile* 1948; *The Doolins of Oklahoma* 1949; *Kiss Tomorrow Goodbye* 1950; *Only the Valiant* 1950; *Rogues of Sherwood Forest* 1950; *Come Fill the Cup* 1951; *I Was a Communist for the FBI* 1951; *The Iron Mistress* 1952; *Mara Maru* 1952; *The Charge at Feather River* 1953; *So This Is Love* 1953; *Them!* 1954; *The McConnell Story* 1955; *Sincerely Yours* 1955; *Young at Heart* 1955; *Santiago* 1956; *The Big Land* 1957; *Bombers B-52* 1957; *The Fiend Who Walked the West* 1958; *Up Periscope* 1959; *Yellowstone Kelly* 1959; *The Sins of Rachel Cade* 1960; *Claudelle Inglish* 1961; *Gold of the Seven Saints* 1961; *Follow That Dream* 1962; *Call Me Bwana* 1963; *Rio Conchos* 1964; *Robin and the 7 Hoods* 1964; *Sylvia* 1964; *Harlow* 1965; *Stagecoach* 1966; *Way… Way Out* 1966; *Chuka* 1967; *In like Flint* 1967; *Tony Rome* 1967; *The Detective* 1968; *Lady in Cement* 1968; *Skullduggery* 1969; *Barquero* 1970; *They Call Me Mister Tibbs!* 1970; *Slaughter's Big Rip-Off* 1973; *Viva Knievel!* 1977

Douglas, Kirk (1916–) *Scalawag* 1973; *Posse* 1975

Doumani, Lorenzo (1962–) *Amore!* 1993; *Storybook* 1995

Dowling, Kevin *The Sum of Us* 1995; *Mojave Moon* 1996; *Last Rites* 1998

Downey Sr, Robert *aka* **Downey, Robert** (1936–) *Putney Swope* 1969; *Greaser's Palace* 1972; *Up the Academy* 1980; *America* 1986; *Too Much Sun* 1990; *Pool Girl* 1997

Dowse, Michael *Fubar* 2002; *It's All Gone Pete Tong* 2004

Doyle, Jim *Going Off, Big Time* 2000; *Re-inventing Eddie* 2002

Dragoti, Stan (1932–) *Dirty Little Billy* 1972; *Love at First Bite* 1979; *Mr Mom* 1983; *The Man with One Red Shoe* 1985; *She's Out of Control* 1989; *Necessary Roughness* 1991

Drake, Jim *Police Academy 4: Citizens on Patrol* 1987; *Cannonball Fever* 1989

Drazan, Anthony (1955–) *Zebrahead* 1992; *Imaginary Crimes* 1994; *Hurlyburly* 1998

Dreifuss, Arthur (1908–1993) *Baby Face Morgan* 1942; *The Last Blitzkrieg* 1958; *Juke Box Rhythm* 1959; *The Quare Fellow* 1962

Dréville, Jean (1906–1997) *A Cage of Nightingales* 1945; *The Seven Deadly Sins* 1952; *La Reine Margot* 1954

Dreyer, Carl Th (1889–1968) *Leaves from Satan's Book* 1919; *The President* 1919; *Master of the House* 1925; *The Passion of Joan of Arc* 1928; *Vampyr* 1932; *Day of Wrath* 1943; *Ordet* 1955; *Gertrud* 1964

Drury, David *Forever Young* 1984; *Defence of the Realm* 1985; *Hostile Waters* 1996

D'Souza, Lawrence *Saajan* 1991; *Balmaa* 1993

Du Chau, Frederik *The Magic Sword: Quest for Camelot* 1997; *Racing Stripes* 2004

Ducastel, Olivier (1962–) *Drôle de Félix* 2000; *Ma Vraie Vie à Rouen* 2002

Duffell, Peter (1924–) *The House That Dripped Blood* 1971; *England Made Me* 1973; *Inside Out* 1975; *Letters to an Unknown Lover* 1985; *King of the Wind* 1989

Dugan, Dennis (1946–) *Problem Child* 1990; *Brain Donors* 1992; *Happy Gilmore* 1996; *Beverly Hills Ninja* 1997; *Big Daddy* 1999; *Evil Woman* 2001; *National Security* 2002

Dugowson, Martine *Mina Tannenbaum* 1993; *Portraits Chinois* 1996

Duguay, Christian *Scanners II: The New Order* 1991; *Live Wire* 1992; *Scanners III: the Takeover* 1992; *Screamers* 1995; *The Assignment* 1997; *The Art of War* 2000; *Extreme Ops* 2003

Duigan, John (1949–) *The Winter of Our Dreams* 1981; *Far East* 1982; *One Night Stand* 1984; *The Year My Voice Broke* 1987; *Flirting* 1989; *Romero* 1989; *Wide Sargasso Sea* 1992; *Sirens* 1994; *The Journey of August King* 1995; *The Leading Man* 1996; *Lawn Dogs* 1997; *Molly* 1999; *The Parole Officer* 2001

Duke, Bill (1943–) *The Killing Floor* 1984; *A Rage in Harlem* 1991; *Deep Cover* 1992; *The Cemetery Club* 1993; *Sister Act 2: Back in the Habit* 1993; *Hoodlum* 1997

Duke, Daryl *Payday* 1972; *I Heard the Owl Call My Name* 1973; *The Silent Partner* 1978; *Hard Feelings* 1981; *Tai-Pan* 1986

Dumont, Bruno (1958–) *La Vie de Jésus* 1996; *L'Humanité* 1999

Duncan, Peter *Children of the Revolution* 1996; *Passion* 1999

Dunham, Duwayne *Homeward Bound: the Incredible Journey* 1993; *Little Giants* 1994

Dunne, Griffin (1955–) *Addicted to Love* 1997; *Practical Magic* 1998

Dunne, Philip (1908–1992) *Prince of Players* 1955; *The View from Pompey's Head* 1955; *Hilda Crane* 1956; *Three Brave Men* 1956; *In Love and War* 1958; *Ten North Frederick* 1958; *Blue Denim* 1959; *Wild in the Country* 1961; *The Inspector* 1962; *Blindfold* 1966

Dunye, Cheryl (1966–) *The Watermelon Woman* 1996; *Stranger Inside* 2001

Dupeyron, François (1950–) *A Strange Place to Meet* 1988; *Your Beating Heart* 1991; *La Machine* 1994; *The Officers' Ward* 2001; *Monsieur Ibrahim and the Flowers of the Koran* 2003

Dupont, E A (1891–1956) *Vaudeville* 1925; *Moulin Rouge* 1928; *Piccadilly* 1929; *Hell's Kitchen* 1939; *The Scarf* 1951; *Return to Treasure Island* 1954

Dutt, Guru (1925–1964) *Aar Paar* 1954; *Mr and Mrs '55* 1955; *Kaagaz Ke Phool* 1959

Dutton, Charles S (1951–) *First Time Felon* 1997; *Against the Ropes* 2003

Duvall, Robert (1931–) *The Apostle* 1997; *Assassination Tango* 2002

Duvivier, Julien (1896–1967) *Poil de Carotte* 1932; *La Belle Equipe* 1936; *The Golem* 1936; *Un Carnet de Bal* 1937; *Pépé le Moko* 1937; *The Great Waltz* 1938; *Marie Antoinette* 1938; *The End of the Day* 1939; *Lydia* 1941; *Tales of Manhattan* 1942; *Flesh and Fantasy* 1943; *The Impostor* 1944; *Anna Karenina* 1947; *The Little World of Don Camillo* 1951; *Black Jack* 1952; *Marianne de Ma Jeunesse* 1955; *Diabolically Yours* 1967

Dwan, Allan (1885–1981) *Robin Hood* 1922; *Stage Struck* 1925; *The Big Noise* 1928; *The Iron Mask* 1929; *What a Widow!* 1930; *Hollywood Party* 1934; *Black Sheep* 1935; *Human Cargo* 1936; *Heidi* 1937; *Josette* 1938; *Rebecca of Sunnybrook Farm* 1938; *Suez* 1938; *Frontier Marshal* 1939; *The Three Musketeers* 1939; *Trail of the Vigilantes* 1940; *Young People* 1940; *Look Who's Laughing* 1941; *Friendly Enemies* 1942; *Here We Go Again* 1942; *Abroad with Two Yanks* 1944; *Up in Mabel's Room* 1944; *Brewster's Millions* 1945; *Getting Gertie's Garter* 1945; *Driftwood* 1946; *Rendezvous with Annie* 1946; *Northwest Outpost* 1947; *Angel in Exile* 1948; *Sands of Iwo Jima* 1949; *I Dream of Jeanie* 1952; *The Woman They Almost Lynched* 1953; *Cattle Queen of Montana* 1954; *Passion* 1954; *Silver Lode* 1954; *Escape to Burma* 1955; *Pearl of the South Pacific* 1955; *Tennessee's Partner* 1955; *Slightly Scarlet* 1956; *The Restless Breed* 1957; *The River's Edge* 1957; *The Most Dangerous Man Alive* 1961

Dylan, Jesse (1966–) *American Pie: the Wedding* 2003; *Kicking & Screaming* 2005

E

Eady, David (1924–) *Three Cases of Murder* 1953; *The Man Who Liked Funerals* 1959; *Faces in the Dark* 1960

Eastman, Allan (1950–) *Crazy Moon* 1986; *Danger Zone* 1996

Eastwood, Clint (1930–) *Play Misty for Me* 1971; *Breezy* 1973; *High Plains Drifter* 1973; *The Eiger Sanction* 1975; *The Outlaw Josey Wales* 1976; *The Gauntlet* 1977; *Bronco Billy* 1980; *Firefox* 1982; *Honkytonk Man* 1982; *Sudden Impact* 1983; *Pale Rider* 1985; *Heartbreak Ridge* 1986; *Bird* 1988; *The Rookie* 1990; *White Hunter, Black Heart* 1990; *Unforgiven* 1992; *A Perfect World* 1993; *The Bridges of Madison County* 1995; *Absolute Power* 1996; *Midnight in the Garden of Good and Evil* 1997; *True Crime* 1999; *Space Cowboys* 2000; *Blood Work* 2002; *Martin Scorsese Presents The Blues: Piano Blues* 2003; *Mystic River* 2003; *Million Dollar Baby* 2004

Eberhardt, Thom *Night of the Comet* 1984; *The Night Before* 1988; *Without a Clue* 1988; *A Cut Above* 1989; *Captain Ron* 1992

Edel, Uli *aka* **Edel, Ulrich** (1947–) *Christiane F* 1981; *Last Exit to Brooklyn* 1989; *Body of Evidence* 1992; *Rasputin* 1996; *Purgatory* 1999; *The Little Vampire* 2000; *Sword of Xanten* 2004

Edwards, Blake (1922–) *Bring Your Smile Along* 1955; *He Laughed Last* 1956; *Mister Cory* 1957; *The Perfect Furlough* 1958; *This Happy Feeling* 1958; *Operation Petticoat* 1959; *High Time* 1960; *Breakfast at Tiffany's* 1961; *Days of Wine and Roses* 1962; *Experiment in Terror* 1962; *The Pink Panther* 1963; *A Shot in the Dark* 1964; *The Great Race* 1965; *What Did You Do in the War, Daddy?* 1966; *Gunn* 1967; *The Party* 1968; *Darling Lili* 1970; *Wild Rovers* 1971; *The Carey Treatment* 1972; *The Return of the Pink Panther* 1974; *The Tamarind Seed* 1974; *The Pink Panther Strikes Again* 1976; *Revenge of the Pink Panther* 1978; *10* 1979; *SOB* 1981; *Trail of the Pink Panther* 1982; *Victor/Victoria* 1982; *The Curse of the Pink Panther* 1983; *The Man Who Loved Women* 1983; *Micki & Maude* 1984; *A Fine Mess* 1986; *That's Life* 1986; *Blind Date* 1987; *Sunset* 1988; *Skin Deep* 1989; *Switch* 1991; *Son of the Pink Panther* 1993

Edwards, Henry (1882–1952) *D'Ye Ken John Peel?* 1934; *Lord Edgware Dies* 1934; *The Man Who Changed His Name* 1934; *The Lad* 1935; *The Private Secretary* 1935; *Scrooge* 1935; *Squibs* 1935; *Vintage Wine* 1935; *In the Soup* 1936; *The Vicar of Bray* 1937

Edzard, Christine (1945–) *Little Dorrit* 1987; *The Fool* 1990; *As You Like It* 1992; *The Children's Midsummer Night's Dream* 2001

Eggleston, Colin (1941–2002) *Long Weekend* 1977; *Sky Pirates* 1986; *Cassandra* 1987

Egleson, Jan *A Shock to the System* 1990; *Hard Evidence* 1994

Egoyan, Atom (1960–) *Family Viewing* 1987; *Speaking Parts* 1989; *The Adjuster* 1991; *Calendar* 1993; *Exotica* 1994; *The Sweet Hereafter* 1997; *Felicia's Journey* 1999; *Ararat* 2002

Eisenstein, Sergei (1898–1948) *Strike* 1924; *The Battleship Potemkin* 1925; *October* 1928; *The General Line* 1929; *Alexander Nevsky* 1938; *Time in the Sun* 1939; *Ivan the Terrible, Part I* 1944; *Ivan the Terrible, Part II* 1946

Eldridge, John (1904–1961) *Brandy for the Parson* 1951; *Conflict of Wings* 1953; *Laxdale Hall* 1953

Elfont, Harry (1968–) *Can't Hardly Wait* 1998; *Josie and the Pussycats* 2001

Elliott, Lang (1950–) *The Private Eyes* 1980; *Cage* 1989

Elliott, Stephan (1964–) *Frauds* 1992; *The Adventures of Priscilla, Queen of the Desert* 1994; *Welcome to Woop Woop* 1997; *Eye of the Beholder* 1999

Ellis, Bob (1942–) *Unfinished Business* 1985; *Warm Nights on a Slow Moving Train* 1986

Ellis, David R (1952–) *Homeward Bound II: Lost in San Francisco* 1996; *Final Destination 2* 2002; *Cellular* 2004

Ellison, Joseph *Don't Go in the House* 1979; *Joey* 1985

Elvey, Maurice (1887–1967) *Hindle Wakes* 1927; *Sally in Our Alley* 1931; *I Lived with You* 1933; *The Wandering Jew* 1933; *The Clairvoyant* 1934; *Love, Life and Laughter* 1934; *The Tunnel* 1935; *The Man in the Mirror* 1936; *Sons of the Sea* 1939; *Under Your Hat* 1940; *The Gentle Sex* 1943; *The Lamp Still Burns* 1943; *Beware of Pity* 1946; *The Late Edwina Black* 1951; *House of Blackmail* 1953; *Dry Rot* 1956

Emlyn, Endaf (1945–) *One Full Moon* 1991; *Leaving Lenin* 1993; *The Making of Maps* 1995

Emmerich, Roland (1955–) *Making Contact* 1985; *Moon 44* 1990; *Universal Soldier* 1992; *Stargate* 1994; *Independence Day* 1996; *Godzilla* 1997; *The Patriot* 2000; *The Day after Tomorrow* 2004

Endfield, Cy *aka* **Endfield, Cyril** *aka* **Raker, Hugh** *aka* **Endfield, C Raker** (1914–1995) *The Sound of Fury* 1950; *The Underworld Story* 1950; *Tarzan's Savage Fury* 1952; *Colonel March Investigates* 1953; *The Limping Man* 1953; *The Master Plan* 1954; *Impulse* 1955; *Child in the House* 1956; *Hell Drivers* 1957; *Sea Fury* 1958; *Jet Storm* 1959; *Mysterious Island* 1961; *Hide and Seek* 1963; *Zulu* 1964; *Sands of the Kalahari* 1965; *De Sade* 1969

English, John (1903–1969) *Murder in the Music Hall* 1946; *Riders in the Sky* 1949; *Mule Train* 1950; *Valley of Fire* 1951

Englund, George (1926–) *The Ugly American* 1963; *Signpost to Murder* 1964; *Zachariah* 1970; *Snow Job* 1972

Enrico, Robert (1931–2001) *The Adventurers* 1968; *Ho!* 1968

Enright, Ray *aka* **Enright, Raymond** (1896–1965) *Havana Widows* 1933; *Dames* 1934; *China Clipper* 1936; *Slim* 1937; *Swing Your Lady* 1937; *Going Places* 1938; *Gold Diggers in Paris* 1938; *Hard to Get* 1938; *Angels Wash Their Faces* 1939; *Naughty but Nice* 1939; *On Your Toes* 1939; *The Wagons Roll at Night* 1941; *Men of Texas* 1942; *Sin Town* 1942; *The Spoilers* 1942; *Gung Ho!* 1943; *The Iron Major* 1943; *China Sky* 1945; *Trail Street* 1947; *Return of the Bad Men* 1948; *South of St Louis* 1949; *Kansas Raiders* 1950; *Montana* 1950; *The Man from Cairo* 1953

Enyedi, Ildiko (1955–) *My 20th Century* 1988; *Magic Hunter* 1994

Ephron, Nora (1941–) *This Is My Life* 1992; *Sleepless in Seattle* 1993; *Mixed Nuts* 1994; *Michael* 1996; *You've Got Mail* 1998

Epstein, Rob *aka* **Epstein, Robert** (1955–) *The Times of Harvey Milk* 1983; *Common Threads: Stories from the Quilt* 1989; *The Celluloid Closet* 1995; *Paragraph 175* 1999

Erdogan, Yilmaz (1967–) *Vizontele* 2001; *Vizontele Tuuba* 2003

Erice, Victor (1940–) *The Spirit of the Beehive* 1973; *El Sur* 1983; *The Quince Tree Sun* 1991; *Ten Minutes Older: the Trumpet* 2002

Erman, John *aka* **Sampson, Bill** (1935–) *Ace Eli and Rodger of the Skies* 1973; *An Early Frost* 1985; *The Attic: the Hiding of Anne Frank* 1988; *Stella* 1990; *The Sunshine Boys* 1997; *The Blackwater Lightship* 2004

Erskine, Chester (1905–1986) *Midnight* 1934; *The Egg and I* 1947; *Androcles and the Lion* 1952; *A Girl in Every Port* 1952

Estevez, Emilio (1962–) *Wisdom* 1986; *Men at Work* 1990; *The War at Home* 1996; *Rated X* 2000

Esway, Alexander (1947–) *Music Hath Charms* 1935; *Conquest of the Air* 1936

Evans, David Mickey *aka* **Evans, David M** (1962–) *The Sandlot* 1993; *First Kid* 1996; *Beethoven's 3rd* 2000; *Beethoven's 4th* 2001

Evans, Marc (1959–) *House of America* 1996; *Resurrection Man* 1997; *My Little Eye* 2002; *Trauma* 2004

Eyre, Richard (1943–) *Loose Connections* 1983; *The Ploughman's Lunch* 1983; *Laughterhouse* 1984; *Iris* 2001; *Stage Beauty* 2004

Fabri, Zoltan (1917–1994) *Merry-Go-Round* 1956; *The Boys of Paul Street* 1968

Faenza, Roberto (1943–) *Order of Death* 1983; *The Bachelor* 1990; *Marianna Ucria* 1997; *The Lost Lover* 1999

Faiman, Peter *"Crocodile" Dundee* 1986; *Driving Me Crazy* 1991

Fairchild, William (1919–2000) *John and Julie* 1955; *The Extra Day* 1956; *The Silent Enemy* 1958

Fairfax, Ferdinand (1944–) *Savage Islands* 1983; *The Rescue* 1988; *True Blue* 1996

Fall, Jim *Trick* 1999; *The Lizzie McGuire Movie* 2003

Famuyiwa, Rick (1973–) *The Wood* 1999; *Brown Sugar* 2002

Fargo, James (1938–) *The Enforcer* 1976; *Caravans* 1978; *Every Which Way but Loose* 1978; *A Game for Vultures* 1979; *Forced Vengeance* 1982

Farrelly, Bobby (1958–) *Kingpin* 1996; *There's Something about Mary* 1998; *Me, Myself & Irene* 2000; *Osmosis Jones* 2001; *Shallow Hal* 2001; *Stuck on You* 2003; *The Perfect Catch* 2005

Farrelly, Peter (1957–) *Dumb and Dumber* 1994; *Kingpin* 1996; *There's Something about Mary* 1998; *Me, Myself & Irene* 2000; *Osmosis Jones* 2001; *Shallow Hal* 2001; *Stuck on You* 2003; *Fever Pitch* 2005

Farrow, John (1904–1963) *The Invisible Menace* 1938; *Five Came Back* 1939; *Full Confession* 1939; *The Saint Strikes Back* 1939; *A Bill of Divorcement* 1940; *The Commandos Strike at Dawn* 1942; *Wake Island* 1942; *China* 1943; *California* 1946; *Two Years before the Mast* 1946; *Blaze of Noon* 1947; *Calcutta* 1947; *The Big Clock* 1948; *Night Has a Thousand Eyes* 1948; *Alias Nick Beal* 1949; *Copper Canyon* 1950; *Where Danger Lives* 1950; *His Kind of Woman* 1951; *Botany Bay* 1952; *Hondo* 1953; *Ride, Vaquero!* 1953; *A Bullet Is Waiting* 1954; *The Sea Chase* 1955; *Back from Eternity* 1956; *The Unholy Wife* 1957; *John Paul Jones* 1959

Fassbinder, Rainer Werner (1946–1982) *Gods of the Plague* 1969; *Love Is Colder Than Death* 1969; *The American Soldier* 1970; *Beware of a Holy Whore* 1970; *Whity* 1970; *Why Does Herr R Run Amok?* 1970; *The Merchant of Four Seasons* 1971; *The Bitter Tears of Petra von Kant* 1972; *Jail Bait* 1972; *Fear Eats the Soul* 1973; *Martha* 1973; *Effi Briest* 1974; *Fox and His Friends* 1975; *Mother Küsters Goes to Heaven* 1975; *Chinese Roulette* 1976; *Fear of Fear* 1976; *I Only Want You to Love Me* 1976; *Satan's Brew* 1976; *Bolwieser* 1977; *Despair* 1978; *Germany in Autumn* 1978; *In a Year of 13 Moons* 1978; *The Marriage of Maria Braun* 1978; *The Third Generation* 1979; *Berlin Alexanderplatz* 1980; *Lili Marleen* 1980; *Lola* 1982; *Querelle* 1982; *Veronika Voss* 1982

Favreau, Jon (1966–) *Made* 2001; *Elf* 2003

Fawcett, John (1968–) *The Boys Club* 1996; *Ginger Snaps* 2000

Fearnley, Neill *A Passion for Murder* 1992; *Dogmatic* 1996

Feist, Felix *aka* **Feist, Felix E** (1906–1965) *Deluge* 1933; *Every Sunday* 1936; *George White's Scandals* 1945; *The Devil Thumbs a Ride* 1947; *The Big Trees* 1952; *This Woman Is Dangerous* 1952; *Donovan's Brain* 1953

Feldman, John *Alligator Eyes* 1990; *Dead Funny* 1995

Feldman, Marty (1933–1982) *The Last Remake of Beau Geste* 1977; *In God We Trust* 1980

Fellini, Federico (1920–1993) *Lights of Variety* 1950; *The White Sheik* 1951; *Love in the City* 1953; *I Vitelloni* 1953; *La Strada* 1954; *The Swindle* 1955; *Nights of Cabiria* 1957; *La Dolce Vita* 1960; *Boccaccio '70* 1961; *8½* 1963; *Juliet of the Spirits* 1965; *Histoires Extraordinaires* 1967; *Satyricon* 1969; *The Clowns* 1970; *Fellini's Roma* 1972; *Amarcord* 1973; *Casanova* 1976;

Orchestra Rehearsal 1978; City of Women 1980; And the Ship Sails On 1983; Ginger & Fred 1986; Intervista 1987

Fenady, Georg (1930–) Arnold 1973; Terror in the Wax Museum 1973

Fenton, Leslie (1902–1978) Tell No Tales 1939; The Man from Dakota 1940; The Saint's Vacation 1941; Tomorrow the World! 1944; Pardon My Past 1945; Lulu Belle 1948; On Our Merry Way 1948; Saigon 1948; Whispering Smith 1948; Streets of Laredo 1949; The Redhead and the Cowboy 1950

Ferguson, Norman (1902–1957) Fantasia 1940; The Three Caballeros 1944

Ferland, Guy (1966–) The Babysitter 1995; Telling Lies in America 1997; Our Guys: Outrage in Glen Ridge 1999; After the Storm 2001; Dirty Dancing 2 2003

Ferrara, Abel (1952–) The Driller Killer 1979; Ms 45 1981; Fear City 1984; China Girl 1987; Cat Chaser 1989; King of New York 1989; Bad Lieutenant 1992; Body Snatchers 1993; Dangerous Game 1993; The Addiction 1994; The Funeral 1996; The Blackout 1997; Subway Stories: Tales from the Underground 1997; New Rose Hotel 1998

Ferrer, José (1909–1992) The Cockleshell Heroes 1955; The Shrike 1955; The Great Man 1956; The High Cost of Loving 1958; I Accuse! 1958; Return to Peyton Place 1961; State Fair 1962

Ferreri, Marco (1928–1997) The Seed of Man 1969; La Grande Bouffe 1973; Bye Bye Monkey 1978; Tales of Ordinary Madness 1981; Storia di Piera 1983

Ferroni, Giorgio aka **Padget, Calvin Jackson** (1908–1981) The Bacchantes 1960; The Trojan War 1961; The Battle of El Alamein 1968

Fessenden, Larry (1963–) Habit 1995; Wendigo 2001

Feyder, Jacques (1885–1948) Faces of Children 1925; The Kiss 1929; Daybreak 1931; Le Grand Jeu 1933; Carnival in Flanders 1935; Knight without Armour 1937

Figgis, Mike (1950–) Stormy Monday 1987; Internal Affairs 1990; Liebestraum 1991; Mr Jones 1993; The Browning Version 1994; Leaving Las Vegas 1995; One Night Stand 1997; The Loss of Sexual Innocence 1999; Miss Julie 1999; Timecode 1999; Hotel 2001; Ten Minutes Older: the Cello 2002; Cold Creek Manor 2003; Martin Scorsese Presents The Blues: Red, White & Blues 2003

Finch, Charles Where Sleeping Dogs Lie 1991; Circle of Passion 1996

Fincher, David (1963–) Alien^3 1992; Se7en 1995; The Game 1997; Fight Club 1999; Panic Room 2002

Findlay, Roberta Snuff 1976; Prime Evil 1988

Finkleman, Ken Airplane II: the Sequel 1982; Head Office 1986

Firstenberg, Sam (1950–) Breakdance 2 – Electric Boogaloo 1984; American Ninja 1985; Avenging Force 1986; Cyborg Cop 1993; Operation Delta Force 1996; Motel Blue 1997

Fischer, Max (1929–) The Lucky Star 1980; Killing 'em Softly 1982; Twist of Fate 1997; Taken 1999

Fisher, Terence (1904–1980) Portrait from Life 1948; The Astonished Heart 1949; Marry Me! 1949; So Long at the Fair 1950; Home to Danger 1951; The Last Page 1952; Mantrap 1952; Stolen Face 1952; Wings of Danger 1952; Blood Orange 1953; Four Sided Triangle 1953; Spaceways 1953; Children Galore 1954; Face the Music 1954; Final Appointment 1954; The Flaw 1954; Mask of Dust 1954; The Stranger Came Home 1954; The Curse of Frankenstein 1957; Kill Me Tomorrow 1957; Horror of Dracula 1958; The Revenge of Frankenstein 1958; The Hound of the Baskervilles 1959; The Man Who Could Cheat Death 1959; The Mummy 1959; The Brides of Dracula 1960; Sword of Sherwood Forest 1960; The Two Faces of Dr Jekyll 1960; The Curse of the Werewolf 1961; The Phantom of the Opera 1962; Sherlock Holmes and the Deadly Necklace 1962; The Earth Dies Screaming 1964; The Gorgon 1964; Dracula – Prince of Darkness 1965; Frankenstein Created Woman 1966; Island of Terror 1966; Night of the Big Heat 1967; The Devil Rides Out 1968; Frankenstein Must Be Destroyed 1969; Frankenstein and the Monster from Hell 1973

Fishman, Bill Tapeheads 1988; Car 54 Where Are You? 1991

Fisk, Jack (1945–) Raggedy Man 1981; Violets Are Blue 1986; Daddy's Dyin'... Who's Got the Will? 1990

Fitzgerald, Thom (1968–) The Hanging Garden 1997; Beefcake 1998

Fitzmaurice, George (1885–1940) The Son of the Sheik 1926; The Barker 1928; Lilac Time 1928; The Devil to Pay 1930; Mata Hari 1931; One Heavenly Night 1931; Strangers May Kiss 1931; The Unholy Garden 1931; As You Desire Me 1932; Rockabye 1932; Suzy 1936; The Emperor's Candlesticks 1937; Live, Love and Learn 1937; Arsene Lupin Returns 1938

Flaherty, Paul 18 Again! 1988; Who's Harry Crumb? 1989

Flaherty, Robert aka **Flaherty, Robert J** (1884–1951) Nanook of the North 1922; Moana 1926; Man of Aran 1934; Elephant Boy 1937; Prelude to War 1943; Louisiana Story 1948

Fleder, Gary (1965–) Things to Do in Denver When You're Dead 1995; Kiss the Girls 1997; Don't Say a Word 2001; Impostor 2001; Runaway Jury 2003

Fleischer, Dave aka **Fleischer, David** (1894–1979) Gulliver's Travels 1939; Hoppity Goes to Town 1941

Fleischer, Richard aka **Fleischer, Richard O** (1916–) Child of Divorce 1946; Bodyguard 1948; So This Is New York 1948; The Clay Pigeon 1949; Armored Car Robbery 1950; The Happy Time 1952; The Narrow Margin 1952; Arena 1953; 20,000 Leagues under the Sea 1954; The Girl in the Red Velvet Swing 1955; Violent Saturday 1955; Bandido 1956; Between Heaven and Hell 1956; The Vikings 1958; Compulsion 1959; These Thousand Hills 1959; Crack in the Mirror 1960; Barabbas 1961; The Big Gamble 1961; Fantastic Voyage 1966; Doctor Dolittle 1967; The Boston Strangler 1968; Che! 1969; 10 Rillington Place 1970; Tora! Tora! Tora! 1970; Blind Terror 1971; The Last Run 1971; The New Centurions 1972; The Don Is Dead 1973; Soylent Green 1973; Mr Majestyk 1974; The Spikes Gang 1974; Mandingo 1975; The Incredible Sarah 1976; The Prince and the Pauper 1977; Ashanti 1979; The Jazz Singer 1980; Tough Enough 1982; Amityville III: the Demon 1983; Conan the Destroyer 1984; Red Sonja 1985; Money Mania 1987

Fleming, Andrew Threesome 1994; The Craft 1996; Dick 1999; The In-Laws 2003

Fleming, Victor (1883–1949) Mantrap 1926; The Way of All Flesh 1927; Abie's Irish Rose 1928; The Virginian 1929; Renegades 1930; Red Dust 1932; The Wet Parade 1932; Blonde Bombshell 1933; The White Sister 1933; Treasure Island 1934; The Farmer Takes a Wife 1935; Reckless 1935; Captains Courageous 1937; Test Pilot 1938; Gone with the Wind 1939; The Wizard of Oz 1939; Dr Jekyll and Mr Hyde 1941; Tortilla Flat 1942; A Guy Named Joe 1944; Adventure 1945; Joan of Arc 1948

Flemyng, Gordon (1934–1995) Solo for Sparrow 1962; Doctor Who and the Daleks 1965; Daleks – Invasion Earth 2150 AD 1966; Great Catherine 1968; The Split 1968; The Last Grenade 1970

Flender, Rodman (1974–) The Unborn 1991; Idle Hands 1999

Flicker, Theodore J (1930–) The Troublemaker 1964; The President's Analyst 1967; Up in the Cellar 1970

Flood, James (1895–1953) Life Begins 1932; Wings in the Dark 1935

Florea, John Invisible Strangler 1976; Where's Willie? 1977

Florentine, Isaac High Voltage 1998; Bridge of Dragons 1999

Florey, Robert (1900–1975) The Cocoanuts 1929; Murders in the Rue Morgue 1932; Ex-Lady 1933; The Florentine Dagger 1935; The Woman in Red 1935; Till We Meet Again 1936; King of Alcatraz 1938; The Face behind the Mask 1941; Meet Boston Blackie 1941; Dangerously They Live 1942; The Desert Song 1944; God Is My Co-Pilot 1945; The Beast with Five Fingers 1946; Tarzan and the Mermaids 1948; Outpost in Morocco 1949

Flynn, John (1931–) The Sergeant 1968; The Jerusalem File 1972; The Outfit 1973; Rolling Thunder 1977; Defiance 1979; Best Seller 1987; Lock Up 1989; Out for Justice 1991; Brainscan 1994; Absence of the Good 1999

Foley, James (1953–) At Close Range 1985; Who's That Girl 1987; After Dark, My Sweet 1990; Glengarry Glen Ross 1992; Two Bits 1995; The Chamber 1996; Fear 1996; The Corruptor 1999; Confidence 2002

Fonda, Peter (1939–) The Hired Hand 1971; Idaho Transfer 1973; Wanda Nevada 1979

Fons, Jorge (1939–) Jory 1972; Midaq Alley 1995

Fontaine, Anne (1959–) Dry Cleaning 1997; Comment J'ai Tué Mon Père 2001; Nathalie... 2003

Forbes, Bryan (1926–) Whistle down the Wind 1961; The L-Shaped Room 1962; Seance on a Wet Afternoon 1964; King Rat 1965; The Wrong Box 1966; The Whisperers 1967; Deadfall 1968; The Madwoman of Chaillot 1969; The Raging Moon 1970; The Stepford Wives 1975; The Slipper and the Rose 1976; International Velvet 1978; Better Late Than Never 1983; The Naked Face 1984

Ford, John aka **Ford, Jack** (1894–1973) Straight Shooting 1917; The Iron Horse 1924; 3 Bad Men 1926; Four Sons 1928; Hangman's House 1928; The Black Watch 1929; Born Reckless 1930; Men without Women 1930; Up the River 1930; Arrowsmith 1931; Air Mail 1932; Flesh 1932; Dr Bull 1933; Pilgrimage 1933; Judge Priest 1934; The Lost Patrol 1934; The World Moves On 1934; The Informer 1935; Steamboat round the Bend 1935; The Whole Town's Talking 1935; Mary of Scotland 1936; The Plough and the Stars 1936; The Prisoner of Shark Island 1936; The Hurricane 1937; Wee Willie Winkie 1937; Four Men and a Prayer 1938; Submarine Patrol 1938; Drums along the Mohawk 1939; Stagecoach 1939; Young Mr Lincoln 1939; The Grapes of Wrath 1940; The Long Voyage Home 1940; How Green Was My Valley 1941; Tobacco Road 1941; The Battle of Midway 1942; They Were Expendable 1945; My Darling Clementine 1946; The Fugitive 1947; Fort Apache 1948; Three Godfathers 1948; She Wore a Yellow Ribbon 1949; Rio Grande 1950; Wagonmaster 1950; When Willie Comes Marching Home 1950; The Quiet Man 1952; What Price Glory? 1952; Mogambo 1953; The Sun Shines Bright 1953; The Long Gray Line 1955; Mister Roberts 1955; The Searchers 1956; The Rising of the Moon 1957; The Wings of Eagles 1957; Gideon's Day 1958; The Last Hurrah 1958; The Horse Soldiers 1959; Sergeant Rutledge 1960; Two Rode Together 1961; How the West Was Won 1962; The Man Who Shot Liberty Valance 1962; Donovan's Reef 1963; Cheyenne Autumn 1964; Young Cassidy 1965; 7 Women 1966

Forde, Eugene (1894–1986) Charlie Chan in London 1934; Charlie Chan at Monte Carlo 1937; Charlie Chan on Broadway 1937; Step Lively, Jeeves 1937; International Settlement 1938; Michael Shayne, Private Detective 1940; Berlin Correspondent 1942

Forde, Walter (1896–1984) The Ghost Train 1931; Rome Express 1932; Bulldog Jack 1934; Chu Chin Chow 1934; Jack Ahoy! 1934; Forever England 1935; King of the Damned 1935; Land without Music 1936; Cheer Boys Cheer 1939; The Four Just Men 1939; Let's Be Famous 1939; Charley's (Big Hearted) Aunt 1940; Sailors Three 1940; Saloon Bar 1940; The Ghost Train 1941; It's That Man Again 1942; Time Flies 1944; The Master of Bankdam 1947; Cardboard Cavalier 1949

Forman, Milos (1932–) Peter and Pavla 1964; A Blonde in Love 1965; The Fireman's Ball 1967; Taking Off 1971; Visions of Eight 1973; One Flew over the Cuckoo's Nest 1975; Hair 1979; Ragtime 1981; Amadeus 1984; Valmont 1989; The People vs Larry Flynt 1996; Man on the Moon 1999

Forster, Marc (1969–) Everything Put Together 2000; Monster's Ball 2001; Finding Neverland 2004

Forsyth, Bill (1946–) That Sinking Feeling 1979; Gregory's Girl 1980; Local Hero 1983; Comfort and Joy 1984; Housekeeping 1987; Breaking In 1989; Being Human 1994; Gregory's Two Girls 1999

Fortenberry, John Jury Duty 1995; A Night at the Roxbury 1998

Fosse, Bob (1927–) Sweet Charity 1968; Cabaret 1972; Lenny 1974; All That Jazz 1979; Star 80 1983

Foster, Giles Consuming Passions 1988; Tree of Hands 1988

Foster, Jodie (1962–) Little Man Tate 1991; Home for the Holidays 1995

Foster, Lewis R (1898–1974) Men o' War 1929; The Man Who Cried Wolf 1937; The Lucky Stiff 1949; Jamaica Run 1953; Crashout 1955; The Bold and the Brave 1956; Dakota Incident 1956; Tonka 1958

Foster, Norman (1900–1976) Fair Warning 1937; Thank You, Mr Moto 1937; Think Fast, Mr Moto 1937; Mr Moto Takes a Chance 1938; Mysterious Mr Moto 1938; Charlie Chan at Treasure Island 1939; Charlie Chan in Reno 1939; Mr Moto Takes a Vacation 1939; Mr Moto's Last Warning 1939; Journey into Fear 1942; Blood on My Hands 1948; Rachel and the Stranger 1948; Tell It to the Judge 1949; Sombrero 1952; Davy Crockett, King of the Wild Frontier 1955; Davy Crockett and the River Pirates 1956

Fowler Jr, Gene (1917–1998) I Was a Teenage Werewolf 1957; Gang War 1958; I Married a Monster from Outer Space 1958; Showdown at Boot Hill 1958; The Oregon Trail 1959; The Rebel Set 1959

Fox, Wallace aka **Fox, Wallace W** (1895–1958) Block Busters 1944; Docks of New York 1945; Mr Muggs Rides Again 1945; Pillow of Death 1945; Wild Beauty 1946

Fraker, William A (1923–) Monte Walsh 1970; A Reflection of Fear 1973; The Legend of the Lone Ranger 1981

Frakes, Jonathan (1952–) Star Trek: First Contact 1996; Star Trek: Insurrection 1998; Clockstoppers 2002; Thunderbirds 2004

Francis, Freddie (1917–) Two and Two Make Six 1961; The Brain 1962; Nightmare 1963; Paranoiac 1963; Dr Terror's House of Horrors 1964; Evil of Frankenstein 1964; Hysteria 1964; The Skull 1965; The Psychopath 1966; The Deadly Bees 1967; They Came from beyond Space 1967; Torture Garden 1967; Dracula Has Risen from the Grave 1968; Mumsy, Nanny, Sonny & Girly 1970; Trog 1970; The Creeping Flesh 1972; Tales from the Crypt 1972; Craze 1973; Tales That Witness Madness 1973; Legend of the Werewolf 1974; The Ghoul 1975; The Doctor and the Devils 1985; Dark Tower 1989

Francis, Karl (1943–) Giro City 1982; Rebecca's Daughters 1991; One of the Hollywood Ten 2000

Francisci, Pietro (1906–) Hercules 1957; Hercules Unchained 1959; The Siege of Syracuse 1959; Hercules, Samson and Ulysses 1963

Franco, Jesus aka **Moutier, Norbert** aka **Franco, Jess** aka **Manera, Franco** (1930–) The Awful Dr Orloff 1962; The Blood of Fu Manchu 1968; The Castle of Fu Manchu 1968; The Bloody Judge 1969; Count Dracula 1970; Vampyros Lesbos 1970; Dracula, Prisoner of Frankenstein 1972; The Female Vampire 1973

Franju, Georges (1912–1987) Eyes without a Face 1959; Thérèse Desqueyroux 1962; Judex 1963; Thomas the Imposter 1964; Shadowman 1973

Frank, Melvin (1913–1988) Callaway Went Thataway 1951; Above and Beyond 1952; Knock on Wood 1954; The Court Jester 1956; That Certain Feeling 1956; The Jayhawkers 1959; Li'l Abner 1959; The Facts of Life 1960; Strange Bedfellows 1965; Buona Sera, Mrs Campbell 1968; A Touch of Class 1973; The Prisoner of Second Avenue 1974; The Duchess and the Dirtwater Fox 1976; Lost and Found 1979; Walk like a Man 1987

Frank, Robert Pull My Daisy 1959; Candy Mountain 1987

Frankel, Cyril (1921–) Devil on Horseback 1954; Man of Africa 1954; It's Great to Be Young 1956; No Time for Tears 1957; Alive and Kicking 1958; Never Take Sweets from a Stranger 1960; Don't Bother to Knock 1961; On the Fiddle 1961; The Very Edge 1962; The Witches 1966; The Trygon Factor 1967; Permission to Kill 1975

Frankenheimer, John (1930–2002) The Young Stranger 1957; The Young Savages 1961; All Fall Down 1962; Birdman of Alcatraz 1962; The Manchurian Candidate 1962; Seven Days in May 1964; The Train 1964; Grand Prix 1966; Seconds 1966; The Fixer 1968; The Extraordinary Seaman 1969; The Gypsy Moths 1969; I Walk the Line 1970; The Horsemen 1971; The Iceman Cometh 1973; Story of a Love Story 1973; 99 and 44/100% Dead 1974; French Connection II 1975; Black Sunday 1976; Prophecy 1979; The Challenge 1982; The Holcroft Covenant 1985; 52 Pick-Up 1986; Dead-Bang 1989; The Fourth War 1990; Year of the Gun 1991; Against the Wall 1994; The Burning Season 1994; The Island of Dr Moreau 1996; Ronin 1998; Deception 2000; Path to War 2002

Franklin, Carl (1949–) Full Fathom Five 1990; One False Move 1992; Devil in a Blue Dress 1995; One True Thing 1998; High Crimes 2002; Out of Time 2003

Franklin, Howard Quick Change 1990; The Public Eye 1992; Larger than Life 1996

Franklin, Richard (1948–) Patrick 1978; Road Games 1981; Psycho II 1983; Cloak and Dagger 1984;

Link 1986; *FX 2* 1991; *Hotel Sorrento* 1994; *Brilliant Lies* 1996

Franklin, Sidney (1893–1972) *The Last of Mrs Cheyney* 1929; *Wild Orchids* 1929; *A Lady's Morals* 1930; *The Guardsman* 1931; *Private Lives* 1931; *Smilin' Through* 1932; *Reunion in Vienna* 1933; *The Barretts of Wimpole Street* 1934; *The Dark Angel* 1935; *The Good Earth* 1937; *The Barretts of Wimpole Street* 1956

Fraser, Harry (1889–1974) *'Neath the Arizona Skies* 1934; *Randy Rides Alone* 1934

Frawley, James (1937–) *The Christian Licorice Store* 1971; *Kid Blue* 1971; *The Big Bus* 1976; *The Muppet Movie* 1979; *Fraternity Vacation* 1985; *The Three Stooges* 2000

Frears, Stephen (1941–) *Gumshoe* 1971; *The Hit* 1984; *My Beautiful Laundrette* 1985; *Prick Up Your Ears* 1987; *Sammy and Rosie Get Laid* 1987; *Dangerous Liaisons* 1988; *The Grifters* 1990; *Accidental Hero* 1992; *The Snapper* 1993; *Mary Reilly* 1995; *The Van* 1996; *The Hi-Lo Country* 1998; *Fail Safe* 2000; *High Fidelity* 2000; *Liam* 2000; *Dirty Pretty Things* 2002

Freda, Riccardo *aka* **Hampton, Robert** (1909–1999) *Les Misérables* 1946; *Lust of the Vampire* 1956; *Caltiki, the Immortal Monster* 1959; *The White Warrior* 1959; *The Horrible Dr Hichcock* 1962; *The Spectre* 1963; *Gold for the Caesars* 1964

Freed, Herb *Beyond Evil* 1980; *Tomboy* 1985

Freedman, Jerrold (1919–) *Kansas City Bomber* 1972; *Borderline* 1980; *Seduced* 1985; *Native Son* 1986

Freeland, Thornton (1898–1987) *Whoopee!* 1930; *Six Cylinder Love* 1931; *Love Affair* 1932; *Flying down to Rio* 1933; *George White's Scandals* 1934; *Accused* 1936; *Over the Moon* 1937; *Hold My Hand* 1938; *The Gang's All Here* 1939; *Meet Me at Dawn* 1946; *The Brass Monkey* 1948; *Dear Mr Prohack* 1949

Freeman, Morgan J (1969–) *Hurricane Streets* 1997; *Desert Blue* 1998; *American Psycho II: All American Girl* 2002

Fregonese, Hugo (1908–1987) *One Way Street* 1950; *Saddle Tramp* 1950; *Apache Drums* 1951; *My Six Convicts* 1952; *Untamed Frontier* 1952; *Blowing Wild* 1953; *Decameron Nights* 1953; *Man in the Attic* 1953; *The Raid* 1954; *Seven Thunders* 1957; *Harry Black and the Tiger* 1958

Freleng, Friz (1906–1995) *Birds Anonymous* 1957; *Looney Looney Looney Bugs Bunny Movie* 1981; *Bugs Bunny 1001 Rabbit Tales* 1982; *Daffy Duck's Movie: Fantastic Island* 1983

French, Harold (1897–1997) *Jeannie* 1941; *Major Barbara* 1941; *The Day Will Dawn* 1942; *Secret Mission* 1942; *Unpublished Story* 1942; *English without Tears* 1944; *Quiet Weekend* 1946; *My Brother Jonathan* 1947; *The Blind Goddess* 1948; *Quartet* 1948; *Adam and Evelyne* 1949; *The Dancing Years* 1949; *Trio* 1950; *Encore* 1951; *The Hour of 13* 1952; *Isn't Life Wonderful!* 1952; *The Man Who Watched Trains Go By* 1952; *Rob Roy, the Highland Rogue* 1953; *Forbidden Cargo* 1954; *The Man Who Loved Redheads* 1954

Frend, Charles (1909–1977) *The Foreman Went to France* 1941; *The Big Blockade* 1942; *San Demetrio London* 1943; *Johnny Frenchman* 1945; *The Loves of Joanna Godden* 1947; *Scott of the Antarctic* 1948; *A Run for Your Money* 1949; *The Magnet* 1950; *The Cruel Sea* 1953; *Lease of Life* 1954; *The Long Arm* 1956; *Barnacle Bill* 1957; *Cone of Silence* 1960; *Girl on Approval* 1962

Freund, Karl (1890–1969) *The Mummy* 1932; *Mad Love* 1935

Freundlich, Bart (1970–) *The Myth of Fingerprints* 1996; *Catch That Kid* 2004

Fridriksson, Fridrik Thor (1954–) *Cold Fever* 1994; *Devil's Island* 1996; *Falcons* 2002

Friedenberg, Richard *The Life and Times of Grizzly Adams* 1974; *The Education of Little Tree* 1997

Friedkin, David (1912–1976) *Hot Summer Night* 1957; *Handle with Care* 1958

Friedkin, William (1939–) *Good Times* 1967; *The Birthday Party* 1968; *The Night They Raided Minsky's* 1968; *The Boys in the Band* 1970; *The French Connection* 1971; *The Exorcist* 1973; *Sorcerer* 1977; *The Brink's Job* 1978; *Cruising* 1980; *Deal of the Century* 1983; *To Live and Die in LA* 1985; *Rampage* 1987; *The Guardian* 1990; *Blue Chips* 1994; *Jade* 1995; *12 Angry Men* 1997; *Rules of Engagement* 2000; *The Hunted* 2002

Friedman, Jeffrey *Common Threads: Stories from the Quilt* 1989; *The Celluloid Closet* 1995; *Paragraph 175* 1999

Friedman, Richard (1951–) *Deathmask* 1984; *Doom Asylum* 1987

Friedman, Seymour (1917–) *Escape Route* 1952; *Khyber Patrol* 1954; *Secret of Treasure Mountain* 1956

Frost, Lee *aka* **Frost, R L** (1935–) *House on Bare Mountain* 1962; *The Thing with Two Heads* 1972; *Dixie Dynamite* 1976

Fruet, William (1933–) *Search and Destroy* 1978; *Killer Party* 1986; *Blue Monkey* 1987

Fuest, Robert (1927–) *Just like a Woman* 1966; *And Soon the Darkness* 1970; *Wuthering Heights* 1970; *The Abominable Dr Phibes* 1971; *Dr Phibes Rises Again* 1972; *The Final Programme* 1973; *The Devil's Rain* 1975

Fukasaku, Kinji (1930–2003) *The Green Slime* 1968; *Tora! Tora! Tora!* 1970; *The Yakuza Papers* 1973; *Virus* 1980; *Battle Royale* 2000; *Battle Royale 2: Requiem* 2003

Fukuda, Jun (1924–2000) *Ebirah, Horror of the Deep* 1966; *Son of Godzilla* 1967; *Godzilla vs Gigan* 1972; *Godzilla vs Megalon* 1973; *Godzilla vs Mechagodzilla* 1974

Fulci, Lucio (1927–1996) *Beatrice Cenci* 1969; *Zombie Flesh Eaters* 1979; *The Black Cat* 1981; *House by the Cemetery* 1981

Fuller, Samuel (1911–1997) *I Shot Jesse James* 1949; *The Baron of Arizona* 1950; *Fixed Bayonets* 1951; *The Steel Helmet* 1951; *Park Row* 1952; *Pickup on South Street* 1953; *Hell and High Water* 1954; *House of Bamboo* 1955; *China Gate* 1957; *Forty Guns* 1957; *Run of the Arrow* 1957; *The Crimson Kimono* 1959; *Verboten!* 1959; *Underworld USA* 1961; *Merrill's Marauders* 1962; *Shock Corridor* 1963; *The Naked Kiss* 1964; *Shark!* 1969; *Dead Pigeon on Beethoven Street* 1972; *The Big Red One* 1980; *White Dog* 1981; *Street of No Return* 1989

Fuqua, Antoine (1966–) *The Replacement Killers* 1998; *Training Day* 2001; *Tears of the Sun* 2003; *King Arthur* 2004

Furie, Sidney J (1933–) *Doctor Blood's Coffin* 1960; *The Boys* 1961; *During One Night* 1961; *Three on a Spree* 1961; *The Young Ones* 1961; *The Leather Boys* 1963; *Wonderful Life* 1964; *The Ipcress File* 1965; *Southwest to Sonora* 1966; *The Naked Runner* 1967; *The Lawyer* 1969; *Little Fauss and Big Halsy* 1970; *Lady Sings the Blues* 1972; *Hit!* 1973; *Sheila Levine Is Dead and Living in New York* 1975; *Gable and Lombard* 1976; *The Boys in Company C* 1978; *The Entity* 1981; *Purple Hearts* 1984; *Iron Eagle* 1985; *Superman IV: the Quest for Peace* 1987; *Iron Eagle II* 1988; *The Taking of Beverly Hills* 1991; *Ladybugs* 1992; *Iron Eagle IV* 1995; *Hollow Point* 1996; *Top of the World* 1997; *In Her Defense* 1998; *Hide and Seek* 2000

Fywell, Tim *Norma Jean & Marilyn* 1996; *I Capture the Castle* 2002

Gabor, Pal (1932–1987) *Angi Vera* 1980; *The Long Ride* 1984

Gabriel, Mike *The Rescuers Down Under* 1990; *Pocahontas* 1995

Gallo, George (1956–) *29th Street* 1991; *Trapped in Paradise* 1994; *Double Take* 2001

Gallo, Vincent (1961–) *Buffalo '66* 1998; *The Brown Bunny* 2003

Gallone, Carmine (1886–1973) *Rigoletto* 1946; *La Forza del Destino* 1949; *Carthage in Flames* 1960

Gance, Abel (1889–1981) *J'Accuse* 1919; *La Roue* 1923; *Napoléon* 1927; *Abel Gance's Beethoven* 1936; *J'Accuse* 1938; *The Battle of Austerlitz* 1960

Gans, Christophe (1960–) *Necronomicon* 1993; *Crying Freeman* 1995; *Brotherhood of the Wolf* 2001

Ganzer, Alvin *When the Boys Meet the Girls* 1965; *Three Bites of the Apple* 1967

Gardner, Cyril (1898–1942) *Grumpy* 1930; *The Royal Family of Broadway* 1930

Gardner, Herb (1934–2003) *The Goodbye People* 1984; *I'm Not Rappaport* 1996

Garnett, Tay (1894–1977) *Her Man* 1930; *Bad Company* 1931; *One Way Passage* 1932; *SOS Iceberg* 1933; *China Seas* 1935; *Love Is News* 1937; *Slave Ship* 1937; *Stand-In* 1937; *Joy of Living* 1938; *Trade Winds* 1938; *Eternally Yours* 1939; *Slightly Honorable* 1939; *Seven Sinners* 1940; *Cheers for Miss Bishop* 1941; *My Favorite Spy* 1942; *Bataan* 1943; *The Cross of Lorraine* 1943; *Mrs Parkington* 1944; *The Valley of Decision* 1945; *The Postman Always Rings Twice* 1946; *A Connecticut Yankee in King Arthur's Court* 1949; *The Fireball* 1950; *Cause for Alarm* 1951; *Soldiers Three* 1951; *One Minute to Zero* 1952; *Main Street to Broadway* 1953; *The Black Knight* 1954; *A Terrible Beauty* 1960; *Cattle King* 1963; *The Delta Factor* 1970; *Challenge to Be Free* 1972

Garris, Mick (1951–) *Critters 2: the Main Course* 1988; *Psycho IV: the Beginning* 1990; *Sleepwalkers* 1992

Gasnier, Louis (1882–1963) *The Virtuous Sin* 1930; *The Last Outpost* 1935; *Reefer Madness* 1936

Gatlif, Tony (1948–) *Les Princes* 1982; *Latcho Drom* 1993; *Gadjo Dilo* 1997; *Exiles* 2004

Gaup, Nils (1955–) *Pathfinder* 1987; *Shipwrecked* 1990; *North Star* 1996

George, Terry *Some Mother's Son* 1996; *Hotel Rwanda* 2004

Gerber, Fred *Rent-a-Kid* 1992; *Family Plan* 1997

Gering, Marion (1901–1977) *Devil and the Deep* 1932; *Madame Butterfly* 1932; *Jennie Gerhardt* 1933; *Thirty-Day Princess* 1934; *Rumba* 1935; *Thunder in the City* 1937

German, Alexei (1938–) *Trial on the Road* 1971; *My Friend Ivan Lapshin* 1982; *Khrustaliov, My Car!* 1998

Germi, Pietro (1904–1974) *Divorce – Italian Style* 1961; *Seduced and Abandoned* 1964; *The Birds, the Bees, and the Italians* 1965; *Alfredo Alfredo* 1971

Geronimi, Clyde (1901–1989) *Victory through Air Power* 1943; *The Three Caballeros* 1944; *Make Mine Music* 1946; *Melody Time* 1948; *The Adventures of Ichabod and Mr Toad* 1949; *Cinderella* 1950; *Alice in Wonderland* 1951; *Peter Pan* 1953; *Lady and the Tramp* 1955; *Sleeping Beauty* 1959; *One Hundred and One Dalmatians* 1960

Gessner, Nicolas (1931–) *Someone behind the Door* 1971; *The Little Girl Who Lives Down the Lane* 1976; *Quicker than the Eye* 1989

Ghai, Subhash (1943–) *Pardes* 1997; *Taal* 1999; *Yaadein* 2001; *Kisna – the Warrior Poet* 2004

Ghobadi, Bahman (1968–) *A Time for Drunken Horses* 2000; *Turtles Can Fly* 2004

Ghosh, Rituparno *Chokher Bali* 2003; *Raincoat* 2004

Giacobetti, Francis *Emmanuelle 2* 1975; *Emmanuelle IV* 1983

Gibbins, Duncan (1952–1993) *Fire with Fire* 1986; *Eve of Destruction* 1991

Gibson, Alan (1938–1987) *Crescendo* 1970; *Dracula AD 1972* 1972; *The Satanic Rites of Dracula* 1973; *Martin's Day* 1984

Gibson, Brian (1944–2004) *Breaking Glass* 1980; *Poltergeist II: the Other Side* 1986; *Tina: What's Love Got to Do with It* 1993; *The Juror* 1996; *Still Crazy* 1998

Gibson, Mel (1956–) *The Man without a Face* 1993; *Braveheart* 1995; *The Passion of the Christ* 2004

Giedroyc, Coky *Stella Does Tricks* 1997; *Women Talking Dirty* 1999

Gilbert, Brian *The Frog Prince* 1984; *Vice Versa* 1988; *Not without My Daughter* 1990; *Tom & Viv* 1994; *Wilde* 1997

Gilbert, Lewis (1920–) *The Scarlet Thread* 1951; *There Is Another Sun* 1951; *Cosh Boy* 1952; *Emergency Call* 1952; *Time Gentlemen Please!* 1952; *Albert, RN* 1953; *The Good Die Young* 1954; *The Sea Shall Not Have Them* 1954; *Reach for the Sky* 1956; *The Admirable Crichton* 1957; *Cast a Dark Shadow* 1957; *A Cry from the Streets* 1957; *Carve Her Name with Pride* 1958; *Ferry to Hong Kong* 1958; *Light Up the Sky* 1960; *Sink the Bismarck!* 1960; *The Greengage Summer* 1961; *HMS Defiant* 1962; *The 7th Dawn* 1964; *Alfie* 1966; *You Only Live Twice* 1967; *The Adventurers* 1970; *Friends* 1971; *Paul and Michelle* 1974; *Operation Daybreak* 1975; *Seven Nights in Japan* 1976; *The Spy Who Loved Me* 1977; *Moonraker* 1979; *Educating Rita* 1983; *Not Quite Jerusalem* 1985; *Shirley Valentine* 1989; *Stepping Out* 1991; *Haunted* 1995; *Before You Go* 2002

Gilbert, Warwick *A Tale of Two Cities* 1984; *Nicholas Nickleby* 1985

Gill (2), Elizabeth *aka* **Gill, Liz** *Gold in the Streets* 1996; *Goldfish Memory* 2003

Gillard, Stuart (1950–) *Paradise* 1982; *Teenage Mutant Ninja Turtles III* 1992; *Rocketman* 1997

Gillespie, Jim *I Know What You Did Last Summer* 1997; *D-Tox* 2001

Gillett, Burt (1891–1971) *Flowers and Trees* 1932; *The Three Little Pigs* 1933

Gilliam, Terry (1940–) *Monty Python and the Holy Grail* 1975; *Jabberwocky* 1977; *Time Bandits* 1981; *Brazil* 1985; *The Adventures of Baron Munchausen* 1988; *The Fisher King* 1991; *Twelve Monkeys* 1995; *Fear and Loathing in Las Vegas* 1998

Gilliat, Sidney (1908–1994) *Millions like Us* 1943; *Waterloo Road* 1944; *The Rake's Progress* 1945; *Green for Danger* 1946; *London Belongs to Me* 1948; *State Secret* 1950; *The Story of Gilbert and Sullivan* 1953; *The Constant Husband* 1955; *Fortune Is a Woman* 1956; *Left, Right and Centre* 1959; *Only Two Can Play* 1961; *The Great St Trinian's Train Robbery* 1966; *Endless Night* 1971

Gilling, John (1912–1985) *No Trace* 1950; *The Quiet Woman* 1950; *The Frightened Man* 1952; *Voice of Merrill* 1952; *Deadly Nightshade* 1953; *Escape by Night* 1953; *Double Exposure* 1954; *The Gilded Cage* 1954; *Tiger by the Tail* 1955; *High Flight* 1957; *Interpol* 1957; *The Man Inside* 1958; *The Bandit of Zhobe* 1959; *The Flesh and the Fiends* 1959; *The Challenge* 1960; *Fury at Smugglers Bay* 1961; *The Pirates of Blood River* 1961; *The Shadow of the Cat* 1961; *The Scarlet Blade* 1963; *The Night Caller* 1965; *The Plague of the Zombies* 1965; *The Mummy's Shroud* 1966; *The Reptile* 1966; *Where the Bullets Fly* 1966

Gilmore, Stuart (1909–1971) *The Virginian* 1946; *The Half-Breed* 1952

Gilroy, Frank D (1925–) *Desperate Characters* 1971; *From Noon till Three* 1976; *Once in Paris* 1978; *The Gig* 1985; *The Luckiest Man in the World* 1989

Giordana, Marco Tullio (1950–) *The Hundred Steps* 2000; *The Best of Youth* 2003

Giovanni, José (1923–2004) *The Last Known Address* 1969; *Two against the Law* 1973; *Boomerang* 1976

Giraldi, Bob (1939–) *National Lampoon's Movie Madness* 1981; *Hiding Out* 1987; *Dinner Rush* 2000

Girard, Bernard (1918–1997) *Dead Heat on a Merry-Go-Round* 1966; *The Mad Room* 1969; *The Mind Snatchers* 1972; *Little Moon & Jud McGraw* 1978

Girard, François (1963–) *Thirty Two Short Films about Glenn Gould* 1993; *The Red Violin* 1998

Girault, Jean (1924–1982) *The Gendarme of St Tropez* 1964; *The Gendarme in New York* 1965; *The Spacemen of St Tropez* 1978; *The Gendarme Wore Skirts* 1982

Girdler, William (1947–1978) *Abby* 1974; *Grizzly* 1976; *Project: Kill* 1976; *Day of the Animals* 1977; *The Manitou* 1978

Girolami, Marino *aka* **Martin, Frank** (1914–1994) *Achilles* 1962; *Zombie Holocaust* 1979

Gist, Robert (1924–1998) *Della* 1965; *An American Dream* 1966

Gitai, Amos (1950–) *Berlin Jerusalem* 1989; *Wadi 1981–1991* 1991; *Golem, the Spirit of Exile* 1992; *Yom Yom* 1998; *Kadosh* 1999; *Kippur* 2000; *11'09"01 – September 11* 2002

Glaser, Paul Michael *aka* **Glaser, Paul M** (1943–) *The Running Man* 1987; *The Cutting Edge* 1992; *The Air Up There* 1993; *Kazaam* 1996

Glatter, Lesli Linka *Now and Then* 1995; *The Proposition* 1998

Glatzer, Richard *Grief* 1993; *The Fluffer* 2001

Glazer, Jonathan (1966–) *Sexy Beast* 2000; *Birth* 2004

Glebas, Francis *Fantasia 2000* 1999; *Piglet's Big Movie* 2003

Glen, John (1932–) *For Your Eyes Only* 1981; *Octopussy* 1983; *A View to a Kill* 1985; *The Living Daylights* 1987; *Licence to Kill* 1989; *Aces: Iron Eagle III* 1992; *Christopher Columbus: the Discovery* 1992; *The Point Men* 2000

Glenville, Peter (1913–1996) *The Prisoner* 1955; *Me and the Colonel* 1958; *Summer and Smoke* 1961; *Term of Trial* 1962; *Becket* 1964; *Hotel Paradiso* 1966; *The Comedians* 1967

Glickenhaus, James (1950–) *The Exterminator* 1980; *The Protector* 1985; *Blue Jean Cop* 1988; *McBain* 1991

Glimcher, Arne (1938–) *The Mambo Kings* 1992; *Just Cause* 1995

Godard, Jean-Luc (1930–) *A Bout de Souffle* 1959; *Le Petit Soldat* 1960; *Une Femme Est une Femme* 1961; *The Seven Deadly Sins* 1961; *RoGoPaG* 1962; *Vivre Sa Vie* 1962; *Les Carabiniers* 1963; *Le Mépris* 1963; *Bande à Part* 1964; *The Married Woman* 1964; *Alphaville* 1965; *Paris Vu Par…* 1965; *Pierrot le Fou* 1965; *Made in USA* 1966; *Masculine Feminine* 1966; *Two or Three Things I Know about Her* 1966; *La Chinoise* 1967; *Far from Vietnam* 1967; *The Oldest Profession* 1967; *Weekend* 1967; *Le Gai*

Savoir 1968; One Plus One 1968; Vent d'Est 1969; Vladimir et Rosa 1970; Tout Va Bien 1972; Number Two 1975; Slow Motion 1980; Passion 1982; First Name: Carmen 1983; Je Vous Salue, Marie 1984; Detective 1985; Grandeur et Décadence d'un Petit Commerce de Cinéma 1986; Soigne Ta Droite 1986; Aria 1987; King Lear – Fear and Loathing 1987; Nouvelle Vague 1990; Hélas pour Moi 1993; JLG/JLG – Self Portrait in December 1994; For Ever Mozart 1996; Eloge de l'Amour 2001; Ten Minutes Older: the Cello 2002; Notre Musique 2004

Goddard, Jim (1936–) Parker 1984; Shanghai Surprise 1986

Godfrey, Peter (1899–1970) The Lone Wolf Spy Hunt 1939; Make Your Own Bed 1944; Christmas in Connecticut 1945; Hotel Berlin 1945; The Two Mrs Carrolls 1945; Cry Wolf 1947; Escape Me Never 1947; The Woman in White 1948; Barricade 1950; The Great Jewel Robber 1950

Golan, Menahem (1929–) What's Good for the Goose 1969; Diamonds 1975; Lepke 1975; The Magician of Lublin 1979; The Apple 1980; Enter the Ninja 1981; Over the Brooklyn Bridge 1983; The Delta Force 1986; Over the Top 1987; Hanna's War 1988; Mack the Knife 1989; Hit the Dutchman 1992

Gold, Jack (1930–) The Bofors Gun 1968; The Reckoning 1969; The National Health 1973; Who? 1974; Man Friday 1975; Aces High 1976; The Medusa Touch 1978; The Sailor's Return 1978; The Chain 1984; Escape from Sobibor 1987; Stones for Ibarra 1988

Goldbacher, Sandra The Governess 1997; Me without You 2001

Goldbeck, Willis (1898–1979) Dr Gillespie's New Assistant 1942; Dr Gillespie's Criminal Case 1943; Three Men in White 1944; Love Laughs at Andy Hardy 1946; Ten Tall Men 1951

Goldberg, Dan aka **Goldberg, Danny** No Nukes 1980; Feds 1988

Goldberg, Eric (1955–) Pocahontas 1995; Fantasia 2000 1999

Goldblatt, Mark Dead Heat 1988; The Punisher 1989

Goldman, Gary (1945–) Stanley's Magic Garden 1994; Thumbelina 1994; Anastasia 1997; Bartok the Magnificent 1999; Titan AE 2000

Goldschmidt, John (1943–) She'll Be Wearing Pink Pyjamas 1984; A Song for Europe 1985

Goldstein, Allan A aka **Goldstein, Allan** Chaindance 1991; Death Wish V: the Face of Death 1994; Memory Run 1995; Home Team 1998; One Way Out 2002

Goldstein, Scott D aka **Goldstein, Scott** Walls of Glass 1985; Ambition 1991

Goldstone, James (1931–) Jigsaw 1968; A Man Called Gannon 1969; Winning 1969; Brother John 1970; The Gang That Couldn't Shoot Straight 1971; Red Sky at Morning 1971; They Only Kill Their Masters 1972; Swashbuckler 1976; Rollercoaster 1977; When Time Ran Out 1980

Goldwyn, Tony (1960–) A Walk on the Moon 1999; Animal Attraction 2001

Gomer, Steve Sunset Park 1996; Barney's Great Adventure 1998

Gomez, Nick (1963–) Laws of Gravity 1992; New Jersey Drive 1995; illtown 1996; Drowning Mona 2000

Gondry, Michel (1963–) Human Nature 2001; Eternal Sunshine of the Spotless Mind 2003

Goode, Frederic Stopover Forever 1964; The Hand of Night 1966

Goodhew, Philip Intimate Relations 1995; Another Life 2000

Goodwins, Leslie (1899–1969) The Girl from Mexico 1939; Let's Make Music 1940; Mexican Spitfire 1940; Ladies' Day 1943; The Mummy's Curse 1944; The Singing Sheriff 1944; Fireman Save My Child 1954

Gopalakrishnan, Adoor (1941–) Rat-Trap 1981; Vidheyan 1993

Gordon, Bert I (1922–) The Amazing Colossal Man 1957; Beginning of the End 1957; The Cyclops 1957; Attack of the Puppet People 1958; Earth vs the Spider 1958; War of the Colossal Beast 1958; The Magic Sword 1962; Village of the Giants 1965; Picture Mommy Dead 1966; The Food of the Gods 1975; Empire of the Ants 1977

Gordon, Bryan Career Opportunities 1991; Pie in the Sky 1995

Gordon, Dennie Joe Dirt 2001; What a Girl Wants 2003; New York Minute 2004

Gordon, Keith (1961–) The Chocolate War 1988; A Midnight Clear 1991; Mother Night 1996; Waking the Dead 2000; The Singing Detective 2003

Gordon, Michael (1911–1993) Crime Doctor 1943; The Web 1947; Another Part of the Forest 1948; The Lady Gambles 1949; Cyrano de Bergerac 1950; I Can Get It for You Wholesale 1951; The Secret of Convict Lake 1951; Pillow Talk 1959; Portrait in Black 1960; Boys' Night Out 1962; For Love or Money 1963; Move Over, Darling 1963; A Very Special Favor 1965; Texas across the River 1966; How Do I Love Thee? 1970

Gordon, Robert (1895–1971) The Joe Louis Story 1953; It Came from beneath the Sea 1955; Damn Citizen 1958; Black Zoo 1963; Tarzan and the Jungle Boy 1968

Gordon, Stuart (1947–) Re-Animator 1985; From Beyond 1986; Dolls 1987; Robot Jox 1989; The Pit and the Pendulum 1991; Fortress 1992; Space Truckers 1996; King of the Ants 2003

Goretta, Claude (1929–) The Invitation 1973; The Lacemaker 1977; The Death of Mario Ricci 1983

Gorin, Jean-Pierre Vladimir et Rosa 1970; Tout Va Bien 1972

Gorris, Marleen (1948–) A Question of Silence 1982; The Last Island 1990; Antonia's Line 1995; Mrs Dalloway 1997; The Luzhin Defence 2000

Goscinny, René (1926–1978) Asterix the Gaul 1967; Asterix and Cleopatra 1968; The 12 Tasks of Asterix 1975

Goslar, Jürgen (1927–) Death in the Sun 1975; Slavers 1977

Gosnell, Raja (1968–) Home Alone 3 1997; Never Been Kissed 1999; Big Momma's House 2000; Scooby-Doo 2002; Scooby-Doo 2: Monsters Unleashed 2004

Gottlieb, Carl (1938–) Caveman 1981; Amazon Women on the Moon 1987

Gottlieb, Lisa Just One of the Guys 1985; Cadillac Ranch 1996

Gottlieb, Michael aka **Smithee, Alan** Mannequin 1987; The Shrimp on the Barbie 1990; Mr Nanny 1992

Gould, Heywood One Good Cop 1991; Trial by Jury 1994

Goulding, Alfred (1896–1972) A Chump at Oxford 1940; The Dark Road 1948

Goulding, Edmund (1891–1959) Sally, Irene and Mary 1925; Love 1927; The Trespasser 1929; The Devil's Holiday 1930; Paramount on Parade 1930; Blondie of the Follies 1932; Grand Hotel 1932; Riptide 1934; That Certain Woman 1937; The Dawn Patrol 1938; White Banners 1938; Dark Victory 1939; The Old Maid 1939; We Are Not Alone 1939; 'Til We Meet Again 1940; The Great Lie 1941; Claudia 1943; The Constant Nymph 1943; Forever and a Day 1943; Of Human Bondage 1946; The Razor's Edge 1946; Nightmare Alley 1947; Everybody Does It 1949; Mister 880 1950; We're Not Married 1952; Teenage Rebel 1956; Mardi Gras 1958

Goursaud, Anne Embrace of the Vampire 1994; Poison Ivy 2 1995; Another $9\frac{1}{2}$ Weeks 1997

Gowariker, Ashutosh Lagaan: Once upon a Time in India 2001; Swades 2004

Graef, Roger (1936–) Pleasure at Her Majesty's 1976; The Secret Policeman's Ball 1980; The Secret Policeman's Other Ball 1982

Graef-Marino, Gustavo (1965–) Johnny 100 Pesos 1993; Diplomatic Siege 1999

Graham, Jo (1892–1976) Always in My Heart 1942; You Can't Escape Forever 1942

Graham, William A aka **Graham, William** (1930–) The Doomsday Flight 1966; Submarine X-1 1967; Waterhole #3 1967; Change of Habit 1969; Cry for Me Billy 1972; Larry 1974; Where the Lilies Bloom 1974; Part 2, Sounder 1976; Return to the Blue Lagoon 1991; Death of a Cheerleader 1994; The Man Who Captured Eichmann 1996

Granier-Deferre, Pierre (1927–) The Widow Couderc 1971; The Last Train 1972; The Trap 1975; A Strange Affair 1981; L'Etoile du Nord 1982

Grant, Lee (1927–) Tell Me a Riddle 1980; Nobody's Child 1986; Staying Together 1989

Grasshoff, Alex (1930–) The Jailbreakers 1960; Smokey and the Good Time Outlaws 1978; A Billion for Boris 1984

Grauman, Walter aka **Grauman, Walter E** (1922–) Lady in a Cage 1964; 633 Squadron 1964; A Rage to Live 1965; The Last Escape 1970

Graver, Gary Trick or Treats 1982; Evil Spirits 1991

Gray, F Gary (1970–) Friday 1995; Set It Off 1996; The Negotiator 1998; The Italian Job 2003; A Man Apart 2003; Be Cool 2005

Gray, James (1969–) Little Odessa 1994; The Yards 2000

Gray, John aka **Gray, John E** Billy Galvin 1986; A Place for Annie 1994; Born to Be Wild 1995; The Glimmer Man 1996; The Hunley 1999

Grayson, Godfrey (1913–1998) Dr Morelle – the Case of the Missing Heiress 1949; Meet Simon Cherry 1949; Room to Let 1949; What the Butler Saw 1950; To Have and to Hold 1951; The Pursuers 1961

Greek, Janet aka **Allen, A K** The Ladies Club 1986; Spellbinder 1988

Green, Alfred E (1889–1960) Little Lord Fauntleroy 1921; Disraeli 1929; The Green Goddess 1930; Smart Money 1931; The Rich Are Always with Us 1932; Union Depot 1932; Baby Face 1933; Dangerous 1935; The Girl from 10th Avenue 1935; Colleen 1936; The League of Frightened Men 1937; Thoroughbreds Don't Cry 1937; The Duke of West Point 1938; The Gracie Allen Murder Case 1939; King of the Turf 1939; East of the River 1940; South of Pago Pago 1940; Mr Winkle Goes to War 1944; A Thousand and One Nights 1945; The Jolson Story 1946; Copacabana 1947; The Fabulous Dorseys 1947; The Girl from Manhattan 1948; They Passed This Way 1948; Sierra 1950; Invasion USA 1952; The Eddie Cantor Story 1953; Top Banana 1953

Green, David (1948–) Car Trouble 1985; Buster 1988; Wings of the Apache 1990

Green, David Gordon (1975–) George Washington 2000; All the Real Girls 2003; Undertow 2004

Green, Guy (1913–) River Beat 1954; Lost 1955; Postmark for Danger 1955; House of Secrets 1956; Sea of Sand 1958; SOS Pacific 1959; The Angry Silence 1960; Light in the Piazza 1961; The Mark 1961; Diamond Head 1962; A Patch of Blue 1965; Pretty Polly 1967; The Magus 1968; A Walk in the Spring Rain 1970; Luther 1974; Once Is Not Enough 1975; The Devil's Advocate 1977

Greenaway, Peter (1942–) The Falls 1980; The Draughtsman's Contract 1982; A Zed & Two Noughts 1985; The Belly of an Architect 1987; Drowning by Numbers 1988; The Cook, the Thief, His Wife and Her Lover 1989; Prospero's Books 1991; The Baby of Macon 1993; The Pillow Book 1995; $8\frac{1}{2}$ Women 1999

Greene, David (1921–2003) The Shuttered Room 1967; Sebastian 1968; The Strange Affair 1968; I Start Counting 1970; The People Next Door 1970; Madame Sin 1972; Godspell 1973; The Count of Monte Cristo 1974; Gray Lady Down 1978; Friendly Fire 1979; Hard Country 1981; Guilty Conscience 1985; The Betty Ford Story 1987

Greene, Max (1918–1985) Hotel Reserve 1944; The Man from Morocco 1944

Greenfield, Luke The Animal 2001; The Girl Next Door 2004

Greengrass, Paul (1955–) Resurrected 1989; The Theory of Flight 1998; Bloody Sunday 2001; The Bourne Supremacy 2004

Greenwald, Maggie (1955–) The Kill-Off 1989; The Ballad of Little Jo 1993; Songcatcher 1999

Greenwald, Robert Xanadu 1980; The Burning Bed 1984; Sweet Hearts Dance 1988; Hear No Evil 1993; Breaking Up 1996; Uncovered: the War on Iraq 2004

Greenwalt, David Secret Admirer 1985; Rude Awakening 1989

Gregg, Colin (1947–) Lamb 1985; We Think the World of You 1988

Greggio, Ezio (1954–) The Silence of the Hams 1993; Screw Loose 1999

Gregoretti, Ugo (1930–) RoGoPaG 1962; The Beautiful Swindlers 1964

Grenier, Marc S Eternal Revenge 1999; Hidden Agenda 2001

Gréville, Edmond T (1906–1966) Noose 1948; The Romantic Age 1949; The House on the Waterfront 1955; Guilty? 1956; Beat Girl 1960; The Hands of Orlac 1960

Grewal, Shani S aka **Grewal, Shani** After Midnight 1990; Double X: the Name of the Game 1991; Guru in Seven 1997

Greyson, John (1960–) Zero Patience 1993; Lilies 1996

Gries, Tom (1922–1977) Will Penny 1967; Number One 1969; 100 Rifles 1969; Fools 1970; The Hawaiians 1970; The Glass House 1972; Journey through Rosebud 1972; Lady Ice 1973; Breakout 1975; Breakheart Pass 1976; The Greatest 1977

Grieve, Andrew (1939–) On the Black Hill 1987; Letters from the East 1995

Griffith, Charles B (1928–) Forbidden Island 1959; Eat My Dust! 1976; Dr Heckyl & Mr Hype 1980

Griffith, D W (1875–1948) The Musketeers of Pig Alley 1912; The Battle of Elderbush 1914; The Battle of the Sexes 1914; Home, Sweet Home 1914; The Birth of a Nation 1915; Intolerance 1916; Hearts of the World 1918; Broken Blossoms 1919; The Fall of Babylon 1919; Way Down East 1920; Dream Street 1921; Orphans of the Storm 1921; America 1924; Isn't Life Wonderful 1924; Sally of the Sawdust 1925; Abraham Lincoln 1930; The Struggle 1931

Griffith, Edward H (1894–1975) Holiday 1930; The Animal Kingdom 1932; Lady with a Past 1932; Ladies in Love 1936; Next Time We Love 1936; Café Metropole 1937; I'll Take Romance 1937; Young and Willing 1942; The Sky's the Limit 1943

Griffiths, Mark Running Hot 1983; Heroes Stand Alone 1989; Cheyenne Warrior 1994; Tactical Assault 1998

Grinde, Nick aka **Grindé, Nicholas** aka **Grinde, Nicholas** (1893–1979) This Modern Age 1931; Shopworn 1932; The Man They Could Not Hang 1939; Million Dollar Legs 1939; Before I Hang 1940

Grofe Jr, Ferde The Proud and the Damned 1972; Day of the Wolves 1973

Grosbard, Ulu (1929–) The Subject Was Roses 1968; Who Is Harry Kellerman, and Why Is He Saying Those Terrible Things about Me? 1971; Straight Time 1978; True Confessions 1981; Falling in Love 1984; Georgia 1995; The Deep End of the Ocean 1999

Gross, Terence Hotel Splendide 1999; The Day the World Ended 2001

Gross, Yoram (1926–) Dot and the Kangaroo 1976; The Little Convict 1980; Blinky Bill 1992

Grossman, Adam Sometimes They Come Back... Again 1996; Carnival of Souls 1999

Guédiguian, Robert (1953–) Marius et Jeannette 1997; A la Place du Coeur 1998; A l'Attaque! 2000; La Ville Est Tranquille 2000; The Last Mitterrand 2005

Guerra, Ruy (1931–) Sweet Hunters 1969; Erendira 1982; Opera do Malandro 1986

Guest, Christopher (1948–) The Big Picture 1989; Attack of the 50 Ft Woman 1993; Waiting for Guffman 1996; Almost Heroes 1998; Best in Show 2000; A Mighty Wind 2003

Guest, Val (1911–) Bees in Paradise 1943; Miss London Ltd 1943; Give Us the Moon 1944; I'll Be Your Sweetheart 1945; Just William's Luck 1947; William at the Circus 1948; Murder at the Windmill 1949; Mr Drake's Duck 1950; Penny Princess 1952; Life with the Lyons 1953; Dance Little Lady 1954; Men of Sherwood Forest 1954; The Runaway Bus 1954; Break in the Circle 1955; The Lyons in Paris 1955; The Quatermass Xperiment 1955; They Can't Hang Me 1955; It's a Wonderful World 1956; The Abominable Snowman 1957; Carry On Admiral 1957; Quatermass II 1957; The Camp on Blood Island 1958; Further up the Creek 1958; Life Is a Circus 1958; Up the Creek 1958; Expresso Bongo 1959; Hell Is a City 1959; Yesterday's Enemy 1959; The Day the Earth Caught Fire 1961; The Full Treatment 1961; Jigsaw 1962; 80,000 Suspects 1963; The Beauty Jungle 1964; Where the Spies Are 1965; Casino Royale 1967; Assignment K 1968; When Dinosaurs Ruled the Earth 1969; Toomorrow 1970; Confessions of a Window Cleaner 1974; Killer Force 1975; The Boys in Blue 1983

Guillermin, John (1925–) Miss Robin Hood 1952; Town on Trial 1956; I Was Monty's Double 1958; The Whole Truth 1958; Tarzan's Greatest Adventure 1959; The Day They Robbed the Bank of England 1960; Never Let Go 1960; Tarzan Goes to India 1962; Waltz of the Toreadors 1962; Guns at Batasi 1964; The Blue Max 1966; House of Cards 1968; New Face in Hell 1968; The Bridge at Remagen 1969; El Condor 1970; Skyjacked 1972; Shaft in Africa 1973; The Towering Inferno 1974; King Kong 1976; Death on the Nile 1978; Sheena 1984; King Kong Lives 1986

Guitry, Sacha (1885–1957) Bonne Chance 1935; The Story of a Cheat 1936; Royal Affairs in Versailles 1953; Napoléon 1955

Gunn, Gilbert (1912–1967) Valley of Song 1953; The Mark of the Hawk 1957; The Strange World of Planet X 1957; Girls at Sea 1958; Operation Bullshine 1959; What a Whopper! 1961

Guterman, Lawrence Cats & Dogs 2001; Son of the Mask 2004

Gutierrez, Sebastian Judas Kiss 1998; She Creature 2001

Gyllenhaal, Stephen (1949–) *Certain Fury* 1985; *Promised a Miracle* 1988; *Evidence of Love* 1990; *Paris Trout* 1991; *Waterland* 1992; *A Dangerous Woman* 1993; *Losing Isaiah* 1995; *The Terror Inside* 1996; *Homegrown* 1998; *Resurrection* 1999

Haas, Charles aka **Haas, Charles F** (1913–) *Showdown at Abilene* 1956; *Star in the Dust* 1956; *Tarzan and the Trappers* 1958; *Wild Heritage* 1958; *The Beat Generation* 1959; *The Big Operator* 1959; *Girls' Town* 1959; *Platinum High School* 1960
Haas, Philip (1954–) *A Day on the Grand Canal with the Emperor of China* 1988; *The Music of Chance* 1993; *Angels and Insects* 1995; *The Blood Oranges* 1997; *Up at the Villa* 1998
Hackford, Taylor (1944–) *The Idolmaker* 1980; *An Officer and a Gentleman* 1982; *Against All Odds* 1984; *White Nights* 1985; *Hail! Hail! Rock 'n' Roll!* 1987; *Everybody's All-American* 1988; *Blood In Blood Out* 1992; *Dolores Claiborne* 1995; *The Devil's Advocate* 1997; *Proof of Life* 2000; *Ray* 2004
Haft, Jeremy *Grizzly Mountain* 1997; *Red Team* 1999
Haggard, Piers (1944–) *Blood on Satan's Claw* 1970; *The Quatermass Conclusion* 1979; *The Fiendish Plot of Dr Fu Manchu* 1980; *Venom* 1981; *A Summer Story* 1987
Hagmann, Stuart (1942–) *The Strawberry Statement* 1970; *Believe in Me* 1971
Haid, Charles (1943–) *Cooperstown* 1993; *Iron Will* 1994; *Buffalo Soldiers* 1997
Haigney, Michael *Pokémon the First Movie: Mewtwo Strikes Back* 1998; *Pokémon the Movie 2000* 1999; *Pokémon 3: Spell of the Unown* 2001
Haines, Randa (1945–) *Children of a Lesser God* 1986; *The Doctor* 1991; *Wrestling Ernest Hemingway* 1993; *Dance with Me* 1998
Haines, Richard W *Class of Nuke 'em High* 1986; *Alien Space Avenger* 1989
Hale, Sonnie (1902–1959) *Gangway* 1937; *Head over Heels in Love* 1937; *Sailing Along* 1938
Hale, William (1937–) *Gunfight in Abilene* 1967; *How I Spent My Summer Vacation* 1967; *Journey to Shiloh* 1967; *SOS Titanic* 1979
Haley Jr, Jack (1934–) *The Love Machine* 1971; *That's Entertainment!* 1974; *That's Dancing!* 1985
Hall, Alexander (1894–1968) *Sinners in the Sun* 1932; *Torch Singer* 1933; *Little Miss Marker* 1934; *Goin' to Town* 1935; *I Am the Law* 1938; *There's Always a Woman* 1938; *The Amazing Mr Williams* 1939; *The Doctor Takes a Wife* 1940; *This Thing Called Love* 1940; *Here Comes Mr Jordan* 1941; *Bedtime Story* 1942; *My Sister Eileen* 1942; *They All Kissed the Bride* 1942; *The Heavenly Body* 1943; *Once upon a Time* 1944; *Down to Earth* 1947; *The Great Lover* 1949; *Love That Brute* 1950; *Because You're Mine* 1952; *Let's Do It Again* 1953; *Forever, Darling* 1956
Hall, Peter (1930–) *Work Is a Four Letter Word* 1968; *A Midsummer Night's Dream* 1969; *Three into Two Won't Go* 1969; *Perfect Friday* 1970; *The Homecoming* 1973; *Akenfield* 1974; *Jacob* 1994; *Never Talk to Strangers* 1995
Haller, Daniel (1928–) *Die, Monster, Die!* 1965; *The Wild Racers* 1968; *The Dunwich Horror* 1970; *Pieces of Dreams* 1970; *Buck Rogers in the 25th Century* 1979
Hallström, Lasse (1946–) *A Lover and His Lass* 1975; *ABBA the Movie* 1977; *Father to Be* 1979; *Happy We* 1983; *My Life as a Dog* 1985; *Once Around* 1991; *What's Eating Gilbert Grape* 1993; *Something to Talk About* 1995; *The Cider House Rules* 1999; *Chocolat* 2000; *The Shipping News* 2001
Halperin, Victor (1895–1983) *Party Girl* 1930; *White Zombie* 1932; *Supernatural* 1933
Hamburg, John (1970–) *Safe Men* 1998; *Along Came Polly* 2004
Hamer, Robert (1911–1963) *Dead of Night* 1945; *Pink String and Sealing Wax* 1945; *It Always Rains on Sunday* 1947; *Kind Hearts and Coronets* 1949; *The Spider and the Fly* 1949; *The Long Memory* 1952; *Father Brown* 1954; *To Paris with Love* 1954; *The Scapegoat* 1959; *School for Scoundrels* 1960
Hamilton, Guy (1922–) *The Intruder* 1953; *The Colditz Story* 1954; *An Inspector Calls* 1954; *Charley Moon* 1956; *Manuela* 1957; *The Devil's Disciple* 1959; *A Touch of Larceny* 1959; *The Best of Enemies* 1961; *Goldfinger* 1964; *The Man in the Middle* 1964; *The Party's Over* 1965; *Funeral in Berlin* 1966; *Battle of Britain* 1969; *Diamonds Are Forever* 1971; *Live and Let Die* 1973; *The Man with the Golden Gun* 1974; *Force 10 from Navarone* 1978; *The Mirror Crack'd* 1980; *Evil under the Sun* 1982; *Remo – Unarmed and Dangerous* 1985
Hamilton, Strathford (1952–) *Blueberry Hill* 1988; *The Set Up* 1995; *The Proposition* 1996
Hamilton, William (1893–1942) *Seven Keys to Baldpate* 1935; *Murder on a Bridle Path* 1936; *Call Out the Marines* 1941
Hamm, Nick *Martha – Meet Frank, Daniel and Laurence* 1997; *Talk of Angels* 1998; *The Hole* 2001; *Godsend* 2003
Hampton, Christopher (1946–) *Carrington* 1995; *The Secret Agent* 1996; *Imagining Argentina* 2003
Hanbury, Victor (1897–1954) *The Avenging Hand* 1936; *Return of a Stranger* 1937; *Hotel Reserve* 1944
Hancock, John (1939–) *Let's Scare Jessica to Death* 1971; *Bang the Drum Slowly* 1973; *California Dreaming* 1979; *Weeds* 1987; *Prancer* 1989
Hancock, John Lee (1957–) *The Rookie* 2002; *The Alamo* 2004
Hand, David aka **Hand, David D** (1900–1986) *Snow White and the Seven Dwarfs* 1937; *Bambi* 1942
Handley, Jim *Fantasia* 1940; *The Reluctant Dragon* 1941
Haneke, Michael (1942–) *The Seventh Continent* 1989; *Benny's Video* 1992; *71 Fragments of a Chronology of Chance* 1994; *Funny Games* 1997; *Code Unknown* 2000; *The Piano Teacher* 2001; *Time of the Wolf* 2003
Hanna, William (1910–2001) *Mouse Trouble* 1944; *The Cat Concerto* 1947; *The Man Called Flintstone* 1966; *Jetsons: the Movie* 1990
Hannam, Ken (1929–) *Sunday Too Far Away* 1974; *Summerfield* 1977; *Dawn!* 1979
Hänsel, Marion (1949–) *Dust* 1985; *Il Maestro* 1989; *Between the Devil and the Deep Blue Sea* 1995
Hanson, Curtis (1945–) *The Arousers* 1970; *Losin' It* 1983; *The Bedroom Window* 1987; *Bad Influence* 1990; *The Hand That Rocks the Cradle* 1992; *The River Wild* 1994; *LA Confidential* 1997; *Wonder Boys* 2000; *8 Mile* 2002
Hardwicke, Catherine (1955–) *Thirteen* 2003; *Lords of Dogtown* 2005
Hardy, Robin (1929–) *The Wicker Man* 1973; *The Fantasist* 1986
Hardy, Rod (1949–) *Thirst* 1979; *Daniel Defoe's Robinson Crusoe* 1996; *Two for Texas* 1998
Hare, David (1947–) *Wetherby* 1985; *Paris by Night* 1988; *Strapless* 1988; *The Designated Mourner* 1997
Harlin, Renny (1959–) *Prison* 1987; *A Nightmare on Elm Street 4: The Dream Master* 1988; *The Adventures of Ford Fairlane* 1990; *Die Hard 2: Die Harder* 1990; *Cliffhanger* 1993; *CutThroat Island* 1995; *The Long Kiss Goodnight* 1996; *Deep Blue Sea* 1999; *Driven* 2001; *Mindhunters* 2003; *Exorcist: the Beginning* 2004
Harlow, John (1896–) *While I Live* 1947; *The Blue Parrot* 1953; *Delayed Action* 1954
Harmon, Robert (1953–) *The Hitcher* 1986; *Eyes of an Angel* 1991; *Nowhere to Run* 1992; *The Crossing* 2000; *They* 2002; *Highwaymen* 2003
Harrington, Curtis aka **Sebastian, John** (1928–) *Night Tide* 1961; *Voyage to the Prehistoric Planet* 1965; *Planet of Blood* 1966; *Games* 1967; *What's the Matter with Helen?* 1971; *Who Slew Auntie Roo?* 1971; *The Killing Kind* 1973; *Ruby* 1977; *Mata Hari* 1985
Harris, Damian (1960–) *The Rachel Papers* 1989; *Deceived* 1991; *Bad Company* 1995; *Mercy* 2000
Harris, James B (1928–) *The Bedford Incident* 1965; *Fast-Walking* 1982; *Cop* 1988; *Boiling Point* 1993
Harris, Mark Jonathan *The Long Way Home* 1996; *Into the Arms of Strangers: Stories of the Kindertransport* 2000
Harris, Trent (1952–) *Rubin & Ed* 1991; *Plan 10 from Outer Space* 1995
Harrison, John Kent *Beautiful Dreamers* 1990; *Old Man* 1997; *What the Deaf Man Heard* 1997; *A House Divided* 2000
Harrison, Matthew (1959–) *Rhythm Thief* 1994; *Kicked in the Head* 1997
Harron, Mary (1953–) *I Shot Andy Warhol* 1995; *American Psycho* 2000
Hart, Harvey (1928–1989) *Bus Riley's Back in Town* 1965; *Dark Intruder* 1965; *The Sweet Ride* 1967; *Fortune and Men's Eyes* 1971; *Shoot* 1976; *The High Country* 1981; *Utilities* 1981
Hartford-Davis, Robert aka **Burrowes, Michael** (1923–1977) *Saturday Night Out* 1963; *The Black Torment* 1964; *Gonks Go Beat* 1965; *The Sandwich Man* 1966; *Corruption* 1968; *The Smashing Bird I Used to Know* 1969; *Incense for the Damned* 1970; *The Fiend* 1971; *The Take* 1974
Hartley, Hal (1959–) *The Unbelievable Truth* 1989; *Trust* 1990; *Simple Men* 1992; *Amateur* 1994; *Flirt* 1995; *Henry Fool* 1997; *The Book of Life* 1998
Hartman, Don (1900–1958) *It Had to Be You* 1947; *Every Girl Should Be Married* 1948; *Holiday Affair* 1949; *It's a Big Country* 1951; *Mr Imperium* 1951
Harvey, Anthony (1931–) *Dutchman* 1966; *The Lion in Winter* 1968; *They Might Be Giants* 1971; *The Abdication* 1974; *The Disappearance of Aimee* 1976; *Eagle's Wing* 1978; *Players* 1979; *The Patricia Neal Story: an Act of Love* 1981; *Grace Quigley* 1984
Harvey, Laurence (1928–1973) *The Ceremony* 1963; *A Dandy in Aspic* 1968; *Welcome to Arrow Beach* 1974
Haskin, Byron (1899–1984) *I Walk Alone* 1947; *Treasure Island* 1950; *Tarzan's Peril* 1951; *Warpath* 1951; *Denver & Rio Grande* 1952; *His Majesty O'Keefe* 1953; *The Naked Jungle* 1953; *The War of the Worlds* 1953; *Long John Silver* 1954; *Conquest of Space* 1955; *The First Texan* 1956; *From the Earth to the Moon* 1958; *Jet over the Atlantic* 1960; *Armored Command* 1961; *Captain Sindbad* 1963; *Robinson Crusoe on Mars* 1964; *The Power* 1968
Hathaway, Henry (1898–1985) *Now and Forever* 1934; *The Lives of a Bengal Lancer* 1935; *Peter Ibbetson* 1935; *Go West, Young Man* 1936; *The Trail of the Lonesome Pine* 1936; *Souls at Sea* 1937; *Spawn of the North* 1938; *The Real Glory* 1939; *Brigham Young* 1940; *Johnny Apollo* 1940; *The Shepherd of the Hills* 1941; *Sundown* 1941; *China Girl* 1942; *Ten Gentlemen from West Point* 1942; *Home in Indiana* 1944; *Wing and a Prayer* 1944; *The House on 92nd Street* 1945; *Nob Hill* 1945; *The Dark Corner* 1946; *13 Rue Madeleine* 1946; *Kiss of Death* 1947; *Call Northside 777* 1948; *Down to the Sea in Ships* 1949; *The Black Rose* 1950; *The Desert Fox* 1951; *Fourteen Hours* 1951; *Rawhide* 1951; *You're in the Navy Now* 1951; *Diplomatic Courier* 1952; *O Henry's Full House* 1952; *Niagara* 1953; *White Witch Doctor* 1953; *Garden of Evil* 1954; *Prince Valiant* 1954; *The Racers* 1955; *Beyond the River* 1956; *23 Paces to Baker Street* 1956; *Legend of the Lost* 1957; *From Hell to Texas* 1958; *Woman Obsessed* 1959; *North to Alaska* 1960; *Seven Thieves* 1960; *How the West Was Won* 1962; *The Magnificent Showman* 1964; *The Sons of Katie Elder* 1965; *Nevada Smith* 1966; *The Last Safari* 1967; *5 Card Stud* 1968; *True Grit* 1969; *Airport* 1970; *Raid on Rommel* 1971; *Shoot Out* 1971; *Hangup* 1973
Hatton, Maurice (?–1997) *Praise Marx and Pass the Ammunition* 1968; *Long Shot* 1978
Hawks, Howard (1896–1977) *Fazil* 1928; *A Girl in Every Port* 1928; *The Criminal Code* 1930; *The Dawn Patrol* 1930; *The Crowd Roars* 1932; *Scarface* 1932; *Tiger Shark* 1932; *Today We Live* 1933; *Twentieth Century* 1934; *Barbary Coast* 1935; *Ceiling Zero* 1935; *Come and Get It* 1936; *The Road to Glory* 1936; *Bringing Up Baby* 1938; *His Girl Friday* 1939; *Only Angels Have Wings* 1939; *Ball of Fire* 1941; *Sergeant York* 1941; *Air Force* 1943; *To Have and Have Not* 1944; *The Big Sleep* 1946; *Red River* 1948; *A Song Is Born* 1948; *I Was a Male War Bride* 1949; *The Big Sky* 1952; *Monkey Business* 1952; *O Henry's Full House* 1952; *Gentlemen Prefer Blondes* 1953; *Land of the Pharaohs* 1955; *Rio Bravo* 1959; *Hatari!* 1962; *Man's Favorite Sport?* 1964; *Red Line 7000* 1965; *El Dorado* 1967; *Rio Lobo* 1970
Hay, John *The Steal* 1994; *There's Only One Jimmy Grimble* 2000
Hay, Will (1888–1949) *The Black Sheep of Whitehall* 1941; *The Goose Steps Out* 1942; *My Learned Friend* 1943
Hayashi, Kaizo (1957–) *Circus Boys* 1989; *The Most Terrible Time in My Life* 1993
Haydn, Richard (1905–1985) *Miss Tatlock's Millions* 1948; *Dear Wife* 1949; *Mr Music* 1950
Hayers, Sidney (1921–2000) *Circus of Horrors* 1960; *Night of the Eagle* 1961; *Payroll* 1961; *This Is My Street* 1963; *Three Hats for Lisa* 1965; *Finders Keepers* 1966; *The Trap* 1966; *Mister Jerico* 1969; *The Southern Star* 1969; *Assault* 1970; *The Firechasers* 1970; *Revenge* 1971; *All Coppers Are...* 1972; *Diagnosis: Murder* 1974; *What Changed Charley Farthing?* 1974
Hayes, Derek *The Miracle Maker* 1999; *Otherworld* 2003
Hayes, John (1930–2000) *Mama's Dirty Girls* 1974; *End of the World* 1977
Hayman, David (1950–) *Silent Scream* 1989; *The Hawk* 1992; *The Near Room* 1995
Haynes, Todd (1961–) *Superstar: the Karen Carpenter Story* 1987; *Poison* 1990; *[Safe]* 1995; *Velvet Goldmine* 1998; *Far from Heaven* 2002
Hazan, Jack *A Bigger Splash* 1974; *Rude Boy* 1980
Heavener, David *Outlaw Force* 1988; *Prime Target* 1991; *Eye of the Stranger* 1993
Hecht, Ben (1894–1964) *Crime without Passion* 1934; *The Scoundrel* 1935; *Angels over Broadway* 1940; *Specter of the Rose* 1946; *Actors and Sin* 1952
Heckerling, Amy (1954–) *Fast Times at Ridgemont High* 1982; *Johnny Dangerously* 1984; *National Lampoon's European Vacation* 1985; *Look Who's Talking* 1989; *Look Who's Talking Too* 1990; *Clueless* 1995; *Loser* 2000
Heerman, Victor (1892–1977) *Animal Crackers* 1930; *Paramount on Parade* 1930
Heffron, Richard T aka **Heffron, Richard** (1930–) *Newman's Law* 1974; *The Rockford Files* 1974; *Futureworld* 1976; *Trackdown* 1976; *Outlaw Blues* 1977; *Foolin' Around* 1980; *I, the Jury* 1982; *Danielle Steel's No Greater Love* 1996
Hegedus, Chris (1952–) *The War Room* 1993; *Down from the Mountain* 2000; *Startup.com* 2001
Heisler, Stuart (1894–1979) *The Biscuit Eater* 1940; *Among the Living* 1941; *The Glass Key* 1942; *Along Came Jones* 1945; *Blue Skies* 1946; *Smash Up – the Story of a Woman* 1947; *Tokyo Joe* 1949; *Tulsa* 1949; *Chain Lightning* 1950; *Dallas* 1950; *Storm Warning* 1950; *Island of Desire* 1952; *The Star* 1953; *Beachhead* 1954; *This Is My Love* 1954; *I Died a Thousand Times* 1955; *The Burning Hills* 1956; *The Lone Ranger* 1956; *Hitler* 1962
Helgeland, Brian (1961–) *Payback* 1998; *A Knight's Tale* 2001; *The Sin Eater* 2002
Hellman, Monte (1932–) *Beast from Haunted Cave* 1959; *Back Door to Hell* 1964; *Flight to Fury* 1966; *Ride in the Whirlwind* 1966; *The Shooting* 1967; *Two-Lane Blacktop* 1971; *Shatter* 1974; *China 9, Liberty 37* 1978
Hemmings, David (1941–2003) *Just a Gigolo* 1978; *The Survivor* 1981; *Treasure of the Yankee Zephyr* 1981; *Dark Horse* 1992
Henderson, John *Loch Ness* 1994; *Bring Me the Head of Mavis Davis* 1997; *Two Men Went to War* 2002
Henenlotter, Frank (1950–) *Basket Case* 1982; *Brain Damage* 1988; *Basket Case 2* 1990; *Frankenhooker* 1990; *Basket Case 3: the Progeny* 1992
Henley, Hobart (1887–1964) *Sinners in Silk* 1924; *The Big Pond* 1930; *Bad Sister* 1931
Henreid, Paul (1908–1992) *Battle Shock* 1956; *Live Fast, Die Young* 1958; *Ballad in Blue* 1964; *Dead Ringer* 1964
Henry, Buck (1930–) *Heaven Can Wait* 1978; *First Family* 1980
Henson, Brian (1963–) *The Muppet Christmas Carol* 1992; *Muppet Treasure Island* 1996
Henson, Jim (1936–1990) *The Great Muppet Caper* 1981; *The Dark Crystal* 1982; *Labyrinth* 1986
Herek, Stephen (1958–) *Critters* 1986; *Bill & Ted's Excellent Adventure* 1988; *Don't Tell Mom the Babysitter's Dead* 1991; *The Mighty Ducks* 1992; *The Three Musketeers* 1993; *Mr Holland's Opus* 1995; *101 Dalmatians* 1996; *Holy Man* 1998; *Rock Star* 2001; *Life or Something like It* 2002; *Man of the House* 2005
Herman, Mark (1954–) *Blame It on the Bellboy* 1992; *Brassed Off* 1996; *Little Voice* 1998; *Purely Belter* 2000; *Hope Springs* 2002
Herman-Wurmfeld, Charles (1966–) *Fanci's Persuasion* 1994; *Kissing Jessica Stein* 2001; *Legally Blonde 2: Red, White & Blonde* 2003
Hernández, Antonio (1953–) *Lisboa* 1999; *The City of No Limits* 2002
Herrington, Rowdy (1951–) *Jack's Back* 1988; *Road House* 1989; *Gladiator* 1992; *Striking*

Distance 1993; A Murder of Crows 1998; The Stickup 2001; Bobby Jones: Stroke of Genius 2004

Hershman, Joel Hold Me, Thrill Me, Kiss Me 1992; Greenfingers 2000

Herskovitz, Marshall (1952–) Jack the Bear 1993; Dangerous Beauty 1997

Herz, Michael (1949–) The Toxic Avenger 1985; The Toxic Avenger, Part II 1988; Sgt Kabukiman NYPD 1991

Herzfeld, John Two of a Kind 1983; 2 Days in the Valley 1996; 15 Minutes 2001

Herzog, Werner (1942–) Signs of Life 1968; Even Dwarfs Started Small 1970; Aguirre, Wrath of God 1972; The Enigma of Kaspar Hauser 1974; Heart of Glass 1976; Stroszek 1977; Woyzeck 1978; Nosferatu, the Vampire 1979; Fitzcarraldo 1982; Where the Green Ants Dream 1984; Cobra Verde 1988; Scream of Stone 1991; Little Dieter Needs to Fly 1997; My Best Fiend 1999; Invincible 2001; Ten Minutes Older: the Trumpet 2002

Hess, Jon Watchers 1988; Alligator II: the Mutation 1991; Excessive Force 1993

Hessler, Gordon (1930–) The Oblong Box 1969; Scream and Scream Again 1969; Cry of the Banshee 1970; Murders in the Rue Morgue 1971; Embassy 1972; The Golden Voyage of Sinbad 1973; The Girl in a Swing 1988; Shogun Warrior 1991

Heston, Charlton (1924–) Antony and Cleopatra 1972; Mother Lode 1982

Heston, Fraser C *aka* **Heston, Fraser** (1955–) Treasure Island 1990; Needful Things 1993; Alaska 1996

Hewitt, Peter *aka* **Hewitt, Pete** (1965–) Bill & Ted's Bogus Journey 1991; Tom and Huck 1995; The Borrowers 1997; Whatever Happened to Harold Smith? 1999; Thunderpants 2002; Garfield 2004

Heyes, Douglas (1919–1993) Kitten with a Whip 1964; Beau Geste 1966

Hibbs, Jesse (1906–1985) The All American 1953; Black Horse Canyon 1954; Rails into Laramie 1954; Ride Clear of Diablo 1954; The Yellow Mountain 1954; The Spoilers 1955; To Hell and Back 1955; Walk the Proud Land 1956; Joe Butterfly 1957; Ride a Crooked Trail 1958

Hickenlooper, George (1964–) Hearts of Darkness: a Film-Maker's Apocalypse 1991; Killing Box 1993; The Low Life 1995; Persons Unknown 1996; Mayor of the Sunset Strip 2003

Hickox, Anthony *aka* **Hickox, Tony** (1959–) Waxwork 1988; Hellraiser III: Hell on Earth 1992; Waxwork II: Lost in Time 1992; Full Eclipse 1993; Warlock: the Armageddon 1993; Prince Valiant 1997; Storm Catcher 1999; Contagion 2000; Jill Rips 2000; Federal Protection 2002

Hickox, Douglas (1929–1988) The Giant Behemoth 1959; Entertaining Mr Sloane 1969; Sitting Target 1972; Theatre of Blood 1973; Brannigan 1975; Sky Riders 1976; Zulu Dawn 1979; The Hound of the Baskervilles 1983

Hickox, James *aka* **Hickox, James D R** Children of the Corn III: Urban Harvest 1995; Blood Surf 2000

Hicks, Scott (1953–) Shine 1996; Snow Falling on Cedars 1999; Hearts in Atlantis 2001

Higgin, Howard (1891–1938) High Voltage 1929; The Leatherneck 1929; The Painted Desert 1931; Hell's House 1932

Higgins, Colin (1941–1988) Foul Play 1978; Nine to Five 1980; The Best Little Whorehouse in Texas 1982

Hill, George *aka* **Hill, George W** (1895–1934) The Big House 1930; Min and Bill 1930; The Secret Six 1931; Hell Divers 1932

Hill, George Roy (1922–2002) Period of Adjustment 1962; Toys in the Attic 1963; The World of Henry Orient 1964; Hawaii 1966; Thoroughly Modern Millie 1967; Butch Cassidy and the Sundance Kid 1969; Slaughterhouse-Five 1972; The Sting 1973; The Great Waldo Pepper 1975; Slap Shot 1977; A Little Romance 1979; The World According to Garp 1982; The Little Drummer Girl 1984; Funny Farm 1988

Hill, Jack (1933–) Spider Baby 1964; House of Evil 1968; Alien Terror 1969; The Big Doll House 1971; The Big Bird Cage 1972; Coffy 1973; Foxy Brown 1974; Switchblade Sisters 1975

Hill, James (1919–1994) The Kitchen 1961; Lunch Hour 1962; Trial and Error 1962; Every Day's a Holiday 1964; A Study in Terror 1965; Born Free 1966; The Corrupt Ones 1966; Captain Nemo and the Underwater City 1969; An Elephant Called Slowly 1969; Black Beauty 1971; The Belstone Fox 1973

Hill, Tim Muppets from Space 1999; Max Keeble's Big Move 2001

Hill, Walter *aka* **Lee, Thomas** (1942–) Hard Times 1975; The Driver 1978; The Warriors 1979; The Long Riders 1980; Southern Comfort 1981; 48 HRS 1982; Streets of Fire 1984; Brewster's Millions 1985; Crossroads 1986; Extreme Prejudice 1987; Red Heat 1988; Johnny Handsome 1989; Another 48 HRS 1990; Trespass 1992; Geronimo: an American Legend 1993; Wild Bill 1995; Last Man Standing 1996; Supernova 2000; Undisputed 2002

Hillcoat, John (1961–) Ghosts… of the Civil Dead 1988; To Have & to Hold 1996

Hiller, Arthur *aka* **Smithee, Alan** (1923–) The Careless Years 1957; Miracle of the White Stallions 1963; The Wheeler Dealers 1963; The Americanization of Emily 1964; Penelope 1966; Promise Her Anything 1966; Tobruk 1966; The Tiger Makes Out 1967; Popi 1969; Love Story 1970; The Out of Towners 1970; The Hospital 1971; Plaza Suite 1971; Man of La Mancha 1972; The Man in the Glass Booth 1975; Silver Streak 1976; WC Fields and Me 1976; The In-Laws 1979; Nightwing 1979; Author! Author! 1982; Making Love 1982; Romantic Comedy 1983; The Lonely Guy 1984; Teachers 1984; Outrageous Fortune 1987; See No Evil, Hear No Evil 1989; Taking Care of Business 1990; Married to It 1991; The Babe 1992; Carpool 1996; Burn Hollywood Burn 1997

Hillyer, Lambert (1889–1969) Dracula's Daughter 1936; The Invisible Ray 1936; Girls Can Play 1937

Hirschbiegel, Oliver (1957–) The Experiment 2000; Downfall 2004

Hiscott, Leslie *aka* **Hiscott, Leslie S** (1894–1968) When London Sleeps 1932; Death on the Set 1935; A Fire Has Been Arranged 1935; The Time of His Life 1955

Hitchcock, Alfred *aka* **Hitchcock, Alfred J** (1899–1980) The Pleasure Garden 1925; The Lodger 1926; Downhill 1927; Easy Virtue 1927; The Ring 1927; Champagne 1928; The Farmer's Wife 1928; Blackmail 1929; The Manxman 1929; Elstree Calling 1930; Juno and the Paycock 1930; Murder 1930; The Skin Game 1931; Number Seventeen 1932; Rich and Strange 1932; Waltzes from Vienna 1933; The Man Who Knew Too Much 1934; The 39 Steps 1935; Sabotage 1936; Secret Agent 1936; Young and Innocent 1937; The Lady Vanishes 1938; Jamaica Inn 1939; Foreign Correspondent 1940; Rebecca 1940; Mr and Mrs Smith 1941; Suspicion 1941; Saboteur 1942; Shadow of a Doubt 1942; Aventure Malgache 1944; Bon Voyage 1944; Lifeboat 1944; Spellbound 1945; Notorious 1946; The Paradine Case 1947; Rope 1948; Stage Fright 1949; Under Capricorn 1949; Strangers on a Train 1951; I Confess 1953; Dial M for Murder 1954; Rear Window 1954; The Trouble with Harry 1954; To Catch a Thief 1955; The Man Who Knew Too Much 1956; The Wrong Man 1956; Vertigo 1958; North by Northwest 1959; Psycho 1960; The Birds 1963; Marnie 1964; Torn Curtain 1966; Topaz 1969; Frenzy 1972; Family Plot 1976

Hitzig, Rupert Night Visitor 1989; Backstreet Dreams 1990

Hively, Jack (1910–1995) The Spellbinder 1939; Anne of Windy Poplars 1940; The Saint Takes Over 1940; The Saint's Double Trouble 1940; The Saint in Palm Springs 1941; Are You with It? 1948

Ho Yim (1952–) The Day the Sun Turned Cold 1994; Kitchen 1997; Pavilion of Women 2000

Hoblit, Gregory (1944–) Roe vs Wade 1989; Class of '61 1993; Primal Fear 1996; Fallen 1998; Frequency 2000; Hart's War 2002

Hodges, Mike *aka* **Hodges, Michael** (1932–) Get Carter 1971; Pulp 1972; The Terminal Man 1974; Flash Gordon 1980; And the Ship Sails On 1983; Morons from Outer Space 1985; A Prayer for the Dying 1987; Black Rainbow 1989; Croupier 1998; I'll Sleep When I'm Dead 2003

Hoffman, Herman (1909–1989) It's a Dog's Life 1955; The Invisible Boy 1957

Hoffman, Michael (1957–) Restless Natives 1985; Promised Land 1988; Some Girls 1988; Soapdish 1991; Restoration 1995; One Fine Day 1996; A Midsummer Night's Dream 1999; The Emperor's Club 2002

Hofmeyr, Gray *aka* **Hofmyer, Gray** Jock of the Bushveld 1988; Out of Darkness 1990

Hogan, David *aka* **Hogan, David Glenn** Barb Wire 1995; Most Wanted 1997

Hogan, James (1891–1943) Bulldog Drummond Escapes 1937; The Last Train from Madrid 1937; Bulldog Drummond's Peril 1938; The Texans 1938; Bulldog Drummond's Bride 1939; Texas Rangers Ride Again 1940

Hogan, P J (1962–) Muriel's Wedding 1994; My Best Friend's Wedding 1997; Unconditional Love 2001; Peter Pan 2003

Holcomb, Rod Chains of Gold 1989; Songs in Ordinary Time 2000

Holden Jones, Amy *aka* **Jones, Amy** (1953–) The Slumber Party Massacre 1982; Love Letters 1983; Maid to Order 1987; The Rich Man's Wife 1996

Holland, Agnieszka (1948–) To Kill a Priest 1988; Europa, Europa 1991; Olivier Olivier 1991; The Secret Garden 1993; Total Eclipse 1995; Washington Square 1997

Holland, Savage Steve (1960–) Better Off Dead 1985; One Crazy Summer 1986; How I Got Into College 1989

Holland, Tom (1943–) Fright Night 1985; Fatal Beauty 1987; Child's Play 1988; The Temp 1993; Stephen King's Thinner 1996

Holmes, Ben (1890–1943) The Plot Thickens 1936; Maid's Night Out 1938; The Saint in New York 1938

Holofcener, Nicole (1960–) Walking and Talking 1996; Lovely & Amazing 2001

Holt, Seth (1923–1971) Nowhere to Go 1958; Taste of Fear 1961; Station Six-Sahara 1962; The Nanny 1965; Danger Route 1967; Blood from the Mummy's Tomb 1971

Holzman, Edward *aka* **Edward R Holzman** Walnut Creek 1996; Sexual Magic 2001

Honda, Inoshiro *aka* **Honda, Ishiro** (1911–1993) Godzilla 1954; The H-Man 1954; Rodan 1956; King Kong vs Godzilla 1962; Mothra 1962; Matango 1963; Frankenstein Conquers the World 1964; Godzilla vs Mothra 1964; Ghidrah, the Three-Headed Monster 1965; Invasion of the Astro-Monster 1965; Destroy All Monsters 1968; Godzilla's Revenge 1969; Latitude Zero 1969; War of the Gargantuas 1970; Terror of Mechagodzilla 1975

Hondo, Med (1936–) Sarraouina 1986; Lumière Noire 1994

Hook, Harry (1960–) The Kitchen Toto 1987; Lord of the Flies 1990; All for Love 1999

Hooks, Kevin (1958–) Heat Wave 1990; Passenger 57 1992; Fled 1996; Black Dog 1998; Glory & Honor 1998; Mutiny 1999

Hooper, Tobe (1943–) The Texas Chain Saw Massacre 1974; Eaten Alive 1976; Salem's Lot 1979; The Funhouse 1981; Poltergeist 1982; Lifeforce 1985; Invaders from Mars 1986; The Texas Chainsaw Massacre Part 2 1986; The Mangler 1994; Crocodile 2000; Toolbox Murders 2003

Hopkins, Ben (1959–) Simon Magus 1998; The Nine Lives of Tomas Katz 1999

Hopkins, Stephen (1959–) A Nightmare on Elm Street 5: The Dream Child 1989; Predator 2 1990; Judgment Night 1993; Blown Away 1994; The Ghost and the Darkness 1996; Lost in Space 1998; Under Suspicion 2000; The Life and Death of Peter Sellers 2003

Hopper, Dennis *aka* **Smithee, Alan** (1936–) Easy Rider 1969; The Last Movie 1971; Out of the Blue 1980; Colors 1988; Catchfire 1989; The Hot Spot 1990; Chasers 1994

Hopper, Jerry (1907–1988) Pony Express 1953; Alaska Seas 1954; Naked Alibi 1954; Secret of the Incas 1954; Never Say Goodbye 1955; One Desire 1955; The Private War of Major Benson 1955; Smoke Signal 1955; The Square Jungle 1955; The Missouri Traveler 1958; Madron 1970

Horn, Leonard (1926–1975) The Magic Garden of Stanley Sweetheart 1970; Corky 1972

Horne, James W *aka* **Horne, James** (1880–1942) College 1927; Big Business 1929; Bonnie Scotland 1935; Thicker than Water 1935; The Bohemian Girl 1936; All over Town 1937; Way Out West 1937

Horner, Harry (1910–1994) Beware, My Lovely 1952; Red Planet Mars 1952; New Faces 1954; A Life in the Balance 1955

Horton, Peter (1953–) Amazon Women on the Moon 1987; The Cure 1995

Hoskins, Bob (1942–) The Raggedy Rawney 1987; Rainbow 1995

Hou Hsiao-Hsien *aka* **Hou Xiaoxian** (1947–) A Summer at Grandpa's 1984; The Time to Live and the Time to Die 1985; Daughter of the Nile 1987; Dust in the Wind 1987; A City of Sadness 1989; The Puppetmaster 1993; Flowers of Shanghai 1998; Cafe Lumière 2003

Hough, John (1941–) Eyewitness 1970; Twins of Evil 1971; Treasure Island 1972; The Legend of Hell House 1973; Dirty Mary Crazy Larry 1974; Escape to Witch Mountain 1975; Brass Target 1978; Return from Witch Mountain 1978; The Watcher in the Woods 1982; Triumphs of a Man Called Horse 1983; Biggles 1986; American Gothic 1987; Howling IV 1988; A Ghost in Monte Carlo 1990; Something to Believe In 1997; Bad Karma 2001

Hovde, Ellen Grey Gardens 1975; Enormous Changes at the Last Minute 1983

Howard, Cy (1915–1993) Lovers and Other Strangers 1970; Every Little Crook and Nanny 1972

Howard, David (1896–1941) Painted Desert 1938; Arizona Legion 1939

Howard, Leslie (1893–1943) Pygmalion 1938; Pimpernel Smith 1941; The First of the Few 1942; The Gentle Sex 1943

Howard, Ron (1954–) Grand Theft Auto 1977; Night Shift 1982; Splash 1984; Cocoon 1985; Gung Ho 1986; Willow 1988; Parenthood 1989; Backdraft 1991; Far and Away 1992; The Paper 1994; Apollo 13 1995; Ransom 1996; Edtv 1999; The Grinch 2000; A Beautiful Mind 2001; The Missing 2003; Cinderella Man 2005

Howard, William K (1899–1954) The Valiant 1929; The First Year 1932; Sherlock Holmes 1932; The Power and the Glory 1933; The Cat and the Fiddle 1934; Evelyn Prentice 1934; This Side of Heaven 1934; Rendezvous 1935; Vanessa, Her Love Story 1935; The Princess Comes Across 1936; Fire over England 1937; The Squeaker 1937; Back Door to Heaven 1939; Johnny Come Lately 1943

Howitt, Peter (1957–) Sliding Doors 1997; Antitrust 2001; Johnny English 2003; Laws of Attraction 2003

Howson, Frank (1952–) Hunting 1992; Flynn 1995

Huang, George Swimming with Sharks 1994; Trojan War 1997

Hudlin, Reginald (1961–) House Party 1990; Boomerang 1992; The Great White Hype 1996; The Ladies Man 2000; Serving Sara 2002

Hudson, Hugh (1936–) Chariots of Fire 1981; Greystoke: the Legend of Tarzan, Lord of the Apes 1984; Revolution 1985; The Road Home 1989; My Life So Far 1999; I Dreamed of Africa 2000

Hughes, Albert (1972–) Menace II Society 1993; Dead Presidents 1995; American Pimp 1999; From Hell 2001

Hughes, Allen (1972–) Menace II Society 1993; Dead Presidents 1995; American Pimp 1999; From Hell 2001

Hughes, Bronwen Harriet the Spy 1996; Forces of Nature 1998; Stander 2003

Hughes, Howard (1905–1976) Hell's Angels 1930; The Outlaw 1943

Hughes, John (1950–) Sixteen Candles 1984; The Breakfast Club 1985; Weird Science 1985; Ferris Bueller's Day Off 1986; Planes, Trains and Automobiles 1987; She's Having a Baby 1988; Uncle Buck 1989; Curly Sue 1991

Hughes, Ken (1922–2001) The Brain Machine 1954; Confession 1955; Joe Macbeth 1955; Little Red Monkey 1955; Timeslip 1955; The Trials of Oscar Wilde 1960; The Small World of Sammy Lee 1963; Of Human Bondage 1964; Drop Dead Darling 1966; Casino Royale 1967; Chitty Chitty Bang Bang 1968; Cromwell 1970; The Internecine Project 1974; Alfie Darling 1975; Sextette 1978

Hughes, Terry Monty Python Live at the Hollywood Bowl 1982; The Butcher's Wife 1991

Hui, Ann *aka* **Hui On-Wah** (1947–) Song of the Exile 1990; Eighteen Springs 1997

Humberstone, H Bruce *aka* **Humberstone, Bruce** (1903–1984) If I Had a Million 1932; Charlie Chan at the Opera 1936; Charlie Chan at the Olympics 1937; Checkers 1937; Pack Up Your Troubles 1939; I Wake Up Screaming 1941; Sun Valley Serenade 1941; Tall, Dark and Handsome 1941; To the Shores of Tripoli 1942; Hello, Frisco, Hello 1943; Pin Up Girl 1944; Wonder Man 1945; Three Little Girls in Blue 1946; Fury at Furnace Creek 1948; Happy Go Lovely 1950; She's Working Her Way through College 1952; The Desert Song 1953; The Purple Mask 1955; Tarzan and the Lost Safari 1956; Tarzan's Fight for Life 1958; Madison Avenue 1962

Hunebelle, André (1896–1985) Le Bossu 1959; The Captain 1960; The Mysteries of Paris 1962; Shadow of Evil 1964

Hung, Sammo (1952–) The Prodigal Son 1983; Wheels on Meals 1984; Mr Nice Guy 1996

Hunsinger, Tom *Boyfriends* 1996; *The Lawless Heart* 2001
Hunt, Peter (1928–2002) *On Her Majesty's Secret Service* 1969; *Gold* 1974; *Shout at the Devil* 1976; *Gulliver's Travels* 1977; *Death Hunt* 1981; *Wild Geese II* 1985; *Assassination* 1986
Hunt, Peter H (1938–) *The Parade* 1984; *Danielle Steel's Secrets* 1992
Hunter, Neil *Boyfriends* 1996; *The Lawless Heart* 2001
Hunter, Tim *Tex* 1982; *Sylvester* 1985; *River's Edge* 1987; *Paint It Black* 1989; *The Saint of Fort Washington* 1993; *The Maker* 1997
Huntington, Lawrence (1900–1968) *Night Boat to Dublin* 1946; *Wanted for Murder* 1946; *The Upturned Glass* 1947; *When the Bough Breaks* 1947; *Mr Perrin and Mr Traill* 1948; *The Franchise Affair* 1950; *Contraband Spain* 1955; *Death Drums along the River* 1963; *The Vulture* 1966
Hurran, Nick *Remember Me?* 1996; *Girls' Night* 1997; *Virtual Sexuality* 1999; *Little Black Book* 2004
Hurst, Brian Desmond (1900–1986) *The Tell-Tale Heart* 1934; *The Lion Has Wings* 1939; *Dangerous Moonlight* 1941; *Hungry Hill* 1946; *The Mark of Cain* 1947; *Trottie True* 1949; *Scrooge* 1951; *Malta Story* 1953; *Simba* 1955; *The Black Tent* 1956; *Dangerous Exile* 1957; *Behind the Mask* 1958; *His and Hers* 1960; *The Playboy of the Western World* 1962
Hurwitz, Harry (1938–1995) *The Projectionist* 1970; *The Comeback Trail* 1972; *Fleshtone* 1994
Hüseyin, Metin *It Was an Accident* 2000; *Anita & Me* 2002
Hussein, Waris (1938–) *A Touch of Love* 1969; *Quackser Fortune Has a Cousin in the Bronx* 1970; *Melody* 1971; *The Possession of Joel Delaney* 1971; *Henry VIII and His Six Wives* 1972; *Surviving* 1985; *Murder between Friends* 1993; *Sixth Happiness* 1997; *Her Best Friend's Husband* 2002
Huston, Danny (1962–) *Mr North* 1988; *Becoming Colette* 1991; *The Maddening* 1995
Huston, John (1906–1987) *The Maltese Falcon* 1941; *Across the Pacific* 1942; *In This Our Life* 1942; *Key Largo* 1948; *The Treasure of the Sierra Madre* 1948; *We Were Strangers* 1949; *The Asphalt Jungle* 1950; *The African Queen* 1951; *The Red Badge of Courage* 1951; *Moulin Rouge* 1952; *Beat the Devil* 1953; *Moby Dick* 1956; *Heaven Knows, Mr Allison* 1957; *The Barbarian and the Geisha* 1958; *The Roots of Heaven* 1958; *The Unforgiven* 1960; *The Misfits* 1961; *Freud* 1962; *The List of Adrian Messenger* 1963; *The Night of the Iguana* 1964; *The Bible...in the Beginning* 1966; *Casino Royale* 1967; *Reflections in a Golden Eye* 1967; *Sinful Davey* 1969; *A Walk with Love and Death* 1969; *The Kremlin Letter* 1970; *Fat City* 1972; *The Life and Times of Judge Roy Bean* 1972; *The Mackintosh Man* 1973; *The Man Who Would Be King* 1975; *Wise Blood* 1979; *Phobia* 1980; *Escape to Victory* 1981; *Annie* 1982; *Under the Volcano* 1984; *Prizzi's Honor* 1985; *The Dead* 1987
Huth, Harold (1892–1967) *East of Piccadilly* 1940; *Night Beat* 1948
Hutton, Brian G (1935–) *Wild Seed* 1965; *The Pad (and How to Use It)* 1966; *Sol Madrid* 1968; *Where Eagles Dare* 1969; *Kelly's Heroes* 1970; *Zee and Co* 1971; *Night Watch* 1973; *The First Deadly Sin* 1980; *High Road to China* 1983
Huyck, Willard *French Postcards* 1979; *Best Defense* 1984; *Howard, a New Breed of Hero* 1986
Hyams, Peter (1943–) *Busting* 1974; *Peeper* 1975; *Capricorn One* 1978; *Hanover Street* 1979; *Outland* 1981; *The Star Chamber* 1983; *2010* 1984; *Running Scared* 1986; *The Presidio* 1988; *Narrow Margin* 1990; *Stay Tuned* 1992; *Timecop* 1994; *Sudden Death* 1995; *The Relic* 1996; *End of Days* 1999; *The Musketeer* 2001
Hytner, Nicholas (1956–) *The Madness of King George* 1995; *The Crucible* 1996; *The Object of My Affection* 1998; *Center Stage* 2000

Ichaso, Leon *Crossover Dreams* 1985; *Sugar Hill* 1993; *Ali: an American Hero* 2000; *Piñero* 2001
Ichikawa, Kon (1915–) *The Burmese Harp* 1956; *Conflagration* 1958; *Fires on the Plain* 1959; *The Key* 1959; *An Actor's Revenge* 1963; *Alone on the Pacific* 1963; *Tokyo Olympiad* 1965; *Visions of Eight* 1973; *The Makioka Sisters* 1983; *The Burmese Harp* 1985
Im Kwon-taek (1936–) *Village in the Mist* 1983; *Chihwaseon (Drunk on Women and Poetry)* 2002
Imamura, Shohei (1926–) *The Profound Desire of the Gods* 1968; *Vengeance Is Mine* 1979; *The Ballad of Narayama* 1983; *Black Rain* 1988; *The Eel* 1997; *Warm Water under a Red Bridge* 2001; *11'09"01 – September 11* 2002
Iñárritu, Alejandro González (1963–) *Amores Perros* 2000; *11'09"01 – September 11* 2002; *21 Grams* 2003
Ingram (1), Rex (1892–1950) *The Four Horsemen of the Apocalypse* 1921; *The Prisoner of Zenda* 1922; *Scaramouche* 1923; *The Arab* 1924; *Mare Nostrum* 1926; *The Garden of Allah* 1927
Ingster, Boris (1913–1978) *Stranger on the Third Floor* 1940; *The Judge Steps Out* 1949
Iosseliani, Otar (1934–) *Les Favoris de la Lune* 1984; *Farewell, Home Sweet Home* 1999; *Monday Morning* 2002
Ireland, Dan *The Whole Wide World* 1996; *The Velocity of Gary* 1998
Irvin, John (1940–) *The Dogs of War* 1980; *Ghost Story* 1981; *Champions* 1983; *Turtle Diary* 1985; *Raw Deal* 1986; *Hamburger Hill* 1987; *Next of Kin* 1989; *Robin Hood* 1990; *Eminent Domain* 1991; *Widows' Peak* 1993; *Freefall* 1994; *A Month by the Lake* 1994; *City of Industry* 1996; *When Trumpets Fade* 1998; *Shiner* 2000; *The Fourth Angel* 2001
Irvin, Sam (1956–) *Guilty as Charged* 1991; *Oblivion* 1993
Irving, David *Rumpelstiltskin* 1986; *The Emperor's New Clothes* 1987; *CHUD II: Bud the Chud* 1989; *Perfume of the Cyclone* 1989
Irving, Richard (1917–1990) *Prescription: Murder* 1968; *Ransom for a Dead Man* 1971; *The Six Million Dollar Man* 1973
Isaac, James aka **Isaac, Jim** (1960–) *House III: The Horror Show* 1989; *Jason X* 2001
Iscove, Robert (1947–) *Rodgers & Hammerstein's Cinderella* 1997; *She's All That* 1999; *Boys and Girls* 2000
Israel, Neal (1945–) *Tunnelvision* 1976; *Americathon* 1979; *Bachelor Party* 1984; *Moving Violations* 1985; *Breaking the Rules* 1992; *Surf Ninjas* 1993
Itami, Juzo (1933–1997) *Death Japanese Style* 1984; *Tampopo* 1986; *A Taxing Woman* 1987; *Minbo – or the Gentle Art of Japanese Extortion* 1992
Ivory, James (1928–) *The Householder* 1963; *Shakespeare Wallah* 1965; *The Guru* 1969; *Bombay Talkie* 1970; *Savages* 1972; *Autobiography of a Princess* 1975; *The Wild Party* 1975; *Roseland* 1977; *The Europeans* 1979; *Hullabaloo over Georgie and Bonnie's Pictures* 1979; *Jane Austen in Manhattan* 1980; *Quartet* 1981; *Heat and Dust* 1982; *The Bostonians* 1984; *A Room with a View* 1985; *Maurice* 1987; *Slaves of New York* 1989; *Mr and Mrs Bridge* 1990; *Howards End* 1992; *The Remains of the Day* 1993; *Jefferson in Paris* 1995; *Surviving Picasso* 1996; *A Soldier's Daughter Never Cries* 1998; *The Golden Bowl* 2000; *Le Divorce* 2003
Izzard, Bryan *Holiday on the Buses* 1973; *Julie and the Cadillacs* 1997

Jackson, David aka **Jackson, David S** *Death Train* 1993; *Night Watch* 1995; *Atomic Train* 1999
Jackson, Douglas aka **Jackson, Doug** *Whispers* 1990; *Midnight in St Petersburg* 1995; *The Ghost* 2000; *Nowhere in Sight* 2000
Jackson, Mick (1943–) *Chattahoochee* 1989; *LA Story* 1991; *The Bodyguard* 1992; *Clean Slate* 1994; *Indictment: the McMartin Trial* 1995; *Volcano* 1997; *Tuesdays with Morrie* 1999; *Live from Baghdad* 2002
Jackson, Pat (1916–) *Encore* 1951; *White Corridors* 1951; *Something Money Can't Buy* 1952; *The Feminine Touch* 1956; *The Birthday Present* 1957; *Virgin Island* 1958; *What a Carve Up!* 1961; *Don't Talk to Strange Men* 1962
Jackson, Peter (1961–) *Bad Taste* 1987; *Meet the Feebles* 1989; *Braindead* 1992; *Heavenly Creatures* 1994; *The Frighteners* 1996; *The Lord of the Rings: The Fellowship of the Ring* 2001; *The Lord of the Rings: The Two Towers* 2002; *The Lord of the Rings: The Return of the King* 2003
Jackson, Wilfred (1906–1988) *The Tortoise and the Hare* 1935; *The Old Mill* 1937; *Fantasia* 1940; *Saludos Amigos* 1943; *Song of the South* 1946; *Melody Time* 1948; *Cinderella* 1950; *Alice in Wonderland* 1951; *Peter Pan* 1953; *Lady and the Tramp* 1955
Jacobs, Alan *Nina Takes a Lover* 1993; *Diary of a Serial Killer* 1997; *American Gun* 2002
Jacoby, Joseph (1942–) *Hurry Up, or I'll Be 30* 1973; *The Great Georgia Bank Hoax* 1977
Jacquot, Benoît (1947–) *The School of Flesh* 1998; *Tosca* 2001
Jaeckin, Just (1940–) *Emmanuelle* 1974; *The Story of O* 1975; *Lady Chatterley's Lover* 1981
Jaglom, Henry (1941–) *A Safe Place* 1971; *Tracks* 1977; *Sitting Ducks* 1979; *National Lampoon's Movie Madness* 1981; *Can She Bake a Cherry Pie?* 1983; *Always* 1985; *Someone to Love* 1987; *Eating* 1990; *Venice/Venice* 1992; *Babyfever* 1994; *Last Summer in the Hamptons* 1995; *Déjà Vu* 1997; *Festival in Cannes* 2001
Jalili, Abolfazl (1957–) *Dance of Dust* 1991; *Don* 1998; *Delbaran* 2001; *Abjad* 2003
James (2), Steve *Hoop Dreams* 1994; *Prefontaine* 1997
Jameson, Jerry *Airport '77* 1977; *Raise the Titanic* 1980; *Starflight One* 1983; *Taken Away* 1996
Jancso, Miklos (1921–) *The Round-Up* 1966; *The Red and the White* 1967
Jankel, Annabel *DOA* 1988; *Super Mario Bros* 1993
Jaoui, Agnès (1964–) *Le Goût des Autres* 1999; *Look at Me* 2004
Jarman, Derek (1942–1994) *Sebastiane* 1976; *Jubilee* 1978; *The Tempest* 1979; *The Angelic Conversation* 1985; *Caravaggio* 1986; *Aria* 1987; *The Last of England* 1987; *War Requiem* 1988; *The Garden* 1990; *Edward II* 1991; *Blue* 1993; *Wittgenstein* 1993
Jarmusch, Jim (1953–) *Permanent Vacation* 1982; *Stranger than Paradise* 1984; *Down by Law* 1986; *Mystery Train* 1989; *Night on Earth* 1992; *Dead Man* 1995; *The Year of the Horse* 1997; *Ghost Dog: the Way of the Samurai* 1999; *Ten Minutes Older: the Trumpet* 2002; *Coffee and Cigarettes* 2003
Jarrott, Charles (1927–) *Anne of the Thousand Days* 1969; *Mary, Queen of Scots* 1971; *Lost Horizon* 1973; *The Dove* 1974; *The Littlest Horse Thieves* 1976; *The Other Side of Midnight* 1977; *The Last Flight of Noah's Ark* 1980; *The Amateur* 1981; *Condorman* 1981; *The Boy in Blue* 1986; *Danielle Steel's Changes* 1991
Jarvilaturi, Ilkka (1961–) *Darkness in Tallinn* 1993; *History Is Made at Night* 1999
Jasny, Vojtech (1925–) *All My Good Countrymen* 1968; *Great Land of the Small* 1987
Jason, Leigh (1904–1979) *The Bride Walks Out* 1936; *New Faces of 1937* 1937; *The Mad Miss Manton* 1938; *Lady for a Night* 1942; *Out of the Blue* 1947
Jason, Will (1899–1970) *Music Man* 1948; *Thief of Damascus* 1952
Jean, Vadim (1966–) *Leon the Pig Farmer* 1992; *Beyond Bedlam* 1993; *Clockwork Mice* 1994; *The Real Howard Spitz* 1998; *One More Kiss* 1999
Jeffrey, Tom (1938–) *Weekend of Shadows* 1978; *The Odd Angry Shot* 1979
Jeffries, Lionel (1926–) *The Railway Children* 1970; *The Amazing Mr Blunden* 1972; *Baxter* 1973; *Wombling Free* 1977; *The Water Babies* 1978
Jeffs, Christine (1963–) *Rain* 2001; *Sylvia* 2003
Jenkins, Michael (1946–) *Rebel* 1985; *The Heartbreak Kid* 1993
Jenson, Vicky *Shrek* 2001; *Shark Tale* 2004
Jessua, Alain (1932–) *Life Upside Down* 1964; *Shock Treatment* 1973; *Armaguedon* 1976; *Les Chiens* 1978; *Frankenstein 90* 1984; *En Toute Innocence* 1987
Jeunet, Jean-Pierre (1955–) *Delicatessen* 1990; *The City of Lost Children* 1995; *Alien: Resurrection* 1997; *Amélie* 2001; *A Very Long Engagement* 2004
Jewison, Norman (1926–) *Forty Pounds of Trouble* 1962; *The Thrill of It All* 1963; *Send Me No Flowers* 1964; *Art of Love* 1965; *The Cincinnati Kid* 1965; *The Russians Are Coming, the Russians Are Coming* 1966; *In the Heat of the Night* 1967; *The Thomas Crown Affair* 1968; *Gaily, Gaily* 1969; *Fiddler on the Roof* 1971; *Jesus Christ Superstar* 1973; *Rollerball* 1975; *FIST* 1978; *...And Justice for All* 1979; *Best Friends* 1982; *A Soldier's Story* 1984; *Agnes of God* 1985; *Moonstruck* 1987; *In Country* 1989; *Other People's Money* 1991; *Only You* 1994; *Bogus* 1996; *The Hurricane* 1999; *Dinner with Friends* 2001; *The Statement* 2003
Jia Zhang Ke (1970–) *Xiao Wu* 1997; *Platform* 2000; *Unknown Pleasures* 2002
Jires, Jaromil (1935–2001) *The Joke* 1968; *Labyrinth* 1991
Joannon, Léo aka **Joannon, Leo** (1904–1969) *Utopia* 1950; *Le Défroqué* 1953
Joanou, Phil (1961–) *Three O'Clock High* 1987; *U2 Rattle and Hum* 1988; *State of Grace* 1990; *Final Analysis* 1992; *Heaven's Prisoners* 1996
Jodorowsky, Alexandro (1929–) *El Topo* 1971; *The Holy Mountain* 1973; *Santa Sangre* 1989; *The Rainbow Thief* 1990
Joffe, Mark (1956–) *Grievous Bodily Harm* 1987; *Nightmaster* 1987; *Spotswood* 1991; *Cosi* 1996; *The Matchmaker* 1997; *The Man Who Sued God* 2001
Joffé, Roland (1945–) *The Killing Fields* 1984; *The Mission* 1986; *Shadow Makers* 1989; *City of Joy* 1992; *The Scarlet Letter* 1995; *Goodbye Lover* 1997; *Vatel* 2000
Johar, Karan (1972–) *Kuch Kuch Hota Hai* 1998; *Kabhi Khushi Kabhie Gham...* 2001
Johnson, Alan *To Be or Not to Be* 1983; *Solarbabies* 1986
Johnson, Clark (1954–) *Boycott* 2001; *SWAT* 2003
Johnson, Kenneth (1942–) *The Incredible Hulk* 1977; *Short Circuit 2* 1988; *Steel* 1997
Johnson, Lamont (1922–) *A Covenant with Death* 1967; *Kona Coast* 1968; *The McKenzie Break* 1970; *A Gunfight* 1971; *The Groundstar Conspiracy* 1972; *You'll Like My Mother* 1972; *The Last American Hero* 1973; *Fear on Trial* 1975; *Lipstick* 1976; *One on One* 1977; *Somebody Killed Her Husband* 1978; *Cattle Annie and Little Britches* 1980; *Spacehunter: Adventures in the Forbidden Zone* 1983; *The Man Next Door* 1996
Johnson, Mark Steven (1964–) *Simon Birch* 1998; *Daredevil* 2003
Johnson, Niall *The Big Swap* 1997; *The Ghost of Greville Lodge* 2000
Johnson, Nunnally (1897–1977) *Black Widow* 1954; *Night People* 1954; *How to Be Very, Very Popular* 1955; *The Man in the Gray Flannel Suit* 1956; *Oh, Men! Oh, Women!* 1957; *The Three Faces of Eve* 1957; *The Man Who Understood Women* 1959; *The Angel Wore Red* 1960
Johnson, Patrick Read (1964–) *Baby's Day Out* 1994; *Angus* 1995
Johnson, Tim *Antz* 1998; *Sinbad: Legend of the Seven Seas* 2003
Johnston, Aaron Kim *The Last Winter* 1989; *For the Moment* 1994
Johnston, Joe (1950–) *Honey, I Shrunk the Kids* 1989; *Rocketeer* 1991; *The Pagemaster* 1994; *Jumanji* 1995; *October Sky* 1999; *Jurassic Park III* 2001; *Hidalgo* 2003
Jolivet, Pierre (1952–) *Force Majeure* 1989; *En Plein Coeur* 1998
Jones, Chuck aka **Jones, Charles M** (1912–2002) *Duck Dodgers in the $24\frac{1}{2}$ Century* 1953; *One Froggy Evening* 1955; *What's Opera, Doc?* 1957; *The Dot and the Line* 1965; *The Phantom Tollbooth* 1969; *The Bugs Bunny/Road Runner Movie* 1979
Jones (3), David aka **Jones, David Hugh** (1934–) *Betrayal* 1982; *84 Charing Cross Road* 1986; *Jacknife* 1988; *The Trial* 1993; *A Christmas Carol* 1999; *Custody of the Heart* 2000
Jones, F Richard (1894–1930) *The Gaucho* 1927; *Bulldog Drummond* 1929
Jones, Harmon (1911–1972) *As Young as You Feel* 1951; *Bloodhounds of Broadway* 1952; *The Pride of St Louis* 1952; *The Kid from Left Field* 1953; *Gorilla at Large* 1954; *Princess of the Nile* 1954; *A Day of Fury* 1956; *Bullwhip* 1958; *Wolf Larsen* 1958
Jones (2), Mark (1953–) *Leprechaun* 1992; *Rumpelstiltskin* 1995
Jones, Terry (1942–) *Monty Python and the Holy Grail* 1975; *Monty Python's Life of Brian* 1979; *Monty Python's The Meaning of Life* 1983; *Personal Services* 1987; *Erik the Viking* 1989; *The Wind in the Willows* 1996
Jonze, Spike (1969–) *Being John Malkovich* 1999; *Adaptation.* 2002
Jordan, Glenn (1936–) *Les Misérables* 1978; *Only When I Laugh* 1981; *The Buddy System* 1984; *Mass Appeal* 1984; *Promise* 1986; *The Boys* 1991; *Barbarians at the Gate* 1993; *Legalese* 1998; *The Long Way Home* 1998; *Night Ride Home* 1999
Jordan, Gregor (1968–) *Two Hands* 1999; *Buffalo Soldiers* 2001; *Ned Kelly* 2003
Jordan, Neil (1950–) *Angel* 1982; *The Company of Wolves* 1984; *Mona Lisa* 1986; *High Spirits* 1988; *We're No Angels* 1989; *The*

Miracle 1990; *The Crying Game* 1992; *Interview with the Vampire: the Vampire Chronicles* 1994; *Michael Collins* 1996; *The Butcher Boy* 1997; *In Dreams* 1998; *The End of the Affair* 1999; *The Good Thief* 2002

Jost, Jon (1943–) *All the Vermeers in New York* 1990; *Sure Fire* 1990; *Frameup* 1993

Judge, Mike (1962–) *Beavis and Butt-head Do America* 1996; *Office Space* 1999

Julien, Isaac (1960–) *Young Soul Rebels* 1991; *Frantz Fanon: Black Skin White Mask* 1996

Junger, Gil *10 Things I Hate about You* 1999; *Black Knight* 2001

Juran, Nathan *aka* **Hertz, Nathan** *aka* **Juran, Nathan H** (1907–2002) *The Black Castle* 1952; *The Golden Blade* 1953; *Gunsmoke* 1953; *Law and Order* 1953; *Tumbleweed* 1953; *Drums across the River* 1954; *The Deadly Mantis* 1957; *Hellcats of the Navy* 1957; *20 Million Miles to Earth* 1957; *Attack of the 50 Foot Woman* 1958; *The Brain from Planet Arous* 1958; *Good Day for a Hanging* 1958; *The 7th Voyage of Sinbad* 1958; *Jack the Giant Killer* 1962; *The Siege of the Saxons* 1963; *East of Sudan* 1964; *First Men in the Moon* 1964; *Land Raiders* 1969

Jutra, Claude (1930–1986) *My Uncle Antoine* 1971; *Kamouraska* 1973

K

Kachyna, Karel (1924–2004) *The Ear* 1969; *The Last Butterfly* 1990

Kaczender, George (1933–) *In Praise of Older Women* 1978; *Agency* 1981; *Chanel Solitaire* 1981; *PrettyKill* 1987; *Danielle Steel's Vanished* 1995

Kadar, Jan (1918–1979) *The Shop on the High Street* 1965; *The Angel Levine* 1970; *Lies My Father Told Me* 1975; *Freedom Road* 1979

Kagan, Jeremy Paul *aka* **Kagan, Jeremy** (1945–) *Heroes* 1977; *Scott Joplin* 1977; *The Big Fix* 1978; *The Chosen* 1981; *The Sting II* 1983; *The Journey of Natty Gann* 1985; *Big Man on Campus* 1989; *By the Sword* 1992; *Roswell* 1994; *The Ballad of Lucy Whipple* 2001

Kahn, Cédric (1966–) *L'Ennui* 1998; *Roberto Succo* 2000; *Red Lights* 2003

Kalatozov, Mikhail *aka* **Kalatozov, Mikhail K** (1903–1973) *The Cranes Are Flying* 1957; *I Am Cuba* 1964; *The Red Tent* 1969

Kane, David *This Year's Love* 1999; *Born Romantic* 2000

Kane, Joseph *aka* **Kane, Joe** (1897–1975) *Billy the Kid Returns* 1938; *Shine On, Harvest Moon* 1938; *The Arizona Kid* 1939; *Rough Riders' Roundup* 1939; *Song of Texas* 1943; *The Yellow Rose of Texas* 1944; *The Cheaters* 1945; *Dakota* 1945; *Flame of the Barbary Coast* 1945; *The Plunderers* 1948; *Hoodlum Empire* 1952; *Ride the Man Down* 1952; *Fair Wind to Java* 1953; *The Maverick Queen* 1955; *The Road to Denver* 1955; *Timberjack* 1955; *Accused of Murder* 1956; *Thunder over Arizona* 1956

Kaneko, Shusuke *aka* **Kaneko, Shu** (1955–) *Summer Vacation: 1999* 1988; *Necronomicon* 1993

Kanew, Jeff *Eddie Macon's Run* 1983; *Revenge of the Nerds* 1984; *Gotcha!* 1985; *Tough Guys* 1986; *Troop Beverly Hills* 1989; *VI Warshawski* 1991

Kang Je-gyu (1962–) *Shiri* 1999; *Brotherhood* 2004

Kanganis, Charles T *Chance* 1990; *A Time to Die* 1991; *Intent to Kill* 1992; *3 Ninjas Kick Back* 1994; *Race the Sun* 1996; *Dennis the Menace Strikes Again* 1998; *K-911* 1999

Kanievska, Marek (1952–) *Another Country* 1984; *Less than Zero* 1987; *Where the Money Is* 2000

Kanin, Garson (1912–1999) *Bachelor Mother* 1939; *The Great Man Votes* 1939; *My Favorite Wife* 1940; *They Knew What They Wanted* 1940; *Tom, Dick and Harry* 1941; *Where It's At* 1969

Kanter, Hal (1918–) *Loving You* 1957; *I Married a Woman* 1958

Kaplan, Deborah *Can't Hardly Wait* 1998; *Josie and the Pussycats* 2001

Kaplan, Jonathan (1947–) *The Slams* 1973; *Truck Turner* 1974; *White Line Fever* 1975; *Mr Billion* 1977; *Over the Edge* 1979; *Heart like a Wheel* 1983; *Project X* 1987; *The Accused* 1988; *Immediate Family* 1989; *Love Field* 1992; *Unlawful Entry* 1992; *Bad Girls* 1994; *Reform School Girl* 1994; *Brokedown Palace* 1999

Kapoor, Raj (1924–1988) *Barsaat* 1949; *Sangam* 1964; *Bobby* 1973

Kapur, Shekhar (1945–) *Mr India* 1986; *Bandit Queen* 1994; *Elizabeth* 1998; *The Four Feathers* 2002

Karbelnikoff, Michael *Mobsters* 1991; *FTW* 1994

Karlson, Phil (1908–1985) *The Shanghai Cobra* 1945; *Dark Alibi* 1946; *Black Gold* 1947; *Ladies of the Chorus* 1949; *Lorna Doone* 1951; *Kansas City Confidential* 1952; *99 River Street* 1953; *They Rode West* 1954; *Five against the House* 1955; *Hell's Island* 1955; *The Phenix City Story* 1955; *Tight Spot* 1955; *The Brothers Rico* 1957; *Gunman's Walk* 1958; *Hell to Eternity* 1960; *Key Witness* 1960; *The Secret Ways* 1961; *The Young Doctors* 1961; *Kid Galahad* 1962; *Rampage* 1963; *The Silencers* 1966; *A Time for Killing* 1967; *The Wrecking Crew* 1969; *Hornet's Nest* 1970; *Ben* 1972; *Walking Tall* 1973; *Framed* 1975

Karn, Bill *Gang Busters* 1955; *Door-to-Door Maniac* 1961

Karson, Eric *The Octagon* 1980; *Hell Camp* 1986; *Black Eagle* 1988

Kasdan, Jake (1975–) *Zero Effect* 1997; *Orange County* 2001

Kasdan, Lawrence (1949–) *Body Heat* 1981; *The Big Chill* 1983; *Silverado* 1985; *The Accidental Tourist* 1988; *I Love You to Death* 1990; *Grand Canyon* 1991; *Wyatt Earp* 1994; *French Kiss* 1995; *Mumford* 1999; *Dreamcatcher* 2003

Kassovitz, Mathieu (1967–) *La Haine* 1995; *The Crimson Rivers* 2000; *Gothika* 2003

Katselas, Milton (1933–) *Butterflies Are Free* 1972; *40 Carats* 1973; *Report to the Commissioner* 1975; *When You Comin' Back, Red Ryder?* 1979

Katzin, Lee H (1935–2002) *Whatever Happened to Aunt Alice?* 1969; *Le Mans* 1971; *The Salzburg Connection* 1972; *World Gone Wild* 1988

Kaufman, Lloyd *aka* **Weil, Samuel** (1945–) *Class of Nuke 'em High* 1986; *The Toxic Avenger, Part II* 1988; *Sgt Kabukiman NYPD* 1991; *Tromeo & Juliet* 1996; *Terror Firmer* 1999

Kaufman, Philip (1936–) *Goldstein* 1963; *Frank's Greatest Adventure* 1967; *The Great Northfield Minnesota Raid* 1972; *The White Dawn* 1974; *Invasion of the Body Snatchers* 1978; *The Wanderers* 1979; *The Right Stuff* 1983; *The Unbearable Lightness of Being* 1988; *Henry & June* 1990; *Rising Sun* 1993; *Quills* 2000; *Twisted* 2003

Kaurismäki, Aki (1957–) *Crime and Punishment* 1983; *Hamlet Goes Business* 1987; *Ariel* 1988; *Leningrad Cowboys Go America* 1989; *I Hired a Contract Killer* 1990; *The Match Factory Girl* 1990; *Leningrad Cowboys Meet Moses* 1993; *Take Care of Your Scarf, Tatjana* 1994; *The Total Balalaika Show* 1994; *Drifting Clouds* 1996; *Juha* 1999; *The Man without a Past* 2002; *Ten Minutes Older: the Trumpet* 2002

Kaurismäki, Mika (1955–) *Tigrero: a Film That Was Never Made* 1994; *LA without a Map* 1998

Käutner, Helmut *aka* **Kautner, Helmut** (1908–1980) *The Last Bridge* 1954; *The Devil's General* 1955; *The Restless Years* 1958; *A Stranger in My Arms* 1959

Kawajiri, Yoshiaki *Lensman* 1984; *Wicked City* 1992

Kawalerowicz, Jerzy (1922–) *The Shadow* 1956; *The Devil and the Nun* 1960; *Pharaoh* 1966

Kay, Stephen *aka* **Kay, Stephen T** *The Last Time I Committed Suicide* 1996; *Get Carter* 2000; *Boogeyman* 2005

Kazan, Elia (1909–2003) *A Tree Grows in Brooklyn* 1945; *Boomerang!* 1947; *Gentleman's Agreement* 1947; *The Sea of Grass* 1947; *Pinky* 1949; *Panic in the Streets* 1950; *A Streetcar Named Desire* 1951; *Viva Zapata!* 1952; *Man on a Tightrope* 1953; *On the Waterfront* 1954; *East of Eden* 1955; *Baby Doll* 1956; *A Face in the Crowd* 1957; *Wild River* 1960; *Splendor in the Grass* 1961; *America, America* 1963; *The Arrangement* 1969; *The Visitors* 1972; *The Last Tycoon* 1976

Keach, James (1948–) *False Identity* 1990; *The Stars Fell on Henrietta* 1995

Keaton, Buster (1895–1966) *Neighbors* 1920; *One Week* 1920; *The Scarecrow* 1920; *The Paleface* 1921; *Day Dreams* 1922; *Our Hospitality* 1923; *The Three Ages* 1923; *The Navigator* 1924; *Sherlock Junior* 1924; *Go West* 1925; *Seven Chances* 1925; *Battling Butler* 1926; *The General* 1927

Keaton, Diane (1946–) *Heaven* 1987; *Wildflower* 1991; *Unstrung Heroes* 1995; *Hanging Up* 2000

Keen, Bob (1960–) *Proteus* 1995; *Shepherd on the Rock* 1995

Keighley, William (1889–1972) *Ladies They Talk About* 1933; *Easy to Love* 1934; *"G" Men* 1935; *Special Agent* 1935; *Bullets or Ballots* 1936; *The Green Pastures* 1936; *The Singing Kid* 1936; *God's Country and the Woman* 1937; *The Prince and the Pauper* 1937; *The Adventures of Robin Hood* 1938; *Each Dawn I Die* 1939; *The Fighting 69th* 1940; *No Time for Comedy* 1940; *Torrid Zone* 1940; *The Bride Came COD* 1941; *Four Mothers* 1941; *The Man Who Came to Dinner* 1941; *George Washington Slept Here* 1942; *The Street with No Name* 1948; *Rocky Mountain* 1950; *Close to My Heart* 1951; *The Master of Ballantrae* 1953

Keller, Patrick (1950–) *London* 1994; *Robinson in Space* 1997

Keller, Harry (1913–1987) *Rose of Cimarron* 1952; *Quantez* 1957; *Day of the Bad Man* 1958; *The Female Animal* 1958; *Voice in the Mirror* 1958; *Seven Ways from Sundown* 1960; *Tammy Tell Me True* 1961; *Six Black Horses* 1962; *Tammy and the Doctor* 1963; *The Brass Bottle* 1964; *In Enemy Country* 1968

Kellett, Bob (1927–) *Up Pompeii* 1971; *Up the Chastity Belt* 1971; *Our Miss Fred* 1972; *Up the Front* 1972; *Don't Just Lie There, Say Something!* 1973; *Are You Being Served?* 1977

Kellino, Roy (1912–1956) *The Last Adventurers* 1937; *The Silken Affair* 1957

Kelljan, Bob *aka* **Kelljchian, Robert** (1930–1982) *The Loves of Count Iorga, Vampire* 1970; *The Return of Count Yorga* 1971; *Scream Blacula Scream* 1973; *Act of Vengeance* 1974

Kellman, Barnet (1947–) *Key Exchange* 1985; *Straight Talk* 1992; *The Adventures of Slappy the Sea Lion* 1998

Kellogg, David (1952–) *Cool as Ice* 1991; *Inspector Gadget* 1999

Kellogg, Ray (1919–1981) *The Giant Gila Monster* 1959; *The Killer Shrews* 1959; *The Green Berets* 1968

Kelly, Gene (1912–1996) *On the Town* 1949; *Singin' in the Rain* 1952; *It's Always Fair Weather* 1955; *The Happy Road* 1956; *Invitation to the Dance* 1956; *The Tunnel of Love* 1958; *Gigot* 1962; *A Guide for the Married Man* 1967; *Hello, Dolly!* 1969; *The Cheyenne Social Club* 1970; *That's Entertainment, Part II* 1976

Kelly, Rory (1961–) *Sleep with Me* 1994; *Some Girls* 1998

Kennedy, Burt (1923–2001) *The Canadians* 1961; *Mail Order Bride* 1963; *The Rounders* 1965; *The Money Trap* 1966; *Return of the Seven* 1966; *The War Wagon* 1967; *Welcome to Hard Times* 1967; *The Good Guys and the Bad Guys* 1969; *Support Your Local Sheriff!* 1969; *Young Billy Young* 1969; *Dirty Dingus Magee* 1970; *The Deserter* 1971; *Hannie Caulder* 1971; *Support Your Local Gunfighter* 1971; *The Train Robbers* 1973; *The Killer inside Me* 1975; *Wolf Lake* 1979; *The Trouble with Spies* 1987; *Once upon a Texas Train* 1988; *Suburban Commando* 1991

Kenton, Erle C (1896–1980) *Island of Lost Souls* 1932; *You're Telling Me!* 1934; *The Ghost of Frankenstein* 1942; *Pardon My Sarong* 1942; *Who Done It?* 1942; *It Ain't Hay* 1943; *House of Frankenstein* 1944; *House of Dracula* 1945

Kern, James V (1909–1966) *The Doughgirls* 1944; *Never Say Goodbye* 1946; *The Second Woman* 1951; *Two Tickets to Broadway* 1951

Kerrigan, Lodge H (1964–) *Clean, Shaven* 1993; *Claire Dolan* 1998

Kershner, Irvin (1923–) *Stakeout on Dope Street* 1958; *The Young Captives* 1958; *The Hoodlum Priest* 1961; *A Face in the Rain* 1963; *The Luck of Ginger Coffey* 1964; *A Fine Madness* 1966; *One Born Every Minute* 1967; *Loving* 1970; *Up the Sandbox* 1972; *SPYS* 1974; *The Return of a Man Called Horse* 1976; *Raid on Entebbe* 1977; *Eyes of Laura Mars* 1978; *Star Wars Episode V: the Empire Strikes Back* 1980; *Never Say Never Again* 1983; *RoboCop 2* 1990

Keshishian, Alek *In Bed with Madonna* 1991; *With Honors* 1994

Keusch, Michael *Lena's Holiday* 1990; *Huck and the King of Hearts* 1993

Khan, Mehboob (1906–1944) *Andaz* 1949; *Mother India* 1957

Khleifi, Michel *Wedding in Galilee* 1987; *Canticle of the Stones* 1990

Kiarostami, Abbas (1940–) *The Traveller* 1974; *Where Is My Friend's House?* 1987; *Close-Up* 1989; *Homework* 1989; *And Life Goes On...* 1991; *Through the Olive Trees* 1994; *A Taste of Cherry* 1997; *The Wind Will Carry Us* 1999; *ABC Africa* 2001; *Ten* 2002; *Five* 2003

Kidron, Beeban (1961–) *Vroom* 1988; *Used People* 1992; *Shades of Fear* 1993; *To Wong Foo, Thanks for Everything, Julie Newmar* 1995; *Amy Foster* 1997; *Bridget Jones: the Edge of Reason* 2004

Kiersch, Fritz *Children of the Corn* 1984; *Tuff Turf* 1984; *Gor* 1987; *Under the Boardwalk* 1988; *Into the Sun* 1992

Kieslowski, Krzysztof (1941–1996) *The Scar* 1976; *Camera Buff* 1979; *No End* 1984; *Blind Chance* 1987; *A Short Film about Killing* 1988; *A Short Film about Love* 1988; *The Double Life of Véronique* 1991; *Three Colours Blue* 1993; *Three Colours White* 1993; *Three Colours Red* 1994

Kikoine, Gérard (1946–) *Dragonard* 1987; *Edge of Sanity* 1989; *Buried Alive* 1990

Killy, Edward *Seven Keys to Baldpate* 1935; *Murder on a Bridle Path* 1936; *Along the Rio Grande* 1941; *Nevada* 1944

Kilner, Clare *Janice Beard 45 WPM* 1999; *The Wedding Date* 2004

Kim Ji-woon (1964–) *The Quiet Family* 1998; *A Tale of Two Sisters* 2003

Kim Ki-Duk (1960–) *The Isle* 2000; *Bad Guy* 2001; *Spring, Summer, Autumn, Winter ... and Spring* 2003; *Samaritan Girl* 2004; *3-iron* 2004

Kimmins, Anthony (1901–1964) *Keep Fit* 1937; *I See Ice* 1938; *It's in the Air* 1938; *Come On George* 1939; *Trouble Brewing* 1939; *Mine Own Executioner* 1947; *Bonnie Prince Charlie* 1948; *Mr Denning Drives North* 1951; *The Captain's Paradise* 1953; *Smiley* 1956; *Smiley Gets a Gun* 1959; *The Amorous Prawn* 1962

King, Allan (1930–) *Warrendale* 1967; *Who Has Seen the Wind* 1977; *Silence of the North* 1981

King, George (1899–1966) *The Crimes of Stephen Hawke* 1936; *Sweeney Todd, the Demon Barber of Fleet Street* 1936; *The Ticket of Leave Man* 1937; *Sexton Blake and the Hooded Terror* 1938; *Crimes at the Dark House* 1939; *The Face at the Window* 1939; *Tomorrow We Live* 1942; *Candlelight in Algeria* 1943; *Gaiety George* 1946; *The Shop at Sly Corner* 1946

King, Henry (1888–1982) *Tol'able David* 1921; *Fury* 1923; *The White Sister* 1923; *Stella Dallas* 1925; *The Winning of Barbara Worth* 1926; *State Fair* 1933; *Marie Galante* 1934; *Way Down East* 1935; *The Country Doctor* 1936; *Lloyd's of London* 1936; *In Old Chicago* 1937; *Alexander's Ragtime Band* 1938; *Jesse James* 1939; *Stanley and Livingstone* 1939; *Chad Hanna* 1940; *Little Old New York* 1940; *Maryland* 1940; *Remember the Day* 1941; *A Yank in the RAF* 1941; *The Black Swan* 1942; *The Song of Bernadette* 1943; *Wilson* 1944; *A Bell for Adano* 1945; *Margie* 1946; *Captain from Castile* 1947; *Prince of Foxes* 1949; *Twelve O'Clock High* 1949; *The Gunfighter* 1950; *David and Bathsheba* 1951; *I'd Climb the Highest Mountain* 1951; *O Henry's Full House* 1952; *The Snows of Kilimanjaro* 1952; *Wait 'til the Sun Shines, Nellie* 1952; *King of the Khyber Rifles* 1953; *Love Is a Many-Splendored Thing* 1955; *Untamed* 1955; *Carousel* 1956; *The Sun Also Rises* 1957; *The Bravados* 1958; *Beloved Infidel* 1959; *This Earth Is Mine* 1959; *Tender Is the Night* 1961

King, Louis (1898–1962) *Charlie Chan in Egypt* 1935; *Bulldog Drummond Comes Back* 1937; *Bulldog Drummond's Revenge* 1937; *Bulldog Drummond in Africa* 1938; *Typhoon* 1940; *The Way of All Flesh* 1940; *Thunderhead – Son of Flicka* 1945; *Smoky* 1946; *Bob, Son of Battle* 1947; *Green Grass of Wyoming* 1948; *Mrs Mike* 1949; *Frenchie* 1950; *Powder River* 1953; *Dangerous Mission* 1954

King, Rick *Hard Choices* 1984; *Hot Shot* 1986; *The Killing Time* 1987; *Forced March* 1989; *Prayer of the Rollerboys* 1990; *Kickboxer III: the Art of War* 1992; *Quick* 1993; *Rules of Obsession* 1994

King, Zalman (1941–) *Two Moon Junction* 1988; *Wild Orchid* 1990; *Wild Orchid 2: Two Shades of Blue* 1992; *Delta of Venus* 1995; *In God's Hands* 1998

Kinney, Jack (1909–1992) *Saludos Amigos* 1943; *Victory through Air Power* 1943; *The Three Caballeros* 1944; *Make Mine Music* 1946; *Fun and Fancy Free* 1947; *Melody Time* 1948; *The Adventures of Ichabod and Mr Toad* 1949

Kinugasa, Teinosuke (1896–1982) *A Page of Madness* 1926; *Gate of Hell* 1953

Kitano, Takeshi (1948–) *Violent Cop* 1989; *Boiling Point* 1990; *A Scene at the Sea* 1991; *Sonatine* 1993; *Kids Return* 1996; *Hana-Bi* 1997; *Kikujiro* 1999; *Brother* 2000; *Dolls* 2002; *Zatoichi* 2003

Kizer, R J (1952–) *The Return of Godzilla* 1984; *Hell Comes to Frogtown* 1988
Kjellin, Alf (1920–1988) *Midas Run* 1969; *The McMasters* 1970
Klane, Robert *Thank God It's Friday* 1978; *Weekend at Bernie's II* 1992
Klapisch, Cédric (1962–) *Un Air de Famille* 1996; *When the Cat's Away...* 1996; *Pot Luck* 2002
Klein, William (1929–) *Far from Vietnam* 1967; *Muhammad Ali, the Greatest* 1974
Kleiser, Randal (1946–) *The Boy in the Plastic Bubble* 1976; *Grease* 1978; *The Blue Lagoon* 1980; *Summer Lovers* 1982; *Grandview, USA* 1984; *Flight of the Navigator* 1986; *Big Top Pee-wee* 1988; *Getting It Right* 1989; *White Fang* 1991; *Honey, I Blew Up the Kid* 1992; *It's My Party* 1996; *Shadow of Doubt* 1998
Klimov, Elem (1933–2003) *Agony* 1975; *Come and See* 1985
Kloves, Steve (1960–) *The Fabulous Baker Boys* 1989; *Flesh and Bone* 1993
Kluge, Alexander (1932–) *Yesterday Girl* 1966; *Germany in Autumn* 1978
Knopf, Edwin H (1899–1981) *Paramount on Parade* 1930; *The Law and the Lady* 1951
Knowles, Bernard (1900–1975) *A Place of One's Own* 1944; *The Magic Bow* 1946; *Easy Money* 1947; *Jassy* 1947; *The Man Within* 1947; *The Lost People* 1949; *The Perfect Woman* 1949; *The Reluctant Widow* 1950; *Park Plaza 605* 1953
Kobayashi, Masaki (1916–1996) *The Thick-Walled Room* 1953; *Somewhere under the Broad Sky* 1954; *The Human Condition* 1958; *Harakiri* 1962; *Kwaidan* 1964; *Rebellion* 1967; *The Empty Table* 1985
Koch, Chris *Snow Day* 2000; *A Guy Thing* 2002
Koch, Howard W (1916–2001) *Shield for Murder* 1954; *Big House, USA* 1955; *The Girl in Black Stockings* 1957; *Untamed Youth* 1957; *Andy Hardy Comes Home* 1958; *Frankenstein – 1970* 1958; *Violent Road* 1958; *Born Reckless* 1959; *The Last Mile* 1959; *Badge 373* 1973
Koepp, David (1964–) *The Trigger Effect* 1996; *Stir of Echoes* 1999; *Secret Window* 2004
Kohli, Kunal *Mujhse Dosti Karoge!* 2002; *Hum Tum* 2004
Kokkinos, Ana (1959–) *Only the Brave* 1994; *Head On* 1997
Kollek, Amos (1947–) *Goodbye New York* 1984; *Forever Lulu* 1987; *High Stakes* 1989; *Double Edge* 1992
Koller, Xavier (1944–) *Journey of Hope* 1990; *Squanto: the Last Great Warrior* 1994
Konchalovsky, Andrei *aka* **Mikhalkov-Konchalovsky, Andrei** (1937–) *The First Teacher* 1965; *Asya's Happiness* 1967; *Sibiriada* 1979; *Maria's Lovers* 1984; *Runaway Train* 1985; *Duet for One* 1986; *Shy People* 1987; *Homer and Eddie* 1989; *Tango & Cash* 1989; *The Inner Circle* 1991; *The Odyssey* 1997; *House of Fools* 2002
Kopple, Barbara (1946–) *Harlan County, USA* 1976; *Wild Man Blues* 1997
Korda, Alexander (1893–1956) *The Private Life of Helen of Troy* 1927; *Marius* 1931; *Wedding Rehearsal* 1932; *The Private Life of Henry VIII* 1933; *The Private Life of Don Juan* 1934; *Rembrandt* 1936; *The Thief of Bagdad* 1940; *That Hamilton Woman* 1941; *Perfect Strangers* 1945; *An Ideal Husband* 1947
Korda, Zoltan (1895–1961) *Sanders of the River* 1935; *Conquest of the Air* 1936; *Forget-Me-Not* 1936; *Elephant Boy* 1937; *The Drum* 1938; *The Four Feathers* 1939; *The Thief of Bagdad* 1940; *Jungle Book* 1942; *Sahara* 1943; *Counter-Attack* 1945; *The Macomber Affair* 1947; *Cry, the Beloved Country* 1951; *Storm over the Nile* 1955
Koreeda, Hirokazu *aka* **Kore-eda, Hirokazu** (1962–) *Maborosi* 1995; *After Life* 1998; *Distance* 2001; *Nobody Knows* 2003
Korine, Harmony (1974–) *Gummo* 1997; *julien donkey-boy* 1999
Korty, John (1936–) *The Autobiography of Miss Jane Pittman* 1974; *Alex and the Gypsy* 1976; *Oliver's Story* 1978; *Twice upon a Time* 1983; *Resting Place* 1986
Kosminsky, Peter *Wuthering Heights* 1992; *White Oleander* 2002
Koster, Henry (1905–1988) *One Hundred Men and a Girl* 1937; *Three Smart Girls* 1937; *The Rage of Paris* 1938; *First Love* 1939; *Three Smart Girls Grow Up* 1939; *It Started with Eve* 1941; *Music for Millions* 1944; *Two Sisters from Boston* 1946; *The Bishop's Wife* 1947; *The Unfinished Dance* 1947; *Come to the Stable* 1949; *The Inspector General* 1949; *Harvey* 1950; *My Blue Heaven* 1950; *Wabash Avenue* 1950; *Mr Belvedere Rings the Bell* 1951; *No Highway* 1951; *My Cousin Rachel* 1952; *O Henry's Full House* 1952; *Stars and Stripes Forever* 1952; *The Robe* 1953; *Desiree* 1954; *Good Morning, Miss Dove* 1955; *A Man Called Peter* 1955; *The Virgin Queen* 1955; *D-Day the Sixth of June* 1956; *The Power and the Prize* 1956; *My Man Godfrey* 1957; *The Naked Maja* 1959; *The Story of Ruth* 1960; *Flower Drum Song* 1961; *Mr Hobbs Takes a Vacation* 1962; *Take Her, She's Mine* 1963; *Dear Brigitte* 1966; *The Singing Nun* 1966
Kotcheff, Ted *aka* **Kotcheff, William T** (1931–) *Tiara Tahiti* 1962; *Life at the Top* 1965; *Two Gentlemen Sharing* 1969; *Billy Two Hats* 1973; *The Apprenticeship of Duddy Kravitz* 1974; *Fun with Dick and Jane* 1977; *Who Is Killing the Great Chefs of Europe?* 1978; *North Dallas Forty* 1979; *First Blood* 1982; *Split Image* 1982; *Uncommon Valor* 1983; *Joshua Then and Now* 1985; *Switching Channels* 1987; *Winter People* 1988; *Weekend at Bernie's* 1989; *Folks!* 1992; *The Shooter* 1994
Kötting, Andrew *Gallivant* 1996; *This Filthy Earth* 2001
Kouf, Jim (1951–) *Miracles* 1985; *Disorganized Crime* 1989; *Gang Related* 1997
Kounen, Jan (1964–) *Dobermann* 1997; *Blueberry* 2004
Kowalchuk, Bill *Rudolph the Red-Nosed Reindeer* 1998; *Rudolph the Red-Nosed Reindeer and the Island of the Misfit Toys* 2001
Kowalski, Bernard L (1929–) *Attack of the Giant Leeches* 1960; *Krakatoa, East of Java* 1969; *Macho Callahan* 1970; *Ssssssss* 1973
Kozintsev, Grigori (1905–1973) *The New Babylon* 1929; *Don Quixote* 1957; *Hamlet* 1964; *King Lear* 1970
Kragh-Jacobsen, Søren (1947–) *The Island on Bird Street* 1997; *Mifune* 1999; *Skagerrak* 2003
Kramer, Lloyd *Before Women Had Wings* 1997; *David and Lisa* 1998
Kramer, Stanley (1913–2001) *Not as a Stranger* 1955; *The Pride and the Passion* 1957; *The Defiant Ones* 1958; *On the Beach* 1959; *Inherit the Wind* 1960; *Judgment at Nuremberg* 1961; *It's a Mad Mad Mad Mad World* 1963; *Ship of Fools* 1965; *Guess Who's Coming to Dinner* 1967; *The Secret of Santa Vittoria* 1969; *RPM – Revolutions per Minute* 1970; *Bless the Beasts and Children* 1971; *Oklahoma Crude* 1973; *The Domino Principle* 1977; *The Runner Stumbles* 1979
Krasna, Norman (1909–1984) *Princess O'Rourke* 1943; *The Big Hangover* 1950; *The Ambassador's Daughter* 1956
Krasny, Paul (1935–2001) *Joe Panther* 1976; *Still Crazy like a Fox* 1987
Krish, John (1923–) *Unearthly Stranger* 1963; *The Wild Affair* 1963; *Decline and Fall... of a Birdwatcher* 1968; *The Man Who Had Power over Women* 1970
Krishnamma, Suri *A Man of No Importance* 1994; *New Year's Day* 1999
Kubrick, Stanley (1928–1999) *Fear and Desire* 1953; *Killer's Kiss* 1955; *The Killing* 1956; *Paths of Glory* 1957; *Spartacus* 1960; *Lolita* 1961; *Dr Strangelove, or How I Learned to Stop Worrying and Love the Bomb* 1963; *2001: a Space Odyssey* 1968; *A Clockwork Orange* 1971; *Barry Lyndon* 1975; *The Shining* 1980; *Full Metal Jacket* 1987; *Eyes Wide Shut* 1999
Kukunoor, Nagesh (1969–) *Hyderabad Blues* 1998; *Bollywood Calling* 2000
Kulik, Buzz (1923–1999) *The Explosive Generation* 1961; *The Yellow Canary* 1963; *Warning Shot* 1967; *Sergeant Ryker* 1968; *Villa Rides* 1968; *Riot* 1969; *Brian's Song* 1971; *Shamus* 1973; *The Lindbergh Kidnapping Case* 1976; *Kill Me If You Can* 1977; *The Hunter* 1980
Kull, Edward (1886–1946) *The New Adventures of Tarzan* 1935; *Tarzan and the Green Goddess* 1938
Kumble, Roger (1966–) *Cruel Intentions* 1999; *Cruel Intentions 2* 2000; *The Sweetest Thing* 2002
Kümel, Harry (1940–) *Daughters of Darkness* 1970; *Malpertuis* 1971
Kurosawa, Akira (1910–1998) *Sanshiro Sugata* 1943; *No Regrets for Our Youth* 1946; *Drunken Angel* 1948; *Stray Dog* 1949; *Rashomon* 1950; *The Idiot* 1951; *Ikiru* 1952; *Seven Samurai* 1954; *I Live in Fear* 1955; *The Lower Depths* 1956; *Throne of Blood* 1957; *The Hidden Fortress* 1958; *The Bad Sleep Well* 1960; *Yojimbo* 1961; *Sanjuro* 1962; *High and Low* 1963; *Red Beard* 1965; *Dodes'ka-Den* 1970; *Dersu Uzala* 1975; *Kagemusha* 1980; *Ran* 1985; *Akira Kurosawa's Dreams* 1990; *Rhapsody in August* 1990; *No, Not Yet* 1993
Kurosawa, Kiyoshi (1955–) *Serpent's Path* 1998; *Eyes of the Spider* 1999; *License to Live* 1999
Kurys, Diane (1948–) *Diabolo Menthe* 1977; *Entre Nous* 1983; *A Man in Love* 1987; *C'est la Vie* 1990; *Après l'Amour* 1992; *Six Days, Six Nights* 1994; *Les Enfants du Siècle* 1999
Kusturica, Emir (1954–) *When Father Was Away on Business* 1985; *Time of the Gypsies* 1988; *Arizona Dream* 1991; *Underground* 1995; *Black Cat, White Cat* 1998; *Super 8 Stories* 2001; *Life Is a Miracle* 2004
Kuzui, Fran Rubel *Tokyo Pop* 1988; *Buffy the Vampire Slayer* 1992
Kwan, Stanley (1957–) *Rouge* 1987; *The Actress* 1992
Kwapis, Ken *Sesame Street Presents: Follow That Bird* 1985; *Vibes* 1988; *He Said, She Said* 1991; *Dunston Checks In* 1996; *The Beautician and the Beast* 1997; *The Sisterhood of the Traveling Pants* 2005
Kwietniowski, Richard (1957–) *Love and Death on Long Island* 1998; *Owning Mahowny* 2002

L

La Cava, Gregory (1892–1952) *Running Wild* 1927; *Big News* 1929; *Laugh and Get Rich* 1931; *The Age of Consent* 1932; *The Half Naked Truth* 1932; *Symphony of Six Million* 1932; *Gabriel over the White House* 1933; *The Affairs of Cellini* 1934; *Gallant Lady* 1934; *What Every Woman Knows* 1934; *Private Worlds* 1935; *She Married Her Boss* 1935; *My Man Godfrey* 1936; *Stage Door* 1937; *Fifth Avenue Girl* 1939; *Primrose Path* 1940; *Unfinished Business* 1941; *Lady in a Jam* 1942; *Living in a Big Way* 1947
Labro, Philippe (1936–) *Without Apparent Motive* 1972; *The Inheritor* 1973; *Right Bank, Left Bank* 1984
LaBute, Neil (1963–) *In the Company of Men* 1997; *Your Friends & Neighbours* 1998; *Nurse Betty* 2000; *Possession* 2002; *The Shape of Things* 2003
Lachman, Harry (1886–1975) *Baby, Take a Bow* 1934; *George White's Scandals* 1934; *Dante's Inferno* 1935; *Charlie Chan at the Circus* 1936; *The Man Who Lived Twice* 1936; *Our Relations* 1936; *Charlie Chan in Rio* 1941
Lacombe, Georges (1902–1990) *Martin Roumagnac* 1946; *The Seven Deadly Sins* 1952; *The Light across the Street* 1956
Lado, Aldo *aka* **Lewis, George B** (1934–) *The Short Night of the Glass Dolls* 1971; *The Humanoid* 1979
Lafia, John *The Blue Iguana* 1988; *Child's Play 2* 1990; *Man's Best Friend* 1993
LaGravenese, Richard (1959–) *Living Out Loud* 1998; *A Decade under the Influence* 2003
Lahiff, Craig (1947–) *Fever* 1988; *Heaven's Burning* 1997; *Black and White* 2002
Laing, John *Beyond Reasonable Doubt* 1980; *Other Halves* 1984
LaLoggia, Frank (1954–) *Fear No Evil* 1980; *Lady in White* 1988; *The Haunted Heart* 1995
Laloux, René (1929–2004) *Fantastic Planet* 1973; *Light Years* 1988
Lam, Ringo *aka* **Lam Ling-Tung** (1954–) *City on Fire* 1987; *Wild Search* 1989; *Full Contact* 1992; *Twin Dragons* 1992; *Maximum Risk* 1996; *Full Alert* 1997; *Replicant* 2001
Lambert, Mary *Siesta* 1987; *Pet Sematary* 1989; *Pet Sematary II* 1992; *The In Crowd* 2000
Lamont, Charles (1898–1993) *Road Agent* 1941; *Hit the Ice* 1943; *The Merry Monahans* 1944; *Frontier Gal* 1945; *Salome, Where She Danced* 1945; *Slave Girl* 1947; *Ma and Pa Kettle* 1949; *Abbott and Costello in the Foreign Legion* 1950; *I Was a Shoplifter* 1950; *Abbott and Costello Meet the Invisible Man* 1951; *Abbott and Costello Meet Captain Kidd* 1952; *Abbott and Costello Go to Mars* 1953; *Abbott and Costello Meet Dr Jekyll and Mr Hyde* 1953; *Abbott and Costello Meet the Keystone Cops* 1955; *Abbott and Costello Meet the Mummy* 1955; *Francis in the Haunted House* 1956
Lamorisse, Albert (1922–1970) *White Mane* 1952; *Red Balloon* 1956
Lancaster, Burt (1913–1994) *The Kentuckian* 1955; *The Midnight Man* 1974
Landers, Lew *aka* **Friedlander, Louis** (1901–1962) *The Raven* 1935; *Stormy* 1935; *Danger Patrol* 1937; *Flight from Glory* 1937; *Annabel Takes a Tour* 1938; *Condemned Women* 1938; *Law of the Underworld* 1938; *Smashing the Rackets* 1938; *Bad Lands* 1939; *The Boogie Man Will Get You* 1942; *The Return of the Vampire* 1943; *Stars on Parade* 1944; *Seven Keys to Baldpate* 1947; *Thunder Mountain* 1947; *Stagecoach Kid* 1949; *Man in the Dark* 1953; *Captain Kidd and the Slave Girl* 1954
Landis, John (1950–) *Schlock* 1971; *The Kentucky Fried Movie* 1977; *National Lampoon's Animal House* 1978; *The Blues Brothers* 1980; *An American Werewolf in London* 1981; *Trading Places* 1983; *Twilight Zone: the Movie* 1983; *Into the Night* 1985; *Spies like Us* 1985; *Three Amigos!* 1986; *Amazon Women on the Moon* 1987; *Coming to America* 1988; *Oscar* 1991; *Innocent Blood* 1992; *Beverly Hills Cop III* 1994; *The Stupids* 1995; *Blues Brothers 2000* 1998; *Susan's Plan* 1998
Landres, Paul (1912–2001) *Last of the Badmen* 1957; *The Flame Barrier* 1958; *The Return of Dracula* 1958; *Go, Johnny, Go!* 1959; *Son of a Gunfighter* 1964
Lane, Andrew *Jake Speed* 1986; *Mortal Passions* 1989
Lane (3), Charles (1953–) *Sidewalk Stories* 1989; *True Identity* 1991
Lane, David *Thunderbirds Are Go!* 1966; *Thunderbird 6* 1968
Lanfield, Sidney (1900–1972) *The Last Gentleman* 1934; *Red Salute* 1935; *King of Burlesque* 1936; *One in a Million* 1936; *Sing, Baby, Sing* 1936; *Thin Ice* 1937; *Wake Up and Live* 1937; *Always Goodbye* 1938; *The Hound of the Baskervilles* 1939; *Second Fiddle* 1939; *Swanee River* 1939; *You'll Never Get Rich* 1941; *My Favorite Blonde* 1942; *Let's Face It* 1943; *The Meanest Man in the World* 1943; *Standing Room Only* 1944; *Bring on the Girls* 1945; *The Well Groomed Bride* 1946; *Where There's Life* 1947; *Station West* 1948; *Sorrowful Jones* 1949; *Follow the Sun: the Ben Hogan Story* 1951; *The Lemon Drop Kid* 1951; *Skirts Ahoy!* 1952
Lang, Fritz (1890–1976) *The Spiders* 1919; *Destiny* 1921; *Dr Mabuse, the Gambler* 1922; *The Nibelungen* 1924; *Metropolis* 1926; *Spies* 1928; *The Woman in the Moon* 1929; *M* 1931; *The Testament of Dr Mabuse* 1932; *Fury* 1936; *You Only Live Once* 1937; *You and Me* 1938; *The Return of Frank James* 1940; *Man Hunt* 1941; *Western Union* 1941; *Hangmen Also Die* 1943; *Ministry of Fear* 1945; *Scarlet Street* 1945; *The Woman in the Window* 1945; *Cloak and Dagger* 1946; *Secret beyond the Door* 1948; *An American Guerrilla in the Philippines* 1950; *House by the River* 1950; *Clash by Night* 1952; *Rancho Notorious* 1952; *The Big Heat* 1953; *The Blue Gardenia* 1953; *Human Desire* 1954; *Moonfleet* 1955; *Beyond a Reasonable Doubt* 1956; *While the City Sleeps* 1956; *The Indian Tomb* 1959; *The Tiger of Eschnapur* 1959; *The Thousand Eyes of Dr Mabuse* 1960
Lang, Perry (1959–) *Little Vegas* 1990; *Men of War* 1995
Lang, Richard *A Change of Seasons* 1980; *The Mountain Men* 1980
Lang, Rocky *All's Fair* 1989; *Race for Glory* 1989
Lang, Walter (1898–1972) *Meet the Baron* 1933; *The Mighty Barnum* 1934; *Hooray for Love* 1935; *Love before Breakfast* 1936; *Wife, Doctor and Nurse* 1937; *The Baroness and the Butler* 1938; *The Little Princess* 1939; *The Blue Bird* 1940; *Star Dust* 1940; *Tin Pan Alley* 1940; *Moon over Miami* 1941; *Weekend in Havana* 1941; *The Magnificent Dope* 1942; *Song of the Islands* 1942; *Coney Island* 1943; *Greenwich Village* 1944; *State Fair* 1945; *Claudia and David* 1946; *Sentimental Journey* 1946; *Mother Wore Tights* 1947; *Sitting Pretty* 1948; *When My Baby Smiles at Me* 1948; *You're My Everything* 1949; *Cheaper by the Dozen* 1950; *The Jackpot* 1950; *On the Riviera* 1951; *With a Song in My Heart* 1952; *Call Me Madam* 1953; *There's No Business like Show Business* 1954; *The King and I* 1956; *Desk Set* 1957; *But Not for Me* 1959; *Can-Can* 1960; *The Marriage-Go-Round* 1960
Langley, Noel (1911–1980) *The Pickwick Papers* 1952; *Our Girl Friday* 1953; *Svengali* 1954
Lanoff, Lawrence *Indecent Behavior* 1993; *Temptress* 1995
Lanza, Anthony M *The Glory Stompers* 1967; *The Incredible Two-Headed Transplant* 1971
Lanzmann, Claude (1925–) *Shoah* 1985; *Sobibor: 14 October 1943, 16:00* 2001
Lapine, James (1949–) *Impromptu* 1991; *Life with Mikey* 1993; *Passion* 1996; *Earthly Possessions* 1999

Larkin, John (1912–1965) *Quiet Please, Murder* 1942; *Circumstantial Evidence* 1945
Larry, Sheldon (1949–) *Terminal Choice* 1983; *A Christmas Romance* 1994; *The Color of Love: Jacey's Story* 2000
Lasseter, John (1957–) *Toy Story* 1995; *A Bug's Life* 1998; *Toy Story 2* 1999
Latham, Larry *An American Tail: the Treasure of Manhattan Island* 1998; *An American Tail: the Mystery of the Night Monster* 2000
Lathan, Stan (1945–) *Beat Street* 1984; *Go Tell It on the Mountain* 1984
Lattuada, Alberto (1914–) *Lights of Variety* 1950; *Love in the City* 1953; *Tempest* 1959; *Fraulein Doktor* 1968
Lau, Andrew *aka* **Lau Wai Keung** *To Live and Die in Tsimshatsui* 1994; *Young and Dangerous* 1996; *A Man Called Hero* 1999; *Infernal Affairs* 2002; *Infernal Affairs II* 2003; *Infernal Affairs 3* 2003
Laughlin, Michael *Strange Invaders* 1983; *Mesmerized* 1984
Laughlin, Tom *aka* **Frank, T C** *aka* **Laughlin, Frank** (1931–) *Born Losers* 1967; *Billy Jack* 1971; *The Trial of Billy Jack* 1974; *The Master Gunfighter* 1975; *Billy Jack Goes to Washington* 1977
Launder, Frank (1907–1997) *Millions like Us* 1943; *Two Thousand Women* 1944; *I See a Dark Stranger* 1946; *Captain Boycott* 1947; *The Blue Lagoon* 1949; *The Happiest Days of Your Life* 1950; *Lady Godiva Rides Again* 1951; *Folly to Be Wise* 1952; *The Belles of St Trinian's* 1954; *Geordie* 1955; *Blue Murder at St Trinian's* 1957; *The Bridal Path* 1959; *The Pure Hell of St Trinian's* 1960; *Joey Boy* 1965; *The Great St Trinian's Train Robbery* 1966; *The Wildcats of St Trinian's* 1980
Lautner, Georges (1926–) *Road to Salina* 1969; *There Was Once a Cop* 1969; *Man in the Trunk* 1973; *Someone Is Bleeding* 1974; *No Problem!* 1975; *To Kill a Rat* 1977; *Double Dare* 1981; *The Professional* 1981; *La Cage aux Folles III: "Elles" Se Marient* 1985
Lauzier, Gérard (1932–) *Petit Con* 1984; *Mon Père Ce Héros* 1991
Lauzon, Jean-Claude (1953–1997) *Night Zoo* 1987; *Léolo* 1992
Laven, Arnold (1922–) *Vice Squad* 1953; *Down Three Dark Streets* 1954; *The Rack* 1956; *The Monster That Challenged the World* 1957; *Slaughter on Tenth Avenue* 1957; *Anna Lucasta* 1958; *Geronimo* 1962; *The Glory Guys* 1965; *Rough Night in Jericho* 1967; *Sam Whiskey* 1969
Law, Clara (1954–) *Autumn Moon* 1992; *Erotique* 1994; *Floating Life* 1996
Lawrence, Quentin (1920–1979) *The Trollenberg Terror* 1958; *Cash on Demand* 1961; *The Man Who Finally Died* 1962; *The Secret of Blood Island* 1964
Lawrence, Ray *Bliss* 1985; *Lantana* 2001
Lawton, J F (1960–) *Cannibal Women in the Avocado Jungle of Death* 1989; *Pizza Man* 1991; *The Hunted* 1995
Lazarus, Ashley *E' Lollipop* 1975; *Golden Rendezvous* 1977
Le Borg, Reginald *aka* **LeBorg, Reginald** (1902–1989) *Calling Dr Death* 1943; *Dead Man's Eyes* 1944; *The Mummy's Ghost* 1944; *Weird Woman* 1944; *Wyoming Mail* 1950; *The Black Sleep* 1956; *The Flight That Disappeared* 1961; *Diary of a Madman* 1963
Le Chanois, Jean-Paul (1909–1985) *La Vie Est à Nous* 1936; *The Case of Dr Laurent* 1957; *Les Misérables* 1957
Leach, Wilford (1929–1988) *The Wedding Party* 1966; *The Pirates of Penzance* 1983
Leacock, Philip (1917–1990) *Appointment in London* 1952; *The Brave Don't Cry* 1952; *The Kidnappers* 1953; *The Spanish Gardener* 1956; *High Tide at Noon* 1957; *Innocent Sinners* 1957; *Take a Giant Step* 1959; *Let No Man Write My Epitaph* 1960; *Reach for Glory* 1962; *13 West Street* 1962; *The War Lover* 1962; *Tamahine* 1963; *Adam's Woman* 1970; *The Birdmen* 1971
Lean, David (1908–1991) *Major Barbara* 1941; *In Which We Serve* 1942; *This Happy Breed* 1944; *Blithe Spirit* 1945; *Brief Encounter* 1945; *Great Expectations* 1946; *Oliver Twist* 1948; *The Passionate Friends* 1948; *Madeleine* 1949; *The Sound Barrier* 1952; *Hobson's Choice* 1953; *Summertime* 1955; *The Bridge on the River Kwai* 1957; *Lawrence of Arabia* 1962; *Doctor Zhivago* 1965; *Ryan's Daughter* 1970; *A Passage to India* 1984
Leconte, Patrice (1947–) *Monsieur Hire* 1989; *The Hairdresser's Husband* 1990; *Tango* 1993; *Le Parfum d'Yvonne* 1994; *Ridicule* 1996; *The Girl on the Bridge* 1999; *La Veuve de Saint-Pierre* 2000; *L'Homme du Train* 2002; *Confidences Trop Intimes* 2004
Leder, Herbert J *Pretty Boy Floyd* 1960; *The Frozen Dead* 1966; *It!* 1966; *The Candy Man* 1969
Leder, Mimi (1952–) *The Peacemaker* 1997; *Deep Impact* 1998; *Pay It Forward* 2000
Leder, Paul (1926–1996) *I Dismember Mama* 1972; *Killing Obsession* 1994
Lederer, Charles (1906–1976) *Fingers at the Window* 1942; *Never Steal Anything Small* 1959
Lederman, D Ross (1895–1972) *Tarzan's Revenge* 1938; *The Body Disappears* 1941; *Shadows on the Stairs* 1941; *Strange Alibi* 1941
Leduc, Paul (1942–) *Reed: Insurgent Mexico* 1971; *Dollar Mambo* 1993
Lee, Ang (1954–) *Pushing Hands* 1991; *The Wedding Banquet* 1993; *Eat Drink Man Woman* 1994; *Sense and Sensibility* 1995; *The Ice Storm* 1997; *Ride with the Devil* 1999; *Crouching Tiger, Hidden Dragon* 2000; *Hulk* 2003
Lee, Damian *Food of the Gods II* 1989; *Abraxas* 1991; *Ski School* 1991; *The Donor* 1994; *Agent Red* 2000
Lee, Jack (1913–2002) *Once a Jolly Swagman* 1948; *The Wooden Horse* 1950; *South of Algiers* 1952; *Turn the Key Softly* 1953; *A Town like Alice* 1956; *Robbery under Arms* 1957; *The Captain's Table* 1958; *Circle of Deception* 1960
Lee, Malcolm D (1970–) *The Best Man* 1999; *Undercover Brother* 2002
Lee, Rowland V (1891–1975) *Paramount on Parade* 1930; *The Return of Dr Fu Manchu* 1930; *The Sign of Four* 1932; *Zoo in Budapest* 1933; *The Count of Monte Cristo* 1934; *Cardinal Richelieu* 1935; *The Three Musketeers* 1935; *Love from a Stranger* 1936; *One Rainy Afternoon* 1936; *The Toast of New York* 1937; *Son of Frankenstein* 1939; *Tower of London* 1939; *Son of Monte Cristo* 1940; *Captain Kidd* 1945
Lee, Spike (1957–) *She's Gotta Have It* 1986; *School Daze* 1988; *Do the Right Thing* 1989; *Mo' Better Blues* 1990; *Jungle Fever* 1991; *Malcolm X* 1992; *Crooklyn* 1994; *Clockers* 1995; *Get on the Bus* 1996; *Girl 6* 1996; *4 Little Girls* 1997; *He Got Game* 1998; *Summer of Sam* 1999; *Bamboozled* 2000; *The Original Kings of Comedy* 2000; *Ten Minutes Older: the Trumpet* 2002; *25th Hour* 2002; *She Hate Me* 2004
Lee Thompson, J (1914–2002) *Murder without Crime* 1950; *The Yellow Balloon* 1952; *The Weak and the Wicked* 1953; *For Better, for Worse* 1954; *An Alligator Named Daisy* 1955; *As Long as They're Happy* 1955; *The Good Companions* 1956; *Yield to the Night* 1956; *Woman in a Dressing Gown* 1957; *Ice Cold in Alex* 1958; *No Trees in the Street* 1958; *North West Frontier* 1959; *Tiger Bay* 1959; *I Aim at the Stars* 1960; *The Guns of Navarone* 1961; *Cape Fear* 1962; *Taras Bulba* 1962; *Kings of the Sun* 1963; *John Goldfarb, Please Come Home* 1964; *What a Way to Go!* 1964; *Return from the Ashes* 1965; *Eye of the Devil* 1966; *Before Winter Comes* 1968; *The Chairman* 1969; *Mackenna's Gold* 1969; *Country Dance* 1970; *Conquest of the Planet of the Apes* 1972; *Battle for the Planet of the Apes* 1973; *Huckleberry Finn* 1974; *The Reincarnation of Peter Proud* 1975; *St Ives* 1976; *The White Buffalo* 1977; *The Greek Tycoon* 1978; *The Passage* 1978; *Caboblanco* 1980; *Happy Birthday to Me* 1981; *10 to Midnight* 1983; *The Ambassador* 1984; *The Evil That Men Do* 1984; *King Solomon's Mines* 1985; *Firewalker* 1986; *Murphy's Law* 1986; *Death Wish 4: the Crackdown* 1987; *Messenger of Death* 1988; *Kinjite: Forbidden Subjects* 1989
Leeds, Herbert I (1900–1984) *The Cisco Kid and the Lady* 1939; *Mr Moto in Danger Island* 1939; *The Return of the Cisco Kid* 1939; *It Shouldn't Happen to a Dog* 1946; *Bunco Squad* 1950
Lehmann, Michael (1957–) *Heathers* 1989; *Hudson Hawk* 1991; *Meet the Applegates* 1991; *Airheads* 1994; *The Truth about Cats and Dogs* 1996; *My Giant* 1998; *40 Days and 40 Nights* 2002
Leifer, Neil *Yesterday's Hero* 1979; *Trading Hearts* 1988
Leigh, Mike (1943–) *Bleak Moments* 1971; *High Hopes* 1988; *Life Is Sweet* 1990; *Naked* 1993; *Secrets & Lies* 1995; *Career Girls* 1997; *Topsy-Turvy* 1999; *All or Nothing* 2002; *Vera Drake* 2004
Leiner, Danny *Dude, Where's My Car?* 2000; *Harold & Kumar Get the Munchies* 2004
Leisen, Mitchell (1898–1972) *Death Takes a Holiday* 1934; *Murder at the Vanities* 1934; *Hands across the Table* 1935; *The Big Broadcast of 1937* 1936; *The Big Broadcast of 1938* 1937; *Easy Living* 1937; *Swing High, Swing Low* 1937; *Artists and Models Abroad* 1938; *Midnight* 1939; *Arise, My Love* 1940; *Remember the Night* 1940; *Hold Back the Dawn* 1941; *I Wanted Wings* 1941; *The Lady Is Willing* 1942; *Take a Letter, Darling* 1942; *No Time for Love* 1943; *Frenchman's Creek* 1944; *Lady in the Dark* 1944; *Practically Yours* 1944; *Kitty* 1945; *To Each His Own* 1946; *Golden Earrings* 1947; *Suddenly It's Spring* 1947; *Dream Girl* 1948; *Bride of Vengeance* 1949; *Captain Carey, USA* 1950; *No Man of Her Own* 1950; *Darling, How Could You!* 1951; *The Mating Season* 1951; *Young Man with Ideas* 1952; *Tonight We Sing* 1953; *Bedevilled* 1955; *The Girl Most Likely* 1957
Leitch, Christopher *Courage Mountain* 1989; *Stolen Youth* 1996
Leland, David (1947–) *Wish You Were Here* 1987; *Checking Out* 1988; *The Big Man* 1990; *The Land Girls* 1997; *Concert for George* 2003
Lelouch, Claude (1937–) *Un Homme et une Femme* 1966; *Far from Vietnam* 1967; *Vivre pour Vivre* 1967; *Visions of Eight* 1973; *And Now My Love* 1974; *Happy New Year* 1974; *Second Chance* 1976; *Another Man, Another Chance* 1977; *Robert et Robert* 1978; *An Adventure for Two* 1979; *Les Uns et les Autres* 1981; *Edith and Marcel* 1983; *Long Live Life* 1984; *A Man and a Woman: 20 Years Later* 1986; *Les Misérables* 1995; *Men, Women: a User's Manual* 1996; *Chance or Coincidence* 1999; *11'09"01 - September 11* 2002
Lembeck, Michael (1948–) *The Santa Clause 2* 2002; *Connie and Carla* 2004
Lemont, John (1914–) *The Shakedown* 1959; *And Women Shall Weep* 1960; *Konga* 1960; *The Frightened City* 1961
Lemorande, Rusty *Journey to the Center of the Earth* 1989; *The Turn of the Screw* 1992
Leni, Paul (1885–1929) *Waxworks* 1924; *The Cat and the Canary* 1927; *The Last Warning* 1928; *The Man Who Laughs* 1928
Lenzi, Umberto *aka* **Milestone, Hank** (1931–) *Sandokan the Great* 1963; *The Pirates of Malaysia* 1964; *From Hell to Victory* 1979; *Cannibal Ferox* 1981
Leonard, Brett *The Lawnmower Man* 1992; *Hideaway* 1995; *Virtuosity* 1995
Leonard, Herbert B (1922–) *The Perils of Pauline* 1967; *Going Home* 1971
Leonard, Robert Z (1889–1968) *The Divorcee* 1930; *The Bachelor Father* 1931; *Susan Lenox: Her Fall and Rise* 1931; *Strange Interlude* 1932; *Dancing Lady* 1933; *Peg o' My Heart* 1933; *After Office Hours* 1935; *Escapade* 1935; *The Great Ziegfeld* 1936; *Piccadilly Jim* 1936; *The Firefly* 1937; *Maytime* 1937; *The Girl of the Golden West* 1938; *Broadway Serenade* 1939; *New Moon* 1940; *Pride and Prejudice* 1940; *Third Finger, Left Hand* 1940; *When Ladies Meet* 1941; *Ziegfeld Girl* 1941; *Stand by for Action* 1942; *The Man from Down Under* 1943; *Marriage Is a Private Affair* 1944; *Week-End at the Waldorf* 1945; *The Secret Heart* 1946; *Cynthia* 1947; *BF's Daughter* 1948; *The Bribe* 1949; *In the Good Old Summertime* 1949; *Nancy Goes to Rio* 1950; *The Clown* 1952; *Everything I Have Is Yours* 1952; *The Great Diamond Robbery* 1953; *Her Twelve Men* 1954; *Beautiful but Dangerous* 1955; *The King's Thief* 1955
Leone, Sergio (1929–1989) *The Colossus of Rhodes* 1961; *Sodom and Gomorrah* 1962; *A Fistful of Dollars* 1964; *For a Few Dollars More* 1965; *The Good, the Bad and the Ugly* 1966; *Once upon a Time in the West* 1968; *A Fistful of Dynamite* 1971; *Once upon a Time in America* 1984
Leong, Po Chih *The Wisdom of Crocodiles* 1998; *Cabin by the Lake* 2000
Lepage, Robert (1957–) *The Confessional* 1995; *Le Polygraphe* 1996; *Nô* 1998; *Possible Worlds* 2000
Lerner, Irving (1909–1976) *Murder by Contract* 1958; *City of Fear* 1959; *Studs Lonigan* 1960; *The Royal Hunt of the Sun* 1969
Lerner, Murray *From Mao to Mozart: Isaac Stern in China* 1980; *Message to Love* 1995
LeRoy, Mervyn (1900–1987) *Five Star Final* 1931; *Little Caesar* 1931; *High Pressure* 1932; *I Am a Fugitive from a Chain Gang* 1932; *Three on a Match* 1932; *Two Seconds* 1932; *Gold Diggers of 1933* 1933; *Hard to Handle* 1933; *Tugboat Annie* 1933; *The World Changes* 1933; *Hi, Nellie!* 1934; *I Found Stella Parish* 1935; *Oil for the Lamps of China* 1935; *Page Miss Glory* 1935; *Sweet Adeline* 1935; *Anthony Adverse* 1936; *Three Men on a Horse* 1936; *The King and the Chorus Girl* 1937; *They Won't Forget* 1937; *Fools for Scandal* 1938; *Escape* 1940; *Waterloo Bridge* 1940; *Blossoms in the Dust* 1941; *Johnny Eager* 1941; *Unholy Partners* 1941; *Random Harvest* 1942; *Madame Curie* 1943; *Thirty Seconds over Tokyo* 1944; *Without Reservations* 1946; *Homecoming* 1948; *Any Number Can Play* 1949; *East Side, West Side* 1949; *Little Women* 1949; *Quo Vadis* 1951; *Lovely to Look At* 1952; *Million Dollar Mermaid* 1952; *Latin Lovers* 1953; *Rose Marie* 1954; *Mister Roberts* 1955; *Strange Lady in Town* 1955; *The Bad Seed* 1956; *Toward the Unknown* 1956; *Home before Dark* 1958; *No Time for Sergeants* 1958; *The FBI Story* 1959; *Wake Me When It's Over* 1960; *The Devil at Four o'Clock* 1961; *A Majority of One* 1961; *Gypsy* 1962; *Mary, Mary* 1963; *Moment to Moment* 1966
Lester, Mark L (1946–) *Truck Stop Women* 1974; *Stunts* 1977; *Roller Boogie* 1979; *Class of 1984* 1982; *Firestarter* 1984; *Commando* 1985; *Armed and Dangerous* 1986; *Class of 1999* 1990; *Showdown in Little Tokyo* 1991; *Double Take* 1997; *Blowback* 1999; *Hitman's Run* 1999
Lester, Richard *aka* **Lester, Dick** (1932–) *The Running, Jumping and Standing Still Film* 1959; *It's Trad, Dad* 1961; *The Mouse on the Moon* 1963; *A Hard Day's Night* 1964; *Help!* 1965; *The Knack... and How to Get It* 1965; *A Funny Thing Happened on the Way to the Forum* 1966; *How I Won the War* 1967; *Petulia* 1968; *The Bed Sitting Room* 1969; *The Three Musketeers* 1973; *The Four Musketeers* 1974; *Juggernaut* 1974; *Royal Flash* 1975; *The Ritz* 1976; *Robin and Marian* 1976; *Butch and Sundance: the Early Days* 1979; *Cuba* 1979; *Superman II* 1980; *Superman III* 1983; *Finders Keepers* 1984; *The Return of the Musketeers* 1989; *Get Back* 1991
Lettich, Sheldon (1962–) *AWOL* 1990; *Double Impact* 1991; *Only the Strong* 1993; *The Order* 2001
Letts, Don *The Punk Rock Movie* 1978; *Dancehall Queen* 1996
Levant, Brian (1952–) *Problem Child 2* 1991; *Beethoven* 1992; *The Flintstones* 1994; *Little Giants* 1994; *Jingle All the Way* 1996; *The Flintstones in Viva Rock Vegas* 2000; *Snow Dogs* 2002; *Are We There Yet?* 2005
Levey, William A (1943–) *The Happy Hooker Goes to Washington* 1977; *Skatetown, USA* 1979; *Lightning the White Stallion* 1986
Levin, Henry (1901–1980) *Cry of the Werewolf* 1944; *The Bandit of Sherwood Forest* 1946; *The Guilt of Janet Ames* 1947; *The Gallant Blade* 1948; *The Man from Colorado* 1948; *And Baby Makes Three* 1949; *Jolson Sings Again* 1949; *Convicted* 1950; *The Petty Girl* 1950; *Belles on Their Toes* 1952; *The Farmer Takes a Wife* 1953; *The President's Lady* 1953; *The Dark Avenger* 1955; *April Love* 1957; *The Lonely Man* 1957; *A Nice Little Bank That Should Be Robbed* 1958; *Holiday for Lovers* 1959; *Journey to the Center of the Earth* 1959; *The Remarkable Mr Pennypacker* 1959; *Where the Boys Are* 1960; *Come Fly with Me* 1962; *If a Man Answers* 1962; *The Wonderful World of the Brothers Grimm* 1962; *Genghis Khan* 1964; *Honeymoon Hotel* 1964; *Murderers' Row* 1966; *The Ambushers* 1967; *The Desperados* 1969; *That Man Bolt* 1973; *The Treasure Seekers* 1977; *Run for the Roses* 1978
Levin, Marc *The Last Party* 1993; *Slam* 1998; *Whiteboys* 1999; *Martin Scorsese Presents the Blues: Godfathers and Sons* 2003
Levin, Peter *Death in the Shadows* 1998; *Homeless to Harvard: the Liz Murray Story* 2003
Levinson, Barry (1942–) *Diner* 1982; *The Natural* 1984; *Young Sherlock Holmes* 1985; *Good Morning, Vietnam* 1987; *Tin Men* 1987; *Rain Man* 1988; *Avalon* 1990; *Bugsy* 1991; *Toys* 1992; *Disclosure* 1994; *Jimmy Hollywood* 1994; *Sleepers* 1996; *Wag the Dog* 1997; *Sphere* 1998; *Liberty Heights* 1999; *An Everlasting Piece* 2000; *Bandits* 2001; *Envy* 2003

Levitow, Abe (1922–1975) *Gay Purr-ee* 1962; *The Phantom Tollbooth* 1969

Levy, Eugene (1946–) *Once upon a Crime* 1992; *Sodbusters* 1994

Levy, Ralph (1920–2001) *Bedtime Story* 1964; *Do Not Disturb* 1965

Levy, Shawn *Big Fat Liar* 2002; *Cheaper by the Dozen* 2003; *Just Married* 2003

Levy, Shuki *Blind Vision* 1992; *Turbo: a Power Rangers Adventure* 1997

Lewin, Albert (1916–1996) *The Moon and Sixpence* 1942; *The Picture of Dorian Gray* 1945; *The Private Affairs of Bel Ami* 1947; *Pandora and the Flying Dutchman* 1950; *Saadia* 1953; *The Living Idol* 1955

Lewin, Ben (1946–) *Georgia* 1988; *The Favour, the Watch and the Very Big Fish* 1991; *Paperback Romance* 1994

Lewis, Herschell Gordon aka **Lewis, Herschell G** (1926–) *Blood Feast* 1963; *Two Thousand Maniacs!* 1964; *Color Me Blood Red* 1965; *The Gruesome Twosome* 1967; *She-Devils on Wheels* 1968; *The Wizard of Gore* 1970; *The Gore-Gore Girls* 1972

Lewis, Jay (1914–1969) *The Baby and the Battleship* 1956; *Invasion Quartet* 1961; *Live Now – Pay Later* 1962

Lewis, Jerry (1926–) *The Bellboy* 1960; *The Errand Boy* 1961; *The Ladies' Man* 1961; *The Nutty Professor* 1963; *The Patsy* 1964; *The Family Jewels* 1965; *Three on a Couch* 1966; *The Big Mouth* 1967; *One More Time* 1970; *Which Way to the Front?* 1970; *Hardly Working* 1981; *Smorgasbord* 1983

Lewis, Joseph H aka **Lewis, Joseph** (1907–2000) *Boys of the City* 1940; *That Gang of Mine* 1940; *Invisible Ghost* 1941; *Pride of the Bowery* 1941; *The Mad Doctor of Market Street* 1942; *The Falcon in San Francisco* 1945; *My Name Is Julia Ross* 1945; *So Dark the Night* 1946; *The Return of October* 1948; *Gun Crazy* 1949; *The Undercover Man* 1949; *A Lady without Passport* 1950; *Desperate Search* 1952; *Retreat, Hell!* 1952; *Cry of the Hunted* 1953; *The Big Combo* 1955; *A Lawless Street* 1955; *Seventh Cavalry* 1956; *The Halliday Brand* 1957; *Terror in a Texas Town* 1958

Lewis (1), Robert (1909–1997) *Ziegfeld Follies* 1944; *Anything Goes* 1956

Lewis, Robert Michael *Agatha Christie's A Caribbean Mystery* 1983; *Agatha Christie's Sparkling Cyanide* 1983

Leytes, Joseph aka **Leytes, Josef** *Valley of Mystery* 1967; *The Counterfeit Killer* 1968

L'Herbier, Marcel (1888–1979) *L'Inhumaine* 1923; *La Nuit Fantastique* 1942

Liapis, Peter *Captured* 1998; *Alone with a Stranger* 2000

Lieberman, Jeff *Blue Sunshine* 1976; *Squirm* 1976; *Just before Dawn* 1980; *Remote Control* 1988

Lieberman, Robert (1941–) *Table for Five* 1983; *All I Want for Christmas* 1991; *Fire in the Sky* 1993; *D3: the Mighty Ducks* 1996

Lifshitz, Sébastien (1968–) *Presque Rien* 2000; *Wild Side* 2004

Lima, Kevin (1962–) *A Goofy Movie* 1995; *Tarzan* 1999; *102 Dalmatians* 2000

Liman, Doug (1965–) *Getting In* 1994; *Swingers* 1996; *Go* 1999; *The Bourne Identity* 2002; *Mr & Mrs Smith* 2005

Lindsay-Hogg, Michael (1940–) *Let It Be* 1970; *Nasty Habits* 1976; *Nazi Hunter: the Beate Klarsfeld Story* 1986; *The Object of Beauty* 1991; *Frankie Starlight* 1995; *The Rolling Stones Rock and Roll Circus* 1995; *Guy* 1996

Link, Caroline (1964–) *Beyond Silence* 1996; *Nowhere in Africa* 2001

Linklater, Richard (1961–) *Slacker* 1989; *Dazed and Confused* 1993; *Before Sunrise* 1995; *subUrbia* 1996; *The Newton Boys* 1998; *Tape* 2001; *Waking Life* 2001; *The School of Rock* 2003; *Before Sunset* 2004

Linson, Art (1942–) *Where the Buffalo Roam* 1980; *The Wild Life* 1984

Lipstadt, Aaron (1952–) *Android* 1982; *City Limits* 1985

Lisberger, Steven (1951–) *Animalympics* 1979; *Tron* 1982; *Hot Pursuit* 1987; *Slipstream* 1989

Little, Dwight H aka **Little, Dwight** *Getting Even* 1986; *Halloween 4: the Return of Michael Myers* 1988; *The Phantom of the Opera* 1989; *Marked for Death* 1990; *Rapid Fire* 1992; *Free Willy 2: the Adventure Home* 1995; *Murder at 1600* 1997; *Anacondas: the Hunt for the Blood Orchid* 2004

Litvak, Anatole aka **Litvak, Major Anatole** (1902–1974) *Mayerling* 1936; *Tovarich* 1937; *The Woman I Love* 1937; *The Amazing Dr Clitterhouse* 1938; *The Sisters* 1938; *Confessions of a Nazi Spy* 1939; *All This, and Heaven Too* 1940; *Castle on the Hudson* 1940; *City for Conquest* 1940; *Blues in the Night* 1941; *Out of the Fog* 1941; *This above All* 1942; *The Battle of Russia* 1943; *Prelude to War* 1943; *The Long Night* 1947; *The Snake Pit* 1948; *Sorry, Wrong Number* 1948; *Decision before Dawn* 1951; *Act of Love* 1953; *The Deep Blue Sea* 1955; *Anastasia* 1956; *The Journey* 1959; *Goodbye Again* 1961; *Five Miles to Midnight* 1963; *The Night of the Generals* 1966; *The Lady in the Car with Glasses and a Gun* 1970

Lizzani, Carlo (1922–) *Love in the City* 1953; *The Dirty Game* 1965; *Kill and Pray* 1967; *The Last Days of Mussolini* 1974

Llosa, Luis *Hour of the Assassin* 1987; *Sniper* 1992; *800 Leagues down the Amazon* 1993; *The Specialist* 1994; *Anaconda* 1997

Lloyd, Frank (1886–1960) *Oliver Twist* 1922; *The Sea Hawk* 1924; *The Divine Lady* 1928; *Drag* 1929; *East Lynne* 1931; *Berkeley Square* 1933; *Cavalcade* 1933; *Mutiny on the Bounty* 1935; *Under Two Flags* 1936; *Wells Fargo* 1937; *If I Were King* 1938; *Rulers of the Sea* 1939; *The Howards of Virginia* 1940; *Forever and a Day* 1943; *Blood on the Sun* 1945; *The Shanghai Story* 1954; *The Last Command* 1955

Lo Wei (1918–1996) *The Big Boss* 1971; *Fist of Fury* 1972

Loach, Ken aka **Loach, Kenneth** (1936–) *Poor Cow* 1967; *Kes* 1969; *Family Life* 1971; *Black Jack* 1979; *Looks and Smiles* 1981; *Fatherland* 1986; *Hidden Agenda* 1990; *Riff-Raff* 1991; *Raining Stones* 1993; *Ladybird Ladybird* 1994; *Land and Freedom* 1995; *Carla's Song* 1996; *My Name Is Joe* 1998; *Bread and Roses* 2000; *The Navigators* 2001; *11'09''01 – September 11* 2002; *Sweet Sixteen* 2002; *Ae Fond Kiss...* 2004

Locke, Sondra (1947–) *Ratboy* 1986; *Impulse* 1990; *Death in Small Doses* 1995

Logan, Joshua (1908–1988) *I Met My Love Again* 1938; *Picnic* 1955; *Bus Stop* 1956; *Sayonara* 1957; *South Pacific* 1958; *Fanny* 1961; *Ensign Pulver* 1964; *Camelot* 1967; *Paint Your Wagon* 1969

Logan, Stanley (1885–1953) *First Lady* 1937; *The Falcon's Brother* 1942

Logothetis, Dimitri *The Closer* 1990; *Body Shot* 1994; *Hungry for You* 1996

Lombardi, Francisco José (1950–) *The City and the Dogs* 1985; *No Mercy* 1994

Lommel, Ulli aka **Van Cleef, Mario** (1944–) *Brainwaves* 1982; *Orbit* 1996

Loncraine, Richard (1946–) *Slade in Flame* 1974; *Full Circle* 1977; *Brimstone and Treacle* 1982; *The Missionary* 1982; *Bellman & True* 1987; *Richard III* 1995; *My House in Umbria* 2002; *Wimbledon* 2004

London, Jerry (1937–) *The Scarlet and the Black* 1983; *Rent-a-Cop* 1988; *Victim of Love* 1991; *I Spy Returns* 1994; *Take Me Home: the John Denver Story* 2000

Long, Stanley aka **Long, Stanley A** *Adventures of a Taxi Driver* 1975; *Adventures of a Private Eye* 1977; *Adventures of a Plumber's Mate* 1978

Lord, Jean-Claude (1943–) *Visiting Hours* 1982; *Eddie and the Cruisers II: Eddie Lives!* 1989

Lorentz, Pare (1905–1992) *The Plow That Broke the Plains* 1934; *The River* 1937

Losey, Joseph aka **Hanbury, Victor** aka **Walton, Joseph** (1909–1984) *The Boy with Green Hair* 1948; *The Lawless* 1950; *The Big Night* 1951; *M* 1951; *The Prowler* 1951; *The Sleeping Tiger* 1954; *A Man on the Beach* 1955; *The Intimate Stranger* 1956; *Time without Pity* 1957; *The Gypsy and the Gentleman* 1958; *Blind Date* 1959; *The Criminal* 1960; *The Damned* 1961; *Eva* 1962; *The Servant* 1963; *King and Country* 1964; *Modesty Blaise* 1966; *Accident* 1967; *Boom* 1968; *Secret Ceremony* 1968; *Figures in a Landscape* 1970; *The Go-Between* 1971; *The Assassination of Trotsky* 1972; *A Doll's House* 1973; *Galileo* 1974; *The Romantic Englishwoman* 1975; *Mr Klein* 1976; *Roads to the South* 1978; *Don Giovanni* 1979; *Steaming* 1985

Lourié, Eugène (1905–1991) *The Beast from 20,000 Fathoms* 1953; *The Colossus of New York* 1958; *The Giant Behemoth* 1959; *Gorgo* 1961

Love, Nick *Goodbye Charlie Bright* 2000; *The Football Factory* 2004

Lovy, Steven *Circuitry Man* 1990; *Plughead Rewired: Circuitry Man II* 1994

Lowney, Declan *Time Will Tell* 1992; *Wild about Harry* 2000

Lowry, Dick *Smokey and the Bandit III* 1983; *Agatha Christie's Murder with Mirrors* 1985; *Unconquered* 1989; *The Price of Vengeance* 1994; *Forgotten Sins* 1996; *In the Line of Duty: Smoke Jumpers* 1996; *Last Stand at Saber River* 1997; *Two Came Back* 1997; *Mr Murder* 1998; *Atomic Train* 1999

Lubin, Arthur (1898–1995) *California Straight Ahead* 1937; *Buck Privates* 1941; *Hold That Ghost* 1941; *In the Navy* 1941; *Keep 'em Flying* 1941; *Ride 'em Cowboy* 1942; *Phantom of the Opera* 1943; *White Savage* 1943; *Ali Baba and the Forty Thieves* 1944; *Francis* 1949; *Impact* 1949; *Francis Goes to the Races* 1951; *Rhubarb* 1951; *Francis Goes to West Point* 1952; *It Grows on Trees* 1952; *Francis Covers the Big Town* 1953; *South Sea Woman* 1953; *Francis Joins the WACS* 1954; *Star of India* 1954; *Footsteps in the Fog* 1955; *Francis in the Navy* 1955; *Lady Godiva* 1955; *The First Travelling Saleslady* 1956; *Escapade in Japan* 1957; *The Incredible Mr Limpet* 1964

Lubitsch, Ernst (1892–1947) *The Oyster Princess* 1919; *Anna Boleyn* 1920; *Rosita* 1923; *The Marriage Circle* 1924; *Kiss Me Again* 1925; *Lady Windermere's Fan* 1925; *So This Is Paris* 1926; *The Student Prince in Old Heidelberg* 1927; *The Patriot* 1928; *Eternal Love* 1929; *The Love Parade* 1929; *Monte Carlo* 1930; *Paramount on Parade* 1930; *The Smiling Lieutenant* 1931; *If I Had a Million* 1932; *The Man I Killed* 1932; *One Hour with You* 1932; *Trouble in Paradise* 1932; *Design for Living* 1933; *The Merry Widow* 1934; *Angel* 1937; *Bluebeard's Eighth Wife* 1938; *Ninotchka* 1939; *The Shop around the Corner* 1940; *That Uncertain Feeling* 1941; *To Be or Not to Be* 1942; *Heaven Can Wait* 1943; *Prelude to War* 1943; *Cluny Brown* 1946; *That Lady in Ermine* 1948

Lucas, George (1945–) *THX 1138* 1971; *American Graffiti* 1973; *Star Wars Episode IV: a New Hope* 1977; *Star Wars Episode I: the Phantom Menace* 1999; *Star Wars Episode II: Attack of the Clones* 2002; *Star Wars Episode III: Revenge of the Sith* 2005

Ludwig, Edward aka **Fuhr, Charles** (1898–1982) *Old Man Rhythm* 1935; *Fatal Lady* 1936; *The Last Gangster* 1937; *That Certain Age* 1938; *Swiss Family Robinson* 1940; *Bomber's Moon* 1943; *The Fighting Seabees* 1944; *The Big Wheel* 1949; *Wake of the Red Witch* 1949; *Big Jim McLain* 1952; *Jivaro* 1954; *The Black Scorpion* 1957

Luhrmann, Baz (1962–) *Strictly Ballroom* 1992; *William Shakespeare's Romeo + Juliet* 1996; *Moulin Rouge!* 2001

Luketic, Robert (1973–) *Legally Blonde* 2001; *Win a Date with Tad Hamilton!* 2004; *Monster-in-Law* 2005

Lumet, Sidney (1924–) *12 Angry Men* 1957; *Stage Struck* 1958; *That Kind of Woman* 1959; *The Fugitive Kind* 1960; *Long Day's Journey into Night* 1962; *Fail-Safe* 1964; *The Hill* 1965; *The Pawnbroker* 1965; *The Deadly Affair* 1966; *The Group* 1966; *The Appointment* 1968; *Bye Bye Braverman* 1968; *The Sea Gull* 1968; *King: a Filmed Record... Montgomery to Memphis* 1970; *Last of the Mobile Hot-Shots* 1970; *The Anderson Tapes* 1971; *Child's Play* 1972; *The Offence* 1972; *Serpico* 1973; *Lovin' Molly* 1974; *Murder on the Orient Express* 1974; *Dog Day Afternoon* 1975; *Network* 1976; *Equus* 1977; *The Wiz* 1978; *Just Tell Me What You Want* 1980; *Prince of the City* 1981; *Deathtrap* 1982; *The Verdict* 1982; *Daniel* 1983; *Garbo Talks* 1984; *The Morning After* 1986; *Power* 1986; *Running on Empty* 1988; *Family Business* 1989; *Q & A* 1990; *A Stranger among Us* 1992; *Guilty as Sin* 1993; *Critical Care* 1997; *Night Falls on Manhattan* 1997; *Gloria* 1998

Luna, Bigas (1946–) *Anguish* 1986; *Lola* 1986; *The Ages of Lulu* 1990; *Jamon Jamon* 1992; *Golden Balls* 1993; *The Tit and the Moon* 1994; *The Chambermaid on the Titanic* 1997

Lupino, Ida (1914–1995) *Outrage* 1950; *Hard, Fast and Beautiful* 1951; *The Bigamist* 1953; *The Hitch-Hiker* 1953; *The Trouble with Angels* 1966

Lurie, Rod (1962–) *Deterrence* 1999; *The Contender* 2000; *The Last Castle* 2001

Luske, Hamilton aka **Luske, Hamilton S** (1903–1968) *Fantasia* 1940; *Pinocchio* 1940; *The Reluctant Dragon* 1941; *Saludos Amigos* 1943; *Make Mine Music* 1946; *Fun and Fancy Free* 1947; *Melody Time* 1948; *So Dear to My Heart* 1949; *Cinderella* 1950; *Alice in Wonderland* 1951; *Peter Pan* 1953; *Lady and the Tramp* 1955; *One Hundred and One Dalmatians* 1960

Lussier, Patrick *Dracula 2001* 2000; *The Prophecy 3: the Ascent* 2000

Lustig, Dana (1963–) *Wedding Bell Blues* 1996; *Kill Me Later* 2001

Lustig, William (1953–) *Hit List* 1988; *Maniac Cop* 1988; *Relentless* 1989; *Maniac Cop 2* 1990

Luther, Miloslav aka **Luther, Slavo** (1945–) *Forget Mozart* 1985; *Angel of Mercy* 1993

Lynch, David (1946–) *Eraserhead* 1976; *The Elephant Man* 1980; *Dune* 1984; *Blue Velvet* 1986; *Wild at Heart* 1990; *Twin Peaks: Fire Walk with Me* 1992; *Lost Highway* 1996; *The Straight Story* 1999; *Mulholland Drive* 2001

Lyne, Adrian (1948–) *Foxes* 1980; *Flashdance* 1983; *Nine $\frac{1}{2}$ Weeks* 1985; *Fatal Attraction* 1987; *Jacob's Ladder* 1990; *Indecent Proposal* 1993; *Lolita* 1997; *Unfaithful* 2002

Lynn, Jonathan (1943–) *Clue* 1985; *Nuns on the Run* 1990; *The Distinguished Gentleman* 1992; *My Cousin Vinny* 1992; *Greedy* 1994; *Sgt Bilko* 1996; *Trial and Error* 1997; *The Whole Nine Yards* 2000; *The Fighting Temptations* 2003

Lynn, Robert (1918–1982) *Postman's Knock* 1961; *Dr Crippen* 1962; *Information Received* 1962

Lyon, Francis D (1905–1996) *The Bob Mathias Story* 1954; *Cult of the Cobra* 1955; *The Great Locomotive Chase* 1956; *Gunsight Ridge* 1957; *The Oklahoman* 1957; *Escort West* 1959; *Tomboy and the Champ* 1961; *Castle of Evil* 1966; *Destination Inner Space* 1966; *The Destructors* 1968; *The Girl Who Knew Too Much* 1969

M

Maas, Dick (1951–) *The Lift* 1983; *Amsterdamned* 1988

McAnuff, Des *Cousin Bette* 1997; *The Adventures of Rocky & Bullwinkle* 1999

MacArthur, Charles (1895–1956) *Crime without Passion* 1934; *The Scoundrel* 1935

Macartney, Sydney (1954–) *The Bridge* 1990; *A Love Divided* 1999

McBride, Jim (1941–) *David Holzman's Diary* 1968; *Hot Times* 1974; *Breathless* 1983; *The Big Easy* 1986; *Great Balls of Fire!* 1989

McCain, Howard *No Dessert Dad, Till You Mow the Lawn* 1994; *When the Bough Breaks 2: Perfect Prey* 1998

McCall, Rod *Paper Hearts* 1993; *Lewis & Clark & George* 1996

McCanlies, Tim (1953–) *Dancer, Texas Pop 81* 1998; *Secondhand Lions* 2003

McCarey, Leo (1898–1969) *Indiscreet* 1931; *The Kid from Spain* 1932; *Duck Soup* 1933; *Belle of the Nineties* 1934; *Six of a Kind* 1934; *Ruggles of Red Gap* 1935; *The Milky Way* 1936; *The Awful Truth* 1937; *Make Way for Tomorrow* 1937; *Love Affair* 1939; *Once upon a Honeymoon* 1942; *Going My Way* 1944; *The Bells of St Mary's* 1945; *Good Sam* 1948; *My Son John* 1952; *An Affair to Remember* 1957; *Rally 'round the Flag, Boys!* 1958; *Satan Never Sleeps* 1962

McCarey, Ray aka **McCarey, Raymond** (1904–1948) *Pack Up Your Troubles* 1932; *Scram!* 1932; *A Gentleman at Heart* 1942; *Atlantic City* 1944; *The Falcon's Alibi* 1946

McCarthy, Michael (1917–1959) *Assassin for Hire* 1951; *John of the Fair* 1952; *Shadow of a Man* 1954; *It's Never Too Late* 1956; *The Traitor* 1957; *Operation Amsterdam* 1958

McCowan, George (1927–1995) *The Face of Fear* 1971; *Frogs* 1972; *The Magnificent Seven Ride!* 1972

McCulloch, Bruce (1961–) *Dog Park* 1998; *Superstar* 1999; *Stealing Harvard* 2002

McDonald, Bruce (1959–) *Roadkill* 1989; *Highway 61* 1992; *Dance Me Outside* 1994

MacDonald, David (1904–1983) *It's Never Too Late to Mend* 1937; *The Brothers* 1947; *Good Time Girl* 1948; *Snowbound* 1948; *The Bad Lord Byron* 1949; *Christopher Columbus* 1949; *Diamond City* 1949; *The Adventurers* 1950; *Cairo Road* 1950; *The Lost Hours* 1952; *Tread Softly* 1952; *Devil Girl from Mars* 1954; *The Moonraker* 1957; *Small Hotel* 1957; *A Lady Mislaid* 1958; *Petticoat Pirates* 1961

McDonald, Frank (1899–1980) *Isle of Fury* 1936; *Smart Blonde* 1936; *Bells of Rosarita* 1945; *My Pal Trigger* 1946; *Bulldog Drummond Strikes Back* 1947; *Thunder Pass* 1954; *The Big Tip*

Off 1955; *Gunfight at Comanche Creek* 1964

Macdonald, Kevin (1967–) *One Day in September* 1999; *Touching the Void* 2003

MacDonald, Peter *Rambo III* 1988; *Mo' Money* 1992; *The NeverEnding Story III* 1994; *Legionnaire* 1998

McDonell, Fergus (1910–1984) *The Small Voice* 1948; *Prelude to Fame* 1950

MacDougall, Ranald (1915–1973) *Queen Bee* 1955; *The World, the Flesh and the Devil* 1959; *The Subterraneans* 1960; *Go Naked in the World* 1961

Macek, Carl *Vampire Hunter D* 1985; *Wicked City* 1992

McEveety, Bernard (1924–2004) *Ride beyond Vengeance* 1966; *Brotherhood of Satan* 1970; *Napoleon and Samantha* 1972; *One Little Indian* 1973; *The Bears and I* 1974

McEveety, Vincent *Firecreek* 1968; *The Million Dollar Duck* 1971; *The Biscuit Eater* 1972; *Charley and the Angel* 1973; *The Castaway Cowboy* 1974; *Superdad* 1974; *The Strongest Man in the World* 1975; *Gus* 1976; *Treasure of Matecumbe* 1976; *Herbie Goes to Monte Carlo* 1977; *The Apple Dumpling Gang Rides Again* 1979; *Herbie Goes Bananas* 1980; *Amy* 1981; *The Watcher in the Woods* 1982

MacFadden, Hamilton (1901–1977) *Riders of the Purple Sage* 1931; *Stand Up and Cheer!* 1934

McGann, William (1893–1977) *The Case of the Black Cat* 1936; *In Old California* 1942

McGehee, Scott *Suture* 1993; *The Deep End* 2001

McGinty Nichol, Joseph *aka* **McG** (1970–) *Charlie's Angels* 2000; *Charlie's Angels: Full Throttle* 2003

McGrath, Douglas (1958–) *Emma* 1996; *Company Man* 2000; *Nicholas Nickleby* 2002

McGrath, Joseph *aka* **McGrath, Joe** (1930–) *Casino Royale* 1967; *The Bliss of Mrs Blossom* 1968; *30 Is a Dangerous Age, Cynthia* 1968; *The Magic Christian* 1969; *Digby, the Biggest Dog in the World* 1973; *The Great McGonagall* 1974; *Rising Damp* 1980

McGuckian, Mary *This Is the Sea* 1996; *Best* 1999

McGuigan, Paul (1963–) *The Acid House* 1998; *Gangster No 1* 2000; *The Reckoning* 2001; *Wicker Park* 2004

McGuire, Don (1919–1999) *Johnny Concho* 1956; *The Delicate Delinquent* 1957

McHenry, Doug *House Party 2* 1991; *Jason's Lyric* 1994

Mackay, David *Route 9* 1998; *Black Point* 2001

Mackendrick, Alexander (1912–1993) *The Man in the White Suit* 1951; *Mandy* 1952; *The Maggie* 1953; *The Ladykillers* 1955; *Sweet Smell of Success* 1957; *Sammy Going South* 1963; *A High Wind in Jamaica* 1965; *Don't Make Waves* 1967; *Oh Dad, Poor Dad, Mama's Hung You in the Closet and I'm Feelin' So Sad* 1967

Mackenzie, David (1966–) *The Last Great Wilderness* 2002; *Young Adam* 2003

Mackenzie, John (1932–) *Unman, Wittering and Zigo* 1971; *The Long Good Friday* 1979; *The Honorary Consul* 1983; *The Innocent* 1984; *The Fourth Protocol* 1987; *Blue Heat* 1990; *Ruby* 1992; *Voyage* 1993; *The Infiltrator* 1995; *Aldrich Ames: Traitor Within* 1998; *When the Sky Falls* 2000

MacKinnon, Gillies (1948–) *Conquest of the South Pole* 1989; *The Playboys* 1992; *A Simple Twist of Fate* 1994; *Small Faces* 1995; *Trojan Eddie* 1996; *Regeneration* 1997; *Hideous Kinky* 1998; *The Escapist* 2002; *Pure* 2002

McLachlan, Duncan *Running Wild* 1992; *The Second Jungle Book* 1997

McLaglen, Andrew V (1920–) *McLintock!* 1963; *Shenandoah* 1965; *Monkeys, Go Home!* 1966; *The Rare Breed* 1966; *The Way West* 1967; *The Ballad of Josie* 1968; *Bandolero!* 1968; *The Devil's Brigade* 1968; *Hellfighters* 1969; *The Undefeated* 1969; *Chisum* 1970; *Dynamite Man from Glory Jail* 1971; *One More Train to Rob* 1971; *something big* 1971; *Cahill, United States Marshal* 1973; *Mitchell* 1975; *The Last Hard Men* 1976; *Breakthrough* 1978; *The Wild Geese* 1978; *North Sea Hijack* 1979; *The Sea Wolves* 1980; *Sahara* 1983; *Return from the River Kwai* 1988

Maclean, Alison (1958–) *Crush* 1992; *Subway Stories: Tales from the Underground* 1997; *Jesus' Son* 1999

McLennan, Don (1949–) *Hard Knocks* 1980; *Slate, Wyn & Me* 1987

McLeod, Norman Z (1898–1964) *Monkey Business* 1931; *Horse Feathers* 1932; *If I Had a Million* 1932; *Alice in Wonderland* 1933; *It's a Gift* 1934; *Pennies from Heaven* 1936; *Topper* 1937; *Merrily We Live* 1938; *There Goes My Heart* 1938; *Remember?* 1939; *Topper Takes a Trip* 1939; *Lady Be Good* 1941; *The Trial of Mary Dugan* 1941; *The Kid from Brooklyn* 1946; *Road to Rio* 1947; *The Secret Life of Walter Mitty* 1947; *Isn't It Romantic* 1948; *The Paleface* 1948; *Let's Dance* 1950; *My Favorite Spy* 1951; *Never Wave at a WAC* 1952; *Casanova's Big Night* 1954; *Alias Jesse James* 1959

McLoughlin, Tom (1950–) *One Dark Night* 1982; *Friday the 13th Part VI: Jason Lives* 1986; *Date with an Angel* 1987; *Sometimes They Come Back* 1991; *Murder of Innocence* 1993; *Leave of Absence* 1994; *The Lies Boys Tell* 1994; *The Haunting of Helen Walker* 1995; *Behind the Mask* 1999

McMullen, Ken (1948–) *Zina* 1985; *1871* 1989

McNally, David *Coyote Ugly* 2000; *Kangaroo Jack* 2003

McNamara, Sean (1962–) *Casper: a Spirited Beginning* 1997; *Casper Meets Wendy* 1998; *3 Ninjas: High Noon at Mega Mountain* 1998; *Raise Your Voice* 2004

McNaught, Bob (1915–1976) *Grand National Night* 1953; *Sea Wife* 1957

MacNaughton, Ian (1925–2002) *And Now for Something Completely Different* 1971; *Monty Python Live at the Hollywood Bowl* 1982

McNaughton, John (1950–) *Henry: Portrait of a Serial Killer* 1986; *The Borrower* 1989; *Sex, Drugs, Rock & Roll* 1991; *Mad Dog and Glory* 1992; *Normal Life* 1995; *Wild Things* 1998; *Lansky* 1999

McPherson, Conor (1970–) *Saltwater* 1999; *The Actors* 2003

McTiernan, John (1951–) *Nomads* 1985; *Predator* 1987; *Die Hard* 1988; *The Hunt for Red October* 1990; *Medicine Man* 1992; *Last Action Hero* 1993; *Die Hard with a Vengeance* 1995; *The 13th Warrior* 1999; *The Thomas Crown Affair* 1999; *Rollerball* 2001; *Basic* 2003

Madden, John (1949–) *Ethan Frome* 1993; *Golden Gate* 1994; *Mrs Brown* 1997; *Shakespeare in Love* 1998; *Captain Corelli's Mandolin* 2001

Maddin, Guy (1956–) *Careful* 1992; *The Twilight of the Ice Nymphs* 1997; *Dracula: Pages from a Virgin's Diary* 2002; *The Saddest Music in the World* 2003

Mailer, Norman (1923–) *Beyond the Law* 1968; *Tough Guys Don't Dance* 1987

Majidi, Majid (1959–) *The Children of Heaven* 1997; *The Color of Paradise* 1999

Mak, Alan *Infernal Affairs* 2002; *Infernal Affairs II* 2003; *Infernal Affairs 3* 2003

Makavejev, Dusan (1932–) *Innocence Unprotected* 1968; *WR – Mysteries of the Organism* 1971; *Montenegro* 1981; *The Coca-Cola Kid* 1985

Makhmalbaf, Mohsen (1952–) *Gabbeh* 1995; *Salaam Cinema* 1995; *A Moment of Innocence* 1996; *Sokhout* 1998; *Kandahar* 2001

Makhmalbaf, Samira (1980–) *The Apple* 1998; *Blackboards* 2000; *11'09''01 – September 11* 2002; *At Five in the Afternoon* 2003

Makin, Kelly (1961–) *National Lampoon's Senior Trip* 1995; *Kids in the Hall: Brain Candy* 1996; *Mickey Blue Eyes* 1999

Makk, Karoly (1925–) *Love* 1971; *Deadly Game* 1982; *Lily in Love* 1985; *The Gambler* 1997

Malenfant, Robert *The Night Caller* 1998; *Facing the Enemy* 2001

Malick, Terrence (1945–) *Badlands* 1973; *Days of Heaven* 1978; *The Thin Red Line* 1998

Malle, Louis (1932–1995) *Le Monde du Silence* 1956; *Lift to the Scaffold* 1957; *Les Amants* 1958; *Zazie dans le Métro* 1960; *A Very Private Affair* 1962; *Le Feu Follet* 1963; *Viva Maria!* 1965; *Histoires Extraordinaires* 1967; *The Thief of Paris* 1967; *Phantom India* 1968; *Le Souffle au Coeur* 1971; *Black Moon* 1974; *Lacombe Lucien* 1974; *Pretty Baby* 1978; *Atlantic City, USA* 1980; *My Dinner with Andre* 1981; *Crackers* 1984; *Alamo Bay* 1985; *God's Country* 1985; *Au Revoir les Enfants* 1987; *Milou en Mai* 1989; *Damage* 1992; *Vanya on 42nd Street* 1994

Malmuth, Bruce (1934–) *Nighthawks* 1981; *Where Are the Children?* 1986; *Hard to Kill* 1989; *Pentathlon* 1994

Malone, Mark *Killer* 1994; *Dead Heat* 2002

Malone, William *Scared to Death* 1980; *House on Haunted Hill* 1999; *FearDotCom* 2002

Mamet, David (1947–) *House of Games* 1987; *Things Change* 1988; *Homicide* 1991; *Oleanna* 1994; *The Spanish Prisoner* 1997; *The Winslow Boy* 1999; *State and Main* 2000; *Heist* 2001; *Spartan* 2004

Mamoulian, Rouben (1897–1987) *Applause* 1929; *City Streets* 1931; *Dr Jekyll and Mr Hyde* 1931; *Love Me Tonight* 1932; *Queen Christina* 1933; *The Song of Songs* 1933; *We Live Again* 1934; *Becky Sharp* 1935; *The Gay Desperado* 1936; *High, Wide and Handsome* 1937; *Golden Boy* 1939; *The Mark of Zorro* 1940; *Blood and Sand* 1941; *Rings on Her Fingers* 1942; *Summer Holiday* 1948; *Silk Stockings* 1957

Manchevski, Milcho (1960–) *Before the Rain* 1994; *Dust* 2001

Mandel, Robert *Independence Day* 1983; *FX: Murder by Illusion* 1985; *Touch and Go* 1986; *School Ties* 1992; *The Substitute* 1996

Mandoki, Luis *Motel* 1983; *Gaby: a True Story* 1987; *White Palace* 1990; *Born Yesterday* 1993; *When a Man Loves a Woman* 1994; *Message in a Bottle* 1998; *Angel Eyes* 2001; *Trapped* 2002

Mandt, Neil (1969–) *Hijacking Hollywood* 1997; *Fortune Hunters* 1999

Manduke, Joseph *Kid Vengeance* 1977; *The Gumshoe Kid* 1990

Mangold, James (1964–) *Heavy* 1995; *Cop Land* 1997; *Girl, Interrupted* 1999; *Kate & Leopold* 2002; *Identity* 2003

Mankiewicz, Joseph L (1909–1993) *Dragonwyck* 1946; *Somewhere in the Night* 1946; *The Ghost and Mrs Muir* 1947; *The Late George Apley* 1947; *House of Strangers* 1949; *A Letter to Three Wives* 1949; *All about Eve* 1950; *No Way Out* 1950; *People Will Talk* 1951; *5 Fingers* 1952; *Julius Caesar* 1953; *The Barefoot Contessa* 1954; *Guys and Dolls* 1955; *The Quiet American* 1958; *Suddenly, Last Summer* 1959; *Cleopatra* 1963; *The Honey Pot* 1967; *King: a Filmed Record... Montgomery to Memphis* 1970; *There Was a Crooked Man...* 1970; *Sleuth* 1972

Mankiewicz, Tom *Dragnet* 1987; *Delirious* 1991

Mann, Anthony (1906–1967) *Dr Broadway* 1942; *The Great Flamarion* 1945; *Two O'Clock Courage* 1945; *The Bamboo Blonde* 1946; *Strange Impersonation* 1946; *Desperate* 1947; *Railroaded* 1947; *T-Men* 1947; *Raw Deal* 1948; *Border Incident* 1949; *Reign of Terror* 1949; *Devil's Doorway* 1950; *The Furies* 1950; *Side Street* 1950; *Winchester '73* 1950; *The Tall Target* 1951; *Bend of the River* 1952; *The Glenn Miller Story* 1953; *The Naked Spur* 1953; *Thunder Bay* 1953; *The Far Country* 1954; *The Last Frontier* 1955; *The Man from Laramie* 1955; *Strategic Air Command* 1955; *Serenade* 1956; *Men in War* 1957; *The Tin Star* 1957; *God's Little Acre* 1958; *Man of the West* 1958; *Cimarron* 1960; *El Cid* 1961; *The Fall of the Roman Empire* 1964; *The Heroes of Telemark* 1965; *A Dandy in Aspic* 1968

Mann, Daniel (1912–1991) *Come Back, Little Sheba* 1952; *About Mrs Leslie* 1954; *I'll Cry Tomorrow* 1955; *The Rose Tattoo* 1955; *The Teahouse of the August Moon* 1956; *Hot Spell* 1958; *The Last Angry Man* 1959; *Butterfield 8* 1960; *The Mountain Road* 1960; *Ada* 1961; *Five Finger Exercise* 1962; *Who's Got the Action?* 1962; *Who's Been Sleeping in My Bed?* 1963; *Judith* 1966; *Our Man Flint* 1966; *For Love of Ivy* 1968; *A Dream of Kings* 1969; *Willard* 1971; *The Revengers* 1972; *Interval* 1973; *Lost in the Stars* 1974; *Matilda* 1978; *Playing for Time* 1980

Mann, Delbert (1920–) *Marty* 1955; *The Bachelor Party* 1957; *Desire under the Elms* 1958; *Separate Tables* 1958; *Middle of the Night* 1959; *The Dark at the Top of the Stairs* 1960; *Lover Come Back* 1961; *The Outsider* 1961; *That Touch of Mink* 1962; *A Gathering of Eagles* 1963; *Dear Heart* 1964; *Mister Buddwing* 1965; *Quick, before It Melts* 1965; *Fitzwilly* 1967; *The Pink Jungle* 1968; *Kidnapped* 1971; *Birch Interval* 1976; *All Quiet on the Western Front* 1979; *Torn between Two Lovers* 1979; *Night Crossing* 1981

Mann, Michael (1943–) *The Jericho Mile* 1979; *Thief* 1981; *The Keep* 1983; *Manhunter* 1986; *The Last of the Mohicans* 1992; *Heat* 1995; *The Insider* 1999; *Ali* 2001; *Collateral* 2004

Mann, Ron (1959–) *Comic Book Confidential* 1988; *Twist* 1992; *Grass* 1999

Marcel, Terry *aka* **Marcel, Terence** (1942–) *There Goes the Bride* 1979; *Hawk the Slayer* 1980; *Jane and the Lost City* 1987; *The Last Seduction 2* 1998

Marcellini, Siro (1921–) *The Secret Mark of D'Artagnan* 1962; *Hero of Babylon* 1963

March, Alex (1921–1989) *Paper Lion* 1968; *The Big Bounce* 1969; *Mastermind* 1976; *The Amazing Captain Nemo* 1978

Marcus, Paul *Break Up* 1998; *Eye of the Killer* 1999

Margheriti, Antonio *aka* **Dawson, Anthony** *aka* **Dawson, Anthony M** (1930–2002) *The Long Hair of Death* 1964; *The Wild, Wild Planet* 1965; *Vengeance* 1968; *Blood Money* 1974; *Flesh for Frankenstein* 1974; *Take a Hard Ride* 1975; *Killer Fish* 1978; *Yor, the Hunter from the Future* 1983; *Codename Wildgeese* 1984

Marin, Edwin L (1899–1951) *The Death Kiss* 1933; *The Casino Murder Case* 1935; *Speed* 1936; *A Christmas Carol* 1938; *Everybody Sing* 1938; *Listen, Darling* 1938; *Fast and Loose* 1939; *Maisie* 1939; *Florian* 1940; *Paris Calling* 1941; *A Gentleman after Dark* 1942; *The Invisible Agent* 1942; *Miss Annie Rooney* 1942; *Show Business* 1944; *Tall in the Saddle* 1944; *Abilene Town* 1945; *Johnny Angel* 1945; *Lady Luck* 1946; *Nocturne* 1946; *Christmas Eve* 1947; *Intrigue* 1947; *Canadian Pacific* 1949; *Fighting Man of the Plains* 1949; *The Younger Brothers* 1949; *The Cariboo Trail* 1950; *Colt .45* 1950; *Fort Worth* 1951; *Sugarfoot* 1951

Marinos, Lex (1949–) *Remember Me* 1985; *Boundaries of the Heart* 1988

Maris, Peter *Diplomatic Immunity* 1991; *Hangfire* 1991

Marker, Chris (1921–) *La Jetée* 1962; *Le Joli Mai* 1962; *Sans Soleil* 1982

Markle, Fletcher (1921–1991) *Jigsaw* 1949; *The Man with a Cloak* 1951; *The Incredible Journey* 1963

Markle, Peter (1952–) *The Personals* 1982; *Hot Dog – The Movie* 1984; *Youngblood* 1986; *BAT-21* 1988; *Nightbreaker* 1989; *Wagons East!* 1994; *The Last Days of Frankie the Fly* 1996

Markowitz, Robert *Voices* 1979; *The Tuskegee Airmen* 1995; *Nicholas' Gift* 1998; *The Pilot's Wife* 2001

Marks, Arthur *Detroit 9000* 1973; *Friday Foster* 1975; *JD's Revenge* 1976

Marks, George Harrison (1926–1997) *Naked as Nature Intended* 1961; *9 Ages of Nakedness* 1969; *Come Play with Me* 1977

Marquand, Richard (1938–1987) *The Legacy* 1978; *Eye of the Needle* 1981; *Star Wars Episode VI: Return of the Jedi* 1983; *Until September* 1984; *Jagged Edge* 1985; *Hearts of Fire* 1987

Marshall, Frank (1947–) *Arachnophobia* 1990; *Alive* 1992; *Congo* 1995

Marshall, Garry (1934–) *Young Doctors in Love* 1982; *The Flamingo Kid* 1984; *Nothing in Common* 1986; *Overboard* 1987; *Beaches* 1988; *Pretty Woman* 1990; *Frankie & Johnny* 1991; *Exit to Eden* 1994; *Dear God* 1996; *The Other Sister* 1999; *Runaway Bride* 1999; *The Princess Diaries* 2001; *The Princess Diaries 2: Royal Engagement* 2004; *Raising Helen* 2004

Marshall, George (1891–1975) *Pack Up Your Troubles* 1932; *Their First Mistake* 1932; *Towed in a Hole* 1932; *In Old Kentucky* 1935; *Life Begins at 40* 1935; *A Message to Garcia* 1936; *Nancy Steele Is Missing* 1937; *The Goldwyn Follies* 1938; *Hold That Co-Ed* 1938; *Destry Rides Again* 1939; *You Can't Cheat an Honest Man* 1939; *The Ghost Breakers* 1940; *When the Daltons Rode* 1940; *Pot o' Gold* 1941; *Texas* 1941; *The Forest Rangers* 1942; *Star Spangled Rhythm* 1942; *Valley of the Sun* 1942; *Riding High* 1943; *True to Life* 1943; *And the Angels Sing* 1944; *Hold That Blonde* 1945; *Incendiary Blonde* 1945; *Murder, He Says* 1945; *The Blue Dahlia* 1946; *Monsieur Beaucaire* 1946; *The Perils of Pauline* 1947; *Variety Girl* 1947; *My Friend Irma* 1949; *Fancy Pants* 1950; *Never a Dull Moment* 1950; *A Millionaire for Christy* 1951; *Houdini* 1953; *Military Policeman* 1953; *Money from Home* 1953; *The Savage* 1953; *Scared Stiff* 1953; *Destry* 1954; *Duel in the Jungle* 1954; *Red Garters* 1954; *Pillars of the Sky* 1956; *Beyond Mombasa* 1957; *Guns of Fort Petticoat* 1957; *The Sad Sack* 1957; *Imitation General* 1958; *The Sheepman* 1958; *The Gazebo* 1959; *It Started with a Kiss* 1959; *The Mating Game* 1959; *Cry for Happy* 1961; *The Happy Thieves* 1962; *How the West Was Won* 1962; *Papa's Delicate Condition* 1963; *Advance to the Rear* 1964; *Boy, Did I Get a Wrong Number* 1966; *Eight on the Lam* 1967; *The Wicked Dreams of*

Paula Schultz 1968; *Hook, Line and Sinker* 1969
Marshall, Neil (1970–) *Dog Soldiers* 2001; *The Descent* 2005
Marshall, Penny (1942–) *Jumpin' Jack Flash* 1986; *Big* 1988; *Awakenings* 1990; *A League of Their Own* 1992; *Renaissance Man* 1994; *The Preacher's Wife* 1996; *Riding in Cars with Boys* 2001
Marshall, Rob (1960–) *Annie* 1999; *Chicago* 2002
Martel, Lucrecia (1966–) *La Cienaga* 2001; *La Niña Santa* 2004
Martin, Charles (1910–) *My Dear Secretary* 1948; *Death of a Scoundrel* 1956; *One Man Jury* 1978
Martin, Eugenio aka **Martin, Gene** (1925–) *Bad Man's River* 1971; *Horror Express* 1972
Martineau, Jacques (1963–) *Drôle de Félix* 2000; *Ma Vraie Vie à Rouen* 2002
Martini, Richard (1955–) *You Can't Hurry Love* 1988; *Limit Up* 1989
Martinson, Leslie H aka **Martinson, Leslie** *The Atomic Kid* 1954; *Black Gold* 1963; *PT 109* 1963; *For Those Who Think Young* 1964; *Batman* 1966; *Fathom* 1967; *Mrs Pollifax – Spy* 1970; *And Millions Will Die!* 1973
Marton, Andrew (1904–1992) *King Solomon's Mines* 1950; *The Devil Makes Three* 1952; *The Wild North* 1952; *Green Fire* 1954; *Gypsy Colt* 1954; *Men of the Fighting Lady* 1954; *Prisoner of War* 1954; *The Longest Day* 1962; *Crack in the World* 1964; *The Thin Red Line* 1964; *Around the World under the Sea* 1965; *Clarence, the Cross-Eyed Lion* 1965; *Africa – Texas Style!* 1967
Marvin, Mike *The Wraith* 1986; *Wishman* 1991
Maselli, Francesco (1930–) *Love in the City* 1953; *Time of Indifference* 1964; *A Fine Pair* 1968
Mason, Herbert (1891–1960) *His Lordship* 1936; *Strange Boarders* 1938; *A Window in London* 1939; *Back Room Boy* 1942
Massot, Joe *Wonderwall* 1968; *The Song Remains the Same* 1976
Masters, Quentin (1946–) *Thumb Tripping* 1972; *The Stud* 1978; *A Dangerous Summer* 1981
Masterson, Peter (1934–) *The Trip to Bountiful* 1985; *Blood Red* 1988; *Full Moon in Blue Water* 1988; *Night Game* 1989; *Convicts* 1991; *The Only Thrill* 1997
Mastorakis, Nico (1941–) *Blind Date* 1984; *Next One* 1984; *Hired to Kill* 1990
Mastroianni, Armand *He Knows You're Alone* 1981; *Distortions* 1987; *Cameron's Closet* 1988; *Desperate Justice* 1993; *One of Her Own* 1994; *Victim of Rage* 1994; *Formula for Death* 1995; *First Daughter* 1999
Maté, Rudolph (1898–1964) *It Had to Be You* 1947; *The Dark Past* 1948; *DOA* 1949; *Branded* 1950; *No Sad Songs for Me* 1950; *Union Station* 1950; *The Prince Who Was a Thief* 1951; *When Worlds Collide* 1951; *Forbidden* 1953; *The Mississippi Gambler* 1953; *Second Chance* 1953; *The Black Shield of Falworth* 1954; *The Siege at Red River* 1954; *The Far Horizons* 1955; *The Violent Men* 1955; *Miracle in the Rain* 1956; *The Rawhide Years* 1956; *Three Violent People* 1956; *The Deep Six* 1958; *For the First Time* 1959; *Seven Seas to Calais* 1962; *The 300 Spartans* 1962
Matthau, Charles (1965–) *Doin' Time on Planet Earth* 1988; *The Grass Harp* 1995; *The Marriage Fool* 1998
Matthews, Paul *The Little Unicorn* 1998; *Merlin the Return* 2000
Maurer, Norman (1926–1986) *The Three Stooges Go around the World in a Daze* 1963; *The Outlaws Is Coming* 1965
Maxwell, Garth *Jack Be Nimble* 1992; *When Love Comes* 1998
Maxwell, Peter (1924–) *Dilemma* 1962; *Serena* 1962; *Impact* 1963; *Run, Rebecca, Run* 1981
Maxwell, Ronald F (1947–) *Little Darlings* 1980; *The Night the Lights Went Out in Georgia* 1981; *Gettysburg* 1993; *Gods and Generals* 2002
May, Bradford *Darkman II: the Return of Durant* 1995; *Darkman III: Die Darkman Die* 1996
May, Elaine (1932–) *A New Leaf* 1971; *The Heartbreak Kid* 1972; *Mikey and Nicky* 1976; *Ishtar* 1987
May, Joe (1880–1954) *Asphalt* 1928; *Heimkehr* 1928; *Confession* 1937; *The House of the Seven Gables* 1940; *The Invisible Man Returns* 1940; *Johnny Doesn't Live Here Anymore* 1944
Maybury, John (1958–) *Love Is the Devil: Study for a Portrait of Francis Bacon* 1998; *The Jacket* 2005
Mayer, Gerald (1919–2001) *Inside Straight* 1951; *The Sellout* 1951; *Bright Road* 1953; *The Marauders* 1955
Mayfield, Les *California Man* 1992; *Miracle on 34th Street* 1994; *Flubber* 1997; *Blue Streak* 1999; *American Outlaws* 2001
Maylam, Tony (1943–) *The Riddle of the Sands* 1978; *The Burning* 1981; *Hero* 1987; *Split Second* 1991
Mayo, Archie (1891–1968) *Doorway to Hell* 1931; *Illicit* 1931; *Svengali* 1931; *Night after Night* 1932; *Ever in My Heart* 1933; *The Mayor of Hell* 1933; *Gambling Lady* 1934; *Bordertown* 1935; *The Case of the Lucky Legs* 1935; *Go into Your Dance* 1935; *The Petrified Forest* 1936; *The Black Legion* 1937; *It's Love I'm After* 1937; *The Adventures of Marco Polo* 1938; *They Shall Have Music* 1939; *Four Sons* 1940; *The House across the Bay* 1940; *Charley's Aunt* 1941; *Confirm or Deny* 1941; *The Great American Broadcast* 1941; *Moontide* 1942; *Orchestra Wives* 1942; *Crash Dive* 1943; *Sweet and Lowdown* 1944; *Angel on My Shoulder* 1946; *A Night in Casablanca* 1946
Mayron, Melanie (1952–) *The Baby-Sitter's Club* 1995; *Slap Her, She's French!* 2001
Maysles, Albert (1933–) *Salesman* 1969; *Gimme Shelter* 1970; *Grey Gardens* 1975
Maysles, David (1931–1987) *Salesman* 1969; *Gimme Shelter* 1970; *Grey Gardens* 1975
Mazursky, Paul (1930–) *Bob & Carol & Ted & Alice* 1969; *Alex in Wonderland* 1970; *Blume in Love* 1973; *Harry and Tonto* 1974; *Next Stop, Greenwich Village* 1976; *An Unmarried Woman* 1978; *Willie and Phil* 1980; *Tempest* 1982; *Moscow on the Hudson* 1984; *Down and Out in Beverly Hills* 1986; *Moon over Parador* 1988; *Enemies, a Love Story* 1989; *Scenes from a Mall* 1991; *The Pickle* 1993; *Faithful* 1996
Mead, Nick *Bank Robber* 1993; *Swing* 1998
Meadows, Shane (1972–) *Smalltime* 1996; *TwentyFourSeven* 1997; *A Room for Romeo Brass* 1999; *Once upon a Time in the Midlands* 2002; *Dead Man's Shoes* 2004
Meckler, Nancy *Sister My Sister* 1994; *Alive and Kicking* 1996
Medak, Peter (1937–) *A Day in the Death of Joe Egg* 1971; *The Ruling Class* 1972; *Ghost in the Noonday Sun* 1973; *The Odd Job* 1978; *The Changeling* 1980; *Zorro, the Gay Blade* 1981; *The Men's Club* 1986; *The Krays* 1990; *Let Him Have It* 1991; *Romeo Is Bleeding* 1992; *Pontiac Moon* 1994; *Species II* 1998
Medem, Julio (1958–) *Vacas* 1991; *The Red Squirrel* 1993; *Tierra* 1995; *The Lovers of the Arctic Circle* 1998; *Sex and Lucia* 2001; *The Basque Ball: Skin against Stone* 2003
Medford, Don (1917–) *To Trap a Spy* 1966; *The Hunting Party* 1971; *The Organization* 1971
Megahy, Francis *Real Life* 1983; *Taffin* 1988; *Red Sun Rising* 1994; *The Disappearance of Kevin Johnson* 1995
Mehrjui, Dariush (1939–) *The Cow* 1969; *Mama's Guest* 2004
Mehta, Deepa (1949–) *Camilla* 1993; *Fire* 1996; *Earth* 1998; *Bollywood/Hollywood* 2002
Mehta, Ketan (1952–) *Mirch Masala* 1987; *Maya* 1992; *Sardar* 1993
Melançon, André (1942–) *The Dog Who Stopped the War* 1984; *Bach and Broccoli* 1986; *Summer of the Colt* 1989
Melchior, Ib (1917–) *The Angry Red Planet* 1959; *The Time Travelers* 1964
Melendez, Bill (1916–) *A Boy Named Charlie Brown* 1969; *Snoopy, Come Home* 1972; *Race for Your Life, Charlie Brown* 1977; *Bon Voyage, Charlie Brown* 1980
Melford, Austin (1884–1971) *Car of Dreams* 1935; *Oh, Daddy!* 1935
Melville, Jean-Pierre (1917–1973) *Le Silence de la Mer* 1947; *Les Enfants Terribles* 1949; *Bob Le Flambeur* 1955; *Two Men in Manhattan* 1959; *Léon Morin, Priest* 1961; *Le Doulos* 1962; *L'Ainé des Ferchaux* 1963; *Le Deuxième Souffle* 1966; *Le Samouraï* 1967; *L'Armée des Ombres* 1969; *The Red Circle* 1970; *Un Flic* 1972
Menaul, Christopher *Feast of July* 1995; *One Kill* 2000
Mendeluk, George (1948–) *The Kidnapping of the President* 1980; *Meatballs III: Summer Job* 1987; *Men of Means* 1997
Mendes, Lothar (1894–1974) *The Four Feathers* 1929; *The Marriage Playground* 1929; *Paramount on Parade* 1930; *Ladies' Man* 1931; *If I Had a Million* 1932; *Payment Deferred* 1932; *Jew Süss* 1934; *The Man Who Could Work Miracles* 1936; *Moonlight Sonata* 1937; *Flight for Freedom* 1943
Mendes, Sam (1965–) *American Beauty* 1999; *Road to Perdition* 2002
Menendez, Ramon *Stand and Deliver* 1988; *Money for Nothing* 1993
Menges, Chris (1940–) *A World Apart* 1987; *CrissCross* 1992; *Second Best* 1993; *The Lost Son* 1998
Menzel, Jirí (1938–) *Closely Observed Trains* 1966; *Capricious Summer* 1968; *Larks on a String* 1969; *Cutting It Short* 1980; *My Sweet Little Village* 1986; *The Last of the Good Old Days* 1989; *The Life and Extraordinary Adventures of Private Ivan Chonkin* 1994; *Ten Minutes Older: the Cello* 2002
Menzies, William Cameron aka **Menzies, William C** (1886–1957) *Chandu the Magician* 1932; *Things to Come* 1936; *The Green Cockatoo* 1937; *The Thief of Bagdad* 1940; *Address Unknown* 1944; *The Whip Hand* 1951; *Invaders from Mars* 1953; *The Maze* 1953
Merchant, Ismail (1936–2005) *In Custody* 1993; *The Proprietor* 1996; *Cotton Mary* 1999; *The Mystic Masseur* 2001
Merhi, Joseph (1953–) *CIA – Codename Alexa* 1992; *Executive Target* 1996
Merhige, E Elias (1964–) *Shadow of the Vampire* 2000; *Suspect Zero* 2004
Merrill, Kieth *The Great American Cowboy* 1973; *Take Down* 1978; *Windwalker* 1980; *Harry's War* 1981
Mészáros, Marta (1931–) *Diary for My Children* 1982; *Diary for My Loves* 1987; *Diary for My Father and Mother* 1990
Metter, Alan *Girls Just Want to Have Fun* 1985; *Back to School* 1986; *Moving* 1988; *Cold Dog Soup* 1989; *Police Academy: Mission to Moscow* 1994
Metzger, Alan *Deadly Vows* 1994; *Carriers* 1998
Meyer, Muffie *Grey Gardens* 1975; *Enormous Changes at the Last Minute* 1983
Meyer, Nicholas (1945–) *Time after Time* 1979; *Star Trek II: the Wrath of Khan* 1982; *Volunteers* 1985; *The Deceivers* 1988; *Company Business* 1991; *Star Trek VI: the Undiscovered Country* 1991
Meyer, Russ (1922–2004) *Immoral Mr Teas* 1959; *Eve and the Handyman* 1961; *Fanny Hill: Memoirs of a Woman of Pleasure* 1964; *Lorna* 1964; *Faster, Pussycat! Kill! Kill!* 1965; *Motor Psycho* 1965; *Mudhoney* 1965; *Common-Law Cabin* 1967; *Good Morning... and Goodbye* 1967; *Finders Keepers, Lovers Weepers* 1968; *Vixen!* 1968; *Cherry, Harry & Raquel* 1969; *Beyond the Valley of the Dolls* 1970; *The Seven Minutes* 1971; *Supervixens* 1975; *Up* 1976; *Beneath the Valley of the Ultra Vixens* 1979
Meyer, Turi (1964–) *Sleepstalker* 1995; *Candyman: Day of the Dead* 1999
Meyers, Nancy (1949–) *The Parent Trap* 1998; *What Women Want* 2001; *Something's Gotta Give* 2003
Michell, Roger (1957–) *Persuasion* 1995; *Titanic Town* 1998; *Notting Hill* 1999; *Changing Lanes* 2002; *The Mother* 2003; *Enduring Love* 2004
Miike, Takashi (1960–) *Audition* 1999; *The Happiness of the Katakuris* 2001; *Ichi the Killer* 2001; *Gozu* 2003
Mikhalkov, Nikita (1945–) *A Slave of Love* 1976; *An Unfinished Piece for Mechanical Piano* 1976; *Oblomov* 1980; *A Private Conversation* 1983; *Dark Eyes* 1987; *Urga* 1990; *Burnt by the Sun* 1995; *The Barber of Siberia* 1999
Miles, Bernard (1907–1991) *Tawny Pipit* 1944; *Chance of a Lifetime* 1950
Miles, Christopher (1939–) *The Virgin and the Gypsy* 1970; *A Time for Loving* 1971; *The Maids* 1974; *That Lucky Touch* 1975; *Priest of Love* 1981; *The Clandestine Marriage* 1999
Milestone, Lewis (1895–1980) *The Kid Brother* 1927; *Two Arabian Knights* 1927; *The Racket* 1928; *All Quiet on the Western Front* 1930; *The Front Page* 1931; *Rain* 1932; *Hallelujah, I'm a Bum* 1933; *The Captain Hates the Sea* 1934; *Anything Goes* 1936; *The General Died at Dawn* 1936; *Of Mice and Men* 1939; *Lucky Partners* 1940; *My Life with Caroline* 1941; *Edge of Darkness* 1943; *The North Star* 1943; *The Purple Heart* 1944; *A Walk in the Sun* 1945; *The Strange Love of Martha Ivers* 1946; *Arch of Triumph* 1948; *No Minor Vices* 1948; *The Red Pony* 1949; *Halls of Montezuma* 1950; *Kangaroo* 1952; *Les Misérables* 1952; *They Who Dare* 1953; *Pork Chop Hill* 1959; *Ocean's Eleven* 1960; *Mutiny on the Bounty* 1962
Milius, John (1944–) *Dillinger* 1973; *The Wind and the Lion* 1975; *Big Wednesday* 1978; *Conan the Barbarian* 1982; *Red Dawn* 1984; *Farewell to the King* 1988; *Flight of the Intruder* 1991
Milland, Ray aka **Milland, R** (1905–1986) *A Man Alone* 1955; *Lisbon* 1956; *The Safecracker* 1958; *Panic in Year Zero* 1962; *Hostile Witness* 1968
Millar, Gavin (1938–) *Dreamchild* 1985; *Complicity* 1999
Millar, Stuart (1929–) *When the Legends Die* 1972; *Rooster Cogburn* 1975
Miller, Claude (1942–) *Garde à Vue* 1981; *An Impudent Girl* 1985; *La Petite Voleuse* 1988; *L'Accompagnatrice* 1992; *Les Enfants de Lumière* 1995; *La Classe de Neige* 1998; *Betty Fisher and Other Stories* 2001
Miller, David (1909–1992) *Billy the Kid* 1941; *Flying Tigers* 1942; *Love Happy* 1949; *Our Very Own* 1950; *Sudden Fear* 1952; *Beautiful Stranger* 1954; *Diane* 1955; *The Opposite Sex* 1956; *The Story of Esther Costello* 1957; *Happy Anniversary* 1959; *Midnight Lace* 1960; *Back Street* 1961; *Lonely Are the Brave* 1962; *Captain Newman, MD* 1963; *Hail, Hero!* 1969; *Executive Action* 1973; *Bittersweet Love* 1976
Miller (1), George (1943–) *The Man from Snowy River* 1982; *The Aviator* 1985; *Les Patterson Saves the World* 1987; *The NeverEnding Story II: the Next Chapter* 1991; *Frozen Assets* 1992; *Over the Hill* 1992; *Andre* 1994; *Daniel Defoe's Robinson Crusoe* 1996; *Zeus and Roxanne* 1997
Miller (2), George (1945–) *Mad Max* 1979; *Mad Max 2* 1981; *Twilight Zone: the Movie* 1983; *Mad Max beyond Thunderdome* 1985; *The Witches of Eastwick* 1987; *Lorenzo's Oil* 1992; *Babe: Pig in the City* 1998
Miller, Harvey (1936–1999) *Bad Medicine* 1985; *Getting Away with Murder* 1996
Miller (2), Michael *Jackson County Jail* 1976; *National Lampoon's Class Reunion* 1982; *Silent Rage* 1982; *Danielle Steel's Daddy* 1991; *Danielle Steel's Palomino* 1991; *Danielle Steel's Heartbeat* 1992; *Danielle Steel's Star* 1993; *Danielle Steel's A Perfect Stranger* 1994; *Danielle Steel's Once in a Lifetime* 1994; *Barbara Taylor Bradford's Everything to Gain* 1996; *Determination of Death* 2001; *Face Value* 2001
Miller, Randall *Class Act* 1992; *Houseguest* 1995; *The 6th Man* 1997
Miller, Robert Ellis (1932–) *Any Wednesday* 1966; *The Heart Is a Lonely Hunter* 1968; *Sweet November* 1968; *The Buttercup Chain* 1970; *The Girl from Petrovka* 1974; *The Baltimore Bullet* 1980; *Reuben, Reuben* 1983; *Hawks* 1988; *Brenda Starr* 1989; *Bed & Breakfast* 1992
Miller, Sam (1962–) *Among Giants* 1998; *Elephant Juice* 1999
Miller, Troy *Jack Frost* 1998; *Dumb and Dumberer: When Harry Met Lloyd* 2003
Milton, Robert (1885–1956) *Outward Bound* 1930; *Westward Passage* 1932
Miner, Steve (1951–) *Friday the 13th Part 2* 1981; *Friday the 13th Part III* 1982; *House* 1986; *Soul Man* 1986; *Warlock* 1989; *Wild Hearts Can't Be Broken* 1991; *Forever Young* 1992; *My Father the Hero* 1994; *Big Bully* 1996; *Halloween H20: 20 Years Later* 1998; *Lake Placid* 1999
Minghella, Anthony (1954–) *Truly Madly Deeply* 1990; *Mr Wonderful* 1992; *The English Patient* 1996; *The Talented Mr Ripley* 1999; *Cold Mountain* 2003
Minkoff, Rob *The Lion King* 1994; *Stuart Little* 1999; *Stuart Little 2* 2002; *The Haunted Mansion* 2003
Minnelli, Vincente (1903–1986) *Cabin in the Sky* 1943; *I Dood It* 1943; *Meet Me in St Louis* 1944; *Ziegfeld Follies* 1944; *The Clock* 1945; *Yolanda and the Thief* 1945; *Undercurrent* 1946; *The Pirate* 1948; *Madame Bovary* 1949; *Father of the Bride* 1950; *An American in Paris* 1951; *Father's Little Dividend* 1951; *The Bad and the Beautiful* 1952; *The Band Wagon* 1953; *The Story of Three Loves* 1953; *Brigadoon* 1954; *The Long, Long Trailer* 1954; *The Cobweb* 1955; *Kismet* 1955; *Lust for Life* 1956; *Tea and Sympathy* 1956; *Designing Woman* 1957; *Gigi* 1958; *The Reluctant Debutante* 1958; *Some Came Running* 1958; *Bells Are Ringing* 1960; *Home from the Hill* 1960; *The Four Horsemen of the Apocalypse* 1962; *Two Weeks in Another Town* 1962; *The Courtship of Eddie's Father* 1963; *Goodbye Charlie* 1964; *The Sandpiper* 1965; *On a Clear Day You Can See Forever* 1970; *A Matter of Time* 1976
Mirkin, David *Romy and Michele's High School Reunion* 1997; *Heartbreakers* 2001

Misumi, Kenji (1921–1975) *Zatoichi* 1962; *Baby Cart at the River Styx* 1972; *Sword of Vengeance* 1972
Mitchell, Mike *Deuce Bigalow: Male Gigolo* 1999; *Surviving Christmas* 2004
Mitchell, Oswald (1890–1949) *Danny Boy* 1941; *The Greed of William Hart* 1948
Miyazaki, Hayao (1941–) *The Castle of Cagliostro* 1979; *Princess Mononoke* 1997; *Spirited Away* 2001
Mizoguchi, Kenji (1898–1956) *The Downfall of Osen* 1935; *Poppy* 1935; *Osaka Elegy* 1936; *Sisters of the Gion* 1936; *The Straits of Love and Hate* 1937; *Story of the Late Chrysanthemums* 1939; *The Loyal 47 Ronin* 1941; *Musashi Miyamoto* 1944; *The Famous Sword* 1945; *Five Women around Utamaro* 1946; *The Victory of Women* 1946; *The Love of Sumako the Actress* 1947; *Women of the Night* 1948; *My Love Has Been Burning* 1949; *The Lady of Musashino* 1951; *Miss Oyu* 1951; *The Life of Oharu* 1952; *Ugetsu Monogatari* 1953; *The Crucified Lovers* 1954; *Sansho the Bailiff* 1954; *The Princess Yang Kwei Fei* 1955; *Street of Shame* 1955; *Tales of the Taira Clan* 1955
Mizrahi, Moshe (1931–) *Rachel's Man* 1975; *Madame Rosa* 1977; *Every Time We Say Goodbye* 1986
Moeller, Philip (?–1958) *The Age of Innocence* 1934; *Break of Hearts* 1935
Moguy, Léonide *aka* **Moguy, Leonide** (1899–1977) *Paris after Dark* 1943; *Action in Arabia* 1944; *Whistle Stop* 1946
Mohamed, Khalid *Fiza* 2000; *Tehzeeb* 2003
Moland, Hans Petter (1955–) *Zero Kelvin* 1995; *Aberdeen* 2000; *The Beautiful Country* 2004
Molander, Gustaf *aka* **Molander, Gustav** (1888–1973) *Swedenhielms* 1935; *Intermezzo* 1936; *Dollar* 1938; *A Woman's Face* 1938; *One Single Night* 1939
Molinaro, Edouard (1928–) *The Seven Deadly Sins* 1961; *Male Hunt* 1964; *Uncle Benjamin* 1969; *Sweet Torture* 1971; *A Pain in the A…!* 1973; *The Pink Telephone* 1975; *La Cage aux Folles* 1978; *La Cage aux Folles II* 1980; *Just the Way You Are* 1984; *Beaumarchais l'Insolent* 1996
Mollo, Andrew (1930–) *It Happened Here* 1963; *Winstanley* 1975
Monger, Christopher (1950–) *Waiting for the Light* 1989; *Just like a Woman* 1992; *The Englishman Who Went up a Hill, but Came down a Mountain* 1995; *Girl from Rio* 2001
Monicelli, Mario (1915–) *Big Deal on Madonna Street* 1958; *The Great War* 1959; *Boccaccio '70* 1961; *The Organizer* 1963; *Casanova '70* 1965; *Lady Liberty* 1971; *Travels with Anita* 1978; *Viva Italia!* 1978; *Let's Hope It's a Girl* 1985
Montagne, Edward J (1912–) *McHale's Navy* 1964; *The Reluctant Astronaut* 1967
Montaldo, Giuliano (1930–) *Grand Slam* 1967; *Sacco and Vanzetti* 1971
Montesi, Jorge (1950–) *Omen IV: the Awakening* 1991; *Soft Deceit* 1994; *Freefall: Flight 174* 1995; *Visitors of the Night* 1995
Montgomery, George (1916–2000) *Samar* 1962; *Satan's Harvest* 1965
Montgomery, Robert (1904–1981) *Lady in the Lake* 1947; *Eye Witness* 1949; *Once More, My Darling* 1949; *The Gallant Hours* 1960
Monton, Vincent *Windrider* 1986; *Fatal Bond* 1991
Moodysson, Lukas (1969–) *Show Me Love* 1998; *Together* 2000; *Lilya 4-Ever* 2002; *A Hole in My Heart* 2004
Moore (3), John (1970–) *Behind Enemy Lines* 2001; *Flight of the Phoenix* 2004
Moore (1), Michael *An Eye for an Eye* 1966; *The Fastest Guitar Alive* 1966; *Paradise, Hawaiian Style* 1966; *Kill a Dragon* 1967
Moore (2), Michael (1954–) *Roger & Me* 1989; *Canadian Bacon* 1995; *The Big One* 1997; *Bowling for Columbine* 2002; *Fahrenheit 9/11* 2004
Moore, Robert (1927–1984) *Murder by Death* 1976; *The Cheap Detective* 1978; *Chapter Two* 1979
Moore, Simon *Under Suspicion* 1991; *Up on the Roof* 1997
Moore, Tom *'Night, Mother* 1986; *Danielle Steel's Fine Things* 1990; *Geppetto* 2000
Moorhouse, Jocelyn (1960–) *Proof* 1991; *How to Make an American Quilt* 1995; *A Thousand Acres* 1997
Mora, Philippe (1949–) *Mad Dog* 1976; *The Return of Captain Invincible* 1983; *A Breed Apart* 1984; *Howling II: Your Sister Is a Werewolf* 1984; *Death of a Soldier* 1985; *The Howling III* 1987; *Communion* 1989; *Art Deco Detective* 1994; *Pterodactyl Woman from Beverly Hills* 1996
Morahan, Andrew *aka* **Morahan, Andy** *Highlander III: the Sorcerer* 1995; *Murder in Mind* 1996
Morahan, Christopher (1929–) *Diamonds for Breakfast* 1968; *All Neat in Black Stockings* 1969; *Clockwise* 1986; *Paper Mask* 1990
Morel, Gaël (1972–) *A Toute Vitesse* 1996; *Le Clan* 2004
Moretti, Nanni (1953–) *Dear Diary* 1994; *Aprile* 1998; *The Son's Room* 2001
Morneau, Louis *Quake!* 1992; *Bats* 1999; *Made Men* 1999
Morris, David Burton (1948–) *Purple Haze* 1982; *Patti Rocks* 1987; *Jersey Girl* 1992; *And the Beat Goes On: the Sonny and Cher Story* 1999; *Come On, Get Happy* 1999
Morris, Ernest (1915–1987) *Echo of Diana* 1963; *Shadow of Fear* 1963; *The Sicilians* 1964; *The Return of Mr Moto* 1965
Morris, Errol (1948–) *The Thin Blue Line* 1988; *The Dark Wind* 1991; *A Brief History of Time* 1992; *Mr Death: the Rise and Fall of Fred A Leuchter Jr* 1999; *The Fog of War: Eleven Lessons from the Life of Robert S McNamara* 2003
Morris, Howard (1919–) *Who's Minding the Mint?* 1967; *With Six You Get Eggroll* 1968; *Don't Drink the Water* 1969; *Goin' Coconuts* 1978
Morrison, Bruce *Constance* 1984; *Shaker Run* 1985
Morrison, Paul *Solomon and Gaenor* 1998; *Wondrous Oblivion* 2003
Morrissey, Paul (1939–) *Flesh* 1968; *Trash* 1970; *Women in Revolt* 1971; *Heat* 1972; *Blood for Dracula* 1974; *Flesh for Frankenstein* 1974; *The Hound of the Baskervilles* 1977; *Mixed Blood* 1984; *Spike of Bensonhurst* 1988
Morse, Hollingsworth *Pufnstuf* 1970; *Daughters of Satan* 1972
Morse, Terry *aka* **Morse, Terrell O** (1906–1984) *Fog Island* 1945; *Dangerous Money* 1946; *Unknown World* 1951; *Godzilla* 1954; *Young Dillinger* 1965
Morton, Rocky *DOA* 1988; *Super Mario Bros* 1993
Mosher, Gregory *A Life in the Theater* 1993; *The Prime Gig* 2000
Mostow, Jonathan (1961–) *Breakdown* 1997; *U-571* 2000; *Terminator 3: Rise of the Machines* 2003
Mowbray, Malcolm *A Private Function* 1984; *Out Cold* 1989; *The Boyfriend School* 1990; *The Revengers' Comedies* 1997
Moxey, John Llewellyn *aka* **Moxey, John** (1925–) *The City of the Dead* 1960; *Foxhole in Cairo* 1960; *Circus of Fear* 1967
Moyle, Allan (1947–) *Times Square* 1980; *Pump Up the Volume* 1990; *The Gun in Betty Lou's Handbag* 1992; *Empire Records* 1995; *XChange* 2000
Mulcahy, Russell (1953–) *Razorback* 1984; *Highlander* 1986; *Highlander II: the Quickening* 1990; *Ricochet* 1991; *Blue Ice* 1992; *The Real McCoy* 1993; *The Shadow* 1994; *Silent Trigger* 1996; *Talos the Mummy* 1997; *Resurrection* 1999; *Swimming Upstream* 2003
Mullan, Peter (1959–) *Orphans* 1998; *The Magdalene Sisters* 2002
Müllerschön, Nikolai (1958–) *Operation Dead End* 1986; *Desperate Measures* 1995
Mulligan, Robert (1925–) *Fear Strikes Out* 1957; *The Great Impostor* 1960; *The Rat Race* 1960; *Come September* 1961; *The Spiral Road* 1962; *To Kill a Mockingbird* 1962; *Love with the Proper Stranger* 1963; *Baby the Rain Must Fall* 1965; *Inside Daisy Clover* 1965; *Up the Down Staircase* 1967; *The Stalking Moon* 1968; *The Pursuit of Happiness* 1971; *Summer of '42* 1971; *The Other* 1972; *Bloodbrothers* 1978; *Same Time, Next Year* 1978; *Kiss Me Goodbye* 1982; *Clara's Heart* 1988; *The Man in the Moon* 1991
Münch, Christopher (1962–) *The Hours and Times* 1992; *Color of a Brisk and Leaping Day* 1996
Munden, Maxwell *House in the Woods* 1957; *The Bank Raiders* 1958
Mundhra, Jag (1946–) *Night Eyes* 1990; *Improper Conduct* 1994
Mune, Ian (1941–) *The End of the Golden Weather* 1992; *What Becomes of the Broken Hearted?* 1999
Munk, Andrzej (1921–1961) *Eroica* 1958; *Passenger* 1963
Munro, Ian *Prejudice* 1988; *Act of Necessity* 1991
Murakami, Jimmy T *Battle beyond the Stars* 1980; *When the Wind Blows* 1986; *Christmas Carol: the Movie* 2001
Murakawa, Toru *Distant Justice* 1992; *New York Cop* 1995
Murlowski, John *Amityville: a New Generation* 1993; *Automatic* 1994; *The Secret Agent Club* 1995; *Santa with Muscles* 1996
Murnau, F W *aka* **Murnau, Friedrich W** (1888–1931) *Nosferatu, a Symphony of Horrors* 1922; *The Last Laugh* 1924; *Faust* 1926; *Tartuffe* 1926; *Sunrise* 1927; *Tabu* 1931
Murphy, Dudley (1897–1968) *The Emperor Jones* 1933; *One Third of a Nation* 1939
Murphy, Geoff (1938–) *Goodbye Pork Pie* 1981; *Utu* 1983; *The Quiet Earth* 1985; *Young Guns II* 1990; *Freejack* 1992; *The Last Outlaw* 1993; *Under Siege 2* 1995; *Fortress 2: Re-entry* 1999; *Race against Time* 2000
Murphy, Pat *Anne Devlin* 1984; *Nora* 1999
Musker, John *Basil the Great Mouse Detective* 1986; *The Little Mermaid* 1989; *Aladdin* 1992; *Hercules* 1997; *Treasure Planet* 2002
Mustan *Baazigar* 1993; *Aitraaz* 2004
Mutrux, Floyd *Aloha, Bobby and Rose* 1975; *American Hot Wax* 1977; *There Goes My Baby* 1994
Myerson, Alan *Steelyard Blues* 1973; *Private Lessons* 1981; *Police Academy 5: Assignment Miami Beach* 1988; *Holiday Affair* 1996

N

Nair, Mira (1957–) *Salaam Bombay!* 1988; *Mississippi Masala* 1991; *The Perez Family* 1995; *Kama Sutra: a Tale of Love* 1996; *Monsoon Wedding* 2001; *11'09"01 – September 11* 2002; *Hysterical Blindness* 2002; *Vanity Fair* 2004
Nakata, Hideo (1961–) *Ring* 1997; *Ring 2* 1998; *Chaos* 1999; *Dark Water* 2002; *The Ring Two* 2004
Nalluri, Bharat (1966–) *Downtime* 1997; *Killing Time* 1998
Narizzano, Silvio (1927–) *Die! Die! My Darling* 1964; *Georgy Girl* 1966; *Blue* 1968; *Loot* 1970; *Why Shoot the Teacher* 1976; *The Class of Miss MacMichael* 1978; *Touchdown* 1981
Natali, Vincenzo (1969–) *Cube* 1997; *Cypher* 2002
Nava, Gregory (1949–) *El Norte* 1983; *A Time of Destiny* 1988; *My Family* 1994; *Selena* 1997; *Why Do Fools Fall in Love?* 1998
Nazarro, Ray (1902–1986) *China Corsair* 1951; *Indian Uprising* 1951; *The Bandits of Corsica* 1953; *Southwest Passage* 1954; *The Hired Gun* 1957
Neame, Ronald (1911–) *Take My Life* 1947; *Golden Salamander* 1949; *The Card* 1952; *The Million Pound Note* 1953; *The Man Who Never Was* 1955; *Windom's Way* 1957; *The Horse's Mouth* 1958; *Tunes of Glory* 1960; *Escape from Zahrain* 1962; *I Could Go On Singing* 1963; *The Chalk Garden* 1964; *Mister Moses* 1965; *Gambit* 1966; *A Man Could Get Killed* 1966; *Prudence and the Pill* 1968; *The Prime of Miss Jean Brodie* 1969; *Scrooge* 1970; *The Poseidon Adventure* 1972; *The Odessa File* 1974; *Meteor* 1979; *Hopscotch* 1980; *First Monday in October* 1981; *Foreign Body* 1986
Needham, Hal (1931–) *Smokey and the Bandit* 1977; *Hooper* 1978; *Cactus Jack* 1979; *Smokey and the Bandit II* 1980; *The Cannonball Run* 1981; *Cannonball Run II* 1983; *Stroker Ace* 1983
Needs, Malcolm *Shoreditch* 2002; *Charlie* 2003
Negulesco, Jean (1900–1993) *The Conspirators* 1944; *The Mask of Dimitrios* 1944; *Humoresque* 1946; *Nobody Lives Forever* 1946; *Three Strangers* 1946; *Deep Valley* 1947; *Johnny Belinda* 1948; *Road House* 1948; *Britannia Mews* 1949; *The Mudlark* 1950; *Three Came Home* 1950; *Lydia Bailey* 1952; *O Henry's Full House* 1952; *Phone Call from a Stranger* 1952; *How to Marry a Millionaire* 1953; *Scandal at Scourie* 1953; *Titanic* 1953; *Three Coins in the Fountain* 1954; *Woman's World* 1954; *Daddy Long Legs* 1955; *The Rains of Ranchipur* 1955; *Boy on a Dolphin* 1957; *A Certain Smile* 1958; *The Gift of Love* 1958; *The Best of Everything* 1959; *Count Your Blessings* 1959; *Jessica* 1962; *The Pleasure Seekers* 1964; *The Heroes* 1968; *Hello – Goodbye* 1970
Neilan, Marshall *aka* **Neilan, Marshall A** (1891–1958) *Rebecca of Sunnybrook Farm* 1917; *Stella Maris* 1918; *Daddy Long Legs* 1919; *Hell's Angels* 1930; *The Lemon Drop Kid* 1934
Neill, Roy William (1887–1946) *The Black Room* 1935; *The Lone Wolf Returns* 1936; *Dr Syn* 1937; *Sherlock Holmes and the Secret Weapon* 1942; *Frankenstein Meets the Wolf Man* 1943; *Sherlock Holmes Faces Death* 1943; *Sherlock Holmes in Washington* 1943; *The House of Fear* 1944; *The Pearl of Death* 1944; *The Scarlet Claw* 1944; *Sherlock Holmes and the Spider Woman* 1944; *Pursuit to Algiers* 1945; *The Woman in Green* 1945; *Black Angel* 1946; *Sherlock Holmes and the Secret Code* 1946; *Terror by Night* 1946
Neilson, James (1909–1979) *Night Passage* 1957; *Bon Voyage!* 1962; *Moon Pilot* 1962; *Dr Syn, Alias the Scarecrow* 1963; *Summer Magic* 1963; *The Moon-Spinners* 1964; *The Legend of Young Dick Turpin* 1965; *The Adventures of Bullwhip Griffin* 1967; *Gentle Giant* 1967; *Where Angels Go...Trouble Follows* 1968; *The First Time* 1969; *Flareup* 1969
Nelson, David (1936–) *A Rare Breed* 1981; *Last Plane Out* 1983
Nelson, Gary *Molly and Lawless John* 1972; *Santee* 1973; *Freaky Friday* 1976; *The Black Hole* 1979; *Jimmy the Kid* 1982; *Agatha Christie's Murder in Three Acts* 1986; *Allan Quatermain and the Lost City of Gold* 1987
Nelson, Gene (1920–1996) *Kissin' Cousins* 1964; *Your Cheatin' Heart* 1964; *Harum Scarum* 1965; *The Cool Ones* 1967
Nelson, Jessie *Corrina, Corrina* 1994; *I Am Sam* 2001
Nelson, Ralph (1916–1987) *Requiem for a Heavyweight* 1962; *Lilies of the Field* 1963; *Soldier in the Rain* 1963; *Fate Is the Hunter* 1964; *Father Goose* 1964; *Once a Thief* 1965; *Duel at Diablo* 1966; *Counterpoint* 1967; *Charly* 1968; *tick… tick… tick…* 1969; *Soldier Blue* 1970; *Flight of the Doves* 1971; *The Wrath of God* 1972; *The Wilby Conspiracy* 1975; *Embryo* 1976; *A Hero Ain't Nothin' but a Sandwich* 1978
Nelson, Tim Blake (1965–) *Eye of God* 1997; *O* 2001
Nesher, Avi *Time Bomb* 1991; *Doppelganger* 1993; *Taxman* 1998
Neumann, Kurt (1908–1958) *Rainbow on the River* 1936; *Espionage* 1937; *Ellery Queen Master Detective* 1940; *The Unknown Guest* 1943; *Tarzan and the Amazons* 1945; *Tarzan and the Leopard Woman* 1946; *Tarzan and the Huntress* 1947; *The Kid from Texas* 1950; *Cattle Drive* 1951; *The Ring* 1952; *Son of Ali Baba* 1952; *Tarzan and the She-Devil* 1953; *Carnival Story* 1954; *Mohawk* 1956; *The Deerslayer* 1957; *Kronos* 1957; *The Fly* 1958
Newby, Chris (1957–) *Anchoress* 1993; *Madagascar Skin* 1995
Newell, Mike (1942–) *The Man in the Iron Mask* 1977; *The Awakening* 1980; *Bad Blood* 1982; *Dance with a Stranger* 1984; *The Good Father* 1986; *Amazing Grace and Chuck* 1987; *Soursweet* 1988; *Enchanted April* 1991; *Into the West* 1992; *An Awfully Big Adventure* 1994; *Four Weddings and a Funeral* 1994; *Donnie Brasco* 1997; *Pushing Tin* 1999; *Mona Lisa Smile* 2003
Newfield, Sam *aka* **Scott, Sherman** *aka* **Stewart, Peter** (1899–1964) *Aces and Eights* 1936; *The Terror of Tiny Town* 1938; *Knight of the Plains* 1939; *The Lone Rider in Ghost Town* 1941; *Sheriff of Sage Valley* 1942; *Frontier Outlaws* 1944; *The Monster Maker* 1944; *The Counterfeiters* 1948; *The Gambler and the Lady* 1952
Newland, John (1917–2000) *That Night* 1957; *The Spy with My Face* 1966; *Who Fears the Devil?* 1972
Newman, Joseph M (1909–) *I'll Get You for This* 1950; *711 Ocean Drive* 1950; *Love Nest* 1951; *Pony Soldier* 1952; *Red Skies of Montana* 1952; *The Human Jungle* 1954; *Kiss of Fire* 1955; *This Island Earth* 1955; *Fort Massacre* 1958; *The Big Circus* 1959; *The Gunfight at Dodge City* 1959; *Tarzan, the Ape Man* 1959; *The George Raft Story* 1961; *King of the Roaring 20s – the Story of Arnold Rothstein* 1961; *A Thunder of Drums* 1961
Newman, Paul (1925–) *Rachel, Rachel* 1968; *Sometimes a Great Notion* 1971; *The Effect of Gamma Rays on Man-in-the-Moon Marigolds* 1972; *Harry and Son* 1984; *The Glass Menagerie* 1987
Newmeyer, Fred C *aka* **Newmeyer, Fred** (1888–1967) *A Sailor-Made Man* 1921; *Safety Last* 1923; *Girl Shy* 1924; *Hot Water* 1924; *The Freshman* 1925; *Fast and Loose* 1930; *General Spanky* 1936
Newton, Joel *Jennifer* 1953; *Main Street to Broadway* 1953
Nibbelink, Phil *An American Tail: Fievel Goes West* 1991; *We're Back! A Dinosaur's Story* 1993
Niblo, Fred (1874–1948) *The Mark of Zorro* 1920; *The Three Musketeers* 1921; *Blood and Sand* 1922; *Ben-Hur: a Tale of the Christ* 1925; *The Temptress* 1926; *Camille* 1927; *The Mysterious Lady* 1928

Niccol, Andrew (1964–) *Gattaca* 1997; *S1MØNE* 2002

Nichetti, Maurizio (1948–) *The Icicle Thief* 1989; *Volere, Volare* 1991

Nichols, Charles A aka **Nichols, C August** *Toot, Whistle, Plunk and Boom* 1953; *Charlotte's Web* 1973

Nichols, Dudley (1895–1960) *Government Girl* 1943; *Sister Kenny* 1946; *Mourning Becomes Electra* 1947

Nichols Jr, George (1897–1939) *Anne of Green Gables* 1934; *Finishing School* 1934; *The Return of Peter Grimm* 1935; *Chatterbox* 1936; *The Adventures of Michael Strogoff* 1937; *Man of Conquest* 1939

Nichols, Mike (1931–) *Who's Afraid of Virginia Woolf?* 1966; *The Graduate* 1967; *Catch-22* 1970; *Carnal Knowledge* 1971; *The Day of the Dolphin* 1973; *The Fortune* 1975; *Silkwood* 1983; *Heartburn* 1986; *Biloxi Blues* 1988; *Working Girl* 1988; *Postcards from the Edge* 1990; *Regarding Henry* 1991; *Wolf* 1994; *The Birdcage* 1996; *Primary Colors* 1998; *What Planet Are You From?* 2000; *Wit* 2001; *Closer* 2004

Nicholson, Jack (1937–) *Drive, He Said* 1971; *Goin' South* 1978; *The Two Jakes* 1990

Nicolaou, Ted *TerrorVision* 1986; *Subspecies* 1991; *Dragonworld* 1994

Nilsson, Rob (1940–) *Signal 7* 1983; *On the Edge* 1985; *Heat and Sunlight* 1988

Nimoy, Leonard (1931–) *Star Trek III: the Search for Spock* 1984; *Star Trek IV: the Voyage Home* 1986; *Three Men and a Baby* 1987; *The Price of Passion* 1988; *Funny about Love* 1990; *Holy Matrimony* 1994

Noé, Gaspar (1963–) *Seul contre Tous* 1998; *Irreversible* 2002

Nolan, Christopher (1970–) *Following* 1998; *Memento* 2000; *Insomnia* 2002; *Batman Begins* 2005

Nolbandov, Sergei (1895–1971) *Ships with Wings* 1942; *Undercover* 1943

Norman, Leslie (1911–1993) *The Night My Number Came Up* 1955; *X the Unknown* 1956; *The Shiralee* 1957; *Dunkirk* 1958; *The Long and the Short and the Tall* 1960; *Season of Passion* 1960; *Spare the Rod* 1961; *Mix Me a Person* 1962

Norrington, Stephen (1965–) *Death Machine* 1994; *Blade* 1998; *The League of Extraordinary Gentlemen* 2003

Norris, Aaron (1951–) *Braddock: Missing in Action III* 1988; *Delta Force 2* 1990; *The Hitman* 1991; *Sidekicks* 1993; *Top Dog* 1995

Norton, Bill L aka **Norton, B W L** aka **Norton, Bill** (1943–) *Cisco Pike* 1971; *More American Graffiti* 1979; *Baby: Secret of the Lost Legend* 1985; *Three for the Road* 1987; *Deadly Whispers* 1995; *Stolen Innocence* 1995; *Thirst* 1998

Nosseck, Max (1902–1972) *Overture to Glory* 1940; *The Brighton Strangler* 1945; *Dillinger* 1945; *Black Beauty* 1946

Nosseck, Noel (1943–) *Dreamer* 1979; *King of the Mountain* 1981; *Tornado!* 1996

Nossiter, Jonathan (1961–) *Resident Alien* 1990; *Sunday* 1997; *Mondovino* 2004

Nostro, Nick aka **Howard, Nick** *Spartacus and the Ten Gladiators* 1964; *One after the Other* 1968

Noujaim, Jehane *Startup.com* 2001; *Control Room* 2004

Noyce, Phillip (1950–) *Newsfront* 1978; *Heatwave* 1981; *Shadows of the Peacock* 1987; *Dead Calm* 1988; *Blind Fury* 1990; *Patriot Games* 1992; *Sliver* 1993; *Clear and Present Danger* 1994; *The Saint* 1997; *The Bone Collector* 1999; *The Quiet American* 2002; *Rabbit-Proof Fence* 2002

Nuchtern, Simon *Snuff* 1976; *Savage Dawn* 1985

Nugent, Elliott (1899–1980) *Life Begins* 1932; *Enter Madame!* 1933; *If I Were Free* 1933; *She Loves Me Not* 1934; *Splendor* 1935; *And So They Were Married* 1936; *The Cat and the Canary* 1939; *Never Say Die* 1939; *Nothing but the Truth* 1941; *The Male Animal* 1942; *The Crystal Ball* 1943; *Up in Arms* 1944; *My Favorite Brunette* 1947; *Welcome Stranger* 1947; *My Girl Tisa* 1948; *The Great Gatsby* 1949; *Mr Belvedere Goes to College* 1949; *Just for You* 1952

Nunez, Victor (1945–) *Gal Young Un* 1979; *A Flash of Green* 1984; *Ruby in Paradise* 1993; *Ulee's Gold* 1997

Nunn, Trevor (1940–) *Lady Jane* 1985; *Twelfth Night* 1996

Nutley, Colin (1944–) *House of Angels* 1992; *House of Angels II: The Second Summer* 1994; *Under the Sun* 1998

Nyby, Christian (1913–1993) *The Thing from Another World* 1951; *Operation CIA* 1965; *First to Fight* 1967

O

O'Bannon, Dan (1946–) *Return of the Living Dead* 1984; *The Resurrected* 1992

Oblowitz, Michael *This World, Then the Fireworks* 1996; *The Breed* 2001

Oboler, Arch (1909–1987) *Strange Holiday* 1942; *Bewitched* 1945; *The Arnelo Affair* 1947; *Five* 1951; *Bwana Devil* 1952; *The Bubble* 1966

O'Brien, Edmond (1915–1985) *Shield for Murder* 1954; *Man-Trap* 1961

Obrow, Jeffrey *The Kindred* 1986; *Bram Stoker's Legend of the Mummy* 1998

O'Connolly, Jim aka **O'Connolly, James** (1926–1987) *The Hi-Jackers* 1963; *Smokescreen* 1964; *Crooks and Coronets* 1969; *The Valley of Gwangi* 1969; *Tower of Evil* 1972

O'Connor, Gavin *Tumbleweeds* 1999; *Miracle* 2004

O'Connor, Pat (1943–) *Cal* 1984; *A Month in the Country* 1987; *Stars and Bars* 1988; *The January Man* 1989; *Fools of Fortune* 1990; *Circle of Friends* 1995; *Inventing the Abbotts* 1997; *Dancing at Lughnasa* 1998; *Sweet November* 2001

Odets, Clifford (1906–1963) *None but the Lonely Heart* 1944; *The Story on Page One* 1959

O'Donnell, Damien *East Is East* 1999; *Heartlands* 2002; *Inside I'm Dancing* 2004

Oedekerk, Steve (1961–) *Ace Ventura: When Nature Calls* 1995; *Nothing to Lose* 1997

O'Fallon, Peter *Suicide Kings* 1997; *A Rumor of Angels* 2000

O'Ferrall, George More (1907–1982) *Angels One Five* 1952; *The Holly and the Ivy* 1952; *The Heart of the Matter* 1953; *Three Cases of Murder* 1953; *The Green Scarf* 1954; *The Woman for Joe* 1955; *The March Hare* 1956

Ogilvie, George (1931–) *Mad Max beyond Thunderdome* 1985; *The Shiralee* 1986

O'Hara, Gerry (1925–) *The Pleasure Girls* 1965; *Maroc 7* 1966; *The Bitch* 1979; *Fanny Hill* 1983

O'Haver, Tommy (1967–) *Billy's Hollywood Screen Kiss* 1998; *Get over It* 2001; *Ella Enchanted* 2004

O'Herlihy, Michael (1919–1997) *The Fighting Prince of Donegal* 1966; *The One and Only, Genuine, Original Family Band* 1968; *Smith!* 1969

O'Keefe, Dennis (1908–1968) *The Diamond* 1954; *Angela* 1955

Olesen, Annette K (1965–) *Minor Mishaps* 2002; *In Your Hands* 2004

Olivera, Hector (1931–) *Funny Dirty Little War* 1983; *Wizards of the Lost Kingdom* 1985

Olivier, Laurence (1907–1989) *Henry V* 1944; *Hamlet* 1948; *Richard III* 1955; *The Prince and the Showgirl* 1957; *Three Sisters* 1970

Olmi, Ermanno (1931–) *Il Posto* 1961; *The Tree of Wooden Clogs* 1978; *Long Live the Lady!* 1987; *The Legend of the Holy Drinker* 1988

O'Neil, Robert Vincent *Paco* 1975; *Angel* 1984; *Avenging Angel* 1985

Ophüls, Marcel (1927–) *Love at Twenty* 1962; *Banana Peel* 1964; *The Sorrow and the Pity* 1969; *A Sense of Loss* 1972; *Hotel Terminus: the Life and Times of Klaus Barbie* 1987

Ophüls, Max (1902–1957) *Liebelei* 1932; *La Signora di Tutti* 1934; *Divine* 1935; *The Exile* 1947; *Letter from an Unknown Woman* 1948; *Caught* 1949; *The Reckless Moment* 1949; *La Ronde* 1950; *Le Plaisir* 1951; *Madame de...* 1953; *Lola Montès* 1955

Orme, Stuart (1954–) *The Wolves of Willoughby Chase* 1988; *The Puppet Masters* 1994

Orr, James (1953–) *Mr Destiny* 1990; *Man of the House* 1994

Ortega, Kenny *The News Boys* 1992; *Hocus Pocus* 1993

Oshii, Mamoru (1951–) *Patlabor: the Mobile Police* 1989; *Ghost in the Shell* 1995; *Avalon* 2000

Oshima, Nagisa (1932–) *Death by Hanging* 1968; *In the Realm of the Senses* 1976; *Merry Christmas Mr Lawrence* 1982; *Max Mon Amour* 1986; *Gohatto* 1999

O'Sullivan, Thaddeus (1947–) *December Bride* 1990; *Nothing Personal* 1995; *Ordinary Decent Criminal* 1999; *The Heart of Me* 2002

Oswald, Gerd (1919–1989) *The Brass Legend* 1956; *A Kiss before Dying* 1956; *Crime of Passion* 1957; *Fury at Showdown* 1957; *Valerie* 1957; *Paris Holiday* 1958; *Screaming Mimi* 1958; *Agent for HARM* 1966; *Eighty Steps to Jonah* 1969; *Bunny O'Hare* 1971

Oswald, Richard aka **Ornstein, Richard** (1880–1963) *The Living Dead* 1932; *The Lovable Cheat* 1949

Othenin-Girard, Dominique *After Darkness* 1985; *Halloween 5: the Revenge of Michael Myers* 1989; *Omen IV: the Awakening* 1991

Ouedraogo, Idrissa (1954–) *Yam Daabo* 1986; *Yaaba* 1989; *Tilaï* 1990; *Samba Traore* 1992; *Le Cri du Coeur* 1994; *Kini and Adams* 1997; *11'09''01 – September 11* 2002

Ouellette, Jean-Paul *The Unnamable* 1988; *The Unnamable Returns* 1992

Oury, Gérard (1919–) *Don't Look Now... We're Being Shot At* 1966; *The Brain* 1969; *Delusions of Grandeur* 1971

Ové, Horace (1939–) *Pressure* 1976; *Playing Away* 1986

Owen, Cliff (1919–1993) *Offbeat* 1960; *A Prize of Arms* 1961; *The Wrong Arm of the Law* 1962; *A Man Could Get Killed* 1966; *That Riviera Touch* 1966; *The Magnificent Two* 1967; *The Vengeance of She* 1968; *Ooh... You Are Awful* 1972; *Steptoe and Son* 1972; *No Sex Please – We're British* 1973; *The Bawdy Adventures of Tom Jones* 1976

Owen, Don (1935–) *Nobody Waved Goodbye* 1964; *Partners* 1976; *Unfinished Business* 1983

Oz, Frank (1944–) *The Dark Crystal* 1982; *The Muppets Take Manhattan* 1984; *Little Shop of Horrors* 1986; *Dirty Rotten Scoundrels* 1988; *What about Bob?* 1991; *HouseSitter* 1992; *The Indian in the Cupboard* 1995; *In & Out* 1997; *Bowfinger* 1999; *The Score* 2001; *The Stepford Wives* 2004

Ozon, François (1967–) *Sitcom* 1997; *Criminal Lovers* 1999; *Water Drops on Burning Rocks* 1999; *Under the Sand* 2000; *8 Women* 2001; *Swimming Pool* 2003; *5x2* 2004

Ozpetek, Ferzan (1959–) *Hamam: the Turkish Bath* 1996; *Harem Suare* 1999; *Le Fate Ignoranti* 2001; *Facing Window* 2003

Ozu, Yasujiro (1903–1963) *Tokyo Chorus* 1931; *I Was Born, but...* 1932; *The Only Son* 1936; *The Brothers and Sisters of the Toda Family* 1941; *There Was a Father* 1942; *Record of a Tenement Gentleman* 1947; *Hen in the Wind* 1948; *Late Spring* 1949; *Early Summer* 1951; *The Flavour of Green Tea over Rice* 1952; *Tokyo Story* 1953; *Early Spring* 1956; *Tokyo Twilight* 1957; *Equinox Flower* 1958; *Floating Weeds* 1959; *Ohayo* 1959; *Late Autumn* 1960; *The End of Summer* 1961; *An Autumn Afternoon* 1962

Pabst, G W (1885–1967) *The Joyless Street* 1925; *Secrets of a Soul* 1926; *The Love of Jeanne Ney* 1927; *Crisis* 1928; *Diary of a Lost Girl* 1929; *Pandora's Box* 1929; *Westfront 1918* 1930; *Kameradschaft* 1931; *The Threepenny Opera* 1931; *Don Quixote* 1932; *Mademoiselle Docteur* 1936; *Paracelsus* 1943

Page, Anthony (1935–) *Inadmissible Evidence* 1968; *Alpha Beta* 1973; *I Never Promised You a Rose Garden* 1977; *Absolution* 1978; *The Lady Vanishes* 1979; *Bill* 1981; *The Patricia Neal Story: an Act of Love* 1981; *Second Serve* 1986

Pagnol, Marcel (1895–1974) *Jofroi* 1933; *Angèle* 1934; *César* 1936; *The Baker's Wife* 1938; *Topaze* 1951; *Manon des Sources* 1952

Pakula, Alan J (1928–1998) *The Sterile Cuckoo* 1969; *Klute* 1971; *Love and Pain and the Whole Damn Thing* 1973; *The Parallax View* 1974; *All the President's Men* 1976; *Comes a Horseman* 1978; *Starting Over* 1979; *Rollover* 1981; *Sophie's Choice* 1982; *Dream Lover* 1986; *Orphans* 1987; *See You in the Morning* 1989; *Presumed Innocent* 1990; *Consenting Adults* 1992; *The Pelican Brief* 1993; *The Devil's Own* 1997

Pal, George (1908–1980) *tom thumb* 1958; *Atlantis, the Lost Continent* 1960; *The Time Machine* 1960; *The Wonderful World of the Brothers Grimm* 1962; *7 Faces of Dr Lao* 1963

Palcy, Euzhan (1958–) *Rue Cases Nègres* 1983; *A Dry White Season* 1989

Palmer, Tony (1941–) *200 Motels* 1971; *Wagner* 1983; *Testimony* 1987; *The Children* 1990

Paltenghi, David (1919–1961) *Orders Are Orders* 1954; *The Love Match* 1955; *Dick Turpin – Highwayman* 1956

Paltrow, Bruce (1943–2002) *A Little Sex* 1981; *Ed McBain's 87th Precinct* 1995; *Duets* 2000

Panahi, Jafar (1960–) *The White Balloon* 1995; *The Circle* 2000; *Crimson Gold* 2003

Panama, Norman (1914–2003) *Callaway Went Thataway* 1951; *Above and Beyond* 1952; *Knock on Wood* 1954; *The Court Jester* 1956; *That Certain Feeling* 1956; *The Baited Trap* 1959; *The Road to Hong Kong* 1962; *Not with My Wife, You Don't!* 1966; *How to Commit Marriage* 1969; *The Maltese Bippy* 1969; *I Will... I Will... for Now* 1976

Panfilov, Gleb (1934–) *The Theme* 1979; *Vassa* 1983

Pang, Danny aka **Pang Brothers** (1965–) *Bangkok Dangerous* 2000; *The Eye* 2002; *The Eye 2* 2004

Pang, Oxide aka **Pang Brothers** (1965–) *Bangkok Dangerous* 2000; *The Eye* 2002; *The Eye 2* 2004

Panh, Rithy (1964–) *Rice People* 1994; *S21: the Khmer Rouge Killing Machine* 2003

Paradjanov, Sergei (1924–1990) *Shadows of Our Forgotten Ancestors* 1964; *The Colour of Pomegranates* 1969; *The Legend of the Suram Fortress* 1984; *Ashik Kerib* 1988

Paragon, John *Double Trouble* 1992; *Ring of the Musketeers* 1994

Parello, Charles aka **Parello, Chuck** *Henry: Portrait of a Serial Killer, Part II* 1996; *Ed Gein* 2000; *The Hillside Strangler* 2004

Paris, Jerry (1925–1986) *Don't Raise the Bridge, Lower the River* 1968; *How Sweet It Is!* 1968; *Never a Dull Moment* 1968; *Viva Max!* 1969; *The Grasshopper* 1970; *Evil Roy Slade* 1971; *Police Academy 2: Their First Assignment* 1985; *Police Academy 3: Back in Training* 1986

Parisot, Dean *Home Fries* 1998; *Galaxy Quest* 1999

Park Chan-wook (1963–) *Sympathy for Mr Vengeance* 2002; *Oldboy* 2003

Parker, Alan (1944–) *Bugsy Malone* 1976; *Midnight Express* 1978; *Fame* 1980; *Pink Floyd – The Wall* 1982; *Shoot the Moon* 1982; *Birdy* 1984; *Angel Heart* 1987; *Mississippi Burning* 1988; *Come See the Paradise* 1990; *The Commitments* 1991; *The Road to Wellville* 1994; *Evita* 1996; *Angela's Ashes* 1999; *The Life of David Gale* 2003

Parker, David (1947–) *Hercules Returns* 1993; *Diana & Me* 1997

Parker, Oliver (1960–) *Othello* 1995; *An Ideal Husband* 1999; *The Importance of Being Earnest* 2002

Parker, Trey (1969–) *Cannibal! the Musical* 1993; *Orgazmo* 1997; *South Park: Bigger, Longer & Uncut* 1999; *Team America: World Police* 2004

Parks, Gordon (1912–) *The Learning Tree* 1969; *Shaft* 1971; *Shaft's Big Score!* 1972; *The Super Cops* 1973; *Leadbelly* 1976

Parks Jr, Gordon (1934–1979) *Superfly* 1972; *Three the Hard Way* 1974; *Aaron Loves Angela* 1975

Parolini, Gianfranco aka **Kramer, Frank** (1930–) *Sartana* 1968; *Adios, Sabata* 1970; *God's Gun* 1977

Parrish, Robert (1916–1995) *Cry Danger* 1951; *The Mob* 1951; *Assignment – Paris* 1952; *My Pal Gus* 1952; *Rough Shoot* 1952; *The San Francisco Story* 1952; *The Purple Plain* 1954; *Lucy Gallant* 1955; *Fire Down Below* 1957; *Saddle the Wind* 1958; *The Wonderful Country* 1959; *In the French Style* 1963; *Up from the Beach* 1965; *The Bobo* 1967; *Casino Royale* 1967; *Duffy* 1968; *Journey to the Far Side of the Sun* 1969; *A Town Called Hell* 1971; *The Marseille Contract* 1974

Parrott, James (1897–1939) *The Two Tars* 1928; *Perfect Day* 1929; *Pardon Us* 1931; *County Hospital* 1932; *The Music Box* 1932; *Twice Two* 1933

Parry, Gordon (1908–1981) *Bond Street* 1948; *The Gay Adventure* 1949; *Now Barabbas Was a Robber* 1949; *Third Time Lucky* 1949; *Tom Brown's Schooldays* 1951; *Women of Twilight* 1952; *Front Page Story* 1953; *Innocents in Paris* 1953; *A Yank in Ermine* 1955; *Sailor Beware!* 1956; *A Touch of the Sun* 1956; *Tread Softly Stranger* 1958; *The Navy Lark* 1959

Pascal, Christine (1953–1996) *La Garce* 1984; *Le Petit Prince A Dit* 1992

Pascal, Gabriel (1894–1954) *Major Barbara* 1941; *Caesar and Cleopatra* 1945

Paskaljevic, Goran (1947–) *Time of Miracles* 1990; *Someone Else's America* 1995; *Cabaret Balkan* 1998

Pasolini, Pier Paolo (1922–1975) *Accattone* 1961; *Mamma Roma* 1962; *RoGoPaG* 1962; *The Gospel According to St Matthew* 1964; *Hawks and Sparrows* 1966; *The Witches* 1966; *Oedipus Rex* 1967; *Theorem* 1968; *Pigsty*

1969; *The Decameron* 1970; *Medea* 1970; *The Canterbury Tales* 1971; *The Arabian Nights* 1974; *Salo, or the 120 Days of Sodom* 1975

Pasquin, John *The Santa Clause* 1994; *Jungle 2 Jungle* 1997; *Joe Somebody* 2001; *Miss Congeniality 2: Armed & Fabulous* 2005

Passer, Ivan (1933–) *Born to Win* 1971; *Law and Disorder* 1974; *Crime and Passion* 1976; *Silver Bears* 1977; *Cutter's Way* 1981; *Creator* 1985; *Haunted Summer* 1988

Pattinson, Michael (1957–) *Ground Zero* 1987; *Almost* 1990; *Virtual Nightmare* 2000

Patzak, Peter (1945–) *Midnight Cop* 1988; *Death of a Schoolboy* 1990

Paul, Steven *Falling in Love Again* 1980; *Slapstick of Another Kind* 1982; *Eternity* 1990

Pawlikowski, Pawel *aka* **Pavlikovsky, Paul** (1957–) *The Stringer* 1997; *Last Resort* 2000; *My Summer of Love* 2004

Payami, Babak (1966–) *Secret Ballot* 2001; *Silence between Two Thoughts* 2003

Payne, Alexander (1961–) *Citizen Ruth* 1996; *Election* 1999; *About Schmidt* 2002; *Sideways* 2004

Payne, Dave *aka* **Payne, David** *Addams Family Reunion* 1998; *Just Can't Get Enough* 2001

Pearce, Richard (1943–) *Heartland* 1979; *Threshold* 1981; *Country* 1984; *No Mercy* 1986; *The Final Days* 1989; *The Long Walk Home* 1990; *Leap of Faith* 1992; *A Family Thing* 1996; *Thicker than Blood* 1998; *Witness Protection* 1999; *South Pacific* 2001; *Martin Scorsese Presents the Blues: The Road to Memphis* 2003

Pearl, Steven *...At First Sight* 1995; *The Substitute 2: School's Out* 1997

Pearson, George (1875–1973) *A Shot in the Dark* 1933; *Open All Night* 1934; *Midnight at Madame Tussaud's* 1936; *Murder by Rope* 1936

Pécas, Max (1925–2003) *I Am a Nymphomaniac* 1971; *I Am Frigid... Why?* 1972

Peckinpah, Sam (1925–1984) *The Deadly Companions* 1961; *Ride the High Country* 1962; *Major Dundee* 1965; *The Wild Bunch* 1969; *The Ballad of Cable Hogue* 1970; *Straw Dogs* 1971; *The Getaway* 1972; *Junior Bonner* 1972; *Pat Garrett and Billy the Kid* 1973; *Bring Me the Head of Alfredo Garcia* 1974; *The Killer Elite* 1975; *Cross of Iron* 1977; *Convoy* 1978; *The Osterman Weekend* 1983

Peerce, Larry (1930–) *One Potato, Two Potato* 1964; *The Big TNT Show* 1966; *The Incident* 1967; *Goodbye, Columbus* 1969; *Ash Wednesday* 1973; *The Other Side of the Mountain* 1975; *Two-Minute Warning* 1976; *The Other Side of the Mountain – Part 2* 1978; *The Bell Jar* 1979; *Why Would I Lie?* 1980; *Love Child* 1982; *Hard to Hold* 1984; *Wired* 1989; *The Court-Martial of Jackie Robinson* 1990; *Breach of Trust* 1999

Peeters, Barbara *Bury Me an Angel* 1972; *Monster* 1980

Pelissier, Anthony (1912–1988) *The History of Mr Polly* 1948; *The Rocking Horse Winner* 1949; *Encore* 1951; *Night without Stars* 1951; *Meet Me Tonight* 1952; *Meet Mr Lucifer* 1953; *Personal Affair* 1953

Pellerin, Jean *For Hire* 1997; *Laserhawk* 1997; *Escape under Pressure* 2000

Pellington, Mark (1965–) *Going All the Way* 1997; *Arlington Road* 1998; *The Mothman Prophecies* 2001

Penn, Arthur (1922–) *The Left Handed Gun* 1958; *The Miracle Worker* 1962; *Mickey One* 1965; *The Chase* 1966; *Bonnie and Clyde* 1967; *Alice's Restaurant* 1969; *Little Big Man* 1970; *Visions of Eight* 1973; *Night Moves* 1975; *The Missouri Breaks* 1976; *Target* 1985; *Dead of Winter* 1987; *Penn & Teller Get Killed* 1989

Penn, Leo (1921–1998) *A Man Called Adam* 1966; *Judgment in Berlin* 1988

Penn, Sean (1960–) *The Indian Runner* 1991; *The Crossing Guard* 1995; *The Pledge* 2000; *11'09''01 – September 11* 2002

Pennebaker, D A (1925–) *Don't Look Back* 1967; *Monterey Pop* 1968; *Ziggy Stardust and the Spiders from Mars* 1982; *The War Room* 1993; *Down from the Mountain* 2000

Pennington-Richards, C M (1911–2005) *The Oracle* 1952; *Inn for Trouble* 1960; *Dentist on the Job* 1961; *Double Bunk* 1961; *Ladies Who Do* 1963; *A Challenge for Robin Hood* 1967

Pepin, Richard *T-Force* 1995; *Darkbreed* 1996

Peploe, Clare *High Season* 1987; *Rough Magic* 1995; *The Triumph of Love* 2001

Peploe, Mark *Afraid of the Dark* 1991; *Victory* 1995

Peralta, Stacy (1957–) *Dogtown and Z-Boys* 2001; *Riding Giants* 2004

Périer, Etienne (1931–) *Bridge to the Sun* 1961; *The Swordsman of Siena* 1962; *When Eight Bells Toll* 1971; *Zeppelin* 1971

Perry, Frank (1930–1995) *David and Lisa* 1962; *Ladybug, Ladybug* 1963; *The Swimmer* 1968; *Last Summer* 1969; *Trilogy* 1969; *Diary of a Mad Housewife* 1970; *Doc* 1971; *Play It As It Lays* 1972; *Rancho Deluxe* 1975; *Mommie Dearest* 1981; *Monsignor* 1982; *Compromising Positions* 1985; *Hello Again* 1987

Peters, Charlie *Passed Away* 1992; *Music from Another Room* 1998

Petersen, Wolfgang (1941–) *Das Boot* 1981; *The NeverEnding Story* 1984; *Enemy Mine* 1985; *Shattered* 1991; *In the Line of Fire* 1993; *Outbreak* 1995; *Air Force One* 1997; *The Perfect Storm* 2000; *Troy* 2004

Peterson, Kristine *Body Chemistry* 1990; *Critters 3* 1991

Petit, Christopher (1949–) *Radio On* 1979; *An Unsuitable Job for a Woman* 1981; *Chinese Boxes* 1984

Petri, Elio (1929–1982) *The Tenth Victim* 1965; *We Still Kill the Old Way* 1967; *Investigation of a Citizen above Suspicion* 1970; *The Working Class Goes to Heaven* 1971

Petrie, Daniel *aka* **Petrie Sr, Daniel** (1920–2004) *The Bramble Bush* 1960; *A Raisin in the Sun* 1961; *The Main Attraction* 1962; *Stolen Hours* 1963; *The Idol* 1966; *The Spy with a Cold Nose* 1966; *The Neptune Factor* 1973; *Buster and Billie* 1974; *Lifeguard* 1976; *The Betsy* 1978; *Resurrection* 1980; *Fort Apache, the Bronx* 1981; *Six Pack* 1982; *Bay Boy* 1984; *The Dollmaker* 1984; *Square Dance* 1987; *Cocoon: the Return* 1988; *Rocket Gibraltar* 1988; *My Name Is Bill W* 1989; *Lassie: a New Generation* 1994; *Inherit the Wind* 1999

Petrie Jr, Daniel (1952–) *Toy Soldiers* 1991; *In the Army Now* 1994; *Framed* 2002

Petrie, Donald *Mystic Pizza* 1988; *Opportunity Knocks* 1990; *Grumpy Old Men* 1993; *The Favor* 1994; *Richie Rich* 1994; *The Associate* 1996; *My Favorite Martian* 1999; *Miss Congeniality* 2000; *How to Lose a Guy in 10 Days* 2003; *Welcome to Mooseport* 2004

Petrovic, Aleksandar (1929–1994) *Three* 1965; *I Even Met Happy Gypsies* 1967

Pevney, Joseph *aka* **Pevney, Joe** (1911–) *Shakedown* 1950; *Undercover Girl* 1950; *Air Cadet* 1951; *Iron Man* 1951; *The Strange Door* 1951; *Flesh and Fury* 1952; *Meet Danny Wilson* 1952; *Back to God's Country* 1953; *Desert Legion* 1953; *Playgirl* 1954; *Three Ring Circus* 1954; *Yankee Pasha* 1954; *Female on the Beach* 1955; *Foxfire* 1955; *Six Bridges to Cross* 1955; *Away All Boats* 1956; *Congo Crossing* 1956; *Istanbul* 1957; *Man of a Thousand Faces* 1957; *The Midnight Story* 1957; *Tammy and the Bachelor* 1957; *Torpedo Run* 1958; *Twilight for the Gods* 1958; *Cash McCall* 1960; *The Crowded Sky* 1960; *The Night of the Grizzly* 1966

Peyser, John (1916–2002) *The Murder Men* 1961; *The Young Warriors* 1967

Pfleghar, Michael (1933–1991) *The Oldest Profession* 1967; *Visions of Eight* 1973

Philips, Lee (1927–1999) *On the Right Track* 1981; *Barnum* 1986

Phillips, Maurice *Riders of the Storm* 1986; *Over Her Dead Body* 1990; *Another You* 1991

Phillips, Stan *A Christmas Carol* 1997; *Madeline: Lost in Paris* 1999

Phillips, Todd (1970–) *Road Trip* 2000; *Old School* 2003; *Starsky & Hutch* 2004

Pialat, Maurice (1925–2003) *L'Enfance Nue* 1968; *The Mouth Agape* 1974; *Loulou* 1980; *To Our Loves* 1984; *Police* 1985; *Sous le Soleil de Satan* 1987; *Van Gogh* 1991

Pichel, Irving (1891–1954) *The Most Dangerous Game* 1932; *She* 1935; *Hudson's Bay* 1940; *The Man I Married* 1940; *Life Begins at 8.30* 1942; *The Pied Piper* 1942; *Happy Land* 1943; *The Moon Is Down* 1943; *And Now Tomorrow* 1944; *Colonel Effingham's Raid* 1945; *A Medal for Benny* 1945; *Tomorrow Is Forever* 1945; *The Bride Wore Boots* 1946; *OSS* 1946; *Temptation* 1946; *Something in the Wind* 1947; *They Won't Believe Me* 1947; *The Miracle of the Bells* 1948; *Mr Peabody and the Mermaid* 1948; *Destination Moon* 1950; *Quicksand* 1950; *Santa Fe* 1951

Pierce, Charles B *The Legend of Boggy Creek* 1972; *Winterhawk* 1975; *Grayeagle* 1977; *The Norseman* 1978; *The Evictors* 1979; *Sacred Ground* 1983; *Hawken's Breed* 1989

Pierson, Arthur (1901–1975) *Dangerous Years* 1947; *The Fighting O'Flynn* 1948; *Home Town Story* 1951

Pierson, Frank *aka* **Pierson, Frank R** (1925–) *The Looking Glass War* 1969; *A Star Is Born* 1976; *King of the Gypsies* 1978; *Truman* 1995; *Dirty Pictures* 2000; *Conspiracy* 2001

Pillsbury, Sam *The Scarecrow* 1982; *Starlight Hotel* 1987; *Zandalee* 1991; *Free Willy 3: the Rescue* 1997

Pintilie, Lucian (1933–) *An Unforgettable Summer* 1994; *Last Stop Paradise* 1998

Pintoff, Ernest (1931–2002) *Harvey Middleman, Fireman* 1965; *Dynamite Chicken* 1971; *Who Killed Mary Whats'ername?* 1971; *Jaguar Lives!* 1979

Piquer Simon, Juan *aka* **Simon, J Piquer** (1934–) *Pieces* 1982; *Sea Devils* 1982

Pirès, Gérard (1942–) *Taxi* 1998; *Steal* 2002

Pirosh, Robert (1910–1989) *Go for Broke!* 1951; *Washington Story* 1952; *Valley of the Kings* 1954; *The Girl Rush* 1955; *Spring Reunion* 1957

Pitof *Vidocq* 2001; *Catwoman* 2004

Planchon, Roger (1931–) *Dandin* 1988; *Lautrec* 1998

Plympton, Bill (1946–) *The Tune* 1992; *I Married a Strange Person* 1997

Poe, Amos *Alphabet City* 1984; *Triple Bogey on a Par Five Hole* 1991

Poiré, Jean-Marie *aka* **Gaubert, Jean-Marie** (1945–) *Les Visiteurs* 1993; *Guardian Angels* 1995; *Les Visiteurs 2: Les Couloirs du Temps* 1998; *Just Visiting* 2001

Poitier, Sidney (1924–) *Buck and the Preacher* 1972; *A Warm December* 1973; *Uptown Saturday Night* 1974; *Let's Do It Again* 1975; *A Piece of the Action* 1977; *Stir Crazy* 1980; *Hanky Panky* 1982; *Ghost Dad* 1990

Polakof, James *Love and the Midnight Auto Supply* 1977; *Balboa* 1982

Polanski, Roman (1933–) *Knife in the Water* 1962; *The Beautiful Swindlers* 1964; *Repulsion* 1965; *Cul-de-Sac* 1966; *The Fearless Vampire Killers* 1967; *Rosemary's Baby* 1968; *Macbeth* 1971; *What?* 1973; *Chinatown* 1974; *The Tenant* 1976; *Tess* 1979; *Pirates* 1986; *Frantic* 1988; *Bitter Moon* 1992; *Death and the Maiden* 1994; *The Ninth Gate* 1999; *The Pianist* 2002

Poliakoff, Stephen (1952–) *Hidden City* 1987; *Close My Eyes* 1991; *Century* 1993; *Food of Love* 1997

Polish, Michael (1972–) *Twin Falls Idaho* 1999; *Jackpot* 2001; *Northfork* 2002

Pollack, Jeff *Above the Rim* 1994; *Booty Call* 1997; *Lost & Found* 1999

Pollack, Sydney (1934–) *The Slender Thread* 1965; *This Property Is Condemned* 1966; *The Scalphunters* 1968; *Castle Keep* 1969; *They Shoot Horses, Don't They?* 1969; *Jeremiah Johnson* 1972; *The Way We Were* 1973; *Three Days of the Condor* 1975; *The Yakuza* 1975; *Bobby Deerfield* 1977; *The Electric Horseman* 1979; *Absence of Malice* 1981; *Tootsie* 1982; *Out of Africa* 1985; *Havana* 1990; *The Firm* 1993; *Sabrina* 1995; *Random Hearts* 1999; *The Interpreter* 2005

Pollock, George (1907–) *Rooney* 1958; *And the Same to You* 1960; *Murder She Said* 1961; *Village of Daughters* 1961; *Kill or Cure* 1962; *Murder at the Gallop* 1963; *Murder Ahoy* 1964; *Murder Most Foul* 1964; *Ten Little Indians* 1965

Polonsky, Abraham (1910–1999) *Force of Evil* 1948; *Tell Them Willie Boy Is Here* 1969; *Romance of a Horse Thief* 1971

Polson, John (1965–) *Siam Sunset* 1999; *Swimfan* 2002; *Hide and Seek* 2005

Pons, Ventura (1945–) *Actresses* 1996; *Beloved/Friend* 1998; *Food of Love* 2002

Pontecorvo, Gillo (1919–) *Kapo* 1959; *The Battle of Algiers* 1965; *Burn!* 1970

Pooh, D J *3 Strikes* 2000; *The Wash* 2001

Pope, Angela *Captives* 1994; *Hollow Reed* 1995

Post, Ted (1918–) *The Legend of Tom Dooley* 1959; *Hang 'Em High* 1968; *Beneath the Planet of the Apes* 1969; *The Baby* 1973; *The Harrad Experiment* 1973; *Magnum Force* 1973; *Whiffs* 1975; *Go Tell the Spartans* 1977; *Good Guys Wear Black* 1977; *Cagney & Lacey* 1981

Potter, H C (1904–1977) *Beloved Enemy* 1936; *The Cowboy and the Lady* 1938; *The Shopworn Angel* 1938; *Blackmail* 1939; *The Story of Vernon and Irene Castle* 1939; *Second Chorus* 1940; *Hellzapoppin'* 1941; *Mr Lucky* 1943; *The Farmer's Daughter* 1946; *Mr Blandings Builds His Dream House* 1948; *The Time of Your Life* 1948; *You Gotta Stay Happy* 1948; *The Miniver Story* 1950; *Three for the Show* 1955; *Top Secret Affair* 1957

Potter, Sally (1949–) *Gold Diggers* 1983; *Orlando* 1992; *The Tango Lesson* 1997; *The Man Who Cried* 2000; *Yes* 2004

Potterton, Gerald *The Railrodder* 1965; *Heavy Metal* 1981

Poulson, Gerry *Under the Doctor* 1976; *Arthur's Dyke* 2001

Powell, Dick (1904–1963) *Split Second* 1953; *The Conqueror* 1956; *You Can't Run Away from It* 1956; *The Enemy Below* 1957; *The Hunters* 1958

Powell, Michael (1905–1990) *Night of the Party* 1934; *The Phantom Light* 1934; *Lazybones* 1935; *The Love Test* 1935; *The Edge of the World* 1937; *The Lion Has Wings* 1939; *The Spy in Black* 1939; *Contraband* 1940; *The Thief of Bagdad* 1940; *49th Parallel* 1941; *One of Our Aircraft Is Missing* 1942; *The Life and Death of Colonel Blimp* 1943; *A Canterbury Tale* 1944; *I Know Where I'm Going!* 1945; *Black Narcissus* 1946; *A Matter of Life and Death* 1946; *The Red Shoes* 1948; *The Small Back Room* 1949; *The Elusive Pimpernel* 1950; *Gone to Earth* 1950; *The Tales of Hoffmann* 1951; *Oh, Rosalinda!!* 1955; *The Battle of the River Plate* 1956; *Ill Met by Moonlight* 1956; *Honeymoon* 1959; *Peeping Tom* 1960; *The Queen's Guards* 1960; *They're a Weird Mob* 1966; *Age of Consent* 1969; *The Boy Who Turned Yellow* 1972

Power, John (1930–) *The Picture Show Man* 1977; *Sound of Love* 1977; *Father* 1990

Prasad, Udayan (1953–) *Brothers in Trouble* 1995; *My Son the Fanatic* 1997; *Gabriel & Me* 2001

Preece, Michael *The Prize Fighter* 1979; *Logan's War: Bound by Honor* 1998; *The President's Man* 2000

Preminger, Otto (1906–1986) *Danger – Love at Work* 1937; *Margin for Error* 1943; *In the Meantime, Darling* 1944; *Laura* 1944; *Fallen Angel* 1945; *A Royal Scandal* 1945; *Centennial Summer* 1946; *Daisy Kenyon* 1947; *Forever Amber* 1947; *That Lady in Ermine* 1948; *The Fan* 1949; *Whirlpool* 1949; *The 13th Letter* 1950; *Where the Sidewalk Ends* 1950; *Angel Face* 1953; *The Moon Is Blue* 1953; *Carmen Jones* 1954; *River of No Return* 1954; *The Court-Martial of Billy Mitchell* 1955; *The Man with the Golden Arm* 1955; *Saint Joan* 1957; *Bonjour Tristesse* 1958; *Anatomy of a Murder* 1959; *Porgy and Bess* 1959; *Exodus* 1960; *Advise and Consent* 1962; *The Cardinal* 1963; *Bunny Lake Is Missing* 1965; *In Harm's Way* 1965; *Hurry Sundown* 1967; *Skidoo* 1968; *Tell Me That You Love Me, Junie Moon* 1970; *Such Good Friends* 1971; *Rosebud* 1975; *The Human Factor* 1979

Pressburger, Emeric (1902–1988) *One of Our Aircraft Is Missing* 1942; *The Life and Death of Colonel Blimp* 1943; *A Canterbury Tale* 1944; *I Know Where I'm Going!* 1945; *Black Narcissus* 1946; *A Matter of Life and Death* 1946; *The Red Shoes* 1948; *The Small Back Room* 1949; *The Elusive Pimpernel* 1950; *Gone to Earth* 1950; *The Tales of Hoffmann* 1951; *Oh, Rosalinda!!* 1955; *The Battle of the River Plate* 1956; *Ill Met by Moonlight* 1956

Pressman, Michael (1950–) *The Great Texas Dynamite Chase* 1976; *The Bad News Bears in Breaking Training* 1977; *Boulevard Nights* 1979; *Those Lips, Those Eyes* 1980; *Some Kind of Hero* 1982; *Doctor Detroit* 1983; *Teenage Mutant Ninja Turtles II: the Secret of the Ooze* 1991; *Quicksand: No Escape* 1992; *To Gillian on Her 37th Birthday* 1996; *To Gillian on Her 37th Birthday* 1996

Preston, Gaylene *Mr Wrong* 1985; *Ruby and Rata* 1990

Preuss, Ruben *Dead on Sight* 1994; *The Art of Murder* 1999

Price, David F (1961–) *Children of the Corn II: the Final Sacrifice* 1993; *Dr Jekyll and Ms Hyde* 1995

Prince (1958–) *Under the Cherry Moon* 1986; *Sign o' the Times* 1987; *Graffiti Bridge* 1990

Prince, Harold *Something for Everyone* 1970; *A Little Night Music* 1977

Prince-Bythewood, Gina (1969–) *Disappearing Acts* 2000; *Love & Basketball* 2000

Prior, David A *Raw Nerve* 1991; *Double Threat* 1992; *Good Cop, Bad Cop* 1993

Priyadarshan *Virasat* 1997; *Hulchul* 2004

Proctor, Elaine *Friends* 1993; *Kin* 2000
Prowse, Andrew *Driving Force* 1988; *Demonstone* 1989
Proyas, Alex (1965–) *The Crow* 1994; *Dark City* 1998; *I, Robot* 2004
Pudovkin, Vsevolod I (1893–1953) *Chess Fever* 1925; *Mother* 1926; *The End of St Petersburg* 1927; *Storm over Asia* 1928
Puenzo, Luis (1946–) *The Official Version* 1985; *Old Gringo* 1989; *The Plague* 1992
Purdy, Jon *Reflections on a Crime* 1994; *Dillinger and Capone* 1995
Pytka, Joe *Let It Ride* 1989; *Space Jam* 1997
Pyun, Albert *The Sword and the Sorcerer* 1982; *Dangerously Close* 1986; *Radioactive Dreams* 1986; *Down Twisted* 1987; *Cyborg* 1989; *Journey to the Center of the Earth* 1989; *Captain America* 1990; *Kickboxer 2: the Road Back* 1990; *Brain Smasher... a Love Story* 1993; *Nemesis* 1993; *Adrenalin: Fear the Rush* 1995; *Mean Guns* 1996; *Omega Doom* 1996; *Postmortem* 1999; *Ticker* 2001

Quay, Stephen (1947–) *Street of Crocodiles* 1986; *Institute Benjamenta, or This Dream People Call Human Life* 1995
Quay, Timothy (1947–) *Street of Crocodiles* 1986; *Institute Benjamenta, or This Dream People Call Human Life* 1995
Quested, John *Philadelphia, Here I Come* 1975; *Loophole* 1980
Quine, Richard (1920–1989) *All Ashore* 1953; *Drive a Crooked Road* 1954; *Pushover* 1954; *So This Is Paris* 1954; *My Sister Eileen* 1955; *Full of Life* 1956; *The Solid Gold Cadillac* 1956; *Operation Mad Ball* 1957; *Bell, Book and Candle* 1958; *It Happened to Jane* 1959; *Strangers When We Meet* 1960; *The World of Suzie Wong* 1960; *The Notorious Landlady* 1962; *Paris When It Sizzles* 1964; *Sex and the Single Girl* 1964; *Get off My Back* 1965; *How to Murder Your Wife* 1965; *Hotel* 1967; *Oh Dad, Poor Dad, Mama's Hung You in the Closet and I'm Feelin' So Sad* 1967; *W* 1974; *The Prisoner of Zenda* 1979
Quintano, Gene (1946–) *For Better or for Worse* 1990; *Why Me?* 1990; *National Lampoon's Loaded Weapon 1* 1993; *Dollar for the Dead* 1998

R

Rademakers, Fons (1920–) *The Assault* 1986; *The Rose Garden* 1989
Radford, Michael (1946–) *Another Time, Another Place* 1983; *Nineteen Eighty-Four* 1984; *White Mischief* 1987; *Il Postino* 1994; *B Monkey* 1996; *Dancing at the Blue Iguana* 2000; *Ten Minutes Older: the Cello* 2002; *William Shakespeare's The Merchant of Venice* 2004
Radler, Robert *Best of the Best* 1989; *Best of the Best II* 1992
Rafelson, Bob (1933–) *Head* 1968; *Five Easy Pieces* 1970; *The King of Marvin Gardens* 1972; *Stay Hungry* 1976; *The Postman Always Rings Twice* 1981; *Black Widow* 1987; *Mountains of the Moon* 1989; *Man Trouble* 1992; *Erotic Tales* 1994; *Blood and Wine* 1996; *Poodle Springs* 1998; *No Good Deed* 2002
Raffill, Stewart (1945–) *The Adventures of the Wilderness Family* 1975; *Across the Great Divide* 1977; *The Sea Gypsies* 1978; *High Risk* 1981; *The Ice Pirates* 1984; *The Philadelphia Experiment* 1984; *Mac and Me* 1988; *Mannequin on the Move* 1991; *Grizzly Falls* 1999
Rafkin, Alan (1928–2001) *Ski Party* 1965; *The Ghost and Mr Chicken* 1966; *The Ride to Hangman's Tree* 1967; *The Shakiest Gun in the West* 1967; *Angel in My Pocket* 1968; *Nobody's Perfect* 1968; *How to Frame a Figg* 1971
Raimi, Sam (1959–) *The Evil Dead* 1983; *Crimewave* 1985; *Evil Dead II* 1987; *Darkman* 1990; *Army of Darkness* 1993; *The Quick and the Dead* 1995; *A Simple Plan* 1998; *For Love of the Game* 1999; *The Gift* 2000; *Spider-Man* 2002; *Spider-Man 2* 2004
Rakoff, Alvin (1937–) *Passport to Shame* 1958; *The Treasure of San Teresa* 1959; *The Comedy Man* 1964; *Crossplot* 1969; *Hoffman* 1970; *Say Hello to Yesterday* 1971; *King Solomon's Treasure* 1977; *City on Fire* 1979
Ramati, Alexander *The Desperate Ones* 1967; *The Assisi Underground* 1985
Ramirez, Robert C *Joseph: King of Dreams* 2000; *Clifford's Really Big Movie* 2004
Ramis, Harold (1944–) *Caddyshack* 1980; *National Lampoon's Vacation* 1983; *Club Paradise* 1986; *Groundhog Day* 1993; *Stuart Saves His Family* 1995; *Multiplicity* 1996; *Analyze This* 1999; *Bedazzled* 2000; *Analyze That* 2002
Ramsay, Lynne (1969–) *Ratcatcher* 1999; *Morvern Callar* 2001
Randall, Addison (1931–2001) *East LA Warriors* 1989; *Chance* 1990
Randel, Tony *Hellbound: Hellraiser II* 1988; *Ticks* 1993; *Fist of the North Star* 1995; *One Good Turn* 1996
Rappeneau, Jean-Paul (1932–) *La Vie de Château* 1965; *Sink or Swim* 1971; *Call Him Savage* 1975; *Cyrano de Bergerac* 1990; *The Horseman on the Roof* 1995; *Bon Voyage* 2003
Rapper, Irving (1898–1999) *One Foot in Heaven* 1941; *Shining Victory* 1941; *The Gay Sisters* 1942; *Now, Voyager* 1942; *The Adventures of Mark Twain* 1944; *The Corn Is Green* 1945; *Rhapsody in Blue* 1945; *Deception* 1946; *Voice of the Turtle* 1947; *Anna Lucasta* 1949; *The Glass Menagerie* 1950; *Another Man's Poison* 1951; *Forever Female* 1953; *Bad for Each Other* 1954; *The Brave One* 1956; *Marjorie Morningstar* 1958; *The Miracle* 1959; *Pontius Pilate* 1961; *Born Again* 1978
Rash, Steve *The Buddy Holly Story* 1978; *Under the Rainbow* 1981; *Can't Buy Me Love* 1987; *Queens Logic* 1991; *Son in Law* 1993; *Eddie* 1996; *Held Up* 1999; *Good Advice* 2001
Ratanaruang, Pen-ek (1962–) *Monrak Transistor* 2001; *Last Life in the Universe* 2003
Rathnam, Mani (1956–) *Roja* 1992; *Bombay* 1995; *Dil Se...* 1998
Ratner, Brett (1970–) *Money Talks* 1997; *Rush Hour* 1998; *The Family Man* 2000; *Rush Hour 2* 2001; *Red Dragon* 2002; *After the Sunset* 2004
Ratoff, Gregory (1897–1960) *Lancer Spy* 1937; *Intermezzo* 1939; *Rose of Washington Square* 1939; *Wife, Husband and Friend* 1939; *I Was an Adventuress* 1940; *Adam Had Four Sons* 1941; *The Corsican Brothers* 1941; *The Men in Her Life* 1941; *Footlight Serenade* 1942; *The Heat's On* 1943; *Irish Eyes Are Smiling* 1944; *Where Do We Go from Here?* 1945; *Do You Love Me?* 1946; *Moss Rose* 1947; *Black Magic* 1949; *That Dangerous Age* 1949; *Taxi* 1953; *Oscar Wilde* 1959
Rawlins, John (1902–1997) *Arabian Nights* 1942; *Sherlock Holmes and the Voice of Terror* 1942; *Sudan* 1945; *Dick Tracy Meets Gruesome* 1947; *Dick Tracy's Dilemma* 1947; *The Arizona Ranger* 1948
Ray, Fred Olen (1954–) *The Alien Dead* 1980; *Armed Response* 1986; *Haunting Fear* 1990
Ray, Nicholas (1911–1979) *They Live by Night* 1948; *Knock on Any Door* 1949; *A Woman's Secret* 1949; *Born to Be Bad* 1950; *In a Lonely Place* 1950; *Flying Leathernecks* 1951; *On Dangerous Ground* 1951; *The Racket* 1951; *The Lusty Men* 1952; *Macao* 1952; *Johnny Guitar* 1954; *Rebel without a Cause* 1955; *Run for Cover* 1955; *Bigger than Life* 1956; *Hot Blood* 1956; *Bitter Victory* 1957; *The True Story of Jesse James* 1957; *Party Girl* 1958; *Wind across the Everglades* 1958; *The Savage Innocents* 1960; *King of Kings* 1961; *55 Days at Peking* 1963; *Lightning over Water* 1980
Ray, Satyajit (1921–1992) *Pather Panchali* 1955; *Aparajito* 1956; *The Music Room* 1958; *The World of Apu* 1959; *Devi* 1960; *Teen Kanya* 1961; *Abhijaan* 1962; *Kangchenjungra* 1962; *The Big City* 1963; *Charulata* 1964; *Days and Nights in the Forest* 1969; *The Adversary* 1970; *Company Limited* 1971; *Distant Thunder* 1973; *The Middleman* 1975; *The Chess Players* 1977; *Sadgati* 1981; *The Home and the World* 1984; *An Enemy of the People* 1989; *Branches of the Tree* 1990; *The Stranger* 1991
Rebane, Bill (1937–) *The Giant Spider Invasion* 1975; *The Alpha Incident* 1977
Red, Eric (1961–) *Cohen and Tate* 1988; *Body Parts* 1991; *Bad Moon* 1996
Redford, Robert (1937–) *Ordinary People* 1980; *The Milagro Beanfield War* 1988; *A River Runs through It* 1992; *Quiz Show* 1994; *The Horse Whisperer* 1998; *The Legend of Bagger Vance* 2000
Reed, Carol (1906–1976) *Bank Holiday* 1938; *Climbing High* 1938; *Penny Paradise* 1938; *The Stars Look Down* 1939; *The Girl in the News* 1940; *Night Train to Munich* 1940; *Kipps* 1941; *The Young Mr Pitt* 1942; *The Way Ahead* 1944; *Odd Man Out* 1946; *The Fallen Idol* 1948; *The Third Man* 1949; *Outcast of the Islands* 1951; *The Man Between* 1953; *A Kid for Two Farthings* 1955; *Trapeze* 1956; *The Key* 1958; *Our Man in Havana* 1959; *The Running Man* 1963; *The Agony and the Ecstasy* 1965; *Oliver!* 1968; *Flap* 1970; *Follow Me* 1971
Reed, Luther (1888–1961) *Rio Rita* 1929; *Hell's Angels* 1930
Reed, Peyton (1964–) *Bring It On* 2000; *Down with Love* 2003
Rees, Clive *The Blockhouse* 1973; *When the Whales Came* 1989
Rees, Jerry *The Brave Little Toaster* 1987; *Too Hot to Handle* 1991
Reeve, Geoffrey (1932–) *Puppet on a Chain* 1970; *Caravan to Vaccares* 1974; *Souvenir* 1987; *Shadow Run* 1998
Reeves, Michael (1944–1969) *The She Beast* 1965; *The Sorcerers* 1967; *Witchfinder General* 1968
Refn, Nicolas Winding (1972–) *Pusher* 1996; *Bleeder* 1999; *Fear X* 2002
Reggio, Godfrey (1940–) *Koyaanisqatsi* 1982; *Powaqqatsi* 1988; *Naqoyqatsi* 2002
Reid, Alastair (1939–) *The Road Builder* 1971; *Something to Hide* 1971; *What Rats Won't Do* 1998
Reid, John *Carry Me Back* 1982; *Leave All Fair* 1985
Reiner, Carl (1922–) *Enter Laughing* 1967; *The Comic* 1969; *Where's Poppa?* 1970; *Oh, God!* 1977; *The One and Only* 1978; *The Jerk* 1979; *Dead Men Don't Wear Plaid* 1982; *The Man with Two Brains* 1983; *All of Me* 1984; *Summer Rental* 1985; *Summer School* 1987; *Bert Rigby, You're a Fool* 1989; *Sibling Rivalry* 1990; *Fatal Instinct* 1993; *That Old Feeling* 1997
Reiner, Jeffrey *Trouble Bound* 1993; *Another Day* 2001
Reiner, Rob (1945–) *This Is Spinal Tap* 1984; *The Sure Thing* 1985; *Stand by Me* 1986; *The Princess Bride* 1987; *When Harry Met Sally...* 1989; *Misery* 1990; *A Few Good Men* 1992; *North* 1994; *The American President* 1995; *Ghosts of Mississippi* 1996; *The Story of Us* 1999; *Alex & Emma* 2003
Reinhardt, Gottfried (1913–1994) *The Story of Three Loves* 1953; *Betrayed* 1954; *Town without Pity* 1961; *Situation Hopeless – but Not Serious* 1965
Reinl, Harald (1908–1986) *The Return of Dr Mabuse* 1961; *The Desperado Trail* 1965; *The Blood Demon* 1967
Reis, Irving (1906–1953) *A Date with the Falcon* 1941; *The Gay Falcon* 1941; *The Big Street* 1942; *The Falcon Takes Over* 1942; *Crack-Up* 1946; *The Bachelor and the Bobby-Soxer* 1947; *All My Sons* 1948; *Enchantment* 1948; *Dancing in the Dark* 1949; *Roseanna McCoy* 1949; *The Four Poster* 1953
Reisch, Walter (1903–1983) *Men Are Not Gods* 1936; *Song of Scheherazade* 1947
Reisner, Allen (1923–2004) *The Day They Gave Babies Away* 1957; *St Louis Blues* 1958
Reisner, Charles *aka* **Reisner, Charles F** (1887–1962) *Steamboat Bill, Jr* 1928; *Hollywood Revue* 1929; *Winter Carnival* 1939; *The Big Store* 1941; *Lost in a Harem* 1944; *Meet the People* 1944
Reisz, Karel (1926–2002) *Saturday Night and Sunday Morning* 1960; *Night Must Fall* 1964; *Morgan – a Suitable Case for Treatment* 1966; *Isadora* 1968; *The Gambler* 1974; *Who'll Stop the Rain?* 1978; *The French Lieutenant's Woman* 1981; *Sweet Dreams* 1985; *Everybody Wins* 1990
Reitherman, Wolfgang (1909–1985) *Sleeping Beauty* 1959; *One Hundred and One Dalmatians* 1960; *The Sword in the Stone* 1963; *The Jungle Book* 1967; *The Aristocats* 1970; *Robin Hood* 1973; *The Rescuers* 1977
Reitman, Ivan (1946–) *Cannibal Girls* 1973; *Meatballs* 1979; *Stripes* 1981; *Ghostbusters* 1984; *Legal Eagles* 1986; *Twins* 1988; *Ghostbusters II* 1989; *Kindergarten Cop* 1990; *Dave* 1993; *Junior* 1994; *Fathers' Day* 1997; *Six Days Seven Nights* 1998; *Evolution* 2001
Reitz, Edgar (1932–) *Germany in Autumn* 1978; *Heimat* 1984; *Heimat 2* 1992; *Heimat 3: a Chronicle of Endings and Beginnings* 2004
Relph, Michael (1915–2004) *Saraband for Dead Lovers* 1948; *The Gentle Gunman* 1952; *I Believe in You* 1952; *The Square Ring* 1953; *The Ship That Died of Shame* 1955; *Rockets Galore* 1958; *Desert Mice* 1959
René, Norman (1951–1996) *Longtime Companion* 1990; *Prelude to a Kiss* 1992; *Reckless* 1995
Renoir, Jean (1894–1979) *Nana* 1926; *La Chienne* 1931; *On Purge Bébé* 1931; *Boudu, Saved from Drowning* 1932; *La Nuit du Carrefour* 1932; *Madame Bovary* 1933; *Le Crime de Monsieur Lange* 1935; *Toni* 1935; *The Lower Depths* 1936; *Une Partie de Campagne* 1936; *La Vie Est à Nous* 1936; *La Grande Illusion* 1937; *La Bête Humaine* 1938; *La Marseillaise* 1938; *La Règle du Jeu* 1939; *Swamp Water* 1941; *This Land Is Mine* 1943; *The Southerner* 1945; *Diary of a Chambermaid* 1946; *The Woman on the Beach* 1947; *The River* 1951; *The Golden Coach* 1953; *French Cancan* 1955; *Elena et les Hommes* 1956; *Lunch on the Grass* 1959; *The Testament of Dr Cordelier* 1959; *The Vanishing Corporal* 1962; *The Little Theatre of Jean Renoir* 1969
Resnais, Alain (1922–) *Nuit et Brouillard* 1955; *Hiroshima, Mon Amour* 1959; *Last Year at Marienbad* 1961; *Muriel* 1963; *La Guerre Est Finie* 1966; *Far from Vietnam* 1967; *Je T'Aime, Je T'Aime* 1968; *Stavisky* 1974; *Providence* 1977; *Mon Oncle d'Amérique* 1980; *Life Is a Bed of Roses* 1983; *Mélo* 1986; *I Want to Go Home* 1989; *Smoking/No Smoking* 1993; *On Connaît la Chanson* 1997; *Pas sur la Bouche* 2003
Reygadas, Carlos (1971–) *Japón* 2002; *Battle in Heaven* 2005
Reynolds, Burt (1936–) *Gator* 1976; *The End* 1978; *Sharky's Machine* 1981; *Stick* 1985; *Hard Time* 1998; *The Last Producer* 2000
Reynolds, Kevin (1952–) *Fandango* 1985; *The Beast of War* 1988; *Robin Hood: Prince of Thieves* 1991; *Rapa Nui* 1994; *Waterworld* 1995; *One Eight Seven* 1997; *The Count of Monte Cristo* 2001
Reynolds, Scott *The Ugly* 1996; *Heaven* 1998
Reynolds, Sheldon (1923–2003) *Foreign Intrigue* 1956; *Assignment to Kill* 1968
Rich, David Lowell (1923–) *Senior Prom* 1958; *Have Rocket, Will Travel* 1959; *Hey Boy! Hey Girl!* 1959; *Madame X* 1966; *The Plainsman* 1966; *Rosie!* 1967; *A Lovely Way to Go* 1968; *Three Guns for Texas* 1968; *Eye of the Cat* 1969; *Runaway!* 1973; *That Man Bolt* 1973; *Airport '79: the Concorde* 1979; *Chu Chu and the Philly Flash* 1981
Rich, John (1925–) *Wives and Lovers* 1963; *The New Interns* 1964; *Roustabout* 1964; *Boeing Boeing* 1965; *Easy Come, Easy Go* 1967
Rich, Matty (1971–) *Straight out of Brooklyn* 1991; *No Ordinary Summer* 1994
Rich, Richard *The Fox and the Hound* 1981; *The Black Cauldron* 1985; *The Swan Princess* 1994; *The King and I* 1999
Rich, Roy (1913–1970) *It's Not Cricket* 1948; *My Brother's Keeper* 1948
Richards, Dick (1936–) *The Culpepper Cattle Co* 1972; *Rafferty and the Gold Dust Twins* 1974; *Farewell, My Lovely* 1975; *March or Die* 1977; *Death Valley* 1982; *Man, Woman and Child* 1983; *Heat* 1987
Richards, Julian *Darklands* 1996; *The Last Horror Movie* 2003
Richardson, Peter (1952–) *The Supergrass* 1985; *Eat the Rich* 1987; *The Pope Must Die* 1991; *Churchill: the Hollywood Years* 2004
Richardson, Tony (1928–1991) *Look Back in Anger* 1959; *The Entertainer* 1960; *Sanctuary* 1961; *A Taste of Honey* 1961; *The Loneliness of the Long Distance Runner* 1962; *Tom Jones* 1963; *The Loved One* 1965; *Mademoiselle* 1966; *The Sailor from Gibraltar* 1967; *The Charge of the Light Brigade* 1968; *Hamlet* 1969; *Laughter in the Dark* 1969; *Ned Kelly* 1970; *A Delicate Balance* 1973; *Dead Cert* 1974; *Joseph Andrews* 1977; *The Border* 1981; *The Hotel New Hampshire* 1984; *Blue Sky* 1991
Richert, William *The American Success Company* 1979; *Winter Kills* 1979; *A Night in the Life of Jimmy Reardon* 1988; *The Man in the Iron Mask* 1997
Richter, W D (1945–) *The Adventures of Buckaroo Banzai across the 8th Dimension* 1984; *Late for Dinner* 1991
Ridley, Philip (1960–) *The Reflecting Skin* 1990; *The Passion of Darkly Noon* 1995
Riefenstahl, Leni (1902–2003) *The Blue Light* 1932; *Triumph of the Will* 1935; *Olympiad* 1938
Rifkin, Adam (1966–) *Never on Tuesday* 1988; *The Dark Backward* 1991; *The Chase* 1994; *Something about Sex* 1998; *Detroit Rock City* 1999
Rilla, Wolf (1920–) *The Black Rider* 1954; *The Blue Peter* 1955; *Stock Car* 1955; *The Scamp*

1957; *Bachelor of Hearts* 1958; *Witness in the Dark* 1959; *Piccadilly Third Stop* 1960; *Village of the Damned* 1960; *Watch It, Sailor!* 1961; *Cairo* 1962; *The World Ten Times Over* 1963
Ripley, Arthur (1895–1961) *The Barber Shop* 1933; *I Met My Love Again* 1938; *The Chase* 1946; *Thunder Road* 1958
Ripoll, Maria *If Only* 1998; *Tortilla Soup* 2001
Ripstein, Arturo (1943–) *Deep Crimson* 1996; *No One Writes to the Colonel* 1999
Risi, Dino (1917–) *Love in the City* 1953; *The Easy Life* 1962; *Le Bambole* 1965; *The Tiger and the Pussycat* 1967; *The Priest's Wife* 1970; *Scent of a Woman* 1974; *Viva Italia!* 1978
Ritchie, Guy (1968–) *Lock, Stock and Two Smoking Barrels* 1998; *Snatch* 2000; *Swept Away* 2002
Ritchie, Michael (1938–2001) *Downhill Racer* 1969; *The Candidate* 1972; *Prime Cut* 1972; *Smile* 1975; *The Bad News Bears* 1976; *Semi-Tough* 1977; *An Almost Perfect Affair* 1979; *Divine Madness* 1980; *The Island* 1980; *The Survivors* 1983; *Fletch* 1985; *The Golden Child* 1986; *Wildcats* 1986; *The Couch Trip* 1988; *Fletch Lives* 1989; *Midnight Sting* 1992; *The Positively True Adventures of the Alleged Texas Cheerleader-Murdering Mom* 1993; *Cops and Robbersons* 1994; *The Scout* 1994; *The Fantasticks* 1995; *A Simple Wish* 1997
Ritt, Martin (1914–1990) *Edge of the City* 1957; *No Down Payment* 1957; *The Long Hot Summer* 1958; *The Black Orchid* 1959; *The Sound and the Fury* 1959; *Five Branded Women* 1960; *Paris Blues* 1961; *Hemingway's Adventures of a Young Man* 1962; *Hud* 1963; *The Outrage* 1964; *The Spy Who Came in from the Cold* 1965; *Hombre* 1967; *The Brotherhood* 1968; *The Great White Hope* 1970; *The Molly Maguires* 1970; *Pete 'n' Tillie* 1972; *Sounder* 1972; *Conrack* 1974; *The Front* 1976; *Casey's Shadow* 1978; *Norma Rae* 1979; *Back Roads* 1981; *Cross Creek* 1983; *Murphy's Romance* 1985; *Nuts* 1987; *Stanley & Iris* 1989
Rivette, Jacques (1928–) *Paris Nous Appartient* 1960; *La Religieuse* 1965; *L'Amour Fou* 1968; *Out 1: Spectre* 1973; *Celine and Julie Go Boating* 1974; *L'Amour par Terre* 1984; *La Belle Noiseuse* 1991; *Jeanne la Pucelle* 1994; *Secret Defense* 1997; *Va Savoir* 2001; *Histoire de Marie et Julien* 2003
Roach, Hal (1892–1992) *Bogus Bandits* 1933; *The Housekeeper's Daughter* 1939; *One Million BC* 1940; *Turnabout* 1940
Roach, Jay (1957–) *Austin Powers: International Man of Mystery* 1997; *Austin Powers: the Spy Who Shagged Me* 1999; *Mystery, Alaska* 1999; *Meet the Parents* 2000; *Austin Powers in Goldmember* 2002; *Meet the Fockers* 2004
Robbe-Grillet, Alain (1922–) *Trans-Europ-Express* 1966; *The Blue Villa* 1994
Robbins, Brian (1964–) *The Show* 1995; *Good Burger* 1997; *Varsity Blues* 1999; *Ready to Rumble* 2000; *Hardball* 2001; *The Perfect Score* 2004
Robbins, Matthew *Corvette Summer* 1978; *Dragonslayer* 1981; *The Legend of Billie Jean* 1985; **batteries not included* 1987; *Bingo* 1991
Robbins, Tim (1958–) *Bob Roberts* 1992; *Dead Man Walking* 1995; *Cradle Will Rock* 1999
Robert, Yves (1920–2002) *War of the Buttons* 1962; *The Tall Blond Man with One Black Shoe* 1972; *The Bit Player* 1973; *Pardon Mon Affaire* 1976; *Le Château de Ma Mère* 1990; *La Gloire de Mon Père* 1990
Roberts, Alan *Young Lady Chatterley* 1976; *The Happy Hooker Goes to Hollywood* 1980; *Round Trip to Heaven* 1992
Roberts, Bill *Fantasia* 1940; *Saludos Amigos* 1943; *The Three Caballeros* 1944; *Fun and Fancy Free* 1947
Roberts, John *War of the Buttons* 1993; *Paulie* 1998
Roberts, Stephen (1917–1999) *If I Had a Million* 1932; *Romance in Manhattan* 1934; *The Man Who Broke the Bank at Monte Carlo* 1935; *Star of Midnight* 1935; *The Ex-Mrs Bradford* 1936
Robertson, Cliff (1925–) *JW Coop* 1971; *The Pilot* 1979
Robertson, John S (1878–1964) *Dr Jekyll and Mr Hyde* 1920; *Tess of the Storm Country* 1922; *Annie Laurie* 1927; *The Single Standard* 1929; *Captain Hurricane* 1935; *Our Little Girl* 1935
Robins, John *Nearest and Dearest* 1972; *That's Your Funeral* 1972; *Love Thy Neighbour* 1973; *The Best of Benny Hill* 1974; *Man about the House* 1974; *Hot Resort* 1985
Robinson, Bruce (1946–) *Withnail & I* 1986; *How to Get Ahead in Advertising* 1989; *Jennifer Eight* 1992
Robinson, John Mark *Roadhouse 66* 1984; *Kid* 1990
Robinson, Phil Alden (1950–) *The Woo Woo Kid* 1987; *Field of Dreams* 1989; *Sneakers* 1992; *Freedom Song* 2000; *The Sum of All Fears* 2002
Robson, Mark (1913–1978) *The Ghost Ship* 1943; *The Seventh Victim* 1943; *Youth Runs Wild* 1944; *Isle of the Dead* 1945; *Bedlam* 1946; *Champion* 1949; *Home of the Brave* 1949; *My Foolish Heart* 1949; *Roughshod* 1949; *Edge of Doom* 1950; *Bright Victory* 1951; *I Want You* 1951; *Return to Paradise* 1953; *The Bridges at Toko-Ri* 1954; *Hell below Zero* 1954; *Phffft!* 1954; *A Prize of Gold* 1955; *Trial* 1955; *The Harder They Fall* 1956; *The Little Hut* 1957; *Peyton Place* 1957; *The Inn of the Sixth Happiness* 1958; *From the Terrace* 1960; *Nine Hours to Rama* 1963; *The Prize* 1963; *Von Ryan's Express* 1965; *Lost Command* 1966; *Valley of the Dolls* 1967; *Daddy's Gone A-Hunting* 1969; *Happy Birthday, Wanda June* 1971; *Limbo* 1972; *Earthquake* 1974; *Avalanche Express* 1979
Rocco, Marc *Dream a Little Dream* 1989; *Where the Day Takes You* 1992; *Murder in the First* 1994
Rocha, Glauber (1938–1981) *Black God, White Devil* 1964; *Antonio das Mortes* 1969
Rochant, Eric (1961–) *A World without Pity* 1989; *Autobus* 1991; *Patriots* 1994
Rochat, Eric *Too Much* 1987; *The 5th Monkey* 1990
Rockwell, Alexandre (1956–) *Sons* 1989; *In the Soup* 1992; *Somebody to Love* 1994; *Four Rooms* 1995
Roddam, Franc (1946–) *Quadrophenia* 1979; *The Lords of Discipline* 1983; *The Bride* 1985; *Aria* 1987; *War Party* 1988; *K2* 1991
Rodriguez, Ismael (1917–2004) *The Beast of Hollow Mountain* 1956; *Tizoc* 1956; *Daniel Boone, Trail Blazer* 1957; *The Important Man* 1961
Rodriguez, Robert (1968–) *El Mariachi* 1992; *Roadracers* 1994; *Desperado* 1995; *Four Rooms* 1995; *From Dusk till Dawn* 1995; *The Faculty* 1998; *SPYkids* 2001; *SPYkids 2: the Island of Lost Dreams* 2002; *Once upon a Time in Mexico* 2003; *SPYkids 3-D: Game Over* 2003; *The Adventures of Sharkboy and Lavagirl in 3-D* 2005; *Sin City* 2005
Roeg, Nicolas (1928–) *Performance* 1970; *Walkabout* 1970; *Don't Look Now* 1973; *The Man Who Fell to Earth* 1976; *Bad Timing* 1980; *Eureka* 1982; *Insignificance* 1985; *Castaway* 1986; *Aria* 1987; *Track 29* 1988; *The Witches* 1989; *Cold Heaven* 1992; *Two Deaths* 1994
Roemer, Michael (1928–) *Nothing but a Man* 1964; *The Plot against Harry* 1969
Roffman, Julian (1919–) *The Bloody Brood* 1959; *The Mask* 1961
Rogell, Albert S (1901–1988) *Atlantic Adventure* 1935; *Start Cheering* 1938; *Argentine Nights* 1940; *The Black Cat* 1941; *Change of Heart* 1943; *War of the Wildcats* 1943; *Heaven Only Knows* 1947; *Northwest Stampede* 1948; *The Admiral Was a Lady* 1950
Rogers, Charles (1890–1960) *Bogus Bandits* 1933; *Babes in Toyland* 1934; *Them Thar Hills!* 1934; *Tit for Tat* 1934; *The Bohemian Girl* 1936
Rogers, James B *aka* **Rogers, J B** *American Pie 2* 2001; *Say It Isn't So* 2001
Rogers, Maclean (1899–1962) *Gert and Daisy's Weekend* 1941; *Variety Jubilee* 1942; *Something in the City* 1950; *Down among the Z-Men* 1952; *Forces' Sweetheart* 1953; *Assignment Redhead* 1956; *Mark of the Phoenix* 1957; *Not Wanted on Voyage* 1957; *You Pay Your Money* 1957
Rogozhkin, Aleksandr *Checkpoint* 1998; *The Cuckoo* 2002
Rohmer, Eric (1920–) *The Sign of Leo* 1959; *The Boulangère de Monceau* 1962; *La Carrière de Suzanne* 1963; *Paris Vu Par…* 1965; *La Collectionneuse* 1967; *My Night with Maud* 1969; *Claire's Knee* 1970; *Love in the Afternoon* 1972; *The Marquise of O* 1976; *Perceval le Gallois* 1978; *The Aviator's Wife* 1980; *Le Beau Mariage* 1982; *Pauline at the Beach* 1983; *Full Moon in Paris* 1984; *Four Adventures of Reinette and Mirabelle* 1986; *The Green Ray* 1986; *My Girlfriend's Boyfriend* 1987; *A Tale of Springtime* 1989; *A Winter's Tale* 1992; *Les Rendez-vous de Paris* 1995; *A Summer's Tale* 1996; *An Autumn Tale* 1998; *The Lady & the Duke* 2001; *Triple Agent* 2003
Roley, Sutton *How to Steal the World* 1968; *The Loners* 1971; *Chosen Survivors* 1974
Rollin, Jean (1938–) *Shiver of the Vampires* 1970; *Lips of Blood* 1975; *Fascination* 1979
Roman, Phil (1930–) *Race for Your Life, Charlie Brown* 1977; *Tom and Jerry: the Movie* 1992
Romanek, Mark (1959–) *Static* 1985; *One Hour Photo* 2001
Romero, Eddie (1924–) *Black Mama, White Mama* 1972; *Twilight People* 1973; *A Case of Honor* 1988
Romero, George A (1940–) *Night of the Living Dead* 1968; *Season of the Witch* 1972; *The Crazies* 1973; *Dawn of the Dead* 1978; *Martin* 1978; *Knightriders* 1981; *Creepshow* 1982; *Day of the Dead* 1985; *Monkey Shines* 1988; *Two Evil Eyes* 1990; *The Dark Half* 1991
Roodt, Darrell James *aka* **Roodt, Darrell** (1963–) *Jobman* 1990; *Sarafina!* 1992; *Father Hood* 1993; *Cry, the Beloved Country* 1995; *Dangerous Ground* 1996
Rooks, Conrad (1934–) *Chappaqua* 1966; *Siddhartha* 1972
Roome, Alfred (1908–1997) *It's Not Cricket* 1948; *My Brother's Keeper* 1948
Rooney, Bethany *Danielle Steel's Mixed Blessings* 1995; *Danielle Steel's Full Circle* 1996; *Danielle Steel's Remembrance* 1996; *Freshman Fall* 1996
Roos, Don (1955–) *The Opposite of Sex* 1998; *Bounce* 2000
Ropelewski, Tom *Madhouse* 1990; *Look Who's Talking Now!* 1993
Rose, Bernard (1960–) *Paperhouse* 1988; *Chicago Joe and the Showgirl* 1989; *Candyman* 1992; *Immortal Beloved* 1994; *Anna Karenina* 1997; *ivansxtc.* 1999
Rosen, Martin *Watership Down* 1978; *The Plague Dogs* 1982; *Season of Dreams* 1987
Rosen, Phil (1888–1951) *The Exquisite Sinner* 1926; *Vanishing Frontier* 1932; *Black Beauty* 1933; *The Sphinx* 1933; *Dangerous Corner* 1934; *Spooks Run Wild* 1941; *Charlie Chan in The Chinese Cat* 1944; *Charlie Chan in the Secret Service* 1944; *Meeting at Midnight* 1944; *The Jade Mask* 1945; *The Red Dragon* 1945; *The Scarlet Clue* 1945
Rosenberg, Stuart *aka* **Smithee, Alan** (1927–) *Murder, Inc* 1960; *Cool Hand Luke* 1967; *The April Fools* 1969; *WUSA* 1970; *Pocket Money* 1972; *The Laughing Policeman* 1973; *The Drowning Pool* 1975; *Voyage of the Damned* 1976; *Love and Bullets* 1978; *The Amityville Horror* 1979; *Brubaker* 1980; *The Pope of Greenwich Village* 1984; *Let's Get Harry* 1986; *My Heroes Have Always Been Cowboys* 1991
Rosenthal, Rick *aka* **Rosenthal, Richard L** (1949–) *Halloween II* 1981; *Bad Boys* 1983; *American Dreamer* 1984; *Russkies* 1987; *Distant Thunder* 1988; *Halloween: Resurrection* 2002
Rosi, Francesco (1922–) *Salvatore Giuliano* 1961; *Hands over the City* 1963; *The Moment of Truth* 1964; *More than a Miracle* 1967; *The Mattei Affair* 1972; *Lucky Luciano* 1973; *Illustrious Corpses* 1976; *Christ Stopped at Eboli* 1979; *Three Brothers* 1980; *Carmen* 1984; *Chronicle of a Death Foretold* 1987; *The Truce* 1997
Rosman, Mark (1959–) *House of Evil* 1983; *Life-Size* 2000; *A Cinderella Story* 2004
Rosmer, Milton (1881–1971) *Dreyfus* 1931; *Maria Marten, or the Murder in the Red Barn* 1935; *Everything Is Thunder* 1936; *The Great Barrier* 1937; *The Challenge* 1938
Ross, Benjamin (1964–) *The Young Poisoner's Handbook* 1994; *RKO 281* 1999
Ross, Gary (1956–) *Pleasantville* 1998; *Seabiscuit* 2003
Ross, Herbert (1927–2001) *Goodbye, Mr Chips* 1969; *The Owl and the Pussycat* 1970; *TR Baskin* 1971; *Play It Again, Sam* 1972; *The Last of Sheila* 1973; *Funny Lady* 1975; *The Sunshine Boys* 1975; *The Seven-Per-Cent Solution* 1976; *The Goodbye Girl* 1977; *The Turning Point* 1977; *California Suite* 1978; *Nijinsky* 1980; *Pennies from Heaven* 1981; *I Ought to Be in Pictures* 1982; *Max Dugan Returns* 1983; *Footloose* 1984; *Protocol* 1984; *Dancers* 1987; *The Secret of My Success* 1987; *Steel Magnolias* 1989; *My Blue Heaven* 1990; *True Colors* 1991; *Undercover Blues* 1993; *Boys on the Side* 1995
Rossellini, Roberto (1906–1977) *Rome, Open City* 1945; *Paisà* 1946; *Germany, Year Zero* 1947; *L'Amore* 1948; *Francis, God's Jester* 1950; *Stromboli* 1950; *Europa '51* 1952; *The Seven Deadly Sins* 1952; *Journey to Italy* 1953; *Fear* 1954; *General Della Rovere* 1959; *RoGoPaG* 1962; *The Rise to Power of Louis XIV* 1966
Rossen, Robert (1908–1966) *Body and Soul* 1947; *Johnny O'Clock* 1947; *All the King's Men* 1949; *The Brave Bulls* 1951; *Mambo* 1954; *Alexander the Great* 1956; *Island in the Sun* 1957; *They Came to Cordura* 1959; *The Hustler* 1961; *Lilith* 1964
Rossi, Franco (1919–2000) *Friends for Life* 1955; *Le Bambole* 1965; *The Witches* 1966
Rosson, Richard (1893–1953) *Behind the Headlines* 1937; *Corvette K-225* 1943
Roth, Bobby (1950–) *Heartbreakers* 1984; *The Man Inside* 1990; *The Switch* 1993; *Kidnapped* 1995; *Devil's Child* 1997; *Her Own Rules* 1998; *A Secret Affair* 1999
Roth, Joe (1948–) *Streets of Gold* 1986; *Coupe de Ville* 1990; *America's Sweethearts* 2001; *Christmas with the Kranks* 2004
Roth, Phillip J *APEX* 1994; *Velocity Trap* 1997
Rotha, Paul (1907–1984) *No Resting Place* 1950; *Cat and Mouse* 1958
Rothkirch, Thilo Graf *The Little Polar Bear* 2001; *Laura's Star* 2004
Rothman, Stephanie (1936–) *The Velvet Vampire* 1971; *Terminal Island* 1973; *Ruby* 1977
Rouse, Russell (1916–1987) *The Well* 1951; *The Thief* 1952; *New York Confidential* 1955; *The Fastest Gun Alive* 1956; *House of Numbers* 1957; *Thunder in the Sun* 1959; *The Oscar* 1966
Rowland, Roy (1910–1995) *Hollywood Party* 1934; *Lost Angel* 1943; *Our Vines Have Tender Grapes* 1945; *Killer McCoy* 1947; *Scene of the Crime* 1949; *The Outriders* 1950; *Bugles in the Afternoon* 1952; *Affair with a Stranger* 1953; *The 5,000 Fingers of Dr T* 1953; *The Moonlighter* 1953; *Rogue Cop* 1954; *Witness to Murder* 1954; *Hit the Deck* 1955; *Many Rivers to Cross* 1955; *Meet Me in Las Vegas* 1956; *These Wilder Years* 1956; *Gun Glory* 1957; *Seven Hills of Rome* 1957; *The Girl Hunters* 1963
Roy, Bimal (1909–1966) *Do Bigha Zameen* 1953; *Yahudi* 1958; *Sujata* 1959; *Bandini* 1963
Rozema, Patricia (1958–) *I've Heard the Mermaids Singing* 1987; *White Room* 1990; *When Night Is Falling* 1995; *Mansfield Park* 1999
Ruane, John (1952–) *Death in Brunswick* 1990; *That Eye, the Sky* 1994; *Dead Letter Office* 1998
Rubbo, Michael (1938–) *The Peanut Butter Solution* 1985; *Tommy Tricker and the Stamp Traveller* 1988
Ruben, J Walter (1899–1942) *The Roadhouse Murder* 1932; *Ace of Aces* 1933; *Success at Any Price* 1934; *Java Head* 1935; *Public Hero No 1* 1935; *Riffraff* 1936; *Trouble for Two* 1936
Ruben, Joseph (1951–) *Joyride* 1977; *GORP* 1980; *Dreamscape* 1984; *The Stepfather* 1986; *True Believer* 1989; *Sleeping with the Enemy* 1991; *The Good Son* 1993; *Money Train* 1995; *Return to Paradise* 1998; *The Forgotten* 2004
Ruben, Katt Shea *aka* **Shea, Katt** *Streets* 1990; *Poison Ivy* 1992; *The Rage: Carrie 2* 1999
Rubin, Bruce Joel *aka* **Rubin, Bruce** (1943–) *Dionysus in '69* 1970; *My Life* 1993
Rudolph, Alan (1943–) *Welcome to LA* 1976; *Remember My Name* 1978; *Roadie* 1980; *Endangered Species* 1982; *Choose Me* 1984; *Songwriter* 1984; *Trouble in Mind* 1985; *Made in Heaven* 1987; *The Moderns* 1988; *Love at Large* 1990; *Mortal Thoughts* 1991; *Equinox* 1992; *Mrs Parker and the Vicious Circle* 1994; *Afterglow* 1997; *Breakfast of Champions* 1999; *Trixie* 2000; *The Secret Lives of Dentists* 2002
Ruggles, Wesley (1889–1972) *Condemned* 1929; *Cimarron* 1931; *No Man of Her Own* 1932; *I'm No Angel* 1933; *Bolero* 1934; *Accent on Youth* 1935; *The Bride Comes Home* 1935; *The Gilded Lily* 1935; *Valiant Is the Word for Carrie* 1936; *I Met Him in Paris* 1937; *True Confession* 1937; *Invitation to Happiness* 1939; *Arizona* 1940; *Too Many Husbands* 1940; *You Belong to Me* 1941; *Somewhere I'll Find You* 1942; *Slightly Dangerous* 1943; *See Here, Private Hargrove* 1944; *London Town* 1946
Ruiz, Raúl *aka* **Ruiz, Raoul** (1941–) *Treasure Island* 1986; *Three Lives and Only One Death* 1996; *Généalogies d'un Crime* 1997; *Shattered Image* 1998; *Time Regained* 1999; *Comédie de l'Innocence* 2000

Rumley, Simon *Strong Language* 1998; *The Truth Game* 2000; *Club le Monde* 2001
Rush, Richard (1930–) *Too Soon to Love* 1960; *Of Love and Desire* 1963; *Hell's Angels on Wheels* 1967; *Thunder Alley* 1967; *Psych-Out* 1968; *Getting Straight* 1970; *Freebie and the Bean* 1974; *The Stunt Man* 1980; *Color of Night* 1994
Russell, Chuck *aka* **Russell, Charles** *A Nightmare on Elm Street 3: Dream Warriors* 1987; *The Blob* 1988; *The Mask* 1994; *Eraser* 1996; *Bless the Child* 2000; *The Scorpion King* 2002
Russell, David O (1959–) *Spanking the Monkey* 1994; *Flirting with Disaster* 1996; *Three Kings* 1999; *I ❤ Huckabees* 2004
Russell, Jay (1960–) *End of the Line* 1987; *My Dog Skip* 1999; *Tuck Everlasting* 2002; *Ladder 49* 2004
Russell, Ken (1927–) *French Dressing* 1964; *Billion Dollar Brain* 1967; *Women in Love* 1969; *The Music Lovers* 1970; *The Boy Friend* 1971; *The Devils* 1971; *Savage Messiah* 1972; *Mahler* 1974; *Lisztomania* 1975; *Tommy* 1975; *Valentino* 1977; *Altered States* 1980; *Crimes of Passion* 1984; *Gothic* 1986; *Aria* 1987; *The Lair of the White Worm* 1988; *The Rainbow* 1988; *Salome's Last Dance* 1988; *Prisoner of Honor* 1991; *Whore* 1991; *Erotic Tales* 1994
Russell, William D (1908–1968) *Dear Ruth* 1947; *The Sainted Sisters* 1948; *Bride for Sale* 1949; *Best of the Badmen* 1951
Ruzowitzky, Stefan (1961–) *The Inheritors* 1997; *Anatomy* 2000
Ryan, Frank (1907–1947) *Call Out the Marines* 1941; *Hers to Hold* 1943; *Can't Help Singing* 1944; *Patrick the Great* 1944; *So Goes My Love* 1946
Ryan, Terence (1948–) *The Brylcreem Boys* 1996; *Puckoon* 2002
Rydell, Mark (1934–) *The Fox* 1967; *The Reivers* 1969; *The Cowboys* 1972; *Cinderella Liberty* 1973; *Harry and Walter Go to New York* 1976; *The Rose* 1979; *On Golden Pond* 1981; *The River* 1984; *For the Boys* 1991; *Intersection* 1994; *Crime of the Century* 1996; *James Dean* 2001
Rymer, Michael (1963–) *Angel Baby* 1995; *In Too Deep* 1999; *Queen of the Damned* 2002

Sachs, William *The Incredible Melting Man* 1977; *Van Nuys Blvd* 1979; *Exterminator 2* 1980; *Galaxina* 1980; *Spooky House* 1999
Safran, Henri (1932–) *Storm Boy* 1976; *Norman Loves Rose* 1982; *Bush Christmas* 1983; *The Wild Duck* 1983
Sagal, Boris (1917–1981) *Twilight of Honor* 1963; *Girl Happy* 1965; *Made in Paris* 1966; *The Helicopter Spies* 1968; *Mosquito Squadron* 1968; *The 1,000 Plane Raid* 1969; *The Harness* 1971; *The Omega Man* 1971; *Sherlock Holmes in New York* 1976
Sagan, Leontine (1899–1974) *Girls in Uniform* 1931; *Gaiety George* 1946
St Clair, Malcolm *aka* **St Clair, Mal** (1897–1952) *The Canary Murder Case* 1929; *Crack-Up* 1936; *Born Reckless* 1937; *The Man in the Trunk* 1942; *The Dancing Masters* 1943; *Jitterbugs* 1943; *The Big Noise* 1944; *The Bullfighters* 1945
St Paul, Stuart *The Scarlet Tunic* 1997; *Devil's Gate* 2002
Saks, Gene (1921–) *Barefoot in the Park* 1967; *The Odd Couple* 1968; *Cactus Flower* 1969; *The Last of the Red Hot Lovers* 1972; *Mame* 1974; *Brighton Beach Memoirs* 1986; *A Touch of Adultery* 1991
Saldanha, Carlos *Ice Age* 2002; *Robots* 2005
Sale, Richard (1911–1993) *A Ticket to Tomahawk* 1950; *Half Angel* 1951; *Let's Make It Legal* 1951; *Meet Me after the Show* 1951; *The Girl Next Door* 1953; *Malaga* 1954; *Gentlemen Marry Brunettes* 1955; *Seven Waves Away* 1957
Salkow, Sidney (1909–2000) *The Lone Wolf Meets a Lady* 1940; *Time Out for Rhythm* 1941; *Shadow of the Eagle* 1950; *Scarlet Angel* 1952; *Prince of Pirates* 1953; *Raiders of the Seven Seas* 1953; *Sitting Bull* 1954; *Las Vegas Shakedown* 1955; *Chicago Confidential* 1957; *Gun Duel in Durango* 1957; *The Iron Sheriff* 1957; *Twice Told Tales* 1963; *The Last Man on Earth* 1964; *The Great Sioux Massacre* 1965
Salles, Walter (1956–) *Central Station* 1998; *Midnight* 1998; *Behind the Sun* 2001; *The Motorcycle Diaries* 2004
Salomon, Mikael (1945–) *A Far Off Place* 1993; *Hard Rain* 1997
Salva, Victor (1958–) *Clownhouse* 1988; *Bad Company* 1994; *Powder* 1995; *Rites of Passage* 1999; *Jeepers Creepers* 2001; *Jeepers Creepers 2* 2003
Salvadori, Pierre (1967–) *Wild Target* 1993; *Les Apprentis* 1995
Salvatores, Gabriele (1950–) *Mediterraneo* 1991; *Puerto Escondido* 1992; *Nirvana* 1996; *I'm Not Scared* 2003
Sanders, Denis (1929–1987) *Crime and Punishment, USA* 1959; *War Hunt* 1962; *One Man's Way* 1964; *Shock Treatment* 1964; *Elvis: That's the Way It Is* 1970
Sandrich, Mark (1900–1945) *Melody Cruise* 1933; *The Gay Divorce* 1934; *Top Hat* 1935; *Follow the Fleet* 1936; *A Woman Rebels* 1936; *Shall We Dance* 1937; *Carefree* 1938; *Buck Benny Rides Again* 1940; *Skylark* 1941; *Holiday Inn* 1942; *So Proudly We Hail* 1943; *Here Come the Waves* 1944; *I Love a Soldier* 1944
Sanford, Arlene *A Very Brady Sequel* 1996; *I'll Be Home for Christmas* 1998
Sangster, Jimmy (1924–) *The Horror of Frankenstein* 1970; *Lust for a Vampire* 1970; *Fear in the Night* 1972
Santell, Alfred (1895–1981) *Body and Soul* 1931; *Daddy Long Legs* 1931; *Polly of the Circus* 1932; *Tess of the Storm Country* 1932; *Winterset* 1936; *Breakfast for Two* 1937; *Internes Can't Take Money* 1937; *Having Wonderful Time* 1938; *Beyond the Blue Horizon* 1942; *The Hairy Ape* 1944; *Jack London* 1944
Santley, Joseph (1899–1971) *The Cocoanuts* 1929; *There Goes the Groom* 1937; *Blond Cheat* 1938; *Music in My Heart* 1940; *Down Mexico Way* 1941; *Chatterbox* 1943; *Brazil* 1944; *Rosie the Riveter* 1944; *Earl Carroll Vanities* 1945
Saperstein, David *A Killing Affair* 1985; *Beyond the Stars* 1988
Sarafian, Deran *Death Warrant* 1990; *Back in the USSR* 1992; *Gunmen* 1994; *Roadflower* 1994; *Terminal Velocity* 1994
Sarafian, Richard C *aka* **Smithee, Alan** (1925–) *Run Wild, Run Free* 1969; *Fragment of Fear* 1970; *Man in the Wilderness* 1971; *Vanishing Point* 1971; *The Lolly-Madonna War* 1973; *The Man Who Loved Cat Dancing* 1973; *The Next Man* 1976; *Sunburn* 1979; *Eye of the Tiger* 1986; *Solar Crisis* 1990
Sargent, Joseph (1925–) *One Spy Too Many* 1966; *The Spy in the Green Hat* 1966; *The Hell with Heroes* 1968; *Colossus: the Forbin Project* 1969; *The Man* 1972; *White Lightning* 1973; *The Taking of Pelham One Two Three* 1974; *MacArthur* 1977; *Goldengirl* 1979; *Coast to Coast* 1980; *Nightmares* 1983; *Jaws the Revenge* 1987; *Day One* 1989; *Caroline?* 1990; *Miss Rose White* 1992; *Mandela and de Klerk* 1997; *Miss Evers' Boys* 1997; *A Lesson Before Dying* 1999; *For Love or Country: the Arturo Sandoval Story* 2000
Sarne, Michael *aka* **Sarne, Mike** (1939–) *Joanna* 1969; *Myra Breckinridge* 1970; *The Punk* 1993; *Glastonbury the Movie* 1995
Sasdy, Peter (1934–) *Taste the Blood of Dracula* 1969; *Countess Dracula* 1970; *Hands of the Ripper* 1971; *Doomwatch* 1972; *Nothing but the Night* 1972; *I Don't Want to Be Born* 1975; *Welcome to Blood City* 1977; *The Lonely Lady* 1983
Saunders, Charles (1904–1997) *Tawny Pipit* 1944; *Death of an Angel* 1951; *Love in Pawn* 1953; *The Hornet's Nest* 1955; *Behind the Headlines* 1956; *Find the Lady* 1956; *The Man without a Body* 1957; *The Woman Eater* 1957; *Naked Fury* 1959; *The Gentle Trap* 1960; *Dangerous Afternoon* 1961; *Danger by My Side* 1962
Saura, Carlos (1932–) *The Hunt* 1966; *Peppermint Frappé* 1967; *Cría Cuervos* 1975; *Mamá Cumple 100 Años* 1979; *Blood Wedding* 1981; *Carmen* 1983; *El Amor Brujo* 1986; *El Dorado* 1988; *Ay, Carmela!* 1990; *Outrage* 1993; *Flamenco* 1995; *Tango* 1998; *Goya in Bordeaux* 1999
Sautet, Claude (1924–2000) *The Big Risk* 1960; *The Things of Life* 1969; *César and Rosalie* 1972; *Vincent, François, Paul and the Others* 1974; *Mado* 1976; *Une Histoire Simple* 1978; *Un Coeur en Hiver* 1992; *Les Enfants de Lumière* 1995; *Nelly & Monsieur Arnaud* 1995
Saville, Philip (1930–) *Stop the World, I Want to Get Off* 1966; *Oedipus the King* 1967; *The Best House in London* 1968; *Secrets* 1971; *Those Glory, Glory Days* 1983; *Shadey* 1985; *Fellow Traveller* 1989; *Metroland* 1997
Saville, Victor (1897–1979) *Kitty* 1928; *Hindle Wakes* 1931; *Friday the Thirteenth* 1933; *The Good Companions* 1933; *Evensong* 1934; *Evergreen* 1934; *I Was a Spy* 1934; *The Dictator* 1935; *First a Girl* 1935; *It's Love Again* 1936; *Dark Journey* 1937; *Storm in a Teacup* 1937; *South Riding* 1938; *Forever and a Day* 1943; *Tonight and Every Night* 1945; *The Green Years* 1946; *Green Dolphin Street* 1947; *If Winter Comes* 1947; *Conspirator* 1949; *Kim* 1950; *Calling Bulldog Drummond* 1951; *The Long Wait* 1954; *The Silver Chalice* 1954
Savoca, Nancy (1959–) *True Love* 1989; *Dogfight* 1991; *Household Saints* 1993; *If These Walls Could Talk* 1996; *The 24 Hour Woman* 1999
Sayadian, Stephen *aka* **Dream, Rinse** *Cafe Flesh* 1982; *Dr Caligari* 1989
Sayles, John (1950–) *Return of the Secaucus Seven* 1980; *Baby It's You* 1983; *Lianna* 1983; *The Brother from Another Planet* 1984; *Matewan* 1987; *Eight Men Out* 1988; *City of Hope* 1991; *Passion Fish* 1992; *The Secret of Roan Inish* 1993; *Lone Star* 1995; *Men with Guns* 1997; *Limbo* 1999; *Sunshine State* 2002; *Casa de los Babys* 2003; *Silver City* 2004
Schaefer, Armand (1898–1967) *The Hurricane Express* 1932; *Sagebrush Trail* 1934
Schaefer, George (1920–1997) *Generation* 1969; *Pendulum* 1969; *Doctors' Wives* 1970; *A War of Children* 1972; *Once upon a Scoundrel* 1973; *An Enemy of the People* 1977; *A Piano for Mrs Cimino* 1982; *Mrs Delafield Wants to Marry* 1986
Schaeffer, Eric (1962–) *If Lucy Fell* 1996; *Fall* 1997
Schaffner, Franklin J *aka* **Schaffner, Franklin** (1920–1989) *The Stripper* 1963; *The Best Man* 1964; *The War Lord* 1965; *The Double Man* 1967; *Planet of the Apes* 1967; *Patton* 1970; *Nicholas and Alexandra* 1971; *Papillon* 1973; *Islands in the Stream* 1976; *The Boys from Brazil* 1978; *Sphinx* 1980; *Yes, Giorgio* 1982; *Lionheart* 1986; *Welcome Home* 1989
Schatzberg, Jerry (1927–) *Puzzle of a Downfall Child* 1970; *The Panic in Needle Park* 1971; *Scarecrow* 1973; *The Seduction of Joe Tynan* 1979; *Honeysuckle Rose* 1980; *Misunderstood* 1984; *No Small Affair* 1984; *Street Smart* 1987; *Reunion* 1989
Scheerer, Robert (1929–) *Adam at 6 AM* 1970; *The World's Greatest Athlete* 1973; *How to Beat the High Cost of Living* 1980
Schell, Maximilian (1930–) *First Love* 1970; *The Pedestrian* 1974; *End of the Game* 1976; *Marlene* 1984
Schenkel, Carl (1948–2003) *Out of Order* 1984; *The Mighty Quinn* 1989; *Silence like Glass* 1989; *Knight Moves* 1992; *Exquisite Tenderness* 1995; *Tarzan and the Lost City* 1998; *Murder on the Orient Express* 2001
Schepisi, Fred (1939–) *The Devil's Playground* 1976; *The Chant of Jimmie Blacksmith* 1978; *Barbarosa* 1982; *Iceman* 1984; *Plenty* 1985; *Roxanne* 1987; *A Cry in the Dark* 1988; *The Russia House* 1990; *Mr Baseball* 1992; *Six Degrees of Separation* 1993; *IQ* 1994; *Fierce Creatures* 1997; *Last Orders* 2001; *It Runs in the Family* 2002
Scherfig, Lone (1959–) *Italian for Beginners* 2000; *Wilbur (Wants to Kill Himself)* 2002
Schertzinger, Victor (1880–1941) *Paramount on Parade* 1930; *Friends and Lovers* 1931; *One Night of Love* 1934; *Something to Sing About* 1937; *The Mikado* 1939; *Rhythm on the River* 1940; *Road to Singapore* 1940; *The Birth of the Blues* 1941; *Kiss the Boys Goodbye* 1941; *Road to Zanzibar* 1941; *The Fleet's In* 1942
Schlamme, Thomas (1952–) *Miss Firecracker* 1989; *Crazy from the Heart* 1991; *So I Married an Axe Murderer* 1993
Schlesinger, John (1926–2003) *A Kind of Loving* 1962; *Billy Liar* 1963; *Darling* 1965; *Far from the Madding Crowd* 1967; *Midnight Cowboy* 1969; *Sunday, Bloody Sunday* 1971; *Visions of Eight* 1973; *The Day of the Locust* 1975; *Marathon Man* 1976; *Yanks* 1979; *Honky Tonk Freeway* 1981; *The Falcon and the Snowman* 1985; *The Believers* 1987; *Madame Sousatzka* 1988; *Pacific Heights* 1990; *The Innocent* 1993; *Eye for an Eye* 1995; *The Next Best Thing* 2000
Schlöndorff, Volker (1939–) *The Lost Honour of Katharina Blum* 1975; *Germany in Autumn* 1978; *The Tin Drum* 1979; *Circle of Deceit* 1981; *Swann in Love* 1984; *Death of a Salesman* 1985; *The Handmaid's Tale* 1990; *Voyager* 1991; *Palmetto* 1998; *The Legends of Rita* 2000; *Ten Minutes Older: the Cello* 2002
Schmidt, Rob (1965–) *Crime + Punishment in Suburbia* 2000; *Wrong Turn* 2003
Schmitz, Oliver *Mapantsula* 1988; *Hijack Stories* 2000
Schmoeller, David (1947–) *Tourist Trap* 1979; *Catacombs* 1988; *Puppet Master* 1989
Schnabel, Julian (1951–) *Basquiat* 1996; *Before Night Falls* 2000
Schneider, Paul *Willy/Milly* 1986; *My Boyfriend's Back* 1989
Schnitzer, Robert Allen *Rebel* 1973; *The Premonition* 1975
Schoedsack, Ernest B (1893–1979) *Grass: a Nation's Battle for Life* 1925; *Chang* 1927; *The Four Feathers* 1929; *The Most Dangerous Game* 1932; *Blind Adventure* 1933; *King Kong* 1933; *Son of Kong* 1933; *Long Lost Father* 1934; *The Last Days of Pompeii* 1935; *Dr Cyclops* 1940; *Mighty Joe Young* 1949
Schoemann, Michael *The Magic Voyage* 1992; *Millionaire Dogs* 1999
Schrader, Paul (1946–) *Blue Collar* 1978; *Hardcore* 1979; *American Gigolo* 1980; *Cat People* 1982; *Mishima: a Life in Four Chapters* 1985; *Light of Day* 1987; *Patty Hearst* 1988; *The Comfort of Strangers* 1991; *Light Sleeper* 1991; *Touch* 1996; *Affliction* 1997; *Forever Mine* 1999; *Auto Focus* 2002
Schroeder, Barbet (1941–) *More* 1969; *The Valley* 1972; *Maîtresse* 1976; *Barfly* 1987; *Reversal of Fortune* 1990; *Single White Female* 1992; *Kiss of Death* 1994; *Before and After* 1996; *Desperate Measures* 1998; *Our Lady of the Assassins* 2000; *Murder by Numbers* 2002
Schroeder, Michael (1952–) *Out of the Dark* 1988; *Damned River* 1989; *Cyborg 2: Glass Shadow* 1993; *Cyborg 3: The Recycler* 1994; *The Glass Cage* 1996
Schultz, Carl (1939–) *Careful, He Might Hear You* 1983; *Travelling North* 1986; *The Seventh Sign* 1988; *Love in Ambush* 1997; *To Walk with Lions* 1999
Schultz, John *Bandwagon* 1995; *Drive Me Crazy* 1999; *Like Mike* 2002; *The Honeymooners* 2005
Schultz, Michael (1938–) *Car Wash* 1976; *Greased Lightning* 1977; *Which Way Is Up?* 1977; *Sgt Pepper's Lonely Hearts Club Band* 1978; *Scavenger Hunt* 1979; *Carbon Copy* 1981; *The Last Dragon* 1985; *Disorderlies* 1987
Schumacher, Joel (1939–) *The Incredible Shrinking Woman* 1981; *DC Cab* 1983; *St Elmo's Fire* 1985; *The Lost Boys* 1987; *Cousins* 1989; *Flatliners* 1990; *Dying Young* 1991; *Falling Down* 1992; *The Client* 1994; *Batman Forever* 1995; *A Time to Kill* 1996; *Batman and Robin* 1997; *8mm* 1999; *Flawless* 1999; *Tigerland* 2000; *Bad Company* 2002; *Phone Booth* 2002; *Veronica Guerin* 2003; *The Phantom of the Opera* 2004
Schünzel, Reinhold (1886–1954) *Viktor und Viktoria* 1933; *Balalaika* 1939; *The Ice Follies of 1939* 1939
Schuster, Harold *aka* **Schuster, Harold D** (1902–1986) *Dinner at the Ritz* 1937; *Wings of the Morning* 1937; *Bomber's Moon* 1943; *My Friend Flicka* 1943; *Marine Raiders* 1944; *The Tender Years* 1947; *So Dear to My Heart* 1949; *Port of Hell* 1954; *Security Risk* 1954; *Tarzan's Hidden Jungle* 1955; *Dragoon Wells Massacre* 1957
Schwartz, Douglas *aka* **Schwartz, Douglas N** *Your Three Minutes Are Up* 1973; *Baywatch the Movie: Forbidden Paradise* 1995
Schwartz, Stefan *Soft Top, Hard Shoulder* 1992; *Shooting Fish* 1997; *The Abduction Club* 2002
Schwarz, Hanns *aka* **Schwartz, Hans** (1888–1945) *The Wonderful Lie of Nina Petrovna* 1929; *The Return of the Scarlet Pimpernel* 1937
Sciamma, Alberto *Killer Tongue* 1996; *Anazapta* 2001
Scola, Ettore (1931–) *Let's Talk About Women* 1964; *Jealousy, Italian Style* 1970; *We All Loved Each Other So Much* 1974; *Down and Dirty* 1976; *A Special Day* 1977; *Viva Italia!* 1978; *Le Bal* 1983; *La Nuit de Varennes* 1983; *Macaroni* 1985; *The Family* 1987
Scorsese, Martin (1942–) *Who's That Knocking at My Door* 1968; *Boxcar Bertha* 1972; *Mean Streets* 1973; *Alice Doesn't Live Here Anymore* 1974; *Taxi Driver* 1976; *New York, New York* 1977; *The Last Waltz* 1978; *Raging Bull* 1980; *The King of Comedy* 1983; *After Hours* 1985; *The Color of Money* 1986; *The Last Temptation of Christ* 1988; *New York Stories* 1989; *GoodFellas* 1990; *Cape Fear* 1991; *The Age of Innocence* 1993; *Casino* 1995; *Kundun* 1997; *Bringing out the Dead* 1999; *My Voyage to Italy* 1999; *Gangs of New York* 2002; *Martin Scorsese Presents The Blues: Feel Like Going Home* 2003; *The Aviator* 2004

Scott, George C (1927–1999) *Rage* 1972; *The Savage Is Loose* 1974

Scott, James (1941–) *Every Picture Tells a Story* 1984; *Loser Takes All* 1990

Scott, Peter Graham (1923–) *Escape Route* 1952; *Account Rendered* 1957; *The Big Chance* 1957; *Devil's Bait* 1959; *Let's Get Married* 1960; *The Pot Carriers* 1962; *Bitter Harvest* 1963; *The Cracksman* 1963; *Father Came Too* 1963; *Mister Ten Per Cent* 1967; *Subterfuge* 1968

Scott, Ridley (1939–) *The Duellists* 1977; *Alien* 1979; *Blade Runner* 1982; *Legend* 1985; *Someone to Watch over Me* 1987; *Black Rain* 1989; *Thelma & Louise* 1991; *1492: Conquest of Paradise* 1992; *White Squall* 1996; *GI Jane* 1997; *Gladiator* 2000; *Black Hawk Down* 2001; *Hannibal* 2001; *Matchstick Men* 2003; *Kingdom of Heaven* 2005

Scott, Tony (1944–) *The Hunger* 1983; *Top Gun* 1986; *Beverly Hills Cop II* 1987; *Days of Thunder* 1990; *Revenge* 1990; *The Last Boy Scout* 1991; *True Romance* 1993; *Crimson Tide* 1995; *The Fan* 1996; *Enemy of the State* 1998; *Spy Game* 2001; *Man on Fire* 2004

Searle, Francis (1909–2002) *A Girl in a Million* 1946; *Celia* 1949; *A Case for PC 49* 1950; *The Rossiter Case* 1950; *Someone at the Door* 1950; *Cloudburst* 1951; *Profile* 1954; *One Way Out* 1955; *Undercover Girl* 1957; *Trouble with Eve* 1959; *Dead Man's Evidence* 1962; *Emergency* 1962; *Gaolbreak* 1962; *Night of the Prowler* 1962; *The Marked One* 1963; *A Hole Lot of Trouble* 1969

Sears, Fred F (1913–1957) *Last Train from Bombay* 1952; *Ambush at Tomahawk Gap* 1953; *The 49th Man* 1953; *Don't Knock the Rock* 1956; *Earth vs the Flying Saucers* 1956; *Rock around the Clock* 1956; *The Werewolf* 1956; *The World Was His Jury* 1957; *Crash Landing* 1958

Seaton, George (1911–1979) *Billy Rose's Diamond Horseshoe* 1945; *Junior Miss* 1945; *Miracle on 34th Street* 1947; *The Shocking Miss Pilgrim* 1947; *Apartment for Peggy* 1948; *Chicken Every Sunday* 1948; *The Big Lift* 1950; *For Heaven's Sake* 1950; *Anything Can Happen* 1952; *Little Boy Lost* 1953; *The Country Girl* 1954; *The Proud and Profane* 1956; *Teacher's Pet* 1958; *The Pleasure of His Company* 1961; *The Counterfeit Traitor* 1962; *The Hook* 1962; *36 Hours* 1964; *What's So Bad About Feeling Good?* 1968; *Airport* 1970; *Showdown* 1973

Sebastian, Beverly *On the Air Live with Captain Midnight* 1979; *Running Cool* 1993

Sebastian, Ferd *On the Air Live with Captain Midnight* 1979; *Running Cool* 1993

Sedgwick, Edward (1892–1953) *The Cameraman* 1928; *Spite Marriage* 1929; *Doughboys* 1930; *Free and Easy* 1930; *Parlor, Bedroom and Bath* 1931; *The Passionate Plumber* 1932; *Speak Easily* 1932; *What – No Beer?* 1933; *Pick a Star* 1937; *The Gladiator* 1938; *A Southern Yankee* 1948

Segal, Alex (1915–1977) *Ransom!* 1956; *All the Way Home* 1963; *Harlow* 1965; *Joy in the Morning* 1965

Segal, Peter *Naked Gun $33\frac{1}{3}$: the Final Insult* 1994; *Tommy Boy* 1995; *My Fellow Americans* 1996; *Nutty Professor 2: the Klumps* 2000; *Anger Management* 2003; *50 First Dates* 2004; *The Longest Yard* 2005

Seidelman, Arthur Allan *aka* **Seidelman, Arthur A** *Hercules in New York* 1969; *Echoes* 1983; *The Caller* 1987; *Rescue Me* 1991; *The Summer of Ben Tyler* 1996; *Grace and Glorie* 1998; *Walking across Egypt* 1999

Seidelman, Susan (1952–) *Smithereens* 1982; *Desperately Seeking Susan* 1985; *Making Mr Right* 1987; *Cookie* 1989; *She-Devil* 1989; *Erotic Tales* 1994; *A Cooler Climate* 1999

Seiler, Lewis (1891–1963) *Charlie Chan in Paris* 1935; *Dust Be My Destiny* 1939; *Hell's Kitchen* 1939; *King of the Underworld* 1939; *You Can't Get Away with Murder* 1939; *It All Came True* 1940; *The Big Shot* 1942; *Pittsburgh* 1942; *Guadalcanal Diary* 1943; *Something for the Boys* 1944; *Molly and Me* 1945; *Breakthrough* 1950; *Women's Prison* 1955; *The True Story of Lynn Stuart* 1957

Seiter, William A *aka* **Seiter, William** (1892–1964) *Sunny* 1930; *If I Had a Million* 1932; *Sons of the Desert* 1933; *The Richest Girl in the World* 1934; *If You Could Only Cook* 1935; *In Person* 1935; *Roberta* 1935; *Dimples* 1936; *The Moon's Our Home* 1936; *Stowaway* 1936; *Life Begins in College* 1937; *This Is My Affair* 1937; *Room Service* 1938; *Sally, Irene and Mary* 1938; *Thanks for Everything* 1938; *Three Blind Mice* 1938; *The First Rebel* 1939; *Susannah of the Mounties* 1939; *Hired Wife* 1940; *It's a Date* 1940; *Appointment for Love* 1941; *Nice Girl?* 1941; *Broadway* 1942; *You Were Never Lovelier* 1942; *A Lady Takes a Chance* 1943; *Belle of the Yukon* 1944; *The Affairs of Susan* 1945; *It's a Pleasure* 1945; *Little Giant* 1946; *Lover Come Back* 1946; *I'll Be Yours* 1947; *One Touch of Venus* 1948; *Up in Central Park* 1948; *The Lady Wants Mink* 1953; *Make Haste to Live* 1954

Seitz, George B (1888–1944) *Danger Lights* 1930; *Buried Loot* 1934; *Kind Lady* 1935; *Woman Wanted* 1935; *The Last of the Mohicans* 1936; *A Family Affair* 1937; *Judge Hardy's Children* 1938; *Love Finds Andy Hardy* 1938; *Out West with the Hardys* 1938; *Yellow Jack* 1938; *You're Only Young Once* 1938; *The Hardys Ride High* 1939; *Judge Hardy and Son* 1939; *Thunder Afloat* 1939; *Andy Hardy Meets Debutante* 1940; *Kit Carson* 1940; *Sky Murder* 1940; *Andy Hardy's Private Secretary* 1941; *Life Begins for Andy Hardy* 1941; *Andy Hardy's Double Life* 1942; *The Courtship of Andy Hardy* 1942; *Andy Hardy's Blonde Trouble* 1944

Sekely, Steve (1899–1979) *Miracle on Main Street* 1940; *Hollow Triumph* 1948; *Cartouche* 1954; *The Day of the Triffids* 1962

Selander, Lesley (1900–1979) *Cherokee Strip* 1940; *The Roundup* 1941; *Belle Starr's Daughter* 1948; *Guns of Hate* 1948; *Rider from Tucson* 1950; *Storm over Wyoming* 1950; *Cavalry Scout* 1951; *Flight to Mars* 1951; *Desert Passage* 1952; *Fort Algiers* 1953; *War Paint* 1953; *Arrow in the Dust* 1954; *The Yellow Tomahawk* 1954; *Shotgun* 1955; *Tall Man Riding* 1955; *The Lone Ranger and the Lost City of Gold* 1958; *Arizona Bushwhackers* 1968

Selick, Henry *The Nightmare before Christmas* 1993; *James and the Giant Peach* 1996; *Monkeybone* 2000

Seltzer, David (1940–) *Lucas* 1986; *Punchline* 1988; *Shining Through* 1992

Selwyn, Edgar (1875–1944) *The Sin of Madelon Claudet* 1931; *Skyscraper Souls* 1932; *Turn Back the Clock* 1933

Sembene, Ousmane (1923–) *Xala* 1974; *Guelwaar* 1992; *Moolaadé* 2004

Semler, Dean (1943–) *Firestorm* 1998; *The Patriot* 1998

Sen, Mrinal (1923–) *And Quiet Rolls the Dawn* 1979; *In Search of Famine* 1980

Sena, Dominic (1949–) *Kalifornia* 1993; *Gone in Sixty Seconds* 2000; *Swordfish* 2001

Serious, Yahoo (1954–) *Young Einstein* 1988; *Reckless Kelly* 1993

Serreau, Coline (1947–) *Pourquoi Pas!* 1977; *3 Men and a Cradle* 1985; *Romuald et Juliette* 1989; *La Crise* 1992

Sewell, Vernon *aka* **Sewell, Vernon Campbell** (1903–2001) *The Silver Fleet* 1943; *The Ghosts of Berkeley Square* 1947; *The Dark Light* 1951; *Ghost Ship* 1952; *Counterspy* 1953; *Where There's a Will* 1955; *Home and Away* 1956; *Rogue's Yarn* 1956; *The Battle of the V1* 1958; *House of Mystery* 1961; *The Man in the Back Seat* 1961; *Strongroom* 1961; *The Wind of Change* 1961; *The Blood Beast Terror* 1967; *Curse of the Crimson Altar* 1968

Shadyac, Tom (1960–) *Ace Ventura: Pet Detective* 1993; *The Nutty Professor* 1996; *Liar Liar* 1997; *Patch Adams* 1998; *Dragonfly* 2002; *Bruce Almighty* 2003

Shane, Maxwell (1905–1983) *Fear in the Night* 1947; *City across the River* 1949; *The Glass Wall* 1953; *The Naked Street* 1955; *Nightmare* 1956

Shankman, Adam *The Wedding Planner* 2001; *A Walk to Remember* 2002; *Bringing Down the House* 2003; *The Pacifier* 2005

Shapiro, Alan *The Crush* 1993; *Flipper* 1996

Shapiro, Craig *Our Lips Are Sealed* 2000; *Winning London* 2001

Shapiro, Ken *The Groove Tube* 1974; *Modern Problems* 1981

Shapiro, Paul (1955–) *Hockey Night* 1984; *Avalanche* 1994; *Murder at Devil's Glen* 1999

Sharman, Jim (1945–) *The Rocky Horror Picture Show* 1975; *Shock Treatment* 1981

Sharp, Don (1922–) *The Golden Disc* 1958; *It's All Happening* 1963; *The Devil-Ship Pirates* 1964; *Curse of the Fly* 1965; *The Face of Fu Manchu* 1965; *Rasputin, the Mad Monk* 1965; *The Brides of Fu Manchu* 1966; *Our Man in Marrakesh* 1966; *Jules Verne's Rocket to the Moon* 1967; *The Violent Enemy* 1969; *Psychomania* 1972; *Dark Places* 1973; *Callan* 1974; *Hennessy* 1975; *The Thirty-Nine Steps* 1978; *Bear Island* 1979; *Secrets of the Phantom Caverns* 1984

Sharp, Ian (1946–) *Who Dares Wins* 1982; *Mrs Caldicot's Cabbage War* 2000

Sharpsteen, Ben (1895–1980) *Pinocchio* 1940; *Dumbo* 1941

Shaughnessy, Alfred (1916–) *Suspended Alibi* 1956; *6.5 Special* 1958; *The Impersonator* 1962

Shavelson, Melville (1917–) *Seven Little Foys* 1955; *Beau James* 1957; *Houseboat* 1958; *The Five Pennies* 1959; *It Started in Naples* 1960; *On the Double* 1961; *The Pigeon That Took Rome* 1962; *A New Kind of Love* 1963; *Cast a Giant Shadow* 1966; *Yours, Mine and Ours* 1968; *The War between Men and Women* 1972; *Mixed Company* 1974

Shaw, Anthony Pullen *aka* **Shaw, Anthony** (1952–) *Mrs 'arris Goes to Paris* 1992; *The Unexpected Mrs Pollifax* 1999

Shaw, Larry *Mortal Fear* 1994; *No One Could Protect Her* 1996; *Wes Craven's Don't Look Down* 1998

Shbib, Bashar (1959–) *Julia Has Two Lovers* 1990; *Lana in Love* 1991

Shear, Barry (1923–1979) *The Karate Killers* 1967; *Wild in the Streets* 1968; *The Todd Killings* 1971; *Across 110th Street* 1972; *The Deadly Trackers* 1973; *Starsky and Hutch* 1975

Shebib, Donald (1938–) *Heartaches* 1981; *The Ascent* 1994

Sheldon, Sidney (1917–) *Dream Wife* 1953; *The Buster Keaton Story* 1957

Shelton, Ron (1945–) *Bull Durham* 1988; *Blaze* 1989; *White Men Can't Jump* 1992; *Cobb* 1994; *Tin Cup* 1996; *Play It to the Bone* 2000; *Dark Blue* 2002; *Hollywood Homicide* 2003

Shepard, Richard *Cool Blue* 1988; *The Linguini Incident* 1991; *Oxygen* 1999

Shepard, Sam (1943–) *Far North* 1988; *Silent Tongue* 1993

Sher, Jack (1913–1988) *The Three Worlds of Gulliver* 1959; *The Wild and the Innocent* 1959; *Love in a Goldfish Bowl* 1961

Sheridan, Jim (1949–) *My Left Foot* 1989; *The Field* 1990; *In the Name of the Father* 1993; *The Boxer* 1997; *In America* 2003

Sherin, Edwin *aka* **Sherin, Ed** (1930–) *Glory Boy* 1971; *Valdez Is Coming* 1971; *Lena: My 100 Children* 1987

Sherman, Gary *aka* **Sherman, Gary A** *Death Line* 1972; *Dead & Buried* 1981; *Vice Squad* 1982; *Wanted Dead or Alive* 1986; *Poltergeist III* 1988

Sherman, George (1908–1991) *Overland Stage Raiders* 1938; *Red River Range* 1938; *Santa Fe Stampede* 1938; *Frontier Horizon* 1939; *Three Texas Steers* 1939; *Wyoming Outlaw* 1939; *The Lady and the Monster* 1944; *The Bandit of Sherwood Forest* 1946; *Personality Kid* 1946; *Black Bart* 1948; *Relentless* 1948; *Calamity Jane and Sam Bass* 1949; *Red Canyon* 1949; *Comanche Territory* 1950; *The Sleeping City* 1950; *Target Unknown* 1951; *Tomahawk* 1951; *Against All Flags* 1952; *The Battle at Apache Pass* 1952; *The Lone Hand* 1953; *War Arrow* 1953; *Border River* 1954; *Dawn at Socorro* 1954; *Johnny Dark* 1954; *Chief Crazy Horse* 1955; *Count Three and Pray* 1955; *The Treasure of Pancho Villa* 1955; *Comanche* 1956; *The Last of the Fast Guns* 1958; *Son of Robin Hood* 1958; *For the Love of Mike* 1960; *Hell Bent for Leather* 1960; *The Wizard of Baghdad* 1960; *The Fiercest Heart* 1961; *Panic Button* 1964; *Big Jake* 1971

Sherman, Lowell (1885–1934) *Bachelor Apartment* 1931; *Broadway through a Keyhole* 1933; *Morning Glory* 1933; *She Done Him Wrong* 1933

Sherman, Vincent (1906–) *The Return of Dr X* 1939; *Saturday's Children* 1940; *Underground* 1941; *All through the Night* 1942; *The Hard Way* 1942; *Old Acquaintance* 1943; *In Our Time* 1944; *Mr Skeffington* 1944; *Nora Prentiss* 1947; *The Unfaithful* 1947; *Adventures of Don Juan* 1948; *The Hasty Heart* 1949; *Backfire* 1950; *The Damned Don't Cry* 1950; *Harriet Craig* 1950; *Goodbye, My Fancy* 1951; *Affair in Trinidad* 1952; *Lone Star* 1952; *The Garment Jungle* 1957; *The Naked Earth* 1958; *The Young Philadelphians* 1959; *Ice Palace* 1960; *A Fever in the Blood* 1961; *The Second Time Around* 1961; *Cervantes* 1968

Sherwood, John (1959–) *The Creature Walks among Us* 1956; *Raw Edge* 1956; *The Monolith Monsters* 1957

Shields (2), Frank (1947–) *Hostage: the Christine Maresch Story* 1982; *Project: Alien* 1990

Shils, Barry *Motorama* 1991; *Wigstock: The Movie* 1995

Shimizu, Takashi (1972–) *The Grudge 2* 2003; *The Grudge: Ju-On* 2003; *The Grudge* 2004; *Marebito* 2004

Shindo, Kaneto (1912–) *The Island* 1961; *Onibaba* 1964

Shire, Talia (1946–) *One Night Stand* 1994; *Before the Night* 1995

Sholder, Jack (1945–) *Alone in the Dark* 1982; *A Nightmare on Elm Street 2: Freddy's Revenge* 1985; *The Hidden* 1987; *Renegades* 1989; *12:01* 1993; *Runaway Car* 1997; *Arachnid* 2001

Sholem, Lee (1913–2000) *Tarzan's Magic Fountain* 1949; *Tarzan and the Slave Girl* 1950; *The Redhead from Wyoming* 1953; *The Stand at Apache River* 1953; *Hell Ship Mutiny* 1957

Shonteff, Lindsay *Devil Doll* 1964; *Licensed to Kill* 1965; *Sumuru* 1967

Shumlin, Herman (1898–1979) *Watch on the Rhine* 1943; *Confidential Agent* 1945

Shyamalan, M Night (1970–) *Wide Awake* 1998; *The Sixth Sense* 1999; *Unbreakable* 2000; *Signs* 2002; *The Village* 2004

Shyer, Charles (1941–) *Irreconcilable Differences* 1984; *Baby Boom* 1987; *Father of the Bride* 1991; *I Love Trouble* 1994; *Father of the Bride Part 2* 1995; *The Affair of the Necklace* 2001; *Alfie* 2004

Sidney (2), George (1916–2002) *Pilot #5* 1943; *Thousands Cheer* 1943; *Bathing Beauty* 1944; *Ziegfeld Follies* 1944; *Anchors Aweigh* 1945; *The Harvey Girls* 1946; *Holiday in Mexico* 1946; *Cass Timberlane* 1947; *The Three Musketeers* 1948; *The Red Danube* 1949; *Annie Get Your Gun* 1950; *Key to the City* 1950; *Show Boat* 1951; *Scaramouche* 1952; *Kiss Me Kate* 1953; *Young Bess* 1953; *Jupiter's Darling* 1955; *The Eddy Duchin Story* 1956; *Jeanne Eagels* 1957; *Pal Joey* 1957; *Pepe* 1960; *Who Was That Lady?* 1960; *Bye Bye Birdie* 1963; *A Ticklish Affair* 1963; *Viva Las Vegas* 1964; *The Swinger* 1966; *Half a Sixpence* 1967

Siegel, David *Suture* 1993; *The Deep End* 2001

Siegel, Don *aka* **Siegel, Donald** *aka* **Smithee, Allen** (1912–1991) *The Verdict* 1946; *The Big Steal* 1949; *Night unto Night* 1949; *The Duel at Silver Creek* 1952; *Count the Hours* 1953; *Private Hell 36* 1954; *Riot in Cell Block 11* 1954; *An Annapolis Story* 1955; *Crime in the Streets* 1956; *Invasion of the Body Snatchers* 1956; *Baby Face Nelson* 1957; *The Gun Runners* 1958; *The Lineup* 1958; *Edge of Eternity* 1959; *Hound Dog Man* 1959; *Flaming Star* 1960; *Hell Is for Heroes* 1962; *The Killers* 1964; *Stranger on the Run* 1967; *Coogan's Bluff* 1968; *Madigan* 1968; *Death of a Gunfighter* 1969; *Two Mules for Sister Sara* 1970; *The Beguiled* 1971; *Dirty Harry* 1971; *Charley Varrick* 1973; *The Black Windmill* 1974; *The Shootist* 1976; *Telefon* 1977; *Escape from Alcatraz* 1979; *Rough Cut* 1980; *Jinxed!* 1982

Signorelli, James *Easy Money* 1983; *Elvira, Mistress of the Dark* 1988

Silberg, Joel *Breakdance* 1984; *Rappin'* 1985; *Bad Guys* 1986; *Lambada* 1990

Silberling, Brad (1965–) *Casper* 1995; *City of Angels* 1998; *Moonlight Mile* 2002; *Lemony Snicket's A Series of Unfortunate Events* 2004

Silver, Joan Micklin (1935–) *Hester Street* 1975; *Between the Lines* 1977; *Chilly Scenes of Winter* 1979; *Crossing Delancey* 1988; *Loverboy* 1989; *A Private Matter* 1992; *Stepkids* 1992; *In the Presence of Mine Enemies* 1997

Silver, Marisa (1960–) *Old Enough* 1984; *Permanent Record* 1988; *Vital Signs* 1990; *He Said, She Said* 1991

Silver, Scott *Johns* 1995; *The Mod Squad* 1999

Silverstein, Elliot (1927–) *Cat Ballou* 1965; *The Happening* 1967; *A Man Called Horse* 1970; *The Car* 1977; *Flashfire* 1993

Simmons, Anthony (1924–) *Your Money or Your Wife* 1960; *Four in the Morning* 1965; *The Optimists of Nine Elms* 1973; *Black Joy* 1977

Simon, Adam (1962–) *Brain Dead* 1990; *Body Chemistry 2: Voice of a Stranger* 1992; *Carnosaur* 1993; *The American Nightmare* 2000

Simon, S Sylvan *aka* **Simon, Sylvan** (1910–1951) *Dancing Co-Ed* 1939; *Four Girls in White* 1939; *Whistling in the Dark* 1941; *Grand Central Murder* 1942; *Rio Rita* 1942; *Whistling in Dixie* 1942; *Salute to the Marines* 1943; *Whistling in Brooklyn* 1943; *Song of the Open Road* 1944; *Abbott and Costello in Hollywood* 1945; *Son of Lassie* 1945; *Bad Bascomb* 1946; *Her Husband's Affairs* 1947; *The Fuller Brush Man* 1948

Simoneau, Yves (1955–) *Perfectly Normal* 1990; *Mother's Boys* 1993; *Free Money* 1998; *36 Hours to Die* 1999

Sinclair, Andrew (1935–) *Under Milk Wood* 1971; *Blue Blood* 1973

Sinclair, Robert B (1905–1970) *Dramatic School* 1938; *Mr and Mrs North* 1941; *That Wonderful Urge* 1948

Singer, Alexander (1932–) *A Cold Wind in August* 1961; *Psyche '59* 1964; *Love Has Many Faces* 1965; *Captain Apache* 1971; *Glass Houses* 1972

Singer, Bryan (1966–) *Public Access* 1993; *The Usual Suspects* 1995; *Apt Pupil* 1997; *X-Men* 2000; *X2* 2003

Singleton, John (1968–) *Boyz N the Hood* 1991; *Poetic Justice* 1993; *Higher Learning* 1995; *Rosewood* 1997; *Shaft* 2000; *Baby Boy* 2001; *2 Fast 2 Furious* 2003

Sinise, Gary (1955–) *Miles from Home* 1988; *Of Mice and Men* 1992

Sinofsky, Bruce (1956–) *Paradise Lost: the Child Murders at Robin Hood Hills* 1996; *Metallica: Some Kind of Monster* 2004

Sinyor, Gary (1962–) *Leon the Pig Farmer* 1992; *Solitaire for 2* 1994; *Stiff Upper Lips* 1997; *The Bachelor* 1999

Siodmak, Robert *aka* **Siodmark, Robert** (1900–1973) *People on Sunday* 1929; *Pièges* 1939; *Fly by Night* 1942; *Son of Dracula* 1943; *Christmas Holiday* 1944; *Cobra Woman* 1944; *Phantom Lady* 1944; *The Suspect* 1944; *The Strange Affair of Uncle Harry* 1945; *The Dark Mirror* 1946; *The Killers* 1946; *The Spiral Staircase* 1946; *Time Out of Mind* 1947; *Cry of the City* 1948; *Criss Cross* 1949; *The File on Thelma Jordon* 1949; *The Great Sinner* 1949; *The Crimson Pirate* 1952; *The Rats* 1955; *The Rough and the Smooth* 1959; *Custer of the West* 1968

Sirk, Douglas *aka* **Sierck, Detlef** (1900–1987) *Pillars of Society* 1935; *Hitler's Madman* 1943; *Summer Storm* 1944; *Thieves' Holiday* 1946; *Lured* 1947; *Sleep, My Love* 1948; *Shockproof* 1949; *Slightly French* 1949; *Mystery Submarine* 1950; *The First Legion* 1951; *The Lady Pays Off* 1951; *Thunder on the Hill* 1951; *Weekend with Father* 1951; *Has Anybody Seen My Gal?* 1952; *Meet Me at the Fair* 1952; *No Room for the Groom* 1952; *All I Desire* 1953; *Take Me to Town* 1953; *Magnificent Obsession* 1954; *Sign of the Pagan* 1954; *Taza, Son of Cochise* 1954; *All That Heaven Allows* 1955; *Captain Lightfoot* 1955; *Never Say Goodbye* 1955; *There's Always Tomorrow* 1956; *Written on the Wind* 1956; *Battle Hymn* 1957; *Interlude* 1957; *The Tarnished Angels* 1957; *A Time to Love and a Time to Die* 1958; *Imitation of Life* 1959

Sitch, Rob (1962–) *The Castle* 1997; *The Dish* 2000

Sivan, Santosh *The Terrorist* 1998; *Asoka* 2001

Sjöberg, Alf (1903–1980) *Torment* 1944; *Miss Julie* 1951

Sjöman, Vilgot (1924–) *My Sister, My Love* 1966; *I Am Curious – Yellow* 1967

Sjöström, Victor *aka* **Seastrom, Victor** (1879–1960) *The Outlaw and His Wife* 1917; *A Dangerous Pledge* 1920; *The Phantom Carriage* 1920; *He Who Gets Slapped* 1924; *The Scarlet Letter* 1926; *The Divine Woman* 1928; *The Wind* 1928; *Under the Red Robe* 1937

Skolimowski, Jerzy (1938–) *The Adventures of Gerard* 1970; *Deep End* 1970; *King, Queen, Knave* 1972; *The Shout* 1978; *Moonlighting* 1982; *Success Is the Best Revenge* 1984; *The Lightship* 1985; *Torrents of Spring* 1989

Sloane, Paul H *aka* **Sloane, Paul** (1893–1963) *Half Shot at Sunrise* 1930; *Consolation Marriage* 1931; *Geronimo* 1939

Sloman, Edward (1887–1972) *Gun Smoke* 1931; *His Woman* 1931

Sluizer, George (1932–) *The Vanishing* 1988; *Utz* 1992; *The Vanishing* 1993

Smart, Ralph (1908–2001) *Bush Christmas* 1947; *Quartet* 1948; *A Boy, a Girl and a Bike* 1949; *Bitter Springs* 1950; *Never Take No for an Answer* 1951; *Curtain Up* 1952

Smight, Jack (1926–2003) *I'd Rather Be Rich* 1964; *The Third Day* 1965; *Harper* 1966; *Kaleidoscope* 1966; *The Secret War of Harry Frigg* 1967; *No Way to Treat a Lady* 1968; *The Illustrated Man* 1969; *Rabbit, Run* 1970; *The Traveling Executioner* 1970; *Frankenstein: the True Story* 1973; *Airport 1975* 1974; *Battle of Midway* 1976; *Damnation Alley* 1977; *Fast Break* 1979; *Loving Couples* 1980; *Number One with a Bullet* 1986

Smith, Charles Martin (1953–) *Trick or Treat* 1986; *Fifty/Fifty* 1991; *Air Bud* 1997

Smith, Chris *American Movie* 1999; *The Yes Men* 2003

Smith, John N *The Masculine Mystique* 1984; *Sitting in Limbo* 1986; *Train of Dreams* 1987; *Dangerous Minds* 1995; *A Cool, Dry Place* 1998

Smith (2), Kevin (1970–) *Clerks* 1994; *Mallrats* 1995; *Chasing Amy* 1996; *Dogma* 1999; *Jay and Silent Bob Strike Back* 2001; *Jersey Girl* 2003

Smith, Mel (1952–) *The Tall Guy* 1989; *Radioland Murders* 1994; *Bean* 1997; *High Heels and Low Lifes* 2001; *Blackball* 2003

Soavi, Michele (1957–) *Stage Fright – Aquarius* 1987; *The Church* 1988; *The Sect* 1991; *Cemetery Man* 1994

Soderbergh, Steven (1963–) *sex, lies, and videotape* 1989; *Kafka* 1991; *King of the Hill* 1993; *The Underneath* 1995; *Gray's Anatomy* 1996; *Schizopolis* 1996; *Out of Sight* 1998; *The Limey* 1999; *Erin Brockovich* 2000; *Traffic* 2000; *Ocean's Eleven* 2001; *Full Frontal* 2002; *Solaris* 2003; *Ocean's Twelve* 2004

Softley, Iain (1958–) *Backbeat* 1993; *Hackers* 1995; *The Wings of the Dove* 1997; *K-PAX* 2001; *The Skeleton Key* 2005

Sokurov, Aleksandr (1951–) *Whispering Pages* 1993; *Mother and Son* 1997; *Moloch* 1999; *Russian Ark* 2002; *Father and Son* 2003

Solanas, Fernando E (1936–) *Tangos, Exilo de Gardel* 1985; *Sur* 1987; *The Voyage* 1991

Soldati, Mario (1906–1999) *The Stranger's Hand* 1953; *Woman of the River* 1955

Sole, Alfred *Alice, Sweet Alice* 1977; *Pandemonium* 1982

Sollima, Sergio (1921–) *Face to Face* 1967; *Violent City* 1970

Solondz, Todd (1960–) *Fear, Anxiety, and Depression* 1989; *Welcome to the Dollhouse* 1995; *Happiness* 1998; *Storytelling* 2001; *Palindromes* 2004

Solt, Andrew *This Is Elvis* 1981; *Imagine: John Lennon* 1988

Sommers, Stephen (1962–) *The Adventures of Huck Finn* 1993; *The Jungle Book* 1994; *Deep Rising* 1998; *The Mummy* 1999; *The Mummy Returns* 2001; *Van Helsing* 2004

Sonnenfeld, Barry (1953–) *The Addams Family* 1991; *Addams Family Values* 1993; *For Love or Money* 1993; *Get Shorty* 1995; *Men in Black* 1997; *Wild Wild West* 1999; *Big Trouble* 2002; *Men in Black 2* 2002

Sorak, Omer Faruk *Vizontele* 2001; *GORA* 2004

Sorin, Carlos (1944–) *Eversmile, New Jersey* 1989; *Historias Mínimas* 2002; *Bombón – El Perro* 2004

Spacey, Kevin (1959–) *Albino Alligator* 1996; *Beyond the Sea* 2004

Sparr, Robert (1915–1969) *More Dead than Alive* 1969; *Once You Kiss a Stranger* 1969

Spence, Richard *Different for Girls* 1996; *New World Disorder* 1999

Spera, Rob *aka* **Spera, Robert** *Witchcraft* 1988; *Sexual Predator* 2001

Spheeris, Penelope (1946–) *The Decline of Western Civilization* 1980; *The Boys Next Door* 1985; *Hollywood Vice Squad* 1986; *Dudes* 1987; *The Decline of Western Civilization Part II: the Metal Years* 1988; *Wayne's World* 1992; *The Beverly Hillbillies* 1993; *The Little Rascals* 1994; *Black Sheep* 1996; *The Decline of Western Civilization Part III* 1997; *Senseless* 1998

Spicer, Bryan *Mighty Morphin Power Rangers: the Movie* 1995; *For Richer or Poorer* 1997; *McHale's Navy* 1997

Spielberg, Steven (1946–) *Duel* 1971; *The Sugarland Express* 1974; *Jaws* 1975; *Close Encounters of the Third Kind* 1977; *1941* 1979; *Raiders of the Lost Ark* 1981; *ET the Extra-Terrestrial* 1982; *Twilight Zone: the Movie* 1983; *Indiana Jones and the Temple of Doom* 1984; *The Color Purple* 1985; *Empire of the Sun* 1987; *Always* 1989; *Indiana Jones and the Last Crusade* 1989; *Hook* 1991; *Jurassic Park* 1993; *Schindler's List* 1993; *Amistad* 1997; *The Lost World: Jurassic Park* 1997; *Saving Private Ryan* 1998; *AI: Artificial Intelligence* 2001; *Catch Me If You Can* 2002; *Minority Report* 2002; *The Terminal* 2004; *War of the Worlds* 2005

Spiers, Bob *Spice World: the Movie* 1997; *That Darn Cat* 1997

Spottiswoode, Roger (1943–) *Terror Train* 1980; *The Pursuit of DB Cooper* 1981; *Under Fire* 1983; *The Best of Times* 1986; *Deadly Pursuit* 1988; *Turner & Hooch* 1989; *Air America* 1990; *Stop! or My Mom Will Shoot* 1992; *And the Band Played On* 1993; *Mesmer* 1994; *Tomorrow Never Dies* 1997; *The 6th Day* 2000; *Ice Bound* 2003

Sprecher, Jill *Clockwatchers* 1997; *13 Conversations about One Thing* 2001

Springsteen, R G (1904–1989) *Come Next Spring* 1956; *Showdown* 1963; *Bullet for a Badman* 1964; *He Rides Tall* 1964; *Taggart* 1964; *Apache Uprising* 1965; *Black Spurs* 1965; *Johnny Reno* 1966; *Waco* 1966; *Hostile Guns* 1967; *Tiger by the Tail* 1970

Spry, Robin (1939–2005) *Keeping Track* 1986; *Obsessed* 1989

Stahl, John M (1886–1950) *Back Street* 1932; *Only Yesterday* 1933; *Imitation of Life* 1934; *Magnificent Obsession* 1935; *Parnell* 1937; *Letter of Introduction* 1938; *When Tomorrow Comes* 1939; *Our Wife* 1941; *Holy Matrimony* 1943; *The Immortal Sergeant* 1943; *The Eve of St Mark* 1944; *The Keys of the Kingdom* 1944; *Leave Her to Heaven* 1945; *The Foxes of Harrow* 1947; *Father Was a Fullback* 1949; *Oh, You Beautiful Doll* 1949

Stallone, Sylvester (1946–) *Paradise Alley* 1978; *Rocky II* 1979; *Rocky III* 1982; *Staying Alive* 1983; *Rocky IV* 1985

Stanley, Richard (1964–) *Hardware* 1990; *Dust Devil* 1992

Starewicz, Ladislaw (1882–1965) *Town Rat, Country Rat* 1923; *The Tale of the Fox* 1931

Stark, Graham (1922–) *Simon, Simon* 1970; *The Magnificent Seven Deadly Sins* 1971

Starrett, Jack (1936–1989) *Run, Angel, Run* 1969; *Slaughter* 1972; *The Strange Vengeance of Rosalie* 1972; *Cleopatra Jones* 1973; *The Gravy Train* 1974; *Race with the Devil* 1975; *A Small Town in Texas* 1976; *Final Chapter – Walking Tall* 1977

Staudte, Wolfgang (1906–1984) *The Murderers Are amongst Us* 1946; *Yesterday's Tomorrow* 1978

Steckler, Ray Dennis (1939–) *The Incredibly Strange Creatures Who Stopped Living and Became Mixed-up Zombies* 1963; *Rat Pfink a Boo Boo* 1965

Stein, Paul L *aka* **Stein, Paul** (1892–1951) *One Romantic Night* 1930; *Blossom Time* 1934; *Heart's Desire* 1935; *Poison Pen* 1939; *The Saint Meets the Tiger* 1943; *Counterblast* 1948

Steinberg, David (1942–) *Paternity* 1981; *Going Berserk* 1983; *The Wrong Guy* 1997

Steinberg, Michael (1959–) *The Waterdance* 1991; *Bodies, Rest and Motion* 1993; *Wicked* 1998

Steinmann, Danny *Savage Streets* 1984; *Friday the 13th: a New Beginning* 1985

Stephenson, John *Animal Farm* 1999; *Five Children and It* 2004

Sterling, Joseph (1916–) *The Case of the Mukkinese Battle Horn* 1955; *Cloak without Dagger* 1955

Stern, Leonard B *aka* **Stern, Leonard** *Just You and Me, Kid* 1979; *Missing Pieces* 1991

Stern, Sandor (1936–) *Pin* 1988; *Amityville: the Evil Escapes* 1989; *Heart of a Child* 1994

Stern, Steven Hilliard (1937–) *The Harrad Summer* 1974; *I Wonder Who's Killing Her Now?* 1975; *Running* 1979; *The Devil and Max Devlin* 1981

Stevens, Art *The Rescuers* 1977; *The Fox and the Hound* 1981

Stevens, David (1940–) *The Clinic* 1982; *Undercover* 1983; *Kansas* 1988

Stevens, George (1904–1975) *Bachelor Bait* 1934; *Alice Adams* 1935; *Annie Oakley* 1935; *Swing Time* 1936; *A Damsel in Distress* 1937; *Quality Street* 1937; *Vivacious Lady* 1938; *Gunga Din* 1939; *Vigil in the Night* 1940; *Penny Serenade* 1941; *The Talk of the Town* 1942; *Woman of the Year* 1942; *The More the Merrier* 1943; *I Remember Mama* 1948; *A Place in the Sun* 1951; *Something to Live For* 1952; *Shane* 1953; *Giant* 1956; *The Diary of Anne Frank* 1959; *The Greatest Story Ever Told* 1965; *The Only Game in Town* 1970

Stevens (1), Leslie (1924–1998) *Hero's Island* 1962; *Incubus* 1965

Stevens, Mark (1915–1994) *Cry Vengeance* 1954; *Timetable* 1956

Stevens, Robert (1921–1998) *The Big Caper* 1957; *Never Love a Stranger* 1958; *I Thank a Fool* 1962; *In the Cool of the Day* 1963

Stevenson, Robert (1905–1986) *The Man Who Changed His Mind* 1936; *Tudor Rose* 1936; *King Solomon's Mines* 1937; *Owd Bob* 1938; *Return to Yesterday* 1940; *Tom Brown's Schooldays* 1940; *Back Street* 1941; *Joan of Paris* 1942; *Forever and a Day* 1943; *Jane Eyre* 1943; *Dishonored Lady* 1947; *To the Ends of the Earth* 1948; *Walk Softly, Stranger* 1949; *The Woman on Pier 13* 1949; *My Forbidden Past* 1951; *The Las Vegas Story* 1952; *Johnny Tremain* 1957; *Old Yeller* 1957; *Darby O'Gill and the Little People* 1959; *Kidnapped* 1960; *The Absent-Minded Professor* 1961; *In Search of the Castaways* 1961; *Son of Flubber* 1962; *Mary Poppins* 1964; *The Misadventures of Merlin Jones* 1964; *The Monkey's Uncle* 1965; *That Darn Cat!* 1965; *Blackbeard's Ghost* 1967; *The Gnome-Mobile* 1967; *The Love Bug* 1969; *Bedknobs and Broomsticks* 1971; *Herbie Rides Again* 1974; *The Island at the Top of the World* 1974; *One of Our Dinosaurs Is Missing* 1975; *The Shaggy DA* 1976

Stewart, Douglas Day *Thief of Hearts* 1984; *Listen to Me* 1989

Stiller, Ben (1965–) *Reality Bites* 1994; *The Cable Guy* 1996; *Zoolander* 2001

Stiller, Mauritz (1883–1928) *Thomas Graal's Best Film* 1917; *Erotikon* 1920; *Gunnar Hede's Saga* 1922; *Gösta Berlings Saga* 1924; *Hotel Imperial* 1927

Stillman, Whit (1952–) *Metropolitan* 1990; *Barcelona* 1994; *The Last Days of Disco* 1998

Stockwell, John (1961–) *crazy/beautiful* 2001; *Blue Crush* 2002

Stoloff, Ben *aka* **Stoloff, Benjamin** (1895–1960) *Palooka* 1934; *Sea Devils* 1937; *Super-Sleuth* 1937; *The Affairs of Annabel* 1938; *Radio City Revels* 1938; *The Bermuda Mystery* 1944

Stone, Andrew L *aka* **Stone, Andrew** (1902–1999) *Stormy Weather* 1943; *Sensations* 1944; *Bedside Manner* 1945; *The Steel Trap* 1952; *The Night Holds Terror* 1955; *Julie* 1956; *Cry Terror* 1958; *The Decks Ran Red* 1958; *The Last Voyage* 1960; *Ring of Fire* 1961; *The Password Is Courage* 1962; *The Secret of My Success* 1965; *Song of Norway* 1970; *The Great Waltz* 1972

Stone, Oliver (1946–) *Seizure* 1974; *The Hand* 1981; *Platoon* 1986; *Salvador* 1986; *Wall Street* 1987; *Talk Radio* 1988; *Born on the Fourth of July* 1989; *The Doors* 1991; *JFK* 1991; *Heaven and Earth* 1993; *Natural Born Killers* 1994; *Nixon* 1995; *U Turn* 1997; *Any Given Sunday* 1999; *Comandante* 2002; *Alexander* 2004

Stopkewich, Lynne (1964–) *Kissed* 1996; *Suspicious River* 2000

Story, Tim (1974–) *Barbershop* 2002; *Taxi* 2004

Strand, Paul (1890–1976) *Manhatta* 1921; *Native Land* 1942

Straub, Jean-Marie (1933–) *Not Reconciled, or Only Violence Helps Where Violence Rules* 1965; *Chronicle of Anna Magdalena Bach* 1968

Strayer, Frank R (1891–1964) *The Vampire Bat* 1933; *Blondie!* 1938

Streisand, Barbra (1942–) *Yentl* 1983; *The Prince of Tides* 1991; *The Mirror Has Two Faces* 1996

Strick, Joseph (1923–) *The Savage Eye* 1959; *The Balcony* 1963; *Ulysses* 1967; *A Portrait of the Artist as a Young Man* 1977

Strock, Herbert L (1918–) *Gog* 1954; *Battle Taxi* 1955; *Blood of Dracula* 1957; *I Was a Teenage Frankenstein* 1957; *How to Make a Monster* 1958; *The Crawling Hand* 1963

Stuart, Mel (1928–) *If It's Tuesday, This Must Be Belgium* 1969; *I Love My... Wife* 1970; *Willy Wonka and the Chocolate Factory* 1971; *One Is a Lonely Number* 1972; *Wattstax* 1972; *Mean Dog Blues* 1978; *The White Lions* 1980

Sturges, John (1911–1992) *The Walking Hills* 1949; *The Capture* 1950; *The Magnificent Yankee* 1950; *Mystery Street* 1950; *Right Cross* 1950; *It's a Big Country* 1951; *Kind Lady* 1951; *The People against O'Hara* 1951; *The Girl in White* 1952; *Escape from Fort Bravo* 1953; *Jeopardy* 1953; *Bad Day at Black Rock* 1955; *The Scarlet Coat* 1955; *Underwater!* 1955; *Backlash* 1956; *Gunfight at the OK Corral* 1957; *The Law and Jake Wade* 1958; *The Old Man and the Sea* 1958; *Last Train from Gun Hill* 1959; *Never So Few* 1959; *The Magnificent Seven* 1960; *By Love Possessed* 1961; *A Girl Named Tamiko* 1962; *Sergeants 3* 1962; *The Great Escape* 1963; *The Hallelujah Trail* 1965; *The Satan Bug* 1965; *Hour of the Gun* 1967; *Ice Station*

Zebra 1968; *Marooned* 1969; *Joe Kidd* 1972; *The Valdez Horses* 1973; *McQ* 1974; *The Eagle Has Landed* 1976

Sturges, Preston (1898–1959) *Christmas in July* 1940; *The Great McGinty* 1940; *The Lady Eve* 1941; *Sullivan's Travels* 1941; *The Palm Beach Story* 1942; *The Great Moment* 1944; *Hail the Conquering Hero* 1944; *The Miracle of Morgan's Creek* 1944; *Unfaithfully Yours* 1948; *The Beautiful Blonde from Bashful Bend* 1949; *Mad Wednesday* 1950; *The Diary of Major Thompson* 1955

Sturridge, Charles (1951–) *Runners* 1983; *Aria* 1987; *A Handful of Dust* 1987; *Where Angels Fear to Tread* 1991; *FairyTale: a True Story* 1997

Styles, Eric *Dreaming of Joseph Lees* 1998; *Relative Values* 2000

Subiela, Eliseo (1944–) *Hombre Mirando al Sudeste* 1986; *Last Images of the Shipwreck* 1989; *The Dark Side of the Heart* 1992

Sugarman, Sara *Mad Cows* 1999; *Very Annie-Mary* 2000; *Confessions of a Teenage Drama Queen* 2004

Sugg, Stewart *Fast Food* 1998; *Kiss Kiss (Bang Bang)* 2001

Sullivan, Kevin Rodney (1959–) *Soul of the Game* 1996; *How Stella Got Her Groove Back* 1998; *Barbershop 2: Back in Business* 2004; *Guess Who* 2005

Summers, Jeremy (1931–) *The Punch and Judy Man* 1962; *Crooks in Cloisters* 1963; *Five Golden Dragons* 1967; *House of a Thousand Dolls* 1967; *The Vengeance of Fu Manchu* 1967

Summers, Walter (1896–1973) *The Return of Bulldog Drummond* 1934; *Music Hath Charms* 1935; *Dark Eyes of London* 1939

Sutherland, A Edward *aka* **Sutherland, Edward** (1895–1974) *It's the Old Army Game* 1926; *The Saturday Night Kid* 1929; *Paramount on Parade* 1930; *Palmy Days* 1931; *International House* 1933; *Murders in the Zoo* 1933; *Mississippi* 1935; *Poppy* 1936; *Every Day's a Holiday* 1937; *The Flying Deuces* 1939; *The Boys from Syracuse* 1940; *The Invisible Woman* 1940; *The Navy Comes Through* 1942; *Dixie* 1943; *Follow the Boys* 1944; *Secret Command* 1944; *Abie's Irish Rose* 1946

Sutherland, Kiefer (1967–) *Last Light* 1993; *Truth or Consequences, NM* 1997

Suzuki, Seijun (1923–) *Gate of Flesh* 1964; *Tokyo Drifter* 1966; *Branded to Kill* 1967

Svankmajer, Jan (1934–) *Alice* 1988; *Faust* 1994; *Conspirators of Pleasure* 1996; *Little Otik* 2000

Svatek, Peter *The Call of the Wild* 1996; *Hemoglobin* 1997

Sverak, Jan (1965–) *Elementary School* 1991; *Kolya* 1996; *Dark Blue World* 2001

Swackhamer, E W (1927–1994) *Man and Boy* 1971; *Spider-Man* 1977

Swaim, Bob (1943–) *La Balance* 1982; *Half Moon Street* 1986; *Masquerade* 1988

Swenson, Charles *aka* **Swenson, Chuck** *The Mouse and His Child* 1977; *Twice upon a Time* 1983

Swift, David (1919–2001) *Pollyanna* 1960; *The Parent Trap* 1961; *The Interns* 1962; *Love Is a Ball* 1963; *Under the Yum Yum Tree* 1963; *Good Neighbor Sam* 1964; *How to Succeed in Business without Really Trying* 1967

Switzer, Michael *Stalking Laura* 1993; *What Love Sees* 1996; *No Higher Love* 1999

Sykes, Peter (1939–) *Demons of the Mind* 1971; *The House in Nightmare Park* 1973; *Steptoe and Son Ride Again* 1973; *To the Devil a Daughter* 1976; *Jesus* 1979

Szabó, István (1938–) *Apa* 1966; *Confidence* 1979; *Mephisto* 1981; *Colonel Redl* 1984; *Hanussen* 1988; *Meeting Venus* 1990; *Sweet Emma Dear Böbe* 1992; *Sunshine* 1999; *Taking Sides* 2001; *Ten Minutes Older: the Cello* 2002; *Being Julia* 2004

Szwarc, Jeannot (1937–) *Extreme Close-Up* 1973; *Bug* 1975; *Jaws 2* 1978; *Somewhere in Time* 1980; *Enigma* 1982; *Supergirl* 1984; *Santa Claus* 1985

T

Tabio, Juan Carlos (1943–) *Plaff!* 1988; *Strawberry and Chocolate* 1993; *The Elephant and the Bicycle* 1995; *Guantanamera* 1995

Tacchella, Jean-Charles (1925–) *Cousin, Cousine* 1975; *L'Homme de Ma Vie* 1992

Takacs, Tibor (1954–) *The Gate* 1987; *Gate II* 1992; *Sanctuary* 1997

Talalay, Rachel *Freddy's Dead: the Final Nightmare* 1991; *Ghost in the Machine* 1993; *Tank Girl* 1995

Tamahori, Lee (1950–) *Once Were Warriors* 1994; *Mulholland Falls* 1996; *The Edge* 1997; *Along Came a Spider* 2001; *Die Another Day* 2002; *xXx: the Next Level* 2005

Tannen (2), William *Flashpoint* 1984; *Deadly Illusion* 1987; *Hero and the Terror* 1988

Tanner, Alain (1929–) *Jonah Who Will Be 25 in the Year 2000* 1976; *Messidor* 1978; *Light Years Away* 1981; *In the White City* 1983; *Woman from Rose Hill* 1989; *The Diary of Lady M* 1992; *Requiem* 1998

Tanovic, Danis (1969–) *No Man's Land* 2001; *11'09''01 – September 11* 2002

Taplitz, Daniel *Commandments* 1996; *Breakin' All the Rules* 2004

Tarantino, Quentin (1963–) *Reservoir Dogs* 1991; *Pulp Fiction* 1994; *Four Rooms* 1995; *Jackie Brown* 1997; *Kill Bill Vol 1* 2003; *Kill Bill Vol 2* 2003

Tarkovsky, Andrei (1932–1986) *Katok i Skrypka* 1961; *Ivan's Childhood* 1962; *Andrei Rublev* 1966; *Solaris* 1972; *Mirror* 1974; *Stalker* 1979; *Nostalgia* 1983; *The Sacrifice* 1986

Tarr, Bela (1955–) *Damnation* 1988; *Werckmeister Harmonies* 2000

Tashlin, Frank (1913–1972) *Son of Paleface* 1952; *Marry Me Again* 1953; *Susan Slept Here* 1954; *Artists and Models* 1955; *The Girl Can't Help It* 1956; *Hollywood or Bust* 1956; *The Lieutenant Wore Skirts* 1956; *Will Success Spoil Rock Hunter?* 1957; *The Geisha Boy* 1958; *Rock-a-Bye Baby* 1958; *Say One for Me* 1959; *Cinderfella* 1960; *Bachelor Flat* 1961; *It'$ Only Money* 1962; *The Man from the Diner's Club* 1963; *Who's Minding the Store?* 1963; *The Disorderly Orderly* 1964; *The Alphabet Murders* 1966; *The Glass Bottom Boat* 1966; *Caprice* 1967; *The Private Navy of Sgt O'Farrell* 1968

Tass, Nadia (1955–) *Malcolm* 1986; *Rikky and Pete* 1988; *The Big Steal* 1990; *Pure Luck* 1991; *Mr Reliable* 1996

Tati, Jacques (1908–1982) *Jour de Fête* 1947; *School for Postmen* 1947; *Monsieur Hulot's Holiday* 1953; *Mon Oncle* 1958; *Playtime* 1967; *Traffic* 1970; *Parade* 1974

Tatoulis, John *In Too Deep* 1990; *The Silver Brumby* 1992

Taurog, Norman (1899–1981) *Huckleberry Finn* 1931; *Skippy* 1931; *If I Had a Million* 1932; *The Phantom President* 1932; *Mrs Wiggs of the Cabbage Patch* 1934; *We're Not Dressing* 1934; *The Big Broadcast of 1936* 1935; *Rhythm on the Range* 1936; *Strike Me Pink* 1936; *You Can't Have Everything* 1937; *The Adventures of Tom Sawyer* 1938; *Boys Town* 1938; *Mad about Music* 1938; *Broadway Melody of 1940* 1940; *Little Nellie Kelly* 1940; *Young Tom Edison* 1940; *Design for Scandal* 1941; *Men of Boys Town* 1941; *A Yank at Eton* 1942; *Girl Crazy* 1943; *Presenting Lily Mars* 1943; *Ziegfeld Follies* 1944; *The Hoodlum Saint* 1946; *The Beginning or the End* 1947; *Words and Music* 1948; *That Midnight Kiss* 1949; *Mrs O'Malley and Mr Malone* 1950; *Please Believe Me* 1950; *The Toast of New Orleans* 1950; *Rich, Young and Pretty* 1951; *The Stooge* 1951; *Jumping Jacks* 1952; *Room for One More* 1952; *The Caddy* 1953; *Living It Up* 1954; *You're Never Too Young* 1955; *The Birds and the Bees* 1956; *Bundle of Joy* 1956; *Pardners* 1956; *The Fuzzy Pink Nightgown* 1957; *Onionhead* 1958; *Don't Give Up the Ship* 1959; *GI Blues* 1960; *Visit to a Small Planet* 1960; *All Hands on Deck* 1961; *Blue Hawaii* 1961; *Girls! Girls! Girls!* 1962; *It Happened at the World's Fair* 1962; *Palm Springs Weekend* 1963; *Dr Goldfoot and the Bikini Machine* 1965; *Sergeant Deadhead* 1965; *Tickle Me* 1965; *Spinout* 1966; *Double Trouble* 1967; *Live a Little, Love a Little* 1968; *Speedway* 1968

Tavernier, Bertrand (1941–) *The Watchmaker of St Paul* 1973; *Deathwatch* 1980; *Clean Slate* 1981; *Sunday in the Country* 1984; *'Round Midnight* 1986; *Life and Nothing But* 1989; *These Foolish Things* 1990; *L.627* 1992; *The Undeclared War* 1992; *D'Artagnan's Daughter* 1994; *The Bait* 1995; *Ca Commence Aujourd'hui* 1999; *Laissez-passer* 2001

Taviani, Paolo (1931–) *Padre Padrone* 1977; *The Night of San Lorenzo* 1981; *Kaos* 1984; *Good Morning, Babylon* 1987; *Night Sun* 1990; *Fiorile* 1993

Taviani, Vittorio (1929–) *Padre Padrone* 1977; *The Night of San Lorenzo* 1981; *Kaos* 1984; *Good Morning, Babylon* 1987; *Night Sun* 1990; *Fiorile* 1993

Taylor, Alan (1965–) *Palookaville* 1995; *The Emperor's New Clothes* 2001

Taylor, Baz (1944–) *Near Mrs* 1990; *Shooting Elizabeth* 1992

Taylor, Don (1920–1998) *Ride the Wild Surf* 1964; *Jack of Diamonds* 1967; *Escape from the Planet of the Apes* 1971; *Tom Sawyer* 1973; *Echoes of a Summer* 1976; *The Great Scout & Cathouse Thursday* 1976; *The Island of Dr Moreau* 1977; *Damien – Omen II* 1978; *The Final Countdown* 1980

Taylor, Finn (1958–) *Dream with the Fishes* 1996; *Cherish* 2002

Taylor, Jud (1940–) *Out of the Darkness* 1985; *Danielle Steel's Kaleidoscope* 1990; *Prophet of Evil* 1993

Taylor, Ray (1888–1952) *Law and Order* 1940; *The Daltons Ride Again* 1945; *The Vigilantes Return* 1947

Taylor (3), Robert *The Nine Lives of Fritz the Cat* 1974; *Heidi's Song* 1982

Taylor, Sam (1895–1958) *Safety Last* 1923; *Girl Shy* 1924; *Hot Water* 1924; *The Freshman* 1925; *For Heaven's Sake* 1926; *My Best Girl* 1927; *Coquette* 1929; *The Taming of the Shrew* 1929; *The Cat's Paw* 1934; *Nothing but Trouble* 1944; *The Monte Carlo Story* 1957

Taymor, Julie (1953–) *Titus* 1999; *Frida* 2002

Teague, Colin *Shooters* 2000; *Spivs* 2003

Teague, Lewis (1938–) *The Lady in Red* 1979; *Alligator* 1980; *Death Vengeance* 1982; *Cujo* 1983; *Cat's Eye* 1984; *The Jewel of the Nile* 1985; *Collision Course* 1987; *Shannon's Deal* 1989; *Navy SEALS* 1990

Téchiné, André (1943–) *The Brontë Sisters* 1979; *Rendez-vous* 1985; *The Scene of the Crime* 1986; *J'Embrasse Pas* 1991; *Ma Saison Préferée* 1993; *Les Roseaux Sauvages* 1994; *Les Voleurs* 1996; *Alice et Martin* 1998; *Far Away* 2001

Temple, Julien (1953–) *The Great Rock 'n' Roll Swindle* 1979; *The Secret Policeman's Other Ball* 1982; *Running Out of Luck* 1985; *Absolute Beginners* 1986; *Aria* 1987; *Earth Girls Are Easy* 1988; *Bullet* 1995; *Vigo: Passion for Life* 1997; *The Filth and the Fury* 2000; *Pandaemonium* 2000

Templeton, George (1906–1980) *The Sundowners* 1950; *A Gift for Heidi* 1958

Tennant, Andy *It Takes Two* 1995; *Fools Rush In* 1997; *Ever After: a Cinderella Story* 1998; *Anna and the King* 1999; *Sweet Home Alabama* 2002; *Hitch* 2005

Tenney, Kevin S *aka* **Tenney, Kevin** *Witchboard* 1987; *Night of the Demons* 1988; *Peacemaker* 1990; *Pinocchio's Revenge* 1996

Tennyson, Pen *aka* **Tennyson, Penrose** (1918–1941) *Convoy* 1940; *The Proud Valley* 1940

Terlesky, John *The Pandora Project* 1998; *Judgment Day* 1999; *Supreme Sanction* 1999; *Chain of Command* 2000; *Guardian* 2000

Teshigahara, Hiroshi (1927–2001) *Pitfall* 1962; *Woman of the Dunes* 1963; *The Face of Another* 1966; *Rikyu* 1989

Tessari, Duccio (1926–1994) *The Heroes* 1972; *Three Tough Guys* 1974; *Zorro* 1975; *Tex and the Lord of the Deep* 1985; *Please Let the Flowers Live* 1986

Tetzlaff, Ted (1903–1995) *Riff-Raff* 1947; *Fighting Father Dunne* 1948; *A Dangerous Profession* 1949; *Johnny Allegro* 1949; *The Window* 1949; *The White Tower* 1950; *Treasure of Lost Canyon* 1952; *Terror on a Train* 1953; *Son of Sinbad* 1955; *The Young Land* 1959

Tewksbury, Peter (1924–2003) *Sunday in New York* 1963; *Emil and the Detectives* 1964; *Stay Away, Joe* 1968; *The Trouble with Girls* 1969

Thiele, William *aka* **Thiele, Wilhelm** (1890–1975) *The Love Waltz* 1930; *London by Night* 1937; *The Ghost Comes Home* 1940; *Tarzan Triumphs* 1943; *Tarzan's Desert Mystery* 1943

Thomas, Betty (1948–) *Only You* 1992; *The Brady Bunch Movie* 1995; *The Late Shift* 1996; *Private Parts* 1997; *Doctor Dolittle* 1998; *28 Days* 2000; *I Spy* 2002

Thomas, Dave (1949–) *Strange Brew* 1983; *The Experts* 1989

Thomas, Gerald (1920–1993) *Circus Friends* 1956; *Time Lock* 1957; *The Vicious Circle* 1957; *Carry On Sergeant* 1958; *The Duke Wore Jeans* 1958; *Carry On Nurse* 1959; *Carry On Teacher* 1959; *Carry On Constable* 1960; *Carry On Regardless* 1960; *No Kidding* 1960; *Please Turn Over* 1960; *Watch Your Stern* 1960; *Raising the Wind* 1961; *Carry On Cruising* 1962; *The Iron Maiden* 1962; *Twice round the Daffodils* 1962; *Carry On Cabby* 1963; *Carry On Jack* 1963; *Nurse on Wheels* 1963; *Carry On Cleo* 1964; *Carry On Spying* 1964; *The Big Job* 1965; *Carry On Cowboy* 1965; *Carry On – Don't Lose Your Head* 1966; *Carry On Screaming* 1966; *Carry On Follow That Camel* 1967; *Carry On Doctor* 1968; *Carry On Up the Khyber* 1968; *Carry On Again Doctor* 1969; *Carry On Camping* 1969; *Carry On Loving* 1970; *Carry On Up the Jungle* 1970; *Carry On at Your Convenience* 1971; *Carry On Henry* 1971; *Bless This House* 1972; *Carry On Abroad* 1972; *Carry On Matron* 1972; *Carry On Girls* 1973; *Carry On Dick* 1974; *Carry On Behind* 1975; *Carry On England* 1976; *That's Carry On* 1977; *Carry On Emmannuelle* 1978; *The Second Victory* 1986; *Carry On Columbus* 1992

Thomas, Ralph (1915–2001) *Once upon a Dream* 1948; *Traveller's Joy* 1949; *The Clouded Yellow* 1950; *Appointment with Venus* 1951; *Venetian Bird* 1952; *A Day to Remember* 1953; *Doctor in the House* 1954; *Mad about Men* 1954; *Above Us the Waves* 1955; *Doctor at Sea* 1955; *Checkpoint* 1956; *The Iron Petticoat* 1956; *Campbell's Kingdom* 1957; *Doctor at Large* 1957; *A Tale of Two Cities* 1957; *The Wind Cannot Read* 1958; *The Thirty-Nine Steps* 1959; *Upstairs and Downstairs* 1959; *Conspiracy of Hearts* 1960; *Doctor in Love* 1960; *No Love for Johnnie* 1960; *No My Darling Daughter* 1961; *A Pair of Briefs* 1961; *The Wild and the Willing* 1962; *Doctor in Distress* 1963; *Hot Enough for June* 1963; *The High Bright Sun* 1965; *Deadlier than the Male* 1966; *Doctor in Clover* 1966; *Nobody Runs Forever* 1968; *Some Girls Do* 1969; *Doctor in Trouble* 1970; *Percy* 1971; *Quest for Love* 1971; *Percy's Progress* 1974; *A Nightingale Sang in Berkeley Square* 1979

Thomas, Ralph L *aka* **Thomas, R L** *Ticket to Heaven* 1981; *Apprentice to Murder* 1988; *Young Ivanhoe* 1994; *Young Connecticut Yankee in King Arthur's Court* 1995

Thompson, Caroline (1956–) *Black Beauty* 1994; *Buddy* 1997; *Snow White* 2001

Thompson, Ernest (1950–) *1969* 1988; *The West Side Waltz* 1995

Thomson, Chris *The Empty Beach* 1985; *The Delinquents* 1989; *Trucks* 1997

Thornton, Billy Bob (1955–) *Sling Blade* 1995; *All the Pretty Horses* 2000

Thorpe, Jerry (1930–) *The Venetian Affair* 1966; *Day of the Evil Gun* 1968; *Company of Killers* 1970

Thorpe, Richard (1896–1991) *Tarzan Escapes* 1936; *Double Wedding* 1937; *Man-Proof* 1937; *Night Must Fall* 1937; *The Crowd Roars* 1938; *Three Loves Has Nancy* 1938; *The Toy Wife* 1938; *The Adventures of Huckleberry Finn* 1939; *Tarzan Finds a Son!* 1939; *The Earl of Chicago* 1940; *Tarzan's Secret Treasure* 1941; *Apache Trail* 1942; *Joe Smith, American* 1942; *Tarzan's New York Adventure* 1942; *White Cargo* 1942; *Above Suspicion* 1943; *Cry Havoc* 1943; *The Thin Man Goes Home* 1944; *Two Girls and a Sailor* 1944; *Thrill of a Romance* 1945; *Fiesta* 1947; *This Time for Keeps* 1947; *A Date with Judy* 1948; *On an Island with You* 1948; *Big Jack* 1949; *Challenge to Lassie* 1949; *Malaya* 1949; *The Black Hand* 1950; *Three Little Words* 1950; *The Great Caruso* 1951; *It's a Big Country* 1951; *Vengeance Valley* 1951; *Carbine Williams* 1952; *Ivanhoe* 1952; *The Prisoner of Zenda* 1952; *All the Brothers Were Valiant* 1953; *The Girl Who Had Everything* 1953; *Knights of the Round Table* 1953; *Athena* 1954; *The Student Prince* 1954; *The Prodigal* 1955; *Quentin Durward* 1955; *Jailhouse Rock* 1957; *Ten Thousand Bedrooms* 1957; *Tip on a Dead Jockey* 1957; *The House of the Seven Hawks* 1959; *Killers of Kilimanjaro* 1960; *The Honeymoon Machine* 1961; *The Horizontal Lieutenant* 1962; *Follow the Boys* 1963; *Fun in Acapulco* 1963; *The Truth about Spring* 1964; *That Funny Feeling* 1965; *The Last Challenge* 1967

Tian Zhuangzhuang (1952–) *Horse Thief* 1986; *The Blue Kite* 1992; *Springtime in a Small Town* 2002

Tickell, Paul *Crush Proof* 1998; *Christie Malry's Own Double-Entry* 2000

Till, Eric (1929–) *Hot Millions* 1968; *The Walking Stick* 1970; *It Shouldn't Happen to a Vet* 1979; *Improper Channels* 1981; *Oh, What a Night* 1992; *Silhouette* 1994; *Murder at My Door* 1996

Tillman Jr, George *Soul Food* 1997; *Men of Honor* 2000

Tinling, James (1889–1967) *Mr Moto's Gamble* 1938; *Riders of the Purple Sage* 1941

Title, Stacy *The Last Supper* 1995; *Let the Devil Wear Black* 1999

Tlatli, Moufida *The Silences of the Palace* 1994; *La Saison des Hommes* 2000

To, Johnny (1955–) *The Heroic Trio* 1992; *Fulltime Killer* 2002
Toback, James (1943–) *Fingers* 1978; *Love and Money* 1982; *Exposed* 1983; *The Pick-Up Artist* 1987; *The Big Bang* 1989; *Two Girls and a Guy* 1997; *Black and White* 1999
Tokar, Norman (1920–1979) *Big Red* 1962; *Sammy, the Way Out Seal* 1962; *Savage Sam* 1963; *Those Calloways* 1964; *A Tiger Walks* 1964; *Follow Me, Boys!* 1966; *The Ugly Dachshund* 1966; *The Happiest Millionaire* 1967; *The Horse in the Gray Flannel Suit* 1968; *The Boatniks* 1970; *Snowball Express* 1972; *The Apple Dumpling Gang* 1974; *Where the Red Fern Grows* 1974; *No Deposit No Return* 1976; *Candleshoe* 1977; *The Cat from Outer Space* 1978
Tolkin, Michael (1950–) *The Rapture* 1991; *The New Age* 1994
Tollin, Mike (1956–) *Summer Catch* 2001; *Radio* 2003
Tong, Stanley (1960–) *Police Story III: Supercop* 1992; *Jackie Chan's First Strike* 1996; *Rumble in the Bronx* 1996; *Mr Magoo* 1997
Topper, Burt *The Strangler* 1964; *The Hard Ride* 1971
Tornatore, Giuseppe (1956–) *Cinema Paradiso* 1988; *Everybody's Fine* 1990; *A Pure Formality* 1994; *The Starmaker* 1994; *The Legend of 1900* 1999; *Malena* 2000
Totten, Robert *aka* **Smithee, Allen** (1937–1995) *Death of a Gunfighter* 1969; *The Wild Country* 1971
Tourneur, Jacques (1904–1977) *Nick Carter, Master Detective* 1939; *Phantom Raiders* 1940; *Cat People* 1942; *I Walked with a Zombie* 1943; *The Leopard Man* 1943; *Days of Glory* 1944; *Experiment Perilous* 1944; *Canyon Passage* 1946; *Build My Gallows High* 1947; *Berlin Express* 1948; *Easy Living* 1949; *Circle of Danger* 1950; *The Flame and the Arrow* 1950; *Stars in My Crown* 1950; *Anne of the Indies* 1951; *Way of a Gaucho* 1952; *Appointment in Honduras* 1953; *Stranger on Horseback* 1955; *Wichita* 1955; *Great Day in the Morning* 1956; *Nightfall* 1956; *Night of the Demon* 1957; *The Fearmakers* 1958; *Timbuktu* 1959; *The Giant of Marathon* 1960; *The Comedy of Terrors* 1964; *City under the Sea* 1965
Tourneur, Maurice (1876–1961) *The Pride of the Clan* 1917; *The Last of the Mohicans* 1920; *The Ship of Lost Men* 1929; *Königsmark* 1935; *Volpone* 1941
Towne, Robert (1936–) *Personal Best* 1982; *Tequila Sunrise* 1988; *Without Limits* 1998
Townsend, Robert (1957–) *Eddie Murphy Raw* 1987; *Hollywood Shuffle* 1987; *The Five Heartbeats* 1991; *The Meteor Man* 1993; *BAPS* 1997; *Little Richard* 2000
Toye, Wendy (1917–) *Three Cases of Murder* 1953; *The Teckman Mystery* 1954; *All for Mary* 1955; *Raising a Riot* 1955; *True as a Turtle* 1956; *We Joined the Navy* 1962
Toynton, Ian *The Maid* 1991; *Annie: a Royal Adventure* 1995
Toyoda, Shiro (1906–1977) *Illusion of Blood* 1965; *Portrait of Hell* 1969
Tran Anh Hung (1962–) *The Scent of Green Papaya* 1993; *Cyclo* 1995; *At the Height of Summer* 1999
Trapero, Pablo (1971–) *El Bonaerense* 2002; *Familia Rodante* 2004
Travolta, Joey (1952–) *Too Hard to Die* 1998; *Partners* 2000
Trenchard-Smith, Brian (1946–) *The Man from Hong Kong* 1975; *Turkey Shoot* 1981; *BMX Bandits* 1983; *Jenny Kissed Me* 1984; *Frog Dreaming* 1985; *Out of the Body* 1988; *Night of the Demons 2* 1994; *Happy Face Murders* 1999; *Britannic* 2000
Trent, John (?–1983) *Homer* 1970; *Sunday in the Country* 1975; *Find the Lady* 1976; *Middle Age Crazy* 1980; *Best Revenge* 1983
Treut, Monika (1954–) *Seduction: the Cruel Woman* 1985; *Virgin Machine* 1988; *My Father Is Coming* 1991; *Erotique* 1994; *Didn't Do It for Love* 1997; *Gendernauts* 1999
Trikonis, Gus *Moonshine County Express* 1977; *The Evil* 1978; *Touched by Love* 1979; *Take This Job and Shove It* 1981; *Dance of the Dwarfs* 1983
Troche, Rose (1964–) *Go Fish* 1994; *Bedrooms and Hallways* 1998; *The Safety of Objects* 2001
Troell, Jan (1931–) *The Emigrants* 1971; *The New Land* 1972; *Zandy's Bride* 1974; *Hurricane* 1979; *Hamsun* 1996
Trousdale, Gary *Beauty and the Beast* 1991; *The Hunchback of Notre Dame* 1996; *Atlantis: the Lost Empire* 2001
Trueba, Fernando (1955–) *Belle Epoque* 1992; *Two Much* 1995; *The Girl of Your Dreams* 1998
Truffaut, François (1932–1984) *The 400 Blows* 1959; *Shoot the Pianist* 1960; *Jules et Jim* 1961; *Love at Twenty* 1962; *La Peau Douce* 1964; *Fahrenheit 451* 1966; *The Bride Wore Black* 1967; *Stolen Kisses* 1968; *Mississippi Mermaid* 1969; *Bed and Board* 1970; *L'Enfant Sauvage* 1970; *Anne and Muriel* 1971; *Une Belle Fille Comme Moi* 1973; *Day for Night* 1973; *The Story of Adèle H* 1975; *Small Change* 1976; *The Man Who Loved Women* 1977; *The Green Room* 1978; *Love on the Run* 1979; *The Last Metro* 1980; *The Woman Next Door* 1981; *Confidentially Yours* 1983
Truman, Michael (1916–1974) *Touch and Go* 1955; *Go to Blazes* 1961; *Girl in the Headlines* 1963; *Daylight Robbery* 1964
Trumbull, Douglas (1942–) *Silent Running* 1971; *Brainstorm* 1983
Tryon, Glenn (1894–1970) *The Law West of Tombstone* 1938; *Beauty for the Asking* 1939
Tsai Ming-liang (1957–) *Rebels of the Neon God* 1992; *Vive L'Amour* 1994; *The River* 1997; *The Hole* 1998; *What Time Is It There?* 2001; *Goodbye, Dragon Inn* 2003
Tsui Hark (1951–) *The Butterfly Murders* 1979; *Zu Warriors* 1983; *Peking Opera Blues* 1986; *A Better Tomorrow III* 1989; *The Master* 1989; *Once upon a Time in China* 1991; *Once upon a Time in China II* 1992; *Twin Dragons* 1992; *Double Team* 1997; *Knock Off* 1998; *Time and Tide* 2000
Tsukamoto, Shinya (1960–) *Tetsuo: the Iron Man* 1989; *Tetsuo II: Body Hammer* 1991; *Tokyo Fist* 1995; *A Snake of June* 2002
Tucci, Stanley (1960–) *Big Night* 1996; *The Impostors* 1998
Tuchner, Michael (1934–) *Villain* 1971; *Fear Is the Key* 1972; *Mister Quilp* 1975; *The Likely Lads* 1976; *Summer of My German Soldier* 1978; *The Hunchback of Notre Dame* 1982; *Adam* 1983; *Trenchcoat* 1983; *Wilt* 1989
Tully, Montgomery (1904–1988) *Boys in Brown* 1949; *The Diamond* 1954; *The Glass Cage* 1955; *The Hypnotist* 1957; *No Road Back* 1957; *Escapement* 1958; *The Third Alibi* 1961; *Clash by Night* 1963; *Master Spy* 1964; *Battle beneath the Earth* 1968
Turman, Lawrence (1926–) *The Marriage of a Young Stockbroker* 1971; *Second Thoughts* 1982
Turner, Ann (1960–) *Celia* 1988; *Hammers over the Anvil* 1992; *Dallas Doll* 1994
Turteltaub, Jon (1964–) *Think Big* 1990; *3 Ninjas* 1992; *Cool Runnings* 1993; *While You Were Sleeping* 1995; *Phenomenon* 1996; *Instinct* 1999; *Disney's The Kid* 2000; *National Treasure* 2004
Tuttle, Frank (1892–1963) *The Canary Murder Case* 1929; *Her Wedding Night* 1930; *Paramount on Parade* 1930; *It Pays to Advertise* 1931; *The Big Broadcast* 1932; *This Is the Night* 1932; *This Reckless Age* 1932; *Roman Scandals* 1933; *Ladies Should Listen* 1934; *All the King's Horses* 1935; *The Glass Key* 1935; *Waikiki Wedding* 1937; *Doctor Rhythm* 1938; *Paris Honeymoon* 1939; *This Gun for Hire* 1942; *Hostages* 1943; *The Hour before the Dawn* 1944; *The Great John L* 1945; *Swell Guy* 1946; *Hell on Frisco Bay* 1955; *A Cry in the Night* 1956
Twist, Derek (1905–1979) *The End of the River* 1947; *Green Grow the Rushes* 1951; *Police Dog* 1955
Twohy, David (1956–) *The Arrival* 1996; *Pitch Black* 1999; *Below* 2002; *The Chronicles of Riddick* 2004
Tykwer, Tom (1965–) *Wintersleepers* 1997; *Run Lola Run* 1998; *The Princess & the Warrior* 2000; *Heaven* 2002

U

Uderzo, Albert (1927–) *Asterix the Gaul* 1967; *Asterix and Cleopatra* 1968; *The 12 Tasks of Asterix* 1975
Ullmann, Liv (1939–) *Sofie* 1992; *Kristin Lavransdatter* 1995; *Private Confessions* 1996; *Faithless* 2000
Ulmer, Edgar G (1900–1972) *People on Sunday* 1929; *The Black Cat* 1934; *Green Fields* 1937; *Bluebeard* 1944; *Detour* 1945; *The Strange Woman* 1946; *Carnegie Hall* 1947; *Ruthless* 1948; *The Man from Planet X* 1951; *The Naked Dawn* 1955; *Daughter of Dr Jekyll* 1957; *Hannibal* 1959; *The Amazing Transparent Man* 1960; *Beyond the Time Barrier* 1960
Underwood, Ron (1959–) *Tremors* 1989; *City Slickers* 1991; *Heart and Souls* 1993; *Speechless* 1994; *Mighty Joe Young* 1998; *Pluto Nash* 2001
Unkrich, Lee (1967–) *Toy Story 2* 1999; *Finding Nemo* 2003
Uno, Michael Toshiyuki *Without Warning: the James Brady Story* 1991; *Dangerous Intentions* 1995
Urban, Stuart (1959–) *Preaching to the Perverted* 1997; *Revelation* 2001
Ustinov, Peter (1921–2004) *School for Secrets* 1946; *Vice Versa* 1947; *Romanoff and Juliet* 1961; *Billy Budd* 1962; *Lady L* 1965; *Hammersmith Is Out* 1972
Uys, Jamie (1921–1996) *The Gods Must Be Crazy* 1980; *The Gods Must Be Crazy II* 1989

V

Vadim, Roger (1928–2000) *And God Created Woman* 1956; *Les Bijoutiers du Clair de Lune* 1957; *Les Liaisons Dangereuses* 1959; *Blood and Roses* 1960; *The Seven Deadly Sins* 1961; *La Ronde* 1964; *The Game Is Over* 1966; *Barbarella* 1967; *Histoires Extraordinaires* 1967; *Pretty Maids All in a Row* 1971; *Don Juan 73, or If Don Juan Were a Woman* 1973; *Night Games* 1979; *The Hot Touch* 1982; *And God Created Woman* 1988
Valdez, Luis (1940–) *Zoot Suit* 1981; *La Bamba* 1987
Van Dormael, Jaco (1957–) *Toto Le Héros* 1991; *The Eighth Day* 1996
Van Dyke, W S *aka* **Van Dyke II, W S** *aka* **Van Dyke II, Major W S** (1889–1943) *White Shadows in the South Seas* 1928; *Guilty Hands* 1931; *Trader Horn* 1931; *Tarzan, the Ape Man* 1932; *Penthouse* 1933; *The Prizefighter and the Lady* 1933; *Forsaking All Others* 1934; *Manhattan Melodrama* 1934; *The Thin Man* 1934; *I Live My Life* 1935; *Naughty Marietta* 1935; *After the Thin Man* 1936; *The Devil Is a Sissy* 1936; *His Brother's Wife* 1936; *Love on the Run* 1936; *Rose Marie* 1936; *San Francisco* 1936; *Personal Property* 1937; *Rosalie* 1937; *They Gave Him a Gun* 1937; *Marie Antoinette* 1938; *Sweethearts* 1938; *Andy Hardy Gets Spring Fever* 1939; *Another Thin Man* 1939; *It's a Wonderful World* 1939; *Bitter Sweet* 1940; *I Love You Again* 1940; *I Take This Woman* 1940; *Dr Kildare's Victory* 1941; *The Feminine Touch* 1941; *Rage in Heaven* 1941; *Shadow of the Thin Man* 1941; *I Married an Angel* 1942; *Journey for Margaret* 1942
Van Horn, Buddy (1929–) *Any Which Way You Can* 1980; *The Dead Pool* 1988; *Pink Cadillac* 1989
Van Peebles, Mario (1958–) *New Jack City* 1991; *Posse* 1993; *Panther* 1995; *Love Kills* 1998; *Baadasssss!* 2003
Van Peebles, Melvin (1932–) *Watermelon Man* 1970; *Sweet Sweetback's Baad Asssss Song* 1971; *Erotic Tales* 1994
Van Sant, Gus (1952–) *Drugstore Cowboy* 1989; *My Own Private Idaho* 1991; *Even Cowgirls Get the Blues* 1993; *To Die For* 1995; *Good Will Hunting* 1997; *Psycho* 1998; *Finding Forrester* 2000; *Gerry* 2001; *Elephant* 2003; *Last Days* 2005
Van Warmerdam, Alex (1952–) *Abel* 1986; *The Northerners* 1992
Vane, Norman Thaddeus *Frightmare* 1981; *Midnight* 1989
Varda, Agnès (1928–) *Cleo from 5 to 7* 1961; *Le Bonheur* 1965; *Les Créatures* 1966; *Far from Vietnam* 1967; *Lions Love* 1969; *One Sings, the Other Doesn't* 1976; *Vagabond* 1985; *Kung-Fu Master* 1987; *Jacquot de Nantes* 1991; *Les Cent et Une Nuits* 1995; *The Gleaners and I* 2000
Varma, Ram Gopal (1961–) *Rangeela* 1995; *Company* 2001; *Bhoot* 2003; *Naach* 2004
Varnel, Marcel (1894–1947) *Chandu the Magician* 1932; *Good Morning, Boys* 1937; *O-Kay for Sound* 1937; *Oh, Mr Porter!* 1937; *Alf's Button Afloat* 1938; *Ask a Policeman* 1938; *Convict 99* 1938; *Hey! Hey! USA* 1938; *Old Bones of the River* 1938; *Band Waggon* 1939; *Where's That Fire?* 1939; *Gasbags* 1940; *Let George Do It* 1940; *Neutral Port* 1940; *The Ghost of St Michael's* 1941; *Hi, Gang!* 1941; *I Thank You* 1941; *It's Turned Out Nice Again* 1941; *South American George* 1941; *King Arthur Was a Gentleman* 1942; *Much Too Shy* 1942; *Bell-Bottom George* 1943; *Get Cracking* 1943; *I Didn't Do It* 1945; *George in Civvy Street* 1946
Veber, Francis (1937–) *Les Compères* 1983; *Three Fugitives* 1989; *Out on a Limb* 1992; *Le Dîner de Cons* 1998; *The Closet* 2001
Verbinski, Gore (1965–) *Mousehunt* 1997; *The Mexican* 2001; *The Ring* 2002; *Pirates of the Caribbean: the Curse of the Black Pearl* 2003
Verbong, Ben (1949–) *The Girl with Red Hair* 1981; *House Call* 1996
Verhoeven, Michael (1938–) *Killing Cars* 1986; *The Nasty Girl* 1990; *My Mother's Courage* 1995
Verhoeven, Paul (1938–) *Business Is Business* 1971; *Turkish Delight* 1973; *Keetje Tippel* 1975; *Soldier of Orange* 1977; *Spetters* 1980; *The Fourth Man* 1983; *Flesh + Blood* 1985; *RoboCop* 1987; *Total Recall* 1990; *Basic Instinct* 1992; *Showgirls* 1995; *Starship Troopers* 1997; *Hollow Man* 2000
Verneuil, Henri (1920–2002) *The Sheep Has Five Legs* 1954; *A Monkey in Winter* 1962; *Any Number Can Win* 1963; *The 25th Hour* 1967; *Guns for San Sebastian* 1968; *The Sicilian Clan* 1969; *The Burglars* 1971; *The Serpent* 1972
Vernoux, Marion (1966–) *Love etc* 1997; *Rien à Faire* 1999
Verona, Stephen (1940–) *The Lords of Flatbush* 1974; *Pipe Dreams* 1976; *Boardwalk* 1979
VeSota, Bruno (1922–1976) *The Female Jungle* 1955; *The Brain Eaters* 1958
Vicas, Victor (1918–1985) *Count Five and Die* 1957; *The Wayward Bus* 1957
Vidor, Charles (1900–1959) *The Arizonian* 1935; *Strangers All* 1935; *Blind Alley* 1939; *The Lady in Question* 1940; *My Son, My Son!* 1940; *Ladies in Retirement* 1941; *They Dare Not Love* 1941; *The Tuttles of Tahiti* 1942; *The Desperadoes* 1943; *Cover Girl* 1944; *Together Again* 1944; *Over 21* 1945; *A Song to Remember* 1945; *Gilda* 1946; *The Loves of Carmen* 1948; *It's a Big Country* 1951; *Hans Christian Andersen* 1952; *Thunder in the East* 1953; *Rhapsody* 1954; *Love Me or Leave Me* 1955; *The Swan* 1956; *A Farewell to Arms* 1957; *The Joker Is Wild* 1957; *Song without End* 1960
Vidor, King (1894–1982) *The Big Parade* 1925; *La Bohème* 1926; *The Crowd* 1928; *The Patsy* 1928; *Show People* 1928; *Hallelujah* 1929; *Billy the Kid* 1930; *The Champ* 1931; *Street Scene* 1931; *Bird of Paradise* 1932; *Cynara* 1932; *The Mask of Fu Manchu* 1932; *The Stranger's Return* 1933; *Our Daily Bread* 1934; *So Red the Rose* 1935; *The Wedding Night* 1935; *The Texas Rangers* 1936; *Stella Dallas* 1937; *The Citadel* 1938; *Comrade X* 1940; *Northwest Passage* 1940; *HM Pulham Esq* 1941; *An American Romance* 1944; *Duel in the Sun* 1946; *On Our Merry Way* 1948; *Beyond the Forest* 1949; *The Fountainhead* 1949; *Lightning Strikes Twice* 1951; *Japanese War Bride* 1952; *Ruby Gentry* 1952; *Man without a Star* 1955; *War and Peace* 1956; *Solomon and Sheba* 1959
Viertel, Berthold (1885–1953) *The Man from Yesterday* 1932; *The Wiser Sex* 1932; *The Passing of the Third Floor Back* 1935; *Rhodes of Africa* 1936
Vieyra, Emilio *Blood of the Virgins* 1967; *Curious Dr Humpp* 1967
Vigo, Jean (1905–1934) *A Propos de Nice* 1930; *Taris* 1931; *Zéro de Conduite* 1933; *L'Atalante* 1934
Vila, Camilo *The Unholy* 1988; *Unlawful Passage* 1994
Vincent, Chuck (1940–1991) *Hollywood Hot Tubs* 1984; *Preppies* 1984; *Warrior Queen* 1986
Vinterberg, Thomas (1969–) *Festen* 1998; *It's All about Love* 2002; *Dear Wendy* 2005
Virgien, Norton *The Rugrats Movie* 1998; *Rugrats Go Wild* 2003
Visconti, Luchino (1906–1976) *Ossessione* 1942; *La Terra Trema* 1947; *Bellissima* 1951; *Senso* 1954; *White Nights* 1957; *Rocco and His Brothers* 1960; *Boccaccio '70* 1961; *The Leopard* 1962; *Of a Thousand Delights* 1965; *The Witches* 1966; *The Stranger* 1967; *The Damned* 1969; *Death in Venice* 1971; *Ludwig* 1973; *Conversation Piece* 1974; *L'Innocente* 1976
Vogel, Virgil W *aka* **Vogel, Virgil** (1919–1996) *The Mole People* 1956; *The Land Unknown* 1957
von Garnier, Katja (1966–) *Making Up* 1992; *Iron Jawed Angels* 2004
von Scherler Mayer, Daisy (1965–) *Party Girl* 1994; *Madeline* 1998; *Woo* 1998; *The Guru* 2002
von Sternberg, Josef (1894–1969) *The Salvation Hunters* 1925; *The Exquisite Sinner* 1926; *Underworld* 1927; *The Docks of New York* 1928; *The Dragnet* 1928; *The Last Command* 1928; *The Case of Lena Smith* 1929; *Thunderbolt* 1929; *The Blue Angel* 1930; *Morocco* 1930; *An American Tragedy* 1931; *Dishonored* 1931; *Blonde Venus* 1932; *Shanghai Express* 1932; *The Scarlet Empress* 1934; *Crime*

and Punishment 1935; *The Devil Is a Woman* 1935; *The King Steps Out* 1936; *Sergeant Madden* 1939; *The Shanghai Gesture* 1941; *Macao* 1952; *The Saga of Anatahan* 1953; *Jet Pilot* 1957
von Stroheim, Erich (1885–1957) *Blind Husbands* 1919; *Foolish Wives* 1920; *Greed* 1925; *The Merry Widow* 1925; *Queen Kelly* 1928; *The Wedding March* 1928; *Hello Sister!* 1933
von Trier, Lars (1956–) *The Element of Crime* 1984; *Medea* 1988; *Europa* 1991; *The Kingdom* 1994; *Breaking the Waves* 1996; *The Idiots* 1998; *Dancer in the Dark* 2000; *Dogville* 2003; *The Five Obstructions* 2003
von Trotta, Margarethe (1942–) *The Lost Honour of Katharina Blum* 1975; *Sisters, or the Balance of Happiness* 1979; *The German Sisters* 1981; *Rosa Luxemburg* 1986; *Three Sisters* 1988; *The Promise* 1994
Vorhaus, Bernard (1904–2000) *Crime on the Hill* 1933; *The Ghost Camera* 1933; *Street Song* 1935; *Dusty Ermine* 1936; *The Last Journey* 1936; *Cotton Queen* 1937; *Meet Dr Christian* 1939; *Three Faces West* 1940; *Lady from Louisiana* 1941
Voss, Kurt (1963–) *Border Radio* 1987; *Genuine Risk* 1990; *Knife Edge* 1990

W

Wachowski, Andy (1967–) *Bound* 1996; *The Matrix* 1999; *The Matrix Reloaded* 2002; *The Matrix Revolutions* 2003
Wachowski, Larry (1965–) *Bound* 1996; *The Matrix* 1999; *The Matrix Reloaded* 2002; *The Matrix Revolutions* 2003
Wacks, Jonathan *Powwow Highway* 1988; *Mystery Date* 1991; *Motherhood* 1993
Wadleigh, Michael (1941–) *Woodstock* 1970; *Wolfen* 1981
Waggner, George (1894–1984) *Man Made Monster* 1941; *The Wolf Man* 1941; *The Fighting Kentuckian* 1949; *Operation Pacific* 1951
Wainwright, Rupert (1962–) *Blank Check* 1994; *Stigmata* 1999
Wajda, Andrzej (1926–) *A Generation* 1954; *Kanal* 1957; *Ashes and Diamonds* 1958; *Love at Twenty* 1962; *Landscape after Battle* 1970; *Man of Marble* 1977; *The Young Ladies of Wilko* 1979; *The Conductor* 1980; *Man of Iron* 1981; *Danton* 1982; *Korczak* 1990; *Miss Nobody* 1997
Walas, Chris (1955–) *The Fly II* 1989; *The Vagrant* 1992
Walker, Giles (1946–) *The Masculine Mystique* 1984; *90 Days* 1986; *Ordinary Magic* 1993; *Never Too Late* 1996
Walker, Hal (1896–1972) *Duffy's Tavern* 1945; *Out of This World* 1945; *Road to Utopia* 1945; *The Stork Club* 1945; *At War with the Army* 1950; *My Friend Irma Goes West* 1950; *Sailor Beware* 1951; *That's My Boy* 1951; *Road to Bali* 1952
Walker, Pete (1935–) *Die Screaming Marianne* 1970; *Tiffany Jones* 1973; *Frightmare* 1974; *House of Whipcord* 1974; *House of Mortal Sin* 1975; *Schizo* 1976; *The Comeback* 1977; *House of the Long Shadows* 1983
Walker, Stuart (1887–1941) *The Eagle and the Hawk* 1933; *White Woman* 1933; *The Mystery of Edwin Drood* 1935
Wallace, Randall *The Man in the Iron Mask* 1997; *We Were Soldiers* 2002
Wallace, Richard (1894–1951) *The Shopworn Angel* 1928; *Man of the World* 1931; *The Masquerader* 1933; *The Little Minister* 1934; *Wedding Present* 1936; *The Young in Heart* 1938; *The Navy Steps Out* 1941; *A Night to Remember* 1942; *Bombardier* 1943; *The Fallen Sparrow* 1943; *Bride by Mistake* 1944; *It's in the Bag* 1945; *Kiss and Tell* 1945; *Because of Him* 1946; *Framed* 1947; *Sinbad the Sailor* 1947; *Tycoon* 1947; *Let's Live a Little* 1948; *Adventure in Baltimore* 1949; *A Kiss for Corliss* 1949
Wallace, Stephen (1943–) *The Boy Who Had Everything* 1984; *Blood Oath* 1990; *Turtle Beach* 1992
Wallace, Tommy Lee *Halloween III: Season of the Witch* 1982; *Aloha Summer* 1988; *Fright Night Part 2* 1988
Waller, Anthony (1959–) *Mute Witness* 1995; *An American Werewolf in Paris* 1997; *The Guilty* 2000
Walls, Tom (1883–1949) *Rookery Nook* 1930; *A Cuckoo in the Nest* 1933; *Fighting Stock* 1935; *Foreign Affaires* 1935; *For Valour* 1937
Walsh, Aisling *Joyriders* 1988; *Song for a Raggy Boy* 2002
Walsh, Raoul aka **Walsh, R A** (1887–1980) *Regeneration* 1915; *The Thief of Bagdad* 1924; *The Lucky Lady* 1926; *What Price Glory* 1926; *The Red Dance* 1928; *Sadie Thompson* 1928; *The Cock-Eyed World* 1929; *In Old Arizona* 1929; *The Big Trail* 1930; *Me and My Gal* 1932; *The Bowery* 1933; *Going Hollywood* 1933; *Big Brown Eyes* 1936; *Klondike Annie* 1936; *Spendthrift* 1936; *You're in the Army Now* 1936; *Artists and Models* 1937; *Jump for Glory* 1937; *College Swing* 1938; *The Roaring Twenties* 1939; *Dark Command* 1940; *They Drive by Night* 1940; *High Sierra* 1941; *Manpower* 1941; *The Strawberry Blonde* 1941; *They Died with Their Boots On* 1941; *Desperate Journey* 1942; *Gentleman Jim* 1942; *Background to Danger* 1943; *Northern Pursuit* 1943; *Uncertain Glory* 1944; *The Horn Blows at Midnight* 1945; *Objective, Burma!* 1945; *Salty O'Rourke* 1945; *The Man I Love* 1946; *Pursued* 1947; *Fighter Squadron* 1948; *Silver River* 1948; *Colorado Territory* 1949; *White Heat* 1949; *Along the Great Divide* 1951; *Captain Horatio Hornblower RN* 1951; *Distant Drums* 1951; *Blackbeard the Pirate* 1952; *Glory Alley* 1952; *The Lawless Breed* 1952; *Sea Devils* 1952; *The World in His Arms* 1952; *Gun Fury* 1953; *A Lion Is in the Streets* 1953; *Saskatchewan* 1954; *Battle Cry* 1955; *The Tall Men* 1955; *The King and Four Queens* 1956; *The Revolt of Mamie Stover* 1956; *Band of Angels* 1957; *The Naked and the Dead* 1958; *The Sheriff of Fractured Jaw* 1958; *A Private's Affair* 1959; *Esther and the King* 1960; *A Distant Trumpet* 1964
Walters, Charles (1911–1982) *Ziegfeld Follies* 1944; *Good News* 1947; *Easter Parade* 1948; *The Barkleys of Broadway* 1949; *Summer Stock* 1950; *Texas Carnival* 1951; *The Belle of New York* 1952; *Dangerous When Wet* 1953; *Easy to Love* 1953; *Lili* 1953; *Torch Song* 1953; *The Glass Slipper* 1955; *The Tender Trap* 1955; *High Society* 1956; *Don't Go Near the Water* 1957; *Ask Any Girl* 1959; *Please Don't Eat the Daisies* 1960; *Two Loves* 1961; *Jumbo* 1962; *The Unsinkable Molly Brown* 1964; *Walk, Don't Run* 1966
Walton, Fred *When a Stranger Calls* 1979; *Hadley's Rebellion* 1984; *April Fool's Day* 1986; *The Rosary Murders* 1987
Wanamaker, Sam (1919–1993) *The File of the Golden Goose* 1969; *The Executioner* 1970; *Catlow* 1971; *Sinbad and the Eye of the Tiger* 1977
Wang, Peter *A Great Wall* 1985; *The Laserman* 1988
Wang, Steve *The Guyver* 1991; *Guyver 2: Dark Hero* 1994; *Drive* 1997
Wang, Wayne (1949–) *Chan Is Missing* 1982; *Dim Sum: a Little Bit of Heart* 1985; *Slam Dance* 1987; *Eat a Bowl of Tea* 1989; *Life Is Cheap... but Toilet Paper Is Expensive* 1990; *The Joy Luck Club* 1993; *Blue in the Face* 1995; *Smoke* 1995; *Chinese Box* 1997; *Anywhere but Here* 1999; *The Center of the World* 2001; *Maid in Manhattan* 2002; *Because of Winn-Dixie* 2004
Wang Xiaoshuai (1966–) *The Days* 1993; *Beijing Bicycle* 2001
Ward, David S (1945–) *Cannery Row* 1982; *Major League* 1989; *King Ralph* 1991; *The Program* 1993; *Major League II* 1994; *Down Periscope* 1996
Ward, Vincent (1956–) *Vigil* 1984; *The Navigator – a Medieval Odyssey* 1988; *Map of the Human Heart* 1992; *What Dreams May Come* 1998
Ware, Clyde (1936–) *No Drums, No Bugles* 1971; *Bad Jim* 1989
Wargnier, Régis (1948–) *Indochine* 1991; *Une Femme Française* 1994; *East-West* 1999
Warhol, Andy (1928–1987) *My Hustler* 1965; *Vinyl* 1965; *Bike Boy* 1967; *The Chelsea Girls* 1967; *Lonesome Cowboys* 1968
Warren, Charles Marquis (1912–1990) *Hellgate* 1952; *Arrowhead* 1953; *Flight to Tangier* 1953; *Seven Angry Men* 1955; *Tension at Table Rock* 1956; *Trooper Hook* 1957; *Cattle Empire* 1958; *Charro!* 1969
Warren, Norman J (1942–) *Satan's Slave* 1976; *Prey* 1977; *Terror* 1979; *Inseminoid* 1981; *Gunpowder* 1985
Waters (2), John (1946–) *Mondo Trasho* 1970; *Multiple Maniacs* 1970; *Pink Flamingos* 1972; *Female Trouble* 1974; *Desperate Living* 1977; *Polyester* 1981; *Hairspray* 1988; *Cry-Baby* 1989; *Serial Mom* 1994; *Pecker* 1998; *Cecil B Demented* 2000; *A Dirty Shame* 2004
Waters, Mark aka **Waters, Mark S** (1964–) *The House of Yes* 1997; *Head over Heels* 2000; *Freaky Friday* 2003; *Mean Girls* 2004
Watkins, Peter (1935–) *The War Game* 1965; *Privilege* 1967; *The Peace Game* 1969; *Punishment Park* 1971
Watt, Harry (1906–1987) *Night Mail* 1936; *Fiddlers Three* 1944; *The Overlanders* 1946; *Eureka Stockade* 1949; *Where No Vultures Fly* 1951; *West of Zanzibar* 1954; *The Siege of Pinchgut* 1959
Waxman, Keoni aka **Black, Darby** *Countdown* 1996; *The Highwayman* 1999; *Sweepers* 1999
Wayans, Keenen Ivory (1958–) *I'm Gonna Git You Sucka* 1988; *A Low Down Dirty Shame* 1994; *Scary Movie* 2000; *Scary Movie 2* 2001; *White Chicks* 2004
Wayne, John (1907–1979) *The Alamo* 1960; *The Green Berets* 1968
Webb, Jack (1920–1982) *Dragnet* 1954; *Pete Kelly's Blues* 1955; *-30-* 1959; *The Last Time I Saw Archie* 1961
Webb, Robert D aka **Webb, Robert** (1903–1990) *Beneath the 12-Mile Reef* 1953; *The Glory Brigade* 1953; *Seven Cities of Gold* 1955; *White Feather* 1955; *Love Me Tender* 1956; *The Proud Ones* 1956; *The Way to the Gold* 1957; *Guns of the Timberland* 1960; *A Little of What You Fancy* 1968
Webb, William *Delta Fever* 1988; *Party Line* 1988
Weber, Bruce (1946–) *Let's Get Lost* 1988; *Chop Suey* 2000
Webster, Nicholas (1922–) *Gone Are the Days* 1963; *Santa Claus Conquers the Martians* 1964
Wedge, Chris *Ice Age* 2002; *Robots* 2005
Weeks, Stephen (1948–) *I, Monster* 1971; *Gawain and the Green Knight* 1973; *Ghost Story* 1974; *Sword of the Valiant* 1984
Weiland, Paul *Leonard, Part 6* 1987; *City Slickers II: the Legend of Curly's Gold* 1994; *Roseanna's Grave* 1996
Weill, Claudia (1947–) *Girlfriends* 1978; *It's My Turn* 1980
Weinstein, Harvey (1952–) *Playing for Keeps* 1986; *Light Years* 1988
Weir, Peter (1944–) *The Cars That Ate Paris* 1974; *Picnic at Hanging Rock* 1975; *The Last Wave* 1977; *The Plumber* 1979; *Gallipoli* 1981; *The Year of Living Dangerously* 1982; *Witness* 1985; *The Mosquito Coast* 1986; *Dead Poets Society* 1989; *Green Card* 1990; *Fearless* 1993; *The Truman Show* 1998; *Master and Commander: the Far Side of the World* 2003
Weis, Don (1922–2000) *It's a Big Country* 1951; *The Affairs of Dobie Gillis* 1953; *I Love Melvin* 1953; *Remains to Be Seen* 1953; *The Adventures of Hajji Baba* 1954; *The Gene Krupa Story* 1959; *Critic's Choice* 1963; *Pajama Party* 1964; *Billie* 1965; *The Ghost in the Invisible Bikini* 1966; *The King's Pirate* 1967; *Did You Hear the One about the Traveling Saleslady?* 1968; *Zero to Sixty* 1978
Weis, Gary *Jimi Hendrix* 1973; *The Rutles – All You Need Is Cash* 1978; *Wholly Moses!* 1980
Weisman, Sam *D2: the Mighty Ducks* 1994; *Bye Bye Love* 1995; *George of the Jungle* 1997; *The Out-of-Towners* 1999; *What's the Worst That Could Happen?* 2001; *Dickie Roberts: Former Child Star* 2003
Weitz, Chris (1970–) *Down to Earth* 2001; *About a Boy* 2002
Weitz, Paul (1966–) *American Pie* 1999; *Down to Earth* 2001; *About a Boy* 2002; *In Good Company* 2004
Welles, Orson (1915–1985) *Citizen Kane* 1941; *The Magnificent Ambersons* 1942; *The Stranger* 1946; *The Lady from Shanghai* 1948; *Macbeth* 1948; *Othello* 1952; *Confidential Report* 1955; *Touch of Evil* 1958; *The Trial* 1962; *Chimes at Midnight* 1966; *The Immortal Story* 1968; *F for Fake* 1973
Wellesley, Gordon (1894–) *Rhythm Serenade* 1943; *The Silver Fleet* 1943
Wellington, David (1963–) *I Love a Man in Uniform* 1993; *Long Day's Journey into Night* 1996; *Blessed Stranger: after Flight 111* 2000
Wellman, William A aka **Wellman, William** (1896–1975) *Wings* 1927; *Beggars of Life* 1928; *Night Nurse* 1931; *Other Men's Women* 1931; *The Public Enemy* 1931; *The Hatchet Man* 1932; *Love Is a Racket* 1932; *The Purchase Price* 1932; *Central Airport* 1933; *Heroes for Sale* 1933; *Looking for Trouble* 1934; *The Call of the Wild* 1935; *The Robin Hood of El Dorado* 1936; *Small Town Girl* 1936; *Nothing Sacred* 1937; *A Star Is Born* 1937; *Men with Wings* 1938; *Beau Geste* 1939; *The Light That Failed* 1939; *The Great Man's Lady* 1942; *Roxie Hart* 1942; *Lady of Burlesque* 1943; *The Ox-Bow Incident* 1943; *Buffalo Bill* 1944; *The Story of GI Joe* 1945; *This Man's Navy* 1945; *Magic Town* 1947; *The Iron Curtain* 1948; *Yellow Sky* 1948; *Battleground* 1949; *The Happy Years* 1950; *The Next Voice You Hear* 1950; *Across the Wide Missouri* 1951; *It's a Big Country* 1951; *Westward the Women* 1951; *Island in the Sky* 1953; *The High and the Mighty* 1954; *Track of the Cat* 1954; *Blood Alley* 1955; *Good-bye, My Lady* 1956; *Hell Bent for Glory* 1957; *Darby's Rangers* 1958
Wells, Audrey (1961–) *Guinevere* 1999; *Under the Tuscan Sun* 2003
Wells, Simon (1961–) *An American Tail: Fievel Goes West* 1991; *We're Back! A Dinosaur's Story* 1993; *Balto* 1995; *The Prince of Egypt* 1998; *The Time Machine* 2002
Wenders, Wim (1945–) *The Goalkeeper's Fear of the Penalty Kick* 1971; *Alice in the Cities* 1974; *Kings of the Road* 1976; *The American Friend* 1977; *Lightning over Water* 1980; *Hammett* 1982; *The State of Things* 1982; *Paris, Texas* 1984; *Wings of Desire* 1987; *Notebook on Cities and Clothes* 1989; *Until the End of the World* 1991; *Faraway, So Close* 1993; *Lisbon Story* 1994; *The End of Violence* 1997; *Buena Vista Social Club* 1998; *The Million Dollar Hotel* 1999; *Ten Minutes Older: the Trumpet* 2002; *Martin Scorsese Presents the Blues: The Soul of a Man* 2003
Wendkos, Paul (1922–) *The Burglar* 1956; *Battle of the Coral Sea* 1959; *Face of a Fugitive* 1959; *Gidget* 1959; *Because They're Young* 1960; *Angel Baby* 1961; *Gidget Goes Hawaiian* 1961; *Gidget Goes to Rome* 1963; *Johnny Tiger* 1966; *Attack on the Iron Coast* 1968; *Guns of the Magnificent Seven* 1969; *Cannon for Cordoba* 1970; *Hell Boats* 1970; *The Mephisto Waltz* 1971; *Special Delivery* 1976
Wenk, Richard *Vamp* 1986; *Just the Ticket* 1998
Werker, Alfred (1896–1975) *Advice to the Lovelorn* 1933; *The House of Rothschild* 1934; *Kidnapped* 1938; *The Adventures of Sherlock Holmes* 1939; *The Reluctant Dragon* 1941; *A-Haunting We Will Go* 1942; *Whispering Ghosts* 1942; *He Walked by Night* 1948; *Sealed Cargo* 1951; *Walk East on Beacon* 1952; *Devil's Canyon* 1953; *The Last Posse* 1953; *Three Hours to Kill* 1954; *At Gunpoint* 1955; *Rebel in Town* 1956
Werner, Peter *Don't Cry, It's Only Thunder* 1982; *No Man's Land* 1987; *The Image* 1990; *The Unspoken Truth* 1995; *Call Me Claus* 2001
Wertmuller, Lina (1928–) *The Seduction of Mimi* 1972; *Swept Away... by an Unusual Destiny in the Blue Sea of August* 1974; *Seven Beauties* 1976; *The End of the World (in Our Usual Bed in a Night Full of Rain)* 1978; *Blood Feud* 1979; *Camorra* 1985; *Francesca and Nunziata* 2001
West, Roland (1885–1952) *The Monster* 1925; *Alibi* 1929; *The Bat Whispers* 1930
West, Simon (1961–) *Con Air* 1997; *The General's Daughter* 1999; *Lara Croft: Tomb Raider* 2001
Weston, Eric *Marvin and Tige* 1983; *The Iron Triangle* 1988; *To Protect and Serve* 1992
Wexler, Haskell (1926–) *Medium Cool* 1969; *Latino* 1985
Whale, James (1896–1957) *Journey's End* 1930; *Frankenstein* 1931; *Waterloo Bridge* 1931; *The Impatient Maiden* 1932; *The Old Dark House* 1932; *The Invisible Man* 1933; *The Kiss before the Mirror* 1933; *By Candlelight* 1934; *One More River* 1934; *Bride of Frankenstein* 1935; *Remember Last Night?* 1935; *Show Boat* 1936; *The Great Garrick* 1937; *Port of Seven Seas* 1938; *Sinners in Paradise* 1938; *Wives under Suspicion* 1938; *Green Hell* 1939; *The Man in the Iron Mask* 1939; *They Dare Not Love* 1941
Whatham, Claude *That'll Be the Day* 1973; *All Creatures Great and Small* 1974; *Swallows and Amazons* 1974; *Sweet William* 1980; *Buddy's Song* 1990
Wheeler, Anne (1946–) *Bye Bye Blues* 1989; *Angel Square* 1990; *The War between Us* 1995
Whelan, Tim (1893–1957) *Aunt Sally* 1933; *It's a Boy* 1933; *The Camels Are Coming* 1934; *Murder Man* 1935; *The Perfect Gentleman* 1935; *The Mill on the Floss* 1937; *Smash and Grab* 1937; *The Divorce of Lady X* 1938; *St Martin's Lane* 1938; *Q Planes* 1939; *Ten Days in Paris* 1939; *The Thief of Bagdad* 1940; *International Lady* 1941; *Seven Days' Leave* 1942; *Twin Beds* 1942; *Higher and Higher* 1943; *Swing Fever* 1943; *Step Lively* 1944; *Badman's Territory* 1946; *This Was a Woman* 1947; *Rage at Dawn* 1955; *Texas Lady* 1955

Whitaker, Forest (1961–) *Waiting to Exhale* 1995; *Hope Floats* 1998; *First Daughter* 2004
White, George (1892–1968) *George White's Scandals* 1934; *George White's 1935 Scandals* 1935
Whitesell, John *Calendar Girl* 1993; *See Spot Run* 2001; *Malibu's Most Wanted* 2003
Whorf, Richard (1906–1966) *Blonde Fever* 1944; *The Hidden Eye* 1945; *The Sailor Takes a Wife* 1945; *Till the Clouds Roll By* 1946; *It Happened in Brooklyn* 1947; *Love from a Stranger* 1947; *Champagne for Caesar* 1950
Wickes, David *Sweeney!* 1976; *Silver Dream Racer* 1980
Wicki, Bernhard (1919–2000) *The Bridge* 1959; *The Longest Day* 1962; *The Visit* 1964; *The Saboteur, Code Name Morituri* 1965
Widerberg, Bo (1930–1997) *The Pram* 1963; *Raven's End* 1963; *Elvira Madigan* 1967; *Adalen 31* 1969; *Joe Hill* 1971; *All Things Fair* 1995
Wiederhorn, Ken *Shock Waves* 1975; *Eyes of a Stranger* 1980; *Meatballs 2* 1984; *Return of the Living Dead Part II* 1988
Wiene, Robert (1981–1938) *The Cabinet of Dr Caligari* 1919; *Hands of Orlac* 1924
Wilcox, Fred M *aka* **Wilcox, Fred** *aka* **Wilcox, Fred McLeod** (1905–1964) *Lassie Come Home* 1943; *Courage of Lassie* 1946; *Hills of Home* 1948; *Three Daring Daughters* 1948; *The Secret Garden* 1949; *Tennessee Champ* 1954; *Forbidden Planet* 1956
Wilcox, Herbert (1892–1977) *Bitter Sweet* 1933; *Nell Gwyn* 1934; *Limelight* 1936; *London Melody* 1937; *Victoria the Great* 1937; *Sixty Glorious Years* 1938; *Nurse Edith Cavell* 1939; *Irene* 1940; *No, No, Nanette* 1940; *Sunny* 1941; *They Flew Alone* 1942; *Forever and a Day* 1943; *Yellow Canary* 1943; *I Live in Grosvenor Square* 1945; *Piccadilly Incident* 1946; *The Courtneys of Curzon Street* 1947; *Elizabeth of Ladymead* 1948; *Spring in Park Lane* 1948; *Maytime in Mayfair* 1949; *Odette* 1950; *The Lady with the Lamp* 1951; *Derby Day* 1952; *Trent's Last Case* 1952; *Trouble in the Glen* 1954; *King's Rhapsody* 1955; *Lilacs in the Spring* 1955; *My Teenage Daughter* 1956; *The Man Who Wouldn't Talk* 1957; *The Heart of a Man* 1959
Wilde, Cornel (1915–1989) *The Devil's Hairpin* 1957; *Maracaibo* 1958; *Lancelot and Guinevere* 1963; *The Naked Prey* 1966; *Beach Red* 1967; *No Blade of Grass* 1970; *Shark's Treasure* 1975
Wilde, Ted (1893–1929) *The Kid Brother* 1927; *Speedy* 1928
Wilder, Billy (1906–2002) *The Major and the Minor* 1942; *Five Graves to Cairo* 1943; *Double Indemnity* 1944; *The Lost Weekend* 1945; *The Emperor Waltz* 1948; *A Foreign Affair* 1948; *Sunset Blvd* 1950; *Ace in the Hole* 1951; *Stalag 17* 1953; *Sabrina* 1954; *The Seven Year Itch* 1955; *Love in the Afternoon* 1957; *The Spirit of St Louis* 1957; *Witness for the Prosecution* 1957; *Some Like It Hot* 1959; *The Apartment* 1960; *One, Two, Three* 1961; *Irma la Douce* 1963; *Kiss Me, Stupid* 1964; *The Fortune Cookie* 1966; *The Private Life of Sherlock Holmes* 1970; *Avanti!* 1972; *The Front Page* 1974; *Fedora* 1978; *Buddy Buddy* 1981
Wilder, Gene (1935–) *The Adventure of Sherlock Holmes' Smarter Brother* 1975; *The World's Greatest Lover* 1977; *The Woman in Red* 1984; *Haunted Honeymoon* 1986
Wilding, Gavin *The Raffle* 1994; *Listen* 1996; *Stag* 1996
Wiles, Gordon (1902–1950) *The Gangster* 1947; *Ginger in the Morning* 1973
Wilkinson, Charles *Quarantine* 1989; *Max* 1994
Williams, Elmo (1913–) *Women without Men* 1956; *Hell Ship Mutiny* 1957; *The Big Gamble* 1961
Williams, Paul (1940–) *The Revolutionary* 1970; *Dealing: or the Berkeley-to-Boston Forty-Brick Lost-Bag Blues* 1971; *The November Men* 1993
Williams, Richard (1933–) *Raggedy Ann and Andy* 1977; *Arabian Knight* 1995
Williams, Tod (1968–) *The Adventures of Sebastian Cole* 1998; *The Door in the Floor* 2004
Willing, Nick *Photographing Fairies* 1997; *Alice in Wonderland* 1999; *Doctor Sleep* 2002
Wills, J Elder *Song of Freedom* 1936; *Big Fella* 1937
Wilson, Hugh (1943–) *Police Academy* 1984; *Rustler's Rhapsody* 1985; *Burglar* 1987; *Guarding Tess* 1994; *The First Wives Club* 1996; *Blast from the Past* 1998; *Dudley Do-Right* 1999
Wilson (2), Jim *Stacy's Knights* 1983; *Head above Water* 1996
Wilson, Richard (1915–1991) *Man with the Gun* 1955; *Raw Wind in Eden* 1958; *Al Capone* 1959; *Pay or Die* 1960; *Invitation to a Gunfighter* 1964; *Three in the Attic* 1968; *Skullduggery* 1969; *It's All True* 1993
Wilson, Sandy (1947–) *My American Cousin* 1985; *American Boyfriends* 1989
Wincer, Simon (1943–) *Harlequin* 1980; *Phar Lap* 1983; *DARYL* 1985; *The Lighthorsemen* 1987; *Quigley Down Under* 1990; *Harley Davidson and the Marlboro Man* 1991; *Free Willy* 1993; *Lightning Jack* 1994; *Operation Dumbo Drop* 1995; *The Phantom* 1996; *Crocodile Dundee in Los Angeles* 2001
Windust, Bretaigne (1906–1960) *June Bride* 1948; *Winter Meeting* 1948; *Perfect Strangers* 1950; *Pretty Baby* 1950; *The Enforcer* 1951; *Face to Face* 1952
Winer, Harry *SpaceCamp* 1986; *House Arrest* 1996
Winick, Gary *Out of the Rain* 1991; *Sweet Nothing* 1995; *The Tic Code* 1998; *Tadpole* 2002; *13 Going on 30* 2004
Winkler, Charles *You Talkin' to Me?* 1987; *Disturbed* 1990
Winkler, Henry (1945–) *Memories of Me* 1988; *Cop and a Half* 1993
Winkler, Irwin (1934–) *Guilty by Suspicion* 1990; *Night and the City* 1992; *The Net* 1995; *At First Sight* 1998; *Life as a House* 2001; *De-Lovely* 2004
Winner, Michael (1935–) *Play It Cool* 1962; *West 11* 1963; *The System* 1964; *You Must Be Joking!* 1965; *I'll Never Forget What's 'Is Name* 1967; *The Jokers* 1967; *Hannibal Brooks* 1968; *The Games* 1970; *Chato's Land* 1971; *Lawman* 1971; *The Mechanic* 1972; *The Nightcomers* 1972; *Scorpio* 1973; *The Stone Killer* 1973; *Death Wish* 1974; *Won Ton Ton, the Dog Who Saved Hollywood* 1976; *The Sentinel* 1977; *The Big Sleep* 1978; *Firepower* 1979; *Death Wish II* 1981; *The Wicked Lady* 1983; *Death Wish 3* 1985; *Appointment with Death* 1988; *A Chorus of Disapproval* 1988; *Bullseye!* 1990; *Dirty Weekend* 1992; *Parting Shots* 1998
Winsor, Terry *aka* **Smithee, Alan** *Party Party* 1983; *Home Front* 1987; *Essex Boys* 1999
Winston, Ron (1932–1973) *Ambush Bay* 1966; *Banning* 1967; *Don't Just Stand There* 1968; *The Gamblers* 1969
Winston, Stan (1946–) *Pumpkinhead* 1988; *Upworld* 1992
Winterbottom, Michael (1961–) *Butterfly Kiss* 1994; *Go Now* 1995; *Jude* 1996; *Welcome to Sarajevo* 1997; *I Want You* 1998; *With or without You* 1999; *Wonderland* 1999; *The Claim* 2000; *24 Hour Party People* 2001; *In This World* 2002; *Code 46* 2003; *9 Songs* 2004
Winters, David (1939–) *Thrashin'* 1986; *Rage to Kill* 1988
Wise, Herbert (1924–) *The Lovers!* 1972; *Skokie* 1981; *Reunion at Fairborough* 1985
Wise, Kirk *Beauty and the Beast* 1991; *The Hunchback of Notre Dame* 1996; *Atlantis: the Lost Empire* 2001
Wise, Robert (1914–) *The Curse of the Cat People* 1944; *The Silent Bell* 1944; *The Body Snatcher* 1945; *A Game of Death* 1945; *Criminal Court* 1946; *Lady of Deceit* 1947; *Blood on the Moon* 1948; *Mystery in Mexico* 1948; *The Set-Up* 1949; *Three Secrets* 1950; *Two Flags West* 1950; *The Day the Earth Stood Still* 1951; *The House on Telegraph Hill* 1951; *The Captive City* 1952; *The Desert Rats* 1953; *Destination Gobi* 1953; *So Big* 1953; *Executive Suite* 1954; *Helen of Troy* 1955; *Somebody Up There Likes Me* 1956; *Tribute to a Bad Man* 1956; *This Could Be the Night* 1957; *Until They Sail* 1957; *I Want to Live!* 1958; *Run Silent, Run Deep* 1958; *Odds against Tomorrow* 1959; *West Side Story* 1961; *Two for the Seesaw* 1962; *The Haunting* 1963; *The Sound of Music* 1965; *The Sand Pebbles* 1966; *Star!* 1968; *The Andromeda Strain* 1970; *Two People* 1973; *The Hindenburg* 1975; *Audrey Rose* 1977; *Star Trek: the Motion Picture* 1979; *Rooftops* 1989; *A Storm in Summer* 2000
Wiseman, Frederick (1930–) *Titicut Follies* 1967; *High School* 1968; *Zoo* 1993
Wishman, Doris (1925–2002) *Nude on the Moon* 1961; *Deadly Weapons* 1974
Witney, William (1915–2002) *Bells of San Angelo* 1947; *Springtime in the Sierras* 1947; *Under California Stars* 1948; *The Far Frontier* 1949; *North of the Great Divide* 1950; *Trail of Robin Hood* 1950; *Twilight in the Sierras* 1950; *The Outcast* 1954; *Santa Fe Passage* 1955; *Stranger at My Door* 1956; *The Bonnie Parker Story* 1958; *The Cool and the Crazy* 1958; *The Secret of the Purple Reef* 1960; *Master of the World* 1961; *Apache Rifles* 1964; *Arizona Raiders* 1965; *40 Guns to Apache Pass* 1966; *I Escaped from Devil's Island* 1973
Wittman, Peter *Play Dead* 1981; *Ellie* 1984
Wolodarsky, Wallace *aka* **Wolodarsky, M Wallace** *Coldblooded* 1995; *Sorority Boys* 2002
Wong, James *Final Destination* 2000; *The One* 2001
Wong Kar-Wai (1958–) *As Tears Go By* 1988; *Days of Being Wild* 1990; *Ashes of Time* 1994; *Chung King Express* 1994; *Fallen Angels* 1995; *Happy Together* 1997; *In the Mood for Love* 2000; *2046* 2004
Wong, Kirk *aka* **Wong, Che Kirk** *aka* **Wong, Che-Kirk** (1949–) *Crime Story* 1993; *Rock 'n' Roll Cop* 1994; *The Big Hit* 1998
Woo, John (1948–) *A Better Tomorrow* 1986; *A Better Tomorrow II* 1987; *The Killer* 1989; *Bullet in the Head* 1990; *Once a Thief* 1991; *Hard-Boiled* 1992; *Hard Target* 1993; *Broken Arrow* 1996; *Face/Off* 1997; *Mission: Impossible 2* 1999; *Windtalkers* 2001; *Paycheck* 2003
Wood, Duncan (1926–1997) *The Bargee* 1964; *Some Will, Some Won't* 1969
Wood Jr, Edward D (1924–1978) *Glen or Glenda* 1953; *Jail Bait* 1954; *Bride of the Monster* 1955; *Night of the Ghouls* 1959; *Plan 9 from Outer Space* 1959; *Hellborn* 1961
Wood, Sam (1883–1949) *The Barbarian* 1933; *Hold Your Man* 1933; *Stamboul Quest* 1934; *Let 'Em Have It* 1935; *A Night at the Opera* 1935; *Whipsaw* 1935; *A Day at the Races* 1937; *Madame X* 1937; *Navy Blue and Gold* 1937; *Goodbye, Mr Chips* 1939; *Raffles* 1939; *Kitty Foyle* 1940; *Our Town* 1940; *The Devil and Miss Jones* 1941; *Kings Row* 1942; *The Pride of the Yankees* 1942; *For Whom the Bell Tolls* 1943; *Casanova Brown* 1944; *Guest Wife* 1945; *Saratoga Trunk* 1945; *Heartbeat* 1946; *Ivy* 1947; *Command Decision* 1948; *Ambush* 1949; *The Stratton Story* 1949
Woodruff, Bille *Honey* 2003; *Beauty Shop* 2005
Woods, Arthur B *aka* **Woods, Arthur** (1904–1944) *Music Hath Charms* 1935; *Busman's Honeymoon* 1940
Woolnough, Jeff *Universal Soldier 2: Brothers in Arms* 1998; *Universal Soldier 3: Unfinished Business* 1998
Workman, Chuck *Cuba Crossing* 1980; *Superstar: the Life and Times of Andy Warhol* 1991
Worsley, Wallace (1878–1944) *The Ace of Hearts* 1921; *The Hunchback of Notre Dame* 1923
Worth, David *Kickboxer* 1989; *The Prophet's Game* 1999; *Time Lapse* 2001
Wortmann, Sönke (1959–) *The Most Desired Man* 1994; *The Miracle of Bern* 2003
Wrede, Casper *aka* **Wrede, Caspar** (1929–1998) *Private Potter* 1963; *One Day in the Life of Ivan Denisovich* 1971; *Ransom* 1975
Wright, Alex *aka* **Wright, Alexander** *Fast Money* 1995; *Styx* 2000
Wright, Basil (1907–1987) *Song of Ceylon* 1934; *Night Mail* 1936
Wright, Edgar (1974–) *A Fistful of Fingers* 1995; *Shaun of the Dead* 2004
Wright, Geoffrey (1961–) *Romper Stomper* 1992; *Cherry Falls* 1999
Wright, Mack V (1894–1965) *Somewhere in Sonora* 1933; *Winds of the Wasteland* 1936; *Hit the Saddle* 1937
Wright, Tenny (1885–1971) *The Big Stampede* 1932; *The Telegraph Trail* 1933
Wright, Thomas J *aka* **Wright, Tom** *Torchlight* 1984; *No Holds Barred* 1989
Wrye, Donald *The Entertainer* 1975; *Ice Castles* 1978; *Divorce Wars* 1982; *Ultimate Betrayal* 1994
Wyler, William *aka* **Wyler, Lt Col William** (1902–1981) *Counsellor-at-Law* 1933; *Glamour* 1934; *The Gay Deception* 1935; *The Good Fairy* 1935; *Come and Get It* 1936; *Dodsworth* 1936; *These Three* 1936; *Dead End* 1937; *Jezebel* 1938; *Raffles* 1939; *Wuthering Heights* 1939; *The Letter* 1940; *The Westerner* 1940; *The Little Foxes* 1941; *Mrs Miniver* 1942; *Memphis Belle* 1943; *The Best Years of Our Lives* 1946; *The Heiress* 1949; *Detective Story* 1951; *Carrie* 1952; *Roman Holiday* 1953; *The Desperate Hours* 1955; *Friendly Persuasion* 1956; *The Big Country* 1958; *Ben-Hur* 1959; *The Children's Hour* 1961; *The Collector* 1965; *How to Steal a Million* 1966; *Funny Girl* 1968; *The Liberation of LB Jones* 1970
Wynorski, Jim *aka* **Andrews, Jay** (1950–) *Big Bad Mama II* 1987; *Not of This Earth* 1988; *The Return of Swamp Thing* 1989; *Transylvania Twist* 1989; *The Haunting of Morella* 1990; *Munchie* 1992; *976-EVIL 2* 1992; *Munchie Strikes Back* 1994; *Desert Thunder* 1998; *The Pandora Project* 1998; *Stealth Fighter* 1999; *Militia* 2000

Y

Yakin, Boaz (1966–) *Fresh* 1994; *A Price above Rubies* 1997; *Remember the Titans* 2000; *Uptown Girls* 2003
Yang, Edward (1947–) *Taipei Story* 1984; *The Terroriser* 1986; *A Brighter Summer Day* 1991; *A One and a Two* 1999
Yarbrough, Jean (1900–1975) *Devil Bat* 1940; *Abbott and Costello in Society* 1944; *Twilight on the Prairie* 1944; *Here Come the Co-Eds* 1945; *The Naughty Nineties* 1945; *Under Western Skies* 1945; *Jack and the Beanstalk* 1952; *Lost in Alaska* 1952
Yates, Peter (1929–) *Summer Holiday* 1962; *One Way Pendulum* 1965; *Robbery* 1967; *Bullitt* 1968; *John and Mary* 1969; *Murphy's War* 1971; *The Hot Rock* 1972; *The Friends of Eddie Coyle* 1973; *For Pete's Sake* 1974; *Mother, Jugs & Speed* 1976; *The Deep* 1977; *Breaking Away* 1979; *Eyewitness* 1981; *The Dresser* 1983; *Krull* 1983; *Eleni* 1985; *The House on Carroll Street* 1987; *Suspect* 1987; *An Innocent Man* 1989; *Year of the Comet* 1992; *Roommates* 1995; *The Run of the Country* 1995; *Curtain Call* 1998; *Don Quixote* 2000
Yeaworth Jr, Irvin S (1926–2004) *The Blob* 1958; *Dinosaurus!* 1960
Yorkin, Bud (1926–) *Come Blow Your Horn* 1963; *Never Too Late* 1965; *Divorce American Style* 1967; *Inspector Clouseau* 1968; *Start the Revolution without Me* 1970; *The Thief Who Came to Dinner* 1973; *Twice in a Lifetime* 1985; *Arthur 2: On the Rocks* 1988; *Love Hurts* 1990
Young, Harold (1897–1970) *The Scarlet Pimpernel* 1934; *The Storm* 1938; *The Mummy's Tomb* 1942; *There's One Born Every Minute* 1942; *The Frozen Ghost* 1944; *The Three Caballeros* 1944
Young (2), Robert *aka* **Young, Robert William** *Vampire Circus* 1971; *The World Is Full of Married Men* 1979; *Hostage* 1992; *Fierce Creatures* 1997; *Captain Jack* 1998
Young, Robert M *aka* **Young, Robert Malcolm** (1924–) *Trauma* 1962; *Keep It Up Downstairs* 1976; *Rich Kids* 1979; *One-Trick Pony* 1980; *The Ballad of Gregorio Cortez* 1983; *Saving Grace* 1985; *Extremities* 1986; *Dominick and Eugene* 1988; *Triumph of the Spirit* 1989; *Talent for the Game* 1991; *Roosters* 1993; *Splitting Heirs* 1993; *Caught* 1996
Young, Roger (1942–) *Magnum: Don't Eat the Snow in Hawaii* 1980; *Lassiter* 1984; *The Squeeze* 1987; *Murder in Mississippi* 1990; *Victim of Beauty* 1991; *Getting Gotti* 1994; *A Knight in Camelot* 1998; *One Special Night* 1999
Young, Terence (1915–1994) *One Night with You* 1948; *Woman Hater* 1948; *They Were Not Divided* 1950; *Valley of Eagles* 1951; *The Red Beret* 1953; *Storm over the Nile* 1955; *That Lady* 1955; *Safari* 1956; *Zarak* 1956; *Action of the Tiger* 1957; *No Time to Die* 1958; *Serious Charge* 1959; *Too Hot to Handle* 1960; *Duel of Champions* 1961; *Dr No* 1962; *From Russia with Love* 1963; *The Amorous Adventures of Moll Flanders* 1965; *The Dirty Game* 1965; *Thunderball* 1965; *The Poppy Is Also a Flower* 1966; *Triple Cross* 1966; *The Rover* 1967; *Wait until Dark* 1967; *Mayerling* 1968; *The Christmas Tree* 1969; *Cold Sweat* 1971; *Red Sun* 1971; *The Valachi Papers* 1972; *The Klansman* 1974; *Bloodline* 1979; *Inchon* 1981; *The Jigsaw Man* 1984
Youngson, Robert (1917–1974) *Days of Thrills and Laughter* 1961; *MGM's Big Parade of Comedy* 1964; *Laurel and Hardy's Laughing 20s* 1965; *4 Clowns* 1970
Yu, Nelson Lik-Wai *aka* **Yu Lik Wai** (1966–) *Love Will Tear Us Apart* 1999; *All Tomorrow's Parties* 2003
Yu, Ronny (1950–) *The Bride with White Hair* 1993; *Warriors of Virtue* 1996; *Bride of Chucky* 1998; *The 51st State* 2001; *Freddy vs Jason* 2003
Yuen, Corey *aka* **Yuen Kwai** *No Retreat, No Surrender* 1985; *The Legend* 1993; *The Legend II*

1993; *The Defender* 1994; *The Enforcer* 1995; *And Now You're Dead* 1998; *So Close* 2002; *The Transporter* 2002
Yuen Woo-Ping (1945–) *Drunken Master* 1978; *Iron Monkey* 1993; *Twin Warriors* 1993
Yuyama, Kunihiko (1952–) *Pokémon the First Movie: Mewtwo Strikes Back* 1998; *Pokémon 3: Spell of the Unown* 2001
Yuzna, Brian (1949–) *Society* 1989; *Bride of Re-Animator* 1991; *Necronomicon* 1993; *Return of the Living Dead III* 1993; *The Dentist* 1996; *The Dentist II* 1998; *Progeny* 1998; *Faust: Love of the Damned* 2001

Z

Zaillian, Steven (1951–) *Innocent Moves* 1993; *A Civil Action* 1998
Zampa, Luigi (1905–1991) *Children of Chance* 1949; *The Masters* 1975; *Tigers in Lipstick* 1979
Zampi, Mario (1903–1963) *Laughter in Paradise* 1951; *Happy Ever After* 1954; *The Naked Truth* 1957; *Too Many Crooks* 1958; *Bottoms Up* 1959
Zanussi, Krzysztof (1939–) *Illumination* 1972; *The Catamount Killing* 1974; *Camouflage* 1977; *The Constant Factor* 1980; *The Contract* 1980; *Imperative* 1982; *A Year of the Quiet Sun* 1984; *The Silent Touch* 1992
Zeffirelli, Franco (1923–) *The Taming of the Shrew* 1967; *Romeo and Juliet* 1968; *Brother Sun, Sister Moon* 1972; *The Champ* 1979; *Endless Love* 1981; *La Traviata* 1982; *Otello* 1986; *Young Toscanini* 1988; *Hamlet* 1990; *Sparrow* 1993; *Jane Eyre* 1996; *Tea with Mussolini* 1998; *Callas Forever* 2002
Zeglio, Primo (1906–) *Morgan the Pirate* 1960; *Seven Seas to Calais* 1962
Zelnik, Fred *aka* **Zelnik, Friedrich** *aka* **Zelnik, Frederick** (1885–1950) *Happy* 1933; *Mister Cinders* 1934; *Southern Roses* 1936
Zeltser, Yuri (1962–) *Eye of the Storm* 1991; *Playmaker* 1994; *Black and White* 1998
Zeman, Karel (1910–1989) *Voyage into Prehistory* 1955; *Invention of Destruction* 1958; *Baron Munchhausen* 1961
Zemeckis, Robert (1952–) *I Wanna Hold Your Hand* 1978; *Used Cars* 1980; *Romancing the Stone* 1984; *Back to the Future* 1985; *Who Framed Roger Rabbit* 1988; *Back to the Future Part II* 1989; *Back to the Future Part III* 1990; *Death Becomes Her* 1992; *Forrest Gump* 1994; *Contact* 1997; *Cast Away* 2000; *What Lies Beneath* 2000; *The Polar Express* 2004
Zetterling, Mai (1925–1994) *Doctor Glas* 1968; *Visions of Eight* 1973; *Scrubbers* 1982
Zhang Yimou (1951–) *Red Sorghum* 1987; *Ju Dou* 1990; *Raise the Red Lantern* 1991; *The Story of Qiu Ju* 1992; *To Live* 1994; *Shanghai Triad* 1995; *Keep Cool* 1997; *Not One Less* 1999; *The Road Home* 1999; *Happy Times* 2001; *Hero* 2002; *House of Flying Daggers* 2004
Zhang Yuan (1963–) *Beijing Bastards* 1993; *Behind the Forbidden City* 1996
Zheng Junli (1911–1969) *Spring River Flows East* 1947; *Crows and Sparrows* 1949
Zhou Xiaowen *Ermo* 1994; *The Emperor's Shadow* 1996
Zidi, Claude (1934–) *Le Cop* 1985; *Le Cop II* 1989; *Asterix and Obelix Take On Caesar* 1999
Zieff, Howard (1943–) *Slither* 1973; *Hearts of the West* 1975; *House Calls* 1978; *The Main Event* 1979; *Private Benjamin* 1980; *Unfaithfully Yours* 1983; *The Dream Team* 1989; *My Girl* 1991; *My Girl 2* 1994
Ziehm, Howard *Flesh Gordon* 1974; *Flesh Gordon Meets the Cosmic Cheerleaders* 1989
Zielinski, Rafal (1957–) *Screwballs* 1983; *Fun* 1994; *National Lampoon's Scuba School* 1994
Zimmerman, Vernon *Deadhead Miles* 1972; *The Unholy Rollers* 1972; *Fade to Black* 1980
Zinnemann, Fred (1907–1997) *Eyes in the Night* 1942; *Kid Glove Killer* 1942; *The Seventh Cross* 1944; *My Brother Talks to Horses* 1946; *The Search* 1948; *Act of Violence* 1949; *The Men* 1950; *Teresa* 1951; *High Noon* 1952; *The Member of the Wedding* 1952; *From Here to Eternity* 1953; *Oklahoma!* 1955; *A Hatful of Rain* 1957; *The Nun's Story* 1959; *The Sundowners* 1960; *Behold a Pale Horse* 1964; *A Man for All Seasons* 1966; *The Day of the Jackal* 1973; *Julia* 1977; *Five Days One Summer* 1982
Zito, Joseph (1949–) *Abduction* 1975; *Friday the 13th: the Final Chapter* 1984; *Missing in Action* 1984; *Invasion USA* 1985; *Red Scorpion* 1989
Zombie, Rob (1966–) *House of 1000 Corpses* 2001; *The Devil's Rejects* 2005
Zondag, Ralph *We're Back! A Dinosaur's Story* 1993; *Dinosaur* 2000
Zucker, David (1947–) *Airplane!* 1980; *Top Secret!* 1984; *Ruthless People* 1986; *The Naked Gun* 1988; *The Naked Gun 2½: the Smell of Fear* 1991; *BASEketball* 1998; *My Boss's Daughter* 2003; *Scary Movie 3* 2003
Zucker, Jerry (1950–) *Airplane!* 1980; *Top Secret!* 1984; *Ruthless People* 1986; *Ghost* 1990; *First Knight* 1995; *Rat Race* 2001
Zugsmith, Albert (1910–1993) *The Private Lives of Adam and Eve* 1959; *Sex Kittens Go to College* 1960; *Confessions of an Opium Eater* 1962
Zulawski, Andrzej (1942–) *Possession* 1981; *La Femme Publique* 1984; *La Fidélité* 2000
Zurinaga, Marcos *Tango Bar* 1988; *The Disappearance of Garcia Lorca* 1997
Zwart, Harald (1965–) *Hamilton* 1998; *One Night at McCool's* 2001; *Agent Cody Banks* 2003
Zwerin, Charlotte (1931–2004) *Gimme Shelter* 1970; *Thelonious Monk: Straight No Chaser* 1988
Zwick, Edward (1953–) *About Last Night...* 1986; *Glory* 1989; *Leaving Normal* 1992; *Legends of the Fall* 1994; *Courage under Fire* 1996; *The Siege* 1998; *The Last Samurai* 2003
Zwick, Joel (1942–) *Second Sight* 1989; *My Big Fat Greek Wedding* 2002; *Fat Albert* 2004
Zwicky, Karl (1958–) *Paws* 1997; *The Magic Pudding* 2000
Zwigoff, Terry (1948–) *Crumb* 1995; *Ghost World* 2001; *Bad Santa* 2003

Actors

A

Aaker, Lee (1943–) *Desperate Search* 1952; *Hondo* 1953; *Jeopardy* 1953
Aaliyah (1979–2001) *Romeo Must Die* 2000; *Queen of the Damned* 2002
Aames, Willie (1960–) *Paradise* 1982; *Zapped!* 1982
Aaron, Caroline (1952–) *A Modern Affair* 1996; *Deconstructing Harry* 1997; *Tuesdays with Morrie* 1999; *Beyond the Sea* 2004
Abatantuono, Diego (1955–) *Christmas Present* 1986; *Puerto Escondido* 1992; *Nirvana* 1996; *The Best Man* 1998; *Children of Hannibal* 1998; *I'm Not Scared* 2003
Abbott, Bruce (1954–) *Re-Animator* 1985; *Bride of Re-Animator* 1991
Abbott, Bud (1895–1974) *Buck Privates* 1941; *Hold That Ghost* 1941; *In the Navy* 1941; *Keep 'em Flying* 1941; *Pardon My Sarong* 1942; *Ride 'em Cowboy* 1942; *Rio Rita* 1942; *Who Done It?* 1942; *Hit the Ice* 1943; *It Ain't Hay* 1943; *Abbott and Costello in Society* 1944; *Lost in a Harem* 1944; *Abbott and Costello in Hollywood* 1945; *Here Come the Co-Eds* 1945; *The Naughty Nineties* 1945; *Little Giant* 1946; *The Time of Their Lives* 1946; *Buck Privates Come Home* 1947; *Abbott and Costello Meet Frankenstein* 1948; *The Noose Hangs High* 1948; *Abbott and Costello Meet the Killer, Boris Karloff* 1949; *Africa Screams* 1949; *Abbott and Costello in the Foreign Legion* 1950; *Abbott and Costello Meet the Invisible Man* 1951; *Abbott and Costello Meet Captain Kidd* 1952; *Jack and the Beanstalk* 1952; *Lost in Alaska* 1952; *Abbott and Costello Go to Mars* 1953; *Abbott and Costello Meet Dr Jekyll and Mr Hyde* 1953; *Abbott and Costello Meet the Keystone Cops* 1955; *Abbott and Costello Meet the Mummy* 1955; *Dance with Me Henry* 1956
Abbott, Diahnne (1945–) *The King of Comedy* 1983; *Love Streams* 1984
Abbott, John (1905–1996) *Conquest of the Air* 1936; *The Falcon in Hollywood* 1944; *Pursuit to Algiers* 1945; *The Bandit of Sherwood Forest* 1946; *Deception* 1946; *The Web* 1947; *The Woman in White* 1948; *Gigi* 1958; *Gambit* 1966; *The Jungle Book* 1967; *Slapstick of Another Kind* 1982
Abbott, Philip (1923–1998) *The Bachelor Party* 1957; *The Invisible Boy* 1957; *The Spiral Road* 1962; *Sweet Bird of Youth* 1962; *Those Calloways* 1964; *Nightmare in Chicago* 1968; *Prophet of Evil* 1993
Abdul-Jabbar, Kareem (1947–) *Game of Death* 1978; *The Fish That Saved Pittsburgh* 1979; *Airplane!* 1980; *Slam Dunk Ernest* 1995
Abel, Alfred (1879–1937) *Dr Mabuse, the Gambler* 1922; *Metropolis* 1926
Abel, Walter (1898–1987) *The Three Musketeers* 1935; *Fury* 1936; *Green Light* 1937; *Law of the Underworld* 1938; *Men with Wings* 1938; *Racket Busters* 1938; *King of the Turf* 1939; *Arise, My Love* 1940; *Michael Shayne, Private Detective* 1940; *Miracle on Main Street* 1940; *Hold Back the Dawn* 1941; *Skylark* 1941; *Beyond the Blue Horizon* 1942; *Holiday Inn* 1942; *Star Spangled Rhythm* 1942; *Wake Island* 1942; *So Proudly We Hail* 1943; *An American Romance* 1944; *Mr Skeffington* 1944; *The Affairs of Susan* 1945; *Kiss and Tell* 1945; *The Kid from Brooklyn* 1946; *13 Rue Madeleine* 1946; *Dream Girl* 1948; *That Lady in Ermine* 1948; *Island in the Sky* 1953; *So This Is Love* 1953; *Night People* 1954; *The Indian Fighter* 1955; *Handle with Care* 1958; *Quick, Let's Get Married* 1964; *Mirage* 1965; *Silent Night, Bloody Night* 1972
Abelanski, Lionel (1964–) *Didier* 1997; *Nationale 7* 1999; *Train of Life* 1999; *Ma Femme Est une Actrice* 2001
Abercrombie, Ian (1936–) *Catacombs* 1988; *Army of Darkness* 1993
Abineri, John (1928–2000) *The McKenzie Break* 1970; *Death Train* 1993
Abkarian, Simon *When the Cat's Away...* 1996; *Almost Peaceful* 2002
Abraham, F Murray (1939–) *The Prisoner of Second Avenue* 1974; *The Sunshine Boys* 1975; *The Ritz* 1976; *The Big Fix* 1978; *Scarface* 1983; *Amadeus* 1984; *The Name of the Rose* 1986; *Beyond the Stars* 1988; *An Innocent Man* 1989; *Slipstream* 1989; *The Bonfire of the Vanities* 1990; *Mobsters* 1991; *Stockade* 1991; *By the Sword* 1992; *Last Action Hero* 1993; *National Lampoon's Loaded Weapon 1* 1993; *Nostradamus* 1993; *Surviving the Game* 1994; *Dillinger and Capone* 1995; *Mighty Aphrodite* 1995; *Children of the Revolution* 1996; *Mimic* 1997; *Star Trek: Insurrection* 1998; *Muppets from Space* 1999; *Finding Forrester* 2000; *Thir13en Ghosts* 2001
Abraham, John (1972–) *Dhoom* 2004; *Kaal* 2005
Abrahams, Jon (1977–) *Meet the Parents* 2000; *Scary Movie* 2000; *They* 2002; *My Boss's Daughter* 2003; *House of Wax* 2004
Abrams, Michele *Victim of Beauty* 1991; *Buffy the Vampire Slayer* 1992; *Cool World* 1992
Abreu, Claudia (1971–) *Four Days in September* 1997; *The Man of the Year* 2002
Abril, Victoria (1959–) *Comin' at Ya* 1981; *I Married a Dead Man* 1983; *The Moon in the Gutter* 1983; *After Darkness* 1985; *Padre Nuestro* 1985; *Max Mon Amour* 1986; *Tie Me Up! Tie Me Down!* 1990; *High Heels* 1991; *Lovers* 1991; *Kika* 1993; *Jimmy Hollywood* 1994; *Gazon Maudit* 1995; *101 Reykjavik* 2000
Absolom, Joe (1978–) *Long Time Dead* 2001; *Extreme Ops* 2003
Abu Warda, Yussef *Cup Final* 1991; *Yom Yom* 1998; *Kadosh* 1999
Accorsi, Stefano (1971–) *Fratelli e Sorelle* 1992; *Captains of April* 2000; *Le Fate Ignoranti* 2001; *The Last Kiss* 2001
Acker, Sharon (1935–) *Lucky Jim* 1957; *Point Blank* 1967; *The First Time* 1969; *Happy Birthday to Me* 1981; *Threshold* 1981
Ackerman, Leslie (1956–) *Law and Disorder* 1974; *Blame It on the Night* 1984
Ackland, Joss (1926–) *A Midsummer Night's Dream* 1961; *Rasputin, the Mad Monk* 1965; *Crescendo* 1970; *The House That Dripped Blood* 1971; *Villain* 1971; *The Mind Snatchers* 1972; *England Made Me* 1973; *Hitler: the Last Ten Days* 1973; *Penny Gold* 1973; *The Black Windmill* 1974; *Great Expectations* 1974; *The Little Prince* 1974; *SPYS* 1974; *One of Our Dinosaurs Is Missing* 1975; *Operation Daybreak* 1975; *Royal Flash* 1975; *Silver Bears* 1977; *A Nightingale Sang in Berkeley Square* 1979; *Saint Jack* 1979; *The Apple* 1980; *Rough Cut* 1980; *Lady Jane* 1985; *A Zed & Two Noughts* 1985; *The Sicilian* 1987; *White Mischief* 1987; *To Kill a Priest* 1988; *Lethal Weapon 2* 1989; *The Bridge* 1990; *The Hunt for Red October* 1990; *Bill & Ted's Bogus Journey* 1991; *The Object of Beauty* 1991; *The Mighty Ducks* 1992; *Nowhere to Run* 1992; *Once upon a Crime* 1992; *The Princess and the Goblin* 1992; *Mother's Boys* 1993; *Jacob* 1994; *Mad Dogs and Englishmen* 1994; *Citizen X* 1995; *D3: the Mighty Ducks* 1996; *Surviving Picasso* 1996; *Amy Foster* 1997; *Firelight* 1997; *Milk* 1999; *Passion of Mind* 2000; *K-19: the Widowmaker* 2002; *No Good Deed* 2002; *I'll Be There* 2003
Ackroyd, David (1940–) *The Mountain Men* 1980; *Memories of Me* 1988; *Dark Angel* 1989; *Love, Cheat & Steal* 1994
Acosta, Rodolfo *aka* **Acosta, Rudolph** *aka* **Acosta, Rudy** (1920–1974) *Appointment in Honduras* 1953; *Hondo* 1953; *Drum Beat* 1954; *Passion* 1954; *A Life in the Balance* 1955; *Bandido* 1956; *Flaming Star* 1960; *Let No Man Write My Epitaph* 1960; *Posse from Hell* 1961; *Return of the Seven* 1966; *Impasse* 1969
Acovone, Jay (1955–) *Cold Steel* 1987; *Quicksand: No Escape* 1992; *Lookin' Italian* 1994
Acquanetta (1921–2004) *Dead Man's Eyes* 1944; *Tarzan and the Leopard Woman* 1946; *The Legend of Grizzly Adams* 1990
Acuff, Eddie (1908–1956) *The Case of the Velvet Claws* 1936; *Law of the Underworld* 1938; *Rough Riders' Roundup* 1939
Adair, Jean (1873–1953) *Advice to the Lovelorn* 1933; *Arsenic and Old Lace* 1944; *Something in the Wind* 1947
Adair, Robert *aka* **A'Dair, Robert** (1900–1954) *Journey's End* 1930; *The Ticket of Leave Man* 1937; *There Is Another Sun* 1951; *Park Plaza 605* 1953
Adam, Ronald (1896–1979) *Strange Boarders* 1938; *Obsession* 1948; *The Lavender Hill Mob* 1951; *Hindle Wakes* 1952; *Assignment Redhead* 1956; *Kill Me Tomorrow* 1957; *The Golden Disc* 1958; *Postman's Knock* 1961
Adams, Amy *Cruel Intentions 2* 2000; *Catch Me If You Can* 2002; *Serving Sara* 2002; *The Wedding Date* 2004
Adams, Beverly (1945–) *How to Fill a Wild Bikini* 1965; *Murderers' Row* 1966; *The Ambushers* 1967; *Torture Garden* 1967
Adams, Brandon *aka* **Adams, Brandon Quintin** (1979–) *Moonwalker* 1988; *The People under the Stairs* 1991; *Ghost in the Machine* 1993; *The Sandlot* 1993
Adams, Brooke (1949–) *Shock Waves* 1975; *Days of Heaven* 1978; *Invasion of the Body Snatchers* 1978; *Cuba* 1979; *A Man, a Woman and a Bank* 1979; *Tell Me a Riddle* 1980; *Utilities* 1981; *The Dead Zone* 1983; *Almost You* 1984; *Key Exchange* 1985; *Man on Fire* 1987; *Sometimes They Come Back* 1991; *The Unborn* 1991; *Gas, Food, Lodging* 1992
Adams, Catlin (1950–) *The Jerk* 1979; *The Jazz Singer* 1980
Adams, Don (1923–) *The Nude Bomb* 1980; *Jimmy the Kid* 1982; *Back to the Beach* 1987
Adams, Dorothy (1900–1988) *The Devil Commands* 1941; *Laura* 1944; *Johnny Concho* 1956; *Peeper* 1975
Adams, Edie (1927–) *The Apartment* 1960; *Lover Come Back* 1961; *Call Me Bwana* 1963; *Love with the Proper Stranger* 1963; *Under the Yum Yum Tree* 1963; *The Best Man* 1964; *Made in Paris* 1966; *The Oscar* 1966; *The Honey Pot* 1967; *Evil Roy Slade* 1971; *The Happy Hooker Goes to Hollywood* 1980
Adams (2), Jane (1965–) *Vital Signs* 1990; *Light Sleeper* 1991; *Kansas City* 1995; *Happiness* 1998; *Songcatcher* 1999; *The Anniversary Party* 2001; *Eternal Sunshine of the Spotless Mind* 2003
Adams, Jill (1930–) *The Young Lovers* 1954; *One Way Out* 1955; *Value for Money* 1955; *Brothers in Law* 1956; *The Green Man* 1956; *The Scamp* 1957
Adams, Joe (1922–) *Carmen Jones* 1954; *Ballad in Blue* 1964
Adams, Joey Lauren *aka* **Adams, Joey** (1971–) *SFW* 1994; *Mallrats* 1995; *Bio-Dome* 1996; *Chasing Amy* 1996; *A Cool, Dry Place* 1998; *Big Daddy* 1999; *Beautiful* 2000; *Jay and Silent Bob Strike Back* 2001
Adams, Julie *aka* **Adams, Julia** (1926–) *Bright Victory* 1951; *Bend of the River* 1952; *Horizons West* 1952; *The Lawless Breed* 1952; *Treasure of Lost Canyon* 1952; *The Man from the Alamo* 1953; *The Mississippi Gambler* 1953; *The Stand at Apache River* 1953; *Creature from the Black Lagoon* 1954; *The Looters* 1955; *One Desire* 1955; *The Private War of Major Benson* 1955; *Six Bridges to Cross* 1955; *Away All Boats* 1956; *Slaughter on Tenth Avenue* 1957; *The Gunfight at Dodge City* 1959; *Tickle Me* 1965; *Valley of Mystery* 1967; *The Last Movie* 1971; *Psychic Killer* 1975
Adams, Kathryn (1920–) *Fifth Avenue Girl* 1939; *Argentine Nights* 1940
Adams, Kim *Ted & Venus* 1991; *Leaving Las Vegas* 1995
Adams, Lynne *Night Zoo* 1987; *Airspeed* 1997; *Twist of Fate* 1997
Adams, Mary (1910–1973) *Blood of Dracula* 1957; *Diary of a Madman* 1963
Adams, Mason (1919–2005) *Omen III: the Final Conflict* 1980; *Adam* 1983; *FX: Murder by Illusion* 1985; *Toy Soldiers* 1991; *Son in Law* 1993
Adams, Maud (1945–) *The Christian Licorice Store* 1971; *The Man with the Golden Gun* 1974; *Killer Force* 1975; *Rollerball* 1975; *Playing for Time* 1980; *Tattoo* 1980; *Target Eagle* 1982; *Octopussy* 1983; *Jane and the Lost City* 1987
Adams, Nick (1931–1968) *The Last Wagon* 1956; *Fury at Showdown* 1957; *No Time for Sergeants* 1958; *Sing, Boy, Sing* 1958; *Teacher's Pet* 1958; *The FBI Story* 1959; *Pillow Talk* 1959; *The Hook* 1962; *The Interns* 1962; *Twilight of Honor* 1963; *Frankenstein Conquers the World* 1964; *The Young Lovers* 1964; *Die, Monster, Die!* 1965; *Invasion of the Astro-Monster* 1965; *Young Dillinger* 1965
Adams, Robert (1906–) *Song of Freedom* 1936; *Old Bones of the River* 1938; *Men of Two Worlds* 1946
Adams, Stanley (1915–1977) *Hell on Frisco Bay* 1955; *Requiem for a Heavyweight* 1962; *Lilies of the Field* 1963; *When the Boys Meet the Girls* 1965; *Thunder Alley* 1967; *The Grasshopper* 1970
Adams, Steve *For Hire* 1997; *Strange Fits of Passion* 1999
Adams, Tom (1938–) *A Prize of Arms* 1961; *Licensed to Kill* 1965; *The Fighting Prince of Donegal* 1966; *Where the Bullets Fly* 1966; *Subterfuge* 1968
Adamson, Christopher *aka* **Adamson, Chris** *Dirty Weekend* 1992; *Razor Blade Smile* 1998; *Lighthouse* 1999
Addams, Dawn (1930–1985) *The Hour of 13* 1952; *Plymouth Adventure* 1952; *The Moon Is Blue* 1953; *Khyber Patrol* 1954; *Return to Treasure Island* 1954; *Secrets d'Alcove* 1954; *A King in New York* 1957; *The Silent Enemy* 1958; *The Treasure of San Teresa* 1959; *The Thousand Eyes of Dr Mabuse* 1960; *The Two Faces of Dr Jekyll* 1960; *Come Fly with Me* 1962; *The Black Tulip* 1963; *Ballad in Blue* 1964; *Where the Bullets Fly* 1966; *Zeta One* 1969; *The Vampire Lovers* 1970; *Vault of Horror* 1973
Addie, Robert (1960–2003) *Excalibur* 1981; *Another Country* 1984; *A Knight in Camelot* 1998
Addy, Mark (1963–) *The Full Monty* 1997; *Jack Frost* 1998; *The Last Yellow* 1999; *The Flintstones in Viva Rock Vegas* 2000; *Down to Earth* 2001; *A Knight's Tale* 2001; *Heartlands* 2002; *The Sin Eater* 2002; *The Time Machine* 2002
Addy, Wesley (1913–1996) *Kiss Me Deadly* 1955; *Timetable* 1956; *Ten Seconds to Hell* 1959; *Hush... Hush, Sweet Charlotte* 1964; *Network* 1976; *The Europeans* 1979; *The Bostonians* 1984; *A Modern Affair* 1996
Adelin, Jean-Claude *Chocolat* 1988; *Annabelle Partagée* 1990
Adelstein, Paul *Bedazzled* 2000; *Intolerable Cruelty* 2003
Ades, Daniel (1932–1992) *The Last Movie* 1971; *Aguirre, Wrath of God* 1972
Adiarte, Patrick (1943–) *The King and I* 1956; *High Time* 1960
Adjani, Isabelle (1955–) *The Story of Adèle H* 1975; *The Tenant* 1976; *The Driver* 1978; *The Brontë Sisters* 1979; *Nosferatu, the Vampire* 1979; *Possession* 1981; *Quartet* 1981; *One Deadly Summer* 1983; *Subway* 1985; *Ishtar* 1987; *Camille Claudel* 1988; *La Reine Margot* 1994; *Diabolique* 1996; *Bon Voyage* 2003; *Monsieur Ibrahim and the Flowers of the Koran* 2003
Adkins, Seth (1989–) *First Do No Harm* 1997; *Geppetto* 2000; *Taming Andrew* 2000
Adler, Bill *Love and the Midnight Auto Supply* 1977; *Van Nuys Blvd* 1979
Adler, Jay (1896–1978) *Cry Danger* 1951; *My Six Convicts* 1952; *The Family Jewels* 1965
Adler, Jerry (1929–) *The Public Eye* 1992; *Manhattan Murder Mystery* 1993; *Getting Away with Murder* 1996; *Six Ways to Sunday* 1997
Adler, Luther (1903–1984) *The Loves of Carmen* 1948; *Saigon* 1948; *DOA* 1949; *House of Strangers* 1949; *Wake of the Red Witch* 1949; *Kiss Tomorrow Goodbye* 1950; *The Desert Fox* 1951; *M* 1951; *Hoodlum Empire* 1952; *Crashout* 1955; *The Girl in the Red Velvet Swing* 1955; *Hot Blood* 1956; *The Last Angry Man* 1959; *The Three Sisters* 1966; *The Brotherhood* 1968; *Live a Little, Steal a Lot* 1974; *The Man in the Glass Booth* 1975; *Absence of Malice* 1981
Adler, Matt (1966–) *Teen Wolf* 1985; *Amazon Women on the Moon* 1987; *North Shore* 1987; *White Water Summer* 1987; *Doin' Time on Planet Earth* 1988
Adler, Robert (1906–1987) *Green Grass of Wyoming* 1948; *Yellow Sky* 1948
Adolphson, Edvin (1893–1979) *Dollar* 1938; *One Single Night* 1939; *Paw* 1959
Adonis, Frank *Eyes of Laura Mars* 1978; *Ace Ventura: Pet Detective* 1993
Adorée, Renée (1898–1933) *Day Dreams* 1922; *The Big Parade* 1925; *The Black Bird* 1926; *La Bohème* 1926; *The Exquisite Sinner* 1926
Adorf, Mario (1930–) *Station Six-Sahara* 1962; *Major Dundee* 1965; *Ghosts – Italian Style* 1967; *The Bird with the Crystal Plumage* 1969; *The Red Tent* 1969; *The Short Night of the Glass Dolls* 1971; *King, Queen, Knave* 1972; *The Italian Connection* 1973; *Without Warning* 1973; *The Lost Honour of Katharina Blum* 1975; *The Tin Drum* 1979; *Lola* 1982; *The Holcroft Covenant* 1985; *The Second Victory* 1986
Adrian, Iris (1912–1994) *Rumba* 1935; *Wild Geese Calling* 1941; *Ladies' Day* 1943; *Lady of Burlesque* 1943; *Bluebeard* 1944; *The Singing Sheriff* 1944; *It's a Pleasure* 1945; *The Stork Club* 1945; *The Bamboo Blonde* 1946; *The Paleface* 1948
Adrian, Max (1903–1973) *Kipps* 1941; *The Young Mr Pitt* 1942; *Pool of London* 1950; *Dr Terror's House of Horrors* 1964; *The Music Lovers* 1970; *The Boy Friend* 1971; *The Devils* 1971
Adway, Dwayne *Death at Clover Bend* 2001; *First Daughter* 2004
Affleck, Ben (1972–) *Danielle Steel's Daddy* 1991; *School Ties* 1992; *Dazed and Confused* 1993; *Glory Daze* 1995; *Mallrats* 1995; *Chasing Amy* 1996; *Going All the Way* 1997; *Good Will Hunting*

1997; Armageddon 1998; Forces of Nature 1998; Phantoms 1998; Shakespeare in Love 1998; Dogma 1999; 200 Cigarettes 1999; Boiler Room 2000; Bounce 2000; Deception 2000; Joseph: King of Dreams 2000; Jay and Silent Bob Strike Back 2001; Pearl Harbor 2001; Changing Lanes 2002; The Sum of All Fears 2002; Daredevil 2003; Gigli 2003; Jersey Girl 2003; Paycheck 2003; Surviving Christmas 2004

Affleck, Casey (1975–) To Die For 1995; Chasing Amy 1996; Race the Sun 1996; Desert Blue 1998; 200 Cigarettes 1999; Committed 2000; Drowning Mona 2000; Gerry 2001; Ocean's Eleven 2001; Soul Survivors 2001; Ocean's Twelve 2004

Agar, John (1921–2002) Fort Apache 1948; Adventure in Baltimore 1949; Sands of Iwo Jima 1949; She Wore a Yellow Ribbon 1949; The Woman on Pier 13 1949; Breakthrough 1950; Along the Great Divide 1951; The Rocket Man 1954; Shield for Murder 1954; Revenge of the Creature 1955; Tarantula 1955; The Mole People 1956; Star in the Dust 1956; Daughter of Dr Jekyll 1957; Attack of the Puppet People 1958; The Brain from Planet Arous 1958; Jet Attack 1958; Of Love and Desire 1963; Johnny Reno 1966; Waco 1966; Miracle Mile 1989

Agashe, Mohan Nishant 1975; Sadgati 1981; Train to Pakistan 1997

Agbayani, Tetchie Gymkata 1985; Rikky and Pete 1988

Agutter, Jenny (1952–) East of Sudan 1964; A Man Could Get Killed 1966; Star! 1968; I Start Counting 1970; The Railway Children 1970; Walkabout 1970; A War of Children 1972; The Eagle Has Landed 1976; Logan's Run 1976; Equus 1977; The Man in the Iron Mask 1977; China 9, Liberty 37 1978; Dominique 1978; The Riddle of the Sands 1978; Sweet William 1980; An American Werewolf in London 1981; Amy 1981; The Survivor 1981; Secret Places 1984; Dark Tower 1989; King of the Wind 1989; Child's Play 2 1990; Freddie as FRO7 1992; The Parole Officer 2001

Aherne, Brian (1902–1985) The Constant Nymph 1933; The Song of Songs 1933; The Fountain 1934; What Every Woman Knows 1934; I Live My Life 1935; Beloved Enemy 1936; Sylvia Scarlett 1936; The Great Garrick 1937; Merrily We Live 1938; Juarez 1939; Hired Wife 1940; The Lady in Question 1940; My Son, My Son! 1940; Vigil in the Night 1940; Skylark 1941; Smilin' Through 1941; My Sister Eileen 1942; A Night to Remember 1942; What a Woman! 1943; The Locket 1946; Smart Woman 1948; I Confess 1953; Titanic 1953; A Bullet Is Waiting 1954; Prince Valiant 1954; The Swan 1956; The Best of Everything 1959; Susan Slade 1961; Lancelot and Guinevere 1963; Rosie! 1967

Ahlstedt, Börje (1939–) I Am Curious – Yellow 1967; A Lover and His Lass 1975; Fanny and Alexander 1982; Best Intentions 1992; Sunday's Children 1992; Saraband 2003

Ahmed, Lalita (1939–) Wild West 1992; Bhaji on the Beach 1993

Ahn, Philip (1911–1978) The General Died at Dawn 1936; China 1943; Back to Bataan 1945; Betrayal from the East 1945; China Sky 1945; The Miracle of the Bells 1948; Hell's Half Acre 1954; Love Is a Many-Splendored Thing 1955; Confessions of an Opium Eater 1962; Shock Corridor 1963; Jonathan Livingston Seagull 1973; Portrait of a Hitman 1977

Ahn Sung-kee (1952–) Village in the Mist 1983; To the Starry Island 1994; Chihwaseon (Drunk on Women and Poetry) 2002

Aidman, Charles (1925–1993) War Hunt 1962; Hour of the Gun 1967; Countdown 1968; Angel, Angel Down We Go 1969; Adam at 6 AM 1970; Kotch 1971; Dirty Little Billy 1972; Zoot Suit 1981

Aiello, Danny (1933–) Fingers 1978; Defiance 1979; Hide in Plain Sight 1980; Chu Chu and the Philly Flash 1981; Fort Apache, the Bronx 1981; Amityville II: the Possession 1982; Deathmask 1984; Old Enough 1984; Once upon a Time in America 1984; Key Exchange 1985; The Protector 1985; The Purple Rose of Cairo 1985; The Stuff 1985; Man on Fire 1987; Moonstruck 1987; The Pick-Up Artist 1987; Radio Days 1987; Do the Right Thing 1989; Harlem Nights 1989; The January Man 1989; The Closer 1990; Jacob's Ladder 1990; Hudson Hawk 1991; Once Around 1991; 29th Street 1991; Mistress 1992; Ruby 1992; The Cemetery Club 1993; Me and the Kid 1993; The Pickle 1993; Leon 1994; Power of Attorney 1994; Pret-a-Porter 1994; The Road Home 1995; Two Much 1995; City Hall 1996; Mojave Moon 1996; 2 Days in the Valley 1996; Bring Me the Head of Mavis Davis 1997; Dinner Rush 2000

Aikawa, Sho (1961–) Serpent's Path 1998; Eyes of the Spider 1999; Gozu 2003

Aiken, Liam (1990–) Henry Fool 1997; Stepmom 1998; Road to Perdition 2002; Good Boy! 2003; Lemony Snicket's A Series of Unfortunate Events 2004

Aikman, Luke (1983–) Fever Pitch 1996; Devil's Gate 2002

Aimée, Anouk aka **Anouk** (1932–) Golden Salamander 1949; The Crimson Curtain 1952; The Bad Liaisons 1955; Contraband Spain 1955; Montparnasse 19 1958; The Journey 1959; La Dolce Vita 1960; Lola 1960; Sodom and Gomorrah 1962; 8½ 1963; Un Homme et une Femme 1966; The Appointment 1968; Justine 1969; Model Shop 1969; Second Chance 1976; The Tragedy of a Ridiculous Man 1981; Long Live Life 1984; Success Is the Best Revenge 1984; A Man and a Woman: 20 Years Later 1986; Bethune: the Making of a Hero 1990; Pret-a-Porter 1994; Men, Women: a User's Manual 1996; LA without a Map 1998; Festival in Cannes 2001

Aimos, Raymond aka **Aimos** (1889–1944) La Belle Equipe 1936; The Golem 1936

Ainley, Anthony (1937–2004) Blood on Satan's Claw 1970; The Land That Time Forgot 1974

Ainley, Richard (1910–1967) As You Like It 1936; Stolen Life 1939; Above Suspicion 1943; I Dood It 1943

Aird, Holly (1969–) Intimate Relations 1995; Fever Pitch 1996; Dreaming of Joseph Lees 1998; The Theory of Flight 1998; The Criminal 1999

Aird, Jane Hunted 1952; Dance Little Lady 1954

Aitken, Maria (1945–) A Fish Called Wanda 1988; The Fool 1990; Jinnah 1998

Ajaye, Franklyn (1949–) Car Wash 1976; Convoy 1978; The Jazz Singer 1980; American Yakuza 1994

Akan, Tarik (1949–) The Herd 1978; Yol 1982; Vizontele Tuuba 2003

Akbag, Demet Vizontele 2001; Vizontele Tuuba 2003; Where's Firuze? 2004

Akbari, Mania Ten 2002; 20 Fingers 2004

Aked, Muriel (1887–1955) Evensong 1934; William at the Circus 1948

Akerman, Chantal (1950–) Je, Tu, Il, Elle 1974; Jeanne Dielman, 23 Quai du Commerce, 1080 Bruxelles 1975

Akers, Andra (1944–2002) Murder à la Mod 1968; Moment by Moment 1978; Desert Hearts 1985

Akin, Philip Iceman 1984; Airborne 1997; Framed 2002

Akinnuoye-Agbaje, Adewale (1967–) Legionnaire 1998; The Bourne Identity 2002

Akins, Claude (1918–1994) Shield for Murder 1954; The Burning Hills 1956; The Lonely Man 1957; The Defiant Ones 1958; Yellowstone Kelly 1959; Comanche Station 1960; Claudelle Inglish 1961; Merrill's Marauders 1962; Black Gold 1963; A Distant Trumpet 1964; The Killers 1964; Incident at Phantom Hill 1966; Return of the Seven 1966; First to Fight 1967; Waterhole #3 1967; The Devil's Brigade 1968; The Great Bank Robbery 1969; Flap 1970; Skyjacked 1972; Battle for the Planet of the Apes 1973; Tentacles 1977; Monster in the Closet 1983; The Curse 1987; Falling from Grace 1992; Seasons of the Heart 1993

Alard, Nelly Eating 1990; Venice/Venice 1992

Alaskey, Joe Bank Robber 1993; Casper 1995; Tweety's High Flying Adventure 2000

Alba, Jessica (1981–) Idle Hands 1999; Honey 2003; Sin City 2005

Alban, Carlo Hurricane Streets 1997; Thicker than Blood 1998

Alberghetti, Anna Maria (1936–) The Medium 1951; The Last Command 1955; Ten Thousand Bedrooms 1957; Cinderfella 1960

Alberni, Luis (1887–1962) The Mad Genius 1931; The Big Stampede 1932; Topaze 1933; One Night of Love 1934; The Gay Deception 1935; The Gilded Lily 1935; Roberta 1935; Colleen 1936; Easy Living 1937; The Great Garrick 1937; When You're in Love 1937

Albers, Hans (1892–1960) The Blue Angel 1930; Baron Münchhausen 1943

Albert, Eddie (1906–2005) On Your Toes 1939; Four Mothers 1941; Out of the Fog 1941; The Wagons Roll at Night 1941; Bombardier 1943; Ladies' Day 1943; Smash Up – the Story of a Woman 1947; Time Out of Mind 1947; You Gotta Stay Happy 1948; The Fuller Brush Girl 1950; Meet Me after the Show 1951; You're in the Navy Now 1951; Actors and Sin 1952; Carrie 1952; Roman Holiday 1953; The Girl Rush 1955; I'll Cry Tomorrow 1955; Oklahoma! 1955; Attack! 1956; The Teahouse of the August Moon 1956; The Joker Is Wild 1957; The Sun Also Rises 1957; The Gun Runners 1958; Orders to Kill 1958; The Roots of Heaven 1958; Beloved Infidel 1959; The Two Little Bears 1961; The Young Doctors 1961; The Longest Day 1962; Madison Avenue 1962; Who's Got the Action? 1962; Captain Newman, MD 1963; Miracle of the White Stallions 1963; 7 Women 1966; The Heartbreak Kid 1972; McQ 1974; The Mean Machine 1974; The Take 1974; The Devil's Rain 1975; Escape to Witch Mountain 1975; Hustle 1975; Whiffs 1975; Birch Interval 1976; Airport '79: the Concorde 1979; Foolin' Around 1980; How to Beat the High Cost of Living 1980; Take This Job and Shove It 1981; Yes, Giorgio 1982; Dreamscape 1984; Head Office 1986

Albert, Edward (1951–) The Fool Killer 1965; Butterflies Are Free 1972; 40 Carats 1973; The Domino Principle 1977; The Purple Taxi 1977; The Greek Tycoon 1978; When Time Ran Out 1980; Butterfly 1982; The House Where Evil Dwells 1982; Ellie 1984; Getting Even 1986; The Rescue 1988; Terminal Entry 1988; Guarding Tess 1994; The Secret Agent Club 1995; Space Marines 1996; The Man in the Iron Mask 1997

Albert, Laura The Unnamable 1988; Dr Caligari 1989

Albert, Shari The Brothers McMullen 1995; No Looking Back 1998

Albertazzi, Giorgio (1923–) Last Year at Marienbad 1961; Eva 1962

Alberti, Guido (1909–1996) 8½ 1963; Hands over the City 1963; Shout Loud, Louder… I Don't Understand 1966; Ten Days' Wonder 1971; What? 1973

Albertini, Giampiero (1927–1991) Burn! 1970; Zorro 1975

Albertson, Frank (1909–1964) Born Reckless 1930; Just Imagine 1930; Men without Women 1930; A Connecticut Yankee 1931; Air Mail 1932; Ever in My Heart 1933; The Last Gentleman 1934; Alice Adams 1935; Kind Lady 1935; Bachelor Mother 1939; When the Daltons Rode 1940; Louisiana Purchase 1941; Man Made Monster 1941; Rosie the Riveter 1944; Nightfall 1956; The Enemy Below 1957

Albertson, Jack (1907–1981) Top Banana 1953; Bring Your Smile Along 1955; Period of Adjustment 1962; Kissin' Cousins 1964; How to Murder Your Wife 1965; One Born Every Minute 1967; How to Save a Marriage and Ruin Your Life 1968; The Subject Was Roses 1968; Rabbit, Run 1970; The Late Liz 1971; Willy Wonka and the Chocolate Factory 1971; The Poseidon Adventure 1972; Dead & Buried 1981; The Fox and the Hound 1981

Albertson, Mabel (1901–1982) Ransom! 1956; Home before Dark 1958; Don't Give Up the Ship 1959; The Gazebo 1959; Period of Adjustment 1962; What's Up, Doc? 1972

Albinus, Jens (1965–) The Idiots 1998; In Your Hands 2004

Albright, Hardie (1903–1975) Jewel Robbery 1932; The Purchase Price 1932; So Big 1932; Red Salute 1935; The Jade Mask 1945; Angel on My Shoulder 1946

Albright, Lola (1925–) Champion 1949; The Magnificent Matador 1955; The Tender Trap 1955; The Monolith Monsters 1957; A Cold Wind in August 1961; Kid Galahad 1962; The Love Cage 1964; Lord Love a Duck 1966; How I Spent My Summer Vacation 1967; The Way West 1967; The Helicopter Spies 1968; Where Were You When the Lights Went Out? 1968

Albright, Wally aka **Albright Jr, Wally** (1925–1999) The Trespasser 1929; Zoo in Budapest 1933

Alcaide, Chris (1923–2004) The Gunslinger 1956; Rock All Night 1957

Alcázar, Damián (1953–) Men with Guns 1997; El Crimen del Padre Amaro 2002

Alda, Alan (1936–) Gone Are the Days 1963; Paper Lion 1968; The Extraordinary Seaman 1969; Jenny 1969; The Mephisto Waltz 1971; The Glass House 1972; To Kill a Clown 1972; Isn't It Shocking? 1973; Kill Me If You Can 1977; California Suite 1978; Same Time, Next Year 1978; The Seduction of Joe Tynan 1979; The Four Seasons 1981; Sweet Liberty 1986; A New Life 1988; Crimes and Misdemeanors 1989; Betsy's Wedding 1990; Whispers in the Dark 1992; And the Band Played On 1993; Manhattan Murder Mystery 1993; Canadian Bacon 1995; Everyone Says I Love You 1996; Flirting with Disaster 1996; Mad City 1997; Murder at 1600 1997; The Object of My Affection 1998; What Women Want 2001; The Aviator 2004

Alda, Robert (1914–1986) Rhapsody in Blue 1945; The Beast with Five Fingers 1946; Cinderella Jones 1946; Cloak and Dagger 1946; The Man I Love 1946; Nora Prentiss 1947; Tarzan and the Slave Girl 1950; Beautiful but Dangerous 1955; Imitation of Life 1959; The Girl Who Knew Too Much 1969; Bittersweet Love 1976; I Will… I Will… for Now 1976

Alda, Rutanya (1945–) The Deer Hunter 1978; Mommie Dearest 1981; Amityville II: the Possession 1982; Racing with the Moon 1984; Apprentice to Murder 1988; Prancer 1989; The Dark Half 1991

Alden, Mary (1883–1946) The Battle of the Sexes 1914; The Birth of a Nation 1915

Alden, Norman (1924–) The Sword in the Stone 1963; Man's Favorite Sport? 1964; The Wild Angels 1966; Good Times 1967; Where Does It Hurt? 1971; Kansas City Bomber 1972

Alderson, Brooke Urban Cowboy 1980; Mike's Murder 1984

Alderson, Erville (1882–1957) America 1924; Isn't Life Wonderful 1924; The Thirteenth Guest 1932

Alderton, John (1940–) The System 1964; Duffy 1968; Hannibal Brooks 1968; Please Sir! 1971; Zardoz 1973; It Shouldn't Happen to a Vet 1979; Clockwork Mice 1994; Mrs Caldicot's Cabbage War 2000; Calendar Girls 2003

Aldon, Mari (1927–) Distant Drums 1951; This Woman Is Dangerous 1952; Mask of Dust 1954; Summertime 1955

Aldredge, Tom (1928–) The Troublemaker 1964; The Rain People 1969; *batteries not included 1987; Other People's Money 1991; What about Bob? 1991; The Adventures of Huck Finn 1993; Passion 1996

Aldridge, Kitty Slipstream 1989; Divorcing Jack 1998

Aldridge, Michael (1920–1994) Bullshot 1983; Shanghai Surprise 1986

Aleandro, Norma (1936–) The Official Version 1985; Gaby: a True Story 1987; Cousins 1989; Son of the Bride 2001; Only Human 2004

Ales, John The Nutty Professor 1996; Spy Hard 1996; Nutty Professor 2: the Klumps 2000

Alexander, Ben (1911–1969) High Pressure 1932; Dragnet 1954; Man in the Shadow 1957

Alexander, Denise Crime in the Streets 1956; The Lindbergh Kidnapping Case 1976

Alexander, Elizabeth (1952–) Summerfield 1977; The Killing of Angel Street 1981

Alexander, Erika (1969–) The Long Walk Home 1990; Love Liza 2001

Alexander, Jace (1964–) Matewan 1987; City of Hope 1991; Mistress 1992; Love and a .45 1994

Alexander, Jane (1939–) The Great White Hope 1970; A Gunfight 1971; The New Centurions 1972; All the President's Men 1976; The Betsy 1978; Kramer vs Kramer 1979; Brubaker 1980; Playing for Time 1980; Night Crossing 1981; Testament 1983; City Heat 1984; Square Dance 1987; The Cider House Rules 1999; Jenifer 2001; The Ring 2002; Sunshine State 2002

Alexander, Jason (1959–) The Burning 1981; The Mosquito Coast 1986; Jacob's Ladder 1990; Pretty Woman 1990; White Palace 1990; I Don't Buy Kisses Anymore 1992; Coneheads 1993; Blankman 1994; North 1994; The Paper 1994; For Better or Worse 1995; The Last Supper 1995; Dunston Checks In 1996; The Hunchback of Notre Dame 1996; Love! Valour! Compassion! 1997; Rodgers & Hammerstein's Cinderella 1997; Something about Sex 1998; The Adventures of Rocky & Bullwinkle 1999; Madeline: Lost in Paris 1999; Shallow Hal 2001

Alexander, John (1897–1982) Arsenic and Old Lace 1944; The Horn Blows at Midnight 1945; The Jolson Story 1946; Where There's Life 1947; The Sleeping City 1950; The Marrying Kind 1952

Alexander, Katherine aka **Alexander, Katharine** (1898–1981) The Barretts of

Wimpole Street 1934; *Death Takes a Holiday* 1934; *Operator 13* 1934; *The Painted Veil* 1934; *After Office Hours* 1935; *She Married Her Boss* 1935; *The Devil Is a Sissy* 1936; *That Certain Woman* 1937; *The Great Man Votes* 1939; *In Name Only* 1939; *Dance, Girl, Dance* 1940; *Kiss and Tell* 1945
Alexander, Khandi (1957–) *Poetic Justice* 1993; *Tina: What's Love Got to Do with It* 1993
Alexander, Richard (1902–1989) *Law and Order* 1932; *Flash Gordon* 1936
Alexander (1), Ross (1907–1937) *The Wiser Sex* 1932; *Flirtation Walk* 1934; *Captain Blood* 1935; *A Midsummer Night's Dream* 1935; *Shipmates Forever* 1935; *China Clipper* 1936
Alexander, Tad (1922–) *Rasputin and the Empress* 1932; *Broadway to Hollywood* 1933
Alexander, Terence (1923–) *The One That Got Away* 1957; *The Square Peg* 1958; *The League of Gentlemen* 1960; *Bitter Harvest* 1963; *Judith* 1966; *Only When I Larf* 1968; *What's Good for the Goose* 1969; *Waterloo* 1970
Alexander, Terry (1947–) *Day of the Dead* 1985; *Conspiracy Theory* 1997
Alexandra, Charlotte *Immoral Tales* 1974; *Goodbye Emmanuelle* 1977
Alexi-Malle, Adam (1964–) *Bowfinger* 1999; *Hidalgo* 2003
Alfonsi, Lidia (1928–) *Morgan the Pirate* 1960; *The Trojan War* 1961; *Black Sabbath* 1963
Alfonso, Yves (1944–) *Made in USA* 1966; *Vladimir et Rosa* 1970
Alford, Phillip (1948–) *To Kill a Mockingbird* 1962; *Shenandoah* 1965
Alfredson, Hans (1931–) *Pippi Longstocking* 1968; *The Emigrants* 1971; *The New Land* 1972; *The Simple-Minded Murderer* 1982
Ali, Muhammad aka **Clay, Cassius** (1942–) *Requiem for a Heavyweight* 1962; *The Greatest* 1977; *Freedom Road* 1979; *Body and Soul* 1981
Ali, Tatyana aka **Ali, Tatyana M** (1979–) *Eddie Murphy Raw* 1987; *Fall into Darkness* 1996
Alice, Mary (1941–) *Beat Street* 1984; *To Sleep with Anger* 1990; *Down in the Delta* 1997; *The Matrix Revolutions* 2003
Alison, Dorothy (1925–1992) *The Maggie* 1953; *Turn the Key Softly* 1953; *Child's Play* 1954; *The Long Arm* 1956; *Reach for the Sky* 1956; *The Scamp* 1957; *The Silken Affair* 1957; *The Man Upstairs* 1958; *Life in Emergency Ward 10* 1959; *Two Living, One Dead* 1961; *Blind Terror* 1971; *Dr Jekyll and Sister Hyde* 1971; *The Amazing Mr Blunden* 1972; *The Winds of Jarrah* 1983; *Rikky and Pete* 1988; *Malpractice* 1989
Allan, Elizabeth (1908–1990) *Ace of Aces* 1933; *Men in White* 1934; *David Copperfield* 1935; *Java Head* 1935; *Mark of the Vampire* 1935; *A Tale of Two Cities* 1935; *The Shadow* 1936; *A Woman Rebels* 1936; *The Adventures of Michael Strogoff* 1937; *Camille* 1937; *Slave Ship* 1937; *Saloon Bar* 1940; *The Great Mr Handel* 1942; *Went the Day Well?* 1942; *That Dangerous Age* 1949; *Folly to Be Wise* 1952; *Front Page Story* 1953; *The Heart of the Matter* 1953; *The Brain Machine* 1954; *Grip of the Strangler* 1958
Allan, Marguerite (1909–) *Blossom Time* 1934; *Doctor's Orders* 1934
Allbritton, Louise (1920–1979) *Pittsburgh* 1942; *Who Done It?* 1942; *Son of Dracula* 1943; *The Egg and I* 1947; *Sitting Pretty* 1948; *Walk a Crooked Mile* 1948; *The Doolins of Oklahoma* 1949
Alldredge, Michael (1940–1997) *The Incredible Melting Man* 1977; *About Last Night...* 1986; *Promise* 1986; *Robot Jox* 1989
Allégret, Catherine (1946–) *The Sleeping Car Murders* 1965; *Last Tango in Paris* 1972; *Burnt Barns* 1973; *Paul and Michelle* 1974; *Chanel Solitaire* 1981; *Nazi Hunter: the Beate Klarsfeld Story* 1986
Allen, Adrianne (1907–1993) *Merrily We Go to Hell* 1932; *The October Man* 1947; *The Final Test* 1953
Allen, Barbara Jo aka **Vague, Vera** (1905–1974) *Kiss the Boys Goodbye* 1941; *Girl Rush* 1944; *Rosie the Riveter* 1944; *Mohawk* 1956; *Sleeping Beauty* 1959
Allen, Chad (1974–) *TerrorVision* 1986; *Murder in New Hampshire* 1991
Allen, Chesney (1894–1982) *A Fire Has Been Arranged* 1935; *O-Kay for Sound* 1937; *Alf's Button Afloat* 1938; *Gasbags* 1940; *We'll Smile Again* 1942; *Dreaming* 1944; *Here Comes the Sun* 1945; *Life Is a Circus* 1958
Allen, Corey (1934–) *Rebel without a Cause* 1955; *The Big Caper* 1957; *Party Girl* 1958; *Key Witness* 1960
Allen, Debbie (1950–) *Fame* 1980; *Jo Jo Dancer, Your Life Is Calling* 1986; *Out of Sync* 1995
Allen, Elizabeth (1934–) *From the Terrace* 1960; *Donovan's Reef* 1963; *The Carey Treatment* 1972
Allen, Fred (1896–1955) *Thanks a Million* 1935; *Sally, Irene and Mary* 1938; *It's in the Bag* 1945; *O Henry's Full House* 1952; *We're Not Married* 1952
Allen, Ginger Lynn (1962–) *Buried Alive* 1990; *Leather Jackets* 1991; *Bound and Gagged: a Love Story* 1992
Allen, Gracie (1902–1964) *The Big Broadcast* 1932; *International House* 1933; *Six of a Kind* 1934; *We're Not Dressing* 1934; *The Big Broadcast of 1936* 1935; *The Big Broadcast of 1937* 1936; *A Damsel in Distress* 1937; *College Swing* 1938; *The Gracie Allen Murder Case* 1939; *Honolulu* 1939; *Mr and Mrs North* 1941
Allen, Jack (1907–1995) *The Four Feathers* 1939; *The Sound Barrier* 1952; *Impulse* 1955; *Man from Tangier* 1957; *Life in Danger* 1959; *The Breaking Point* 1961
Allen, Joan (1956–) *Manhunter* 1986; *Peggy Sue Got Married* 1986; *Tucker: the Man and His Dream* 1988; *In Country* 1989; *Without Warning: the James Brady Story* 1991; *Ethan Frome* 1993; *Innocent Moves* 1993; *Josh and SAM* 1993; *Mad Love* 1995; *Nixon* 1995; *The Crucible* 1996; *Face/Off* 1997; *The Ice Storm* 1997; *Pleasantville* 1998; *The Contender* 2000; *When the Sky Falls* 2000; *The Notebook* 2003; *The Bourne Supremacy* 2004; *Yes* 2004
Allen, Judith (1911–1996) *This Day and Age* 1933; *Bright Eyes* 1934; *The Old-Fashioned Way* 1934
Allen, Karen (1951–) *The Wanderers* 1979; *Cruising* 1980; *A Small Circle of Friends* 1980; *Raiders of the Lost Ark* 1981; *Shoot the Moon* 1982; *Split Image* 1982; *Starman* 1984; *Until September* 1984; *Backfire* 1987; *The Glass Menagerie* 1987; *Scrooged* 1988; *Animal Behavior* 1989; *The Turning* 1992; *Ghost in the Machine* 1993; *King of the Hill* 1993; *The Sandlot* 1993; *Voyage* 1993; *Wind River* 1999; *The Perfect Storm* 2000; *In the Bedroom* 2001
Allen, Keith (1953–) *Loose Connections* 1983; *The Supergrass* 1985; *Comrades: a Lanternist's Account of the Tolpuddle Martyrs and What Became of Them* 1986; *Chicago Joe and the Showgirl* 1989; *Kafka* 1991; *Rebecca's Daughters* 1991; *Carry On Columbus* 1992; *Beyond Bedlam* 1993; *Second Best* 1993; *The Young Americans* 1993; *Captives* 1994; *Loch Ness* 1994; *Shallow Grave* 1994; *Blue Juice* 1995; *Rancid Aluminium* 1999; *Ma Femme Est une Actrice* 2001; *Agent Cody Banks 2: Destination London* 2003; *De-Lovely* 2004
Allen, Lester (1891–1949) *The Heat's On* 1943; *The Great Flamarion* 1945
Allen, Marty (1922–) *The Last of the Secret Agents* 1966; *Mister Jerico* 1969
Allen, Nancy (1950–) *Carrie* 1976; *I Wanna Hold Your Hand* 1978; *Home Movies* 1979; *1941* 1979; *Dressed to Kill* 1980; *Blow Out* 1981; *Strange Invaders* 1983; *The Buddy System* 1984; *Not for Publication* 1984; *The Philadelphia Experiment* 1984; *RoboCop* 1987; *Poltergeist III* 1988; *Limit Up* 1989; *RoboCop 2* 1990; *RoboCop 3* 1993; *Patriots* 1994; *Dusting Cliff 7* 1996
Allen, Patrick (1927–) *Dial M for Murder* 1954; *Confession* 1955; *High Hell* 1957; *The Man Who Wouldn't Talk* 1957; *I Was Monty's Double* 1958; *Tread Softly Stranger* 1958; *Never Take Sweets from a Stranger* 1960; *Night of the Big Heat* 1967; *The Body Stealers* 1969; *When Dinosaurs Ruled the Earth* 1969; *Puppet on a Chain* 1970; *The Sea Wolves* 1980
Allen, Penelope aka **Allen, Penny** *Scarecrow* 1973; *Dog Day Afternoon* 1975; *On the Nickel* 1979
Allen, Rae (1926–) *Damn Yankees* 1958; *Where's Poppa?* 1970
Allen, Rex (1920–1999) *Trail of Robin Hood* 1950; *For the Love of Mike* 1960; *The Incredible Journey* 1963; *Charlotte's Web* 1973
Allen, Robert (1906–1998) *The Black Room* 1935; *Crime and Punishment* 1935; *Terror in the City* 1963
Allen, Ronald (1930–1991) *A Night to Remember* 1958; *The Projected Man* 1966; *Hell Boats* 1970; *Eat the Rich* 1987
Allen, Rosalind *Children of the Corn II: the Final Sacrifice* 1993; *Ticks* 1993; *Pinocchio's Revenge* 1996
Allen, Sheila (1932–) *Children of the Damned* 1964; *The Alphabet Murders* 1966; *Viva Knievel!* 1977; *Pascali's Island* 1988
Allen, Sian Barbara (1946–) *You'll Like My Mother* 1972; *Billy Two Hats* 1973; *The Lindbergh Kidnapping Case* 1976
Allen, Steve (1921–2000) *The Benny Goodman Story* 1955; *Warning Shot* 1967; *Where Were You When the Lights Went Out?* 1968; *The Comic* 1969
Allen, Tim (1953–) *The Santa Clause* 1994; *Toy Story* 1995; *For Richer or Poorer* 1997; *Jungle 2 Jungle* 1997; *Galaxy Quest* 1999; *Toy Story 2* 1999; *Joe Somebody* 2001; *Big Trouble* 2002; *The Santa Clause 2* 2002; *Christmas with the Kranks* 2004
Allen, Todd (1960–) *Witchboard* 1987; *Brothers in Arms* 1988; *Pinocchio's Revenge* 1996; *The Apostle* 1997
Allen, Woody (1935–) *What's New, Pussycat?* 1965; *What's Up, Tiger Lily?* 1966; *Casino Royale* 1967; *Take the Money and Run* 1969; *Bananas* 1971; *Everything You Always Wanted to Know about Sex ... but Were Afraid to Ask* 1972; *Play It Again, Sam* 1972; *Sleeper* 1973; *Love and Death* 1975; *The Front* 1976; *Annie Hall* 1977; *Manhattan* 1979; *Stardust Memories* 1980; *A Midsummer Night's Sex Comedy* 1982; *Zelig* 1983; *Broadway Danny Rose* 1984; *Hannah and Her Sisters* 1986; *King Lear – Fear and Loathing* 1987; *Radio Days* 1987; *Crimes and Misdemeanors* 1989; *New York Stories* 1989; *Scenes from a Mall* 1991; *Shadows and Fog* 1991; *Husbands and Wives* 1992; *Manhattan Murder Mystery* 1993; *Mighty Aphrodite* 1995; *Everyone Says I Love You* 1996; *Deconstructing Harry* 1997; *The Sunshine Boys* 1997; *Antz* 1998; *The Impostors* 1998; *Sweet and Lowdown* 1999; *Company Man* 2000; *Picking Up the Pieces* 2000; *Small Time Crooks* 2000; *The Curse of the Jade Scorpion* 2001; *Hollywood Ending* 2002; *Anything Else* 2003
Allenby, Frank (1898–1953) *The Black Sheep of Whitehall* 1941; *Madame Bovary* 1949; *Soldiers Three* 1951
Allende, Fernando (1954–) *Agatha Christie's Murder in Three Acts* 1986; *Naked Lies* 1997
Allerson, Alexander (1930–) *The McKenzie Break* 1970; *Chinese Roulette* 1976; *I Only Want You to Love Me* 1976; *Despair* 1978
Alley, Kirstie (1951–) *Star Trek II: the Wrath of Khan* 1982; *Champions* 1983; *Blind Date* 1984; *Runaway* 1984; *Summer School* 1987; *Deadly Pursuit* 1988; *Look Who's Talking* 1989; *Loverboy* 1989; *Look Who's Talking Too* 1990; *Madhouse* 1990; *Sibling Rivalry* 1990; *Look Who's Talking Now!* 1993; *David's Mother* 1994; *It Takes Two* 1995; *Village of the Damned* 1995; *Sticks and Stones* 1996; *Deconstructing Harry* 1997; *For Richer or Poorer* 1997; *Drop Dead Gorgeous* 1999
Allgood, Sara (1883–1950) *Blackmail* 1929; *Juno and the Paycock* 1930; *Lazybones* 1935; *It's Love Again* 1936; *Southern Roses* 1936; *Storm in a Teacup* 1937; *How Green Was My Valley* 1941; *That Hamilton Woman* 1941; *Life Begins at 8.30* 1942; *Roxie Hart* 1942; *The War against Mrs Hadley* 1942; *Jane Eyre* 1943; *The Lodger* 1944; *Kitty* 1945; *The Strange Affair of Uncle Harry* 1945; *The Spiral Staircase* 1946; *The Fabulous Dorseys* 1947; *Mother Wore Tights* 1947; *My Wild Irish Rose* 1947; *The Accused* 1949; *Cheaper by the Dozen* 1950
Allister, Claud aka **Allister, Claude** (1888–1970) *Bulldog Drummond* 1929; *Monte Carlo* 1930; *The Return of Bulldog Drummond* 1934; *Those Were the Days* 1934; *Confirm or Deny* 1941
Allnutt, Wendy (1946–) *Oh! What a Lovely War* 1969; *All Coppers Are...* 1972; *From beyond the Grave* 1973
Allred, Corbin (1979–) *Quest of the Delta Knights* 1993; *Diamonds* 1999
Allwyn, Astrid (1905–1978) *Love Affair* 1932; *The White Parade* 1934; *Accent on Youth* 1935; *Hands across the Table* 1935; *Dimples* 1936; *Follow the Fleet* 1936; *Love Affair* 1939; *Miracles for Sale* 1939
Allyson, June (1917–) *Best Foot Forward* 1943; *Girl Crazy* 1943; *Meet the People* 1944; *Music for Millions* 1944; *Two Girls and a Sailor* 1944; *The Sailor Takes a Wife* 1945; *The Secret Heart* 1946; *Two Sisters from Boston* 1946; *Good News* 1947; *High Barbaree* 1947; *The Three Musketeers* 1948; *Little Women* 1949; *The Stratton Story* 1949; *Right Cross* 1950; *The Girl in White* 1952; *Battle Circus* 1953; *The Glenn Miller Story* 1953; *Remains to Be Seen* 1953; *Executive Suite* 1954; *Woman's World* 1954; *The McConnell Story* 1955; *The Shrike* 1955; *Strategic Air Command* 1955; *The Opposite Sex* 1956; *You Can't Run Away from It* 1956; *Interlude* 1957; *My Man Godfrey* 1957; *A Stranger in My Arms* 1959; *They Only Kill Their Masters* 1972
Almagor, Gila (1939–) *Sallah* 1964; *Every Time We Say Goodbye* 1986; *The Summer of Aviya* 1988
Alonso, Chelo (1933–) *The Sign of the Gladiator* 1958; *Goliath and the Barbarians* 1959; *Morgan the Pirate* 1960
Alonso, Ernesto (1919–) *Wuthering Heights* 1953; *The Criminal Life of Archibaldo de la Cruz* 1955
Alonso, Maria Conchita (1957–) *Moscow on the Hudson* 1984; *A Fine Mess* 1986; *Touch and Go* 1986; *Extreme Prejudice* 1987; *The Running Man* 1987; *Colors* 1988; *Vampire's Kiss* 1988; *Predator 2* 1990; *McBain* 1991; *The House of the Spirits* 1993; *Roosters* 1993; *Caught* 1996; *Chain of Command* 2000
Alper, Murray (1904–1984) *Down Mexico Way* 1941; *Security Risk* 1954
Alt, Carol (1960–) *Ring of Steel* 1994; *Body Armor* 1996; *Private Parts* 1997
Alterio, Ernesto (1970–) *The Other Side of the Bed* 2002; *Football Days* 2003
Alterio, Héctor (1929–) *Camila* 1984; *The Official Version* 1985; *Summer of the Colt* 1989; *I, the Worst of All* 1990; *Son of the Bride* 2001
Altman, Bruce *Regarding Henry* 1991; *My New Gun* 1992; *Rookie of the Year* 1993; *To Gillian on Her 37th Birthday* 1996; *LIE* 2001; *Matchstick Men* 2003
Alvarado, Don (1904–1967) *Rio Rita* 1929; *Beau Ideal* 1931; *Lady with a Past* 1932; *Black Beauty* 1933; *The Devil Is a Woman* 1935; *The Big Steal* 1949
Alvarado, Magali *Salsa* 1988; *Mi Vida Loca* 1993
Alvarado, Trini (1967–) *Rich Kids* 1979; *Times Square* 1980; *Mrs Soffel* 1984; *Satisfaction* 1988; *Stella* 1990; *American Friends* 1991; *The Babe* 1992; *Little Women* 1994; *The Perez Family* 1995; *The Frighteners* 1996; *Paulie* 1998
Alvarez, Ana (1969–) *La Madre Muerta* 1993; *Cha-Cha-Cha* 1998
Alvin, John (1917–) *The Fighting Sullivans* 1944; *Objective, Burma!* 1945; *The Beast with Five Fingers* 1946
Alvina, Anicée (1954–) *Friends* 1971; *Paul and Michelle* 1974
Alzado, Lyle (1949–1992) *The Double McGuffin* 1979; *Ernest Goes to Camp* 1987; *Destroyer* 1988
Amalric, Mathieu (1965–) *Ma Vie Sexuelle* 1996; *Alice et Martin* 1998; *Late August, Early September* 1998; *Kings & Queen* 2004
Amandes, Tom (1956–) *The Long Kiss Goodnight* 1996; *Brokedown Palace* 1999
Amann, Betty (1906–1990) *Asphalt* 1928; *Rich and Strange* 1932
Ambler, Joss (1900–1959) *Come On George* 1939; *Trouble Brewing* 1939; *The Black Sheep of Whitehall* 1941; *Much Too Shy* 1942; *Here Comes the Sun* 1945; *Ghost Ship* 1952; *The Long Arm* 1956
Ameche, Don (1908–1993) *Ladies in Love* 1936; *One in a Million* 1936; *In Old Chicago* 1937; *Love Is News* 1937; *You Can't Have Everything* 1937; *Alexander's Ragtime Band* 1938; *Happy Landing* 1938; *Josette* 1938; *Hollywood Cavalcade* 1939; *Midnight* 1939; *The Story of Alexander Graham Bell* 1939; *Swanee River* 1939; *The Three Musketeers* 1939; *Down Argentine Way* 1940; *Four Sons* 1940; *Lillian Russell* 1940; *Confirm or Deny* 1941; *The Feminine Touch* 1941; *Kiss the Boys Goodbye* 1941; *Moon over Miami* 1941; *That Night in Rio* 1941; *The Magnificent Dope* 1942; *Happy Land* 1943; *Heaven Can Wait* 1943; *Greenwich Village* 1944; *Wing and a Prayer* 1944; *Guest Wife* 1945; *So Goes My Love* 1946; *That's My Man* 1947; *Sleep, My Love* 1948; *Slightly French* 1949; *A Fever in the Blood* 1961; *Picture Mommy Dead* 1966; *The Boatniks* 1970; *Suppose They Gave a War and Nobody Came?* 1970; *Trading Places* 1983; *Cocoon* 1985; *Pals* 1986; *Bigfoot and the Hendersons* 1987; *Cocoon: the Return* 1988; *Coming to America* 1988; *Things Change* 1988; *Oddball Hall* 1990; *Oscar* 1991; *Folks!* 1992; *Homeward Bound: the Incredible Journey* 1993; *Corrina, Corrina* 1994
Amédée (1923–) *Jeux Interdits* 1953; *Gates of Paris* 1957
Amendola, Claudio (1963–) *La Scorta* 1993; *The Horseman on*

the Roof 1995; Strong Hands 1997
America, Paul (1944–) *My Hustler* 1965; *Ciao! Manhattan* 1973
Ames, Adrienne (1907–1947) *Sinners in the Sun* 1932; *The Death Kiss* 1933; *George White's Scandals* 1934; *You're Telling Me!* 1934; *Black Sheep* 1935; *Woman Wanted* 1935
Ames, Joyce *Hello, Dolly!* 1969; *The Todd Killings* 1971
Ames, Leon *aka* **Waycoff, Leon** (1902–1993) *Murders in the Rue Morgue* 1932; *Mysterious Mr Moto* 1938; *Mr Moto in Danger Island* 1939; *Crime Doctor* 1943; *The Iron Major* 1943; *Meet Me in St Louis* 1944; *The Thin Man Goes Home* 1944; *Son of Lassie* 1945; *Yolanda and the Thief* 1945; *The Postman Always Rings Twice* 1946; *Lady in the Lake* 1947; *Merton of the Movies* 1947; *Song of the Thin Man* 1947; *On an Island with You* 1948; *The Velvet Touch* 1948; *Ambush* 1949; *Little Women* 1949; *Scene of the Crime* 1949; *The Big Hangover* 1950; *The Happy Years* 1950; *Watch the Birdie* 1950; *Cattle Drive* 1951; *On Moonlight Bay* 1951; *Angel Face* 1953; *By the Light of the Silvery Moon* 1953; *Let's Do It Again* 1953; *From the Terrace* 1960; *The Absent-Minded Professor* 1961; *Son of Flubber* 1962; *The Misadventures of Merlin Jones* 1964; *The Monkey's Uncle* 1965; *Hammersmith Is Out* 1972; *Testament* 1983; *Jake Speed* 1986; *Peggy Sue Got Married* 1986
Ames, Ramsay (1919–1998) *Calling Dr Death* 1943; *Ali Baba and the Forty Thieves* 1944; *The Mummy's Ghost* 1944
Ames, Robert (1889–1931) *The Trespasser* 1929; *Holiday* 1930
Amick, Mädchen (1970–) *The Borrower* 1989; *The Boyfriend School* 1990; *Sleepwalkers* 1992; *Twin Peaks: Fire Walk with Me* 1992; *Dream Lover* 1993; *Love, Cheat & Steal* 1994; *Trapped in Paradise* 1994; *Twist of Fate* 1997; *The Hunted* 1998; *Hangman* 2000; *The List* 2000
Amidou (1942–) *Man in the Trunk* 1973; *Sorcerer* 1977
Amis, Suzy (1962–) *The Big Town* 1987; *Plain Clothes* 1988; *Rocket Gibraltar* 1988; *Twister* 1989; *Where the Heart Is* 1990; *Rich in Love* 1992; *The Ballad of Little Jo* 1993; *Two Small Bodies* 1993; *Blown Away* 1994; *Nadja* 1995; *The Usual Suspects* 1995; *Cadillac Ranch* 1996; *One Good Turn* 1996; *Last Stand at Saber River* 1997; *Firestorm* 1998; *Judgment Day* 1999
Amos, John (1941–) *The World's Greatest Athlete* 1973; *Let's Do It Again* 1975; *Touched by Love* 1979; *The Beastmaster* 1982; *Dance of the Dwarfs* 1983; *American Flyers* 1985; *Coming to America* 1988; *Lock Up* 1989; *Die Hard 2: Die Harder* 1990; *Two Evil Eyes* 1990; *Mac* 1992; *Disappearing Acts* 2000
Amplas, John *Martin* 1978; *Midnight* 1980
Amsterdam, Morey (1908–1996) *Machine Gun Kelly* 1958; *Beach Party* 1963; *The Horse in the Gray Flannel Suit* 1968
Amstutz, Roland (1942–1997) *Slow Motion* 1980; *Nouvelle Vague* 1990
Amurri, Eva (1985–) *The Banger Sisters* 2002; *Saved!* 2004
Anand, Dev (1923–) *Shai'r* 1949; *Munimji* 1955; *Tere Ghar Ke Saamne* 1963
Anand, Tinnu *Bombay* 1995; *Kyun! Ho Gaya Na …* 2004
Anaya, Elena (1975–) *Sex and Lucia* 2001; *Van Helsing* 2004
Anconina, Richard (1953–) *Love Songs* 1984; *Police* 1985; *Would I Lie to You?* 1997
Anders, Glenn (1889–1981) *Laughter* 1930; *The Lady from Shanghai* 1948; *M* 1951; *Tarzan's Peril* 1951
Anders, Luana (1940–1996) *Reform School Girl* 1957; *Night Tide* 1961; *The Pit and the Pendulum* 1961; *Dementia 13* 1963; *That Cold Day in the Park* 1969; *Greaser's Palace* 1972; *When the Legends Die* 1972; *The Killing Kind* 1973; *Border Radio* 1987; *Limit Up* 1989
Anders, Merry (1932–) *The Night Runner* 1957; *Violent Road* 1958; *Beauty and the Beast* 1962; *The Time Travelers* 1964; *Tickle Me* 1965
Andersen, Bridgette (1975–) *Savannah Smiles* 1982; *Fever Pitch* 1985; *Too Much* 1987
Andersen, Elga (1939–1994) *A Global Affair* 1964; *Le Mans* 1971
Anderson, Anthony (1970–) *Romeo Must Die* 2000; *Exit Wounds* 2001; *Two Can Play That Game* 2001; *Barbershop* 2002; *Agent Cody Banks 2: Destination London* 2003; *Cradle 2 the Grave* 2003; *Kangaroo Jack* 2003; *Malibu's Most Wanted* 2003; *Scary Movie 3* 2003
Anderson, Daphne (1922–) *The Beggar's Opera* 1953; *Hobson's Choice* 1953
Anderson, Dion *Roe vs Wade* 1989; *Dying Young* 1991
Anderson, Donna (1925–) *On the Beach* 1959; *Inherit the Wind* 1960
Anderson, Eddie "Rochester" (1905–1977) *What Price Hollywood?* 1932; *The Green Pastures* 1936; *Three Men on a Horse* 1936; *Buck Benny Rides Again* 1940; *The Birth of the Blues* 1941; *Cabin in the Sky* 1943; *The Meanest Man in the World* 1943; *Broadway Rhythm* 1944; *Brewster's Millions* 1945; *The Sailor Takes a Wife* 1945
Anderson, Erika (1965–) *A Nightmare on Elm Street 5: The Dream Child* 1989; *Zandalee* 1991; *Quake!* 1992
Anderson, Esther *The Touchables* 1968; *Two Gentlemen Sharing* 1969; *A Warm December* 1973
Anderson, Gene (1931–1965) *The Shakedown* 1959; *The Day the Earth Caught Fire* 1961; *The Break* 1962
Anderson, Gillian (1968–) *The Turning* 1992; *Princess Mononoke* 1997; *Chicago Cab* 1998; *The Mighty* 1998; *Playing by Heart* 1998; *The X-Files* 1998; *The House of Mirth* 2000
Anderson, Herbert (1917–1994) *The Body Disappears* 1941; *The Male Animal* 1942; *The Benny Goodman Story* 1955; *My Man Godfrey* 1957
Anderson (2), James (1921–1969) *Along the Great Divide* 1951; *Five* 1951; *Ruby Gentry* 1952; *The Connection* 1961; *Take the Money and Run* 1969
Anderson, Jean (1908–2001) *The Romantic Age* 1949; *The Kidnappers* 1953; *A Town like Alice* 1956; *Lucky Jim* 1957; *Robbery under Arms* 1957; *SOS Pacific* 1959; *Spare the Rod* 1961; *Waltz of the Toreadors* 1962; *The Three Lives of Thomasina* 1963; *The Road Builder* 1971; *The Lady Vanishes* 1979; *Leon the Pig Farmer* 1992
Anderson, John (1922–1992) *Ride the High Country* 1962; *The Hallelujah Trail* 1965; *Namu, the Killer Whale* 1966; *A Covenant with Death* 1967; *Welcome to Hard Times* 1967; *Day of the Evil Gun* 1968; *5 Card Stud* 1968; *The Great Bank Robbery* 1969; *A Man Called Gannon* 1969; *Young Billy Young* 1969; *Soldier Blue* 1970; *Molly and Lawless John* 1972; *Executive Action* 1973; *The Dove* 1974; *Zoot Suit* 1981; *Danielle Steel's Daddy* 1991
Anderson, Judith (1898–1992) *Rebecca* 1940; *All through the Night* 1942; *Kings Row* 1942; *Edge of Darkness* 1943; *Stage Door Canteen* 1943; *Laura* 1944; *And Then There Were None* 1945; *Diary of a Chambermaid* 1946; *Specter of the Rose* 1946; *The Strange Love of Martha Ivers* 1946; *Pursued* 1947; *The Red House* 1947; *Tycoon* 1947; *The Furies* 1950; *Salome* 1953; *Cat on a Hot Tin Roof* 1958; *Cinderfella* 1960; *Don't Bother to Knock* 1961; *A Man Called Horse* 1970
Anderson, Kevin (1960–) *Orphans* 1987; *Miles from Home* 1988; *In Country* 1989; *Liebestraum* 1991; *Sleeping with the Enemy* 1991; *Hoffa* 1992; *The Night We Never Met* 1993; *Rising Sun* 1993; *Eye of God* 1997; *Firelight* 1997; *A Thousand Acres* 1997; *Gregory's Two Girls* 1999
Anderson, Lindsay (1923–1994) *Inadmissible Evidence* 1968; *Chariots of Fire* 1981
Anderson, Loni (1946–) *Stroker Ace* 1983; *All Dogs Go to Heaven* 1989; *Munchie* 1992; *Munchie Strikes Back* 1994; *A Night at the Roxbury* 1998; *3 Ninjas: High Noon at Mega Mountain* 1998
Anderson, Mary (1921–) *Cheers for Miss Bishop* 1941; *Lifeboat* 1944; *To Each His Own* 1946; *The Underworld Story* 1950
Anderson, Melissa Sue *aka* **Anderson, Melissa** (1962–) *Happy Birthday to Me* 1981; *Chattanooga Choo Choo* 1984; *Dead Men Don't Die* 1991
Anderson, Melody (1955–) *Flash Gordon* 1980; *Dead & Buried* 1981; *The Boy in Blue* 1986; *Firewalker* 1986; *Cannonball Fever* 1989
Anderson Jr, Michael (1943–) *The Sundowners* 1960; *In Search of the Castaways* 1961; *Play It Cool* 1962; *Reach for Glory* 1962; *Dear Heart* 1964; *The Glory Guys* 1965; *Major Dundee* 1965; *The Sons of Katie Elder* 1965; *Logan's Run* 1976; *Sunset Grill* 1992
Anderson, Michael J (1953–) *Great Land of the Small* 1987; *Mulholland Drive* 2001; *Snow White* 2001
Anderson, Miles (1953–) *Gunbus* 1986; *Cry Freedom* 1987; *Fast Food* 1998; *The King Is Alive* 2000
Anderson, Pamela *aka* **Anderson Lee, Pamela** (1967–) *Good Cop, Bad Cop* 1993; *Snapdragon* 1993; *Barb Wire* 1995; *Baywatch the Movie: Forbidden Paradise* 1995; *Naked Souls* 1995
Anderson, Richard (1926–) *The Magnificent Yankee* 1950; *Scaramouche* 1952; *Escape from Fort Bravo* 1953; *Give a Girl a Break* 1953; *I Love Melvin* 1953; *A Cry in the Night* 1956; *Forbidden Planet* 1956; *The Buster Keaton Story* 1957; *Paths of Glory* 1957; *The Long Hot Summer* 1958; *Compulsion* 1959; *The Gunfight at Dodge City* 1959; *Johnny Cool* 1963; *Kitten with a Whip* 1964; *Seconds* 1966; *The Ride to Hangman's Tree* 1967; *The Honkers* 1971; *The Glass Shield* 1995
Anderson (2), Robert (1923–) *The Night Runner* 1957; *Buchanan Rides Alone* 1958
Anderson, Rona (1926–) *Sleeping Car to Trieste* 1948; *Floodtide* 1949; *Home to Danger* 1951; *Scrooge* 1951; *The Black Rider* 1954; *Double Exposure* 1954; *The Flaw* 1954; *Shadow of a Man* 1954; *Little Red Monkey* 1955; *Stock Car* 1955; *The Bay of Saint Michel* 1963; *Devils of Darkness* 1964
Anderson, Sam *Critters 2: the Main Course* 1988; *The Man Next Door* 1996
Anderson, Stanley (1939–) *He Said, She Said* 1991; *Arlington Road* 1998; *S1MØNE* 2002
Anderson, Sylvia *Thunderbirds Are Go!* 1966; *Thunderbird 6* 1968
Anderson, Warner (1911–1976) *Destination Tokyo* 1943; *Abbott and Costello in Hollywood* 1945; *Objective, Burma!* 1945; *My Reputation* 1946; *High Wall* 1947; *The Lucky Stiff* 1949; *Destination Moon* 1950; *Santa Fe* 1951; *The Last Posse* 1953; *A Lion Is in the Streets* 1953; *The Star* 1953; *Drum Beat* 1954; *The Yellow Tomahawk* 1954; *The Blackboard Jungle* 1955; *A Lawless Street* 1955; *The Violent Men* 1955; *The Lineup* 1958; *Armored Command* 1961; *Rio Conchos* 1964
Andersson, Bibi (1935–) *Smiles of a Summer Night* 1955; *The Seventh Seal* 1957; *So Close to Life* 1957; *Wild Strawberries* 1957; *The Magician* 1958; *The Devil's Eye* 1960; *Square of Violence* 1961; *All These Women* 1964; *Duel at Diablo* 1966; *My Sister, My Love* 1966; *Persona* 1966; *A Passion* 1969; *The Kremlin Letter* 1970; *The Touch* 1971; *Scenes from a Marriage* 1973; *An Enemy of the People* 1977; *I Never Promised You a Rose Garden* 1977; *Airport '79: the Concorde* 1979; *Quintet* 1979; *Exposed* 1983; *Babette's Feast* 1987
Andersson, Harriet (1932–) *Summer with Monika* 1952; *Sawdust and Tinsel* 1953; *Lesson in Love* 1954; *Dreams* 1955; *Smiles of a Summer Night* 1955; *Through a Glass Darkly* 1961; *All These Women* 1964; *The Deadly Affair* 1966; *Cries and Whispers* 1972; *Dogville* 2003
Andes, Keith (1920–) *Blackbeard the Pirate* 1952; *Clash by Night* 1952; *Split Second* 1953; *Away All Boats* 1956; *Back from Eternity* 1956; *Pillars of the Sky* 1956; *The Girl Most Likely* 1957; *Interlude* 1957; *Damn Citizen* 1958
Ando, Masanobu (1975–) *Kids Return* 1996; *Battle Royale* 2000
Andorai, Peter (1948–) *Confidence* 1979; *Mephisto* 1981; *My 20th Century* 1988; *Sweet Emma Dear Böbe* 1992
Andre, Annette (1939–) *This Is My Street* 1963; *A Funny Thing Happened on the Way to the Forum* 1966
Andre, Carole *Face to Face* 1967; *Yor, the Hunter from the Future* 1983
André, Marcel (1885–1974) *La Belle et la Bête* 1946; *Les Parents Terribles* 1948; *Les Mains Sales* 1951
Andréani, Jean-Pierre *Goto, l'Ile d'Amour* 1968; *The Story of O* 1975
Andreeff, Starr (1964–) *Out of the Dark* 1988; *The Terror Within* 1988; *Amityville Dollhouse* 1996
Andress, Ursula (1936–) *Dr No* 1962; *4 for Texas* 1963; *Fun in Acapulco* 1963; *Nightmare in the Sun* 1964; *Once Before I Die* 1965; *She* 1965; *The Tenth Victim* 1965; *Up to His Ears* 1965; *What's New, Pussycat?* 1965; *The Blue Max* 1966; *Casino Royale* 1967; *The Southern Star* 1969; *Perfect Friday* 1970; *Red Sun* 1971; *The Loves and Times of Scaramouche* 1976; *The Fifth Musketeer* 1979; *Tigers in Lipstick* 1979; *Clash of the Titans* 1981; *Cremaster 5* 1997
Andreu, Simon (1941–) *Bad Man's River* 1971; *Triumphs of a Man Called Horse* 1983; *Crystal Heart* 1987; *Blood and Sand* 1989; *Prince of Shadows* 1991; *El Mar* 1999
Andrews, Anthony (1948–) *A War of Children* 1972; *Take Me High* 1973; *Operation Daybreak* 1975; *The Scarlet Pimpernel* 1982; *Agatha Christie's Sparkling Cyanide* 1983; *Under the Volcano* 1984; *The Holcroft Covenant* 1985; *The Second Victory* 1986; *The Lighthorsemen* 1987; *Hanna's War* 1988; *Lost in Siberia* 1991; *Haunted* 1995
Andrews, Barry *Dracula Has Risen from the Grave* 1968; *Blood on Satan's Claw* 1970
Andrews, Brian *Halloween* 1978; *The Great Santini* 1979
Andrews, Carol *The Bullfighters* 1945; *Blue Skies* 1946
Andrews, Dana (1909–1992) *Kit Carson* 1940; *Belle Starr* 1941; *Swamp Water* 1941; *Tobacco Road* 1941; *Berlin Correspondent* 1942; *Crash Dive* 1943; *The North Star* 1943; *The Ox-Bow Incident* 1943; *Laura* 1944; *The Purple Heart* 1944; *Up in Arms* 1944; *Wing and a Prayer* 1944; *Fallen Angel* 1945; *State Fair* 1945; *A Walk in the Sun* 1945; *The Best Years of Our Lives* 1946; *Canyon Passage* 1946; *Boomerang!* 1947; *Daisy Kenyon* 1947; *Night Song* 1947; *The Iron Curtain* 1948; *No Minor Vices* 1948; *Britannia Mews* 1949; *My Foolish Heart* 1949; *Edge of Doom* 1950; *Where the Sidewalk Ends* 1950; *The Frogmen* 1951; *I Want You* 1951; *Sealed Cargo* 1951; *Assignment – Paris* 1952; *Duel in the Jungle* 1954; *Elephant Walk* 1954; *Three Hours to Kill* 1954; *Smoke Signal* 1955; *Strange Lady in Town* 1955; *Beyond a Reasonable Doubt* 1956; *Comanche* 1956; *While the City Sleeps* 1956; *Night of the Demon* 1957; *Spring Reunion* 1957; *Zero Hour!* 1957; *The Fearmakers* 1958; *The Crowded Sky* 1960; *Madison Avenue* 1962; *Crack in the World* 1964; *Battle of the Bulge* 1965; *Brainstorm* 1965; *In Harm's Way* 1965; *The Loved One* 1965; *The Satan Bug* 1965; *Spy in Your Eye* 1965; *The Frozen Dead* 1966; *Johnny Reno* 1966; *The Devil's Brigade* 1968; *Innocent Bystanders* 1972; *Airport 1975* 1974; *Take a Hard Ride* 1975; *The Last Tycoon* 1976; *Good Guys Wear Black* 1977; *Born Again* 1978; *The Pilot* 1979
Andrews, David (1952–) *Some People* 1962; *A Place to Go* 1963; *Cherry 2000* 1988; *Graveyard Shift* 1990; *Wyatt Earp* 1994; *Under Pressure* 1997; *Mistaken Identity* 1999; *Terminator 3: Rise of the Machines* 2003
Andrews, Dean *The Navigators* 2001; *My Summer of Love* 2004
Andrews, Edward (1914–1985) *The Phenix City Story* 1955; *The Harder They Fall* 1956; *Tea and Sympathy* 1956; *Tension at Table Rock* 1956; *These Wilder Years* 1956; *Three Brave Men* 1956; *Hot Summer Night* 1957; *Trooper Hook* 1957; *Elmer Gantry* 1960; *The Absent-Minded Professor* 1961; *Love in a Goldfish Bowl* 1961; *The Young Savages* 1961; *Forty Pounds of Trouble* 1962; *The Thrill of It All* 1963; *The Brass Bottle* 1964; *Kisses for My President* 1964; *Send Me No Flowers* 1964; *A Tiger Walks* 1964; *Youngblood Hawke* 1964; *Fluffy* 1965; *The Glass Bottom Boat* 1966; *The Trouble with Girls* 1969; *How to Frame a Figg* 1971; *Avanti!* 1972; *The Seniors* 1978
Andrews, Harry (1911–1989) *The Red Beret* 1953; *The Black Knight* 1954; *The Man Who Loved Redheads* 1954; *Helen of Troy* 1955; *Alexander the Great* 1956; *A Hill in Korea* 1956; *Moby Dick* 1956; *Saint Joan* 1957; *Ice Cold in Alex* 1958; *The Devil's Disciple* 1959; *Circle of Deception* 1960; *Barabbas* 1961; *The Best of Enemies* 1961; *The Inspector* 1962; *Reach for Glory* 1962; *55 Days at Peking* 1963; *The Informers* 1963; *Nine Hours to Rama* 1963; *Nothing but the Best* 1963; *633 Squadron* 1964; *The System* 1964; *The Truth about Spring* 1964; *The Agony and the Ecstasy* 1965; *The Hill* 1965; *Sands of the Kalahari* 1965; *The Deadly Affair* 1966; *The Long Duel* 1966; *Modesty Blaise* 1966; *Danger Route* 1967; *I'll Never Forget What's 'Is Name* 1967; *The Jokers* 1967; *The Charge of the Light Brigade* 1968; *A Dandy in Aspic* 1968; *The Night They Raided Minsky's* 1968; *The Sea Gull* 1968; *Entertaining Mr Sloane* 1969; *A Nice Girl like Me* 1969; *Play Dirty* 1969; *The Southern Star* 1969; *Country Dance* 1970; *Too Late the Hero* 1970; *Wuthering Heights* 1970; *I Want What I Want* 1971; *Man of La Mancha* 1972; *The Nightcomers* 1972; *The Ruling Class* 1972; *The Mackintosh Man* 1973; *Theatre of Blood* 1973; *The Internecine Project* 1974; *The Blue Bird* 1976; *The Passover Plot* 1976; *Equus* 1977; *The Prince and the Pauper* 1977; *The Big*

Sleep 1978; *Death on the Nile* 1978; *The Medusa Touch* 1978; *SOS Titanic* 1979; *Mesmerized* 1984

Andrews, Jason *Last Exit to Brooklyn* 1989; *Federal Hill* 1994; *Rhythm Thief* 1994

Andrews, Julie (1935–) *The Americanization of Emily* 1964; *Mary Poppins* 1964; *The Sound of Music* 1965; *Hawaii* 1966; *Torn Curtain* 1966; *Thoroughly Modern Millie* 1967; *Star!* 1968; *Darling Lili* 1970; *The Tamarind Seed* 1974; *10* 1979; *Little Miss Marker* 1980; *SOB* 1981; *Victor/Victoria* 1982; *The Man Who Loved Women* 1983; *Duet for One* 1986; *That's Life* 1986; *A Touch of Adultery* 1991; *One Special Night* 1999; *Relative Values* 2000; *The Princess Diaries* 2001; *The Princess Diaries 2: Royal Engagement* 2004; *Shrek 2* 2004

Andrews, Laverne aka **Andrews Sisters, The** (1915–1967) *Argentine Nights* 1940; *Buck Privates* 1941; *In the Navy* 1941; *Private Buckaroo* 1942

Andrews, Maxene aka **Andrews Sisters, The** (1916–1995) *Argentine Nights* 1940; *Buck Privates* 1941; *In the Navy* 1941; *Private Buckaroo* 1942

Andrews, Naveen (1969–) *Wild West* 1992; *The English Patient* 1996; *Kama Sutra: a Tale of Love* 1996; *Bombay Boys* 1998; *Mighty Joe Young* 1998; *Rollerball* 2001; *Bride & Prejudice* 2004

Andrews, Patty aka **Andrews Sisters, The** (1920–) *Argentine Nights* 1940; *Buck Privates* 1941; *In the Navy* 1941; *Private Buckaroo* 1942

Andrews, Russell *The In-Laws* 2003; *The Punisher* 2004

Andrews, Shawn *Dazed and Confused* 1993; *City of Ghosts* 2002

Andrews, Stanley (1891–1969) *Forbidden Valley* 1938; *Shine On, Harvest Moon* 1938; *Strange Alibi* 1941

Andrews, Tod aka **Ames, Michael** (1914–1972) *Voodoo Man* 1944; *Outrage* 1950; *From Hell It Came* 1957

Anémone (1950–) *Death in a French Garden* 1985; *Le Grand Chemin* 1987; *Le Petit Prince A Dit* 1992; *Lautrec* 1998

Angarano, Michael (1987–) *The Brainiacs.com* 2000; *Dear Wendy* 2005; *Lords of Dogtown* 2005

Angarita, Gustavo *Time to Die* 1985; *The Snail's Strategy* 1993

Angarola, Richard *Gambit* 1966; *Three the Hard Way* 1974

Angel, Heather (1909–1986) *Berkeley Square* 1933; *Pilgrimage* 1933; *The Informer* 1935; *The Mystery of Edwin Drood* 1935; *The Perfect Gentleman* 1935; *The Three Musketeers* 1935; *The Last of the Mohicans* 1936; *Bulldog Drummond Escapes* 1937; *Bulldog Drummond in Africa* 1938; *Bulldog Drummond's Bride* 1939; *Pride and Prejudice* 1940; *Shadows on the Stairs* 1941; *The Undying Monster* 1942; *Lifeboat* 1944; *The Saxon Charm* 1948; *Peter Pan* 1953; *The Premature Burial* 1962

Angel, Mikel *The Hard Ride* 1971; *Evil Spirits* 1991

Angel, Vanessa (1963–) *Kingpin* 1996; *Kissing a Fool* 1998; *Made Men* 1999; *G-Men from Hell* 2000; *Partners* 2000

Angeli, Pier (1932–1971) *The Light Touch* 1951; *Teresa* 1951; *The Devil Makes Three* 1952; *Sombrero* 1952; *The Story of Three Loves* 1953; *The Silver Chalice* 1954; *Somebody Up There Likes Me* 1956; *Merry Andrew* 1958; *SOS Pacific* 1959; *The Angry Silence* 1960; *Sodom and Gomorrah* 1962; *Shadow of Evil* 1964; *Battle of the Bulge* 1965; *Spy in Your Eye* 1965

Angelis, Michael *A Nightingale Sang in Berkeley Square* 1979; *No Surrender* 1986

Angelis, Paul *Yellow Submarine* 1968; *Hussy* 1979

Angelou, Maya (1928–) *Poetic Justice* 1993; *How to Make an American Quilt* 1995

Angelus, Muriel (1909–2004) *Hindle Wakes* 1931; *The Light That Failed* 1939; *The Great McGinty* 1940

Anger, Kenneth (1927–) *A Midsummer Night's Dream* 1935; *Fireworks* 1947; *Invocation of My Demon Brother* 1969; *Lucifer Rising* 1981

Angers, Avril (1922–) *The Brass Monkey* 1948; *The Green Man* 1956; *Women without Men* 1956; *Be My Guest* 1965; *The Family Way* 1966; *Three Bites of the Apple* 1967; *Two a Penny* 1968

Anglade, Jean-Hugues (1955–) *Subway* 1985; *Betty Blue* 1986; *Nikita* 1990; *Killing Zoe* 1993; *La Reine Margot* 1994; *Nelly & Monsieur Arnaud* 1995; *Maximum Risk* 1996; *En Face* 1999; *The Best Day of My Life* 2002; *Taking Lives* 2004

Anglim, Philip (1953–) *Testament* 1983; *Haunted Summer* 1988; *The Man Inside* 1990; *Milena* 1990

Angulo, Alex (1953–) *Acción Mutante* 1993; *The Day of the Beast* 1995; *Dying of Laughter* 1999

Anholt, Christien (1971–) *Reunion* 1989; *One against the Wind* 1991; *Preaching to the Perverted* 1997

Aniston, Jennifer (1969–) *Leprechaun* 1992; *Dream for an Insomniac* 1996; *She's the One* 1996; *Picture Perfect* 1997; *'Til There Was You* 1997; *The Object of My Affection* 1998; *The Iron Giant* 1999; *Office Space* 1999; *The Good Girl* 2001; *Rock Star* 2001; *Bruce Almighty* 2003; *Along Came Polly* 2004

Anka, Paul (1941–) *Girls' Town* 1959; *The Private Lives of Adam and Eve* 1959; *Look in Any Window* 1961; *The Longest Day* 1962; *Ordinary Magic* 1993

Ankers, Evelyn (1918–1985) *Hold That Ghost* 1941; *The Wolf Man* 1941; *The Ghost of Frankenstein* 1942; *Sherlock Holmes and the Voice of Terror* 1942; *Hers to Hold* 1943; *Son of Dracula* 1943; *The Frozen Ghost* 1944; *The Invisible Man's Revenge* 1944; *The Pearl of Death* 1944; *Weird Woman* 1944; *Black Beauty* 1946; *Tarzan's Magic Fountain* 1949

Ankri, Etti *Witness in the War Zone* 1986; *Burning Memory* 1988

Ankrum, Morris (1896–1964) *Buck Benny Rides Again* 1940; *Cherokee Strip* 1940; *Desire Me* 1947; *Lady in the Lake* 1947; *Colorado Territory* 1949; *In a Lonely Place* 1950; *The Redhead and the Cowboy* 1950; *Along the Great Divide* 1951; *Son of Ali Baba* 1952; *The Moonlighter* 1953; *Apache* 1954; *Cattle Queen of Montana* 1954; *Southwest Passage* 1954; *Taza, Son of Cochise* 1954; *Vera Cruz* 1954; *Tennessee's Partner* 1955; *Earth vs the Flying Saucers* 1956; *Beginning of the End* 1957; *Drango* 1957; *Kronos* 1957; *The Saga of Hemp Brown* 1958

Ann-Margret (1941–) *Pocketful of Miracles* 1961; *State Fair* 1962; *Bye Bye Birdie* 1963; *Kitten with a Whip* 1964; *The Pleasure Seekers* 1964; *Viva Las Vegas* 1964; *Bus Riley's Back in Town* 1965; *The Cincinnati Kid* 1965; *Once a Thief* 1965; *Made in Paris* 1966; *Murderers' Row* 1966; *Stagecoach* 1966; *The Swinger* 1966; *The Tiger and the Pussycat* 1967; *RPM – Revolutions per Minute* 1970; *Carnal Knowledge* 1971; *The Outside Man* 1973; *The Train Robbers* 1973; *Tommy* 1975; *The Twist* 1976; *Joseph Andrews* 1977; *The Last Remake of Beau Geste* 1977; *The Cheap Detective* 1978; *Magic* 1978; *Cactus Jack* 1979; *Middle Age Crazy* 1980; *I Ought to Be in Pictures* 1982; *Lookin' to Get Out* 1982; *The Return of the Soldier* 1982; *Twice in a Lifetime* 1985; *52 Pick-Up* 1986; *A Tiger's Tale* 1987; *A New Life* 1988; *The News Boys* 1992; *Grumpy Old Men* 1993; *Grumpier Old Men* 1996; *Any Given Sunday* 1999; *Happy Face Murders* 1999; *The Last Producer* 2000; *Taxi* 2004

Annabella (1909–1996) *Le Million* 1931; *Caravan* 1934; *Dinner at the Ritz* 1937; *Under the Red Robe* 1937; *Wings of the Morning* 1937; *The Baroness and the Butler* 1938; *Hôtel du Nord* 1938; *Suez* 1938; *Bomber's Moon* 1943; *13 Rue Madeleine* 1946

Annis, Francesca (1944–) *The Cat Gang* 1959; *No Kidding* 1960; *Crooks in Cloisters* 1963; *Saturday Night Out* 1963; *Flipper's New Adventure* 1964; *Murder Most Foul* 1964; *The Pleasure Girls* 1965; *The Walking Stick* 1970; *Macbeth* 1971; *Penny Gold* 1973; *Krull* 1983; *Dune* 1984; *Under the Cherry Moon* 1986; *The Debt Collector* 1999; *Milk* 1999; *Onegin* 1999

Ansara, Michael (1922–) *Soldiers Three* 1951; *The Diamond Queen* 1953; *Serpent of the Nile* 1953; *Bengal Brigade* 1954; *Princess of the Nile* 1954; *Abbott and Costello Meet the Mummy* 1955; *The Lone Ranger* 1956; *Last of the Badmen* 1957; *The Tall Stranger* 1957; *The Comancheros* 1961; *Voyage to the Bottom of the Sea* 1961; *Quick, Let's Get Married* 1964; *Harum Scarum* 1965; *And Now Miguel* 1966; *How I Spent My Summer Vacation* 1967; *Daring Game* 1968; *The Destructors* 1968; *The Pink Jungle* 1968; *Sol Madrid* 1968; *The Bears and I* 1974; *The Message* 1976; *Day of the Animals* 1977; *The Manitou* 1978; *Assassination* 1986; *Border Shootout* 1990

Anspach, Susan (1939–) *Five Easy Pieces* 1970; *Play It Again, Sam* 1972; *Blume in Love* 1973; *The Big Fix* 1978; *Running* 1979; *The Devil and Max Devlin* 1981; *Montenegro* 1981; *Misunderstood* 1984; *Blue Monkey* 1987

Ant, Adam (1954–) *Jubilee* 1978; *Nomads* 1985; *Cold Steel* 1987; *Slam Dance* 1987; *World Gone Wild* 1988; *Trust Me* 1989; *Lover's Knot* 1995

Anthony, Lysette (1963–) *Krull* 1983; *The Emperor's New Clothes* 1987; *Without a Clue* 1988; *A Ghost in Monte Carlo* 1990; *The Pleasure Principle* 1991; *Switch* 1991; *Husbands and Wives* 1992; *The Hour of the Pig* 1993; *Look Who's Talking Now!* 1993; *Dr Jekyll and Ms Hyde* 1995; *Dracula: Dead and Loving It* 1995; *Talos the Mummy* 1997; *The Evil beneath Loch Ness* 2001

Anthony, Marc (1969–) *Big Night* 1996; *The Substitute* 1996; *Bringing out the Dead* 1999; *Man on Fire* 2004

Anthony, Ray (1922–) *The Beat Generation* 1959; *The Big Operator* 1959; *Girls' Town* 1959

Antin, Steve (1956–) *The Accused* 1988; *Without You I'm Nothing* 1990

Antonelli, Laura (1941–) *Dr Goldfoot and the Girl Bombs* 1966; *Sink or Swim* 1971; *Without Apparent Motive* 1972; *L'Innocente* 1976; *Tigers in Lipstick* 1979

Antonio, Lou (1934–) *America, America* 1963; *Cool Hand Luke* 1967

Antonov, Aleksander aka **Antonov, Aleksandr** (1898–1962) *Strike* 1924; *The Battleship Potemkin* 1925

Antonutti, Omero (1935–) *Padre Padrone* 1977; *The Night of San Lorenzo* 1981; *El Sur* 1983; *Kaos* 1984; *Good Morning, Babylon* 1987; *El Dorado* 1988

Antony, Scott (1950–) *Savage Messiah* 1972; *The Mutations* 1973; *Dead Cert* 1974

Antrim, Harry *Let's Live a Little* 1948; *Act of Violence* 1949; *Ma and Pa Kettle* 1949; *The Bounty Hunter* 1954; *Teacher's Pet* 1958

Anwar, Gabrielle (1969–) *Teen Agent* 1991; *Wild Hearts Can't Be Broken* 1991; *Scent of a Woman* 1992; *Body Snatchers* 1993; *For Love or Money* 1993; *The Three Musketeers* 1993; *Innocent Lies* 1995; *Things to Do in Denver When You're Dead* 1995; *The Guilty* 2000; *Without Malice* 2000

Anys, Georgette (1909–1993) *Little Boy Lost* 1953; *La Traversée de Paris* 1956; *Bon Voyage!* 1962

Anzilotti, Perry *Crossworlds* 1996; *Air Bud: Golden Receiver* 1998

Aparicio, Rafaela (1906–1996) *Mamá Cumple 100 Años* 1979; *El Sur* 1983; *Padre Nuestro* 1985

Apfel, Oscar (1878–1938) *The Texan* 1930; *Inspiration* 1931; *The Bowery* 1933

Appel, Anna (1888–1963) *Symphony of Six Million* 1932; *Green Fields* 1937

Appel, Peter *Leon* 1994; *Six Ways to Sunday* 1997; *Tadpole* 2002

Appleby, Shiri (1978–) *Swimfan* 2002; *Undertow* 2004

Applegate, Christina (1971–) *Streets* 1990; *Don't Tell Mom the Babysitter's Dead* 1991; *Wild Bill* 1995; *The Big Hit* 1998; *Jane Austen's Mafia* 1998; *The Brutal Truth* 1999; *Just Visiting* 2001; *The Sweetest Thing* 2002; *Grand Theft Parsons* 2003; *View from the Top* 2003; *Wonderland* 2003; *Anchorman: the Legend of Ron Burgundy* 2004; *Surviving Christmas* 2004

Aquino, Amy *Alan & Naomi* 1992; *Danielle Steel's Once in a Lifetime* 1994; *Boys on the Side* 1995

Aragón, Angélica *A Walk in the Clouds* 1995; *El Crimen del Padre Amaro* 2002

Arahanga, Julian *Once Were Warriors* 1994; *Broken English* 1996; *What Becomes of the Broken Hearted?* 1999

Arana, Tomas aka **Arana, Thomas** (1959–) *The Church* 1988; *The Sect* 1991; *The Bodyguard* 1992

Aranda, Angel (1934–) *The Colossus of Rhodes* 1961; *Planet of the Vampires* 1965

Arashi, Kanjuro *The Profound Desire of the Gods* 1968; *Zatoichi Meets Yojimbo* 1970

Arata (1974–) *After Life* 1998; *Distance* 2001; *Ping Pong* 2002

Aratama, Michiyo (1930–) *Conflagration* 1958; *The Human Condition* 1958; *The End of Summer* 1961; *Kwaidan* 1964

Arau, Alfonso (1932–) *Scandalous John* 1971; *Romancing the Stone* 1984; *Stones for Ibarra* 1988; *Committed* 2000

Arbuckle, Roscoe "Fatty" aka **Arbuckle, Roscoe** (1887–1933) *The Butcher Boy* 1917; *Hollywood* 1923; *Go West* 1925

Arbus, Allan (1918–) *The Christian Licorice Store* 1971; *Greaser's Palace* 1972; *Coffy* 1973; *The Electric Horseman* 1979; *The Last Married Couple in America* 1980

Arcand, Denys (1941–) *Jesus of Montreal* 1989; *Léolo* 1992

Arcand, Gabriel (1949–) *Agnes of God* 1985; *The Decline of the American Empire* 1986; *The Revolving Doors* 1988; *Post Mortem* 1999

Archard, Bernard (1916–) *The List of Adrian Messenger* 1963; *Play Dirty* 1969; *The Horror of Frankenstein* 1970; *Dad's Army* 1971

Archer, Anne (1947–) *The Honkers* 1971; *Cancel My Reservation* 1972; *The All-American Boy* 1973; *The Blue Knight* 1973; *Lifeguard* 1976; *Trackdown* 1976; *Good Guys Wear Black* 1977; *Paradise Alley* 1978; *Hero at Large* 1980; *Raise the Titanic* 1980; *Green Ice* 1981; *Too Scared to Scream* 1982; *The Naked Face* 1984; *The Check Is in the Mail* 1986; *Fatal Attraction* 1987; *Love at Large* 1990; *Narrow Margin* 1990; *Eminent Domain* 1991; *Family Prayers* 1991; *Body of Evidence* 1992; *Patriot Games* 1992; *Short Cuts* 1993; *Clear and Present Danger* 1994; *Mojave Moon* 1996; *Nico the Unicorn* 1998; *The Art of War* 2000; *Rules of Engagement* 2000; *Whispers: an Elephant's Tale* 2000; *Man of the House* 2005

Archer, Barbara *The Feminine Touch* 1956; *Stranger's Meeting* 1957

Archer, John (1915–1999) *Sherlock Holmes in Washington* 1943; *The Lost Moment* 1947; *Colorado Territory* 1949; *White Heat* 1949; *Destination Moon* 1950; *The Great Jewel Robber* 1950; *High Lonesome* 1950; *Best of the Badmen* 1951; *My Favorite Spy* 1951; *Santa Fe* 1951; *The Big Trees* 1952; *Rock around the Clock* 1956; *Decision at Sundown* 1957; *City of Fear* 1959; *Blue Hawaii* 1961; *Apache Rifles* 1964

Archer, Karen *Giro City* 1982; *Forever Young* 1984

Archibald, Stephen *My Childhood* 1972; *My Ain Folk* 1973; *My Way Home* 1978

Ardant, Fanny (1949–) *Les Chiens* 1978; *The Woman Next Door* 1981; *Confidentially Yours* 1983; *Life Is a Bed of Roses* 1983; *Swann in Love* 1984; *Mélo* 1986; *Le Paltoquet* 1986; *The Family* 1987; *Three Sisters* 1988; *Australia* 1989; *Afraid of the Dark* 1991; *Le Colonel Chabert* 1994; *Beyond the Clouds* 1995; *Ridicule* 1996; *Elizabeth* 1998; *Le Libertin* 2000; *8 Women* 2001; *Callas Forever* 2002; *Nathalie...* 2003

Arden, Eve (1908–1990) *Stage Door* 1937; *Having Wonderful Time* 1938; *Letter of Introduction* 1938; *At the Circus* 1939; *Eternally Yours* 1939; *Comrade X* 1940; *No, No, Nanette* 1940; *Manpower* 1941; *That Uncertain Feeling* 1941; *Whistling in the Dark* 1941; *Ziegfeld Girl* 1941; *Bedtime Story* 1942; *Change of Heart* 1943; *Let's Face It* 1943; *Cover Girl* 1944; *The Doughgirls* 1944; *Patrick the Great* 1944; *Earl Carroll Vanities* 1945; *Mildred Pierce* 1945; *Pan-Americana* 1945; *The Kid from Brooklyn* 1946; *My Reputation* 1946; *Night and Day* 1946; *The Arnelo Affair* 1947; *Song of Scheherazade* 1947; *The Unfaithful* 1947; *Voice of the Turtle* 1947; *One Touch of Venus* 1948; *My Dream Is Yours* 1949; *Paid in Full* 1950; *Tea for Two* 1950; *Goodbye, My Fancy* 1951; *We're Not Married* 1952; *The Lady Wants Mink* 1953; *Anatomy of a Murder* 1959; *The Dark at the Top of the Stairs* 1960; *The Strongest Man in the World* 1975; *Under the Rainbow* 1981; *Grease 2* 1982; *Pandemonium* 1982

Arden, Robert (1922–) *Confidential Report* 1955; *Joe Macbeth* 1955; *Omen III: the Final Conflict* 1980

Arditi, Pierre (1944–) *Mélo* 1986; *Smoking/No Smoking* 1993; *Men, Women: a User's Manual* 1996; *On Connaît la Chanson* 1997; *Chance or Coincidence* 1999; *Pas sur la Bouche* 2003

Arena, Maurizio (1933–1979) *Le Bambole* 1965; *The Corrupt Ones* 1966

Arenas, Reynaldo aka **Arenas, Reinaldo** *Hour of the Assassin* 1987; *Sniper* 1992

Arenberg, Lee (1962–) *Cross My Heart* 1987; *Dungeons & Dragons* 2000

Arestrup, Niels (1949–) *Je, Tu, Il, Elle* 1974; *Second Chance* 1976; *Meeting Venus* 1990

Argento, Asia (1975–) *The Church* 1988; *Trauma* 1993; *Il Cielo è Sempre Più Blu* 1995; *B Monkey* 1996; *The Stendhal Syndrome* 1996; *New Rose Hotel* 1998; *The Phantom of the Opera* 1998; *xXx* 2002; *The Heart Is Deceitful above All Things* 2004; *Last Days* 2005

Argenziano, Carmen (1943–) *Punishment Park* 1971; *The Hot Box* 1972; *The Accused* 1988; *Stand and Deliver* 1988; *Red Scorpion* 1989; *Unlawful Entry* 1992; *Final Combination* 1993; *The Burning Season* 1994; *Identity* 2003

Argo, Victor aka **Argo, Vic** (1934–2004) *Boxcar Bertha* 1972; *Mean Streets* 1973; *King*

of New York 1989; *McBain* 1991; *Bad Lieutenant* 1992; *Dangerous Game* 1993; *Household Saints* 1993; *Next Stop Wonderland* 1998; *Angel Eyes* 2001
Argue, David (1959–) *Gallipoli* 1981; *BMX Bandits* 1983; *Backlash* 1986; *Hercules Returns* 1993; *Angel Baby* 1995
Arias, Imanol (1956–) *Labyrinth of Passion* 1982; *Camila* 1984; *The Flower of My Secret* 1995
Arima, Ineko (1932–) *Tokyo Twilight* 1957; *Equinox Flower* 1958; *The Human Condition* 1958
Arizmendi, Yareli *Like Water for Chocolate* 1993; *The Big Green* 1995
Arkin, Adam (1956–) *Chu Chu and the Philly Flash* 1981; *Full Moon High* 1982; *Personal Foul* 1987; *The Doctor* 1991; *Halloween H20: 20 Years Later* 1998; *Thirst* 1998; *A Slight Case of Murder* 1999; *Hanging Up* 2000; *Hitch* 2005
Arkin, Alan (1934–) *The Russians Are Coming, the Russians Are Coming* 1966; *Wait until Dark* 1967; *Woman Times Seven* 1967; *The Heart Is a Lonely Hunter* 1968; *Inspector Clouseau* 1968; *Popi* 1969; *Catch-22* 1970; *Little Murders* 1971; *Deadhead Miles* 1972; *The Last of the Red Hot Lovers* 1972; *Freebie and the Bean* 1974; *Rafferty and the Gold Dust Twins* 1974; *Hearts of the West* 1975; *The Seven-Per-Cent Solution* 1976; *Fire Sale* 1977; *The In-Laws* 1979; *The Magician of Lublin* 1979; *The Last Unicorn* 1980; *Simon* 1980; *Chu Chu and the Philly Flash* 1981; *Improper Channels* 1981; *The Return of Captain Invincible* 1983; *Bad Medicine* 1985; *Big Trouble* 1985; *Joshua Then and Now* 1985; *Escape from Sobibor* 1987; *Coupe de Ville* 1990; *Edward Scissorhands* 1990; *Havana* 1990; *Rocketeer* 1991; *Glengarry Glen Ross* 1992; *Cooperstown* 1993; *Indian Summer* 1993; *North* 1994; *The Jerky Boys* 1995; *Steal Big, Steal Little* 1995; *Mother Night* 1996; *Four Days in September* 1997; *Gattaca* 1997; *Grosse Pointe Blank* 1997; *Slums of Beverly Hills* 1998; *Jakob the Liar* 1999; *Varian's War* 2000; *America's Sweethearts* 2001; *13 Conversations about One Thing* 2001
Arkin, David (1941–1990) *I Love You, Alice B Toklas* 1968; *Up in the Cellar* 1970; *The Long Goodbye* 1973; *Nashville* 1975
Arledge, John (1906–1947) *Daddy Long Legs* 1931; *Flirtation Walk* 1934; *Murder on a Bridle Path* 1936; *You Can't Cheat an Honest Man* 1939
Arlen, Richard (1898–1976) *Wings* 1927; *Beggars of Life* 1928; *The Four Feathers* 1929; *Thunderbolt* 1929; *The Virginian* 1929; *Gun Smoke* 1931; *Island of Lost Souls* 1932; *Tiger Shark* 1932; *Alice in Wonderland* 1933; *Let 'Em Have It* 1935; *Artists and Models* 1937; *The Great Barrier* 1937; *The Lady and the Monster* 1944; *When My Baby Smiles at Me* 1948; *The Mountain* 1956; *Warlock* 1959; *The Last Time I Saw Archie* 1961; *Apache Uprising* 1965; *Black Spurs* 1965; *The Bounty Killer* 1965
Arletty (1898–1992) *Hôtel du Nord* 1938; *Le Jour Se Lève* 1939; *Les Visiteurs du Soir* 1942; *Les Enfants du Paradis* 1945; *No Exit* 1954
Arliss, Florence (1871–1950) *Disraeli* 1929; *The King's Vacation* 1933
Arliss, George (1868–1946) *Disraeli* 1929; *The Green Goddess* 1930; *The Man Who Played God* 1932; *A Successful Calamity* 1932; *The King's Vacation* 1933; *The House of Rothschild* 1934; *The Last Gentleman* 1934; *Cardinal Richelieu* 1935; *The Tunnel* 1935; *His Lordship* 1936; *Dr Syn* 1937
Armendáriz, Pedro (1912–1963) *Portrait of Maria* 1943; *The Fugitive* 1947; *Fort Apache* 1948; *Three Godfathers* 1948; *Tulsa* 1949; *We Were Strangers* 1949; *El Bruto* 1952; *Border River* 1954; *Diane* 1955; *The Conqueror* 1956; *Manuela* 1957; *The Wonderful Country* 1959; *Francis of Assisi* 1961; *Captain Sindbad* 1963; *From Russia with Love* 1963
Armendáriz Jr, Pedro *aka* **Armendáriz, Pedro** (1930–) *Macho Callahan* 1970; *The Magnificent Seven Ride!* 1972; *The Deadly Trackers* 1973; *Chosen Survivors* 1974; *Survival Run* 1979; *Agatha Christie's Murder in Three Acts* 1986; *Old Gringo* 1989; *Highway Patrolman* 1991; *El Crimen del Padre Amaro* 2002
Armetta, Henry (1888–1945) *The Unholy Garden* 1931; *A Farewell to Arms* 1932; *Bogus Bandits* 1933; *What – No Beer?* 1933; *The Black Cat* 1934; *Magnificent Obsession* 1935; *Princess O'Hara* 1935; *Dust Be My Destiny* 1939
Armstrong, Alun (1946–) *Get Carter* 1971; *Krull* 1983; *That Summer of White Roses* 1989; *White Hunter, Black Heart* 1990; *American Friends* 1991; *London Kills Me* 1991; *Split Second* 1991; *Blue Ice* 1992; *An Awfully Big Adventure* 1994; *Black Beauty* 1994; *The Saint* 1997; *Onegin* 1999; *With or without You* 1999; *Harrison's Flowers* 2000; *Strictly Sinatra* 2000; *It's All about Love* 2002; *Millions* 2004; *Van Helsing* 2004
Armstrong, Bess (1953–) *The Four Seasons* 1981; *Jekyll and Hyde… Together Again* 1982; *High Road to China* 1983; *Jaws III* 1983; *Nothing in Common* 1986; *Second Sight* 1989; *Dream Lover* 1993; *The Skateboard Kid* 1993; *The Lies Boys Tell* 1994; *Danielle Steel's Mixed Blessings* 1995; *Stolen Innocence* 1995; *Forgotten Sins* 1996; *Freshman Fall* 1996; *That Darn Cat* 1997; *Pecker* 1998; *Her Best Friend's Husband* 2002
Armstrong, Bridget *The Amorous Prawn* 1962; *For the Love of Benji* 1977
Armstrong, Curtis (1953–) *Risky Business* 1983; *Revenge of the Nerds* 1984; *Bad Medicine* 1985; *The Clan of the Cave Bear* 1986; *One Crazy Summer* 1986; *Big Bully* 1996
Armstrong, Kerry (1958–) *The Getting of Wisdom* 1977; *Hunting* 1992; *Lantana* 2001
Armstrong, Louis (1900–1971) *Pennies from Heaven* 1936; *Artists and Models* 1937; *Every Day's a Holiday* 1937; *Going Places* 1938; *Cabin in the Sky* 1943; *Atlantic City* 1944; *Here Comes the Groom* 1951; *Glory Alley* 1952; *High Society* 1956; *The Beat Generation* 1959; *The Five Pennies* 1959; *Paris Blues* 1961; *A Man Called Adam* 1966; *Hello, Dolly!* 1969
Armstrong, R G (1917–) *From Hell to Texas* 1958; *No Name on the Bullet* 1959; *Ten Who Dared* 1960; *Ride the High Country* 1962; *He Rides Tall* 1964; *El Dorado* 1967; *Eighty Steps to Jonah* 1969; *The Great White Hope* 1970; *JW Coop* 1971; *The Great Northfield Minnesota Raid* 1972; *My Name Is Nobody* 1973; *Running Wild* 1973; *White Lightning* 1973; *Race with the Devil* 1975; *Stay Hungry* 1976; *The Car* 1977; *Mr Billion* 1977; *The Pack* 1977; *Fast Charlie: the Moonbeam Rider* 1978; *Where the Buffalo Roam* 1980; *The Pursuit of DB Cooper* 1981; *Raggedy Man* 1981; *Hammett* 1982; *Children of the Corn* 1984; *Jocks* 1986; *Warlock: the Armageddon* 1993
Armstrong, Robert (1890–1973) *A Girl in Every Port* 1928; *Big News* 1929; *The Leatherneck* 1929; *Danger Lights* 1930; *The Iron Man* 1931; *The Lost Squadron* 1932; *The Most Dangerous Game* 1932; *The Penguin Pool Murder* 1932; *Blind Adventure* 1933; *King Kong* 1933; *Son of Kong* 1933; *Palooka* 1934; *"G" Men* 1935; *Remember Last Night?* 1935; *The Ex-Mrs Bradford* 1936; *Winter Carnival* 1939; *Dive Bomber* 1941; *Baby Face Morgan* 1942; *My Favorite Spy* 1942; *Action in Arabia* 1944; *Blood on the Sun* 1945; *Criminal Court* 1946; *The Paleface* 1948; *Return of the Bad Men* 1948; *The Lucky Stiff* 1949; *Mighty Joe Young* 1949
Armstrong, Todd (1939–1993) *Jason and the Argonauts* 1963; *King Rat* 1965; *Dead Heat on a Merry-Go-Round* 1966; *A Time for Killing* 1967
Arnall, Julia (1931–) *Lost* 1955; *House of Secrets* 1956; *The Man without a Body* 1957; *Mark of the Phoenix* 1957
Arnatt, John (1917–1999) *House of Blackmail* 1953; *Only Two Can Play* 1961; *The Third Alibi* 1961; *Shadow of Fear* 1963; *Licensed to Kill* 1965; *Where the Bullets Fly* 1966; *A Challenge for Robin Hood* 1967; *Crucible of Terror* 1971
Arnaud, Yvonne (1892–1958) *A Cuckoo in the Nest* 1933; *Neutral Port* 1940; *Tomorrow We Live* 1942; *The Ghosts of Berkeley Square* 1947; *Mon Oncle* 1958
Arnaz, Desi (1917–1986) *Too Many Girls* 1940; *The Navy Comes Through* 1942; *The Long, Long Trailer* 1954; *Forever, Darling* 1956; *The Escape Artist* 1982
Arnaz Jr, Desi (1953–) *Red Sky at Morning* 1971; *Billy Two Hats* 1973; *Marco* 1973; *Joyride* 1977; *A Wedding* 1978; *House of the Long Shadows* 1983
Arnaz, Lucie (1951–) *Billy Jack Goes to Washington* 1977; *The Jazz Singer* 1980; *Second Thoughts* 1982
Arndt, Adelheid *Chinese Boxes* 1984; *Rosa Luxemburg* 1986
Arndt, Denis *Distant Thunder* 1988; *Basic Instinct* 1992
Arne, Peter (1920–1983) *For Those in Peril* 1943; *The Cockleshell Heroes* 1955; *Timeslip* 1955; *The Moonraker* 1957; *Stranger's Meeting* 1957; *Intent to Kill* 1958; *Conspiracy of Hearts* 1960; *Sands of the Desert* 1960; *The Treasure of Monte Cristo* 1960; *The Hellfire Club* 1961; *Girl in the Headlines* 1963; *The Black Torment* 1964; *Battle beneath the Earth* 1968; *The Oblong Box* 1969; *The Return of the Pink Panther* 1974
Arness, James *aka* **Arness, Jim** (1923–) *Sierra* 1950; *Stars in My Crown* 1950; *Wagonmaster* 1950; *Wyoming Mail* 1950; *Cavalry Scout* 1951; *Iron Man* 1951; *The People against O'Hara* 1951; *The Thing from Another World* 1951; *Big Jim McLain* 1952; *Hellgate* 1952; *Horizons West* 1952; *Hondo* 1953; *Island in the Sky* 1953; *The Lone Hand* 1953; *Her Twelve Men* 1954; *Them!* 1954; *Many Rivers to Cross* 1955; *The Sea Chase* 1955; *The First Travelling Saleslady* 1956; *Alias Jesse James* 1959
Arnold, Edward (1890–1956) *The Barbarian* 1933; *I'm No Angel* 1933; *Jennie Gerhardt* 1933; *Roman Scandals* 1933; *The White Sister* 1933; *Sadie McKee* 1934; *Thirty-Day Princess* 1934; *Cardinal Richelieu* 1935; *Crime and Punishment* 1935; *The Glass Key* 1935; *Remember Last Night?* 1935; *Come and Get It* 1936; *Meet Nero Wolfe* 1936; *Easy Living* 1937; *The Toast of New York* 1937; *The Crowd Roars* 1938; *You Can't Take It with You* 1938; *Idiot's Delight* 1939; *Mr Smith Goes to Washington* 1939; *Slightly Honorable* 1939; *The Earl of Chicago* 1940; *Johnny Apollo* 1940; *Lillian Russell* 1940; *Daniel and the Devil* 1941; *Design for Scandal* 1941; *Johnny Eager* 1941; *Meet John Doe* 1941; *Nothing but the Truth* 1941; *The Penalty* 1941; *Unholy Partners* 1941; *Eyes in the Night* 1942; *The War against Mrs Hadley* 1942; *The Youngest Profession* 1943; *Kismet* 1944; *Mrs Parkington* 1944; *Standing Room Only* 1944; *The Hidden Eye* 1945; *Week-End at the Waldorf* 1945; *My Brother Talks to Horses* 1946; *Dear Ruth* 1947; *The Hucksters* 1947; *Command Decision* 1948; *Three Daring Daughters* 1948; *Big Jack* 1949; *Dear Wife* 1949; *Take Me Out to the Ball Game* 1949; *Annie Get Your Gun* 1950; *The Yellow Cab Man* 1950; *Belles on Their Toes* 1952; *City That Never Sleeps* 1953; *Living It Up* 1954; *The Ambassador's Daughter* 1956
Arnold, Henry (1961–) *Heimat 2* 1992; *Heimat 3: a Chronicle of Endings and Beginnings* 2004
Arnold, Keri (1987–) *The Darkest Light* 1999; *This Is Not a Love Song* 2002
Arnold, Marcelle (1917–) *The Bride Is Too Beautiful* 1956; *The Seven Deadly Sins* 1961
Arnold, Mark (1957–) *Teen Wolf* 1985; *Threesome* 1994
Arnold, Tom (1959–) *Accidental Hero* 1992; *Undercover Blues* 1993; *True Lies* 1994; *Nine Months* 1995; *The Stupids* 1995; *Big Bully* 1996; *Carpool* 1996; *Touch* 1996; *McHale's Navy* 1997; *Animal Factory* 2000; *Shriek If You Know What I Did Last Friday the 13th* 2000; *Exit Wounds* 2001; *Cradle 2 the Grave* 2003; *Soul Plane* 2004
Arnold, Victor (1936–) *Shaft* 1971; *The Seven-Ups* 1973; *The Protector* 1985
Arnoul, Françoise (1931–) *French Cancan* 1955; *The Little Theatre of Jean Renoir* 1969
Arnt, Charles (1908–1990) *Take a Letter, Darling* 1942; *Bride for Sale* 1949
Aronson, Judie *Friday the 13th: the Final Chapter* 1984; *American Ninja* 1985; *Weird Science* 1985
Arora, Amrita *Kitne Door… Kitne Paas* 2001; *Awara Paagal Deewana* 2002; *Ek Aur Ek Gyarah* 2003
Arquette, Alexis (1969–) *Death of a Schoolboy* 1990; *Terminal Bliss* 1990; *Jumpin' at the Boneyard* 1991; *Jack Be Nimble* 1992; *Of Mice and Men* 1992; *Grief* 1993; *Threesome* 1994; *Frank and Jesse* 1995; *Sometimes They Come Back… Again* 1996; *I Think I Do* 1997; *Bride of Chucky* 1998; *Love Kills* 1998; *The Wedding Singer* 1998; *Spun* 2002
Arquette, David (1971–) *Buffy the Vampire Slayer* 1992; *Killing Box* 1993; *Fall Time* 1994; *Roadflower* 1994; *Roadracers* 1994; *Johns* 1995; *Wild Bill* 1995; *Beautiful Girls* 1996; *Dream with the Fishes* 1996; *Scream* 1996; *The Alarmist* 1997; *Scream 2* 1997; *Free Money* 1998; *Never Been Kissed* 1999; *Ravenous* 1999; *The Runner* 1999; *Scream 3* 1999; *Ready to Rumble* 2000; *The Shrink Is In* 2000; *3000 Miles to Graceland* 2000; *Eight Legged Freaks* 2001; *See Spot Run* 2001; *It's a Very Merry Muppet Christmas Movie* 2002; *Never Die Alone* 2004; *The Adventures of Sharkboy and Lavagirl in 3-D* 2005
Arquette, Lewis (1935–2001) *Nobody's Fool* 1986; *The Linguini Incident* 1991; *Waiting for Guffman* 1996; *The Alarmist* 1997; *Almost Heroes* 1998
Arquette, Patricia (1968–) *A Nightmare on Elm Street 3: Dream Warriors* 1987; *Far North* 1988; *Prayer of the Rollerboys* 1990; *The Indian Runner* 1991; *Wildflower* 1991; *Ethan Frome* 1993; *Trouble Bound* 1993; *True Romance* 1993; *Ed Wood* 1994; *Holy Matrimony* 1994; *Beyond Rangoon* 1995; *Flirting with Disaster* 1996; *Infinity* 1996; *Lost Highway* 1996; *The Secret Agent* 1996; *Goodbye Lover* 1997; *Nightwatch* 1997; *The Hi-Lo Country* 1998; *Bringing out the Dead* 1999; *Stigmata* 1999; *Little Nicky* 2000; *Human Nature* 2001; *Holes* 2003
Arquette, Rosanna (1959–) *SOB* 1981; *Baby It's You* 1983; *The Parade* 1984; *After Hours* 1985; *The Aviator* 1985; *Desperately Seeking Susan* 1985; *Silverado* 1985; *8 Million Ways to Die* 1986; *Nobody's Fool* 1986; *Amazon Women on the Moon* 1987; *The Big Blue* 1988; *Promised a Miracle* 1988; *Black Rainbow* 1989; *New York Stories* 1989; *Almost* 1990; *Flight of the Intruder* 1991; *The Linguini Incident* 1991; *In the Deep Woods* 1992; *Nowhere to Run* 1992; *Pulp Fiction* 1994; *Search and Destroy* 1995; *Crash* 1996; *Gone Fishin'* 1997; *Liar* 1997; *Buffalo '66* 1998; *Hope Floats* 1998; *I'm Losing You* 1998; *Mistaken Identity* 1999; *Palmer's Pick-Up* 1999; *Sugar Town* 1999; *The Whole Nine Yards* 2000; *Diary of a Sex Addict* 2001; *Good Advice* 2001
Arredondo, Jeri *Spirit of the Eagle* 1991; *Silent Tongue* 1993; *Color of a Brisk and Leaping Day* 1996
Arrick, Rose *Mikey and Nicky* 1976; *Those Lips, Those Eyes* 1980
Arrighi, Nike (1946–) *The Devil Rides Out* 1968; *Day for Night* 1973
Artaud, Antonin (1896–1948) *Napoléon* 1927; *The Passion of Joan of Arc* 1928
Arthur, Beatrice (1923–) *Lovers and Other Strangers* 1970; *Mame* 1974; *For Better or Worse* 1995
Arthur, George K (1889–1985) *Hollywood* 1923; *The Salvation Hunters* 1925; *The Exquisite Sinner* 1926
Arthur, Jean (1905–1991) *Seven Chances* 1925; *The Canary Murder Case* 1929; *The Saturday Night Kid* 1929; *Danger Lights* 1930; *Paramount on Parade* 1930; *The Return of Dr Fu Manchu* 1930; *If You Could Only Cook* 1935; *Public Hero No 1* 1935; *The Whole Town's Talking* 1935; *The Ex-Mrs Bradford* 1936; *Mr Deeds Goes to Town* 1936; *The Plainsman* 1936; *Easy Living* 1937; *History Is Made at Night* 1937; *You Can't Take It with You* 1938; *Mr Smith Goes to Washington* 1939; *Only Angels Have Wings* 1939; *Arizona* 1940; *Too Many Husbands* 1940; *The Devil and Miss Jones* 1941; *The Talk of the Town* 1942; *A Lady Takes a Chance* 1943; *The More the Merrier* 1943; *A Foreign Affair* 1948; *Shane* 1953
Arthur, Johnny (1883–1951) *The Monster* 1925; *The Desert Song* 1929; *The Bride Comes Home* 1935; *Road to Singapore* 1940
Arthur, Maureen (1934–) *How to Succeed in Business without Really Trying* 1967; *Thunder Alley* 1967; *The Wicked Dreams of Paula Schultz* 1968; *How to Commit Marriage* 1969; *The Love God?* 1969
Arthur, Robert (1925–) *Mother Wore Tights* 1947; *Nora Prentiss* 1947; *Green Grass of Wyoming* 1948; *Yellow Sky* 1948; *Mother Is a Freshman* 1949; *Twelve O'Clock High* 1949; *September Affair* 1950; *Air Cadet* 1951; *Belles on Their Toes* 1952; *Just for You* 1952; *The Ring* 1952; *Hellcats of the Navy* 1957
Asano, Tadanobu (1973–) *Maborosi* 1995; *Gohatto* 1999; *Distance* 2001; *Ichi the Killer* 2001; *Cafe Lumiere* 2003; *Last Life in the Universe* 2003; *Zatoichi* 2003
Ascaride, Ariane (1954–) *Marius et Jeannette* 1997; *A la Place du Coeur* 1998; *A l'Attaque!* 2000; *Drôle de Félix* 2000; *La Ville Est Tranquille* 2000; *Ma Vraie Vie à Rouen* 2002; *A Common Thread* 2004
Asche, Oscar (1871–1936) *Don Quixote* 1932; *The Private Secretary* 1935; *Scrooge* 1935
Asensi, Neus (1965–) *The Girl of Your Dreams* 1998; *Arachnid* 2001
Ash, Leslie (1960–) *Quadrophenia* 1979; *The Curse of the Pink Panther* 1983; *Shadey* 1985
Ash, William (1977–) *Fanny & Elvis* 1999; *Mad about Mambo* 1999

Ashbourne, Lorraine *Distant Voices, Still Lives* 1988; *Fever Pitch* 1996; *The Martins* 2001

Ashbrook, Dana (1967–) *Return of the Living Dead Part II* 1988; *Waxwork* 1988

Ashbrook, Daphne (1966–) *Quiet Cool* 1986; *Automatic* 1994

Ashby, Linden (1960–) *Wyatt Earp* 1994; *Mortal Kombat* 1995; *Shelter* 1997; *Judgment Day* 1999; *Facing the Enemy* 2001

Ashcroft, Peggy (1907–1991) *The Wandering Jew* 1933; *The 39 Steps* 1935; *Rhodes of Africa* 1936; *Quiet Wedding* 1940; *The Nun's Story* 1959; *Tell Me Lies* 1967; *Secret Ceremony* 1968; *Three into Two Won't Go* 1969; *Sunday, Bloody Sunday* 1971; *The Pedestrian* 1974; *Joseph Andrews* 1977; *Hullabaloo over Georgie and Bonnie's Pictures* 1979; *A Passage to India* 1984; *When the Wind Blows* 1986; *Madame Sousatzka* 1988

Asher, Jane (1946–) *The Greengage Summer* 1961; *The Prince and the Pauper* 1962; *Girl in the Headlines* 1963; *The Masque of the Red Death* 1964; *Alfie* 1966; *The Winter's Tale* 1966; *The Buttercup Chain* 1970; *Deep End* 1970; *Henry VIII and His Six Wives* 1972; *Runners* 1983; *Dreamchild* 1985; *Paris by Night* 1988

Asherson, Renée *aka* **Ascherson, Renee** (1920–) *Henry V* 1944; *The Way Ahead* 1944; *The Way to the Stars* 1945; *Once a Jolly Swagman* 1948; *The Cure for Love* 1949; *The Small Back Room* 1949; *Pool of London* 1950; *The Magic Box* 1951; *Malta Story* 1953; *The Day the Earth Caught Fire* 1961; *The Smashing Bird I Used to Know* 1969; *Grey Owl* 1999; *The Others* 2001

Ashfield, Kate *The War Zone* 1999; *Christie Malry's Own Double-Entry* 2000; *The Low Down* 2000; *Late Night Shopping* 2001; *Pure* 2002; *Spivs* 2003; *Fakers* 2004; *Shaun of the Dead* 2004

Ashikawa, Makoto *Violent Cop* 1989; *Boiling Point* 1990

Ashley, Edward (1904–2000) *Bitter Sweet* 1940; *Sky Murder* 1940; *Come Live with Me* 1941; *The Black Swan* 1942; *Dick Tracy Meets Gruesome* 1947; *Tarzan and the Mermaids* 1948; *Macao* 1952

Ashley, Elizabeth (1939–) *The Carpetbaggers* 1964; *Ship of Fools* 1965; *The Third Day* 1965; *The Face of Fear* 1971; *The Marriage of a Young Stockbroker* 1971; *Paperback Hero* 1972; *Golden Needles* 1974; *92 in the Shade* 1975; *Rancho Deluxe* 1975; *The Great Scout & Cathouse Thursday* 1976; *Coma* 1977; *Paternity* 1981; *Split Image* 1982; *Vampire's Kiss* 1988; *Sleeping Together* 1997; *Happiness* 1998; *Just the Ticket* 1998

Ashley, John (1934–1997) *Dragstrip Girl* 1957; *Motorcycle Gang* 1957; *Suicide Battalion* 1958; *Beach Party* 1963; *Hud* 1963; *Bikini Beach* 1964; *Muscle Beach Party* 1964; *Beach Blanket Bingo* 1965; *Sergeant Deadhead* 1965; *Young Dillinger* 1965; *Twilight People* 1973

Ashton, Frederick (1904–1988) *The Tales of Hoffmann* 1951; *The Tales of Beatrix Potter* 1971

Ashton, John (1948–) *Beverly Hills Cop* 1984; *King Kong Lives* 1986; *Beverly Hills Cop II* 1987; *Some Kind of Wonderful* 1987; *Midnight Run* 1988; *I Want to Go Home* 1989; *Little Big League* 1994; *The Shooter* 1994; *Fast Money* 1995; *Meet the Deedles* 1998; *Instinct* 1999

Ashton, Joseph *The Education of Little Tree* 1997; *The Adventures of Slappy the Sea Lion* 1998

Ashton, Sylvia (1880–1940) *Why Change Your Wife?* 1920; *Greed* 1925; *The Barker* 1928

Ashton-Griffiths, Roger (1957–) *Haunted Honeymoon* 1986; *Seven Minutes* 1989; *Devil's Gate* 2002; *Gangs of New York* 2002

Askew, Luke (1937–) *The Green Berets* 1968; *Flareup* 1969; *The Culpepper Cattle Co* 1972; *The Great Northfield Minnesota Raid* 1972; *The Magnificent Seven Ride!* 1972; *Part 2 Walking Tall* 1975; *Posse* 1975; *Wanda Nevada* 1979; *The Warrior and the Sorceress* 1983; *Traveller* 1997; *Frailty* 2001

Askey, Arthur (1900–1982) *Band Waggon* 1939; *Charley's (Big Hearted) Aunt* 1940; *The Ghost Train* 1941; *I Thank You* 1941; *Back Room Boy* 1942; *King Arthur Was a Gentleman* 1942; *Bees in Paradise* 1943; *Miss London Ltd* 1943; *The Love Match* 1955; *Make Mine a Million* 1959; *Rosie Dixon: Night Nurse* 1978

Askin, Leon (1907–2005) *Desert Legion* 1953; *South Sea Woman* 1953; *Knock on Wood* 1954; *Valley of the Kings* 1954; *One, Two, Three* 1961; *Sherlock Holmes and the Deadly Necklace* 1962; *Do Not Disturb* 1965; *A Fine Pair* 1968; *The Wicked Dreams of Paula Schultz* 1968; *Frightmare* 1981

Askwith, Robin (1950–) *Bless This House* 1972; *Tower of Evil* 1972; *Horror Hospital* 1973; *Confessions of a Window Cleaner* 1974; *Confessions of a Pop Performer* 1975; *Confessions of a Driving Instructor* 1976; *Confessions from a Holiday Camp* 1977; *Let's Get Laid* 1977; *Stand Up Virgin Soldiers* 1977; *Britannia Hospital* 1982

Aslan, Grégoire (1908–1982) *The Adventurers* 1950; *Act of Love* 1953; *Joe Macbeth* 1955; *Celui Qui Doit Mourir* 1957; *The Roots of Heaven* 1958; *Sea Fury* 1958; *The Three Worlds of Gulliver* 1959; *The Criminal* 1960; *Killers of Kilimanjaro* 1960; *The Rebel* 1960; *Under Ten Flags* 1960; *The Devil at Four o'Clock* 1961; *Invasion Quartet* 1961; *King of Kings* 1961; *Village of Daughters* 1961; *The Happy Thieves* 1962; *Crooks in Cloisters* 1963; *Paris When It Sizzles* 1964; *The High Bright Sun* 1965; *Lost Command* 1966; *A Man Could Get Killed* 1966; *Moment to Moment* 1966; *Our Man in Marrakesh* 1966; *The 25th Hour* 1967; *A Flea in Her Ear* 1968; *Marry Me! Marry Me!* 1968; *You Can't Win 'em All* 1970; *The Golden Voyage of Sinbad* 1973; *The Girl from Petrovka* 1974; *The Return of the Pink Panther* 1974

Asner, Edward *aka* **Asner, Ed** (1929–) *The Murder Men* 1961; *The Satan Bug* 1965; *The Slender Thread* 1965; *The Doomsday Flight* 1966; *The Venetian Affair* 1966; *El Dorado* 1967; *Gunn* 1967; *Change of Habit* 1969; *Halls of Anger* 1970; *They Call Me Mister Tibbs!* 1970; *Skin Game* 1971; *The Todd Killings* 1971; *Gus* 1976; *Fort Apache, the Bronx* 1981; *O'Hara's Wife* 1982; *Daniel* 1983; *Happily Ever After* 1990; *JFK* 1991; *Gypsy* 1993; *A Christmas Carol* 1997; *Hard Rain* 1997; *Payback* 1997; *The Bachelor* 1999; *The Animal* 2001; *Elf* 2003

Asparagus, Fred (1947–1998) *Three Amigos!* 1986; *Just the Ticket* 1998

Assante, Armand (1949–) *Paradise Alley* 1978; *Prophecy* 1979; *Little Darlings* 1980; *Private Benjamin* 1980; *I, the Jury* 1982; *Love and Money* 1982; *Unfaithfully Yours* 1983; *Belizaire the Cajun* 1985; *The Penitent* 1988; *Animal Behavior* 1989; *Eternity* 1990; *Q & A* 1990; *Too Hot to Handle* 1991; *1492: Conquest of Paradise* 1992; *Hoffa* 1992; *The Mambo Kings* 1992; *Fatal Instinct* 1993; *Trial by Jury* 1994; *Judge Dredd* 1995; *Striptease* 1996; *The Odyssey* 1997; *The Hunley* 1999; *The Road to El Dorado* 2000; *After the Storm* 2001; *Federal Protection* 2002; *Citizen Verdict* 2003

Ast, Pat (1941–2001) *Heat* 1972; *The Duchess and the Dirtwater Fox* 1976; *Reform School Girls* 1986

Astaire, Fred (1899–1987) *Dancing Lady* 1933; *Flying down to Rio* 1933; *The Gay Divorce* 1934; *Roberta* 1935; *Top Hat* 1935; *Follow the Fleet* 1936; *Swing Time* 1936; *A Damsel in Distress* 1937; *Shall We Dance* 1937; *Carefree* 1938; *The Story of Vernon and Irene Castle* 1939; *Broadway Melody of 1940* 1940; *Second Chorus* 1940; *You'll Never Get Rich* 1941; *Holiday Inn* 1942; *You Were Never Lovelier* 1942; *The Sky's the Limit* 1943; *Ziegfeld Follies* 1944; *Yolanda and the Thief* 1945; *Blue Skies* 1946; *Easter Parade* 1948; *The Barkleys of Broadway* 1949; *Let's Dance* 1950; *Three Little Words* 1950; *Royal Wedding* 1951; *The Belle of New York* 1952; *The Band Wagon* 1953; *Daddy Long Legs* 1955; *Funny Face* 1957; *Silk Stockings* 1957; *On the Beach* 1959; *The Pleasure of His Company* 1961; *The Notorious Landlady* 1962; *Paris When It Sizzles* 1964; *Finian's Rainbow* 1968; *Midas Run* 1969; *The Towering Inferno* 1974; *The Amazing Dobermans* 1976; *That's Entertainment, Part II* 1976; *The Purple Taxi* 1977; *Ghost Story* 1981

Asther, Nils (1897–1981) *Laugh, Clown, Laugh* 1928; *Our Dancing Daughters* 1928; *The Single Standard* 1929; *Wild Orchids* 1929; *The Bitter Tea of General Yen* 1933; *If I Were Free* 1933; *By Candlelight* 1934; *Dr Kildare's Wedding Day* 1941; *Bluebeard* 1944

Asti, Adriana (1933–) *Accattone* 1961; *Before the Revolution* 1964; *Le Fantôme de la Liberté* 1974; *The Inheritance* 1976; *The Best of Youth* 2003

Astin, John (1930–) *That Touch of Mink* 1962; *The Wheeler Dealers* 1963; *Candy* 1968; *Viva Max!* 1969; *Evil Roy Slade* 1971; *Every Little Crook and Nanny* 1972; *Get to Know Your Rabbit* 1972; *Freaky Friday* 1976; *National Lampoon's European Vacation* 1985; *Return of the Killer Tomatoes* 1988; *Huck and the King of Hearts* 1993; *The Frighteners* 1996

Astin, MacKenzie (1973–) *The Garbage Pail Kids Movie* 1987; *Iron Will* 1994; *Dream for an Insomniac* 1996; *In Love and War* 1996; *The Last Days of Disco* 1998; *The Mating Habits of the Earthbound Human* 1999; *Stranger than Fiction* 1999

Astin, Sean (1971–) *The Goonies* 1985; *Like Father, like Son* 1987; *White Water Summer* 1987; *Staying Together* 1989; *The War of the Roses* 1989; *Memphis Belle* 1990; *Toy Soldiers* 1991; *California Man* 1992; *Where the Day Takes You* 1992; *Rudy* 1993; *Safe Passage* 1994; *The Low Life* 1995; *Bulworth* 1998; *Deterrence* 1999; *The Last Producer* 2000; *The Lord of the Rings: The Fellowship of the Ring* 2001; *The Lord of the Rings: The Two Towers* 2002; *The Lord of the Rings: The Return of the King* 2003; *50 First Dates* 2004

Astor, Gertrude (1887–1977) *Hollywood* 1923; *Stage Struck* 1925; *The Strong Man* 1926; *The Cat and the Canary* 1927

Astor, Mary (1906–1987) *Hollywood* 1923; *Don Q, Son of Zorro* 1925; *Don Juan* 1926; *Two Arabian Knights* 1927; *Holiday* 1930; *Other Men's Women* 1931; *The Sin Ship* 1931; *The Lost Squadron* 1932; *Red Dust* 1932; *A Successful Calamity* 1932; *Jennie Gerhardt* 1933; *The Kennel Murder Case* 1933; *The Little Giant* 1933; *The World Changes* 1933; *The Case of the Howling Dog* 1934; *Easy to Love* 1934; *Upper World* 1934; *Page Miss Glory* 1935; *And So They Were Married* 1936; *Dodsworth* 1936; *The Hurricane* 1937; *The Prisoner of Zenda* 1937; *Listen, Darling* 1938; *Paradise for Three* 1938; *There's Always a Woman* 1938; *Midnight* 1939; *Brigham Young* 1940; *Turnabout* 1940; *The Great Lie* 1941; *The Maltese Falcon* 1941; *Across the Pacific* 1942; *The Palm Beach Story* 1942; *Thousands Cheer* 1943; *Blonde Fever* 1944; *Meet Me in St Louis* 1944; *Claudia and David* 1946; *Cass Timberlane* 1947; *Cynthia* 1947; *Desert Fury* 1947; *Fiesta* 1947; *Act of Violence* 1949; *Any Number Can Play* 1949; *Little Women* 1949; *A Kiss before Dying* 1956; *The Power and the Prize* 1956; *The Devil's Hairpin* 1957; *This Happy Feeling* 1958; *A Stranger in My Arms* 1959; *Return to Peyton Place* 1961; *Hush... Hush, Sweet Charlotte* 1964; *Youngblood Hawke* 1964

Ates, Roscoe *aka* **Ates, Rosco** (1892–1962) *The Champ* 1931; *Freaks* 1932; *Alice in Wonderland* 1933; *What – No Beer?* 1933; *Three Texas Steers* 1939

Atherton, William (1947–) *Class of '44* 1973; *The Sugarland Express* 1974; *The Day of the Locust* 1975; *The Hindenburg* 1975; *Looking for Mr Goodbar* 1977; *Ghostbusters* 1984; *Real Genius* 1985; *No Mercy* 1986; *Die Hard* 1988; *Buried Alive* 1990; *Die Hard 2: Die Harder* 1990; *Grim Prairie Tales* 1990; *The Pelican Brief* 1993; *Formula for Death* 1995; *Frank and Jesse* 1995; *Bio-Dome* 1996; *Mad City* 1997; *Executive Power* 1998

Atkin, Harvey (1942–) *Meatballs* 1979; *Visiting Hours* 1982; *Love and Death on Long Island* 1998

Atkine, Feodor (1948–) *Love and Death* 1975; *Le Beau Mariage* 1982; *Pauline at the Beach* 1983; *Leave All Fair* 1985; *Lola* 1986; *Nazi Hunter: the Beate Klarsfeld Story* 1986; *Sarraouina* 1986; *El Dorado* 1988; *High Heels* 1991; *Three Lives and Only One Death* 1996

Atkins, Christopher (1961–) *The Blue Lagoon* 1980; *The Pirate Movie* 1982; *A Night in Heaven* 1983; *Listen to Me* 1989; *Die Watching* 1993; *The Little Unicorn* 1998

Atkins, Eileen (1934–) *Inadmissible Evidence* 1968; *I Don't Want to Be Born* 1975; *Equus* 1977; *Oliver Twist* 1982; *The Dresser* 1983; *Let Him Have It* 1991; *Wolf* 1994; *Jack & Sarah* 1995; *The Avengers* 1998; *Women Talking Dirty* 1999; *Gosford Park* 2001; *Wit* 2001; *What a Girl Wants* 2003; *Vanity Fair* 2004

Atkins, Tom (1935–) *Special Delivery* 1976; *The Fog* 1980; *Halloween III: Season of the Witch* 1982; *Lethal Weapon* 1987; *Maniac Cop* 1988

Atkinson, Frank (1893–1963) *Ladies' Man* 1931; *The Green Cockatoo* 1937

Atkinson, Jayne (1959–) *Free Willy* 1993; *Blank Check* 1994; *The Village* 2004

Atkinson, Kate *The Hard Word* 2002; *Japanese Story* 2003

Atkinson, Rowan (1955–) *The Tall Guy* 1989; *The Witches* 1989; *Hot Shots! Part Deux* 1993; *Four Weddings and a Funeral* 1994; *The Lion King* 1994; *Bean* 1997; *Maybe Baby* 1999; *Rat Race* 2001; *Scooby-Doo* 2002; *Johnny English* 2003; *Love Actually* 2003

Attal, Henri *Les Biches* 1968; *Juste avant la Nuit* 1971

Attal, Yvan (1965–) *A World without Pity* 1989; *Autobus* 1991; *Après l'Amour* 1992; *Patriots* 1994; *Portraits Chinois* 1996; *Love etc* 1997; *The Criminal* 1999; *With or without You* 1999; *Ma Femme Est une Actrice* 2001; *Bon Voyage* 2003; *The Interpreter* 2005

Attaway, Ruth (1910–1987) *Porgy and Bess* 1959; *Conrack* 1974; *Being There* 1979

Attenborough, Richard (1923–) *In Which We Serve* 1942; *Journey Together* 1944; *Dancing with Crime* 1946; *A Matter of Life and Death* 1946; *School for Secrets* 1946; *Brighton Rock* 1947; *The Man Within* 1947; *The Guinea Pig* 1948; *London Belongs to Me* 1948; *Boys in Brown* 1949; *The Lost People* 1949; *Morning Departure* 1950; *The Gift Horse* 1951; *The Magic Box* 1951; *Father's Doing Fine* 1952; *Eight O'Clock Walk* 1953; *The Ship That Died of Shame* 1955; *The Baby and the Battleship* 1956; *Brothers in Law* 1956; *Private's Progress* 1956; *The Scamp* 1957; *Danger Within* 1958; *Dunkirk* 1958; *The Man Upstairs* 1958; *Sea of Sand* 1958; *I'm All Right Jack* 1959; *Jet Storm* 1959; *SOS Pacific* 1959; *The Angry Silence* 1960; *The League of Gentlemen* 1960; *All Night Long* 1961; *Only Two Can Play* 1961; *Trial and Error* 1962; *The Great Escape* 1963; *Guns at Batasi* 1964; *Seance on a Wet Afternoon* 1964; *The Third Secret* 1964; *The Flight of the Phoenix* 1965; *The Sand Pebbles* 1966; *Doctor Dolittle* 1967; *The Bliss of Mrs Blossom* 1968; *Only When I Larf* 1968; *The Magic Christian* 1969; *The Last Grenade* 1970; *Loot* 1970; *A Severed Head* 1970; *10 Rillington Place* 1970; *And Then There Were None* 1974; *Brannigan* 1975; *Conduct Unbecoming* 1975; *Rosebud* 1975; *The Chess Players* 1977; *The Human Factor* 1979; *Jurassic Park* 1993; *Miracle on 34th Street* 1994; *Hamlet* 1996; *The Lost World: Jurassic Park* 1997; *Elizabeth* 1998; *Puckoon* 2002

Atterbury, Malcolm (1907–1992) *Crime in the Streets* 1956; *Blood of Dracula* 1957; *How to Make a Monster* 1958; *Cattle King* 1963; *The Learning Tree* 1969; *Emperor of the North* 1973

Atterton, Edward *Britannic* 2000; *Relative Values* 2000

Attwell, Michael *Buster* 1988; *Bodywork* 1999

Atwater, Barry (1918–1978) *The True Story of Lynn Stuart* 1957; *Pork Chop Hill* 1959

Atwill, Lionel (1885–1946) *Doctor X* 1932; *Murders in the Zoo* 1933; *Mystery of the Wax Museum* 1933; *The Secret of Madame Blanche* 1933; *The Song of Songs* 1933; *The Sphinx* 1933; *The Vampire Bat* 1933; *The Age of Innocence* 1934; *Nana* 1934; *One More River* 1934; *Stamboul Quest* 1934; *Captain Blood* 1935; *The Devil Is a Woman* 1935; *Mark of the Vampire* 1935; *Murder Man* 1935; *Rendezvous* 1935; *Till We Meet Again* 1936; *The Great Garrick* 1937; *Lancer Spy* 1937; *The Last Train from Madrid* 1937; *The Great Waltz* 1938; *Three Comrades* 1938; *Balalaika* 1939; *The Hound of the Baskervilles* 1939; *Mr Moto Takes a Vacation* 1939; *The Secret of Dr Kildare* 1939; *Son of Frankenstein* 1939; *The Three Musketeers* 1939; *Boom Town* 1940; *Johnny Apollo* 1940; *Man Made Monster* 1941; *The Ghost of Frankenstein* 1942; *The Mad Doctor of Market Street* 1942; *Pardon My Sarong* 1942; *Sherlock Holmes and the Secret Weapon* 1942; *To Be or Not to Be* 1942; *Frankenstein Meets the Wolf Man* 1943; *House of Frankenstein* 1944; *Fog Island* 1945; *House of Dracula* 1945

Atzmon, Anat (1958–) *Lemon Popsicle* 1978; *Every Time We Say Goodbye* 1986; *Double Edge* 1992

Atzorn, Robert (1945–) *From the Life of the Marionettes* 1980; *The Beautiful End of This World* 1983

Auberjonois, René (1940–) *Lilith* 1964; *Petulia* 1968; *MASH* 1969; *Brewster McCloud* 1970; *The Birdmen* 1971; *McCabe and Mrs Miller* 1971; *Images* 1972; *Pete 'n' Tillie* 1972; *The Big Bus* 1976; *King Kong* 1976; *Eyes of Laura Mars* 1978; *Where the Buffalo Roam* 1980; *3:15* 1986; *Walker* 1987; *Police Academy 5: Assignment Miami Beach* 1988; *The Feud* 1989; *The Little Mermaid* 1989; *Little Nemo: Adventures in Slumberland* 1992; *The Ballad of Little Jo* 1993; *Los Locos* 1997; *An American Tail: the Treasure of Manhattan Island* 1998; *Cats Don't Dance* 1998;

Geppetto 2000; *The Cat Returns* 2002
Aubert, Lenore (1913–1993) *They Got Me Covered* 1943; *Action in Arabia* 1944; *I Wonder Who's Kissing Her Now* 1947; *Abbott and Costello Meet Frankenstein* 1948; *Abbott and Costello Meet the Killer, Boris Karloff* 1949
Aubrey, Anne (1937–) *No Time to Die* 1958; *The Bandit of Zhobe* 1959; *Killers of Kilimanjaro* 1960; *Let's Get Married* 1960
Aubrey, James (1947–) *Lord of the Flies* 1963; *Terror* 1979; *Forever Young* 1984; *Riders of the Storm* 1986
Aubrey, Juliet (1969–) *Jacob* 1994; *Go Now* 1995; *Food of Love* 1997; *Still Crazy* 1998; *The Lost Lover* 1999; *Iris* 2001
Aubuchon, Jacques (1924–1991) *Gun Glory* 1957; *Short Cut to Hell* 1957; *The Way to the Gold* 1957; *Thunder Road* 1958; *Wild and Wonderful* 1964
Auclair, Michel aka **Auclair, Michael** (1922–1988) *La Belle et la Bête* 1946; *Funny Face* 1957; *Sink or Swim* 1971; *Story of a Love Story* 1973; *Three Men to Destroy* 1980
Audley, Eleanor (1905–1991) *Cinderella* 1950; *Sleeping Beauty* 1959
Audley, Maxine (1923–1992) *The Sleeping Tiger* 1954; *A King in New York* 1957; *Hell Is a City* 1959; *Peeping Tom* 1960; *The Trials of Oscar Wilde* 1960; *Petticoat Pirates* 1961; *The Brain* 1962; *A Jolly Bad Fellow* 1964; *The Battle of the Villa Fiorita* 1965; *House of Cards* 1968; *Sinful Davey* 1969
Audran, Stéphane (1932–) *The Sign of Leo* 1959; *Les Bonnes Femmes* 1960; *Bluebeard* 1962; *Paris Vu Par...* 1965; *The Champagne Murders* 1966; *Les Biches* 1968; *La Femme Infidèle* 1968; *Le Boucher* 1969; *The Lady in the Car with Glasses and a Gun* 1970; *La Rupture* 1970; *Juste avant la Nuit* 1971; *The Discreet Charm of the Bourgeoisie* 1972; *Without Apparent Motive* 1972; *Les Noces Rouges* 1973; *And Then There Were None* 1974; *Vincent, François, Paul and the Others* 1974; *The Black Bird* 1975; *The Twist* 1976; *Blood Relatives* 1977; *The Devil's Advocate* 1977; *Silver Bears* 1977; *To Kill a Rat* 1977; *Violette Nozière* 1977; *Eagle's Wing* 1978; *The Big Red One* 1980; *Clean Slate* 1981; *Le Choc* 1982; *Bay Boy* 1984; *The Blood of Others* 1984; *Cop au Vin* 1984; *La Cage aux Folles III: "Elles" Se Marient* 1985; *Babette's Feast* 1987; *Sons* 1989; *The Turn of the Screw* 1992; *Maximum Risk* 1996; *Madeline* 1998
Auer, Mischa (1905–1967) *Paramount on Parade* 1930; *Delicious* 1931; *Tarzan the Fearless* 1933; *Bulldog Drummond Strikes Back* 1934; *Stamboul Quest* 1934; *I Dream Too Much* 1935; *My Man Godfrey* 1936; *Winterset* 1936; *One Hundred Men and a Girl* 1937; *Pick a Star* 1937; *Three Smart Girls* 1937; *Vogues of 1938* 1937; *The Rage of Paris* 1938; *Sweethearts* 1938; *You Can't Take It with You* 1938; *Destry Rides Again* 1939; *East Side of Heaven* 1939; *Seven Sinners* 1940; *Trail of the Vigilantes* 1940; *The Flame of New Orleans* 1941; *Hellzapoppin'* 1941; *Twin Beds* 1942; *Lady in the Dark* 1944; *Up in Mabel's Room* 1944; *And Then There Were None* 1945; *Brewster's Millions* 1945; *A Royal Scandal* 1945; *Sentimental Journey* 1946; *Confidential Report* 1955; *The Monte Carlo Story* 1957; *We Joined the Navy* 1962; *Drop Dead Darling* 1966
Auger, Claudine (1942–) *Le Masque de Fer* 1962; *Yoyo* 1964; *That Man George* 1965; *Thunderball* 1965; *Triple Cross* 1966; *Bay of Blood* 1971; *Travels with Anita* 1978; *Secret Places* 1984; *Salt on Our Skin* 1992
August, Pernilla aka **Wallgren, Pernilla** (1958–) *Fanny and Alexander* 1982; *Best Intentions* 1992; *Jerusalem* 1996; *Private Confessions* 1996; *The Last Contract* 1998; *Star Wars Episode I: the Phantom Menace* 1999; *Star Wars Episode II: Attack of the Clones* 2002; *Daybreak* 2003
Ault, Marie (1870–1951) *The Lodger* 1926; *Hindle Wakes* 1927; *Kitty* 1928; *They Knew Mr Knight* 1945
Aumont, Jean-Pierre (1913–2001) *Drôle de Drame* 1937; *Hôtel du Nord* 1938; *The Cross of Lorraine* 1943; *Heartbeat* 1946; *Song of Scheherazade* 1947; *Siren of Atlantis* 1948; *The Gay Adventure* 1949; *Lili* 1953; *Royal Affairs in Versailles* 1953; *Charge of the Lancers* 1954; *Napoléon* 1955; *Hilda Crane* 1956; *The Devil at Four o'Clock* 1961; *Five Miles to Midnight* 1963; *Cauldron of Blood* 1967; *Castle Keep* 1969; *Day for Night* 1973; *The Happy Hooker* 1975; *Mahogany* 1975; *Something Short of Paradise* 1979; *The Blood of Others* 1984; *Becoming Colette* 1991; *Jefferson in Paris* 1995; *The Proprietor* 1996
Aumont, Michel (1936–) *Nada* 1974; *Pourquoi Pas!* 1977; *To Kill a Rat* 1977; *Les Compères* 1983; *Dangerous Moves* 1984; *Sunday in the Country* 1984; *Angel Dust* 1987; *Le Cop II* 1989; *A Shadow of Doubt* 1992; *The King of Paris* 1995; *Man Is a Woman* 1998
Aumont, Tina aka **Marquand, Tina** (1946–) *The Game Is Over* 1966; *Partner* 1968; *Lifespan* 1975; *Casanova* 1976; *Illustrious Corpses* 1976; *A Matter of Time* 1976
Aureli, Andrea (1923–) *Duel of Champions* 1961; *Tiger of the Seven Seas* 1962
Aussey, Germaine (1909–1979) *A Nous la Liberté* 1931; *The Golem* 1936
Austin, Albert (1881–1953) *Behind the Screen* 1916; *The Pawnshop* 1916; *The Cure* 1917; *The Immigrant* 1917
Austin, Charlotte (1933–) *The Farmer Takes a Wife* 1953; *Desiree* 1954; *Gorilla at Large* 1954; *How to Be Very, Very Popular* 1955; *The Bride and the Beast* 1958
Austin, Jerry (1892–1976) *Saratoga Trunk* 1945; *Adventures of Don Juan* 1948
Austin, Karen *Summer Rental* 1985; *The Ladies Club* 1986; *Far from Home* 1989
Austin, Pamela aka **Austin, Pam** (1942–) *Kissin' Cousins* 1964; *The Perils of Pauline* 1967; *Evil Roy Slade* 1971
Austin, William (1884–1975) *It* 1927; *County Hospital* 1932; *Alice in Wonderland* 1933
Auteuil, Daniel (1950–) *Jean de Florette* 1986; *Manon des Sources* 1986; *Le Paltoquet* 1986; *Romuald et Juliette* 1989; *Un Coeur en Hiver* 1992; *Ma Saison Préferée* 1993; *Une Femme Française* 1994; *La Reine Margot* 1994; *La Séparation* 1994; *The Eighth Day* 1996; *Les Voleurs* 1996; *Le Bossu* 1997; *Lucie Aubrac* 1997; *The Lost Son* 1998; *The Escort* 1999; *The Girl on the Bridge* 1999; *La Veuve de Saint-Pierre* 2000; *The Closet* 2001; *Petites Coupures* 2002
Autry, Alan (1952–) *Roadhouse 66* 1984; *World Gone Wild* 1988
Autry, Gene (1907–1998) *Down Mexico Way* 1941; *Riders in the Sky* 1949; *Mule Train* 1950; *Valley of Fire* 1951; *Blue Canadian Rockies* 1952; *Last of the Pony Riders* 1953; *On Top of Old Smoky* 1953; *Winning of the West* 1953; *Alias Jesse James* 1959
Avalon, Frankie (1940–) *The Alamo* 1960; *Guns of the Timberland* 1960; *Sail a Crooked Ship* 1961; *Voyage to the Bottom of the Sea* 1961; *Panic in Year Zero* 1962; *Beach Party* 1963; *The Castilian* 1963; *Bikini Beach* 1964; *Muscle Beach Party* 1964; *Pajama Party* 1964; *Beach Blanket Bingo* 1965; *Dr Goldfoot and the Bikini Machine* 1965; *How to Fill a Wild Bikini* 1965; *I'll Take Sweden* 1965; *Sergeant Deadhead* 1965; *Ski Party* 1965; *Fireball 500* 1966; *Sumuru* 1967; *Skidoo* 1968; *The Haunted House of Horror* 1969; *The Take* 1974; *Back to the Beach* 1987
Avalos, Luis (1946–) *Hot Stuff* 1979; *Fires Within* 1991
Avery, James (1948–) *Beastmaster 2: through the Portal of Time* 1991; *Death of a Cheerleader* 1994
Avery (2), Margaret *Hell Up in Harlem* 1973; *Scott Joplin* 1977; *Which Way Is Up?* 1977; *The Lathe of Heaven* 1979; *The Color Purple* 1985; *Blueberry Hill* 1988; *Heat Wave* 1990; *The Set Up* 1995; *White Man's Burden* 1995
Avery, Val (1924–) *Hud* 1963; *Faces* 1968; *A Dream of Kings* 1969; *The Anderson Tapes* 1971; *Minnie and Moskowitz* 1971; *Black Caesar* 1973; *The Laughing Policeman* 1973; *Heroes* 1977; *Continental Divide* 1981; *Touchdown* 1981; *Jinxed!* 1982; *Easy Money* 1983
Aviles, Angel *Mi Vida Loca* 1993; *Scorpion Spring* 1995
Aviles, Rick (1953–1995) *Ghost* 1990; *The Saint of Fort Washington* 1993
Avital, Mili (1972–) *Stargate* 1994; *Dead Man* 1995; *Kissing a Fool* 1998; *Polish Wedding* 1998; *After the Storm* 2001
Avonde, Richard *Captain Carey, USA* 1950; *The 49th Man* 1953
Awaji, Keiko (1933–) *Stray Dog* 1949; *The Bridges at Toko-Ri* 1954; *Illusion of Blood* 1965
Awashima, Chikage (1924–) *Early Summer* 1951; *The Flavour of Green Tea over Rice* 1952; *Early Spring* 1956
Axberg, Eddie (1947–) *The Emigrants* 1971; *The New Land* 1972
Axton, Hoyt (1938–1999) *The Black Stallion* 1979; *Endangered Species* 1982; *Liar's Moon* 1982; *The Black Stallion Returns* 1983; *Heart like a Wheel* 1983; *Gremlins* 1984; *Disorganized Crime* 1989; *We're No Angels* 1989; *Buried Alive* 1990; *King Cobra* 1999
Ayars, Ann (1918–1995) *Dr Kildare's Victory* 1941; *Apache Trail* 1942; *The Youngest Profession* 1943; *The Tales of Hoffmann* 1951
Aycox, Nicki Lynn aka **Aycox, Nicki** (1975–) *Slap Her, She's French!* 2001; *Jeepers Creepers 2* 2003
Aykroyd, Dan (1952–) *1941* 1979; *The Blues Brothers* 1980; *Neighbors* 1981; *Doctor Detroit* 1983; *Trading Places* 1983; *Twilight Zone: the Movie* 1983; *Ghostbusters* 1984; *Nothing Lasts Forever* 1984; *Into the Night* 1985; *Spies like Us* 1985; *Dragnet* 1987; *Caddyshack II* 1988; *The Couch Trip* 1988; *The Great Outdoors* 1988; *My Stepmother Is an Alien* 1988; *Driving Miss Daisy* 1989; *Ghostbusters II* 1989; *Loose Cannons* 1990; *My Girl* 1991; *Nothing but Trouble* 1991; *Chaplin* 1992; *Sneakers* 1992; *This Is My Life* 1992; *Coneheads* 1993; *Exit to Eden* 1994; *My Girl 2* 1994; *North* 1994; *Rainbow* 1995; *Tommy Boy* 1995; *Celtic Pride* 1996; *Feeling Minnesota* 1996; *Getting Away with Murder* 1996; *My Fellow Americans* 1996; *Sgt Bilko* 1996; *Grosse Pointe Blank* 1997; *Antz* 1998; *Blues Brothers 2000* 1998; *Susan's Plan* 1998; *Diamonds* 1999; *The House of Mirth* 2000; *Loser* 2000; *Stardom* 2000; *The Curse of the Jade Scorpion* 2001; *Evolution* 2001; *Pearl Harbor* 2001; *Crossroads* 2002; *Bright Young Things* 2003; *Christmas with the Kranks* 2004; *50 First Dates* 2004
Aylesworth, Arthur (1883–1946) *The Plot Thickens* 1936; *Test Pilot* 1938
Aylmer, Felix (1889–1979) *The Ghost Camera* 1933; *The Clairvoyant* 1934; *Doctor's Orders* 1934; *As You Like It* 1936; *Dusty Ermine* 1936; *Seven Sinners* 1936; *The Shadow* 1936; *Tudor Rose* 1936; *The Mill on the Floss* 1937; *The Vicar of Bray* 1937; *Sixty Glorious Years* 1938; *Charley's (Big Hearted) Aunt* 1940; *The Black Sheep of Whitehall* 1941; *The Ghost of St Michael's* 1941; *Hi, Gang!* 1941; *I Thank You* 1941; *The Saint's Vacation* 1941; *South American George* 1941; *The Young Mr Pitt* 1942; *The Demi-Paradise* 1943; *Time Flies* 1944; *The Way to the Stars* 1945; *The Wicked Lady* 1945; *The Magic Bow* 1946; *The Years Between* 1946; *The Ghosts of Berkeley Square* 1947; *A Man about the House* 1947; *The Man Within* 1947; *The October Man* 1947; *The Calendar* 1948; *Hamlet* 1948; *Edward, My Son* 1949; *Eye Witness* 1949; *Trio* 1950; *The Lady with the Lamp* 1951; *The Man Who Watched Trains Go By* 1952; *Knights of the Round Table* 1953; *The Master of Ballantrae* 1953; *The Angel Who Pawned Her Harp* 1954; *Anastasia* 1956; *Loser Takes All* 1956; *Saint Joan* 1957; *The Doctor's Dilemma* 1958; *The Two-Headed Spy* 1958; *The Mummy* 1959; *The Hands of Orlac* 1960; *Never Take Sweets from a Stranger* 1960; *The Boys* 1961; *The Road to Hong Kong* 1962; *The Running Man* 1963; *The Chalk Garden* 1964; *Hostile Witness* 1968
Aylward, John *Buddy* 1997; *Path to War* 2002
Aynesworth, Alan (1864–1959) *Love, Life and Laughter* 1934; *The Last Days of Dolwyn* 1949
Ayres, Leah (1957–) *The Burning* 1981; *Eddie Macon's Run* 1983; *Bloodsport* 1987
Ayres, Lew aka **Ayres, Lewis** (1908–1996) *Big News* 1929; *The Kiss* 1929; *All Quiet on the Western Front* 1930; *Doorway to Hell* 1931; *The Iron Man* 1931; *The Impatient Maiden* 1932; *State Fair* 1933; *The Last Train from Madrid* 1937; *Holiday* 1938; *Young Dr Kildare* 1938; *Broadway Serenade* 1939; *Calling Dr Kildare* 1939; *The Ice Follies of 1939* 1939; *Remember?* 1939; *The Secret of Dr Kildare* 1939; *Dr Kildare Goes Home* 1940; *Dr Kildare's Crisis* 1940; *Dr Kildare's Strange Case* 1940; *Dr Kildare's Victory* 1941; *Dr Kildare's Wedding Day* 1941; *The People vs Dr Kildare* 1941; *Fingers at the Window* 1942; *The Dark Mirror* 1946; *The Unfaithful* 1947; *Johnny Belinda* 1948; *The Capture* 1950; *Donovan's Brain* 1953; *Advise and Consent* 1962; *The Carpetbaggers* 1964; *The Biscuit Eater* 1972; *The Man* 1972; *Battle for the Planet of the Apes* 1973; *End of the World* 1977; *Damien – Omen II* 1978; *Salem's Lot* 1979
Ayres, Robert (1914–1968) *Night without Stars* 1951; *To Have and to Hold* 1951; *Cosh Boy* 1952; *13 East Street* 1952; *Delayed Action* 1954; *River Beat* 1954; *Time Lock* 1957; *First Man into Space* 1958; *A Night to Remember* 1958; *The Sicilians* 1964; *Battle beneath the Earth* 1968
Ayres, Rosalind (1946–) *That'll Be the Day* 1973; *Little Malcolm and His Struggle Against the Eunuchs* 1974; *Stardust* 1974; *Beautiful People* 1999
Azabal, Lubna *Far Away* 2001; *Almost Peaceful* 2002; *Exiles* 2004
Azaria, Hank (1964–) *Cool Blue* 1988; *Quiz Show* 1994; *The Birdcage* 1996; *Anastasia* 1997; *Godzilla* 1997; *Great Expectations* 1997; *Grosse Pointe Blank* 1997; *Celebrity* 1998; *Homegrown* 1998; *Bartok the Magnificent* 1999; *Cradle Will Rock* 1999; *Mystery, Alaska* 1999; *Mystery Men* 1999; *Tuesdays with Morrie* 1999; *Fail Safe* 2000; *America's Sweethearts* 2001; *Shattered Glass* 2003; *Along Came Polly* 2004; *Dodgeball: a True Underdog Story* 2004
Azéma, Sabine (1955–) *Life Is a Bed of Roses* 1983; *Sunday in the Country* 1984; *Mélo* 1986; *Life and Nothing But* 1989; *Smoking/No Smoking* 1993; *Le Bonheur Est dans le Pré* 1995; *Mon Homme* 1996; *On Connaît la Chanson* 1997; *La Bûche* 1999; *The Officers' Ward* 2001; *Pas sur la Bouche* 2003
Azito, Tony (1949–1995) *The Pirates of Penzance* 1983; *Bloodhounds of Broadway* 1989; *Necronomicon* 1993
Azmi, Shabana (1948–) *Ankur* 1974; *Nishant* 1975; *The Chess Players* 1977; *Junoon* 1978; *Mandi* 1983; *Madame Sousatzka* 1988; *Disha* 1990; *Immaculate Conception* 1991; *City of Joy* 1992; *Son of the Pink Panther* 1993; *Fire* 1996; *Side Streets* 1998; *Tehzeeb* 2003
Azmi, Tanvi *Vidheyan* 1993; *English, August* 1994
Aznavour, Charles (1924–) *Shoot the Pianist* 1960; *Le Testament d'Orphée* 1960; *Candy* 1968; *The Last Shot* 1969; *The Adventurers* 1970; *The Games* 1970; *The Blockhouse* 1973; *And Then There Were None* 1974; *Sky Riders* 1976; *The Twist* 1976; *The Tin Drum* 1979; *Edith and Marcel* 1983; *Long Live Life* 1984; *Il Maestro* 1989; *Ararat* 2002
Azzara, Candy aka **Azzara, Candice** (1945–) *House Calls* 1978; *Fatso* 1979; *Divorce Wars* 1982; *Easy Money* 1983; *Doin' Time on Planet Earth* 1988

B

Baal, Karin (1940–) *Hannibal Brooks* 1968; *Berlin Alexanderplatz* 1980; *Deadly Game* 1982; *Lola* 1982; *Thousand Eyes* 1984
Baas, Balduin (1922–) *Orchestra Rehearsal* 1978; *Mischief* 1983
Babatunde, Obba aka **Babatundé, Obba** *Miami Blues* 1990; *The Importance of Being Earnest* 1992; *Introducing Dorothy Dandridge* 1999; *Life* 1999; *After the Sunset* 2004
Babbar, Raj (1952–) *Maya* 1992; *Shikaar – the Musical Thriller* 2004; *Bunty Aur Babli* 2005
Babcock, Barbara (1937–) *The Black Marble* 1980; *The Lords of Discipline* 1983; *That Was Then... This Is Now* 1985; *Happy Together* 1989; *Far and Away* 1992
Babe, Fabienne (1962–) *Fatherland* 1986; *Les Voleurs* 1996
Bacall, Lauren (1924–) *To Have and Have Not* 1944; *Confidential Agent* 1945; *The Big Sleep* 1946; *Two Guys from Milwaukee* 1946; *Dark Passage* 1947; *Key Largo* 1948; *Bright Leaf* 1950; *Young Man with a Horn* 1950; *How to Marry a Millionaire* 1953; *Woman's World* 1954; *Blood Alley* 1955; *The Cobweb* 1955; *Written on the Wind* 1956; *Designing Woman* 1957; *The Gift of Love* 1958; *North West Frontier* 1959; *Sex and the Single Girl* 1964; *Shock Treatment* 1964; *Harper* 1966; *Murder on the Orient Express* 1974; *The Shootist* 1976; *HEALTH* 1980; *The Fan* 1981; *Appointment with Death* 1988; *Mr North* 1988; *Tree of Hands* 1988; *Misery* 1990; *All I Want for Christmas* 1991; *Pret-a-Porter* 1994; *The Mirror Has Two Faces* 1996; *My Fellow Americans* 1996; *Diamonds* 1999; *Madeline: Lost in Paris* 1999; *Dogville* 2003; *Birth* 2004
Bacall, Michael *Wait until Spring, Bandini* 1989; *Manic* 2001
Baccaloni, Salvatore aka **Baccaloni** (1900–1969) *Full of Life* 1956; *Merry Andrew* 1958; *Rock-a-Bye Baby* 1958; *Fanny* 1961; *The Pigeon That Took Rome* 1962
Bach, Barbara (1947–) *The Short Night of the Glass Dolls* 1971;

The Spy Who Loved Me 1977; *Force 10 from Navarone* 1978; *The Humanoid* 1979; *Jaguar Lives!* 1979; *Caveman* 1981; *Give My Regards to Broad Street* 1984
Bach, Catherine (1954–) *Thunderbolt and Lightfoot* 1974; *Driving Force* 1988; *Masters of Menace* 1990
Bach, John *Battletruck* 1982; *Georgia* 1988; *Blood Oath* 1990
Bachar, Dian (1971–) *Orgazmo* 1997; *BASEketball* 1998
Bacharach, Burt (1929–) *Austin Powers: International Man of Mystery* 1997; *Austin Powers: the Spy Who Shagged Me* 1999
Bachchan, Abhishek (1976–) *Kuch Naa Kaho* 2003; *LOC Kargil* 2003; *Main Prem Ki Diwani Hoon* 2003; *Dhoom* 2004; *Hum Tum* 2004; *Naach* 2004; *Run* 2004; *Bunty Aur Babli* 2005
Bachchan, Amitabh (1942–) *Sholay* 1975; *Kabhi Kabhie* 1976; *Hum* 1991; *Hindustan Ki Kasam* 1999; *Mohabbatein* 2000; *Aks* 2001; *Kabhi Khushi Kabhie Gham...* 2001; *Armaan* 2003; *Baghban* 2003; *Khakee* 2003; *Black* 2004; *Deewaar: Let's Bring Our Heroes Home* 2004; *Dev* 2004; *Kyun! Ho Gaya Na ...* 2004; *Lakshya* 2004; *Veer-Zaara* 2004; *Bunty Aur Babli* 2005; *WAQT: the Race Against Time* 2005
Bachchan, Jaya *aka* **Bhaduri, Jaya** (1948–) *The Big City* 1963; *Fiza* 2000; *Kabhi Khushi Kabhie Gham...* 2001; *Koi Mere Dil Se Pooche* 2001; *Kal Ho Naa Ho* 2003
Bachelor, Stephanie (1912–1996) *Earl Carroll Vanities* 1945; *Springtime in the Sierras* 1947
Backer, Brian (1956–) *The Burning* 1981; *Fast Times at Ridgemont High* 1982; *Moving Violations* 1985
Backus, Georgia (1900–1983) *Apache Drums* 1951; *Cause for Alarm* 1951
Backus, Jim (1913–1989) *A Dangerous Profession* 1949; *The Great Lover* 1949; *Bright Victory* 1951; *Half Angel* 1951; *I'll See You in My Dreams* 1951; *Iron Man* 1951; *M* 1951; *The Man with a Cloak* 1951; *Don't Bother to Knock* 1952; *Angel Face* 1953; *Francis in the Navy* 1955; *Rebel without a Cause* 1955; *The Square Jungle* 1955; *When Magoo Flew* 1955; *The Girl He Left Behind* 1956; *The Great Man* 1956; *Meet Me in Las Vegas* 1956; *You Can't Run Away from It* 1956; *Man of a Thousand Faces* 1957; *Top Secret Affair* 1957; *The High Cost of Loving* 1958; *Macabre* 1958; *Ask Any Girl* 1959; *The Big Operator* 1959; *A Private's Affair* 1959; *The Wild and the Innocent* 1959; *Ice Palace* 1960; *The Horizontal Lieutenant* 1962; *My Six Loves* 1962; *The Wonderful World of the Brothers Grimm* 1962; *Zotz* 1962; *Johnny Cool* 1963; *Sunday in New York* 1963; *The Wheeler Dealers* 1963; *Advance to the Rear* 1964; *John Goldfarb, Please Come Home* 1964; *Billie* 1965; *Fluffy* 1965; *Where Were You When the Lights Went Out?* 1968; *Hello Down There* 1969; *The Cockeyed Cowboys of Calico County* 1970; *Myra Breckinridge* 1970; *Now You See Him, Now You Don't* 1972; *Crazy Mama* 1975; *Friday Foster* 1975; *Good Guys Wear Black* 1977; *Pete's Dragon* 1977; *Slapstick of Another Kind* 1982
Baclanova, Olga (1899–1974) *The Docks of New York* 1928; *Freaks* 1932; *Claudia* 1943
Bacon, Irving (1893–1965) *Internes Can't Take Money* 1937; *Blondie!* 1938; *The Howards of Virginia* 1940; *A Guy Named Joe* 1944; *Under Western Skies* 1945; *Cause for Alarm* 1951; *Room for One More* 1952; *The Glenn Miller Story* 1953; *Black Horse Canyon* 1954; *A Star Is Born* 1954; *At Gunpoint* 1955
Bacon, Kevin (1958–) *National Lampoon's Animal House* 1978; *Friday the 13th* 1980; *Hero at Large* 1980; *Diner* 1982; *Enormous Changes at the Last Minute* 1983; *Footloose* 1984; *Quicksilver* 1986; *End of the Line* 1987; *Planes, Trains and Automobiles* 1987; *White Water Summer* 1987; *Criminal Law* 1988; *She's Having a Baby* 1988; *The Big Picture* 1989; *Tremors* 1989; *Flatliners* 1990; *He Said, She Said* 1991; *JFK* 1991; *Pyrates* 1991; *Queens Logic* 1991; *A Few Good Men* 1992; *The Air Up There* 1993; *Murder in the First* 1994; *The River Wild* 1994; *Apollo 13* 1995; *Balto* 1995; *Sleepers* 1996; *Picture Perfect* 1997; *Telling Lies in America* 1997; *Digging to China* 1998; *Wild Things* 1998; *My Dog Skip* 1999; *Stir of Echoes* 1999; *Hollow Man* 2000; *Novocaine* 2001; *Trapped* 2002; *In the Cut* 2003; *Mystic River* 2003; *The Woodsman* 2004; *Beauty Shop* 2005
Bacon, Lloyd (1890–1955) *The Tramp* 1915; *Behind the Screen* 1916
Bacon, Max (1904–1969) *King Arthur Was a Gentleman* 1942; *Bees in Paradise* 1943; *Miss London Ltd* 1943; *Give Us the Moon* 1944; *Privilege* 1967
Bacri, Jean-Pierre (1951–) *Entre Nous* 1983; *Subway* 1985; *C'est la Vie* 1990; *L'Homme de Ma Vie* 1992; *Un Air de Famille* 1996; *Didier* 1997; *On Connaît la Chanson* 1997; *Place Vendôme* 1998; *Le Goût des Autres* 1999; *Look at Me* 2004
Badalucco, Michael (1954–) *Mac* 1992; *Leon* 1994; *The Search for One-Eye Jimmy* 1996; *Stolen Hearts* 1996; *Love Walked In* 1997; *O Brother, Where Art Thou?* 2000; *The Man Who Wasn't There* 2001
Baddeley, Angela (1904–1976) *The Ghost Train* 1931; *Those Were the Days* 1934
Baddeley, Hermione (1906–1986) *Brighton Rock* 1947; *No Room at the Inn* 1948; *Quartet* 1948; *Dear Mr Prohack* 1949; *Passport to Pimlico* 1949; *The Woman in Question* 1950; *Scrooge* 1951; *There Is Another Sun* 1951; *Tom Brown's Schooldays* 1951; *Cosh Boy* 1952; *The Pickwick Papers* 1952; *Time Gentlemen Please!* 1952; *Counterspy* 1953; *The Belles of St Trinian's* 1954; *Room at the Top* 1958; *Jet Storm* 1959; *Let's Get Married* 1960; *Midnight Lace* 1960; *Rag Doll* 1960; *Information Received* 1962; *Mary Poppins* 1964; *The Unsinkable Molly Brown* 1964; *Do Not Disturb* 1965; *Harlow* 1965; *Marriage on the Rocks* 1965; *The Adventures of Bullwhip Griffin* 1967; *The Happiest Millionaire* 1967; *The Aristocats* 1970; *Up the Front* 1972; *CHOMPS* 1979; *The Secret of NIMH* 1982
Badel, Alan (1923–1982) *Salome* 1953; *Three Cases of Murder* 1953; *Magic Fire* 1956; *Bitter Harvest* 1963; *This Sporting Life* 1963; *Children of the Damned* 1964; *Arabesque* 1966; *Otley* 1968; *Where's Jack?* 1969; *The Adventurers* 1970; *The Day of the Jackal* 1973; *Luther* 1974; *Telefon* 1977; *Agatha* 1978; *The Riddle of the Sands* 1978; *Nijinsky* 1980
Badel, Sarah (1943–) *Not without My Daughter* 1990; *Mrs Dalloway* 1997; *Cotton Mary* 1999
Bader, Diedrich (1966–) *The Beverly Hillbillies* 1993; *Office Space* 1999; *The Country Bears* 2002; *Napoleon Dynamite* 2004
Badham, Mary (1952–) *To Kill a Mockingbird* 1962; *This Property Is Condemned* 1966
Badie, Laurence (1934–) *Jeux Interdits* 1953; *Muriel* 1963
Badland, Annette *Jabberwocky* 1977; *Anchoress* 1993; *Captives* 1994; *Angels and Insects* 1995; *Caught in the Act* 1996; *Little Voice* 1998
Bae Doo-na *Sympathy for Mr Vengeance* 2002; *Take Care of My Cat* 2002
Baer, Buddy (1915–1986) *Africa Screams* 1949; *The Big Sky* 1952; *Jack and the Beanstalk* 1952; *Dream Wife* 1953; *Fair Wind to Java* 1953; *Slightly Scarlet* 1956
Baer, Harry (1947–) *Gods of the Plague* 1969; *Whity* 1970; *Jail Bait* 1972; *Ludwig – Requiem for a Virgin King* 1972; *Fox and His Friends* 1975; *The Third Generation* 1979; *La Amiga* 1988
Baer, Max (1909–1959) *The Prizefighter and the Lady* 1933; *Over She Goes* 1937; *The Navy Comes Through* 1942; *Ladies' Day* 1943; *Africa Screams* 1949; *Bride for Sale* 1949; *The Harder They Fall* 1956
Baer Jr, Max (1937–) *A Time for Killing* 1967; *The Birdmen* 1971; *Macon County Line* 1973
Baer, Parley (1914–2002) *Comanche Territory* 1950; *Gypsy* 1962; *Bedtime Story* 1964; *Two on a Guillotine* 1964; *The Ugly Dachshund* 1966
Baeyens, Dominique *Karnaval* 1998; *Les Convoyeurs Attendent* 1999
Bagdasarian, Carol *The Octagon* 1980; *The Aurora Encounter* 1985
Bagdasarian, Ross *aka* **Seville, David** (1919–1972) *Alaska Seas* 1954; *Rear Window* 1954; *The Proud and Profane* 1956
Bagdonas, Vladas *Come and See* 1985; *House of Fools* 2002
Bagley, Lorri (1973–) *Trick* 1999; *The Stepford Wives* 2004
Bahns, Maxine (1971–) *The Brothers McMullen* 1995; *She's the One* 1996; *Cutaway* 2000
Bai Ling (1970–) *Red Corner* 1997; *Anna and the King* 1999; *The Breed* 2001; *The Beautiful Country* 2004; *She Hate Me* 2004; *Sky Captain and the World of Tomorrow* 2004
Bailey, G W (1945–) *Police Academy* 1984; *Runaway* 1984; *Rustler's Rhapsody* 1985; *Warning Sign* 1985; *Short Circuit* 1986; *Burglar* 1987; *Mannequin* 1987; *Police Academy 5: Assignment Miami Beach* 1988; *Dead before Dawn* 1993; *Police Academy: Mission to Moscow* 1994
Bailey, John (1914–1989) *Celia* 1949; *Meet Simon Cherry* 1949
Bailey, Marion *Don't Get Me Started* 1994; *All or Nothing* 2002
Bailey, Pearl (1918–1990) *Carmen Jones* 1954; *That Certain Feeling* 1956; *St Louis Blues* 1958; *Porgy and Bess* 1959; *All the Fine Young Cannibals* 1960; *The Landlord* 1970; *Norman... Is That You?* 1976; *The Fox and the Hound* 1981
Bailey, Raymond (1904–1980) *Congo Crossing* 1956; *The Incredible Shrinking Man* 1957; *The Lineup* 1958; *Vertigo* 1958; *The Gallant Hours* 1960
Bailey, Robin (1919–1991) *Portrait of Clare* 1950; *Catch Us If You Can* 1965; *Blind Terror* 1971; *Jane and the Lost City* 1987
Bailey-Gates, Charles *Knight Moves* 1992; *Exquisite Tenderness* 1995
Bain, Barbara (1931–) *Trust Me* 1989; *Gideon* 1999; *Panic* 2000; *American Gun* 2002
Bain, Conrad (1923–) *CHOMPS* 1979; *Postcards from the Edge* 1990
Bainter, Fay (1892–1968) *This Side of Heaven* 1934; *Make Way for Tomorrow* 1937; *Quality Street* 1937; *Jezebel* 1938; *The Shining Hour* 1938; *White Banners* 1938; *Daughters Courageous* 1939; *A Bill of Divorcement* 1940; *Maryland* 1940; *Our Town* 1940; *Young Tom Edison* 1940; *Babes on Broadway* 1941; *Journey for Margaret* 1942; *The War against Mrs Hadley* 1942; *Woman of the Year* 1942; *Cry Havoc* 1943; *The Heavenly Body* 1943; *The Human Comedy* 1943; *Presenting Lily Mars* 1943; *Salute to the Marines* 1943; *Dark Waters* 1944; *State Fair* 1945; *The Kid from Brooklyn* 1946; *The Virginian* 1946; *Deep Valley* 1947; *The Secret Life of Walter Mitty* 1947; *Give My Regards to Broadway* 1948; *June Bride* 1948; *Close to My Heart* 1951; *The President's Lady* 1953; *The Children's Hour* 1961
Baio, Jimmy (1962–) *The Bad News Bears in Breaking Training* 1977; *Playing for Keeps* 1986
Baio, Scott (1961–) *Bugsy Malone* 1976; *Skatetown, USA* 1979; *Foxes* 1980; *Zapped!* 1982; *Danielle Steel's Mixed Blessings* 1995; *Face Value* 2001; *Cursed* 2005
Baird, Anthony (1920–) *Dead of Night* 1945; *Night Comes Too Soon* 1949
Baird, Harry (1931–2005) *Offbeat* 1960; *Station Six-Sahara* 1962; *The Oblong Box* 1969
Baird, Jimmy (1945–) *The Return of Dracula* 1958; *The Black Orchid* 1959
Bairstow, Scott (1970–) *White Fang 2: Myth of the White Wolf* 1994; *Wild America* 1997; *Two for Texas* 1998; *Tuck Everlasting* 2002
Baisho, Mitsuko (1946–) *Vengeance Is Mine* 1979; *Akira Kurosawa's Dreams* 1990; *The Eel* 1997; *Warm Water under a Red Bridge* 2001
Baitz, Jon Robin (1961–) *Last Summer in the Hamptons* 1995; *One Fine Day* 1996
Bajema, Don *Signal 7* 1983; *Heat and Sunlight* 1988
Bajpai, Manoj *Bandit Queen* 1994; *Zubeidaa* 2000; *Aks* 2001; *Road* 2002
Bakalyan, Richard *aka* **Bakalyan, Dick** (1931–) *The Delicate Delinquent* 1957; *The Delinquents* 1957; *Dino* 1957; *The Bonnie Parker Story* 1958; *The Cool and the Crazy* 1958; *The Computer Wore Tennis Shoes* 1969; *Return from Witch Mountain* 1978; *Blame It on the Night* 1984
Bakare, Ariyon *The Secret Laughter of Women* 1998; *Dead Bolt Dead* 1999
Baker, Art (1898–1966) *Abie's Irish Rose* 1946; *The Beginning or the End* 1947; *Homecoming* 1948; *Walk a Crooked Mile* 1948
Baker, Benny (1907–1994) *Thanks a Million* 1935; *Up in Arms* 1944; *Boy, Did I Get a Wrong Number* 1966; *Jory* 1972
Baker, Blanche (1956–) *French Postcards* 1979; *Nobody's Child* 1986; *The Handmaid's Tale* 1990; *Dead Funny* 1995
Baker, Carroll (1931–) *Easy to Love* 1953; *Baby Doll* 1956; *Giant* 1956; *The Big Country* 1958; *But Not for Me* 1959; *The Miracle* 1959; *Bridge to the Sun* 1961; *How the West Was Won* 1962; *Station Six-Sahara* 1962; *The Carpetbaggers* 1964; *Cheyenne Autumn* 1964; *Sylvia* 1964; *The Greatest Story Ever Told* 1965; *Harlow* 1965; *Mister Moses* 1965; *Jack of Diamonds* 1967; *Captain Apache* 1971; *Bad* 1976; *The World Is Full of Married Men* 1979; *The Watcher in the Woods* 1982; *Star 80* 1983; *The Secret Diary of Sigmund Freud* 1984; *Native Son* 1986; *Ironweed* 1987; *Kindergarten Cop* 1990; *Blonde Fist* 1991; *Desperate Measures* 1995; *The Game* 1997
Baker, David Aaron (1963–) *The Tao of Steve* 2000; *Melinda and Melinda* 2004
Baker, Diane (1938–) *The Best of Everything* 1959; *The Diary of Anne Frank* 1959; *Journey to the Center of the Earth* 1959; *Tess of the Storm Country* 1960; *The Wizard of Baghdad* 1960; *Hemingway's Adventures of a Young Man* 1962; *The 300 Spartans* 1962; *Nine Hours to Rama* 1963; *The Prize* 1963; *Stolen Hours* 1963; *Strait-Jacket* 1963; *Marnie* 1964; *Della* 1965; *Mirage* 1965; *The Horse in the Gray Flannel Suit* 1968; *Krakatoa, East of Java* 1969; *Baker's Hawk* 1976; *The Pilot* 1979; *The Closer* 1990; *Imaginary Crimes* 1994; *The Net* 1995; *The Cable Guy* 1996; *Murder at 1600* 1997; *About Sarah* 1998
Baker, Dylan (1958–) *Planes, Trains and Automobiles* 1987; *The Wizard of Loneliness* 1988; *The Long Walk Home* 1990; *Delirious* 1991; *Love Potion No 9* 1992; *Disclosure* 1994; *True Blue* 1996; *Happiness* 1998; *Oxygen* 1999; *Simply Irresistible* 1999; *Thirteen Days* 2000; *Along Came a Spider* 2001; *Head of State* 2003; *Kinsey* 2004; *Hide and Seek* 2005
Baker, Fay (1894–1954) *Tell It to the Judge* 1949; *The Company She Keeps* 1950; *The House on Telegraph Hill* 1951; *Don't Knock the Rock* 1956; *Sorority Girl* 1957
Baker, Frank (1892–1980) *The New Adventures of Tarzan* 1935; *Tarzan and the Green Goddess* 1938
Baker, George (1931–) *The Intruder* 1953; *The Dam Busters* 1954; *The Ship That Died of Shame* 1955; *The Woman for Joe* 1955; *The Extra Day* 1956; *The Feminine Touch* 1956; *A Hill in Korea* 1956; *The Moonraker* 1957; *No Time for Tears* 1957; *Tread Softly Stranger* 1958; *Lancelot and Guinevere* 1963; *Curse of the Fly* 1965; *Goodbye, Mr Chips* 1969; *Justine* 1969; *On Her Majesty's Secret Service* 1969; *The Executioner* 1970; *A Warm December* 1973; *The Thirty-Nine Steps* 1978; *For Queen and Country* 1988
Baker, Henry Judd *aka* **Baker, Henry** *Seizure* 1974; *Clean and Sober* 1988
Baker, Hylda (1908–1986) *Saturday Night and Sunday Morning* 1960; *Up the Junction* 1967; *Oliver!* 1968; *Nearest and Dearest* 1972
Baker, Joby (1935–) *Gidget* 1959; *The Last Angry Man* 1959; *Key Witness* 1960; *The Wackiest Ship in the Army* 1961; *Gidget Goes to Rome* 1963; *Girl Happy* 1965; *When the Boys Meet the Girls* 1965; *Blackbeard's Ghost* 1967; *Valley of Mystery* 1967; *Superdad* 1974
Baker, Joe (1928–2001) *Where the Bullets Fly* 1966; *Pocahontas* 1995
Baker, Joe Don (1936–) *Guns of the Magnificent Seven* 1969; *Adam at 6 AM* 1970; *Welcome Home, Soldier Boys* 1971; *Wild Rovers* 1971; *Junior Bonner* 1972; *Charley Varrick* 1973; *The Outfit* 1973; *Walking Tall* 1973; *Golden Needles* 1974; *Framed* 1975; *Mitchell* 1975; *The Pack* 1977; *Wacko* 1981; *The Natural* 1984; *Fletch* 1985; *Getting Even* 1986; *The Killing Time* 1987; *Leonard, Part 6* 1987; *The Living Daylights* 1987; *Criminal Law* 1988; *The Children* 1990; *Cape Fear* 1991; *The Distinguished Gentleman* 1992; *Complex of Fear* 1993; *Reality Bites* 1994; *Ring of Steel* 1994; *Congo* 1995; *GoldenEye* 1995; *Panther* 1995; *The Underneath* 1995; *Tomorrow Never Dies* 1997
Baker, Kathy (1950–) *A Killing Affair* 1985; *Nobody's Child* 1986; *Street Smart* 1987; *Clean and Sober* 1988; *Jacknife* 1988; *Dad* 1989; *Edward Scissorhands* 1990; *The Image* 1990; *Mister Frost* 1990; *Article 99* 1992; *Jennifer Eight* 1992; *Mad Dog and Glory* 1992; *Lush Life* 1993; *To Gillian on Her 37th Birthday* 1996; *Inventing the Abbotts* 1997; *The Cider House Rules* 1999; *Things You Can Tell Just by Looking at Her* 2000; *The Glass House* 2001; *Assassination Tango* 2002; *Cold Mountain* 2003; *13 Going on 30* 2004
Baker (1), Kenny (1912–1985) *The Goldwyn Follies* 1938; *Radio City Revels* 1938; *At the Circus* 1939; *The Mikado* 1939; *The Harvey Girls* 1946
Baker (2), Kenny (1934–) *Star Wars Episode IV: a New Hope* 1977; *Star Wars Episode V: the Empire Strikes Back* 1980; *Time Bandits* 1981; *Star Wars Episode VI: Return of the Jedi* 1983; *UFO* 1993; *Star Wars Episode I: the Phantom Menace* 1999; *Star Wars Episode II: Attack of the*

Clones 2002; *Star Wars Episode III: Revenge of the Sith* 2005
Baker, Mark (?–1972) *The Flying Scot* 1957; *Raggedy Ann and Andy* 1977
Baker, Phil (1896–1963) *The Goldwyn Follies* 1938; *The Gang's All Here* 1943
Baker, Ray *aka* **Baker, Raymond** (1948–) *Nobody's Child* 1986; *Everybody's All-American* 1988; *Heart Condition* 1990; *Masters of Menace* 1990; *Hexed* 1993; *Camp Nowhere* 1994; *Anywhere but Here* 1999
Baker, Rick *aka* **Baker, Richard A** (1950–) *King Kong* 1976; *The Kentucky Fried Movie* 1977
Baker, Simon (1969–) *Smoke Signals* 1998; *Ride with the Devil* 1999; *Spooky House* 1999; *Red Planet* 2000; *Sunset Strip* 2000; *The Affair of the Necklace* 2001; *The Ring Two* 2004
Baker, Stanley (1928–1976) *Captain Horatio Hornblower RN* 1951; *Home to Danger* 1951; *The Cruel Sea* 1953; *Knights of the Round Table* 1953; *The Red Beret* 1953; *Beautiful Stranger* 1954; *The Good Die Young* 1954; *Hell below Zero* 1954; *Helen of Troy* 1955; *Richard III* 1955; *Alexander the Great* 1956; *Checkpoint* 1956; *Child in the House* 1956; *A Hill in Korea* 1956; *Campbell's Kingdom* 1957; *Hell Drivers* 1957; *Sea Fury* 1958; *Violent Playground* 1958; *The Angry Hills* 1959; *Blind Date* 1959; *Hell Is a City* 1959; *Jet Storm* 1959; *Yesterday's Enemy* 1959; *The Criminal* 1960; *The Guns of Navarone* 1961; *A Prize of Arms* 1961; *Eva* 1962; *The Man Who Finally Died* 1962; *Sodom and Gomorrah* 1962; *In the French Style* 1963; *Zulu* 1964; *Sands of the Kalahari* 1965; *Accident* 1967; *Robbery* 1967; *Where's Jack?* 1969; *The Games* 1970; *The Last Grenade* 1970; *Perfect Friday* 1970; *Popsy-Pop* 1970; *Innocent Bystanders* 1972; *Zorro* 1975
Baker, Tom (1934–) *The Canterbury Tales* 1971; *Nicholas and Alexandra* 1971; *Frankenstein: the True Story* 1973; *The Golden Voyage of Sinbad* 1973; *The Mutations* 1973; *Vault of Horror* 1973; *Wholly Moses!* 1980; *Dungeons & Dragons* 2000; *The Magic Roundabout* 2005
Baker-Denny, Simon (1969–) *Judas Kiss* 1998; *Restaurant* 1998
Bakewell, William (1908–1993) *Gold Diggers of Broadway* 1929; *All Quiet on the Western Front* 1930; *Dance, Fools, Dance* 1931; *Guilty Hands* 1931; *Lucky Devils* 1933; *Strangers All* 1935; *The Capture* 1950; *Davy Crockett, King of the Wild Frontier* 1955
Bakke, Brenda (1963–) *Gunhed* 1989; *Solar Crisis* 1990; *Hot Shots! Part Deux* 1993; *Twogether* 1994; *Tales from the Crypt: Demon Knight* 1995; *Shelter* 1997; *Trucks* 1997
Bako, Brigitte (1970–) *I Love a Man in Uniform* 1993; *Double Take* 1997; *Primary Suspect* 2000
Bakri, Muhamad *aka* **Bacri, Muhamad** *Beyond the Walls* 1984; *Cup Final* 1991; *Double Edge* 1992
Baku, Shango *Black Joy* 1977; *Rage* 1999
Bakula, Scott (1954–) *Sibling Rivalry* 1990; *Necessary Roughness* 1991; *Color of Night* 1994; *Rules of Obsession* 1994; *Lord of Illusions* 1995; *Cats Don't Dance* 1998; *Major League: Back to the Minors* 1998; *American Beauty* 1999; *Life as a House* 2001
Balaban, Bob *aka* **Balaban, Robert** (1945–) *Catch-22* 1970; *Bank Shot* 1974; *Report to the Commissioner* 1975; *Close Encounters of the Third Kind* 1977; *Girlfriends* 1978; *Altered States* 1980; *Absence of Malice* 1981; *Whose Life Is It Anyway?* 1981; *2010* 1984; *End of the Line* 1987; *Dead-Bang* 1989; *For Love or Money* 1993; *Pie in the Sky* 1995; *The Late Shift* 1996; *Waiting for Guffman* 1996; *Deconstructing Harry* 1997; *Jakob the Liar* 1999; *Three to Tango* 1999; *Best in Show* 2000; *Ghost World* 2001; *Gosford Park* 2001; *The Majestic* 2001; *The Mexican* 2001; *A Mighty Wind* 2003
Balaski, Belinda (1947–) *The Food of the Gods* 1975; *Cannonball* 1976; *The Howling* 1981
Balasko, Josiane (1952–) *Le Maître d'Ecole* 1981; *Trop Belle pour Toi* 1989; *A Shadow of Doubt* 1992; *Gazon Maudit* 1995; *Le Libertin* 2000
Baldini, Renato (1921–) *The White Warrior* 1959; *Esther and the King* 1960
Baldwin, A Michael (1964–) *Phantasm* 1978; *Phantasm III – Lord of the Dead* 1994
Baldwin, Adam (1962–) *My Bodyguard* 1980; *DC Cab* 1983; *Hadley's Rebellion* 1984; *Bad Guys* 1986; *3:15* 1986; *Full Metal Jacket* 1987; *The Chocolate War* 1988; *Cohen and Tate* 1988; *Next of Kin* 1989; *Radio Flyer* 1992; *Where the Day Takes You* 1992; *Bitter Harvest* 1993; *Cold Sweat* 1993; *800 Leagues down the Amazon* 1993; *How to Make an American Quilt* 1995; *Lover's Knot* 1995; *In the Line of Duty: Smoke Jumpers* 1996; *Independence Day* 1996; *Farewell, My Love* 1999; *Jackpot* 2001
Baldwin, Alec (1958–) *Forever Lulu* 1987; *Beetle Juice* 1988; *Married to the Mob* 1988; *She's Having a Baby* 1988; *Talk Radio* 1988; *Working Girl* 1988; *Great Balls of Fire!* 1989; *Alice* 1990; *The Hunt for Red October* 1990; *Miami Blues* 1990; *Too Hot to Handle* 1991; *Glengarry Glen Ross* 1992; *Prelude to a Kiss* 1992; *Malice* 1993; *The Getaway* 1994; *The Shadow* 1994; *Ghosts of Mississippi* 1996; *Heaven's Prisoners* 1996; *The Juror* 1996; *Looking for Richard* 1996; *The Edge* 1997; *Mercury Rising* 1998; *Outside Providence* 1999; *State and Main* 2000; *Thomas and the Magic Railroad* 2000; *Cats & Dogs* 2001; *Final Fantasy: the Spirits Within* 2001; *Pearl Harbor* 2001; *The Royal Tenenbaums* 2001; *The Cooler* 2002; *Path to War* 2002; *Dr Seuss' The Cat in the Hat* 2003; *Along Came Polly* 2004; *The Aviator* 2004; *The SpongeBob SquarePants Movie* 2004
Baldwin, Daniel (1960–) *Car 54 Where Are You?* 1991; *Harley Davidson and the Marlboro Man* 1991; *Knight Moves* 1992; *Attack of the 50 Ft Woman* 1993; *Dead on Sight* 1994; *Desert Thunder* 1998; *Love Kills* 1998; *The Pandora Project* 1998; *Phoenix* 1998; *Vampires* 1998; *In Pursuit* 2000; *King of the Ants* 2003; *Paparazzi* 2004
Baldwin, Dick *Life Begins in College* 1937; *International Settlement* 1938; *Mr Moto's Gamble* 1938
Baldwin, Peter (1931–) *Short Cut to Hell* 1957; *I Married a Monster from Outer Space* 1958; *Teacher's Pet* 1958; *The Spectre* 1963
Baldwin, Stephen (1966–) *The Beast of War* 1988; *Last Exit to Brooklyn* 1989; *Bitter Harvest* 1993; *Posse* 1993; *8 Seconds* 1994; *Fall Time* 1994; *A Simple Twist of Fate* 1994; *Threesome* 1994; *Under the Hula Moon* 1995; *The Usual Suspects* 1995; *Bio-Dome* 1996; *Fled* 1996; *Mr Murder* 1998; *One Tough Cop* 1998; *Scarred City* 1998; *Absence of the Good* 1999; *Cutaway* 2000; *The Flintstones in Viva Rock Vegas* 2000; *Mercy* 2000; *XChange* 2000
Baldwin, Walter (1887–1977) *Together Again* 1944; *Winter Meeting* 1948
Baldwin, William (1963–) *Flatliners* 1990; *Internal Affairs* 1990; *Backdraft* 1991; *Three of Hearts* 1992; *Sliver* 1993; *Curdled* 1995; *Fair Game* 1995; *A Pyromaniac's Love Story* 1995; *Shattered Image* 1998; *Virus* 1998; *Primary Suspect* 2000; *Relative Values* 2000
Bale, Christian (1975–) *Empire of the Sun* 1987; *Mio in the Land of Faraway* 1987; *Treasure Island* 1990; *The News Boys* 1992; *Swing Kids* 1993; *Little Women* 1994; *Prince of Jutland* 1994; *Pocahontas* 1995; *The Portrait of a Lady* 1996; *The Secret Agent* 1996; *Metroland* 1997; *All the Little Animals* 1998; *Velvet Goldmine* 1998; *A Midsummer Night's Dream* 1999; *American Psycho* 2000; *Shaft* 2000; *Captain Corelli's Mandolin* 2001; *Reign of Fire* 2001; *Equilibrium* 2002; *Laurel Canyon* 2002; *The Machinist* 2003; *Batman Begins* 2005
Balenda, Carla (1925–) *Sealed Cargo* 1951; *The Whip Hand* 1951; *Prince of Pirates* 1953
Balfour, Betty (1903–1978) *Champagne* 1928; *Evergreen* 1934; *Forever England* 1935; *Squibs* 1935; *29 Acacia Avenue* 1945
Balfour, Michael (1918–1997) *The Small Voice* 1948; *A Case for PC 49* 1950; *The Quiet Woman* 1950; *13 East Street* 1952; *Albert, RN* 1953; *Fiend without a Face* 1957; *The Monster of Highgate Ponds* 1961; *The Oblong Box* 1969; *Revenge of Billy the Kid* 1991
Balibar, Jeanne (1968–) *Late August, Early September* 1998; *Comédie de l'Innocence* 2000; *Va Savoir* 2001; *Code 46* 2003; *Clean* 2004
Balin, Ina (1937–1990) *The Black Orchid* 1959; *From the Terrace* 1960; *The Comancheros* 1961; *The Young Doctors* 1961; *The Patsy* 1964; *Charro!* 1969; *The Projectionist* 1970; *The Comeback Trail* 1972
Balint, Eszter (1966–) *Stranger than Paradise* 1984; *The Linguini Incident* 1991
Balk, Fairuza (1974–) *Return to Oz* 1985; *Valmont* 1989; *Gas, Food, Lodging* 1992; *Imaginary Crimes* 1994; *Tollbooth* 1994; *Things to Do in Denver When You're Dead* 1995; *The Craft* 1996; *The Island of Dr Moreau* 1996; *American Perfekt* 1997; *The Maker* 1997; *American History X* 1998; *The Waterboy* 1998; *Almost Famous* 2000; *Personal Velocity* 2001
Ball, Angeline *The Commitments* 1991; *Brothers in Trouble* 1995; *Trojan Eddie* 1996; *The Gambler* 1997; *The General* 1998; *bl,.m* 2003
Ball, Lucille (1911–1989) *The Affairs of Cellini* 1934; *Broadway Bill* 1934; *I Dream Too Much* 1935; *Old Man Rhythm* 1935; *Roberta* 1935; *Chatterbox* 1936; *Follow the Fleet* 1936; *Stage Door* 1937; *The Affairs of Annabel* 1938; *Annabel Takes a Tour* 1938; *Go Chase Yourself* 1938; *Having Wonderful Time* 1938; *Joy of Living* 1938; *Room Service* 1938; *Beauty for the Asking* 1939; *Five Came Back* 1939; *That's Right – You're Wrong* 1939; *Dance, Girl, Dance* 1940; *Too Many Girls* 1940; *Look Who's Laughing* 1941; *The Navy Steps Out* 1941; *The Big Street* 1942; *Seven Days' Leave* 1942; *Valley of the Sun* 1942; *Best Foot Forward* 1943; *DuBarry Was a Lady* 1943; *Meet the People* 1944; *Ziegfeld Follies* 1944; *Without Love* 1945; *The Dark Corner* 1946; *Easy to Wed* 1946; *Lover Come Back* 1946; *Her Husband's Affairs* 1947; *Lured* 1947; *Easy Living* 1949; *Miss Grant Takes Richmond* 1949; *Sorrowful Jones* 1949; *Fancy Pants* 1950; *The Fuller Brush Girl* 1950; *The Long, Long Trailer* 1954; *Forever, Darling* 1956; *The Facts of Life* 1960; *Critic's Choice* 1963; *Yours, Mine and Ours* 1968; *Mame* 1974
Ball, Nicholas (1946–) *Overlord* 1975; *Lifeforce* 1985; *Croupier* 1998; *Out of Depth* 1998
Ball, Suzan (1933–1955) *Untamed Frontier* 1952; *City beneath the Sea* 1953; *East of Sumatra* 1953; *War Arrow* 1953; *Chief Crazy Horse* 1955
Ball, Vincent (1923–) *The Black Rider* 1954; *The Blue Peter* 1955; *Blood of the Vampire* 1958; *Sea of Sand* 1958; *Dentist in the Chair* 1960; *Season of Passion* 1960; *A Matter of WHO* 1961; *Echo of Diana* 1963; *Breaker Morant* 1979; *Phar Lap* 1983
Ballard, Kaye (1926–) *The Girl Most Likely* 1957; *The Ritz* 1976; *Falling in Love Again* 1980; *Pandemonium* 1982; *Eternity* 1990; *Baby Geniuses* 1999; *Fortune Hunters* 1999
Ballerini, Edoardo (1970–) *The Pest* 1997; *Dinner Rush* 2000
Balmer, Jean-François (1946–) *A Strange Affair* 1981; *Polar* 1984; *Golden Eighties* 1986; *Madame Bovary* 1991; *Beaumarchais l'Insolent* 1996; *Rien Ne Va Plus* 1997
Balpêtré, Antoine (1898–1963) *Nous Sommes Tous des Assassins* 1952; *Le Rouge et le Noir* 1954; *Lust of the Vampire* 1956
Balsam, Martin *aka* **Balsam, Marty** (1919–1996) *On the Waterfront* 1954; *Time Limit* 1957; *12 Angry Men* 1957; *Marjorie Morningstar* 1958; *Al Capone* 1959; *Middle of the Night* 1959; *Psycho* 1960; *Ada* 1961; *Breakfast at Tiffany's* 1961; *Cape Fear* 1962; *Captive City* 1962; *Who's Been Sleeping in My Bed?* 1963; *The Carpetbaggers* 1964; *Seven Days in May* 1964; *The Bedford Incident* 1965; *Harlow* 1965; *A Thousand Clowns* 1965; *After the Fox* 1966; *Hombre* 1967; *The Good Guys and the Bad Guys* 1969; *Trilogy* 1969; *Catch-22* 1970; *Little Big Man* 1970; *Tora! Tora! Tora!* 1970; *The Anderson Tapes* 1971; *The Man* 1972; *The Six Million Dollar Man* 1973; *The Stone Killer* 1973; *Summer Wishes, Winter Dreams* 1973; *Murder on the Orient Express* 1974; *The Taking of Pelham One Two Three* 1974; *Mitchell* 1975; *All the President's Men* 1976; *The Lindbergh Kidnapping Case* 1976; *Two-Minute Warning* 1976; *Raid on Entebbe* 1977; *The Sentinel* 1977; *Silver Bears* 1977; *Cuba* 1979; *There Goes the Bride* 1979; *The Salamander* 1981; *The Goodbye People* 1984; *Death Wish 3* 1985; *St Elmo's Fire* 1985; *The Delta Force* 1986; *Second Serve* 1986; *Private Investigations* 1987; *Two Evil Eyes* 1990; *Cape Fear* 1991; *The Silence of the Hams* 1993
Balsam, Talia (1960–) *The Kindred* 1986; *Private Investigations* 1987; *The Woo Woo Kid* 1987; *Trust Me* 1989
Balsan, Humbert (1954–2005) *Lancelot du Lac* 1974; *Loulou* 1980
Balson, Allison (1969–) *Legend of the White Horse* 1985; *Best Seller* 1987
Baltz, Kirk *Reservoir Dogs* 1991; *Bulworth* 1998
Bamber, David (1954–) *High Hopes* 1988; *I Capture the Castle* 2002
Bamman, Gerry (1941–) *The Secret of My Success* 1987; *Lorenzo's Oil* 1992; *Superstar* 1999
Bana, Eric (1968–) *Chopper* 2000; *Black Hawk Down* 2001; *The Nugget* 2002; *Finding Nemo* 2003; *Hulk* 2003; *Troy* 2004
Bancroft, Anne (1931–2005) *Don't Bother to Knock* 1952; *The Kid from Left Field* 1953; *Tonight We Sing* 1953; *Treasure of the Golden Condor* 1953; *Demetrius and the Gladiators* 1954; *Gorilla at Large* 1954; *The Raid* 1954; *The Last Frontier* 1955; *A Life in the Balance* 1955; *The Naked Street* 1955; *New York Confidential* 1955; *Nightfall* 1956; *Walk the Proud Land* 1956; *The Girl in Black Stockings* 1957; *The Restless Breed* 1957; *The Miracle Worker* 1962; *The Pumpkin Eater* 1964; *The Slender Thread* 1965; *7 Women* 1966; *The Graduate* 1967; *Young Winston* 1972; *The Prisoner of Second Avenue* 1974; *The Hindenburg* 1975; *Lipstick* 1976; *The Turning Point* 1977; *Fatso* 1979; *The Elephant Man* 1980; *To Be or Not to Be* 1983; *Garbo Talks* 1984; *Agnes of God* 1985; *84 Charing Cross Road* 1986; *'Night, Mother* 1986; *Torch Song Trilogy* 1988; *Bert Rigby, You're a Fool* 1989; *Broadway Bound* 1991; *Honeymoon in Vegas* 1992; *Love Potion No 9* 1992; *The Assassin* 1993; *Malice* 1993; *Mr Jones* 1993; *Point of No Return* 1993; *Home for the Holidays* 1995; *How to Make an American Quilt* 1995; *Homecoming* 1996; *Sunchaser* 1996; *Critical Care* 1997; *GI Jane* 1997; *Great Expectations* 1997; *Antz* 1998; *Up at the Villa* 1998; *Keeping the Faith* 2000; *Heartbreakers* 2001
Bancroft, Bradford *Dangerously Close* 1986; *Damned River* 1989
Bancroft, Cameron (1967–) *Love and Human Remains* 1993; *Sleeping Together* 1997; *LA without a Map* 1998
Bancroft, George (1882–1956) *The Pony Express* 1925; *Underworld* 1927; *The Docks of New York* 1928; *The Dragnet* 1928; *Thunderbolt* 1929; *Mr Deeds Goes to Town* 1936; *Wedding Present* 1936; *Angels with Dirty Faces* 1938; *Submarine Patrol* 1938; *Each Dawn I Die* 1939; *Green Hell* 1939; *Rulers of the Sea* 1939; *Stagecoach* 1939; *North West Mounted Police* 1940; *When the Daltons Rode* 1940; *Young Tom Edison* 1940; *Texas* 1941; *Syncopation* 1942; *Whistling in Dixie* 1942
Banderas, Antonio (1960–) *Matador* 1986; *The Law of Desire* 1987; *Women on the Verge of a Nervous Breakdown* 1988; *Tie Me Up! Tie Me Down!* 1990; *The Mambo Kings* 1992; *The House of the Spirits* 1993; *Outrage* 1993; *Philadelphia* 1993; *Interview with the Vampire: the Vampire Chronicles* 1994; *Of Love and Shadows* 1994; *Assassins* 1995; *Desperado* 1995; *Four Rooms* 1995; *Miami Rhapsody* 1995; *Never Talk to Strangers* 1995; *Two Much* 1995; *Evita* 1996; *The Mask of Zorro* 1998; *The 13th Warrior* 1999; *The Body* 2000; *Play It to the Bone* 2000; *Original Sin* 2001; *SPYkids* 2001; *Ballistic: Ecks vs Sever* 2002; *Femme Fatale* 2002; *Frida* 2002; *SPYkids 2: the Island of Lost Dreams* 2002; *Imagining Argentina* 2003; *Once upon a Time in Mexico* 2003; *SPYkids 3-D: Game Over* 2003; *Shrek 2* 2004
Banderet, Pierre *Marius et Jeannette* 1997; *A l'Attaque!* 2000
Bando, Kotaro (1911–1981) *Five Women around Utamaro* 1946; *Gate of Hell* 1953
Banerjee, Victor *aka* **Bannerjee, Victor** (1946–) *Hullabaloo over Georgie and Bonnie's Pictures* 1979; *The Home and the World* 1984; *A Passage to India* 1984; *Foreign Body* 1986; *Bitter Moon* 1992; *Bhoot* 2003
Banes, Lisa (1955–) *The Hotel New Hampshire* 1984; *Marie: a True Story* 1985; *Cocktail* 1988; *Sudden Fury* 1993
Bang, Joy (1947–) *Cisco Pike* 1971; *Dealing: or the Berkeley-to-Boston Forty-Brick Lost-Bag Blues* 1971; *Play It Again, Sam* 1972
Bankhead, Tallulah (1902–1968) *My Sin* 1931; *Tarnished Lady* 1931; *Devil and the Deep* 1932; *Faithless* 1932; *Stage Door Canteen* 1943; *Lifeboat* 1944; *A Royal Scandal* 1945; *Main Street to Broadway* 1953; *Die! Die! My Darling* 1964
Banks (2), Elizabeth (1975–) *Swept Away* 2002; *Seabiscuit* 2003
Banks, Joan (1918–1998) *Bright Victory* 1951; *My Pal Gus* 1952

Banks, Jonathan (1947–) *Beverly Hills Cop* 1984; *Armed and Dangerous* 1986; *Cold Steel* 1987; *For Better or for Worse* 1990; *Freejack* 1992; *Boiling Point* 1993; *Body Shot* 1994; *Darkbreed* 1996; *Flipper* 1996; *Dollar for the Dead* 1998; *Crocodile Dundee in Los Angeles* 2001
Banks, Leslie (1890–1952) *The Most Dangerous Game* 1932; *The Man Who Knew Too Much* 1934; *Night of the Party* 1934; *Sanders of the River* 1935; *The Tunnel* 1935; *Fire over England* 1937; *21 Days* 1937; *Wings of the Morning* 1937; *The Arsenal Stadium Mystery* 1939; *Jamaica Inn* 1939; *Sons of the Sea* 1939; *Busman's Honeymoon* 1940; *Neutral Port* 1940; *Cottage to Let* 1941; *Ships with Wings* 1942; *Went the Day Well?* 1942; *Henry V* 1944; *Eye Witness* 1949; *Madeleine* 1949; *The Small Back Room* 1949
Banks, Richard *The Killing Zone* 1998; *Small Time Obsession* 2000
Banks, Tyra (1973–) *Higher Learning* 1995; *Love Stinks* 1999; *Coyote Ugly* 2000; *Life-Size* 2000
Banky, Vilma (1898–1991) *The Eagle* 1925; *The Son of the Sheik* 1926; *The Winning of Barbara Worth* 1926
Bannen, Ian (1928–1999) *The Long Arm* 1956; *Miracle in Soho* 1957; *Behind the Mask* 1958; *Carlton-Browne of the FO* 1958; *A French Mistress* 1960; *Suspect* 1960; *Station Six-Sahara* 1962; *Psyche '59* 1964; *The Flight of the Phoenix* 1965; *The Hill* 1965; *Mister Moses* 1965; *Rotten to the Core* 1965; *Penelope* 1966; *The Sailor from Gibraltar* 1967; *Lock Up Your Daughters!* 1969; *Too Late the Hero* 1970; *The Deserter* 1971; *Fright* 1971; *Doomwatch* 1972; *The Offence* 1972; *From beyond the Grave* 1973; *The Mackintosh Man* 1973; *The Voyage* 1974; *Bite the Bullet* 1975; *The Driver's Seat* 1975; *Sweeney!* 1976; *Eye of the Needle* 1981; *The Watcher in the Woods* 1982; *Gorky Park* 1983; *The Prodigal* 1983; *Defence of the Realm* 1985; *Lamb* 1985; *The Courier* 1987; *Hope and Glory* 1987; *The Big Man* 1990; *Ghost Dad* 1990; *George's Island* 1991; *Damage* 1992; *A Pin for the Butterfly* 1994; *Braveheart* 1995; *Something to Believe In* 1997; *Waking Ned* 1998; *Best* 1999; *To Walk with Lions* 1999
Banner, Jill *Spider Baby* 1964; *The President's Analyst* 1967
Banner, John (1910–1973) *The Blue Angel* 1959; *Hitler* 1962; *The Wicked Dreams of Paula Schultz* 1968
Bannerjee, Haradhan *The Big City* 1963; *Branches of the Tree* 1990
Bannerjee, Kanu (1905–1985) *Pather Panchali* 1955; *Aparajito* 1956
Bannerjee, Karuna *aka* **Bannerji, Karuna** (1919–2001) *Pather Panchali* 1955; *Aparajito* 1956; *Devi* 1960; *Kangchenjunga* 1962
Bannerjee, Satya *aka* **Bannerji, Satya** *The Middleman* 1975; *And Quiet Rolls the Dawn* 1979
Bannister, Reggie *Phantasm* 1978; *Phantasm II* 1988; *Phantasm III – Lord of the Dead* 1994
Bannon, Jim (1911–1984) *Framed* 1947; *The Man from Colorado* 1948; *Unknown World* 1951
Bansagi, Ildiko (1947–) *Confidence* 1979; *Mephisto* 1981; *The Long Ride* 1984; *Hanussen* 1988; *Diary for My Father and Mother* 1990; *Ten Minutes Older: the Cello* 2002
Baptiste, Thomas (1936–) *Sunday, Bloody Sunday* 1971; *Ama* 1991
Baragrey, John (1918–1975) *Shockproof* 1949; *Tall Man Riding* 1955; *Pardners* 1956; *The Colossus of New York* 1958; *Gamera the Invincible* 1965
Baranovskaya, Vera (1885–1935) *Mother* 1926; *The End of St Petersburg* 1927
Baranski, Christine (1952–) *Playing for Time* 1980; *Lovesick* 1983; *Crackers* 1984; *Nine ½ Weeks* 1985; *Reversal of Fortune* 1990; *Addams Family Values* 1993; *Life with Mikey* 1993; *The Night We Never Met* 1993; *Hostile Hostages* 1994; *Jeffrey* 1995; *The Birdcage* 1996; *Bulworth* 1998; *The Odd Couple II* 1998; *Bowfinger* 1999; *The Grinch* 2000; *Chicago* 2002; *The Guru* 2002; *Marci X* 2003; *Welcome to Mooseport* 2004
Barantini, Philip (1980–) *The Escapist* 2002; *Ned Kelly* 2003
Barash, Olivia (1965–) *Repo Man* 1984; *Tuff Turf* 1984; *Patty Hearst* 1988
Barbareschi, Luca (1956–) *Cannibal Holocaust* 1979; *Il Cielo è Sempre Più Blu* 1995
Barbeau, Adrienne (1945–) *The Fog* 1980; *The Cannonball Run* 1981; *Escape from New York* 1981; *Creepshow* 1982; *Swamp Thing* 1982; *Next One* 1984; *Seduced* 1985; *Cannibal Women in the Avocado Jungle of Death* 1989; *Two Evil Eyes* 1990
Barber, Ellen *Dealing: or the Berkeley-to-Boston Forty-Brick Lost-Bag Blues* 1971; *The Premonition* 1975
Barber, Frances (1958–) *A Zed & Two Noughts* 1985; *Castaway* 1986; *Prick Up Your Ears* 1987; *Sammy and Rosie Get Laid* 1987; *We Think the World of You* 1988; *Secret Friends* 1991; *Young Soul Rebels* 1991; *Soft Top, Hard Shoulder* 1992; *Photographing Fairies* 1997; *Still Crazy* 1998; *The Escort* 1999; *Esther Kahn* 2000; *Shiner* 2000; *The Children's Midsummer Night's Dream* 2001; *Superstition* 2001; *Suzie Gold* 2003
Barber, Glynis (1955–) *Terror* 1979; *Yesterday's Hero* 1979; *Tangier* 1982; *The Hound of the Baskervilles* 1983; *The Wicked Lady* 1983; *Edge of Sanity* 1989; *Déjà Vu* 1997
Barberini, Urbano (1962–) *Otello* 1986; *Gor* 1987; *Opera* 1987; *Torrents of Spring* 1989
Barbier, Christian (1924–) *Trans-Europ-Express* 1966; *L'Armée des Ombres* 1969
Barbier, George (1864–1945) *The Big Pond* 1930; *Girls about Town* 1931; *The Smiling Lieutenant* 1931; *The Big Broadcast* 1932; *No Man of Her Own* 1932; *No One Man* 1932; *One Hour with You* 1932; *The Phantom President* 1932; *Tillie and Gus* 1933; *Turn Back the Clock* 1933; *The Cat's Paw* 1934; *The Merry Widow* 1934; *Life Begins at 40* 1935; *Old Man Rhythm* 1935; *The Milky Way* 1936; *The Princess Comes Across* 1936; *Spendthrift* 1936; *Wife vs Secretary* 1936; *On the Avenue* 1937; *Waikiki Wedding* 1937; *The Adventures of Marco Polo* 1938; *Hold That Co-Ed* 1938; *Little Miss Broadway* 1938; *My Lucky Star* 1938; *Tarzan's Revenge* 1938; *Remember?* 1939; *Wife, Husband and Friend* 1939; *Weekend in Havana* 1941; *The Magnificent Dope* 1942; *Song of the Islands* 1942
Barbour, Joyce (1901–1977) *Sabotage* 1936; *Housemaster* 1938; *Saloon Bar* 1940
Barboza, Richard *Small Time* 1990; *Erotic Tales* 1994
Barbuscia, Lisa (1971–) *Almost Heroes* 1998; *Highlander: Endgame* 2000
Barcis, Artur *No End* 1984; *A Short Film about Love* 1988
Barclay, Joan (1914–2002) *Ladies' Day* 1943; *The Falcon Out West* 1944; *The Shanghai Cobra* 1945
Barclay, Stephen *aka* **Barclay, Steve** (1918–1994) *The Great Flamarion* 1945; *Fool's Gold* 1946
Barcroft, Roy (1902–1969) *My Pal Trigger* 1946; *Springtime in the Sierras* 1947; *The Far Frontier* 1949; *North of the Great Divide* 1950; *Ride the Man Down* 1952; *Six Black Horses* 1962
Bard, Ben (1893–1974) *7th Heaven* 1927; *The Ghost Ship* 1943; *The Seventh Victim* 1943; *Youth Runs Wild* 1944
Bard, Katharine (1916–1983) *The Decks Ran Red* 1958; *The Interns* 1962; *Inside Daisy Clover* 1965; *How to Save a Marriage and Ruin Your Life* 1968
Bardem, Javier (1969–) *The Ages of Lulu* 1990; *Jamon Jamon* 1992; *Golden Balls* 1993; *Mouth to Mouth* 1995; *Live Flesh* 1997; *Perdita Durango* 1997; *Before Night Falls* 2000; *Second Skin* 2000; *The Dancer Upstairs* 2002; *Mondays in the Sun* 2002; *Collateral* 2004; *The Sea Inside* 2004
Bardem, Pilar (1939–) *Vacas* 1991; *Live Flesh* 1997
Bardette, Trevor (1902–1977) *Dick Tracy* 1945; *The Man from Bitter Ridge* 1955; *Dragoon Wells Massacre* 1957; *The Monolith Monsters* 1957; *Thunder Road* 1958
Bardini, Aleksander (1913–1995) *Landscape after Battle* 1970; *No End* 1984; *The Double Life of Véronique* 1991; *Prince of Shadows* 1991; *The Silent Touch* 1992
Bardot, Brigitte (1934–) *Act of Love* 1953; *Royal Affairs in Versailles* 1953; *Doctor at Sea* 1955; *Les Grandes Manoeuvres* 1955; *Helen of Troy* 1955; *And God Created Woman* 1956; *The Bride Is Too Beautiful* 1956; *The Light across the Street* 1956; *Les Bijoutiers du Clair de Lune* 1957; *Une Parisienne* 1957; *Le Testament d'Orphée* 1960; *La Vérité* 1960; *A Very Private Affair* 1962; *Le Mépris* 1963; *Viva Maria!* 1965; *Dear Brigitte* 1966; *Masculine Feminine* 1966; *Histoires Extraordinaires* 1967; *Shalako* 1968; *Don Juan 73, or If Don Juan Were a Woman* 1973
Bardot, Mijanou (1939–) *Sex Kittens Go to College* 1960; *La Collectionneuse* 1967
Barea, Ramón (1949–) *La Madre Muerta* 1993; *The Other Side of the Bed* 2002; *Torremolinos 73* 2003
Bareikis, Arija (1966–) *The Naked Man* 1998; *Deuce Bigalow: Male Gigolo* 1999
Bari, Lynn (1913–1989) *Always Goodbye* 1938; *Mr Moto's Gamble* 1938; *Pack Up Your Troubles* 1939; *The Return of the Cisco Kid* 1939; *Kit Carson* 1940; *Blood and Sand* 1941; *Sun Valley Serenade* 1941; *China Girl* 1942; *The Falcon Takes Over* 1942; *The Magnificent Dope* 1942; *Orchestra Wives* 1942; *Hello, Frisco, Hello* 1943; *Sweet and Lowdown* 1944; *Captain Eddie* 1945; *Home Sweet Homicide* 1946; *Margie* 1946; *Nocturne* 1946; *I'd Climb the Highest Mountain* 1951; *Has Anybody Seen My Gal?* 1952; *I Dream of Jeanie* 1952; *Francis Joins the WACS* 1954; *Abbott and Costello Meet the Keystone Cops* 1955; *Damn Citizen* 1958; *Trauma* 1962
Barker, Eric (1912–1990) *Brothers in Law* 1956; *Happy Is the Bride* 1957; *Carry On Sergeant* 1958; *Left, Right and Centre* 1959; *Carry On Constable* 1960; *Dentist in the Chair* 1960; *The Pure Hell of St Trinian's* 1960; *Watch Your Stern* 1960; *Dentist on the Job* 1961; *Nearly a Nasty Accident* 1961; *On the Fiddle* 1961; *Raising the Wind* 1961; *On the Beat* 1962; *The Bargee* 1964; *Carry On Spying* 1964
Barker, Jess (1912–2000) *Government Girl* 1943; *Cover Girl* 1944; *The Daltons Ride Again* 1945; *Scarlet Street* 1945; *This Love of Ours* 1945; *The Time of Their Lives* 1946; *Marry Me Again* 1953; *Shack Out on 101* 1955
Barker, Lex (1919–1973) *Return of the Bad Men* 1948; *The Velvet Touch* 1948; *Tarzan's Magic Fountain* 1949; *Tarzan and the Slave Girl* 1950; *Tarzan's Peril* 1951; *Tarzan's Savage Fury* 1952; *Tarzan and the She-Devil* 1953; *Thunder over the Plains* 1953; *The Yellow Mountain* 1954; *The Man from Bitter Ridge* 1955; *Away All Boats* 1956; *The Deerslayer* 1957; *The Girl in Black Stockings* 1957; *La Dolce Vita* 1960; *The Return of Dr Mabuse* 1961; *The Executioner of Venice* 1963; *The Desperado Trail* 1965; *The Blood Demon* 1967; *Woman Times Seven* 1967
Barker, Ronnie (1929–) *Kill or Cure* 1962; *Father Came Too* 1963; *The Bargee* 1964; *Robin and Marian* 1976; *Porridge* 1979; *My House in Umbria* 2002
Barkin, Ellen (1954–) *Diner* 1982; *Tender Mercies* 1982; *Daniel* 1983; *Eddie and the Cruisers* 1983; *Enormous Changes at the Last Minute* 1983; *Terminal Choice* 1983; *The Adventures of Buckaroo Banzai across the 8th Dimension* 1984; *Harry and Son* 1984; *Desert Bloom* 1985; *The Big Easy* 1986; *Down by Law* 1986; *Siesta* 1987; *Johnny Handsome* 1989; *Sea of Love* 1989; *Switch* 1991; *Into the West* 1992; *Mac* 1992; *Man Trouble* 1992; *This Boy's Life* 1993; *Bad Company* 1995; *Wild Bill* 1995; *The Fan* 1996; *Trigger Happy* 1996; *Before Women Had Wings* 1997; *Fear and Loathing in Las Vegas* 1998; *Drop Dead Gorgeous* 1999; *Crime + Punishment in Suburbia* 2000; *Mercy* 2000; *Animal Attraction* 2001; *Palindromes* 2004; *She Hate Me* 2004
Barkworth, Peter (1929–) *No My Darling Daughter* 1961; *Two a Penny* 1968; *The Littlest Horse Thieves* 1976; *International Velvet* 1978; *Champions* 1983
Barlow, Reginald (1866–1943) *The Age of Consent* 1932; *The Wet Parade* 1932
Barnard, Ivor (1887–1953) *Sally in Our Alley* 1931; *The Saint's Vacation* 1941; *Great Expectations* 1946; *Esther Waters* 1948; *Beat the Devil* 1953
Barnes, Barry K (1906–1965) *The Return of the Scarlet Pimpernel* 1937; *The Girl in the News* 1940; *Bedelia* 1946; *Dancing with Crime* 1946
Barnes, Binnie (1905–1998) *The Private Life of Henry VIII* 1933; *The Private Life of Don Juan* 1934; *Rendezvous* 1935; *The Last of the Mohicans* 1936; *Small Town Girl* 1936; *Broadway Melody of 1938* 1937; *Three Smart Girls* 1937; *The Adventures of Marco Polo* 1938; *The Divorce of Lady X* 1938; *Holiday* 1938; *Thanks for Everything* 1938; *Three Blind Mice* 1938; *Frontier Marshal* 1939; *The Three Musketeers* 1939; *Wife, Husband and Friend* 1939; *This Thing Called Love* 1940; *'Til We Meet Again* 1940; *Call Out the Marines* 1941; *Skylark* 1941; *I Married an Angel* 1942; *In Old California* 1942; *The Man from Down Under* 1943; *Barbary Coast Gent* 1944; *The Hour before the Dawn* 1944; *Up in Mabel's Room* 1944; *Getting Gertie's Garter* 1945; *It's in the Bag* 1945; *The Spanish Main* 1945; *The Time of Their Lives* 1946; *If Winter Comes* 1947; *Shadow of the Eagle* 1950; *Decameron Nights* 1953; *Malaga* 1954; *The Trouble with Angels* 1966; *Where Angels Go...Trouble Follows* 1968; *40 Carats* 1973
Barnes, Chris (1965–) *The Bad News Bears in Breaking Training* 1977; *Angel of Fury* 1991
Barnes, Christopher Daniel *aka* **Barnes, C D** (1972–) *American Dreamer* 1984; *The Little Mermaid* 1989; *The Brady Bunch Movie* 1995; *A Very Brady Sequel* 1996
Barnes, Joanna (1934–) *Violent Road* 1958; *Tarzan, the Ape Man* 1959; *The Parent Trap* 1961; *Goodbye Charlie* 1964; *Don't Make Waves* 1967; *The War Wagon* 1967; *I Wonder Who's Killing Her Now?* 1975
Barnes, Priscilla (1955–) *The Seniors* 1978; *Erotique* 1994; *The Crossing Guard* 1995; *The Killing Grounds* 1997; *Alone with a Stranger* 2000
Barnes, Susan *Repo Man* 1984; *Stranded* 1987; *Meet the Applegates* 1991; *Mistaken Identity* 1999; *Where the Money Is* 2000
Barnes, Walter (1918–1998) *Escape to Witch Mountain* 1975; *Every Which Way but Loose* 1978
Barnett, Griff (1884–1958) *The Tender Years* 1947; *Apartment for Peggy* 1948; *Holiday Affair* 1949; *Cattle Drive* 1951
Barnett, Vince (1902–1977) *Flesh* 1932; *Scarface* 1932; *Tiger Shark* 1932; *The Death Kiss* 1933; *The Prizefighter and the Lady* 1933; *The Affairs of Cellini* 1934; *Black Fury* 1935; *The Falcon's Alibi* 1946; *The Killers* 1946; *Mule Train* 1950; *Girl on the Run* 1958
Barney, Jay (1913–1985) *Battle Taxi* 1955; *The Shrike* 1955
Barney, Matthew (1967–) *Cremaster 4* 1994; *Cremaster 5* 1997; *Cremaster 2* 1999; *Cremaster 3* 2002
Baron, Geraldine *Human Highway* 1982; *The City Girl* 1984
Baron, Joanne *Crazy in Love* 1992; *Pet Shop* 1995
Baron, Lita (1929–) *Jungle Jim* 1948; *Red Sundown* 1956
Baron, Lynda (1942–) *Hands of the Ripper* 1971; *Tiffany Jones* 1973
Baron, Sandy (1937–2001) *Sweet November* 1968; *Targets* 1968; *If It's Tuesday, This Must Be Belgium* 1969; *The Out of Towners* 1970; *Straight Time* 1978; *Birdy* 1984; *Vamp* 1986; *Motorama* 1991
Barondes, Elizabeth *Oscar* 1991; *Adrenalin: Fear the Rush* 1995; *Love to Kill* 1997; *Sexual Predator* 2001
Barondess, Barbara (1907–2000) *Hold Your Man* 1933; *The Plot Thickens* 1936
Baronova, Irina (1919–) *Florian* 1940; *Train of Events* 1949
Barr, Byron (1917–1966) *Double Indemnity* 1944; *The Affairs of Susan* 1945; *Love Letters* 1945; *Pitfall* 1948
Barr, Douglas (1949–) *Hue and Cry* 1947; *Dance Hall* 1950
Barr, Jean-Marc (1960–) *Hope and Glory* 1987; *The Big Blue* 1988; *Europa* 1991; *The Plague* 1992; *Breaking the Waves* 1996; *The Scarlet Tunic* 1997; *All for Love* 1999; *Dogville* 2003
Barr, Patrick (1908–1985) *Midnight at Madame Tussaud's* 1936; *The Return of the Scarlet Pimpernel* 1937; *Let's Be Famous* 1939; *Death of an Angel* 1951; *To Have and to Hold* 1951; *You're Only Young Twice* 1952; *Escape by Night* 1953; *The Vanquished* 1953; *The Brain Machine* 1954; *The Dam Busters* 1954; *Duel in the Jungle* 1954; *It's Never Too Late* 1956; *Next to No Time* 1958; *Guns in the Heather* 1969; *The Satanic Rites of Dracula* 1973; *House of Whipcord* 1974; *The Godsend* 1980
Barr, Roseanne *aka* **Arnold, Roseanne** (1952–) *She-Devil* 1989; *Look Who's Talking Too* 1990; *Even Cowgirls Get the Blues* 1993; *Blue in the Face* 1995; *Home on the Range* 2004
Barra, Gianfranco (1940–) *Avanti!* 1972; *Screw Loose* 1999
Barranco, Maria (1961–) *Women on the Verge of a Nervous Breakdown* 1988; *The Ages of Lulu* 1990; *The Red Squirrel* 1993; *The Butterfly Effect* 1995; *Mouth to Mouth* 1995
Barrat, Robert (1889–1970) *Heroes for Sale* 1933; *The Kennel Murder Case* 1933; *Gambling Lady* 1934; *Hi, Nellie!* 1934; *Upper World* 1934; *Bordertown* 1935; *The Florentine Dagger* 1935; *Murder Man* 1935; *Village Tale* 1935; *The Country Doctor* 1936; *The Last of the Mohicans* 1936; *Mary of Scotland* 1936; *The Trail of the Lonesome Pine* 1936; *The Black Legion* 1937; *God's Country and the Woman* 1937; *The Life of Emile Zola* 1937; *The Texans* 1938; *Bad Lands* 1939; *The Cisco Kid and the Lady* 1939; *The First Rebel* 1939; *Man of Conquest* 1939;

The Return of the Cisco Kid 1939; *The Man from Dakota* 1940; *Northwest Passage* 1940; *Riders of the Purple Sage* 1941; *Bomber's Moon* 1943; *The Adventures of Mark Twain* 1944; *The Great John L* 1945; *Road to Utopia* 1945; *Relentless* 1948; *Canadian Pacific* 1949; *An American Guerrilla in the Philippines* 1950; *The Baron of Arizona* 1950; *Distant Drums* 1951; *Tall Man Riding* 1955
Barrault, Jean-Louis (1910–1994) *Abel Gance's Beethoven* 1936; *Drôle de Drame* 1937; *Les Enfants du Paradis* 1945; *The Testament of Dr Cordelier* 1959; *Chappaqua* 1966; *La Nuit de Varennes* 1983
Barrault, Marie-Christine (1944–) *My Night with Maud* 1969; *Cousin, Cousine* 1975; *The Medusa Touch* 1978; *Perceval le Gallois* 1978; *Stardust Memories* 1980; *Table for Five* 1983; *Swann in Love* 1984
Barrett, Brendon Ryan (1986–) *Casper: a Spirited Beginning* 1997; *Durango Kids* 2000
Barrett, Caitlin *Little Bigfoot* 1995; *Durango Kids* 2000
Barrett, Edith (1907–1977) *Ladies in Retirement* 1941; *Lady for a Night* 1942; *The Ghost Ship* 1943; *I Walked with a Zombie* 1943; *Molly and Me* 1945; *The Lady Gambles* 1949
Barrett, Jacinda *The Human Stain* 2003; *Bridget Jones: the Edge of Reason* 2004; *Ladder 49* 2004
Barrett, Jane (1923–1969) *Eureka Stockade* 1949; *The Sword and the Rose* 1952; *Time Gentlemen Please!* 1952
Barrett, Laurinda *The Wrong Man* 1956; *The Heart Is a Lonely Hunter* 1968
Barrett, Majel aka **Roddenberry, Majel Barrett** (1939–) *Love in a Goldfish Bowl* 1961; *Star Trek: the Motion Picture* 1979; *Star Trek IV: the Voyage Home* 1986; *Star Trek: Nemesis* 2002
Barrett, Nancy (1941–) *House of Dark Shadows* 1970; *Night of Dark Shadows* 1971; *Belizaire the Cajun* 1985
Barrett, Nitchie *Preppies* 1984; *A Time to Die* 1991
Barrett, Ray (1926–) *The Reptile* 1966; *Thunderbirds Are Go!* 1966; *Revenge* 1971; *Don's Party* 1976; *The Chant of Jimmie Blacksmith* 1978; *Where the Green Ants Dream* 1984; *The Empty Beach* 1985; *Rebel* 1985; *Relatives* 1985; *Waiting* 1990; *Hotel Sorrento* 1994; *Brilliant Lies* 1996; *Hotel de Love* 1996; *Heaven's Burning* 1997
Barrett (1), Sean (1940–) *Four Sided Triangle* 1953; *Bang! You're Dead* 1954
Barrett, Tim (1928–1990) *Where the Bullets Fly* 1966; *The Deadly Bees* 1967; *A Hole Lot of Trouble* 1969; *White Cargo* 1973
Barrett, Tony (1916–1974) *Dick Tracy Meets Gruesome* 1947; *Guns of Hate* 1948; *Mystery in Mexico* 1948
Barretta, Bill *Muppets from Space* 1999; *It's a Very Merry Muppet Christmas Movie* 2002
Barrie, Amanda (1939–) *Carry On Cabby* 1963; *Carry On Cleo* 1964; *I've Gotta Horse* 1965
Barrie, Barbara (1931–) *One Potato, Two Potato* 1964; *Summer of My German Soldier* 1978; *The Bell Jar* 1979; *Breaking Away* 1979; *End of the Line* 1987; *Real Men* 1987; *Judy Berlin* 1999
Barrie, Chris aka **Barrie, Christopher** (1960–) *Testimony* 1987; *Lara Croft: Tomb Raider* 2001; *Lara Croft Tomb Raider: the Cradle of Life* 2003
Barrie, John (1917–1980) *Life for Ruth* 1962; *The File of the Golden Goose* 1969
Barrie, Mona (1909–1964) *Charlie Chan in London* 1934; *One Night of Love* 1934; *King of Burlesque* 1936; *Love on the Run* 1936; *I Met Him in Paris* 1937; *Something to Sing About* 1937; *I Take This Woman* 1940; *Never Give a Sucker an Even Break* 1941
Barrie, Wendy (1912–1978) *Wedding Rehearsal* 1932; *The Private Life of Henry VIII* 1933; *Speed* 1936; *Dead End* 1937; *I Am the Law* 1938; *Five Came Back* 1939; *The Hound of the Baskervilles* 1939; *The Saint Strikes Back* 1939; *The Saint Takes Over* 1940; *A Date with the Falcon* 1941; *The Gay Falcon* 1941; *The Saint in Palm Springs* 1941
Barrier, Edgar (1907–1964) *They Dare Not Love* 1941; *Phantom of the Opera* 1943; *Cobra Woman* 1944; *Cornered* 1945; *A Game of Death* 1945; *Tarzan and the Leopard Woman* 1946; *Macbeth* 1948; *To the Ends of the Earth* 1948; *The Whip Hand* 1951; *Count the Hours* 1953; *The Golden Blade* 1953; *Princess of the Nile* 1954
Barrier, Maurice (1934–) *Police Story* 1975; *Black and White in Color* 1976; *Life and Nothing But* 1989
Barrile, Anthony *Hamburger Hill* 1987; *Kiss Me, Guido* 1997
Barrit, Desmond *A Midsummer Night's Dream* 1996; *A Christmas Carol* 1999
Barron, Dana (1968–) *National Lampoon's Vacation* 1983; *Death Wish 4: the Crackdown* 1987; *The Man in the Iron Mask* 1997
Barron, Keith (1936–) *The Firechasers* 1970; *Nothing but the Night* 1972; *The Land That Time Forgot* 1974; *La Passione* 1996
Barry, Bruce (1934–) *ABBA the Movie* 1977; *Patrick* 1978; *The Good Wife* 1986
Barry, Donald aka **Barry, Don** aka **Barry, Don "Red"** (1912–1980) *The Duke of West Point* 1938; *Wyoming Outlaw* 1939; *The Purple Heart* 1944; *Bells of Rosarita* 1945; *The Twinkle in God's Eye* 1955; *Seven Men from Now* 1956; *Gun Duel in Durango* 1957; *Frankenstein – 1970* 1958; *Born Reckless* 1959; *Walk on the Wild Side* 1962; *Apache Uprising* 1965; *The Shakiest Gun in the West* 1967
Barry, Gene (1921–) *The War of the Worlds* 1953; *Alaska Seas* 1954; *Naked Alibi* 1954; *Red Garters* 1954; *The Purple Mask* 1955; *Soldier of Fortune* 1955; *Back from Eternity* 1956; *China Gate* 1957; *The 27th Day* 1957; *Thunder Road* 1958; *Maroc 7* 1966; *Prescription: Murder* 1968; *Subterfuge* 1968; *The Second Coming of Suzanne* 1974; *These Old Broads* 2001; *War of the Worlds* 2005
Barry, Gerald *The Lad* 1935; *Cheer Up!* 1936; *The Crimes of Stephen Hawke* 1936
Barry, Hilda (1885–1979) *John of the Fair* 1952; *House of Mortal Sin* 1975
Barry, Jason (1975–) *Noose* 1997; *When the Sky Falls* 2000
Barry, Joan (1903–1989) *Rich and Strange* 1932; *Rome Express* 1932
Barry, Matthew (1962–) *La Luna* 1979; *The Wraith* 1986
Barry, Neill (1965–) *Old Enough* 1984; *Joey* 1985; *Heat* 1987; *OC and Stiggs* 1987
Barry, Patricia (1930–) *Safe at Home* 1962; *Sammy, the Way Out Seal* 1962; *Dear Heart* 1964; *Kitten with a Whip* 1964; *Send Me No Flowers* 1964; *The Marriage of a Young Stockbroker* 1971
Barry, Phyllis (1909–) *Cynara* 1932; *What – No Beer?* 1933; *The Moonstone* 1934; *Shadows on the Stairs* 1941
Barry, Raymond J aka **Barry, Ray** aka **Barry, Raymond** (1939–) *You Better Watch Out* 1980; *Year of the Dragon* 1985; *Three for the Road* 1987; *Cop* 1988; *Born on the Fourth of July* 1989; *K2* 1991; *Rapid Fire* 1992; *The Turning* 1992; *Cool Runnings* 1993; *Hostile Hostages* 1994; *Dead Man Walking* 1995; *Sudden Death* 1995; *The Chamber* 1996; *Flubber* 1997; *New Port South* 2001; *Training Day* 2001
Barry, Roukietou *Yaaba* 1989; *Tilaï* 1990
Barry, Tony (1941–) *Beyond Reasonable Doubt* 1980; *Hard Knocks* 1980; *Goodbye Pork Pie* 1981; *The Settlement* 1982; *We of the Never Never* 1982; *The Coca-Cola Kid* 1985; *Frog Dreaming* 1985; *Shame* 1987; *Jack Be Nimble* 1992; *Doing Time for Patsy Cline* 1997
Barrymore, Deborah (1963–) *Lionheart* 1986; *Bullseye!* 1990
Barrymore, Drew (1975–) *Altered States* 1980; *ET the Extra-Terrestrial* 1982; *Cat's Eye* 1984; *Firestarter* 1984; *Irreconcilable Differences* 1984; *A Conspiracy of Love* 1987; *Far from Home* 1989; *See You in the Morning* 1989; *Motorama* 1991; *Guncrazy* 1992; *No Place to Hide* 1992; *Poison Ivy* 1992; *Waxwork II: Lost in Time* 1992; *Doppelganger* 1993; *Bad Girls* 1994; *Batman Forever* 1995; *Boys on the Side* 1995; *Mad Love* 1995; *Everyone Says I Love You* 1996; *Scream* 1996; *Best Men* 1997; *Wishful Thinking* 1997; *Ever After: a Cinderella Story* 1998; *Home Fries* 1998; *The Wedding Singer* 1998; *Never Been Kissed* 1999; *Charlie's Angels* 2000; *Titan AE* 2000; *Donnie Darko* 2001; *Freddy Got Fingered* 2001; *Riding in Cars with Boys* 2001; *Confessions of a Dangerous Mind* 2002; *Charlie's Angels: Full Throttle* 2003; *Our House* 2003; *50 First Dates* 2004; *The Perfect Catch* 2005
Barrymore, Ethel (1879–1959) *Rasputin and the Empress* 1932; *None but the Lonely Heart* 1944; *The Farmer's Daughter* 1946; *The Spiral Staircase* 1946; *Moss Rose* 1947; *Night Song* 1947; *The Paradine Case* 1947; *Moonrise* 1948; *Portrait of Jennie* 1948; *The Great Sinner* 1949; *Pinky* 1949; *The Red Danube* 1949; *That Midnight Kiss* 1949; *It's a Big Country* 1951; *Kind Lady* 1951; *The Secret of Convict Lake* 1951; *Deadline – USA* 1952; *Just for You* 1952; *Main Street to Broadway* 1953; *The Story of Three Loves* 1953; *Young at Heart* 1955; *Johnny Trouble* 1957
Barrymore, John (1882–1942) *Dr Jekyll and Mr Hyde* 1920; *Don Juan* 1926; *When a Man Loves* 1926; *Eternal Love* 1929; *The Show of Shows* 1929; *Moby Dick* 1930; *The Mad Genius* 1931; *Svengali* 1931; *Arsene Lupin* 1932; *A Bill of Divorcement* 1932; *Grand Hotel* 1932; *Rasputin and the Empress* 1932; *Counsellor-at-Law* 1933; *Dinner at Eight* 1933; *Night Flight* 1933; *Reunion in Vienna* 1933; *Topaze* 1933; *Long Lost Father* 1934; *Twentieth Century* 1934; *Romeo and Juliet* 1936; *Bulldog Drummond Comes Back* 1937; *Bulldog Drummond's Revenge* 1937; *Maytime* 1937; *True Confession* 1937; *Bulldog Drummond's Peril* 1938; *Hold That Co-Ed* 1938; *Marie Antoinette* 1938; *Spawn of the North* 1938; *The Great Man Votes* 1939; *Midnight* 1939; *The Invisible Woman* 1940; *Playmates* 1941
Barrymore, John Drew aka **Barrymore Jr, John** (1932–2004) *High Lonesome* 1950; *The Sundowners* 1950; *The Big Night* 1951; *Thunderbirds* 1952; *While the City Sleeps* 1956; *High School Confidential* 1958; *Never Love a Stranger* 1958; *The Cossacks* 1959; *Pontius Pilate* 1961; *The Trojan War* 1961
Barrymore, Lionel (1878–1954) *America* 1924; *The Lucky Lady* 1926; *The Temptress* 1926; *Sadie Thompson* 1928; *West of Zanzibar* 1928; *Hollywood Revue* 1929; *The Mysterious Island* 1929; *Free and Easy* 1930; *A Free Soul* 1931; *Guilty Hands* 1931; *Mata Hari* 1931; *Arsene Lupin* 1932; *Grand Hotel* 1932; *The Man I Killed* 1932; *Rasputin and the Empress* 1932; *Dinner at Eight* 1933; *Night Flight* 1933; *The Stranger's Return* 1933; *The Girl from Missouri* 1934; *This Side of Heaven* 1934; *Treasure Island* 1934; *Ah, Wilderness!* 1935; *David Copperfield* 1935; *The Little Colonel* 1935; *Mark of the Vampire* 1935; *Public Hero No 1* 1935; *The Return of Peter Grimm* 1935; *The Devil-Doll* 1936; *The Gorgeous Hussy* 1936; *The Road to Glory* 1936; *Camille* 1937; *Captains Courageous* 1937; *A Family Affair* 1937; *Navy Blue and Gold* 1937; *Saratoga* 1937; *Test Pilot* 1938; *A Yank at Oxford* 1938; *You Can't Take It with You* 1938; *Young Dr Kildare* 1938; *Calling Dr Kildare* 1939; *The Secret of Dr Kildare* 1939; *Dr Kildare Goes Home* 1940; *Dr Kildare's Crisis* 1940; *Dr Kildare's Strange Case* 1940; *Dr Kildare's Victory* 1941; *Dr Kildare's Wedding Day* 1941; *Lady Be Good* 1941; *The Penalty* 1941; *The People vs Dr Kildare* 1941; *Calling Dr Gillespie* 1942; *Dr Gillespie's New Assistant* 1942; *Tennessee Johnson* 1942; *Dr Gillespie's Criminal Case* 1943; *Dragon Seed* 1944; *A Guy Named Joe* 1944; *Since You Went Away* 1944; *Three Men in White* 1944; *The Valley of Decision* 1945; *Duel in the Sun* 1946; *It's a Wonderful Life* 1946; *The Secret Heart* 1946; *Key Largo* 1948; *Down to the Sea in Ships* 1949; *Malaya* 1949; *Right Cross* 1950; *Lone Star* 1952
Barsi, Judith (1977–1988) *Jaws the Revenge* 1987; *All Dogs Go to Heaven* 1989
Bartel, Paul (1938–2000) *Hollywood Boulevard* 1976; *Rock 'n' Roll High School* 1979; *Eating Raoul* 1982; *Trick or Treats* 1982; *Sesame Street Presents: Follow That Bird* 1985; *Killer Party* 1986; *Out of the Dark* 1988; *Pucker Up and Bark like a Dog* 1989; *Desire & Hell at Sunset Motel* 1991; *The Pope Must Die* 1991; *Shelf Life* 1993; *The Usual Suspects* 1995; *Basquiat* 1996; *Escape from LA* 1996; *Devil's Child* 1997; *Billy's Hollywood Screen Kiss* 1998
Bartenieff, George (1933–) *Dead End Kids* 1986; *The Laserman* 1988
Barth, Eddie (1931–) *Boardwalk* 1979; *Fame* 1980
Bartha, Justin *Gigli* 2003; *National Treasure* 2004
Barthelmess, Richard (1895–1963) *Broken Blossoms* 1919; *Way Down East* 1920; *Tol'able David* 1921; *Fury* 1923; *Drag* 1929; *The Dawn Patrol* 1930; *The Finger Points* 1931; *The Last Flight* 1931; *Cabin in the Cotton* 1932; *Central Airport* 1933; *Heroes for Sale* 1933; *Only Angels Have Wings* 1939; *The Spoilers* 1942
Bartholomew, Freddie (1924–1992) *Anna Karenina* 1935; *David Copperfield* 1935; *The Devil Is a Sissy* 1936; *Little Lord Fauntleroy* 1936; *Lloyd's of London* 1936; *Captains Courageous* 1937; *Kidnapped* 1938; *Listen, Darling* 1938; *Swiss Family Robinson* 1940; *Tom Brown's Schooldays* 1940; *A Yank at Eton* 1942
Bartlett, Bennie (1927–1999) *The Texas Rangers* 1936; *The Great Man Votes* 1939; *Let's Make Music* 1940; *Clancy Street Boys* 1943; *Jungle Gents* 1954
Bartlett, Bonnie (1929–) *Love Letters* 1983; *Twins* 1988; *The Lies Boys Tell* 1994; *Shiloh* 1996; *Tuesdays with Morrie* 1999
Bartlett, Martine (1925–) *Kansas City Bomber* 1972; *Aloha, Bobby and Rose* 1975
Bartlett, Robin (1951–) *Playing for Time* 1980; *Deceived* 1991; *Regarding Henry* 1991; *Teen Agent* 1991; *12:01* 1993; *Dangerous Minds* 1995; *Honey, We Shrunk Ourselves* 1997
Bartok, Eva (1926–1998) *The Crimson Pirate* 1952; *Venetian Bird* 1952; *Front Page Story* 1953; *Park Plaza 605* 1953; *Spaceways* 1953; *Break in the Circle* 1955; *Special Delivery* 1955; *Ten Thousand Bedrooms* 1957; *Operation Amsterdam* 1958; *SOS Pacific* 1959; *Beyond the Curtain* 1960; *Blood and Black Lace* 1964
Bartok, Jayce *subUrbia* 1996; *Murder at Devil's Glen* 1999
Barton, James (1890–1962) *Captain Hurricane* 1935; *The Shepherd of the Hills* 1941; *Yellow Sky* 1948; *The Daughter of Rosie O'Grady* 1950; *Wabash Avenue* 1950; *Golden Girl* 1951; *Here Comes the Groom* 1951; *The Scarf* 1951; *Quantez* 1957; *The Misfits* 1961
Barton, Margaret (1926–) *Brief Encounter* 1945; *The Romantic Age* 1949; *The Happy Family* 1952
Barton, Mischa (1986–) *Lawn Dogs* 1997; *The Sixth Sense* 1999; *A Ring of Endless Light* 2002; *Octane* 2003
Barton, Peter (1956–) *Hell Night* 1981; *Friday the 13th: the Final Chapter* 1984
Bartusiak, Skye McCole (1992–) *Witness Protection* 1999; *Don't Say a Word* 2001; *Boogeyman* 2005
Barty, Billy (1924–2000) *The Undead* 1957; *Harum Scarum* 1965; *Pufnstuf* 1970; *WC Fields and Me* 1976; *Under the Rainbow* 1981; *Night Patrol* 1984; *Legend* 1985; *Rumpelstiltskin* 1986; *Masters of the Universe* 1987; *Willow* 1988; *Life Stinks* 1991
Baryshnikov, Mikhail (1948–) *The Turning Point* 1977; *White Nights* 1985; *Dancers* 1987; *Company Business* 1991
Basaraba, Gary (1959–) *One Magic Christmas* 1985; *Sweet Dreams* 1985; *No Mercy* 1986; *The Dark Wind* 1991; *Fried Green Tomatoes at the Whistle Stop Cafe* 1991; *For Their Own Good* 1993
Basch, Felix (1882–1944) *The Falcon in Danger* 1943; *Hostages* 1943
Basco, Dante (1975–) *Fist of the North Star* 1995; *The Debut* 2000
Basco, Dion (1977–) *The Debut* 2000; *Dahmer* 2002
Basehart, Richard (1914–1984) *Cry Wolf* 1947; *He Walked by Night* 1948; *Reign of Terror* 1949; *Roseanna McCoy* 1949; *Tension* 1949; *Decision before Dawn* 1951; *Fixed Bayonets* 1951; *Fourteen Hours* 1951; *The House on Telegraph Hill* 1951; *The Stranger's Hand* 1953; *Cartouche* 1954; *The Good Die Young* 1954; *La Strada* 1954; *The Swindle* 1955; *The Extra Day* 1956; *The Intimate Stranger* 1956; *Moby Dick* 1956; *Time Limit* 1957; *The Brothers Karamazov* 1958; *Five Branded Women* 1960; *For the Love of Mike* 1960; *Portrait in Black* 1960; *Hitler* 1962; *The Satan Bug* 1965; *The Birdmen* 1971; *Chato's Land* 1971; *City beneath the Sea* 1971; *Rage* 1972; *And Millions Will Die!* 1973; *Mansion of the Doomed* 1975; *The Great Georgia Bank Hoax* 1977; *The Island of Dr Moreau* 1977; *Being There* 1979
Basil, Toni (1948–) *Easy Rider* 1969; *Rockula* 1989; *Eating* 1990
Basilashvili, Oleg (1934–) *A Slave of Love* 1976; *Autumn Marathon* 1979; *A Station for Two* 1983
Basinger, Kim (1953–) *Hard Country* 1981; *Mother Lode* 1982; *The Man Who Loved Women* 1983; *Never Say Never Again* 1983; *The Natural* 1984; *Fool for Love* 1985; *Nine ½ Weeks* 1985; *No Mercy* 1986; *Blind Date* 1987; *Nadine* 1987; *My Stepmother Is an Alien* 1988; *Batman* 1989; *Too Hot to Handle* 1991; *Cool World* 1992; *Final Analysis* 1992; *The Real McCoy* 1993; *Wayne's World 2* 1993; *The Getaway* 1994; *Pret-a-Porter* 1994; *LA Confidential* 1997; *Bless the Child* 2000; *I Dreamed of Africa* 2000; *8 Mile* 2002; *People I Know* 2002; *Cellular* 2004; *The Door in the Floor* 2004
Baskin, Elya (1951–) *The Name of the Rose* 1986; *Streets of Gold* 1986

Basler, Antoine *Les Rendez-vous de Paris* 1995; *Dobermann* 1997
Basler, Marianne (1964–) *A Soldier's Tale* 1988; *Farinelli il Castrato* 1994; *Va Savoir* 2001
Bass, Alfie (1921–1987) *The Hasty Heart* 1949; *Brandy for the Parson* 1951; *The Lavender Hill Mob* 1951; *The Square Ring* 1953; *Top of the Form* 1953; *The Angel Who Pawned Her Harp* 1954; *Svengali* 1954; *The Bespoke Overcoat* 1955; *Jumping for Joy* 1955; *A Kid for Two Farthings* 1955; *Behind the Headlines* 1956; *Child in the House* 1956; *Hell Drivers* 1957; *No Road Back* 1957; *I Was Monty's Double* 1958; *The Millionairess* 1960; *The Sandwich Man* 1966; *The Fearless Vampire Killers* 1967; *Up the Junction* 1967; *The Magnificent Seven Deadly Sins* 1971; *Come Play with Me* 1977
Basserman, Albert *aka* **Bassermann, Albert** (1867–1952) *A Dispatch from Reuters* 1940; *Escape* 1940; *Foreign Correspondent* 1940; *Knute Rockne – All American* 1940; *The Shanghai Gesture* 1941; *A Woman's Face* 1941; *Fly by Night* 1942; *The Moon and Sixpence* 1942; *Once upon a Honeymoon* 1942; *Reunion in France* 1942; *Madame Curie* 1943; *Rhapsody in Blue* 1945; *The Searching Wind* 1946; *Escape Me Never* 1947; *The Red Shoes* 1948
Bassett, Angela (1958–) *Boyz N the Hood* 1991; *City of Hope* 1991; *Critters 4* 1992; *Malcolm X* 1992; *Passion Fish* 1992; *Tina: What's Love Got to Do with It* 1993; *Strange Days* 1995; *Vampire in Brooklyn* 1995; *Waiting to Exhale* 1995; *Contact* 1997; *How Stella Got Her Groove Back* 1998; *Music of the Heart* 1999; *Boesman & Lena* 2000; *Supernova* 2000; *Whispers: an Elephant's Tale* 2000; *The Score* 2001; *Sunshine State* 2002
Bassett, Linda *Waiting for the Moon* 1987; *East Is East* 1999; *The Martins* 2001; *Calendar Girls* 2003; *Spivs* 2003
Bastedo, Alexandra (1946–) *The Ghoul* 1975; *Find the Lady* 1976
Bastos, Othon (1933–) *The Given Word* 1962; *Black God, White Devil* 1964; *Antonio das Mortes* 1969; *Central Station* 1998
Bat-Adam, Michal *Rachel's Man* 1975; *Madame Rosa* 1977; *The Ambassador* 1984
Bataille, Sylvia (1912–1993) *Le Crime de Monsieur Lange* 1935; *Une Partie de Campagne* 1936
Batalov, Alexei (1928–) *The Cranes Are Flying* 1957; *The Lady with the Little Dog* 1960; *Moscow Distrusts Tears* 1979
Batcheff, Pierre (1901–1932) *The Chess Player* 1927; *Un Chien Andalou* 1928
Bate, Anthony (1929–) *A Prize of Arms* 1961; *Stopover Forever* 1964; *Ghost Story* 1974; *Eminent Domain* 1991
Bateman, Charles *Brotherhood of Satan* 1970; *Interval* 1973
Bateman, Jason (1969–) *Breaking the Rules* 1992; *Love Stinks* 1999; *One Way Out* 2002; *The Sweetest Thing* 2002; *Starsky & Hutch* 2004
Bateman, Justine (1966–) *Satisfaction* 1988; *The Closer* 1990; *Primary Motive* 1992; *The Night We Never Met* 1993
Bates, Alan (1934–2003) *The Entertainer* 1960; *Whistle down the Wind* 1961; *A Kind of Loving* 1962; *The Caretaker* 1963; *Nothing but the Best* 1963; *The Running Man* 1963; *Zorba the Greek* 1964; *Georgy Girl* 1966; *King of Hearts* 1966; *Far from the Madding Crowd* 1967; *The Fixer* 1968; *Women in Love* 1969; *Three Sisters* 1970; *A Day in the Death of Joe Egg* 1971; *The Go-Between* 1971; *Butley* 1973; *Story of a Love Story* 1973; *In Celebration* 1974; *Royal Flash* 1975; *The Shout* 1978; *An Unmarried Woman* 1978; *The Rose* 1979; *Nijinsky* 1980; *Quartet* 1981; *Britannia Hospital* 1982; *The Return of the Soldier* 1982; *The Wicked Lady* 1983; *Duet for One* 1986; *A Prayer for the Dying* 1987; *We Think the World of You* 1988; *Dr M* 1989; *Force Majeure* 1989; *Hamlet* 1990; *Mister Frost* 1990; *Secret Friends* 1991; *Shuttlecock* 1991; *Silent Tongue* 1993; *The Grotesque* 1995; *The Cherry Orchard* 1998; *Nicholas' Gift* 1998; *St Patrick: the Irish Legend* 2000; *Gosford Park* 2001; *The Mothman Prophecies* 2001; *Evelyn* 2002; *The Sum of All Fears* 2002; *The Statement* 2003
Bates, Barbara (1925–1969) *Strange Holiday* 1942; *June Bride* 1948; *The Inspector General* 1949; *All about Eve* 1950; *Cheaper by the Dozen* 1950; *Quicksand* 1950; *I'd Climb the Highest Mountain* 1951; *Let's Make It Legal* 1951; *The Secret of Convict Lake* 1951; *Belles on Their Toes* 1952; *All Ashore* 1953; *The Caddy* 1953; *Rhapsody* 1954; *House of Secrets* 1956; *Town on Trial* 1956
Bates, Florence (1888–1954) *Rebecca* 1940; *Son of Monte Cristo* 1940; *The Chocolate Soldier* 1941; *Love Crazy* 1941; *Strange Alibi* 1941; *The Tuttles of Tahiti* 1942; *Slightly Dangerous* 1943; *Belle of the Yukon* 1944; *Kismet* 1944; *San Antonio* 1945; *Saratoga Trunk* 1945; *Claudia and David* 1946; *Diary of a Chambermaid* 1946; *Desire Me* 1947; *The Secret Life of Walter Mitty* 1947; *My Dear Secretary* 1948; *Portrait of Jennie* 1948; *Winter Meeting* 1948; *The Judge Steps Out* 1949; *A Letter to Three Wives* 1949; *On the Town* 1949; *Lullaby of Broadway* 1951; *The Second Woman* 1951; *The San Francisco Story* 1952
Bates, Granville (1882–1940) *Midnight* 1934; *Poppy* 1936; *The Affairs of Annabel* 1938
Bates, Kathy (1948–) *Straight Time* 1978; *Come Back to the Five and Dime, Jimmy Dean, Jimmy Dean* 1982; *Arthur 2: On the Rocks* 1988; *High Stakes* 1989; *Roe vs Wade* 1989; *Dick Tracy* 1990; *Men Don't Leave* 1990; *Misery* 1990; *White Palace* 1990; *At Play in the Fields of the Lord* 1991; *Fried Green Tomatoes at the Whistle Stop Cafe* 1991; *Shadows and Fog* 1991; *Prelude to a Kiss* 1992; *Used People* 1992; *A Home of Our Own* 1993; *Hostages* 1993; *Angus* 1995; *Dolores Claiborne* 1995; *The West Side Waltz* 1995; *Diabolique* 1996; *The Late Shift* 1996; *The War at Home* 1996; *Amy Foster* 1997; *Titanic* 1997; *A Civil Action* 1998; *Primary Colors* 1998; *The Waterboy* 1998; *Annie* 1999; *American Outlaws* 2001; *Love Liza* 2001; *Unconditional Love* 2001; *About Schmidt* 2002; *Dragonfly* 2002; *Around the World in 80 Days* 2004; *Little Black Book* 2004
Bates, Michael (1920–1978) *Don't Raise the Bridge, Lower the River* 1968; *Salt & Pepper* 1968; *Patton* 1970; *A Clockwork Orange* 1971; *No Sex Please – We're British* 1973
Bates, Ralph (1940–1991) *The Horror of Frankenstein* 1970; *Lust for a Vampire* 1970; *Dr Jekyll and Sister Hyde* 1971; *Fear in the Night* 1972; *Persecution* 1974; *I Don't Want to Be Born* 1975; *Letters to an Unknown Lover* 1985; *King of the Wind* 1989
Bates Post, Guy (1875–1968) *Fatal Lady* 1936; *Till We Meet Again* 1936
Bateson, Timothy (1926–) *The Mouse That Roared* 1959; *There Was a Crooked Man* 1960; *It's Trad, Dad* 1961; *The Anniversary* 1968; *Autobiography of a Princess* 1975
Batinkoff, Randall (1968–) *For Keeps* 1987; *School Ties* 1992; *Walking and Talking* 1996; *Dead Man's Curve* 1997; *The Peacemaker* 1997; *The Last Marshal* 1999
Battaglia, Matt (1965–) *Army of One* 1993; *Universal Soldier 2: Brothers in Arms* 1998; *Universal Soldier 3: Unfinished Business* 1998
Battaglia, Rik *aka* **Battaglia, Rick** (1930–) *Woman of the River* 1955; *Hannibal* 1959; *Esther and the King* 1960; *Don't Bother to Knock* 1961; *Sandokan the Great* 1963; *The Desperado Trail* 1965; *This Man Can't Die* 1967; *A Fistful of Dynamite* 1971
Batten, John (1903–1993) *The Love Waltz* 1930; *For Those in Peril* 1943
Battista, Lloyd *Last Plane Out* 1983; *Round Trip to Heaven* 1992
Battley, David *That's Your Funeral* 1972; *Krull* 1983
Bauchau, Patrick (1938–) *La Collectionneuse* 1967; *The State of Things* 1982; *Emmanuelle IV* 1983; *Entre Nous* 1983; *Choose Me* 1984; *Lola* 1986; *The Music Teacher* 1988; *Australia* 1989; *Erreur de jeunesse* 1989; *The Rapture* 1991; *Every Breath* 1993; *Lisbon Story* 1994; *The New Age* 1994; *Twin Falls Idaho* 1999; *Secretary* 2001; *Panic Room* 2002; *The Five Obstructions* 2003
Bauche, Vanessa (1973–) *Highway Patrolman* 1991; *Amores Perros* 2000
Bauer, Belinda (1951–) *The American Success Company* 1979; *Winter Kills* 1979; *The Rosary Murders* 1987; *Act of Piracy* 1990; *RoboCop 2* 1990; *Poison Ivy 2* 1995
Bauer, Chris *aka* **Bauer, Christopher** *8mm* 1999; *The Hunley* 1999
Bauer, David *The Double Man* 1967; *Embassy* 1972
Bauer, Richard *Good to Go* 1986; *The Sicilian* 1987
Bauer, Steven *aka* **Bauer, Steve** (1956–) *Scarface* 1983; *Thief of Hearts* 1984; *Running Scared* 1986; *The Beast of War* 1988; *Gleaming the Cube* 1988; *A Row of Crows* 1991; *Raising Cain* 1992; *Snapdragon* 1993; *Improper Conduct* 1994; *Woman of Desire* 1994; *Wild Side* 1995; *The Blackout* 1997; *Naked Lies* 1997; *Traffic* 2000
Bauleo, Ricardo *Blood of the Virgins* 1967; *Curious Dr Humpp* 1967
Baumann, Katherine *aka* **Baumann, Kathy** (1948–) *The Thing with Two Heads* 1972; *99 and 44/100% Dead* 1974
Baur, Harry (1880–1943) *Poil de Carotte* 1932; *Les Misérables* 1934; *Crime and Punishment* 1935; *Moscow Nights* 1935; *Abel Gance's Beethoven* 1936; *The Golem* 1936; *Un Carnet de Bal* 1937; *Volpone* 1941
Bavier, Frances (1903–1989) *The Day the Earth Stood Still* 1951; *Man in the Attic* 1953; *A Nice Little Bank That Should Be Robbed* 1958
Baxendale, Helen (1969–) *Macbeth* 1997; *Ordinary Decent Criminal* 1999; *Skagerrak* 2003
Baxley, Barbara (1923–1990) *The Savage Eye* 1959; *All Fall Down* 1962; *Countdown* 1968; *Nashville* 1975; *Norma Rae* 1979
Baxter, Alan (1908–1976) *Big Brown Eyes* 1936; *Boy Slaves* 1938; *I Met My Love Again* 1938; *Each Dawn I Die* 1939; *Spirit of the People* 1940; *Shadow of the Thin Man* 1941; *China Girl* 1942; *Saboteur* 1942; *Pilot #5* 1943; *The Set-Up* 1949; *The True Story of Jesse James* 1957; *The Restless Years* 1958; *Face of a Fugitive* 1959; *This Property Is Condemned* 1966
Baxter, Anne (1923–1985) *Charley's Aunt* 1941; *Swamp Water* 1941; *The Magnificent Ambersons* 1942; *The Pied Piper* 1942; *Crash Dive* 1943; *Five Graves to Cairo* 1943; *The North Star* 1943; *The Eve of St Mark* 1944; *The Fighting Sullivans* 1944; *Guest in the House* 1944; *Sunday Dinner for a Soldier* 1944; *A Royal Scandal* 1945; *Angel on My Shoulder* 1946; *The Razor's Edge* 1946; *Smoky* 1946; *Blaze of Noon* 1947; *Mother Wore Tights* 1947; *Homecoming* 1948; *Yellow Sky* 1948; *You're My Everything* 1949; *All about Eve* 1950; *A Ticket to Tomahawk* 1950; *Follow the Sun: the Ben Hogan Story* 1951; *O Henry's Full House* 1952; *The Blue Gardenia* 1953; *I Confess* 1953; *Carnival Story* 1954; *Bedevilled* 1955; *One Desire* 1955; *The Spoilers* 1955; *The Come On* 1956; *The Ten Commandments* 1956; *Three Violent People* 1956; *Chase a Crooked Shadow* 1957; *Cimarron* 1960; *Season of Passion* 1960; *Mix Me a Person* 1962; *Walk on the Wild Side* 1962; *The Busy Body* 1967; *Stranger on the Run* 1967; *Dynamite Man from Glory Jail* 1971; *The Late Liz* 1971; *Jane Austen in Manhattan* 1980
Baxter, Jane (1909–1996) *The Constant Nymph* 1933; *Blossom Time* 1934; *The Clairvoyant* 1934; *Night of the Party* 1934; *We Live Again* 1934; *Dusty Ermine* 1936; *Ships with Wings* 1942; *Death of an Angel* 1951
Baxter, Keith (1933–) *Chimes at Midnight* 1966; *Ash Wednesday* 1973; *Golden Rendezvous* 1977
Baxter, Lynsey (1965–) *The French Lieutenant's Woman* 1981; *Real Life* 1983; *The Pleasure Principle* 1991
Baxter, Meredith *aka* **Baxter Birney, Meredith** (1947–) *Ben* 1972; *All the President's Men* 1976; *Bittersweet Love* 1976; *The Rape of Richard Beck* 1985; *Darkness before Dawn* 1992; *Mary Higgins Clark's Let Me Call You Sweetheart* 1997; *Murder on the Orient Express* 2001
Baxter, Stanley (1926–) *Very Important Person* 1961; *Crooks Anonymous* 1962; *The Fast Lady* 1963; *Father Came Too* 1963; *Joey Boy* 1965
Baxter, Warner (1891–1951) *West of Zanzibar* 1928; *In Old Arizona* 1929; *Renegades* 1930; *The Cisco Kid* 1931; *Daddy Long Legs* 1931; *The Squaw Man* 1931; *42nd Street* 1933; *Penthouse* 1933; *Broadway Bill* 1934; *Stand Up and Cheer!* 1934; *King of Burlesque* 1936; *The Prisoner of Shark Island* 1936; *The Road to Glory* 1936; *The Robin Hood of El Dorado* 1936; *Slave Ship* 1937; *Vogues of 1938* 1937; *Wife, Doctor and Nurse* 1937; *Kidnapped* 1938; *The Return of the Cisco Kid* 1939; *Wife, Husband and Friend* 1939; *Adam Had Four Sons* 1941; *Crime Doctor* 1943; *Lady in the Dark* 1944
Bay, Frances *The Pit and the Pendulum* 1991; *Single White Female* 1992; *Happy Gilmore* 1996
Baye, Nathalie (1948–) *Day for Night* 1973; *The Mouth Agape* 1974; *The Man Who Loved Women* 1977; *The Green Room* 1978; *Slow Motion* 1980; *A Strange Affair* 1981; *La Balance* 1982; *The Return of Martin Guerre* 1982; *I Married a Dead Man* 1983; *Right Bank, Left Bank* 1984; *Detective* 1985; *En Toute Innocence* 1987; *C'est la Vie* 1990; *The Man Inside* 1990; *The Lie* 1992; *La Machine* 1994; *Food of Love* 1997; *Venus Beauty Institute* 1998; *Une Liaison Pornographique* 1999; *Catch Me If You Can* 2002; *The Flower of Evil* 2002
Bayldon, Geoffrey (1924–) *Sky West and Crooked* 1965; *Where the Spies Are* 1965; *Casino Royale* 1967; *To Sir, with Love* 1967; *Two a Penny* 1968; *Tales from the Crypt* 1972; *The Monster Club* 1980; *Madame Sousatzka* 1988; *Asterix Conquers America* 1994
Bayley, Hilda (1883–1955) *Much Too Shy* 1942; *Home Sweet Home* 1945
Bayliss, Peter (1927–2002) *House of Cards* 1968; *30 Is a Dangerous Age, Cynthia* 1968; *Vampira* 1975
Baylor, Hal (1918–1998) *Big Jim McLain* 1952; *This Is My Love* 1954; *A Boy and His Dog* 1975
Bayly, Lorraine (1944–) *Ride a Wild Pony* 1976; *The Man from Snowy River* 1982
Baynaud, Erwan (1983–) *La Machine* 1994; *East-West* 1999
Bazinet, Brenda *Dancing in the Dark* 1986; *Thicker than Blood* 1993; *No Higher Love* 1999
Bazlen, Brigid (1944–1989) *The Honeymoon Machine* 1961; *King of Kings* 1961
Beach, Adam (1972–) *Dance Me Outside* 1994; *Squanto: the Last Great Warrior* 1994; *A Boy Called Hate* 1995; *Smoke Signals* 1998; *Joe Dirt* 2001; *Windtalkers* 2001
Beach, Michael (1963–) *In a Shallow Grave* 1988; *Late for Dinner* 1991; *Stockade* 1991; *One False Move* 1992; *Bad Company* 1995; *Waiting to Exhale* 1995; *A Family Thing* 1996; *Casualties* 1997; *Soul Food* 1997; *Made Men* 1999
Beacham, Stephanie (1947–) *Dracula AD 1972* 1972; *The Nightcomers* 1972; *And Now the Screaming Starts!* 1973; *House of Mortal Sin* 1975; *Schizo* 1976; *Inseminoid* 1981; *The Wolves of Willoughby Chase* 1988; *Troop Beverly Hills* 1989; *Danielle Steel's Secrets* 1992; *Wedding Bell Blues* 1996; *Unconditional Love* 2001
Beal, John (1909–1997) *The Little Minister* 1934; *Break of Hearts* 1935; *Les Misérables* 1935; *Danger Patrol* 1937; *Double Wedding* 1937; *Madame X* 1937; *I Am the Law* 1938; *Port of Seven Seas* 1938; *The Cat and the Canary* 1939; *Edge of Darkness* 1943; *My Six Convicts* 1952; *Remains to Be Seen* 1953; *That Night* 1957; *Ten Who Dared* 1960; *Amityville III: the Demon* 1983
Beale, Simon Russell (1961–) *Orlando* 1992; *Persuasion* 1995
Beals, Jennifer (1963–) *Flashdance* 1983; *The Bride* 1985; *The Gamble* 1988; *Vampire's Kiss* 1988; *Dr M* 1989; *Sons* 1989; *Day of Atonement* 1992; *In the Soup* 1992; *Dead on Sight* 1994; *Dear Diary* 1994; *Arabian Knight* 1995; *Devil in a Blue Dress* 1995; *Let It Be Me* 1995; *The Search for One-Eye Jimmy* 1996; *The Prophecy II* 1997; *Wishful Thinking* 1997; *The Last Days of Disco* 1998; *A House Divided* 2000; *Militia* 2000; *Without Malice* 2000; *After the Storm* 2001; *Roger Dodger* 2002; *Runaway Jury* 2003; *Catch That Kid* 2004
Bean, Orson (1928–) *How to Be Very, Very Popular* 1955; *Twinky* 1969; *Being John Malkovich* 1999
Bean, Sean (1959–) *Caravaggio* 1986; *Stormy Monday* 1987; *War Requiem* 1988; *Windprints* 1989; *The Field* 1990; *Patriot Games* 1992; *Shopping* 1993; *Black Beauty* 1994; *Jacob* 1994; *GoldenEye* 1995; *When Saturday Comes* 1995; *Airborne* 1997; *Anna Karenina* 1997; *Ronin* 1998; *Essex Boys* 1999; *Don't Say a Word* 2001; *The Lord of the Rings: The Fellowship of the Ring* 2001; *Equilibrium* 2002; *National Treasure* 2004; *Troy* 2004
Béart, Emmanuelle (1965–) *Manon des Sources* 1986; *Date with an Angel* 1987; *La Belle Noiseuse* 1991; *J'Embrasse Pas* 1991; *Un Coeur en Hiver* 1992; *L'Enfer* 1994; *Une Femme Française* 1994; *Nelly & Monsieur Arnaud* 1995; *Mission: Impossible* 1996; *La Bûche* 1999; *Elephant Juice* 1999; *Time Regained* 1999; *Les Destinées Sentimentales* 2000; *8 Women* 2001; *Histoire de Marie et Julien* 2003; *Nathalie…* 2003
Beasley, John (1943–) *The Apostle* 1997; *Lost Souls* 2000; *Walking Tall* 2004
Beaton, Norman (1934–1994) *Pressure* 1976; *Black Joy* 1977; *Real Life* 1983; *Playing Away* 1986

Beatty, May (1880–1945) *Mad Love* 1935; *The Adventures of Sherlock Holmes* 1939
Beatty, Ned (1937–) *Deliverance* 1972; *The Life and Times of Judge Roy Bean* 1972; *The Last American Hero* 1973; *The Thief Who Came to Dinner* 1973; *White Lightning* 1973; *Nashville* 1975; *WW and the Dixie Dancekings* 1975; *All the President's Men* 1976; *The Big Bus* 1976; *Mikey and Nicky* 1976; *Network* 1976; *Silver Streak* 1976; *Exorcist II: The Heretic* 1977; *The Great Georgia Bank Hoax* 1977; *Gray Lady Down* 1978; *Superman* 1978; *The American Success Company* 1979; *Friendly Fire* 1979; *1941* 1979; *Promises in the Dark* 1979; *Wise Blood* 1979; *Hopscotch* 1980; *Superman II* 1980; *The Incredible Shrinking Woman* 1981; *The Toy* 1982; *Stroker Ace* 1983; *Restless Natives* 1985; *The Big Easy* 1986; *The Fourth Protocol* 1987; *Switching Channels* 1987; *The Trouble with Spies* 1987; *Midnight Crossing* 1988; *Physical Evidence* 1988; *The Purple People Eater* 1988; *The Unholy* 1988; *Chattahoochee* 1989; *Time Trackers* 1989; *Angel Square* 1990; *Captain America* 1990; *Going Under* 1990; *Repossessed* 1990; *Hear My Song* 1991; *Blind Vision* 1992; *Prelude to a Kiss* 1992; *Motherhood* 1993; *Rudy* 1993; *Radioland Murders* 1994; *Just Cause* 1995; *He Got Game* 1998; *Cookie's Fortune* 1999; *Life* 1999; *Thunderpants* 2002
Beatty, Robert (1909–1992) *San Demetrio London* 1943; *Odd Man Out* 1946; *Against the Wind* 1947; *Another Shore* 1948; *Counterblast* 1948; *Portrait from Life* 1948; *Calling Bulldog Drummond* 1951; *Captain Horatio Hornblower RN* 1951; *The Magic Box* 1951; *The Gentle Gunman* 1952; *The Oracle* 1952; *Wings of Danger* 1952; *Albert, RN* 1953; *Man on a Tightrope* 1953; *The Net* 1953; *The Square Ring* 1953; *The Loves of Three Queens* 1954; *Out of the Clouds* 1954; *Postmark for Danger* 1955; *Tarzan and the Lost Safari* 1956; *Something of Value* 1957; *Time Lock* 1957; *The Shakedown* 1959; *The Amorous Prawn* 1962; *2001: a Space Odyssey* 1968; *Where Eagles Dare* 1969; *The Spaceman and King Arthur* 1979
Beatty, Warren (1937–) *The Roman Spring of Mrs Stone* 1961; *Splendor in the Grass* 1961; *All Fall Down* 1962; *Lilith* 1964; *Mickey One* 1965; *Kaleidoscope* 1966; *Promise Her Anything* 1966; *Bonnie and Clyde* 1967; *The Only Game in Town* 1970; *Dollars* 1971; *McCabe and Mrs Miller* 1971; *The Parallax View* 1974; *The Fortune* 1975; *Shampoo* 1975; *Heaven Can Wait* 1978; *Reds* 1981; *Ishtar* 1987; *Dick Tracy* 1990; *Bugsy* 1991; *Love Affair* 1994; *Bulworth* 1998; *Town & Country* 2001
Beaumont, Diana (1909–1964) *When London Sleeps* 1932; *Let George Do It* 1940; *Home at Seven* 1952
Beaumont, Hugh (1909–1982) *The Seventh Victim* 1943; *The Blue Dahlia* 1946; *Railroaded* 1947; *The Counterfeiters* 1948; *The Mole People* 1956
Beaumont, Kathryn (1938–) *On an Island with You* 1948; *Alice in Wonderland* 1951; *Peter Pan* 1953
Beaumont, Lucy (1873–1937) *A Free Soul* 1931; *His Double Life* 1933; *The Devil-Doll* 1936
Beaumont, Susan (1936–) *Eyewitness* 1956; *Innocent Sinners* 1957; *The Spaniard's Curse* 1958; *The Man Who Liked Funerals* 1959
Beauvois, Xavier (1967–) *Don't Forget You're Going to Die* 1995; *Le Vent de la Nuit* 1999
Beauvy, Nicolas (1958–) *Rage* 1972; *Take Down* 1978; *The Toolbox Murders* 1978
Beavers, Louise (1902–1962) *What Price Hollywood?* 1932; *Imitation of Life* 1934; *Rainbow on the River* 1936; *Belle Starr* 1941; *The Vanishing Virginian* 1941; *Holiday Inn* 1942; *Barbary Coast Gent* 1944; *Lover Come Back* 1946; *Good Sam* 1948; *Mr Blandings Builds His Dream House* 1948; *My Blue Heaven* 1950; *Good-bye, My Lady* 1956
Beck, Jennifer *Tightrope* 1984; *Troll* 1986; *Gypsy* 1993
Beck, John (1943–) *Mrs Pollifax – Spy* 1970; *Paperback Hero* 1972; *Pat Garrett and Billy the Kid* 1973; *Sleeper* 1973; *Rollerball* 1975; *The Big Bus* 1976; *Audrey Rose* 1977; *The Other Side of Midnight* 1977; *Deadly Illusion* 1987; *A Row of Crows* 1991
Beck, Julian (1925–1985) *Oedipus Rex* 1967; *Poltergeist II: the Other Side* 1986
Beck, Kimberly (1958–) *Roller Boogie* 1979; *Friday the 13th: the Final Chapter* 1984
Beck, Michael (1949–) *The Warriors* 1979; *Xanadu* 1980; *Battletruck* 1982; *The Golden Seal* 1983; *Triumphs of a Man Called Horse* 1983; *Chiller* 1985
Beck, Stanley (1936–) *John and Mary* 1969; *Lenny* 1974
Beck, Thomas (1909–1995) *Charlie Chan in Egypt* 1935; *Charlie Chan in Paris* 1935; *Charlie Chan at the Opera* 1936; *Crack-Up* 1936; *White Fang* 1936; *Heidi* 1937; *Thank You, Mr Moto* 1937; *Think Fast, Mr Moto* 1937
Beck, Vincent (1924–1984) *Santa Claus Conquers the Martians* 1964; *Don't Just Stand There* 1968
Beckel, Graham (1955–) *The Paper Chase* 1973; *The Road Home* 1989; *Welcome Home, Roxy Carmichael* 1990; *Liebestraum* 1991; *Jennifer Eight* 1992; *Murder of Innocence* 1993; *Black Dog* 1998; *Blue Streak* 1999; *Northfork* 2002
Becker, Belinda *The Sticky Fingers of Time* 1997; *Life and Debt* 2001
Becker, Gerry (1950–) *The Public Eye* 1992; *Donnie Brasco* 1997; *The Hunley* 1999; *Man on the Moon* 1999; *Mickey Blue Eyes* 1999
Becker, Gretchen *Firehead* 1991; *Huck and the King of Hearts* 1993
Becker, Meret (1969–) *The Promise* 1994; *Painted Angels* 1997
Beckett, James *Rotten to the Core* 1965; *Poor Cow* 1967
Beckett, Scotty (1929–1968) *Dante's Inferno* 1935; *Listen, Darling* 1938; *My Favorite Wife* 1940; *Circumstantial Evidence* 1945; *Cynthia* 1947; *The Happy Years* 1950
Beckinsale, Kate (1973–) *One against the Wind* 1991; *Much Ado about Nothing* 1993; *Prince of Jutland* 1994; *Haunted* 1995; *Shooting Fish* 1997; *The Last Days of Disco* 1998; *Brokedown Palace* 1999; *The Golden Bowl* 2000; *Pearl Harbor* 2001; *Serendipity* 2001; *Laurel Canyon* 2002; *Underworld* 2003; *The Aviator* 2004; *Van Helsing* 2004
Beckinsale, Richard (1947–1979) *The Lovers!* 1972; *Rentadick* 1972; *Porridge* 1979
Beckley, Tony (1927–1980) *The Penthouse* 1967; *The Long Day's Dying* 1968; *The Lost Continent* 1968; *The Italian Job* 1969; *Assault* 1970; *The Fiend* 1971; *Diagnosis: Murder* 1974; *Gold* 1974; *When a Stranger Calls* 1979
Beckley, William *The Collector* 1965; *Young Lady Chatterley* 1976
Beckman, Henry (1925–) *The Harness* 1971; *The Brood* 1979
Beckwith, Reginald (1908–1965) *Scott of the Antarctic* 1948; *Mr Drake's Duck* 1950; *Another Man's Poison* 1951; *Penny Princess* 1952; *Genevieve* 1953; *The Million Pound Note* 1953; *Dance Little Lady* 1954; *Lease of Life* 1954; *Men of Sherwood Forest* 1954; *The Runaway Bus* 1954; *Break in the Circle* 1955; *The Lyons in Paris* 1955; *They Can't Hang Me* 1955; *A Yank in Ermine* 1955; *A Touch of the Sun* 1956; *Night of the Demon* 1957; *The Captain's Table* 1958; *Next to No Time* 1958; *Up the Creek* 1958; *Bottoms Up* 1959; *Desert Mice* 1959; *The Thirty-Nine Steps* 1959; *The Night We Got the Bird* 1960; *There Was a Crooked Man* 1960; *The Day the Earth Caught Fire* 1961; *Dentist on the Job* 1961; *Double Bunk* 1961; *Night of the Eagle* 1961; *The Password Is Courage* 1962
Becwar, George (1917–1970) *Bride of the Monster* 1955; *War of the Colossal Beast* 1958
Bedard, Irene (1967–) *Squanto: the Last Great Warrior* 1994; *Pocahontas* 1995; *Pocahontas II: Journey to a New World* 1998; *Smoke Signals* 1998; *Two for Texas* 1998
Beddoe, Don (1891–1991) *The Amazing Mr Williams* 1939; *The Man They Could Not Hang* 1939; *The Face behind the Mask* 1941; *Sweetheart of the Campus* 1941; *Texas* 1941; *Unholy Partners* 1941; *The Boogie Man Will Get You* 1942; *The Bachelor and the Bobby-Soxer* 1947; *Buck Privates Come Home* 1947; *The Lady Gambles* 1949; *The Company She Keeps* 1950; *Carson City* 1952; *Bullwhip* 1958; *The Boy Who Caught a Crook* 1961; *Jack the Giant Killer* 1962
Bedelia, Bonnie (1946–) *The Gypsy Moths* 1969; *They Shoot Horses, Don't They?* 1969; *Lovers and Other Strangers* 1970; *The Strange Vengeance of Rosalie* 1972; *The Big Fix* 1978; *Salem's Lot* 1979; *Heart like a Wheel* 1983; *Death of an Angel* 1985; *The Boy Who Could Fly* 1986; *Violets Are Blue* 1986; *The Stranger* 1987; *Die Hard* 1988; *The Prince of Pennsylvania* 1988; *Shadow Makers* 1989; *Die Hard 2: Die Harder* 1990; *Presumed Innocent* 1990; *Needful Things* 1993; *Speechless* 1994; *Judicial Consent* 1995; *Homecoming* 1996; *Bad Manners* 1998; *Gloria* 1998; *Anywhere but Here* 1999
Bedell, Rodney *The Gruesome Twosome* 1967; *She-Devils on Wheels* 1968
Bedford, Barbara (1903–1981) *The Last of the Mohicans* 1920; *Tumbleweeds* 1925; *Tol'able David* 1930
Bedford, Brian (1935–) *Miracle in Soho* 1957; *Grand Prix* 1966; *The Pad (and How to Use It)* 1966; *Robin Hood* 1973; *Nixon* 1995
Bedi, Kabir (1945–) *The Thief of Baghdad* 1978; *Ashanti* 1979; *Octopussy* 1983; *The Beast of War* 1988; *Terminal Entry* 1988
Bedoya, Alfonso (1904–1957) *Angel in Exile* 1948; *The Treasure of the Sierra Madre* 1948; *Border Incident* 1949; *Streets of Laredo* 1949; *The Stranger Wore a Gun* 1953; *The Big Country* 1958
Beeby, Bruce (1923–) *The Limping Man* 1953; *The Man in the Road* 1957; *Serena* 1962
Beecher, Janet (1884–1955) *The Last Gentleman* 1934; *The Mighty Barnum* 1934; *The Dark Angel* 1935; *So Red the Rose* 1935; *Village Tale* 1935; *Love before Breakfast* 1936; *Big City* 1937; *The Story of Vernon and Irene Castle* 1939; *The Gay Caballero* 1940; *The Mark of Zorro* 1940; *The Lady Eve* 1941
Beena *Kitne Door... Kitne Paas* 2001; *Khushi* 2002
Beery, Noah *aka* **Beery Sr, Noah** (1884–1946) *The Mark of Zorro* 1920; *Beau Geste* 1926; *Beau Sabreur* 1928; *Noah's Ark* 1928; *The Four Feathers* 1929; *Renegades* 1930; *Tol'able David* 1930; *Under a Texas Moon* 1930; *Riders of the Purple Sage* 1931; *The Big Stampede* 1932; *The Kid from Spain* 1932; *She Done Him Wrong* 1933; *Caravan* 1934; *The Trail Beyond* 1934; *King of the Damned* 1935; *The Avenging Hand* 1936; *Someone at the Door* 1936; *Clancy Street Boys* 1943; *Barbary Coast Gent* 1944; *Block Busters* 1944; *This Man's Navy* 1945
Beery Jr, Noah *aka* **Beery, Noah** (1913–1994) *The Trail Beyond* 1934; *Stormy* 1935; *Trouble at Midnight* 1937; *Forbidden Valley* 1938; *Bad Lands* 1939; *Of Mice and Men* 1939; *Frontier Badmen* 1943; *Gung Ho!* 1943; *The Daltons Ride Again* 1945; *Under Western Skies* 1945; *Red River* 1948; *The Doolins of Oklahoma* 1949; *Two Flags West* 1950; *The Cimarron Kid* 1951; *War Arrow* 1953; *The Yellow Tomahawk* 1954; *White Feather* 1955; *The Fastest Gun Alive* 1956; *Jubal* 1956; *Decision at Sundown* 1957; *Escort West* 1959; *Guns of the Timberland* 1960; *7 Faces of Dr Lao* 1963; *The Cockeyed Cowboys of Calico County* 1970; *Little Fauss and Big Halsy* 1970; *Smash-Up Alley* 1972; *Walking Tall* 1973; *The Spikes Gang* 1974; *Part 2 Walking Tall* 1975
Beery, Wallace (1885–1949) *The Last of the Mohicans* 1920; *Robin Hood* 1922; *The Three Ages* 1923; *The Sea Hawk* 1924; *The Lost World* 1925; *The Pony Express* 1925; *Beggars of Life* 1928; *The Big House* 1930; *Billy the Kid* 1930; *A Lady's Morals* 1930; *Min and Bill* 1930; *The Champ* 1931; *The Secret Six* 1931; *Flesh* 1932; *Grand Hotel* 1932; *Hell Divers* 1932; *The Bowery* 1933; *Dinner at Eight* 1933; *Tugboat Annie* 1933; *The Mighty Barnum* 1934; *Treasure Island* 1934; *Viva Villa!* 1934; *Ah, Wilderness!* 1935; *China Seas* 1935; *A Message to Garcia* 1936; *Slave Ship* 1937; *Bad Man of Brimstone* 1938; *Port of Seven Seas* 1938; *Sergeant Madden* 1939; *Thunder Afloat* 1939; *The Man from Dakota* 1940; *Salute to the Marines* 1943; *Barbary Coast Gent* 1944; *This Man's Navy* 1945; *Bad Bascomb* 1946; *A Date with Judy* 1948; *Big Jack* 1949
Beesley, Max (1971–) *The Match* 1999; *It Was an Accident* 2000; *Glitter* 2001; *Kill Me Later* 2001; *Anita & Me* 2002
Beghe, Jason (1960–) *Monkey Shines* 1988; *Thelma & Louise* 1991; *Jimmy Hollywood* 1994; *GI Jane* 1997; *Taming Andrew* 2000
Beglau, Bibiana *The Legends of Rita* 2000; *Ten Minutes Older: the Cello* 2002
Begley, Ed (1901–1970) *Sitting Pretty* 1948; *Sorry, Wrong Number* 1948; *The Street with No Name* 1948; *It Happens Every Spring* 1949; *Tulsa* 1949; *Backfire* 1950; *Dark City* 1950; *Saddle Tramp* 1950; *Stars in My Crown* 1950; *Wyoming Mail* 1950; *Boots Malone* 1951; *On Dangerous Ground* 1951; *Deadline – USA* 1952; *Lone Star* 1952; *The Turning Point* 1952; *Patterns* 1956; *12 Angry Men* 1957; *Odds against Tomorrow* 1959; *The Green Helmet* 1960; *Sweet Bird of Youth* 1962; *The Unsinkable Molly Brown* 1964; *The Oscar* 1966; *Billion Dollar Brain* 1967; *Warning Shot* 1967; *Firecreek* 1968; *Hang 'Em High* 1968; *Wild in the Streets* 1968; *Road to Salina* 1969; *The Violent Enemy* 1969; *The Dunwich Horror* 1970
Begley Jr, Ed (1949–) *Showdown* 1973; *Blue Collar* 1978; *The One and Only* 1978; *The In-Laws* 1979; *Private Lessons* 1981; *Cat People* 1982; *Eating Raoul* 1982; *Get Crazy* 1983; *Protocol* 1984; *Transylvania 6-5000* 1985; *Amazon Women on the Moon* 1987; *The Accidental Tourist* 1988; *Scenes from the Class Struggle In Beverly Hills* 1989; *She-Devil* 1989; *Meet the Applegates* 1991; *Dark Horse* 1992; *Cooperstown* 1993; *Even Cowgirls Get the Blues* 1993; *Greedy* 1994; *The Pagemaster* 1994; *Renaissance Man* 1994; *Two Much Trouble* 1995; *The Late Shift* 1996; *Santa with Muscles* 1996; *Addams Family Reunion* 1998; *I'm Losing You* 1998; *Diary of a Sex Addict* 2001; *Get over It* 2001; *A Mighty Wind* 2003
Behan, Paudge *Snakes & Ladders* 1996; *A Secret Affair* 1999
Behets, Briony (1951–) *Long Weekend* 1977; *Cassandra* 1987
Behr, Dani (1975–) *Like It Is* 1997; *Rancid Aluminium* 1999; *Goodbye Charlie Bright* 2000
Behr, Jason (1973–) *Rites of Passage* 1999; *The Grudge* 2004
Behrens, Bernard *The Changeling* 1980; *Zero Patience* 1993
Behrens, Sam (1950–) *And You Thought Your Parents Were Weird* 1991; *Alive* 1992
Beirute, Yerye *Battle Shock* 1956; *Alien Terror* 1969
Bekassy, Stephen (1910–1995) *A Song to Remember* 1945; *Arch of Triumph* 1948; *Black Magic* 1949; *Hell and High Water* 1954; *Calypso Joe* 1957
Bel Geddes, Barbara (1922–) *The Long Night* 1947; *Blood on the Moon* 1948; *I Remember Mama* 1948; *Caught* 1949; *Panic in the Streets* 1950; *Fourteen Hours* 1951; *Vertigo* 1958; *The Five Pennies* 1959; *Five Branded Women* 1960; *By Love Possessed* 1961; *The Todd Killings* 1971
Belafonte, Harry (1927–) *Bright Road* 1953; *Carmen Jones* 1954; *Island in the Sun* 1957; *Odds against Tomorrow* 1959; *The World, the Flesh and the Devil* 1959; *The Angel Levine* 1970; *King: a Filmed Record... Montgomery to Memphis* 1970; *Buck and the Preacher* 1972; *Uptown Saturday Night* 1974; *Kansas City* 1995; *White Man's Burden* 1995; *Robert Altman's Jazz '34: Remembrances of Kansas City Swing* 1996
Belafonte, Shari *aka* **Belafonte-Harper, Shari** (1954–) *Cannonball Fever* 1989; *Fire, Ice and Dynamite* 1990
Belasco, Leon (1902–1988) *Everybody Does It* 1949; *Love Happy* 1949; *Jalopy* 1953
Belcher, Charles (1872–1943) *Rosita* 1923; *The Thief of Bagdad* 1924; *The Black Pirate* 1926
Belford, Christine (1949–) *The Groundstar Conspiracy* 1972; *Pocket Money* 1972; *Agatha Christie's Sparkling Cyanide* 1983; *Christine* 1983; *The Ladies Club* 1986
Belita (1923–) *The Gangster* 1947; *The Man on the Eiffel Tower* 1949; *Never Let Me Go* 1953
Belkhadra, Karim *La Haine* 1995; *The Crimson Rivers* 2000; *Room to Rent* 2000
Bell, Ann (1940–) *A Midsummer Night's Dream* 1961; *Stopover Forever* 1964; *The Witches* 1966; *The Reckoning* 1969; *Champions* 1983; *When Saturday Comes* 1995
Bell, Arnold (1988–) *Doss House* 1933; *The Greed of William Hart* 1948; *The Master Plan* 1954
Bell, Dan *Brothers in Arms* 1988; *The Shot* 1996
Bell, Edward *The Premonition* 1975; *Gymkata* 1985
Bell, James (1891–1973) *White Woman* 1933; *Holiday Inn* 1942; *I Walked with a Zombie* 1943; *The Leopard Man* 1943; *My Friend Flicka* 1943; *Thunderhead – Son of Flicka* 1945; *The Company She Keeps* 1950; *Red Mountain* 1951; *Japanese War Bride* 1952; *About Mrs Leslie* 1954; *The City Is Dark* 1954; *A Lawless Street* 1955; *Texas Lady* 1955; *-30-* 1959
Bell, Jamie (1986–) *Billy Elliot* 2000; *Deathwatch* 2002; *Nicholas Nickleby* 2002; *Undertow* 2004; *Dear Wendy* 2005
Bell, Kristen (1980–) *The Cat Returns* 2002; *Spartan* 2004
Bell, Marie (1900–1985) *Le Grand Jeu* 1933; *Un Carnet de Bal* 1937; *La Bonne Soupe* 1963; *Hotel Paradiso* 1966
Bell, Marshall (1944–) *Twins* 1988; *Total Recall* 1990; *Leather Jackets* 1991; *The Vagrant* 1992; *The Brave* 1997; *Virus* 1998; *Mercy* 2000

Bell, Nicholas *Father* 1990; *Hotel Sorrento* 1994; *Dead Letter Office* 1998
Bell, Tobin *False Identity* 1990; *The Quick and the Dead* 1995; *Serial Killer* 1996; *Overnight Delivery* 1997; *Brown's Requiem* 1998; *The Road to El Dorado* 2000; *Saw* 2004
Bell, Tom (1932–) *The Kitchen* 1961; *Payroll* 1961; *A Prize of Arms* 1961; *HMS Defiant* 1962; *The L-Shaped Room* 1962; *Ballad in Blue* 1964; *He Who Rides a Tiger* 1965; *In Enemy Country* 1968; *The Long Day's Dying* 1968; *Lock Up Your Daughters!* 1969; *The Violent Enemy* 1969; *Quest for Love* 1971; *Royal Flash* 1975; *The Sailor's Return* 1978; *The Innocent* 1984; *Wish You Were Here* 1987; *Resurrected* 1989; *The Krays* 1990; *Let Him Have It* 1991; *Prospero's Books* 1991; *Feast of July* 1995; *Amy Foster* 1997; *Preaching to the Perverted* 1997; *Swing* 1998; *Lava* 2000; *Long Time Dead* 2001; *My Kingdom* 2001; *Devil's Gate* 2002
Bell Calloway, Vanessa (1957–) *Bebe's Kids* 1992; *Tina: What's Love Got to Do with It* 1993; *No Ordinary Summer* 1994; *Love Don't Cost a Thing* 2003
Bella, Rachael (1984–) *Household Saints* 1993; *The Blood Oranges* 1997
Bellamy, Bill (1965–) *How to Be a Player* 1997; *Love Jones* 1997; *Love Stinks* 1999; *Buying the Cow* 2000; *The Brothers* 2001
Bellamy, Madge (1899–1990) *The Iron Horse* 1924; *White Zombie* 1932; *Charlie Chan in London* 1934
Bellamy, Ralph (1904–1991) *The Secret Six* 1931; *Air Mail* 1932; *Forbidden* 1932; *Ace of Aces* 1933; *Blind Adventure* 1933; *Ever in My Heart* 1933; *Picture Snatcher* 1933; *Spitfire* 1934; *This Man Is Mine* 1934; *Hands across the Table* 1935; *The Wedding Night* 1935; *The Man Who Lived Twice* 1936; *The Awful Truth* 1937; *Boy Meets Girl* 1938; *Carefree* 1938; *Fools for Scandal* 1938; *Trade Winds* 1938; *Blind Alley* 1939; *His Girl Friday* 1939; *Brother Orchid* 1940; *Dance, Girl, Dance* 1940; *Ellery Queen Master Detective* 1940; *Affectionately Yours* 1941; *Dive Bomber* 1941; *Footsteps in the Dark* 1941; *The Wolf Man* 1941; *The Ghost of Frankenstein* 1942; *Lady in a Jam* 1942; *Men of Texas* 1942; *Stage Door Canteen* 1943; *Guest in the House* 1944; *Lady on a Train* 1945; *The Court-Martial of Billy Mitchell* 1955; *Sunrise at Campobello* 1960; *The Professionals* 1966; *Rosemary's Baby* 1968; *Doctors' Wives* 1970; *Cancel My Reservation* 1972; *The Boy in the Plastic Bubble* 1976; *Oh, God!* 1977; *Trading Places* 1983; *Amazon Women on the Moon* 1987; *Disorderlies* 1987; *Coming to America* 1988; *The Price of Passion* 1988; *Pretty Woman* 1990
Bellaver, Harry (1905–1993) *No Way Out* 1950; *Perfect Strangers* 1950; *Something to Live For* 1952; *Miss Sadie Thompson* 1953; *Love Me or Leave Me* 1955; *The Birds and the Bees* 1956; *Serenade* 1956; *The Brothers Rico* 1957; *The Old Man and the Sea* 1958; *One Potato, Two Potato* 1964; *Blue Collar* 1978; *Hero at Large* 1980
Belle, Camilla (1986–) *Annie: a Royal Adventure* 1995; *Poison Ivy 2* 1995; *Marshal Law* 1996
Beller, Kathleen (1955–) *Something for Joey* 1977; *The Betsy* 1978; *Promises in the Dark* 1979; *Fort Apache, the Bronx* 1981; *The Sword and the Sorcerer* 1982; *Time Trackers* 1989
Belli, Agostina (1949–) *Bluebeard* 1972; *The Seduction of Mimi* 1972; *Scent of a Woman* 1974; *Holocaust 2000* 1977; *The Purple Taxi* 1977
Bellingham, Lynda (1948–) *Sweeney!* 1976; *Stand Up Virgin Soldiers* 1977; *Bodywork* 1999; *Devil's Gate* 2002
Bellini, Francesca *Bachelor Flat* 1961; *Who's Minding the Store?* 1963
Bellman, Gina (1966–) *Secret Friends* 1991; *Leon the Pig Farmer* 1992; *Silent Trigger* 1996; *7 Days to Live* 2000; *Married/Unmarried* 2001
Bello, Maria (1967–) *Payback* 1998; *Permanent Midnight* 1998; *Coyote Ugly* 2000; *Duets* 2000; *Auto Focus* 2002; *The Cooler* 2002; *Secret Window* 2004; *Silver City* 2004; *Assault on Precinct 13* 2005; *A History of Violence* 2005
Bellows, Gil (1967–) *Love and a .45* 1994; *The Shawshank Redemption* 1994; *Miami Rhapsody* 1995; *Snow White: a Tale of Terror* 1996; *The Substance of Fire* 1996; *Judas Kiss* 1998; *Beautiful Joe* 2000
Bellucci, Monica (1968–) *L'Appartement* 1996; *Dobermann* 1997; *Malena* 2000; *Under Suspicion* 2000; *Asterix & Obelix: Mission Cleopatra* 2001; *Brotherhood of the Wolf* 2001; *Irreversible* 2002; *The Matrix Reloaded* 2002; *The Matrix Revolutions* 2003; *Tears of the Sun* 2003; *The Passion of the Christ* 2004; *She Hate Me* 2004
Bellwood, Pamela (1951–) *Hangar 18* 1980; *Serial* 1980; *Agatha Christie's Sparkling Cyanide* 1983
Belmadi, Yasmine (1976–) *Criminal Lovers* 1999; *Who Killed Bambi?* 2003; *Wild Side* 2004
Belmondo, Jean-Paul (1933–) *A Bout de Souffle* 1959; *Web of Passion* 1959; *The Big Risk* 1960; *Two Women* 1960; *Cartouche* 1961; *Une Femme Est une Femme* 1961; *Léon Morin, Priest* 1961; *Le Doulos* 1962; *A Monkey in Winter* 1962; *L'Ainé des Ferchaux* 1963; *Banana Peel* 1964; *Male Hunt* 1964; *That Man from Rio* 1964; *Pierrot le Fou* 1965; *Up to His Ears* 1965; *Is Paris Burning?* 1966; *Casino Royale* 1967; *The Thief of Paris* 1967; *Ho!* 1968; *The Brain* 1969; *Mississippi Mermaid* 1969; *Borsalino* 1970; *The Burglars* 1971; *Sink or Swim* 1971; *The Inheritor* 1973; *Stavisky* 1974; *The Professional* 1981; *Hold-Up* 1985; *Les Misérables* 1995
Belmont, Lara *The War Zone* 1999; *Long Time Dead* 2001
Belmore, Bertha (1882–1953) *Broken Blossoms* 1936; *In the Soup* 1936; *Please Teacher* 1937; *Hold My Hand* 1938
Belmore, Lionel (1867–1953) *Oliver Twist* 1922; *The Three Ages* 1923; *The Matinee Idol* 1928; *Monte Carlo* 1930; *The Rogue Song* 1930; *Frankenstein* 1931; *One Heavenly Night* 1931; *Berkeley Square* 1933
Beltran, Robert (1953–) *Eating Raoul* 1982; *Lone Wolf McQuade* 1983; *Night of the Comet* 1984; *Latino* 1985; *Gaby: a True Story* 1987; *Slam Dance* 1987; *Scenes from the Class Struggle in Beverly Hills* 1989
Beltran, Susana *Blood of the Virgins* 1967; *Curious Dr Humpp* 1967
Belushi, James aka **Belushi, Jim** (1954–) *Thief* 1981; *Trading Places* 1983; *The Man with One Red Shoe* 1985; *About Last Night...* 1986; *Jumpin' Jack Flash* 1986; *Little Shop of Horrors* 1986; *Salvador* 1986; *The Principal* 1987; *Real Men* 1987; *Red Heat* 1988; *Homer and Eddie* 1989; *K-9* 1989; *Mr Destiny* 1990; *Taking Care of Business* 1990; *Curly Sue* 1991; *Only the Lonely* 1991; *Diary of a Hitman* 1992; *Once upon a Crime* 1992; *Traces of Red* 1992; *Canadian Bacon* 1995; *Destiny Turns on the Radio* 1995; *The Pebble and the Penguin* 1995; *Separate Lives* 1995; *Gold in the Streets* 1996; *Jingle All the Way* 1996; *Race the Sun* 1996; *Gang Related* 1997; *Wag the Dog* 1997; *Angel's Dance* 1999; *K-911* 1999; *Made Men* 1999; *Return to Me* 2000; *Joe Somebody* 2001; *One Way Out* 2002
Belushi, John (1949–1982) *Goin' South* 1978; *National Lampoon's Animal House* 1978; *The Rutles – All You Need Is Cash* 1978; *1941* 1979; *Old Boyfriends* 1979; *The Blues Brothers* 1980; *Continental Divide* 1981; *Neighbors* 1981
Belvaux, Lucas (1961–) *Cop au Vin* 1984; *Madame Bovary* 1991; *[One] Cavale* 2002; *[Three] Après la Vie* 2002; *[Two] Un Couple Epatant* 2002
Belzer, Richard (1944–) *The Groove Tube* 1974; *America* 1986; *Missing Pieces* 1991; *Off and Running* 1991; *The Puppet Masters* 1994; *Get on the Bus* 1996
Ben-Victor, Paul *Body Parts* 1991; *Trouble Bound* 1993; *The Corruptor* 1999; *The Three Stooges* 2000
Benben, Brian (1956–) *Dark Angel* 1989; *Mortal Sins* 1989; *Radioland Murders* 1994
Benchley, Robert (1889–1945) *Dancing Lady* 1933; *China Seas* 1935; *Piccadilly Jim* 1936; *Live, Love and Learn* 1937; *Foreign Correspondent* 1940; *Hired Wife* 1940; *Nice Girl?* 1941; *You'll Never Get Rich* 1941; *Bedtime Story* 1942; *I Married a Witch* 1942; *The Major and the Minor* 1942; *Take a Letter, Darling* 1942; *Young and Willing* 1942; *Flesh and Fantasy* 1943; *The Sky's the Limit* 1943; *Practically Yours* 1944; *See Here, Private Hargrove* 1944; *It's in the Bag* 1945; *Kiss and Tell* 1945; *Pan-Americana* 1945; *Road to Utopia* 1945; *The Stork Club* 1945; *Week-End at the Waldorf* 1945; *Blue Skies* 1946; *The Bride Wore Boots* 1946
Bender, Dawn aka **Anderson, Dawn** (1937–1975) *The Actress* 1953; *Teenagers from Outer Space* 1959
Bender, Russ (1910–1969) *The Amazing Colossal Man* 1957; *Motorcycle Gang* 1957; *Suicide Battalion* 1958; *War of the Colossal Beast* 1958
Bendix, William (1906–1964) *The Glass Key* 1942; *Star Spangled Rhythm* 1942; *Wake Island* 1942; *Woman of the Year* 1942; *China* 1943; *The Crystal Ball* 1943; *Guadalcanal Diary* 1943; *Hostages* 1943; *Abroad with Two Yanks* 1944; *Greenwich Village* 1944; *The Hairy Ape* 1944; *Lifeboat* 1944; *A Bell for Adano* 1945; *It's in the Bag* 1945; *The Blue Dahlia* 1946; *The Dark Corner* 1946; *Sentimental Journey* 1946; *Two Years before the Mast* 1946; *Blaze of Noon* 1947; *Calcutta* 1947; *I'll Be Yours* 1947; *The Web* 1947; *Where There's Life* 1947; *The Babe Ruth Story* 1948; *The Time of Your Life* 1948; *The Big Steal* 1949; *A Connecticut Yankee in King Arthur's Court* 1949; *Streets of Laredo* 1949; *Detective Story* 1951; *Blackbeard the Pirate* 1952; *A Girl in Every Port* 1952; *Macao* 1952; *Dangerous Mission* 1954; *Crashout* 1955; *The Deep Six* 1958; *The Rough and the Smooth* 1959; *For Love or Money* 1963
Benedetti, Caprice *Italian Movie* 1994; *Sleeping Together* 1997
Benedetti, Pierre *La Bête* 1975; *Heroines of Evil* 1979
Benedict, Billy (1917–1999) *Ghosts in the Night* 1943; *Block Busters* 1944; *Bowery Champs* 1944; *Come Out Fighting* 1945; *Docks of New York* 1945; *Mr Muggs Rides Again* 1945
Benedict, Brooks (1896–1968) *The Freshman* 1925; *Speedy* 1928; *Gun Smoke* 1931; *What Price Hollywood?* 1932
Benedict, Dirk (1945–) *Georgia, Georgia* 1972; *Ssssss* 1973; *W* 1974; *Battlestar Galactica* 1978; *Scavenger Hunt* 1979; *The November Conspiracy* 1995; *Alaska* 1996; *Waking Up Horton* 1997
Benedict, Paul (1938–) *Taking Off* 1971; *Deadhead Miles* 1972; *Jeremiah Johnson* 1972; *The Goodbye Girl* 1977; *The Man with Two Brains* 1983; *Arthur 2: On the Rocks* 1988; *The Freshman* 1990; *The Addams Family* 1991; *Attack of the 50 Ft Woman* 1993
Benedict, Richard (1916–1984) *OSS* 1946; *Ace in the Hole* 1951; *Jalopy* 1953; *Beginning of the End* 1957
Benet, Marianne *Shake Hands with the Devil* 1959; *The Boy Who Stole a Million* 1960; *A Terrible Beauty* 1960
Beneyton, Yves *Weekend* 1967; *The Lacemaker* 1977; *Letters to an Unknown Lover* 1985; *Eminent Domain* 1991; *Rogue Trader* 1998
Benfield, John *Hidden Agenda* 1990; *24 Hours in London* 1999; *You're Dead* 1999
Benge, Wilson (1875–1955) *Bulldog Drummond* 1929; *The Bat Whispers* 1930; *Charley's Aunt* 1930; *The Lady Eve* 1941
Bengell, Norma (1935–) *The Given Word* 1962; *Planet of the Vampires* 1965; *The Color of Destiny* 1986
Benguigui, Jean (1944–) *La Garce* 1984; *Salut Cousin!* 1996
Benham, Joan (1918–1981) *King's Rhapsody* 1955; *Murder Ahoy* 1964; *Perfect Friday* 1970
Bénichou, Maurice (1943–) *Fausto* 1992; *Drôle de Félix* 2000; *Time of the Wolf* 2003
Benicio, Murilo (1972–) *Woman on Top* 2000; *The Man of the Year* 2002
Benigni, Roberto (1952–) *La Luna* 1979; *Tigers in Lipstick* 1979; *Tigers in Lipstick* 1979; *Down by Law* 1986; *Johnny Stecchino* 1991; *Night on Earth* 1992; *Son of the Pink Panther* 1993; *Life Is Beautiful* 1997; *Asterix and Obelix Take On Caesar* 1999; *Pinocchio* 2002; *Coffee and Cigarettes* 2003
Bening, Annette (1958–) *The Great Outdoors* 1988; *Valmont* 1989; *The Grifters* 1990; *Guilty by Suspicion* 1990; *Postcards from the Edge* 1990; *Bugsy* 1991; *Regarding Henry* 1991; *Love Affair* 1994; *The American President* 1995; *Richard III* 1995; *Mars Attacks!* 1996; *In Dreams* 1998; *The Siege* 1998; *American Beauty* 1999; *What Planet Are You From?* 2000; *Open Range* 2003; *Being Julia* 2004
Benjamin, Christopher (1934–) *The Plague Dogs* 1982; *Treasure Island* 1998
Benjamin, Paul *Across 110th Street* 1972; *The Deadly Trackers* 1973; *Leadbelly* 1976; *Escape from Alcatraz* 1979; *Some Kind of Hero* 1982; *Last Rites* 1998; *The Station Agent* 2003
Benjamin, Richard (1938–) *Goodbye, Columbus* 1969; *Catch-22* 1970; *Diary of a Mad Housewife* 1970; *The Marriage of a Young Stockbroker* 1971; *Portnoy's Complaint* 1972; *The Last of Sheila* 1973; *Westworld* 1973; *The Sunshine Boys* 1975; *House Calls* 1978; *Love at First Bite* 1979; *Scavenger Hunt* 1979; *Witches' Brew* 1979; *First Family* 1980; *How to Beat the High Cost of Living* 1980; *The Last Married Couple in America* 1980; *Saturday the 14th* 1981; *Deconstructing Harry* 1997; *The Pentagon Wars* 1998; *Marci X* 2003
Bennent, Anne (1963–) *Swann in Love* 1984; *71 Fragments of a Chronology of Chance* 1994
Bennent, David (1968–) *The Tin Drum* 1979; *Legend* 1985
Bennent, Heinz (1921–) *The Lost Honour of Katharina Blum* 1975; *The Serpent's Egg* 1977; *The Last Metro* 1980; *Possession* 1981; *The Death of Mario Ricci* 1983; *Une Femme Française* 1994
Bennes, John *Black Rainbow* 1989; *Stephen King's The Night Flier* 1997
Bennett, Alan (1934–) *Pleasure at Her Majesty's* 1976; *Long Shot* 1978; *In Love and War* 1996
Bennett, Belle (1891–1932) *Stella Dallas* 1925; *The Way of All Flesh* 1927; *The Iron Mask* 1929
Bennett, Brian (1940–) *Wonderful Life* 1964; *Finders Keepers* 1966
Bennett, Bruce aka **Brix, Herman** (1909–) *The New Adventures of Tarzan* 1935; *A Million to One* 1937; *Tarzan and the Green Goddess* 1938; *Before I Hang* 1940; *The More the Merrier* 1943; *Sahara* 1943; *Mildred Pierce* 1945; *The Man I Love* 1946; *A Stolen Life* 1946; *Dark Passage* 1947; *Nora Prentiss* 1947; *Silver River* 1948; *The Treasure of the Sierra Madre* 1948; *The Doctor and the Girl* 1949; *Task Force* 1949; *The Younger Brothers* 1949; *Mystery Street* 1950; *Shakedown* 1950; *Angels in the Outfield* 1951; *Sudden Fear* 1952; *The Big Tip Off* 1955; *Strategic Air Command* 1955; *Beyond the River* 1956; *Three Violent People* 1956; *Daniel Boone, Trail Blazer* 1957; *The Alligator People* 1959; *The Cosmic Man* 1959; *The Outsider* 1961
Bennett, Charles (1899–1995) *Tillie's Punctured Romance* 1914; *America* 1924
Bennett, Constance (1904–1965) *The Goose Woman* 1925; *Sally, Irene and Mary* 1925; *Lady with a Past* 1932; *Rockabye* 1932; *What Price Hollywood?* 1932; *Our Betters* 1933; *The Affairs of Cellini* 1934; *After Office Hours* 1935; *Everything Is Thunder* 1936; *Ladies in Love* 1936; *Topper* 1937; *Merrily We Live* 1938; *Topper Takes a Trip* 1939; *Two-Faced Woman* 1941; *Sin Town* 1942; *Centennial Summer* 1946; *The Unsuspected* 1947; *Smart Woman* 1948; *As Young as You Feel* 1951; *Madame X* 1966
Bennett, Enid (1895–1969) *Robin Hood* 1922; *The Sea Hawk* 1924; *Skippy* 1931; *Waterloo Bridge* 1931; *Intermezzo* 1939; *Meet Dr Christian* 1939
Bennett, Hywel (1944–) *The Family Way* 1966; *Twisted Nerve* 1968; *The Virgin Soldiers* 1969; *The Buttercup Chain* 1970; *Loot* 1970; *Endless Night* 1971; *Percy* 1971; *Witness in the War Zone* 1986; *Deadly Advice* 1993; *Nasty Neighbours* 2000; *One for the Road* 2003
Bennett, Jeff aka **Bennett, Jeff Glen** *Lady and the Tramp II: Scamp's Adventure* 2000; *Scooby-Doo and the Alien Invaders* 2000; *Return to Never Land* 2002
Bennett, Jill (1931–1990) *Hell below Zero* 1954; *Lust for Life* 1956; *The Criminal* 1960; *The Nanny* 1965; *The Skull* 1965; *The Charge of the Light Brigade* 1968; *Inadmissible Evidence* 1968; *Julius Caesar* 1970; *I Want What I Want* 1971; *Mister Quilp* 1975; *Full Circle* 1977; *For Your Eyes Only* 1981; *Britannia Hospital* 1982; *Lady Jane* 1985; *Hawks* 1988; *The Sheltering Sky* 1990
Bennett, Jimmy (1996–) *The Heart Is Deceitful above All Things* 2004; *Hostage* 2004; *The Amityville Horror* 2005
Bennett, Joan (1910–1990) *Bulldog Drummond* 1929; *Disraeli* 1929; *Moby Dick* 1930; *Me and My Gal* 1932; *Little Women* 1933; *The Man Who Broke the Bank at Monte Carlo* 1935; *Mississippi* 1935; *Private Worlds* 1935; *Big Brown Eyes* 1936; *Wedding Present* 1936; *Vogues of 1938* 1937; *Artists and Models Abroad* 1938; *I Met My Love Again* 1938; *The Texans* 1938; *Trade Winds* 1938; *Green Hell* 1939; *The Housekeeper's Daughter* 1939; *The Man in the Iron Mask* 1939; *The House across the Bay* 1940; *The Man I Married* 1940; *Son of Monte Cristo* 1940; *Confirm or Deny* 1941; *Man Hunt* 1941; *Wild Geese Calling* 1941; *Twin Beds* 1942; *Margin for Error* 1943; *Colonel Effingham's Raid* 1945; *Nob Hill* 1945; *Scarlet Street* 1945; *The Woman in the Window* 1945; *The Macomber Affair* 1947; *The Woman on the Beach* 1947; *Hollow Triumph* 1948; *Secret beyond the Door* 1948; *The Reckless Moment* 1949; *Father of*

the Bride 1950; *For Heaven's Sake* 1950; *Father's Little Dividend* 1951; *We're No Angels* 1955; *There's Always Tomorrow* 1956; *Desire in the Dust* 1960; *House of Dark Shadows* 1970; *Suspiria* 1976; *Divorce Wars* 1982
Bennett, John (1928–2005) *The House That Dripped Blood* 1971; *The House in Nightmare Park* 1973; *Watership Down* 1978
Bennett, Leila *The First Year* 1932; *Taxi!* 1932; *Tiger Shark* 1932
Bennett, Marjorie (1896–1982) *Limelight* 1952; *What Ever Happened to Baby Jane?* 1962; *Games* 1967
Bennett, Nigel (1949–) *Soft Deceit* 1994; *Sanctuary* 1997; *The Pilot's Wife* 2001; *Cypher* 2002
Bennett, Richard (1873–1944) *Arrowsmith* 1931; *If I Had a Million* 1932; *This Reckless Age* 1932; *Nana* 1934; *The Magnificent Ambersons* 1942
Bennett, Rosalind *Dealers* 1989; *Smack and Thistle* 1989
Benny, Jack (1894–1974) *Hollywood Revue* 1929; *Broadway Melody of 1936* 1935; *The Big Broadcast of 1937* 1936; *Artists and Models* 1937; *Artists and Models Abroad* 1938; *Buck Benny Rides Again* 1940; *Charley's Aunt* 1941; *George Washington Slept Here* 1942; *To Be or Not to Be* 1942; *The Meanest Man in the World* 1943; *Hollywood Canteen* 1944; *The Horn Blows at Midnight* 1945; *It's in the Bag* 1945; *Without Reservations* 1946; *Somebody Loves Me* 1952; *The Man* 1972
Benrath, Martin (1926–2000) *The Saboteur, Code Name Morituri* 1965; *From the Life of the Marionettes* 1980; *Stalingrad* 1992
Benrubi, Abraham (1969–) *The Program* 1993; *Open Range* 2003; *Without a Paddle* 2004
Benson, Deborah *September 30, 1955* 1977; *Just before Dawn* 1980
Benson, George (1911–1983) *Keep Fit* 1937; *The Creeping Flesh* 1972
Benson, Jodi (1961–) *The Little Mermaid* 1989; *Thumbelina* 1994; *Joseph: King of Dreams* 2000; *Lady and the Tramp II: Scamp's Adventure* 2000; *The Little Mermaid II: Return to the Sea* 2000
Benson, Lucille (1914–1984) *Little Fauss and Big Halsy* 1970; *Duel* 1971; *Tom Sawyer* 1973; *Huckleberry Finn* 1974
Benson, Martin (1918–) *I'll Get You for This* 1950; *Assassin for Hire* 1951; *The Dark Light* 1951; *West of Zanzibar* 1954; *The King and I* 1956; *The Flesh Is Weak* 1957; *Man from Tangier* 1957; *The Strange World of Planet X* 1957; *Oscar Wilde* 1959; *The Gentle Trap* 1960; *Gorgo* 1961; *Satan Never Sleeps* 1962; *Goldfinger* 1964; *The Magnificent Two* 1967; *Battle beneath the Earth* 1968; *The Omen* 1976
Benson, Perry *Annie: a Royal Adventure* 1995; *Final Cut* 1998; *Last Resort* 2000
Benson, Robby (1956–) *Jory* 1972; *Jeremy* 1973; *Lucky Lady* 1975; *Ode to Billy Joe* 1976; *One on One* 1977; *Ice Castles* 1978; *Walk Proud* 1979; *Die Laughing* 1980; *Tribute* 1980; *The Chosen* 1981; *National Lampoon's Movie Madness* 1981; *Harry and Son* 1984; *Rent-a-Cop* 1988; *Modern Love* 1990; *Beauty and the Beast* 1991; *Beauty and the Beast: the Enchanted Christmas* 1997; *Dragonheart: a New Beginning* 1999
Benson, Roy *Sweet and Lowdown* 1944; *Billy Rose's Diamond Horseshoe* 1945
Bentine, Michael (1922–1996) *Down among the Z-Men* 1952; *Forces' Sweetheart* 1953; *Raising a Riot* 1955; *We Joined the Navy* 1962; *The Sandwich Man* 1966; *Rentadick* 1972
Bentivoglio, Fabrizio (1957–) *Apartment Zero* 1988; *Eternity and a Day* 1998
Bentley, Beverly *Scent of Mystery* 1960; *Beyond the Law* 1968
Bentley, Dick (1907–1995) *Desert Mice* 1959; *And the Same to You* 1960; *In the Doghouse* 1961; *Tamahine* 1963; *The Adventures of Barry McKenzie* 1972; *Barry McKenzie Holds His Own* 1974
Bentley, John (1916–) *The Hills of Donegal* 1947; *The Happiest Days of Your Life* 1950; *The Lost Hours* 1952; *Tread Softly* 1952; *Double Exposure* 1954; *Final Appointment* 1954; *The Flaw* 1954; *Profile* 1954; *River Beat* 1954; *Confession* 1955; *Istanbul* 1957; *Submarine Seahawk* 1959; *The Singer Not the Song* 1960
Bentley, Wes (1978–) *American Beauty* 1999; *The Claim* 2000; *Soul Survivors* 2001; *The Four Feathers* 2002
Benton, Jerome *Purple Rain* 1984; *Under the Cherry Moon* 1986; *Graffiti Bridge* 1990
Benton, Mark (1965–) *Career Girls* 1997; *Mr In-Between* 2001
Benton, Susanne (1948–) *That Cold Day in the Park* 1969; *A Boy and His Dog* 1975
Benussi, Femi (1948–) *Hawks and Sparrows* 1966; *Hatchet for the Honeymoon* 1969
Benz, Julie (1972–) *Jawbreaker* 1999; *Shriek If You Know What I Did Last Friday the 13th* 2000
Benzali, Daniel (1950–) *Messenger of Death* 1988; *A Day in October* 1991; *Murder at 1600* 1997; *All the Little Animals* 1998; *Screwed* 2000; *Dead Heat* 2002
Beranger, George (1893–1973) *Broken Blossoms* 1919; *Road House* 1948
Bercek, Aleksandar (1950–) *Cabaret Balkan* 1998; *Life Is a Miracle* 2004
Bercovici, Luca (1957–) *Frightmare* 1981; *Parasite* 1982; *American Flyers* 1985; *Clean and Sober* 1988; *Mortal Passions* 1989; *K2* 1991; *Mission of Justice* 1992; *Drop Zone* 1994; *The Big Squeeze* 1996
Beregi, Oscar (1876–1965) *Anything Can Happen* 1952; *Desert Legion* 1953; *Panic in the City* 1968
Berenger, Tom (1950–) *Looking for Mr Goodbar* 1977; *The Sentinel* 1977; *In Praise of Older Women* 1978; *Butch and Sundance: the Early Days* 1979; *The Dogs of War* 1980; *The Big Chill* 1983; *Eddie and the Cruisers* 1983; *Fear City* 1984; *Rustler's Rhapsody* 1985; *Platoon* 1986; *Someone to Watch over Me* 1987; *Betrayed* 1988; *Deadly Pursuit* 1988; *Last Rites* 1988; *Born on the Fourth of July* 1989; *Major League* 1989; *The Field* 1990; *Love at Large* 1990; *At Play in the Fields of the Lord* 1991; *Shattered* 1991; *Sniper* 1992; *Gettysburg* 1993; *Sliver* 1993; *Chasers* 1994; *Major League II* 1994; *Last of the Dogmen* 1995; *The Substitute* 1996; *The Gingerbread Man* 1997; *A Murder of Crows* 1998; *Shadow of Doubt* 1998; *Diplomatic Siege* 1999; *In the Company of Spies* 1999; *Cutaway* 2000; *D-Tox* 2001; *Training Day* 2001
Berens, Harold (1903–1995) *Live Now – Pay Later* 1962; *Hear My Song* 1991
Berenson, Marisa (1946–) *Death in Venice* 1971; *Cabaret* 1972; *Barry Lyndon* 1975; *Casanova & Co* 1976; *Killer Fish* 1978; *Playing for Time* 1980; *SOB* 1981; *The Secret Diary of Sigmund Freud* 1984; *Perfume of the Cyclone* 1989; *White Hunter, Black Heart* 1990
Beresford, Harry (1864–1944) *Doctor X* 1932; *High Pressure* 1932; *The Sign of the Cross* 1932; *I Cover the Waterfront* 1933; *Murders in the Zoo* 1933; *Follow the Fleet* 1936; *Klondike Annie* 1936
Berg, Peter (1964–) *Never on Tuesday* 1988; *Race for Glory* 1989; *Shocker* 1989; *Genuine Risk* 1990; *Crooked Hearts* 1991; *Late for Dinner* 1991; *A Midnight Clear* 1991; *Aspen Extreme* 1993; *Fire in the Sky* 1993; *The Last Seduction* 1993; *FTW* 1994; *Girl 6* 1996; *The Great White Hype* 1996; *Cop Land* 1997; *Corky Romano* 2001; *Collateral* 2004
Bergé, Francine (1940–) *Judex* 1963; *La Ronde* 1964; *La Religieuse* 1965; *Une Histoire Simple* 1978
Bergen, Candice (1946–) *The Group* 1966; *The Sand Pebbles* 1966; *The Day the Fish Came Out* 1967; *Vivre pour Vivre* 1967; *The Magus* 1968; *The Adventurers* 1970; *Getting Straight* 1970; *Soldier Blue* 1970; *Carnal Knowledge* 1971; *The Hunting Party* 1971; *TR Baskin* 1971; *11 Harrowhouse* 1974; *Bite the Bullet* 1975; *The Wind and the Lion* 1975; *The Domino Principle* 1977; *The End of the World (in Our Usual Bed in a Night Full of Rain)* 1978; *Oliver's Story* 1978; *Starting Over* 1979; *Rich and Famous* 1981; *Gandhi* 1982; *Stick* 1985; *Miss Congeniality* 2000; *Sweet Home Alabama* 2002; *The In-Laws* 2003; *View from the Top* 2003
Bergen, Edgar (1903–1978) *The Goldwyn Follies* 1938; *You Can't Cheat an Honest Man* 1939; *Look Who's Laughing* 1941; *Here We Go Again* 1942; *Song of the Open Road* 1944; *Fun and Fancy Free* 1947; *I Remember Mama* 1948; *Don't Make Waves* 1967
Bergen, Polly (1930–) *At War with the Army* 1950; *The Stooge* 1951; *That's My Boy* 1951; *Warpath* 1951; *Arena* 1953; *Cry of the Hunted* 1953; *Escape from Fort Bravo* 1953; *Cape Fear* 1962; *The Caretakers* 1963; *Move Over, Darling* 1963; *Kisses for My President* 1964; *Making Mr Right* 1987; *Cry-Baby* 1989; *Leave of Absence* 1994; *Dr Jekyll and Ms Hyde* 1995; *In the Blink of an Eye* 1996
Bergen, Tushka (1969–) *Swing Kids* 1993; *Barcelona* 1994
Berger, Helmut (1944–) *The Damned* 1969; *The Garden of the Finzi-Continis* 1971; *Ash Wednesday* 1973; *Ludwig* 1973; *Conversation Piece* 1974; *The Romantic Englishwoman* 1975; *Salon Kitty* 1976; *Victory at Entebbe* 1976; *Mad Dog Murderer* 1977; *Deadly Game* 1982; *Code Name: Emerald* 1985
Bergé, Nicole (1935–1967) *The Ripening Seed* 1953; *Shoot the Pianist* 1960; *The Siege of Sidney Street* 1960
Berger, Senta (1941–) *The Secret Ways* 1961; *Sherlock Holmes and the Deadly Necklace* 1962; *The Victors* 1963; *The Glory Guys* 1965; *Major Dundee* 1965; *Cast a Giant Shadow* 1966; *Our Man in Marrakesh* 1966; *The Quiller Memorandum* 1966; *The Spy with My Face* 1966; *The Ambushers* 1967; *Diabolically Yours* 1967; *De Sade* 1969; *The Swiss Conspiracy* 1975; *Killing Cars* 1986
Berger, Toni (1921–2005) *The Serpent's Egg* 1977; *Sugarbaby* 1985
Berger, William (1928–1993) *Face to Face* 1967; *Sartana* 1968; *Today It's Me… Tomorrow You!* 1968; *Sabata* 1969; *Three Tough Guys* 1974; *Keoma* 1976; *Hercules* 1983; *Hercules II* 1983; *Tex and the Lord of the Deep* 1985; *Dr M* 1989
Bergerac, Jacques (1927–) *Beautiful Stranger* 1954; *Les Girls* 1957; *Gigi* 1958; *Thunder in the Sun* 1959; *Achilles* 1962; *The Unkissed Bride* 1966
Bergere, Lee (1924–) *Bob & Carol & Ted & Alice* 1969; *Time Trackers* 1989
Berggren, Thommy (1937–) *The Pram* 1963; *Raven's End* 1963; *Elvira Madigan* 1967; *Joe Hill* 1971; *Sunday's Children* 1992
Berghof, Herbert (1909–1990) *Assignment – Paris* 1952; *5 Fingers* 1952; *Red Planet Mars* 1952; *Dark Victory* 1976; *Those Lips, Those Eyes* 1980; *Times Square* 1980; *Target* 1985
Bergin, Patrick (1954–) *The Courier* 1987; *Taffin* 1988; *Mountains of the Moon* 1989; *Robin Hood* 1990; *Love Crimes* 1991; *Sleeping with the Enemy* 1991; *Highway to Hell* 1992; *Map of the Human Heart* 1992; *Patriot Games* 1992; *Soft Deceit* 1994; *Lawnmower Man 2: Beyond Cyberspace* 1995; *The Proposition* 1996; *The Island on Bird Street* 1997; *Treasure Island* 1998; *The Invisible Circus* 2000; *Merlin the Return* 2000; *St Patrick: the Irish Legend* 2000; *When the Sky Falls* 2000; *The Evil beneath Loch Ness* 2001; *Silent Grace* 2001; *bl,.m* 2003; *Ella Enchanted* 2004
Bergman, Henry (1868–1946) *Behind the Screen* 1916; *The Pawnshop* 1916; *Sunnyside* 1919; *The Idle Class* 1921; *The Circus* 1928; *Modern Times* 1936
Bergman, Ingrid (1915–1982) *The Count of the Old Town* 1935; *Swedenhielms* 1935; *Walpurgis Night* 1935; *Intermezzo* 1936; *Dollar* 1938; *A Woman's Face* 1938; *Intermezzo* 1939; *One Single Night* 1939; *June Night* 1940; *Adam Had Four Sons* 1941; *Dr Jekyll and Mr Hyde* 1941; *Rage in Heaven* 1941; *Casablanca* 1942; *For Whom the Bell Tolls* 1943; *Gaslight* 1944; *The Bells of St Mary's* 1945; *Saratoga Trunk* 1945; *Spellbound* 1945; *Notorious* 1946; *Arch of Triumph* 1948; *Joan of Arc* 1948; *Under Capricorn* 1949; *Stromboli* 1950; *Europa '51* 1952; *Journey to Italy* 1953; *Fear* 1954; *Anastasia* 1956; *Elena et les Hommes* 1956; *Indiscreet* 1958; *The Inn of the Sixth Happiness* 1958; *Goodbye Again* 1961; *The Visit* 1964; *The Yellow Rolls-Royce* 1964; *Cactus Flower* 1969; *A Walk in the Spring Rain* 1970; *The Hideaways* 1973; *Murder on the Orient Express* 1974; *A Matter of Time* 1976; *Autumn Sonata* 1978
Bergman, Mary Kay (1961–1999) *The Hunchback of Notre Dame* 1996; *South Park: Bigger, Longer & Uncut* 1999; *Scooby-Doo and the Alien Invaders* 2000
Bergman, Sandahl (1951–) *All That Jazz* 1979; *Conan the Barbarian* 1982; *Red Sonja* 1985; *Hell Comes to Frogtown* 1988; *Raw Nerve* 1991; *Body of Influence* 1993
Bergner, Elisabeth aka **Bergner, Elizabeth** (1900–1986) *Ariane* 1931; *The Rise of Catherine the Great* 1934; *Escape Me Never* 1935; *As You Like It* 1936; *Stolen Life* 1939; *Paris Calling* 1941; *Cry of the Banshee* 1970; *The Pedestrian* 1974
Bergström, Helena (1964–) *House of Angels* 1992; *House of Angels II: The Second Summer* 1994; *Still Crazy* 1998; *Under the Sun* 1998
Beristain, Luis (1918–1962) *El* 1953; *The Exterminating Angel* 1962
Berkel, Christian (1957–) *The Serpent's Egg* 1977; *The Experiment* 2000; *Downfall* 2004
Berkeley, Ballard (1904–1988) *The Last Adventurers* 1937; *The Blue Parrot* 1953; *Child's Play* 1954; *Impact* 1963
Berkeley, Xander (1958–) *The Fabulous Baker Boys* 1989; *Short Time* 1990; *Candyman* 1992; *Roswell* 1994; *Apollo 13* 1995; *Barb Wire* 1995; *Poison Ivy 2* 1995; *[Safe]* 1995; *If These Walls Could Talk* 1996; *Persons Unknown* 1996; *Air Force One* 1997; *Gattaca* 1997; *Universal Soldier – the Return* 1999; *Shanghai Noon* 2000
Berkley, Elizabeth (1973–) *Showgirls* 1995; *The First Wives Club* 1996; *The Real Blonde* 1997; *Taxman* 1998; *The Curse of the Jade Scorpion* 2001; *Roger Dodger* 2002
Berkoff, Steven (1937–) *A Clockwork Orange* 1971; *Barry Lyndon* 1975; *The Passenger* 1975; *McVicar* 1980; *Outland* 1981; *Octopussy* 1983; *Beverly Hills Cop* 1984; *Rambo: First Blood, Part II* 1985; *Revolution* 1985; *Absolute Beginners* 1986; *Under the Cherry Moon* 1986; *Prisoner of Rio* 1988; *The Krays* 1990; *Decadence* 1993; *Fair Game* 1995; *Flynn* 1995; *Another $9\frac{1}{2}$ Weeks* 1997; *Legionnaire* 1998; *Rancid Aluminium* 1999; *Beginner's Luck* 2001; *9 Dead Gay Guys* 2001; *Steal* 2002; *Charlie* 2003
Berle, Milton (1908–2002) *New Faces of 1937* 1937; *Radio City Revels* 1938; *Sun Valley Serenade* 1941; *Tall, Dark and Handsome* 1941; *A Gentleman at Heart* 1942; *Whispering Ghosts* 1942; *Margin for Error* 1943; *Always Leave Them Laughing* 1949; *Let's Make Love* 1960; *It's a Mad Mad Mad Mad World* 1963; *Journey back to Oz* 1964; *The Loved One* 1965; *The Oscar* 1966; *The Happening* 1967; *Who's Minding the Mint?* 1967; *Where Angels Go…Trouble Follows* 1968; *Can Heironymus Merkin Ever Forget Mercy Humppe and Find True Happiness?* 1969; *Evil Roy Slade* 1971; *Lepke* 1975; *Smorgasbord* 1983; *Storybook* 1995
Berléand, François (1952–) *Au Revoir les Enfants* 1987; *Milou en Mai* 1989; *Place Vendôme* 1998; *Romance* 1998; *The School of Flesh* 1998; *The Transporter* 2002; *The Chorus* 2004
Berley, André (1890–1936) *Hara-Kiri* 1928; *The Passion of Joan of Arc* 1928
Berlin, Jeannie (1949–) *The Baby Maker* 1970; *Bone* 1972; *The Heartbreak Kid* 1972; *Sheila Levine Is Dead and Living in New York* 1975; *In the Spirit* 1990
Berling, Charles (1958–) *Salt on Our Skin* 1992; *Ridicule* 1996; *Dry Cleaning* 1997; *Love etc* 1997; *L'Ennui* 1998; *Those Who Love Me Can Take the Train* 1998; *The Bridge* 1999; *Comédie de l'Innocence* 2000; *Les Destinées Sentimentales* 2000; *Stardom* 2000; *Comment J'ai Tué Mon Père* 2001; *Demonlover* 2002
Berling, Peter (1934–) *Aguirre, Wrath of God* 1972; *Haunted Summer* 1988; *Francesco* 1989
Berlinger, Warren (1937–) *Teenage Rebel* 1956; *Blue Denim* 1959; *Because They're Young* 1960; *All Hands on Deck* 1961; *The Wackiest Ship in the Army* 1961; *Billie* 1965; *Thunder Alley* 1967; *Lepke* 1975; *The Four Deuces* 1976; *Outlaw Force* 1988; *Accidental Hero* 1992
Berman, Marc *Noir et Blanc* 1986; *The Last Island* 1990; *Autobus* 1991; *The Voyage* 1991; *The Girl from Paris* 2001
Berman, Shelley (1926–) *The Best Man* 1964; *Divorce American Style* 1967; *Every Home Should Have One* 1970; *Beware! The Blob* 1971; *Teen Witch* 1989
Berman, Susan *Smithereens* 1982; *Making Mr Right* 1987
Bernal, Gael García (1978–) *Amores Perros* 2000; *Y Tu Mamá También* 2001; *El Crimen del Padre Amaro* 2002; *I'm with Lucy* 2002; *Dot the i* 2003; *Bad Education* 2004; *The Motorcycle Diaries* 2004
Bernard, Carl *The Silver Darlings* 1947; *The Hour of Decision* 1957
Bernard, Ed (1939–) *Across 110th Street* 1972; *Blue Thunder* 1983
Bernard, Jason (1938–1996) *Going Home* 1971; *All of Me* 1984; *No Way Out* 1986; *Paint It Black* 1989; *While You Were Sleeping* 1995; *Liar Liar* 1997
Bernardi, Herschel (1923–1986) *Murder by Contract* 1958; *The Savage Eye* 1959; *A Cold Wind in August* 1961; *Irma la Douce* 1963; *Love with the Proper Stranger* 1963; *The Front* 1976; *No Deposit No Return* 1976
Berner, Sara (1912–1969) *Rear Window* 1954; *Spring Reunion* 1957
Bernhard, Sandra (1955–) *Cheech and Chong's Nice Dreams*

1981; *The King of Comedy* 1983; *Sesame Street Presents: Follow That Bird* 1985; *Track 29* 1988; *Without You I'm Nothing* 1990; *Hudson Hawk* 1991; *Dallas Doll* 1994; *Burn Hollywood Burn* 1997; *Wrongfully Accused* 1998; *Dinner Rush* 2000

Bernhardsson, Lena-Pia *Elvis! Elvis!* 1977; *The Simple-Minded Murderer* 1982

Bernsen, Corbin (1954–) *Hello Again* 1987; *Bert Rigby, You're a Fool* 1989; *Disorganized Crime* 1989; *Major League* 1989; *Shattered* 1991; *Frozen Assets* 1992; *Final Mission* 1993; *Killing Box* 1993; *Major League II* 1994; *Ring of the Musketeers* 1994; *Silhouette* 1994; *Dangerous Intentions* 1995; *Temptress* 1995; *Danielle Steel's Full Circle* 1996; *The Dentist* 1996; *The Great White Hype* 1996; *The Dentist II* 1998; *Major League: Back to the Minors* 1998; *The Misadventures of Margaret* 1998

Berrell, George (1849–1933) *Straight Shooting* 1917; *Pollyanna* 1920

Berri, Claude (1934–) *Les Bonnes Femmes* 1960; *Marry Me! Marry Me!* 1968

Berridge, Elizabeth (1962–) *The Funhouse* 1981; *Amadeus* 1984; *Five Corners* 1987; *When the Party's Over* 1992

Berroyer, Jackie *aka* **Berroyer, Jacky** (1946–) *L'Eau Froide* 1994; *Rien Ne Va Plus* 1997; *Le Clan* 2004; *A Common Thread* 2004; *The Ordeal* 2004

Berry, Halle (1968–) *Jungle Fever* 1991; *The Last Boy Scout* 1991; *Boomerang* 1992; *Father Hood* 1993; *The Program* 1993; *The Flintstones* 1994; *Losing Isaiah* 1995; *Executive Decision* 1996; *Race the Sun* 1996; *The Rich Man's Wife* 1996; *BAPS* 1997; *Bulworth* 1998; *Why Do Fools Fall in Love?* 1998; *Introducing Dorothy Dandridge* 1999; *X-Men* 2000; *Monster's Ball* 2001; *Swordfish* 2001; *Die Another Day* 2002; *Gothika* 2003; *X2* 2003; *Catwoman* 2004; *Robots* 2005

Berry, John (1917–1999) *Golden Eighties* 1986; *A Man in Love* 1987

Berry, Jules (1883–1951) *Le Crime de Monsieur Lange* 1935; *Le Jour Se Lève* 1939; *Les Visiteurs du Soir* 1942

Berry, Ken (1933–) *Hello Down There* 1969; *Herbie Rides Again* 1974; *The Cat from Outer Space* 1978

Berry, Richard (1950–) *Le Grand Pardon* 1981; *La Balance* 1982; *La Garce* 1984; *Brothers in Arms* 1990; *C'est la Vie* 1990; *Day of Atonement* 1992; *Le Petit Prince A Dit* 1992; *The Bait* 1995

Berryman, Dorothée (1948–) *The Decline of the American Empire* 1986; *A Paper Wedding* 1989; *Taken* 1999; *The Barbarian Invasions* 2003

Berryman, Michael (1948–) *The Hills Have Eyes* 1977; *The Hills Have Eyes Part II* 1985; *Armed Response* 1986; *Haunting Fear* 1990; *Auntie Lee's Meat Pies* 1991; *Evil Spirits* 1991; *The Guyver* 1991

Bertheau, Julien (1910–1995) *La Vie Est à Nous* 1936; *Celà S'Appelle l'Aurore* 1956; *Madame* 1961; *The Discreet Charm of the Bourgeoisie* 1972; *Le Fantôme de la Liberté* 1974; *Verdict* 1974; *That Obscure Object of Desire* 1977

Berthelsen, Anders W (1969–) *Mifune* 1999; *Italian for Beginners* 2000; *The Weight of Water* 2000

Berti, Marina (1924–2002) *Prince of Foxes* 1949; *Marie Antoinette* 1956; *Madame* 1961; *A Face in the Rain* 1963

Bertie, Diego (1967–) *Full Fathom Five* 1990; *No Mercy* 1994

Bertin, Pierre (1891–1984) *Orphée* 1950; *Elena et les Hommes* 1956; *The Stranger* 1967

Bertin, Roland *The Brontë Sisters* 1979; *Diva* 1981; *Cyrano de Bergerac* 1990; *The Hairdresser's Husband* 1990; *La Fille de l'Air* 1992; *Lumière Noire* 1994

Bertinelli, Valerie (1960–) *CHOMPS* 1979; *Number One with a Bullet* 1986; *Murder of Innocence* 1993; *The Haunting of Helen Walker* 1995

Bertish, Suzanne (1953–) *Hearts of Fire* 1987; *Venice/Venice* 1992

Berto, Juliet (1947–1990) *La Chinoise* 1967; *Le Gai Savoir* 1968; *Vladimir et Rosa* 1970; *Out 1: Spectre* 1973; *Celine and Julie Go Boating* 1974; *Mr Klein* 1976

Bertorelli, Toni *The Prince of Homburg* 1997; *Strong Hands* 1997; *Elvjs & Merilijn* 1998; *The Passion of the Christ* 2004

Bervoets, Gene *aka* **Bervoets, Eugene** *The Vanishing* 1988; *Anchoress* 1993

Besch, Bibi (1942–1996) *The Pack* 1977; *Star Trek II: the Wrath of Khan* 1982; *The Lonely Lady* 1983; *Who's That Girl* 1987

Besnéhard, Dominique *To Our Loves* 1984; *The Lie* 1992

Bessell, Ted (1935–1996) *Billie* 1965; *Don't Drink the Water* 1969

Besserer, Eugenie (1868–1934) *The Jazz Singer* 1927; *Madame X* 1929; *Thunderbolt* 1929

Bessho, Tetsuya (1965–) *Solar Crisis* 1990; *Godzilla vs Mothra* 1992

Best, Ahmed (1974–) *Star Wars Episode II: Attack of the Clones* 2002; *Star Wars Episode III: Revenge of the Sith* 2005

Best, Alyson (1960–) *Man of Flowers* 1984; *Relatives* 1985

Best, Edna (1900–1974) *Escape* 1930; *The Key* 1934; *The Man Who Knew Too Much* 1934; *South Riding* 1938; *Intermezzo* 1939; *A Dispatch from Reuters* 1940; *Swiss Family Robinson* 1940; *The Ghost and Mrs Muir* 1947; *The Iron Curtain* 1948

Best, James (1926–) *Kansas Raiders* 1950; *The Cimarron Kid* 1951; *Seven Angry Men* 1955; *Hot Summer Night* 1957; *Last of the Badmen* 1957; *The Left Handed Gun* 1958; *The Naked and the Dead* 1958; *Cast a Long Shadow* 1959; *The Killer Shrews* 1959; *Ride Lonesome* 1959; *Verboten!* 1959; *The Mountain Road* 1960; *Black Gold* 1963; *Shock Corridor* 1963; *Black Spurs* 1965; *Three on a Couch* 1966; *Sounder* 1972; *Ode to Billy Joe* 1976; *Rolling Thunder* 1977; *Hooper* 1978

Best, Willie (1913–1962) *The Littlest Rebel* 1935; *The Bride Walks Out* 1936; *The Ghost Breakers* 1940; *Nothing but the Truth* 1941; *Whispering Ghosts* 1942; *The Red Dragon* 1945; *The Bride Wore Boots* 1946; *Dangerous Money* 1946

Beswick, Martine *aka* **Beswicke, Martine** (1941–) *Thunderball* 1965; *One Million Years BC* 1966; *The Penthouse* 1967; *Dr Jekyll and Sister Hyde* 1971; *Seizure* 1974; *The Happy Hooker Goes to Hollywood* 1980; *Evil Spirits* 1991; *Trancers II: The Return of Jack Deth* 1991; *Wide Sargasso Sea* 1992

Bethmann, Sabine (1931–) *The Indian Tomb* 1959; *The Tiger of Eschnapur* 1959

Bettany, Paul (1971–) *Dead Babies* 2000; *Gangster No 1* 2000; *A Beautiful Mind* 2001; *Kiss Kiss (Bang Bang)* 2001; *A Knight's Tale* 2001; *The Reckoning* 2001; *The Heart of Me* 2002; *Dogville* 2003; *Master and Commander: the Far Side of the World* 2003; *Wimbledon* 2004

Bettenfeld, Dominique *Dobermann* 1997; *A Very Long Engagement* 2004

Bettger, Lyle (1915–2003) *No Man of Her Own* 1950; *Union Station* 1950; *The First Legion* 1951; *Denver & Rio Grande* 1952; *The Greatest Show on Earth* 1952; *All I Desire* 1953; *Forbidden* 1953; *The Great Sioux Uprising* 1953; *Carnival Story* 1954; *Destry* 1954; *Drums across the River* 1954; *The Sea Chase* 1955; *The Lone Ranger* 1956; *Showdown at Abilene* 1956; *Gunfight at the OK Corral* 1957; *Guns of the Timberland* 1960; *The Fastest Guitar Alive* 1966; *Johnny Reno* 1966; *Impasse* 1969; *The Seven Minutes* 1971

Betti, Laura (1934–2004) *RoGoPaG* 1962; *Theorem* 1968; *Hatchet for the Honeymoon* 1969; *The Canterbury Tales* 1971; *1900* 1976; *La Luna* 1979; *The Art of Love* 1983; *Courage Mountain* 1989; *Marianna Ucria* 1997

Bettin, Val *Basil the Great Mouse Detective* 1986; *Aladdin and the King of Thieves* 1996

Bettis, Angela (1975–) *Sparrow* 1993; *Bless the Child* 2000; *Toolbox Murders* 2003

Bettis, Valerie (1919–1982) *Affair in Trinidad* 1952; *Let's Do It Again* 1953

Bettoja, Franca (1936–) *Duel of Champions* 1961; *The Last Man on Earth* 1964; *Sandokan against the Leopard of Sarawak* 1964

Betz, Carl (1921–1978) *Inferno* 1953; *Powder River* 1953

Betz, Matthew (1881–1938) *The Unholy Three* 1925; *The Wedding March* 1928

Betzler, Geri (1966–) *Fear* 1988; *Amityville: the Evil Escapes* 1989

Bevan, Billy (1887–1957) *High Voltage* 1929; *Journey's End* 1930; *Payment Deferred* 1932; *The Lost Patrol* 1934; *Another Dawn* 1937

Bevan, Stewart *The Ghoul* 1975; *House of Mortal Sin* 1975

Bevans, Clem (1879–1963) *Thunder Afloat* 1939; *Saboteur* 1942; *The Yearling* 1946; *Big Jack* 1949; *The Boy from Oklahoma* 1954

Beverly, Helen *Green Fields* 1937; *Overture to Glory* 1940; *Meeting at Midnight* 1944

Bevis, Leslie *The Squeeze* 1987; *Alien Nation* 1988; *The November Men* 1993

Bewes, Rodney (1938–) *A Prize of Arms* 1961; *Billy Liar* 1963; *Decline and Fall... of a Birdwatcher* 1968; *Spring and Port Wine* 1969; *The Likely Lads* 1976; *Jabberwocky* 1977; *Saint Jack* 1979; *The Spaceman and King Arthur* 1979; *The Wildcats of St Trinian's* 1980

Bexton, Nathan (1977–) *Nowhere* 1997; *Go* 1999; *The In Crowd* 2000

Bey, Marki (1946–) *The Landlord* 1970; *Hangup* 1973; *Sugar Hill* 1974

Bey, Turhan (1920–) *Shadows on the Stairs* 1941; *Arabian Nights* 1942; *The Mummy's Tomb* 1942; *Background to Danger* 1943; *White Savage* 1943; *Ali Baba and the Forty Thieves* 1944; *Dragon Seed* 1944; *Sudan* 1945; *Out of the Blue* 1947; *Prisoners of the Casbah* 1953

Beyer, Alexander (1975–) *The Legends of Rita* 2000; *Sophiiie!* 2002; *Good Bye Lenin!* 2003

Beyer, Brad (1973–) *Trick* 1999; *Sorority Boys* 2002

Beyer, Troy (1965–) *Disorderlies* 1987; *Rooftops* 1989; *Weekend at Bernie's II* 1992; *Eddie* 1996; *BAPS* 1997; *Let's Talk about Sex* 1998

Beymer, Richard *aka* **Beymer, Dick** (1939–) *Indiscretion of an American Wife* 1954; *Johnny Tremain* 1957; *The Diary of Anne Frank* 1959; *High Time* 1960; *Bachelor Flat* 1961; *West Side Story* 1961; *Five Finger Exercise* 1962; *Hemingway's Adventures of a Young Man* 1962; *The Longest Day* 1962; *The Stripper* 1963; *The Face* 1996

Bezace, Didier (1946–) *La Petite Voleuse* 1988; *L.627* 1992; *Les Voleurs* 1996; *The Chambermaid on the Titanic* 1997

Bhaskar, Sanjeev (1964–) *The Mystic Masseur* 2001; *Anita & Me* 2002; *The Guru* 2002

Bhasker *aka* **Patel, Bhasker** *Wild West* 1992; *Brothers in Trouble* 1995; *My Son the Fanatic* 1997

Bhatti, Ahsen *Brothers in Trouble* 1995; *Sixth Happiness* 1997

Bianchi, Daniela *From Russia with Love* 1963; *Operation Kid Brother* 1967

Bibb, Leon (1926–) *For Love of Ivy* 1968; *The Lost Man* 1969; *Dead Wrong* 1983

Bibb, Leslie (1973–) *The Skulls* 2000; *See Spot Run* 2001

Biberman, Abner (1909–1977) *Whispering Ghosts* 1942; *Betrayal from the East* 1945; *Elephant Walk* 1954; *Knock on Wood* 1954

Bice, Robert (1914–1968) *Invasion USA* 1952; *Three for the Show* 1955

Bichir, Bruno (1967–) *Highway Patrolman* 1991; *Midaq Alley* 1995

Bichir, Demian (1963–) *'Til Death* 1993; *Sex, Shame and Tears* 1999

Bick, Stewart *Grey Owl* 1999; *One Special Night* 1999; *Taken* 1999; *36 Hours to Die* 1999; *A Walk on the Moon* 1999; *Danger beneath the Sea* 2001; *Life in the Balance* 2001

Bickford, Charles (1889–1967) *Dynamite* 1929; *Anna Christie* 1930; *The Squaw Man* 1931; *This Day and Age* 1933; *White Woman* 1933; *Little Miss Marker* 1934; *The Farmer Takes a Wife* 1935; *The Plainsman* 1936; *High, Wide and Handsome* 1937; *The Storm* 1938; *Of Mice and Men* 1939; *Tarzan's New York Adventure* 1942; *Mr Lucky* 1943; *The Song of Bernadette* 1943; *Wing and a Prayer* 1944; *Captain Eddie* 1945; *Fallen Angel* 1945; *Duel in the Sun* 1946; *The Farmer's Daughter* 1946; *Brute Force* 1947; *The Woman on the Beach* 1947; *The Babe Ruth Story* 1948; *Command Decision* 1948; *Johnny Belinda* 1948; *They Passed This Way* 1948; *Roseanna McCoy* 1949; *Whirlpool* 1949; *Branded* 1950; *Riding High* 1950; *Jim Thorpe – All-American* 1951; *The Last Posse* 1953; *A Star Is Born* 1954; *The Court-Martial of Billy Mitchell* 1955; *Not as a Stranger* 1955; *Prince of Players* 1955; *You Can't Run Away from It* 1956; *Mister Cory* 1957; *The Big Country* 1958; *The Unforgiven* 1960; *Days of Wine and Roses* 1962; *Della* 1965; *A Big Hand for a Little Lady* 1966

Bideau, Jean-Luc (1940–) *State of Siege* 1972; *The Invitation* 1973; *Jonah Who Will Be 25 in the Year 2000* 1976; *D'Artagnan's Daughter* 1994

Biehn, Michael (1956–) *The Fan* 1981; *The Lords of Discipline* 1983; *The Terminator* 1984; *Aliens* 1986; *Rampage* 1987; *In a Shallow Grave* 1988; *The Seventh Sign* 1988; *The Abyss* 1989; *Navy SEALS* 1990; *K2* 1991; *Terminator 2: Judgment Day* 1991; *Time Bomb* 1991; *Deadfall* 1993; *Tombstone* 1993; *Jade* 1995; *Mojave Moon* 1996; *The Rock* 1996; *American Dragons* 1997; *Dead Men Can't Dance* 1997; *Susan's Plan* 1998; *Cherry Falls* 1999; *The Art of War* 2000; *Clockstoppers* 2002

Biel, Jessica (1982–) *Ulee's Gold* 1997; *I'll Be Home for Christmas* 1998; *Summer Catch* 2001; *The Rules of Attraction* 2002; *The Texas Chainsaw Massacre* 2003; *Blade: Trinity* 2004; *Cellular* 2004

Bierbichler, Josef (1945–) *Heart of Glass* 1976; *Wintersleepers* 1997; *The Farewell – Brecht's Last Summer* 2000

Bieri, Ramon (1931–) *The Andromeda Strain* 1970; *Brother John* 1970; *The Grasshopper* 1970; *The Honkers* 1971; *Badlands* 1973; *Sorcerer* 1977; *The Frisco Kid* 1979; *Vibes* 1988

Bierko, Craig (1965–) *Danielle Steel's Star* 1993; *The Long Kiss Goodnight* 1996; *'Til There Was You* 1997; *Sour Grapes* 1998; *The Suburbans* 1999; *The Thirteenth Floor* 1999; *I'm with Lucy* 2002; *Dickie Roberts: Former Child Star* 2003; *Cinderella Man* 2005

Biesk, Adam *Meet the Applegates* 1991; *Gas, Food, Lodging* 1992

Bigagli, Claudio (1955–) *The Night of San Lorenzo* 1981; *Kaos* 1984; *Mediterraneo* 1991; *Fiorile* 1993

Biggins, Christopher (1948–) *The Rocky Horror Picture Show* 1975; *The Tempest* 1979; *Decadence* 1993; *Asterix Conquers America* 1994

Biggs, Jason (1978–) *American Pie* 1999; *Boys and Girls* 2000; *Loser* 2000; *American Pie 2* 2001; *Evil Woman* 2001; *American Pie: the Wedding* 2003; *Anything Else* 2003; *Jersey Girl* 2003

Biggs, Julie *Nobody Waved Goodbye* 1964; *Unfinished Business* 1983

Bigham, Lexie *aka* **Bigham, Lexie D** (1968–1995) *South Central* 1992; *High School High* 1996

Bikel, Theodore (1924–) *The African Queen* 1951; *A Day to Remember* 1953; *The Kidnappers* 1953; *Never Let Me Go* 1953; *Forbidden Cargo* 1954; *The Young Lovers* 1954; *Above Us the Waves* 1955; *The Enemy Below* 1957; *The Pride and the Passion* 1957; *The Defiant Ones* 1958; *I Want to Live!* 1958; *The Angry Hills* 1959; *The Blue Angel* 1959; *A Dog of Flanders* 1959; *Woman Obsessed* 1959; *My Fair Lady* 1964; *Sands of the Kalahari* 1965; *The Russians Are Coming, the Russians Are Coming* 1966; *The Desperate Ones* 1967; *Sweet November* 1968; *My Side of the Mountain* 1969; *Darker than Amber* 1970; *The Little Ark* 1971; *200 Motels* 1971; *Victory at Entebbe* 1976; *Prince Jack* 1984; *Dark Tower* 1989; *The Final Days* 1989; *Benefit of the Doubt* 1993; *Shadow Conspiracy* 1996

Bilginer, Haluk (1954–) *Harem Suare* 1999; *Where's Firuze?* 2004

Bilis, Teddy (1913–1998) *Celui Qui Doit Mourir* 1957; *The Testament of Dr Cordelier* 1959

Bill, Tony (1940–) *Come Blow Your Horn* 1963; *Soldier in the Rain* 1963; *Marriage on the Rocks* 1965; *None but the Brave* 1965; *Ice Station Zebra* 1968; *Never a Dull Moment* 1968; *Flap* 1970; *Shampoo* 1975; *Heart Beat* 1979; *Less than Zero* 1987

Billerey, Raoul *L'Enfance Nue* 1968; *An Impudent Girl* 1985; *Le Grand Chemin* 1987; *La Petite Voleuse* 1988; *D'Artagnan's Daughter* 1994

Billett, Don *Prince of the City* 1981; *Gloria* 1998

Billing, Roy *Dallas Doll* 1994; *Siam Sunset* 1999; *The Dish* 2000

Billings, Earl *Stakeout* 1987; *One False Move* 1992; *Antwone Fisher* 2002; *American Splendor* 2003

Billingsley, Barbara (1922–) *The Careless Years* 1957; *Leave It to Beaver* 1997

Billingsley, Jennifer *Lady in a Cage* 1964; *Welcome Home, Soldier Boys* 1971; *White Lightning* 1973

Billingsley, Peter (1971–) *Paternity* 1981; *Death Valley* 1982; *A Christmas Story* 1983; *The Dirt Bike Kid* 1986; *Russkies* 1987; *Beverly Hills Brats* 1989

Binder, Mike (1958–) *The Sex Monster* 1998; *Londinium* 1999; *The Search for John Gissing* 2001

Binder, Sybilla (1898–1962) *Blanche Fury* 1948; *Counterblast* 1948

Bindon, John (1943–1993) *Poor Cow* 1967; *Performance* 1970

Bing, Herman (1889–1947) *The Guardsman* 1931; *The Mighty Barnum* 1934; *The King Steps Out* 1936; *Every Day's a Holiday* 1937; *Maytime* 1937; *Bluebeard's Eighth Wife* 1938; *Dumbo* 1941

Bingham, Barbara *Deathmask* 1984; *Friday the 13th Part VIII: Jason Takes Manhattan* 1989

Binns, Edward (1916–1990) *Vice Squad* 1953; *Beyond a Reasonable Doubt* 1956; *12 Angry Men* 1957; *Desire in the Dust* 1960; *The Americanization of Emily* 1964; *Fail-Safe* 1964; *Lovin' Molly* 1974; *Night Moves* 1975;

Oliver's Story 1978; *The Verdict* 1982
Binoche, Juliette (1964–) *Je Vous Salue, Marie* 1984; *Rendez-vous* 1985; *The Night Is Young* 1986; *The Unbearable Lightness of Being* 1988; *Les Amants du Pont-Neuf* 1990; *Damage* 1992; *Wuthering Heights* 1992; *Three Colours Blue* 1993; *The Horseman on the Roof* 1995; *The English Patient* 1996; *Alice et Martin* 1998; *Les Enfants du Siècle* 1999; *Chocolat* 2000; *Code Unknown* 2000; *La Veuve de Saint-Pierre* 2000
Biraud, Maurice (1922–1982) *Any Number Can Win* 1963; *The Last Train* 1972
Birch, Paul (1913–1969) *The War of the Worlds* 1953; *Ride Clear of Diablo* 1954; *Apache Woman* 1955; *The Beast with a Million Eyes* 1955; *Five Guns West* 1955; *The Day the World Ended* 1956; *Not of This Earth* 1956; *The 27th Day* 1957; *The World Was His Jury* 1957; *Queen of Outer Space* 1958; *Two Rode Together* 1961
Birch, Thora (1982–) *The Purple People Eater* 1988; *All I Want for Christmas* 1991; *Paradise* 1991; *Patriot Games* 1992; *Hocus Pocus* 1993; *Monkey Trouble* 1994; *Now and Then* 1995; *Alaska* 1996; *American Beauty* 1999; *Night Ride Home* 1999; *Dungeons & Dragons* 2000; *Ghost World* 2001; *The Hole* 2001; *Homeless to Harvard: the Liz Murray Story* 2003; *Silver City* 2004
Bird, Billie (1908–2002) *Somebody Loves Me* 1952; *Too Soon to Love* 1960
Bird, John (1936–) *The Best House in London* 1968; *30 Is a Dangerous Age, Cynthia* 1968; *Take a Girl like You* 1970; *Pleasure at Her Majesty's* 1976
Bird, Norman (1919–2005) *Man in the Moon* 1960; *Cash on Demand* 1961; *The Secret Partner* 1961; *Victim* 1961; *Whistle down the Wind* 1961; *Bitter Harvest* 1963; *80,000 Suspects* 1963; *The Bargee* 1964; *The Beauty Jungle* 1964; *The Black Torment* 1964; *The Hill* 1965; *Sky West and Crooked* 1965; *Ooh... You Are Awful* 1972; *The Lord of the Rings* 1978
Bird, Richard (1894–1986) *The Halfway House* 1943; *Don't Take It to Heart* 1944
Birdsall, Jesse (1963–) *Wish You Were Here* 1987; *Getting It Right* 1989; *Beyond Bedlam* 1993
Birell, Tala (1907–1958) *Crime and Punishment* 1935; *The Lone Wolf Returns* 1936; *Bringing Up Baby* 1938; *The Monster Maker* 1944
Birkett, Jack *aka* **Orlando** *Jubilee* 1978; *The Tempest* 1979
Birkin, Jane (1946–) *Blowup* 1966; *Kaleidoscope* 1966; *The Swimming Pool* 1968; *Wonderwall* 1968; *Romance of a Horse Thief* 1971; *Dark Places* 1973; *Don Juan 73, or If Don Juan Were a Woman* 1973; *Death on the Nile* 1978; *Evil under the Sun* 1982; *L'Amour par Terre* 1984; *Dust* 1985; *Leave All Fair* 1985; *Soigne Ta Droite* 1986; *Kung-Fu Master* 1987; *These Foolish Things* 1990; *La Belle Noiseuse* 1991; *Between the Devil and the Deep Blue Sea* 1995; *On Connaît la Chanson* 1997; *A Soldier's Daughter Never Cries* 1998; *The Last September* 1999; *Merci Docteur Rey* 2002
Birman, Serafima (1890–1976) *Ivan the Terrible, Part I* 1944; *Ivan the Terrible, Part II* 1946
Birney, David (1939–) *Caravan to Vaccares* 1974; *Trial by Combat* 1976; *Oh God! Book II* 1980; *PrettyKill* 1987
Bishop, Debbie *aka* **Bishop, Debby** *Scrubbers* 1982; *Sid and Nancy* 1986
Bishop, Ed (1932–2005) *Brass Target* 1978; *SOS Titanic* 1979; *Saturn 3* 1980; *The Unexpected Mrs Pollifax* 1999
Bishop (1), Jennifer *The Female Bunch* 1969; *Impulse* 1975
Bishop, Joey (1918–) *The Naked and the Dead* 1958; *Onionhead* 1958; *Ocean's Eleven* 1960; *Pepe* 1960; *Sergeants 3* 1962; *Johnny Cool* 1963; *Texas across the River* 1966; *Who's Minding the Mint?* 1967; *The Delta Force* 1986; *Betsy's Wedding* 1990
Bishop, Julie *aka* **Wells, Jacqueline** (1914–2001) *Tarzan the Fearless* 1933; *Tillie and Gus* 1933; *The Black Cat* 1934; *The Bohemian Girl* 1936; *Girls Can Play* 1937; *Action in the North Atlantic* 1943; *Northern Pursuit* 1943; *Rhapsody in Blue* 1945; *Cinderella Jones* 1946; *Murder in the Music Hall* 1946; *Westward the Women* 1951; *The Big Land* 1957
Bishop, Kelly (1944–) *An Unmarried Woman* 1978; *Dirty Dancing* 1987
Bishop, Kevin (1980–) *Muppet Treasure Island* 1996; *Food of Love* 2002; *Pot Luck* 2002
Bishop, Larry (1947–) *Shanks* 1974; *CHOMPS* 1979; *Trigger Happy* 1996; *Underworld* 1996
Bishop, Piers *Tomorrow at Ten* 1962; *Ballad in Blue* 1964
Bishop, William (1918–1959) *Anna Lucasta* 1949; *The Walking Hills* 1949; *Harriet Craig* 1950; *Lorna Doone* 1951; *The Redhead from Wyoming* 1953; *Short Cut to Hell* 1957; *The Oregon Trail* 1959
Bisio, Claudio (1957–) *Mediterraneo* 1991; *Puerto Escondido* 1992
Bisley, Steve (1951–) *Mad Max* 1979; *The Chain Reaction* 1980; *Silver City* 1984; *The Big Steal* 1990; *Over the Hill* 1992
Bisoglio, Val (1926–) *Linda Lovelace for President* 1975; *The Frisco Kid* 1979
Bissell, Whit (1909–1996) *Brute Force* 1947; *He Walked by Night* 1948; *Anna Lucasta* 1949; *Wyoming Mail* 1950; *The Atomic Kid* 1954; *Creature from the Black Lagoon* 1954; *Riot in Cell Block 11* 1954; *The Shanghai Story* 1954; *Shack Out on 101* 1955; *I Was a Teenage Frankenstein* 1957; *I Was a Teenage Werewolf* 1957; *Johnny Tremain* 1957; *The Tall Stranger* 1957; *The Young Stranger* 1957; *No Name on the Bullet* 1959; *The Time Machine* 1960; *Hud* 1963; *Seven Days in May* 1964; *Psychic Killer* 1975
Bisset, Donald (1911–1995) *Murder in the Cathedral* 1952; *Little Red Monkey* 1955
Bisset, Jacqueline (1944–) *Casino Royale* 1967; *The Sweet Ride* 1967; *Bullitt* 1968; *The Detective* 1968; *The First Time* 1969; *Airport* 1970; *The Grasshopper* 1970; *Believe in Me* 1971; *The Mephisto Waltz* 1971; *Secrets* 1971; *The Life and Times of Judge Roy Bean* 1972; *Day for Night* 1973; *The Thief Who Came to Dinner* 1973; *Murder on the Orient Express* 1974; *End of the Game* 1976; *St Ives* 1976; *The Deep* 1977; *The Greek Tycoon* 1978; *Who Is Killing the Great Chefs of Europe?* 1978; *When Time Ran Out* 1980; *Inchon* 1981; *Rich and Famous* 1981; *Class* 1983; *Under the Volcano* 1984; *High Season* 1987; *Scenes from the Class Struggle in Beverly Hills* 1989; *Wild Orchid* 1990; *The Maid* 1991; *Leave of Absence* 1994; *La Cérémonie* 1995; *Dangerous Beauty* 1997; *Let the Devil Wear Black* 1999; *New Year's Day* 1999; *Britannic* 2000
Bissett, Josie (1970–) *Danielle Steel's Secrets* 1992; *Deadly Vows* 1994
Bisson, Chris (1975–) *East Is East* 1999; *Chicken Tikka Masala* 2005
Bissonnette, Joel *Boulevard* 1994; *Suspicious River* 2000
Biswas, Chhabi (1900–1962) *The Music Room* 1958; *Devi* 1960; *Kangchenjunga* 1962
Biswas, Seema *Bandit Queen* 1994; *Bhoot* 2003
Bixby, Bill (1934–1993) *Irma la Douce* 1963; *Ride beyond Vengeance* 1966; *Clambake* 1967; *Speedway* 1968; *The Apple Dumpling Gang* 1974; *The Incredible Hulk* 1977; *The Incredible Hulk Returns* 1988; *The Trial of the Incredible Hulk* 1989; *The Death of the Incredible Hulk* 1990
Bjelogrlic, Dragan (1963–) *Hey Babu Riba* 1986; *Pretty Village Pretty Flame* 1996
Björk *aka* **Gudmundsdottir, Björk** (1965–) *The Juniper Tree* 1990; *Dancer in the Dark* 2000
Björk, Anita (1923–) *Miss Julie* 1951; *Waiting Women* 1952; *Night People* 1954; *Square of Violence* 1961; *Private Confessions* 1996
Bjork, Halvar (1928–2000) *The New Land* 1972; *Autumn Sonata* 1978
Björnstrand, Gunnar (1909–1986) *It Rains on Our Love* 1946; *Waiting Women* 1952; *Lesson in Love* 1954; *Dreams* 1955; *Smiles of a Summer Night* 1955; *The Seventh Seal* 1957; *Wild Strawberries* 1957; *The Magician* 1958; *The Devil's Eye* 1960; *Through a Glass Darkly* 1961; *Winter Light* 1962; *My Sister, My Love* 1966; *Persona* 1966; *Shame* 1968; *The Rite* 1969; *Face to Face* 1976; *Autumn Sonata* 1978; *Fanny and Alexander* 1982
Black, Isobel (1943–) *The Magnificent Two* 1967; *10 Rillington Place* 1970; *Twins of Evil* 1971
Black, Jack (1969–) *The NeverEnding Story III* 1994; *The Cable Guy* 1996; *Jesus' Son* 1999; *High Fidelity* 2000; *Evil Woman* 2001; *Orange County* 2001; *Shallow Hal* 2001; *Ice Age* 2002; *Envy* 2003; *The School of Rock* 2003; *Shark Tale* 2004
Black, Jennifer *Local Hero* 1983; *Heavenly Pursuits* 1986
Black, Karen (1942–) *You're a Big Boy Now* 1966; *Easy Rider* 1969; *Hard Contract* 1969; *Five Easy Pieces* 1970; *Born to Win* 1971; *Cisco Pike* 1971; *Drive, He Said* 1971; *A Gunfight* 1971; *Portnoy's Complaint* 1972; *The Outfit* 1973; *Airport 1975* 1974; *The Great Gatsby* 1974; *Law and Disorder* 1974; *Rhinoceros* 1974; *The Day of the Locust* 1975; *Nashville* 1975; *Burnt Offerings* 1976; *Crime and Passion* 1976; *Family Plot* 1976; *Capricorn One* 1978; *In Praise of Older Women* 1978; *Killer Fish* 1978; *Chanel Solitaire* 1981; *Separate Ways* 1981; *Come Back to the Five and Dime, Jimmy Dean, Jimmy Dean* 1982; *Can She Bake a Cherry Pie?* 1983; *Martin's Day* 1984; *Savage Dawn* 1985; *Invaders from Mars* 1986; *It's Alive III: Island of the Alive* 1987; *The Invisible Kid* 1988; *Out of the Dark* 1988; *Homer and Eddie* 1989; *The Children* 1990; *Haunting Fear* 1990; *Auntie Lee's Meat Pies* 1991; *Evil Spirits* 1991; *Rubin & Ed* 1991; *Bound and Gagged: a Love Story* 1992; *Plan 10 from Outer Space* 1995; *House of 1000 Corpses* 2001
Black, Lucas (1982–) *Sling Blade* 1995; *Crazy in Alabama* 1999; *All the Pretty Horses* 2000; *Friday Night Lights* 2004
Black, Maurice (1891–1938) *Smart Money* 1931; *I Cover the Waterfront* 1933
Blackburn, Richard *Eating Raoul* 1982; *Not for Publication* 1984; *Under the Piano* 1995
Blackman, Honor (1926–) *Daughter of Darkness* 1948; *Quartet* 1948; *A Boy, a Girl and a Bike* 1949; *Conspirator* 1949; *Diamond City* 1949; *So Long at the Fair* 1950; *Green Grow the Rushes* 1951; *The Glass Cage* 1955; *Suspended Alibi* 1956; *Account Rendered* 1957; *You Pay Your Money* 1957; *A Night to Remember* 1958; *The Rainbow Jacket* 1958; *The Square Peg* 1958; *A Matter of WHO* 1961; *Serena* 1962; *Jason and the Argonauts* 1963; *Goldfinger* 1964; *Life at the Top* 1965; *The Secret of My Success* 1965; *Moment to Moment* 1966; *A Twist of Sand* 1967; *Shalako* 1968; *Twinky* 1969; *The Last Grenade* 1970; *The Virgin and the Gypsy* 1970; *Fright* 1971; *something big* 1971; *To the Devil a Daughter* 1976; *The Cat and the Canary* 1979; *Talos the Mummy* 1997; *To Walk with Lions* 1999; *Bridget Jones's Diary* 2001
Blackman, Joan (1938–) *Good Day for a Hanging* 1958; *Career* 1959; *The Great Impostor* 1960; *Visit to a Small Planet* 1960; *Blue Hawaii* 1961; *Kid Galahad* 1962; *Twilight of Honor* 1963; *Daring Game* 1968; *The Destructors* 1968; *Macon County Line* 1973
Blackmer, Sidney (1895–1973) *Deluge* 1933; *The Count of Monte Cristo* 1934; *This Man Is Mine* 1934; *The Little Colonel* 1935; *Streamline Express* 1935; *Charlie Chan at Monte Carlo* 1937; *The Last Gangster* 1937; *Thank You, Mr Moto* 1937; *This Is My Affair* 1937; *Wife, Doctor and Nurse* 1937; *Suez* 1938; *Trade Winds* 1938; *Maryland* 1940; *Cheers for Miss Bishop* 1941; *Down Mexico Way* 1941; *Love Crazy* 1941; *Quiet Please, Murder* 1942; *War of the Wildcats* 1943; *The Lady and the Monster* 1944; *People Will Talk* 1951; *The San Francisco Story* 1952; *Washington Story* 1952; *Johnny Dark* 1954; *The View from Pompey's Head* 1955; *Accused of Murder* 1956; *Beyond a Reasonable Doubt* 1956; *High Society* 1956; *Tammy and the Bachelor* 1957; *How to Murder Your Wife* 1965; *Joy in the Morning* 1965; *A Covenant with Death* 1967; *Rosemary's Baby* 1968
Blackthorne, Paul (1969–) *The Truth Game* 2000; *Lagaan: Once upon a Time in India* 2001
Blackwood, Vas *Arthur's Hallowed Ground* 1985; *Babymother* 1998; *Lock, Stock and Two Smoking Barrels* 1998; *Mean Machine* 2001; *9 Dead Gay Guys* 2001; *The Escapist* 2002; *Creep* 2004
Blades, Rubén (1948–) *Crossover Dreams* 1985; *Critical Condition* 1987; *Fatal Beauty* 1987; *The Milagro Beanfield War* 1988; *Disorganized Crime* 1989; *The Lemon Sisters* 1989; *Predator 2* 1990; *The Two Jakes* 1990; *Crazy from the Heart* 1991; *The Super* 1991; *Color of Night* 1994; *Scorpion Spring* 1995; *Chinese Box* 1997; *The Devil's Own* 1997; *Cradle Will Rock* 1999; *All the Pretty Horses* 2000; *Assassination Tango* 2002; *Imagining Argentina* 2003; *Once upon a Time in Mexico* 2003
Blain, Gérard (1930–2000) *Le Beau Serge* 1958; *Young Husbands* 1958; *Les Cousins* 1959; *Hatari!* 1962; *La Bonne Soupe* 1963; *The American Friend* 1977
Blaine, Vivian (1921–1995) *Jitterbugs* 1943; *Greenwich Village* 1944; *Something for the Boys* 1944; *Nob Hill* 1945; *State Fair* 1945; *Three Little Girls in Blue* 1946; *Skirts Ahoy!* 1952; *Guys and Dolls* 1955; *The Cracker Factory* 1979
Blair, Barbara *Hold My Hand* 1938; *Bedelia* 1946
Blair, Betsy (1923–) *The Guilt of Janet Ames* 1947; *Kind Lady* 1951; *Marty* 1955; *Calle Mayor* 1956; *Il Grido* 1957; *The Halliday Brand* 1957; *All Night Long* 1961; *A Delicate Balance* 1973; *Descent into Hell* 1986; *Betrayed* 1988
Blair, Isla (1944–) *Real Life* 1983; *Valmont* 1989; *The Monk* 1990; *The Match* 1999
Blair, Janet (1921–) *Broadway* 1942; *My Sister Eileen* 1942; *Once upon a Time* 1944; *Tonight and Every Night* 1945; *The Fabulous Dorseys* 1947; *The Black Arrow* 1948; *The Fuller Brush Man* 1948; *Night of the Eagle* 1961; *Boys' Night Out* 1962; *The One and Only, Genuine, Original Family Band* 1968
Blair, Linda (1959–) *The Exorcist* 1973; *Airport 1975* 1974; *Victory at Entebbe* 1976; *Exorcist II: The Heretic* 1977; *Roller Boogie* 1979; *Hell Night* 1981; *Chained Heat* 1983; *Night Patrol* 1984; *Savage Streets* 1984; *Red Heat* 1985; *Silent Assassins* 1988; *Witchcraft* 1989; *Repossessed* 1990; *Fatal Bond* 1991; *Scream* 1996
Blair, Lionel (1934–) *The Main Attraction* 1962; *A Hard Day's Night* 1964
Blair, Selma (1972–) *Brown's Requiem* 1998; *Girl* 1998; *Cruel Intentions* 1999; *Down to You* 2000; *Kill Me Later* 2001; *Legally Blonde* 2001; *Storytelling* 2001; *A Guy Thing* 2002; *The Sweetest Thing* 2002; *A Dirty Shame* 2004; *Hellboy* 2004; *In Good Company* 2004
Blake, Amanda (1929–1989) *Stars in My Crown* 1950; *Scarlet Angel* 1952; *Lili* 1953; *The Adventures of Hajji Baba* 1954; *A Star Is Born* 1954; *The Glass Slipper* 1955; *The Boost* 1988
Blake, Catherine *The Dark Light* 1951; *Tale of a Vampire* 1992
Blake, Geoffrey (1962–) *Critters 3* 1991; *FernGully: the Last Rainforest* 1992; *The Philadelphia Experiment 2* 1993; *Entertaining Angels: the Dorothy Day Story* 1996; *Max Q: Emergency Landing* 1998
Blake, Jon (1958–) *Early Frost* 1981; *The Lighthorsemen* 1987
Blake, Julia (1936–) *Patrick* 1978; *Lonely Hearts* 1981; *Man of Flowers* 1984; *Travelling North* 1986; *Georgia* 1988; *Father* 1990; *Mushrooms* 1995; *Hotel de Love* 1996; *Innocence* 2000
Blake, Katharine *aka* **Blake, Kathryn** (1928–1991) *Assassin for Hire* 1951; *Anne of the Thousand Days* 1969
Blake, Larry J *aka* **Blake, Larry** (1914–1982) *Trouble at Midnight* 1937; *The Trap* 1947; *Earth vs the Flying Saucers* 1956; *Demon Seed* 1977
Blake, Madge (1899–1969) *The Prowler* 1951; *Batman* 1966
Blake, Pamela *aka* **Pearce, Adele** (1918–) *Wyoming Outlaw* 1939; *The Unknown Guest* 1943
Blake, Rachael *Paws* 1997; *The Three Stooges* 2000; *Lantana* 2001
Blake, Robert *aka* **Blake, Bobby** (1933–) *China Girl* 1942; *The Big Noise* 1944; *The Horn Blows at Midnight* 1945; *Pork Chop Hill* 1959; *Town without Pity* 1961; *PT 109* 1963; *This Property Is Condemned* 1966; *In Cold Blood* 1967; *Tell Them Willie Boy Is Here* 1969; *Corky* 1972; *Electra Glide in Blue* 1973; *Busting* 1974; *Coast to Coast* 1980; *Money Train* 1995; *Lost Highway* 1996
Blakely, Colin (1930–1987) *The Informers* 1963; *The Long Ships* 1963; *This Sporting Life* 1963; *A Man for All Seasons* 1966; *The Spy with a Cold Nose* 1966; *Charlie Bubbles* 1967; *The Day the Fish Came Out* 1967; *Decline and Fall... of a Birdwatcher* 1968; *The Vengeance of She* 1968; *Alfred the Great* 1969; *The Private Life of Sherlock Holmes* 1970; *Something to Hide* 1971; *The National Health* 1973; *Galileo* 1974; *Murder on the Orient Express* 1974; *Love among the Ruins* 1975; *The Pink Panther Strikes Again* 1976; *Equus* 1977; *It Shouldn't Happen to a Vet* 1979; *The Dogs of War* 1980; *Loophole* 1980; *Nijinsky* 1980; *Evil under the Sun* 1982
Blakely, Gene (1922–1987) *Battle of the Coral Sea* 1959; *Beach Red* 1967
Blakely, Susan (1950–) *Savages* 1972; *The Lords of Flatbush* 1974; *The Towering Inferno* 1974; *Capone* 1975; *Report to the Commissioner* 1975; *Airport '79: the Concorde* 1979; *Dreamer* 1979; *Over the Top* 1987; *Wildflower* 1991
Blakeney, Olive (1903–1959) *Gangway* 1937; *That Uncertain Feeling* 1941; *Experiment Perilous* 1944
Blakley, Ronee (1946–) *Nashville* 1975; *The Private Files of J Edgar Hoover* 1977; *The Driver* 1978; *Good Luck, Miss Wyckoff* 1979; *The Baltimore Bullet* 1980; *A*

Nightmare on Elm Street 1984; *A Return to Salem's Lot* 1987

Blanc, Dominique (1962–) *Milou en Mai* 1989; *Indochine* 1991; *La Reine Margot* 1994; *Total Eclipse* 1995; *A Soldier's Daughter Never Cries* 1998; *The Pornographer* 2001; *[One] Cavale* 2002; *[Three] Après la Vie* 2002; *[Two] Un Couple Epatant* 2002

Blanc, Manuel (1968–) *J'Embrasse Pas* 1991; *The King of Paris* 1995; *Beaumarchais l'Insolent* 1996

Blanc, Mel (1908–1989) *A Wild Hare* 1940; *Neptune's Daughter* 1949; *Duck Dodgers in the $24\frac{1}{2}$ Century* 1953; *Birds Anonymous* 1957; *What's Opera, Doc?* 1957; *The Man Called Flintstone* 1966; *The Phantom Tollbooth* 1969; *Scalawag* 1973; *Buck Rogers in the 25th Century* 1979; *The Bugs Bunny/Road Runner Movie* 1979; *Looney Looney Looney Bugs Bunny Movie* 1981; *Bugs Bunny 1001 Rabbit Tales* 1982; *Daffy Duck's Movie: Fantastic Island* 1983; *Daffy Duck's Quackbusters* 1988; *Who Framed Roger Rabbit* 1988; *Jetsons: the Movie* 1990

Blanc, Michel (1952–) *Tenue de Soirée* 1986; *Monsieur Hire* 1989; *Uranus* 1990; *The Favour, the Watch and the Very Big Fish* 1991; *Merci la Vie* 1991; *Prospero's Books* 1991; *Summer Things* 2002

Blancard, René (1897–1965) *A Cage of Nightingales* 1945; *Calle Mayor* 1956

Blanchar, Dominique (1927–) *Decision before Dawn* 1951; *L'Avventura* 1960

Blanchar, Pierre (1892–1963) *The Chess Player* 1927; *Crime and Punishment* 1935; *Mademoiselle Docteur* 1936; *Un Carnet de Bal* 1937; *La Symphonie Pastorale* 1946

Blanchard, Mari (1927–1970) *Abbott and Costello Go to Mars* 1953; *Black Horse Canyon* 1954; *Destry* 1954; *Rails into Laramie* 1954; *Son of Sinbad* 1955; *Twice Told Tales* 1963

Blanchard, Rachel (1976–) *Young Ivanhoe* 1994; *Road Trip* 2000; *Sugar & Spice* 2001; *Without a Paddle* 2004

Blanchard, Ron *Caddie* 1976; *Warming Up* 1983

Blanche, Roland (1943–1999) *Les Compères* 1983; *Trop Belle pour Toi* 1989

Blanchett, Cate (1969–) *Oscar and Lucinda* 1997; *Paradise Road* 1997; *Thank God He Met Lizzie* 1997; *Elizabeth* 1998; *An Ideal Husband* 1999; *Pushing Tin* 1999; *The Talented Mr Ripley* 1999; *The Gift* 2000; *The Man Who Cried* 2000; *Bandits* 2001; *Charlotte Gray* 2001; *The Lord of the Rings: The Fellowship of the Ring* 2001; *The Shipping News* 2001; *Heaven* 2002; *The Lord of the Rings: The Two Towers* 2002; *Coffee and Cigarettes* 2003; *The Lord of the Rings: The Return of the King* 2003; *The Missing* 2003; *Veronica Guerin* 2003; *The Aviator* 2004; *The Life Aquatic with Steve Zissou* 2004

Blancke, Sandrine *Toto Le Héros* 1991; *A Shadow of Doubt* 1992

Blandick, Clara (1880–1962) *Romance* 1930; *Tom Sawyer* 1930; *Huckleberry Finn* 1931; *Rockabye* 1932; *The Bitter Tea of General Yen* 1933; *Ever in My Heart* 1933; *Turn Back the Clock* 1933; *The Girl from Missouri* 1934; *The Adventures of Huckleberry Finn* 1939; *The Wizard of Oz* 1939; *Frontier Gal* 1945; *Pillow of Death* 1945

Blane, Sally (1910–1997) *Advice to the Lovelorn* 1933; *Crime on the Hill* 1933

Blankfield, Mark (1950–) *Jekyll and Hyde... Together Again* 1982; *Robin Hood: Men in Tights* 1993; *Dracula: Dead and Loving It* 1995

Blanks, Billy (1956–) *Bloodfist* 1989; *Time Bomb* 1991; *Back in Action* 1993; *TC 2000* 1993; *Expect No Mercy* 1995

Blasco, Txema *Vacas* 1991; *Tierra* 1995

Blaser, Brandon *The Butter Cream Gang* 1991; *Secret of Treasure Mountain* 1993

Blatt, Melanie (1975–) *Dog Eat Dog* 2000; *Honest* 2000

Blau, Martin Maria *Ginger & Fred* 1986; *Heimat 2* 1992

Blavette, Charles (1902–1967) *Jofroi* 1933; *Toni* 1935; *Stormy Waters* 1941

Blech, Hans Christian (1925–1993) *Decision before Dawn* 1951; *The Visit* 1964; *The Saboteur, Code Name Morituri* 1965; *Les Innocents aux Mains Sales* 1975; *Knife in the Head* 1978; *Colonel Redl* 1984

Bledel, Alexis (1981–) *Tuck Everlasting* 2002; *The Sisterhood of the Traveling Pants* 2005

Bleeth, Yasmine (1968–) *Baywatch the Movie: Forbidden Paradise* 1995; *The Face* 1996; *BASEketball* 1998

Bleibtreu, Moritz (1971–) *Knockin' on Heaven's Door* 1997; *Run Lola Run* 1998; *The Experiment* 2000; *Taking Sides* 2001

Blendick, James *Shoot* 1976; *Utilities* 1981

Blessed, Brian (1937–) *Till Death Us Do Part* 1968; *Country Dance* 1970; *The Trojan Women* 1971; *Henry VIII and His Six Wives* 1972; *Man of La Mancha* 1972; *High Road to China* 1983; *The Hound of the Baskervilles* 1983; *Asterix and the Big Fight* 1989; *Henry V* 1989; *Prisoner of Honor* 1991; *Robin Hood: Prince of Thieves* 1991; *Back in the USSR* 1992; *Freddie as FRO7* 1992; *Chasing the Deer* 1994; *The Bruce* 1996; *Hamlet* 1996; *Macbeth* 1997; *Star Wars Episode I: the Phantom Menace* 1999; *Tarzan* 1999

Blethyn, Brenda (1946–) *The Witches* 1989; *A River Runs through It* 1992; *Secrets & Lies* 1995; *Remember Me?* 1996; *Girls' Night* 1997; *Little Voice* 1998; *Music from Another Room* 1998; *Night Train* 1998; *RKO 281* 1999; *Saving Grace* 2000; *Lovely & Amazing* 2001; *Sonny* 2002; *The Wild Thornberrys Movie* 2003; *Beyond the Sea* 2004; *A Way of Life* 2004; *On a Clear Day* 2005; *Pooh's Heffalump Movie* 2005

Blick, Newton (1899–1965) *The Long Arm* 1956; *The Gypsy and the Gentleman* 1958; *Morgan – a Suitable Case for Treatment* 1966

Blicker, Jason *American Boyfriends* 1989; *Baby on Board* 1993; *Superstar* 1999; *Owning Mahowny* 2002

Blier, Bernard (1916–1989) *Hôtel du Nord* 1938; *Le Jour Se Lève* 1939; *La Nuit Fantastique* 1942; *Quai des Orfèvres* 1947; *Secrets d'Alcove* 1954; *Les Misérables* 1957; *The Great War* 1959; *La Bonne Soupe* 1963; *The Organizer* 1963; *Male Hunt* 1964; *Casanova '70* 1965; *Uncle Benjamin* 1969; *Catch Me a Spy* 1971; *The Tall Blond Man with One Black Shoe* 1972; *Buffet Froid* 1979

Bliss, Boti Ann *Warlock III: the End of Innocence* 1999; *Bundy* 2002

Bliss, Caroline (1961–) *The Living Daylights* 1987; *Licence to Kill* 1989

Bloch, Bernard *Hidden Agenda* 1990; *The Cow and the President* 2000

Blocker, Dan (1928–1972) *Come Blow Your Horn* 1963; *Lady in Cement* 1968; *The Cockeyed Cowboys of Calico County* 1970

Blodgett, Michael (1940–) *Beyond the Valley of the Dolls* 1970; *The Velvet Vampire* 1971

Blondell, Joan (1909–1979) *Blonde Crazy* 1931; *God's Gift to Women* 1931; *Illicit* 1931; *Night Nurse* 1931; *Other Men's Women* 1931; *The Public Enemy* 1931; *The Crowd Roars* 1932; *Lawyer Man* 1932; *Make Me a Star* 1932; *Three on a Match* 1932; *Union Depot* 1932; *Footlight Parade* 1933; *Gold Diggers of 1933* 1933; *Havana Widows* 1933; *Dames* 1934; *He Was Her Man* 1934; *Bullets or Ballots* 1936; *Colleen* 1936; *Gold Diggers of 1937* 1936; *Stage Struck* 1936; *Three Men on a Horse* 1936; *The King and the Chorus Girl* 1937; *The Perfect Specimen* 1937; *Stand-In* 1937; *There's Always a Woman* 1938; *The Amazing Mr Williams* 1939; *East Side of Heaven* 1939; *Topper Returns* 1941; *Lady for a Night* 1942; *Cry Havoc* 1943; *Adventure* 1945; *A Tree Grows in Brooklyn* 1945; *Christmas Eve* 1947; *Nightmare Alley* 1947; *For Heaven's Sake* 1950; *The Blue Veil* 1951; *Desk Set* 1957; *Lizzie* 1957; *This Could Be the Night* 1957; *Will Success Spoil Rock Hunter?* 1957; *Angel Baby* 1961; *Advance to the Rear* 1964; *The Cincinnati Kid* 1965; *Ride beyond Vengeance* 1966; *The Spy in the Green Hat* 1966; *Waterhole #3* 1967; *Kona Coast* 1968; *Stay Away, Joe* 1968; *Support Your Local Gunfighter* 1971; *Opening Night* 1977; *The Glove* 1978; *The Champ* 1979

Bloom, Claire (1931–) *The Blind Goddess* 1948; *Limelight* 1952; *Innocents in Paris* 1953; *The Man Between* 1953; *Richard III* 1955; *Alexander the Great* 1956; *The Brothers Karamazov* 1958; *The Buccaneer* 1958; *Look Back in Anger* 1959; *The Chapman Report* 1962; *The Wonderful World of the Brothers Grimm* 1962; *80,000 Suspects* 1963; *The Haunting* 1963; *The Outrage* 1964; *The Spy Who Came in from the Cold* 1965; *Charly* 1968; *The Illustrated Man* 1969; *Three into Two Won't Go* 1969; *A Severed Head* 1970; *Red Sky at Morning* 1971; *A Doll's House* 1973; *Islands in the Stream* 1976; *Clash of the Titans* 1981; *Déjà Vu* 1984; *Sammy and Rosie Get Laid* 1987; *Crimes and Misdemeanors* 1989; *The Princess and the Goblin* 1992; *Mad Dogs and Englishmen* 1994; *Mighty Aphrodite* 1995; *Daylight* 1996; *What the Deaf Man Heard* 1997; *Wrestling with Alligators* 1998; *The Lady in Question* 1999; *Imagining Argentina* 2003

Bloom (1), John (1945–1999) *Dracula vs Frankenstein* 1970; *The Incredible Two-Headed Transplant* 1971

Bloom, Orlando (1977–) *Black Hawk Down* 2001; *The Lord of the Rings: The Fellowship of the Ring* 2001; *The Lord of the Rings: The Two Towers* 2002; *The Calcium Kid* 2003; *The Lord of the Rings: The Return of the King* 2003; *Ned Kelly* 2003; *Pirates of the Caribbean: the Curse of the Black Pearl* 2003; *Troy* 2004; *Kingdom of Heaven* 2005

Bloom, Verna (1939–) *Medium Cool* 1969; *The Hired Hand* 1971; *Badge 373* 1973; *High Plains Drifter* 1973; *National Lampoon's Animal House* 1978; *Playing for Time* 1980; *Honkytonk Man* 1982; *After Hours* 1985; *The Journey of Natty Gann* 1985; *The Last Temptation of Christ* 1988

Blore, Eric (1887–1959) *Tarnished Lady* 1931; *The Gay Divorce* 1934; *Folies Bergère* 1935; *The Good Fairy* 1935; *I Dream Too Much* 1935; *I Live My Life* 1935; *Old Man Rhythm* 1935; *Seven Keys to Baldpate* 1935; *Top Hat* 1935; *The Ex-Mrs Bradford* 1936; *Piccadilly Jim* 1936; *Swing Time* 1936; *The Adventures of Michael Strogoff* 1937; *Breakfast for Two* 1937; *It's Love I'm After* 1937; *Quality Street* 1937; *Shall We Dance* 1937; *Joy of Living* 1938; *Swiss Miss* 1938; *The Boys from Syracuse* 1940; *The Lone Wolf Meets a Lady* 1940; *The Man Who Wouldn't Talk* 1940; *Music in My Heart* 1940; *'Til We Meet Again* 1940; *Confirm or Deny* 1941; *The Lady Eve* 1941; *Road to Zanzibar* 1941; *The Shanghai Gesture* 1941; *Sullivan's Travels* 1941; *The Moon and Sixpence* 1942; *The Sky's the Limit* 1943; *Abie's Irish Rose* 1946; *Romance on the High Seas* 1948; *The Adventures of Ichabod and Mr Toad* 1949; *Love Happy* 1949

Blossom, Roberts (1924–) *Slaughterhouse-Five* 1972; *Deranged* 1974; *Citizens Band* 1977; *Close Encounters of the Third Kind* 1977; *Escape from Alcatraz* 1979; *Resurrection* 1980; *Reuben, Reuben* 1983; *Candy Mountain* 1987; *The Last Temptation of Christ* 1988; *Always* 1989; *Home Alone* 1990

Blount, Lisa (1957–) *September 30, 1955* 1977; *Dead & Buried* 1981; *An Officer and a Gentleman* 1982; *Secrets of the Phantom Caverns* 1984; *Radioactive Dreams* 1986; *Nightflyers* 1987; *Prince of Darkness* 1987; *Out Cold* 1989; *Blind Fury* 1990; *Femme Fatale* 1991; *Murder between Friends* 1993; *Judicial Consent* 1995; *Box of Moonlight* 1996

Blucas, Marc (1972–) *The Mating Habits of the Earthbound Human* 1999; *I Capture the Castle* 2002; *They* 2002; *The Alamo* 2004; *First Daughter* 2004

Blue, Ben (1901–1975) *Artists and Models* 1937; *College Swing* 1938; *Paris Honeymoon* 1939; *For Me and My Gal* 1942; *Broadway Rhythm* 1944; *Two Sisters from Boston* 1946

Blue, Callum *Devil's Gate* 2002; *The Princess Diaries 2: Royal Engagement* 2004

Blue, Jean (1972–) *The Overlanders* 1946; *Bitter Springs* 1950

Blue, Monte (1890–1963) *Orphans of the Storm* 1921; *The Marriage Circle* 1924; *Kiss Me Again* 1925; *So This Is Paris* 1926; *White Shadows in the South Seas* 1928; *The Lives of a Bengal Lancer* 1935; *Hell Town* 1937; *A Million to One* 1937; *Silver River* 1948; *The Younger Brothers* 1949; *Apache* 1954

Bluhm, Brady (1983–) *Two Much Trouble* 1995; *Alone in the Woods* 1996; *Winnie the Pooh's Most Grand Adventure* 1997

Blum, Jack *Meatballs* 1979; *Happy Birthday to Me* 1981

Blum, Mark (1950–) *Desperately Seeking Susan* 1985; *"Crocodile" Dundee* 1986; *Blind Date* 1987; *"Crocodile" Dundee II* 1988; *The Presidio* 1988; *Indictment: the McMartin Trial* 1995; *You Can Thank Me Later* 1998

Blumenfeld, Alan *Out Cold* 1989; *Ed McBain's 87th Precinct* 1995

Blundell, Graeme (1945–) *Alvin Purple* 1973; *Don's Party* 1976; *Weekend of Shadows* 1978; *The Odd Angry Shot* 1979; *The Year My Voice Broke* 1987; *Idiot Box* 1996

Blunt, Erin (1963–) *The Bad News Bears in Breaking Training* 1977; *The Bad News Bears Go to Japan* 1978

Bluteau, Lothaire (1957–) *Jesus of Montreal* 1989; *Black Robe* 1991; *Mrs 'arris Goes to Paris* 1992; *Orlando* 1992; *The Silent Touch* 1992; *The Confessional* 1995; *I Shot Andy Warhol* 1995; *Other Voices, Other Rooms* 1995; *Bent* 1996; *Dead Heat* 2002

Bluthal, John (1929–) *The Knack... and How to Get It* 1965; *Carry On Follow That Camel* 1967; *The Bliss of Mrs Blossom* 1968; *Digby, the Biggest Dog in the World* 1973

Blyden, Larry (1925–1975) *The Bachelor Party* 1957; *Kiss Them for Me* 1957; *On a Clear Day You Can See Forever* 1970

Blye, Maggie *aka* **Blye, Margaret** *Waterhole #3* 1967; *Diamonds for Breakfast* 1968; *The Italian Job* 1969; *Every Little Crook and Nanny* 1972; *Hard Times* 1975; *Final Chapter – Walking Tall* 1977; *The Entity* 1981; *Liar's Moon* 1982; *Mischief* 1985

Blyth, Ann (1928–) *The Merry Monahans* 1944; *Mildred Pierce* 1945; *Swell Guy* 1946; *Brute Force* 1947; *Killer McCoy* 1947; *Another Part of the Forest* 1948; *Mr Peabody and the Mermaid* 1948; *Once More, My Darling* 1949; *Red Canyon* 1949; *Our Very Own* 1950; *The Great Caruso* 1951; *Thunder on the Hill* 1951; *One Minute to Zero* 1952; *The World in His Arms* 1952; *All the Brothers Were Valiant* 1953; *Rose Marie* 1954; *The Student Prince* 1954; *The King's Thief* 1955; *Kismet* 1955; *The Buster Keaton Story* 1957; *The Helen Morgan Story* 1957

Blythe, Janus *The Hills Have Eyes* 1977; *The Hills Have Eyes Part II* 1985

Blythe, John (1921–1993) *Bon Voyage* 1944; *The Frightened Man* 1952; *Gaolbreak* 1962

Blythe, Peter (1934–2004) *Frankenstein Created Woman* 1966; *A Challenge for Robin Hood* 1967; *Carrington* 1995; *The Luzhin Defence* 2000

Boardman, Eleanor (1898–1991) *Sinners in Silk* 1924; *The Crowd* 1928; *The Squaw Man* 1931

Boatman, Michael *aka* **Boatman, Michael Patrick** (1964–) *Hamburger Hill* 1987; *The Glass Shield* 1995

Boatman, Ross *Hard Men* 1996; *Bring Me the Head of Mavis Davis* 1997

Bobby, Anne (1967–) *Nightbreed* 1990; *Finding North* 1997

Boccardo, Delia (1948–) *Inspector Clouseau* 1968; *Panhandle Calibre 38* 1972; *Snow Job* 1972; *Massacre in Rome* 1973; *Tentacles* 1977

Bochner, Hart (1956–) *Islands in the Stream* 1976; *Breaking Away* 1979; *Terror Train* 1980; *Rich and Famous* 1981; *Apartment Zero* 1988; *Die Hard* 1988; *Fellow Traveller* 1989; *Mr Destiny* 1990; *Mad at the Moon* 1992; *Batman: Mask of the Phantasm* 1993; *Complex of Fear* 1993; *The Innocent* 1993; *Break Up* 1998; *Urban Legends: Final Cut* 2000; *Liberty Stands Still* 2002

Bochner, Lloyd (1924–) *The Night Walker* 1964; *Harlow* 1965; *Point Blank* 1967; *Stranger on the Run* 1967; *Tony Rome* 1967; *The Detective* 1968; *The Horse in the Gray Flannel Suit* 1968; *Tiger by the Tail* 1970; *Ulzana's Raid* 1972; *The Hot Touch* 1982; *The Lonely Lady* 1983; *Crystal Heart* 1987; *Millennium* 1989; *The Naked Gun $2\frac{1}{2}$: the Smell of Fear* 1991; *Bram Stoker's Legend of the Mummy* 1998

Bodison, Wolfgang (1966–) *The Expert* 1994; *Freeway* 1996

Bodnia, Kim (1965–) *Nightwatch* 1994; *Pusher* 1996; *Bleeder* 1999; *Dragonflies* 2001

Bodrov Jr, Sergei (1971–2002) *Prisoner of the Mountains* 1996; *Brother* 1997; *The Stringer* 1997; *East-West* 1999; *War* 2002

Boen, Earl (1945–) *The Man with Two Brains* 1983; *The Terminator* 1984; *Terminator 2: Judgment Day* 1991; *The Dentist* 1996; *Terminator 3: Rise of the Machines* 2003

Boes, Richard *Permanent Vacation* 1982; *Johnny Suede* 1991; *Dead Man* 1995

Bogaert, Lucienne (1892–1983) *Les Dames du Bois de Boulogne* 1946; *Maigret Sets a Trap* 1957

Bogarde, Dirk (1921–1999) *Dancing with Crime* 1946; *Esther Waters* 1948; *Once a Jolly Swagman* 1948; *Quartet* 1948; *The Blue Lamp* 1949; *Boys in Brown* 1949; *Dear Mr Prohack* 1949; *So Long at the Fair* 1950; *The Woman in Question* 1950; *Appointment in London* 1952; *The Gentle Gunman* 1952; *Hunted* 1952; *Penny Princess* 1952; *Desperate Moment* 1953; *They Who Dare* 1953; *Doctor in the House* 1954; *For Better, for Worse* 1954; *The Sea Shall Not Have Them* 1954; *The Sleeping Tiger* 1954; *Doctor at Sea* 1955; *Simba* 1955; *Ill Met by Moonlight* 1956; *The Spanish Gardener* 1956; *Campbell's Kingdom* 1957; *Cast a Dark Shadow* 1957; *Doctor at Large* 1957; *A Tale of Two Cities* 1957; *The Doctor's Dilemma* 1958; *The Wind Cannot Read* 1958; *Libel* 1959; *The Angel Wore Red* 1960; *The Singer*

Not the Song 1960; Song without End 1960; Victim 1961; HMS Defiant 1962; The Password Is Courage 1962; We Joined the Navy 1962; Doctor in Distress 1963; Hot Enough for June 1963; I Could Go On Singing 1963; The Mind Benders 1963; The Servant 1963; King and Country 1964; Darling 1965; The High Bright Sun 1965; Modesty Blaise 1966; Accident 1967; Our Mother's House 1967; The Fixer 1968; Sebastian 1968; The Damned 1969; Justine 1969; Oh! What a Lovely War 1969; Death in Venice 1971; The Serpent 1972; The Night Porter 1973; Permission to Kill 1975; A Bridge Too Far 1977; Providence 1977; Despair 1978; The Patricia Neal Story: an Act of Love 1981; These Foolish Things 1990

Bogart, Humphrey (1899–1957) Up the River 1930; Bad Sister 1931; Body and Soul 1931; Love Affair 1932; Three on a Match 1932; Midnight 1934; Bullets or Ballots 1936; China Clipper 1936; Isle of Fury 1936; The Petrified Forest 1936; The Black Legion 1937; Dead End 1937; The Great O'Malley 1937; Kid Galahad 1937; Marked Woman 1937; San Quentin 1937; Stand-In 1937; Swing Your Lady 1937; The Amazing Dr Clitterhouse 1938; Angels with Dirty Faces 1938; Racket Busters 1938; Dark Victory 1939; Invisible Stripes 1939; King of the Underworld 1939; The Oklahoma Kid 1939; The Return of Dr X 1939; The Roaring Twenties 1939; You Can't Get Away with Murder 1939; Brother Orchid 1940; It All Came True 1940; They Drive by Night 1940; Virginia City 1940; High Sierra 1941; The Maltese Falcon 1941; The Wagons Roll at Night 1941; Across the Pacific 1942; All through the Night 1942; The Big Shot 1942; Casablanca 1942; Action in the North Atlantic 1943; Sahara 1943; Thank Your Lucky Stars 1943; Passage to Marseille 1944; To Have and Have Not 1944; Conflict 1945; The Two Mrs Carrolls 1945; The Big Sleep 1946; Two Guys from Milwaukee 1946; Dark Passage 1947; Dead Reckoning 1947; Key Largo 1948; The Treasure of the Sierra Madre 1948; Knock on Any Door 1949; Tokyo Joe 1949; Chain Lightning 1950; In a Lonely Place 1950; The African Queen 1951; The Enforcer 1951; Sirocco 1951; Deadline – USA 1952; Battle Circus 1953; Beat the Devil 1953; The Love Lottery 1953; The Barefoot Contessa 1954; The Caine Mutiny 1954; Sabrina 1954; The Desperate Hours 1955; The Left Hand of God 1955; We're No Angels 1955; The Harder They Fall 1956

Bogatyrev, Yuri An Unfinished Piece for Mechanical Piano 1976; Oblomov 1980

Bogdanovich, Peter (1939–) Targets 1968; Saint Jack 1979; Mr Jealousy 1997; Festival in Cannes 2001

Bogosian, Eric (1953–) Talk Radio 1988; Suffering Bastards 1989; Sex, Drugs, Rock & Roll 1991; Arabian Knight 1995; Dolores Claiborne 1995; Under Siege 2 1995; Beavis and Butt-head Do America 1996; The Substance of Fire 1996; Deconstructing Harry 1997; Gossip 1999; Ararat 2002; Wonderland 2003

Bohm, Hark (1939–) The American Soldier 1970; Effi Briest 1974; Lili Marleen 1980

Böhm, Karlheinz aka **Boehm, Carl** aka **Boehm, Karl** aka **Bohm, Karl-Heinz** (1928–) Peeping Tom 1960; Too Hot to Handle 1960; The Magnificent Rebel 1961; Come Fly with Me 1962; The Wonderful World of the Brothers Grimm 1962; The Venetian Affair 1966; Martha 1973; Fox and His Friends 1975; Mother Küsters Goes to Heaven 1975

Bohm, Marquard Beware of a Holy Whore 1970; Kings of the Road 1976; Satan's Brew 1976

Bohnen, Roman (1894–1949) Of Mice and Men 1939; They Dare Not Love 1941; The Song of Bernadette 1943; The Hairy Ape 1944; Counter-Attack 1945; The Strange Love of Martha Ivers 1946; Arch of Triumph 1948

Bohrer, Corinne (1959–) Vice Versa 1988; Star Kid 1997

Bohringer, Richard (1942–) Diva 1981; Le Grand Pardon 1981; I Married a Dead Man 1983; Death in a French Garden 1985; Subway 1985; Kamikaze 1986; Le Paltoquet 1986; Le Grand Chemin 1987; The Cook, the Thief, His Wife and Her Lover 1989; L'Accompagnatrice 1992; Tango 1993; Le Cri du Coeur 1994; Le Parfum d'Yvonne 1994; Would I Lie to You? 1997; Crime Spree 2002

Bohringer, Romane (1973–) Kamikaze 1986; L'Accompagnatrice 1992; Les Nuits Fauves 1992; Mina Tannenbaum 1993; Total Eclipse 1995; L'Appartement 1996; Portraits Chinois 1996; The Chambermaid on the Titanic 1997; Vigo: Passion for Life 1997; The King Is Alive 2000

Boht, Jean (1936–) Arthur's Hallowed Ground 1985; The Girl in a Swing 1988; To Die For 1994

Bois, Curt (1901–1991) The Great Waltz 1938; Hold Back the Dawn 1941; That Night in Rio 1941; The Tuttles of Tahiti 1942; The Woman in White 1948; Caught 1949; The Lovable Cheat 1949; Wings of Desire 1987

Boisson, Christine (1957–) Emmanuelle 1974; Identification of a Woman 1982; The Passage 1986; En Face 1999; The Truth about Charlie 2002

Boitel, Jeanne (1904–1987) Marie Antoinette 1956; Maigret Sets a Trap 1957

Bolam, James (1938–) The Kitchen 1961; A Kind of Loving 1962; The Loneliness of the Long Distance Runner 1962; Murder Most Foul 1964; Otley 1968; Crucible of Terror 1971; In Celebration 1974; The Likely Lads 1976; The Plague Dogs 1982; Clockwork Mice 1994; The Island on Bird Street 1997; Stella Does Tricks 1997; The End of the Affair 1999; It Was an Accident 2000; To Kill a King 2003

Boland, Eddie (1883–1935) Oliver Twist 1922; The Kid Brother 1927; The Miracle Woman 1931

Boland, Mary (1880–1965) Four Frightened People 1934; Six of a Kind 1934; Ruggles of Red Gap 1935; Danger – Love at Work 1937; There Goes the Groom 1937; Artists and Models Abroad 1938; The Women 1939; New Moon 1940; Pride and Prejudice 1940; In Our Time 1944; Nothing but Trouble 1944; Guilty Bystander 1950

Boles, John (1895–1969) Fazil 1928; The Last Warning 1928; The Desert Song 1929; Rio Rita 1929; The King of Jazz 1930; Frankenstein 1931; One Heavenly Night 1931; Back Street 1932; Only Yesterday 1933; The Age of Innocence 1934; The White Parade 1934; Curly Top 1935; The Littlest Rebel 1935; Craig's Wife 1936; A Message to Garcia 1936; Stella Dallas 1937; Sinners in Paradise 1938; Thousands Cheer 1943

Bolger, Franklin aka **Bolger, Franklin H** Common-Law Cabin 1967; Cherry, Harry & Raquel 1969

Bolger, Ray (1904–1987) Rosalie 1937; Sweethearts 1938; The Wizard of Oz 1939; Sunny 1941; Forever and a Day 1943; The Harvey Girls 1946; Look for the Silver Lining 1949; April in Paris 1952; Babes in Toyland 1961; The Entertainer 1975; The Runner Stumbles 1979

Bolkan, Florinda (1941–) Investigation of a Citizen above Suspicion 1970; The Last Valley 1971; A Man to Respect 1972; Royal Flash 1975; Prisoner of Rio 1988; Some Girls 1988

Bollain, Iciar (1967–) El Sur 1983; Land and Freedom 1995

Bolling, Tiffany (1947–) The Marriage of a Young Stockbroker 1971; The Wild Party 1975; Kingdom of the Spiders 1977

Bollman, Ryan (1972–) Children of the Corn II: the Final Sacrifice 1993; The NeverEnding Story III 1994; True Blue 1996

Bologna, Joseph (1936–) Cops and Robbers 1973; Mixed Company 1974; The Big Bus 1976; Chapter Two 1979; Torn between Two Lovers 1979; My Favorite Year 1982; Blame It on Rio 1984; The Woman in Red 1984; Transylvania 6-5000 1985; Coupe de Ville 1990; Alligator II: the Mutation 1991; Jersey Girl 1992; Love Is All There Is 1996; Big Daddy 1999

Bolt, David Phobia 1980; The Grace of God 1998

Bompoil, Michel Didier 1997; Dry Cleaning 1997; Le Secret 2000

Bon Jovi, Jon (1962–) Moonlight and Valentino 1995; The Leading Man 1996; Little City 1997; Homegrown 1998; No Looking Back 1998; Pay It Forward 2000; U-571 2000

Bonacelli, Paolo (1939–) Salo, or the 120 Days of Sodom 1975; Illustrious Corpses 1976; Midnight Express 1978; Christ Stopped at Eboli 1979; The Oberwald Mystery 1980; Camorra 1985; Francesco 1989; Johnny Stecchino 1991

Bonaiuto, Anna (1950–) Fratelli e Sorelle 1992; L'Amore Molesto 1995

Bonamy, Olivia (1974–) Boys on the Beach 1998; The Captive 2000; Read My Lips 2001

Bonanova, Fortunio (1893–1969) Citizen Kane 1941; Five Graves to Cairo 1943; Ali Baba and the Forty Thieves 1944; The Red Dragon 1945; Where Do We Go from Here? 1945; Romance on the High Seas 1948; Whirlpool 1949; An Affair to Remember 1957; The Saga of Hemp Brown 1958; Thunder in the Sun 1959

Bonar, Ivan (1924–1988) MacArthur 1977; Same Time, Next Year 1978

Bond, Derek (1919–) The Loves of Joanna Godden 1947; Nicholas Nickleby 1947; Uncle Silas 1947; Broken Journey 1948; Scott of the Antarctic 1948; The Weaker Sex 1948; Christopher Columbus 1949; Marry Me! 1949; The Quiet Woman 1950; Tony Draws a Horse 1950; The Hour of 13 1952; Trouble in Store 1953; Stranger from Venus 1954; Svengali 1954; Rogue's Yarn 1956; Wonderful Life 1964; Press for Time 1966; When Eight Bells Toll 1971

Bond III, James Go Tell It on the Mountain 1984; Def by Temptation 1990

Bond, Lillian aka **Bond, Lilian** (1908–1991) Air Mail 1932; Fireman Save My Child 1932; The Old Dark House 1932; Blond Cheat 1938; The Housekeeper's Daughter 1939

Bond, Raleigh (1935–1989) The Black Marble 1980; Nightmares 1983

Bond, Raymond (1885–1972) Outrage 1950; The Man from Planet X 1951

Bond, Samantha (1962–) Erik the Viking 1989; GoldenEye 1995; Tomorrow Never Dies 1997; What Rats Won't Do 1998; Die Another Day 2002; Strings 2004; Yes 2004

Bond, Sheila The Marrying Kind 1952; The Spirit of St Louis 1957

Bond, Sudie (1928–1984) Tomorrow 1972; Come Back to the Five and Dime, Jimmy Dean, Jimmy Dean 1982; Enormous Changes at the Last Minute 1983

Bond, Ward (1903–1960) The Man Who Lived Twice 1936; Submarine Patrol 1938; The Cisco Kid and the Lady 1939; The Girl from Mexico 1939; Buck Benny Rides Again 1940; Kit Carson 1940; The Long Voyage Home 1940; The Maltese Falcon 1941; A Man Betrayed 1941; Manpower 1941; Sergeant York 1941; The Shepherd of the Hills 1941; The Falcon Takes Over 1942; Gentleman Jim 1942; Sin Town 1942; Ten Gentlemen from West Point 1942; Hello, Frisco, Hello 1943; The Fighting Sullivans 1944; A Guy Named Joe 1944; Home in Indiana 1944; Tall in the Saddle 1944; Dakota 1945; They Were Expendable 1945; Canyon Passage 1946; It's a Wonderful Life 1946; My Darling Clementine 1946; The Fugitive 1947; Unconquered 1947; Fort Apache 1948; Joan of Arc 1948; Three Godfathers 1948; The Time of Your Life 1948; Kiss Tomorrow Goodbye 1950; Only the Valiant 1950; Riding High 1950; Wagonmaster 1950; On Dangerous Ground 1951; Operation Pacific 1951; Hellgate 1952; The Quiet Man 1952; Thunderbirds 1952; Blowing Wild 1953; Hondo 1953; The Moonlighter 1953; The Bob Mathias Story 1954; Gypsy Colt 1954; Johnny Guitar 1954; The Long Gray Line 1955; A Man Alone 1955; Mister Roberts 1955; Dakota Incident 1956; Pillars of the Sky 1956; The Searchers 1956; The Halliday Brand 1957; The Wings of Eagles 1957; China Doll 1958; Alias Jesse James 1959; Rio Bravo 1959

Bondarchuk, Sergei (1920–1994) Othello 1955; Destiny of a Man 1959; War and Peace 1966; The Battle of Neretva 1969

Bondi, Beulah (1892–1981) Arrowsmith 1931; Street Scene 1931; The Stranger's Return 1933; Finishing School 1934; The Painted Veil 1934; The Good Fairy 1935; The Gorgeous Hussy 1936; The Invisible Ray 1936; The Moon's Our Home 1936; The Trail of the Lonesome Pine 1936; Make Way for Tomorrow 1937; Of Human Hearts 1938; The Sisters 1938; Vivacious Lady 1938; Mr Smith Goes to Washington 1939; Our Town 1940; Remember the Night 1940; One Foot in Heaven 1941; Penny Serenade 1941; The Shepherd of the Hills 1941; Watch on the Rhine 1943; And Now Tomorrow 1944; I Love a Soldier 1944; The Very Thought of You 1944; Back to Bataan 1945; The Southerner 1945; It's a Wonderful Life 1946; Sister Kenny 1946; The Sainted Sisters 1948; The Snake Pit 1948; Reign of Terror 1949; So Dear to My Heart 1949; The Furies 1950; Lone Star 1952; Latin Lovers 1953; Track of the Cat 1954; Back from Eternity 1956; The Unholy Wife 1957; Tammy Tell Me True 1961; The Wonderful World of the Brothers Grimm 1962; Tammy and the Doctor 1963

Bonds, De'Aundre (1976–) Get on the Bus 1996; Sunset Park 1996; The Wood 1999

Bonet, Lisa (1967–) Angel Heart 1987; Bank Robber 1993; Final Combination 1993; Enemy of the State 1998; High Fidelity 2000; Biker Boyz 2003

Bonetti, Massimo The Night of San Lorenzo 1981; Night Sun 1990

Bonham-Carter, Crispin Annie: a Royal Adventure 1995; Basil 1998

Bonham Carter, Helena (1966–) Lady Jane 1985; A Room with a View 1985; La Maschera 1988; Francesco 1989; Getting It Right 1989; Hamlet 1990; Where Angels Fear to Tread 1991; Howards End 1992; Mary Shelley's Frankenstein 1994; Margaret's Museum 1995; Mighty Aphrodite 1995; Portraits Chinois 1996; Twelfth Night 1996; Keep the Aspidistra Flying 1997; The Revengers' Comedies 1997; The Wings of the Dove 1997; The Theory of Flight 1998; Fight Club 1999; Women Talking Dirty 1999; Novocaine 2001; Planet of the Apes 2001; The Heart of Me 2002; Live from Baghdad 2002; Big Fish 2003

Bonifant, J Evan aka **Bonifant, Evan** (1985–) 3 Ninjas Kick Back 1994; Blues Brothers 2000 1998

Bonilla, Jesús (1955–) The Girl of Your Dreams 1998; La Comunidad 2000

Bonnaffé, Jacques (1958–) First Name: Carmen 1983; Venus Beauty Institute 1998; Va Savoir 2001; Les Diables 2002

Bonnaire, Sandrine (1967–) To Our Loves 1984; Police 1985; Vagabond 1985; Sous le Soleil de Satan 1987; Monsieur Hire 1989; Captive of the Desert 1990; The Plague 1992; Jeanne la Pucelle 1994; La Cérémonie 1995; Circle of Passion 1996; Secret Defense 1997; The Colour of Lies 1999; East-West 1999; Confidences Trop Intimes 2004

Bonner, Priscilla (1898–1996) The Strong Man 1926; Long Pants 1927

Bonner, Tony (1943–) Eyewitness 1970; You Can't Win 'em All 1970; Creatures the World Forgot 1971; Money Movers 1978; The Man from Snowy River 1982; The Lighthorsemen 1987; Quigley Down Under 1990

Bonner, William Run, Angel, Run 1969; The Hard Ride 1971

Bonnevie, Maria (1973–) Jerusalem 1996; Insomnia 1997; Dragonflies 2001; I Am David 2003; Reconstruction 2003

Bonneville, Hugh (1963–) Notting Hill 1999; Blow Dry 2000; The Emperor's New Clothes 2001; Iris 2001; Stage Beauty 2004

Bonney, John Paranoiac 1963; Saturday Night Out 1963

Bono, Sonny (1935–1898) Wild on the Beach 1965; Good Times 1967; Escape to Athena 1979; Airplane II: the Sequel 1982; Balboa 1982; Troll 1986; Hairspray 1988; First Kid 1996

Bonsall, Brian (1981–) Father Hood 1993; Blank Check 1994

Bonvoisin, Bérangère Hôtel du Paradis 1986; Good Morning, Babylon 1987; Docteur Petiot 1990

Booke, Sorrell (1930–1994) Gone Are the Days 1963; Black like Me 1964; The Love Cage 1964; Up the Down Staircase 1967; Bye Bye Braverman 1968; Slaughterhouse-Five 1972; What's Up, Doc? 1972; The Iceman Cometh 1973; Bank Shot 1974; The Take 1974; Freaky Friday 1976; Special Delivery 1976

Boone, Pat (1934–) April Love 1957; Mardi Gras 1958; Journey to the Center of the Earth 1959; All Hands on Deck 1961; The Main Attraction 1962; State Fair 1962; The Yellow Canary 1963; Goodbye Charlie 1964; The Greatest Story Ever Told 1965; The Perils of Pauline 1967

Boone, Richard (1917–1981) Halls of Montezuma 1950; Call Me Mister 1951; Kangaroo 1952; Red Skies of Montana 1952; Way of a Gaucho 1952; Beneath the 12-Mile Reef 1953; The Robe 1953; Dragnet 1954; The Raid 1954; The Siege at Red River 1954; Man without a Star 1955; Away All Boats 1956; Star in the Dust 1956; The Garment Jungle 1957; Lizzie 1957; The Tall T 1957; The Alamo 1960; A Thunder of Drums 1961; Rio Conchos 1964; The War Lord 1965; Hombre 1967; Kona Coast 1968; The Night of the Following Day 1968; The Arrangement 1969; The Kremlin Letter 1970; Madron 1970; Big Jake 1971; Against a Crooked Sky 1975; The Shootist 1976; God's Gun 1977; The Big Sleep 1978; Winter Kills 1979; The Bushido Blade 1981

Boone Junior, Mark (1955–) Trees Lounge 1996; Vampires 1998; Buddy Boy 1999; Everything Put Together 2000; Memento 2000; 2 Fast 2 Furious 2003

Boorem, Mika (1987–) Hearts in Atlantis 2001; Blue Crush 2002; Dirty Dancing 2 2003; Sleepover 2004

Boorman, Charley (1966–) *The Emerald Forest* 1985; *The Bunker* 2001
Booth, Anthony (1937–) *Pit of Darkness* 1961; *The L-Shaped Room* 1962; *The Hi-Jackers* 1963; *Corruption* 1968; *Till Death Us Do Part* 1968; *Neither the Sea nor the Sand* 1972; *Confessions of a Window Cleaner* 1974; *Confessions of a Pop Performer* 1975; *Confessions of a Driving Instructor* 1976; *Confessions from a Holiday Camp* 1977; *Revengers Tragedy* 2002
Booth, Bronwen (1966–) *For Hire* 1997; *Glory & Honor* 1998
Booth, Connie (1941–) *And Now for Something Completely Different* 1971; *Monty Python and the Holy Grail* 1975; *The Hound of the Baskervilles* 1983; *Hawks* 1988; *High Spirits* 1988; *Smack and Thistle* 1989; *American Friends* 1991; *Leon the Pig Farmer* 1992
Booth, James (1930–) *Let's Get Married* 1960; *The Trials of Oscar Wilde* 1960; *In the Doghouse* 1961; *Sparrows Can't Sing* 1962; *French Dressing* 1964; *Zulu* 1964; *The Secret of My Success* 1965; *Robbery* 1967; *The Bliss of Mrs Blossom* 1968; *Fraulein Doktor* 1968; *Adam's Woman* 1970; *Darker than Amber* 1970; *Macho Callahan* 1970; *The Man Who Had Power over Women* 1970; *Revenge* 1971; *Rentadick* 1972; *Penny Gold* 1973; *That'll Be the Day* 1973; *Zorro, the Gay Blade* 1981; *Avenging Force* 1986; *Bad Guys* 1986
Booth, Karin (1923–1992) *The Unfinished Dance* 1947; *The Cariboo Trail* 1950; *Charge of the Lancers* 1954; *The Crooked Sky* 1957; *The World Was His Jury* 1957; *Beloved Infidel* 1959; *Juke Box Rhythm* 1959
Booth, Lindy (1979–) *American Psycho II: All American Girl* 2002; *Her Best Friend's Husband* 2002; *Wrong Turn* 2003; *Dawn of the Dead* 2004
Booth, Shirley (1907–1992) *Come Back, Little Sheba* 1952; *About Mrs Leslie* 1954; *Hot Spell* 1958; *The Matchmaker* 1958
Boothe, Powers (1949–) *Southern Comfort* 1981; *A Breed Apart* 1984; *Red Dawn* 1984; *The Emerald Forest* 1985; *Extreme Prejudice* 1987; *Blue Sky* 1991; *Rapid Fire* 1992; *Tombstone* 1993; *Nixon* 1995; *Sudden Death* 1995; *U Turn* 1997; *Men of Honor* 2000; *Frailty* 2001; *Sin City* 2005
Boratto, Caterina (1915–) *Juliet of the Spirits* 1965; *The Tiger and the Pussycat* 1967; *Salo, or the 120 Days of Sodom* 1975
Borboni, Paola (1900–1995) *Arabella* 1967; *La Cage aux Folles II* 1980; *Yes, Giorgio* 1982
Borchers, Cornell (1925–) *The Big Lift* 1950; *The Divided Heart* 1954; *Never Say Goodbye* 1955; *Istanbul* 1957
Borden, Eugene (1897–1971) *So Dark the Night* 1946; *An American in Paris* 1951
Borden, Lynn (1939–) *Black Mama, White Mama* 1972; *This Is a Hijack* 1973
Boreanaz, David (1969–) *Valentine* 2001; *I'm with Lucy* 2002
Borell, Louis (1905–1973) *The Avenging Hand* 1936; *Head over Heels in Love* 1937; *Over the Moon* 1937
Borg, Veda Ann (1915–1973) *San Quentin* 1937; *Miracle on Main Street* 1940; *The Penalty* 1941; *The Unknown Guest* 1943; *The Big Noise* 1944; *The Falcon in Hollywood* 1944; *Fog Island* 1945; *Rider from Tucson* 1950; *Big Jim McLain* 1952; *Three Sailors and a Girl* 1953; *You're Never Too Young* 1955; *The Fearmakers* 1958; *Thunder in the Sun* 1959
Borge, Victor (1909–2000) *Higher and Higher* 1943; *The King of Comedy* 1983
Borgeaud, Nelly (1931–2004) *Celà S'Appelle l'Aurore* 1956; *Mississippi Mermaid* 1969; *The Man Who Loved Women* 1977; *Mon Oncle d'Amérique* 1980; *Dandin* 1988; *L'Accompagnatrice* 1992
Borgese, Sal (1937–) *Adios, Sabata* 1970; *Flight of the Innocent* 1993
Borgnine, Ernest (1917–) *China Corsair* 1951; *The Mob* 1951; *From Here to Eternity* 1953; *The Stranger Wore a Gun* 1953; *The Bounty Hunter* 1954; *Demetrius and the Gladiators* 1954; *Johnny Guitar* 1954; *Vera Cruz* 1954; *Bad Day at Black Rock* 1955; *The Last Command* 1955; *Marty* 1955; *Run for Cover* 1955; *The Square Jungle* 1955; *Violent Saturday* 1955; *The Best Things in Life Are Free* 1956; *The Catered Affair* 1956; *Jubal* 1956; *Three Brave Men* 1956; *The Badlanders* 1958; *Torpedo Run* 1958; *The Vikings* 1958; *Pay or Die* 1960; *Season of Passion* 1960; *Barabbas* 1961; *Go Naked in the World* 1961; *McHale's Navy* 1964; *The Flight of the Phoenix* 1965; *The Oscar* 1966; *Chuka* 1967; *The Dirty Dozen* 1967; *Ice Station Zebra* 1968; *The Legend of Lylah Clare* 1968; *The Split* 1968; *The Wild Bunch* 1969; *The Adventurers* 1970; *A Bullet for Sandoval* 1970; *Suppose They Gave a War and Nobody Came?* 1970; *Bunny O'Hare* 1971; *Hannie Caulder* 1971; *Willard* 1971; *The Poseidon Adventure* 1972; *The Revengers* 1972; *Emperor of the North* 1973; *The Neptune Factor* 1973; *Law and Disorder* 1974; *The Devil's Rain* 1975; *Hustle* 1975; *Sunday in the Country* 1975; *Shoot* 1976; *The Greatest* 1977; *The Prince and the Pauper* 1977; *Convoy* 1978; *All Quiet on the Western Front* 1979; *The Black Hole* 1979; *The Double McGuffin* 1979; *When Time Ran Out* 1980; *Deadly Blessing* 1981; *Escape from New York* 1981; *High Risk* 1981; *Young Warriors* 1983; *Codename Wildgeese* 1984; *Spike of Bensonhurst* 1988; *Any Man's Death* 1990; *All Dogs Go to Heaven 2* 1996; *Gattaca* 1997; *McHale's Navy* 1997; *BASEketball* 1998; *Small Soldiers* 1998; *Blueberry* 2004
Borisenko, Don *During One Night* 1961; *Nine Hours to Rama* 1963
Borkan, Gene *Dealing: or the Berkeley-to-Boston Forty-Brick Lost-Bag Blues* 1971; *The All-American Boy* 1973
Borland, Barlowe (1877–1948) *Bluebeard's Eighth Wife* 1938; *The Hound of the Baskervilles* 1939
Boros, Ferike (1880–1951) *Once upon a Honeymoon* 1942; *The Pied Piper* 1942
Borowitz, Katherine *Fellow Traveller* 1989; *Men of Respect* 1990; *Mac* 1992; *The Man Who Wasn't There* 2001
Borrego, Jesse (1962–) *Blood In Blood Out* 1992; *Mi Vida Loca* 1993; *I Like It like That* 1994
Bory, Jean-Marc (1934–2001) *Les Amants* 1958; *RoGoPaG* 1962
Bosch, Johnny Yong (1976–) *Mighty Morphin Power Rangers: the Movie* 1995; *Turbo: a Power Rangers Adventure* 1997
Bosco, Philip (1930–) *Catholic Boys* 1985; *The Money Pit* 1985; *Walls of Glass* 1985; *Children of a Lesser God* 1986; *Suspect* 1987; *Three Men and a Baby* 1987; *The Dream Team* 1989; *The Luckiest Man in the World* 1989; *Blue Steel* 1990; *FX 2* 1991; *True Colors* 1991; *Against the Wall* 1994; *Angie* 1994; *Milk Money* 1994; *It Takes Two* 1995; *My Best Friend's Wedding* 1997; *Carriers* 1998; *Wonder Boys* 2000
Bosé, Lucia (1931–) *Chronicle of a Love* 1950; *La Signora senza Camelie* 1953; *Death of a Cyclist* 1955; *Celà S'Appelle l'Aurore* 1956; *Harem Suare* 1999
Bose, Miguel (1956–) *Suspiria* 1976; *High Heels* 1991; *Gazon Maudit* 1995
Bose, Rahul (1968–) *English, August* 1994; *Bombay Boys* 1998; *Split Wide Open* 1999; *Mumbai Matinee* 2003
Bosetti, Giulio (1930–) *Imperial Venus* 1963; *Gold for the Caesars* 1964
Bosic, Andrea *Sandokan the Great* 1963; *The Pirates of Malaysia* 1964
Bosley, Tom (1927–) *Love with the Proper Stranger* 1963; *The World of Henry Orient* 1964; *The Secret War of Harry Frigg* 1967; *Yours, Mine and Ours* 1968; *Mixed Company* 1974; *O'Hara's Wife* 1982; *Money Mania* 1987; *Wicked Stepmother* 1989
Bossell, Simon *Spider & Rose* 1994; *Hotel de Love* 1996; *Aberration* 1997
Bostwick, Barry (1945–) *Fantastic Planet* 1973; *The Rocky Horror Picture Show* 1975; *Weekend at Bernie's II* 1992; *800 Leagues down the Amazon* 1993; *Danielle Steel's Once in a Lifetime* 1994; *The Secret Agent Club* 1995; *Spy Hard* 1996
Boswall, John *Three Men and a Little Lady* 1990; *The Statement* 2003
Boswell, Connee (1907–1996) *Syncopation* 1942; *Senior Prom* 1958
Bosworth, Hobart (1867–1943) *The Big Parade* 1925; *Annie Laurie* 1927; *Hangman's House* 1928; *Eternal Love* 1929; *The Show of Shows* 1929; *Abraham Lincoln* 1930; *The Devil's Holiday* 1930; *Just Imagine* 1930; *Mammy* 1930; *Dirigible* 1931; *This Modern Age* 1931; *General Spanky* 1936
Bosworth, Kate (1983–) *Blue Crush* 2002; *The Rules of Attraction* 2002; *Wonderland* 2003; *Beyond the Sea* 2004; *Win a Date with Tad Hamilton!* 2004
Boteler, Wade (1888–1943) *Big News* 1929; *Billy the Kid Returns* 1938
Botsford, Sara (1953–) *Murder by Phone* 1982; *Still of the Night* 1982; *The Gunrunner* 1984; *Our Guys: Outrage in Glen Ridge* 1999
Bottoms, Joseph (1954–) *The Dove* 1974; *Crime and Passion* 1976; *The Black Hole* 1979; *Cloud Dancer* 1979; *King of the Mountain* 1981; *Blind Date* 1984
Bottoms, Sam (1955–) *The Last Picture Show* 1971; *Class of '44* 1973; *Zandy's Bride* 1974; *The Outlaw Josey Wales* 1976; *Apocalypse Now* 1979; *Bronco Billy* 1980; *Prime Risk* 1985
Bottoms, Timothy (1950–) *Johnny Got His Gun* 1971; *The Last Picture Show* 1971; *Love and Pain and the Whole Damn Thing* 1973; *The Paper Chase* 1973; *The White Dawn* 1974; *Operation Daybreak* 1975; *A Small Town in Texas* 1976; *Rollercoaster* 1977; *The Other Side of the Mountain – Part 2* 1978; *Hurricane* 1979; *The High Country* 1981; *Hambone and Hillie* 1984; *Secrets of the Phantom Caverns* 1984; *The Fantasist* 1986; *Invaders from Mars* 1986; *Mio in the Land of Faraway* 1987; *A Case of Honor* 1988; *The Drifter* 1988; *Return from the River Kwai* 1988; *Texasville* 1990; *Horses and Champions* 1994; *The Man in the Iron Mask* 1997; *Elephant* 2003; *The Girl Next Door* 2004
Bouajila, Sami (1966–) *The Siege* 1998; *Drôle de Félix* 2000
Bouchet, Barbara (1943–) *Agent for HARM* 1966; *Casino Royale* 1967; *Danger Route* 1967; *Gangs of New York* 2002
Bouchey, Willis (1907–1977) *Red Planet Mars* 1952; *The Big Heat* 1953; *The McConnell Story* 1955; *The Night Runner* 1957; *The Sheepman* 1958; *Sergeant Rutledge* 1960
Bouchez, Elodie (1973–) *Les Roseaux Sauvages* 1994; *Les Roseaux Sauvages* 1994; *A Toute Vitesse* 1996; *Clubbed to Death* 1996; *The Dream Life of Angels* 1998; *Lovers* 1999
Boudet, Jacques *Waiting for the Moon* 1987; *Farinelli il Castrato* 1994; *Marius et Jeannette* 1997; *A l'Attaque!* 2000; *La Ville Est Tranquille* 2000
Bouise, Jean (1929–1989) *I Am Cuba* 1964; *The Things of Life* 1969; *The Confession* 1970; *Edith and Marcel* 1983; *The Last Battle* 1983; *The Big Blue* 1988
Bouix, Evelyne (1956–) *Les Misérables* 1982; *Edith and Marcel* 1983; *Long Live Life* 1984; *A Man and a Woman: 20 Years Later* 1986
Boujenah, Michel (1952–) *3 Men and a Cradle* 1985; *Les Misérables* 1995
Boulanger, Daniel (1922–) *A Bout de Souffle* 1959; *The Bride Wore Black* 1967; *Bed and Board* 1970
Boulter, Rosalyn (1917–1997) *Return of a Stranger* 1937; *George in Civvy Street* 1946
Boulton, Matthew (1893–1962) *Sabotage* 1936; *They Met in Bombay* 1941; *The Brighton Strangler* 1945; *The Woman in Green* 1945; *Bulldog Drummond Strikes Back* 1947; *Last Train from Bombay* 1952
Bouquet, Carole (1957–) *That Obscure Object of Desire* 1977; *Buffet Froid* 1979; *For Your Eyes Only* 1981; *Trop Belle pour Toi* 1989; *A Business Affair* 1993; *Lucie Aubrac* 1997; *En Plein Coeur* 1998; *The Bridge* 1999; *Summer Things* 2002; *Red Lights* 2003
Bouquet, Michel (1926–) *Nuit et Brouillard* 1955; *The Bride Wore Black* 1967; *The Road to Corinth* 1967; *La Femme Infidèle* 1968; *Mississippi Mermaid* 1969; *Borsalino* 1970; *La Rupture* 1970; *Juste avant la Nuit* 1971; *Malpertuis* 1971; *The Serpent* 1972; *Two against the Law* 1973; *Les Misérables* 1982; *Cop au Vin* 1984; *Toto Le Héros* 1991; *Tous les Matins du Monde* 1991; *Elisa* 1994; *Comment J'ai Tué Mon Père* 2001; *The Last Mitterrand* 2005
Bourdin, Lise (1925–) *Woman of the River* 1955; *Love in the Afternoon* 1957; *The Last Blitzkrieg* 1958
Bourne, Whitney (1914–1988) *Crime without Passion* 1934; *Flight from Glory* 1937; *The Mad Miss Manton* 1938; *Beauty for the Asking* 1939
Bourneuf, Philip (1908–1979) *The Big Night* 1951; *Beyond a Reasonable Doubt* 1956
Bourvil aka **Bourvil, André** (1917–1970) *La Traversée de Paris* 1956; *Les Misérables* 1957; *Le Bossu* 1959; *The Captain* 1960; *The Dirty Game* 1965; *Don't Look Now... We're Being Shot At* 1966; *The Brain* 1969; *The Christmas Tree* 1969; *Monte Carlo or Bust* 1969; *The Red Circle* 1970
Boutefeu, Nathalie *Port Djema* 1997; *Le Chignon d'Olga* 2002; *Son Frère* 2003; *Kings & Queen* 2004
Boutsikaris, Dennis (1952–) **batteries not included* 1987; *The Dream Team* 1989; *The Boy Who Cried Bitch* 1991; *Boys on the Side* 1995; *Taken* 1999; *Custody of the Heart* 2000; *They Crawl* 2001
Bouvier, Jean-Pierre (1948–) *Goodbye Emmanuelle* 1977; *Ma Saison Préferée* 1993
Bova, Raoul (1971–) *Francesca and Nunziata* 2001; *Avenging Angelo* 2002; *Facing Window* 2003; *Under the Tuscan Sun* 2003; *AVP: Alien vs Predator* 2004
Bovasso, Julie (1930–1991) *Saturday Night Fever* 1977; *Willie and Phil* 1980; *Daniel* 1983; *Staying Alive* 1983; *Wise Guys* 1986; *Moonstruck* 1987
Bovell, Brian (1959–) *Babylon* 1980; *Playing Away* 1986
Bow, Clara (1905–1965) *Kiss Me Again* 1925; *Mantrap* 1926; *It* 1927; *Wings* 1927; *The Saturday Night Kid* 1929; *The Wild Party* 1929; *Her Wedding Night* 1930; *Paramount on Parade* 1930
Bowdon, Dorris (1915–) *Drums along the Mohawk* 1939; *The Grapes of Wrath* 1940; *The Moon Is Down* 1943
Bowe, David *UHF* 1989; *Heavyweights* 1995
Bowe, Rosemarie (1932–) *The Adventures of Hajji Baba* 1954; *The View from Pompey's Head* 1955
Bowen, Julie (1970–) *Happy Gilmore* 1996; *An American Werewolf in Paris* 1997; *Joe Somebody* 2001
Bowen, Michael *Valley Girl* 1983; *Echo Park* 1985; *The Check Is in the Mail* 1986; *Less than Zero* 1987; *Mortal Passions* 1989; *Season of Fear* 1989; *Kid* 1990; *True Crime* 1995; *Excess Baggage* 1997; *Jackie Brown* 1997; *Walking Tall* 2004
Bowens, Malick *Out of Africa* 1985; *Bopha!* 1993; *Harem Suare* 1999; *Tears of the Sun* 2003
Bower, Antoinette (1932–) *Prom Night* 1980; *The Evil That Men Do* 1984
Bower, Tom *The Ballad of Gregorio Cortez* 1983; *The Lightship* 1985; *Distant Thunder* 1988; *Promised a Miracle* 1988; *True Believer* 1989; *Talent for the Game* 1991; *Raising Cain* 1992; *The Ballad of Little Jo* 1993; *Against the Wall* 1994; *Far from Home: the Adventures of Yellow Dog* 1994; *White Man's Burden* 1995; *Buffalo Soldiers* 1997; *Poodle Springs* 1998; *High Crimes* 2002
Bowers, John (1893–1936) *The Ace of Hearts* 1921; *Say It with Songs* 1929
Bowers, Lally (1917–1984) *We Joined the Navy* 1962; *The Chalk Garden* 1964
Bowie, David (1947–) *The Man Who Fell to Earth* 1976; *Just a Gigolo* 1978; *Christiane F* 1981; *Merry Christmas Mr Lawrence* 1982; *The Hunger* 1983; *Into the Night* 1985; *Absolute Beginners* 1986; *Labyrinth* 1986; *The Last Temptation of Christ* 1988; *The Linguini Incident* 1991; *Twin Peaks: Fire Walk with Me* 1992; *Basquiat* 1996
Bowker, Judi (1954–) *Brother Sun, Sister Moon* 1972; *East of Elephant Rock* 1976; *Clash of the Titans* 1981; *The Shooting Party* 1984
Bowler, Norman (1932–) *Submarine X-1* 1967; *Renegade* 1987
Bowles, Peter (1936–) *Three Hats for Lisa* 1965; *Blowup* 1966; *The Charge of the Light Brigade* 1968; *Laughter in the Dark* 1969; *Eyewitness* 1970; *A Day in the Death of Joe Egg* 1971; *Endless Night* 1971; *The Offence* 1972; *The Legend of Hell House* 1973; *For the Love of Benji* 1977; *The Steal* 1994; *One of the Hollywood Ten* 2000
Bowman, Lee (1914–1979) *I Met Him in Paris* 1937; *Internes Can't Take Money* 1937; *Having Wonderful Time* 1938; *Dancing Co-Ed* 1939; *Fast and Furious* 1939; *Love Affair* 1939; *Miracles for Sale* 1939; *Florian* 1940; *Third Finger, Left Hand* 1940; *Buck Privates* 1941; *Design for Scandal* 1941; *Kid Glove Killer* 1942; *Bataan* 1943; *Cover Girl* 1944; *Up in Mabel's Room* 1944; *Tonight and Every Night* 1945; *Smash Up – the Story of a Woman* 1947; *My Dream Is Yours* 1949; *House by the River* 1950; *Youngblood Hawke* 1964
Bown, Paul (1957–) *Morons from Outer Space* 1985; *Butterfly Kiss* 1994
Bowz, Eddie *Hit the Dutchman* 1992; *The Fear* 1995; *Family Plan* 1997
Boxer, John (1909–1982) *Mr Drake's Duck* 1950; *The Bridge on the River Kwai* 1957
Boxleitner, Bruce (1950–) *The Baltimore Bullet* 1980; *Tron* 1982; *Diplomatic Immunity* 1991; *Kuffs* 1991; *The Babe* 1992; *Double Jeopardy* 1992; *Life in the Balance* 2001
Boyar, Sully (1923–2001) *Dog Day Afternoon* 1975; *Car Wash* 1976; *The Jazz Singer* 1980; *Best Seller* 1987; *The Lemon Sisters* 1989

Boyce, Alan *Permanent Record* 1988; *Totally F***ed Up* 1993
Boyd, Billy (1968–) *The Lord of the Rings: The Fellowship of the Ring* 2001; *The Lord of the Rings: The Two Towers* 2002; *The Lord of the Rings: The Return of the King* 2003; *Master and Commander: the Far Side of the World* 2003; *Seed of Chucky* 2004; *On a Clear Day* 2005
Boyd, Dorothy (1907–) *The Constant Nymph* 1928; *A Shot in the Dark* 1933
Boyd, Guy (1942–) *Ticket to Heaven* 1981; *Streamers* 1983; *Body Double* 1984; *Flashpoint* 1984; *Target* 1985; *Blue Heat* 1990
Boyd, Jan Gan *A Chorus Line* 1985; *Assassination* 1986
Boyd, Jenna (1993–) *Dickie Roberts: Former Child Star* 2003; *The Missing* 2003; *The Sisterhood of the Traveling Pants* 2005
Boyd, Jimmy (1939–) *Platinum High School* 1960; *The Two Little Bears* 1961
Boyd, Stephen (1928–1977) *An Alligator Named Daisy* 1955; *The Man Who Never Was* 1955; *Les Bijoutiers du Clair de Lune* 1957; *Seven Thunders* 1957; *Seven Waves Away* 1957; *The Bravados* 1958; *Ben-Hur* 1959; *The Best of Everything* 1959; *Woman Obsessed* 1959; *The Big Gamble* 1961; *The Inspector* 1962; *Jumbo* 1962; *Imperial Venus* 1963; *The Fall of the Roman Empire* 1964; *Genghis Khan* 1964; *The Third Secret* 1964; *The Bible...in the Beginning* 1966; *Fantastic Voyage* 1966; *The Oscar* 1966; *The Poppy Is Also a Flower* 1966; *Assignment K* 1968; *Shalako* 1968; *Slaves* 1969; *Kill!* 1972; *Montana Trap* 1976; *The Squeeze* 1977
Boyd, Susan *Rover Dangerfield* 1991; *An American Tail: the Mystery of the Night Monster* 2000
Boyd (1), William *aka* **Boyd, Bill** (1898–1972) *The Road to Yesterday* 1925; *Two Arabian Knights* 1927; *High Voltage* 1929; *The Leatherneck* 1929; *City Streets* 1931; *The Painted Desert* 1931; *Lucky Devils* 1933; *Hopalong Cassidy* 1935; *The Devil's Playground* 1946; *Fool's Gold* 1946; *The Marauders* 1947; *The Dead Don't Dream* 1948; *False Paradise* 1948; *Silent Conflict* 1948
Boyd, William "Stage" (1889–1935) *Gun Smoke* 1931; *The Wiser Sex* 1932; *Laughing at Life* 1933
Boyer, Charles (1897–1978) *The Man from Yesterday* 1932; *Red-Headed Woman* 1932; *The Battle* 1934; *Caravan* 1934; *Break of Hearts* 1935; *Private Worlds* 1935; *The Garden of Allah* 1936; *Mayerling* 1936; *Conquest* 1937; *History Is Made at Night* 1937; *Tovarich* 1937; *Algiers* 1938; *Love Affair* 1939; *When Tomorrow Comes* 1939; *All This, and Heaven Too* 1940; *Appointment for Love* 1941; *Back Street* 1941; *Hold Back the Dawn* 1941; *Tales of Manhattan* 1942; *The Constant Nymph* 1943; *Flesh and Fantasy* 1943; *Gaslight* 1944; *Together Again* 1944; *Confidential Agent* 1945; *La Bataille du Rail* 1946; *Cluny Brown* 1946; *Arch of Triumph* 1948; *The 13th Letter* 1950; *The First Legion* 1951; *The Happy Time* 1952; *Madame de...* 1953; *Thunder in the East* 1953; *The Cobweb* 1955; *Lucky to Be a Woman* 1955; *Nana* 1955; *Une Parisienne* 1957; *The Buccaneer* 1958; *Fanny* 1961; *The Four Horsemen of the Apocalypse* 1962; *Love Is a Ball* 1963; *A Very Special Favor* 1965; *How to Steal a Million* 1966; *Is Paris Burning?* 1966; *Barefoot in the Park* 1967; *Casino Royale* 1967; *The April Fools* 1969; *The Madwoman of Chaillot* 1969; *Lost Horizon* 1973; *Stavisky* 1974; *A Matter of Time* 1976
Boyer, Myriam (1948–) *Jonah Who Will Be 25 in the Year 2000* 1976; *Golden Eighties* 1986
Boylan, Mary (1913–1984) *Bad* 1976; *Heartland* 1979
Boyle, Lara Flynn (1971–) *Poltergeist III* 1988; *How I Got Into College* 1989; *May Wine* 1990; *The Rookie* 1990; *The Dark Backward* 1991; *Eye of the Storm* 1991; *Mobsters* 1991; *Equinox* 1992; *Red Rock West* 1992; *Wayne's World* 1992; *Where the Day Takes You* 1992; *The Temp* 1993; *Baby's Day Out* 1994; *Jacob* 1994; *The Road to Wellville* 1994; *Threesome* 1994; *The Big Squeeze* 1996; *Afterglow* 1997; *Happiness* 1998; *Susan's Plan* 1998; *Men in Black 2* 2002
Boyle, Peter (1933–) *Joe* 1970; *Kid Blue* 1971; *TR Baskin* 1971; *The Candidate* 1972; *The Friends of Eddie Coyle* 1973; *Ghost in the Noonday Sun* 1973; *Slither* 1973; *Steelyard Blues* 1973; *Young Frankenstein* 1974; *Swashbuckler* 1976; *Taxi Driver* 1976; *The Brink's Job* 1978; *FIST* 1978; *Beyond the Poseidon Adventure* 1979; *Hardcore* 1979; *In God We Trust* 1980; *Where the Buffalo Roam* 1980; *Outland* 1981; *Hammett* 1982; *Yellowbeard* 1983; *Johnny Dangerously* 1984; *Turk 182!* 1985; *Surrender* 1987; *Walker* 1987; *Red Heat* 1988; *Cannonball Fever* 1989; *The Dream Team* 1989; *Kickboxer 2: the Road Back* 1990; *Men of Respect* 1990; *Solar Crisis* 1990; *Killer* 1994; *The Shadow* 1994; *Born to Be Wild* 1995; *Exquisite Tenderness* 1995; *While You Were Sleeping* 1995; *That Darn Cat* 1997; *Doctor Dolittle* 1998; *Monster's Ball* 2001; *The Cat Returns* 2002; *Scooby-Doo 2: Monsters Unleashed* 2004
Bozonnet, Marcel (1944–) *Right Bank, Left Bank* 1984; *Jeanne la Pucelle* 1994
Bozzuffi, Marcel (1929–1988) *Le Deuxième Souffle* 1966; *The French Connection* 1971; *Images* 1972; *The Valdez Horses* 1973; *Caravan to Vaccares* 1974; *The Marseille Contract* 1974; *Illustrious Corpses* 1976; *La Cage aux Folles II* 1980; *Identification of a Woman* 1982
Bracco, Elizabeth *Mystery Train* 1989; *Jumpin' at the Boneyard* 1991; *Trees Lounge* 1996
Bracco, Lorraine (1954–) *Someone to Watch over Me* 1987; *The Dream Team* 1989; *Sea of Love* 1989; *Sing* 1989; *GoodFellas* 1990; *Switch* 1991; *Talent for the Game* 1991; *Medicine Man* 1992; *Radio Flyer* 1992; *Traces of Red* 1992; *Even Cowgirls Get the Blues* 1993; *Being Human* 1994; *Getting Gotti* 1994; *The Basketball Diaries* 1995; *Custody of the Heart* 2000; *Riding in Cars with Boys* 2001
Bracey, Sidney *aka* **Bracy, Sidney** (1877–1942) *The Black Bird* 1926; *The Cameraman* 1928; *Queen Kelly* 1928
Bracken, Eddie (1920–2002) *Too Many Girls* 1940; *The Fleet's In* 1942; *Star Spangled Rhythm* 1942; *Young and Willing* 1942; *Happy Go Lucky* 1943; *Hail the Conquering Hero* 1944; *The Miracle of Morgan's Creek* 1944; *Bring on the Girls* 1945; *Duffy's Tavern* 1945; *Hold That Blonde* 1945; *Out of This World* 1945; *Summer Stock* 1950; *Two Tickets to Broadway* 1951; *We're Not Married* 1952; *Shinbone Alley* 1971; *National Lampoon's Vacation* 1983; *Rookie of the Year* 1993
Bradbury, Kitty (1875–1945) *Our Hospitality* 1923; *The Pilgrim* 1923
Braddell, Maurice (1900–1990) *Things to Come* 1936; *Flesh* 1968; *Women in Revolt* 1971
Bradecki, Tadeusz (1955–) *Camera Buff* 1979; *The Constant Factor* 1980
Braden, Bernard (1916–1993) *Love in Pawn* 1953; *Jet Storm* 1959; *The Day the Earth Caught Fire* 1961; *Two and Two Make Six* 1961
Bradford, Jesse (1979–) *The Boy Who Cried Bitch* 1991; *King of the Hill* 1993; *Far from Home: the Adventures of Yellow Dog* 1994; *Hackers* 1995; *William Shakespeare's Romeo + Juliet* 1996; *A Soldier's Daughter Never Cries* 1998; *Cherry Falls* 1999; *Bring It On* 2000; *Clockstoppers* 2002; *Swimfan* 2002
Bradford, Marshall (1885–1971) *Hellgate* 1952; *I Was a Teenage Frankenstein* 1957
Bradford, Richard (1937–) *Goin' South* 1978; *Hammett* 1982; *Running Hot* 1983; *The Legend of Billie Jean* 1985; *The Mean Season* 1985; *The Trip to Bountiful* 1985; *Resting Place* 1986; *The Untouchables* 1987; *Little Nikita* 1988; *The Milagro Beanfield War* 1988; *Permanent Record* 1988; *Sunset* 1988; *Night Game* 1989; *Internal Affairs* 1990; *Ambition* 1991; *Cold Heaven* 1992; *Dr Giggles* 1992; *Just the Ticket* 1998
Bradin, Jean *Champagne* 1928; *Moulin Rouge* 1928
Bradley, Cathleen *About Adam* 2000; *Silent Grace* 2001
Bradley (2), David *aka* **Bradley, Dai** (1955–) *Kes* 1969; *Malachi's Cove* 1973; *Absolution* 1978
Bradley (3), David (1942–) *Left Luggage* 1997; *Tom's Midnight Garden* 1998; *The King Is Alive* 2000; *Gabriel & Me* 2001; *Harry Potter and the Philosopher's Stone* 2001; *This Is Not a Love Song* 2002
Bradley, Doug (1954–) *Hellraiser* 1987; *Hellbound: Hellraiser II* 1988; *Hellraiser III: Hell on Earth* 1992; *Shepherd on the Rock* 1995; *Hellraiser: Bloodline* 1996; *Killer Tongue* 1996
Bradley, Grace (1913–) *The Cat's Paw* 1934; *Old Man Rhythm* 1935; *Anything Goes* 1936; *You're In the Army Now* 1936; *Wake Up and Live* 1937
Bradley, Leslie (1907–1974) *Time Flies* 1944; *Waterloo Road* 1944; *Just William's Luck* 1947; *No Orchids for Miss Blandish* 1948; *A Case for PC 49* 1950; *The Crimson Pirate* 1952; *The Iron Glove* 1954; *Kiss of Fire* 1955; *Lady Godiva* 1955; *Seven Cities of Gold* 1955; *Attack of the Crab Monsters* 1957; *Teenage Caveman* 1958; *The Sad Horse* 1959
Bradna, Olympe (1920–) *Souls at Sea* 1937; *South of Pago Pago* 1940
Bradshaw, Carl *The Harder They Come* 1972; *The Lunatic* 1992; *Third World Cop* 1999
Bradshaw, Cathryn *Bert Rigby, You're a Fool* 1989; *The Mother* 2003
Brady, Alice (1892–1972) *Broadway to Hollywood* 1933; *When Ladies Meet* 1933; *The Gay Divorce* 1934; *Gold Diggers of 1935* 1935; *Let 'Em Have It* 1935; *Go West, Young Man* 1936; *My Man Godfrey* 1936; *In Old Chicago* 1937; *One Hundred Men and a Girl* 1937; *Three Smart Girls* 1937; *Joy of Living* 1938; *Young Mr Lincoln* 1939; *Zenobia* 1939
Brady, Moya *Life Is Sweet* 1990; *Middleton's Changeling* 1997
Brady, Orla (1961–) *A Love Divided* 1999; *Silent Grace* 2001; *Fogbound* 2002
Brady, Patti (1939–) *Never Say Goodbye* 1946; *Two Guys from Milwaukee* 1946
Brady, Scott (1924–1985) *He Walked by Night* 1948; *The Gal Who Took the West* 1949; *Port of New York* 1949; *Undertow* 1949; *I Was a Shoplifter* 1950; *Kansas Raiders* 1950; *Undercover Girl* 1950; *The Model and the Marriage Broker* 1951; *Bloodhounds of Broadway* 1952; *Bronco Buster* 1952; *Untamed Frontier* 1952; *Johnny Guitar* 1954; *Gentlemen Marry Brunettes* 1955; *The Maverick Queen* 1955; *Mohawk* 1956; *The Restless Breed* 1957; *John Goldfarb, Please Come Home* 1964; *Black Spurs* 1965; *Castle of Evil* 1966; *Destination Inner Space* 1966; *Arizona Bushwhackers* 1968; *Dollars* 1971; *The Loners* 1971; *The China Syndrome* 1979
Brady, Wayne (1972–) *Geppetto* 2000; *Clifford's Really Big Movie* 2004
Braeden, Eric *aka* **Gudegast, Hans** (1942–) *Dayton's Devils* 1968; *Colossus: the Forbin Project* 1969; *100 Rifles* 1969; *Escape from the Planet of the Apes* 1971; *Lady Ice* 1973; *The Ambulance* 1990; *Meet the Deedles* 1998
Braff, Zach (1975–) *The Broken Hearts Club: a Romantic Comedy* 2000; *Garden State* 2003
Braga, Sonia (1950–) *Dona Flor and Her Two Husbands* 1977; *Gabriela* 1983; *Kiss of the Spider Woman* 1985; *The Milagro Beanfield War* 1988; *Moon over Parador* 1988; *The Rookie* 1990; *Roosters* 1993; *The Burning Season* 1994; *Two Deaths* 1994; *From Dusk till Dawn 3: the Hangman's Daughter* 2000; *Angel Eyes* 2001; *Empire* 2002
Braithwaite, Lilian *Downhill* 1927; *A Man about the House* 1947
Brajovic, Vojislav (1949–) *Tito and Me* 1992; *Cabaret Balkan* 1998
Brambell, Wilfrid *aka* **Bramble, Wilfred** (1912–1985) *Another Shore* 1948; *The Boys* 1961; *Crooks in Cloisters* 1963; *The Small World of Sammy Lee* 1963; *A Hard Day's Night* 1964; *Where the Bullets Fly* 1966; *Witchfinder General* 1968; *Some Will, Some Won't* 1969; *Steptoe and Son* 1972; *Holiday on the Buses* 1973; *Steptoe and Son Ride Again* 1973; *The Terence Davies Trilogy* 1984
Branagh, Kenneth (1960–) *High Season* 1987; *A Month in the Country* 1987; *Henry V* 1989; *Dead Again* 1991; *Peter's Friends* 1992; *Much Ado about Nothing* 1993; *Swing Kids* 1993; *Mary Shelley's Frankenstein* 1994; *Othello* 1995; *Hamlet* 1996; *The Gingerbread Man* 1997; *Celebrity* 1998; *The Proposition* 1998; *The Theory of Flight* 1998; *Universal Horror* 1998; *Love's Labour's Lost* 1999; *Wild Wild West* 1999; *The Road to El Dorado* 2000; *Conspiracy* 2001; *Harry Potter and the Chamber of Secrets* 2002; *Rabbit-Proof Fence* 2002; *Five Children and It* 2004
Brancato, Lillo *aka* **Brancato Jr, Lillo** *A Bronx Tale* 1993; *Renaissance Man* 1994
Branch, Sarah (1938–) *Sands of the Desert* 1960; *Sword of Sherwood Forest* 1960
Brand, Neville (1921–1992) *DOA* 1949; *Only the Valiant* 1950; *The Mob* 1951; *Kansas City Confidential* 1952; *Kansas City Confidential* 1952; *Gun Fury* 1953; *Stalag 17* 1953; *Riot in Cell Block 11* 1954; *The Prodigal* 1955; *Love Me Tender* 1956; *Mohawk* 1956; *The Lonely Man* 1957; *The Tin Star* 1957; *The Way to the Gold* 1957; *Cry Terror* 1958; *Five Gates to Hell* 1959; *The Adventures of Huckleberry Finn* 1960; *The George Raft Story* 1961; *The Last Sunset* 1961; *Birdman of Alcatraz* 1962; *Hero's Island* 1962; *That Darn Cat!* 1965; *Three Guns for Texas* 1968; *Backtrack* 1969; *The Desperados* 1969; *Cahill, United States Marshal* 1973; *The Deadly Trackers* 1973; *Scalawag* 1973; *This Is a Hijack* 1973; *Psychic Killer* 1975; *Eaten Alive* 1976; *Five Days from Home* 1978; *The Ninth Configuration* 1979; *Without Warning* 1980
Brandauer, Klaus Maria (1944–) *The Salzburg Connection* 1972; *Mephisto* 1981; *Never Say Never Again* 1983; *Colonel Redl* 1984; *The Lightship* 1985; *Out of Africa* 1985; *Streets of Gold* 1986; *Burning Secret* 1988; *Hanussen* 1988; *Seven Minutes* 1989; *The Russia House* 1990; *Becoming Colette* 1991; *White Fang* 1991; *Introducing Dorothy Dandridge* 1999; *Druids* 2001
Brandenburg, Larry (1948–) *The Santa Clause* 1994; *What the #$*! Do We Know!?* 2004
Brandis, Jonathan (1976–2003) *Stepfather II* 1989; *The NeverEnding Story II: the Next Chapter* 1991; *Ladybugs* 1992; *Sidekicks* 1993; *Fall into Darkness* 1996; *Two Came Back* 1997; *Outside Providence* 1999
Brando, Jocelyn (1919–) *The Big Heat* 1953; *Nightfall* 1956; *The Ugly American* 1963; *Bus Riley's Back in Town* 1965
Brando, Luisina *Miss Mary* 1986; *We Don't Want to Talk about It* 1993
Brando, Marlon (1924–2004) *The Men* 1950; *A Streetcar Named Desire* 1951; *Viva Zapata!* 1952; *Julius Caesar* 1953; *The Wild One* 1953; *Desiree* 1954; *On the Waterfront* 1954; *Guys and Dolls* 1955; *The Teahouse of the August Moon* 1956; *Sayonara* 1957; *The Young Lions* 1958; *The Fugitive Kind* 1960; *One-Eyed Jacks* 1961; *Mutiny on the Bounty* 1962; *The Ugly American* 1963; *Bedtime Story* 1964; *The Saboteur, Code Name Morituri* 1965; *The Chase* 1966; *Southwest to Sonora* 1966; *A Countess from Hong Kong* 1967; *Reflections in a Golden Eye* 1967; *Candy* 1968; *The Night of the Following Day* 1968; *Burn!* 1970; *The Godfather* 1972; *Last Tango in Paris* 1972; *The Nightcomers* 1972; *The Missouri Breaks* 1976; *Superman* 1978; *Apocalypse Now* 1979; *The Formula* 1980; *A Dry White Season* 1989; *The Freshman* 1990; *Christopher Columbus: the Discovery* 1992; *Don Juan DeMarco* 1995; *The Island of Dr Moreau* 1996; *The Brave* 1997; *Free Money* 1998; *The Score* 2001
Brandon, Clark (1958–) *My Tutor* 1983; *Fast Food* 1989
Brandon, David *All Hands on Deck* 1961; *State Fair* 1962; *Stage Fright – Aquarius* 1987
Brandon, Henry *aka* **Kleinbach, Henry** (1912–1990) *Babes in Toyland* 1934; *Westbound Limited* 1937; *Cattle Drive* 1951; *Tarzan and the She-Devil* 1953; *War Arrow* 1953; *Vera Cruz* 1954; *Bandido* 1956; *Comanche* 1956; *The Searchers* 1956; *The Land Unknown* 1957
Brandon, Michael (1945–) *Lovers and Other Strangers* 1970; *Jennifer on My Mind* 1971; *FM* 1977; *Promises in the Dark* 1979; *A Change of Seasons* 1980; *Shattering the Silence* 1992; *Déjà Vu* 1997; *Contagion* 2000
Brandt, Carolyn *The Incredibly Strange Creatures Who Stopped Living and Became Mixed-up Zombies* 1963; *Rat Pfink a Boo Boo* 1965
Brandt, Janet *A Cold Wind in August* 1961; *Hit!* 1973; *Sheila Levine Is Dead and Living in New York* 1975
Brandy *aka* **Norwood, Brandy** (1979–) *Rodgers & Hammerstein's Cinderella* 1997; *I Still Know What You Did Last Summer* 1998; *Double Platinum* 1999; *Osmosis Jones* 2001
Branice, Ligia *Goto, l'Ile d'Amour* 1968; *Blanche* 1971; *Behind Convent Walls* 1977
Brännström, Brasse (1945–) *A Lover and His Lass* 1975; *Happy We* 1983
Bransfield, Marjorie *Easy Wheels* 1989; *Abraxas* 1991
Brantford, Mickey (1911–) *The Phantom Light* 1934; *The Last Journey* 1936
Brantley, Betsy (1955–) *Five Days One Summer* 1982; *Another Country* 1984; *Dark Angel* 1989; *Havana* 1990; *Shepherd on the Rock* 1995; *Schizopolis* 1996; *Washington Square* 1997; *Rogue Trader* 1998
Braschi, Nicoletta (1960–) *Down by Law* 1986; *Mystery Train* 1989; *Johnny Stecchino* 1991; *Life Is Beautiful* 1997; *Pinocchio* 2002

Brascia, John *White Christmas* 1954; *Walking Tall* 1973

Brasno, George (1911–1982) *The Mighty Barnum* 1934; *Charlie Chan at the Circus* 1936

Brass, Steffani *Dawg* 2001; *Bundy* 2002

Brassard, Marie *Le Polygraphe* 1996; *Nô* 1998

Brasselle, Keefe (1923–1981) *It's a Big Country* 1951; *A Place in the Sun* 1951; *Skirts Ahoy!* 1952; *The Eddie Cantor Story* 1953; *Bring Your Smile Along* 1955

Brasseur, Claude (1936–) *The Vanishing Corporal* 1962; *Banana Peel* 1964; *Bande à Part* 1964; *The Loser* 1971; *The Heroes* 1972; *Une Belle Fille Comme Moi* 1973; *Someone Is Bleeding* 1974; *Pardon Mon Affaire* 1976; *Une Histoire Simple* 1978; *The Police War* 1979; *Detective* 1985; *Descent into Hell* 1986; *Dandin* 1988; *The Edge of the Horizon* 1993

Brasseur, Pierre (1903–1972) *Caravan* 1934; *Le Quai des Brumes* 1938; *Les Enfants du Paradis* 1945; *Les Portes de la Nuit* 1946; *Les Mains Sales* 1951; *Napoléon* 1955; *Gates of Paris* 1957; *Eyes without a Face* 1959; *Where the Hot Wind Blows!* 1959; *Carthage in Flames* 1960; *La Vie de Château* 1965; *King of Hearts* 1966; *Goto, l'Ile d'Amour* 1968; *Sink or Swim* 1971

Bratt, Benjamin (1963–) *Chains of Gold* 1989; *Bright Angel* 1990; *One Good Cop* 1991; *Blood In Blood Out* 1992; *Demolition Man* 1993; *The River Wild* 1994; *The Last Producer* 2000; *Miss Congeniality* 2000; *The Next Best Thing* 2000; *Red Planet* 2000; *After the Storm* 2001; *Piñero* 2001; *Catwoman* 2004; *The Woodsman* 2004

Braugher, André (1962–) *Glory* 1989; *The Court-Martial of Jackie Robinson* 1990; *The Tuskegee Airmen* 1995; *Get on the Bus* 1996; *City of Angels* 1998; *A Better Way to Die* 2000; *Duets* 2000; *Frequency* 2000; *Standing in the Shadows of Motown* 2002

Braun, Judith (1930–) *Horizons West* 1952; *Red Ball Express* 1952

Braun, Pinkas (1922–) *The Door with Seven Locks* 1962; *City of Fear* 1965; *The Last Escape* 1970

Brauss, Arthur *Dollars* 1971; *The Goalkeeper's Fear of the Penalty Kick* 1971; *Montana Trap* 1976; *Knight Moves* 1992

Bray, Robert (1917–1983) *Return of the Bad Men* 1948; *Stagecoach Kid* 1949; *Bus Stop* 1956; *The Traitor* 1957; *Never Love a Stranger* 1958

Brazeau, Jay (1953–) *We're No Angels* 1989; *Slam Dunk Ernest* 1995; *Kissed* 1996; *Air Bud* 1997; *Trucks* 1997

Brazzi, Rossano (1916–1994) *We the Living* 1942; *Little Women* 1949; *Volcano* 1950; *The Barefoot Contessa* 1954; *Three Coins in the Fountain* 1954; *Angela* 1955; *Summertime* 1955; *Loser Takes All* 1956; *Interlude* 1957; *Legend of the Lost* 1957; *The Story of Esther Costello* 1957; *A Certain Smile* 1958; *South Pacific* 1958; *Count Your Blessings* 1959; *The Siege of Syracuse* 1959; *Light in the Piazza* 1961; *Rome Adventure* 1962; *The Battle of the Villa Fiorita* 1965; *The Bobo* 1967; *Woman Times Seven* 1967; *The Italian Job* 1969; *Krakatoa, East of Java* 1969; *The Adventurers* 1970; *Mr Kingstreet's War* 1970; *The Great Waltz* 1972; *Omen III: the Final Conflict* 1980; *Fear City* 1984

Breakston, George (1920–1973) *No Greater Glory* 1934; *The Return of Peter Grimm* 1935

Brecher, Egon (1880–1946) *The Black Cat* 1934; *They Dare Not Love* 1941; *So Dark the Night* 1946

Breck, Jonathan *Jeepers Creepers* 2001; *Jeepers Creepers 2* 2003

Breck, Kathleen *West 11* 1963; *The Frozen Dead* 1966

Breck, Peter (1929–) *The Crawling Hand* 1963; *Shock Corridor* 1963; *The Glory Guys* 1965; *Benji* 1974; *Highway 61* 1992

Bredice, Leticia *Nine Queens* 2000; *The City of No Limits* 2002

Bredin, Patricia *Left, Right and Centre* 1959; *The Treasure of Monte Cristo* 1960

Breen, Patrick *For Love or Money* 1993; *Sweet Nothing* 1995; *Galaxy Quest* 1999; *Just a Kiss* 2002; *Stark Raving Mad* 2002

Breese, Edmund (1871–1936) *The Hatchet Man* 1932; *Madame Butterfly* 1932; *Duck Soup* 1933

Bregman, Tracy aka **Bregman, Tracey** (1963–) *Happy Birthday to Me* 1981; *The Concrete Jungle* 1982

Brejchova, Jana (1940–) *Baron Munchhausen* 1961; *End of a Priest* 1969

Brel, Jacques (1929–1978) *Uncle Benjamin* 1969; *A Pain in the A...!* 1973

Bremer, Lucille (1917–1996) *Meet Me in St Louis* 1944; *Yolanda and the Thief* 1945; *Till the Clouds Roll By* 1946; *Ruthless* 1948

Bremner, Ewen (1971–) *Heavenly Pursuits* 1986; *Conquest of the South Pole* 1989; *As You Like It* 1992; *Naked* 1993; *Trainspotting* 1995; *The Life of Stuff* 1997; *The Acid House* 1998; *Mojo* 1998; *julien donkey-boy* 1999; *Snatch* 2000; *Black Hawk Down* 2001; *The Reckoning* 2001; *16 Years of Alcohol* 2003; *Welcome to the Jungle* 2003; *AVP: Alien vs Predator* 2004

Brendel, El (1890–1964) *Wings* 1927; *Sunny Side Up* 1929; *The Big Trail* 1930; *Just Imagine* 1930; *Delicious* 1931; *The Beautiful Blonde from Bashful Bend* 1949

Brendemühl, Alex (1972–) *A Bench in the Park* 1998; *The Hours of the Day* 2003

Brendler, Julia (1975–) *Flight of the Albatross* 1995; *Moondance* 1995

Brennan, Brid *Anne Devlin* 1984; *Trojan Eddie* 1996; *Dancing at Lughnasa* 1998; *Felicia's Journey* 1999

Brennan, Eileen (1935–) *The Last Picture Show* 1971; *The Blue Knight* 1973; *Scarecrow* 1973; *The Sting* 1973; *Daisy Miller* 1974; *At Long Last Love* 1975; *Hustle* 1975; *Murder by Death* 1976; *FM* 1977; *The Great Smokey Roadblock* 1977; *The Cheap Detective* 1978; *Private Benjamin* 1980; *Clue* 1985; *The New Adventures of Pippi Longstocking* 1988; *Sticky Fingers* 1988; *Stella* 1990; *Texasville* 1990; *White Palace* 1990; *I Don't Buy Kisses Anymore* 1992; *The Lies Boys Tell* 1994; *Reckless* 1995; *If These Walls Could Talk* 1996; *Changing Habits* 1997; *Jeepers Creepers* 2001

Brennan, Michael (1912–1982) *Blackout* 1950; *Morning Departure* 1950; *They Were Not Divided* 1950; *13 East Street* 1952; *It's a Grand Life* 1953; *Up to His Neck* 1954; *Not Wanted on Voyage* 1957

Brennan, Walter (1894–1974) *The King of Jazz* 1930; *Law and Order* 1932; *Barbary Coast* 1935; *The Man on the Flying Trapeze* 1935; *Public Hero No 1* 1935; *Seven Keys to Baldpate* 1935; *The Wedding Night* 1935; *Banjo on My Knee* 1936; *Come and Get It* 1936; *Fury* 1936; *The Adventures of Tom Sawyer* 1938; *The Buccaneer* 1938; *The Cowboy and the Lady* 1938; *Kentucky* 1938; *The Texans* 1938; *Stanley and Livingstone* 1939; *The Story of Vernon and Irene Castle* 1939; *They Shall Have Music* 1939; *Maryland* 1940; *Northwest Passage* 1940; *The Westerner* 1940; *Meet John Doe* 1941; *Nice Girl?* 1941; *Sergeant York* 1941; *Swamp Water* 1941; *The Pride of the Yankees* 1942; *Stand by for Action* 1942; *Hangmen Also Die* 1943; *The North Star* 1943; *Slightly Dangerous* 1943; *Home in Indiana* 1944; *The Princess and the Pirate* 1944; *To Have and Have Not* 1944; *Dakota* 1945; *Centennial Summer* 1946; *Driftwood* 1946; *My Darling Clementine* 1946; *Nobody Lives Forever* 1946; *A Stolen Life* 1946; *Blood on the Moon* 1948; *Red River* 1948; *Task Force* 1949; *A Ticket to Tomahawk* 1950; *Along the Great Divide* 1951; *Best of the Badmen* 1951; *Drums across the River* 1954; *The Far Country* 1954; *Four Guns to the Border* 1954; *At Gunpoint* 1955; *Bad Day at Black Rock* 1955; *Come Next Spring* 1956; *Good-bye, My Lady* 1956; *The Proud Ones* 1956; *Tammy and the Bachelor* 1957; *The Way to the Gold* 1957; *Rio Bravo* 1959; *How the West Was Won* 1962; *Those Calloways* 1964; *The Oscar* 1966; *The Gnome-Mobile* 1967; *Who's Minding the Mint?* 1967; *The One and Only, Genuine, Original Family Band* 1968; *Support Your Local Sheriff!* 1969

Brenneman, Amy (1964–) *Bye Bye Love* 1995; *Heat* 1995; *Daylight* 1996; *Fear* 1996; *Your Friends & Neighbours* 1998; *The Suburbans* 1999; *Things You Can Tell Just by Looking at Her* 2000

Brenner, Dori (1946–2000) *Summer Wishes, Winter Dreams* 1973; *Next Stop, Greenwich Village* 1976; *Altered States* 1980; *Infinity* 1996

Brent, Eve aka **Brent Ashe, Eve** *Tarzan and the Trappers* 1958; *Tarzan's Fight for Life* 1958; *Going Berserk* 1983; *Garfield* 2004

Brent, Evelyn (1899–1975) *Underworld* 1927; *Beau Sabreur* 1928; *The Dragnet* 1928; *The Last Command* 1928; *Broadway* 1929; *High Pressure* 1932; *The Law West of Tombstone* 1938; *The Seventh Victim* 1943

Brent, George (1904–1979) *The Purchase Price* 1932; *The Rich Are Always with Us* 1932; *So Big* 1932; *Baby Face* 1933; *Female* 1933; *42nd Street* 1933; *The Painted Veil* 1934; *Stamboul Quest* 1934; *Front Page Woman* 1935; *In Person* 1935; *Special Agent* 1935; *God's Country and the Woman* 1937; *Gold Is Where You Find It* 1938; *Jezebel* 1938; *Racket Busters* 1938; *Dark Victory* 1939; *The Old Maid* 1939; *The Rains Came* 1939; *The Fighting 69th* 1940; *'Til We Meet Again* 1940; *The Great Lie* 1941; *International Lady* 1941; *They Dare Not Love* 1941; *The Gay Sisters* 1942; *In This Our Life* 1942; *Twin Beds* 1942; *You Can't Escape Forever* 1942; *Experiment Perilous* 1944; *The Affairs of Susan* 1945; *Tomorrow Is Forever* 1945; *Lover Come Back* 1946; *My Reputation* 1946; *The Spiral Staircase* 1946; *Temptation* 1946; *Christmas Eve* 1947; *Out of the Blue* 1947; *Slave Girl* 1947; *Bride for Sale* 1949; *Red Canyon* 1949; *The Last Page* 1952; *Born Again* 1978

Brent, Romney (1902–1976) *Dinner at the Ritz* 1937; *Head over Heels in Love* 1937; *Under the Red Robe* 1937; *Let George Do It* 1940; *Adventures of Don Juan* 1948; *Screaming Mimi* 1958

Breon, Edmund aka **Breon, Edmond** (1882–1951) *Mister Cinders* 1934; *Keep Fit* 1937; *Crackerjack* 1938; *Casanova Brown* 1944; *The Woman in the Window* 1945; *Sherlock Holmes and the Secret Code* 1946

Breslin, Abigail (1996–) *Signs* 2002; *Raising Helen* 2004

Breslin, Patricia aka **Breslin, Pat** *Go, Man, Go!* 1953; *Andy Hardy Comes Home* 1958; *Homicidal* 1961; *I Saw What You Did* 1965

Breslin, Spencer (1992–) *Disney's The Kid* 2000; *The Santa Clause 2* 2002; *Dr Seuss' The Cat in the Hat* 2003; *Raising Helen* 2004

Bressart, Felix (1890–1949) *Ninotchka* 1939; *Swanee River* 1939; *Bitter Sweet* 1940; *Comrade X* 1940; *Escape* 1940; *The Shop around the Corner* 1940; *Third Finger, Left Hand* 1940; *Blossoms in the Dust* 1941; *Crossroads* 1942; *To Be or Not to Be* 1942; *Blonde Fever* 1944; *Greenwich Village* 1944; *Without Love* 1945; *I've Always Loved You* 1946

Bresslaw, Bernard (1933–1993) *Blood of the Vampire* 1958; *Too Many Crooks* 1958; *It's All Happening* 1963; *Carry On Cowboy* 1965; *Carry On Screaming* 1966; *Morgan – a Suitable Case for Treatment* 1966; *Carry On Follow That Camel* 1967; *Carry On Doctor* 1968; *Carry On Up the Khyber* 1968; *Carry On Camping* 1969; *Moon Zero Two* 1969; *Carry On Loving* 1970; *Carry On Up the Jungle* 1970; *Carry On at Your Convenience* 1971; *Up Pompeii* 1971; *Carry On Abroad* 1972; *Carry On Matron* 1972; *Carry On Girls* 1973; *Carry On Dick* 1974; *Carry On Behind* 1975; *One of Our Dinosaurs Is Missing* 1975; *Jabberwocky* 1977; *Hawk the Slayer* 1980; *Krull* 1983; *Asterix and the Big Fight* 1989

Brestoff, Richard *Car Wash* 1976; *The Entity* 1981; *The Man with Two Brains* 1983

Brett, Danielle *Jill Rips* 2000; *Rated X* 2000

Brett, Jeremy (1935–1995) *The Very Edge* 1962; *The Wild and the Willing* 1962; *Girl in the Headlines* 1963; *My Fair Lady* 1964; *Mad Dogs and Englishmen* 1994

Brewster, Diane (1931–1991) *Courage of Black Beauty* 1957; *The Invisible Boy* 1957; *Quantrill's Raiders* 1958; *Torpedo Run* 1958; *The Man in the Net* 1959; *The Young Philadelphians* 1959

Brewster, Jordana (1980–) *The Faculty* 1998; *The Invisible Circus* 2000; *The Fast and the Furious* 2001

Brewster, Paget (1969–) *Let's Talk about Sex* 1998; *Max Q: Emergency Landing* 1998; *One True Love* 2000; *The Specials* 2000

Breznahan, Tom (1965–) *Twice Dead* 1988; *Diplomatic Immunity* 1991; *Ski School* 1991

Brialy, Jean-Claude (1933–) *Le Beau Serge* 1958; *Les Cousins* 1959; *Paris Nous Appartient* 1960; *Cleo from 5 to 7* 1961; *Une Femme Est une Femme* 1961; *La Bonne Soupe* 1963; *Male Hunt* 1964; *La Ronde* 1964; *King of Hearts* 1966; *The Bride Wore Black* 1967; *The Oldest Profession* 1967; *Claire's Knee* 1970; *Le Fantôme de la Liberté* 1974; *Robert et Robert* 1978; *Edith and Marcel* 1983; *La Nuit de Varennes* 1983; *An Impudent Girl* 1985; *Inspecteur Lavardin* 1986; *Le Cop II* 1989; *Une Femme Française* 1994; *Portraits Chinois* 1996

Brian, David (1914–1993) *Beyond the Forest* 1949; *Flamingo Road* 1949; *Intruder in the Dust* 1949; *Breakthrough* 1950; *The Damned Don't Cry* 1950; *The Great Jewel Robber* 1950; *Fort Worth* 1951; *Inside Straight* 1951; *Million Dollar Mermaid* 1952; *Springfield Rifle* 1952; *This Woman Is Dangerous* 1952; *Ambush at Tomahawk Gap* 1953; *Dawn at Socorro* 1954; *The High and the Mighty* 1954; *Timberjack* 1955; *Accused of Murder* 1956; *The First Travelling Saleslady* 1956; *Castle of Evil* 1966; *The Rare Breed* 1966; *The Destructors* 1968; *The Girl Who Knew Too Much* 1969

Brian, Mary (1906–2002) *Beau Geste* 1926; *Running Wild* 1927; *The Marriage Playground* 1929; *The Virginian* 1929; *The Royal Family of Broadway* 1930; *The Front Page* 1931; *Gun Smoke* 1931; *Blessed Event* 1932; *Hard to Handle* 1933; *Charlie Chan in Paris* 1935; *The Man on the Flying Trapeze* 1935; *The Amazing Quest of Ernest Bliss* 1936; *Spendthrift* 1936

Briant, Shane (1946–) *Demons of the Mind* 1971; *Captain Kronos: Vampire Hunter* 1972; *Frankenstein and the Monster from Hell* 1973; *Lady Chatterley's Lover* 1981; *Constance* 1984; *Shaker Run* 1985; *Cassandra* 1987; *Grievous Bodily Harm* 1987; *Till There Was You* 1990; *Tunnel Vision* 1994

Brice, Fanny (1891–1951) *Everybody Sing* 1938; *Ziegfeld Follies* 1944

Brice, Pierre (1929–) *The Cossacks* 1959; *The Bacchantes* 1960; *The Desperado Trail* 1965

Brice, Ron *Fresh* 1994; *The Keeper* 1995; *Ripe* 1996

Bridge, Al aka **Bridge, Alan** (1891–1957) *Law and Order* 1936; *The Falcon's Alibi* 1946

Bridges, Beau (1941–) *The Red Pony* 1949; *The Explosive Generation* 1961; *Village of the Giants* 1965; *The Incident* 1967; *For Love of Ivy* 1968; *Gaily, Gaily* 1969; *Adam's Woman* 1970; *The Landlord* 1970; *The Christian Licorice Store* 1971; *Child's Play* 1972; *Hammersmith Is Out* 1972; *Your Three Minutes Are Up* 1973; *Lovin' Molly* 1974; *One Summer Love* 1975; *The Other Side of the Mountain* 1975; *Swashbuckler* 1976; *Two-Minute Warning* 1976; *Greased Lightning* 1977; *The Fifth Musketeer* 1979; *Norma Rae* 1979; *The Runner Stumbles* 1979; *Silver Dream Racer* 1980; *Honky Tonk Freeway* 1981; *Night Crossing* 1981; *Love Child* 1982; *Heart like a Wheel* 1983; *The Hotel New Hampshire* 1984; *The Killing Time* 1987; *The Wild Pair* 1987; *The Iron Triangle* 1988; *Seven Hours to Judgment* 1988; *Everybody's Baby: the Rescue of Jessica McClure* 1989; *The Fabulous Baker Boys* 1989; *Daddy's Dyin'... Who's Got the Will?* 1990; *Married to It* 1991; *Wildflower* 1991; *Without Warning: the James Brady Story* 1991; *The Positively True Adventures of the Alleged Texas Cheerleader-Murdering Mom* 1993; *Sidekicks* 1993; *Rocketman* 1997; *The Second Civil War* 1997; *Inherit the Wind* 1999; *Songs in Ordinary Times* 2000

Bridges, Chris "Ludacris" (1977–) *2 Fast 2 Furious* 2003; *Crash* 2004

Bridges, Jeff (1949–) *Halls of Anger* 1970; *The Last Picture Show* 1971; *Bad Company* 1972; *Fat City* 1972; *The Iceman Cometh* 1973; *The Last American Hero* 1973; *The Lolly-Madonna War* 1973; *Thunderbolt and Lightfoot* 1974; *Hearts of the West* 1975; *Rancho Deluxe* 1975; *King Kong* 1976; *Stay Hungry* 1976; *Somebody Killed Her Husband* 1978; *The American Success Company* 1979; *Winter Kills* 1979; *Heaven's Gate* 1980; *The Last Unicorn* 1980; *Cutter's Way* 1981; *Kiss Me Goodbye* 1982; *Tron* 1982; *Against All Odds* 1984; *Starman* 1984; *Jagged Edge* 1985; *8 Million Ways to Die* 1986; *The Morning After* 1986; *Nadine* 1987; *Tucker: the Man and His Dream* 1988; *Cold Feet* 1989; *The Fabulous Baker Boys* 1989; *See You in the Morning* 1989; *Texasville* 1990; *The Fisher King* 1991; *American Heart* 1992; *Fearless* 1993; *The Vanishing* 1993; *Blown Away* 1994; *Wild Bill* 1995; *The Mirror Has Two Faces* 1996; *White Squall* 1996; *The Big Lebowski* 1997; *Arlington Road* 1998; *The Muse* 1999; *Simpatico* 1999; *The Contender* 2000; *K-PAX* 2001; *Lost in La Mancha* 2002; *Masked and Anonymous* 2003; *Seabiscuit* 2003; *The Door in the Floor* 2004

Bridges, Lloyd (1913–1998) *They Dare Not Love* 1941; *The Heat's On* 1943; *Sahara* 1943; *The Master Race* 1944; *Abilene Town* 1945; *Miss Susie Slagle's* 1945; *Strange Confession* 1945; *A Walk in the Sun* 1945; *Ramrod* 1947; *Calamity Jane and Sam Bass* 1949; *Home of the Brave* 1949; *Red Canyon* 1949; *Colt .45* 1950;

The Sound of Fury 1950; *The White Tower* 1950; *High Noon* 1952; *Last of the Comanches* 1952; *Plymouth Adventure* 1952; *The Kid from Left Field* 1953; *The Limping Man* 1953; *Pride of the Blue Grass* 1954; *Apache Woman* 1955; *Wichita* 1955; *The Rainmaker* 1956; *The Goddess* 1958; *Around the World under the Sea* 1965; *Attack on the Iron Coast* 1968; *Daring Game* 1968; *The Happy Ending* 1969; *Running Wild* 1973; *Bear Island* 1979; *The Fifth Musketeer* 1979; *Airplane!* 1980; *Airplane II: the Sequel* 1982; *Weekend Warriors* 1986; *The Wild Pair* 1987; *Tucker: the Man and His Dream* 1988; *Winter People* 1988; *Cousins* 1989; *Joe versus the Volcano* 1990; *Hot Shots!* 1991; *Honey, I Blew Up the Kid* 1992; *Hot Shots! Part Deux* 1993; *Blown Away* 1994; *The Other Woman* 1994; *Jane Austen's Mafia* 1998

Bridges, Penny Bae *Space Jam* 1997; *The Color of Love: Jacey's Story* 2000

Briers, Richard (1934–) *Bottoms Up* 1959; *A Matter of WHO* 1961; *The Girl on the Boat* 1962; *The Bargee* 1964; *Fathom* 1967; *Rentadick* 1972; *Watership Down* 1978; *A Chorus of Disapproval* 1988; *Henry V* 1989; *Much Ado about Nothing* 1993; *Mary Shelley's Frankenstein* 1994; *In the Bleak Midwinter* 1995; *Hamlet* 1996; *Love's Labour's Lost* 1999; *Unconditional Love* 2001; *Peter Pan* 2003

Brieux, Bernard *Hit List* 1984; *Petit Con* 1984

Briggs, Johnny (1935–) *Light Up the Sky* 1960; *The Wind of Change* 1961; *The Last Escape* 1970

Briggs, Matt (1883–1962) *Advice to the Lovelorn* 1933; *The Dancing Masters* 1943; *The Meanest Man in the World* 1943; *The Ox-Bow Incident* 1943

Bright, Cameron (1993–) *Godsend* 2003; *Birth* 2004

Bright, Richard (1937–) *Lions Love* 1969; *The Panic in Needle Park* 1971; *The Getaway* 1972; *Marathon Man* 1976; *On the Yard* 1978; *Two of a Kind* 1983; *The Ambulance* 1990; *Who's the Man?* 1993; *Sweet Nothing* 1995

Brightwell, Paul *The Innocent Sleep* 1995; *Sliding Doors* 1997

Briguglia, Paolo *The Hundred Steps* 2000; *Good Morning, Night* 2003

Brill, Patti (1923–1963) *Girl Rush* 1944; *Music in Manhattan* 1944

Brimble, Nick *Frankenstein Unbound* 1990; *Robin Hood: Prince of Thieves* 1991; *Loch Ness* 1994; *Gone Fishin'* 1997; *7 Days to Live* 2000

Brimley, Wilford (1934–) *The China Syndrome* 1979; *The Electric Horseman* 1979; *Death Valley* 1982; *Tender Mercies* 1982; *The Thing* 1982; *Tough Enough* 1982; *High Road to China* 1983; *10 to Midnight* 1983; *Country* 1984; *Harry and Son* 1984; *The Hotel New Hampshire* 1984; *The Natural* 1984; *The Stone Boy* 1984; *Cocoon* 1985; *Remo – Unarmed and Dangerous* 1985; *End of the Line* 1987; *Cocoon: the Return* 1988; *Eternity* 1990; *The Firm* 1993; *Hard Target* 1993; *Last of the Dogmen* 1995; *My Fellow Americans* 1996

Brine, Adrian (1936–) *The Girl with Red Hair* 1981; *Vincent and Theo* 1990; *Between the Devil and the Deep Blue Sea* 1995

Brinegar, Paul (1917–1995) *Cattle Empire* 1958; *How to Make a Monster* 1958

Brinkley, John *The Mobster* 1958; *A Bucket of Blood* 1959

Brinkley, Ritch *Cabin Boy* 1994; *Breakdown* 1997

Brisbane, Syd *Bad Boy Bubby* 1993; *Dead Letter Office* 1998

Brisbane, William *There Goes the Groom* 1937; *Maid's Night Out* 1938

Brisbin, David *Dead End Kids* 1986; *Kiss Daddy Good Night* 1987

Briscoe, Brent (1961–) *Another Day in Paradise* 1998; *A Simple Plan* 1998; *Mulholland Drive* 2001

Brissac, Virginia (1894–1979) *Dark Victory* 1939; *The Ghost Breakers* 1940; *The Scarlet Clue* 1945; *About Mrs Leslie* 1954

Brisson, Carl (1893–1958) *The Ring* 1927; *The Manxman* 1929; *Murder at the Vanities* 1934; *All the King's Horses* 1935

Britt, May (1936–) *The Hunters* 1958; *The Young Lions* 1958; *The Blue Angel* 1959; *Murder, Inc* 1960

Brittany, Morgan (1951–) *The Prodigal* 1983; *Body Armor* 1996

Britton, Barbara (1919–1980) *Young and Willing* 1942; *So Proudly We Hail* 1943; *Till We Meet Again* 1944; *Captain Kidd* 1945; *The Great John L* 1945; *The Virginian* 1946; *I Shot Jesse James* 1949; *Champagne for Caesar* 1950; *Bwana Devil* 1952; *Ride the Man Down* 1952; *Ain't Misbehavin'* 1955; *The Spoilers* 1955

Britton, Connie (1968–) *No Looking Back* 1998; *Friday Night Lights* 2004

Britton, Pamela *aka* **Britton, Pam** (1923–1974) *Anchors Aweigh* 1945; *DOA* 1949; *Watch the Birdie* 1950

Britton, Tony (1924–) *The Birthday Present* 1957; *Behind the Mask* 1958; *Operation Amsterdam* 1958; *The Heart of a Man* 1959; *The Rough and the Smooth* 1959; *Suspect* 1960; *The Break* 1962; *Dr Syn, Alias the Scarecrow* 1963; *There's a Girl in My Soup* 1970; *Sunday, Bloody Sunday* 1971; *The Day of the Jackal* 1973; *Night Watch* 1973; *The People That Time Forgot* 1977; *Agatha* 1978

Bro, Nicolas (1972–) *The Green Butchers* 2003; *Reconstruction* 2003

Broadbent, Jim (1949–) *Brazil* 1985; *Running Out of Luck* 1985; *The Good Father* 1986; *Vroom* 1988; *Life Is Sweet* 1990; *Enchanted April* 1991; *The Crying Game* 1992; *Widows' Peak* 1993; *Bullets over Broadway* 1994; *Princess Caraboo* 1994; *Richard III* 1995; *Rough Magic* 1995; *The Secret Agent* 1996; *Smilla's Feeling for Snow* 1996; *The Borrowers* 1997; *The Avengers* 1998; *Little Voice* 1998; *Topsy-Turvy* 1999; *Bridget Jones's Diary* 2001; *Iris* 2001; *Moulin Rouge!* 2001; *Gangs of New York* 2002; *Nicholas Nickleby* 2002; *Bright Young Things* 2003; *Tooth* 2003; *Around the World in 80 Days* 2004; *Bridget Jones: the Edge of Reason* 2004; *Vanity Fair* 2004; *The Magic Roundabout* 2005; *Robots* 2005; *Valiant* 2005

Broadhurst, Kent (1940–) *Stars and Bars* 1988; *The Dark Half* 1991

Brocco, Peter (1903–1992) *Appointment with Murder* 1948; *The Balcony* 1963

Brochard, Jean (1893–1972) *Clochemerle* 1948; *Dieu A Besoin des Hommes* 1950; *Les Diaboliques* 1954

Brochet, Anne (1966–) *Masques* 1987; *Cyrano de Bergerac* 1990; *Tous les Matins du Monde* 1991; *Driftwood* 1996; *Dust* 2001; *Histoire de Marie et Julien* 2003; *Confidences Trop Intimes* 2004

Brock, Phil (1953–) *POW the Escape* 1986; *The Allnighter* 1987; *Date with an Angel* 1987

Brock, Stanley (1931–1991) *Tin Men* 1987; *UHF* 1989

Brocksmith, Roy (1945–2001) *Killer Fish* 1978; *Tales of Ordinary Madness* 1981; *Total Recall* 1990; *Nickel & Dime* 1991; *Kull the Conqueror* 1997

Brockwell, Gladys (1894–1929) *Oliver Twist* 1922; *Long Pants* 1927; *Lights of New York* 1928

Broderick, Beth (1959–) *Hard Evidence* 1994; *Man of the Year* 1995

Broderick, Helen (1891–1959) *Top Hat* 1935; *The Bride Walks Out* 1936; *Murder on a Bridle Path* 1936; *Swing Time* 1936; *Radio City Revels* 1938; *The Rage of Paris* 1938; *Naughty but Nice* 1939; *No, No, Nanette* 1940; *Nice Girl?* 1941; *Because of Him* 1946

Broderick, James (1927–1982) *Girl of the Night* 1960; *Alice's Restaurant* 1969; *The Todd Killings* 1971; *The Taking of Pelham One Two Three* 1974; *Dog Day Afternoon* 1975

Broderick, Matthew (1962–) *Max Dugan Returns* 1983; *WarGames* 1983; *Ladyhawke* 1985; *1918* 1985; *Ferris Bueller's Day Off* 1986; *Project X* 1987; *Biloxi Blues* 1988; *Torch Song Trilogy* 1988; *Family Business* 1989; *Glory* 1989; *The Freshman* 1990; *Out on a Limb* 1992; *A Life in the Theater* 1993; *The Night We Never Met* 1993; *The Lion King* 1994; *Mrs Parker and the Vicious Circle* 1994; *The Road to Wellville* 1994; *Arabian Knight* 1995; *The Cable Guy* 1996; *Infinity* 1996; *Addicted to Love* 1997; *Godzilla* 1997; *Election* 1999; *Inspector Gadget* 1999; *You Can Count on Me* 1999; *Good Boy!* 2003; *The Stepford Wives* 2004

Brodie, Kevin (1952–) *The Night of the Grizzly* 1966; *The Giant Spider Invasion* 1975

Brodie, Steve (1919–1992) *A Walk in the Sun* 1945; *Badman's Territory* 1946; *Criminal Court* 1946; *The Falcon's Adventure* 1946; *Build My Gallows High* 1947; *Crossfire* 1947; *Desperate* 1947; *Thunder Mountain* 1947; *Trail Street* 1947; *The Arizona Ranger* 1948; *Bodyguard* 1948; *Guns of Hate* 1948; *Return of the Bad Men* 1948; *Station West* 1948; *The Big Wheel* 1949; *Home of the Brave* 1949; *The Admiral Was a Lady* 1950; *Armored Car Robbery* 1950; *Winchester '73* 1950; *M* 1951; *The Steel Helmet* 1951; *The Sword of Monte Cristo* 1951; *The Beast from 20,000 Fathoms* 1953; *Donovan's Brain* 1953; *Gun Duel in Durango* 1957; *Sierra Baron* 1958; *A Girl Named Tamiko* 1962; *Of Love and Desire* 1963; *The Giant Spider Invasion* 1975; *Delta Pi* 1985; *The Wizard of Speed and Time* 1988

Brodsky, Vlastimil (1920–2002) *All My Good Countrymen* 1968; *Capricious Summer* 1968; *End of a Priest* 1969; *Jacob the Liar* 1974

Brody, Adrien (1976–) *The Boy Who Cried Bitch* 1991; *Bullet* 1995; *Six Ways to Sunday* 1997; *Restaurant* 1998; *Liberty Heights* 1999; *Oxygen* 1999; *Summer of Sam* 1999; *Bread and Roses* 2000; *Harrison's Flowers* 2000; *The Affair of the Necklace* 2001; *Dummy* 2002; *The Pianist* 2002; *The Singing Detective* 2003; *The Village* 2004; *The Jacket* 2005

Brody, Estelle (1900–1995) *Hindle Wakes* 1927; *Kitty* 1928

Brogi, Giulio *The Spider's Stratagem* 1970; *Voyage to Cythera* 1984

Brolin, James (1940–) *Von Ryan's Express* 1965; *Skyjacked* 1972; *Westworld* 1973; *Gable and Lombard* 1976; *The Car* 1977; *Capricorn One* 1978; *The Amityville Horror* 1979; *Night of the Juggler* 1980; *High Risk* 1981; *Bad Jim* 1989; *Ted & Venus* 1991; *Gas, Food, Lodging* 1992; *Paper Hearts* 1993; *The Expert* 1994; *Traffic* 2000; *Antwone Fisher* 2002; *Catch Me If You Can* 2002; *A Guy Thing* 2002; *The Master of Disguise* 2002

Brolin, Josh (1968–) *The Goonies* 1985; *Thrashin'* 1986; *Roadflower* 1994; *Bed of Roses* 1995; *Flirting with Disaster* 1996; *Mimic* 1997; *Nightwatch* 1997; *Best Laid Plans* 1999; *The Mod Squad* 1999; *Hollow Man* 2000; *Milwaukee, Minnesota* 2002

Bromberg, J Edward (1903–1951) *Stowaway* 1936; *Under Two Flags* 1936; *Charlie Chan on Broadway* 1937; *Fair Warning* 1937; *Seventh Heaven* 1937; *The Baroness and the Butler* 1938; *Four Men and a Prayer* 1938; *Mr Moto Takes a Chance* 1938; *Suez* 1938; *Hollywood Cavalcade* 1939; *Wife, Husband and Friend* 1939; *The Mark of Zorro* 1940; *The Return of Frank James* 1940; *Strange Cargo* 1940; *The Invisible Agent* 1942; *Life Begins at 8.30* 1942; *Tennessee Johnson* 1942; *Lady of Burlesque* 1943; *Son of Dracula* 1943; *Pillow of Death* 1945; *Cloak and Dagger* 1946; *I Shot Jesse James* 1949; *Guilty Bystander* 1950

Bromfield, John (1922–) *Rope of Sand* 1949; *Easy to Love* 1953; *Revenge of the Creature* 1955

Bromley, Dorothy (1935–) *It's Great to Be Young* 1956; *A Touch of the Sun* 1956

Bromley, Sheila *aka* **Mannors, Sheila** (1911–2003) *The Cocaine Fiends* 1935; *Westward Ho* 1935

Bron, Eleanor (1940–) *Help!* 1965; *Alfie* 1966; *Bedazzled* 1967; *Two for the Road* 1967; *A Touch of Love* 1969; *Women in Love* 1969; *The National Health* 1973; *Pleasure at Her Majesty's* 1976; *The Hound of the Baskervilles* 1983; *Turtle Diary* 1985; *The Attic: the Hiding of Anne Frank* 1988; *Deadly Advice* 1993; *Black Beauty* 1994; *A Little Princess* 1995; *The House of Mirth* 2000; *Iris* 2001; *The Heart of Me* 2002; *Wimbledon* 2004

Bronson, Betty (1906–1971) *Ben-Hur: a Tale of the Christ* 1925; *The Singing Fool* 1928; *The Naked Kiss* 1964

Bronson, Charles *aka* **Buchinski, Charles** *aka* **Buchinsky, Charles** (1921–2003) *The Mob* 1951; *The People against O'Hara* 1951; *My Six Convicts* 1952; *Pat and Mike* 1952; *Red Skies of Montana* 1952; *House of Wax* 1953; *Miss Sadie Thompson* 1953; *Apache* 1954; *The City Is Dark* 1954; *Drum Beat* 1954; *Riding Shotgun* 1954; *Tennessee Champ* 1954; *Vera Cruz* 1954; *Big House, USA* 1955; *Jubal* 1956; *Run of the Arrow* 1957; *Gang War* 1958; *Machine Gun Kelly* 1958; *Showdown at Boot Hill* 1958; *Never So Few* 1959; *The Magnificent Seven* 1960; *Master of the World* 1961; *A Thunder of Drums* 1961; *X-15* 1961; *Kid Galahad* 1962; *4 for Texas* 1963; *The Great Escape* 1963; *Battle of the Bulge* 1965; *The Sandpiper* 1965; *This Property Is Condemned* 1966; *The Dirty Dozen* 1967; *Guns for San Sebastian* 1968; *Once upon a Time in the West* 1968; *Villa Rides* 1968; *Twinky* 1969; *Rider on the Rain* 1970; *Violent City* 1970; *You Can't Win 'em All* 1970; *Chato's Land* 1971; *Cold Sweat* 1971; *Red Sun* 1971; *Someone behind the Door* 1971; *The Mechanic* 1972; *The Valachi Papers* 1972; *The Stone Killer* 1973; *The Valdez Horses* 1973; *Death Wish* 1974; *Mr Majestyk* 1974; *Breakout* 1975; *Hard Times* 1975; *Breakheart Pass* 1976; *From Noon till Three* 1976; *St Ives* 1976; *Raid on Entebbe* 1977; *Telefon* 1977; *The White Buffalo* 1977; *Love and Bullets* 1978; *Borderline* 1980; *Caboblanco* 1980; *Death Hunt* 1981; *Death Wish II* 1981; *10 to Midnight* 1983; *The Evil That Men Do* 1984; *Death Wish 3* 1985; *Assassination* 1986; *Murphy's Law* 1986; *Death Wish 4: the Crackdown* 1987; *Messenger of Death* 1988; *Kinjite: Forbidden Subjects* 1989; *The Indian Runner* 1991; *Death Wish V: the Face of Death* 1994

Brook, Claudio (1929–1995) *The Young One* 1960; *The Exterminating Angel* 1962; *Simon of the Desert* 1965; *Don't Look Now... We're Being Shot At* 1966; *Jory* 1972; *Interval* 1973; *Alucarda* 1975; *The Return of a Man Called Horse* 1976; *Cronos* 1992

Brook, Clive (1887–1974) *Underworld* 1927; *The Four Feathers* 1929; *Anybody's Woman* 1930; *Paramount on Parade* 1930; *East Lynne* 1931; *Tarnished Lady* 1931; *The Man from Yesterday* 1932; *Shanghai Express* 1932; *Sherlock Holmes* 1932; *Cavalcade* 1933; *If I Were Free* 1933; *Gallant Lady* 1934; *The Dictator* 1935; *Convoy* 1940; *Freedom Radio* 1940; *Return to Yesterday* 1940; *The List of Adrian Messenger* 1963

Brook, Faith (1922–) *Jungle Book* 1942; *The Intimate Stranger* 1956; *Chase a Crooked Shadow* 1957; *The Thirty-Nine Steps* 1959; *To Sir, with Love* 1967; *The Smashing Bird I Used to Know* 1969; *Walk a Crooked Path* 1969; *North Sea Hijack* 1979; *Eye of the Needle* 1981

Brook, Irina (1962–) *The Girl in the Picture* 1985; *Captive* 1986; *The Fool* 1990

Brook, Isabel *Faust: Love of the Damned* 2001; *About a Boy* 2002

Brook, Jayne (1962–) *Clean Slate* 1994; *Ed* 1996; *Last Dance* 1996

Brook, Lyndon (1926–2004) *The Purple Plain* 1954; *One Way Out* 1955; *Reach for the Sky* 1956; *The Spanish Gardener* 1956; *The Gypsy and the Gentleman* 1958; *Invasion* 1965; *Who?* 1974

Brook-Jones, Elwyn (1911–1962) *Bonnie Prince Charlie* 1948; *It's Hard to Be Good* 1948; *The Gilded Cage* 1954; *Rogue's Yarn* 1956; *Passport to Shame* 1958

Brooke, Hillary (1914–1999) *Sherlock Holmes Faces Death* 1943; *Standing Room Only* 1944; *The Enchanted Cottage* 1945; *Ministry of Fear* 1945; *Road to Utopia* 1945; *The Woman in Green* 1945; *Strange Impersonation* 1946; *The Strange Woman* 1946; *The Fuller Brush Man* 1948; *Africa Screams* 1949; *The Admiral Was a Lady* 1950; *Abbott and Costello Meet Captain Kidd* 1952; *Invaders from Mars* 1953; *Bengazi* 1955; *The Man Who Knew Too Much* 1956

Brooke Jr, Michael *The Magnet* 1950; *The Long Arm* 1956

Brooke, Paul (1944–) *The Lair of the White Worm* 1988; *The Fool* 1990; *Lighthouse* 1999

Brooke, Tyler (1886–1943) *Fazil* 1928; *Dynamite* 1929; *Monte Carlo* 1930; *Hallelujah, I'm a Bum* 1933

Brooke, Walter (1914–1986) *Conquest of Space* 1955; *The Graduate* 1967; *Sergeant Ryker* 1968; *Zigzag* 1970

Brooke-Taylor, Tim (1940–) *Twelve plus One* 1969; *Pleasure at Her Majesty's* 1976

Brookes, Jacqueline (1930–) *The Gambler* 1974; *Last Embrace* 1979; *The Entity* 1981; *Without a Trace* 1983; *The Good Son* 1993

Brooks, Aimee (1976–) *Critters 3* 1991; *Monster Man* 2003

Brooks, Albert (1947–) *Taxi Driver* 1976; *Real Life* 1979; *Private Benjamin* 1980; *Modern Romance* 1981; *Twilight Zone: the Movie* 1983; *Unfaithfully Yours* 1983; *Lost in America* 1985; *Broadcast News* 1987; *Defending Your Life* 1991; *I'll Do Anything* 1994; *The Scout* 1994; *Mother* 1996; *Critical Care* 1997; *Out of Sight* 1998; *The Muse* 1999; *My First Mister* 2001; *Finding Nemo* 2003; *The In-Laws* 2003

Brooks, Avery (1948–) *American History X* 1998; *The Big Hit* 1998; *15 Minutes* 2001

Brooks, Claude *Solarbabies* 1986; *Hiding Out* 1987

Brooks, Foster (1912–2001) *Cactus Jack* 1979; *Smorgasbord* 1983

Brooks, Geraldine (1925–1977) *Cry Wolf* 1947; *Possessed* 1947; *Challenge to Lassie* 1949; *The Reckless Moment* 1949; *The Younger Brothers* 1949; *Volcano* 1950; *Johnny Tiger* 1966; *Mr Ricco* 1975

Brooks, Hazel (1924–) *Body and Soul* 1947; *Sleep, My Love* 1948

Brooks, Jean (1915–1963) *The Falcon and the Co-Eds* 1943; *The Falcon in Danger* 1943; *The Leopard Man* 1943; *The Seventh Victim* 1943; *The Falcon in Hollywood* 1944; *Youth Runs Wild* 1944

Brooks, Joel (1949–) *Skin Deep* 1989; *Indecent Proposal* 1993

Brooks, Leslie (1922–) *You Were Never Lovelier* 1942; *Cover Girl* 1944; *Tonight and Every Night* 1945; *Hollow Triumph* 1948
Brooks, Louise (1906–1985) *It's the Old Army Game* 1926; *Beggars of Life* 1928; *A Girl in Every Port* 1928; *The Canary Murder Case* 1929; *Diary of a Lost Girl* 1929; *Pandora's Box* 1929; *Prix de Beauté* 1930; *God's Gift to Women* 1931; *It Pays to Advertise* 1931; *Overland Stage Raiders* 1938
Brooks, Mel (1926–) *Putney Swope* 1969; *The Twelve Chairs* 1970; *Blazing Saddles* 1974; *Silent Movie* 1976; *High Anxiety* 1977; *History of the World Part 1* 1981; *To Be or Not to Be* 1983; *Spaceballs* 1987; *Look Who's Talking Too* 1990; *Life Stinks* 1991; *Robin Hood: Men in Tights* 1993; *The Little Rascals* 1994; *Dracula: Dead and Loving It* 1995; *Screw Loose* 1999; *Robots* 2005
Brooks, Phyllis (1915–1995) *Little Miss Broadway* 1938; *Rebecca of Sunnybrook Farm* 1938; *Charlie Chan in Reno* 1939; *The Shanghai Gesture* 1941; *The Unseen* 1945
Brooks, Rand (1918–2003) *The Devil's Playground* 1946; *Fool's Gold* 1946; *The Marauders* 1947; *The Dead Don't Dream* 1948; *False Paradise* 1948; *Silent Conflict* 1948; *Ladies of the Chorus* 1949; *Comanche Station* 1960
Brooks, Randy *Assassination* 1986; *8 Million Ways to Die* 1986; *Colors* 1988; *Reservoir Dogs* 1991
Brooks, Ray (1939–) *Some People* 1962; *The Knack... and How to Get It* 1965; *Daleks – Invasion Earth 2150 AD* 1966; *The Last Grenade* 1970; *Assassin* 1973; *Tiffany Jones* 1973; *House of Whipcord* 1974
Brooks, Richard (1912–1992) *Good to Go* 1986; *The Hidden* 1987; *Blue Jean Cop* 1988; *84 Charlie Mopic* 1989; *Shocker* 1989; *To Sleep with Anger* 1990; *The Crow: City of Angels* 1996
Brooks, Victor *Cover Girl Killer* 1959; *Life in Danger* 1959; *Give Us Tomorrow* 1978
Brophy, Anthony *The Run of the Country* 1995; *Snow White: a Tale of Terror* 1996; *The Last Bus Home* 1997
Brophy, Brian *Brain Dead* 1990; *Love to Kill* 1997
Brophy, Edward *aka* **Brophy, Edward S** (1895–1960) *The Cameraman* 1928; *Doughboys* 1930; *The Champ* 1931; *What – No Beer?* 1933; *Evelyn Prentice* 1934; *Mad Love* 1935; *Great Guy* 1936; *Spendthrift* 1936; *Strike Me Pink* 1936; *The Adventures of Michael Strogoff* 1937; *The Last Gangster* 1937; *The Amazing Mr Williams* 1939; *Golden Boy* 1939; *Kid Nightingale* 1939; *Dance, Girl, Dance* 1940; *The Invisible Woman* 1940; *Dumbo* 1941; *The Gay Falcon* 1941; *Broadway* 1942; *Larceny, Inc* 1942; *It Happened Tomorrow* 1944; *The Falcon in San Francisco* 1945; *The Falcon's Adventure* 1946; *The Last Hurrah* 1958
Brophy, Kevin (1953–) *The Long Riders* 1980; *Hell Night* 1981
Brosnan, Pierce (1953–) *The Long Good Friday* 1979; *Nomads* 1985; *The Fourth Protocol* 1987; *The Deceivers* 1988; *Taffin* 1988; *Mister Johnson* 1991; *Victim of Love* 1991; *The Lawnmower Man* 1992; *Live Wire* 1992; *Death Train* 1993; *Mrs Doubtfire* 1993; *Love Affair* 1994; *The Disappearance of Kevin Johnson* 1995; *GoldenEye* 1995; *Night Watch* 1995; *Daniel Defoe's Robinson Crusoe* 1996; *Mars Attacks!* 1996; *The Mirror Has Two Faces* 1996; *Dante's Peak* 1997; *The Magic Sword: Quest for Camelot* 1997; *The Nephew* 1997; *Tomorrow Never Dies* 1997; *Grey Owl* 1999; *The Match* 1999; *The Thomas Crown Affair* 1999; *The World Is Not Enough* 1999; *The Tailor of Panama* 2000; *Die Another Day* 2002; *Evelyn* 2002; *Laws of Attraction* 2003; *After the Sunset* 2004
Brosset, Claude (1943–) *The Outsider* 1983; *Le Cop* 1985
Brothers, Dr Joyce (1928–) *Oh God! Book II* 1980; *The Lonely Guy* 1984; *Age Isn't Everything* 1991
Brough, Mary (1863–1934) *Rookery Nook* 1930; *A Cuckoo in the Nest* 1933
Brousse, Liliane *Maniac* 1962; *Paranoiac* 1963
Browder, Ben (1965–) *A Kiss before Dying* 1991; *Danielle Steel's Secrets* 1992
Brower, Jordan (1981–) *Sticks and Stones* 1996; *Night Ride Home* 1999
Brown, Barbara (1902–1975) *Hollywood Canteen* 1944; *Personality Kid* 1946; *Born Yesterday* 1950; *Home Town Story* 1951; *Jack and the Beanstalk* 1952; *An Annapolis Story* 1955; *Gonks Go Beat* 1965
Brown, Barry (1951–1978) *Flesh* 1968; *Bad Company* 1972; *Daisy Miller* 1974
Brown, Bille *The Dish* 2000; *The Man Who Sued God* 2001
Brown, Blair (1948–) *Altered States* 1980; *One-Trick Pony* 1980; *Continental Divide* 1981; *A Flash of Green* 1984; *Stealing Home* 1988; *Strapless* 1988; *Passed Away* 1992; *Dogville* 2003
Brown, Bobby (1969–) *Panther* 1995; *A Thin Line between Love and Hate* 1996
Brown, Bryan (1947–) *The Irishman* 1978; *Money Movers* 1978; *Newsfront* 1978; *Breaker Morant* 1979; *Cathy's Child* 1979; *The Odd Angry Shot* 1979; *Blood Money* 1980; *The Winter of Our Dreams* 1981; *Far East* 1982; *Give My Regards to Broad Street* 1984; *Kim* 1984; *Parker* 1984; *The Empty Beach* 1985; *FX: Murder by Illusion* 1985; *Rebel* 1985; *The Good Wife* 1986; *The Shiralee* 1986; *Tai-Pan* 1986; *Cocktail* 1988; *Gorillas in the Mist* 1988; *Blood Oath* 1990; *FX 2* 1991; *Blame It on the Bellboy* 1992; *Dead Heart* 1996; *Grizzly Falls* 1999; *Two Hands* 1999; *Risk* 2000; *Styx* 2000; *Dirty Deeds* 2002; *Along Came Polly* 2004
Brown, Charles D (1887–1949) *Gold Diggers of 1937* 1936; *The Duke of West Point* 1938; *The Shopworn Angel* 1938; *Kid Nightingale* 1939; *Brother Orchid* 1940; *The Big Sleep* 1946; *The Killers* 1946; *The Senator Was Indiscreet* 1947; *Smash Up – the Story of a Woman* 1947
Brown, Clancy (1959–) *The Bride* 1985; *Highlander* 1986; *Extreme Prejudice* 1987; *Deadly Pursuit* 1988; *Season of Fear* 1989; *Waiting for the Light* 1989; *Blue Steel* 1990; *Ambition* 1991; *Pet Sematary II* 1992; *Last Light* 1993; *The Shawshank Redemption* 1994; *Flubber* 1997; *Starship Troopers* 1997; *The Hurricane* 1999; *In the Company of Spies* 1999; *Snow White* 2001; *Normal* 2002; *The SpongeBob SquarePants Movie* 2004
Brown, D W *Weekend Pass* 1984; *Mischief* 1985
Brown, Dwier (1959–) *House II: the Second Story* 1987; *Field of Dreams* 1989; *The Guardian* 1990; *The Cutting Edge* 1992; *Mom and Dad Save the World* 1992; *Dennis the Menace Strikes Again* 1998
Brown, Eric (1964–) *Private Lessons* 1981; *They're Playing With Fire* 1984
Brown, Garrett M *aka* **Brown, Garrett** *Zelig* 1983; *Uncle Buck* 1989
Brown, Georg Stanford (1943–) *The Comedians* 1967; *Bullitt* 1968; *Dayton's Devils* 1968; *Colossus: the Forbin Project* 1969; *Black Jack* 1972; *The Man* 1972; *Stir Crazy* 1980
Brown, Georgia (1933–1992) *The Fixer* 1968; *Lock Up Your Daughters!* 1969; *The Raging Moon* 1970; *Nothing but the Night* 1972; *Galileo* 1974; *The Bawdy Adventures of Tom Jones* 1976; *Victim of Love* 1991
Brown, Henry *The Man in the Glass Booth* 1975; *Stepfather II* 1989
Brown (1), James (1920–1992) *Corvette K-225* 1943; *Going My Way* 1944; *Objective, Burma!* 1945; *Sands of Iwo Jima* 1949; *The Younger Brothers* 1949; *Chain Lightning* 1950; *The Fireball* 1950; *Montana* 1950; *The Pride of St Louis* 1952; *The Woman They Almost Lynched* 1953; *A Star Is Born* 1954; *Targets* 1968
Brown (2), James (1933–) *The Blues Brothers* 1980; *Rocky IV* 1985; *Blues Brothers 2000* 1998; *Holy Man* 1998
Brown, Janet (1924–) *Floodtide* 1949; *For Your Eyes Only* 1981
Brown, Jim (1935–) *Rio Conchos* 1964; *Dark of the Sun* 1967; *The Dirty Dozen* 1967; *Ice Station Zebra* 1968; *The Split* 1968; *100 Rifles* 1969; *Riot* 1969; *tick... tick... tick...* 1969; *El Condor* 1970; *The Grasshopper* 1970; *Slaughter* 1972; *I Escaped from Devil's Island* 1973; *The Slams* 1973; *Slaughter's Big Rip-Off* 1973; *Three the Hard Way* 1974; *Take a Hard Ride* 1975; *Kid Vengeance* 1977; *Fingers* 1978; *Pacific Inferno* 1979; *The Running Man* 1987; *Crack House* 1989; *Original Gangstas* 1996; *He Got Game* 1998; *Any Given Sunday* 1999; *She Hate Me* 2004
Brown (2), Joe (1941–) *What a Crazy World* 1963; *Three Hats for Lisa* 1965; *Mona Lisa* 1986
Brown, Joe E *aka* **Brown, Joe** (1892–1973) *Sunny Side Up* 1929; *Fireman Save My Child* 1932; *A Midsummer Night's Dream* 1935; *The Gladiator* 1938; *Chatterbox* 1943; *Pin Up Girl* 1944; *The Tender Years* 1947; *Show Boat* 1951; *Some Like It Hot* 1959; *The Comedy of Terrors* 1964
Brown, John *Hans Christian Andersen* 1952; *Master Spy* 1964; *Doctor Who and the Daleks* 1965
Brown, Johnny Mack *aka* **Brown, John Mack** *aka* **Mack Brown, John** (1904–1974) *The Divine Woman* 1928; *Our Dancing Daughters* 1928; *A Woman of Affairs* 1928; *Coquette* 1929; *The Single Standard* 1929; *The Valiant* 1929; *Billy the Kid* 1930; *The Last Flight* 1931; *The Secret Six* 1931; *Vanishing Frontier* 1932; *Female* 1933; *Belle of the Nineties* 1934; *Hell Town* 1937; *Law and Order* 1940; *Apache Uprising* 1965; *The Bounty Killer* 1965
Brown, Jophery (1945–) *The Bingo Long Travelling All-Stars and Motor Kings* 1976; *The Squeeze* 1987; *Sudden Death* 1995
Brown, Juanita *Caged Heat* 1974; *Foxy Brown* 1974
Brown, Judith *aka* **Brown, Judy** *The Big Doll House* 1971; *Women in Cages* 1972; *Slaughter's Big Rip-Off* 1973
Brown, Julie (1958–) *Earth Girls Are Easy* 1988; *Shakes the Clown* 1991; *The Opposite Sex and How to Live with Them* 1993; *Raining Stones* 1993
Brown, Kenneth *aka* **Buddy** (1932–) *Never Give a Sucker an Even Break* 1941; *Bomber's Moon* 1943
Brown, Kimberly J (1984–) *Tumbleweeds* 1999; *Bringing Down the House* 2003
Brown (2), Lew (1925–) *Crime and Punishment, USA* 1959; *Grand Theft Auto* 1977
Brown, Lou *The Irishman* 1978; *Alison's Birthday* 1979
Brown, Pamela (1917–1975) *One of Our Aircraft Is Missing* 1942; *I Know Where I'm Going!* 1945; *The Tales of Hoffmann* 1951; *Personal Affair* 1953; *Richard III* 1955; *Lust for Life* 1956; *The Scapegoat* 1959; *Cleopatra* 1963; *Becket* 1964; *Secret Ceremony* 1968; *Figures in a Landscape* 1970; *On a Clear Day You Can See Forever* 1970; *Wuthering Heights* 1970; *The Road Builder* 1971; *Lady Caroline Lamb* 1972; *Dracula* 1974
Brown, Pat Crawford *Elvira, Mistress of the Dark* 1988; *Stuck on You* 2003
Brown, Peter (1935–) *Darby's Rangers* 1958; *Merrill's Marauders* 1962; *Kitten with a Whip* 1964; *Ride the Wild Surf* 1964; *A Tiger Walks* 1964; *Three Guns for Texas* 1968; *Backtrack* 1969; *Act of Vengeance* 1974; *Foxy Brown* 1974; *The Concrete Jungle* 1982; *The Aurora Encounter* 1985; *Demonstone* 1989
Brown, Phil (1916–) *Calling Dr Gillespie* 1942; *The Killers* 1946; *Without Reservations* 1946; *If You Knew Susie* 1948; *Obsession* 1948; *A King in New York* 1957; *The Adding Machine* 1969; *Valdez Is Coming* 1971
Brown, Ralph (1960–) *Withnail & I* 1986; *Buster* 1988; *Diamond Skulls* 1989; *Impromptu* 1991; *Alien³* 1992; *Wayne's World 2* 1993; *Don't Get Me Started* 1994; *Up 'n' Under* 1997; *Mean Machine* 2001; *The Final Curtain* 2002; *I'll Be There* 2003; *Exorcist: the Beginning* 2004
Brown, Reb (1948–) *Fast Break* 1979; *Uncommon Valor* 1983; *Yor, the Hunter from the Future* 1983; *Howling II: Your Sister Is a Werewolf* 1984; *Death of a Soldier* 1985; *Distant Thunder* 1988; *Cage* 1989
Brown, Rob (1984–) *Finding Forrester* 2000; *Coach Carter* 2005
Brown, Robert (1918–2003) *Time Gentlemen Please!* 1952; *The Abominable Snowman* 1957; *The Steel Bayonet* 1957; *The Flame Barrier* 1958; *Passport to Shame* 1958; *Tower of London* 1962; *One Million Years BC* 1966; *Octopussy* 1983; *A View to a Kill* 1985; *The Living Daylights* 1987; *Licence to Kill* 1989
Brown, Roger Aaron *Tall Tale* 1994; *DNA* 1996
Brown, Roy "Chubby" (1945–) *UFO* 1993; *Chubby Down Under and Other Sticky Regions* 1998
Brown, Russ (1896–1993) *Damn Yankees* 1958; *South Pacific* 1958; *It Happened to Jane* 1959
Brown, Ruth (1928–) *Hairspray* 1988; *Shake, Rattle and Rock* 1994
Brown, Samantha *New Jersey Drive* 1995; *Double Platinum* 1999
Brown, Sharon *A Chorus Line* 1985; *For Keeps* 1987
Brown, Stanley *aka* **Taylor, Brad** (1914–2001) *The Face behind the Mask* 1941; *Atlantic City* 1944
Brown, Thomas Wilson *aka* **Brown, Thomas** (1972–) *Honey, I Shrunk the Kids* 1989; *Welcome Home* 1989; *Welcome Home, Roxy Carmichael* 1990; *Midnight Sting* 1992
Brown, Timothy *aka* **Brown, Tim** (1937–) *Nashville* 1975; *Pacific Inferno* 1979
Brown, Tom (1913–1990) *Hell's Highway* 1932; *Central Airport* 1933; *Anne of Green Gables* 1934; *Judge Priest* 1934; *This Side of Heaven* 1934; *Black Sheep* 1935; *The Man Who Cried Wolf* 1937; *Maytime* 1937; *Navy Blue and Gold* 1937; *The Duke of West Point* 1938; *Merrily We Live* 1938; *The Storm* 1938; *Sergeant Madden* 1939; *There's One Born Every Minute* 1942; *Buck Privates Come Home* 1947; *Fireman Save My Child* 1954
Brown, Vanessa (1928–1999) *The Foxes of Harrow* 1947; *The Ghost and Mrs Muir* 1947; *The Late George Apley* 1947; *Mother Wore Tights* 1947; *Big Jack* 1949; *The Heiress* 1949; *Tarzan and the Slave Girl* 1950; *The Bad and the Beautiful* 1952; *The Fighter* 1952; *Rosie!* 1967
Brown, Wally (1904–1961) *Girl Rush* 1944; *Step Lively* 1944; *From This Day Forward* 1946; *Holiday for Lovers* 1959; *The Absent-Minded Professor* 1961
Browne, Coral (1913–1991) *We're Going to Be Rich* 1938; *Let George Do It* 1940; *Piccadilly Incident* 1946; *The Courtneys of Curzon Street* 1947; *Beautiful Stranger* 1954; *Auntie Mame* 1958; *Go to Blazes* 1961; *The Roman Spring of Mrs Stone* 1961; *Dr Crippen* 1962; *Tamahine* 1963; *The Night of the Generals* 1966; *The Killing of Sister George* 1968; *The Ruling Class* 1972; *Theatre of Blood* 1973; *American Dreamer* 1984; *Dreamchild* 1985
Browne, Irene (1891–1965) *The Letter* 1929; *Berkeley Square* 1933; *Peg o' My Heart* 1933; *Meet Me at Dawn* 1946; *Barnacle Bill* 1957; *Serious Charge* 1959
Browne, Kathie *aka* **Brown, Kathy** (1939–2003) *Smash-Up Alley* 1972; *Happy Mother's Day... Love, George* 1973
Browne, Leslie (1958–) *The Turning Point* 1977; *Nijinsky* 1980; *Dancers* 1987
Browne, Roscoe Lee (1925–) *The Connection* 1961; *Black like Me* 1964; *Uptight* 1968; *Topaz* 1969; *The Liberation of LB Jones* 1970; *Cisco Pike* 1971; *The Cowboys* 1972; *The World's Greatest Athlete* 1973; *Uptown Saturday Night* 1974; *Logan's Run* 1976; *Nothing Personal* 1980; *Oliver & Company* 1988; *Babe* 1995; *Last Summer in the Hamptons* 1995; *The Pompatus of Love* 1995; *Dear God* 1996
Browning, Alistair *Merry Christmas Mr Lawrence* 1982; *Rain* 2001
Browning, Emily (1988–) *The Man Who Sued God* 2001; *Lemony Snicket's A Series of Unfortunate Events* 2004
Browning, Ricou (1930–) *Creature from the Black Lagoon* 1954; *Revenge of the Creature* 1955
Brubaker, Robert *Apache Rifles* 1964; *40 Guns to Apache Pass* 1966
Bruce, Betty (1920–1974) *Gypsy* 1962; *Island of Love* 1963
Bruce, Brenda (1918–1996) *While the Sun Shines* 1946; *When the Bough Breaks* 1947; *The Final Test* 1953; *Behind the Mask* 1958; *Law and Disorder* 1958; *Peeping Tom* 1960; *Nightmare* 1963; *The Uncle* 1964; *All Creatures Great and Small* 1974; *Swallows and Amazons* 1974; *The Man in the Iron Mask* 1977; *Steaming* 1985; *December Bride* 1990; *Splitting Heirs* 1993
Bruce, Carol (1919–) *Keep 'em Flying* 1941; *Planes, Trains and Automobiles* 1987
Bruce, Cheryl Lynn *Music Box* 1989; *Daughters of the Dust* 1991
Bruce, Colin *Crusoe* 1988; *The Dead Can't Lie* 1988
Bruce, David (1914–1976) *Calling Dr Death* 1943; *Can't Help Singing* 1944; *Christmas Holiday* 1944; *Salome, Where She Danced* 1945
Bruce, Nigel (1895–1953) *I Was a Spy* 1934; *The Scarlet Pimpernel* 1934; *Stand Up and Cheer!* 1934; *Treasure Island* 1934; *Becky Sharp* 1935; *The Man Who Broke the Bank at Monte Carlo* 1935; *She* 1935; *The Charge of the Light Brigade* 1936; *The Trail of the Lonesome Pine* 1936; *Under Two Flags* 1936; *The White Angel* 1936; *The Last of Mrs Cheyney* 1937; *Thunder in the City* 1937; *Kidnapped* 1938; *The Adventures of Sherlock Holmes* 1939; *The Hound of the Baskervilles* 1939; *The Rains Came* 1939; *The Blue Bird* 1940; *A Dispatch from Reuters* 1940; *Rebecca* 1940; *Susan and God* 1940; *The Chocolate Soldier* 1941; *Suspicion* 1941; *Journey for Margaret* 1942; *Roxie Hart* 1942; *Sherlock Holmes and the Secret Weapon* 1942; *Sherlock Holmes and the Voice of Terror* 1942; *This above All* 1942; *Lassie Come Home* 1943; *Sherlock Holmes Faces Death* 1943; *Sherlock Holmes in Washington* 1943; *Frenchman's*

Creek 1944; *The House of Fear* 1944; *The Pearl of Death* 1944; *The Scarlet Claw* 1944; *Sherlock Holmes and the Spider Woman* 1944; *The Corn Is Green* 1945; *Pursuit to Algiers* 1945; *Son of Lassie* 1945; *The Two Mrs Carrolls* 1945; *The Woman in Green* 1945; *Sherlock Holmes and the Secret Code* 1946; *Terror by Night* 1946; *The Exile* 1947; *Julia Misbehaves* 1948; *Bwana Devil* 1952; *Limelight* 1952; *World for Ransom* 1953

Bruce, Virginia (1910–1982) *Dangerous Corner* 1934; *The Mighty Barnum* 1934; *Escapade* 1935; *Let 'Em Have It* 1935; *Murder Man* 1935; *Born to Dance* 1936; *The Great Ziegfeld* 1936; *Wife, Doctor and Nurse* 1937; *Arsene Lupin Returns* 1938; *Bad Man of Brimstone* 1938; *There Goes My Heart* 1938; *Yellow Jack* 1938; *Hired Wife* 1940; *The Invisible Woman* 1940; *Careful, Soft Shoulder* 1942; *Pardon My Sarong* 1942; *Action in Arabia* 1944; *Brazil* 1944; *Night Has a Thousand Eyes* 1948; *Strangers When We Meet* 1960

Brücher, Christine *A la Place du Coeur* 1998; *La Ville Est Tranquille* 2000

Bruckner, Agnes (1985–) *Blue Car* 2001; *Murder by Numbers* 2002

Bruel, Patrick (1959–) *Force Majeure* 1989; *Brothers in Arms* 1990; *Lost & Found* 1999

Brühl, Daniel (1978–) *Good Bye Lenin!* 2003; *The Edukators* 2004; *Ladies in Lavender* 2004

Brühl, Heidi (1942–1991) *Captain Sindbad* 1963; *The Eiger Sanction* 1975

Brundin, Bo (1937–) *The Great Waldo Pepper* 1975; *Late for Dinner* 1991

Brunetti, Argentina *The Brothers Rico* 1957; *The Midnight Story* 1957

Bruni-Tedeschi, Valéria (1964–) *Mon Homme* 1996; *Those Who Love Me Can Take the Train* 1998; *The Colour of Lies* 1999; *Rien à Faire* 1999; *Ten Minutes Older: the Cello* 2002; *5x2* 2004

Brunius, Jacques aka **Borel, Jacques** (1906–1967) *Une Partie de Campagne* 1936; *Sea Devils* 1952; *South of Algiers* 1952

Brunning, Nancy *When Love Comes* 1998; *What Becomes of the Broken Hearted?* 1999

Bruno, Dylan (1972–) *When Trumpets Fade* 1998; *The Rage: Carrie 2* 1999; *The Simian Line* 2000; *Where the Heart Is* 2000; *The One* 2001

Brunot, André (1879–1973) *Hôtel du Nord* 1938; *Pièges* 1939; *Le Rouge et le Noir* 1954

Bruns, Philip aka **Bruns, Phil** (1931–) *The Out of Towners* 1970; *Corvette Summer* 1978; *Return of the Living Dead Part II* 1988

Bryan, Arthur Q (1899–1959) *A Wild Hare* 1940; *What's Opera, Doc?* 1957

Bryan, Dora (1924–) *No Room at the Inn* 1948; *Once upon a Dream* 1948; *Adam and Evelyne* 1949; *The Blue Lamp* 1949; *The Cure for Love* 1949; *The Interrupted Journey* 1949; *Now Barabbas Was a Robber* 1949; *Traveller's Joy* 1949; *Circle of Danger* 1950; *No Trace* 1950; *The Quiet Woman* 1950; *Something in the City* 1950; *The Gift Horse* 1951; *Lady Godiva Rides Again* 1951; *The Scarlet Thread* 1951; *Miss Robin Hood* 1952; *13 East Street* 1952; *Time Gentlemen Please!* 1952; *Women of Twilight* 1952; *The Intruder* 1953; *Mad about Men* 1954; *You Know What Sailors Are* 1954; *As Long as They're Happy* 1955; *Child in the House* 1956; *The Man Who Wouldn't Talk* 1957; *Carry On Sergeant* 1958; *Desert Mice* 1959; *Operation Bullshine* 1959; *The Night We Got the Bird* 1960; *A Taste of Honey* 1961; *The Great St Trinian's Train Robbery* 1966; *The Sandwich Man* 1966; *Two a Penny* 1968; *Hands of the Ripper* 1971; *Up the Front* 1972; *Apartment Zero* 1988

Bryan, Jane (1918–) *The Case of the Black Cat* 1936; *Confession* 1937; *Kid Galahad* 1937; *Marked Woman* 1937; *The Sisters* 1938; *A Slight Case of Murder* 1938; *Each Dawn I Die* 1939; *Invisible Stripes* 1939; *The Old Maid* 1939; *We Are Not Alone* 1939

Bryant, Joy (1976–) *Antwone Fisher* 2002; *Baadasssss!* 2003; *Honey* 2003; *The Skeleton Key* 2005

Bryant, Michael (1928–2002) *The Mind Benders* 1963; *Torture Garden* 1967; *Goodbye, Mr Chips* 1969; *Mumsy, Nanny, Sonny & Girly* 1970; *The Ruling Class* 1972; *Caravan to Vaccares* 1974; *The Miracle Maker* 1999

Bryant, Nana (1888–1955) *Atlantic Adventure* 1935; *The King Steps Out* 1936; *The Man Who Lived Twice* 1936; *Meet Nero Wolfe* 1936; *Pennies from Heaven* 1936; *The League of Frightened Men* 1937; *Man-Proof* 1937; *The Adventures of Tom Sawyer* 1938; *Her Husband's Affairs* 1947; *Possessed* 1947; *Ladies of the Chorus* 1949; *Follow the Sun: the Ben Hogan Story* 1951; *The Outcast* 1954

Bryant, William (1924–2001) *The Other Side of the Mountain* 1975; *Corvette Summer* 1978; *The Other Side of the Mountain – Part 2* 1978

Bryar, Paul (1910–1985) *Easy to Love* 1953; *The Bob Mathias Story* 1954; *Vertigo* 1958

Bryce, Scott *Stalking Laura* 1993; *Up Close & Personal* 1996

Bryggman, Larry (1938–) *Die Hard with a Vengeance* 1995; *Spy Game* 2001

Brygmann, Lars *The Inheritance* 2003; *Someone like Hodder* 2003

Bryniarski, Andrew (1969–) *Cyborg 3: The Recycler* 1994; *The Texas Chainsaw Massacre* 2003

Brynner, Yul (1915–1985) *Port of New York* 1949; *Anastasia* 1956; *The King and I* 1956; *The Ten Commandments* 1956; *The Brothers Karamazov* 1958; *The Buccaneer* 1958; *The Journey* 1959; *Once More, with Feeling* 1959; *Solomon and Sheba* 1959; *The Sound and the Fury* 1959; *The Magnificent Seven* 1960; *Surprise Package* 1960; *Le Testament d'Orphée* 1960; *Escape from Zahrain* 1962; *Taras Bulba* 1962; *Kings of the Sun* 1963; *Flight from Ashiya* 1964; *Invitation to a Gunfighter* 1964; *The Saboteur, Code Name Morituri* 1965; *Cast a Giant Shadow* 1966; *The Long Duel* 1966; *The Poppy Is Also a Flower* 1966; *Return of the Seven* 1966; *Triple Cross* 1966; *The Double Man* 1967; *Villa Rides* 1968; *The Battle of Neretva* 1969; *The File of the Golden Goose* 1969; *The Madwoman of Chaillot* 1969; *The Magic Christian* 1969; *Adios, Sabata* 1970; *Catlow* 1971; *The Light at the Edge of the World* 1971; *Romance of a Horse Thief* 1971; *Fuzz* 1972; *The Serpent* 1972; *Westworld* 1973; *The Ultimate Warrior* 1975; *Futureworld* 1976

Brynolfsson, Reine (1953–) *House of Angels* 1992; *House of Angels II: The Second Summer* 1994; *Jerusalem* 1996; *Les Misérables* 1997; *The Last Contract* 1998; *Kitchen Stories* 2003

Buccella, Maria Grazia aka **Buccella, Maria** (1940–) *The Dirty Game* 1965; *Dead Run* 1967; *Villa Rides* 1968

Bucci, Flavio (1947–) *Suspiria* 1976; *Tex and the Lord of the Deep* 1985

Buccille, Ashley (1986–) *Dusting Cliff 7* 1996; *Phenomenon* 1996

Buchanan, Edgar (1903–1979) *Too Many Husbands* 1940; *Penny Serenade* 1941; *Texas* 1941; *You Belong to Me* 1941; *The Talk of the Town* 1942; *The Desperadoes* 1943; *Bride by Mistake* 1944; *Buffalo Bill* 1944; *Abilene Town* 1945; *The Bandit of Sherwood Forest* 1946; *Framed* 1947; *The Sea of Grass* 1947; *The Black Arrow* 1948; *The Man from Colorado* 1948; *Red Canyon* 1949; *The Walking Hills* 1949; *The Big Hangover* 1950; *Cheaper by the Dozen* 1950; *Devil's Doorway* 1950; *Cave of Outlaws* 1951; *Rawhide* 1951; *The Big Trees* 1952; *Shane* 1953; *Beautiful but Dangerous* 1954; *Dawn at Socorro* 1954; *Destry* 1954; *Human Desire* 1954; *Make Haste to Live* 1954; *Rage at Dawn* 1955; *Wichita* 1955; *Come Next Spring* 1956; *Day of the Bad Man* 1958; *The Sheepman* 1958; *Edge of Eternity* 1959; *Tammy Tell Me True* 1961; *Ride the High Country* 1962; *A Ticklish Affair* 1963; *The Man from Button Willow* 1965; *The Rounders* 1965; *Gunpoint* 1966; *Welcome to Hard Times* 1967; *Angel in My Pocket* 1968; *Benji* 1974

Buchanan, Ian (1957–) *The Cool Surface* 1993; *Panic Room* 2002

Buchanan, Jack (1891–1957) *Monte Carlo* 1930; *When Knights Were Bold* 1936; *Smash and Grab* 1937; *The Gang's All Here* 1939; *The Band Wagon* 1953; *As Long as They're Happy* 1955; *The Diary of Major Thompson* 1955; *Josephine and Men* 1955

Buchanan, Robert *That Sinking Feeling* 1979; *Gregory's Girl* 1980

Buchanan, Simone (1968–) *Run, Rebecca, Run* 1981; *Shame* 1987

Buchholz, Horst (1932–2003) *Tiger Bay* 1959; *The Magnificent Seven* 1960; *Fanny* 1961; *One, Two, Three* 1961; *The Empty Canvas* 1963; *Nine Hours to Rama* 1963; *Cervantes* 1968; *The Great Waltz* 1972; *The Catamount Killing* 1974; *Raid on Entebbe* 1977; *The Amazing Captain Nemo* 1978; *Avalanche Express* 1979; *From Hell to Victory* 1979; *Sahara* 1983; *Code Name: Emerald* 1985; *Aces: Iron Eagle III* 1992; *Faraway, So Close* 1993; *Life Is Beautiful* 1997; *The Enemy* 2000

Buck, David (1936–1989) *The Mummy's Shroud* 1966; *Deadfall* 1968; *Mosquito Squadron* 1968

Buckler, John (1906–1936) *The Black Room* 1935; *Tarzan Escapes* 1936

Buckley, Betty (1947–) *Carrie* 1976; *Tender Mercies* 1982; *Wild Thing* 1987; *Another Woman* 1988; *Frantic* 1988; *Simply Irresistible* 1999

Buckley, Keith (1941–) *Spring and Port Wine* 1969; *Dr Phibes Rises Again* 1972; *Hanover Street* 1979; *Gunbus* 1986; *Half Moon Street* 1986

Bueno, Gustavo *The City and the Dogs* 1985; *The Motorcycle Diaries* 2004

Buetel, Jack (1915–1989) *The Outlaw* 1943; *Best of the Badmen* 1951; *The Half-Breed* 1952; *Rose of Cimarron* 1952

Buferd, Marilyn (1925–1990) *Les Belles de Nuit* 1952; *The Unearthly* 1957

Buffalo Bill Jr aka **Wilsey, Jay** (1896–1961) *'Neath the Arizona Skies* 1934; *Texas Terror* 1935

Bugallo, Celso *Mondays in the Sun* 2002; *The Sea Inside* 2004

Buggy, Niall *Zardoz* 1973; *King David* 1985

Buhagiar, Valerie (1964–) *Roadkill* 1989; *Highway 61* 1992

Buhr, Gérard (1928–1988) *Bob Le Flambeur* 1955; *Five Days One Summer* 1982

Bujeau, Christian *Les Visiteurs 2: Les Couloirs du Temps* 1998; *The Cow and the President* 2000

Bujold, Geneviève (1942–) *La Guerre Est Finie* 1966; *King of Hearts* 1966; *The Thief of Paris* 1967; *Anne of the Thousand Days* 1969; *Act of the Heart* 1970; *The Trojan Women* 1971; *Kamouraska* 1973; *Earthquake* 1974; *Alex and the Gypsy* 1976; *Obsession* 1976; *Swashbuckler* 1976; *Another Man, Another Chance* 1977; *Coma* 1977; *Murder by Decree* 1978; *The Last Flight of Noah's Ark* 1980; *Monsignor* 1982; *Choose Me* 1984; *Tightrope* 1984; *Trouble in Mind* 1985; *Dead Ringers* 1988; *The Moderns* 1988; *A Paper Wedding* 1989; *The Dance Goes On* 1990; *False Identity* 1990; *Oh, What a Night* 1992; *The Adventures of Pinocchio* 1996; *The House of Yes* 1997; *Last Night* 1998; *You Can Thank Me Later* 1998

Bull, Peter (1912–1984) *Saraband for Dead Lovers* 1948; *The African Queen* 1951; *Dr Strangelove, or How I Learned to Stop Worrying and Love the Bomb* 1963; *The Old Dark House* 1963; *Licensed to Kill* 1965; *Doctor Dolittle* 1967; *The Tempest* 1979

Bull, Richard (1924–) *The Secret Life of an American Wife* 1968; *A Different Story* 1978

Bulloch, Jeremy aka **Bullock, Jeremy** *The Cat Gang* 1959; *Summer Holiday* 1962; *Hoffman* 1970; *Can You Keep It Up for a Week?* 1974

Bullock, Sandra (1964–) *Who Shot Patakango?* 1989; *Love Potion No 9* 1992; *Me and the Mob* 1992; *When the Party's Over* 1992; *Demolition Man* 1993; *The Thing Called Love* 1993; *The Vanishing* 1993; *Wrestling Ernest Hemingway* 1993; *Speed* 1994; *The Net* 1995; *While You Were Sleeping* 1995; *In Love and War* 1996; *Stolen Hearts* 1996; *A Time to Kill* 1996; *Speed 2: Cruise Control* 1997; *Forces of Nature* 1998; *Hope Floats* 1998; *Practical Magic* 1998; *The Prince of Egypt* 1998; *Gun Shy* 2000; *Miss Congeniality* 2000; *28 Days* 2000; *Divine Secrets of the Ya-Ya Sisterhood* 2002; *Murder by Numbers* 2002; *Two Weeks Notice* 2002; *Crash* 2004; *Miss Congeniality 2: Armed & Fabulous* 2005

Buloff, Joseph (1899–1985) *Let's Make Music* 1940; *Carnegie Hall* 1947; *The Loves of Carmen* 1948; *A Kiss in the Dark* 1949; *Silk Stockings* 1957

Bunce, Alan (1902–1965) *The Last Mile* 1959; *Sunrise at Campobello* 1960; *Homicidal* 1961

Bunce, Stuart *Bring Me the Head of Mavis Davis* 1997; *Regeneration* 1997; *The Lost Lover* 1999

Bunel, Marie *Arsène Lupin* 2004; *The Chorus* 2004

Bunker, Edward aka **Bunker, Eddie** (1933–) *Reservoir Dogs* 1991; *Animal Factory* 2000

Bunnage, Avis (1923–1990) *The L-Shaped Room* 1962; *The Loneliness of the Long Distance Runner* 1962; *Sparrows Can't Sing* 1962; *What a Crazy World* 1963; *Rotten to the Core* 1965; *The Whisperers* 1967; *No Surrender* 1986; *The Krays* 1990

Bunston, Herbert (1874–1935) *The Last of Mrs Cheyney* 1929; *Dracula* 1931; *The Moonstone* 1934

Buono, Cara (1974–) *The Cowboy Way* 1994; *Kicking and Screaming* 1995; *Killer: a Journal of Murder* 1995; *Next Stop Wonderland* 1998; *Hulk* 2003

Buono, Victor (1938–1982) *What Ever Happened to Baby Jane?* 1962; *4 for Texas* 1963; *Hush... Hush, Sweet Charlotte* 1964; *Robin and the 7 Hoods* 1964; *The Strangler* 1964; *Young Dillinger* 1965; *The Silencers* 1966; *Who's Minding the Mint?* 1967; *Beneath the Planet of the Apes* 1969; *The Wrath of God* 1972; *Arnold* 1973; *The Evil* 1978; *The Man with Bogart's Face* 1980

Bupp, Tommy aka **Bupp, Tom** (1925–1983) *It's a Gift* 1934; *Hey! Hey! USA* 1938

Burden, Hugh (1913–1985) *One of Our Aircraft Is Missing* 1942; *The Way Ahead* 1944; *Fame Is the Spur* 1947; *Ghost Ship* 1952; *No Love for Johnnie* 1960; *The Secret Partner* 1961; *Blood from the Mummy's Tomb* 1971; *The Ruling Class* 1972; *The House in Nightmare Park* 1973

Burfield, Kim *Bloomfield* 1969; *Treasure Island* 1972

Burgard, Christopher *Twice Dead* 1988; *84 Charlie Mopic* 1989

Burgers, Michele *Friends* 1993; *Jump the Gun* 1996

Burgess, Dorothy (1907–1961) *In Old Arizona* 1929; *Taxi!* 1932; *Hold Your Man* 1933; *Ladies They Talk About* 1933; *Village Tale* 1935

Buric, Zlatko (1953–) *Pusher* 1996; *Bleeder* 1999

Burke, Alfred (1918–) *Bitter Victory* 1957; *The Angry Silence* 1960; *Children of the Damned* 1964; *The Nanny* 1965; *The Night Caller* 1965; *Guns in the Heather* 1969; *One Day in the Life of Ivan Denisovich* 1971; *Kim* 1984

Burke, Billie (1885–1970) *A Bill of Divorcement* 1932; *Christopher Strong* 1933; *Dinner at Eight* 1933; *Only Yesterday* 1933; *Finishing School* 1934; *Forsaking All Others* 1934; *After Office Hours* 1935; *Becky Sharp* 1935; *Splendor* 1935; *Craig's Wife* 1936; *Piccadilly Jim* 1936; *The Bride Wore Red* 1937; *Navy Blue and Gold* 1937; *Parnell* 1937; *Topper* 1937; *Everybody Sing* 1938; *Merrily We Live* 1938; *The Young in Heart* 1938; *Eternally Yours* 1939; *Remember?* 1939; *Topper Takes a Trip* 1939; *The Wizard of Oz* 1939; *Zenobia* 1939; *The Ghost Comes Home* 1940; *Irene* 1940; *The Man Who Came to Dinner* 1941; *Topper Returns* 1941; *They All Kissed the Bride* 1942; *The Cheaters* 1945; *And Baby Makes Three* 1949; *The Barkleys of Broadway* 1949; *Father of the Bride* 1950; *Father's Little Dividend* 1951; *The Young Philadelphians* 1959; *Sergeant Rutledge* 1960

Burke, Billy *Jane Austen's Mafia* 1998; *Wes Craven's Don't Look Down* 1998; *Without Limits* 1998; *Komodo* 1999; *Ladder 49* 2004

Burke, Brandon *The Odd Angry Shot* 1979; *Mushrooms* 1995

Burke, Georgia (1880–1985) *Anna Lucasta* 1958; *The Cool World* 1963

Burke, James (1886–1968) *Lady by Choice* 1934; *Great Guy* 1936; *The Dawn Patrol* 1938; *Ellery Queen Master Detective* 1940; *Little Nellie Kelly* 1940; *The Saint Takes Over* 1940

Burke, Kathleen (1913–1980) *Island of Lost Souls* 1932; *Murders in the Zoo* 1933; *The Lives of a Bengal Lancer* 1935

Burke, Kathy (1964–) *Scrubbers* 1982; *Eat the Rich* 1987; *Nil by Mouth* 1997; *Dancing at Lughnasa* 1998; *Elizabeth* 1998; *This Year's Love* 1999; *Kevin & Perry Go Large* 2000; *Love, Honour and Obey* 2000; *The Martins* 2001; *Anita & Me* 2002; *Once upon a Time in the Midlands* 2002

Burke, Marie (1894–1980) *Odette* 1950; *Miracle in Soho* 1957

Burke, Marylouise *Series 7: the Contenders* 2001; *Sideways* 2004

Burke, Michelle aka **Thomas, Michelle Rene** (1973–) *Coneheads* 1993; *Dazed and Confused* 1993; *Midnight in St Petersburg* 1995

Burke, Patricia (1917–2003) *While I Live* 1947; *Dilemma* 1962; *The Impersonator* 1962

Burke, Paul (1926–) *Della* 1965; *Valley of the Dolls* 1967; *The Thomas Crown Affair* 1968; *Daddy's Gone A-Hunting* 1969; *Once You Kiss a Stranger* 1969; *Psychic Killer* 1975

Burke, Robert aka **Burke, Robert John** (1961–) *The Unbelievable Truth* 1989; *Rambling Rose* 1991; *Dust Devil* 1992; *Simple Men* 1992; *A Far Off Place* 1993; *RoboCop 3* 1993; *Killer: a Journal of Murder* 1995; *Fled* 1996; *If Lucy Fell* 1996; *Stephen King's Thinner* 1996; *Hide and Seek* 2005

Burke, Simon (1961–) *The Devil's Playground* 1976; *The Irishman* 1978; *The Clinic* 1982; *Slate, Wyn & Me* 1987; *Passion* 1999

Burke, Walter (1908–1984) *Jack the Giant Killer* 1962; *The Three Stooges Go around the World in a Daze* 1963; *The Stone Killer* 1973

Burkley, Dennis (1945–) *Heroes* 1977; *Mask* 1985; *Murphy's Romance* 1985; *Pass the Ammo* 1988; *Lambada* 1990; *The Doors* 1991; *Son in Law* 1993; *Tin Cup* 1996; *Possums* 1998
Burlinson, Tom (1956–) *The Man from Snowy River* 1982; *Phar Lap* 1983; *Flesh + Blood* 1985; *Windrider* 1986; *The Time Guardian* 1987; *Return to Snowy River* 1988
Burmester, Leo (1944–) *Odd Jobs* 1986; *The Abyss* 1989; *A Perfect World* 1993; *The Neon Bible* 1995; *Old Man* 1997
Burnaby, Davy (1881–1949) *A Shot in the Dark* 1933; *Boys Will Be Boys* 1935; *Song of the Road* 1937
Burnett, Carol (1933–) *Pete 'n' Tillie* 1972; *The Front Page* 1974; *A Wedding* 1978; *Friendly Fire* 1979; *HEALTH* 1980; *Chu Chu and the Philly Flash* 1981; *The Four Seasons* 1981; *Annie* 1982; *Between Friends* 1983; *Noises Off* 1992; *The Marriage Fool* 1998
Burnette, Olivia (1977–) *Planes, Trains and Automobiles* 1987; *Hard Promises* 1991; *A Murderous Affair* 1992; *Eye for an Eye* 1995
Burnette, Smiley (1911–1967) *Billy the Kid Returns* 1938; *Down Mexico Way* 1941; *Last of the Pony Riders* 1953; *On Top of Old Smoky* 1953
Burnham, Edward *To Sir, with Love* 1967; *The Abominable Dr Phibes* 1971
Burnham, Jeremy *Bachelor of Hearts* 1958; *Law and Disorder* 1958
Burns, Bob (1893–1956) *The Big Broadcast of 1937* 1936; *Rhythm on the Range* 1936; *Waikiki Wedding* 1937; *Wells Fargo* 1937; *Radio City Revels* 1938; *Belle of the Yukon* 1944
Burns, Carol (1947–) *Bad Blood* 1982; *Dusty* 1982
Burns, Catherine *aka* **Burns, Cathy** (1945–) *Last Summer* 1969; *Red Sky at Morning* 1971
Burns, David (1902–1971) *Smash and Grab* 1937; *Hey! Hey! USA* 1938; *The Gang's All Here* 1939; *The Saint in London* 1939; *Knock on Wood* 1954; *It's Always Fair Weather* 1955; *Let's Make Love* 1960; *Who Is Harry Kellerman, and Why Is He Saying Those Terrible Things about Me?* 1971
Burns, Edward (1968–) *The Brothers McMullen* 1995; *She's the One* 1996; *No Looking Back* 1998; *Saving Private Ryan* 1998; *Sidewalks of New York* 2000; *15 Minutes* 2001; *Ash Wednesday* 2002; *Confidence* 2002; *Life or Something like It* 2002
Burns, George (1896–1996) *The Big Broadcast* 1932; *International House* 1933; *Six of a Kind* 1934; *We're Not Dressing* 1934; *The Big Broadcast of 1936* 1935; *The Big Broadcast of 1937* 1936; *A Damsel in Distress* 1937; *College Swing* 1938; *Honolulu* 1939; *The Sunshine Boys* 1975; *Oh, God!* 1977; *Sgt Pepper's Lonely Hearts Club Band* 1978; *Going in Style* 1979; *Just You and Me, Kid* 1979; *Oh God! Book II* 1980; *Oh, God! You Devil* 1984; *18 Again!* 1988; *Radioland Murders* 1994
Burns, Heather (1974–) *Miss Congeniality* 2000; *Two Weeks Notice* 2002; *Miss Congeniality 2: Armed & Fabulous* 2005
Burns, Jack (1933–) *The Night They Raided Minsky's* 1968; *Sour Grapes* 1998
Burns, Jere (1954–) *Hit List* 1988; *Greedy* 1994; *My Giant* 1998; *Life-Size* 2000; *Crocodile Dundee in Los Angeles* 2001
Burns, Larry *The Hornet's Nest* 1955; *Count Five and Die* 1957
Burns, Marilyn (1956–) *The Texas Chain Saw Massacre* 1974; *Eaten Alive* 1976
Burns, Marion (1907–1993) *Me and My Gal* 1932; *The Dawn Rider* 1935; *Paradise Canyon* 1935
Burns, Mark (1936–) *The Charge of the Light Brigade* 1968; *The Adventures of Gerard* 1970; *The Virgin and the Gypsy* 1970; *Death in Venice* 1971; *A Time for Loving* 1971; *The Maids* 1974; *The Bitch* 1979; *Bullseye!* 1990
Burns, Martha *Never Talk to Strangers* 1995; *Long Day's Journey into Night* 1996; *The Life before This* 1999
Burns, Megan *Liam* 2000; *28 Days Later...* 2002
Burns, Michael (1947–) *40 Guns to Apache Pass* 1966; *Journey to Shiloh* 1967; *Stranger on the Run* 1967; *That Cold Day in the Park* 1969; *Thumb Tripping* 1972; *Santee* 1973
Burns, Paul E (1881–1967) *The Woman on Pier 13* 1949; *Montana* 1950
Burr, Raymond (1917–1993) *Without Reservations* 1946; *Desperate* 1947; *Pitfall* 1948; *Raw Deal* 1948; *Ruthless* 1948; *Sleep, My Love* 1948; *Station West* 1948; *Walk a Crooked Mile* 1948; *Black Magic* 1949; *Bride of Vengeance* 1949; *Love Happy* 1949; *Red Light* 1949; *Key to the City* 1950; *His Kind of Woman* 1951; *M* 1951; *A Place in the Sun* 1951; *The Whip Hand* 1951; *Horizons West* 1952; *Mara Maru* 1952; *Meet Danny Wilson* 1952; *The Bandits of Corsica* 1953; *The Blue Gardenia* 1953; *Fort Algiers* 1953; *Serpent of the Nile* 1953; *Tarzan and the She-Devil* 1953; *Casanova's Big Night* 1954; *Godzilla* 1954; *Gorilla at Large* 1954; *Khyber Patrol* 1954; *Passion* 1954; *Rear Window* 1954; *Thunder Pass* 1954; *Count Three and Pray* 1955; *A Man Alone* 1955; *You're Never Too Young* 1955; *The Brass Legend* 1956; *A Cry in the Night* 1956; *Great Day in the Morning* 1956; *Secret of Treasure Mountain* 1956; *Affair in Havana* 1957; *Crime of Passion* 1957; *Desire in the Dust* 1960; *New Face in Hell* 1968; *Tomorrow Never Comes* 1977; *Out of the Blue* 1980; *Airplane II: the Sequel* 1982; *The Return of Godzilla* 1984; *Delirious* 1991
Burrell, Sheila (1922–) *The Rossiter Case* 1950; *Cloudburst* 1951; *Colonel March Investigates* 1953; *Paranoiac* 1963; *The Woodlanders* 1997
Burress, Hedy (1973–) *Foxfire* 1996; *If These Walls Could Talk* 1996; *Cabin by the Lake* 2000
Burroughs, Jackie (1939–) *Heavy Metal* 1981; *The Grey Fox* 1982; *The Care Bears Movie* 1985; *Hemoglobin* 1997; *Willard* 2003
Burroughs, William S (1914–1997) *Chappaqua* 1966; *Drugstore Cowboy* 1989
Burrows, Saffron (1973–) *Welcome II the Terrordome* 1994; *Circle of Friends* 1995; *Hotel de Love* 1996; *Deep Blue Sea* 1999; *The Loss of Sexual Innocence* 1999; *Miss Julie* 1999; *Timecode* 1999; *Wing Commander* 1999; *Gangster No 1* 2000; *Enigma* 2001; *Hotel* 2001; *Tempted* 2001; *Frida* 2002; *Troy* 2004
Burruano, Luigi Maria *The Hundred Steps* 2000; *Benzina* 2001
Burstyn, Ellen *aka* **McRae, Ellen** (1932–) *For Those Who Think Young* 1964; *Goodbye Charlie* 1964; *Alex in Wonderland* 1970; *The Last Picture Show* 1971; *The King of Marvin Gardens* 1972; *The Exorcist* 1973; *Alice Doesn't Live Here Anymore* 1974; *Harry and Tonto* 1974; *Providence* 1977; *A Dream of Passion* 1978; *Same Time, Next Year* 1978; *Resurrection* 1980; *Silence of the North* 1981; *The Ambassador* 1984; *Surviving* 1985; *Twice in a Lifetime* 1985; *Hanna's War* 1988; *Dying Young* 1991; *The Cemetery Club* 1993; *Shattered Trust* 1993; *Getting Gotti* 1994; *When a Man Loves a Woman* 1994; *The Baby-Sitter's Club* 1995; *How to Make an American Quilt* 1995; *Roommates* 1995; *The Spitfire Grill* 1996; *Liar* 1997; *Playing by Heart* 1998; *You Can Thank Me Later* 1998; *Night Ride Home* 1999; *Walking across Egypt* 1999; *Requiem for a Dream* 2000; *The Yards* 2000; *Divine Secrets of the Ya-Ya Sisterhood* 2002; *Red Dragon* 2002
Burton, Clarence (1882–1933) *The Navigator* 1924; *The Unholy Three* 1930
Burton, Corey (1955–) *The Hunchback of Notre Dame* 1996; *Atlantis: the Lost Empire* 2001; *Cinderella II: Dreams Come True* 2002; *Return to Never Land* 2002
Burton, Frederick (1871–1957) *The Big Trail* 1930; *An American Tragedy* 1931; *One Way Passage* 1932; *The Wet Parade* 1932; *The Man from Dakota* 1940
Burton, Kate (1957–) *Big Trouble in Little China* 1986; *August* 1995; *Swimfan* 2002; *Unfaithful* 2002
Burton, LeVar (1957–) *The Hunter* 1980; *Star Trek: Generations* 1994; *Star Trek: First Contact* 1996; *Star Trek: Insurrection* 1998; *Star Trek: Nemesis* 2002
Burton, Martin (1904–1976) *Ladies' Man* 1931; *When Ladies Meet* 1933
Burton, Norman *aka* **Burton, Normann** (1923–2003) *Diamonds Are Forever* 1971; *Save the Tiger* 1973; *The Terminal Man* 1974; *The Reincarnation of Peter Proud* 1975; *The Gumball Rally* 1976; *Scorchy* 1976; *Mausoleum* 1983; *Crimes of Passion* 1984; *Bloodsport* 1987
Burton, Peter *What the Butler Saw* 1950; *The Wooden Horse* 1950; *Dr No* 1962
Burton, Richard (1925–1984) *The Last Days of Dolwyn* 1949; *Now Barabbas Was a Robber* 1949; *Waterfront* 1950; *Green Grow the Rushes* 1951; *My Cousin Rachel* 1952; *The Desert Rats* 1953; *The Robe* 1953; *Prince of Players* 1955; *The Rains of Ranchipur* 1955; *Alexander the Great* 1956; *Bitter Victory* 1957; *Sea Wife* 1957; *Look Back in Anger* 1959; *The Bramble Bush* 1960; *Ice Palace* 1960; *A Midsummer Night's Dream* 1961; *The Longest Day* 1962; *Cleopatra* 1963; *The VIPs* 1963; *Becket* 1964; *Hamlet* 1964; *The Night of the Iguana* 1964; *The Sandpiper* 1965; *The Spy Who Came in from the Cold* 1965; *What's New, Pussycat?* 1965; *Who's Afraid of Virginia Woolf?* 1966; *The Comedians* 1967; *Doctor Faustus* 1967; *The Taming of the Shrew* 1967; *Boom* 1968; *Candy* 1968; *Anne of the Thousand Days* 1969; *Staircase* 1969; *Where Eagles Dare* 1969; *Raid on Rommel* 1971; *Under Milk Wood* 1971; *Villain* 1971; *The Assassination of Trotsky* 1972; *Bluebeard* 1972; *Hammersmith Is Out* 1972; *Massacre in Rome* 1973; *Brief Encounter* 1974; *The Klansman* 1974; *The Voyage* 1974; *Equus* 1977; *Exorcist II: The Heretic* 1977; *Absolution* 1978; *Breakthrough* 1978; *The Medusa Touch* 1978; *The Wild Geese* 1978; *Lovespell* 1979; *Circle of Two* 1980; *Wagner* 1983; *Nineteen Eighty-Four* 1984
Burton, Robert (1895–1964) *Above and Beyond* 1952; *Desperate Search* 1952; *Confidentially Connie* 1953; *Cry of the Hunted* 1953; *The Girl Who Had Everything* 1953; *A Man Called Peter* 1955; *The Brass Legend* 1956; *The Hired Gun* 1957; *I Was a Teenage Frankenstein* 1957; *The Gallant Hours* 1960
Burton, Tony *Assault on Precinct 13* 1976; *The Bingo Long Travelling All-Stars and Motor Kings* 1976; *Heroes* 1977; *Rocky II* 1979; *Inside Moves: the Guys from Max's Bar* 1980; *Rocky IV* 1985; *Rocky V* 1990; *Mission of Justice* 1992
Burton, Wendell (1947–) *The Sterile Cuckoo* 1969; *Fortune and Men's Eyes* 1971
Burtwell, Frederick (1900–1948) *Dr Syn* 1937; *The Silver Fleet* 1943; *I'll Be Your Sweetheart* 1945
Bury, Sean (1954–) *Friends* 1971; *Paul and Michelle* 1974
Buryak, Zoya (1966–) *The Cold Summer of 1953* 1987; *The Life and Extraordinary Adventures of Private Ivan Chonkin* 1994; *Checkpoint* 1998
Busby, Tom (1936–2003) *During One Night* 1961; *Heavenly Pursuits* 1986
Buscemi, Steve (1957–) *Parting Glances* 1985; *Heart* 1987; *Kiss Daddy Good Night* 1987; *Call Me* 1988; *Heart of Midnight* 1988; *Bloodhounds of Broadway* 1989; *King of New York* 1989; *Mystery Train* 1989; *New York Stories* 1989; *Slaves of New York* 1989; *Miller's Crossing* 1990; *Barton Fink* 1991; *Billy Bathgate* 1991; *Reservoir Dogs* 1991; *Tales from the Darkside: the Movie* 1991; *Zandalee* 1991; *CrissCross* 1992; *In the Soup* 1992; *Me and the Mob* 1992; *The Last Outlaw* 1993; *Motherhood* 1993; *Rising Sun* 1993; *Twenty Bucks* 1993; *Airheads* 1994; *Floundering* 1994; *Pulp Fiction* 1994; *Somebody to Love* 1994; *Desperado* 1995; *Fargo* 1995; *Kansas City* 1995; *Living in Oblivion* 1995; *Things to Do in Denver When You're Dead* 1995; *Escape from LA* 1996; *The Search for One-Eye Jimmy* 1996; *Trees Lounge* 1996; *The Big Lebowski* 1997; *Con Air* 1997; *The Real Blonde* 1997; *Armageddon* 1998; *The Impostors* 1998; *Big Daddy* 1999; *Animal Factory* 2000; *28 Days* 2000; *Domestic Disturbance* 2001; *Double Whammy* 2001; *Final Fantasy: the Spirits Within* 2001; *Ghost World* 2001; *Monsters, Inc* 2001; *The Laramie Project* 2002; *Mr Deeds* 2002; *SPYkids 2: the Island of Lost Dreams* 2002; *Coffee and Cigarettes* 2003; *Home on the Range* 2004
Busch, Ernst (1900–1980) *Kameradschaft* 1931; *Kühle Wampe* 1931
Busch, Mae (1897–1946) *Foolish Wives* 1920; *The Unholy Three* 1925; *Fazil* 1928; *Alibi* 1929; *Their First Mistake* 1932; *Sons of the Desert* 1933; *Oliver the Eighth* 1934; *Them Thar Hills!* 1934; *Tit for Tat* 1934; *The Bohemian Girl* 1936
Busey, Gary *aka* **Busey, Garey** (1944–) *The Last American Hero* 1973; *The Lolly-Madonna War* 1973; *Thunderbolt and Lightfoot* 1974; *The Gumball Rally* 1976; *A Star Is Born* 1976; *Big Wednesday* 1978; *The Buddy Holly Story* 1978; *Straight Time* 1978; *Carny* 1980; *Foolin' Around* 1980; *Barbarosa* 1982; *DC Cab* 1983; *Insignificance* 1985; *Silver Bullet* 1985; *Eye of the Tiger* 1986; *Let's Get Harry* 1986; *Bulletproof* 1987; *Lethal Weapon* 1987; *Hider in the House* 1989; *Act of Piracy* 1990; *Predator 2* 1990; *My Heroes Have Always Been Cowboys* 1991; *Point Break* 1991; *Under Siege* 1992; *Rookie of the Year* 1993; *Chasers* 1994; *Drop Zone* 1994; *Surviving the Game* 1994; *Acts of Love* 1995; *Black Sheep* 1996; *Lethal Tender* 1996; *Lost Highway* 1996; *Sticks and Stones* 1996; *Diary of a Serial Killer* 1997; *Fear and Loathing in Las Vegas* 1998; *Soldier* 1998; *Too Hard to Die* 1998; *Universal Soldier 2: Brothers in Arms* 1998; *Universal Soldier 3: Unfinished Business* 1998; *Gang Law* 1999; *Jacob Two Two Meets the Hooded Fang* 1999; *A Crack in the Floor* 2000; *G-Men from Hell* 2000
Busey, Jake (1972–) *SFW* 1994; *Starship Troopers* 1997; *Home Fries* 1998; *Held Up* 1999; *Tomcats* 2000; *Identity* 2003; *Christmas with the Kranks* 2004
Busfield, Timothy (1960–) *Revenge of the Nerds* 1984; *Field of Dreams* 1989; *Sneakers* 1992; *Murder between Friends* 1993; *The Skateboard Kid* 1993; *Striking Distance* 1993; *Little Big League* 1994; *Kidnapped* 1995; *First Kid* 1996; *Buffalo Soldiers* 1997; *Trucks* 1997; *Erasable You* 1998; *National Security* 2002
Bush, Billy Green *aka* **Bush, Billy "Green"** (1935–) *Five Easy Pieces* 1970; *Welcome Home, Soldier Boys* 1971; *The Culpepper Cattle Co* 1972; *Electra Glide in Blue* 1973; *Alice Doesn't Live Here Anymore* 1974; *The Jericho Mile* 1979; *Tom Horn* 1980; *The River* 1984; *Critters* 1986
Bush, Grand L *aka* **Bush, Grand** (1955–) *Hard Feelings* 1981; *Freejack* 1992
Bush, James (1907–1987) *The Arizonian* 1935; *The Return of Peter Grimm* 1935; *Strangers All* 1935; *You Can't Cheat an Honest Man* 1939
Bushell, Anthony (1904–1997) *Disraeli* 1929; *Journey's End* 1930; *Five Star Final* 1931; *Crime on the Hill* 1933; *The Ghoul* 1933; *The Scarlet Pimpernel* 1934; *Dusty Ermine* 1936; *Dark Journey* 1937; *The Return of the Scarlet Pimpernel* 1937; *The Arsenal Stadium Mystery* 1939; *The Miniver Story* 1950; *The Long Dark Hall* 1951; *The Red Beret* 1953; *The Black Knight* 1954; *The Purple Plain* 1954; *The Battle of the River Plate* 1956; *The Black Tent* 1956; *Bitter Victory* 1957; *A Night to Remember* 1958; *The Wind Cannot Read* 1958
Bushman, Ralph *aka* **Bushman Jr, Francis X** (1903–1978) *Our Hospitality* 1923; *Four Sons* 1928
Busia, Akosua (1968–) *The Color Purple* 1985; *Native Son* 1986
Bussières, Pascale (1968–) *Sonatine* 1984; *When Night Is Falling* 1995; *The Twilight of the Ice Nymphs* 1997; *The Five Senses* 1999; *Girls Can't Swim* 1999; *XChange* 2000; *Petites Coupures* 2002
Bussières, Raymond (1907–1982) *Les Portes de la Nuit* 1946; *Casque d'Or* 1952; *Gates of Paris* 1957; *Paris When It Sizzles* 1964
Busta Rhymes (1972–) *The Rugrats Movie* 1998; *Finding Forrester* 2000; *Shaft* 2000; *Narc* 2001; *Halloween: Resurrection* 2002
Butel, Mitchell *Dark City* 1998; *Strange Fits of Passion* 1999; *The Bank* 2001
Butler, David (1894–1979) *7th Heaven* 1927; *The Corpse* 1969
Butler, Gerard (1969–) *Mrs Brown* 1997; *Fast Food* 1998; *One More Kiss* 1999; *Dracula 2001* 2000; *Shooters* 2000; *Reign of Fire* 2001; *Dear Frankie* 2003; *Lara Croft Tomb Raider: the Cradle of Life* 2003; *Timeline* 2003; *The Phantom of the Opera* 2004
Butler, Jean (1971–) *The Brylcreem Boys* 1996; *Goldfish Memory* 2003
Butler, Jimmy (1921–1945) *No Greater Glory* 1934; *Romance in Manhattan* 1934
Butler, Josephine *Out of Depth* 1998; *The Lawless Heart* 2001
Butler, Tom *Confidential* 1986; *Scanners II: The New Order* 1991; *Ernest Rides Again* 1993
Butler, William *Friday the 13th Part VII: the New Blood* 1988; *Leatherface: the Texas Chainsaw Massacre III* 1990; *Night of the Living Dead* 1990
Butler, Yancy (1970–) *Hard Target* 1993; *Drop Zone* 1994; *Fast Money* 1995; *Let It Be Me* 1995; *Doomsday Man* 1998
Butrick, Merritt (1959–1989) *Star Trek II: the Wrath of Khan* 1982; *Star Trek III: the Search for Spock* 1984; *Shy People* 1987
Butterworth, Charles (1896–1946) *Illicit* 1931; *The Mad Genius* 1931; *Love Me Tonight* 1932; *Penthouse* 1933; *Bulldog Drummond Strikes Back* 1934; *The Cat and the Fiddle* 1934; *Forsaking All Others* 1934; *Magnificent Obsession* 1935; *The Moon's Our Home* 1936; *Rainbow on the River* 1936; *Every Day's a Holiday* 1937; *Swing High, Swing Low* 1937; *The Boys from Syracuse* 1940; *Second Chorus* 1940; *Road Show* 1941; *This Is*

the Army 1943; *The Bermuda Mystery* 1944

Butterworth, Donna *The Family Jewels* 1965; *Paradise, Hawaiian Style* 1966

Butterworth, Peter (1919–1979) *Mr Drake's Duck* 1950; *tom thumb* 1958; *Live Now – Pay Later* 1962; *Doctor in Distress* 1963; *Carry On Cowboy* 1965; *Carry On – Don't Lose Your Head* 1966; *Carry On Follow That Camel* 1967; *Carry On Doctor* 1968; *Carry On Camping* 1969; *Bless This House* 1972; *Carry On Abroad* 1972; *Carry On Girls* 1973; *Carry On Dick* 1974; *Carry On Behind* 1975; *Carry On England* 1976; *Carry On Emmannuelle* 1978

Buttons, Red (1919–) *Sayonara* 1957; *Imitation General* 1958; *The Big Circus* 1959; *Five Weeks in a Balloon* 1962; *Gay Purr-ee* 1962; *Hatari!* 1962; *The Longest Day* 1962; *A Ticklish Affair* 1963; *Your Cheatin' Heart* 1964; *Harlow* 1965; *Up from the Beach* 1965; *Stagecoach* 1966; *They Shoot Horses, Don't They?* 1969; *Who Killed Mary Whats'ername?* 1971; *The Poseidon Adventure* 1972; *Gable and Lombard* 1976; *Pete's Dragon* 1977; *Viva Knievel!* 1977; *CHOMPS* 1979; *When Time Ran Out* 1980; *Leave 'em Laughing* 1981; *Reunion at Fairborough* 1985; *18 Again!* 1988; *The Ambulance* 1990; *It Could Happen to You* 1994; *The Story of Us* 1999

Buttram, Pat (1917–1994) *Riders in the Sky* 1949; *Mule Train* 1950; *Valley of Fire* 1951; *Blue Canadian Rockies* 1952; *Twilight of Honor* 1963; *Roustabout* 1964; *Back to the Future Part III* 1990

Buy, Margherita (1962–) *Il Cielo è Sempre Più Blu* 1995; *Not of This World* 1998; *Le Fate Ignoranti* 2001; *The Best Day of My Life* 2002

Buzzi, Ruth (1936–) *Cactus Jack* 1979; *Skatetown, USA* 1979; *Bad Guys* 1986; *Pound Puppies and the Legend of Big Paw* 1988; *Wishful Thinking* 1990

Byers, Kate *Staggered* 1993; *Career Girls* 1997

Bygraves, Max (1922–) *Tom Brown's Schooldays* 1951; *Charley Moon* 1956; *A Cry from the Streets* 1957; *Bobbikins* 1959; *Spare the Rod* 1961

Byington, Spring (1893–1971) *Little Women* 1933; *Ah, Wilderness!* 1935; *Way Down East* 1935; *The Charge of the Light Brigade* 1936; *Stage Struck* 1936; *Theodora Goes Wild* 1936; *A Family Affair* 1937; *Green Light* 1937; *The Buccaneer* 1938; *You Can't Take It with You* 1938; *The Story of Alexander Graham Bell* 1939; *The Blue Bird* 1940; *Lucky Partners* 1940; *The Devil and Miss Jones* 1941; *Meet John Doe* 1941; *The Vanishing Virginian* 1941; *When Ladies Meet* 1941; *The Affairs of Martha* 1942; *Rings on Her Fingers* 1942; *Roxie Hart* 1942; *The War against Mrs Hadley* 1942; *Heaven Can Wait* 1943; *The Heavenly Body* 1943; *Presenting Lily Mars* 1943; *I'll Be Seeing You* 1944; *The Enchanted Cottage* 1945; *Salty O'Rourke* 1945; *Thrill of a Romance* 1945; *Dragonwyck* 1946; *My Brother Talks to Horses* 1946; *Cynthia* 1947; *It Had to Be You* 1947; *Living in a Big Way* 1947; *Singapore* 1947; *BF's Daughter* 1948; *The Big Wheel* 1949; *In the Good Old Summertime* 1949; *Walk Softly, Stranger* 1949; *Devil's Doorway* 1950; *Please Believe Me* 1950; *Angels in the Outfield* 1951; *Because You're Mine* 1952; *No Room for the Groom* 1952; *The Rocket Man* 1954; *Please Don't Eat the Daisies* 1960

Bykov, Rolan (1929–1998) *The Commissar* 1967; *Trial on the Road* 1971

Byner, John (1938–) *The Great Smokey Roadblock* 1977; *Stroker Ace* 1983; *The Black Cauldron* 1985; *Transylvania 6-5000* 1985

Bynes, Amanda (1986–) *Big Fat Liar* 2002; *What a Girl Wants* 2003; *Robots* 2005

Byrd, Eugene (1975–) *Murder in Mississippi* 1990; *Whiteboys* 1999; *8 Mile* 2002; *Anacondas: the Hunt for the Blood Orchid* 2004

Byrd, Ralph (1909–1952) *Careful, Soft Shoulder* 1942; *Jungle Book* 1942; *Moontide* 1942; *Dick Tracy Meets Gruesome* 1947; *Dick Tracy's Dilemma* 1947

Byrd, Thomas Jefferson aka **Byrd, Tom** (1960–) *Clockers* 1995; *Get on the Bus* 1996; *Bamboozled* 2000

Byrge, Bill *Ernest Goes to Jail* 1990; *Ernest Scared Stupid* 1991

Byrne, Anne *The End of the World (in Our Usual Bed in a Night Full of Rain)* 1978; *Manhattan* 1979; *Why Would I Lie?* 1980

Byrne, Eddie (1911–1982) *Lady Godiva Rides Again* 1951; *The Gentle Gunman* 1952; *Time Gentlemen Please!* 1952; *Beautiful Stranger* 1954; *Children Galore* 1954; *The Divided Heart* 1954; *Happy Ever After* 1954; *Trouble in the Glen* 1954; *One Way Out* 1955; *The Man in the Sky* 1956; *Floods of Fear* 1958; *Jack the Ripper* 1958; *The Mummy* 1959; *The Shakedown* 1959; *The Break* 1962; *The Cracksman* 1963; *Island of Terror* 1966; *All Coppers Are...* 1972

Byrne, Gabriel (1950–) *The Outsider* 1979; *Excalibur* 1981; *The Keep* 1983; *Defence of the Realm* 1985; *Gothic* 1986; *Lionheart* 1986; *The Courier* 1987; *Hello Again* 1987; *Julia and Julia* 1987; *Siesta* 1987; *A Soldier's Tale* 1988; *Diamond Skulls* 1989; *Miller's Crossing* 1990; *Shipwrecked* 1990; *Cool World* 1992; *Into the West* 1992; *The Assassin* 1993; *A Dangerous Woman* 1993; *Point of No Return* 1993; *Little Women* 1994; *Prince of Jutland* 1994; *A Simple Twist of Fate* 1994; *Trial by Jury* 1994; *Dead Man* 1995; *Frankie Starlight* 1995; *The Usual Suspects* 1995; *The Brylcreem Boys* 1996; *Last of the High Kings* 1996; *Smilla's Feeling for Snow* 1996; *This Is the Sea* 1996; *Trigger Happy* 1996; *The End of Violence* 1997; *The Man in the Iron Mask* 1997; *Enemy of the State* 1998; *Polish Wedding* 1998; *End of Days* 1999; *Stigmata* 1999; *Ghost Ship* 2002; *Spider* 2002; *Vanity Fair* 2004; *Assault on Precinct 13* 2005

Byrne, Michael (1922–) *Butley* 1973; *Champions* 1983; *The Infiltrator* 1995; *The Island on Bird Street* 1997; *Battlefield Earth* 2000; *Gangs of New York* 2002

Byrne, Rose (1979–) *Dallas Doll* 1994; *Two Hands* 1999; *My Mother Frank* 2000; *City of Ghosts* 2002; *I Capture the Castle* 2002; *The Rage in Placid Lake* 2002; *The Night We Called It a Day* 2003; *Troy* 2004; *Wicker Park* 2004

Byrnes, Edd aka **Byrnes, Edward** (1933–) *Johnny Trouble* 1957; *Reform School Girl* 1957; *Darby's Rangers* 1958; *Girl on the Run* 1958; *Yellowstone Kelly* 1959; *The Secret Invasion* 1964; *Stardust* 1974; *Troop Beverly Hills* 1989

Byrnes, Jim (1948–) *Omen IV: the Awakening* 1991; *Highlander: Endgame* 2000

Byron, Arthur aka **Byron, A S** (1872–1943) *The Mummy* 1932; *Gabriel over the White House* 1933; *The Mayor of Hell* 1933; *20,000 Years in Sing Sing* 1933; *Fog over Frisco* 1934; *The House of Rothschild* 1934; *Marie Galante* 1934; *The Secret Bride* 1934; *The Casino Murder Case* 1935; *Oil for the Lamps of China* 1935; *The Whole Town's Talking* 1935

Byron, Jean (1926–) *The Magnetic Monster* 1953; *Serpent of the Nile* 1953; *Flareup* 1969

Byron, Kathleen (1922–) *Black Narcissus* 1946; *A Matter of Life and Death* 1946; *Madness of the Heart* 1949; *The Small Back Room* 1949; *Prelude to Fame* 1950; *The Reluctant Widow* 1950; *The Scarlet Thread* 1951; *Tom Brown's Schooldays* 1951; *The Gambler and the Lady* 1952; *Young Bess* 1953; *Profile* 1954; *Night of the Eagle* 1961; *Twins of Evil* 1971; *The Abdication* 1974; *Saving Private Ryan* 1998

Byron, Walter (1899–1972) *Queen Kelly* 1928; *The Last Flight* 1931; *Sinners in the Sun* 1932; *Three Wise Girls* 1932; *British Agent* 1934; *Folies Bergère* 1935

C

Caan, James (1939–) *Lady in a Cage* 1964; *The Glory Guys* 1965; *Red Line 7000* 1965; *El Dorado* 1967; *Games* 1967; *Journey to Shiloh* 1967; *Submarine X-1* 1967; *Countdown* 1968; *The Rain People* 1969; *Rabbit, Run* 1970; *Brian's Song* 1971; *TR Baskin* 1971; *The Godfather* 1972; *Cinderella Liberty* 1973; *Slither* 1973; *Freebie and the Bean* 1974; *The Gambler* 1974; *Funny Lady* 1975; *The Killer Elite* 1975; *Rollerball* 1975; *Harry and Walter Go to New York* 1976; *Another Man, Another Chance* 1977; *A Bridge Too Far* 1977; *Comes a Horseman* 1978; *Little Moon & Jud McGraw* 1978; *Chapter Two* 1979; *Hide in Plain Sight* 1980; *Thief* 1981; *Les Uns et les Autres* 1981; *Kiss Me Goodbye* 1982; *Gardens of Stone* 1987; *Alien Nation* 1988; *Dick Tracy* 1990; *Misery* 1990; *The Dark Backward* 1991; *For the Boys* 1991; *Honeymoon in Vegas* 1992; *Flesh and Bone* 1993; *The Program* 1993; *A Boy Called Hate* 1995; *Bottle Rocket* 1996; *Bulletproof* 1996; *Eraser* 1996; *North Star* 1996; *Poodle Springs* 1998; *Mickey Blue Eyes* 1999; *This Is My Father* 1999; *The Way of the Gun* 2000; *The Yards* 2000; *City of Ghosts* 2002; *Dogville* 2003; *Elf* 2003

Caan, Scott (1976–) *A Boy Called Hate* 1995; *Black and White* 1999; *Varsity Blues* 1999; *Ready to Rumble* 2000; *American Outlaws* 2001; *Novocaine* 2001; *Ocean's Eleven* 2001; *Sonny* 2002; *Ocean's Twelve* 2004

Caba, Emilio Gutiérrez (1942–) *The Hunt* 1966; *La Comunidad* 2000

Cabot, Bruce (1904–1972) *The Roadhouse Murder* 1932; *Ann Vickers* 1933; *King Kong* 1933; *Lucky Devils* 1933; *Finishing School* 1934; *Murder on the Blackboard* 1934; *Let 'Em Have It* 1935; *Fury* 1936; *The Robin Hood of El Dorado* 1936; *Sinners in Paradise* 1938; *Smashing the Rackets* 1938; *Dodge City* 1939; *Susan and God* 1940; *The Flame of New Orleans* 1941; *Sundown* 1941; *The Desert Song* 1944; *Fallen Angel* 1945; *Salty O'Rourke* 1945; *Smoky* 1946; *Angel and the Badman* 1947; *Sorrowful Jones* 1949; *Fancy Pants* 1950; *Best of the Badmen* 1951; *Lost in Alaska* 1952; *The Quiet American* 1958; *The Sheriff of Fractured Jaw* 1958; *Goliath and the Barbarians* 1959; *The Comancheros* 1961; *Hatari!* 1962; *Black Spurs* 1965; *The War Wagon* 1967; *The Green Berets* 1968; *Hellfighters* 1969; *Chisum* 1970; *Big Jake* 1971; *Diamonds Are Forever* 1971

Cabot, Sebastian (1918–1977) *Kismet* 1955; *Westward Ho the Wagons!* 1956; *Dragoon Wells Massacre* 1957; *Johnny Tremain* 1957; *Omar Khayyam* 1957; *Terror in a Texas Town* 1958; *The Angry Hills* 1959; *The Time Machine* 1960; *The Sword in the Stone* 1963; *Twice-Told Tales* 1963; *The Family Jewels* 1965; *The Jungle Book* 1967

Cabot, Susan (1927–1986) *Tomahawk* 1951; *The Battle at Apache Pass* 1952; *The Duel at Silver Creek* 1952; *Son of Ali Baba* 1952; *Gunsmoke* 1953; *Ride Clear of Diablo* 1954; *Sorority Girl* 1957; *Viking Women and the Sea Serpent* 1957; *Fort Massacre* 1958; *Machine Gun Kelly* 1958; *War of the Satellites* 1958; *The Wasp Woman* 1959

Cadeau, Lally *Between Friends* 1983; *Separate Vacations* 1986

Cadell, Jean (1884–1967) *David Copperfield* 1935; *Love from a Stranger* 1936; *Pygmalion* 1938; *Quiet Wedding* 1940; *Whisky Galore!* 1949; *The Late Edwina Black* 1951; *The Little Hut* 1957

Cadieux, Anne-Marie *The Confessional* 1995; *Nô* 1998; *Four Days* 1999

Cady, Frank (1915–) *Ace in the Hole* 1951; *Let's Make It Legal* 1951; *Zandy's Bride* 1974

Caesar, Adolph (1933–1986) *A Soldier's Story* 1984; *The Color Purple* 1985; *Club Paradise* 1986

Caesar, Harry (1928–1994) *Emperor of the North* 1973; *The Mean Machine* 1974; *A Small Circle of Friends* 1980; *Breakdance 2 – Electric Boogaloo* 1984; *Bird on a Wire* 1990

Caesar, Sid (1922–) *The Guilt of Janet Ames* 1947; *It's a Mad Mad Mad Mad World* 1963; *The Busy Body* 1967; *Airport 1975* 1974; *Silent Movie* 1976; *Fire Sale* 1977; *The Cheap Detective* 1978; *The Fiendish Plot of Dr Fu Manchu* 1980; *History of the World Part 1* 1981; *Grease 2* 1982; *Over the Brooklyn Bridge* 1983; *The Emperor's New Clothes* 1987

Caffrey, Peter *Angel* 1982; *I Went Down* 1997; *A Love Divided* 1999

Caffrey, Sean (1940–) *I Was Happy Here* 1966; *When Dinosaurs Ruled the Earth* 1969

Caffrey, Stephen (1961–) *Longtime Companion* 1990; *Murder of Innocence* 1993; *Formula for Death* 1995

Cage, Nicolas (1964–) *Rumble Fish* 1983; *Valley Girl* 1983; *Birdy* 1984; *The Cotton Club* 1984; *Racing with the Moon* 1984; *The Boy in Blue* 1986; *Peggy Sue Got Married* 1986; *Moonstruck* 1987; *Raising Arizona* 1987; *Never on Tuesday* 1988; *Vampire's Kiss* 1988; *Wild at Heart* 1990; *Wings of the Apache* 1990; *Zandalee* 1991; *Honeymoon in Vegas* 1992; *Red Rock West* 1992; *Amos & Andrew* 1993; *Deadfall* 1993; *Guarding Tess* 1994; *It Could Happen to You* 1994; *Kiss of Death* 1994; *Trapped in Paradise* 1994; *Leaving Las Vegas* 1995; *The Rock* 1996; *Con Air* 1997; *Face/Off* 1997; *City of Angels* 1998; *Snake Eyes* 1998; *Bringing out the Dead* 1999; *8mm* 1999; *The Family Man* 2000; *Gone in Sixty Seconds* 2000; *Captain Corelli's Mandolin* 2001; *Christmas Carol: the Movie* 2001; *Windtalkers* 2001; *Adaptation.* 2002; *Sonny* 2002; *Matchstick Men* 2003; *National Treasure* 2004

Cagney, James (1899–1986) *Blonde Crazy* 1931; *Doorway to Hell* 1931; *Other Men's Women* 1931; *The Public Enemy* 1931; *Smart Money* 1931; *The Crowd Roars* 1932; *Taxi!* 1932; *Footlight Parade* 1933; *Hard to Handle* 1933; *Lady Killer* 1933; *The Mayor of Hell* 1933; *Picture Snatcher* 1933; *He Was Her Man* 1934; *Here Comes the Navy* 1934; *Jimmy the Gent* 1934; *Ceiling Zero* 1935; *Devil Dogs of the Air* 1935; *Frisco Kid* 1935; *"G" Men* 1935; *The Irish in Us* 1935; *A Midsummer Night's Dream* 1935; *Mutiny on the Bounty* 1935; *Great Guy* 1936; *Something to Sing About* 1937; *Angels with Dirty Faces* 1938; *Boy Meets Girl* 1938; *Each Dawn I Die* 1939; *The Oklahoma Kid* 1939; *The Roaring Twenties* 1939; *City for Conquest* 1940; *The Fighting 69th* 1940; *Torrid Zone* 1940; *The Bride Came COD* 1941; *The Strawberry Blonde* 1941; *Captains of the Clouds* 1942; *Yankee Doodle Dandy* 1942; *Johnny Come Lately* 1943; *Blood on the Sun* 1945; *13 Rue Madeleine* 1946; *The Time of Your Life* 1948; *White Heat* 1949; *Kiss Tomorrow Goodbye* 1950; *The West Point Story* 1950; *Come Fill the Cup* 1951; *What Price Glory?* 1952; *A Lion Is in the Streets* 1953; *Love Me or Leave Me* 1955; *Mister Roberts* 1955; *Run for Cover* 1955; *Seven Little Foys* 1955; *These Wilder Years* 1956; *Tribute to a Bad Man* 1956; *Man of a Thousand Faces* 1957; *Never Steal Anything Small* 1959; *Shake Hands with the Devil* 1959; *The Gallant Hours* 1960; *One, Two, Three* 1961; *Arizona Bushwhackers* 1968; *Ragtime* 1981

Cagney, Jeanne (1908–1984) *Yankee Doodle Dandy* 1942; *The Time of Your Life* 1948; *Quicksand* 1950; *Don't Bother to Knock* 1952; *A Lion Is in the Streets* 1953; *Man of a Thousand Faces* 1957

Cagney, William aka **Cagney, Bill** (1902–1988) *Ace of Aces* 1933; *Palooka* 1934; *Kiss Tomorrow Goodbye* 1950

Cahill, Barry *Daddy's Gone A-Hunting* 1969; *Coffy* 1973; *Grand Theft Auto* 1977

Caicedo, Franklin *The Color of Destiny* 1986; *The Voyage* 1991

Cain, Dean (1966–) *The Stone Boy* 1984; *Best Men* 1997; *Futuresport* 1998; *The Broken Hearts Club: a Romantic Comedy* 2000; *Flight of Fancy* 2000; *Militia* 2000; *Firetrap* 2001; *Out of Time* 2003

Caine, Henry (1888–1962) *The Ghost Train* 1931; *Number Seventeen* 1932

Caine, Howard (1926–1993) *The Man from the Diner's Club* 1963; *Watermelon Man* 1970

Caine, Michael (1933–) *A Hill in Korea* 1956; *Sailor Beware!* 1956; *How to Murder a Rich Uncle* 1957; *The Steel Bayonet* 1957; *Carve Her Name with Pride* 1958; *Danger Within* 1958; *The Key* 1958; *Passport to Shame* 1958; *The Two-Headed Spy* 1958; *The Bulldog Breed* 1960; *Foxhole in Cairo* 1960; *The Day the Earth Caught Fire* 1961; *Solo for Sparrow* 1962; *The Wrong Arm of the Law* 1962; *Zulu* 1964; *The Ipcress File* 1965; *Alfie* 1966; *Funeral in Berlin* 1966; *Gambit* 1966; *The Wrong Box* 1966; *Billion Dollar Brain* 1967; *Hurry Sundown* 1967; *Woman Times Seven* 1967; *Deadfall* 1968; *The Magus* 1968; *Battle of Britain* 1969; *The Italian Job* 1969; *Play Dirty* 1969; *Simon, Simon* 1970; *Too Late the Hero* 1970; *Get Carter* 1971; *Kidnapped* 1971; *The Last Valley* 1971; *Zee and Co* 1971; *Pulp* 1972; *Sleuth* 1972; *The Black Windmill* 1974; *The Marseille Contract* 1974; *The Man Who Would Be King* 1975; *Peeper* 1975; *The Romantic Englishwoman* 1975; *The Wilby Conspiracy* 1975; *The Eagle Has Landed* 1976; *Harry and Walter Go to New York* 1976; *A Bridge Too Far* 1977; *Silver Bears* 1977; *California Suite* 1978; *The Swarm* 1978; *Ashanti* 1979; *Beyond the Poseidon Adventure* 1979; *Dressed to Kill* 1980; *The Island* 1980; *Escape to Victory* 1981; *The Hand* 1981; *Deathtrap* 1982; *Educating Rita* 1983; *The Honorary Consul* 1983; *Blame It on Rio* 1984; *The Jigsaw Man* 1984; *The Holcroft Covenant* 1985; *Water* 1985; *Half Moon Street* 1986; *Hannah and Her Sisters* 1986; *Mona Lisa* 1986; *Sweet Liberty* 1986; *The Whistle Blower* 1986; *The Fourth Protocol* 1987; *Hero* 1987; *Jaws the Revenge* 1987; *Surrender* 1987; *Dirty Rotten Scoundrels* 1988; *Without a Clue* 1988; *Bullseye!* 1990; *Mr Destiny* 1990; *A Shock to the System* 1990; *Blue Ice* 1992; *The Muppet Christmas Carol* 1992; *Noises Off* 1992; *On Deadly Ground* 1994; *Bullet to Beijing* 1995; *Midnight in St Petersburg* 1995; *Blood and Wine* 1996; *Mandela and de Klerk* 1997; *Curtain Call* 1998; *Little Voice* 1998; *Shadow Run* 1998; *The Cider House Rules* 1999; *Get*

Carter 2000; *Miss Congeniality* 2000; *Quills* 2000; *Shiner* 2000; *Last Orders* 2001; *Austin Powers in Goldmember* 2002; *The Quiet American* 2002; *The Actors* 2003; *Secondhand Lions* 2003; *The Statement* 2003; *Around the Bend* 2004; *Batman Begins* 2005
Cairney, John (1930–) *Windom's Way* 1957; *A Night to Remember* 1958; *Operation Bullshine* 1959; *The Devil-Ship Pirates* 1964
Cake, Jonathan (1968–) *Honest* 2000; *The One and Only* 2001
Calamai, Clara (1915–1998) *Ossessione* 1942; *White Nights* 1957; *Deep Red* 1975
Calder, David (1946–) *Defence of the Realm* 1985; *American Friends* 1991; *Mr In-Between* 2001
Calderon, Paul *aka* **Calderone, Paul** *King of New York* 1989; *Sea of Love* 1989; *Bad Lieutenant* 1992; *CrissCross* 1992; *The Addiction* 1994; *Sweet Nothing* 1995; *Oxygen* 1999; *Girlfight* 2000; *21 Grams* 2003
Caldicot, Richard (1908–1995) *One Good Turn* 1954; *The Fool* 1990
Caldwell, Zoe (1933–) *The Purple Rose of Cairo* 1985; *Lilo & Stitch* 2002
Calfa, Don (1940–) *Return of the Living Dead* 1984; *Weekend at Bernie's* 1989; *Chopper Chicks in Zombietown* 1990
Calfan, Nicole (1947–) *The Burglars* 1971; *Permission to Kill* 1975; *Les Chiens* 1978; *Max Mon Amour* 1986
Calhern, Louis (1895–1956) *Blonde Crazy* 1931; *Duck Soup* 1933; *20,000 Years in Sing Sing* 1933; *The Affairs of Cellini* 1934; *The Count of Monte Cristo* 1934; *The Arizonian* 1935; *The Last Days of Pompeii* 1935; *Woman Wanted* 1935; *The Gorgeous Hussy* 1936; *Fast Company* 1938; *Up in Arms* 1944; *Notorious* 1946; *Arch of Triumph* 1948; *The Red Danube* 1949; *The Red Pony* 1949; *Annie Get Your Gun* 1950; *The Asphalt Jungle* 1950; *Devil's Doorway* 1950; *A Life of Her Own* 1950; *The Magnificent Yankee* 1950; *Nancy Goes to Rio* 1950; *The Man with a Cloak* 1951; *The Prisoner of Zenda* 1952; *Washington Story* 1952; *We're Not Married* 1952; *Confidentially Connie* 1953; *Julius Caesar* 1953; *Latin Lovers* 1953; *Remains to Be Seen* 1953; *Athena* 1954; *Betrayed* 1954; *Executive Suite* 1954; *Men of the Fighting Lady* 1954; *Rhapsody* 1954; *The Student Prince* 1954; *The Blackboard Jungle* 1955; *The Prodigal* 1955; *Forever, Darling* 1956; *High Society* 1956
Calhoun, Monica (1971–) *Bagdad Café* 1987; *The Players Club* 1998; *The Best Man* 1999
Calhoun, Rory (1922–1999) *The Red House* 1947; *A Ticket to Tomahawk* 1950; *I'd Climb the Highest Mountain* 1951; *Meet Me after the Show* 1951; *Way of a Gaucho* 1952; *With a Song in My Heart* 1952; *How to Marry a Millionaire* 1953; *Powder River* 1953; *A Bullet Is Waiting* 1954; *Dawn at Socorro* 1954; *Four Guns to the Border* 1954; *River of No Return* 1954; *The Yellow Tomahawk* 1954; *Ain't Misbehavin'* 1955; *The Looters* 1955; *The Spoilers* 1955; *The Treasure of Pancho Villa* 1955; *Raw Edge* 1956; *Red Sundown* 1956; *The Big Caper* 1957; *The Hired Gun* 1957; *The Saga of Hemp Brown* 1958; *The Treasure of Monte Cristo* 1960; *The Colossus of Rhodes* 1961; *A Face in the Rain* 1963; *Apache Uprising* 1965; *Black Spurs* 1965; *Dayton's Devils* 1968; *Night of the Lepus* 1972; *Love and the Midnight Auto Supply* 1977; *Motel Hell* 1980; *Angel* 1984; *Avenging Angel* 1985; *Hell Comes to Frogtown* 1988; *Bad Jim* 1989; *Pure Country* 1992
Call, Joseph (1950–) *Saturday Night Fever* 1977; *The Competition* 1980; *The Lonely Lady* 1983
Call, R D *Unconquered* 1989; *Young Guns II* 1990; *Other People's Money* 1991; *Jack Reed: Badge of Honor* 1993; *Waterworld* 1995; *Logan's War: Bound by Honor* 1998; *Murder by Numbers* 2002
Callahan, James (1930–) *Lady Sings the Blues* 1972; *Outlaw Blues* 1977; *The Burning Bed* 1984
Callahan, Margaret (1910–1981) *Seven Keys to Baldpate* 1935; *The Last Outlaw* 1936
Callan, K (1942–) *A Touch of Class* 1973; *The Unborn* 1991
Callan, Michael (1935–) *They Came to Cordura* 1959; *Because They're Young* 1960; *Gidget Goes Hawaiian* 1961; *Mysterious Island* 1961; *Bon Voyage!* 1962; *The Interns* 1962; *13 West Street* 1962; *The New Interns* 1964; *Cat Ballou* 1965; *You Must Be Joking!* 1965; *The Magnificent Seven Ride!* 1972; *Frasier, the Sensuous Lion* 1973; *Lepke* 1975; *The Cat and the Canary* 1979
Callard, Kay (1933–) *They Who Dare* 1953; *Find the Lady* 1956; *The Flying Scot* 1957; *The Hypnotist* 1957; *Undercover Girl* 1957; *Escapement* 1958
Calleia, Joseph (1897–1975) *Public Hero No 1* 1935; *After the Thin Man* 1936; *His Brother's Wife* 1936; *Riffraff* 1936; *Algiers* 1938; *Bad Man of Brimstone* 1938; *Full Confession* 1939; *Golden Boy* 1939; *My Little Chickadee* 1940; *Sundown* 1941; *The Glass Key* 1942; *Jungle Book* 1942; *The Cross of Lorraine* 1943; *The Conspirators* 1944; *Deadline at Dawn* 1946; *Gilda* 1946; *Noose* 1948; *The Noose Hangs High* 1948; *They Passed This Way* 1948; *Branded* 1950; *Captain Carey, USA* 1950; *The Light Touch* 1951; *Valentino* 1951; *The Iron Mistress* 1952; *The Caddy* 1953; *The Treasure of Pancho Villa* 1955; *Underwater!* 1955; *Hot Blood* 1956; *Serenade* 1956; *Wild Is the Wind* 1957; *The Light in the Forest* 1958; *Touch of Evil* 1958; *The Alamo* 1960
Callie, Dayton *Executive Target* 1996; *The Last Days of Frankie the Fly* 1996
Callis, James (1971–) *Beginner's Luck* 2001; *Bridget Jones's Diary* 2001; *Bridget Jones: the Edge of Reason* 2004
Callow, Simon (1949–) *Amadeus* 1984; *A Room with a View* 1985; *The Good Father* 1986; *Maurice* 1987; *Mr and Mrs Bridge* 1990; *Postcards from the Edge* 1990; *Soft Top, Hard Shoulder* 1992; *Four Weddings and a Funeral* 1994; *Street Fighter* 1994; *Ace Ventura: When Nature Calls* 1995; *Jefferson in Paris* 1995; *James and the Giant Peach* 1996; *The Scarlet Tunic* 1997; *Bedrooms and Hallways* 1998; *Shakespeare in Love* 1998; *Christmas Carol: the Movie* 2001; *Merci Docteur Rey* 2002; *Thunderpants* 2002; *Bright Young Things* 2003; *The Phantom of the Opera* 2004
Calloway, Cab (1907–1994) *International House* 1933; *Stormy Weather* 1943; *St Louis Blues* 1958; *The Blues Brothers* 1980
Calthrop, Donald (1888–1940) *Blackmail* 1929; *The Ghost Train* 1931; *FP1* 1932; *Rome Express* 1932; *The Clairvoyant* 1934; *The Phantom Light* 1934; *Scrooge* 1935; *Broken Blossoms* 1936; *The Man Who Changed His Mind* 1936
Calvé, Jean-François *Marguerite de la Nuit* 1955; *The Bride Is Too Beautiful* 1956
Calvert, Bill *Six Weeks* 1982; *CHUD II: Bud the Chud* 1989
Calvert, John (1911–) *Appointment with Murder* 1948; *Devil's Cargo* 1948; *Search for Danger* 1949
Calvert, Phyllis (1915–2002) *Let George Do It* 1940; *Neutral Port* 1940; *Kipps* 1941; *Uncensored* 1942; *The Young Mr Pitt* 1942; *The Man in Grey* 1943; *Fanny by Gaslight* 1944; *Madonna of the Seven Moons* 1944; *Two Thousand Women* 1944; *They Were Sisters* 1945; *The Magic Bow* 1946; *Men of Two Worlds* 1946; *The Root of All Evil* 1946; *Time Out of Mind* 1947; *Broken Journey* 1948; *Appointment with Danger* 1950; *Mr Denning Drives North* 1951; *Mandy* 1952; *The Net* 1953; *Child in the House* 1956; *It's Never Too Late* 1956; *Indiscreet* 1958; *A Lady Mislaid* 1958; *Oscar Wilde* 1959; *The Battle of the Villa Fiorita* 1965; *Twisted Nerve* 1968; *Oh! What a Lovely War* 1969; *The Walking Stick* 1970
Calvet, Corinne (1925–2001) *Rope of Sand* 1949; *My Friend Irma Goes West* 1950; *When Willie Comes Marching Home* 1950; *On the Riviera* 1951; *Peking Express* 1951; *Sailor Beware* 1951; *What Price Glory?* 1952; *Flight to Tangier* 1953; *Powder River* 1953; *Thunder in the East* 1953; *The Far Country* 1954; *So This Is Paris* 1954; *Hemingway's Adventures of a Young Man* 1962; *Apache Uprising* 1965
Calvin, Henry (1918–1975) *Toby Tyler, or Ten Weeks with a Circus* 1960; *Babes in Toyland* 1961
Calvin, John *California Dreaming* 1979; *Foolin' Around* 1980; *Critters 3* 1991; *The Magic Bubble* 1992; *Dragonworld* 1994
Cámara, Javier (1967–) *Talk to Her* 2001; *Torremolinos 73* 2003; *Bad Education* 2004
Camardiel, Roberto (1917–1986) *Adios Gringo* 1965; *Django Kill* 1967
Camaso, Claudio *aka* **Volonté, Claudio** (?–1977) *Vengeance* 1968; *Bay of Blood* 1971
Cambridge, Godfrey (1933–1976) *Gone Are the Days* 1963; *The President's Analyst* 1967; *The Biggest Bundle of Them All* 1968; *Bye Bye Braverman* 1968; *Cotton Comes to Harlem* 1970; *Watermelon Man* 1970; *Beware! The Blob* 1971; *The Biscuit Eater* 1972; *Friday Foster* 1975; *Whiffs* 1975; *Scott Joplin* 1977
Cameron, Candace *aka* **Cameron Bure, Candace** (1976–) *Visitors of the Night* 1995; *Freshman Fall* 1996
Cameron, Dean (1962–) *Summer School* 1987; *Rockula* 1989; *Men at Work* 1990; *Ski School* 1991; *Sleep with Me* 1994
Cameron, Earl (1917–) *Pool of London* 1950; *Emergency Call* 1952; *The Woman for Joe* 1955; *Sapphire* 1959; *Flame in the Streets* 1961; *Tarzan's Three Challenges* 1963; *Guns at Batasi* 1964; *A Warm December* 1973; *The Interpreter* 2005
Cameron, Hugh (1879–1941) *For the Love of Mike* 1927; *One Heavenly Night* 1931
Cameron, Kirk (1970–) *Like Father, like Son* 1987; *Listen to Me* 1989
Cameron, Rod (1910–1983) *Riding High* 1943; *Frontier Gal* 1945; *Salome, Where She Danced* 1945; *Belle Starr's Daughter* 1948; *The Plunderers* 1948; *Cavalry Scout* 1951; *Ride the Man Down* 1952; *Southwest Passage* 1954; *Santa Fe Passage* 1955; *Passport to Treason* 1956; *Escapement* 1958; *The Bounty Killer* 1965; *Evel Knievel* 1971
Camilleri, Mickey *aka* **Camilleri, Micki** *Return Home* 1989; *The Last Days of Chez Nous* 1992
Camilleri, Terry (1949–) *The Cars That Ate Paris* 1974; *Bill & Ted's Excellent Adventure* 1988; *Encounter at Raven's Gate* 1988
Camp, Colleen (1953–) *Smile* 1975; *Death Game* 1976; *Love and the Midnight Auto Supply* 1977; *Game of Death* 1978; *They All Laughed* 1981; *Smokey and the Bandit III* 1983; *Joy of Sex* 1984; *DARYL* 1985; *Police Academy 2: Their First Assignment* 1985; *Walk like a Man* 1987; *Illegally Yours* 1988; *Track 29* 1988; *Wicked Stepmother* 1989; *The Magic Bubble* 1992; *The Vagrant* 1992; *Sliver* 1993; *Die Hard with a Vengeance* 1995; *Trapped* 2002
Camp, Hamilton (1934–) *The Perils of Pauline* 1967; *All Night Long* 1981; *Twice upon a Time* 1983; *Meatballs 2* 1984
Campanella, Joseph (1927–) *The Young Lovers* 1964; *The St Valentine's Day Massacre* 1967; *Ben* 1972; *Hangar 18* 1980; *Earthbound* 1981; *Body Chemistry* 1990; *The Glass Cage* 1996
Campbell, Beatrice (1922–1979) *Meet Me at Dawn* 1946; *Silent Dust* 1948; *No Place for Jennifer* 1949; *Now Barabbas Was a Robber* 1949; *Last Holiday* 1950; *The Mudlark* 1950; *Laughter in Paradise* 1951; *Grand National Night* 1953; *The Master of Ballantrae* 1953
Campbell, Bill *aka* **Campbell, William** *aka* **Campbell, Billy** (1959–) *Rocketeer* 1991; *Bram Stoker's Dracula* 1992; *Lover's Knot* 1995; *The Brylcreem Boys* 1996; *The Second Jungle Book* 1997; *Max Q: Emergency Landing* 1998; *Enough* 2002
Campbell, Bruce (1958–) *The Evil Dead* 1983; *Crimewave* 1985; *Evil Dead II* 1987; *Maniac Cop* 1988; *Maniac Cop 2* 1990; *Lunatics: a Love Story* 1991; *Waxwork II: Lost in Time* 1992; *Army of Darkness* 1993; *The Hudsucker Proxy* 1994; *Tornado!* 1996; *From Dusk till Dawn II: Texas Blood Money* 1999; *Bubba Ho-tep* 2002; *Serving Sara* 2002
Campbell, Cheryl (1949–) *Hawk the Slayer* 1980; *McVicar* 1980; *Chariots of Fire* 1981; *Greystoke: the Legend of Tarzan, Lord of the Apes* 1984; *The Shooting Party* 1984
Campbell, Colin (1883–1966) *The Leather Boys* 1963; *Saturday Night Out* 1963; *The High Bright Sun* 1965
Campbell, Eric (1878–1917) *Behind the Screen* 1916; *The Rink* 1916; *The Vagabond* 1916; *The Cure* 1917; *The Immigrant* 1917
Campbell, G Smokey *Bagdad Café* 1987; *Fear of a Black Hat* 1992
Campbell, Glen (1936–) *The Cool Ones* 1967; *True Grit* 1969; *Uphill All the Way* 1985; *Rock-a-Doodle* 1990
Campbell, John *The Fighting Sullivans* 1944; *Sweet and Lowdown* 1944
Campbell, Judy (1916–2004) *Convoy* 1940; *East of Piccadilly* 1940; *Saloon Bar* 1940; *Green for Danger* 1946; *Bonnie Prince Charlie* 1948; *There's a Girl in My Soup* 1970
Campbell, Julia (1963–) *Opportunity Knocks* 1990; *Diary of a Serial Killer* 1997; *Romy and Michele's High School Reunion* 1997; *Poodle Springs* 1998; *A Slight Case of Murder* 1999
Campbell, Ken (1941–) *The Tempest* 1979; *Letter to Brezhnev* 1985; *Hard Men* 1996; *Creep* 2004
Campbell, Louise (1911–1997) *Bulldog Drummond Comes Back* 1937; *Bulldog Drummond's Revenge* 1937; *Bulldog Drummond's Peril* 1938; *Men with Wings* 1938; *The Star Maker* 1939; *Anne of Windy Poplars* 1940
Campbell, Mrs Patrick (1865–1940) *One More River* 1934; *Riptide* 1934; *Crime and Punishment* 1935
Campbell, Naomi (1970–) *Cool as Ice* 1991; *Miami Rhapsody* 1995; *Girl 6* 1996; *Burn Hollywood Burn* 1997; *Fat Slags* 2004
Campbell, Neil *aka* **Little Nell** (1953–) *Lisztomania* 1975; *The Rocky Horror Picture Show* 1975; *Shock Treatment* 1981
Campbell, Neve (1973–) *The Craft* 1996; *Scream* 1996; *Scream 2* 1997; *54* 1998; *Wild Things* 1998; *Scream 3* 1999; *Three to Tango* 1999; *Drowning Mona* 2000; *Panic* 2000; *The Company* 2003; *Churchill: the Hollywood Years* 2004
Campbell, Nicholas (1952–) *The Amateur* 1981; *Killing 'em Softly* 1982; *Terminal Choice* 1983; *Certain Fury* 1985; *Rampage* 1987; *Bordertown Cafe* 1991; *Naked Lunch* 1991; *Butterbox Babies* 1995; *The Boys Club* 1996; *Danielle Steel's No Greater Love* 1996; *Happy Face Murders* 1999
Campbell, Paul *The Lunatic* 1992; *Dancehall Queen* 1996; *Third World Cop* 1999
Campbell, Rob *The Crucible* 1996; *Hostile Waters* 1996; *Boys Don't Cry* 1999
Campbell, Scott Michael *Radioland Murders* 1994; *Flight of the Phoenix* 2004
Campbell, Tisha (1968–) *Little Shop of Horrors* 1986; *School Daze* 1988; *Rooftops* 1989; *House Party* 1990; *House Party 3* 1994
Campbell, William (1926–) *The Breaking Point* 1950; *Breakthrough* 1950; *Operation Pacific* 1951; *Battle Circus* 1953; *Big Leaguer* 1953; *Escape from Fort Bravo* 1953; *Man without a Star* 1955; *Running Wild* 1955; *Backlash* 1956; *Love Me Tender* 1956; *The Naked and the Dead* 1958; *The Sheriff of Fractured Jaw* 1958; *Dementia 13* 1963; *The Secret Invasion* 1964; *Pretty Maids All in a Row* 1971
Campbell Moore, Stephen *Bright Young Things* 2003; *A Good Woman* 2004
Campeau, Frank (1864–1943) *3 Bad Men* 1926; *Abraham Lincoln* 1930
Campion, Cris (1966–) *Pirates* 1986; *Beyond Therapy* 1987
Campo, Wally *Machine Gun Kelly* 1958; *Beast from Haunted Cave* 1959
Campos, Rafael (1936–1985) *Trial* 1955; *Tonka* 1958; *Lady in a Cage* 1964; *Where the Buffalo Roam* 1980; *The Return of Josey Wales* 1986
Campos, Victor *Newman's Law* 1974; *The Master Gunfighter* 1975; *Five Days from Home* 1978
Canale, Gianna Maria (1927–) *The Man from Cairo* 1953; *Lust of the Vampire* 1956; *Hercules* 1957; *The Whole Truth* 1958; *Queen of the Pirates* 1960; *The Treasure of Monte Cristo* 1960; *Tiger of the Seven Seas* 1962
Canals, Maria *aka* **Canals, María** (1966–) *The Master of Disguise* 2002; *Imagining Argentina* 2003
Canary, David (1938–) *Posse* 1975; *Shark's Treasure* 1975
Candelier, Isabelle *News from the Good Lord* 1996; *Strange Gardens* 2003
Candido, Candy (1913–1999) *Sleeping Beauty* 1959; *Basil the Great Mouse Detective* 1986
Candy, John (1950–1994) *Find the Lady* 1976; *The Silent Partner* 1978; *Lost and Found* 1979; *1941* 1979; *The Blues Brothers* 1980; *Heavy Metal* 1981; *Stripes* 1981; *Going Berserk* 1983; *National Lampoon's Vacation* 1983; *Splash* 1984; *Brewster's Millions* 1985; *Sesame Street Presents: Follow That Bird* 1985; *Summer Rental* 1985; *Volunteers* 1985; *Armed and Dangerous* 1986; *Little Shop of Horrors* 1986; *Planes, Trains and Automobiles* 1987; *Spaceballs* 1987; *The Great Outdoors* 1988; *Hot to Trot* 1988; *Cannonball Fever* 1989; *Uncle Buck* 1989; *Who's Harry Crumb?* 1989; *Home Alone* 1990; *The Rescuers Down Under* 1990; *Career Opportunities* 1991; *Delirious* 1991; *JFK* 1991; *Nothing but Trouble* 1991; *Only the Lonely* 1991; *Once upon a Crime* 1992; *Cool Runnings* 1993; *Wagons East!* 1994; *Canadian Bacon* 1995
Cane, Charles (1899–1973) *Dead Reckoning* 1947; *The Guilt of Janet Ames* 1947; *Revenge of the Creature* 1955
Canerday, Natalie *One False Move* 1992; *Sling Blade* 1995
Canet, Guillaume (1973–) *En Plein Coeur* 1998; *The Beach*

2000; *La Fidélité* 2000; *Vidocq* 2001; *Love Me If You Dare* 2003
Canfield, Gene *The Boy Who Cried Bitch* 1991; *Love Walked In* 1997
Cannavale, Bobby (1971–) *The Station Agent* 2003; *Shall We Dance* 2004
Cannon, Dyan *aka* **Cannon, Diane** (1937–) *The Rise and Fall of Legs Diamond* 1960; *This Rebel Breed* 1960; *Bob & Carol & Ted & Alice* 1969; *Doctors' Wives* 1970; *The Anderson Tapes* 1971; *The Burglars* 1971; *The Love Machine* 1971; *Such Good Friends* 1971; *The Last of Sheila* 1973; *Shamus* 1973; *Heaven Can Wait* 1978; *Revenge of the Pink Panther* 1978; *Coast to Coast* 1980; *Honeysuckle Rose* 1980; *Author! Author!* 1982; *Deathtrap* 1982; *Caddyshack II* 1988; *The End of Innocence* 1990; *The Pickle* 1993; *8 Heads in a Duffel Bag* 1997; *Out to Sea* 1997; *That Darn Cat* 1997
Cannon, Esma (1896–1974) *The Last Adventurers* 1937; *Holiday Camp* 1947; *Sailor Beware!* 1956; *Carry On Regardless* 1960; *Raising the Wind* 1961; *What a Carve Up!* 1961; *On the Beat* 1962; *We Joined the Navy* 1962; *Carry On Cabby* 1963
Cannon, J D (1922–2005) *An American Dream* 1966; *Cool Hand Luke* 1967; *Krakatoa, East of Java* 1969; *The 1,000 Plane Raid* 1969; *Scorpio* 1973; *Death Wish II* 1981
Cannon, Nick (1980–) *Drumline* 2002; *Love Don't Cost a Thing* 2003
Cannon, Wanda *The Last Winter* 1989; *For the Moment* 1994; *They* 2002
Canonica, Sibylle (1957–) *Waller's Last Walk* 1989; *Beyond Silence* 1996; *Mostly Martha* 2001
Canova, Judy (1916–1983) *Artists and Models* 1937; *Chatterbox* 1943; *The Adventures of Huckleberry Finn* 1960
Cantafora, Antonio (1943–) *Baron Blood* 1972; *Gabriela* 1983
Cantinflas (1911–1993) *Around the World in 80 Days* 1956; *Pepe* 1960
Cantó, Toni (1965–) *All about My Mother* 1999; *You're My Hero* 2003
Cantona, Eric (1966–) *Le Bonheur Est dans le Pré* 1995; *The Children of the Marshland* 1998; *Elizabeth* 1998
Cantor, Eddie (1892–1964) *Whoopee!* 1930; *Palmy Days* 1931; *The Kid from Spain* 1932; *Roman Scandals* 1933; *Kid Millions* 1934; *Strike Me Pink* 1936; *Thank Your Lucky Stars* 1943; *Show Business* 1944; *If You Knew Susie* 1948
Canutt, Yakima (1895–1986) *Riders of Destiny* 1933; *The Telegraph Trail* 1933; *Blue Steel* 1934; *The Lucky Texan* 1934; *The Man from Utah* 1934; *'Neath the Arizona Skies* 1934; *Randy Rides Alone* 1934; *Sagebrush Trail* 1934; *The Star Packer* 1934; *West of the Divide* 1934; *The Dawn Rider* 1935; *The Lawless Frontier* 1935; *Paradise Canyon* 1935; *Westward Ho* 1935; *Trouble in Texas* 1937; *Wyoming Outlaw* 1939
Capaldi, Peter (1958–) *Local Hero* 1983; *Dangerous Liaisons* 1988; *The Lair of the White Worm* 1988; *December Bride* 1990; *Soft Top, Hard Shoulder* 1992; *Captives* 1994; *Shooting Fish* 1997; *What Rats Won't Do* 1998; *Mrs Caldicot's Cabbage War* 2000; *Max* 2002
Capell, Peter (1912–1986) *Walk East on Beacon* 1952; *The Burglar* 1956; *A Gift for Heidi* 1958; *For the First Time* 1959; *One, Two, Three* 1961; *Sorcerer* 1977
Caplan, Twink *Look Who's Talking* 1989; *Clueless* 1995
Capodice, John *The Hard Way* 1991; *Honeymoon in Vegas* 1992; *Ringmaster* 1998
Capolicchio, Lino (1943–) *The Garden of the Finzi-Continis* 1971; *The Last Days of Mussolini* 1974; *Noi Tre* 1984; *Fratelli e Sorelle* 1992; *Fiorile* 1993
Capote, Truman (1924–1984) *Trilogy* 1969; *Murder by Death* 1976
Capotorto, Carl (1959–) *American Blue Note* 1989; *Mac* 1992
Capra, Francis (1983–) *A Bronx Tale* 1993; *Free Willy 2: the Adventure Home* 1995; *Kazaam* 1996; *A Simple Wish* 1997
Capri, Ahna *aka* **Capri, Anna** (1945–) *Kisses for My President* 1964; *One of Our Spies Is Missing* 1966; *Brotherhood of Satan* 1970; *Payday* 1972; *Enter the Dragon* 1973
Capri, Alaina *Common-Law Cabin* 1967; *Good Morning... and Goodbye* 1967
Caprioli, Vittorio (1921–1989) *General Della Rovere* 1959; *A Full Day's Work* 1973; *The Tragedy of a Ridiculous Man* 1981
Capshaw, Jessica (1976–) *A Secret Sin* 1997; *The Love Letter* 1999; *Valentine* 2001
Capshaw, Kate (1953–) *A Little Sex* 1981; *Best Defense* 1984; *Dreamscape* 1984; *Indiana Jones and the Temple of Doom* 1984; *Windy City* 1984; *Power* 1986; *SpaceCamp* 1986; *Black Rain* 1989; *Love at Large* 1990; *My Heroes Have Always Been Cowboys* 1991; *Love Affair* 1994; *How to Make an American Quilt* 1995; *Just Cause* 1995; *The Alarmist* 1997; *A Secret Sin* 1997; *The Love Letter* 1999
Capucine (1933–1990) *North to Alaska* 1960; *Song without End* 1960; *The Lion* 1962; *Walk on the Wild Side* 1962; *The Pink Panther* 1963; *The 7th Dawn* 1964; *What's New, Pussycat?* 1965; *The Honey Pot* 1967; *Fraulein Doktor* 1968; *Satyricon* 1969; *Red Sun* 1971; *The Con Artists* 1976; *Arabian Adventure* 1979; *From Hell to Victory* 1979; *Jaguar Lives!* 1979; *Trail of the Pink Panther* 1982; *The Curse of the Pink Panther* 1983
Cara, Irene (1957–) *Aaron Loves Angela* 1975; *Fame* 1980; *Killing 'em Softly* 1982; *DC Cab* 1983; *City Heat* 1984; *Certain Fury* 1985; *Happily Ever After* 1990; *The Magic Voyage* 1992
Carafotes, Paul *Touchdown* 1981; *All the Right Moves* 1983; *Journey to the Center of the Earth* 1989
Caramitru, Ion (1942–) *Two Deaths* 1994; *Amen.* 2002
Caravaca, Eric (1970–) *The Officers' Ward* 2001; *Novo* 2002; *Son Frère* 2003
Carax, Léos (1960–) *King Lear – Fear and Loathing* 1987; *Process* 2004
Carbone, Antony (1927–) *A Bucket of Blood* 1959; *The Last Woman on Earth* 1960; *The Pit and the Pendulum* 1961
Cardellini, Linda (1975–) *Dee Snider's Strangeland* 1998; *Scooby-Doo* 2002; *Scooby-Doo 2: Monsters Unleashed* 2004
Cardenas, Elsa *The Brave One* 1956; *For the Love of Mike* 1960; *Fun in Acapulco* 1963; *Of Love and Desire* 1963; *Taggart* 1964
Cardinal, Ben *Avalanche* 1994; *Alaska* 1996
Cardinal, Tantoo (1951–) *Dances with Wolves* 1990; *Black Robe* 1991; *Silent Tongue* 1993; *Where the Rivers Flow North* 1993; *Legends of the Fall* 1994; *Sioux City* 1994; *The Education of Little Tree* 1997; *Smoke Signals* 1998
Cardinale, Claudia (1939–) *Big Deal on Madonna Street* 1958; *Upstairs and Downstairs* 1959; *The Battle of Austerlitz* 1960; *Rocco and His Brothers* 1960; *Cartouche* 1961; *The Leopard* 1962; *8½* 1963; *The Pink Panther* 1963; *The Magnificent Showman* 1964; *Time of Indifference* 1964; *Of a Thousand Delights* 1965; *Blindfold* 1966; *Lost Command* 1966; *The Professionals* 1966; *Don't Make Waves* 1967; *A Fine Pair* 1968; *The Hell with Heroes* 1968; *Once upon a Time in the West* 1968; *The Red Tent* 1969; *The Adventures of Gerard* 1970; *Popsy-Pop* 1970; *Conversation Piece* 1974; *Escape to Athena* 1979; *Immortal Bachelor* 1980; *La Pelle* 1981; *The Salamander* 1981; *Fitzcarraldo* 1982; *A Man in Love* 1987
Cardone, Nathalie (1967–) *A Strange Place to Meet* 1988; *L'Enfer* 1994
Cardwell, James (1920–1954) *The Fighting Sullivans* 1944; *Sweet and Lowdown* 1944; *The Shanghai Cobra* 1945; *He Walked by Night* 1948
Carette, Julien *aka* **Carette** (1897–1966) *La Grande Illusion* 1937; *Gribouille* 1937; *La Bête Humaine* 1938; *La Règle du Jeu* 1939
Carewe, Arthur Edmund (1884–1937) *The Cat and the Canary* 1927; *Doctor X* 1932
Carey, Amie *subUrbia* 1996; *Dog Park* 1998
Carey, Drew (1958–) *Geppetto* 2000; *Play It to the Bone* 2000; *Robots* 2005
Carey, Harry *aka* **Carey Sr, Harry** (1878–1947) *The Musketeers of Pig Alley* 1912; *Straight Shooting* 1917; *The Trail of '98* 1929; *Trader Horn* 1931; *Law and Order* 1932; *The Last Outlaw* 1936; *Valiant Is the Word for Carrie* 1936; *Born Reckless* 1937; *Danger Patrol* 1937; *Kid Galahad* 1937; *Souls at Sea* 1937; *King of Alcatraz* 1938; *The Law West of Tombstone* 1938; *You and Me* 1938; *Mr Smith Goes to Washington* 1939; *They Knew What They Wanted* 1940; *Among the Living* 1941; *The Shepherd of the Hills* 1941; *Sundown* 1941; *The Spoilers* 1942; *Air Force* 1943; *Happy Land* 1943; *The Great Moment* 1944; *Angel and the Badman* 1947; *The Sea of Grass* 1947; *Red River* 1948
Carey Jr, Harry *aka* **Carey, Harry** (1921–) *Pursued* 1947; *Red River* 1948; *Three Godfathers* 1948; *She Wore a Yellow Ribbon* 1949; *So Dear to My Heart* 1949; *Copper Canyon* 1950; *Rio Grande* 1950; *Wagonmaster* 1950; *Warpath* 1951; *Beneath the 12-Mile Reef* 1953; *Silver Lode* 1954; *The Long Gray Line* 1955; *The Searchers* 1956; *Seventh Cavalry* 1956; *The River's Edge* 1957; *Escort West* 1959; *The Undefeated* 1969; *Dirty Dingus Magee* 1970; *Take a Hard Ride* 1975; *Nickelodeon* 1976; *The Long Riders* 1980; *UFOria* 1980; *Endangered Species* 1982; *Mask* 1985; *The Whales of August* 1987; *Cherry 2000* 1988; *Illegally Yours* 1988; *Bad Jim* 1989; *Breaking In* 1989; *Back to the Future Part III* 1990
Carey, Joyce (1898–1993) *In Which We Serve* 1942; *Blithe Spirit* 1945; *Brief Encounter* 1945; *The October Man* 1947; *The Astonished Heart* 1949; *The Chiltern Hundreds* 1949; *Cry, the Beloved Country* 1951; *The Rough and the Smooth* 1959; *Let's Get Married* 1960; *Greyfriars Bobby* 1961; *A Nice Girl like Me* 1969
Carey, Leonard (1887–1977) *Laughter* 1930; *Rebecca* 1940
Carey, Macdonald *aka* **Carey, MacDonald** (1913–1994) *Dr Broadway* 1942; *Shadow of a Doubt* 1942; *Star Spangled Rhythm* 1942; *Take a Letter, Darling* 1942; *Wake Island* 1942; *Suddenly It's Spring* 1947; *Dream Girl* 1948; *Bride of Vengeance* 1949; *The Great Gatsby* 1949; *Streets of Laredo* 1949; *Comanche Territory* 1950; *Copper Canyon* 1950; *The Lawless* 1950; *Mystery Submarine* 1950; *Cave of Outlaws* 1951; *Let's Make It Legal* 1951; *Meet Me after the Show* 1951; *Count the Hours* 1953; *Malaga* 1954; *Stranger at My Door* 1956; *Blue Denim* 1959; *The Damned* 1961; *Tammy and the Doctor* 1963; *End of the World* 1977
Carey, Mariah (1970–) *The Bachelor* 1999; *Glitter* 2001; *Wisegirls* 2001
Carey, Michele (1943–) *El Dorado* 1967; *The Sweet Ride* 1967; *Live a Little, Love a Little* 1968; *Dirty Dingus Magee* 1970; *Scandalous John* 1971
Carey, Olive (1896–1988) *The Searchers* 1956; *Run of the Arrow* 1957
Carey, Philip *aka* **Carey, Phil** (1925–) *I Was a Communist for the FBI* 1951; *Operation Pacific* 1951; *Springfield Rifle* 1952; *This Woman Is Dangerous* 1952; *Calamity Jane* 1953; *Gun Fury* 1953; *Pushover* 1954; *They Rode West* 1954; *Count Three and Pray* 1955; *The Long Gray Line* 1955; *Screaming Mimi* 1958; *Tonka* 1958; *Black Gold* 1963; *Dead Ringer* 1964; *The Time Travelers* 1964; *The Great Sioux Massacre* 1965; *Three Guns for Texas* 1968; *Backtrack* 1969; *Once You Kiss a Stranger* 1969; *The Seven Minutes* 1971; *Fighting Mad* 1976
Carey, Ron (1935–) *The Out of Towners* 1970; *Dynamite Chicken* 1971; *Silent Movie* 1976; *High Anxiety* 1977; *Fatso* 1979; *History of the World Part 1* 1981
Carey, Timothy *aka* **Carey, Timothy Agoglia** (1929–1994) *White Witch Doctor* 1953; *Paths of Glory* 1957; *A Time for Killing* 1967; *Waterhole #3* 1967; *Head* 1968; *Minnie and Moskowitz* 1971; *The Outfit* 1973; *The Killing of a Chinese Bookie* 1976
Cargill, Patrick (1918–1996) *The Hi-Jackers* 1963; *A Countess from Hong Kong* 1967; *Inspector Clouseau* 1968; *Every Home Should Have One* 1970; *Up Pompeii* 1971; *Father Dear Father* 1972; *The Picture Show Man* 1977
Carhart, Timothy (1953–) *Pink Cadillac* 1989; *Thelma & Louise* 1991; *Quicksand: No Escape* 1992; *Beverly Hills Cop III* 1994; *Candyman: Farewell to the Flesh* 1995; *Black Sheep* 1996; *In the Line of Duty: Smoke Jumpers* 1996
Carides, Gia (1964–) *Bliss* 1985; *Backlash* 1986; *Daydream Believer* 1991; *Strictly Ballroom* 1992; *Paperback Romance* 1994; *Bad Company* 1995; *Brilliant Lies* 1996; *Austin Powers: the Spy Who Shagged Me* 1999; *A Secret Affair* 1999; *My Big Fat Greek Wedding* 2002
Carides, Zoe (1962–) *Death in Brunswick* 1990; *Brilliant Lies* 1996
Caridi, Carmine (1933–) *The Gambler* 1974; *Prince of the City* 1981; *Life Stinks* 1991; *Top Dog* 1995
Cariou, Len (1939–) *A Little Night Music* 1977; *The Four Seasons* 1981; *Surviving* 1985; *Lady in White* 1988; *Never Talk to Strangers* 1995; *The Summer of Ben Tyler* 1996; *Thirteen Days* 2000; *About Schmidt* 2002; *Secret Window* 2004
Carle, Richard (1871–1941) *Fireman Save My Child* 1932; *The Bride Comes Home* 1935; *Anything Goes* 1936; *Spendthrift* 1936; *Remember?* 1939
Carleton, Claire (1913–1966) *Witness to Murder* 1954; *The Buster Keaton Story* 1957
Carlin, George (1937–) *With Six You Get Eggroll* 1968; *Car Wash* 1976; *Outrageous Fortune* 1987; *Bill & Ted's Excellent Adventure* 1988; *Bill & Ted's Bogus Journey* 1991; *The Prince of Tides* 1991; *Dogma* 1999; *Jay and Silent Bob Strike Back* 2001; *Jersey Girl* 2003; *Scary Movie 3* 2003
Carlin, Lynn (1930–) *Faces* 1968; *tick... tick... tick...* 1969; *Taking Off* 1971; *Wild Rovers* 1971; *Dead of Night* 1972; *Baxter* 1973
Carlini, Paolo (1922–1979) *Roman Holiday* 1953; *It Started in Naples* 1960; *Chronicle of Anna Magdalena Bach* 1968
Carlisi, Olimpia *Casanova* 1976; *The Tragedy of a Ridiculous Man* 1981
Carlisle, Anne (1956–) *Liquid Sky* 1982; *Blind Alley* 1984
Carlisle, Kitty (1910–) *Murder at the Vanities* 1934; *She Loves Me Not* 1934; *A Night at the Opera* 1935
Carlisle, Mary (1916–) *Palooka* 1934; *This Side of Heaven* 1934; *Kind Lady* 1935; *Doctor Rhythm* 1938; *Dance, Girl, Dance* 1940; *Baby Face Morgan* 1942
Carlqvist, Margit *aka* **Carlquist, Margit** (1932–) *To Joy* 1950; *Smiles of a Summer Night* 1955
Carlson, Karen (1945–) *The Candidate* 1972; *Matilda* 1978; *The Octagon* 1980; *The Man Next Door* 1998
Carlson, Les (1933–) *Shoot* 1976; *Videodrome* 1982; *The Fly* 1986
Carlson, Richard (1912–1977) *The Duke of West Point* 1938; *Dancing Co-Ed* 1939; *Winter Carnival* 1939; *The Ghost Breakers* 1940; *The Howards of Virginia* 1940; *No, No, Nanette* 1940; *Too Many Girls* 1940; *Back Street* 1941; *Hold That Ghost* 1941; *The Little Foxes* 1941; *The Affairs of Martha* 1942; *Fly by Night* 1942; *White Cargo* 1942; *The Man from Down Under* 1943; *Presenting Lily Mars* 1943; *Young Ideas* 1943; *So Well Remembered* 1947; *King Solomon's Mines* 1950; *The Sound of Fury* 1950; *The Blue Veil* 1951; *A Millionaire for Christy* 1951; *Valentino* 1951; *Retreat, Hell!* 1952; *All I Desire* 1953; *It Came from Outer Space* 1953; *The Magnetic Monster* 1953; *The Maze* 1953; *Seminole* 1953; *Creature from the Black Lagoon* 1954; *Bengazi* 1955; *The Last Command* 1955; *The Helen Morgan Story* 1957; *Della* 1965; *Kid Rodelo* 1966; *The Power* 1968; *The Valley of Gwangi* 1969
Carlson, Veronica (1944–) *Dracula Has Risen from the Grave* 1968; *Frankenstein Must Be Destroyed* 1969; *The Horror of Frankenstein* 1970; *The Ghoul* 1975
Carlyle, Richard *The Valiant* 1929; *Torpedo Run* 1958
Carlyle, Robert (1961–) *Silent Scream* 1989; *Riff-Raff* 1991; *Priest* 1994; *Go Now* 1995; *Trainspotting* 1995; *Carla's Song* 1996; *Face* 1997; *The Full Monty* 1997; *Angela's Ashes* 1999; *Plunkett & Macleane* 1999; *Ravenous* 1999; *The World Is Not Enough* 1999; *The Beach* 2000; *There's Only One Jimmy Grimble* 2000; *The 51st State* 2001; *To End All Wars* 2001; *Black and White* 2002; *Once upon a Time in the Midlands* 2002
Carmel, Roger C (1932–1986) *Goodbye Charlie* 1964; *Alvarez Kelly* 1966; *Gambit* 1966; *The Venetian Affair* 1966; *Skullduggery* 1969; *Myra Breckinridge* 1970; *Breezy* 1973; *Thunder and Lightning* 1977; *Hardly Working* 1981
Carmen, Julie (1960–) *Gloria* 1980; *Night of the Juggler* 1980; *Last Plane Out* 1983; *Blue City* 1986; *Fright Night Part 2* 1988; *The Milagro Beanfield War* 1988; *The Penitent* 1988; *Paint It Black* 1989; *Cold Heaven* 1992; *In the Mouth of Madness* 1994
Carmet, Jean (1920–1994) *The Vanishing Corporal* 1962; *The Little Theatre of Jean Renoir* 1969; *The Tall Blond Man with One Black Shoe* 1972; *Black and White in Color* 1976; *Violette Nozière* 1977; *Buffet Froid* 1979; *Circle of Deceit* 1981; *Les Misérables* 1982; *Merci la Vie* 1991; *Germinal* 1993
Carmi, Vera (1914–1969) *Sunday in August* 1949; *Friends for Life* 1955
Carmichael, Hoagy (1899–1981) *To Have and Have Not* 1944; *Johnny Angel* 1945; *The Best Years of Our Lives* 1946; *Night Song* 1947; *Young Man with a Horn* 1950; *Belles on Their Toes* 1952; *The Las Vegas Story* 1952; *Timberjack* 1955
Carmichael, Ian (1920–) *Dear Mr Prohack* 1949; *Betrayed* 1954; *The Colditz Story* 1954; *Simon and Laura* 1955; *Storm over the Nile* 1955; *The Big Money* 1956; *Brothers in Law* 1956; *Private's*

Progress 1956; Happy Is the Bride 1957; Lucky Jim 1957; I'm All Right Jack 1959; Left, Right and Centre 1959; Light Up the Sky 1960; School for Scoundrels 1960; Double Bunk 1961; The Amorous Prawn 1962; Heavens Above! 1963; Hide and Seek 1963; Smashing Time 1967; The Magnificent Seven Deadly Sins 1971; From beyond the Grave 1973; The Lady Vanishes 1979; Diamond Skulls 1989

Carminati, Tullio (1894–1971) Gallant Lady 1934; One Night of Love 1934; London Melody 1937; Roman Holiday 1953; A Breath of Scandal 1960; The Swordsman of Siena 1962

Carmine, Michael (1959–1989) *batteries not included 1987; Leviathan 1989

Carnelutti, Francesco The Belly of an Architect 1987; The Sin Eater 2002

Carnera, Primo (1906–1967) The Prizefighter and the Lady 1933; A Kid for Two Farthings 1955; Hercules Unchained 1959

Carney, Alan (1909–1973) Mr Lucky 1943; Girl Rush 1944; Step Lively 1944; Li'l Abner 1959

Carney, Art (1918–2003) The Yellow Rolls-Royce 1964; Harry and Tonto 1974; WW and the Dixie Dancekings 1975; Won Ton Ton, the Dog Who Saved Hollywood 1976; The Late Show 1977; House Calls 1978; Defiance 1979; Going in Style 1979; Sunburn 1979; Roadie 1980; Steel 1980; Take This Job and Shove It 1981; Better Late Than Never 1983; Firestarter 1984; The Naked Face 1984; Last Action Hero 1993

Carney, George (1887–1947) Love on the Dole 1941; In Which We Serve 1942; I Know Where I'm Going! 1945; Good Time Girl 1948

Carnovsky, Morris (1897–1992) The City 1939; Edge of Darkness 1943; Address Unknown 1944; The Master Race 1944; Cornered 1945; Our Vines Have Tender Grapes 1945; Rhapsody in Blue 1945; Dead Reckoning 1947; Dishonored Lady 1947; Siren of Atlantis 1948; Gun Crazy 1949; Thieves' Highway 1949; Cyrano de Bergerac 1950; The Second Woman 1951; The Gambler 1974

Caroit, Philippe The Aviator's Wife 1980; En Toute Innocence 1987

Carol, Cindy Gidget Goes to Rome 1963; Dear Brigitte 1966

Carol, Joan Mr Moto's Last Warning 1939; Ghost Ship 1952

Carol, Martine (1922–1967) Les Belles de Nuit 1952; Madame du Barry 1954; Secrets d'Alcove 1954; The Diary of Major Thompson 1955; Lola Montès 1955; Nana 1955; Action of the Tiger 1957; Ten Seconds to Hell 1959; The Battle of Austerlitz 1960; Violent Summer 1961

Caron, Leslie (1931–) An American in Paris 1951; The Man with a Cloak 1951; Glory Alley 1952; Lili 1953; The Story of Three Loves 1953; Daddy Long Legs 1955; The Glass Slipper 1955; Gaby 1956; The Doctor's Dilemma 1958; Gigi 1958; The Man Who Understood Women 1959; The Battle of Austerlitz 1960; The Subterraneans 1960; Fanny 1961; Guns of Darkness 1962; The L-Shaped Room 1962; Father Goose 1964; A Very Special Favor 1965; Is Paris Burning? 1966; Promise Her Anything 1966; Madron 1970; The Man Who Loved Women 1977; Valentino 1977; Goldengirl 1979; The Contract 1980; Imperative 1982; Dangerous Moves 1984; Courage Mountain 1989; Damage 1992; Funny Bones 1994; Let It Be Me 1995; Chocolat 2000; Murder on the Orient Express 2001; Le Divorce 2003

Carotenuto, Memmo (1908–1980) Umberto D 1952; Bread, Love and Dreams 1953; Big Deal on Madonna Street 1958

Carpenter, Carleton (1926–) Vengeance Valley 1951; Take the High Ground 1953; Up Periscope 1959

Carpenter, Ken Spirit of the Eagle 1991; Hellraiser III: Hell on Earth 1992

Carpenter, Paul (1921–1964) Face the Music 1954; Shadow of a Man 1954; The Stranger Came Home 1954; The Young Lovers 1954; The Hornet's Nest 1955; Stock Car 1955; Behind the Headlines 1956; Fire Maidens from Outer Space 1956; The Hypnotist 1957; No Road Back 1957; Undercover Girl 1957; Intent to Kill 1958

Carpentieri, Renato (1943–) Open Doors 1990; Puerto Escondido 1992; The Stolen Children 1992

Carr, Alexander (1878–1946) The Death Kiss 1933; Christmas in July 1940

Carr, Darleen (1950–) The Jungle Book 1967; The Beguiled 1971; Runaway! 1973

Carr (1), Jane (1909–1957) Lord Edgware Dies 1934; Those Were the Days 1934; The Lad 1935

Carr, Marian San Quentin 1946; The Devil Thumbs a Ride 1947; World for Ransom 1953; Indestructible Man 1956

Carr, Mary (1874–1973) Lights of New York 1928; Kept Husbands 1931; Pack Up Your Troubles 1932

Carr, Paul (1934–) Jamboree 1957; Posse from Hell 1961; Ben 1972; Executive Action 1973

Carradine, David (1936–) Taggart 1964; The Violent Ones 1967; The Good Guys and the Bad Guys 1969; Young Billy Young 1969; Macho Callahan 1970; The McMasters 1970; Boxcar Bertha 1972; Death Race 2000 1975; Bound for Glory 1976; Cannonball 1976; The Serpent's Egg 1977; Thunder and Lightning 1977; Deathsport 1978; Fast Charlie: the Moonbeam Rider 1978; Gray Lady Down 1978; The Silent Flute 1978; Cloud Dancer 1979; The Long Riders 1980; Americana 1981; Q – the Winged Serpent 1982; Trick or Treats 1982; Lone Wolf McQuade 1983; The Warrior and the Sorceress 1983; Armed Response 1986; POW the Escape 1986; Bird on a Wire 1990; Think Big 1990; Distant Justice 1992; Double Trouble 1992; Roadside Prophets 1992; Waxwork II: Lost in Time 1992; Jailbreak 1997; Last Stand at Saber River 1997; An American Tail: the Treasure of Manhattan Island 1998; Kill Bill Vol 1 2003; Kill Bill Vol 2 2003

Carradine, John (1906–1988) The Garden of Allah 1936; Mary of Scotland 1936; The Prisoner of Shark Island 1936; White Fang 1936; Winterset 1936; Captains Courageous 1937; Danger – Love at Work 1937; The Hurricane 1937; The Last Gangster 1937; Nancy Steele Is Missing 1937; Thank You, Mr Moto 1937; This Is My Affair 1937; Alexander's Ragtime Band 1938; Four Men and a Prayer 1938; International Settlement 1938; Kentucky Moonshine 1938; Kidnapped 1938; Of Human Hearts 1938; Submarine Patrol 1938; Drums along the Mohawk 1939; Five Came Back 1939; Frontier Marshal 1939; The Hound of the Baskervilles 1939; Jesse James 1939; Mr Moto's Last Warning 1939; Stagecoach 1939; The Three Musketeers 1939; Brigham Young 1940; Chad Hanna 1940; The Grapes of Wrath 1940; The Return of Frank James 1940; Blood and Sand 1941; Man Hunt 1941; Swamp Water 1941; Western Union 1941; Reunion in France 1942; Son of Fury 1942; Whispering Ghosts 1942; Hitler's Madman 1943; The Adventures of Mark Twain 1944; Barbary Coast Gent 1944; Bluebeard 1944; House of Frankenstein 1944; The Invisible Man's Revenge 1944; The Mummy's Ghost 1944; Voodoo Man 1944; Captain Kidd 1945; Fallen Angel 1945; House of Dracula 1945; It's in the Bag 1945; The Private Affairs of Bel Ami 1947; Casanova's Big Night 1954; Johnny Guitar 1954; Thunder Pass 1954; The Female Jungle 1955; The Kentuckian 1955; Stranger on Horseback 1955; The Black Sleep 1956; The Ten Commandments 1956; Hell Ship Mutiny 1957; The True Story of Jesse James 1957; The Unearthly 1957; Showdown at Boot Hill 1958; The Cosmic Man 1959; The Oregon Trail 1959; The Adventures of Huckleberry Finn 1960; Sex Kittens Go to College 1960; Tarzan the Magnificent 1960; The Man Who Shot Liberty Valance 1962; Cheyenne Autumn 1964; The Patsy 1964; Billy the Kid vs Dracula 1966; The Hostage 1966; Munster, Go Home! 1966; Blood of Dracula's Castle 1967; The Good Guys and the Bad Guys 1969; The Trouble with Girls 1969; The McMasters 1970; Myra Breckinridge 1970; The Seven Minutes 1971; Shinbone Alley 1971; Boxcar Bertha 1972; Everything You Always Wanted to Know about Sex ... but Were Afraid to Ask 1972; Silent Night, Bloody Night 1972; The House of Seven Corpses 1973; Terror in the Wax Museum 1973; The Killer inside Me 1975; Shock Waves 1975; The Last Tycoon 1976; The Shootist 1976; Crash! 1977; Golden Rendezvous 1977; Satan's Cheerleaders 1977; The Sentinel 1977; The White Buffalo 1977; The Monster Club 1980; The Howling 1981; The Nesting 1981; The Scarecrow 1982; The Secret of NIMH 1982; House of the Long Shadows 1983; Monster in the Closet 1983; The Ice Pirates 1984; Peggy Sue Got Married 1986; Buried Alive 1990

Carradine, Keith (1949–) McCabe and Mrs Miller 1971; Emperor of the North 1973; Idaho Transfer 1973; Thieves like Us 1974; Nashville 1975; Welcome to LA 1976; The Duellists 1977; Pretty Baby 1978; An Almost Perfect Affair 1979; Old Boyfriends 1979; The Long Riders 1980; Southern Comfort 1981; Choose Me 1984; Maria's Lovers 1984; Trouble in Mind 1985; Backfire 1987; The Moderns 1988; Stones for Ibarra 1988; Cold Feet 1989; Street of No Return 1989; The Bachelor 1990; Daddy's Dyin'... Who's Got the Will? 1990; The Ballad of the Sad Café 1991; CrissCross 1992; Andre 1994; The Tie That Binds 1995; Wild Bill 1995; Last Stand at Saber River 1997; A Thousand Acres 1997; Night Ride Home 1999; Falcons 2002

Carradine, Robert (1954–) Mean Streets 1973; Aloha, Bobby and Rose 1975; Cannonball 1976; Jackson County Jail 1976; Joyride 1977; Orca ... Killer Whale 1977; Coming Home 1978; The Big Red One 1980; The Long Riders 1980; Heartaches 1981; Wavelength 1983; Just the Way You Are 1984; Revenge of the Nerds 1984; Number One with a Bullet 1986; Buy & Cell 1988; All's Fair 1989; Rude Awakening 1989; Palmer's Pick-Up 1999; Max Keeble's Big Move 2001; The Lizzie McGuire Movie 2003

Carré, Isabelle (1971–) The Children of the Marshland 1998; La Bûche 1999; Les Enfants du Siècle 1999; He Loves Me... He Loves Me Not 2002

Carrel, Dany (1935–) Les Possédées 1955; Gates of Paris 1957; The Hands of Orlac 1960

Carrera, Barbara (1951–) The Master Gunfighter 1975; Embryo 1976; The Island of Dr Moreau 1977; When Time Ran Out 1980; Condorman 1981; I, the Jury 1982; Lone Wolf McQuade 1983; Never Say Never Again 1983; Wild Geese II 1985; Love at Stake 1987; Loverboy 1989; Wicked Stepmother 1989; Love Is All There Is 1996; Waking Up Horton 1997

Carrere, Tia (1967–) Aloha Summer 1988; Fatal Mission 1990; Harley Davidson and the Marlboro Man 1991; Showdown in Little Tokyo 1991; Wayne's World 1992; Quick 1993; Rising Sun 1993; Wayne's World 2 1993; True Lies 1994; Hostile Intentions 1995; Jury Duty 1995; High School High 1996; Hollow Point 1996; Kull the Conqueror 1997; Top of the World 1997; Scarred City 1998; 20 Dates 1998; Merlin the Return 2000; Lilo & Stitch 2002

Carrey, Jim (1962–) Finders Keepers 1984; Once Bitten 1985; Peggy Sue Got Married 1986; Earth Girls Are Easy 1988; Pink Cadillac 1989; Ace Ventura: Pet Detective 1993; Dumb and Dumber 1994; The Mask 1994; Ace Ventura: When Nature Calls 1995; Batman Forever 1995; The Cable Guy 1996; Liar Liar 1997; The Truman Show 1998; Man on the Moon 1999; The Grinch 2000; Me, Myself & Irene 2000; The Majestic 2001; Bruce Almighty 2003; Eternal Sunshine of the Spotless Mind 2003; Lemony Snicket's A Series of Unfortunate Events 2004

Carrier, Albert Bengazi 1955; The Secret Life of an American Wife 1968

Carrier, Corey (1980–) After Dark, My Sweet 1990; The Adventures of Pinocchio 1996

Carrière, Jean-Claude (1931–) The Diary of a Chambermaid 1964; Jaya Ganga 1996

Carrière, Mathieu (1950–) Malpertuis 1971; Don Juan 73, or If Don Juan Were a Woman 1973; The Aviator's Wife 1980; Bay Boy 1984; Christopher Columbus: the Discovery 1992; A Girl Called Rosemarie 1996; Arsène Lupin 2004

Carrillo, Elpidia (1963–) The Border 1981; The Honorary Consul 1983; Salvador 1986; Predator 1987; My Family 1994; The Brave 1997; Bread and Roses 2000

Carrillo, Leo (1880–1961) Four Frightened People 1934; The Gay Bride 1934; Manhattan Melodrama 1934; If You Could Only Cook 1935; In Caliente 1935; The Gay Desperado 1936; History Is Made at Night 1937; Blockade 1938; The Girl of the Golden West 1938; Too Hot to Handle 1938; Lillian Russell 1940; Road Agent 1941; Men of Texas 1942; Sin Town 1942; Frontier Badmen 1943; Phantom of the Opera 1943; Ghost Catchers 1944; Under Western Skies 1945; The Fugitive 1947

Carrol, Regina (1943–1992) The Female Bunch 1969; Dracula vs Frankenstein 1970

Carroll, Beeson Lady Liberty 1971; Spacehunter: Adventures in the Forbidden Zone 1983; Crimes of the Heart 1986

Carroll, Diahann (1935–) Carmen Jones 1954; Porgy and Bess 1959; Paris Blues 1961; The Split 1968; Claudine 1974; The Five Heartbeats 1991

Carroll, Janet (1940–) Risky Business 1983; Memories of Me 1988; Family Business 1989; Talent for the Game 1991; Destiny Turns on the Radio 1995

Carroll, Joan (1932–) Anne of Windy Poplars 1940; Meet Me in St Louis 1944; Tomorrow the World! 1944; The Bells of St Mary's 1945

Carroll, John (1906–1979) Go West 1940; Hired Wife 1940; Phantom Raiders 1940; Susan and God 1940; Lady Be Good 1941; Sunny 1941; Flying Tigers 1942; Rio Rita 1942; Change of Heart 1943; The Youngest Profession 1943; Bedside Manner 1945; Fiesta 1947; Angel in Exile 1948; The Farmer Takes a Wife 1953; Decision at Sundown 1957

Carroll, Leo G (1892–1972) London by Night 1937; Tower of London 1939; Wuthering Heights 1939; Rebecca 1940; The House on 92nd Street 1945; Spellbound 1945; Song of Love 1947; Time Out of Mind 1947; Enchantment 1948; Father of the Bride 1950; The Happy Years 1950; The Desert Fox 1951; The First Legion 1951; Strangers on a Train 1951; The Snows of Kilimanjaro 1952; Treasure of the Golden Condor 1953; Tarantula 1955; We're No Angels 1955; The Swan 1956; North by Northwest 1959; The Parent Trap 1961; That Funny Feeling 1965; One of Our Spies Is Missing 1966; One Spy Too Many 1966; The Spy in the Green Hat 1966; The Spy with My Face 1966; The Helicopter Spies 1968

Carroll, Madeleine (1906–1987) Escape 1930; I Was a Spy 1934; The World Moves On 1934; The Dictator 1935; The 39 Steps 1935; The General Died at Dawn 1936; Lloyd's of London 1936; Secret Agent 1936; On the Avenue 1937; The Prisoner of Zenda 1937; Blockade 1938; My Son, My Son! 1940; North West Mounted Police 1940; My Favorite Blonde 1942; The Fan 1949

Carroll, Nancy (1904–1965) Abie's Irish Rose 1928; The Shopworn Angel 1928; The Devil's Holiday 1930; Laughter 1930; Paramount on Parade 1930; The Man I Killed 1932; Scarlet Dawn 1932; The Kiss before the Mirror 1933; Atlantic Adventure 1935; That Certain Age 1938; There Goes My Heart 1938

Carroll, Pat (1927–) With Six You Get Eggroll 1968; The Little Mermaid 1989; Songcatcher 1999; The Little Mermaid II: Return to the Sea 2000

Carroll, Rocky The Chase 1994; Crimson Tide 1995; Best Laid Plans 1999

Carrot Top (1967–) Chairman of the Board 1998; Dennis the Menace Strikes Again 1998

Carruthers, Ben aka **Carruthers, Benito** (1936–1983) Shadows 1959; Goldstein 1963; A High Wind in Jamaica 1965; Frank's Greatest Adventure 1967; Riot 1969

Carry III, Julius J (1952–) The Last Dragon 1985; World Gone Wild 1988

Carson, Charles (1885–1977) Dreyfus 1931; Blossom Time 1934; Sixty Glorious Years 1938; We're Going to Be Rich 1938; Cry, the Beloved Country 1951; The Dam Busters 1954; Bobbikins 1959

Carson, Hunter (1975–) Paris, Texas 1984; Invaders from Mars 1986

Carson, Jack (1910–1963) Stage Door 1937; Stand-In 1937; Carefree 1938; Go Chase Yourself 1938; Law of the Underworld 1938; The Saint in New York 1938; Vivacious Lady 1938; I Take This Woman 1940; Lucky Partners 1940; Blues in the Night 1941; The Bride Came COD 1941; Love Crazy 1941; Mr and Mrs Smith 1941; The Strawberry Blonde 1941; Gentleman Jim 1942; The Hard Way 1942; Larceny, Inc 1942; The Male Animal 1942; Princess O'Rourke 1943; Arsenic and Old Lace 1944; The Doughgirls 1944; Make Your Own Bed 1944; Shine On, Harvest Moon 1944; Mildred Pierce 1945; Roughly Speaking 1945; Two Guys from Milwaukee 1946; Romance on the High Seas 1948; It's a Great Feeling 1949; My Dream Is Yours 1949; Bright Leaf 1950; Dangerous When Wet 1953; Phffft! 1954; Red Garters 1954; A Star Is Born 1954; Ain't Misbehavin' 1955; Beyond the River 1956; The Tarnished Angels 1957; Cat on a Hot Tin Roof 1958; Rally 'round the Flag, Boys! 1958; The Bramble Bush 1960; King of the Roaring 20s – the Story of Arnold Rothstein 1961; Sammy, the Way Out Seal 1962; The Night Caller 1965

Carson, Jean aka **Carson, Jeannie** (1928–) A Date with a Dream 1948; Love in Pawn 1953; An Alligator Named Daisy 1955; As Long as They're Happy 1955; Rockets Galore 1958

Carson, John (1927–) Master Spy 1964; Smokescreen 1964; The

Plague of the Zombies 1965; *Captain Kronos: Vampire Hunter* 1972; *Out of Darkness* 1990
Carson, John David (1952–) *Pretty Maids All in a Row* 1971; *The Savage Is Loose* 1974; *Empire of the Ants* 1977
Carson, L M Kit (1947–) *David Holzman's Diary* 1968; *Running on Empty* 1988
Carson, Lisa Nicole (1969–) *Devil in a Blue Dress* 1995; *Eve's Bayou* 1997; *Love Jones* 1997
Carson, Shawn *The Funhouse* 1981; *Something Wicked This Way Comes* 1983
Carsten, Peter (1929–) *Dark of the Sun* 1967; *Zeppelin* 1971
Carstensen, Margit (1940–) *The Bitter Tears of Petra von Kant* 1972; *Martha* 1973; *Mother Küsters Goes to Heaven* 1975; *Chinese Roulette* 1976; *Fear of Fear* 1976; *Satan's Brew* 1976; *The Third Generation* 1979; *Possession* 1981
Cartaxo, Marcelia *Hour of the Star* 1985; *Madame Sata* 2002
Carter, Ben (1907–1946) *Tin Pan Alley* 1940; *Dark Alibi* 1946
Carter, Finn *How I Got Into College* 1989; *Tremors* 1989
Carter, Helena (1923–2000) *Intrigue* 1947; *Something in the Wind* 1947; *Time Out of Mind* 1947; *The Fighting O'Flynn* 1948; *Kiss Tomorrow Goodbye* 1950; *Double Crossbones* 1951; *Fort Worth* 1951; *Bugles in the Afternoon* 1952; *Invaders from Mars* 1953
Carter, Jack (1923–) *The Horizontal Lieutenant* 1962; *The Extraordinary Seaman* 1969; *The Resurrection of Zachary Wheeler* 1971; *The Amazing Dobermans* 1976; *The Happy Hooker Goes to Washington* 1977; *The Glove* 1978; *Alligator* 1980; *Separate Ways* 1981; *Hambone and Hillie* 1984; *The Opposite Sex and How to Live with Them* 1993
Carter, Janis (1913–1994) *Framed* 1947; *And Baby Makes Three* 1949; *Miss Grant Takes Richmond* 1949; *Slightly French* 1949; *The Woman on Pier 13* 1949; *A Woman of Distinction* 1950; *My Forbidden Past* 1951; *Santa Fe* 1951; *The Half-Breed* 1952
Carter, Jason (1960–) *The Emperor's New Clothes* 1987; *Georgia* 1995
Carter, Jim *A Private Function* 1984; *Haunted Honeymoon* 1986; *A Month in the Country* 1987; *The Rainbow* 1988; *Soursweet* 1988; *Blame It on the Bellboy* 1992; *The Hour of the Pig* 1993; *Black Beauty* 1994; *The Grotesque* 1995; *The Madness of King George* 1995; *Brassed Off* 1996; *Keep the Aspidistra Flying* 1997; *Vigo: Passion for Life* 1997; *Legionnaire* 1998; *Shakespeare in Love* 1998; *The Little Vampire* 2000; *Heartlands* 2002; *16 Years of Alcohol* 2003
Carter, Louise (1875–1957) *Hell's Highway* 1932; *Madame Butterfly* 1932; *Jennie Gerhardt* 1933; *You're Telling Me!* 1934
Carter, Lynda (1951–) *Danielle Steel's Daddy* 1991; *Super Troopers* 2001
Carter, Nell (1948–2003) *Modern Problems* 1981; *Bebe's Kids* 1992; *The Grass Harp* 1995; *The Proprietor* 1996
Carter, Reggie *Dr No* 1962; *The Lunatic* 1992
Carter, T K (1956–) *Seems like Old Times* 1980; *Southern Comfort* 1981; *The Thing* 1982; *Doctor Detroit* 1983; *Runaway Train* 1985; *He's My Girl* 1987; *Ski Patrol* 1989; *Baadasssss!* 2003
Carter, Terry (1929–) *Abby* 1974; *Foxy Brown* 1974; *Battlestar Galactica* 1978
Carter, Thomas *Almost Summer* 1977; *Whose Life Is It Anyway?* 1981
Cartlidge, Katrin (1961–2002) *Naked* 1993; *Before the Rain* 1994; *Breaking the Waves* 1996; *Career Girls* 1997; *The Cherry Orchard* 1998; *Claire Dolan* 1998; *Hi-Life* 1998; *The Lost Son* 1998; *Hotel Splendide* 1999; *The Weight of Water* 2000; *From Hell* 2001
Carton, Pauline (1884–1974) *The Blood of a Poet* 1930; *Bonne Chance* 1935
Cartwright, Nancy (1959–) *Yellow Pages* 1984; *Pound Puppies and the Legend of Big Paw* 1988; *Rugrats Go Wild* 2003
Cartwright, Veronica (1949–) *The Children's Hour* 1961; *The Birds* 1963; *One Man's Way* 1964; *Inserts* 1975; *Goin' South* 1978; *Invasion of the Body Snatchers* 1978; *Alien* 1979; *The Right Stuff* 1983; *My Man Adam* 1985; *Flight of the Navigator* 1986; *Wisdom* 1986; *Valentino Returns* 1987; *The Witches of Eastwick* 1987; *False Identity* 1990; *Candyman: Farewell to the Flesh* 1995; *Money Talks* 1997; *Scary Movie 2* 2001; *Just Married* 2003
Caruso, Anthony aka **Caruso, Tony** (1916–2003) *The Asphalt Jungle* 1950; *Tarzan and the Slave Girl* 1950; *Desert Legion* 1953; *Fort Algiers* 1953; *The Boy from Oklahoma* 1954; *Cattle Queen of Montana* 1954; *Phantom of the Rue Morgue* 1954; *Jail Busters* 1955; *Tennessee's Partner* 1955; *Baby Face Nelson* 1957; *The Big Land* 1957; *The Badlanders* 1958; *Fort Massacre* 1958; *Never Steal Anything Small* 1959; *The Most Dangerous Man Alive* 1961; *The Legend of Grizzly Adams* 1990
Caruso, David (1956–) *First Blood* 1982; *An Officer and a Gentleman* 1982; *Thief of Hearts* 1984; *Blue City* 1986; *China Girl* 1987; *Twins* 1988; *King of New York* 1989; *Hudson Hawk* 1991; *Mad Dog and Glory* 1992; *Kiss of Death* 1994; *Jade* 1995; *Body Count* 1997; *Deadlocked* 2000; *Proof of Life* 2000; *Black Point* 2001; *Session 9* 2001
Carver, Brent (1952–) *Millennium* 1989; *Lilies* 1996; *Ararat* 2002
Carver, Lynne aka **Carver, Lynn** (1909–1955) *The Bride Wore Red* 1937; *Maytime* 1937; *A Christmas Carol* 1938; *Everybody Sing* 1938; *Young Dr Kildare* 1938; *The Adventures of Huckleberry Finn* 1939; *Bitter Sweet* 1940; *Broadway Melody of 1940* 1940
Carver, Mary (1924–) *Best Seller* 1987; *[Safe]* 1995
Carvey, Dana (1955–) *Tough Guys* 1986; *Moving* 1988; *Opportunity Knocks* 1990; *Wayne's World* 1992; *Wayne's World 2* 1993; *Clean Slate* 1994; *The Road to Wellville* 1994; *Trapped in Paradise* 1994; *The Shot* 1996; *The Master of Disguise* 2002
Casar, Amira (1971–) *Angel Sharks* 1997; *Would I Lie to You?* 1997; *Pourquoi Pas Moi?* 1999; *Comment J'ai Tué Mon Père* 2001; *Murder on the Orient Express* 2001; *Anatomy of Hell* 2003; *Sylvia* 2003
Casarès, Maria (1922–1996) *Les Enfants du Paradis* 1945; *Les Dames du Bois de Boulogne* 1946; *Orphée* 1950; *Le Testament d'Orphée* 1960; *Someone Else's America* 1995
Case, Kathleen (1938–) *Last of the Pony Riders* 1953; *Human Desire* 1954; *Running Wild* 1955
Casella, Max (1967–) *Sgt Bilko* 1996; *Analyze This* 1999; *The Little Mermaid II: Return to the Sea* 2000
Caselli, Chiara (1967–) *My Own Private Idaho* 1991; *Beyond the Clouds* 1995; *The Vivero Letter* 1998; *Garage Olimpo* 1999; *Ripley's Game* 2002
Casey, Bernie (1939–) *Guns of the Magnificent Seven* 1969; *Brian's Song* 1971; *Boxcar Bertha* 1972; *Hit Man* 1972; *Cleopatra Jones* 1973; *The Man Who Fell to Earth* 1976; *Brothers* 1977; *Sharky's Machine* 1981; *Never Say Never Again* 1983; *Spies like Us* 1985; *Backfire* 1987; *I'm Gonna Git You Sucka* 1988; *Rent-a-Cop* 1988; *Chains of Gold* 1989; *Another 48 HRS* 1990; *The Cemetery Club* 1993; *The Glass Shield* 1995; *The Simple Life of Noah Dearborn* 1999
Casey, Lawrence P aka **Casey, Lawrence** aka **Casey, Larry** *Acapulco Gold* 1976; *Good Guys Wear Black* 1977
Cash, Johnny (1932–2003) *Door-to-Door Maniac* 1961; *A Gunfight* 1971
Cash, Rosalind (1938–1995) *The Omega Man* 1971; *Hickey and Boggs* 1972; *The New Centurions* 1972; *Uptown Saturday Night* 1974; *The Class of Miss MacMichael* 1978; *Go Tell It on the Mountain* 1984
Cashman, Michael (1950–) *I've Gotta Horse* 1965; *Unman, Wittering and Zigo* 1971; *Zee and Co* 1971
Casini, Stefania (1949–) *Blood for Dracula* 1974; *Bad* 1976; *Suspiria* 1976; *The Belly of an Architect* 1987
Casnoff, Philip (1955–) *GORP* 1980; *Kiss Tomorrow Goodbye* 2000
Caso, Mark *Teenage Mutant Ninja Turtles II: the Secret of the Ooze* 1991; *Teenage Mutant Ninja Turtles III* 1992
Caspary, Tina aka **Caspary, Katrina** *Can't Buy Me Love* 1987; *Mac and Me* 1988
Cass, Peggy (1924–1999) *The Marrying Kind* 1952; *Auntie Mame* 1958; *Gidget Goes Hawaiian* 1961
Cassavetes, John (1929–1989) *Taxi* 1953; *The Night Holds Terror* 1955; *Crime in the Streets* 1956; *Affair in Havana* 1957; *Edge of the City* 1957; *Saddle the Wind* 1958; *Virgin Island* 1958; *The Killers* 1964; *The Dirty Dozen* 1967; *Rosemary's Baby* 1968; *If It's Tuesday, This Must Be Belgium* 1969; *Husbands* 1970; *Capone* 1975; *Mikey and Nicky* 1976; *Two-Minute Warning* 1976; *Opening Night* 1977; *Brass Target* 1978; *The Fury* 1978; *Whose Life Is It Anyway?* 1981; *Tempest* 1982; *Marvin and Tige* 1983; *Love Streams* 1984
Cassavetes, Katherine (1896–1983) *Minnie and Moskowitz* 1971; *A Woman under the Influence* 1974
Cassavetes, Nick (1959–) *Black Moon Rising* 1985; *Quiet Cool* 1986; *The Wraith* 1986; *Body of Influence* 1993; *Mrs Parker and the Vicious Circle* 1994; *Twogether* 1994; *Face/Off* 1997; *The Astronaut's Wife* 1999
Cassel, Jean-Pierre (1932–) *The Vanishing Corporal* 1962; *The Beautiful Swindlers* 1964; *Those Magnificent Men in Their Flying Machines* 1965; *Is Paris Burning?* 1966; *L'Armée des Ombres* 1969; *Oh! What a Lovely War* 1969; *La Rupture* 1970; *Malpertuis* 1971; *The Discreet Charm of the Bourgeoisie* 1972; *Baxter* 1973; *Murder on the Orient Express* 1974; *Doctor Françoise Gailland* 1975; *That Lucky Touch* 1975; *The Twist* 1976; *Who Is Killing the Great Chefs of Europe?* 1978; *From Hell to Victory* 1979; *Mister Frost* 1990; *The Favour, the Watch and the Very Big Fish* 1991; *The Maid* 1991; *Pétain* 1992; *La Cérémonie* 1995; *The Crimson Rivers* 2000
Cassel, Seymour (1935–) *Too Late Blues* 1961; *Faces* 1968; *The Revolutionary* 1970; *Minnie and Moskowitz* 1971; *Death Game* 1976; *The Killing of a Chinese Bookie* 1976; *Scott Joplin* 1977; *Valentino* 1977; *Convoy* 1978; *California Dreaming* 1979; *The Mountain Men* 1980; *Love Streams* 1984; *Eye of the Tiger* 1986; *Tin Men* 1987; *Johnny Be Good* 1988; *Plain Clothes* 1988; *Track 29* 1988; *Cold Dog Soup* 1989; *White Fang* 1991; *Chain of Desire* 1992; *Diary of a Hitman* 1992; *In the Soup* 1992; *Boiling Point* 1993; *Indecent Proposal* 1993; *Trouble Bound* 1993; *Chasers* 1994; *Hand Gun* 1994; *Tollbooth* 1994; *Dream for an Insomniac* 1996; *This World, Then the Fireworks* 1996; *Motel Blue* 1997; *Relax... It's Just Sex* 1998; *Rushmore* 1998; *Animal Factory* 2000; *Bartleby* 2000; *Sonny* 2002; *Stealing Harvard* 2002; *The Life Aquatic with Steve Zissou* 2004
Cassel, Vincent (1967–) *La Haine* 1995; *L'Appartement* 1996; *Dobermann* 1997; *Guest House Paradiso* 1999; *Joan of Arc* 1999; *The Crimson Rivers* 2000; *Birthday Girl* 2001; *Brotherhood of the Wolf* 2001; *Read My Lips* 2001; *The Reckoning* 2001; *Shrek* 2001; *Irreversible* 2002; *Blueberry* 2004; *Ocean's Twelve* 2004
Cassell, Alan (1932–) *Cathy's Child* 1979; *Harlequin* 1980; *The Settlement* 1982
Cassell, Wally (1915–1992) *The Story of GI Joe* 1945; *Saigon* 1948; *Sands of Iwo Jima* 1949; *We Were Strangers* 1949; *White Heat* 1949; *Princess of the Nile* 1954; *The Come On* 1956; *Until They Sail* 1957
Casseus, Gabriel *New Jersey Drive* 1995; *Get on the Bus* 1996; *Black Dog* 1998; *Fallen* 1998
Cassidy, Elaine (1980–) *The Sun, the Moon and the Stars* 1995; *Felicia's Journey* 1999; *Disco Pigs* 2001; *The Others* 2001
Cassidy, Jack (1927–1976) *Look in Any Window* 1961; *The Cockeyed Cowboys of Calico County* 1970; *Bunny O'Hare* 1971; *The Eiger Sanction* 1975; *WC Fields and Me* 1976
Cassidy, Joanna (1944–) *The Outfit* 1973; *Bank Shot* 1974; *The Late Show* 1977; *Stunts* 1977; *The Glove* 1978; *Night Games* 1979; *Under Fire* 1983; *Club Paradise* 1986; *The Fourth Protocol* 1987; *1969* 1988; *Who Framed Roger Rabbit* 1988; *The Package* 1989; *May Wine* 1990; *Where the Heart Is* 1990; *Don't Tell Mom the Babysitter's Dead* 1991; *Barbarians at the Gate* 1993; *Vampire in Brooklyn* 1995; *Chain Reaction* 1996; *Loved* 1996; *The Second Civil War* 1997; *Executive Power* 1998; *John Carpenter's Ghosts of Mars* 2001
Cassidy, Patrick (1961–) *Love at Stake* 1987; *Longtime Companion* 1990
Cassidy, Ted (1932–1979) *Butch Cassidy and the Sundance Kid* 1969; *Mackenna's Gold* 1969; *The Slams* 1973; *Goin' Coconuts* 1978
Casson, Lewis (1875–1969) *Escape* 1930; *Crime on the Hill* 1933
Castaldi, Jean-Pierre (1944–) *French Connection II* 1975; *Le Cop II* 1989; *A Touch of Adultery* 1991
Castañeda, Luis Aceves (1913–1973) *Mexican Bus Ride* 1951; *Wuthering Heights* 1953
Castel, France (1943–) *Une Histoire Inventée* 1990; *Karmina* 1996
Castel, Lou (1943–) *Fists in the Pocket* 1965; *A Bullet for the General* 1966; *Kill and Pray* 1967; *Beware of a Holy Whore* 1970; *Nada* 1974; *Killer Nun* 1978; *Treasure Island* 1986; *Irma Vep* 1996
Castellaneta, Dan (1958–) *My Giant* 1998; *Laughter on the 23rd Floor* 2000; *Recess: School's Out* 2001; *Hey Arnold! the Movie* 2002; *Dr Seuss' The Cat in the Hat* 2003
Castellano, Richard (1933–1988) *Lovers and Other Strangers* 1970; *The Godfather* 1972; *Night of the Juggler* 1980
Castellanos, Vincent (1962–) *The Crow: City of Angels* 1996; *Anaconda* 1997; *The Last Marshal* 1999; *Primary Suspect* 2000
Castellitto, Sergio (1953–) *The Big Blue* 1988; *Three Sisters* 1988; *The Starmaker* 1994; *Portraits Chinois* 1996; *Mostly Martha* 2001; *Va Savoir* 2001; *Don't Move* 2004
Castello, Don (1894–1942) *The New Adventures of Tarzan* 1935; *Tarzan and the Green Goddess* 1938
Castelnuovo, Nino (1936–) *The Umbrellas of Cherbourg* 1964; *Les Créatures* 1966; *A Pain in the A...!* 1973; *Loving in the Rain* 1974
Castelot, Jacques (1914–1989) *Les Mains Sales* 1951; *Nana* 1955; *One Night at the Music Hall* 1956
Castile, Christopher (1980–) *Beethoven* 1992; *Beethoven's 2nd* 1993
Castillo, Enrique aka **Castillo, Enrique J** *Borderline* 1980; *Blood In Blood Out* 1992; *The Hi-Lo Country* 1998
Castillo, Gloria (1933–) *Runaway Daughters* 1956; *Invasion of the Saucer Men* 1957; *Reform School Girl* 1957; *Teenage Monster* 1958
Castle, Don (1917–1966) *Out West with the Hardys* 1938; *Wake Island* 1942; *The Big Land* 1957
Castle, John (1940–) *Blowup* 1966; *The Lion in Winter* 1968; *Antony and Cleopatra* 1972; *Man of La Mancha* 1972; *Eagle's Wing* 1978; *Dealers* 1989; *RoboCop 3* 1993; *Sparrow* 1993
Castle, Mary (1931–) *The Lawless Breed* 1952; *Gunsmoke* 1953; *The Jailbreakers* 1960
Castle, Peggie (1927–1973) *Payment on Demand* 1951; *The Prince Who Was a Thief* 1951; *Invasion USA* 1952; *I, the Jury* 1953; *99 River Street* 1953; *The Long Wait* 1954; *The Yellow Tomahawk* 1954; *Tall Man Riding* 1955; *Miracle in the Rain* 1956; *The Oklahoma Woman* 1956; *Beginning of the End* 1957; *Seven Hills of Rome* 1957
Castle, Roy (1932–1994) *Dr Terror's House of Horrors* 1964; *Doctor Who and the Daleks* 1965; *The Plank* 1967; *Carry On Up the Khyber* 1968; *Legend of the Werewolf* 1974
Catania, Antonio (1952–) *Puerto Escondido* 1992; *Bread and Tulips* 2000
Cater, John (1932–) *Loot* 1970; *Captain Kronos: Vampire Hunter* 1972; *Rising Damp* 1980
Cates, Georgina (1975–) *An Awfully Big Adventure* 1994; *Frankie Starlight* 1995; *Stiff Upper Lips* 1997; *Clay Pigeons* 1998
Cates, Phoebe (1963–) *Fast Times at Ridgemont High* 1982; *Paradise* 1982; *Private School* 1983; *Gremlins* 1984; *Date with an Angel* 1987; *Bright Lights, Big City* 1988; *Shag* 1988; *Heart of Dixie* 1989; *Gremlins 2: the New Batch* 1990; *Drop Dead Fred* 1991; *Bodies, Rest and Motion* 1993; *Princess Caraboo* 1994; *The Anniversary Party* 2001
Catherwood, Emma *Large* 2000; *My Kingdom* 2001; *Spirit Trap* 2005
Cathey, Reg E (1958–) *Boycott* 2001; *The Machinist* 2003
Catillon, Brigitte *La Lectrice* 1988; *Un Coeur en Hiver* 1992; *Artemisia* 1997; *Le Goût des Autres* 1999
Catlett, Mary Jo (1938–) *Serial Mom* 1994; *Bram Stoker's Legend of the Mummy* 1998
Catlett, Walter (1889–1960) *The Front Page* 1931; *Rain* 1932; *Banjo on My Knee* 1936; *Cain and Mabel* 1936; *Danger – Love at Work* 1937; *Every Day's a Holiday* 1937; *Love Is News* 1937; *On the Avenue* 1937; *Bringing Up Baby* 1938; *Going Places* 1938; *Kid Nightingale* 1939; *Zaza* 1939; *Change of Heart* 1943; *His Butler's Sister* 1943; *I'll Be Yours* 1947; *Are You with It?* 1948; *The Boy with Green Hair* 1948
Caton, Juliette (1975–) *The Last Temptation of Christ* 1988; *Courage Mountain* 1989; *Small Time Obsession* 2000
Caton, Michael (1943–) *Monkey Grip* 1983; *The Castle* 1997; *The Animal* 2001
Cattrall, Kim (1956–) *Tribute* 1980; *Porky's* 1981; *Ticket to Heaven* 1981; *Police Academy* 1984; *City Limits* 1985; *Hold-Up* 1985; *Turk 182!* 1985; *Big Trouble in Little China* 1986; *Mannequin* 1987; *Masquerade* 1988; *Midnight Crossing* 1988;

Palais Royale 1988; *The Return of the Musketeers* 1989; *The Bonfire of the Vanities* 1990; *For Better or for Worse* 1990; *Split Second* 1991; *Star Trek VI: the Undiscovered Country* 1991; *Live Nude Girls* 1995; *Baby Geniuses* 1999; *36 Hours to Die* 1999; *15 Minutes* 2001; *Crossroads* 2002

Caubère, Philippe (1950–) *Le Château de Ma Mère* 1990; *La Gloire de Mon Père* 1990

Cauchy, Daniel (1930–) *Bob Le Flambeur* 1955; *The Gendarme of St Tropez* 1964

Caulfield, Joan (1922–1991) *Miss Susie Slagle's* 1945; *Blue Skies* 1946; *Monsieur Beaucaire* 1946; *Dear Ruth* 1947; *The Unsuspected* 1947; *Welcome Stranger* 1947; *The Sainted Sisters* 1948; *Dear Wife* 1949; *The Petty Girl* 1950; *The Rains of Ranchipur* 1955; *Cattle King* 1963; *The Daring Dobermans* 1973

Caulfield, Maxwell (1959–) *Grease 2* 1982; *Electric Dreams* 1984; *The Parade* 1984; *The Boys Next Door* 1985; *Project: Alien* 1990; *Gettysburg* 1993; *Empire Records* 1995; *The Real Blonde* 1997; *Facing the Enemy* 2001

Caussimon, Jean-Roger (1918–1985) *French Cancan* 1955; *The House on the Waterfront* 1955

Cavadini, Cathy *aka* **Cavadini, Catherine** *An American Tail: Fievel Goes West* 1991; *The Powerpuff Girls* 2002

Cavalli, Valeria *Everybody's Fine* 1990; *Double Team* 1997

Cavanagh, Megan *A League of Their Own* 1992; *Robin Hood: Men in Tights* 1993; *Jimmy Neutron: Boy Genius* 2001

Cavanagh, Paul *aka* **Cavanaugh, Paul** (1888–1964) *The Devil to Pay* 1930; *The Squaw Man* 1931; *A Bill of Divorcement* 1932; *The Kennel Murder Case* 1933; *The Sin of Nora Moran* 1933; *Tarzan and His Mate* 1934; *Goin' to Town* 1935; *Splendor* 1935; *I Take This Woman* 1940; *The Case of the Black Parrot* 1941; *Shadows on the Stairs* 1941; *The Hard Way* 1942; *The House of Fear* 1944; *The Scarlet Claw* 1944; *The Woman in Green* 1945; *The Verdict* 1946; *Dishonored Lady* 1947; *Secret beyond the Door* 1948; *Rogues of Sherwood Forest* 1950; *The Strange Door* 1951; *The All American* 1953; *The Mississippi Gambler* 1953; *Khyber Patrol* 1954; *Francis in the Haunted House* 1956; *Women without Men* 1956

Cavanaugh, Christine *Babe* 1995; *The Rugrats Movie* 1998; *Rugrats in Paris: the Movie* 2000

Cavanaugh, Hobart (1886–1950) *I Cover the Waterfront* 1933; *Hi, Nellie!* 1934; *The Key* 1934; *A Midsummer Night's Dream* 1935; *Wings in the Dark* 1935; *Cain and Mabel* 1936; *Stage Struck* 1936; *Wife vs Secretary* 1936; *The Great O'Malley* 1937; *Rose of Washington Square* 1939; *Black Angel* 1946; *Up in Central Park* 1948; *A Letter to Three Wives* 1949

Cavanaugh, Michael (1942–) *The Gauntlet* 1977; *Forced Vengeance* 1982

Cavazos, Lumi (1969–) *Like Water for Chocolate* 1993; *Bottle Rocket* 1996; *Sugar Town* 1999

Cave, Nick (1957–) *Ghosts... of the Civil Dead* 1988; *Johnny Suede* 1991

Cavell, Marc (1929–) *Thunder in the East* 1953; *The Wild Angels* 1966

Caven, Ingrid (1943–) *Gods of the Plague* 1969; *The American Soldier* 1970; *Mother Küsters Goes to Heaven* 1975; *Fear of Fear* 1976; *Satan's Brew* 1976; *In a Year of 13 Moons* 1978

Cavendish, Nicola *Angel Square* 1990; *Air Bud* 1997

Caviezel, Jim *aka* **Caviezel, James** (1968–) *GI Jane* 1997; *The Thin Red Line* 1998; *Ride with the Devil* 1999; *Frequency* 2000; *Pay It Forward* 2000; *Angel Eyes* 2001; *The Count of Monte Cristo* 2001; *High Crimes* 2002; *Highwaymen* 2003; *I Am David* 2003; *Bobby Jones: Stroke of Genius* 2004; *The Final Cut* 2004; *The Passion of the Christ* 2004

Cavina, Gianni (1940–) *Noi Tre* 1984; *Christmas Present* 1986

Cawdron, Robert (1921–1998) *Street of Shadows* 1953; *Saturday Night and Sunday Morning* 1960

Cawthorn, Joseph (1868–1949) *The Taming of the Shrew* 1929; *Love Me Tonight* 1932; *White Zombie* 1932; *Glamour* 1934; *Sweet Adeline* 1935; *One Rainy Afternoon* 1936

Cazale, John (1936–1978) *The Conversation* 1974; *The Godfather, Part II* 1974; *Dog Day Afternoon* 1975; *The Deer Hunter* 1978

Cazenove, Christopher (1945–) *Royal Flash* 1975; *East of Elephant Rock* 1976; *Eye of the Needle* 1981; *Heat and Dust* 1982; *Until September* 1984; *Mata Hari* 1985; *The Fantasist* 1986; *Souvenir* 1987; *Three Men and a Little Lady* 1990; *Aces: Iron Eagle III* 1992; *The Proprietor* 1996; *Shadow Run* 1998; *Contagion* 2000; *Beginner's Luck* 2001; *A Knight's Tale* 2001

Ceccaldi, Daniel (1927–2003) *Bed and Board* 1970; *Love in the Afternoon* 1972; *The Pink Telephone* 1975

Cecchi, Carlo (1939–) *La Scorta* 1993; *Hamam: the Turkish Bath* 1996; *The Red Violin* 1998

Cecil, Jonathan (1939–) *Under the Doctor* 1976; *Thirteen at Dinner* 1985; *Agatha Christie's Murder in Three Acts* 1986; *Dead Man's Folly* 1986

Cecil, Nora (1878–1951) *The Old-Fashioned Way* 1934; *The Unknown Guest* 1943

Cedar, Jon *The Manitou* 1978; *Death Hunt* 1981; *Murder in Mind* 1996

Cederlund, Gosta (1888–1980) *Torment* 1944; *It Rains on Our Love* 1946

Cedric the Entertainer *aka* **Cedric "The Entertainer"** (1964–) *Ride* 1998; *Barbershop* 2002; *Serving Sara* 2002; *Intolerable Cruelty* 2003; *Barbershop 2: Back in Business* 2004; *Johnson Family Vacation* 2004; *Be Cool* 2005; *The Honeymooners* 2005; *Madagascar* 2005; *Man of the House* 2005

Celano, Guido (1905–1988) *Four Steps in the Clouds* 1942; *Never Take No for an Answer* 1951; *The Man from Cairo* 1953; *The Loves of Three Queens* 1954; *Seven Hills of Rome* 1957

Célarié, Clémentine (1957–) *Betty Blue* 1986; *Le Cri du Coeur* 1994; *The Lawless Heart* 2001

Cele, Henry (1949–) *Out of Darkness* 1990; *Curse III: Blood Sacrifice* 1991

Celi, Adolfo (1922–1986) *That Man from Rio* 1964; *The Agony and the Ecstasy* 1965; *Thunderball* 1965; *The Bobo* 1967; *Danger: Diabolik* 1967; *Grand Slam* 1967; *The Honey Pot* 1967; *Operation Kid Brother* 1967; *Midas Run* 1969; *Fragment of Fear* 1970; *In Search of Gregory* 1970; *Murders in the Rue Morgue* 1971; *Hitler: the Last Ten Days* 1973; *The Italian Connection* 1973; *And Then There Were None* 1974; *Le Fantôme de la Liberté* 1974; *The Next Man* 1976; *Monsignor* 1982

Celinska, Stanislawa (1947–) *Landscape after Battle* 1970; *Miss Nobody* 1997

Celio, Teco *Three Colours Red* 1994; *The Truce* 1997

Celli, Teresa (1924–) *Border Incident* 1949; *The Black Hand* 1950; *Right Cross* 1950

Cellier, Antoinette (1913–1981) *Music Hath Charms* 1935; *The Great Barrier* 1937; *Bees in Paradise* 1943; *The End of the River* 1947

Cellier, Caroline (1945–) *Que la Bête Meure* 1969; *Sweet Torture* 1971; *A Pain in the A...!* 1973; *Petit Con* 1984; *Farinelli il Castrato* 1994

Cellier, Frank (1884–1948) *Doss House* 1933; *The Passing of the Third Floor Back* 1935; *The 39 Steps* 1935; *The Man Who Changed His Mind* 1936; *Rhodes of Africa* 1936; *Tudor Rose* 1936; *You're In the Army Now* 1936; *The Black Sheep of Whitehall* 1941; *Love on the Dole* 1941; *Give Us the Moon* 1944; *Quiet Weekend* 1946; *The Blind Goddess* 1948

Cellier, Peter (1940–1994) *Man about the House* 1974; *Man Friday* 1975; *And the Ship Sails On* 1983

Cepek, Petr *Cutting It Short* 1980; *My Sweet Little Village* 1986; *Faust* 1994

Cerra, Saturno *Valentina* 1982; *1919* 1983

Cerval, Claude (1921–1975) *Bob Le Flambeur* 1955; *Le Beau Serge* 1958; *Les Cousins* 1959; *The Big Risk* 1960; *Ophélia* 1962

Cervantes, Gary *Boulevard Nights* 1979; *A Low Down Dirty Shame* 1994

Cervera Jr, Jorge *aka* **Cervera, Jorge** *The Longshot* 1986; *Real Women Have Curves* 2002

Cervi, Gino (1901–1974) *Four Steps in the Clouds* 1942; *Les Misérables* 1946; *The Little World of Don Camillo* 1951; *La Signora senza Camelie* 1953; *Indiscretion of an American Wife* 1954; *The Naked Maja* 1959; *The Siege of Syracuse* 1959; *Becket* 1964

Cervi, Valentina (1974–) *Artemisia* 1997; *Children of Hannibal* 1998; *Rien sur Robert* 1998; *James Dean* 2001

Cervo, Pascal (1977–) *A Toute Vitesse* 1996; *Skin of Man, Heart of Beast* 1999

Cesana, Renzo (1907–1970) *Stromboli* 1950; *For the First Time* 1959

Chabat, Alain (1958–) *Six Days, Six Nights* 1994; *Gazon Maudit* 1995; *Didier* 1997; *Le Goût des Autres* 1999; *Asterix & Obelix: Mission Cleopatra* 2001

Chabert, Lacey (1982–) *An American Tail: the Treasure of Manhattan Island* 1998; *Lost in Space* 1998; *An American Tail: the Mystery of the Night Monster* 2000; *The Wild Thornberrys Movie* 2003; *Mean Girls* 2004

Chabrol, Claude (1930–) *Les Bonnes Femmes* 1960; *Paris Vu Par...* 1965; *The Road to Corinth* 1967; *Les Biches* 1968; *Polar* 1984

Chabrol, Thomas (1963–) *Rien Ne Va Plus* 1997; *The Flower of Evil* 2002

Chadbon, Tom (1946–) *The Beast Must Die* 1974; *Dance with a Stranger* 1984

Chadov, Alexei (1981–) *War* 2002; *Night Watch* 2004

Chadwick, Cyril *The Iron Horse* 1924; *The Black Watch* 1929; *The Last of Mrs Cheyney* 1929

Chadwick, June (1950–) *Agatha Christie's Sparkling Cyanide* 1983; *Distortions* 1987

Chagrin, Julian *aka* **Joy-Chagrin, Julian** (1940–) *Alfred the Great* 1969; *The Emperor's New Clothes* 1987

Chahine, Youssef (1926–) *Cairo Station* 1958; *Alexandria Encore* 1990

Chakiris, George *aka* **Kerris, George** (1933–) *Meet Me in Las Vegas* 1956; *Two and Two Make Six* 1961; *West Side Story* 1961; *Diamond Head* 1962; *Kings of the Sun* 1963; *Flight from Ashiya* 1964; *633 Squadron* 1964; *The High Bright Sun* 1965; *The Theft of the Mona Lisa* 1965; *The Young Girls of Rochefort* 1967; *The Big Cube* 1969

Chakravarty, Lily *aka* **Chakraborty, Lily** *The Middleman* 1975; *Branches of the Tree* 1990; *Chokher Bali* 2003

Chaliapin Jr, Feodor *aka* **Chaliapin, Feodor** (1907–1992) *The Name of the Rose* 1986; *The Church* 1988; *Stanley & Iris* 1989; *The King's Whore* 1990; *The Inner Circle* 1991

Chalmers, Thomas (1884–1966) *The Plow That Broke the Plains* 1934; *The River* 1937; *All the Way Home* 1963; *The Outrage* 1964

Chamas, Mohamad *West Beirut* 1998; *Blind Flight* 2003

Chamberlain, Cyril (1909–1974) *Impulse* 1955; *Tiger by the Tail* 1955; *The Great St Trinian's Train Robbery* 1966

Chamberlain, Richard (1935–) *The Secret of the Purple Reef* 1960; *A Thunder of Drums* 1961; *Twilight of Honor* 1963; *Joy in the Morning* 1965; *Petulia* 1968; *The Madwoman of Chaillot* 1969; *Julius Caesar* 1970; *The Music Lovers* 1970; *Lady Caroline Lamb* 1972; *The Three Musketeers* 1973; *The Count of Monte Cristo* 1974; *The Four Musketeers* 1974; *The Towering Inferno* 1974; *The Slipper and the Rose* 1976; *The Last Wave* 1977; *The Man in the Iron Mask* 1977; *The Swarm* 1978; *Murder by Phone* 1982; *King Solomon's Mines* 1985; *Allan Quatermain and the Lost City of Gold* 1987; *The Return of the Musketeers* 1989

Chamberlin, Howland *aka* **Chamberlain, Howland** (1911–1984) *The Web* 1947; *Force of Evil* 1948; *The Big Night* 1951; *Kramer vs Kramer* 1979

Chamberlin, Lee (1938–) *Let's Do It Again* 1975; *Beat Street* 1984

Chambers, Justin (1970–) *The Musketeer* 2001; *The Wedding Planner* 2001; *Leo* 2002

Chambers (1), Michael *aka* **Chambers, Michael "Boogaloo Shrimp"** *Breakdance* 1984; *Breakdance 2 – Electric Boogaloo* 1984

Chambliss, Woodrow (1914–1981) *Wild Seed* 1965; *Cry for Me Billy* 1972

Champa, Jo (1969–) *The Family* 1987; *Out for Justice* 1991

Champion, Gower (1919–1980) *Show Boat* 1951; *Everything I Have Is Yours* 1952; *Lovely to Look At* 1952; *Give a Girl a Break* 1953; *Jupiter's Darling* 1955; *Three for the Show* 1955

Champion, Jean (1914–2001) *The Umbrellas of Cherbourg* 1964; *Day for Night* 1973; *The Invitation* 1973

Champion, Marge (1921–) *Show Boat* 1951; *Everything I Have Is Yours* 1952; *Lovely to Look At* 1952; *Give a Girl a Break* 1953; *Jupiter's Darling* 1955; *Three for the Show* 1955; *The Party* 1968; *The Swimmer* 1968

Champion, Michael *aka* **Champion, Mike** *False Identity* 1990; *Total Recall* 1990

Chan, Anthony *Mr Vampire* 1986; *Twin Dragons* 1992

Chan, Dennis *Kickboxer* 1989; *Kickboxer 2: the Road Back* 1990; *Kickboxer III: the Art of War* 1992

Chan, Jackie (1954–) *Drunken Master* 1978; *The Young Master* 1979; *The Big Brawl* 1980; *The Cannonball Run* 1981; *Cannonball Run II* 1983; *Project A* 1983; *Wheels on Meals* 1984; *Police Story* 1985; *The Protector* 1985; *The Armour of God* 1986; *Police Story 2* 1986; *Project A: Part II* 1987; *Operation Condor: the Armour of God II* 1990; *Police Story III: Supercop* 1992; *Twin Dragons* 1992; *Crime Story* 1993; *Thunderbolt* 1995; *Jackie Chan's First Strike* 1996; *Mr Nice Guy* 1996; *Rumble in the Bronx* 1996; *Burn Hollywood Burn* 1997; *Jackie Chan's Who Am I?* 1998; *Rush Hour* 1998; *Gen-X Cops* 1999; *Gorgeous* 1999; *Shanghai Noon* 2000; *The Accidental Spy* 2001; *Rush Hour 2* 2001; *Shanghai Knights* 2002; *The Tuxedo* 2002; *The Medallion* 2003; *Around the World in 80 Days* 2004

Chan, Jacqui *The World of Suzie Wong* 1960; *Krakatoa, East of Java* 1969

Chan, Jordan (1967–) *Young and Dangerous* 1996; *Kitchen* 1997; *And Now You're Dead* 1998

Chan, Michael Paul *Thousand Pieces of Gold* 1990; *The Big Tease* 1999

Chan, Philip *aka* **Chan, Philip Yan Kin** *Bloodsport* 1987; *Double Impact* 1991; *Hard-Boiled* 1992; *Twin Dragons* 1992

Chance, Naomi (1930–) *The Gambler and the Lady* 1952; *Wings of Danger* 1952; *Blood Orange* 1953; *Suspended Alibi* 1956

Chancellor, Anna (1964–) *Staggered* 1993; *Four Weddings and a Funeral* 1994; *Heart* 1997; *The Man Who Knew Too Little* 1997; *Crush* 2001; *Agent Cody Banks 2: Destination London* 2003; *The Dreamers* 2003; *What a Girl Wants* 2003; *The Hitchhiker's Guide to the Galaxy* 2005

Chandler, Chick (1905–1988) *Melody Cruise* 1933; *Murder on a Honeymoon* 1935; *Born Reckless* 1937; *Mr Moto Takes a Chance* 1938; *Swanee River* 1939; *Baby Face Morgan* 1942; *The Big Shot* 1942; *Johnny Doesn't Live Here Anymore* 1944; *Do You Love Me?* 1946; *Nightmare in the Sun* 1964

Chandler, Estee *The Emerald Forest* 1985; *Terminal Bliss* 1990

Chandler, George (1898–1985) *Arizona* 1940; *Strange Impersonation* 1946

Chandler, Helen (1906–1965) *Outward Bound* 1930; *Daybreak* 1931; *Dracula* 1931; *The Last Flight* 1931; *Christopher Strong* 1933; *The Worst Woman in Paris?* 1933; *Long Lost Father* 1934; *The Unfinished Symphony* 1934

Chandler, Jeff (1918–1961) *Broken Arrow* 1950; *Two Flags West* 1950; *Bird of Paradise* 1951; *Double Crossbones* 1951; *Iron Man* 1951; *The Battle at Apache Pass* 1952; *Red Ball Express* 1952; *East of Sumatra* 1953; *The Great Sioux Uprising* 1953; *War Arrow* 1953; *Sign of the Pagan* 1954; *Yankee Pasha* 1954; *Female on the Beach* 1955; *Foxfire* 1955; *The Spoilers* 1955; *Away All Boats* 1956; *Pillars of the Sky* 1956; *Drango* 1957; *Jeanne Eagels* 1957; *Man in the Shadow* 1957; *The Lady Takes a Flyer* 1958; *Raw Wind in Eden* 1958; *The Jayhawkers* 1959; *A Stranger in My Arms* 1959; *Ten Seconds to Hell* 1959; *Thunder in the Sun* 1959; *Return to Peyton Place* 1961; *Merrill's Marauders* 1962

Chandler, Joan (1923–1979) *Humoresque* 1946; *Rope* 1948

Chandler, John Davis *aka* **Chandler, John** (1937–) *Mad Dog Coll* 1961; *Ride the High Country* 1962; *Once a Thief* 1965; *The Good Guys and the Bad Guys* 1969; *Part 2 Walking Tall* 1975; *Scorchy* 1976

Chandler, Kyle (1965–) *Pure Country* 1992; *Angel's Dance* 1999

Chandler, Lane (1899–1972) *The Single Standard* 1929; *Sagebrush Trail* 1934; *Winds of the Wasteland* 1936; *Return to Treasure Island* 1954

Chandos, John (1917–1987) *Next of Kin* 1942; *The Long Memory* 1952; *One Way Out* 1955; *The Battle of the River Plate* 1956; *The Green Man* 1956

Chandrasekhar, Jay *Super Troopers* 2001; *Broken Lizard's Club Dread* 2004

Chaney, Lon (1883–1930) *The Ace of Hearts* 1921; *Oliver Twist* 1922; *The Hunchback of Notre Dame* 1923; *He Who Gets Slapped* 1924; *The Monster* 1925; *The Phantom of the Opera* 1925; *The Unholy Three* 1925; *The Black Bird* 1926; *The Road to Mandalay* 1926; *London after Midnight* 1927; *The Unknown* 1927; *Laugh, Clown, Laugh* 1928; *West of Zanzibar* 1928; *The Unholy Three* 1930

Chaney Jr, Lon *aka* **Chaney, Creighton** *aka* **Chaney, Lon** (1906–1973) *Bird of Paradise* 1932; *Lucky Devils* 1933; *Josette* 1938; *Frontier Marshal* 1939; *Of Mice and Men* 1939; *Union Pacific*

1939; *One Million BC* 1940; *Billy the Kid* 1941; *Man Made Monster* 1941; *The Wolf Man* 1941; *The Ghost of Frankenstein* 1942; *The Mummy's Tomb* 1942; *Calling Dr Death* 1943; *Frankenstein Meets the Wolf Man* 1943; *Frontier Badmen* 1943; *Son of Dracula* 1943; *Cobra Woman* 1944; *Dead Man's Eyes* 1944; *Follow the Boys* 1944; *The Frozen Ghost* 1944; *Ghost Catchers* 1944; *House of Frankenstein* 1944; *The Mummy's Curse* 1944; *The Mummy's Ghost* 1944; *Weird Woman* 1944; *The Daltons Ride Again* 1945; *Here Come the Co-Eds* 1945; *House of Dracula* 1945; *Pillow of Death* 1945; *Strange Confession* 1945; *My Favorite Brunette* 1947; *Abbott and Costello Meet Frankenstein* 1948; *The Counterfeiters* 1948; *Only the Valiant* 1950; *Inside Straight* 1951; *The Black Castle* 1952; *High Noon* 1952; *Springfield Rifle* 1952; *Thief of Damascus* 1952; *A Lion Is in the Streets* 1953; *Raiders of the Seven Seas* 1953; *The Boy from Oklahoma* 1954; *Casanova's Big Night* 1954; *Jivaro* 1954; *Passion* 1954; *Big House, USA* 1955; *I Died a Thousand Times* 1955; *The Indian Fighter* 1955; *Not as a Stranger* 1955; *The Black Sleep* 1956; *Indestructible Man* 1956; *Pardners* 1956; *The Cyclops* 1957; *Daniel Boone, Trail Blazer* 1957; *The Defiant Ones* 1958; *Money, Women and Guns* 1958; *The Alligator People* 1959; *Night of the Ghouls* 1959; *The Haunted Palace* 1963; *Spider Baby* 1964; *Apache Uprising* 1965; *Black Spurs* 1965; *Johnny Reno* 1966; *The Female Bunch* 1969; *Dracula vs Frankenstein* 1970

Chang Chen (1976–) *Happy Together* 1997; *Crouching Tiger, Hidden Dragon* 2000; *Chinese Odyssey 2002* 2002

Chang, Sylvia (1953–) *Soursweet* 1988; *Eat Drink Man Woman* 1994; *The Red Violin* 1998

Channing, Carol (1921–) *The First Travelling Saleslady* 1956; *Thoroughly Modern Millie* 1967; *Skidoo* 1968; *Shinbone Alley* 1971; *Happily Ever After* 1990

Channing, Stockard (1944–) *The Fortune* 1975; *The Big Bus* 1976; *The Cheap Detective* 1978; *Grease* 1978; *The Fish That Saved Pittsburgh* 1979; *Without a Trace* 1983; *Heartburn* 1986; *The Men's Club* 1986; *A Time of Destiny* 1988; *Staying Together* 1989; *Married to It* 1991; *Meet the Applegates* 1991; *Bitter Moon* 1992; *Six Degrees of Separation* 1993; *David's Mother* 1994; *Moll Flanders* 1995; *Smoke* 1995; *To Wong Foo, Thanks for Everything, Julie Newmar* 1995; *The First Wives Club* 1996; *Up Close & Personal* 1996; *Practical Magic* 1998; *Twilight* 1998; *Isn't She Great* 1999; *Where the Heart Is* 2000; *The Business of Strangers* 2001; *Life or Something like It* 2002; *Anything Else* 2003; *Bright Young Things* 2003; *Le Divorce* 2003

Chao, Rosalind (1949–) *The Big Brawl* 1980; *An Eye for an Eye* 1981; *Thousand Pieces of Gold* 1990; *The End of Violence* 1997; *What Dreams May Come* 1998; *Freaky Friday* 2003

Chao, Winston *The Wedding Banquet* 1993; *Eat Drink Man Woman* 1994

Chapa, Damian (1963–) *Blood In Blood Out* 1992; *Under Siege* 1992; *Final Combination* 1993; *Street Fighter* 1994; *Sometimes They Come Back... for More* 1998; *Bad Karma* 2001

Chapin, Billy (1943–) *The Kid from Left Field* 1953; *Naked Alibi* 1954; *The Night of the Hunter* 1955; *Tension at Table Rock* 1956

Chapin, Miles (1954–) *Bless the Beasts and Children* 1971; *French Postcards* 1979; *Buddy Buddy* 1981; *The Funhouse* 1981; *Pandemonium* 1982; *Get Crazy* 1983

Chaplin, Ben (1970–) *The Remains of the Day* 1993; *Feast of July* 1995; *The Truth about Cats and Dogs* 1996; *Washington Square* 1997; *The Thin Red Line* 1998; *Lost Souls* 2000; *Birthday Girl* 2001; *Murder by Numbers* 2002; *Stage Beauty* 2004

Chaplin, Carmen *The Serpent's Kiss* 1997; *Pourquoi Pas Moi?* 1999

Chaplin, Charles *aka* **Chaplin, Charlie** (1889–1977) *Tillie's Punctured Romance* 1914; *His New Job* 1915; *The Tramp* 1915; *Work* 1915; *Behind the Screen* 1916; *The Floorwalker* 1916; *The Pawnshop* 1916; *The Rink* 1916; *The Vagabond* 1916; *The Cure* 1917; *The Immigrant* 1917; *Shoulder Arms* 1918; *A Day's Pleasure* 1919; *Sunnyside* 1919; *The Idle Class* 1921; *The Kid* 1921; *Pay Day* 1922; *Hollywood* 1923; *The Pilgrim* 1923; *A Woman of Paris* 1923; *The Gold Rush* 1925; *The Circus* 1928; *Show People* 1928; *City Lights* 1931; *Modern Times* 1936; *The Great Dictator* 1940; *Monsieur Verdoux* 1947; *Limelight* 1952; *A King in New York* 1957

Chaplin Jr, Charles (1925–1968) *Limelight* 1952; *The Beat Generation* 1959; *The Big Operator* 1959

Chaplin, Christopher (1962–) *Death of a Schoolboy* 1990; *Labyrinth* 1991

Chaplin, Geraldine (1944–) *Limelight* 1952; *Doctor Zhivago* 1965; *Peppermint Frappé* 1967; *Stranger in the House* 1967; *The Hawaiians* 1970; *ZPG: Zero Population Growth* 1971; *Innocent Bystanders* 1972; *The Four Musketeers* 1974; *Cría Cuervos* 1975; *Nashville* 1975; *Buffalo Bill and the Indians, or Sitting Bull's History Lesson* 1976; *Welcome to LA* 1976; *Roseland* 1977; *Remember My Name* 1978; *A Wedding* 1978; *Mamá Cumple 100 Años* 1979; *The Mirror Crack'd* 1980; *Les Uns et les Autres* 1981; *Life Is a Bed of Roses* 1983; *L'Amour par Terre* 1984; *White Mischief* 1987; *The Moderns* 1988; *The Return of the Musketeers* 1989; *The Children* 1990; *Chaplin* 1992; *The Age of Innocence* 1993; *Home for the Holidays* 1995; *Jane Eyre* 1996; *Cousin Bette* 1997; *The Odyssey* 1997; *To Walk with Lions* 1999; *Talk to Her* 2001; *The City of No Limits* 2002

Chaplin, Josephine (1949–) *Limelight* 1952; *Shadowman* 1973

Chaplin, Syd *aka* **Chaplin, Sydney** (1885–1965) *Shoulder Arms* 1918; *A Day's Pleasure* 1919; *Pay Day* 1922; *The Pilgrim* 1923

Chaplin, Sydney (1926–) *Limelight* 1952; *Confession* 1955; *Land of the Pharaohs* 1955; *Quantez* 1957; *A Countess from Hong Kong* 1967; *Ho!* 1968; *The Adding Machine* 1969; *Satan's Cheerleaders* 1977

Chapman, Constance (1912–2003) *Say Hello to Yesterday* 1971; *In Celebration* 1974; *Hedda* 1975; *Clockwise* 1986

Chapman, Edward (1901–1977) *Juno and the Paycock* 1930; *Murder* 1930; *The Skin Game* 1931; *Blossom Time* 1934; *The Man Who Could Work Miracles* 1936; *Rembrandt* 1936; *Someone at the Door* 1936; *Things to Come* 1936; *Poison Pen* 1939; *Convoy* 1940; *The Proud Valley* 1940; *It's Turned Out Nice Again* 1941; *They Flew Alone* 1941; *Ships with Wings* 1942; *It Always Rains on Sunday* 1947; *The October Man* 1947; *The History of Mr Polly* 1948; *Mr Perrin and Mr Traill* 1948; *Madeleine* 1949; *The Spider and the Fly* 1949; *Gone to Earth* 1950; *The Card* 1952; *Folly to Be Wise* 1952; *Mandy* 1952; *A Day to Remember* 1953; *A Yank in Ermine* 1955; *Bhowani Junction* 1956; *X the Unknown* 1956; *Just My Luck* 1957; *The Square Peg* 1958; *Oscar Wilde* 1959; *The Bulldog Breed* 1960; *School for Scoundrels* 1960; *A Stitch in Time* 1963; *The Early Bird* 1965

Chapman, Graham (1941–1989) *The Magic Christian* 1969; *Doctor in Trouble* 1970; *And Now for Something Completely Different* 1971; *Monty Python and the Holy Grail* 1975; *Pleasure at Her Majesty's* 1976; *The Odd Job* 1978; *Monty Python's Life of Brian* 1979; *Monty Python Live at the Hollywood Bowl* 1982; *Monty Python's The Meaning of Life* 1983; *Yellowbeard* 1983; *Still Crazy like a Fox* 1987

Chapman, Lonny (1921–) *Baby Doll* 1956; *The Stalking Moon* 1968; *The Reivers* 1969; *Take the Money and Run* 1969; *I Walk the Line* 1970; *The Cowboys* 1972; *Where the Red Fern Grows* 1974; *52 Pick-Up* 1986

Chapman, Marguerite (1918–1999) *The Body Disappears* 1941; *Counter-Attack* 1945; *Pardon My Past* 1945; *The Gallant Blade* 1948; *Relentless* 1948; *Kansas Raiders* 1950; *Flight to Mars* 1951; *Bloodhounds of Broadway* 1952; *The Last Page* 1952; *The Seven Year Itch* 1955; *The Amazing Transparent Man* 1960

Chapman, Mark Lindsay *Separate Lives* 1995; *Bram Stoker's Legend of the Mummy* 1998

Chapman, Sean *Party Party* 1983; *Hellraiser* 1987; *For Queen and Country* 1988; *Hellbound: Hellraiser II* 1988; *One of the Hollywood Ten* 2000

Chappelle, Dave (1973–) *Robin Hood: Men in Tights* 1993; *Getting In* 1994; *The Nutty Professor* 1996; *Half-Baked* 1998; *Woo* 1998; *You've Got Mail* 1998; *Blue Streak* 1999; *Screwed* 2000; *Undercover Brother* 2002

Chappey, Antoine *Pour Rire!* 1996; *I'm Going Home* 2001; *5x2* 2004

Charbonneau, Patricia (1959–) *Desert Hearts* 1985; *Call Me* 1988; *Brain Dead* 1990; *K2* 1991; *One Special Night* 1999

Charendoff, Tara *aka* **Strong, Tara** (1973–) *The Little Mermaid II: Return to the Sea* 2000; *Rugrats in Paris: the Movie* 2000; *Spirited Away* 2001; *Ice Age* 2002; *The Powerpuff Girls* 2002; *Rugrats Go Wild* 2003

Charisse, Cyd (1921–) *Ziegfeld Follies* 1944; *The Harvey Girls* 1946; *Fiesta* 1947; *The Unfinished Dance* 1947; *On an Island with You* 1948; *East Side, West Side* 1949; *The Kissing Bandit* 1949; *Tension* 1949; *Singin' in the Rain* 1952; *Sombrero* 1952; *The Wild North* 1952; *The Band Wagon* 1953; *Brigadoon* 1954; *Deep in My Heart* 1954; *It's Always Fair Weather* 1955; *Meet Me in Las Vegas* 1956; *Silk Stockings* 1957; *Party Girl* 1958; *Twilight for the Gods* 1958; *Two Weeks in Another Town* 1962; *Maroc 7* 1966; *The Silencers* 1966; *Warlords of Atlantis* 1978

Charles, Josh (1971–) *Dead Poets Society* 1989; *Murder in Mississippi* 1990; *Don't Tell Mom the Babysitter's Dead* 1991; *Cooperstown* 1993; *Threesome* 1994; *Coldblooded* 1995; *Pie in the Sky* 1995; *Crosswords* 1996; *Norma Jean & Marilyn* 1996; *Little City* 1997; *SWAT* 2003

Charles, Ray (1930–2004) *Ballad in Blue* 1964; *The Blues Brothers* 1980; *Limit Up* 1989

Charleson, Ian (1949–1990) *Jubilee* 1978; *Chariots of Fire* 1981; *Greystoke: the Legend of Tarzan, Lord of the Apes* 1984; *Car Trouble* 1985; *Opera* 1987

Charlesworth, John (1934–1960) *Scrooge* 1951; *Tom Brown's Schooldays* 1951; *John of the Fair* 1952; *The Blue Peter* 1955

Charlita *The Brave Bulls* 1951; *Bela Lugosi Meets a Brooklyn Gorilla* 1952; *Ride, Vaquero!* 1953; *The Naked Dawn* 1955

Charmetant, Christian *News from the Good Lord* 1996; *Le Libertin* 2000

Charney, Jordan (1937–) *Witches' Brew* 1979; *Do You Remember Love* 1985

Charney, Kim (1945–) *Suddenly* 1954; *Quantrill's Raiders* 1958; *Hey Boy! Hey Girl!* 1959

Charo (1941–) *Tiger by the Tail* 1970; *Airport '79: the Concorde* 1979; *Moon over Parador* 1988

Charpin, Fernand (1887–1944) *Marius* 1931; *Fanny* 1932; *César* 1936; *Pépé le Moko* 1937

Charrier, Jacques (1936–) *Les Tricheurs* 1958; *The Seven Deadly Sins* 1961; *Les Créatures* 1966

Charters, Spencer (1875–1943) *Whoopee!* 1930; *Palmy Days* 1931; *Jewel Robbery* 1932; *Spendthrift* 1936; *Forbidden Valley* 1938; *Three Faces West* 1940

Chartoff, Melanie (1955–) *The Rugrats Movie* 1998; *Rugrats Go Wild* 2003

Chase, Alden (1902–1982) *The Little Colonel* 1935; *The Lone Rider in Ghost Town* 1941

Chase, Annazette *Truck Turner* 1974; *Part 2, Sounder* 1976

Chase, Charley (1893–1940) *Sons of the Desert* 1933; *Laurel and Hardy's Laughing 20s* 1965; *4 Clowns* 1970

Chase, Cheryl *Rugrats in Paris: the Movie* 2000; *Rugrats Go Wild* 2003

Chase, Chevy (1943–) *The Groove Tube* 1974; *Tunnelvision* 1976; *Foul Play* 1978; *Caddyshack* 1980; *Oh, Heavenly Dog!* 1980; *Seems like Old Times* 1980; *Modern Problems* 1981; *Under the Rainbow* 1981; *Deal of the Century* 1983; *National Lampoon's Vacation* 1983; *Fletch* 1985; *National Lampoon's European Vacation* 1985; *Sesame Street Presents: Follow That Bird* 1985; *Spies like Us* 1985; *Three Amigos!* 1986; *Caddyshack II* 1988; *The Couch Trip* 1988; *Funny Farm* 1988; *Fletch Lives* 1989; *National Lampoon's Christmas Vacation* 1989; *Nothing but Trouble* 1991; *Memoirs of an Invisible Man* 1992; *Cops and Robbersons* 1994; *Man of the House* 1994; *Vegas Vacation* 1997; *Dirty Work* 1998; *Snow Day* 2000; *Orange County* 2001

Chase, Daveigh (1990–) *Spirited Away* 2001; *Lilo & Stitch* 2002

Chase, Ilka (1900–1978) *The Animal Kingdom* 1932; *Now, Voyager* 1942; *No Time for Love* 1943; *Miss Tatlock's Millions* 1948; *Johnny Dark* 1954

Chase (1), Stephen *aka* **Chase, Steven** (1902–1982) *Cavalry Scout* 1951; *My Favorite Spy* 1951; *When Worlds Collide* 1951; *The Great Sioux Uprising* 1953; *The Blob* 1958

Chatel, Peter (1943–1986) *Martha* 1973; *Fox and His Friends* 1975

Chatterjee, Anil (1928–) *The Cloud Capped Star* 1960; *Teen Kanya* 1961; *Kangchenjunga* 1962; *The Big City* 1963

Chatterjee, Dhritiman *aka* **Chaterji, Dhritiman** (1946–) *The Adversary* 1970; *In Search of Famine* 1980; *36 Chowringhee Lane* 1982; *An Enemy of the People* 1989; *The Stranger* 1991; *Black* 2004

Chatterjee, Soumitra (1934–) *The World of Apu* 1959; *Devi* 1960; *Teen Kanya* 1961; *Abhijaan* 1962; *Charulata* 1964; *Days and Nights in the Forest* 1969; *Distant Thunder* 1973; *The Home and the World* 1984; *An Enemy of the People* 1989; *Branches of the Tree* 1990

Chatterton, Ruth (1893–1961) *Madame X* 1929; *Anybody's Woman* 1930; *Paramount on Parade* 1930; *Sarah and Son* 1930; *The Rich Are Always with Us* 1932; *Female* 1933; *Dodsworth* 1936

Chattopadhyay, Harindranath *The Householder* 1963; *Tere Ghar Ke Saamne* 1963; *Company Limited* 1971

Chau, François (1959–) *Teenage Mutant Ninja Turtles II: the Secret of the Ooze* 1991; *Beverly Hills Ninja* 1997

Chaudhary, Mahima *Pardes* 1997; *Baghban* 2003

Chaulet, Emmanuelle *My Girlfriend's Boyfriend* 1987; *All the Vermeers in New York* 1990

Chaumette, Monique (1927–) *La Grande Bouffe* 1973; *Sunday in the Country* 1984; *Masques* 1987

Chautard, Emile *aka* **Chautard, Emil** (1881–1934) *Shanghai Express* 1932; *The Devil's in Love* 1933

Chaykin, Maury (1949–) *Of Unknown Origin* 1983; *Def-Con 4* 1984; *Harry and Son* 1984; *Wild Thing* 1987; *Stars and Bars* 1988; *Breaking In* 1989; *Cold Comfort* 1989; *Millennium* 1989; *Dances with Wolves* 1990; *Mr Destiny* 1990; *The Adjuster* 1991; *George's Island* 1991; *Accidental Hero* 1992; *Leaving Normal* 1992; *Camilla* 1993; *Money for Nothing* 1993; *Whale Music* 1994; *CutThroat Island* 1995; *Devil in a Blue Dress* 1995; *Unstrung Heroes* 1995; *Mousehunt* 1997; *The Sweet Hereafter* 1997; *Jerry and Tom* 1998; *Love and Death on Long Island* 1998; *The Mask of Zorro* 1998; *Entrapment* 1999; *Jacob Two Two Meets the Hooded Fang* 1999; *Mystery, Alaska* 1999; *The Art of War* 2000; *Bartleby* 2000; *Varian's War* 2000; *What's Cooking?* 2000; *Owning Mahowny* 2002; *Being Julia* 2004

Chazel, Marie-Anne (1951–) *Les Visiteurs* 1993; *Les Visiteurs 2: Les Couloirs du Temps* 1998

Cheadle, Don (1964–) *Hamburger Hill* 1987; *Colors* 1988; *Roadside Prophets* 1992; *Lush Life* 1993; *Devil in a Blue Dress* 1995; *Boogie Nights* 1997; *Rosewood* 1997; *Volcano* 1997; *Out of Sight* 1998; *The Rat Pack* 1998; *A Lesson Before Dying* 1999; *Mission to Mars* 1999; *Fail Safe* 2000; *The Family Man* 2000; *Traffic* 2000; *Manic* 2001; *Ocean's Eleven* 2001; *Swordfish* 2001; *The United States of Leland* 2002; *After the Sunset* 2004; *The Assassination of Richard Nixon* 2004; *Crash* 2004; *Hotel Rwanda* 2004; *Ocean's Twelve* 2004

Checchi, Andrea (1916–1974) *La Signora senza Camelie* 1953; *The Mask of Satan* 1960; *The Thousand Eyes of Dr Mabuse* 1960; *Two Women* 1960; *A Bullet for the General* 1966

Cheek, Molly *Torn between Two Lovers* 1979; *American Pie: the Wedding* 2003

Cheirel, Micheline (1917–) *Carnival in Flanders* 1935; *La Belle Equipe* 1936; *Cornered* 1945; *So Dark the Night* 1946

Chekhov, Michael (1891–1955) *Spellbound* 1945; *Abie's Irish Rose* 1946; *Specter of the Rose* 1946; *Rhapsody* 1954

Chelton, Tsilla (1918–) *Shanks* 1974; *Tatie Danielle* 1990

Chen Chao-jung *Rebels of the Neon God* 1992; *Eat Drink Man Woman* 1994; *Vive L'Amour* 1994

Chen Dao Ming (1955–) *Hero* 2002; *Infernal Affairs 3* 2003

Chen, Edison (1980–) *Infernal Affairs* 2002; *Infernal Affairs II* 2003; *Infernal Affairs 3* 2003

Chen, Joan (1961–) *Tai-Pan* 1986; *The Last Emperor* 1987; *The Salute of the Jugger* 1989; *Where Sleeping Dogs Lie* 1991; *Turtle Beach* 1992; *Heaven and Earth* 1993; *Golden Gate* 1994; *On Deadly Ground* 1994; *The Hunted* 1995; *Wild Side* 1995; *What's Cooking?* 2000

Chen, Kelly (1973–) *Tokyo Raiders* 2000; *Infernal Affairs* 2002; *Infernal Affairs 3* 2003

Chen, Tina *Alice's Restaurant* 1969; *The Hawaiians* 1970; *Three Days of the Condor* 1975

Chen Xiangqi *aka* **Chen Shiang-chyi** *The River* 1997; *What Time Is It There?* 2001; *Goodbye, Dragon Inn* 2003

Cheng, Adam (1947–) *Zu Warriors* 1983; *The Legend II* 1993

Cheng, Ekin (1967–) *A Man Called Hero* 1999; *Tokyo Raiders* 2000
Cheng, Kent (1951–) *Sex and Zen* 1992; *Crime Story* 1993; *The Defender* 1994
Cheng, Sammi *Infernal Affairs* 2002; *Infernal Affairs 3* 2003
Cher (1946–) *Wild on the Beach* 1965; *Good Times* 1967; *Chastity* 1969; *Come Back to the Five and Dime, Jimmy Dean, Jimmy Dean* 1982; *Silkwood* 1983; *Mask* 1985; *Moonstruck* 1987; *Suspect* 1987; *The Witches of Eastwick* 1987; *Mermaids* 1990; *Faithful* 1996; *If These Walls Could Talk* 1996; *Tea with Mussolini* 1998; *Stuck on You* 2003
Chéreau, Patrice (1944–) *Danton* 1982; *The Last of the Mohicans* 1992; *Lucie Aubrac* 1997; *Time of the Wolf* 2003
Cherkassov, Nikolai (1903–1966) *Alexander Nevsky* 1938; *Ivan the Terrible, Part I* 1944; *Ivan the Terrible, Part II* 1946; *Don Quixote* 1957
Cherrill, Virginia (1908–1996) *City Lights* 1931; *Delicious* 1931
Cherry, Helen (1915–2001) *Adam and Evelyne* 1949; *Morning Departure* 1950; *They Were Not Divided* 1950; *Young Wives' Tale* 1951; *Three Cases of Murder* 1953; *High Flight* 1957; *Tomorrow at Ten* 1962; *Flipper's New Adventure* 1964; *Hard Contract* 1969; *11 Harrowhouse* 1974
Cherry, Jonathan *Final Destination 2* 2002; *House of the Dead* 2003
Chesebro, George (1888–1959) *The Lone Rider in Ghost Town* 1941; *Trail of Robin Hood* 1950
Chesney, Arthur (1882–1949) *The Lodger* 1926; *Please Teacher* 1937
Chester, Colby *Executive Action* 1973; *The Dove* 1974; *Salvador* 1986
Chester, Craig (1965–) *Swoon* 1992; *Grief* 1993; *Kiss Me, Guido* 1997; *The Misadventures of Margaret* 1998
Chester, Vanessa Lee (1984–) *A Little Princess* 1995; *Harriet the Spy* 1996
Chestnut, Morris (1969–) *Boyz N the Hood* 1991; *Under Siege 2* 1995; *GI Jane* 1997; *The Best Man* 1999; *The Brothers* 2001; *Two Can Play That Game* 2001; *Half Past Dead* 2002; *Like Mike* 2002; *Anacondas: the Hunt for the Blood Orchid* 2004; *Breakin' All the Rules* 2004; *Ladder 49* 2004
Cheung, Daphne *China Cry* 1990; *Peggy Su!* 1997
Cheung, George Kee *The Amsterdam Kill* 1978; *High Voltage* 1998
Cheung, Jacky (1960–) *As Tears Go By* 1988; *Bullet in the Head* 1990; *A Chinese Ghost Story II* 1990; *Once upon a Time in China* 1991; *To Live and Die in Tsimshatsui* 1994
Cheung, Leslie *aka* **Cheung, Leslie Kwok-Wing** (1956–2003) *A Better Tomorrow* 1986; *A Better Tomorrow II* 1987; *A Chinese Ghost Story* 1987; *Rouge* 1987; *A Chinese Ghost Story II* 1990; *Days of Being Wild* 1990; *Once a Thief* 1991; *The Bride with White Hair* 1993; *Farewell My Concubine* 1993; *Ashes of Time* 1994; *Temptress Moon* 1996; *Happy Together* 1997
Cheung, Maggie *aka* **Cheung Man Yuk, Maggie** *aka* **Cheung Man-Yuk** *aka* **Cheung Man-Yuk, Maggie** (1964–) *Police Story* 1985; *Police Story 2* 1986; *Project A: Part II* 1987; *As Tears Go By* 1988; *A Better Tomorrow III* 1989; *Days of Being Wild* 1990; *Song of the Exile* 1990; *The Actress* 1992; *The Heroic Trio* 1992; *Police Story III: Supercop* 1992; *Twin Dragons* 1992; *Ashes of Time* 1994; *Irma Vep* 1996; *Chinese Box* 1997; *In the Mood for Love* 2000; *Hero* 2002; *Clean* 2004; *2046* 2004
Cheung, Roy *aka* **Cheung Yiu-Yeung, Roy** *Wild Search* 1989; *To Live and Die in Tsimshatsui* 1994; *Beast Cops* 1998
Chevalier, Maurice (1888–1972) *The Love Parade* 1929; *The Big Pond* 1930; *Paramount on Parade* 1930; *The Smiling Lieutenant* 1931; *Love Me Tonight* 1932; *One Hour with You* 1932; *The Merry Widow* 1934; *Folies Bergère* 1935; *Pièges* 1939; *Man about Town* 1947; *Love in the Afternoon* 1957; *Gigi* 1958; *Count Your Blessings* 1959; *A Breath of Scandal* 1960; *Can-Can* 1960; *Pepe* 1960; *Fanny* 1961; *In Search of the Castaways* 1961; *Jessica* 1962; *I'd Rather Be Rich* 1964; *Panic Button* 1964; *Monkeys, Go Home!* 1966
Chevit, Maurice (1923–) *The Hairdresser's Husband* 1990; *Voyages* 1999
Chew, Laureen *Chan Is Missing* 1982; *Dim Sum: a Little Bit of Heart* 1985
Chiaki, Minoru (1917–1999) *Rashomon* 1950; *Seven Samurai* 1954; *Godzilla Raids Again* 1955; *Throne of Blood* 1957; *The Hidden Fortress* 1958
Chiang, David *The Legend of the 7 Golden Vampires* 1974; *Once upon a Time in China II* 1992
Chiao, Roy (1927–1999) *Golden Needles* 1974; *Indiana Jones and the Temple of Doom* 1984; *The Protector* 1985; *Bloodsport* 1987
Chiarella, Jorge *No Mercy* 1994; *The Motorcycle Diaries* 2004
Chiari, Walter (1924–1991) *Bellissima* 1951; *Nana* 1955; *The Little Hut* 1957; *Bonjour Tristesse* 1958; *Let's Talk About Women* 1964; *They're a Weird Mob* 1966; *The Valachi Papers* 1972
Chiaureli, Sofiko (1937–) *The Colour of Pomegranates* 1969; *Ashik Kerib* 1988
Chiba, Sonny *aka* **Chiba, Shinichi** (1939–) *The Street Fighter* 1974; *Virus* 1980; *The Bushido Blade* 1981; *Aces: Iron Eagle III* 1992; *Kill Bill Vol 1* 2003
Chieffo, Michael *Heroes Stand Alone* 1989; *The Big Squeeze* 1996
Chiklis, Michael (1963–) *Wired* 1989; *Taxman* 1998; *The Three Stooges* 2000; *Spirited Away* 2001
Chilcott, Barbara *The Trap* 1966; *Lies My Father Told Me* 1975
Child, Jeremy (1944–) *Privilege* 1967; *Sir Henry at Rawlinson End* 1980; *Taffin* 1988
Chiles, Linden (1933–) *Incident at Phantom Hill* 1966; *Counterpoint* 1967; *Eye of the Cat* 1969
Chiles, Lois (1947–) *The Way We Were* 1973; *The Great Gatsby* 1974; *Coma* 1977; *Death on the Nile* 1978; *Moonraker* 1979; *Raw Courage* 1984; *Sweet Liberty* 1986; *Broadcast News* 1987; *Lush Life* 1993; *The Babysitter* 1995; *Curdled* 1995
Chilvers, Simon (1939–) *The Naked Country* 1985; *Sky Pirates* 1986; *Ground Zero* 1987; *Mushrooms* 1995
Chin Siu-hou *Twin Warriors* 1993; *Fist of Legend* 1994
Ching, William *aka* **Ching, Bill** (1913–1989) *DOA* 1949; *Never Wave at a WAC* 1952; *Pat and Mike* 1952; *Give a Girl a Break* 1953; *The Moonlighter* 1953; *Scared Stiff* 1953; *The Magnificent Matador* 1955; *Tall Man Riding* 1955
Chinlund, Nick (1961–) *Con Air* 1997; *Mr Magoo* 1997; *Resurrection* 1999; *Tears of the Sun* 2003; *The Chronicles of Riddick* 2004
Chironi, Graciana *El Bonaerense* 2002; *Familia Rodante* 2004
Chisholm, Gregory *aka* **Chisholm, Greg** *Shuttlecock* 1991; *One for the Road* 2003
Chistyakov, A (1880–1942) *The End of St Petersburg* 1927; *Storm over Asia* 1928
Chitty, Erik (1906–1977) *First Men in the Moon* 1964; *Please Sir!* 1971
Chlumsky, Anna (1980–) *My Girl* 1991; *The Mommy Market* 1994; *My Girl 2* 1994; *Gold Diggers: the Secret of Bear Mountain* 1995
Cho Jae-Hyeon *The Isle* 2000; *Bad Guy* 2001
Cho, John (1972–) *Pavilion of Women* 2000; *Harold & Kumar Get the Munchies* 2004
Choate, Tim (1954–2004) *The Europeans* 1979; *Jane Austen in Manhattan* 1980; *Def-Con 4* 1984
Choi Min-sik (1962–) *The Quiet Family* 1998; *Shiri* 1999; *Chihwaseon (Drunk on Women and Poetry)* 2002; *Oldboy* 2003
Chong, Marcus (1967–) *Panther* 1995; *The Matrix* 1999
Chong, Rae Dawn (1961–) *Quest for Fire* 1981; *Beat Street* 1984; *Choose Me* 1984; *Fear City* 1984; *American Flyers* 1985; *City Limits* 1985; *The Color Purple* 1985; *Commando* 1985; *Running Out of Luck* 1985; *Soul Man* 1986; *The Principal* 1987; *The Squeeze* 1987; *The Borrower* 1989; *Chaindance* 1991; *Tales from the Darkside: the Movie* 1991; *When the Party's Over* 1992; *Time Runner* 1993; *Boulevard* 1994; *Power of Attorney* 1994; *Crying Freeman* 1995; *Hideaway* 1995
Chong, Tommy *aka* **Chong, Thomas** (1938–) *Cheech & Chong's Up in Smoke* 1978; *Cheech and Chong's Next Movie* 1980; *Cheech and Chong's Nice Dreams* 1981; *Things Are Tough All Over* 1982; *Cheech & Chong's Still Smokin'* 1983; *Yellowbeard* 1983; *Cheech & Chong's The Corsican Brothers* 1984; *After Hours* 1985; *National Lampoon's Senior Trip* 1995; *Half-Baked* 1998
Chopra, Prem *Upkaar* 1967; *Bobby* 1973; *Hindustan Ki Kasam* 1999; *Koi... Mil Gaya* 2003; *Shikaar – the Musical Thriller* 2004
Chopra, Priyanka (1982–) *Aitraaz* 2004; *Mujhse Shaadi Karogi* 2004; *WAQT: the Race Against Time* 2005
Chopra, Uday (1973–) *Mohabbatein* 2000; *Mujhse Dosti Karoge!* 2002; *Supari* 2003; *Dhoom* 2004
Choudhury, Sarita (1966–) *Mississippi Masala* 1991; *Wild West* 1992; *Kama Sutra: a Tale of Love* 1996; *Subway Stories: Tales from the Underground* 1997; *A Perfect Murder* 1998; *Just a Kiss* 2002
Choureau, Etchika (1923–) *The Vanquished* 1953; *Hell Bent for Glory* 1957; *Darby's Rangers* 1958
Chow, China (1974–) *The Big Hit* 1998; *Head over Heels* 2000
Chow, Stephen (1962–) *Shaolin Soccer* 2001; *Kung Fu Hustle* 2004
Chow, Valerie *aka* **Shane, Rachel** *Chung King Express* 1994; *Bridge of Dragons* 1999
Chow Yun-Fat (1955–) *A Better Tomorrow* 1986; *A Better Tomorrow II* 1987; *City on Fire* 1987; *Spiritual Love* 1987; *A Better Tomorrow III* 1989; *The Killer* 1989; *Wild Search* 1989; *Once a Thief* 1991; *Full Contact* 1992; *Hard-Boiled* 1992; *The Replacement Killers* 1998; *Anna and the King* 1999; *The Corruptor* 1999; *Crouching Tiger, Hidden Dragon* 2000; *Bulletproof Monk* 2002
Chowdhry, Navin *Madame Sousatzka* 1988; *King of the Wind* 1989; *The Seventh Coin* 1993
Chowdhry, Ranjit *Lonely in America* 1990; *Mississippi Masala* 1991; *Camilla* 1993; *Fire* 1996; *Bollywood/Hollywood* 2002
Chriqui, Emmanuelle (1977–) *Snow Day* 2000; *On the Line* 2001; *Wrong Turn* 2003
Christensen, Carol *The Big Show* 1961; *The Three Stooges in Orbit* 1962
Christensen, Erika (1982–) *Traffic* 2000; *The Banger Sisters* 2002; *Swimfan* 2002; *The Perfect Score* 2004
Christensen, Hayden (1981–) *Life as a House* 2001; *Star Wars Episode II: Attack of the Clones* 2002; *Shattered Glass* 2003; *Star Wars Episode III: Revenge of the Sith* 2005
Christensen, Jesper (1948–) *Sofie* 1992; *Minor Mishaps* 2002; *The Interpreter* 2005
Christian, Claudia (1965–) *The Hidden* 1987; *Clean and Sober* 1988; *Never on Tuesday* 1988; *Danielle Steel's Kaleidoscope* 1990; *Maniac Cop 2* 1990; *Think Big* 1990; *The Dark Backward* 1991; *Upworld* 1992; *Hexed* 1993; *Atlantis: the Lost Empire* 2001; *Half Past Dead* 2002
Christian, Kurt (1950–) *The Golden Voyage of Sinbad* 1973; *Sinbad and the Eye of the Tiger* 1977
Christian, Linda (1923–) *Tarzan and the Mermaids* 1948; *The Happy Time* 1952; *The House of the Seven Hawks* 1959; *The VIPs* 1963; *The Moment of Truth* 1964
Christians, Mady (1900–1951) *Escapade* 1935; *Tender Comrade* 1943; *Address Unknown* 1944; *All My Sons* 1948; *Letter from an Unknown Woman* 1948
Christie, Audrey (1912–1989) *Keeper of the Flame* 1942; *Carousel* 1956; *Splendor in the Grass* 1961; *Frankie & Johnny* 1966; *Mame* 1974
Christie, Julie (1941–) *Crooks Anonymous* 1962; *Billy Liar* 1963; *The Fast Lady* 1963; *Darling* 1965; *Doctor Zhivago* 1965; *Young Cassidy* 1965; *Fahrenheit 451* 1966; *Far from the Madding Crowd* 1967; *Petulia* 1968; *In Search of Gregory* 1970; *The Go-Between* 1971; *McCabe and Mrs Miller* 1971; *Don't Look Now* 1973; *Shampoo* 1975; *Demon Seed* 1977; *Heaven Can Wait* 1978; *Heat and Dust* 1982; *The Return of the Soldier* 1982; *Gold Diggers* 1983; *Miss Mary* 1986; *Power* 1986; *Fools of Fortune* 1990; *DragonHeart* 1996; *Hamlet* 1996; *Afterglow* 1997; *The Miracle Maker* 1999; *I'm with Lucy* 2002; *Finding Neverland* 2004; *Troy* 2004
Christine, Virginia (1920–1996) *The Mummy's Curse* 1944; *Invasion of the Body Snatchers* 1956; *Nightmare* 1956; *Three Brave Men* 1956; *One Man's Way* 1964; *Billy the Kid vs Dracula* 1966
Christmas, Eric (1916–2000) *Harold and Maude* 1972; *An Enemy of the People* 1977; *Attack of the Killer Tomatoes* 1978; *Middle Age Crazy* 1980; *The Philadelphia Experiment* 1984; *Home Is Where the Hart Is* 1987; *Air Bud* 1997; *Mousehunt* 1997
Christophe, Françoise (1925–) *Le Testament d'Orphée* 1960; *King of Hearts* 1966; *Borsalino* 1970
Christophe, Pascale *Immoral Tales* 1974; *Piaf: the Sparrow of Pigalle* 1974; *Heroines of Evil* 1979
Christopher, Dennis (1955–) *September 30, 1955* 1977; *A Wedding* 1978; *Breaking Away* 1979; *California Dreaming* 1979; *Fade to Black* 1980; *Chariots of Fire* 1981; *Don't Cry, It's Only Thunder* 1982; *Jake Speed* 1986; *A Sinful Life* 1989; *Circuitry Man* 1990; *Dead Women in Lingerie* 1990; *Doppelganger* 1993; *Plughead Rewired: Circuitry Man II* 1994; *The Ballad of Lucy Whipple* 2001
Christopher, Jordan (1942–) *Return of the Seven* 1966; *Angel, Angel Down We Go* 1969; *The Sidelong Glances of a Pigeon Kicker* 1970
Christopher, Thom (1940–) *Space Raiders* 1983; *Wizards of the Lost Kingdom* 1985
Christy, Dorothy (1906–1977) *Parlor, Bedroom and Bath* 1931; *Sons of the Desert* 1933
Christy, Eileen (1927–) *I Dream of Jeanie* 1952; *Thunderbirds* 1952
Chrystall, Belle (1910–2003) *Hindle Wakes* 1931; *Friday the Thirteenth* 1933; *Scotland Yard Mystery* 1933; *The Edge of the World* 1937; *Poison Pen* 1939
Chun Shih *A Touch of Zen* 1969; *Goodbye, Dragon Inn* 2003
Chung, Cherie *aka* **Chung, Cherry Cho-Hung** (1960–) *The Dead and the Deadly* 1983; *Peking Opera Blues* 1986; *Spiritual Love* 1987; *Wild Search* 1989; *Once a Thief* 1991
Chung, David *Missing in Action 2: the Beginning* 1985; *The Ballad of Little Jo* 1993; *Color of a Brisk and Leaping Day* 1996
Chung Lam *The Killer* 1989; *Life Is Cheap... but Toilet Paper Is Expensive* 1990
Church, Thomas Haden (1960–) *George of the Jungle* 1997; *Free Money* 1998; *Mr Murder* 1998; *The Specials* 2000; *3000 Miles to Graceland* 2000; *Sideways* 2004
Churchill, Berton (1876–1940) *The Big Stampede* 1932; *Cabin in the Cotton* 1932; *I Am a Fugitive from a Chain Gang* 1932; *Dr Bull* 1933; *Heroes for Sale* 1933; *The Little Giant* 1933; *Bachelor Bait* 1934; *Steamboat round the Bend* 1935; *Daughters Courageous* 1939
Churchill, Diana (1913–1994) *Foreign Affaires* 1935; *Housemaster* 1938; *The History of Mr Polly* 1948; *Scott of the Antarctic* 1948; *The Winter's Tale* 1966
Churchill, Donald (1930–1991) *Victim* 1961; *The Hound of the Baskervilles* 1983
Churchill, Marguerite (1909–2000) *They Had to See Paris* 1929; *The Valiant* 1929; *The Big Trail* 1930; *Born Reckless* 1930; *Quick Millions* 1931; *Riders of the Purple Sage* 1931; *Dracula's Daughter* 1936; *The Walking Dead* 1936; *Bunco Squad* 1950
Churchill, Sarah (1914–1982) *Royal Wedding* 1951; *Serious Charge* 1959
Churikova, Inna (1943–) *The Theme* 1979; *Vassa* 1983
Ciamaca, Julien *Le Château de Ma Mère* 1990; *La Gloire de Mon Père* 1990
Ciannelli, Eduardo *aka* **Cianelli, Eduardo** *aka* **Ciannelli, Edward** (1887–1969) *Reunion in Vienna* 1933; *Winterset* 1936; *Criminal Lawyer* 1937; *The League of Frightened Men* 1937; *Marked Woman* 1937; *Super-Sleuth* 1937; *Law of the Underworld* 1938; *Bulldog Drummond's Bride* 1939; *Gunga Din* 1939; *Foreign Correspondent* 1940; *Kitty Foyle* 1940; *The Mummy's Hand* 1940; *Strange Cargo* 1940; *Dr Broadway* 1942; *You Can't Escape Forever* 1942; *Flight for Freedom* 1943; *They Got Me Covered* 1943; *Dillinger* 1945; *The Lost Moment* 1947; *Seven Keys to Baldpate* 1947; *Volcano* 1950; *The People against O'Hara* 1951; *The Stranger's Hand* 1953; *The Vanquished* 1953; *Mambo* 1954; *Houseboat* 1958; *Monster from Green Hell* 1958; *The Spy in the Green Hat* 1966; *Boot Hill* 1969
Cibrian, Eddie (1973–) *Logan's War: Bound by Honor* 1998; *But I'm a Cheerleader* 1999
Ciccolella, Jude *Blue Jean Cop* 1988; *Mad Love* 1995
Ciepielewska, Anna (1936–) *The Devil and the Nun* 1960; *Passenger* 1963
Cigoli, Emilio (1909–1980) *We the Living* 1942; *The Children Are Watching Us* 1943; *Sunday in August* 1949
Cilento, Diane (1933–) *Wings of Danger* 1952; *The Angel Who Pawned Her Harp* 1954; *Passage Home* 1955; *The Woman for Joe* 1955; *The Admirable Crichton* 1957; *The Truth about Women* 1958; *Jet Storm* 1959; *The Full Treatment* 1961; *The Naked Edge* 1961; *I Thank a Fool* 1962; *Tom Jones* 1963; *Rattle of a Simple Man* 1964; *The Third Secret* 1964; *The Agony and the Ecstasy* 1965; *Hombre* 1967; *ZPG: Zero Population Growth* 1971; *Hitler: the Last Ten Days* 1973; *The Wicker Man* 1973; *The Boy Who Had Everything* 1984
Cilliers, Jana *A Game for Vultures* 1979; *Quest for Love* 1988
Cimino, Leonardo *Jeremy* 1973; *Amityville II: the Possession*

1982; *Monsignor* 1982; *Penn & Teller Get Killed* 1989
Cintra, Luis Miguel (1949–) *Tall Stories* 1990; *The Divine Comedy* 1992; *Abraham Valley* 1993; *Here on Earth* 1993; *The Convent* 1995; *Un Filme Falado* 2003
Cioffi, Charles (1935–) *Klute* 1971; *Shaft* 1971; *The Don Is Dead* 1973; *The Thief Who Came to Dinner* 1973; *Time after Time* 1979; *Missing* 1981; *All the Right Moves* 1983; *Remo – Unarmed and Dangerous* 1985
Citran, Roberto (1955–) *Il Cielo è Sempre Più Blu* 1995; *Nora* 1999
Citti, Franco (1935–) *Accattone* 1961; *Mamma Roma* 1962; *Kill and Pray* 1967; *Oedipus Rex* 1967; *The Decameron* 1970; *The Arabian Nights* 1974
Citti, Marc *The Lie* 1992; *The Music Freelancers* 1998
Claire, Cyrielle *aka* **Clair, Cyrielle** (1955–) *Sword of the Valiant* 1984; *Code Name: Emerald* 1985; *Triple Agent* 2003
Claire, Imogen *The Lair of the White Worm* 1988; *I Hired a Contract Killer* 1990
Claire, Ina (1892–1985) *The Royal Family of Broadway* 1930; *Ninotchka* 1939; *Claudia* 1943
Clanton, Ralph (1914–) *Cyrano de Bergerac* 1950; *They Were Not Divided* 1950; *The 27th Day* 1957
Clare, Diane (1938–) *Ice Cold in Alex* 1958; *The Reluctant Debutante* 1958; *Let's Get Married* 1960; *The Haunting* 1963; *The Plague of the Zombies* 1965; *The Hand of Night* 1966; *The Vulture* 1966
Clare, Mary (1894–1970) *The Constant Nymph* 1928; *Hindle Wakes* 1931; *The Constant Nymph* 1933; *The Clairvoyant* 1934; *Lorna Doone* 1934; *The Mill on the Floss* 1937; *Young and Innocent* 1937; *The Challenge* 1938; *The Citadel* 1938; *Climbing High* 1938; *The Lady Vanishes* 1938; *Old Bill and Son* 1940; *The Night Has Eyes* 1942; *My Brother Jonathan* 1947; *The Three Weird Sisters* 1948; *The Black Rose* 1950; *The Beggar's Opera* 1953; *Mambo* 1954
Clare, Phyllis (1908–1947) *The Roadhouse Murder* 1932; *Aunt Sally* 1933
Clariond, Aimé (1894–1960) *Monsieur Vincent* 1947; *Marie Antoinette* 1956
Clark, Anthony (1964–) *Dogfight* 1991; *The Thing Called Love* 1993
Clark, Blake (1946–) *Fast Food* 1989; *Shakes the Clown* 1991; *The Waterboy* 1998; *50 First Dates* 2004
Clark, Bobby (1946–) *The Happy Road* 1956; *Gun Duel in Durango* 1957
Clark, Bryan *Pizza Man* 1991; *Without Warning: the James Brady Story* 1991
Clark, Candy (1947–) *Fat City* 1972; *American Graffiti* 1973; *The Man Who Fell to Earth* 1976; *Citizens Band* 1977; *The Big Sleep* 1978; *More American Graffiti* 1979; *When You Comin' Back, Red Ryder?* 1979; *Q – the Winged Serpent* 1982; *Amityville III: the Demon* 1983; *Blue Thunder* 1983; *Cat's Eye* 1984; *Hambone and Hillie* 1984; *The Blob* 1988; *Cool as Ice* 1991; *Cherry Falls* 1999
Clark, Christie (1973–) *Danielle Steel's Changes* 1991; *Children of the Corn II: the Final Sacrifice* 1993
Clark, Cliff (1889–1953) *Miracles for Sale* 1939; *Stranger on the Third Floor* 1940; *Strange Alibi* 1941; *The Wagons Roll at Night* 1941; *The Falcon's Brother* 1942; *Kid Glove Killer* 1942; *The Falcon and the Co-Eds* 1943; *The Falcon in Danger* 1943; *The Falcon Out West* 1944; *The Stratton Story* 1949
Clark, Dane (1913–1998) *Action in the North Atlantic* 1943; *Destination Tokyo* 1943; *Hollywood Canteen* 1944; *The Very Thought of You* 1944; *God Is My Co-Pilot* 1945; *Pride of the Marines* 1945; *A Stolen Life* 1946; *Deep Valley* 1947; *Moonrise* 1948; *Backfire* 1950; *Barricade* 1950; *Highly Dangerous* 1950; *The Gambler and the Lady* 1952; *Go, Man, Go!* 1953; *Port of Hell* 1954; *Thunder Pass* 1954; *The McMasters* 1970; *The Face of Fear* 1971; *Last Rites* 1988
Clark, Dick (1929–) *Because They're Young* 1960; *The Young Doctors* 1961
Clark, Ernest (1912–1994) *The Dam Busters* 1954; *The Baby and the Battleship* 1956; *The Safecracker* 1958; *Tomorrow at Ten* 1962; *The Devil-Ship Pirates* 1964; *It!* 1966; *Salt & Pepper* 1968
Clark, Fred (1914–1968) *The Unsuspected* 1947; *Cry of the City* 1948; *Alias Nick Beal* 1949; *Flamingo Road* 1949; *The Jackpot* 1950; *Mrs O'Malley and Mr Malone* 1950; *Sunset Blvd* 1950; *The Lemon Drop Kid* 1951; *Meet Me after the Show* 1951; *Dreamboat* 1952; *Here Come the Girls* 1953; *How to Marry a Millionaire* 1953; *Living It Up* 1954; *Abbott and Costello Meet the Keystone Cops* 1955; *Daddy Long Legs* 1955; *How to Be Very, Very Popular* 1955; *Back from Eternity* 1956; *The Birds and the Bees* 1956; *Miracle in the Rain* 1956; *The Solid Gold Cadillac* 1956; *Don't Go Near the Water* 1957; *Joe Butterfly* 1957; *Auntie Mame* 1958; *Mardi Gras* 1958; *It Started with a Kiss* 1959; *The Mating Game* 1959; *Bells Are Ringing* 1960; *Visit to a Small Planet* 1960; *Hemingway's Adventures of a Young Man* 1962; *Zotz* 1962; *Move Over, Darling* 1963; *The Curse of the Mummy's Tomb* 1964; *John Goldfarb, Please Come Home* 1964; *Dr Goldfoot and the Bikini Machine* 1965; *Sergeant Deadhead* 1965; *When the Boys Meet the Girls* 1965; *The Horse in the Gray Flannel Suit* 1968; *Skidoo* 1968
Clark, Harvey (1885–1938) *Camille* 1927; *Red-Headed Woman* 1932; *Man's Castle* 1933
Clark, Jameson (1907–1984) *The Brave Don't Cry* 1952; *Laxdale Hall* 1953; *The Battle of the Sexes* 1960; *Ring of Bright Water* 1969
Clark, Ken (1932–) *Six Bridges to Cross* 1955; *Between Heaven and Hell* 1956; *Attack of the Giant Leeches* 1960
Clark, Marlene *Slaughter* 1972; *Ganja and Hess* 1973; *The Beast Must Die* 1974; *Switchblade Sisters* 1975
Clark, Matt (1936–) *The Bridge at Remagen* 1969; *White Lightning* 1973; *The Terminal Man* 1974; *Kid Vengeance* 1977; *The Driver* 1978; *Brubaker* 1980; *An Eye for an Eye* 1981; *The Legend of the Lone Ranger* 1981; *Honkytonk Man* 1982; *Love Letters* 1983; *Country* 1984; *Tuff Turf* 1984; *Out of the Darkness* 1985; *Return to Oz* 1985; *Class Action* 1991; *Frozen Assets* 1992; *Barbarians at the Gate* 1993; *Dead before Dawn* 1993; *The Haunted Heart* 1995
Clark, Oliver (1939–) *End of the Road* 1970; *Deadhead Miles* 1972; *A Star Is Born* 1976; *Ernest Saves Christmas* 1988
Clark, Petula (1932–) *I Know Where I'm Going!* 1945; *London Town* 1946; *Easy Money* 1947; *Vice Versa* 1947; *Here Come the Huggetts* 1948; *Vote for Huggett* 1948; *Don't Ever Leave Me* 1949; *The Huggetts Abroad* 1949; *The Romantic Age* 1949; *Dance Hall* 1950; *White Corridors* 1951; *The Card* 1952; *Made in Heaven* 1952; *The Runaway Bus* 1954; *That Woman Opposite* 1957; *Finian's Rainbow* 1968; *Goodbye, Mr Chips* 1969
Clark, Roger (1909–1978) *You Belong to Me* 1941; *The Lady Is Willing* 1942; *Detour* 1945; *Angel Baby* 1961
Clark, Spencer Treat (1987–) *Arlington Road* 1998; *Unbreakable* 2000; *Mystic River* 2003
Clark, Susan (1940–) *Banning* 1967; *Coogan's Bluff* 1968; *Colossus: the Forbin Project* 1969; *Skullduggery* 1969; *Tell Them Willie Boy Is Here* 1969; *Skin Game* 1971; *Valdez Is Coming* 1971; *Showdown* 1973; *The Apple Dumpling Gang* 1974; *The Midnight Man* 1974; *Night Moves* 1975; *City on Fire* 1979; *Hill's Angels* 1979; *Promises in the Dark* 1979; *Porky's* 1981; *Butterbox Babies* 1995
Clarke, Angela (1969–) *Mrs Mike* 1949; *Captain Carey, USA* 1950; *Beneath the 12-Mile Reef* 1953; *Houdini* 1953; *Seven Little Foys* 1955; *Dancin' thru the Dark* 1989; *Blonde Fist* 1991; *Land and Freedom* 1995
Clarke, Betty Ross *aka* **Clarke, Betsy Ross** *aka* **Clark, Betty Ross** (1896–1947) *Judge Hardy's Children* 1938; *Love Finds Andy Hardy* 1938
Clarke, Caitlin (1952–2004) *Dragonslayer* 1981; *Penn & Teller Get Killed* 1989; *Blown Away* 1994
Clarke, David (1908–2004) *The Narrow Margin* 1952; *The Great St Louis Bank Robbery* 1959
Clarke, Gage *aka* **Clark, Gage** (1900–1964) *Nightmare* 1956; *Fury at Showdown* 1957; *The Return of Dracula* 1958
Clarke, Hope (1943–) *Book of Numbers* 1972; *A Piece of the Action* 1977
Clarke, Jason *Risk* 2000; *Rabbit-Proof Fence* 2002
Clarke, Jean *There Was a Crooked Man* 1960; *Goodbye Again* 1961
Clarke (2), John (1948–) *Footrot Flats: the Dog's Tale* 1986; *Blood Oath* 1990; *Death in Brunswick* 1990
Clarke, Kathy Keira *The Most Fertile Man in Ireland* 1999; *Bloody Sunday* 2001
Clarke, Mae (1907–1992) *Frankenstein* 1931; *The Public Enemy* 1931; *Waterloo Bridge* 1931; *The Impatient Maiden* 1932; *The Penguin Pool Murder* 1932; *Three Wise Girls* 1932; *Penthouse* 1933; *Turn Back the Clock* 1933; *Nana* 1934; *This Side of Heaven* 1934; *Great Guy* 1936; *Flying Tigers* 1942
Clarke, Margi (1954–) *Letter to Brezhnev* 1985; *I Hired a Contract Killer* 1990; *Loser Takes All* 1990; *Blonde Fist* 1991; *Revengers Tragedy* 2002; *School for Seduction* 2004
Clarke, Melinda *aka* **Clarke, Mindy** *Return of the Living Dead III* 1993; *Killer Tongue* 1996; *Spawn* 1997
Clarke, Robert (1920–2005) *A Game of Death* 1945; *Outrage* 1950; *Hard, Fast and Beautiful* 1951; *The Man from Planet X* 1951; *The Astounding She-Monster* 1958; *Hideous Sun Demon* 1959; *Beyond the Time Barrier* 1960; *Midnight Movie Massacre* 1987
Clarke, Robin *The Prize Fighter* 1979; *Inseminoid* 1981
Clarke, Warren (1947–) *A Clockwork Orange* 1971; *Hawk the Slayer* 1980; *Firefox* 1982; *Real Life* 1983; *Lassiter* 1984; *Top Secret!* 1984; *Crusoe* 1988; *ID* 1994; *Blow Dry* 2000; *Greenfingers* 2000; *Arthur's Dyke* 2001
Clarke-Smith, D A (1888–1959) *Friday the Thirteenth* 1933; *The Ghoul* 1933; *Murder by Rope* 1936; *Southern Roses* 1936; *Flying 55* 1939
Clarkson, Lana (1962–2003) *Blind Date* 1984; *The Haunting of Morella* 1990
Clarkson, Patricia (1960–) *The Dead Pool* 1988; *Everybody's All-American* 1988; *Rocket Gibraltar* 1988; *Aunt Julia and the Scriptwriter* 1990; *Jumanji* 1995; *High Art* 1998; *Simply Irresistible* 1999; *The Safety of Objects* 2001; *Wendigo* 2001; *Far from Heaven* 2002; *Pieces of April* 2002; *Welcome to Collinwood* 2002; *All the Real Girls* 2003; *Dogville* 2003; *The Station Agent* 2003; *Miracle* 2004
Clary, Robert (1926–) *Thief of Damascus* 1952; *New Faces* 1954
Clash, Kevin (1960–) *Teenage Mutant Ninja Turtles II: the Secret of the Ooze* 1991; *The Adventures of Elmo in Grouchland* 1999
Clausen, Claus (1899–1989) *Westfront 1918* 1930; *The Devil Makes Three* 1952
Clavering, Eric (1901–1989) *Where's That Fire?* 1939; *To Kill a Clown* 1972
Clavier, Christian (1952–) *Les Visiteurs* 1993; *Guardian Angels* 1995; *Les Visiteurs 2: Les Couloirs du Temps* 1998; *Asterix and Obelix Take On Caesar* 1999; *Asterix & Obelix: Mission Cleopatra* 2001; *Just Visiting* 2001
Clay, Andrew Dice *aka* **Clay, Andrew** *aka* **Silverstein, Andrew** (1958–) *Wacko* 1981; *Casual Sex?* 1988; *The Adventures of Ford Fairlane* 1990; *Brain Smasher... a Love Story* 1993; *One Night at McCool's* 2001
Clay, Juanin (1949–1995) *The Legend of the Lone Ranger* 1981; *The Long Summer of George Adams* 1982; *WarGames* 1983
Clay, Nicholas (1946–2000) *The Road Builder* 1971; *The Darwin Adventure* 1972; *Victor Frankenstein* 1977; *Lovespell* 1979; *Excalibur* 1981; *Lady Chatterley's Lover* 1981; *Evil under the Sun* 1982; *The Hound of the Baskervilles* 1983; *Lionheart* 1986
Clay, Philippe (1927–) *French Cancan* 1955; *The Hunchback of Notre Dame* 1956; *Shanks* 1974; *The Music Freelancers* 1998
Clayburgh, Jill (1944–) *The Wedding Party* 1966; *The Thief Who Came to Dinner* 1973; *The Terminal Man* 1974; *Gable and Lombard* 1976; *Silver Streak* 1976; *Semi-Tough* 1977; *An Unmarried Woman* 1978; *La Luna* 1979; *Starting Over* 1979; *It's My Turn* 1980; *First Monday in October* 1981; *I'm Dancing as Fast as I Can* 1982; *Where Are the Children?* 1986; *Shy People* 1987; *Day of Atonement* 1992; *Rich in Love* 1992; *Whispers in the Dark* 1992; *Naked in New York* 1994; *Going All the Way* 1997
Clayton, Jan (1917–1983) *The Llano Kid* 1939; *This Man's Navy* 1945
Clayton, John *Unfinished Business* 1985; *Warm Nights on a Slow Moving Train* 1986; *High Tide* 1987; *Boundaries of the Heart* 1988; *Out of the Body* 1988; *Cappuccino* 1989
Clayton, Merry *Blame It on the Night* 1984; *Maid to Order* 1987
Clayworth, June (1912–1993) *Criminal Court* 1946; *Dick Tracy Meets Gruesome* 1947; *Bodyguard* 1948; *Sons of the Musketeers* 1951; *The Marriage-Go-Round* 1960
Cleere, John *War of the Buttons* 1993; *My Friend Joe* 1996
Cleese, John (1939–) *The Bliss of Mrs Blossom* 1968; *Interlude* 1968; *The Magic Christian* 1969; *The Rise and Rise of Michael Rimmer* 1970; *And Now for Something Completely Different* 1971; *Monty Python and the Holy Grail* 1975; *Pleasure at Her Majesty's* 1976; *Monty Python's Life of Brian* 1979; *The Great Muppet Caper* 1981; *Time Bandits* 1981; *Monty Python Live at the Hollywood Bowl* 1982; *Privates on Parade* 1982; *Monty Python's The Meaning of Life* 1983; *Yellowbeard* 1983; *Silverado* 1985; *Clockwise* 1986; *A Fish Called Wanda* 1988; *The Big Picture* 1989; *Erik the Viking* 1989; *An American Tail: Fievel Goes West* 1991; *Splitting Heirs* 1993; *The Jungle Book* 1994; *Mary Shelley's Frankenstein* 1994; *The Swan Princess* 1994; *The Wind in the Willows* 1996; *Fierce Creatures* 1997; *George of the Jungle* 1997; *Parting Shots* 1998; *Isn't She Great* 1999; *The Out-of-Towners* 1999; *The World Is Not Enough* 1999; *The Magic Pudding* 2000; *Harry Potter and the Philosopher's Stone* 2001; *Pluto Nash* 2001; *Rat Race* 2001; *Die Another Day* 2002; *Harry Potter and the Chamber of Secrets* 2002; *Charlie's Angels: Full Throttle* 2003; *Around the World in 80 Days* 2004; *Shrek 2* 2004; *Valiant* 2005
Clem, Jimmy *Grayeagle* 1977; *The Evictors* 1979
Clemens, Paul (1958–) *Promises in the Dark* 1979; *They're Playing With Fire* 1984
Clemenson, Christian (1959–) *Broadcast News* 1987; *Bad Influence* 1990; *Accidental Hero* 1992
Clément, Andrée (1894–1960) *La Symphonie Pastorale* 1946; *Dieu A Besoin des Hommes* 1950
Clément, Aurore (1945–) *Lacombe Lucien* 1974; *Les Rendez-vous d'Anna* 1978; *Travels with Anita* 1978; *Apocalypse Now* 1979; *El Sur* 1983; *Paris, Texas* 1984; *The Captive* 2000; *Bon Voyage* 2003; *The Bridesmaid* 2004
Clément, Coralie *Diabolo Menthe* 1977; *The Aviator's Wife* 1980
Clement, Jennifer *The Raffle* 1994; *waydowntown* 2000
Clementi, Margareth *Medea* 1970; *Casanova* 1976
Clémenti, Pierre (1942–1999) *Belle de Jour* 1967; *The Milky Way* 1968; *Partner* 1968; *The Conformist* 1969; *Pigsty* 1969; *Steppenwolf* 1974; *Quartet* 1981; *Exposed* 1983; *Hideous Kinky* 1998
Clements, John (1910–1988) *South Riding* 1938; *The Four Feathers* 1939; *Convoy* 1940; *Ships with Wings* 1942; *Tomorrow We Live* 1942; *Undercover* 1943; *Train of Events* 1949; *The Silent Enemy* 1958; *The Mind Benders* 1963; *Oh! What a Lovely War* 1969
Clements, Stanley *aka* **Clements, Stanley "Stash"** (1926–1981) *Tall, Dark and Handsome* 1941; *Salty O'Rourke* 1945; *Destination Murder* 1950; *Boots Malone* 1951; *Military Policeman* 1953
Clennon, David *aka* **Clennon, Dave** (1943–) *Go Tell the Spartans* 1977; *Being There* 1979; *Ladies and Gentlemen, the Fabulous Stains* 1981; *Missing* 1981; *The Thing* 1982; *Star 80* 1983; *Falling in Love* 1984; *Sweet Dreams* 1985; *Legal Eagles* 1986; *He's My Girl* 1987; *Betrayed* 1988; *The Couch Trip* 1988; *Downtown* 1990; *Light Sleeper* 1991
Cléry, Corinne (1950–) *The Story of O* 1975; *The Con Artists* 1976; *The Humanoid* 1979; *Moonraker* 1979; *Yor, the Hunter from the Future* 1983; *The Gamble* 1988
Cleveland, Carol (1943–) *And Now for Something Completely Different* 1971; *Pleasure at Her Majesty's* 1976; *Monty Python Live at the Hollywood Bowl* 1982
Cleveland, George (1886–1957) *Blue Steel* 1934; *The Man from Utah* 1934; *The Star Packer* 1934; *The Navy Steps Out* 1941; *Seven Miles from Alcatraz* 1942; *Abroad with Two Yanks* 1944; *The Yellow Rose of Texas* 1944; *Pillow of Death* 1945; *Angel on My Shoulder* 1946; *Courage of Lassie* 1946; *Little Giant* 1946; *Wild Beauty* 1946; *The Plunderers* 1948
Clevenot, Philippe (1942–2001) *Celine and Julie Go Boating* 1974; *Roselyne and the Lions* 1989; *The Hairdresser's Husband* 1990
Cliff, Jimmy (1948–) *The Harder They Come* 1972; *Club Paradise* 1986
Cliff, John (1918–) *Back to God's Country* 1953; *I Was a Teenage Frankenstein* 1957
Cliff, Laddie (1891–1937) *Happy* 1933; *Over She Goes* 1937
Clifford, Colleen (1898–1996) *Careful, He Might Hear You* 1983; *Frauds* 1992

Clifford, Jefferson (1892–1959) *Confession* 1955; *The Bridal Path* 1959

Clift, Montgomery (1920–1966) *Red River* 1948; *The Search* 1948; *The Heiress* 1949; *The Big Lift* 1950; *A Place in the Sun* 1951; *From Here to Eternity* 1953; *I Confess* 1953; *Indiscretion of an American Wife* 1954; *Raintree County* 1957; *Lonelyhearts* 1958; *The Young Lions* 1958; *Suddenly, Last Summer* 1959; *Wild River* 1960; *Judgment at Nuremberg* 1961; *The Misfits* 1961; *Freud* 1962; *The Defector* 1966

Climent, Joaquín *Goya in Bordeaux* 1999; *Mondays in the Sun* 2002

Climo, Brett (1964–) *Relatives* 1985; *Blackwater Trail* 1995

Cline, Edward *aka* **Cline, Eddie** *aka* **Cline, Edward F** (1892–1961) *Neighbors* 1920; *The Scarecrow* 1920; *Day Dreams* 1922

Clinton, Roger (1956–) *The Revenge of Pumpkinhead – Blood Wings* 1994; *Bio-Dome* 1996

Clitheroe, Jimmy (1916–1973) *Rhythm Serenade* 1943; *Jules Verne's Rocket to the Moon* 1967

Clive, Colin (1898–1937) *Journey's End* 1930; *Frankenstein* 1931; *Christopher Strong* 1933; *The Key* 1934; *One More River* 1934; *Bride of Frankenstein* 1935; *Clive of India* 1935; *The Girl from 10th Avenue* 1935; *Mad Love* 1935; *The Man Who Broke the Bank at Monte Carlo* 1935; *History Is Made at Night* 1937; *The Woman I Love* 1937

Clive, E E (1879–1940) *Charlie Chan in London* 1934; *Long Lost Father* 1934; *Atlantic Adventure* 1935; *The Mystery of Edwin Drood* 1935; *Isle of Fury* 1936; *Libeled Lady* 1936; *Tarzan Escapes* 1936; *Trouble for Two* 1936; *Bulldog Drummond Comes Back* 1937; *Bulldog Drummond Escapes* 1937; *Bulldog Drummond's Revenge* 1937; *Live, Love and Learn* 1937; *Personal Property* 1937; *Arsene Lupin Returns* 1938; *Bulldog Drummond in Africa* 1938; *Bulldog Drummond's Peril* 1938; *The Adventures of Sherlock Holmes* 1939; *Bachelor Mother* 1939; *Bulldog Drummond's Bride* 1939; *The Earl of Chicago* 1940

Clive, John (1938–) *Yellow Submarine* 1968; *A Clockwork Orange* 1971; *Never Too Young to Rock* 1975

Clooney, George (1961–) *Return of the Killer Tomatoes* 1988; *Red Surf* 1990; *The Magic Bubble* 1992; *From Dusk till Dawn* 1995; *One Fine Day* 1996; *Batman and Robin* 1997; *The Peacemaker* 1997; *Out of Sight* 1998; *The Thin Red Line* 1998; *South Park: Bigger, Longer & Uncut* 1999; *Three Kings* 1999; *Fail Safe* 2000; *O Brother, Where Art Thou?* 2000; *The Perfect Storm* 2000; *Ocean's Eleven* 2001; *SPYkids* 2001; *Confessions of a Dangerous Mind* 2002; *Welcome to Collinwood* 2002; *Intolerable Cruelty* 2003; *Solaris* 2003; *Ocean's Twelve* 2004

Clooney, Rosemary (1928–2002) *Here Come the Girls* 1953; *Deep in My Heart* 1954; *Red Garters* 1954; *White Christmas* 1954

Cloos, Hans Peter *Germany in Autumn* 1978; *Les Favoris de la Lune* 1984

Close, Glenn (1947–) *The World According to Garp* 1982; *The Big Chill* 1983; *The Natural* 1984; *The Stone Boy* 1984; *Jagged Edge* 1985; *Maxie* 1985; *Fatal Attraction* 1987; *Dangerous Liaisons* 1988; *Light Years* 1988; *Stones for Ibarra* 1988; *Immediate Family* 1989; *Hamlet* 1990; *Meeting Venus* 1990; *Reversal of Fortune* 1990; *The House of the Spirits* 1993; *The Paper* 1994; *Mary Reilly* 1995; *Mars Attacks!* 1996; *101 Dalmatians* 1996; *Air Force One* 1997; *In & Out* 1997; *In the Gloaming* 1997; *Paradise Road* 1997; *Cookie's Fortune* 1999; *Tarzan* 1999; *102 Dalmatians* 2000; *Things You Can Tell Just by Looking at Her* 2000; *The Ballad of Lucy Whipple* 2001; *The Safety of Objects* 2001; *South Pacific* 2001; *Le Divorce* 2003; *The Stepford Wives* 2004

Closser Hale, Louise (1872–1933) *Platinum Blonde* 1931; *The Man Who Played God* 1932; *Shanghai Express* 1932; *The Barbarian* 1933; *Today We Live* 1933; *The White Sister* 1933

Cloutier, Suzanne (1927–2003) *Derby Day* 1952; *Othello* 1952; *Doctor in the House* 1954

Clouzot, Vera (1921–1960) *The Wages of Fear* 1953; *Les Diaboliques* 1954; *Les Espions* 1957

Clunes, Alec (1912–1970) *Saloon Bar* 1940; *Quentin Durward* 1955; *Richard III* 1955; *Tiger in the Smoke* 1956; *Tomorrow at Ten* 1962

Clunes, Martin (1963–) *The Russia House* 1990; *Carry On Columbus* 1992; *Staggered* 1993; *The Revengers' Comedies* 1997; *The Acid House* 1998; *Shakespeare in Love* 1998; *Saving Grace* 2000

Clutesi, George (1988–) *I Heard the Owl Call My Name* 1973; *Prophecy* 1979

Cluzet, François (1955–) *Le Cheval d'Orgeuil* 1980; *One Deadly Summer* 1983; *'Round Midnight* 1986; *Une Affaire de Femmes* 1988; *Chocolat* 1988; *Force Majeure* 1989; *Trop Belle pour Toi* 1989; *Olivier Olivier* 1991; *L'Enfer* 1994; *Les Apprentis* 1995; *French Kiss* 1995; *Rien Ne Va Plus* 1997; *Late August, Early September* 1998

Clyde, Andy (1892–1967) *Million Dollar Legs* 1932; *The Little Minister* 1934; *Annie Oakley* 1935; *Bad Lands* 1939; *Cherokee Strip* 1940; *The Devil's Playground* 1946; *Fool's Gold* 1946; *The Marauders* 1947; *The Dead Don't Dream* 1948; *False Paradise* 1948; *Silent Conflict* 1948; *The Road to Denver* 1955

Clyde, Jeremy (1941–) *Wilt* 1989; *Kaspar Hauser* 1993

Clyde, June (1909–1987) *Back Street* 1932; *Tess of the Storm Country* 1932; *Land without Music* 1936; *Night without Stars* 1951; *Treasure Hunt* 1952

Coates, Kim *Palais Royale* 1988; *Cold Front* 1989; *The Amityville Curse* 1990; *Dead before Dawn* 1993; *Carpool* 1996; *Lethal Tender* 1996; *Airborne* 1997; *Auggie Rose* 2000; *Battlefield Earth* 2000; *XChange* 2000; *Open Range* 2003; *Hostage* 2004

Coates, Phyllis (1927–) *I Was a Teenage Frankenstein* 1957; *Cattle Empire* 1958

Cobanoglu, Necmettin (1953–) *Yol* 1982; *Journey of Hope* 1990

Cobb, Lee J (1911–1976) *Golden Boy* 1939; *This Thing Called Love* 1940; *Men of Boys Town* 1941; *Paris Calling* 1941; *The Moon Is Down* 1943; *The Song of Bernadette* 1943; *Anna and the King of Siam* 1946; *Boomerang!* 1947; *Captain from Castile* 1947; *Johnny O'Clock* 1947; *Call Northside 777* 1948; *The Dark Past* 1948; *The Miracle of the Bells* 1948; *Thieves' Highway* 1949; *Sirocco* 1951; *The Fighter* 1952; *Gorilla at Large* 1954; *On the Waterfront* 1954; *Yankee Pasha* 1954; *The Left Hand of God* 1955; *The Racers* 1955; *The Road to Denver* 1955; *The Man in the Gray Flannel Suit* 1956; *The Garment Jungle* 1957; *The Three Faces of Eve* 1957; *12 Angry Men* 1957; *The Brothers Karamazov* 1958; *Man of the West* 1958; *Party Girl* 1958; *The Baited Trap* 1959; *But Not for Me* 1959; *Green Mansions* 1959; *Exodus* 1960; *The Four Horsemen of the Apocalypse* 1962; *How the West Was Won* 1962; *Come Blow Your Horn* 1963; *Our Man Flint* 1966; *In like Flint* 1967; *Coogan's Bluff* 1968; *They Came to Rob Las Vegas* 1968; *Mackenna's Gold* 1969; *The Liberation of LB Jones* 1970; *Macho Callahan* 1970; *Lawman* 1971; *The Exorcist* 1973; *The Man Who Loved Cat Dancing* 1973; *That Lucky Touch* 1975

Cobb, Randall "Tex" (1950–) *Uncommon Valor* 1983; *The Golden Child* 1986; *Critical Condition* 1987; *Buy & Cell* 1988; *Fletch Lives* 1989; *Blind Fury* 1990; *Ernest Goes to Jail* 1990; *Raw Nerve* 1991; *Midnight Sting* 1992

Cobbs, Bill *aka* **Cobbs, William** (1935–) *The Brother from Another Planet* 1984; *Dominick and Eugene* 1988; *The People under the Stairs* 1991; *The Bodyguard* 1992; *The Hudsucker Proxy* 1994; *Ed* 1996; *Air Bud* 1997; *Hope Floats* 1998; *I Still Know What You Did Last Summer* 1998

Cobo, Eva *aka* **Cobo de Garcia, Eva** (1967–) *Matador* 1986; *Operation Condor: the Armour of God II* 1990

Cobo, Roberto (1930–2002) *Los Olvidados* 1950; *Mexican Bus Ride* 1951

Coburn, Charles (1877–1961) *Of Human Hearts* 1938; *Vivacious Lady* 1938; *Yellow Jack* 1938; *Bachelor Mother* 1939; *Idiot's Delight* 1939; *In Name Only* 1939; *Made for Each Other* 1939; *Stanley and Livingstone* 1939; *The Story of Alexander Graham Bell* 1939; *Edison, the Man* 1940; *Florian* 1940; *Road to Singapore* 1940; *Three Faces West* 1940; *The Devil and Miss Jones* 1941; *HM Pulham Esq* 1941; *The Lady Eve* 1941; *Our Wife* 1941; *George Washington Slept Here* 1942; *In This Our Life* 1942; *Kings Row* 1942; *The Constant Nymph* 1943; *Forever and a Day* 1943; *Heaven Can Wait* 1943; *The More the Merrier* 1943; *Princess O'Rourke* 1943; *Knickerbocker Holiday* 1944; *Together Again* 1944; *Wilson* 1944; *Colonel Effingham's Raid* 1945; *Over 21* 1945; *Rhapsody in Blue* 1945; *A Royal Scandal* 1945; *The Green Years* 1946; *Lured* 1947; *The Paradine Case* 1947; *BF's Daughter* 1948; *Green Grass of Wyoming* 1948; *The Doctor and the Girl* 1949; *Everybody Does It* 1949; *The Gal Who Took the West* 1949; *Impact* 1949; *Mr Music* 1950; *Has Anybody Seen My Gal?* 1952; *Monkey Business* 1952; *Gentlemen Prefer Blondes* 1953; *Trouble along the Way* 1953; *The Long Wait* 1954; *The Rocket Man* 1954; *How to Be Very, Very Popular* 1955; *The Power and the Prize* 1956; *Town on Trial* 1956; *How to Murder a Rich Uncle* 1957; *John Paul Jones* 1959; *The Remarkable Mr Pennypacker* 1959; *A Stranger in My Arms* 1959; *Pepe* 1960

Coburn, James (1928–2002) *Face of a Fugitive* 1959; *Ride Lonesome* 1959; *The Magnificent Seven* 1960; *The Murder Men* 1961; *Hell Is for Heroes* 1962; *Charade* 1963; *The Great Escape* 1963; *The Americanization of Emily* 1964; *A High Wind in Jamaica* 1965; *The Loved One* 1965; *Major Dundee* 1965; *Dead Heat on a Merry-Go-Round* 1966; *Our Man Flint* 1966; *What Did You Do in the War, Daddy?* 1966; *In like Flint* 1967; *The President's Analyst* 1967; *Waterhole #3* 1967; *Candy* 1968; *Duffy* 1968; *Hard Contract* 1969; *Last of the Mobile Hot-Shots* 1970; *A Fistful of Dynamite* 1971; *The Honkers* 1971; *The Carey Treatment* 1972; *Harry in Your Pocket* 1973; *The Last of Sheila* 1973; *Pat Garrett and Billy the Kid* 1973; *The Internecine Project* 1974; *Bite the Bullet* 1975; *Hard Times* 1975; *Battle of Midway* 1976; *The Last Hard Men* 1976; *Sky Riders* 1976; *Cross of Iron* 1977; *Firepower* 1979; *Goldengirl* 1979; *The Baltimore Bullet* 1980; *Loving Couples* 1980; *High Risk* 1981; *Looker* 1981; *Martin's Day* 1984; *Death of a Soldier* 1985; *Young Guns II* 1990; *Hudson Hawk* 1991; *Deadfall* 1993; *Sister Act 2: Back in the Habit* 1993; *Maverick* 1994; *The Disappearance of Kevin Johnson* 1995; *The Set Up* 1995; *Eraser* 1996; *Keys to Tulsa* 1996; *The Nutty Professor* 1996; *Skeletons* 1996; *Affliction* 1997; *The Second Civil War* 1997; *Mr Murder* 1998; *Payback* 1998; *Monsters, Inc* 2001; *American Gun* 2002; *Snow Dogs* 2002

Coca, Imogene (1908–2001) *Under the Yum Yum Tree* 1963; *National Lampoon's Vacation* 1983; *Nothing Lasts Forever* 1984

Cochran, Robert *Moscow Nights* 1935; *Sanders of the River* 1935; *Scrooge* 1935; *The Man Who Could Work Miracles* 1936

Cochran, Steve (1917–1965) *Wonder Man* 1945; *The Chase* 1946; *The Kid from Brooklyn* 1946; *Copacabana* 1947; *A Song Is Born* 1948; *White Heat* 1949; *Dallas* 1950; *The Damned Don't Cry* 1950; *Storm Warning* 1950; *Jim Thorpe – All-American* 1951; *Back to God's Country* 1953; *The Desert Song* 1953; *Carnival Story* 1954; *Private Hell 36* 1954; *Come Next Spring* 1956; *Il Grido* 1957; *The Mobster* 1958; *Quantrill's Raiders* 1958; *The Beat Generation* 1959; *The Big Operator* 1959; *The Deadly Companions* 1961; *Of Love and Desire* 1963

Cochrane, Rory (1972–) *Dazed and Confused* 1993; *Love and a .45* 1994; *Empire Records* 1995; *The Low Life* 1995; *Black and White* 1998; *The Prime Gig* 2000; *Sunset Strip* 2000; *Hart's War* 2002

Cockburn, Arlene *The Winter Guest* 1996; *The Governess* 1997

Cockrell, Gary *Lolita* 1961; *The War Lover* 1962

Coco, James (1930–1987) *Ensign Pulver* 1964; *Generation* 1969; *End of the Road* 1970; *Tell Me That You Love Me, Junie Moon* 1970; *A New Leaf* 1971; *Such Good Friends* 1971; *Man of La Mancha* 1972; *The Wild Party* 1975; *Murder by Death* 1976; *Bye Bye Monkey* 1978; *The Cheap Detective* 1978; *Scavenger Hunt* 1979; *Wholly Moses!* 1980; *Only When I Laugh* 1981; *Hunk* 1987

Cocteau, Jean (1889–1963) *The Blood of a Poet* 1930; *Les Parents Terribles* 1948; *Les Enfants Terribles* 1949; *Orphée* 1950; *Le Testament d'Orphée* 1960

Coduri, Camille (1966–) *Hawks* 1988; *Nuns on the Run* 1990; *King Ralph* 1991

Cody, Iron Eyes (1907–1999) *Sitting Bull* 1954; *Gun for a Coward* 1957; *The Great Sioux Massacre* 1965; *El Condor* 1970; *Grayeagle* 1977; *Ernest Goes to Camp* 1987

Cody, Kathleen (1953–) *Charley and the Angel* 1973; *Superdad* 1974

Cody, Lew (1884–1934) *What a Widow!* 1930; *Dishonored* 1931; *Sporting Blood* 1931; *Sitting Pretty* 1933

Coe, Barry (1934–) *The Bravados* 1958; *But Not for Me* 1959; *A Private's Affair* 1959; *One Foot in Hell* 1960; *The Wizard of Baghdad* 1960; *The 300 Spartans* 1962; *Jaws 2* 1978

Coe, George *Kramer vs Kramer* 1979; *The First Deadly Sin* 1980; *The Amateur* 1981; *The Entity* 1981; *A Flash of Green* 1984; *Remo – Unarmed and Dangerous* 1985; *Best Seller* 1987; *Blind Date* 1987; *My Name Is Bill W* 1989; *The End of Innocence* 1990; *Nick and Jane* 1996; *Big Eden* 2000

Coe, Peter (1929–1987) *House of Frankenstein* 1944; *The Mummy's Curse* 1944; *Hellgate* 1952; *Road to Bali* 1952

Coeur, Paul *aka* **Jolicoeur, Paul** *The High Country* 1981; *Cool Runnings* 1993

Coffey, Denise (1936–) *Waltz of the Toreadors* 1962; *Georgy Girl* 1966; *Sir Henry at Rawlinson End* 1980; *Another Time, Another Place* 1983

Coffey, Scott (1967–) *Satisfaction* 1988; *Shag* 1988; *The Temp* 1993

Coffin, Frederick (1943–2003) *Hard to Kill* 1989; *VI Warshawski* 1991

Cohen, J J *aka* **Cohen, Jeffrey Jay** *Fire with Fire* 1986; *The Principal* 1987

Cohen, Lynn *Manhattan Murder Mystery* 1993; *Vanya on 42nd Street* 1994; *Hurricane Streets* 1997

Cohen, Sacha Baron (1970–) *Ali G indahouse* 2002; *Madagascar* 2005

Cohen, Scott (1964–) *The Mambo Kings* 1992; *Kissing Jessica Stein* 2001

Colantoni, Enrico (1963–) *Galaxy Quest* 1999; *Stigmata* 1999; *James Dean* 2001; *Criminal* 2004

Colasanto, Nicholas (1924–1985) *Fat City* 1972; *Raging Bull* 1980

Colbert, Claudette (1905–1996) *For the Love of Mike* 1927; *The Big Pond* 1930; *Manslaughter* 1930; *His Woman* 1931; *Honor among Lovers* 1931; *The Smiling Lieutenant* 1931; *The Man from Yesterday* 1932; *The Phantom President* 1932; *The Sign of the Cross* 1932; *The Wiser Sex* 1932; *I Cover the Waterfront* 1933; *Torch Singer* 1933; *Cleopatra* 1934; *Four Frightened People* 1934; *Imitation of Life* 1934; *It Happened One Night* 1934; *The Bride Comes Home* 1935; *The Gilded Lily* 1935; *Private Worlds* 1935; *She Married Her Boss* 1935; *Under Two Flags* 1936; *I Met Him in Paris* 1937; *Tovarich* 1937; *Bluebeard's Eighth Wife* 1938; *Drums along the Mohawk* 1939; *It's a Wonderful World* 1939; *Midnight* 1939; *Zaza* 1939; *Arise, My Love* 1940; *Boom Town* 1940; *Remember the Day* 1941; *Skylark* 1941; *The Palm Beach Story* 1942; *No Time for Love* 1943; *So Proudly We Hail* 1943; *Practically Yours* 1944; *Since You Went Away* 1944; *Guest Wife* 1945; *Tomorrow Is Forever* 1945; *The Secret Heart* 1946; *Without Reservations* 1946; *The Egg and I* 1947; *Sleep, My Love* 1948; *Bride for Sale* 1949; *Three Came Home* 1950; *Let's Make It Legal* 1951; *Thunder on the Hill* 1951; *The Planter's Wife* 1952; *Royal Affairs in Versailles* 1953; *Texas Lady* 1955; *Parrish* 1961

Colbert, Robert *aka* **Colbert, Bob** (1931–) *Have Rocket, Will Travel* 1959; *The Lawyer* 1969; *City beneath the Sea* 1971

Colby, Anita (1914–1992) *Cover Girl* 1944; *Brute Force* 1947

Cole, Carol *The Mad Room* 1969; *Model Shop* 1969

Cole, Gary (1957–) *In the Line of Fire* 1993; *The Switch* 1993; *The Brady Bunch Movie* 1995; *A Very Brady Sequel* 1996; *Gang Related* 1997; *I'll Be Home for Christmas* 1998; *A Simple Plan* 1998; *Office Space* 1999; *One Hour Photo* 2001; *I Spy* 2002; *The Ring Two* 2004; *Win a Date with Tad Hamilton!* 2004

Cole, George (1925–) *Cottage to Let* 1941; *My Brother's Keeper* 1948; *Quartet* 1948; *The Spider and the Fly* 1949; *Gone to Earth* 1950; *Lady Godiva Rides Again* 1951; *Laughter in Paradise* 1951; *Scrooge* 1951; *The Happy Family* 1952; *The Intruder* 1953; *Our Girl Friday* 1953; *Will Any Gentleman...?* 1953; *The Belles of St Trinian's* 1954; *Happy Ever After* 1954; *The Constant Husband* 1955; *A Prize of Gold* 1955; *Quentin Durward* 1955; *Where There's a Will* 1955; *The Green Man* 1956; *It's a Wonderful World* 1956; *Blue Murder at St Trinian's* 1957; *Too Many Crooks* 1958; *The Bridal Path* 1959; *The Pure Hell of St Trinian's* 1960; *Cleopatra* 1963; *Dr Syn, Alias the Scarecrow* 1963; *The Legend of Young Dick Turpin* 1965; *One Way Pendulum* 1965; *The Great St Trinian's Train Robbery* 1966; *The Vampire Lovers* 1970; *Fright* 1971; *Take Me High* 1973; *Gone in 60 Seconds* 1974; *The Blue*

Bird 1976; *Double Nickels* 1977; *Mary Reilly* 1995; *The Ghost of Greville Lodge* 2000
Cole, Nat King (1919–1965) *The Blue Gardenia* 1953; *China Gate* 1957; *Istanbul* 1957; *St Louis Blues* 1958
Cole, Natalie (1950–) *Fugitive from Justice* 1996; *Cats Don't Dance* 1998
Cole, Olivia (1942–) *Heroes* 1977; *Some Kind of Hero* 1982; *Go Tell It on the Mountain* 1984
Coleby, Robert (1947–) *The Plumber* 1979; *Now and Forever* 1983
Coleman, Charles (1885–1951) *The Rage of Paris* 1938; *That Certain Age* 1938
Coleman, Charlotte (1968–2001) *Four Weddings and a Funeral* 1994; *The Young Poisoner's Handbook* 1994; *Different for Girls* 1996; *If Only* 1998; *Beautiful People* 1999; *Bodywork* 1999
Coleman, Dabney (1932–) *The Slender Thread* 1965; *This Property Is Condemned* 1966; *The Scalphunters* 1968; *Downhill Racer* 1969; *I Love My... Wife* 1970; *Cinderella Liberty* 1973; *The Dove* 1974; *The Other Side of the Mountain* 1975; *Rolling Thunder* 1977; *North Dallas Forty* 1979; *How to Beat the High Cost of Living* 1980; *Nine to Five* 1980; *Nothing Personal* 1980; *Modern Problems* 1981; *On Golden Pond* 1981; *Tootsie* 1982; *Young Doctors in Love* 1982; *WarGames* 1983; *Cloak and Dagger* 1984; *The Man with One Red Shoe* 1985; *Dragnet* 1987; *Hot to Trot* 1988; *Short Time* 1990; *Where the Heart Is* 1990; *Meet the Applegates* 1991; *Paydirt* 1992; *Amos & Andrew* 1993; *The Beverly Hillbillies* 1993; *Judicial Consent* 1995; *Kidnapped* 1995; *You've Got Mail* 1998; *Taken* 1999; *Recess: School's Out* 2001; *Moonlight Mile* 2002
Coleman, Frank J *Behind the Screen* 1916; *The Cure* 1917
Coleman, Gary (1968–) *On the Right Track* 1981; *Jimmy the Kid* 1982; *Dirty Work* 1998
Coleman, Holliston (1992–) *Supreme Sanction* 1999; *Bless the Child* 2000
Coleman, Marilyn *Which Way Is Up?* 1977; *Remember My Name* 1978
Coleman, Nancy (1917–2000) *Dangerously They Live* 1942; *Desperate Journey* 1942; *The Gay Sisters* 1942; *Kings Row* 1942; *Edge of Darkness* 1943; *In Our Time* 1944; *Devotion* 1946; *Mourning Becomes Electra* 1947
Coleman, Renée *aka* **Coleman, Renee** *Pentathlon* 1994; *Waiting for Michelangelo* 1995
Coleridge, Ethel (1883–1976) *Rookery Nook* 1930; *Penny Paradise* 1938
Coles, Michael (1936–) *Solo for Sparrow* 1962; *Doctor Who and the Daleks* 1965; *A Touch of Love* 1969; *I Want What I Want* 1971; *Dracula AD 1972* 1972; *The Satanic Rites of Dracula* 1973
Colgan, Eileen *Quackser Fortune Has a Cousin in the Bronx* 1970; *The Secret of Roan Inish* 1993
Colicos, John (1928–2000) *Anne of the Thousand Days* 1969; *Raid on Rommel* 1971; *Red Sky at Morning* 1971; *The Wrath of God* 1972; *Scorpio* 1973; *Breaking Point* 1976; *Drum* 1976; *King Solomon's Treasure* 1977; *Phobia* 1980; *The Postman Always Rings Twice* 1981; *Nowhere to Hide* 1987
Colin, Grégoire (1975–) *Olivier Olivier* 1991; *Before the Rain* 1994; *Secret Defense* 1997; *The Dream Life of Angels* 1998; *Beau Travail* 1999; *Sex Is Comedy* 2002; *Vendredi Soir* 2002
Colin, Ian (1910–) *It's Never Too Late to Mend* 1937; *The Big Chance* 1957
Colin, Margaret (1957–) *Something Wild* 1986; *Like Father, like Son* 1987; *Three Men and a Baby* 1987; *True Believer* 1989; *Martians Go Home* 1990; *The Butcher's Wife* 1991; *Amos & Andrew* 1993; *Independence Day* 1996; *The Devil's Own* 1997; *The Adventures of Sebastian Cole* 1998; *Hit and Run* 1999; *Blue Car* 2001; *Unfaithful* 2002; *First Daughter* 2004
Colleano, Bonar (1924–1958) *A Matter of Life and Death* 1946; *Wanted for Murder* 1946; *While the Sun Shines* 1946; *Good Time Girl* 1948; *Once a Jolly Swagman* 1948; *One Night with You* 1948; *Give Us This Day* 1949; *Dance Hall* 1950; *Pool of London* 1950; *Eight Iron Men* 1952; *Escape by Night* 1953; *The Sea Shall Not Have Them* 1954; *Joe Macbeth* 1955; *Zarak* 1956; *Fire Down Below* 1957; *Interpol* 1957; *The Man Inside* 1958; *No Time to Die* 1958
Collet, Christopher (1968–) *Firstborn* 1984; *The Deadly Game* 1986; *Prayer of the Rollerboys* 1990
Collet, Pierre (1914–1977) *The Invitation* 1973; *French Connection II* 1975
Collette, Toni (1972–) *Spotswood* 1991; *Muriel's Wedding* 1994; *Arabian Knight* 1995; *Cosi* 1996; *Emma* 1996; *The Pallbearer* 1996; *Clockwatchers* 1997; *Diana & Me* 1997; *The James Gang* 1997; *The Boys* 1998; *Velvet Goldmine* 1998; *8½ Women* 1999; *Hotel Splendide* 1999; *The Sixth Sense* 1999; *The Magic Pudding* 2000; *Shaft* 2000; *Dinner with Friends* 2001; *About a Boy* 2002; *Changing Lanes* 2002; *Dirty Deeds* 2002; *The Hours* 2002; *Japanese Story* 2003; *Connie and Carla* 2004
Colley, Don Pedro (1938–) *THX 1138* 1971; *Sugar Hill* 1974
Colley, Kenneth *aka* **Colley, Ken** (1937–) *The Music Lovers* 1970; *The Triple Echo* 1972; *Giro City* 1982; *The Scarlet and the Black* 1983; *The Whistle Blower* 1986; *A Summer Story* 1987; *I Hired a Contract Killer* 1990; *The Last Island* 1990; *Prisoner of Honor* 1991; *Brassed Off* 1996; *Shadow Run* 1998; *Hold Back the Night* 1999
Collier, Constance (1878–1955) *A Damsel in Distress* 1937; *Stage Door* 1937; *Thunder in the City* 1937; *Zaza* 1939; *Kitty* 1945; *The Dark Corner* 1946; *Monsieur Beaucaire* 1946; *An Ideal Husband* 1947; *The Perils of Pauline* 1947; *The Girl from Manhattan* 1948; *Rope* 1948; *Whirlpool* 1949
Collier, Don (1928–) *Safe at Home* 1962; *Flap* 1970
Collier, Lois (1919–1999) *Cobra Woman* 1944; *The Naughty Nineties* 1945; *A Night in Casablanca* 1946; *Wild Beauty* 1946; *Slave Girl* 1947
Collier, Patience (1910–1987) *Countess Dracula* 1970; *Every Home Should Have One* 1970; *Perfect Friday* 1970
Collier Sr, William (1866–1944) *Up the River* 1930; *The Bride Comes Home* 1935; *Murder Man* 1935; *Invitation to Happiness* 1939; *Miracle on Main Street* 1940
Collier Jr, William *aka* **Collier, William** (1902–1987) *The Lucky Lady* 1926; *Rain or Shine* 1930; *Cimarron* 1931; *Little Caesar* 1931; *Street Scene* 1931
Collin, John (1931–1987) *The Witches* 1966; *Before Winter Comes* 1968; *The Last Escape* 1970; *All Creatures Great and Small* 1974; *Tess* 1979
Collinge, Patricia (1892–1974) *The Little Foxes* 1941; *Shadow of a Doubt* 1942; *Tender Comrade* 1943; *Casanova Brown* 1944; *Teresa* 1951; *Washington Story* 1952; *The Nun's Story* 1959
Collings, Anne *The Mask* 1961; *Seven Alone* 1974
Collins Jr, Clifton *aka* **Gonzalez, Clifton Gonzalez** (1970–) *Fortress* 1992; *One Eight Seven* 1997; *Light It Up* 1999; *Price of Glory* 2000; *Tigerland* 2000; *Traffic* 2000; *The Last Castle* 2001; *Mindhunters* 2003
Collins, Eddie (1884–1940) *Drums along the Mohawk* 1939; *Young Mr Lincoln* 1939; *The Blue Bird* 1940
Collins, Elaine *Up* 1976; *Soft Top, Hard Shoulder* 1992
Collins, Gary (1938–) *Angel in My Pocket* 1968; *Killer Fish* 1978; *Hangar 18* 1980; *Danielle Steel's Secrets* 1992
Collins, Greg *Cool World* 1992; *Walnut Creek* 1996
Collins, Jackie (1939–) *Barnacle Bill* 1957; *Undercover Girl* 1957; *During One Night* 1961
Collins, Joan (1933–) *Judgement Deferred* 1951; *Lady Godiva Rides Again* 1951; *Cosh Boy* 1952; *I Believe in You* 1952; *Decameron Nights* 1953; *Our Girl Friday* 1953; *The Square Ring* 1953; *Turn the Key Softly* 1953; *The Good Die Young* 1954; *The Girl in the Red Velvet Swing* 1955; *Land of the Pharaohs* 1955; *The Virgin Queen* 1955; *The Opposite Sex* 1956; *Island in the Sun* 1957; *Sea Wife* 1957; *Stopover Tokyo* 1957; *The Wayward Bus* 1957; *The Bravados* 1958; *Rally 'round the Flag, Boys!* 1958; *Esther and the King* 1960; *Seven Thieves* 1960; *The Road to Hong Kong* 1962; *Warning Shot* 1967; *Subterfuge* 1968; *Can Heironymus Merkin Ever Forget Mercy Humppe and Find True Happiness?* 1969; *If It's Tuesday, This Must Be Belgium* 1969; *The Executioner* 1970; *Up in the Cellar* 1970; *Quest for Love* 1971; *Revenge* 1971; *Fear in the Night* 1972; *Tales from the Crypt* 1972; *Dark Places* 1973; *Tales That Witness Madness* 1973; *Alfie Darling* 1975; *I Don't Want to Be Born* 1975; *The Bawdy Adventures of Tom Jones* 1976; *Empire of the Ants* 1977; *The Big Sleep* 1978; *The Stud* 1978; *Zero to Sixty* 1978; *The Bitch* 1979; *A Game for Vultures* 1979; *Sunburn* 1979; *Nutcracker* 1982; *Decadence* 1993; *Annie: a Royal Adventure* 1995; *In the Bleak Midwinter* 1995; *The Clandestine Marriage* 1999; *The Flintstones in Viva Rock Vegas* 2000; *These Old Broads* 2001
Collins, Kevin *The Garden* 1990; *Edward II* 1991; *Wittgenstein* 1993
Collins, Lewis (1946–) *Who Dares Wins* 1982; *Codename Wildgeese* 1984; *A Ghost in Monte Carlo* 1990
Collins, Patricia *Bear Island* 1979; *Circle of Two* 1980; *Speaking Parts* 1989
Collins, Paul (1937–) *Peter Pan* 1953; *Mother* 1996
Collins, Pauline (1940–) *Shirley Valentine* 1989; *City of Joy* 1992; *My Mother's Courage* 1995; *Paradise Road* 1997; *Mrs Caldicot's Cabbage War* 2000
Collins, Phil (1951–) *Buster* 1988; *Hook* 1991; *Frauds* 1992; *And the Band Played On* 1993; *Balto* 1995; *The Jungle Book 2* 2003
Collins, Ray (1889–1965) *Citizen Kane* 1941; *The Big Street* 1942; *The Commandos Strike at Dawn* 1942; *The Magnificent Ambersons* 1942; *Crime Doctor* 1943; *The Human Comedy* 1943; *Salute to the Marines* 1943; *Whistling in Brooklyn* 1943; *Can't Help Singing* 1944; *The Eve of St Mark* 1944; *See Here, Private Hargrove* 1944; *The Hidden Eye* 1945; *Leave Her to Heaven* 1945; *Miss Susie Slagle's* 1945; *Badman's Territory* 1946; *Crack-Up* 1946; *The Bachelor and the Bobby-Soxer* 1947; *A Double Life* 1947; *The Senator Was Indiscreet* 1947; *For the Love of Mary* 1948; *Good Sam* 1948; *Homecoming* 1948; *The Man from Colorado* 1948; *The Fountainhead* 1949; *Francis* 1949; *The Heiress* 1949; *Paid in Full* 1950; *Summer Stock* 1950; *The Racket* 1951; *Vengeance Valley* 1951; *You're in the Navy Now* 1951; *Young Man with Ideas* 1952; *Column South* 1953; *The Desert Song* 1953; *The Kid from Left Field* 1953; *Bad for Each Other* 1954; *Never Say Goodbye* 1955; *Texas Lady* 1955; *The Solid Gold Cadillac* 1956; *Touch of Evil* 1958
Collins, Roberta *The Big Doll House* 1971; *The Unholy Rollers* 1972; *Women in Cages* 1972; *Caged Heat* 1974; *Death Race 2000* 1975; *School Spirit* 1985
Collins, Russell (1897–1965) *Shockproof* 1949; *Miss Sadie Thompson* 1953; *The Last Frontier* 1955; *The Enemy Below* 1957
Collins, Stephen (1947–) *All the President's Men* 1976; *Between the Lines* 1977; *Face of a Stranger* 1978; *Star Trek: the Motion Picture* 1979; *Loving Couples* 1980; *Brewster's Millions* 1985; *Jumpin' Jack Flash* 1986; *On Dangerous Ground* 1986; *Stella* 1990; *My New Gun* 1992; *Drive Me Crazy* 1999
Collison, Frank (1950–) *Hope Springs* 2002; *The Whole Ten Yards* 2004
Collyer, June *Hangman's House* 1928; *Charley's Aunt* 1930
Colman, Ronald (1891–1958) *The White Sister* 1923; *Lady Windermere's Fan* 1925; *Stella Dallas* 1925; *Beau Geste* 1926; *The Winning of Barbara Worth* 1926; *Bulldog Drummond* 1929; *Condemned* 1929; *The Devil to Pay* 1930; *Raffles* 1930; *Arrowsmith* 1931; *The Unholy Garden* 1931; *Cynara* 1932; *The Masquerader* 1933; *Bulldog Drummond Strikes Back* 1934; *Clive of India* 1935; *The Man Who Broke the Bank at Monte Carlo* 1935; *A Tale of Two Cities* 1935; *Under Two Flags* 1936; *Lost Horizon* 1937; *The Prisoner of Zenda* 1937; *If I Were King* 1938; *The Light That Failed* 1939; *Lucky Partners* 1940; *My Life with Caroline* 1941; *Random Harvest* 1942; *The Talk of the Town* 1942; *Kismet* 1944; *A Double Life* 1947; *The Late George Apley* 1947; *Champagne for Caesar* 1950; *The Story of Mankind* 1957
Colmans, Edward (1908–1977) *Thief of Damascus* 1952; *Diary of a Madman* 1963
Colomby, Scott (1952–) *Caddyshack* 1980; *Porky's II: The Next Day* 1983; *Porky's Revenge* 1985
Colon, Alex (1941–1995) *Death of an Angel* 1985; *Invasion USA* 1985; *Red Scorpion* 1989
Colon, Miriam (1945–) *Thunder Island* 1963; *Southwest to Sonora* 1966; *Back Roads* 1981; *Scarface* 1983
Colonna, Jerry (1904–1986) *Road to Singapore* 1940; *Atlantic City* 1944; *Make Mine Music* 1946; *Alice in Wonderland* 1951; *Andy Hardy Comes Home* 1958
Colosimo, Clara (1922–1994) *Alfredo Alfredo* 1971; *Orchestra Rehearsal* 1978; *Vampire in Venice* 1987
Colosimo, Vince (1966–) *Chopper* 2000; *Lantana* 2001; *The Hard Word* 2002; *The Nugget* 2002
Colpeyn, Louisa *aka* **Colpeyn, Luisa** *Bande à Part* 1964; *Marry Me! Marry Me!* 1968
Colton, Jacque Lynn *Uphill All the Way* 1985; *Heartbreak Hotel* 1988
Coltrane, Robbie (1950–) *Scrubbers* 1982; *Krull* 1983; *Loose Connections* 1983; *Chinese Boxes* 1984; *Defence of the Realm* 1985; *National Lampoon's European Vacation* 1985; *The Supergrass* 1985; *Caravaggio* 1986; *Mona Lisa* 1986; *Eat the Rich* 1987; *Bert Rigby, You're a Fool* 1989; *Henry V* 1989; *Let It Ride* 1989; *Nuns on the Run* 1990; *Perfectly Normal* 1990; *The Pope Must Die* 1991; *Triple Bogey on a Par Five Hole* 1991; *Oh, What a Night* 1992; *The Adventures of Huck Finn* 1993; *GoldenEye* 1995; *Buddy* 1997; *Montana* 1997; *Message in a Bottle* 1998; *Alice in Wonderland* 1999; *The World Is Not Enough* 1999; *From Hell* 2001; *Harry Potter and the Philosopher's Stone* 2001; *Harry Potter and the Chamber of Secrets* 2002; *Harry Potter and the Prisoner of Azkaban* 2004; *Ocean's Twelve* 2004
Colvig, Pinto (1892–1967) *The Three Little Pigs* 1933; *Snow White and the Seven Dwarfs* 1937
Colvin, Jack *The Incredible Hulk* 1977; *Child's Play* 1988; *The Incredible Hulk Returns* 1988
Combeau, Muriel *Romuald et Juliette* 1989; *Near Mrs* 1990
Combs, Holly Marie (1973–) *Sweet Hearts Dance* 1988; *Dr Giggles* 1992; *Danielle Steel's A Perfect Stranger* 1994; *Swearing Allegiance* 1997
Combs, Jeffrey (1954–) *Re-Animator* 1985; *From Beyond* 1986; *Bride of Re-Animator* 1991; *The Pit and the Pendulum* 1991; *Trancers II: The Return of Jack Deth* 1991; *Necronomicon* 1993; *Love and a .45* 1994; *The Frighteners* 1996; *Faust: Love of the Damned* 2001; *FearDotCom* 2002
Combs, Sean (1969–) *Made* 2001; *Monster's Ball* 2001
Comer, Anjanette (1942–) *The Loved One* 1965; *Quick, before It Melts* 1965; *Southwest to Sonora* 1966; *Banning* 1967; *Guns for San Sebastian* 1968; *In Enemy Country* 1968; *The Firechasers* 1970; *Rabbit, Run* 1970; *The Baby* 1973; *Lepke* 1975; *Fire Sale* 1977; *The Long Summer of George Adams* 1982
Comer, John (1924–1984) *The Family Way* 1966; *There's a Girl in My Soup* 1970; *The Lovers!* 1972
Comerate, Sheridan *Crash Landing* 1958; *Live Fast, Die Young* 1958
Comingore, Dorothy (1913–1971) *Citizen Kane* 1941; *The Hairy Ape* 1944; *The Big Night* 1951
Como, Perry (1912–2001) *Something for the Boys* 1944; *Words and Music* 1948
Compson, Betty (1897–1974) *The Pony Express* 1925; *The Barker* 1928; *The Docks of New York* 1928; *The Great Gabbo* 1929
Compton, Fay (1894–1978) *Waltzes from Vienna* 1933; *The Mill on the Floss* 1937; *The Prime Minister* 1940; *Odd Man Out* 1946; *Esther Waters* 1948; *London Belongs to Me* 1948; *Britannia Mews* 1949; *Laughter in Paradise* 1951; *Othello* 1952; *The Vanquished* 1953; *Double Cross* 1955; *The Story of Esther Costello* 1957; *The Haunting* 1963; *The Virgin and the Gypsy* 1970
Compton, Joyce (1907–1997) *The Wild Party* 1929; *The Awful Truth* 1937; *Artists and Models Abroad* 1938; *Rose of Washington Square* 1939; *Let's Make Music* 1940; *Sky Murder* 1940; *The Villain Still Pursued Her* 1940; *Bedtime Story* 1942; *Christmas in Connecticut* 1945; *Scared to Death* 1947
Compton, Juliette (1899–1989) *Anybody's Woman* 1930; *Morocco* 1930; *Devil and the Deep* 1932; *No One Man* 1932; *Westward Passage* 1932; *The Masquerader* 1933; *Peg o' My Heart* 1933
Compton, O'Neal (1951–) *Attack of the 50 Ft Woman* 1993; *Murder between Friends* 1993; *Roadracers* 1994; *Kill Me Later* 2001
Conant, Oliver (1955–) *Summer of '42* 1971; *Class of '44* 1973
Conaway, Jeff (1950–) *Grease* 1978; *The Patriot* 1986; *Elvira, Mistress of the Dark* 1988; *A Time to Die* 1991
Condra, Julie (1970–) *Crying Freeman* 1995; *Danielle Steel's Mixed Blessings* 1995; *Screw Loose* 1999
Congdon, James *The Left Handed Gun* 1958; *The Gardener* 1972
Conklin, Chester (1888–1971) *Tillie's Punctured Romance* 1914; *Greed* 1925; *The Big Noise* 1928; *The Virginian* 1929; *Her Majesty Love* 1931; *Hallelujah, I'm a Bum* 1933; *Modern Times* 1936; *The Perils of Pauline* 1947; *The Beast with a Million Eyes* 1955
Conklin, Peggy (1912–2003) *The Devil Is a Sissy* 1936; *Having Wonderful Time* 1938

Conley, Brian (1961–) *Circus* 1999; *Arthur's Dyke* 2001

Conlin, Jimmy aka **Conlin, James** (1884–1962) *Rose Marie* 1936; *Seven Keys to Baldpate* 1947; *Knock on Any Door* 1949; *Tulsa* 1949; *Mad Wednesday* 1950

Conn, Didi (1951–) *Almost Summer* 1977; *Raggedy Ann and Andy* 1977; *You Light Up My Life* 1977; *Grease 2* 1982; *Thomas and the Magic Railroad* 2000

Connell, Maureen (1931–) *The Abominable Snowman* 1957; *Lucky Jim* 1957; *Next to No Time* 1958; *Danger by My Side* 1962

Connelly, Christopher aka **Connelly, Chris** (1941–1988) *Corky* 1972; *They Only Kill Their Masters* 1972; *Hawmps* 1976; *The Norseman* 1978; *Earthbound* 1981; *Liar's Moon* 1982

Connelly, Edward (1859–1928) *Camille* 1921; *Sinners in Silk* 1924; *The Torrent* 1926

Connelly, Erwin (1879–1931) *Sherlock Junior* 1924; *Go West* 1925; *Seven Chances* 1925

Connelly, Jennifer (1970–) *Labyrinth* 1986; *Some Girls* 1988; *The Hot Spot* 1990; *Career Opportunities* 1991; *Rocketeer* 1991; *The Heart of Justice* 1992; *Of Love and Shadows* 1994; *Higher Learning* 1995; *Mulholland Falls* 1996; *Inventing the Abbotts* 1997; *Dark City* 1998; *Pollock* 2000; *Requiem for a Dream* 2000; *Waking the Dead* 2000; *A Beautiful Mind* 2001; *House of Sand and Fog* 2003; *Hulk* 2003

Connery, Jason (1962–) *The Lords of Discipline* 1983; *The Boy Who Had Everything* 1984; *Bullet to Beijing* 1995; *Midnight in St Petersburg* 1995; *Macbeth* 1997; *Urban Ghost Story* 1998; *Shanghai Noon* 2000

Connery, Neil *Operation Kid Brother* 1967; *The Body Stealers* 1969

Connery, Sean (1930–) *Lilacs in the Spring* 1955; *Action of the Tiger* 1957; *Hell Drivers* 1957; *No Road Back* 1957; *Time Lock* 1957; *Another Time, Another Place* 1958; *A Night to Remember* 1958; *Darby O'Gill and the Little People* 1959; *Tarzan's Greatest Adventure* 1959; *The Frightened City* 1961; *On the Fiddle* 1961; *Dr No* 1962; *The Longest Day* 1962; *From Russia with Love* 1963; *Goldfinger* 1964; *Marnie* 1964; *Woman of Straw* 1964; *The Hill* 1965; *Thunderball* 1965; *A Fine Madness* 1966; *You Only Live Twice* 1967; *Shalako* 1968; *The Red Tent* 1969; *The Molly Maguires* 1970; *The Anderson Tapes* 1971; *Diamonds Are Forever* 1971; *The Offence* 1972; *Zardoz* 1973; *Murder on the Orient Express* 1974; *The Man Who Would Be King* 1975; *Ransom* 1975; *The Wind and the Lion* 1975; *The Next Man* 1976; *Robin and Marian* 1976; *A Bridge Too Far* 1977; *The First Great Train Robbery* 1978; *Cuba* 1979; *Meteor* 1979; *Outland* 1981; *Time Bandits* 1981; *Five Days One Summer* 1982; *The Man with the Deadly Lens* 1982; *Never Say Never Again* 1983; *Sword of the Valiant* 1984; *Highlander* 1986; *The Name of the Rose* 1986; *The Untouchables* 1987; *Memories of Me* 1988; *The Presidio* 1988; *Family Business* 1989; *Indiana Jones and the Last Crusade* 1989; *Highlander II: the Quickening* 1990; *The Hunt for Red October* 1990; *The Russia House* 1990; *Robin Hood: Prince of Thieves* 1991; *Medicine Man* 1992; *A Good Man in Africa* 1993; *Rising Sun* 1993; *First Knight* 1995; *Just Cause* 1995; *DragonHeart* 1996; *The Rock* 1996; *The Avengers* 1998; *Playing by Heart* 1998; *Entrapment* 1999; *Finding Forrester* 2000; *The League of Extraordinary Gentlemen* 2003

Connick Jr, Harry (1967–) *Memphis Belle* 1990; *Little Man Tate* 1991; *Copycat* 1995; *Excess Baggage* 1997; *Hope Floats* 1998; *The Iron Giant* 1999; *The Simian Line* 2000; *South Pacific* 2001

Connolly, Andrew *Joyriders* 1988; *Mad Dogs and Englishmen* 1994

Connolly, Billy (1942–) *Absolution* 1978; *Bullshot* 1983; *Water* 1985; *The Big Man* 1990; *Indecent Proposal* 1993; *Pocahontas* 1995; *Muppet Treasure Island* 1996; *Middleton's Changeling* 1997; *Mrs Brown* 1997; *Paws* 1997; *The Impostors* 1998; *Still Crazy* 1998; *The Boondock Saints* 1999; *The Debt Collector* 1999; *Beautiful Joe* 2000; *An Everlasting Piece* 2000; *Gabriel & Me* 2001; *The Man Who Sued God* 2001; *White Oleander* 2002; *The Last Samurai* 2003; *Timeline* 2003; *Lemony Snicket's A Series of Unfortunate Events* 2004

Connolly, Kevin (1974–) *Alan & Naomi* 1992; *Antwone Fisher* 2002; *The Notebook* 2003

Connolly, Walter (1887–1940) *Washington Merry-Go-Round* 1932; *The Bitter Tea of General Yen* 1933; *Lady for a Day* 1933; *Man's Castle* 1933; *Broadway Bill* 1934; *The Captain Hates the Sea* 1934; *It Happened One Night* 1934; *Lady by Choice* 1934; *Twentieth Century* 1934; *So Red the Rose* 1935; *The King Steps Out* 1936; *Libeled Lady* 1936; *First Lady* 1937; *The Good Earth* 1937; *The League of Frightened Men* 1937; *Nancy Steele Is Missing* 1937; *Nothing Sacred* 1937; *Four's a Crowd* 1938; *Start Cheering* 1938; *Too Hot to Handle* 1938; *The Adventures of Huckleberry Finn* 1939; *Fifth Avenue Girl* 1939

Connor, Edric (1915–1968) *Cry, the Beloved Country* 1951; *West of Zanzibar* 1954; *Virgin Island* 1958; *4 for Texas* 1963; *Only When I Larf* 1968

Connor, Kenneth (1918–1992) *The Ladykillers* 1955; *Carry On Sergeant* 1958; *Carry On Nurse* 1959; *Carry On Teacher* 1959; *Make Mine a Million* 1959; *Carry On Constable* 1960; *Carry On Regardless* 1960; *Dentist in the Chair* 1960; *His and Hers* 1960; *Watch Your Stern* 1960; *Dentist on the Job* 1961; *Nearly a Nasty Accident* 1961; *What a Carve Up!* 1961; *Carry On Cruising* 1962; *Carry On Cabby* 1963; *Carry On Cleo* 1964; *Gonks Go Beat* 1965; *Captain Nemo and the Underwater City* 1969; *Carry On Up the Jungle* 1970; *Carry On Henry* 1971; *Carry On Abroad* 1972; *Carry On Matron* 1972; *Carry On Girls* 1973; *Carry On Dick* 1974; *Carry On Behind* 1975; *Carry On England* 1976; *Carry On Emmannuelle* 1978

Connors, Chuck (1921–1992) *Pat and Mike* 1952; *South Sea Woman* 1953; *The Human Jungle* 1954; *Naked Alibi* 1954; *Good Morning, Miss Dove* 1955; *The Hired Gun* 1957; *Old Yeller* 1957; *The Big Country* 1958; *The Lady Takes a Flyer* 1958; *Geronimo* 1962; *Flipper* 1963; *Move Over, Darling* 1963; *Get off My Back* 1965; *Ride beyond Vengeance* 1966; *Captain Nemo and the Underwater City* 1969; *The Birdmen* 1971; *The Deserter* 1971; *Pancho Villa* 1971; *Support Your Local Gunfighter* 1971; *Embassy* 1972; *The Proud and the Damned* 1972; *Soylent Green* 1973; *99 and 44/100% Dead* 1974; *Tourist Trap* 1979; *Virus* 1980; *Airplane II: the Sequel* 1982; *Balboa* 1982; *Target Eagle* 1982; *Once upon a Texas Train* 1988; *Salmonberries* 1991

Connors, Mike aka **Connors, Touch** aka **Connors, Michael** (1925–) *Sudden Fear* 1952; *The 49th Man* 1953; *Five Guns West* 1955; *The Twinkle in God's Eye* 1955; *The Day the World Ended* 1956; *Shake, Rattle and Rock!* 1957; *Voodoo Woman* 1957; *Live Fast, Die Young* 1958; *Suicide Battalion* 1958; *Good Neighbor Sam* 1964; *Panic Button* 1964; *Where Love Has Gone* 1964; *Harlow* 1965; *Situation Hopeless – but Not Serious* 1965; *Stagecoach* 1966; *Avalanche Express* 1979; *Too Scared to Scream* 1982; *Gideon* 1999

Conrad, Chris *Airborne* 1993; *The Next Karate Kid* 1994

Conrad, David (1967–) *The Wizard of Speed and Time* 1988; *Snow White: a Tale of Terror* 1996; *Return to Paradise* 1998

Conrad, Jess (1940–) *Konga* 1960; *Rag Doll* 1960; *The Boys* 1961; *The Punk* 1993

Conrad, Michael (1925–1983) *They Shoot Horses, Don't They?* 1969; *Un Flic* 1972; *Scream Blacula Scream* 1973; *The Mean Machine* 1974; *W* 1974; *Starsky and Hutch* 1975

Conrad, Robert (1935–) *Palm Springs Weekend* 1963; *Young Dillinger* 1965; *Live a Little, Steal a Lot* 1974; *The Lady in Red* 1979; *The Man with the Deadly Lens* 1982; *Jingle All the Way* 1996

Conrad, William (1920–1994) *The Killers* 1946; *Body and Soul* 1947; *Sorry, Wrong Number* 1948; *They Passed This Way* 1948; *East Side, West Side* 1949; *Tension* 1949; *One Way Street* 1950; *Cry Danger* 1951; *The Sword of Monte Cristo* 1951; *Cry of the Hunted* 1953; *The Naked Jungle* 1953; *Five against the House* 1955; *The Conqueror* 1956; *Johnny Concho* 1956; *–30–* 1959; *Moonshine County Express* 1977; *Killing Cars* 1986

Conried, Hans (1917–1982) *A Lady Takes a Chance* 1943; *The Senator Was Indiscreet* 1947; *My Friend Irma* 1949; *The Affairs of Dobie Gillis* 1953; *The 5,000 Fingers of Dr T* 1953; *Peter Pan* 1953; *Davy Crockett, King of the Wild Frontier* 1955; *The Birds and the Bees* 1956; *Bus Stop* 1956; *The Monster That Challenged the World* 1957; *Rock-a-Bye Baby* 1958; *Juke Box Rhythm* 1959; *My Six Loves* 1962; *The Patsy* 1964

Conroy, Frances (1953–) *Rocket Gibraltar* 1988; *The Neon Bible* 1995; *Murder in a Small Town* 1999; *Maid in Manhattan* 2002; *Catwoman* 2004

Conroy, Frank (1890–1964) *Bad Company* 1931; *Possessed* 1931; *The White Parade* 1934; *The Call of the Wild* 1935; *Charlie Chan in Egypt* 1935; *All My Sons* 1948; *Lightning Strikes Twice* 1951; *The Last Mile* 1959; *The Bramble Bush* 1960

Conroy, Ruaidhri (1979–) *Into the West* 1992; *Clockwork Mice* 1994; *Moondance* 1995; *Nothing Personal* 1995; *The Van* 1996

Considine, John (1938–) *Buffalo Bill and the Indians, or Sitting Bull's History Lesson* 1976; *Trouble in Mind* 1985; *Hell Camp* 1986; *Tinseltown* 1997

Considine, Paddy (1974–) *A Room for Romeo Brass* 1999; *Last Resort* 2000; *24 Hour Party People* 2001; *Doctor Sleep* 2002; *In America* 2003; *Dead Man's Shoes* 2004; *My Summer of Love* 2004; *Cinderella Man* 2005

Considine, Tim (1940–) *The Clown* 1952; *Her Twelve Men* 1954; *The Private War of Major Benson* 1955; *The Shaggy Dog* 1959; *Sunrise at Campobello* 1960; *The Daring Dobermans* 1973

Constance, Nathan (1979–) *A Kind of Hush* 1998; *Dog Eat Dog* 2000

Constantin, Michel (1924–2003) *Le Trou* 1959; *The Last Known Address* 1969; *There Was Once a Cop* 1969; *Violent City* 1970; *Cold Sweat* 1971; *Man in the Trunk* 1973

Constantine, Eddie (1917–1993) *One Night at the Music Hall* 1956; *Passport to Shame* 1958; *SOS Pacific* 1959; *The Treasure of San Teresa* 1959; *Cleo from 5 to 7* 1961; *The Seven Deadly Sins* 1961; *As If It Were Raining* 1963; *Alphaville* 1965; *Beware of a Holy Whore* 1970; *It Lives Again* 1978; *The Long Good Friday* 1979; *The Third Generation* 1979; *Europa* 1991

Constantine, Michael (1927–) *The Hustler* 1961; *Quick, before It Melts* 1965; *Skidoo* 1968; *Don't Drink the Water* 1969; *If It's Tuesday, This Must Be Belgium* 1969; *The Reivers* 1969; *Summer of My German Soldier* 1978; *Hill's Angels* 1979; *The Woo Woo Kid* 1987; *My Life* 1993; *The Juror* 1996; *My Big Fat Greek Wedding* 2002

Conte, John (1915–) *Lost in a Harem* 1944; *The Man with the Golden Arm* 1955; *Trauma* 1962

Conte, Richard (1910–1975) *Guadalcanal Diary* 1943; *The Purple Heart* 1944; *A Bell for Adano* 1945; *Captain Eddie* 1945; *A Walk in the Sun* 1945; *Somewhere in the Night* 1946; *13 Rue Madeleine* 1946; *The Other Love* 1947; *Call Northside 777* 1948; *Cry of the City* 1948; *Big Jack* 1949; *House of Strangers* 1949; *Thieves' Highway* 1949; *Whirlpool* 1949; *The Sleeping City* 1950; *The Fighter* 1952; *The Blue Gardenia* 1953; *Desert Legion* 1953; *Mask of Dust* 1954; *Bengazi* 1955; *The Big Combo* 1955; *The Big Tip Off* 1955; *I'll Cry Tomorrow* 1955; *Little Red Monkey* 1955; *New York Confidential* 1955; *Full of Life* 1956; *The Brothers Rico* 1957; *This Angry Age* 1957; *They Came to Cordura* 1959; *Ocean's Eleven* 1960; *Who's Been Sleeping in My Bed?* 1963; *The Magnificent Showman* 1964; *Get off My Back* 1965; *Assault on a Queen* 1966; *Hotel* 1967; *Tony Rome* 1967; *Lady in Cement* 1968; *The Godfather* 1972

Conti, Albert (1887–1967) *The Eagle* 1925; *One Romantic Night* 1930; *Lady with a Past* 1932; *Topaze* 1933; *The Black Cat* 1934

Conti, Tom (1941–) *Galileo* 1974; *Slade in Flame* 1974; *The Duellists* 1977; *Full Circle* 1977; *Merry Christmas Mr Lawrence* 1982; *Reuben, Reuben* 1983; *American Dreamer* 1984; *Miracles* 1985; *Saving Grace* 1985; *Heavenly Pursuits* 1986; *Nazi Hunter: the Beate Klarsfeld Story* 1986; *Beyond Therapy* 1987; *Shirley Valentine* 1989; *That Summer of White Roses* 1989; *Someone Else's America* 1995; *Something to Believe In* 1997; *Don't Go Breaking My Heart* 1999; *The Enemy* 2000

Conti, Ugo *Mediterraneo* 1991; *Children of Hannibal* 1998

Contreras, Luis (1950–) *Blue City* 1986; *Straight to Hell* 1987

Contreras, Patricio (1947–) *Old Gringo* 1989; *After the Storm* 1990; *La Frontera* 1991; *Of Love and Shadows* 1994

Converse, Frank (1938–) *The Pilot* 1979; *The Bushido Blade* 1981; *Everybody Wins* 1990; *Primary Motive* 1992

Converse-Roberts, William *1918* 1985; *Drive Me Crazy* 1999

Convy, Bert (1933–1991) *Semi-Tough* 1977; *Jennifer* 1978; *Hero at Large* 1980

Conway, Gary (1938–) *I Was a Teenage Frankenstein* 1957; *How to Make a Monster* 1958; *Young Guns of Texas* 1962; *Once Is Not Enough* 1975

Conway, Kevin (1942–) *Believe in Me* 1971; *Slaughterhouse-Five* 1972; *FIST* 1978; *Paradise Alley* 1978; *The Lathe of Heaven* 1979; *Flashpoint* 1984; *Homeboy* 1988; *One Good Cop* 1991; *Rambling Rose* 1991; *Jennifer Eight* 1992; *Lawnmower Man 2: Beyond Cyberspace* 1995; *Black Knight* 2001; *Gods and Generals* 2002

Conway, Morgan (1903–1981) *Looking for Trouble* 1934; *The Spellbinder* 1939; *Brother Orchid* 1940; *The Saint Takes Over* 1940; *Dick Tracy* 1945; *Dick Tracy vs Cueball* 1946

Conway, Pat (1931–1981) *An Annapolis Story* 1955; *Geronimo* 1962

Conway, Russ (1913–1978) *Jennifer* 1953; *The Looters* 1955; *Interval* 1973

Conway, Tim (1933–) *McHale's Navy* 1964; *The World's Greatest Athlete* 1973; *The Apple Dumpling Gang* 1974; *Gus* 1976; *The Shaggy DA* 1976; *The Billion Dollar Hobo* 1978; *The Apple Dumpling Gang Rides Again* 1979; *The Prize Fighter* 1979; *The Private Eyes* 1980; *The Longshot* 1986; *Dear God* 1996; *Air Bud: Golden Receiver* 1998

Conway, Tom (1904–1967) *Sky Murder* 1940; *Lady Be Good* 1941; *Mr and Mrs North* 1941; *Tarzan's Secret Treasure* 1941; *The Trial of Mary Dugan* 1941; *Cat People* 1942; *The Falcon's Brother* 1942; *Rio Rita* 1942; *The Falcon and the Co-Eds* 1943; *The Falcon in Danger* 1943; *The Falcon Strikes Back* 1943; *I Walked with a Zombie* 1943; *The Seventh Victim* 1943; *The Falcon in Hollywood* 1944; *The Falcon in Mexico* 1944; *The Falcon Out West* 1944; *The Falcon in San Francisco* 1945; *Two O'Clock Courage* 1945; *Criminal Court* 1946; *The Falcon's Adventure* 1946; *The Falcon's Alibi* 1946; *Whistle Stop* 1946; *One Touch of Venus* 1948; *Painting the Clouds with Sunshine* 1951; *Blood Orange* 1953; *Park Plaza 605* 1953; *Peter Pan* 1953; *Tarzan and the She-Devil* 1953; *Death of a Scoundrel* 1956; *The She-Creature* 1956; *Voodoo Woman* 1957; *The Atomic Submarine* 1960

Coogan, Jackie (1914–1984) *A Day's Pleasure* 1919; *The Kid* 1921; *Oliver Twist* 1922; *Tom Sawyer* 1930; *Huckleberry Finn* 1931; *College Swing* 1938; *Million Dollar Legs* 1939; *The Buster Keaton Story* 1957; *The Joker Is Wild* 1957; *Lonelyhearts* 1958; *The Beat Generation* 1959; *The Big Operator* 1959; *Sex Kittens Go to College* 1960; *The Shakiest Gun in the West* 1967; *Marlowe* 1969; *Sherlock Holmes in New York* 1976; *Dr Heckyl & Mr Hype* 1980; *The Escape Artist* 1982

Coogan, Keith (1970–) *Hiding Out* 1987; *A Night on the Town* 1987; *Under the Boardwalk* 1988; *Cheetah* 1989; *Cousins* 1989; *Don't Tell Mom the Babysitter's Dead* 1991; *Toy Soldiers* 1991; *Forever* 1993

Coogan, Richard (1914–) *Three Hours to Kill* 1954; *The Revolt of Mamie Stover* 1956

Coogan, Steve (1965–) *The Indian in the Cupboard* 1995; *The Wind in the Willows* 1996; *The Revengers' Comedies* 1997; *The Parole Officer* 2001; *24 Hour Party People* 2001; *Coffee and Cigarettes* 2003; *Around the World in 80 Days* 2004; *Ella Enchanted* 2004

Cook, A J (1978–) *The Virgin Suicides* 1999; *Final Destination 2* 2002

Cook, Carole *The Incredible Mr Limpet* 1964; *The Gauntlet* 1977; *Summer Lovers* 1982; *Grandview, USA* 1984; *Home on the Range* 2004

Cook, Clyde (1891–1984) *The Docks of New York* 1928; *The Taming of the Shrew* 1929; *The Man from Down Under* 1943

Cook, Donald (1901–1961) *The Mad Genius* 1931; *The Public Enemy* 1931; *The Man Who Played God* 1932; *The Penguin Pool Murder* 1932; *Baby Face* 1933; *Jennie Gerhardt* 1933; *The Kiss before the Mirror* 1933; *The World Changes* 1933; *Long Lost Father* 1934; *Viva Villa!* 1934; *The Casino Murder Case* 1935; *Confidential* 1935; *Show Boat* 1936; *Patrick the Great* 1944; *Here Come the Co-Eds* 1945; *Our Very Own* 1950

Cook Jr, Elisha aka **Cook, Elisha** (1903–1995) *Love Is News* 1937; *They Won't Forget* 1937; *My Lucky Star* 1938; *Stranger on the Third Floor* 1940; *Hellzapoppin'* 1941; *I Wake Up Screaming* 1941; *The Maltese Falcon* 1941; *A-Haunting We Will Go* 1942; *A Gentleman at Heart* 1942; *Dark Waters* 1944; *Phantom Lady* 1944; *Up in Arms* 1944; *Dillinger* 1945; *The Big*

Sleep 1946; *The Falcon's Alibi* 1946; *Lady of Deceit* 1947; *The Long Night* 1947; *Don't Bother to Knock* 1952; *Shane* 1953; *Thunder over the Plains* 1953; *Drum Beat* 1954; *The Killing* 1956; *Baby Face Nelson* 1957; *Chicago Confidential* 1957; *The Lonely Man* 1957; *Plunder Road* 1957; *House on Haunted Hill* 1958; *Platinum High School* 1960; *Black Zoo* 1963; *The Haunted Palace* 1963; *The Spy in the Green Hat* 1966; *The Great Bank Robbery* 1969; *El Condor* 1970; *Electra Glide in Blue* 1973; *The Outfit* 1973; *The Black Bird* 1975; *Winterhawk* 1975; *St Ives* 1976; *1941* 1979; *Carny* 1980; *Harry's War* 1981; *Leave 'em Laughing* 1981; *National Lampoon's Movie Madness* 1981; *Hammett* 1982
Cook, Paul (1956–) *The Great Rock 'n' Roll Swindle* 1979; *Ladies and Gentlemen, the Fabulous Stains* 1981
Cook, Peter (1938–1995) *The Wrong Box* 1966; *Bedazzled* 1967; *A Dandy in Aspic* 1968; *The Bed Sitting Room* 1969; *Monte Carlo or Bust* 1969; *The Rise and Rise of Michael Rimmer* 1970; *The Adventures of Barry McKenzie* 1972; *Find the Lady* 1976; *Pleasure at Her Majesty's* 1976; *The Hound of the Baskervilles* 1977; *Yellowbeard* 1983; *Supergirl* 1984; *Whoops Apocalypse* 1986; *The Princess Bride* 1987; *Without a Clue* 1988; *Getting It Right* 1989; *Black Beauty* 1994
Cook, Rachael Leigh (1979–) *The Baby-Sitter's Club* 1995; *Tom and Huck* 1995; *Carpool* 1996; *The Eighteenth Angel* 1997; *The House of Yes* 1997; *The Naked Man* 1998; *Strike!* 1998; *She's All That* 1999; *Blow Dry* 2000; *Get Carter* 2000; *Antitrust* 2001; *Josie and the Pussycats* 2001; *29 Palms* 2002
Cook, Ron *Secrets & Lies* 1995; *Topsy-Turvy* 1999; *Lucky Break* 2001; *Thunderbirds* 2004; *On a Clear Day* 2005
Cook, Tommy (1930–) *Tarzan and the Leopard Woman* 1946; *Cry of the City* 1948; *An American Guerrilla in the Philippines* 1950
Cooke, Baldwin (1888–1953) *County Hospital* 1932; *Twice Two* 1933
Cooke, Chris aka **Cooke, Christopher** *The Unbelievable Truth* 1989; *Simple Men* 1992; *I Married a Strange Person* 1997
Cooke, Keith *China O'Brien* 1988; *Born to Ride* 1991
Cookson, Georgina (1918–) *The Naked Truth* 1957; *Your Money or Your Wife* 1960; *Walk a Crooked Path* 1969
Cooley, Hallam (1895–1971) *The Monster* 1925; *Sporting Blood* 1931
Coolidge, Jennifer (1963–) *The Adventures of Slappy the Sea Lion* 1998; *American Pie* 1999; *Best in Show* 2000; *Down to Earth* 2001; *Legally Blonde* 2001; *Legally Blonde 2: Red, White & Blonde* 2003; *A Mighty Wind* 2003; *A Cinderella Story* 2004; *Robots* 2005
Coolio (1963–) *Burn Hollywood Burn* 1997; *Judgment Day* 1999; *In Pursuit* 2000; *Shriek If You Know What I Did Last Friday the 13th* 2000
Coombs, Pat (1930–2002) *Dad's Army* 1971; *Adolf Hitler – My Part in His Downfall* 1972; *Ooh… You Are Awful* 1972
Cooney, Kevin (1945–) *The Trip to Bountiful* 1985; *Full Moon in Blue Water* 1988
Cooney, Ray (1932–) *Not Now Darling* 1972; *Not Now, Comrade* 1976
Cooper, Alice (1948–) *Sgt Pepper's Lonely Hearts Club Band* 1978; *Sextette* 1978; *Prince of Darkness* 1987
Cooper, Ben (1930–) *The Woman They Almost Lynched* 1953; *Johnny Guitar* 1954; *The Outcast* 1954; *The Rose Tattoo* 1955; *Rebel in Town* 1956; *Gunfight at Comanche Creek* 1964; *Arizona Raiders* 1965
Cooper, Camille aka **Cooper, Cami** *Like Father, like Son* 1987; *Shocker* 1989; *Meet the Applegates* 1991; *Lawnmower Man 2: Beyond Cyberspace* 1995
Cooper, Charles *The Wrong Man* 1956; *A Dog's Best Friend* 1960
Cooper, Chris (1951–) *Matewan* 1987; *Guilty by Suspicion* 1990; *Thousand Pieces of Gold* 1990; *City of Hope* 1991; *This Boy's Life* 1993; *Boys* 1995; *Lone Star* 1995; *Money Train* 1995; *Breast Men* 1997; *Great Expectations* 1997; *The Horse Whisperer* 1998; *American Beauty* 1999; *October Sky* 1999; *Me, Myself & Irene* 2000; *The Patriot* 2000; *Adaptation.* 2002; *The Bourne Identity* 2002; *My House in Umbria* 2002; *Seabiscuit* 2003; *Silver City* 2004
Cooper, Clancy (1906–1975) *Distant Drums* 1951; *A Gift for Heidi* 1958
Cooper, Garry *Quadrophenia* 1979; *Caravaggio* 1986
Cooper, Gary (1901–1961) *The Winning of Barbara Worth* 1926; *It* 1927; *Wings* 1927; *Beau Sabreur* 1928; *Lilac Time* 1928; *The Shopworn Angel* 1928; *The Virginian* 1929; *Morocco* 1930; *Paramount on Parade* 1930; *The Texan* 1930; *City Streets* 1931; *Fighting Caravans* 1931; *His Woman* 1931; *Devil and the Deep* 1932; *A Farewell to Arms* 1932; *If I Had a Million* 1932; *Alice in Wonderland* 1933; *Design for Living* 1933; *Today We Live* 1933; *Now and Forever* 1934; *Operator 13* 1934; *The Lives of a Bengal Lancer* 1935; *Peter Ibbetson* 1935; *The Wedding Night* 1935; *Desire* 1936; *The General Died at Dawn* 1936; *Mr Deeds Goes to Town* 1936; *The Plainsman* 1936; *Souls at Sea* 1937; *The Adventures of Marco Polo* 1938; *Bluebeard's Eighth Wife* 1938; *The Cowboy and the Lady* 1938; *Beau Geste* 1939; *The Real Glory* 1939; *North West Mounted Police* 1940; *The Westerner* 1940; *Ball of Fire* 1941; *Meet John Doe* 1941; *Sergeant York* 1941; *The Pride of the Yankees* 1942; *For Whom the Bell Tolls* 1943; *Casanova Brown* 1944; *The Story of Dr Wassell* 1944; *Along Came Jones* 1945; *Saratoga Trunk* 1945; *Cloak and Dagger* 1946; *Unconquered* 1947; *Variety Girl* 1947; *Good Sam* 1948; *The Fountainhead* 1949; *It's a Great Feeling* 1949; *Task Force* 1949; *Bright Leaf* 1950; *Dallas* 1950; *Distant Drums* 1951; *You're in the Navy Now* 1951; *High Noon* 1952; *Springfield Rifle* 1952; *Blowing Wild* 1953; *Return to Paradise* 1953; *Garden of Evil* 1954; *Vera Cruz* 1954; *The Court-Martial of Billy Mitchell* 1955; *Friendly Persuasion* 1956; *Love in the Afternoon* 1957; *Man of the West* 1958; *Ten North Frederick* 1958; *Alias Jesse James* 1959; *The Hanging Tree* 1959; *They Came to Cordura* 1959; *The Wreck of the Mary Deare* 1959; *The Naked Edge* 1961
Cooper, George (1892–1943) *The Barker* 1928; *Lilac Time* 1928; *The Trail of '98* 1929; *Renegades* 1930; *Think Fast, Mr Moto* 1937; *Crossfire* 1947; *Roughshod* 1949
Cooper, George A (1894–1947) *Violent Playground* 1958; *Hell Is a City* 1959; *Nightmare* 1963; *The Strange Affair* 1968; *The Rise and Rise of Michael Rimmer* 1970
Cooper, Gladys (1888–1971) *Kitty Foyle* 1940; *Rebecca* 1940; *The Black Cat* 1941; *The Gay Falcon* 1941; *That Hamilton Woman* 1941; *Now, Voyager* 1942; *This above All* 1942; *Mr Lucky* 1943; *The Song of Bernadette* 1943; *Mrs Parkington* 1944; *The White Cliffs of Dover* 1944; *Love Letters* 1945; *The Valley of Decision* 1945; *Beware of Pity* 1946; *The Green Years* 1946; *The Bishop's Wife* 1947; *Homecoming* 1948; *The Pirate* 1948; *Madame Bovary* 1949; *The Secret Garden* 1949; *Sons of the Musketeers* 1951; *Thunder on the Hill* 1951; *The Man Who Loved Redheads* 1954; *Separate Tables* 1958; *The List of Adrian Messenger* 1963; *My Fair Lady* 1964; *The Happiest Millionaire* 1967; *A Nice Girl like Me* 1969
Cooper, Jackie (1921–) *The Champ* 1931; *Skippy* 1931; *The Bowery* 1933; *Broadway to Hollywood* 1933; *Treasure Island* 1934; *The Devil Is a Sissy* 1936; *That Certain Age* 1938; *White Banners* 1938; *The Return of Frank James* 1940; *Ziegfeld Girl* 1941; *Men of Texas* 1942; *The Navy Comes Through* 1942; *Syncopation* 1942; *The Love Machine* 1971; *Chosen Survivors* 1974; *Superman* 1978; *Superman II* 1980; *Superman III* 1983; *Superman IV: the Quest for Peace* 1987; *Surrender* 1987
Cooper, Jeanne (1928–) *The Man from the Alamo* 1953; *The Redhead from Wyoming* 1953; *Five Steps to Danger* 1957; *Plunder Road* 1957; *The Intruder* 1961; *Black Zoo* 1963; *Kansas City Bomber* 1972
Cooper, Jeff *Born Losers* 1967; *Sharaz* 1968; *The Silent Flute* 1978
Cooper, Justin (1988–) *Liar Liar* 1997; *Dennis the Menace Strikes Again* 1998
Cooper, Maggie *An Eye for an Eye* 1981; *Divorce Wars* 1982
Cooper, Maxine *Kiss Me Deadly* 1955; *Autumn Leaves* 1956
Cooper, Melville (1896–1973) *The Great Garrick* 1937; *Tovarich* 1937; *The Adventures of Robin Hood* 1938; *The Dawn Patrol* 1938; *Garden of the Moon* 1938; *Gold Diggers in Paris* 1938; *Blind Alley* 1939; *Rebecca* 1940; *Too Many Husbands* 1940; *The Lady Eve* 1941; *You Belong to Me* 1941; *Life Begins at 8.30* 1942; *Change of Heart* 1943; *Holy Matrimony* 1943; *The Immortal Sergeant* 1943; *Heartbeat* 1946; *13 Rue Madeleine* 1946; *Love Happy* 1949; *Father of the Bride* 1950; *Let's Dance* 1950; *The Petty Girl* 1950; *The Underworld Story* 1950; *The King's Thief* 1955; *Bundle of Joy* 1956; *From the Earth to the Moon* 1958
Cooper, Richard (1893–1947) *The Black Abbot* 1934; *Lord Edgware Dies* 1934
Cooper, Terence (1928–1997) *Calculated Risk* 1963; *Sylvia* 1984; *The Shrimp on the Barbie* 1990
Cooper, Tommy (1922–1984) *And the Same to You* 1960; *The Plank* 1967
Coote, Jonathan *Razor Blade Smile* 1998; *The Last Horror Movie* 2003
Coote, Robert (1909–1982) *Blond Cheat* 1938; *Bad Lands* 1939; *Mr Moto's Last Warning* 1939; *Vigil in the Night* 1940; *The Commandos Strike at Dawn* 1942; *A Matter of Life and Death* 1946; *The Exile* 1947; *The Ghost and Mrs Muir* 1947; *Berlin Express* 1948; *The Elusive Pimpernel* 1950; *Soldiers Three* 1951; *Othello* 1952; *Scaramouche* 1952; *The Horse's Mouth* 1958; *Merry Andrew* 1958; *The League of Gentlemen* 1960; *A Man Could Get Killed* 1966; *The Swinger* 1966; *The Cool Ones* 1967; *Prudence and the Pill* 1968; *Theatre of Blood* 1973
Cope, Kenneth (1934–) *Naked Fury* 1959; *The Damned* 1961; *Tomorrow at Ten* 1962; *Night of the Big Heat* 1967; *Carry On Matron* 1972; *Rentadick* 1972; *George and Mildred* 1980; *Captives* 1994
Copeland, James aka **Copeland, Jimmy** (1923–) *Innocents in Paris* 1953; *The Maggie* 1953; *Mask of Dust* 1954
Copeland, Joan (1922–) *The Goddess* 1958; *Cagney & Lacey* 1981; *A Little Sex* 1981; *Happy New Year* 1987; *The Laserman* 1988; *Brother Bear* 2003
Copley, Peter (1915–) *Golden Salamander* 1949; *The Sword and the Rose* 1952; *Victim* 1961; *King and Country* 1964; *The Knack… and How to Get It* 1965
Copley, Teri (1961–) *Transylvania Twist* 1989; *Masters of Menace* 1990; *Brain Donors* 1992
Coppola, Alicia (1968–) *Velocity Trap* 1997; *Framed* 2002
Coppola, Marc (1958–) *Dracula's Widow* 1988; *Deadfall* 1993
Coppola, Sofia (1971–) *Peggy Sue Got Married* 1986; *The Godfather Part III* 1990; *Star Wars Episode I: the Phantom Menace* 1999
Corbet, Brady (1988–) *Thirteen* 2003; *Mysterious Skin* 2004; *Thunderbirds* 2004
Corbett, Glenn (1930–1993) *The Crimson Kimono* 1959; *All the Young Men* 1960; *The Mountain Road* 1960; *Homicidal* 1961; *The Pirates of Blood River* 1961; *Shenandoah* 1965; *Guns in the Heather* 1969; *Chisum* 1970; *Dead Pigeon on Beethoven Street* 1972
Corbett, Gretchen (1947–) *Let's Scare Jessica to Death* 1971; *The Other Side of the Mountain – Part 2* 1978; *Jaws of Satan* 1979
Corbett, Harry H (1925–1982) *Floods of Fear* 1958; *Cover Girl Killer* 1959; *The Shakedown* 1959; *Ladies Who Do* 1963; *Sammy Going South* 1963; *What a Crazy World* 1963; *The Bargee* 1964; *Rattle of a Simple Man* 1964; *Joey Boy* 1965; *Carry On Screaming* 1966; *The Sandwich Man* 1966; *Crooks and Coronets* 1969; *The Magnificent Seven Deadly Sins* 1971; *Steptoe and Son* 1972; *Steptoe and Son Ride Again* 1973; *Percy's Progress* 1974; *Adventures of a Private Eye* 1977; *Jabberwocky* 1977; *Silver Dream Racer* 1980
Corbett, John (1961–) *Wedding Bell Blues* 1996; *Volcano* 1997; *Prancer Returns* 2001; *Serendipity* 2001; *My Big Fat Greek Wedding* 2002; *Raise Your Voice* 2004; *Raising Helen* 2004
Corbett, Leonora (1907–1960) *The Constant Nymph* 1933; *Heart's Desire* 1935; *Under Your Hat* 1940
Corbett, Ronnie (1930–) *You're Only Young Twice* 1952; *Top of the Form* 1953; *Rockets Galore* 1958; *Casino Royale* 1967; *Some Will, Some Won't* 1969; *The Rise and Rise of Michael Rimmer* 1970; *No Sex Please – We're British* 1973; *Fierce Creatures* 1997
Corbin, Barry (1940–) *Stir Crazy* 1980; *Urban Cowboy* 1980; *Honkytonk Man* 1982; *Six Pack* 1982; *WarGames* 1983; *Hard Traveling* 1985; *My Science Project* 1985; *Nothing in Common* 1986; *Critters 2: the Main Course* 1988; *Who's Harry Crumb?* 1989; *Ghost Dad* 1990; *The Hot Spot* 1990; *Short Time* 1990; *Career Opportunities* 1991; *Curdled* 1995; *Formula for Death* 1995; *Solo* 1996; *Held Up* 1999; *Death at Clover Bend* 2001
Corby, Ellen (1913–1999) *I Remember Mama* 1948; *Caged* 1950; *Harriet Craig* 1950; *On Moonlight Bay* 1951; *Shane* 1953; *The Bowery Boys Meet the Monsters* 1954; *Illegal* 1955; *Macabre* 1958; *Vertigo* 1958; *Visit to a Small Planet* 1960; *The Strangler* 1964; *The Night of the Grizzly* 1966
Corcoran, Donna (1942–) *Angels in the Outfield* 1951; *Don't Bother to Knock* 1952; *Million Dollar Mermaid* 1952; *Young Man with Ideas* 1952; *Dangerous When Wet* 1953; *Scandal at Scourie* 1953; *Gypsy Colt* 1954
Corcoran, Kevin (1949–) *Old Yeller* 1957; *The Shaggy Dog* 1959; *Swiss Family Robinson* 1960; *Toby Tyler, or Ten Weeks with a Circus* 1960; *Babes in Toyland* 1961; *Savage Sam* 1963; *A Tiger Walks* 1964
Corcoran, Noreen (1943–) *I Love Melvin* 1953; *Tanganyika* 1954
Cord, Alex (1931–) *Get off My Back* 1965; *Stagecoach* 1966; *The Brotherhood* 1968; *The Last Grenade* 1970; *Chosen Survivors* 1974; *Grayeagle* 1977; *Sidewinder One* 1977; *CIA – Codename Alexa* 1992
Corday, Mara (1932–) *Drums across the River* 1954; *So This Is Paris* 1954; *Foxfire* 1955; *The Man from Bitter Ridge* 1955; *Man without a Star* 1955; *Tarantula* 1955; *A Day of Fury* 1956; *Raw Edge* 1956; *The Black Scorpion* 1957
Corday, Rita aka **Croset, Paula** aka **Corday, Paula** (1920–1992) *The Falcon and the Co-Eds* 1943; *The Falcon Strikes Back* 1943; *The Falcon in Hollywood* 1944; *The Body Snatcher* 1945; *The Falcon in San Francisco* 1945; *Dick Tracy vs Cueball* 1946; *The Falcon's Alibi* 1946; *The Exile* 1947; *The Sword of Monte Cristo* 1951; *Because You're Mine* 1952; *The Black Castle* 1952
Cordero, Joaquin (1926–) *A Woman without Love* 1951; *The River and Death* 1954
Cording, Harry (1891–1954) *The Patriot* 1928; *Arizona Legion* 1939; *Law and Order* 1940
Cording, John *One Day in the Life of Ivan Denisovich* 1971; *Ransom* 1975
Corduner, Allan *Topsy-Turvy* 1999; *Kiss Kiss (Bang Bang)* 2001; *Food of Love* 2002; *Moonlight Mile* 2002; *De-Lovely* 2004
Cordy, Annie (1928–) *Rider on the Rain* 1970; *La Rupture* 1970
Cordy, Raymond (1898–1956) *A Nous la Liberté* 1931; *La Belle Equipe* 1936; *Les Belles de Nuit* 1952
Corey, Isabelle (1929–) *Bob Le Flambeur* 1955; *It Happened in Rome* 1956; *Aphrodite Goddess of Love* 1957
Corey, Jeff (1914–2002) *My Friend Flicka* 1943; *Kidnapped* 1948; *City across the River* 1949; *Home of the Brave* 1949; *Roughshod* 1949; *The Next Voice You Hear* 1950; *Only the Valiant* 1950; *The Outriders* 1950; *The Prince Who Was a Thief* 1951; *Red Mountain* 1951; *The Balcony* 1963; *Lady in a Cage* 1964; *Mickey One* 1965; *Once a Thief* 1965; *Seconds* 1966; *In Cold Blood* 1967; *The Boston Strangler* 1968; *Butch Cassidy and the Sundance Kid* 1969; *Impasse* 1969; *True Grit* 1969; *Getting Straight* 1970; *Little Big Man* 1970; *They Call Me Mister Tibbs!* 1970; *Catlow* 1971; *Shoot Out* 1971; *The Premonition* 1975; *Moonshine County Express* 1977; *Butch and Sundance: the Early Days* 1979; *Bird on a Wire* 1990; *Surviving the Game* 1994
Corey, Wendell (1914–1968) *Desert Fury* 1947; *I Walk Alone* 1947; *The Search* 1948; *Sorry, Wrong Number* 1948; *The Accused* 1949; *Any Number Can Play* 1949; *The File on Thelma Jordon* 1949; *Holiday Affair* 1949; *The Furies* 1950; *Harriet Craig* 1950; *No Sad Songs for Me* 1950; *Rich, Young and Pretty* 1951; *Carbine Williams* 1952; *The Wild North* 1952; *Jamaica Run* 1953; *Hell's Half Acre* 1954; *Rear Window* 1954; *The Big Knife* 1955; *The Bold and the Brave* 1956; *The Killer Is Loose* 1956; *The Rack* 1956; *The Rainmaker* 1956; *Loving You* 1957; *The Light in the Forest* 1958; *Alias Jesse James* 1959; *Agent for HARM* 1966; *Picture Mommy Dead* 1966; *Waco* 1966
Corley, Annie *The Bridges of Madison County* 1995; *Box of Moonlight* 1996; *Free Willy 3: the Rescue* 1997; *Here on Earth* 2000; *Monster* 2003
Corley, Pat (1930–) *The Black Marble* 1980; *Night Shift* 1982; *Against All Odds* 1984
Cormack, Danielle *Siam Sunset* 1999; *The Price of Milk* 2000
Cormack, Lynne *Too Outrageous!* 1987; *Dead Ringers* 1988
Corman, Maddie (1969–) *The Adventures of Ford Fairlane* 1990; *My New Gun* 1992; *Mickey Blue Eyes* 1999; *Jenifer* 2001

Corman, Roger (1926–) *War of the Satellites* 1958; *Cannonball* 1976; *The State of Things* 1982; *Scream 3* 1999
Cornell, Ellie (1963–) *Halloween 4: the Return of Michael Myers* 1988; *Halloween 5: the Revenge of Michael Myers* 1989; *House of the Dead* 2003
Cornillac, Clovis *Karnaval* 1998; *Carnages* 2002; *A Very Long Engagement* 2004
Cornish, Abbie (1982–) *The Monkey's Mask* 2000; *Somersault* 2004
Cornthwaite, Robert (1917–) *The Thing from Another World* 1951; *The War of the Worlds* 1953; *The Spirit of St Louis* 1957; *Ten Seconds to Hell* 1959; *Waterhole #3* 1967
Cornwell, Judy (1942–) *The Wild Racers* 1968; *Country Dance* 1970; *Every Home Should Have One* 1970; *Wuthering Heights* 1970; *Who Slew Auntie Roo?* 1971; *Santa Claus* 1985; *Persuasion* 1995
Corr, Andrea (1974–) *Evita* 1996; *The Magic Sword: Quest for Camelot* 1997
Corradi, Nelly (1914–1968) *La Signora di Tutti* 1934; *The Barber of Seville* 1946; *La Forza del Destino* 1949
Corraface, Georges *aka* **Corraface, George** (1952–) *Not without My Daughter* 1990; *Impromptu* 1991; *Christopher Columbus: the Discovery* 1992; *Escape from LA* 1996
Corri, Adrienne (1930–) *The Romantic Age* 1949; *The River* 1951; *The Kidnappers* 1953; *Devil Girl from Mars* 1954; *Lease of Life* 1954; *Behind the Headlines* 1956; *The Feminine Touch* 1956; *The Big Chance* 1957; *The Rough and the Smooth* 1959; *The Hellfire Club* 1961; *Corridors of Blood* 1962; *A Study in Terror* 1965; *Africa – Texas Style!* 1967; *The Viking Queen* 1967; *Moon Zero Two* 1969; *A Clockwork Orange* 1971; *Vampire Circus* 1971; *Madhouse* 1974; *Rosebud* 1975
Corri, Nick *Gotcha!* 1985; *Slaves of New York* 1989; *Candyman: Day of the Dead* 1999
Corrieri, Sergio *I Am Cuba* 1964; *Memories of Underdevelopment* 1968
Corrigan, Kevin (1969–) *Zebrahead* 1992; *The Last Good Time* 1994; *Rhythm Thief* 1994; *Bandwagon* 1995; *Walking and Talking* 1996; *Henry Fool* 1997; *Kicked in the Head* 1997; *Slums of Beverly Hills* 1998
Corrigan, Lloyd (1900–1969) *The Ghost Breakers* 1940; *The Lady in Question* 1940; *The Great Man's Lady* 1942; *Hitler's Children* 1943; *Tarzan's Desert Mystery* 1943; *Rosie the Riveter* 1944; *The Chase* 1946; *And Baby Makes Three* 1949; *Dancing in the Dark* 1949; *Cyrano de Bergerac* 1950; *My Friend Irma Goes West* 1950; *When Willie Comes Marching Home* 1950; *Son of Paleface* 1952; *Marry Me Again* 1953; *The Bowery Boys Meet the Monsters* 1954
Corrigan, Ray "Crash" (1902–1976) *Hit the Saddle* 1937; *Overland Stage Raiders* 1938; *Red River Range* 1938; *Santa Fe Stampede* 1938; *Frontier Horizon* 1939; *Three Texas Steers* 1939; *Wyoming Outlaw* 1939; *It! The Terror from beyond Space* 1958
Corseaut, Aneta *aka* **Corsaut, Aneta** (1933–1995) *The Blob* 1958; *The Toolbox Murders* 1978
Corsini, Silvana *Accattone* 1961; *Mamma Roma* 1962
Cort, Bud (1950–) *Brewster McCloud* 1970; *Gas-s-s-s, or It Became Necessary to Destroy the World in Order to Save It* 1970; *The Strawberry Statement* 1970; *The Traveling Executioner* 1970; *Harold and Maude* 1972; *Why Shoot the Teacher* 1976; *Die Laughing* 1980; *She Dances Alone* 1981; *Love Letters* 1983; *Electric Dreams* 1984; *Maria's Lovers* 1984; *The Secret Diary of Sigmund Freud* 1984; *Love at Stake* 1987; *The Chocolate War* 1988; *Out of the Dark* 1988; *Brain Dead* 1990; *Going Under* 1990; *Ted & Venus* 1991; *Theodore Rex* 1995; *But I'm a Cheerleader* 1999; *Dogma* 1999; *The Million Dollar Hotel* 1999; *Pollock* 2000; *South of Heaven, West of Hell* 2000; *The Life Aquatic with Steve Zissou* 2004
Cortese, Joe (1949–) *Death Collector* 1976; *Monsignor* 1982; *Deadly Illusion* 1987; *The Closer* 1990; *Ruby* 1992; *To Protect and Serve* 1992; *Against the Ropes* 2003
Cortese, Valentina *aka* **Cortesa, Valentina** (1924–) *Les Misérables* 1946; *Black Magic* 1949; *The Glass Mountain* 1949; *Malaya* 1949; *Thieves' Highway* 1949; *Shadow of the Eagle* 1950; *The House on Telegraph Hill* 1951; *The Secret People* 1951; *The Barefoot Contessa* 1954; *Le Amiche* 1955; *Magic Fire* 1956; *Barabbas* 1961; *Square of Violence* 1961; *The Visit* 1964; *The Legend of Lylah Clare* 1968; *First Love* 1970; *The Assassination of Trotsky* 1972; *Brother Sun, Sister Moon* 1972; *Day for Night* 1973; *The Adventures of Baron Munchausen* 1988
Cortez, Julia *The Adventures of Priscilla, Queen of the Desert* 1994; *Mighty Morphin Power Rangers: the Movie* 1995
Cortez, Ricardo (1899–1977) *The Pony Express* 1925; *The Torrent* 1926; *The Private Life of Helen of Troy* 1927; *The Younger Generation* 1929; *Her Man* 1930; *Bad Company* 1931; *Dangerous Female* 1931; *Illicit* 1931; *Flesh* 1932; *No One Man* 1932; *Symphony of Six Million* 1932; *Torch Singer* 1933; *Mandalay* 1934; *Wonder Bar* 1934; *Frisco Kid* 1935; *Special Agent* 1935; *The Case of the Black Cat* 1936; *The Walking Dead* 1936; *Charlie Chan in Reno* 1939; *Mr Moto's Last Warning* 1939; *The Locket* 1946; *Mystery in Mexico* 1948; *Bunco Squad* 1950
Corti, Jesse *Revenge* 1990; *Beauty and the Beast* 1991
Cosby, Bill (1937–) *Man and Boy* 1971; *Hickey and Boggs* 1972; *Uptown Saturday Night* 1974; *Let's Do It Again* 1975; *Mother, Jugs & Speed* 1976; *A Piece of the Action* 1977; *California Suite* 1978; *The Devil and Max Devlin* 1981; *Leonard, Part 6* 1987; *Ghost Dad* 1990; *The Meteor Man* 1993; *I Spy Returns* 1994; *Jack* 1996; *Fat Albert* 2004
Cosgrove, Daniel (1970–) *They Crawl* 2001; *Van Wilder: Party Liaison* 2002
Cosgrove, Douglas *Lady Killer* 1933; *Winds of the Wasteland* 1936
Cosmo, James (1948–) *Stormy Monday* 1987; *Braveheart* 1995; *Trainspotting* 1995; *Emma* 1996; *Sunset Heights* 1996; *Urban Ghost Story* 1998; *The Match* 1999; *One More Kiss* 1999; *Honest* 2000; *To End All Wars* 2001; *Man Dancin'* 2003; *One Last Chance* 2003; *Skagerrak* 2003
Cossart, Ernest (1876–1951) *Accent on Youth* 1935; *The Scoundrel* 1935; *Desire* 1936; *The Great Ziegfeld* 1936; *Angel* 1937; *Lady of the Tropics* 1939; *The Light That Failed* 1939; *Never Say Die* 1939; *A Bill of Divorcement* 1940; *Kitty Foyle* 1940; *Knickerbocker Holiday* 1944; *Love from a Stranger* 1947
Cossins, James (1933–1997) *The Anniversary* 1968; *The Rise and Rise of Michael Rimmer* 1970; *Wuthering Heights* 1970; *Fear in the Night* 1972
Costa, James *Joe the King* 1999; *LIE* 2001
Costa, Mary (1930–) *Marry Me Again* 1953; *The Big Caper* 1957; *Sleeping Beauty* 1959; *The Great Waltz* 1972
Costa-Gavras (1933–) *Madame Rosa* 1977; *The Stupids* 1995
Costanzo, Paulo (1978–) *Road Trip* 2000; *40 Days and 40 Nights* 2002
Costanzo, Robert *The Lightship* 1985; *Delusion* 1991; *Man's Best Friend* 1993; *Underworld* 1996; *Air Bud: Golden Receiver* 1998
Costello, Anthony (1938–1983) *Blue* 1968; *Night Moves* 1975
Costello, Dolores *aka* **Barrymore, Dolores Costello** (1905–1979) *When a Man Loves* 1926; *Noah's Ark* 1928; *Little Lord Fauntleroy* 1936; *King of the Turf* 1939; *The Magnificent Ambersons* 1942
Costello (1), Don (1901–1945) *A-Haunting We Will Go* 1942; *Crime Doctor* 1943; *A Lady Takes a Chance* 1943; *The Whistler* 1944
Costello, Elvis (1954–) *Americathon* 1979; *No Surrender* 1986; *Straight to Hell* 1987; *Austin Powers: the Spy Who Shagged Me* 1999
Costello, Helene (1903–1957) *Don Juan* 1926; *Lights of New York* 1928
Costello, Lou (1906–1959) *Buck Privates* 1941; *Hold That Ghost* 1941; *In the Navy* 1941; *Keep 'em Flying* 1941; *Pardon My Sarong* 1942; *Ride 'em Cowboy* 1942; *Rio Rita* 1942; *Who Done It?* 1942; *Hit the Ice* 1943; *It Ain't Hay* 1943; *Abbott and Costello in Society* 1944; *Lost in a Harem* 1944; *Abbott and Costello in Hollywood* 1945; *Here Come the Co-Eds* 1945; *The Naughty Nineties* 1945; *Little Giant* 1946; *The Time of Their Lives* 1946; *Buck Privates Come Home* 1947; *Abbott and Costello Meet Frankenstein* 1948; *The Noose Hangs High* 1948; *Abbott and Costello Meet the Killer, Boris Karloff* 1949; *Africa Screams* 1949; *Abbott and Costello in the Foreign Legion* 1950; *Abbott and Costello Meet the Invisible Man* 1951; *Abbott and Costello Meet Captain Kidd* 1952; *Jack and the Beanstalk* 1952; *Lost in Alaska* 1952; *Abbott and Costello Go to Mars* 1953; *Abbott and Costello Meet Dr Jekyll and Mr Hyde* 1953; *Abbott and Costello Meet the Keystone Cops* 1955; *Abbott and Costello Meet the Mummy* 1955; *Dance with Me Henry* 1956
Costello, Ward *Terror from the Year 5,000* 1958; *The Gallant Hours* 1960; *MacArthur* 1977; *Return from Witch Mountain* 1978; *Goldengirl* 1979
Costelloe, John *Me and the Mob* 1992; *Kazaam* 1996
Coster, Nicolas *aka* **Coster, Nicholas** (1934–) *My Blood Runs Cold* 1965; *MacArthur* 1977; *The Big Fix* 1978; *Slow Dancing in the Big City* 1978; *The Electric Horseman* 1979; *Just You and Me, Kid* 1979; *Reds* 1981; *Danielle Steel's Full Circle* 1996
Coster-Waldau, Nikolaj *aka* **Waldau, Nikolaj** *aka* **Coster Waldau, Nikolaj** (1970–) *Nightwatch* 1994; *Bent* 1996; *Enigma* 2001; *Wimbledon* 2004
Costigan, George *The Sailor's Return* 1978; *Rita, Sue and Bob Too* 1987; *Shirley Valentine* 1989; *The Hawk* 1992; *Girls' Night* 1997
Costner, Kevin (1955–) *Sizzle Beach, USA* 1974; *Chasing Dreams* 1982; *Night Shift* 1982; *Stacy's Knights* 1983; *Testament* 1983; *The Gunrunner* 1984; *American Flyers* 1985; *Fandango* 1985; *Silverado* 1985; *No Way Out* 1986; *The Untouchables* 1987; *Bull Durham* 1988; *Field of Dreams* 1989; *Dances with Wolves* 1990; *Revenge* 1990; *JFK* 1991; *Robin Hood: Prince of Thieves* 1991; *The Bodyguard* 1992; *A Perfect World* 1993; *The War* 1994; *Wyatt Earp* 1994; *Waterworld* 1995; *Tin Cup* 1996; *The Postman* 1997; *Message in a Bottle* 1998; *For Love of the Game* 1999; *Play It to the Bone* 2000; *Thirteen Days* 2000; *3000 Miles to Graceland* 2000; *Dragonfly* 2002; *Open Range* 2003
Cote, Tina *Mean Guns* 1996; *Omega Doom* 1996
Cotillard, Marion (1975–) *Taxi* 1998; *Taxi 2* 2000; *Big Fish* 2003; *Love Me If You Dare* 2003; *Innocence* 2004; *A Very Long Engagement* 2004
Cotten, Joseph (1905–1994) *Citizen Kane* 1941; *Lydia* 1941; *Journey into Fear* 1942; *The Magnificent Ambersons* 1942; *Shadow of a Doubt* 1942; *Hers to Hold* 1943; *Gaslight* 1944; *I'll Be Seeing You* 1944; *Since You Went Away* 1944; *Love Letters* 1945; *Duel in the Sun* 1946; *The Farmer's Daughter* 1946; *Portrait of Jennie* 1948; *Beyond the Forest* 1949; *The Third Man* 1949; *Under Capricorn* 1949; *Walk Softly, Stranger* 1949; *September Affair* 1950; *Two Flags West* 1950; *Half Angel* 1951; *The Man with a Cloak* 1951; *Peking Express* 1951; *The Steel Trap* 1952; *Untamed Frontier* 1952; *Niagara* 1953; *Special Delivery* 1955; *Beyond the River* 1956; *The Killer Is Loose* 1956; *The Halliday Brand* 1957; *From the Earth to the Moon* 1958; *Touch of Evil* 1958; *The Angel Wore Red* 1960; *The Last Sunset* 1961; *Hush... Hush, Sweet Charlotte* 1964; *The Great Sioux Massacre* 1965; *The Money Trap* 1966; *The Oscar* 1966; *Jack of Diamonds* 1967; *Petulia* 1968; *Latitude Zero* 1969; *The Grasshopper* 1970; *Tora! Tora! Tora!* 1970; *The Abominable Dr Phibes* 1971; *City beneath the Sea* 1971; *Baron Blood* 1972; *A Delicate Balance* 1973; *F for Fake* 1973; *Soylent Green* 1973; *The Lindbergh Kidnapping Case* 1976; *Airport '77* 1977; *Twilight's Last Gleaming* 1977; *Caravans* 1978; *The Hearse* 1980; *Heaven's Gate* 1980; *The Survivor* 1981
Cottençon, Fanny (1957–) *L'Etoile du Nord* 1982; *Golden Eighties* 1986; *Angel Dust* 1987
Cotterill, Chrissie (1955–) *Scrubbers* 1982; *Nil by Mouth* 1997; *Underground* 1998; *Weak at Denise* 2000
Cotterill, Ralph (1932–) *The Chain Reaction* 1980; *The Survivor* 1981; *Burke and Wills* 1985; *Lorca and the Outlaws* 1985; *The Howling III* 1987; *Bad Boy Bubby* 1993
Cottet, Mia (1968–) *Romy and Michele's High School Reunion* 1997; *The Tuxedo* 2002
Cotton, Oliver (1944–) *Oliver Twist* 1982; *Eleni* 1985; *Hiding Out* 1987; *Christopher Columbus: the Discovery* 1992; *The Innocent Sleep* 1995; *The Dancer Upstairs* 2002
Cottrell, Mickey *Paper Hearts* 1993; *Apt Pupil* 1997
Coughlan, Marisa (1973–) *Gossip* 1999; *Teaching Mrs Tingle* 1999; *Freddy Got Fingered* 2001; *Super Troopers* 2001
Coulouris, George (1903–1989) *The Lady in Question* 1940; *Citizen Kane* 1941; *Watch on the Rhine* 1943; *Between Two Worlds* 1944; *The Master Race* 1944; *Mr Skeffington* 1944; *None but the Lonely Heart* 1944; *Confidential Agent* 1945; *Hotel Berlin* 1945; *Lady on a Train* 1945; *A Song to Remember* 1945; *California* 1946; *Nobody Lives Forever* 1946; *The Verdict* 1946; *Where There's Life* 1947; *Sleep, My Love* 1948; *A Southern Yankee* 1948; *Appointment with Venus* 1951; *Outcast of the Islands* 1951; *Venetian Bird* 1952; *A Day to Remember* 1953; *The Heart of the Matter* 1953; *Duel in the Jungle* 1954; *Mask of Dust* 1954; *The Runaway Bus* 1954; *The Teckman Mystery* 1954; *The Big Money* 1956; *Tarzan and the Lost Safari* 1956; *Kill Me Tomorrow* 1957; *The Man without a Body* 1957; *The Woman Eater* 1957; *Law and Disorder* 1958; *Son of Robin Hood* 1958; *The Boy Who Stole a Million* 1960; *Surprise Package* 1960; *Fury at Smugglers Bay* 1961; *The Crooked Road* 1964; *The Skull* 1965; *Arabesque* 1966; *Land Raiders* 1969; *Blood from the Mummy's Tomb* 1971; *The Final Programme* 1973; *Papillon* 1973; *Shout at the Devil* 1976; *The Long Good Friday* 1979
Coulson, Bernie *The Accused* 1988; *Eddie and the Cruisers II: Eddie Lives!* 1989; *The Highwayman* 1999; *Cabin by the Lake* 2000
Coupland, Diana (1930–) *Spring and Port Wine* 1969; *The Twelve Chairs* 1970; *The Best Pair of Legs in the Business* 1972; *Bless This House* 1972; *Operation Daybreak* 1975
Courau, Clotilde *aka* **Courau, Clothilde** (1969–) *Map of the Human Heart* 1992; *The Pickle* 1993; *Elisa* 1994; *The Bait* 1995; *Deterrence* 1999; *En Face* 1999; *Milk* 1999; *Almost Peaceful* 2002; *La Mentale* 2002
Courcel, Nicole (1930–) *No Exit* 1954; *The Case of Dr Laurent* 1957; *Sundays and Cybèle* 1962
Courcet, Richard *Clubbed to Death* 1996; *Beau Travail* 1999
Court, Hazel (1926–) *Dreaming* 1944; *Carnival* 1946; *Gaiety George* 1946; *Meet Me at Dawn* 1946; *Holiday Camp* 1947; *Bond Street* 1948; *Ghost Ship* 1952; *Counterspy* 1953; *Devil Girl from Mars* 1954; *Behind the Headlines* 1956; *The Curse of Frankenstein* 1957; *The Hour of Decision* 1957; *The Man Who Could Cheat Death* 1959; *The Shakedown* 1959; *Doctor Blood's Coffin* 1960; *The Premature Burial* 1962; *The Raven* 1963; *The Masque of the Red Death* 1964
Courtenay, Tom (1937–) *The Loneliness of the Long Distance Runner* 1962; *Billy Liar* 1963; *Private Potter* 1963; *King and Country* 1964; *Doctor Zhivago* 1965; *King Rat* 1965; *Operation Crossbow* 1965; *The Night of the Generals* 1966; *The Day the Fish Came Out* 1967; *A Dandy in Aspic* 1968; *Otley* 1968; *Catch Me a Spy* 1971; *One Day in the Life of Ivan Denisovich* 1971; *I Heard the Owl Call My Name* 1973; *The Dresser* 1983; *Happy New Year* 1987; *Leonard, Part 6* 1987; *The Last Butterfly* 1990; *Let Him Have It* 1991; *The Boy from Mercury* 1996; *Whatever Happened to Harold Smith?* 1999; *Last Orders* 2001; *Nicholas Nickleby* 2002
Courtland, Jerome (1926–) *Together Again* 1944; *Kiss and Tell* 1945; *The Man from Colorado* 1948; *Battleground* 1949; *Tokyo Joe* 1949; *A Woman of Distinction* 1950; *Santa Fe* 1951; *Tonka* 1958
Courtneidge, Cicely (1893–1980) *The Ghost Train* 1931; *Aunt Sally* 1933; *The Perfect Gentleman* 1935; *Under Your Hat* 1940; *The L-Shaped Room* 1962; *Not Now Darling* 1972
Courtney, Alex (1940–) *Enter the Ninja* 1981; *Murder between Friends* 1993
Courtney, Chuck *aka* **Courtney, Charles** (1930–2000) *Teenage Monster* 1958; *Billy the Kid vs Dracula* 1966
Courtney, Inez (1908–1975) *Break of Hearts* 1935; *Beauty for the Asking* 1939; *The Shop around the Corner* 1940
Coustas, Mary (1964–) *Nirvana Street Murder* 1990; *Hercules Returns* 1993
Covert, Allen *aka* **Covert, Alan** (1964–) *Bulletproof* 1996; *Happy Gilmore* 1996; *The Wedding Singer* 1998; *Big Daddy* 1999; *Little Nicky* 2000; *50 First Dates* 2004
Cowan, Jerome (1897–1972) *Beloved Enemy* 1936; *New Faces of 1937* 1937; *Shall We Dance* 1937; *Vogues of 1938* 1937; *There's Always a Woman* 1938; *East Side of Heaven* 1939; *The Gracie Allen Murder Case* 1939; *The Saint Strikes Back* 1939; *Castle on the Hudson* 1940; *Torrid Zone* 1940; *Victory* 1940; *Affectionately Yours* 1941; *The Great Lie* 1941; *Kiss the Boys Goodbye* 1941; *The Maltese Falcon* 1941; *A Gentleman at Heart* 1942; *Moontide* 1942;

Ladies' Day 1943; Guest in the House 1944; Fog Island 1945; Getting Gertie's Garter 1945; Deadline at Dawn 1946; My Reputation 1946; Cry Wolf 1947; Dangerous Years 1947; Miracle on 34th Street 1947; Riff-Raff 1947; The Unfaithful 1947; So This Is New York 1948; Always Leave Them Laughing 1949; Dallas 1950; The Fuller Brush Girl 1950; Young Man with a Horn 1950; Have Rocket, Will Travel 1959; All in a Night's Work 1960; Black Zoo 1963; The Gnome-Mobile 1967

Coward, Noël (1899–1973) Hearts of the World 1918; The Scoundrel 1935; In Which We Serve 1942; The Astonished Heart 1949; Around the World in 80 Days 1956; Our Man in Havana 1959; Surprise Package 1960; Paris When It Sizzles 1964; Bunny Lake Is Missing 1965; Boom 1968; The Italian Job 1969

Cowl, Jane (1884–1950) Once More, My Darling 1949; No Man of Her Own 1950; Payment on Demand 1951

Cowling, Bruce (1919–1986) Ambush 1949; Battleground 1949; The Stratton Story 1949; A Lady without Passport 1950; Cause for Alarm 1951; The Battle at Apache Pass 1952

Cowper, Nicola (1967–) Dreamchild 1985; Lionheart 1986; Journey to the Center of the Earth 1989

Cox, Alan (1970–) Young Sherlock Holmes 1985; Death of a Schoolboy 1990; Mrs Dalloway 1997

Cox, Alex (1954–) Dead Beat 1994; The Winner 1996; Perdita Durango 1997

Cox, Brian (1946–) In Celebration 1974; Manhunter 1986; Hidden Agenda 1990; Terminal Bliss 1990; Iron Will 1994; Prince of Jutland 1994; Rob Roy 1995; Chain Reaction 1996; The Glimmer Man 1996; The Long Kiss Goodnight 1996; The Boxer 1997; Kiss the Girls 1997; Desperate Measures 1998; Poodle Springs 1998; Rushmore 1998; Complicity 1999; The Corruptor 1999; For Love of the Game 1999; Mad about Mambo 1999; The Minus Man 1999; Saltwater 1999; A Shot at Glory 2000; Strictly Sinatra 2000; The Affair of the Necklace 2001; LIE 2001; The Reckoning 2001; Super Troopers 2001; Adaptation. 2002; The Bourne Identity 2002; The Ring 2002; The Rookie 2002; The Trials of Henry Kissinger 2002; 25th Hour 2002; X2 2003; The Bourne Supremacy 2004; Troy 2004

Cox, Charlie (1982–) Dot the i 2003; William Shakespeare's The Merchant of Venice 2004

Cox, Courteney aka **Cox Arquette, Courteney** (1964–) Down Twisted 1987; Masters of the Universe 1987; Cocoon: the Return 1988; Shaking the Tree 1990; Ace Ventura: Pet Detective 1993; The Opposite Sex and How to Live with Them 1993; Commandments 1996; Scream 1996; Scream 2 1997; The Runner 1999; Scream 3 1999; The Shrink Is In 2000; 3000 Miles to Graceland 2000; Get Well Soon 2001

Cox, Jennifer Elise (1973–) The Brady Bunch Movie 1995; Sometimes They Come Back... Again 1996; A Very Brady Sequel 1996

Cox, Paul (1940–) Golden Braid 1991; Careful 1992

Cox, Richard (1948–) Cruising 1980; King of the Mountain 1981; Zombie High 1987

Cox, Ronny (1938–) Deliverance 1972; The Mind Snatchers 1972; Bound for Glory 1976; Gray Lady Down 1978; Harper Valley PTA 1978; The Onion Field 1979; Taps 1981; Some Kind of Hero 1982; Tangier 1982; Beverly Hills Cop 1984; Raw Courage 1984; Vision Quest 1985; Hollywood Vice Squad 1986; Beverly Hills Cop II 1987; RoboCop 1987; One Man Force 1989; Captain America 1990; Loose Cannons 1990; Total Recall 1990; Scissors 1991; Murder at 1600 1997; Forces of Nature 1998

Cox, Veanne Miss Firecracker 1989; Rodgers & Hammerstein's Cinderella 1997; Beethoven's 4th 2001

Cox, Wally (1924–1973) State Fair 1962; Spencer's Mountain 1963; Fate Is the Hunter 1964; The Yellow Rolls-Royce 1964; The Bedford Incident 1965; The Saboteur, Code Name Morituri 1965; The Boatniks 1970; The Cockeyed Cowboys of Calico County 1970; The Barefoot Executive 1971

Coy, Johnny (1920–1973) Bring on the Girls 1945; Top Banana 1953

Coy, Jonathan (1953–) The Wolves of Willoughby Chase 1988; Conspiracy 2001; Shoreditch 2002

Coy, Walter (1909–1974) Barricade 1950; The Lusty Men 1952; Cult of the Cobra 1955

Coyle, Brendan Ailsa 1994; The Last Bus Home 1997; I Could Read the Sky 1999; Conspiracy 2001

Coyote, Peter (1942–) Southern Comfort 1981; ET the Extra-Terrestrial 1982; Endangered Species 1982; Cross Creek 1983; Slayground 1983; Strangers Kiss 1983; Heartbreakers 1984; Jagged Edge 1985; The Legend of Billie Jean 1985; A Man in Love 1987; Outrageous Fortune 1987; Season of Dreams 1987; Heart of Midnight 1988; Unconquered 1989; The Man Inside 1990; Crooked Hearts 1991; Bitter Moon 1992; Kika 1993; That Eye, the Sky 1994; Moonlight and Valentino 1995; Seeds of Doubt 1996; Unforgettable 1996; Route 9 1998; Sphere 1998; Two for Texas 1998; Random Hearts 1999; Erin Brockovich 2000; Femme Fatale 2002; Northfork 2002; A Walk to Remember 2002; Bon Voyage 2003; Enron: the Smartest Guys in the Room 2005

Cozart, Cylk (1957–) White Men Can't Jump 1992; Conspiracy Theory 1997; Three to Tango 1999

Crabbe, Larry "Buster" aka **Crabbe, Buster** aka **Crabbe, Larry** (1907–1983) Island of Lost Souls 1932; Tarzan the Fearless 1933; You're Telling Me! 1934; Flash Gordon 1936; Million Dollar Legs 1939; Sheriff of Sage Valley 1942; Frontier Outlaws 1944; Arizona Raiders 1965; The Bounty Killer 1965; The Comeback Trail 1972; The Alien Dead 1980

Crabtree, Michael Tender Mercies 1982; Whore 1991

Cracknell, Ruth (1925–2002) Kokoda Crescent 1989; Spider & Rose 1994

Craig, Alec (1878–1945) Vivacious Lady 1938; Sherlock Holmes and the Spider Woman 1944

Craig, Carolyn (1934–1970) Fury at Showdown 1957; Gunsight Ridge 1957; House on Haunted Hill 1958; Studs Lonigan 1960

Craig, Catherine (1917–) Here Come the Waves 1944; Appointment with Murder 1948

Craig, Daniel (1968–) Love Is the Devil: Study for a Portrait of Francis Bacon 1998; Hotel Splendide 1999; The Trench 1999; I Dreamed of Africa 2000; Some Voices 2000; Lara Croft: Tomb Raider 2001; Road to Perdition 2002; Ten Minutes Older: the Cello 2002; The Mother 2003; Sylvia 2003; Enduring Love 2004; Layer Cake 2004; The Jacket 2005

Craig, Davina The Ghost Camera 1933; Dusty Ermine 1936; Sweeney Todd, the Demon Barber of Fleet Street 1936

Craig, Diane (1949–) Double Deal 1981; Travelling North 1986

Craig, Helen The Snake Pit 1948; They Live by Night 1948

Craig, James (1912–1985) Kitty Foyle 1940; Law and Order 1940; Daniel and the Devil 1941; Friendly Enemies 1942; Seven Miles from Alcatraz 1942; Valley of the Sun 1942; The Heavenly Body 1943; The Human Comedy 1943; Lost Angel 1943; Kismet 1944; Marriage Is a Private Affair 1944; Our Vines Have Tender Grapes 1945; Northwest Stampede 1948; A Lady without Passport 1950; Side Street 1950; The Strip 1951; The Cyclops 1957; Shoot-Out at Medicine Bend 1957; Arizona Bushwhackers 1968

Craig, Michael (1928–) The Black Tent 1956; Eyewitness 1956; House of Secrets 1956; Yield to the Night 1956; Campbell's Kingdom 1957; High Tide at Noon 1957; Nor the Moon by Night 1958; Sea of Sand 1958; The Silent Enemy 1958; Life in Emergency Ward 10 1959; Sapphire 1959; Upstairs and Downstairs 1959; The Angry Silence 1960; Cone of Silence 1960; Doctor in Love 1960; Mysterious Island 1961; No My Darling Daughter 1961; A Pair of Briefs 1961; Payroll 1961; Captive City 1962; The Iron Maiden 1962; Life for Ruth 1962; Stolen Hours 1963; Life at the Top 1965; Of a Thousand Delights 1965; Modesty Blaise 1966; Star! 1968; The Royal Hunt of the Sun 1969; Twinky 1969; Country Dance 1970; A Town Called Hell 1971; Vault of Horror 1973; Ride a Wild Pony 1976; The Irishman 1978; Turkey Shoot 1981

Craig, Nell (1891–1965) Dr Kildare's Victory 1941; Dr Gillespie's New Assistant 1942; Dr Gillespie's Criminal Case 1943

Craig, Wendy (1934–) The Mind Benders 1963; The Servant 1963; The Nanny 1965; Just like a Woman 1966; I'll Never Forget What's 'Is Name 1967

Craig, Yvonne (1937–) The Gene Krupa Story 1959; The Young Land 1959; High Time 1960; By Love Possessed 1961; Kissin' Cousins 1964; Ski Party 1965; One of Our Spies Is Missing 1966; One Spy Too Many 1966; How to Frame a Figg 1971

Craigie, Ingrid The Dead 1987; Da 1988

Crain, Jeanne (1925–2003) Home in Indiana 1944; In the Meantime, Darling 1944; Winged Victory 1944; Leave Her to Heaven 1945; State Fair 1945; Centennial Summer 1946; Margie 1946; Apartment for Peggy 1948; You Were Meant for Me 1948; The Fan 1949; A Letter to Three Wives 1949; Pinky 1949; Cheaper by the Dozen 1950; The Model and the Marriage Broker 1951; People Will Talk 1951; Belles on Their Toes 1952; O Henry's Full House 1952; Duel in the Jungle 1954; Gentlemen Marry Brunettes 1955; Man without a Star 1955; The Fastest Gun Alive 1956; The Joker Is Wild 1957; Guns of the Timberland 1960; Nefertite, Queen of the Nile 1961; Pontius Pilate 1961; Madison Avenue 1962; Skyjacked 1972

Cramer, Joey (1974–) Runaway 1984; Flight of the Navigator 1986

Cramer, Marc (1918–1988) Bride by Mistake 1944; First Yank into Tokyo 1945; Isle of the Dead 1945; Pan-Americana 1945; Those Endearing Young Charms 1945

Cramer, Richard aka **Cramer, Rychard** (1889–1960) Pack Up Your Troubles 1932; Scram! 1932; Knight of the Plains 1939; Saps at Sea 1940

Crampton, Barbara (1962–) Re-Animator 1985; From Beyond 1986; Robot Wars 1993; Space Truckers 1996

Crane, Bob (1928–1978) The Wicked Dreams of Paula Schultz 1968; Superdad 1974; Gus 1976

Crane, Norma (1928–1973) Tea and Sympathy 1956; All in a Night's Work 1960; The Sweet Ride 1967; They Call Me Mister Tibbs! 1970; Fiddler on the Roof 1971

Crane, Rachel Two-Bits and Pepper 1995; Wildly Available 1996

Crane, Richard (1918–1969) Happy Land 1943; None Shall Escape 1944; Winning of the West 1953; The Alligator People 1959; The Boy Who Caught a Crook 1961

Cranham, Kenneth (1944–) Brother Sun, Sister Moon 1972; Joseph Andrews 1977; Dead Man's Folly 1986; Chocolat 1988; Hellbound: Hellraiser II 1988; Stealing Heaven 1988; Prospero's Books 1991; Under Suspicion 1991; Tale of a Vampire 1992; The Last Yellow 1999; The Most Fertile Man in Ireland 1999; Women Talking Dirty 1999; Gangster No 1 2000; Two Men Went to War 2002; Blackball 2003; Man Dancin' 2003; Layer Cake 2004; Trauma 2004

Cranitch, Lorcan (1969–) Food of Love 1997; Dancing at Lughnasa 1998; Night Train 1998; Titanic Town 1998

Crauchet, Paul (1920–) Ho! 1968; The Swimming Pool 1968; L'Armée des Ombres 1969; Un Flic 1972; Without Apparent Motive 1972; Burnt Barns 1973; Hit List 1984; La Gloire de Mon Père 1990; The King's Whore 1990

Cravat, Nick (1911–1994) The Flame and the Arrow 1950; The Crimson Pirate 1952; Run Silent, Run Deep 1958; The Island of Dr Moreau 1977

Craven, Eddie (1909–1991) The Gilded Lily 1935; The Invisible Menace 1938

Craven, Frank (1875–1945) He Was Her Man 1934; Barbary Coast 1935; Small Town Girl 1936; You're Only Young Once 1938; Miracles for Sale 1939; City for Conquest 1940; Our Town 1940; Pittsburgh 1942; Son of Dracula 1943; Jack London 1944

Craven, Gemma (1950–) The Slipper and the Rose 1976; Wagner 1983; Double X: the Name of the Game 1991; The Mystery of Edwin Drood 1993; The Last Bus Home 1997

Craven, John (1916–1995) Count the Hours 1953; Security Risk 1954

Craven, Matt (1956–) Happy Birthday to Me 1981; Palais Royale 1988; Jacob's Ladder 1990; K2 1991; Indian Summer 1993; Killer 1994; Crimson Tide 1995; The Final Cut 1995; Never Too Late 1996; Masterminds 1997; Varian's War 2000; The Life of David Gale 2003; The Statement 2003; Timeline 2003; The Clearing 2004; Assault on Precinct 13 2005

Craven, Wes (1939–) Wes Craven's New Nightmare 1994; The Fear 1995; Scream 1996

Crawford, Andrew (1917–) The Brothers 1947; Boys in Brown 1949; Diamond City 1949; Trottie True 1949; Morning Departure 1950

Crawford, Anne (1920–1956) Millions like Us 1943; Two Thousand Women 1944; They Were Sisters 1945; Bedelia 1946; Caravan 1946; The Master of Bankdam 1947; The Blind Goddess 1948; Daughter of Darkness 1948; It's Hard to Be Good 1948; Night Beat 1948; Tony Draws a Horse 1950; Trio 1950; Thunder on the Hill 1951; Knights of the Round Table 1953; Mad about Men 1954

Crawford, Broderick (1911–1986) Woman Chases Man 1937; Start Cheering 1938; Beau Geste 1939; Eternally Yours 1939; The Real Glory 1939; Slightly Honorable 1939; Seven Sinners 1940; Texas Rangers Ride Again 1940; Trail of the Vigilantes 1940; When the Daltons Rode 1940; The Black Cat 1941; Broadway 1942; Larceny, Inc 1942; Men of Texas 1942; Sin Town 1942; Black Angel 1946; Slave Girl 1947; The Time of Your Life 1948; All the King's Men 1949; Anna Lucasta 1949; A Kiss in the Dark 1949; Night unto Night 1949; Born Yesterday 1950; Convicted 1950; The Mob 1951; Last of the Comanches 1952; Lone Star 1952; Stop, You're Killing Me 1952; The Last Posse 1953; Down Three Dark Streets 1954; Human Desire 1954; Night People 1954; Big House, USA 1955; New York Confidential 1955; Not as a Stranger 1955; The Swindle 1955; Between Heaven and Hell 1956; The Fastest Gun Alive 1956; The Decks Ran Red 1958; Square of Violence 1961; Convicts Four 1962; The Castilian 1963; Up from the Beach 1965; Kid Rodelo 1966; The Oscar 1966; The Vulture 1966; Embassy 1972; Terror in the Wax Museum 1973; The Private Files of J Edgar Hoover 1977; A Little Romance 1979; Harlequin 1980; Liar's Moon 1982

Crawford, Cindy (1966–) Fair Game 1995; The Simian Line 2000

Crawford, Clayne (1978–) Swimfan 2002; A Walk to Remember 2002; A Love Song for Bobby Long 2004

Crawford, Joan (1904–1977) Sally, Irene and Mary 1925; Tramp, Tramp, Tramp 1926; The Unknown 1927; Our Dancing Daughters 1928; Hollywood Revue 1929; Our Modern Maidens 1929; Dance, Fools, Dance 1931; Laughing Sinners 1931; Possessed 1931; This Modern Age 1931; Grand Hotel 1932; Rain 1932; Dancing Lady 1933; Today We Live 1933; Chained 1934; Forsaking All Others 1934; Sadie McKee 1934; I Live My Life 1935; The Gorgeous Hussy 1936; Love on the Run 1936; The Bride Wore Red 1937; The Last of Mrs Cheyney 1937; Mannequin 1937; The Shining Hour 1938; The Ice Follies of 1939 1939; The Women 1939; Strange Cargo 1940; Susan and God 1940; When Ladies Meet 1941; A Woman's Face 1941; Reunion in France 1942; They All Kissed the Bride 1942; Above Suspicion 1943; Hollywood Canteen 1944; Mildred Pierce 1945; Humoresque 1946; Daisy Kenyon 1947; Possessed 1947; Flamingo Road 1949; It's a Great Feeling 1949; The Damned Don't Cry 1950; Harriet Craig 1950; Goodbye, My Fancy 1951; Sudden Fear 1952; This Woman Is Dangerous 1952; Torch Song 1953; Johnny Guitar 1954; Female on the Beach 1955; Queen Bee 1955; Autumn Leaves 1956; The Story of Esther Costello 1957; The Best of Everything 1959; What Ever Happened to Baby Jane? 1962; The Caretakers 1963; Strait-Jacket 1963; Della 1965; I Saw What You Did 1965; Berserk 1967; The Karate Killers 1967; Trog 1970

Crawford, John (1926–) Courage of Black Beauty 1957; Floods of Fear 1958; Orders to Kill 1958; Hell Is a City 1959; Solomon and Sheba 1959; Piccadilly Third Stop 1960; The Impersonator 1962; Night Moves 1975; The Enforcer 1976; Outlaw Blues 1977; Tilt 1978

Crawford, Johnny (1946–) Village of the Giants 1965; El Dorado 1967; The Great Texas Dynamite Chase 1976

Crawford, Katherine (1944–) The Doomsday Flight 1966; A Walk in the Spring Rain 1970

Crawford, Michael (1942–) A French Mistress 1960; The War Lover 1962; Two Left Feet 1963; The Knack... and How to Get It 1965; A Funny Thing Happened on the Way to the Forum 1966; How I Won the War 1967; The Jokers 1967; Hello, Dolly! 1969; The Games 1970; Hello – Goodbye 1970; Alice's Adventures in Wonderland 1972; Condorman 1981; Once upon a Forest 1992

Crawford, Rachael (1969–) *Rude* 1995; *When Night Is Falling* 1995
Crayne, Dani *Ain't Misbehavin'* 1955; *Shoot-Out at Medicine Bend* 1957
Craze, Michael (1942–1998) *Two Left Feet* 1963; *Neither the Sea nor the Sand* 1972; *Satan's Slave* 1976; *Terror* 1979
Creed-Miles, Charlie (1972–) *The Punk* 1993; *Nil by Mouth* 1997; *Essex Boys* 1999; *The Last Yellow* 1999
Cregar, Laird (1916–1944) *Hudson's Bay* 1940; *Blood and Sand* 1941; *Charley's Aunt* 1941; *I Wake Up Screaming* 1941; *The Black Swan* 1942; *Joan of Paris* 1942; *Rings on Her Fingers* 1942; *Ten Gentlemen from West Point* 1942; *This Gun for Hire* 1942; *Heaven Can Wait* 1943; *Hello, Frisco, Hello* 1943; *Holy Matrimony* 1943; *The Lodger* 1944; *Hangover Square* 1945
Crehan, Joseph (1883–1966) *Front Page Woman* 1935; *Special Agent* 1935; *Girls Can Play* 1937; *Meeting at Midnight* 1944; *Dick Tracy* 1945; *Dangerous Money* 1946; *Dick Tracy vs Cueball* 1946; *Dick Tracy Meets Gruesome* 1947; *Roadblock* 1951
Creley, Jack (1926–2004) *The Canadians* 1961; *Videodrome* 1982
Cremer, Bruno (1929–) *The Stranger* 1967; *Without Warning* 1973; *The Flesh of the Orchid* 1974; *Sorcerer* 1977; *Une Histoire Simple* 1978; *Tenue de Soirée* 1986; *Noce Blanche* 1989; *Brothers in Arms* 1990; *Under the Sand* 2000
Cremieux, Henri (1896–1980) *Orphée* 1950; *Le Testament d'Orphée* 1960
Crenna, Richard (1926–2003) *It Grows on Trees* 1952; *The Pride of St Louis* 1952; *John Goldfarb, Please Come Home* 1964; *Made in Paris* 1966; *The Sand Pebbles* 1966; *Wait until Dark* 1967; *Star!* 1968; *Marooned* 1969; *Midas Run* 1969; *Doctors' Wives* 1970; *Catlow* 1971; *The Deserter* 1971; *Red Sky at Morning* 1971; *Un Flic* 1972; *Breakheart Pass* 1976; *The Evil* 1978; *Body Heat* 1981; *First Blood* 1982; *Table for Five* 1983; *The Flamingo Kid* 1984; *Rambo: First Blood, Part II* 1985; *The Rape of Richard Beck* 1985; *Summer Rental* 1985; *Rambo III* 1988; *Leviathan* 1989; *Hot Shots! Part Deux* 1993; *Shattered Family* 1993; *Jade* 1995; *A Pyromaniac's Love Story* 1995; *Sabrina* 1995; *Wrongfully Accused* 1998
Crews, Laura Hope (1879–1942) *Blind Adventure* 1933; *Ever in My Heart* 1933; *The Silver Cord* 1933; *The Age of Innocence* 1934; *Escapade* 1935; *Angel* 1937; *Camille* 1937; *Doctor Rhythm* 1938; *Gone with the Wind* 1939; *The Star Maker* 1939; *One Foot in Heaven* 1941
Crews, Terry (1968–) *The 6th Day* 2000; *Serving Sara* 2002; *Baadasssss!* 2003; *White Chicks* 2004
Crewson, Wendy (1956–) *The Doctor* 1991; *Folks!* 1992; *The Good Son* 1993; *Corrina, Corrina* 1994; *The Santa Clause* 1994; *To Gillian on Her 37th Birthday* 1996; *Air Force One* 1997; *The Eighteenth Angel* 1997; *Gang Related* 1997; *Bicentennial Man* 1999; *Mercy* 2000; *The Santa Clause 2* 2002; *The Clearing* 2004
Cribbins, Bernard (1928–) *Make Mine a Million* 1959; *Tommy the Toreador* 1959; *Two Way Stretch* 1960; *The World of Suzie Wong* 1960; *The Best of Enemies* 1961; *The Girl on the Boat* 1962; *The Wrong Arm of the Law* 1962; *Carry On Jack* 1963; *Crooks in Cloisters* 1963; *The Mouse on the Moon* 1963; *Carry On Spying* 1964; *She* 1965; *You Must Be Joking!* 1965; *Daleks – Invasion Earth 2150 AD* 1966; *The Sandwich Man* 1966; *Casino Royale* 1967; *Don't Raise the Bridge, Lower the River* 1968; *The Railway Children* 1970; *Frenzy* 1972; *The Water Babies* 1978; *Carry On Columbus* 1992; *Blackball* 2003
Crider, Missy *aka* **Crider, Melissa** (1974–) *Desperate Justice* 1993; *A Boy Called Hate* 1995; *The Sex Monster* 1998; *Frailty* 2001; *Gigli* 2003
Crisa, Erno (1924–1968) *Plein Soleil* 1960; *Brennus – Enemy of Rome* 1963
Crisham, Walter (1906–1985) *No Orchids for Miss Blandish* 1948; *The Beachcomber* 1954
Crisp, Donald (1880–1974) *The Battle of the Sexes* 1914; *Broken Blossoms* 1919; *Don Q, Son of Zorro* 1925; *The Black Pirate* 1926; *Svengali* 1931; *Red Dust* 1932; *The Key* 1934; *The Little Minister* 1934; *What Every Woman Knows* 1934; *Mutiny on the Bounty* 1935; *Oil for the Lamps of China* 1935; *The Charge of the Light Brigade* 1936; *Mary of Scotland* 1936; *The White Angel* 1936; *A Woman Rebels* 1936; *Confession* 1937; *The Life of Emile Zola* 1937; *Parnell* 1937; *That Certain Woman* 1937; *The Amazing Dr Clitterhouse* 1938; *The Dawn Patrol* 1938; *Jezebel* 1938; *Daughters Courageous* 1939; *Juarez* 1939; *The Oklahoma Kid* 1939; *The Old Maid* 1939; *The Private Lives of Elizabeth and Essex* 1939; *Wuthering Heights* 1939; *Brother Orchid* 1940; *City for Conquest* 1940; *Dr Ehrlich's Magic Bullet* 1940; *Knute Rockne – All American* 1940; *The Sea Hawk* 1940; *Dr Jekyll and Mr Hyde* 1941; *How Green Was My Valley* 1941; *Shining Victory* 1941; *The Battle of Midway* 1942; *The Gay Sisters* 1942; *Lassie Come Home* 1943; *The Adventures of Mark Twain* 1944; *National Velvet* 1944; *The Uninvited* 1944; *Son of Lassie* 1945; *The Valley of Decision* 1945; *Hills of Home* 1948; *Whispering Smith* 1948; *Challenge to Lassie* 1949; *Bright Leaf* 1950; *Home Town Story* 1951; *Prince Valiant* 1954; *The Long Gray Line* 1955; *The Man from Laramie* 1955; *Drango* 1957; *The Last Hurrah* 1958; *Saddle the Wind* 1958; *A Dog of Flanders* 1959; *Pollyanna* 1960; *Greyfriars Bobby* 1961; *Spencer's Mountain* 1963
Crisp, Quentin (1908–1999) *The Bride* 1985; *Orlando* 1992; *Naked in New York* 1994
Cristal, Linda (1934–) *Comanche* 1956; *The Fiend Who Walked the West* 1958; *The Last of the Fast Guns* 1958; *The Perfect Furlough* 1958; *The Alamo* 1960; *Two Rode Together* 1961; *Panic in the City* 1968; *Mr Majestyk* 1974; *Love and the Midnight Auto Supply* 1977
Cristal, Perla (1937–) *The Awful Dr Orloff* 1962; *Sharaz* 1968
Cristofer, Michael (1945–) *The Entertainer* 1975; *An Enemy of the People* 1977; *The Little Drummer Girl* 1984
Crivello, Anthony *Spellbinder* 1988; *Dillinger and Capone* 1995
Crocker, Barry (1935–) *The Adventures of Barry McKenzie* 1972; *Barry McKenzie Holds His Own* 1974
Croft, Colin (1919–) *High Hell* 1957; *The Wild Duck* 1983
Croft, Peter (1917–) *King of the Damned* 1935; *The Goose Steps Out* 1942
Croiset, Max (1912–1993) *A Dog of Flanders* 1959; *The Little Ark* 1971
Cromwell, James (1940–) *The Man with Two Brains* 1983; *Tank* 1984; *Explorers* 1985; *The Babe* 1992; *Babe* 1995; *Eraser* 1996; *The People vs Larry Flynt* 1996; *Star Trek: First Contact* 1996; *The Education of Little Tree* 1997; *LA Confidential* 1997; *Babe: Pig in the City* 1998; *Deep Impact* 1998; *The Bachelor* 1999; *The General's Daughter* 1999; *The Green Mile* 1999; *RKO 281* 1999; *A Slight Case of Murder* 1999; *Snow Falling on Cedars* 1999; *Fail Safe* 2000; *Space Cowboys* 2000; *Spirit: Stallion of the Cimarron* 2002; *The Sum of All Fears* 2002; *Blackball* 2003; *I, Robot* 2004; *The Longest Yard* 2005
Cromwell, John (1888–1979) *Top Secret Affair* 1957; *3 Women* 1977
Cromwell, Richard (1910–1960) *Tol'able David* 1930; *The Age of Consent* 1932; *Emma* 1932; *The Strange Love of Molly Louvain* 1932; *This Day and Age* 1933; *Life Begins at 40* 1935; *The Lives of a Bengal Lancer* 1935; *Poppy* 1936; *Jezebel* 1938; *The Villain Still Pursued Her* 1940; *Baby Face Morgan* 1942
Cronauer, Gail *Positive ID* 1986; *The Newton Boys* 1998
Cronenberg, David (1943–) *The Fly* 1986; *Nightbreed* 1990; *The Stupids* 1995; *To Die For* 1995; *Extreme Measures* 1996; *The Grace of God* 1998; *Last Night* 1998; *Jason X* 2001
Cronin, Jeanette *The Shrimp on the Barbie* 1990; *The Boys* 1998; *The Three Stooges* 2000
Cronyn, Hume (1911–2003) *Shadow of a Doubt* 1942; *The Cross of Lorraine* 1943; *Lifeboat* 1944; *The Seventh Cross* 1944; *The Sailor Takes a Wife* 1945; *The Green Years* 1946; *The Postman Always Rings Twice* 1946; *The Beginning or the End* 1947; *Brute Force* 1947; *People Will Talk* 1951; *Sunrise at Campobello* 1960; *Cleopatra* 1963; *Hamlet* 1964; *The Arrangement* 1969; *Gaily, Gaily* 1969; *There Was a Crooked Man...* 1970; *Conrack* 1974; *The Parallax View* 1974; *Honky Tonk Freeway* 1981; *Rollover* 1981; *The World According to Garp* 1982; *Impulse* 1984; *Brewster's Millions* 1985; *Cocoon* 1985; **batteries not included* 1987; *Cocoon: the Return* 1988; *Day One* 1989; *Broadway Bound* 1991; *Camilla* 1993; *The Pelican Brief* 1993; *Marvin's Room* 1996; *12 Angry Men* 1997
Crook, Mackenzie (1971–) *Sex Lives of the Potato Men* 2003; *Churchill: the Hollywood Years* 2004; *William Shakespeare's The Merchant of Venice* 2004
Cropper, Linda *Blackrock* 1997; *Passion* 1999
Crosbie, Annette (1934–) *Sky West and Crooked* 1965; *Follow Me* 1971; *The Slipper and the Rose* 1976; *Hawk the Slayer* 1980; *Ordeal by Innocence* 1984; *The Pope Must Die* 1991; *Leon the Pig Farmer* 1992; *Solitaire for 2* 1994; *Shooting Fish* 1997; *The Debt Collector* 1999; *Calendar Girls* 2003
Crosby, Bing (1904–1977) *The King of Jazz* 1930; *The Big Broadcast* 1932; *Going Hollywood* 1933; *She Loves Me Not* 1934; *We're Not Dressing* 1934; *The Big Broadcast of 1936* 1935; *Mississippi* 1935; *Anything Goes* 1936; *Pennies from Heaven* 1936; *Rhythm on the Range* 1936; *Waikiki Wedding* 1937; *Doctor Rhythm* 1938; *East Side of Heaven* 1939; *Paris Honeymoon* 1939; *The Star Maker* 1939; *Rhythm on the River* 1940; *Road to Singapore* 1940; *The Birth of the Blues* 1941; *Road to Zanzibar* 1941; *Holiday Inn* 1942; *My Favorite Blonde* 1942; *Road to Morocco* 1942; *Star Spangled Rhythm* 1942; *Dixie* 1943; *Going My Way* 1944; *Here Come the Waves* 1944; *The Princess and the Pirate* 1944; *The Bells of St Mary's* 1945; *Duffy's Tavern* 1945; *Out of This World* 1945; *Road to Utopia* 1945; *Blue Skies* 1946; *My Favorite Brunette* 1947; *The Road to Hollywood* 1947; *Road to Rio* 1947; *Variety Girl* 1947; *Welcome Stranger* 1947; *The Emperor Waltz* 1948; *The Adventures of Ichabod and Mr Toad* 1949; *A Connecticut Yankee in King Arthur's Court* 1949; *Mr Music* 1950; *Riding High* 1950; *Here Comes the Groom* 1951; *The Greatest Show on Earth* 1952; *Just for You* 1952; *Road to Bali* 1952; *Little Boy Lost* 1953; *Scared Stiff* 1953; *The Country Girl* 1954; *White Christmas* 1954; *Anything Goes* 1956; *High Society* 1956; *Alias Jesse James* 1959; *Say One for Me* 1959; *High Time* 1960; *Let's Make Love* 1960; *Pepe* 1960; *The Road to Hong Kong* 1962; *Robin and the 7 Hoods* 1964; *Stagecoach* 1966
Crosby, Bob (1913–1993) *Let's Make Music* 1940; *See Here, Private Hargrove* 1944; *The Singing Sheriff* 1944; *Two Tickets to Broadway* 1951; *Senior Prom* 1958; *The Five Pennies* 1959
Crosby, Cathy Lee (1944–) *The Laughing Policeman* 1973; *Trackdown* 1976; *The Dark* 1979; *Untamed Love* 1994; *The Real Howard Spitz* 1998
Crosby, Denise (1957–) *Miracle Mile* 1989; *Pet Sematary* 1989; *Max* 1994; *Jackie Brown* 1997; *Executive Power* 1998
Crosby, Gary (1933–1995) *Mardi Gras* 1958; *Holiday for Lovers* 1959; *A Private's Affair* 1959; *Battle at Bloody Beach* 1961; *Girl Happy* 1965
Crosby, Mary (1959–) *Last Plane Out* 1983; *The Ice Pirates* 1984; *Tapeheads* 1988; *Quicker than the Eye* 1989; *Body Chemistry* 1990; *Eating* 1990; *The Night Caller* 1998
Crosby, Norm (1927–) *Amore!* 1993; *Adam Sandler's Eight Crazy Nights* 2003
Crosman, Henrietta (1861–1944) *The Royal Family of Broadway* 1930; *Pilgrimage* 1933; *The Dark Angel* 1935; *The Moon's Our Home* 1936; *Personal Property* 1937
Cross, Ben (1947–) *Chariots of Fire* 1981; *The Assisi Underground* 1985; *Paperhouse* 1988; *The Unholy* 1988; *Live Wire* 1992; *Cold Sweat* 1993; *The Ascent* 1994; *The Criminal Mind* 1995; *First Knight* 1995; *Temptress* 1995; *Turbulence* 1997; *The Order* 2001; *Exorcist: the Beginning* 2004
Cross, Harley (1978–) *Where Are the Children?* 1986; *The Believers* 1987; *Cohen and Tate* 1988; *Stanley & Iris* 1989; *The Boy Who Cried Bitch* 1991; *Perdita Durango* 1997; *Shriek If You Know What I Did Last Friday the 13th* 2000
Cross, Hugh (1925–) *Just William's Luck* 1947; *William at the Circus* 1948; *Seven Days to Noon* 1950
Cross, Joseph (1986–) *Desperate Measures* 1998; *Jack Frost* 1998; *Wide Awake* 1998
Cross, Murphy (1950–) *Torn between Two Lovers* 1979; *Victim of Love* 1991
Crosse, Rupert (1927–1973) *Wild Seed* 1965; *Ride in the Whirlwind* 1966; *The Reivers* 1969
Crothers, Scatman *aka* **Crothers, Benjamin "Scatman"** *aka* **Crothers, Sherman "Scatman"** (1910–1986) *Meet Me at the Fair* 1952; *East of Sumatra* 1953; *The Sins of Rachel Cade* 1960; *Three on a Couch* 1966; *The Aristocats* 1970; *The King of Marvin Gardens* 1972; *Detroit 9000* 1973; *Black Belt Jones* 1974; *Friday Foster* 1975; *One Flew over the Cuckoo's Nest* 1975; *Silver Streak* 1976; *The Cheap Detective* 1978; *Mean Dog Blues* 1978; *Scavenger Hunt* 1979; *Bronco Billy* 1980; *The Shining* 1980; *Zapped!* 1982; *Two of a Kind* 1983; *The Journey of Natty Gann* 1985
Crouse, Lindsay (1948–) *Between the Lines* 1977; *Slap Shot* 1977; *The Verdict* 1982; *Daniel* 1983; *Iceman* 1984; *Places in the Heart* 1984; *House of Games* 1987; *Communion* 1989; *Desperate Hours* 1990; *Being Human* 1994; *Bye Bye Love* 1995; *The Indian in the Cupboard* 1995; *The Arrival* 1996; *If These Walls Could Talk* 1996; *The Juror* 1996; *Prefontaine* 1997; *Progeny* 1998; *The Insider* 1999; *Impostor* 2001; *Cherish* 2002
Crow, Ashley (1960–) *The Good Son* 1993; *Little Big League* 1994
Crowden, Graham (1922–) *Leo the Last* 1970; *The Rise and Rise of Michael Rimmer* 1970; *The Road Builder* 1971; *Something to Hide* 1971; *Up the Chastity Belt* 1971; *The Ruling Class* 1972; *The Final Programme* 1973; *The Abdication* 1974; *The Little Prince* 1974; *Hardcore* 1977; *Britannia Hospital* 1982; *The Missionary* 1982; *The Company of Wolves* 1984; *Code Name: Emerald* 1985; *Possession* 2002
Crowe, Eileen (1899–1978) *The Plough and the Stars* 1936; *Hungry Hill* 1946; *The Rising of the Moon* 1957
Crowe, Russell (1964–) *Blood Oath* 1990; *Proof* 1991; *Spotswood* 1991; *Hammers over the Anvil* 1992; *Romper Stomper* 1992; *The Silver Brumby* 1992; *For the Moment* 1994; *The Quick and the Dead* 1995; *Rough Magic* 1995; *The Sum of Us* 1995; *Virtuosity* 1995; *Breaking Up* 1996; *No Way Back* 1996; *Heaven's Burning* 1997; *LA Confidential* 1997; *The Insider* 1999; *Mystery, Alaska* 1999; *Gladiator* 2000; *Proof of Life* 2000; *A Beautiful Mind* 2001; *Master and Commander: the Far Side of the World* 2003; *Cinderella Man* 2005
Crowe, Sara (1967–) *Carry On Columbus* 1992; *Caught in the Act* 1996
Crowell, Josephine (1849–1932) *Home, Sweet Home* 1914; *Intolerance* 1916; *Hearts of the World* 1918; *Hot Water* 1924; *Mantrap* 1926
Crowley, Kathleen (1931–) *The Female Jungle* 1955; *Westward Ho the Wagons!* 1956; *The Flame Barrier* 1958; *The Rebel Set* 1959; *Showdown* 1963; *The Lawyer* 1969
Crowley, Matt (1904–1983) *The Mob* 1951; *April Love* 1957
Crowley, Pat *aka* **Crowley, Patricia** (1929–) *Forever Female* 1953; *Money from Home* 1953; *Red Garters* 1954; *The Square Jungle* 1955; *Hollywood or Bust* 1956; *There's Always Tomorrow* 1956; *Walk the Proud Land* 1956; *Key Witness* 1960; *The Wheeler Dealers* 1963; *To Trap a Spy* 1966; *The Biscuit Eater* 1972
Croze, Marie-Josée (1970–) *Maelström* 2000; *Ararat* 2002; *The Barbarian Invasions* 2003
Crudup, Billy (1968–) *Sleepers* 1996; *Inventing the Abbotts* 1997; *Noose* 1997; *Princess Mononoke* 1997; *The Hi-Lo Country* 1998; *Without Limits* 1998; *Jesus' Son* 1999; *Almost Famous* 2000; *Waking the Dead* 2000; *Charlotte Gray* 2001; *Big Fish* 2003; *Stage Beauty* 2004
Cruickshank, Andrew (1907–1988) *Eye Witness* 1949; *There Was a Crooked Man* 1960; *El Cid* 1961; *Greyfriars Bobby* 1961; *We Joined the Navy* 1962; *Murder Most Foul* 1964
Cruise, Tom (1962–) *Endless Love* 1981; *Taps* 1981; *All the Right Moves* 1983; *Losin' It* 1983; *The Outsiders* 1983; *Risky Business* 1983; *Legend* 1985; *The Color of Money* 1986; *Top Gun* 1986; *Cocktail* 1988; *Rain Man* 1988; *Born on the Fourth of July* 1989; *Days of Thunder* 1990; *Far and Away* 1992; *A Few Good Men* 1992; *The Firm* 1993; *Interview with the Vampire: the Vampire Chronicles* 1994; *Jerry Maguire* 1996; *Mission: Impossible* 1996; *Eyes Wide Shut* 1999; *Magnolia* 1999; *Mission: Impossible 2* 1999; *Vanilla Sky* 2001; *Minority Report* 2002; *The Last Samurai* 2003; *Collateral* 2004; *War of the Worlds* 2005
Crutchley, Jeremy *A Good Man in Africa* 1993; *The Mangler* 1994
Crutchley, Rosalie (1920–1997) *Take My Life* 1947; *Prelude to Fame* 1950; *The Sword and the Rose* 1952; *Miracle in Soho* 1957; *Seven Thunders* 1957; *A Tale of Two Cities* 1957; *Beyond This Place* 1959; *The Nun's Story* 1959; *No Love for Johnnie* 1960; *Greyfriars Bobby* 1961; *Girl in the Headlines* 1963; *The Haunting* 1963; *Wuthering Heights* 1970;

Blood from the Mummy's Tomb 1971; *Creatures the World Forgot* 1971; *Who Slew Auntie Roo?* 1971; *And Now the Screaming Starts!* 1973; *The House in Nightmare Park* 1973; *Mahler* 1974; *The Fool* 1990; *Four Weddings and a Funeral* 1994
Cruttenden, Abigail (1969–) *P'Tang, Yang, Kipperbang* 1982; *Hideous Kinky* 1998
Cruttwell, Greg *Naked* 1993; *2 Days in the Valley* 1996; *George of the Jungle* 1997
Cruz, Alexis (1974–) *Rooftops* 1989; *Stargate* 1994
Cruz, Ernesto Gómez (1933–) *Reed: Insurgent Mexico* 1971; *El Norte* 1983; *Midaq Alley* 1995; *El Crimen del Padre Amaro* 2002
Cruz, Lito (1941–) *Sur* 1987; *La Amiga* 1988
Cruz, Penélope (1974–) *Belle Epoque* 1992; *Jamon Jamon* 1992; *Live Flesh* 1997; *Open Your Eyes* 1997; *The Girl of Your Dreams* 1998; *The Hi-Lo Country* 1998; *If Only* 1998; *Talk of Angels* 1998; *All about My Mother* 1999; *All the Pretty Horses* 2000; *Woman on Top* 2000; *Blow* 2001; *Captain Corelli's Mandolin* 2001; *Vanilla Sky* 2001; *Gothika* 2003; *Masked and Anonymous* 2003; *Don't Move* 2004; *Sahara* 2004
Cruz, Raymond *The Substitute* 1996; *From Dusk till Dawn II: Texas Blood Money* 1999
Cruz, Wilson (1973–) *All over Me* 1996; *Supernova* 2000; *Party Monster* 2003
Cryer, Jon (1965–) *No Small Affair* 1984; *Pretty in Pink* 1986; *Dudes* 1987; *Hiding Out* 1987; *Home Front* 1987; *OC and Stiggs* 1987; *Superman IV: the Quest for Peace* 1987; *Penn & Teller Get Killed* 1989; *Hot Shots!* 1991; *The Pompatus of Love* 1995; *Holy Man* 1998
Crystal, Billy (1947–) *Animalympics* 1979; *This Is Spinal Tap* 1984; *Running Scared* 1986; *The Princess Bride* 1987; *Throw Momma from the Train* 1987; *Memories of Me* 1988; *When Harry Met Sally...* 1989; *City Slickers* 1991; *Mr Saturday Night* 1992; *City Slickers II: the Legend of Curly's Gold* 1994; *Forget Paris* 1995; *Deconstructing Harry* 1997; *Fathers' Day* 1997; *My Giant* 1998; *The Adventures of Rocky & Bullwinkle* 1999; *Analyze This* 1999; *America's Sweethearts* 2001; *Monsters, Inc* 2001; *Analyze That* 2002
Cserhalmi, Gyorgy (1948–) *Mephisto* 1981; *Zelary* 2003
Csokas, Marton (1966–) *Broken English* 1996; *The Monkey's Mask* 2000; *Rain* 2001; *xXx* 2002; *Kangaroo Jack* 2003; *The Bourne Supremacy* 2004; *Kingdom of Heaven* 2005
Cucciolla, Riccardo (1932–1999) *Grand Slam* 1967; *Sacco and Vanzetti* 1971; *Un Flic* 1972; *Borsalino and Co* 1974
Cucinotta, Maria Grazia (1969–) *Il Postino* 1994; *The Day of the Beast* 1995; *Picking Up the Pieces* 2000
Cugat, Xavier (1900–1990) *Holiday in Mexico* 1946; *A Date with Judy* 1948; *Neptune's Daughter* 1949
Cuka, Frances (1936–) *Henry VIII and His Six Wives* 1972; *The Attic: the Hiding of Anne Frank* 1988
Culkin, Kieran (1982–) *Father of the Bride* 1991; *Nowhere to Run* 1992; *It Runs in the Family* 1994; *Father of the Bride Part 2* 1995; *The Mighty* 1998; *She's All That* 1999; *The Dangerous Lives of Altar Boys* 2001; *Igby Goes Down* 2002
Culkin, Macaulay (1980–) *Rocket Gibraltar* 1988; *Uncle Buck* 1989; *Home Alone* 1990; *Jacob's Ladder* 1990; *My Girl* 1991; *Only the Lonely* 1991; *Home Alone 2: Lost in New York* 1992; *George Balanchine's The Nutcracker* 1993; *The Good Son* 1993; *Getting Even with Dad* 1994; *The Pagemaster* 1994; *Richie Rich* 1994; *Party Monster* 2003; *Saved!* 2004
Culkin, Rory (1989–) *You Can Count on Me* 1999; *Igby Goes Down* 2002; *It Runs in the Family* 2002; *Signs* 2002; *Mean Creek* 2004
Cullen, Brett (1956–) *By the Sword* 1992; *Leaving Normal* 1992; *Complex of Fear* 1993; *Prehysteria!* 1993; *Something to Talk About* 1995; *The Terror Inside* 1996
Cullen, Max (1940–) *Sunday Too Far Away* 1974; *Summerfield* 1977; *My Brilliant Career* 1979; *Hard Knocks* 1980; *Boundaries of the Heart* 1988; *Rough Diamonds* 1994; *Kiss or Kill* 1997; *The Nugget* 2002
Cullen, Peter *Heidi's Song* 1982; *Winnie the Pooh's Most Grand Adventure* 1997; *The Tigger Movie* 2000; *Piglet's Big Movie* 2003; *Pooh's Heffalump Movie* 2005
Culley, Frederick (1879–1942) *Conquest of the Air* 1936; *The Four Feathers* 1939; *Uncensored* 1942
Cullum, John (1930–) *All the Way Home* 1963; *The Prodigal* 1983; *Held Up* 1999
Cullum, John David *aka* **Cullum, J D** (1966–) *Willy/Milly* 1986; *Ambition* 1991
Culp, Robert (1930–) *Sammy, the Way Out Seal* 1962; *PT 109* 1963; *Sunday in New York* 1963; *The Raiders* 1964; *Rhino!* 1964; *Bob & Carol & Ted & Alice* 1969; *Hannie Caulder* 1971; *Hickey and Boggs* 1972; *The Castaway Cowboy* 1974; *Inside Out* 1975; *Breaking Point* 1976; *The Great Scout & Cathouse Thursday* 1976; *Sky Riders* 1976; *Goldengirl* 1979; *National Lampoon's Movie Madness* 1981; *Turk 182!* 1985; *Big Bad Mama II* 1987; *Pucker Up and Bark like a Dog* 1989; *The Pelican Brief* 1993; *I Spy Returns* 1994; *Most Wanted* 1997; *Farewell, My Love* 1999
Culp, Steven (1955–) *Jason Goes to Hell: the Final Friday* 1993; *Thirteen Days* 2000; *The Emperor's Club* 2002
Culver, Roland (1900–1984) *French without Tears* 1939; *The Day Will Dawn* 1942; *The First of the Few* 1942; *Secret Mission* 1942; *Unpublished Story* 1942; *The Life and Death of Colonel Blimp* 1943; *English without Tears* 1944; *Give Us the Moon* 1944; *Dead of Night* 1945; *Perfect Strangers* 1945; *To Each His Own* 1946; *Wanted for Murder* 1946; *Down to Earth* 1947; *Singapore* 1947; *The Emperor Waltz* 1948; *Isn't It Romantic* 1948; *The Great Lover* 1949; *Trio* 1950; *Encore* 1951; *Hotel Sahara* 1951; *The Late Edwina Black* 1951; *Folly to Be Wise* 1952; *The Hour of 13* 1952; *Rough Shoot* 1952; *Betrayed* 1954; *The Man Who Loved Redheads* 1954; *The Teckman Mystery* 1954; *An Alligator Named Daisy* 1955; *The Ship That Died of Shame* 1955; *Touch and Go* 1955; *Safari* 1956; *The Hypnotist* 1957; *The Vicious Circle* 1957; *Next to No Time* 1958; *Rockets Galore* 1958; *A Pair of Briefs* 1961; *Term of Trial* 1962; *A Man Could Get Killed* 1966; *In Search of Gregory* 1970; *The Legend of Hell House* 1973
Cumming, Alan (1965–) *Black Beauty* 1994; *Circle of Friends* 1995; *Emma* 1996; *Buddy* 1997; *Romy and Michele's High School Reunion* 1997; *Spice World: the Movie* 1997; *Annie* 1999; *Eyes Wide Shut* 1999; *Plunkett & Macleane* 1999; *Titus* 1999; *Company Man* 2000; *The Flintstones in Viva Rock Vegas* 2000; *Get Carter* 2000; *The Anniversary Party* 2001; *Josie and the Pussycats* 2001; *SPYkids* 2001; *Nicholas Nickleby* 2002; *X2* 2003; *Son of the Mask* 2004
Cumming, Dorothy (1899–1983) *The King of Kings* 1927; *The Divine Woman* 1928; *Kitty* 1928; *Our Dancing Daughters* 1928; *The Wind* 1928
Cummings, Constance (1910–) *The Criminal Code* 1930; *American Madness* 1932; *Movie Crazy* 1932; *Night after Night* 1932; *Washington Merry-Go-Round* 1932; *Broadway through a Keyhole* 1933; *The Mind Reader* 1933; *Glamour* 1934; *Looking for Trouble* 1934; *This Man Is Mine* 1934; *Remember Last Night?* 1935; *Seven Sinners* 1936; *Busman's Honeymoon* 1940; *The Foreman Went to France* 1941; *Blithe Spirit* 1945; *John and Julie* 1955; *The Intimate Stranger* 1956; *The Battle of the Sexes* 1960; *In the Cool of the Day* 1963; *Sammy Going South* 1963; *Dead Man's Folly* 1986
Cummings, Jim (1953–) *The Lion King* 1994; *Balto* 1995; *A Goofy Movie* 1995; *Winnie the Pooh's Most Grand Adventure* 1997; *The Road to El Dorado* 2000; *The Tigger Movie* 2000; *The Jungle Book 2* 2003; *Piglet's Big Movie* 2003; *Pooh's Heffalump Movie* 2005
Cummings, Robert *aka* **Cummings, Bob** (1908–1990) *So Red the Rose* 1935; *The Last Train from Madrid* 1937; *Souls at Sea* 1937; *Wells Fargo* 1937; *The Texans* 1938; *Three Smart Girls Grow Up* 1939; *The Devil and Miss Jones* 1941; *It Started with Eve* 1941; *Moon over Miami* 1941; *Kings Row* 1942; *Saboteur* 1942; *Flesh and Fantasy* 1943; *Princess O'Rourke* 1943; *The Bride Wore Boots* 1946; *The Chase* 1946; *Heaven Only Knows* 1947; *The Lost Moment* 1947; *Let's Live a Little* 1948; *Sleep, My Love* 1948; *The Accused* 1949; *Reign of Terror* 1949; *Tell It to the Judge* 1949; *For Heaven's Sake* 1950; *Paid in Full* 1950; *The Petty Girl* 1950; *Marry Me Again* 1953; *Dial M for Murder* 1954; *Lucky Me* 1954; *How to Be Very, Very Popular* 1955; *My Geisha* 1962; *Beach Party* 1963; *The Carpetbaggers* 1964; *What a Way to Go!* 1964; *Promise Her Anything* 1966; *Stagecoach* 1966; *Five Golden Dragons* 1967
Cummings, Susan *Secret of Treasure Mountain* 1956; *Verboten!* 1959
Cummins, Peggy (1925–) *English without Tears* 1944; *The Late George Apley* 1947; *Moss Rose* 1947; *Green Grass of Wyoming* 1948; *Gun Crazy* 1949; *That Dangerous Age* 1949; *The Love Lottery* 1953; *Meet Mr Lucifer* 1953; *To Dorothy, a Son* 1954; *The March Hare* 1956; *Carry On Admiral* 1957; *Hell Drivers* 1957; *Night of the Demon* 1957; *The Captain's Table* 1958; *Dentist in the Chair* 1960; *Your Money or Your Wife* 1960; *In the Doghouse* 1961
Cummins, Peter (1931–) *Sunday Too Far Away* 1974; *Storm Boy* 1976; *Double Deal* 1981; *Kangaroo* 1986
Cunningham, Anne (1937–) *Bitter Harvest* 1963; *This Sporting Life* 1963
Cunningham, Cecil (1888–1959) *Anybody's Woman* 1930; *The Awful Truth* 1937; *Blond Cheat* 1938; *Wives under Suspicion* 1938; *Above Suspicion* 1943
Cunningham, Colin (1967–) *The 6th Day* 2000; *Elektra* 2005
Cunningham, Danny *Loaded* 1994; *24 Hour Party People* 2001
Cunningham, Jack (1912–1967) *Dublin Nightmare* 1958; *The Quare Fellow* 1962
Cunningham, Liam (1961–) *First Knight* 1995; *A Little Princess* 1995; *Jude* 1996; *The Life of Stuff* 1997; *A Love Divided* 1999; *When the Sky Falls* 2000; *Dog Soldiers* 2001; *Revelation* 2001; *The Abduction Club* 2002; *The Card Player* 2004
Cunningham, Neil *The Tempest* 1979; *The Draughtsman's Contract* 1982
Cuny, Alain (1908–1994) *Les Visiteurs du Soir* 1942; *La Signora senza Camelie* 1953; *The Hunchback of Notre Dame* 1956; *Les Amants* 1958; *La Dolce Vita* 1960; *Banana Peel* 1964; *Satyricon* 1969; *Emmanuelle* 1974; *Illustrious Corpses* 1976; *Christ Stopped at Eboli* 1979; *Detective* 1985; *Camille Claudel* 1988
Cupisti, Barbara *Stage Fright – Aquarius* 1987; *The Church* 1988
Curran, Lynette (1945–) *Bliss* 1985; *The Year My Voice Broke* 1987; *The Delinquents* 1989; *Mushrooms* 1995; *Road to Nhill* 1997; *The Boys* 1998; *Japanese Story* 2003; *Somersault* 2004
Curran, Tony (1968–) *The 13th Warrior* 1999; *The League of Extraordinary Gentlemen* 2003; *Flight of the Phoenix* 2004
Curreri, Lee *Fame* 1980; *Crystal Heart* 1987
Currie, Cherie (1959–) *Foxes* 1980; *Parasite* 1982; *Wavelength* 1983
Currie, Finlay (1878–1968) *Mister Cinders* 1934; *Command Performance* 1937; *The Edge of the World* 1937; *The Day Will Dawn* 1942; *Thunder Rock* 1942; *The Bells Go Down* 1943; *Great Expectations* 1946; *School for Secrets* 1946; *The Brothers* 1947; *My Brother Jonathan* 1947; *Bonnie Prince Charlie* 1948; *The History of Mr Polly* 1948; *Mr Perrin and Mr Traill* 1948; *Sleeping Car to Trieste* 1948; *The Black Rose* 1950; *The Mudlark* 1950; *Treasure Island* 1950; *People Will Talk* 1951; *Quo Vadis* 1951; *Kangaroo* 1952; *Stars and Stripes Forever* 1952; *Walk East on Beacon* 1952; *Rob Roy, the Highland Rogue* 1953; *Treasure of the Golden Condor* 1953; *Captain Lightfoot* 1955; *Footsteps in the Fog* 1955; *King's Rhapsody* 1955; *Zarak* 1956; *Dangerous Exile* 1957; *The Little Hut* 1957; *Saint Joan* 1957; *The Naked Earth* 1958; *Ben-Hur* 1959; *Tempest* 1959; *The Angel Wore Red* 1960; *Kidnapped* 1960; *Go to Blazes* 1961; *Corridors of Blood* 1962; *The Inspector* 1962; *Billy Liar* 1963; *The Cracksman* 1963; *Murder at the Gallop* 1963; *The Three Lives of Thomasina* 1963; *West 11* 1963; *Bunny Lake Is Missing* 1965
Currie, Gordon (1965–) *Listen* 1996; *Ripe* 1996; *Laserhawk* 1997; *Dog Park* 1998; *waydowntown* 2000; *Highwaymen* 2003
Currie, Sondra *Mama's Dirty Girls* 1974; *The Concrete Jungle* 1982
Currier, Mary (1904–1957) *The Falcon in Mexico* 1944; *Stars on Parade* 1944
Curry, Stephen *The Castle* 1997; *Cut* 2000; *The Nugget* 2002
Curry, Tim (1946–) *The Rocky Horror Picture Show* 1975; *The Shout* 1978; *Times Square* 1980; *Annie* 1982; *Oliver Twist* 1982; *The Ploughman's Lunch* 1983; *Clue* 1985; *Legend* 1985; *Pass the Ammo* 1988; *The Hunt for Red October* 1990; *Oscar* 1991; *FernGully: the Last Rainforest* 1992; *Passed Away* 1992; *National Lampoon's Loaded Weapon 1* 1993; *The Three Musketeers* 1993; *The Shadow* 1994; *Congo* 1995; *Lover's Knot* 1995; *The Pebble and the Penguin* 1995; *Muppet Treasure Island* 1996; *Beauty and the Beast: the Enchanted Christmas* 1997; *A Christmas Carol* 1997; *McHale's Navy* 1997; *Addams Family Reunion* 1998; *The Rugrats Movie* 1998; *Bartok the Magnificent* 1999; *Four Dogs Playing Poker* 1999; *Charlie's Angels* 2000; *Lion of Oz* 2000; *Sorted* 2000; *Scary Movie 2* 2001; *The Cat Returns* 2002; *The Wild Thornberrys Movie* 2003; *Kinsey* 2004; *Valiant* 2005
Curtin, Jane (1947–) *How to Beat the High Cost of Living* 1980; *Divorce Wars* 1982; *OC and Stiggs* 1987; *Coneheads* 1993; *Antz* 1998
Curtin, Valerie (1945–) *A Different Story* 1978; *Big Trouble* 1985; *Maxie* 1985
Curtis, Alan (1909–1953) *Mannequin* 1937; *The Duke of West Point* 1938; *Hollywood Cavalcade* 1939; *Sergeant Madden* 1939; *Four Sons* 1940; *Buck Privates* 1941; *High Sierra* 1941; *Gung Ho!* 1943; *Hitler's Madman* 1943; *The Invisible Man's Revenge* 1944; *Phantom Lady* 1944; *The Daltons Ride Again* 1945; *The Naughty Nineties* 1945
Curtis, Amelia *aka* **Shankley, Amelia** (1972–) *Red Riding Hood* 1987; *Janice Beard 45 WPM* 1999; *South West Nine* 2001; *FearDotCom* 2002
Curtis, Cliff (1968–) *Desperate Remedies* 1993; *Deep Rising* 1998; *Virus* 1998; *Three Kings* 1999; *Collateral Damage* 2001; *Whale Rider* 2002
Curtis, Donald (1915–1997) *Phffft!* 1954; *It Came from beneath the Sea* 1955; *Earth vs the Flying Saucers* 1956
Curtis, Jackie (1947–1985) *Flesh* 1968; *Women in Revolt* 1971
Curtis, Jamie Lee (1958–) *Halloween* 1978; *The Fog* 1980; *Prom Night* 1980; *Terror Train* 1980; *Halloween II* 1981; *Road Games* 1981; *Love Letters* 1983; *Trading Places* 1983; *Grandview, USA* 1984; *Perfect* 1985; *Amazing Grace and Chuck* 1987; *A Man in Love* 1987; *Dominick and Eugene* 1988; *A Fish Called Wanda* 1988; *Blue Steel* 1990; *My Girl* 1991; *Queens Logic* 1991; *Forever Young* 1992; *Mother's Boys* 1993; *My Girl 2* 1994; *True Lies* 1994; *House Arrest* 1996; *Fierce Creatures* 1997; *Halloween H20: 20 Years Later* 1998; *Homegrown* 1998; *Nicholas' Gift* 1998; *Virus* 1998; *Drowning Mona* 2000; *The Tailor of Panama* 2000; *Rudolph the Red-Nosed Reindeer and the Island of the Misfit Toys* 2001; *Halloween: Resurrection* 2002; *Freaky Friday* 2003; *Christmas with the Kranks* 2004
Curtis, Keene (1925–) *Macbeth* 1948; *The Buddy System* 1984; *Lambada* 1990
Curtis, Ken (1916–1991) *The Searchers* 1956; *The Wings of Eagles* 1957; *The Missouri Traveler* 1958; *The Killer Shrews* 1959; *Once upon a Texas Train* 1988
Curtis, Mickey (1938–) *Fires on the Plain* 1959; *Gunhed* 1989
Curtis, Robin (1956–) *Star Trek III: the Search for Spock* 1984; *Star Trek IV: the Voyage Home* 1986; *Darkbreed* 1996; *Santa with Muscles* 1996
Curtis, Tony *aka* **Curtis, Anthony** *aka* **Curtis, James** (1925–) *City across the River* 1949; *Criss Cross* 1949; *Francis* 1949; *Johnny Stool Pigeon* 1949; *The Lady Gambles* 1949; *I Was a Shoplifter* 1950; *Kansas Raiders* 1950; *Sierra* 1950; *Winchester '73* 1950; *The Prince Who Was a Thief* 1951; *Flesh and Fury* 1952; *Meet Danny Wilson* 1952; *No Room for the Groom* 1952; *Son of Ali Baba* 1952; *The All American* 1953; *Forbidden* 1953; *Houdini* 1953; *Beachhead* 1954; *The Black Shield of Falworth* 1954; *Johnny Dark* 1954; *So This Is Paris* 1954; *The Purple Mask* 1955; *Six Bridges to Cross* 1955; *The Square Jungle* 1955; *The Rawhide Years* 1956; *Trapeze* 1956; *The Midnight Story* 1957; *Mister Cory* 1957; *Sweet Smell of Success* 1957; *The Defiant Ones* 1958; *Kings Go Forth* 1958; *The Perfect Furlough* 1958; *The Vikings* 1958; *Operation Petticoat* 1959; *Some Like It Hot* 1959; *The Great Impostor* 1960; *Pepe* 1960; *The Rat Race* 1960; *Spartacus* 1960; *Who Was That Lady?* 1960; *The Outsider* 1961; *Forty Pounds of Trouble* 1962; *Taras Bulba* 1962; *Captain Newman, MD* 1963; *The List of Adrian Messenger* 1963; *Goodbye Charlie* 1964; *Paris When It Sizzles* 1964; *Sex and the Single Girl* 1964; *Wild and Wonderful* 1964; *Boeing Boeing* 1965; *The Great Race* 1965; *Chamber of Horrors* 1966; *Drop Dead Darling* 1966; *Not with My Wife, You Don't!* 1966; *Don't Make Waves* 1967; *On My Way to the Crusades, I Met a Girl Who...*

1967; The Boston Strangler 1968; Rosemary's Baby 1968; Monte Carlo or Bust 1969; Suppose They Gave a War and Nobody Came? 1970; You Can't Win 'em All 1970; The Count of Monte Cristo 1974; Lepke 1975; Casanova & Co 1976; The Last Tycoon 1976; The Bad News Bears Go to Japan 1978; The Manitou 1978; Sextette 1978; Title Shot 1979; Little Miss Marker 1980; The Mirror Crack'd 1980; Balboa 1982; Brainwaves 1982; Where Is Parsifal? 1983; Insignificance 1985; Agatha Christie's Murder in Three Acts 1986; Lobster Man from Mars 1989; Midnight 1989; Prime Target 1991; Naked in New York 1994; Play It to the Bone 2000

Curtis, Yvette A Warm December 1973; Claudine 1974

Curtis-Hall, Vondie (1956–) Heat Wave 1990; Passion Fish 1992; Crooklyn 1994; DROP Squad 1994; Broken Arrow 1996; Gridlock'd 1996; Heaven's Prisoners 1996; Eve's Bayou 1997; Ali: an American Hero 2000; Freedom Song 2000

Curtright, Jorja (1923–1985) Whistle Stop 1946; The Revolt of Mamie Stover 1956

Curzi, Pierre (1946–) Maria Chapdelaine 1982; The Decline of the American Empire 1986; The Barbarian Invasions 2003

Curzon, George (1898–1976) Scotland Yard Mystery 1933; Lorna Doone 1934; Java Head 1935; Young and Innocent 1937; Sexton Blake and the Hooded Terror 1938; Q Planes 1939

Cusack, Ann (1961–) A League of Their Own 1992; Multiplicity 1996

Cusack, Cyril (1910–1993) Odd Man Out 1946; Esther Waters 1948; Once a Jolly Swagman 1948; The Blue Lagoon 1949; The Small Back Room 1949; The Elusive Pimpernel 1950; Gone to Earth 1950; The Blue Veil 1951; The Secret of Convict Lake 1951; Soldiers Three 1951; Saadia 1953; Passage Home 1955; Ill Met by Moonlight 1956; Jacqueline 1956; The March Hare 1956; The Spanish Gardener 1956; The Man in the Road 1957; Miracle in Soho 1957; The Rising of the Moon 1957; Floods of Fear 1958; Gideon's Day 1958; Shake Hands with the Devil 1959; A Terrible Beauty 1960; I Thank a Fool 1962; Waltz of the Toreadors 1962; 80,000 Suspects 1963; The Spy Who Came in from the Cold 1965; Where the Spies Are 1965; Fahrenheit 451 1966; I Was Happy Here 1966; Oedipus the King 1967; The Taming of the Shrew 1967; Country Dance 1970; King Lear 1970; Sacco and Vanzetti 1971; Harold and Maude 1972; The Day of the Jackal 1973; The Homecoming 1973; The Italian Connection 1973; The Abdication 1974; Les Misérables 1978; Lovespell 1979; True Confessions 1981; Nineteen Eighty-Four 1984; Little Dorrit 1987; The Fool 1990; As You Like It 1992; Far and Away 1992

Cusack, Joan (1962–) My Bodyguard 1980; Sixteen Candles 1984; The Allnighter 1987; Broadcast News 1987; Married to the Mob 1988; Stars and Bars 1988; Working Girl 1988; Men Don't Leave 1990; My Blue Heaven 1990; Accidental Hero 1992; Toys 1992; Addams Family Values 1993; Corrina, Corrina 1994; Nine Months 1995; Two Much 1995; Mr Wrong 1996; Grosse Pointe Blank 1997; In & Out 1997; A Smile like Yours 1997; Arlington Road 1998; Cradle Will Rock 1999; Runaway Bride 1999; Toy Story 2 1999; High Fidelity 2000; Where the Heart Is 2000; It's a Very Merry Muppet Christmas Movie 2002; The School of Rock 2003; Looney Tunes: Back in Action 2004; Raising Helen 2004

Cusack, John (1966–) Class 1983; Sixteen Candles 1984; Better Off Dead 1985; The Journey of Natty Gann 1985; The Sure Thing 1985; One Crazy Summer 1986; Stand by Me 1986; Hot Pursuit 1987; Eight Men Out 1988; Tapeheads 1988; Say Anything... 1989; Shadow Makers 1989; The Grifters 1990; Shadows and Fog 1991; True Colors 1991; Bob Roberts 1992; Map of the Human Heart 1992; Roadside Prophets 1992; Money for Nothing 1993; Bullets over Broadway 1994; Floundering 1994; The Road to Wellville 1994; City Hall 1996; Anastasia 1997; Con Air 1997; Grosse Pointe Blank 1997; Midnight in the Garden of Good and Evil 1997; Chicago Cab 1998; The Thin Red Line 1998; Being John Malkovich 1999; Cradle Will Rock 1999; The Jack Bull 1999; Pushing Tin 1999; This Is My Father 1999; High Fidelity 2000; America's Sweethearts 2001; Serendipity 2001; Max 2002; Identity 2003; Runaway Jury 2003

Cusack, Niamh (1959–) Paris by Night 1988; Fools of Fortune 1990; The Playboys 1992; The Closer You Get 2000

Cusack, Sinead (1948–) Hoffman 1970; Revenge 1971; The Last Remake of Beau Geste 1977; Rocket Gibraltar 1988; Venus Peter 1989; Bad Behaviour 1992; The Cement Garden 1992; Waterland 1992; Sparrow 1993; Stealing Beauty 1995; The Nephew 1997; My Mother Frank 2000; Passion of Mind 2000; I Capture the Castle 2002

Cushing, Peter (1913–1994) The Man in the Iron Mask 1939; A Chump at Oxford 1940; Vigil in the Night 1940; Hamlet 1948; The Black Knight 1954; The End of the Affair 1954; Alexander the Great 1956; Magic Fire 1956; The Abominable Snowman 1957; The Curse of Frankenstein 1957; Time without Pity 1957; Horror of Dracula 1958; The Revenge of Frankenstein 1958; Violent Playground 1958; The Flesh and the Fiends 1959; The Hound of the Baskervilles 1959; The Mummy 1959; The Brides of Dracula 1960; Cone of Silence 1960; Suspect 1960; Sword of Sherwood Forest 1960; Cash on Demand 1961; Fury at Smugglers Bay 1961; The Hellfire Club 1961; The Naked Edge 1961; The Man Who Finally Died 1962; Dr Terror's House of Horrors 1964; Evil of Frankenstein 1964; The Gorgon 1964; Doctor Who and the Daleks 1965; She 1965; The Skull 1965; Daleks – Invasion Earth 2150 AD 1966; Frankenstein Created Woman 1966; Island of Terror 1966; The Blood Beast Terror 1967; Night of the Big Heat 1967; Torture Garden 1967; Corruption 1968; Frankenstein Must Be Destroyed 1969; Scream and Scream Again 1969; Incense for the Damned 1970; One More Time 1970; The Vampire Lovers 1970; The House That Dripped Blood 1971; I, Monster 1971; Twins of Evil 1971; Asylum 1972; The Creeping Flesh 1972; Dracula AD 1972 1972; Fear in the Night 1972; Horror Express 1972; Nothing but the Night 1972; Tales from the Crypt 1972; And Now the Screaming Starts! 1973; Frankenstein and the Monster from Hell 1973; From beyond the Grave 1973; The Satanic Rites of Dracula 1973; The Beast Must Die 1974; The Legend of the 7 Golden Vampires 1974; Legend of the Werewolf 1974; Madhouse 1974; Shatter 1974; The Ghoul 1975; Shock Waves 1975; At the Earth's Core 1976; Trial by Combat 1976; Star Wars Episode IV: a New Hope 1977; The Uncanny 1977; Arabian Adventure 1979; A Touch of the Sun 1979; House of the Long Shadows 1983; Sword of the Valiant 1984; Top Secret! 1984; Biggles 1986

Cuthbert, Elisha (1982–) Airspeed 1997; The Girl Next Door 2004; House of Wax 2004

Cuthbertson, Allan (1920–1988) Carrington VC 1954; Cloak without Dagger 1955; Double Cross 1955; Postmark for Danger 1955; Dick Turpin – Highwayman 1956; Room at the Top 1958; Tunes of Glory 1960; On the Double 1961; Solo for Sparrow 1962; The Informers 1963; The Running Man 1963; Tamahine 1963; The 7th Dawn 1964; The Body Stealers 1969; Captain Nemo and the Underwater City 1969

Cuthbertson, Iain (1930–) The Railway Children 1970; The Assam Garden 1985; Gorillas in the Mist 1988; Chasing the Deer 1994; Strictly Sinatra 2000

Cutter, Lise Buy & Cell 1988; Havana 1990; Nickel & Dime 1991; Fleshtone 1994

Cutting, Richard H (1912–1972) Attack of the Crab Monsters 1957; Rock All Night 1957; The World Was His Jury 1957

Cutts, Patricia aka **Wayne, Patricia** (1926–1974) Eye Witness 1949; The Man Who Loved Redheads 1954; Merry Andrew 1958; Battle of the Coral Sea 1959; The Tingler 1959

Cuvelier, Marcel The Wanderer 1967; Kamouraska 1973

Cybulski, Zbigniew (1927–1967) A Generation 1954; Ashes and Diamonds 1958; The Saragossa Manuscript 1964

Cypher, Jon (1932–) Believe in Me 1971; Valdez Is Coming 1971; Lady Ice 1973; The Food of the Gods 1975

Cyphers, Charles (1939–) Coming Home 1978; Halloween 1978; Halloween II 1981

Cyr, Myriam (1960–) Gothic 1986; Species II 1998

Czerny, Henry (1959–) Cold Sweat 1993; Clear and Present Danger 1994; When Night Is Falling 1995; Mission: Impossible 1996; The Ice Storm 1997; Death in the Shadows 1998; Glory & Honor 1998; Eye of the Killer 1999; Possessed 2000

Czinkoczi, Zsuzsa Diary for My Children 1982; Diary for My Loves 1987; Diary for My Father and Mother 1990

Czyplonka, Hansa Kaspar Hauser 1993; Beyond Silence 1996

D M X (1970–) Romeo Must Die 2000; Exit Wounds 2001; Cradle 2 the Grave 2003; Never Die Alone 2004

Da Cunha, Gerson Electric Moon 1992; Cotton Mary 1999

Da Silva, Howard (1909–1986) The Lost Weekend 1945; The Blue Dahlia 1946; Two Years before the Mast 1946; Blaze of Noon 1947; Unconquered 1947; They Live by Night 1948; Border Incident 1949; The Great Gatsby 1949; The Underworld Story 1950; Wyoming Mail 1950; M 1951; David and Lisa 1962; The Outrage 1964; Nevada Smith 1966; Mommie Dearest 1981; Garbo Talks 1984

Dabas, Parvin Monsoon Wedding 2001; The Perfect Husband 2003

Dabney, Augusta (1918–) That Night 1957; The Heartbreak Kid 1972; Violets Are Blue 1986

D'Abo, Maryam (1960–) Xtro 1983; The Living Daylights 1987; Leon the Pig Farmer 1992; The Browning Version 1994; Solitaire for 2 1994; The Point Men 2000

D'Abo, Olivia (1967–) Bolero 1984; Conan the Destroyer 1984; Beyond the Stars 1988; The Assassin 1993; Bank Robber 1993; Point of No Return 1993; Wayne's World 2 1993; Clean Slate 1994; Greedy 1994; The Last Good Time 1994; The Big Green 1995; Kicking and Screaming 1995; Live Nude Girls 1995; The Velocity of Gary 1998; Soccer Dog: the Movie 1999; The Enemy 2000

Dacascos, Mark (1964–) Only the Strong 1993; Double Dragon 1994; Crying Freeman 1995; DNA 1996; Drive 1997; Sanctuary 1997; No Code of Conduct 1998; Brotherhood of the Wolf 2001; Cradle 2 the Grave 2003

Dacla, Corinne Captive 1986; Brothers in Arms 1990

Dacqmine, Jacques (1923–) Web of Passion 1959; The Big Risk 1960; Inspecteur Lavardin 1986; Mélo 1986

Dade, Frances (1910–1968) Grumpy 1930; Raffles 1930; Dracula 1931

Dafoe, Willem (1955–) The Loveless 1981; Roadhouse 66 1984; Streets of Fire 1984; To Live and Die in LA 1985; Platoon 1986; The Last Temptation of Christ 1988; Mississippi Burning 1988; Saigon 1988; Born on the Fourth of July 1989; Cry-Baby 1989; Triumph of the Spirit 1989; Wild at Heart 1990; Flight of the Intruder 1991; Light Sleeper 1991; Body of Evidence 1992; White Sands 1992; Faraway, So Close 1993; Clear and Present Danger 1994; Tom & Viv 1994; Victory 1995; Basquiat 1996; The English Patient 1996; Affliction 1997; Speed 2: Cruise Control 1997; Lulu on the Bridge 1998; New Rose Hotel 1998; The Boondock Saints 1999; eXistenZ 1999; American Psycho 2000; Animal Factory 2000; Pavilion of Women 2000; Shadow of the Vampire 2000; The Reckoning 2001; Auto Focus 2002; Spider-Man 2002; Finding Nemo 2003; Once upon a Time in Mexico 2003; The Clearing 2004; The Life Aquatic with Steve Zissou 2004; xXx: the Next Level 2005

Dagover, Lil (1897–1980) The Cabinet of Dr Caligari 1919; The Spiders 1919; Destiny 1921; Tartuffe 1926; Congress Dances 1931; The Pedestrian 1974

Dahl, Arlene (1924–) My Wild Irish Rose 1947; A Southern Yankee 1948; Ambush 1949; Reign of Terror 1949; Scene of the Crime 1949; The Outriders 1950; Three Little Words 1950; Watch the Birdie 1950; Inside Straight 1951; Desert Legion 1953; The Diamond Queen 1953; Here Come the Girls 1953; Jamaica Run 1953; Bengal Brigade 1954; Woman's World 1954; Fortune Is a Woman 1956; Slightly Scarlet 1956; Journey to the Center of the Earth 1959; Kisses for My President 1964; Land Raiders 1969

Dahlbeck, Eva (1920–) Waiting Women 1952; Lesson in Love 1954; Dreams 1955; Smiles of a Summer Night 1955; So Close to Life 1957; The Counterfeit Traitor 1962; All These Women 1964; Les Créatures 1966

Daike, Yuko Kikujiro 1999; Zatoichi 2003

Dailey, Dan aka **Dailey Jr, Dan** (1914–1978) Lady Be Good 1941; Mother Wore Tights 1947; Chicken Every Sunday 1948; Give My Regards to Broadway 1948; When My Baby Smiles at Me 1948; You Were Meant for Me 1948; You're My Everything 1949; My Blue Heaven 1950; A Ticket to Tomahawk 1950; When Willie Comes Marching Home 1950; Call Me Mister 1951; I Can Get It for You Wholesale 1951; Meet Me at the Fair 1952; The Pride of St Louis 1952; What Price Glory? 1952; The Girl Next Door 1953; The Kid from Left Field 1953; Taxi 1953; There's No Business like Show Business 1954; It's Always Fair Weather 1955; The Best Things in Life Are Free 1956; Meet Me in Las Vegas 1956; Oh, Men! Oh, Women! 1957; The Wayward Bus 1957; The Wings of Eagles 1957; Pepe 1960; Hemingway's Adventures of a Young Man 1962; The Private Files of J Edgar Hoover 1977

Dailey, Irene (1920–) Daring Game 1968; The Grissom Gang 1971

Daily, Elizabeth aka **Daily, E G** (1962–) Wacko 1981; The Escape Artist 1982; One Dark Night 1982; Valley Girl 1983; No Small Affair 1984; Fandango 1985; Pee-wee's Big Adventure 1985; Driving Me Crazy 1991; Babe: Pig in the City 1998; The Rugrats Movie 1998; Rugrats in Paris: the Movie 2000; The Powerpuff Girls 2002; Rugrats Go Wild 2003

Dainton, Patricia (1930–) The Dancing Years 1949; Tread Softly 1952; No Road Back 1957; The Passionate Stranger 1957; Witness in the Dark 1959; The Third Alibi 1961

Dalban, Max (1908–1960) Boudu, Saved from Drowning 1932; Toni 1935; Clochemerle 1948

Dalbert, Suzanne (1927–1970) The Accused 1949; Target Unknown 1951; The 49th Man 1953

D'Albie, Julian The Gay Adventure 1949; The Lady with the Lamp 1951

Dale, Cynthia (1961–) Heavenly Bodies 1985; The Boy in Blue 1986

Dale, Esther (1885–1961) Crime without Passion 1934; Curly Top 1935; Private Worlds 1935; The Wedding Night 1935; The Awful Truth 1937; Condemned Women 1938; Blackmail 1939; Unfinished Business 1941; Dangerously They Live 1942; Bedside Manner 1945; Margie 1946; Smoky 1946; The Unfinished Dance 1947; Holiday Affair 1949; Ma and Pa Kettle 1949

Dale, Jennifer (1955–) Ticket to Heaven 1981; Of Unknown Origin 1983; Separate Vacations 1986; Something about Love 1987; The Adjuster 1991; Whale Music 1994

Dale, Jim (1935–) Raising the Wind 1961; Carry On Cabby 1963; Carry On Cleo 1964; Carry On Spying 1964; The Big Job 1965; Carry On Cowboy 1965; Carry On – Don't Lose Your Head 1966; Carry On Screaming 1966; The Winter's Tale 1966; Carry On Follow That Camel 1967; The Plank 1967; Carry On Doctor 1968; Carry On Again Doctor 1969; Lock Up Your Daughters! 1969; Adolf Hitler – My Part in His Downfall 1972; Digby, the Biggest Dog in the World 1973; The National Health 1973; Joseph Andrews 1977; Pete's Dragon 1977; Hot Lead and Cold Feet 1978; The Spaceman and King Arthur 1979; Carry On Columbus 1992

Dale, Virginia (1917–1994) Buck Benny Rides Again 1940; Kiss the Boys Goodbye 1941; Holiday Inn 1942

Daley, Cass (1915–1975) The Fleet's In 1942; Riding High 1943; Out of This World 1945

Dalio, Marcel aka **Dalio** (1900–1983) Les Affaires Publiques 1934; La Grande Illusion 1937; La Règle du Jeu 1939; The Shanghai Gesture 1941; Paris after Dark 1943; The Desert Song 1944; Snowbound 1948; On the Riviera 1951; Rich, Young and Pretty 1951; Black Jack 1952; Flight to Tangier 1953; Lucky Me 1954; Sabrina 1954; Razzia sur la Chnouf 1955; Hell Bent for Glory 1957; Tip on a Dead Jockey 1957; The Perfect Furlough 1958; The Man Who Understood Women 1959; The Big Risk 1960; Can-Can 1960; Cartouche 1961; The List of Adrian Messenger 1963; How to Steal a Million 1966; The 25th Hour 1967; How Sweet It Is! 1968; La Bête 1975

Dalkowska, Ewa (1947–) A Year of the Quiet Sun 1984; Korczak 1990

Dall, Evelyn (1914–) King Arthur Was a Gentleman 1942; Miss London Ltd 1943; Time Flies 1944

Dall, John (1918–1971) The Corn Is Green 1945; Something in the Wind 1947; Another Part of the Forest 1948; Rope 1948; Gun Crazy 1949; Atlantis, the Lost Continent 1960

Dallas, Charlene Rancho Deluxe 1975; The Great Georgia Bank Hoax 1977

Dalle, Béatrice (1964–) *Betty Blue* 1986; *La Fille de l'Air* 1992; *Night on Earth* 1992; *Six Days, Six Nights* 1994; *Clubbed to Death* 1996; *The Blackout* 1997; *Trouble Every Day* 2000; *Time of the Wolf* 2003; *Clean* 2004; *Process* 2004
Dallesandro, Joe (1948–) *Flesh* 1968; *Lonesome Cowboys* 1968; *Trash* 1970; *The Gardener* 1972; *Heat* 1972; *Black Moon* 1974; *Blood for Dracula* 1974; *Flesh for Frankenstein* 1974; *The Streetwalker* 1976; *Killer Nun* 1978; *Critical Condition* 1987; *Sunset* 1988; *Cry-Baby* 1989; *Guncrazy* 1992; *Wild Orchid 2: Two Shades of Blue* 1992; *Beefcake* 1998; *LA without a Map* 1998; *The Limey* 1999
Dallimore, Maurice (1912–1973) *The Three Stooges Go around the World in a Daze* 1963; *The Collector* 1965
D'Aloja, Francesca *Apartment Zero* 1988; *Hamam: the Turkish Bath* 1996
Dalton, Abby (1935–) *Rock All Night* 1957; *Viking Women and the Sea Serpent* 1957; *Stakeout on Dope Street* 1958; *The Plainsman* 1966
Dalton, Audrey (1934–) *My Cousin Rachel* 1952; *Titanic* 1953; *Casanova's Big Night* 1954; *Drum Beat* 1954; *Confession* 1955; *The Prodigal* 1955; *The Monster That Challenged the World* 1957; *This Other Eden* 1959; *Mr Sardonicus* 1961; *The Bounty Killer* 1965
Dalton, Darren (1965–) *Red Dawn* 1984; *Brotherhood of Justice* 1986
Dalton, Timothy (1944–) *The Lion in Winter* 1968; *Cromwell* 1970; *Wuthering Heights* 1970; *Mary, Queen of Scots* 1971; *Permission to Kill* 1975; *Agatha* 1978; *Sextette* 1978; *Flash Gordon* 1980; *Chanel Solitaire* 1981; *The Doctor and the Devils* 1985; *The Living Daylights* 1987; *Hawks* 1988; *Brenda Starr* 1989; *Licence to Kill* 1989; *The King's Whore* 1990; *Rocketeer* 1991; *Naked in New York* 1994; *The Beautician and the Beast* 1997; *Made Men* 1999; *Bitter Suite* 2000; *Possessed* 2000; *American Outlaws* 2001; *Looney Tunes: Back in Action* 2004
Daltrey, Roger (1944–) *Lisztomania* 1975; *Tommy* 1975; *The Legacy* 1978; *McVicar* 1980; *Mack the Knife* 1989; *Buddy's Song* 1990; *Cold Justice* 1991; *Teen Agent* 1991; *Lightning Jack* 1994; *Like It Is* 1997; *Best* 1999; *Dark Prince – the Legend of Dracula* 2000
Daly, Eileen *Razor Blade Smile* 1998; *Sacred Flesh* 2000; *Cradle of Fear* 2001
Daly, James (1918–1978) *The Young Stranger* 1957; *I Aim at the Stars* 1960; *Planet of the Apes* 1967; *The Big Bounce* 1969; *The Resurrection of Zachary Wheeler* 1971
Daly, Mark (1887–1957) *Doss House* 1933; *Command Performance* 1937; *Good Morning, Boys* 1937
Daly, Timothy *aka* **Daly, Tim** (1956–) *Diner* 1982; *Made in Heaven* 1987; *Spellbinder* 1988; *Love or Money* 1990; *Year of the Comet* 1992; *Denise Calls Up* 1995; *Dr Jekyll and Ms Hyde* 1995; *The Associate* 1996; *The Object of My Affection* 1998; *A House Divided* 2000; *Against the Ropes* 2003; *Basic* 2003
Daly, Tyne (1946–) *John and Mary* 1969; *Larry* 1974; *The Entertainer* 1975; *The Enforcer* 1976; *Telefon* 1977; *Cagney & Lacey* 1981; *Zoot Suit* 1981; *The Aviator* 1985; *Movers and Shakers* 1985; *The Autumn Heart* 1998; *Absence of the Good* 1999; *The Simian Line* 2000
Dalya, Jacqueline (1918–1980) *The Gay Caballero* 1940; *Mystery in Mexico* 1948
Damas, Bertila *Fires Within* 1991; *Nothing but Trouble* 1991
d'Amboise, Jacques (1934–) *Seven Brides for Seven Brothers* 1954; *The Best Things in Life Are Free* 1956; *Off Beat* 1986
Damita, Lili (1901–1994) *The Cock-Eyed World* 1929; *Fighting Caravans* 1931; *Friends and Lovers* 1931; *This Is the Night* 1932; *Frisco Kid* 1935
Damon, Gabriel (1976–) *The Land before Time* 1988; *RoboCop 2* 1990; *Iron Maze* 1991; *Little Nemo: Adventures in Slumberland* 1992
Damon, Mark (1933–) *Between Heaven and Hell* 1956; *The Fall of the House of Usher* 1960; *This Rebel Breed* 1960; *Beauty and the Beast* 1962; *Black Sabbath* 1963; *Ringo and His Golden Pistol* 1966; *Kill and Pray* 1967; *Anzio* 1968
Damon, Matt (1970–) *School Ties* 1992; *Geronimo: an American Legend* 1993; *Glory Daze* 1995; *Chasing Amy* 1996; *Courage under Fire* 1996; *Good Will Hunting* 1997; *John Grisham's The Rainmaker* 1997; *Rounders* 1998; *Saving Private Ryan* 1998; *Dogma* 1999; *The Talented Mr Ripley* 1999; *All the Pretty Horses* 2000; *The Legend of Bagger Vance* 2000; *Titan AE* 2000; *Gerry* 2001; *Jay and Silent Bob Strike Back* 2001; *Ocean's Eleven* 2001; *The Bourne Identity* 2002; *Spirit: Stallion of the Cimarron* 2002; *Jersey Girl* 2003; *Stuck on You* 2003; *The Bourne Supremacy* 2004; *EuroTrip* 2004; *Ocean's Twelve* 2004
Damone, Vic (1928–) *Rich, Young and Pretty* 1951; *Athena* 1954; *Deep in My Heart* 1954; *Hit the Deck* 1955; *Kismet* 1955; *Hell to Eternity* 1960
Damus, Mike (1979–) *Lost in Yonkers* 1993; *A Pig's Tale* 1994
Dana, Bill (1924–) *The Harrad Summer* 1974; *I Wonder Who's Killing Her Now?* 1975
Dana, Leora (1923–1983) *3:10 to Yuma* 1957; *Kings Go Forth* 1958; *A Gathering of Eagles* 1963; *Change of Habit* 1969; *Wild Rovers* 1971; *Amityville III: the Demon* 1983
Danare, Malcolm (1962–) *The Curse* 1987; *Popcorn* 1991
Dance, Charles (1946–) *For Your Eyes Only* 1981; *Plenty* 1985; *The Golden Child* 1986; *Good Morning, Babylon* 1987; *Hidden City* 1987; *White Mischief* 1987; *Pascali's Island* 1988; *Alien³* 1992; *Century* 1993; *Last Action Hero* 1993; *China Moon* 1994; *Exquisite Tenderness* 1995; *Michael Collins* 1996; *Space Truckers* 1996; *The Blood Oranges* 1997; *In the Presence of Mine Enemies* 1997; *Hilary and Jackie* 1998; *What Rats Won't Do* 1998; *Don't Go Breaking My Heart* 1999; *Dark Blue World* 2001; *Gosford Park* 2001; *Ali G indahouse* 2002; *Black and White* 2002; *Swimming Pool* 2003
Dancy, Hugh (1975–) *Ella Enchanted* 2004; *King Arthur* 2004
D'Andrea, Tom (1909–1998) *Humoresque* 1946; *Dark Passage* 1947; *Fighter Squadron* 1948; *Silver River* 1948; *Tension* 1949; *The Next Voice You Hear* 1950
Dandridge, Dorothy (1923–1965) *Lady from Louisiana* 1941; *Sun Valley Serenade* 1941; *Sundown* 1941; *Ride 'em Cowboy* 1942; *Change of Heart* 1943; *Atlantic City* 1944; *Tarzan's Peril* 1951; *Bright Road* 1953; *Remains to Be Seen* 1953; *Carmen Jones* 1954; *Island in the Sun* 1957; *The Decks Ran Red* 1958; *Porgy and Bess* 1959; *Moment of Danger* 1960; *The Murder Men* 1961
Dane, Karl (1886–1934) *The Big Parade* 1925; *La Bohème* 1926; *The Scarlet Letter* 1926; *The Son of the Sheik* 1926; *The Trail of '98* 1929; *The Big House* 1930; *Billy the Kid* 1930
Dane, Lawrence (1937–) *Find the Lady* 1976; *Bear Island* 1979; *Running* 1979; *Head On* 1980; *Nothing Personal* 1980; *Scanners* 1980; *Happy Birthday to Me* 1981; *Of Unknown Origin* 1983; *Darkman II: the Return of Durant* 1995; *National Lampoon's Senior Trip* 1995; *Bride of Chucky* 1998
Dane, Patricia *aka* **Dane, Pat** (1918–1995) *Johnny Eager* 1941; *Life Begins for Andy Hardy* 1941; *Grand Central Murder* 1942; *Rio Rita* 1942; *I Dood It* 1943; *Are You with It?* 1948
Daneman, Paul (1925–2001) *Time without Pity* 1957; *Zulu* 1964; *Oh! What a Lovely War* 1969
Danes, Claire (1979–) *Little Women* 1994; *Home for the Holidays* 1995; *How to Make an American Quilt* 1995; *To Gillian on Her 37th Birthday* 1996; *William Shakespeare's Romeo + Juliet* 1996; *I Love You, I Love You Not* 1997; *John Grisham's The Rainmaker* 1997; *Les Misérables* 1997; *Princess Mononoke* 1997; *U Turn* 1997; *Polish Wedding* 1998; *Brokedown Palace* 1999; *The Mod Squad* 1999; *The Hours* 2002; *Igby Goes Down* 2002; *It's All about Love* 2002; *Terminator 3: Rise of the Machines* 2003; *Stage Beauty* 2004
Danese, Shera (1950–) *Risky Business* 1983; *The Ladies Club* 1986; *The Magic Bubble* 1992
Danet, Jean (1924–2001) *Diary of a Country Priest* 1950; *The Hunchback of Notre Dame* 1956
D'Angelo, Angelo *BMX Bandits* 1983; *The Big Steal* 1990
D'Angelo, Beverly (1953–) *First Love* 1977; *The Sentinel* 1977; *Every Which Way but Loose* 1978; *Hair* 1979; *Highpoint* 1979; *Coal Miner's Daughter* 1980; *Honky Tonk Freeway* 1981; *Paternity* 1981; *National Lampoon's Vacation* 1983; *Finders Keepers* 1984; *Big Trouble* 1985; *National Lampoon's European Vacation* 1985; *Aria* 1987; *Maid to Order* 1987; *The Woo Woo Kid* 1987; *High Spirits* 1988; *Trading Hearts* 1988; *Cold Front* 1989; *National Lampoon's Christmas Vacation* 1989; *Daddy's Dyin'... Who's Got the Will?* 1990; *The Miracle* 1990; *The Pope Must Die* 1991; *Man Trouble* 1992; *The Switch* 1993; *Lightning Jack* 1994; *Eye for an Eye* 1995; *Two Much Trouble* 1995; *Pterodactyl Woman from Beverly Hills* 1996; *Vegas Vacation* 1997; *American History X* 1998; *A Rat's Tale* 1998; *Lansky* 1999; *Sugar Town* 1999
D'Angelo, Mirella (1956–) *Tenebrae* 1982; *Hercules* 1983; *Apartment Zero* 1988; *Hard Men* 1996
Dangerfield, Rodney (1921–2004) *The Projectionist* 1970; *Caddyshack* 1980; *Easy Money* 1983; *Back to School* 1986; *Rover Dangerfield* 1991; *Ladybugs* 1992; *Natural Born Killers* 1994; *Casper: a Spirited Beginning* 1997; *Little Nicky* 2000
Dangler, Anita (1922–2000) *Law and Disorder* 1974; *Slow Dancing in the Big City* 1978; *Hero at Large* 1980
Dani (1944–) *Day for Night* 1973; *Love on the Run* 1979
Daniel, Brittany (1976–) *Joe Dirt* 2001; *Broken Lizard's Club Dread* 2004; *White Chicks* 2004
Daniel, Roger (1924–) *Boy Slaves* 1938; *King of the Turf* 1939
Daniell, Isa *Camorra* 1985; *Macaroni* 1985
Daniell, Henry (1894–1963) *Camille* 1937; *Madame X* 1937; *Holiday* 1938; *We Are Not Alone* 1939; *The Great Dictator* 1940; *The Philadelphia Story* 1940; *The Sea Hawk* 1940; *Sherlock Holmes and the Voice of Terror* 1942; *Jane Eyre* 1943; *Sherlock Holmes in Washington* 1943; *The Suspect* 1944; *The Body Snatcher* 1945; *The Woman in Green* 1945; *The Bandit of Sherwood Forest* 1946; *The Exile* 1947; *Song of Love* 1947; *Siren of Atlantis* 1948; *Lust for Life* 1956; *Les Girls* 1957; *Mister Cory* 1957; *Witness for the Prosecution* 1957; *From the Earth to the Moon* 1958; *The Comancheros* 1961; *Madison Avenue* 1962
Danielle, Suzanne (1957–) *Carry On Emmannuelle* 1978; *Long Shot* 1978; *The Boys in Blue* 1983
Daniels, Alex *Cyborg* 1989; *Star Kid* 1997
Daniels, Anthony (1946–) *Star Wars Episode IV: a New Hope* 1977; *The Lord of the Rings* 1978; *Star Wars Episode V: the Empire Strikes Back* 1980; *Star Wars Episode VI: Return of the Jedi* 1983; *I Bought a Vampire Motorcycle* 1989; *Star Wars Episode I: the Phantom Menace* 1999; *Star Wars Episode II: Attack of the Clones* 2002; *Star Wars Episode III: Revenge of the Sith* 2005
Daniels, Bebe (1901–1971) *Male and Female* 1919; *Why Change Your Wife?* 1920; *Rio Rita* 1929; *Dangerous Female* 1931; *Counsellor-at-Law* 1933; *42nd Street* 1933; *Hi, Gang!* 1941; *Life with the Lyons* 1953; *The Lyons in Paris* 1955
Daniels, Ben (1964–) *Beautiful Thing* 1995; *I Want You* 1998; *Madeline* 1998; *Passion in the Desert* 1998; *Fanny & Elvis* 1999; *Britannic* 2000; *Conspiracy* 2001; *Married/Unmarried* 2001; *Fogbound* 2002
Daniels, Erin *House of 1000 Corpses* 2001; *One Hour Photo* 2001
Daniels Jr, Henry H *Meet Me in St Louis* 1944; *Bewitched* 1945
Daniels, Jeff (1955–) *Terms of Endearment* 1983; *Marie: a True Story* 1985; *The Purple Rose of Cairo* 1985; *Heartburn* 1986; *Something Wild* 1986; *The House on Carroll Street* 1987; *Checking Out* 1988; *Sweet Hearts Dance* 1988; *Arachnophobia* 1990; *Love Hurts* 1990; *Welcome Home, Roxy Carmichael* 1990; *The Butcher's Wife* 1991; *Paydirt* 1992; *Gettysburg* 1993; *Dumb and Dumber* 1994; *Speed* 1994; *Fly Away Home* 1996; *101 Dalmatians* 1996; *2 Days in the Valley* 1996; *Trial and Error* 1997; *Pleasantville* 1998; *My Favorite Martian* 1999; *The Crossing* 2000; *Blood Work* 2002; *Gods and Generals* 2002; *The Hours* 2002; *Because of Winn-Dixie* 2004; *Imaginary Heroes* 2004
Daniels, Mark (1916–1990) *The Vanishing Virginian* 1941; *Candyman* 1992
Daniels, Phil (1958–) *The Class of Miss MacMichael* 1978; *Quadrophenia* 1979; *Scum* 1979; *Breaking Glass* 1980; *Number One* 1984; *The Bride* 1985; *Bad Behaviour* 1992; *Still Crazy* 1998; *Chicken Run* 2000; *Goodbye Charlie Bright* 2000; *Nasty Neighbours* 2000
Daniels, William (1927–) *Ladybug, Ladybug* 1963; *A Thousand Clowns* 1965; *The Graduate* 1967; *Two for the Road* 1967; *Marlowe* 1969; *The Parallax View* 1974; *Black Sunday* 1976; *Oh, God!* 1977; *The One and Only* 1978; *Sunburn* 1979; *The Blue Lagoon* 1980; *All Night Long* 1981; *Blind Date* 1987; *Her Alibi* 1989
Danielson, Lynn *Out of the Dark* 1988; *Nickel & Dime* 1991
Daniely, Lisa (1930–) *Hindle Wakes* 1952; *Tiger by the Tail* 1955; *The Man in the Road* 1957; *Souvenir* 1987
Dankan (1959–) *Ikinai* 1998; *Eyes of the Spider* 1999
Danker, Eli *The Little Drummer Girl* 1984; *Impulse* 1990; *Upworld* 1992
Danner, Blythe (1944–) *To Kill a Clown* 1972; *Lovin' Molly* 1974; *Hearts of the West* 1975; *Futureworld* 1976; *The Great Santini* 1979; *Man, Woman and Child* 1983; *Guilty Conscience* 1985; *Brighton Beach Memoirs* 1986; *Another Woman* 1988; *Alice* 1990; *Mr and Mrs Bridge* 1990; *The Prince of Tides* 1991; *Husbands and Wives* 1992; *Leave of Absence* 1994; *Homage* 1995; *Napoleon* 1995; *To Wong Foo, Thanks for Everything, Julie Newmar* 1995; *The Myth of Fingerprints* 1996; *Mad City* 1997; *Forces of Nature* 1998; *No Looking Back* 1998; *The Proposition* 1998; *The Love Letter* 1999; *The Invisible Circus* 2000; *Meet the Parents* 2000; *Sylvia* 2003; *Meet the Fockers* 2004
Danning, Sybil (1952–) *Death in the Sun* 1975; *God's Gun* 1977; *Battle beyond the Stars* 1980; *Cuba Crossing* 1980; *The Salamander* 1981; *Chained Heat* 1983; *Hercules* 1983; *Howling II: Your Sister Is a Werewolf* 1984; *They're Playing With Fire* 1984; *Reform School Girls* 1986; *Warrior Queen* 1986; *Amazon Women on the Moon* 1987
Dano, Paul *aka* **Dano, Paul Franklin** (1984–) *LIE* 2001; *The Girl Next Door* 2004; *Taking Lives* 2004
Dano, Royal (1922–1994) *Undercover Girl* 1950; *The Red Badge of Courage* 1951; *The Trouble with Harry* 1954; *Tension at Table Rock* 1956; *Crime of Passion* 1957; *Man in the Shadow* 1957; *Trooper Hook* 1957; *Man of the West* 1958; *Saddle the Wind* 1958; *Face of Fire* 1959; *Never Steal Anything Small* 1959; *Posse from Hell* 1961; *Gunpoint* 1966; *Backtrack* 1969; *Cahill, United States Marshal* 1973; *Electra Glide in Blue* 1973; *Big Bad Mama* 1974; *The Wild Party* 1975; *Something Wicked This Way Comes* 1983; *Teachers* 1984; *House II: the Second Story* 1987; *Killer Klowns from Outer Space* 1988; *Once upon a Texas Train* 1988
Danon, Géraldine (1968–) *Erreur de jeunesse* 1989; *The Old Lady Who Walked in the Sea* 1991
Danova, Cesare (1926–1992) *Crossed Swords* 1954; *The Man Who Understood Women* 1959; *Tarzan, the Ape Man* 1959; *Tender Is the Night* 1961; *Cleopatra* 1963; *Gidget Goes to Rome* 1963; *Viva Las Vegas* 1964; *Boy, Did I Get a Wrong Number* 1966; *Chamber of Horrors* 1966; *Che!* 1969; *Mean Streets* 1973; *Scorchy* 1976; *Tentacles* 1977
Danson, Ted (1947–) *The Onion Field* 1979; *Body Heat* 1981; *Creepshow* 1982; *Little Treasure* 1985; *A Fine Mess* 1986; *Just between Friends* 1986; *Three Men and a Baby* 1987; *Cousins* 1989; *Dad* 1989; *Three Men and a Little Lady* 1990; *Made in America* 1993; *Getting Even with Dad* 1994; *Loch Ness* 1994; *Pontiac Moon* 1994; *Homegrown* 1998; *Jerry and Tom* 1998; *Saving Private Ryan* 1998; *Mumford* 1999
Dante, Joe (1946–) *Cannonball* 1976; *Sleepwalkers* 1992
Dante, Michael (1931–) *Westbound* 1959; *Seven Thieves* 1960; *Apache Rifles* 1964; *The Naked Kiss* 1964; *Arizona Raiders* 1965; *Willard* 1971; *Winterhawk* 1975; *Beyond Evil* 1980; *Cage* 1989
Dantine, Helmut (1917–1982) *Edge of Darkness* 1943; *Northern Pursuit* 1943; *Passage to Marseille* 1944; *Hotel Berlin* 1945; *Stranger from Venus* 1954; *War and Peace* 1956; *Tempest* 1959; *Bring Me the Head of Alfredo Garcia* 1974
Danton, Ray (1931–1992) *Chief Crazy Horse* 1955; *I'll Cry Tomorrow* 1955; *The Looters* 1955; *The Spoilers* 1955; *The Night Runner* 1957; *Onionhead* 1958; *Too Much, Too Soon* 1958; *The Beat Generation* 1959; *The Big Operator* 1959; *Yellowstone Kelly* 1959; *Ice Palace* 1960; *The Rise and Fall of Legs Diamond* 1960; *A Fever in the Blood* 1961; *The George Raft Story* 1961; *A Majority of One* 1961; *Sandokan against the Leopard of Sarawak* 1964; *Sandokan Fights Back* 1964
Danza, Tony (1951–) *Going Ape!* 1981; *She's Out of Control* 1989; *Angels in the Outfield* 1994; *Deadly Whispers* 1995; *illtown*

1996; *Love to Kill* 1997; *12 Angry Men* 1997
Danziger, Maia *The Kirlian Witness* 1978; *The Magician of Lublin* 1979; *Dr Heckyl & Mr Hype* 1980
Dapkunaite, Ingeborga (1963–) *Katia Ismailova* 1994; *Burnt by the Sun* 1995; *Letters from the East* 1995; *War* 2002; *Kiss of Life* 2003
D'Arbanville, Patti *aka* **D'Arbanville-Quinn, Patti** (1951–) *Flesh* 1968; *Big Wednesday* 1978; *The Main Event* 1979; *Time after Time* 1979; *The Fifth Floor* 1980; *Modern Problems* 1981; *The Boys Next Door* 1985; *Real Genius* 1985; *Call Me* 1988; *Fresh Horses* 1988; *Wired* 1989; *The Fan* 1996; *Personal Velocity* 2001
Darbo, Patrika (1948–) *Daddy's Dyin'... Who's Got the Will?* 1990; *Leaving Normal* 1992; *The Vagrant* 1992; *Fast Money* 1995
Darby, Kim (1947–) *Generation* 1969; *True Grit* 1969; *The Strawberry Statement* 1970; *The Grissom Gang* 1971; *The One and Only* 1978; *Better Off Dead* 1985; *Halloween 6: the Curse of Michael Myers* 1995
Darc, Mireille (1938–) *Weekend* 1967; *Monte Carlo or Bust* 1969; *There Was Once a Cop* 1969; *The Tall Blond Man with One Black Shoe* 1972; *Man in the Trunk* 1973; *Someone Is Bleeding* 1974; *The Pink Telephone* 1975; *To Kill a Rat* 1977
Darcel, Denise (1925–) *Tarzan and the Slave Girl* 1950; *Westward the Women* 1951; *Young Man with Ideas* 1952; *Dangerous When Wet* 1953; *Vera Cruz* 1954
Darcey, Janine (1917–1993) *French without Tears* 1939; *Rififi* 1955
D'Arcy, Alex *aka* **D'Arcy, Alexandre** *aka* **D'Arcy, Alexander** (1908–1996) *A Nous la Liberté* 1931; *The Awful Truth* 1937; *Topper Takes a Trip* 1939; *How to Marry a Millionaire* 1953; *Man on a Tightrope* 1953; *Fanny Hill: Memoirs of a Woman of Pleasure* 1964; *Blood of Dracula's Castle* 1967; *Dead Pigeon on Beethoven Street* 1972
D'Arcy, James (1975–) *The Trench* 1999; *Revelation* 2001; *Dot the i* 2003; *Master and Commander: the Far Side of the World* 2003; *Exorcist: the Beginning* 2004
D'Arcy, Roy (1894–1969) *The Merry Widow* 1925; *La Bohème* 1926; *The Temptress* 1926; *The Last Warning* 1928; *The Black Watch* 1929
Darden, Severn (1929–1995) *Frank's Greatest Adventure* 1967; *The President's Analyst* 1967; *The Mad Room* 1969; *Model Shop* 1969; *The Hired Hand* 1971; *Conquest of the Planet of the Apes* 1972; *Who Fears the Devil?* 1972; *Battle for the Planet of the Apes* 1973; *Jackson County Jail* 1976; *Wanda Nevada* 1979; *In God We Trust* 1980; *Saturday the 14th* 1981; *The Telephone* 1988
Dare, John *Girl on Approval* 1962; *The Impersonator* 1962
Darel, Dominique (1950–1978) *The Big Showdown* 1972; *Blood for Dracula* 1974
Darel, Florence (1968–) *A Tale of Springtime* 1989; *Fausto* 1992
Darien, Frank (1876–1955) *Bad Girl* 1931; *The Outlaw* 1943
Darin, Bobby *aka* **Darin, Robert** (1936–1973) *Pepe* 1960; *Come September* 1961; *Too Late Blues* 1961; *Hell Is for Heroes* 1962; *If a Man Answers* 1962; *Pressure Point* 1962; *State Fair* 1962; *Captain Newman, MD* 1963; *That Funny Feeling* 1965; *Gunfight in Abilene* 1967; *Stranger in the House* 1967; *The Happy Ending* 1969; *Happy Mother's Day... Love, George* 1973
Darin, Ricardo (1957–) *Nine Queens* 2000; *Son of the Bride* 2001
Dark, Christopher *aka* **Dark, Chris** (1920–1971) *Suddenly* 1954; *World without End* 1955; *Baby Face Nelson* 1957; *The Halliday Brand* 1957; *Scandalous John* 1971
Darling, Candy (1946–1974) *Flesh* 1968; *Women in Revolt* 1971; *Silent Night, Bloody Night* 1972
Darling, Joan (1935–) *The Troublemaker* 1964; *Frank's Greatest Adventure* 1967
Darmon, Gérard (1948–) *Les Princes* 1982; *Betty Blue* 1986; *Day of Atonement* 1992; *The Tit and the Moon* 1994; *Asterix & Obelix: Mission Cleopatra* 2001; *The Good Thief* 2002
Darnell, Linda (1921–1965) *Brigham Young* 1940; *Chad Hanna* 1940; *The Mark of Zorro* 1940; *Star Dust* 1940; *Blood and Sand* 1941; *The Song of Bernadette* 1943; *Buffalo Bill* 1944; *It Happened Tomorrow* 1944; *Summer Storm* 1944; *Sweet and Lowdown* 1944; *Fallen Angel* 1945; *The Great John L* 1945; *Hangover Square* 1945; *Anna and the King of Siam* 1946; *Centennial Summer* 1946; *My Darling Clementine* 1946; *Forever Amber* 1947; *Unfaithfully Yours* 1948; *Everybody Does It* 1949; *A Letter to Three Wives* 1949; *Slattery's Hurricane* 1949; *No Way Out* 1950; *The 13th Letter* 1950; *Two Flags West* 1950; *The Lady Pays Off* 1951; *Blackbeard the Pirate* 1952; *Island of Desire* 1952; *Second Chance* 1953; *This Is My Love* 1954; *Dakota Incident* 1956; *Zero Hour!* 1957; *Black Spurs* 1965
Darren, James (1936–) *The Brothers Rico* 1957; *Operation Mad Ball* 1957; *Gunman's Walk* 1958; *The Gene Krupa Story* 1959; *Gidget* 1959; *All the Young Men* 1960; *Let No Man Write My Epitaph* 1960; *Gidget Goes Hawaiian* 1961; *The Guns of Navarone* 1961; *Diamond Head* 1962; *Gidget Goes to Rome* 1963; *For Those Who Think Young* 1964
Darrieux, Danielle (1917–) *Club de Femmes* 1936; *Mayerling* 1936; *The Rage of Paris* 1938; *La Ronde* 1950; *Le Plaisir* 1951; *Rich, Young and Pretty* 1951; *5 Fingers* 1952; *Madame de...* 1953; *Le Rouge et le Noir* 1954; *Napoléon* 1955; *Alexander the Great* 1956; *The Greengage Summer* 1961; *Bluebeard* 1962; *The Young Girls of Rochefort* 1967; *The Scene of the Crime* 1986; *8 Women* 2001
Darro, Frankie (1917–1976) *The Mad Genius* 1931; *The Mayor of Hell* 1933; *No Greater Glory* 1934
Darroussin, Jean-Pierre (1953–) *L'Eau Froide* 1994; *Un Air de Famille* 1996; *A la Place du Coeur* 1998; *La Bûche* 1999; *A l'Attaque!* 2000; *La Ville Est Tranquille* 2000; *Red Lights* 2003; *A Very Long Engagement* 2004
Darrow, Barbara (1931–) *The Mountain* 1956; *Queen of Outer Space* 1958
Darrow, Henry (1933–) *Badge 373* 1973; *Where's Willie?* 1977; *Walk Proud* 1979; *Losin' It* 1983; *Blue Heat* 1990
Darrow, John (1907–1980) *The Racket* 1928; *Hell's Angels* 1930
Darrow, Tony *GoodFellas* 1990; *Me and the Mob* 1992; *Small Time Crooks* 2000
Darvas, Lili (1906–1974) *Meet Me in Las Vegas* 1956; *Love* 1971
Darvi, Bella (1928–1971) *Hell and High Water* 1954; *The Racers* 1955
Darwell, Jane (1879–1967) *Tom Sawyer* 1930; *Bright Eyes* 1934; *Change of Heart* 1934; *The White Parade* 1934; *Curly Top* 1935; *Life Begins at 40* 1935; *Captain January* 1936; *The Country Doctor* 1936; *Craig's Wife* 1936; *Poor Little Rich Girl* 1936; *White Fang* 1936; *Love Is News* 1937; *Slave Ship* 1937; *Wife, Doctor and Nurse* 1937; *Little Miss Broadway* 1938; *Jesse James* 1939; *Brigham Young* 1940; *Chad Hanna* 1940; *The Grapes of Wrath* 1940; *Miracle on Main Street* 1940; *Daniel and the Devil* 1941; *All through the Night* 1942; *The Battle of Midway* 1942; *The Ox-Bow Incident* 1943; *Tender Comrade* 1943; *Music in Manhattan* 1944; *I Live in Grosvenor Square* 1945; *Three Godfathers* 1948; *Red Canyon* 1949; *Caged* 1950; *The Daughter of Rosie O'Grady* 1950; *Wagonmaster* 1950; *The Lemon Drop Kid* 1951; *Affair with a Stranger* 1953; *The Bigamist* 1953; *Mary Poppins* 1964
Dary, René (1905–1974) *Honour among Thieves* 1954; *Goto, l'Ile d'Amour* 1968
Das, Nandita (1969–) *Fire* 1996; *Earth* 1998; *Aks* 2001; *Supari* 2003
Dash, Stacey (1966–) *Enemy Territory* 1987; *Moving* 1988; *Mo' Money* 1992; *Renaissance Man* 1994; *Clueless* 1995
Dassin, Jules *aka* **Vita, Perlo** (1911–) *Rififi* 1955; *Never on Sunday* 1960
Dasté, Jean (1904–1994) *Boudu, Saved from Drowning* 1932; *Zéro de Conduite* 1933; *L'Atalante* 1934; *La Vie Est à Nous* 1936; *La Grande Illusion* 1937; *La Guerre Est Finie* 1966; *The Green Room* 1978; *Noce Blanche* 1989
Datcher, Alex *Passenger 57* 1992; *The Expert* 1994
Dattilo, Kristin (1970–) *Pyrates* 1991; *Some Girls* 1998
Dauphin, Claude (1903–1978) *English without Tears* 1944; *Le Plaisir* 1951; *April in Paris* 1952; *Casque d'Or* 1952; *Innocents in Paris* 1953; *Little Boy Lost* 1953; *Phantom of the Rue Morgue* 1954; *The Bad Liaisons* 1955; *The Quiet American* 1958; *The Full Treatment* 1961; *Tiara Tahiti* 1962; *Lady L* 1965; *Barbarella* 1967; *Two for the Road* 1967; *Hard Contract* 1969; *The Madwoman of Chaillot* 1969; *Rosebud* 1975; *Madame Rosa* 1977; *Les Misérables* 1978
Davalos, Dominique *Howard, a New Breed of Hero* 1986; *Salvation! Have You Said Your Prayers Today?* 1987
Davalos, Elyssa *The Apple Dumpling Gang Rides Again* 1979; *Herbie Goes Bananas* 1980
Davalos, Richard (1935–) *East of Eden* 1955; *The Sea Chase* 1955; *The Cabinet of Caligari* 1962; *Hot Stuff* 1979
Davenport, A Bromley (1867–1946) *When London Sleeps* 1932; *A Shot in the Dark* 1933
Davenport, Harry (1866–1949) *My Sin* 1931; *The Cowboy and the Lady* 1938; *The Hunchback of Notre Dame* 1939; *Made for Each Other* 1939; *All This, and Heaven Too* 1940; *Lucky Partners* 1940; *Too Many Husbands* 1940; *The Bride Came COD* 1941; *One Foot in Heaven* 1941; *That Uncertain Feeling* 1941; *Ten Gentlemen from West Point* 1942; *The Amazing Mrs Holliday* 1943; *Government Girl* 1943; *Princess O'Rourke* 1943; *Jack London* 1944; *Kismet* 1944; *Meet Me in St Louis* 1944; *The Thin Man Goes Home* 1944; *Pardon My Past* 1945; *This Love of Ours* 1945; *Claudia and David* 1946; *Courage of Lassie* 1946; *Lady Luck* 1946; *The Bachelor and the Bobby-Soxer* 1947; *For the Love of Mary* 1948; *That Lady in Ermine* 1948; *Three Daring Daughters* 1948; *Down to the Sea in Ships* 1949; *The Forsyte Saga* 1949; *Tell It to the Judge* 1949
Davenport, Jack (1973–) *Talos the Mummy* 1997; *The Wisdom of Crocodiles* 1998; *The Talented Mr Ripley* 1999; *The Bunker* 2001; *Pirates of the Caribbean: the Curse of the Black Pearl* 2003; *The Wedding Date* 2004
Davenport, Nigel (1928–) *Lunch Hour* 1962; *In the Cool of the Day* 1963; *Ladies Who Do* 1963; *The Third Secret* 1964; *Sands of the Kalahari* 1965; *A Man for All Seasons* 1966; *Sebastian* 1968; *Play Dirty* 1969; *The Royal Hunt of the Sun* 1969; *Sinful Davey* 1969; *The Virgin Soldiers* 1969; *The Mind of Mr Soames* 1970; *No Blade of Grass* 1970; *The Last Valley* 1971; *Mary, Queen of Scots* 1971; *Villain* 1971; *Living Free* 1972; *Phase IV* 1973; *Dracula* 1974; *The Island of Dr Moreau* 1977; *Stand Up Virgin Soldiers* 1977; *Zulu Dawn* 1979; *Chariots of Fire* 1981; *Nighthawks* 1981; *Greystoke: the Legend of Tarzan, Lord of the Apes* 1984; *Caravaggio* 1986; *Without a Clue* 1988
Davey, Belinda *Death of a Soldier* 1985; *Proof* 1991
Davi, Robert (1953–) *The Goonies* 1985; *Raw Deal* 1986; *Wild Thing* 1987; *Action Jackson* 1988; *Licence to Kill* 1989; *Maniac Cop 2* 1990; *Peacemaker* 1990; *The Taking of Beverly Hills* 1991; *Christopher Columbus: the Discovery* 1992; *Wild Orchid 2: Two Shades of Blue* 1992; *Quick* 1993; *Son of the Pink Panther* 1993; *Cops and Robbersons* 1994; *Showgirls* 1995; *The Hot Chick* 2002
David, Angel *Mixed Blood* 1984; *The Crow* 1994; *The Substitute 2: School's Out* 1997; *Two Girls and a Guy* 1997
David, Clifford *The Last Mile* 1959; *The Party's Over* 1965; *Resurrection* 1980
David, Eleanor (1956–) *Pink Floyd – The Wall* 1982; *The Scarlet Pimpernel* 1982; *Comfort and Joy* 1984; *Sylvia* 1984; *84 Charing Cross Road* 1986; *Ladder of Swords* 1988; *The Wolves of Willoughby Chase* 1988; *London Kills Me* 1991
David, Joanna (1947–) *Secret Friends* 1991; *Cotton Mary* 1999
David, Keith (1954–) *The Thing* 1982; *Platoon* 1986; *Bird* 1988; *Saigon* 1988; *They Live* 1988; *Always* 1989; *Marked for Death* 1990; *Men at Work* 1990; *Article 99* 1992; *Final Analysis* 1992; *The Last Outlaw* 1993; *The Puppet Masters* 1994; *Clockers* 1995; *Dead Presidents* 1995; *Johns* 1995; *Executive Target* 1996; *Flipping* 1996; *Volcano* 1997; *Armageddon* 1998; *Pitch Black* 1999; *Requiem for a Dream* 2000; *Where the Heart Is* 2000; *Final Fantasy: the Spirits Within* 2001; *Novocaine* 2001; *Agent Cody Banks* 2003; *Head of State* 2003; *Hollywood Homicide* 2003; *The Chronicles of Riddick* 2004; *Mr & Mrs Smith* 2005
David, Mario (1930–1996) *Les Bonnes Femmes* 1960; *L'Enfer* 1994
David, Michael *Let's Make Love* 1960; *The Fiercest Heart* 1961; *Anita* 1973
David, Thayer (1927–1978) *A Time to Love and a Time to Die* 1958; *Wolf Larsen* 1958; *Journey to the Center of the Earth* 1959; *The Story of Ruth* 1960; *House of Dark Shadows* 1970; *Night of Dark Shadows* 1971; *Savages* 1972; *Save the Tiger* 1973; *The Eiger Sanction* 1975; *Peeper* 1975; *The Duchess and the Dirtwater Fox* 1976; *Rocky* 1976; *Spider-Man* 1977
Davidovich, Lolita (1961–) *Blaze* 1989; *The Inner Circle* 1991; *The Object of Beauty* 1991; *Leap of Faith* 1992; *Raising Cain* 1992; *Boiling Point* 1993; *Younger and Younger* 1993; *Cobb* 1994; *Intersection* 1994; *For Better or Worse* 1995; *Indictment: the McMartin Trial* 1995; *Jungle 2 Jungle* 1997; *Gods and Monsters* 1998; *Four Days* 1999; *Mystery, Alaska* 1999; *Play It to the Bone* 2000; *Dark Blue* 2002; *Hollywood Homicide* 2003
Davidson, Eileen (1959–) *House of Evil* 1983; *Easy Wheels* 1989; *Eternity* 1990
Davidson, Holly *Food of Love* 1997; *Final Cut* 1998
Davidson, Jack *Shock Waves* 1975; *Baby It's You* 1983; *The Autumn Heart* 1998
Davidson, Jaye (1968–) *The Crying Game* 1992; *Stargate* 1994
Davidson, John (1886–1968) *The Happiest Millionaire* 1967; *The One and Only, Genuine, Original Family Band* 1968; *Airport '79: the Concorde* 1979; *The Squeeze* 1987
Davidson, Tommy (1965–) *Ace Ventura: When Nature Calls* 1995; *Booty Call* 1997; *Woo* 1998; *Bamboozled* 2000; *Santa Who?* 2000; *Juwanna Mann* 2002
Davidson, William B (1888–1947) *The Singing Kid* 1936; *Man Made Monster* 1941
Davidtz, Embeth (1966–) *Army of Darkness* 1993; *Schindler's List* 1993; *Murder in the First* 1994; *Feast of July* 1995; *Matilda* 1996; *The Gingerbread Man* 1997; *Fallen* 1998; *Last Rites* 1998; *Simon Magus* 1998; *Bicentennial Man* 1999; *Mansfield Park* 1999; *Bridget Jones's Diary* 2001; *The Hole* 2001; *Thir13en Ghosts* 2001; *The Emperor's Club* 2002
Davies, Betty Ann (1910–1955) *It Always Rains on Sunday* 1947; *The History of Mr Polly* 1948; *The Passionate Friends* 1948; *Outcast of the Islands* 1951; *Cosh Boy* 1952; *Meet Me Tonight* 1952; *Grand National Night* 1953; *The Belles of St Trinian's* 1954
Davies, Brian *Convoy* 1978; *American Gigolo* 1980; *Masquerade* 1988
Davies, Jeremy (1969–) *Nell* 1994; *Spanking the Monkey* 1994; *Going All the Way* 1997; *A Secret Sin* 1997; *Saving Private Ryan* 1998; *Up at the Villa* 1998; *The Million Dollar Hotel* 1999; *Ravenous* 1999; *Secretary* 2001; *29 Palms* 2002; *Dogville* 2003; *Solaris* 2003
Davies, John Howard (1939–) *Oliver Twist* 1948; *The Rocking Horse Winner* 1949; *Tom Brown's Schooldays* 1951
Davies, Marion (1897–1961) *The Patsy* 1928; *Show People* 1928; *Hollywood Revue* 1929; *The Bachelor Father* 1931; *Blondie of the Follies* 1932; *Polly of the Circus* 1932; *Going Hollywood* 1933; *Peg o' My Heart* 1933; *Operator 13* 1934; *Page Miss Glory* 1935; *Cain and Mabel* 1936
Davies, Richard (1915–1994) *Private Buckaroo* 1942; *The Falcon in Danger* 1943; *Please Sir!* 1971; *Blue Blood* 1973
Davies, Rudi *The Lonely Passion of Judith Hearne* 1987; *Resurrected* 1989; *Frankie Starlight* 1995
Davies, Rupert (1916–1976) *The Traitor* 1957; *Devil's Bait* 1959; *The Criminal* 1960; *The Uncle* 1964; *The Spy Who Came in from the Cold* 1965; *Five Golden Dragons* 1967; *Submarine X-1* 1967; *Curse of the Crimson Altar* 1968; *Dracula Has Risen from the Grave* 1968; *Witchfinder General* 1968; *The Firechasers* 1970; *The Night Visitor* 1970; *Zeppelin* 1971; *Frightmare* 1974
Davies, Stephen *Inserts* 1975; *Hanoi Hilton* 1987; *Dillinger and Capone* 1995
Davies, Windsor (1930–) *Adolf Hitler – My Part in His Downfall* 1972; *Carry On Behind* 1975; *Carry On England* 1976; *Confessions of a Driving Instructor* 1976; *Not Now, Comrade* 1976; *Old Scores* 1991
Davion, Alexander *aka* **Davion, Alex** (1929–) *Paranoiac* 1963; *The Plague of the Zombies* 1965; *Valley of the Dolls* 1967; *Incense for the Damned* 1970
Davis, Altovise *Pipe Dreams* 1976; *Kingdom of the Spiders* 1977
Davis, Bette (1908–1989) *Bad Sister* 1931; *Waterloo Bridge* 1931; *Cabin in the Cotton* 1932; *Hell's House* 1932; *The Man Who Played God* 1932; *The Rich Are Always with Us* 1932; *So Big* 1932; *Three on a Match* 1932; *Bureau of Missing Persons* 1933; *Ex-Lady* 1933; *20,000 Years in Sing Sing* 1933; *Fashions of 1934* 1934; *Fog over Frisco* 1934; *Jimmy the Gent* 1934; *Of Human Bondage* 1934; *Bordertown* 1935; *Dangerous*

1935; *Front Page Woman* 1935; *The Girl from 10th Avenue* 1935; *Special Agent* 1935; *The Petrified Forest* 1936; *Satan Met a Lady* 1936; *It's Love I'm After* 1937; *Kid Galahad* 1937; *Marked Woman* 1937; *That Certain Woman* 1937; *Jezebel* 1938; *The Sisters* 1938; *Dark Victory* 1939; *Juarez* 1939; *The Old Maid* 1939; *The Private Lives of Elizabeth and Essex* 1939; *All This, and Heaven Too* 1940; *The Letter* 1940; *The Bride Came COD* 1941; *The Great Lie* 1941; *The Little Foxes* 1941; *The Man Who Came to Dinner* 1941; *In This Our Life* 1942; *Now, Voyager* 1942; *Old Acquaintance* 1943; *Watch on the Rhine* 1943; *Hollywood Canteen* 1944; *Mr Skeffington* 1944; *The Corn Is Green* 1945; *Deception* 1946; *A Stolen Life* 1946; *June Bride* 1948; *Winter Meeting* 1948; *Beyond the Forest* 1949; *All about Eve* 1950; *Another Man's Poison* 1951; *Payment on Demand* 1951; *Phone Call from a Stranger* 1952; *The Star* 1953; *The Virgin Queen* 1955; *The Catered Affair* 1956; *Storm Center* 1956; *John Paul Jones* 1959; *The Scapegoat* 1959; *Pocketful of Miracles* 1961; *What Ever Happened to Baby Jane?* 1962; *The Empty Canvas* 1963; *Dead Ringer* 1964; *Hush... Hush, Sweet Charlotte* 1964; *Where Love Has Gone* 1964; *The Nanny* 1965; *The Anniversary* 1968; *Connecting Rooms* 1969; *Bunny O'Hare* 1971; *Madame Sin* 1972; *Burnt Offerings* 1976; *The Disappearance of Aimee* 1976; *Death on the Nile* 1978; *Return from Witch Mountain* 1978; *A Piano for Mrs Cimino* 1982; *The Watcher in the Woods* 1982; *Agatha Christie's Murder with Mirrors* 1985; *The Whales of August* 1987; *Wicked Stepmother* 1989

Davis, Brad (1949–1991) *Midnight Express* 1978; *A Small Circle of Friends* 1980; *Chariots of Fire* 1981; *Querelle* 1982; *Cold Steel* 1987; *Heart* 1987; *Rosalie Goes Shopping* 1989; *Hangfire* 1991

Davis, Carole (1953–) *Mannequin* 1987; *The Princess Academy* 1987; *The Shrimp on the Barbie* 1990

Davis, Charles (1925–1990) *The Man from Planet X* 1951; *The Desert Rats* 1953; *Five Steps to Danger* 1957

Davis, Clifton (1945–) *Lost in the Stars* 1974; *Scott Joplin* 1977

Davis, Daniel (1945–) *K-9* 1989; *Havana* 1990

Davis, Don S *aka* **Davis, Don** (1942–) *Omen IV: the Awakening* 1991; *Avalanche* 1994; *Max* 1994

Davis, Essie *The Custodian* 1993; *Dad and Dave: on Our Selection* 1995; *River Street* 1996; *Blackrock* 1997; *The Sound of One Hand Clapping* 1998; *Code 46* 2003; *Girl with a Pearl Earring* 2003

Davis, Gail (1925–1997) *The Far Frontier* 1949; *Valley of Fire* 1951; *Blue Canadian Rockies* 1952; *On Top of Old Smoky* 1953; *Winning of the West* 1953; *Alias Jesse James* 1959; *Race for Your Life, Charlie Brown* 1977

Davis, Geena (1957–) *Tootsie* 1982; *Fletch* 1985; *Transylvania 6-5000* 1985; *The Fly* 1986; *The Accidental Tourist* 1988; *Beetle Juice* 1988; *Earth Girls Are Easy* 1988; *Quick Change* 1990; *Thelma & Louise* 1991; *Accidental Hero* 1992; *A League of Their Own* 1992; *Angie* 1994; *Speechless* 1994; *CutThroat Island* 1995; *The Long Kiss Goodnight* 1996; *Stuart Little* 1999; *Stuart Little 2* 2002

Davis, Gene *aka* **Davis, Eugene M** *Night Games* 1979; *10 to Midnight* 1983; *Fear X* 2002

Davis, George (1889–1965) *The Circus* 1928; *The Kiss* 1929; *I Met Him in Paris* 1937

Davis, Harry (1907–1993) *America, America* 1963; *One of Our Spies Is Missing* 1966; *Rollercoaster* 1977

Davis, Hope (1964–) *Guy* 1996; *Mr Wrong* 1996; *The Myth of Fingerprints* 1996; *Arlington Road* 1998; *The Daytrippers* 1998; *The Impostors* 1998; *Next Stop Wonderland* 1998; *Mumford* 1999; *Hearts in Atlantis* 2001; *About Schmidt* 2002; *The Secret Lives of Dentists* 2002; *American Splendor* 2003; *Duma* 2005

Davis, Jim *aka* **Davis, James** (1915–1981) *Winter Meeting* 1948; *The Cariboo Trail* 1950; *Cavalry Scout* 1951; *The Big Sky* 1952; *Ride the Man Down* 1952; *Rose of Cimarron* 1952; *The Outcast* 1954; *Timberjack* 1955; *Women without Men* 1956; *The Restless Breed* 1957; *Monster from Green Hell* 1958; *Alias Jesse James* 1959; *Dracula vs Frankenstein* 1970; *Monte Walsh* 1970; *Bad Company* 1972; *Comes a Horseman* 1978; *The Day Time Ended* 1980

Davis, Joan (1907–1961) *Life Begins in College* 1937; *On the Avenue* 1937; *Thin Ice* 1937; *Hold That Co-Ed* 1938; *Josette* 1938; *Just around the Corner* 1938; *My Lucky Star* 1938; *Sally, Irene and Mary* 1938; *Hold That Ghost* 1941; *Sun Valley Serenade* 1941; *Show Business* 1944; *George White's Scandals* 1945; *If You Knew Susie* 1948; *Love That Brute* 1950

Davis, Johnnie *aka* **Davis, Johnnie "Scat"** (1910–1983) *Hollywood Hotel* 1937; *Garden of the Moon* 1938; *Knickerbocker Holiday* 1944

Davis, Judy (1955–) *My Brilliant Career* 1979; *Heatwave* 1981; *The Winter of Our Dreams* 1981; *Who Dares Wins* 1982; *A Passage to India* 1984; *Kangaroo* 1986; *High Tide* 1987; *Georgia* 1988; *Barton Fink* 1991; *Impromptu* 1991; *Naked Lunch* 1991; *One against the Wind* 1991; *Where Angels Fear to Tread* 1991; *Husbands and Wives* 1992; *On My Own* 1992; *Hostile Hostages* 1994; *The New Age* 1994; *Absolute Power* 1996; *Blood and Wine* 1996; *Children of the Revolution* 1996; *Deconstructing Harry* 1997; *Celebrity* 1998; *A Cooler Climate* 1999; *The Man Who Sued God* 2001; *Swimming Upstream* 2003

Davis, Julia (1966–) *Wilbur (Wants to Kill Himself)* 2002; *Sex Lives of the Potato Men* 2003

Davis, Kristin (1965–) *Doom Asylum* 1987; *Atomic Train* 1999; *Take Me Home: the John Denver Story* 2000; *The Adventures of Sharkboy and Lavagirl in 3-D* 2005

Davis, Lucy (1973–) *Sex Lives of the Potato Men* 2003; *Shaun of the Dead* 2004

Davis, Mac (1942–) *North Dallas Forty* 1979; *The Sting II* 1983; *Possums* 1998; *Jackpot* 2001

Davis, Matthew *aka* **Davis, Matt** (1978–) *Tigerland* 2000; *Urban Legends: Final Cut* 2000; *Legally Blonde* 2001; *Below* 2002; *Blue Crush* 2002

Davis, Mildred (1900–1969) *A Sailor-Made Man* 1921; *Safety Last* 1923

Davis, Nancy *aka* **Reagan, Nancy** (1921–) *The Doctor and the Girl* 1949; *East Side, West Side* 1949; *The Next Voice You Hear* 1950; *It's a Big Country* 1951; *Donovan's Brain* 1953; *Hellcats of the Navy* 1957; *Crash Landing* 1958

Davis, Nathan *aka* **Davis, Nate** *Code of Silence* 1985; *Flowers in the Attic* 1987; *Dunston Checks In* 1996; *Holes* 2003

Davis, Ossie (1917–2005) *The Cardinal* 1963; *Gone Are the Days* 1963; *Shock Treatment* 1964; *The Hill* 1965; *A Man Called Adam* 1966; *The Scalphunters* 1968; *Sam Whiskey* 1969; *Slaves* 1969; *Hot Stuff* 1979; *Harry and Son* 1984; *Avenging Angel* 1985; *School Daze* 1988; *Do the Right Thing* 1989; *Joe versus the Volcano* 1990; *Jungle Fever* 1991; *Gladiator* 1992; *Grumpy Old Men* 1993; *I'm Not Rappaport* 1996; *Miss Evers' Boys* 1997; *12 Angry Men* 1997; *Doctor Dolittle* 1998; *Dinosaur* 2000; *Bubba Ho-tep* 2002; *Baadasssss!* 2003; *She Hate Me* 2004

Davis Jr, Owen (1907–1949) *They Had to See Paris* 1929; *Murder on a Bridle Path* 1936; *The Plot Thickens* 1936

Davis, Philip *aka* **Davis, Phil** (1953–) *Quadrophenia* 1979; *The Bounty* 1984; *Comrades: a Lanternist's Account of the Tolpuddle Martyrs and What Became of Them* 1986; *High Hopes* 1988; *Blue Ice* 1992; *Face* 1997; *Photographing Fairies* 1997; *Still Crazy* 1998; *Vera Drake* 2004

Davis, Roger (1939–) *House of Dark Shadows* 1970; *Ruby* 1977

Davis, Sammi (1964–) *Mona Lisa* 1986; *Hope and Glory* 1987; *A Prayer for the Dying* 1987; *Consuming Passions* 1988; *The Lair of the White Worm* 1988; *The Rainbow* 1988; *Knife Edge* 1990

Davis Jr, Sammy (1925–1990) *Anna Lucasta* 1958; *Porgy and Bess* 1959; *Ocean's Eleven* 1960; *Pepe* 1960; *Convicts Four* 1962; *Sergeants 3* 1962; *Johnny Cool* 1963; *Nightmare in the Sun* 1964; *Robin and the 7 Hoods* 1964; *A Man Called Adam* 1966; *Salt & Pepper* 1968; *Sweet Charity* 1968; *One More Time* 1970; *Little Moon & Jud McGraw* 1978; *Sammy Stops the World* 1978; *The Cannonball Run* 1981; *Heidi's Song* 1982; *Cannonball Run II* 1983; *Smorgasbord* 1983; *Moon over Parador* 1988; *Tap* 1989

Davis, Sonny Carl *aka* **Davis, Sonny** *Roadie* 1980; *Thelma & Louise* 1991

Davis, Stringer (1896–1973) *Murder at the Gallop* 1963; *Murder Ahoy* 1964; *Murder Most Foul* 1964

Davis, Ursula *Brennus – Enemy of Rome* 1963; *Spartacus and the Ten Gladiators* 1964

Davis, Viola *The Pentagon Wars* 1998; *The Shrink Is In* 2000; *Antwone Fisher* 2002; *Far from Heaven* 2002; *Solaris* 2003

Davis, Viveka *Shoot the Moon* 1982; *Home Front* 1987; *Stalking Laura* 1993

Davis, Warwick (1970–) *Willow* 1988; *Leprechaun* 1992; *Prince Valiant* 1997; *The New Adventures of Pinocchio* 1999; *Snow White* 2001

Davis, William B (1938–) *Heart of a Child* 1994; *The X-Files* 1998; *The Proposal* 2000

Davison, Bruce (1946–) *Last Summer* 1969; *The Strawberry Statement* 1970; *Willard* 1971; *The Jerusalem File* 1972; *Ulzana's Raid* 1972; *The Affair* 1973; *Mame* 1974; *Grand Jury* 1976; *Mother, Jugs & Speed* 1976; *Brass Target* 1978; *Summer of My German Soldier* 1978; *The Lathe of Heaven* 1979; *High Risk* 1981; *Crimes of Passion* 1984; *Spies like Us* 1985; *The Ladies Club* 1986; *Longtime Companion* 1990; *Desperate Justice* 1993; *Short Cuts* 1993; *Six Degrees of Separation* 1993; *Far from Home: the Adventures of Yellow Dog* 1994; *The Baby-Sitter's Club* 1995; *The Cure* 1995; *Homage* 1995; *The Crucible* 1996; *Grace of My Heart* 1996; *Apt Pupil* 1997; *At First Sight* 1998; *Paulie* 1998; *The King Is Alive* 2000; *X-Men* 2000; *crazy/beautiful* 2001; *Summer Catch* 2001; *Dahmer* 2002; *High Crimes* 2002; *Runaway Jury* 2003; *X2* 2003

Davison, Davey (1942–) *The Strangler* 1964; *Angel, Angel Down We Go* 1969; *No Drums, No Bugles* 1971

Davison, Peter (1951–) *Black Beauty* 1994; *Parting Shots* 1998

Davoli, Andrew *Knockaround Guys* 2001; *Welcome to Collinwood* 2002

Davoli, Ninetto (1948–) *Hawks and Sparrows* 1966; *Oedipus Rex* 1967; *The Decameron* 1970; *The Arabian Nights* 1974

Davy, Jean (1911–2001) *Le Masque de Fer* 1962; *Eloge de l'Amour* 2001

Dawber, Pam (1951–) *Stay Tuned* 1992; *I'll Remember April* 1999

Dawson, Anthony *aka* **Dawson, Tony** (1916–1992) *The Queen of Spades* 1948; *The Wooden Horse* 1950; *The Long Dark Hall* 1951; *Valley of Eagles* 1951; *Dial M for Murder* 1954; *Action of the Tiger* 1957; *The Hour of Decision* 1957; *Grip of the Strangler* 1958; *Libel* 1959; *Tiger Bay* 1959; *Offbeat* 1960; *The Curse of the Werewolf* 1961; *Dr No* 1962; *Seven Seas to Calais* 1962; *Pirates* 1986

Dawson, Hal K (1896–1987) *Dr Socrates* 1935; *Billy Rose's Diamond Horseshoe* 1945; *Cattle Empire* 1958

Dawson, Kamala *aka* **Lopez, Kamala** *aka* **Lopez-Dawson, Kamala** *Born in East LA* 1987; *Break of Dawn* 1988; *The Burning Season* 1994; *Erotique* 1994; *Lightning Jack* 1994

Dawson, Richard (1932–) *Munster, Go Home!* 1966; *The Running Man* 1987

Dawson, Rosario (1979–) *kids* 1995; *He Got Game* 1998; *Light It Up* 1999; *Down to You* 2000; *Sidewalks of New York* 2000; *Josie and the Pussycats* 2001; *Pluto Nash* 2001; *Ash Wednesday* 2002; *Men in Black 2* 2002; *25th Hour* 2002; *Shattered Glass* 2003; *Welcome to the Jungle* 2003; *Alexander* 2004; *Sin City* 2005

Day, Dennis (1912–1988) *Buck Benny Rides Again* 1940; *Music in Manhattan* 1944; *Golden Girl* 1951; *The Girl Next Door* 1953

Day, Doris (1924–) *Romance on the High Seas* 1948; *It's a Great Feeling* 1949; *My Dream Is Yours* 1949; *Storm Warning* 1950; *Tea for Two* 1950; *The West Point Story* 1950; *Young Man with a Horn* 1950; *I'll See You in My Dreams* 1951; *Lullaby of Broadway* 1951; *On Moonlight Bay* 1951; *April in Paris* 1952; *By the Light of the Silvery Moon* 1953; *Calamity Jane* 1953; *Lucky Me* 1954; *Love Me or Leave Me* 1955; *Young at Heart* 1955; *Julie* 1956; *The Man Who Knew Too Much* 1956; *The Pajama Game* 1957; *Teacher's Pet* 1958; *The Tunnel of Love* 1958; *It Happened to Jane* 1959; *Pillow Talk* 1959; *Midnight Lace* 1960; *Please Don't Eat the Daisies* 1960; *Lover Come Back* 1961; *Jumbo* 1962; *That Touch of Mink* 1962; *Move Over, Darling* 1963; *The Thrill of It All* 1963; *Send Me No Flowers* 1964; *Do Not Disturb* 1965; *The Glass Bottom Boat* 1966; *Caprice* 1967; *The Ballad of Josie* 1968; *Where Were You When the Lights Went Out?* 1968; *With Six You Get Eggroll* 1968

Day, Frances (1907–1984) *Oh, Daddy!* 1935; *Fiddlers Three* 1944; *Tread Softly* 1952

Day, Josette (1914–1978) *Club de Femmes* 1936; *La Belle et la Bête* 1946; *Les Parents Terribles* 1948

Day, Laraine *aka* **Johnson, Laraine** (1917–) *Painted Desert* 1938; *Arizona Legion* 1939; *Calling Dr Kildare* 1939; *The Secret of Dr Kildare* 1939; *Sergeant Madden* 1939; *Tarzan Finds a Son!* 1939; *Dr Kildare Goes Home* 1940; *Dr Kildare's Crisis* 1940; *Dr Kildare's Strange Case* 1940; *Foreign Correspondent* 1940; *I Take This Woman* 1940; *My Son, My Son!* 1940; *Dr Kildare's Wedding Day* 1941; *The People vs Dr Kildare* 1941; *The Trial of Mary Dugan* 1941; *Unholy Partners* 1941; *Fingers at the Window* 1942; *Journey for Margaret* 1942; *Mr Lucky* 1943; *Bride by Mistake* 1944; *The Story of Dr Wassell* 1944; *Keep Your Powder Dry* 1945; *Those Endearing Young Charms* 1945; *The Locket* 1946; *Tycoon* 1947; *My Dear Secretary* 1948; *The Woman on Pier 13* 1949; *The High and the Mighty* 1954; *The Third Voice* 1960

Day, Larry (1963–) *Demon House* 1997; *Dead Silent* 1999

Day, Marceline (1907–2000) *London after Midnight* 1927; *The Cameraman* 1928; *The Wild Party* 1929; *The Telegraph Trail* 1933

Day, Matt (1971–) *Muriel's Wedding* 1994; *Love and Other Catastrophes* 1996; *Doing Time for Patsy Cline* 1997; *Kiss or Kill* 1997

Day, Morris (1957–) *Purple Rain* 1984; *The Adventures of Ford Fairlane* 1990; *Graffiti Bridge* 1990

Day, Vera (1939–) *It's a Great Day* 1955; *A Kid for Two Farthings* 1955; *Quatermass II* 1957; *The Woman Eater* 1957; *Grip of the Strangler* 1958; *Too Many Crooks* 1958; *Up the Creek* 1958; *Trouble with Eve* 1959; *And the Same to You* 1960; *Watch It, Sailor!* 1961; *Saturday Night Out* 1963

Day George, Lynda *aka* **Day, Lynda** (1944–) *The Gentle Rain* 1966; *Day of the Animals* 1977; *The Amazing Captain Nemo* 1978; *Beyond Evil* 1980; *Pieces* 1982; *Young Warriors* 1983

Day-Lewis, Daniel (1957–) *The Bounty* 1984; *My Beautiful Laundrette* 1985; *A Room with a View* 1985; *Nanou* 1986; *Stars and Bars* 1988; *The Unbearable Lightness of Being* 1988; *Eversmile, New Jersey* 1989; *My Left Foot* 1989; *The Last of the Mohicans* 1992; *The Age of Innocence* 1993; *In the Name of the Father* 1993; *The Crucible* 1996; *The Boxer* 1997; *Gangs of New York* 2002

Dayan, Assi *aka* **Dayan, Assaf** (1945–) *A Walk with Love and Death* 1969; *The Sellout* 1975; *Beyond the Walls* 1984; *Time of Favor* 2000

Dayton, Dan (1923–1999) *At War with the Army* 1950; *The Turning Point* 1952

De Acutis, William (1957–1991) *Nine ½ Weeks* 1985; *Chattahoochee* 1989

de Almeida, Joaquim (1957–) *The Honorary Consul* 1983; *Good Morning, Babylon* 1987; *Clear and Present Danger* 1994; *Only You* 1994; *Desperado* 1995; *Dollar for the Dead* 1998; *Captains of April* 2000; *Behind Enemy Lines* 2001

De Baer, Jean *A Flash of Green* 1984; *84 Charing Cross Road* 1986

de Bankole, Isaach (1957–) *Chocolat* 1988; *Night on Earth* 1992; *The Keeper* 1995; *Ghost Dog: the Way of the Samurai* 1999; *Coffee and Cigarettes* 2003

de Banzie, Brenda (1915–1981) *Hobson's Choice* 1953; *The Purple Plain* 1954; *As Long as They're Happy* 1955; *Doctor at Sea* 1955; *A Kid for Two Farthings* 1955; *House of Secrets* 1956; *The Man Who Knew Too Much* 1956; *Passport to Shame* 1958; *Too Many Crooks* 1958; *The Thirty-Nine Steps* 1959; *The Entertainer* 1960; *Flame in the Streets* 1961; *The Mark* 1961; *A Pair of Briefs* 1961; *The Pink Panther* 1963; *Pretty Polly* 1967

de Blas, Manuel (1941–) *A Bullet for Sandoval* 1970; *Callas Forever* 2002

de Boer, Nicole (1970–) *Cube* 1997; *Rated X* 2000

de Bray, Yvonne (1889–1954) *Eternal Love* 1943; *Les Parents Terribles* 1948; *Olivia* 1950

de Brulier, Nigel (1877–1948) *The Three Musketeers* 1921; *Salome* 1922; *The Hunchback of Notre Dame* 1923; *Moby Dick* 1930; *The Three Musketeers* 1935

De Burgh, Celia (1958–) *The Getting of Wisdom* 1977; *Sound of Love* 1977; *Phar Lap* 1983

De Cadenet, Amanda (1972–) *The Rachel Papers* 1989; *Four Rooms* 1995; *Fall* 1997

De Capitani, Grace (1959–) *Le Cop* 1985; *Le Cop II* 1989

De Carlo, Yvonne (1922–) *True to Life* 1943; *Practically Yours* 1944; *Frontier Gal* 1945; *Salome, Where*

She Danced 1945; *Brute Force* 1947; *Slave Girl* 1947; *Song of Scheherazade* 1947; *Black Bart* 1948; *Casbah* 1948; *Calamity Jane and Sam Bass* 1949; *Criss Cross* 1949; *The Gal Who Took the West* 1949; *Hotel Sahara* 1951; *Tomahawk* 1951; *The San Francisco Story* 1952; *Scarlet Angel* 1952; *Sea Devils* 1952; *Sombrero* 1952; *The Captain's Paradise* 1953; *Fort Algiers* 1953; *Border River* 1954; *Happy Ever After* 1954; *Passion* 1954; *Shotgun* 1955; *Death of a Scoundrel* 1956; *Magic Fire* 1956; *Raw Edge* 1956; *The Ten Commandments* 1956; *Band of Angels* 1957; *The Sword and the Cross* 1958; *Timbuktu* 1959; *McLintock!* 1963; *A Global Affair* 1964; *Munster, Go Home!* 1966; *Hostile Guns* 1967; *Arizona Bushwhackers* 1968; *The Power* 1968; *The Delta Factor* 1970; *The Seven Minutes* 1971; *Satan's Cheerleaders* 1977; *Play Dead* 1981; *Liar's Moon* 1982; *American Gothic* 1987; *Seasons of the Heart* 1993

de Casalis, Jeanne (1897–1966) *Nell Gwyn* 1934; *Sailors Three* 1940; *Cottage to Let* 1941; *Woman Hater* 1948

De Castro, Isabel (1931–) *Tall Stories* 1990; *Here on Earth* 1993

de Caunes, Antoine (1953–) *Man Is a Woman* 1998; *The Colour of Lies* 1999

De Cordoba, Pedro (1881–1950) *Girl Loves Boy* 1937; *Devil's Island* 1940; *The Ghost Breakers* 1940; *Tarzan Triumphs* 1943; *Comanche Territory* 1950

de Cordova, Arturo (1908–1973) *For Whom the Bell Tolls* 1943; *Hostages* 1943; *Frenchman's Creek* 1944; *Duffy's Tavern* 1945; *Incendiary Blonde* 1945; *A Medal for Benny* 1945; *El* 1953

De Corsia, Ted (1903–1973) *The Lady from Shanghai* 1948; *The Naked City* 1948; *It Happens Every Spring* 1949; *Three Secrets* 1950; *The Enforcer* 1951; *Man in the Dark* 1953; *Ride, Vaquero!* 1953; *The City Is Dark* 1954; *20,000 Leagues under the Sea* 1954; *The Big Combo* 1955; *The Conqueror* 1956; *The Killing* 1956; *Showdown at Abilene* 1956; *Slightly Scarlet* 1956; *Baby Face Nelson* 1957

De Filippo, Eduardo (1900–1984) *The Seven Deadly Sins* 1952; *Shout Loud, Louder... I Don't Understand* 1966

De Filippo, Peppino (1903–1980) *Lights of Variety* 1950; *Boccaccio '70* 1961

de Fougerolles, Hélène (1973–) *Va Savoir* 2001; *Innocence* 2004

de France, Cécile (1976–) *Pot Luck* 2002; *Switchblade Romance* 2003; *Around the World in 80 Days* 2004

De Funès, Louis (1914–1983) *The Sheep Has Five Legs* 1954; *La Traversée de Paris* 1956; *The Gendarme of St Tropez* 1964; *The Gendarme in New York* 1965; *Don't Look Now... We're Being Shot At* 1966; *Delusions of Grandeur* 1971; *The Spacemen of St Tropez* 1978; *The Gendarme Wore Skirts* 1982

De Grasse, Sam (1875–1953) *Blind Husbands* 1919; *Robin Hood* 1922; *The Black Pirate* 1926; *When a Man Loves* 1926

de Havilland, Olivia aka **de Haviland, Olivia** (1916–) *Captain Blood* 1935; *The Irish in Us* 1935; *A Midsummer Night's Dream* 1935; *Anthony Adverse* 1936; *The Charge of the Light Brigade* 1936; *The Great Garrick* 1937; *It's Love I'm After* 1937; *The Adventures of Robin Hood* 1938; *Four's a Crowd* 1938; *Gold Is Where You Find It* 1938; *Hard to Get* 1938; *Dodge City* 1939; *Gone with the Wind* 1939; *The Private Lives of Elizabeth and Essex* 1939; *Raffles* 1939; *Santa Fe Trail* 1940; *Hold Back the Dawn* 1941; *The Strawberry Blonde* 1941; *They Died with Their Boots On* 1941; *In This Our Life* 1942; *The Male Animal* 1942; *Government Girl* 1943; *Princess O'Rourke* 1943; *The Dark Mirror* 1946; *Devotion* 1946; *To Each His Own* 1946; *The Well Groomed Bride* 1946; *The Snake Pit* 1948; *The Heiress* 1949; *My Cousin Rachel* 1952; *Not as a Stranger* 1955; *That Lady* 1955; *The Ambassador's Daughter* 1956; *The Proud Rebel* 1958; *Libel* 1959; *Light in the Piazza* 1961; *Hush... Hush, Sweet Charlotte* 1964; *Lady in a Cage* 1964; *The Adventurers* 1970; *Pope Joan* 1972; *Airport '77* 1977; *The Swarm* 1978; *The Fifth Musketeer* 1979

De Keyser, David *Leo the Last* 1970; *Leon the Pig Farmer* 1992; *The Designated Mourner* 1997; *Sunshine* 1999

De Kova, Frank (1910–1981) *Shack Out on 101* 1955; *Teenage Caveman* 1958; *Atlantis, the Lost Continent* 1960; *The Wild Country* 1971; *The Mechanic* 1972; *Frasier, the Sensuous Lion* 1973; *The Slams* 1973

de la Brosse, Simon (1965–1998) *Pauline at the Beach* 1983; *La Petite Voleuse* 1988; *Loser Takes All* 1990

de la Fontaine, Agathe (1971–) *Another 9½ Weeks* 1997; *Train of Life* 1999

De La Paz, Danny (1957–) *Boulevard Nights* 1979; *Barbarosa* 1982; *City Limits* 1985; *3:15* 1986; *The Wild Pair* 1987; *American Me* 1992

De La Pena, George (1955–) *Nijinsky* 1980; *Kuffs* 1991; *Brain Donors* 1992

de la Tour, Frances (1945–) *Our Miss Fred* 1972; *Wombling Free* 1977; *Rising Damp* 1980; *Agatha Christie's Murder with Mirrors* 1985; *Loser Takes All* 1990; *The Cherry Orchard* 1998

De Lacy, Philippe (1917–1995) *The Student Prince in Old Heidelberg* 1927; *Sarah and Son* 1930

de Lancie, John (1948–) *The Hand That Rocks the Cradle* 1992; *Fearless* 1993; *Woman on Top* 2000

De Lint, Derek (1950–) *Soldier of Orange* 1977; *The Assault* 1986; *Mascara* 1987; *Stealing Heaven* 1988; *The Unbearable Lightness of Being* 1988

De Luca, Lorella (1940–) *The Swindle* 1955; *The Sign of the Gladiator* 1958

de Marney, Derrick (1906–1978) *Land without Music* 1936; *Things to Come* 1936; *Young and Innocent* 1937; *Flying 55* 1939; *Dangerous Moonlight* 1941; *Uncle Silas* 1947; *Sleeping Car to Trieste* 1948

de Medeiros, Maria (1965–) *1871* 1989; *Henry & June* 1990; *The Divine Comedy* 1992; *L'Homme de Ma Vie* 1992; *Golden Balls* 1993; *Pulp Fiction* 1994; *News from the Good Lord* 1996; *Le Polygraphe* 1996; *Captains of April* 2000; *My Life without Me* 2002; *The Saddest Music in the World* 2003

de Mendoza, Alberto aka **Mendoza, Albert** (1923–) *That Man George* 1965; *A Bullet for Sandoval* 1970; *Delusions of Grandeur* 1971; *Horror Express* 1972; *Open Season* 1974; *What Changed Charley Farthing?* 1974

De Metz, Danielle *Return of the Fly* 1959; *Gidget Goes to Rome* 1963; *Raid on Rommel* 1971

De Monaghan, Laurence *Claire's Knee* 1970; *Story of a Love Story* 1973

de Montalembert, Thibault *Love etc* 1997; *Lovers* 1999; *The Pornographer* 2001; *In My Skin* 2002

De Mornay, Rebecca (1962–) *Risky Business* 1983; *Testament* 1983; *Runaway Train* 1985; *The Slugger's Wife* 1985; *The Trip to Bountiful* 1985; *Beauty and the Beast* 1987; *And God Created Woman* 1988; *Feds* 1988; *Dealers* 1989; *Backdraft* 1991; *The Hand That Rocks the Cradle* 1992; *Guilty as Sin* 1993; *The Three Musketeers* 1993; *Never Talk to Strangers* 1995; *Night Ride Home* 1999; *Raise Your Voice* 2004; *Lords of Dogtown* 2005

De Niro, Robert aka **DeNero, Robert** (1943–) *Trois Chambres à Manhattan* 1965; *The Wedding Party* 1966; *Greetings* 1968; *Sam's Song* 1969; *Bloody Mama* 1970; *Hi, Mom!* 1970; *Born to Win* 1971; *The Gang That Couldn't Shoot Straight* 1971; *Jennifer on My Mind* 1971; *Bang the Drum Slowly* 1973; *Mean Streets* 1973; *The Godfather, Part II* 1974; *The Last Tycoon* 1976; *1900* 1976; *Taxi Driver* 1976; *New York, New York* 1977; *The Deer Hunter* 1978; *Raging Bull* 1980; *True Confessions* 1981; *The King of Comedy* 1983; *Falling in Love* 1984; *Once upon a Time in America* 1984; *Brazil* 1985; *The Mission* 1986; *Angel Heart* 1987; *The Untouchables* 1987; *Jacknife* 1988; *Midnight Run* 1988; *Stanley & Iris* 1989; *We're No Angels* 1989; *Awakenings* 1990; *GoodFellas* 1990; *Guilty by Suspicion* 1990; *Backdraft* 1991; *Cape Fear* 1991; *Mad Dog and Glory* 1992; *Mistress* 1992; *Night and the City* 1992; *A Bronx Tale* 1993; *This Boy's Life* 1993; *Mary Shelley's Frankenstein* 1994; *Casino* 1995; *Heat* 1995; *The Fan* 1996; *Marvin's Room* 1996; *Sleepers* 1996; *Cop Land* 1997; *Great Expectations* 1997; *Jackie Brown* 1997; *Wag the Dog* 1997; *Ronin* 1998; *The Adventures of Rocky & Bullwinkle* 1999; *Analyze This* 1999; *Flawless* 1999; *Meet the Parents* 2000; *Men of Honor* 2000; *15 Minutes* 2001; *The Score* 2001; *Analyze That* 2002; *City by the Sea* 2002; *Showtime* 2002; *Godsend* 2003; *Meet the Fockers* 2004; *Shark Tale* 2004; *Hide and Seek* 2005

de Palma, Rossy (1965–) *Women on the Verge of a Nervous Breakdown* 1988; *Kika* 1993; *The Flower of My Secret* 1995

de Penguern, Artus (1957–) *Amélie* 2001; *Grégoire Moulin* 2001

De Rienzo, Libero *A Ma Soeur!* 2001; *My House in Umbria* 2002

De Rita, Joe (1909–1993) *Have Rocket, Will Travel* 1959; *The Three Stooges in Orbit* 1962; *The Three Stooges Meet Hercules* 1962; *The Three Stooges Go around the World in a Daze* 1963; *The Outlaws Is Coming* 1965

de Rossi, Portia aka **Di Rossi, Portia** (1973–) *Sirens* 1994; *Girl* 1998; *The Night We Called It a Day* 2003; *Cursed* 2005

De Sade, Ana *The Return of a Man Called Horse* 1976; *Triumphs of a Man Called Horse* 1983

De Salvo, Anne (1949–) *My Favorite Year* 1982; *Compromising Positions* 1985; *Perfect* 1985; *Burglar* 1987; *Spike of Bensonhurst* 1988; *Taking Care of Business* 1990

De Santis, Eliana *The Monk* 1972; *Les Noces Rouges* 1973

De Santis, Joe aka **De Santis, Joseph** (1909–1989) *The Man with a Cloak* 1951; *Deadline – USA* 1952; *Full of Life* 1956; *Tension at Table Rock* 1956; *Dino* 1957; *Jeanne Eagels* 1957; *The Unholy Wife* 1957; *Al Capone* 1959; *A Cold Wind in August* 1961; *And Now Miguel* 1966; *The Professionals* 1966; *Blue* 1968

De Sapio, Francesca *Blood Red* 1988; *Torrents of Spring* 1989

De Sica, Vittorio (1902–1974) *Bread, Love and Dreams* 1953; *Madame de...* 1953; *Gold of Naples* 1954; *Secrets d'Alcove* 1954; *The Miller's Wife* 1955; *Too Bad She's Bad* 1955; *It Happened in Rome* 1956; *A Farewell to Arms* 1957; *The Monte Carlo Story* 1957; *General Della Rovere* 1959; *The Angel Wore Red* 1960; *It Started in Naples* 1960; *The Millionairess* 1960; *The Amorous Adventures of Moll Flanders* 1965; *The Biggest Bundle of Them All* 1968; *The Shoes of the Fisherman* 1968; *Twelve plus One* 1969; *Snow Job* 1972; *Blood for Dracula* 1974; *Blood for Dracula* 1974; *We All Loved Each Other So Much* 1974

De Soto, Rosana (1950–) *La Bamba* 1987; *Stand and Deliver* 1988; *Family Business* 1989

De Souza, Edward (1933–) *The Phantom of the Opera* 1962; *The Return of the Soldier* 1982

De Turckheim, Charlotte (1955–) *Le Maître d'Ecole* 1981; *Right Bank, Left Bank* 1984; *Mon Père Ce Héros* 1991

de Van, Marina (1971–) *Sitcom* 1997; *In My Skin* 2002

De Villalonga, José-Luis aka **Vilallonga** (1920–) *Breakfast at Tiffany's* 1961; *Cleo from 5 to 7* 1961; *Any Number Can Win* 1963; *Darling* 1965; *The Burglars* 1971

De Vito, Francesco *I Am David* 2003; *The Passion of the Christ* 2004

de Vries, Dolf (1937–) *Turkish Delight* 1973; *The Fourth Man* 1983

de Wilde, Brandon (1942–1972) *The Member of the Wedding* 1952; *Shane* 1953; *Good-bye, My Lady* 1956; *Night Passage* 1957; *The Missouri Traveler* 1958; *Blue Denim* 1959; *All Fall Down* 1962; *Hud* 1963; *Those Calloways* 1964; *In Harm's Way* 1965; *The Deserter* 1971; *Black Jack* 1972

de Wit, Jacqueline (1912–1998) *Meeting at Midnight* 1944; *Little Giant* 1946; *Wild Beauty* 1946; *The Great Jewel Robber* 1950; *All That Heaven Allows* 1955; *Tea and Sympathy* 1956; *Twice Told Tales* 1963

De Wolfe, Billy (1907–1974) *Dixie* 1943; *Miss Susie Slagle's* 1945; *Blue Skies* 1946; *Dear Ruth* 1947; *The Perils of Pauline* 1947; *Isn't It Romantic* 1948; *Dear Wife* 1949; *Tea for Two* 1950; *Lullaby of Broadway* 1951; *Call Me Madam* 1953; *Billie* 1965

De Wolff, Francis (1913–1984) *The Kidnappers* 1953; *The Diamond* 1954; *Geordie* 1955; *King's Rhapsody* 1955; *The Hound of the Baskervilles* 1959; *The Man Who Could Cheat Death* 1959; *The Two Faces of Dr Jekyll* 1960; *From Russia with Love* 1963; *The World Ten Times Over* 1963; *Devil Doll* 1964; *Licensed to Kill* 1965

de Woolfson, Luke *Large* 2000; *Late Night Shopping* 2001

De Young, Cliff (1945–) *The Lindbergh Kidnapping Case* 1976; *Shock Treatment* 1981; *The Hunger* 1983; *Independence Day* 1983; *Protocol* 1984; *FX: Murder by Illusion* 1985; *Secret Admirer* 1985; *Flight of the Navigator* 1986; *Fear* 1988; *Pulse* 1988; *Rude Awakening* 1989; *Flashback* 1990; *Dr Giggles* 1992; *The Craft* 1996

Déa, Marie (1919–1992) *Pièges* 1939; *Les Visiteurs du Soir* 1942; *Orphée* 1950

Deacon, Brian (1949–) *The Triple Echo* 1972; *Jesus* 1979; *A Zed & Two Noughts* 1985

Deacon, Kim (1959–) *The Getting of Wisdom* 1977; *Rebel* 1985

Deacon, Richard (1921–1984) *Abbott and Costello Meet the Mummy* 1955; *Blackbeard's Ghost* 1967; *The Gnome-Mobile* 1967; *The Happy Hooker Goes to Hollywood* 1980

Deakin, Julia *Mr Love* 1985; *Dancin' thru the Dark* 1989; *Between Two Women* 2000

Deakins, Lucy (1971–) *The Boy Who Could Fly* 1986; *Cheetah* 1989; *There Goes My Baby* 1994

Dean, Allison *Coming to America* 1988; *Ruby in Paradise* 1993

Dean, Bill (1921–2000) *Family Life* 1971; *Night Watch* 1973

Dean, Felicity *Steaming* 1985; *The Whistle Blower* 1986

Dean, Isabel (1918–1997) *The Passionate Friends* 1948; *The Story of Gilbert and Sullivan* 1953; *Out of the Clouds* 1954; *Virgin Island* 1958; *Light in the Piazza* 1961; *Ransom* 1975; *Rough Cut* 1980; *Five Days One Summer* 1982

Dean, James (1931–1955) *Sailor Beware* 1951; *Has Anybody Seen My Gal?* 1952; *East of Eden* 1955; *Rebel without a Cause* 1955; *Giant* 1956

Dean, Julia (1878–1952) *The Curse of the Cat People* 1944; *Nightmare Alley* 1947

Dean, Laura (1963–) *Fame* 1980; *Almost You* 1984

Dean, Loren (1969–) *Billy Bathgate* 1991; *1492: Conquest of Paradise* 1992; *The Passion of Darkly Noon* 1995; *Mrs Winterbourne* 1996; *The End of Violence* 1997; *Gattaca* 1997; *Rosewood* 1997; *Mumford* 1999; *Space Cowboys* 2000; *The War Bride* 2001

Dean, Margia (1921–) *The Quatermass Xperiment* 1955; *Villa!* 1958; *The Secret of the Purple Reef* 1960; *The Big Show* 1961

Dean, Rick aka **Dean, Richard** *Heroes Stand Alone* 1989; *Quake!* 1992; *Cheyenne Warrior* 1994

Dean, Ron *Cocktail* 1988; *Cold Justice* 1991

Deane, Lezlie *976-EVIL* 1988; *Freddy's Dead: the Final Nightmare* 1991; *To Protect and Serve* 1992

Dear, Elizabeth *The Greengage Summer* 1961; *The Battle of the Villa Fiorita* 1965

Dearing, Edgar (1893–1974) *Free and Easy* 1930; *They Gave Him a Gun* 1937

Dearman, Glynn (1939–1997) *The Small Voice* 1948; *Scrooge* 1951; *Four Sided Triangle* 1953

Deayton, Angus (1956–) *Elizabeth* 1998; *Fat Slags* 2004

Debar, Andrée (1926–) *The House on the Waterfront* 1955; *Guilty?* 1956

Debbouze, Jamel (1975–) *Boys on the Beach* 1998; *Asterix & Obelix: Mission Cleopatra* 2001

DeBell, Kristine (1954–) *Meatballs* 1979; *The Big Brawl* 1980

DeBello, James (1980–) *Detroit Rock City* 1999; *Crime + Punishment in Suburbia* 2000; *Cabin Fever* 2002

DeBenning, Burr *Beach Red* 1967; *Sweet November* 1968; *City beneath the Sea* 1971; *The Face of Fear* 1971; *The Incredible Melting Man* 1977; *The Amazing Captain Nemo* 1978

DeBroux, Lee *Run, Angel, Run* 1969; *Hangfire* 1991; *The Day the World Ended* 2001

Debucourt, Jean (1894–1958) *Abel Gance's Beethoven* 1936; *Mayerling* 1936; *Devil in the Flesh* 1947; *Monsieur Vincent* 1947; *The Eagle Has Two Heads* 1948; *Madame de...* 1953; *The Witches of Salem* 1957

DeCamp, Rosemary (1910–2001) *Hold Back the Dawn* 1941; *Jungle Book* 1942; *Yankee Doodle Dandy* 1942; *This Is the Army* 1943; *The Merry Monahans* 1944; *Practically Yours* 1944; *Blood on the Sun* 1945; *Pride of the Marines* 1945; *Rhapsody in Blue* 1945; *From This Day Forward* 1946; *Two Guys from Milwaukee* 1946; *Nora Prentiss* 1947; *Look for the Silver Lining* 1949; *Night unto Night* 1949; *The Story of Seabiscuit* 1949; *On Moonlight Bay* 1951; *Treasure of Lost Canyon* 1952; *By the Light of the Silvery Moon* 1953; *Main Street to Broadway* 1953; *So This Is Love* 1953; *13 Ghosts* 1959; *Saturday the 14th* 1981

Dechent, Antonio *Intacto* 2001; *Carmen* 2003; *You're My Hero* 2003

Decker, Diana (1926–) *Fiddlers Three* 1944; *When You Come Home* 1947; *Murder at the Windmill* 1949; *Knave of Hearts* 1954; *A Yank in Ermine* 1955; *Lolita* 1961; *Devils of Darkness* 1964

Deckers, Eugene (1917–1977) *Highly Dangerous* 1950; *Hotel Sahara* 1951; *Foreign Intrigue* 1956; *Seven Thunders* 1957; *North West Frontier* 1959

Deckert, Blue *Getting Even* 1986; *Muhammad Ali: King of the World* 2000

Decleir, Jan (1946–) *Daens* 1992; *Antonia's Line* 1995;

Character 1997; Running Free 1999
Decomble, Guy (1910–1964) Jour de Fête 1947; Bob Le Flambeur 1955; Les Cousins 1959; The 400 Blows 1959
Dee, Frances (1907–2004) An American Tragedy 1931; If I Had a Million 1932; Love Is a Racket 1932; This Reckless Age 1932; Little Women 1933; The Silver Cord 1933; Finishing School 1934; Of Human Bondage 1934; Becky Sharp 1935; The Gay Deception 1935; Souls at Sea 1937; Wells Fargo 1937; If I Were King 1938; A Man Betrayed 1941; So Ends Our Night 1941; Happy Land 1943; I Walked with a Zombie 1943; Patrick the Great 1944; The Private Affairs of Bel Ami 1947; They Passed This Way 1948; Payment on Demand 1951; Gypsy Colt 1954
Dee, Jack (1962–) The Steal 1994; Londinium 1999; Spivs 2003
Dee, Ruby (1924–) The Tall Target 1951; Go, Man, Go! 1953; Edge of the City 1957; St Louis Blues 1958; Take a Giant Step 1959; A Raisin in the Sun 1961; The Balcony 1963; Gone Are the Days 1963; The Incident 1967; Uptight 1968; King: a Filmed Record... Montgomery to Memphis 1970; Buck and the Preacher 1972; Cat People 1982; Do the Right Thing 1989; The Court-Martial of Jackie Robinson 1990; Jungle Fever 1991; Cop and a Half 1993; A Simple Wish 1997; Baby Geniuses 1999; A Storm in Summer 2000
Dee, Sandra (1942–2005) Until They Sail 1957; The Reluctant Debutante 1958; The Restless Years 1958; Gidget 1959; Imitation of Life 1959; The Snow Queen 1959; A Stranger in My Arms 1959; A Summer Place 1959; The Wild and the Innocent 1959; Portrait in Black 1960; Come September 1961; Romanoff and Juliet 1961; Tammy Tell Me True 1961; If a Man Answers 1962; Take Her, She's Mine 1963; Tammy and the Doctor 1963; I'd Rather Be Rich 1964; That Funny Feeling 1965; A Man Could Get Killed 1966; Rosie! 1967; The Dunwich Horror 1970
Deering, Olive (1918–1986) Samson and Delilah 1949; Shock Treatment 1964
Deezen, Eddie (1957–) Midnight Madness 1980; Delta Pi 1985; Money Mania 1987; Rock-a-Doodle 1990; The Polar Express 2004
DeFore, Don (1917–1993) The Affairs of Susan 1945; The Stork Club 1945; Without Reservations 1946; It Happened on Fifth Avenue 1947; Romance on the High Seas 1948; My Friend Irma 1949; Dark City 1950; A Girl in Every Port 1952; No Room for the Groom 1952; She's Working Her Way through College 1952; Battle Hymn 1957; A Time to Love and a Time to Die 1958; The Facts of Life 1960
DeGeneres, Ellen (1958–) Coneheads 1993; Mr Wrong 1996; Goodbye Lover 1997; Edtv 1999; The Love Letter 1999; If These Walls Could Talk 2 2000; Finding Nemo 2003
Degermark, Pia (1949–) Elvira Madigan 1967; The Looking Glass War 1969
DeGrazia, Julio Funny Dirty Little War 1983; The Stranger 1987
DeHaven, Gloria aka **De Haven, Gloria** (1924–) Best Foot Forward 1943; Broadway Rhythm 1944; Step Lively 1944; The Thin Man Goes Home 1944; Two Girls and a Sailor 1944; Summer Holiday 1948; The Doctor and the Girl 1949; Scene of the Crime 1949; Summer Stock 1950; Three Little Words 1950; The Yellow Cab Man 1950; Two Tickets to Broadway 1951; So This Is Paris 1954; The Girl Rush 1955; Out to Sea 1997
Dehner, John (1915–1992) China Corsair 1951; Ten Tall Men 1951; Desert Passage 1952; Fort Algiers 1953; Powder River 1953; Apache 1954; The Bowery Boys Meet the Monsters 1954; The King's Thief 1955; The Man from Bitter Ridge 1955; The Scarlet Coat 1955; The Girl in Black Stockings 1957; The Iron Sheriff 1957; Trooper Hook 1957; The Left Handed Gun 1958; Man of the West 1958; Cast a Long Shadow 1959; Timbuktu 1959; The Canadians 1961; Critic's Choice 1963; The Helicopter Spies 1968; Dirty Dingus Magee 1970; Tiger by the Tail 1970; The Killer inside Me 1975; Creator 1985; Jagged Edge 1985
Dekker, Albert (1904–1968) Beau Geste 1939; Paris Honeymoon 1939; Dr Cyclops 1940; Seven Sinners 1940; Strange Cargo 1940; Among the Living 1941; Honky Tonk 1941; The Forest Rangers 1942; In Old California 1942; Once upon a Honeymoon 1942; Wake Island 1942; War of the Wildcats 1943; Experiment Perilous 1944; Hold That Blonde 1945; Incendiary Blonde 1945; Salome, Where She Danced 1945; California 1946; The Killers 1946; Two Years before the Mast 1946; Cass Timberlane 1947; Gentleman's Agreement 1947; Slave Girl 1947; Fury at Furnace Creek 1948; Lulu Belle 1948; Bride of Vengeance 1949; Search for Danger 1949; Tarzan's Magic Fountain 1949; Destination Murder 1950; The Kid from Texas 1950; Wait 'til the Sun Shines, Nellie 1952; East of Eden 1955; Illegal 1955; Kiss Me Deadly 1955; Middle of the Night 1959; Suddenly, Last Summer 1959; These Thousand Hills 1959; The Wonderful Country 1959; Gamera the Invincible 1965
Dekker, Thomas (1987–) An American Tail: the Treasure of Manhattan Island 1998; An American Tail: the Mystery of the Night Monster 2000
del Lago, Alicia Tizoc 1956; El Norte 1983
Del Mar, Maria (1964–) Cold Sweat 1993; Price of Glory 2000
Del Pozo, Angel (1934–) Pancho Villa 1971; Treasure Island 1972
Del Prete, Duilio (1938–1998) The Assassination of Trotsky 1972; Daisy Miller 1974; At Long Last Love 1975
Del Rey, Geraldo (1930–1993) The Given Word 1962; Black God, White Devil 1964
Del Rey, Pilar Black Horse Canyon 1954; And Now Miguel 1966
Del Rio, Dolores (1905–1983) What Price Glory 1926; The Red Dance 1928; The Trail of '98 1929; Bird of Paradise 1932; Flying down to Rio 1933; Madame Du Barry 1934; Wonder Bar 1934; In Caliente 1935; Accused 1936; Lancer Spy 1937; International Settlement 1938; The Man from Dakota 1940; Journey into Fear 1942; Portrait of Maria 1943; The Fugitive 1947; Flaming Star 1960; Cheyenne Autumn 1964; More than a Miracle 1967; The Children of Sanchez 1978
Del Sol, Laura (1961–) Carmen 1983; The Hit 1984; El Amor Brujo 1986; Killing Dad 1989
Del Toro, Benicio (1967–) Big Top Pee-wee 1988; Licence to Kill 1989; Christopher Columbus: the Discovery 1992; Fearless 1993; Golden Balls 1993; Money for Nothing 1993; China Moon 1994; Swimming with Sharks 1994; The Usual Suspects 1995; Basquiat 1996; The Fan 1996; The Funeral 1996; Excess Baggage 1997; Fear and Loathing in Las Vegas 1998; The Pledge 2000; Snatch 2000; Traffic 2000; The Way of the Gun 2000; The Hunted 2002; 21 Grams 2003; Sin City 2005
Delahaye, Michel (1929–) Alphaville 1965; Shiver of the Vampires 1970; Une Belle Fille Comme Moi 1973
Delair, Suzy (1916–) Quai des Orfèvres 1947; Utopia 1950; Gervaise 1956; Rocco and His Brothers 1960
Delamare, Lise (1913–) La Marseillaise 1938; Monsieur Vincent 1947; Les Grandes Manoeuvres 1955; Lola Montès 1955
Delamere, Matthew Under the Skin 1997; $8\frac{1}{2}$ Women 1999
Delamere, Victorien Le Château de Ma Mère 1990; La Gloire de Mon Père 1990
Delaney, Cathleen The Dead 1987; The Miracle 1990
Delaney, Joan The President's Analyst 1967; Don't Drink the Water 1969; Bunny O'Hare 1971
Delaney, Kim (1961–) That Was Then... This Is Now 1985; The Drifter 1988; Body Parts 1991; Hangfire 1991; Darkman II: the Return of Durant 1995; Temptress 1995; Serial Killer 1996; Devil's Child 1997
Delaney, Maureen (1888–1961) Another Shore 1948; Jacqueline 1956; The Scamp 1957; Tread Softly Stranger 1958
Delano, Michael (1940–) Catlow 1971; Not of This Earth 1988
Delany, Dana (1956–) The Adventures of Mowgli 1967; Almost You 1984; Where the River Runs Black 1986; Masquerade 1988; Patty Hearst 1988; Light Sleeper 1991; HouseSitter 1992; Batman: Mask of the Phantasm 1993; The Enemy Within 1994; Exit to Eden 1994; Live Nude Girls 1995; Fly Away Home 1996; Wide Awake 1998; Resurrection 1999
Delevanti, Cyril (1887–1975) The Night of the Iguana 1964; The Killing of Sister George 1968
Delfosse, Raoul The Burglars 1971; The Frog Prince 1984
Delgado, Roger (1918–1973) The Road to Hong Kong 1962; Hot Enough for June 1963; The Mummy's Shroud 1966
Dell, Gabriel (1919–1988) Dead End 1937; Angels with Dirty Faces 1938; Angels Wash Their Faces 1939; Hell's Kitchen 1939; Block Busters 1944; Bowery Champs 1944; Follow the Leader 1944; Come Out Fighting 1945; Who Is Harry Kellerman, and Why Is He Saying Those Terrible Things about Me? 1971; Framed 1975; The Escape Artist 1982
Dell, Myrna (1924–) The Falcon's Adventure 1946; Nocturne 1946; Guns of Hate 1948; The Gal Who Took the West 1949; The Judge Steps Out 1949; Roughshod 1949; Search for Danger 1949; Destination Murder 1950
Delle Piane, Carlo (1936–) What? 1973; Noi Tre 1984; Christmas Present 1986
Dell'Isola, Patrick Rien à Faire 1999; Roberto Succo 2000
Delmont, Edouard aka **Delmont** (1883–1955) Angèle 1934; Toni 1935; The Sheep Has Five Legs 1954
Delon, Alain (1935–) Plein Soleil 1960; Rocco and His Brothers 1960; The Eclipse 1962; The Leopard 1962; Any Number Can Win 1963; The Black Tulip 1963; The Love Cage 1964; The Yellow Rolls-Royce 1964; Once a Thief 1965; Is Paris Burning? 1966; Lost Command 1966; Texas across the River 1966; Diabolically Yours 1967; Histoires Extraordinaires 1967; Le Samouraï 1967; The Adventurers 1968; The Girl on a Motorcycle 1968; The Swimming Pool 1968; The Sicilian Clan 1969; Borsalino 1970; The Red Circle 1970; Red Sun 1971; Take It Easy 1971; The Widow Couderc 1971; The Assassination of Trotsky 1972; Un Flic 1972; Burnt Barns 1973; Scorpio 1973; Shock Treatment 1973; Two against the Law 1973; Borsalino and Co 1974; Someone Is Bleeding 1974; Police Story 1975; Zorro 1975; Armaguedon 1976; Boomerang 1976; Mr Klein 1976; To Kill a Rat 1977; Airport '79: the Concorde 1979; Three Men to Destroy 1980; Le Choc 1982; Swann in Love 1984; The Passage 1986; Nouvelle Vague 1990
Delon, Nathalie (1938–) Le Samouraï 1967; Take It Easy 1971; When Eight Bells Toll 1971; Bluebeard 1972; The Monk 1972; The Romantic Englishwoman 1975
DeLorenzo, Michael (1959–) Somebody to Love 1994; Phantoms 1998
Delorme, Danièle (1926–) Les Misérables 1957; Mitsou 1957; Cleo from 5 to 7 1961; Hoa-Binh 1970; Pardon Mon Affaire 1976
Delpy, Albert The Hairdresser's Husband 1990; Before Sunset 2004
Delpy, Julie (1969–) Detective 1985; The Night Is Young 1986; Europa, Europa 1991; Voyager 1991; Killing Zoe 1993; Three Colours White 1993; The Three Musketeers 1993; Younger and Younger 1993; Before Sunrise 1995; An American Werewolf in Paris 1997; LA without a Map 1998; But I'm a Cheerleader 1999; Beginner's Luck 2001; Waking Life 2001; Villa des Roses 2002; Before Sunset 2004
Deltgen, René (1909–1979) Special Delivery 1955; The Tiger of Eschnapur 1959
Delubac, Jacqueline (1910–1997) Bonne Chance 1935; The Story of a Cheat 1936
DeLuise, Dom (1933–) The Glass Bottom Boat 1966; The Busy Body 1967; What's So Bad About Feeling Good? 1968; The Twelve Chairs 1970; Evil Roy Slade 1971; Who Is Harry Kellerman, and Why Is He Saying Those Terrible Things about Me? 1971; Every Little Crook and Nanny 1972; The Adventure of Sherlock Holmes' Smarter Brother 1975; Silent Movie 1976; The World's Greatest Lover 1977; The Cheap Detective 1978; The End 1978; Sextette 1978; Fatso 1979; Hot Stuff 1979; The Last Married Couple in America 1980; Smokey and the Bandit II 1980; Wholly Moses! 1980; The Cannonball Run 1981; History of the World Part 1 1981; The Best Little Whorehouse in Texas 1982; The Secret of NIMH 1982; Cannonball Run II 1983; Johnny Dangerously 1984; An American Tail 1986; Haunted Honeymoon 1986; Spaceballs 1987; Oliver & Company 1988; All Dogs Go to Heaven 1989; Happily Ever After 1990; Loose Cannons 1990; An American Tail: Fievel Goes West 1991; The Magic Voyage 1992; Munchie 1992; Robin Hood: Men in Tights 1993; The Silence of the Hams 1993; The Skateboard Kid 1993; Munchie Strikes Back 1994; Stanley's Magic Garden 1994; All Dogs Go to Heaven 2 1996; An American Tail: the Treasure of Manhattan Island 1998; The Secret of NIMH II: Timmy to the Rescue 1998; Baby Geniuses 1999; An American Tail: the Mystery of the Night Monster 2000; The Brainiacs.com 2000; Lion of Oz 2000
DeLuise, Michael (1970–) California Man 1992; Wayne's World 1992; The Man without a Face 1993; The Shot 1996
DeLuise, Peter (1966–) Solarbabies 1986; Rescue Me 1991
Demange, Paul School for Postmen 1947; Clochemerle 1948
Demarest, William (1892–1983) The Jazz Singer 1927; Hands across the Table 1935; Murder Man 1935; Wedding Present 1936; Easy Living 1937; Rosalie 1937; Christmas in July 1940; The Great McGinty 1940; The Devil and Miss Jones 1941; The Lady Eve 1941; Sullivan's Travels 1941; All through the Night 1942; Life Begins at 8.30 1942; Pardon My Sarong 1942; Stage Door Canteen 1943; True to Life 1943; The Great Moment 1944; Hail the Conquering Hero 1944; The Miracle of Morgan's Creek 1944; Once upon a Time 1944; Along Came Jones 1945; Pardon My Past 1945; Salty O'Rourke 1945; The Jolson Story 1946; The Perils of Pauline 1947; Night Has a Thousand Eyes 1948; On Our Merry Way 1948; The Sainted Sisters 1948; Whispering Smith 1948; Jolson Sings Again 1949; Sorrowful Jones 1949; Never a Dull Moment 1950; Riding High 1950; When Willie Comes Marching Home 1950; The First Legion 1951; The Strip 1951; What Price Glory? 1952; Dangerous When Wet 1953; Escape from Fort Bravo 1953; Here Come the Girls 1953; The Lady Wants Mink 1953; The Yellow Mountain 1954; The Far Horizons 1955; Hell on Frisco Bay 1955; Jupiter's Darling 1955; Lucy Gallant 1955; The Private War of Major Benson 1955; Sincerely Yours 1955; The Mountain 1956; The Rawhide Years 1956; Pepe 1960; Son of Flubber 1962; Viva Las Vegas 1964; That Darn Cat! 1965
Demazis, Orane (1904–1991) Marius 1931; Fanny 1932; Angèle 1934; César 1936
Demetral, Chris (1976–) Sometimes They Come Back 1991; Blank Check 1994
Demick, Irina (1936–) The Visit 1964; Up from the Beach 1965; Prudence and the Pill 1968; The Sicilian Clan 1969
DeMille, Cecil B (1881–1959) Hollywood 1923; Free and Easy 1930; Star Spangled Rhythm 1942; Son of Paleface 1952; The Buster Keaton Story 1957
DeMille, Katherine (1911–1995) Belle of the Nineties 1934; All the King's Horses 1935; The Black Room 1935; The Crusades 1935; Banjo on My Knee 1936; Charlie Chan at the Olympics 1937; Black Gold 1947; Unconquered 1947
Demongeot, Mylène aka **Nicole, Mylene** (1936–) It's a Wonderful World 1956; The Witches of Salem 1957; Bonjour Tristesse 1958; Upstairs and Downstairs 1959; The Giant of Marathon 1960; The Singer Not the Song 1960; Under Ten Flags 1960; Doctor in Distress 1963; Gold for the Caesars 1964; The Private Navy of Sgt O'Farrell 1968; Twelve plus One 1969
Dempsey, Jack (1895–1983) The Prizefighter and the Lady 1933; Military Policeman 1953; Requiem for a Heavyweight 1962
Dempsey, Patrick (1966–) Catholic Boys 1985; Can't Buy Me Love 1987; Meatballs III: Summer Job 1987; The Woo Woo Kid 1987; In a Shallow Grave 1988; Some Girls 1988; Happy Together 1989; Loverboy 1989; Coupe de Ville 1990; Mobsters 1991; Run 1991; Bank Robber 1993; For Better and for Worse 1993; With Honors 1994; Outbreak 1995; Pool Girl 1997; Something about Sex 1998; Scream 3 1999; The Emperor's Club 2002; Sweet Home Alabama 2002; Iron Jawed Angels 2004
Dempster, Carol (1901–1991) Dream Street 1921; America 1924; Isn't Life Wonderful 1924; Sally of the Sawdust 1925
DeMunn, Jeffrey (1947–) Enormous Changes at the Last Minute 1983; Windy City 1984; Warning Sign 1985; The Hitcher 1986; Betrayed 1988; The Blob 1988; Blaze 1989; Eyes of an Angel 1991; Barbarians at the Gate 1993; Citizen X 1995; Killer: a Journal of Murder 1995; Rocketman 1997; Turbulence 1997; The Majestic 2001
Demy, Mathieu (1972–) Kung-Fu Master 1987; Les Cent et Une Nuits 1995
Denberg, Susan (1944–) An American Dream 1966; Frankenstein Created Woman 1966
Dench, Judi (1934–) The Third Secret 1964; Four in the Morning 1965; He Who Rides a Tiger 1965; A Study in Terror 1965; A Midsummer Night's Dream 1969; Dead Cert 1974; Luther 1974; The Angelic Conversation 1985; A Room with a View 1985; Wetherby 1985; 84 Charing Cross Road 1986; A Handful of Dust 1987; Henry V 1989; GoldenEye 1995;

Jack & Sarah 1995; Hamlet 1996; Mrs Brown 1997; Tomorrow Never Dies 1997; Shakespeare in Love 1998; Tea with Mussolini 1998; The World Is Not Enough 1999; Chocolat 2000; Into the Arms of Strangers: Stories of the Kindertransport 2000; Iris 2001; The Shipping News 2001; Die Another Day 2002; The Importance of Being Earnest 2002; The Chronicles of Riddick 2004; Home on the Range 2004; Ladies in Lavender 2004

Deneuve, Catherine (1943–) The Beautiful Swindlers 1964; Male Hunt 1964; The Umbrellas of Cherbourg 1964; Repulsion 1965; La Vie de Château 1965; Les Créatures 1966; Belle de Jour 1967; The Young Girls of Rochefort 1967; La Chamade 1968; Mayerling 1968; The April Fools 1969; Mississippi Mermaid 1969; The Magic Donkey 1970; Tristana 1970; Un Flic 1972; The Lady with Red Boots 1974; Call Him Savage 1975; Hustle 1975; Second Chance 1976; March or Die 1977; Ecoute Voir... 1978; An Adventure for Two 1979; Je Vous Aime 1980; The Last Metro 1980; Choice of Arms 1981; Le Choc 1982; The Hunger 1983; Fort Saganne 1984; Love Songs 1984; Let's Hope It's a Girl 1985; The Scene of the Crime 1986; A Strange Place to Meet 1988; Indochine 1991; Ma Saison Préferée 1993; The Convent 1995; Les Voleurs 1996; Généalogies d'un Crime 1997; Place Vendôme 1998; East-West 1999; Pola X 1999; Time Regained 1999; Le Vent de la Nuit 1999; Dancer in the Dark 2000; 8 Women 2001; I'm Going Home 2001; The Musketeer 2001; Un Filme Falado 2003; Kings & Queen 2004

Denham, Maurice (1909–2002) Daybreak 1946; Captain Boycott 1947; Take My Life 1947; Blanche Fury 1948; The Blind Goddess 1948; It's Not Cricket 1948; Oliver Twist 1948; Once upon a Dream 1948; A Boy, a Girl and a Bike 1949; Landfall 1949; Madness of the Heart 1949; The Spider and the Fly 1949; Traveller's Joy 1949; Eight O'Clock Walk 1953; The Net 1953; Terror on a Train 1953; Animal Farm 1954; Carrington VC 1954; The Purple Plain 1954; Doctor at Sea 1955; Simon and Laura 1955; Checkpoint 1956; 23 Paces to Baker Street 1956; Barnacle Bill 1957; Night of the Demon 1957; The Captain's Table 1958; Sink the Bismarck! 1960; Two Way Stretch 1960; Invasion Quartet 1961; HMS Defiant 1962; The Very Edge 1962; Paranoiac 1963; Hysteria 1964; The 7th Dawn 1964; The Legend of Young Dick Turpin 1965; The Nanny 1965; The Night Caller 1965; The Alphabet Murders 1966; The Long Duel 1966; Danger Route 1967; Torture Garden 1967; Attack on the Iron Coast 1968; The Best House in London 1968; Midas Run 1969; Some Girls Do 1969; Countess Dracula 1970; The Virgin and the Gypsy 1970; Sunday, Bloody Sunday 1971; Luther 1974; Shout at the Devil 1976; The Chain 1984; Mr Love 1985; 84 Charing Cross Road 1986

Denicourt, Marianne (1966–) La Belle Noiseuse 1991; Ma Vie Sexuelle 1996; The Lost Son 1998; Me without You 2001

Denis, Jacques (1943–) The Watchmaker of St Paul 1973; Jonah Who Will Be 25 in the Year 2000 1976; Chocolat 1988

Denison, Anthony John (1950–) Little Vegas 1990; Full Eclipse 1993; The Harvest 1993; Getting Gotti 1994; Men of War 1995; No One Could Protect Her 1996

Denison, Michael (1915–1998) Hungry Hill 1946; My Brother Jonathan 1947; The Blind Goddess 1948; The Glass Mountain 1949; Landfall 1949; The Franchise Affair 1950; Angels One Five 1952; The Importance of Being Earnest 1952; Contraband Spain 1955; The Truth about Women 1958; Faces in the Dark 1960; Shadowlands 1993

Denman, Tony (1979–) Fargo 1995; Poor White Trash 2000; Sorority Boys 2002

Dennehy, Brian (1939–) Semi-Tough 1977; Foul Play 1978; Butch and Sundance: the Early Days 1979; The Jericho Mile 1979; 10 1979; Little Miss Marker 1980; Skokie 1981; First Blood 1982; Split Image 1982; Gorky Park 1983; Never Cry Wolf 1983; The River Rat 1984; Cocoon 1985; FX: Murder by Illusion 1985; Silverado 1985; The Check Is in the Mail 1986; Legal Eagles 1986; The Belly of an Architect 1987; Best Seller 1987; Miles from Home 1988; Return to Snowy River 1988; Day One 1989; Seven Minutes 1989; Blue Heat 1990; Evidence of Love 1990; Presumed Innocent 1990; FX 2 1991; Gladiator 1992; Jack Reed: Badge of Honor 1993; Prophet of Evil 1993; Jack Reed: a Search for Justice 1994; Leave of Absence 1994; Jack Reed: One of Our Own 1995; The Stars Fell on Henrietta 1995; Tommy Boy 1995; Jack Reed: Death and Vengeance 1996; William Shakespeare's Romeo + Juliet 1996; A Father's Betrayal 1997; Fail Safe 2000; Summer Catch 2001; Stolen Summer 2002; She Hate Me 2004; Assault on Precinct 13 2005

Dennen, Barry (1938–) Jesus Christ Superstar 1973; Brannigan 1975; The Dark Crystal 1982

Denner, Charles (1926–1995) Bluebeard 1962; Life Upside Down 1964; The Bride Wore Black 1967; Z 1968; Une Belle Fille Comme Moi 1973; The Inheritor 1973; And Now My Love 1974; Mado 1976; Second Chance 1976; The Man Who Loved Women 1977; Robert et Robert 1978; Golden Eighties 1986

Denning, Richard (1914–1998) Adam Had Four Sons 1941; Beyond the Blue Horizon 1942; The Glass Key 1942; Quiet Please, Murder 1942; Black Beauty 1946; No Man of Her Own 1950; Weekend with Father 1951; Scarlet Angel 1952; The 49th Man 1953; The Glass Web 1953; Creature from the Black Lagoon 1954; Jivaro 1954; Creature with the Atom Brain 1955; The Magnificent Matador 1955; Assignment Redhead 1956; The Day the World Ended 1956; The Oklahoma Woman 1956; An Affair to Remember 1957; The Black Scorpion 1957; The Lady Takes a Flyer 1958; Twice Told Tales 1963

Dennis, Les (1954–) Intimate Relations 1995; Large 2000

Dennis, Nick (1904–1980) Sirocco 1951; A Streetcar Named Desire 1951; Ten Tall Men 1951; Anything Can Happen 1952; Eight Iron Men 1952; The Glory Brigade 1953; Man in the Dark 1953; Kiss Me Deadly 1955; Too Late Blues 1961; Gunpoint 1966

Dennis, Sandy (1937–1992) Splendor in the Grass 1961; The Three Sisters 1966; Who's Afraid of Virginia Woolf? 1966; The Fox 1967; Up the Down Staircase 1967; Sweet November 1968; That Cold Day in the Park 1969; A Touch of Love 1969; The Out of Towners 1970; Mr Sycamore 1974; God Told Me to 1976; Nasty Habits 1976; The Four Seasons 1981; Come Back to the Five and Dime, Jimmy Dean, Jimmy Dean 1982; Another Woman 1988; 976-EVIL 1988; Parents 1988; The Indian Runner 1991

Denny, Reginald (1891–1967) A Lady's Morals 1930; Madam Satan 1930; Parlor, Bedroom and Bath 1931; Private Lives 1931; The Barbarian 1933; Only Yesterday 1933; The Lost Patrol 1934; Of Human Bondage 1934; One More River 1934; The Richest Girl in the World 1934; The World Moves On 1934; Anna Karenina 1935; Remember Last Night? 1935; Bulldog Drummond Comes Back 1937; Bulldog Drummond Escapes 1937; Bulldog Drummond's Revenge 1937; Bulldog Drummond in Africa 1938; Bulldog Drummond's Peril 1938; Bulldog Drummond's Bride 1939; Rebecca 1940; Seven Sinners 1940; Appointment for Love 1941; Captains of the Clouds 1942; Sherlock Holmes and the Voice of Terror 1942; Christmas Eve 1947; Escape Me Never 1947; The Macomber Affair 1947; My Favorite Brunette 1947; The Secret Life of Walter Mitty 1947; Abbott and Costello Meet Dr Jekyll and Mr Hyde 1953; World for Ransom 1953; Cat Ballou 1965

Denny, Susan (1934–) The Pursuers 1961; The Sicilians 1964

Denton, Christa The Burning Bed 1984; The Gate 1987

Denton, Crahan (1914–1966) The Great St Louis Bank Robbery 1959; The Young One 1960; Birdman of Alcatraz 1962; Hud 1963; Bus Riley's Back in Town 1965

Denver, Bob (1935–) For Those Who Think Young 1964; The Sweet Ride 1967; Who's Minding the Mint? 1967; Did You Hear the One about the Traveling Saleslady? 1968

Denzongpa, Danny (1948–) Hum 1991; Seven Years in Tibet 1997; Asoka 2001; Shikaar – the Musical Thriller 2004

Deol, Esha (1971–) Koi Mere Dil Se Pooche 2001; Na Tum Jaano Na Hum 2002; Dhoom 2004; Kaal 2005

Depardieu, Elisabeth (1941–) Jean de Florette 1986; Manon des Sources 1986

Depardieu, Gérard aka **Depardieu, Gerard** (1948–) Les Valseuses 1974; Vincent, François, Paul and the Others 1974; Maîtresse 1976; 1900 1976; Get out Your Handkerchiefs 1977; Bye Bye Monkey 1978; Les Chiens 1978; Buffet Froid 1979; Je Vous Aime 1980; The Last Metro 1980; Loulou 1980; Mon Oncle d'Amérique 1980; Choice of Arms 1981; The Woman Next Door 1981; Danton 1982; The Return of Martin Guerre 1982; Les Compères 1983; The Moon in the Gutter 1983; Fort Saganne 1984; Right Bank, Left Bank 1984; Police 1985; Jean de Florette 1986; Tenue de Soirée 1986; Sous le Soleil de Satan 1987; Camille Claudel 1988; A Strange Place to Meet 1988; I Want to Go Home 1989; Trop Belle pour Toi 1989; Cyrano de Bergerac 1990; Green Card 1990; Uranus 1990; Merci la Vie 1991; Mon Père Ce Héros 1991; Tous les Matins du Monde 1991; 1492: Conquest of Paradise 1992; Germinal 1993; Hélas pour Moi 1993; Le Colonel Chabert 1994; Elisa 1994; La Machine 1994; My Father the Hero 1994; A Pure Formality 1994; Guardian Angels 1995; The Horseman on the Roof 1995; Bogus 1996; Hamlet 1996; The Secret Agent 1996; Unhook the Stars 1996; The Man in the Iron Mask 1997; Asterix and Obelix Take On Caesar 1999; The Bridge 1999; 102 Dalmatians 2000; Vatel 2000; Asterix & Obelix: Mission Cleopatra 2001; The Closet 2001; Vidocq 2001; City of Ghosts 2002; Crime Spree 2002; Bon Voyage 2003; Nathalie... 2003

Depardieu, Guillaume (1971–) Tous les Matins du Monde 1991; Wild Target 1993; Les Apprentis 1995; Pola X 1999; Process 2004

Depp, Johnny (1963–) A Nightmare on Elm Street 1984; Private Resort 1985; Platoon 1986; Cry-Baby 1989; Edward Scissorhands 1990; Arizona Dream 1991; Benny and Joon 1993; What's Eating Gilbert Grape 1993; Ed Wood 1994; Dead Man 1995; Don Juan DeMarco 1995; Nick of Time 1995; The Brave 1997; Donnie Brasco 1997; Fear and Loathing in Las Vegas 1998; LA without a Map 1998; The Astronaut's Wife 1999; The Ninth Gate 1999; Sleepy Hollow 1999; Before Night Falls 2000; Chocolat 2000; The Man Who Cried 2000; Blow 2001; From Hell 2001; Once upon a Time in Mexico 2003; Pirates of the Caribbean: the Curse of the Black Pearl 2003; Finding Neverland 2004; The Libertine 2004; Secret Window 2004

Dequenne, Emilie (1981–) Rosetta 1999; Brotherhood of the Wolf 2001

Derangère, Grégori The Officers' Ward 2001; Bon Voyage 2003

Derek, Bo (1956–) Orca ... Killer Whale 1977; 10 1979; A Change of Seasons 1980; Tarzan, the Ape Man 1981; Bolero 1984; Ghosts Can't Do It 1990; Woman of Desire 1994; Tommy Boy 1995; Life in the Balance 2001; The Master of Disguise 2002; Malibu's Most Wanted 2003

Derek, John (1926–1998) All the King's Men 1949; Knock on Any Door 1949; Rogues of Sherwood Forest 1950; Thunderbirds 1952; Ambush at Tomahawk Gap 1953; The Last Posse 1953; Prince of Pirates 1953; The Adventures of Hajji Baba 1954; The Outcast 1954; An Annapolis Story 1955; Prince of Players 1955; Run for Cover 1955; The Ten Commandments 1956; The Flesh Is Weak 1957; Fury at Showdown 1957; High Hell 1957; Omar Khayyam 1957; Exodus 1960; Nightmare in the Sun 1964; Once Before I Die 1965

Dermithe, Edouard (1925–1995) Les Enfants Terribles 1949; Orphée 1950; Le Testament d'Orphée 1960

Dern, Bruce (1936–) Wild River 1960; Marnie 1964; The Wild Angels 1966; Rebel Rousers 1967; The St Valentine's Day Massacre 1967; The Trip 1967; The War Wagon 1967; Waterhole #3 1967; Will Penny 1967; Hang 'Em High 1968; Psych-Out 1968; Castle Keep 1969; Number One 1969; Support Your Local Sheriff! 1969; They Shoot Horses, Don't They? 1969; Bloody Mama 1970; Drive, He Said 1971; The Incredible Two-Headed Transplant 1971; Silent Running 1971; The Cowboys 1972; The King of Marvin Gardens 1972; Thumb Tripping 1972; The Laughing Policeman 1973; The Great Gatsby 1974; Posse 1975; Smile 1975; Black Sunday 1976; Family Plot 1976; The Twist 1976; Won Ton Ton, the Dog Who Saved Hollywood 1976; Coming Home 1978; The Driver 1978; Middle Age Crazy 1980; Tattoo 1980; That Championship Season 1982; On the Edge 1985; The Big Town 1987; 1969 1988; World Gone Wild 1988; The 'Burbs 1989; After Dark, My Sweet 1990; The Court-Martial of Jackie Robinson 1990; Midnight Sting 1992; Wild Bill 1995; Down Periscope 1996; Small Soldiers 1998; When the Bough Breaks 2: Perfect Prey 1998; The Haunting 1999; All the Pretty Horses 2000; The Glass House 2001; Milwaukee, Minnesota 2002; Monster 2003

Dern, Laura (1966–) Ladies and Gentlemen, the Fabulous Stains 1981; Teachers 1984; Mask 1985; Smooth Talk 1985; Blue Velvet 1986; Haunted Summer 1988; Shadow Makers 1989; Wild at Heart 1990; Rambling Rose 1991; Jurassic Park 1993; A Perfect World 1993; Citizen Ruth 1996; October Sky 1999; Dr T & the Women 2000; Focus 2001; I Am Sam 2001; Jurassic Park III 2001; Novocaine 2001; We Don't Live Here Anymore 2003

Derr, Richard (1918–1992) A Gentleman at Heart 1942; The Secret Heart 1946; When Worlds Collide 1951; Something to Live For 1952; Terror Is a Man 1959

Derricks, Cleavant (1953–) Moscow on the Hudson 1984; The Slugger's Wife 1985; Off Beat 1986

Derryberry, Debi Whispers: an Elephant's Tale 2000; Jimmy Neutron: Boy Genius 2001

Des Barres, Michael (1948–) Ghoulies 1985; Nightflyers 1987; Pink Cadillac 1989; Sugar Town 1999; Diary of a Sex Addict 2001; Catch That Kid 2004

Desailly, Jean (1920–) La Symphonie Pastorale 1946; Les Grandes Manoeuvres 1955; Maigret Sets a Trap 1957; Violent Summer 1961; Le Doulos 1962; La Peau Douce 1964

DeSando, Anthony Federal Hill 1994; Party Girl 1994; Kiss Me, Guido 1997

DeSantis, Stanley (1954–) The Truth about Cats and Dogs 1996; Clockwatchers 1997

Desarthe, Gérard (1945–) The Police War 1979; Uranus 1990; Daens 1992

Descas, Alex (1958–) Le Cri du Coeur 1994; Harem Suare 1999; Trouble Every Day 2000; Coffee and Cigarettes 2003

Deschamps, Hubert (1923–1998) Zazie dans le Métro 1960; Le Feu Follet 1963; The Mouth Agape 1974

Deschanel, Zooey (1980–) Mumford 1999; Almost Famous 2000; The Good Girl 2001; Manic 2001; The New Guy 2002; All the Real Girls 2003; Elf 2003; The Hitchhiker's Guide to the Galaxy 2005

Descher, Sandy (1948–) It Grows on Trees 1952; A Gift for Heidi 1958

Desiderio, Robert Oh, God! You Devil 1984; A Cut Above 1989

Desmond, Florence (1905–1993) Sally in Our Alley 1931; No Limit 1935; Accused 1936; Keep Your Seats, Please 1936; Three Came Home 1950; Charley Moon 1956

Desmond, Johnny (1920–1985) China Doll 1958; The Bubble 1966

Desmonde, Jerry (1908–1967) London Town 1946; Cardboard Cavalier 1949; Trouble in Store 1953; The Angel Who Pawned Her Harp 1954; Man of the Moment 1955; Up in the World 1956; Follow a Star 1959; A Stitch in Time 1963; The Early Bird 1965

Desni, Tamara (1913–) Jack Ahoy! 1934; Fire over England 1937; The Squeaker 1937; Send for Paul Temple 1946; The Hills of Donegal 1947

Desny, Ivan aka **Desny, Yvan** (1928–2002) Madeleine 1949; La Signora senza Camelie 1953; Lola Montès 1955; Anastasia 1956; Is Anna Anderson Anastasia? 1956; Song without End 1960; The Magnificent Rebel 1961; Sherlock Holmes and the Deadly Necklace 1962; Kidnapped to Mystery Island 1964; Paper Tiger 1974; The Marriage of Maria Braun 1978; Lola 1982; J'Embrasse Pas 1991

Desselle, Natalie BAPS 1997; How to Be a Player 1997; Rodgers & Hammerstein's Cinderella 1997

Deste, Luli (1901–1951) Thunder in the City 1937; The Case of the Black Parrot 1941

Detmer, Amanda (1971–) Boys and Girls 2000; Final Destination 2000; Evil Woman 2001; Big Fat Liar 2002

Detmers, Maruschka (1962–) First Name: Carmen 1983; Hanna's War 1988; The Mambo Kings 1992; Love in the Strangest Way 1994; The Shooter 1994

Deutsch, Ernst (1890–1969) The Golem 1920; The Third Man 1949

Dev, Rahul Asoka 2001; Awara Paagal Deewana 2002; 23rd March 1931: Shaheed 2002; Supari 2003

Devane, William (1939–) Glory Boy 1971; Lady Liberty 1971; McCabe and Mrs Miller 1971; The Pursuit of Happiness 1971; Fear on Trial 1975; Report to the Commissioner 1975; Family Plot 1976; Marathon Man 1976; The

Bad News Bears in Breaking Training 1977; *Rolling Thunder* 1977; *The Dark* 1979; *Yanks* 1979; *Honky Tonk Freeway* 1981; *Testament* 1983; *Hadley's Rebellion* 1984; *Victim of Beauty* 1991; *Prophet of Evil* 1993; *Formula for Death* 1995; *Freefall: Flight 174* 1995; *Night Watch* 1995; *Forgotten Sins* 1996; *Payback* 1998; *Hollow Man* 2000; *Poor White Trash* 2000; *Space Cowboys* 2000

Devereaux, Ed (1925–2003) *Watch Your Stern* 1960; *The Password Is Courage* 1962; *Live It Up* 1963; *They're a Weird Mob* 1966; *Pressure* 1976; *Money Movers* 1978

Devgan, Ajay (1967–) *Hindustan Ki Kasam* 1999; *Hum Dil De Chuke Sanam* 1999; *Company* 2001; *Bhoot* 2003; *Khakee* 2003; *LOC Kargil* 2003; *Masti* 2004; *Raincoat* 2004; *Kaal* 2005

Devi, Kamala *Geronimo* 1962; *The Brass Bottle* 1964

Devillers, Renée (1903–2001) *J'Accuse* 1938; *Thérèse Desqueyroux* 1962

Devine, Aidan *Trucks* 1997; *Ice Bound* 2003

Devine, Andy (1905–1977) *The Impatient Maiden* 1932; *The Man from Yesterday* 1932; *Three Wise Girls* 1932; *Dr Bull* 1933; *Upper World* 1934; *The Farmer Takes a Wife* 1935; *In Old Chicago* 1937; *A Star Is Born* 1937; *You're a Sweetheart* 1937; *Doctor Rhythm* 1938; *Men with Wings* 1938; *The Storm* 1938; *Yellow Jack* 1938; *Geronimo* 1939; *Never Say Die* 1939; *Stagecoach* 1939; *Little Old New York* 1940; *Torrid Zone* 1940; *Trail of the Vigilantes* 1940; *When the Daltons Rode* 1940; *The Flame of New Orleans* 1941; *Road Agent* 1941; *Sin Town* 1942; *Corvette K-225* 1943; *Frontier Badmen* 1943; *Ali Baba and the Forty Thieves* 1944; *Ghost Catchers* 1944; *Frontier Gal* 1945; *Sudan* 1945; *Canyon Passage* 1946; *Bells of San Angelo* 1947; *Slave Girl* 1947; *Springtime in the Sierras* 1947; *The Vigilantes Return* 1947; *Under California Stars* 1948; *The Far Frontier* 1949; *Never a Dull Moment* 1950; *The Red Badge of Courage* 1951; *Slaughter Trail* 1951; *Thunder Pass* 1954; *Pete Kelly's Blues* 1955; *The Adventures of Huckleberry Finn* 1960; *Two Rode Together* 1961; *The Man Who Shot Liberty Valance* 1962; *The Ballad of Josie* 1968; *Myra Breckinridge* 1970; *Robin Hood* 1973; *The Mouse and His Child* 1977

Devine, George (1910–1966) *The Beggar's Opera* 1953; *Tom Jones* 1963

Devine, Loretta (1949–) *Sticky Fingers* 1988; *Waiting to Exhale* 1995; *The Preacher's Wife* 1996; *Down in the Delta* 1997; *Love Kills* 1998; *Urban Legend* 1998; *Introducing Dorothy Dandridge* 1999; *Freedom Song* 2000; *Urban Legends: Final Cut* 2000; *I Am Sam* 2001

DeVito, Danny (1944–) *Lady Liberty* 1971; *Hurry Up, or I'll Be 30* 1973; *Scalawag* 1973; *One Flew over the Cuckoo's Nest* 1975; *Goin' South* 1978; *Going Ape!* 1981; *Terms of Endearment* 1983; *Johnny Dangerously* 1984; *Romancing the Stone* 1984; *The Jewel of the Nile* 1985; *Head Office* 1986; *My Little Pony* 1986; *Ruthless People* 1986; *Wise Guys* 1986; *Throw Momma from the Train* 1987; *Tin Men* 1987; *Twins* 1988; *The War of the Roses* 1989; *Other People's Money* 1991; *Batman Returns* 1992; *Hoffa* 1992; *Jack the Bear* 1993; *Look Who's Talking Now!* 1993; *Junior* 1994; *Renaissance Man* 1994; *Get Shorty* 1995; *Mars Attacks!* 1996; *Matilda* 1996; *Hercules* 1997; *John Grisham's The Rainmaker* 1997; *LA Confidential* 1997; *Space Jam* 1997; *Living Out Loud* 1998; *The Big Kahuna* 1999; *Man on the Moon* 1999; *The Virgin Suicides* 1999; *Drowning Mona* 2000; *Screwed* 2000; *Heist* 2001; *What's the Worst That Could Happen?* 2001; *Death to Smoochy* 2002; *Anything Else* 2003; *Be Cool* 2005

Devlin, Alan *Angel* 1982; *The Lonely Passion of Judith Hearne* 1987; *The Playboys* 1992; *High Boot Benny* 1993; *Song for a Raggy Boy* 2002; *bl,.m* 2003

Devlin, J G (1907–1991) *Sir Henry at Rawlinson End* 1980; *No Surrender* 1986; *The Miracle* 1990

Devlin, William (1911–1987) *Blood of the Vampire* 1958; *The Shuttered Room* 1967

Devon, Laura (1940–) *Goodbye Charlie* 1964; *Red Line 7000* 1965; *Chamber of Horrors* 1966; *A Covenant with Death* 1967; *Gunn* 1967

Devon, Richard (1931–) *Viking Women and the Sea Serpent* 1957; *War of the Satellites* 1958

Devos, Emmanuelle (1964–) *Ma Vie Sexuelle* 1996; *Esther Kahn* 2000; *Read My Lips* 2001; *Petites Coupures* 2002; *Kings & Queen* 2004

Devry, Elaine (1935–) *Man-Trap* 1961; *Diary of a Madman* 1963; *A Guide for the Married Man* 1967; *The Cheyenne Social Club* 1970; *Bless the Beasts and Children* 1971

Dewaere, Patrick (1947–1982) *Les Valseuses* 1974; *Get out Your Handkerchiefs* 1977

Dewhurst, Colleen (1924–1993) *The Nun's Story* 1959; *A Fine Madness* 1966; *The Last Run* 1971; *The Cowboys* 1972; *McQ* 1974; *Annie Hall* 1977; *Ice Castles* 1978; *When a Stranger Calls* 1979; *Tribute* 1980; *The Dead Zone* 1983; *The Boy Who Could Fly* 1986; *Danielle Steel's Kaleidoscope* 1990; *Dying Young* 1991; *Bed & Breakfast* 1992

Dexter, Alan (1918–1983) *Forbidden* 1953; *Time Limit* 1957; *Paint Your Wagon* 1969

Dexter, Anthony (1913–2001) *Valentino* 1951; *Captain Kidd and the Slave Girl* 1954; *Fire Maidens from Outer Space* 1956; *He Laughed Last* 1956; *The Parson and the Outlaw* 1957

Dexter, Aubrey (1898–1958) *The Love Test* 1935; *Please Teacher* 1937

Dexter, Brad (1917–2002) *The Las Vegas Story* 1952; *Macao* 1952; *99 River Street* 1953; *House of Bamboo* 1955; *Between Heaven and Hell* 1956; *Beyond the River* 1956; *The Oklahoman* 1957; *Run Silent, Run Deep* 1958; *Last Train from Gun Hill* 1959; *The Magnificent Seven* 1960; *The George Raft Story* 1961; *X-15* 1961; *Taras Bulba* 1962; *Johnny Cool* 1963; *Kings of the Sun* 1963; *Invitation to a Gunfighter* 1964; *Bus Riley's Back in Town* 1965; *None but the Brave* 1965; *Von Ryan's Express* 1965; *Blindfold* 1966; *Jory* 1972; *Vigilante Force* 1975

Dexter, William (1974–) *The Knack... and How to Get It* 1965; *The Hand of Night* 1966

Dey, Dipankar *The Middleman* 1975; *In Search of Famine* 1980; *An Enemy of the People* 1989; *Branches of the Tree* 1990; *The Stranger* 1991

Dey, Susan (1952–) *Skyjacked* 1972; *First Love* 1977; *Looker* 1981; *Echo Park* 1985

Dharkar, Ayesha aka **Dharker, Ayesha** (1977–) *City of Joy* 1992; *The Terrorist* 1998; *Split Wide Open* 1999; *The Mystic Masseur* 2001

Dharmendra (1935–) *Bandini* 1963; *Sholay* 1975; *Dharam Veer* 1977

Di Stefano, Andrea *The Prince of Homburg* 1997; *The Phantom of the Opera* 1998; *Before Night Falls* 2000; *Angela* 2002

Diamantidou, Despo (1916–2004) *A Dream of Passion* 1978; *Hard Goodbyes: My Father* 2002

Diamond, Neil (1941–) *The Jazz Singer* 1980; *Evil Woman* 2001

Diamond, Reed aka **Diamond, Reed Edward** (1964–) *Memphis Belle* 1990; *Danielle Steel's Full Circle* 1996; *A Father's Betrayal* 1997

Diamond, Selma (1920–1985) *Bang the Drum Slowly* 1973; *All of Me* 1984

Diaz, Cameron (1972–) *The Mask* 1994; *The Last Supper* 1995; *Feeling Minnesota* 1996; *Head above Water* 1996; *Keys to Tulsa* 1996; *She's the One* 1996; *A Life Less Ordinary* 1997; *My Best Friend's Wedding* 1997; *Fear and Loathing in Las Vegas* 1998; *There's Something about Mary* 1998; *Very Bad Things* 1998; *Any Given Sunday* 1999; *Being John Malkovich* 1999; *Charlie's Angels* 2000; *The Invisible Circus* 2000; *Things You Can Tell Just by Looking at Her* 2000; *Shrek* 2001; *Slackers* 2001; *Vanilla Sky* 2001; *Gangs of New York* 2002; *The Sweetest Thing* 2002; *Charlie's Angels: Full Throttle* 2003; *Shrek 2* 2004

Diaz, Guillermo *Party Girl* 1994; *Stonewall* 1995; *High School High* 1996; *I'm Not Rappaport* 1996; *I Think I Do* 1997; *Half-Baked* 1998

Diaz, Vic (1932–) *Operation CIA* 1965; *Bloodfist* 1989

Dibbs, Kem (1917–1996) *The Twinkle in God's Eye* 1955; *Daniel Boone, Trail Blazer* 1957

Diberti, Luigi (1939–) *The Seduction of Mimi* 1972; *The Oberwald Mystery* 1980; *The Stendhal Syndrome* 1996

DiCaprio, Leonardo (1974–) *Critters 3* 1991; *Poison Ivy* 1992; *This Boy's Life* 1993; *What's Eating Gilbert Grape* 1993; *The Basketball Diaries* 1995; *The Quick and the Dead* 1995; *Total Eclipse* 1995; *Marvin's Room* 1996; *William Shakespeare's Romeo + Juliet* 1996; *The Man in the Iron Mask* 1997; *Titanic* 1997; *Celebrity* 1998; *The Beach* 2000; *Catch Me If You Can* 2002; *Gangs of New York* 2002; *The Aviator* 2004

DiCenzo, George *Going Home* 1971; *The Frisco Kid* 1979; *Starflight One* 1983; *About Last Night...* 1986; *Walk like a Man* 1987; *18 Again!* 1988; *Sing* 1989; *Tempted* 2001

DiCicco, Bobby (1955–) *I Wanna Hold Your Hand* 1978; *The Big Red One* 1980; *Night Shift* 1982; *The Philadelphia Experiment* 1984; *Tiger Warsaw* 1988

Dick, Andy (1965–) *...And God Spoke* 1993; *In the Army Now* 1994; *Best Men* 1997

Dick, Douglas (1920–) *The Searching Wind* 1946; *Casbah* 1948; *Saigon* 1948; *The Accused* 1949; *Home of the Brave* 1949; *The Red Badge of Courage* 1951; *Something to Live For* 1952; *The Oklahoman* 1957

Dickens, Kim (1965–) *Great Expectations* 1997; *Truth or Consequences, NM* 1997; *Zero Effect* 1997; *Mercury Rising* 1998; *Hollow Man* 2000; *House of Sand and Fog* 2003

Dickerson, George *Space Raiders* 1983; *Blue Velvet* 1986; *Death Wish 4: the Crackdown* 1987; *After Dark, My Sweet* 1990; *Death Warrant* 1990

Dickey, Lucinda *Breakdance* 1984; *Breakdance 2 – Electric Boogaloo* 1984

Dickinson, Angie (1931–) *Lucky Me* 1954; *Man with the Gun* 1955; *Tension at Table Rock* 1956; *Calypso Joe* 1957; *China Gate* 1957; *Shoot-Out at Medicine Bend* 1957; *Cry Terror* 1958; *I Married a Woman* 1958; *Rio Bravo* 1959; *The Bramble Bush* 1960; *Ocean's Eleven* 1960; *The Sins of Rachel Cade* 1960; *A Fever in the Blood* 1961; *Jessica* 1962; *Rome Adventure* 1962; *Captain Newman, MD* 1963; *The Killers* 1964; *Art of Love* 1965; *Cast a Giant Shadow* 1966; *The Chase* 1966; *The Poppy Is Also a Flower* 1966; *The Last Challenge* 1967; *Point Blank* 1967; *Sam Whiskey* 1969; *Young Billy Young* 1969; *Pretty Maids All in a Row* 1971; *The Resurrection of Zachary Wheeler* 1971; *The Outside Man* 1973; *Big Bad Mama* 1974; *Dressed to Kill* 1980; *Charlie Chan and the Curse of the Dragon Queen* 1981; *Death Hunt* 1981; *Big Bad Mama II* 1987; *Once upon a Texas Train* 1988; *Even Cowgirls Get the Blues* 1993; *The Maddening* 1995; *Sabrina* 1995; *The Sun, the Moon and the Stars* 1995; *Danielle Steel's Remembrance* 1996; *Duets* 2000; *Pay It Forward* 2000

Dickson, Gloria (1916–1945) *They Won't Forget* 1937; *Gold Diggers in Paris* 1938; *Racket Busters* 1938; *They Made Me a Criminal* 1939; *This Thing Called Love* 1940; *Lady of Burlesque* 1943

Dickson, Neil *Biggles* 1986; *Lionheart* 1986; *King of the Wind* 1989

Diddley, Bo (1928–) *Trading Places* 1983; *Eddie and the Cruisers II: Eddie Lives!* 1989; *Rockula* 1989

Diefenthal, Frédéric (1968–) *Taxi* 1998; *Taxi 2* 2000

Diego, Gabino (1966–) *Ay, Carmela!* 1990; *Belle Epoque* 1992; *Two Much* 1995

Diego, Juan (1942–) *Los Santos Inocentes* 1984; *Jarrapellejos* 1987; *Cabeza de Vaca* 1990; *Jamon Jamon* 1992; *Torremolinos 73* 2003

Diehl, John (1956–) *Angel* 1984; *City Limits* 1985; *Kickboxer 2: the Road Back* 1990; *Madhouse* 1990; *Motorama* 1991; *A Row of Crows* 1991; *Whore* 1991; *Mo' Money* 1992; *Stargate* 1994; *Three Wishes* 1995; *Casualties* 1997; *Anywhere but Here* 1999; *Jurassic Park III* 2001

Dierkes, John (1905–1975) *Macbeth* 1948; *The Red Badge of Courage* 1951; *The Moonlighter* 1953; *The Naked Jungle* 1953; *Shane* 1953; *Daughter of Dr Jekyll* 1957; *The Hanging Tree* 1959

Dierkop, Charles (1936–) *The Face of Fear* 1971; *The Hot Box* 1972; *Messenger of Death* 1988

Diesel, Vin (1967–) *Saving Private Ryan* 1998; *The Iron Giant* 1999; *Pitch Black* 1999; *Boiler Room* 2000; *The Fast and the Furious* 2001; *Knockaround Guys* 2001; *xXx* 2002; *A Man Apart* 2003; *The Chronicles of Riddick* 2004; *The Pacifier* 2005

Diessl, Gustav (1899–1948) *Crisis* 1928; *Westfront 1918* 1930; *The Testament of Dr Mabuse* 1932

Dieterle, William aka **Dieterle, Wilhelm** (1893–1972) *Waxworks* 1924; *Faust* 1926

Dietrich, Dena (1928–) *The Wild Party* 1975; *On the Air Live with Captain Midnight* 1979

Dietrich, Marlene (1901–1992) *The Joyless Street* 1925; *The Ship of Lost Men* 1929; *Three Loves* 1929; *The Blue Angel* 1930; *Morocco* 1930; *Dishonored* 1931; *Blonde Venus* 1932; *Shanghai Express* 1932; *The Song of Songs* 1933; *The Scarlet Empress* 1934; *The Devil Is a Woman* 1935; *Desire* 1936; *The Garden of Allah* 1936; *Angel* 1937; *Knight without Armour* 1937; *Destry Rides Again* 1939; *Seven Sinners* 1940; *The Flame of New Orleans* 1941; *Manpower* 1941; *The Lady Is Willing* 1942; *Pittsburgh* 1942; *The Spoilers* 1942; *Follow the Boys* 1944; *Kismet* 1944; *Martin Roumagnac* 1946; *Golden Earrings* 1947; *A Foreign Affair* 1948; *Jigsaw* 1949; *Stage Fright* 1949; *No Highway* 1951; *Rancho Notorious* 1952; *Around the World in 80 Days* 1956; *The Monte Carlo Story* 1957; *Witness for the Prosecution* 1957; *Touch of Evil* 1958; *Judgment at Nuremberg* 1961; *The Black Fox* 1962; *Paris When It Sizzles* 1964; *Just a Gigolo* 1978; *Marlene* 1984

Diffring, Anton (1918–1989) *Albert, RN* 1953; *Park Plaza 605* 1953; *Double Cross* 1955; *I Am a Camera* 1955; *The Black Tent* 1956; *House of Secrets* 1956; *The Crooked Sky* 1957; *Mark of the Phoenix* 1957; *The Traitor* 1957; *The Man Who Could Cheat Death* 1959; *Circus of Horrors* 1960; *The Heroes of Telemark* 1965; *The Blue Max* 1966; *Fahrenheit 451* 1966; *Counterpoint* 1967; *The Double Man* 1967; *Where Eagles Dare* 1969; *Zeppelin* 1971; *Dead Pigeon on Beethoven Street* 1972; *The Beast Must Die* 1974; *Shatter* 1974; *Operation Daybreak* 1975; *The Swiss Conspiracy* 1975; *Montana Trap* 1976; *Operation Dead End* 1986

Digard, Uschi aka **Lillimor, Astrid** (1948–) *Cherry, Harry & Raquel* 1969; *Supervixens* 1975; *Beneath the Valley of the Ultra Vixens* 1979

Digges, Dudley (1879–1947) *Condemned* 1929; *Outward Bound* 1930; *Dangerous Female* 1931; *The First Year* 1932; *The Hatchet Man* 1932; *Tess of the Storm Country* 1932; *The Emperor Jones* 1933; *The King's Vacation* 1933; *The Mayor of Hell* 1933; *What Every Woman Knows* 1934; *China Seas* 1935; *Kind Lady* 1935; *Mutiny on the Bounty* 1935; *The General Died at Dawn* 1936; *Valiant Is the Word for Carrie* 1936; *Love Is News* 1937; *The Light That Failed* 1939; *Raffles* 1939; *The Searching Wind* 1946

Diggs, Taye (1972–) *How Stella Got Her Groove Back* 1998; *The Best Man* 1999; *House on Haunted Hill* 1999; *The Wood* 1999; *The Way of the Gun* 2000; *Brown Sugar* 2002; *Chicago* 2002; *Equilibrium* 2002; *Just a Kiss* 2002; *Basic* 2003; *Malibu's Most Wanted* 2003

Dignam, Arthur (1939–) *Petersen* 1974; *The Devil's Playground* 1976; *Cathy's Child* 1979; *Grendel, Grendel, Grendel* 1981; *We of the Never Never* 1982; *The Wild Duck* 1983; *Beneath Clouds* 2002

Dignam, Basil (1905–1979) *Seven Seas to Calais* 1962; *80,000 Suspects* 1963

Dignam, Mark (1909–1989) *The Siege of the Saxons* 1963; *Hamlet* 1969; *Dead Cert* 1974

Dillane, Stephen (1957–) *Hamlet* 1990; *Stolen Hearts* 1996; *Déjà Vu* 1997; *Firelight* 1997; *Welcome to Sarajevo* 1997; *The Darkest Light* 1999; *Ordinary Decent Criminal* 1999; *The Parole Officer* 2001; *Spy Game* 2001; *The Hours* 2002; *The Truth about Charlie* 2002; *King Arthur* 2004

Dillard, Victoria (1969–) *Ricochet* 1991; *Deep Cover* 1992; *Out of Sync* 1995; *The Best Man* 1999

Dillaway, Donald aka **Dillaway, Don** (1903–1982) *Min and Bill* 1930; *Body and Soul* 1931; *Platinum Blonde* 1931; *The Animal Kingdom* 1932; *Pack Up Your Troubles* 1932; *The Little Giant* 1933; *The Magnificent Ambersons* 1942

Diller, Phyllis (1917–) *Boy, Did I Get a Wrong Number* 1966; *Mad Monster Party* 1966; *Eight on the Lam* 1967; *Did You Hear the One about the Traveling Saleslady?* 1968; *The Private Navy of Sgt O'Farrell* 1968; *The Adding Machine* 1969; *Pucker Up and Bark like a Dog* 1989; *Happily Ever After* 1990; *The Silence of the Hams* 1993; *A Bug's Life* 1998

Dillman, Bradford aka **Dillman, Brad** (1930–) *A Certain Smile* 1958; *In Love and War* 1958; *Compulsion* 1959; *Circle of Deception* 1960; *Crack in the Mirror* 1960; *Francis of Assisi* 1961; *Sanctuary* 1961; *A Rage to Live* 1965; *The Plainsman* 1966; *The Helicopter Spies* 1968; *Jigsaw* 1968; *Sergeant Ryker* 1968; *The Bridge at Remagen* 1969; *Brother John* 1970; *Suppose They Gave a War and Nobody Came?* 1970; *Escape from the Planet of the Apes* 1971; *The Mephisto Waltz* 1971; *The Resurrection of Zachary Wheeler* 1971; *The Iceman Cometh* 1973; *The Way We Were* 1973; *Chosen Survivors* 1974; *Gold* 1974; *99*

and 44/100% Dead 1974; *Bug* 1975; *The Enforcer* 1976; *Mastermind* 1976; *The Amsterdam Kill* 1978; *Love and Bullets* 1978; *Piranha* 1978; *Sudden Impact* 1983; *Heroes Stand Alone* 1989; *The Heart of Justice* 1992
Dillon, Edward *aka* **Dillon, Eddie** (1879–1933) *The Broadway Melody* 1929; *The Iron Man* 1931
Dillon, Kevin (1965–) *No Big Deal* 1983; *Catholic Boys* 1985; *Platoon* 1986; *The Blob* 1988; *Remote Control* 1988; *The Rescue* 1988; *War Party* 1988; *Immediate Family* 1989; *The Doors* 1991; *A Midnight Clear* 1991; *No Escape* 1994; *True Crime* 1995; *Stag* 1996
Dillon, Matt (1964–) *Over the Edge* 1979; *Little Darlings* 1980; *My Bodyguard* 1980; *Liar's Moon* 1982; *Tex* 1982; *The Outsiders* 1983; *Rumble Fish* 1983; *The Flamingo Kid* 1984; *Rebel* 1985; *Target* 1985; *Native Son* 1986; *The Big Town* 1987; *Kansas* 1988; *Bloodhounds of Broadway* 1989; *Drugstore Cowboy* 1989; *A Kiss before Dying* 1991; *Mr Wonderful* 1992; *Singles* 1992; *The Saint of Fort Washington* 1993; *Golden Gate* 1994; *Frankie Starlight* 1995; *To Die For* 1995; *Albino Alligator* 1996; *Beautiful Girls* 1996; *Grace of My Heart* 1996; *In & Out* 1997; *There's Something about Mary* 1998; *Wild Things* 1998; *One Night at McCool's* 2001; *City of Ghosts* 2002; *Crash* 2004
Dillon, Melinda (1939–) *The April Fools* 1969; *Bound for Glory* 1976; *Close Encounters of the Third Kind* 1977; *FIST* 1978; *Absence of Malice* 1981; *A Christmas Story* 1983; *Songwriter* 1984; *Bigfoot and the Hendersons* 1987; *Nightbreaker* 1989; *Staying Together* 1989; *Captain America* 1990; *The Prince of Tides* 1991; *Sioux City* 1994; *To Wong Foo, Thanks for Everything, Julie Newmar* 1995; *Magnolia* 1999
Dillon, Paul *Kiss Daddy Good Night* 1987; *Blink* 1994; *CutThroat Island* 1995; *Chicago Cab* 1998
Dimitriades, Alex (1973–) *The Heartbreak Kid* 1993; *Head On* 1997; *La Spagnola* 2001; *Ghost Ship* 2002
Dinehart, Alan (1889–1944) *Girls about Town* 1931; *Lawyer Man* 1932; *Washington Merry-Go-Round* 1932; *Bureau of Missing Persons* 1933; *The Sin of Nora Moran* 1933; *Supernatural* 1933; *Baby, Take a Bow* 1934; *The Cat's Paw* 1934; *Jimmy the Gent* 1934; *Dante's Inferno* 1935; *Born to Dance* 1936; *Human Cargo* 1936; *Step Lively, Jeeves* 1937; *This Is My Affair* 1937; *Fast and Loose* 1939; *Second Fiddle* 1939; *The Heat's On* 1943; *Sweet Rosie O'Grady* 1943; *What a Woman!* 1943; *The Whistler* 1944
Dingle, Charles (1887–1956) *The Little Foxes* 1941; *Unholy Partners* 1941; *Somewhere I'll Find You* 1942; *The Talk of the Town* 1942; *Lady of Burlesque* 1943; *Home in Indiana* 1944; *Together Again* 1944; *Guest Wife* 1945; *A Medal for Benny* 1945; *The Beast with Five Fingers* 1946; *Cinderella Jones* 1946; *Sister Kenny* 1946; *My Favorite Brunette* 1947; *If You Knew Susie* 1948; *Big Jack* 1949; *Never Wave at a WAC* 1952
Dingo, Ernie (1956–) *"Crocodile" Dundee II* 1988; *Until the End of the World* 1991; *Dead Heart* 1996
Dinome, Jerry (1958–) *Tomboy* 1985; *Dangerously Close* 1986
Dinsdale, Reece (1959–) *A Private Function* 1984; *ID* 1994; *Hamlet* 1996
Dione, Rose (1875–1936) *Salome* 1922; *Freaks* 1932
Dionisi, Stefano (1966–) *Farinelli il Castrato* 1994; *The Truce* 1997; *Shooting the Moon* 1998; *Les Enfants du Siècle* 1999; *The Loss of Sexual Innocence* 1999
Dionisotti, Paola *The Sailor's Return* 1978; *Vigo: Passion for Life* 1997; *The Tichborne Claimant* 1998
DiSanti, John *Eyes of a Stranger* 1980; *PK and the Kid* 1982
Dishy, Bob *aka* **Dishy, Robert** *The Tiger Makes Out* 1967; *Lovers and Other Strangers* 1970; *I Wonder Who's Killing Her Now?* 1975; *The Big Bus* 1976; *First Family* 1980; *Author! Author!* 1982; *Brighton Beach Memoirs* 1986; *Critical Condition* 1987; *Used People* 1992; *Thicker than Blood* 1993; *Don Juan DeMarco* 1995; *Judy Berlin* 1999
Disney, Walt (1901–1966) *Steamboat Willie* 1928; *Fun and Fancy Free* 1947
DiSpina, Teresa *Reform School Girl* 1994; *The Big Squeeze* 1996
Distel, Sacha (1933–2004) *La Bonne Soupe* 1963; *Without Apparent Motive* 1972
Ditson, Harry *The Sender* 1982; *Back in the USSR* 1992
Divine (1945–1988) *Mondo Trasho* 1970; *Multiple Maniacs* 1970; *Pink Flamingos* 1972; *Female Trouble* 1974; *The Alternative Miss World* 1980; *Polyester* 1981; *Lust in the Dust* 1984; *Trouble in Mind* 1985; *Hairspray* 1988; *Out of the Dark* 1988
Divoff, Andrew (1955–) *Another 48 HRS* 1990; *Graveyard Shift* 1990; *Toy Soldiers* 1991; *Back in the USSR* 1992; *Oblivion* 1993; *Running Cool* 1993; *A Low Down Dirty Shame* 1994; *Adrenalin: Fear the Rush* 1995; *Wishmaster* 1997; *Captured* 1998; *Stealth Fighter* 1999; *Faust: Love of the Damned* 2001
Dix, Richard (1894–1949) *The Ten Commandments* 1923; *Cimarron* 1931; *Hell's Highway* 1932; *The Lost Squadron* 1932; *Ace of Aces* 1933; *The Arizonian* 1935; *The Tunnel* 1935; *Man of Conquest* 1939; *Cherokee Strip* 1940; *The Roundup* 1941; *The Ghost Ship* 1943; *The Whistler* 1944
Dix, William (1956–) *The Nanny* 1965; *Doctor Dolittle* 1967
Dixit, Madhuri (1967–) *Saajan* 1991; *Hum Tumhare Hain Sanam* 2000; *Devdas* 2002
Dixon, Billie *Lions Love* 1969; *The Lady in the Car with Glasses and a Gun* 1970
Dixon, Donna (1957–) *Doctor Detroit* 1983; *Spies like Us* 1985; *The Couch Trip* 1988; *Cannonball Fever* 1989
Dixon, Ivan (1931–) *The Murder Men* 1961; *A Raisin in the Sun* 1961; *Nothing but a Man* 1964; *A Patch of Blue* 1965; *Suppose They Gave a War and Nobody Came?* 1970
Dixon, James *It's Alive* 1974; *It Lives Again* 1978; *Q – the Winged Serpent* 1982; *The Stuff* 1985; *It's Alive III: Island of the Alive* 1987
Dixon, Jean (1896–1981) *The Kiss before the Mirror* 1933; *She Married Her Boss* 1935; *My Man Godfrey* 1936; *Swing High, Swing Low* 1937; *You Only Live Once* 1937; *Holiday* 1938; *Joy of Living* 1938
Dixon, Jill *Just My Luck* 1957; *A Night to Remember* 1958
Dixon, Joan (1930–1995) *Bunco Squad* 1950; *Roadblock* 1951; *Desert Passage* 1952
Dixon, Lee (1914–1953) *Gold Diggers of 1937* 1936; *Angel and the Badman* 1947
Dixon, MacIntyre (1931–) *Starting Over* 1979; *Funny Farm* 1988
Dixon, Reg (1914–1983) *Love in Pawn* 1953; *No Smoking* 1954
Djalili, Omid (1965–) *The Calcium Kid* 2003; *Sky Captain and the World of Tomorrow* 2004
Djola, Badja (1948–2005) *The Lightship* 1985; *The Serpent and the Rainbow* 1987; *An Innocent Man* 1989; *A Rage in Harlem* 1991; *Who's the Man?* 1993; *Heaven's Prisoners* 1996; *Deterrence* 1999
Dmochowski, Mariusz (1930–1992) *The Scar* 1976; *Camouflage* 1977
Dobie, Alan (1932–) *The Long Day's Dying* 1968; *Alfred the Great* 1969; *The Chairman* 1969
Dobkin, Lawrence (1919–2002) *The Gene Krupa Story* 1959; *The Cabinet of Caligari* 1962; *Geronimo* 1962
Dobrowolska, Gosia (1958–) *Silver City* 1984; *A Woman's Tale* 1991; *Careful* 1992; *The Nun and the Bandit* 1992; *Erotic Tales* 1994
Dobson, Anita (1949–) *Beyond Bedlam* 1993; *Darkness Falls* 1998; *Charlie* 2003
Dobson, James (1920–1987) *The Tall Stranger* 1957; *Jet Attack* 1958; *Impulse* 1975
Dobson, Peter (1964–) *Last Exit to Brooklyn* 1989; *Sing* 1989; *Too Hot to Handle* 1991; *Where the Day Takes You* 1992; *The Big Squeeze* 1996; *The Frighteners* 1996; *Norma Jean & Marilyn* 1996
Dobson, Tamara (1947–) *Cleopatra Jones* 1973; *Cleopatra Jones and the Casino of Gold* 1975; *Norman... Is That You?* 1976; *Chained Heat* 1983
Dobtcheff, Vernon (1934–) *Condorman* 1981; *Berlin Jerusalem* 1989; *Venice/Venice* 1992; *M Butterfly* 1993; *Déjà Vu* 1997; *All for Love* 1999; *The Order* 2001; *Before Sunset* 2004
Dr Dre (1965–) *Who's the Man?* 1993; *Set It Off* 1996; *Ride* 1998; *Training Day* 2001; *The Wash* 2001
Dodd, Claire (1908–1973) *Lawyer Man* 1932; *Ex-Lady* 1933; *Hard to Handle* 1933; *Gambling Lady* 1934; *The Glass Key* 1935; *Roberta* 1935; *The Case of the Velvet Claws* 1936; *Fast Company* 1938; *Three Loves Has Nancy* 1938; *Slightly Honorable* 1939; *In the Navy* 1941; *The Mad Doctor of Market Street* 1942
Dodsworth, John (1910–1964) *Here Comes the Sun* 1945; *The Maze* 1953
Doe, John (1954–) *Border Radio* 1987; *Slam Dance* 1987; *Great Balls of Fire!* 1989; *Without You I'm Nothing* 1990; *Pure Country* 1992; *Roadside Prophets* 1992; *Georgia* 1995; *Sugar Town* 1999
Doermer, Christian (1935–) *Love at Twenty* 1962; *Joanna* 1969
Doherty, Shannen (1971–) *Night Shift* 1982; *The Secret of NIMH* 1982; *Girls Just Want to Have Fun* 1985; *Heathers* 1989; *Mallrats* 1995; *Another Day* 2001; *Jay and Silent Bob Strike Back* 2001; *The Battle of Mary Kay* 2002
Dolan, Michael (1965–) *Hamburger Hill* 1987; *Light of Day* 1987; *Biloxi Blues* 1988; *The Turning* 1992
Doleman, Guy (1923–1996) *The Ipcress File* 1965; *Thunderball* 1965; *Funeral in Berlin* 1966; *The Idol* 1966; *Billion Dollar Brain* 1967; *The Deadly Bees* 1967; *A Twist of Sand* 1967; *Early Frost* 1981
Dolenz, Ami (1969–) *She's Out of Control* 1989; *Rescue Me* 1991; *Ticks* 1993; *The Revenge of Pumpkinhead – Blood Wings* 1994
Dolenz, George (1908–1963) *Enter Arsene Lupin* 1944; *My Cousin Rachel* 1952; *Scared Stiff* 1953; *Sign of the Pagan* 1954; *A Bullet for Joey* 1955; *The Purple Mask* 1955; *The Sad Sack* 1957; *Timbuktu* 1959; *Look in Any Window* 1961
Dolenz, Micky *aka* **Dolenz, Mickey** (1945–) *Head* 1968; *Linda Lovelace for President* 1975; *Night of the Strangler* 1975
Doll, Birgit (1958–) *Please Let the Flowers Live* 1986; *The Second Victory* 1986; *The Seventh Continent* 1989
Doll, Dora (1922–) *Honour among Thieves* 1954; *Calle Mayor* 1956; *Black and White in Color* 1976; *Boomerang* 1976; *L'Enfer* 1994
Dolman, Richard (1895–) *Looking on the Bright Side* 1931; *The Man Who Changed His Name* 1934; *Southern Roses* 1936
Domasin, Larry (1955–) *Fun in Acapulco* 1963; *Island of the Blue Dolphins* 1964
Dombasle, Arielle (1955–) *Le Beau Mariage* 1982; *Pauline at the Beach* 1983; *The Blue Villa* 1994; *Three Lives and Only One Death* 1996; *L'Ennui* 1998; *Le Libertin* 2000
Domeier, Richard *Evil Dead II* 1987; *The Unnamable Returns* 1992
Domergue, Faith (1925–1999) *Where Danger Lives* 1950; *The Duel at Silver Creek* 1952; *The Great Sioux Uprising* 1953; *This Is My Love* 1954; *Cult of the Cobra* 1955; *It Came from beneath the Sea* 1955; *Santa Fe Passage* 1955; *This Island Earth* 1955; *Timeslip* 1955; *Escort West* 1959; *Voyage to the Prehistoric Planet* 1965; *The Gamblers* 1969; *The House of Seven Corpses* 1973
Dominczyk, Dagmara (1976–) *The Count of Monte Cristo* 2001; *Rock Star* 2001; *They* 2002
Domingo, Placido (1941–) *La Traviata* 1982; *Carmen* 1984; *Otello* 1986
Dominguez, Columba (1929–) *The River and Death* 1954; *The Important Man* 1961
Dominguez D, Berta *Where Is Parsifal?* 1983; *The Rainbow Thief* 1990
Dominguez, Wade (1966–1999) *City of Industry* 1996; *Shadow of Doubt* 1998; *Taxman* 1998
Dominici, Arturo (1918–1992) *Hercules* 1957; *Goliath and the Barbarians* 1959; *The Mask of Satan* 1960; *The Trojan War* 1961; *Investigation of a Citizen above Suspicion* 1970
Dommartin, Solveig (1961–) *Wings of Desire* 1987; *Until the End of the World* 1991; *Faraway, So Close* 1993
Donahue, Elinor (1937–) *Love Is Better Than Ever* 1951; *Girls' Town* 1959
Donahue, Heather (1974–) *The Blair Witch Project* 1998; *Boys and Girls* 2000
Donahue, Troy (1936–2001) *The Tarnished Angels* 1957; *Live Fast, Die Young* 1958; *Monster on the Campus* 1958; *Wild Heritage* 1958; *A Summer Place* 1959; *The Crowded Sky* 1960; *Parrish* 1961; *Susan Slade* 1961; *Rome Adventure* 1962; *Palm Springs Weekend* 1963; *A Distant Trumpet* 1964; *My Blood Runs Cold* 1965; *Jules Verne's Rocket to the Moon* 1967; *Seizure* 1974; *Grandview, USA* 1984; *Cry-Baby* 1989; *Double Trouble* 1992
Donald, James (1917–1993) *The Way Ahead* 1944; *Broken Journey* 1948; *The Small Voice* 1948; *Edward, My Son* 1949; *Trottie True* 1949; *Cage of Gold* 1950; *Brandy for the Parson* 1951; *The Gift Horse* 1951; *White Corridors* 1951; *The Pickwick Papers* 1952; *The Net* 1953; *Beau Brummell* 1954; *Lust for Life* 1956; *The Bridge on the River Kwai* 1957; *The Vikings* 1958; *Third Man on the Mountain* 1959; *The Great Escape* 1963; *King Rat* 1965; *The Jokers* 1967; *Quatermass and the Pit* 1967; *The Royal Hunt of the Sun* 1969
Donaldson, Ted (1933–) *Mr Winkle Goes to War* 1944; *Once upon a Time* 1944; *A Tree Grows in Brooklyn* 1945; *Personality Kid* 1946
Donat, Peter (1928–) *Glory Boy* 1971; *A Different Story* 1978; *The China Syndrome* 1979; *Highpoint* 1979; *Ladies and Gentlemen, the Fabulous Stains* 1981; *Bay Boy* 1984; *Unfinished Business...* 1987; *Skin Deep* 1989; *The War of the Roses* 1989; *The Babe* 1992; *The Game* 1997; *Red Corner* 1997; *The Deep End* 2001
Donat, Robert (1905–1958) *The Private Life of Henry VIII* 1933; *The Count of Monte Cristo* 1934; *The Ghost Goes West* 1935; *The 39 Steps* 1935; *Knight without Armour* 1937; *The Citadel* 1938; *Goodbye, Mr Chips* 1939; *The Young Mr Pitt* 1942; *The Adventures of Tartu* 1943; *Perfect Strangers* 1945; *Captain Boycott* 1947; *The Winslow Boy* 1948; *The Cure for Love* 1949; *The Magic Box* 1951; *Lease of Life* 1954; *The Inn of the Sixth Happiness* 1958
Donath, Ludwig (1900–1967) *The Jolson Story* 1946; *To the Ends of the Earth* 1948; *Jolson Sings Again* 1949; *Mystery Submarine* 1950; *Torn Curtain* 1966
Donde, Manuel *The Treasure of the Sierra Madre* 1948; *Mexican Bus Ride* 1951; *El* 1953
Doniol-Valcroze, Jacques (1920–1989) *Out 1: Spectre* 1973; *Jeanne Dielman, 23 Quai du Commerce, 1080 Bruxelles* 1975; *Goodbye Emmanuelle* 1977
Donlan, James (1888–1938) *Big News* 1929; *Belle of the Nineties* 1934
Donlan, Yolande (1920–) *Traveller's Joy* 1949; *Mr Drake's Duck* 1950; *Penny Princess* 1952; *They Can't Hang Me* 1955; *Tarzan and the Lost Safari* 1956; *Expresso Bongo* 1959; *Jigsaw* 1962; *80,000 Suspects* 1963
Donlevy, Brian (1899–1972) *Barbary Coast* 1935; *Crack-Up* 1936; *Human Cargo* 1936; *Strike Me Pink* 1936; *Born Reckless* 1937; *This Is My Affair* 1937; *We're Going to Be Rich* 1938; *Beau Geste* 1939; *Destry Rides Again* 1939; *The First Rebel* 1939; *Jesse James* 1939; *Union Pacific* 1939; *Brigham Young* 1940; *The Great McGinty* 1940; *When the Daltons Rode* 1940; *Billy the Kid* 1941; *The Birth of the Blues* 1941; *I Wanted Wings* 1941; *A Gentleman after Dark* 1942; *The Glass Key* 1942; *The Great Man's Lady* 1942; *Stand by for Action* 1942; *Wake Island* 1942; *Hangmen Also Die* 1943; *An American Romance* 1944; *The Miracle of Morgan's Creek* 1944; *Duffy's Tavern* 1945; *Canyon Passage* 1946; *Two Years before the Mast* 1946; *The Virginian* 1946; *The Beginning or the End* 1947; *Heaven Only Knows* 1947; *Killer McCoy* 1947; *Kiss of Death* 1947; *Song of Scheherazade* 1947; *Command Decision* 1948; *A Southern Yankee* 1948; *Impact* 1949; *The Lucky Stiff* 1949; *Kansas Raiders* 1950; *Shakedown* 1950; *Slaughter Trail* 1951; *Hoodlum Empire* 1952; *Ride the Man Down* 1952; *The Woman They Almost Lynched* 1953; *The Big Combo* 1955; *The Quatermass Xperiment* 1955; *A Cry in the Night* 1956; *Quatermass II* 1957; *Cowboy* 1958; *Juke Box Rhythm* 1959; *Never So Few* 1959; *The Errand Boy* 1961; *Curse of the Fly* 1965; *Gamera the Invincible* 1965; *How to Fill a Wild Bikini* 1965; *Waco* 1966; *Five Golden Dragons* 1967; *Hostile Guns* 1967; *Arizona Bushwhackers* 1968
Donlin, Mike (1878–1933) *Beggars of Life* 1928; *The Iron Man* 1931
Donnadieu, Bernard-Pierre (1949–) *The Return of Martin Guerre* 1982; *Max Mon Amour* 1986; *The Vanishing* 1988; *Shadow of the Wolf* 1992; *Druids* 2001
Donnell, Jeff (1921–1988) *The Boogie Man Will Get You* 1942; *A Night to Remember* 1942; *Stars on Parade* 1944; *Over 21* 1945; *Easy Living* 1949; *Roughshod* 1949; *Stagecoach Kid* 1949; *Walk Softly, Stranger* 1949; *The Fuller Brush Girl* 1950; *In a Lonely Place* 1950; *Because You're Mine* 1952; *Thief of Damascus* 1952; *The Blue Gardenia* 1953; *So This Is Love* 1953; *Guns of Fort Petticoat* 1957; *Sweet Smell of Success* 1957; *The Iron Maiden* 1962
Donnelly, Donal (1931–) *The Knack... and How to Get It* 1965; *The Mind of Mr Soames* 1970; *Waterloo* 1970; *The Dead* 1987; *Squanto: the Last Great Warrior* 1994; *Korea* 1995
Donnelly, Ruth (1896–1982) *Blessed Event* 1932; *Bureau of Missing Persons* 1933; *Ever in My Heart* 1933; *Female* 1933; *Hard to Handle* 1933; *Mandalay* 1934; *Hands across the Table* 1935;

Red Salute 1935; *Fatal Lady* 1936; *The Affairs of Annabel* 1938; *Annabel Takes a Tour* 1938; *A Slight Case of Murder* 1938; *The Amazing Mr Williams* 1939; *My Little Chickadee* 1940; *The Roundup* 1941; *You Belong to Me* 1941; *The Bells of St Mary's* 1945; *Cinderella Jones* 1946; *Where the Sidewalk Ends* 1950; *I'd Climb the Highest Mountain* 1951; *A Lawless Street* 1955; *Autumn Leaves* 1956; *The Way to the Gold* 1957
Donner, Robert (1931–) *Vanishing Point* 1971; *The Man Who Loved Cat Dancing* 1973; *Five Days from Home* 1978; *Under the Rainbow* 1981; *Allan Quatermain and the Lost City of Gold* 1987
D'Onofrio, Vincent *aka* **D'Onofrio, Vincent Phillip** (1959–) *Full Metal Jacket* 1987; *A Night on the Town* 1987; *Mystic Pizza* 1988; *The Salute of the Jugger* 1989; *Naked Tango* 1990; *Crooked Hearts* 1991; *Dying Young* 1991; *Fires Within* 1991; *Mr Wonderful* 1992; *The Player* 1992; *Salt on Our Skin* 1992; *Household Saints* 1993; *Being Human* 1994; *Ed Wood* 1994; *Imaginary Crimes* 1994; *Strange Days* 1995; *Stuart Saves His Family* 1995; *Feeling Minnesota* 1996; *Good Luck* 1996; *Guy* 1996; *The Whole Wide World* 1996; *The Winner* 1996; *Men in Black* 1997; *Claire Dolan* 1998; *The Newton Boys* 1998; *The Velocity of Gary* 1998; *The Thirteenth Floor* 1999; *The Cell* 2000; *The Dangerous Lives of Altar Boys* 2001; *Impostor* 2001; *The Salton Sea* 2002
Donohoe, Amanda (1962–) *Castaway* 1986; *Foreign Body* 1986; *The Lair of the White Worm* 1988; *The Rainbow* 1988; *Diamond Skulls* 1989; *Paper Mask* 1990; *The Madness of King George* 1995; *Liar Liar* 1997; *I'm Losing You* 1998; *A Knight in Camelot* 1998; *The Real Howard Spitz* 1998; *Stardust* 1998; *Wild about Harry* 2000
Donovan (1946–) *If It's Tuesday, This Must Be Belgium* 1969; *The Pied Piper* 1971
Donovan, Jason (1968–) *Blood Oath* 1990; *Rough Diamonds* 1994; *The Sun, the Moon and the Stars* 1995; *Sorted* 2000
Donovan, King (1918–1987) *One Way Street* 1950; *The Enforcer* 1951; *Easy to Love* 1953; *The Magnetic Monster* 1953; *Private Hell 36* 1954; *Invasion of the Body Snatchers* 1956; *The Defiant Ones* 1958
Donovan (2), Martin (1957–) *Hard Choices* 1984; *Julia Has Two Lovers* 1990; *Trust* 1990; *Simple Men* 1992; *Quick* 1993; *Amateur* 1994; *Flirt* 1995; *Hollow Reed* 1995; *Nadja* 1995; *The Portrait of a Lady* 1996; *The Book of Life* 1998; *Heaven* 1998; *Living Out Loud* 1998; *The Opposite of Sex* 1998; *When Trumpets Fade* 1998; *Onegin* 1999; *Custody of the Heart* 2000; *Insomnia* 2002; *The United States of Leland* 2002; *Agent Cody Banks* 2003; *Saved!* 2004
Donovan, Tate (1963–) *SpaceCamp* 1986; *Clean and Sober* 1988; *Dead-Bang* 1989; *Memphis Belle* 1990; *Equinox* 1992; *Little Noises* 1992; *Love Potion No 9* 1992; *Ethan Frome* 1993; *Holy Matrimony* 1994; *Hercules* 1997; *G-Men from Hell* 2000; *Get Well Soon* 2001
Donovan, Terence (1939–) *Money Movers* 1978; *Breaker Morant* 1979; *The Winds of Jarrah* 1983; *Emma's War* 1985
Dontsov, Sergei *aka* **Dreiden, Sergei** (1941–) *The Fountain* 1988; *Russian Ark* 2002
Doody, Alison (1966–) *Taffin* 1988; *Indiana Jones and the Last Crusade* 1989; *Ring of the Musketeers* 1994
Doohan, James (1920–) *Pretty Maids All in a Row* 1971; *Star Trek: the Motion Picture* 1979; *Star Trek II: the Wrath of Khan* 1982; *Star Trek III: the Search for Spock* 1984; *Star Trek IV: the Voyage Home* 1986; *Star Trek V: the Final Frontier* 1989; *Star Trek VI: the Undiscovered Country* 1991; *Double Trouble* 1992; *Star Trek: Generations* 1994
Dooley, Paul (1928–) *A Wedding* 1978; *Breaking Away* 1979; *A Perfect Couple* 1979; *Rich Kids* 1979; *HEALTH* 1980; *Popeye* 1980; *Paternity* 1981; *Endangered Species* 1982; *Kiss Me Goodbye* 1982; *Monster in the Closet* 1983; *Strange Brew* 1983; *Big Trouble* 1985; *OC and Stiggs* 1987; *Last Rites* 1988; *Flashback* 1990; *Shakes the Clown* 1991; *Cooperstown* 1993; *The Underneath* 1995; *Loved* 1996; *Telling Lies in America* 1997; *Guinevere* 1999; *Runaway Bride* 1999; *Insomnia* 2002
Doonan, Patric (1925–1958) *The Blue Lamp* 1949; *Blackout* 1950; *The Net* 1953; *Seagulls over Sorrento* 1954
DoQui, Robert (1934–) *Coffy* 1973; *Nashville* 1975; *Part 2 Walking Tall* 1975; *Good to Go* 1986; *RoboCop* 1987
Dor, Christiane *Poil de Carotte* 1932; *Madame Bovary* 1933
Dor, Karin (1936–) *The Face of Fu Manchu* 1965; *The Blood Demon* 1967; *You Only Live Twice* 1967; *Topaz* 1969
Doran, Ann (1911–2000) *Blondie!* 1938; *Blind Alley* 1939; *Penny Serenade* 1941; *Here Come the Waves* 1944; *I Love a Soldier* 1944; *Pride of the Marines* 1945; *Roughly Speaking* 1945; *The Strange Love of Martha Ivers* 1946; *Fear in the Night* 1947; *Magic Town* 1947; *Pitfall* 1948; *No Sad Songs for Me* 1950; *Love Is Better Than Ever* 1951; *Tomahawk* 1951; *So This Is Love* 1953; *The Bob Mathias Story* 1954; *Rebel without a Cause* 1955; *It! The Terror from beyond Space* 1958; *Violent Road* 1958; *Voice in the Mirror* 1958; *The Brass Bottle* 1964; *Kitten with a Whip* 1964; *All Night Long* 1981
Doran, Johnny (1962–) *The Hideaways* 1973; *Treasure of Matecumbe* 1976
Doran, Mary (1907–1995) *The Broadway Melody* 1929; *The Criminal Code* 1930; *The Divorcee* 1930
Doran, Richard *The Harrad Summer* 1974; *Hollywood Boulevard* 1976
Dorat, Charles *La Belle Equipe* 1936; *The Golem* 1936
Doré, Edna (1922–) *High Hopes* 1988; *Nil by Mouth* 1997; *Weak at Denise* 2000
Dorff, Stephen (1973–) *The Gate* 1987; *The Power of One* 1991; *Rescue Me* 1991; *Backbeat* 1993; *Judgment Night* 1993; *SFW* 1994; *I Shot Andy Warhol* 1995; *Innocent Lies* 1995; *Reckless* 1995; *Blood and Wine* 1996; *City of Industry* 1996; *Space Truckers* 1996; *Blade* 1998; *Earthly Possessions* 1999; *Cecil B Demented* 2000; *FearDotCom* 2002; *Steal* 2002; *Cold Creek Manor* 2003
Dorfman, David (1993–) *Panic* 2000; *The Ring* 2002; *The Texas Chainsaw Massacre* 2003; *The Ring Two* 2004
Doria, Diogo (1953–) *The Divine Comedy* 1992; *Journey to the Beginning of the World* 1997
Doria, Jorge *The Lady from the Shanghai Cinema* 1987; *The Man of the Year* 2002
Doria, Malena (?–1999) *Little Treasure* 1985; *Highway Patrolman* 1991
Dorléac, Françoise (1942–1967) *Genghis Khan* 1964; *Male Hunt* 1964; *La Peau Douce* 1964; *That Man from Rio* 1964; *Where the Spies Are* 1965; *Cul-de-Sac* 1966; *Billion Dollar Brain* 1967; *The Young Girls of Rochefort* 1967
Dorn, Dolores (1934–) *The Bounty Hunter* 1954; *Phantom of the Rue Morgue* 1954; *Underworld USA* 1961; *13 West Street* 1962; *Truck Stop Women* 1974; *Tell Me a Riddle* 1980
Dorn, Michael (1952–) *Star Trek: Generations* 1994; *Star Trek: First Contact* 1996; *Star Trek: Insurrection* 1998; *The Prophet's Game* 1999; *Shadow Hours* 2000; *Star Trek: Nemesis* 2002
Dorn, Philip (1901–1975) *Escape* 1940; *Tarzan's Secret Treasure* 1941; *Underground* 1941; *Calling Dr Gillespie* 1942; *Random Harvest* 1942; *Reunion in France* 1942; *Paris after Dark* 1943; *Blonde Fever* 1944; *Passage to Marseille* 1944; *I've Always Loved You* 1946; *I Remember Mama* 1948; *The Fighting Kentuckian* 1949; *Sealed Cargo* 1951
Dorne, Sandra (1925–1992) *Hindle Wakes* 1952; *13 East Street* 1952; *Police Dog* 1955; *The Bank Raiders* 1958; *Devil Doll* 1964; *All Coppers Are…* 1972
Dorning, Robert (1914–1989) *Die! Die! My Darling* 1964; *Ups and Downs of a Handyman* 1975
Doro, Mino (1903–) *Duel of Champions* 1961; *Sandokan Fights Back* 1964
Dors, Diana (1931–1984) *Dancing with Crime* 1946; *The Calendar* 1948; *Good Time Girl* 1948; *Here Come the Huggetts* 1948; *It's Not Cricket* 1948; *Oliver Twist* 1948; *Vote for Huggett* 1948; *A Boy, a Girl and a Bike* 1949; *Diamond City* 1949; *Dance Hall* 1950; *Lady Godiva Rides Again* 1951; *The Last Page* 1952; *It's a Grand Life* 1953; *The Weak and the Wicked* 1953; *An Alligator Named Daisy* 1955; *As Long as They're Happy* 1955; *A Kid for Two Farthings* 1955; *Value for Money* 1955; *Yield to the Night* 1956; *The Unholy Wife* 1957; *I Married a Woman* 1958; *Passport to Shame* 1958; *Tread Softly Stranger* 1958; *Scent of Mystery* 1960; *King of the Roaring 20s – the Story of Arnold Rothstein* 1961; *On the Double* 1961; *West 11* 1963; *The Sandwich Man* 1966; *Berserk* 1967; *Danger Route* 1967; *Deep End* 1970; *There's a Girl in My Soup* 1970; *Hannie Caulder* 1971; *The Pied Piper* 1971; *The Amazing Mr Blunden* 1972; *Nothing but the Night* 1972; *Craze* 1973; *From beyond the Grave* 1973; *Steptoe and Son Ride Again* 1973; *The Amorous Milkman* 1974; *Adventures of a Taxi Driver* 1975; *Keep It Up Downstairs* 1976; *Adventures of a Private Eye* 1977; *Steaming* 1985
D'Orsay, Fifi (1904–1983) *They Had to See Paris* 1929; *Going Hollywood* 1933
Dorsey, Jimmy (1904–1957) *The Fabulous Dorseys* 1947; *Music Man* 1948
Dorsey, Joe (1925–) *Brainstorm* 1983; *The Philadelphia Experiment* 1984
Dorsey, Tommy (1905–1956) *Presenting Lily Mars* 1943; *The Fabulous Dorseys* 1947
Dorziat, Gabrielle (1880–1979) *Mayerling* 1936; *The End of the Day* 1939; *Monsieur Vincent* 1947; *Les Parents Terribles* 1948; *Act of Love* 1953; *Little Boy Lost* 1953; *Gigot* 1962; *A Monkey in Winter* 1962
Dossett, John *Longtime Companion* 1990; *That Night* 1992
Dotrice, Karen (1955–) *The Three Lives of Thomasina* 1963; *Mary Poppins* 1964; *The Gnome-Mobile* 1967; *The Thirty-Nine Steps* 1978
Dotrice, Michele (1947–) *The Witches* 1966; *And Soon the Darkness* 1970; *Blood on Satan's Claw* 1970; *Not Now, Comrade* 1976
Dotrice, Roy (1923–) *A Twist of Sand* 1967; *Lock Up Your Daughters!* 1969; *The Buttercup Chain* 1970; *One of Those Things* 1970; *Toomorrow* 1970; *Tales from the Crypt* 1972; *Amadeus* 1984; *Cheech & Chong's The Corsican Brothers* 1984; *The Cutting Edge* 1992; *Swimming with Sharks* 1994; *The Scarlet Letter* 1995
Doucet, Catherine *aka* **Doucet, Catharine** (1875–1958) *Little Man, What Now?* 1934; *Accent on Youth* 1935; *Poppy* 1936; *These Three* 1936; *When You're in Love* 1937; *There's One Born Every Minute* 1942
Doucette, John (1921–1994) *Cavalry Scout* 1951; *Beachhead* 1954; *Gang War* 1958; *The Fastest Guitar Alive* 1966; *One Little Indian* 1973; *Fighting Mad* 1976
Doug, Doug E (1970–) *Hangin' with the Homeboys* 1991; *Cool Runnings* 1993; *Operation Dumbo Drop* 1995; *That Darn Cat* 1997; *Eight Legged Freaks* 2001
Douglas, Angela (1940–) *Some People* 1962; *It's All Happening* 1963; *The Comedy Man* 1964; *Carry On Cowboy* 1965; *Carry On Follow That Camel* 1967; *Digby, the Biggest Dog in the World* 1973
Douglas, Burt *Handle with Care* 1958; *The Law and Jake Wade* 1958
Douglas, Craig *It's Trad, Dad* 1961; *The Painted Smile* 1961
Douglas, Diana (1923–) *The Indian Fighter* 1955; *It Runs in the Family* 2002
Douglas, Don *aka* **Douglas, Donald** (1905–1945) *The Great Gabbo* 1929; *Smashing the Rackets* 1938; *I Love You Again* 1940; *Behind the Rising Sun* 1943; *The Falcon Out West* 1944; *Show Business* 1944; *Tall in the Saddle* 1944
Douglas, Donna (1933–) *Career* 1959; *Frankie & Johnny* 1966
Douglas, Eric (1958–2004) *A Gunfight* 1971; *Tomboy* 1985
Douglas, Howard (1896–) *No Limit* 1935; *Night Comes Too Soon* 1949
Douglas, Illeana (1965–) *Cape Fear* 1991; *Alive* 1992; *Grief* 1993; *Search and Destroy* 1995; *To Die For* 1995; *Grace of My Heart* 1996; *Wedding Bell Blues* 1996; *Picture Perfect* 1997; *Message in a Bottle* 1998; *Happy, Texas* 1999; *Lansky* 1999; *Stir of Echoes* 1999; *The Next Best Thing* 2000; *Ghost World* 2001; *Dummy* 2002; *The New Guy* 2002
Douglas, Jack (1927–) *Carry On Abroad* 1972; *Carry On Girls* 1973; *Carry On Dick* 1974; *Carry On Behind* 1975; *Carry On England* 1976; *Carry On Emmannuelle* 1978; *The Boys in Blue* 1983
Douglas, James *GI Blues* 1960; *A Thunder of Drums* 1961
Douglas, Kirk (1916–) *The Strange Love of Martha Ivers* 1946; *Build My Gallows High* 1947; *I Walk Alone* 1947; *Mourning Becomes Electra* 1947; *My Dear Secretary* 1948; *Champion* 1949; *A Letter to Three Wives* 1949; *The Glass Menagerie* 1950; *Young Man with a Horn* 1950; *Ace in the Hole* 1951; *Along the Great Divide* 1951; *Detective Story* 1951; *The Bad and the Beautiful* 1952; *The Big Sky* 1952; *The Big Trees* 1952; *Act of Love* 1953; *The Juggler* 1953; *The Story of Three Loves* 1953; *20,000 Leagues under the Sea* 1954; *Ulysses* 1954; *The Indian Fighter* 1955; *Man without a Star* 1955; *The Racers* 1955; *Lust for Life* 1956; *Gunfight at the OK Corral* 1957; *Paths of Glory* 1957; *Top Secret Affair* 1957; *The Vikings* 1958; *The Devil's Disciple* 1959; *Last Train from Gun Hill* 1959; *Spartacus* 1960; *Strangers When We Meet* 1960; *The Last Sunset* 1961; *Town without Pity* 1961; *The Hook* 1962; *Lonely Are the Brave* 1962; *Two Weeks in Another Town* 1962; *For Love or Money* 1963; *The List of Adrian Messenger* 1963; *Seven Days in May* 1964; *The Heroes of Telemark* 1965; *In Harm's Way* 1965; *Cast a Giant Shadow* 1966; *Is Paris Burning?* 1966; *The War Wagon* 1967; *The Way West* 1967; *The Brotherhood* 1968; *A Lovely Way to Go* 1968; *The Arrangement* 1969; *There Was a Crooked Man…* 1970; *Catch Me a Spy* 1971; *A Gunfight* 1971; *The Light at the Edge of the World* 1971; *A Man to Respect* 1972; *Scalawag* 1973; *Once Is Not Enough* 1975; *Posse* 1975; *Victory at Entebbe* 1976; *Holocaust 2000* 1977; *The Fury* 1978; *Cactus Jack* 1979; *Home Movies* 1979; *The Final Countdown* 1980; *Saturn 3* 1980; *The Man from Snowy River* 1982; *Eddie Macon's Run* 1983; *Tough Guys* 1986; *Oscar* 1991; *Greedy* 1994; *The Lies Boys Tell* 1994; *Diamonds* 1999; *It Runs in the Family* 2002
Douglas, Melvyn (1901–1981) *As You Desire Me* 1932; *The Old Dark House* 1932; *The Wiser Sex* 1932; *Counsellor-at-Law* 1933; *The Vampire Bat* 1933; *Dangerous Corner* 1934; *Annie Oakley* 1935; *She Married Her Boss* 1935; *And So They Were Married* 1936; *The Gorgeous Hussy* 1936; *The Lone Wolf Returns* 1936; *Theodora Goes Wild* 1936; *Angel* 1937; *Captains Courageous* 1937; *I Met Him in Paris* 1937; *I'll Take Romance* 1937; *Arsene Lupin Returns* 1938; *Fast Company* 1938; *The Shining Hour* 1938; *That Certain Age* 1938; *There's Always a Woman* 1938; *The Toy Wife* 1938; *The Amazing Mr Williams* 1939; *Ninotchka* 1939; *Tell No Tales* 1939; *Third Finger, Left Hand* 1940; *This Thing Called Love* 1940; *Too Many Husbands* 1940; *Our Wife* 1941; *That Uncertain Feeling* 1941; *Two-Faced Woman* 1941; *A Woman's Face* 1941; *They All Kissed the Bride* 1942; *The Guilt of Janet Ames* 1947; *The Sea of Grass* 1947; *Mr Blandings Builds His Dream House* 1948; *The Great Sinner* 1949; *A Woman's Secret* 1949; *My Forbidden Past* 1951; *Billy Budd* 1962; *Hud* 1963; *Advance to the Rear* 1964; *The Americanization of Emily* 1964; *Hotel* 1967; *I Never Sang for My Father* 1969; *The Candidate* 1972; *One Is a Lonely Number* 1972; *The Tenant* 1976; *Twilight's Last Gleaming* 1977; *Being There* 1979; *The Seduction of Joe Tynan* 1979; *The Changeling* 1980; *Tell Me a Riddle* 1980; *Ghost Story* 1981; *The Hot Touch* 1982
Douglas, Michael (1944–) *Hail, Hero!* 1969; *Adam at 6 AM* 1970; *Napoleon and Samantha* 1972; *Coma* 1977; *The China Syndrome* 1979; *Running* 1979; *It's My Turn* 1980; *The Star Chamber* 1983; *Romancing the Stone* 1984; *A Chorus Line* 1985; *The Jewel of the Nile* 1985; *Fatal Attraction* 1987; *Wall Street* 1987; *Black Rain* 1989; *The War of the Roses* 1989; *Basic Instinct* 1992; *Falling Down* 1992; *Shining Through* 1992; *Disclosure* 1994; *The American President* 1995; *The Ghost and the Darkness* 1996; *The Game* 1997; *A Perfect Murder* 1998; *One Day in September* 1999; *Traffic* 2000; *Wonder Boys* 2000; *Don't Say a Word* 2001; *One Night at McCool's* 2001; *It Runs in the Family* 2002; *The In-Laws* 2003
Douglas, Paul (1907–1959) *Everybody Does It* 1949; *It Happens Every Spring* 1949; *A Letter to Three Wives* 1949; *The Big Lift* 1950; *Love That Brute* 1950; *Panic in the Streets* 1950; *Angels in the Outfield* 1951; *Fourteen Hours* 1951; *Clash by Night* 1952; *Never Wave at a WAC* 1952; *We're Not Married* 1952; *Forever Female* 1953; *The Maggie* 1953; *Executive Suite* 1954; *Green Fire* 1954; *Joe Macbeth* 1955; *The Solid Gold Cadillac* 1956; *Beau James* 1957; *This Could Be the Night* 1957; *The Mating Game* 1959
Douglas, Robert (1909–1999) *London Melody* 1937; *Over the Moon* 1937; *The Challenge* 1938; *The Lion Has Wings* 1939; *The End of the River* 1947; *Adventures of Don Juan* 1948; *The Fountainhead* 1949; *Barricade* 1950; *The Flame and the Arrow* 1950; *Kim* 1950; *Mystery Submarine* 1950; *Sons of the*

Musketeers 1951; Target Unknown 1951; Thunder on the Hill 1951; Ivanhoe 1952; The Desert Rats 1953; Fair Wind to Java 1953; Flight to Tangier 1953; King Richard and the Crusaders 1954; Saskatchewan 1954; Good Morning, Miss Dove 1955; The Scarlet Coat 1955; Tarzan, the Ape Man 1959; Secret Ceremony 1968
Douglas, Sarah (1952–) The People That Time Forgot 1977; Superman II 1980; Conan the Destroyer 1984; The Return of Swamp Thing 1989; Beastmaster 2: through the Portal of Time 1991
Douglas, Shirley Dead Ringers 1988; Barney's Great Adventure 1998; A House Divided 2000
Douglas, Suzzanne (1957–) Tap 1989; Jason's Lyric 1994; No Ordinary Summer 1994; How Stella Got Her Groove Back 1998
Douglas, Warren (1911–1997) Murder on the Waterfront 1943; Pride of the Marines 1945
Douglass, Robyn (1953–) Breaking Away 1979; Partners 1982; Romantic Comedy 1983; The Lonely Guy 1984
Dourdan, Gary (1966–) Alien: Resurrection 1997; Scarred City 1998; Muhammad Ali: King of the World 2000; Impostor 2001
Dourif, Brad (1950–) One Flew over the Cuckoo's Nest 1975; Eyes of Laura Mars 1978; Wise Blood 1979; Heaven's Gate 1980; Ragtime 1981; Dune 1984; Blue Velvet 1986; Fatal Beauty 1987; Child's Play 1988; Mississippi Burning 1988; Child's Play 2 1990; The Exorcist III 1990; Graveyard Shift 1990; Grim Prairie Tales 1990; Hidden Agenda 1990; Knife Edge 1990; Body Parts 1991; Chaindance 1991; Child's Play 3 1991; Jungle Fever 1991; London Kills Me 1991; Scream of Stone 1991; Critters 4 1992; Amos & Andrew 1993; Trauma 1993; Color of Night 1994; Death Machine 1994; Murder in the First 1994; Nightwatch 1997; Bride of Chucky 1998; Brown's Requiem 1998; Progeny 1998; Senseless 1998; Urban Legend 1998; The Ghost 2000; The Prophecy 3: the Ascent 2000; Shadow Hours 2000; Seed of Chucky 2004
Dove, Billie (1900–1997) The Black Pirate 1926; Blondie of the Follies 1932
Dow, Peggy (1928–) Undertow 1949; Harvey 1950; Shakedown 1950; The Sleeping City 1950; Bright Victory 1951; I Want You 1951
Dowd, Ann Bushwhacked 1995; All over Me 1996; Shiloh 1996; Apt Pupil 1997; Garden State 2003
Dowie, Freda Distant Voices, Still Lives 1988; The Monk 1990; Butterfly Kiss 1994
Dowling, Constance (1920–1969) Knickerbocker Holiday 1944; Up in Arms 1944; Black Angel 1946; The Well Groomed Bride 1946; Gog 1954
Dowling, Doris (1923–2004) The Lost Weekend 1945; The Blue Dahlia 1946; Bitter Rice 1949
Dowling, Joan (1928–1954) No Room at the Inn 1948; Train of Events 1949; Murder without Crime 1950; Pool of London 1950; Women of Twilight 1952
Dowling, Kathryn Diner 1982; Ultimate Betrayal 1994
Dowling, Rachael aka **Dowling, Rachel** The Dead 1987; Bogwoman 1997; The Tichborne Claimant 1998
Down, Lesley-Anne (1954–) Assault 1970; Countess Dracula 1970; Pope Joan 1972; From beyond the Grave 1973; Scalawag 1973; Brannigan 1975; The Pink Panther Strikes Again 1976; A Little Night Music 1977; The Betsy 1978; The First Great Train Robbery 1978; Hanover Street 1979; Rough Cut 1980; Sphinx 1980; The Hunchback of Notre Dame 1982; Nomads 1985; Death Wish V: the Face of Death 1994; Munchie Strikes Back 1994; The Secret Agent Club 1995
Downer, David (1948–) The Killing of Angel Street 1981; Norman Loves Rose 1982
Downey Sr, Robert (1936–) Is There Sex after Death? 1971; To Live and Die in LA 1985; Johnny Be Good 1988
Downey Jr, Robert (1965–) Baby It's You 1983; Tuff Turf 1984; Weird Science 1985; America 1986; Back to School 1986; Less than Zero 1987; The Pick-Up Artist 1987; Johnny Be Good 1988; 1969 1988; Chances Are 1989; True Believer 1989; Air America 1990; Too Much Sun 1990; Soapdish 1991; Chaplin 1992; Heart and Souls 1993; The Last Party 1993; Short Cuts 1993; Hail Caesar 1994; Natural Born Killers 1994; Only You 1994; Home for the Holidays 1995; Restoration 1995; Richard III 1995; Danger Zone 1996; The Gingerbread Man 1997; One Night Stand 1997; Pool Girl 1997; Two Girls and a Guy 1997; In Dreams 1998; US Marshals 1998; Black and White 1999; Bowfinger 1999; Wonder Boys 2000; Gothika 2003; The Singing Detective 2003
Downing, Vernon (1913–1973) Clive of India 1935; Sherlock Holmes and the Spider Woman 1944
Downs, Cathy (1924–1976) The Dark Corner 1946; My Darling Clementine 1946; The Noose Hangs High 1948; The Sundowners 1950; The Big Tip Off 1955; The Oklahoma Woman 1956; The She-Creature 1956; The Amazing Colossal Man 1957
Downs, Johnny (1913–1994) Pigskin Parade 1936; Adam Had Four Sons 1941; Twilight on the Prairie 1944
Dowse, Denise (1958–) Bio-Dome 1996; Coach Carter 2005
Doyen, Jacqueline Entre Nous 1983; The Frog Prince 1984
Doyle, David (1925–1997) Paper Lion 1968; The April Fools 1969; Loving 1970; The Comeback 1977; Love or Money 1990
Doyle Kennedy, Maria aka **Doyle, Maria** The Commitments 1991; The General 1998; Gregory's Two Girls 1999; I Could Read the Sky 1999; Miss Julie 1999
Doyle, Kevin The Courier 1987; A Midsummer Night's Dream 1996
Doyle, Shawn Frequency 2000; Don't Say a Word 2001
Doyle, Tony (1941–2000) Loophole 1980; Who Dares Wins 1982; Eat the Peach 1986; Secret Friends 1991; A Love Divided 1999
Doyle-Murray, Brian (1945–) Modern Problems 1981; JFK 1991; Wayne's World 1992; Groundhog Day 1993; Cabin Boy 1994; Jury Duty 1995; Dennis the Menace Strikes Again 1998; Legalese 1998; Snow Dogs 2002
Drache, Heinz (1923–2002) The Door with Seven Locks 1962; The Brides of Fu Manchu 1966; Circus of Fear 1967
Drago, Billy (1949–) Windwalker 1980; The Untouchables 1987; Delta Force 2 1990; Diplomatic Immunity 1991; Guncrazy 1992; Cyborg 2: Glass Shadow 1993; The Outfit 1993; Soccer Dog: the Movie 1999; Mysterious Skin 2004
Drake, Betsy (1923–) Every Girl Should Be Married 1948; Dancing in the Dark 1949; Pretty Baby 1950; The Second Woman 1951; Room for One More 1952; Will Success Spoil Rock Hunter? 1957; Intent to Kill 1958; Next to No Time 1958; Clarence, the Cross-Eyed Lion 1965
Drake, Charles (1914–1994) Air Force 1943; Conflict 1945; A Night in Casablanca 1946; The Tender Years 1947; Tarzan's Magic Fountain 1949; Comanche Territory 1950; Harvey 1950; I Was a Shoplifter 1950; Winchester '73 1950; Air Cadet 1951; Red Ball Express 1952; Treasure of Lost Canyon 1952; The Glenn Miller Story 1953; Gunsmoke 1953; It Came from Outer Space 1953; The Lone Hand 1953; War Arrow 1953; All That Heaven Allows 1955; To Hell and Back 1955; Walk the Proud Land 1956; Jeanne Eagels 1957; Until They Sail 1957; No Name on the Bullet 1959; Back Street 1961; Tammy Tell Me True 1961; Showdown 1963; Dear Heart 1964; Valley of the Dolls 1967; The Counterfeit Killer 1968; Hail, Hero! 1969; The Seven Minutes 1971
Drake, Charlie (1925–) Sands of the Desert 1960; Petticoat Pirates 1961; The Cracksman 1963; Mister Ten Per Cent 1967
Drake, Claudia Bedside Manner 1945; Detour 1945; Calypso Joe 1957
Drake, Dona (1914–1989) Louisiana Purchase 1941; Road to Morocco 1942; Without Reservations 1946; Another Part of the Forest 1948; So This Is New York 1948; Beyond the Forest 1949; The Doolins of Oklahoma 1949; Valentino 1951; Kansas City Confidential 1952; The Bandits of Corsica 1953; Princess of the Nile 1954
Drake, Fabia (1904–1990) Not Wanted on Voyage 1957; Girls at Sea 1958; Operation Bullshine 1959; Valmont 1989
Drake, Frances (1908–2000) Bolero 1934; Forsaking All Others 1934; Ladies Should Listen 1934; Mad Love 1935; Les Misérables 1935; The Invisible Ray 1936; There's Always a Woman 1938; It's a Wonderful World 1939; I Take This Woman 1940; The Affairs of Martha 1942
Drake, Gabrielle (1944–) Connecting Rooms 1969; There's a Girl in My Soup 1970
Drake, Larry (1950–) Darkman 1990; Murder in New Hampshire 1991; Dr Giggles 1992; Darkman II: the Return of Durant 1995; The Journey of August King 1995; Bean 1997; Overnight Delivery 1997; Desert Heat 1999
Drake, Tom (1918–1982) Meet Me in St Louis 1944; Two Girls and a Sailor 1944; This Man's Navy 1945; Courage of Lassie 1946; The Green Years 1946; The Beginning or the End 1947; Cass Timberlane 1947; I'll Be Yours 1947; Hills of Home 1948; Words and Music 1948; Mr Belvedere Goes to College 1949; Scene of the Crime 1949; The Cyclops 1957; Money, Women and Guns 1958; Warlock 1959; The Bramble Bush 1960; Johnny Reno 1966
Draper, Paul (1909–1996) Colleen 1936; The Time of Your Life 1948
Draper, Polly (1956–) Danielle Steel's Heartbeat 1992; A Million to Juan 1994; Gold Diggers: the Secret of Bear Mountain 1995; The Tic Code 1998
Drasbaek, Laura (1974–) Pusher 1996; Okay 2002
Dravic, Milena (1940–) The Battle of Neretva 1969; WR – Mysteries of the Organism 1971
Dray, Albert La Balance 1982; Crime Spree 2002
Drayton, Alfred (1881–1949) Friday the Thirteenth 1933; It's a Boy 1933; Jack Ahoy! 1934; The Dictator 1935; First a Girl 1935; Look Up and Laugh 1935; Oh, Daddy! 1935; Banana Ridge 1941; The Halfway House 1943; Don't Take It to Heart 1944; They Knew Mr Knight 1945; Nicholas Nickleby 1947
Drescher, Fran (1957–) American Hot Wax 1977; GORP 1980; Doctor Detroit 1983; Cadillac Man 1990; Car 54 Where Are You? 1991; Jack 1996; The Beautician and the Beast 1997; Picking Up the Pieces 2000
Dresdel, Sonia (1909–1976) This Was a Woman 1947; While I Live 1947; The Fallen Idol 1948; The Clouded Yellow 1950; The Break 1962
Dresser, Louise (1878–1965) Ruggles of Red Gap 1923; The Eagle 1925; The Goose Woman 1925; Mammy 1930; Dr Bull 1933; State Fair 1933; The Scarlet Empress 1934; The World Moves On 1934
Dressler, Lieux (1930–) Truck Stop Women 1974; Kingdom of the Spiders 1977
Dressler, Marie (1869–1934) Tillie's Punctured Romance 1914; The Divine Lady 1928; The Patsy 1928; Hollywood Revue 1929; Anna Christie 1930; Min and Bill 1930; One Romantic Night 1930; Emma 1932; Dinner at Eight 1933; Tugboat Annie 1933
Drew, Ellen (1915–2003) If I Were King 1938; French without Tears 1939; Geronimo 1939; The Gracie Allen Murder Case 1939; Buck Benny Rides Again 1940; Christmas in July 1940; Texas Rangers Ride Again 1940; Our Wife 1941; My Favorite Spy 1942; The Impostor 1944; China Sky 1945; Isle of the Dead 1945; Johnny O'Clock 1947; The Man from Colorado 1948; The Baron of Arizona 1950; Stars in My Crown 1950; Man in the Saddle 1951
Drew, Roland (1900–1988) The Bermuda Mystery 1944; Two O'Clock Courage 1945
Drew, Sarah (1980–) Daria the Movie: Is It Fall Yet? 2000; Radio 2003
Drexel, Ruth (1930–) Jail Bait 1972; The Marquise of O 1976
Dreyfus, James (1964–) Thin Ice 1994; Boyfriends 1996; Notting Hill 1999; Fat Slags 2004
Dreyfus, Jean-Claude (1946–) Heroines of Evil 1979; Delicatessen 1990; La Fille de l'Air 1992; Pétain 1992; The City of Lost Children 1995; The Lady & the Duke 2001; Two Brothers 2004; A Very Long Engagement 2004
Dreyfuss, Richard (1947–) Hello Down There 1969; American Graffiti 1973; Dillinger 1973; The Apprenticeship of Duddy Kravitz 1974; The Second Coming of Suzanne 1974; Inserts 1975; Jaws 1975; Victory at Entebbe 1976; Close Encounters of the Third Kind 1977; The Goodbye Girl 1977; The Big Fix 1978; The Competition 1980; Whose Life Is It Anyway? 1981; The Buddy System 1984; Down and Out in Beverly Hills 1986; Stand by Me 1986; Nuts 1987; Stakeout 1987; Tin Men 1987; Moon over Parador 1988; Always 1989; Let It Ride 1989; Postcards from the Edge 1990; Rosencrantz and Guildenstern Are Dead 1990; Once Around 1991; Prisoner of Honor 1991; What about Bob? 1991; Another Stakeout 1993; Lost in Yonkers 1993; Silent Fall 1994; The American President 1995; Mr Holland's Opus 1995; The Call of the Wild 1996; James and the Giant Peach 1996; Trigger Happy 1996; Night Falls on Manhattan 1997; Krippendorf's Tribe 1998; Lansky 1999; Fail Safe 2000; The Old Man Who Read Love Stories 2000; Rudolph the Red-Nosed Reindeer and the Island of the Misfit Toys 2001; Silver City 2004
Drier, Moosie (1964–) The War between Men and Women 1972; American Hot Wax 1977
Drinkwater, Carol (1948–) The Shout 1978; Father 1990
Driscoll, Bobby (1937–1968) The Fighting Sullivans 1944; From This Day Forward 1946; So Goes My Love 1946; Song of the South 1946; So Dear to My Heart 1949; The Window 1949; Treasure Island 1950; The Happy Time 1952; Peter Pan 1953
Driscoll, Patricia (1927–) Charley Moon 1956; The Wackiest Ship in the Army 1961
Drivas, Robert (1938–1986) Cool Hand Luke 1967; The Illustrated Man 1969; Where It's At 1969; God Told Me to 1976
Driver, Betty (1920–) Boots! Boots! 1934; Penny Paradise 1938; Let's Be Famous 1939
Driver, Edgar (1887–1964) Doss House 1933; Song of the Road 1937
Driver, Minnie (1970–) Circle of Friends 1995; Big Night 1996; Sleepers 1996; Good Will Hunting 1997; The Governess 1997; Grosse Pointe Blank 1997; Hard Rain 1997; Princess Mononoke 1997; An Ideal Husband 1999; South Park: Bigger, Longer & Uncut 1999; Tarzan 1999; Beautiful 2000; Return to Me 2000; High Heels and Low Lifes 2001; Hope Springs 2002; Owning Mahowny 2002; Ella Enchanted 2004; The Phantom of the Opera 2004
Drouot, Jean-Claude Le Bonheur 1965; Laughter in the Dark 1969; The Light at the Edge of the World 1971
Dru, Joanne (1922–1996) Abie's Irish Rose 1946; Red River 1948; All the King's Men 1949; She Wore a Yellow Ribbon 1949; 711 Ocean Drive 1950; Wagonmaster 1950; Mr Belvedere Rings the Bell 1951; Vengeance Valley 1951; My Pal Gus 1952; The Pride of St Louis 1952; Forbidden 1953; Thunder Bay 1953; The Siege at Red River 1954; Southwest Passage 1954; Three Ring Circus 1954; The Dark Avenger 1955; Hell on Frisco Bay 1955; Sincerely Yours 1955; Drango 1957; The Light in the Forest 1958; The Wild and the Innocent 1959; Sylvia 1964
Drukarova, Dinara (1976–) Don't Move, Die and Rise Again 1989; Of Freaks and Men 1998
Drummond, Alice Awakenings 1990; Pieces of April 2002
Drury, James (1934–) Good Day for a Hanging 1958; Ten Who Dared 1960; Toby Tyler, or Ten Weeks with a Circus 1960; Ride the High Country 1962; The Young Warriors 1967; Backtrack 1969
Drynan, Jeanie Cappuccino 1989; Muriel's Wedding 1994; Paperback Hero 1998; Soft Fruit 1999
du Maurier, Gerald (1873–1934) Escape 1930; Scotland Yard Mystery 1933; I Was a Spy 1934; Jew Süss 1934; The Rise of Catherine the Great 1934
Duane, Michael (1914–) Dr Gillespie's Criminal Case 1943; Personality Kid 1946; The Prince of Thieves 1948
Dubbins, Don (1928–1991) These Wilder Years 1956; Tribute to a Bad Man 1956; From the Earth to the Moon 1958; The Illustrated Man 1969
Dube, Desmond The Long Run 2000; Hotel Rwanda 2004
Duberg, Axel (1927–) The Devil's Eye 1960; The Virgin Spring 1960
Dubey, Satyadev Nishant 1975; Maya 1992
Dubois, Marie (1937–) Shoot the Pianist 1960; Une Femme Est une Femme 1961; Jules et Jim 1961; La Ronde 1964; Don't Look Now… We're Being Shot At 1966; The Thief of Paris 1967; Vincent, François, Paul and the Others 1974; L'Innocente 1976; Mon Oncle d'Amérique 1980; Descent into Hell 1986
DuBois, Marta Boulevard Nights 1979; The Trial of the Incredible Hulk 1989; Dead Badge 1995
Dubost, Paulette (1911–) La Règle du Jeu 1939; Lola Montès 1955; Le Bossu 1959; Viva Maria! 1965; The Last Metro 1980
Dubov, Paul (1918–1979) China Gate 1957; Voodoo Woman 1957; Verboten! 1959; The Atomic Submarine 1960; Underworld USA 1961
DuBrey, Claire (1892–1993) Gabriel over the White House 1933; The Sin of Nora Moran 1933
Duby, Jacques (1922–) Thérèse Raquin 1953; Piaf: the Sparrow of Pigalle 1974
Duchaussoy, Michel (1938–) La Femme Infidèle 1968; Que la Bête Meure 1969; Shock Treatment 1973; Nada 1974; Armaguedon 1976; Fort Saganne 1984; Milou

en Mai 1989; Road to Ruin 1992; La Veuve de Saint-Pierre 2000; Amen. 2002; La Mentale 2002; The Bridesmaid 2004; Confidences Trop Intimes 2004
Duchesne, Roger (1906–1996) The Golem 1936; Bob Le Flambeur 1955
Duchovny, David (1960–) Bad Influence 1990; Julia Has Two Lovers 1990; Don't Tell Mom the Babysitter's Dead 1991; The Rapture 1991; Beethoven 1992; Chaplin 1992; Ruby 1992; Venice/Venice 1992; Kalifornia 1993; Playing God 1997; The X-Files 1998; Return to Me 2000; Evolution 2001; Zoolander 2001; Full Frontal 2002; Connie and Carla 2004
Duclos, Philippe The Bait 1995; Ma Mère 2004
Ducommun, Rick (1949–) The 'Burbs 1989; Ghost in the Machine 1993; Groundhog Day 1993; Dogmatic 1996
Dudgeon, Neil Different for Girls 1996; It Was an Accident 2000
Dudikoff, Michael (1954–) American Ninja 1985; Avenging Force 1986; Radioactive Dreams 1986; River of Death 1989; Rescue Me 1991; In Her Defense 1998; The Silencer 1999
Dudley, Doris (1917–1985) A Woman Rebels 1936; The Moon and Sixpence 1942
Dudley Ward, Penelope (1919–1982) Escape Me Never 1935; Moscow Nights 1935; Convoy 1940; The Demi-Paradise 1943
Duel, Pete (1940–1971) The Hell with Heroes 1968; Generation 1969; Cannon for Cordoba 1970
Duell, William (1923–) Deadhead Miles 1972; Grace Quigley 1984
Duering, Carl (1923–) Arabesque 1966; Duffy 1968; A Clockwork Orange 1971
Duff, Amanda (1914–) Just around the Corner 1938; Mr Moto in Danger Island 1939; The Devil Commands 1941
Duff, Hilary (1987–) Casper Meets Wendy 1998; Agent Cody Banks 2003; Cheaper by the Dozen 2003; The Lizzie McGuire Movie 2003; A Cinderella Story 2004; Raise Your Voice 2004
Duff, Howard (1917–1990) All My Sons 1948; The Naked City 1948; Calamity Jane and Sam Bass 1949; Johnny Stool Pigeon 1949; Red Canyon 1949; Shakedown 1950; Jennifer 1953; Spaceways 1953; Private Hell 36 1954; Tanganyika 1954; The Yellow Mountain 1954; Women's Prison 1955; While the City Sleeps 1956; Boys' Night Out 1962; Panic in the City 1968; Kramer vs Kramer 1979; Monster in the Closet 1983; No Way Out 1986; Too Much Sun 1990
Duffy, Julia (1951–) Wacko 1981; Intolerable Cruelty 2003
Duffy, Karen (1962–) Blank Check 1994; Dumb and Dumber 1994; Memory Run 1995
Dufilho, Jacques (1914–) War of the Buttons 1962; A Full Day's Work 1973; Black and White in Color 1976; Le Cheval d'Orgeuil 1980; Pétain 1992
Dugan, Dennis (1946–) Norman... Is That You? 1976; The Spaceman and King Arthur 1979; The Howling 1981; Can't Buy Me Love 1987; The New Adventures of Pippi Longstocking 1988; Happy Gilmore 1996
Dugan, Tom (1889–1955) Lights of New York 1928; Drag 1929; Pennies from Heaven 1936; Wife vs Secretary 1936; The Lone Wolf Spy Hunt 1939; To Be or Not to Be 1942; Take Me Out to the Ball Game 1949; Painting the Clouds with Sunshine 1951; Twogether 1994
Dugay, Yvette aka **Duguay, Yvette** (1932–) The Cimarron Kid 1951; The People against O'Hara 1951; Francis Covers the Big Town 1953; Cattle Queen of Montana 1954
Duggan, Andrew (1923–1988) Decision at Sundown 1957; Westbound 1959; The Chapman Report 1962; House of Women 1962; Merrill's Marauders 1962; Palm Springs Weekend 1963; The Incredible Mr Limpet 1964; The Glory Guys 1965; In like Flint 1967; The Secret War of Harry Frigg 1967; Skin Game 1971; Bone 1972; The Bears and I 1974; It's Alive 1974; It Lives Again 1978; A Return to Salem's Lot 1987
Duggan, Tom (1915–1969) Frankenstein – 1970 1958; Born Reckless 1959
Duk Kim, Randall Anna and the King 1999; The Matrix Reloaded 2002
Dukakis, Olympia (1931–) John and Mary 1969; The Idolmaker 1980; National Lampoon's Movie Madness 1981; Walls of Glass 1985; Moonstruck 1987; Working Girl 1988; Dad 1989; Look Who's Talking 1989; Steel Magnolias 1989; In the Spirit 1990; Look Who's Talking Too 1990; Over the Hill 1992; The Cemetery Club 1993; Look Who's Talking Now! 1993; I Love Trouble 1994; Dead Badge 1995; The Haunted Heart 1995; Jeffrey 1995; Mighty Aphrodite 1995; Mr Holland's Opus 1995; Jerusalem 1996; Never Too Late 1996; Picture Perfect 1997; Jane Austen's Mafia 1998
Duke, Bill (1943–) Car Wash 1976; American Gigolo 1980; Commando 1985; No Man's Land 1987; Predator 1987; Action Jackson 1988; Street of No Return 1989; Bird on a Wire 1990; Menace II Society 1993; Payback 1998; Exit Wounds 2001; National Security 2002
Duke, Patty aka **Duke Astin, Patty** (1946–) Happy Anniversary 1959; The Miracle Worker 1962; Billie 1965; Valley of the Dolls 1967; You'll Like My Mother 1972; The Swarm 1978; Willy/Milly 1986; Amityville: the Evil Escapes 1989; Everybody's Baby: the Rescue of Jessica McClure 1989; Prelude to a Kiss 1992; One Woman's Courage 1994
Dukes, David (1945–2000) The Wild Party 1975; A Little Romance 1979; The First Deadly Sin 1980; Only When I Laugh 1981; Without a Trace 1983; The Men's Club 1986; Rawhead Rex 1986; Date with an Angel 1987; See You in the Morning 1989; Me and the Kid 1993; Norma Jean & Marilyn 1996; Tinseltown 1997; Gods and Monsters 1998; Supreme Sanction 1999
Duléry, Antoine The Chinese Connection 1988; Grégoire Moulin 2001
Dullaghan (1), John Sweet Sweetback's Baad Asssss Song 1971; The Thing with Two Heads 1972
Dullea, Keir (1936–) The Hoodlum Priest 1961; David and Lisa 1962; Mail Order Bride 1963; The Thin Red Line 1964; Bunny Lake Is Missing 1965; Madame X 1966; The Fox 1967; 2001: a Space Odyssey 1968; De Sade 1969; Paperback Hero 1972; Pope Joan 1972; Black Christmas 1974; Paul and Michelle 1974; Full Circle 1977; Welcome to Blood City 1977; Brainwaves 1982; Blind Date 1984; Next One 1984; 2010 1984; Oh, What a Night 1992; The Audrey Hepburn Story 2000
Dullin, Charles (1885–1949) The Chess Player 1927; Mademoiselle Docteur 1936; Quai des Orfèvres 1947
Dumas, Roger (1932–) The Bride Is Too Beautiful 1956; La Femme Publique 1984; Masques 1987
Dumas, Sandrine (1957–) Hit List 1984; Beyond Therapy 1987; The Legend of the Holy Drinker 1988
Dumbrille, Douglass aka **Dumbrille, Douglas** (1890–1974) His Woman 1931; Blondie of the Follies 1932; Broadway Bill 1934; Fog over Frisco 1934; Hi, Nellie! 1934; The Secret Bride 1934; Stamboul Quest 1934; Cardinal Richelieu 1935; Crime and Punishment 1935; The Lives of a Bengal Lancer 1935; Naughty Marietta 1935; Peter Ibbetson 1935; The Lone Wolf Returns 1936; Mr Deeds Goes to Town 1936; The Princess Comes Across 1936; The Emperor's Candlesticks 1937; The Firefly 1937; The Buccaneer 1938; Fast Company 1938; Kentucky 1938; Charlie Chan at Treasure Island 1939; Mr Moto in Danger Island 1939; Tell No Tales 1939; The Three Musketeers 1939; Thunder Afloat 1939; Michael Shayne, Private Detective 1940; South of Pago Pago 1940; The Roundup 1941; Ten Gentlemen from West Point 1942; DuBarry Was a Lady 1943; The Frozen Ghost 1944; Lost in a Harem 1944; Uncertain Glory 1944; A Medal for Benny 1945; Pardon My Past 1945; Road to Utopia 1945; Christmas Eve 1947; Dishonored Lady 1947; Tell It to the Judge 1949; Abbott and Costello in the Foreign Legion 1950; A Millionaire for Christy 1951; Apache War Smoke 1952; Son of Paleface 1952; World for Ransom 1953; Shake, Rattle and Rock! 1957; Shock Treatment 1964
Dumke, Ralph (1899–1964) All the King's Men 1949; The Breaking Point 1950; The Fireball 1950; Where Danger Lives 1950; Boots Malone 1951; Alaska Seas 1954; Invasion of the Body Snatchers 1956; The Solid Gold Cadillac 1956
Dumont, José (1950–) Hour of the Star 1985; Behind the Sun 2001
Dumont, Margaret (1889–1965) The Cocoanuts 1929; Animal Crackers 1930; Duck Soup 1933; A Night at the Opera 1935; A Day at the Races 1937; Dramatic School 1938; At the Circus 1939; The Big Store 1941; Never Give a Sucker an Even Break 1941; The Dancing Masters 1943; Billy Rose's Diamond Horseshoe 1945; The Horn Blows at Midnight 1945; Little Giant 1946; Stop, You're Killing Me 1952; Shake, Rattle and Rock! 1957; Zotz 1962
Dumont, Ulises (1937–) Sur 1987; Wind with the Gone 1998
Dun, Dennis Big Trouble in Little China 1986; The Last Emperor 1987; Prince of Darkness 1987; Thousand Pieces of Gold 1990
Duna, Steffi (1910–1992) Anthony Adverse 1936; Pagliacci 1936; Phantom Raiders 1940
Dunaway, Faye (1941–) Bonnie and Clyde 1967; The Happening 1967; Hurry Sundown 1967; A Place for Lovers 1968; The Thomas Crown Affair 1968; The Arrangement 1969; The Extraordinary Seaman 1969; Little Big Man 1970; Puzzle of a Downfall Child 1970; The Deadly Trap 1971; Doc 1971; Oklahoma Crude 1973; The Three Musketeers 1973; Chinatown 1974; The Four Musketeers 1974; The Towering Inferno 1974; Three Days of the Condor 1975; The Disappearance of Aimee 1976; Network 1976; Voyage of the Damned 1976; Eyes of Laura Mars 1978; The Champ 1979; The First Deadly Sin 1980; Mommie Dearest 1981; The Wicked Lady 1983; Ordeal by Innocence 1984; Supergirl 1984; Thirteen at Dinner 1985; Barfly 1987; Burning Secret 1988; The Gamble 1988; Midnight Crossing 1988; Wait until Spring, Bandini 1989; The Handmaid's Tale 1990; Arizona Dream 1991; Scorchers 1991; Double Edge 1992; The Temp 1993; Don Juan DeMarco 1995; Albino Alligator 1996; The Chamber 1996; Dunston Checks In 1996; Gia 1998; Joan of Arc 1999; The Thomas Crown Affair 1999; The Yards 2000; The Rules of Attraction 2002
Dunbar, Adrian (1958–) Dealers 1989; Hear My Song 1991; The Crying Game 1992; Widows' Peak 1993; Innocent Lies 1995; The Near Room 1995; The General 1998; Shooters 2000; The Wedding Tackle 2000; Wild about Harry 2000; Triggermen 2002
Dunbar, Dixie (1919–1991) One in a Million 1936; Pigskin Parade 1936
Duncan, Andrew Loving 1970; The Hospital 1971; Slap Shot 1977; An Unmarried Woman 1978; A Little Romance 1979; The Gig 1985; Home Front 1987
Duncan, Archie (1914–1979) The Gorbals Story 1949; Counterspy 1953; Rob Roy, the Highland Rogue 1953; Trouble in the Glen 1954; Tess of the Storm Country 1960; Lancelot and Guinevere 1963
Duncan, Carmen (1942–) Harlequin 1980; Turkey Shoot 1981; Now and Forever 1983
Duncan, Kenne (1903–1972) My Pal Trigger 1946; On Top of Old Smoky 1953; The Astounding She-Monster 1958; Night of the Ghouls 1959; Hellborn 1961
Duncan, Lindsay (1950–) Loose Connections 1983; Prick Up Your Ears 1987; The Reflecting Skin 1990; Body Parts 1991; City Hall 1996; A Midsummer Night's Dream 1996; An Ideal Husband 1999; Mansfield Park 1999; Star Wars Episode I: the Phantom Menace 1999; AfterLife 2003; Under the Tuscan Sun 2003
Duncan, Michael Clarke (1957–) The Green Mile 1999; The Whole Nine Yards 2000; Planet of the Apes 2001; See Spot Run 2001; The Scorpion King 2002; Daredevil 2003; Racing Stripes 2004
Duncan, Pamela Attack of the Crab Monsters 1957; The Undead 1957
Duncan, Rachel (1985–) Two Much Trouble 1995; Amityville Dollhouse 1996; Last Stand at Saber River 1997
Duncan, Sandy (1946–) The Million Dollar Duck 1971; The Cat from Outer Space 1978; The Fox and the Hound 1981; My Boyfriend's Back 1989; Rock-a-Doodle 1990
Duncan, Todd (1903–1998) Syncopation 1942; Unchained 1955
Dundas, Jennie The Hotel New Hampshire 1984; Mrs Soffel 1984
Dunford, Christine Reversal of Fortune 1990; Ulee's Gold 1997
Dunham, Joanna (1936–) The Breaking Point 1961; Dangerous Afternoon 1961; The House That Dripped Blood 1971
Dunham, Katherine (1912–) Stormy Weather 1943; Mambo 1954
Dunn, Clive (1920–) She'll Have to Go 1961; Just like a Woman 1966; The Bliss of Mrs Blossom 1968; The Magic Christian 1969; Dad's Army 1971
Dunn, Emma (1875–1966) Manslaughter 1930; The Texan 1930; Bad Sister 1931; This Modern Age 1931; Hell's House 1932; The Wet Parade 1932; George White's 1935 Scandals 1935; The Cowboy and the Lady 1938; Young Dr Kildare 1938; The Llano Kid 1939; Dr Kildare's Crisis 1940; Dr Kildare's Strange Case 1940; The Penalty 1941; Life with Father 1947
Dunn, Harvey B (1894–1968) Bride of the Monster 1955; Teenagers from Outer Space 1959
Dunn, James (1905–1967) Bad Girl 1931; Hello Sister! 1933; Baby, Take a Bow 1934; Bright Eyes 1934; Change of Heart 1934; George White's 1935 Scandals 1935; Government Girl 1943; A Tree Grows in Brooklyn 1945; Killer McCoy 1947; The Bramble Bush 1960; Hemingway's Adventures of a Young Man 1962
Dunn, Josephine (1906–1983) The Singing Fool 1928; Our Modern Maidens 1929
Dunn, Kevin (1956–) Blue Steel 1990; The Bonfire of the Vanities 1990; Hot Shots! 1991; Only the Lonely 1991; Chaplin 1992; 1492: Conquest of Paradise 1992; Dave 1993; Little Big League 1994; Unforgivable 1995; Chain Reaction 1996; The Terror Inside 1996; Godzilla 1997; Picture Perfect 1997; The Second Civil War 1997; The 6th Man 1997; Almost Heroes 1998; Snake Eyes 1998; Stir of Echoes 1999
Dunn, Liam (1916–1976) What's Up, Doc? 1972; Blazing Saddles 1974; Peeper 1975
Dunn, Michael (1934–1973) You're a Big Boy Now 1966; Boom 1968; No Way to Treat a Lady 1968; The Mutations 1973; The Abdication 1974
Dunn, Nora (1952–) Miami Blues 1990; The Last Supper 1995; Air Bud: Golden Receiver 1998; Three Kings 1999; Max Keeble's Big Move 2001; Laws of Attraction 2003
Dunn, Roger No Higher Love 1999; Owning Mahowny 2002
Dunn-Hill, John Bullet to Beijing 1995; Wilder 2000
Dunne, Griffin (1955–) Chilly Scenes of Winter 1979; An American Werewolf in London 1981; Almost You 1984; Johnny Dangerously 1984; After Hours 1985; Who's That Girl 1987; The Big Blue 1988; My Girl 1991; Stepkids 1992; Straight Talk 1992; The Pickle 1993; I Like It like That 1994; Search and Destroy 1995; 40 Days and 40 Nights 2002
Dunne, Irene (1898–1990) Bachelor Apartment 1931; Cimarron 1931; Consolation Marriage 1931; Back Street 1932; Symphony of Six Million 1932; Ann Vickers 1933; If I Were Free 1933; The Secret of Madame Blanche 1933; The Silver Cord 1933; The Age of Innocence 1934; This Man Is Mine 1934; Magnificent Obsession 1935; Roberta 1935; Sweet Adeline 1935; Show Boat 1936; Theodora Goes Wild 1936; The Awful Truth 1937; High, Wide and Handsome 1937; Joy of Living 1938; Invitation to Happiness 1939; Love Affair 1939; When Tomorrow Comes 1939; My Favorite Wife 1940; Penny Serenade 1941; Unfinished Business 1941; Lady in a Jam 1942; A Guy Named Joe 1944; Together Again 1944; The White Cliffs of Dover 1944; Over 21 1945; Anna and the King of Siam 1946; Life with Father 1947; I Remember Mama 1948; The Mudlark 1950; Never a Dull Moment 1950; It Grows on Trees 1952
Dunne, Robin (1976–) Cruel Intentions 2 2000; American Psycho II: All American Girl 2002
Dunne, Steve aka **Dunne, Michael** aka **Dunne, Stephen** (1918–1977) Junior Miss 1945; The Dark Past 1948; Above and Beyond 1952; Home before Dark 1958; I Married a Woman 1958; The Explosive Generation 1961
Dunning, Ruth (1911–1983) It's a Great Day 1955; And Women Shall Weep 1960; Dangerous Afternoon 1961; Hoffman 1970; The House in Nightmare Park 1973
Dunnock, Mildred (1901–1991) The Corn Is Green 1945; Death of a Salesman 1951; I Want You 1951; The Girl in White 1952; The Jazz Singer 1952; Bad for Each Other 1954; The Trouble with Harry 1954; Baby Doll 1956; Love Me Tender 1956; The Nun's Story 1959; The Story on Page One 1959; Butterfield 8 1960; Sweet Bird of Youth 1962; Behold a Pale Horse 1964; 7 Women 1966; Whatever Happened to Aunt Alice? 1969; One Summer Love 1975; The Pick-Up Artist 1987
Dunsmore, Rosemary Dancing in the Dark 1986; The Boys 1991
Dunst, Kirsten (1982–) Interview with the Vampire: the Vampire Chronicles 1994; Little Women 1994; Jumanji 1995; Mother Night 1996; Anastasia 1997; Wag the Dog 1997; Small Soldiers 1998; Strike! 1998; The Devil's Arithmetic 1999; Dick 1999; Drop Dead Gorgeous 1999; The Virgin Suicides 1999; Bring It On 2000;

The Cat's Meow 2001; *crazy/beautiful* 2001; *Get over It* 2001; *Levity* 2002; *Spider-Man* 2002; *Eternal Sunshine of the Spotless Mind* 2003; *Mona Lisa Smile* 2003; *Spider-Man 2* 2004; *Wimbledon* 2004
Duperey, Anny (1947–) *Two or Three Things I Know about Her* 1966; *Without Warning* 1973; *Stavisky* 1974; *No Problem!* 1975; *Pardon Mon Affaire* 1976; *Bobby Deerfield* 1977; *Le Grand Pardon* 1981; *Les Compères* 1983
DuPois, Starletta *Hollywood Shuffle* 1987; *Convicts* 1991
Dupontel, Albert (1964–) *A Self-Made Hero* 1995; *Irreversible* 2002
Duprez, June (1918–1984) *The Four Feathers* 1939; *The Lion Has Wings* 1939; *The Spy in Black* 1939; *The Thief of Bagdad* 1940; *None but the Lonely Heart* 1944; *And Then There Were None* 1945; *The Brighton Strangler* 1945; *Calcutta* 1947
Dupuis, Paul (1913–1976) *Johnny Frenchman* 1945; *Against the Wind* 1947; *Sleeping Car to Trieste* 1948; *Madness of the Heart* 1949; *The Romantic Age* 1949; *The Reluctant Widow* 1950
Dupuis, Roy (1963–) *Being at Home with Claude* 1992; *Screamers* 1995; *Waiting for Michelangelo* 1995; *Hemoglobin* 1997
Durang, Christopher (1949–) *Penn & Teller Get Killed* 1989; *Simply Irresistible* 1999
Durante, Jimmy (1893–1980) *Blondie of the Follies* 1932; *The Passionate Plumber* 1932; *The Phantom President* 1932; *Speak Easily* 1932; *The Wet Parade* 1932; *Broadway to Hollywood* 1933; *Meet the Baron* 1933; *What – No Beer?* 1933; *George White's Scandals* 1934; *Hollywood Party* 1934; *Palooka* 1934; *Land without Music* 1936; *Little Miss Broadway* 1938; *Sally, Irene and Mary* 1938; *Start Cheering* 1938; *The Man Who Came to Dinner* 1941; *Music for Millions* 1944; *Two Girls and a Sailor* 1944; *Two Sisters from Boston* 1946; *It Happened in Brooklyn* 1947; *This Time for Keeps* 1947; *On an Island with You* 1948; *Pepe* 1960; *Jumbo* 1962
Durbin, Deanna (1921–) *Every Sunday* 1936; *One Hundred Men and a Girl* 1937; *Three Smart Girls* 1937; *Mad about Music* 1938; *That Certain Age* 1938; *First Love* 1939; *Three Smart Girls Grow Up* 1939; *It's a Date* 1940; *It Started with Eve* 1941; *Nice Girl?* 1941; *The Amazing Mrs Holliday* 1943; *Hers to Hold* 1943; *His Butler's Sister* 1943; *Can't Help Singing* 1944; *Christmas Holiday* 1944; *Lady on a Train* 1945; *Because of Him* 1946; *I'll Be Yours* 1947; *Something in the Wind* 1947; *For the Love of Mary* 1948; *Up in Central Park* 1948
Duret, Marc (1957–) *The Big Blue* 1988; *Nikita* 1990; *La Haine* 1995
Düringer, Annemarie *aka* **Düringer, Anne-Marie** (1925–) *Count Five and Die* 1957; *The Lacemaker* 1977; *Veronika Voss* 1982
Duris, Romain (1974–) *Gadjo Dilo* 1997; *Pot Luck* 2002; *Arsène Lupin* 2004; *Exiles* 2004
Durkin, Junior (1915–1935) *Tom Sawyer* 1930; *Huckleberry Finn* 1931; *Hell's House* 1932
Durning, Charles *aka* **Durnham, Charles** (1933–) *Harvey Middleman, Fireman* 1965; *Hi, Mom!* 1970; *I Walk the Line* 1970; *Dealing: or the Berkeley-to-Boston Forty-Brick Lost-Bag Blues* 1971; *Deadhead Miles* 1972; *Sisters* 1973; *The Sting* 1973; *Dog Day Afternoon* 1975; *The Hindenburg* 1975; *Breakheart Pass* 1976; *Harry and Walter Go to New York* 1976; *The Choirboys* 1977; *An Enemy of the People* 1977; *Twilight's Last Gleaming* 1977; *The Fury* 1978; *The Greek Tycoon* 1978; *Tilt* 1978; *North Dallas Forty* 1979; *Starting Over* 1979; *When a Stranger Calls* 1979; *Die Laughing* 1980; *The Final Countdown* 1980; *Sharky's Machine* 1981; *True Confessions* 1981; *The Best Little Whorehouse in Texas* 1982; *Tootsie* 1982; *To Be or Not to Be* 1983; *Two of a Kind* 1983; *Mass Appeal* 1984; *Big Trouble* 1985; *Death of a Salesman* 1985; *The Man with One Red Shoe* 1985; *Stand Alone* 1985; *Stick* 1985; *Solarbabies* 1986; *Tough Guys* 1986; *Where the River Runs Black* 1986; *Happy New Year* 1987; *The Rosary Murders* 1987; *A Tiger's Tale* 1987; *Cop* 1988; *Far North* 1988; *Brenda Starr* 1989; *Cat Chaser* 1989; *Dick Tracy* 1990; *Project: Alien* 1990; *VI Warshawski* 1991; *The Music of Chance* 1993; *The Hudsucker Proxy* 1994; *Home for the Holidays* 1995; *The Last Supper* 1995; *One Fine Day* 1996; *Spy Hard* 1996; *Shelter* 1997; *Hard Time* 1998; *Hi-Life* 1998; *Jerry and Tom* 1998; *The Last Producer* 2000; *O Brother, Where Art Thou?* 2000; *State and Main* 2000
Durock, Dick *Swamp Thing* 1982; *The Return of Swamp Thing* 1989
Durr, Jason (1968–) *Young Soul Rebels* 1991; *Killer Tongue* 1996
Dury, Ian (1942–2000) *Number One* 1984; *Rocinante* 1986; *Hearts of Fire* 1987; *The Raggedy Rawney* 1987; *The Cook, the Thief, His Wife and Her Lover* 1989; *After Midnight* 1990; *Split Second* 1991; *The Crow: City of Angels* 1996; *Middleton's Changeling* 1997; *Underground* 1998
Duryea, Dan (1907–1968) *The Little Foxes* 1941; *Sahara* 1943; *Mrs Parkington* 1944; *None but the Lonely Heart* 1944; *Along Came Jones* 1945; *The Great Flamarion* 1945; *Lady on a Train* 1945; *Ministry of Fear* 1945; *Scarlet Street* 1945; *The Woman in the Window* 1945; *Black Angel* 1946; *Another Part of the Forest* 1948; *Black Bart* 1948; *Criss Cross* 1949; *Johnny Stool Pigeon* 1949; *One Way Street* 1950; *The Underworld Story* 1950; *Winchester '73* 1950; *Thunder Bay* 1953; *World for Ransom* 1953; *Rails into Laramie* 1954; *Ride Clear of Diablo* 1954; *Silver Lode* 1954; *This Is My Love* 1954; *Foxfire* 1955; *The Marauders* 1955; *The Burglar* 1956; *Battle Hymn* 1957; *Night Passage* 1957; *Slaughter on Tenth Avenue* 1957; *Platinum High School* 1960; *Six Black Horses* 1962; *He Rides Tall* 1964; *Taggart* 1964; *The Bounty Killer* 1965; *Incident at Phantom Hill* 1966; *Five Golden Dragons* 1967; *Stranger on the Run* 1967
Dusay, Marj (1936–) *Sweet November* 1968; *Breezy* 1973; *MacArthur* 1977; *Love Walked In* 1997
Duse, Vittorio (1916–) *Ossessione* 1942; *Mad Dog Murderer* 1977; *Queen of Hearts* 1989
Dusek, Jaroslav (1961–) *Divided We Fall* 2000; *Zelary* 2003
Dusenberry, Ann (1953–) *Jaws 2* 1978; *Heart Beat* 1979; *Cutter's Way* 1981
Dushku, Eliza (1980–) *That Night* 1992; *This Boy's Life* 1993; *True Lies* 1994; *Bye Bye Love* 1995; *Race the Sun* 1996; *Bring It On* 2000; *Soul Survivors* 2001; *City by the Sea* 2002; *The New Guy* 2002; *Wrong Turn* 2003
Dussollier, André (1946–) *Une Belle Fille Comme Moi* 1973; *And Now My Love* 1974; *Perceval le Gallois* 1978; *Le Beau Mariage* 1982; *L'Amour par Terre* 1984; *Just the Way You Are* 1984; *3 Men and a Cradle* 1985; *Mélo* 1986; *Un Coeur en Hiver* 1992; *Le Colonel Chabert* 1994; *On Connaît la Chanson* 1997; *The Children of the Marshland* 1998; *Vidocq* 2001; *Strange Gardens* 2003
Dutronc, Jacques (1943–) *Mado* 1976; *An Adventure for Two* 1979; *Slow Motion* 1980; *Van Gogh* 1991; *Place Vendôme* 1998; *Merci pour le Chocolat* 2000; *Summer Things* 2002
Dutt, Guru (1925–1964) *Aar Paar* 1954; *Mr and Mrs '55* 1955; *Kaagaz Ke Phool* 1959
Dutt, Sanjay (1959–) *Saajan* 1991; *Chal Mere Bhai* 2000; *Ek Aur Ek Gyarah* 2003; *LOC Kargil* 2003; *Deewaar: Let's Bring Our Heroes Home* 2004; *Parineeta* 2005
Dutt, Sunil (1930–2005) *Ek Hi Rasta* 1956; *Mother India* 1957; *Sadhna* 1958; *Sujata* 1959; *Waqt* 1965
Dutt, Utpal (1929–1993) *Shakespeare Wallah* 1965; *The Guru* 1969; *Bombay Talkie* 1970; *The Stranger* 1991
Duttine, John (1949–) *Who Dares Wins* 1982; *The Hawk* 1992
Dutton, Charles S *aka* **Dutton, Charles** (1951–) *"Crocodile" Dundee II* 1988; *Jacknife* 1988; *Q & A* 1990; *Mississippi Masala* 1991; *Alien³* 1992; *The Distinguished Gentleman* 1992; *Menace II Society* 1993; *Rudy* 1993; *Jack Reed: a Search for Justice* 1994; *A Low Down Dirty Shame* 1994; *Surviving the Game* 1994; *Cry, the Beloved Country* 1995; *Jack Reed: One of Our Own* 1995; *Nick of Time* 1995; *Jack Reed: Death and Vengeance* 1996; *A Time to Kill* 1996; *Mimic* 1997; *Black Dog* 1998; *Cookie's Fortune* 1999; *Random Hearts* 1999; *Deadlocked* 2000; *For Love or Country: the Arturo Sandoval Story* 2000; *D-Tox* 2001; *Against the Ropes* 2003; *Gothika* 2003; *Secret Window* 2004
Dutton, Tim *Tom & Viv* 1994; *Darkness Falls* 1998; *All for Love* 1999; *Tooth* 2003
Duval, Daniel (1944–) *Will It Snow for Christmas?* 1996; *Le Vent de la Nuit* 1999; *Time of the Wolf* 2003; *Process* 2004
Duval, James (1973–) *Totally F***ed Up* 1993; *Doom Generation* 1995; *Nowhere* 1997
Duval, Paulette *The Exquisite Sinner* 1926; *The Divine Woman* 1928
DuVall, Clea (1977–) *The Faculty* 1998; *The Astronaut's Wife* 1999; *But I'm a Cheerleader* 1999; *Girl, Interrupted* 1999; *John Carpenter's Ghosts of Mars* 2001; *13 Conversations about One Thing* 2001; *The Laramie Project* 2002; *Identity* 2003; *21 Grams* 2003; *The Grudge* 2004
Duvall, Robert (1931–) *To Kill a Mockingbird* 1962; *Captain Newman, MD* 1963; *Nightmare in the Sun* 1964; *The Chase* 1966; *Bullitt* 1968; *Countdown* 1968; *The Detective* 1968; *MASH* 1969; *The Rain People* 1969; *True Grit* 1969; *The Revolutionary* 1970; *Lawman* 1971; *THX 1138* 1971; *The Godfather* 1972; *The Great Northfield Minnesota Raid* 1972; *Joe Kidd* 1972; *Tomorrow* 1972; *Badge 373* 1973; *Lady Ice* 1973; *The Outfit* 1973; *The Conversation* 1974; *The Godfather, Part II* 1974; *Breakout* 1975; *The Killer Elite* 1975; *The Eagle Has Landed* 1976; *Network* 1976; *The Seven-Per-Cent Solution* 1976; *The Greatest* 1977; *The Betsy* 1978; *Invasion of the Body Snatchers* 1978; *Apocalypse Now* 1979; *The Great Santini* 1979; *The Pursuit of DB Cooper* 1981; *True Confessions* 1981; *Tender Mercies* 1982; *The Natural* 1984; *The Stone Boy* 1984; *Belizaire the Cajun* 1985; *The Lightship* 1985; *Let's Get Harry* 1986; *Hotel Colonial* 1987; *Colors* 1988; *Days of Thunder* 1990; *The Handmaid's Tale* 1990; *A Show of Force* 1990; *Convicts* 1991; *Rambling Rose* 1991; *Falling Down* 1992; *The News Boys* 1992; *The Plague* 1992; *Geronimo: an American Legend* 1993; *Wrestling Ernest Hemingway* 1993; *The Paper* 1994; *The Scarlet Letter* 1995; *Something to Talk About* 1995; *The Stars Fell on Henrietta* 1995; *A Family Thing* 1996; *The Man Who Captured Eichmann* 1996; *Phenomenon* 1996; *The Apostle* 1997; *The Gingerbread Man* 1997; *A Civil Action* 1998; *Deep Impact* 1998; *Gone in Sixty Seconds* 2000; *A Shot at Glory* 2000; *The 6th Day* 2000; *John Q* 2001; *Assassination Tango* 2002; *Gods and Generals* 2002; *Open Range* 2003; *Secondhand Lions* 2003; *Kicking & Screaming* 2005
Duvall, Shelley (1949–) *Brewster McCloud* 1970; *McCabe and Mrs Miller* 1971; *Thieves like Us* 1974; *Nashville* 1975; *Annie Hall* 1977; *3 Women* 1977; *Popeye* 1980; *The Shining* 1980; *Time Bandits* 1981; *Roxanne* 1987; *Suburban Commando* 1991; *The Portrait of a Lady* 1996; *Changing Habits* 1997; *Rocketman* 1997; *Talos the Mummy* 1997; *The Twilight of the Ice Nymphs* 1997; *Casper Meets Wendy* 1998; *Home Fries* 1998
Dux, Pierre (1908–1990) *Monsieur Vincent* 1947; *Les Grandes Manoeuvres* 1955; *Goodbye Again* 1961; *Z* 1968; *Three Men to Destroy* 1980
Dvorak, Ann (1912–1979) *Hollywood Revue* 1929; *The Crowd Roars* 1932; *Love Is a Racket* 1932; *Scarface* 1932; *The Strange Love of Molly Louvain* 1932; *Three on a Match* 1932; *Dr Socrates* 1935; *"G" Men* 1935; *Thanks a Million* 1935; *The Case of the Stuttering Bishop* 1937; *Merrily We Live* 1938; *Blind Alley* 1939; *Abilene Town* 1945; *Flame of the Barbary Coast* 1945; *The Long Night* 1947; *Out of the Blue* 1947; *The Private Affairs of Bel Ami* 1947; *A Life of Her Own* 1950; *Mrs O'Malley and Mr Malone* 1950; *Our Very Own* 1950; *The Secret of Convict Lake* 1951
Dwan, Dorothy (1906–1981) *The Wizard of Oz* 1925; *Hills of Kentucky* 1927
Dwire, Earl (1883–1940) *Randy Rides Alone* 1934; *The Star Packer* 1934; *The Trail Beyond* 1934; *The Lawless Frontier* 1935; *Trouble in Texas* 1937; *The Arizona Kid* 1939
Dwyer, Hilary (1945–) *Witchfinder General* 1968; *The Body Stealers* 1969; *The Oblong Box* 1969; *Two Gentlemen Sharing* 1969; *Cry of the Banshee* 1970; *Wuthering Heights* 1970
Dwyer, Leslie (1906–1986) *The Way Ahead* 1944; *When the Bough Breaks* 1947; *The Calendar* 1948; *The Bad Lord Byron* 1949; *A Boy, a Girl and a Bike* 1949; *Judgement Deferred* 1951; *There Is Another Sun* 1951; *Hindle Wakes* 1952; *The Hour of 13* 1952; *The Black Rider* 1954; *Cloak without Dagger* 1955; *Where There's a Will* 1955; *Left, Right and Centre* 1959; *A Hole Lot of Trouble* 1969
Dyall, Franklin (1874–1950) *Easy Virtue* 1927; *Conquest of the Air* 1936
Dyall, Valentine (1908–1985) *Dr Morelle – the Case of the Missing Heiress* 1949; *Night Comes Too Soon* 1949; *Room to Let* 1949; *Suspended Alibi* 1956; *The City of the Dead* 1960; *The Haunting* 1963
d'Yd, Jean *The Passion of Joan of Arc* 1928; *Martin Roumagnac* 1946
Dye, Cameron (1967–) *Valley Girl* 1983; *Joy of Sex* 1984; *Fraternity Vacation* 1985; *Stranded* 1987; *Out of the Dark* 1988
Dye, Dale (1944–) *Kid* 1990; *Wings of the Apache* 1990; *Mission: Impossible* 1996; *Operation Delta Force II: Mayday* 1998
Dyer, Danny *Human Traffic* 1999; *The Trench* 1999; *Goodbye Charlie Bright* 2000; *Greenfingers* 2000; *High Heels and Low Lifes* 2001; *The Football Factory* 2004
Dyktynski, Matthew *Love and Other Catastrophes* 1996; *Japanese Story* 2003
Dylan, Bob (1941–) *Pat Garrett and Billy the Kid* 1973; *Hearts of Fire* 1987; *Masked and Anonymous* 2003
Dymon Jr, Frankie *Some People* 1962; *One Plus One* 1968
Dyne, Aminta (1887–1964) *Molly and Me* 1945; *Blood on My Hands* 1948
Dyneley, Peter (1921–1977) *Hell below Zero* 1954; *The Golden Disc* 1958; *The Whole Truth* 1958; *House of Mystery* 1961; *Thunderbirds Are Go!* 1966; *Thunderbird 6* 1968
Dyrholm, Trine (1972–) *Festen* 1998; *In Your Hands* 2004
Dysart, Richard *aka* **Dysart, Richard A** (1929–) *The Lost Man* 1969; *The Autobiography of Miss Jane Pittman* 1974; *The Terminal Man* 1974; *An Enemy of the People* 1977; *Being There* 1979; *Meteor* 1979; *Prophecy* 1979; *The Thing* 1982; *The Falcon and the Snowman* 1985; *Mask* 1985; *Pale Rider* 1985; *Warning Sign* 1985; *Day One* 1989; *Back to the Future Part III* 1990; *Truman* 1995; *Hard Rain* 1997
Dyson, Noel (1916–1995) *Press for Time* 1966; *Mister Ten Per Cent* 1967; *Father Dear Father* 1972
Dzundza, George (1945–) *The Deer Hunter* 1978; *Skokie* 1981; *Streamers* 1983; *Best Defense* 1984; *The Rape of Richard Beck* 1985; *No Mercy* 1986; *No Way Out* 1986; *The Beast of War* 1988; *Impulse* 1990; *White Hunter, Black Heart* 1990; *The Butcher's Wife* 1991; *Basic Instinct* 1992; *The Enemy Within* 1994; *Crimson Tide* 1995; *Dangerous Minds* 1995; *That Darn Cat* 1997; *Species II* 1998; *Instinct* 1999; *Determination of Death* 2001; *City by the Sea* 2002

E

Eadie, Nicholas (1958–) *Celia* 1988; *Return to Snowy River* 1988
Eagan, Daisy (1979–) *Losing Isaiah* 1995; *Ripe* 1996
Eagger, Victoria *The Nun and the Bandit* 1992; *Diana & Me* 1997
Ealy, Michael (1973–) *2 Fast 2 Furious* 2003; *Barbershop 2: Back in Business* 2004; *Never Die Alone* 2004
Earle, Edward (1882–1972) *The Wind* 1928; *Spite Marriage* 1929
Earles, Harry (1902–1985) *The Unholy Three* 1925; *The Unholy Three* 1930; *Freaks* 1932
East, Jeff (1957–) *Tom Sawyer* 1973; *Huckleberry Finn* 1974; *The Hazing* 1977; *Deadly Blessing* 1981; *Pumpkinhead* 1988
Easterbrook, Leslie (1951–) *Police Academy* 1984; *Police Academy 3: Back in Training* 1986; *Police Academy 4: Citizens on Patrol* 1987; *Police Academy 5: Assignment Miami Beach* 1988; *Police Academy 6: City under Siege* 1989; *Police Academy: Mission to Moscow* 1994; *The Devil's Rejects* 2005
Eastham, Richard (1918–) *There's No Business like Show Business* 1954; *Toby Tyler, or Ten Weeks with a Circus* 1960; *Not with My Wife, You Don't!* 1966
Easton, Robert (1930–) *Mr Sycamore* 1974; *The Giant Spider Invasion* 1975
Easton, Sheena (1959–) *Indecent Proposal* 1993; *All Dogs Go to Heaven 2* 1996
Eastwood, Alison (1972–) *Tightrope* 1984; *Absolute Power* 1996; *Midnight in the Garden of Good and Evil* 1997; *Black and White* 1998
Eastwood, Clint (1930–) *Francis in the Navy* 1955; *Lady Godiva* 1955; *Revenge of the Creature* 1955; *Tarantula* 1955; *Away All Boats* 1956; *The First Travelling Saleslady* 1956; *Star in the Dust* 1956; *Escapade in Japan* 1957; *Hell Bent for Glory* 1957; *A Fistful of Dollars* 1964; *For a Few Dollars More* 1965; *The Good, the Bad and the Ugly* 1966; *The Witches*

1966; *Coogan's Bluff* 1968; *Hang 'Em High* 1968; *Paint Your Wagon* 1969; *Where Eagles Dare* 1969; *Kelly's Heroes* 1970; *Two Mules for Sister Sara* 1970; *The Beguiled* 1971; *Dirty Harry* 1971; *Play Misty for Me* 1971; *Joe Kidd* 1972; *High Plains Drifter* 1973; *Magnum Force* 1973; *Thunderbolt and Lightfoot* 1974; *The Eiger Sanction* 1975; *The Enforcer* 1976; *The Outlaw Josey Wales* 1976; *The Gauntlet* 1977; *Every Which Way but Loose* 1978; *Escape from Alcatraz* 1979; *Any Which Way You Can* 1980; *Bronco Billy* 1980; *Firefox* 1982; *Honkytonk Man* 1982; *Sudden Impact* 1983; *City Heat* 1984; *Tightrope* 1984; *Pale Rider* 1985; *Heartbreak Ridge* 1986; *The Dead Pool* 1988; *Pink Cadillac* 1989; *The Rookie* 1990; *White Hunter, Black Heart* 1990; *Unforgiven* 1992; *In the Line of Fire* 1993; *A Perfect World* 1993; *The Bridges of Madison County* 1995; *Casper* 1995; *Absolute Power* 1996; *True Crime* 1999; *Space Cowboys* 2000; *Blood Work* 2002; *Million Dollar Baby* 2004

Eaton, Shirley (1936–) *The Love Match* 1955; *Charley Moon* 1956; *Sailor Beware!* 1956; *Three Men in a Boat* 1956; *Doctor at Large* 1957; *The Naked Truth* 1957; *Carry On Sergeant* 1958; *Further up the Creek* 1958; *Life Is a Circus* 1958; *Carry On Nurse* 1959; *Dentist on the Job* 1961; *Nearly a Nasty Accident* 1961; *What a Carve Up!* 1961; *The Girl Hunters* 1963; *Goldfinger* 1964; *Rhino!* 1964; *Around the World under the Sea* 1965; *Ten Little Indians* 1965; *Eight on the Lam* 1967; *Sumuru* 1967; *The Blood of Fu Manchu* 1968

Eberhardt, Norma *Live Fast, Die Young* 1958; *The Return of Dracula* 1958

Ebersole, Christine (1953–) *Amadeus* 1984; *Thief of Hearts* 1984; *Mac and Me* 1988; *Ghost Dad* 1990; *Folks!* 1992; *My Girl 2* 1994; *Richie Rich* 1994; *Pie in the Sky* 1995; *Black Sheep* 1996; *Double Platinum* 1999; *My Favorite Martian* 1999

Ebsen, Buddy (1908–2003) *Broadway Melody of 1936* 1935; *Banjo on My Knee* 1936; *Captain January* 1936; *Broadway Melody of 1938* 1937; *The Girl of the Golden West* 1938; *My Lucky Star* 1938; *Yellow Jack* 1938; *Night People* 1954; *Davy Crockett, King of the Wild Frontier* 1955; *Attack!* 1956; *Between Heaven and Hell* 1956; *Davy Crockett and the River Pirates* 1956; *Breakfast at Tiffany's* 1961; *The Interns* 1962; *Mail Order Bride* 1963; *The One and Only, Genuine, Original Family Band* 1968; *The Beverly Hillbillies* 1993

Eburne, Maude (1875–1960) *The Bat Whispers* 1930; *The Guardsman* 1931; *Her Majesty Love* 1931; *Indiscreet* 1931; *Ladies They Talk About* 1933; *The Vampire Bat* 1933; *Ruggles of Red Gap* 1935; *Among the Living* 1941; *You Belong to Me* 1941; *The Boogie Man Will Get You* 1942; *Rosie the Riveter* 1944

Eccles, Aimee *aka* **Eccles, Amy** *Little Big Man* 1970; *Marco* 1973; *The Concrete Jungle* 1982

Eccles, Ted *aka* **Eccles, Teddy** (1955–) *My Side of the Mountain* 1969; *The Honkers* 1971

Eccleston, Christopher *aka* **Eccleston, Chris** (1964–) *Let Him Have It* 1991; *Anchoress* 1993; *Shallow Grave* 1994; *Jude* 1996; *Heart* 1997; *A Price above Rubies* 1997; *Elizabeth* 1998; *eXistenZ* 1999; *With or without You* 1999; *Gone in Sixty Seconds* 2000; *The Invisible Circus* 2000; *The Others* 2001; *Strumpet* 2001; *Revengers Tragedy* 2002; *28 Days Later…* 2002

Echanove, Juan (1961–) *Shooting Elizabeth* 1992; *The Flower of My Secret* 1995

Echevarría, Emilio *Amores Perros* 2000; *The Alamo* 2004

Eckhart, Aaron (1968–) *In the Company of Men* 1997; *Thursday* 1998; *Your Friends & Neighbours* 1998; *Any Given Sunday* 1999; *Molly* 1999; *Erin Brockovich* 2000; *Nurse Betty* 2000; *The Pledge* 2000; *The Core* 2002; *Possession* 2002; *Paycheck* 2003; *Suspect Zero* 2004

Eckstine, Billy (1914–1993) *Skirts Ahoy!* 1952; *Jo Jo Dancer, Your Life Is Calling* 1986

Ecoffey, Jean-Philippe (1959–) *Nanou* 1986; *Woman from Rose Hill* 1989; *Henry & June* 1990; *Mina Tannenbaum* 1993; *L'Appartement* 1996; *Ma Vie en Rose* 1997; *Daybreak* 2000

Eddington, Paul (1927–1995) *The Devil Rides Out* 1968; *Baxter* 1973

Eddison, Robert (1908–1991) *The Angel Who Pawned Her Harp* 1954; *The Boy Who Turned Yellow* 1972; *American Friends* 1991

Eddy, Duane (1938–) *Because They're Young* 1960; *A Thunder of Drums* 1961

Eddy, Helen Jerome (1897–1990) *Rebecca of Sunnybrook Farm* 1917; *Pollyanna* 1920; *Skippy* 1931; *Madame Butterfly* 1932; *Klondike Annie* 1936

Eddy, Nelson (1901–1967) *Broadway to Hollywood* 1933; *Dancing Lady* 1933; *Naughty Marietta* 1935; *Rose Marie* 1936; *Maytime* 1937; *Rosalie* 1937; *The Girl of the Golden West* 1938; *Sweethearts* 1938; *Balalaika* 1939; *Bitter Sweet* 1940; *New Moon* 1940; *The Chocolate Soldier* 1941; *I Married an Angel* 1942; *Phantom of the Opera* 1943; *Knickerbocker Holiday* 1944; *Make Mine Music* 1946; *Northwest Outpost* 1947

Edelman, Gregg (1958–) *Green Card* 1990; *Passion* 1996

Edelman, Herb *aka* **Edelman, Herbert** (1930–1996) *Barefoot in the Park* 1967; *I Love You, Alice B Toklas* 1968; *The Odd Couple* 1968; *The War between Men and Women* 1972; *The Way We Were* 1973; *Hearts of the West* 1975; *The Yakuza* 1975; *Goin' Coconuts* 1978; *On the Right Track* 1981; *Smorgasbord* 1983

Eden, Barbara (1934–) *A Private's Affair* 1959; *Flaming Star* 1960; *All Hands on Deck* 1961; *Voyage to the Bottom of the Sea* 1961; *Five Weeks in a Balloon* 1962; *The Wonderful World of the Brothers Grimm* 1962; *7 Faces of Dr Lao* 1963; *The Yellow Canary* 1963; *The Brass Bottle* 1964; *The New Interns* 1964; *Quick, Let's Get Married* 1964; *Ride the Wild Surf* 1964; *The Amazing Dobermans* 1976; *Harper Valley PTA* 1978; *Chattanooga Choo Choo* 1984

Eden, Mark (1928–) *Seance on a Wet Afternoon* 1964; *The Pleasure Girls* 1965; *Attack on the Iron Coast* 1968; *Curse of the Crimson Altar* 1968

Edeson, Robert (1868–1931) *The Prisoner of Zenda* 1922; *The King of Kings* 1927

Edgerton, Joel (1974–) *The Hard Word* 2002; *Ned Kelly* 2003; *The Night We Called It a Day* 2003

Edmond, J Trevor (1969–) *Return of the Living Dead III* 1993; *The Revenge of Pumpkinhead – Blood Wings* 1994

Edmond, Valerie *One More Kiss* 1999; *Saving Grace* 2000

Edmondson, Adrian (1957–) *The Supergrass* 1985; *Eat the Rich* 1987; *Guest House Paradiso* 1999

Edney, Beatie (1962–) *Highlander* 1986; *Mister Johnson* 1991; *In the Name of the Father* 1993; *Mesmer* 1994; *Highlander: Endgame* 2000

Edson, Richard (1954–) *Stranger than Paradise* 1984; *Platoon* 1986; *Do the Right Thing* 1989; *Eyes of an Angel* 1991; *Joey Breaker* 1993; *Super Mario Bros* 1993; *Love, Cheat & Steal* 1994; *Jury Duty* 1995; *The Winner* 1996; *Double Tap* 1997

Edwall, Allan (1924–1997) *Winter Light* 1962; *The Emigrants* 1971; *The New Land* 1972; *Elvis! Elvis!* 1977; *Fanny and Alexander* 1982; *The Sacrifice* 1986

Edwards, Alan (1892–1954) *The White Sister* 1933; *If You Could Only Cook* 1935; *The Gentle Trap* 1960

Edwards, Anthony (1962–) *Fast Times at Ridgemont High* 1982; *Heart like a Wheel* 1983; *Revenge of the Nerds* 1984; *Gotcha!* 1985; *The Sure Thing* 1985; *Top Gun* 1986; *Hawks* 1988; *Mr North* 1988; *How I Got Into College* 1989; *Miracle Mile* 1989; *Downtown* 1990; *Pet Sematary II* 1992; *Charlie's Ghost Story* 1994; *The Client* 1994; *Playing by Heart* 1998; *Don't Go Breaking My Heart* 1999; *Northfork* 2002; *The Forgotten* 2004; *Thunderbirds* 2004

Edwards, Bill *aka* **Edwards, Billy** (1918–1999) *Hail the Conquering Hero* 1944; *The Virginian* 1946; *First Man into Space* 1958; *The Primitives* 1962; *The War Lover* 1962

Edwards, Bruce (1914–2002) *The Fallen Sparrow* 1943; *The Iron Major* 1943; *Bride by Mistake* 1944; *Betrayal from the East* 1945

Edwards, Cliff (1895–1971) *Doughboys* 1930; *Dance, Fools, Dance* 1931; *Laughing Sinners* 1931; *Parlor, Bedroom and Bath* 1931; *The Sin of Madelon Claudet* 1931; *Hell Divers* 1932; *George White's Scandals* 1934; *George White's 1935 Scandals* 1935; *Red Salute* 1935; *Saratoga* 1937; *They Gave Him a Gun* 1937; *His Girl Friday* 1939; *Maisie* 1939; *Pinocchio* 1940; *Dumbo* 1941; *Seven Miles from Alcatraz* 1942; *The Falcon Strikes Back* 1943; *Fun and Fancy Free* 1947

Edwards, Daryl *The Brother from Another Planet* 1984; *Blue Jean Cop* 1988

Edwards, Glynn (1931–) *The Hi-Jackers* 1963; *Smokescreen* 1964; *Zulu* 1964; *The Blood Beast Terror* 1967; *All Coppers Are…* 1972; *Rising Damp* 1980

Edwards, Henry (1882–1952) *East of Piccadilly* 1940; *Take My Life* 1947; *The Brass Monkey* 1948; *Oliver Twist* 1948; *The Rossiter Case* 1950

Edwards, Hilton (1903–1982) *Othello* 1952; *Cat and Mouse* 1958; *The Quare Fellow* 1962; *Half a Sixpence* 1967

Edwards, James (1918–1970) *Home of the Brave* 1949; *Bright Victory* 1951; *The Steel Helmet* 1951; *The Member of the Wedding* 1952; *The Joe Louis Story* 1953; *Battle Hymn* 1957; *Anna Lucasta* 1958; *Tarzan's Fight for Life* 1958; *Pork Chop Hill* 1959

Edwards, Jennifer (1959–) *Hook, Line and Sinker* 1969; *SOB* 1981; *A Fine Mess* 1986; *That's Life* 1986; *Perfect Match* 1987; *Sunset* 1988; *All's Fair* 1989; *Son of the Pink Panther* 1993

Edwards, Jimmy (1920–1988) *Murder at the Windmill* 1949; *Treasure Hunt* 1952; *Innocents in Paris* 1953; *Three Men in a Boat* 1956; *Bottoms Up* 1959; *Nearly a Nasty Accident* 1961; *The Plank* 1967; *The Bed Sitting Room* 1969

Edwards, Lance *Peacemaker* 1990; *A Woman, Her Men and Her Futon* 1992

Edwards, Luke (1980–) *Guilty by Suspicion* 1990; *Mother's Boys* 1993; *Little Big League* 1994

Edwards, Mark (1942–) *Blood from the Mummy's Tomb* 1971; *Tower of Evil* 1972

Edwards, Maudie (1906–1991) *I'll Be Your Sweetheart* 1945; *Only Two Can Play* 1961

Edwards, Meredith (1917–1999) *A Run for Your Money* 1949; *The Magnet* 1950; *There Is Another Sun* 1951; *Where No Vultures Fly* 1951; *The Gambler and the Lady* 1952; *The Last Page* 1952; *The Conquest of Everest* 1953; *A Day to Remember* 1953; *Devil on Horseback* 1954; *Final Appointment* 1954; *Mask of Dust* 1954; *Circus Friends* 1956; *Dunkirk* 1958; *Escapement* 1958; *This Is My Street* 1963; *Gulliver's Travels* 1977

Edwards, Penny (1928–1998) *North of the Great Divide* 1950; *Trail of Robin Hood* 1950; *Pony Soldier* 1952; *Powder River* 1953

Edwards, Snitz (1862–1937) *The Thief of Bagdad* 1924; *The Phantom of the Opera* 1925; *Seven Chances* 1925; *Battling Butler* 1926; *College* 1927; *The Mysterious Island* 1929

Edwards, Stacy (1965–) *In the Company of Men* 1997; *Black and White* 1999; *Four Dogs Playing Poker* 1999; *Driven* 2001; *Prancer Returns* 2001

Edwards, Vince *aka* **Edwards, Vincent** (1928–1996) *Sailor Beware* 1951; *The Night Holds Terror* 1955; *The Killing* 1956; *Serenade* 1956; *The Hired Gun* 1957; *Murder by Contract* 1958; *City of Fear* 1959; *The Victors* 1963; *The Devil's Brigade* 1968; *The Desperados* 1969; *Deal of the Century* 1983; *Space Raiders* 1983; *The Gumshoe Kid* 1990; *The Fear* 1995

Efron, Marshall (1938–) *Dynamite Chicken* 1971; *Is There Sex after Death?* 1971; *Twice upon a Time* 1983

Egan, Aeryk *Shrunken Heads* 1994; *The Cure* 1995

Egan, Eddie (1930–1995) *Badge 373* 1973; *Out of the Darkness* 1985; *Cold Steel* 1987

Egan, Peter (1946–) *The Hireling* 1973; *Callan* 1974; *Hennessy* 1975; *The Wedding Date* 2004

Egan, Richard (1921–1987) *Kansas Raiders* 1950; *Undercover Girl* 1950; *The Devil Makes Three* 1952; *One Minute to Zero* 1952; *The Glory Brigade* 1953; *The Kid from Left Field* 1953; *Split Second* 1953; *Gog* 1954; *Khyber Patrol* 1954; *Seven Cities of Gold* 1955; *Underwater!* 1955; *Untamed* 1955; *The View from Pompey's Head* 1955; *Violent Saturday* 1955; *Love Me Tender* 1956; *The Revolt of Mamie Stover* 1956; *Tension at Table Rock* 1956; *Slaughter on Tenth Avenue* 1957; *The Hunters* 1958; *Voice in the Mirror* 1958; *A Summer Place* 1959; *These Thousand Hills* 1959; *Esther and the King* 1960; *Pollyanna* 1960; *The 300 Spartans* 1962; *Chubasco* 1967; *Valley of Mystery* 1967; *The Destructors* 1968; *The Big Cube* 1969; *Day of the Wolves* 1973; *The Amsterdam Kill* 1978

Egan, Susan (1970–) *Hercules* 1997; *Spirited Away* 2001

Ege, Julie (1943–) *Every Home Should Have One* 1970; *Creatures the World Forgot* 1971; *The Magnificent Seven Deadly Sins* 1971; *Up Pompeii* 1971; *Go for a Take* 1972; *Not Now Darling* 1972; *Rentadick* 1972; *Craze* 1973; *The Mutations* 1973; *The Amorous Milkman* 1974; *The Legend of the 7 Golden Vampires* 1974; *Percy's Progress* 1974

Eggar, Samantha (1939–) *Dr Crippen* 1962; *The Wild and the Willing* 1962; *Doctor in Distress* 1963; *Psyche '59* 1964; *The Collector* 1965; *Return from the Ashes* 1965; *Walk, Don't Run* 1966; *Doctor Dolittle* 1967; *The Lady in the Car with Glasses and a Gun* 1970; *The Molly Maguires* 1970; *The Walking Stick* 1970; *The Light at the Edge of the World* 1971; *The Seven-Per-Cent Solution* 1976; *Why Shoot the Teacher* 1976; *The Uncanny* 1977; *Welcome to Blood City* 1977; *The Brood* 1979; *The Exterminator* 1980; *The Hot Touch* 1982; *A Ghost in Monte Carlo* 1990; *Dark Horse* 1992; *The Magic Voyage* 1992; *Barbara Taylor Bradford's Everything to Gain* 1996; *Hercules* 1997; *The Astronaut's Wife* 1999

Egger, Josef (1889–1966) *A Fistful of Dollars* 1964; *For a Few Dollars More* 1965

Eggert, Nicole (1972–) *Kinjite: Forbidden Subjects* 1989; *The Haunting of Morella* 1990; *Siberia* 1998

Eggerth, Marta (1912–) *The Unfinished Symphony* 1934; *For Me and My Gal* 1942; *Presenting Lily Mars* 1943

Egi, Stan *Come See the Paradise* 1990; *Rising Sun* 1993; *Golden Gate* 1994

Ehara, Tatsuyoshi *Red Beard* 1965; *Rebellion* 1967

Ehle, Jennifer (1969–) *Backbeat* 1993; *Paradise Road* 1997; *Wilde* 1997; *Bedrooms and Hallways* 1998; *Sunshine* 1999; *This Year's Love* 1999; *Possession* 2002

Ehlers, Jerome (1958–) *Deadly* 1991; *Fatal Bond* 1991; *Cubbyhouse* 2001

Eichhorn, Lisa (1952–) *The Europeans* 1979; *Yanks* 1979; *Why Would I Lie?* 1980; *Cutter's Way* 1981; *Agatha Christie's Murder in Three Acts* 1986; *Hell Camp* 1986; *Grim Prairie Tales* 1990; *Moon 44* 1990; *King of the Hill* 1993; *The Vanishing* 1993; *First Kid* 1996; *A Modern Affair* 1996; *Sticks and Stones* 1996

Eidsvold, Gard B (1966–) *Zero Kelvin* 1995; *Hamsun* 1996; *The Magnetist's Fifth Winter* 1999

Eigeman, Chris *aka* **Eigeman, Christopher** (1965–) *Metropolitan* 1990; *Barcelona* 1994; *Kicking and Screaming* 1995; *Mr Jealousy* 1997; *The Last Days of Disco* 1998; *Maid in Manhattan* 2002

Eikenberry, Jill (1947–) *Between the Lines* 1977; *Hide in Plain Sight* 1980; *Arthur* 1981; *The Deadly Game* 1986; *My Boyfriend's Back* 1989; *The Other Woman* 1994; *Taken Away* 1996

Eilbacher, Cindy (1958–) *The Big Bounce* 1969; *Shanks* 1974

Eilbacher, Lisa (1957–) *Spider-Man* 1977; *Run for the Roses* 1978; *On the Right Track* 1981; *An Officer and a Gentleman* 1982; *10 to Midnight* 1983; *Beverly Hills Cop* 1984; *Leviathan* 1989; *Live Wire* 1992

Eilber, Janet (1951–) *Romantic Comedy* 1983; *Hard to Hold* 1984

Eilers, Sally (1908–1978) *Doughboys* 1930; *Bad Girl* 1931; *Parlor, Bedroom and Bath* 1931; *Central Airport* 1933; *State Fair* 1933; *Remember Last Night?* 1935; *Strike Me Pink* 1936; *Danger Patrol* 1937; *Condemned Women* 1938; *Full Confession* 1939

Eisenberg, Aron (1969–) *Amityville: the Evil Escapes* 1989; *House III: The Horror Show* 1989; *Pterodactyl Woman from Beverly Hills* 1996

Eisenberg, Hallie Kate (1992–) *Nicholas' Gift* 1998; *Paulie* 1998; *Beautiful* 2000

Eisenberg, Jesse (1983–) *Roger Dodger* 2002; *Cursed* 2005

Eisenberg, Ned *The Burning* 1981; *Moving Violations* 1985; *A Murderous Affair* 1992; *Last Man Standing* 1996

Eisenmann, Ike (1962–) *Escape to Witch Mountain* 1975; *Return from Witch Mountain* 1978; *GoBots: Battle of the Rocklords* 1986

Eisley, Anthony *aka* **Eisley, Fred** (1925–2003) *The Wasp Woman* 1959; *The Naked Kiss* 1964; *The Navy vs the Night Monsters* 1966; *Dracula vs Frankenstein* 1970

Ejiofor, Chiwetel (1976–) *GMT Greenwich Mean Time* 1998; *It Was an Accident* 2000; *Dirty Pretty Things* 2002; *Melinda and Melinda* 2004; *She Hate Me* 2004

Ejogo, Carmen (1975–) *I Want You* 1998; *Love's Labour's Lost* 1999; *Boycott* 2001; *What's the Worst That Could Happen?* 2001

Ek, Anders (1916–1979) *Sawdust and Tinsel* 1953; *The Rite* 1969

Ekberg, Anita (1931–) *Abbott and Costello Go to Mars* 1953; *Artists and Models* 1955; *Blood Alley* 1955; *Back from Eternity* 1956; *Hollywood or Bust* 1956; *War and Peace* 1956; *Zarak* 1956; *Interpol* 1957; *Valerie* 1957; *The Man Inside* 1958; *Paris Holiday* 1958; *Screaming*

Mimi 1958; *The Sign of the Gladiator* 1958; *La Dolce Vita* 1960; *Boccaccio '70* 1961; *The Mongols* 1961; *Call Me Bwana* 1963; *4 for Texas* 1963; *The Alphabet Murders* 1966; *Way... Way Out* 1966; *Woman Times Seven* 1967; *If It's Tuesday, This Must Be Belgium* 1969; *Killer Nun* 1978; *Intervista* 1987

Ekborg, Lars (1926–1969) *Summer with Monika* 1952; *The Magician* 1958

Ekerot, Bengt (1920–1971) *The Seventh Seal* 1957; *The Magician* 1958

Ekland, Britt *aka* **Ekman, Brita** (1942–) *The Happy Thieves* 1962; *After the Fox* 1966; *The Bobo* 1967; *The Double Man* 1967; *The Night They Raided Minsky's* 1968; *Endless Night* 1971; *Get Carter* 1971; *Percy* 1971; *A Time for Loving* 1971; *Asylum* 1972; *Baxter* 1973; *The Wicker Man* 1973; *The Man with the Golden Gun* 1974; *Royal Flash* 1975; *Casanova & Co* 1976; *High Velocity* 1977; *King Solomon's Treasure* 1977; *Slavers* 1977; *The Monster Club* 1980; *Dead Wrong* 1983; *Fraternity Vacation* 1985; *Scandal* 1988; *The Children* 1990

Eklund, Bengt (1925–1998) *Night Is My Future* 1948; *Port of Call* 1948; *Three Strange Loves* 1949

Eklund, Jakob (1962–) *House of Angels* 1992; *Daybreak* 2003

Ekman (1), Gösta (1890–1938) *Faust* 1926; *Swedenhielms* 1935; *Intermezzo* 1936

Ekman, Hasse (1915–2004) *Intermezzo* 1936; *The Devil's Wanton* 1949; *Three Strange Loves* 1949

Ekman, John (1880–1949) *The Outlaw and His Wife* 1917; *To Joy* 1950

Elam, Jack (1916–2003) *An American Guerrilla in the Philippines* 1950; *High Lonesome* 1950; *One Way Street* 1950; *The Sundowners* 1950; *Bird of Paradise* 1951; *Rawhide* 1951; *Kansas City Confidential* 1952; *Rancho Notorious* 1952; *The Ring* 1952; *Appointment in Honduras* 1953; *Count the Hours* 1953; *The Moonlighter* 1953; *Ride, Vaquero!* 1953; *Cattle Queen of Montana* 1954; *The Far Country* 1954; *Princess of the Nile* 1954; *Ride Clear of Diablo* 1954; *Artists and Models* 1955; *Kismet* 1955; *The Man from Laramie* 1955; *Tarzan's Hidden Jungle* 1955; *Thunder over Arizona* 1956; *Dragoon Wells Massacre* 1957; *The Gun Runners* 1958; *Edge of Eternity* 1959; *The Night of the Grizzly* 1966; *The Rare Breed* 1966; *The Last Challenge* 1967; *The Way West* 1967; *Never a Dull Moment* 1968; *Support Your Local Sheriff!* 1969; *The Cockeyed Cowboys of Calico County* 1970; *Dirty Dingus Magee* 1970; *Rio Lobo* 1970; *Hannie Caulder* 1971; *The Last Rebel* 1971; *Support Your Local Gunfighter* 1971; *The Wild Country* 1971; *Pat Garrett and Billy the Kid* 1973; *Hawmps* 1976; *Grayeagle* 1977; *Hot Lead and Cold Feet* 1978; *The Norseman* 1978; *The Apple Dumpling Gang Rides Again* 1979; *Cactus Jack* 1979; *The Cannonball Run* 1981; *Jinxed!* 1982; *Sacred Ground* 1983; *The Aurora Encounter* 1985; *Once upon a Texas Train* 1988; *Hawken's Breed* 1989; *Suburban Commando* 1991

Elbaz, Vincent (1971–) *Would I Lie to You?* 1997; *Almost Peaceful* 2002

Elcar, Dana (1927–2005) *The Fool Killer* 1965; *The Learning Tree* 1969; *Adam at 6 AM* 1970; *Soldier Blue* 1970; *Zigzag* 1970; *The Great Northfield Minnesota Raid* 1972; *Report to the Commissioner* 1975; *WC Fields and Me* 1976; *Good Luck, Miss Wyckoff* 1979; *The Nude Bomb* 1980; *Buddy Buddy* 1981; *Condorman* 1981; *All of Me* 1984; *2010* 1984; *Agatha Christie's Murder in Three Acts* 1986

Eldard, Ron (1965–) *True Love* 1989; *The Last Supper* 1995; *Sex and the Other Man* 1995; *Sleepers* 1996; *When Trumpets Fade* 1998; *The Runner* 1999; *Ghost Ship* 2002; *Just a Kiss* 2002; *House of Sand and Fog* 2003

Elder, Ann *One of Our Spies Is Missing* 1966; *Don't Make Waves* 1967

Eldredge, John (1917–1960) *Flirtation Walk* 1934; *Dangerous* 1935; *The Girl from 10th Avenue* 1935; *Oil for the Lamps of China* 1935; *The Woman in Red* 1935; *His Brother's Wife* 1936; *Charlie Chan at the Olympics* 1937; *Blind Alley* 1939; *King of the Underworld* 1939

Eldridge, Florence (1901–1988) *The Divorcee* 1930; *Mary of Scotland* 1936; *Another Part of the Forest* 1948; *Christopher Columbus* 1949; *Inherit the Wind* 1960

Electra, Carmen (1972–) *The Mating Habits of the Earthbound Human* 1999; *Scary Movie* 2000; *My Boss's Daughter* 2003; *Starsky & Hutch* 2004

Elejalde, Karra (1960–) *Vacas* 1991; *La Madre Muerta* 1993; *Tierra* 1995

Eleniak, Erika (1969–) *ET the Extra-Terrestrial* 1982; *Under Siege* 1992; *The Beverly Hillbillies* 1993; *Chasers* 1994; *A Pyromaniac's Love Story* 1995; *Tales from the Crypt Presents: Bordello of Blood* 1996; *The Pandora Project* 1998; *Stealth Fighter* 1999

Elerick, John *Dark Victory* 1976; *Embryo* 1976

Eles, Sandor (1936–) *Evil of Frankenstein* 1964; *And Soon the Darkness* 1970; *Countess Dracula* 1970

Elfman, Jenna (1971–) *Krippendorf's Tribe* 1998; *Edtv* 1999; *Keeping the Faith* 2000; *Town & Country* 2001; *Clifford's Really Big Movie* 2004; *Looney Tunes: Back in Action* 2004

Elg, Taina (1931–) *Diane* 1955; *Gaby* 1956; *Les Girls* 1957; *Imitation General* 1958; *The Thirty-Nine Steps* 1959; *The Bacchantes* 1960; *Hercules in New York* 1969

Elgar, Avril (1932–) *Ladies Who Do* 1963; *Betrayal* 1982

Elias, Alix *John and Mary* 1969; *A Night in Heaven* 1983; *True Stories* 1986; *Munchies* 1987

Elias, Hector *The Master Gunfighter* 1975; *Heroes* 1977; *Losin' It* 1983; *Buddy Boy* 1999; *Envy* 2003

Elic, Josip *The Producers* 1968; *Dirty Little Billy* 1972

Elise, Christine (1965–) *Child's Play 2* 1990; *Body Snatchers* 1993; *Boiling Point* 1993

Elise, Kimberly (1971–) *Set It Off* 1996; *Beloved* 1998; *John Q* 2001; *The Manchurian Candidate* 2004

Elizabeth, Shannon (1973–) *Scary Movie* 2000; *Tomcats* 2000; *American Pie 2* 2001; *Jay and Silent Bob Strike Back* 2001; *Thir13en Ghosts* 2001; *Johnson Family Vacation* 2004

Elizondo, Hector (1936–) *Born to Win* 1971; *Valdez Is Coming* 1971; *Deadhead Miles* 1972; *Pocket Money* 1972; *The Taking of Pelham One Two Three* 1974; *Report to the Commissioner* 1975; *Thieves* 1977; *Cuba* 1979; *American Gigolo* 1980; *The Fan* 1981; *Young Doctors in Love* 1982; *The Flamingo Kid* 1984; *Out of the Darkness* 1985; *Private Resort* 1985; *Nothing in Common* 1986; *Chains of Gold* 1989; *Leviathan* 1989; *Pretty Woman* 1990; *Taking Care of Business* 1990; *Final Approach* 1991; *Frankie & Johnny* 1991; *Necessary Roughness* 1991; *Paydirt* 1992; *Being Human* 1994; *Beverly Hills Cop III* 1994; *Exit to Eden* 1994; *Getting Even with Dad* 1994; *Perfect Alibi* 1994; *Dear God* 1996; *Turbulence* 1997; *Runaway Bride* 1999; *The Princess Diaries* 2001; *Tortilla Soup* 2001; *The Princess Diaries 2: Royal Engagement* 2004; *Raising Helen* 2004

Ellerbe, Harry (1905–1992) *Murder on a Honeymoon* 1935; *So Red the Rose* 1935; *The Magnetic Monster* 1953; *The Fall of the House of Usher* 1960

Elliot, Biff (1923–) *I, the Jury* 1953; *Good Morning, Miss Dove* 1955; *The Dark* 1979

Elliot, Laura *Strangers on a Train* 1951; *Jamaica Run* 1953

Elliot, Mike *Eden Valley* 1994; *Billy Elliot* 2000

Elliott (2), Alison (1970–) *Indictment: the McMartin Trial* 1995; *The Underneath* 1995; *The Spitfire Grill* 1996; *The Wings of the Dove* 1997; *The Eternal* 1998; *Birth* 2004

Elliott, Bill *aka* **Elliott, Gordon** *aka* **Elliott, Wild Bill** (1903–1965) *The Case of the Black Cat* 1936; *The Case of the Velvet Claws* 1936; *Bells of Rosarita* 1945

Elliott, Bob (1923–) *Author! Author!* 1982; *Quick Change* 1990

Elliott, Chris (1960–) *Gremloids* 1990; *CB4* 1993; *Groundhog Day* 1993; *Cabin Boy* 1994; *Kingpin* 1996; *There's Something about Mary* 1998; *Snow Day* 2000

Elliott, David James (1960–) *Holiday Affair* 1996; *The Shrink Is In* 2000

Elliott, Denholm (1922–1992) *Dear Mr Prohack* 1949; *The Holly and the Ivy* 1952; *The Sound Barrier* 1952; *The Cruel Sea* 1953; *The Heart of the Matter* 1953; *They Who Dare* 1953; *Lease of Life* 1954; *The Man Who Loved Redheads* 1954; *The Night My Number Came Up* 1955; *Scent of Mystery* 1960; *Station Six-Sahara* 1962; *Nothing but the Best* 1963; *The High Bright Sun* 1965; *King Rat* 1965; *You Must Be Joking!* 1965; *Alfie* 1966; *Maroc 7* 1966; *The Spy with a Cold Nose* 1966; *Here We Go round the Mulberry Bush* 1967; *The Night They Raided Minsky's* 1968; *The Sea Gull* 1968; *The Rise and Rise of Michael Rimmer* 1970; *Too Late the Hero* 1970; *The House That Dripped Blood* 1971; *Percy* 1971; *Quest for Love* 1971; *Madame Sin* 1972; *A Doll's House* 1973; *Vault of Horror* 1973; *The Apprenticeship of Duddy Kravitz* 1974; *Percy's Progress* 1974; *Partners* 1976; *Robin and Marian* 1976; *To the Devil a Daughter* 1976; *The Hound of the Baskervilles* 1977; *The Boys from Brazil* 1978; *Sweeney 2* 1978; *Cuba* 1979; *A Game for Vultures* 1979; *Saint Jack* 1979; *Zulu Dawn* 1979; *Bad Timing* 1980; *Rising Damp* 1980; *Raiders of the Lost Ark* 1981; *Brimstone and Treacle* 1982; *The Missionary* 1982; *The Hound of the Baskervilles* 1983; *Trading Places* 1983; *The Wicked Lady* 1983; *A Private Function* 1984; *The Razor's Edge* 1984; *Defence of the Realm* 1985; *A Room with a View* 1985; *Mrs Delafield Wants to Marry* 1986; *The Whoopee Boys* 1986; *Maurice* 1987; *September* 1987; *Return from the River Kwai* 1988; *Stealing Heaven* 1988; *Indiana Jones and the Last Crusade* 1989; *Killing Dad* 1989; *One against the Wind* 1991; *Scorchers* 1991; *Toy Soldiers* 1991; *Noises Off* 1992

Elliott, Robert (1879–1951) *Lights of New York* 1928; *The Divorcee* 1930; *Dangerous Female* 1931; *Doorway to Hell* 1931; *The Finger Points* 1931; *Trade Winds* 1938; *The Saint Strikes Back* 1939; *The Devil's Playground* 1946

Elliott, Ross (1917–1999) *Tarantula* 1955; *Wild Seed* 1965

Elliott, Sam (1944–) *The Adventures of Mowgli* 1967; *Frogs* 1972; *Molly and Lawless John* 1972; *The Blue Knight* 1973; *Lifeguard* 1976; *The Legacy* 1978; *Mask* 1985; *Fatal Beauty* 1987; *Blue Jean Cop* 1988; *Prancer* 1989; *Road House* 1989; *Sibling Rivalry* 1990; *Rush* 1991; *Gettysburg* 1993; *Tombstone* 1993; *The Final Cut* 1995; *Dogwatch* 1997; *The Hi-Lo Country* 1998; *The Contender* 2000; *Fail Safe* 2000; *We Were Soldiers* 2002; *Hulk* 2003

Elliott, Shawn *aka* **Elliot, Shawn** *Crossover Dreams* 1985; *Hurricane Streets* 1997; *13 Conversations about One Thing* 2001

Elliott, Stephen *aka* **Elliot, Stephen** (1918–2005) *Three Hours to Kill* 1954; *The Hospital* 1971; *Report to the Commissioner* 1975; *Arthur* 1981; *Cutter's Way* 1981; *Roadhouse 66* 1984; *Assassination* 1986; *Walk like a Man* 1987; *Arthur 2: On the Rocks* 1988; *Taking Care of Business* 1990

Elliott, William (1934–1983) *Where Does It Hurt?* 1971; *Coffy* 1973; *Hangup* 1973

Ellis, Aunjanue *Girls Town* 1996; *Men of Honor* 2000; *Lovely & Amazing* 2001; *Undercover Brother* 2002; *Ray* 2004

Ellis, Bob (1942–) *Man of Flowers* 1984; *Unfinished Business* 1985

Ellis, Chris (1956–) *Bean* 1997; *Armageddon* 1998; *The Watcher* 2000

Ellis, Diane (1909–1930) *High Voltage* 1929; *Laughter* 1930

Ellis, Edward (1870–1952) *I Am a Fugitive from a Chain Gang* 1932; *The Last Gentleman* 1934; *The Return of Peter Grimm* 1935; *Village Tale* 1935; *Chatterbox* 1936; *Fury* 1936; *The Texas Rangers* 1936; *Little Miss Broadway* 1938; *Man of Conquest* 1939; *A Man Betrayed* 1941

Ellis, James (1931–) *No Surrender* 1986; *Priest* 1994; *Resurrection Man* 1997

Ellis, Mary (1897–2003) *All the King's Horses* 1935; *Fatal Lady* 1936

Ellis, Patricia (1916–1970) *Three on a Match* 1932; *The King's Vacation* 1933; *Picture Snatcher* 1933; *The World Changes* 1933; *Easy to Love* 1934; *The Case of the Lucky Legs* 1935; *Step Lively, Jeeves* 1937; *Blockheads* 1938

Ellis, Robert (1933–1973) *Broadway* 1929; *The McConnell Story* 1955; *Space Master X 7* 1958

Ellison, James *aka* **Ellison, Jimmy** (1910–1993) *Hopalong Cassidy* 1935; *The Plainsman* 1936; *Vivacious Lady* 1938; *Fifth Avenue Girl* 1939; *Zenobia* 1939; *Anne of Windy Poplars* 1940; *Charley's Aunt* 1941; *Careful, Soft Shoulder* 1942; *The Undying Monster* 1942; *I Walked with a Zombie* 1943; *Johnny Doesn't Live Here Anymore* 1944

Elmaleh, Gad (1971–) *Salut Cousin!* 1996; *Man Is a Woman* 1998

Elmaloglou, Rebekah (1974–) *In Too Deep* 1990; *Back of Beyond* 1995

Elphick, Michael (1946–2002) *Hamlet* 1969; *Where's Jack?* 1969; *The Buttercup Chain* 1970; *Blind Terror* 1971; *The First Great Train Robbery* 1978; *The Odd Job* 1978; *The Elephant Man* 1980; *Gorky Park* 1983; *The Element of Crime* 1984; *Ordeal by Innocence* 1984; *Arthur's Hallowed Ground* 1985; *Withnail & I* 1986; *I Bought a Vampire Motorcycle* 1989; *Buddy's Song* 1990; *Let Him Have It* 1991

Elsner, Hannelore (1942–) *Parker* 1984; *Please Let the Flowers Live* 1986; *A Girl Called Rosemarie* 1996; *No Place to Go* 2000

Elsom, Isobel (1893–1981) *Ladies in Retirement* 1941; *You Were Never Lovelier* 1942; *The Two Mrs Carrolls* 1945; *The Unseen* 1945; *Two Sisters from Boston* 1946; *Escape Me Never* 1947; *Love from a Stranger* 1947; *Love Is a Many-Splendored Thing* 1955; *Rock-a-Bye Baby* 1958; *The Second Time Around* 1961; *My Fair Lady* 1964

Elwes, Cary (1962–) *Another Country* 1984; *Oxford Blues* 1984; *Lady Jane* 1985; *The Princess Bride* 1987; *Never on Tuesday* 1988; *Glory* 1989; *Days of Thunder* 1990; *Hot Shots!* 1991; *Leather Jackets* 1991; *Bram Stoker's Dracula* 1992; *The Crush* 1993; *Robin Hood: Men in Tights* 1993; *The Jungle Book* 1994; *Twister* 1996; *Kiss the Girls* 1997; *Liar Liar* 1997; *The Magic Sword: Quest for Camelot* 1997; *The Pentagon Wars* 1998; *Cradle Will Rock* 1999; *Race against Time* 2000; *Shadow of the Vampire* 2000; *The Cat's Meow* 2001; *The Cat Returns* 2002; *Ella Enchanted* 2004; *Saw* 2004

Ely, Ron (1938–) *The Remarkable Mr Pennypacker* 1959; *Once Before I Die* 1965; *The Night of the Grizzly* 1966; *Tarzan's Deadly Silence* 1970; *Doc Savage: the Man of Bronze* 1975; *Slavers* 1977

Embry, Ethan *aka* **Randall, Ethan** (1978–) *All I Want for Christmas* 1991; *Driving Me Crazy* 1991; *A Far Off Place* 1993; *Empire Records* 1995; *That Thing You Do!* 1996; *Vegas Vacation* 1997; *Can't Hardly Wait* 1998; *Dancer, Texas Pop 81* 1998; *Sweet Home Alabama* 2002; *They* 2002; *Timeline* 2003

Emerson, Faye (1917–1983) *The Hard Way* 1942; *Between Two Worlds* 1944; *The Desert Song* 1944; *The Mask of Dimitrios* 1944; *Uncertain Glory* 1944; *The Very Thought of You* 1944; *Hotel Berlin* 1945; *Nobody Lives Forever* 1946; *Guilty Bystander* 1950

Emerson, Hope (1897–1960) *Cry of the City* 1948; *Adam's Rib* 1949; *Dancing in the Dark* 1949; *Caged* 1950; *Double Crossbones* 1951; *Westward the Women* 1951; *The Lady Wants Mink* 1953; *Untamed* 1955; *Guns of Fort Petticoat* 1957

Emerton, Roy (1892–1944) *Lorna Doone* 1934; *Everything Is Thunder* 1936; *Big Fella* 1937; *Dr Syn* 1937; *The Last Adventurers* 1937

Emery, Dick (1917–1983) *The Case of the Mukkinese Battle Horn* 1955; *Light Up the Sky* 1960; *The Fast Lady* 1963; *The Big Job* 1965; *Yellow Submarine* 1968; *Loot* 1970; *Ooh... You Are Awful* 1972; *Find the Lady* 1976

Emery, Gilbert (1875–1945) *A Lady's Morals* 1930; *Sarah and Son* 1930; *Ladies' Man* 1931; *Now and Forever* 1934; *Goin' to Town* 1935; *Magnificent Obsession* 1935; *The Return of the Vampire* 1943; *The Brighton Strangler* 1945

Emery, John (1905–1964) *Eyes in the Night* 1942; *The Silent Bell* 1944; *Blood on the Sun* 1945; *The Spanish Main* 1945; *Spellbound* 1945; *The Woman in White* 1948; *Frenchie* 1950; *Double Crossbones* 1951; *The Mad Magician* 1954; *A Lawless Street* 1955; *Forever, Darling* 1956; *The Girl Can't Help It* 1956; *Kronos* 1957; *Ten North Frederick* 1958

Emery, Katherine (1906–1980) *Eyes in the Night* 1942; *Isle of the Dead* 1945; *Untamed Frontier* 1952; *The Maze* 1953

Emery, Tania (1976–) *The Truth Game* 2000; *Club le Monde* 2001

Emhardt, Robert (1914–1994) *3:10 to Yuma* 1957; *The Badlanders* 1958; *The Intruder* 1961; *Underworld USA* 1961; *Hostile Guns* 1967; *Change of Habit* 1969; *Alex and the Gypsy* 1976; *Fraternity Row* 1977

Emil, Michael *Tracks* 1977; *Sitting Ducks* 1979; *Can She Bake a Cherry Pie?* 1983; *Insignificance* 1985; *Someone to Love* 1987

Emile, Taungaroa *Once Were Warriors* 1994; *Flight of the Albatross* 1995

Emilfork, Daniel (1924–) *Lady L* 1965; *Kill!* 1972; *The City of Lost Children* 1995

Emmanuel, Takis *Elektra* 1962; *Zorba the Greek* 1964; *The Magus* 1968; *The Golden Voyage of Sinbad* 1973; *Caddie* 1976

Emmerich, Noah (1966–) *Beautiful Girls* 1996; *The Truman*

Show 1998; *Frequency* 2000; *Love & Sex* 2000; *Windtalkers* 2001; *Beyond Borders* 2003; *Miracle* 2004
Emney, Fred (1900–1980) *Hold My Hand* 1938; *Just William* 1939
Empson, Tameka *Beautiful Thing* 1995; *Food of Love* 1997; *Babymother* 1998
Endre, Lena (1955–) *Best Intentions* 1992; *Kristin Lavransdatter* 1995; *Jerusalem* 1996; *Faithless* 2000
Enfield, Harry (1961–) *Kevin & Perry Go Large* 2000; *Tooth* 2003; *Churchill: the Hollywood Years* 2004
Engel, Georgia (1948–) *Taking Off* 1971; *The Outside Man* 1973; *The Care Bears Movie* 1985
Engel, Roy (1913–1980) *The Man from Planet X* 1951; *The Naked Dawn* 1955; *A Dog's Best Friend* 1960
Engel, Susan (1935–) *King Lear* 1970; *Butley* 1973
England, Audie (1971–) *Delta of Venus* 1995; *One Good Turn* 1996; *Free Enterprise* 1998
England, Sue (1928–) *This Love of Ours* 1945; *Kidnapped* 1948
English, Arthur (1919–1995) *The Hi-Jackers* 1963; *For the Love of Ada* 1972; *Malachi's Cove* 1973; *Are You Being Served?* 1977; *The Boys in Blue* 1983
English, Maria (1935–) *Shield for Murder* 1954; *Runaway Daughters* 1956; *The She-Creature* 1956; *Voodoo Woman* 1957
Englund, Robert (1949–) *Buster and Billie* 1974; *Eaten Alive* 1976; *St Ives* 1976; *Stay Hungry* 1976; *The Great Smokey Roadblock* 1977; *The Fifth Floor* 1980; *Dead & Buried* 1981; *Don't Cry, It's Only Thunder* 1982; *Starflight One* 1983; *A Nightmare on Elm Street* 1984; *A Nightmare on Elm Street 2: Freddy's Revenge* 1985; *A Nightmare on Elm Street 3: Dream Warriors* 1987; *A Nightmare on Elm Street 4: The Dream Master* 1988; *A Nightmare on Elm Street 5: The Dream Child* 1989; *The Phantom of the Opera* 1989; *The Adventures of Ford Fairlane* 1990; *Freddy's Dead: the Final Nightmare* 1991; *The Mangler* 1994; *Mortal Fear* 1994; *Wes Craven's New Nightmare* 1994; *Killer Tongue* 1996; *Wishmaster* 1997; *Dee Snider's Strangeland* 1998; *Meet the Deedles* 1998; *Urban Legend* 1998; *Python* 2000; *Freddy vs Jason* 2003
Enos, John *aka* **Enos III, John** (1962–) *Bullet* 1995; *Dead of Night* 1997; *Dead Sexy* 2001
Enriquez, Rene (1933–1990) *The Evil That Men Do* 1984; *Bulletproof* 1987
Ensign, Michael (1944–) *Buddy Buddy* 1981; *House* 1986; *Life Stinks* 1991; *Born Yesterday* 1993; *Children of the Corn III: Urban Harvest* 1995
Epps, Mike *Next Friday* 1999; *The Fighting Temptations* 2003; *Resident Evil: Apocalypse* 2004; *The Honeymooners* 2005
Epps, Omar (1973–) *Juice* 1991; *The Program* 1993; *Major League II* 1994; *Higher Learning* 1995; *First Time Felon* 1997; *Scream 2* 1997; *Breakfast of Champions* 1999; *In Too Deep* 1999; *The Mod Squad* 1999; *The Wood* 1999; *Brother* 2000; *Dracula 2001* 2000; *Love & Basketball* 2000; *Against the Ropes* 2003; *Alfie* 2004
Erbe, Kathryn (1966–) *What about Bob?* 1991; *Rich in Love* 1992; *D2: the Mighty Ducks* 1994; *Kiss of Death* 1994; *Dream with the Fishes* 1996; *Stir of Echoes* 1999
Ercy, Elizabeth *Phaedra* 1962; *The Sorcerers* 1967
Erdman, Richard (1925–) *The Admiral Was a Lady* 1950; *The Men* 1950; *Cry Danger* 1951; *The Stooge* 1951; *The San Francisco Story* 1952; *The Blue Gardenia* 1953; *Stalag 17* 1953; *Bengazi* 1955; *Francis in the Navy* 1955; *Face of Fire* 1959; *Namu, the Killer Whale* 1966; *Heidi's Song* 1982; *Tomboy* 1985
Erdogan, Yilmaz (1967–) *Vizontele* 2001; *Vizontele Tuuba* 2003
Ergun, Halil (1946–) *Yol* 1982; *Hamam: the Turkish Bath* 1996
Erhard, Bernard *GoBots: Battle of the Rocklords* 1986; *Little Nemo: Adventures in Slumberland* 1992
Erickson, Ethan (1973–) *Two-Bits and Pepper* 1995; *The In Crowd* 2000
Erickson, Leif (1911–1986) *Waikiki Wedding* 1937; *HM Pulham Esq* 1941; *Nothing but the Truth* 1941; *Arabian Nights* 1942; *Pardon My Sarong* 1942; *Joan of Arc* 1948; *The Snake Pit* 1948; *Sorry, Wrong Number* 1948; *Johnny Stool Pigeon* 1949; *Dallas* 1950; *Stella* 1950; *Three Secrets* 1950; *The Cimarron Kid* 1951; *Sailor Beware* 1951; *Abbott and Costello Meet Captain Kidd* 1952; *Never Wave at a WAC* 1952; *Fort Algiers* 1953; *Invaders from Mars* 1953; *On the Waterfront* 1954; *The Fastest Gun Alive* 1956; *Star in the Dust* 1956; *Tea and Sympathy* 1956; *Istanbul* 1957; *Kiss Them for Me* 1957; *Twilight for the Gods* 1958; *Strait-Jacket* 1963; *Roustabout* 1964; *I Saw What You Did* 1965; *Mirage* 1965; *Man and Boy* 1971; *Abduction* 1975; *Winterhawk* 1975
Ericson, John (1926–) *Teresa* 1951; *Green Fire* 1954; *Rhapsody* 1954; *The Student Prince* 1954; *Bad Day at Black Rock* 1955; *Forty Guns* 1957; *Day of the Bad Man* 1958; *Pretty Boy Floyd* 1960; *Under Ten Flags* 1960; *7 Faces of Dr Lao* 1963; *The Destructors* 1968; *Bedknobs and Broomsticks* 1971; *Crash!* 1977
Erikson, Leif (1911–1986) *Conquest* 1937; *One Third of a Nation* 1939
Erkekli, Altan (1955–) *Vizontele* 2001; *Vizontele Tuuba* 2003; *Anlat Istanbul* 2005
Ermey, R Lee *aka* **Ermey, Lee** *aka* **Ermey, Ronald Lee** (1944–) *The Boys in Company C* 1978; *Purple Hearts* 1984; *Full Metal Jacket* 1987; *Mississippi Burning* 1988; *Demonstone* 1989; *Fletch Lives* 1989; *Kid* 1990; *Toy Soldiers* 1991; *Body Snatchers* 1993; *Hexed* 1993; *Sommersby* 1993; *Love Is a Gun* 1994; *Murder in the First* 1994; *On Deadly Ground* 1994; *Dead Man Walking* 1995; *Se7en* 1995; *Soul of the Game* 1996; *Dead Men Can't Dance* 1997; *Prefontaine* 1997; *Switchback* 1997; *Toy Story 2* 1999; *Evil Woman* 2001; *Taking Sides* 2001; *The Texas Chainsaw Massacre* 2003; *Willard* 2003; *Man of the House* 2005
Ernst, Ole (1940–) *Possessed* 1999; *Okay* 2002
Errickson, Krista (1964–) *Little Darlings* 1980; *Jekyll and Hyde... Together Again* 1982; *Mortal Passions* 1989
Errol, Leon (1881–1951) *Her Majesty Love* 1931; *One Heavenly Night* 1931; *Alice in Wonderland* 1933; *We're Not Dressing* 1934; *Princess O'Hara* 1935; *Dancing Co-Ed* 1939; *The Girl from Mexico* 1939; *Mexican Spitfire* 1940; *Never Give a Sucker an Even Break* 1941; *Higher and Higher* 1943; *The Invisible Man's Revenge* 1944; *Twilight on the Prairie* 1944; *Under Western Skies* 1945; *The Noose Hangs High* 1948
Erskine, Marilyn (1926–) *Westward the Women* 1951; *Above and Beyond* 1952; *The Girl in White* 1952; *The Eddie Cantor Story* 1953
Ertmanis, Victor *Paris France* 1993; *Brainscan* 1994
Erwin, Bill (1914–) *Somewhere in Time* 1980; *The Land before Time* 1988; *Silent Assassins* 1988; *Desert Heat* 1999
Erwin, Stuart (1903–1967) *The Big Broadcast* 1932; *Make Me a Star* 1932; *Going Hollywood* 1933; *Hold Your Man* 1933; *International House* 1933; *The Stranger's Return* 1933; *Bachelor Bait* 1934; *Chained* 1934; *Palooka* 1934; *Viva Villa!* 1934; *After Office Hours* 1935; *Ceiling Zero* 1935; *Pigskin Parade* 1936; *Checkers* 1937; *I'll Take Romance* 1937; *Slim* 1937; *Three Blind Mice* 1938; *Hollywood Cavalcade* 1939; *When the Daltons Rode* 1940; *The Bride Came COD* 1941; *Heaven Only Knows* 1947; *For the Love of Mike* 1960; *The Misadventures of Merlin Jones* 1964
Eshley, Norman (1945–) *The Immortal Story* 1968; *Blind Terror* 1971; *House of Mortal Sin* 1975; *George and Mildred* 1980
Esmond, Annie (1873–1945) *Thunder in the City* 1937; *Gert and Daisy's Weekend* 1941
Esmond, Carl (1908–2004) *Blossom Time* 1934; *Evensong* 1934; *The Dawn Patrol* 1938; *Thunder Afloat* 1939; *The Navy Comes Through* 1942; *Margin for Error* 1943; *Address Unknown* 1944; *Experiment Perilous* 1944; *The Master Race* 1944; *The Story of Dr Wassell* 1944; *Ministry of Fear* 1945; *This Love of Ours* 1945; *Without Love* 1945; *Lover Come Back* 1946; *Smash Up – the Story of a Woman* 1947; *Walk a Crooked Mile* 1948; *Mystery Submarine* 1950; *The World in His Arms* 1952; *Thunder in the Sun* 1959; *Brushfire!* 1962; *Agent for HARM* 1966
Esmond, Jill (1908–1990) *The Skin Game* 1931; *FP1* 1932; *The Pied Piper* 1942; *Casanova Brown* 1944; *The Bandit of Sherwood Forest* 1946; *Bedelia* 1946; *A Man Called Peter* 1955
Esposito, Giancarlo (1958–) *School Daze* 1988; *Do the Right Thing* 1989; *King of New York* 1989; *Mo' Better Blues* 1990; *Harley Davidson and the Marlboro Man* 1991; *Bob Roberts* 1992; *Night on Earth* 1992; *Fresh* 1994; *The Keeper* 1995; *Reckless* 1995; *Smoke* 1995; *The Usual Suspects* 1995; *Nothing to Lose* 1997; *Stardust* 1998; *Thirst* 1998; *Twilight* 1998; *Monkeybone* 2000; *Piñero* 2001
Esposito, Gianni *French Cancan* 1955; *Celà S'Appelle l'Aurore* 1956; *Les Misérables* 1957; *Paris Nous Appartient* 1960
Esposito, Jennifer (1973–) *Summer of Sam* 1999; *Dracula 2001* 2000; *The Proposal* 2000; *Don't Say a Word* 2001; *The Master of Disguise* 2002; *Breakin' All the Rules* 2004; *Crash* 2004; *Taxi* 2004
Essell, Eileen *Our House* 2003; *Finding Neverland* 2004
Essex, David (1947–) *All Coppers Are...* 1972; *That'll Be the Day* 1973; *Stardust* 1974; *Silver Dream Racer* 1980; *Shogun Warrior* 1991
Estefan, Gloria (1957–) *Music of the Heart* 1999; *For Love or Country: the Arturo Sandoval Story* 2000
Estes, Will (1978–) *The Road Home* 1995; *New Port South* 2001
Esteve, María (1974–) *The Other Side of the Bed* 2002; *Football Days* 2003
Estevez, Emilio (1962–) *Tex* 1982; *Nightmares* 1983; *The Outsiders* 1983; *Repo Man* 1984; *The Breakfast Club* 1985; *St Elmo's Fire* 1985; *That Was Then... This Is Now* 1985; *Maximum Overdrive* 1986; *Wisdom* 1986; *Stakeout* 1987; *Never on Tuesday* 1988; *Young Guns* 1988; *Nightbreaker* 1989; *Men at Work* 1990; *Young Guns II* 1990; *Freejack* 1992; *The Mighty Ducks* 1992; *Another Stakeout* 1993; *Judgment Night* 1993; *National Lampoon's Loaded Weapon 1* 1993; *D2: the Mighty Ducks* 1994; *D3: the Mighty Ducks* 1996; *The War at Home* 1996; *Dollar for the Dead* 1998; *Rated X* 2000
Estevez, Joe *Eye of the Stranger* 1993; *Orbit* 1996
Estevez, Renée (1967–) *Running Wild* 1992; *Paper Hearts* 1993; *Storm* 1999
Estrada, Erik (1949–) *The New Centurions* 1972; *Trackdown* 1976; *Where Is Parsifal?* 1983; *Hour of the Assassin* 1987; *A Show of Force* 1990; *King Cobra* 1999
Etaix, Pierre (1928–) *Pickpocket* 1959; *Yoyo* 1964
Eure, Wesley (1955–) *The Toolbox Murders* 1978; *CHOMPS* 1979
Evans, Alice (1974–) *102 Dalmatians* 2000; *The Abduction Club* 2002; *Blackball* 2003
Evans, Art *Leadbelly* 1976; *A Soldier's Story* 1984; *Jo Jo Dancer, Your Life Is Calling* 1986; *Native Son* 1986; *Ruthless People* 1986; *White of the Eye* 1986; *School Daze* 1988; *The Mighty Quinn* 1989; *Die Hard 2: Die Harder* 1990; *Downtown* 1990; *Trespass* 1992; *Metro* 1997
Evans, Barry (1943–1997) *Here We Go round the Mulberry Bush* 1967; *Die Screaming Marianne* 1970; *Adventures of a Taxi Driver* 1975; *Under the Doctor* 1976
Evans, Charles *Black Beauty* 1946; *The Dark Mirror* 1946; *It Had to Be You* 1947
Evans, Chris (1981–) *Not Another Teen Movie* 2001; *Cellular* 2004; *The Perfect Score* 2004
Evans, Clifford (1912–1985) *The Foreman Went to France* 1941; *Love on the Dole* 1941; *The Saint Meets the Tiger* 1943; *The Silver Darlings* 1947; *While I Live* 1947; *Escape Route* 1952; *Valley of Song* 1953; *The Gilded Cage* 1954; *Passport to Treason* 1956; *Violent Playground* 1958; *The Curse of the Werewolf* 1961; *The Long Ships* 1963
Evans, Dale (1912–2001) *War of the Wildcats* 1943; *The Yellow Rose of Texas* 1944; *Bells of Rosarita* 1945; *My Pal Trigger* 1946; *Bells of San Angelo* 1947; *Twilight in the Sierras* 1950
Evans, Daniel (1974–) *A Midsummer Night's Dream* 1996; *Otherworld* 2003
Evans, Edith *aka* **Evans, Dame Edith** (1888–1976) *The Queen of Spades* 1948; *The Last Days of Dolwyn* 1949; *The Importance of Being Earnest* 1952; *Look Back in Anger* 1959; *The Nun's Story* 1959; *Tom Jones* 1963; *The Chalk Garden* 1964; *Young Cassidy* 1965; *Fitzwilly* 1967; *The Whisperers* 1967; *Prudence and the Pill* 1968; *Crooks and Coronets* 1969; *The Madwoman of Chaillot* 1969; *Scrooge* 1970; *Craze* 1973; *A Doll's House* 1973; *The Slipper and the Rose* 1976
Evans, Edward (1914–2001) *Valley of Song* 1953; *It's a Great Day* 1955; *One More Time* 1970
Evans, Estelle *To Kill a Mockingbird* 1962; *The Learning Tree* 1969
Evans, Evans (1936–) *All Fall Down* 1962; *Bonnie and Clyde* 1967; *Story of a Love Story* 1973
Evans, Gene (1922–1998) *Fixed Bayonets* 1951; *Force of Arms* 1951; *The Steel Helmet* 1951; *Mutiny* 1952; *Park Row* 1952; *Thunderbirds* 1952; *Donovan's Brain* 1953; *The Golden Blade* 1953; *Cattle Queen of Montana* 1954; *Hell and High Water* 1954; *The Long Wait* 1954; *Crashout* 1955; *The Helen Morgan Story* 1957; *The Sad Sack* 1957; *Damn Citizen* 1958; *Money, Women and Guns* 1958; *The Giant Behemoth* 1959; *The Hangman* 1959; *Operation Petticoat* 1959; *Gold of the Seven Saints* 1961; *Shock Corridor* 1963; *Apache Uprising* 1965; *Waco* 1966; *The War Wagon* 1967; *Walking Tall* 1973
Evans, Joan (1934–) *Roseanna McCoy* 1949; *Edge of Doom* 1950; *Our Very Own* 1950; *It Grows on Trees* 1952; *Skirts Ahoy!* 1952; *Column South* 1953; *The Outcast* 1954; *No Name on the Bullet* 1959
Evans, John (1934–) *I've Heard the Mermaids Singing* 1987; *Lena: My 100 Children* 1987
Evans, Josh (1971–) *Born on the Fourth of July* 1989; *The Doors* 1991
Evans, Lee (1965–) *Funny Bones* 1994; *The Fifth Element* 1997; *Mousehunt* 1997; *There's Something about Mary* 1998; *The Ladies Man* 2000; *The Martins* 2001; *Freeze Frame* 2003; *The Medallion* 2003; *The Magic Roundabout* 2005
Evans, Linda (1942–) *Those Calloways* 1964; *Beach Blanket Bingo* 1965; *The Klansman* 1974; *Mitchell* 1975; *Avalanche Express* 1979; *Tom Horn* 1980
Evans, Madge (1909–1981) *Guilty Hands* 1931; *Sporting Blood* 1931; *Broadway to Hollywood* 1933; *Dinner at Eight* 1933; *Hallelujah, I'm a Bum* 1933; *The Mayor of Hell* 1933; *Stand Up and Cheer!* 1934; *What Every Woman Knows* 1934; *David Copperfield* 1935; *The Tunnel* 1935; *Pennies from Heaven* 1936; *Piccadilly Jim* 1936; *Espionage* 1937; *Sinners in Paradise* 1938
Evans, Maurice (1901–1989) *Wedding Rehearsal* 1932; *Kind Lady* 1951; *Androcles and the Lion* 1952; *The Story of Gilbert and Sullivan* 1953; *The War Lord* 1965; *One of Our Spies Is Missing* 1966; *Jack of Diamonds* 1967; *Planet of the Apes* 1967; *Rosemary's Baby* 1968; *Beneath the Planet of the Apes* 1969; *The Body Stealers* 1969; *Terror in the Wax Museum* 1973
Evans (1), Michael (1926–) *Blackout* 1950; *The 1,000 Plane Raid* 1969
Evans, Monica *The Odd Couple* 1968; *Robin Hood* 1973
Evans, Peggy (1925–) *The Blue Lamp* 1949; *Calling Bulldog Drummond* 1951
Evans, Reg (1925–) *Kitty and the Bagman* 1982; *Mesmerized* 1984
Evans, Rex (1903–1969) *The Brighton Strangler* 1945; *Merry Andrew* 1958
Evans, Richard (1935–) *Too Soon to Love* 1960; *Dirty Little Billy* 1972; *Islands in the Stream* 1976
Evans, Robert *aka* **Evans, Bob** (1930–) *Lydia Bailey* 1952; *Man of a Thousand Faces* 1957; *The Sun Also Rises* 1957; *The Fiend Who Walked the West* 1958; *The Best of Everything* 1959; *Burn Hollywood Burn* 1997; *The Kid Stays in the Picture* 2001
Evans, Troy (1948–) *Kuffs* 1991; *Under Siege* 1992; *Ace Ventura: Pet Detective* 1993; *It Runs in the Family* 1994
Evanson, Edith (1900–1980) *The Jade Mask* 1945; *Rope* 1948; *The Magnificent Yankee* 1950
Eve (1978–) *Barbershop* 2002; *Barbershop 2: Back in Business* 2004; *The Woodsman* 2004
Eve, Trevor (1951–) *Dracula* 1979; *Aspen Extreme* 1993; *Don't Get Me Started* 1994; *Possession* 2002
Evelyn, Judith (1913–1967) *The 13th Letter* 1950; *Rear Window* 1954; *Female on the Beach* 1955; *Hilda Crane* 1956; *The Brothers Karamazov* 1958; *The Tingler* 1959
Everest, Barbara (1890–1968) *When London Sleeps* 1932; *The Lad* 1935; *Old Mother Riley* 1937; *Gaslight* 1944; *The Uninvited* 1944; *Wanted for Murder* 1946; *Children of Chance* 1949; *Madeleine* 1949; *Tony Draws a Horse* 1950; *The Safecracker* 1958; *The Man Who Finally Died* 1962; *Nurse on Wheels* 1963
Everett, Chad (1936–) *Claudelle Inglish* 1961; *Rome Adventure* 1962; *Get Yourself a College Girl* 1964; *Johnny Tiger* 1966; *Made in Paris* 1966; *The Singing Nun* 1966; *First to Fight* 1967; *The Last Challenge* 1967; *The Firechasers* 1970; *Airplane II: the Sequel* 1982; *Fever Pitch* 1985; *Heroes Stand Alone* 1989; *Psycho* 1998; *Mulholland Drive* 2001
Everett, Rupert (1959–) *Real Life* 1983; *Another Country* 1984; *Dance with a Stranger* 1984; *Duet for One* 1986; *Chronicle of a Death Foretold* 1987; *Hearts of*

Fire 1987; The Comfort of Strangers 1991; Cemetery Man 1994; Pret-a-Porter 1994; The Madness of King George 1995; B Monkey 1996; Dunston Checks In 1996; My Best Friend's Wedding 1997; Shakespeare in Love 1998; An Ideal Husband 1999; Inspector Gadget 1999; A Midsummer Night's Dream 1999; Paragraph 175 1999; The Next Best Thing 2000; Unconditional Love 2001; The Importance of Being Earnest 2002; To Kill a King 2003; The Wild Thornberrys Movie 2003; Shrek 2 2004; Stage Beauty 2004

Everett, Tom Leatherface: the Texas Chainsaw Massacre III 1990; xXx 2002

Everhard, Nancy (1959–) DeepStar Six 1989; Demonstone 1989; The Trial of the Incredible Hulk 1989

Everhart, Angie (1969–) Executive Target 1996; Tales from the Crypt Presents: Bordello of Blood 1996; Another $9\frac{1}{2}$ Weeks 1997; The Stray 1999; Sexual Predator 2001

Evers, Jason (1922–2005) The Brain That Wouldn't Die 1959; Pretty Boy Floyd 1960; The Illustrated Man 1969; Escape from the Planet of the Apes 1971; Basket Case 2 1990

Evigan, Greg (1953–) DeepStar Six 1989; One of Her Own 1994

Evison, Pat (1924–) Tim 1979; The Clinic 1982; The Silent One 1984; Emma's War 1985

Ewart, John (1928–1994) The Picture Show Man 1977; Newsfront 1978; Bush Christmas 1983; Frog Dreaming 1985

Ewell, Dwight Flirt 1995; Stonewall 1995; Chasing Amy 1996

Ewell, Tom (1909–1994) Adam's Rib 1949; An American Guerrilla in the Philippines 1950; A Life of Her Own 1950; Mr Music 1950; Lost in Alaska 1952; The Seven Year Itch 1955; The Girl Can't Help It 1956; The Lieutenant Wore Skirts 1956; A Nice Little Bank That Should Be Robbed 1958; Tender Is the Night 1961; State Fair 1962; Suppose They Gave a War and Nobody Came? 1970; They Only Kill Their Masters 1972; Easy Money 1983

Ewing, Barbara Dracula Has Risen from the Grave 1968; Eye of the Needle 1981; When the Whales Came 1989

Ewing, Diana Eighty Steps to Jonah 1969; Play It As It Lays 1972; The Way We Were 1973

Eyer, Richard (1945–) The Desperate Hours 1955; Sincerely Yours 1955; Come Next Spring 1956; Friendly Persuasion 1956; The Invisible Boy 1957; The 7th Voyage of Sinbad 1958

Eyre, Peter (1942–) Hedda 1975; Dragonslayer 1981; Princess Caraboo 1994

Eythe, William (1918–1957) The Ox-Bow Incident 1943; The Song of Bernadette 1943; The Eve of St Mark 1944; Wing and a Prayer 1944; Colonel Effingham's Raid 1945; The House on 92nd Street 1945; A Royal Scandal 1945; Centennial Summer 1946; Meet Me at Dawn 1946

Eziashi, Maynard Mister Johnson 1991; Twenty-One 1991; Bopha! 1993; Ace Ventura: When Nature Calls 1995

F

Fabares, Shelley (1944–) Never Say Goodbye 1955; Ride the Wild Surf 1964; Girl Happy 1965; Spinout 1966; Clambake 1967; Brian's Song 1971; Hot Pursuit 1987; Love or Money 1990

Fabbri, Jacques (1925–1997) Le Défroqué 1953; Diva 1981

Fabian aka **Forte, Fabian** (1942–) Hound Dog Man 1959; High Time 1960; North to Alaska 1960; Love in a Goldfish Bowl 1961; Five Weeks in a Balloon 1962; The Longest Day 1962; Mr Hobbs Takes a Vacation 1962; Ride the Wild Surf 1964; Ten Little Indians 1965; Dear Brigitte 1966; Dr Goldfoot and the Girl Bombs 1966; Fireball 500 1966; Thunder Alley 1967; The Wild Racers 1968; Get Crazy 1983

Fabian, Françoise (1932–) The Thief of Paris 1967; My Night with Maud 1969; The Bit Player 1973; Out 1: Spectre 1973; Happy New Year 1974; Reunion 1989; La Bûche 1999; 5x2 2004

Fabray, Nanette (1920–) The Band Wagon 1953; The Happy Ending 1969; The Cockeyed Cowboys of Calico County 1970; Harper Valley PTA 1978; Amy 1981

Fabre, Saturnin (1884–1961) La Nuit Fantastique 1942; Les Portes de la Nuit 1946

Fabregas, Manolo (1920–1996) Captain Scarlett 1953; The Candy Man 1969; Two Mules for Sister Sara 1970

Fabrizi, Aldo (1905–1990) Rome, Open City 1945; Francis, God's Jester 1950; The Angel Wore Red 1960

Fabrizi, Franco (1926–1995) I Vitelloni 1953; Le Amiche 1955; The Swindle 1955; Duel of Champions 1961; The Birds, the Bees, and the Italians 1965; Ginger & Fred 1986

Fabrizi, Mario (1925–1963) The Running, Jumping and Standing Still Film 1959; The Punch and Judy Man 1962

Facinelli, Peter (1973–) Touch Me 1997; Can't Hardly Wait 1998; Dancer, Texas Pop 81 1998; Telling You 1998; The Big Kahuna 1999; Honest 2000; Supernova 2000; Tempted 2001; The Scorpion King 2002

Fackeldey, Gisela (1923–1987) The Bitter Tears of Petra von Kant 1972; Martha 1973

Fagerbakke, Bill (1957–) Lady and the Tramp II: Scamp's Adventure 2000; The SpongeBob SquarePants Movie 2004

Faget, Huguette (1922–) The Last Stage 1947; Le Beau Mariage 1982

Fahey, Jeff (1954–) Psycho III 1986; Backfire 1987; Blue Heat 1990; Impulse 1990; White Hunter, Black Heart 1990; Body Parts 1991; Iron Maze 1991; The Lawnmower Man 1992; Quick 1993; Freefall 1994; Woman of Desire 1994; Wyatt Earp 1994; Darkman III: Die Darkman Die 1996; Lethal Tender 1996; Operation Delta Force 1996; Too Hard to Die 1998

Fahey, Myrna (1933–1973) Face of a Fugitive 1959; The Fall of the House of Usher 1960

Fairbank, Christopher Anazapta 2001; The Bunker 2001

Fairbanks, Douglas (1883–1939) The Mark of Zorro 1920; The Three Musketeers 1921; Robin Hood 1922; Hollywood 1923; The Thief of Bagdad 1924; Don Q, Son of Zorro 1925; The Black Pirate 1926; The Gaucho 1927; Show People 1928; The Iron Mask 1929; The Taming of the Shrew 1929; The Private Life of Don Juan 1934

Fairbanks Jr, Douglas (1909–2000) Stella Dallas 1925; The Barker 1928; A Woman of Affairs 1928; Our Modern Maidens 1929; The Show of Shows 1929; The Dawn Patrol 1930; Outward Bound 1930; Party Girl 1930; Little Caesar 1931; Love Is a Racket 1932; Scarlet Dawn 1932; Union Depot 1932; Morning Glory 1933; The Rise of Catherine the Great 1934; Success at Any Price 1934; Accused 1936; Jump for Glory 1937; The Prisoner of Zenda 1937; Having Wonderful Time 1938; Joy of Living 1938; The Rage of Paris 1938; The Young in Heart 1938; Green Hell 1939; Gunga Din 1939; Rulers of the Sea 1939; Angels over Broadway 1940; The Corsican Brothers 1941; The Exile 1947; Sinbad the Sailor 1947; The Fighting O'Flynn 1948; That Lady in Ermine 1948; Mr Drake's Duck 1950; State Secret 1950; Ghost Story 1981

Fairbrass, Craig (1964–) For Queen and Country 1988; Beyond Bedlam 1993; Cliffhanger 1993; Proteus 1995; Darklands 1996; Killing Time 1998; Weak at Denise 2000

Fairbrother, Sydney (1872–1941) The Private Secretary 1935; King Solomon's Mines 1937

Fairchild, Max Death of a Soldier 1985; The Howling III 1987; The Salute of the Jugger 1989

Fairchild, Morgan (1950–) Deadly Illusion 1987; Midnight Cop 1988; Gospa 1995; Holy Man 1998

Faire, Virginia Brown (1904–1980) The Temptress 1926; West of the Divide 1934

Fairman, Michael (1934–) Forces of Nature 1998; Thirteen Days 2000

Faison, Donald Adeosun aka **Faison, Donald** (1974–) Clueless 1995; New Jersey Drive 1995; Trippin' 1999; Remember the Titans 2000; Big Fat Liar 2002; Uptown Girls 2003

Faison, Frankie aka **Faison, Frankie R** (1949–) Exterminator 2 1980; Sommersby 1993; The Rich Man's Wife 1996; Julian Po 1997; The Thomas Crown Affair 1999; Hannibal 2001; 13 Conversations about One Thing 2001; Gods and Generals 2002; Red Dragon 2002; Showtime 2002; Highwaymen 2003; In Good Company 2004; White Chicks 2004

Faison, Sandy aka **Faison, Sandra** The Sterile Cuckoo 1969; All the Right Moves 1983

Faith, Adam (1940–2003) Beat Girl 1960; Never Let Go 1960; What a Whopper! 1961; Mix Me a Person 1962; Stardust 1974; Yesterday's Hero 1979; Foxes 1980; McVicar 1980

Faithfull, Marianne (1946–) I'll Never Forget What's 'Is Name 1967; The Girl on a Motorcycle 1968; Hamlet 1969; Ghost Story 1974; Lucifer Rising 1981; The Turn of the Screw 1992; Shopping 1993; Moondance 1995; Intimacy 2000

Fajardo, Eduardo (1918–) Tizoc 1956; A Professional Gun 1968

Falana, Lola (1942–) The Liberation of LB Jones 1970; The Klansman 1974

Falco, Edie (1954–) The Unbelievable Truth 1989; Trust 1990; Laws of Gravity 1992; The Addiction 1994; Hurricane Streets 1997; The Sunshine Boys 1997; Judy Berlin 1999; Jenifer 2001; Sunshine State 2002

Falcon, André (1924–) Stolen Kisses 1968; A Full Day's Work 1973; The Streetwalker 1976

Falk, Lisanne Heathers 1989; Shattered Image 1998

Falk, Peter (1927–) Wind across the Everglades 1958; The Bloody Brood 1959; Murder, Inc 1960; Pretty Boy Floyd 1960; The Secret of the Purple Reef 1960; Pocketful of Miracles 1961; Pressure Point 1962; The Balcony 1963; Robin and the 7 Hoods 1964; The Great Race 1965; Penelope 1966; Luv 1967; Anzio 1968; Prescription: Murder 1968; Castle Keep 1969; Husbands 1970; Ransom for a Dead Man 1971; A Woman under the Influence 1974; Mikey and Nicky 1976; Murder by Death 1976; The Brink's Job 1978; The Cheap Detective 1978; The In-Laws 1979; The California Dolls 1981; The Great Muppet Caper 1981; Big Trouble 1985; Happy New Year 1987; The Princess Bride 1987; Wings of Desire 1987; Vibes 1988; Cookie 1989; Aunt Julia and the Scriptwriter 1990; In the Spirit 1990; Faraway, So Close 1993; Roommates 1995; The Sunshine Boys 1997; A Storm in Summer 2000; Corky Romano 2001; Made 2001; Undisputed 2002; Shark Tale 2004

Falk, Rossella (1926–) $8\frac{1}{2}$ 1963; Modesty Blaise 1966; The Legend of Lylah Clare 1968

Fallon, Jimmy (1974–) Anything Else 2003; Taxi 2004; The Perfect Catch 2005

Fallon, Siobhan aka **Hogan, Siobhan Fallon** (1972–) Only You 1994; Fools Rush In 1997; The Negotiator 1998; Daddy Day Care 2003

Fann, Al (1925–) Parasite 1982; Frankie & Johnny 1991; Stop! or My Mom Will Shoot 1992

Fanning, Dakota (1994–) I Am Sam 2001; Trapped 2002; Dr Seuss' The Cat in the Hat 2003; Uptown Girls 2003; Man on Fire 2004; Hide and Seek 2005; War of the Worlds 2005

Fanning, Elle (1998–) Because of Winn-Dixie 2004; The Door in the Floor 2004

Fanning, Neil Scooby-Doo 2002; Scooby-Doo 2: Monsters Unleashed 2004

Fantoni, Sergio (1930–) Esther and the King 1960; The Giant of Marathon 1960; Do Not Disturb 1965; Von Ryan's Express 1965; What Did You Do in the War, Daddy? 1966; Diabolically Yours 1967; Hornet's Nest 1970; The Belly of an Architect 1987

Faracy, Stephanie (1949–) When You Comin' Back, Red Ryder? 1979; The Great Outdoors 1988

Faraldo, Daniel Trenchcoat 1983; Nico 1988

Farebrother, Violet (1888–1969) Easy Virtue 1927; The Woman for Joe 1955; Fortune Is a Woman 1956

Farentino, Debrah (1961–) Mortal Sins 1989; Son of the Pink Panther 1993

Farentino, James (1938–) Psychomania 1964; The War Lord 1965; The Pad (and How to Use It) 1966; Banning 1967; The Ride to Hangman's Tree 1967; Rosie! 1967; The Final Countdown 1980; Dead & Buried 1981; Her Alibi 1989; One Woman's Courage 1994; Bulletproof 1996

Farès, Nadia Love in the Strangest Way 1994; The Crimson Rivers 2000

Fargas, Antonio (1946–) Putney Swope 1969; Believe in Me 1971; Cisco Pike 1971; Across 110th Street 1972; Cleopatra Jones 1973; Conrack 1974; Foxy Brown 1974; Starsky and Hutch 1975; Car Wash 1976; Next Stop, Greenwich Village 1976; Pretty Baby 1978; Crimewave 1985; Blue Jean Cop 1988; I'm Gonna Git You Sucka 1988; The Borrower 1989; Whore 1991

Farina, Dennis (1944–) Thief 1981; The Killing Floor 1984; Manhunter 1986; Midnight Run 1988; Men of Respect 1990; Romeo Is Bleeding 1992; Another Stakeout 1993; Striking Distance 1993; Little Big League 1994; One Woman's Courage 1994; Get Shorty 1995; Eddie 1996; That Old Feeling 1997; Out of Sight 1998; The Mod Squad 1999; Deception 2000; Sidewalks of New York 2000; Snatch 2000; Big Trouble 2002; Stealing Harvard 2002; Paparazzi 2004

Faris, Anna (1976–) Scary Movie 2000; Scary Movie 2 2001; The Hot Chick 2002; Lost in Translation 2003; Scary Movie 3 2003

Farley, Chris (1964–1997) Coneheads 1993; Airheads 1994; Tommy Boy 1995; Black Sheep 1996; Beverly Hills Ninja 1997; Almost Heroes 1998; Dirty Work 1998

Farley, James aka **Farley, Jim** (1882–1947) The General 1927; Westward Ho 1935

Farley, John Black Sheep 1996; Beverly Hills Ninja 1997; The Straight Story 1999

Farley, Kevin aka **Farley, Kevin P** (1965–) Black Sheep 1996; Beverly Hills Ninja 1997; The Straight Story 1999

Farley, Morgan (1898–1988) The Devil's Holiday 1930; Barricade 1950; The Wild North 1952

Farmer, Bill A Goofy Movie 1995; Casper: a Spirited Beginning 1997

Farmer, Frances (1913–1970) Come and Get It 1936; Rhythm on the Range 1936; The Toast of New York 1937; South of Pago Pago 1940; Among the Living 1941; Son of Fury 1942

Farmer, Gary (1953–) Powwow Highway 1988; The Dark Wind 1991; Dead Man 1995; Smoke Signals 1998; The Score 2001

Farmer, Mimsy (1945–) Spencer's Mountain 1963; The Wild Racers 1968; More 1969; Road to Salina 1969; Two against the Law 1973; The Black Cat 1981; The Death of Mario Ricci 1983; Codename Wildgeese 1984

Farmer, Suzan (1943–) Die, Monster, Die! 1965; Dracula – Prince of Darkness 1965; Rasputin, the Mad Monk 1965

Farmer, Virginia (1898–1988) Born to Be Bad 1950; Cyrano de Bergerac 1950; The Men 1950; Darling, How Could You! 1951

Farmiga, Vera (1973–) Return to Paradise 1998; Autumn in New York 2000; The Opportunists 2000; Dummy 2002

Farnsworth, Richard (1920–2000) Comes a Horseman 1978; Resurrection 1980; Tom Horn 1980; The Legend of the Lone Ranger 1981; The Grey Fox 1982; Independence Day 1983; The Natural 1984; Rhinestone 1984; Into the Night 1985; Sylvester 1985; Misery 1990; The Two Jakes 1990; Highway to Hell 1992; The Getaway 1994; The Straight Story 1999

Farnum, William (1876–1953) A Connecticut Yankee 1931; The Painted Desert 1931; Supernatural 1933; The Count of Monte Cristo 1934; Santa Fe Stampede 1938; Shine On, Harvest Moon 1938; The Perils of Pauline 1947; Trail of Robin Hood 1950; Lone Star 1952

Farr, Derek (1912–1986) Freedom Radio 1940; Quiet Wedding 1940; Quiet Weekend 1946; The Shop at Sly Corner 1946; Wanted for Murder 1946; Conspiracy in Teheran 1947; Bond Street 1948; Noose 1948; Silent Dust 1948; Murder without Crime 1950; Young Wives' Tale 1951; Eight O'Clock Walk 1953; Front Page Story 1953; Bang! You're Dead 1954; The Dam Busters 1954; Value for Money 1955; Town on Trial 1956; Doctor at Large 1957; The Man in the Road 1957; The Vicious Circle 1957; The Truth about Women 1958; The Projected Man 1966

Farr, Felicia (1932–) The First Texan 1956; Jubal 1956; The Last Wagon 1956; Timetable 1956; 3:10 to Yuma 1957; Onionhead 1958; Hell Bent for Leather 1960; Kiss Me, Stupid 1964; The Venetian Affair 1966; Kotch 1971; Charley Varrick 1973; That's Life 1986

Farr, Jamie (1934–) Who's Minding the Mint? 1967; The Cannonball Run 1981; Cannonball Run II 1983; Happy Hour 1987; Curse II: The Bite 1989

Farrar, David (1908–1995) Danny Boy 1941; Went the Day Well? 1942; For Those in Peril 1943; Black Narcissus 1946; Frieda 1947; Mr Perrin and Mr Traill 1948; Diamond City 1949; The Small Back Room 1949; Cage of Gold 1950; Gone to Earth 1950; The Late Edwina Black 1951; Night without Stars 1951; The Black Shield of Falworth 1954; Duel in the Jungle 1954; Escape to Burma 1955; Lilacs in the Spring 1955; Lost 1955; Pearl of the South Pacific 1955; The Sea Chase 1955; The Woman and the Hunter 1957; I Accuse! 1958; Son of Robin Hood 1958; Solomon and Sheba 1959; Beat Girl 1960; The 300 Spartans 1962

Farrell, Charles (1901–1990) 7th Heaven 1927; Fazil 1928; The Red Dance 1928; Street Angel 1928; Sunny Side Up 1929; Body and Soul 1931; Delicious 1931; The First Year 1932; Tess of the Storm Country 1932; Change of Heart 1934; Boys Will Be Boys 1935; Moonlight Sonata 1937;

Just around the Corner 1938; *Bell-Bottom George* 1943; *Final Appointment* 1954; *The Hornet's Nest* 1955; *Hidden Homicide* 1958
Farrell (2), Colin aka **Farrell, Colin J** (1976–) *The War Zone* 1999; *Tigerland* 2000; *American Outlaws* 2001; *Hart's War* 2002; *Minority Report* 2002; *Phone Booth* 2002; *The Recruit* 2002; *Daredevil* 2003; *interMission* 2003; *SWAT* 2003; *Veronica Guerin* 2003; *Alexander* 2004; *A Home at the End of the World* 2004
Farrell, Glenda (1904–1971) *Little Caesar* 1931; *I Am a Fugitive from a Chain Gang* 1932; *Life Begins* 1932; *Bureau of Missing Persons* 1933; *Havana Widows* 1933; *Lady for a Day* 1933; *Man's Castle* 1933; *Mystery of the Wax Museum* 1933; *Hi, Nellie!* 1934; *The Secret Bride* 1934; *Go into Your Dance* 1935; *Gold Diggers of 1935* 1935; *In Caliente* 1935; *Gold Diggers of 1937* 1936; *Smart Blonde* 1936; *Breakfast for Two* 1937; *Hollywood Hotel* 1937; *Johnny Eager* 1941; *The Talk of the Town* 1942; *Twin Beds* 1942; *Lulu Belle* 1948; *Apache War Smoke* 1952; *Secret of the Incas* 1954; *Susan Slept Here* 1954; *The Girl in the Red Velvet Swing* 1955; *Middle of the Night* 1959; *The Disorderly Orderly* 1964; *Kissin' Cousins* 1964; *Tiger by the Tail* 1970
Farrell, Nicholas *Chariots of Fire* 1981; *Playing Away* 1986; *In the Bleak Midwinter* 1995; *Othello* 1995; *Hamlet* 1996; *Twelfth Night* 1996; *Legionnaire* 1998; *Beautiful People* 1999; *Arthur's Dyke* 2001; *Bloody Sunday* 2001
Farrell, Paul (1893–1975) *The Rising of the Moon* 1957; *A Clockwork Orange* 1971
Farrell, Sharon (1946–) *The Spy with My Face* 1966; *A Lovely Way to Go* 1968; *Marlowe* 1969; *The Reivers* 1969; *It's Alive* 1974; *The Premonition* 1975; *The Fifth Floor* 1980; *Out of the Blue* 1980; *The Stunt Man* 1980; *Separate Ways* 1981; *One Man Force* 1989
Farrell, Terry (1963–) *Back to School* 1986; *Hellraiser III: Hell on Earth* 1992; *Danielle Steel's Star* 1993; *Red Sun Rising* 1994; *One True Love* 2000
Farrell, Timothy (1923–1989) *Glen or Glenda* 1953; *Jail Bait* 1954
Farrell, Tommy (1921–2004) *At War with the Army* 1950; *Meet Danny Wilson* 1952
Farrow, Mia (1945–) *Guns at Batasi* 1964; *A Dandy in Aspic* 1968; *Rosemary's Baby* 1968; *Secret Ceremony* 1968; *John and Mary* 1969; *Blind Terror* 1971; *Follow Me* 1971; *The Great Gatsby* 1974; *Full Circle* 1977; *Avalanche* 1978; *Death on the Nile* 1978; *A Wedding* 1978; *Hurricane* 1979; *The Last Unicorn* 1980; *A Midsummer Night's Sex Comedy* 1982; *Zelig* 1983; *Broadway Danny Rose* 1984; *Supergirl* 1984; *The Purple Rose of Cairo* 1985; *Hannah and Her Sisters* 1986; *Radio Days* 1987; *September* 1987; *Another Woman* 1988; *Crimes and Misdemeanors* 1989; *New York Stories* 1989; *Alice* 1990; *Shadows and Fog* 1991; *Husbands and Wives* 1992; *Widows' Peak* 1993; *Miami Rhapsody* 1995; *Reckless* 1995; *Private Parts* 1997; *Forget Me Never* 1999
Farrow, Tisa (1951–) *Homer* 1970; *And Hope to Die* 1972; *Fingers* 1978; *Search and Destroy* 1978; *Zombie Flesh Eaters* 1979
Fassbinder, Rainer Werner (1946–1982) *Gods of the Plague* 1969; *Love Is Colder Than Death* 1969; *The American Soldier* 1970; *Beware of a Holy Whore* 1970; *Whity* 1970; *Fear Eats the Soul* 1973; *Fox and His Friends* 1975; *Kamikaze 1989* 1983
Fatone, Joey (1977–) *On the Line* 2001; *My Big Fat Greek Wedding* 2002
Faulds, Andrew (1923–2000) *The One That Got Away* 1957; *Blood of the Vampire* 1958
Faulkner, Edward *Tickle Me* 1965; *Hellfighters* 1969
Faulkner, James (1948–) *The Great Waltz* 1972; *The Abdication* 1974; *Death in the Sun* 1975; *Real Life* 1983; *The Maid* 1991; *A Kid in Aladdin's Palace* 1997; *Vigo: Passion for Life* 1997; *All the Little Animals* 1998; *Agent Cody Banks 2: Destination London* 2003
Faulkner, Keith *The Man in the Back Seat* 1961; *Strongroom* 1961
Faulkner, Lisa (1973–) *The Lover* 1992; *A Feast at Midnight* 1994
Faure, Julia *Love Me If You Dare* 2003; *Process* 2004
Favino, Pierfrancesco *The Last Kiss* 2001; *The Keys to the House* 2004
Favreau, Jon (1966–) *Rudy* 1993; *PCU* 1994; *Just Your Luck* 1996; *Persons Unknown* 1996; *Swingers* 1996; *Very Bad Things* 1998; *Love & Sex* 2000; *The Replacements* 2000; *Made* 2001; *Daredevil* 2003; *Something's Gotta Give* 2003; *Wimbledon* 2004
Fawcett, Alan *A Conspiracy of Love* 1987; *Afterglow* 1997; *Hidden Agenda* 2001
Fawcett, Farrah aka **Fawcett-Majors, Farrah** (1947–) *Myra Breckinridge* 1970; *Logan's Run* 1976; *Somebody Killed Her Husband* 1978; *Sunburn* 1979; *Saturn 3* 1980; *The Cannonball Run* 1981; *The Burning Bed* 1984; *Extremities* 1986; *Nazi Hunter: the Beate Klarsfeld Story* 1986; *See You in the Morning* 1989; *Man of the House* 1994; *The Apostle* 1997; *Dr T & the Women* 2000
Fawcett, George (1860–1939) *Flesh and the Devil* 1926; *The Son of the Sheik* 1926; *Love* 1927; *The Private Life of Helen of Troy* 1927; *The Wedding March* 1928; *Ladies of Leisure* 1930
Fawdon, Michele (1947–) *Cathy's Child* 1979; *Unfinished Business* 1985; *Travelling North* 1986
Fay, Frank (1897–1961) *The Show of Shows* 1929; *Under a Texas Moon* 1930; *God's Gift to Women* 1931; *Nothing Sacred* 1937; *They Knew What They Wanted* 1940; *Love Nest* 1951
Faye, Alice (1915–1998) *George White's Scandals* 1934; *George White's 1935 Scandals* 1935; *King of Burlesque* 1936; *Poor Little Rich Girl* 1936; *Sing, Baby, Sing* 1936; *Stowaway* 1936; *In Old Chicago* 1937; *On the Avenue* 1937; *Wake Up and Live* 1937; *You Can't Have Everything* 1937; *You're a Sweetheart* 1937; *Alexander's Ragtime Band* 1938; *Sally, Irene and Mary* 1938; *Hollywood Cavalcade* 1939; *Rose of Washington Square* 1939; *Lillian Russell* 1940; *Little Old New York* 1940; *Tin Pan Alley* 1940; *The Great American Broadcast* 1941; *That Night in Rio* 1941; *Weekend in Havana* 1941; *The Gang's All Here* 1943; *Hello, Frisco, Hello* 1943; *Fallen Angel* 1945; *State Fair* 1962; *The Magic of Lassie* 1978
Faye, Herbie (1899–1980) *Top Banana* 1953; *Requiem for a Heavyweight* 1962
Faye, Janina *Don't Talk to Strange Men* 1962; *The Beauty Jungle* 1964; *The Dance of Death* 1969
Faye, Julia (1893–1966) *The Ten Commandments* 1923; *Dynamite* 1929; *Samson and Delilah* 1949
Faylen, Frank (1905–1985) *It's a Wonderful Life* 1946; *The Perils of Pauline* 1947; *Road to Rio* 1947; *Suddenly It's Spring* 1947; *Welcome Stranger* 1947; *Blood on the Moon* 1948; *Whispering Smith* 1948; *Convicted* 1950; *Copper Canyon* 1950; *Detective Story* 1951; *Hangman's Knot* 1952; *The Lusty Men* 1952; *The Sniper* 1952; *99 River Street* 1953; *Riot in Cell Block 11* 1954; *The Looters* 1955; *The McConnell Story* 1955; *Seventh Cavalry* 1956; *Dino* 1957; *Gunfight at the OK Corral* 1957; *Fluffy* 1965; *The Monkey's Uncle* 1965; *When the Boys Meet the Girls* 1965
Faysse, Dominique *Your Beating Heart* 1991; *L'Eau Froide* 1994
Fazenda, Louise (1895–1962) *Noah's Ark* 1928; *The Desert Song* 1929; *Rain or Shine* 1930; *Gun Smoke* 1931; *Alice in Wonderland* 1933; *Colleen* 1936; *Swing Your Lady* 1937
Fearn, Sheila (1940–) *The Likely Lads* 1976; *George and Mildred* 1980
Featherstone, Angela (1965–) *Zero Effect* 1997; *The Wedding Singer* 1998; *200 Cigarettes* 1999; *The Guilty* 2000; *Soul Survivors* 2001; *Federal Protection* 2002; *One Way Out* 2002
Feder, Frédérique *Acción Mutante* 1993; *Three Colours Red* 1994
Feeney, Caroleen *Denise Calls Up* 1995; *Cadillac Ranch* 1996; *Bad Manners* 1998
Fehmiu, Bekim (1936–) *I Even Met Happy Gypsies* 1967; *The Adventurers* 1970; *The Deserter* 1971; *Permission to Kill* 1975; *Black Sunday* 1976; *Salon Kitty* 1976
Fehr, Brendan (1977–) *The Forsaken* 2001; *Biker Boyz* 2003
Fehr, Oded (1970–) *Deuce Bigalow: Male Gigolo* 1999; *The Mummy Returns* 2001; *Resident Evil: Apocalypse* 2004
Feig, Paul (1962–) *Zombie High* 1987; *Ski Patrol* 1989; *Heavyweights* 1995
Feinberg, Ron *Brian's Song* 1971; *A Boy and His Dog* 1975
Feinstein, Alan (1941–) *Joe Panther* 1976; *Looking for Mr Goodbar* 1977
Feld, Fritz (1900–1993) *The Affairs of Annabel* 1938; *Bringing Up Baby* 1938; *Go Chase Yourself* 1938; *Gold Diggers in Paris* 1938; *I Was an Adventuress* 1940; *I've Always Loved You* 1946; *The World's Greatest Lover* 1977; *Heidi's Song* 1982
Felder, Clarence *Slayground* 1983; *The Killing Floor* 1984; *Ruthless People* 1986; *The Hidden* 1987
Feldman, Andrea (1948–1972) *Trash* 1970; *Heat* 1972
Feldman, Corey (1971–) *Friday the 13th: the Final Chapter* 1984; *The Goonies* 1985; *Stand by Me* 1986; *The Lost Boys* 1987; *License to Drive* 1988; *The 'Burbs* 1989; *Dream a Little Dream* 1989; *The Magic Voyage* 1992; *Round Trip to Heaven* 1992; *National Lampoon's Scuba School* 1994; *Tales from the Crypt Presents: Bordello of Blood* 1996; *Fortune Hunters* 1999
Feldman, Marty (1933–1982) *The Bed Sitting Room* 1969; *Every Home Should Have One* 1970; *Young Frankenstein* 1974; *The Adventure of Sherlock Holmes' Smarter Brother* 1975; *Silent Movie* 1976; *The Last Remake of Beau Geste* 1977; *In God We Trust* 1980; *Slapstick of Another Kind* 1982; *Yellowbeard* 1983
Feldon, Barbara (1941–) *Fitzwilly* 1967; *Smile* 1975; *No Deposit No Return* 1976
Feldshuh, Tovah (1952–) *The Idolmaker* 1980; *Daniel* 1983; *Brewster's Millions* 1985; *A Day in October* 1991; *A Walk on the Moon* 1999; *Kissing Jessica Stein* 2001
Felix, Maria (1914–2002) *French Cancan* 1955; *Tizoc* 1956; *La Fièvre Monte à el Pao* 1959
Fell, Norman (1924–1998) *Pork Chop Hill* 1959; *The Killers* 1964; *Bullitt* 1968; *Sergeant Ryker* 1968; *If It's Tuesday, This Must Be Belgium* 1969; *The Boatniks* 1970; *The Stone Killer* 1973; *Cleopatra Jones and the Casino of Gold* 1975; *The End* 1978; *On the Right Track* 1981; *Paternity* 1981; *For the Boys* 1991
Fellini, Federico (1920–1993) *L'Amore* 1948; *Alex in Wonderland* 1970; *Fellini's Roma* 1972; *We All Loved Each Other So Much* 1974; *Intervista* 1987
Fellowes, Julian (1950–) *The Scarlet Pimpernel* 1982; *Baby: Secret of the Lost Legend* 1985; *Fellow Traveller* 1989; *Damage* 1992; *Shadowlands* 1993
Fellowes, Rockliffe (1883–1950) *Regeneration* 1915; *Monkey Business* 1931
Fellows, Edith (1923–) *She Married Her Boss* 1935; *And So They Were Married* 1936; *Pennies from Heaven* 1936; *Music in My Heart* 1940
Felmy, Hansjörg aka **Felmy, Hansjoerg** (1931–) *Station Six-Sahara* 1962; *Torn Curtain* 1966
Felton, Felix (1911–1972) *Night Was Our Friend* 1951; *It's Trad, Dad* 1961
Felton, Tom (1987–) *Anna and the King* 1999; *Harry Potter and the Philosopher's Stone* 2001; *Harry Potter and the Chamber of Secrets* 2002
Felton, Verna (1890–1966) *Dumbo* 1941; *Cinderella* 1950; *The Gunfighter* 1950; *Alice in Wonderland* 1951; *Don't Bother to Knock* 1952; *Lady and the Tramp* 1955; *The Oklahoman* 1957; *Sleeping Beauty* 1959; *Guns of the Timberland* 1960; *The Jungle Book* 1967
Fenemore, Hilda (1919–) *The Tommy Steele Story* 1957; *The Wind of Change* 1961
Fenn, Sherilyn (1965–) *Just One of the Guys* 1985; *Thrashin'* 1986; *The Wraith* 1986; *Zombie High* 1987; *Two Moon Junction* 1988; *Backstreet Dreams* 1990; *Desire & Hell at Sunset Motel* 1991; *Diary of a Hitman* 1992; *Of Mice and Men* 1992; *Ruby* 1992; *Three of Hearts* 1992; *Boxing Helena* 1993; *Fatal Instinct* 1993; *Darkness Falls* 1998; *The United States of Leland* 2002
Fennec, Sylvie (1947–) *En Toute Innocence* 1987; *The Music Teacher* 1988
Fennelly, Parker (1891–1988) *The Trouble with Harry* 1954; *Angel in My Pocket* 1968
Fenton, Frank (1906–1957) *Buffalo Bill* 1944; *Hold That Blonde* 1945; *The Clay Pigeon* 1949
Fenton, Lance *Night of the Demons* 1988; *Heathers* 1989
Fenton, Leslie (1902–1978) *The Dragnet* 1928; *The Public Enemy* 1931; *FP1* 1932; *The Hatchet Man* 1932; *The Strange Love of Molly Louvain* 1932; *Lady Killer* 1933; *Marie Galante* 1934; *Star of Midnight* 1935; *Boys Town* 1938
Fenton, Sarah-Jane *The Bachelor* 1990; *A Good Man in Africa* 1993
Fenwick, Perry (1962–) *Party Party* 1983; *ID* 1994
Feore, Colm (1958–) *Beautiful Dreamers* 1990; *Bethune: the Making of a Hero* 1990; *Thirty Two Short Films about Glenn Gould* 1993; *Truman* 1995; *Night Falls on Manhattan* 1997; *The Wrong Guy* 1997; *City of Angels* 1998; *The Red Violin* 1998; *Forget Me Never* 1999; *Titus* 1999; *Pearl Harbor* 2001; *Chicago* 2002; *National Security* 2002; *The Sum of All Fears* 2002; *Highwaymen* 2003; *Paycheck* 2003; *The Chronicles of Riddick* 2004
Ferch, Heino (1963–) *Who's Afraid of Red Yellow Blue?* 1990; *Lucie Aubrac* 1997; *Wintersleepers* 1997; *Run Lola Run* 1998; *Extreme Ops* 2003; *Downfall* 2004
Ferdin, Pamelyn (1959–) *A Boy Named Charlie Brown* 1969; *The Beguiled* 1971; *Happy Birthday, Wanda June* 1971; *The Mephisto Waltz* 1971; *The Toolbox Murders* 1978
Ferguson, Anna *Tokyo Cowboy* 1994; *Dangerous Intentions* 1995
Ferguson, Craig (1962–) *The Big Tease* 1999; *Born Romantic* 2000; *Saving Grace* 2000; *I'll Be There* 2003
Ferguson, Frank (1899–1978) *Abbott and Costello Meet Frankenstein* 1948; *Caught* 1949; *Gun Duel in Durango* 1957; *Andy Hardy Comes Home* 1958
Ferguson, Jessie Lawrence (1941–) *Darkman* 1990; *To Protect and Serve* 1992
Ferguson, John Pyper aka **Ferguson, John** *Pin* 1988; *Every Breath* 1993
Ferguson, Matthew (1973–) *On My Own* 1992; *Love and Human Remains* 1993; *Lilies* 1996
Ferguson, Myles (1981–2000) *Avalanche* 1994; *Spooky House* 1999
Ferjac, Anouk (1932–) *Vivre pour Vivre* 1967; *Je T'Aime, Je T'Aime* 1968; *Que la Bête Meure* 1969; *Piaf: the Sparrow of Pigalle* 1974; *Diabolo Menthe* 1977
Fernandel (1903–1971) *On Purge Bébé* 1931; *Angèle* 1934; *Un Carnet de Bal* 1937; *The Little World of Don Camillo* 1951; *Topaze* 1951; *The Sheep Has Five Legs* 1954; *Paris Holiday* 1958
Fernández, Ana *Solas* 1998; *The City of No Limits* 2002
Fernandez, Emilio (1904–1986) *The Reward* 1965; *Return of the Seven* 1966; *Southwest to Sonora* 1966; *The Wild Bunch* 1969; *Bring Me the Head of Alfredo Garcia* 1974
Fernandez, Jaime (1937–2005) *The Adventures of Robinson Crusoe* 1952; *The River and Death* 1954; *A Bullet for the General* 1966; *Guns for San Sebastian* 1968
Fernandez, Jesus *Simon of the Desert* 1965; *Tristana* 1970
Fernandez, Juan *"Crocodile" Dundee II* 1988; *Kinjite: Forbidden Subjects* 1989; *Extralarge: Moving Target* 1990; *A Show of Force* 1990; *Solas* 1998; *Fausto 5.0* 2001; *A Man Apart* 2003
Fernside, John *The Overlanders* 1946; *Bush Christmas* 1947; *Eureka Stockade* 1949
Ferraday, Lisa *China Corsair* 1951; *The Belle of New York* 1952; *Last Train from Bombay* 1952; *Death of a Scoundrel* 1956
Ferrara, Abel aka **Laine, Jimmy** (1952–) *The Driller Killer* 1979; *Ms 45* 1981
Ferratti, Rebecca (1964–) *Gor* 1987; *Cyborg 3: The Recycler* 1994
Ferrell, Conchata (1943–) *Heartland* 1979; *Where the River Runs Black* 1986; *For Keeps* 1987; *Mystic Pizza* 1988; *Chains of Gold* 1989; *True Romance* 1993; *Stranger Inside* 2001; *Mr Deeds* 2002
Ferrell, Tyra *Lady Beware* 1987; *Boyz N the Hood* 1991; *Equinox* 1992; *White Men Can't Jump* 1992; *Poetic Justice* 1993; *The Perfect Score* 2004
Ferrell, Will (1967–) *A Night at the Roxbury* 1998; *Austin Powers: the Spy Who Shagged Me* 1999; *Dick* 1999; *The Suburbans* 1999; *Superstar* 1999; *Drowning Mona* 2000; *The Ladies Man* 2000; *Jay and Silent Bob Strike Back* 2001; *Zoolander* 2001; *Elf* 2003; *Old School* 2003; *Anchorman: the Legend of Ron Burgundy* 2004; *Melinda and Melinda* 2004; *Kicking & Screaming* 2005
Ferréol, Andréa (1947–) *La Grande Bouffe* 1973; *Despair* 1978; *The Last Metro* 1980; *Three Brothers* 1980; *Letters to an Unknown Lover* 1985; *A Zed & Two Noughts* 1985; *Francesco* 1989; *Il Maestro* 1989; *Street of No Return* 1989; *Wings of Fame* 1990; *The Edge of the Horizon* 1993
Ferrer, José (1909–1992) *Joan of Arc* 1948; *Whirlpool* 1949; *Crisis* 1950; *Cyrano de Bergerac* 1950; *Anything Can Happen* 1952; *Moulin Rouge* 1952; *Miss Sadie Thompson* 1953; *The Caine Mutiny* 1954; *Deep in My Heart* 1954; *The Cockleshell Heroes* 1955; *The Shrike* 1955; *The Great Man* 1956; *The High Cost of Loving* 1958; *I Accuse!* 1958; *Lawrence of Arabia* 1962; *Nine Hours to Rama* 1963; *The Greatest Story Ever Told* 1965; *Ship of Fools* 1965; *Enter Laughing* 1967; *Cervantes* 1968; *E' Lollipop* 1975; *Paco* 1975; *The Big Bus* 1976; *Crash!* 1977; *The*

Private Files of J Edgar Hoover 1977; *The Sentinel* 1977; *Who Has Seen the Wind* 1977; *Zoltan... Hound of Dracula* 1977; *The Amazing Captain Nemo* 1978; *Fedora* 1978; *The Swarm* 1978; *The Fifth Musketeer* 1979; *The Big Brawl* 1980; *Gideon's Trumpet* 1980; *A Midsummer Night's Sex Comedy* 1982; *To Be or Not to Be* 1983; *Dune* 1984; *The Evil That Men Do* 1984; *Seduced* 1985; *Hired to Kill* 1990
Ferrer, Leilani aka **Ferrer, Leilani Sarelle** (1966–) *Barbarians at the Gate* 1993; *The Harvest* 1993
Ferrer, Lupita (1947–) *The Children of Sanchez* 1978; *Balboa* 1982
Ferrer, Mel (1917–) *Born to Be Bad* 1950; *The Brave Bulls* 1951; *Rancho Notorious* 1952; *Scaramouche* 1952; *Knights of the Round Table* 1953; *Lili* 1953; *Saadia* 1953; *Oh, Rosalinda!!* 1955; *Elena et les Hommes* 1956; *War and Peace* 1956; *The Sun Also Rises* 1957; *The World, the Flesh and the Devil* 1959; *Blood and Roses* 1960; *The Hands of Orlac* 1960; *The Longest Day* 1962; *The Fall of the Roman Empire* 1964; *Paris When It Sizzles* 1964; *Sex and the Single Girl* 1964; *A Time for Loving* 1971; *Brannigan* 1975; *Eaten Alive* 1976; *The Amazing Captain Nemo* 1978; *The Norseman* 1978; *Yesterday's Tomorrow* 1978; *The Fifth Floor* 1980; *Lili Marleen* 1980; *The Visitor* 1980; *Deadly Game* 1982; *Seduced* 1985
Ferrer, Miguel (1955–) *RoboCop* 1987; *DeepStar Six* 1989; *Shannon's Deal* 1989; *The Guardian* 1990; *Another Stakeout* 1993; *The Assassin* 1993; *The Harvest* 1993; *Hot Shots! Part Deux* 1993; *It's All True* 1993; *Point of No Return* 1993; *Blank Check* 1994; *Jack Reed: a Search for Justice* 1994; *The Disappearance of Garcia Lorca* 1997; *Stephen King's The Night Flier* 1997; *Mulan* 1998; *Traffic* 2000; *The Manchurian Candidate* 2004
Ferrera, America (1984–) *Real Women Have Curves* 2002; *The Sisterhood of the Traveling Pants* 2005
Ferreri, Marco (1928–1997) *Casanova '70* 1965; *Pigsty* 1969
Ferrero, Martin (1946–) *I Ought to Be in Pictures* 1982; *Stop! or My Mom Will Shoot* 1992; *Jurassic Park* 1993; *The Tailor of Panama* 2000
Ferret, Eve *Foreign Body* 1986; *Haunted Honeymoon* 1986
Ferri, Claudia *The Assignment* 1997; *Mambo Italiano* 2003
Ferrier, Noel (1920–1997) *Alvin Purple* 1973; *Turkey Shoot* 1981; *The Year of Living Dangerously* 1982
Ferrigno, Lou (1952–) *The Incredible Hulk* 1977; *Hercules* 1983; *Hercules II* 1983; *The Incredible Hulk Returns* 1988; *All's Fair* 1989; *Cage* 1989; *The Trial of the Incredible Hulk* 1989; *The Death of the Incredible Hulk* 1990; *Hangfire* 1991; *...And God Spoke* 1993; *Hulk* 2003
Ferris, Barbara (1942–) *A Place to Go* 1963; *Children of the Damned* 1964; *The System* 1964; *Catch Us If You Can* 1965; *Interlude* 1968; *A Nice Girl like Me* 1969; *The Krays* 1990
Ferris, Pam (1948–) *Matilda* 1996; *Death to Smoochy* 2002
Ferro, Turi (1921–2001) *The Seduction of Mimi* 1972; *Blood Feud* 1979
Ferry, David *The Last Winter* 1989; *Darkman II: the Return of Durant* 1995
Ferzetti, Gabriele (1925–) *Le Amiche* 1955; *L'Avventura* 1960; *Jessica* 1962; *Imperial Venus* 1963; *Trois Chambres à Manhattan* 1965; *We Still Kill the Old Way* 1967; *Once upon a Time in the West* 1968; *On Her Majesty's Secret Service* 1969; *The Confession* 1970; *Hitler: the Last Ten Days* 1973; *The Night Porter* 1973; *End of the Game* 1976; *A Matter of Time* 1976; *Julia and Julia* 1987
Fetchit, Stepin aka **Fetchit, Step'n** aka **Fetchit, Stepin'** (1902–1985) *Fox Movietone Follies of 1929* 1929; *Judge Priest* 1934; *Stand Up and Cheer!* 1934; *Steamboat round the Bend* 1935; *Dimples* 1936; *Love Is News* 1937; *Zenobia* 1939; *Bend of the River* 1952; *The Sun Shines Bright* 1953
Fetty, Darrell *The Wind and the Lion* 1975; *Stunts* 1977; *Big Wednesday* 1978; *Blood Beach* 1981
Feuer, Debra *Moment by Moment* 1978; *To Live and Die in LA* 1985; *Homeboy* 1988
Feuerstein, Mark (1971–) *The Muse* 1999; *Woman on Top* 2000; *What Women Want* 2001
Feuillère, Edwige (1907–1998) *The Eagle Has Two Heads* 1948; *Woman Hater* 1948; *Olivia* 1950; *The Ripening Seed* 1953; *The Flesh of the Orchid* 1974
Feulner, Miles *A Home of Our Own* 1993; *Little Big League* 1994
Ffrangcon-Davies, Gwen (1891–1992) *The Witches* 1966; *The Devil Rides Out* 1968; *Leo the Last* 1970
Flander, Lewis (1938–) *Dr Jekyll and Sister Hyde* 1971; *Dr Phibes Rises Again* 1972; *The Abdication* 1974; *Georgia* 1988
Fichtner, William (1956–) *The Underneath* 1995; *Albino Alligator* 1996; *Contact* 1997; *Drowning Mona* 2000; *Passion of Mind* 2000; *The Perfect Storm* 2000; *Black Hawk Down* 2001; *Equilibrium* 2002; *Crash* 2004; *The Longest Yard* 2005
Fiddis, Shelby *Things Are Tough All Over* 1982; *Cheech & Chong's The Corsican Brothers* 1984
Fiedler, John (1925–) *12 Angry Men* 1957; *A Raisin in the Sun* 1961; *The Odd Couple* 1968; *Winnie the Pooh's Most Grand Adventure* 1997; *The Tigger Movie* 2000; *Piglet's Big Movie* 2003; *Pooh's Heffalump Movie* 2005
Field, Alexander (1892–1971) *When London Sleeps* 1932; *Limelight* 1936; *Dark Eyes of London* 1939; *Naked Fury* 1959
Field, Ben (1878–1939) *When London Sleeps* 1932; *The Clairvoyant* 1934
Field, Betty (1913–1973) *Of Mice and Men* 1939; *Victory* 1940; *Blues in the Night* 1941; *The Shepherd of the Hills* 1941; *Kings Row* 1942; *Flesh and Fantasy* 1943; *The Great Moment* 1944; *Tomorrow the World!* 1944; *The Southerner* 1945; *The Great Gatsby* 1949; *Picnic* 1955; *Bus Stop* 1956; *Butterfield 8* 1960; *Birdman of Alcatraz* 1962; *7 Women* 1966; *Coogan's Bluff* 1968; *How to Save a Marriage and Ruin Your Life* 1968
Field, Chelsea (1957–) *Prison* 1987; *Skin Deep* 1989; *The Dark Half* 1991; *Harley Davidson and the Marlboro Man* 1991; *The Last Boy Scout* 1991; *Dust Devil* 1992; *Complex of Fear* 1993; *Snapdragon* 1993; *Andre* 1994; *Rules of Obsession* 1994; *Indictment: the McMartin Trial* 1995; *Flipper* 1996; *Wicked* 1998
Field, David aka **Field, Dave** *Ghosts... of the Civil Dead* 1988; *Dad and Dave: on Our Selection* 1995; *To Have & to Hold* 1996; *Two Hands* 1999; *Chopper* 2000; *The Night We Called It a Day* 2003
Field, Mary (1896–1968) *Shadows on the Stairs* 1941; *The Crystal Ball* 1943; *A Lady Takes a Chance* 1943; *The Affairs of Susan* 1945; *Ride a Crooked Trail* 1958; *Seven Ways from Sundown* 1960
Field, Sally (1946–) *The Way West* 1967; *Stay Hungry* 1976; *Heroes* 1977; *Smokey and the Bandit* 1977; *The End* 1978; *Hooper* 1978; *Beyond the Poseidon Adventure* 1979; *Norma Rae* 1979; *Smokey and the Bandit II* 1980; *Absence of Malice* 1981; *Back Roads* 1981; *Kiss Me Goodbye* 1982; *Places in the Heart* 1984; *Murphy's Romance* 1985; *Surrender* 1987; *Punchline* 1988; *Steel Magnolias* 1989; *Not without My Daughter* 1990; *Soapdish* 1991; *Homeward Bound: the Incredible Journey* 1993; *Mrs Doubtfire* 1993; *Forrest Gump* 1994; *Eye for an Eye* 1995; *Homeward Bound II: Lost in San Francisco* 1996; *A Cooler Climate* 1999; *Where the Heart Is* 2000; *Say It Isn't So* 2001; *Legally Blonde 2: Red, White & Blonde* 2003
Field, Shirley Anne aka **Field, Shirley Ann** (1936–) *It's Never Too Late* 1956; *Horrors of the Black Museum* 1959; *Beat Girl* 1960; *The Entertainer* 1960; *Man in the Moon* 1960; *Peeping Tom* 1960; *Saturday Night and Sunday Morning* 1960; *The Damned* 1961; *Lunch Hour* 1962; *The War Lover* 1962; *Kings of the Sun* 1963; *Alfie* 1966; *Doctor in Clover* 1966; *My Beautiful Laundrette* 1985; *Shag* 1988; *Getting It Right* 1989; *The Rachel Papers* 1989; *Hear My Song* 1991; *UFO* 1993; *A Monkey's Tale* 1999; *Christie Malry's Own Double-Entry* 2000
Field, Sid (1904–1950) *London Town* 1946; *Cardboard Cavalier* 1949
Field, Todd (1964–) *A Cut Above* 1989; *Ruby in Paradise* 1993; *Sleep with Me* 1994; *Frank and Jesse* 1995; *Walking and Talking* 1996; *Broken Vessels* 1998; *Eyes Wide Shut* 1999; *Stranger than Fiction* 1999; *New Port South* 2001
Field, Virginia (1917–1992) *Lloyd's of London* 1936; *Thank You, Jeeves* 1936; *Charlie Chan at Monte Carlo* 1937; *Lancer Spy* 1937; *London by Night* 1937; *Think Fast, Mr Moto* 1937; *The Cisco Kid and the Lady* 1939; *Mr Moto Takes a Vacation* 1939; *Mr Moto's Last Warning* 1939; *Dance, Girl, Dance* 1940; *Hudson's Bay* 1940; *Waterloo Bridge* 1940; *The Crystal Ball* 1943; *Christmas Eve* 1947; *The Imperfect Lady* 1947; *Dream Girl* 1948; *The Lady Pays Off* 1951; *Weekend with Father* 1951; *The Explosive Generation* 1961; *The Earth Dies Screaming* 1964
Fielding, Dorothy *Kiss Me Goodbye* 1982; *Fright Night* 1985
Fielding, Edward (1875–1945) *The Major and the Minor* 1942; *What a Woman!* 1943; *Dead Man's Eyes* 1944
Fielding, Emma (1971–) *The Scarlet Tunic* 1997; *Pandaemonium* 2000
Fielding, Fenella (1930–) *Follow a Star* 1959; *Foxhole in Cairo* 1960; *In the Doghouse* 1961; *The Old Dark House* 1963; *Carry On Screaming* 1966; *Doctor in Clover* 1966; *Drop Dead Darling* 1966; *Lock Up Your Daughters!* 1969; *Dougal and the Blue Cat* 1970; *Guest House Paradiso* 1999; *Beginner's Luck* 2001
Fielding, Marjorie (1892–1956) *Quiet Wedding* 1940; *The Demi-Paradise* 1943; *Yellow Canary* 1943; *Quiet Weekend* 1946; *Easy Money* 1947; *Spring in Park Lane* 1948; *The Chiltern Hundreds* 1949; *Conspirator* 1949; *The Franchise Affair* 1950; *Portrait of Clare* 1950; *The Lavender Hill Mob* 1951; *Mandy* 1952; *The Net* 1953
Fielding, Tom *Model Shop* 1969; *A Walk in the Spring Rain* 1970
Fields, Christopher John *Alien³* 1992; *Devil's Child* 1997
Fields, Gracie (1898–1979) *Looking on the Bright Side* 1931; *Sally in Our Alley* 1931; *Love, Life and Laughter* 1934; *Sing as We Go* 1934; *Look Up and Laugh* 1935; *The Show Goes On* 1937; *We're Going to Be Rich* 1938; *Shipyard Sally* 1939; *Holy Matrimony* 1943; *Stage Door Canteen* 1943; *Molly and Me* 1945
Fields, Stanley (1884–1941) *City Streets* 1931; *Little Caesar* 1931; *Riders of the Purple Sage* 1931; *The Gay Desperado* 1936; *All over Town* 1937; *Way Out West* 1937; *Pack Up Your Troubles* 1939; *New Moon* 1940
Fields, Tony aka **Fields, Tony Dean** (1958–1995) *Trick or Treat* 1986; *Dance Academy* 1988; *Backstreet Dreams* 1990
Fields, W C (1879–1946) *Sally of the Sawdust* 1925; *It's the Old Army Game* 1926; *Running Wild* 1927; *Her Majesty Love* 1931; *The Dentist* 1932; *If I Had a Million* 1932; *Million Dollar Legs* 1932; *Alice in Wonderland* 1933; *The Barber Shop* 1933; *International House* 1933; *Tillie and Gus* 1933; *It's a Gift* 1934; *Mrs Wiggs of the Cabbage Patch* 1934; *The Old-Fashioned Way* 1934; *Six of a Kind* 1934; *You're Telling Me!* 1934; *David Copperfield* 1935; *The Man on the Flying Trapeze* 1935; *Mississippi* 1935; *Poppy* 1936; *The Big Broadcast of 1938* 1937; *You Can't Cheat an Honest Man* 1939; *The Bank Dick* 1940; *My Little Chickadee* 1940; *Never Give a Sucker an Even Break* 1941; *Follow the Boys* 1944; *Sensations* 1944; *Song of the Open Road* 1944
Fiennes, Joseph (1970–) *Stealing Beauty* 1995; *Martha – Meet Frank, Daniel and Laurence* 1997; *Elizabeth* 1998; *Shakespeare in Love* 1998; *Forever Mine* 1999; *Rancid Aluminium* 1999; *Dust* 2001; *Enemy at the Gates* 2001; *Killing Me Softly* 2001; *Leo* 2002; *Sinbad: Legend of the Seven Seas* 2003; *William Shakespeare's The Merchant of Venice* 2004
Fiennes, Ralph (1962–) *Wuthering Heights* 1992; *The Baby of Macon* 1993; *Schindler's List* 1993; *Quiz Show* 1994; *Strange Days* 1995; *The English Patient* 1996; *Oscar and Lucinda* 1997; *The Avengers* 1998; *The Prince of Egypt* 1998; *The End of the Affair* 1999; *The Miracle Maker* 1999; *Onegin* 1999; *Sunshine* 1999; *Maid in Manhattan* 2002; *Red Dragon* 2002; *Spider* 2002
Fiermonte, Enzo (1908–1993) *Romeo and Juliet* 1954; *Angela* 1955; *A Black Veil for Lisa* 1969
Fierstein, Harvey (1954–) *The Times of Harvey Milk* 1983; *Torch Song Trilogy* 1988; *The Harvest* 1993; *Mrs Doubtfire* 1993; *Bullets over Broadway* 1994; *Dr Jekyll and Ms Hyde* 1995; *Independence Day* 1996; *Kull the Conqueror* 1997; *Mulan* 1998; *Safe Men* 1998; *Death to Smoochy* 2002; *Our House* 2003
Figueroa, Efrain *Star Maps* 1997; *Desperate Measures* 1998
Figueroa, Reuben aka **Figueroa, Ruben** (1958–) *Popi* 1969; *Who Says I Can't Ride a Rainbow?* 1971
Fillmore, Clyde (1875–1946) *The More the Merrier* 1943; *Laura* 1944
Fimple, Dennis (1940–2002) *Truck Stop Women* 1974; *Smokey and the Good Time Outlaws* 1978; *The Evictors* 1979; *Hawken's Breed* 1989
Finch, Jon (1941–) *The Vampire Lovers* 1970; *Macbeth* 1971; *Frenzy* 1972; *Lady Caroline Lamb* 1972; *The Final Programme* 1973; *Diagnosis: Murder* 1974; *Death on the Nile* 1978; *Breaking Glass* 1980; *Giro City* 1982; *Darklands* 1996; *Anazapta* 2001; *Kingdom of Heaven* 2005
Finch, Peter (1916–1977) *Train of Events* 1949; *The Miniver Story* 1950; *The Story of Robin Hood and His Merrie Men* 1952; *The Heart of the Matter* 1953; *The Story of Gilbert and Sullivan* 1953; *Elephant Walk* 1954; *Father Brown* 1954; *The Dark Avenger* 1955; *Josephine and Men* 1955; *Passage Home* 1955; *Simon and Laura* 1955; *The Battle of the River Plate* 1956; *A Town like Alice* 1956; *Robbery under Arms* 1957; *The Shiralee* 1957; *Windom's Way* 1957; *Operation Amsterdam* 1958; *The Nun's Story* 1959; *Kidnapped* 1960; *No Love for Johnnie* 1960; *The Sins of Rachel Cade* 1960; *The Trials of Oscar Wilde* 1960; *I Thank a Fool* 1962; *Girl with Green Eyes* 1963; *In the Cool of the Day* 1963; *The Pumpkin Eater* 1964; *The Flight of the Phoenix* 1965; *Judith* 1966; *10:30 PM Summer* 1966; *Far from the Madding Crowd* 1967; *The Legend of Lylah Clare* 1968; *The Red Tent* 1969; *Something to Hide* 1971; *Sunday, Bloody Sunday* 1971; *Bequest to the Nation* 1972; *England Made Me* 1973; *Lost Horizon* 1973; *The Abdication* 1974; *Network* 1976; *Raid on Entebbe* 1977
Fine, Harry *The Ghosts of Berkeley Square* 1947; *To Have and to Hold* 1951
Fine, Larry (1902–1975) *Meet the Baron* 1933; *Hollywood Party* 1934; *Time Out for Rhythm* 1941; *Have Rocket, Will Travel* 1959; *The Three Stooges in Orbit* 1962; *The Three Stooges Meet Hercules* 1962; *The Three Stooges Go around the World in a Daze* 1963; *The Outlaws Is Coming* 1965
Fine, Travis (1968–) *Child's Play 3* 1991; *Vanished without a Trace* 1993
Fink, John *Ransom for a Dead Man* 1971; *The Carey Treatment* 1972
Finlay, Frank (1926–) *The Informers* 1963; *Private Potter* 1963; *The Wild Affair* 1963; *The Comedy Man* 1964; *Othello* 1965; *A Study in Terror* 1965; *The Deadly Bees* 1967; *I'll Never Forget What's 'Is Name* 1967; *The Jokers* 1967; *Robbery* 1967; *Inspector Clouseau* 1968; *Twisted Nerve* 1968; *Assault* 1970; *Cromwell* 1970; *The Molly Maguires* 1970; *Gumshoe* 1971; *Neither the Sea nor the Sand* 1972; *Sitting Target* 1972; *Shaft in Africa* 1973; *The Three Musketeers* 1973; *The Four Musketeers* 1974; *Murder by Decree* 1978; *The Thief of Baghdad* 1978; *The Wild Geese* 1978; *Enigma* 1982; *The Return of the Soldier* 1982; *The Ploughman's Lunch* 1983; *Nineteen Nineteen* 1984; *Lifeforce* 1985; *King of the Wind* 1989; *The Return of the Musketeers* 1989; *Sparrow* 1993; *Gospa* 1995; *Stiff Upper Lips* 1997; *Dreaming of Joseph Lees* 1998; *The Martins* 2001; *The Pianist* 2002; *The Statement* 2003
Finlayson, James (1887–1953) *Big Business* 1929; *Men o' War* 1929; *The Dawn Patrol* 1930; *Pardon Us* 1931; *Pack Up Your Troubles* 1932; *Bogus Bandits* 1933; *Bonnie Scotland* 1935; *Thicker than Water* 1935; *The Bohemian Girl* 1936; *All over Town* 1937; *Way Out West* 1937; *Blockheads* 1938; *A Chump at Oxford* 1940; *Saps at Sea* 1940; *The Perils of Pauline* 1947; *The Crazy World of Laurel and Hardy* 1964; *Laurel and Hardy's Laughing 20s* 1965
Finley, Cameron (1987–) *Leave It to Beaver* 1997; *Hope Floats* 1998; *Bitter Suite* 2000; *One True Love* 2000
Finley, William (1944–) *Murder à la Mod* 1968; *Dionysus in '69* 1970; *Sisters* 1973; *Phantom of the Paradise* 1974; *Eaten Alive* 1976; *Silent Rage* 1982
Finn, John aka **Finn, John Joseph** (1952–) *Glory* 1989; *Cover-Up* 1991; *Quicksand: No Escape* 1992; *Blown Away* 1994; *Turbulence* 1997; *Atomic Train* 1999; *Deadlocked* 2000; *Analyze That* 2002; *The Hunted* 2002
Finnerty, Warren (1925–1974) *The Connection* 1961; *Easy Rider* 1969
Finney, Albert (1936–) *The Entertainer* 1960; *Saturday Night and Sunday Morning* 1960; *Tom Jones* 1963; *The Victors* 1963; *Night Must Fall* 1964; *Charlie Bubbles* 1967; *Two for the Road* 1967; *The Picasso Summer* 1969; *Scrooge* 1970; *Gumshoe* 1971; *Alpha Beta* 1973; *Murder on the Orient Express* 1974; *The Duellists* 1977; *Loophole* 1980; *Looker* 1981; *Wolfen* 1981; *Annie*

1982; *Shoot the Moon* 1982; *The Dresser* 1983; *Under the Volcano* 1984; *Orphans* 1987; *The Image* 1990; *Miller's Crossing* 1990; *The Playboys* 1992; *Rich in Love* 1992; *The Browning Version* 1994; *A Man of No Importance* 1994; *The Run of the Country* 1995; *Washington Square* 1997; *Breakfast of Champions* 1999; *Simpatico* 1999; *Erin Brockovich* 2000; *Traffic* 2000; *Big Fish* 2003

Finocchiaro, Angela (1955–) *Volere, Volare* 1991; *Don't Move* 2004

Finsterer, Anni *To Have & to Hold* 1996; *Strange Fits of Passion* 1999

Fiore, Elena *The Seduction of Mimi* 1972; *Seven Beauties* 1976

Fiorentino, Linda (1960–) *After Hours* 1985; *Gotcha!* 1985; *Vision Quest* 1985; *The Moderns* 1988; *Queens Logic* 1991; *Shout* 1991; *Chain of Desire* 1992; *The Last Seduction* 1993; *Charlie's Ghost Story* 1994; *Fixing the Shadow* 1994; *Jade* 1995; *Larger than Life* 1996; *Unforgettable* 1996; *Body Count* 1997; *Kicked in the Head* 1997; *Men in Black* 1997; *Dogma* 1999; *Ordinary Decent Criminal* 1999; *What Planet Are You From?* 2000; *Where the Money Is* 2000; *Liberty Stands Still* 2002

Firbank, Ann *Behind the Mask* 1958; *The Servant* 1963; *Accident* 1967; *One of Those Things* 1970; *A Severed Head* 1970

Firestone, Eddie (1920–) *The Brass Legend* 1956; *The Great Locomotive Chase* 1956; *The Law and Jake Wade* 1958; *Two for the Seesaw* 1962; *Duel* 1971; *Play It As It Lays* 1972; *The Stone Killer* 1973

Firestone, Roy (1953–) *Daffy Duck's Quackbusters* 1988; *Good Luck* 1996

Firth, Anne *aka* **Firth, Annie** (1918–) *The First of the Few* 1942; *The Goose Steps Out* 1942; *Bell-Bottom George* 1943; *Demobbed* 1944; *Scott of the Antarctic* 1948

Firth, Colin (1960–) *Another Country* 1984; *Nineteen Nineteen* 1984; *A Month in the Country* 1987; *Apartment Zero* 1988; *Valmont* 1989; *Wings of Fame* 1990; *Femme Fatale* 1991; *Hostages* 1993; *The Hour of the Pig* 1993; *Playmaker* 1994; *Circle of Friends* 1995; *The English Patient* 1996; *Fever Pitch* 1996; *A Thousand Acres* 1997; *The Secret Laughter of Women* 1998; *Shakespeare in Love* 1998; *Londinium* 1999; *My Life So Far* 1999; *Relative Values* 2000; *Bridget Jones's Diary* 2001; *Conspiracy* 2001; *Hope Springs* 2002; *The Importance of Being Earnest* 2002; *Girl with a Pearl Earring* 2003; *Love Actually* 2003; *What a Girl Wants* 2003; *Bridget Jones: the Edge of Reason* 2004; *Trauma* 2004

Firth, Julian *Scum* 1979; *Oxford Blues* 1984

Firth, Peter (1953–) *Diamonds on Wheels* 1973; *Aces High* 1976; *Equus* 1977; *Joseph Andrews* 1977; *Tess* 1979; *When You Comin' Back, Red Ryder?* 1979; *Letter to Brezhnev* 1985; *Lifeforce* 1985; *Born of Fire* 1987; *Prisoner of Rio* 1988; *Tree of Hands* 1988; *The Hunt for Red October* 1990; *The Pleasure Principle* 1991; *Prisoner of Honor* 1991; *Shadowlands* 1993; *White Angel* 1993; *An Awfully Big Adventure* 1994; *Mighty Joe Young* 1998; *Chill Factor* 1999

Fischer, Kai (1934–) *The Hellfire Club* 1961; *The Goalkeeper's Fear of the Penalty Kick* 1971

Fischer, Kate (1973–) *Sirens* 1994; *Blood Surf* 2000

Fischer, Vera (1950–) *Quilombo* 1984; *The 5th Monkey* 1990

Fish (1958–) *Chasing the Deer* 1994; *The Jacket* 2005

Fish, Nancy (1938–) *Birdy* 1984; *The Exorcist III* 1990; *Death Becomes Her* 1992; *Ghost in the Machine* 1993; *Reflections on a Crime* 1994

Fishburne, Laurence *aka* **Fishburne, Larry** (1961–) *Apocalypse Now* 1979; *Rumble Fish* 1983; *The Cotton Club* 1984; *Quicksilver* 1986; *A Nightmare on Elm Street 3: Dream Warriors* 1987; *Red Heat* 1988; *School Daze* 1988; *King of New York* 1989; *Boyz N the Hood* 1991; *Class Action* 1991; *Stockade* 1991; *Deep Cover* 1992; *Innocent Moves* 1993; *Tina: What's Love Got to Do with It* 1993; *Bad Company* 1995; *Higher Learning* 1995; *Just Cause* 1995; *Othello* 1995; *The Tuskegee Airmen* 1995; *Fled* 1996; *Event Horizon* 1997; *Hoodlum* 1997; *Miss Evers' Boys* 1997; *The Matrix* 1999; *Osmosis Jones* 2001; *The Matrix Reloaded* 2002; *Biker Boyz* 2003; *The Matrix Revolutions* 2003; *Mystic River* 2003; *Assault on Precinct 13* 2005

Fisher, Carrie (1956–) *Shampoo* 1975; *Star Wars Episode IV: a New Hope* 1977; *The Blues Brothers* 1980; *Star Wars Episode V: the Empire Strikes Back* 1980; *Under the Rainbow* 1981; *Star Wars Episode VI: Return of the Jedi* 1983; *Garbo Talks* 1984; *The Man with One Red Shoe* 1985; *Hannah and Her Sisters* 1986; *Hollywood Vice Squad* 1986; *Amazon Women on the Moon* 1987; *The Time Guardian* 1987; *Appointment with Death* 1988; *The 'Burbs* 1989; *Loverboy* 1989; *When Harry Met Sally…* 1989; *Sibling Rivalry* 1990; *Drop Dead Fred* 1991; *Soapdish* 1991; *This Is My Life* 1992; *Scream 3* 1999; *Heartbreakers* 2001; *Jay and Silent Bob Strike Back* 2001; *Wonderland* 2003

Fisher, Cindy *Liar's Moon* 1982; *The Stone Boy* 1984

Fisher, Eddie (1928–) *Bundle of Joy* 1956; *Butterfield 8* 1960; *Nothing Lasts Forever* 1984

Fisher, Frances (1952–) *Can She Bake a Cherry Pie?* 1983; *Heart* 1987; *Patty Hearst* 1988; *Pink Cadillac* 1989; *Welcome Home, Roxy Carmichael* 1990; *Unforgiven* 1992; *Attack of the 50 Ft Woman* 1993; *Babyfever* 1994; *The Stars Fell on Henrietta* 1995; *Female Perversions* 1996; *Titanic* 1997; *Wild America* 1997; *The Big Tease* 1999; *The Audrey Hepburn Story* 2000; *Blue Car* 2001; *House of Sand and Fog* 2003; *Laws of Attraction* 2003

Fisher, Gregor (1953–) *Another Time, Another Place* 1983; *Nineteen Eighty-Four* 1984; *The Girl in the Picture* 1985; *To Kill a Priest* 1988

Fisher, Isla (1976–) *Scooby-Doo* 2002; *Wedding Crashers* 2005

Fisher, Joely (1967–) *Thirst* 1998; *When the Bough Breaks 2: Perfect Prey* 1998; *Inspector Gadget* 1999

Fisher, Thomas *The Nine Lives of Tomas Katz* 1999; *The Truth Game* 2000; *Shanghai Knights* 2002

Fisher, Tricia Leigh (1969–) *CHUD II: Bud the Chud* 1989; *Hostile Intentions* 1995

Fisk, Schuyler (1982–) *The Baby-Sitter's Club* 1995; *My Friend Joe* 1996; *Snow Day* 2000; *Orange County* 2001

Fiske, Robert (1899–1944) *Old Louisiana* 1938; *Along the Rio Grande* 1941

Fitzgerald, Barry (1888–1961) *The Plough and the Stars* 1936; *Bringing Up Baby* 1938; *The Dawn Patrol* 1938; *Full Confession* 1939; *The Saint Strikes Back* 1939; *The Long Voyage Home* 1940; *How Green Was My Valley* 1941; *The Sea Wolf* 1941; *Tarzan's Secret Treasure* 1941; *The Amazing Mrs Holliday* 1943; *Corvette K-225* 1943; *Going My Way* 1944; *None but the Lonely Heart* 1944; *And Then There Were None* 1945; *Duffy's Tavern* 1945; *The Stork Club* 1945; *California* 1946; *Two Years before the Mast* 1946; *Welcome Stranger* 1947; *Miss Tatlock's Millions* 1948; *The Naked City* 1948; *The Sainted Sisters* 1948; *The Story of Seabiscuit* 1949; *Union Station* 1950; *The Quiet Man* 1952; *Happy Ever After* 1954; *The Catered Affair* 1956; *Rooney* 1958

Fitzgerald, Ciaran (1983–) *Into the West* 1992; *The Boxer* 1997

Fitzgerald, Ella (1917–1996) *Ride 'em Cowboy* 1942; *Pete Kelly's Blues* 1955; *St Louis Blues* 1958; *Let No Man Write My Epitaph* 1960

Fitzgerald, Geraldine (1914–) *The Lad* 1935; *The Mill on the Floss* 1937; *Dark Victory* 1939; *Wuthering Heights* 1939; *'Til We Meet Again* 1940; *Shining Victory* 1941; *The Gay Sisters* 1942; *Watch on the Rhine* 1943; *Wilson* 1944; *The Strange Affair of Uncle Harry* 1945; *Nobody Lives Forever* 1946; *OSS* 1946; *Three Strangers* 1946; *The Late Edwina Black* 1951; *Ten North Frederick* 1958; *The Fiercest Heart* 1961; *The Pawnbroker* 1965; *The Last American Hero* 1973; *Harry and Tonto* 1974; *Echoes of a Summer* 1976; *Bye Bye Monkey* 1978; *Lovespell* 1979; *Arthur* 1981; *Easy Money* 1983; *Do You Remember Love* 1985; *Poltergeist II: the Other Side* 1986; *Arthur 2: On the Rocks* 1988

Fitzgerald, Glenn *A Price above Rubies* 1997; *The Sixth Sense* 1999; *The Believer* 2001; *Series 7: the Contenders* 2001

Fitz-Gerald, Lewis (1958–) *We of the Never Never* 1982; *The Boy Who Had Everything* 1984; *The More Things Change* 1985; *The Shiralee* 1986; *Warm Nights on a Slow Moving Train* 1986; *Spider & Rose* 1994; *Dead Heart* 1996; *Pitch Black* 1999

Fitzgerald, Nuala *The Brood* 1979; *Circle of Two* 1980

FitzGerald, Tara (1968–) *Hear My Song* 1991; *A Man of No Importance* 1994; *Sirens* 1994; *The Englishman Who Went up a Hill, but Came down a Mountain* 1995; *Brassed Off* 1996; *New World Disorder* 1999; *Rancid Aluminium* 1999; *Dark Blue World* 2001; *I Capture the Castle* 2002; *Five Children and It* 2004

Fitzgerald, Walter (1896–1976) *San Demetrio London* 1943; *Great Day* 1944; *This Was a Woman* 1947; *Blanche Fury* 1948; *The Fallen Idol* 1948; *Edward, My Son* 1949; *Treasure Island* 1950; *The Net* 1953; *Our Girl Friday* 1953; *Personal Affair* 1953; *Lease of Life* 1954; *The Man in the Sky* 1956; *The Birthday Present* 1957; *Something of Value* 1957; *The Camp on Blood Island* 1958; *Darby O'Gill and the Little People* 1959; *HMS Defiant* 1962

Fitzpatrick, Colleen *aka* **Fitzpatrick, Colleen Ann** (1970–) *Hairspray* 1988; *Dracula 2001* 2000

Fitzpatrick, Gabrielle *Blackwater Trail* 1995; *Mr Nice Guy* 1996; *Farewell, My Love* 1999

Fitzpatrick, Leo (1978–) *kids* 1995; *Personal Velocity* 2001

Fitzpatrick, Neil *Ground Zero* 1987; *A Cry in the Dark* 1988

Fitzroy, Emily (1860–1954) *Love* 1927; *The Case of Lena Smith* 1929; *Don Quixote* 1932

Fluzat, Allen *Benji* 1974; *For the Love of Benji* 1977

Fix, Paul (1901–1983) *Somewhere in Sonora* 1933; *Zoo in Budapest* 1933; *The Desert Trail* 1935; *The Plot Thickens* 1936; *Dr Cyclops* 1940; *Down Mexico Way* 1941; *The Unknown Guest* 1943; *Tall in the Saddle* 1944; *Angel in Exile* 1948; *The Plunderers* 1948; *Wake of the Red Witch* 1949; *Warpath* 1951; *Ride the Man Down* 1952; *Blood Alley* 1955; *The Bad Seed* 1956; *Santiago* 1956; *Toward the Unknown* 1956; *The Devil's Hairpin* 1957; *Hell Bent for Glory* 1957; *Jet Pilot* 1957; *Mail Order Bride* 1963; *Baby the Rain Must Fall* 1965; *An Eye for an Eye* 1966; *Day of the Evil Gun* 1968; *Zabriskie Point* 1970; *Night of the Lepus* 1972; *Grayeagle* 1977; *Wanda Nevada* 1979

Flacks, Niki (1943–) *Raggedy Ann and Andy* 1977; *The Lathe of Heaven* 1979

Flaherty, Joe (1941–) *Going Berserk* 1983; *Sesame Street Presents: Follow That Bird* 1985; *One Crazy Summer* 1986; *Blue Monkey* 1987; *Cannonball Fever* 1989; *A Pig's Tale* 1994; *The Wrong Guy* 1997

Flaherty, Lanny *Winter People* 1988; *The Ballad of the Sad Café* 1991; *Sommersby* 1993

Flamand, Didier (1947–) *Erreur de jeunesse* 1989; *Merci Docteur Rey* 2002

Flanagan, Bud (1896–1968) *A Fire Has Been Arranged* 1935; *O-Kay for Sound* 1937; *Alf's Button Afloat* 1938; *Gasbags* 1940; *We'll Smile Again* 1942; *Dreaming* 1944; *Here Comes the Sun* 1945; *Life Is a Circus* 1958; *The Wild Affair* 1963

Flanagan, Fionnula *aka* **Flanagan, Fionnuala** (1941–) *Sinful Davey* 1969; *Mad at the Moon* 1992; *Money for Nothing* 1993; *Some Mother's Son* 1996; *Waking Ned* 1998; *A Secret Affair* 1999; *With or without You* 1999; *The Others* 2001; *Divine Secrets of the Ya-Ya Sisterhood* 2002; *Tears of the Sun* 2003

Flanagan, John (1947–) *Sweeney 2* 1978; *Arthur's Hallowed Ground* 1985

Flanagan, Markus *aka* **Flanigan, Markus** (1964–) *Biloxi Blues* 1988; *Holiday in the Sun* 2001

Flanagan, Tommy (1965–) *Ratcatcher* 1999; *Strictly Sinatra* 2000; *AVP: Alien vs Predator* 2004; *Trauma* 2004

Flanders, Ed (1934–1995) *MacArthur* 1977; *The Ninth Configuration* 1979; *Salem's Lot* 1979; *The Pursuit of DB Cooper* 1981; *True Confessions* 1981; *The Final Days* 1989; *The Exorcist III* 1990; *Bye Bye Love* 1995

Flanery, Sean Patrick (1965–) *The Grass Harp* 1995; *Powder* 1995; *Just Your Luck* 1996; *Best Men* 1997; *Suicide Kings* 1997; *Girl* 1998; *Body Shots* 1999; *The Boondock Saints* 1999; *Simply Irresistible* 1999; *D-Tox* 2001

Flaus, John (1934–) *Blood Money* 1980; *In Too Deep* 1990

Flavin, James (1906–1976) *Corvette K-225* 1943; *Abroad with Two Yanks* 1944; *Laura* 1944; *Uncertain Glory* 1944; *Angel on My Shoulder* 1946; *Desert Fury* 1947; *The Fabulous Dorseys* 1947; *Destination Murder* 1950; *Francis in the Haunted House* 1956; *In Cold Blood* 1967

Flea (1962–) *Dudes* 1987; *The Blue Iguana* 1988; *The Wild Thornberrys Movie* 2003

Fleet, James (1954–) *Blue Black Permanent* 1992; *Four Weddings and a Funeral* 1994; *The Butterfly Effect* 1995; *Sense and Sensibility* 1995; *Remember Me?* 1996; *Milk* 1999; *Kevin & Perry Go Large* 2000; *Charlotte Gray* 2001; *Two Men Went to War* 2002; *Blackball* 2003

Fleetwood, Susan (1944–1995) *Clash of the Titans* 1981; *Heat and Dust* 1982; *Young Sherlock Holmes* 1985; *The Sacrifice* 1986; *Dream Demon* 1988; *The Krays* 1990; *Persuasion* 1995

Fleischer, Charles (1950–) *Who Framed Roger Rabbit* 1988; *Back to the Future Part II* 1989; *We're Back! A Dinosaur's Story* 1993; *Gridlock'd* 1996; *G-Men from Hell* 2000; *The Polar Express* 2004

Fleiss, Noah (1984–) *Josh and SAM* 1993; *Under Pressure* 1997; *Joe the King* 1999

Fleming, Eric (1925–1966) *Conquest of Space* 1955; *Queen of Outer Space* 1958; *The Glass Bottom Boat* 1966

Fleming, Ian (1888–1969) *They Met in the Dark* 1943; *I Didn't Do It* 1945; *George in Civvy Street* 1946

Fleming, Rhonda (1923–) *Abilene Town* 1945; *Spellbound* 1945; *The Spiral Staircase* 1946; *Build My Gallows High* 1947; *A Connecticut Yankee in King Arthur's Court* 1949; *The Great Lover* 1949; *The Redhead and the Cowboy* 1950; *Cry Danger* 1951; *Inferno* 1953; *Pony Express* 1953; *Serpent of the Nile* 1953; *Jivaro* 1954; *Yankee Pasha* 1954; *Tennessee's Partner* 1955; *The Killer Is Loose* 1956; *Slightly Scarlet* 1956; *While the City Sleeps* 1956; *The Buster Keaton Story* 1957; *Gun Glory* 1957; *Gunfight at the OK Corral* 1957; *Bullwhip* 1958; *Home before Dark* 1958; *Alias Jesse James* 1959; *The Big Circus* 1959; *The Crowded Sky* 1960; *Backtrack* 1969; *The Nude Bomb* 1980

Flemyng, Jason (1966–) *The Jungle Book* 1994; *Hollow Reed* 1995; *Alive and Kicking* 1996; *The James Gang* 1997; *The Life of Stuff* 1997; *Deep Rising* 1998; *Lock, Stock and Two Smoking Barrels* 1998; *The Red Violin* 1998; *The Body* 2000; *Snatch* 2000; *Anazapta* 2001; *The Bunker* 2001; *From Hell* 2001; *Mean Machine* 2001; *Rock Star* 2001; *Below* 2002; *The League of Extraordinary Gentlemen* 2003; *Aaltra* 2004; *Seed of Chucky* 2004

Flemyng, Robert (1912–1995) *Head over Heels in Love* 1937; *The Guinea Pig* 1948; *The Blue Lamp* 1949; *Conspirator* 1949; *The Man Who Never Was* 1955; *Funny Face* 1957; *Windom's Way* 1957; *Blind Date* 1959; *A Touch of Larceny* 1959; *The Horrible Dr Hichcock* 1962; *The Blood Beast Terror* 1967; *The Body Stealers* 1969; *The Darwin Adventure* 1972

Fletcher, Bramwell (1904–1988) *Raffles* 1930; *Svengali* 1931; *The Mummy* 1932; *The Scarlet Pimpernel* 1934; *The Undying Monster* 1942; *White Cargo* 1942; *The Immortal Sergeant* 1943

Fletcher, Brendan (1981–) *Trucks* 1997; *The Five Senses* 1999; *Rollercoaster* 1999; *Freddy vs Jason* 2003; *The Final Cut* 2004

Fletcher, Dexter (1966–) *Revolution* 1985; *Gothic* 1986; *Lionheart* 1986; *The Raggedy Rawney* 1987; *The Rachel Papers* 1989; *Lock, Stock and Two Smoking Barrels* 1998; *Below* 2002; *Stander* 2003

Fletcher, Jay *Born to Win* 1971; *California Split* 1974

Fletcher, Louise (1934–) *Thieves like Us* 1974; *One Flew over the Cuckoo's Nest* 1975; *Exorcist II: The Heretic* 1977; *The Cheap Detective* 1978; *The Lady in Red* 1979; *The Magician of Lublin* 1979; *The Lucky Star* 1980; *Brainstorm* 1983; *Strange Invaders* 1983; *Firestarter* 1984; *Invaders from Mars* 1986; *Nobody's Fool* 1986; *Flowers in the Attic* 1987; *Two Moon Junction* 1988; *Blue Steel* 1990; *Shadowzone* 1990; *Blind Vision* 1992; *Tollbooth* 1994; *Virtuosity* 1995; *High School High* 1996; *Breast Men* 1997; *Love to Kill* 1997; *Love Kills* 1998; *Cruel Intentions* 1999; *The Devil's Arithmetic* 1999; *A Map of the World* 1999; *Big Eden* 2000

Flicker, Theodore J *aka* **Flicker, Ted** (1930–) *The Troublemaker* 1964; *The Legend of the Lone Ranger* 1981

Flint, Helen (1898–1967) *The Black Legion* 1937; *Sea Devils* 1937; *Step Lively, Jeeves* 1937

Flint, Katja (1960–) *The Democratic Terrorist* 1992; *A Girl Called Rosemarie* 1996

Flint, Sam (1882–1980) *Winds of the Wasteland* 1936; *Abbott and Costello Meet the Keystone Cops* 1955; *The Big Tip Off* 1955

Flippen, Jay C (1898–1971) *They Live by Night* 1948; *Oh, You Beautiful Doll* 1949; *A Woman's Secret* 1949; *Love That Brute* 1950; *Two Flags West* 1950; *Winchester '73* 1950; *Flying Leathernecks* 1951; *The Lemon Drop Kid* 1951; *The People against O'Hara* 1951; *The Las Vegas Story* 1952; *Devil's Canyon* 1953; *East of Sumatra* 1953; *Thunder Bay* 1953; *The Wild One* 1953; *Carnival Story* 1954; *The Far Country* 1954; *Kismet* 1955;

Man without a Star 1955; Oklahoma! 1955; Six Bridges to Cross 1955; Strategic Air Command 1955; The Killing 1956; Seventh Cavalry 1956; The Deerslayer 1957; The Halliday Brand 1957; Hot Summer Night 1957; Jet Pilot 1957; The Midnight Story 1957; The Restless Breed 1957; Run of the Arrow 1957; From Hell to Texas 1958; Wild River 1960; Hellfighters 1969; The Seven Minutes 1971

Floberg, Bjørn (1947–) Insomnia 1997; The Last Contract 1998; Kitchen Stories 2003

Flockhart, Calista (1964–) Getting In 1994; The Birdcage 1996; Telling Lies in America 1997; A Midsummer Night's Dream 1999; Things You Can Tell Just by Looking at Her 2000

Flon, Suzanne (1918–2005) Moulin Rouge 1952; Thou Shalt Not Kill 1961; A Monkey in Winter 1962; The Trial 1962; The Train 1964; The Silent One 1973; Loving in the Rain 1974; Boomerang 1976; Mr Klein 1976; One Deadly Summer 1983; En Toute Innocence 1987; The Children of the Marshland 1998; The Flower of Evil 2002; Strange Gardens 2003; The Bridesmaid 2004

Florance, Sheila (1916–1991) Cactus 1986; Nirvana Street Murder 1990; A Woman's Tale 1991

Florelle aka **Florelle, Odette** (1901–1974) Les Misérables 1934; Le Crime de Monsieur Lange 1935

Flower, George "Buck" (1937–2004) Across the Great Divide 1977; They Live 1988; Masters of Menace 1990

Fluegel, Darlanne (1956–) Battle beyond the Stars 1980; To Live and Die in LA 1985; Running Scared 1986; Tough Guys 1986; Bulletproof 1987; Lock Up 1989; Project: Alien 1990; Scanner Cop 1994; Darkman III: Die Darkman Die 1996

Fluellen, Joel (1907–1990) Monster from Green Hell 1958; The Learning Tree 1969; The Great White Hope 1970

Flynn, Bill Kill and Kill Again 1981; Saturday Night at the Palace 1987

Flynn, Colleen (1962–) Late for Dinner 1991; The Temp 1993; Devil's Child 1997

Flynn, Errol (1909–1959) Captain Blood 1935; The Charge of the Light Brigade 1936; Another Dawn 1937; Green Light 1937; The Perfect Specimen 1937; The Prince and the Pauper 1937; The Adventures of Robin Hood 1938; The Dawn Patrol 1938; Four's a Crowd 1938; The Sisters 1938; Dodge City 1939; The Private Lives of Elizabeth and Essex 1939; Santa Fe Trail 1940; The Sea Hawk 1940; Virginia City 1940; Dive Bomber 1941; Footsteps in the Dark 1941; They Died with Their Boots On 1941; Desperate Journey 1942; Gentleman Jim 1942; Edge of Darkness 1943; Northern Pursuit 1943; Uncertain Glory 1944; Objective, Burma! 1945; San Antonio 1945; Never Say Goodbye 1946; Cry Wolf 1947; Escape Me Never 1947; Adventures of Don Juan 1948; Silver River 1948; The Forsyte Saga 1949; It's a Great Feeling 1949; Kim 1950; Montana 1950; Rocky Mountain 1950; Adventures of Captain Fabian 1951; Against All Flags 1952; Mara Maru 1952; The Master of Ballantrae 1953; Crossed Swords 1954; The Dark Avenger 1955; King's Rhapsody 1955; Lilacs in the Spring 1955; Istanbul 1957; The Sun Also Rises 1957; The Roots of Heaven 1958; Too Much, Too Soon 1958

Flynn, Jerome (1963–) A Summer Story 1987; Edward II 1991; Best 1999

Flynn, Joe (1925–1974) The Last Time I Saw Archie 1961; McHale's Navy 1964; Divorce American Style 1967; Did You Hear the One about the Traveling Saleslady? 1968; The Computer Wore Tennis Shoes 1969; The Love Bug 1969; The Barefoot Executive 1971; How to Frame a Figg 1971; The Million Dollar Duck 1971; Now You See Him, Now You Don't 1972; Superdad 1974; The Strongest Man in the World 1975; The Rescuers 1977

Flynn, Miriam National Lampoon's Class Reunion 1982; For Keeps 1987; 18 Again! 1988; National Lampoon's Christmas Vacation 1989; Babe 1995

Flynn, Steven Without Warning: the James Brady Story 1991; Ulee's Gold 1997

Foà, Arnoldo (1916–) Angela 1955; The Angel Wore Red 1960; The Captain 1960; The Trial 1962

Focas, Spiros (1937–) Shaft in Africa 1973; The Jewel of the Nile 1985; Rambo III 1988

Foch, Nina (1924–) The Return of the Vampire 1943; Cry of the Werewolf 1944; My Name Is Julia Ross 1945; A Song to Remember 1945; The Guilt of Janet Ames 1947; Johnny O'Clock 1947; The Dark Past 1948; Johnny Allegro 1949; The Undercover Man 1949; An American in Paris 1951; Scaramouche 1952; Sombrero 1952; Young Man with Ideas 1952; Executive Suite 1954; Four Guns to the Border 1954; Illegal 1955; You're Never Too Young 1955; The Ten Commandments 1956; Three Brave Men 1956; Cash McCall 1960; Spartacus 1960; Prescription: Murder 1968; Such Good Friends 1971; Mahogany 1975; Jennifer 1978; Hush 1998; Shadow of Doubt 1998

Fogel, Vladimir (1902–1929) Chess Fever 1925; By the Law 1926; The House on Trubnaya Square 1928

Foley, Dave (1963–) Kids in the Hall: Brain Candy 1996; The Wrong Guy 1997; Blast from the Past 1998; A Bug's Life 1998; Dick 1999; Monkeybone 2000; Stark Raving Mad 2002

Foley, Jeremy (1983–) Casper: a Spirited Beginning 1997; Dante's Peak 1997; Casper Meets Wendy 1998; Soccer Dog: the Movie 1999

Foley, Scott (1973–) Scream 3 1999; Below 2002

Folland, Alison (1978–) To Die For 1995; All over Me 1996; Boys Don't Cry 1999; Milwaukee, Minnesota 2002

Follows, Megan (1968–) Hockey Night 1984; Silver Bullet 1985; Season of Dreams 1987; The Nutcracker Prince 1990; Under the Piano 1995

Fonda, Bridget (1964–) Aria 1987; Light Years 1988; Scandal 1988; Shag 1988; Strapless 1988; You Can't Hurry Love 1988; Frankenstein Unbound 1990; The Godfather Part III 1990; Doc Hollywood 1991; Drop Dead Fred 1991; Iron Maze 1991; Leather Jackets 1991; Out of the Rain 1991; Single White Female 1992; Singles 1992; Army of Darkness 1993; The Assassin 1993; Bodies, Rest and Motion 1993; Camilla 1993; Little Buddha 1993; Point of No Return 1993; It Could Happen to You 1994; The Road to Wellville 1994; Balto 1995; Rough Magic 1995; City Hall 1996; Grace of My Heart 1996; Touch 1996; In the Gloaming 1997; Jackie Brown 1997; Mr Jealousy 1997; Break Up 1998; A Simple Plan 1998; Finding Graceland 1999; Lake Placid 1999; Monkeybone 2000; South of Heaven, West of Hell 2000; Kiss of the Dragon 2001

Fonda, Henry (1905–1982) The Farmer Takes a Wife 1935; I Dream Too Much 1935; Way Down East 1935; The Moon's Our Home 1936; Spendthrift 1936; The Trail of the Lonesome Pine 1936; Slim 1937; That Certain Woman 1937; Wings of the Morning 1937; You Only Live Once 1937; Blockade 1938; I Met My Love Again 1938; Jezebel 1938; The Mad Miss Manton 1938; Spawn of the North 1938; Drums along the Mohawk 1939; Jesse James 1939; The Story of Alexander Graham Bell 1939; Young Mr Lincoln 1939; Chad Hanna 1940; The Grapes of Wrath 1940; Lillian Russell 1940; The Return of Frank James 1940; The Lady Eve 1941; Wild Geese Calling 1941; You Belong to Me 1941; The Battle of Midway 1942; The Big Street 1942; The Magnificent Dope 1942; The Male Animal 1942; Rings on Her Fingers 1942; Tales of Manhattan 1942; The Immortal Sergeant 1943; The Ox-Bow Incident 1943; My Darling Clementine 1946; Daisy Kenyon 1947; The Fugitive 1947; The Long Night 1947; Fort Apache 1948; On Our Merry Way 1948; Jigsaw 1949; Mister Roberts 1955; War and Peace 1956; The Wrong Man 1956; The Tin Star 1957; 12 Angry Men 1957; Stage Struck 1958; The Man Who Understood Women 1959; Warlock 1959; Advise and Consent 1962; How the West Was Won 1962; The Longest Day 1962; Spencer's Mountain 1963; The Best Man 1964; Fail-Safe 1964; Sex and the Single Girl 1964; Battle of the Bulge 1965; The Dirty Game 1965; In Harm's Way 1965; The Rounders 1965; A Big Hand for a Little Lady 1966; Stranger on the Run 1967; Welcome to Hard Times 1967; The Boston Strangler 1968; Firecreek 1968; Madigan 1968; Once upon a Time in the West 1968; Yours, Mine and Ours 1968; The Cheyenne Social Club 1970; There Was a Crooked Man... 1970; Too Late the Hero 1970; Sometimes a Great Notion 1971; The Serpent 1972; Ash Wednesday 1973; My Name Is Nobody 1973; The Last Days of Mussolini 1974; Battle of Midway 1976; The Great Smokey Roadblock 1977; Rollercoaster 1977; Tentacles 1977; Fedora 1978; City on Fire 1979; Meteor 1979; Wanda Nevada 1979; Gideon's Trumpet 1980; On Golden Pond 1981

Fonda, Jane (1937–) The Chapman Report 1962; Period of Adjustment 1962; Walk on the Wild Side 1962; In the Cool of the Day 1963; Sunday in New York 1963; The Love Cage 1964; La Ronde 1964; Cat Ballou 1965; Any Wednesday 1966; The Chase 1966; The Game Is Over 1966; Barbarella 1967; Barefoot in the Park 1967; Histoires Extraordinaires 1967; Hurry Sundown 1967; They Shoot Horses, Don't They? 1969; Klute 1971; FTA 1972; Tout Va Bien 1972; A Doll's House 1973; Steelyard Blues 1973; The Blue Bird 1976; Fun with Dick and Jane 1977; Julia 1977; California Suite 1978; Comes a Horseman 1978; Coming Home 1978; The China Syndrome 1979; The Electric Horseman 1979; Nine to Five 1980; On Golden Pond 1981; Rollover 1981; The Dollmaker 1984; Agnes of God 1985; The Morning After 1986; Leonard, Part 6 1987; Old Gringo 1989; Stanley & Iris 1989; Monster-in-Law 2005

Fonda, Peter (1939–) Tammy and the Doctor 1963; The Victors 1963; Lilith 1964; The Young Lovers 1964; The Wild Angels 1966; Histoires Extraordinaires 1967; The Trip 1967; Easy Rider 1969; The Hired Hand 1971; The Last Movie 1971; Two People 1973; Dirty Mary Crazy Larry 1974; Open Season 1974; Killer Force 1975; 92 in the Shade 1975; Race with the Devil 1975; Fighting Mad 1976; Futureworld 1976; Outlaw Blues 1977; High-ballin' 1978; Wanda Nevada 1979; The Cannonball Run 1981; Split Image 1982; Dance of the Dwarfs 1983; Certain Fury 1985; Hawken's Breed 1989; The Rose Garden 1989; Fatal Mission 1990; Deadfall 1993; Love and a .45 1994; Nadja 1995; Shadow of the Past 1995; Escape from LA 1996; Ulee's Gold 1997; The Limey 1999; South of Heaven, West of Hell 2000; Thomas and the Magic Railroad 2000; The Laramie Project 2002; The Heart Is Deceitful above All Things 2004

Fondacaro, Phil (1958–) Troll 1986; The Garbage Pail Kids Movie 1987

Fong, Benson (1916–1987) Charlie Chan in The Chinese Cat 1944; Charlie Chan in the Secret Service 1944; The Red Dragon 1945; The Scarlet Clue 1945; The Shanghai Cobra 1945; Dark Alibi 1946; Deception 1946; Peking Express 1951; His Majesty O'Keefe 1953; Flower Drum Song 1961; Girls! Girls! Girls! 1962; Our Man Flint 1966; The Love Bug 1969; Oliver's Story 1978

Fontaine, Frank (1920–1978) Stella 1950; The Model and the Marriage Broker 1951

Fontaine, Joan (1917–) A Damsel in Distress 1937; A Million to One 1937; Quality Street 1937; Blond Cheat 1938; The Duke of West Point 1938; Maid's Night Out 1938; Gunga Din 1939; Man of Conquest 1939; The Women 1939; Rebecca 1940; Suspicion 1941; This above All 1942; The Constant Nymph 1943; Jane Eyre 1943; Frenchman's Creek 1944; The Affairs of Susan 1945; From This Day Forward 1946; Ivy 1947; Blood on My Hands 1948; The Emperor Waltz 1948; Letter from an Unknown Woman 1948; You Gotta Stay Happy 1948; Born to Be Bad 1950; September Affair 1950; Darling, How Could You! 1951; Ivanhoe 1952; Something to Live For 1952; The Bigamist 1953; Decameron Nights 1953; Flight to Tangier 1953; Casanova's Big Night 1954; Beyond a Reasonable Doubt 1956; Serenade 1956; Island in the Sun 1957; Until They Sail 1957; A Certain Smile 1958; South Pacific 1958; Tender Is the Night 1961; Voyage to the Bottom of the Sea 1961; The Witches 1966

Fonteney, Catherine (1879–1966) Poil de Carotte 1932; Divine 1935

Foody, Ralph (?–1999) Code of Silence 1985; Cold Justice 1991

Foran, Dick aka **Foran, Richard** (1910–1979) Dangerous 1935; Shipmates Forever 1935; The Petrified Forest 1936; The Black Legion 1937; The Perfect Specimen 1937; Boy Meets Girl 1938; Four Daughters 1938; Daughters Courageous 1939; The House of the Seven Gables 1940; The Mummy's Hand 1940; My Little Chickadee 1940; Keep 'em Flying 1941; Road Agent 1941; Unfinished Business 1941; The Mummy's Tomb 1942; Private Buckaroo 1942; Ride 'em Cowboy 1942; Guest Wife 1945; Chicago Confidential 1957; The Fearmakers 1958; Violent Road 1958; The Atomic Submarine 1960; Studs Lonigan 1960; Taggart 1964

Foray, June (1919–) Daffy Duck's Movie: Fantastic Island 1983; Duck Tales: the Movie – Treasure of the Lost Lamp 1990; Thumbelina 1994; The Adventures of Rocky & Bullwinkle 1999; Tweety's High Flying Adventure 2000

Forbes, Bryan (1926–) Appointment in London 1952; Sea Devils 1952; The World in His Arms 1952; The Colditz Story 1954; An Inspector Calls 1954; Passage Home 1955; The Baby and the Battleship 1956; Satellite in the Sky 1956; Quatermass II 1957; The Key 1958; The League of Gentlemen 1960; The Guns of Navarone 1961; Restless Natives 1985

Forbes, Mary (1883–1974) Sunny Side Up 1929; The Devil to Pay 1930; Blonde Bombshell 1933; We Live Again 1934; Tender Comrade 1943

Forbes, Meriel (1913–2000) Come On George 1939; The Bells Go Down 1943; Home at Seven 1952

Forbes, Michelle (1967–) Kalifornia 1993; Roadflower 1994; Swimming with Sharks 1994; Escape from LA 1996

Forbes, Ralph (1902–1951) Beau Geste 1926; The Trail of '98 1929; The Green Goddess 1930; Her Wedding Night 1930; The Bachelor Father 1931; Beau Ideal 1931; Smilin' Through 1932; The Barretts of Wimpole Street 1934; The Fountain 1934; Riptide 1934; Streamline Express 1935; Piccadilly Jim 1936; The Last of Mrs Cheyney 1937; Annabel Takes a Tour 1938; Kidnapped 1938; Frenchman's Creek 1944

Forbes, Scott aka **Dallas, Julian** (1920–1997) This Was a Woman 1947; Rocky Mountain 1950; Operation Pacific 1951; The Mind of Mr Soames 1970

Ford, Alan The Squeeze 1977; Snatch 2000; Exorcist: the Beginning 2004

Ford, Constance (1923–1993) The Last Hunt 1956; The Iron Sheriff 1957; A Summer Place 1959; Claudelle Inglish 1961; All Fall Down 1962; The Cabinet of Caligari 1962; House of Women 1962; Rome Adventure 1962; 99 and 44/100% Dead 1974

Ford, Dorothy (1923–) On Our Merry Way 1948; Jack and the Beanstalk 1952

Ford, Faith (1964–) You Talkin' to Me? 1987; Sometimes They Come Back... for More 1998; The Pacifier 2005

Ford, Francis (1881–1953) Charlie Chan at the Circus 1936; Bad Lands 1939; South of Pago Pago 1940; The Ox-Bow Incident 1943; The Plunderers 1948; The Far Frontier 1949; The Sun Shines Bright 1953

Ford, Fritz The Bridge at Remagen 1969; Challenge to Be Free 1972

Ford, Glenn (1916–) The Lady in Question 1940; So Ends Our Night 1941; Texas 1941; The Desperadoes 1943; Gilda 1946; A Stolen Life 1946; Framed 1947; The Loves of Carmen 1948; The Man from Colorado 1948; The Return of October 1948; The Doctor and the Girl 1949; The Undercover Man 1949; Convicted 1950; The Redhead and the Cowboy 1950; The White Tower 1950; Follow the Sun: the Ben Hogan Story 1951; The Secret of Convict Lake 1951; Affair in Trinidad 1952; Young Man with Ideas 1952; Appointment in Honduras 1953; The Big Heat 1953; The Man from the Alamo 1953; Terror on a Train 1953; Human Desire 1954; The Americano 1955; The Blackboard Jungle 1955; Interrupted Melody 1955; Trial 1955; The Violent Men 1955; The Fastest Gun Alive 1956; Jubal 1956; Ransom! 1956; The Teahouse of the August Moon 1956; Don't Go Near the Water 1957; 3:10 to Yuma 1957; Cowboy 1958; Imitation General 1958; The Sheepman 1958; Torpedo Run 1958; The Gazebo 1959; It Started with a Kiss 1959; Cimarron 1960; Cry for Happy 1961; Pocketful of Miracles 1961; Experiment in Terror 1962; The Four Horsemen of the Apocalypse 1962; The Courtship of Eddie's Father 1963; Love Is a Ball 1963; Advance to the Rear 1964; Dear Heart 1964; Fate Is the Hunter 1964; The Rounders 1965; Is Paris Burning? 1966; The Money Trap 1966; Rage 1966; The Last Challenge 1967; A Time for Killing 1967; Day of the Evil Gun 1968; Smith! 1969; Santee 1973; Battle of Midway 1976; Superman 1978; Virus 1980; The Visitor 1980; Happy Birthday to Me 1981; Border Shootout 1990; Raw Nerve 1991

Ford, Harrison (1942–) Dead Heat on a Merry-Go-Round 1966; Journey to Shiloh 1967; A Time for Killing 1967; Getting Straight 1970; American Graffiti 1973; The Conversation 1974; Heroes 1977;

Star Wars Episode IV: a New Hope 1977; *Force 10 from Navarone* 1978; *Apocalypse Now* 1979; *The Frisco Kid* 1979; *Hanover Street* 1979; *More American Graffiti* 1979; *Star Wars Episode V: the Empire Strikes Back* 1980; *Raiders of the Lost Ark* 1981; *Blade Runner* 1982; *Star Wars Episode VI: Return of the Jedi* 1983; *Indiana Jones and the Temple of Doom* 1984; *Witness* 1985; *The Mosquito Coast* 1986; *Frantic* 1988; *Working Girl* 1988; *Indiana Jones and the Last Crusade* 1989; *Presumed Innocent* 1990; *Regarding Henry* 1991; *Patriot Games* 1992; *The Fugitive* 1993; *Clear and Present Danger* 1994; *Jimmy Hollywood* 1994; *Sabrina* 1995; *Air Force One* 1997; *The Devil's Own* 1997; *Six Days Seven Nights* 1998; *Random Hearts* 1999; *What Lies Beneath* 2000; *K-19: the Widowmaker* 2002; *Hollywood Homicide* 2003

Ford, John *aka* **Ford, Jack** (1894–1973) *The Birth of a Nation* 1915; *His Lordship* 1936; *The Tales of Hoffmann* 1951

Ford, Maria (1966–) *The Haunting of Morella* 1990; *Ring of Fire* 1991; *The Unnamable Returns* 1992

Ford, Mick *The Sailor's Return* 1978; *Scum* 1979; *Light Years Away* 1981

Ford, Paul (1901–1976) *Perfect Strangers* 1950; *The Teahouse of the August Moon* 1956; *The Matchmaker* 1958; *The Missouri Traveler* 1958; *The Music Man* 1962; *Who's Got the Action?* 1962; *Never Too Late* 1965; *A Big Hand for a Little Lady* 1966; *The Russians Are Coming, the Russians Are Coming* 1966; *The Comedians* 1967

Ford, Ross (1923–1988) *Challenge to Lassie* 1949; *Force of Arms* 1951; *Blue Canadian Rockies* 1952; *Project Moonbase* 1953; *Reform School Girl* 1957

Ford, Ruth (1915–) *Murder on the Waterfront* 1943; *Circumstantial Evidence* 1945; *Strange Impersonation* 1946; *Act One* 1963; *Play It As It Lays* 1972; *Too Scared to Scream* 1982

Ford, Wallace *aka* **Ford, Wally** (1898–1966) *Possessed* 1931; *The Beast of the City* 1932; *Freaks* 1932; *The Wet Parade* 1932; *Employees' Entrance* 1933; *The Lost Patrol* 1934; *The Informer* 1935; *The Whole Town's Talking* 1935; *You're in the Army Now* 1936; *The Mummy's Hand* 1940; *Blues in the Night* 1941; *A Man Betrayed* 1941; *All through the Night* 1942; *The Mummy's Tomb* 1942; *Seven Days' Leave* 1942; *Shadow of a Doubt* 1942; *Secret Command* 1944; *Blood on the Sun* 1945; *The Great John L* 1945; *Black Angel* 1946; *Crack-Up* 1946; *Dead Reckoning* 1947; *Magic Town* 1947; *T-Men* 1947; *Belle Starr's Daughter* 1948; *The Set-Up* 1949; *The Breaking Point* 1950; *Harvey* 1950; *He Ran All the Way* 1951; *Painting the Clouds with Sunshine* 1951; *Warpath* 1951; *Flesh and Fury* 1952; *Beautiful but Dangerous* 1954; *The Boy from Oklahoma* 1954; *Destry* 1954; *Three Ring Circus* 1954; *A Lawless Street* 1955; *Lucy Gallant* 1955; *The Man from Laramie* 1955; *The Maverick Queen* 1955; *The Spoilers* 1955; *Wichita* 1955; *The First Texan* 1956; *Johnny Concho* 1956; *The Rainmaker* 1956; *Thunder over Arizona* 1956; *The Matchmaker* 1958; *Warlock* 1959; *Tess of the Storm Country* 1960; *A Patch of Blue* 1965

Ford Davies, Oliver *Titanic Town* 1998; *Star Wars Episode I: the Phantom Menace* 1999; *Johnny English* 2003; *The Mother* 2003

Foree, Ken (1941–) *Dawn of the Dead* 1978; *From Beyond* 1986; *Leatherface: the Texas Chainsaw Massacre III* 1990; *Without You I'm Nothing* 1990; *Hangfire* 1991; *The Dentist* 1996

Foreman, Deborah (1962–) *Valley Girl* 1983; *April Fool's Day* 1986; *My Chauffeur* 1986; *3:15* 1986; *Destroyer* 1988; *Waxwork* 1988; *The Experts* 1989; *Lobster Man from Mars* 1989; *Lunatics: a Love Story* 1991

Foreman, Jamie (1958–) *Gangster No 1* 2000; *Goodbye Charlie Bright* 2000; *Saving Grace* 2000; *I'll Sleep When I'm Dead* 2003; *The Football Factory* 2004; *Layer Cake* 2004

Forest, Michael (1929–) *Beast from Haunted Cave* 1959; *Atlas* 1960; *Deathwatch* 1966; *100 Rifles* 1969; *The Loves and Times of Scaramouche* 1976; *The Message* 1976

Forke, Farrah (1967–) *Complex of Fear* 1993; *Hitman's Run* 1999

Forlani, Claire (1972–) *Mallrats* 1995; *Basquiat* 1996; *The Last Time I Committed Suicide* 1996; *Basil* 1998; *Meet Joe Black* 1998; *Boys and Girls* 2000; *Antitrust* 2001; *Triggermen* 2002; *The Medallion* 2003; *Bobby Jones: Stroke of Genius* 2004

Forman, Carol (1919–1997) *The Falcon's Adventure* 1946; *San Quentin* 1946

Forman, Joey (1929–1982) *The Twinkle in God's Eye* 1955; *The Wicked Dreams of Paula Schultz* 1968

Forman, Milos (1932–) *Heartburn* 1986; *Keeping the Faith* 2000

Formby, Beryl (?–1960) *Boots! Boots!* 1934; *Off the Dole* 1935

Formby, George (1904–1961) *Boots! Boots!* 1934; *No Limit* 1935; *Off the Dole* 1935; *Keep Your Seats, Please* 1936; *Keep Fit* 1937; *I See Ice* 1938; *It's in the Air* 1938; *Come On George* 1939; *Trouble Brewing* 1939; *Let George Do It* 1940; *Spare a Copper* 1940; *It's Turned Out Nice Again* 1941; *South American George* 1941; *Much Too Shy* 1942; *Bell-Bottom George* 1943; *Get Cracking* 1943; *I Didn't Do It* 1945; *George in Civvy Street* 1946

Forner, Lola (1960–) *Wheels on Meals* 1984; *The Armour of God* 1986

Foronjy, Richard (1937–) *Prince of the City* 1981; *The Morning After* 1986; *Odd Jobs* 1986; *Midnight Run* 1988

Forqué, Verónica (1955–) *What Have I Done to Deserve This?* 1984; *Kika* 1993

Forquet, Philippe (1940–) *In the French Style* 1963; *Take Her, She's Mine* 1963

Forrest, Christine *Martin* 1978; *Knightriders* 1981; *Monkey Shines* 1988

Forrest, Frederic (1936–) *When the Legends Die* 1972; *The Don Is Dead* 1973; *The Conversation* 1974; *The Gravy Train* 1974; *Larry* 1974; *Permission to Kill* 1975; *The Missouri Breaks* 1976; *It Lives Again* 1978; *Apocalypse Now* 1979; *The Rose* 1979; *Hammett* 1982; *One from the Heart* 1982; *The Parade* 1984; *The Stone Boy* 1984; *Return* 1985; *Where Are the Children?* 1986; *Season of Dreams* 1987; *Valentino Returns* 1987; *The Dead Can't Lie* 1988; *Tucker: the Man and His Dream* 1988; *Cat Chaser* 1989; *Music Box* 1989; *The Two Jakes* 1990; *Falling Down* 1992; *Hidden Fears* 1993; *Trauma* 1993; *Against the Wall* 1994; *Lassie: a New Generation* 1994; *One Night Stand* 1994; *Before the Night* 1995; *The Brave* 1997; *Point Blank* 1997; *Whatever* 1998; *Militia* 2000; *Shadow Hours* 2000; *Path to War* 2002

Forrest, Sally (1928–) *Mystery Street* 1950; *Hard, Fast and Beautiful* 1951; *The Strange Door* 1951; *The Strip* 1951; *Vengeance Valley* 1951; *Son of Sinbad* 1955; *While the City Sleeps* 1956

Forrest, Steve (1924–) *Dream Wife* 1953; *So Big* 1953; *Take the High Ground* 1953; *Phantom of the Rue Morgue* 1954; *Prisoner of War* 1954; *Rogue Cop* 1954; *Bedevilled* 1955; *The Living Idol* 1955; *It Happened to Jane* 1959; *Flaming Star* 1960; *Heller in Pink Tights* 1960; *The Second Time Around* 1961; *The Yellow Canary* 1963; *The Late Liz* 1971; *The Wild Country* 1971; *North Dallas Forty* 1979; *Mommie Dearest* 1981; *Spies like Us* 1985; *Amazon Women on the Moon* 1987; *Killer: a Journal of Murder* 1995

Forster, Robert (1941–) *Reflections in a Golden Eye* 1967; *The Stalking Moon* 1968; *Justine* 1969; *Medium Cool* 1969; *Pieces of Dreams* 1970; *Journey through Rosebud* 1972; *The Don Is Dead* 1973; *Stunts* 1977; *The Black Hole* 1979; *Alligator* 1980; *Hollywood Harry* 1985; *The Delta Force* 1986; *Peacemaker* 1990; *Diplomatic Immunity* 1991; *29th Street* 1991; *American Yakuza* 1994; *American Perfekt* 1997; *Jackie Brown* 1997; *Psycho* 1998; *Rear Window* 1998; *Me, Myself & Irene* 2000; *Supernova* 2000; *Human Nature* 2001; *Mulholland Drive* 2001; *Grand Theft Parsons* 2003

Forster, Rudolf (1884–1968) *Ariane* 1931; *The Threepenny Opera* 1931

Forster-Jones, Glenna *Joanna* 1969; *Leo the Last* 1970

Forsyth, Bruce (1928–) *Star!* 1968; *Can Heironymus Merkin Ever Forget Mercy Humppe and Find True Happiness?* 1969; *Bedknobs and Broomsticks* 1971; *The Magnificent Seven Deadly Sins* 1971; *House!* 2000

Forsyth, Rosemary (1944–) *Shenandoah* 1965; *The War Lord* 1965; *Texas across the River* 1966; *Whatever Happened to Aunt Alice?* 1969; *Where It's At* 1969; *How Do I Love Thee?* 1970; *City beneath the Sea* 1971; *Gray Lady Down* 1978; *Disclosure* 1994; *Girl* 1998

Forsythe, Drew (1950–) *Annie's Coming Out* 1984; *Burke and Wills* 1985

Forsythe, Henderson (1917–) *Dead of Night* 1972; *End of the Line* 1987

Forsythe, John (1918–) *The Captive City* 1952; *Escape from Fort Bravo* 1953; *The Glass Web* 1953; *The Trouble with Harry* 1954; *The Ambassador's Daughter* 1956; *Kitten with a Whip* 1964; *Madame X* 1966; *In Cold Blood* 1967; *The Happy Ending* 1969; *Topaz* 1969; *...And Justice for All* 1979; *Scrooged* 1988; *Charlie's Angels* 2000; *Charlie's Angels: Full Throttle* 2003

Forsythe, William *aka* **Forsythe, Bill** (1955–) *Once upon a Time in America* 1984; *The Lightship* 1985; *Savage Dawn* 1985; *Extreme Prejudice* 1987; *Raising Arizona* 1987; *Weeds* 1987; *Patty Hearst* 1988; *Dead-Bang* 1989; *Sons* 1989; *Torrents of Spring* 1989; *Dick Tracy* 1990; *Out for Justice* 1991; *Stone Cold* 1991; *The Waterdance* 1991; *American Me* 1992; *The Gun in Betty Lou's Handbag* 1992; *Palookaville* 1995; *Things to Do in Denver When You're Dead* 1995; *Virtuosity* 1995; *The Rock* 1996; *The Substitute* 1996; *Dollar for the Dead* 1998; *Firestorm* 1998; *Deuce Bigalow: Male Gigolo* 1999; *Four Days* 1999; *G-Men from Hell* 2000; *Luck of the Draw* 2000; *City by the Sea* 2002; *The Devil's Rejects* 2005

Fortescue, Kenneth *High Flight* 1957; *The Brides of Fu Manchu* 1966

Fortier, Robert (1926–2005) *Incubus* 1965; *3 Women* 1977

Fortineau, Thierry *Your Beating Heart* 1991; *La Fille de l'Air* 1992; *L'Homme de Ma Vie* 1992

Fortune, John (1939–) *Pleasure at Her Majesty's* 1976; *Bloodbath at the House of Death* 1983; *Calendar Girls* 2003

Forwood, Anthony (1915–1988) *Meet Simon Cherry* 1949; *The Gambler and the Lady* 1952

Fosse, Bob *aka* **Fosse, Robert** (1927–) *The Affairs of Dobie Gillis* 1953; *Give a Girl a Break* 1953; *Kiss Me Kate* 1953; *My Sister Eileen* 1955; *Damn Yankees* 1958; *The Little Prince* 1974; *Thieves* 1977

Fossey, Brigitte (1946–) *Jeux Interdits* 1953; *The Happy Road* 1956; *The Wanderer* 1967; *Les Valseuses* 1974; *The Man Who Loved Women* 1977; *Quintet* 1979; *Enigma* 1982; *Imperative* 1982; *The Last Butterfly* 1990

Foster, Ami (1975–) *Troop Beverly Hills* 1989; *Danielle Steel's Changes* 1991

Foster, Barry (1931–2002) *Sea Fury* 1958; *Sea of Sand* 1958; *Surprise Package* 1960; *King and Country* 1964; *The Family Way* 1966; *Robbery* 1967; *Inspector Clouseau* 1968; *Twisted Nerve* 1968; *The Guru* 1969; *Ryan's Daughter* 1970; *Frenzy* 1972; *Sweeney!* 1976; *Heat and Dust* 1982; *The Whistle Blower* 1986; *King of the Wind* 1989

Foster, Ben (1980–) *Liberty Heights* 1999; *Get over It* 2001; *The Heart Is Deceitful above All Things* 2004; *Hostage* 2004; *The Punisher* 2004

Foster, Blake (1985–) *Turbo: a Power Rangers Adventure* 1997; *Kids World* 2001

Foster, Dianne (1928–) *The Quiet Woman* 1950; *Isn't Life Wonderful!* 1952; *The Lost Hours* 1952; *The Steel Key* 1953; *Bad for Each Other* 1954; *Drive a Crooked Road* 1954; *Three Hours to Kill* 1954; *The Kentuckian* 1955; *The Violent Men* 1955; *The Brothers Rico* 1957; *Night Passage* 1957; *The Deep Six* 1958; *Gideon's Day* 1958; *The Last Hurrah* 1958; *King of the Roaring 20s – the Story of Arnold Rothstein* 1961

Foster, Dudley (1925–1973) *Moon Zero Two* 1969; *Where's Jack?* 1969; *Dulcima* 1971

Foster, Gloria (1936–) *The Cool World* 1963; *Nothing but a Man* 1964; *The Angel Levine* 1970; *Man and Boy* 1971; *Leonard, Part 6* 1987; *The Matrix* 1999; *The Matrix Reloaded* 2002

Foster, Jodie (1962–) *Kansas City Bomber* 1972; *Napoleon and Samantha* 1972; *One Little Indian* 1973; *Tom Sawyer* 1973; *Alice Doesn't Live Here Anymore* 1974; *Bugsy Malone* 1976; *Echoes of a Summer* 1976; *Freaky Friday* 1976; *The Little Girl Who Lives Down the Lane* 1976; *Taxi Driver* 1976; *Candleshoe* 1977; *Carny* 1980; *Foxes* 1980; *O'Hara's Wife* 1982; *The Blood of Others* 1984; *The Hotel New Hampshire* 1984; *Mesmerized* 1984; *Five Corners* 1987; *Siesta* 1987; *The Accused* 1988; *Stealing Home* 1988; *Catchfire* 1989; *Little Man Tate* 1991; *Shadows and Fog* 1991; *The Silence of the Lambs* 1991; *Sommersby* 1993; *Maverick* 1994; *Nell* 1994; *Contact* 1997; *Anna and the King* 1999; *The Dangerous Lives of Altar Boys* 2001; *Panic Room* 2002; *A Very Long Engagement* 2004

Foster, Julia (1942–) *The Loneliness of the Long Distance Runner* 1962; *The Small World of Sammy Lee* 1963; *Two Left Feet* 1963; *The Bargee* 1964; *The System* 1964; *One Way Pendulum* 1965; *Alfie* 1966; *Half a Sixpence* 1967; *Simon, Simon* 1970; *Percy* 1971; *All Coppers Are...* 1972; *The Great McGonagall* 1974

Foster, Meg (1948–) *Adam at 6 AM* 1970; *Thumb Tripping* 1972; *A Different Story* 1978; *Carny* 1980; *Ticket to Heaven* 1981; *The Osterman Weekend* 1983; *The Emerald Forest* 1985; *Masters of the Universe* 1987; *They Live* 1988; *Leviathan* 1989; *Relentless* 1989; *Stepfather II* 1989; *Blind Fury* 1990; *Diplomatic Immunity* 1991; *Relentless 2: Dead On* 1991; *Best of the Best II* 1992; *Hidden Fears* 1993; *Oblivion* 1993; *Shrunken Heads* 1994; *Space Marines* 1996

Foster, Norman (1900–1976) *It Pays to Advertise* 1931; *Skyscraper Souls* 1932; *Pilgrimage* 1933; *State Fair* 1933; *Fatal Lady* 1936

Foster, Phil (1914–1985) *Conquest of Space* 1955; *Bang the Drum Slowly* 1973

Foster, Phoebe (1896–1975) *Tarnished Lady* 1931; *Our Betters* 1933; *Anna Karenina* 1935

Foster, Preston *aka* **Foster, Preston S** (1900–1970) *Doctor X* 1932; *I Am a Fugitive from a Chain Gang* 1932; *Two Seconds* 1932; *Ladies They Talk About* 1933; *Annie Oakley* 1935; *The Arizonian* 1935; *The Informer* 1935; *The Last Days of Pompeii* 1935; *Strangers All* 1935; *Love before Breakfast* 1936; *The Plough and the Stars* 1936; *First Lady* 1937; *Sea Devils* 1937; *The Storm* 1938; *Submarine Patrol* 1938; *Geronimo* 1939; *North West Mounted Police* 1940; *The Roundup* 1941; *Unfinished Business* 1941; *A Gentleman after Dark* 1942; *Guadalcanal Diary* 1943; *My Friend Flicka* 1943; *The Bermuda Mystery* 1944; *Thunderhead – Son of Flicka* 1945; *The Valley of Decision* 1945; *The Harvey Girls* 1946; *Ramrod* 1947; *I Shot Jesse James* 1949; *The Big Night* 1951; *Tomahawk* 1951; *Kansas City Confidential* 1952; *I, the Jury* 1953; *Law and Order* 1953; *The Time Travelers* 1964; *Chubasco* 1967

Foster, Susanna (1924–) *Phantom of the Opera* 1943; *Detour* 1992

Fouldes, Angela *The Small Voice* 1948; *The Secret People* 1951

Foulger, Byron (1899–1968) *Arizona* 1940; *Circumstantial Evidence* 1945; *The Magnetic Monster* 1953; *The River's Edge* 1957

Foulk, Robert (1908–1989) *The 49th Man* 1953; *Last of the Badmen* 1957

Foundas, George (1924–) *Stella* 1955; *Never on Sunday* 1960; *Zorba the Greek* 1964

Fourçade, Christian *Little Boy Lost* 1953; *The Captain* 1960

Fowlds, Derek *aka* **Fowldes, Derek** (1937–) *We Joined the Navy* 1962; *East of Sudan* 1964; *Frankenstein Created Woman* 1966; *Hotel Paradiso* 1966; *The Smashing Bird I Used to Know* 1969; *Tower of Evil* 1972; *Over the Hill* 1992

Fowler, Harry (1926–) *Went the Day Well?* 1942; *Hue and Cry* 1947; *I Believe in You* 1952; *Conflict of Wings* 1953; *A Day to Remember* 1953; *Up to His Neck* 1954; *The Blue Peter* 1955; *Stock Car* 1955; *Behind the Headlines* 1956; *Fire Maidens from Outer Space* 1956; *Booby Trap* 1957; *Clash by Night* 1963; *Sir Henry at Rawlinson End* 1980

Fowley, Douglas *aka* **Fowley, Douglas V** (1911–1998) *Big Brown Eyes* 1936; *Charlie Chan on Broadway* 1937; *On the Avenue* 1937; *Mr Moto's Gamble* 1938; *Charlie Chan at Treasure Island* 1939; *Jitterbugs* 1943; *Desperate* 1947; *Scared to Death* 1947; *Mighty Joe Young* 1949; *Search for Danger* 1949; *Armored Car Robbery* 1950; *Bunco Squad* 1950; *Mrs O'Malley and Mr Malone* 1950; *Rider from Tucson* 1950; *Tarzan's Peril* 1951; *Singin' in the Rain* 1952; *Cat-women of the Moon* 1953; *The Naked Jungle* 1953; *Bandido* 1956; *A Gift for Heidi* 1958; *From Noon till Three* 1976

Fox, Bernard (1927–) *One of Our Spies Is Missing* 1966; *The Private Eyes* 1980

Fox, Colin *Food of the Gods II* 1989; *Beautiful Dreamers* 1990; *Scanners III: the Takeover* 1992

Fox, David *Ordinary Magic* 1993; *When Night Is Falling* 1995; *The Saddest Music in the World* 2003

Fox, Edward (1937–) *The Mind Benders* 1963; *The Frozen Dead* 1966; *I'll Never Forget What's 'Is Name* 1967; *The Jokers* 1967; *The Naked Runner* 1967; *Skullduggery* 1969; *The Go-Between* 1971; *The Day of the*

Jackal 1973; A Doll's House 1973; Galileo 1974; A Bridge Too Far 1977; The Duellists 1977; Soldier of Orange 1977; The Squeeze 1977; The Big Sleep 1978; Force 10 from Navarone 1978; The Cat and the Canary 1979; The Mirror Crack'd 1980; Gandhi 1982; The Dresser 1983; Never Say Never Again 1983; The Bounty 1984; The Shooting Party 1984; Wild Geese II 1985; Return from the River Kwai 1988; Robin Hood 1990; A Feast at Midnight 1994; A Month by the Lake 1994; Prince Valiant 1997; The Importance of Being Earnest 2002; Nicholas Nickleby 2002; Stage Beauty 2004

Fox, Huckleberry (1975–) Terms of Endearment 1983; American Dreamer 1984; Misunderstood 1984

Fox, James aka **Fox, William** (1939–) The Magnet 1950; The Lavender Hill Mob 1951; The Servant 1963; Tamahine 1963; King Rat 1965; Those Magnificent Men in Their Flying Machines 1965; The Chase 1966; Arabella 1967; Thoroughly Modern Millie 1967; Duffy 1968; Isadora 1968; Performance 1970; Runners 1983; Greystoke: the Legend of Tarzan, Lord of the Apes 1984; A Passage to India 1984; Absolute Beginners 1986; Comrades: a Lanternist's Account of the Tolpuddle Martyrs and What Became of Them 1986; The Whistle Blower 1986; High Season 1987; Farewell to the King 1988; The Mighty Quinn 1989; The Russia House 1990; Afraid of the Dark 1991; As You Like It 1992; Hostage 1992; Patriot Games 1992; The Remains of the Day 1993; Circle of Passion 1996; Anna Karenina 1997; Jinnah 1998; Shadow Run 1998; Up at the Villa 1998; Mickey Blue Eyes 1999; The Golden Bowl 2000; Sexy Beast 2000; The Mystic Masseur 2001; The Prince & Me 2004

Fox, Jorja aka **Fox, Jorjan** (1968–) The Kill-Off 1989; Velocity Trap 1997

Fox, Kerry (1966–) An Angel at My Table 1990; The Last Days of Chez Nous 1992; Friends 1993; Country Life 1994; Shallow Grave 1994; The Hanging Garden 1997; Welcome to Sarajevo 1997; The Sound of One Hand Clapping 1998; The Wisdom of Crocodiles 1998; The Darkest Light 1999; Fanny & Elvis 1999; To Walk with Lions 1999; Intimacy 2000; The Point Men 2000; Black and White 2002

Fox, Laurence The Hole 2001; Deathwatch 2002

Fox, Matthew (1966–) My Boyfriend's Back 1993; Behind the Mask 1999

Fox, Michael (1921–1996) Last Train from Bombay 1952; The Magnetic Monster 1953; Top Secret Affair 1957; War of the Satellites 1958

Fox, Michael J (1961–) Midnight Madness 1980; Class of 1984 1982; Back to the Future 1985; Teen Wolf 1985; Light of Day 1987; The Secret of My Success 1987; Bright Lights, Big City 1988; Back to the Future Part II 1989; Casualties of War 1989; Back to the Future Part III 1990; Doc Hollywood 1991; The Hard Way 1991; For Love or Money 1993; Homeward Bound: the Incredible Journey 1993; Life with Mikey 1993; Where the Rivers Flow North 1993; Greedy 1994; The American President 1995; Blue in the Face 1995; Coldblooded 1995; The Frighteners 1996; Homeward Bound II: Lost in San Francisco 1996; Mars Attacks! 1996; Stuart Little 1999; Atlantis: the Lost Empire 2001; Stuart Little 2 2002

Fox, Sidney (1910–1942) Bad Sister 1931; Six Cylinder Love 1931; Don Quixote 1932; Murders in the Rue Morgue 1932; Midnight 1934

Fox, Virginia (1902–1982) Neighbors 1920; The Paleface 1921

Fox, Vivica A (1964–) Independence Day 1996; Set It Off 1996; Booty Call 1997; Soul Food 1997; Why Do Fools Fall in Love? 1998; Idle Hands 1999; Two Can Play That Game 2001; Boat Trip 2002; Juwanna Mann 2002; Kill Bill Vol 1 2003; Ella Enchanted 2004

Foxe, Earle (1891–1973) Four Sons 1928; Hangman's House 1928; Dance, Fools, Dance 1931

Foxworth, Robert (1941–) Invisible Strangler 1976; Treasure of Matecumbe 1976; Airport '77 1977; Damien – Omen II 1978; Prophecy 1979; The Black Marble 1980; Beyond the Stars 1988

Foxx, Jamie (1967–) The Truth about Cats and Dogs 1996; Booty Call 1997; The Players Club 1998; Any Given Sunday 1999; Held Up 1999; Ali 2001; Breakin' All the Rules 2004; Collateral 2004; Ray 2004; Redemption 2004

Foxx, Redd (1922–1991) Cotton Comes to Harlem 1970; Norman... Is That You? 1976; Harlem Nights 1989

Foy Jr, Eddie (1905–1983) The Case of the Black Parrot 1941; Dixie 1943; And the Angels Sing 1944; The Farmer Takes a Wife 1953; Lucky Me 1954; Seven Little Foys 1955; The Pajama Game 1957; Bells Are Ringing 1960; Gidget Goes Hawaiian 1961; 30 Is a Dangerous Age, Cynthia 1968

Foyt, Victoria Babyfever 1994; Last Summer in the Hamptons 1995; Déjà Vu 1997

Frain, James (1969–) Loch Ness 1994; Nothing Personal 1995; Daniel Defoe's Robinson Crusoe 1996; Rasputin 1996; Vigo: Passion for Life 1997; Hilary and Jackie 1998; What Rats Won't Do 1998; Sunshine 1999; Deception 2000; Where the Heart Is 2000; The Count of Monte Cristo 2001; Path to War 2002

Frakes, Jonathan (1952–) Star Trek: Generations 1994; Star Trek: First Contact 1996; Star Trek: Insurrection 1998; Star Trek: Nemesis 2002

Frame, Grazina What a Crazy World 1963; Every Day's a Holiday 1964

France, C V (1868–1949) The Skin Game 1931; Lord Edgware Dies 1934; Scrooge 1935; Victoria the Great 1937; If I Were King 1938; Strange Boarders 1938; A Yank at Oxford 1938; Cheer Boys Cheer 1939; Ten Days in Paris 1939; Went the Day Well? 1942

Francen, Victor (1888–1977) J'Accuse 1938; The End of the Day 1939; Hold Back the Dawn 1941; Ten Gentlemen from West Point 1942; The Tuttles of Tahiti 1942; The Conspirators 1944; The Desert Song 1944; In Our Time 1944; Passage to Marseille 1944; Confidential Agent 1945; San Antonio 1945; The Beast with Five Fingers 1946; Night and Day 1946; Adventures of Captain Fabian 1951; Hell and High Water 1954; Bedevilled 1955; Fanny 1961

Francey, Micheline (1919–1969) The Raven 1943; A Cage of Nightingales 1945

Franchi, Franco (1928–1992) Dr Goldfoot and the Girl Bombs 1966; War Italian Style 1966; Kaos 1984

Francine, Francis Flaming Creatures 1963; Lonesome Cowboys 1968

Franciosa, Anthony aka **Franciosa, Tony** (1928–) A Face in the Crowd 1957; A Hatful of Rain 1957; This Could Be the Night 1957; Wild Is the Wind 1957; The Long Hot Summer 1958; Career 1959; The Naked Maja 1959; The Story on Page One 1959; Go Naked in the World 1961; Period of Adjustment 1962; The Pleasure Seekers 1964; Rio Conchos 1964; Assault on a Queen 1966; A Man Could Get Killed 1966; The Swinger 1966; Fathom 1967; The Sweet Ride 1967; In Enemy Country 1968; A Man Called Gannon 1969; Across 110th Street 1972; Ghost in the Noonday Sun 1973; The Drowning Pool 1975; Firepower 1979; The World Is Full of Married Men 1979; Death Wish II 1981; Tenebrae 1982; Backstreet Dreams 1990; Double Threat 1992; City Hall 1996

Francis, Alec B aka **Francis, Alec** (1867–1934) Camille 1927; Feet First 1930; Outward Bound 1930; Mata Hari 1931

Francis, Anne aka **Francis, Anne Lloyd** (1930–) Dreamboat 1952; Lydia Bailey 1952; A Lion Is in the Streets 1953; The Rocket Man 1954; Rogue Cop 1954; Susan Slept Here 1954; Bad Day at Black Rock 1955; The Blackboard Jungle 1955; The Scarlet Coat 1955; Forbidden Planet 1956; Don't Go Near the Water 1957; The Hired Gun 1957; The Crowded Sky 1960; Girl of the Night 1960; Brainstorm 1965; The Satan Bug 1965; Funny Girl 1968; Hook, Line and Sinker 1969; Impasse 1969; The Love God? 1969; More Dead than Alive 1969; Pancho Villa 1971; Born Again 1978; Return 1985; Little Vegas 1990

Francis, Arlene (1908–2001) All My Sons 1948; One, Two, Three 1961; The Thrill of It All 1963

Francis, Connie (1938–) Where the Boys Are 1960; Follow the Boys 1963; When the Boys Meet the Girls 1965

Francis, Derek (1923–1984) The Hi-Jackers 1963; The Tomb of Ligeia 1964; Press for Time 1966; What's Good for the Goose 1969

Francis, Dick (1889–1949) Dreaming 1944; Here Comes the Sun 1945

Francis, Jan (1951–) Dracula 1979; Champions 1983

Francis, Kay (1899–1968) The Marriage Playground 1929; Raffles 1930; The Virtuous Sin 1930; Girls about Town 1931; Guilty Hands 1931; Ladies' Man 1931; Cynara 1932; Jewel Robbery 1932; One Way Passage 1932; Trouble in Paradise 1932; British Agent 1934; Mandalay 1934; Wonder Bar 1934; I Found Stella Parish 1935; The White Angel 1936; Another Dawn 1937; Confession 1937; First Lady 1937; In Name Only 1939; King of the Underworld 1939; It's a Date 1940; When the Daltons Rode 1940; Charley's Aunt 1941; The Feminine Touch 1941; Always in My Heart 1942

Francis, Noel (1906–1959) Bachelor Apartment 1931; Blonde Crazy 1931; Smart Money 1931; I Am a Fugitive from a Chain Gang 1932

Francis, Raymond Carrington VC 1954; Double Cross 1955

Francis, Robert (1930–1955) The Caine Mutiny 1954; They Rode West 1954; The Long Gray Line 1955

Franciscus, James (1934–1991) The Outsider 1961; Miracle of the White Stallions 1963; Youngblood Hawke 1964; Beneath the Planet of the Apes 1969; Marooned 1969; The Valley of Gwangi 1969; Hell Boats 1970; Cat o'Nine Tails 1971; Jonathan Livingston Seagull 1973; The Amazing Dobermans 1976; Good Guys Wear Black 1977; The Greek Tycoon 1978; Killer Fish 1978; City on Fire 1979; When Time Ran Out 1980; Butterfly 1982

Francks, Don (1932–) Finian's Rainbow 1968; Terminal Choice 1983

Franco, James (1978–) James Dean 2001; City by the Sea 2002; Sonny 2002; Spider-Man 2002; The Company 2003; Spider-Man 2 2004

François, Emilie Sense and Sensibility 1995; Paws 1997

François, Jacques (1920–2003) South of Algiers 1952; To Paris with Love 1954; Les Grandes Manoeuvres 1955; The Gendarme Wore Skirts 1982; North Star 1996

Frank, Ben (1934–1990) Death Wish II 1981; Hollywood Vice Squad 1986

Frank, Gary (1905–1975) Enemy Territory 1987; Untamed Love 1994; Death in Small Doses 1995

Frank, Horst (1929–1999) Thou Shalt Not Kill 1961; Dead Run 1967; The Big Showdown 1972; Cold Blood 1975; Death in the Sun 1975

Frank, Jason David (1973–) Mighty Morphin Power Rangers: the Movie 1995; Turbo: a Power Rangers Adventure 1997

Frankel, Mark (1962–1996) Leon the Pig Farmer 1992; Solitaire for 2 1994; Roseanna's Grave 1996

Franken, Steve (1932–) Which Way to the Front? 1970; Avalanche 1978

Frankeur, Paul (1905–1975) Jour de Fête 1947; Nous Sommes Tous des Assassins 1952; Honour among Thieves 1954; Nana 1955; A Monkey in Winter 1962; The Theft of the Mona Lisa 1965; The Milky Way 1968; The Discreet Charm of the Bourgeoisie 1972

Frankfather, William (1944–1998) Alamo Bay 1985; Cool World 1992

Frankham, David aka **Frankham, Dave** (1926–) Return of the Fly 1959; One Hundred and One Dalmatians 1960; Master of the World 1961

Franklin, Aretha (1942–) The Blues Brothers 1980; Blues Brothers 2000 1998

Franklin, Diane Amityville II: the Possession 1982; Better Off Dead 1985; TerrorVision 1986

Franklin, Pamela (1949–) The Innocents 1961; The Lion 1962; Flipper's New Adventure 1964; The Third Secret 1964; A Tiger Walks 1964; The Nanny 1965; Our Mother's House 1967; The Night of the Following Day 1968; The Prime of Miss Jean Brodie 1969; Sinful Davey 1969; And Soon the Darkness 1970; Ace Eli and Rodger of the Skies 1973; The Legend of Hell House 1973; The Food of the Gods 1975

Franklyn, Leo (1897–1975) The Night We Dropped a Clanger 1959; And the Same to You 1960; The Night We Got the Bird 1960

Franklyn, William (1926–) The Flesh Is Weak 1957; Quatermass II 1957; That Woman Opposite 1957; Pit of Darkness 1961; The Intelligence Men 1965; Cul-de-Sac 1966; Ooh... You Are Awful 1972; The Satanic Rites of Dracula 1973; Nutcracker 1982

Franks, Chloe (1959–) Who Slew Auntie Roo? 1971; A Little Night Music 1977

Franky G The Italian Job 2003; Wonderland 2003

Franz, Arthur (1920–) Abbott and Costello Meet the Invisible Man 1951; Flight to Mars 1951; Eight Iron Men 1952; The Member of the Wedding 1952; The Sniper 1952; The Eddie Cantor Story 1953; Invaders from Mars 1953; Bad for Each Other 1954; Battle Taxi 1955; Beyond a Reasonable Doubt 1956; The Devil's Hairpin 1957; Hellcats of the Navy 1957; The Unholy Wife 1957; The Flame Barrier 1958; Monster on the Campus 1958; Woman Obsessed 1959; The Atomic Submarine 1960; The Human Factor 1975; That Championship Season 1982

Franz, Dennis (1944–) Dressed to Kill 1980; Blow Out 1981; Psycho II 1983; Body Double 1984; A Fine Mess 1986; The Package 1989; Die Hard 2: Die Harder 1990; American Buffalo 1995; City of Angels 1998

Franz, Eduard (1902–1983) Hollow Triumph 1948; Outpost in Morocco 1949; Wake of the Red Witch 1949; Whirlpool 1949; The Magnificent Yankee 1950; Everything I Have Is Yours 1952; The Jazz Singer 1952; Dream Wife 1953; Latin Lovers 1953; Beachhead 1954; Broken Lance 1954; Sign of the Pagan 1954; Lady Godiva 1955; White Feather 1955; The Burning Hills 1956; A Certain Smile 1958; The Last of the Fast Guns 1958; Beauty and the Beast 1962

Franz, Elizabeth (1941–) Jacknife 1988; Christmas with the Kranks 2004

Frappat, Francis Noir et Blanc 1986; Erreur de jeunesse 1989; Requiem 1998

Fraser, Bill (1908–1987) The Captain's Paradise 1953; Orders Are Orders 1954; The Man Who Liked Funerals 1959; I've Gotta Horse 1965; Joey Boy 1965; Masquerade 1965; The Best House in London 1968; Captain Nemo and the Underwater City 1969; Up Pompeii 1971; Up the Chastity Belt 1971; That's Your Funeral 1972; Up the Front 1972; The Amorous Milkman 1974

Fraser, Brendan (1968–) California Man 1992; School Ties 1992; Twenty Bucks 1993; Younger and Younger 1993; Airheads 1994; The Scout 1994; With Honors 1994; The Passion of Darkly Noon 1995; Mrs Winterbourne 1996; George of the Jungle 1997; Blast from the Past 1998; Gods and Monsters 1998; Dudley Do-Right 1999; The Mummy 1999; Bedazzled 2000; Monkeybone 2000; The Mummy Returns 2001; The Quiet American 2002; Crash 2004; Looney Tunes: Back in Action 2004

Fraser, Brent The Chocolate War 1988; Wild Orchid 2: Two Shades of Blue 1992

Fraser, David Teenage Mutant Ninja Turtles III 1992; Airborne 1997

Fraser, Duncan Watchers 1988; The Reflecting Skin 1990; Needful Things 1993; Alaska 1996; Unforgettable 1996

Fraser, Elisabeth (1920–2005) One Foot in Heaven 1941; So Big 1953; Young at Heart 1955; The Tunnel of Love 1958; Ask Any Girl 1959; Sammy, the Way Out Seal 1962; Two for the Seesaw 1962; A Patch of Blue 1965

Fraser, Helen (1942–) Billy Liar 1963; The Uncle 1964; Something to Hide 1971

Fraser, Hugh The Draughtsman's Contract 1982; 101 Dalmatians 1996

Fraser, John (1931–) Valley of Song 1953; The Dam Busters 1954; Touch and Go 1955; The Good Companions 1956; The Wind Cannot Read 1958; The Trials of Oscar Wilde 1960; Tunes of Glory 1960; El Cid 1961; Fury at Smugglers Bay 1961; Waltz of the Toreadors 1962; Tamahine 1963; Repulsion 1965; A Study in Terror 1965; Doctor in Clover 1966; Isadora 1968; Schizo 1976

Fraser, Laura (1976–) Small Faces 1995; Cousin Bette 1997; Left Luggage 1997; Divorcing Jack 1998; The Match 1999; Titus 1999; Virtual Sexuality 1999; Whatever Happened to Harold Smith? 1999; Kevin & Perry Go Large 2000; A Knight's Tale 2001; Devil's Gate 2002; 16 Years of Alcohol 2003

Fraser, Liz (1933–) Desert Mice 1959; I'm All Right Jack 1959; The Night We Dropped a Clanger 1959; Carry On Regardless 1960; Doctor in Love 1960; The Night We Got the Bird 1960; The Rebel 1960; Two Way Stretch 1960; Double Bunk 1961; The Painted Smile 1961; A Pair of Briefs 1961; Raising the Wind 1961; Watch It, Sailor! 1961; The Amorous Prawn 1962; Carry On Cruising 1962; Live Now – Pay Later 1962; Carry On Cabby 1963; The Americanization of Emily 1964; Every Day's a Holiday 1964; Up the Junction 1967; Dad's Army 1971; Adventures of a Taxi Driver 1975; Carry On Behind 1975; Confessions of a Driving Instructor 1976; Under the Doctor 1976; Adventures of a Private Eye

1977; *Rosie Dixon: Night Nurse* 1978; *Chicago Joe and the Showgirl* 1989

Fraser, Richard (1913–1971) *A Yank in the RAF* 1941; *The Picture of Dorian Gray* 1945; *Bedlam* 1946

Fraser, Ronald (1930–1997) *The Long and the Short and the Tall* 1960; *The Best of Enemies* 1961; *The Pot Carriers* 1962; *The Punch and Judy Man* 1962; *Crooks in Cloisters* 1963; *Girl in the Headlines* 1963; *Private Potter* 1963; *The Beauty Jungle* 1964; *Daylight Robbery* 1964; *The Flight of the Phoenix* 1965; *Fathom* 1967; *The Whisperers* 1967; *The Killing of Sister George* 1968; *Sebastian* 1968; *Sinful Davey* 1969; *The Rise and Rise of Michael Rimmer* 1970; *Too Late the Hero* 1970; *The Magnificent Seven Deadly Sins* 1971; *Ooh... You Are Awful* 1972; *Rentadick* 1972; *Paper Tiger* 1974; *Swallows and Amazons* 1974; *Come Play with Me* 1977; *Hardcore* 1977; *Tangier* 1982; *Let Him Have It* 1991; *The Mystery of Edwin Drood* 1993

Fraser, Sally *It's a Dog's Life* 1955; *It Conquered the World* 1956; *Roadracers* 1958; *War of the Colossal Beast* 1958

Fraser, Shelagh (1922–2000) *The History of Mr Polly* 1948; *Raising a Riot* 1955

Fratkin, Stuart (1963–) *Ski School* 1991; *Prehysteria!* 1993

Frawley, James (1937–) *Ladybug, Ladybug* 1963; *The Troublemaker* 1964

Frawley, John *The Devil's Playground* 1976; *Dallas Doll* 1994

Frawley, William (1887–1966) *Bolero* 1934; *The Lemon Drop Kid* 1934; *Desire* 1936; *The General Died at Dawn* 1936; *The Princess Comes Across* 1936; *Strike Me Pink* 1936; *Something to Sing About* 1937; *Mad about Music* 1938; *The Adventures of Huckleberry Finn* 1939; *Rose of Washington Square* 1939; *Rhythm on the River* 1940; *The Bride Came COD* 1941; *Footsteps in the Dark* 1941; *Gentleman Jim* 1942; *Roxie Hart* 1942; *Whistling in Brooklyn* 1943; *The Fighting Seabees* 1944; *Flame of the Barbary Coast* 1945; *I Wonder Who's Kissing Her Now* 1947; *Miracle on 34th Street* 1947; *Mother Wore Tights* 1947; *The Babe Ruth Story* 1948; *The Girl from Manhattan* 1948; *Abbott and Costello Meet the Invisible Man* 1951; *The Lemon Drop Kid* 1951; *Rhubarb* 1951; *Rancho Notorious* 1952; *Safe at Home* 1962

Frazee, Jane (1918–1985) *Buck Privates* 1941; *Hellzapoppin'* 1941; *Rosie the Riveter* 1944; *Springtime in the Sierras* 1947; *Under California Stars* 1948

Frazer, Dan *Lilies of the Field* 1963; *Cleopatra Jones* 1973; *The Super Cops* 1973

Frazer, Robert (1891–1944) *White Zombie* 1932; *The Trail Beyond* 1934

Frazer, Rupert *The Shooting Party* 1984; *The Girl in a Swing* 1988

Frazier, Ron *Rollover* 1981; *The Road Home* 1989; *Shadow Makers* 1989

Frazier, Sheila (1948–) *Superfly* 1972; *The Super Cops* 1973; *Three the Hard Way* 1974

Frechette, Peter (1956–) *Grease 2* 1982; *No Small Affair* 1984; *The Unholy* 1988; *Empire City* 1991

Fréchette, Richard *The Confessional* 1995; *Nô* 1998

Fred, Gunnel (1955–) *Ake and His World* 1984; *Saraband* 2003

Frederici, Blanche (1878–1933) *Sadie Thompson* 1928; *The Trespasser* 1929; *Billy the Kid* 1930; *Mata Hari* 1931; *Night Nurse* 1931; *A Farewell to Arms* 1932; *If I Had a Million* 1932; *The Barbarian* 1933; *Secrets* 1933; *It Happened One Night* 1934

Frederick, Lynne (1954–1994) *No Blade of Grass* 1970; *Nicholas and Alexandra* 1971; *Vampire Circus* 1971; *The Amazing Mr Blunden* 1972; *Henry VIII and His Six Wives* 1972; *Phase IV* 1973; *Schizo* 1976; *Voyage of the Damned* 1976; *The Prisoner of Zenda* 1979

Frederick, Pauline (1883–1938) *This Modern Age* 1931; *Thank You, Mr Moto* 1937

Frederick, Vicki (1954–) *The California Dolls* 1981; *A Chorus Line* 1985; *Scissors* 1991

Freed, Alan (1922–1965) *Don't Knock the Rock* 1956; *Rock around the Clock* 1956; *Go, Johnny, Go!* 1959

Freed, Bert (1919–1994) *The Company She Keeps* 1950; *Where the Sidewalk Ends* 1950; *Detective Story* 1951; *Red Mountain* 1951; *Men of the Fighting Lady* 1954; *The Gazebo* 1959; *Billy Jack* 1971; *Evel Knievel* 1971

Freeman Jr, Al (1934–) *Dutchman* 1966; *The Lost Man* 1969; *Seven Hours to Judgment* 1988; *Malcolm X* 1992; *Down in the Delta* 1997

Freeman, Alan (1927–) *Dr Terror's House of Horrors* 1964; *Sebastian* 1968

Freeman, Howard (1899–1967) *Hitler's Madman* 1943; *Margin for Error* 1943; *Slightly Dangerous* 1943; *Once upon a Time* 1944; *Abilene Town* 1945; *The Blue Dahlia* 1946; *The Long Night* 1947; *Letter from an Unknown Woman* 1948; *Perfect Strangers* 1950; *Double Dynamite* 1951; *Million Dollar Mermaid* 1952

Freeman, J E *Hard Traveling* 1985; *Miller's Crossing* 1990; *Dream with the Fishes* 1996

Freeman, Joan (1941–) *Panic in Year Zero* 1962; *Tower of London* 1962; *The Three Stooges Go around the World in a Daze* 1963; *Roustabout* 1964; *The Rounders* 1965; *The Fastest Guitar Alive* 1966; *The Reluctant Astronaut* 1967

Freeman, K Todd *The End of Violence* 1997; *Grosse Pointe Blank* 1997

Freeman, Kathleen (1919–2001) *Love Is Better Than Ever* 1951; *The Fly* 1958; *The Ladies' Man* 1961; *Madison Avenue* 1962; *The Nutty Professor* 1963; *The Disorderly Orderly* 1964; *The Rounders* 1965; *Three on a Couch* 1966; *Your Three Minutes Are Up* 1973; *The Blues Brothers* 1980; *Nickel & Dime* 1991; *Reckless Kelly* 1993; *Naked Gun $33\frac{1}{3}$: the Final Insult* 1994; *...At First Sight* 1995; *Shrek* 2001

Freeman, Martin (1971–) *Ali G indahouse* 2002; *The Hitchhiker's Guide to the Galaxy* 2005

Freeman, Mona (1926–) *Till We Meet Again* 1944; *Together Again* 1944; *Junior Miss* 1945; *Black Beauty* 1946; *Dear Ruth* 1947; *Mother Wore Tights* 1947; *Isn't It Romantic* 1948; *Dear Wife* 1949; *The Heiress* 1949; *Streets of Laredo* 1949; *Branded* 1950; *Copper Canyon* 1950; *I Was a Shoplifter* 1950; *Darling, How Could You!* 1951; *Flesh and Fury* 1952; *Jumping Jacks* 1952; *Thunderbirds* 1952; *Angel Face* 1953; *Battle Cry* 1955; *The Road to Denver* 1955; *Dragoon Wells Massacre* 1957; *The World Was His Jury* 1957

Freeman, Morgan (1937–) *Who Says I Can't Ride a Rainbow?* 1971; *Brubaker* 1980; *Eyewitness* 1981; *Harry and Son* 1984; *Teachers* 1984; *Marie: a True Story* 1985; *That Was Then... This Is Now* 1985; *Resting Place* 1986; *Street Smart* 1987; *Clean and Sober* 1988; *Driving Miss Daisy* 1989; *Glory* 1989; *Johnny Handsome* 1989; *Lean on Me* 1989; *The Bonfire of the Vanities* 1990; *The Power of One* 1991; *Robin Hood: Prince of Thieves* 1991; *Unforgiven* 1992; *The Shawshank Redemption* 1994; *Moll Flanders* 1995; *Outbreak* 1995; *Se7en* 1995; *Chain Reaction* 1996; *The Long Way Home* 1996; *Amistad* 1997; *Hard Rain* 1997; *Kiss the Girls* 1997; *Deep Impact* 1998; *Nurse Betty* 2000; *Under Suspicion* 2000; *Along Came a Spider* 2001; *High Crimes* 2002; *Levity* 2002; *The Sum of All Fears* 2002; *Bruce Almighty* 2003; *Dreamcatcher* 2003; *The Big Bounce* 2004; *Million Dollar Baby* 2004; *Batman Begins* 2005; *Unleashed* 2005

Freeman, Paul (1943–) *The Dogs of War* 1980; *Raiders of the Lost Ark* 1981; *An Unsuitable Job for a Woman* 1981; *The Sender* 1982; *Shanghai Surprise* 1986; *A World Apart* 1987; *Prisoner of Rio* 1988; *Without a Clue* 1988; *The Last Island* 1990; *May Wine* 1990; *Eminent Domain* 1991; *Aces: Iron Eagle III* 1992; *Just like a Woman* 1992; *Mighty Morphin Power Rangers: the Movie* 1995; *Double Team* 1997; *The Devil's Arithmetic* 1999

Frees, Paul (1920–1986) *Riot in Cell Block 11* 1954; *Suddenly* 1954; *Francis in the Haunted House* 1956; *Space Master X 7* 1958; *The Snow Queen* 1959; *Gay Purr-ee* 1962

Frégis, Lucien *Monsieur Hulot's Holiday* 1953; *Mon Oncle* 1958

Freindlikh, Alisa (1934–) *Agony* 1975; *Stalker* 1979; *Katia Ismailova* 1994

Freiss, Stéphane (1960–) *Vagabond* 1985; *The King's Whore* 1990; *Betty Fisher and Other Stories* 2001; *Crime Spree* 2002; *Monsieur N* 2003; *5x2* 2004

Frémont, Thierry *Merci la Vie* 1991; *Femme Fatale* 2002

French, Bruce *Pipe Dreams* 1976; *Black Eagle* 1988

French, Dawn (1957–) *The Supergrass* 1985; *Eat the Rich* 1987; *The Adventures of Pinocchio* 1996; *Maybe Baby* 1999; *Milk* 1999

French, Harold (1897–1997) *When London Sleeps* 1932; *A Fire Has Been Arranged* 1935

French, Leslie (1904–1999) *Orders to Kill* 1958; *The Singer Not the Song* 1960; *The Leopard* 1962; *More than a Miracle* 1967

French, Valerie (1931–1990) *Jubal* 1956; *Secret of Treasure Mountain* 1956; *Decision at Sundown* 1957; *The Garment Jungle* 1957; *The 27th Day* 1957; *Shalako* 1968

French, Victor (1934–1989) *Charro!* 1969; *Rio Lobo* 1970; *Chato's Land* 1971; *Wild Rovers* 1971; *The Other* 1972; *Touchdown* 1981

Fresnay, Pierre (1897–1975) *Marius* 1931; *Fanny* 1932; *The Man Who Knew Too Much* 1934; *Königsmark* 1935; *César* 1936; *Mademoiselle Docteur* 1936; *La Grande Illusion* 1937; *The Raven* 1943; *Monsieur Vincent* 1947; *Dieu A Besoin des Hommes* 1950; *Le Défroqué* 1953

Fresson, Bernard (1931–2002) *Hiroshima, Mon Amour* 1959; *Je T'Aime, Je T'Aime* 1968; *The Lady in the Car with Glasses and a Gun* 1970; *French Connection II* 1975; *The Tenant* 1976; *To Each His Own Hell* 1977; *Right Bank, Left Bank* 1984; *Street of No Return* 1989; *Place Vendôme* 1998

Frewer, Matt (1958–) *Cannonball Fever* 1989; *Far from Home* 1989; *Honey, I Shrunk the Kids* 1989; *Short Time* 1990; *The Taking of Beverly Hills* 1991; *The Positively True Adventures of the Alleged Texas Cheerleader-Murdering Mom* 1993; *Lawnmower Man 2: Beyond Cyberspace* 1995; *National Lampoon's Senior Trip* 1995; *Breast Men* 1997; *A Home at the End of the World* 2004

Frey, Barbara *Love at Twenty* 1962; *Kill and Pray* 1967

Frey, Leonard (1938–1988) *The Magic Christian* 1969; *The Boys in the Band* 1970; *Fiddler on the Roof* 1971; *Tattoo* 1980; *Where the Buffalo Roam* 1980

Frey, Nathaniel (1913–1970) *Kiss Them for Me* 1957; *Damn Yankees* 1958; *What's So Bad About Feeling Good?* 1968

Frey, Sami (1937–) *La Vérité* 1960; *Cleo from 5 to 7* 1961; *Thérèse Desqueyroux* 1962; *Bande à Part* 1964; *Sink or Swim* 1971; *César and Rosalie* 1972; *Pourquoi Pas!* 1977; *Ecoute Voir...* 1978; *The Little Drummer Girl* 1984; *Black Widow* 1987; *D'Artagnan's Daughter* 1994; *Traps* 1994

Fricker, Brenda (1944–) *My Left Foot* 1989; *The Field* 1990; *Utz* 1992; *Deadly Advice* 1993; *So I Married an Axe Murderer* 1993; *Angels in the Outfield* 1994; *A Man of No Importance* 1994; *Moll Flanders* 1995; *Swann* 1996; *A Time to Kill* 1996; *Masterminds* 1997; *Painted Angels* 1997; *Resurrection Man* 1997; *Resurrection* 1999; *The War Bride* 2001; *Veronica Guerin* 2003; *Inside I'm Dancing* 2004; *Trauma* 2004

Frid, Jonathan (1924–) *House of Dark Shadows* 1970; *Seizure* 1974

Fridh, Gertrud (1921–1984) *A Ship to India* 1947; *The Magician* 1958; *The Devil's Eye* 1960

Friedman, Peter *You Better Watch Out* 1980; *The Seventh Sign* 1988; *Single White Female* 1992; *Blink* 1994; *[Safe]* 1995

Friedman, Shraga (1923–1970) *Sallah* 1964; *Bloomfield* 1969

Friedrich, John *Almost Summer* 1977; *The Wanderers* 1979; *A Small Circle of Friends* 1980

Friel, Anna (1976–) *The Land Girls* 1997; *The Stringer* 1997; *Rogue Trader* 1998; *All for Love* 1999; *Mad Cows* 1999; *A Midsummer Night's Dream* 1999; *An Everlasting Piece* 2000; *Sunset Strip* 2000; *Me without You* 2001; *The War Bride* 2001; *Timeline* 2003

Friels, Colin (1952–) *Monkey Grip* 1983; *The Gold and Glory* 1984; *Kangaroo* 1986; *Malcolm* 1986; *Warm Nights on a Slow Moving Train* 1986; *Grievous Bodily Harm* 1987; *Ground Zero* 1987; *High Tide* 1987; *Darkman* 1990; *Class Action* 1991; *Dingo* 1991; *A Good Man in Africa* 1993; *Angel Baby* 1995; *Back of Beyond* 1995; *Cosi* 1996; *Mr Reliable* 1996; *Dark City* 1998; *The Man Who Sued God* 2001; *Black and White* 2002

Friend, Philip (1915–1987) *The Bells Go Down* 1943; *Great Day* 1944; *Enchantment* 1948; *Thunder on the Hill* 1951; *Background* 1953; *Desperate Moment* 1953; *The Diamond* 1954; *Cloak without Dagger* 1955; *Dick Turpin – Highwayman* 1956; *Son of Robin Hood* 1958; *The Vulture* 1966

Frinton, Freddie (1911–1968) *Forces' Sweetheart* 1953; *What a Whopper!* 1961

Frisch, Arno *Benny's Video* 1992; *Funny Games* 1997

Frith, Rebecca *Love Serenade* 1996; *Me Myself I* 1999; *Strange Planet* 1999

Fritsch, Willy (1901–1973) *Spies* 1928; *The Woman in the Moon* 1929; *Congress Dances* 1931

Frizzell, Lou (1920–1979) *The Stalking Moon* 1968; *Duel* 1971; *Hickey and Boggs* 1972; *The Other* 1972

Fröbe, Gert aka **Froebe, Gert** aka **Frobe, Gert** (1913–1988) *Celui Qui Doit Mourir* 1957; *Too Many Lovers* 1957; *The Thousand Eyes of Dr Mabuse* 1960; *The Return of Dr Mabuse* 1961; *Banana Peel* 1964; *Goldfinger* 1964; *A High Wind in Jamaica* 1965; *Those Magnificent Men in Their Flying Machines* 1965; *Triple Cross* 1966; *Jules Verne's Rocket to the Moon* 1967; *Chitty Chitty Bang Bang* 1968; *Monte Carlo or Bust* 1969; *Dollars* 1971; *Ludwig* 1973; *Shadowman* 1973; *And Then There Were None* 1974; *The Serpent's Egg* 1977

Froboess, Cornelia aka **Froboess, Conny** (1943–) *The Vanishing Corporal* 1962; *Veronika Voss* 1982

Fröhlich, Gustav (1902–1987) *Metropolis* 1926; *Asphalt* 1928; *Heimkehr* 1928

Froler, Samuel (1957–) *Best Intentions* 1992; *Private Confessions* 1996

Fröling, Ewa (1952–) *Fanny and Alexander* 1982; *The Ox* 1991; *Letters from the East* 1995

Frome, Milton (1908–1989) *Go, Johnny, Go!* 1959; *The Swinger* 1966

Frost, Lindsay (1962–) *Dead Heat* 1988; *Danielle Steel's Palomino* 1991; *In the Line of Duty: Smoke Jumpers* 1996; *Death in the Shadows* 1998; *The Ring* 2002

Frost, Sadie (1968–) *Diamond Skulls* 1989; *Bram Stoker's Dracula* 1992; *Shopping* 1993; *Splitting Heirs* 1993; *Magic Hunter* 1994; *A Pyromaniac's Love Story* 1995; *Captain Jack* 1998; *Final Cut* 1998; *Rancid Aluminium* 1999; *Love, Honour and Obey* 2000

Frost, Terry (1906–1993) *The Monster Maker* 1944; *Valley of Fire* 1951

Frot, Catherine (1956–) *Un Air de Famille* 1996; *Le Dîner de Cons* 1998; *La Nouvelle Eve* 1999; *[One] Cavale* 2002; *[Three] Après la Vie* 2002; *[Two] Un Couple Epatant* 2002

Fry, Stephen (1957–) *The Good Father* 1986; *Peter's Friends* 1992; *IQ* 1994; *The Steal* 1994; *The Wind in the Willows* 1996; *Wilde* 1997; *A Civil Action* 1998; *The Tichborne Claimant* 1998; *Londinium* 1999; *Whatever Happened to Harold Smith?* 1999; *Relative Values* 2000; *Gosford Park* 2001; *Thunderpants* 2002; *Bright Young Things* 2003; *Le Divorce* 2003; *The Life and Death of Peter Sellers* 2003; *Tooth* 2003; *The Hitchhiker's Guide to the Galaxy* 2005

Frye, Dwight (1899–1943) *Dracula* 1931; *Frankenstein* 1931; *The Vampire Bat* 1933; *Atlantic Adventure* 1935

Frye, Soleil Moon (1976–) *The Revenge of Pumpkinhead – Blood Wings* 1994; *Piranhas* 1996; *Motel Blue* 1997

Frye, Virgil *Dr Heckyl & Mr Hype* 1980; *Running Hot* 1983

Fuchs, Leo (1910–1994) *The Frisco Kid* 1979; *Avalon* 1990

Fudge, Alan (1944–) *Two People* 1973; *Bug* 1975; *Chapter Two* 1979; *My Demon Lover* 1987

Fugard, Athol (1932–) *Meetings with Remarkable Men* 1979; *The Killing Fields* 1984

Fugit, Patrick (1982–) *Almost Famous* 2000; *Spun* 2002; *White Oleander* 2002; *Saved!* 2004

Fuji, Takako (1972–) *The Grudge 2* 2003; *The Grudge: Ju-On* 2003

Fujiki, Yu (1931–) *King Kong vs Godzilla* 1962; *Godzilla vs Mothra* 1964; *War of the Gargantuas* 1970

Fujioka, John (1925–) *The Last Flight of Noah's Ark* 1980; *They Call Me Bruce* 1982; *A Conspiracy of Love* 1987

Fujita, Susumu (1912–1991) *Sanshiro Sugata* 1943; *No Regrets for Our Youth* 1946; *Escapade in Japan* 1957; *The Hidden Fortress* 1958; *Yojimbo* 1961

Fujiwara, Kamatari (1905–1985) *Seven Samurai* 1954; *The Hidden Fortress* 1958; *Mickey One* 1965

Fujiwara, Tatsuya (1982–) *Battle Royale* 2000; *Battle Royale 2: Requiem* 2003

Fujiwara, Toshizo *A Scene at the Sea* 1991; *Mr Baseball* 1992

Fukada, Kyoko *Ring 2* 1998; *Dolls* 2002

Fulford, Christopher *Resurrected* 1989; *Bedrooms and Hallways* 1998; *One of the Hollywood Ten* 2000; *D-Tox* 2001; *Millions* 2004

Fulger, Holly *God's Will* 1989; *Lover's Knot* 1995

Fuller, Dale (1885–1948) *The Wedding March* 1928; *Twentieth Century* 1934

Fuller, Dolores (1923–) *Glen or Glenda* 1953; *Jail Bait* 1954

Fuller, Kurt (1952–) *Elvira, Mistress of the Dark* 1988; *Miracle Mile* 1989; *No Holds Barred* 1989; *Bingo* 1991; *Eve of*

Destruction 1991; *Calendar Girl* 1993; *Reflections on a Crime* 1994; *Diamonds* 1999; *Auto Focus* 2002; *Anger Management* 2003

Fuller, Lance (1928–2001) *Cattle Queen of Montana* 1954; *Apache Woman* 1955; *Pearl of the South Pacific* 1955; *This Island Earth* 1955; *Runaway Daughters* 1956; *Secret of Treasure Mountain* 1956; *The She-Creature* 1956; *Slightly Scarlet* 1956; *Voodoo Woman* 1957; *The Bride and the Beast* 1958

Fuller, Penny (1940–) *A Piano for Mrs Cimino* 1982; *Miss Rose White* 1992; *The Color of Love: Jacey's Story* 2000

Fuller, Robert (1934–) *The Brain from Planet Arous* 1958; *Incident at Phantom Hill* 1966; *Return of the Seven* 1966; *Whatever Happened to Aunt Alice?* 1969; *The Hard Ride* 1971; *Mustang Country* 1976; *Separate Ways* 1981

Fuller, Samuel *aka* **Fuller, Sam** (1911–1997) *Pierrot le Fou* 1965; *The Last Movie* 1971; *The American Friend* 1977; *1941* 1979; *Slapstick of Another Kind* 1982; *The State of Things* 1982; *A Return to Salem's Lot* 1987; *Sons* 1989; *Somebody to Love* 1994

Fullerton, Fiona (1956–) *Run Wild, Run Free* 1969; *Nicholas and Alexandra* 1971; *Alice's Adventures in Wonderland* 1972; *A View to a Kill* 1985; *A Ghost in Monte Carlo* 1990

Fulton, Rad (1934–) *Hell Bent for Leather* 1960; *The Last Sunset* 1961; *No My Darling Daughter* 1961

Fulton, Rikki (1924–2004) *Gorky Park* 1983; *Local Hero* 1983; *Comfort and Joy* 1984; *The Girl in the Picture* 1985

Fulton, Soren *A Ring of Endless Light* 2002; *Thunderbirds* 2004

Funicello, Annette *aka* **Annette** (1942–) *The Shaggy Dog* 1959; *Babes in Toyland* 1961; *Beach Party* 1963; *Bikini Beach* 1964; *The Misadventures of Merlin Jones* 1964; *Muscle Beach Party* 1964; *Pajama Party* 1964; *Beach Blanket Bingo* 1965; *Dr Goldfoot and the Bikini Machine* 1965; *How to Fill a Wild Bikini* 1965; *The Monkey's Uncle* 1965; *Ski Party* 1965; *Fireball 500* 1966; *Thunder Alley* 1967; *Head* 1968; *Back to the Beach* 1987

Funk, Terry (1944–) *Paradise Alley* 1978; *Over the Top* 1987

Furia, Giacomo (1925–) *Gold of Naples* 1954; *Boccaccio '70* 1961

Furlong, Edward (1977–) *Terminator 2: Judgment Day* 1991; *American Heart* 1992; *Pet Sematary II* 1992; *A Home of Our Own* 1993; *Brainscan* 1994; *Little Odessa* 1994; *The Grass Harp* 1995; *Before and After* 1996; *American History X* 1998; *Pecker* 1998; *Detroit Rock City* 1999; *Animal Factory* 2000

Furlong, John *Mudhoney* 1965; *Common-Law Cabin* 1967; *The Man Next Door* 1998

Furman, Rosa (?–1999) *Guns for San Sebastian* 1968; *Deep Crimson* 1996

Fürmann, Benno (1972–) *Anatomy* 2000; *The Princess & the Warrior* 2000; *My House in Umbria* 2002; *The Sin Eater* 2002; *Sword of Xanten* 2004

Furneaux, Yvonne (1928–) *The Master of Ballantrae* 1953; *Le Amiche* 1955; *The Dark Avenger* 1955; *Lisbon* 1956; *The Mummy* 1959; *La Dolce Vita* 1960; *Repulsion* 1965; *The Champagne Murders* 1966

Furness, Betty (1916–1994) *Dangerous Corner* 1934; *Magnificent Obsession* 1935; *Swing Time* 1936; *Fair Warning* 1937

Furness, Deborra-Lee (1960–) *Jenny Kissed Me* 1984; *Shame* 1987; *Blue Heat* 1990; *Waiting* 1990; *Voyager* 1991; *Angel Baby* 1995

Furst, Joseph *The High Bright Sun* 1965; *The Brides of Fu Manchu* 1966; *Diamonds Are Forever* 1971

Furst, Stephen (1955–) *National Lampoon's Animal House* 1978; *Take Down* 1978; *Midnight Madness* 1980; *National Lampoon's Class Reunion* 1982; *Silent Rage* 1982; *The Dream Team* 1989; *Shake, Rattle and Rock* 1994; *American Yakuza 2: Back to Back* 1996; *The Little Mermaid II: Return to the Sea* 2000

Furtado, Ruy (1919–1991) *Recollections of the Yellow House* 1989; *The Divine Comedy* 1992

Furth, George (1932–) *What's So Bad About Feeling Good?* 1968; *Butch Cassidy and the Sundance Kid* 1969; *The Man with Two Brains* 1983

Fury, Billy (1941–1983) *Play It Cool* 1962; *I've Gotta Horse* 1965; *That'll Be the Day* 1973

Futterman, Dan (1967–) *Stepkids* 1992; *Class of '61* 1993; *The Birdcage* 1996; *Shooting Fish* 1997; *Thicker than Blood* 1998; *Enough* 2002

Fyffe, Will (1885–1947) *Happy* 1933; *Cotton Queen* 1937; *Owd Bob* 1938; *Rulers of the Sea* 1939; *Neutral Port* 1940; *The Prime Minister* 1940; *The Brothers* 1947

G

G Q *On the Line* 2001; *Drumline* 2002

Gaal, Franciska (1904–1972) *The Buccaneer* 1938; *Paris Honeymoon* 1939

Gabel, Martin (1912–1986) *M* 1951; *Deadline – USA* 1952; *The Thief* 1952; *The James Dean Story* 1957; *Tip on a Dead Jockey* 1957; *Goodbye Charlie* 1964; *Marnie* 1964; *Divorce American Style* 1967; *Lady in Cement* 1968; *The First Deadly Sin* 1980

Gabel, Scilla (1938–) *Tarzan's Greatest Adventure* 1959; *The White Warrior* 1959; *Queen of the Pirates* 1960; *Village of Daughters* 1961; *Modesty Blaise* 1966

Gabin, Jean (1904–1976) *La Belle Equipe* 1936; *The Lower Depths* 1936; *La Grande Illusion* 1937; *Pépé le Moko* 1937; *La Bête Humaine* 1938; *Le Quai des Brumes* 1938; *Le Jour Se Lève* 1939; *Stormy Waters* 1941; *Moontide* 1942; *The Impostor* 1944; *Martin Roumagnac* 1946; *Le Plaisir* 1951; *Honour among Thieves* 1954; *French Cancan* 1955; *The House on the Waterfront* 1955; *Napoléon* 1955; *Razzia sur la Chnouf* 1955; *La Traversée de Paris* 1956; *The Case of Dr Laurent* 1957; *Maigret Sets a Trap* 1957; *Les Misérables* 1957; *A Monkey in Winter* 1962; *Any Number Can Win* 1963; *The Sicilian Clan* 1969; *Two against the Law* 1973; *Verdict* 1974

Gable, Christopher (1940–1998) *The Music Lovers* 1970; *The Boy Friend* 1971; *The Slipper and the Rose* 1976; *The Rainbow* 1988

Gable, Clark (1901–1960) *Dance, Fools, Dance* 1931; *The Finger Points* 1931; *A Free Soul* 1931; *Laughing Sinners* 1931; *The Painted Desert* 1931; *Possessed* 1931; *The Secret Six* 1931; *Sporting Blood* 1931; *Susan Lenox: Her Fall and Rise* 1931; *Hell Divers* 1932; *No Man of Her Own* 1932; *Polly of the Circus* 1932; *Red Dust* 1932; *Strange Interlude* 1932; *Dancing Lady* 1933; *Hold Your Man* 1933; *Night Flight* 1933; *The White Sister* 1933; *Chained* 1934; *Forsaking All Others* 1934; *It Happened One Night* 1934; *Manhattan Melodrama* 1934; *Men in White* 1934; *After Office Hours* 1935; *The Call of the Wild* 1935; *China Seas* 1935; *Mutiny on the Bounty* 1935; *Cain and Mabel* 1936; *Love on the Run* 1936; *San Francisco* 1936; *Wife vs Secretary* 1936; *Parnell* 1937; *Saratoga* 1937; *Test Pilot* 1938; *Too Hot to Handle* 1938; *Gone with the Wind* 1939; *Idiot's Delight* 1939; *Boom Town* 1940; *Comrade X* 1940; *Strange Cargo* 1940; *Honky Tonk* 1941; *They Met in Bombay* 1941; *Somewhere I'll Find You* 1942; *Adventure* 1945; *The Hucksters* 1947; *Command Decision* 1948; *Homecoming* 1948; *Any Number Can Play* 1949; *Key to the City* 1950; *To Please a Lady* 1950; *Across the Wide Missouri* 1951; *Callaway Went Thataway* 1951; *Lone Star* 1952; *Mogambo* 1953; *Never Let Me Go* 1953; *Betrayed* 1954; *Soldier of Fortune* 1955; *The Tall Men* 1955; *The King and Four Queens* 1956; *Band of Angels* 1957; *Run Silent, Run Deep* 1958; *Teacher's Pet* 1958; *But Not for Me* 1959; *It Started in Naples* 1960; *The Misfits* 1961

Gabor, Eva (1919–1995) *Captain Kidd and the Slave Girl* 1954; *The Last Time I Saw Paris* 1954; *The Mad Magician* 1954; *Artists and Models* 1955; *My Man Godfrey* 1957; *Gigi* 1958; *The Truth about Women* 1958; *It Started with a Kiss* 1959; *A New Kind of Love* 1963; *Youngblood Hawke* 1964; *The Aristocats* 1970; *The Rescuers* 1977; *The Princess Academy* 1987; *The Rescuers Down Under* 1990

Gabor, Miklos (1919–1998) *Somewhere in Europe* 1947; *Apa* 1966

Gabor, Zsa Zsa (1917–) *Lovely to Look At* 1952; *Moulin Rouge* 1952; *We're Not Married* 1952; *Lili* 1953; *Three Ring Circus* 1954; *Death of a Scoundrel* 1956; *The Man Who Wouldn't Talk* 1957; *Queen of Outer Space* 1958; *Touch of Evil* 1958; *For the First Time* 1959; *Pepe* 1960; *The Road to Hong Kong* 1962; *Drop Dead Darling* 1966; *Picture Mommy Dead* 1966; *Jack of Diamonds* 1967; *Up the Front* 1972; *Happily Ever After* 1990; *The Beverly Hillbillies* 1993

Gabriel, John (1931–) *The Hunters* 1958; *The Cat Gang* 1959

Gabriello, André *aka* **Gabriello** (1896–1975) *The Lower Depths* 1936; *Une Partie de Campagne* 1936

Gadd, Renee *aka* **Gadd, Renée** (1908–2003) *Happy* 1933; *The Man in the Mirror* 1936

Gaden, John (1941–) *Children of the Revolution* 1996; *Thank God He Met Lizzie* 1997

Gades, Antonio (1936–2004) *Blood Wedding* 1981; *Carmen* 1983; *El Amor Brujo* 1986

Gael, Anna *Zeta One* 1969; *Blue Blood* 1973

Gaffney, Liam *Curtain Up* 1952; *Street of Shadows* 1953

Gaffney, Mo (1958–) *Other People's Money* 1991; *The Shot* 1996

Gage, Erford (1912–1945) *The Falcon Strikes Back* 1943; *The Seventh Victim* 1943; *The Curse of the Cat People* 1944

Gage, Kevin *Double Tap* 1997; *Point Blank* 1997; *Dee Snider's Strangeland* 1998; *Paparazzi* 2004

Gage, Patricia *Rabid* 1976; *Perfectly Normal* 1990

Gago, Jenny (1953–) *Old Gringo* 1989; *My Family* 1994

Gail, Jane (1890–1963) *Traffic in Souls* 1913; *20,000 Leagues under the Sea* 1916

Gail, Max (1943–) *DC Cab* 1983; *Heartbreakers* 1984; *Where Are the Children?* 1986; *Judgment in Berlin* 1988; *The Switch* 1993; *Mortal Fear* 1994; *Pontiac Moon* 1994; *Sodbusters* 1994; *Good Luck* 1996

Gaines, Boyd (1953–) *Fame* 1980; *The Sure Thing* 1985; *Heartbreak Ridge* 1986; *Call Me* 1988; *I'm Not Rappaport* 1996

Gaines, Lynn *Quest for Love* 1988; *Jobman* 1990

Gaines, Richard (1904–1975) *The More the Merrier* 1943; *The Enchanted Cottage* 1945; *Do You Love Me?* 1946; *So Goes My Love* 1946; *Dangerous Years* 1947; *Flight to Mars* 1951; *Marry Me Again* 1953; *Love Me or Leave Me* 1955; *Five Steps to Danger* 1957

Gainey, M C *Leap of Faith* 1992; *Citizen Ruth* 1996; *Breakdown* 1997; *Happy, Texas* 1999; *The Country Bears* 2002; *Wonderland* 2003; *Broken Lizard's Club Dread* 2004; *Sideways* 2004; *Are We There Yet?* 2005

Gains, Courtney (1965–) *Children of the Corn* 1984; *Can't Buy Me Love* 1987; *The 'Burbs* 1989; *King Cobra* 1999

Gainsbourg, Charlotte (1971–) *Love Songs* 1984; *An Impudent Girl* 1985; *Kung-Fu Master* 1987; *La Petite Voleuse* 1988; *Night Sun* 1990; *Autobus* 1991; *Merci la Vie* 1991; *The Cement Garden* 1992; *Jane Eyre* 1996; *Love etc* 1997; *La Bûche* 1999; *Ma Femme Est une Actrice* 2001; *21 Grams* 2003

Gainsbourg, Serge (1928–1991) *The Looters* 1966; *Romance of a Horse Thief* 1971; *Je Vous Aime* 1980

Gajos, Janusz (1939–) *The Contract* 1980; *Interrogation* 1982; *Three Colours White* 1993

Galabru, Michel (1924–) *The Gendarme of St Tropez* 1964; *The Gendarme in New York* 1965; *La Cage aux Folles* 1978; *The Spacemen of St Tropez* 1978; *La Cage aux Folles II* 1980; *Choice of Arms* 1981; *Double Dare* 1981; *The Gendarme Wore Skirts* 1982; *One Deadly Summer* 1983; *La Cage aux Folles III: "Elles" Se Marient* 1985; *Subway* 1985; *Kamikaze* 1986; *Soigne Ta Droite* 1986; *Uranus* 1990; *Asterix and Obelix Take On Caesar* 1999

Galbraith, Alastair *Conquest of the South Pole* 1989; *The Debt Collector* 1999; *Intimacy* 2000

Gale, David (1936–1991) *Gold Diggers* 1983; *Re-Animator* 1985; *Bride of Re-Animator* 1991; *The Guyver* 1991

Gale, Lorena *Barnum* 1986; *Behind the Mask* 1999

Galecki, Johnny (1975–) *National Lampoon's Christmas Vacation* 1989; *Sudden Fury* 1993; *Murder at My Door* 1996; *Bean* 1997; *Suicide Kings* 1997; *The Opposite of Sex* 1998; *Bounce* 2000

Galiena, Anna (1954–) *The Hairdresser's Husband* 1990; *Jamon Jamon* 1992; *Being Human* 1994; *The Leading Man* 1996; *Three Lives and Only One Death* 1996

Galik, Denise *Melvin and Howard* 1980; *Monster* 1980; *Eye of the Tiger* 1986

Galindo, Nacho (1973–) *Gypsy Colt* 1954; *Thunder over Arizona* 1956; *Born Reckless* 1959

Galipeau, Annie *Map of the Human Heart* 1992; *Grey Owl* 1999

Gallacher, Frank (1943–) *Deadly* 1991; *Dallas Doll* 1994; *Dark City* 1998

Gallagher, Bronagh (1972–) *The Commitments* 1991; *Mary Reilly* 1995; *Painted Angels* 1997; *The Most Fertile Man in Ireland* 1999; *Wild about Harry* 2000; *Skagerrak* 2003

Gallagher, David (1985–) *Look Who's Talking Now!* 1993; *Phenomenon* 1996

Gallagher, Megan (1960–) *The Ambulance* 1990; *Fugitive from Justice* 1996

Gallagher, Peter (1955–) *The Idolmaker* 1980; *Summer Lovers* 1982; *Dreamchild* 1985; *High Spirits* 1988; *sex, lies, and videotape* 1989; *Milena* 1990; *Late for Dinner* 1991; *The Player* 1992; *Malice* 1993; *Mother's Boys* 1993; *Short Cuts* 1993; *The Underneath* 1995; *While You Were Sleeping* 1995; *Last Dance* 1996; *To Gillian on Her 37th Birthday* 1996; *The Man Who Knew Too Little* 1997; *American Beauty* 1999; *House on Haunted Hill* 1999; *Center Stage* 2000; *The Last Debate* 2000; *The Adventures of Tom Thumb and Thumbelina* 2002; *Mr Deeds* 2002

Gallagher, Richard "Skeets" *aka* **Gallagher, Skeets** (1891–1955) *Her Wedding Night* 1930; *It Pays to Advertise* 1931; *Possessed* 1931; *Bird of Paradise* 1932; *Merrily We Go to Hell* 1932; *Bachelor Bait* 1934; *Riptide* 1934; *Espionage* 1937

Gallagher, Sean *La Passione* 1996; *Elephant Juice* 1999

Galland, Jean (1887–1967) *Le Plaisir* 1951; *Madame de...* 1953

Gallaudet, John (1903–1983) *Pennies from Heaven* 1936; *Girls Can Play* 1937; *Holiday Inn* 1942; *Julie* 1956; *The Decks Ran Red* 1958; *In Cold Blood* 1967

Gallian, Ketti (1912–1972) *Marie Galante* 1934; *Espionage* 1937; *Shall We Dance* 1937

Galligan, Zach (1963–) *Gremlins* 1984; *Nothing Lasts Forever* 1984; *Surviving* 1985; *Waxwork* 1988; *Mortal Passions* 1989; *Gremlins 2: the New Batch* 1990; *Round Trip to Heaven* 1992; *Waxwork II: Lost in Time* 1992; *Cyborg 3: The Recycler* 1994; *Ice* 1994

Gallo, Michaela (1990–) *Beethoven's 3rd* 2000; *Beethoven's 4th* 2001

Gallo, Vincent (1961–) *Arizona Dream* 1991; *The House of the Spirits* 1993; *Palookaville* 1995; *The Funeral* 1996; *Truth or Consequences, NM* 1997; *Buffalo '66* 1998; *LA without a Map* 1998; *Confessions of a Trickbaby* 1999; *Hide and Seek* 2000; *Trouble Every Day* 2000; *Get Well Soon* 2001; *The Brown Bunny* 2003

Galloway, Don (1937–) *The Rare Breed* 1966; *Gunfight in Abilene* 1967; *The Ride to Hangman's Tree* 1967; *Rough Night in Jericho* 1967; *The Big Chill* 1983; *Two Moon Junction* 1988

Galvani, Graziella *Kapo* 1959; *Pierrot le Fou* 1965

Gam, Rita (1928–) *The Thief* 1952; *Saadia* 1953; *Night People* 1954; *Sign of the Pagan* 1954; *Magic Fire* 1956; *Mohawk* 1956; *Sierra Baron* 1958; *Hannibal* 1959; *King of Kings* 1961; *Klute* 1971; *Shoot Out* 1971; *The Gardener* 1972; *Distortions* 1987; *Midnight* 1989

Gamble, Mason (1986–) *Dennis* 1993; *Bad Moon* 1996; *Arlington Road* 1998; *Rushmore* 1998

Gamble, Warburton (1893–1945) *By Candlelight* 1934; *Spare a Copper* 1940

Gamblin, Jacques (1957–) *The Children of the Marshland* 1998; *The Colour of Lies* 1999; *Laissez-passer* 2001; *Carnages* 2002

Gamboa, Joonee (1936–) *Demonstone* 1989; *Fatal Mission* 1990

Gambon, Michael (1940–) *Nothing but the Night* 1972; *The Beast Must Die* 1974; *Turtle Diary* 1985; *Paris by Night* 1988; *The Cook, the Thief, His Wife and Her Lover* 1989; *Missing Link* 1989; *The Rachel Papers* 1989; *Mobsters* 1991; *Toys* 1992; *The Browning Version* 1994; *Clean Slate* 1994; *A Man of No Importance* 1994; *Squanto: the Last Great Warrior* 1994; *Two Deaths* 1994; *Bullet to Beijing* 1995; *The Innocent Sleep* 1995; *Mary Reilly* 1995; *Midnight in St Petersburg* 1995; *Nothing Personal* 1995; *The Gambler* 1997; *The Wings of the Dove* 1997; *Dancing at Lughnasa* 1998; *The Insider* 1999; *The Last September* 1999; *A Monkey's Tale* 1999; *Plunkett & Macleane* 1999; *Sleepy Hollow* 1999; *Charlotte Gray* 2001; *Christmas Carol: the Movie* 2001; *Gosford Park* 2001; *High Heels and Low Lifes* 2001; *Ali G indahouse* 2002; *Path to War* 2002; *The Actors* 2003; *Deep Blue* 2003; *Open Range* 2003; *Sylvia* 2003; *Being Julia* 2004; *Harry Potter and the Prisoner of Azkaban* 2004; *Layer Cake* 2004; *The Life Aquatic with Steve Zissou* 2004; *Sky Captain and the World of Tomorrow* 2004

Gammell, Robin *Lipstick* 1976; *Full Circle* 1977; *Highpoint* 1979; *Circle of Two* 1980; *Murder by Phone* 1982; *Project X* 1987; *Bone Daddy* 1998; *Last Night* 1998

Gammon, James (1940–) *The 1,000 Plane Raid* 1969; *The Ballad of Gregorio Cortez* 1983; *Hard Traveling* 1985; *Made in Heaven* 1987; *The Milagro Beanfield War* 1988; *Major League* 1989; *Roe vs Wade* 1989; *Coupe de Ville* 1990; *Revenge* 1990; *CrissCross* 1992; *Leaving Normal* 1992; *The Adventures of Huck Finn* 1993; *Cabin Boy* 1994; *Major League II* 1994; *Truman* 1995; *Traveller* 1997; *The Iron Giant* 1999; *The Country Bears* 2002; *Life or Something like It* 2002; *Cold Mountain* 2003

Gampu, Ken (1929–2003) *The Naked Prey* 1966; *Kill and Kill Again* 1981; *King Solomon's Mines* 1985

Ganatra, Nitin Chandra *aka* **Ganatra, Nitin** *Guru in Seven* 1997; *Second Generation* 1999; *Bride & Prejudice* 2004

Gandolfini, James (1961–) *Money for Nothing* 1993; *True Romance* 1993; *Angie* 1994; *Italian Movie* 1994; *Terminal Velocity* 1994; *Crimson Tide* 1995; *Get Shorty* 1995; *The Juror* 1996; *Night Falls on Manhattan* 1997; *Perdita Durango* 1997; *She's So Lovely* 1997; *12 Angry Men* 1997; *A Civil Action* 1998; *Fallen* 1998; *8mm* 1999; *The Last Castle* 2001; *The Man Who Wasn't There* 2001; *The Mexican* 2001; *Surviving Christmas* 2004

Ganios, Tony (1959–) *The Wanderers* 1979; *Continental Divide* 1981; *Porky's* 1981; *Porky's II: The Next Day* 1983; *Porky's Revenge* 1985; *The Taking of Beverly Hills* 1991

Ganoung, Richard *Parting Glances* 1985; *Billy's Hollywood Screen Kiss* 1998

Gant, Richard (1940–) *Rocky V* 1990; *Stone Cold* 1991; *Divorcing Jack* 1998; *Nutty Professor 2: the Klumps* 2000

Ganz, Bruno (1941–) *The Marquise of O* 1976; *The American Friend* 1977; *The Boys from Brazil* 1978; *Knife in the Head* 1978; *Nosferatu, the Vampire* 1979; *Circle of Deceit* 1981; *In the White City* 1983; *Wings of Desire* 1987; *Strapless* 1988; *The Last Days of Chez Nous* 1992; *Faraway, So Close* 1993; *Eternity and a Day* 1998; *Bread and Tulips* 2000; *Downfall* 2004; *The Manchurian Candidate* 2004

Garai, Romola (1982–) *I Capture the Castle* 2002; *Dirty Dancing 2* 2003; *Inside I'm Dancing* 2004; *Vanity Fair* 2004

Garas, Kaz (1940–) *The Last Safari* 1967; *Ben* 1972

Garber, Matthew (1956–1977) *Mary Poppins* 1964; *The Gnome-Mobile* 1967

Garber, Victor (1949–) *Godspell* 1973; *Light Sleeper* 1991; *Sleepless in Seattle* 1993; *Exotica* 1994; *Mary Higgins Clark's Let Me Call You Sweetheart* 1997; *Rodgers & Hammerstein's Cinderella* 1997; *Annie* 1999; *Laughter on the 23rd Floor* 2000; *Call Me Claus* 2001; *Legally Blonde* 2001; *Tuck Everlasting* 2002

Garbo, Greta (1905–1990) *The Joyless Street* 1925; *Flesh and the Devil* 1926; *The Temptress* 1926; *The Torrent* 1926; *Love* 1927; *The Divine Woman* 1928; *The Mysterious Lady* 1928; *A Woman of Affairs* 1928; *The Kiss* 1929; *The Single Standard* 1929; *Wild Orchids* 1929; *Anna Christie* 1930; *Romance* 1930; *Inspiration* 1931; *Mata Hari* 1931; *Susan Lenox: Her Fall and Rise* 1931; *As You Desire Me* 1932; *Grand Hotel* 1932; *Queen Christina* 1933; *The Painted Veil* 1934; *Anna Karenina* 1935; *Camille* 1937; *Conquest* 1937; *Ninotchka* 1939; *Two-Faced Woman* 1941

Garcés, Paula (1974–) *Clockstoppers* 2002; *Marci X* 2003; *Harold & Kumar Get the Munchies* 2004; *Man of the House* 2005

Garcia, Adam (1973–) *Bootmen* 2000; *Coyote Ugly* 2000; *Riding in Cars with Boys* 2001; *Confessions of a Teenage Drama Queen* 2004

Garcia, Allan (1887–1938) *The Circus* 1928; *City Lights* 1931

Garcia, Andres *House of Evil* 1968; *Tintorera* 1977

Garcia, Andy (1956–) *A Night in Heaven* 1983; *The Mean Season* 1985; *8 Million Ways to Die* 1986; *The Untouchables* 1987; *Stand and Deliver* 1988; *Black Rain* 1989; *The Godfather Part III* 1990; *Internal Affairs* 1990; *A Show of Force* 1990; *Dead Again* 1991; *Accidental Hero* 1992; *Jennifer Eight* 1992; *When a Man Loves a Woman* 1994; *Steal Big, Steal Little* 1995; *Things to Do in Denver When You're Dead* 1995; *The Disappearance of Garcia Lorca* 1997; *Hoodlum* 1997; *Night Falls on Manhattan* 1997; *Desperate Measures* 1998; *Just the Ticket* 1998; *For Love or Country: the Arturo Sandoval Story* 2000; *Ocean's Eleven* 2001; *Confidence* 2002; *Twisted* 2003; *Ocean's Twelve* 2004

Garcia, José (1966–) *Would I Lie to You?* 1997; *En Face* 1999; *Extension du Domaine de la Lutte* 1999

Garcia, Juan *Blowing Wild* 1953; *The Tall Men* 1955

Garcia, Luis Alberto *The Last Supper* 1976; *Plaff!* 1988; *Adorable Lies* 1991; *The Elephant and the Bicycle* 1995; *Guantanamera* 1995

Garcia, Nicole (1946–) *Mon Oncle d'Amérique* 1980; *Les Uns et les Autres* 1981; *Order of Death* 1983; *Death in a French Garden* 1985; *Betty Fisher and Other Stories* 2001; *Histoire de Marie et Julien* 2003

Garcia, Stella *The Last Movie* 1971; *Joe Kidd* 1972

Garcia, Stenio (1933–) *At Play in the Fields of the Lord* 1991; *Me, You, Them* 2000

Garcin, Ginette (1928–) *Cousin, Cousine* 1975; *L'Homme de Ma Vie* 1992

Garcin, Henri (1929–) *La Vie de Château* 1965; *Someone behind the Door* 1971; *Kill!* 1972; *Verdict* 1974; *An Almost Perfect Affair* 1979; *The Woman Next Door* 1981; *Abel* 1986; *Les Cent et Une Nuits* 1995; *The Eighth Day* 1996; *The Music Freelancers* 1998

Garde, Betty (1905–1989) *Call Northside 777* 1948; *Cry of the City* 1948; *Caged* 1950; *The Prince Who Was a Thief* 1951

Gardenia, Vincent (1922–1992) *Mad Dog Coll* 1961; *Cold Turkey* 1969; *Jenny* 1969; *Where's Poppa?* 1970; *Little Murders* 1971; *Bang the Drum Slowly* 1973; *Lucky Luciano* 1973; *Death Wish* 1974; *The Front Page* 1974; *Fire Sale* 1977; *Greased Lightning* 1977; *Heaven Can Wait* 1978; *Firepower* 1979; *Home Movies* 1979; *The Last Flight of Noah's Ark* 1980; *Death Wish II* 1981; *Movers and Shakers* 1985; *Little Shop of Horrors* 1986; *Moonstruck* 1987; *Skin Deep* 1989; *The Super* 1991

Gardiner, Reginald (1903–1980) *A Damsel in Distress* 1937; *The Flying Deuces* 1939; *The Doctor Takes a Wife* 1940; *The Great Dictator* 1940; *The Man Who Came to Dinner* 1941; *My Life with Caroline* 1941; *Sundown* 1941; *A Yank in the RAF* 1941; *Captains of the Clouds* 1942; *Claudia* 1943; *The Immortal Sergeant* 1943; *Sweet Rosie O'Grady* 1943; *Christmas in Connecticut* 1945; *The Dolly Sisters* 1945; *The Horn Blows at Midnight* 1945; *Molly and Me* 1945; *Cluny Brown* 1946; *Do You Love Me?* 1946; *I Wonder Who's Kissing Her Now* 1947; *Fury at Furnace Creek* 1948; *That Lady in Ermine* 1948; *That Wonderful Urge* 1948; *Halls of Montezuma* 1950; *Wabash Avenue* 1950; *Androcles and the Lion* 1952; *Black Widow* 1954; *Ain't Misbehavin'* 1955; *The Birds and the Bees* 1956; *Rock-a-Bye Baby* 1958; *Back Street* 1961; *Do Not Disturb* 1965

Gardner, Ava (1922–1990) *Calling Dr Gillespie* 1942; *Joe Smith, American* 1942; *Kid Glove Killer* 1942; *Reunion in France* 1942; *Ghosts in the Night* 1943; *Hitler's Madman* 1943; *Pilot #5* 1943; *Swing Fever* 1943; *Young Ideas* 1943; *Three Men in White* 1944; *Two Girls and a Sailor* 1944; *The Killers* 1946; *Whistle Stop* 1946; *The Hucksters* 1947; *Singapore* 1947; *One Touch of Venus* 1948; *The Bribe* 1949; *East Side, West Side* 1949; *The Great Sinner* 1949; *Pandora and the Flying Dutchman* 1950; *My Forbidden Past* 1951; *Show Boat* 1951; *Lone Star* 1952; *The Snows of Kilimanjaro* 1952; *The Band Wagon* 1953; *Knights of the Round Table* 1953; *Mogambo* 1953; *Ride, Vaquero!* 1953; *The Barefoot Contessa* 1954; *Bhowani Junction* 1956; *The Little Hut* 1957; *The Sun Also Rises* 1957; *The Naked Maja* 1959; *On the Beach* 1959; *The Angel Wore Red* 1960; *55 Days at Peking* 1963; *The Night of the Iguana* 1964; *Seven Days in May* 1964; *The Bible...in the Beginning* 1966; *Mayerling* 1968; *The Life and Times of Judge Roy Bean* 1972; *Earthquake* 1974; *Permission to Kill* 1975; *The Blue Bird* 1976; *The Cassandra Crossing* 1976; *The Sentinel* 1977; *City on Fire* 1979; *The Kidnapping of the President* 1980; *Priest of Love* 1981; *Regina* 1982

Gardner, Joan (1914–1999) *Wedding Rehearsal* 1932; *The Private Life of Don Juan* 1934; *The Scarlet Pimpernel* 1934; *Forget-Me-Not* 1936; *The Man Who Could Work Miracles* 1936; *Dark Journey* 1937; *The Challenge* 1938

Garfield, Allen *aka* **Garfield, Alan** *aka* **Goorwitz, Allen** (1939–) *Greetings* 1968; *Hi, Mom!* 1970; *The Owl and the Pussycat* 1970; *Believe in Me* 1971; *The Organization* 1971; *The Candidate* 1972; *Get to Know Your Rabbit* 1972; *Slither* 1973; *Busting* 1974; *The Conversation* 1974; *The Front Page* 1974; *Nashville* 1975; *Paco* 1975; *Gable and Lombard* 1976; *Mother, Jugs & Speed* 1976; *The Brink's Job* 1978; *Skateboard* 1978; *One-Trick Pony* 1980; *The Stunt Man* 1980; *Continental Divide* 1981; *Leave 'em Laughing* 1981; *One from the Heart* 1982; *The State of Things* 1982; *The Black Stallion Returns* 1983; *Get Crazy* 1983; *The Cotton Club* 1984; *Irreconcilable Differences* 1984; *Teachers* 1984; *Desert Bloom* 1985; *Beverly Hills Cop II* 1987; *Let It Ride* 1989; *Night Visitor* 1989; *Family Prayers* 1991; *Cyborg 2: Glass Shadow* 1993; *Patriots* 1994; *Wild Side* 1995; *Crime of the Century* 1996; *Diabolique* 1996; *Absence of the Good* 1999; *The Majestic* 2001

Garfield, John (1913–1952) *Daughters Courageous* 1939; *Dust Be My Destiny* 1939; *Four Wives* 1939; *Juarez* 1939; *They Made Me a Criminal* 1939; *Castle on the Hudson* 1940; *East of the River* 1940; *Saturday's Children* 1940; *Out of the Fog* 1941; *The Sea Wolf* 1941; *Dangerously They Live* 1942; *Tortilla Flat* 1942; *Air Force* 1943; *Destination Tokyo* 1943; *The Fallen Sparrow* 1943; *Thank Your Lucky Stars* 1943; *Between Two Worlds* 1944; *Hollywood Canteen* 1944; *Pride of the Marines* 1945; *Humoresque* 1946; *Nobody Lives Forever* 1946; *The Postman Always Rings Twice* 1946; *Body and Soul* 1947; *Daisy Kenyon* 1947; *Gentleman's Agreement* 1947; *Force of Evil* 1948; *Jigsaw* 1949; *We Were Strangers* 1949; *The Breaking Point* 1950; *He Ran All the Way* 1951

Garfunkel, Art *aka* **Garfunkel, Arthur** (1941–) *Catch-22* 1970; *Carnal Knowledge* 1971; *Bad Timing* 1980; *Good to Go* 1986; *Boxing Helena* 1993

Gargan, Edward *aka* **Gargan, Ed** (1902–1964) *Danger Patrol* 1937; *The Falcon Takes Over* 1942; *The Falcon and the Co-Eds* 1943; *The Falcon in Danger* 1943; *The Falcon Out West* 1944

Gargan, William (1905–1979) *The Animal Kingdom* 1932; *Rain* 1932; *Lucky Devils* 1933; *British Agent* 1934; *Four Frightened People* 1934; *Black Fury* 1935; *The Milky Way* 1936; *You Only Live Once* 1937; *You're a Sweetheart* 1937; *The Crowd Roars* 1938; *The Housekeeper's Daughter* 1939; *Star Dust* 1940; *They Knew What They Wanted* 1940; *Turnabout* 1940; *Cheers for Miss Bishop* 1941; *I Wake Up Screaming* 1941; *Keep 'em Flying* 1941; *Miss Annie Rooney* 1942; *Swing Fever* 1943; *The Canterville Ghost* 1944; *The Bells of St Mary's* 1945; *Murder in the Music Hall* 1946; *Strange Impersonation* 1946; *Swell Guy* 1946; *Till the End of Time* 1946; *The Rawhide Years* 1956

Garity, Troy (1973–) *Bandits* 2001; *Barbershop* 2002; *Milwaukee, Minnesota* 2002; *Barbershop 2: Back in Business* 2004

Garko, Gabriel (1974–) *Le Fate Ignoranti* 2001; *Callas Forever* 2002

Garko, Gianni *aka* **Garko, John** (1935–) *Kapo* 1959; *The Mongols* 1961; *Pontius Pilate* 1961; *Sartana* 1968; *Sartana, Angel of Death* 1969; *The Heroes* 1972

Garland, Beverly *aka* **Campbell, Beverly** (1926–) *DOA* 1949; *The Gunslinger* 1956; *It Conquered the World* 1956; *Not of This Earth* 1956; *Chicago Confidential* 1957; *The Joker Is Wild* 1957; *The Saga of Hemp Brown* 1958; *The Alligator People* 1959; *Twice Told Tales* 1963; *Pretty Poison* 1968; *The Mad Room* 1969; *Where the Red Fern Grows* 1974; *Sixth and Main* 1977; *Roller Boogie* 1979; *It's My Turn* 1980

Garland, Judy (1922–1969) *Every Sunday* 1936; *Pigskin Parade* 1936; *Broadway Melody of 1938* 1937; *Thoroughbreds Don't Cry* 1937; *Everybody Sing* 1938; *Listen, Darling* 1938; *Love Finds Andy Hardy* 1938; *Babes in Arms* 1939; *The Wizard of Oz* 1939; *Andy Hardy Meets Debutante* 1940; *Little Nellie Kelly* 1940; *Strike Up the Band* 1940; *Babes on Broadway* 1941; *Life Begins for Andy Hardy* 1941; *Ziegfeld Girl* 1941; *For Me and My Gal* 1942; *Girl Crazy* 1943; *Presenting Lily Mars* 1943; *Meet Me in St Louis* 1944; *Ziegfeld Follies* 1944; *The Clock* 1945; *The Harvey Girls* 1946; *Till the Clouds Roll By* 1946; *Easter Parade* 1948; *The Pirate* 1948; *Words and Music* 1948; *In the Good Old Summertime* 1949; *Summer Stock* 1950; *A Star Is Born* 1954; *Pepe* 1960; *Judgment at Nuremberg* 1961; *A Child Is Waiting* 1962; *Gay Purr-ee* 1962; *I Could Go On Singing* 1963

Garland, Richard (1927–1969) *Rage at Dawn* 1955; *Attack of the Crab Monsters* 1957; *The Undead* 1957; *Panic in Year Zero* 1962

Garlington, Lee (1953–) *Cobra* 1986; *Psycho III* 1986; *Evidence of Love* 1990; *My Life* 1993; *Reflections on a Crime* 1994; *The Babysitter* 1995

Garner, Alice (1969–) *Monkey Grip* 1983; *Love and Other Catastrophes* 1996; *Strange Planet* 1999

Garner, James (1928–) *The Girl He Left Behind* 1956; *Toward the Unknown* 1956; *Sayonara* 1957; *Shoot-Out at Medicine Bend* 1957; *Darby's Rangers* 1958; *Alias Jesse James* 1959; *Up Periscope* 1959; *Cash McCall* 1960; *The Children's Hour* 1961; *Boys' Night Out* 1962; *The Great Escape* 1963; *Move Over, Darling* 1963; *The Thrill of It All* 1963; *The Wheeler Dealers* 1963; *The Americanization of Emily* 1964; *36 Hours* 1964; *Art of Love* 1965; *Mister Buddwing* 1965; *Duel at Diablo* 1966; *Grand Prix* 1966; *A Man Could Get Killed* 1966; *Hour of the Gun* 1967; *How Sweet It Is!* 1968; *The Pink Jungle* 1968; *Marlowe* 1969; *Support Your Local Sheriff!* 1969; *Skin Game* 1971; *Support Your Local Gunfighter* 1971; *They Only Kill Their Masters* 1972; *One Little Indian* 1973; *The Castaway Cowboy* 1974; *The Rockford Files* 1974; *HEALTH* 1980; *The Fan* 1981; *The Long Summer of George Adams* 1982; *Victor/Victoria* 1982; *Tank* 1984; *Murphy's Romance* 1985; *Promise* 1986; *Sunset* 1988; *My Name Is Bill W* 1989; *The Distinguished Gentleman* 1992; *Barbarians at the Gate* 1993; *Fire in the Sky* 1993; *Maverick* 1994; *My Fellow Americans* 1996; *Legalese* 1998; *Twilight* 1998; *One Special Night* 1999; *The Last Debate* 2000; *Space Cowboys* 2000; *Atlantis: the Lost Empire* 2001; *Divine Secrets of the Ya-Ya Sisterhood* 2002; *The Notebook* 2003

Garner, Jennifer (1973–) *Mr Magoo* 1997; *Washington Square* 1997; *Dude, Where's My Car?* 2000; *Catch Me If You Can* 2002; *Daredevil* 2003; *13 Going on 30* 2004; *Elektra* 2005

Garner, Peggy Ann (1931–1984) *Jane Eyre* 1943; *Junior Miss* 1945; *Nob Hill* 1945; *A Tree Grows in Brooklyn* 1945; *Home Sweet Homicide* 1946; *Bob, Son of Battle* 1947; *Daisy Kenyon* 1947; *The Lovable Cheat* 1949; *Teresa* 1951; *Black Widow* 1954

Garnett, Gale (1942–) *Mad Monster Party* 1966; *Tribute* 1980

Garofalo, Janeane (1964–) *Reality Bites* 1994; *Bye Bye Love* 1995; *Coldblooded* 1995; *The Cable Guy* 1996; *Larger than Life* 1996; *Touch* 1996; *The Truth about Cats and Dogs* 1996; *Cop Land* 1997; *The Matchmaker* 1997; *Romy and Michele's High School Reunion* 1997; *Clay Pigeons* 1998; *Dog Park* 1998; *Permanent Midnight* 1998; *Dogma* 1999; *The Minus Man* 1999; *Mystery Men* 1999; *200 Cigarettes* 1999; *Titan AE* 2000; *The Search for John Gissing* 2001; *Big Trouble* 2002; *The Laramie Project* 2002; *Wonderland* 2003

Garr, Teri (1949–) *The Cool Ones* 1967; *Head* 1968; *The Conversation* 1974; *Young Frankenstein* 1974; *Won Ton Ton, the Dog Who Saved Hollywood* 1976; *Close Encounters of the Third Kind* 1977; *Oh, God!* 1977; *The Black Stallion* 1979; *Witches' Brew* 1979; *Honky Tonk Freeway* 1981; *The Escape Artist* 1982; *One from the Heart* 1982; *Tootsie* 1982; *The Black Stallion Returns* 1983; *Mr Mom* 1983; *The Sting II* 1983; *Firstborn* 1984; *After Hours* 1985; *Miracles* 1985; *Full Moon in Blue Water* 1988; *Let It Ride* 1989; *Out Cold* 1989; *Waiting for the Light* 1989; *Short Time* 1990; *Mom and Dad Save the World* 1992; *Dumb and Dumber* 1994; *Perfect Alibi* 1994; *Pret-a-Porter* 1994; *Michael* 1996; *Changing Habits* 1997; *A Simple Wish* 1997; *Casper Meets Wendy* 1998; *Dick* 1999; *Ghost World* 2001

Garralaga, Martin (1894–1981) *A Message to Garcia* 1936; *They Passed This Way* 1948; *The Bribe* 1949; *The Ring* 1952

Garrani, Ivo (1924–) *Aphrodite Goddess of Love* 1957; *Hercules* 1957; *General Della Rovere* 1959; *The Giant of Marathon* 1960; *The Mask of Satan* 1960; *Morgan the Pirate* 1960; *The Rover* 1967; *The Sicilian Cross* 1976

Garrel, Louis (1983–) *The Dreamers* 2003; *Ma Mère* 2004

Garrel, Maurice (1923–) *Nada* 1974; *Son Frère* 2003; *Kings & Queen* 2004
Garrett, Betty (1919–) *Words and Music* 1948; *Neptune's Daughter* 1949; *On the Town* 1949; *Take Me Out to the Ball Game* 1949; *My Sister Eileen* 1955; *The Long Way Home* 1998
Garrett, Eliza *Schlock* 1971; *Love Is a Gun* 1994
Garrett, Leif (1961–) *Part 2 Walking Tall* 1975; *Final Chapter – Walking Tall* 1977; *God's Gun* 1977; *Kid Vengeance* 1977; *Skateboard* 1978; *The Outsiders* 1983; *Shaker Run* 1985; *Delta Fever* 1988; *Party Line* 1988
Garrett, Patsy (1921–) *Benji* 1974; *For the Love of Benji* 1977
Garrick, John (1902–1966) *Just Imagine* 1930; *Song o' My Heart* 1930; *Bad Company* 1931; *Chu Chin Chow* 1934; *D'Ye Ken John Peel?* 1934; *Street Song* 1935
Garrick, Rian *Battle of the Coral Sea* 1959; *Edge of Eternity* 1959
Garrison, Miranda (1950–) *Salsa* 1988; *Mack the Knife* 1989
Garrison, Sean (1937–) *Violent Road* 1958; *Bridge to the Sun* 1961; *Moment to Moment* 1966
Garrone, Riccardo (1926–) *Pontius Pilate* 1961; *Eva* 1962; *The Swordsman of Siena* 1962
Garson, Greer (1908–1996) *Goodbye, Mr Chips* 1939; *Remember?* 1939; *Pride and Prejudice* 1940; *Blossoms in the Dust* 1941; *When Ladies Meet* 1941; *Mrs Miniver* 1942; *Random Harvest* 1942; *Madame Curie* 1943; *Mrs Parkington* 1944; *Adventure* 1945; *The Valley of Decision* 1945; *Desire Me* 1947; *Julia Misbehaves* 1948; *The Forsyte Saga* 1949; *The Miniver Story* 1950; *The Law and the Lady* 1951; *Julius Caesar* 1953; *Scandal at Scourie* 1953; *Her Twelve Men* 1954; *Strange Lady in Town* 1955; *Pepe* 1960; *Sunrise at Campobello* 1960; *The Singing Nun* 1966; *The Happiest Millionaire* 1967
Garson, Willie (1964–) *Every Breath* 1993; *Untamed Heart* 1993; *Fortress 2: Re-entry* 1999; *The Perfect Catch* 2005
Garth, David (1920–1988) *John of the Fair* 1952; *Neither the Sea nor the Sand* 1972
Gartin, Christopher *No Big Deal* 1983; *Danielle Steel's Changes* 1991; *Johns* 1995; *Tremors II: Aftershocks* 1995
Garwood, John *Hell's Angels on Wheels* 1967; *The Stunt Man* 1980
Gary, Lorraine (1937–) *Jaws* 1975; *I Never Promised You a Rose Garden* 1977; *Jaws 2* 1978; *Just You and Me, Kid* 1979; *1941* 1979; *Jaws the Revenge* 1987
Gascoine, Jill (1937–) *Confessions of a Pop Performer* 1975; *King of the Wind* 1989
Gaspar, Dominique *Virgin Machine* 1988; *My Father Is Coming* 1991
Gassman, Alessandro (1965–) *Snow White* 1989; *Golden Balls* 1993; *A Month by the Lake* 1994; *Hamam: the Turkish Bath* 1996
Gassman, Vittorio (1922–2000) *Bitter Rice* 1949; *Sombrero* 1952; *Cry of the Hunted* 1953; *The Glass Wall* 1953; *Mambo* 1954; *Rhapsody* 1954; *Beautiful but Dangerous* 1955; *War and Peace* 1956; *Big Deal on Madonna Street* 1958; *The Great War* 1959; *The Miracle* 1959; *Tempest* 1959; *Barabbas* 1961; *The Easy Life* 1962; *Let's Talk About Women* 1964; *The Dirty Game* 1965; *Ghosts – Italian Style* 1967; *The Tiger and the Pussycat* 1967; *Woman Times Seven* 1967; *Twelve plus One* 1969; *Scent of a Woman* 1974; *We All Loved Each Other So Much* 1974; *Viva Italia!* 1978; *A Wedding* 1978; *Quintet* 1979; *Immortal Bachelor* 1980; *The Nude Bomb* 1980; *Sharky's Machine* 1981; *Tempest* 1982; *Life Is a Bed of Roses* 1983; *The Family* 1987; *Sleepers* 1996
Gastdorf, Johanna *The Miracle of Bern* 2003; *Sophie Scholl – The Final Days* 2005
Gasteyer, Ana (1967–) *Dick* 1999; *Woman on Top* 2000; *Mean Girls* 2004
Gastoni, Lisa (1935–) *The Baby and the Battleship* 1956; *Three Men in a Boat* 1956; *Man from Tangier* 1957; *Intent to Kill* 1958; *The Breaking Point* 1961; *Eva* 1962; *RoGoPaG* 1962; *The Wild, Wild Planet* 1965; *The Man Who Laughs* 1966; *The Last Days of Mussolini* 1974
Gates, Larry (1915–1996) *Above and Beyond* 1952; *Glory Alley* 1952; *Has Anybody Seen My Gal?* 1952; *Francis Covers the Big Town* 1953; *Take Me to Town* 1953; *Invasion of the Body Snatchers* 1956; *The Brothers Rico* 1957; *Jeanne Eagels* 1957; *The Strange One* 1957; *Cat on a Hot Tin Roof* 1958; *One Foot in Hell* 1960; *Ada* 1961; *The Hoodlum Priest* 1961; *Underworld USA* 1961; *The Young Savages* 1961; *Toys in the Attic* 1963; *The Sand Pebbles* 1966
Gates, Nancy (1926–) *The Master Race* 1944; *Nevada* 1944; *Sons of the Musketeers* 1951; *The Member of the Wedding* 1952; *Hell's Half Acre* 1954; *Suddenly* 1954; *Stranger on Horseback* 1955; *World without End* 1955; *The Brass Legend* 1956; *Death of a Scoundrel* 1956; *Some Came Running* 1958; *The Gunfight at Dodge City* 1959; *Comanche Station* 1960
Gateson, Marjorie (1891–1977) *The King's Vacation* 1933; *Chained* 1934; *Goin' to Town* 1935; *Big Brown Eyes* 1936; *Vogues of 1938* 1937; *Geronimo* 1939; *The Sky's the Limit* 1943
Gatiss, Mark *Sex Lives of the Potato Men* 2003; *The League of Gentlemen's Apocalypse* 2005
Gatliff, Frank (1927–1990) *The Ipcress File* 1965; *Déjà Vu* 1984
Gatlin, Jerry *An Eye for an Eye* 1966; *The Train Robbers* 1973
Gaubert, Danièle (1943–1987) *Flight from Ashiya* 1964; *Snow Job* 1972
Gauge, Alexander (1914–1960) *Murder in the Cathedral* 1952; *The Pickwick Papers* 1952; *Counterspy* 1953; *House of Blackmail* 1953; *Double Exposure* 1954
Gauthier, Vincent *The Green Ray* 1986; *Nazi Hunter: the Beate Klarsfeld Story* 1986
Gautier, Dick (1937–) *Black Jack* 1972; *Billy Jack Goes to Washington* 1977; *Fun with Dick and Jane* 1977
Gautier, Jean-Yves *The Promise* 1994; *Three Lives and Only One Death* 1996; *Journey to the Beginning of the World* 1997
Gava, Cassandra *High Road to China* 1983; *The Amityville Curse* 1990
Gaven, Jean (1922–) *Obsession* 1954; *Rider on the Rain* 1970; *And Hope to Die* 1972; *The Story of O* 1975
Gavin, Erica (1949–) *Vixen!* 1968; *Beyond the Valley of the Dolls* 1970; *Caged Heat* 1974
Gavin, John (1928–) *Quantez* 1957; *A Time to Love and a Time to Die* 1958; *Imitation of Life* 1959; *A Breath of Scandal* 1960; *Midnight Lace* 1960; *Psycho* 1960; *Spartacus* 1960; *Back Street* 1961; *Romanoff and Juliet* 1961; *Tammy Tell Me True* 1961; *Thoroughly Modern Millie* 1967; *The Madwoman of Chaillot* 1969
Gawthorne, Peter (1884–1962) *The Camels Are Coming* 1934; *No Limit* 1935; *The Amazing Quest of Ernest Bliss* 1936; *Good Morning, Boys* 1937; *The Last Adventurers* 1937; *The Ticket of Leave Man* 1937; *Alf's Button Afloat* 1938; *Ask a Policeman* 1938; *Convict 99* 1938; *Band Waggon* 1939; *Flying 55* 1939; *Where's That Fire?* 1939; *I Thank You* 1941; *Pimpernel Smith* 1941
Gaxton, William (1890–1963) *It's the Old Army Game* 1926; *Best Foot Forward* 1943; *The Heat's On* 1943; *Billy Rose's Diamond Horseshoe* 1945
Gaye, Gregory (1900–1993) *Renegades* 1930; *Charlie Chan at the Opera* 1936; *Dodsworth* 1936; *Ninotchka* 1939; *Black Magic* 1949; *Creature with the Atom Brain* 1955; *The Eddy Duchin Story* 1956
Gaye, Lisa (1935–) *Drums across the River* 1954; *Rock around the Clock* 1956; *Shake, Rattle and Rock!* 1957; *Ten Thousand Bedrooms* 1957; *Castle of Evil* 1966; *The Violent Ones* 1967
Gaye, Nona (1974–) *The Matrix Reloaded* 2002; *The Polar Express* 2004; *xXx: the Next Level* 2005
Gayet, Julie (1972–) *Les Cent et Une Nuits* 1995; *Sélect Hôtel* 1996; *Pourquoi Pas Moi?* 1999; *Almost Peaceful* 2002
Gayheart, Rebecca (1972–) *Urban Legend* 1998; *Jawbreaker* 1999; *From Dusk till Dawn 3: the Hangman's Daughter* 2000; *Shadow Hours* 2000
Gayle, Jackie (1926–2002) *Tin Men* 1987; *Plain Clothes* 1988; *Bert Rigby, You're a Fool* 1989
Gayle, Monica *Switchblade Sisters* 1975; *Love and the Midnight Auto Supply* 1977
Gaylor, Anna (1932–) *Seven Thunders* 1957; *Nor the Moon by Night* 1958; *Life Upside Down* 1964
Gaynes, George (1917–) *Dead Men Don't Wear Plaid* 1982; *Tootsie* 1982; *Micki & Maude* 1984; *Police Academy* 1984; *Police Academy 4: Citizens on Patrol* 1987; *Police Academy 5: Assignment Miami Beach* 1988; *Police Academy: Mission to Moscow* 1994; *Vanya on 42nd Street* 1994
Gaynor, Janet (1906–1984) *7th Heaven* 1927; *Sunrise* 1927; *Street Angel* 1928; *Sunny Side Up* 1929; *Daddy Long Legs* 1931; *Delicious* 1931; *The First Year* 1932; *Tess of the Storm Country* 1932; *State Fair* 1933; *Change of Heart* 1934; *The Farmer Takes a Wife* 1935; *Ladies in Love* 1936; *Small Town Girl* 1936; *A Star Is Born* 1937; *Three Loves Has Nancy* 1938; *The Young in Heart* 1938
Gaynor, Mitzi (1930–) *My Blue Heaven* 1950; *Golden Girl* 1951; *Bloodhounds of Broadway* 1952; *The I Don't Care Girl* 1952; *We're Not Married* 1952; *There's No Business like Show Business* 1954; *Anything Goes* 1956; *The Birds and the Bees* 1956; *Les Girls* 1957; *The Joker Is Wild* 1957; *South Pacific* 1958; *Happy Anniversary* 1959; *Surprise Package* 1960; *For Love or Money* 1963
Gayson, Eunice (1931–) *Dance Hall* 1950; *To Have and to Hold* 1951; *Dance Little Lady* 1954; *Out of the Clouds* 1954; *Zarak* 1956; *Carry On Admiral* 1957; *The Revenge of Frankenstein* 1958; *Dr No* 1962; *From Russia with Love* 1963
Gazelle, Wendy *Hot Pursuit* 1987; *Sammy and Rosie Get Laid* 1987; *The In Crowd* 1988; *Triumph of the Spirit* 1989; *The Net* 1995
Gazzara, Ben (1930–) *The Strange One* 1957; *Anatomy of a Murder* 1959; *The Young Doctors* 1961; *Captive City* 1962; *Convicts Four* 1962; *A Rage to Live* 1965; *The Bridge at Remagen* 1969; *If It's Tuesday, This Must Be Belgium* 1969; *Husbands* 1970; *King: a Filmed Record… Montgomery to Memphis* 1970; *The Neptune Factor* 1973; *Capone* 1975; *The Killing of a Chinese Bookie* 1976; *Voyage of the Damned* 1976; *High Velocity* 1977; *Opening Night* 1977; *Bloodline* 1979; *Saint Jack* 1979; *Inchon* 1981; *Tales of Ordinary Madness* 1981; *They All Laughed* 1981; *An Early Frost* 1985; *Quicker than the Eye* 1989; *Road House* 1989; *Shadow Conspiracy* 1996; *Stag* 1996; *The Spanish Prisoner* 1997; *Buffalo '66* 1998; *Happiness* 1998; *The Thomas Crown Affair* 1999; *The List* 2000; *Hysterical Blindness* 2002; *Dogville* 2003
Gazzo, Michael V aka **Gazzo, Michael** (1923–1995) *The Godfather, Part II* 1974; *Black Sunday* 1976; *Fingers* 1978; *Alligator* 1980; *Back Roads* 1981; *Body and Soul* 1981; *Fear City* 1984; *Cookie* 1989
Ge You *Farewell My Concubine* 1993; *To Live* 1994; *The Emperor's Shadow* 1996; *Eighteen Springs* 1997; *Keep Cool* 1997; *Big Shot's Funeral* 2001
Ge Zhijun *The Story of Qiu Ju* 1992; *Ermo* 1994
Gear, Luella (1897–1980) *Carefree* 1938; *Phffft!* 1954
Gearon, Valerie (1937–2003) *Nine Hours to Rama* 1963; *Invasion* 1965; *Anne of the Thousand Days* 1969
Geary, Anthony (1947–) *Disorderlies* 1987; *You Can't Hurry Love* 1988; *Crack House* 1989; *UHF* 1989; *Scorchers* 1991
Geary, Karl (1972–) *Nadja* 1995; *Gold in the Streets* 1996; *The Eternal* 1998; *Hamlet* 2000
Gebert, Gordon (1941–) *Holiday Affair* 1949; *The House on Telegraph Hill* 1951; *The Narrow Margin* 1952
Gedeck, Martina (1961–) *Life Is All You Get* 1998; *Mostly Martha* 2001
Gedrick, Jason (1965–) *The Heavenly Kid* 1985; *Iron Eagle* 1985; *Season of Dreams* 1987; *Promised Land* 1988; *Rooftops* 1989; *Backdraft* 1991; *Summer Catch* 2001
Gee, Robbie (1970–) *Mean Machine* 2001; *Underworld* 2003
Geer, Ellen (1941–) *Kotch* 1971; *Harold and Maude* 1972; *Over the Edge* 1979; *Hard Traveling* 1985
Geer, Will (1902–1978) *Anna Lucasta* 1949; *Intruder in the Dust* 1949; *Johnny Allegro* 1949; *Broken Arrow* 1950; *Comanche Territory* 1950; *The Kid from Texas* 1950; *To Please a Lady* 1950; *Winchester '73* 1950; *Bright Victory* 1951; *Double Crossbones* 1951; *The Tall Target* 1951; *Salt of the Earth* 1954; *Seconds* 1966; *In Cold Blood* 1967; *Bandolero!* 1968; *The Reivers* 1969; *Brother John* 1970; *Pieces of Dreams* 1970; *Jeremiah Johnson* 1972; *Napoleon and Samantha* 1972; *Executive Action* 1973; *Isn't It Shocking?* 1973; *The Billion Dollar Hobo* 1978
Geeson, Judy (1948–) *Berserk* 1967; *Here We Go round the Mulberry Bush* 1967; *To Sir, with Love* 1967; *Prudence and the Pill* 1968; *Three into Two Won't Go* 1969; *Two Gentlemen Sharing* 1969; *The Executioner* 1970; *One of Those Things* 1970; *10 Rillington Place* 1970; *Doomwatch* 1972; *Fear in the Night* 1972; *Diagnosis: Murder* 1974; *Percy's Progress* 1974; *Adventures of a Taxi Driver* 1975; *Brannigan* 1975; *Carry On England* 1976; *The Eagle Has Landed* 1976; *Dominique* 1978; *Inseminoid* 1981; *Everything Put Together* 2000
Geeson, Sally (1950–) *What's Good for the Goose* 1969; *Bless This House* 1972
Gégauff, Paul (1922–1983) *Weekend* 1967; *Une Partie de Plaisir* 1974
Gehman, Martha *The Legend of Billie Jean* 1985; *A Kiss before Dying* 1991; *Threesome* 1994
Geislerova, Anna (1976–) *Return of the Idiot* 1999; *Zelary* 2003
Geldof, Bob (1954–) *Pink Floyd – The Wall* 1982; *Number One* 1984; *Diana & Me* 1997
Gélin, Daniel (1921–2002) *Dieu A Besoin des Hommes* 1950; *La Ronde* 1950; *Les Mains Sales* 1951; *Le Plaisir* 1951; *Napoléon* 1955; *The Man Who Knew Too Much* 1956; *Too Many Lovers* 1957; *Carthage in Flames* 1960; *Le Souffle au Coeur* 1971; *Killing Cars* 1986; *Dandin* 1988
Gellar, Sarah Michelle aka **Gellar, Sarah** (1977–) *High Stakes* 1989; *I Know What You Did Last Summer* 1997; *Scream 2* 1997; *Small Soldiers* 1998; *Cruel Intentions* 1999; *Simply Irresistible* 1999; *Scooby-Doo* 2002; *The Grudge* 2004; *Scooby-Doo 2: Monsters Unleashed* 2004
Gemma, Giuliano (1938–) *A Man to Respect* 1972; *Somewhere beyond Love* 1974; *Tex and the Lord of the Deep* 1985
Genaro, Tony *Tremors* 1989; *Phenomenon* 1996; *Tremors 3: Back to Perfection* 2001
Genest, Emile (1921–2003) *Big Red* 1962; *The Incredible Journey* 1963; *Rampage* 1963
Géniat, Marcelle (1879–1959) *Crime and Punishment* 1935; *La Belle Equipe* 1936; *Le Défroqué* 1953
Génin, René *Le Jour Se Lève* 1939; *A Cage of Nightingales* 1945
Genn, Leo (1905–1978) *Ten Days in Paris* 1939; *Henry V* 1944; *Green for Danger* 1946; *Mourning Becomes Electra* 1947; *The Snake Pit* 1948; *The Velvet Touch* 1948; *No Place for Jennifer* 1949; *The Miniver Story* 1950; *The Wooden Horse* 1950; *Quo Vadis* 1951; *Plymouth Adventure* 1952; *Personal Affair* 1953; *The Red Beret* 1953; *The Green Scarf* 1954; *Moby Dick* 1956; *Beyond Mombasa* 1957; *The Steel Bayonet* 1957; *I Accuse!* 1958; *No Time to Die* 1958; *Too Hot to Handle* 1960; *Ten Little Indians* 1965; *Circus of Fear* 1967; *The Bloody Judge* 1969; *Die Screaming Marianne* 1970; *The Silent One* 1973
Genovese, Mike *Code of Silence* 1985; *From Hollywood to Deadwood* 1989
Gentle, Lili *Will Success Spoil Rock Hunter?* 1957; *Sing, Boy, Sing* 1958; *Mr Hobbs Takes a Vacation* 1962
Gentry, Minnie (1915–1993) *Georgia, Georgia* 1972; *Black Caesar* 1973; *Def by Temptation* 1990
Gentry, Race (1934–) *Black Horse Canyon* 1954; *The Bold and the Brave* 1956
Geoffrey, Paul *Excalibur* 1981; *Zina* 1985
Geoffreys, Stephen (1964–) *Fraternity Vacation* 1985; *Fright Night* 1985; *976-EVIL* 1988; *Moon 44* 1990
George, Chief Dan (1899–1981) *Smith!* 1969; *Little Big Man* 1970; *Dan Candy's Law* 1973; *The Bears and I* 1974; *Harry and Tonto* 1974; *The Outlaw Josey Wales* 1976
George, Christopher (1929–1983) *The Gentle Rain* 1966; *Project X* 1968; *The 1,000 Plane Raid* 1969; *Chisum* 1970; *The Delta Factor* 1970; *Tiger by the Tail* 1970; *I Escaped from Devil's Island* 1973; *The Train Robbers* 1973; *Dixie Dynamite* 1976; *Grizzly* 1976; *Day of the Animals* 1977; *The Exterminator* 1980; *Enter the Ninja* 1981; *Pieces* 1982
George, Florence (1915–) *College Swing* 1938; *Tell No Tales* 1939
George, Gladys (1900–1954) *Valiant Is the Word for Carrie* 1936; *Madame X* 1937; *They Gave Him a Gun* 1937; *Marie Antoinette* 1938; *The Roaring Twenties* 1939; *The House across the Bay* 1940; *The Way of All Flesh* 1940; *The Maltese Falcon* 1941; *The Hard Way* 1942; *The Crystal Ball* 1943; *Christmas Holiday* 1944; *Flamingo Road* 1949; *Bright Leaf* 1950; *Undercover Girl* 1950; *He Ran All the Way* 1951; *Lullaby of Broadway* 1951
George, Götz (1938–) *The Blood of Fu Manchu* 1968; *The Beautiful End of This World* 1983; *Out of Order* 1984; *Schtonk!* 1992
George, Heinrich (1893–1945) *Berlin Alexanderplatz* 1931; *Pillars of Society* 1935
George, Jan *Gods of the Plague* 1969; *The American Soldier* 1970
George, Maude (1888–1963) *Foolish Wives* 1920; *The Wedding March* 1928
George, Melissa (1976–) *Dark City* 1998; *The Limey* 1999; *New*

Port South 2001; Sugar & Spice 2001; The Amityville Horror 2005

George, Muriel (1883–1965) Limelight 1936; Song of the Road 1937; Went the Day Well? 1942; Last Holiday 1950

George, Richard (1898–) John of the Fair 1952; Ghost in the Shell 1995

George, Susan (1950–) The Sorcerers 1967; The Strange Affair 1968; All Neat in Black Stockings 1969; The Looking Glass War 1969; Spring and Port Wine 1969; Twinky 1969; Die Screaming Marianne 1970; Eyewitness 1970; Fright 1971; Straw Dogs 1971; Dirty Mary Crazy Larry 1974; Mandingo 1975; Out of Season 1975; A Small Town in Texas 1976; Tintorera 1977; Tomorrow Never Comes 1977; Enter the Ninja 1981; Venom 1981; The House Where Evil Dwells 1982; The Jigsaw Man 1984; Lightning the White Stallion 1986; That Summer of White Roses 1989

Georges-Picot, Olga (1944–1997) Je T'Aime, Je T'Aime 1968; The Man Who Haunted Himself 1970; Persecution 1974; Goodbye Emmanuelle 1977

Georgeson, Tom No Surrender 1986; A Fish Called Wanda 1988; Downtime 1997; The Land Girls 1997; Man Dancin' 2003

Geraghty, Carmelita (1901–1966) The Pleasure Garden 1925; My Best Girl 1927

Geraghty, Marita Sleeping with the Enemy 1991; This Is My Life 1992; Groundhog Day 1993; Desperate Measures 1995

Gérald, Jim (1889–1958) An Italian Straw Hat 1927; Adventures of Captain Fabian 1951; The Crimson Curtain 1952

Geray, Steven *aka* **Geray, Steve** (1904–1973) The Moon and Sixpence 1942; Cornered 1945; Gilda 1946; So Dark the Night 1946; The Unfaithful 1947; The Dark Past 1948; Once More, My Darling 1949; A Lady without Passport 1950; The Big Sky 1952; The Golden Blade 1953; Jesse James Meets Frankenstein's Daughter 1966

Gere, Richard (1949–) Report to the Commissioner 1975; Looking for Mr Goodbar 1977; Bloodbrothers 1978; Days of Heaven 1978; Yanks 1979; American Gigolo 1980; An Officer and a Gentleman 1982; Breathless 1983; The Honorary Consul 1983; The Cotton Club 1984; King David 1985; No Mercy 1986; Power 1986; Miles from Home 1988; Internal Affairs 1990; Pretty Woman 1990; Rhapsody in August 1990; Final Analysis 1992; And the Band Played On 1993; Mr Jones 1993; Sommersby 1993; Intersection 1994; First Knight 1995; Primal Fear 1996; The Jackal 1997; Red Corner 1997; Runaway Bride 1999; Autumn in New York 2000; Dr T & the Women 2000; The Mothman Prophecies 2001; Chicago 2002; Unfaithful 2002; Shall We Dance 2004

Geret, Georges *aka* **Géret, Georges** (1924–1996) The Diary of a Chambermaid 1964; Dead Run 1967; The Stranger 1967; They Came to Rob Las Vegas 1968; Z 1968

Gerini, Claudia (1971–) Francesca and Nunziata 2001; Don't Move 2004; The Passion of the Christ 2004

Germaine, Mary (1933–) Cloudburst 1951; Father's Doing Fine 1952; House of Blackmail 1953

Germann, Greg (1962–) Jesus' Son 1999; The Last Producer 2000; Down to Earth 2001; Joe Somebody 2001

Germon, Nane (1909–) La Belle et la Bête 1946; Les Biches 1968

Gerrish, Frank (1963–) Secret of Treasure Mountain 1993; Rigoletto 1995

Gerritsen, Lisa (1957–) The War between Men and Women 1972; Mixed Company 1974

Gerroll, Daniel (1951–) 84 Charing Cross Road 1986; Happy New Year 1987; Big Business 1988; Drop Dead Fred 1991; A Far Off Place 1993

Gerry, Alex (1904–1993) The Jazz Singer 1952; The Eddie Cantor Story 1953; The Come On 1956; The Bellboy 1960

Gersak, Savina Curse II: The Bite 1989; Death Train 1989

Gershon, Gina (1962–) 3:15 1986; Cocktail 1988; Red Heat 1988; Suffering Bastards 1989; Out for Justice 1991; Miss Rose White 1992; Joey Breaker 1993; Showgirls 1995; Bound 1996; This World, Then the Fireworks 1996; Touch 1996; Face/Off 1997; Black and White 1998; I'm Losing You 1998; Legalese 1998; Lulu on the Bridge 1998; One Tough Cop 1998; Palmetto 1998; Guinevere 1999; The Insider 1999; Driven 2001; Demonlover 2002

Gerson, Betty Lou (1914–1999) The Fly 1958; One Hundred and One Dalmatians 1960

Gerstle, Frank (1915–1970) Gang Busters 1955; Top Secret Affair 1957; Submarine Seahawk 1959; The Wasp Woman 1959

Gert, Valeska (1892–1978) The Joyless Street 1925; The Threepenny Opera 1931

Gertz, Jami (1965–) Alphabet City 1984; Mischief 1985; Crossroads 1986; Quicksilver 1986; Solarbabies 1986; Less than Zero 1987; The Lost Boys 1987; Listen to Me 1989; Renegades 1989; Silence like Glass 1989; The Boyfriend School 1990; Sibling Rivalry 1990; Jersey Girl 1992; Twister 1996

Gervais, Ricky (1961–) Dog Eat Dog 2000; Valiant 2005

Getty, Balthazar *aka* **Getty, Paul Balthazar** (1975–) Lord of the Flies 1990; Young Guns II 1990; December 1991; My Heroes Have Always Been Cowboys 1991; The Pope Must Die 1991; Where the Day Takes You 1992; Dead Beat 1994; Lost Highway 1996; Four Dogs Playing Poker 1999; Shadow Hours 2000; The Center of the World 2001; Ladder 49 2004

Getty, Estelle (1923–) Mask 1985; Mannequin 1987; Stop! or My Mom Will Shoot 1992; Fortune Hunters 1999

Getz, John (1947–) Tattoo 1980; Blood Simple 1983; Thief of Hearts 1984; The Fly 1986; The Fly II 1989; Men at Work 1990; Curly Sue 1991; Don't Tell Mom the Babysitter's Dead 1991; Playmaker 1994; Rules of Obsession 1994; Untamed Love 1994; Shadow of the Past 1995; Stolen Youth 1996

Ghosh, Robi (1931–1997) Abhijaan 1962; Days and Nights in the Forest 1969

Ghostley, Alice (1926–) New Faces 1954; One Born Every Minute 1967; With Six You Get Eggroll 1968; Viva Max! 1969; Ace Eli and Rodger of the Skies 1973; Gator 1976; Not for Publication 1984; Palmer's Pick-Up 1999; Whispers: an Elephant's Tale 2000

Gialelis, Stathis (1939–) America, America 1963; Blue 1968; The Children of Sanchez 1978

Giamatti, Paul (1967–) Private Parts 1997; The Negotiator 1998; Safe Men 1998; Man on the Moon 1999; Big Momma's House 2000; Duets 2000; Planet of the Apes 2001; Storytelling 2001; Big Fat Liar 2002; Confidence 2002; Thunderpants 2002; American Splendor 2003; Paycheck 2003; Sideways 2004; Cinderella Man 2005

Giambalvo, Louis (1945–) See No Evil, Hear No Evil 1989; Flashfire 1993

Giannini, Adriano (1971–) Swept Away 2002; Sinbad: Legend of the Seven Seas 2003; The Consequences of Love 2004

Giannini, Giancarlo (1942–) Anzio 1968; Jealousy, Italian Style 1970; The Seduction of Mimi 1972; Swept Away... by an Unusual Destiny in the Blue Sea of August 1974; L'Innocente 1976; Seven Beauties 1976; The End of the World (in Our Usual Bed in a Night Full of Rain) 1978; Travels with Anita 1978; Blood Feud 1979; Immortal Bachelor 1980; Lili Marleen 1980; American Dreamer 1984; Fever Pitch 1985; Saving Grace 1985; Blood Red 1988; New York Stories 1989; Once upon a Crime 1992; Jacob 1994; A Walk in the Clouds 1995; The Disappearance of Garcia Lorca 1997; Mimic 1997; Francesca and Nunziata 2001; Hannibal 2001; Darkness 2002; Eugenio 2002; My House in Umbria 2002; Man on Fire 2004

Giatti, Ian (1977–) The Great Outdoors 1988; The Rescue 1988

Gibb, Cynthia (1963–) Salvador 1986; Youngblood 1986; Malone 1987; Jack's Back 1988; Short Circuit 2 1988; Death Warrant 1990; Gypsy 1993; Holiday Affair 1996

Gibb, Donald Bloodsport 1987; Bloodsport II: The Next Kumite 1996

Gibney, Susan Unforgivable 1995; Cabin by the Lake 2000

Gibson, Donal (1958–) Emma's War 1985; Fatal Bond 1991

Gibson, Henry (1935–) Evil Roy Slade 1971; Charlotte's Web 1973; The Long Goodbye 1973; Nashville 1975; The Last Remake of Beau Geste 1977; A Perfect Couple 1979; The Blues Brothers 1980; HEALTH 1980; The Incredible Shrinking Woman 1981; Monster in the Closet 1983; Switching Channels 1987; The 'Burbs 1989; Tom and Jerry: the Movie 1992; Color of a Brisk and Leaping Day 1996; Magnolia 1999

Gibson, Hoot (1892–1962) Straight Shooting 1917; The Last Outlaw 1936; The Horse Soldiers 1959

Gibson, Mel (1956–) Mad Max 1979; Tim 1979; Attack Force Z 1981; Gallipoli 1981; Mad Max 2 1981; The Year of Living Dangerously 1982; The Bounty 1984; Mrs Soffel 1984; The River 1984; Mad Max beyond Thunderdome 1985; Lethal Weapon 1987; Tequila Sunrise 1988; Lethal Weapon 2 1989; Air America 1990; Bird on a Wire 1990; Hamlet 1990; Forever Young 1992; Lethal Weapon 3 1992; The Man without a Face 1993; Maverick 1994; Braveheart 1995; Casper 1995; Pocahontas 1995; Ransom 1996; Conspiracy Theory 1997; FairyTale: a True Story 1997; Lethal Weapon 4 1998; Payback 1998; The Million Dollar Hotel 1999; Chicken Run 2000; The Patriot 2000; What Women Want 2001; Signs 2002; We Were Soldiers 2002; The Singing Detective 2003; Paparazzi 2004

Gibson, Thomas (1962–) Far and Away 1992; Love and Human Remains 1993; Barcelona 1994; Devil's Child 1997; Stardom 2000

Gibson, Tyrese *aka* **Tyrese** (1978–) Baby Boy 2001; 2 Fast 2 Furious 2003; Flight of the Phoenix 2004

Gibson, Virginia (1928–) Stop, You're Killing Me 1952; Athena 1954

Gibson, Wynne (1899–1987) City Streets 1931; Man of the World 1931; If I Had a Million 1932; Night after Night 1932; The Captain Hates the Sea 1934; Miracle on Main Street 1940

Gidley, Pamela (1966–) Thrashin' 1986; The Blue Iguana 1988; Cherry 2000 1988; Permanent Record 1988; Disturbed 1990; Liebestraum 1991; Highway to Hell 1992; Paper Hearts 1993; Freefall 1994; SFW 1994; Aberration 1997; Jane Austen's Mafia 1998; The Little Vampire 2000

Gidwani, Kitu Dance of the Wind 1997; Earth 1998

Giehse, Thérèse (1898–1975) Black Moon 1974; Lacombe Lucien 1974

Gielgud, John (1904–2000) The Good Companions 1933; Secret Agent 1936; The Prime Minister 1940; Julius Caesar 1953; Romeo and Juliet 1954; Richard III 1955; Around the World in 80 Days 1956; The Barretts of Wimpole Street 1956; Saint Joan 1957; To Die in Madrid 1963; Becket 1964; The Loved One 1965; Chimes at Midnight 1966; Assignment to Kill 1968; The Charge of the Light Brigade 1968; Sebastian 1968; The Shoes of the Fisherman 1968; Oh! What a Lovely War 1969; Julius Caesar 1970; Eagle in a Cage 1971; Frankenstein: the True Story 1973; Lost Horizon 1973; 11 Harrowhouse 1974; Galileo 1974; Gold 1974; Murder on the Orient Express 1974; Aces High 1976; Joseph Andrews 1977; A Portrait of the Artist as a Young Man 1977; Providence 1977; Les Misérables 1978; Murder by Decree 1978; Caligula 1979; The Human Factor 1979; The Conductor 1980; The Elephant Man 1980; The Formula 1980; Sphinx 1980; Arthur 1981; Chariots of Fire 1981; Lion of the Desert 1981; Priest of Love 1981; Gandhi 1982; The Hunchback of Notre Dame 1982; Invitation to the Wedding 1983; Scandalous 1983; The Scarlet and the Black 1983; Wagner 1983; The Wicked Lady 1983; The Shooting Party 1984; Leave All Fair 1985; Plenty 1985; The Whistle Blower 1986; Appointment with Death 1988; Arthur 2: On the Rocks 1988; Getting It Right 1989; Loser Takes All 1990; The Power of One 1991; Prospero's Books 1991; Shining Through 1992; Haunted 1995; DragonHeart 1996; Hamlet 1996; The Portrait of a Lady 1996; Shine 1996; The Magic Sword: Quest for Camelot 1997; Elizabeth 1998; The Tichborne Claimant 1998

Gierasch, Stefan (1926–) Jeremiah Johnson 1972; What's Up, Doc? 1972; High Plains Drifter 1973; Blood Beach 1981; Perfect 1985; Shannon's Deal 1989; Jack the Bear 1993

Gifford, Alan (1905–1989) The Flying Scot 1957; Time Lock 1957; Screaming Mimi 1958; Phase IV 1973

Gifford, Frances (1920–1994) Beyond the Blue Horizon 1942; Cry Havoc 1943; Tarzan Triumphs 1943; Marriage Is a Private Affair 1944; Thrill of a Romance 1945; The Arnelo Affair 1947; Riding High 1950

Gifford, Frank (1930–) Up Periscope 1959; Viva Knievel! 1977

Gifford, Gloria DC Cab 1983; Vice Versa 1988

Gift, Roland (1963–) Sammy and Rosie Get Laid 1987; Scandal 1988

Giglio, Sandro (1900–1979) Assignment – Paris 1952; The War of the Worlds 1953

Gil, Ariadna (1969–) Belle Epoque 1992; Second Skin 2000

Gil, Vincent (1939–) Encounter at Raven's Gate 1988; Ghosts... of the Civil Dead 1988; Body Melt 1993

Gilbert, Andrew S *aka* **Gilbert, Andrew** Mortgage 1989; Kiss or Kill 1997; Paperback Hero 1998; Mullet 2001

Gilbert, Billy (1894–1971) County Hospital 1932; The Music Box 1932; Pack Up Your Troubles 1932; Their First Mistake 1932; Towed in a Hole 1932; Them Thar Hills! 1934; The Bride Walks Out 1936; Poor Little Rich Girl 1936; Espionage 1937; One Hundred Men and a Girl 1937; Rosalie 1937; Snow White and the Seven Dwarfs 1937; Blockheads 1938; Happy Landing 1938; Maid's Night Out 1938; My Lucky Star 1938; His Girl Friday 1939; The Great Dictator 1940; Lucky Partners 1940; No, No, Nanette 1940; Seven Sinners 1940; The Villain Still Pursued Her 1940; Weekend in Havana 1941; Song of the Islands 1942; Stage Door Canteen 1943; Anchors Aweigh 1945; Fun and Fancy Free 1947; Bride of Vengeance 1949

Gilbert, Helen (1915–1995) Andy Hardy Gets Spring Fever 1939; The Secret of Dr Kildare 1939; Florian 1940; Beyond the Blue Horizon 1942; The Falcon Takes Over 1942

Gilbert, Joanne Red Garters 1954; The Great Man 1956; The High Cost of Loving 1958

Gilbert, Jody (1916–1979) House by the River 1950; Willard 1971

Gilbert (1), John (1895–1936) He Who Gets Slapped 1924; The Big Parade 1925; The Merry Widow 1925; La Bohème 1926; Flesh and the Devil 1926; Love 1927; Show People 1928; A Woman of Affairs 1928; Hollywood Revue 1929; Queen Christina 1933; The Captain Hates the Sea 1934

Gilbert, Lou (1909–1978) Goldstein 1963; Frank's Greatest Adventure 1967; The Great White Hope 1970; Jennifer on My Mind 1971

Gilbert, Marcus Biggles 1986; A Ghost in Monte Carlo 1990; Army of Darkness 1993

Gilbert, Melissa (1964–) Sylvester 1985; Shattered Trust 1993; Her Own Rules 1998; Mistaken Identity 1999

Gilbert, Paul (1918–1976) So This Is Paris 1954; You Can't Run Away from It 1956

Gilbert, Philip (1931–2004) Bachelor of Hearts 1958; The Frozen Dead 1966

Gilbert, Sara (1975–) Poison Ivy 1992; Dead Beat 1994; Desert Blue 1998; Light It Up 1999; Riding in Cars with Boys 2001

Gilborn, Steven [Safe] 1995; About Sarah 1998

Gilchrist, Connie (1901–1985) A Woman's Face 1941; Apache Trail 1942; Act of Violence 1949; A Letter to Three Wives 1949; A Ticket to Tomahawk 1950; Flesh and Fury 1952; The Half-Breed 1952; Houdini 1953; It Should Happen to You 1954; Long John Silver 1954; Say One for Me 1959; The Misadventures of Merlin Jones 1964; Two on a Guillotine 1964; Tickle Me 1965

Gilford, Jack (1907–1990) Mister Buddwing 1965; A Funny Thing Happened on the Way to the Forum 1966; Enter Laughing 1967; The Incident 1967; Catch-22 1970; They Might Be Giants 1971; Save the Tiger 1973; Wholly Moses! 1980; Caveman 1981; Cocoon 1985; Cocoon: the Return 1988

Gill, Basil (1877–1955) The Wandering Jew 1933; Knight without Armour 1937

Gill, John Something for Everyone 1970; That Summer of White Roses 1989

Gill, Tom (1916–1971) Something in the City 1950; Behind the Headlines 1956; Up the Creek 1958

Gillain, Marie (1975–) Mon Père Ce Héros 1991; The Bait 1995; Le Bossu 1997; Harem Suare 1999; Laissez-passer 2001

Gillen, Aidan (1958–) Circle of Friends 1995; Gold in the Streets 1996; Some Mother's Son 1996; Mojo 1998; Buddy Boy 1999; The Low Down 2000; My Kingdom 2001; The Final Curtain 2002; Shanghai Knights 2002

Gillespie, Dana The People That Time Forgot 1977; Bad Timing 1980; Scrubbers 1982

Gillett, Aden The Winslow Boy 1999; Shadow of the Vampire 2000

Gillette, Anita (1936–) Boys on the Side 1995; Larger than Life 1996

Gilliam, Burton Thunderbolt and Lightfoot 1974; Quake! 1992

Gilliam, Seth Jefferson in Paris 1995; Courage under Fire 1996

Gilliam, Stu (1943–) Brothers 1977; Return from Witch Mountain 1978

Gilliam, Terry (1940–) *And Now for Something Completely Different* 1971; *Monty Python and the Holy Grail* 1975; *Pleasure at Her Majesty's* 1976; *Monty Python's Life of Brian* 1979; *Monty Python Live at the Hollywood Bowl* 1982; *Monty Python's The Meaning of Life* 1983
Gilliard Jr, Larry *aka* **Gilliard Jr, Lawrence** *Straight out of Brooklyn* 1991; *The Substitute 2: School's Out* 1997; *Next Stop Wonderland* 1998; *The Waterboy* 1998; *Simply Irresistible* 1999; *Cecil B Demented* 2000
Gillie, Jean (1915–1949) *The Gentle Sex* 1943; *The Saint Meets the Tiger* 1943; *Tawny Pipit* 1944
Gilliland, Richard (1950–) *Bug* 1975; *Happy Hour* 1987; *Evidence of Love* 1990; *Shattering the Silence* 1992; *The Lies Boys Tell* 1994; *The Man Next Door* 1996; *Dogwatch* 1997; *Star Kid* 1997
Gillin, Hugh (1925–2004) *Psycho II* 1983; *Psycho III* 1986; *Doin' Time on Planet Earth* 1988
Gilling, Rebecca (1953–) *The Naked Country* 1985; *Heaven Tonight* 1990
Gillingwater, Claude *aka* **Gillingwater Sr, Claude** (1870–1939) *Little Lord Fauntleroy* 1921; *Daddy Long Legs* 1931; *Tess of the Storm Country* 1932; *The Prisoner of Shark Island* 1936; *Just around the Corner* 1938
Gillis, Ann *aka* **Gillis, Anne** (1927–) *The Adventures of Tom Sawyer* 1938; *Nice Girl?* 1941; *Abbott and Costello in Society* 1944; *The Cheaters* 1945
Gillmer, Caroline *Hotel Sorrento* 1994; *Paws* 1997; *The Monkey's Mask* 2000
Gillmore, Margalo (1897–1986) *The Happy Years* 1950; *Perfect Strangers* 1950; *Cause for Alarm* 1951; *Gaby* 1956
Gilman, Sam (1915–1985) *Macon County Line* 1973; *Every Which Way but Loose* 1978
Gilmore, Craig *The Living End* 1992; *Totally F***ed Up* 1993
Gilmore, Lowell (1906–1960) *Days of Glory* 1944; *Johnny Angel* 1945; *The Picture of Dorian Gray* 1945; *Calcutta* 1947; *The Black Arrow* 1948; *Dream Girl* 1948; *King Solomon's Mines* 1950; *Rogues of Sherwood Forest* 1950; *Roadblock* 1951; *Lone Star* 1952; *Comanche* 1956
Gilmore, Peter (1931–) *I've Gotta Horse* 1965; *The Abominable Dr Phibes* 1971; *Warlords of Atlantis* 1978
Gilmore, Virginia (1919–1986) *Swamp Water* 1941; *Tall, Dark and Handsome* 1941; *Western Union* 1941; *Berlin Correspondent* 1942; *Orchestra Wives* 1942; *Walk East on Beacon* 1952
Gilmour, Ian (1955–) *The Odd Angry Shot* 1979; *A Dangerous Summer* 1981; *The Boy Who Had Everything* 1984; *Malpractice* 1989
Gilpin, Jack (1951–) *Something Wild* 1986; *Funny Farm* 1988; *Reversal of Fortune* 1990
Gilpin, Marc (1966–) *Where's Willie?* 1977; *Earthbound* 1981
Gilpin, Peri (1961–) *Laughter on the 23rd Floor* 2000; *Final Fantasy: the Spirits Within* 2001
Gimenez Cacho, Daniel *aka* **Giménez-Cacho, Daniel** (1961–) *Cabeza de Vaca* 1990; *Deep Crimson* 1996; *Bad Education* 2004
Ging, Jack (1931–) *Tess of the Storm Country* 1960; *High Plains Drifter* 1973; *Ssssss* 1973; *Where the Red Fern Grows* 1974
Gingold, Hermione (1897–1987) *Someone at the Door* 1936; *Cosh Boy* 1952; *The Pickwick Papers* 1952; *Our Girl Friday* 1953; *Around the World in 80 Days* 1956; *Bell, Book and Candle* 1958; *Gigi* 1958; *The Naked Edge* 1961; *Gay Purr-ee* 1962; *The Music Man* 1962; *I'd Rather Be Rich* 1964; *Harvey Middleman, Fireman* 1965; *Munster, Go Home!* 1966; *Promise Her Anything* 1966; *Jules Verne's Rocket to the Moon* 1967; *A Little Night Music* 1977
Ginsberg, Allen (1926–1997) *Pull My Daisy* 1959; *Chappaqua* 1966
Ginty, Robert (1948–) *Coming Home* 1978; *The Exterminator* 1980; *Exterminator 2* 1980; *The Alchemist* 1981; *Loverboy* 1989; *Madhouse* 1990; *Harley Davidson and the Marlboro Man* 1991
Gio, Frank *Me and the Mob* 1992; *Assassination Tango* 2002
Giordani, Rocky *After Dark, My Sweet* 1990; *Cop and a Half* 1993
Giordano, Domiziana (1960–) *Nostalgia* 1983; *Zina* 1985; *Nouvelle Vague* 1990; *Interview with the Vampire: the Vampire Chronicles* 1994
Giorgelli, Gabriella (1942–) *The Organizer* 1963; *The Beautiful Swindlers* 1964
Giorgetti, Florence (1944–) *La Grande Bouffe* 1973; *The Lacemaker* 1977
Girard, Philippe *Wild Target* 1993; *Les Apprentis* 1995
Girard, Rémy (1950–) *The Decline of the American Empire* 1986; *Jesus of Montreal* 1989; *The Barbarian Invasions* 2003
Girardon, Michèle (1938–1975) *The Sign of Leo* 1959; *The Seven Deadly Sins* 1961; *The Boulangère de Monceau* 1962; *Hatari!* 1962
Girardot, Annie (1931–) *Maigret Sets a Trap* 1957; *Rocco and His Brothers* 1960; *La Bonne Soupe* 1963; *The Organizer* 1963; *The Dirty Game* 1965; *Trois Chambres à Manhattan* 1965; *The Witches* 1966; *Vivre pour Vivre* 1967; *The Seed of Man* 1969; *Shock Treatment* 1973; *Doctor Françoise Gailland* 1975; *To Each His Own Hell* 1977; *Hit List* 1984; *The Piano Teacher* 2001
Girardot, Etienne (1856–1939) *Twentieth Century* 1934; *Breakfast for Two* 1937; *Port of Seven Seas* 1938; *Fast and Loose* 1939; *The Story of Vernon and Irene Castle* 1939
Girardot, Hippolyte (1955–) *First Name: Carmen* 1983; *Manon des Sources* 1986; *A World without Pity* 1989; *Hors la Vie* 1991; *Après l'Amour* 1992; *La Fille de l'Air* 1992; *Le Parfum d'Yvonne* 1994; *Jump Tomorrow* 2001; *Kings & Queen* 2004
Giraud, Roland (1942–) *3 Men and a Cradle* 1985; *Mister Frost* 1990
Giraudeau, Bernard (1947–) *Le Grand Pardon* 1981; *Angel Dust* 1987; *Après l'Amour* 1992; *Ridicule* 1996; *Marquise* 1997; *Water Drops on Burning Rocks* 1999
Girling, Cindy *The Kidnapping of the President* 1980; *Heart of a Child* 1994
Girotti, Massimo (1918–2003) *Ossessione* 1942; *Chronicle of a Love* 1950; *Senso* 1954; *Marguerite de la Nuit* 1955; *It Happened in Rome* 1956; *Duel of the Titans* 1961; *Imperial Venus* 1963; *Gold for the Caesars* 1964; *Theorem* 1968; *The Red Tent* 1969; *Medea* 1970; *Baron Blood* 1972; *L'Innocente* 1976; *The Art of Love* 1983; *Facing Window* 2003
Gish, Annabeth (1971–) *Desert Bloom* 1985; *Hiding Out* 1987; *Mystic Pizza* 1988; *Shag* 1988; *Coupe de Ville* 1990; *The Last Supper* 1995; *Beautiful Girls* 1996; *What Love Sees* 1996; *Steel* 1997; *Double Jeopardy* 1999; *No Higher Love* 1999; *SLC Punk!* 1999; *Buying the Cow* 2000
Gish, Dorothy (1898–1968) *Home, Sweet Home* 1914; *Hearts of the World* 1918; *Orphans of the Storm* 1921; *Fury* 1923; *Centennial Summer* 1946; *The Cardinal* 1963
Gish, Lillian (1893–1993) *The Musketeers of Pig Alley* 1912; *The Battle of Elderbush* 1914; *The Battle of the Sexes* 1914; *Home, Sweet Home* 1914; *The Birth of a Nation* 1915; *Intolerance* 1916; *Hearts of the World* 1918; *Broken Blossoms* 1919; *Way Down East* 1920; *Orphans of the Storm* 1921; *The White Sister* 1923; *La Bohème* 1926; *The Scarlet Letter* 1926; *Annie Laurie* 1927; *The Wind* 1928; *One Romantic Night* 1930; *His Double Life* 1933; *The Commandos Strike at Dawn* 1942; *Miss Susie Slagle's* 1945; *Duel in the Sun* 1946; *Portrait of Jennie* 1948; *The Cobweb* 1955; *The Night of the Hunter* 1955; *Orders to Kill* 1958; *The Unforgiven* 1960; *Follow Me, Boys!* 1966; *The Comedians* 1967; *Warning Shot* 1967; *A Wedding* 1978; *Hambone and Hillie* 1984; *Sweet Liberty* 1986; *The Whales of August* 1987
Gish, Sheila (1942–2005) *A Day in the Death of Joe Egg* 1971; *Highlander* 1986; *Mansfield Park* 1999; *Highlander: Endgame* 2000
Gist, Robert (1924–1998) *The Band Wagon* 1953; *D-Day the Sixth of June* 1956
Gittins, Paul *Other Halves* 1984; *The End of the Golden Weather* 1992; *Exposure* 2000
Giuffre, Aldo (1924–) *The Best of Enemies* 1961; *Hercules, Samson and Ulysses* 1963; *Ghosts – Italian Style* 1967; *The Heroes* 1972
Giuffrè, Carlo (1928–) *Madame* 1961; *Pinocchio* 2002
Giuntoli, Neil *Child's Play* 1988; *The Borrower* 1989; *Henry: Portrait of a Serial Killer, Part II* 1996; *Palmer's Pick-Up* 1999
Giustini, Carlo *aka* **Justin, Charles** (1923–) *The Passionate Stranger* 1957; *The Savage Innocents* 1960; *The Wild, Wild Planet* 1965
Givens, Robin (1964–) *A Rage in Harlem* 1991; *Boomerang* 1992; *Blankman* 1994; *Foreign Student* 1994; *Dangerous Intentions* 1995; *The Face* 1996; *Head of State* 2003
Givney, Kathryn (1897–1978) *My Friend Irma* 1949; *Lightning Strikes Twice* 1951; *Operation Pacific* 1951; *Three Coins in the Fountain* 1954; *Congo Crossing* 1956
Givot, George (1903–1984) *Step Lively, Jeeves* 1937; *Behind the Rising Sun* 1943; *DuBarry Was a Lady* 1943; *The Falcon and the Co-Eds* 1943; *Riff-Raff* 1947; *April in Paris* 1952; *Three Sailors and a Girl* 1953; *China Gate* 1957
Gladwin, Joe (1906–1987) *Night Must Fall* 1964; *Work Is a Four Letter Word* 1968; *Nearest and Dearest* 1972
Glaser, Paul Michael *aka* **Glaser, Michael** (1943–) *Fiddler on the Roof* 1971; *Starsky and Hutch* 1975; *Phobia* 1980; *Something's Gotta Give* 2003
Glass, Ned (1906–1984) *Jennifer* 1953; *The Rebel Set* 1959; *West Side Story* 1961; *Experiment in Terror* 1962; *Kid Galahad* 1962; *Charade* 1963; *The All-American Boy* 1973
Glasser, Isabel *Forever Young* 1992; *Pure Country* 1992; *Exquisite Tenderness* 1995; *Tactical Assault* 1998
Glasser, Phillip (1978–) *An American Tail* 1986; *An American Tail: Fievel Goes West* 1991; *Stanley's Magic Garden* 1994
Glaubrecht, Frank *The Bridge* 1959; *Codename Wildgeese* 1984
Glaudini, Robert *The Alchemist* 1981; *Parasite* 1982
Glave, Matthew *The Wedding Singer* 1998; *Mutiny* 1999
Gleason, Jackie (1916–1987) *All through the Night* 1942; *Larceny, Inc* 1942; *Orchestra Wives* 1942; *Springtime in the Rockies* 1942; *The Hustler* 1961; *Gigot* 1962; *Requiem for a Heavyweight* 1962; *Papa's Delicate Condition* 1963; *Soldier in the Rain* 1963; *Skidoo* 1968; *Don't Drink the Water* 1969; *How to Commit Marriage* 1969; *How Do I Love Thee?* 1970; *Mr Billion* 1977; *Smokey and the Bandit* 1977; *Smokey and the Bandit II* 1980; *The Toy* 1982; *Smokey and the Bandit III* 1983; *The Sting II* 1983; *Nothing in Common* 1986
Gleason, James (1886–1959) *Her Man* 1930; *A Free Soul* 1931; *Blondie of the Follies* 1932; *The Penguin Pool Murder* 1932; *Murder on the Blackboard* 1934; *Murder on a Honeymoon* 1935; *The Ex-Mrs Bradford* 1936; *Murder on a Bridle Path* 1936; *The Plot Thickens* 1936; *On Your Toes* 1939; *Affectionately Yours* 1941; *A Date with the Falcon* 1941; *Here Comes Mr Jordan* 1941; *Meet John Doe* 1941; *The Falcon Takes Over* 1942; *Footlight Serenade* 1942; *My Gal Sal* 1942; *Crash Dive* 1943; *Arsenic and Old Lace* 1944; *A Guy Named Joe* 1944; *Once upon a Time* 1944; *The Clock* 1945; *This Man's Navy* 1945; *A Tree Grows in Brooklyn* 1945; *Home Sweet Homicide* 1946; *The Hoodlum Saint* 1946; *Lady Luck* 1946; *The Well Groomed Bride* 1946; *The Bishop's Wife* 1947; *Down to Earth* 1947; *Tycoon* 1947; *The Return of October* 1948; *Smart Woman* 1948; *When My Baby Smiles at Me* 1948; *Miss Grant Takes Richmond* 1949; *The Jackpot* 1950; *Key to the City* 1950; *Riding High* 1950; *The Yellow Cab Man* 1950; *Come Fill the Cup* 1951; *I'll See You in My Dreams* 1951; *Forever Female* 1953; *Suddenly* 1954; *The Girl Rush* 1955; *The Night of the Hunter* 1955; *Star in the Dust* 1956; *Loving You* 1957; *Man in the Shadow* 1957; *Spring Reunion* 1957; *The Last Hurrah* 1958; *Rock-a-Bye Baby* 1958
Gleason, Joanna (1950–) *Crimes and Misdemeanors* 1989; *The Boys* 1991; *FX 2* 1991; *American Perfekt* 1997
Gleason, Lucille Webster (1888–1947) *Girls about Town* 1931; *Rhythm on the Range* 1936
Gleason, Paul (1944–) *Doc Savage: the Man of Bronze* 1975; *He Knows You're Alone* 1981; *The Pursuit of DB Cooper* 1981; *Trading Places* 1983; *The Breakfast Club* 1985; *Forever Lulu* 1987; *Home Front* 1987; *Die Hard* 1988; *Johnny Be Good* 1988; *Night Game* 1989; *Wishman* 1991; *Running Cool* 1993; *Money Talks* 1997
Gleckler, Robert (1887–1939) *The Glass Key* 1935; *Whipsaw* 1935
Gleeson, Brendan (1954–) *The Snapper* 1993; *Braveheart* 1995; *A Further Gesture* 1996; *Trojan Eddie* 1996; *I Went Down* 1997; *Turbulence* 1997; *The General* 1998; *Lake Placid* 1999; *Saltwater* 1999; *Harrison's Flowers* 2000; *The Tailor of Panama* 2000; *Wild about Harry* 2000; *AI: Artificial Intelligence* 2001; *Dark Blue* 2002; *Gangs of New York* 2002; *28 Days Later…* 2002; *Cold Mountain* 2003; *Troy* 2004; *The Village* 2004; *Kingdom of Heaven* 2005
Gleeson, Paul *Komodo* 1999; *Virtual Nightmare* 2000
Glen, Georgie *Mrs Brown* 1997; *Calendar Girls* 2003
Glen, Iain (1961–) *Gorillas in the Mist* 1988; *Paris by Night* 1988; *Mountains of the Moon* 1989; *Silent Scream* 1989; *Fools of Fortune* 1990; *Rosencrantz and Guildenstern Are Dead* 1990; *The Young Americans* 1993; *Beautiful Creatures* 2000; *Gabriel & Me* 2001; *Lara Croft: Tomb Raider* 2001; *Darkness* 2002; *Song for a Raggy Boy* 2002; *Kingdom of Heaven* 2005
Glenaan, Kenneth *aka* **Glenaan, Kenny** *Silent Scream* 1989; *This Is Not a Love Song* 2002
Glendenning, Candace *Nicholas and Alexandra* 1971; *Satan's Slave* 1976
Glenister, Philip *ID* 1994; *Calendar Girls* 2003
Glenn, Jason *The Butter Cream Gang* 1991; *Secret of Treasure Mountain* 1993
Glenn, Roy *aka* **Glenn Sr, Roy E** (1914–1971) *Carmen Jones* 1954; *Guess Who's Coming to Dinner* 1967
Glenn, Scott (1942–) *The Baby Maker* 1970; *Fighting Mad* 1976; *Apocalypse Now* 1979; *Cattle Annie and Little Britches* 1980; *Urban Cowboy* 1980; *The Challenge* 1982; *Personal Best* 1982; *The Keep* 1983; *The Right Stuff* 1983; *The River* 1984; *Silverado* 1985; *Wild Geese II* 1985; *Man on Fire* 1987; *Saigon* 1988; *Miss Firecracker* 1989; *The Hunt for Red October* 1990; *Backdraft* 1991; *My Heroes Have Always Been Cowboys* 1991; *The Silence of the Lambs* 1991; *Tall Tale* 1994; *Reckless* 1995; *Absolute Power* 1996; *Carla's Song* 1996; *Courage under Fire* 1996; *Firestorm* 1998; *The Last Marshal* 1999; *Vertical Limit* 2000; *Buffalo Soldiers* 2001; *The Shipping News* 2001; *Training Day* 2001
Glenville, Peter (1913–1996) *Uncensored* 1942; *Madonna of the Seven Moons* 1944; *Good Time Girl* 1948
Glick, Stacey *Brighton Beach Memoirs* 1986; *Three O'Clock High* 1987
Glover, Brian (1934–1997) *Kes* 1969; *Sweeney!* 1976; *Trial by Combat* 1976; *An American Werewolf in London* 1981; *The Company of Wolves* 1984; *To Kill a Priest* 1988; *Kafka* 1991; *Alien*^{3} 1992; *Leon the Pig Farmer* 1992; *1942: a Love Story* 1994; *Prince of Jutland* 1994; *Bob's Weekend* 1996; *Snow White: a Tale of Terror* 1996; *Stiff Upper Lips* 1997
Glover, Bruce (1932–) *Diamonds Are Forever* 1971; *One Little Indian* 1973; *Walking Tall* 1973; *Part 2 Walking Tall* 1975; *Stunts* 1977; *Big Bad Mama II* 1987; *Ghost Town* 1988; *Hider in the House* 1989; *Chaindance* 1991; *Warlock: the Armageddon* 1993
Glover, Crispin (1964–) *My Tutor* 1983; *Friday the 13th: the Final Chapter* 1984; *Teachers* 1984; *Back to the Future* 1985; *River's Edge* 1987; *Twister* 1989; *Where the Heart Is* 1990; *Wild at Heart* 1990; *Rubin & Ed* 1991; *Little Noises* 1992; *Even Cowgirls Get the Blues* 1993; *What's Eating Gilbert Grape* 1993; *Chasers* 1994; *Dead Man* 1995; *The People vs Larry Flynt* 1996; *Bartleby* 2000; *Charlie's Angels* 2000; *Nurse Betty* 2000; *Like Mike* 2002; *Charlie's Angels: Full Throttle* 2003; *Willard* 2003
Glover, Danny (1947–) *Chu Chu and the Philly Flash* 1981; *Iceman* 1984; *Places in the Heart* 1984; *The Color Purple* 1985; *Silverado* 1985; *Witness* 1985; *Lethal Weapon* 1987; *BAT-21* 1988; *Lethal Weapon 2* 1989; *Predator 2* 1990; *To Sleep with Anger* 1990; *Flight of the Intruder* 1991; *Grand Canyon* 1991; *Pure Luck* 1991; *A Rage in Harlem* 1991; *Lethal Weapon 3* 1992; *Bopha!* 1993; *The Saint of Fort Washington* 1993; *Angels in the Outfield* 1994; *Operation Dumbo Drop* 1995; *Buffalo Soldiers* 1997; *Gone Fishin'* 1997; *John Grisham's The Rainmaker* 1997; *Switchback* 1997; *Antz* 1998; *Beloved* 1998; *Lethal Weapon 4* 1998; *The Prince of Egypt* 1998; *Boesman & Lena* 2000; *Freedom Song* 2000; *The Royal Tenenbaums* 2001; *Saw* 2004
Glover, Edmund (1911–1978) *The Ghost Ship* 1943; *Marine Raiders* 1944
Glover, Joan *The Neon Bible* 1995; *Lolita* 1997
Glover, John (1944–) *Somebody Killed Her Husband* 1978; *The American Success Company* 1979; *Last Embrace* 1979; *The Mountain Men* 1980; *A Little Sex* 1981; *The Evil That Men Do* 1984; *A Flash of Green* 1984; *An Early Frost* 1985; *A Killing Affair* 1985; *White Nights* 1985; *52 Pick-Up* 1986; *Willy/Milly* 1986; *The Chocolate War* 1988; *Masquerade* 1988; *Rocket Gibraltar* 1988; *Scrooged* 1988;

Gremlins 2: the New Batch 1990; Motherhood 1993; Automatic 1994; In the Mouth of Madness 1994; Love! Valour! Compassion! 1997; Payback 1998

Glover, Julian (1935–) Girl with Green Eyes 1963; I Was Happy Here 1966; Theatre of Death 1966; Quatermass and the Pit 1967; The Magus 1968; The Adding Machine 1969; Alfred the Great 1969; The Last Grenade 1970; The Rise and Rise of Michael Rimmer 1970; Dead Cert 1974; Luther 1974; For Your Eyes Only 1981; Heat and Dust 1982; Kim 1984; Hearts of Fire 1987; Indiana Jones and the Last Crusade 1989; Treasure Island 1990; King Ralph 1991; The Infiltrator 1995; Vatel 2000; Two Men Went to War 2002; Strings 2004

Glover, Savion (1973–) Tap 1989; Bamboozled 2000

Glowna, Vadim (1941–) Cross of Iron 1977; Germany in Autumn 1978; No Place to Go 2000

Glynn, Carlin (1940–) Continental Divide 1981; The Trip to Bountiful 1985; Blood Red 1988; Night Game 1989; Convicts 1991; Judy Berlin 1999

Glynne, Mary (1898–1954) The Good Companions 1933; Scrooge 1935

Gobbi, Tito (1913–1984) The Barber of Seville 1946; Rigoletto 1946; Pagliacci 1948; La Forza del Destino 1949; The Glass Mountain 1949

Gobel, George (1919–1991) The Birds and the Bees 1956; I Married a Woman 1958; Ellie 1984

Godard, Jean-Luc (1930–) A Bout de Souffle 1959; The Sign of Leo 1959; Le Petit Soldat 1960; Cleo from 5 to 7 1961; RoGoPaG 1962; Vivre Sa Vie 1962; Bande à Part 1964; The Defector 1966; Two or Three Things I Know about Her 1966; Vladimir et Rosa 1970; Number Two 1975; First Name: Carmen 1983; Soigne Ta Droite 1986; King Lear – Fear and Loathing 1987; Notre Musique 2004

Goddard, Paulette (1911–1990) Pack Up Your Troubles 1932; Modern Times 1936; Dramatic School 1938; The Young in Heart 1938; The Cat and the Canary 1939; The Women 1939; The Ghost Breakers 1940; The Great Dictator 1940; North West Mounted Police 1940; Second Chorus 1940; Hold Back the Dawn 1941; Nothing but the Truth 1941; Pot o' Gold 1941; The Forest Rangers 1942; Reap the Wild Wind 1942; Star Spangled Rhythm 1942; The Crystal Ball 1943; So Proudly We Hail 1943; I Love a Soldier 1944; Standing Room Only 1944; Duffy's Tavern 1945; Kitty 1945; Diary of a Chambermaid 1946; An Ideal Husband 1947; Suddenly It's Spring 1947; Unconquered 1947; Variety Girl 1947; On Our Merry Way 1948; Anna Lucasta 1949; Bride of Vengeance 1949; Vice Squad 1953; Charge of the Lancers 1954; The Stranger Came Home 1954; Time of Indifference 1964

Godfrey, Derek (1924–1983) Guns of Darkness 1962; The Vengeance of She 1968; A Midsummer Night's Dream 1969; Hands of the Ripper 1971

Godfrey, Patrick Heat and Dust 1982; Ever After: a Cinderella Story 1998

Godfrey, Peter (1899–1970) Good Morning, Boys 1937; Dr Jekyll and Mr Hyde 1941

Godfrey, Renee (1919–1964) Bedside Manner 1945; Terror by Night 1946

Godin, Maurice White Room 1990; Danielle Steel's Vanished 1995

Godrèche, Judith (1972–) Tango 1993; The Man in the Iron Mask 1997; Pot Luck 2002

Godridge, Constance First a Girl 1935; Murder by Rope 1936; Return of a Stranger 1937

Godsell, Vanda (1919–1990) The Brain Machine 1954; The Hour of Decision 1957; Bitter Harvest 1963; Clash by Night 1963; This Sporting Life 1963; The Earth Dies Screaming 1964

Godunov, Alexander (1949–1995) The Money Pit 1985; Witness 1985; Die Hard 1988; The Runestone 1991; Waxwork II: Lost in Time 1992

Goelz, Dave (1946–) The Muppet Movie 1979; The Great Muppet Caper 1981; The Muppets Take Manhattan 1984; The Muppet Christmas Carol 1992; Muppet Treasure Island 1996; Muppets from Space 1999; It's a Very Merry Muppet Christmas Movie 2002

Goethals, Angela (1977–) Heartbreak Hotel 1988; Triple Bogey on a Par Five Hole 1991; VI Warshawski 1991

Goetz, Peter Michael (1941–) Best Defense 1984; Beer 1985; Jumpin' Jack Flash 1986; My Little Girl 1986; Promise 1986; Dad 1989; Infinity 1996

Goetzke, Bernhard (1884–1964) Destiny 1921; Dr Mabuse, the Gambler 1922

Goggins, Walton The Apostle 1997; Shanghai Noon 2000

Going, Joanna (1963–) Wyatt Earp 1994; Inventing the Abbotts 1997; Little City 1997; Heaven 1998; Phantoms 1998

Golan, Gila (1940–) Our Man Flint 1966; Three on a Couch 1966; The Valley of Gwangi 1969

Gold, Brandy (1977–) Wildcats 1986; Amityville: the Evil Escapes 1989

Gold, Jimmy (1886–1967) O-Kay for Sound 1937; Alf's Button Afloat 1938; Gasbags 1940; Life Is a Circus 1958

Gold, Tracey (1969–) Shoot the Moon 1982; Stolen Innocence 1995

Goldberg, Adam (1970–) Dazed and Confused 1993; The Prophecy 1994; Saving Private Ryan 1998; Sunset Strip 2000; All over the Guy 2001; A Beautiful Mind 2001; The Salton Sea 2002; How to Lose a Guy in 10 Days 2003

Goldberg, Bill (1966–) Ready to Rumble 2000; Looney Tunes: Back in Action 2004

Goldberg, Whoopi (1949–) The Color Purple 1985; Jumpin' Jack Flash 1986; Burglar 1987; Fatal Beauty 1987; Clara's Heart 1988; The Telephone 1988; Homer and Eddie 1989; Ghost 1990; The Long Walk Home 1990; Soapdish 1991; The Player 1992; Sarafina! 1992; Sister Act 1992; Made in America 1993; Sister Act 2: Back in the Habit 1993; Corrina, Corrina 1994; The Lion King 1994; The Little Rascals 1994; Naked in New York 1994; The Pagemaster 1994; Star Trek: Generations 1994; Boys on the Side 1995; Moonlight and Valentino 1995; Theodore Rex 1995; The Associate 1996; Bogus 1996; Eddie 1996; Ghosts of Mississippi 1996; Burn Hollywood Burn 1997; A Christmas Carol 1997; In & Out 1997; In the Gloaming 1997; Rodgers & Hammerstein's Cinderella 1997; How Stella Got Her Groove Back 1998; A Knight in Camelot 1998; Rudolph the Red-Nosed Reindeer 1998; The Rugrats Movie 1998; The Adventures of Rocky & Bullwinkle 1999; Alice in Wonderland 1999; The Deep End of the Ocean 1999; Girl, Interrupted 1999; Monkeybone 2000; Call Me Claus 2001; Rat Race 2001; It's a Very Merry Muppet Christmas Movie 2002; Star Trek: Nemesis 2002; Racing Stripes 2004

Goldblatt, Harold (?–1982) The Big Gamble 1961; The Reluctant Saint 1962; The Mind Benders 1963; The Running Man 1963; The Scarlet Blade 1963; The Reptile 1966

Goldblum, Jeff (1952–) Death Wish 1974; Nashville 1975; St Ives 1976; Special Delivery 1976; Between the Lines 1977; The Sentinel 1977; Invasion of the Body Snatchers 1978; Remember My Name 1978; Thank God It's Friday 1978; Threshold 1981; The Big Chill 1983; The Adventures of Buckaroo Banzai across the 8th Dimension 1984; Into the Night 1985; Silverado 1985; Transylvania 6-5000 1985; The Fly 1986; Beyond Therapy 1987; Earth Girls Are Easy 1988; Vibes 1988; The Tall Guy 1989; Mister Frost 1990; The Favour, the Watch and the Very Big Fish 1991; Deep Cover 1992; Shooting Elizabeth 1992; Jurassic Park 1993; Lush Life 1993; Hideaway 1995; Nine Months 1995; Powder 1995; The Great White Hype 1996; Independence Day 1996; Trigger Happy 1996; The Lost World: Jurassic Park 1997; Holy Man 1998; The Prince of Egypt 1998; Auggie Rose 2000; One of the Hollywood Ten 2000; Cats & Dogs 2001; Igby Goes Down 2002; The Life Aquatic with Steve Zissou 2004

Golden, Annie (1951–) Hair 1979; Forever Lulu 1987; The Pebble and the Penguin 1995

Golden, Geoffrey This Other Eden 1959; December Bride 1990

Goldie, Wyndham (1897–1957) Under the Red Robe 1937; Old Bones of the River 1938; The Girl in the News 1940; The Strange World of Planet X 1957

Goldin, Ricky Paull (1968–) The Blob 1988; Lambada 1990; Pastime 1991

Goldman, Danny The World's Greatest Athlete 1973; Where the Buffalo Roam 1980

Goldner, Charles (1900–1955) Give Us This Day 1949; The Rocking Horse Winner 1949; Third Time Lucky 1949; I'll Get You for This 1950; Shadow of the Eagle 1950; The Secret People 1951; South of Algiers 1952; The Captain's Paradise 1953; Duel in the Jungle 1954

Goldoni, Lelia (1937–) Shadows 1959; Hysteria 1964; Theatre of Death 1966; Alice Doesn't Live Here Anymore 1974; The Disappearance of Aimee 1976; Bloodbrothers 1978; Touchdown 1981

Goldstein, Jenette (1960–) Aliens 1986; Near Dark 1987

Goldthwait, Bobcat aka **Goldthwait, Bob** (1962–) Police Academy 2: Their First Assignment 1985; One Crazy Summer 1986; Police Academy 3: Back in Training 1986; Burglar 1987; Police Academy 4: Citizens on Patrol 1987; Hot to Trot 1988; Scrooged 1988; Shakes the Clown 1991; American Yakuza 2: Back to Back 1996; G-Men from Hell 2000; Lion of Oz 2000

Goldwyn, Tony (1960–) Ghost 1990; Kuffs 1991; Traces of Red 1992; The Pelican Brief 1993; Reckless 1995; Truman 1995; The Substance of Fire 1996; Kiss the Girls 1997; Tarzan 1999; Bounce 2000; The 6th Day 2000; An American Rhapsody 2001; The Last Samurai 2003

Golino, Valeria (1966–) Big Top Pee-wee 1988; Rain Man 1988; Three Sisters 1988; Torrents of Spring 1989; The King's Whore 1990; Hot Shots! 1991; The Indian Runner 1991; Year of the Gun 1991; Puerto Escondido 1992; Hot Shots! Part Deux 1993; Clean Slate 1994; Immortal Beloved 1994; Leaving Las Vegas 1995; Shooting the Moon 1998; Side Streets 1998; Harem Suare 1999; Things You Can Tell Just by Looking at Her 2000; Frida 2002; Respiro 2002

Golonka, Arlene (1939–) Harvey Middleman, Fireman 1965; The Busy Body 1967; Hang 'Em High 1968; The In-Laws 1979; The Last Married Couple in America 1980; Separate Ways 1981; My Tutor 1983; The Gumshoe Kid 1990; Skeletons 1996

Gombell, Minna (1892–1973) Bad Girl 1931; The First Year 1932; Hello Sister! 1933; The Lemon Drop Kid 1934; The Merry Widow 1934; The Thin Man 1934; Banjo on My Knee 1936; Blockheads 1938; Johnny Doesn't Live Here Anymore 1944

Gomez, Carlos Hostile Intentions 1995; In the Blink of an Eye 1996; Fools Rush In 1997

Gomez, Carmelo Vacas 1991; The Red Squirrel 1993; Tierra 1995; Secrets of the Heart 1997; Living It Up 2000

Gómez, Fernando Fernán (1921–) The Spirit of the Beehive 1973; Mamá Cumple 100 Años 1979; Belle Epoque 1992; Butterfly's Tongue 1999; The City of No Limits 2002

Gomez, Ian (1964–) My Big Fat Greek Wedding 2002; Connie and Carla 2004

Gomez, Jaime aka **Gomez, Jaime P** (1965–) Untamed Love 1994; Solo 1996

Gómez, José Luis (1940–) Rowing with the Wind 1987; Prince of Shadows 1991

Gomez, Panchito (1963–) Paco 1975; Run for the Roses 1978; Max Dugan Returns 1983

Gomez, Thomas (1905–1971) Sherlock Holmes and the Voice of Terror 1942; Who Done It? 1942; White Savage 1943; Abbott and Costello in Society 1944; Dead Man's Eyes 1944; Patrick the Great 1944; Phantom Lady 1944; The Daltons Ride Again 1945; Swell Guy 1946; Johnny O'Clock 1947; Singapore 1947; Angel in Exile 1948; Casbah 1948; Force of Evil 1948; Key Largo 1948; Come to the Stable 1949; Sorrowful Jones 1949; That Midnight Kiss 1949; The Woman on Pier 13 1949; The Furies 1950; Kim 1950; Anne of the Indies 1951; The Sellout 1951; Macao 1952; The Merry Widow 1952; Pony Soldier 1952; The Adventures of Hajji Baba 1954; Las Vegas Shakedown 1955; The Looters 1955; The Magnificent Matador 1955; The Conqueror 1956; Trapeze 1956; But Not for Me 1959; Stay Away, Joe 1968

Gonzales, George (1967–) The Bad News Bears in Breaking Training 1977; The Bad News Bears Go to Japan 1978

Gonzalez, Carmelita Mexican Bus Ride 1951; Motel 1983

Gonzalez, Rick (1979–) The Rookie 2002; Coach Carter 2005

Gonzalez-Gonzales, Pedro aka **Gonzalez, Pedro** (1926–) I Died a Thousand Times 1955; Hook, Line and Sinker 1969

Goodall, Caroline (1959–) Hook 1991; The Silver Brumby 1992; Cliffhanger 1993; Schindler's List 1993; Disclosure 1994; Hotel Sorrento 1994; White Squall 1996; Casualties 1997; The Princess Diaries 2001; Chasing Liberty 2004

Goodall, Louise Carla's Song 1996; My Name Is Joe 1998; Aberdeen 2000

Goodfellow, Joan Buster and Billie 1974; A Flash of Green 1984

Gooding Jr, Cuba (1968–) Boyz N the Hood 1991; Gladiator 1992; Judgment Night 1993; Lightning Jack 1994; Losing Isaiah 1995; Outbreak 1995; The Tuskegee Airmen 1995; Jerry Maguire 1996; As Good as It Gets 1997; A Murder of Crows 1998; What Dreams May Come 1998; Chill Factor 1999; Instinct 1999; Men of Honor 2000; Pearl Harbor 2001; Rat Race 2001; Boat Trip 2002; Snow Dogs 2002; The Fighting Temptations 2003; Radio 2003; Home on the Range 2004

Goodliffe, Michael (1914–1976) The Wooden Horse 1950; Sea Devils 1952; Front Page Story 1953; The End of the Affair 1954; The Battle of the River Plate 1956; The One That Got Away 1957; Up the Creek 1958; The Thirty-Nine Steps 1959; Conspiracy of Hearts 1960; Peeping Tom 1960; The Day the Earth Caught Fire 1961; Jigsaw 1962; 80,000 Suspects 1963; The Gorgon 1964; The 7th Dawn 1964; 633 Squadron 1964; Henry VIII and His Six Wives 1972; To the Devil a Daughter 1976

Goodman, Benny (1909–1986) The Big Broadcast of 1937 1936; Hollywood Hotel 1937; Sweet and Lowdown 1944; A Song Is Born 1948

Goodman, Dody (1915–) Bedtime Story 1964; Max Dugan Returns 1983; Splash 1984; Private Resort 1985; Cool as Ice 1991; Frozen Assets 1992

Goodman, Henry The Saint 1997; The Final Curtain 2002

Goodman, John (1952–) Eddie Macon's Run 1983; Maria's Lovers 1984; Sweet Dreams 1985; The Big Easy 1986; True Stories 1986; Burglar 1987; Raising Arizona 1987; Everybody's All-American 1988; Punchline 1988; Always 1989; Sea of Love 1989; Arachnophobia 1990; Stella 1990; Barton Fink 1991; King Ralph 1991; The Babe 1992; Born Yesterday 1993; Matinee 1993; We're Back! A Dinosaur's Story 1993; The Flintstones 1994; Pie in the Sky 1995; Mother Night 1996; The Big Lebowski 1997; The Borrowers 1997; Blues Brothers 2000 1998; Fallen 1998; Rudolph the Red-Nosed Reindeer 1998; Bringing out the Dead 1999; The Jack Bull 1999; The Runner 1999; Coyote Ugly 2000; The Emperor's New Groove 2000; O Brother, Where Art Thou? 2000; What Planet Are You From? 2000; Monsters, Inc 2001; My First Mister 2001; One Night at McCool's 2001; Storytelling 2001; Dirty Deeds 2002; The Jungle Book 2 2003; Masked and Anonymous 2003; Beyond the Sea 2004; Clifford's Really Big Movie 2004

Goodrich, Deborah Just One of the Guys 1985; April Fool's Day 1986; Remote Control 1988

Goodrow, Garry The Connection 1961; Steelyard Blues 1973

Goodwin, Alexander (1987–) Box of Moonlight 1996; Mimic 1997

Goodwin, Angela (1925–) Julia and Julia 1987; The Consequences of Love 2004

Goodwin, Bill (1910–1958) Riding High 1943; Bathing Beauty 1944; The Stork Club 1945; The Jolson Story 1946; To Each His Own 1946; Heaven Only Knows 1947; So This Is New York 1948; It's a Great Feeling 1949; Jolson Sings Again 1949; The Atomic Kid 1954; Lucky Me 1954; Bundle of Joy 1956

Goodwin, Ginnifer Mona Lisa Smile 2003; Win a Date with Tad Hamilton! 2004

Goodwin (1), Harold (1902–1987) College 1927; The Cameraman 1928; Flight 1929; Dirigible 1931

Goodwin (2), Harold (1917–2004) Angels One Five 1952; Barnacle Bill 1957; Sea Wife 1957; The Hi-Jackers 1963

Goodwin, Laurel (1942–) Girls! Girls! Girls! 1962; Papa's Delicate Condition 1963

Goodwin, Raven (1992–) Lovely & Amazing 2001; The Station Agent 2003

Goorjian, Michael (1971–) David's Mother 1994; Hard Rain 1997; SLC Punk! 1999

Gopal, Ram (1917–2003) The Planter's Wife 1952; The Purple Plain 1954; The Blue Peter 1955

Gorcey, Bernard (1886–1955) Abie's Irish Rose 1928; No Minor Vices 1948; Jalopy 1953; The Bowery Boys Meet the Monsters 1954; Jungle Gents 1954; Jail Busters 1955

Gorcey, David aka **Condon, David** (1921–1984) Sergeant Madden 1939; That Gang of Mine 1940; Pride of the Bowery 1941; Spooks Run Wild 1941; Jungle Gents 1954

Gorcey, Leo (1915–1969) Dead End 1937; Mannequin 1937; Angels with Dirty Faces 1938; Angels Wash Their Faces 1939; Hell's Kitchen 1939; They Made Me a Criminal 1939; Boys of the City 1940; That Gang of Mine 1940; Pride of the Bowery 1941; Spooks Run Wild 1941; Clancy

Street Boys 1943; *Ghosts in the Night* 1943; *Block Busters* 1944; *Bowery Champs* 1944; *Follow the Leader* 1944; *Come Out Fighting* 1945; *Docks of New York* 1945; *Mr Muggs Rides Again* 1945; *So This Is New York* 1948; *Jalopy* 1953; *The Bowery Boys Meet the Monsters* 1954; *Jungle Gents* 1954; *Jail Busters* 1955
Gordon, Barbara *Dead Ringers* 1988; *White Room* 1990
Gordon (1), Bruce *Elephant Boy* 1937; *Love Happy* 1949
Gordon, C Henry (1883–1940) *Renegades* 1930; *Mata Hari* 1931; *Hell's Highway* 1932; *Rasputin and the Empress* 1932; *Scarface* 1932; *The Devil's in Love* 1933; *Gabriel over the White House* 1933; *Penthouse* 1933; *Turn Back the Clock* 1933; *Stamboul Quest* 1934; *The Charge of the Light Brigade* 1936; *Charlie Chan at the Olympics* 1937; *Conquest* 1937; *Stand-In* 1937; *Tarzan's Revenge* 1938; *The Return of the Cisco Kid* 1939
Gordon, Claire *And Women Shall Weep* 1960; *Beat Girl* 1960; *Konga* 1960
Gordon, Clarke *A Cold Wind in August* 1961; *Impasse* 1969; *Glass Houses* 1972
Gordon, Colin (1911–1972) *Traveller's Joy* 1949; *Green Grow the Rushes* 1951; *Folly to Be Wise* 1952; *Up to His Neck* 1954; *Little Red Monkey* 1955; *The Extra Day* 1956; *Up in the World* 1956; *The One That Got Away* 1957; *Virgin Island* 1958; *Bobbikins* 1959; *House of Mystery* 1961; *In the Doghouse* 1961; *Night of the Eagle* 1961; *Strongroom* 1961; *Three on a Spree* 1961; *Don't Raise the Bridge, Lower the River* 1968
Gordon, Don (1926–) *Bullitt* 1968; *The Gamblers* 1969; *Cannon for Cordoba* 1970; *WUSA* 1970; *The Last Movie* 1971; *ZPG: Zero Population Growth* 1971; *Slaughter* 1972; *The Mack* 1973; *Papillon* 1973; *Omen III: the Final Conflict* 1980; *The Borrower* 1989; *Skin Deep* 1989
Gordon, Dorothy *The Silver Fleet* 1943; *House of Whipcord* 1974
Gordon, Eve (1960–) *Avalon* 1990; *The Boys* 1991; *Paradise* 1991; *Leaving Normal* 1992; *Honey, We Shrunk Ourselves* 1997; *I'll Be Home for Christmas* 1998; *Come On, Get Happy* 1999
Gordon, Gale (1906–1995) *Here We Go Again* 1942; *Francis Covers the Big Town* 1953; *Don't Give Up the Ship* 1959; *All in a Night's Work* 1960; *Visit to a Small Planet* 1960; *All Hands on Deck* 1961; *Sergeant Deadhead* 1965; *Speedway* 1968
Gordon, Gavin (1901–1983) *Romance* 1930; *American Madness* 1932; *The Bitter Tea of General Yen* 1933; *Black Beauty* 1933; *Hard to Handle* 1933; *Mystery of the Wax Museum* 1933; *The Scarlet Empress* 1934; *Bordertown* 1935; *Bride of Frankenstein* 1935; *The Bat* 1959
Gordon, Hannah (1941–) *Spring and Port Wine* 1969; *Alfie Darling* 1975; *Watership Down* 1978; *The Elephant Man* 1980
Gordon, Harold (1919–1959) *The Jazz Singer* 1952; *Viva Zapata!* 1952; *East of Eden* 1955
Gordon, Hilary (1977–) *The Mosquito Coast* 1986; *The Great Outdoors* 1988
Gordon, Huntley (1887–1956) *The Marriage Playground* 1929; *Anybody's Woman* 1930
Gordon, Keith (1961–) *Home Movies* 1979; *Dressed to Kill* 1980; *Christine* 1983; *The Legend of Billie Jean* 1985; *Static* 1985; *Back to School* 1986
Gordon, Leo (1922–2000) *Gun Fury* 1953; *Hondo* 1953; *Riot in Cell Block 11* 1954; *The Yellow Mountain* 1954; *Seven Angry Men* 1955; *Tennessee's Partner* 1955; *Great Day in the Morning* 1956; *Seventh Cavalry* 1956; *Baby Face Nelson* 1957; *The Restless Breed* 1957; *Quantrill's Raiders* 1958; *Ride a Crooked Trail* 1958; *Escort West* 1959; *The Jayhawkers* 1959; *Tarzan Goes to India* 1962; *The Haunted Palace* 1963; *Kings of the Sun* 1963; *Beau Geste* 1966; *Tobruk* 1966; *Hostile Guns* 1967; *My Name Is Nobody* 1973; *Savage Dawn* 1985
Gordon, Mary (1882–1963) *The Irish in Us* 1935; *The Great O'Malley* 1937; *Pot o' Gold* 1941; *Little Giant* 1946
Gordon, Nora (1894–1970) *Night Was Our Friend* 1951; *Police Dog* 1955; *Woman in a Dressing Gown* 1957
Gordon, Rebecca (1977–) *The Mosquito Coast* 1986; *The Great Outdoors* 1988
Gordon, Ruth (1896–1985) *Dr Ehrlich's Magic Bullet* 1940; *Spirit of the People* 1940; *Two-Faced Woman* 1941; *Action in the North Atlantic* 1943; *Edge of Darkness* 1943; *Inside Daisy Clover* 1965; *Lord Love a Duck* 1966; *Rosemary's Baby* 1968; *Whatever Happened to Aunt Alice?* 1969; *Where's Poppa?* 1970; *Harold and Maude* 1972; *Isn't It Shocking?* 1973; *The Big Bus* 1976; *Every Which Way but Loose* 1978; *Boardwalk* 1979; *Any Which Way You Can* 1980; *My Bodyguard* 1980; *Jimmy the Kid* 1982; *Delta Pi* 1985; *Maxie* 1985; *The Trouble with Spies* 1987
Gordon, Susan (1949–) *The Five Pennies* 1959; *Picture Mommy Dead* 1966
Gordon-Levitt, Joseph (1981–) *Danielle Steel's Changes* 1991; *Angels in the Outfield* 1994; *Holy Matrimony* 1994; *Roadflower* 1994; *The Juror* 1996; *Halloween H20: 20 Years Later* 1998; *10 Things I Hate about You* 1999; *Manic* 2001; *Treasure Planet* 2002; *Mysterious Skin* 2004
Gordon-Sinclair, John *aka* **Sinclair, Gordon John** (1962–) *That Sinking Feeling* 1979; *Gregory's Girl* 1980; *The Girl in the Picture* 1985; *Erik the Viking* 1989; *The Brylcreem Boys* 1996; *Gregory's Two Girls* 1999
Gore, Sandy (1951–) *Undercover* 1983; *Remember Me* 1985
Gorg, Galyn *America 3000* 1986; *Dance Academy* 1988
Gorham, Mel (1959–) *Blue in the Face* 1995; *Curdled* 1995; *Wishful Thinking* 1997; *The Center of the World* 2001
Goring, Marius (1912–1998) *Flying 55* 1939; *The Spy in Black* 1939; *Pastor Hall* 1940; *A Matter of Life and Death* 1946; *Night Boat to Dublin* 1946; *Take My Life* 1947; *Mr Perrin and Mr Traill* 1948; *The Red Shoes* 1948; *Circle of Danger* 1950; *Highly Dangerous* 1950; *Odette* 1950; *Pandora and the Flying Dutchman* 1950; *The Man Who Watched Trains Go By* 1952; *Rough Shoot* 1952; *The Barefoot Contessa* 1954; *Break in the Circle* 1955; *Quentin Durward* 1955; *Ill Met by Moonlight* 1956; *The Moonraker* 1957; *I Was Monty's Double* 1958; *Son of Robin Hood* 1958; *The Treasure of San Teresa* 1959; *Beyond the Curtain* 1960; *The Inspector* 1962; *The Crooked Road* 1964; *Up from the Beach* 1965; *The 25th Hour* 1967; *The Girl on a Motorcycle* 1968; *Subterfuge* 1968; *First Love* 1970; *Zeppelin* 1971
Gorintin, Esther *Voyages* 1999; *Carnages* 2002; *Since Otar Left* 2003
Gorman, Bud (1921–) *Bowery Champs* 1944; *Follow the Leader* 1944; *Docks of New York* 1945; *Mr Muggs Rides Again* 1945
Gorman, Cliff (1936–2002) *The Boys in the Band* 1970; *Cops and Robbers* 1973; *Rosebud* 1975; *An Unmarried Woman* 1978; *All That Jazz* 1979; *Night of the Juggler* 1980; *Angel* 1984; *Night and the City* 1992; *Ghost Dog: the Way of the Samurai* 1999
Gorman, Robert Hy *aka* **Gorman, Robert** (1980–) *The Accidental Tourist* 1988; *Sometimes They Come Back* 1991; *Leprechaun* 1992; *Mr Nanny* 1992
Gorney, Karen Lynn (1945–) *Saturday Night Fever* 1977; *Ripe* 1996
Gorshin, Frank (1933–2005) *Dragstrip Girl* 1957; *Invasion of the Saucer Men* 1957; *Bells Are Ringing* 1960; *Studs Lonigan* 1960; *The George Raft Story* 1961; *Ring of Fire* 1961; *Sail a Crooked Ship* 1961; *Batman* 1966; *Skidoo* 1968; *Hot Resort* 1985; *Uphill All the Way* 1985; *Hollywood Vice Squad* 1986; *Midnight* 1989; *Hail Caesar* 1994; *Twelve Monkeys* 1995; *The Twilight of the Ice Nymphs* 1997; *Beethoven's 3rd* 2000; *Luck of the Draw* 2000
Gortner, Marjoe (1944–) *Earthquake* 1974; *The Food of the Gods* 1975; *Acapulco Gold* 1976; *Sidewinder One* 1977; *When You Comin' Back, Red Ryder?* 1979; *Mausoleum* 1983
Gosling, Ryan (1980–) *The Believer* 2001; *Murder by Numbers* 2002; *The United States of Leland* 2002; *The Notebook* 2003
Goss, Luke (1968–) *two days, nine lives* 2000; *Blade II* 2002; *Charlie* 2003
Gosselaar, Mark-Paul (1974–) *Freshman Fall* 1996; *Dead Man on Campus* 1998
Gossett Jr, Louis *aka* **Gossett, Louis** (1936–) *A Raisin in the Sun* 1961; *The Landlord* 1970; *Skin Game* 1971; *Travels with My Aunt* 1972; *The Laughing Policeman* 1973; *The White Dawn* 1974; *JD's Revenge* 1976; *The River Niger* 1976; *The Choirboys* 1977; *The Deep* 1977; *An Officer and a Gentleman* 1982; *Jaws III* 1983; *Finders Keepers* 1984; *Enemy Mine* 1985; *Iron Eagle* 1985; *Firewalker* 1986; *The Principal* 1987; *Iron Eagle II* 1988; *The Punisher* 1989; *Cover-Up* 1991; *Toy Soldiers* 1991; *Aces: Iron Eagle III* 1992; *Midnight Sting* 1992; *Flashfire* 1993; *A Good Man in Africa* 1993; *Blue Chips* 1994; *Iron Eagle IV* 1995; *Bram Stoker's Legend of the Mummy* 1998; *The Highwayman* 1999; *Strange Justice* 1999; *The Color of Love: Jacey's Story* 2000
Gostukhin, Vladimir (1946–) *The Ascent* 1976; *Urga* 1990
Gotell, Walter (1924–1997) *The African Queen* 1951; *The Bandit of Zhobe* 1959; *The Treasure of San Teresa* 1959; *The Damned* 1961; *The Road to Hong Kong* 1962; *From Russia with Love* 1963; *The Spy Who Loved Me* 1977; *The Stud* 1978; *Octopussy* 1983; *A View to a Kill* 1985
Gothard, Michael (1939–1993) *Up the Junction* 1967; *The Devils* 1971; *Who Slew Auntie Roo?* 1971; *The Valley* 1972; *Warlords of Atlantis* 1978; *For Your Eyes Only* 1981; *Lifeforce* 1985
Gottfried, Gilbert (1955–) *Never on Tuesday* 1988; *The Adventures of Ford Fairlane* 1990; *Problem Child* 1990; *Problem Child 2* 1991; *Aladdin* 1992; *Aladdin and the King of Thieves* 1996
Gottschalk, Ferdinand (1869–1944) *The Sign of the Cross* 1932; *Female* 1933; *The Man Who Broke the Bank at Monte Carlo* 1935
Gough, Lloyd (1907–1984) *All My Sons* 1948; *Black Bart* 1948; *A Southern Yankee* 1948; *That Wonderful Urge* 1948; *Tension* 1949; *Storm Warning* 1950; *Sunset Blvd* 1950; *The Scarf* 1951; *Glory Boy* 1971
Gough, Michael (1917–) *Anna Karenina* 1947; *Blanche Fury* 1948; *Saraband for Dead Lovers* 1948; *No Resting Place* 1950; *The Man in the White Suit* 1951; *Night Was Our Friend* 1951; *The Sword and the Rose* 1952; *Rob Roy, the Highland Rogue* 1953; *Richard III* 1955; *Ill Met by Moonlight* 1956; *House in the Woods* 1957; *Horror of Dracula* 1958; *Horrors of the Black Museum* 1959; *Konga* 1960; *Mr Topaze* 1961; *What a Carve Up!* 1961; *The Phantom of the Opera* 1962; *Black Zoo* 1963; *Tamahine* 1963; *The Skull* 1965; *Berserk* 1967; *They Came from beyond Space* 1967; *Curse of the Crimson Altar* 1968; *The Corpse* 1969; *Women in Love* 1969; *Trog* 1970; *The Go-Between* 1971; *Henry VIII and His Six Wives* 1972; *Savage Messiah* 1972; *Horror Hospital* 1973; *The Legend of Hell House* 1973; *Galileo* 1974; *Satan's Slave* 1976; *The Boys from Brazil* 1978; *The Dresser* 1983; *Oxford Blues* 1984; *Top Secret!* 1984; *Out of Africa* 1985; *Caravaggio* 1986; *The Serpent and the Rainbow* 1987; *Strapless* 1988; *Batman* 1989; *The Garden* 1990; *Let Him Have It* 1991; *Batman Returns* 1992; *The Hour of the Pig* 1993; *Wittgenstein* 1993; *Batman Forever* 1995; *The Haunting of Helen Walker* 1995; *Batman and Robin* 1997; *All for Love* 1999
Gould, Elliott (1938–) *Quick, Let's Get Married* 1964; *The Night They Raided Minsky's* 1968; *Bob & Carol & Ted & Alice* 1969; *MASH* 1969; *Getting Straight* 1970; *I Love My... Wife* 1970; *Little Murders* 1971; *The Touch* 1971; *The Long Goodbye* 1973; *Busting* 1974; *California Split* 1974; *SPYS* 1974; *Who?* 1974; *Whiffs* 1975; *Harry and Walter Go to New York* 1976; *I Will... I Will... for Now* 1976; *A Bridge Too Far* 1977; *Capricorn One* 1978; *Matilda* 1978; *The Silent Partner* 1978; *Escape to Athena* 1979; *The Lady Vanishes* 1979; *Falling in Love Again* 1980; *The Last Flight of Noah's Ark* 1980; *The Devil and Max Devlin* 1981; *Over the Brooklyn Bridge* 1983; *The Naked Face* 1984; *The Telephone* 1988; *The Big Picture* 1989; *The Lemon Sisters* 1989; *Night Visitor* 1989; *Bugsy* 1991; *Dead Men Don't Die* 1991; *Amore!* 1993; *A Boy Called Hate* 1995; *The Glass Shield* 1995; *Kicking and Screaming* 1995; *Let It Be Me* 1995; *The November Conspiracy* 1995; *City of Industry* 1996; *American History X* 1998; *The Big Hit* 1998; *Picking Up the Pieces* 2000; *Ocean's Eleven* 2001; *The Cat Returns* 2002; *Puckoon* 2002; *Ocean's Twelve* 2004
Gould, Harold (1923–) *Project X* 1968; *The Lawyer* 1969; *Mrs Pollifax – Spy* 1970; *Ransom for a Dead Man* 1971; *Where Does It Hurt?* 1971; *The Sting* 1973; *The Strongest Man in the World* 1975; *The Big Bus* 1976; *Silent Movie* 1976; *The One and Only* 1978; *Seems like Old Times* 1980; *Mrs Delafield Wants to Marry* 1986; *Playing for Keeps* 1986; *Romero* 1989; *Brown's Requiem* 1998; *My Giant* 1998; *The Master of Disguise* 2002; *Freaky Friday* 2003
Gould, Jason (1966–) *Say Anything...* 1989; *The Prince of Tides* 1991
Goulet, Robert (1933–) *Gay Purr-ee* 1962; *Honeymoon Hotel* 1964; *I'd Rather Be Rich* 1964; *Atlantic City, USA* 1980; *Beetle Juice* 1988; *The Naked Gun* $2\frac{1}{2}$*: the Smell of Fear* 1991; *Mr Wrong* 1996; *G-Men from Hell* 2000; *Recess: School's Out* 2001
Goullet, Arthur *Hey! Hey! USA* 1938; *Caravan* 1946
Gourmet, Olivier (1963–) *La Promesse* 1996; *Nationale 7* 1999; *Rosetta* 1999; *Read My Lips* 2001; *The Son* 2002; *Time of the Wolf* 2003
Govinda (1958–) *Tan-Badan* 1986; *Anari No 1* 1999; *Ek Aur Ek Gyarah* 2003
Gowland, Gibson *aka* **Gibson-Gowland, T H** (1877–1951) *Blind Husbands* 1919; *Greed* 1925; *The Phantom of the Opera* 1925; *The Mysterious Island* 1929; *SOS Iceberg* 1933; *Cotton Queen* 1937
Goyette, Patrick *The Confessional* 1995; *Le Polygraphe* 1996
Goz, Harry (1932–2003) *Bill* 1981; *Mommie Dearest* 1981
Gozlino, Paolo *Vengeance* 1968; *Django the Bastard* 1970
Grable, Betty (1916–1973) *Melody Cruise* 1933; *The Gay Divorce* 1934; *Old Man Rhythm* 1935; *Follow the Fleet* 1936; *Pigskin Parade* 1936; *College Swing* 1938; *Million Dollar Legs* 1939; *Down Argentine Way* 1940; *Tin Pan Alley* 1940; *I Wake Up Screaming* 1941; *Moon over Miami* 1941; *A Yank in the RAF* 1941; *Footlight Serenade* 1942; *Song of the Islands* 1942; *Springtime in the Rockies* 1942; *Coney Island* 1943; *Sweet Rosie O'Grady* 1943; *Pin Up Girl* 1944; *Billy Rose's Diamond Horseshoe* 1945; *The Dolly Sisters* 1945; *Mother Wore Tights* 1947; *The Shocking Miss Pilgrim* 1947; *That Lady in Ermine* 1948; *When My Baby Smiles at Me* 1948; *The Beautiful Blonde from Bashful Bend* 1949; *My Blue Heaven* 1950; *Wabash Avenue* 1950; *Call Me Mister* 1951; *Meet Me after the Show* 1951; *The Farmer Takes a Wife* 1953; *How to Marry a Millionaire* 1953; *How to Be Very, Very Popular* 1955; *Three for the Show* 1955
Grabol, Sofie (1968–) *The Wolf at the Door* 1986; *The Silent Touch* 1992; *Nightwatch* 1994; *Mifune* 1999
Grabowski, Norman *The Monkey's Uncle* 1965; *Blackbeard's Ghost* 1967
Grace, April (1962–) *Finding Forrester* 2000; *The Assassination of Richard Nixon* 2004
Grace, Carol (1925–2003) *Gangster Story* 1959; *Mikey and Nicky* 1976
Grace, Nickolas (1949–) *Heat and Dust* 1982; *Dream Demon* 1988; *Salome's Last Dance* 1988; *Tom & Viv* 1994; *Two Deaths* 1994; *Shooting Fish* 1997; *Puckoon* 2002
Grace, Topher (1978–) *In Good Company* 2004; *Win a Date with Tad Hamilton!* 2004
Gracen, Elizabeth (1960–) *The Death of the Incredible Hulk* 1990; *Marked for Death* 1990; *Final Mission* 1993
Gracia, Sancho (1936–) *La Comunidad* 2000; *El Crimen del Padre Amaro* 2002
Grad, Geneviève (1944–) *Violent Summer* 1961; *Hero of Babylon* 1963; *Sandokan the Great* 1963; *The Gendarme of St Tropez* 1964; *The Gendarme in New York* 1965
Graetz, Paul (1889–1937) *Blossom Time* 1934; *Bulldog Jack* 1934; *Jew Süss* 1934; *Heart's Desire* 1935; *Isle of Fury* 1936
Graf, David (1950–2001) *The Long Summer of George Adams* 1982; *Police Academy* 1984; *Police Academy 2: Their First Assignment* 1985; *Police Academy 3: Back in Training* 1986; *Love at Stake* 1987; *Police Academy 4: Citizens on Patrol* 1987; *Police Academy 5: Assignment Miami Beach* 1988; *Police Academy 6: City under Siege* 1989; *Police Academy: Mission to Moscow* 1994
Graff, Todd (1959–) *Not Quite Jerusalem* 1985; *Five Corners* 1987; *Dominick and Eugene* 1988; *The Abyss* 1989; *An Innocent Man* 1989; *Opportunity Knocks* 1990
Graff, Wilton (1903–1969) *Bulldog Drummond Strikes Back* 1947; *The Dark Past* 1948; *Miss Sadie Thompson* 1953
Graham, Aimee (1971–) *Reform School Girl* 1994; *Perdita Durango* 1997
Graham, David *Thunderbirds Are Go!* 1966; *Thunderbird 6* 1968
Graham, Gerrit *aka* **Chud, Bud T** (1949–) *Greetings* 1968; *Hi, Mom!* 1970; *Phantom of the Paradise* 1974; *Cannonball* 1976; *Special Delivery* 1976; *Demon Seed* 1977; *Home Movies* 1979; *Used Cars* 1980; *National Lampoon's Class Reunion* 1982; *TerrorVision* 1986; *It's Alive III: Island of the Alive* 1987; *Big Man on Campus* 1989; *CHUD II: Bud the Chud* 1989; *Perfume of the Cyclone* 1989; *Child's Play 2* 1990; *The Philadelphia Experiment 2* 1993

Graham, Heather (1970–) *License to Drive* 1988; *Drugstore Cowboy* 1989; *Guilty as Charged* 1991; *Shout* 1991; *Midnight Sting* 1992; *The Ballad of Little Jo* 1993; *Even Cowgirls Get the Blues* 1993; *Six Degrees of Separation* 1993; *Entertaining Angels: the Dorothy Day Story* 1996; *Swingers* 1996; *Boogie Nights* 1997; *Nowhere* 1997; *Two Girls and a Guy* 1997; *Lost in Space* 1998; *Austin Powers: the Spy Who Shagged Me* 1999; *Bowfinger* 1999; *Committed* 2000; *Sidewalks of New York* 2000; *From Hell* 2001; *Killing Me Softly* 2001; *Say It Isn't So* 2001; *The Guru* 2002; *Hope Springs* 2002

Graham, Julie (1967–) *The Near Room* 1995; *Preaching to the Perverted* 1997; *Bedrooms and Hallways* 1998; *With or without You* 1999; *Some Voices* 2000

Graham, Lauren (1967–) *Nightwatch* 1997; *One True Thing* 1998; *Bad Santa* 2003; *The Pacifier* 2005

Graham, Morland (1891–1949) *Old Bill and Son* 1940; *The Ghost Train* 1941; *Gaiety George* 1946; *The Upturned Glass* 1947; *Bonnie Prince Charlie* 1948; *Esther Waters* 1948

Graham (2), Richard *Return from the River Kwai* 1988; *ID* 1994; *Arthur's Dyke* 2001

Graham, Stephen (1973–) *Downtime* 1997; *Gangs of New York* 2002; *American Cousins* 2003

Graham, William *Just William's Luck* 1947; *William at the Circus* 1948

Grahame, Gloria (1925–1981) *Blonde Fever* 1944; *Without Love* 1945; *It's a Wonderful Life* 1946; *Crossfire* 1947; *It Happened in Brooklyn* 1947; *Merton of the Movies* 1947; *Roughshod* 1949; *A Woman's Secret* 1949; *In a Lonely Place* 1950; *The Bad and the Beautiful* 1952; *The Greatest Show on Earth* 1952; *Macao* 1952; *Sudden Fear* 1952; *The Big Heat* 1953; *The Glass Wall* 1953; *Man on a Tightrope* 1953; *Prisoners of the Casbah* 1953; *The Good Die Young* 1954; *Human Desire* 1954; *Naked Alibi* 1954; *The Cobweb* 1955; *The Man Who Never Was* 1955; *Not as a Stranger* 1955; *Oklahoma!* 1955; *Odds against Tomorrow* 1959; *Ride beyond Vengeance* 1966; *The Loners* 1971; *The Todd Killings* 1971; *Mama's Dirty Girls* 1974; *Mansion of the Doomed* 1975; *Chilly Scenes of Winter* 1979; *A Nightingale Sang in Berkeley Square* 1979; *Melvin and Howard* 1980; *The Nesting* 1981

Grahame, Margot (1911–1982) *Rookery Nook* 1930; *The Arizonian* 1935; *The Informer* 1935; *The Three Musketeers* 1935; *The Adventures of Michael Strogoff* 1937; *Criminal Lawyer* 1937; *The Buccaneer* 1938; *Broken Journey* 1948; *Black Magic* 1949; *The Romantic Age* 1949; *The Crimson Pirate* 1952; *Venetian Bird* 1952; *The Beggar's Opera* 1953; *Orders Are Orders* 1954

Grainger, Gawn (1940–) *Mastermind* 1976; *August* 1995; *Love and Death on Long Island* 1998

Grammer, Kelsey (1954–) *Down Periscope* 1996; *Anastasia* 1997; *The Pentagon Wars* 1998; *The Real Howard Spitz* 1998; *Animal Farm* 1999; *Bartok the Magnificent* 1999; *Toy Story 2* 1999; *15 Minutes* 2001

Gran, Albert (1862–1932) *7th Heaven* 1927; *Four Sons* 1928; *Employees' Entrance* 1933

Grana, Sam *The Masculine Mystique* 1984; *90 Days* 1986

Granach, Alexander (1893–1945) *Nosferatu, a Symphony of Horrors* 1922; *Kameradschaft* 1931; *Ninotchka* 1939; *Joan of Paris* 1942; *Hangmen Also Die* 1943

Granados, Daisy *Memories of Underdevelopment* 1968; *Plaff!* 1988; *The Elephant and the Bicycle* 1995

Granados, Rosario (1925–1997) *The Great Madcap* 1949; *A Woman without Love* 1951

Grand'Henry, Philippe *Les Convoyeurs Attendent* 1999; *The Ordeal* 2004

Grandinetti, Darío (1959–) *The Dark Side of the Heart* 1992; *Talk to Her* 2001

Granger, Farley (1925–) *The North Star* 1943; *The Purple Heart* 1944; *Enchantment* 1948; *Rope* 1948; *They Live by Night* 1948; *Roseanna McCoy* 1949; *Edge of Doom* 1950; *Our Very Own* 1950; *Side Street* 1950; *I Want You* 1951; *Strangers on a Train* 1951; *Hans Christian Andersen* 1952; *O Henry's Full House* 1952; *The Story of Three Loves* 1953; *Senso* 1954; *The Girl in the Red Velvet Swing* 1955; *The Naked Street* 1955; *They Call Me Trinity* 1970; *The Serpent* 1972; *Arnold* 1973; *Deathmask* 1984; *The Imagemaker* 1986

Granger, Michael (1923–1981) *Tarzan and the She-Devil* 1953; *Creature with the Atom Brain* 1955; *Murder by Contract* 1958

Granger, Stewart (1913–1993) *Convoy* 1940; *Secret Mission* 1942; *The Lamp Still Burns* 1943; *The Man in Grey* 1943; *Fanny by Gaslight* 1944; *Love Story* 1944; *Madonna of the Seven Moons* 1944; *Waterloo Road* 1944; *Caesar and Cleopatra* 1945; *Caravan* 1946; *The Magic Bow* 1946; *Captain Boycott* 1947; *Blanche Fury* 1948; *Saraband for Dead Lovers* 1948; *Woman Hater* 1948; *Adam and Evelyne* 1949; *King Solomon's Mines* 1950; *The Light Touch* 1951; *Soldiers Three* 1951; *The Prisoner of Zenda* 1952; *Scaramouche* 1952; *The Wild North* 1952; *All the Brothers Were Valiant* 1953; *Salome* 1953; *Young Bess* 1953; *Beau Brummell* 1954; *Green Fire* 1954; *Footsteps in the Fog* 1955; *Moonfleet* 1955; *Bhowani Junction* 1956; *The Last Hunt* 1956; *Gun Glory* 1957; *The Little Hut* 1957; *Harry Black and the Tiger* 1958; *The Whole Truth* 1958; *North to Alaska* 1960; *The Secret Partner* 1961; *Sodom and Gomorrah* 1962; *The Swordsman of Siena* 1962; *The Crooked Road* 1964; *The Secret Invasion* 1964; *The Last Safari* 1967; *The Trygon Factor* 1967; *The Wild Geese* 1978

Granstedt, Greta (1907–1987) *Crime without Passion* 1934; *The Eddie Cantor Story* 1953; *The Return of Dracula* 1958

Grant, Beth (1949–) *Love Field* 1992; *City Slickers II: the Legend of Curly's Gold* 1994; *To Wong Foo, Thanks for Everything, Julie Newmar* 1995; *Dance with Me* 1998; *The Rookie* 2002; *Matchstick Men* 2003

Grant, Bob (1932–2003) *On the Buses* 1971; *Mutiny on the Buses* 1972; *Holiday on the Buses* 1973

Grant, Cary (1904–1986) *Blonde Venus* 1932; *Devil and the Deep* 1932; *Madame Butterfly* 1932; *Merrily We Go to Hell* 1932; *Sinners in the Sun* 1932; *This Is the Night* 1932; *Alice in Wonderland* 1933; *The Eagle and the Hawk* 1933; *Enter Madame!* 1933; *I'm No Angel* 1933; *She Done Him Wrong* 1933; *Kiss and Make-Up* 1934; *Ladies Should Listen* 1934; *Thirty-Day Princess* 1934; *The Last Outpost* 1935; *Wings in the Dark* 1935; *The Amazing Quest of Ernest Bliss* 1936; *Big Brown Eyes* 1936; *Suzy* 1936; *Sylvia Scarlett* 1936; *Wedding Present* 1936; *The Awful Truth* 1937; *The Toast of New York* 1937; *Topper* 1937; *When You're in Love* 1937; *Bringing Up Baby* 1938; *Holiday* 1938; *Gunga Din* 1939; *His Girl Friday* 1939; *In Name Only* 1939; *Only Angels Have Wings* 1939; *Topper Takes a Trip* 1939; *The Howards of Virginia* 1940; *My Favorite Wife* 1940; *The Philadelphia Story* 1940; *Penny Serenade* 1941; *Suspicion* 1941; *Once upon a Honeymoon* 1942; *The Talk of the Town* 1942; *Destination Tokyo* 1943; *Mr Lucky* 1943; *Arsenic and Old Lace* 1944; *None but the Lonely Heart* 1944; *Once upon a Time* 1944; *Night and Day* 1946; *Notorious* 1946; *Without Reservations* 1946; *The Bachelor and the Bobby-Soxer* 1947; *The Bishop's Wife* 1947; *Every Girl Should Be Married* 1948; *Mr Blandings Builds His Dream House* 1948; *I Was a Male War Bride* 1949; *Crisis* 1950; *People Will Talk* 1951; *Monkey Business* 1952; *Room for One More* 1952; *Dream Wife* 1953; *To Catch a Thief* 1955; *An Affair to Remember* 1957; *Kiss Them for Me* 1957; *The Pride and the Passion* 1957; *Houseboat* 1958; *Indiscreet* 1958; *North by Northwest* 1959; *Operation Petticoat* 1959; *The Grass Is Greener* 1960; *That Touch of Mink* 1962; *Charade* 1963; *Father Goose* 1964; *Walk, Don't Run* 1966

Grant, Cy *Sea Wife* 1957; *Shaft in Africa* 1973; *At the Earth's Core* 1976

Grant, David Marshall aka **Grant, David** (1955–) *French Postcards* 1979; *Happy Birthday, Gemini* 1980; *American Flyers* 1985; *The Big Town* 1987; *BAT-21* 1988; *Air America* 1990; *Three Wishes* 1995; *The Stepford Wives* 2004

Grant, Faye (1957–) *The January Man* 1989; *Omen IV: the Awakening* 1991; *Traces of Red* 1992; *Drive Me Crazy* 1999

Grant, Hugh (1960–) *Maurice* 1987; *Rowing with the Wind* 1987; *White Mischief* 1987; *The Dawning* 1988; *The Lair of the White Worm* 1988; *The Big Man* 1990; *Impromptu* 1991; *Bitter Moon* 1992; *Night Train to Venice* 1993; *The Remains of the Day* 1993; *An Awfully Big Adventure* 1994; *Four Weddings and a Funeral* 1994; *Sirens* 1994; *The Englishman Who Went up a Hill, but Came down a Mountain* 1995; *Nine Months* 1995; *Restoration* 1995; *Sense and Sensibility* 1995; *Extreme Measures* 1996; *Mickey Blue Eyes* 1999; *Notting Hill* 1999; *Small Time Crooks* 2000; *Bridget Jones's Diary* 2001; *About a Boy* 2002; *Two Weeks Notice* 2002; *Love Actually* 2003; *Bridget Jones: the Edge of Reason* 2004

Grant, Kathryn (1933–) *The Phenix City Story* 1955; *The Brothers Rico* 1957; *Guns of Fort Petticoat* 1957; *Mister Cory* 1957; *Operation Mad Ball* 1957; *Gunman's Walk* 1958; *The 7th Voyage of Sinbad* 1958; *Anatomy of a Murder* 1959; *The Big Circus* 1959

Grant, Kirby (1914–1985) *Red River Range* 1938; *Abbott and Costello in Society* 1944; *Ghost Catchers* 1944

Grant, Lawrence (1870–1952) *Bulldog Drummond* 1929; *The Unholy Garden* 1931; *The Mask of Fu Manchu* 1932; *Shanghai Express* 1932; *Speak Easily* 1932; *By Candlelight* 1934; *Under the Red Robe* 1937

Grant, Lee (1927–) *Detective Story* 1951; *Middle of the Night* 1959; *The Balcony* 1963; *Terror in the City* 1963; *In the Heat of the Night* 1967; *Valley of the Dolls* 1967; *Buona Sera, Mrs Campbell* 1968; *The Big Bounce* 1969; *Marooned* 1969; *The Landlord* 1970; *Plaza Suite* 1971; *Ransom for a Dead Man* 1971; *Portnoy's Complaint* 1972; *The Internecine Project* 1974; *Shampoo* 1975; *Voyage of the Damned* 1976; *Airport '77* 1977; *Damien – Omen II* 1978; *The Swarm* 1978; *When You Comin' Back, Red Ryder?* 1979; *Little Miss Marker* 1980; *Charlie Chan and the Curse of the Dragon Queen* 1981; *Visiting Hours* 1982; *A Billion for Boris* 1984; *Teachers* 1984; *The Big Town* 1987; *Defending Your Life* 1991; *It's My Party* 1996; *The Substance of Fire* 1996; *Mulholland Drive* 2001

Grant, Leon W *Beat Street* 1984; *Playing for Keeps* 1986

Grant, Oliver "Power" aka **Power Belly** 1998; *Black and White* 1999

Grant, Richard E (1957–) *Withnail & I* 1986; *Hidden City* 1987; *How to Get Ahead in Advertising* 1989; *Killing Dad* 1989; *Mountains of the Moon* 1989; *Warlock* 1989; *Henry & June* 1990; *Hudson Hawk* 1991; *LA Story* 1991; *Bram Stoker's Dracula* 1992; *The Player* 1992; *The Age of Innocence* 1993; *Prêt-a-Porter* 1994; *Jack & Sarah* 1995; *The Portrait of a Lady* 1996; *Twelfth Night* 1996; *Food of Love* 1997; *Keep the Aspidistra Flying* 1997; *The Serpent's Kiss* 1997; *Spice World: the Movie* 1997; *All for Love* 1999; *A Christmas Carol* 1999; *The Match* 1999; *The Miracle Maker* 1999; *The Little Vampire* 2000; *Strictly Sinatra* 2000; *Gosford Park* 2001; *Monsieur N* 2003; *Tooth* 2003

Grant, Rodney A (1959–) *Dances with Wolves* 1990; *Geronimo: an American Legend* 1993; *Wagons East!* 1994; *The Killing Grounds* 1997; *The Jack Bull* 1999

Grant, Salim (1977–) *Ghost Dad* 1990; *The Hitman* 1991

Grantham, Leslie (1947–) *Shadow Run* 1998; *Lava* 2000; *The Wedding Tackle* 2000; *Charlie* 2003

Granville, Bonita (1923–1988) *These Three* 1936; *Hard to Get* 1938; *Merrily We Live* 1938; *Nancy Drew – Detective* 1938; *White Banners* 1938; *Angels Wash Their Faces* 1939; *The Mortal Storm* 1940; *Third Finger, Left Hand* 1940; *The People vs Dr Kildare* 1941; *The Glass Key* 1942; *Now, Voyager* 1942; *Seven Miles from Alcatraz* 1942; *Syncopation* 1942; *Hitler's Children* 1943; *Andy Hardy's Blonde Trouble* 1944; *Song of the Open Road* 1944; *Youth Runs Wild* 1944; *Love Laughs at Andy Hardy* 1946; *The Lone Ranger* 1956

Grapewin, Charley aka **Grapewin, Charles** (1869–1956) *Hell's House* 1932; *The Kiss before the Mirror* 1933; *Pilgrimage* 1933; *Torch Singer* 1933; *Anne of Green Gables* 1934; *Ah, Wilderness!* 1935; *Alice Adams* 1935; *Libeled Lady* 1936; *The Petrified Forest* 1936; *Big City* 1937; *Captains Courageous* 1937; *A Family Affair* 1937; *The Good Earth* 1937; *Artists and Models Abroad* 1938; *Listen, Darling* 1938; *Of Human Hearts* 1938; *The Shopworn Angel* 1938; *Dust Be My Destiny* 1939; *The Wizard of Oz* 1939; *Ellery Queen Master Detective* 1940; *The Grapes of Wrath* 1940; *Johnny Apollo* 1940; *Rhythm on the River* 1940; *Texas Rangers Ride Again* 1940; *They Died with Their Boots On* 1941; *Tobacco Road* 1941; *Atlantic City* 1944; *Follow the Boys* 1944

Graves, George (1876–1949) *Those Were the Days* 1934; *Heart's Desire* 1935

Graves (1), Peter (1911–1994) *King Arthur Was a Gentleman* 1942; *Bees in Paradise* 1943; *Miss London Ltd* 1943; *Give Us the Moon* 1944; *I'll Be Your Sweetheart* 1945; *Gaiety George* 1946; *Spring in Park Lane* 1948; *Maytime in Mayfair* 1949; *Derby Day* 1952; *The Admirable Crichton* 1957

Graves (2), Peter (1925–) *Red Planet Mars* 1952; *Beneath the 12-Mile Reef* 1953; *East of Sumatra* 1953; *Stalag 17* 1953; *War Paint* 1953; *The Raid* 1954; *The Yellow Tomahawk* 1954; *The Court-Martial of Billy Mitchell* 1955; *Lilacs in the Spring* 1955; *The Naked Street* 1955; *The Night of the Hunter* 1955; *Wichita* 1955; *It Conquered the World* 1956; *Beginning of the End* 1957; *Wolf Larsen* 1958; *A Stranger in My Arms* 1959; *A Rage to Live* 1965; *Texas across the River* 1966; *Valley of Mystery* 1967; *The Ballad of Josie* 1968; *Sergeant Ryker* 1968; *The Adventurers* 1970; *Survival Run* 1979; *Airplane!* 1980; *Airplane II: the Sequel* 1982; *Savannah Smiles* 1982; *Number One with a Bullet* 1986; *These Old Broads* 2001

Graves, Ralph (1900–1977) *Dream Street* 1921; *Flight* 1929; *Ladies of Leisure* 1930; *Dirigible* 1931; *Three Texas Steers* 1939

Graves, Rupert (1963–) *A Room with a View* 1985; *A Handful of Dust* 1987; *Maurice* 1987; *The Children* 1990; *Where Angels Fear to Tread* 1991; *Damage* 1992; *The Innocent Sleep* 1995; *Intimate Relations* 1995; *The Madness of King George* 1995; *Different for Girls* 1996; *Mrs Dalloway* 1997; *The Revengers' Comedies* 1997; *Dreaming of Joseph Lees* 1998; *Room to Rent* 2000; *Extreme Ops* 2003

Graves, Teresa (1949–2002) *That Man Bolt* 1973; *Vampira* 1975

Gravet, Fernand aka **Graavey, Fernand** aka **Gravey, Fernand** (1904–1970) *Bitter Sweet* 1933; *The King and the Chorus Girl* 1937; *Fools for Scandal* 1938; *The Great Waltz* 1938; *La Nuit Fantastique* 1942; *La Ronde* 1950; *Mitsou* 1957; *How to Steal a Million* 1966

Gravina, Carla (1941–) *Big Deal on Madonna Street* 1958; *Five Branded Women* 1960; *Alfredo Alfredo* 1971; *Without Apparent Motive* 1972; *The Bit Player* 1973; *The Inheritor* 1973; *And Now My Love* 1974; *Boomerang* 1976

Gravina, Cesare (1858–1954) *The Divine Woman* 1928; *The Wedding March* 1928

Gray, Billy (1938–) *The Day the Earth Stood Still* 1951; *On Moonlight Bay* 1951; *All I Desire* 1953; *By the Light of the Silvery Moon* 1953; *The Girl Next Door* 1953; *Some Like It Hot* 1959; *The Explosive Generation* 1961; *Two for the Seesaw* 1962; *The Navy vs the Night Monsters* 1966

Gray, Bruce *Between Friends* 1983; *Odd Birds* 1985; *Dragnet* 1987

Gray, Carole (1940–) *The Young Ones* 1961; *Devils of Darkness* 1964; *Curse of the Fly* 1965; *The Brides of Fu Manchu* 1966; *Island of Terror* 1966

Gray, Charles (1928–2000) *Tommy the Toreador* 1959; *Man in the Moon* 1960; *Masquerade* 1965; *The Night of the Generals* 1966; *The Secret War of Harry Frigg* 1967; *The Devil Rides Out* 1968; *Mosquito Squadron* 1968; *The File of the Golden Goose* 1969; *9 Ages of Nakedness* 1969; *The Executioner* 1970; *Diamonds Are Forever* 1971; *The Beast Must Die* 1974; *The Rocky Horror Picture Show* 1975; *Seven Nights in Japan* 1976; *The Legacy* 1978; *Shock Treatment* 1981; *The Jigsaw Man* 1984; *The Tichborne Claimant* 1998

Gray, Coleen (1922–) *Kiss of Death* 1947; *Nightmare Alley* 1947; *Fury at Furnace Creek* 1948; *Red River* 1948; *I'll Get You for This* 1950; *Riding High* 1950; *The Sleeping City* 1950; *Apache Drums* 1951; *Kansas City Confidential* 1952; *Arrow in the Dust* 1954; *Las Vegas Shakedown* 1955; *Tennessee's Partner* 1955; *The Twinkle in God's Eye* 1955; *Death of a Scoundrel* 1956; *The Killing* 1956; *Star in the Dust* 1956; *The Leech Woman* 1960; *New Face in Hell* 1968; *The Late Liz* 1971

Gray, David Barry *Mr Wonderful* 1992; *Cops and Robbersons* 1994; *Lawn Dogs* 1997

Gray, Dolores (1924–) *It's Always Fair Weather* 1955; *Kismet* 1955; *The Opposite Sex* 1956; *Designing Woman* 1957

Gray, Donald (1914–1978) *The Four Feathers* 1939; *We'll Meet Again* 1942; *Island of Desire* 1952; *Timeslip* 1955

Gray, Dulcie (1919–) *A Place of One's Own* 1944; *They Were Sisters* 1945; *Wanted for Murder* 1946; *The Years Between* 1946; *A Man about the House* 1947; *Mine Own Executioner* 1947; *My*

Brother Jonathan 1947; *The Glass Mountain* 1949; *The Franchise Affair* 1950; *Angels One Five* 1952; *A Man Could Get Killed* 1966
Gray, Erin (1950–) *Buck Rogers in the 25th Century* 1979; *Six Pack* 1982; *Jason Goes to Hell: the Final Friday* 1993; *T-Force* 1995; *Death at Clover Bend* 2001
Gray, Eve (1900–1983) *Moulin Rouge* 1928; *Death on the Set* 1935; *The Vicar of Bray* 1937
Gray, Gary (1936–) *Rachel and the Stranger* 1948; *The Next Voice You Hear* 1950
Gray, Lawrence (1898–1970) *Stage Struck* 1925; *The Patsy* 1928; *Sunny* 1930; *Man of the World* 1931
Gray, Lorna aka **Booth, Adrian** (1918–) *Red River Range* 1938; *The Man They Could Not Hang* 1939; *The Plunderers* 1948
Gray, Nadia (1923–1994) *The Spider and the Fly* 1949; *Night without Stars* 1951; *Valley of Eagles* 1951; *Crossed Swords* 1954; *One Night at the Music Hall* 1956; *Une Parisienne* 1957; *The Captain's Table* 1958; *La Dolce Vita* 1960; *Mr Topaze* 1961; *Maniac* 1962; *The Crooked Road* 1964; *The Naked Runner* 1967; *The Oldest Profession* 1967; *Two for the Road* 1967
Gray, Robert (1940–) *Elvis – the Movie* 1979; *UFOria* 1980
Gray, Sally (1916–) *Cheer Up!* 1936; *Over She Goes* 1937; *Hold My Hand* 1938; *The Saint in London* 1939; *A Window in London* 1939; *Dangerous Moonlight* 1941; *The Saint's Vacation* 1941; *Green for Danger* 1946; *The Mark of Cain* 1947; *They Made Me a Fugitive* 1947; *Obsession* 1948; *Silent Dust* 1948; *Escape Route* 1952; *The Keeper* 1976
Gray, Sam *You Better Watch Out* 1980; *Heart* 1987
Gray, Spalding (1941–2004) *Hard Choices* 1984; *The Killing Fields* 1984; *True Stories* 1986; *Swimming to Cambodia* 1987; *Beaches* 1988; *Clara's Heart* 1988; *The Image* 1990; *Straight Talk* 1992; *King of the Hill* 1993; *The Paper* 1994; *Bad Company* 1995; *Beyond Rangoon* 1995; *Diabolique* 1996; *Gray's Anatomy* 1996; *Bliss* 1997; *Kate & Leopold* 2002
Gray, Vernon *A Day to Remember* 1953; *To Paris with Love* 1954; *The Gold Express* 1955
Gray, Vivean *Picnic at Hanging Rock* 1975; *The Last Wave* 1977
Gray, Willoughby (1916–1993) *Stranger from Venus* 1954; *Absolution* 1978
Grayson, Diane (1948–) *The Prime of Miss Jean Brodie* 1969; *Blind Terror* 1971
Grayson, Jerry *Bullet* 1995; *Striptease* 1996
Grayson, Kathryn (1922–) *Andy Hardy's Private Secretary* 1941; *The Vanishing Virginian* 1941; *Rio Rita* 1942; *Thousands Cheer* 1943; *Ziegfeld Follies* 1944; *Anchors Aweigh* 1945; *Two Sisters from Boston* 1946; *It Happened in Brooklyn* 1947; *The Kissing Bandit* 1949; *That Midnight Kiss* 1949; *The Toast of New Orleans* 1950; *Show Boat* 1951; *Lovely to Look At* 1952; *The Desert Song* 1953; *Kiss Me Kate* 1953; *So This Is Love* 1953; *The Vagabond King* 1956
Greco, José (1918–2000) *Sombrero* 1952; *Ship of Fools* 1965; *The Proud and the Damned* 1972
Greco, Juliette aka **Gréco, Juliette** (1927–) *Orphée* 1950; *Elena et les Hommes* 1956; *The Sun Also Rises* 1957; *Bonjour Tristesse* 1958; *The Naked Earth* 1958; *The Roots of Heaven* 1958; *Crack in the Mirror* 1960; *The Big Gamble* 1961
Green, Adolph (1915–2002) *Simon* 1980; *Lily in Love* 1985; *I Want to Go Home* 1989
Green, Brian Austin (1973–) *Kid* 1990; *Stolen Youth* 1996
Green, Danny (1903–1973) *Someone at the Door* 1950; *The Ladykillers* 1955; *Assignment Redhead* 1956; *The 7th Voyage of Sinbad* 1958; *The Old Dark House* 1963
Green, Dorothy *Face of a Fugitive* 1959; *The Six Million Dollar Man* 1973
Green, Eva (1980–) *The Dreamers* 2003; *Arsène Lupin* 2004; *Kingdom of Heaven* 2005
Green, Garard (1924–2004) *Profile* 1954; *Emergency* 1962
Green, Gilbert (1914–1984) *Dark Intruder* 1965; *Executive Action* 1973
Green, Harry (1892–1958) *This Day and Age* 1933; *The Cisco Kid and the Lady* 1939; *A King in New York* 1957; *Next to No Time* 1958
Green, Kerri (1967–) *The Goonies* 1985; *Summer Rental* 1985; *Lucas* 1986; *Three for the Road* 1987
Green, Marika *Pickpocket* 1959; *Emmanuelle* 1974
Green, Martyn (1899–1975) *The Mikado* 1939; *The Story of Gilbert and Sullivan* 1953; *A Lovely Way to Go* 1968
Green, Mitzi (1920–1969) *Paramount on Parade* 1930; *Tom Sawyer* 1930; *Huckleberry Finn* 1931; *Skippy* 1931; *Bloodhounds of Broadway* 1952; *Lost in Alaska* 1952
Green, Nigel (1924–1972) *Witness in the Dark* 1959; *Sword of Sherwood Forest* 1960; *Pit of Darkness* 1961; *The Man Who Finally Died* 1962; *Saturday Night Out* 1963; *The Masque of the Red Death* 1964; *Zulu* 1964; *The Face of Fu Manchu* 1965; *The Ipcress File* 1965; *The Skull* 1965; *Deadlier than the Male* 1966; *Khartoum* 1966; *Tobruk* 1966; *Africa – Texas Style!* 1967; *The Pink Jungle* 1968; *Play Dirty* 1969; *The Wrecking Crew* 1969; *Countess Dracula* 1970; *The Ruling Class* 1972; *Gawain and the Green Knight* 1973
Green, Seth (1974–) *A Billion for Boris* 1984; *The Hotel New Hampshire* 1984; *Willy/Milly* 1986; *Can't Buy Me Love* 1987; *Radio Days* 1987; *Big Business* 1988; *My Stepmother Is an Alien* 1988; *Airborne* 1993; *Ticks* 1993; *Austin Powers: International Man of Mystery* 1997; *Austin Powers: the Spy Who Shagged Me* 1999; *Idle Hands* 1999; *Web of Lies* 1999; *Knockaround Guys* 2001; *Austin Powers in Goldmember* 2002; *The Italian Job* 2003; *Party Monster* 2003; *Scooby-Doo 2: Monsters Unleashed* 2004; *Without a Paddle* 2004
Green, Teddy *The Young Ones* 1961; *Summer Holiday* 1962
Green, Tom (1971–) *Freddy Got Fingered* 2001; *Stealing Harvard* 2002
Greene, Angela (1923–1978) *Shotgun* 1955; *The Cosmic Man* 1959
Greene, Daniel (1921–) *Weekend Warriors* 1986; *Elvira, Mistress of the Dark* 1988
Greene, David (1921–2003) *The Small Voice* 1948; *The Wooden Horse* 1950; *The Dark Light* 1951
Greene, Ellen (1952–) *Next Stop, Greenwich Village* 1976; *Little Shop of Horrors* 1986; *Talk Radio* 1988; *Pump Up the Volume* 1990; *Rock-a-Doodle* 1990; *Stepping Out* 1991; *Leon* 1994; *Naked Gun $33\frac{1}{3}$: the Final Insult* 1994; *Wagons East!* 1994; *Killer: a Journal of Murder* 1995; *One Fine Day* 1996
Greene (2), Graham (1952–) *Dances with Wolves* 1990; *Clearcut* 1992; *Thunderheart* 1992; *Benefit of the Doubt* 1993; *Camilla* 1993; *Cooperstown* 1993; *Huck and the King of Hearts* 1993; *Maverick* 1994; *Die Hard with a Vengeance* 1995; *The Education of Little Tree* 1997; *Shattered Image* 1998; *The Green Mile* 1999
Greene, Leon *A Challenge for Robin Hood* 1967; *The Devil Rides Out* 1968
Greene, Lorne (1915–1987) *The Silver Chalice* 1954; *Tight Spot* 1955; *Autumn Leaves* 1956; *The Buccaneer* 1958; *The Gift of Love* 1958; *The Last of the Fast Guns* 1958; *The Baited Trap* 1959; *The Harness* 1971; *Earthquake* 1974; *Battlestar Galactica* 1978; *Heidi's Song* 1982
Greene, Michael (1934–) *Americana* 1981; *Lost in America* 1985; *To Live and Die in LA* 1985; *Stranded* 1987; *Moon over Parador* 1988; *Eve of Destruction* 1991; *Rubin & Ed* 1991
Greene, Michele (1962–) *Heart of a Child* 1994; *Determination of Death* 2001
Greene, Peter *Laws of Gravity* 1992; *Clean, Shaven* 1993; *Judgment Night* 1993; *The Mask* 1994; *Pulp Fiction* 1994; *Bang* 1995; *The Rich Man's Wife* 1996; *Double Tap* 1997; *Blue Streak* 1999; *Shadow Hours* 2000
Greene, Richard (1918–1985) *Four Men and a Prayer* 1938; *Kentucky* 1938; *My Lucky Star* 1938; *Submarine Patrol* 1938; *The Hound of the Baskervilles* 1939; *The Little Princess* 1939; *Stanley and Livingstone* 1939; *I Was an Adventuress* 1940; *Little Old New York* 1940; *Unpublished Story* 1942; *Yellow Canary* 1943; *Don't Take It to Heart* 1944; *Gaiety George* 1946; *Forever Amber* 1947; *The Fighting O'Flynn* 1948; *The Fan* 1949; *Now Barabbas Was a Robber* 1949; *That Dangerous Age* 1949; *Shadow of the Eagle* 1950; *Lorna Doone* 1951; *The Black Castle* 1952; *The Bandits of Corsica* 1953; *Captain Scarlett* 1953; *Contraband Spain* 1955; *Beyond the Curtain* 1960; *Sword of Sherwood Forest* 1960; *The Blood of Fu Manchu* 1968; *The Castle of Fu Manchu* 1968; *Tales from the Crypt* 1972
Greenleaf, Raymond (1892–1963) *Harriet Craig* 1950; *Storm Warning* 1950; *A Millionaire for Christy* 1951; *Angel Face* 1953; *The Bandits of Corsica* 1953; *Three Sailors and a Girl* 1953
Greenlees, Billy aka **Greenlees, William** *That Sinking Feeling* 1979; *Gregory's Girl* 1980
Greenstreet, Sydney (1879–1954) *The Maltese Falcon* 1941; *They Died with Their Boots On* 1941; *Across the Pacific* 1942; *Casablanca* 1942; *Background to Danger* 1943; *Between Two Worlds* 1944; *The Conspirators* 1944; *Hollywood Canteen* 1944; *The Mask of Dimitrios* 1944; *Passage to Marseille* 1944; *Christmas in Connecticut* 1945; *Conflict* 1945; *Devotion* 1946; *Three Strangers* 1946; *The Verdict* 1946; *The Hucksters* 1947; *Ruthless* 1948; *The Velvet Touch* 1948; *The Woman in White* 1948; *Flamingo Road* 1949; *It's a Great Feeling* 1949; *Malaya* 1949
Greenwood, Bruce (1956–) *Wild Orchid* 1990; *Passenger 57* 1992; *Exotica* 1994; *Heart of a Child* 1994; *Danielle Steel's Mixed Blessings* 1995; *The Sweet Hereafter* 1997; *Disturbing Behaviour* 1998; *The Lost Son* 1998; *Double Jeopardy* 1999; *Here on Earth* 2000; *Hide and Seek* 2000; *Rules of Engagement* 2000; *Thirteen Days* 2000; *Ararat* 2002; *Below* 2002; *The Core* 2002; *Swept Away* 2002; *Hollywood Homicide* 2003; *Being Julia* 2004; *I, Robot* 2004; *Racing Stripes* 2004
Greenwood, Charlotte (1890–1978) *Palmy Days* 1931; *Parlor, Bedroom and Bath* 1931; *Down Argentine Way* 1940; *Star Dust* 1940; *Young People* 1940; *Moon over Miami* 1941; *Tall, Dark and Handsome* 1941; *Springtime in the Rockies* 1942; *The Gang's All Here* 1943; *Home in Indiana* 1944; *Up in Mabel's Room* 1944; *Driftwood* 1946; *Oh, You Beautiful Doll* 1949; *Dangerous When Wet* 1953
Greenwood, Joan (1921–1987) *The Gentle Sex* 1943; *They Knew Mr Knight* 1945; *A Girl in a Million* 1946; *The Man Within* 1947; *The October Man* 1947; *Saraband for Dead Lovers* 1948; *The Bad Lord Byron* 1949; *Kind Hearts and Coronets* 1949; *Whisky Galore!* 1949; *The Man in the White Suit* 1951; *Young Wives' Tale* 1951; *The Importance of Being Earnest* 1952; *Father Brown* 1954; *Knave of Hearts* 1954; *Moonfleet* 1955; *Stage Struck* 1958; *Mysterious Island* 1961; *The Amorous Prawn* 1962; *The Moon-Spinners* 1964; *The Hound of the Baskervilles* 1977; *The Uncanny* 1977; *The Water Babies* 1978; *Little Dorrit* 1987
Greer, Dabbs (1917–) *Affair with a Stranger* 1953; *Riot in Cell Block 11* 1954; *It! The Terror from beyond Space* 1958; *The Cheyenne Social Club* 1970
Greer, Jane aka **Greer, Bettejane** (1924–2001) *Dick Tracy* 1945; *Two O'Clock Courage* 1945; *The Bamboo Blonde* 1946; *The Falcon's Alibi* 1946; *They Won't Believe Me* 1947; *Station West* 1948; *The Big Steal* 1949; *The Company She Keeps* 1950; *You're in the Navy Now* 1951; *The Clown* 1952; *Desperate Search* 1952; *Run for the Sun* 1956; *Man of a Thousand Faces* 1957; *Where Love Has Gone* 1964; *Billie* 1965; *The Outfit* 1973; *Against All Odds* 1984; *Immediate Family* 1989
Greer, Judy aka **Greer, Judy Evans** (1971–) *Jawbreaker* 1999; *The Specials* 2000; *The Wedding Planner* 2001; *What Women Want* 2001; *Adaptation.* 2002; *The Cat Returns* 2002; *13 Going on 30* 2004; *The Village* 2004; *Cursed* 2005
Greer, Michael (1943–) *The Magic Garden of Stanley Sweetheart* 1970; *Fortune and Men's Eyes* 1971
Gregg, Bradley *Stand by Me* 1986; *Class of 1999* 1990; *Madhouse* 1990; *Eye of the Storm* 1991; *Fire in the Sky* 1993
Gregg, Christina *Cover Girl Killer* 1959; *Rag Doll* 1960; *Don't Talk to Strange Men* 1962
Gregg, Clark (1964–) *Lana in Love* 1991; *The Adventures of Sebastian Cole* 1998; *State and Main* 2000; *Lovely & Amazing* 2001; *The Human Stain* 2003; *In Good Company* 2004
Gregg, Everley (1903–1959) *The Private Life of Henry VIII* 1933; *The Ghost Goes West* 1935; *Pygmalion* 1938; *Brief Encounter* 1945
Gregg, Hubert (1914–2004) *29 Acacia Avenue* 1945; *The Root of All Evil* 1946; *The Story of Robin Hood and His Merrie Men* 1952; *The Maggie* 1953; *Final Appointment* 1954; *Doctor at Sea* 1955; *Simon and Laura* 1955
Gregg, John (1940–) *Heatwave* 1981; *To End All Wars* 2001
Gregg, Virginia (1916–1986) *Dragnet* 1954; *Love Is a Many-Splendored Thing* 1955; *Crime in the Streets* 1956; *The Hanging Tree* 1959; *Spencer's Mountain* 1963; *Two on a Guillotine* 1964; *Joy in the Morning* 1965; *A Walk in the Spring Rain* 1970
Greggio, Ezio (1954–) *The Silence of the Hams* 1993; *Screw Loose* 1999
Greggory, Pascal (1954–) *The Brontë Sisters* 1979; *Pauline at the Beach* 1983; *Lucie Aubrac* 1997; *Those Who Love Me Can Take the Train* 1998; *Joan of Arc* 1999; *Time Regained* 1999; *La Fidélité* 2000; *Arsène Lupin* 2004
Gregory, Andre aka **Gregory, André** (1934–) *My Dinner with Andre* 1981; *Protocol* 1984; *Street Smart* 1987; *The Last Temptation of Christ* 1988; *Some Girls* 1988; *The Linguini Incident* 1991; *Vanya on 42nd Street* 1994; *Last Summer in the Hamptons* 1995
Gregory, Celia *Agatha* 1978; *The Inside Man* 1984; *The Baby of Macon* 1993
Gregory, David *Gaolbreak* 1962; *The Hi-Jackers* 1963; *The Marked One* 1963
Gregory, James (1911–2002) *Nightfall* 1956; *The Big Caper* 1957; *Gun Glory* 1957; *The Young Stranger* 1957; *Onionhead* 1958; *Al Capone* 1959; *Hey Boy! Hey Girl!* 1959; *The Manchurian Candidate* 1962; *Two Weeks in Another Town* 1962; *PT 109* 1963; *Twilight of Honor* 1963; *A Distant Trumpet* 1964; *Quick, before It Melts* 1965; *Murderers' Row* 1966; *The Silencers* 1966; *The Ambushers* 1967; *Clambake* 1967; *Beneath the Planet of the Apes* 1969; *The Love God?* 1969; *The Late Liz* 1971; *The Million Dollar Duck* 1971; *Shoot Out* 1971
Gregory, Leo *Octane* 2003; *Suzie Gold* 2003
Gregory, Thea (1929–) *Profile* 1954; *Satellite in the Sky* 1956
Gregson, John (1919–1975) *The Lavender Hill Mob* 1951; *Angels One Five* 1952; *The Brave Don't Cry* 1952; *The Holly and the Ivy* 1952; *The Titfield Thunderbolt* 1952; *Venetian Bird* 1952; *Conflict of Wings* 1953; *Genevieve* 1953; *Three Cases of Murder* 1953; *The Weak and the Wicked* 1953; *To Dorothy, a Son* 1954; *Above Us the Waves* 1955; *Value for Money* 1955; *The Battle of the River Plate* 1956; *Jacqueline* 1956; *True as a Turtle* 1956; *Miracle in Soho* 1957; *The Captain's Table* 1958; *Rooney* 1958; *Sea of Sand* 1958; *SOS Pacific* 1959; *Faces in the Dark* 1960; *The Treasure of Monte Cristo* 1960; *The Frightened City* 1961; *Live Now – Pay Later* 1962; *Tomorrow at Ten* 1962; *Fright* 1971
Gregson Wagner, Natasha (1970–) *Dead Beat* 1994; *Wes Craven's Mind Ripper* 1995; *Lost Highway* 1996; *Two Girls and a Guy* 1997; *Another Day in Paradise* 1998; *Stranger than Fiction* 1999; *High Fidelity* 2000; *Play It to the Bone* 2000; *Wonderland* 2003
Greig, Robert (1880–1958) *Love Me Tonight* 1932; *The Devil-Doll* 1936; *Rose Marie* 1936; *The Lady Eve* 1941; *Sullivan's Travels* 1941
Greist, Kim (1958–) *CHUD* 1984; *Brazil* 1985; *Manhunter* 1986; *Throw Momma from the Train* 1987; *Punchline* 1988; *Why Me?* 1990; *Homeward Bound: the Incredible Journey* 1993; *Roswell* 1994; *Houseguest* 1995; *Homeward Bound II: Lost in San Francisco* 1996
Grenfell, Joyce (1910–1979) *The Demi-Paradise* 1943; *The Lamp Still Burns* 1943; *While the Sun Shines* 1946; *A Run for Your Money* 1949; *Stage Fright* 1949; *The Happiest Days of Your Life* 1950; *Laughter in Paradise* 1951; *The Pickwick Papers* 1952; *Genevieve* 1953; *The Million Pound Note* 1953; *The Belles of St Trinian's* 1954; *Forbidden Cargo* 1954; *The Good Companions* 1956; *Blue Murder at St Trinian's* 1957; *Happy Is the Bride* 1957; *The Pure Hell of St Trinian's* 1960; *The Old Dark House* 1963; *The Americanization of Emily* 1964; *The Yellow Rolls-Royce* 1964
Grenier, Adrian (1976–) *The Adventures of Sebastian Cole* 1998; *Drive Me Crazy* 1999; *Cecil B Demented* 2000
Grenier, Zach (1954–) *Liebestraum* 1991; *Maximum Risk* 1996
Gress, Googy *Maxie* 1985; *Promised Land* 1988; *Vibes* 1988
Gretsch, Joel (1963–) *The Legend of Bagger Vance* 2000; *The Emperor's Club* 2002
Grévill, Laurent (1961–) *Jack & Sarah* 1995; *Look at Me* 2004
Grey, Anne (1907–) *Number Seventeen* 1932; *The Wandering Jew* 1933; *Bonnie Scotland* 1935
Grey, Denise (1896–1996) *Devil in the Flesh* 1947; *Carve Her Name with Pride* 1958

Grey, Jennifer (1960–) *Red Dawn* 1984; *American Flyers* 1985; *Ferris Bueller's Day Off* 1986; *Dirty Dancing* 1987; *Light Years* 1988; *Bloodhounds of Broadway* 1989; *Murder in Mississippi* 1990; *Wind* 1992; *Lover's Knot* 1995; *The West Side Waltz* 1995
Grey, Joel (1932–) *Cabaret* 1972; *Buffalo Bill and the Indians, or Sitting Bull's History Lesson* 1976; *The Seven-Per-Cent Solution* 1976; *Remo – Unarmed and Dangerous* 1985; *Kafka* 1991; *The Music of Chance* 1993; *The Fantasticks* 1995; *A Christmas Carol* 1999; *Dancer in the Dark* 2000
Grey, Nan (1918–1993) *Dracula's Daughter* 1936; *Three Smart Girls* 1937; *The Storm* 1938; *Three Smart Girls Grow Up* 1939; *Tower of London* 1939; *The House of the Seven Gables* 1940; *The Invisible Man Returns* 1940
Grey, Shirley (1910–1981) *Back Street* 1932; *The Hurricane Express* 1932; *The Little Giant* 1933
Grey, Virginia (1917–2004) *Another Thin Man* 1939; *Broadway Serenade* 1939; *Thunder Afloat* 1939; *The Big Store* 1941; *Mr and Mrs North* 1941; *Whistling in the Dark* 1941; *Grand Central Murder* 1942; *Tarzan's New York Adventure* 1942; *Sweet Rosie O'Grady* 1943; *Flame of the Barbary Coast* 1945; *Jungle Jim* 1948; *So This Is New York* 1948; *The Bullfighter and the Lady* 1951; *Slaughter Trail* 1951; *All That Heaven Allows* 1955; *The Rose Tattoo* 1955; *Accused of Murder* 1956; *Crime of Passion* 1957; *Jeanne Eagels* 1957; *The Restless Years* 1958; *No Name on the Bullet* 1959; *Portrait in Black* 1960; *Bachelor in Paradise* 1961; *Back Street* 1961; *Tammy Tell Me True* 1961; *Black Zoo* 1963; *The Naked Kiss* 1964; *Love Has Many Faces* 1965
Grey, Zena (1988–) *Snow Day* 2000; *Max Keeble's Big Move* 2001
Greyeyes, Michael (1967–) *Dance Me Outside* 1994; *Race against Time* 2000
Gribbon, Harry (1885–1961) *The Cameraman* 1928; *The Mysterious Island* 1929
Grieco, Richard (1965–) *Mobsters* 1991; *Teen Agent* 1991; *A Night at the Roxbury* 1998; *Sexual Predator* 2001
Griem, Helmut (1932–2004) *The Damned* 1969; *The McKenzie Break* 1970; *Cabaret* 1972; *Ludwig* 1973; *Breakthrough* 1978; *Germany in Autumn* 1978; *Les Rendez-vous d'Anna* 1978; *The Second Victory* 1986
Grier, David Alan (1955–) *Streamers* 1983; *A Soldier's Story* 1984; *Beer* 1985; *Amazon Women on the Moon* 1987; *Boomerang* 1992; *Blankman* 1994; *In the Army Now* 1994; *Jumanji* 1995; *McHale's Navy* 1997; *Top of the World* 1997; *Return to Me* 2000; *3 Strikes* 2000; *Baadasssss!* 2003; *The Woodsman* 2004
Grier, Pam (1949–) *The Big Doll House* 1971; *The Big Bird Cage* 1972; *Black Mama, White Mama* 1972; *Hit Man* 1972; *Women in Cages* 1972; *Coffy* 1973; *Scream Blacula Scream* 1973; *Twilight People* 1973; *Foxy Brown* 1974; *Friday Foster* 1975; *Drum* 1976; *Greased Lightning* 1977; *Fort Apache, the Bronx* 1981; *Tough Enough* 1982; *Something Wicked This Way Comes* 1983; *On the Edge* 1985; *Stand Alone* 1985; *The Allnighter* 1987; *Nico* 1988; *The Package* 1989; *Class of 1999* 1990; *Escape from LA* 1996; *Original Gangstas* 1996; *Serial Killer* 1996; *Jackie Brown* 1997; *Holy Smoke* 1999; *In Too Deep* 1999; *Jawbreaker* 1999; *Snow Day* 2000; *Wilder* 2000; *Bones* 2001; *John Carpenter's Ghosts of Mars* 2001; *Pluto Nash* 2001
Grier, Rosey *aka* **Grier, Roosevelt** (1932–) *Skyjacked* 1972; *The Thing with Two Heads* 1972; *The Glove* 1978
Gries, Jonathan *aka* **Gries, Jon** (1957–) *TerrorVision* 1986; *Fright Night Part 2* 1988; *Kill Me Again* 1989; *Pucker Up and Bark like a Dog* 1989; *Get Shorty* 1995; *Casualties* 1997; *Jackpot* 2001; *Northfork* 2002; *Welcome to the Jungle* 2003; *Napoleon Dynamite* 2004
Grieve, Helen *The Overlanders* 1946; *Bush Christmas* 1947
Grifasi, Joe (1944–) *On the Yard* 1978; *Something Short of Paradise* 1979; *Hide in Plain Sight* 1980; *Still of the Night* 1982; *FX: Murder by Illusion* 1985; *The Feud* 1989; *Primary Motive* 1992; *Benny and Joon* 1993; *Heavy* 1995; *One Fine Day* 1996; *Sunday* 1997; *The Naked Man* 1998
Griffeth, Simone (1955–) *Death Race 2000* 1975; *Hot Target* 1985; *The Patriot* 1986
Griffies, Ethel (1878–1975) *Waterloo Bridge* 1931; *We Live Again* 1934; *Crackerjack* 1938; *Stranger on the Third Floor* 1940; *Billy Liar* 1963; *The Birds* 1963
Griffin, David (1943–) *The Blood Beast Terror* 1967; *Trog* 1970
Griffin, Eddie (1968–) *The Meteor Man* 1993; *The Walking Dead* 1995; *Deuce Bigalow: Male Gigolo* 1999; *Double Take* 2001; *John Q* 2001; *Undercover Brother* 2002
Griffin, Josephine (1928–) *The Man Who Never Was* 1955; *Postmark for Danger* 1955; *The Extra Day* 1956; *The Spanish Gardener* 1956
Griffin, Luke *The Disappearance of Finbar* 1996; *St Patrick: the Irish Legend* 2000
Griffin, Lynne (1953–) *Black Christmas* 1974; *Strange Brew* 1983
Griffin, Merv (1925–) *So This Is Love* 1953; *The Boy from Oklahoma* 1954; *Phantom of the Rue Morgue* 1954; *Hello Down There* 1969; *Slapstick of Another Kind* 1982; *The Lonely Guy* 1984
Griffin, Robert *aka* **Griffin, Robert E** (1902–1960) *Barricade* 1950; *Gunsight Ridge* 1957; *Monster from Green Hell* 1958
Griffith, Andy (1926–) *A Face in the Crowd* 1957; *No Time for Sergeants* 1958; *Onionhead* 1958; *The Second Time Around* 1961; *Angel in My Pocket* 1968; *Hearts of the West* 1975; *Rustler's Rhapsody* 1985; *Spy Hard* 1996
Griffith, Anthony *Panther* 1995; *Tales from the Hood* 1995; *Dead Man's Curve* 1997
Griffith, Gordon (1907–1958) *Tarzan of the Apes* 1918; *Little Annie Rooney* 1925
Griffith, Hugh (1912–1980) *Neutral Port* 1940; *Kind Hearts and Coronets* 1949; *The Last Days of Dolwyn* 1949; *A Run for Your Money* 1949; *Gone to Earth* 1950; *The Titfield Thunderbolt* 1952; *The Beggar's Opera* 1953; *The Sleeping Tiger* 1954; *Passage Home* 1955; *The Good Companions* 1956; *Lucky Jim* 1957; *Ben-Hur* 1959; *The Story on Page One* 1959; *The Day They Robbed the Bank of England* 1960; *Exodus* 1960; *The Counterfeit Traitor* 1962; *The Inspector* 1962; *Mutiny on the Bounty* 1962; *Term of Trial* 1962; *Hide and Seek* 1963; *Tom Jones* 1963; *The Bargee* 1964; *The Amorous Adventures of Moll Flanders* 1965; *How to Steal a Million* 1966; *Oh Dad, Poor Dad, Mama's Hung You in the Closet and I'm Feelin' So Sad* 1967; *On My Way to the Crusades, I Met a Girl Who...* 1967; *The Sailor from Gibraltar* 1967; *The Fixer* 1968; *Oliver!* 1968; *Cry of the Banshee* 1970; *Start the Revolution without Me* 1970; *The Abominable Dr Phibes* 1971; *Who Slew Auntie Roo?* 1971; *Dr Phibes Rises Again* 1972; *Craze* 1973; *The Final Programme* 1973; *Take Me High* 1973; *What?* 1973; *Legend of the Werewolf* 1974; *Luther* 1974; *Casanova & Co* 1976; *The Passover Plot* 1976
Griffith, James (1916–1993) *Apache Drums* 1951; *Eight Iron Men* 1952; *Red Skies of Montana* 1952; *Tribute to a Bad Man* 1956; *Bullwhip* 1958; *The Amazing Transparent Man* 1960; *Lorna* 1964; *Seven Alone* 1974
Griffith, Kenneth (1921–) *The Shop at Sly Corner* 1946; *Blue Scar* 1947; *Waterfront* 1950; *The Prisoner* 1955; *The Two-Headed Spy* 1958; *Circus of Horrors* 1960; *A French Mistress* 1960; *Rag Doll* 1960; *Only Two Can Play* 1961; *The Painted Smile* 1961; *Payroll* 1961; *Rotten to the Core* 1965; *The Bobo* 1967; *The Whisperers* 1967; *Great Catherine* 1968; *The Gamblers* 1969; *Revenge* 1971; *The House in Nightmare Park* 1973; *Callan* 1974; *SPYS* 1974; *Sky Riders* 1976; *Who Dares Wins* 1982; *The Englishman Who Went up a Hill, but Came down a Mountain* 1995
Griffith, Kristin *Interiors* 1978; *The Europeans* 1979; *The Long Way Home* 1998
Griffith, Melanie (1957–) *The Harrad Experiment* 1973; *The Drowning Pool* 1975; *Night Moves* 1975; *Smile* 1975; *Joyride* 1977; *One on One* 1977; *Roar* 1981; *Body Double* 1984; *Fear City* 1984; *Something Wild* 1986; *Stormy Monday* 1987; *Cherry 2000* 1988; *The Milagro Beanfield War* 1988; *Working Girl* 1988; *The Bonfire of the Vanities* 1990; *In the Spirit* 1990; *Pacific Heights* 1990; *Paradise* 1991; *Shining Through* 1992; *A Stranger among Us* 1992; *Born Yesterday* 1993; *Milk Money* 1994; *Nobody's Fool* 1994; *Now and Then* 1995; *Two Much* 1995; *Mulholland Falls* 1996; *Lolita* 1997; *Another Day in Paradise* 1998; *Celebrity* 1998; *Shadow of Doubt* 1998; *Crazy in Alabama* 1999; *RKO 281* 1999; *Cecil B Demented* 2000; *Stuart Little 2* 2002; *The Night We Called It a Day* 2003
Griffith, Raymond (1894–1937) *Hands Up!* 1926; *All Quiet on the Western Front* 1930
Griffith, Thomas Ian (1962–) *The Karate Kid III* 1989; *Excessive Force* 1993; *Hollow Point* 1996; *Kull the Conqueror* 1997; *Vampires* 1998; *The Unexpected Mrs Pollifax* 1999; *Black Point* 2001
Griffith, Tracy (1965–) *Fast Food* 1989; *The First Power* 1990; *The Finest Hour* 1991
Griffiths, Jane (1929–1975) *The Million Pound Note* 1953; *The Green Scarf* 1954; *Shadow of a Man* 1954; *The Traitor* 1957; *Tread Softly Stranger* 1958; *The Third Alibi* 1961; *Dead Man's Evidence* 1962; *The Impersonator* 1962
Griffiths, Lucy (1919–1982) *Children Galore* 1954; *The Third Alibi* 1961
Griffiths, Rachel (1968–) *Muriel's Wedding* 1994; *Children of the Revolution* 1996; *Cosi* 1996; *Jude* 1996; *To Have & to Hold* 1996; *My Best Friend's Wedding* 1997; *My Son the Fanatic* 1997; *Among Giants* 1998; *Divorcing Jack* 1998; *Hilary and Jackie* 1998; *Me Myself I* 1999; *Blow Dry* 2000; *Very Annie-Mary* 2000; *Blow* 2001; *The Adventures of Tom Thumb and Thumbelina* 2002; *The Hard Word* 2002; *The Rookie* 2002
Griffiths, Richard (1947–) *Chariots of Fire* 1981; *Gorky Park* 1983; *Greystoke: the Legend of Tarzan, Lord of the Apes* 1984; *A Private Function* 1984; *Shanghai Surprise* 1986; *Withnail & I* 1986; *King Ralph* 1991; *The Naked Gun $2\frac{1}{2}$: the Smell of Fear* 1991; *Blame It on the Bellboy* 1992; *Funny Bones* 1994; *Guarding Tess* 1994; *Sleepy Hollow* 1999; *Harry Potter and the Philosopher's Stone* 2001; *Harry Potter and the Chamber of Secrets* 2002; *Stage Beauty* 2004
Griggs, Camila *Forced Vengeance* 1982; *Bar Girls* 1994
Grimaldi, Dan *Don't Go in the House* 1979; *Joey* 1985
Grimes, Frank *The Outsider* 1979; *Britannia Hospital* 1982; *The Whales of August* 1987; *Crystalstone* 1988; *The Dive* 1989
Grimes, Gary (1955–) *Summer of '42* 1971; *The Culpepper Cattle Co* 1972; *Cahill, United States Marshal* 1973; *Class of '44* 1973; *The Spikes Gang* 1974; *Gus* 1976
Grimes, Scott (1971–) *Critters* 1986; *Critters 2: the Main Course* 1988
Grimes, Tammy (1934–) *Three Bites of the Apple* 1967; *Play It As It Lays* 1972; *Somebody Killed Her Husband* 1978; *The Runner Stumbles* 1979; *Can't Stop the Music* 1980; *The Last Unicorn* 1980; *America* 1986; *A Modern Affair* 1996; *High Art* 1998
Grimm, Oliver (1948–) *The Magnificent Rebel* 1961; *Reach for Glory* 1962
Grinberg, Anouk (1963–) *Merci la Vie* 1991; *A Self-Made Hero* 1995; *Mon Homme* 1996
Grinko, Nikolai (1920–1989) *Andrei Rublev* 1966; *Stalker* 1979
Grint, Rupert (1988–) *Harry Potter and the Philosopher's Stone* 2001; *Harry Potter and the Chamber of Secrets* 2002; *Thunderpants* 2002; *Harry Potter and the Prisoner of Azkaban* 2004
Grives, Steven (1951–) *Inseminoid* 1981; *Jenny Kissed Me* 1984; *Scooby-Doo* 2002
Grizzard, George (1928–) *Advise and Consent* 1962; *Warning Shot* 1967; *Happy Birthday, Wanda June* 1971; *Comes a Horseman* 1978; *Seems like Old Times* 1980; *The Man with the Deadly Lens* 1982; *Bachelor Party* 1984; *Caroline?* 1990; *Small Time Crooks* 2000
Grodin, Charles (1935–) *Catch-22* 1970; *The Heartbreak Kid* 1972; *11 Harrowhouse* 1974; *King Kong* 1976; *Thieves* 1977; *Heaven Can Wait* 1978; *Sunburn* 1979; *It's My Turn* 1980; *Seems like Old Times* 1980; *The Great Muppet Caper* 1981; *The Incredible Shrinking Woman* 1981; *The Lonely Guy* 1984; *The Woman in Red* 1984; *Movers and Shakers* 1985; *Ishtar* 1987; *The Couch Trip* 1988; *Midnight Run* 1988; *You Can't Hurry Love* 1988; *Taking Care of Business* 1990; *Beethoven* 1992; *Beethoven's 2nd* 1993; *Dave* 1993; *Heart and Souls* 1993; *So I Married an Axe Murderer* 1993; *It Runs in the Family* 1994
Grody, Kathryn (1946–) *Parents* 1988; *The Lemon Sisters* 1989
Groener, Harry (1951–) *Buddy Boy* 1999; *The Day the World Ended* 2001; *About Schmidt* 2002
Grogan, Clare *aka* **Grogan, C P** (1962–) *Gregory's Girl* 1980; *Comfort and Joy* 1984
Groh, David (1941–) *A Hero Ain't Nothin' but a Sandwich* 1978; *Hot Shot* 1986; *Blowback* 1999
Groom, Sam *The Baby Maker* 1970; *Run for the Roses* 1978
Gross, Arye (1960–) *Just One of the Guys* 1985; *Soul Man* 1986; *House II: the Second Story* 1987; *The Couch Trip* 1988; *The Experts* 1989; *Coupe de Ville* 1990; *Shaking the Tree* 1990; *For the Boys* 1991; *A Midnight Clear* 1991; *Hexed* 1993; *The Opposite Sex and How to Live with Them* 1993; *Mother Night* 1996; *Tinseltown* 1997; *Big Eden* 2000
Gross, Edan *And You Thought Your Parents Were Weird* 1991; *Best of the Best II* 1992
Gross, Mary (1953–) *Casual Sex?* 1988; *The Couch Trip* 1988; *Feds* 1988; *Troop Beverly Hills* 1989
Gross, Michael (1947–) *Big Business* 1988; *Tremors* 1989; *Cool as Ice* 1991; *Alan & Naomi* 1992; *Avalanche* 1994; *The Price of Vengeance* 1994; *Tremors II: Aftershocks* 1995; *Sometimes They Come Back... Again* 1996; *Tremors 3: Back to Perfection* 2001
Gross, Paul (1959–) *Cold Comfort* 1989; *Aspen Extreme* 1993; *Whale Music* 1994
Grossmann, Mechthild *Berlin Alexanderplatz* 1980; *Seduction: the Cruel Woman* 1985
Grove, Richard *Army of Darkness* 1993; *Scanner Cop* 1994
Grover, Edward *aka* **Grover, Ed** (1932–) *Who?* 1974; *Report to the Commissioner* 1975
Grover, Gulshan *Rangeela* 1995; *Ek Aur Ek Gyarah* 2003
Groves, Fred (1880–1955) *Sally in Our Alley* 1931; *The Ghost Camera* 1933; *The Challenge* 1938; *An Ideal Husband* 1947
Groves, Marianne *Fausto* 1992; *The Chambermaid on the Titanic* 1997
Grubb, Robert (1950–) *My Brilliant Career* 1979; *Gallipoli* 1981; *Remember Me* 1985
Grubbs, Gary *The Burning Bed* 1984; *JFK* 1991; *Gone Fishin'* 1997; *The Astronaut's Wife* 1999; *Double Take* 2001
Gruffudd, Ioan (1974–) *Wilde* 1997; *Solomon and Gaenor* 1998; *Another Life* 2000; *102 Dalmatians* 2000; *Shooters* 2000; *Very Annie-Mary* 2000; *King Arthur* 2004
Gründgens, Gustaf (1899–1963) *M* 1931; *Liebelei* 1932
Gruner, Mark (1958–) *Fantastic Planet* 1973; *Jaws 2* 1978
Gruner, Olivier (1960–) *Nemesis* 1993; *Automatic* 1994; *Velocity Trap* 1997
Grüning, Ilka *aka* **Gruning, Ilka** (1876–1964) *Secrets of a Soul* 1926; *Friendly Enemies* 1942
Guadagni, Nicky *White Room* 1990; *Cube* 1997
Guard, Christopher (1953–) *A Little Night Music* 1977; *The Lord of the Rings* 1978; *Dead Man's Folly* 1986; *The Haunting of Helen Walker* 1995
Guard, Dominic (1956–) *The Go-Between* 1971; *Bequest to the Nation* 1972; *Picnic at Hanging Rock* 1975; *Absolution* 1978; *The Lord of the Rings* 1978; *An Unsuitable Job for a Woman* 1981
Guardino, Harry (1925–1995) *Houseboat* 1958; *The Five Pennies* 1959; *Pork Chop Hill* 1959; *Five Branded Women* 1960; *King of Kings* 1961; *Hell Is for Heroes* 1962; *The Pigeon That Took Rome* 1962; *Rhino!* 1964; *The Adventures of Bullwhip Griffin* 1967; *Valley of Mystery* 1967; *The Hell with Heroes* 1968; *Jigsaw* 1968; *Madigan* 1968; *Lovers and Other Strangers* 1970; *Dirty Harry* 1971; *Red Sky at Morning* 1971; *They Only Kill Their Masters* 1972; *Capone* 1975; *Whiffs* 1975; *The Enforcer* 1976; *St Ives* 1976; *Rollercoaster* 1977; *Matilda* 1978; *Goldengirl* 1979; *Any Which Way You Can* 1980
Guastaferro, Vincent *Eyes of an Angel* 1991; *Homicide* 1991; *Sweet and Lowdown* 1999
Guérin, François *Mitsou* 1957; *Eyes without a Face* 1959
Guerra, Blanca (1953–) *Motel* 1983; *Separate Vacations* 1986; *Santa Sangre* 1989; *Danzón* 1991
Guerra, Castulo *Stick* 1985; *Terminator 2: Judgment Day* 1991
Guerra, Saverio *The Winner* 1996; *Summer of Sam* 1999
Guerrasio, John *Jane Austen in Manhattan* 1980; *Boo, Zino and the Snurks* 2004
Guerrero, Evelyn (1949–) *Cheech and Chong's Next Movie* 1980; *Cheech and Chong's Nice Dreams* 1981; *Things Are Tough All Over* 1982
Guers, Paul (1927–) *Bay of the Angels* 1963; *Le Parfum d'Yvonne* 1994
Guest, Christopher (1948–) *Girlfriends* 1978; *The Long Riders* 1980; *Heartbeeps* 1981; *A Piano for Mrs Cimino* 1982; *This Is Spinal Tap* 1984; *Little Shop of Horrors* 1986; *Beyond Therapy* 1987; *The Princess Bride* 1987; *Sticky Fingers* 1988; *Waiting for Guffman* 1996; *Best in Show* 2000; *A Mighty Wind* 2003
Guest, Lance (1960–) *Halloween II* 1981; *I Ought to Be in Pictures*

1982; *The Last Starfighter* 1984; *The Roommate* 1984; *Jaws the Revenge* 1987; *The Wizard of Loneliness* 1988

Guest, Nicholas *The Long Riders* 1980; *Appointment with Death* 1988; *Wind Dancer* 1991; *Forever* 1993; *Adrenalin: Fear the Rush* 1995

Guevara, Nacha *Miss Mary* 1986; *The Dark Side of the Heart* 1992

Gugino, Carla (1971–) *Son in Law* 1993; *This Boy's Life* 1993; *The War at Home* 1996; *Judas Kiss* 1998; *Snake Eyes* 1998; *The Center of the World* 2001; *The One* 2001; *She Creature* 2001; *SPYkids* 2001; *SPYkids 2: the Island of Lost Dreams* 2002; *The Singing Detective* 2003; *SPYkids 3-D: Game Over* 2003; *Sin City* 2005

Guidall, George *Golden Gate* 1994; *The Impostors* 1998

Guilbert, Jean-Claude *aka* **Guilbert, J C** *Au Hasard, Balthazar* 1966; *Mouchette* 1966

Guild, Nancy (1925–1999) *Somewhere in the Night* 1946; *Give My Regards to Broadway* 1948; *Black Magic* 1949; *Abbott and Costello Meet the Invisible Man* 1951; *Francis Covers the Big Town* 1953

Guilfoyle (1), Paul (1902–1961) *Winterset* 1936; *The Adventures of Michael Strogoff* 1937; *Behind the Headlines* 1937; *Flight from Glory* 1937; *Super-Sleuth* 1937; *The Woman I Love* 1937; *Law of the Underworld* 1938; *The Saint in New York* 1938; *Remember the Night* 1940; *The Saint Takes Over* 1940; *The Saint in Palm Springs* 1941; *The Woman on Pier 13* 1949; *Apache* 1954; *Chief Crazy Horse* 1955

Guilfoyle (2), Paul (1955–) *Billy Galvin* 1986; *Howard, a New Breed of Hero* 1986; *Dealers* 1989; *Cadillac Man* 1990; *True Colors* 1991; *Final Analysis* 1992; *Mother's Boys* 1993; *Little Odessa* 1994; *Celtic Pride* 1996; *Extreme Measures* 1996; *Striptease* 1996; *Air Force One* 1997; *LA Confidential* 1997; *Primary Colors* 1998; *Session 9* 2001; *Live from Baghdad* 2002

Guillaume, Robert (1932–) *Seems like Old Times* 1980; *Prince Jack* 1984; *Wanted Dead or Alive* 1986; *Lean on Me* 1989; *Death Warrant* 1990; *The Meteor Man* 1993; *The Lion King* 1994; *The Adventures of Tom Thumb and Thumbelina* 2002; *Big Fish* 2003

Guillemin, Sophie (1977–) *L'Ennui* 1998; *Harry, He's Here to Help* 2000; *He Loves Me... He Loves Me Not* 2002

Guillen-Cuervo, Fernando *aka* **Guillen, Fernando** *aka* **Guillén, Fernando** (1963–) *La Señora* 1987; *Women on the Verge of a Nervous Breakdown* 1988; *The Ages of Lulu* 1990; *Acción Mutante* 1993; *A Business Affair* 1993; *Mouth to Mouth* 1995

Guillory, Sienna (1975–) *Sorted* 2000; *two days, nine lives* 2000; *Kiss Kiss (Bang Bang)* 2001; *Late Night Shopping* 2001; *Superstition* 2001; *The Principles of Lust* 2002; *The Time Machine* 2002; *Resident Evil: Apocalypse* 2004

Guinan, Francis *Shining Through* 1992; *Guinevere* 1999

Guinee, Tim *Tai-Pan* 1986; *American Blue Note* 1989; *Once Around* 1991; *The Pompatus of Love* 1995; *Vampires* 1998; *Impostor* 2001; *Personal Velocity* 2001; *Ladder 49* 2004

Guinness, Alec (1914–2000) *Evensong* 1934; *Great Expectations* 1946; *Oliver Twist* 1948; *Kind Hearts and Coronets* 1949; *A Run for Your Money* 1949; *Last Holiday* 1950; *The Mudlark* 1950; *The Lavender Hill Mob* 1951; *The Man in the White Suit* 1951; *The Card* 1952; *The Captain's Paradise* 1953; *Malta Story* 1953; *Father Brown* 1954; *To Paris with Love* 1954; *The Ladykillers* 1955; *The Prisoner* 1955; *The Swan* 1956; *Barnacle Bill* 1957; *The Bridge on the River Kwai* 1957; *The Horse's Mouth* 1958; *Our Man in Havana* 1959; *The Scapegoat* 1959; *Tunes of Glory* 1960; *A Majority of One* 1961; *HMS Defiant* 1962; *Lawrence of Arabia* 1962; *The Fall of the Roman Empire* 1964; *Doctor Zhivago* 1965; *Situation Hopeless – but Not Serious* 1965; *Hotel Paradiso* 1966; *The Quiller Memorandum* 1966; *The Comedians* 1967; *Cromwell* 1970; *Scrooge* 1970; *Brother Sun, Sister Moon* 1972; *Hitler: the Last Ten Days* 1973; *Murder by Death* 1976; *Star Wars Episode IV: a New Hope* 1977; *Raise the Titanic* 1980; *Star Wars Episode V: the Empire Strikes Back* 1980; *Lovesick* 1983; *Star Wars Episode VI: Return of the Jedi* 1983; *A Passage to India* 1984; *A Handful of Dust* 1987; *Little Dorrit* 1987; *Kafka* 1991; *Mute Witness* 1995

Guiomar, Julien (1928–) *King of Hearts* 1966; *The Thief of Paris* 1967; *Take It Easy* 1971; *Mado* 1976; *Double Dare* 1981; *Le Cop* 1985; *Léolo* 1992

Guiry, Tom *aka* **Guiry, Thomas** (1981–) *The Sandlot* 1993; *Shattered Family* 1993; *Strike!* 1998; *Wrestling with Alligators* 1998; *Ride with the Devil* 1999; *Songs in Ordinary Time* 2000; *Tigerland* 2000; *Mystic River* 2003

Guisol, Henri (1904–1994) *Le Crime de Monsieur Lange* 1935; *Drôle de Drame* 1937; *Lola Montès* 1955

Guitry, Sacha (1885–1957) *Bonne Chance* 1935; *The Story of a Cheat* 1936; *Royal Affairs in Versailles* 1953; *Napoléon* 1955

Guizar, Tito (1908–1999) *The Llano Kid* 1939; *Brazil* 1944

Gulager, Clu (1928–) *The Killers* 1964; *And Now Miguel* 1966; *Winning* 1969; *Company of Killers* 1970; *The Last Picture Show* 1971; *The Glass House* 1972; *Molly and Lawless John* 1972; *McQ* 1974; *The Other Side of Midnight* 1977; *A Force of One* 1979; *Touched by Love* 1979; *The Initiation* 1984; *Return of the Living Dead* 1984; *A Nightmare on Elm Street 2: Freddy's Revenge* 1985; *Prime Risk* 1985; *The Hidden* 1987; *I'm Gonna Git You Sucka* 1988; *Tapeheads* 1988

Gulp, Elsi *In the Belly of the Whale* 1984; *Sugarbaby* 1985

Gulpilil, David *aka* **Gulpilil** (1954–) *Walkabout* 1970; *Mad Dog* 1976; *Storm Boy* 1976; *The Last Wave* 1977; *"Crocodile" Dundee* 1986; *Rabbit-Proof Fence* 2002

Gummersall, Devon (1978–) *Lured Innocence* 1999; *Wind River* 1999

Gunn, Judy (1915–1991) *The Love Test* 1935; *The Private Secretary* 1935; *Vintage Wine* 1935; *In the Soup* 1936; *The Last Journey* 1936

Gunn, Moses (1929–1993) *Eagle in a Cage* 1971; *Shaft* 1971; *Wild Rovers* 1971; *The Hot Rock* 1972; *Shaft's Big Score!* 1972; *Aaron Loves Angela* 1975; *Rollerball* 1975; *Remember My Name* 1978; *The Ninth Configuration* 1979; *Ragtime* 1981; *The Killing Floor* 1984; *The NeverEnding Story* 1984; *Certain Fury* 1985; *Heartbreak Ridge* 1986; *Leonard, Part 6* 1987; *The Luckiest Man in the World* 1989

Gunn, Peter *Resurrected* 1989; *Blue Juice* 1995; *Brassed Off* 1996

Gunther, Dan *Denise Calls Up* 1995; *Lewis & Clark & George* 1996

Günther, Ernst (1933–1999) *House of Angels* 1992; *House of Angels II: The Second Summer* 1994

Gunton, Bob (1945–) *Rollover* 1981; *Static* 1985; *Matewan* 1987; *Unconquered* 1989; *Missing Pieces* 1991; *Demolition Man* 1993; *Roswell* 1994; *The Shawshank Redemption* 1994; *Ace Ventura: When Nature Calls* 1995; *Broken Arrow* 1996; *The Glimmer Man* 1996; *Buffalo Soldiers* 1997; *Changing Habits* 1997; *Patch Adams* 1998; *Bats* 1999; *Boat Trip* 2002

Gupta, Neena *In Custody* 1993; *Cotton Mary* 1999

Gur, Alizia *The Hand of Night* 1966; *Kill a Dragon* 1967; *Tarzan and the Jungle Boy* 1968

Gurchenko, Lyudmila (1935–) *Sibiriada* 1979; *Dream Flights* 1983; *A Station for Two* 1983

Gurie, Sigrid (1911–1969) *The Adventures of Marco Polo* 1938; *Algiers* 1938; *Three Faces West* 1940

Gurney, Sharon *The Corpse* 1969; *Death Line* 1972

Gurry, Eric *Bad Boys* 1983; *Willy/Milly* 1986

Gurwitch, Annabelle *Kiss Daddy Good Night* 1987; *Pizza Man* 1991

Guthrie, Arlo (1947–) *Alice's Restaurant* 1969; *Roadside Prophets* 1992

Guthrie, Tyrone (1900–1971) *St Martin's Lane* 1938; *Vessel of Wrath* 1938

Gutierrez, Zaide Silvia *El Norte* 1983; *Highway Patrolman* 1991

Guttenberg, Steve (1958–) *The Chicken Chronicles* 1977; *Something for Joey* 1977; *The Boys from Brazil* 1978; *Players* 1979; *Can't Stop the Music* 1980; *Diner* 1982; *Police Academy* 1984; *Bad Medicine* 1985; *Cocoon* 1985; *Police Academy 2: Their First Assignment* 1985; *Police Academy 3: Back in Training* 1986; *Short Circuit* 1986; *Amazon Women on the Moon* 1987; *The Bedroom Window* 1987; *Police Academy 4: Citizens on Patrol* 1987; *Surrender* 1987; *Three Men and a Baby* 1987; *Cocoon: the Return* 1988; *High Spirits* 1988; *The Boyfriend School* 1990; *Three Men and a Little Lady* 1990; *The Big Green* 1995; *Home for the Holidays* 1995; *It Takes Two* 1995; *Airborne* 1997; *Casper: a Spirited Beginning* 1997; *Zeus and Roxanne* 1997; *Home Team* 1998

Gutteridge, Lucy (1956–) *Top Secret!* 1984; *The Trouble with Spies* 1987; *Grief* 1993

Gutteridge, Melanie *GMT Greenwich Mean Time* 1998; *Large* 2000; *Long Time Dead* 2001

Guy, Jasmine (1964–) *Harlem Nights* 1989; *Cats Don't Dance* 1998; *Guinevere* 1999

Guyler, Deryck (1914–1999) *A Hard Day's Night* 1964; *The Big Job* 1965; *Please Sir!* 1971

Guzman, Luis *aka* **Guzmán, Luis** (1956–) *Q & A* 1990; *The Hard Way* 1991; *Jumpin' at the Boneyard* 1991; *Carlito's Way* 1993; *The Substitute* 1996; *The Bone Collector* 1999; *The Limey* 1999; *Magnolia* 1999; *Traffic* 2000; *The Count of Monte Cristo* 2001; *Double Whammy* 2001; *Pluto Nash* 2001; *Confidence* 2002; *Punch-Drunk Love* 2002; *The Salton Sea* 2002; *Welcome to Collinwood* 2002; *Anger Management* 2003; *Dumb and Dumberer: When Harry Met Lloyd* 2003

Gwaltney, Jack (1960–) *Casualties of War* 1989; *Vital Signs* 1990; *Risk* 1993

Gwenn, Edmund (1875–1959) *Hindle Wakes* 1931; *The Skin Game* 1931; *Friday the Thirteenth* 1933; *The Good Companions* 1933; *Waltzes from Vienna* 1933; *I Was a Spy* 1934; *Java Head* 1935; *Anthony Adverse* 1936; *Sylvia Scarlett* 1936; *The Walking Dead* 1936; *Parnell* 1937; *Penny Paradise* 1938; *South Riding* 1938; *A Yank at Oxford* 1938; *Cheer Boys Cheer* 1939; *The Doctor Takes a Wife* 1940; *The Earl of Chicago* 1940; *Foreign Correspondent* 1940; *Pride and Prejudice* 1940; *Charley's Aunt* 1941; *Cheers for Miss Bishop* 1941; *The Devil and Miss Jones* 1941; *Random Harvest* 1942; *A Yank at Eton* 1942; *Forever and a Day* 1943; *Lassie Come Home* 1943; *The Meanest Man in the World* 1943; *Between Two Worlds* 1944; *The Keys of the Kingdom* 1944; *Bewitched* 1945; *Of Human Bondage* 1946; *Undercurrent* 1946; *Bob, Son of Battle* 1947; *Green Dolphin Street* 1947; *Life with Father* 1947; *Miracle on 34th Street* 1947; *Apartment for Peggy* 1948; *Hills of Home* 1948; *Challenge to Lassie* 1949; *For Heaven's Sake* 1950; *Mister 880* 1950; *Pretty Baby* 1950; *A Woman of Distinction* 1950; *Peking Express* 1951; *Les Misérables* 1952; *The Bigamist* 1953; *The Student Prince* 1954; *Them!* 1954; *The Trouble with Harry* 1954; *It's a Dog's Life* 1955

Gwillim, Jack (1909–2001) *The Battle of the River Plate* 1956; *The One That Got Away* 1957; *North West Frontier* 1959; *Circus of Horrors* 1960; *Sword of Sherwood Forest* 1960; *A Midsummer Night's Dream* 1961; *Jason and the Argonauts* 1963; *The Curse of the Mummy's Tomb* 1964; *Clash of the Titans* 1981

Gwynn, Michael (1916–1976) *The Revenge of Frankenstein* 1958; *Village of the Damned* 1960; *Jason and the Argonauts* 1963; *The Scars of Dracula* 1970

Gwynne, Anne (1918–2003) *The Black Cat* 1941; *Road Agent* 1941; *Broadway* 1942; *Men of Texas* 1942; *Ride 'em Cowboy* 1942; *Sin Town* 1942; *Frontier Badmen* 1943; *House of Frankenstein* 1944; *Weird Woman* 1944; *Dick Tracy Meets Gruesome* 1947; *Teenage Monster* 1958

Gwynne, Fred (1926–1993) *On the Waterfront* 1954; *Munster, Go Home!* 1966; *La Luna* 1979; *Simon* 1980; *So Fine* 1981; *The Cotton Club* 1984; *Water* 1985; *The Boy Who Could Fly* 1986; *Off Beat* 1986; *Fatal Attraction* 1987; *Ironweed* 1987; *The Land before Time* 1988; *Disorganized Crime* 1989; *Pet Sematary* 1989; *My Cousin Vinny* 1992

Gwynne, Haydn *The Pleasure Principle* 1991; *Remember Me?* 1996

Gwynne, Michael C (1942–) *Payday* 1972; *Harry in Your Pocket* 1973; *The Terminal Man* 1974; *Special Delivery* 1976; *Butch and Sundance: the Early Days* 1979; *Seduced* 1985; *Blue Heat* 1990

Gwynne, Peter *Tim* 1979; *Remember Me* 1985; *Kick* 1999

Gyllenhaal, Jake *aka* **Gyllenhaal, Jacob** (1980–) *A Dangerous Woman* 1993; *October Sky* 1999; *Bubble Boy* 2001; *Donnie Darko* 2001; *The Good Girl* 2001; *Lovely & Amazing* 2001; *Moonlight Mile* 2002; *The Day after Tomorrow* 2004

Gyllenhaal, Maggie (1977–) *A Dangerous Woman* 1993; *Resurrection* 1999; *Cecil B Demented* 2000; *Donnie Darko* 2001; *Secretary* 2001; *Adaptation.* 2002; *Confessions of a Dangerous Mind* 2002; *40 Days and 40 Nights* 2002; *Casa de los Babys* 2003; *Mona Lisa Smile* 2003; *Criminal* 2004

Gyngell, Kim (1952–) *Just Us* 1986; *Grievous Bodily Harm* 1987; *Boulevard of Broken Dreams* 1988; *Heaven Tonight* 1990; *Holidays on the River Yarra* 1991; *Love and Other Catastrophes* 1996

Gynt, Greta (1916–2000) *Sexton Blake and the Hooded Terror* 1938; *The Arsenal Stadium Mystery* 1939; *Dark Eyes of London* 1939; *Crooks' Tour* 1940; *The Common Touch* 1941; *It's That Man Again* 1942; *Tomorrow We Live* 1942; *London Town* 1946; *Dear Murderer* 1947; *Easy Money* 1947; *Take My Life* 1947; *The Calendar* 1948; *Mr Perrin and Mr Traill* 1948; *Shadow of the Eagle* 1950; *Soldiers Three* 1951; *Forbidden Cargo* 1954; *The Blue Peter* 1955

Haas, Dolly (1910–1994) *Broken Blossoms* 1936; *I Confess* 1953

Haas, Hugo (1901–1968) *Days of Glory* 1944; *Summer Storm* 1944; *Dakota* 1945; *Holiday in Mexico* 1946; *Northwest Outpost* 1947; *Casbah* 1948; *For the Love of Mary* 1948; *My Girl Tisa* 1948; *The Fighting Kentuckian* 1949; *King Solomon's Mines* 1950; *Lizzie* 1957

Haas, Lukas (1976–) *Testament* 1983; *Witness* 1985; *Solarbabies* 1986; *Lady in White* 1988; *The Wizard of Loneliness* 1988; *Music Box* 1989; *See You in the Morning* 1989; *Convicts* 1991; *Rambling Rose* 1991; *Alan & Naomi* 1992; *Leap of Faith* 1992; *Boys* 1995; *Johns* 1995; *Everyone Says I Love You* 1996; *David and Lisa* 1998; *Breakfast of Champions* 1999; *Running Free* 1999; *Long Time Dead* 2001; *Last Days* 2005

Haberle, Sean *Deadly Whispers* 1995; *Exquisite Tenderness* 1995

Habich, Matthias (1940–) *Imperative* 1982; *Beyond Silence* 1996; *Nowhere in Africa* 2001; *Downfall* 2004

Hack, Olivia (1983–) *The Brady Bunch Movie* 1995; *A Very Brady Sequel* 1996

Hack, Shelley (1952–) *The Stepfather* 1986; *Troll* 1986; *Shattering the Silence* 1992; *Freefall: Flight 174* 1995

Hackett, Buddy (1924–2003) *Fireman Save My Child* 1954; *God's Little Acre* 1958; *All Hands on Deck* 1961; *The Music Man* 1962; *It's a Mad Mad Mad Mad World* 1963; *The Love Bug* 1969; *The Little Mermaid* 1989; *Paulie* 1998; *The Little Mermaid II: Return to the Sea* 2000

Hackett, Claire *Dancin' thru the Dark* 1989; *Liam* 2000

Hackett, Joan (1934–1983) *The Group* 1966; *Will Penny* 1967; *Assignment to Kill* 1968; *Support Your Local Sheriff!* 1969; *The Last of Sheila* 1973; *The Terminal Man* 1974; *Treasure of Matecumbe* 1976; *One-Trick Pony* 1980; *Only When I Laugh* 1981; *The Long Summer of George Adams* 1982

Hackman, Gene (1930–) *Mad Dog Coll* 1961; *Lilith* 1964; *Hawaii* 1966; *Banning* 1967; *Bonnie and Clyde* 1967; *A Covenant with Death* 1967; *First to Fight* 1967; *The Split* 1968; *Downhill Racer* 1969; *The Gypsy Moths* 1969; *I Never Sang for My Father* 1969; *Marooned* 1969; *Riot* 1969; *Doctors' Wives* 1970; *Cisco Pike* 1971; *The French Connection* 1971; *The Hunting Party* 1971; *The Poseidon Adventure* 1972; *Prime Cut* 1972; *Scarecrow* 1973; *The Conversation* 1974; *Young Frankenstein* 1974; *Zandy's Bride* 1974; *Bite the Bullet* 1975; *French Connection II* 1975; *Lucky Lady* 1975; *Night Moves* 1975; *A Bridge Too Far* 1977; *The Domino Principle* 1977; *March or Die* 1977; *Superman* 1978; *Superman II* 1980; *All Night Long* 1981; *Reds* 1981; *Eureka* 1982; *Uncommon Valor* 1983; *Under Fire* 1983; *Misunderstood* 1984; *Target* 1985; *Twice in a Lifetime* 1985; *Hoosiers* 1986; *No Way Out* 1986; *Power* 1986; *Superman IV: the Quest for Peace* 1987; *Another Woman* 1988; *BAT-21* 1988; *Full Moon in Blue Water* 1988; *Mississippi Burning* 1988; *The Package* 1989; *Loose Cannons* 1990; *Narrow Margin* 1990; *Postcards from the Edge* 1990; *Class Action* 1991; *Company Business* 1991; *Unforgiven* 1992; *The Firm* 1993; *Geronimo: an American Legend* 1993; *Wyatt Earp* 1994; *Crimson Tide* 1995; *Get Shorty* 1995; *The Quick and the Dead* 1995; *Absolute Power* 1996; *The Birdcage* 1996; *The Chamber* 1996; *Extreme Measures* 1996; *Antz* 1998; *Enemy of the State*

1998; *Twilight* 1998; *The Replacements* 2000; *Under Suspicion* 2000; *Behind Enemy Lines* 2001; *Heartbreakers* 2001; *Heist* 2001; *The Mexican* 2001; *The Royal Tenenbaums* 2001; *Runaway Jury* 2003; *Welcome to Mooseport* 2004
Haddon, Dayle (1949–) *Paperback Hero* 1972; *The World's Greatest Athlete* 1973; *North Dallas Forty* 1979; *Love Songs* 1984; *Cyborg* 1989
Haddrick, Ron (1929–) *Dawn!* 1979; *Quigley Down Under* 1990
Haden, Sara (1897–1981) *Anne of Green Gables* 1934; *Mad Love* 1935; *Magnificent Obsession* 1935; *Captain January* 1936; *Poor Little Rich Girl* 1936; *Out West with the Hardys* 1938; *Andy Hardy Gets Spring Fever* 1939; *Judge Hardy and Son* 1939; *Andy Hardy Meets Debutante* 1940; *The Shop around the Corner* 1940; *Life Begins for Andy Hardy* 1941; *Andy Hardy's Double Life* 1942; *The Courtship of Andy Hardy* 1942; *Andy Hardy's Blonde Trouble* 1944; *Love Laughs at Andy Hardy* 1946; *Andy Hardy Comes Home* 1958
Hadley, Reed (1911–1974) *Circumstantial Evidence* 1945; *The Dark Corner* 1946; *It Shouldn't Happen to a Dog* 1946; *I Shot Jesse James* 1949; *The Baron of Arizona* 1950; *Dallas* 1950; *The Half-Breed* 1952; *Big House, USA* 1955
Hagan, Molly (1962–) *Some Kind of Wonderful* 1987; *The Dentist* 1996; *Ringmaster* 1998; *Election* 1999
Hageman, Richard (1882–1966) *The Toast of New Orleans* 1950; *The Great Caruso* 1951; *Rhapsody* 1954
Hagen, Jean (1923–1977) *Adam's Rib* 1949; *Ambush* 1949; *The Asphalt Jungle* 1950; *A Life of Her Own* 1950; *Side Street* 1950; *Carbine Williams* 1952; *Singin' in the Rain* 1952; *Arena* 1953; *Latin Lovers* 1953; *The Big Knife* 1955; *Spring Reunion* 1957; *The Shaggy Dog* 1959; *Sunrise at Campobello* 1960; *Panic in Year Zero* 1962; *Dead Ringer* 1964
Hagen, Ross (1938–) *Speedway* 1968; *Avenging Angel* 1985; *Armed Response* 1986
Hagen, Uta (1919–2004) *The Other* 1972; *The Boys from Brazil* 1978; *Reversal of Fortune* 1990
Hagerthy, Ron *I Was a Communist for the FBI* 1951; *The Hostage* 1966
Hagerty, Julie (1955–) *Airplane!* 1980; *Airplane II: the Sequel* 1982; *A Midsummer Night's Sex Comedy* 1982; *Goodbye New York* 1984; *Bad Medicine* 1985; *Lost in America* 1985; *Aria* 1987; *Beyond Therapy* 1987; *What about Bob?* 1991; *Noises Off* 1992; *U Turn* 1997; *The Story of Us* 1999; *Freddy Got Fingered* 2001; *Storytelling* 2001
Hagerty, Michael G aka **Hagerty, Michael** (1953–) *Overboard* 1987; *Speed 2: Cruise Control* 1997; *Best Laid Plans* 1999
Haggerty, Dan (1941–) *The Life and Times of Grizzly Adams* 1974; *King of the Mountain* 1981; *Elves* 1989; *Chance* 1990; *Spirit of the Eagle* 1991; *The Magic Voyage* 1992; *Grizzly Mountain* 1997
Haggerty, Don (1914–1988) *Armored Car Robbery* 1950; *Storm over Wyoming* 1950; *The Sundowners* 1950; *Cause for Alarm* 1951; *Bronco Buster* 1952; *Cry Vengeance* 1954; *Cattle Empire* 1958; *The Resurrection of Zachary Wheeler* 1971
Hagiwara, Masato (1971–) *Chaos* 1999; *Cafe Lumiere* 2003
Hagman, Larry (1931–) *Ensign Pulver* 1964; *Fail-Safe* 1964; *The Group* 1966; *Up in the Cellar* 1970; *Beware! The Blob* 1971; *Harry and Tonto* 1974; *Stardust* 1974; *The Big Bus* 1976; *Mother, Jugs & Speed* 1976; *Superman* 1978; *SOB* 1981; *Primary Colors* 1998
Hagney, Frank (1884–1973) *The General* 1927; *The Lone Rider in Ghost Town* 1941
Hahn, Archie *Meatballs 2* 1984; *Amazon Women on the Moon* 1987
Hahn, Jess (1922–1998) *The Sign of Leo* 1959; *Cartouche* 1961; *The Trial* 1962; *Topkapi* 1964; *The Night of the Following Day* 1968
Hahn, Kathryn (1974–) *Anchorman: the Legend of Ron Burgundy* 2004; *Win a Date with Tad Hamilton!* 2004; *A Lot like Love* 2005
Hald, Charles (1943–) *Oliver's Story* 1978; *Who'll Stop the Rain?* 1978; *Altered States* 1980; *Divorce Wars* 1982; *Cop* 1988; *The Rescue* 1988; *Nightbreed* 1990; *Storyville* 1992; *Cooperstown* 1993; *For Their Own Good* 1993; *Home on the Range* 2004
Halduk, Stacy (1968–) *Danielle Steel's A Perfect Stranger* 1994; *Desert Thunder* 1998
Haig, Sid (1939–) *Spider Baby* 1964; *The Big Doll House* 1971; *THX 1138* 1971; *The Big Bird Cage* 1972; *Black Mama, White Mama* 1972; *Coffy* 1973; *Chu Chu and the Philly Flash* 1981; *Genuine Risk* 1990; *Lambada! The Forbidden Dance* 1990; *House of 1000 Corpses* 2001; *The Devil's Rejects* 2005
Haigh, Kenneth (1929–) *My Teenage Daughter* 1956; *High Flight* 1957; *Cleopatra* 1963; *A Hard Day's Night* 1964; *The Deadly Affair* 1966; *A Lovely Way to Go* 1968; *Eagle in a Cage* 1971; *Robin and Marian* 1976; *The Bitch* 1979; *Wild Geese II* 1985; *Shuttlecock* 1991
Haim, Corey (1972–) *Firstborn* 1984; *Murphy's Romance* 1985; *Silver Bullet* 1985; *Lucas* 1986; *The Lost Boys* 1987; *License to Drive* 1988; *Watchers* 1988; *Dream a Little Dream* 1989; *The Dream Machine* 1990; *Prayer of the Rollerboys* 1990; *Oh, What a Night* 1992; *National Lampoon's Scuba School* 1994; *Never Too Late* 1996; *Without Malice* 2000
Haines, Donald (1941–) *No Greater Glory* 1934; *That Gang of Mine* 1940; *Pride of the Bowery* 1941; *Spooks Run Wild* 1941
Haines, Larry (1918–) *The Odd Couple* 1968; *The Seven-Ups* 1973
Haines, Patricia (?–1976) *The Night Caller* 1965; *Walk a Crooked Path* 1969
Haines, William (1900–1973) *Little Annie Rooney* 1925; *Sally, Irene and Mary* 1925; *Show People* 1928
Haji *Faster, Pussycat! Kill! Kill!* 1965; *Motor Psycho* 1965; *Good Morning… and Goodbye* 1967
Hale, Alan (1892–1950) *The Four Horsemen of the Apocalypse* 1921; *Robin Hood* 1922; *The Covered Wagon* 1923; *The Leatherneck* 1929; *The Sin of Madelon Claudet* 1931; *Susan Lenox: Her Fall and Rise* 1931; *Union Depot* 1932; *It Happened One Night* 1934; *Little Man, What Now?* 1934; *The Little Minister* 1934; *The Lost Patrol* 1934; *Of Human Bondage* 1934; *The Good Fairy* 1935; *The Last Days of Pompeii* 1935; *A Message to Garcia* 1936; *Our Relations* 1936; *God's Country and the Woman* 1937; *Jump for Glory* 1937; *The Prince and the Pauper* 1937; *Stella Dallas* 1937; *The Adventures of Marco Polo* 1938; *The Adventures of Robin Hood* 1938; *Algiers* 1938; *Four Men and a Prayer* 1938; *Listen, Darling* 1938; *Dodge City* 1939; *Dust Be My Destiny* 1939; *Green Hell* 1939; *The Man in the Iron Mask* 1939; *On Your Toes* 1939; *The Private Lives of Elizabeth and Essex* 1939; *The Fighting 69th* 1940; *Santa Fe Trail* 1940; *The Sea Hawk* 1940; *They Drive by Night* 1940; *Virginia City* 1940; *Footsteps in the Dark* 1941; *Manpower* 1941; *The Strawberry Blonde* 1941; *Captains of the Clouds* 1942; *Desperate Journey* 1942; *Gentleman Jim* 1942; *Action in the North Atlantic* 1943; *Destination Tokyo* 1943; *This Is the Army* 1943; *The Adventures of Mark Twain* 1944; *Make Your Own Bed* 1944; *God Is My Co-Pilot* 1945; *Hotel Berlin* 1945; *Roughly Speaking* 1945; *The Man I Love* 1946; *Night and Day* 1946; *My Wild Irish Rose* 1947; *Pursued* 1947; *Adventures of Don Juan* 1948; *My Girl Tisa* 1948; *Always Leave Them Laughing* 1949; *The Inspector General* 1949; *South of St Louis* 1949; *The Younger Brothers* 1949; *Colt .45* 1950; *Rogues of Sherwood Forest* 1950; *Stars in My Crown* 1950
Hale Jr, Alan aka **Hale, Alan** (1918–1990) *Sweetheart of the Campus* 1941; *Music Man* 1948; *Riders in the Sky* 1949; *The West Point Story* 1950; *Home Town Story* 1951; *Sons of the Musketeers* 1951; *The Big Trees* 1952; *Wait 'til the Sun Shines, Nellie* 1952; *Captain Kidd and the Slave Girl* 1954; *Destry* 1954; *The Iron Glove* 1954; *A Man Alone* 1955; *Many Rivers to Cross* 1955; *Young at Heart* 1955; *The Killer Is Loose* 1956; *Battle Hymn* 1957; *The True Story of Jesse James* 1957; *Up Periscope* 1959; *The Iron Maiden* 1962; *The Crawling Hand* 1963; *Bullet for a Badman* 1964; *Hang 'Em High* 1968; *Tiger by the Tail* 1970; *The Giant Spider Invasion* 1975; *The Fifth Musketeer* 1979; *Hambone and Hillie* 1984
Hale, Barbara (1921–) *Higher and Higher* 1943; *The Falcon in Hollywood* 1944; *The Falcon Out West* 1944; *First Yank into Tokyo* 1945; *Lady Luck* 1946; *The Boy with Green Hair* 1948; *And Baby Makes Three* 1949; *The Clay Pigeon* 1949; *Jolson Sings Again* 1949; *The Window* 1949; *The Jackpot* 1950; *Lorna Doone* 1951; *Last of the Comanches* 1952; *A Lion Is in the Streets* 1953; *The Lone Hand* 1953; *Seminole* 1953; *The Far Horizons* 1955; *Unchained* 1955; *Seventh Cavalry* 1956; *The Oklahoman* 1957; *The Giant Spider Invasion* 1975; *Big Wednesday* 1978
Hale, Binnie (1899–1984) *The Phantom Light* 1934; *Love from a Stranger* 1936
Hale, Creighton (1882–1965) *The Marriage Circle* 1924; *Annie Laurie* 1927; *The Cat and the Canary* 1927; *The Masquerader* 1933; *The Perils of Pauline* 1947
Hale, Diana *My Friend Flicka* 1943; *Thunderhead – Son of Flicka* 1945
Hale, Elvi (1931–) *True as a Turtle* 1956; *Happy Is the Bride* 1957; *The Navy Lark* 1959
Hale, Georgia (1903–1985) *The Gold Rush* 1925; *The Salvation Hunters* 1925
Hale, Georgina (1943–) *The Devils* 1971; *Eagle in a Cage* 1971; *Butley* 1973; *Mahler* 1974; *The World Is Full of Married Men* 1979; *McVicar* 1980; *Castaway* 1986; *Beyond Bedlam* 1993; *Preaching to the Perverted* 1997
Hale, Jean *Psychomania* 1964; *Taggart* 1964; *In like Flint* 1967; *The St Valentine's Day Massacre* 1967
Hale, Jennifer *Scooby-Doo and the Alien Invaders* 2000; *Cinderella II: Dreams Come True* 2002; *The Powerpuff Girls* 2002
Hale, Jonathan (1891–1966) *Charlie Chan at the Olympics* 1937; *Madame X* 1937; *Blondie!* 1938; *The Saint in New York* 1938; *The Amazing Mr Williams* 1939; *In Name Only* 1939; *The Saint Strikes Back* 1939; *The Saint Takes Over* 1940; *The Saint's Double Trouble* 1940; *The Saint in Palm Springs* 1941; *Strange Alibi* 1941; *Joe Smith, American* 1942; *Miss Annie Rooney* 1942; *Dead Man's Eyes* 1944; *Hollywood Canteen* 1944; *Her Husband's Affairs* 1947; *The Vigilantes Return* 1947; *Silver River* 1948; *Strangers on a Train* 1951
Hale, Richard (1893–1981) *Knickerbocker Holiday* 1944; *None Shall Escape* 1944; *Abilene Town* 1945; *The Other Love* 1947; *The Man with a Cloak* 1951; *The Miracle of Our Lady of Fatima* 1952; *The Diamond Queen* 1953; *Julius Caesar* 1953
Hale, Sonnie (1902–1959) *Friday the Thirteenth* 1933; *Evergreen* 1934; *First a Girl* 1935; *It's Love Again* 1936; *Let's Be Famous* 1939; *Fiddlers Three* 1944; *London Town* 1946
Haley, Bill (1925–1981) *Don't Knock the Rock* 1956; *Rock around the Clock* 1956
Haley, Brian (1963–) *Into the Sun* 1992; *Baby's Day Out* 1994
Haley, Jack (1899–1979) *Sitting Pretty* 1933; *Pigskin Parade* 1936; *Poor Little Rich Girl* 1936; *Danger – Love at Work* 1937; *Pick a Star* 1937; *Wake Up and Live* 1937; *Alexander's Ragtime Band* 1938; *Hold That Co-Ed* 1938; *Rebecca of Sunnybrook Farm* 1938; *Thanks for Everything* 1938; *The Wizard of Oz* 1939; *Moon over Miami* 1941; *Beyond the Blue Horizon* 1942; *Higher and Higher* 1943; *George White's Scandals* 1945
Haley, Jackie Earle (1961–) *The Bad News Bears* 1976; *The Bad News Bears in Breaking Training* 1977; *Damnation Alley* 1977; *The Bad News Bears Go to Japan* 1978; *Breaking Away* 1979; *Losin' It* 1983
Hall, Albert aka **Hall, Albert P** (1937–) *Leadbelly* 1976; *Apocalypse Now* 1979; *Betrayed* 1988; *Malcolm X* 1992; *Rookie of the Year* 1993; *Devil in a Blue Dress* 1995; *Get on the Bus* 1996; *Beloved* 1998
Hall, Anthony Michael (1968–) *National Lampoon's Vacation* 1983; *Sixteen Candles* 1984; *The Breakfast Club* 1985; *Weird Science* 1985; *Johnny Be Good* 1988; *Edward Scissorhands* 1990; *Into the Sun* 1992; *Upworld* 1992; *Six Degrees of Separation* 1993; *Hail Caesar* 1994; *Exit in Red* 1996; *The Killing Grounds* 1997; *Eternal Revenge* 1999; *Freddy Got Fingered* 2001; *61** 2001
Hall, Arsenio (1956–) *Coming to America* 1988; *Harlem Nights* 1989; *Blankman* 1994
Hall, Berta (1909–1999) *Port of Call* 1948; *My Sister, My Love* 1966
Hall, Brad (1958–) *Limit Up* 1989; *The Guardian* 1990
Hall, Bug (1965–) *The Little Rascals* 1994; *The Stupids* 1995; *Honey, We Shrunk Ourselves* 1997
Hall, Charlie (1899–1959) *The Music Box* 1932; *Twice Two* 1933; *Them Thar Hills!* 1934; *Tit for Tat* 1934; *Thicker than Water* 1935; *Saps at Sea* 1940
Hall, Grayson (1927–1985) *Satan in High Heels* 1962; *The Night of the Iguana* 1964; *Adam at 6 AM* 1970; *End of the Road* 1970; *House of Dark Shadows* 1970; *Night of Dark Shadows* 1971
Hall, Hanna (1987–) *Homecoming* 1996; *The Virgin Suicides* 1999
Hall (1), Henry (1876–1954) *Feet First* 1930; *The Ape* 1940
Hall, Huntz (1920–1999) *Dead End* 1937; *Angels with Dirty Faces* 1938; *Angels Wash Their Faces* 1939; *Hell's Kitchen* 1939; *The Return of Dr X* 1939; *They Made Me a Criminal* 1939; *Spooks Run Wild* 1941; *Private Buckaroo* 1942; *Clancy Street Boys* 1943; *Ghosts in the Night* 1943; *Block Busters* 1944; *Bowery Champs* 1944; *Follow the Leader* 1944; *Come Out Fighting* 1945; *Docks of New York* 1945; *Mr Muggs Rides Again* 1945; *A Walk in the Sun* 1945; *Jalopy* 1953; *The Bowery Boys Meet the Monsters* 1954; *Jungle Gents* 1954; *Jail Busters* 1955; *Gentle Giant* 1967; *Herbie Rides Again* 1974; *Valentino* 1977; *Auntie Lee's Meat Pies* 1991
Hall, Irma P (1937–) *A Family Thing* 1996; *Buddy* 1997; *Midnight in the Garden of Good and Evil* 1997; *Steel* 1997; *Patch Adams* 1998; *A Lesson Before Dying* 1999; *Collateral* 2004; *The Ladykillers* 2004
Hall, James (1900–1940) *Hotel Imperial* 1927; *Four Sons* 1928; *The Canary Murder Case* 1929; *The Case of Lena Smith* 1929; *The Saturday Night Kid* 1929; *Hell's Angels* 1930
Hall, Jerry (1956–) *Running Out of Luck* 1985; *Batman* 1989; *Diana & Me* 1997; *Merci Docteur Rey* 2002; *Tooth* 2003
Hall, Jon aka **Locher, Charles** (1913–1979) *Charlie Chan in Shanghai* 1935; *The Hurricane* 1937; *Kit Carson* 1940; *South of Pago Pago* 1940; *Arabian Nights* 1942; *The Invisible Agent* 1942; *The Tuttles of Tahiti* 1942; *White Savage* 1943; *Ali Baba and the Forty Thieves* 1944; *Cobra Woman* 1944; *The Invisible Man's Revenge* 1944; *Lady in the Dark* 1944; *Sudan* 1945; *The Vigilantes Return* 1947; *The Prince of Thieves* 1948; *China Corsair* 1951; *Last Train from Bombay* 1952; *Hell Ship Mutiny* 1957; *Forbidden Island* 1959
Hall, Juanita (1901–1968) *South Pacific* 1958; *Flower Drum Song* 1961
Hall, Kevin Peter (1955–1991) *One Dark Night* 1982; *Monster in the Closet* 1983; *Bigfoot and the Hendersons* 1987; *Predator* 1987; *Predator 2* 1990
Hall, Philip Baker (1931–) *Secret Honor* 1984; *Three O'Clock High* 1987; *How I Got Into College* 1989; *Live Wire* 1992; *Kiss of Death* 1994; *Hard Eight* 1996; *Psycho* 1998; *Rush Hour* 1998; *Cradle Will Rock* 1999; *The Insider* 1999; *Let the Devil Wear Black* 1999; *Magnolia* 1999; *The Talented Mr Ripley* 1999; *The Contender* 2000; *Lost Souls* 2000; *Rules of Engagement* 2000; *Path to War* 2002; *The Sum of All Fears* 2002; *Bruce Almighty* 2003; *Dogville* 2003; *In Good Company* 2004; *The Amityville Horror* 2005
Hall, Porter (1888–1953) *The Thin Man* 1934; *The General Died at Dawn* 1936; *The Petrified Forest* 1936; *The Plainsman* 1936; *Satan Met a Lady* 1936; *Bulldog Drummond Escapes* 1937; *Make Way for Tomorrow* 1937; *True Confession* 1937; *Wells Fargo* 1937; *Bulldog Drummond's Peril* 1938; *Men with Wings* 1938; *His Girl Friday* 1939; *Arizona* 1940; *Dark Command* 1940; *Trail of the Vigilantes* 1940; *Sullivan's Travels* 1941; *The Desperadoes* 1943; *Double Indemnity* 1944; *Going My Way* 1944; *The Great Moment* 1944; *The Miracle of Morgan's Creek* 1944; *Standing Room Only* 1944; *Kiss and Tell* 1945; *Murder, He Says* 1945; *Miracle on 34th Street* 1947; *Singapore* 1947; *That Wonderful Urge* 1948; *The Beautiful Blonde from Bashful Bend* 1949; *Intruder in the Dust* 1949; *Ace in the Hole* 1951; *Pony Express* 1953; *Vice Squad* 1953; *Return to Treasure Island* 1954
Hall, Regina (1971–) *Disappearing Acts* 2000; *Scary Movie* 2000; *Scary Movie 2* 2001; *Malibu's Most Wanted* 2003; *The Honeymooners* 2005
Hall, Ruth (1910–2003) *Monkey Business* 1931; *The Kid from Spain* 1932; *Ride Him, Cowboy* 1932
Hall, Scott H *Blood Feast* 1963; *Color Me Blood Red* 1965
Hall, Thurston (1883–1958) *The Black Room* 1935; *Hooray for Love* 1935; *The Lone Wolf Returns* 1936; *The Man Who Lived Twice* 1936; *Theodora Goes Wild* 1936; *The Affairs of Annabel* 1938; *The Amazing Dr Clitterhouse* 1938; *Dancing Co-Ed* 1939; *The Star Maker* 1939; *The Blue Bird* 1940; *The Lone Wolf Meets a Lady* 1940; *The Great Man's Lady* 1942; *I Dood It* 1943; *Without Reservations* 1946; *Black Gold* 1947; *It Had to Be You*

1947; *The Secret Life of Walter Mitty* 1947; *The Unfinished Dance* 1947; *Up in Central Park* 1948; *Stagecoach Kid* 1949
Hall, Winter (1872–1947) *A Romance of the Redwoods* 1917; *Kitty* 1928
Hall, Zooey (1946–) *Fortune and Men's Eyes* 1971; *I Dismember Mama* 1972
Hall-Davis, Lillian (1897–1933) *The Ring* 1927; *The Farmer's Wife* 1928
Hallahan, Charles (1943–1997) *Going in Style* 1979; *PK and the Kid* 1982; *The Thing* 1982; *Twilight Zone: the Movie* 1983; *Vision Quest* 1985; *Warlock: the Armageddon* 1993; *Jack Reed: a Search for Justice* 1994; *The Rich Man's Wife* 1996; *Dante's Peak* 1997
Hallam, John (1941–) *A Walk with Love and Death* 1969; *Murphy's War* 1971; *The Offence* 1972; *Dragonslayer* 1981; *When the Whales Came* 1989
Hallaren, Jane *Hero at Large* 1980; *Body Heat* 1981; *Modern Romance* 1981; *Lianna* 1983; *A Night in the Life of Jimmy Reardon* 1988
Hallatt, May (1876–1969) *The Gold Express* 1955; *Dangerous Afternoon* 1961
Halldorsson, Gisli (1927–1988) *Cold Fever* 1994; *Devil's Island* 1996
Hallett, Neil *The Brain Machine* 1954; *Can You Keep It Up for a Week?* 1974
Hallick, Tom (1941–) *The Amazing Captain Nemo* 1978; *A Rare Breed* 1981
Halliday, Bryant (1928–1996) *Devil Doll* 1964; *The Projected Man* 1966; *Tower of Evil* 1972
Halliday, John (1880–1947) *Consolation Marriage* 1931; *The Age of Consent* 1932; *Bird of Paradise* 1932; *The Impatient Maiden* 1932; *Finishing School* 1934; *The Dark Angel* 1935; *Peter Ibbetson* 1935; *Desire* 1936; *Fatal Lady* 1936; *Arsene Lupin Returns* 1938; *Blockade* 1938; *That Certain Age* 1938; *Intermezzo* 1939; *The Philadelphia Story* 1940; *Lydia* 1941
Halloran, John *Blood on the Sun* 1945; *The Deerslayer* 1957
Hallyday, Johnny (1943–) *Detective* 1985; *The Iron Triangle* 1988; *Crime Spree* 2002; *L'Homme du Train* 2002
Halop, Billy (1920–1976) *Dead End* 1937; *Angels with Dirty Faces* 1938; *Angels Wash Their Faces* 1939; *Dust Be My Destiny* 1939; *Hell's Kitchen* 1939; *They Made Me a Criminal* 1939; *You Can't Get Away with Murder* 1939; *Tom Brown's Schooldays* 1940; *Dangerous Years* 1947
Halpin, Luke (1948–) *Flipper* 1963; *Flipper's New Adventure* 1964; *Shock Waves* 1975; *Flipper* 1996
Halprin, Daria *Zabriskie Point* 1970; *The Jerusalem File* 1972
Halsey, Brett *aka* **Ford, Montgomery** (1933–) *The Cry Baby Killer* 1958; *The Best of Everything* 1959; *Return of the Fly* 1959; *Submarine Seahawk* 1959; *The Atomic Submarine* 1960; *Desire in the Dust* 1960; *Return to Peyton Place* 1961; *Twice Told Tales* 1963; *Spy in Your Eye* 1965; *Today It's Me... Tomorrow You!* 1968; *Four Times That Night* 1972; *Expect No Mercy* 1995
Halsey, Michael *Mean Guns* 1996; *Postmortem* 1999
Halton, Charles (1876–1959) *Woman Chases Man* 1937; *Bluebeard's Eighth Wife* 1938; *Dr Cyclops* 1940; *Stranger on the Third Floor* 1940; *Mr and Mrs Smith* 1941; *Across the Pacific* 1942; *Whispering Ghosts* 1942; *Because of Him* 1946; *Three Little Girls in Blue* 1946
Hama, Mie (1943–) *King Kong vs Godzilla* 1962; *The Beautiful Swindlers* 1964; *What's Up, Tiger Lily?* 1966; *You Only Live Twice* 1967
Hamel, Veronica (1945–) *Cannonball* 1976; *Beyond the Poseidon Adventure* 1979; *A New Life* 1988; *Taking Care of Business* 1990; *In the Blink of an Eye* 1996; *Determination of Death* 2001
Hamer, Gerald (1886–1972) *Blond Cheat* 1938; *The Scarlet Claw* 1944
Hamill, John *The Beast in the Cellar* 1970; *No Blade of Grass* 1970; *Trog* 1970
Hamill, Mark (1951–) *Star Wars Episode IV: a New Hope* 1977; *Wizards* 1977; *Corvette Summer* 1978; *The Big Red One* 1980; *Star Wars Episode V: the Empire Strikes Back* 1980; *The Night the Lights Went Out in Georgia* 1981; *Star Wars Episode VI: Return of the Jedi* 1983; *Slipstream* 1989; *The Guyver* 1991; *Time Runner* 1993; *The Raffle* 1994; *Village of the Damned* 1995; *Laserhawk* 1997; *Hamilton* 1998; *Walking across Egypt* 1999; *Joseph: King of Dreams* 2000; *Scooby-Doo and the Alien Invaders* 2000; *Jay and Silent Bob Strike Back* 2001
Hamilton, Bernie (1928–) *The Young One* 1960; *Captain Sindbad* 1963; *One Potato, Two Potato* 1964; *The Organization* 1971; *Hammer* 1972
Hamilton, Gay *A Challenge for Robin Hood* 1967; *Barry Lyndon* 1975
Hamilton, George (1939–) *The Well* 1951; *Crime and Punishment, USA* 1959; *All the Fine Young Cannibals* 1960; *Home from the Hill* 1960; *Where the Boys Are* 1960; *Angel Baby* 1961; *By Love Possessed* 1961; *Light in the Piazza* 1961; *A Thunder of Drums* 1961; *Two Weeks in Another Town* 1962; *Act One* 1963; *The Victors* 1963; *Your Cheatin' Heart* 1964; *That Man George* 1965; *Viva Maria!* 1965; *Jack of Diamonds* 1967; *A Time for Killing* 1967; *The Power* 1968; *Evel Knievel* 1971; *The Man Who Loved Cat Dancing* 1973; *Once Is Not Enough* 1975; *The Happy Hooker Goes to Washington* 1977; *Sextette* 1978; *From Hell to Victory* 1979; *Love at First Bite* 1979; *Zorro, the Gay Blade* 1981; *The Godfather Part III* 1990; *Doc Hollywood* 1991; *Once upon a Crime* 1992; *Amore!* 1993; *Danielle Steel's Vanished* 1995; *8 Heads in a Duffel Bag* 1997; *Casper Meets Wendy* 1998; *The Little Unicorn* 1998; *Hollywood Ending* 2002
Hamilton, Hale (1883–1942) *The Champ* 1931; *Strangers May Kiss* 1931; *Susan Lenox: Her Fall and Rise* 1931; *Black Beauty* 1933; *Employees' Entrance* 1933; *After Office Hours* 1935
Hamilton, Josh (1968–) *Alive* 1992; *With Honors* 1994; *Kicking and Screaming* 1995; *The House of Yes* 1997
Hamilton, Kipp (1934–1981) *Good Morning, Miss Dove* 1955; *War of the Gargantuas* 1970
Hamilton, Leigh *A Man, a Woman and a Bank* 1979; *PK and the Kid* 1982
Hamilton, Linda (1956–) *Children of the Corn* 1984; *The Terminator* 1984; *Black Moon Rising* 1985; *King Kong Lives* 1986; *Mr Destiny* 1990; *Terminator 2: Judgment Day* 1991; *Silent Fall* 1994; *Separate Lives* 1995; *Shadow Conspiracy* 1996; *Dante's Peak* 1997
Hamilton, Lisa Gay (1964–) *Jackie Brown* 1997; *Beloved* 1998; *True Crime* 1999; *A House Divided* 2000; *The Truth about Charlie* 2002
Hamilton, Margaret (1902–1985) *Way Down East* 1935; *Chatterbox* 1936; *The Moon's Our Home* 1936; *I'll Take Romance* 1937; *You Only Live Once* 1937; *A Slight Case of Murder* 1938; *The Wizard of Oz* 1939; *The Invisible Woman* 1940; *My Little Chickadee* 1940; *The Villain Still Pursued Her* 1940; *The Affairs of Martha* 1942; *Twin Beds* 1942; *George White's Scandals* 1945; *Driftwood* 1946; *The Red Pony* 1949; *Mad Wednesday* 1950; *Wabash Avenue* 1950; *People Will Talk* 1951; *13 Ghosts* 1959; *Rosie!* 1967; *The Anderson Tapes* 1971
Hamilton, Murray (1923–1986) *The Girl He Left Behind* 1956; *Toward the Unknown* 1956; *The Spirit of St Louis* 1957; *Houseboat* 1958; *No Time for Sergeants* 1958; *Too Much, Too Soon* 1958; *The FBI Story* 1959; *The Hustler* 1961; *An American Dream* 1966; *The Graduate* 1967; *The Boston Strangler* 1968; *The Brotherhood* 1968; *No Way to Treat a Lady* 1968; *If It's Tuesday, This Must Be Belgium* 1969; *The Harness* 1971; *The Way We Were* 1973; *The Drowning Pool* 1975; *Jaws* 1975; *Casey's Shadow* 1978; *Jaws 2* 1978; *1941* 1979; *Brubaker* 1980
Hamilton, Neil (1899–1984) *America* 1924; *Isn't Life Wonderful* 1924; *Beau Geste* 1926; *The Patriot* 1928; *The Dawn Patrol* 1930; *The Return of Dr Fu Manchu* 1930; *Laughing Sinners* 1931; *The Sin of Madelon Claudet* 1931; *Strangers May Kiss* 1931; *This Modern Age* 1931; *The Animal Kingdom* 1932; *Payment Deferred* 1932; *Tarzan, the Ape Man* 1932; *The Wet Parade* 1932; *What Price Hollywood?* 1932; *Tarzan and His Mate* 1934; *Southern Roses* 1936; *The Saint Strikes Back* 1939; *Betrayed* 1944; *Batman* 1966
Hamilton, Richard (1920–) *Ladybug, Ladybug* 1963; *Greetings* 1968; *Pals* 1986; *In Country* 1989; *On Deadly Ground* 1994
Hamilton, Suzanna (1960–) *Brimstone and Treacle* 1982; *Nineteen Eighty-Four* 1984; *Out of Africa* 1985; *Wetherby* 1985; *Tale of a Vampire* 1992
Hamlett, Dilys (1928–2002) *Assault* 1970; *Diagnosis: Murder* 1974; *What Changed Charley Farthing?* 1974
Hamlin, Harry (1951–) *Clash of the Titans* 1981; *King of the Mountain* 1981; *Making Love* 1982; *The Hunted* 1998
Hammond, Darrell (1960–) *The King and I* 1999; *New York Minute* 2004
Hammond, Earl *Satan in High Heels* 1962; *Light Years* 1988
Hammond, Kay (1909–1980) *The Trespasser* 1929; *Abraham Lincoln* 1930; *Blithe Spirit* 1945
Hammond, Nicholas (1950–) *The Sound of Music* 1965; *Spider-Man* 1977; *The Rage in Placid Lake* 2002
Hammond, Peter (1923–) *They Knew Mr Knight* 1945; *Holiday Camp* 1947; *Vote for Huggett* 1948; *The Adventurers* 1950; *The Reluctant Widow* 1950; *Confession* 1955; *X the Unknown* 1956
Hammond, Virginia (1893–1972) *Anybody's Woman* 1930; *No One Man* 1932
Hamnett, Olivia *The Last Wave* 1977; *The Earthling* 1980
Hamon, Lucienne *Force Majeure* 1989; *Becoming Colette* 1991
Hampden, Walter (1879–1955) *The Hunchback of Notre Dame* 1939; *All This, and Heaven Too* 1940; *They Died with Their Boots On* 1941; *5 Fingers* 1952; *Treasure of the Golden Condor* 1953; *Sabrina* 1954; *The Silver Chalice* 1954; *The Prodigal* 1955; *Strange Lady in Town* 1955; *The Vagabond King* 1956
Hampshire, Susan (1938–) *During One Night* 1961; *The Three Lives of Thomasina* 1963; *Night Must Fall* 1964; *Wonderful Life* 1964; *The Fighting Prince of Donegal* 1966; *The Trygon Factor* 1967; *Monte Carlo or Bust* 1969; *The Violent Enemy* 1969; *Malpertuis* 1971; *A Time for Loving* 1971; *Living Free* 1972; *Neither the Sea nor the Sand* 1972
Hampton, James *aka* **Hampton, Jim** (1936–) *The Mean Machine* 1974; *WW and the Dixie Dancekings* 1975; *Hawmps* 1976; *The China Syndrome* 1979; *Condorman* 1981; *Teen Wolf* 1985; *Sling Blade* 1995
Hampton, Paul (1945–) *Senior Prom* 1958; *More Dead than Alive* 1969; *Lady Sings the Blues* 1972; *Hit!* 1973; *Shivers* 1975
Han, Maggie (1959–) *The Last Emperor* 1987; *Open Season* 1995
Hanauer, Terri *Communion* 1989; *The Rapture* 1991
Hanayagi, Shotaro (1894–1965) *Story of the Late Chrysanthemums* 1939; *The Famous Sword* 1945
Hancock, Herbie (1940–) *'Round Midnight* 1986; *Indecent Proposal* 1993
Hancock, John (1939–) *The Black Marble* 1980; *Collision Course* 1987; *The Bonfire of the Vanities* 1990; *Why Me?* 1990
Hancock, Lou *Evil Dead II* 1987; *Miracle Mile* 1989
Hancock, Sheila (1933–) *Light Up the Sky* 1960; *The Girl on the Boat* 1962; *Twice round the Daffodils* 1962; *Carry On Cleo* 1964; *The Moon-Spinners* 1964; *Night Must Fall* 1964; *The Anniversary* 1968; *Take a Girl like You* 1970; *The Wildcats of St Trinian's* 1980; *Buster* 1988; *Hawks* 1988; *Asterix and the Big Fight* 1989; *Three Men and a Little Lady* 1990; *A Business Affair* 1993; *Love and Death on Long Island* 1998; *Hold Back the Night* 1999; *Yes* 2004
Hancock, Tony (1924–1968) *Orders Are Orders* 1954; *The Rebel* 1960; *The Punch and Judy Man* 1962; *Those Magnificent Men in Their Flying Machines* 1965; *The Wrong Box* 1966
Handl, Irene (1901–1987) *Strange Boarders* 1938; *The Girl in the News* 1940; *Uncensored* 1942; *Rhythm Serenade* 1943; *Give Us the Moon* 1944; *Brief Encounter* 1945; *The Hills of Donegal* 1947; *Adam and Evelyne* 1949; *Cardboard Cavalier* 1949; *The Perfect Woman* 1949; *Stage Fright* 1949; *Mad about Men* 1954; *A Kid for Two Farthings* 1955; *Brothers in Law* 1956; *It's Never Too Late* 1956; *Who Done It?* 1956; *Small Hotel* 1957; *Desert Mice* 1959; *I'm All Right Jack* 1959; *Doctor in Love* 1960; *A French Mistress* 1960; *Make Mine Mink* 1960; *The Night We Got the Bird* 1960; *No Kidding* 1960; *The Pure Hell of St Trinian's* 1960; *The Rebel* 1960; *School for Scoundrels* 1960; *Two Way Stretch* 1960; *Double Bunk* 1961; *Watch It, Sailor!* 1961; *Heavens Above!* 1963; *Morgan – a Suitable Case for Treatment* 1966; *Smashing Time* 1967; *Wonderwall* 1968; *The Italian Job* 1969; *Doctor in Trouble* 1970; *On a Clear Day You Can See Forever* 1970; *The Private Life of Sherlock Holmes* 1970; *For the Love of Ada* 1972; *Confessions of a Driving Instructor* 1976; *Adventures of a Private Eye* 1977; *Come Play with Me* 1977; *The Hound of the Baskervilles* 1977; *The Last Remake of Beau Geste* 1977; *Stand Up Virgin Soldiers* 1977
Handley, Tommy (1894–1949) *Elstree Calling* 1930; *It's That Man Again* 1942; *Time Flies* 1944
Handy, James *Burglar* 1987; *Bird* 1988; *K-9* 1989; *Rocketeer* 1991; *K-911* 1999; *Ash Wednesday* 2002
Haney, Anne (1934–2001) *Liar Liar* 1997; *Psycho* 1998
Haney, Carol (1924–1964) *Invitation to the Dance* 1956; *The Pajama Game* 1957
Hanft, Helen *Stardust Memories* 1980; *License to Drive* 1988
Hanin, Roger (1925–) *A Bout de Souffle* 1959; *Rocco and His Brothers* 1960; *They Came to Rob Las Vegas* 1968; *Sweet Torture* 1971; *The Revengers* 1972; *Le Grand Pardon* 1981; *Day of Atonement* 1992
Hankin, Larry (1945–) *Thumb Tripping* 1972; *Escape from Alcatraz* 1979; *Ratboy* 1986; *Out on a Limb* 1992; *Billy Madison* 1995
Hanks, Colin (1977–) *Get over It* 2001; *Orange County* 2001
Hanks, Tom (1956–) *He Knows You're Alone* 1981; *Bachelor Party* 1984; *Splash* 1984; *The Man with One Red Shoe* 1985; *The Money Pit* 1985; *Volunteers* 1985; *Every Time We Say Goodbye* 1986; *Nothing in Common* 1986; *Dragnet* 1987; *Big* 1988; *Punchline* 1988; *The 'Burbs* 1989; *Turner & Hooch* 1989; *The Bonfire of the Vanities* 1990; *Joe versus the Volcano* 1990; *A League of Their Own* 1992; *Radio Flyer* 1992; *Philadelphia* 1993; *Sleepless in Seattle* 1993; *Forrest Gump* 1994; *Apollo 13* 1995; *Toy Story* 1995; *That Thing You Do!* 1996; *Saving Private Ryan* 1998; *You've Got Mail* 1998; *The Green Mile* 1999; *Toy Story 2* 1999; *Cast Away* 2000; *Catch Me If You Can* 2002; *Road to Perdition* 2002; *The Ladykillers* 2004; *The Polar Express* 2004; *The Terminal* 2004
Hanley, Jimmy (1918–1970) *Boys Will Be Boys* 1935; *Forever England* 1935; *Cotton Queen* 1937; *Housemaster* 1938; *Gaslight* 1940; *The Way Ahead* 1944; *29 Acacia Avenue* 1945; *Holiday Camp* 1947; *The Master of Bankdam* 1947; *Here Come the Huggetts* 1948; *It's Hard to Be Good* 1948; *The Blue Lamp* 1949; *Boys in Brown* 1949; *Don't Ever Leave Me* 1949; *The Huggetts Abroad* 1949; *Room to Let* 1949; *The Black Rider* 1954; *Satellite in the Sky* 1956
Hanley, Katie *Godspell* 1973; *Xanadu* 1980
Hann-Byrd, Adam (1982–) *Little Man Tate* 1991; *The Ice Storm* 1997; *Halloween H20: 20 Years Later* 1998
Hannah, Daryl (1960–) *Hard Country* 1981; *Blade Runner* 1982; *Summer Lovers* 1982; *The Pope of Greenwich Village* 1984; *Splash* 1984; *The Clan of the Cave Bear* 1986; *Legal Eagles* 1986; *Roxanne* 1987; *Wall Street* 1987; *High Spirits* 1988; *Steel Magnolias* 1989; *Steel Magnolias* 1989; *Crazy People* 1990; *At Play in the Fields of the Lord* 1991; *Memoirs of an Invisible Man* 1992; *Attack of the 50 Ft Woman* 1993; *Grumpy Old Men* 1993; *The Little Rascals* 1994; *The Tie That Binds* 1995; *Two Much* 1995; *Grumpier Old Men* 1996; *The Last Days of Frankie the Fly* 1996; *The Gingerbread Man* 1997; *The Real Blonde* 1997; *Addams Family Reunion* 1998; *Hi-Life* 1998; *Rear Window* 1998; *Diplomatic Siege* 1999; *My Favorite Martian* 1999; *Dancing at the Blue Iguana* 2000; *Hide and Seek* 2000; *Jackpot* 2001; *Northfork* 2002; *A Walk to Remember* 2002; *Casa de los Babys* 2003; *Kill Bill Vol 1* 2003; *Kill Bill Vol 2* 2003; *Silver City* 2004
Hannah, John (1962–) *Four Weddings and a Funeral* 1994; *The Final Cut* 1995; *The Innocent Sleep* 1995; *Madagascar Skin* 1995; *The James Gang* 1997; *Resurrection Man* 1997; *Sliding Doors* 1997; *Circus* 1999; *The Hurricane* 1999; *The Mummy* 1999; *Pandaemonium* 2000; *The Mummy Returns* 2001; *Before You Go* 2002; *I'm with Lucy* 2002
Hannah, Page (1964–) *My Man Adam* 1985; *Shag* 1988
Hannen, Nicholas (1881–1972) *FP1* 1932; *The Dictator* 1935
Hannigan, Alyson (1974–) *My Stepmother Is an Alien* 1988; *Dead Man on Campus* 1998; *American Pie* 1999; *Boys and Girls* 2000; *American Pie 2* 2001; *American Pie: the Wedding* 2003
Hanover, Donna (1950–) *The People vs Larry Flynt* 1996; *Series 7: the Contenders* 2001
Hanray, Lawrence *aka* **Hanray, Laurence** (1874–1947) *Street Song* 1935; *The Man Who Could Work Miracles* 1936; *It's Never Too Late to Mend* 1937; *Moonlight Sonata* 1937; *My Learned Friend* 1943; *Mine Own Executioner* 1947

Hansen, Gale (1969–) *Dead Poets Society* 1989; *Shaking the Tree* 1990; *The Finest Hour* 1991
Hansen, Myrna (1934–) *Cult of the Cobra* 1955; *Man without a Star* 1955
Hansen, Patti (1956–) *They All Laughed* 1981; *Hard to Hold* 1984
Hansen, William (1911–1975) *The Member of the Wedding* 1952; *Fail-Safe* 1964; *Save the Tiger* 1973; *The Terminal Man* 1974
Hanson, Lars (1886–1965) *Erotikon* 1920; *Gösta Berlings Saga* 1924; *Flesh and the Devil* 1926; *The Scarlet Letter* 1926; *The Divine Woman* 1928; *Heimkehr* 1928; *The Wind* 1928; *Walpurgis Night* 1935
Hanson, Peter *aka* **Hansen, Peter** (1922–) *Branded* 1950; *Darling, How Could You!* 1951; *When Worlds Collide* 1951; *The Savage* 1953; *A Bullet for Joey* 1955
Hanzlik, Jaromir (1948–) *Cutting It Short* 1980; *The Last of the Good Old Days* 1989
Hara, Setsuko (1920–) *No Regrets for Our Youth* 1946; *Late Spring* 1949; *Early Summer* 1951; *The Idiot* 1951; *Tokyo Story* 1953; *Tokyo Twilight* 1957; *Late Autumn* 1960; *The End of Summer* 1961
Harada, Mieko (1958–) *Ran* 1985; *Akira Kurosawa's Dreams* 1990
Harareet, Haya (1931–) *Ben-Hur* 1959; *The Secret Partner* 1961; *The Interns* 1962
Harari, Clément (1919–) *Monkeys, Go Home!* 1966; *Shadowman* 1973; *Once in Paris* 1978; *Train of Life* 1999
Harbord, Carl (1908–1958) *Heart's Desire* 1935; *Sherlock Holmes and the Secret Code* 1946; *The Macomber Affair* 1947
Harcourt, James (1873–1951) *The Old Curiosity Shop* 1934; *The Avenging Hand* 1936; *Return of a Stranger* 1937; *Night Train to Munich* 1940; *Obsession* 1948
Harden, Jacques *Gervaise* 1956; *The Long Absence* 1961
Harden, Marcia Gay (1959–) *Miller's Crossing* 1990; *Late for Dinner* 1991; *Crush* 1992; *Used People* 1992; *Safe Passage* 1994; *The Spitfire Grill* 1996; *Spy Hard* 1996; *Flubber* 1997; *Desperate Measures* 1998; *Meet Joe Black* 1998; *Pollock* 2000; *Space Cowboys* 2000; *Casa de los Babys* 2003; *Mona Lisa Smile* 2003; *Mystic River* 2003; *Welcome to Mooseport* 2004
Hardie, Kate (1969–) *Runners* 1983; *Mona Lisa* 1986; *Tree of Hands* 1988; *Melancholia* 1989; *The Krays* 1990; *Jack & Sarah* 1995; *Heart* 1997; *Croupier* 1998
Hardie, Russell (1904–1973) *Broadway to Hollywood* 1933; *Operator 13* 1934; *In Old Kentucky* 1935; *Camille* 1937
Hardin, Jerry (1929–) *Chilly Scenes of Winter* 1979; *Heartland* 1979; *Wolf Lake* 1979; *Missing* 1981; *Honkytonk Man* 1982; *Warning Sign* 1985; *Wanted Dead or Alive* 1986; *Blaze* 1989; *The Hot Spot* 1990; *Murder of Innocence* 1993
Hardin, Melora (1967–) *Soul Man* 1986; *Big Man on Campus* 1989; *Lambada* 1990; *Reckless Kelly* 1993; *Erasable You* 1998; *The Hot Chick* 2002
Hardin, Ty (1930–) *Merrill's Marauders* 1962; *PT 109* 1963; *Palm Springs Weekend* 1963; *Battle of the Bulge* 1965; *Berserk* 1967; *Ragan* 1967; *Custer of the West* 1968; *Acquasanta Joe* 1971; *The Last Rebel* 1971; *Bad Jim* 1989
Harding, Ann (1901–1981) *Condemned* 1929; *Holiday* 1930; *East Lynne* 1931; *The Animal Kingdom* 1932; *Westward Passage* 1932; *When Ladies Meet* 1933; *The Fountain* 1934; *Gallant Lady* 1934; *Peter Ibbetson* 1935; *Love from a Stranger* 1936; *Eyes in the Night* 1942; *Mission to Moscow* 1943; *Those Endearing Young Charms* 1945; *Christmas Eve* 1947; *The Magnificent Yankee* 1950; *The Man in the Gray Flannel Suit* 1956
Harding, Gilbert (1907–1960) *The Gentle Gunman* 1952; *The Oracle* 1952
Harding, John *Crime and Punishment, USA* 1959; *This Property Is Condemned* 1966
Harding, Kay *The Mummy's Curse* 1944; *The Scarlet Claw* 1944
Harding, Lyn (1867–1952) *The Constant Nymph* 1933; *The Man Who Changed His Name* 1934; *An Old Spanish Custom* 1935; *The Man Who Changed His Mind* 1936; *Fire over England* 1937; *Goodbye, Mr Chips* 1939
Hardison, Kadeem (1965–) *Def by Temptation* 1990; *White Men Can't Jump* 1992; *Gunmen* 1994; *Renaissance Man* 1994; *Panther* 1995; *Vampire in Brooklyn* 1995; *Drive* 1997; *The 6th Man* 1997
Hardwicke, Cedric *aka* **Hardwicke, Sir Cedric** (1893–1964) *Dreyfus* 1931; *Rome Express* 1932; *The Ghoul* 1933; *Jew Süss* 1934; *Nell Gwyn* 1934; *Becky Sharp* 1935; *Les Misérables* 1935; *Things to Come* 1936; *Tudor Rose* 1936; *Green Light* 1937; *King Solomon's Mines* 1937; *The Hunchback of Notre Dame* 1939; *Stanley and Livingstone* 1939; *The Howards of Virginia* 1940; *The Invisible Man Returns* 1940; *Tom Brown's Schooldays* 1940; *Victory* 1940; *Sundown* 1941; *Suspicion* 1941; *The Commandos Strike at Dawn* 1942; *The Ghost of Frankenstein* 1942; *The Invisible Agent* 1942; *Valley of the Sun* 1942; *The Cross of Lorraine* 1943; *Forever and a Day* 1943; *The Moon Is Down* 1943; *The Keys of the Kingdom* 1944; *The Lodger* 1944; *Wilson* 1944; *Wing and a Prayer* 1944; *Beware of Pity* 1946; *Sentimental Journey* 1946; *The Imperfect Lady* 1947; *Ivy* 1947; *Lured* 1947; *Nicholas Nickleby* 1947; *Tycoon* 1947; *I Remember Mama* 1948; *Rope* 1948; *The Winslow Boy* 1948; *A Connecticut Yankee in King Arthur's Court* 1949; *Now Barabbas Was a Robber* 1949; *The White Tower* 1950; *The Desert Fox* 1951; *Mr Imperium* 1951; *Botany Bay* 1952; *Salome* 1953; *The War of the Worlds* 1953; *Diane* 1955; *Helen of Troy* 1955; *Richard III* 1955; *Gaby* 1956; *The Power and the Prize* 1956; *The Ten Commandments* 1956; *The Vagabond King* 1956; *Baby Face Nelson* 1957; *Five Weeks in a Balloon* 1962; *The Pumpkin Eater* 1964
Hardwicke, Edward *aka* **Hardwick, Edward** (1932–) *The Odd Job* 1978; *Baby: Secret of the Lost Legend* 1985; *Shadowlands* 1993; *The Scarlet Letter* 1995; *Photographing Fairies* 1997
Hardy, Jonathan (1940–) *The Devil's Playground* 1976; *Lonely Hearts* 1981
Hardy, Oliver (1892–1957) *The Three Ages* 1923; *The Wizard of Oz* 1925; *The Two Tars* 1928; *Big Business* 1929; *Hollywood Revue* 1929; *Men o' War* 1929; *Perfect Day* 1929; *The Rogue Song* 1930; *Pardon Us* 1931; *County Hospital* 1932; *The Music Box* 1932; *Pack Up Your Troubles* 1932; *Scram!* 1932; *Their First Mistake* 1932; *Towed in a Hole* 1932; *Bogus Bandits* 1933; *Sons of the Desert* 1933; *Twice Two* 1933; *Babes in Toyland* 1934; *Hollywood Party* 1934; *Oliver the Eighth* 1934; *Them Thar Hills!* 1934; *Tit for Tat* 1934; *Bonnie Scotland* 1935; *Thicker than Water* 1935; *The Bohemian Girl* 1936; *Our Relations* 1936; *Pick a Star* 1937; *Way Out West* 1937; *Blockheads* 1938; *Swiss Miss* 1938; *The Flying Deuces* 1939; *Zenobia* 1939; *A Chump at Oxford* 1940; *Saps at Sea* 1940; *Great Guns* 1941; *A-Haunting We Will Go* 1942; *The Dancing Masters* 1943; *Jitterbugs* 1943; *The Big Noise* 1944; *Nothing but Trouble* 1944; *The Bullfighters* 1945; *The Fighting Kentuckian* 1949; *Utopia* 1950; *The Crazy World of Laurel and Hardy* 1964; *Laurel and Hardy's Laughing 20s* 1965; *4 Clowns* 1970
Hardy, Robert (1925–) *Berserk* 1967; *Demons of the Mind* 1971; *Psychomania* 1972; *Dark Places* 1973; *Gawain and the Green Knight* 1973; *The Silent One* 1973; *The Shooting Party* 1984; *Paris by Night* 1988; *A Feast at Midnight* 1994; *Mary Shelley's Frankenstein* 1994; *Sense and Sensibility* 1995; *The Tichborne Claimant* 1998
Hardy, Sam (1883–1935) *The Big Noise* 1928; *Big News* 1929; *The Miracle Woman* 1931; *Ann Vickers* 1933; *Aunt Sally* 1933; *King Kong* 1933; *The Gay Bride* 1934; *Break of Hearts* 1935
Hardy, Sophie (1944–) *The Desperado Trail* 1965; *Three Hats for Lisa* 1965; *The Trygon Factor* 1967
Hardy, Tom (1977–) *The Reckoning* 2001; *Star Trek: Nemesis* 2002; *Dot the i* 2003; *Layer Cake* 2004
Hare, Doris (1905–2000) *A Place to Go* 1963; *On the Buses* 1971; *Mutiny on the Buses* 1972; *Holiday on the Buses* 1973; *Confessions of a Pop Performer* 1975; *Confessions of a Driving Instructor* 1976; *Confessions from a Holiday Camp* 1977; *Nuns on the Run* 1990
Hare, Lumsden (1875–1964) *The Black Watch* 1929; *Svengali* 1931; *His Double Life* 1933; *The Little Minister* 1934; *The World Moves On* 1934; *Folies Bergère* 1935; *She* 1935; *Northwest Passage* 1940; *Shadows on the Stairs* 1941; *Forever and a Day* 1943; *The Fighting O'Flynn* 1948
Hare, Robertson *aka* **Hare, J Robertson** (1891–1979) *Rookery Nook* 1930; *A Cuckoo in the Nest* 1933; *Friday the Thirteenth* 1933; *Car of Dreams* 1935; *Fighting Stock* 1935; *Foreign Affaires* 1935; *Oh, Daddy!* 1935; *Banana Ridge* 1941; *Our Girl Friday* 1953; *The Night We Got the Bird* 1960; *Crooks Anonymous* 1962
Hare, Will (1916–1997) *The Effect of Gamma Rays on Man-in-the-Moon Marigolds* 1972; *The Electric Horseman* 1979; *Enter the Ninja* 1981; *Grim Prairie Tales* 1990
Harelik, Mark (1951–) *Upworld* 1992; *Election* 1999
Harens, Dean (1920–1996) *Christmas Holiday* 1944; *The Suspect* 1944; *Crack-Up* 1946
Härenstam, Magnus (1941–) *Father to Be* 1979; *Happy We* 1983
Harewood, David (1965–) *The Hawk* 1992; *Strings* 2004
Harewood, Dorian (1950–) *Gray Lady Down* 1978; *Looker* 1981; *Against All Odds* 1984; *The Falcon and the Snowman* 1985; *Full Metal Jacket* 1987; *Pacific Heights* 1990; *Sudden Death* 1995; *12 Angry Men* 1997; *Levity* 2002; *Gothika* 2003
Harfouch, Corinna (1954–) *The Promise* 1994; *Downfall* 2004
Hargreaves, John (1945–1996) *Don's Party* 1976; *Long Weekend* 1977; *The Odd Angry Shot* 1979; *Beyond Reasonable Doubt* 1980; *The Killing of Angel Street* 1981; *Careful, He Might Hear You* 1983; *My First Wife* 1984; *Malcolm* 1986; *Sky Pirates* 1986; *Cry Freedom* 1987; *Boundaries of the Heart* 1988; *Country Life* 1994; *Hotel Sorrento* 1994
Harker, Gordon (1885–1967) *Champagne* 1928; *The Farmer's Wife* 1928; *Escape* 1930; *Rome Express* 1932; *Friday the Thirteenth* 1933; *The Phantom Light* 1934; *Boys Will Be Boys* 1935; *The Lad* 1935; *Squibs* 1935; *Saloon Bar* 1940; *29 Acacia Avenue* 1945; *Derby Day* 1952; *Bang! You're Dead* 1954; *Out of the Clouds* 1954; *A Touch of the Sun* 1956; *Small Hotel* 1957; *Left, Right and Centre* 1959
Harker, Susannah (1965–) *Surviving Picasso* 1996; *Intimacy* 2000; *Offending Angels* 2000
Harker, Wiley *Crimewave* 1985; *Guilty Conscience* 1985
Harkins, John (1932–1999) *The Tiger Makes Out* 1967; *Popi* 1969; *Acapulco Gold* 1976; *The Cracker Factory* 1979; *Absence of Malice* 1981; *Six Weeks* 1982; *Amityville III: the Demon* 1983; *Birdy* 1984
Harlan, Otis (1865–1940) *Broadway* 1929; *Ride Him, Cowboy* 1932; *The Telegraph Trail* 1933; *Snow White and the Seven Dwarfs* 1937
Harlow, Jean (1911–1937) *The Love Parade* 1929; *The Saturday Night Kid* 1929; *Hell's Angels* 1930; *City Lights* 1931; *The Iron Man* 1931; *Platinum Blonde* 1931; *The Public Enemy* 1931; *The Secret Six* 1931; *The Beast of the City* 1932; *Red Dust* 1932; *Red-Headed Woman* 1932; *Three Wise Girls* 1932; *Blonde Bombshell* 1933; *Dinner at Eight* 1933; *Hold Your Man* 1933; *The Girl from Missouri* 1934; *China Seas* 1935; *Reckless* 1935; *Libeled Lady* 1936; *Riffraff* 1936; *Suzy* 1936; *Wife vs Secretary* 1936; *Personal Property* 1937; *Saratoga* 1937; *The Crazy World of Laurel and Hardy* 1964
Harlow, Shalom (1973–) *Head over Heels* 2000; *How to Lose a Guy in 10 Days* 2003
Harmon, Angie (1972–) *Good Advice* 2001; *Agent Cody Banks* 2003
Harmon, Mark (1951–) *Comes a Horseman* 1978; *Beyond the Poseidon Adventure* 1979; *Let's Get Harry* 1986; *Summer School* 1987; *The Presidio* 1988; *Stealing Home* 1988; *Till There Was You* 1990; *Cold Heaven* 1992; *Wyatt Earp* 1994; *The Last Supper* 1995; *Magic in the Water* 1995; *Casualties* 1997; *Fear and Loathing in Las Vegas* 1998; *I'll Remember April* 1999; *Freaky Friday* 2003; *Chasing Liberty* 2004
Harmon, Pat (1886–1958) *Hot Water* 1924; *The Freshman* 1925
Harnick, Aaron (1969–) *Happy Together* 1989; *Judy Berlin* 1999
Harnois, Elisabeth (1979–) *One Magic Christmas* 1985; *Where Are the Children?* 1986
Harnos, Christine *aka* **Harnos, Christina** *The Rescue* 1988; *Cold Dog Soup* 1989
Harolde, Ralf (1899–1974) *Check and Double Check* 1930; *Smart Money* 1931; *Deluge* 1933; *I'm No Angel* 1933; *Picture Snatcher* 1933; *He Was Her Man* 1934
Harper, Frank *A Room for Romeo Brass* 1999; *Shiner* 2000; *The Football Factory* 2004
Harper, Gerald (1929–) *The Admirable Crichton* 1957; *The Lady Vanishes* 1979
Harper, Hill (1973–) *Get on the Bus* 1996; *The Nephew* 1997; *Hav Plenty* 1998; *He Got Game* 1998; *The Skulls* 2000
Harper, Jessica (1949–) *Phantom of the Paradise* 1974; *Inserts* 1975; *Suspiria* 1976; *The Evictors* 1979; *Stardust Memories* 1980; *Pennies from Heaven* 1981; *Shock Treatment* 1981; *My Favorite Year* 1982; *The Imagemaker* 1986; *The Blue Iguana* 1988; *Big Man on Campus* 1989
Harper, Tess (1950–) *Tender Mercies* 1982; *Amityville III: the Demon* 1983; *Crimes of the Heart* 1986; *Ishtar* 1987; *Criminal Law* 1988; *Far North* 1988; *Her Alibi* 1989; *Unconquered* 1989; *Daddy's Dyin'... Who's Got the Will?* 1990; *The Man in the Moon* 1991; *My Heroes Have Always Been Cowboys* 1991; *My New Gun* 1992; *The Turning* 1992; *Death in Small Doses* 1995; *The In Crowd* 2000
Harper, Valerie (1940–) *Freebie and the Bean* 1974; *Chapter Two* 1979; *The Last Married Couple in America* 1980; *Blame It on Rio* 1984; *Death of a Cheerleader* 1994
Harrelson, Brett *The People vs Larry Flynt* 1996; *Dee Snider's Strangeland* 1998; *From Dusk till Dawn II: Texas Blood Money* 1999
Harrelson, Woody (1962–) *Wildcats* 1986; *Cool Blue* 1988; *Doc Hollywood* 1991; *Ted & Venus* 1991; *White Men Can't Jump* 1992; *Indecent Proposal* 1993; *The Cowboy Way* 1994; *Natural Born Killers* 1994; *Money Train* 1995; *Kingpin* 1996; *The People vs Larry Flynt* 1996; *Sunchaser* 1996; *Wag the Dog* 1997; *Welcome to Sarajevo* 1997; *The Hi-Lo Country* 1998; *Palmetto* 1998; *The Thin Red Line* 1998; *Edtv* 1999; *Grass* 1999; *Play It to the Bone* 2000; *Anger Management* 2003; *After the Sunset* 2004; *She Hate Me* 2004
Harrigan, William (1894–1966) *Born Reckless* 1930; *The Invisible Man* 1933; *"G" Men* 1935; *Whipsaw* 1935; *Back Door to Heaven* 1939; *Desert Fury* 1947; *Flying Leathernecks* 1951
Harring, Laura *aka* **Herring, Laura** *aka* **Harring, Laura Elena** (1964–) *Lambada! The Forbidden Dance* 1990; *Mulholland Drive* 2001; *Willard* 2003; *The Punisher* 2004
Harrington, Desmond (1976–) *The Hole* 2001; *My First Mister* 2001; *Ghost Ship* 2002; *Wrong Turn* 2003
Harrington, Kate (1903–1978) *Rachel, Rachel* 1968; *Child's Play* 1972
Harrington, Laura (1958–) *The City Girl* 1984; *Maximum Overdrive* 1986; *What's Eating Gilbert Grape* 1993
Harrington, Pat (1929–) *Stage Struck* 1958; *Easy Come, Easy Go* 1967; *The President's Analyst* 1967; *The Affair* 1973
Harrington, Richard *Leaving Lenin* 1993; *House of America* 1996
Harris, Barbara (1935–) *A Thousand Clowns* 1965; *Oh Dad, Poor Dad, Mama's Hung You in the Closet and I'm Feelin' So Sad* 1967; *Plaza Suite* 1971; *Who Is Harry Kellerman, and Why Is He Saying Those Terrible Things about Me?* 1971; *The War between Men and Women* 1972; *Mixed Company* 1974; *Family Plot* 1976; *Freaky Friday* 1976; *Movie Movie* 1978; *Hill's Angels* 1979; *The Seduction of Joe Tynan* 1979; *Peggy Sue Got Married* 1986; *Nice Girls Don't Explode* 1987; *Dirty Rotten Scoundrels* 1988
Harris, Brad (1933–) *The Mutations* 1973; *Hercules* 1983
Harris, Bruklin *Dangerous Minds* 1995; *Girls Town* 1996
Harris, Danielle (1977–) *Halloween 4: the Return of Michael Myers* 1988; *Halloween 5: the Revenge of Michael Myers* 1989; *Marked for Death* 1990; *The Last Boy Scout* 1991; *American Yakuza 2: Back to Back* 1996; *The Wild Thornberrys Movie* 2003
Harris, David *The Warriors* 1979; *Purple Hearts* 1984; *A Soldier's Story* 1984
Harris, Ed (1950–) *Borderline* 1980; *Knightriders* 1981; *Creepshow* 1982; *The Right Stuff* 1983; *Under Fire* 1983; *A Flash of Green* 1984; *Places in the Heart* 1984; *Swing Shift* 1984; *Alamo Bay* 1985; *Code Name: Emerald* 1985; *Sweet Dreams* 1985; *Walker* 1987; *Jacknife* 1988; *To Kill a Priest* 1988; *The Abyss* 1989; *State of Grace* 1990; *Paris Trout* 1991; *Glengarry Glen Ross* 1992; *The Firm* 1993; *Needful Things* 1993; *China Moon* 1994; *Milk Money* 1994; *Apollo 13* 1995; *Eye for an Eye* 1995; *Just Cause* 1995; *Nixon* 1995; *Absolute Power* 1996; *The Rock* 1996; *Stepmom* 1998; *The Truman Show* 1998; *Pollock* 2000; *The Prime Gig* 2000; *Waking the Dead* 2000; *A Beautiful Mind* 2001; *Buffalo Soldiers* 2001; *Enemy at the Gates* 2001; *The Hours* 2002; *The Human Stain* 2003; *Radio* 2003; *A History of Violence* 2005

Harris, Estelle (1932–) *Chairman of the Board* 1998; *Good Advice* 2001

Harris, Fox (1936–1988) *Repo Man* 1984; *Dr Caligari* 1989

Harris (2), George *Camilla* 1993; *Layer Cake* 2004; *The Interpreter* 2005

Harris, Jared (1961–) *The Public Eye* 1992; *Tall Tale* 1994; *Blue in the Face* 1995; *I Shot Andy Warhol* 1995; *Nadja* 1995; *B Monkey* 1996; *Gold in the Streets* 1996; *Chinese Box* 1997; *Sunday* 1997; *The Eternal* 1998; *Happiness* 1998; *Lost in Space* 1998; *Shadow Magic* 2000; *Dummy* 2002; *Igby Goes Down* 2002; *Mr Deeds* 2002; *Sylvia* 2003; *Resident Evil: Apocalypse* 2004

Harris, Jet (1939–) *The Young Ones* 1961; *Summer Holiday* 1962

Harris, Jo Ann *The Beguiled* 1971; *Act of Vengeance* 1974

Harris, Jonathan (1914–2002) *Botany Bay* 1952; *A Bug's Life* 1998; *Toy Story 2* 1999

Harris, Julie (1925–) *The Member of the Wedding* 1952; *East of Eden* 1955; *I Am a Camera* 1955; *The Truth about Women* 1958; *Requiem for a Heavyweight* 1962; *The Haunting* 1963; *Harper* 1966; *You're a Big Boy Now* 1966; *Reflections in a Golden Eye* 1967; *The Split* 1968; *The People Next Door* 1970; *The Hiding Place* 1975; *Voyage of the Damned* 1976; *The Bell Jar* 1979; *Gorillas in the Mist* 1988; *The Dark Half* 1991; *HouseSitter* 1992; *Vanished without a Trace* 1993; *Acts of Love* 1995; *Bad Manners* 1998; *The First of May* 2000

Harris, Julius *aka* **Harris, Julius W** (1923–2004) *Nothing but a Man* 1964; *Shaft's Big Score!* 1972; *Superfly* 1972; *Trouble Man* 1972; *Black Caesar* 1973; *Hell Up in Harlem* 1973; *Live and Let Die* 1973; *Islands in the Stream* 1976; *Victory at Entebbe* 1976; *Prayer of the Rollerboys* 1990; *Shrunken Heads* 1994

Harris, Lara *No Man's Land* 1987; *Blood Red* 1988; *The Fourth War* 1990

Harris, Laura (1976–) *The Faculty* 1998; *The Highwayman* 1999

Harris, Mel (1957–) *Wanted Dead or Alive* 1986; *Cameron's Closet* 1988; *K-9* 1989; *Wind Dancer* 1991; *Suture* 1993; *The Pagemaster* 1994; *Ultimate Betrayal* 1994; *Firetrap* 2001

Harris (2), Michael *aka* **Harris, M K** *Genuine Risk* 1990; *Knife Edge* 1990; *Bar Girls* 1994; *Sleepstalker* 1995

Harris, Moira *The Fantasist* 1986; *Breakdown* 1997; *Chicago Cab* 1998

Harris, Naomie (1976–) *Living in Hope* 2001; *28 Days Later...* 2002; *After the Sunset* 2004; *Trauma* 2004

Harris, Neil Patrick (1973–) *Clara's Heart* 1988; *The Purple People Eater* 1988; *Sudden Fury* 1993; *Starship Troopers* 1997; *The Proposition* 1998; *The Next Best Thing* 2000; *Undercover Brother* 2002; *Harold & Kumar Get the Munchies* 2004

Harris, Paul (1917–1985) *All Night Long* 1961; *The Slams* 1973; *Truck Turner* 1974

Harris, Phil (1904–1995) *Melody Cruise* 1933; *Buck Benny Rides Again* 1940; *Wabash Avenue* 1950; *The High and the Mighty* 1954; *Anything Goes* 1956; *Good-bye, My Lady* 1956; *The Wheeler Dealers* 1963; *The Patsy* 1964; *The Cool Ones* 1967; *The Jungle Book* 1967; *The Aristocats* 1970; *Robin Hood* 1973; *Rock-a-Doodle* 1990

Harris, Richard (1932–2002) *Alive and Kicking* 1958; *The Wreck of the Mary Deare* 1959; *The Long and the Short and the Tall* 1960; *A Terrible Beauty* 1960; *The Guns of Navarone* 1961; *Mutiny on the Bounty* 1962; *This Sporting Life* 1963; *The Red Desert* 1964; *The Heroes of Telemark* 1965; *Major Dundee* 1965; *The Bible...in the Beginning* 1966; *Hawaii* 1966; *Camelot* 1967; *Caprice* 1967; *Bloomfield* 1969; *Cromwell* 1970; *A Man Called Horse* 1970; *The Molly Maguires* 1970; *Man in the Wilderness* 1971; *The Deadly Trackers* 1973; *Juggernaut* 1974; *99 and 44/100% Dead* 1974; *The Cassandra Crossing* 1976; *Echoes of a Summer* 1976; *The Return of a Man Called Horse* 1976; *Robin and Marian* 1976; *Golden Rendezvous* 1977; *Gulliver's Travels* 1977; *Orca ... Killer Whale* 1977; *The Wild Geese* 1978; *A Game for Vultures* 1979; *Highpoint* 1979; *Tarzan, the Ape Man* 1981; *Triumphs of a Man Called Horse* 1983; *Martin's Day* 1984; *King of the Wind* 1989; *Mack the Knife* 1989; *The Field* 1990; *Patriot Games* 1992; *Unforgiven* 1992; *Silent Tongue* 1993; *Wrestling Ernest Hemingway* 1993; *Cry, the Beloved Country* 1995; *Smilla's Feeling for Snow* 1996; *This Is the Sea* 1996; *Trojan Eddie* 1996; *The Barber of Siberia* 1999; *Grizzly Falls* 1999; *To Walk with Lions* 1999; *Gladiator* 2000; *The Count of Monte Cristo* 2001; *Harry Potter and the Philosopher's Stone* 2001; *My Kingdom* 2001; *Harry Potter and the Chamber of Secrets* 2002

Harris, Robert (1900–1995) *Undercover* 1943; *That Lady* 1955; *The Big Caper* 1957; *Decline and Fall... of a Birdwatcher* 1968; *Ransom* 1975

Harris, Robert H (1911–1981) *The Invisible Boy* 1957; *How to Make a Monster* 1958

Harris, Rosemary (1930–) *Beau Brummell* 1954; *The Shiralee* 1957; *A Flea in Her Ear* 1968; *The Boys from Brazil* 1978; *The Ploughman's Lunch* 1983; *The Bridge* 1990; *Tom & Viv* 1994; *My Life So Far* 1999; *Sunshine* 1999; *Blow Dry* 2000; *Spider-Man* 2002; *Spider-Man 2* 2004

Harris, Rossie *aka* **Harris, Ross** (1969–) *Another Man, Another Chance* 1977; *Testament* 1983

Harris, Sean *24 Hour Party People* 2001; *Creep* 2004; *Trauma* 2004

Harris, Stacy (1918–1973) *Appointment with Danger* 1950; *The Great Sioux Uprising* 1953; *Dragnet* 1954; *Comanche* 1956; *The Hunters* 1958

Harris, Steve (1965–) *The Mod Squad* 1999; *The Skulls* 2000

Harris, Theresa (1909–1985) *Baby Face* 1933; *Our Wife* 1941

Harris, Zelda *Crooklyn* 1994; *The Baby-Sitter's Club* 1995

Harrison, Cathryn (1960–) *Images* 1972; *Black Moon* 1974; *The Dresser* 1983; *Duet for One* 1986

Harrison, George (1943–2001) *A Hard Day's Night* 1964; *Help!* 1965; *The Rutles – All You Need Is Cash* 1978; *Shanghai Surprise* 1986

Harrison, Gregory (1950–) *Fraternity Row* 1977; *Razorback* 1984; *Seduced* 1985; *North Shore* 1987; *Body Chemistry 2: Voice of a Stranger* 1992; *Sudden Fury* 1993; *A Christmas Romance* 1994; *Mortal Fear* 1994; *Air Bud: Golden Receiver* 1998; *First Daughter* 1999

Harrison, Jenilee (1959–) *Tank* 1984; *Curse III: Blood Sacrifice* 1991

Harrison, Kathleen (1892–1995) *The Ghoul* 1933; *Night Must Fall* 1937; *Bank Holiday* 1938; *The Ghost Train* 1941; *I Thank You* 1941; *Much Too Shy* 1942; *The Shop at Sly Corner* 1946; *Wanted for Murder* 1946; *Holiday Camp* 1947; *Bond Street* 1948; *Here Come the Huggetts* 1948; *Vote for Huggett* 1948; *The Winslow Boy* 1948; *The Gay Adventure* 1949; *The Huggetts Abroad* 1949; *Now Barabbas Was a Robber* 1949; *Trio* 1950; *Waterfront* 1950; *Scrooge* 1951; *The Happy Family* 1952; *The Pickwick Papers* 1952; *Turn the Key Softly* 1953; *All for Mary* 1955; *Lilacs in the Spring* 1955; *Where There's a Will* 1955; *The Big Money* 1956; *Home and Away* 1956; *It's a Wonderful World* 1956; *Cast a Dark Shadow* 1957; *A Cry from the Streets* 1957; *Seven Thunders* 1957; *Alive and Kicking* 1958; *On the Fiddle* 1961; *The Fast Lady* 1963; *West 11* 1963; *Lock Up Your Daughters!* 1969

Harrison, Linda (1945–) *A Guide for the Married Man* 1967; *Planet of the Apes* 1967; *Beneath the Planet of the Apes* 1969

Harrison, Noel (1934–) *The Best of Enemies* 1961; *Where the Spies Are* 1965; *Take a Girl like You* 1970

Harrison, Rex (1908–1990) *Men Are Not Gods* 1936; *Over the Moon* 1937; *Storm in a Teacup* 1937; *The Citadel* 1938; *St Martin's Lane* 1938; *Ten Days in Paris* 1939; *Night Train to Munich* 1940; *Major Barbara* 1941; *Blithe Spirit* 1945; *I Live in Grosvenor Square* 1945; *The Rake's Progress* 1945; *Anna and the King of Siam* 1946; *The Foxes of Harrow* 1947; *The Ghost and Mrs Muir* 1947; *Unfaithfully Yours* 1948; *The Long Dark Hall* 1951; *The Four Poster* 1953; *King Richard and the Crusaders* 1954; *The Constant Husband* 1955; *The Reluctant Debutante* 1958; *Midnight Lace* 1960; *The Happy Thieves* 1962; *Cleopatra* 1963; *My Fair Lady* 1964; *The Yellow Rolls-Royce* 1964; *The Agony and the Ecstasy* 1965; *Doctor Dolittle* 1967; *The Honey Pot* 1967; *A Flea in Her Ear* 1968; *Staircase* 1969; *The Prince and the Pauper* 1977; *Ashanti* 1979; *The Fifth Musketeer* 1979

Harrison, Richard (1935–) *Master of the World* 1961; *One after the Other* 1968; *Vengeance* 1968; *Mad Dog Murderer* 1977

Harrison, Susan (1938–) *Sweet Smell of Success* 1957; *Key Witness* 1960

Harrold, Jamie *I Think I Do* 1997; *The Score* 2001

Harrold, Kathryn (1950–) *Nightwing* 1979; *The Hunter* 1980; *Modern Romance* 1981; *The Pursuit of DB Cooper* 1981; *The Sender* 1982; *Yes, Giorgio* 1982; *Heartbreakers* 1984; *Into the Night* 1985; *Raw Deal* 1986

Harron, John (1903–1939) *Laugh and Get Rich* 1931; *White Zombie* 1932

Harron, Robert (1893–1920) *The Battle of Elderbush* 1914; *The Battle of the Sexes* 1914; *Intolerance* 1916; *Hearts of the World* 1918

Harrow, Lisa (1943–) *All Creatures Great and Small* 1974; *It Shouldn't Happen to a Vet* 1979; *Omen III: the Final Conflict* 1980; *Other Halves* 1984; *Shaker Run* 1985; *The Last Days of Chez Nous* 1992; *That Eye, the Sky* 1994; *Sunday* 1997

Harry, Deborah *aka* **Harry, Debbie** (1945–) *Union City* 1980; *Downtown 81* 1981; *Videodrome* 1982; *Forever Lulu* 1987; *Hairspray* 1988; *Satisfaction* 1988; *Tales from the Darkside: the Movie* 1991; *Dead Beat* 1994; *Heavy* 1995; *Six Ways to Sunday* 1997; *The Fluffer* 2001; *My Life without Me* 2002; *Spun* 2002

Hart, David (1954–) *Before Women Had Wings* 1997; *Liam* 2000

Hart, Diane (1926–2002) *Happy Go Lovely* 1950; *Father's Doing Fine* 1952; *You're Only Young Twice* 1952; *Dick Turpin – Highwayman* 1956

Hart, Dolores (1938–) *Loving You* 1957; *Wild Is the Wind* 1957; *King Creole* 1958; *Lonelyhearts* 1958; *Where the Boys Are* 1960; *Francis of Assisi* 1961; *Sail a Crooked Ship* 1961; *Come Fly with Me* 1962; *The Inspector* 1962

Hart, Dorothy (1922–2004) *The Countess of Monte Cristo* 1948; *The Naked City* 1948; *Calamity Jane and Sam Bass* 1949; *Undertow* 1949; *I Was a Communist for the FBI* 1951; *Tarzan's Savage Fury* 1952

Hart, Ian (1964–) *The Hours and Times* 1992; *Backbeat* 1993; *Clockwork Mice* 1994; *The Englishman Who Went up a Hill, but Came down a Mountain* 1995; *Hollow Reed* 1995; *Land and Freedom* 1995; *Nothing Personal* 1995; *B Monkey* 1996; *Daniel Defoe's Robinson Crusoe* 1996; *Gold in the Streets* 1996; *Michael Collins* 1996; *The Butcher Boy* 1997; *Noose* 1997; *Enemy of the State* 1998; *Mojo* 1998; *Best* 1999; *The End of the Affair* 1999; *This Year's Love* 1999; *Wonderland* 1999; *Aberdeen* 2000; *Born Romantic* 2000; *The Closer You Get* 2000; *Liam* 2000; *Strictly Sinatra* 2000; *Harry Potter and the Philosopher's Stone* 2001; *Killing Me Softly* 2001; *Blind Flight* 2003; *Finding Neverland* 2004; *Strings* 2004

Hart, John (1917–) *The Man Who Loved Redheads* 1954; *The Legend of the Lone Ranger* 1981

Hart, Kevin *Lone Wolf* 1988; *Soul Plane* 2004

Hart, Linda *Stella* 1990; *Tin Cup* 1996

Hart, Melissa Joan (1976–) *Two Came Back* 1997; *Can't Hardly Wait* 1998; *Drive Me Crazy* 1999; *Recess: School's Out* 2001

Hart, Richard (1915–1951) *Desire Me* 1947; *Green Dolphin Street* 1947; *BF's Daughter* 1948; *Reign of Terror* 1949

Hart, Roxanne (1952–) *Oh, God! You Devil* 1984; *Highlander* 1986; *Pulse* 1988; *Once Around* 1991

Hart, Susan (1941–) *City under the Sea* 1965; *Dr Goldfoot and the Bikini Machine* 1965

Hart, Teddy (1897–1971) *After the Thin Man* 1936; *Three Men on a Horse* 1936; *A Girl in Every Port* 1952; *Mickey One* 1965

Hartley, John *Million Dollar Legs* 1939; *The Way of All Flesh* 1940

Hartley, Mariette (1940–) *Ride the High Country* 1962; *Marnie* 1964; *Marooned* 1969; *Barquero* 1970; *The Return of Count Yorga* 1971; *The Magnificent Seven Ride!* 1972; *Improper Channels* 1981; *O'Hara's Wife* 1982; *1969* 1988; *Freefall: Flight 174* 1995

Hartley, Ted (1935–) *Walk, Don't Run* 1966; *Barefoot in the Park* 1967; *High Plains Drifter* 1973

Hartman, David (1935–) *The Ballad of Josie* 1968; *Did You Hear the One about the Traveling Saleslady?* 1968; *The Island at the Top of the World* 1974

Hartman, Elizabeth (1941–1987) *A Patch of Blue* 1965; *The Group* 1966; *You're a Big Boy Now* 1966; *The Fixer* 1968; *The Beguiled* 1971; *Walking Tall* 1973; *Full Moon High* 1982; *The Secret of NIMH* 1982

Hartman, Margot *The Curse of the Living Corpse* 1964; *Psychomania* 1964

Hartman, Paul (1904–1973) *Sunny* 1941; *Soldier in the Rain* 1963

Hartman, Phil (1948–1998) *Blind Date* 1987; *The Brave Little Toaster* 1987; *CB4* 1993; *Coneheads* 1993; *So I Married an Axe Murderer* 1993; *Greedy* 1994; *Houseguest* 1995; *Jingle All the Way* 1996; *Sgt Bilko* 1996; *The Second Civil War* 1997; *Small Soldiers* 1998

Hartnell, William *aka* **Hartnell, Billy** (1908–1975) *Midnight at Madame Tussaud's* 1936; *The Bells Go Down* 1943; *The Way Ahead* 1944; *Brighton Rock* 1947; *The Lost People* 1949; *Now Barabbas Was a Robber* 1949; *Will Any Gentleman...?* 1953; *Double Cross* 1955; *Footsteps in the Fog* 1955; *Josephine and Men* 1955; *Private's Progress* 1956; *Yangtse Incident* 1956; *Hell Drivers* 1957; *The Hypnotist* 1957; *Carry On Sergeant* 1958; *The Mouse That Roared* 1959; *The Night We Dropped a Clanger* 1959; *And the Same to You* 1960; *Piccadilly Third Stop* 1960; *Tomorrow at Ten* 1962; *This Sporting Life* 1963; *The World Ten Times Over* 1963

Hartnett, Josh (1978–) *The Faculty* 1998; *Halloween H20: 20 Years Later* 1998; *The Virgin Suicides* 1999; *Blow Dry* 2000; *Here on Earth* 2000; *Black Hawk Down* 2001; *O* 2001; *Pearl Harbor* 2001; *Town & Country* 2001; *40 Days and 40 Nights* 2002; *Hollywood Homicide* 2003; *Wicker Park* 2004; *Sin City* 2005

Harvey, Don *The Beast of War* 1988; *Casualties of War* 1989; *American Heart* 1992; *The Glass Shield* 1995; *Men of War* 1995; *Tank Girl* 1995

Harvey, Forrester (1884–1945) *Guilty Hands* 1931; *Red Dust* 1932; *Tarzan, the Ape Man* 1932; *The Eagle and the Hawk* 1933; *Tarzan and His Mate* 1934; *Thoroughbreds Don't Cry* 1937; *Little Nellie Kelly* 1940

Harvey, John (1911–1982) *Pin Up Girl* 1944; *X the Unknown* 1956; *The Deadly Bees* 1967

Harvey, Laurence (1928–1973) *Landfall* 1949; *Cairo Road* 1950; *The Scarlet Thread* 1951; *There Is Another Sun* 1951; *I Believe in You* 1952; *Women of Twilight* 1952; *Innocents in Paris* 1953; *The Good Die Young* 1954; *King Richard and the Crusaders* 1954; *Romeo and Juliet* 1954; *I Am a Camera* 1955; *Storm over the Nile* 1955; *Three Men in a Boat* 1956; *Room at the Top* 1958; *The Silent Enemy* 1958; *The Truth about Women* 1958; *Expresso Bongo* 1959; *The Alamo* 1960; *Butterfield 8* 1960; *The Long and the Short and the Tall* 1960; *Summer and Smoke* 1961; *Two Loves* 1961; *A Girl Named Tamiko* 1962; *The Manchurian Candidate* 1962; *Walk on the Wild Side* 1962; *The Wonderful World of the Brothers Grimm* 1962; *The Ceremony* 1963; *The Running Man* 1963; *Of Human Bondage* 1964; *The Outrage* 1964; *Darling* 1965; *Life at the Top* 1965; *The Spy with a Cold Nose* 1966; *The Winter's Tale* 1966; *A Dandy in Aspic* 1968; *The Magic Christian* 1969; *WUSA* 1970; *Night Watch* 1973; *Welcome to Arrow Beach* 1974

Harvey, Lilian *aka* **Harvey, Lillian** (1906–1968) *The Love Waltz* 1930; *Congress Dances* 1931

Harvey, Morris (1877–1944) *Sing as We Go* 1934; *The Love Test* 1935; *Squibs* 1935

Harvey, Paul (1882–1955) *Advice to the Lovelorn* 1933; *The Walking Dead* 1936; *Meet Dr Christian* 1939; *Never Say Die* 1939; *Arizona* 1940; *Side Street* 1950; *April in Paris* 1952; *Dreamboat* 1952; *Calamity Jane* 1953; *Three for the Show* 1955

Harvey, Phil *The Land Unknown* 1957; *The Monolith Monsters* 1957; *Monster on the Campus* 1958

Harvey, Rodney (1967–1998) *Salsa* 1988; *My Own Private Idaho* 1991

Harvey, Steve (1956–) *The Fighting Temptations* 2003; *Love Don't Cost a Thing* 2003; *Johnson Family Vacation* 2004

Harvey, Terence *Gunbus* 1986; *The Phantom of the Opera* 1989

Harvey, Tom *The Luck of Ginger Coffey* 1964; *Strange Brew* 1983

Harvey, Verna *The Nightcomers* 1972; *Assassin* 1973

Hasegawa, Kazuo (1908–1984) *Gate of Hell* 1953; *The Crucified Lovers* 1954; *An Actor's Revenge* 1963

Haskell, David (1948–2000) *Godspell* 1973; *Body Double* 1984

Haskell, Peter (1934–) *The Cracker Factory* 1979; *Child's Play 3* 1991

Hassall, Imogen (1942–1980) *The Long Duel* 1966; *El Condor* 1970; *Incense for the Damned* 1970; *Mumsy, Nanny, Sonny & Girly* 1970; *White Cargo* 1973

Hassan, Tamer (1968–) *The Calcium Kid* 2003; *The Football Factory* 2004

Hasse, O E (1903–1978) *The Big Lift* 1950; *Decision before Dawn* 1951; *I Confess* 1953; *Betrayed*

1954; Above Us the Waves 1955; Les Espions 1957; Trois Chambres à Manhattan 1965; State of Siege 1972

Hassel, Danny A Nightmare on Elm Street 4: The Dream Master 1988; A Nightmare on Elm Street 5: The Dream Child 1989

Hasselhoff, David (1952–) Witchcraft 1989; Avalanche 1994; Ring of the Musketeers 1994; Baywatch the Movie: Forbidden Paradise 1995; The Big Tease 1999; Layover 2000; One True Love 2000; The SpongeBob SquarePants Movie 2004

Hassett, Marilyn (1947–) The Other Side of the Mountain 1975; Two-Minute Warning 1976; The Other Side of the Mountain – Part 2 1978; The Bell Jar 1979; Messenger of Death 1988

Hasso, Signe (1910–2002) Journey for Margaret 1942; The Seventh Cross 1944; The Story of Dr Wassell 1944; The House on 92nd Street 1945; Johnny Angel 1945; Thieves' Holiday 1946; A Double Life 1947; Where There's Life 1947; To the Ends of the Earth 1948; Crisis 1950; Picture Mommy Dead 1966; A Reflection of Fear 1973; The Black Bird 1975; Sherlock Holmes in New York 1976

Hastings, Bob (1925–) Did You Hear the One about the Traveling Saleslady? 1968; The All-American Boy 1973

Hatch, Richard *aka* **Hatch, Richard L** (1945–) Battlestar Galactica 1978; Charlie Chan and the Curse of the Dragon Queen 1981; Party Line 1988; The Ghost 2000

Hatcher, Mary Variety Girl 1947; Isn't It Romantic 1948; The Big Wheel 1949

Hatcher, Teri (1964–) The Big Picture 1989; Tango & Cash 1989; Soapdish 1991; Straight Talk 1992; Brain Smasher… a Love Story 1993; The Cool Surface 1993; Heaven's Prisoners 1996; 2 Days in the Valley 1996; Tomorrow Never Dies 1997; SPYkids 2001

Hatfield, Hurd (1918–1998) Dragon Seed 1944; The Picture of Dorian Gray 1945; Diary of a Chambermaid 1946; The Beginning or the End 1947; The Unsuspected 1947; Destination Murder 1950; Tarzan and the Slave Girl 1950; The Left Handed Gun 1958; El Cid 1961; King of Kings 1961; Harlow 1965; Mickey One 1965; The Boston Strangler 1968; Von Richthofen and Brown 1971; King David 1985; Crimes of the Heart 1986; Her Alibi 1989

Hathaway, Anne (1982–) The Princess Diaries 2001; The Cat Returns 2002; Nicholas Nickleby 2002; Ella Enchanted 2004; The Princess Diaries 2: Royal Engagement 2004

Hathaway, Noah (1971–) Battlestar Galactica 1978; The NeverEnding Story 1984; Troll 1986

Hatosy, Shawn (1975–) The Faculty 1998; Anywhere but Here 1999; The Joyriders 1999; Outside Providence 1999; Witness Protection 1999; Down to You 2000; The Cooler 2002; A Guy Thing 2002

Hattab, Yoram (1966–) Kadosh 1999; Kippur 2000

Hatton, Raymond (1887–1971) A Romance of the Redwoods 1917; Male and Female 1919; The Ace of Hearts 1921; The Hunchback of Notre Dame 1923; The Squaw Man 1931; Law and Order 1932; Polly of the Circus 1932; Vanishing Frontier 1932; Lady Killer 1933; The Texans 1938; Frontier Horizon 1939; Rough Riders' Roundup 1939; Wyoming Outlaw 1939; Black Gold 1947; Thunder Pass 1954; Invasion of the Saucer Men 1957; Motorcycle Gang 1957

Haudepin, Didier (1951–) L'Innocente 1976; Ecoute Voir… 1978

Haudepin, Sabine (1955–) Jules et Jim 1961; The Last Metro 1980; Force Majeure 1989

Hauer, Rutger (1944–) Turkish Delight 1973; Cold Blood 1975; Keetje Tippel 1975; The Wilby Conspiracy 1975; Soldier of Orange 1977; Spetters 1980; Chanel Solitaire 1981; Nighthawks 1981; Blade Runner 1982; Eureka 1982; The Osterman Weekend 1983; A Breed Apart 1984; Flesh + Blood 1985; Ladyhawke 1985; The Hitcher 1986; Wanted Dead or Alive 1986; Escape from Sobibor 1987; The Legend of the Holy Drinker 1988; Bloodhounds of Broadway 1989; The Salute of the Jugger 1989; Blind Fury 1990; Split Second 1991; Buffy the Vampire Slayer 1992; Nostradamus 1993; Voyage 1993; The Beans of Egypt, Maine 1994; Surviving the Game 1994; The Call of the Wild 1996; Crossworlds 1996; Hostile Waters 1996; Omega Doom 1996; Hemoglobin 1997; Bone Daddy 1998; Simon Magus 1998; Tactical Assault 1998; New World Disorder 1999; Wilder 2000; Confessions of a Dangerous Mind 2002; Batman Begins 2005; Sin City 2005

Haupt, Ullrich *aka* **Haupt, Ulrich** (1887–1931) Morocco 1930; The Unholy Garden 1931

Hauser, Cole (1975–) School Ties 1992; Higher Learning 1995; All over Me 1996; The Hi-Lo Country 1998; Pitch Black 1999; Hart's War 2002; White Oleander 2002; Tears of the Sun 2003; 2 Fast 2 Furious 2003; Paparazzi 2004

Hauser, Fay Marvin and Tige 1983; Jo Jo Dancer, Your Life Is Calling 1986; Candyman: Farewell to the Flesh 1995

Hauser, Wings (1948–) Vice Squad 1982; Deadly Force 1983; Mutant 1984; Tough Guys Don't Dance 1987; Beastmaster 2: through the Portal of Time 1991; Tales from the Hood 1995

Havens, Richie (1941–) Catch My Soul 1973; Greased Lightning 1977; Hearts of Fire 1987

Haver, June (1926–) Home in Indiana 1944; Irish Eyes Are Smiling 1944; The Dolly Sisters 1945; Where Do We Go from Here? 1945; Three Little Girls in Blue 1946; I Wonder Who's Kissing Her Now 1947; Look for the Silver Lining 1949; Oh, You Beautiful Doll 1949; The Daughter of Rosie O'Grady 1950; Love Nest 1951; The Girl Next Door 1953

Haver, Phyllis (1899–1960) What Price Glory 1926; The Way of All Flesh 1927

Havers, Nigel (1949–) Chariots of Fire 1981; A Passage to India 1984; Burke and Wills 1985; The Whistle Blower 1986; Empire of the Sun 1987; Farewell to the King 1988; The Burning Season 1994; The Life and Death of Peter Sellers 2003

Havill, Andrew The Heart of Me 2002; Sylvia 2003

Havoc, June (1916–) Hello, Frisco, Hello 1943; No Time for Love 1943; Brewster's Millions 1945; Gentleman's Agreement 1947; Intrigue 1947; The Iron Curtain 1948; When My Baby Smiles at Me 1948; Follow the Sun: the Ben Hogan Story 1951; Can't Stop the Music 1980; A Return to Salem's Lot 1987

Hawdon, Robin (1939–) When Dinosaurs Ruled the Earth 1969; Zeta One 1969

Hawes, Keeley (1977–) Complicity 1999; The Last September 1999

Hawke, Ethan (1970–) Explorers 1985; Dad 1989; Dead Poets Society 1989; A Midnight Clear 1991; Mystery Date 1991; White Fang 1991; Alive 1992; Rich in Love 1992; Waterland 1992; Floundering 1994; Reality Bites 1994; White Fang 2: Myth of the White Wolf 1994; Before Sunrise 1995; Search and Destroy 1995; Gattaca 1997; Great Expectations 1997; The Newton Boys 1998; Joe the King 1999; Snow Falling on Cedars 1999; Hamlet 2000; Tape 2001; Training Day 2001; Waking Life 2001; Before Sunset 2004; Taking Lives 2004; Assault on Precinct 13 2005

Hawkes, John (1959–) Roadracers 1994; Hardball 2001; Identity 2003

Hawkins, Frank The Crooked Sky 1957; Information Received 1962

Hawkins, Jack *aka* **Hawkins, 2nd Lt Jack** (1910–1973) I Lived with You 1933; A Shot in the Dark 1933; Next of Kin 1942; Bonnie Prince Charlie 1948; The Fallen Idol 1948; The Small Back Room 1949; The Adventurers 1950; The Black Rose 1950; The Elusive Pimpernel 1950; State Secret 1950; No Highway 1951; Angels One Five 1952; Home at Seven 1952; Mandy 1952; The Planter's Wife 1952; The Cruel Sea 1953; Front Page Story 1953; The Intruder 1953; Malta Story 1953; The Seekers 1954; Land of the Pharaohs 1955; The Prisoner 1955; Touch and Go 1955; Fortune Is a Woman 1956; The Long Arm 1956; The Man in the Sky 1956; The Bridge on the River Kwai 1957; Gideon's Day 1958; The Two-Headed Spy 1958; Ben-Hur 1959; The League of Gentlemen 1960; Two Loves 1961; Five Finger Exercise 1962; Lawrence of Arabia 1962; Rampage 1963; Guns at Batasi 1964; The Third Secret 1964; Zulu 1964; Lord Jim 1965; Masquerade 1965; Judith 1966; Great Catherine 1968; Shalako 1968; Monte Carlo or Bust 1969; Oh! What a Lovely War 1969; Twinky 1969; The Adventures of Gerard 1970; Waterloo 1970; Kidnapped 1971; When Eight Bells Toll 1971; Sin 1972; Tales That Witness Madness 1973; Theatre of Blood 1973

Hawkins, Screamin' Jay (1929–2000) Mystery Train 1989; Perdita Durango 1997

Hawley, Richard Paper Marriage 1991; Captives 1994

Hawn, Goldie *aka* **Hawn, Goldie Jeanne** (1945–) The One and Only, Genuine, Original Family Band 1968; Cactus Flower 1969; There's a Girl in My Soup 1970; Dollars 1971; Butterflies Are Free 1972; The Girl from Petrovka 1974; The Sugarland Express 1974; Shampoo 1975; The Duchess and the Dirtwater Fox 1976; Foul Play 1978; Travels with Anita 1978; Private Benjamin 1980; Seems like Old Times 1980; Best Friends 1982; Protocol 1984; Swing Shift 1984; Wildcats 1986; Overboard 1987; Bird on a Wire 1990; Deceived 1991; CrissCross 1992; Death Becomes Her 1992; HouseSitter 1992; Everyone Says I Love You 1996; The First Wives Club 1996; The Out-of-Towners 1999; Town & Country 2001; The Banger Sisters 2002

Haworth, Jill (1945–) The Mysteries of Paris 1962; In Harm's Way 1965; It! 1966; The Haunted House of Horror 1969; Tower of Evil 1972; The Mutations 1973

Hawthorne, Denys The Chinese Connection 1988; Emma 1996

Hawthorne, Elizabeth Jack Be Nimble 1992; Exposure 2000

Hawthorne, Nigel (1929–2001) Sweeney 2 1978; The Hunchback of Notre Dame 1982; The Plague Dogs 1982; The Chain 1984; The Black Cauldron 1985; Turtle Diary 1985; King of the Wind 1989; Freddie as FRO7 1992; Demolition Man 1993; The Madness of King George 1995; Richard III 1995; Murder in Mind 1996; Twelfth Night 1996; Amistad 1997; Madeline 1998; The Object of My Affection 1998; The Clandestine Marriage 1999; A Reasonable Man 1999; Tarzan 1999; The Winslow Boy 1999; Call Me Claus 2001

Hawtrey, Charles (1914–1988) Where's That Fire? 1939; The Ghost of St Michael's 1941; The Goose Steps Out 1942; A Canterbury Tale 1944; Room to Let 1949; Brandy for the Parson 1951; You're Only Young Twice 1952; Timeslip 1955; The March Hare 1956; Who Done It? 1956; Carry On Sergeant 1958; Carry On Nurse 1959; Carry On Teacher 1959; Carry On Constable 1960; Carry On Regardless 1960; Inn for Trouble 1960; Please Turn Over 1960; Dentist on the Job 1961; What a Whopper! 1961; Carry On Cabby 1963; Carry On Jack 1963; Carry On Cleo 1964; Carry On Spying 1964; Carry On Cowboy 1965; Carry On – Don't Lose Your Head 1966; Carry On Screaming 1966; Carry On Follow That Camel 1967; Carry On Doctor 1968; Carry On Up the Khyber 1968; Carry On Again Doctor 1969; Carry On Camping 1969; Zeta One 1969; Carry On Loving 1970; Carry On Up the Jungle 1970; Carry On at Your Convenience 1971; Carry On Henry 1971; Carry On Abroad 1972; Carry On Matron 1972

Hay, Alexandra (1944–1993) Model Shop 1969; One Man Jury 1978

Hay, Will (1888–1949) Those Were the Days 1934; Boys Will Be Boys 1935; Where There's a Will 1936; Windbag the Sailor 1936; Good Morning, Boys 1937; Oh, Mr Porter! 1937; Ask a Policeman 1938; Convict 99 1938; Hey! Hey! USA 1938; Old Bones of the River 1938; Where's That Fire? 1939; The Black Sheep of Whitehall 1941; The Ghost of St Michael's 1941; The Big Blockade 1942; The Goose Steps Out 1942; My Learned Friend 1943

Hayakawa, Sessue (1889–1973) The Cheat 1915; Tokyo Joe 1949; Three Came Home 1950; House of Bamboo 1955; The Bridge on the River Kwai 1957; The Geisha Boy 1958; Green Mansions 1959; Hell to Eternity 1960; Swiss Family Robinson 1960

Hayama, Masao (1925–) The Only Son 1936; The Brothers and Sisters of the Toda Family 1941

Hayashi, Marc Chan Is Missing 1982; The Laserman 1988

Hayden, Harry (1884–1955) The Meanest Man in the World 1943; The Unknown Guest 1943; Two Sisters from Boston 1946; Double Dynamite 1951

Hayden, Linda (1953–) Taste the Blood of Dracula 1969; Blood on Satan's Claw 1970; Something to Hide 1971; Confessions of a Window Cleaner 1974; Madhouse 1974; Exposé 1975; Vampira 1975; Confessions from a Holiday Camp 1977; Let's Get Laid 1977

Hayden, Nora Plunder Road 1957; The Angry Red Planet 1959

Hayden, Peter Shaker Run 1985; Footrot Flats: the Dog's Tale 1986

Hayden, Sterling (1916–1986) Blaze of Noon 1947; The Asphalt Jungle 1950; Denver & Rio Grande 1952; Hellgate 1952; So Big 1953; The Star 1953; Take Me to Town 1953; Arrow in the Dust 1954; The City Is Dark 1954; Johnny Guitar 1954; Naked Alibi 1954; Prince Valiant 1954; Suddenly 1954; Battle Taxi 1955; The Last Command 1955; Shotgun 1955; Timberjack 1955; The Come On 1956; The Killing 1956; Crime of Passion 1957; Five Steps to Danger 1957; The Iron Sheriff 1957; Valerie 1957; Zero Hour! 1957; Terror in a Texas Town 1958; Dr Strangelove, or How I Learned to Stop Worrying and Love the Bomb 1963; Hard Contract 1969; Sweet Hunters 1969; Loving 1970; The Godfather 1972; The Final Programme 1973; The Long Goodbye 1973; 1900 1976; King of the Gypsies 1978; The Outsider 1979; Winter Kills 1979; Nine to Five 1980; Venom 1981

Haydn, Richard *aka* **Rancyd, Richard** (1905–1985) No Time for Love 1943; Adventure 1945; Forever Amber 1947; The Foxes of Harrow 1947; The Late George Apley 1947; Singapore 1947; The Emperor Waltz 1948; Miss Tatlock's Millions 1948; Sitting Pretty 1948; Alice in Wonderland 1951; The Merry Widow 1952; Money from Home 1953; Never Let Me Go 1953; Her Twelve Men 1954; Jupiter's Darling 1955; Twilight for the Gods 1958; The Lost World 1960; Please Don't Eat the Daisies 1960; Five Weeks in a Balloon 1962; Mutiny on the Bounty 1962; Clarence, the Cross-Eyed Lion 1965; The Sound of Music 1965; The Adventures of Bullwhip Griffin 1967; Young Frankenstein 1974

Haydon, Julie (1910–1994) The Age of Innocence 1934; The Scoundrel 1935; A Family Affair 1937

Haye, Helen (1874–1957) The Skin Game 1931; The Dictator 1935; The 39 Steps 1935; Cotton Queen 1937; Wings of the Morning 1937; The Spy in Black 1939; Kipps 1941; A Place of One's Own 1944; Third Time Lucky 1949; Hobson's Choice 1953; Lilacs in the Spring 1955; My Teenage Daughter 1956; Action of the Tiger 1957; The Gypsy and the Gentleman 1958

Hayek, Salma (1966–) Roadracers 1994; Desperado 1995; Fair Game 1995; Four Rooms 1995; From Dusk till Dawn 1995; Midaq Alley 1995; Breaking Up 1996; Fled 1996; Fools Rush In 1997; The Faculty 1998; 54 1998; The Velocity of Gary 1998; Dogma 1999; No One Writes to the Colonel 1999; Timecode 1999; Wild Wild West 1999; Living It Up 2000; Hotel 2001; Frida 2002; Once upon a Time in Mexico 2003; After the Sunset 2004

Hayenga, Jeff The Prince of Pennsylvania 1988; The Unborn 1991

Hayes, Allison (1930–1977) Sign of the Pagan 1954; Count Three and Pray 1955; The Gunslinger 1956; Mohawk 1956; The Undead 1957; The Unearthly 1957; Attack of the 50 Foot Woman 1958

Hayes, Anthony (1977–) The Boys 1998; Bootmen 2000

Hayes, Bernadene (1903–1987) Great Guy 1936; The Emperor's Candlesticks 1937; Girl Loves Boy 1937; Trouble at Midnight 1937; Dick Tracy's Dilemma 1947; Bunco Squad 1950

Hayes, George "Gabby" *aka* **Hayes, George** (1885–1969) Riders of Destiny 1933; Blue Steel 1934; The Lucky Texan 1934; The Man from Utah 1934; 'Neath the Arizona Skies 1934; Randy Rides Alone 1934; The Star Packer 1934; West of the Divide 1934; The Lawless Frontier 1935; Texas Terror 1935; Land without Music 1936; The Arizona Kid 1939; Come On George 1939; Dark Command 1940; War of the Wildcats 1943; Tall in the Saddle 1944; Bells of Rosarita 1945; Badman's Territory 1946; My Pal Trigger 1946; Trail Street 1947; Return of the Bad Men 1948; The Cariboo Trail 1950

Hayes, Grace (1895–1989) Babes in Arms 1939; Always Leave Them Laughing 1949

Hayes, Helen (1900–1993) Arrowsmith 1931; The Sin of Madelon Claudet 1931; A Farewell to Arms 1932; Night Flight 1933; The White Sister 1933; What Every Woman Knows 1934; Vanessa, Her Love Story 1935; Stage Door Canteen 1943; My Son John 1952; Anastasia 1956; Airport 1970; Herbie Rides Again 1974; One of Our Dinosaurs Is Missing 1975; Victory at Entebbe 1976; Candleshoe 1977; Agatha Christie's A Caribbean Mystery 1983; Agatha Christie's Murder with Mirrors 1985

Hayes, Isaac (1942–) Three Tough Guys 1974; Truck Turner 1974; Escape from New York 1981; I'm Gonna Git You Sucka 1988; Guilty as Charged 1991; Prime Target 1991; Oblivion 1993; Posse 1993; Robin Hood: Men in Tights 1993; It Could Happen to You 1994; Out of Sync

1995; *Flipper* 1996; *illtown* 1996; *Six Ways to Sunday* 1997; *South Park: Bigger, Longer & Uncut* 1999; *Dr Dolittle 2* 2001
Hayes, Linda (1922–1995) *The Girl from Mexico* 1939; *The Spellbinder* 1939; *Mexican Spitfire* 1940; *The Saint in Palm Springs* 1941
Hayes, Margaret *aka* **Hayes, Maggie** (1916–) *The Blackboard Jungle* 1955; *Violent Saturday* 1955; *Beyond the River* 1956; *Omar Khayyam* 1957; *Damn Citizen* 1958; *Good Day for a Hanging* 1958; *The Beat Generation* 1959; *Girls' Town* 1959; *House of Women* 1962; *13 West Street* 1962
Hayes, Melvyn (1935–) *No Trees in the Street* 1958; *Bottoms Up* 1959; *The Young Ones* 1961; *Summer Holiday* 1962; *Crooks in Cloisters* 1963; *Wonderful Life* 1964; *Carry On England* 1976
Hayes, Patricia (1909–1996) *Went the Day Well?* 1942; *The Sicilians* 1964; *Can Heironymus Merkin Ever Forget Mercy Humppe and Find True Happiness?* 1969; *Goodbye, Mr Chips* 1969; *The Best of Benny Hill* 1974; *The NeverEnding Story* 1984; *Little Dorrit* 1987; *A Fish Called Wanda* 1988; *War Requiem* 1988; *Willow* 1988; *The Fool* 1990; *The Last Island* 1990
Hayes, Peter Lind (1915–1998) *Playmates* 1941; *Seven Days' Leave* 1942; *The Senator Was Indiscreet* 1947; *The 5,000 Fingers of Dr T* 1953; *Once You Kiss a Stranger* 1969
Hayes, Sean *aka* **Hayes, Sean P** (1970–) *Billy's Hollywood Screen Kiss* 1998; *Cats & Dogs* 2001; *Pieces of April* 2002; *Dr Seuss' The Cat in the Hat* 2003; *Win a Date with Tad Hamilton!* 2004
Haygarth, Tony *aka* **Haygarth, Anthony** (1945–) *Unman, Wittering and Zigo* 1971; *Dracula* 1979; *A Private Function* 1984; *The Dressmaker* 1988; *Tree of Hands* 1988; *London Kills Me* 1991; *The Infiltrator* 1995; *Amy Foster* 1997; *The Woodlanders* 1997; *Fakers* 2004
Hayman, Cyd (1944–) *Percy* 1971; *The Godsend* 1980
Hayman, David (1950–) *Eye of the Needle* 1981; *Heavenly Pursuits* 1986; *Sid and Nancy* 1986; *Hope and Glory* 1987; *Venus Peter* 1989; *The Near Room* 1995; *Regeneration* 1997; *Ordinary Decent Criminal* 1999; *The Last Great Wilderness* 2002
Haymes, Bob *aka* **Stanton, Robert** (1923–1989) *Mr Winkle Goes to War* 1944; *Abbott and Costello in Hollywood* 1945
Haymes, Dick (1918–1980) *Dramatic School* 1938; *Irish Eyes Are Smiling* 1944; *Billy Rose's Diamond Horseshoe* 1945; *State Fair* 1945; *Do You Love Me?* 1946; *The Shocking Miss Pilgrim* 1947; *One Touch of Venus* 1948; *Up in Central Park* 1948; *All Ashore* 1953
Haynes, Linda (1947–) *Latitude Zero* 1969; *The Drowning Pool* 1975; *Rolling Thunder* 1977
Haynes, Lloyd (1934–1986) *Good Guys Wear Black* 1977; *The Greatest* 1977
Haynes, Roberta (1929–) *The Fighter* 1952; *Gun Fury* 1953; *Return to Paradise* 1953; *Hell Ship Mutiny* 1957
Haynie, Jim *Country* 1984; *Hard Traveling* 1985; *On the Edge* 1985; *Pretty in Pink* 1986; *Jack's Back* 1988; *Dark Angel* 1989; *From Hollywood to Deadwood* 1989; *Staying Together* 1989; *Too Much Sun* 1990; *Sleepwalkers* 1992; *The Bridges of Madison County* 1995
Hays, Kathryn (1933–) *Ladybug, Ladybug* 1963; *Ride beyond Vengeance* 1966; *Counterpoint* 1967
Hays, Robert (1947–) *Airplane!* 1980; *Take This Job and Shove It* 1981; *Utilities* 1981; *Airplane II: the Sequel* 1982; *Scandalous* 1983; *Trenchcoat* 1983; *Cat's Eye* 1984; *For Better or for Worse* 1990; *Fifty/Fifty* 1991; *Good Cop, Bad Cop* 1993; *Homeward Bound: the Incredible Journey* 1993; *No Dessert Dad, Till You Mow the Lawn* 1994; *Danielle Steel's Vanished* 1995; *Homeward Bound II: Lost in San Francisco* 1996; *An American Tail: the Mystery of the Night Monster* 2000
Haysbert, Dennis (1955–) *Love Field* 1992; *Mr Baseball* 1992; *Suture* 1993; *Major League II* 1994; *Waiting to Exhale* 1995; *Absolute Power* 1996; *Major League: Back to the Minors* 1998; *The Minus Man* 1999; *Random Hearts* 1999; *The Thirteenth Floor* 1999; *Love & Basketball* 2000; *What's Cooking?* 2000; *Far from Heaven* 2002; *Sinbad: Legend of the Seven Seas* 2003
Hayter, James (1907–1983) *Big Fella* 1937; *Sailors Three* 1940; *The End of the River* 1947; *Once a Jolly Swagman* 1948; *The Blue Lagoon* 1949; *Trio* 1950; *Tom Brown's Schooldays* 1951; *The Crimson Pirate* 1952; *The Pickwick Papers* 1952; *The Story of Robin Hood and His Merrie Men* 1952; *A Day to Remember* 1953; *Four Sided Triangle* 1953; *Will Any Gentleman...?* 1953; *Beau Brummell* 1954; *Land of the Pharaohs* 1955; *The Big Money* 1956; *It's a Wonderful World* 1956; *Seven Waves Away* 1957; *Gideon's Day* 1958; *The Thirty-Nine Steps* 1959; *A Challenge for Robin Hood* 1967
Hayward, David (1969–) *The Hazing* 1977; *Van Nuys Blvd* 1979
Hayward, Louis (1909–1985) *The Love Test* 1935; *Anthony Adverse* 1936; *Trouble for Two* 1936; *The Woman I Love* 1937; *Condemned Women* 1938; *The Duke of West Point* 1938; *The Rage of Paris* 1938; *The Saint in New York* 1938; *The Man in the Iron Mask* 1939; *Dance, Girl, Dance* 1940; *My Son, My Son!* 1940; *Son of Monte Cristo* 1940; *Ladies in Retirement* 1941; *And Then There Were None* 1945; *The Strange Woman* 1946; *The Black Arrow* 1948; *Ruthless* 1948; *Walk a Crooked Mile* 1948; *House by the River* 1950; *Chuka* 1967
Hayward, Susan (1918–1975) *Hollywood Hotel* 1937; *The Amazing Dr Clitterhouse* 1938; *The Sisters* 1938; *Beau Geste* 1939; *Adam Had Four Sons* 1941; *Among the Living* 1941; *The Forest Rangers* 1942; *I Married a Witch* 1942; *Reap the Wild Wind* 1942; *Star Spangled Rhythm* 1942; *Young and Willing* 1942; *Change of Heart* 1943; *And Now Tomorrow* 1944; *The Fighting Seabees* 1944; *The Hairy Ape* 1944; *Jack London* 1944; *Canyon Passage* 1946; *Deadline at Dawn* 1946; *The Lost Moment* 1947; *Smash Up – the Story of a Woman* 1947; *They Won't Believe Me* 1947; *The Saxon Charm* 1948; *House of Strangers* 1949; *My Foolish Heart* 1949; *Tulsa* 1949; *David and Bathsheba* 1951; *I Can Get It for You Wholesale* 1951; *I'd Climb the Highest Mountain* 1951; *Rawhide* 1951; *The Lusty Men* 1952; *The Snows of Kilimanjaro* 1952; *With a Song in My Heart* 1952; *The President's Lady* 1953; *White Witch Doctor* 1953; *Demetrius and the Gladiators* 1954; *Garden of Evil* 1954; *I'll Cry Tomorrow* 1955; *Soldier of Fortune* 1955; *Untamed* 1955; *The Conqueror* 1956; *Top Secret Affair* 1957; *I Want to Live!* 1958; *Thunder in the Sun* 1959; *Woman Obsessed* 1959; *The Marriage-Go-Round* 1960; *Ada* 1961; *Back Street* 1961; *I Thank a Fool* 1962; *Stolen Hours* 1963; *Where Love Has Gone* 1964; *The Honey Pot* 1967; *Valley of the Dolls* 1967; *The Revengers* 1972
Haywood, Chris (1949–) *Breaker Morant* 1979; *Attack Force Z* 1981; *Heatwave* 1981; *The Clinic* 1982; *The Man from Snowy River* 1982; *Man of Flowers* 1984; *Razorback* 1984; *The Coca-Cola Kid* 1985; *A Street to Die* 1985; *Dogs in Space* 1986; *Malcolm* 1986; *The Navigator – a Medieval Odyssey* 1988; *Island* 1989; *Quigley Down Under* 1990; *Golden Braid* 1991; *A Woman's Tale* 1991; *The Nun and the Bandit* 1992; *Blackrock* 1997; *Kiss or Kill* 1997
Haywood, Roy *Bronco Bullfrog* 1970; *Looks and Smiles* 1981
Hayworth, Rita *aka* **Cansino, Rita** (1918–1987) *Charlie Chan in Egypt* 1935; *Dante's Inferno* 1935; *Human Cargo* 1936; *Meet Nero Wolfe* 1936; *Girls Can Play* 1937; *Hit the Saddle* 1937; *Trouble in Texas* 1937; *Old Louisiana* 1938; *There's Always a Woman* 1938; *Who Killed Gail Preston?* 1938; *The Lone Wolf Spy Hunt* 1939; *Only Angels Have Wings* 1939; *Angels over Broadway* 1940; *The Lady in Question* 1940; *Music in My Heart* 1940; *Susan and God* 1940; *Affectionately Yours* 1941; *Blood and Sand* 1941; *The Strawberry Blonde* 1941; *You'll Never Get Rich* 1941; *My Gal Sal* 1942; *Tales of Manhattan* 1942; *You Were Never Lovelier* 1942; *Cover Girl* 1944; *Tonight and Every Night* 1945; *Gilda* 1946; *Down to Earth* 1947; *The Lady from Shanghai* 1948; *The Loves of Carmen* 1948; *Affair in Trinidad* 1952; *Miss Sadie Thompson* 1953; *Salome* 1953; *Fire Down Below* 1957; *Pal Joey* 1957; *Separate Tables* 1958; *The Story on Page One* 1959; *They Came to Cordura* 1959; *The Happy Thieves* 1962; *The Magnificent Showman* 1964; *The Money Trap* 1966; *The Poppy Is Also a Flower* 1966; *The Rover* 1967; *Road to Salina* 1969; *The Wrath of God* 1972
Haze, Jonathan (1929–) *Five Guns West* 1955; *The Gunslinger* 1956; *Not of This Earth* 1956; *Stakeout on Dope Street* 1958; *Forbidden Island* 1959; *The Little Shop of Horrors* 1960
Hazell, Hy (1919–1970) *Celia* 1949; *Forces' Sweetheart* 1953; *Trouble with Eve* 1959
Hazlehurst, Noni (1954–) *Monkey Grip* 1983; *The Shiralee* 1986; *Waiting* 1990
He Caifei *Raise the Red Lantern* 1991; *Temptress Moon* 1996
Head, Anthony (1954–) *Lady Chatterley's Lover* 1981; *Fat Slags* 2004
Head, Edith (1907–1981) *Lucy Gallant* 1955; *The Pleasure of His Company* 1961; *The Oscar* 1966
Head, Murray (1946–) *Sunday, Bloody Sunday* 1971; *Gawain and the Green Knight* 1973
Headey, Lena (1976–) *Waterland* 1992; *Century* 1993; *The Jungle Book* 1994; *The Grotesque* 1995; *Face* 1997; *Mrs Dalloway* 1997; *If Only* 1998; *Gossip* 1999; *Onegin* 1999; *Aberdeen* 2000; *Anazapta* 2001; *The Parole Officer* 2001; *Possession* 2002; *Ripley's Game* 2002; *The Actors* 2003
Headly, Glenne (1955–) *Eleni* 1985; *Making Mr Right* 1987; *Nadine* 1987; *Dirty Rotten Scoundrels* 1988; *Paperhouse* 1988; *Dick Tracy* 1990; *Mortal Thoughts* 1991; *And the Band Played On* 1993; *Ordinary Magic* 1993; *Getting Even with Dad* 1994; *Mr Holland's Opus* 1995; *Sgt Bilko* 1996; *2 Days in the Valley* 1996; *Babe: Pig in the City* 1998; *Breakfast of Champions* 1999; *Timecode* 1999; *Bartleby* 2000; *What's the Worst That Could Happen?* 2001; *Around the Bend* 2004; *Confessions of a Teenage Drama Queen* 2004
Heald, Anthony (1944–) *Orphans* 1987; *Outrageous Fortune* 1987; *The Silence of the Lambs* 1991; *Bushwhacked* 1995; *Deep Rising* 1998; *8mm* 1999; *Red Dragon* 2002
Healey, Myron (1922–) *Count Three and Pray* 1955; *Gang Busters* 1955; *Rage at Dawn* 1955; *The Unearthly* 1957; *The Incredible Melting Man* 1977
Healy, Darren *Crush Proof* 1998; *Disco Pigs* 2001
Healy, David (1932–1995) *The Sign of Four* 1983; *The Unbelievable Truth* 1989
Healy, Dorian *For Queen and Country* 1988; *Young Soul Rebels* 1991
Healy, Mary (1918–) *Second Fiddle* 1939; *Star Dust* 1940; *The 5,000 Fingers of Dr T* 1953
Healy, Ted (1896–1937) *Blonde Bombshell* 1933; *Dancing Lady* 1933; *Meet the Baron* 1933; *Hollywood Party* 1934; *Operator 13* 1934; *The Casino Murder Case* 1935; *Mad Love* 1935; *Reckless* 1935; *San Francisco* 1936; *Sing, Baby, Sing* 1936; *Speed* 1936; *Hollywood Hotel* 1937
Healy, Tim (1952–) *Shadow Run* 1998; *Purely Belter* 2000; *School for Seduction* 2004
Heard, John (1946–) *Between the Lines* 1977; *First Love* 1977; *On the Yard* 1978; *Chilly Scenes of Winter* 1979; *Heart Beat* 1979; *Cutter's Way* 1981; *Cat People* 1982; *Too Scared to Scream* 1982; *Best Revenge* 1983; *CHUD* 1984; *After Hours* 1985; *Catholic Boys* 1985; *The Trip to Bountiful* 1985; *Beaches* 1988; *Betrayed* 1988; *Big* 1988; *The Milagro Beanfield War* 1988; *The Seventh Sign* 1988; *The Telephone* 1988; *The Package* 1989; *Awakenings* 1990; *The End of Innocence* 1990; *Home Alone* 1990; *Mindwalk* 1990; *Deceived* 1991; *Rambling Rose* 1991; *Gladiator* 1992; *Home Alone 2: Lost in New York* 1992; *Radio Flyer* 1992; *Waterland* 1992; *The Pelican Brief* 1993; *Before and After* 1996; *My Fellow Americans* 1996; *One Eight Seven* 1997; *Desert Blue* 1998; *Executive Power* 1998; *Snake Eyes* 1998; *Animal Factory* 2000; *Pollock* 2000; *The Pilot's Wife* 2001; *White Chicks* 2004
Hearn, Ann *The Dollmaker* 1984; *The Accused* 1988; *Omen IV: the Awakening* 1991; *My Father the Hero* 1994; *The War at Home* 1996
Hearn, George (1934–) *A Piano for Mrs Cimino* 1982; *See You in the Morning* 1989; *The Vanishing* 1993; *Annie: a Royal Adventure* 1995; *All Dogs Go to Heaven 2* 1996; *The Devil's Own* 1997; *Barney's Great Adventure* 1998
Hearne, Richard (1908–1979) *Miss London Ltd* 1943; *Something in the City* 1950; *Miss Robin Hood* 1952; *The Time of His Life* 1955
Hearst, Patricia (1954–) *Cry-Baby* 1989; *Serial Mom* 1994; *Bio-Dome* 1996; *Pecker* 1998; *A Dirty Shame* 2004
Heath, Gordon (1918–1991) *Animal Farm* 1954; *Sapphire* 1959; *Asterix vs Caesar* 1985
Heather, Jean (1921–) *Double Indemnity* 1944; *Going My Way* 1944; *Murder, He Says* 1945
Heatherley, Clifford (1888–1937) *Champagne* 1928; *Bitter Sweet* 1933
Heatherly, May *Love and Pain and the Whole Damn Thing* 1973; *Crystal Heart* 1987
Heatherton, Joey (1944–) *Twilight of Honor* 1963; *Where Love Has Gone* 1964; *My Blood Runs Cold* 1965; *Bluebeard* 1972; *The Happy Hooker Goes to Washington* 1977
Heavener, David *Outlaw Force* 1988; *Prime Target* 1991; *Eye of the Stranger* 1993
Hebert, Chris (1973–) *The Last Starfighter* 1984; *The Check Is in the Mail* 1986
Heche, Anne (1969–) *The Adventures of Huck Finn* 1993; *Against the Wall* 1994; *Milk Money* 1994; *Pie in the Sky* 1995; *Wild Side* 1995; *If These Walls Could Talk* 1996; *The Juror* 1996; *Walking and Talking* 1996; *Donnie Brasco* 1997; *I Know What You Did Last Summer* 1997; *Subway Stories: Tales from the Underground* 1997; *Volcano* 1997; *Wag the Dog* 1997; *Psycho* 1998; *Return to Paradise* 1998; *Six Days Seven Nights* 1998; *Auggie Rose* 2000; *One Kill* 2000; *John Q* 2001; *Birth* 2004
Hecht, Ben (1894–1964) *The Scoundrel* 1935; *Specter of the Rose* 1946
Hecht, Gina (1953–) *Night Shift* 1982; *Unfinished Business...* 1987; *One Night Stand* 1994
Hecht, Jessica (1965–) *The Forgotten* 2004; *Sideways* 2004
Heckart, Eileen (1919–2001) *The Bad Seed* 1956; *Bus Stop* 1956; *Miracle in the Rain* 1956; *Somebody Up There Likes Me* 1956; *Hot Spell* 1958; *Heller in Pink Tights* 1960; *My Six Loves* 1962; *Up the Down Staircase* 1967; *No Way to Treat a Lady* 1968; *Butterflies Are Free* 1972; *Zandy's Bride* 1974; *The Hiding Place* 1975; *Burnt Offerings* 1976; *Heartbreak Ridge* 1986; *Ultimate Betrayal* 1994
Hedaya, Dan (1940–) *Night of the Juggler* 1980; *Endangered Species* 1982; *Blood Simple* 1983; *The Hunger* 1983; *Tightrope* 1984; *Commando* 1985; *Running Scared* 1986; *Wise Guys* 1986; *Aunt Julia and the Scriptwriter* 1990; *Joe versus the Volcano* 1990; *The Addams Family* 1991; *Mr Wonderful* 1992; *Benny and Joon* 1993; *Rookie of the Year* 1993; *Clueless* 1995; *To Die For* 1995; *The Usual Suspects* 1995; *Daylight* 1996; *The First Wives Club* 1996; *Freeway* 1996; *Marvin's Room* 1996; *Alien: Resurrection* 1997; *A Life Less Ordinary* 1997; *The Second Civil War* 1997; *A Civil Action* 1998; *A Night at the Roxbury* 1998; *Dick* 1999; *The Hurricane* 1999; *Shaft* 2000; *Mulholland Drive* 2001; *Swimfan* 2002; *American Cousins* 2003
Hedin, Serene *Windwalker* 1980; *Sacred Ground* 1983; *Hawken's Breed* 1989
Hedison, David *aka* **Hedison, Al** (1927–) *The Enemy Below* 1957; *The Fly* 1958; *Son of Robin Hood* 1958; *The Lost World* 1960; *Live and Let Die* 1973; *North Sea Hijack* 1979; *The Naked Face* 1984
Hedley, Jack (1930–) *Left, Right and Centre* 1959; *Make Mine Mink* 1960; *The Very Edge* 1962; *In the French Style* 1963; *The Scarlet Blade* 1963; *Of Human Bondage* 1964; *The Secret of Blood Island* 1964; *How I Won the War* 1967; *The Anniversary* 1968; *Brief Encounter* 1974
Hedren, Tippi *aka* **Hedren, "Tippi"** (1935–) *The Petty Girl* 1950; *The Birds* 1963; *Marnie* 1964; *Satan's Harvest* 1965; *A Countess from Hong Kong* 1967; *Mr Kingstreet's War* 1970; *Tiger by the Tail* 1970; *The Harrad Experiment* 1973; *Roar* 1981; *Pacific Heights* 1990; *Citizen Ruth* 1996; *Break Up* 1998; *I Woke Up Early the Day I Died* 1998
Heffernan, John (1934–) *Puzzle of a Downfall Child* 1970; *The Sting* 1973
Heffley, Wayne (1927–) *Crime and Punishment, USA* 1959; *Submarine Seahawk* 1959
Heffner, Kyle T *Flashdance* 1983; *Runaway Train* 1985
Heflin, Marta *A Star Is Born* 1976; *A Perfect Couple* 1979; *Come Back to the Five and Dime, Jimmy Dean, Jimmy Dean* 1982
Heflin, Nora *Fantastic Planet* 1973; *Chilly Scenes of Winter* 1979
Heflin, Van (1910–1971) *A Woman Rebels* 1936; *Flight from Glory* 1937; *Back Door to Heaven* 1939; *Santa Fe Trail* 1940; *The Feminine Touch* 1941; *HM Pulham Esq* 1941; *Johnny Eager* 1941; *Grand Central Murder* 1942; *Kid Glove Killer* 1942; *Tennessee Johnson* 1942; *Presenting Lily Mars* 1943; *The Strange Love of Martha Ivers* 1946; *Till the Clouds Roll By* 1946; *Green Dolphin Street* 1947; *Possessed* 1947; *BF's Daughter* 1948; *The Three Musketeers* 1948; *Act of Violence* 1949; *East Side, West Side* 1949; *Madame Bovary* 1949; *The Prowler* 1951; *Tomahawk* 1951;

Weekend with Father 1951; *My Son John* 1952; *South of Algiers* 1952; *Shane* 1953; *Black Widow* 1954; *The Raid* 1954; *Tanganyika* 1954; *Woman's World* 1954; *Battle Cry* 1955; *Count Three and Pray* 1955; *Patterns* 1956; *3:10 to Yuma* 1957; *Gunman's Walk* 1958; *Tempest* 1959; *They Came to Cordura* 1959; *Five Branded Women* 1960; *Under Ten Flags* 1960; *Once a Thief* 1965; *Stagecoach* 1966; *The Big Bounce* 1969; *Airport* 1970

Heggie, O P (1879–1936) *The Letter* 1929; *One Romantic Night* 1930; *East Lynne* 1931; *Smilin' Through* 1932; *Zoo in Budapest* 1933; *Anne of Green Gables* 1934; *The Count of Monte Cristo* 1934; *Midnight* 1934

Hehir, Peter (1949–) *A Street to Die* 1985; *Kangaroo* 1986

Heigl, Katherine (1978–) *That Night* 1992; *My Father the Hero* 1994; *Under Siege 2* 1995; *Prince Valiant* 1997; *Bride of Chucky* 1998; *Valentine* 2001

Heilbron, Lorna *The Creeping Flesh* 1972; *The Girl in a Swing* 1988

Heineman, Laurie *Save the Tiger* 1973; *The Lady in Red* 1979

Heinz, Gerard (1904–1972) *Caravan* 1946; *The Lost People* 1949; *That Dangerous Age* 1949; *Traveller's Joy* 1949; *Desperate Moment* 1953

Held, Ingrid *Gunbus* 1986; *The Last Butterfly* 1990; *Après l'Amour* 1992

Heldfond, Susan *Why Would I Lie?* 1980; *Love and Money* 1982

Helgenberger, Marg (1958–) *After Midnight* 1989; *The Cowboy Way* 1994; *Bad Boys* 1995; *Species* 1995; *Fire Down Below* 1997; *Species II* 1998; *Happy Face Murders* 1999; *Erin Brockovich* 2000; *In Good Company* 2004

Hélia, Jenny *Toni* 1935; *La Bête Humaine* 1938

Hell, Erik (1911–1973) *Port of Call* 1948; *A Passion* 1969; *The Rite* 1969

Heller, Ariane *Up the Sandbox* 1972; *Mixed Company* 1974

Heller, Barbara *Hey Boy! Hey Girl!* 1959; *The Comic* 1969

Hellman, Jaclyn aka **Hellman, Jacqueline** *Flight to Fury* 1966; *Two-Lane Blacktop* 1971

Helm, Anne (1938–) *Follow That Dream* 1962; *The Interns* 1962; *The Iron Maiden* 1962; *The Magic Sword* 1962; *The Unkissed Bride* 1966

Helm, Brigitte (1906–1996) *Metropolis* 1926; *Alraune* 1927; *The Love of Jeanne Ney* 1927; *Crisis* 1928; *The Wonderful Lie of Nina Petrovna* 1929

Helm, Fay (1913–2003) *Blondie!* 1938; *Calling Dr Death* 1943; *Phantom Lady* 1944; *The Falcon in San Francisco* 1945

Helm, Levon (1943–) *Coal Miner's Daughter* 1980; *Best Revenge* 1983; *The Dollmaker* 1984; *Smooth Talk* 1985; *End of the Line* 1987; *Staying Together* 1989; *Feeling Minnesota* 1996

Helmond, Katherine (1934–) *Larry* 1974; *Family Plot* 1976; *Time Bandits* 1981; *Brazil* 1985; *Shadey* 1985; *Overboard* 1987; *Lady in White* 1988; *Amore!* 1993; *Living in Fear* 2001

Helmore, Tom (1904–1995) *Trouble along the Way* 1953; *Lucy Gallant* 1955; *Designing Woman* 1957; *Vertigo* 1958; *Count Your Blessings* 1959; *The Time Machine* 1960; *Flipper's New Adventure* 1964

Helpmann, Robert (1909–1986) *Caravan* 1946; *The Red Shoes* 1948; *The Tales of Hoffmann* 1951; *The Big Money* 1956; *The Iron Petticoat* 1956; *The Quiller Memorandum* 1966; *Alice's Adventures in Wonderland* 1972; *Don Quixote* 1973; *Patrick* 1978

Helton, Percy (1894–1971) *The Set-Up* 1949; *Jail Busters* 1955

Hemblen, David *Family Viewing* 1987; *Short Circuit 2* 1988; *Speaking Parts* 1989; *The Adjuster* 1991; *I Love a Man in Uniform* 1993; *Brainscan* 1994; *Exotica* 1994; *Mesmer* 1994; *Hollow Point* 1996; *Rollerball* 2001

Hembrow, Mark (1955–) *High Tide* 1987; *Out of the Body* 1988; *Return to Snowy River* 1988; *The Last Island* 1990; *Redheads* 1992

Hemingway, Margaux (1955–1996) *Lipstick* 1976; *Killer Fish* 1978; *They Call Me Bruce* 1982; *Over the Brooklyn Bridge* 1983

Hemingway, Mariel (1961–) *Lipstick* 1976; *Manhattan* 1979; *Personal Best* 1982; *Star 80* 1983; *Creator* 1985; *The Mean Season* 1985; *Superman IV: the Quest for Peace* 1987; *Sunset* 1988; *Delirious* 1991; *Falling from Grace* 1992; *Bad Moon* 1996; *Deconstructing Harry* 1997; *The Sex Monster* 1998; *First Daughter* 1999; *Londinium* 1999

Hemmings, David (1941–2003) *The Painted Smile* 1961; *The Wind of Change* 1961; *Some People* 1962; *Live It Up* 1963; *Two Left Feet* 1963; *The System* 1964; *Be My Guest* 1965; *Blowup* 1966; *Eye of the Devil* 1966; *Barbarella* 1967; *Camelot* 1967; *The Best House in London* 1968; *The Charge of the Light Brigade* 1968; *The Long Day's Dying* 1968; *Only When I Larf* 1968; *Alfred the Great* 1969; *Fragment of Fear* 1970; *The Walking Stick* 1970; *The Love Machine* 1971; *Unman, Wittering and Zigo* 1971; *Juggernaut* 1974; *Deep Red* 1975; *Mister Quilp* 1975; *Islands in the Stream* 1976; *Blood Relatives* 1977; *The Disappearance* 1977; *The Prince and the Pauper* 1977; *The Squeeze* 1977; *Just a Gigolo* 1978; *Murder by Decree* 1978; *Power Play* 1978; *Thirst* 1979; *Beyond Reasonable Doubt* 1980; *Harlequin* 1980; *Man, Woman and Child* 1983; *The Rainbow* 1988; *Last Orders* 2001; *Mean Machine* 2001; *Spy Game* 2001; *Gangs of New York* 2002; *The League of Extraordinary Gentlemen* 2003; *The Night We Called It a Day* 2003

Hempel, Anouska (1941–) *The Scars of Dracula* 1970; *Tiffany Jones* 1973

Hemsley, Estelle (1887–1968) *Take a Giant Step* 1959; *America, America* 1963; *Baby the Rain Must Fall* 1965

Hemsley, Sherman (1938–) *Love at First Bite* 1979; *Mr Nanny* 1992; *Screwed* 2000

Hendel, Paolo (1952–) *The Night of San Lorenzo* 1981; *Three Sisters* 1988

Henderson, Albert (1915–2004) *Greaser's Palace* 1972; *Big Top Pee-wee* 1988

Henderson, Bill (1925–) *Trouble Man* 1972; *Inside Moves: the Guys from Max's Bar* 1980; *Continental Divide* 1981; *Murphy's Law* 1986; *Wisdom* 1986; *Trippin'* 1999

Henderson, Dell (1883–1956) *The Crowd* 1928; *The Patsy* 1928; *Show People* 1928

Henderson, Don (1931–1997) *Callan* 1974; *The Ghoul* 1975; *The Island* 1980; *The Chinese Connection* 1988; *As You Like It* 1992; *The Baby of Macon* 1993; *White Angel* 1993; *No Escape* 1994

Henderson, Florence (1934–) *Song of Norway* 1970; *Shakes the Clown* 1991

Henderson, Marcia (1929–1987) *All I Desire* 1953; *Back to God's Country* 1953; *The Glass Web* 1953; *Thunder Bay* 1953; *Naked Alibi* 1954; *Timbuktu* 1959; *A Dog's Best Friend* 1960

Henderson, Martin (1974–) *Kick* 1999; *The Ring* 2002; *Skagerrak* 2003; *Torque* 2003; *Bride & Prejudice* 2004

Henderson, Shirley (1966–) *Salt on Our Skin* 1992; *Topsy-Turvy* 1999; *Wonderland* 1999; *The Claim* 2000; *Bridget Jones's Diary* 2001; *24 Hour Party People* 2001; *Doctor Sleep* 2002; *Harry Potter and the Chamber of Secrets* 2002; *Once upon a Time in the Midlands* 2002; *Villa des Roses* 2002; *Wilbur (Wants to Kill Himself)* 2002; *AfterLife* 2003; *American Cousins* 2003; *interMission* 2003; *Bridget Jones: the Edge of Reason* 2004; *Yes* 2004

Henderson, Ty *The Competition* 1980; *Happy Hour* 1987

Hendrickson, Benjamin *Manhunter* 1986; *Spanking the Monkey* 1994

Hendrix, Elaine (1971–) *Romy and Michele's High School Reunion* 1997; *The Parent Trap* 1998; *Superstar* 1999; *What the #$*! Do We Know!?* 2004

Hendrix, Wanda (1928–1981) *Confidential Agent* 1945; *Welcome Stranger* 1947; *Miss Tatlock's Millions* 1948; *Prince of Foxes* 1949; *The Admiral Was a Lady* 1950; *Captain Carey, USA* 1950; *Saddle Tramp* 1950; *Sierra* 1950; *South of Algiers* 1952; *The Last Posse* 1953; *The Boy Who Caught a Crook* 1961

Hendry, Gloria (1945–) *Black Caesar* 1973; *Hell Up in Harlem* 1973; *Live and Let Die* 1973; *Slaughter's Big Rip-Off* 1973; *Black Belt Jones* 1974; *The Revenge of Pumpkinhead – Blood Wings* 1994

Hendry, Ian (1931–1984) *Live Now – Pay Later* 1962; *Girl in the Headlines* 1963; *This Is My Street* 1963; *The Beauty Jungle* 1964; *Children of the Damned* 1964; *The Hill* 1965; *Repulsion* 1965; *The Sandwich Man* 1966; *Journey to the Far Side of the Sun* 1969; *The Southern Star* 1969; *The McKenzie Break* 1970; *Get Carter* 1971; *All Coppers Are...* 1972; *Captain Kronos: Vampire Hunter* 1972; *The Jerusalem File* 1972; *Tales from the Crypt* 1972; *Assassin* 1973; *Theatre of Blood* 1973; *The Internecine Project* 1974; *The Passenger* 1975; *The Bitch* 1979; *McVicar* 1980

Henfrey, Janet *She'll Be Wearing Pink Pyjamas* 1984; *The Nine Lives of Tomas Katz* 1999

Henie, Sonja (1912–1969) *One in a Million* 1936; *Thin Ice* 1937; *Happy Landing* 1938; *My Lucky Star* 1938; *Second Fiddle* 1939; *Sun Valley Serenade* 1941; *Wintertime* 1943; *It's a Pleasure* 1945; *The Countess of Monte Cristo* 1948

Henley, Barry "Shabaka" aka **Henley, Barry Shabaka** *Collateral* 2004; *The Terminal* 2004

Henner, Marilu (1952–) *Between the Lines* 1977; *Bloodbrothers* 1978; *Hammett* 1982; *The Man Who Loved Women* 1983; *Johnny Dangerously* 1984; *Perfect* 1985; *Rustler's Rhapsody* 1985; *Chains of Gold* 1989; *LA Story* 1991; *Noises Off* 1992

Hennessy, Jill (1969–) *RoboCop 3* 1993; *Most Wanted* 1997; *A Smile like Yours* 1997; *Komodo* 1999; *Molly* 1999; *Exit Wounds* 2001

Henney, Del *Straw Dogs* 1971; *Brannigan* 1975

Henning, Eva (1920–) *The Devil's Wanton* 1949; *Three Strange Loves* 1949

Henning, Uno (1895–1970) *The Love of Jeanne Ney* 1927; *Three Loves* 1929

Henreid, Paul (1908–1992) *Goodbye, Mr Chips* 1939; *Night Train to Munich* 1940; *Casablanca* 1942; *Joan of Paris* 1942; *Now, Voyager* 1942; *Between Two Worlds* 1944; *The Conspirators* 1944; *In Our Time* 1944; *The Spanish Main* 1945; *Deception* 1946; *Devotion* 1946; *Of Human Bondage* 1946; *Song of Love* 1947; *Hollow Triumph* 1948; *Rope of Sand* 1949; *Mantrap* 1952; *Stolen Face* 1952; *Thief of Damascus* 1952; *Deep in My Heart* 1954; *Battle Shock* 1956; *Ten Thousand Bedrooms* 1957; *Holiday for Lovers* 1959; *Never So Few* 1959; *The Four Horsemen of the Apocalypse* 1962; *Operation Crossbow* 1965; *The Madwoman of Chaillot* 1969; *Exorcist II: The Heretic* 1977

Henriksen, Lance (1940–) *Mansion of the Doomed* 1975; *Damien – Omen II* 1978; *The Visitor* 1980; *Piranha II: the Spawning* 1981; *The Right Stuff* 1983; *The Terminator* 1984; *Jagged Edge* 1985; *Savage Dawn* 1985; *Aliens* 1986; *On Dangerous Ground* 1986; *Near Dark* 1987; *Hit List* 1988; *Pumpkinhead* 1988; *House III: The Horror Show* 1989; *Johnny Handsome* 1989; *The Pit and the Pendulum* 1991; *Stone Cold* 1991; *Alien^3* 1992; *Jennifer Eight* 1992; *Excessive Force* 1993; *Hard Target* 1993; *Man's Best Friend* 1993; *The Outfit* 1993; *Bad Company* 1994; *Boulevard* 1994; *Color of Night* 1994; *No Escape* 1994; *The Criminal Mind* 1995; *Dead Man* 1995; *Powder* 1995; *The Quick and the Dead* 1995; *Wes Craven's Mind Ripper* 1995; *Dusting Cliff 7* 1996; *Scream 3* 1999; *Tarzan* 1999; *AVP: Alien vs Predator* 2004

Henrikson, Anders (1896–1965) *A Woman's Face* 1938; *The Devil's Wanton* 1949

Henriksson, Krister (1946–) *Faithless* 2000; *Reconstruction* 2003

Henritze, Bette *Other People's Money* 1991; *Judy Berlin* 1999

Henry, Buck (1930–) *The Troublemaker* 1964; *Catch-22* 1970; *Is There Sex after Death?* 1971; *Taking Off* 1971; *The Man Who Fell to Earth* 1976; *Heaven Can Wait* 1978; *Old Boyfriends* 1979; *First Family* 1980; *Gloria* 1980; *Eating Raoul* 1982; *Aria* 1987; *Rude Awakening* 1989; *Defending Your Life* 1991; *The Linguini Incident* 1991; *Even Cowgirls Get the Blues* 1993; *Grumpy Old Men* 1993; *Curtain Call* 1998; *I'm Losing You* 1998; *Breakfast of Champions* 1999; *Town & Country* 2001

Henry, Charlotte (1913–1980) *Alice in Wonderland* 1933; *Babes in Toyland* 1934; *The Last Gentleman* 1934; *Charlie Chan at the Opera* 1936

Henry, Gloria (1923–) *Bulldog Drummond Strikes Back* 1947; *Johnny Allegro* 1949; *Miss Grant Takes Richmond* 1949; *Riders in the Sky* 1949; *Rancho Notorious* 1952; *Gang War* 1958

Henry, Gregg (1952–) *Mean Dog Blues* 1978; *Just before Dawn* 1980; *Body Double* 1984; *The Patriot* 1986; *Raising Cain* 1992; *Payback* 1998; *Layover* 2000; *Ballistic: Ecks vs Sever* 2002; *Femme Fatale* 2002

Henry, Guy *Caught in the Act* 1996; *Bright Young Things* 2003

Henry, Hank (1906–1981) *Pal Joey* 1957; *Pepe* 1960; *Robin and the 7 Hoods* 1964; *The Only Game in Town* 1970

Henry, Judith *Germinal* 1993; *Les Apprentis* 1995

Henry, Justin (1971–) *Kramer vs Kramer* 1979; *Martin's Day* 1984; *Sixteen Candles* 1984; *Sweet Hearts Dance* 1988

Henry, Louise (1912–) *Reckless* 1935; *Remember Last Night?* 1935; *There Goes the Groom* 1937

Henry, Martha (1938–) *Dancing in the Dark* 1986; *Long Day's Journey into Night* 1996; *Clean* 2004

Henry, Mike (1939–) *Tarzan and the Valley of Gold* 1966; *Tarzan and the Great River* 1967; *Tarzan and the Jungle Boy* 1968; *More Dead than Alive* 1969; *Smokey and the Bandit* 1977; *Smokey and the Bandit III* 1983

Henry, Thomas Browne aka **Henry, Tom Browne** aka **Henry, Thomas B** (1907–1980) *Earth vs the Flying Saucers* 1956; *Blood of Dracula* 1957; *20 Million Miles to Earth* 1957; *The Brain from Planet Arous* 1958; *Showdown at Boot Hill* 1958; *Space Master X 7* 1958

Henry, Victor (1943–1985) *The Sorcerers* 1967; *All Neat in Black Stockings* 1969

Henry, William (1918–1982) *Tarzan Escapes* 1936; *Madame X* 1937; *Four Men and a Prayer* 1938; *Geronimo* 1939; *The Way of All Flesh* 1940; *The Adventures of Mark Twain* 1944; *Secret of the Incas* 1954

Henshall, Douglas (1967–) *Angels and Insects* 1995; *Kull the Conqueror* 1997; *Fast Food* 1998; *If Only* 1998; *Orphans* 1998; *This Year's Love* 1999; *The Lawless Heart* 2001; *It's All about Love* 2002

Hensley, Pamela (1950–) *Rollerball* 1975; *Buck Rogers in the 25th Century* 1979

Henson, Brian (1963–) *Return to Oz* 1985; *Labyrinth* 1986

Henson, Elden (1977–) *The Mighty* 1998; *Idle Hands* 1999; *Manic* 2001; *The Butterfly Effect* 2003; *Dumb and Dumberer: When Harry Met Lloyd* 2003

Henson, Gladys (1897–1982) *The Captive Heart* 1946; *The Blue Lamp* 1949; *The Cure for Love* 1949; *Train of Events* 1949; *Dance Hall* 1950; *The Magnet* 1950; *Lady Godiva Rides Again* 1951; *Derby Day* 1952; *The Leather Boys* 1963

Henson, Jim (1936–1990) *The Muppet Movie* 1979; *The Great Muppet Caper* 1981; *The Muppets Take Manhattan* 1984; *Sesame Street Presents: Follow That Bird* 1985

Henson, Leslie (1891–1957) *It's a Boy* 1933; *Oh, Daddy!* 1935; *Home and Away* 1956

Henson, Nicky (1945–) *Witchfinder General* 1968; *Crooks and Coronets* 1969; *There's a Girl in My Soup* 1970; *All Coppers Are...* 1972; *Psychomania* 1972; *Penny Gold* 1973; *Vampira* 1975; *The Bawdy Adventures of Tom Jones* 1976; *Me without You* 2001

Henstridge, Natasha (1974–) *Adrenalin: Fear the Rush* 1995; *Species* 1995; *Maximum Risk* 1996; *Dog Park* 1998; *Species II* 1998; *A Better Way to Die* 2000; *Bounce* 2000; *The Whole Nine Yards* 2000; *John Carpenter's Ghosts of Mars* 2001; *Steal* 2002; *The Whole Ten Yards* 2004

Hepburn, Audrey (1929–1993) *Laughter in Paradise* 1951; *The Lavender Hill Mob* 1951; *The Secret People* 1951; *Young Wives' Tale* 1951; *Roman Holiday* 1953; *Sabrina* 1954; *War and Peace* 1956; *Funny Face* 1957; *Love in the Afternoon* 1957; *Green Mansions* 1959; *The Nun's Story* 1959; *The Unforgiven* 1960; *Breakfast at Tiffany's* 1961; *The Children's Hour* 1961; *Charade* 1963; *My Fair Lady* 1964; *Paris When It Sizzles* 1964; *How to Steal a Million* 1966; *Two for the Road* 1967; *Wait until Dark* 1967; *Robin and Marian* 1976; *Bloodline* 1979; *They All Laughed* 1981; *Always* 1989

Hepburn, Katharine (1907–2003) *A Bill of Divorcement* 1932; *Christopher Strong* 1933; *Little Women* 1933; *Morning Glory* 1933; *The Little Minister* 1934; *Spitfire* 1934; *Alice Adams* 1935; *Break of Hearts* 1935; *Mary of Scotland* 1936; *Sylvia Scarlett* 1936; *A Woman Rebels* 1936; *Quality Street* 1937; *Stage Door* 1937; *Bringing Up Baby* 1938; *Holiday* 1938; *The Philadelphia Story* 1940; *Keeper of the Flame* 1942; *Woman of the Year* 1942; *Stage Door Canteen* 1943; *Dragon Seed* 1944; *Without Love* 1945; *Undercurrent* 1946; *The Sea of Grass* 1947; *Song of Love* 1947; *State of the Union* 1948; *Adam's Rib* 1949; *The African Queen* 1951; *Pat and Mike* 1952; *Summertime* 1955; *The Iron Petticoat* 1956; *The Rainmaker* 1956; *Desk Set* 1957; *Suddenly, Last Summer* 1959; *Long Day's Journey into Night* 1962; *Guess Who's Coming to Dinner* 1967; *The Lion in Winter* 1968; *The Madwoman of Chaillot* 1969; *The Trojan Women* 1971; *A Delicate Balance* 1973; *Love among the Ruins* 1975; *Rooster Cogburn* 1975; *The Great Balloon Adventure* 1978; *On Golden Pond*

1981; *Grace Quigley* 1984; *Mrs Delafield Wants to Marry* 1986; *Love Affair* 1994

Hepton, Bernard (1925–) *Henry VIII and His Six Wives* 1972; *The Plague Dogs* 1982; *Shadey* 1985; *Stealing Heaven* 1988; *Eminent Domain* 1991

Herbert, Charles (1948–) *The Colossus of New York* 1958; *The Fly* 1958; *13 Ghosts* 1959

Herbert, Holmes (1882–1956) *When a Man Loves* 1926; *The Kiss* 1929; *Madame X* 1929; *Say It with Songs* 1929; *Dr Jekyll and Mr Hyde* 1931; *Accent on Youth* 1935; *Mark of the Vampire* 1935; *Calling Dr Death* 1943; *The House of Fear* 1944; *Bulldog Drummond Strikes Back* 1947; *Johnny Belinda* 1948; *Anne of the Indies* 1951

Herbert, Hugh (1887–1952) *Danger Lights* 1930; *Friends and Lovers* 1931; *Laugh and Get Rich* 1931; *The Sin Ship* 1931; *Faithless* 1932; *Bureau of Missing Persons* 1933; *Dames* 1934; *Easy to Love* 1934; *Fashions of 1934* 1934; *Fog over Frisco* 1934; *Sweet Adeline* 1935; *Colleen* 1936; *One Rainy Afternoon* 1936; *Hollywood Hotel* 1937; *The Perfect Specimen* 1937; *Four's a Crowd* 1938; *Gold Diggers in Paris* 1938; *The Great Waltz* 1938; *Eternally Yours* 1939; *The Villain Still Pursued Her* 1940; *The Black Cat* 1941; *Hellzapoppin'* 1941; *There's One Born Every Minute* 1942; *Kismet* 1944; *Music for Millions* 1944; *The Girl from Manhattan* 1948; *On Our Merry Way* 1948; *So This Is New York* 1948; *A Song Is Born* 1948; *The Beautiful Blonde from Bashful Bend* 1949

Herbert, Leon *Double X: the Name of the Game* 1991; *Emotional Backgammon* 2003

Herbert, Percy (1920–1992) *The Cockleshell Heroes* 1955; *Barnacle Bill* 1957; *Sea of Sand* 1958; *Serious Charge* 1959; *Mutiny on the Bounty* 1962; *Carry On Jack* 1963; *The Cracksman* 1963; *Joey Boy* 1965; *One Million Years BC* 1966; *Tobruk* 1966; *Too Late the Hero* 1970; *Captain Apache* 1971; *The Fiend* 1971; *Man in the Wilderness* 1971; *Doomwatch* 1972

Herd, Richard (1932–) *Wolf Lake* 1979; *Trancers* 1985; *Gleaming the Cube* 1988

Hériat, Philippe (1898–1971) *L'Inhumaine* 1923; *Divine* 1935

Herlie, Eileen (1919–) *Hamlet* 1948; *Isn't Life Wonderful!* 1952; *The Story of Gilbert and Sullivan* 1953; *For Better, for Worse* 1954; *Hamlet* 1964; *The Sea Gull* 1968

Herlitzka, Roberto (1937–) *La Maschera* 1988; *Marianna Ucria* 1997; *Good Morning, Night* 2003

Herman, David (1968–) *Office Space* 1999; *Dude, Where's My Car?* 2000

Hermann, Irm *aka* **Herrmann, Irm** (1942–) *The Merchant of Four Seasons* 1971; *The Bitter Tears of Petra von Kant* 1972; *Fear Eats the Soul* 1973; *Mother Küsters Goes to Heaven* 1975; *Fear of Fear* 1976; *Ten Minutes Older: the Cello* 2002

Hernandez, Jay (1978–) *crazy/beautiful* 2001; *The Rookie* 2002; *Torque* 2003; *Friday Night Lights* 2004

Hernandez, Juano (1901–1970) *Intruder in the Dust* 1949; *The Breaking Point* 1950; *Young Man with a Horn* 1950; *Kiss Me Deadly* 1955; *Trial* 1955; *Ransom!* 1956; *The Mark of the Hawk* 1957; *Something of Value* 1957; *Sergeant Rutledge* 1960; *The Sins of Rachel Cade* 1960; *Two Loves* 1961; *Hemingway's Adventures of a Young Man* 1962; *The Extraordinary Seaman* 1969; *The Reivers* 1969; *They Call Me Mister Tibbs!* 1970

Heron, Blake (1982–) *Shiloh* 1996; *Wind River* 1999

Herrand, Marcel (1897–1953) *Les Visiteurs du Soir* 1942; *Les Enfants du Paradis* 1945; *Martin Roumagnac* 1946; *Fanfan la Tulipe* 1951

Herrier, Mark *Porky's* 1981; *Porky's II: The Next Day* 1983; *Tank* 1984; *Porky's Revenge* 1985

Herrmann, Edward (1943–) *The Day of the Dolphin* 1973; *The Paper Chase* 1973; *The Great Waldo Pepper* 1975; *Brass Target* 1978; *Take Down* 1978; *Freedom Road* 1979; *Hill's Angels* 1979; *Harry's War* 1981; *A Little Sex* 1981; *Reds* 1981; *Death Valley* 1982; *Mrs Soffel* 1984; *Compromising Positions* 1985; *The Man with One Red Shoe* 1985; *The Lost Boys* 1987; *Overboard* 1987; *Big Business* 1988; *Born Yesterday* 1993; *My Boyfriend's Back* 1993; *Foreign Student* 1994; *Richie Rich* 1994; *Soul of the Game* 1996; *What Love Sees* 1996; *Frank Lloyd Wright* 1997; *Atomic Train* 1999; *Walking across Egypt* 1999; *The Cat's Meow* 2001; *James Dean* 2001; *The Emperor's Club* 2002; *Intolerable Cruelty* 2003

Hersent, Philippe (1912–1982) *The Sword and the Cross* 1958; *The Giant of Marathon* 1960

Hershey, Barbara *aka* **Seagull, Barbara** (1948–) *With Six You Get Eggroll* 1968; *Last Summer* 1969; *The Baby Maker* 1970; *The Liberation of LB Jones* 1970; *Dealing: or the Berkeley-to-Boston Forty-Brick Lost-Bag Blues* 1971; *The Pursuit of Happiness* 1971; *Boxcar Bertha* 1972; *Diamonds* 1975; *The Last Hard Men* 1976; *Trial by Combat* 1976; *The Stunt Man* 1980; *Americana* 1981; *The Entity* 1981; *Take This Job and Shove It* 1981; *The Right Stuff* 1983; *The Natural* 1984; *Hannah and Her Sisters* 1986; *Hoosiers* 1986; *Shy People* 1987; *Tin Men* 1987; *A World Apart* 1987; *Beaches* 1988; *The Last Temptation of Christ* 1988; *Aunt Julia and the Scriptwriter* 1990; *Evidence of Love* 1990; *Defenseless* 1991; *Paris Trout* 1991; *Falling Down* 1992; *The Public Eye* 1992; *A Dangerous Woman* 1993; *Splitting Heirs* 1993; *Swing Kids* 1993; *Last of the Dogmen* 1995; *The Pallbearer* 1996; *The Portrait of a Lady* 1996; *A Soldier's Daughter Never Cries* 1998; *Breakfast of Champions* 1999; *Passion* 1999; *Lantana* 2001

Hersholt, Jean (1886–1956) *Tess of the Storm Country* 1922; *Sinners in Silk* 1924; *Don Q, Son of Zorro* 1925; *Greed* 1925; *Stella Dallas* 1925; *The Student Prince in Old Heidelberg* 1927; *Abie's Irish Rose* 1928; *The Younger Generation* 1929; *Daybreak* 1931; *Private Lives* 1931; *The Sin of Madelon Claudet* 1931; *Susan Lenox: Her Fall and Rise* 1931; *The Beast of the City* 1932; *Emma* 1932; *Flesh* 1932; *Grand Hotel* 1932; *The Mask of Fu Manchu* 1932; *Skyscraper Souls* 1932; *Dinner at Eight* 1933; *The Cat and the Fiddle* 1934; *The Fountain* 1934; *Men in White* 1934; *The Painted Veil* 1934; *Break of Hearts* 1935; *Mark of the Vampire* 1935; *The Country Doctor* 1936; *His Brother's Wife* 1936; *One in a Million* 1936; *Heidi* 1937; *Seventh Heaven* 1937; *Alexander's Ragtime Band* 1938; *Happy Landing* 1938; *Meet Dr Christian* 1939; *Mr Moto in Danger Island* 1939; *Stage Door Canteen* 1943; *Run for Cover* 1955

Herter, Gerard *Caltiki, the Immortal Monster* 1959; *The White Warrior* 1959; *Adios, Sabata* 1970

Hervey, Irene (1910–1998) *The Stranger's Return* 1933; *Charlie Chan in Shanghai* 1935; *The League of Frightened Men* 1937; *East Side of Heaven* 1939; *The Boys from Syracuse* 1940; *Mr Peabody and the Mermaid* 1948; *The Lucky Stiff* 1949; *A Cry in the Night* 1956; *Crash Landing* 1958; *Cactus Flower* 1969

Herzog, Werner (1942–) *Man of Flowers* 1984; *Little Dieter Needs to Fly* 1997; *julien donkey-boy* 1999; *My Best Fiend* 1999

Heslov, Grant (1963–) *Congo* 1995; *Black Sheep* 1996; *Dante's Peak* 1997; *The Scorpion King* 2002

Hess, David *aka* **Hess, David A** (1942–) *Last House on the Left* 1972; *Avalanche Express* 1979; *Swamp Thing* 1982

Hess, Sandra *Mortal Kombat: Annihilation* 1997; *Face Value* 2001

Hesseman, Howard (1940–) *Steelyard Blues* 1973; *The Sunshine Boys* 1975; *Jackson County Jail* 1976; *Tunnelvision* 1976; *Honky Tonk Freeway* 1981; *Private Lessons* 1981; *Doctor Detroit* 1983; *Police Academy 2: Their First Assignment* 1985; *Flight of the Navigator* 1986; *My Chauffeur* 1986; *Heat* 1987; *Murder in New Hampshire* 1991; *Rubin & Ed* 1991; *Munchie Strikes Back* 1994; *Out of Sync* 1995; *Gridlock'd* 1996; *About Schmidt* 2002

Heston, Charlton (1924–) *Dark City* 1950; *The Greatest Show on Earth* 1952; *Ruby Gentry* 1952; *Arrowhead* 1953; *The Naked Jungle* 1953; *Pony Express* 1953; *The President's Lady* 1953; *The Savage* 1953; *Bad for Each Other* 1954; *Secret of the Incas* 1954; *The Far Horizons* 1955; *Lucy Gallant* 1955; *The Private War of Major Benson* 1955; *The Ten Commandments* 1956; *Three Violent People* 1956; *The Big Country* 1958; *The Buccaneer* 1958; *Touch of Evil* 1958; *Ben-Hur* 1959; *The Wreck of the Mary Deare* 1959; *El Cid* 1961; *Diamond Head* 1962; *The Pigeon That Took Rome* 1962; *55 Days at Peking* 1963; *The Agony and the Ecstasy* 1965; *The Greatest Story Ever Told* 1965; *Major Dundee* 1965; *The War Lord* 1965; *Khartoum* 1966; *The Adventures of Mowgli* 1967; *Counterpoint* 1967; *Planet of the Apes* 1967; *Will Penny* 1967; *Beneath the Planet of the Apes* 1969; *Number One* 1969; *The Hawaiians* 1970; *Julius Caesar* 1970; *King: a Filmed Record... Montgomery to Memphis* 1970; *The Omega Man* 1971; *Antony and Cleopatra* 1972; *Call of the Wild* 1972; *Skyjacked* 1972; *Soylent Green* 1973; *The Three Musketeers* 1973; *Airport 1975* 1974; *Earthquake* 1974; *The Four Musketeers* 1974; *Battle of Midway* 1976; *The Last Hard Men* 1976; *Two-Minute Warning* 1976; *The Prince and the Pauper* 1977; *Gray Lady Down* 1978; *The Awakening* 1980; *The Mountain Men* 1980; *Mother Lode* 1982; *Almost an Angel* 1990; *Solar Crisis* 1990; *Treasure Island* 1990; *Tombstone* 1993; *In the Mouth of Madness* 1994; *True Lies* 1994; *Alaska* 1996; *Hamlet* 1996; *Hercules* 1997; *Armageddon* 1998; *Any Given Sunday* 1999; *Gideon* 1999; *Cats & Dogs* 2001; *The Order* 2001; *Town & Country* 2001

Hetherington, Jason (1965–) *Complicity* 1999; *Aberdeen* 2000

Hewer, John *Assassin for Hire* 1951; *Colonel March Investigates* 1953; *Mister Ten Per Cent* 1967

Hewett, Christopher (1922–2001) *The Producers* 1968; *Ratboy* 1986

Hewitt, Alan (1915–1986) *Days of Wine and Roses* 1962; *That Touch of Mink* 1962; *The Misadventures of Merlin Jones* 1964; *How to Murder Your Wife* 1965; *The Computer Wore Tennis Shoes* 1969; *The Barefoot Executive* 1971

Hewitt, Henry (1885–1968) *Sailors Three* 1940; *The Black Sheep of Whitehall* 1941

Hewitt, Jennifer Love *aka* **Hewitt, Love** (1979–) *Munchie* 1992; *Sister Act 2: Back in the Habit* 1993; *House Arrest* 1996; *I Know What You Did Last Summer* 1997; *Trojan War* 1997; *Can't Hardly Wait* 1998; *I Still Know What You Did Last Summer* 1998; *Telling You* 1998; *The Suburbans* 1999; *The Audrey Hepburn Story* 2000; *Heartbreakers* 2001; *The Adventures of Tom Thumb and Thumbelina* 2002; *The Tuxedo* 2002; *Garfield* 2004

Hewitt, Martin (1958–) *Endless Love* 1981; *Killer Party* 1986; *Two Moon Junction* 1988

Hewitt, Sean *The Sender* 1982; *Wild Thing* 1987; *Swann* 1996

Hewlett, David (1968–) *Pin* 1988; *Where the Heart Is* 1990; *Desire & Hell at Sunset Motel* 1991; *Scanners II: The New Order* 1991; *Cube* 1997; *Cypher* 2002

Heyburn, Weldon *Speed* 1936; *Charlie Chan in The Chinese Cat* 1944

Heydt, Louis Jean (1905–1960) *The Great McGinty* 1940; *Let's Make Music* 1940; *The Great Moment* 1944; *The Big Sleep* 1946; *Roadblock* 1951; *The Boy from Oklahoma* 1954; *Stranger at My Door* 1956

Heyerdahl, Christopher *Silent Trigger* 1996; *The Peacekeeper* 1997; *Nowhere in Sight* 2000

Heyes, Herbert (1889–1958) *Union Station* 1950; *Bedtime for Bonzo* 1951; *A Place in the Sun* 1951; *Carbine Williams* 1952; *Park Row* 1952; *Something to Live For* 1952; *Seven Little Foys* 1955

Heyman, Barton (1937–1996) *Let's Scare Jessica to Death* 1971; *Valdez Is Coming* 1971; *Static* 1985; *Billy Galvin* 1986

Heywood, Anne (1932–) *Dangerous Exile* 1957; *Floods of Fear* 1958; *Violent Playground* 1958; *The Heart of a Man* 1959; *Upstairs and Downstairs* 1959; *Carthage in Flames* 1960; *A Terrible Beauty* 1960; *Petticoat Pirates* 1961; *The Brain* 1962; *The Very Edge* 1962; *The Fox* 1967; *The Chairman* 1969; *Midas Run* 1969; *I Want What I Want* 1971; *Good Luck, Miss Wyckoff* 1979; *Secrets of the Phantom Caverns* 1984

Heywood, Pat (1927–) *Romeo and Juliet* 1968; *Mumsy, Nanny, Sonny & Girly* 1970; *10 Rillington Place* 1970; *Wish You Were Here* 1987; *Young Toscanini* 1988

Hiatt, Philippa *The Bells Go Down* 1943; *The Halfway House* 1943; *George in Civvy Street* 1946

Hibbert, Geoffrey (1922–1969) *The Common Touch* 1941; *Love on the Dole* 1941; *In Which We Serve* 1942; *Gaolbreak* 1962

Hibler, Winston *White Wilderness* 1958; *Jungle Cat* 1959; *King of the Grizzlies* 1969

Hickey, John Benjamin *Only You* 1994; *Eddie* 1996; *Finding North* 1997; *Love! Valour! Compassion!* 1997; *The Bone Collector* 1999; *The Anniversary Party* 2001

Hickey, Tom *Fools of Fortune* 1990; *Raining Stones* 1993; *Gold in the Streets* 1996; *Possession* 2002; *Inside I'm Dancing* 2004

Hickey, William (1928–1997) *A Hatful of Rain* 1957; *The Producers* 1968; *Happy Birthday, Wanda June* 1971; *92 in the Shade* 1975; *Mikey and Nicky* 1976; *Wise Blood* 1979; *Prizzi's Honor* 1985; *Walls of Glass* 1985; *The Name of the Rose* 1986; *One Crazy Summer* 1986; *Da* 1988; *Pink Cadillac* 1989; *Puppet Master* 1989; *Sea of Love* 1989; *Sons* 1989; *Starlight* 1989; *Any Man's Death* 1990; *My Blue Heaven* 1990; *The Runestone* 1991; *Tales from the Darkside: the Movie* 1991; *The Nightmare before Christmas* 1993; *The Jerky Boys* 1995; *The Maddening* 1995; *Love Is All There Is* 1996; *Mousehunt* 1997

Hickland, Catherine (1956–) *Ghost Town* 1988; *Witchcraft* 1989

Hickman, Bill (1921–1986) *The French Connection* 1971; *The Seven-Ups* 1973

Hickman, Darryl (1931–) *Men of Boys Town* 1941; *Joe Smith, American* 1942; *Kiss and Tell* 1945; *Salty O'Rourke* 1945; *Fighting Father Dunne* 1948; *A Kiss for Corliss* 1949; *The Happy Years* 1950; *Lightning Strikes Twice* 1951; *Destination Gobi* 1953; *Southwest Passage* 1954; *Tea and Sympathy* 1956; *The Iron Sheriff* 1957; *The Tingler* 1959

Hickman, Dwayne (1934–) *Cat Ballou* 1965; *Dr Goldfoot and the Bikini Machine* 1965; *How to Fill a Wild Bikini* 1965; *Ski Party* 1965

Hicks, Catherine (1951–) *Death Valley* 1982; *Better Late Than Never* 1983; *Garbo Talks* 1984; *The Razor's Edge* 1984; *Fever Pitch* 1985; *Peggy Sue Got Married* 1986; *Star Trek IV: the Voyage Home* 1986; *Like Father, like Son* 1987; *Souvenir* 1987; *Child's Play* 1988; *She's Out of Control* 1989; *Dillinger and Capone* 1995; *Eight Days a Week* 1996

Hicks, Danny *aka* **Hicks, Dan** *Evil Dead II* 1987; *Darkman* 1990

Hicks, Michele (1973–) *Twin Falls Idaho* 1999; *Everything Put Together* 2000

Hicks, Russell (1895–1957) *Charlie Chan in Shanghai* 1935; *The Woman in Red* 1935; *Follow the Fleet* 1936; *The Big Broadcast of 1938* 1937; *Kentucky* 1938; *Swanee River* 1939; *The Bank Dick* 1940; *Flame of the Barbary Coast* 1945; *A Game of Death* 1945; *The Bandit of Sherwood Forest* 1946; *The Black Arrow* 1948; *The Flying Saucer* 1949

Hicks, Seymour (1871–1949) *Scrooge* 1935; *Vintage Wine* 1935; *Busman's Honeymoon* 1940; *Pastor Hall* 1940

Hicks, Taral (1975–) *A Bronx Tale* 1993; *Belly* 1998

Hickson, Joan (1906–1998) *Love from a Stranger* 1936; *Don't Take It to Heart* 1944; *This Was a Woman* 1947; *The Guinea Pig* 1948; *Seven Days to Noon* 1950; *The Card* 1952; *Hindle Wakes* 1952; *Deadly Nightshade* 1953; *Mad about Men* 1954; *Jumping for Joy* 1955; *Child in the House* 1956; *The Extra Day* 1956; *Port of Escape* 1956; *Sea Wife* 1957; *Law and Disorder* 1958; *Upstairs and Downstairs* 1959; *Carry On Regardless* 1960; *No Kidding* 1960; *Please Turn Over* 1960; *Murder She Said* 1961; *I Thank a Fool* 1962; *Nurse on Wheels* 1963; *Carry On Loving* 1970; *A Day in the Death of Joe Egg* 1971; *Carry On Girls* 1973; *Confessions of a Window Cleaner* 1974; *The Wicked Lady* 1983; *Clockwise* 1986; *King of the Wind* 1989; *Century* 1993

Higashiyama, Chieko (1890–1980) *Early Summer* 1951; *Tokyo Story* 1953

Higgins, Anthony *aka* **Corlan, Anthony** (1947–) *Taste the Blood of Dracula* 1969; *A Walk with Love and Death* 1969; *Something for Everyone* 1970; *Quartet* 1981; *Raiders of the Lost Ark* 1981; *The Draughtsman's Contract* 1982; *She'll Be Wearing Pink Pyjamas* 1984; *The Bride* 1985; *Young Sherlock Holmes* 1985; *Max Mon Amour* 1986; *The Bridge* 1990; *One against the Wind* 1991; *For Love or Money* 1993; *Nostradamus* 1993; *Alive and Kicking* 1996

Higgins, Clare *Nineteen Nineteen* 1984; *Hellraiser* 1987; *Hellbound: Hellraiser II* 1988; *Bad Behaviour* 1992; *Thin Ice* 1994; *Small Faces* 1995

Higgins, John Michael (1962–) *The Late Shift* 1996; *Best in Show* 2000; *A Mighty Wind* 2003

Higgins, Jonathan *Life in the Balance* 2001; *No Good Deed* 2002

Higgins, Michael (1921–) *Terror in the City* 1963; *The Arrangement* 1969; *Wanda* 1971; *The Conversation* 1974; *An Enemy of the People* 1977; *The Black Stallion* 1979; *A Midsummer Night's Sex Comedy* 1982; *Angel Heart* 1987

Highmore, Freddie (1992–) *Finding Neverland* 2004; *Five Children and It* 2004; *Two Brothers* 2004

Hiken, Gerald (1927–) *The Goddess* 1958; *The Three Sisters* 1966
Hilary, Jennifer (1942–) *The Heroes of Telemark* 1965; *The Idol* 1966; *Five Days One Summer* 1982
Hill, Amy (1953–) *Dim Sum: a Little Bit of Heart* 1985; *Dr Seuss' The Cat in the Hat* 2003; *50 First Dates* 2004
Hill, Arthur (1922–) *The Scarlet Thread* 1951; *The Deep Blue Sea* 1955; *In the Cool of the Day* 1963; *The Ugly American* 1963; *Harper* 1966; *Moment to Moment* 1966; *Petulia* 1968; *The Chairman* 1969; *The Andromeda Strain* 1970; *Rabbit, Run* 1970; *The Pursuit of Happiness* 1971; *The Killer Elite* 1975; *Futureworld* 1976; *The Champ* 1979; *A Little Romance* 1979; *The Amateur* 1981; *Making Love* 1982; *Something Wicked This Way Comes* 1983; *One Magic Christmas* 1985
Hill, Benny (1925–1992) *Who Done It?* 1956; *Light Up the Sky* 1960; *Those Magnificent Men in Their Flying Machines* 1965; *Chitty Chitty Bang Bang* 1968; *The Italian Job* 1969; *The Best of Benny Hill* 1974
Hill, Bernard (1944–) *The Sailor's Return* 1978; *The Bounty* 1984; *The Chain* 1984; *Restless Natives* 1985; *No Surrender* 1986; *Bellman & True* 1987; *Drowning by Numbers* 1988; *Mountains of the Moon* 1989; *Shirley Valentine* 1989; *Double X: the Name of the Game* 1991; *Madagascar Skin* 1995; *Shepherd on the Rock* 1995; *The Ghost and the Darkness* 1996; *The Wind in the Willows* 1996; *Titanic* 1997; *The Criminal* 1999; *The Loss of Sexual Innocence* 1999; *A Midsummer Night's Dream* 1999; *True Crime* 1999; *Going Off, Big Time* 2000; *The Lord of the Rings: The Two Towers* 2002; *The Scorpion King* 2002; *Gothika* 2003; *The Lord of the Rings: The Return of the King* 2003; *Wimbledon* 2004; *The League of Gentlemen's Apocalypse* 2005
Hill, Craig (1927–) *Detective Story* 1951; *Fixed Bayonets* 1951; *The I Don't Care Girl* 1952; *What Price Glory?* 1952; *The Siege at Red River* 1954; *The Flight That Disappeared* 1961; *The Swinger* 1966
Hill, Dana (1964–1996) *Shoot the Moon* 1982; *Cross Creek* 1983; *National Lampoon's European Vacation* 1985; *Rover Dangerfield* 1991; *Tom and Jerry: the Movie* 1992
Hill, Dave *Slade in Flame* 1974; *The Draughtsman's Contract* 1982; *The Raggedy Rawney* 1987
Hill, Harry *Crazy Moon* 1986; *Shadow of the Wolf* 1992
Hill, Lauryn (1975–) *Sister Act 2: Back in the Habit* 1993; *Restaurant* 1998
Hill, Marianna *aka* **Hill, Mariana** (1941–) *Red Line 7000* 1965; *Paradise, Hawaiian Style* 1966; *Medium Cool* 1969; *El Condor* 1970; *The Traveling Executioner* 1970; *Thumb Tripping* 1972; *The Baby* 1973; *High Plains Drifter* 1973; *Blood Beach* 1981
Hill, Matt *Teenage Mutant Ninja Turtles III* 1992; *A Monkey's Tale* 1999
Hill, Melanie (1963–) *The Hawk* 1992; *When Saturday Comes* 1995; *Brassed Off* 1996
Hill, Steven (1922–) *The Goddess* 1958; *A Child Is Waiting* 1962; *The Slender Thread* 1965; *It's My Turn* 1980; *Rich and Famous* 1981; *Yentl* 1983; *Garbo Talks* 1984; *Heartburn* 1986; *Legal Eagles* 1986; *The Boost* 1988; *White Palace* 1990; *Billy Bathgate* 1991
Hill, Terence *aka* **Girotti, Mario** (1939–) *The Sword and the Cross* 1958; *Hannibal* 1959; *The Leopard* 1962; *Seven Seas to Calais* 1962; *Ace High* 1968; *Boot Hill* 1969; *They Call Me Trinity* 1970; *My Name Is Nobody* 1973; *March or Die* 1977; *Mr Billion* 1977; *Renegade* 1987
Hill, Thelma (1906–1938) *The Two Tars* 1928; *The Miracle Woman* 1931
Hillaire, Marcel (1908–1988) *Sabrina* 1954; *Take the Money and Run* 1969
Hiller, Wendy (1912–2003) *Pygmalion* 1938; *Major Barbara* 1941; *I Know Where I'm Going!* 1945; *Outcast of the Islands* 1951; *Sailor of the King* 1953; *How to Murder a Rich Uncle* 1957; *Something of Value* 1957; *Separate Tables* 1958; *Sons and Lovers* 1960; *Toys in the Attic* 1963; *A Man for All Seasons* 1966; *Murder on the Orient Express* 1974; *The Cat and the Canary* 1979; *The Elephant Man* 1980; *Making Love* 1982; *The Lonely Passion of Judith Hearne* 1987
Hillerman, John (1932–) *Paper Moon* 1973; *Chinatown* 1974; *At Long Last Love* 1975; *Lucky Lady* 1975; *Kill Me If You Can* 1977; *Sunburn* 1979; *Magnum: Don't Eat the Snow in Hawaii* 1980
Hillie, Verna (1914–1997) *The Star Packer* 1934; *The Trail Beyond* 1934; *Princess O'Hara* 1935
Hillman, Richard (1974–) *Palmer's Pick-Up* 1999; *Teenage Caveman* 2001
Hills, Gillian (1946–) *Beat Girl* 1960; *Blowup* 1966; *Demons of the Mind* 1971
Hilton, George (1934–) *The Battle of El Alamein* 1968; *A Bullet for Sandoval* 1970
Hilton-Jacobs, Lawrence (1953–) *Claudine* 1974; *East LA Warriors* 1989; *Indecent Behavior* 1993
Hinchley, Pippa (1966–) *Secret Places* 1984; *The Dressmaker* 1988
Hinde, Madeline *The Smashing Bird I Used to Know* 1969; *Incense for the Damned* 1970; *The Fiend* 1971; *The Last Valley* 1971; *Brief Encounter* 1974
Hindle, Art (1948–) *Black Christmas* 1974; *A Small Town in Texas* 1976; *Invasion of the Body Snatchers* 1978; *The Brood* 1979; *The Octagon* 1980; *Raw Courage* 1984
Hindman, Earl (1942–2003) *The Parallax View* 1974; *The Taking of Pelham One Two Three* 1974; *Greased Lightning* 1977
Hinds, Ciaran (1953–) *December Bride* 1990; *Hostages* 1993; *Circle of Friends* 1995; *Persuasion* 1995; *Some Mother's Son* 1996; *The Life of Stuff* 1997; *Oscar and Lucinda* 1997; *The Lost Son* 1998; *Titanic Town* 1998; *The Lost Lover* 1999; *The Weight of Water* 2000; *The Sum of All Fears* 2002; *Calendar Girls* 2003; *Lara Croft Tomb Raider: the Cradle of Life* 2003; *The Statement* 2003; *Veronica Guerin* 2003; *The Phantom of the Opera* 2004
Hinds, Samuel S *aka* **Hinds, Samuel** (1875–1948) *Deluge* 1933; *Gabriel over the White House* 1933; *Private Worlds* 1935; *The Raven* 1935; *Rendezvous* 1935; *She* 1935; *Strangers All* 1935; *His Brother's Wife* 1936; *Rhythm on the Range* 1936; *Navy Blue and Gold* 1937; *Stage Door* 1937; *Forbidden Valley* 1938; *The Storm* 1938; *Test Pilot* 1938; *Wives under Suspicion* 1938; *You Can't Take It with You* 1938; *Young Dr Kildare* 1938; *Calling Dr Kildare* 1939; *The Secret of Dr Kildare* 1939; *The Boys from Syracuse* 1940; *Dr Kildare Goes Home* 1940; *Dr Kildare's Strange Case* 1940; *It's a Date* 1940; *Seven Sinners* 1940; *Back Street* 1941; *Blossoms in the Dust* 1941; *Dr Kildare's Wedding Day* 1941; *Man Made Monster* 1941; *Road Agent* 1941; *The Shepherd of the Hills* 1941; *Grand Central Murder* 1942; *Kid Glove Killer* 1942; *Lady in a Jam* 1942; *Ride 'em Cowboy* 1942; *Hers to Hold* 1943; *Son of Dracula* 1943; *Cobra Woman* 1944; *The Singing Sheriff* 1944; *The Strange Affair of Uncle Harry* 1945; *The Boy with Green Hair* 1948; *The Bribe* 1949
Hines, Damon *Lethal Weapon* 1987; *Lethal Weapon 3* 1992
Hines, Gregory (1946–2003) *History of the World Part 1* 1981; *Wolfen* 1981; *Deal of the Century* 1983; *The Cotton Club* 1984; *White Nights* 1985; *Running Scared* 1986; *Saigon* 1988; *Tap* 1989; *Eve of Destruction* 1991; *A Rage in Harlem* 1991; *Renaissance Man* 1994; *Waiting to Exhale* 1995; *Good Luck* 1996; *The Preacher's Wife* 1996; *Trigger Happy* 1996; *Subway Stories: Tales from the Underground* 1997; *The Tic Code* 1998; *Things You Can Tell Just by Looking at Her* 2000
Hingle, Pat (1923–) *No Down Payment* 1957; *The Strange One* 1957; *Splendor in the Grass* 1961; *All the Way Home* 1963; *The Ugly American* 1963; *Nevada Smith* 1966; *Hang 'Em High* 1968; *Jigsaw* 1968; *Sol Madrid* 1968; *Bloody Mama* 1970; *WUSA* 1970; *The Carey Treatment* 1972; *One Little Indian* 1973; *Running Wild* 1973; *The Super Cops* 1973; *The Gauntlet* 1977; *Elvis – the Movie* 1979; *Norma Rae* 1979; *Going Berserk* 1983; *Sudden Impact* 1983; *Brewster's Millions* 1985; *The Falcon and the Snowman* 1985; *The Rape of Richard Beck* 1985; *Maximum Overdrive* 1986; *Baby Boom* 1987; *The Land before Time* 1988; *Batman* 1989; *Everybody's Baby: the Rescue of Jessica McClure* 1989; *The Grifters* 1990; *Lightning Jack* 1994; *Batman Forever* 1995; *Truman* 1995; *A Thousand Acres* 1997
Hinkley, Tommy (1958–) *Back to the Beach* 1987; *The Little Vampire* 2000
Hinnant, Skip (1940–) *Fritz the Cat* 1972; *The Nine Lives of Fritz the Cat* 1974
Hintermann, Carlo (1923–1988) *A Breath of Scandal* 1960; *A Black Veil for Lisa* 1969
Hinz, Michael *The Bridge* 1959; *Four Times That Night* 1972
Hira, Mikijiro (1933–) *The Face of Another* 1966; *The Empty Table* 1985
Hirata, Akihiko (1927–1984) *Godzilla* 1954; *The H-Man* 1954; *Terror of Mechagodzilla* 1975
Hird, Thora (1911–2003) *The Big Blockade* 1942; *Next of Kin* 1942; *Went the Day Well?* 1942; *Once a Jolly Swagman* 1948; *Portrait from Life* 1948; *The Weaker Sex* 1948; *A Boy, a Girl and a Bike* 1949; *Boys in Brown* 1949; *Conspirator* 1949; *The Cure for Love* 1949; *Fools Rush In* 1949; *Madness of the Heart* 1949; *Maytime in Mayfair* 1949; *The Magnet* 1950; *Emergency Call* 1952; *The Frightened Man* 1952; *The Long Memory* 1952; *The Lost Hours* 1952; *Time Gentlemen Please!* 1952; *A Day to Remember* 1953; *Personal Affair* 1953; *Turn the Key Softly* 1953; *One Good Turn* 1954; *Lost* 1955; *The Love Match* 1955; *The Quatermass Xperiment* 1955; *Simon and Laura* 1955; *The Good Companions* 1956; *Home and Away* 1956; *Sailor Beware!* 1956; *Women without Men* 1956; *Further up the Creek* 1958; *The Entertainer* 1960; *A Kind of Loving* 1962; *Term of Trial* 1962; *Rattle of a Simple Man* 1964; *Some Will, Some Won't* 1969; *The Nightcomers* 1972; *Consuming Passions* 1988; *Julie and the Cadillacs* 1997
Hirdwall, Ingvar (1934–) *Raven's End* 1963; *Daybreak* 2003
Hirsch, Elroy "Crazylegs" (1923–2004) *Unchained* 1955; *Zero Hour!* 1957
Hirsch, Emile (1985–) *The Dangerous Lives of Altar Boys* 2001; *The Emperor's Club* 2002; *The Girl Next Door* 2004; *Imaginary Heroes* 2004; *Lords of Dogtown* 2005
Hirsch, Judd (1935–) *King of the Gypsies* 1978; *Ordinary People* 1980; *Without a Trace* 1983; *The Goodbye People* 1984; *Teachers* 1984; *Running on Empty* 1988; *Independence Day* 1996; *A Beautiful Mind* 2001
Hirsch, Robert (1925–) *The Hunchback of Notre Dame* 1956; *Shock Treatment* 1973
Hirschmüller, Hans *Love Is Colder Than Death* 1969; *The Merchant of Four Seasons* 1971
Hirt, Christianne *For the Moment* 1994; *Tokyo Cowboy* 1994; *Firestorm* 1998
Hirt, Eléonore *A Very Private Affair* 1962; *Seven Nights in Japan* 1976; *Get out Your Handkerchiefs* 1977; *La Nuit de Varennes* 1983
Hitchcock, Patricia (1928–) *Stage Fright* 1949; *Strangers on a Train* 1951
Hjejle, Iben (1971–) *Mifune* 1999; *High Fidelity* 2000; *The Emperor's New Clothes* 2001; *Skagerrak* 2003
Hjelm, Keve (1922–2004) *Raven's End* 1963; *Best Intentions* 1992
Hoag, Judith (1968–) *Danielle Steel's Fine Things* 1990; *Teenage Mutant Ninja Turtles* 1990
Hoath, Florence (1984–) *A Pin for the Butterfly* 1994; *The Haunting of Helen Walker* 1995; *Innocent Lies* 1995; *FairyTale: a True Story* 1997; *The Governess* 1997; *Tom's Midnight Garden* 1998
Hobart, Deborah (1950–) *The Real McCoy* 1993; *Gordy* 1994
Hobart, Rose (1906–2000) *Dr Jekyll and Mr Hyde* 1931; *Mr and Mrs North* 1941; *A Gentleman at Heart* 1942; *The Brighton Strangler* 1945; *Conflict* 1945; *Claudia and David* 1946; *The Farmer's Daughter* 1946
Hobbes, Halliwell (1877–1962) *Charley's Aunt* 1930; *Grumpy* 1930; *Dr Jekyll and Mr Hyde* 1931; *The Masquerader* 1933; *British Agent* 1934; *The Key* 1934; *Cardinal Richelieu* 1935; *Charlie Chan in Shanghai* 1935; *The Earl of Chicago* 1940; *Sherlock Holmes Faces Death* 1943
Hobbs, Jack (1893–1968) *No Limit* 1935; *It's in the Air* 1938
Hobbs, Peter *The Lady in Red* 1979; *The Man with Two Brains* 1983
Hobbs, Rebecca *The Ugly* 1996; *Siam Sunset* 1999
Hobel, Mara (1971–) *The Hand* 1981; *Mommie Dearest* 1981
Hobson, Valerie (1917–1998) *Bride of Frankenstein* 1935; *The Mystery of Edwin Drood* 1935; *Jump for Glory* 1937; *The Drum* 1938; *Q Planes* 1939; *The Spy in Black* 1939; *Contraband* 1940; *Unpublished Story* 1942; *The Adventures of Tartu* 1943; *Great Expectations* 1946; *The Years Between* 1946; *Blanche Fury* 1948; *The Small Voice* 1948; *The Interrupted Journey* 1949; *Kind Hearts and Coronets* 1949; *The Rocking Horse Winner* 1949; *Train of Events* 1949; *The Card* 1952; *Meet Me Tonight* 1952; *Voice of Merrill* 1952; *Background* 1953; *Knave of Hearts* 1954
Hodder, Kane (1951–) *Friday the 13th Part VII: the New Blood* 1988; *Friday the 13th Part VIII: Jason Takes Manhattan* 1989; *Jason Goes to Hell: the Final Friday* 1993; *Wishmaster* 1997; *Jason X* 2001
Hodge, Douglas (1960–) *Salome's Last Dance* 1988; *Dealers* 1989; *Diamond Skulls* 1989; *Buddy's Song* 1990
Hodge, Kate *Leatherface: the Texas Chainsaw Massacre III* 1990; *Rapid Fire* 1992; *The Hidden II* 1993
Hodge, Patricia (1946–) *Betrayal* 1982; *Just Ask for Diamond* 1988; *Sunset* 1988; *The Leading Man* 1996; *Before You Go* 2002
Hodges, Eddie (1947–) *A Hole in the Head* 1959; *The Adventures of Huckleberry Finn* 1960; *Summer Magic* 1963; *The Happiest Millionaire* 1967
Hodges, Horace (1865–1951) *Escape* 1930; *London Melody* 1937; *The Show Goes On* 1937
Hodges, Tom *aka* **Hodges, Thomas E** (1965–) *Lucas* 1986; *Critters 2: the Main Course* 1988; *Excessive Force* 1993; *Vanished without a Trace* 1993; *Heavyweights* 1995
Hodgins, Earle *aka* **Hodgins, Earl** (1893–1964) *Paradise Canyon* 1935; *Aces and Eights* 1936; *Silent Conflict* 1948
Hodgson, Leyland (1894–1949) *Enter Arsene Lupin* 1944; *Bedlam* 1946
Hodiak, John (1914–1955) *Lifeboat* 1944; *Marriage Is a Private Affair* 1944; *Sunday Dinner for a Soldier* 1944; *A Bell for Adano* 1945; *The Harvey Girls* 1946; *Somewhere in the Night* 1946; *The Arnelo Affair* 1947; *Desert Fury* 1947; *Love from a Stranger* 1947; *Command Decision* 1948; *Homecoming* 1948; *Ambush* 1949; *Battleground* 1949; *The Bribe* 1949; *Malaya* 1949; *A Lady without Passport* 1950; *The Miniver Story* 1950; *Across the Wide Missouri* 1951; *The People against O'Hara* 1951; *The Sellout* 1951; *Ambush at Tomahawk Gap* 1953; *Trial* 1955
Hoey, Dennis (1893–1960) *The Good Companions* 1933; *Chu Chin Chow* 1934; *Sherlock Holmes and the Secret Weapon* 1942; *Bomber's Moon* 1943; *Sherlock Holmes Faces Death* 1943; *The House of Fear* 1944; *The Pearl of Death* 1944; *Sherlock Holmes and the Spider Woman* 1944; *Kitty* 1945; *A Thousand and One Nights* 1945; *Anna and the King of Siam* 1946; *Terror by Night* 1946; *Golden Earrings* 1947; *Where There's Life* 1947
Hoey, Iris (1885–1979) *Those Were the Days* 1934; *Just William* 1939
Hofer, Johanna (1896–1988) *The Lost One* 1951; *I Only Want You to Love Me* 1976
Hoff, Halvard *Leaves from Satan's Book* 1919; *The President* 1919
Hoffman, Basil (1941–) *My Favorite Year* 1982; *Communion* 1989; *Lambada* 1990
Hoffman, David (1904–1961) *Flesh and Fantasy* 1943; *The Beast with Five Fingers* 1946; *Desire Me* 1947
Hoffman, Dustin (1937–) *The Graduate* 1967; *Madigan's Millions* 1967; *The Tiger Makes Out* 1967; *John and Mary* 1969; *Midnight Cowboy* 1969; *Little Big Man* 1970; *Alfredo Alfredo* 1971; *Straw Dogs* 1971; *Who Is Harry Kellerman, and Why Is He Saying Those Terrible Things about Me?* 1971; *Papillon* 1973; *Lenny* 1974; *All the President's Men* 1976; *Marathon Man* 1976; *Agatha* 1978; *Straight Time* 1978; *Kramer vs Kramer* 1979; *Tootsie* 1982; *Death of a Salesman* 1985; *Ishtar* 1987; *Rain Man* 1988; *Common Threads: Stories from the Quilt* 1989; *Family Business* 1989; *Dick Tracy* 1990; *Billy Bathgate* 1991; *Hook* 1991; *Accidental Hero* 1992; *American Buffalo* 1995; *Outbreak* 1995; *Sleepers* 1996; *Mad City* 1997; *Wag the Dog* 1997; *Sphere* 1998; *Joan of Arc* 1999; *Confidence* 2002; *Moonlight Mile* 2002; *Runaway Jury* 2003; *Finding Neverland* 2004; *I ❤ Huckabees* 2004; *Meet the Fockers* 2004; *Racing Stripes* 2004
Hoffman, Elizabeth *Fear No Evil* 1980; *Dante's Peak* 1997
Hoffman, Jane (1911–2004) *Ladybug, Ladybug* 1963; *Up the Sandbox* 1972; *Static* 1985
Hoffman, Linda *The Dentist* 1996; *Captured* 1998; *The Dentist II* 1998
Hoffman, Otto (1879–1944) *The Criminal Code* 1930; *Captain Hurricane* 1935
Hoffman, Philip Seymour *aka* **Hoffman, Philip S** (1967–) *Triple Bogey on a Par Five Hole* 1991; *Leap of Faith* 1992; *Scent of a Woman* 1992; *Joey Breaker* 1993; *When a Man Loves a Woman* 1994; *Hard Eight* 1996; *Twister*

1996; *The Big Lebowski* 1997; *Montana* 1997; *Happiness* 1998; *Next Stop Wonderland* 1998; *Patch Adams* 1998; *Flawless* 1999; *Magnolia* 1999; *The Talented Mr Ripley* 1999; *State and Main* 2000; *Love Liza* 2001; *Owning Mahowny* 2002; *Punch-Drunk Love* 2002; *Red Dragon* 2002; *25th Hour* 2002; *Cold Mountain* 2003; *Along Came Polly* 2004

Hoffman, Thom (1957–) *The Fourth Man* 1983; *Force Majeure* 1989; *Orlando* 1992

Hoffmann, Gaby *aka* **Hoffman, Gaby** (1982–) *Field of Dreams* 1989; *Uncle Buck* 1989; *This Is My Life* 1992; *The Man without a Face* 1993; *Now and Then* 1995; *Everyone Says I Love You* 1996; *Volcano* 1997; *Strike!* 1998; *Black and White* 1999

Hoffmann, Robert (1939–) *Grand Slam* 1967; *Assignment K* 1968; *A Black Veil for Lisa* 1969

Hofheimer, Charlie *Boys* 1995; *Fathers' Day* 1997

Hofschneider, Marco (1969–) *Europa, Europa* 1991; *Foreign Student* 1994; *The Island of Dr Moreau* 1996

Hogan, Bosco *Zardoz* 1973; *A Portrait of the Artist as a Young Man* 1977; *Anne Devlin* 1984

Hogan, Hulk *aka* **Hogan, Terry "Hulk"** (1953–) *Rocky III* 1982; *No Holds Barred* 1989; *Suburban Commando* 1991; *Mr Nanny* 1992; *The Secret Agent Club* 1995; *Santa with Muscles* 1996; *3 Ninjas: High Noon at Mega Mountain* 1998

Hogan, Jack (1929–) *The Bonnie Parker Story* 1958; *The Legend of Tom Dooley* 1959

Hogan (3), Michael *The Peanut Butter Solution* 1985; *Palais Royale* 1988; *Clearcut* 1992; *Stay Tuned* 1992

Hogan, Pat (1920–1966) *Davy Crockett, King of the Wild Frontier* 1955; *The Last Frontier* 1955; *Secret of Treasure Mountain* 1956

Hogan, Paul (1939–) *"Crocodile" Dundee* 1986; *"Crocodile" Dundee II* 1988; *Almost an Angel* 1990; *Lightning Jack* 1994; *Flipper* 1996; *Crocodile Dundee in Los Angeles* 2001

Hogan, Robert *The Lady in Red* 1979; *Prince Jack* 1984

Hogan, Susan *The Brood* 1979; *Title Shot* 1979; *Phobia* 1980; *Narrow Margin* 1990; *Bordertown Cafe* 1991; *White Fang* 1991; *Visitors of the Night* 1995; *A Father's Choice* 2000

Hoger, Hannelore (1942–) *The Lost Honour of Katharina Blum* 1975; *Germany in Autumn* 1978

Hogg, Ian (1937–) *Tell Me Lies* 1967; *Dead Cert* 1974; *Hennessy* 1975; *The Legacy* 1978; *Lady Jane* 1985; *The Pleasure Principle* 1991; *A Pin for the Butterfly* 1994

Hohl, Arthur (1889–1964) *Baby Face* 1933; *Man's Castle* 1933; *Cleopatra* 1934; *Jimmy the Gent* 1934; *Lady by Choice* 1934; *Romance in Manhattan* 1934; *Atlantic Adventure* 1935; *Village Tale* 1935; *The Whole Town's Talking* 1935; *The Adventures of Sherlock Holmes* 1939; *Blackmail* 1939; *The Scarlet Claw* 1944; *Sherlock Holmes and the Spider Woman* 1944; *The Vigilantes Return* 1947

Holbrook, Hal (1925–) *The Group* 1966; *Wild in the Streets* 1968; *The Great White Hope* 1970; *The People Next Door* 1970; *They Only Kill Their Masters* 1972; *Jonathan Livingston Seagull* 1973; *Magnum Force* 1973; *The Girl from Petrovka* 1974; *All the President's Men* 1976; *Battle of Midway* 1976; *Julia* 1977; *Capricorn One* 1978; *The Fog* 1980; *The Kidnapping of the President* 1980; *Creepshow* 1982; *The Star Chamber* 1983; *Wall Street* 1987; *The Unholy* 1988; *Day One* 1989; *Fletch Lives* 1989; *Evidence of Love* 1990; *The Firm* 1993; *Acts of Love* 1995; *Operation Delta Force* 1996; *Eye of God* 1997; *Cats Don't Dance* 1998; *Hush* 1998; *The Bachelor* 1999; *Men of Honor* 2000; *Waking the Dead* 2000; *The Majestic* 2001

Holcomb, Sarah *Walk Proud* 1979; *Caddyshack* 1980; *Happy Birthday, Gemini* 1980

Holcombe, Harry (1906–1987) *Kisses for My President* 1964; *The Fortune Cookie* 1966; *Foxy Brown* 1974

Holden, Alexandra (1977–) *Dancer, Texas Pop 81* 1998; *Sugar & Spice* 2001; *American Gun* 2002; *The Hot Chick* 2002; *Dead End* 2003

Holden, Fay (1895–1973) *Bulldog Drummond Escapes* 1937; *Judge Hardy's Children* 1938; *Love Finds Andy Hardy* 1938; *Out West with the Hardys* 1938; *Sweethearts* 1938; *You're Only Young Once* 1938; *Andy Hardy Gets Spring Fever* 1939; *The Hardys Ride High* 1939; *Judge Hardy and Son* 1939; *Sergeant Madden* 1939; *Andy Hardy Meets Debutante* 1940; *Andy Hardy's Private Secretary* 1941; *Blossoms in the Dust* 1941; *Dr Kildare's Wedding Day* 1941; *HM Pulham Esq* 1941; *Life Begins for Andy Hardy* 1941; *Andy Hardy's Double Life* 1942; *The Courtship of Andy Hardy* 1942; *Andy Hardy's Blonde Trouble* 1944; *Love Laughs at Andy Hardy* 1946; *Whispering Smith* 1948; *Samson and Delilah* 1949; *The Big Hangover* 1950; *Andy Hardy Comes Home* 1958

Holden, Frankie J (1952–) *High Tide* 1987; *Return Home* 1989; *Hammers over the Anvil* 1992

Holden, Gloria (1908–1991) *Dracula's Daughter* 1936; *The Life of Emile Zola* 1937; *This Thing Called Love* 1940; *A Gentleman after Dark* 1942; *Miss Annie Rooney* 1942; *Strange Holiday* 1942; *Behind the Rising Sun* 1943; *Dream Wife* 1953; *The Eddy Duchin Story* 1956

Holden, Jan (1931–) *Assignment Redhead* 1956; *The Primitives* 1962

Holden, Jennifer *Jailhouse Rock* 1957; *Gang War* 1958

Holden, Joyce (1930–) *Bronco Buster* 1952; *The Werewolf* 1956; *Terror from the Year 5,000* 1958

Holden, Laurie (1972–) *Separate Vacations* 1986; *Expect No Mercy* 1995; *The Majestic* 2001

Holden, Marjean *The Philadelphia Experiment 2* 1993; *Automatic* 1994

Holden, Scott (1946–) *Panhandle Calibre 38* 1972; *The Revengers* 1972

Holden (1), William (1872–1932) *The Trespasser* 1929; *Holiday* 1930; *What a Widow!* 1930; *Dance, Fools, Dance* 1931

Holden (2), William (1918–1981) *Golden Boy* 1939; *Invisible Stripes* 1939; *Arizona* 1940; *Our Town* 1940; *I Wanted Wings* 1941; *Texas* 1941; *The Fleet's In* 1942; *Young and Willing* 1942; *Blaze of Noon* 1947; *Dear Ruth* 1947; *Variety Girl* 1947; *Apartment for Peggy* 1948; *The Dark Past* 1948; *The Man from Colorado* 1948; *Rachel and the Stranger* 1948; *Dear Wife* 1949; *Miss Grant Takes Richmond* 1949; *Streets of Laredo* 1949; *Born Yesterday* 1950; *Sunset Blvd* 1950; *Union Station* 1950; *Boots Malone* 1951; *Force of Arms* 1951; *The Turning Point* 1952; *Escape from Fort Bravo* 1953; *Forever Female* 1953; *The Moon Is Blue* 1953; *Stalag 17* 1953; *The Bridges at Toko-Ri* 1954; *The Country Girl* 1954; *Executive Suite* 1954; *Sabrina* 1954; *Samurai* 1954; *Love Is a Many-Splendored Thing* 1955; *Picnic* 1955; *The Proud and Profane* 1956; *Toward the Unknown* 1956; *The Bridge on the River Kwai* 1957; *The Key* 1958; *The Horse Soldiers* 1959; *The World of Suzie Wong* 1960; *The Counterfeit Traitor* 1962; *The Lion* 1962; *Satan Never Sleeps* 1962; *Paris When It Sizzles* 1964; *The 7th Dawn* 1964; *Alvarez Kelly* 1966; *Casino Royale* 1967; *The Devil's Brigade* 1968; *The Christmas Tree* 1969; *The Wild Bunch* 1969; *Wild Rovers* 1971; *The Revengers* 1972; *The Blue Knight* 1973; *Breezy* 1973; *Open Season* 1974; *The Towering Inferno* 1974; *Network* 1976; *Damien – Omen II* 1978; *Fedora* 1978; *Ashanti* 1979; *Escape to Athena* 1979; *The Earthling* 1980; *When Time Ran Out* 1980; *SOB* 1981

Holder, Geoffrey (1930–) *Live and Let Die* 1973; *Swashbuckler* 1976; *Annie* 1982; *Boomerang* 1992; *Chance or Coincidence* 1999

Holder, Roy (1946–) *Whistle down the Wind* 1961; *Loot* 1970; *Psychomania* 1972

Holding, Thomas (1880–1929) *The Three Musketeers* 1921; *Ruggles of Red Gap* 1923

Holgado, Ticky (1944–2004) *Delicatessen* 1990; *Gazon Maudit* 1995; *A Very Long Engagement* 2004

Holiday, Hope (1938–) *The Apartment* 1960; *The Rounders* 1965

Holland, Anthony (1928–1988) *Frank's Greatest Adventure* 1967; *Lucky Lady* 1975; *The Lonely Lady* 1983

Holland, John *Ladies' Man* 1931; *The Girl in Black Stockings* 1957

Hollander, Tom (1969–) *Some Mother's Son* 1996; *Martha – Meet Frank, Daniel and Laurence* 1997; *Bedrooms and Hallways* 1998; *The Clandestine Marriage* 1999; *Maybe Baby* 1999; *Enigma* 2001; *The Lawless Heart* 2001; *Possession* 2002; *The Libertine* 2004; *Paparazzi* 2004

Holles, Antony (1901–1950) *Limelight* 1936; *Smash and Grab* 1937; *The Dark Road* 1948

Holliday, Judy (1922–1965) *Winged Victory* 1944; *Adam's Rib* 1949; *Born Yesterday* 1950; *The Marrying Kind* 1952; *It Should Happen to You* 1954; *Phffft!* 1954; *Full of Life* 1956; *The Solid Gold Cadillac* 1956; *Bells Are Ringing* 1960

Holliday, Polly (1937–) *The One and Only* 1978; *Gremlins* 1984; *Mrs Doubtfire* 1993

Holliman, Earl (1928–) *The Bridges at Toko-Ri* 1954; *Broken Lance* 1954; *Tennessee Champ* 1954; *I Died a Thousand Times* 1955; *The Burning Hills* 1956; *Forbidden Planet* 1956; *The Rainmaker* 1956; *Don't Go Near the Water* 1957; *Gunfight at the OK Corral* 1957; *Trooper Hook* 1957; *Hot Spell* 1958; *The Baited Trap* 1959; *Last Train from Gun Hill* 1959; *Visit to a Small Planet* 1960; *Armored Command* 1961; *The Sons of Katie Elder* 1965; *A Covenant with Death* 1967; *Anzio* 1968; *The Power* 1968; *The Biscuit Eater* 1972; *Sharky's Machine* 1981

Holloman, Laurel (1971–) *The Incredibly True Adventures of Two Girls in Love* 1995; *The Myth of Fingerprints* 1996; *Tumbleweeds* 1999

Holloway, Ann *Two a Penny* 1968; *Father Dear Father* 1972

Holloway, Stanley (1890–1982) *D'Ye Ken John Peel?* 1934; *Sing as We Go* 1934; *Squibs* 1935; *Cotton Queen* 1937; *The Vicar of Bray* 1937; *Champagne Charlie* 1944; *This Happy Breed* 1944; *The Way Ahead* 1944; *Brief Encounter* 1945; *The Way to the Stars* 1945; *Carnival* 1946; *Meet Me at Dawn* 1946; *Wanted for Murder* 1946; *Nicholas Nickleby* 1947; *Another Shore* 1948; *Hamlet* 1948; *Noose* 1948; *One Night with You* 1948; *Snowbound* 1948; *Passport to Pimlico* 1949; *The Perfect Woman* 1949; *Lady Godiva Rides Again* 1951; *The Lavender Hill Mob* 1951; *The Magic Box* 1951; *The Happy Family* 1952; *Meet Me Tonight* 1952; *The Titfield Thunderbolt* 1952; *The Beggar's Opera* 1953; *A Day to Remember* 1953; *Meet Mr Lucifer* 1953; *An Alligator Named Daisy* 1955; *Jumping for Joy* 1955; *Alive and Kicking* 1958; *No Trees in the Street* 1958; *No Love for Johnnie* 1960; *On the Fiddle* 1961; *My Fair Lady* 1964; *In Harm's Way* 1965; *Ten Little Indians* 1965; *The Sandwich Man* 1966; *The Private Life of Sherlock Holmes* 1970; *Flight of the Doves* 1971; *Up the Front* 1972

Holloway, Sterling (1905–1992) *Faithless* 1932; *Advice to the Lovelorn* 1933; *When Ladies Meet* 1933; *The Merry Widow* 1934; *Life Begins at 40* 1935; *Remember the Night* 1940; *Cheers for Miss Bishop* 1941; *Dumbo* 1941; *A Walk in the Sun* 1945; *Make Mine Music* 1946; *The Beautiful Blonde from Bashful Bend* 1949; *Alice in Wonderland* 1951; *Shake, Rattle and Rock!* 1957; *The Jungle Book* 1967; *Live a Little, Love a Little* 1968; *The Aristocats* 1970; *Thunder and Lightning* 1977

Holly, Ellen (1931–) *Take a Giant Step* 1959; *Cops and Robbers* 1973; *School Daze* 1988

Holly, Lauren (1963–) *The Adventures of Ford Fairlane* 1990; *Dragon: the Bruce Lee Story* 1993; *Dumb and Dumber* 1994; *Sabrina* 1995; *Beautiful Girls* 1996; *Down Periscope* 1996; *A Smile like Yours* 1997; *Turbulence* 1997; *No Looking Back* 1998; *The Last Producer* 2000; *Spirited Away* 2001; *What Women Want* 2001

Holm, Astrid (1893–1961) *The Phantom Carriage* 1920; *Master of the House* 1925

Holm, Celeste (1919–) *Three Little Girls in Blue* 1946; *Gentleman's Agreement* 1947; *Chicken Every Sunday* 1948; *Road House* 1948; *The Snake Pit* 1948; *Come to the Stable* 1949; *Everybody Does It* 1949; *A Letter to Three Wives* 1949; *All about Eve* 1950; *Champagne for Caesar* 1950; *The Tender Trap* 1955; *High Society* 1956; *Bachelor Flat* 1961; *Tom Sawyer* 1973; *Bittersweet Love* 1976; *The Private Files of J Edgar Hoover* 1977; *Three Men and a Baby* 1987

Holm, Claus (1918–1996) *The Indian Tomb* 1959; *The Tiger of Eschnapur* 1959

Holm, Ian (1931–) *The Bofors Gun* 1968; *The Fixer* 1968; *A Midsummer Night's Dream* 1969; *Oh! What a Lovely War* 1969; *A Severed Head* 1970; *Mary, Queen of Scots* 1971; *Young Winston* 1972; *The Homecoming* 1973; *Juggernaut* 1974; *Robin and Marian* 1976; *Shout at the Devil* 1976; *The Man in the Iron Mask* 1977; *March or Die* 1977; *Les Misérables* 1978; *The Thief of Baghdad* 1978; *Alien* 1979; *All Quiet on the Western Front* 1979; *SOS Titanic* 1979; *Chariots of Fire* 1981; *Time Bandits* 1981; *The Return of the Soldier* 1982; *Dance with a Stranger* 1984; *Greystoke: the Legend of Tarzan, Lord of the Apes* 1984; *Laughterhouse* 1984; *Brazil* 1985; *Dreamchild* 1985; *Wetherby* 1985; *Another Woman* 1988; *Henry V* 1989; *Hamlet* 1990; *Kafka* 1991; *Naked Lunch* 1991; *Blue Ice* 1992; *The Hour of the Pig* 1993; *Loch Ness* 1994; *Mary Shelley's Frankenstein* 1994; *The Madness of King George* 1995; *Big Night* 1996; *The Fifth Element* 1997; *Night Falls on Manhattan* 1997; *The Sweet Hereafter* 1997; *Simon Magus* 1998; *Animal Farm* 1999; *eXistenZ* 1999; *The Match* 1999; *The Miracle Maker* 1999; *Beautiful Joe* 2000; *Bless the Child* 2000; *Esther Kahn* 2000; *The Emperor's New Clothes* 2001; *From Hell* 2001; *The Lord of the Rings: The Fellowship of the Ring* 2001; *Garden State* 2003; *The Aviator* 2004; *The Day after Tomorrow* 2004

Holm, Sonia (1922–1974) *Miranda* 1947; *Broken Journey* 1948; *The Calendar* 1948; *The Bad Lord Byron* 1949; *13 East Street* 1952

Holman, Clare *Afraid of the Dark* 1991; *Let Him Have It* 1991; *Tom & Viv* 1994

Holman, Vincent (1886–1962) *Love Story* 1944; *The Sound Barrier* 1952

Holmen, Kjersti (1956–) *Orion's Belt* 1985; *Bloody Angels* 1998

Holmes, Katie (1978–) *The Ice Storm* 1997; *Disturbing Behaviour* 1998; *Go* 1999; *Teaching Mrs Tingle* 1999; *The Gift* 2000; *Wonder Boys* 2000; *Phone Booth* 2002; *Pieces of April* 2002; *The Singing Detective* 2003; *First Daughter* 2004; *Batman Begins* 2005

Holmes, Phillips (1907–1942) *The Criminal Code* 1930; *The Devil's Holiday* 1930; *Grumpy* 1930; *Her Man* 1930; *An American Tragedy* 1931; *The Man I Killed* 1932; *Penthouse* 1933; *The Secret of Madame Blanche* 1933; *Caravan* 1934; *Nana* 1934; *Chatterbox* 1936; *General Spanky* 1936; *Housemaster* 1938

Holmes, Stuart (1887–1971) *The Prisoner of Zenda* 1922; *When a Man Loves* 1926; *Belle of the Nineties* 1934

Holmes, Taylor (1872–1959) *Boomerang!* 1947; *Kiss of Death* 1947; *Nightmare Alley* 1947; *The Plunderers* 1948; *Act of Violence* 1949; *Rhubarb* 1951; *Beware, My Lovely* 1952; *Gentlemen Prefer Blondes* 1953; *The Outcast* 1954; *Sleeping Beauty* 1959

Holmes, Wendell (1915–1962) *Good Day for a Hanging* 1958; *But Not for Me* 1959

Holt, Charlene (1939–) *Man's Favorite Sport?* 1964; *Red Line 7000* 1965; *El Dorado* 1967

Holt, Jack (1888–1951) *Flight* 1929; *Dirigible* 1931; *The Littlest Rebel* 1935; *San Francisco* 1936; *Cat People* 1942; *They Were Expendable* 1945; *The Chase* 1946; *My Pal Trigger* 1946; *The Arizona Ranger* 1948; *Task Force* 1949; *Trail of Robin Hood* 1950; *Across the Wide Missouri* 1951

Holt, Jany (1912–) *Abel Gance's Beethoven* 1936; *The Golem* 1936; *The Lower Depths* 1936; *Les Anges du Péché* 1943

Holt, Jennifer (1920–1997) *Private Buckaroo* 1942; *Under Western Skies* 1945

Holt, Jim (1956–) *Fever* 1988; *Backsliding* 1991

Holt, Patrick (1912–1993) *The Mark of Cain* 1947; *When the Bough Breaks* 1947; *Portrait from Life* 1948; *A Boy, a Girl and a Bike* 1949; *Boys in Brown* 1949; *Marry Me!* 1949; *13 East Street* 1952; *Men of Sherwood Forest* 1954; *The Stranger Came Home* 1954; *The Dark Avenger* 1955; *The Girl in the Picture* 1956; *Suspended Alibi* 1956; *I Was Monty's Double* 1958; *Night of the Prowler* 1962; *Serena* 1962; *The Vulture* 1966; *No Blade of Grass* 1970; *Psychomania* 1972

Holt, Sandrine (1972–) *Black Robe* 1991; *Dance Me Outside* 1994; *Rapa Nui* 1994; *Resident Evil: Apocalypse* 2004

Holt, Tim (1918–1973) *Stella Dallas* 1937; *Gold Is Where You Find It* 1938; *The Law West of Tombstone* 1938; *Fifth Avenue Girl* 1939; *Stagecoach* 1939; *Swiss Family Robinson* 1940; *Along the Rio Grande* 1941; *Back Street* 1941; *The Magnificent Ambersons* 1942; *Hitler's Children* 1943; *My Darling Clementine* 1946; *Thunder Mountain* 1947; *The Arizona Ranger* 1948; *Guns of Hate* 1948; *The Treasure of the Sierra Madre* 1948; *Stagecoach Kid* 1949; *Rider from Tucson* 1950; *Storm over Wyoming* 1950; *His Kind of Woman* 1951; *Desert Passage* 1952; *The Monster That Challenged the World* 1957

Holt, Ula *The New Adventures of Tarzan* 1935; *Tarzan and the Green Goddess* 1938

Holton, Mark *Pee-wee's Big Adventure* 1985; *Leprechaun* 1992

Holub, Miroslav *aka* **Holub, Miloslav** (1915–1999) *Invention of Destruction* 1958; *The Ear* 1969

Holzboer, Max aka **Holzboer, Dr Max** *The Blue Light* 1932; *SOS Iceberg* 1933

Homeier, Skip aka **Homeier, Skippy** (1930–) *Tomorrow the World!* 1944; *The Gunfighter* 1950; *Halls of Montezuma* 1950; *Fixed Bayonets* 1951; *Sealed Cargo* 1951; *Has Anybody Seen My Gal?* 1952; *Beachhead* 1954; *Cry Vengeance* 1954; *At Gunpoint* 1955; *The Road to Denver* 1955; *The Burning Hills* 1956; *Stranger at My Door* 1956; *Thunder over Arizona* 1956; *No Road Back* 1957; *The Tall T* 1957; *Day of the Bad Man* 1958; *Comanche Station* 1960; *Showdown* 1963; *Bullet for a Badman* 1964; *The Ghost and Mr Chicken* 1966

Homolka, Oscar aka **Homolka, Oskar** (1898–1978) *Everything Is Thunder* 1936; *Rhodes of Africa* 1936; *Sabotage* 1936; *Comrade X* 1940; *The Invisible Woman* 1940; *Seven Sinners* 1940; *Ball of Fire* 1941; *Rage in Heaven* 1941; *Hostages* 1943; *Mission to Moscow* 1943; *The Shop at Sly Corner* 1946; *I Remember Mama* 1948; *Anna Lucasta* 1949; *The White Tower* 1950; *Prisoner of War* 1954; *The Seven Year Itch* 1955; *War and Peace* 1956; *A Farewell to Arms* 1957; *The Key* 1958; *Tempest* 1959; *Mr Sardonicus* 1961; *Boys' Night Out* 1962; *The Wonderful World of the Brothers Grimm* 1962; *The Long Ships* 1963; *Joy in the Morning* 1965; *Funeral in Berlin* 1966; *Billion Dollar Brain* 1967; *The Happening* 1967; *Assignment to Kill* 1968; *The Madwoman of Chaillot* 1969; *The Executioner* 1970; *Song of Norway* 1970; *The Tamarind Seed* 1974

Hong, James (1929–) *Yes, Giorgio* 1982; *Missing in Action* 1984; *Big Trouble in Little China* 1986; *The Golden Child* 1986; *Black Widow* 1987; *Vice Versa* 1988; *Tango & Cash* 1989; *Shadowzone* 1990; *Wayne's World 2* 1993; *Bloodsport II: The Next Kumite* 1996; *Broken Vessels* 1998; *The Art of War* 2000

Hood, Ed *My Hustler* 1965; *Bike Boy* 1967; *The Chelsea Girls* 1967

Hood, Noel (1910–1979) *The Curse of Frankenstein* 1957; *How to Murder a Rich Uncle* 1957; *The Inn of the Sixth Happiness* 1958

Hooks, Brian *Runaway Car* 1997; *3 Strikes* 2000; *Soul Plane* 2004

Hooks, Kevin (1958–) *Sounder* 1972; *Aaron Loves Angela* 1975; *A Hero Ain't Nothin' but a Sandwich* 1978; *Take Down* 1978

Hooks, Robert (1937–) *Hurry Sundown* 1967; *Last of the Mobile Hot-Shots* 1970; *Trouble Man* 1972; *Aaron Loves Angela* 1975; *Fast-Walking* 1982; *Passenger 57* 1992; *Fled* 1996

Hoosier, Trula *Sidewalk Stories* 1989; *Daughters of the Dust* 1991

Hootkins, William (1948–) *Zina* 1985; *Biggles* 1986; *American Gothic* 1987; *Hardware* 1990; *Hear My Song* 1991; *The Pope Must Die* 1991; *Dust Devil* 1992; *Death Machine* 1994; *This World, Then the Fireworks* 1996

Hope, Bob (1903–2003) *The Big Broadcast of 1938* 1937; *College Swing* 1938; *The Cat and the Canary* 1939; *Never Say Die* 1939; *Some Like It Hot* 1939; *The Ghost Breakers* 1940; *Road to Singapore* 1940; *Louisiana Purchase* 1941; *Nothing but the Truth* 1941; *Road to Zanzibar* 1941; *My Favorite Blonde* 1942; *Road to Morocco* 1942; *Star Spangled Rhythm* 1942; *Let's Face It* 1943; *They Got Me Covered* 1943; *The Princess and the Pirate* 1944; *Road to Utopia* 1945; *Monsieur Beaucaire* 1946; *My Favorite Brunette* 1947; *Road to Rio* 1947; *Variety Girl* 1947; *Where There's Life* 1947; *The Paleface* 1948; *The Great Lover* 1949; *Sorrowful Jones* 1949; *Fancy Pants* 1950; *The Lemon Drop Kid* 1951; *My Favorite Spy* 1951; *The Greatest Show on Earth* 1952; *Road to Bali* 1952; *Son of Paleface* 1952; *Here Come the Girls* 1953; *Military Policeman* 1953; *Scared Stiff* 1953; *Casanova's Big Night* 1954; *Seven Little Foys* 1955; *The Iron Petticoat* 1956; *That Certain Feeling* 1956; *Beau James* 1957; *Paris Holiday* 1958; *Alias Jesse James* 1959; *The Five Pennies* 1959; *The Facts of Life* 1960; *Bachelor in Paradise* 1961; *The Road to Hong Kong* 1962; *Call Me Bwana* 1963; *Critic's Choice* 1963; *A Global Affair* 1964; *I'll Take Sweden* 1965; *Boy, Did I Get a Wrong Number* 1966; *The Oscar* 1966; *Eight on the Lam* 1967; *The Private Navy of Sgt O'Farrell* 1968; *How to Commit Marriage* 1969; *Cancel My Reservation* 1972; *Spies like Us* 1985

Hope, Leslie (1965–) *Kansas* 1988; *Talk Radio* 1988; *Men at Work* 1990; *Doppelganger* 1993; *Paris France* 1993; *Fun* 1994

Hope, Nicholas (1959–) *Bad Boy Bubby* 1993; *The Darkest Light* 1999

Hope, Richard *Laughterhouse* 1984; *Bellman & True* 1987; *My Brother Tom* 2001

Hope, Vida (1918–1963) *They Made Me a Fugitive* 1947; *Vice Versa* 1947; *Green Grow the Rushes* 1951; *The Man in the White Suit* 1951; *Women of Twilight* 1952

Hope, William *Aliens* 1986; *Hellbound: Hellraiser II* 1988

Hopkins, Anthony (1937–) *The Lion in Winter* 1968; *Hamlet* 1969; *The Looking Glass War* 1969; *When Eight Bells Toll* 1971; *Young Winston* 1972; *A Doll's House* 1973; *All Creatures Great and Small* 1974; *The Girl from Petrovka* 1974; *Juggernaut* 1974; *Dark Victory* 1976; *The Lindbergh Kidnapping Case* 1976; *Victory at Entebbe* 1976; *Audrey Rose* 1977; *A Bridge Too Far* 1977; *International Velvet* 1978; *Magic* 1978; *A Change of Seasons* 1980; *The Elephant Man* 1980; *The Hunchback of Notre Dame* 1982; *The Bounty* 1984; *Guilty Conscience* 1985; *84 Charing Cross Road* 1986; *The Good Father* 1986; *A Chorus of Disapproval* 1988; *The Dawning* 1988; *Desperate Hours* 1990; *The Silence of the Lambs* 1991; *Spotswood* 1991; *Bram Stoker's Dracula* 1992; *Chaplin* 1992; *Freejack* 1992; *Howards End* 1992; *The Innocent* 1993; *The Remains of the Day* 1993; *Shadowlands* 1993; *The Trial* 1993; *Legends of the Fall* 1994; *The Road to Wellville* 1994; *August* 1995; *Nixon* 1995; *Surviving Picasso* 1996; *Amistad* 1997; *The Edge* 1997; *The Mask of Zorro* 1998; *Meet Joe Black* 1998; *Instinct* 1999; *Mission: Impossible 2* 1999; *Titus* 1999; *The Grinch* 2000; *Hannibal* 2001; *Hearts in Atlantis* 2001; *Bad Company* 2002; *Red Dragon* 2002; *The Human Stain* 2003; *Alexander* 2004

Hopkins, Bo (1942–) *The Culpepper Cattle Co* 1972; *American Graffiti* 1973; *The Man Who Loved Cat Dancing* 1973; *White Lightning* 1973; *The Killer Elite* 1975; *Posse* 1975; *A Small Town in Texas* 1976; *Tentacles* 1977; *Midnight Express* 1978; *More American Graffiti* 1979; *The Fifth Floor* 1980; *Mutant* 1984; *The Ballad of Little Jo* 1993; *Cheyenne Warrior* 1994; *The November Conspiracy* 1995; *Shadow of the Past* 1995; *U Turn* 1997; *The Newton Boys* 1998; *From Dusk till Dawn II: Texas Blood Money* 1999; *A Crack in the Floor* 2000; *South of Heaven, West of Hell* 2000

Hopkins, Harold (1944–) *Age of Consent* 1969; *Don's Party* 1976; *The Picture Show Man* 1977; *The Club* 1980; *Gallipoli* 1981; *Monkey Grip* 1983

Hopkins, Jermaine aka **Hopkins, Jermaine "Big Hugg"** (1973–) *Lean on Me* 1989; *Juice* 1991; *How to Be a Player* 1997

Hopkins, Joan (1915–) *We Dive at Dawn* 1943; *The Weaker Sex* 1948

Hopkins, Miriam (1902–1972) *Fast and Loose* 1930; *Dr Jekyll and Mr Hyde* 1931; *The Smiling Lieutenant* 1931; *Trouble in Paradise* 1932; *Design for Living* 1933; *The Stranger's Return* 1933; *The Richest Girl in the World* 1934; *She Loves Me Not* 1934; *Barbary Coast* 1935; *Becky Sharp* 1935; *Splendor* 1935; *Men Are Not Gods* 1936; *These Three* 1936; *Woman Chases Man* 1937; *The Woman I Love* 1937; *The Old Maid* 1939; *Virginia City* 1940; *A Gentleman after Dark* 1942; *Old Acquaintance* 1943; *The Heiress* 1949; *The Mating Season* 1951; *Carrie* 1952; *The Children's Hour* 1961; *Fanny Hill: Memoirs of a Woman of Pleasure* 1964; *The Chase* 1966

Hopkins, Nikita *The Tigger Movie* 2000; *Piglet's Big Movie* 2003; *Pooh's Heffalump Movie* 2005

Hopkins, Telma (1948–) *Trancers* 1985; *Trancers II: The Return of Jack Deth* 1991

Hoppe, Rolf (1930–) *Mephisto* 1981; *Schtonk!* 1992; *Palmetto* 1998

Hopper, Dennis (1936–) *I Died a Thousand Times* 1955; *Rebel without a Cause* 1955; *Giant* 1956; *Gunfight at the OK Corral* 1957; *From Hell to Texas* 1958; *The Young Land* 1959; *Key Witness* 1960; *Night Tide* 1961; *The Sons of Katie Elder* 1965; *Planet of Blood* 1966; *Cool Hand Luke* 1967; *The Glory Stompers* 1967; *The Trip* 1967; *Hang 'Em High* 1968; *Panic in the City* 1968; *Easy Rider* 1969; *True Grit* 1969; *Kid Blue* 1971; *The Last Movie* 1971; *Mad Dog* 1976; *The American Friend* 1977; *Tracks* 1977; *Apocalypse Now* 1979; *Out of the Blue* 1980; *King of the Mountain* 1981; *Human Highway* 1982; *The Osterman Weekend* 1983; *Rumble Fish* 1983; *The Inside Man* 1984; *My Science Project* 1985; *Running Out of Luck* 1985; *Blue Velvet* 1986; *Hoosiers* 1986; *Riders of the Storm* 1986; *The Texas Chainsaw Massacre Part 2* 1986; *Black Widow* 1987; *OC and Stiggs* 1987; *The Pick-Up Artist* 1987; *River's Edge* 1987; *Straight to Hell* 1987; *Blood Red* 1988; *Catchfire* 1989; *Chattahoochee* 1989; *Flashback* 1990; *Eye of the Storm* 1991; *The Indian Runner* 1991; *Paris Trout* 1991; *The Heart of Justice* 1992; *Red Rock West* 1992; *Boiling Point* 1993; *Super Mario Bros* 1993; *True Romance* 1993; *Speed* 1994; *Acts of Love* 1995; *Search and Destroy* 1995; *Waterworld* 1995; *Basquiat* 1996; *The Last Days of Frankie the Fly* 1996; *Space Truckers* 1996; *The Blackout* 1997; *Top of the World* 1997; *Meet the Deedles* 1998; *Edtv* 1999; *Jesus' Son* 1999; *Lured Innocence* 1999; *The Prophet's Game* 1999; *Luck of the Draw* 2000; *Knockaround Guys* 2001; *Ticker* 2001; *Leo* 2002; *The Night We Called It a Day* 2003; *Inside Deep Throat* 2005

Hopper, Hal (1912–1970) *Lorna* 1964; *Mudhoney* 1965

Hopper, Hedda (1890–1966) *Sinners in Silk* 1924; *Wings* 1927; *The Last of Mrs Cheyney* 1929; *Holiday* 1930; *As You Desire Me* 1932; *Skyscraper Souls* 1932; *Speak Easily* 1932; *Pilgrimage* 1933; *Alice Adams* 1935; *Dracula's Daughter* 1936; *Nothing Sacred* 1937; *Topper* 1937; *Vogues of 1938* 1937; *Maid's Night Out* 1938; *Tarzan's Revenge* 1938; *Midnight* 1939; *The Women* 1939; *The Oscar* 1966

Hopper, Victoria (1909–) *The Constant Nymph* 1933; *Lorna Doone* 1934; *The Mill on the Floss* 1937

Hopper, William (1915–1970) *Track of the Cat* 1954; *Conquest of Space* 1955; *Rebel without a Cause* 1955; *The Bad Seed* 1956; *Good-bye, My Lady* 1956; *The Deadly Mantis* 1957; *20 Million Miles to Earth* 1957

Hopton, Russell (1900–1945) *Arrowsmith* 1931; *The Miracle Woman* 1931; *Air Mail* 1932; *Law and Order* 1932; *Lady Killer* 1933; *The Little Giant* 1933; *He Was Her Man* 1934; *Star of Midnight* 1935; *Wings in the Dark* 1935

Hordern, Michael (1911–1995) *School for Secrets* 1946; *The Astonished Heart* 1949; *Highly Dangerous* 1950; *Trio* 1950; *Scrooge* 1951; *Tom Brown's Schooldays* 1951; *The Card* 1952; *The Hour of 13* 1952; *Grand National Night* 1953; *Personal Affair* 1953; *The Beachcomber* 1954; *You Know What Sailors Are* 1954; *The Dark Avenger* 1955; *The Man Who Never Was* 1955; *The Night My Number Came Up* 1955; *Storm over the Nile* 1955; *Alexander the Great* 1956; *The Baby and the Battleship* 1956; *The Spanish Gardener* 1956; *Windom's Way* 1957; *Girls at Sea* 1958; *I Was Monty's Double* 1958; *The Spaniard's Curse* 1958; *Man in the Moon* 1960; *Moment of Danger* 1960; *Sink the Bismarck!* 1960; *El Cid* 1961; *Dr Syn, Alias the Scarecrow* 1963; *Genghis Khan* 1964; *The Yellow Rolls-Royce* 1964; *A Funny Thing Happened on the Way to the Forum* 1966; *Khartoum* 1966; *How I Won the War* 1967; *I'll Never Forget What's 'Is Name* 1967; *The Jokers* 1967; *The Taming of the Shrew* 1967; *Anne of the Thousand Days* 1969; *The Bed Sitting Room* 1969; *Some Will, Some Won't* 1969; *Where Eagles Dare* 1969; *Demons of the Mind* 1971; *The Pied Piper* 1971; *The Possession of Joel Delaney* 1971; *Up Pompeii* 1971; *Alice's Adventures in Wonderland* 1972; *England Made Me* 1973; *Theatre of Blood* 1973; *Lucky Lady* 1975; *Mister Quilp* 1975; *Royal Flash* 1975; *The Slipper and the Rose* 1976; *Joseph Andrews* 1977; *The Medusa Touch* 1978; *Watership Down* 1978; *The Wildcats of St Trinian's* 1980; *The Missionary* 1982; *Oliver Twist* 1982; *Yellowbeard* 1983; *Lady Jane* 1985; *Comrades: a Lanternist's Account of the Tolpuddle Martyrs and What Became of Them* 1986; *Labyrinth* 1986; *The Trouble with Spies* 1987; *Diamond Skulls* 1989; *Freddie as FRO7* 1992

Horino, Tad *Pacific Inferno* 1979; *Galaxina* 1980

Horn, Camilla (1903–1996) *Faust* 1926; *Eternal Love* 1929

Horne, David (1898–1970) *Crimes at the Dark House* 1939; *The First of the Few* 1942; *Don't Take It to Heart* 1944; *The Man from Morocco* 1944; *The Seventh Veil* 1945; *The Wicked Lady* 1945; *It's Hard to Be Good* 1948; *Once upon a Dream* 1948; *The Sheriff of Fractured Jaw* 1958

Horne, Geoffrey (1933–) *The Bridge on the River Kwai* 1957; *Bonjour Tristesse* 1958; *Tempest* 1959

Horne, Lena (1917–) *Cabin in the Sky* 1943; *Stormy Weather* 1943; *Swing Fever* 1943; *Broadway Rhythm* 1944; *Ziegfeld Follies* 1944; *Death of a Gunfighter* 1969; *The Wiz* 1978

Horne, Victoria (1920–2003) *Pillow of Death* 1945; *Harvey* 1950

Horneff, Wil (1979–) *Ghost in the Machine* 1993; *Born to Be Wild* 1995

Horner, Penelope *Half a Sixpence* 1967; *The Man Who Had Power over Women* 1970; *Dracula* 1974

Horney, Brigitte (1911–1988) *Baron Münchhausen* 1943; *The Trygon Factor* 1967

Horovitch, David (1945–) *An Unsuitable Job for a Woman* 1981; *Solomon and Gaenor* 1998; *Max* 2002

Horovitz, Adam (1966–) *The Road Home* 1989; *Roadside Prophets* 1992

Horrocks, Jane (1964–) *The Dressmaker* 1988; *The Wolves of Willoughby Chase* 1988; *Getting It Right* 1989; *The Witches* 1989; *Life Is Sweet* 1990; *Memphis Belle* 1990; *Deadly Advice* 1993; *Second Best* 1993; *Bring Me the Head of Mavis Davis* 1997; *Little Voice* 1998; *Born Romantic* 2000; *Chicken Run* 2000; *Lion of Oz* 2000; *Christmas Carol: the Movie* 2001

Horsfall, Bernard (1930–) *On Her Majesty's Secret Service* 1969; *Gold* 1974

Horsford, Anna Maria (1948–) *An Almost Perfect Affair* 1979; *Times Square* 1980; *Bill* 1981; *The Fan* 1981; *Friday* 1995; *Dear God* 1996; *Nutty Professor 2: the Klumps* 2000

Horsley, John (1920–) *Deadly Nightshade* 1953; *Double Exposure* 1954; *Circus Friends* 1956; *Night of the Prowler* 1962; *Serena* 1962

Horsley, Lee (1955–) *The Sword and the Sorcerer* 1982; *Danielle Steel's Palomino* 1991; *Unlawful Passage* 1994

Horton, Edward Everett aka **Horton, Edward** (1886–1970) *Ruggles of Red Gap* 1923; *La Bohème* 1926; *Holiday* 1930; *The Front Page* 1931; *Six Cylinder Love* 1931; *Trouble in Paradise* 1932; *Alice in Wonderland* 1933; *Design for Living* 1933; *It's a Boy* 1933; *Easy to Love* 1934; *The Gay Divorce* 1934; *Kiss and Make-Up* 1934; *Ladies Should Listen* 1934; *The Merry Widow* 1934; *Success at Any Price* 1934; *All the King's Horses* 1935; *The Devil Is a Woman* 1935; *In Caliente* 1935; *The Private Secretary* 1935; *Top Hat* 1935; *The Man in the Mirror* 1936; *The Singing Kid* 1936; *Angel* 1937; *Danger – Love at Work* 1937; *The Great Garrick* 1937; *The King and the Chorus Girl* 1937; *Lost Horizon* 1937; *The Perfect Specimen* 1937; *Shall We Dance* 1937; *Bluebeard's Eighth Wife* 1938; *College Swing* 1938; *Holiday* 1938; *The Gang's All Here* 1939; *Paris Honeymoon* 1939; *That's Right – You're Wrong* 1939; *The Body Disappears* 1941; *Here Comes Mr Jordan* 1941; *Sunny* 1941; *Ziegfeld Girl* 1941; *I Married an Angel* 1942; *The Magnificent Dope* 1942; *Springtime in the Rockies* 1942; *The Gang's All Here* 1943; *Thank Your Lucky Stars* 1943; *Arsenic and Old Lace* 1944; *Brazil* 1944; *Summer Storm* 1944; *Lady on a Train* 1945; *Cinderella Jones* 1946; *Down to Earth* 1947; *Her Husband's Affairs* 1947; *Pocketful of Miracles* 1961; *Sex and the Single Girl* 1964; *The Perils of Pauline* 1967; *Cold Turkey* 1969

Horton, Helen (1928–) *The Mark of the Hawk* 1957; *Phase IV* 1973; *Alien* 1979

Horton, Louisa (1924–) *All My Sons* 1948; *Walk East on Beacon* 1952

Horton, Peter (1953–) *Children of the Corn* 1984; *Where the River Runs Black* 1986; *Side Out* 1990; *2 Days in the Valley* 1996

Horton, Robert (1924–) *When Knights Were Bold* 1936; *Apache War Smoke* 1952; *Pony Soldier* 1952; *Arena* 1953; *Bright Road* 1953; *Men of the Fighting Lady* 1954; *The Green Slime* 1968

Horwitz, Dominique (1957–) *Stalingrad* 1992; *Night Shapes* 1999

Hoshi, Shizuko *Come See the Paradise* 1990; *M Butterfly* 1993

Hoshi, Yuriko (1943–) *Godzilla vs Mothra* 1964; *Ghidrah, the Three-Headed Monster* 1965

Hoskins, Bob (1942–) *Up the Front* 1972; *The National Health* 1973; *Inserts* 1975; *The Long Good Friday* 1979; *Zulu Dawn* 1979; *Pink Floyd – The Wall* 1982; *The Honorary Consul* 1983; *The Cotton Club* 1984; *Lassiter* 1984; *Brazil* 1985; *Mona Lisa* 1986; *Sweet Liberty* 1986; *The Lonely Passion of Judith Hearne* 1987; *A Prayer for the Dying*

1987; *The Raggedy Rawney* 1987; *Who Framed Roger Rabbit* 1988; *Heart Condition* 1990; *Mermaids* 1990; *The Favour, the Watch and the Very Big Fish* 1991; *Hook* 1991; *The Inner Circle* 1991; *Shattered* 1991; *Passed Away* 1992; *Super Mario Bros* 1993; *Balto* 1995; *Nixon* 1995; *Rainbow* 1995; *Michael* 1996; *The Secret Agent* 1996; *Cousin Bette* 1997; *TwentyFourSeven* 1997; *Captain Jack* 1998; *Parting Shots* 1998; *Felicia's Journey* 1999; *A Room for Romeo Brass* 1999; *Don Quixote* 2000; *Live Virgin* 2000; *Enemy at the Gates* 2001; *Last Orders* 2001; *Maid in Manhattan* 2002; *Beyond the Sea* 2004; *Son of the Mask* 2004; *Vanity Fair* 2004; *Unleashed* 2005

Hossein, Robert (1927–) *Madame* 1961; *Shadow of Evil* 1964; *The Dirty Game* 1965; *The Battle of El Alamein* 1968; *The Last Shot* 1969; *The Burglars* 1971; *Don Juan 73, or If Don Juan Were a Woman* 1973; *Le Grand Pardon* 1981; *The Professional* 1981; *Les Uns et les Autres* 1981; *Wax Mask* 1997

Hotchkis, Joan (1927–) *The Late Liz* 1971; *Breezy* 1973; *Ode to Billy Joe* 1976; *Old Boyfriends* 1979

Hotton, Donald *The Hearse* 1980; *One Dark Night* 1982; *Brainstorm* 1983

Houghton, Katharine (1945–) *Guess Who's Coming to Dinner* 1967; *The Gardener* 1972; *Ethan Frome* 1993

Hounsou, Djimon (1964–) *Amistad* 1997; *Gladiator* 2000; *The Four Feathers* 2002; *Biker Boyz* 2003; *In America* 2003; *Lara Croft Tomb Raider: the Cradle of Life* 2003; *Blueberry* 2004; *Beauty Shop* 2005; *Constantine* 2005

House, Billy (1890–1961) *Bedlam* 1946; *The Egg and I* 1947; *Trail Street* 1947; *Rogues of Sherwood Forest* 1950; *Where Danger Lives* 1950

Houseman, John (1902–1988) *The Paper Chase* 1973; *Rollerball* 1975; *Three Days of the Condor* 1975; *St Ives* 1976; *The Cheap Detective* 1978; *Old Boyfriends* 1979; *The Fog* 1980; *Gideon's Trumpet* 1980; *My Bodyguard* 1980; *Wholly Moses!* 1980; *Ghost Story* 1981; *Murder by Phone* 1982; *Another Woman* 1988; *Bright Lights, Big City* 1988

Houser, Jerry (1952–) *Summer of '42* 1971; *Bad Company* 1972; *Class of '44* 1973; *Slap Shot* 1977; *Magic* 1978; *Another You* 1991

Housman, Arthur (1888–1942) *The Singing Fool* 1928; *Scram!* 1932

Houston, Donald (1923–1991) *The Blue Lagoon* 1949; *A Run for Your Money* 1949; *Dance Hall* 1950; *The Red Beret* 1953; *Doctor in the House* 1954; *The Flaw* 1954; *Double Cross* 1955; *Find the Lady* 1956; *The Girl in the Picture* 1956; *Yangtse Incident* 1956; *Danger Within* 1958; *The Man Upstairs* 1958; *Room at the Top* 1958; *The Mark* 1961; *Maniac* 1962; *The Prince and the Pauper* 1962; *The 300 Spartans* 1962; *Twice round the Daffodils* 1962; *Carry On Jack* 1963; *Doctor in Distress* 1963; *633 Squadron* 1964; *A Study in Terror* 1965; *The Viking Queen* 1967; *Where Eagles Dare* 1969; *Sunstruck* 1972

Houston, Glyn (1926–) *The Cruel Sea* 1953; *Turn the Key Softly* 1953; *River Beat* 1954; *The Sleeping Tiger* 1954; *The Wind of Change* 1961; *Emergency* 1962; *Solo for Sparrow* 1962; *A Stitch in Time* 1963; *Old Scores* 1991; *The Mystery of Edwin Drood* 1993

Houston, Marques aka **Houston, Marques B** (1981–) *Fat Albert* 2004; *You Got Served* 2004

Houston, Renee (1902–1980) *Old Bill and Son* 1940; *Two Thousand Women* 1944; *Lady Godiva Rides Again* 1951; *The Big Money* 1956; *A Town like Alice* 1956; *Time without Pity* 1957; *The Horse's Mouth* 1958; *The Flesh and the Fiends* 1959; *And the Same to You* 1960; *No My Darling Daughter* 1961; *Three on a Spree* 1961; *Repulsion* 1965; *Cul-de-Sac* 1966; *Legend of the Werewolf* 1974

Houston, Whitney (1963–) *The Bodyguard* 1992; *Waiting to Exhale* 1995; *The Preacher's Wife* 1996; *Rodgers & Hammerstein's Cinderella* 1997

Hoven, Adrian (1922–1981) *Foxhole in Cairo* 1960; *I Aim at the Stars* 1960; *Fox and His Friends* 1975; *Inside Out* 1975; *Fear of Fear* 1976

Howard, Adam Coleman *Quiet Cool* 1986; *Slaves of New York* 1989

Howard, Alan (1937–) *Oxford Blues* 1984; *Strapless* 1988; *The Cook, the Thief, His Wife and Her Lover* 1989; *The Secret Rapture* 1993

Howard, Andrew *Rancid Aluminium* 1999; *Shooters* 2000; *Mr In-Between* 2001

Howard, Arliss (1955–) *The Prodigal* 1983; *The Lightship* 1985; *Full Metal Jacket* 1987; *Plain Clothes* 1988; *Tequila Sunrise* 1988; *Men Don't Leave* 1990; *CrissCross* 1992; *Ruby* 1992; *Wilder Napalm* 1993; *Erotic Tales* 1994; *The Infiltrator* 1995; *Johns* 1995; *To Wong Foo, Thanks for Everything, Julie Newmar* 1995; *Beyond the Call* 1996; *The Man Who Captured Eichmann* 1996; *The Lost World: Jurassic Park* 1997; *Old Man* 1997; *A Map of the World* 1999; *Birth* 2004

Howard (2), Arthur (1910–1995) *Bottoms Up* 1959; *Paradisio* 1962; *The Love Cage* 1964; *Steptoe and Son* 1972

Howard, Clint (1959–) *An Eye for an Eye* 1966; *Gentle Giant* 1967; *The Jungle Book* 1967; *The Wild Country* 1971; *Eat My Dust!* 1976; *Rock 'n' Roll High School* 1979; *Night Shift* 1982; *The Wraith* 1986; *Disturbed* 1990; *Body Chemistry 2: Voice of a Stranger* 1992; *Carnosaur* 1993; *Cheyenne Warrior* 1994; *Dillinger and Capone* 1995; *Santa with Muscles* 1996; *The Dentist II* 1998; *Edtv* 1999; *The Grinch* 2000; *House of the Dead* 2003

Howard, Curly (1903–1952) *Hollywood Party* 1934; *Time Out for Rhythm* 1941

Howard, Esther (1892–1965) *Detour* 1945; *Dick Tracy vs Cueball* 1946; *The Falcon's Alibi* 1946; *Lady of Deceit* 1947

Howard, Jean *Claudia* 1943; *The Bermuda Mystery* 1944

Howard (1), John (1913–1995) *Valiant Is the Word for Carrie* 1936; *Bulldog Drummond Comes Back* 1937; *Bulldog Drummond's Revenge* 1937; *Lost Horizon* 1937; *Bulldog Drummond in Africa* 1938; *Bulldog Drummond's Peril* 1938; *Bulldog Drummond's Bride* 1939; *Green Hell* 1939; *The Invisible Woman* 1940; *The Man from Dakota* 1940; *The Philadelphia Story* 1940; *Texas Rangers Ride Again* 1940; *The Undying Monster* 1942; *Love from a Stranger* 1947; *The Fighting Kentuckian* 1949; *Make Haste to Live* 1954; *Destination Inner Space* 1966

Howard (2), John (1952–) *The Club* 1980; *Bush Christmas* 1983; *Young Einstein* 1988

Howard, Joyce (1922–) *Freedom Radio* 1940; *The Common Touch* 1941; *Love on the Dole* 1941; *Back Room Boy* 1942; *The Night Has Eyes* 1942; *The Gentle Sex* 1943; *They Met in the Dark* 1943; *They Knew Mr Knight* 1945

Howard, Kathleen (1879–1956) *Death Takes a Holiday* 1934; *It's a Gift* 1934; *You're Telling Me!* 1934; *The Man on the Flying Trapeze* 1935; *Young People* 1940; *Blossoms in the Dust* 1941; *The Navy Steps Out* 1941; *Sweetheart of the Campus* 1941; *Take a Letter, Darling* 1942; *Laura* 1944

Howard, Ken (1944–) *Tell Me That You Love Me, Junie Moon* 1970; *Such Good Friends* 1971; *The Strange Vengeance of Rosalie* 1972; *Second Thoughts* 1982; *Murder in New Hampshire* 1991; *Oscar* 1991; *The Net* 1995; *At First Sight* 1998; *Tactical Assault* 1998

Howard, Kevyn Major *Alien Nation* 1988; *War Party* 1988

Howard, Kyle (1978–) *House Arrest* 1996; *Skeletons* 1996; *Baby Geniuses* 1999

Howard, Leslie (1893–1943) *Outward Bound* 1930; *A Free Soul* 1931; *The Animal Kingdom* 1932; *Smilin' Through* 1932; *Berkeley Square* 1933; *Secrets* 1933; *British Agent* 1934; *Of Human Bondage* 1934; *The Scarlet Pimpernel* 1934; *The Petrified Forest* 1936; *Romeo and Juliet* 1936; *It's Love I'm After* 1937; *Stand-In* 1937; *Pygmalion* 1938; *Gone with the Wind* 1939; *Intermezzo* 1939; *49th Parallel* 1941; *Pimpernel Smith* 1941; *The First of the Few* 1942

Howard, Mary (1912–1989) *All over Town* 1937; *Four Girls in White* 1939; *Spirit of the People* 1940; *Billy the Kid* 1941; *Riders of the Purple Sage* 1941; *Swamp Water* 1941

Howard, Michael (1916–1988) *I See a Dark Stranger* 1946; *Out of the Clouds* 1954; *The Baby and the Battleship* 1956

Howard, Moe (1897–1975) *Meet the Baron* 1933; *Hollywood Party* 1934; *Time Out for Rhythm* 1941; *Have Rocket, Will Travel* 1959; *The Three Stooges in Orbit* 1962; *The Three Stooges Meet Hercules* 1962; *The Three Stooges Go around the World in a Daze* 1963; *The Outlaws Is Coming* 1965

Howard, Norah (1901–1968) *Love, Life and Laughter* 1934; *Car of Dreams* 1935; *The Last Adventurers* 1937; *Two Loves* 1961

Howard, Rance (1928–) *Gentle Giant* 1967; *Where the Lilies Bloom* 1974; *Eat My Dust!* 1976; *Limit Up* 1989; *A Crack in the Floor* 2000; *Toolbox Murders* 2003

Howard, Ron aka **Howard, Ronny** aka **Howard, Ronnie** (1954–) *The Journey* 1959; *Door-to-Door Maniac* 1961; *The Music Man* 1962; *The Courtship of Eddie's Father* 1963; *Village of the Giants* 1965; *The Wild Country* 1971; *American Graffiti* 1973; *Happy Mother's Day... Love, George* 1973; *The Spikes Gang* 1974; *Eat My Dust!* 1976; *The Shootist* 1976; *Grand Theft Auto* 1977; *More American Graffiti* 1979

Howard, Ronald (1918–1996) *While the Sun Shines* 1946; *My Brother Jonathan* 1947; *Bond Street* 1948; *Night Beat* 1948; *Now Barabbas Was a Robber* 1949; *Portrait of Clare* 1950; *Assassin for Hire* 1951; *The Browning Version* 1951; *Night Was Our Friend* 1951; *Drango* 1957; *House in the Woods* 1957; *Gideon's Day* 1958; *No Trees in the Street* 1958; *The Monster of Highgate Ponds* 1961; *Live Now – Pay Later* 1962; *The Bay of Saint Michel* 1963; *Nurse on Wheels* 1963; *The Siege of the Saxons* 1963; *The Curse of the Mummy's Tomb* 1964; *Africa – Texas Style!* 1967; *The Hunting Party* 1971

Howard, Shemp (1895–1955) *The Bank Dick* 1940; *Arabian Nights* 1942; *Private Buckaroo* 1942

Howard, Susan (1944–) *Moonshine County Express* 1977; *Sidewinder One* 1977

Howard, Terrence aka **Howard, Terrence Dashon** (1969–) *Mr Holland's Opus* 1995; *Sunset Park* 1996; *Best Laid Plans* 1999; *The Best Man* 1999; *Big Momma's House* 2000; *Muhammad Ali: King of the World* 2000; *Angel Eyes* 2001; *Boycott* 2001; *Hart's War* 2002; *Crash* 2004

Howard, Traylor (1966–) *Dirty Work* 1998; *Son of the Mask* 2004

Howard, Trevor (1916–1988) *Brief Encounter* 1945; *The Way to the Stars* 1945; *Green for Danger* 1946; *I See a Dark Stranger* 1946; *So Well Remembered* 1947; *They Made Me a Fugitive* 1947; *The Passionate Friends* 1948; *Golden Salamander* 1949; *The Third Man* 1949; *The Clouded Yellow* 1950; *Odette* 1950; *The Gift Horse* 1951; *Outcast of the Islands* 1951; *The Heart of the Matter* 1953; *The Stranger's Hand* 1953; *The Cockleshell Heroes* 1955; *Around the World in 80 Days* 1956; *Run for the Sun* 1956; *Interpol* 1957; *Manuela* 1957; *The Key* 1958; *The Roots of Heaven* 1958; *Moment of Danger* 1960; *Sons and Lovers* 1960; *The Lion* 1962; *Mutiny on the Bounty* 1962; *Father Goose* 1964; *The Man in the Middle* 1964; *Operation Crossbow* 1965; *The Saboteur, Code Name Morituri* 1965; *Von Ryan's Express* 1965; *The Liquidator* 1966; *The Long Duel* 1966; *The Poppy Is Also a Flower* 1966; *Triple Cross* 1966; *Pretty Polly* 1967; *The Charge of the Light Brigade* 1968; *Battle of Britain* 1969; *Twinky* 1969; *The Night Visitor* 1970; *Ryan's Daughter* 1970; *Catch Me a Spy* 1971; *Kidnapped* 1971; *Mary, Queen of Scots* 1971; *The Offence* 1972; *Pope Joan* 1972; *Craze* 1973; *A Doll's House* 1973; *Ludwig* 1973; *The Count of Monte Cristo* 1974; *11 Harrowhouse* 1974; *Persecution* 1974; *Who?* 1974; *Conduct Unbecoming* 1975; *Death in the Sun* 1975; *Hennessy* 1975; *Aces High* 1976; *The Bawdy Adventures of Tom Jones* 1976; *The Last Remake of Beau Geste* 1977; *Slavers* 1977; *Stevie* 1978; *Superman* 1978; *Hurricane* 1979; *Meteor* 1979; *The Sea Wolves* 1980; *Sir Henry at Rawlinson End* 1980; *Windwalker* 1980; *Light Years Away* 1981; *Gandhi* 1982; *The Missionary* 1982; *Sword of the Valiant* 1984; *Dust* 1985; *Foreign Body* 1986; *White Mischief* 1987; *The Dawning* 1988; *The Unholy* 1988

Howard, Vanessa *The Blood Beast Terror* 1967; *Here We Go round the Mulberry Bush* 1967; *Mumsy, Nanny, Sonny & Girly* 1970; *The Rise and Rise of Michael Rimmer* 1970

Howarth, Kevin *The Big Swap* 1997; *Razor Blade Smile* 1998; *The Last Horror Movie* 2003

Howat, Clark *The Glass Web* 1953; *Billy Jack* 1971

Howell, C Thomas aka **Howell, Tom** (1966–) *ET the Extra-Terrestrial* 1982; *The Outsiders* 1983; *Grandview, USA* 1984; *Red Dawn* 1984; *Tank* 1984; *Secret Admirer* 1985; *The Hitcher* 1986; *Soul Man* 1986; *A Tiger's Tale* 1987; *Young Toscanini* 1988; *The Return of the Musketeers* 1989; *Kid* 1990; *Side Out* 1990; *Nickel & Dime* 1991; *Breaking the Rules* 1992; *That Night* 1992; *To Protect and Serve* 1992; *Gettysburg* 1993; *Mad Dogs and Englishmen* 1994; *Fortune Hunters* 1999; *Gang Law* 1999; *Hitman's Run* 1999; *Red Team* 1999; *Gods and Generals* 2002; *The Hillside Strangler* 2004

Howell, Hoke (1930–1997) *Grand Theft Auto* 1977; *The Alarmist* 1997

Howell, Kenneth (1913–1966) *The Eagle and the Hawk* 1933; *Pride of the Bowery* 1941

Howells, Ursula (1922–) *The Oracle* 1952; *The Gilded Cage* 1954; *They Can't Hang Me* 1955; *Account Rendered* 1957; *The Sicilians* 1964; *Mumsy, Nanny, Sonny & Girly* 1970

Howerd, Frankie (1922–1992) *The Runaway Bus* 1954; *Jumping for Joy* 1955; *The Ladykillers* 1955; *A Touch of the Sun* 1956; *Further up the Creek* 1958; *Watch It, Sailor!* 1961; *The Great St Trinian's Train Robbery* 1966; *Carry On Doctor* 1968; *Carry On Up the Jungle* 1970; *Up Pompeii* 1971; *Up the Chastity Belt* 1971; *Up the Front* 1972; *The House in Nightmare Park* 1973; *Sgt Pepper's Lonely Hearts Club Band* 1978

Howes, Bobby (1895–1972) *Please Teacher* 1937; *Happy Go Lovely* 1950

Howes, Hans aka **Howes, Hans R** *Fire and Ice* 1983; *Terminal Velocity* 1994

Howes, Reed (1900–1964) *The Singing Fool* 1928; *The Dawn Rider* 1935; *Paradise Canyon* 1935; *A Million to One* 1937; *The Lone Rider in Ghost Town* 1941

Howes, Sally Ann (1930–) *The Halfway House* 1943; *Dead of Night* 1945; *Pink String and Sealing Wax* 1945; *Anna Karenina* 1947; *Nicholas Nickleby* 1947; *The History of Mr Polly* 1948; *Fools Rush In* 1949; *The Admirable Crichton* 1957; *Chitty Chitty Bang Bang* 1968

Howland, Jobyna (1880–1936) *Rockabye* 1932; *Topaze* 1933

Howlett, Noel (1901–1984) *Serious Charge* 1959; *Murder at the Gallop* 1963; *Please Sir!* 1971

Howlin, Olin (1886–1959) *Belle Starr* 1941; *The Blob* 1958

Howman, Karl (1952–) *Babylon* 1980; *Party Party* 1983

Hoyos, Cristina *Blood Wedding* 1981; *Carmen* 1983; *El Amor Brujo* 1986

Hoyos, Rodolfo aka **Hoyos Jr, Rodolfo** (1896–1980) *Gypsy Colt* 1954; *The Americano* 1955; *The Brave One* 1956; *Villa!* 1958

Hoyt, Arthur (1874–1953) *Camille* 1921; *The Lost World* 1925; *Shanghai Madness* 1933; *It Happened One Night* 1934; *The Great McGinty* 1940; *Sullivan's Travels* 1941

Hoyt, John (1905–1991) *OSS* 1946; *Brute Force* 1947; *My Favorite Brunette* 1947; *The Unfaithful* 1947; *To the Ends of the Earth* 1948; *Winter Meeting* 1948; *The Bribe* 1949; *Everybody Does It* 1949; *The Lady Gambles* 1949; *The Company She Keeps* 1950; *The Lawless* 1950; *When Worlds Collide* 1951; *The Blackboard Jungle* 1955; *The Purple Mask* 1955; *The Come On* 1956; *The Conqueror* 1956; *Death of a Scoundrel* 1956; *Forever, Darling* 1956; *Mohawk* 1956; *Attack of the Puppet People* 1958; *Merrill's Marauders* 1962; *The Man with the X-Ray Eyes* 1963; *The Time Travelers* 1964; *Operation CIA* 1965; *Duel at Diablo* 1966; *Flesh Gordon* 1974

Hrusinsky, Rudolf (1921–1994) *Baron Munchhausen* 1961; *Capricious Summer* 1968; *The Cremator* 1968; *Cutting It Short* 1980; *My Sweet Little Village* 1986; *The Last of the Good Old Days* 1989; *Elementary School* 1991

Hu, Kelly (1968–) *The Scorpion King* 2002; *Cradle 2 the Grave* 2003

Hubbard, John aka **Allan, Anthony** (1914–1988) *Dramatic School* 1938; *The Housekeeper's Daughter* 1939; *Maisie* 1939; *One Million BC* 1940; *Turnabout* 1940; *Our Wife* 1941; *Road Show* 1941; *You'll Never Get Rich* 1941; *The Mummy's Tomb* 1942; *Chatterbox* 1943; *Up in Mabel's Room* 1944; *The Bullfighter and the Lady* 1951; *Escort West* 1959; *Gunfight at Comanche Creek* 1964

Hubbert, Cork *Caveman* 1981; *Under the Rainbow* 1981; *Not for Publication* 1984; *Legend* 1985; *The Ballad of the Sad Café* 1991

Huber, Harold (1904–1959) *He Was Her Man* 1934; *The Gay Desperado* 1936; *Klondike Annie* 1936; *Charlie Chan at Monte Carlo* 1937; *Charlie Chan on Broadway* 1937; *Going Places* 1938; *Mysterious Mr Moto* 1938; *Kit Carson* 1940; *Charlie Chan in Rio* 1941; *Down Mexico Way* 1941; *A Gentleman after Dark* 1942; *Crime Doctor* 1943

Hubley, Season (1951–) *Catch My Soul* 1973; *The Lolly-Madonna War* 1973; *Elvis – the Movie* 1979; *Hardcore* 1979; *Vice Squad*

1982; *Agatha Christie's A Caribbean Mystery* 1983; *PrettyKill* 1987
Hubley, Whip (1957–) *Russkies* 1987; *Desire & Hell at Sunset Motel* 1991; *Lake Consequence* 1992
Hubschmid, Paul (1917–2001) *The Indian Tomb* 1959; *The Tiger of Eschnapur* 1959; *Funeral in Berlin* 1966; *In Enemy Country* 1968; *Skullduggery* 1969
Huckabee, Cooper *Urban Cowboy* 1980; *The Funhouse* 1981; *The Curse* 1987; *Cohen and Tate* 1988; *Night Eyes* 1990
Hudd, Roy (1936–) *The Blood Beast Terror* 1967; *The Magnificent Seven Deadly Sins* 1971; *Up Pompeii* 1971; *Up the Chastity Belt* 1971; *A Kind of Hush* 1998; *Purely Belter* 2000
Hudd, Walter (1897–1963) *Rembrandt* 1936; *Elephant Boy* 1937; *I Know Where I'm Going!* 1945; *The Two-Headed Spy* 1958
Huddleston, David (1930–) *Brian's Song* 1971; *Bad Company* 1972; *Billy Two Hats* 1973; *Blazing Saddles* 1974; *The Klansman* 1974; *McQ* 1974; *Breakheart Pass* 1976; *Sherlock Holmes in New York* 1976; *GORP* 1980; *Smokey and the Bandit II* 1980; *Santa Claus* 1985; *Frantic* 1988; *The Big Lebowski* 1997; *The Man Next Door* 1998; *G-Men from Hell* 2000
Hudson, Ernie (1945–) *Spacehunter: Adventures in the Forbidden Zone* 1983; *Ghostbusters* 1984; *Collision Course* 1987; *Weeds* 1987; *Ghostbusters II* 1989; *Leviathan* 1989; *The Hand That Rocks the Cradle* 1992; *Sugar Hill* 1993; *Airheads* 1994; *The Cowboy Way* 1994; *The Crow* 1994; *Speechless* 1994; *The Basketball Diaries* 1995; *Congo* 1995; *Just Your Luck* 1996; *Operation Delta Force* 1996; *The Substitute* 1996; *Tornado!* 1996; *Mr Magoo* 1997; *Shark Attack* 1999; *Stealth Fighter* 1999; *Miss Congeniality* 2000; *The Watcher* 2000; *Miss Congeniality 2: Armed & Fabulous* 2005
Hudson, Gary (1956–) *Indecent Behavior* 1993; *Serial Killer* 1996; *Eye of the Killer* 1999
Hudson (1), John (1922–) *The Cimarron Kid* 1951; *The Battle at Apache Pass* 1952; *Return to Paradise* 1953; *Silver Lode* 1954; *The Marauders* 1955
Hudson, Kate (1979–) *Desert Blue* 1998; *Gossip* 1999; *200 Cigarettes* 1999; *About Adam* 2000; *Almost Famous* 2000; *Dr T & the Women* 2000; *The Four Feathers* 2002; *Alex & Emma* 2003; *Le Divorce* 2003; *How to Lose a Guy in 10 Days* 2003; *Raising Helen* 2004; *The Skeleton Key* 2005
Hudson, Rochelle (1914–1972) *Hell's Highway* 1932; *Dr Bull* 1933; *Bachelor Bait* 1934; *Imitation of Life* 1934; *The Mighty Barnum* 1934; *Curly Top* 1935; *Life Begins at 40* 1935; *Les Misérables* 1935; *Way Down East* 1935; *Poppy* 1936; *Born Reckless* 1937; *Mr Moto Takes a Chance* 1938; *Meet Boston Blackie* 1941; *Devil's Cargo* 1948; *Rebel without a Cause* 1955; *Strait-Jacket* 1963; *The Night Walker* 1964
Hudson, Rock (1925–1985) *Fighter Squadron* 1948; *Undertow* 1949; *I Was a Shoplifter* 1950; *One Way Street* 1950; *Shakedown* 1950; *Winchester '73* 1950; *Bright Victory* 1951; *Iron Man* 1951; *Tomahawk* 1951; *Bend of the River* 1952; *Has Anybody Seen My Gal?* 1952; *Horizons West* 1952; *The Lawless Breed* 1952; *Scarlet Angel* 1952; *Sea Devils* 1952; *Back to God's Country* 1953; *The Golden Blade* 1953; *Gun Fury* 1953; *Seminole* 1953; *Bengal Brigade* 1954; *Magnificent Obsession* 1954; *Taza, Son of Cochise* 1954; *All That Heaven Allows* 1955; *Captain Lightfoot* 1955; *Never Say Goodbye* 1955; *One Desire* 1955; *Giant* 1956; *Written on the Wind* 1956; *Battle Hymn* 1957; *A Farewell to Arms* 1957; *Something of Value* 1957; *The Tarnished Angels* 1957; *Twilight for the Gods* 1958; *Pillow Talk* 1959; *This Earth Is Mine* 1959; *Come September* 1961; *The Last Sunset* 1961; *Lover Come Back* 1961; *The Spiral Road* 1962; *A Gathering of Eagles* 1963; *Man's Favorite Sport?* 1964; *Send Me No Flowers* 1964; *Strange Bedfellows* 1965; *A Very Special Favor* 1965; *Blindfold* 1966; *Seconds* 1966; *Tobruk* 1966; *A Fine Pair* 1968; *Ice Station Zebra* 1968; *The Undefeated* 1969; *Darling Lili* 1970; *Hornet's Nest* 1970; *Pretty Maids All in a Row* 1971; *Showdown* 1973; *Embryo* 1976; *Avalanche* 1978; *The Mirror Crack'd* 1980; *The Ambassador* 1984
Hudson, Toni *Just One of the Guys* 1985; *Prime Risk* 1985; *Leatherface: the Texas Chainsaw Massacre III* 1990
Hudson, William (1925–1974) *The Amazing Colossal Man* 1957; *Attack of the 50 Foot Woman* 1958
Hues, Matthias *Dark Angel* 1989; *Diplomatic Immunity* 1991; *Mission of Justice* 1992; *TC 2000* 1993; *Alone in the Woods* 1996
Huet, Henri-Jacques (1930–) *A Bout de Souffle* 1959; *Le Petit Soldat* 1960; *Violent Summer* 1961
Huff, Neal *The Wedding Banquet* 1993; *Love Walked In* 1997
Huffman, David (1945–1985) *FIST* 1978; *Ice Castles* 1978; *The Onion Field* 1979; *Wolf Lake* 1979; *Blood Beach* 1981; *Firefox* 1982; *Agatha Christie's Sparkling Cyanide* 1983; *Last Plane Out* 1983
Huffman, Felicity (1962–) *Quicksand: No Escape* 1992; *The Spanish Prisoner* 1997; *Path to War* 2002; *Raising Helen* 2004
Hugh-Kelly, Daniel (1954–) *Cujo* 1983; *Nowhere to Hide* 1987; *The Good Son* 1993; *Danielle Steel's No Greater Love* 1996
Hughes, Barnard (1915–) *Midnight Cowboy* 1969; *The Hospital* 1971; *Deadhead Miles* 1972; *Rage* 1972; *Sisters* 1973; *Kill Me If You Can* 1977; *First Monday in October* 1981; *Best Friends* 1982; *Tron* 1982; *Agatha Christie's A Caribbean Mystery* 1983; *Maxie* 1985; *Where Are the Children?* 1986; *The Lost Boys* 1987; *Da* 1988; *Doc Hollywood* 1991; *Sister Act 2: Back in the Habit* 1993; *The Odd Couple II* 1998
Hughes, Carol (1915–1995) *Stage Struck* 1936; *Three Men on a Horse* 1936; *The Red Dragon* 1945; *Stagecoach Kid* 1949
Hughes, Finola (1960–) *Nutcracker* 1982; *Staying Alive* 1983; *Aspen Extreme* 1993
Hughes, Geoffrey (1944–) *Yellow Submarine* 1968; *Adolf Hitler – My Part in His Downfall* 1972
Hughes, Hazel (1913–1974) *Lunch Hour* 1962; *A Stitch in Time* 1963
Hughes, Helen *The Lucky Star* 1980; *Middle Age Crazy* 1980; *Visiting Hours* 1982; *The Amityville Curse* 1990
Hughes, Jason *House!* 2000; *Shooters* 2000; *Killing Me Softly* 2001
Hughes, John (1950–) *That Sinking Feeling* 1979; *The Breakfast Club* 1985
Hughes, Kathleen (1928–) *Mr Belvedere Goes to College* 1949; *The Glass Web* 1953; *The Golden Blade* 1953; *Dawn at Socorro* 1954; *Cult of the Cobra* 1955
Hughes, Kirsten *Jane and the Lost City* 1987; *The Kitchen Toto* 1987
Hughes, Laura Leigh aka **Hughes, Laura** *The Betty Ford Story* 1987; *Cold Fever* 1994
Hughes, Lloyd (1897–1958) *Tess of the Storm Country* 1922; *The Sea Hawk* 1924; *The Lost World* 1925; *The Mysterious Island* 1929; *Moby Dick* 1930
Hughes, Mary Beth (1919–1995) *Four Sons* 1940; *Star Dust* 1940; *Charlie Chan in Rio* 1941; *The Ox-Bow Incident* 1943; *The Great Flamarion* 1945; *Riders in the Sky* 1949; *Young Man with a Horn* 1950; *Close to My Heart* 1951
Hughes, Miko (1986–) *Pet Sematary* 1989; *Jack the Bear* 1993; *Wes Craven's New Nightmare* 1994; *Mercury Rising* 1998
Hughes, Roddy (1891–1970) *Cheer Up!* 1936; *The Ghost of St Michael's* 1941; *The Dark Road* 1948; *Escape Route* 1952
Hughes, Sean (1965–) *Snakes & Ladders* 1996; *Fast Food* 1998; *Puckoon* 2002
Hughes, Tresa (1929–) *The Lolly-Madonna War* 1973; *Summer Wishes, Winter Dreams* 1973; *Fame* 1980
Hughes, Wendy (1952–) *Petersen* 1974; *Newsfront* 1978; *My Brilliant Career* 1979; *A Dangerous Summer* 1981; *Lonely Hearts* 1981; *Careful, He Might Hear You* 1983; *My First Wife* 1984; *Remember Me* 1985; *Warm Nights on a Slow Moving Train* 1986; *Happy New Year* 1987; *Shadows of the Peacock* 1987; *Boundaries of the Heart* 1988; *Wild Orchid 2: Two Shades of Blue* 1992; *Princess Caraboo* 1994; *Paradise Road* 1997; *The Man Who Sued God* 2001
Hughley, D L (1963–) *The Brothers* 2001; *Soul Plane* 2004
Hugueny, Sharon (1944–1996) *Parrish* 1961; *The Young Lovers* 1964
Hulson, Steve *The Full Monty* 1997; *Prometheus* 1998; *The Navigators* 2001
Hulbert, Claude (1900–1964) *Bulldog Jack* 1934; *Sailors Three* 1940; *The Ghost of St Michael's* 1941; *My Learned Friend* 1943
Hulbert, Jack (1892–1978) *The Ghost Train* 1931; *Bulldog Jack* 1934; *The Camels Are Coming* 1934; *Jack Ahoy!* 1934; *Under Your Hat* 1940; *Not Now Darling* 1972
Hulce, Tom aka **Hulce, Thomas** (1953–) *September 30, 1955* 1977; *National Lampoon's Animal House* 1978; *Those Lips, Those Eyes* 1980; *Amadeus* 1984; *Echo Park* 1985; *Slam Dance* 1987; *Dominick and Eugene* 1988; *Black Rainbow* 1989; *Parenthood* 1989; *Murder in Mississippi* 1990; *The Inner Circle* 1991; *Fearless* 1993; *Mary Shelley's Frankenstein* 1994; *The Hunchback of Notre Dame* 1996
Hulett, Otto (1898–1983) *The Mob* 1951; *Carbine Williams* 1952; *Ambush at Tomahawk Gap* 1953; *City That Never Sleeps* 1953
Hulette, Gladys (1896–1991) *Tol'able David* 1921; *The Iron Horse* 1924
Hull, Dianne (1949–) *The Magic Garden of Stanley Sweetheart* 1970; *Aloha, Bobby and Rose* 1975; *The Fifth Floor* 1980; *You Better Watch Out* 1980; *The New Adventures of Pippi Longstocking* 1988
Hull, Henry (1890–1977) *Midnight* 1934; *Boys Town* 1938; *Paradise for Three* 1938; *Three Comrades* 1938; *Yellow Jack* 1938; *Jesse James* 1939; *Miracles for Sale* 1939; *Nick Carter, Master Detective* 1939; *The Return of the Cisco Kid* 1939; *Stanley and Livingstone* 1939; *My Son, My Son!* 1940; *The Return of Frank James* 1940; *High Sierra* 1941; *Lifeboat* 1944; *Objective, Burma!* 1945; *Deep Valley* 1947; *High Barbaree* 1947; *Mourning Becomes Electra* 1947; *Fighter Squadron* 1948; *Colorado Territory* 1949; *The Fountainhead* 1949; *The Great Gatsby* 1949; *Treasure of Lost Canyon* 1952; *Inferno* 1953; *The Last Posse* 1953; *Thunder over the Plains* 1953; *Man with the Gun* 1955; *The Buccaneer* 1958; *The Proud Rebel* 1958; *The Sheriff of Fractured Jaw* 1958; *The Oregon Trail* 1959; *Master of the World* 1961; *The Fool Killer* 1965
Hull, Josephine (1884–1957) *Arsenic and Old Lace* 1944; *Harvey* 1950
Hull, Warren (1903–1974) *The Walking Dead* 1936; *The Lone Wolf Meets a Lady* 1940
Hulme, Anthony (1910–) *Send for Paul Temple* 1946; *The Three Weird Sisters* 1948
Humbert, George (1880–1963) *Daughters Courageous* 1939; *Boys of the City* 1940
Hume, Benita (1906–1967) *The Constant Nymph* 1928; *Only Yesterday* 1933; *The Worst Woman in Paris?* 1933; *Jew Süss* 1934; *The Private Life of Don Juan* 1934; *The Gay Deception* 1935; *Rainbow on the River* 1936; *Suzy* 1936; *Tarzan Escapes* 1936; *The Last of Mrs Cheyney* 1937
Humphrey, Renee (1975–) *Fun* 1994; *French Kiss* 1995; *Mallrats* 1995; *Cadillac Ranch* 1996; *The Sex Monster* 1998
Humphreys, Cecil (1883–1947) *The Unfinished Symphony* 1934; *Königsmark* 1935; *Accused* 1936; *Wuthering Heights* 1939; *Desire Me* 1947
Humphries, Barry aka **Everage, Dame Edna** (1934–) *Bedazzled* 1967; *The Bliss of Mrs Blossom* 1968; *The Adventures of Barry McKenzie* 1972; *Barry McKenzie Holds His Own* 1974; *Percy's Progress* 1974; *Side by Side* 1975; *Pleasure at Her Majesty's* 1976; *The Getting of Wisdom* 1977; *Shock Treatment* 1981; *The Howling III* 1987; *Les Patterson Saves the World* 1987; *Napoleon* 1995; *The Leading Man* 1996; *Pterodactyl Woman from Beverly Hills* 1996; *Welcome to Woop Woop* 1997; *Nicholas Nickleby* 2002; *Finding Nemo* 2003
Humphries, Tessa *Cassandra* 1987; *Out of the Body* 1988
Hung, Sammo aka **Hung, Samo Kam-Bo** (1952–) *The Dead and the Deadly* 1983; *The Prodigal Son* 1983; *Project A* 1983; *Zu Warriors* 1983; *Wheels on Meals* 1984
Hunnicutt, Arthur (1911–1979) *Abroad with Two Yanks* 1944; *Broken Arrow* 1950; *A Ticket to Tomahawk* 1950; *Distant Drums* 1951; *The Red Badge of Courage* 1951; *Sugarfoot* 1951; *The Big Sky* 1952; *The Lusty Men* 1952; *Devil's Canyon* 1953; *Split Second* 1953; *Beautiful but Dangerous* 1954; *The French Line* 1954; *The Last Command* 1955; *The Tall T* 1957; *Born Reckless* 1959; *Apache Uprising* 1965; *Cat Ballou* 1965; *El Dorado* 1967; *Harry and Tonto* 1974; *The Spikes Gang* 1974
Hunnicutt, Gayle (1943–) *New Face in Hell* 1968; *Eye of the Cat* 1969; *Marlowe* 1969; *Fragment of Fear* 1970; *The Legend of Hell House* 1973; *Scorpio* 1973; *The Sellout* 1975; *Once in Paris* 1978; *Target* 1985; *Dream Lover* 1986; *Silence like Glass* 1989
Hunt, Bonnie (1964–) *Beethoven* 1992; *Beethoven's 2nd* 1993; *Only You* 1994; *Jumanji* 1995; *Getting Away with Murder* 1996; *Jerry Maguire* 1996; *Subway Stories: Tales from the Underground* 1997; *A Bug's Life* 1998; *Kissing a Fool* 1998; *The Green Mile* 1999; *Random Hearts* 1999; *Return to Me* 2000; *Stolen Summer* 2002; *Cheaper by the Dozen* 2003
Hunt, Brad *Dream with the Fishes* 1996; *Fire Down Below* 1997; *Cherish* 2002
Hunt, David (1954–) *The Dead Pool* 1988; *Murder on the Orient Express* 2001
Hunt, Eleanor (1910–1981) *Whoopee!* 1930; *Blue Steel* 1934
Hunt, Gareth (1943–) *The World Is Full of Married Men* 1979; *Bloodbath at the House of Death* 1983; *A Chorus of Disapproval* 1988; *A Ghost in Monte Carlo* 1990; *Parting Shots* 1998
Hunt, Helen (1963–) *Rollercoaster* 1977; *Girls Just Want to Have Fun* 1985; *Trancers* 1985; *Peggy Sue Got Married* 1986; *Project X* 1987; *Next of Kin* 1989; *Murder in New Hampshire* 1991; *Queens Logic* 1991; *Trancers II: The Return of Jack Deth* 1991; *The Waterdance* 1991; *Bob Roberts* 1992; *Mr Saturday Night* 1992; *Only You* 1992; *Kiss of Death* 1994; *Twister* 1996; *As Good as It Gets* 1997; *Cast Away* 2000; *Dr T & the Women* 2000; *Pay It Forward* 2000; *The Curse of the Jade Scorpion* 2001; *What Women Want* 2001; *A Good Woman* 2004
Hunt, Jimmy (1939–) *Pitfall* 1948; *The Capture* 1950; *Weekend with Father* 1951; *Invaders from Mars* 1953; *The Lone Hand* 1953
Hunt, Linda (1945–) *The Year of Living Dangerously* 1982; *The Bostonians* 1984; *Dune* 1984; *Eleni* 1985; *Silverado* 1985; *Waiting for the Moon* 1987; *She-Devil* 1989; *Kindergarten Cop* 1990; *Teen Agent* 1991; *Twenty Bucks* 1993; *Younger and Younger* 1993; *Pret-a-Porter* 1994; *Pocahontas* 1995; *The Relic* 1996; *Pocahontas II: Journey to a New World* 1998; *Dragonfly* 2002
Hunt, Marsha (1917–) *Hell Town* 1937; *Ellery Queen Master Detective* 1940; *Pride and Prejudice* 1940; *Blossoms in the Dust* 1941; *The Penalty* 1941; *The Trial of Mary Dugan* 1941; *Unholy Partners* 1941; *The Affairs of Martha* 1942; *Joe Smith, American* 1942; *Kid Glove Killer* 1942; *Cry Havoc* 1943; *The Human Comedy* 1943; *Lost Angel* 1943; *Pilot #5* 1943; *Bride by Mistake* 1944; *Music for Millions* 1944; *None Shall Escape* 1944; *The Valley of Decision* 1945; *Carnegie Hall* 1947; *Smash Up – the Story of a Woman* 1947; *Raw Deal* 1948; *Actors and Sin* 1952; *The Happy Time* 1952; *Bombers B-52* 1957; *Blue Denim* 1959; *Johnny Got His Gun* 1971
Hunt, Marsha A (1947–) *Dracula AD 1972* 1972; *Britannia Hospital* 1982; *The Sender* 1982; *Howling II: Your Sister Is a Werewolf* 1984
Hunt, Martita (1900–1969) *Friday the Thirteenth* 1933; *First a Girl* 1935; *When Knights Were Bold* 1936; *Good Morning, Boys* 1937; *Trouble Brewing* 1939; *East of Piccadilly* 1940; *The Man in Grey* 1943; *The Wicked Lady* 1945; *Great Expectations* 1946; *Anna Karenina* 1947; *The Fan* 1949; *Folly to Be Wise* 1952; *It Started in Paradise* 1952; *The Story of Robin Hood and His Merrie Men* 1952; *Treasure Hunt* 1952; *King's Rhapsody* 1955; *Anastasia* 1956; *The March Hare* 1956; *Three Men in a Boat* 1956; *The Admirable Crichton* 1957; *Dangerous Exile* 1957; *Les Espions* 1957; *Me and the Colonel* 1958; *Bottoms Up* 1959; *The Brides of Dracula* 1960; *Song without End* 1960; *Mr Topaze* 1961; *The Wonderful World of the Brothers Grimm* 1962; *Becket* 1964; *The Unsinkable Molly Brown* 1964; *Bunny Lake Is Missing* 1965; *The Best House in London* 1968
Hunt, William Dennis aka **Hunt, William** *Flesh Gordon* 1974; *Flesh Gordon Meets the Cosmic Cheerleaders* 1989
Hunter, Bill (1940–) *Mad Dog* 1976; *Newsfront* 1978; *Weekend of Shadows* 1978; *Dead Man's Float* 1980; *Hard Knocks* 1980; *Gallipoli* 1981; *Heatwave* 1981; *The Hit* 1984; *Death of a Soldier* 1985; *Rebel* 1985; *Sky Pirates* 1986; *Fever* 1988; *Rikky and Pete* 1988; *Deadly* 1991; *The Last Days of Chez Nous* 1992; *Strictly Ballroom* 1992; *The Custodian* 1993; *The Adventures of Priscilla, Queen of the Desert* 1994; *Muriel's Wedding* 1994; *Race the Sun* 1996; *River Street* 1996; *Kangaroo Jack* 2003
Hunter, Henry (1907–1985) *Westbound Limited* 1937; *The Boy Who Caught a Crook* 1961

Hunter, Holly (1958–) *The Burning* 1981; *Swing Shift* 1984; *Broadcast News* 1987; *End of the Line* 1987; *Raising Arizona* 1987; *Always* 1989; *Animal Behavior* 1989; *Miss Firecracker* 1989; *Roe vs Wade* 1989; *Once Around* 1991; *Crazy in Love* 1992; *The Firm* 1993; *The Piano* 1993; *The Positively True Adventures of the Alleged Texas Cheerleader-Murdering Mom* 1993; *Copycat* 1995; *Home for the Holidays* 1995; *Crash* 1996; *A Life Less Ordinary* 1997; *Living Out Loud* 1998; *Jesus' Son* 1999; *Timecode* 1999; *O Brother, Where Art Thou?* 2000; *Things You Can Tell Just by Looking at Her* 2000; *Levity* 2002; *Moonlight Mile* 2002; *Thirteen* 2003; *The Incredibles* 2004; *Little Black Book* 2004
Hunter, Ian (1900–1975) *Downhill* 1927; *The Ring* 1927; *Sally in Our Alley* 1931; *The Sign of Four* 1932; *Night of the Party* 1934; *The Phantom Light* 1934; *The Girl from 10th Avenue* 1935; *I Found Stella Parish* 1935; *Lazybones* 1935; *A Midsummer Night's Dream* 1935; *The Devil Is a Sissy* 1936; *The White Angel* 1936; *Another Dawn* 1937; *Confession* 1937; *That Certain Woman* 1937; *The Adventures of Robin Hood* 1938; *Always Goodbye* 1938; *The Sisters* 1938; *Broadway Serenade* 1939; *The Little Princess* 1939; *Maisie* 1939; *Tarzan Finds a Son!* 1939; *Tower of London* 1939; *Bitter Sweet* 1940; *Broadway Melody of 1940* 1940; *The Long Voyage Home* 1940; *Strange Cargo* 1940; *Andy Hardy's Private Secretary* 1941; *Billy the Kid* 1941; *Come Live with Me* 1941; *Dr Jekyll and Mr Hyde* 1941; *Smilin' Through* 1941; *Ziegfeld Girl* 1941; *A Yank at Eton* 1942; *Bedelia* 1946; *Edward, My Son* 1949; *Appointment in London* 1952; *It Started in Paradise* 1952; *Eight O'Clock Walk* 1953; *The Battle of the River Plate* 1956; *Fortune Is a Woman* 1956; *Rockets Galore* 1958; *North West Frontier* 1959; *The Bulldog Breed* 1960; *Doctor Blood's Coffin* 1960; *Guns of Darkness* 1962
Hunter, Jeffrey *aka* **Hunter, Jeff** (1925–1969) *The Frogmen* 1951; *Belles on Their Toes* 1952; *Dreamboat* 1952; *Red Skies of Montana* 1952; *Sailor of the King* 1953; *Princess of the Nile* 1954; *Seven Angry Men* 1955; *Seven Cities of Gold* 1955; *White Feather* 1955; *The Great Locomotive Chase* 1956; *A Kiss before Dying* 1956; *The Proud Ones* 1956; *The Searchers* 1956; *Count Five and Die* 1957; *Gun for a Coward* 1957; *No Down Payment* 1957; *The True Story of Jesse James* 1957; *The Way to the Gold* 1957; *In Love and War* 1958; *The Last Hurrah* 1958; *Hell to Eternity* 1960; *Key Witness* 1960; *Sergeant Rutledge* 1960; *King of Kings* 1961; *Man-Trap* 1961; *The Longest Day* 1962; *Gold for the Caesars* 1964; *Brainstorm* 1965; *Custer of the West* 1968; *The Private Navy of Sgt O'Farrell* 1968
Hunter, Kaki (1955–) *Roadie* 1980; *Whose Life Is It Anyway?* 1981; *Porky's II: The Next Day* 1983; *Just the Way You Are* 1984; *Porky's Revenge* 1985
Hunter, Kelly *Being Human* 1994; *Hollow Reed* 1995
Hunter, Kim (1922–2002) *The Seventh Victim* 1943; *Tender Comrade* 1943; *Betrayed* 1944; *A Matter of Life and Death* 1946; *A Streetcar Named Desire* 1951; *Anything Can Happen* 1952; *Deadline – USA* 1952; *Storm Center* 1956; *The Young Stranger* 1957; *Money, Women and Guns* 1958; *Lilith* 1964; *Planet of the Apes* 1967; *Beneath the Planet of the Apes* 1969; *Escape from the Planet of the Apes* 1971; *Skokie* 1981; *The Kindred* 1986; *Two Evil Eyes* 1990; *A Price above Rubies* 1997
Hunter, Russell (1925–2004) *The Gorbals Story* 1949; *Callan* 1974; *American Cousins* 2003
Hunter, Tab (1931–) *Island of Desire* 1952; *Return to Treasure Island* 1954; *Track of the Cat* 1954; *Battle Cry* 1955; *The Sea Chase* 1955; *The Burning Hills* 1956; *The Girl He Left Behind* 1956; *Hell Bent for Glory* 1957; *Damn Yankees* 1958; *Gunman's Walk* 1958; *That Kind of Woman* 1959; *They Came to Cordura* 1959; *The Pleasure of His Company* 1961; *Ride the Wild Surf* 1964; *City under the Sea* 1965; *The Loved One* 1965; *Hostile Guns* 1967; *The Arousers* 1970; *The Life and Times of Judge Roy Bean* 1972; *Polyester* 1981; *Pandemonium* 1982; *Lust in the Dust* 1984; *Cameron's Closet* 1988; *Out of the Dark* 1988; *Dark Horse* 1992
Huntington, Sam (1982–) *Jungle 2 Jungle* 1997; *Detroit Rock City* 1999; *Sleepover* 2004
Huntley, Raymond (1904–1990) *Freedom Radio* 1940; *The Ghost of St Michael's* 1941; *The Ghost Train* 1941; *Pimpernel Smith* 1941; *The Way Ahead* 1944; *I See a Dark Stranger* 1946; *School for Secrets* 1946; *Broken Journey* 1948; *It's Hard to Be Good* 1948; *Mr Perrin and Mr Traill* 1948; *The Long Dark Hall* 1951; *Mr Denning Drives North* 1951; *The Last Page* 1952; *Laxdale Hall* 1953; *Orders Are Orders* 1954; *The Constant Husband* 1955; *Brothers in Law* 1956; *The Green Man* 1956; *Carlton-Browne of the FO* 1958; *Room at the Top* 1958; *Bottoms Up* 1959; *The Mummy* 1959; *A French Mistress* 1960; *Sands of the Desert* 1960; *Suspect* 1960; *On the Beat* 1962; *The Black Torment* 1964; *Hostile Witness* 1968; *The Adding Machine* 1969; *That's Your Funeral* 1972
Huppert, Isabelle (1955–) *Les Valseuses* 1974; *Doctor Françoise Gailland* 1975; *The Lacemaker* 1977; *Violette Nozière* 1977; *The Brontë Sisters* 1979; *Heaven's Gate* 1980; *Loulou* 1980; *Slow Motion* 1980; *Clean Slate* 1981; *Passion* 1982; *Entre Nous* 1983; *Storia di Piera* 1983; *La Garce* 1984; *Cactus* 1986; *The Bedroom Window* 1987; *Une Affaire de Femmes* 1988; *Madame Bovary* 1991; *Après l'Amour* 1992; *The Flood* 1993; *Amateur* 1994; *La Séparation* 1994; *La Cérémonie* 1995; *Rien Ne Va Plus* 1997; *The School of Flesh* 1998; *Comédie de l'Innocence* 2000; *Les Destinées Sentimentales* 2000; *Merci pour le Chocolat* 2000; *8 Women* 2001; *The Piano Teacher* 2001; *Time of the Wolf* 2003; *I ♥ Huckabees* 2004; *Ma Mère* 2004
Hurlbut, Gladys (1898–1988) *The Long, Long Trailer* 1954; *A Man Called Peter* 1955
Hurley, Elizabeth (1965–) *Aria* 1987; *Rowing with the Wind* 1987; *Passenger 57* 1992; *Beyond Bedlam* 1993; *Mad Dogs and Englishmen* 1994; *Dangerous Ground* 1996; *Austin Powers: International Man of Mystery* 1997; *Permanent Midnight* 1998; *Austin Powers: the Spy Who Shagged Me* 1999; *Edtv* 1999; *My Favorite Martian* 1999; *Bedazzled* 2000; *The Weight of Water* 2000; *Dawg* 2001; *Double Whammy* 2001; *Serving Sara* 2002
Hursey, Sherry (1940–) *Friendly Fire* 1979; *Bring It On* 2000
Hurst, Brandon (1866–1947) *Dr Jekyll and Mr Hyde* 1920; *The Hunchback of Notre Dame* 1923; *The Thief of Bagdad* 1924; *Annie Laurie* 1927; *Love* 1927; *Murders in the Rue Morgue* 1932
Hurst, Paul (1888–1953) *Bad Company* 1931; *The Secret Six* 1931; *The Big Stampede* 1932; *The Sphinx* 1933; *Josette* 1938; *Bad Lands* 1939; *Topper Takes a Trip* 1939; *The Westerner* 1940; *Girl Rush* 1944
Hurst, Rick (1946–) *Tunnelvision* 1976; *Going Ape!* 1981
Hurst, Ryan (1976–) *Remember the Titans* 2000; *The Ladykillers* 2004
Hurst, Veronica (1931–) *Laughter in Paradise* 1951; *Angels One Five* 1952; *The Maze* 1953; *Will Any Gentleman...?* 1953; *Bang! You're Dead* 1954; *The Gilded Cage* 1954; *Dead Man's Evidence* 1962; *Licensed to Kill* 1965
Hurt, John (1940–) *The Wild and the Willing* 1962; *This Is My Street* 1963; *A Man for All Seasons* 1966; *Before Winter Comes* 1968; *Sinful Davey* 1969; *In Search of Gregory* 1970; *10 Rillington Place* 1970; *The Pied Piper* 1971; *Little Malcolm and His Struggle Against the Eunuchs* 1974; *The Ghoul* 1975; *East of Elephant Rock* 1976; *The Disappearance* 1977; *The Lord of the Rings* 1978; *Midnight Express* 1978; *The Shout* 1978; *Watership Down* 1978; *Alien* 1979; *The Elephant Man* 1980; *Heaven's Gate* 1980; *Night Crossing* 1981; *Partners* 1982; *The Plague Dogs* 1982; *Champions* 1983; *The Osterman Weekend* 1983; *The Hit* 1984; *Nineteen Eighty-Four* 1984; *Success Is the Best Revenge* 1984; *After Darkness* 1985; *The Black Cauldron* 1985; *Jake Speed* 1986; *Rocinante* 1986; *Aria* 1987; *From the Hip* 1987; *Spaceballs* 1987; *Vincent: the Life and Death of Vincent Van Gogh* 1987; *White Mischief* 1987; *Scandal* 1988; *Windprints* 1989; *The Field* 1990; *Frankenstein Unbound* 1990; *King Ralph* 1991; *Lapse of Memory* 1992; *Even Cowgirls Get the Blues* 1993; *Second Best* 1993; *Shades of Fear* 1993; *Dead Man* 1995; *Rob Roy* 1995; *Wild Bill* 1995; *Contact* 1997; *All the Little Animals* 1998; *Love and Death on Long Island* 1998; *Night Train* 1998; *A Monkey's Tale* 1999; *You're Dead* 1999; *Lost Souls* 2000; *The Tigger Movie* 2000; *Captain Corelli's Mandolin* 2001; *Harry Potter and the Philosopher's Stone* 2001; *Miranda* 2001; *Owning Mahowny* 2002; *Hellboy* 2004; *The Skeleton Key* 2005; *Valiant* 2005
Hurt, Mary Beth (1948–) *Interiors* 1978; *Chilly Scenes of Winter* 1979; *A Change of Seasons* 1980; *The World According to Garp* 1982; *Compromising Positions* 1985; *DARYL* 1985; *Parents* 1988; *Slaves of New York* 1989; *Defenseless* 1991; *Light Sleeper* 1991; *The Age of Innocence* 1993; *My Boyfriend's Back* 1993; *Six Degrees of Separation* 1993; *Affliction* 1997; *Bringing out the Dead* 1999
Hurt, William (1950–) *Altered States* 1980; *Body Heat* 1981; *Eyewitness* 1981; *The Big Chill* 1983; *Gorky Park* 1983; *Kiss of the Spider Woman* 1985; *Children of a Lesser God* 1986; *Broadcast News* 1987; *The Accidental Tourist* 1988; *A Time of Destiny* 1988; *Alice* 1990; *I Love You to Death* 1990; *The Doctor* 1991; *Until the End of the World* 1991; *Mr Wonderful* 1992; *The Plague* 1992; *Second Best* 1993; *Trial by Jury* 1994; *Smoke* 1995; *Jane Eyre* 1996; *Loved* 1996; *Michael* 1996; *Dark City* 1998; *Lost in Space* 1998; *One True Thing* 1998; *The Proposition* 1998; *The Miracle Maker* 1999; *Sunshine* 1999; *Contagion* 2000; *The Simian Line* 2000; *Varian's War* 2000; *AI: Artificial Intelligence* 2001; *Changing Lanes* 2002; *Tuck Everlasting* 2002; *The Village* 2004; *A History of Violence* 2005
Huss, Toby *Down Periscope* 1996; *Bedazzled* 2000
Hussenot, Olivier (1913–1978) *Fanfan la Tulipe* 1951; *Maigret Sets a Trap* 1957
Hussey, Olivia (1951–) *The Battle of the Villa Fiorita* 1965; *Romeo and Juliet* 1968; *Lost Horizon* 1973; *Black Christmas* 1974; *Death on the Nile* 1978; *The Cat and the Canary* 1979; *The Man with Bogart's Face* 1980; *Virus* 1980; *Turkey Shoot* 1981; *Distortions* 1987; *Psycho IV: the Beginning* 1990; *Quest of the Delta Knights* 1993
Hussey, Ruth (1914–2005) *Man-Proof* 1937; *Another Thin Man* 1939; *Blackmail* 1939; *Fast and Furious* 1939; *Maisie* 1939; *Flight Command* 1940; *Northwest Passage* 1940; *The Philadelphia Story* 1940; *Susan and God* 1940; *HM Pulham Esq* 1941; *Our Wife* 1941; *Tennessee Johnson* 1942; *Tender Comrade* 1943; *Marine Raiders* 1944; *The Uninvited* 1944; *Bedside Manner* 1945; *The Great Gatsby* 1949; *Mr Music* 1950; *That's My Boy* 1951; *Stars and Stripes Forever* 1952; *The Lady Wants Mink* 1953; *The Facts of Life* 1960
Huster, Francis (1947–) *Second Chance* 1976; *Another Man, Another Chance* 1977; *Edith and Marcel* 1983; *I Married a Dead Man* 1983; *La Femme Publique* 1984; *Le Dîner de Cons* 1998
Huston, Anjelica (1951–) *Hamlet* 1969; *Sinful Davey* 1969; *A Walk with Love and Death* 1969; *The Last Tycoon* 1976; *Swashbuckler* 1976; *The Postman Always Rings Twice* 1981; *The Ice Pirates* 1984; *This Is Spinal Tap* 1984; *Prizzi's Honor* 1985; *The Dead* 1987; *Gardens of Stone* 1987; *A Handful of Dust* 1987; *Mr North* 1988; *Crimes and Misdemeanors* 1989; *Enemies, a Love Story* 1989; *The Witches* 1989; *The Grifters* 1990; *The Addams Family* 1991; *Addams Family Values* 1993; *And the Band Played On* 1993; *Manhattan Murder Mystery* 1993; *The Crossing Guard* 1995; *The Perez Family* 1995; *Buffalo '66* 1998; *Ever After: a Cinderella Story* 1998; *Phoenix* 1998; *Agnes Browne* 1999; *The Golden Bowl* 2000; *The Royal Tenenbaums* 2001; *Blood Work* 2002; *Daddy Day Care* 2003; *Iron Jawed Angels* 2004; *The Life Aquatic with Steve Zissou* 2004
Huston, Danny (1962–) *Anna Karenina* 1997; *ivansxtc.* 1999; *Hotel* 2001; *21 Grams* 2003; *The Aviator* 2004; *Birth* 2004; *Silver City* 2004
Huston, John (1906–1987) *The Treasure of the Sierra Madre* 1948; *The Cardinal* 1963; *The List of Adrian Messenger* 1963; *The Bible...in the Beginning* 1966; *Casino Royale* 1967; *Candy* 1968; *De Sade* 1969; *Myra Breckinridge* 1970; *The Deserter* 1971; *Man in the Wilderness* 1971; *The Life and Times of Judge Roy Bean* 1972; *Battle for the Planet of the Apes* 1973; *Chinatown* 1974; *Breakout* 1975; *The Wind and the Lion* 1975; *Sherlock Holmes in New York* 1976; *Tentacles* 1977; *Winter Kills* 1979; *Wise Blood* 1979; *Head On* 1980; *The Visitor* 1980; *Cannery Row* 1982; *The Black Cauldron* 1985
Huston, Virginia (1925–1981) *Nocturne* 1946; *Build My Gallows High* 1947; *The Doolins of Oklahoma* 1949; *Flamingo Road* 1949; *Flight to Mars* 1951; *Tarzan's Peril* 1951
Huston, Walter (1884–1950) *The Virginian* 1929; *Abraham Lincoln* 1930; *The Criminal Code* 1930; *The Virtuous Sin* 1930; *American Madness* 1932; *The Beast of the City* 1932; *Law and Order* 1932; *Rain* 1932; *The Wet Parade* 1932; *Ann Vickers* 1933; *Gabriel over the White House* 1933; *The Prizefighter and the Lady* 1933; *The Tunnel* 1935; *Dodsworth* 1936; *Rhodes of Africa* 1936; *Of Human Hearts* 1938; *The Light That Failed* 1939; *Daniel and the Devil* 1941; *The Shanghai Gesture* 1941; *Swamp Water* 1941; *Always in My Heart* 1942; *In This Our Life* 1942; *Yankee Doodle Dandy* 1942; *The Battle of Russia* 1943; *Edge of Darkness* 1943; *Mission to Moscow* 1943; *The North Star* 1943; *The Outlaw* 1943; *Prelude to War* 1943; *Dragon Seed* 1944; *And Then There Were None* 1945; *Dragonwyck* 1946; *Duel in the Sun* 1946; *Summer Holiday* 1948; *The Treasure of the Sierra Madre* 1948; *The Great Sinner* 1949; *The Furies* 1950
Hutchence, Michael (1960–1997) *Dogs in Space* 1986; *Frankenstein Unbound* 1990
Hutcheson, David (1905–1976) *The Love Test* 1935; *The Life and Death of Colonel Blimp* 1943; *Vice Versa* 1947; *Woman Hater* 1948; *Something Money Can't Buy* 1952
Hutchings, Geoffrey *Clockwise* 1986; *Wish You Were Here* 1987; *It's All about Love* 2002
Hutchins, Will (1932–) *Hell Bent for Glory* 1957; *No Time for Sergeants* 1958; *Claudelle Inglish* 1961; *Merrill's Marauders* 1962; *Clambake* 1967; *The Shooting* 1967
Hutchinson, Josephine (1903–1998) *Oil for the Lamps of China* 1935; *The Story of Louis Pasteur* 1936; *Son of Frankenstein* 1939; *My Son, My Son!* 1940; *Tom Brown's Schooldays* 1940; *Somewhere in the Night* 1946; *The Tender Years* 1947; *Adventure in Baltimore* 1949; *Love Is Better Than Ever* 1951; *Ruby Gentry* 1952; *Miracle in the Rain* 1956; *Gun for a Coward* 1957; *Sing, Boy, Sing* 1958; *Walk like a Dragon* 1960; *Baby the Rain Must Fall* 1965
Hutchison, Doug (1960–) *The Chocolate War* 1988; *The Green Mile* 1999; *No Good Deed* 2002; *The Salton Sea* 2002
Hutchison, Fiona (1960–) *Biggles* 1986; *American Gothic* 1987
Hutchison, Ken *Straw Dogs* 1971; *The Wrath of God* 1972; *Sweeney 2* 1978; *Ladyhawke* 1985; *Blonde Fist* 1991
Huth, Harold (1892–1967) *Rome Express* 1932; *The Ghoul* 1933; *The Camels Are Coming* 1934
Hutton, Betty (1921–) *The Fleet's In* 1942; *Star Spangled Rhythm* 1942; *Happy Go Lucky* 1943; *Let's Face It* 1943; *And the Angels Sing* 1944; *Here Come the Waves* 1944; *The Miracle of Morgan's Creek* 1944; *Duffy's Tavern* 1945; *Incendiary Blonde* 1945; *The Stork Club* 1945; *The Perils of Pauline* 1947; *Dream Girl* 1948; *Annie Get Your Gun* 1950; *Let's Dance* 1950; *Sailor Beware* 1951; *The Greatest Show on Earth* 1952; *Somebody Loves Me* 1952; *Spring Reunion* 1957
Hutton, Jim (1933–1979) *The Subterraneans* 1960; *Where the Boys Are* 1960; *Bachelor in Paradise* 1961; *The Honeymoon Machine* 1961; *The Horizontal Lieutenant* 1962; *Period of Adjustment* 1962; *The Hallelujah Trail* 1965; *Major Dundee* 1965; *Never Too Late* 1965; *Walk, Don't Run* 1966; *Who's Minding the Mint?* 1967; *The Green Berets* 1968; *Hellfighters* 1969; *Psychic Killer* 1975
Hutton, Lauren (1943–) *Paper Lion* 1968; *Little Fauss and Big Halsy* 1970; *Pieces of Dreams* 1970; *The Gambler* 1974; *Gator* 1976; *Welcome to LA* 1976; *Viva Knievel!* 1977; *American Gigolo* 1980; *Paternity* 1981; *Zorro, the Gay Blade* 1981; *Starflight One* 1983; *Lassiter* 1984; *Once Bitten* 1985; *Malone* 1987; *Guilty as Charged* 1991; *Missing Pieces* 1991; *My Father the Hero* 1994; *A Rat's Tale* 1998
Hutton, Marion (1919–1987) *Orchestra Wives* 1942; *Abbott and Costello in Society* 1944; *Love Happy* 1949
Hutton, Robert (1920–1994) *Destination Tokyo* 1943; *Hollywood Canteen* 1944; *Roughly Speaking* 1945; *Time Out of Mind* 1947; *And Baby Makes Three* 1949; *The Man on the Eiffel Tower* 1949; *The Younger Brothers* 1949; *The Racket* 1951; *Slaughter Trail* 1951; *The Steel Helmet* 1951; *Man from Tangier* 1957; *The Man without a Body* 1957; *The Colossus of New York* 1958; *Showdown at Boot Hill* 1958; *Cinderfella* 1960; *The Jailbreakers* 1960; *The Sicilians* 1964; *The Vulture* 1966; *They*

Came from beyond Space 1967; *Torture Garden* 1967
Hutton, Timothy (1960–) *Friendly Fire* 1979; *Ordinary People* 1980; *Taps* 1981; *Daniel* 1983; *Iceman* 1984; *The Falcon and the Snowman* 1985; *Turk 182!* 1985; *Made in Heaven* 1987; *Everybody's All-American* 1988; *A Time of Destiny* 1988; *Torrents of Spring* 1989; *Q & A* 1990; *The Dark Half* 1991; *The Temp* 1993; *French Kiss* 1995; *Beautiful Girls* 1996; *City of Industry* 1996; *The Substance of Fire* 1996; *Playing God* 1997; *Aldrich Ames: Traitor Within* 1998; *Deterrence* 1999; *The General's Daughter* 1999; *Sunshine State* 2002; *Kinsey* 2004; *Secret Window* 2004
Huxtable, Judy *The Psychopath* 1966; *The Touchables* 1968; *Scream and Scream Again* 1969; *Die Screaming Marianne* 1970
Hyams, Leila (1905–1977) *Spite Marriage* 1929; *The Big House* 1930; *The Big Broadcast* 1932; *Freaks* 1932; *Island of Lost Souls* 1932; *Red-Headed Woman* 1932; *Ruggles of Red Gap* 1935
Hyatt, Bobby *He Ran All the Way* 1951; *Gypsy Colt* 1954
Hyde, Jonathan (1947–) *Deadly Advice* 1993; *Being Human* 1994; *I Spy Returns* 1994; *Richie Rich* 1994; *Jumanji* 1995; *Anaconda* 1997; *The Mummy* 1999
Hyde-White, Alex (1958–) *Biggles* 1986; *The Phantom of the Opera* 1989; *Time Trackers* 1989; *Pretty Woman* 1990
Hyde White, Wilfrid *aka* **Hyde-White, Wilfrid** (1903–1991) *Murder by Rope* 1936; *Elephant Boy* 1937; *Poison Pen* 1939; *It's Turned Out Nice Again* 1941; *The Demi-Paradise* 1943; *While the Sun Shines* 1946; *The Winslow Boy* 1948; *Adam and Evelyne* 1949; *Britannia Mews* 1949; *Conspirator* 1949; *Golden Salamander* 1949; *The Man on the Eiffel Tower* 1949; *The Third Man* 1949; *Highly Dangerous* 1950; *Last Holiday* 1950; *Mr Drake's Duck* 1950; *Trio* 1950; *The Browning Version* 1951; *Mr Denning Drives North* 1951; *The Million Pound Note* 1953; *The Story of Gilbert and Sullivan* 1953; *Betrayed* 1954; *Duel in the Jungle* 1954; *To Dorothy, a Son* 1954; *John and Julie* 1955; *Quentin Durward* 1955; *The March Hare* 1956; *My Teenage Daughter* 1956; *Tarzan and the Lost Safari* 1956; *The Silken Affair* 1957; *That Woman Opposite* 1957; *The Vicious Circle* 1957; *The Rainbow Jacket* 1958; *Up the Creek* 1958; *Carry On Nurse* 1959; *Libel* 1959; *Life in Emergency Ward 10* 1959; *North West Frontier* 1959; *His and Hers* 1960; *Let's Make Love* 1960; *Two Way Stretch* 1960; *Ada* 1961; *In Search of the Castaways* 1961; *On the Double* 1961; *On the Fiddle* 1961; *Crooks Anonymous* 1962; *John Goldfarb, Please Come Home* 1964; *My Fair Lady* 1964; *Ten Little Indians* 1965; *You Must Be Joking!* 1965; *Chamber of Horrors* 1966; *The Liquidator* 1966; *Our Man in Marrakesh* 1966; *The Sandwich Man* 1966; *Sumuru* 1967; *New Face in Hell* 1968; *Gaily, Gaily* 1969; *The Magic Christian* 1969; *Skullduggery* 1969; *Fragment of Fear* 1970; *King Solomon's Treasure* 1977; *The Cat and the Canary* 1979; *A Touch of the Sun* 1979; *In God We Trust* 1980; *Oh God! Book II* 1980; *Tarzan, the Ape Man* 1981; *The Toy* 1982; *Fanny Hill* 1983
Hyer, Martha (1924–) *Thunder Mountain* 1947; *The Clay Pigeon* 1949; *Roughshod* 1949; *Abbott and Costello Go to Mars* 1953; *So Big* 1953; *Cry Vengeance* 1954; *Down Three Dark Streets* 1954; *Lucky Me* 1954; *Sabrina* 1954; *Francis in the Navy* 1955; *Kiss of Fire* 1955; *Red Sundown* 1956; *Showdown at Abilene* 1956; *Battle Hymn* 1957; *The Delicate Delinquent* 1957; *Mister Cory* 1957; *My Man Godfrey* 1957; *Houseboat* 1958; *Paris Holiday* 1958; *Some Came Running* 1958; *The Best of Everything* 1959; *The Big Fisherman* 1959; *Desire in the Dust* 1960; *Ice Palace* 1960; *The Last Time I Saw Archie* 1961; *A Girl Named Tamiko* 1962; *The Man from the Diner's Club* 1963; *Wives and Lovers* 1963; *Bikini Beach* 1964; *The Carpetbaggers* 1964; *First Men in the Moon* 1964; *The Sons of Katie Elder* 1965; *The Night of the Grizzly* 1966; *Picture Mommy Dead* 1966; *War Italian Style* 1966; *The Happening* 1967; *House of a Thousand Dolls* 1967; *Crossplot* 1969; *Once You Kiss a Stranger* 1969; *Day of the Wolves* 1973
Hyland, Diana (1936–1977) *One Man's Way* 1964; *Jigsaw* 1968; *The Boy in the Plastic Bubble* 1976
Hylands, Scott (1943–) *Daddy's Gone A-Hunting* 1969; *Fools* 1970; *Bittersweet Love* 1976; *The Boys in Company C* 1978; *Freefall: Flight 174* 1995
Hylton, Jane (1926–1979) *Daybreak* 1946; *It Always Rains on Sunday* 1947; *Here Come the Huggetts* 1948; *My Brother's Keeper* 1948; *Dance Hall* 1950; *The Quiet Woman* 1950; *It Started in Paradise* 1952; *The Weak and the Wicked* 1953; *You Pay Your Money* 1957; *Devil's Bait* 1959; *Circus of Horrors* 1960; *House of Mystery* 1961
Hylton, Richard (1920–1962) *Halls of Montezuma* 1950; *Fixed Bayonets* 1951; *The Pride of St Louis* 1952
Hymer, Warren (1906–1948) *Fox Movietone Follies of 1929* 1929; *Born Reckless* 1930; *Men without Women* 1930; *Up the River* 1930; *One Way Passage* 1932; *20,000 Years in Sing Sing* 1933; *She Loves Me Not* 1934; *Confidential* 1935; *Mr Deeds Goes to Town* 1936; *Rhythm on the Range* 1936; *You Only Live Once* 1937; *Bluebeard's Eighth Wife* 1938; *You and Me* 1938; *Destry Rides Again* 1939; *Mr Moto in Danger Island* 1939; *The Birth of the Blues* 1941; *Baby Face Morgan* 1942; *Dr Broadway* 1942
Hyson, Dorothy (1914–1996) *The Ghoul* 1933; *Happy* 1933; *Sing as We Go* 1934; *Spare a Copper* 1940
Hytten, Olaf (1888–1955) *Kitty* 1928; *Blond Cheat* 1938; *Bells of San Angelo* 1947

I

Ibarra, Mirta *aka* **Ibarra, Mirtha** *Adorable Lies* 1991; *Strawberry and Chocolate* 1993; *Guantanamera* 1995
Ice Cube (1969–) *Boyz N the Hood* 1991; *Trespass* 1992; *CB4* 1993; *Friday* 1995; *The Glass Shield* 1995; *Higher Learning* 1995; *Dangerous Ground* 1996; *Anaconda* 1997; *I Got the Hook Up* 1998; *The Players Club* 1998; *Next Friday* 1999; *Three Kings* 1999; *John Carpenter's Ghosts of Mars* 2001; *Barbershop* 2002; *Torque* 2003; *Barbershop 2: Back in Business* 2004; *Are We There Yet?* 2005; *xXx: the Next Level* 2005
Ice-T *aka* **Ice T** (1958–) *New Jack City* 1991; *Ricochet* 1991; *Trespass* 1992; *CB4* 1993; *Who's the Man?* 1993; *Surviving the Game* 1994; *Johnny Mnemonic* 1995; *Tank Girl* 1995; *Mean Guns* 1996; *Jacob Two Two Meets the Hooded Fang* 1999; *Judgment Day* 1999; *Stealth Fighter* 1999; *Guardian* 2000; *Luck of the Draw* 2000
Ichikawa, Raizo (1931–1969) *Tales of the Taira Clan* 1955; *Conflagration* 1958
Ichikawa, Yui (1986–) *The Grudge 2* 2003; *The Grudge: Ju-On* 2003
Idle, Eric (1943–) *And Now for Something Completely Different* 1971; *Monty Python and the Holy Grail* 1975; *The Rutles – All You Need Is Cash* 1978; *Monty Python's Life of Brian* 1979; *Monty Python Live at the Hollywood Bowl* 1982; *Monty Python's The Meaning of Life* 1983; *Yellowbeard* 1983; *National Lampoon's European Vacation* 1985; *Transformers – The Movie* 1986; *The Adventures of Baron Munchausen* 1988; *Nuns on the Run* 1990; *Too Much Sun* 1990; *Missing Pieces* 1991; *Mom and Dad Save the World* 1992; *Splitting Heirs* 1993; *Casper* 1995; *The Wind in the Willows* 1996; *Burn Hollywood Burn* 1997; *The Magic Sword: Quest for Camelot* 1997; *Rudolph the Red-Nosed Reindeer* 1998; *The Secret of NIMH II: Timmy to the Rescue* 1998; *Dudley Do-Right* 1999; *South Park: Bigger, Longer & Uncut* 1999; *102 Dalmatians* 2000; *Ella Enchanted* 2004
Ifans, Rhys (1968–) *Heart* 1997; *Twin Town* 1997; *Dancing at Lughnasa* 1998; *Janice Beard 45 WPM* 1999; *Notting Hill* 1999; *Rancid Aluminium* 1999; *You're Dead* 1999; *Kevin & Perry Go Large* 2000; *Little Nicky* 2000; *Love, Honour and Obey* 2000; *The Replacements* 2000; *Christmas Carol: the Movie* 2001; *The 51st State* 2001; *Hotel* 2001; *Human Nature* 2001; *The Shipping News* 2001; *Once upon a Time in the Midlands* 2002; *Enduring Love* 2004; *Vanity Fair* 2004
Igawa, Hisashi (1936–) *Pitfall* 1962; *Dodes'ka-Den* 1970; *Ran* 1985; *Boiling Point* 1990; *Rhapsody in August* 1990; *No, Not Yet* 1993
Iglesias, Eugene *aka* **Iglesias, Gene** (1926–) *The Brave Bulls* 1951; *The Duel at Silver Creek* 1952; *Taza, Son of Cochise* 1954; *The Naked Dawn* 1955; *Underwater!* 1955; *Safe at Home* 1962
Ihnat, Steve (1934–1972) *Hour of the Gun* 1967; *Countdown* 1968; *Kona Coast* 1968; *Zigzag* 1970
Iida, Choko *Tokyo Chorus* 1931; *The Only Son* 1936; *Record of a Tenement Gentleman* 1947
Illig, Rolf (1925–) *Swing* 1983; *Alpine Fire* 1985; *Waller's Last Walk* 1989; *Salt on Our Skin* 1992
Illing, Peter (1899–1966) *Eureka Stockade* 1949; *I'll Get You for This* 1950; *Outcast of the Islands* 1951; *Mask of Dust* 1954; *The Battle of the River Plate* 1956; *Bhowani Junction* 1956; *Passport to Treason* 1956; *Miracle in Soho* 1957; *Escapement* 1958; *The Angry Hills* 1959; *Sands of the Desert* 1960; *Echo of Diana* 1963; *Devils of Darkness* 1964
Ilyin, Vladimir (1947–) *Lost in Siberia* 1991; *The Life and Extraordinary Adventures of Private Ivan Chonkin* 1994; *The Stringer* 1997
Iman (1955–) *The Human Factor* 1979; *No Way Out* 1986; *Surrender* 1987; *House Party 2* 1991; *The Linguini Incident* 1991; *Star Trek VI: the Undiscovered Country* 1991; *Exit to Eden* 1994
Imhof, Roger (1875–1958) *The Farmer Takes a Wife* 1935; *Riffraff* 1936; *Girl Loves Boy* 1937
Imhoff, Gary *The Seniors* 1978; *Thumbelina* 1994
Imperioli, Michael (1966–) *Household Saints* 1993; *Hand Gun* 1994; *Postcards from America* 1994; *Sweet Nothing* 1995; *Girl 6* 1996; *Last Man Standing* 1996; *Shark Tale* 2004
Imrie, Celia (1952–) *Blue Black Permanent* 1992; *In the Bleak Midwinter* 1995; *The Borrowers* 1997; *Hilary and Jackie* 1998; *Star Wars Episode I: the Phantom Menace* 1999; *Bridget Jones's Diary* 2001; *Revelation* 2001; *Heartlands* 2002; *Thunderpants* 2002; *Calendar Girls* 2003
Inaba, Yoshio (1921–1998) *Seven Samurai* 1954; *Harakiri* 1962
Ince, Ralph (1881–1937) *Little Caesar* 1931; *Law and Order* 1932
Inclan, Miguel (1900–1956) *Fort Apache* 1948; *Indian Uprising* 1951
Inescort, Frieda (1900–1976) *If You Could Only Cook* 1935; *Another Dawn* 1937; *The Great O'Malley* 1937; *Beauty for the Asking* 1939; *Tarzan Finds a Son!* 1939; *Pride and Prejudice* 1940; *Shadows on the Stairs* 1941; *Sunny* 1941; *The Trial of Mary Dugan* 1941; *You'll Never Get Rich* 1941; *Mission to Moscow* 1943; *The Return of the Vampire* 1943; *The Judge Steps Out* 1949; *Foxfire* 1955; *The Eddy Duchin Story* 1956; *Senior Prom* 1958; *The Alligator People* 1959
Ingalls, Joyce (1950–) *The Man Who Would Not Die* 1975; *Paradise Alley* 1978; *Deadly Force* 1983
Ingerman, Randi (1967–) *Let's Talk about Sex* 1998; *Screw Loose* 1999
Ingham, Barrie (1934–) *Doctor Who and the Daleks* 1965; *A Challenge for Robin Hood* 1967; *Basil the Great Mouse Detective* 1986
Ingram, Jack (1902–1969) *Frontier Outlaws* 1944; *Lost in Alaska* 1952; *Five Guns West* 1955
Ingram (2), Rex (1895–1969) *The Green Pastures* 1936; *The Adventures of Huckleberry Finn* 1939; *The Thief of Bagdad* 1940; *Cabin in the Sky* 1943; *Sahara* 1943; *Dark Waters* 1944; *A Thousand and One Nights* 1945; *Moonrise* 1948; *Congo Crossing* 1956; *Anna Lucasta* 1958; *Escort West* 1959; *Your Cheatin' Heart* 1964
Ingrassia, Ciccio (1923–2003) *Dr Goldfoot and the Girl Bombs* 1966; *War Italian Style* 1966; *Amarcord* 1973; *Kaos* 1984
Inkijinoff, Valery (1895–) *The Battle* 1934; *The Indian Tomb* 1959; *The Tiger of Eschnapur* 1959; *Up to His Ears* 1965
Innes, George (1938–) *Gumshoe* 1971; *Master and Commander: the Far Side of the World* 2003
Innes, Neil (1944–) *The Rutles – All You Need Is Cash* 1978; *Monty Python Live at the Hollywood Bowl* 1982
Interlenghi, Franco (1931–) *Shoeshine* 1946; *Sunday in August* 1949; *The Little World of Don Camillo* 1951; *The Vanquished* 1953; *I Vitelloni* 1953; *Young Husbands* 1958
Iosseliani, Otar (1934–) *Farewell, Home Sweet Home* 1999; *Monday Morning* 2002
Ireland, Anthony (1902–1957) *Jump for Glory* 1937; *The Gambler and the Lady* 1952
Ireland, Celia *Dad and Dave: on Our Selection* 1995; *My Mother Frank* 2000
Ireland, Jill (1936–1990) *The Big Money* 1956; *Three Men in a Boat* 1956; *Hell Drivers* 1957; *Robbery under Arms* 1957; *Twice round the Daffodils* 1962; *Rider on the Rain* 1970; *Violent City* 1970; *Cold Sweat* 1971; *Someone behind the Door* 1971; *The Mechanic* 1972; *The Valachi Papers* 1972; *The Valdez Horses* 1973; *Breakout* 1975; *Hard Times* 1975; *Breakheart Pass* 1976; *From Noon till Three* 1976; *Love and Bullets* 1978; *Death Wish II* 1981; *Assassination* 1986
Ireland, John (1914–1992) *A Walk in the Sun* 1945; *My Darling Clementine* 1946; *The Gangster* 1947; *Railroaded* 1947; *Raw Deal* 1948; *Red River* 1948; *A Southern Yankee* 1948; *All the King's Men* 1949; *Anna Lucasta* 1949; *The Doolins of Oklahoma* 1949; *I Shot Jesse James* 1949; *Roughshod* 1949; *The Walking Hills* 1949; *Red Mountain* 1951; *The Scarf* 1951; *Vengeance Valley* 1951; *The 49th Man* 1953; *The Good Die Young* 1954; *Security Risk* 1954; *Southwest Passage* 1954; *The Glass Cage* 1955; *Queen Bee* 1955; *The Gunslinger* 1956; *Gunfight at the OK Corral* 1957; *Party Girl* 1958; *Faces in the Dark* 1960; *Wild in the Country* 1961; *Brushfire!* 1962; *The Ceremony* 1963; *55 Days at Peking* 1963; *The Fall of the Roman Empire* 1964; *I Saw What You Did* 1965; *Arizona Bushwhackers* 1968; *The Adventurers* 1970; *The House of Seven Corpses* 1973; *Welcome to Arrow Beach* 1974; *Farewell, My Lovely* 1975; *The Swiss Conspiracy* 1975; *Love and the Midnight Auto Supply* 1977; *Maniac* 1977; *Satan's Cheerleaders* 1977; *Tomorrow Never Comes* 1977; *On the Air Live with Captain Midnight* 1979; *Martin's Day* 1984; *Thunder Run* 1986; *Waxwork II: Lost in Time* 1992
Ireland, Kathy (1963–) *Journey to the Center of the Earth* 1989; *Mom and Dad Save the World* 1992; *Amore!* 1993; *National Lampoon's Loaded Weapon 1* 1993
Irons, Jeremy (1948–) *The French Lieutenant's Woman* 1981; *Betrayal* 1982; *Moonlighting* 1982; *The Wild Duck* 1983; *Swann in Love* 1984; *The Mission* 1986; *A Chorus of Disapproval* 1988; *Dead Ringers* 1988; *Australia* 1989; *Reversal of Fortune* 1990; *Kafka* 1991; *Damage* 1992; *Waterland* 1992; *The House of the Spirits* 1993; *M Butterfly* 1993; *The Lion King* 1994; *Die Hard with a Vengeance* 1995; *Stealing Beauty* 1995; *Chinese Box* 1997; *Lolita* 1997; *The Man in the Iron Mask* 1997; *Dungeons & Dragons* 2000; *The Fourth Angel* 2001; *Callas Forever* 2002; *The Time Machine* 2002; *Being Julia* 2004; *William Shakespeare's The Merchant of Venice* 2004; *Kingdom of Heaven* 2005
Ironside, Michael (1950–) *High-ballin'* 1978; *Scanners* 1980; *Visiting Hours* 1982; *Spacehunter: Adventures in the Forbidden Zone* 1983; *Top Gun* 1986; *Extreme Prejudice* 1987; *Nowhere to Hide* 1987; *Watchers* 1988; *Highlander II: the Quickening* 1990; *Total Recall* 1990; *Chaindance* 1991; *McBain* 1991; *Guncrazy* 1992; *A Passion for Murder* 1992; *The Vagrant* 1992; *Father Hood* 1993; *The Next Karate Kid* 1994; *Red Sun Rising* 1994; *The Glass Shield* 1995; *Starship Troopers* 1997; *Chicago Cab* 1998; *Desert Blue* 1998; *Crime + Punishment in Suburbia* 2000; *The Machinist* 2003
Irvine, Andrea *Ailsa* 1994; *Gold in the Streets* 1996
Irvine, Robin (1901–1933) *Downhill* 1927; *Easy Virtue* 1927; *The Ship of Lost Men* 1929
Irving, Amy (1953–) *Carrie* 1976; *The Fury* 1978; *Voices* 1979; *The Competition* 1980; *Honeysuckle Rose* 1980; *Yentl* 1983; *Micki & Maude* 1984; *Rumpelstiltskin* 1986; *Crossing Delancey* 1988; *Who Framed Roger Rabbit* 1988; *A Show of Force* 1990; *An American Tail: Fievel Goes West* 1991; *Benefit of the Doubt* 1993; *Acts of Love* 1995; *I'm Not Rappaport* 1996; *Deconstructing Harry* 1997; *One Tough Cop* 1998; *The Rage: Carrie 2* 1999; *Traffic* 2000; *13 Conversations about One Thing* 2001; *Tuck Everlasting* 2002; *Hide and Seek* 2005
Irving, George (1874–1961) *Bringing Up Baby* 1938; *Maid's Night Out* 1938
Irving, George S (1922–) *Deadly Hero* 1976; *Raggedy Ann and Andy* 1977
Irving, Margaret (1898–1988) *Charlie Chan at the Opera* 1936; *Abbott and Costello in Society* 1944
Irwin, Bill *aka* **Irwin, William** (1950–) *My Blue Heaven* 1990; *Scenes from a Mall* 1991; *Stepping Out* 1991; *Subway Stories: Tales from the Underground* 1997; *The Grinch* 2000
Irwin, Charles (1887–1969) *Bob, Son of Battle* 1947; *The Iron Glove* 1954
Irwin, Tom (1956–) *Light of Day* 1987; *Deceived* 1991; *Mr Jones* 1993; *Holiday Affair* 1996; *No*

Higher Love 1999; *Snow White* 2001

Isaacs, Jason (1963–) *Solitaire for 2* 1994; *DragonHeart* 1996; *Event Horizon* 1997; *Armageddon* 1998; *Divorcing Jack* 1998; *Soldier* 1998; *All for Love* 1999; *The End of the Affair* 1999; *The Patriot* 2000; *Black Hawk Down* 2001; *Sweet November* 2001; *Harry Potter and the Chamber of Secrets* 2002; *The Tuxedo* 2002; *Peter Pan* 2003

Isaak, Chris (1956–) *The Silence of the Lambs* 1991; *Twin Peaks: Fire Walk with Me* 1992; *Little Buddha* 1993; *Grace of My Heart* 1996; *That Thing You Do!* 1996; *A Dirty Shame* 2004

Isabel, Margarita *Danzón* 1991; *Cronos* 1992

Isabelle, Katharine *aka* **Murray, Kate** (1982–) *The Last Winter* 1989; *Ginger Snaps* 2000; *Freddy vs Jason* 2003

Iseya, Yusuke (1976–) *Distance* 2001; *Casshern* 2004

Ishibashi, Renji (1941–) *The Sea Is Watching* 2002; *Gozu* 2003

Ishibashi, Ryo *American Yakuza* 1994; *Blue Tiger* 1994; *American Yakuza 2: Back to Back* 1996; *Kids Return* 1996; *Audition* 1999

Ishihama, Akira (1935–) *Somewhere under the Broad Sky* 1954; *The Human Condition* 1958; *Harakiri* 1962

Israel, Neal (1945–) *It's Alive III: Island of the Alive* 1987; *Look Who's Talking Too* 1990

Issyanov, Ravil *aka* **Isyanov, Ravil** *Back in the USSR* 1992; *Arachnid* 2001

Ito, Emi (1941–) *Mothra* 1962; *Godzilla vs Mothra* 1964

Ito, Robert (1931–) *The Adventures of Buckaroo Banzai across the 8th Dimension* 1984; *The War between Us* 1995

Ito, Yumi (1946–) *Mothra* 1962; *Godzilla vs Mothra* 1964

Ito, Yunosuke *The Burmese Harp* 1956; *The Ballad of Narayama* 1958

Iturbi, José (1895–1980) *Thousands Cheer* 1943; *Music for Millions* 1944; *Anchors Aweigh* 1945; *Holiday in Mexico* 1946; *Three Daring Daughters* 1948; *That Midnight Kiss* 1949

Itzin, Gregory *The Fabulous Baker Boys* 1989; *Born to Be Wild* 1995; *Original Sin* 2001

Iures, Marcel (1951–) *Mission: Impossible* 1996; *The Peacemaker* 1997; *Amen.* 2002; *Hart's War* 2002; *Layer Cake* 2004

Ivan, Rosalind (1884–1959) *The Suspect* 1944; *The Corn Is Green* 1945; *Pillow of Death* 1945; *Pursuit to Algiers* 1945; *Scarlet Street* 1945; *The Verdict* 1946; *Elephant Walk* 1954

Ivanek, Zeljko (1957–) *The Sender* 1982; *Mass Appeal* 1984; *Donnie Brasco* 1997; *A Civil Action* 1998; *The Rat Pack* 1998

Ivernel, Daniel (1920–1999) *Madame du Barry* 1954; *Ulysses* 1954; *Sundays and Cybèle* 1962; *The Diary of a Chambermaid* 1964; *That Man George* 1965; *Borsalino and Co* 1974

Ivers, Robert (1934–2003) *The Delicate Delinquent* 1957; *Short Cut to Hell* 1957; *I Married a Monster from Outer Space* 1958; *GI Blues* 1960

Ives, Burl (1909–1995) *Smoky* 1946; *Green Grass of Wyoming* 1948; *Station West* 1948; *So Dear to My Heart* 1949; *Sierra* 1950; *East of Eden* 1955; *The Power and the Prize* 1956; *The Big Country* 1958; *Cat on a Hot Tin Roof* 1958; *Desire under the Elms* 1958; *Wind across the Everglades* 1958; *Day of the Outlaw* 1959; *Our Man in Havana* 1959; *Let No Man Write My Epitaph* 1960; *The Spiral Road* 1962; *Summer Magic* 1963; *The Brass Bottle* 1964; *Ensign Pulver* 1964; *Jules Verne's Rocket to the Moon* 1967; *The McMasters* 1970; *Baker's Hawk* 1976; *Just You and Me, Kid* 1979; *Earthbound* 1981; *White Dog* 1981; *Uphill All the Way* 1985; *Two Moon Junction* 1988

Ivey, Dana (1942–) *Explorers* 1985; *Dirty Rotten Scoundrels* 1988; *The Addams Family* 1991; *The Adventures of Huck Finn* 1993; *Guilty as Sin* 1993; *Simon Birch* 1998; *Walking across Egypt* 1999; *Disney's The Kid* 2000; *Two Weeks Notice* 2002; *Legally Blonde 2: Red, White & Blonde* 2003

Ivey, Judith (1951–) *Harry and Son* 1984; *The Lonely Guy* 1984; *The Woman in Red* 1984; *Compromising Positions* 1985; *Brighton Beach Memoirs* 1986; *Hello Again* 1987; *In Country* 1989; *Everybody Wins* 1990; *Love Hurts* 1990; *The Devil's Advocate* 1997; *Washington Square* 1997; *What the Deaf Man Heard* 1997

Ivgi, Moshe (1953–) *Cup Final* 1991; *Yom Yom* 1998

Ivo, Tommy (1936–) *Treasure of Lost Canyon* 1952; *Dragstrip Girl* 1957

Iwashita, Shima (1941–) *An Autumn Afternoon* 1962; *Harakiri* 1962; *Twin Sisters of Kyoto* 1963; *The Empty Table* 1985

Izay, Victor *Billy Jack* 1971; *The Trial of Billy Jack* 1974

Izzard, Eddie (1962–) *The Secret Agent* 1996; *The Avengers* 1998; *Velvet Goldmine* 1998; *Circus* 1999; *The Criminal* 1999; *Shadow of the Vampire* 2000; *The Cat's Meow* 2001; *Revengers Tragedy* 2002; *Blueberry* 2004; *Five Children and It* 2004; *Ocean's Twelve* 2004

Ja Rule *aka* **Atkins, Jeffrey "Ja Rule"** (1976–) *Half Past Dead* 2002; *Assault on Precinct 13* 2005

Jackman, Hugh (1968–) *Paperback Hero* 1998; *X-Men* 2000; *Animal Attraction* 2001; *Swordfish* 2001; *Kate & Leopold* 2002; *X2* 2003; *Van Helsing* 2004

Jackson, Anne (1926–) *The Tiger Makes Out* 1967; *How to Save a Marriage and Ruin Your Life* 1968; *The Secret Life of an American Wife* 1968; *Dirty Dingus Magee* 1970; *Zigzag* 1970; *Nasty Habits* 1976; *The Bell Jar* 1979; *The Shining* 1980; *Leave 'em Laughing* 1981; *Sam's Son* 1984; *Folks!* 1992

Jackson, Barry (1938–) *The Bofors Gun* 1968; *Alfred the Great* 1969; *Diamonds on Wheels* 1973; *Mr Love* 1985

Jackson, Brad *April Love* 1957; *Viking Women and the Sea Serpent* 1957

Jackson, Freda (1909–1990) *Beware of Pity* 1946; *No Room at the Inn* 1948; *Women of Twilight* 1952; *The Flesh Is Weak* 1957; *The Brides of Dracula* 1960; *The Shadow of the Cat* 1961; *West 11* 1963; *Die, Monster, Die!* 1965; *The Valley of Gwangi* 1969

Jackson, Glenda (1936–) *Marat/Sade* 1966; *Tell Me Lies* 1967; *Women in Love* 1969; *The Music Lovers* 1970; *Mary, Queen of Scots* 1971; *Sunday, Bloody Sunday* 1971; *Bequest to the Nation* 1972; *The Triple Echo* 1972; *A Touch of Class* 1973; *The Maids* 1974; *Hedda* 1975; *The Romantic Englishwoman* 1975; *The Incredible Sarah* 1976; *Nasty Habits* 1976; *The Class of Miss MacMichael* 1978; *House Calls* 1978; *Stevie* 1978; *Lost and Found* 1979; *HEALTH* 1980; *Hopscotch* 1980; *The Patricia Neal Story: an Act of Love* 1981; *Giro City* 1982; *The Return of the Soldier* 1982; *Turtle Diary* 1985; *Beyond Therapy* 1987; *Business as Usual* 1987; *The Rainbow* 1988; *Salome's Last Dance* 1988; *King of the Wind* 1989

Jackson, Gordon (1923–1990) *The Foreman Went to France* 1941; *Millions like Us* 1943; *San Demetrio London* 1943; *Pink String and Sealing Wax* 1945; *The Captive Heart* 1946; *Against the Wind* 1947; *Eureka Stockade* 1949; *Floodtide* 1949; *Whisky Galore!* 1949; *Bitter Springs* 1950; *Happy Go Lovely* 1950; *The Love Lottery* 1953; *Meet Mr Lucifer* 1953; *Passage Home* 1955; *The Quatermass Xperiment* 1955; *The Baby and the Battleship* 1956; *Sailor Beware!* 1956; *Women without Men* 1956; *Hell Drivers* 1957; *Seven Waves Away* 1957; *Rockets Galore* 1958; *Blind Date* 1959; *The Bridal Path* 1959; *Devil's Bait* 1959; *The Navy Lark* 1959; *Yesterday's Enemy* 1959; *Cone of Silence* 1960; *Tunes of Glory* 1960; *Greyfriars Bobby* 1961; *Mutiny on the Bounty* 1962; *The Great Escape* 1963; *The Long Ships* 1963; *Daylight Robbery* 1964; *The Ipcress File* 1965; *The Fighting Prince of Donegal* 1966; *Danger Route* 1967; *Hamlet* 1969; *The Prime of Miss Jean Brodie* 1969; *Run Wild, Run Free* 1969; *Scrooge* 1970; *Kidnapped* 1971; *Madame Sin* 1972; *Golden Rendezvous* 1977; *The Medusa Touch* 1978; *The Shooting Party* 1984; *Gunpowder* 1985; *The Whistle Blower* 1986

Jackson, Harry (1923–1973) *The Night Runner* 1957; *The True Story of Lynn Stuart* 1957

Jackson, Janet (1966–) *Poetic Justice* 1993; *Nutty Professor 2: the Klumps* 2000

Jackson, Jay *Days of Thrills and Laughter* 1961; *Laurel and Hardy's Laughing 20s* 1965

Jackson, John M (1950–) *Career Opportunities* 1991; *Eve of Destruction* 1991; *Sudden Fury* 1993; *The Glimmer Man* 1996

Jackson, Jonathan (1982–) *Camp Nowhere* 1994; *The Deep End of the Ocean* 1999; *Insomnia* 2002; *Tuck Everlasting* 2002; *Dirty Dancing 2* 2003

Jackson, Joshua (1978–) *The Mighty Ducks* 1992; *Andre* 1994; *Magic in the Water* 1995; *D3: the Mighty Ducks* 1996; *Apt Pupil* 1997; *Urban Legend* 1998; *Cruel Intentions* 1999; *Gossip* 1999; *The Skulls* 2000; *The Safety of Objects* 2001; *Racing Stripes* 2004; *Cursed* 2005

Jackson, Kate (1949–) *Night of Dark Shadows* 1971; *Limbo* 1972; *Thunder and Lightning* 1977; *Making Love* 1982; *Loverboy* 1989; *Hard Evidence* 1994

Jackson, Leonard (1928–) *Ganja and Hess* 1973; *The Brother from Another Planet* 1984

Jackson, Mary (1910–) *Targets* 1968; *A Family Thing* 1996

Jackson (3), Michael (1958–) *The Wiz* 1978; *Moonwalker* 1988

Jackson, Peter (1961–) *Bad Taste* 1987; *Braindead* 1992

Jackson, Philip (1948–) *High Hopes* 1988; *Bad Behaviour* 1992; *Brassed Off* 1996; *Little Voice* 1998; *Mike Bassett: England Manager* 2001

Jackson, Ray (1931–1989) *The Final Test* 1953; *Dunkirk* 1958

Jackson, Roger L *Scream 3* 1999; *The Powerpuff Girls* 2002

Jackson, Rose *aka* **Jackson, Rosemarie** *Hangin' with the Homeboys* 1991; *Dead Presidents* 1995

Jackson, Samuel L *aka* **Jackson, Sam** (1948–) *Eddie Murphy Raw* 1987; *School Daze* 1988; *Do the Right Thing* 1989; *Betsy's Wedding* 1990; *Def by Temptation* 1990; *The Exorcist III* 1990; *A Shock to the System* 1990; *Johnny Suede* 1991; *Juice* 1991; *Jumpin' at the Boneyard* 1991; *Jungle Fever* 1991; *Patriot Games* 1992; *White Sands* 1992; *Amos & Andrew* 1993; *Jurassic Park* 1993; *Menace II Society* 1993; *National Lampoon's Loaded Weapon 1* 1993; *True Romance* 1993; *Against the Wall* 1994; *Fresh* 1994; *Hail Caesar* 1994; *Kiss of Death* 1994; *Pulp Fiction* 1994; *Die Hard with a Vengeance* 1995; *Fluke* 1995; *Losing Isaiah* 1995; *The Great White Hype* 1996; *Hard Eight* 1996; *The Long Kiss Goodnight* 1996; *The Search for One-Eye Jimmy* 1996; *A Time to Kill* 1996; *Eve's Bayou* 1997; *Jackie Brown* 1997; *One Eight Seven* 1997; *The Negotiator* 1998; *Out of Sight* 1998; *The Red Violin* 1998; *Sphere* 1998; *Deep Blue Sea* 1999; *Star Wars Episode I: the Phantom Menace* 1999; *Rules of Engagement* 2000; *Shaft* 2000; *Unbreakable* 2000; *The 51st State* 2001; *Changing Lanes* 2002; *No Good Deed* 2002; *Star Wars Episode II: Attack of the Clones* 2002; *xXx* 2002; *Basic* 2003; *Kill Bill Vol 2* 2003; *SWAT* 2003; *Twisted* 2003; *The Incredibles* 2004; *Coach Carter* 2005; *Star Wars Episode III: Revenge of the Sith* 2005; *xXx: the Next Level* 2005

Jackson, Selmer (1888–1971) *Stars on Parade* 1944; *Autumn Leaves* 1956

Jackson, Sherry (1942–) *The Miracle of Our Lady of Fatima* 1952; *Trouble along the Way* 1953; *Come Next Spring* 1956; *Wild on the Beach* 1965; *Gunn* 1967

Jackson, Stoney (1960–) *Blind Vision* 1992; *By the Sword* 1992; *Trespass* 1992

Jackson, Thomas E *aka* **Jackson, Thomas** (1886–1967) *Broadway* 1929; *Little Caesar* 1931; *The Woman in the Window* 1945

Jackson, Victoria (1959–) *Casual Sex?* 1988; *Family Business* 1989; *UHF* 1989

Jacob, Catherine (1959–) *Tatie Danielle* 1990; *Merci la Vie* 1991; *Mon Père Ce Héros* 1991; *Nine Months* 1994; *Who Killed Bambi?* 2003

Jacob, Irène (1966–) *Erreur de jeunesse* 1989; *The Double Life of Véronique* 1991; *The Secret Garden* 1993; *Three Colours Red* 1994; *All Men Are Mortal* 1995; *Beyond the Clouds* 1995; *Othello* 1995; *Victory* 1995; *Incognito* 1997; *US Marshals* 1998; *History Is Made at Night* 1999; *Londinium* 1999; *My Life So Far* 1999

Jacobi, Derek (1938–) *Othello* 1965; *Three Sisters* 1970; *Blue Blood* 1973; *The Day of the Jackal* 1973; *The Odessa File* 1974; *The Medusa Touch* 1978; *The Human Factor* 1979; *Enigma* 1982; *The Hunchback of Notre Dame* 1982; *The Secret of NIMH* 1982; *Little Dorrit* 1987; *Henry V* 1989; *The Fool* 1990; *Dead Again* 1991; *Hamlet* 1996; *Basil* 1998; *Love Is the Devil: Study for a Portrait of Francis Bacon* 1998; *Up at the Villa* 1998; *The Body* 2000; *Gladiator* 2000; *The Children's Midsummer Night's Dream* 2001; *Gosford Park* 2001; *Revelation* 2001; *Revengers Tragedy* 2002; *Two Men Went to War* 2002; *Cloud Cuckoo Land* 2004; *Strings* 2004

Jacobi, Lou (1913–) *The Diary of Anne Frank* 1959; *Irma la Douce* 1963; *The Last of the Secret Agents* 1966; *Everything You Always Wanted to Know about Sex ... but Were Afraid to Ask* 1972; *Roseland* 1977; *The Magician of Lublin* 1979; *The Lucky Star* 1980; *My Favorite Year* 1982; *Avalon* 1990; *I Don't Buy Kisses Anymore* 1992; *IQ* 1994

Jacobs, Martin *Over the Hill* 1992; *Turtle Beach* 1992

Jacobs, Paula *She'll Be Wearing Pink Pyjamas* 1984; *The Remains of the Day* 1993

Jacobs, Steve *aka* **Jacobs, Steven** (1967–) *Shadows of the Peacock* 1987; *Kokoda Crescent* 1989; *Father* 1990; *To Have & to Hold* 1996

Jacobson, Dean *Lobster Man from Mars* 1989; *Child's Play 3* 1991

Jacobsson, Ulla (1929–1982) *Smiles of a Summer Night* 1955; *Zulu* 1964; *The Heroes of Telemark* 1965; *Fox and His Friends* 1975

Jacoby, Billy (1969–) *The Beastmaster* 1982; *Just One of the Guys* 1985

Jacoby, Bobby (1973–) *Tremors* 1989; *Meet the Applegates* 1991; *Night of the Demons 2* 1994

Jacoby, Scott (1956–) *Baxter* 1973; *The Little Girl Who Lives Down the Lane* 1976; *Love and the Midnight Auto Supply* 1977

Jacott, Carlos *Kicking and Screaming* 1995; *Mr Jealousy* 1997; *Being John Malkovich* 1999

Jacques, Hattie (1924–1980) *Trottie True* 1949; *Chance of a Lifetime* 1950; *Scrooge* 1951; *The Pickwick Papers* 1952; *Our Girl Friday* 1953; *Carry On Sergeant* 1958; *The Square Peg* 1958; *Carry On Nurse* 1959; *Carry On Teacher* 1959; *Follow a Star* 1959; *The Navy Lark* 1959; *Carry On Constable* 1960; *Carry On Regardless* 1960; *Make Mine Mink* 1960; *School for Scoundrels* 1960; *Watch Your Stern* 1960; *In the Doghouse* 1961; *She'll Have to Go* 1961; *Carry On Cabby* 1963; *The Bobo* 1967; *The Plank* 1967; *Carry On Doctor* 1968; *Carry On Again Doctor* 1969; *Carry On Camping* 1969; *Crooks and Coronets* 1969; *The Magic Christian* 1969; *Monte Carlo or Bust* 1969; *Carry On Loving* 1970; *Carry On at Your Convenience* 1971; *Carry On Abroad* 1972; *Carry On Matron* 1972; *Carry On Dick* 1974

Jacques, Sylvain *Those Who Love Me Can Take the Train* 1998; *Son Frère* 2003

Jacques, Yves (1956–) *The Decline of the American Empire* 1986; *Jesus of Montreal* 1989; *The Barbarian Invasions* 2003

Jade, Claude (1948–) *Stolen Kisses* 1968; *Topaz* 1969; *Uncle Benjamin* 1969; *Bed and Board* 1970; *Love on the Run* 1979

Jaeckel, Richard (1926–1997) *Guadalcanal Diary* 1943; *Wing and a Prayer* 1944; *Come Back, Little Sheba* 1952; *My Son John* 1952; *Big Leaguer* 1953; *The Shanghai Story* 1954; *Attack!* 1956; *3:10 to Yuma* 1957; *Cowboy* 1958; *The Gun Runners* 1958; *The Lineup* 1958; *The Naked and the Dead* 1958; *The Gallant Hours* 1960; *Platinum High School* 1960; *Town without Pity* 1961; *Nightmare in the Sun* 1964; *Once Before I Die* 1965; *The Dirty Dozen* 1967; *The Devil's Brigade* 1968; *The Green Slime* 1968; *Latitude Zero* 1969; *Chisum* 1970; *Sometimes a Great Notion* 1971; *Ulzana's Raid* 1972; *The Outfit* 1973; *Pat Garrett and Billy the Kid* 1973; *Chosen Survivors* 1974; *The Drowning Pool* 1975; *Part 2 Walking Tall* 1975; *Grizzly* 1976; *Day of the Animals* 1977; *The Dark* 1979; *Pacific Inferno* 1979; *Herbie Goes Bananas* 1980; *The California Dolls* 1981; *Cold River* 1982; *Starman* 1984; *Black Moon Rising* 1985; *Delta Force 2* 1990

Jaeger, Frederick (1928–2004) *The Black Tent* 1956; *One of Those Things* 1970

Jaenicke, Hannes (1960–) *Out of Order* 1984; *Operation Dead End* 1986; *The Hunted* 1998

Jaffe, Carl (1902–1974) *I Didn't Do It* 1945; *State Secret* 1950; *Desperate Moment* 1953; *Park Plaza 605* 1953; *Child's Play* 1954; *The Traitor* 1957; *Escapement* 1958; *First Man into Space* 1958; *Subway in the Sky* 1958

Jaffe, Chapelle *Who Has Seen the Wind* 1977; *Confidential* 1986

Jaffe, Sam (1891–1984) *The Scarlet Empress* 1934; *We Live Again* 1934; *Lost Horizon* 1937; *Gunga Din* 1939; *Stage Door Canteen* 1943; *13 Rue Madeleine* 1946; *The Accused* 1949; *Rope of Sand* 1949; *The Asphalt Jungle* 1950; *The Day the Earth Stood Still* 1951; *I Can Get It for You Wholesale* 1951; *Les Espions* 1957; *The Barbarian and the Geisha* 1958; *Ben-Hur* 1959; *Guns for San Sebastian* 1968; *The Great Bank Robbery* 1969; *The Dunwich Horror* 1970; *Bedknobs and Broomsticks* 1971; *Battle beyond the Stars* 1980; *Gideon's Trumpet* 1980

Jaffer, Melissa (1936–) *Caddie* 1976; *Ride a Wild Pony* 1976;

Weekend of Shadows 1978; The Gold and Glory 1984
Jaffrey, Madhur (1933–) Shakespeare Wallah 1965; The Guru 1969; Autobiography of a Princess 1975; Heat and Dust 1982; The Assam Garden 1985; The Perfect Murder 1988; Vanya on 42nd Street 1994; ABCD 1999; Cotton Mary 1999
Jaffrey, Saeed (1929–) The Horsemen 1971; The Man Who Would Be King 1975; The Wilby Conspiracy 1975; The Chess Players 1977; Hullabaloo over Georgie and Bonnie's Pictures 1979; Sphinx 1980; Mandi 1983; A Passage to India 1984; The Razor's Edge 1984; My Beautiful Laundrette 1985; The Deceivers 1988; After Midnight 1990; Henna 1990; Masala 1991; Balmaa 1993; Guru in Seven 1997; The Journey 1997; Second Generation 1999; Mr In-Between 2001; Chicken Tikka Masala 2005
Jagger, Bianca (1945–) The Rutles – All You Need Is Cash 1978; The American Success Company 1979; The Cannonball Run 1981
Jagger, Dean (1903–1991) Wings in the Dark 1935; Having Wonderful Time 1938; Brigham Young 1940; The Men in Her Life 1941; Western Union 1941; Valley of the Sun 1942; Betrayed 1944; I Live in Grosvenor Square 1945; Driftwood 1946; Sister Kenny 1946; Pursued 1947; Twelve O'Clock High 1949; Sierra 1950; Rawhide 1951; Warpath 1951; Denver & Rio Grande 1952; It Grows on Trees 1952; My Son John 1952; The Robe 1953; Private Hell 36 1954; White Christmas 1954; Bad Day at Black Rock 1955; It's a Dog's Life 1955; The Great Man 1956; Red Sundown 1956; Three Brave Men 1956; X the Unknown 1956; Forty Guns 1957; King Creole 1958; The Proud Rebel 1958; The Nun's Story 1959; Cash McCall 1960; Elmer Gantry 1960; The Honeymoon Machine 1961; Parrish 1961; Jumbo 1962; First to Fight 1967; Day of the Evil Gun 1968; Firecreek 1968; Smith! 1969; The Kremlin Letter 1970; Tiger by the Tail 1970; Vanishing Point 1971; The Glass House 1972; I Heard the Owl Call My Name 1973; End of the World 1977; Game of Death 1978; Alligator 1980; Gideon's Trumpet 1980
Jagger, Mick (1943–) Ned Kelly 1970; Performance 1970; Running Out of Luck 1985; Freejack 1992; Bent 1996
Jaglom, Henry (1941–) Psych-Out 1968; Drive, He Said 1971; The Last Movie 1971; Sitting Ducks 1979; Always 1985; Someone to Love 1987; Venice/Venice 1992; Last Summer in the Hamptons 1995
Jakub, Lisa (1978–) Rambling Rose 1991; Matinee 1993; Mrs Doubtfire 1993; A Pig's Tale 1994; The Beautician and the Beast 1997; Painted Angels 1997
Jalal, Farida The Chess Players 1977; Dilwale Dulhania Le Jayenge 1995; Raja Hindustani 1996; Garv: Pride & Honour 2004
James, Anthony (1942–) The Last Days of Dolwyn 1949; Return from Witch Mountain 1978; Wacko 1981; Nightmares 1983; World Gone Wild 1988; The Naked Gun $2\frac{1}{2}$: the Smell of Fear 1991
James, Brion (1945–1999) Blue Sunshine 1976; Southern Comfort 1981; Blade Runner 1982; The Ballad of Gregorio Cortez 1983; A Breed Apart 1984; Crimewave 1985; Enemy Mine 1985; Armed and Dangerous 1986; Cherry 2000 1988; DOA 1988; House III: The Horror Show 1989; Red Scorpion 1989; Tango & Cash 1989; Another 48 HRS 1990; Over Her Dead Body 1990; Wishman 1991; The Player 1992; Brain Smasher… a Love Story 1993; Striking Distance 1993; Time Runner 1993; Art Deco Detective 1994; Bad Company 1994; Cabin Boy 1994; FTW 1994; Pterodactyl Woman from Beverly Hills 1996; The Fifth Element 1997; Brown's Requiem 1998; Farewell, My Love 1999
James, Clifton (1921–) David and Lisa 1962; Experiment in Terror 1962; Black like Me 1964; Cool Hand Luke 1967; The Reivers 1969; The Biscuit Eater 1972; The New Centurions 1972; The Last Detail 1973; Live and Let Die 1973; Bank Shot 1974; Buster and Billie 1974; The Man with the Golden Gun 1974; Rancho Deluxe 1975; Silver Streak 1976; The Bad News Bears in Breaking Training 1977; Caboblanco 1980; Eight Men Out 1988
James, Dalton (1971–) California Man 1992; My Father the Hero 1994
James, Geraldine (1950–) Sweet William 1980; The Wolves of Willoughby Chase 1988; The Tall Guy 1989; The Bridge 1990; Prince of Shadows 1991; Teen Agent 1991; Moll Flanders 1995; The Man Who Knew Too Little 1997; The Luzhin Defence 2000; Calendar Girls 2003
James, Godfrey The Land That Time Forgot 1974; At the Earth's Core 1976
James, Harry (1916–1983) Private Buckaroo 1942; Springtime in the Rockies 1942; Do You Love Me? 1946
James, Jesse (1989–) Message in a Bottle 1998; A Dog of Flanders 1999; Slap Her, She's French! 2001; The Amityville Horror 2005
James, Lennie Among Giants 1998; Elephant Juice 1999; Lucky Break 2001; 24 Hour Party People 2001
James, Oliver (1980–) What a Girl Wants 2003; Raise Your Voice 2004
James, Oscar Pressure 1976; Black Joy 1977
James, Sidney (1913–1976) No Orchids for Miss Blandish 1948; Last Holiday 1950; Lady Godiva Rides Again 1951; The Lavender Hill Mob 1951; Emergency Call 1952; Father's Doing Fine 1952; I Believe in You 1952; Miss Robin Hood 1952; Time Gentlemen Please! 1952; The Titfield Thunderbolt 1952; Venetian Bird 1952; The Yellow Balloon 1952; Escape by Night 1953; Park Plaza 605 1953; The Square Ring 1953; The Weak and the Wicked 1953; Will Any Gentleman…? 1953; Father Brown 1954; For Better, for Worse 1954; Orders Are Orders 1954; Seagulls over Sorrento 1954; The Deep Blue Sea 1955; The Glass Cage 1955; It's a Great Day 1955; Joe Macbeth 1955; John and Julie 1955; A Kid for Two Farthings 1955; Dry Rot 1956; The Extra Day 1956; The Iron Petticoat 1956; Trapeze 1956; Campbell's Kingdom 1957; Hell Drivers 1957; A King in New York 1957; Quatermass II 1957; The Shiralee 1957; The Smallest Show on Earth 1957; The Story of Esther Costello 1957; I Was Monty's Double 1958; The Man Inside 1958; The Rainbow Jacket 1958; The Silent Enemy 1958; Too Many Crooks 1958; Desert Mice 1959; Make Mine a Million 1959; Tommy the Toreador 1959; Upstairs and Downstairs 1959; And the Same to You 1960; Carry On Constable 1960; Carry On Regardless 1960; The Green Helmet 1960; The Pure Hell of St Trinian's 1960; Watch Your Stern 1960; Double Bunk 1961; Raising the Wind 1961; What a Carve Up! 1961; What a Whopper! 1961; Carry On Cruising 1962; We Joined the Navy 1962; Carry On Cabby 1963; Carry On Cleo 1964; The Big Job 1965; Carry On Cowboy 1965; Three Hats for Lisa 1965; Carry On – Don't Lose Your Head 1966; Where the Bullets Fly 1966; Carry On Doctor 1968; Carry On Up the Khyber 1968; Carry On Again Doctor 1969; Carry On Camping 1969; Carry On Loving 1970; Carry On Up the Jungle 1970; Carry On at Your Convenience 1971; Carry On Henry 1971; Bless This House 1972; Carry On Abroad 1972; Carry On Matron 1972; Carry On Girls 1973; Carry On Dick 1974
James (1), Steve (1955–1993) The Exterminator 1980; The Brother from Another Planet 1984; American Ninja 1985; To Live and Die in LA 1985; Avenging Force 1986; POW the Escape 1986; Hero and the Terror 1988; I'm Gonna Git You Sucka 1988; Johnny Be Good 1988; McBain 1991; Weekend at Bernie's II 1992
James, Walter (1882–1946) Little Annie Rooney 1925; Battling Butler 1926; The Kid Brother 1927
Jameson, Joyce (1932–1987) Tales of Terror 1962; The Balcony 1963; The Comedy of Terrors 1964; Scorchy 1976
Jameson, Pauline (1920–) Two Living, One Dead 1961; Crooks Anonymous 1962; I Could Go On Singing 1963
Janda, Krystyna (1955–) Man of Marble 1977; The Conductor 1980; Man of Iron 1981; Interrogation 1982
Jane, Thomas aka **Jane, Tom** (1969–) The Crow: City of Angels 1996; The Last Time I Committed Suicide 1996; Thursday 1998; The Velocity of Gary 1998; Deep Blue Sea 1999; Molly 1999; Under Suspicion 2000; Original Sin 2001; 61* 2001; The Sweetest Thing 2002; Dreamcatcher 2003; Stander 2003; The Punisher 2004
Jang Dong-gun aka **Jang Dong-Keon** (1972–) Nowhere to Hide 1999; Brotherhood 2004
Janis, Conrad (1928–) Margie 1946; The Happy Hooker 1975; The Duchess and the Dirtwater Fox 1976; The Buddy Holly Story 1978; Oh God! Book II 1980; The November Conspiracy 1995
Jankowski, Oleg aka **Jankowskij, Oleg** (1944–) My 20th Century 1988; Mute Witness 1995
Janney, Allison (1960–) Dead Funny 1995; First Do No Harm 1997; David and Lisa 1998; The Object of My Affection 1998; Six Days Seven Nights 1998; American Beauty 1999; Drop Dead Gorgeous 1999; The Hours 2002; Finding Nemo 2003
Janney, Leon (1917–1980) Doorway to Hell 1931; The Last Mile 1959; Charly 1968
Janney, William (1908–1992) The Dawn Patrol 1930; A Successful Calamity 1932; Bonnie Scotland 1935
Jannings, Emil (1884–1950) Anna Boleyn 1920; The Last Laugh 1924; Waxworks 1924; Vaudeville 1925; Faust 1926; Tartuffe 1926; The Way of All Flesh 1927; The Last Command 1928; The Patriot 1928; The Blue Angel 1930
Jansen, Tom (1945–) Suite 16 1994; The Gambler 1997
Janson, Horst (1935–) The McKenzie Break 1970; Murphy's War 1971; Captain Kronos: Vampire Hunter 1972
Janssen, David (1930–1980) Chief Crazy Horse 1955; Cult of the Cobra 1955; Francis in the Navy 1955; Never Say Goodbye 1955; The Square Jungle 1955; Francis in the Haunted House 1956; The Girl He Left Behind 1956; Showdown at Abilene 1956; Hell Bent for Glory 1957; Hell to Eternity 1960; King of the Roaring 20s – the Story of Arnold Rothstein 1961; Man-Trap 1961; Ring of Fire 1961; My Six Loves 1962; Warning Shot 1967; The Green Berets 1968; The Shoes of the Fisherman 1968; Generation 1969; Marooned 1969; Where It's At 1969; Macho Callahan 1970; Once Is Not Enough 1975; The Swiss Conspiracy 1975; Two-Minute Warning 1976; Golden Rendezvous 1977; SOS Titanic 1979; Inchon 1981
Janssen, Eilene aka **Janssen, Eileen** (1937–) On Our Merry Way 1948; About Mrs Leslie 1954
Janssen, Famke (1964–) GoldenEye 1995; Lord of Illusions 1995; City of Industry 1996; The Gingerbread Man 1997; Noose 1997; Celebrity 1998; Deep Rising 1998; The Faculty 1998; Rounders 1998; Circus 1999; House on Haunted Hill 1999; Love & Sex 2000; X-Men 2000; Don't Say a Word 2001; Made 2001; I Spy 2002; X2 2003; Hide and Seek 2005
January, Lois (1913–) By Candlelight 1934; The Cocaine Fiends 1935
Jaoui, Agnès (1964–) Un Air de Famille 1996; On Connaît la Chanson 1997; Le Goût des Autres 1999; Look at Me 2004
Jaray, Hans (1906–1990) The Love of Jeanne Ney 1927; The Unfinished Symphony 1934; Lydia 1941; Carnegie Hall 1947
Jaregard, Ernst-Hugo (1928–1998) Europa 1991; The Kingdom 1994
Jarman Jr, Claude (1934–) The Yearling 1946; High Barbaree 1947; Intruder in the Dust 1949; Roughshod 1949; The Outriders 1950; Rio Grande 1950; Hangman's Knot 1952; Fair Wind to Java 1953
Jarmusch, Jim (1953–) Leningrad Cowboys Go America 1989; In the Soup 1992; Blue in the Face 1995; Sling Blade 1995
Jarratt, John (1952–) Sound of Love 1977; The Odd Angry Shot 1979; The Settlement 1982; We of the Never Never 1982; The Naked Country 1985; Dead Heart 1996
Järrel, Stig (1910–1998) Torment 1944; The Devil's Eye 1960
Jarvet, Juri (1919–1995) King Lear 1970; Solaris 1972; Khrustaliov, My Car! 1998
Jarvis, Graham (1930–2003) RPM – Revolutions per Minute 1970; The Traveling Executioner 1970; Middle Age Crazy 1980; Weekend Warriors 1986; Parents 1988; Misery 1990
Jason, David (1940–) White Cargo 1973; Wombling Free 1977; The Odd Job 1978
Jason, Harvey (1940–) Oklahoma Crude 1973; The Gumball Rally 1976
Jason, Peter (1950–) Trick or Treats 1982; Alien Nation 1988; They Live 1988
Jason, Rick (1926–2000) Sombrero 1952; This Is My Love 1954; The Lieutenant Wore Skirts 1956; The Wayward Bus 1957; Sierra Baron 1958; Color Me Dead 1969; Day of the Wolves 1973
Jason, Sybil (1929–) I Found Stella Parish 1935; The Singing Kid 1936; The Great O'Malley 1937; The Little Princess 1939
Jasper, Star True Love 1989; Hand Gun 1994
Jasso, Stephen (1984–) Teenage Caveman 2001; Ken Park 2002
Jay, Ernest (1893–1957) Broken Blossoms 1936; School for Secrets 1946
Jay, Ricky (1948–) Things Change 1988; The Spanish Prisoner 1997; Tomorrow Never Dies 1997; Last Days 2005
Jay, Tony Tom and Jerry: the Movie 1992; The Jungle Book 2 2003
Jayne, Jennifer (1932–) It's a Grand Life 1953; The Trollenberg Terror 1958; On the Beat 1962; Clash by Night 1963; Hysteria 1964; They Came from beyond Space 1967
Jayston, Michael (1935–) A Midsummer Night's Dream 1969; Follow Me 1971; Nicholas and Alexandra 1971; Alice's Adventures in Wonderland 1972; Bequest to the Nation 1972; Craze 1973; The Homecoming 1973; Tales That Witness Madness 1973; The Internecine Project 1974; Dominique 1978
Jean, Gloria (1927–) Never Give a Sucker an Even Break 1941; Ghost Catchers 1944; Copacabana 1947
Jean-Baptiste, Marianne (1967–) Secrets & Lies 1995; Mr Jealousy 1997; A Murder of Crows 1998; New Year's Day 1999; The 24 Hour Woman 1999; The Cell 2000; 28 Days 2000; Spy Game 2001
Jeanmaire, Zizi aka **Jeanmaire** (1924–) Hans Christian Andersen 1952; Anything Goes 1956; One Night at the Music Hall 1956; Too Many Lovers 1957
Jeans, Isabel (1891–1985) Downhill 1927; Easy Virtue 1927; Tovarich 1937; Fools for Scandal 1938; Garden of the Moon 1938; Banana Ridge 1941; Suspicion 1941; Great Day 1944; It Happened in Rome 1956; Gigi 1958; A Breath of Scandal 1960; Heavens Above! 1963
Jeans, Ursula (1906–1973) Cavalcade 1933; Friday the Thirteenth 1933; I Lived with You 1933; The Man in the Mirror 1936; Dark Journey 1937; Over the Moon 1937; Storm in a Teacup 1937; Gaiety George 1946; The Weaker Sex 1948; The Dam Busters 1954; The Night My Number Came Up 1955; North West Frontier 1959; The Green Helmet 1960; The Queen's Guards 1960; The Battle of the Villa Fiorita 1965
Jeavons, Colin (1929–) Bartleby 1971; Diagnosis: Murder 1974; The Island 1980; Secret Friends 1991
Jeayes, Allan (1885–1963) The Ghost Train 1931; The Camels Are Coming 1934; Königsmark 1935; Rembrandt 1936; Elephant Boy 1937; The Green Cockatoo 1937; The Squeaker 1937; The Four Feathers 1939; The Stars Look Down 1939; Convoy 1940; Pimpernel Smith 1941; Blanche Fury 1948
Jeevan Tarana 1951; Ek Hi Rasta 1956; Naya Daur 1957
Jefford, Barbara (1930–) A Midsummer Night's Dream 1961; Ulysses 1967; The Shoes of the Fisherman 1968; A Midsummer Night's Dream 1969; Lust for a Vampire 1970; And the Ship Sails On 1983; Reunion 1989; When the Whales Came 1989; Where Angels Fear to Tread 1991; The Ninth Gate 1999
Jeffrey, Peter (1929–1999) if… 1968; Anne of the Thousand Days 1969; Ring of Bright Water 1969; The Abominable Dr Phibes 1971; The Horsemen 1971; The Odessa File 1974; The Return of the Pink Panther 1974; Britannia Hospital 1982; The Adventures of Baron Munchausen 1988
Jeffreys, Anne (1923–) Nevada 1944; Dick Tracy 1945; Dillinger 1945; Those Endearing Young Charms 1945; Dick Tracy vs Cueball 1946; Riff-Raff 1947; Trail Street 1947; Return of the Bad Men 1948; Panic in the City 1968
Jeffreys, Ellis (1872–1943) Limelight 1936; Return of a Stranger 1937
Jeffries, Fran (1939–) Sex and the Single Girl 1964; Harum Scarum 1965
Jeffries, Lionel (1926–) The Black Rider 1954; The Colditz Story 1954; No Smoking 1954; All for Mary 1955; Jumping for Joy 1955; The Quatermass Xperiment 1955; The Baby and the Battleship 1956; The Man in the Sky 1956; Blue Murder at St Trinian's 1957; Doctor at Large 1957; The Hour of Decision 1957; The Vicious Circle 1957; Behind the Mask 1958; Further up the Creek 1958; Law and Disorder 1958; Life Is a Circus 1958; Orders to Kill 1958; The Revenge of Frankenstein 1958; Bobbikins 1959; The Nun's Story 1959; Let's Get Married 1960; Please Turn Over 1960; Tarzan the Magnificent 1960; The Trials of Oscar Wilde 1960; Two Way Stretch 1960; Fanny 1961; Kill or Cure 1962; The Notorious Landlady 1962; Operation Snatch 1962; The Wrong Arm of the Law 1962; Call Me Bwana 1963; The

Long Ships 1963; *The Scarlet Blade* 1963; *First Men in the Moon* 1964; *Murder Ahoy* 1964; *The Truth about Spring* 1964; *The Secret of My Success* 1965; *You Must Be Joking!* 1965; *Drop Dead Darling* 1966; *The Spy with a Cold Nose* 1966; *Camelot* 1967; *Jules Verne's Rocket to the Moon* 1967; *Oh Dad, Poor Dad, Mama's Hung You in the Closet and I'm Feelin' So Sad* 1967; *Chitty Chitty Bang Bang* 1968; *Twinky* 1969; *Eyewitness* 1970; *Who Slew Auntie Roo?* 1971; *What Changed Charley Farthing?* 1974; *Royal Flash* 1975; *Wombling Free* 1977; *The Prisoner of Zenda* 1979; *Better Late Than Never* 1983; *A Chorus of Disapproval* 1988

Jehanne, Edith *The Chess Player* 1927; *The Love of Jeanne Ney* 1927

Jemison, Anna *aka* **Monticelli, Anna Maria** *Heatwave* 1981; *Smash Palace* 1981; *Silver City* 1984; *The Empty Beach* 1985

Jemison, Eddie *Schizopolis* 1996; *Ocean's Twelve* 2004

Jendly, Roger *Jonah Who Will Be 25 in the Year 2000* 1976; *Woman from Rose Hill* 1989

Jenesky, George *Alien Nation* 1988; *Inside Edge* 1992

Jenkins, Allen (1900–1974) *Blessed Event* 1932; *I Am a Fugitive from a Chain Gang* 1932; *Lawyer Man* 1932; *Bureau of Missing Persons* 1933; *Hard to Handle* 1933; *Havana Widows* 1933; *The Mayor of Hell* 1933; *The Mind Reader* 1933; *The Case of the Howling Dog* 1934; *Jimmy the Gent* 1934; *The Case of the Lucky Legs* 1935; *The Irish in Us* 1935; *Cain and Mabel* 1936; *The Singing Kid* 1936; *Three Men on a Horse* 1936; *Dead End* 1937; *Marked Woman* 1937; *The Perfect Specimen* 1937; *Swing Your Lady* 1937; *The Amazing Dr Clitterhouse* 1938; *Fools for Scandal* 1938; *Going Places* 1938; *Gold Diggers in Paris* 1938; *Hard to Get* 1938; *Racket Busters* 1938; *A Slight Case of Murder* 1938; *Destry Rides Again* 1939; *Five Came Back* 1939; *Naughty but Nice* 1939; *Brother Orchid* 1940; *Tin Pan Alley* 1940; *A Date with the Falcon* 1941; *Dive Bomber* 1941; *Footsteps in the Dark* 1941; *The Gay Falcon* 1941; *Time Out for Rhythm* 1941; *Eyes in the Night* 1942; *The Falcon Takes Over* 1942; *They All Kissed the Bride* 1942; *Lady on a Train* 1945; *Wonder Man* 1945; *The Senator Was Indiscreet* 1947; *The Big Wheel* 1949; *Robin and the 7 Hoods* 1964; *The Spy in the Green Hat* 1966

Jenkins, Jackie "Butch" *aka* **Jenkins, "Butch"** (1937–) *National Velvet* 1944; *Our Vines Have Tender Grapes* 1945; *My Brother Talks to Horses* 1946; *Summer Holiday* 1948

Jenkins, Ken *Matewan* 1987; *Air America* 1990; *Thirst* 1998

Jenkins, Megs (1917–1998) *Millions like Us* 1943; *Green for Danger* 1946; *The History of Mr Polly* 1948; *Saraband for Dead Lovers* 1948; *A Boy, a Girl and a Bike* 1949; *The Secret People* 1951; *Personal Affair* 1953; *Trouble in Store* 1953; *Tiger Bay* 1959; *The Green Helmet* 1960; *The Innocents* 1961; *Life for Ruth* 1962; *Murder Most Foul* 1964; *The Smashing Bird I Used to Know* 1969

Jenkins, Rebecca (1959–) *Bye Bye Blues* 1989; *Bob Roberts* 1992; *Clearcut* 1992

Jenkins, Richard (1953–) *The Witches of Eastwick* 1987; *Little Nikita* 1988; *Blaze* 1989; *Sea of Love* 1989; *Trapped in Paradise* 1994; *Wolf* 1994; *The Indian in the Cupboard* 1995; *Eddie* 1996; *Flirting with Disaster* 1996; *Eye of God* 1997; *The Man Who Wasn't There* 2001; *Say It Isn't So* 2001; *Changing Lanes* 2002; *The Core* 2002; *Stealing Harvard* 2002; *Intolerable Cruelty* 2003; *Shall We Dance* 2004

Jenks, Frank (1902–1962) *The Storm* 1938; *Back Street* 1941; *The Flame of New Orleans* 1941; *Seven Miles from Alcatraz* 1942; *Rosie the Riveter* 1944; *Christmas in Connecticut* 1945

Jenn, Michael *Another Country* 1984; *Unleashed* 2005

Jenney, Lucinda (1954–) *The Whoopee Boys* 1986; *Wired* 1989; *Thelma & Louise* 1991; *American Heart* 1992; *Matinee* 1993; *Stephen King's Thinner* 1996; *First Time Felon* 1997; *GI Jane* 1997; *The Mothman Prophecies* 2001

Jennings, Alex (1957–) *A Midsummer Night's Dream* 1996; *The Wings of the Dove* 1997; *The Hunley* 1999; *The Four Feathers* 2002

Jennings, Brent *Witness* 1985; *The Serpent and the Rainbow* 1987; *The Price of Vengeance* 1994; *A Lesson Before Dying* 1999

Jennings, Claudia (1949–1979) *The Unholy Rollers* 1972; *Truck Stop Women* 1974; *The Great Texas Dynamite Chase* 1976; *Moonshine County Express* 1977; *Deathsport* 1978

Jennings, DeWitt (1879–1937) *Fox Movietone Follies of 1929* 1929; *The Valiant* 1929; *The Criminal Code* 1930; *Min and Bill* 1930; *Little Man, What Now?* 1934

Jens, Arnette *aka* **Jens Zerbe, Arnette** *The Balcony* 1963; *Cloud Dancer* 1979

Jens, Salome (1935–) *Terror from the Year 5,000* 1958; *Angel Baby* 1961; *The Fool Killer* 1965; *Seconds* 1966; *Savages* 1972; *Cloud Dancer* 1979; *Harry's War* 1981

Jensen (2), David (1952–) *Schizopolis* 1996; *A Love Song for Bobby Long* 2004

Jensen, Maren (1957–) *Battlestar Galactica* 1978; *Deadly Blessing* 1981

Jensen, Todd *Cyborg Cop* 1993; *Operation Delta Force* 1996; *Operation Delta Force II: Mayday* 1998

Jenson, Roy (1935–) *Cry for Me Billy* 1972; *Journey through Rosebud* 1972; *Chinatown* 1974; *The Wind and the Lion* 1975; *Breakheart Pass* 1976; *The Duchess and the Dirtwater Fox* 1976

Jenson, Sasha *Dazed and Confused* 1993; *Bad Company* 1994

Jentsch, Julia (1978–) *The Edukators* 2004; *Sophie Scholl – The Final Days* 2005

Jergens, Adele (1917–2002) *A Thousand and One Nights* 1945; *Down to Earth* 1947; *The Dark Past* 1948; *The Prince of Thieves* 1948; *Ladies of the Chorus* 1949; *Slightly French* 1949; *Armored Car Robbery* 1950; *The Sound of Fury* 1950; *Abbott and Costello Meet the Invisible Man* 1951; *Sugarfoot* 1951; *Somebody Loves Me* 1952; *Fireman Save My Child* 1954; *The Day the World Ended* 1956; *Runaway Daughters* 1956

Jergens, Diane (1937–) *The Bob Mathias Story* 1954; *High School Confidential* 1958; *Sing, Boy, Sing* 1958; *The FBI Story* 1959

Jerrold, Mary (1877–1955) *Friday the Thirteenth* 1933; *Doctor's Orders* 1934; *Mr Perrin and Mr Traill* 1948; *The Queen of Spades* 1948; *Woman Hater* 1948; *Top of the Form* 1953

Jessel, George (1898–1981) *Juke Box Rhythm* 1959; *Can Heironymus Merkin Ever Forget Mercy Humppe and Find True Happiness?* 1969

Jessel, Patricia (1920–1968) *The Man Upstairs* 1958; *The City of the Dead* 1960; *A Funny Thing Happened on the Way to the Forum* 1966

Jessie, DeWayne *Halls of Anger* 1970; *DC Cab* 1983

Jeter, Michael (1952–2003) *The Fisher King* 1991; *Sister Act 2: Back in the Habit* 1993; *Drop Zone* 1994; *Waterworld* 1995; *Air Bud* 1997; *The Naked Man* 1998; *Thursday* 1998; *The Green Mile* 1999; *Jakob the Liar* 1999; *Jurassic Park III* 2001; *Welcome to Collinwood* 2002; *Open Range* 2003; *The Polar Express* 2004

Jewel, Jimmy (1909–1995) *Rhythm Serenade* 1943; *Nearest and Dearest* 1972; *Arthur's Hallowed Ground* 1985; *Rocinante* 1986; *The Krays* 1990

Jewell, Isabel (1909–1972) *Advice to the Lovelorn* 1933; *Counsellor-at-Law* 1933; *Design for Living* 1933; *Evelyn Prentice* 1934; *Ceiling Zero* 1935; *Big Brown Eyes* 1936; *Go West, Young Man* 1936; *The Man Who Lived Twice* 1936; *Valiant Is the Word for Carrie* 1936; *Lost Horizon* 1937; *Marked Woman* 1937; *The Falcon and the Co-Eds* 1943; *The Leopard Man* 1943; *The Seventh Victim* 1943; *The Merry Monahans* 1944; *Badman's Territory* 1946; *Lady of Deceit* 1947; *Belle Starr's Daughter* 1948; *The Arousers* 1970; *Ciao! Manhattan* 1973

Jhangiani, Preeti (1980–) *Mohabbatein* 2000; *Awara Paagal Deewana* 2002

Jhulka, Ayesha *Balmaa* 1993; *Run* 2004

Jhutti, Ronny *Immaculate Conception* 1991; *Wild West* 1992

Jiang Wen (1963–) *Red Sorghum* 1987; *The Emperor's Shadow* 1996; *Keep Cool* 1997; *Devils on the Doorstep* 2000; *The Missing Gun* 2002

Jillette, Penn *aka* **Penn** (1955–) *My Chauffeur* 1986; *Penn & Teller Get Killed* 1989; *Fantasia 2000* 1999

Jillian, Ann (1950–) *Sammy, the Way Out Seal* 1962; *Heart of a Child* 1994

Jimenez, Juan Antonio *Blood Wedding* 1981; *Carmen* 1983; *El Amor Brujo* 1986

Jiminez, Soledad *aka* **Jimenez, Soledad** (1874–1966) *Bordertown* 1935; *The Robin Hood of El Dorado* 1936

Jin, Elaine *A Brighter Summer Day* 1991; *A One and a Two* 1999

Jobert, Marlène (1943–) *Masculine Feminine* 1966; *The Last Known Address* 1969; *Rider on the Rain* 1970; *Catch Me a Spy* 1971; *Sink or Swim* 1971; *Ten Days' Wonder* 1971; *The Evil Trap* 1975; *The Police War* 1979

Jodorowsky, Alexandro (1929–) *El Topo* 1971; *The Holy Mountain* 1973

Johann, Zita (1904–1993) *The Struggle* 1931; *The Mummy* 1932; *Tiger Shark* 1932; *The Sin of Nora Moran* 1933

Johansen, David (1950–) *Candy Mountain* 1987; *Scrooged* 1988; *Let It Ride* 1989; *Car 54 Where Are You?* 1991; *Desire & Hell at Sunset Motel* 1991; *Tales from the Darkside: the Movie* 1991; *Freejack* 1992; *Nick and Jane* 1996

Johansson, Scarlett (1984–) *The Horse Whisperer* 1998; *My Brother the Pig* 1999; *An American Rhapsody* 2001; *Eight Legged Freaks* 2001; *Ghost World* 2001; *The Man Who Wasn't There* 2001; *Girl with a Pearl Earring* 2003; *Lost in Translation* 2003; *A Good Woman* 2004; *In Good Company* 2004; *A Love Song for Bobby Long* 2004; *The Perfect Score* 2004; *The SpongeBob SquarePants Movie* 2004

Johar, I S (1920–1984) *Harry Black and the Tiger* 1958; *North West Frontier* 1959; *Death on the Nile* 1978

John, Elton (1947–) *Tommy* 1975; *The Road to El Dorado* 2000

John, Errol (1924–1988) *The Sins of Rachel Cade* 1960; *PT 109* 1963; *Guns at Batasi* 1964; *Assault on a Queen* 1966

John, Georg *The Spiders* 1919; *Dr Mabuse, the Gambler* 1922

John, Gottfried (1942–) *Mother Küsters Goes to Heaven* 1975; *In a Year of 13 Moons* 1978; *The Marriage of Maria Braun* 1978; *Berlin Alexanderplatz* 1980; *Chinese Boxes* 1984; *Wings of Fame* 1990; *Institute Benjamenta, or This Dream People Call Human Life* 1995; *Asterix and Obelix Take On Caesar* 1999

John, Karl (1905–1977) *The Lost One* 1951; *The Devil's General* 1955

John, Rosamund (1913–1998) *The First of the Few* 1942; *The Gentle Sex* 1943; *The Lamp Still Burns* 1943; *Tawny Pipit* 1944; *The Way to the Stars* 1945; *Green for Danger* 1946; *Fame Is the Spur* 1947; *The Upturned Glass* 1947; *When the Bough Breaks* 1947; *No Place for Jennifer* 1949

Johnes, Alexandra *Zelly and Me* 1988; *The NeverEnding Story II: the Next Chapter* 1991

Johns, Glynis (1923–) *South Riding* 1938; *49th Parallel* 1941; *The Adventures of Tartu* 1943; *The Halfway House* 1943; *Perfect Strangers* 1945; *Frieda* 1947; *An Ideal Husband* 1947; *Miranda* 1947; *Dear Mr Prohack* 1949; *Third Time Lucky* 1949; *State Secret* 1950; *Appointment with Venus* 1951; *Encore* 1951; *The Magic Box* 1951; *No Highway* 1951; *The Card* 1952; *The Sword and the Rose* 1952; *Personal Affair* 1953; *Rob Roy, the Highland Rogue* 1953; *The Weak and the Wicked* 1953; *The Beachcomber* 1954; *Mad about Men* 1954; *The Seekers* 1954; *Josephine and Men* 1955; *The Court Jester* 1956; *Loser Takes All* 1956; *The Day They Gave Babies Away* 1957; *Another Time, Another Place* 1958; *Shake Hands with the Devil* 1959; *The Sundowners* 1960; *The Cabinet of Caligari* 1962; *The Chapman Report* 1962; *Papa's Delicate Condition* 1963; *Mary Poppins* 1964; *Dear Brigitte* 1966; *Don't Just Stand There* 1968; *Lock Up Your Daughters!* 1969; *Under Milk Wood* 1971; *Vault of Horror* 1973; *Zelly and Me* 1988; *Nukie* 1992; *Hostile Hostages* 1994; *While You Were Sleeping* 1995; *Superstar* 1999

Johns, Harriette (1921–) *An Ideal Husband* 1947; *Edward, My Son* 1949

Johns, Mervyn (1899–1992) *Saloon Bar* 1940; *Next of Kin* 1942; *Went the Day Well?* 1942; *The Bells Go Down* 1943; *The Halfway House* 1943; *My Learned Friend* 1943; *San Demetrio London* 1943; *Dead of Night* 1945; *Pink String and Sealing Wax* 1945; *They Knew Mr Knight* 1945; *The Captive Heart* 1946; *Captain Boycott* 1947; *Easy Money* 1947; *Counterblast* 1948; *Diamond City* 1949; *Edward, My Son* 1949; *Tony Draws a Horse* 1950; *Scrooge* 1951; *The Oracle* 1952; *The Master of Ballantrae* 1953; *Valley of Song* 1953; *Romeo and Juliet* 1954; *The Blue Peter* 1955; *1984* 1955; *Find the Lady* 1956; *The Intimate Stranger* 1956; *The Vicious Circle* 1957; *Once More, with Feeling* 1959; *Never Let Go* 1960; *The Day of the Triffids* 1962; *80,000 Suspects* 1963; *The Old Dark House* 1963; *The Heroes of Telemark* 1965

Johns, Stratford (1925–2002) *The Great St Trinian's Train Robbery* 1966; *The Plank* 1967; *The Fiendish Plot of Dr Fu Manchu* 1980; *George and Mildred* 1980; *Dance with a Stranger* 1984; *Car Trouble* 1985; *Wild Geese II* 1985; *The Lair of the White Worm* 1988; *Salome's Last Dance* 1988; *Splitting Heirs* 1993

Johnson, Adrienne-Joi *aka* **Johnson, A J** *House Party* 1990; *Double Trouble* 1992; *Baby Boy* 2001

Johnson, Anne-Marie (1960–) *Hollywood Shuffle* 1987; *Robot Jox* 1989; *True Identity* 1991

Johnson, Anthony *aka* **Johnson, A J** *BAPS* 1997; *I Got the Hook Up* 1998; *The Players Club* 1998

Johnson, Arch (1924–1997) *Gun Glory* 1957; *GI Blues* 1960; *The Explosive Generation* 1961; *The Cheyenne Social Club* 1970; *Napoleon and Samantha* 1972; *Walking Tall* 1973; *Deathmask* 1984

Johnson, Arnold (1922–2000) *Putney Swope* 1969; *My Demon Lover* 1987

Johnson, Arte (1929–) *Love at First Bite* 1979; *Evil Spirits* 1991; *Munchie* 1992

Johnson, Ashley (1983–) *AWOL* 1990; *Annie: a Royal Adventure* 1995; *Dancer, Texas Pop 81* 1998; *Recess: School's Out* 2001; *What Women Want* 2001

Johnson, Ben (1918–1996) *Mighty Joe Young* 1949; *She Wore a Yellow Ribbon* 1949; *Rio Grande* 1950; *Wagonmaster* 1950; *Shane* 1953; *Ten Who Dared* 1960; *One-Eyed Jacks* 1961; *Tomboy and the Champ* 1961; *Will Penny* 1967; *Hang 'Em High* 1968; *The Undefeated* 1969; *The Wild Bunch* 1969; *Chisum* 1970; *Kid Blue* 1971; *The Last Picture Show* 1971; *something big* 1971; *Corky* 1972; *The Getaway* 1972; *Junior Bonner* 1972; *Dillinger* 1973; *Runaway!* 1973; *The Train Robbers* 1973; *The Sugarland Express* 1974; *Bite the Bullet* 1975; *Hustle* 1975; *Breakheart Pass* 1976; *Grayeagle* 1977; *The Greatest* 1977; *The Swarm* 1978; *The Hunter* 1980; *Terror Train* 1980; *Tex* 1982; *Champions* 1983; *Red Dawn* 1984; *Let's Get Harry* 1986; *Cherry 2000* 1988; *My Heroes Have Always Been Cowboys* 1991; *Radio Flyer* 1992; *Angels in the Outfield* 1994; *The Evening Star* 1996

Johnson, Bill (1916–1957) *It's a Pleasure* 1945; *Keep Your Powder Dry* 1945; *Savage Islands* 1983; *The Texas Chainsaw Massacre Part 2* 1986

Johnson, Brad (1959–) *Always* 1989; *Flight of the Intruder* 1991; *The Philadelphia Experiment 2* 1993; *Victim of Rage* 1994

Johnson, Celia (1908–1982) *In Which We Serve* 1942; *This Happy Breed* 1944; *Brief Encounter* 1945; *The Astonished Heart* 1949; *The Holly and the Ivy* 1952; *I Believe in You* 1952; *The Captain's Paradise* 1953; *A Kid for Two Farthings* 1955; *The Good Companions* 1956; *The Prime of Miss Jean Brodie* 1969; *Les Misérables* 1978

Johnson, Chic (1891–1962) *All over Town* 1937; *Hellzapoppin'* 1941; *Ghost Catchers* 1944

Johnson, Chubby (1903–1974) *Treasure of Lost Canyon* 1952; *Back to God's Country* 1953; *Calamity Jane* 1953; *Law and Order* 1953; *Cattle Queen of Montana* 1954; *The River's Edge* 1957

Johnson, Clark (1954–) *Killing 'em Softly* 1982; *Wild Thing* 1987; *Rude* 1995

Johnson, Don (1950–) *Good Morning... and Goodbye* 1967; *The Magic Garden of Stanley Sweetheart* 1970; *Zachariah* 1970; *The Harrad Experiment* 1973; *A Boy and His Dog* 1975; *Return to Macon County* 1975; *Sweet Hearts Dance* 1988; *Dead-Bang* 1989; *The Hot Spot* 1990; *Harley Davidson and the Marlboro Man* 1991; *Paradise* 1991; *Born Yesterday* 1993; *Guilty as Sin* 1993; *Tin Cup* 1996; *Goodbye Lover* 1997

Johnson, Dots *aka* **Johnson, Dotts** (1913–1986) *Paisà* 1946; *The Joe Louis Story* 1953

Johnson, Dyke *Ride Lonesome* 1959; *Comanche Station* 1960

Johnson, Fred (1899–1971) *Native Land* 1942; *Break in the Circle* 1955; *Doctor Blood's Coffin* 1960

Johnson, Georgann *Short Cut to Hell* 1957; *The Hideaways* 1973; *Murphy's Romance* 1985

Johnson, Jason (1907–1977) *The Butter Cream Gang* 1991; *Secret of Treasure Mountain* 1993

Johnson, Karl (1924–1993) *Jubilee* 1978; *The Tempest* 1979; *Avenging Force* 1986; *Close My Eyes* 1991; *Wittgenstein* 1993; *Love Is the Devil: Study for a*

Portrait of Francis Bacon 1998; *Pure* 2002
Johnson, Katie (1878–1957) *The Last Adventurers* 1937; *Death of an Angel* 1951; *The Ladykillers* 1955; *How to Murder a Rich Uncle* 1957
Johnson, Kay (1904–1975) *Dynamite* 1929; *Billy the Kid* 1930; *Madam Satan* 1930; *American Madness* 1932; *Of Human Bondage* 1934; *This Man Is Mine* 1934; *Village Tale* 1935; *White Banners* 1938; *The Real Glory* 1939
Johnson, Kelly *Goodbye Pork Pie* 1981; *Carry Me Back* 1982
Johnson, Kurt R *Jane Austen in Manhattan* 1980; *The Fan* 1981
Johnson, Lamont (1922–) *The Human Jungle* 1954; *The Brothers Rico* 1957; *Live Virgin* 2000
Johnson, Laura (1957–) *Chiller* 1985; *Paper Hearts* 1993; *Trauma* 1993; *Judge & Jury* 1995; *And the Beat Goes On: the Sonny and Cher Story* 1999
Johnson, Lynn-Holly (1958–) *Ice Castles* 1978; *For Your Eyes Only* 1981; *The Watcher in the Woods* 1982
Johnson, Melodie (1943–) *The Ride to Hangman's Tree* 1967; *Coogan's Bluff* 1968
Johnson, Michelle (1965–) *Blame It on Rio* 1984; *Waxwork* 1988; *Genuine Risk* 1990; *Wishful Thinking* 1990; *Dr Giggles* 1992; *Far and Away* 1992; *Body Shot* 1994; *The Donor* 1994; *The Glimmer Man* 1996; *Eternal Revenge* 1999
Johnson, Mike *Get Cracking* 1943; *George in Civvy Street* 1946
Johnson, Noble (1881–1978) *The Navigator* 1924; *Hands Up!* 1926; *The Four Feathers* 1929; *The Most Dangerous Game* 1932; *Murders in the Rue Morgue* 1932; *King Kong* 1933; *She* 1935; *The Ghost Breakers* 1940; *A Game of Death* 1945
Johnson, Rafer (1935–) *The Fiercest Heart* 1961; *Wild in the Country* 1961; *Tarzan and the Jungle Boy* 1968; *The Last Grenade* 1970
Johnson, Reggie *Platoon* 1986; *Seven Hours to Judgment* 1988
Johnson, Richard (1927–) *Never So Few* 1959; *Cairo* 1962; *80,000 Suspects* 1963; *The Haunting* 1963; *The Pumpkin Eater* 1964; *The Amorous Adventures of Moll Flanders* 1965; *Operation Crossbow* 1965; *Deadlier than the Male* 1966; *Khartoum* 1966; *Danger Route* 1967; *Oedipus the King* 1967; *The Rover* 1967; *A Twist of Sand* 1967; *Some Girls Do* 1969; *Julius Caesar* 1970; *Sin* 1972; *Hennessy* 1975; *Aces High* 1976; *A Nightingale Sang in Berkeley Square* 1979; *Zombie Flesh Eaters* 1979; *The Monster Club* 1980; *Secrets of the Phantom Caverns* 1984; *Turtle Diary* 1985; *Treasure Island* 1990; *Milk* 1999
Johnson, Rita (1913–1965) *London by Night* 1937; *Man-Proof* 1937; *Letter of Introduction* 1938; *Smashing the Rackets* 1938; *Broadway Serenade* 1939; *Nick Carter, Master Detective* 1939; *Edison, the Man* 1940; *Appointment for Love* 1941; *Here Comes Mr Jordan* 1941; *The Major and the Minor* 1942; *My Friend Flicka* 1943; *The Affairs of Susan* 1945; *The Naughty Nineties* 1945; *Pardon My Past* 1945; *Thunderhead – Son of Flicka* 1945; *They Won't Believe Me* 1947; *The Big Clock* 1948; *Sleep, My Love* 1948
Johnson, Robin (1964–) *Times Square* 1980; *DOA* 1988
Johnson, Russell (1924–) *It Came from Outer Space* 1953; *Law and Order* 1953; *Seminole* 1953; *The Stand at Apache River* 1953; *Tumbleweed* 1953; *Ride Clear of Diablo* 1954; *This Island Earth* 1955; *Attack of the Crab Monsters* 1957; *Courage of Black Beauty* 1957; *The Saga of Hemp Brown* 1958
Johnson, Sunny (1953–1984) *Dr Heckyl & Mr Hype* 1980; *Flashdance* 1983
Johnson, Tor (1903–1971) *Bride of the Monster* 1955; *The Black Sleep* 1956; *The Unearthly* 1957; *Night of the Ghouls* 1959
Johnson, Van (1916–) *Too Many Girls* 1940; *Dr Gillespie's New Assistant* 1942; *Somewhere I'll Find You* 1942; *The War against Mrs Hadley* 1942; *Dr Gillespie's Criminal Case* 1943; *The Human Comedy* 1943; *Pilot #5* 1943; *A Guy Named Joe* 1944; *Thirty Seconds over Tokyo* 1944; *Three Men in White* 1944; *Two Girls and a Sailor* 1944; *The White Cliffs of Dover* 1944; *Thrill of a Romance* 1945; *Week-End at the Waldorf* 1945; *Easy to Wed* 1946; *High Barbaree* 1947; *Command Decision* 1948; *State of the Union* 1948; *Battleground* 1949; *In the Good Old Summertime* 1949; *Mother Is a Freshman* 1949; *Scene of the Crime* 1949; *The Big Hangover* 1950; *Go for Broke!* 1951; *It's a Big Country* 1951; *Plymouth Adventure* 1952; *Washington Story* 1952; *Confidentially Connie* 1953; *Easy to Love* 1953; *Remains to Be Seen* 1953; *Brigadoon* 1954; *The Caine Mutiny* 1954; *The End of the Affair* 1954; *The Last Time I Saw Paris* 1954; *Men of the Fighting Lady* 1954; *The Siege at Red River* 1954; *Beyond the River* 1956; *Miracle in the Rain* 1956; *23 Paces to Baker Street* 1956; *Action of the Tiger* 1957; *The Last Blitzkrieg* 1958; *Subway in the Sky* 1958; *Beyond This Place* 1959; *Wives and Lovers* 1963; *The Doomsday Flight* 1966; *Divorce American Style* 1967; *Where Angels Go...Trouble Follows* 1968; *Yours, Mine and Ours* 1968; *Company of Killers* 1970; *The Kidnapping of the President* 1980; *The Purple Rose of Cairo* 1985
Johnson, Wil *Babymother* 1998; *South West Nine* 2001; *Emotional Backgammon* 2003
Johnston, Amy *The Buddy Holly Story* 1978; *Jennifer* 1978
Johnston, J J *Things Change* 1988; *K-911* 1999
Johnston, John Dennis *A Breed Apart* 1984; *Communion* 1989; *Pink Cadillac* 1989; *Art Deco Detective* 1994
Johnston, Johnny (1914–1996) *Unchained* 1955; *Rock around the Clock* 1956
Johnston, Kristen (1967–) *Austin Powers: the Spy Who Shagged Me* 1999; *The Flintstones in Viva Rock Vegas* 2000
Johnston, Margaret (1917–2002) *A Man about the House* 1947; *Portrait of Clare* 1950; *The Magic Box* 1951; *Knave of Hearts* 1954; *Touch and Go* 1955; *Night of the Eagle* 1961; *Girl in the Headlines* 1963; *The Psychopath* 1966; *Sebastian* 1968
Johnston, Oliver (1888–1966) *The Hypnotist* 1957; *A King in New York* 1957; *A Touch of Larceny* 1959; *Dr Crippen* 1962; *The Tomb of Ligeia* 1964; *It!* 1966; *A Countess from Hong Kong* 1967
Johnston, Sue (1943–) *Brassed Off* 1996; *Face* 1997; *New Year's Day* 1999
Jokovic, Mirjana (1967–) *Eversmile, New Jersey* 1989; *Underground* 1995; *Cabaret Balkan* 1998; *Side Streets* 1998
Jolie, Angelina (1975–) *Cyborg 2: Glass Shadow* 1993; *Hackers* 1995; *Foxfire* 1996; *Love Is All There Is* 1996; *Mojave Moon* 1996; *Playing God* 1997; *Gia* 1998; *Playing by Heart* 1998; *The Bone Collector* 1999; *Girl, Interrupted* 1999; *Pushing Tin* 1999; *Gone in Sixty Seconds* 2000; *Lara Croft: Tomb Raider* 2001; *Original Sin* 2001; *Life or Something like It* 2002; *Beyond Borders* 2003; *Lara Croft Tomb Raider: the Cradle of Life* 2003; *Alexander* 2004; *Shark Tale* 2004; *Sky Captain and the World of Tomorrow* 2004; *Taking Lives* 2004; *Mr & Mrs Smith* 2005
Jolson, Al (1886–1950) *The Jazz Singer* 1927; *The Singing Fool* 1928; *Say It with Songs* 1929; *Mammy* 1930; *Hallelujah, I'm a Bum* 1933; *Wonder Bar* 1934; *Go into Your Dance* 1935; *The Singing Kid* 1936; *Rose of Washington Square* 1939; *Swanee River* 1939
Jones, Allan (1908–1992) *A Night at the Opera* 1935; *Show Boat* 1936; *A Day at the Races* 1937; *The Firefly* 1937; *Everybody Sing* 1938; *The Boys from Syracuse* 1940
Jones, Angela *Naked as Nature Intended* 1961; *Curdled* 1995
Jones, Angus T *See Spot Run* 2001; *The Rookie* 2002; *Bringing Down the House* 2003
Jones, Barry (1893–1981) *Dancing with Crime* 1946; *Madeleine* 1949; *The Clouded Yellow* 1950; *Seven Days to Noon* 1950; *Appointment with Venus* 1951; *White Corridors* 1951; *Plymouth Adventure* 1952; *Return to Paradise* 1953; *Brigadoon* 1954; *Demetrius and the Gladiators* 1954; *The Glass Slipper* 1955; *Alexander the Great* 1956; *Saint Joan* 1957; *The Safecracker* 1958; *The Thirty-Nine Steps* 1959
Jones, Bruce (1953–) *Raining Stones* 1993; *Bob's Weekend* 1996; *The Full Monty* 1997
Jones, Carolyn (1929–1983) *House of Wax* 1953; *Shield for Murder* 1954; *The Tender Trap* 1955; *Invasion of the Body Snatchers* 1956; *Baby Face Nelson* 1957; *The Bachelor Party* 1957; *Johnny Trouble* 1957; *King Creole* 1958; *Marjorie Morningstar* 1958; *Career* 1959; *A Hole in the Head* 1959; *Last Train from Gun Hill* 1959; *The Man in the Net* 1959; *Ice Palace* 1960; *Sail a Crooked Ship* 1961; *How the West Was Won* 1962; *A Ticklish Affair* 1963; *Color Me Dead* 1969; *The Dance of Death* 1969; *Eaten Alive* 1976; *Good Luck, Miss Wyckoff* 1979
Jones, Cherry (1956–) *Light of Day* 1987; *Julian Po* 1997; *Cradle Will Rock* 1999; *The Lady in Question* 1999; *Murder in a Small Town* 1999; *Erin Brockovich* 2000; *Signs* 2002; *The Village* 2004
Jones, Christopher (1941–) *Chubasco* 1967; *Three in the Attic* 1968; *Wild in the Streets* 1968; *The Looking Glass War* 1969; *Ryan's Daughter* 1970
Jones, Claude Earl *Impulse* 1984; *Bride of Re-Animator* 1991
Jones, Clifton (1942–) *Only When I Larf* 1968; *Sheena* 1984
Jones, Dean (1931–) *Tea and Sympathy* 1956; *These Wilder Years* 1956; *Jailhouse Rock* 1957; *Until They Sail* 1957; *Handle with Care* 1958; *Imitation General* 1958; *Torpedo Run* 1958; *Never So Few* 1959; *Under the Yum Yum Tree* 1963; *The New Interns* 1964; *Two on a Guillotine* 1964; *That Darn Cat!* 1965; *Any Wednesday* 1966; *Monkeys, Go Home!* 1966; *The Ugly Dachshund* 1966; *Blackbeard's Ghost* 1967; *The Horse in the Gray Flannel Suit* 1968; *The Love Bug* 1969; *The Million Dollar Duck* 1971; *Snowball Express* 1972; *The Shaggy DA* 1976; *Herbie Goes to Monte Carlo* 1977; *Born Again* 1978; *Other People's Money* 1991; *Beethoven* 1992; *That Darn Cat* 1997
Jones, Dickie *aka* **Jones, Dick** (1927–) *Pinocchio* 1940; *Rocky Mountain* 1950; *Fort Worth* 1951; *Last of the Pony Riders* 1953; *The Cool and the Crazy* 1958
Jones, Duane (1937–1988) *Night of the Living Dead* 1968; *Ganja and Hess* 1973
Jones, Eddie *Year of the Dragon* 1985; *Apprentice to Murder* 1988; *Ed McBain's 87th Precinct* 1995; *Return to Me* 2000; *Seabiscuit* 2003
Jones, Emrys (1915–1972) *One of Our Aircraft Is Missing* 1942; *Blue Scar* 1947; *This Was a Woman* 1947; *The Small Back Room* 1949; *Deadly Nightshade* 1953; *Three Cases of Murder* 1953; *Serena* 1962
Jones, Freddie (1927–) *Marat/Sade* 1966; *The Bliss of Mrs Blossom* 1968; *Otley* 1968; *Frankenstein Must Be Destroyed* 1969; *Assault* 1970; *Doctor in Trouble* 1970; *Antony and Cleopatra* 1972; *Sitting Target* 1972; *The Satanic Rites of Dracula* 1973; *All Creatures Great and Small* 1974; *Never Too Young to Rock* 1975; *Zulu Dawn* 1979; *The Elephant Man* 1980; *Firefox* 1982; *And the Ship Sails On* 1983; *Krull* 1983; *Dune* 1984; *Firestarter* 1984; *The Black Cauldron* 1985; *Young Sherlock Holmes* 1985; *Consuming Passions* 1988; *The Last Butterfly* 1990; *The NeverEnding Story III* 1994; *House!* 2000; *Ladies in Lavender* 2004
Jones, Gemma (1942–) *The Devils* 1971; *On the Black Hill* 1987; *Paperhouse* 1988; *Feast of July* 1995; *Sense and Sensibility* 1995; *Wilde* 1997; *Captain Jack* 1998; *The Theory of Flight* 1998; *The Winslow Boy* 1999; *Bridget Jones's Diary* 2001; *Bridget Jones: the Edge of Reason* 2004
Jones, Gordon (1911–1963) *Red Salute* 1935; *Strike Me Pink* 1936; *Sea Devils* 1937; *Among the Living* 1941; *The Feminine Touch* 1941; *Flying Tigers* 1942; *The Secret Life of Walter Mitty* 1947; *Tokyo Joe* 1949; *North of the Great Divide* 1950; *Trail of Robin Hood* 1950; *Smoke Signal* 1955
Jones, Grace (1952–) *Gordon's War* 1973; *Conan the Destroyer* 1984; *A View to a Kill* 1985; *Vamp* 1986; *Siesta* 1987; *Straight to Hell* 1987; *Boomerang* 1992; *Palmer's Pick-Up* 1999
Jones, Griffith (1910–) *The Rise of Catherine the Great* 1934; *Escape Me Never* 1935; *First a Girl* 1935; *The Mill on the Floss* 1937; *Return of a Stranger* 1937; *A Yank at Oxford* 1938; *The Four Just Men* 1939; *Uncensored* 1942; *The Rake's Progress* 1945; *The Wicked Lady* 1945; *Miranda* 1947; *They Made Me a Fugitive* 1947; *Once upon a Dream* 1948; *Account Rendered* 1957; *Not Wanted on Voyage* 1957; *Hidden Homicide* 1958
Jones, Hannah *Blackmail* 1929; *Piccadilly* 1929
Jones, Helen *Bliss* 1985; *Waiting* 1990
Jones, Henry (1912–1999) *The Bad Seed* 1956; *The Girl Can't Help It* 1956; *The Girl He Left Behind* 1956; *3:10 to Yuma* 1957; *Will Success Spoil Rock Hunter?* 1957; *Vertigo* 1958; *The Bramble Bush* 1960; *Cash McCall* 1960; *Angel Baby* 1961; *Never Too Late* 1965; *Angel in My Pocket* 1968; *Project X* 1968; *Butch Cassidy and the Sundance Kid* 1969; *Support Your Local Sheriff!* 1969; *The Cockeyed Cowboys of Calico County* 1970; *Skin Game* 1971; *Support Your Local Gunfighter* 1971; *Napoleon and Samantha* 1972; *The Outfit* 1973; *Tom Sawyer* 1973; *Nine to Five* 1980; *Deathtrap* 1982; *Arachnophobia* 1990; *The Grifters* 1990; *Over Her Dead Body* 1990
Jones (2), Jack (1938–) *Juke Box Rhythm* 1959; *The Comeback* 1977; *Airplane II: the Sequel* 1982
Jones, James Earl (1931–) *Dr Strangelove, or How I Learned to Stop Worrying and Love the Bomb* 1963; *The Comedians* 1967; *End of the Road* 1970; *The Great White Hope* 1970; *King: a Filmed Record... Montgomery to Memphis* 1970; *The Man* 1972; *Claudine* 1974; *The Bingo Long Travelling All-Stars and Motor Kings* 1976; *Deadly Hero* 1976; *The River Niger* 1976; *Swashbuckler* 1976; *Exorcist II: The Heretic* 1977; *The Greatest* 1977; *The Last Remake of Beau Geste* 1977; *A Piece of the Action* 1977; *Star Wars Episode IV: a New Hope* 1977; *Star Wars Episode V: the Empire Strikes Back* 1980; *The Bushido Blade* 1981; *Conan the Barbarian* 1982; *Star Wars Episode VI: Return of the Jedi* 1983; *City Limits* 1985; *My Little Girl* 1986; *Soul Man* 1986; *Allan Quatermain and the Lost City of Gold* 1987; *Gardens of Stone* 1987; *Matewan* 1987; *Coming to America* 1988; *Best of the Best* 1989; *Field of Dreams* 1989; *Three Fugitives* 1989; *The Ambulance* 1990; *Grim Prairie Tales* 1990; *Heat Wave* 1990; *The Hunt for Red October* 1990; *Convicts* 1991; *Scorchers* 1991; *Patriot Games* 1992; *Sneakers* 1992; *Excessive Force* 1993; *The Meteor Man* 1993; *The Sandlot* 1993; *Sommersby* 1993; *Clean Slate* 1994; *The Lion King* 1994; *Cry, the Beloved Country* 1995; *Jefferson in Paris* 1995; *A Family Thing* 1996; *Good Luck* 1996; *Casper: a Spirited Beginning* 1997; *Gang Related* 1997; *The Second Civil War* 1997; *What the Deaf Man Heard* 1997; *Fantasia 2000* 1999; *Star Wars Episode III: Revenge of the Sith* 2005
Jones, January (1978–) *American Pie: the Wedding* 2003; *Dirty Dancing 2* 2003
Jones, Jeffrey (1947–) *Easy Money* 1983; *Amadeus* 1984; *Transylvania 6-5000* 1985; *Ferris Bueller's Day Off* 1986; *Howard, a New Breed of Hero* 1986; *Beetle Juice* 1988; *Without a Clue* 1988; *Valmont* 1989; *Who's Harry Crumb?* 1989; *Over Her Dead Body* 1990; *Mom and Dad Save the World* 1992; *Out on a Limb* 1992; *Stay Tuned* 1992; *Ed Wood* 1994; *The Crucible* 1996; *The Devil's Advocate* 1997; *The Pest* 1997; *Ravenous* 1999; *Sleepy Hollow* 1999; *Stuart Little* 1999; *Dr Dolittle 2* 2001; *Heartbreakers* 2001
Jones, Jennifer *aka* **Isley, Phyllis** (1919–) *Frontier Horizon* 1939; *The Song of Bernadette* 1943; *Since You Went Away* 1944; *Love Letters* 1945; *Cluny Brown* 1946; *Duel in the Sun* 1946; *Portrait of Jennie* 1948; *Madame Bovary* 1949; *We Were Strangers* 1949; *Gone to Earth* 1950; *Carrie* 1952; *Ruby Gentry* 1952; *Beat the Devil* 1953; *Indiscretion of an American Wife* 1954; *Good Morning, Miss Dove* 1955; *Love Is a Many-Splendored Thing* 1955; *The Barretts of Wimpole Street* 1956; *The Man in the Gray Flannel Suit* 1956; *A Farewell to Arms* 1957; *Tender Is the Night* 1961; *The Idol* 1966; *Angel, Angel Down We Go* 1969; *The Towering Inferno* 1974
Jones, Jocelyn *The Great Texas Dynamite Chase* 1976; *Tourist Trap* 1979
Jones, L Q *aka* **McQueen, Justus E** (1927–) *An Annapolis Story* 1955; *Battle Cry* 1955; *Santiago* 1956; *Toward the Unknown* 1956; *Men in War* 1957; *Buchanan Rides Alone* 1958; *Torpedo Run* 1958; *Battle of the Coral Sea* 1959; *Ten Who Dared* 1960; *Hell Is for Heroes* 1962; *Ride the High Country* 1962; *Showdown* 1963; *Apache Rifles* 1964; *Stay Away, Joe* 1968; *Backtrack* 1969; *The Ballad of Cable Hogue* 1970; *Brotherhood of Satan* 1970; *The McMasters* 1970; *The Hunting Party* 1971; *Smash-Up Alley* 1972; *White Line Fever* 1975; *Winterhawk* 1975; *Mother, Jugs & Speed* 1976; *Fast Charlie: the Moonbeam Rider* 1978; *Lone Wolf McQuade* 1983; *Sacred Ground* 1983; *Bulletproof* 1987; *River of Death* 1989; *The Legend of Grizzly Adams* 1990; *Lightning Jack* 1994; *The Edge* 1997; *The Mask of Zorro* 1998; *The Patriot* 1998; *The Jack Bull* 1999
Jones, Mark Lewis *Paper Mask* 1990; *Solomon and Gaenor* 1998; *Master and Commander: the Far Side of the World* 2003
Jones, Morgan *Apache Woman* 1955; *Not of This Earth* 1956
Jones, Nicholas (1946–) *The Blockhouse* 1973; *Daisy Miller* 1974
Jones, Orlando (1968–) *Liberty Heights* 1999; *Magnolia* 1999;

Bedazzled 2000; *The Replacements* 2000; *Double Take* 2001; *Evolution* 2001; *Say It Isn't So* 2001; *Drumline* 2002; *The Time Machine* 2002; *Biker Boyz* 2003

Jones, Paul (1942–) *Privilege* 1967; *Demons of the Mind* 1971

Jones, Peter (1920–2000) *The Blue Lagoon* 1949; *Miss Robin Hood* 1952; *The Yellow Balloon* 1952; *A Day to Remember* 1953; *Private's Progress* 1956; *Never Let Go* 1960; *School for Scoundrels* 1960; *Nearly a Nasty Accident* 1961; *Just like a Woman* 1966; *The Sandwich Man* 1966; *Carry On England* 1976; *Milk* 1999

Jones, Quincy (1933–) *A Great Day in Harlem* 1994; *Fantasia 2000* 1999

Jones, Renee *Friday the 13th Part VI: Jason Lives* 1986; *Talkin' Dirty after Dark* 1991

Jones, Richard T (1972–) *Renaissance Man* 1994; *The Trigger Effect* 1996; *Event Horizon* 1997; *The Wood* 1999; *Auggie Rose* 2000; *Moonlight Mile* 2002; *Phone Booth* 2002; *Twisted* 2003

Jones, Robert Earl (1911–) *Cold River* 1982; *Starlight* 1989

Jones, Sam *aka* **Jones, Sam J** (1954–) *10* 1979; *Flash Gordon* 1980; *My Chauffeur* 1986; *Jane and the Lost City* 1987; *Driving Force* 1988; *Silent Assassins* 1988; *American Strays* 1996

Jones, Samantha *Wait until Dark* 1967; *Get to Know Your Rabbit* 1972

Jones, Shirley (1934–) *Oklahoma!* 1955; *Carousel* 1956; *April Love* 1957; *Bobbikins* 1959; *Never Steal Anything Small* 1959; *Elmer Gantry* 1960; *Pepe* 1960; *Two Rode Together* 1961; *The Music Man* 1962; *The Courtship of Eddie's Father* 1963; *A Ticklish Affair* 1963; *Bedtime Story* 1964; *Fluffy* 1965; *The Secret of My Success* 1965; *The Happy Ending* 1969; *The Cheyenne Social Club* 1970; *Beyond the Poseidon Adventure* 1979; *Tank* 1984; *Gideon* 1999

Jones, Simon (1950–) *Giro City* 1982; *American Friends* 1991; *Miracle on 34th Street* 1994

Jones, Steve (1955–) *The Great Rock 'n' Roll Swindle* 1979; *Ladies and Gentlemen, the Fabulous Stains* 1981

Jones, Sue *Blood Money* 1980; *Dead Man's Float* 1980

Jones, Tamala (1974–) *Booty Call* 1997; *Little Richard* 2000; *On the Line* 2001; *Two Can Play That Game* 2001; *Head of State* 2003

Jones, Terry (1942–) *And Now for Something Completely Different* 1971; *Monty Python and the Holy Grail* 1975; *Pleasure at Her Majesty's* 1976; *Monty Python's Life of Brian* 1979; *Monty Python Live at the Hollywood Bowl* 1982; *Monty Python's The Meaning of Life* 1983; *Erik the Viking* 1989; *The Wind in the Willows* 1996; *Help, I'm a Fish!* 2000

Jones, Tom (1940–) *Mars Attacks!* 1996; *Agnes Browne* 1999

Jones, Tommy Lee *aka* **Jones, Tom Lee** (1946–) *Love Story* 1970; *Jackson County Jail* 1976; *Rolling Thunder* 1977; *The Betsy* 1978; *Eyes of Laura Mars* 1978; *Coal Miner's Daughter* 1980; *Back Roads* 1981; *Savage Islands* 1983; *The River Rat* 1984; *Black Moon Rising* 1985; *The Big Town* 1987; *Stormy Monday* 1987; *The Dead Can't Lie* 1988; *The Package* 1989; *Wings of the Apache* 1990; *Blue Sky* 1991; *JFK* 1991; *Under Siege* 1992; *The Fugitive* 1993; *Heaven and Earth* 1993; *House of Cards* 1993; *Blown Away* 1994; *The Client* 1994; *Cobb* 1994; *Natural Born Killers* 1994; *Batman Forever* 1995; *Men in Black* 1997; *Volcano* 1997; *Small Soldiers* 1998; *US Marshals* 1998; *Double Jeopardy* 1999; *Rules of Engagement* 2000; *Space Cowboys* 2000; *The Hunted* 2002; *Men in Black 2* 2002; *The Missing* 2003; *Man of the House* 2005

Jones, Vinnie (1965–) *Lock, Stock and Two Smoking Barrels* 1998; *Snatch* 2000; *Mean Machine* 2001; *Swordfish* 2001; *Tooth* 2003; *The Big Bounce* 2004; *EuroTrip* 2004

Jones-Davies, Sue *Radio On* 1979; *Elenya* 1992; *Solomon and Gaenor* 1998

Jonz, Jo D *First Time Felon* 1997; *Deadlocked* 2000

Jordan, Bobby *aka* **Jordan, Bobbie** (1923–1965) *Dead End* 1937; *Angels with Dirty Faces* 1938; *Angels Wash Their Faces* 1939; *Dust Be My Destiny* 1939; *Hell's Kitchen* 1939; *They Made Me a Criminal* 1939; *Boys of the City* 1940; *That Gang of Mine* 1940; *Young Tom Edison* 1940; *Pride of the Bowery* 1941; *Spooks Run Wild* 1941; *Clancy Street Boys* 1943; *Ghosts in the Night* 1943; *Bowery Champs* 1944

Jordan, Dorothy (1906–1988) *Min and Bill* 1930; *Cabin in the Cotton* 1932; *Hell Divers* 1932; *The Lost Squadron* 1932; *The Roadhouse Murder* 1932; *The Wet Parade* 1932

Jordan, Elliott *Fogbound* 2002; *New Town Original* 2004

Jordan, Jim (1896–1988) *Look Who's Laughing* 1941; *Here We Go Again* 1942

Jordan, Joanne Moore *Faces* 1968; *The Dunwich Horror* 1970; *Bury Me an Angel* 1972; *I Dismember Mama* 1972

Jordan, Marian (1896–1961) *Look Who's Laughing* 1941; *Here We Go Again* 1942

Jordan, Michael (1963–) *Space Jam* 1997; *Hardball* 2001

Jordan, Patrick (1923–) *Rag Doll* 1960; *Dilemma* 1962; *The Marked One* 1963; *The Last Escape* 1970

Jordan, Richard (1938–1993) *Valdez Is Coming* 1971; *The Friends of Eddie Coyle* 1973; *Kamouraska* 1973; *Rooster Cogburn* 1975; *The Yakuza* 1975; *Logan's Run* 1976; *Interiors* 1978; *Les Misérables* 1978; *A Nightingale Sang in Berkeley Square* 1979; *Old Boyfriends* 1979; *Raise the Titanic* 1980; *Dune* 1984; *A Flash of Green* 1984; *The Mean Season* 1985; *The Men's Club* 1986; *Solarbabies* 1986; *The Secret of My Success* 1987; *Romero* 1989; *The Hunt for Red October* 1990; *Heaven Is a Playground* 1991; *Shout* 1991; *Time Bomb* 1991; *Gettysburg* 1993

Jordan, William *A Man Called Horse* 1970; *The Buddy Holly Story* 1978; *Kingpin* 1996

Jorgensen, Ann Eleonora (1965–) *Italian for Beginners* 2000; *In Your Hands* 2004

Jorgensen, Bodil (1961–) *Agnus Dei* 1997; *The Idiots* 1998; *The Green Butchers* 2003

Jory, Victor (1902–1982) *Renegades* 1930; *The Devil's in Love* 1933; *He Was Her Man* 1934; *Madame Du Barry* 1934; *A Midsummer Night's Dream* 1935; *Streamline Express* 1935; *Meet Nero Wolfe* 1936; *First Lady* 1937; *The Adventures of Tom Sawyer* 1938; *Man of Conquest* 1939; *Susannah of the Mounties* 1939; *Cherokee Strip* 1940; *The Lone Wolf Meets a Lady* 1940; *Charlie Chan in Rio* 1941; *The Unknown Guest* 1943; *The Gallant Blade* 1948; *The Loves of Carmen* 1948; *Canadian Pacific* 1949; *Fighting Man of the Plains* 1949; *South of St Louis* 1949; *A Woman's Secret* 1949; *The Capture* 1950; *The Cariboo Trail* 1950; *Cave of Outlaws* 1951; *Son of Ali Baba* 1952; *Cat-women of the Moon* 1953; *The Man from the Alamo* 1953; *Valley of the Kings* 1954; *Death of a Scoundrel* 1956; *The Fugitive Kind* 1960; *The Miracle Worker* 1962; *Jigsaw* 1968; *Flap* 1970; *A Time for Dying* 1971; *Frasier, the Sensuous Lion* 1973; *Papillon* 1973

Joseph, Allen *Eraserhead* 1976; *Marathon Man* 1976

Joseph, Paterson *The Beach* 2000; *Greenfingers* 2000; *The Long Run* 2000

Josephson, Erland (1923–) *So Close to Life* 1957; *The Magician* 1958; *The Hour of the Wolf* 1967; *A Passion* 1969; *Cries and Whispers* 1972; *Scenes from a Marriage* 1973; *Face to Face* 1976; *Autumn Sonata* 1978; *Montenegro* 1981; *Fanny and Alexander* 1982; *Nostalgia* 1983; *After the Rehearsal* 1984; *Saving Grace* 1985; *The Sacrifice* 1986; *Hanussen* 1988; *The Unbearable Lightness of Being* 1988; *The Ox* 1991; *Prospero's Books* 1991; *Sofie* 1992; *Kristin Lavransdatter* 1995; *Ulysses' Gaze* 1995; *Faithless* 2000; *Saraband* 2003

Joshua, Larry *The Burning* 1981; *A Midnight Clear* 1991; *Sugar Hill* 1993

Joslyn, Allyn (1901–1981) *They Won't Forget* 1937; *The Shining Hour* 1938; *Fast and Furious* 1939; *The Great McGinty* 1940; *No Time for Comedy* 1940; *This Thing Called Love* 1940; *The Affairs of Martha* 1942; *Bedtime Story* 1942; *My Sister Eileen* 1942; *Heaven Can Wait* 1943; *The Immortal Sergeant* 1943; *Young Ideas* 1943; *Bride by Mistake* 1944; *The Impostor* 1944; *Sweet and Lowdown* 1944; *Colonel Effingham's Raid* 1945; *The Horn Blows at Midnight* 1945; *Junior Miss* 1945; *It Shouldn't Happen to a Dog* 1946; *The Shocking Miss Pilgrim* 1947; *If You Knew Susie* 1948; *Moonrise* 1948; *Harriet Craig* 1950; *The Jazz Singer* 1952; *I Love Melvin* 1953; *The Fastest Gun Alive* 1956; *Nightmare in the Sun* 1964

Jostyn, Jennifer *Telling You* 1998; *House of 1000 Corpses* 2001

Jourdan, Louis (1919–) *The Paradine Case* 1947; *Letter from an Unknown Woman* 1948; *No Minor Vices* 1948; *Madame Bovary* 1949; *Anne of the Indies* 1951; *Bird of Paradise* 1951; *The Happy Time* 1952; *Decameron Nights* 1953; *Three Coins in the Fountain* 1954; *The Bride Is Too Beautiful* 1956; *Julie* 1956; *The Swan* 1956; *Dangerous Exile* 1957; *Gigi* 1958; *The Best of Everything* 1959; *Can-Can* 1960; *The VIPs* 1963; *Made in Paris* 1966; *Cervantes* 1968; *A Flea in Her Ear* 1968; *The Count of Monte Cristo* 1974; *The Man in the Iron Mask* 1977; *Silver Bears* 1977; *Double Deal* 1981; *Swamp Thing* 1982; *Octopussy* 1983; *The Return of Swamp Thing* 1989; *Year of the Comet* 1992

Jouvet, Louis (1887–1951) *Carnival in Flanders* 1935; *The Lower Depths* 1936; *Mademoiselle Docteur* 1936; *Un Carnet de Bal* 1937; *Drôle de Drame* 1937; *Hôtel du Nord* 1938; *La Marseillaise* 1938; *The End of the Day* 1939; *Volpone* 1941; *Quai des Orfèvres* 1947

Jovovich, Milla (1975–) *Kuffs* 1991; *Return to the Blue Lagoon* 1991; *Chaplin* 1992; *Dazed and Confused* 1993; *The Fifth Element* 1997; *He Got Game* 1998; *Joan of Arc* 1999; *The Million Dollar Hotel* 1999; *The Claim* 2000; *Zoolander* 2001; *Dummy* 2002; *No Good Deed* 2002; *Resident Evil* 2002; *Resident Evil: Apocalypse* 2004

Joy, Leatrice (1893–1985) *The Ace of Hearts* 1921; *The Ten Commandments* 1923; *First Love* 1939; *Love Nest* 1951

Joy, Mark *Black Rainbow* 1989; *Pecker* 1998

Joy, Nicholas (1894–1964) *The Iron Curtain* 1948; *And Baby Makes Three* 1949; *Native Son* 1951; *Affair with a Stranger* 1953

Joy, Robert (1951–) *Atlantic City, USA* 1980; *Ragtime* 1981; *Amityville III: the Demon* 1983; *Terminal Choice* 1983; *Desperately Seeking Susan* 1985; *Millennium* 1989; *The Dark Half* 1991; *Harriet the Spy* 1996

Joyce, Alice (1890–1955) *Stella Dallas* 1925; *Beau Geste* 1926; *The Green Goddess* 1930

Joyce, Brenda (1917–) *The Rains Came* 1939; *Little Old New York* 1940; *Maryland* 1940; *Whispering Ghosts* 1942; *Pillow of Death* 1945; *Strange Confession* 1945; *Tarzan and the Amazons* 1945; *Little Giant* 1946; *Tarzan and the Leopard Woman* 1946; *Tarzan and the Huntress* 1947; *Tarzan and the Mermaids* 1948; *Tarzan's Magic Fountain* 1949

Joyce, Elaine (1945–) *How to Frame a Figg* 1971; *Motel Hell* 1980; *Uphill All the Way* 1985; *Trick or Treat* 1986

Joyce, Paddy (1923–2000) *The Girl in the Picture* 1956; *The Cat Gang* 1959

Joyce, Patricia *The Visitors* 1972; *The Catamount Killing* 1974

Joyce, Yootha (1927–1980) *Die! Die! My Darling* 1964; *Stranger in the House* 1967; *The Road Builder* 1971; *Nearest and Dearest* 1972; *Man about the House* 1974; *George and Mildred* 1980

Joyner, Michelle *Grim Prairie Tales* 1990; *Traces of Red* 1992; *Shadow of the Past* 1995

Judd, Ashley (1968–) *Kuffs* 1991; *Ruby in Paradise* 1993; *Heat* 1995; *Normal Life* 1995; *The Passion of Darkly Noon* 1995; *Smoke* 1995; *Norma Jean & Marilyn* 1996; *Kiss the Girls* 1997; *A Secret Sin* 1997; *Simon Birch* 1998; *Double Jeopardy* 1999; *Eye of the Beholder* 1999; *Where the Heart Is* 2000; *Animal Attraction* 2001; *Divine Secrets of the Ya-Ya Sisterhood* 2002; *Frida* 2002; *High Crimes* 2002; *Twisted* 2003; *De-Lovely* 2004

Judd, Edward (1932–) *The Day the Earth Caught Fire* 1961; *The Long Ships* 1963; *Stolen Hours* 1963; *The World Ten Times Over* 1963; *First Men in the Moon* 1964; *Invasion* 1965; *Strange Bedfellows* 1965; *Island of Terror* 1966; *The Vengeance of She* 1968; *Living Free* 1972; *Assassin* 1973; *Vault of Horror* 1973; *The Boys in Blue* 1983; *The Hound of the Baskervilles* 1983; *The Kitchen Toto* 1987

Judels, Charles (1882–1969) *Sweetheart of the Campus* 1941; *Baby Face Morgan* 1942

Judge, Arline (1912–1974) *The Age of Consent* 1932; *Looking for Trouble* 1934; *George White's 1935 Scandals* 1935; *King of Burlesque* 1936; *One in a Million* 1936; *Pigskin Parade* 1936; *Valiant Is the Word for Carrie* 1936; *The Lady Is Willing* 1942; *Song of Texas* 1943; *Mad Wednesday* 1950; *The Crawling Hand* 1963

Judge, Mike (1962–) *Beavis and Butt-head Do America* 1996; *SPYkids 2: the Island of Lost Dreams* 2002; *SPYkids 3-D: Game Over* 2003

Juerging, Arno (1947–) *Blood for Dracula* 1974; *Flesh for Frankenstein* 1974

Julia, Raul (1940–1994) *The Organization* 1971; *The Panic in Needle Park* 1971; *The Gumball Rally* 1976; *Eyes of Laura Mars* 1978; *The Escape Artist* 1982; *One from the Heart* 1982; *Tempest* 1982; *Compromising Positions* 1985; *Kiss of the Spider Woman* 1985; *The Morning After* 1986; *Moon over Parador* 1988; *The Penitent* 1988; *Tango Bar* 1988; *Tequila Sunrise* 1988; *Trading Hearts* 1988; *Mack the Knife* 1989; *Romero* 1989; *Frankenstein Unbound* 1990; *Havana* 1990; *Presumed Innocent* 1990; *The Rookie* 1990; *The Addams Family* 1991; *The Plague* 1992; *Addams Family Values* 1993; *The Burning Season* 1994; *Street Fighter* 1994

Julian, Janet (1959–) *On Dangerous Ground* 1986; *King of New York* 1989; *Heaven Is a Playground* 1991

Julien, Max *Psych-Out* 1968; *Getting Straight* 1970; *The Mack* 1973

Julien, Sandra *aka* **Jullien, Sandra** (1950–) *Shiver of the Vampires* 1970; *I Am Frigid... Why?* 1972

Junco, Tito (1915–1983) *A Woman without Love* 1951; *Death in the Garden* 1956

Junco, Victor (1917–1988) *Bandido* 1956; *La Fièvre Monte à el Pao* 1959

Jungmann, Eric (1981–) *Winning London* 2001; *Monster Man* 2003

Junkin, John (1930–) *A Hard Day's Night* 1964; *Simon, Simon* 1970; *Rosie Dixon: Night Nurse* 1978

Jurado, Katy (1927–2002) *The Bullfighter and the Lady* 1951; *El Bruto* 1952; *High Noon* 1952; *Arrowhead* 1953; *Broken Lance* 1954; *Trial* 1955; *Trapeze* 1956; *Dragoon Wells Massacre* 1957; *The Badlanders* 1958; *Barabbas* 1961; *One-Eyed Jacks* 1961; *A Covenant with Death* 1967; *Stay Away, Joe* 1968; *Once upon a Scoundrel* 1973; *Pat Garrett and Billy the Kid* 1973; *The Children of Sanchez* 1978; *Under the Volcano* 1984

Jurasik, Peter (1950–) *Born Again* 1978; *Tron* 1982

Jurgens, Curt *aka* **Jürgens, Curd** (1912–1982) *The Devil's General* 1955; *The Rats* 1955; *And God Created Woman* 1956; *Bitter Victory* 1957; *The Enemy Below* 1957; *Les Espions* 1957; *Ferry to Hong Kong* 1958; *The Inn of the Sixth Happiness* 1958; *Me and the Colonel* 1958; *This Happy Feeling* 1958; *The Blue Angel* 1959; *I Aim at the Stars* 1960; *Hide and Seek* 1963; *Miracle of the White Stallions* 1963; *Of Love and Desire* 1963; *Psyche '59* 1964; *Lord Jim* 1965; *The Karate Killers* 1967; *The Heroes* 1968; *The Assassination Bureau* 1969; *Battle of Britain* 1969; *The Battle of Neretva* 1969; *Hello – Goodbye* 1970; *The Mephisto Waltz* 1971; *Kill!* 1972; *Soft Beds, Hard Battles* 1973; *Vault of Horror* 1973; *The Twist* 1976; *The Spy Who Loved Me* 1977; *Breakthrough* 1978; *Just a Gigolo* 1978; *Goldengirl* 1979

Justice, Katherine (1942–) *The Way West* 1967; *5 Card Stud* 1968; *Prescription: Murder* 1968; *Limbo* 1972; *Frasier, the Sensuous Lion* 1973

Justin, John (1917–2002) *The Thief of Bagdad* 1940; *The Gentle Sex* 1943; *The Sound Barrier* 1952; *King of the Khyber Rifles* 1953; *The Man Who Loved Redheads* 1954; *Seagulls over Sorrento* 1954; *The Teckman Mystery* 1954; *Untamed* 1955; *Guilty?* 1956; *Safari* 1956

Justine, William *Gang Busters* 1955; *The Bride and the Beast* 1958

Justini, Carlo (1923–) *Intent to Kill* 1958; *The Siege of Pinchgut* 1959

K

Kaa, Wi Kuki *Utu* 1983; *Ngati* 1987

Kaaren, Suzanne (1912–2004) *A Million to One* 1937; *Devil Bat* 1940

Kaas, Nikolaj Lie (1973–) *The Idiots* 1998; *Open Hearts* 2002; *The Green Butchers* 2003; *Reconstruction* 2003; *Brothers* 2004

Kaci, Nadia *Bab El-Oued City* 1994; *Ca Commence Aujourd'hui* 1999; *Nationale 7* 1999

Kaczmarek, Jane (1955–) *Falling in Love* 1984; *The Heavenly Kid* 1985; *DOA* 1988; *Vice Versa* 1988; *All's Fair* 1989; *Wildly Available* 1996; *Jenifer* 2001

Kadochnikov, Pavel (1915–1988) *Ivan the Terrible, Part I* 1944; *Ivan the Terrible, Part II* 1946

Kady, Charlotte *These Foolish Things* 1990; *L.627* 1992; *D'Artagnan's Daughter* 1994; *Laissez-passer* 2001

Kagan, Elaine *By the Sword* 1992; *Babyfever* 1994

Kagan, Marilyn (1951–) *Foxes* 1980; *The Initiation* 1984; *The Ladies Club* 1986
Kagawa, Kyoko (1931–) *The Crucified Lovers* 1954; *Sansho the Bailiff* 1954; *The Lower Depths* 1956; *Mothra* 1962; *High and Low* 1963; *No, Not Yet* 1993
Kagawa, Teruyuki (1965–) *Serpent's Path* 1998; *Devils on the Doorstep* 2000
Kagen, David *Friday the 13th Part VI: Jason Lives* 1986; *Body Chemistry* 1990
Kahan, Steve *aka* **Kahan, Stephen** *Inside Moves: the Guys from Max's Bar* 1980; *Lethal Weapon* 1987; *Lethal Weapon 2* 1989; *Lethal Weapon 3* 1992; *Warlock: the Armageddon* 1993; *Assassins* 1995; *Conspiracy Theory* 1997; *Lethal Weapon 4* 1998
Kahn, Madeline (1942–1999) *What's Up, Doc?* 1972; *The Hideaways* 1973; *Paper Moon* 1973; *Blazing Saddles* 1974; *Young Frankenstein* 1974; *The Adventure of Sherlock Holmes' Smarter Brother* 1975; *At Long Last Love* 1975; *Won Ton Ton, the Dog Who Saved Hollywood* 1976; *High Anxiety* 1977; *The Cheap Detective* 1978; *First Family* 1980; *Happy Birthday, Gemini* 1980; *Simon* 1980; *Wholly Moses!* 1980; *History of the World Part 1* 1981; *Slapstick of Another Kind* 1982; *City Heat* 1984; *Clue* 1985; *An American Tail* 1986; *My Little Pony* 1986; *Betsy's Wedding* 1990; *Mixed Nuts* 1994; *A Bug's Life* 1998; *Judy Berlin* 1999
Kaidanovsky, Alexander (1946–1995) *Stalker* 1979; *Magic Hunter* 1994
Kain, Khalil (1965–) *Juice* 1991; *Renaissance Man* 1994; *Bones* 2001
Kajol (1975–) *Baazigar* 1993; *Dilwale Dulhania Le Jayenge* 1995; *Sapnay* 1997; *Kuch Kuch Hota Hai* 1998; *Kabhi Khushi Kabhie Gham...* 2001
Kalem, Toni *The Wanderers* 1979; *Silent Rage* 1982; *Billy Galvin* 1986
Kalember, Patricia (1957–) *Danielle Steel's Kaleidoscope* 1990; *Stepkids* 1992; *A Far Off Place* 1993; *The Unspoken Truth* 1995; *Signs* 2002
Kaler, Berwick *Go Now* 1995; *Jude* 1996
Kalfon, Jean-Pierre (1938–) *Weekend* 1967; *L'Amour Fou* 1968; *The Valley* 1972; *The Lady Cop* 1979; *Condorman* 1981; *A Strange Affair* 1981; *Confidentially Yours* 1983; *L'Amour par Terre* 1984; *Le Cri du Hibou* 1987
Kallianiotes, Helena *Kansas City Bomber* 1972; *Stay Hungry* 1976; *Eureka* 1982
Kalyagin, Aleksandr (1942–) *A Slave of Love* 1976; *An Unfinished Piece for Mechanical Piano* 1976
Kamekona, Danny (1935–1996) *The Karate Kid Part II* 1986; *Robot Jox* 1989
Kamen, Milt (1921–1977) *The Out of Towners* 1970; *This Is a Hijack* 1973
Kaminska, Ida (1899–1980) *The Shop on the High Street* 1965; *The Angel Levine* 1970
Kammer, Salome (1959–) *Heimat 2* 1992; *Heimat 3: a Chronicle of Endings and Beginnings* 2004
Kampers, Fritz (1891–1950) *Westfront 1918* 1930; *Kameradschaft* 1931
Kanaly, Steve (1946–) *Dillinger* 1973; *Act of Vengeance* 1974; *The Sugarland Express* 1974; *The Wind and the Lion* 1975; *Balboa* 1982
Kanaoka, Nobu (1959–) *Tetsuo: the Iron Man* 1989; *Tetsuo II: Body Hammer* 1991
Kane, Carol (1952–) *Carnal Knowledge* 1971; *Desperate Characters* 1971; *The Last Detail* 1973; *Dog Day Afternoon* 1975; *Hester Street* 1975; *Annie Hall* 1977; *Valentino* 1977; *The World's Greatest Lover* 1977; *When a Stranger Calls* 1979; *Norman Loves Rose* 1982; *Pandemonium* 1982; *Over the Brooklyn Bridge* 1983; *The Secret Diary of Sigmund Freud* 1984; *Transylvania 6-5000* 1985; *Jumpin' Jack Flash* 1986; *Ishtar* 1987; *License to Drive* 1988; *Scrooged* 1988; *Sticky Fingers* 1988; *The Lemon Sisters* 1989; *Flashback* 1990; *My Blue Heaven* 1990; *Ted & Venus* 1991; *In the Soup* 1992; *Addams Family Values* 1993; *Baby on Board* 1993; *Even Cowgirls Get the Blues* 1993; *Napoleon* 1995; *Theodore Rex* 1995; *Two Much Trouble* 1995; *American Strays* 1996; *Big Bully* 1996; *The Pallbearer* 1996; *Sunset Park* 1996; *Trees Lounge* 1996; *Gone Fishin'* 1997; *Jawbreaker* 1999; *The Shrink Is In* 2000; *My First Mister* 2001; *Confessions of a Teenage Drama Queen* 2004; *The Pacifier* 2005
Kane, Christian (1974–) *Life or Something like It* 2002; *Just Married* 2003; *Secondhand Lions* 2003; *Taxi* 2004
Kane, Eddie (1889–1969) *The Mummy* 1932; *All over Town* 1937
Kane, Jackson D *Showdown* 1973; *The Man Who Fell to Earth* 1976
Kane, Marjorie *aka* **Kane, Margie "Babe"** *aka* **Kane, "Babe"** (1909–1992) *The Great Gabbo* 1929; *The Dentist* 1932
Kane, Michael *Lonely Are the Brave* 1962; *The Bedford Incident* 1965
Kane, Tom *The Powerpuff Girls* 2002; *The Wild Thornberrys Movie* 2003
Kaneko, Nobuo *Ikiru* 1952; *The Yakuza Papers* 1973; *The Return of Godzilla* 1984
Kaneshiro, Takeshi (1973–) *Chung King Express* 1994; *Fallen Angels* 1995; *House of Flying Daggers* 2004
Kani, John (1943–) *Saturday Night at the Palace* 1987; *Sarafina!* 1992; *The Ghost and the Darkness* 1996; *Kini and Adams* 1997; *The Tichborne Claimant* 1998
Kanner, Alexis (1942–2003) *Connecting Rooms* 1969; *Crossplot* 1969; *Kings and Desperate Men* 1981
Kanter, Marin *Ladies and Gentlemen, the Fabulous Stains* 1981; *The Loveless* 1981; *Endangered Species* 1982
Kants, Ivar (1949–) *The Plumber* 1979; *Jenny Kissed Me* 1984; *Silver City* 1984; *The Naked Country* 1985
Kao Jai *Daughter of the Nile* 1987; *A City of Sadness* 1989
Kapelos, John (1956–) *The Breakfast Club* 1985; *My Man Adam* 1985; *Roxanne* 1987; *The Boost* 1988; *All's Fair* 1989; *The Deep End of the Ocean* 1999; *Shallow Ground* 2004
Kaplan, Marvin (1924–) *Angels in the Outfield* 1951; *I Can Get It for You Wholesale* 1951
Kapoor, Anil (1959–) *Mr India* 1986; *1942: a Love Story* 1994; *Virasat* 1997; *Taal* 1999; *Armaan* 2003
Kapoor, Annu *Sardar* 1993; *Aitraaz* 2004; *Raincoat* 2004
Kapoor, Kareena (1980–) *Asoka* 2001; *Kabhi Khushi Kabhie Gham...* 2001; *Yaadein* 2001; *Khushi* 2002; *Mujhse Dosti Karoge!* 2002; *Main Prem Ki Diwani Hoon* 2003; *Aitraaz* 2004; *Dev* 2004; *Hulchul* 2004
Kapoor, Karishma *aka* **Kapoor, Karisma** (1974–) *Raja Hindustani* 1996; *Chal Mere Bhai* 2000; *Fiza* 2000; *Zubeidaa* 2000; *Shakti – the Power* 2002
Kapoor, Pincho *Bombay Talkie* 1970; *Siddhartha* 1972
Kapoor, Raj (1924–1988) *Andaz* 1949; *Barsaat* 1949; *Chori Chori* 1956; *Anari* 1959; *Sangam* 1964; *Teesri Kasam* 1966
Kapoor, Rishi (1952–) *Bobby* 1973; *Kabhi Kabhie* 1976; *Henna* 1990; *Tehzeeb* 2003; *Hum Tum* 2004
Kapoor, Sanjay (1965–) *Koi Mere Dil Se Pooche* 2001; *Shakti – the Power* 2002
Kapoor, Shashi (1938–) *The Householder* 1963; *Shakespeare Wallah* 1965; *Waqt* 1965; *Pretty Polly* 1967; *Bombay Talkie* 1970; *Siddhartha* 1972; *Kabhi Kabhie* 1976; *Junoon* 1978; *Heat and Dust* 1982; *Sammy and Rosie Get Laid* 1987; *The Deceivers* 1988; *In Custody* 1993; *Jinnah* 1998; *Side Streets* 1998
Kapoor, Tusshar (1976–) *Khakee* 2003; *Gayab* 2004
Kaprisky, Valérie (1963–) *Breathless* 1983; *La Femme Publique* 1984; *Milena* 1990
Kapur, Pankaj *Roja* 1992; *Main Prem Ki Diwani Hoon* 2003
Kapur, Rajit *The Making of the Mahatma* 1995; *Train to Pakistan* 1997
Karaman, Bushra *Wedding in Galilee* 1987; *Canticle of the Stones* 1990
Karanovic, Mirjana (1957–) *When Father Was Away on Business* 1985; *Underground* 1995
Karen, Anna (1936–) *On the Buses* 1971; *Mutiny on the Buses* 1972; *Holiday on the Buses* 1973
Karen, James (1923–) *Hercules in New York* 1969; *Frances* 1982; *Return of the Living Dead* 1984; *Invaders from Mars* 1986; *Return of the Living Dead Part II* 1988; *The Unborn* 1991; *Apt Pupil* 1997
Karewicz, Emil (1923–) *The Shadow* 1956; *Kanal* 1957
Karin, Rita (1919–1993) *Sophie's Choice* 1982; *Enemies, a Love Story* 1989
Karina, Anna (1940–) *Le Petit Soldat* 1960; *Cleo from 5 to 7* 1961; *Une Femme Est une Femme* 1961; *She'll Have to Go* 1961; *Vivre Sa Vie* 1962; *Bande à Part* 1964; *La Ronde* 1964; *Alphaville* 1965; *Pierrot le Fou* 1965; *La Religieuse* 1965; *Made in USA* 1966; *The Oldest Profession* 1967; *The Stranger* 1967; *Before Winter Comes* 1968; *The Magus* 1968; *Justine* 1969; *Laughter in the Dark* 1969; *The Salzburg Connection* 1972; *Chinese Roulette* 1976; *Regina* 1982; *Treasure Island* 1986
Karlatos, Olga (1947–) *Zombie Flesh Eaters* 1979; *Purple Rain* 1984
Karlen, John (1933–) *Daughters of Darkness* 1970; *House of Dark Shadows* 1970; *Night of Dark Shadows* 1971; *A Small Town in Texas* 1976; *Pennies from Heaven* 1981; *Impulse* 1984; *Racing with the Moon* 1984; *Native Son* 1986; *The Dark Wind* 1991; *Surf Ninjas* 1993
Karlin, Miriam (1925–) *The Deep Blue Sea* 1955; *The Entertainer* 1960; *The Millionairess* 1960; *Watch It, Sailor!* 1961; *Ladies Who Do* 1963; *The Small World of Sammy Lee* 1963; *The Bargee* 1964; *Just like a Woman* 1966; *A Clockwork Orange* 1971; *Mahler* 1974; *Utz* 1992; *The Man Who Cried* 2000; *Suzie Gold* 2003
Karloff, Boris *aka* ? *aka* **Karloff** (1887–1969) *The Last of the Mohicans* 1920; *Two Arabian Knights* 1927; *The Criminal Code* 1930; *Five Star Final* 1931; *Frankenstein* 1931; *The Mad Genius* 1931; *Smart Money* 1931; *The Mask of Fu Manchu* 1932; *The Mummy* 1932; *The Old Dark House* 1932; *Scarface* 1932; *The Ghoul* 1933; *The Black Cat* 1934; *The House of Rothschild* 1934; *The Lost Patrol* 1934; *The Black Room* 1935; *Bride of Frankenstein* 1935; *The Raven* 1935; *Charlie Chan at the Opera* 1936; *The Invisible Ray* 1936; *The Man Who Changed His Mind* 1936; *The Walking Dead* 1936; *The Invisible Menace* 1938; *The Man They Could Not Hang* 1939; *Son of Frankenstein* 1939; *Tower of London* 1939; *The Ape* 1940; *Before I Hang* 1940; *Devil's Island* 1940; *You'll Find Out* 1940; *The Devil Commands* 1941; *The Boogie Man Will Get You* 1942; *House of Frankenstein* 1944; *The Body Snatcher* 1945; *Isle of the Dead* 1945; *Bedlam* 1946; *Dick Tracy Meets Gruesome* 1947; *Lured* 1947; *The Secret Life of Walter Mitty* 1947; *Unconquered* 1947; *Abbott and Costello Meet the Killer, Boris Karloff* 1949; *The Strange Door* 1951; *The Black Castle* 1952; *Abbott and Costello Meet Dr Jekyll and Mr Hyde* 1953; *Colonel March Investigates* 1953; *Frankenstein – 1970* 1958; *Grip of the Strangler* 1958; *Corridors of Blood* 1962; *Black Sabbath* 1963; *The Raven* 1963; *The Terror* 1963; *Bikini Beach* 1964; *The Comedy of Terrors* 1964; *Die, Monster, Die!* 1965; *The Ghost in the Invisible Bikini* 1966; *Mad Monster Party* 1966; *The Venetian Affair* 1966; *Cauldron of Blood* 1967; *The Sorcerers* 1967; *Curse of the Crimson Altar* 1968; *House of Evil* 1968; *Targets* 1968; *Alien Terror* 1969
Karlsen, John *Le Bambole* 1965; *The She Beast* 1965; *Screw Loose* 1999
Karlweis, Oscar (1894–1956) *Anything Can Happen* 1952; *5 Fingers* 1952; *Meet Me in Las Vegas* 1956
Karns, Roscoe (1893–1970) *The Shopworn Angel* 1928; *Dirigible* 1931; *Today We Live* 1933; *It Happened One Night* 1934; *Twentieth Century* 1934; *Front Page Woman* 1935; *Wings in the Dark* 1935; *Cain and Mabel* 1936; *You and Me* 1938; *Dancing Co-Ed* 1939; *Saturday's Children* 1940; *They Drive by Night* 1940; *That's My Man* 1947; *Devil's Cargo* 1948; *Man's Favorite Sport?* 1964
Karr, Mabel (1934–2001) *The Colossus of Rhodes* 1961; *Killer Tongue* 1996
Karr, Sarah Rose (1984–) *Beethoven* 1992; *Beethoven's 2nd* 1993
Karras, Alex (1935–) *Blazing Saddles* 1974; *FM* 1977; *Victor/Victoria* 1982; *Against All Odds* 1984
Kartalian, Buck (1922–) *Gymkata* 1985; *Checkpoint* 1987; *Eight Days a Week* 1996
Kartheiser, Vincent (1979–) *Alaska* 1996; *Masterminds* 1997; *Another Day in Paradise* 1998; *Strike!* 1998; *Crime + Punishment in Suburbia* 2000
Karvan, Claudia (1973–) *High Tide* 1987; *The Big Steal* 1990; *Redheads* 1992; *The Heartbreak Kid* 1993; *Flynn* 1995; *Paperback Hero* 1998; *Passion* 1999; *Strange Planet* 1999; *Risk* 2000
Karyo, Tcheky (1953–) *The Outsider* 1983; *Full Moon in Paris* 1984; *The Bear* 1988; *Australia* 1989; *Nikita* 1990; *1492: Conquest of Paradise* 1992; *Nostradamus* 1993; *Bad Boys* 1995; *Crying Freeman* 1995; *GoldenEye* 1995; *Operation Dumbo Drop* 1995; *To Have & to Hold* 1996; *Addicted to Love* 1997; *Dobermann* 1997; *Joan of Arc* 1999; *My Life So Far* 1999; *Wing Commander* 1999; *The Patriot* 2000; *Le Roi Danse* 2000; *Saving Grace* 2000; *Kiss of the Dragon* 2001; *The Core* 2002; *The Good Thief* 2002; *Blueberry* 2004; *Taking Lives* 2004; *A Very Long Engagement* 2004
Kasdorf, Lenore (1948–) *Missing in Action* 1984; *Kid* 1990
Kasem, Casey (1933–) *The Incredible Two-Headed Transplant* 1971; *Rugrats in Paris: the Movie* 2000
Kashfi, Anna (1934–) *The Mountain* 1956; *Battle Hymn* 1957; *Cowboy* 1958
Kaskanis, Dora *Only the Brave* 1994; *Head On* 1997
Kasket, Harold (1926–2002) *The 7th Voyage of Sinbad* 1958; *The Boy Who Stole a Million* 1960; *Sands of the Desert* 1960
Kassir, John (1962–) *Tales from the Crypt Presents: Bordello of Blood* 1996; *The Three Stooges* 2000
Kassovitz, Mathieu (1967–) *See How They Fall* 1993; *A Self-Made Hero* 1995; *Mon Homme* 1996; *News from the Good Lord* 1996; *Amélie* 2001; *Birthday Girl* 2001; *Amen.* 2002
Kastner, Daphna (1961–) *Eating* 1990; *Julia Has Two Lovers* 1990; *Lana in Love* 1991; *Venice/Venice* 1992
Kastner, Peter (1944–) *Nobody Waved Goodbye* 1964; *Unfinished Business* 1983
Kasznar, Kurt (1913–1979) *The Light Touch* 1951; *Anything Can Happen* 1952; *Glory Alley* 1952; *All the Brothers Were Valiant* 1953; *Give a Girl a Break* 1953; *The Great Diamond Robbery* 1953; *Kiss Me Kate* 1953; *Lili* 1953; *Ride, Vaquero!* 1953; *The Last Time I Saw Paris* 1954; *Valley of the Kings* 1954; *My Sister Eileen* 1955; *Anything Goes* 1956; *A Farewell to Arms* 1957; *Legend of the Lost* 1957; *Arms and the Man* 1958; *For the First Time* 1959; *The Ambushers* 1967; *The King's Pirate* 1967; *The Perils of Pauline* 1967
Katarina, Anna *The Salute of the Jugger* 1989; *Omega Doom* 1996; *The Game* 1997
Katch, Kurt (1896–1958) *Berlin Correspondent* 1942; *Ali Baba and the Forty Thieves* 1944; *Abbott and Costello Meet the Mummy* 1955
Kates, Kimberley (1971–) *Shadow of Doubt* 1998; *Blue Valley Songbird* 1999
Kath, Katherine (1928–) *Moulin Rouge* 1952; *A Touch of the Sun* 1956; *The Man Who Wouldn't Talk* 1957; *Seven Thunders* 1957; *Subway in the Sky* 1958; *Gigot* 1962; *The High Bright Sun* 1965
Kato, Masaya (1963–) *Drive* 1997; *Brother* 2000
Katsaros, Andonia *Age of Consent* 1969; *Time after Time* 1979
Katsu, Shintaro (1931–1997) *Zatoichi* 1962; *Zatoichi Meets Yojimbo* 1970
Katsulas, Andreas (1946–) *Someone to Watch over Me* 1987; *Communion* 1989; *Next of Kin* 1989; *The Death of the Incredible Hulk* 1990; *True Identity* 1991; *Blame It on the Bellboy* 1992; *New York Cop* 1995
Katt, Nicky (1970–) *The Babysitter* 1995; *subUrbia* 1996; *One True Thing* 1998; *Phantoms* 1998; *The Limey* 1999; *Boiler Room* 2000; *The Way of the Gun* 2000; *Full Frontal* 2002; *Insomnia* 2002; *Secondhand Lions* 2003
Katt, William (1955–) *Carrie* 1976; *First Love* 1977; *Big Wednesday* 1978; *Butch and Sundance: the Early Days* 1979; *Baby: Secret of the Lost Legend* 1985; *House* 1986; *Double X: the Name of the Game* 1991; *Tollbooth* 1994; *Piranhas* 1996; *Determination of Death* 2001
Kattan, Chris (1970–) *A Night at the Roxbury* 1998; *House on Haunted Hill* 1999; *Monkeybone* 2000; *Corky Romano* 2001; *Undercover Brother* 2002
Katz, Omri (1976–) *Hocus Pocus* 1993; *Matinee* 1993
Kaufman, Andy (1949–1984) *In God We Trust* 1980; *Heartbeeps* 1981
Kaufman, Maurice (1928–) *Die! Die! My Darling* 1964; *The Abominable Dr Phibes* 1971
Kaufmann, Christine (1944–) *The Last Days of Pompeii* 1960; *Constantine and the Cross* 1961; *Town without Pity* 1961; *The Swordsman of Siena* 1962; *Taras Bulba* 1962; *Wild and Wonderful* 1964; *Murders in the Rue Morgue* 1971; *Swing* 1983
Kaufmann, Günther *Gods of the Plague* 1969; *Whity* 1970; *The Third Generation* 1979; *Querelle* 1982; *Kamikaze 1989* 1983
Kaufmann, Maurice (1928–1997) *Find the Lady* 1956; *The Girl in the Picture* 1956; *The Giant Behemoth* 1959; *Gorgo* 1961; *House of Mystery* 1961; *Bloomfield* 1969
Kaushal, Kamini *Shaheed* 1948; *Upkaar* 1967
Kava, Caroline *Year of the Dragon* 1985; *Nobody's Child* 1986; *Little Nikita* 1988; *Born on the Fourth of July* 1989; *The Terror Inside* 1996
Kavanagh, John *The Country Girls* 1983; *Cal* 1984; *The Fantasist* 1986; *Bellman & True* 1987; *Joyriders* 1988; *Fools of Fortune*

1990; Widows' Peak 1993; A Love Divided 1999

Kavli, Karin (1906–1990) Walpurgis Night 1935; A Woman's Face 1938

Kavner, Julie (1951–) National Lampoon's Movie Madness 1981; Hannah and Her Sisters 1986; Radio Days 1987; Surrender 1987; New York Stories 1989; Awakenings 1990; Shadows and Fog 1991; This Is My Life 1992; I'll Do Anything 1994; Forget Paris 1995; Deconstructing Harry 1997; Judy Berlin 1999

Kawahara, Takashi Eat the Peach 1986; Road to Ruin 1992

Kawarazaki, Chojuro The Loyal 47 Ronin 1941; Musashi Miyamoto 1944

Kawazu, Seizaburo (1908–1983) The Straits of Love and Hate 1937; Yojimbo 1961

Kay, Beatrice (1907–1986) Billy Rose's Diamond Horseshoe 1945; Underworld USA 1961; A Time for Dying 1971

Kay, Bernard (1928–) Doctor Zhivago 1965; The Shuttered Room 1967; They Came from beyond Space 1967; Interlude 1968; Trog 1970

Kay, Billy (1984–) Bitter Suite 2000; LIE 2001

Kay, Charles (1930–) Bachelor of Hearts 1958; Amadeus 1984

Kay, Mary Ellen (1929–) The Long Wait 1954; Thunder Pass 1954; Francis in the Haunted House 1956; Runaway Daughters 1956

Kay, Melody Camp Nowhere 1994; The NeverEnding Story III 1994

Kayama, Yuzo (1937–) Sanjuro 1962; Red Beard 1965

Kaye, Caren (1951–) Cuba Crossing 1980; My Tutor 1983

Kaye, Celia (1941–) Island of the Blue Dolphins 1964; Wild Seed 1965; The Final Comedown 1972

Kaye, Clarissa aka **Kaye-Mason, Clarissa** (1931–1994) Age of Consent 1969; The Good Wife 1986

Kaye, Danny (1913–1987) Up in Arms 1944; Wonder Man 1945; The Kid from Brooklyn 1946; The Secret Life of Walter Mitty 1947; A Song Is Born 1948; The Inspector General 1949; It's a Great Feeling 1949; On the Riviera 1951; Hans Christian Andersen 1952; Knock on Wood 1954; White Christmas 1954; The Court Jester 1956; Me and the Colonel 1958; Merry Andrew 1958; The Five Pennies 1959; On the Double 1961; The Man from the Diner's Club 1963; The Madwoman of Chaillot 1969; Skokie 1981

Kaye, Davy (1916–1998) The Wrong Arm of the Law 1962; Crooks in Cloisters 1963; The World Ten Times Over 1963; Satan's Harvest 1965; The Biggest Bundle of Them All 1968

Kaye, Lila (1929–) An American Werewolf in London 1981; Nuns on the Run 1990; Mrs 'arris Goes to Paris 1992; Dragonworld 1994

Kaye, Norman (1927–) Lonely Hearts 1981; Man of Flowers 1984; Where the Green Ants Dream 1984; Relatives 1985; Unfinished Business 1985; Cactus 1986; Warm Nights on a Slow Moving Train 1986; Boundaries of the Heart 1988; Island 1989; Golden Braid 1991; A Woman's Tale 1991; The Nun and the Bandit 1992; Turtle Beach 1992; Bad Boy Bubby 1993

Kaye, Paul (1965–) Blackball 2003; Spivs 2003; It's All Gone Pete Tong 2004

Kaye, Stubby (1918–1997) Guys and Dolls 1955; You Can't Run Away from It 1956; Li'l Abner 1959; Forty Pounds of Trouble 1962; The Way West 1967; Sweet Charity 1968; Can Heironymus Merkin Ever Forget Mercy Humppe and Find True Happiness? 1969; The Cockeyed Cowboys of Calico County 1970; Who Framed Roger Rabbit 1988

Kazan, Elia (1909–2003) City for Conquest 1940; Blues in the Night 1941

Kazan, Lainie (1942–) Dayton's Devils 1968; Lady in Cement 1968; Romance of a Horse Thief 1971; My Favorite Year 1982; One from the Heart 1982; Lust in the Dust 1984; The Journey of Natty Gann 1985; The Delta Force 1986; Bigfoot and the Hendersons 1987; Beaches 1988; Out of the Dark 1988; Eternity 1990; 29th Street 1991; I Don't Buy Kisses Anymore 1992; The Associate 1996; Love Is All There Is 1996; The Big Hit 1998; My Big Fat Greek Wedding 2002; Gigli 2003

Kazann, Zitto Beyond Evil 1980; Ghost Town 1988; Criminal 2004

Keach, James (1948–) FM 1977; Hurricane 1979; The Long Riders 1980; Love Letters 1983; National Lampoon's Vacation 1983; The Razor's Edge 1984; Moving Violations 1985; Stand Alone 1985; Wildcats 1986; The Experts 1989; The Dance Goes On 1990

Keach, Stacy (1941–) The Heart Is a Lonely Hunter 1968; Brewster McCloud 1970; End of the Road 1970; The Traveling Executioner 1970; Doc 1971; Fat City 1972; The Life and Times of Judge Roy Bean 1972; The New Centurions 1972; The Gravy Train 1974; Luther 1974; Watched 1974; Conduct Unbecoming 1975; James Dean – the First American Teenager 1975; The Killer inside Me 1975; The Sicilian Cross 1976; The Squeeze 1977; Cheech & Chong's Up in Smoke 1978; Gray Lady Down 1978; The Ninth Configuration 1979; The Long Riders 1980; Cheech and Chong's Nice Dreams 1981; Road Games 1981; Butterfly 1982; That Championship Season 1982; Class of 1999 1990; False Identity 1990; Milena 1990; Sunset Grill 1992; Batman: Mask of the Phantasm 1993; Good Cop, Bad Cop 1993; Young Ivanhoe 1994; Escape from LA 1996; American History X 1998; Militia 2000

Kean, Marie (1922–1994) Rooney 1958; The Big Gamble 1961; Girl with Green Eyes 1963; I Was Happy Here 1966; Ryan's Daughter 1970; Barry Lyndon 1975; The Lonely Passion of Judith Hearne 1987

Keane, Edward (1884–1959) The Singing Kid 1936; Devil's Island 1940

Keane, James (1952–) Cannery Row 1982; Assassination Tango 2002

Keane, Kerrie Second Serve 1986; Distant Thunder 1988; Malarek 1989; Obsessed 1989

Keane, Robert Emmett aka **Keane, Robert E** (1883–1981) Laugh and Get Rich 1931; The Spellbinder 1939; The Saint Takes Over 1940; The Red Dragon 1945; Fool's Gold 1946; Fear in the Night 1947

Kearns, Billy aka **Kearns, Bill** (1923–1992) Plein Soleil 1960; Playtime 1967; Asterix vs Caesar 1985; Asterix in Britain 1986

Keating, Larry (1896–1963) Three Secrets 1950; Follow the Sun: the Ben Hogan Story 1951; The Light Touch 1951; The Mating Season 1951; When Worlds Collide 1951; Above and Beyond 1952; Carson City 1952; Inferno 1953; Gypsy Colt 1954; The Buster Keaton Story 1957; Stopover Tokyo 1957; The Wayward Bus 1957; Who Was That Lady? 1960

Keaton, Buster (1895–1966) The Butcher Boy 1917; Neighbors 1920; One Week 1920; The Saphead 1920; The Scarecrow 1920; The Paleface 1921; Day Dreams 1922; Our Hospitality 1923; The Three Ages 1923; The Navigator 1924; Sherlock Junior 1924; Go West 1925; Seven Chances 1925; Battling Butler 1926; College 1927; The General 1927; The Cameraman 1928; Steamboat Bill, Jr 1928; Hollywood Revue 1929; Spite Marriage 1929; Doughboys 1930; Free and Easy 1930; Parlor, Bedroom and Bath 1931; The Passionate Plumber 1932; Speak Easily 1932; What – No Beer? 1933; An Old Spanish Custom 1935; The Villain Still Pursued Her 1940; Forever and a Day 1943; In the Good Old Summertime 1949; The Lovable Cheat 1949; You're My Everything 1949; Limelight 1952; Around the World in 80 Days 1956; The Adventures of Huckleberry Finn 1960; Pajama Party 1964; Beach Blanket Bingo 1965; Film 1965; How to Fill a Wild Bikini 1965; The Railrodder 1965; Sergeant Deadhead 1965; A Funny Thing Happened on the Way to the Forum 1966; War Italian Style 1966; 4 Clowns 1970; The Golden Age of Buster Keaton 1975

Keaton, Diane (1946–) Lovers and Other Strangers 1970; The Godfather 1972; Play It Again, Sam 1972; Sleeper 1973; The Godfather, Part II 1974; Love and Death 1975; Harry and Walter Go to New York 1976; I Will... I Will... for Now 1976; Annie Hall 1977; Looking for Mr Goodbar 1977; Interiors 1978; Manhattan 1979; Reds 1981; Shoot the Moon 1982; The Little Drummer Girl 1984; Mrs Soffel 1984; Crimes of the Heart 1986; Baby Boom 1987; Radio Days 1987; The Price of Passion 1988; The Lemon Sisters 1989; The Godfather Part III 1990; Father of the Bride 1991; Look Who's Talking Now! 1993; Manhattan Murder Mystery 1993; Father of the Bride Part 2 1995; The First Wives Club 1996; Marvin's Room 1996; The Only Thrill 1997; The Other Sister 1999; Hanging Up 2000; Town & Country 2001; Something's Gotta Give 2003

Keaton, Joe aka **Keaton, Joseph** (1867–1946) Neighbors 1920; The Scarecrow 1920; Day Dreams 1922; Our Hospitality 1923; Sherlock Junior 1924; Go West 1925

Keaton, Michael (1951–) Night Shift 1982; Mr Mom 1983; Johnny Dangerously 1984; Gung Ho 1986; Touch and Go 1986; The Squeeze 1987; Beetle Juice 1988; Clean and Sober 1988; Batman 1989; The Dream Team 1989; Pacific Heights 1990; One Good Cop 1991; Batman Returns 1992; Much Ado about Nothing 1993; My Life 1993; The Paper 1994; Speechless 1994; Multiplicity 1996; Jackie Brown 1997; Desperate Measures 1998; Jack Frost 1998; Out of Sight 1998; A Shot at Glory 2000; Live from Baghdad 2002; First Daughter 2004; White Noise 2004

Keats, Steven (1945–1994) The Friends of Eddie Coyle 1973; Death Wish 1974; The Gambler 1974; Hester Street 1975; Black Sunday 1976; The American Success Company 1979; Silent Rage 1982; Turk 182! 1985; Eternity 1990

Keays-Byrne, Hugh (1947–) The Man from Hong Kong 1975; Mad Max 1979; The Chain Reaction 1980; Lorca and the Outlaws 1985; Kangaroo 1986; Les Patterson Saves the World 1987; The Salute of the Jugger 1989

Kechiouche, Salim (1979–) A Toute Vitesse 1996; Criminal Lovers 1999; Le Clan 2004

Kedrova, Lila (1918–2000) Razzia sur la Chnouf 1955; Calle Mayor 1956; Montparnasse 19 1958; Zorba the Greek 1964; A High Wind in Jamaica 1965; Torn Curtain 1966; A Time for Loving 1971; Soft Beds, Hard Battles 1973; The Tenant 1976; Tell Me a Riddle 1980; Sword of the Valiant 1984

Keefer, Don (1916–) Riot in Cell Block 11 1954; Ace Eli and Rodger of the Skies 1973

Keegan, Andrew (1979–) Camp Nowhere 1994; 10 Things I Hate about You 1999; The Broken Hearts Club: a Romantic Comedy 2000; O 2001; Teenage Caveman 2001

Keehne, Virginya Ticks 1993; The Dentist 1996

Keel, Howard aka **Keel, Harold** (1917–2004) The Small Voice 1948; Annie Get Your Gun 1950; Across the Wide Missouri 1951; Callaway Went Thataway 1951; Show Boat 1951; Texas Carnival 1951; Desperate Search 1952; Lovely to Look At 1952; Calamity Jane 1953; Kiss Me Kate 1953; Ride, Vaquero! 1953; Deep in My Heart 1954; Rose Marie 1954; Seven Brides for Seven Brothers 1954; Jupiter's Darling 1955; Kismet 1955; Floods of Fear 1958; The Big Fisherman 1959; Armored Command 1961; The Day of the Triffids 1962; The Man from Button Willow 1965; Waco 1966; The War Wagon 1967; Arizona Bushwhackers 1968

Keeler, Ruby (1909–1993) Footlight Parade 1933; 42nd Street 1933; Gold Diggers of 1933 1933; Dames 1934; Flirtation Walk 1934; Go into Your Dance 1935; Shipmates Forever 1935; Colleen 1936; Sweetheart of the Campus 1941

Keen, Diane (1946–) Here We Go round the Mulberry Bush 1967; Sweeney! 1976; Silver Dream Racer 1980; Thirteen at Dinner 1985

Keen, Geoffrey (1918–) It's Hard to Be Good 1948; Chance of a Lifetime 1950; Cry, the Beloved Country 1951; Green Grow the Rushes 1951; Hunted 1952; The Long Memory 1952; Genevieve 1953; The Maggie 1953; Rob Roy, the Highland Rogue 1953; Turn the Key Softly 1953; Carrington VC 1954; The Divided Heart 1954; Face the Music 1954; The Glass Cage 1955; Passage Home 1955; Postmark for Danger 1955; Storm over the Nile 1955; House of Secrets 1956; The Long Arm 1956; Sailor Beware! 1956; Yield to the Night 1956; The Birthday Present 1957; Nowhere to Go 1958; Devil's Bait 1959; Horrors of the Black Museum 1959; The Scapegoat 1959; The Angry Silence 1960; Sink the Bismarck! 1960; Spare the Rod 1961; Live Now – Pay Later 1962; The Spiral Road 1962; Dr Syn, Alias the Scarecrow 1963; The Mind Benders 1963; Born Free 1966; Berserk 1967; Taste the Blood of Dracula 1969; Sacco and Vanzetti 1971; Doomwatch 1972; Living Free 1972; The Spy Who Loved Me 1977; Octopussy 1983

Keen, Malcolm (1888–1970) The Lodger 1926; The Manxman 1929; The Great Mr Handel 1942; Operation Amsterdam 1958; Two and Two Make Six 1961; Life for Ruth 1962

Keen, Noah Battle for the Planet of the Apes 1973; Gable and Lombard 1976

Keen, Pat A Kind of Loving 1962; Clockwise 1986; Without a Clue 1988

Keena, Monica (1979–) Ripe 1996; Snow White: a Tale of Terror 1996; First Daughter 1999; Crime + Punishment in Suburbia 2000; The Simian Line 2000; Freddy vs Jason 2003; Man of the House 2005

Keenan, Will Tromeo & Juliet 1996; Terror Firmer 1999

Keene, Tom aka **Duryea, George** aka **Powers, Richard** (1896–1963) Tol'able David 1930; Our Daily Bread 1934; Old Louisiana 1938; San Quentin 1946; Thunder Mountain 1947; Return of the Bad Men 1948; Storm over Wyoming 1950; Trail of Robin Hood 1950; Plan 9 from Outer Space 1959

Keener, Catherine (1961–) Johnny Suede 1991; Living in Oblivion 1995; Box of Moonlight 1996; If These Walls Could Talk 1996; Walking and Talking 1996; The Real Blonde 1997; Your Friends & Neighbours 1998; Being John Malkovich 1999; 8mm 1999; Simpatico 1999; Lovely & Amazing 2001; Death to Smoochy 2002; Full Frontal 2002; S1MØNE 2002; The Interpreter 2005

Keeslar, Matt (1972–) Safe Passage 1994; The Run of the Country 1995; Mr Magoo 1997; The Last Days of Disco 1998; Scream 3 1999; Splendor 1999

Kehler, Jack One Eight Seven 1997; Love Liza 2001; Big Trouble 2002; The Perfect Catch 2005

Kehoe, Jack (1938–) Serpico 1973; Law and Disorder 1974; On the Nickel 1979; The Untouchables 1987; Young Guns II 1990

Keim, Betty Lou (1938–) Teenage Rebel 1956; These Wilder Years 1956; The Wayward Bus 1957

Keim, Claire (1975–) The Girl 1999; Le Roi Danse 2000

Keir, Andrew (1926–1997) The Brave Don't Cry 1952; Suspended Alibi 1956; The Pirates of Blood River 1961; Cleopatra 1963; The Devil-Ship Pirates 1964; Dracula – Prince of Darkness 1965; Daleks – Invasion Earth 2150 AD 1966; The Fighting Prince of Donegal 1966; The Long Duel 1966; Quatermass and the Pit 1967; The Viking Queen 1967; Attack on the Iron Coast 1968; The Royal Hunt of the Sun 1969; Adam's Woman 1970; The Last Grenade 1970; The Night Visitor 1970; Blood from the Mummy's Tomb 1971; Zeppelin 1971; Absolution 1978; Lion of the Desert 1981; Dragonworld 1994; Rob Roy 1995

Keita, Balla Moussa aka **Keita, Balamoussa** Yeelen 1987; Ta Dona 1991

Keitel, Harvey (1939–) Who's That Knocking at My Door 1968; Mean Streets 1973; Alice Doesn't Live Here Anymore 1974; Buffalo Bill and the Indians, or Sitting Bull's History Lesson 1976; Mother, Jugs & Speed 1976; Taxi Driver 1976; Welcome to LA 1976; The Duellists 1977; Blue Collar 1978; Eagle's Wing 1978; Fingers 1978; Bad Timing 1980; Deathwatch 1980; Saturn 3 1980; The Border 1981; Exposed 1983; La Nuit de Varennes 1983; Order of Death 1983; Falling in Love 1984; Camorra 1985; The Men's Club 1986; Off Beat 1986; Wise Guys 1986; The Pick-Up Artist 1987; The Last Temptation of Christ 1988; The January Man 1989; Two Evil Eyes 1990; The Two Jakes 1990; Bugsy 1991; Mortal Thoughts 1991; Reservoir Dogs 1991; Thelma & Louise 1991; Bad Lieutenant 1992; Sister Act 1992; The Assassin 1993; Dangerous Game 1993; The Piano 1993; Point of No Return 1993; Rising Sun 1993; The Young Americans 1993; Imaginary Crimes 1994; Monkey Trouble 1994; Pulp Fiction 1994; Somebody to Love 1994; Blue in the Face 1995; Clockers 1995; From Dusk till Dawn 1995; Smoke 1995; Ulysses' Gaze 1995; City of Industry 1996; Head above Water 1996; Cop Land 1997; FairyTale: a True Story 1997; Lulu on the Bridge 1998; Finding Graceland 1999; Holy Smoke 1999; Three Seasons 1999; Fail Safe 2000; Little Nicky 2000; U-571 2000; Taking Sides 2001; Crime Spree 2002; Red Dragon 2002; National Treasure 2004; Be Cool 2005

Keith, Brian (1921–1997) Arrowhead 1953; Alaska Seas 1954; Jivaro 1954; Five against the House 1955; Tight Spot 1955; The Violent Men 1955; Nightfall 1956; Storm Center 1956; Chicago Confidential 1957; Dino 1957; Run of the Arrow 1957; Sierra Baron 1958; Villa! 1958; Violent Road 1958; The Young Philadelphians 1959; Ten Who Dared 1960; The Deadly Companions 1961; The Parent Trap 1961; Moon Pilot 1962; Savage Sam 1963; The Pleasure Seekers 1964; The Raiders 1964; Those Calloways 1964; A Tiger Walks 1964; The Hallelujah Trail

1965; *Nevada Smith* 1966; *The Rare Breed* 1966; *The Russians Are Coming, the Russians Are Coming* 1966; *Way... Way Out* 1966; *Reflections in a Golden Eye* 1967; *With Six You Get Eggroll* 1968; *Gaily, Gaily* 1969; *Krakatoa, East of Java* 1969; *The McKenzie Break* 1970; *Suppose They Gave a War and Nobody Came?* 1970; *Scandalous John* 1971; *something big* 1971; *The Wind and the Lion* 1975; *The Yakuza* 1975; *Joe Panther* 1976; *Nickelodeon* 1976; *Hooper* 1978; *Meteor* 1979; *The Mountain Men* 1980; *Charlie Chan and the Curse of the Dragon Queen* 1981; *Sharky's Machine* 1981; *Death before Dishonor* 1987; *Welcome Home* 1989; *Wind Dancer* 1991
Keith, David (1954–) *The Rose* 1979; *Brubaker* 1980; *Back Roads* 1981; *Take This Job and Shove It* 1981; *An Officer and a Gentleman* 1982; *Independence Day* 1983; *The Lords of Discipline* 1983; *Firestarter* 1984; *White of the Eye* 1986; *Heartbreak Hotel* 1988; *The Two Jakes* 1990; *Off and Running* 1991; *Running Wild* 1992; *Good Cop, Bad Cop* 1993; *Gold Diggers: the Secret of Bear Mountain* 1995; *Judge & Jury* 1995; *Poodle Springs* 1998; *When the Bough Breaks 2: Perfect Prey* 1998; *Men of Honor* 2000; *U-571* 2000; *Behind Enemy Lines* 2001; *Death at Clover Bend* 2001; *The Stickup* 2001; *Daredevil* 2003; *Raise Your Voice* 2004
Keith, Ian (1899–1960) *The Divine Lady* 1928; *The Big Trail* 1930; *The Sin Ship* 1931; *The Sign of the Cross* 1932; *Queen Christina* 1933; *Cleopatra* 1934; *Dangerous Corner* 1934; *The Crusades* 1935; *The Three Musketeers* 1935; *The Buccaneer* 1938; *Charlie Chan in The Chinese Cat* 1944; *Under Western Skies* 1945; *Dick Tracy vs Cueball* 1946; *Dick Tracy's Dilemma* 1947; *Nightmare Alley* 1947; *The Black Shield of Falworth* 1954; *It Came from beneath the Sea* 1955
Keith, Penelope (1940–) *Every Home Should Have One* 1970; *Rentadick* 1972; *Ghost Story* 1974; *The Hound of the Baskervilles* 1977; *Priest of Love* 1981
Keith (1), Robert (1898–1966) *Boomerang!* 1947; *My Foolish Heart* 1949; *Branded* 1950; *Edge of Doom* 1950; *Fourteen Hours* 1951; *I Want You* 1951; *Somebody Loves Me* 1952; *Battle Circus* 1953; *Devil's Canyon* 1953; *The Wild One* 1953; *Drum Beat* 1954; *Guys and Dolls* 1955; *Love Me or Leave Me* 1955; *Underwater!* 1955; *Young at Heart* 1955; *Between Heaven and Hell* 1956; *Ransom!* 1956; *Written on the Wind* 1956; *Men in War* 1957; *My Man Godfrey* 1957; *The Lineup* 1958; *Tempest* 1959; *Duel of Champions* 1961; *Posse from Hell* 1961
Keith, Rosalind (1912–2000) *The Glass Key* 1935; *Theodora Goes Wild* 1936
Keith, Sheila (1920–2004) *Frightmare* 1974; *House of Whipcord* 1974; *House of Mortal Sin* 1975; *The Comeback* 1977
Keith-Johnston, Colin (1896–1980) *Berkeley Square* 1933; *Blood on My Hands* 1948
Kellaway, Cecil aka **Kelloway, Cecil** (1891–1973) *Blond Cheat* 1938; *Maid's Night Out* 1938; *Intermezzo* 1939; *Brother Orchid* 1940; *The House of the Seven Gables* 1940; *The Invisible Man Returns* 1940; *Mexican Spitfire* 1940; *The Mummy's Hand* 1940; *Phantom Raiders* 1940; *Appointment for Love* 1941; *I Married a Witch* 1942; *Take a Letter, Darling* 1942; *The Crystal Ball* 1943; *It Ain't Hay* 1943; *And Now Tomorrow* 1944; *Frenchman's Creek* 1944; *Practically Yours* 1944; *Kitty* 1945; *Love Letters* 1945; *Easy to Wed* 1946; *Monsieur Beaucaire* 1946; *The Postman Always Rings Twice* 1946; *Unconquered* 1947; *Portrait of Jennie* 1948; *Down to the Sea in Ships* 1949; *Harvey* 1950; *Kim* 1950; *Francis Goes to the Races* 1951; *Half Angel* 1951; *The Beast from 20,000 Fathoms* 1953; *Thunder in the East* 1953; *Female on the Beach* 1955; *Interrupted Melody* 1955; *Johnny Trouble* 1957; *The Proud Rebel* 1958; *The Private Lives of Adam and Eve* 1959; *The Shaggy Dog* 1959; *Tammy Tell Me True* 1961; *Zotz* 1962; *The Cardinal* 1963; *Hush... Hush, Sweet Charlotte* 1964; *The Adventures of Bullwhip Griffin* 1967; *Guess Who's Coming to Dinner* 1967; *Getting Straight* 1970
Keller, Hiram (1944–1997) *Satyricon* 1969; *Lifespan* 1975
Keller, Marthe (1945–) *The Loser* 1971; *And Now My Love* 1974; *Black Sunday* 1976; *Marathon Man* 1976; *Bobby Deerfield* 1977; *Fedora* 1978; *The Formula* 1980; *The Amateur* 1981; *Rouge Baiser* 1985; *Dark Eyes* 1987; *Lapse of Memory* 1992; *The School of Flesh* 1998
Kellerman, Barbara (1949–) *Satan's Slave* 1976; *The Quatermass Conclusion* 1979; *The Monster Club* 1980; *The Sea Wolves* 1980
Kellerman, Sally (1938–) *Reform School Girl* 1957; *The Boston Strangler* 1968; *The April Fools* 1969; *MASH* 1969; *Brewster McCloud* 1970; *The Last of the Red Hot Lovers* 1972; *Lost Horizon* 1973; *A Reflection of Fear* 1973; *Slither* 1973; *Rafferty and the Gold Dust Twins* 1974; *The Big Bus* 1976; *Welcome to LA* 1976; *The Mouse and His Child* 1977; *A Little Romance* 1979; *Foxes* 1980; *Head On* 1980; *Loving Couples* 1980; *Serial* 1980; *Moving Violations* 1985; *Back to School* 1986; *That's Life* 1986; *Meatballs III: Summer Job* 1987; *Someone to Love* 1987; *Three for the Road* 1987; *You Can't Hurry Love* 1988; *All's Fair* 1989; *Limit Up* 1989; *Happily Ever After* 1990; *Doppelganger* 1993; *Younger and Younger* 1993; *Pret-a-Porter* 1994; *Live Virgin* 2000
Kelley, Alice *Against All Flags* 1952; *Francis Goes to West Point* 1952
Kelley, Barry (1908–1991) *Knock on Any Door* 1949; *Ma and Pa Kettle* 1949; *The Undercover Man* 1949; *The Asphalt Jungle* 1950; *The Black Hand* 1950; *The Capture* 1950; *Right Cross* 1950; *711 Ocean Drive* 1950; *Wabash Avenue* 1950; *Francis Goes to the Races* 1951; *The Well* 1951; *Carrie* 1952; *Law and Order* 1953; *South Sea Woman* 1953; *The Shanghai Story* 1954; *The Tall Stranger* 1957; *Buchanan Rides Alone* 1958; *The Extraordinary Seaman* 1969
Kelley, DeForest (1920–1999) *Fear in the Night* 1947; *Variety Girl* 1947; *Malaya* 1949; *Illegal* 1955; *Tension at Table Rock* 1956; *Gunfight at the OK Corral* 1957; *The Law and Jake Wade* 1958; *Warlock* 1959; *Gunfight at Comanche Creek* 1964; *Where Love Has Gone* 1964; *Apache Uprising* 1965; *Waco* 1966; *Night of the Lepus* 1972; *Star Trek: the Motion Picture* 1979; *Star Trek II: the Wrath of Khan* 1982; *Star Trek III: the Search for Spock* 1984; *Star Trek IV: the Voyage Home* 1986; *Star Trek V: the Final Frontier* 1989; *Star Trek VI: the Undiscovered Country* 1991
Kelley, James T (1854–1933) *The Rink* 1916; *The Cure* 1917
Kelley, Sheila (1964–) *Some Girls* 1988; *Breaking In* 1989; *Mortal Passions* 1989; *Pure Luck* 1991; *Singles* 1992; *Rules of Obsession* 1994; *Matchstick Men* 2003
Kellin, Mike (1922–1983) *At War with the Army* 1950; *Hell Is for Heroes* 1962; *Invitation to a Gunfighter* 1964; *The Boston Strangler* 1968; *Riot* 1969; *Freebie and the Bean* 1974; *On the Yard* 1978; *Just before Dawn* 1980; *So Fine* 1981
Kellino, Pamela aka **Mason, Pamela** (1916–1996) *The Upturned Glass* 1947; *Sex Kittens Go to College* 1960; *Door-to-Door Maniac* 1961; *The Navy vs the Night Monsters* 1966
Kellogg, Bruce (1910–1967) *Barbary Coast Gent* 1944; *Unknown World* 1951
Kellogg, John (1916–2000) *Johnny O'Clock* 1947; *Twelve O'Clock High* 1949; *Bunco Squad* 1950; *The Greatest Show on Earth* 1952; *Go Naked in the World* 1961; *Violets Are Blue* 1986; *Orphans* 1987
Kelly, Barbara *Love in Pawn* 1953; *Jet Storm* 1959
Kelly (1), Brian (1931–2005) *Thunder Island* 1963; *Around the World under the Sea* 1965; *Company of Killers* 1970
Kelly, Carol *Daniel Boone, Trail Blazer* 1957; *Terror in a Texas Town* 1958
Kelly, Claire (1934–) *The Badlanders* 1958; *Party Girl* 1958; *Ask Any Girl* 1959; *A Guide for the Married Man* 1967
Kelly, Clare (?–2001) *Georgy Girl* 1966; *All Neat in Black Stockings* 1969; *And Soon the Darkness* 1970
Kelly (2), Craig (1970–) *Beyond Bedlam* 1993; *The Young Americans* 1993; *When Saturday Comes* 1995
Kelly, David (1929–) *Pirates* 1986; *Joyriders* 1988; *Into the West* 1992; *The Run of the Country* 1995; *Waking Ned* 1998; *Greenfingers* 2000; *Mean Machine* 2001
Kelly, David Patrick (1952–) *Dreamscape* 1984; *Commando* 1985; *Penn & Teller Get Killed* 1989; *The Adventures of Ford Fairlane* 1990; *Crooklyn* 1994; *The Crow* 1994; *Heavy* 1995; *Last Man Standing* 1996; *Trojan War* 1997; *K-PAX* 2001
Kelly, Dean Lennox *The Low Down* 2000; *Deathwatch* 2002
Kelly, Dermot (1918–) *Devil's Bait* 1959; *The Quare Fellow* 1962
Kelly, Frank (1938–) *Rat* 2000; *Evelyn* 2002
Kelly, Gene (1912–1996) *For Me and My Gal* 1942; *The Cross of Lorraine* 1943; *DuBarry Was a Lady* 1943; *Pilot #5* 1943; *Thousands Cheer* 1943; *Christmas Holiday* 1944; *Cover Girl* 1944; *Ziegfeld Follies* 1944; *Anchors Aweigh* 1945; *Living in a Big Way* 1947; *The Pirate* 1948; *The Three Musketeers* 1948; *Words and Music* 1948; *On the Town* 1949; *Take Me Out to the Ball Game* 1949; *The Black Hand* 1950; *Summer Stock* 1950; *An American in Paris* 1951; *It's a Big Country* 1951; *Love Is Better Than Ever* 1951; *The Devil Makes Three* 1952; *Singin' in the Rain* 1952; *Brigadoon* 1954; *Deep in My Heart* 1954; *Seagulls over Sorrento* 1954; *It's Always Fair Weather* 1955; *The Happy Road* 1956; *Invitation to the Dance* 1956; *Les Girls* 1957; *Marjorie Morningstar* 1958; *Inherit the Wind* 1960; *Let's Make Love* 1960; *What a Way to Go!* 1964; *The Young Girls of Rochefort* 1967; *40 Carats* 1973; *That's Entertainment, Part II* 1976; *Viva Knievel!* 1977; *Xanadu* 1980
Kelly, Grace aka **Princess Grace of Monaco** (1928–1982) *High Noon* 1952; *Mogambo* 1953; *The Bridges at Toko-Ri* 1954; *The Country Girl* 1954; *Dial M for Murder* 1954; *Green Fire* 1954; *Rear Window* 1954; *To Catch a Thief* 1955; *High Society* 1956; *The Swan* 1956; *The Poppy Is Also a Flower* 1966; *The Children of Theatre Street* 1977
Kelly, Ian *In Love and War* 1996; *War* 2002
Kelly, Jack (1927–1992) *No Room for the Groom* 1952; *Gunsmoke* 1953; *Law and Order* 1953; *The Redhead from Wyoming* 1953; *The Stand at Apache River* 1953; *Drive a Crooked Road* 1954; *Cult of the Cobra* 1955; *The Night Holds Terror* 1955; *To Hell and Back* 1955; *Forbidden Planet* 1956; *A Fever in the Blood* 1961; *Young Billy Young* 1969
Kelly, Jean Louisa (1972–) *Uncle Buck* 1989; *The Fantasticks* 1995
Kelly, Jim (1946–) *Enter the Dragon* 1973; *Black Belt Jones* 1974; *Golden Needles* 1974; *Three the Hard Way* 1974; *Take a Hard Ride* 1975
Kelly (3), John *Tarzan and the Valley of Gold* 1966; *Two Mules for Sister Sara* 1970; *Buck and the Preacher* 1972
Kelly, Judy (1913–1991) *Crime on the Hill* 1933; *The Black Abbot* 1934; *Over She Goes* 1937; *Tomorrow We Live* 1942; *Dead of Night* 1945; *Dancing with Crime* 1946
Kelly, Kathleen (1912–) *Heart's Desire* 1935; *The Avenging Hand* 1936
Kelly, Moira (1968–) *The Boy Who Cried Bitch* 1991; *Chaplin* 1992; *The Cutting Edge* 1992; *Twin Peaks: Fire Walk with Me* 1992; *The Lion King* 1994; *Little Odessa* 1994; *With Honors* 1994; *The Tie That Binds* 1995; *Entertaining Angels: the Dorothy Day Story* 1996; *Unhook the Stars* 1996; *Changing Habits* 1997; *Dangerous Beauty* 1997; *Love Walked In* 1997; *Hi-Life* 1998; *The Safety of Objects* 2001
Kelly, Nancy (1921–1995) *Submarine Patrol* 1938; *Frontier Marshal* 1939; *Jesse James* 1939; *Stanley and Livingstone* 1939; *Fly by Night* 1942; *Friendly Enemies* 1942; *To the Shores of Tripoli* 1942; *Tarzan's Desert Mystery* 1943; *Show Business* 1944; *Betrayal from the East* 1945; *Murder in the Music Hall* 1946; *The Bad Seed* 1956
Kelly, Patsy (1910–1981) *Going Hollywood* 1933; *The Girl from Missouri* 1934; *Go into Your Dance* 1935; *Thanks a Million* 1935; *Pigskin Parade* 1936; *Sing, Baby, Sing* 1936; *Pick a Star* 1937; *Wake Up and Live* 1937; *The Cowboy and the Lady* 1938; *Merrily We Live* 1938; *There Goes My Heart* 1938; *Broadway Limited* 1941; *Playmates* 1941; *Road Show* 1941; *Topper Returns* 1941; *In Old California* 1942; *Ladies' Day* 1943; *The Crowded Sky* 1960; *Please Don't Eat the Daisies* 1960; *The Naked Kiss* 1964; *Freaky Friday* 1976; *Hill's Angels* 1979
Kelly (1), Paul (1899–1956) *Broadway through a Keyhole* 1933; *Public Hero No 1* 1935; *Star of Midnight* 1935; *Invisible Stripes* 1939; *Flight Command* 1940; *The Howards of Virginia* 1940; *Call Out the Marines* 1941; *Mr and Mrs North* 1941; *Flying Tigers* 1942; *Tarzan's New York Adventure* 1942; *Dead Man's Eyes* 1944; *Crossfire* 1947; *Fear in the Night* 1947; *The File on Thelma Jordon* 1949; *Frenchie* 1950; *Side Street* 1950; *Springfield Rifle* 1952; *Gunsmoke* 1953; *Split Second* 1953; *The High and the Mighty* 1954; *Johnny Dark* 1954; *The Square Jungle* 1955; *Storm Center* 1956
Kelly, Paula (1943–) *Sweet Charity* 1968; *The Andromeda Strain* 1970; *Trouble Man* 1972; *Three Tough Guys* 1974
Kelly, Roz (1943–) *The Owl and the Pussycat* 1970; *Full Moon High* 1982
Kelly, Sam (1943–) *Blue Ice* 1992; *All or Nothing* 2002
Kelly, Sean *High Flight* 1957; *The Man Inside* 1958; *The Green Helmet* 1960
Kelly, Tommy (1925–) *The Adventures of Tom Sawyer* 1938; *They Shall Have Music* 1939
Kelsall, Moultrie (1901–1980) *The Dark Avenger* 1955; *Violent Playground* 1958; *The Battle of the Sexes* 1960; *The Birthday Party* 1968
Kelsey, Linda (1946–) *Something for Joey* 1977; *Shattered Family* 1993; *Sudden Fury* 1993
Kelton, Pert (1907–1968) *The Bowery* 1933; *Bachelor Bait* 1934; *Annie Oakley* 1935; *Hooray for Love* 1935; *The Music Man* 1962; *The Comic* 1969
Kemble-Cooper, Violet aka **Kemble Cooper, Violet** (1886–1961) *Vanessa, Her Love Story* 1935; *The Invisible Ray* 1936
Kemmer, Edward (1921–2004) *Calypso Joe* 1957; *Earth vs the Spider* 1958
Kemmerling, Warren aka **Kemmerling, Warren J** (1928–2005) *Trauma* 1962; *The Lawyer* 1969; *Brother John* 1970; *Hit!* 1973; *Eat My Dust!* 1976; *Family Plot* 1976; *Close Encounters of the Third Kind* 1977; *The Dark* 1979
Kemp, Elizabeth *He Knows You're Alone* 1981; *Eating* 1990
Kemp, Gary (1960–) *The Krays* 1990; *Paper Marriage* 1991; *The Bodyguard* 1992; *Killing Zoe* 1993; *Magic Hunter* 1994; *Dog Eat Dog* 2000
Kemp, Jeremy (1934–) *Operation Crossbow* 1965; *The Blue Max* 1966; *A Twist of Sand* 1967; *Assignment K* 1968; *The Strange Affair* 1968; *Darling Lili* 1970; *Eyewitness* 1970; *The Games* 1970; *The Belstone Fox* 1973; *The Blockhouse* 1973; *East of Elephant Rock* 1976; *The Seven-Per-Cent Solution* 1976; *The Treasure Seekers* 1977; *The Return of the Soldier* 1982; *Top Secret!* 1984; *Prisoner of Honor* 1991; *Angels and Insects* 1995
Kemp, Lindsay *Savage Messiah* 1972; *The Wicker Man* 1973
Kemp, Martin (1961–) *The Krays* 1990; *Daydream Believer* 1991; *Waxwork II: Lost in Time* 1992; *Aspen Extreme* 1993; *Murder between Friends* 1993; *Embrace of the Vampire* 1994; *Fleshtone* 1994; *Monk Dawson* 1997; *Sugar Town* 1999
Kemp, Will (1977–) *Mindhunters* 2003; *Van Helsing* 2004
Kemp-Welch, Joan (1906–1999) *Busman's Honeymoon* 1940; *They Flew Alone* 1941
Kempe, Will *Pledge Night* 1990; *Hit the Dutchman* 1992
Kemper, Charles (1900–1950) *The Southerner* 1945; *Belle Starr's Daughter* 1948; *Fighting Father Dunne* 1948; *Yellow Sky* 1948; *Adventure in Baltimore* 1949; *The Doolins of Oklahoma* 1949; *A Ticket to Tomahawk* 1950; *Wagonmaster* 1950; *Where Danger Lives* 1950; *On Dangerous Ground* 1951
Kempson, Rachel (1910–2003) *The Captive Heart* 1946; *The Third Secret* 1964; *Georgy Girl* 1966; *The Charge of the Light Brigade* 1968; *A Touch of Love* 1969; *Two Gentlemen Sharing* 1969; *The Virgin Soldiers* 1969; *Out of Africa* 1985
Kendal, Felicity (1946–) *Shakespeare Wallah* 1965; *Valentino* 1977; *We're Back! A Dinosaur's Story* 1993; *Parting Shots* 1998
Kendal, Geoffrey (1910–1998) *Shakespeare Wallah* 1965; *36 Chowringhee Lane* 1982
Kendal, Jennifer (1934–1984) *Bombay Talkie* 1970; *Junoon* 1978; *36 Chowringhee Lane* 1982
Kendall, Cy aka **Kendall, Cyrus W** (1898–1953) *The Saint Takes Over* 1940; *Tarzan's New York Adventure* 1942; *Charlie Chan in The Chinese Cat* 1944; *Laura* 1944
Kendall, Henry (1897–1962) *Rich and Strange* 1932; *The Ghost Camera* 1933; *Death on the Set* 1935; *The Amazing Quest of Ernest Bliss* 1936; *The Shadow* 1936; *29 Acacia Avenue* 1945; *Voice of Merrill* 1952; *An Alligator Named Daisy* 1955
Kendall, Kay (1926–1959) *London Town* 1946; *Dance Hall* 1950; *Lady Godiva Rides Again* 1951; *Curtain Up* 1952; *It Started in Paradise* 1952; *Wings of Danger* 1952; *Genevieve* 1953; *Meet Mr Lucifer* 1953; *The Square Ring* 1953; *Street of Shadows*

1953; *Doctor in the House* 1954; *The Constant Husband* 1955; *Quentin Durward* 1955; *Simon and Laura* 1955; *Les Girls* 1957; *The Reluctant Debutante* 1958; *Once More, with Feeling* 1959

Kendall, Suzy (1944–) *The Sandwich Man* 1966; *Circus of Fear* 1967; *The Penthouse* 1967; *To Sir, with Love* 1967; *Up the Junction* 1967; *Fraulein Doktor* 1968; *30 Is a Dangerous Age, Cynthia* 1968; *The Bird with the Crystal Plumage* 1969; *The Gamblers* 1969; *Assault* 1970; *Darker than Amber* 1970; *Fear Is the Key* 1972; *Craze* 1973; *Adventures of a Private Eye* 1977

Kenin, Alexa (1962–1985) *Honkytonk Man* 1982; *A Piano for Mrs Cimino* 1982; *Animal Behavior* 1989

Kennedy, Arthur (1914–1990) *City for Conquest* 1940; *High Sierra* 1941; *Strange Alibi* 1941; *They Died with Their Boots On* 1941; *Desperate Journey* 1942; *Air Force* 1943; *Devotion* 1946; *Boomerang!* 1947; *Champion* 1949; *The Walking Hills* 1949; *The Window* 1949; *The Glass Menagerie* 1950; *Bright Victory* 1951; *Red Mountain* 1951; *Bend of the River* 1952; *The Girl in White* 1952; *The Lusty Men* 1952; *Rancho Notorious* 1952; *Crashout* 1955; *The Desperate Hours* 1955; *Impulse* 1955; *The Man from Laramie* 1955; *The Naked Dawn* 1955; *Trial* 1955; *The Rawhide Years* 1956; *Peyton Place* 1957; *Some Came Running* 1958; *Twilight for the Gods* 1958; *A Summer Place* 1959; *Elmer Gantry* 1960; *Barabbas* 1961; *Claudelle Inglish* 1961; *Murder She Said* 1961; *Hemingway's Adventures of a Young Man* 1962; *Lawrence of Arabia* 1962; *Cheyenne Autumn* 1964; *Joy in the Morning* 1965; *Fantastic Voyage* 1966; *Nevada Smith* 1966; *Anzio* 1968; *Day of the Evil Gun* 1968; *Hail, Hero!* 1969; *Shark!* 1969; *Glory Boy* 1971; *The Living Dead at the Manchester Morgue* 1974; *The Sentinel* 1977; *The Humanoid* 1979

Kennedy, Deborah *Tim* 1979; *The Sum of Us* 1995; *Idiot Box* 1996; *Swimming Upstream* 2003

Kennedy, Douglas (1915–1973) *Fighting Man of the Plains* 1949; *South of St Louis* 1949; *The Cariboo Trail* 1950; *Montana* 1950; *China Corsair* 1951; *Last Train from Bombay* 1952; *Cry Vengeance* 1954; *Sitting Bull* 1954; *The Land Unknown* 1957; *Last of the Badmen* 1957; *The Bonnie Parker Story* 1958; *The Lone Ranger and the Lost City of Gold* 1958; *The Amazing Transparent Man* 1960

Kennedy, Edgar (1890–1948) *The Two Tars* 1928; *Perfect Day* 1929; *Murder on the Blackboard* 1934; *Woman Wanted* 1935; *The Robin Hood of El Dorado* 1936; *Three Men on a Horse* 1936; *Double Wedding* 1937; *Super-Sleuth* 1937; *True Confession* 1937; *Hey! Hey! USA* 1938; *The Falcon Strikes Back* 1943; *Hitler's Madman* 1943; *It Happened Tomorrow* 1944; *Unfaithfully Yours* 1948; *My Dream Is Yours* 1949; *Mad Wednesday* 1950; *Laurel and Hardy's Laughing 20s* 1965

Kennedy, George (1925–) *Lonely Are the Brave* 1962; *Charade* 1963; *The Man from the Diner's Club* 1963; *Strait-Jacket* 1963; *Hush... Hush, Sweet Charlotte* 1964; *Island of the Blue Dolphins* 1964; *In Harm's Way* 1965; *Mirage* 1965; *Shenandoah* 1965; *The Sons of Katie Elder* 1965; *Cool Hand Luke* 1967; *The Dirty Dozen* 1967; *Hurry Sundown* 1967; *The Ballad of Josie* 1968; *Bandolero!* 1968; *The Boston Strangler* 1968; *The Pink Jungle* 1968; *Gaily, Gaily* 1969; *The Good Guys and the Bad Guys* 1969; *Guns of the Magnificent Seven* 1969; *tick... tick... tick...* 1969; *Airport* 1970; *Dirty Dingus Magee* 1970; *Zigzag* 1970; *Dynamite Man from Glory Jail* 1971; *Cahill, United States Marshal* 1973; *Lost Horizon* 1973; *Airport 1975* 1974; *Earthquake* 1974; *Thunderbolt and Lightfoot* 1974; *The Eiger Sanction* 1975; *The Human Factor* 1975; *Airport '77* 1977; *Brass Target* 1978; *Death on the Nile* 1978; *Mean Dog Blues* 1978; *Search and Destroy* 1978; *Airport '79: the Concorde* 1979; *The Double McGuffin* 1979; *Just before Dawn* 1980; *Steel* 1980; *Virus* 1980; *Modern Romance* 1981; *A Rare Breed* 1981; *Wacko* 1981; *Bolero* 1984; *Chattanooga Choo Choo* 1984; *Savage Dawn* 1985; *The Delta Force* 1986; *Radioactive Dreams* 1986; *Creepshow 2* 1987; *The Naked Gun* 1988; *The Terror Within* 1988; *Brain Dead* 1990; *Hired to Kill* 1990; *Hangfire* 1991; *The Naked Gun $2\frac{1}{2}$: the Smell of Fear* 1991; *Distant Justice* 1992; *Naked Gun $33\frac{1}{3}$: the Final Insult* 1994; *Cats Don't Dance* 1998; *Dennis the Menace Strikes Again* 1998; *Small Soldiers* 1998

Kennedy, Gerard (1932–) *Newsfront* 1978; *Body Melt* 1993

Kennedy, Gordon *Just like a Woman* 1992; *With or without You* 1999

Kennedy, Graham (1934–2005) *The Odd Angry Shot* 1979; *The Club* 1980; *The Return of Captain Invincible* 1983; *The Killing Fields* 1984; *Travelling North* 1986

Kennedy, Jamie (1970–) *Scream* 1996; *Clockwatchers* 1997; *Scream 2* 1997; *Bowfinger* 1999; *Three Kings* 1999; *The Specials* 2000; *Max Keeble's Big Move* 2001; *Malibu's Most Wanted* 2003; *Son of the Mask* 2004

Kennedy, Jo (1960–) *Tender Hooks* 1988; *Golden Braid* 1991

Kennedy, Leon Isaac (1949–) *Penitentiary* 1979; *Body and Soul* 1981; *Too Scared to Scream* 1982; *Lone Wolf McQuade* 1983; *Hollywood Vice Squad* 1986

Kennedy, Madge (1891–1987) *The Marrying Kind* 1952; *The Catered Affair* 1956; *Lust for Life* 1956; *A Nice Little Bank That Should Be Robbed* 1958

Kennedy, Merle (1967–) *Nemesis* 1993; *Night of the Demons 2* 1994

Kennedy, Merna (1908–1944) *The Circus* 1928; *Broadway* 1929; *Lady with a Past* 1932

Kennedy, Mimi (1949–) *Pump Up the Volume* 1990; *Buddy* 1997

Kennedy, Neil *Sebastiane* 1976; *Jubilee* 1978

Kennedy, Patricia (1917–) *The Getting of Wisdom* 1977; *My Brilliant Career* 1979; *Country Life* 1994; *Road to Nhill* 1997

Kennedy, Tom (1885–1965) *Mantrap* 1926; *Big News* 1929; *Monkey Business* 1931; *Smart Blonde* 1936; *Go Chase Yourself* 1938; *Change of Heart* 1943; *Invasion USA* 1952

Kenney, Horace (1890–1955) *Love, Life and Laughter* 1934; *We'll Smile Again* 1942

Kenney, James (1930–1982) *Outcast of the Islands* 1951; *Cosh Boy* 1952; *The Gentle Gunman* 1952; *Above Us the Waves* 1955; *The Love Match* 1955; *Hidden Homicide* 1958

Kenney, June *Sorority Girl* 1957; *Viking Women and the Sea Serpent* 1957; *Attack of the Puppet People* 1958

Kenny, Tom *Shakes the Clown* 1991; *The Powerpuff Girls* 2002; *The SpongeBob SquarePants Movie* 2004

Kensit, Patsy (1968–) *The Blue Bird* 1976; *Hanover Street* 1979; *Absolute Beginners* 1986; *A Chorus of Disapproval* 1988; *Chicago Joe and the Showgirl* 1989; *Lethal Weapon 2* 1989; *Prince of Shadows* 1991; *Time Bomb* 1991; *Twenty-One* 1991; *Blame It on the Bellboy* 1992; *The Turn of the Screw* 1992; *Bitter Harvest* 1993; *Full Eclipse* 1993; *Tunnel Vision* 1994; *Angels and Insects* 1995; *Grace of My Heart* 1996; *Best* 1999; *Janice Beard 45 WPM* 1999; *Bad Karma* 2001; *The One and Only* 2001

Kent, Barbara (1906–) *Flesh and the Devil* 1926; *Feet First* 1930; *Indiscreet* 1931; *Old Man Rhythm* 1935

Kent, Crauford aka **Kent, Crawford** (1881–1953) *The Unholy Three* 1930; *Body and Soul* 1931; *The Thirteenth Guest* 1932

Kent, Jean (1921–) *Bees in Paradise* 1943; *Champagne Charlie* 1944; *Fanny by Gaslight* 1944; *Madonna of the Seven Moons* 1944; *Two Thousand Women* 1944; *Caravan* 1946; *Carnival* 1946; *The Magic Bow* 1946; *The Loves of Joanna Godden* 1947; *The Man Within* 1947; *Bond Street* 1948; *Good Time Girl* 1948; *Sleeping Car to Trieste* 1948; *Trottie True* 1949; *The Reluctant Widow* 1950; *The Woman in Question* 1950; *The Browning Version* 1951; *The Lost Hours* 1952; *Grip of the Strangler* 1958; *Beyond This Place* 1959; *Please Turn Over* 1960; *Shout at the Devil* 1976

Kent, Robert (1908–1955) *Dimples* 1936; *Born Reckless* 1937; *Nancy Steele Is Missing* 1937; *Step Lively, Jeeves* 1937; *The Gladiator* 1938; *Mr Moto Takes a Chance* 1938; *East Side of Heaven* 1939; *One Million BC* 1940

Kente, Dambisa *Friends* 1993; *Cry, the Beloved Country* 1995

Kenworthy, Michael (1974–) *'Night, Mother* 1986; *Return of the Living Dead Part II* 1988

Kenzle, Leila (1960–) *Dogmatic* 1996; *Identity* 2003

Kercheval, Ken (1935–) *Pretty Poison* 1968; *The Seven-Ups* 1973; *The Patricia Neal Story: an Act of Love* 1981

Kerima (1925–) *Outcast of the Islands* 1951; *The Quiet American* 1958

Kermack, Paul (?–1990) *My Childhood* 1972; *My Ain Folk* 1973; *My Way Home* 1978

Kerman, Robert aka **Bolla, Richard** *Cannibal Holocaust* 1979; *Cannibal Ferox* 1981

Kern, Peter (1949–) *Ludwig – Requiem for a Virgin King* 1972; *Despair* 1978; *Virgin Machine* 1988

Kernan, David (1938–) *Gaolbreak* 1962; *Mix Me a Person* 1962; *Zulu* 1964

Kerns, Joanna (1953–) *Cross My Heart* 1987; *Shattering the Silence* 1992; *Mortal Fear* 1994; *No Dessert Dad, Till You Mow the Lawn* 1994; *No One Could Protect Her* 1996

Kerr, Bill (1922–) *Appointment in London* 1952; *You Know What Sailors Are* 1954; *Port of Escape* 1956; *The Captain's Table* 1958; *The Wrong Arm of the Law* 1962; *Gallipoli* 1981; *Dusty* 1982; *The Pirate Movie* 1982; *The Settlement* 1982; *Razorback* 1984; *Vigil* 1984; *The Coca-Cola Kid* 1985; *Great Expectations* 1985; *Relatives* 1985; *Kokoda Crescent* 1989; *Over the Hill* 1992

Kerr, Deborah (1921–) *Hatter's Castle* 1941; *Love on the Dole* 1941; *Major Barbara* 1941; *The Day Will Dawn* 1942; *The Life and Death of Colonel Blimp* 1943; *Perfect Strangers* 1945; *Black Narcissus* 1946; *I See a Dark Stranger* 1946; *The Hucksters* 1947; *If Winter Comes* 1947; *Edward, My Son* 1949; *King Solomon's Mines* 1950; *Please Believe Me* 1950; *Quo Vadis* 1951; *The Prisoner of Zenda* 1952; *Dream Wife* 1953; *From Here to Eternity* 1953; *Julius Caesar* 1953; *Thunder in the East* 1953; *Young Bess* 1953; *The End of the Affair* 1954; *The King and I* 1956; *The Proud and Profane* 1956; *Tea and Sympathy* 1956; *An Affair to Remember* 1957; *Heaven Knows, Mr Allison* 1957; *Bonjour Tristesse* 1958; *Separate Tables* 1958; *Beloved Infidel* 1959; *Count Your Blessings* 1959; *The Journey* 1959; *The Grass Is Greener* 1960; *The Sundowners* 1960; *The Innocents* 1961; *The Naked Edge* 1961; *The Chalk Garden* 1964; *The Night of the Iguana* 1964; *Marriage on the Rocks* 1965; *Eye of the Devil* 1966; *Casino Royale* 1967; *Prudence and the Pill* 1968; *The Arrangement* 1969; *The Gypsy Moths* 1969; *The Assam Garden* 1985; *Reunion at Fairborough* 1985

Kerr, E Katherine (1937–) *Reuben, Reuben* 1983; *Suspect* 1987; *The Impostors* 1998

Kerr, Frederick (1858–1933) *The Devil to Pay* 1930; *Raffles* 1930; *Frankenstein* 1931; *Friends and Lovers* 1931; *Waterloo Bridge* 1931

Kerr, John (1931–) *The Cobweb* 1955; *Gaby* 1956; *Tea and Sympathy* 1956; *South Pacific* 1958; *The Crowded Sky* 1960; *Girl of the Night* 1960; *The Pit and the Pendulum* 1961

Kerridge, Linda (1959–) *Fade to Black* 1980; *Strangers Kiss* 1983; *Mixed Blood* 1984; *Down Twisted* 1987

Kerridge, Mary (1914–1999) *The Blue Peter* 1955; *Richard III* 1955; *The Duke Wore Jeans* 1958

Kerrigan, J M aka **Kerrigan, Jim** (1884–1964) *Song o' My Heart* 1930; *The Lost Patrol* 1934; *The General Died at Dawn* 1936; *Lloyd's of London* 1936; *Spendthrift* 1936; *Young Tom Edison* 1940; *Appointment for Love* 1941; *The Fighting Seabees* 1944; *The Spanish Main* 1945; *Abie's Irish Rose* 1946; *Black Beauty* 1946; *The Fighting O'Flynn* 1948; *Mrs Mike* 1949; *The Wild North* 1952

Kerrigan, Patricia *Joyriders* 1988; *To Kill a King* 2003

Kerry, Norman (1889–1956) *The Hunchback of Notre Dame* 1923; *The Phantom of the Opera* 1925; *Annie Laurie* 1927; *The Unknown* 1927; *Bachelor Apartment* 1931

Kerwin, Brian (1949–) *Hometown USA* 1979; *Murphy's Romance* 1985; *King Kong Lives* 1986; *Torch Song Trilogy* 1988; *Hard Promises* 1991; *Love Field* 1992; *Gold Diggers: the Secret of Bear Mountain* 1995; *Getting Away with Murder* 1996; *Jack* 1996; *The Myth of Fingerprints* 1996; *Mr Jealousy* 1997

Kerwin, Lance (1960–) *Salem's Lot* 1979; *Enemy Mine* 1985

Kerwin, Maureen (1949–) *The Inheritor* 1973; *The Marseille Contract* 1974; *Misunderstood* 1984; *Reunion* 1989

Kerwin, William aka **Wood, Thomas** *Blood Feast* 1963; *Two Thousand Maniacs!* 1964

Kestelman, Sara (1944–) *Zardoz* 1973; *Lisztomania* 1975; *Lady Jane* 1985

Kestner, Boyd (1964–) *Entertaining Angels: the Dorothy Day Story* 1996; *The Art of Murder* 1999

Keuning, Mark *Dark City* 1950; *Three Came Home* 1950

Keyes, Evelyn (1919–) *Before I Hang* 1940; *The Lady in Question* 1940; *The Face behind the Mask* 1941; *Here Comes Mr Jordan* 1941; *Ladies in Retirement* 1941; *The Desperadoes* 1943; *A Thousand and One Nights* 1945; *The Jolson Story* 1946; *Johnny O'Clock* 1947; *Enchantment* 1948; *Mrs Mike* 1949; *Iron Man* 1951; *The Prowler* 1951; *Rough Shoot* 1952; *99 River Street* 1953; *Hell's Half Acre* 1954; *The Seven Year Itch* 1955; *A Return to Salem's Lot* 1987

Keyes, Irwin (1952–) *The Private Eyes* 1980; *Disturbed* 1990

Keyloun, Mark (1960–) *Mike's Murder* 1984; *Separate Vacations* 1986

Keymas, George (1894–1967) *Santa Fe Passage* 1955; *Thunder over Arizona* 1956

Khambatta, Persis (1950–1998) *The Wilby Conspiracy* 1975; *Star Trek: the Motion Picture* 1979; *Nighthawks* 1981

Khan, Aamir (1965–) *Rangeela* 1995; *Raja Hindustani* 1996; *Earth* 1998; *Lagaan: Once upon a Time in India* 2001

Khan, Amjad (1940–1992) *Sholay* 1975; *The Chess Players* 1977

Khan, Arbaaz (1972–) *Garv: Pride & Honour* 2004; *Hulchul* 2004

Khan, Fardeen (1974–) *Kitne Door... Kitne Paas* 2001; *Khushi* 2002; *Dev* 2004

Khan, Saif Ali (1970–) *Na Tum Jaano Na Hum* 2002; *Kal Ho Naa Ho* 2003; *LOC Kargil* 2003; *Hum Tum* 2004; *Parineeta* 2005

Khan, Salman (1965–) *Saajan* 1991; *Jab Pyaar Kisise Hota Hai* 1998; *Kuch Kuch Hota Hai* 1998; *Hum Dil De Chuke Sanam* 1999; *Chal Mere Bhai* 2000; *Hum Tumhare Hain Sanam* 2000; *Baghban* 2003; *Garv: Pride & Honour* 2004; *Mujhse Shaadi Karogi* 2004

Khan, Shah Rukh aka **Khan, Shahrukh** (1965–) *Maya* 1992; *Baazigar* 1993; *Dilwale Dulhania Le Jayenge* 1995; *Pardes* 1997; *Dil Se...* 1998; *Kuch Kuch Hota Hai* 1998; *Hum Tumhare Hain Sanam* 2000; *Mohabbatein* 2000; *Asoka* 2001; *Kabhi Khushi Kabhie Gham...* 2001; *Devdas* 2002; *Shakti – the Power* 2002; *Kal Ho Naa Ho* 2003; *Main Hoon Na* 2004; *Swades* 2004; *Veer-Zaara* 2004

Khan, Shaheen *Bhaji on the Beach* 1993; *Hollow Reed* 1995

Khanjian, Arsinée (1958–) *Family Viewing* 1987; *Speaking Parts* 1989; *The Adjuster* 1991; *Calendar* 1993; *Exotica* 1994; *The Sweet Hereafter* 1997; *Felicia's Journey* 1999; *A Ma Soeur!* 2001; *Ararat* 2002

Khanna, Akshaye (1975–) *Taal* 1999; *LOC Kargil* 2003; *Deewaar: Let's Bring Our Heroes Home* 2004; *Hulchul* 2004

Khanna, Rahul (1972–) *Earth* 1998; *Bollywood/Hollywood* 2002

Kharbanda, Kulbhushan *Nishant* 1975; *Junoon* 1978; *Mandi* 1983; *Fire* 1996; *Earth* 1998; *Lagaan: Once upon a Time in India* 2001; *Monsoon Wedding* 2001; *I – Proud to Be an Indian* 2003

Kher, Anupam (1945–) *Hum* 1991; *Jab Pyaar Kisise Hota Hai* 1998; *Bend It like Beckham* 2001; *Bride & Prejudice* 2004; *Garv: Pride & Honour* 2004

Kheradmand, Farhad *And Life Goes On...* 1991; *Through the Olive Trees* 1994

Khote, Durga (1905–1991) *Mughal-e-Azam* 1960; *The Householder* 1963

Khouri, Makram *Canticle of the Stones* 1990; *Double Edge* 1992

Khumalo, Leleti (1970–) *Sarafina!* 1992; *Cry, the Beloved Country* 1995

Kibbee, Guy (1882–1956) *Blonde Crazy* 1931; *City Streets* 1931; *Laughing Sinners* 1931; *Man of the World* 1931; *The Crowd Roars* 1932; *Fireman Save My Child* 1932; *High Pressure* 1932; *Rain* 1932; *Scarlet Dawn* 1932; *The Strange Love of Molly Louvain* 1932; *Taxi!* 1932; *Two Seconds* 1932; *Union Depot* 1932; *Footlight Parade* 1933; *42nd Street* 1933; *Gold Diggers of 1933* 1933; *Havana Widows* 1933; *Lady for a Day* 1933; *The World Changes* 1933; *Dames* 1934; *Easy to Love* 1934; *Wonder Bar* 1934; *Captain Blood* 1935; *Captain January* 1936; *Little Lord Fauntleroy* 1936; *Three Men on a Horse* 1936; *Bad Man of Brimstone* 1938; *Joy of Living* 1938; *Of Human Hearts* 1938; *Three Comrades* 1938; *Three Loves Has Nancy* 1938; *Babes in Arms* 1939; *It's a Wonderful World* 1939; *Mr Smith Goes to Washington* 1939; *Chad Hanna* 1940; *Our Town* 1940; *Design for Scandal* 1941; *It Started with Eve* 1941; *Miss Annie Rooney* 1942; *There's One Born Every Minute* 1942; *Whistling in Dixie* 1942; *Girl Crazy* 1943; *The Horn Blows at Midnight* 1945; *Three Godfathers* 1948

Kibbee, Milton (1896–1970) *Strange Holiday* 1942; *Betrayed* 1944
Kiberlain, Sandrine (1968–) *Patriots* 1994; *A Self-Made Hero* 1995; *L'Appartement* 1996; *Beaumarchais l'Insolent* 1996; *Rien sur Robert* 1998; *Betty Fisher and Other Stories* 2001
Kidd, Michael (1919–) *It's Always Fair Weather* 1955; *Smile* 1975
Kidder, Margot (1948–) *Gaily, Gaily* 1969; *Quackser Fortune Has a Cousin in the Bronx* 1970; *Sisters* 1973; *Black Christmas* 1974; *The Gravy Train* 1974; *92 in the Shade* 1975; *The Reincarnation of Peter Proud* 1975; *Superman* 1978; *The Amityville Horror* 1979; *Superman II* 1980; *Willie and Phil* 1980; *Heartaches* 1981; *Some Kind of Hero* 1982; *Superman III* 1983; *Trenchcoat* 1983; *Little Treasure* 1985; *GoBots: Battle of the Rocklords* 1986; *Keeping Track* 1986; *Superman IV: the Quest for Peace* 1987; *White Room* 1990; *One Woman's Courage* 1994; *Young Ivanhoe* 1994
Kidman, Nicole (1967–) *BMX Bandits* 1983; *Bush Christmas* 1983; *Windrider* 1986; *Nightmaster* 1987; *Dead Calm* 1988; *Flirting* 1989; *Days of Thunder* 1990; *Billy Bathgate* 1991; *Far and Away* 1992; *Malice* 1993; *My Life* 1993; *Batman Forever* 1995; *To Die For* 1995; *The Portrait of a Lady* 1996; *The Peacemaker* 1997; *Practical Magic* 1998; *Eyes Wide Shut* 1999; *Birthday Girl* 2001; *Moulin Rouge!* 2001; *The Others* 2001; *The Hours* 2002; *Panic Room* 2002; *Cold Mountain* 2003; *Dogville* 2003; *The Human Stain* 2003; *Birth* 2004; *The Stepford Wives* 2004; *The Interpreter* 2005
Kidnie, James *Run* 1991; *Gate II* 1992; *Resurrection* 1999
Kiel, Richard (1939–) *Lassie's Great Adventure* 1963; *Silver Streak* 1976; *The Spy Who Loved Me* 1977; *Force 10 from Navarone* 1978; *The Humanoid* 1979; *Moonraker* 1979; *So Fine* 1981; *Pale Rider* 1985; *Think Big* 1990; *Happy Gilmore* 1996
Kieling, Wolfgang (1924–1985) *Torn Curtain* 1966; *House of a Thousand Dolls* 1967; *The Vengeance of Fu Manchu* 1967; *Out of Order* 1984
Kier, Udo (1944–) *Mark of the Devil* 1970; *The Salzburg Connection* 1972; *Blood for Dracula* 1974; *Flesh for Frankenstein* 1974; *Exposé* 1975; *The Story of O* 1975; *Suspiria* 1976; *Bolwieser* 1977; *The Third Generation* 1979; *Lili Marleen* 1980; *Seduction: the Cruel Woman* 1985; *Medea* 1988; *Europa* 1991; *Ace Ventura: Pet Detective* 1993; *For Love or Money* 1993; *Barb Wire* 1995; *The Adventures of Pinocchio* 1996; *Breaking the Waves* 1996; *Prince Valiant* 1997; *Blade* 1998; *History Is Made at Night* 1999; *The New Adventures of Pinocchio* 1999; *Possessed* 1999; *Dancer in the Dark* 2000; *Shadow of the Vampire* 2000; *Invincible* 2001; *Revelation* 2001; *FearDotCom* 2002; *Dogville* 2003; *Surviving Christmas* 2004
Kieu Chinh (1939–) *Operation CIA* 1965; *Welcome Home* 1989; *The Joy Luck Club* 1993
Kiger, Robby (1973–) *Table for Five* 1983; *Children of the Corn* 1984; *The Monster Squad* 1987; *Welcome Home, Roxy Carmichael* 1990
Kilbride, Percy (1888–1964) *White Woman* 1933; *George Washington Slept Here* 1942; *Fallen Angel* 1945; *The Southerner* 1945; *State Fair* 1945; *The Well Groomed Bride* 1946; *The Egg and I* 1947; *Riff-Raff* 1947; *Black Bart* 1948; *You Were Meant for Me* 1948; *Ma and Pa Kettle* 1949; *Riding High* 1950
Kilburn, Terry aka **Kilburn, Terence** (1926–) *A Christmas Carol* 1938; *The Adventures of Sherlock Holmes* 1939; *Goodbye, Mr Chips* 1939; *They Shall Have Music* 1939; *Swiss Family Robinson* 1940; *Black Beauty* 1946; *Bulldog Drummond Strikes Back* 1947; *Fiend without a Face* 1957
Kiley, Richard (1922–1999) *The Mob* 1951; *Eight Iron Men* 1952; *The Sniper* 1952; *Pickup on South Street* 1953; *The Blackboard Jungle* 1955; *The Phenix City Story* 1955; *Pendulum* 1969; *The Little Prince* 1974; *Looking for Mr Goodbar* 1977; *Endless Love* 1981; *Do You Remember Love* 1985; *The Final Days* 1989
Kilian, Victor aka **Killian, Victor** (1891–1979) *Riffraff* 1936; *The Road to Glory* 1936; *Fair Warning* 1937; *The League of Frightened Men* 1937; *The Adventures of Tom Sawyer* 1938; *Only Angels Have Wings* 1939; *Dr Cyclops* 1940; *Young Tom Edison* 1940; *A Date with the Falcon* 1941; *Northwest Stampede* 1948; *I Shot Jesse James* 1949; *Unknown World* 1951
Kilmer, Val (1959–) *Top Secret!* 1984; *Real Genius* 1985; *Top Gun* 1986; *Willow* 1988; *Kill Me Again* 1989; *The Doors* 1991; *Thunderheart* 1992; *The Real McCoy* 1993; *Tombstone* 1993; *True Romance* 1993; *Batman Forever* 1995; *Heat* 1995; *The Ghost and the Darkness* 1996; *The Island of Dr Moreau* 1996; *The Saint* 1997; *At First Sight* 1998; *The Prince of Egypt* 1998; *Joe the King* 1999; *Pollock* 2000; *Red Planet* 2000; *The Salton Sea* 2002; *Mindhunters* 2003; *The Missing* 2003; *Wonderland* 2003; *Alexander* 2004; *Spartan* 2004
Kilner, Kevin (1958–) *Danielle Steel's Heartbeat* 1992; *Home Alone 3* 1997; *The Brainiacs.com* 2000
Kilpatrick, Lincoln (1932–2004) *The Omega Man* 1971; *The Master Gunfighter* 1975; *Deadly Force* 1983; *Prison* 1987; *Fortress* 1992
Kilpatrick, Patrick *Insignificance* 1985; *Russkies* 1987; *Death Warrant* 1990; *3 Ninjas Knuckle Up* 1995; *Free Willy 3: the Rescue* 1997; *Palmer's Pick-Up* 1999
Kim, Evan aka **Kim, Evan C** *Go Tell the Spartans* 1977; *Hollywood Vice Squad* 1986; *The Dead Pool* 1988
Kim, Jacqueline *Volcano* 1997; *Brokedown Palace* 1999
Kim Yu-Seok *Whispering Corridors* 1998; *The Isle* 2000
Kimbrough, Clint (1933–1996) *Hot Spell* 1958; *Bloody Mama* 1970
Kime, Jeffrey *The State of Things* 1982; *Treasure Island* 1986
Kimura, Isao aka **Kimura, Ko** (1923–1881) *Stray Dog* 1949; *Seven Samurai* 1954
Kincaid, Aron (1940–) *The Ghost in the Invisible Bikini* 1966; *The Proud and the Damned* 1972
Kind, Richard (1956–) *Tom and Jerry: the Movie* 1992; *Quest of the Delta Knights* 1993; *A Bug's Life* 1998
King, Adrienne *Friday the 13th* 1980; *Friday the 13th Part 2* 1981
King, Alan (1927–2004) *The Girl He Left Behind* 1956; *Miracle in the Rain* 1956; *The Helen Morgan Story* 1957; *On the Fiddle* 1961; *Bye Bye Braverman* 1968; *The Anderson Tapes* 1971; *Just Tell Me What You Want* 1980; *Author! Author!* 1982; *I, the Jury* 1982; *Cat's Eye* 1984; *You Talkin' to Me?* 1987; *Memories of Me* 1988; *Enemies, a Love Story* 1989; *Night and the City* 1992; *Casino* 1995; *The Infiltrator* 1995; *Rush Hour 2* 2001
King, Andrea (1919–2003) *God Is My Co-Pilot* 1945; *Hotel Berlin* 1945; *Roughly Speaking* 1945; *The Beast with Five Fingers* 1946; *The Man I Love* 1946; *My Wild Irish Rose* 1947; *Mr Peabody and the Mermaid* 1948; *I Was a Shoplifter* 1950; *The Lemon Drop Kid* 1951; *Red Planet Mars* 1952; *The World in His Arms* 1952
King (2), Charles (1895–1957) *The Lone Rider in Ghost Town* 1941; *Frontier Outlaws* 1944
King, Claude (1875–1941) *Arrowsmith* 1931; *Long Lost Father* 1934
King, Dave (1929–) *Go to Blazes* 1961; *The Long Good Friday* 1979; *Revolution* 1985
King, Don (1932–) *Head Office* 1986; *The Devil's Advocate* 1997
King, Edith (1898–1963) *Blaze of Noon* 1947; *Calcutta* 1947; *Belle Starr's Daughter* 1948; *The Gallant Blade* 1948
King, Erik *Casualties of War* 1989; *Joey Breaker* 1993; *Desperate Measures* 1998
King, Jaime (1979–) *Slackers* 2001; *Bulletproof Monk* 2002; *White Chicks* 2004; *Sin City* 2005
King (1), Joseph (1883–1951) *Bullets or Ballots* 1936; *The Case of the Velvet Claws* 1936; *The Walking Dead* 1936; *God's Country and the Woman* 1937; *San Quentin* 1937
King, Mabel (1932–1999) *The Wiz* 1978; *The Jerk* 1979
King, Perry (1948–) *The Possession of Joel Delaney* 1971; *The Lords of Flatbush* 1974; *Mandingo* 1975; *The Wild Party* 1975; *Bad* 1976; *Lipstick* 1976; *The Choirboys* 1977; *A Different Story* 1978; *Search and Destroy* 1978; *The Cracker Factory* 1979; *Class of 1984* 1982; *Danielle Steel's Kaleidoscope* 1990; *Switch* 1991
King, Regina (1971–) *Poetic Justice* 1993; *Friday* 1995; *Jerry Maguire* 1996; *A Thin Line between Love and Hate* 1996; *Enemy of the State* 1998; *How Stella Got Her Groove Back* 1998; *Mighty Joe Young* 1998; *Down to Earth* 2001; *Daddy Day Care* 2003; *Legally Blonde 2: Red, White & Blonde* 2003; *A Cinderella Story* 2004; *Ray* 2004; *Miss Congeniality 2: Armed & Fabulous* 2005
King, Stephen (1947–) *Knightriders* 1981; *Creepshow* 1982; *Sleepwalkers* 1992
King, Tony *Gordon's War* 1973; *Hell Up in Harlem* 1973; *Report to the Commissioner* 1975
King, Wright (1923–) *The Young Guns* 1956; *Journey through Rosebud* 1972
King, Zalman (1941–) *Blue Sunshine* 1976; *The Passover Plot* 1976; *Tell Me a Riddle* 1980
King-Wood, David (1913–2003) *Men of Sherwood Forest* 1954; *The Stranger Came Home* 1954; *The Quatermass Xperiment* 1955; *Jamboree* 1957
Kingsford, Walter (1881–1958) *The Mystery of Edwin Drood* 1935; *The Invisible Ray* 1936; *Trouble for Two* 1936; *I'll Take Romance* 1937; *Carefree* 1938; *Young Dr Kildare* 1938; *Calling Dr Kildare* 1939; *The Man in the Iron Mask* 1939; *Miracles for Sale* 1939; *The Devil and Miss Jones* 1941; *Dr Kildare's Victory* 1941; *Dr Kildare's Wedding Day* 1941; *Unholy Partners* 1941; *Fingers at the Window* 1942; *Fly by Night* 1942; *My Favorite Blonde* 1942; *Bomber's Moon* 1943; *Dr Gillespie's Criminal Case* 1943; *Flight for Freedom* 1943; *The Velvet Touch* 1948; *Slattery's Hurricane* 1949
Kingsley, Ben (1943–) *Fear Is the Key* 1972; *Betrayal* 1982; *Gandhi* 1982; *Harem* 1985; *Turtle Diary* 1985; *Maurice* 1987; *Testimony* 1987; *Pascali's Island* 1988; *Without a Clue* 1988; *Slipstream* 1989; *The Children* 1990; *The 5th Monkey* 1990; *Bugsy* 1991; *Freddie as FRO7* 1992; *Sneakers* 1992; *Dave* 1993; *Innocent Moves* 1993; *Schindler's List* 1993; *Death and the Maiden* 1994; *Species* 1995; *Twelfth Night* 1996; *The Assignment* 1997; *Photographing Fairies* 1997; *Parting Shots* 1998; *Alice in Wonderland* 1999; *Spooky House* 1999; *Rules of Engagement* 2000; *Sexy Beast* 2000; *What Planet Are You From?* 2000; *AI: Artificial Intelligence* 2001; *The Triumph of Love* 2001; *Tuck Everlasting* 2002; *House of Sand and Fog* 2003; *Suspect Zero* 2004; *Thunderbirds* 2004
Kingston, Alex (1963–) *The Cook, the Thief, His Wife and Her Lover* 1989; *Carrington* 1995; *The Infiltrator* 1995; *Croupier* 1998; *Essex Boys* 1999
Kinkade, Amelia (1959–) *Night of the Demons* 1988; *Night of the Demons 2* 1994; *Demon House* 1997
Kinlan, Laurence (1983–) *Saltwater* 1999; *Ned Kelly* 2003
Kinmont, Kathleen (1965–) *Bride of Re-Animator* 1991; *CIA – Codename Alexa* 1992; *Dead of Night* 1997
Kinnear, Greg (1963–) *Blankman* 1994; *Sabrina* 1995; *Dear God* 1996; *As Good as It Gets* 1997; *A Smile like Yours* 1997; *You've Got Mail* 1998; *Mystery Men* 1999; *The Gift* 2000; *Loser* 2000; *Nurse Betty* 2000; *What Planet Are You From?* 2000; *Animal Attraction* 2001; *Dinner with Friends* 2001; *Auto Focus* 2002; *We Were Soldiers* 2002; *Godsend* 2003; *Stuck on You* 2003; *Robots* 2005
Kinnear, Roy (1934–1988) *Sparrows Can't Sing* 1962; *Tiara Tahiti* 1962; *A Place to Go* 1963; *The Small World of Sammy Lee* 1963; *French Dressing* 1964; *Help!* 1965; *The Hill* 1965; *The Deadly Affair* 1966; *How I Won the War* 1967; *The Bed Sitting Room* 1969; *Lock Up Your Daughters!* 1969; *Taste the Blood of Dracula* 1969; *The Firechasers* 1970; *On a Clear Day You Can See Forever* 1970; *Scrooge* 1970; *The Pied Piper* 1971; *Willy Wonka and the Chocolate Factory* 1971; *Madame Sin* 1972; *That's Your Funeral* 1972; *The Three Musketeers* 1973; *The Amorous Milkman* 1974; *Barry McKenzie Holds His Own* 1974; *The Adventure of Sherlock Holmes' Smarter Brother* 1975; *One of Our Dinosaurs Is Missing* 1975; *Royal Flash* 1975; *Not Now, Comrade* 1976; *Herbie Goes to Monte Carlo* 1977; *The Hound of the Baskervilles* 1977; *The Last Remake of Beau Geste* 1977; *Watership Down* 1978; *Hawk the Slayer* 1980; *Hammett* 1982; *The Boys in Blue* 1983; *Pirates* 1986; *Just Ask for Diamond* 1988; *The Return of the Musketeers* 1989; *The Princess and the Goblin* 1992
Kinnell, Murray (1889–1954) *The Purchase Price* 1932; *Zoo in Budapest* 1933; *Anne of Green Gables* 1934; *Think Fast, Mr Moto* 1937
Kinney, Terry (1954–) *No Mercy* 1986; *Talent for the Game* 1991; *Body Snatchers* 1993; *The Firm* 1993; *Devil in a Blue Dress* 1995; *Fly Away Home* 1996; *Wes Craven's Don't Look Down* 1998; *Oxygen* 1999; *The House of Mirth* 2000; *Save the Last Dance* 2000
Kinsey, Lance (1960–) *Police Academy 6: City under Siege* 1989; *Masters of Menace* 1990; *Dollar for the Dead* 1998
Kinskey, Leonid (1903–1998) *Duck Soup* 1933; *The Great Waltz* 1938; *Ball of Fire* 1941; *Broadway Limited* 1941; *That Night in Rio* 1941; *Weekend in Havana* 1941; *Lady for a Night* 1942; *Can't Help Singing* 1944; *The Fighting Seabees* 1944
Kinski, Klaus (1926–1991) *A Time to Love and a Time to Die* 1958; *The Door with Seven Locks* 1962; *Doctor Zhivago* 1965; *For a Few Dollars More* 1965; *The Pleasure Girls* 1965; *A Bullet for the General* 1966; *Our Man in Marrakesh* 1966; *Circus of Fear* 1967; *Five Golden Dragons* 1967; *Grand Slam* 1967; *The Great Silence* 1967; *Sumuru* 1967; *Sartana* 1968; *Sartana, Angel of Death* 1969; *Count Dracula* 1970; *Aguirre, Wrath of God* 1972; *Lifespan* 1975; *To Kill a Rat* 1977; *Woyzeck* 1978; *Nosferatu, the Vampire* 1979; *Buddy Buddy* 1981; *Venom* 1981; *Android* 1982; *Fitzcarraldo* 1982; *Love and Money* 1982; *Codename Wildgeese* 1984; *The Little Drummer Girl* 1984; *The Secret Diary of Sigmund Freud* 1984; *Vampire in Venice* 1987; *Cobra Verde* 1988
Kinski, Nastassja aka **Kinski, Nastassia** (1959–) *To the Devil a Daughter* 1976; *Tess* 1979; *Cat People* 1982; *One from the Heart* 1982; *Exposed* 1983; *The Moon in the Gutter* 1983; *Unfaithfully Yours* 1983; *The Hotel New Hampshire* 1984; *Maria's Lovers* 1984; *Paris, Texas* 1984; *Harem* 1985; *Revolution* 1985; *Torrents of Spring* 1989; *Night Sun* 1990; *Faraway, So Close* 1993; *Terminal Velocity* 1994; *Fathers' Day* 1997; *One Night Stand* 1997; *Savior* 1997; *The Lost Son* 1998; *Playing by Heart* 1998; *Susan's Plan* 1998; *Your Friends & Neighbours* 1998; *Bitter Suite* 2000; *The Claim* 2000; *A Storm in Summer* 2000; *An American Rhapsody* 2001; *The Day the World Ended* 2001; *Diary of a Sex Addict* 2001; *Town & Country* 2001
Kinsolving, Lee (1938–1974) *The Dark at the Top of the Stairs* 1960; *The Explosive Generation* 1961
Kirac, Guven (1968–) *Head-On* 2003; *Anlat Istanbul* 2005
Kirby, Bruno aka **Kirby Jr, Bruno** (1949–) *Cinderella Liberty* 1973; *The Harrad Experiment* 1973; *Superdad* 1974; *Almost Summer* 1977; *Between the Lines* 1977; *Borderline* 1980; *Where the Buffalo Roam* 1980; *Modern Romance* 1981; *Birdy* 1984; *This Is Spinal Tap* 1984; *Good Morning, Vietnam* 1987; *Tin Men* 1987; *The In Crowd* 1988; *Bert Rigby, You're a Fool* 1989; *We're No Angels* 1989; *When Harry Met Sally...* 1989; *The Freshman* 1990; *City Slickers* 1991; *Golden Gate* 1994; *The Basketball Diaries* 1995; *Donnie Brasco* 1997; *History Is Made at Night* 1999
Kirby, Michael (1925–) *The Countess of Monte Cristo* 1948; *The Silent Partner* 1978; *Swoon* 1992
Kirienko, Zinaida (1933–) *And Quiet Flows the Don* 1957; *Destiny of a Man* 1959
Kirk, Phyllis (1926–) *Mrs O'Malley and Mr Malone* 1950; *Our Very Own* 1950; *The Iron Mistress* 1952; *House of Wax* 1953; *Thunder over the Plains* 1953; *The City Is Dark* 1954; *River Beat* 1954; *Back from Eternity* 1956; *Johnny Concho* 1956; *The Sad Sack* 1957; *That Woman Opposite* 1957
Kirk, Tommy aka **Kirk, Tom** (1941–) *Old Yeller* 1957; *The Shaggy Dog* 1959; *The Snow Queen* 1959; *Swiss Family Robinson* 1960; *The Absent-Minded Professor* 1961; *Babes in Toyland* 1961; *Bon Voyage!* 1962; *Son of Flubber* 1962; *Savage Sam* 1963; *The Misadventures of Merlin Jones* 1964; *Pajama Party* 1964; *The Monkey's Uncle* 1965; *Village of the Giants* 1965; *The Ghost in the Invisible Bikini* 1966; *The Unkissed Bride* 1966
Kirkland, Alexander (1901–) *Tarnished Lady* 1931; *Strange Interlude* 1932; *Black Beauty* 1933
Kirkland, Muriel (1903–1971) *Hold Your Man* 1933; *Little Man, What Now?* 1934; *Nana* 1934; *The White Parade* 1934
Kirkland, Sally (1944–) *Blue* 1968; *Going Home* 1971; *A Star Is Born* 1976; *Human Highway* 1982; *Anna* 1987; *Best of the Best* 1989; *Cold Feet* 1989; *High Stakes* 1989; *Paint It Black* 1989; *Bullseye!* 1990; *Heat Wave* 1990; *Revenge* 1990; *Two Evil Eyes* 1990; *Double Jeopardy* 1992; *Double Threat* 1992; *Hit the Dutchman* 1992; *Primary Motive* 1992; *Eye of the Stranger* 1993; *Forever* 1993; *Paper Hearts* 1993; *Gunmen* 1994; *Edtv* 1999
Kirkwood, Jack (1894–1964) *Fancy Pants* 1950; *Never a Dull Moment* 1950

Kirkwood, Pat (1921–) *Band Waggon* 1939; *Come On George* 1939
Kirshner, Mia (1976–) *Love and Human Remains* 1993; *Exotica* 1994; *The Crow: City of Angels* 1996; *Anna Karenina* 1997; *Mad City* 1997; *Not Another Teen Movie* 2001
Kirwan, Dervla (1971–) *December Bride* 1990; *With or without You* 1999; *School for Seduction* 2004
Kirwan, Kitty *The Vicar of Bray* 1937; *Odd Man Out* 1946
Kiser, Terry (1939–) *Rachel, Rachel* 1968; *Fast Charlie: the Moonbeam Rider* 1978; *Rich Kids* 1979; *Six Pack* 1982; *Friday the 13th Part VII: the New Blood* 1988; *Weekend at Bernie's* 1989; *Mannequin on the Move* 1991; *Into the Sun* 1992; *Weekend at Bernie's II* 1992; *Pet Shop* 1995
Kishi, Keiko (1932–) *The Thick-Walled Room* 1953; *Early Spring* 1956; *Kwaidan* 1964; *The Yakuza* 1975; *Mastermind* 1976; *The Makioka Sisters* 1983
Kishimoto, Kayoko (1960–) *Hana-Bi* 1997; *Kikujiro* 1999
Kitabayashi, Tanie *The Burmese Harp* 1956; *The Key* 1959; *The Burmese Harp* 1985
Kitaen, Tawny (1961–) *Bachelor Party* 1984; *Crystal Heart* 1987; *Happy Hour* 1987; *Witchboard* 1987
Kitamura, Kazuo (1927–) *The Profound Desire of the Gods* 1968; *Black Rain* 1988; *Warm Water under a Red Bridge* 2001
Kitano, Takeshi *aka* **Takeshi** *aka* **Takeshi, "Beat"** (1948–) *Merry Christmas Mr Lawrence* 1982; *Violent Cop* 1989; *Sonatine* 1993; *Johnny Mnemonic* 1995; *Hana-Bi* 1997; *Gohatto* 1999; *Kikujiro* 1999; *Battle Royale* 2000; *Brother* 2000; *Battle Royale 2: Requiem* 2003; *Zatoichi* 2003
Kitchen, Michael (1948–) *Out of Africa* 1985; *The Dive* 1989; *Fools of Fortune* 1990; *The Russia House* 1990; *Enchanted April* 1991; *Hostage* 1992; *Mrs Dalloway* 1997; *The Last Contract* 1998; *New Year's Day* 1999
Kitosch, Cole *Texas Adios* 1966; *Killer Calibre 32* 1967
Kitsuwan, Suppakorn *Tears of the Black Tiger* 2000; *Monrak Transistor* 2001
Kitt, Eartha (1928–) *Casbah* 1948; *New Faces* 1954; *The Mark of the Hawk* 1957; *Anna Lucasta* 1958; *St Louis Blues* 1958; *Get off My Back* 1965; *Up the Chastity Belt* 1971; *Friday Foster* 1975; *Dragonard* 1987; *Erik the Viking* 1989; *Ernest Scared Stupid* 1991; *Boomerang* 1992; *Harriet the Spy* 1996; *The Emperor's New Groove* 2000; *Holes* 2003
Kitzmiller, John (1913–1965) *Dolina Mira* 1956; *The Naked Earth* 1958; *Dr No* 1962; *The Son of Captain Blood* 1962
Kjellin, Alf *aka* **Kent, Christopher** (1920–1988) *Torment* 1944; *Madame Bovary* 1949; *Summer Interlude* 1950; *My Six Convicts* 1952; *The Juggler* 1953; *Two Living, One Dead* 1961; *Assault on a Queen* 1966; *Ice Station Zebra* 1968
Kjellman, Björn (1963–) *Best Intentions* 1992; *The Premonition* 1992; *All Things Fair* 1995
Klaussner, Burghart (1949–) *Good Bye Lenin!* 2003; *The Edukators* 2004
Klauzner, Uri Ran *Kadosh* 1999; *Kippur* 2000
Klein, Chris (1979–) *American Pie* 1999; *Election* 1999; *Here on Earth* 2000; *American Pie 2* 2001; *Rollerball* 2001; *Say It Isn't So* 2001; *The United States of Leland* 2002; *We Were Soldiers* 2002
Klein, Nita *Muriel* 1963; *Total Eclipse* 1995
Klein, Robert (1942–) *The Thirteenth Guest* 1932; *The Landlord* 1970; *The Owl and the Pussycat* 1970; *The Pursuit of Happiness* 1971; *Hooper* 1978; *The Bell Jar* 1979; *The Last Unicorn* 1980; *Mixed Nuts* 1994; *Jeffrey* 1995; *The Safety of Objects* 2001; *Two Weeks Notice* 2002; *How to Lose a Guy in 10 Days* 2003
Klein-Rogge, Rudolf (1888–1955) *Destiny* 1921; *Dr Mabuse, the Gambler* 1922; *Metropolis* 1926; *Spies* 1928; *The Testament of Dr Mabuse* 1932
Klemperer, Werner (1920–2000) *Five Steps to Danger* 1957; *Kiss Them for Me* 1957; *Dark Intruder* 1965; *Ship of Fools* 1965; *The Wicked Dreams of Paula Schultz* 1968
Kline, Kevin (1947–) *Sophie's Choice* 1982; *The Big Chill* 1983; *The Pirates of Penzance* 1983; *Silverado* 1985; *Violets Are Blue* 1986; *Cry Freedom* 1987; *A Fish Called Wanda* 1988; *The January Man* 1989; *I Love You to Death* 1990; *Grand Canyon* 1991; *Soapdish* 1991; *Chaplin* 1992; *Consenting Adults* 1992; *Dave* 1993; *George Balanchine's The Nutcracker* 1993; *Princess Caraboo* 1994; *French Kiss* 1995; *The Hunchback of Notre Dame* 1996; *Fierce Creatures* 1997; *The Ice Storm* 1997; *In & Out* 1997; *A Midsummer Night's Dream* 1999; *Wild Wild West* 1999; *The Road to El Dorado* 2000; *The Anniversary Party* 2001; *Life as a House* 2001; *Orange County* 2001; *The Emperor's Club* 2002; *De-Lovely* 2004
Kling, Heidi (1967–) *The Mighty Ducks* 1992; *Out on a Limb* 1992; *D3: the Mighty Ducks* 1996
Klugman, Jack (1922–) *Timetable* 1956; *12 Angry Men* 1957; *Cry Terror* 1958; *Days of Wine and Roses* 1962; *Act One* 1963; *I Could Go On Singing* 1963; *The Yellow Canary* 1963; *The Detective* 1968; *The Split* 1968; *Goodbye, Columbus* 1969; *Who Says I Can't Ride a Rainbow?* 1971; *Two-Minute Warning* 1976
Knaggs, Skelton (1911–1955) *The Ghost Ship* 1943; *Terror by Night* 1946; *Dick Tracy Meets Gruesome* 1947
Knapp, Evalyn (1908–1981) *Smart Money* 1931; *Fireman Save My Child* 1932; *High Pressure* 1932; *A Successful Calamity* 1932; *Vanishing Frontier* 1932; *Confidential* 1935
Knaup, Herbert (1956–) *Waller's Last Walk* 1989; *Run Lola Run* 1998
Knepper, Robert *aka* **Knepper, Rob** *Wild Thing* 1987; *DOA* 1988; *Renegades* 1989; *Gas, Food, Lodging* 1992; *Where the Day Takes You* 1992; *When the Bough Breaks* 1993; *Dead of Night* 1997; *The Stringer* 1997; *Absence of the Good* 1999; *Love & Sex* 2000
Knight, David (1928–) *Out of the Clouds* 1954; *The Young Lovers* 1954; *Lost* 1955; *Eyewitness* 1956; *Across the Bridge* 1957; *The Battle of the V1* 1958; *Nightmare* 1963; *Who Shot Patakango?* 1989
Knight, Don (1933–1997) *The Hell with Heroes* 1968; *The Hawaiians* 1970; *something big* 1971; *Swamp Thing* 1982
Knight, Esmond (1906–1987) *Waltzes from Vienna* 1933; *Pagliacci* 1936; *The Vicar of Bray* 1937; *The Arsenal Stadium Mystery* 1939; *Contraband* 1940; *The Halfway House* 1943; *The Silver Fleet* 1943; *Henry V* 1944; *Black Narcissus* 1946; *The End of the River* 1947; *Uncle Silas* 1947; *The Red Shoes* 1948; *Gone to Earth* 1950; *The River* 1951; *The Battle of the V1* 1958; *Peeping Tom* 1960; *The Winter's Tale* 1966; *The Boy Who Turned Yellow* 1972; *Robin and Marian* 1976; *The Element of Crime* 1984
Knight, Fuzzy (1901–1976) *The Cowboy and the Lady* 1938; *Spawn of the North* 1938; *Law and Order* 1940; *My Little Chickadee* 1940; *The Singing Sheriff* 1944; *Frontier Gal* 1945; *The Bounty Killer* 1965
Knight, Gladys (1944–) *Pipe Dreams* 1976; *Twenty Bucks* 1993; *Hollywood Homicide* 2003
Knight, Michael E (1959–) *Date with an Angel* 1987; *Hexed* 1993
Knight, Shirley *aka* **Knight Hopkins, Shirley** (1937–) *The Dark at the Top of the Stairs* 1960; *House of Women* 1962; *Sweet Bird of Youth* 1962; *Flight from Ashiya* 1964; *Dutchman* 1966; *The Group* 1966; *The Counterfeit Killer* 1968; *Petulia* 1968; *The Rain People* 1969; *Secrets* 1971; *Juggernaut* 1974; *Beyond the Poseidon Adventure* 1979; *Endless Love* 1981; *The Sender* 1982; *Desperate Justice* 1993; *Indictment: the McMartin Trial* 1995; *Stuart Saves His Family* 1995; *Diabolique* 1996; *If These Walls Could Talk* 1996; *As Good as It Gets* 1997; *Angel Eyes* 2001; *Divine Secrets of the Ya-Ya Sisterhood* 2002
Knight, Ted (1923–1986) *Nightmare in Chicago* 1968; *Caddyshack* 1980
Knight, Trenton (1982–) *Charlie's Ghost Story* 1994; *Munchie Strikes Back* 1994
Knight, Wayne (1955–) *Dead Again* 1991; *Jurassic Park* 1993; *To Die For* 1995; *For Richer or Poorer* 1997; *Space Jam* 1997
Knight, Wyatt (1955–) *Porky's* 1981; *Porky's II: The Next Day* 1983; *Porky's Revenge* 1985
Knightley, Keira (1985–) *Bend It like Beckham* 2001; *The Hole* 2001; *Love Actually* 2003; *Pirates of the Caribbean: the Curse of the Black Pearl* 2003; *King Arthur* 2004; *The Jacket* 2005
Knott, Andrew (1979–) *The Secret Garden* 1993; *Black Beauty* 1994
Knotts, Don (1924–) *No Time for Sergeants* 1958; *Wake Me When It's Over* 1960; *The Last Time I Saw Archie* 1961; *Move Over, Darling* 1963; *The Incredible Mr Limpet* 1964; *The Ghost and Mr Chicken* 1966; *The Reluctant Astronaut* 1967; *The Shakiest Gun in the West* 1967; *The Love God?* 1969; *How to Frame a Figg* 1971; *The Apple Dumpling Gang* 1974; *Gus* 1976; *No Deposit No Return* 1976; *Herbie Goes to Monte Carlo* 1977; *Hot Lead and Cold Feet* 1978; *The Apple Dumpling Gang Rides Again* 1979; *The Prize Fighter* 1979; *The Private Eyes* 1980; *Pleasantville* 1998
Knowlden, Marilyn (1927–) *Les Misérables* 1935; *The Way of All Flesh* 1940
Knowles, Beyoncé (1981–) *Austin Powers in Goldmember* 2002; *The Fighting Temptations* 2003
Knowles, Patric (1911–1995) *The Charge of the Light Brigade* 1936; *It's Love I'm After* 1937; *The Adventures of Robin Hood* 1938; *Four's a Crowd* 1938; *Another Thin Man* 1939; *Beauty for the Asking* 1939; *The Spellbinder* 1939; *Anne of Windy Poplars* 1940; *A Bill of Divorcement* 1940; *The Wolf Man* 1941; *Lady in a Jam* 1942; *Sin Town* 1942; *Who Done It?* 1942; *Frankenstein Meets the Wolf Man* 1943; *Hit the Ice* 1943; *Kitty* 1945; *The Bride Wore Boots* 1946; *Monsieur Beaucaire* 1946; *OSS* 1946; *Of Human Bondage* 1946; *Ivy* 1947; *Dream Girl* 1948; *Isn't It Romantic* 1948; *The Big Steal* 1949; *Three Came Home* 1950; *Mutiny* 1952; *Tarzan's Savage Fury* 1952; *Jamaica Run* 1953; *World for Ransom* 1953; *Khyber Patrol* 1954; *Band of Angels* 1957; *Auntie Mame* 1958
Knox, Alexander (1907–1995) *Cheer Boys Cheer* 1939; *The Sea Wolf* 1941; *This above All* 1942; *None Shall Escape* 1944; *Wilson* 1944; *Over 21* 1945; *Sister Kenny* 1946; *The Judge Steps Out* 1949; *Tokyo Joe* 1949; *I'd Climb the Highest Mountain* 1951; *Man in the Saddle* 1951; *Europa '51* 1952; *The Divided Heart* 1954; *The Sleeping Tiger* 1954; *The Night My Number Came Up* 1955; *Reach for the Sky* 1956; *Chase a Crooked Shadow* 1957; *Hidden Fear* 1957; *High Tide at Noon* 1957; *Intent to Kill* 1958; *Operation Amsterdam* 1958; *Passionate Summer* 1958; *The Two-Headed Spy* 1958; *The Vikings* 1958; *Oscar Wilde* 1959; *The Wreck of the Mary Deare* 1959; *Crack in the Mirror* 1960; *The Damned* 1961; *The Longest Day* 1962; *In the Cool of the Day* 1963; *Crack in the World* 1964; *The Man in the Middle* 1964; *Woman of Straw* 1964; *Mister Moses* 1965; *Khartoum* 1966; *The Psychopath* 1966; *Accident* 1967; *The 25th Hour* 1967; *Fraulein Doktor* 1968; *Shalako* 1968; *Villa Rides* 1968; *Skullduggery* 1969; *Puppet on a Chain* 1970; *Holocaust 2000* 1977
Knox, Elyse (1917–) *The Mummy's Tomb* 1942; *Hit the Ice* 1943; *Black Gold* 1947
Knox, Mickey (1922–) *Knock on Any Door* 1949; *White Heat* 1949; *Beyond the Law* 1968; *Cemetery Man* 1994
Knox, Teddy (1894–1974) *O-Kay for Sound* 1937; *Alf's Button Afloat* 1938; *Gasbags* 1940; *Life Is a Circus* 1958
Knox, Terence (1946–) *Distortions* 1987; *Children of the Corn II: the Final Sacrifice* 1993; *Forever* 1993; *Stolen Innocence* 1995
Knoxville, Johnny (1971–) *Big Trouble* 2002; *Jackass: the Movie* 2002; *Men in Black 2* 2002; *Grand Theft Parsons* 2003; *A Dirty Shame* 2004; *Walking Tall* 2004; *Lords of Dogtown* 2005
Knudsen, Peggy (1923–1980) *The Big Sleep* 1946; *Humoresque* 1946; *A Stolen Life* 1946; *The Unfaithful* 1947; *Good Morning, Miss Dove* 1955; *Unchained* 1955; *Beyond the River* 1956; *Hilda Crane* 1956; *Istanbul* 1957
Knudson, Barbara *Meet Danny Wilson* 1952; *The Cry Baby Killer* 1958
Knuth, Gustav (1901–1987) *The Rats* 1955; *Heidi* 1965
Kober, Jeff *Alien Nation* 1988; *The First Power* 1990; *Automatic* 1994; *Tank Girl* 1995; *Logan's War: Bound by Honor* 1998
Kobiela, Bogumil (1932–1969) *Ashes and Diamonds* 1958; *Eroica* 1958
Koch, Marianne (1931–) *The Devil's General* 1955; *Death Drums along the River* 1963; *A Fistful of Dollars* 1964
Koch, Peter *aka* **Koch, Pete** *Sunset Grill* 1992; *Body Shot* 1994
Köchl, Edda *The Goalkeeper's Fear of the Penalty Kick* 1971; *Alice in the Cities* 1974
Kodet, Jiri (1937–) *Buttoners* 1997; *Mandragora* 1997; *Divided We Fall* 2000
Koechner, David (1962–) *My Boss's Daughter* 2003; *Anchorman: the Legend of Ron Burgundy* 2004
Koehler, Frederick *aka* **Koehler, Fred** (1975–) *Mr Mom* 1983; *The Positively True Adventures of the Alleged Texas Cheerleader-Murdering Mom* 1993
Koenig, Mende *Docks of New York* 1945; *Mr Muggs Rides Again* 1945
Koenig, Walter (1936–) *Star Trek: the Motion Picture* 1979; *Star Trek II: the Wrath of Khan* 1982; *Star Trek III: the Search for Spock* 1984; *Star Trek IV: the Voyage Home* 1986; *Star Trek V: the Final Frontier* 1989; *Star Trek VI: the Undiscovered Country* 1991; *Star Trek: Generations* 1994
Kogure, Michiyo (1918–1990) *Drunken Angel* 1948; *The Flavour of Green Tea over Rice* 1952; *Street of Shame* 1955; *Tales of the Taira Clan* 1955
Kohler, Fred *aka* **Kohler Sr, Fred** (1889–1938) *The Iron Horse* 1924; *Riders of the Purple Sage* 1925; *Underworld* 1927; *The Way of All Flesh* 1927; *The Dragnet* 1928; *The Case of Lena Smith* 1929; *The Leatherneck* 1929; *Say It with Songs* 1929; *Fighting Caravans* 1931; *Other Men's Women* 1931; *Deluge* 1933; *Goin' to Town* 1935; *Billy the Kid Returns* 1938; *Forbidden Valley* 1938; *Painted Desert* 1938
Köhler, Juliane (1965–) *Aimée and Jaguar* 1999; *Nowhere in Africa* 2001; *Downfall* 2004
Kohner, Susan (1936–) *To Hell and Back* 1955; *The Last Wagon* 1956; *Dino* 1957; *Trooper Hook* 1957; *The Big Fisherman* 1959; *The Gene Krupa Story* 1959; *Imitation of Life* 1959; *All the Fine Young Cannibals* 1960; *By Love Possessed* 1961; *Freud* 1962
Koirala, Manisha (1970–) *1942: a Love Story* 1994; *Bombay* 1995; *Dil Se...* 1998; *Hindustan Ki Kasam* 1999; *Company* 2001
Koivula, Pertti (1961–) *The Unknown Soldier* 1983; *A Summer by the River* 1998
Koizumi, Hiroshi (1926–) *Godzilla Raids Again* 1955; *Mothra* 1962; *Matango* 1963; *Godzilla vs Mothra* 1964; *Ghidrah, the Three-Headed Monster* 1965
Kojo, Nikola (1969–) *Pretty Village Pretty Flame* 1996; *Life Is a Miracle* 2004
Kolb, Clarence (1875–1964) *The Toast of New York* 1937; *The Law West of Tombstone* 1938; *The Amazing Mr Williams* 1939; *His Girl Friday* 1939; *Honolulu* 1939; *No Time for Comedy* 1940; *Nothing but the Truth* 1941; *True to Life* 1943; *Standing Room Only* 1944; *Adam's Rib* 1949
Kolk, Scott (1905–1993) *All Quiet on the Western Front* 1930; *My Sin* 1931
Kolker, Henry (1870–1947) *The Valiant* 1929; *Jewel Robbery* 1932; *Baby Face* 1933; *Meet the Baron* 1933; *The Power and the Glory* 1933; *The Black Room* 1935; *Mad Love* 1935; *Great Guy* 1936; *The Cowboy and the Lady* 1938; *Holiday* 1938; *The Invisible Menace* 1938; *Too Hot to Handle* 1938
Kolldehoff, Reinhard *aka* **Kolldehoff, Rene** *aka* **Kolldehoff, Reinhardt** *aka* **Kolldehof, Rene** (1914–1995) *A Man to Respect* 1972; *Borsalino and Co* 1974; *The Romantic Englishwoman* 1975; *Shout at the Devil* 1976
Kollek, Amos *Goodbye New York* 1984; *Double Edge* 1992
Komorowska, Liliana *Scanners III: the Takeover* 1992; *The Assignment* 1997; *The Art of War* 2000
Komorowska, Maja (1937–) *The Young Ladies of Wilko* 1979; *The Contract* 1980; *A Year of the Quiet Sun* 1984
Konstam, Phyllis (1907–1976) *Murder* 1930; *The Skin Game* 1931
Koock, Guich (1944–) *Seven* 1979; *American Ninja* 1985; *Square Dance* 1987
Kopache, Thomas *Liebestraum* 1991; *Stigmata* 1999
Kopecky, Milos (1922–1996) *Baron Munchhausen* 1961; *Labyrinth* 1991
Kopell, Bernie (1933–) *Black Jack* 1972; *Missing Pieces* 1991
Kopernikus, Nicolaj (1967–) *Okay* 2002; *In Your Hands* 2004
Kopins, Karen *Creator* 1985; *Once Bitten* 1985; *Jake Speed* 1986
Korff, Arnold (1870–1944) *Diary of a Lost Girl* 1929; *Doughboys* 1930; *The Royal Family of Broadway* 1930; *All the King's Horses* 1935
Korkes, Jon *Little Murders* 1971; *The Day of the Dolphin* 1973; *Jaws of Satan* 1979
Korman, Harvey (1927–) *Lord Love a Duck* 1966; *Three Bites of the Apple* 1967; *Don't Just Stand There* 1968; *The April Fools* 1969; *Blazing Saddles* 1974; *Huckleberry Finn* 1974; *High Anxiety* 1977; *Americathon* 1979; *Herbie Goes Bananas* 1980; *History of the World Part 1* 1981; *Trail of the Pink Panther* 1982; *The Curse of the Pink Panther* 1983; *The Longshot* 1986; *Munchies* 1987; *Dracula: Dead and Loving It* 1995; *The Secret of NIMH II: Timmy to the Rescue*

1998; *The Flintstones in Viva Rock Vegas* 2000
Korsmo, Charlie (1978–) *Dick Tracy* 1990; *Men Don't Leave* 1990; *The Doctor* 1991; *Hook* 1991; *What about Bob?* 1991; *Can't Hardly Wait* 1998
Kortner, Fritz (1892–1970) *Hands of Orlac* 1924; *Pandora's Box* 1929; *The Ship of Lost Men* 1929; *Three Loves* 1929; *Chu Chin Chow* 1934; *Evensong* 1934
Korvin, Charles (1907–1998) *Enter Arsene Lupin* 1944; *This Love of Ours* 1945; *Temptation* 1946; *Berlin Express* 1948; *Lydia Bailey* 1952; *Tarzan's Savage Fury* 1952; *The Man Who Had Power over Women* 1970
Koscina, Sylva (1933–1994) *Hercules* 1957; *Young Husbands* 1958; *Hercules Unchained* 1959; *The Siege of Syracuse* 1959; *Jessica* 1962; *Le Masque de Fer* 1962; *The Swordsman of Siena* 1962; *Hot Enough for June* 1963; *Let's Talk About Women* 1964; *Juliet of the Spirits* 1965; *Deadlier than the Male* 1966; *The Secret War of Harry Frigg* 1967; *Three Bites of the Apple* 1967; *A Lovely Way to Go* 1968; *The Battle of Neretva* 1969; *Hornet's Nest* 1970; *The Italian Connection* 1973; *Lisa and the Devil* 1976
Kosleck, Martin (1907–1994) *Berlin Correspondent* 1942; *Fly by Night* 1942; *Bomber's Moon* 1943; *The Frozen Ghost* 1944; *The Mummy's Curse* 1944; *Pursuit to Algiers* 1945; *Hitler* 1962; *The Flesh Eaters* 1964; *Agent for HARM* 1966
Koslo, Paul (1944–) *The Omega Man* 1971; *Vanishing Point* 1971; *Welcome Home, Soldier Boys* 1971; *Joe Kidd* 1972; *Mr Majestyk* 1974; *Tomorrow Never Comes* 1977; *A Night in the Life of Jimmy Reardon* 1988; *Robot Jox* 1989; *Judge & Jury* 1995
Kossoff, David (1919–2005) *Svengali* 1954; *The Young Lovers* 1954; *The Bespoke Overcoat* 1955; *A Kid for Two Farthings* 1955; *1984* 1955; *The Woman for Joe* 1955; *House of Secrets* 1956; *The Iron Petticoat* 1956; *Who Done It?* 1956; *Count Five and Die* 1957; *Innocent Sinners* 1957; *Indiscreet* 1958; *The House of the Seven Hawks* 1959; *Jet Storm* 1959; *The Journey* 1959; *The Mouse That Roared* 1959; *Conspiracy of Hearts* 1960; *Inn for Trouble* 1960; *The Two Faces of Dr Jekyll* 1960; *The Mouse on the Moon* 1963; *Ring of Spies* 1963
Kosugi, Sho (1948–) *Enter the Ninja* 1981; *Aloha Summer* 1988; *Black Eagle* 1988; *Blind Fury* 1990; *Shogun Warrior* 1991
Kotamanidou, Eva (1936–) *The Travelling Players* 1975; *Trilogy: the Weeping Meadow* 2004
Koteas, Elias (1961–) *One Magic Christmas* 1985; *Some Kind of Wonderful* 1987; *Blood Red* 1988; *Full Moon in Blue Water* 1988; *Tucker: the Man and His Dream* 1988; *Malarek* 1989; *Almost an Angel* 1990; *Desperate Hours* 1990; *Look Who's Talking Too* 1990; *Teenage Mutant Ninja Turtles* 1990; *The Adjuster* 1991; *Chain of Desire* 1992; *Teenage Mutant Ninja Turtles III* 1992; *Camilla* 1993; *Cyborg 2: Glass Shadow* 1993; *Exotica* 1994; *Power of Attorney* 1994; *The Prophecy* 1994; *Crash* 1996; *Gattaca* 1997; *Fallen* 1998; *Living Out Loud* 1998; *The Thin Red Line* 1998; *Harrison's Flowers* 2000; *Lost Souls* 2000; *Collateral Damage* 2001; *Novocaine* 2001; *Ararat* 2002
Kotto, Yaphet (1937–) *Nothing but a Man* 1964; *5 Card Stud* 1968; *The Thomas Crown Affair* 1968; *The Liberation of LB Jones* 1970; *Man and Boy* 1971; *Across 110th Street* 1972; *Bone* 1972; *Live and Let Die* 1973; *Truck Turner* 1974; *Friday Foster* 1975; *Report to the Commissioner* 1975; *Shark's Treasure* 1975; *Drum* 1976; *Raid on Entebbe* 1977; *Blue Collar* 1978; *Alien* 1979; *Brubaker* 1980; *Death Vengeance* 1982; *The Star Chamber* 1983; *Warning Sign* 1985; *Eye of the Tiger* 1986; *PrettyKill* 1987; *The Running Man* 1987; *Midnight Run* 1988; *Terminal Entry* 1988; *Freddy's Dead: the Final Nightmare* 1991; *Hangfire* 1991; *Intent to Kill* 1992; *The Puppet Masters* 1994; *Dead Badge* 1995; *Out of Sync* 1995; *Stolen Hearts* 1996
Kouberskaya, Irina *Diary for My Loves* 1987; *Diary for My Father and Mother* 1990
Koumani, Maya *Undercover Girl* 1957; *Hidden Homicide* 1958
Kovack, Nancy (1935–) *Diary of a Madman* 1963; *Jason and the Argonauts* 1963; *The Great Sioux Massacre* 1965; *The Outlaws Is Coming* 1965; *Frankie & Johnny* 1966; *Tarzan and the Valley of Gold* 1966; *Marooned* 1969
Kovacs, Ernie (1919–1962) *Operation Mad Ball* 1957; *Bell, Book and Candle* 1958; *It Happened to Jane* 1959; *Our Man in Havana* 1959; *North to Alaska* 1960; *Pepe* 1960; *Strangers When We Meet* 1960; *Wake Me When It's Over* 1960; *Sail a Crooked Ship* 1961
Kove, Martin aka **Kove, Marty** aka **Kove, Martin L** (1946–) *Women in Revolt* 1971; *Death Race 2000* 1975; *Seven* 1979; *The Karate Kid* 1984; *The Karate Kid III* 1989; *The Outfit* 1993; *Judge & Jury* 1995; *Grizzly Mountain* 1997
Kowalski, Wladyslaw (1936–) *The Double Life of Véronique* 1991; *Avalon* 2000
Kowanko, Pete aka **Kowanko, Peter** *Sylvester* 1985; *Date with an Angel* 1987
Kozak, Harley Jane aka **Kozak, Harley** (1957–) *House of Evil* 1983; *Parenthood* 1989; *Arachnophobia* 1990; *Side Out* 1990; *All I Want for Christmas* 1991; *Necessary Roughness* 1991; *The Taking of Beverly Hills* 1991; *The Favor* 1994; *Magic in the Water* 1995; *Unforgivable* 1995; *Stolen Youth* 1996
Kozlowski, Linda (1958–) *"Crocodile" Dundee* 1986; *"Crocodile" Dundee II* 1988; *Pass the Ammo* 1988; *Almost an Angel* 1990; *Village of the Damned* 1995; *Crocodile Dundee in Los Angeles* 2001
Kozlowski, Piotr *Korczak* 1990; *Europa, Europa* 1991
Krabbé, Jeroen (1944–) *Soldier of Orange* 1977; *Spetters* 1980; *The Fourth Man* 1983; *Turtle Diary* 1985; *No Mercy* 1986; *The Living Daylights* 1987; *A World Apart* 1987; *Crossing Delancey* 1988; *Scandal* 1988; *Melancholia* 1989; *The Punisher* 1989; *Robin Hood* 1990; *Till There Was You* 1990; *Kafka* 1991; *The Prince of Tides* 1991; *King of the Hill* 1993; *Farinelli il Castrato* 1994; *Immortal Beloved* 1994; *The Disappearance of Garcia Lorca* 1997; *Left Luggage* 1997; *The Odyssey* 1997; *An Ideal Husband* 1999; *Fogbound* 2002; *Ocean's Twelve* 2004
Kraft, Scott *For the Moment* 1994; *The Stupids* 1995
Krakowski, Jane (1968–) *Stepping Out* 1991; *Mrs Winterbourne* 1996; *Dance with Me* 1998; *The Flintstones in Viva Rock Vegas* 2000; *Marci X* 2003; *Alfie* 2004
Kramer, Eric Allan aka **Kramer, Eric** *The Incredible Hulk Returns* 1988; *Robin Hood: Men in Tights* 1993
Kramer, Jeffrey aka **Kramer, Jeffrey C** (1952–) *Jaws* 1975; *Hollywood Boulevard* 1976; *Jaws 2* 1978; *Halloween II* 1981; *Santa Claus* 1985; *Hero and the Terror* 1988
Krause, Brian (1972–) *December* 1991; *Return to the Blue Lagoon* 1991; *Sleepwalkers* 1992; *Naked Souls* 1995
Krauss, Werner (1884–1959) *The Cabinet of Dr Caligari* 1919; *Waxworks* 1924; *The Joyless Street* 1925; *Nana* 1926; *Secrets of a Soul* 1926; *Tartuffe* 1926; *Paracelsus* 1943
Kretschmann, Thomas (1962–) *Stalingrad* 1992; *The Stendhal Syndrome* 1996; *Prince Valiant* 1997; *Blade II* 2002; *The Pianist* 2002; *Downfall* 2004; *Resident Evil: Apocalypse* 2004
Kreuger, Kurt (1916–) *The Silent Bell* 1944; *The Dark Corner* 1946; *Unfaithfully Yours* 1948; *Fear* 1954; *The Enemy Below* 1957
Kreuk, Kristin (1982–) *Snow White* 2001; *EuroTrip* 2004
Kreuzer, Lisa (1945–) *Kings of the Road* 1976; *The American Friend* 1977; *Radio On* 1979; *Berlin Jerusalem* 1989
Kriegel, David *Alive* 1992; *Quest of the Delta Knights* 1993
Krige, Alice (1955–) *Chariots of Fire* 1981; *Ghost Story* 1981; *King David* 1985; *Second Serve* 1986; *Barfly* 1987; *Haunted Summer* 1988; *See You in the Morning* 1989; *Sleepwalkers* 1992; *Jack Reed: Badge of Honor* 1993; *Institute Benjamenta, or This Dream People Call Human Life* 1995; *Star Trek: First Contact* 1996; *A Father's Betrayal* 1997; *The Twilight of the Ice Nymphs* 1997; *In the Company of Spies* 1999; *The Little Vampire* 2000; *Superstition* 2001
Kristel, Sylvia (1952–) *Emmanuelle* 1974; *Emmanuelle 2* 1975; *The Streetwalker* 1976; *Goodbye Emmanuelle* 1977; *Airport '79: the Concorde* 1979; *The Fifth Musketeer* 1979; *Tigers in Lipstick* 1979; *The Nude Bomb* 1980; *Lady Chatterley's Lover* 1981; *Private Lessons* 1981; *Emmanuelle IV* 1983; *Private School* 1983; *Mata Hari* 1985; *Red Heat* 1985; *Dracula's Widow* 1988
Kristen, Marta (1945–) *Savage Sam* 1963; *Terminal Island* 1973
Kristofferson, Kris (1936–) *Cisco Pike* 1971; *The Last Movie* 1971; *Blume in Love* 1973; *Pat Garrett and Billy the Kid* 1973; *Alice Doesn't Live Here Anymore* 1974; *Bring Me the Head of Alfredo Garcia* 1974; *Vigilante Force* 1975; *The Sailor Who Fell from Grace with the Sea* 1976; *A Star Is Born* 1976; *Semi-Tough* 1977; *Convoy* 1978; *Freedom Road* 1979; *Heaven's Gate* 1980; *Rollover* 1981; *Flashpoint* 1984; *Songwriter* 1984; *Trouble in Mind* 1985; *Big Top Pee-wee* 1988; *Millennium* 1989; *Perfume of the Cyclone* 1989; *Welcome Home* 1989; *No Place to Hide* 1992; *Paper Hearts* 1993; *Sodbusters* 1994; *Lone Star* 1995; *The Road Home* 1995; *Fire Down Below* 1997; *Girls' Night* 1997; *Blade* 1998; *Dance with Me* 1998; *Payback* 1998; *A Soldier's Daughter Never Cries* 1998; *Two for Texas* 1998; *The Joyriders* 1999; *Limbo* 1999; *D-Tox* 2001; *Blade II* 2002; *Blade: Trinity* 2004; *The Jacket* 2005
Kroeger, Berry (1912–1991) *Cry of the City* 1948; *The Dark Past* 1948; *The Iron Curtain* 1948; *Act of Violence* 1949; *Black Magic* 1949; *Down to the Sea in Ships* 1949; *Gun Crazy* 1949; *The Sword of Monte Cristo* 1951; *Blood Alley* 1955; *Atlantis, the Lost Continent* 1960; *Seven Thieves* 1960; *Demon Seed* 1977
Król, Joachim (1957–) *The Most Desired Man* 1994; *The Princess & the Warrior* 2000
Kroner, Jozef aka **Kroner, Josef** (1924–1998) *The Shop on the High Street* 1965; *Deadly Game* 1982
Kruger, Alma (1871–1960) *Craig's Wife* 1936; *These Three* 1936; *One Hundred Men and a Girl* 1937; *Vogues of 1938* 1937; *The Toy Wife* 1938; *Calling Dr Kildare* 1939; *Dr Kildare's Strange Case* 1940; *Dr Kildare's Victory* 1941; *The People vs Dr Kildare* 1941; *Calling Dr Gillespie* 1942; *Dr Gillespie's New Assistant* 1942; *Saboteur* 1942; *Dr Gillespie's Criminal Case* 1943; *Three Men in White* 1944; *Do You Love Me?* 1946
Kruger, Diane (1976–) *National Treasure* 2004; *Troy* 2004; *Wicker Park* 2004
Kruger, Hardy (1928–) *The One That Got Away* 1957; *Bachelor of Hearts* 1958; *Blind Date* 1959; *Hatari!* 1962; *Sundays and Cybèle* 1962; *The Flight of the Phoenix* 1965; *The Defector* 1966; *The Battle of Neretva* 1969; *The Red Tent* 1969; *The Secret of Santa Vittoria* 1969; *Paper Tiger* 1974; *Barry Lyndon* 1975; *Montana Trap* 1976; *A Bridge Too Far* 1977; *To Each His Own Hell* 1977; *The Wild Geese* 1978; *The Inside Man* 1984
Kruger, Otto (1885–1974) *Ever in My Heart* 1933; *The Prizefighter and the Lady* 1933; *Turn Back the Clock* 1933; *Chained* 1934; *Gallant Lady* 1934; *Men in White* 1934; *Treasure Island* 1934; *Vanessa, Her Love Story* 1935; *Dracula's Daughter* 1936; *They Won't Forget* 1937; *Housemaster* 1938; *I Am the Law* 1938; *Another Thin Man* 1939; *Black Eyes* 1939; *The Gang's All Here* 1939; *A Dispatch from Reuters* 1940; *Dr Ehrlich's Magic Bullet* 1940; *The Man I Married* 1940; *The Men in Her Life* 1941; *Friendly Enemies* 1942; *Saboteur* 1942; *Hitler's Children* 1943; *Stage Door Canteen* 1943; *Tarzan's Desert Mystery* 1943; *Cover Girl* 1944; *Farewell My Lovely* 1944; *Earl Carroll Vanities* 1945; *The Great John L* 1945; *Wonder Man* 1945; *Duel in the Sun* 1946; *Lulu Belle* 1948; *711 Ocean Drive* 1950; *Valentino* 1951; *High Noon* 1952; *Black Widow* 1954; *Magnificent Obsession* 1954; *The Colossus of New York* 1958; *The Young Philadelphians* 1959; *Cash McCall* 1960
Krumholtz, David (1978–) *Life with Mikey* 1993; *The Santa Clause* 1994; *Slums of Beverly Hills* 1998; *10 Things I Hate about You* 1999; *Sidewalks of New York* 2000; *The Santa Clause 2* 2002; *Harold & Kumar Get the Munchies* 2004
Krupa, Olek *Black Rainbow* 1989; *Mac* 1992; *Home Alone 3* 1997; *Stardust* 1998; *Blue Streak* 1999; *Behind Enemy Lines* 2001
Kruschen, Jack (1922–2002) *Cry Terror* 1958; *The Decks Ran Red* 1958; *The Angry Red Planet* 1959; *The Apartment* 1960; *The Last Voyage* 1960; *Cape Fear* 1962; *Follow That Dream* 1962; *McLintock!* 1963; *The Unsinkable Molly Brown* 1964; *Harlow* 1965; *Caprice* 1967; *The Million Dollar Duck* 1971; *Freebie and the Bean* 1974; *Satan's Cheerleaders* 1977
Kubo, Akira (1926–) *Matango* 1963; *Invasion of the Astro-Monster* 1965; *Son of Godzilla* 1967; *Destroy All Monsters* 1968
Kudoh, Youki (1971–) *Mystery Train* 1989; *Picture Bride* 1994; *Heaven's Burning* 1997; *Snow Falling on Cedars* 1999
Kudrow, Lisa (1963–) *The Unborn* 1991; *Two Much Trouble* 1995; *Mother* 1996; *Clockwatchers* 1997; *Romy and Michele's High School Reunion* 1997; *The Opposite of Sex* 1998; *Analyze This* 1999; *Hanging Up* 2000; *All over the Guy* 2001; *Dr Dolittle 2* 2001; *Analyze That* 2002; *Marci X* 2003; *Wonderland* 2003
Kuga, Yoshiko (1931–) *The Idiot* 1951; *Somewhere under the Broad Sky* 1954; *Tales of the Taira Clan* 1955; *Ohayo* 1959
Kulky, Henry (1911–1965) *The 5,000 Fingers of Dr T* 1953; *Abbott and Costello Meet the Keystone Cops* 1955
Kulle, Jarl (1927–1997) *Waiting Women* 1952; *The Devil's Eye* 1960; *All These Women* 1964; *Dear John* 1964; *My Sister, My Love* 1966; *Fanny and Alexander* 1982; *Babette's Feast* 1987
Kulp, Nancy (1921–1991) *The Three Faces of Eve* 1957; *The Two Little Bears* 1961; *The Night of the Grizzly* 1966
Kuluva, Will (1917–1990) *Odds against Tomorrow* 1959; *Go Naked in the World* 1961; *The Spiral Road* 1962; *To Trap a Spy* 1966
Kumar, Akshay (1967–) *Awara Paagal Deewana* 2002; *Khakee* 2003; *Aitraaz* 2004; *Mujhse Shaadi Karogi* 2004; *WAQT: the Race Against Time* 2005
Kumar, Ashok (1911–2001) *Ek Hi Rasta* 1956; *Kanoon* 1960; *Bandini* 1963; *Pakeezah* 1971
Kumar, Dilip (1922–) *Shaheed* 1948; *Andaz* 1949; *Babul* 1950; *Tarana* 1951; *Naya Daur* 1957; *Yahudi* 1958; *Mughal-e-Azam* 1960
Kumar, Raaj *Mother India* 1957; *Waqt* 1965; *Pakeezah* 1971
Kumar, Rajendra (1929–) *Mother India* 1957; *Kanoon* 1960; *Sangam* 1964
Kumar, Sanjeev (1937–1985) *Sholay* 1975; *The Chess Players* 1977
Kumari, Meena *Baiju Bawra* 1952; *Ek Hi Rasta* 1956; *Yahudi* 1958; *Pakeezah* 1971
Kunene, Vusi *Cry, the Beloved Country* 1995; *Kini and Adams* 1997; *A Reasonable Man* 1999
Kunis, Mila (1983–) *Piranhas* 1996; *American Psycho II: All American Girl* 2002
Kunstmann, Doris (1944–) *Hitler: the Last Ten Days* 1973; *Funny Games* 1997
Kuosmanen, Sakari *Drifting Clouds* 1996; *Juha* 1999; *The Man without a Past* 2002
Kupchenko, Irina (1948–) *A Private Conversation* 1983; *Lonely Woman Seeks Lifetime Companion* 1987
Kurata, Yasuaki *Fist of Legend* 1994; *So Close* 2002
Kuroki, Hitomi *Lost Paradise* 1997; *Dark Water* 2002
Kurts, Alwyn (1915–2000) *And Millions Will Die!* 1973; *Tim* 1979; *The Earthling* 1980; *Spotswood* 1991
Kurtz, Marcia Jean *Believe in Me* 1971; *Born to Win* 1971; *The Panic in Needle Park* 1971
Kurtz, Swoosie (1944–) *First Love* 1977; *Oliver's Story* 1978; *The World According to Garp* 1982; *Agatha Christie's A Caribbean Mystery* 1983; *Against All Odds* 1984; *Guilty Conscience* 1985; *True Stories* 1986; *Wildcats* 1986; *Bright Lights, Big City* 1988; *Dangerous Liaisons* 1988; *Vice Versa* 1988; *Stanley & Iris* 1989; *The Image* 1990; *A Shock to the System* 1990; *The Positively True Adventures of the Alleged Texas Cheerleader-Murdering Mom* 1993; *Reality Bites* 1994; *Storybook* 1995; *Citizen Ruth* 1996; *Liar Liar* 1997; *Bubble Boy* 2001; *Get over It* 2001; *The Rules of Attraction* 2002; *Our House* 2003
Kusatsu, Clyde (1948–) *The Choirboys* 1977; *Shanghai Surprise* 1986; *Made in America* 1993; *Top Dog* 1995
Kussman, Dylan *Dead Poets Society* 1989; *Wild Hearts Can't Be Broken* 1991
Kusturica, Emir (1954–) *La Veuve de Saint-Pierre* 2000; *The Good Thief* 2002
Kutcher, Ashton (1978–) *Down to You* 2000; *Dude, Where's My Car?* 2000; *The Butterfly Effect* 2003; *Just Married* 2003; *My Boss's Daughter* 2003; *Guess Who* 2005; *A Lot like Love* 2005
Kuter, Kay E (1925–2003) *Watermelon Man* 1970; *The Last Starfighter* 1984; *Zombie High* 1987
Kuzyk, Mimi (1952–) *The Kiss* 1988; *Cannonball Fever* 1989; *The Final Cut* 2004
Kwan, Nancy (1939–) *The World of Suzie Wong* 1960; *Flower Drum Song* 1961; *The Main Attraction* 1962; *Tamahine* 1963; *The Wild Affair* 1963; *Fate Is the Hunter* 1964; *Honeymoon Hotel* 1964; *The Corrupt Ones* 1966; *Drop Dead Darling* 1966; *Lt Robin Crusoe, USN* 1966; *Nobody's Perfect* 1968; *The Girl Who Knew Too Much* 1969; *The Wrecking Crew* 1969; *The McMasters* 1970; *Project: Kill* 1976; *Cold Dog Soup*

1989; *Dragon: the Bruce Lee Story* 1993
Kwan, Rosamund *aka* **Kwan, Rosamund Chi-Lam** (1962–) *The Armour of God* 1986; *Once upon a Time in China* 1991; *Once upon a Time in China II* 1992; *Big Shot's Funeral* 2001
Kwouk, Burt *aka* **Kwouk, Bert** (1930–) *The Inn of the Sixth Happiness* 1958; *Satan Never Sleeps* 1962; *A Shot in the Dark* 1964; *Curse of the Fly* 1965; *The Return of the Pink Panther* 1974; *The Pink Panther Strikes Again* 1976; *Revenge of the Pink Panther* 1978; *Trail of the Pink Panther* 1982; *The Curse of the Pink Panther* 1983; *Plenty* 1985; *Empire of the Sun* 1987; *I Bought a Vampire Motorcycle* 1989; *Race for Glory* 1989; *Leon the Pig Farmer* 1992; *Shooting Elizabeth* 1992; *Son of the Pink Panther* 1993; *Bullet to Beijing* 1995; *Peggy Su!* 1997; *Kiss of the Dragon* 2001
Kydd, Sam (1917–1982) *Trent's Last Case* 1952; *Devil on Horseback* 1954; *Final Appointment* 1954; *Circus Friends* 1956; *The Treasure of Monte Cristo* 1960; *Island of Terror* 1966; *Steptoe and Son Ride Again* 1973; *Yesterday's Hero* 1979
Kyle, Jackson *Aria* 1987; *A Handful of Dust* 1987
Kyo, Machiko (1924–) *Rashomon* 1950; *Gate of Hell* 1953; *Ugetsu Monogatari* 1953; *The Princess Yang Kwei Fei* 1955; *Street of Shame* 1955; *The Teahouse of the August Moon* 1956; *Floating Weeds* 1959; *The Key* 1959; *The Face of Another* 1966
Kyser, Kay (1897–1985) *That's Right – You're Wrong* 1939; *You'll Find Out* 1940; *Playmates* 1941; *My Favorite Spy* 1942; *Swing Fever* 1943

L

L L Cool J *aka* **Smith, James Todd** (1968–) *The Hard Way* 1991; *Toys* 1992; *Out of Sync* 1995; *Touch* 1996; *Halloween H20: 20 Years Later* 1998; *Woo* 1998; *Any Given Sunday* 1999; *Deep Blue Sea* 1999; *In Too Deep* 1999; *Rollerball* 2001; *Mindhunters* 2003; *SWAT* 2003
La Plante, Laura (1904–1996) *The Cat and the Canary* 1927; *The Last Warning* 1928; *The King of Jazz* 1930; *God's Gift to Women* 1931; *Spring Reunion* 1957
La Rocque, Rod (1896–1969) *The Ten Commandments* 1923; *Our Modern Maidens* 1929; *One Romantic Night* 1930; *SOS Iceberg* 1933; *Till We Meet Again* 1936
La Roy, Rita (1907–1993) *Blonde Venus* 1932; *Sinners in the Sun* 1932
La Salle, Eriq (1962–) *Rappin'* 1985; *Coming to America* 1988; *Jacob's Ladder* 1990; *DROP Squad* 1994; *One Hour Photo* 2001
La Verne, Lucille (1869–1945) *Pilgrimage* 1933; *The Mighty Barnum* 1934; *Snow White and the Seven Dwarfs* 1937
Laage, Barbara (1925–1988) *Act of Love* 1953; *Guilty?* 1956; *The Happy Road* 1956; *Bed and Board* 1970
Labarthe, André S *aka* **Labarthe, André** (1931–) *Vivre Sa Vie* 1962; *L'Amour Fou* 1968
Labbé, Patrick (1970–) *Coyote* 1992; *Chance or Coincidence* 1999
LaBelle, Patti (1944–) *A Soldier's Story* 1984; *Sing* 1989
LaBeouf, Shia (1986–) *Charlie's Angels: Full Throttle* 2003; *Holes* 2003; *Constantine* 2005
Laborit, Emmanuelle (1971–) *Beyond Silence* 1996; *Marianna Ucria* 1997
Laborteaux, Matthew (1966–) *A Woman under the Influence* 1974; *Deadly Friend* 1986
Labourdette, Elina (1919–) *Les Dames du Bois de Boulogne* 1946; *To Paris with Love* 1954; *The Truth about Women* 1958; *Lola* 1960
Labourier, Dominique *Celine and Julie Go Boating* 1974; *Jonah Who Will Be 25 in the Year 2000* 1976
Labuda, Marian (1944–) *My Sweet Little Village* 1986; *The Last of the Good Old Days* 1989; *Meeting Venus* 1990
Labyorteaux, Patrick (1965–) *Terminal Entry* 1988; *Heathers* 1989; *Ski School* 1991
Lacey, Catherine (1904–1979) *Poison Pen* 1939; *Pink String and Sealing Wax* 1945; *Carnival* 1946; *The October Man* 1947; *Whisky Galore!* 1949; *Innocent Sinners* 1957; *Crack in the Mirror* 1960; *The Servant* 1963; *The Sorcerers* 1967; *The Private Life of Sherlock Holmes* 1970
Lacey, Ingrid *The Funny Man* 1994; *In Love and War* 1996
Lacey, Ronald (1935–1991) *The Boys* 1961; *Take a Girl like You* 1970; *Crucible of Terror* 1971; *Gawain and the Green Knight* 1973; *Raiders of the Lost Ark* 1981; *Firefox* 1982; *The Hound of the Baskervilles* 1983; *Trenchcoat* 1983; *Sword of the Valiant* 1984; *Red Sonja* 1985; *Gunbus* 1986
Lacher, Taylor *Mr Majestyk* 1974; *Baker's Hawk* 1976; *Spirit of the Eagle* 1991
Lachow, Stan *The Gig* 1985; *The Luckiest Man in the World* 1989
Lack, Simon (1915–1980) *Sons of the Sea* 1939; *The Proud Valley* 1940; *The Silver Darlings* 1947
Lack, Stephen (1946–) *Head On* 1980; *Scanners* 1980; *Blind Alley* 1984; *Dead Ringers* 1988; *All the Vermeers in New York* 1990
Lacroix, Ghalia *The Silences of the Palace* 1994; *For Ever Mozart* 1996
LaCroix, Lisa *aka* **Lacroix, Lisa** *Dance Me Outside* 1994; *Les Convoyeurs Attendent* 1999
LaCroix, Peter *The Hunted* 1998; *The Silencer* 1999
Ladd, Alan (1913–1964) *Island of Lost Souls* 1932; *Pigskin Parade* 1936; *Hell Town* 1937; *The Goldwyn Follies* 1938; *Rulers of the Sea* 1939; *The Howards of Virginia* 1940; *The Black Cat* 1941; *The Glass Key* 1942; *Joan of Paris* 1942; *Star Spangled Rhythm* 1942; *This Gun for Hire* 1942; *China* 1943; *And Now Tomorrow* 1944; *Duffy's Tavern* 1945; *Salty O'Rourke* 1945; *The Blue Dahlia* 1946; *OSS* 1946; *Two Years before the Mast* 1946; *Calcutta* 1947; *My Favorite Brunette* 1947; *Variety Girl* 1947; *Saigon* 1948; *Whispering Smith* 1948; *The Great Gatsby* 1949; *Appointment with Danger* 1950; *Branded* 1950; *Captain Carey, USA* 1950; *Red Mountain* 1951; *Botany Bay* 1952; *The Iron Mistress* 1952; *Desert Legion* 1953; *The Red Beret* 1953; *Shane* 1953; *Thunder in the East* 1953; *The Black Knight* 1954; *Drum Beat* 1954; *Hell below Zero* 1954; *Saskatchewan* 1954; *Hell on Frisco Bay* 1955; *The McConnell Story* 1955; *A Cry in the Night* 1956; *Santiago* 1956; *The Big Land* 1957; *Boy on a Dolphin* 1957; *The Badlanders* 1958; *The Deep Six* 1958; *The Proud Rebel* 1958; *The Man in the Net* 1959; *All the Young Men* 1960; *Guns of the Timberland* 1960; *One Foot in Hell* 1960; *Duel of Champions* 1961; *13 West Street* 1962; *The Carpetbaggers* 1964
Ladd, Alana (1943–) *Guns of the Timberland* 1960; *Duel of Champions* 1961; *Young Guns of Texas* 1962
Ladd, Cheryl (1951–) *Now and Forever* 1983; *Purple Hearts* 1984; *Millennium* 1989; *Danielle Steel's Changes* 1991; *Poison Ivy* 1992; *Dead before Dawn* 1993; *A Dog of Flanders* 1999; *Her Best Friend's Husband* 2002
Ladd, David (1947–) *The Big Land* 1957; *The Proud Rebel* 1958; *A Dog of Flanders* 1959; *The Sad Horse* 1959; *Death Line* 1972; *Jonathan Livingston Seagull* 1973
Ladd, Diane (1939–) *Rebel Rousers* 1967; *The Reivers* 1969; *Macho Callahan* 1970; *White Lightning* 1973; *Alice Doesn't Live Here Anymore* 1974; *Chinatown* 1974; *Embryo* 1976; *All Night Long* 1981; *Something Wicked This Way Comes* 1983; *Black Widow* 1987; *Plain Clothes* 1988; *National Lampoon's Christmas Vacation* 1989; *Wild at Heart* 1990; *A Kiss before Dying* 1991; *Rambling Rose* 1991; *Hold Me, Thrill Me, Kiss Me* 1992; *Carnosaur* 1993; *The Cemetery Club* 1993; *Father Hood* 1993; *Forever* 1993; *The Haunted Heart* 1995; *Citizen Ruth* 1996; *Primary Colors* 1998; *28 Days* 2000
Ladd, Jordan (1975–) *Embrace of the Vampire* 1994; *Cabin Fever* 2002; *Broken Lizard's Club Dread* 2004
Laffan, Patricia (1919–) *Quo Vadis* 1951; *Escape Route* 1952; *Rough Shoot* 1952; *Devil Girl from Mars* 1954; *23 Paces to Baker Street* 1956; *Hidden Homicide* 1958
LaFleur, Art *aka* **La Fleur, Art** (1943–) *Trancers* 1985; *Air America* 1990; *Death Warrant* 1990; *Oscar* 1991; *Jack the Bear* 1993; *Man of the House* 1994; *First Kid* 1996
Lafont, Bernadette (1938–) *Le Beau Serge* 1958; *Web of Passion* 1959; *Les Bonnes Femmes* 1960; *Male Hunt* 1964; *Catch Me a Spy* 1971; *Une Belle Fille Comme Moi* 1973; *La Maman et la Putain* 1973; *Out 1: Spectre* 1973; *An Impudent Girl* 1985; *Inspecteur Lavardin* 1986; *Masques* 1987; *Waiting for the Moon* 1987; *Dingo* 1991; *Généalogies d'un Crime* 1997; *Rien sur Robert* 1998
Lafont, Jean-Philippe *Carmen* 1984; *Babette's Feast* 1987
Laforêt, Marie (1939–) *Plein Soleil* 1960; *Male Hunt* 1964; *Jack of Diamonds* 1967; *Tangos, Exilo de Gardel* 1985
Lafortune, Roc (1956–) *The Minion* 1998; *The List* 2000
Lagercrantz, Marika (1954–) *The Dive* 1989; *All Things Fair* 1995
Lagerwall, Sture (1908–1964) *Walpurgis Night* 1935; *The Devil's Eye* 1960
Lagrange, Valérie (1942–) *Morgan the Pirate* 1960; *La Ronde* 1964; *Up to His Ears* 1965; *Un Homme et une Femme* 1966; *Weekend* 1967; *The Valley* 1972
Laguna, Sylvie *Delicatessen* 1990; *Road to Ruin* 1992
Lahaie, Brigitte (1955–) *Fascination* 1979; *The Ordeal* 2004
Lahr, Bert (1895–1967) *Josette* 1938; *Just around the Corner* 1938; *The Wizard of Oz* 1939; *Zaza* 1939; *Ship Ahoy* 1942; *Meet the People* 1944; *Always Leave Them Laughing* 1949; *Rose Marie* 1954
Lahti, Christine (1950–) *...And Justice for All* 1979; *Ladies and Gentlemen, the Fabulous Stains* 1981; *Whose Life Is It Anyway?* 1981; *Swing Shift* 1984; *Just between Friends* 1986; *Housekeeping* 1987; *Season of Dreams* 1987; *Running on Empty* 1988; *A Cut Above* 1989; *Funny about Love* 1990; *Crazy from the Heart* 1991; *The Doctor* 1991; *Leaving Normal* 1992; *Hideaway* 1995; *Pie in the Sky* 1995; *Subway Stories: Tales from the Underground* 1997; *The Pilot's Wife* 2001
Lai, Leon *aka* **Lai Ming** (1966–) *Fallen Angels* 1995; *Eighteen Springs* 1997; *Infernal Affairs 3* 2003
Lail, Leah (1966–) *Heavyweights* 1995; *Something about Sex* 1998
Laine, Cleo (1927–) *The Roman Spring of Mrs Stone* 1961; *The Third Alibi* 1961
Laine, Frankie (1913–) *Bring Your Smile Along* 1955; *He Laughed Last* 1956
Laing, Stuart (1969–) *The Truth Game* 2000; *Cradle of Fear* 2001; *South West Nine* 2001; *Butterfly Man* 2002
Laird, Jenny (1917–2001) *Just William* 1939; *Black Narcissus* 1946; *Village of the Damned* 1960
Lake, Arthur (1905–1987) *Indiscreet* 1931; *Topper* 1937; *Blondie!* 1938
Lake, Don *Blue Monkey* 1987; *Short Circuit 2* 1988
Lake, Florence (1904–1980) *The Rogue Song* 1930; *Romance* 1930
Lake, Ricki (1968–) *Hairspray* 1988; *Cry-Baby* 1989; *Last Exit to Brooklyn* 1989; *Where the Day Takes You* 1992; *Serial Mom* 1994; *Mrs Winterbourne* 1996
Lake, Veronica (1919–1973) *Hold Back the Dawn* 1941; *I Wanted Wings* 1941; *Sullivan's Travels* 1941; *The Glass Key* 1942; *I Married a Witch* 1942; *Star Spangled Rhythm* 1942; *This Gun for Hire* 1942; *So Proudly We Hail* 1943; *The Hour before the Dawn* 1944; *Bring on the Girls* 1945; *Duffy's Tavern* 1945; *Hold That Blonde* 1945; *Miss Susie Slagle's* 1945; *Out of This World* 1945; *The Blue Dahlia* 1946; *Ramrod* 1947; *Isn't It Romantic* 1948; *Saigon* 1948; *The Sainted Sisters* 1948; *Slattery's Hurricane* 1949; *Flesh Feast* 1970
Lally, Mick *The Fantasist* 1986; *Fools of Fortune* 1990; *The Secret of Roan Inish* 1993; *Circle of Friends* 1995
Lam Ching Ying (1952–1997) *The Prodigal Son* 1983; *Mr Vampire* 1986
Lamarr, Hedy *aka* **Kiesler, Hedy** (1913–2000) *Ecstasy* 1933; *Algiers* 1938; *Lady of the Tropics* 1939; *Boom Town* 1940; *Comrade X* 1940; *I Take This Woman* 1940; *Come Live with Me* 1941; *HM Pulham Esq* 1941; *Ziegfeld Girl* 1941; *Crossroads* 1942; *Tortilla Flat* 1942; *White Cargo* 1942; *The Heavenly Body* 1943; *The Conspirators* 1944; *Experiment Perilous* 1944; *The Strange Woman* 1946; *Dishonored Lady* 1947; *Let's Live a Little* 1948; *Samson and Delilah* 1949; *Copper Canyon* 1950; *A Lady without Passport* 1950; *My Favorite Spy* 1951; *The Loves of Three Queens* 1954; *The Story of Mankind* 1957; *The Female Animal* 1958
Lamas, Fernando (1915–1982) *The Law and the Lady* 1951; *Rich, Young and Pretty* 1951; *The Merry Widow* 1952; *Dangerous When Wet* 1953; *The Diamond Queen* 1953; *The Girl Who Had Everything* 1953; *Jivaro* 1954; *Rose Marie* 1954; *The Girl Rush* 1955; *The Lost World* 1960; *Kill a Dragon* 1967; *Valley of Mystery* 1967; *The Violent Ones* 1967; *Backtrack* 1969; *100 Rifles* 1969; *The Cheap Detective* 1978
Lamas, Lorenzo (1958–) *Take Down* 1978; *CIA – Codename Alexa* 1992
Lamb, Gil (1906–1995) *The Fleet's In* 1942; *Riding High* 1943; *Practically Yours* 1944
Lamb, Larry *Shadey* 1985; *Buster* 1988; *Essex Boys* 1999; *Fakers* 2004
Lambert, Anne Louise *aka* **Lambert, Anne** (1956–) *Picnic at Hanging Rock* 1975; *The Draughtsman's Contract* 1982
Lambert, Christopher *aka* **Lambert, Christophe** (1957–) *Greystoke: the Legend of Tarzan, Lord of the Apes* 1984; *Love Songs* 1984; *Subway* 1985; *Highlander* 1986; *The Sicilian* 1987; *To Kill a Priest* 1988; *Highlander II: the Quickening* 1990; *Why Me?* 1990; *Fortress* 1992; *Knight Moves* 1992; *Gunmen* 1994; *Roadflower* 1994; *Adrenalin: Fear the Rush* 1995; *Highlander III: the Sorcerer* 1995; *The Hunted* 1995; *Mortal Kombat* 1995; *Mean Guns* 1996; *Nirvana* 1996; *North Star* 1996; *Fortress 2: Re-entry* 1999; *Gideon* 1999; *Resurrection* 1999; *Highlander: Endgame* 2000; *The Point Men* 2000; *Druids* 2001
Lambert, Jack (1920–) *Abilene Town* 1945; *Dick Tracy's Dilemma* 1947; *The Unsuspected* 1947; *Belle Starr's Daughter* 1948; *Eureka Stockade* 1949; *Floodtide* 1949; *North of the Great Divide* 1950; *The Lost Hours* 1952; *Scared Stiff* 1953; *At Gunpoint* 1955; *Run for Cover* 1955; *Storm over the Nile* 1955; *Machine Gun Kelly* 1958; *The Bridal Path* 1959; *Neither the Sea nor the Sand* 1972
Lambert, Paul (1922–1997) *The Big Mouth* 1967; *Play It As It Lays* 1972; *Mama's Dirty Girls* 1974
Lamberts, Heath (1941–2005) *To Kill a Clown* 1972; *Ordinary Magic* 1993
Lamble, Lloyd (1914–) *Suspended Alibi* 1956; *Blue Murder at St Trinian's* 1957; *The Bank Raiders* 1958
Lamont, Duncan (1918–1978) *The Golden Coach* 1953; *The Teckman Mystery* 1954; *Passage Home* 1955; *The Devil-Ship Pirates* 1964; *Evil of Frankenstein* 1964; *Arabesque* 1966; *The Witches* 1966; *Quatermass and the Pit* 1967; *The Creeping Flesh* 1972
Lamont, Molly (1910–2000) *The Awful Truth* 1937; *The Suspect* 1944; *So Goes My Love* 1946; *Scared to Death* 1947
Lamont, Nicholas *aka* **Lamont, Nick** *The Long Day Closes* 1992; *Going Off, Big Time* 2000
Lamorisse, Pascal (1950–) *White Mane* 1952; *Red Balloon* 1956
LaMotta, John *American Ninja* 1985; *Lookin' Italian* 1994
Lamour, Dorothy (1914–1996) *The Big Broadcast of 1938* 1937; *High, Wide and Handsome* 1937; *The Hurricane* 1937; *The Last Train from Madrid* 1937; *Swing High, Swing Low* 1937; *Spawn of the North* 1938; *Chad Hanna* 1940; *Johnny Apollo* 1940; *Road to Singapore* 1940; *Typhoon* 1940; *Road to Zanzibar* 1941; *Beyond the Blue Horizon* 1942; *The Fleet's In* 1942; *Road to Morocco* 1942; *Star Spangled Rhythm* 1942; *Dixie* 1943; *Riding High* 1943; *They Got Me Covered* 1943; *And the Angels Sing* 1944; *Duffy's Tavern* 1945; *A Medal for Benny* 1945; *Road to Utopia* 1945; *My Favorite Brunette* 1947; *Road to Rio* 1947; *Variety Girl* 1947; *The Girl from Manhattan* 1948; *Lulu Belle* 1948; *On Our Merry Way* 1948; *The Lucky Stiff* 1949; *Slightly French* 1949; *Here Comes the Groom* 1951; *The Greatest Show on Earth* 1952; *Road to Bali* 1952; *The Road to Hong Kong* 1962; *Donovan's Reef* 1963; *Pajama Party* 1964; *Creepshow 2* 1987
Lampe, Jutta *Sisters, or the Balance of Happiness* 1979; *The German Sisters* 1981
Lampert, Zohra (1937–) *Pay or Die* 1960; *Hey, Let's Twist!* 1961; *Posse from Hell* 1961; *Splendor in the Grass* 1961; *Bye Bye Braverman* 1968; *Let's Scare Jessica to Death* 1971; *Opening Night* 1977; *Alphabet City* 1984; *American Blue Note* 1989; *Stanley & Iris* 1989; *The Last Good Time* 1994
Lampkin, Charles (1913–1989) *Five* 1951; *Hammer* 1972
Lampley, Oni Faida *Lone Star* 1995; *First Do No Harm* 1997
Lampreave, Chus *Dark Habits* 1983; *What Have I Done to Deserve This?* 1984; *Matador* 1986; *The Flower of My Secret* 1995
Lamprecht, Günter *aka* **Lamprecht, Günther** (1930–) *Berlin Alexanderplatz* 1980; *Rouge Baiser* 1985
Lancaster, Burt (1913–1994) *The Killers* 1946; *Brute Force* 1947; *Desert Fury* 1947; *I Walk Alone* 1947; *All My Sons* 1948; *Blood on My Hands* 1948; *Sorry, Wrong Number* 1948; *Criss Cross* 1949; *Rope of Sand* 1949; *The Flame and the Arrow* 1950; *Mister 880* 1950; *Jim Thorpe – All-American*

1951; *Ten Tall Men* 1951; *Vengeance Valley* 1951; *Come Back, Little Sheba* 1952; *The Crimson Pirate* 1952; *From Here to Eternity* 1953; *His Majesty O'Keefe* 1953; *South Sea Woman* 1953; *Apache* 1954; *Vera Cruz* 1954; *The Kentuckian* 1955; *The Rose Tattoo* 1955; *The Rainmaker* 1956; *Trapeze* 1956; *Gunfight at the OK Corral* 1957; *Sweet Smell of Success* 1957; *Run Silent, Run Deep* 1958; *Separate Tables* 1958; *The Devil's Disciple* 1959; *Elmer Gantry* 1960; *The Unforgiven* 1960; *Judgment at Nuremberg* 1961; *The Young Savages* 1961; *Birdman of Alcatraz* 1962; *A Child Is Waiting* 1962; *The Leopard* 1962; *The List of Adrian Messenger* 1963; *Seven Days in May* 1964; *The Train* 1964; *The Hallelujah Trail* 1965; *The Professionals* 1966; *The Scalphunters* 1968; *The Swimmer* 1968; *Castle Keep* 1969; *The Gypsy Moths* 1969; *Airport* 1970; *King: a Filmed Record... Montgomery to Memphis* 1970; *Lawman* 1971; *Valdez Is Coming* 1971; *Ulzana's Raid* 1972; *Executive Action* 1973; *Scorpio* 1973; *Conversation Piece* 1974; *The Midnight Man* 1974; *Moses* 1975; *Buffalo Bill and the Indians, or Sitting Bull's History Lesson* 1976; *The Cassandra Crossing* 1976; *1900* 1976; *Victory at Entebbe* 1976; *Go Tell the Spartans* 1977; *The Island of Dr Moreau* 1977; *Twilight's Last Gleaming* 1977; *Zulu Dawn* 1979; *Atlantic City, USA* 1980; *Cattle Annie and Little Britches* 1980; *La Pelle* 1981; *Local Hero* 1983; *The Osterman Weekend* 1983; *Little Treasure* 1985; *Barnum* 1986; *Tough Guys* 1986; *Rocket Gibraltar* 1988; *Field of Dreams* 1989

Lancaster, Stuart (1920–2000) *Faster, Pussycat! Kill! Kill!* 1965; *Mudhoney* 1965; *Good Morning... and Goodbye* 1967

Lanchester, Elsa (1902–1986) *The Private Life of Henry VIII* 1933; *Bride of Frankenstein* 1935; *David Copperfield* 1935; *The Ghost Goes West* 1935; *Naughty Marietta* 1935; *Rembrandt* 1936; *Vessel of Wrath* 1938; *Ladies in Retirement* 1941; *Son of Fury* 1942; *Tales of Manhattan* 1942; *Lassie Come Home* 1943; *The Razor's Edge* 1946; *The Spiral Staircase* 1946; *The Bishop's Wife* 1947; *Northwest Outpost* 1947; *The Big Clock* 1948; *Come to the Stable* 1949; *The Inspector General* 1949; *The Secret Garden* 1949; *Frenchie* 1950; *Mystery Street* 1950; *The Petty Girl* 1950; *Androcles and the Lion* 1952; *Dreamboat* 1952; *Les Misérables* 1952; *Hell's Half Acre* 1954; *Three Ring Circus* 1954; *The Glass Slipper* 1955; *Witness for the Prosecution* 1957; *Bell, Book and Candle* 1958; *Honeymoon Hotel* 1964; *Mary Poppins* 1964; *Pajama Party* 1964; *That Darn Cat!* 1965; *Blackbeard's Ghost* 1967; *Easy Come, Easy Go* 1967; *Willard* 1971; *Arnold* 1973; *Terror in the Wax Museum* 1973; *Murder by Death* 1976; *Die Laughing* 1980

Land, Geoffrey *The Female Bunch* 1969; *Against a Crooked Sky* 1975

Landau, David (1878–1935) *Street Scene* 1931; *Horse Feathers* 1932; *I Am a Fugitive from a Chain Gang* 1932; *Lawyer Man* 1932; *Polly of the Circus* 1932; *The Purchase Price* 1932; *Taxi!* 1932; *Gabriel over the White House* 1933; *She Done Him Wrong* 1933; *Judge Priest* 1934

Landau, Juliet (1965–) *Theodore Rex* 1995; *Toolbox Murders* 2003

Landau, Martin (1931–) *The Gazebo* 1959; *North by Northwest* 1959; *Pork Chop Hill* 1959; *Stagecoach to Dancer's Rock* 1962; *Cleopatra* 1963; *The Greatest Story Ever Told* 1965; *The Hallelujah Trail* 1965; *Nevada Smith* 1966; *They Call Me Mister Tibbs!* 1970; *A Town Called Hell* 1971; *Meteor* 1979; *Without Warning* 1980; *Alone in the Dark* 1982; *Treasure Island* 1986; *Delta Fever* 1988; *Tucker: the Man and His Dream* 1988; *Crimes and Misdemeanors* 1989; *Paint It Black* 1989; *Firehead* 1991; *Mistress* 1992; *No Place to Hide* 1992; *Eye of the Stranger* 1993; *Sliver* 1993; *12:01* 1993; *Ed Wood* 1994; *Intersection* 1994; *The Adventures of Pinocchio* 1996; *City Hall* 1996; *BAPS* 1997; *Rounders* 1998; *The X-Files* 1998; *Edtv* 1999; *The Joyriders* 1999; *The New Adventures of Pinocchio* 1999; *Ready to Rumble* 2000; *Shiner* 2000; *The Majestic* 2001; *Hollywood Homicide* 2003

Landen, Dinsdale (1932–2003) *Operation Snatch* 1962; *We Joined the Navy* 1962; *Mosquito Squadron* 1968; *Every Home Should Have One* 1970; *Digby, the Biggest Dog in the World* 1973; *International Velvet* 1978; *Morons from Outer Space* 1985; *The Steal* 1994

Landers, Audrey (1959–) *A Chorus Line* 1985; *Getting Even* 1986

Landers, Harry (1921–) *Guilty Bystander* 1950; *Drive a Crooked Road* 1954

Landes, Michael (1972–) *When the Party's Over* 1992; *Danielle Steel's No Greater Love* 1996; *Dream for an Insomniac* 1996; *Final Destination 2* 2002

Landfield, Timothy *Cheetah* 1989; *Without Warning: the James Brady Story* 1991

Landgard, Janet *The Swimmer* 1968; *Land Raiders* 1969

Landgré, Inga (1927–) *Crisis* 1945; *Dreams* 1955

Landgrebe, Gudrun (1950–) *Colonel Redl* 1984; *Snow White* 1989; *Milena* 1990

Landham, Sonny (1941–) *Firewalker* 1986; *Predator* 1987; *Lock Up* 1989; *Best of the Best II* 1992

Landi, Elissa (1904–1948) *Body and Soul* 1931; *The Sign of the Cross* 1932; *Enter Madame!* 1933; *The Masquerader* 1933; *By Candlelight* 1934; *The Count of Monte Cristo* 1934; *Königsmark* 1935; *After the Thin Man* 1936

Landi, Marla (1937–) *The Hornet's Nest* 1955; *Across the Bridge* 1957; *Dublin Nightmare* 1958; *First Man into Space* 1958; *The Hound of the Baskervilles* 1959; *The Pirates of Blood River* 1961

Landi, Sal *Savage Streets* 1984; *Rover Dangerfield* 1991

Landis, Carole (1919–1948) *Hollywood Hotel* 1937; *Three Texas Steers* 1939; *One Million BC* 1940; *Turnabout* 1940; *I Wake Up Screaming* 1941; *Moon over Miami* 1941; *Road Show* 1941; *Topper Returns* 1941; *A Gentleman at Heart* 1942; *My Gal Sal* 1942; *Orchestra Wives* 1942; *Wintertime* 1943; *Secret Command* 1944; *It Shouldn't Happen to a Dog* 1946; *Thieves' Holiday* 1946; *Out of the Blue* 1947; *The Brass Monkey* 1948; *Noose* 1948

Landis, Jessie Royce (1904–1972) *Mr Belvedere Goes to College* 1949; *My Foolish Heart* 1949; *To Catch a Thief* 1955; *The Girl He Left Behind* 1956; *The Swan* 1956; *My Man Godfrey* 1957; *I Married a Woman* 1958; *North by Northwest* 1959; *A Private's Affair* 1959; *Goodbye Again* 1961; *Bon Voyage!* 1962; *Boys' Night Out* 1962; *Critic's Choice* 1963; *Gidget Goes to Rome* 1963

Landis, John (1950–) *Schlock* 1971; *1941* 1979; *Into the Night* 1985; *Body Chemistry 2: Voice of a Stranger* 1992; *Sleepwalkers* 1992; *Venice/Venice* 1992; *Diamonds* 1999

Landis, Monte *aka* **Landis, Monty** *Targets* 1968; *Pee-wee's Big Adventure* 1985

Landis, Nina *Rikky and Pete* 1988; *Komodo* 1999

Lando, Joe (1961–) *Seeds of Doubt* 1996; *No Code of Conduct* 1998

Landon, Laurene (1958–) *The California Dolls* 1981; *I, the Jury* 1982; *America 3000* 1986; *Armed Response* 1986; *It's Alive III: Island of the Alive* 1987; *Maniac Cop* 1988; *Maniac Cop 2* 1990

Landon, Michael (1936–1991) *I Was a Teenage Werewolf* 1957; *Maracaibo* 1958; *The Legend of Tom Dooley* 1959; *Sam's Son* 1984

Landone, Avice (1910–1976) *True as a Turtle* 1956; *Gaolbreak* 1962; *The Leather Boys* 1963; *This Is My Street* 1963; *The Adventures of Barry McKenzie* 1972

Landry, Gérard (1914–) *La Bête Humaine* 1938; *Night without Stars* 1951; *Trapeze* 1956

Landry, Karen *The Personals* 1982; *Patti Rocks* 1987

Landsburg, Valerie (1958–) *Thank God It's Friday* 1978; *One of Her Own* 1994

Lane, Abbe (1932–) *Ride Clear of Diablo* 1954; *The Americano* 1955; *Maracaibo* 1958

Lane, Allan *aka* **Lane, Allan "Rocky"** (1904–1973) *Charlie Chan at the Olympics* 1937; *The Law West of Tombstone* 1938; *Maid's Night Out* 1938; *The Spellbinder* 1939; *Bells of Rosarita* 1945; *Trail of Robin Hood* 1950; *The Saga of Hemp Brown* 1958

Lane (1), Charles (1869–1945) *Dr Jekyll and Mr Hyde* 1920; *The White Sister* 1923; *The Winning of Barbara Worth* 1926; *Sadie Thompson* 1928; *The Canary Murder Case* 1929

Lane (2), Charles *aka* **Levison, Charles** (1905–) *Blonde Crazy* 1931; *Advice to the Lovelorn* 1933; *Twentieth Century* 1934; *The Affairs of Dobie Gillis* 1953; *The Juggler* 1953; *Teacher's Pet* 1958; *But Not for Me* 1959; *Good Neighbor Sam* 1964; *Billie* 1965; *The Ugly Dachshund* 1966; *What's So Bad About Feeling Good?* 1968

Lane (3), Charles (1953–) *Sidewalk Stories* 1989; *True Identity* 1991; *Posse* 1993

Lane, Colin *Broken Harvest* 1994; *The Blood Oranges* 1997

Lane, Diane (1965–) *A Little Romance* 1979; *Touched by Love* 1979; *Cattle Annie and Little Britches* 1980; *Ladies and Gentlemen, the Fabulous Stains* 1981; *National Lampoon's Movie Madness* 1981; *Six Pack* 1982; *The Outsiders* 1983; *Rumble Fish* 1983; *The Cotton Club* 1984; *Streets of Fire* 1984; *The Big Town* 1987; *Lady Beware* 1987; *Vital Signs* 1990; *Chaplin* 1992; *Knight Moves* 1992; *My New Gun* 1992; *Indian Summer* 1993; *Judge Dredd* 1995; *Wild Bill* 1995; *Jack* 1996; *Trigger Happy* 1996; *Murder at 1600* 1997; *The Only Thrill* 1997; *Grace and Glorie* 1998; *My Dog Skip* 1999; *A Walk on the Moon* 1999; *The Perfect Storm* 2000; *The Glass House* 2001; *Hardball* 2001; *Unfaithful* 2002; *Under the Tuscan Sun* 2003

Lane, Jocelyn *aka* **Lane, Jackie** (1937–) *Goodbye Again* 1961; *Two and Two Make Six* 1961; *Operation Snatch* 1962; *Tickle Me* 1965; *Incident at Phantom Hill* 1966; *Land Raiders* 1969

Lane, Lenita (1901–1995) *The Mad Magician* 1954; *The Bat* 1959

Lane, Lola (1909–1981) *Fox Movietone Follies of 1929* 1929; *Murder on a Honeymoon* 1935; *Hollywood Hotel* 1937; *Marked Woman* 1937; *Four Daughters* 1938; *Daughters Courageous* 1939; *Four Wives* 1939; *Four Mothers* 1941; *Deadline at Dawn* 1946

Lane, Mara (1930–) *Decameron Nights* 1953; *Angela* 1955

Lane, Mike *aka* **Lane, Michael** *The Harder They Fall* 1956; *Hero of Babylon* 1963; *Stryker* 1983

Lane, Nathan (1956–) *Frankie & Johnny* 1991; *He Said, She Said* 1991; *Life with Mikey* 1993; *The Lion King* 1994; *Jeffrey* 1995; *The Birdcage* 1996; *Mousehunt* 1997; *At First Sight* 1998; *Isn't She Great* 1999; *Love's Labour's Lost* 1999; *Stuart Little* 1999; *Laughter on the 23rd Floor* 2000; *Titan AE* 2000; *Trixie* 2000; *Nicholas Nickleby* 2002; *Stuart Little 2* 2002; *Win a Date with Tad Hamilton!* 2004

Lane, Priscilla (1917–1995) *Four Daughters* 1938; *Daughters Courageous* 1939; *Dust Be My Destiny* 1939; *Four Wives* 1939; *The Roaring Twenties* 1939; *Blues in the Night* 1941; *Four Mothers* 1941; *Million Dollar Baby* 1941; *Saboteur* 1942; *The Meanest Man in the World* 1943; *Arsenic and Old Lace* 1944; *Bodyguard* 1948

Lane, Richard (1899–1982) *Flight from Glory* 1937; *Go Chase Yourself* 1938; *Mr Moto in Danger Island* 1939; *The Biscuit Eater* 1940; *Hellzapoppin'* 1941; *Meet Boston Blackie* 1941; *Riders of the Purple Sage* 1941; *Arabian Nights* 1942; *Dr Broadway* 1942; *Ride 'em Cowboy* 1942; *Corvette K-225* 1943; *The Bermuda Mystery* 1944; *Brazil* 1944; *Mr Winkle Goes to War* 1944; *The Bullfighters* 1945; *Two O'Clock Courage* 1945; *Take Me Out to the Ball Game* 1949

Lane, Rosemary (1914–1974) *Hollywood Hotel* 1937; *Four Daughters* 1938; *Gold Diggers in Paris* 1938; *Daughters Courageous* 1939; *Four Wives* 1939; *The Oklahoma Kid* 1939; *The Return of Dr X* 1939; *The Boys from Syracuse* 1940; *Four Mothers* 1941; *Time Out for Rhythm* 1941; *Chatterbox* 1943

Lane, Rusty (1899–1986) *Bigger than Life* 1956; *Johnny Tremain* 1957

Laneuville, Eric (1952–) *The Omega Man* 1971; *Black Belt Jones* 1974; *A Force of One* 1979

Lang, Harold (1923–1971) *Cairo Road* 1950; *Cloudburst* 1951; *Wings of Danger* 1952; *Dance Little Lady* 1954; *It's a Wonderful World* 1956

Lang, June (1915–) *Bonnie Scotland* 1935; *Captain January* 1936; *The Country Doctor* 1936; *The Road to Glory* 1936; *Nancy Steele Is Missing* 1937; *Wee Willie Winkie* 1937; *International Settlement* 1938; *Footlight Serenade* 1942

Lang, Katherine Kelly (1961–) *The Night Stalker* 1985; *Delta Fever* 1988

lang, kd (1961–) *Salmonberries* 1991; *Eye of the Beholder* 1999

Lang, Perry (1959–) *Alligator* 1980; *Body and Soul* 1981; *O'Hara's Wife* 1982; *Sahara* 1983; *Jocks* 1986; *Little Vegas* 1990; *Jennifer Eight* 1992

Lang, Robert (1934–2004) *Othello* 1965; *The Dance of Death* 1969; *Night Watch* 1973; *Hawks* 1988

Lang, Stephen (1952–) *Death of a Salesman* 1985; *Twice in a Lifetime* 1985; *Manhunter* 1986; *Project X* 1987; *Last Exit to Brooklyn* 1989; *Another You* 1991; *The Hard Way* 1991; *Darkness before Dawn* 1992; *Gettysburg* 1993; *Guilty as Sin* 1993; *Murder between Friends* 1993; *Tall Tale* 1994; *The Amazing Panda Adventure* 1995; *Lone Star* 1995; *Shadow Conspiracy* 1996; *Fire Down Below* 1997; *Niagara Niagara* 1997; *The Proposal* 2000; *Trixie* 2000; *Gods and Generals* 2002; *The I Inside* 2003

Langan, Glenn *aka* **Langan, Glen** (1917–1991) *Something for the Boys* 1944; *A Bell for Adano* 1945; *Hangover Square* 1945; *Dragonwyck* 1946; *Margie* 1946; *Sentimental Journey* 1946; *Forever Amber* 1947; *Fury at Furnace Creek* 1948; *The Snake Pit* 1948; *The Amazing Colossal Man* 1957

Langdon, Harry (1884–1944) *The Strong Man* 1926; *Tramp, Tramp, Tramp* 1926; *Long Pants* 1927; *Hallelujah, I'm a Bum* 1933; *Atlantic Adventure* 1935; *Zenobia* 1939; *Block Busters* 1944

Langdon, Libby *Federal Hill* 1994; *A Shot at Glory* 2000

Langdon, Sue Ane *aka* **Langdon, Sue Ann** *aka* **Langdon, Sue Anne** (1936–) *Roustabout* 1964; *The Rounders* 1965; *When the Boys Meet the Girls* 1965; *Frankie & Johnny* 1966; *A Guide for the Married Man* 1967; *The Cheyenne Social Club* 1970; *The Evictors* 1979; *Without Warning* 1980; *Hawken's Breed* 1989

Lange, Artie (1967–) *Dirty Work* 1998; *The Bachelor* 1999; *Lost & Found* 1999

Lange, Carl (1909–1999) *The Desperado Trail* 1965; *The Blood Demon* 1967

Lange, Hope (1931–2003) *Bus Stop* 1956; *Peyton Place* 1957; *The True Story of Jesse James* 1957; *In Love and War* 1958; *The Young Lions* 1958; *The Best of Everything* 1959; *Pocketful of Miracles* 1961; *Wild in the Country* 1961; *Love Is a Ball* 1963; *Jigsaw* 1968; *Death Wish* 1974; *I Am the Cheese* 1983; *The Prodigal* 1983; *A Nightmare on Elm Street 2: Freddy's Revenge* 1985; *Blue Velvet* 1986; *Aunt Julia and the Scriptwriter* 1990; *Dead before Dawn* 1993

Lange, Jessica (1949–) *King Kong* 1976; *All That Jazz* 1979; *How to Beat the High Cost of Living* 1980; *The Postman Always Rings Twice* 1981; *Frances* 1982; *Tootsie* 1982; *Country* 1984; *Sweet Dreams* 1985; *Crimes of the Heart* 1986; *Everybody's All-American* 1988; *Far North* 1988; *Music Box* 1989; *Men Don't Leave* 1990; *Blue Sky* 1991; *Cape Fear* 1991; *Night and the City* 1992; *Losing Isaiah* 1995; *Rob Roy* 1995; *Cousin Bette* 1997; *A Thousand Acres* 1997; *Hush* 1998; *Titus* 1999; *Normal* 2002; *Big Fish* 2003; *Masked and Anonymous* 2003

Langella, Frank (1940–) *Diary of a Mad Housewife* 1970; *The Twelve Chairs* 1970; *The Deadly Trap* 1971; *The Wrath of God* 1972; *Dracula* 1979; *Sphinx* 1980; *Those Lips, Those Eyes* 1980; *The Men's Club* 1986; *Masters of the Universe* 1987; *And God Created Woman* 1988; *True Identity* 1991; *Dave* 1993; *Brainscan* 1994; *Junior* 1994; *Bad Company* 1995; *CutThroat Island* 1995; *Eddie* 1996; *Lolita* 1997; *I'm Losing You* 1998; *Small Soldiers* 1998; *The Ninth Gate* 1999; *Stardom* 2000; *Sweet November* 2001

Langenkamp, Heather (1964–) *A Nightmare on Elm Street* 1984; *A Nightmare on Elm Street 3: Dream Warriors* 1987; *Shocker* 1989; *Wes Craven's New Nightmare* 1994

Langer, A J (1974–) *The People under the Stairs* 1991; *Escape from LA* 1996; *Meet the Deedles* 1998

Langford, Frances (1914–) *Born to Dance* 1936; *Too Many Girls* 1940; *Girl Rush* 1944; *The Bamboo Blonde* 1946

Langlet, Amanda *Pauline at the Beach* 1983; *A Summer's Tale* 1996; *Triple Agent* 2003

Langlois, Lisa (1959–) *Blood Relatives* 1977; *Phobia* 1980; *Class of 1984* 1982; *Joy of Sex* 1984; *The Slugger's Wife* 1985

Langrick, Margaret (1971–) *My American Cousin* 1985; *Bigfoot and the Hendersons* 1987; *American Boyfriends* 1989; *Cold Comfort* 1989; *Death of a Cheerleader* 1994; *Sweet Angel Mine* 1996

Langrishe, Caroline (1958–) *Eagle's Wing* 1978; *Hawks* 1988; *Rogue Trader* 1998; *Kisna – the Warrior Poet* 2004

Langston, Murray *Night Patrol* 1984; *Wishful Thinking* 1990

Langton, Brooke (1970–) *Listen* 1996; *The Replacements* 2000

Langton, Paul (1913–1980) *The Hidden Eye* 1945; *They Were*

Expendable 1945; *Till the Clouds Roll By* 1946; *Big Leaguer* 1953; *Chicago Confidential* 1957; *The Incredible Shrinking Man* 1957; *The Cosmic Man* 1959

Lanning, Frank (1872–1945) *The Kid Brother* 1927; *The Unknown* 1927

Lanoux, Victor (1936–) *Two against the Law* 1973; *Cousin, Cousine* 1975; *Pardon Mon Affaire* 1976; *Un Moment d'Egarement* 1977; *Les Chiens* 1978; *The Scene of the Crime* 1986

Lansbury, Angela (1925–) *Gaslight* 1944; *National Velvet* 1944; *The Picture of Dorian Gray* 1945; *The Harvey Girls* 1946; *The Hoodlum Saint* 1946; *If Winter Comes* 1947; *The Private Affairs of Bel Ami* 1947; *State of the Union* 1948; *The Three Musketeers* 1948; *The Red Danube* 1949; *Samson and Delilah* 1949; *Kind Lady* 1951; *Mutiny* 1952; *Remains to Be Seen* 1953; *A Lawless Street* 1955; *The Purple Mask* 1955; *The Court Jester* 1956; *The Reluctant Debutante* 1958; *A Breath of Scandal* 1960; *The Dark at the Top of the Stairs* 1960; *Season of Passion* 1960; *Blue Hawaii* 1961; *All Fall Down* 1962; *The Manchurian Candidate* 1962; *In the Cool of the Day* 1963; *Dear Heart* 1964; *The World of Henry Orient* 1964; *The Amorous Adventures of Moll Flanders* 1965; *The Greatest Story Ever Told* 1965; *Harlow* 1965; *Mister Buddwing* 1965; *Something for Everyone* 1970; *Bedknobs and Broomsticks* 1971; *Death on the Nile* 1978; *The Lady Vanishes* 1979; *The Last Unicorn* 1980; *The Mirror Crack'd* 1980; *The Pirates of Penzance* 1983; *The Company of Wolves* 1984; *Beauty and the Beast* 1991; *Mrs 'arris Goes to Paris* 1992; *Anastasia* 1997; *Beauty and the Beast: the Enchanted Christmas* 1997; *Fantasia 2000* 1999; *The Unexpected Mrs Pollifax* 1999; *The Blackwater Lightship* 2004

Lansing, Joi (1928–1972) *The Brave One* 1956; *The Atomic Submarine* 1960

Lansing, Robert (1929–1994) *A Gathering of Eagles* 1963; *Under the Yum Yum Tree* 1963; *An Eye for an Eye* 1966; *Namu, the Killer Whale* 1966; *The Grissom Gang* 1971; *Black Jack* 1972; *Acapulco Gold* 1976; *Bittersweet Love* 1976; *Empire of the Ants* 1977

Lanvin, Gérard (1949–) *Choice of Arms* 1981; *Double Dare* 1981; *A Strange Affair* 1981; *Mon Homme* 1996; *En Plein Coeur* 1998; *Le Goût des Autres* 1999

Lanza, Mario (1921–1959) *That Midnight Kiss* 1949; *The Toast of New Orleans* 1950; *The Great Caruso* 1951; *Because You're Mine* 1952; *The Student Prince* 1954; *Serenade* 1956; *Seven Hills of Rome* 1957; *For the First Time* 1959

LaPaglia, Anthony (1959–) *Mortal Sins* 1989; *Slaves of New York* 1989; *Betsy's Wedding* 1990; *He Said, She Said* 1991; *One Good Cop* 1991; *29th Street* 1991; *Innocent Blood* 1992; *Whispers in the Dark* 1992; *The Custodian* 1993; *So I Married an Axe Murderer* 1993; *The Client* 1994; *Killer* 1994; *Mixed Nuts* 1994; *Paperback Romance* 1994; *Empire Records* 1995; *Brilliant Lies* 1996; *Commandments* 1996; *Trees Lounge* 1996; *Phoenix* 1998; *Lansky* 1999; *Sweet and Lowdown* 1999; *Autumn in New York* 2000; *Company Man* 2000; *The House of Mirth* 2000; *The Bank* 2001; *Lantana* 2001; *Dead Heat* 2002; *I'm with Lucy* 2002; *The Salton Sea* 2002

Lapaine, Daniel *Polish Wedding* 1998; *Brokedown Palace* 1999; *Elephant Juice* 1999; *The Abduction Club* 2002

Laplace, Victor (1943–) *Funny Dirty Little War* 1983; *La Amiga* 1988

Lapointe, Jean (1935–) *Une Histoire Inventée* 1990; *Never Too Late* 1996

Lapotaire, Jane (1944–) *Crescendo* 1970; *Antony and Cleopatra* 1972; *The Asphyx* 1972; *Eureka* 1982; *Lady Jane* 1985; *Surviving Picasso* 1996; *There's Only One Jimmy Grimble* 2000

Larbi, Doghmi *The Man Who Would Be King* 1975; *The Black Stallion* 1979

Larch, John (1922–) *Seven Men from Now* 1956; *The Careless Years* 1957; *Man in the Shadow* 1957; *Quantez* 1957; *The Saga of Hemp Brown* 1958; *Miracle of the White Stallions* 1963; *Hail, Hero!* 1969; *The Wrecking Crew* 1969; *Dirty Harry* 1971; *Play Misty for Me* 1971; *Santee* 1973

Laresca, Vincent (1974–) *Juice* 1991; *Ripe* 1996; *Forever Mine* 1999; *Empire* 2002

Larive, Léon *aka* **Larive** (1886–1961) *Zéro de Conduite* 1933; *La Marseillaise* 1938

Larken, Sheila (1944–) *Dangerous Intentions* 1995; *Behind the Mask* 1999

Larkin, Chris *Angels and Insects* 1995; *Master and Commander: the Far Side of the World* 2003

Larkin, John (1912–1965) *Those Calloways* 1964; *The Satan Bug* 1965

Larkin, Linda (1970–) *Aladdin* 1992; *Aladdin and the King of Thieves* 1996

LaRoche, Mary *The Lineup* 1958; *Gidget* 1959; *The Swinger* 1966

Laroque, Michèle (1960–) *Tango* 1993; *Ma Vie en Rose* 1997; *The Closet* 2001

Larquey, Pierre (1884–1962) *Madame Bovary* 1933; *The Raven* 1943; *Topaze* 1951; *Les Diaboliques* 1954

Larroquette, John (1947–) *Green Ice* 1981; *Stripes* 1981; *Choose Me* 1984; *Meatballs 2* 1984; *Summer Rental* 1985; *Blind Date* 1987; *Second Sight* 1989; *Madhouse* 1990; *Richie Rich* 1994

Larsen, Ham *The Adventures of the Wilderness Family* 1975; *Mountain Family Robinson* 1979

Larsen, Keith (1925–) *War Paint* 1953; *Arrow in the Dust* 1954; *Security Risk* 1954; *Chief Crazy Horse* 1955; *Wichita* 1955; *Last of the Badmen* 1957

Larsen, Thomas Bo (1963–) *Festen* 1998; *Torremolinos 73* 2003

Larson, Christine (1918–1973) *Valley of Fire* 1951; *Last Train from Bombay* 1952

Larson, Darrell (1951–) *Kotch* 1971; *UFOria* 1980; *Brainstorm* 1983; *Mike's Murder* 1984; *City Limits* 1985; *Twice in a Lifetime* 1985; *Eye for an Eye* 1995

Larter, Ali (1976–) *House on Haunted Hill* 1999; *Final Destination* 2000; *American Outlaws* 2001; *Legally Blonde* 2001; *Final Destination 2* 2002; *A Lot like Love* 2005

LaRue, Jack *aka* **La Rue, Jack** (1902–1984) *A Farewell to Arms* 1932; *The Kennel Murder Case* 1933; *The Gang's All Here* 1939; *Follow the Leader* 1944; *Cornered* 1945; *Road to Utopia* 1945; *My Favorite Brunette* 1947; *No Orchids for Miss Blandish* 1948; *For Heaven's Sake* 1950; *Robin and the 7 Hoods* 1964; *The Spy in the Green Hat* 1966

Lasalle, Martin *aka* **Lassalle, Martin** *aka* **Lasalle, Martino** *Pickpocket* 1959; *Alamo Bay* 1985

Lascher, David (1872–) *Victim of Rage* 1994; *White Squall* 1996

Laser, Dieter *The Lost Honour of Katharina Blum* 1975; *Germany in Autumn* 1978; *The Man Inside* 1990

Lassander, Dagmar (1943–) *Hatchet for the Honeymoon* 1969; *The Black Cat* 1981

Lasser, Louise (1939–) *What's Up, Tiger Lily?* 1966; *Bananas* 1971; *Such Good Friends* 1971; *Everything You Always Wanted to Know about Sex ... but Were Afraid to Ask* 1972; *Isn't It Shocking?* 1973; *Slither* 1973; *In God We Trust* 1980; *Crimewave* 1985; *Surrender* 1987; *Rude Awakening* 1989; *Sing* 1989; *Frankenhooker* 1990; *Happiness* 1998; *Requiem for a Dream* 2000

Lassez, Sarah *Roosters* 1993; *The Blackout* 1997; *In Pursuit* 2000

Lassgård, Rolf (1955–) *Under the Sun* 1998; *The Magnetist's Fifth Winter* 1999

Lassick, Sydney *aka* **Lassick, Sidney** (1922–2003) *One Flew over the Cuckoo's Nest* 1975; *The Billion Dollar Hobo* 1978; *Alligator* 1980; *Ratboy* 1986; *Cool as Ice* 1991; *Shakes the Clown* 1991; *Deep Cover* 1992

Latell, Lyle (1905–1967) *Dick Tracy* 1945; *Dick Tracy vs Cueball* 1946; *Dick Tracy Meets Gruesome* 1947; *Dick Tracy's Dilemma* 1947

Latessa, Dick *Shattered Trust* 1993; *Stigmata* 1999

Latham, Louise *Marnie* 1964; *Adam at 6 AM* 1970; *The Harness* 1971; *White Lightning* 1973; *The Sugarland Express* 1974; *Mass Appeal* 1984; *Crazy from the Heart* 1991; *Paradise* 1991; *Love Field* 1992

Lathan, Sanaa (1971–) *The Best Man* 1999; *Disappearing Acts* 2000; *Love & Basketball* 2000; *Brown Sugar* 2002; *Out of Time* 2003; *AVP: Alien vs Predator* 2004

Lathouris, Nico *Death in Brunswick* 1990; *The Heartbreak Kid* 1993

Latimer, Hugh (1913–) *Someone at the Door* 1950; *Ghost Ship* 1952; *Counterspy* 1953; *Rogue's Yarn* 1956; *The Strange World of Planet X* 1957; *The Gentle Trap* 1960

Latimer, Louise (1916–) *Murder on a Bridle Path* 1936; *The Plot Thickens* 1936; *California Straight Ahead* 1937

Latimore, Frank (1925–1998) *In the Meantime, Darling* 1944; *The Dolly Sisters* 1945; *13 Rue Madeleine* 1946; *Three Little Girls in Blue* 1946; *Black Magic* 1949; *Plein Soleil* 1960; *The Sergeant* 1968; *Patton* 1970

Lattanzi, Matt (1959–) *Rich and Famous* 1981; *My Tutor* 1983; *Blueberry Hill* 1988

Lau, Andy (1961–) *As Tears Go By* 1988; *Fulltime Killer* 2002; *Infernal Affairs* 2002; *Infernal Affairs 3* 2003; *House of Flying Daggers* 2004

Lau, Carina (1964–) *Days of Being Wild* 1990; *The Actress* 1992; *Flowers of Shanghai* 1998; *Infernal Affairs II* 2003; *2046* 2004

Lau Ching Wan (1964–) *I've Got You, Babe* 1994; *Black Mask* 1996; *Full Alert* 1997

Lau Siu-Ming *Eat a Bowl of Tea* 1989; *Kitchen* 1997

Lauchlan, Agnes (1905–1993) *Oh, Mr Porter!* 1937; *The Spy in Black* 1939

Laudenbach, Philippe *Confidentially Yours* 1983; *Four Adventures of Reinette and Mirabelle* 1986

Lauer, Andrew *aka* **Lauer, Andy** (1965–) *Never on Tuesday* 1988; *Screamers* 1995

Laughlin, John *Crimes of Passion* 1984; *Footloose* 1984; *Midnight Crossing* 1988; *Improper Conduct* 1994; *American Yakuza 2: Back to Back* 1996

Laughlin, Teresa *The Trial of Billy Jack* 1974; *Billy Jack Goes to Washington* 1977

Laughlin, Tom (1931–) *These Wilder Years* 1956; *The Delinquents* 1957; *Senior Prom* 1958; *Gidget* 1959; *Born Losers* 1967; *Billy Jack* 1971; *The Trial of Billy Jack* 1974; *The Master Gunfighter* 1975; *Billy Jack Goes to Washington* 1977

Laughton, Charles (1899–1962) *Piccadilly* 1929; *Devil and the Deep* 1932; *If I Had a Million* 1932; *Island of Lost Souls* 1932; *The Old Dark House* 1932; *Payment Deferred* 1932; *The Sign of the Cross* 1932; *The Private Life of Henry VIII* 1933; *White Woman* 1933; *The Barretts of Wimpole Street* 1934; *Les Misérables* 1935; *Mutiny on the Bounty* 1935; *Ruggles of Red Gap* 1935; *Rembrandt* 1936; *St Martin's Lane* 1938; *Vessel of Wrath* 1938; *The Hunchback of Notre Dame* 1939; *Jamaica Inn* 1939; *They Knew What They Wanted* 1940; *It Started with Eve* 1941; *Stand by for Action* 1942; *Tales of Manhattan* 1942; *The Tuttles of Tahiti* 1942; *Forever and a Day* 1943; *The Man from Down Under* 1943; *This Land Is Mine* 1943; *The Canterville Ghost* 1944; *The Suspect* 1944; *Captain Kidd* 1945; *Because of Him* 1946; *The Paradine Case* 1947; *Arch of Triumph* 1948; *The Big Clock* 1948; *The Girl from Manhattan* 1948; *The Bribe* 1949; *The Man on the Eiffel Tower* 1949; *The Blue Veil* 1951; *The Strange Door* 1951; *Abbott and Costello Meet Captain Kidd* 1952; *O Henry's Full House* 1952; *Hobson's Choice* 1953; *Salome* 1953; *Young Bess* 1953; *Witness for the Prosecution* 1957; *Spartacus* 1960; *Under Ten Flags* 1960; *Advise and Consent* 1962

Launer, S John (1919–) *Creature with the Atom Brain* 1955; *The Werewolf* 1956; *Marnie* 1964

Lauper, Cyndi (1953–) *Vibes* 1988; *Off and Running* 1991; *Life with Mikey* 1993; *The Opportunists* 2000

Laurance, Matthew (1950–) *Eddie and the Cruisers* 1983; *Eddie and the Cruisers II: Eddie Lives!* 1989

Laurance, Mitchell (1950–) *A Conspiracy of Love* 1987; *Stepfather II* 1989; *The Runestone* 1991; *The Hand That Rocks the Cradle* 1992

Laure, Carole (1951–) *Get out Your Handkerchiefs* 1977; *Maria Chapdelaine* 1982; *Heartbreakers* 1984

Laure, Odette (1917–2004) *Mitsou* 1957; *These Foolish Things* 1990

Laurel, Stan *aka* **Laurel, Stanley** (1890–1965) *The Two Tars* 1928; *Big Business* 1929; *Hollywood Revue* 1929; *Men o' War* 1929; *Perfect Day* 1929; *The Rogue Song* 1930; *Pardon Us* 1931; *County Hospital* 1932; *The Music Box* 1932; *Pack Up Your Troubles* 1932; *Scram!* 1932; *Their First Mistake* 1932; *Towed in a Hole* 1932; *Bogus Bandits* 1933; *Sons of the Desert* 1933; *Twice Two* 1933; *Babes in Toyland* 1934; *Hollywood Party* 1934; *Oliver the Eighth* 1934; *Them Thar Hills!* 1934; *Tit for Tat* 1934; *Bonnie Scotland* 1935; *Thicker than Water* 1935; *The Bohemian Girl* 1936; *Our Relations* 1936; *Pick a Star* 1937; *Way Out West* 1937; *Blockheads* 1938; *Swiss Miss* 1938; *The Flying Deuces* 1939; *A Chump at Oxford* 1940; *Saps at Sea* 1940; *Great Guns* 1941; *A-Haunting We Will Go* 1942; *The Dancing Masters* 1943; *Jitterbugs* 1943; *The Big Noise* 1944; *Nothing but Trouble* 1944; *The Bullfighters* 1945; *Utopia* 1950; *The Crazy World of Laurel and Hardy* 1964; *Laurel and Hardy's Laughing 20s* 1965; *4 Clowns* 1970

Lauren, Rod (1940–) *Black Zoo* 1963; *The Crawling Hand* 1963; *Once Before I Die* 1965

Lauren, Tammy (1968–) *The Last Flight of Noah's Ark* 1980; *Wishmaster* 1997

Lauren, Veronica (1980–) *Homeward Bound: the Incredible Journey* 1993; *Homeward Bound II: Lost in San Francisco* 1996

Laurence, Ashley *aka* **Lauren, Ashley** (1971–) *Hellraiser* 1987; *Hellbound: Hellraiser II* 1988; *A Murder of Crows* 1998; *Warlock III: the End of Innocence* 1999

Laurence (1), Michael *Piccadilly Incident* 1946; *Elizabeth of Ladymead* 1948; *Return to Glennascaul* 1951; *Othello* 1952

Laurenson, James (1940–) *Assault* 1970; *The Monster Club* 1980; *Pink Floyd – The Wall* 1982; *Heartbreakers* 1984; *Dead Bolt Dead* 1999; *AfterLife* 2003

Lauria, Dan (1947–) *Stakeout* 1987; *No One Could Protect Her* 1996; *Dogwatch* 1997; *Hangman* 2000

Laurie, Hugh (1959–) *Strapless* 1988; *Peter's Friends* 1992; *A Pin for the Butterfly* 1994; *Sense and Sensibility* 1995; *101 Dalmatians* 1996; *The Borrowers* 1997; *Cousin Bette* 1997; *The Man in the Iron Mask* 1997; *Maybe Baby* 1999; *Stuart Little* 1999; *Girl from Rio* 2001; *Stuart Little 2* 2002; *Flight of the Phoenix* 2004; *Valiant* 2005

Laurie, John (1897–1980) *Juno and the Paycock* 1930; *The 39 Steps* 1935; *As You Like It* 1936; *The Edge of the World* 1937; *Convoy* 1940; *The Ghost of St Michael's* 1941; *The Lamp Still Burns* 1943; *The Way Ahead* 1944; *I Know Where I'm Going!* 1945; *School for Secrets* 1946; *The Brothers* 1947; *Jassy* 1947; *Mine Own Executioner* 1947; *Bonnie Prince Charlie* 1948; *Floodtide* 1949; *Happy Go Lovely* 1950; *No Trace* 1950; *Pandora and the Flying Dutchman* 1950; *Treasure Island* 1950; *Laughter in Paradise* 1951; *Island of Desire* 1952; *Tread Softly* 1952; *Campbell's Kingdom* 1957; *Kidnapped* 1960; *The Siege of the Saxons* 1963; *The Reptile* 1966; *Dad's Army* 1971

Laurie, Piper (1932–) *Francis Goes to the Races* 1951; *The Prince Who Was a Thief* 1951; *Has Anybody Seen My Gal?* 1952; *No Room for the Groom* 1952; *Son of Ali Baba* 1952; *The Golden Blade* 1953; *The Mississippi Gambler* 1953; *Dangerous Mission* 1954; *Dawn at Socorro* 1954; *Johnny Dark* 1954; *Ain't Misbehavin'* 1955; *Smoke Signal* 1955; *Until They Sail* 1957; *The Hustler* 1961; *Carrie* 1976; *Ruby* 1977; *Tim* 1979; *Return to Oz* 1985; *Children of a Lesser God* 1986; *Promise* 1986; *Distortions* 1987; *Appointment with Death* 1988; *Tiger Warsaw* 1988; *Dream a Little Dream* 1989; *Other People's Money* 1991; *Rich in Love* 1992; *Trauma* 1993; *Wrestling Ernest Hemingway* 1993; *The Crossing Guard* 1995; *The Grass Harp* 1995; *In the Blink of an Eye* 1996; *The Faculty* 1998; *Inherit the Wind* 1999; *Palmer's Pick-Up* 1999; *Possessed* 2000

Laurier, Charlotte (1966–) *Une Histoire Inventée* 1990; *2 Seconds* 1998

Lauter, Ed (1940–) *Executive Action* 1973; *The Last American Hero* 1973; *The Mean Machine* 1974; *Breakheart Pass* 1976; *Family Plot* 1976; *King Kong* 1976; *The Chicken Chronicles* 1977; *Magic* 1978; *The Jericho Mile* 1979; *The Amateur* 1981; *Eureka* 1982; *Cujo* 1983; *Finders Keepers* 1984; *Lassiter* 1984; *Death Wish 3* 1985; *3:15* 1986; *Youngblood* 1986; *Gleaming the Cube* 1988; *Rocketeer* 1991; *School Ties* 1992; *Trial by Jury* 1994; *Wagons East!* 1994; *Dollar for the Dead* 1998; *Farewell, My Love* 1999; *Seabiscuit* 2003

Lauter, Harry (1914–1990) *Valley of Fire* 1951; *Return to Treasure Island* 1954; *The Werewolf* 1956; *Hellcats of the Navy* 1957; *The Cry Baby Killer* 1958; *Ambush Bay* 1966

Lauterbach, Heiner (1953–) *Men...* 1985; *A Girl Called Rosemarie* 1996

Lavanant, Dominique (1944–) *Love Songs* 1984; *Rendez-vous* 1985; *3 Men and a Cradle* 1985; *Kamikaze* 1986

Lavant, Denis (1961–) *The Night Is Young* 1986; *Les Amants du Pont-Neuf* 1990; *Beau Travail* 1999; *Married/Unmarried* 2001

Lavender, Ian (1946–) *Dad's Army* 1971; *Adventures of a Taxi*

Driver 1975; *Adventures of a Private Eye* 1977
Laverick, June (1931–) *It Happened in Rome* 1956; *The Duke Wore Jeans* 1958; *The Gypsy and the Gentleman* 1958; *Son of Robin Hood* 1958; *The Flesh and the Fiends* 1959; *Follow a Star* 1959
Lavi, Daliah (1940–) *The Return of Dr Mabuse* 1961; *Violent Summer* 1961; *Lord Jim* 1965; *Ten Little Indians* 1965; *The Silencers* 1966; *The Spy with a Cold Nose* 1966; *Nobody Runs Forever* 1968; *Some Girls Do* 1969; *Catlow* 1971
Lavia, Gabriele (1942–) *Deep Red* 1975; *The Legend of 1900* 1999
Lavin, Linda (1937–) *Lena: My 100 Children* 1987; *I Want to Go Home* 1989
Lavoine, Marc *L'Enfer* 1994; *The Good Thief* 2002
LaVorgna, Adam (1981–) *The Beautician and the Beast* 1997; *I'll Be Home for Christmas* 1998
Law, John Phillip (1937–) *Barbarella* 1967; *Danger: Diabolik* 1967; *Death Rides a Horse* 1967; *Hurry Sundown* 1967; *The Sergeant* 1968; *Skidoo* 1968; *The Hawaiians* 1970; *The Love Machine* 1971; *Von Richthofen and Brown* 1971; *The Golden Voyage of Sinbad* 1973; *Open Season* 1974; *The Cassandra Crossing* 1976; *Attack Force Z* 1981; *Tarzan, the Ape Man* 1981; *A Case of Honor* 1988
Law, Jude (1972–) *Shopping* 1993; *Bent* 1996; *Gattaca* 1997; *I Love You, I Love You Not* 1997; *Midnight in the Garden of Good and Evil* 1997; *Wilde* 1997; *Final Cut* 1998; *Music from Another Room* 1998; *The Wisdom of Crocodiles* 1998; *eXistenZ* 1999; *The Talented Mr Ripley* 1999; *Love, Honour and Obey* 2000; *AI: Artificial Intelligence* 2001; *Enemy at the Gates* 2001; *Road to Perdition* 2002; *Cold Mountain* 2003; *Alfie* 2004; *The Aviator* 2004; *Closer* 2004; *I ❤ Huckabees* 2004; *Lemony Snicket's A Series of Unfortunate Events* 2004; *Sky Captain and the World of Tomorrow* 2004
Law, Phyllida (1932–) *Tree of Hands* 1988; *Peter's Friends* 1992; *Much Ado about Nothing* 1993; *Before the Rain* 1994; *Emma* 1996; *The Winter Guest* 1996; *Anna Karenina* 1997; *The Lost Lover* 1999; *Mad Cows* 1999; *Milk* 1999; *The Time Machine* 2002; *Two Men Went to War* 2002; *I'll Be There* 2003; *Tooth* 2003
Lawford, Betty (1910–1960) *Love before Breakfast* 1936; *Criminal Lawyer* 1937; *The Devil Thumbs a Ride* 1947
Lawford, Christopher (1955–) *Blankman* 1994; *Kiss Me, Guido* 1997
Lawford, Peter (1923–1984) *A Yank at Eton* 1942; *Paris after Dark* 1943; *Pilot #5* 1943; *The Sky's the Limit* 1943; *The Canterville Ghost* 1944; *The White Cliffs of Dover* 1944; *The Picture of Dorian Gray* 1945; *Son of Lassie* 1945; *Cluny Brown* 1946; *My Brother Talks to Horses* 1946; *Two Sisters from Boston* 1946; *Good News* 1947; *It Happened in Brooklyn* 1947; *Easter Parade* 1948; *Julia Misbehaves* 1948; *On an Island with You* 1948; *Little Women* 1949; *The Red Danube* 1949; *Please Believe Me* 1950; *Royal Wedding* 1951; *The Hour of 13* 1952; *Kangaroo* 1952; *It Should Happen to You* 1954; *Never So Few* 1959; *Exodus* 1960; *Ocean's Eleven* 1960; *Pepe* 1960; *Advise and Consent* 1962; *The Longest Day* 1962; *Sergeants 3* 1962; *Dead Ringer* 1964; *Sylvia* 1964; *Harlow* 1965; *A Man Called Adam* 1966; *The Oscar* 1966; *Dead Run* 1967; *How I Spent My Summer Vacation* 1967; *Buona Sera, Mrs Campbell* 1968; *Salt & Pepper* 1968; *Skidoo* 1968; *The April Fools* 1969; *Hook, Line and Sinker* 1969; *One More Time* 1970; *They Only Kill Their Masters* 1972; *Rosebud* 1975; *Body and Soul* 1981; *Where Is Parsifal?* 1983
Lawless, Lucy (1968–) *EuroTrip* 2004; *Boogeyman* 2005
Lawley, Yvonne (1914–1999) *Death in Brunswick* 1990; *Ruby and Rata* 1990
Lawlor, Sean *Reefer and the Model* 1988; *The Disappearance of Finbar* 1996
Lawrance, Jody *aka* **Lawrence, Jody** (1930–1986) *Ten Tall Men* 1951; *All Ashore* 1953; *Hot Spell* 1958; *Stagecoach to Dancer's Rock* 1962
Lawrence, Andre (1939–) *The Pleasure Seekers* 1964; *And Hope to Die* 1972
Lawrence, Barbara (1928–) *Margie* 1946; *Give My Regards to Broadway* 1948; *The Street with No Name* 1948; *Unfaithfully Yours* 1948; *You Were Meant for Me* 1948; *A Letter to Three Wives* 1949; *Mother Is a Freshman* 1949; *Thieves' Highway* 1949; *Two Tickets to Broadway* 1951; *Arena* 1953; *Her Twelve Men* 1954; *Oklahoma!* 1955; *Kronos* 1957; *Man in the Shadow* 1957
Lawrence, Bruno (1941–1995) *Smash Palace* 1981; *Treasure of the Yankee Zephyr* 1981; *Battletruck* 1982; *Utu* 1983; *The Quiet Earth* 1985; *Grievous Bodily Harm* 1987; *Rikky and Pete* 1988; *Spotswood* 1991; *Jack Be Nimble* 1992
Lawrence, David *aka* **Lawrence, Dave** *Fubar* 2002; *It's All Gone Pete Tong* 2004
Lawrence, Delphi (1926–) *Blood Orange* 1953; *Double Cross* 1955; *The Gold Express* 1955; *The Feminine Touch* 1956; *Just My Luck* 1957; *Stranger's Meeting* 1957; *Son of Robin Hood* 1958; *Too Many Crooks* 1958; *The Man Who Could Cheat Death* 1959; *The Last Challenge* 1967
Lawrence, Elizabeth (1922–2000) *We're No Angels* 1989; *Sleeping with the Enemy* 1991
Lawrence, Gertrude (1898–1952) *Men Are Not Gods* 1936; *Rembrandt* 1936; *Stage Door Canteen* 1943; *The Glass Menagerie* 1950
Lawrence, Jim *The High Country* 1981; *Fubar* 2002
Lawrence, Joey (1976–) *Summer Rental* 1985; *Oliver & Company* 1988; *Pulse* 1988; *Chains of Gold* 1989
Lawrence, Josie (1959–) *Riders of the Storm* 1986; *Enchanted April* 1991
Lawrence (1), Marc (1910–) *Blind Alley* 1939; *The Housekeeper's Daughter* 1939; *Sergeant Madden* 1939; *Johnny Apollo* 1940; *Hold That Ghost* 1941; *Hit the Ice* 1943; *Dillinger* 1945; *Key Largo* 1948; *Calamity Jane and Sam Bass* 1949; *Jigsaw* 1949; *The Asphalt Jungle* 1950; *The Black Hand* 1950; *Johnny Tiger* 1966; *The Man with the Golden Gun* 1974; *Marathon Man* 1976; *Goin' Coconuts* 1978; *Hot Stuff* 1979; *Ruby* 1992; *From Dusk till Dawn* 1995
Lawrence, Martin (1965–) *House Party* 1990; *House Party 2* 1991; *Talkin' Dirty after Dark* 1991; *Boomerang* 1992; *Bad Boys* 1995; *A Thin Line between Love and Hate* 1996; *Nothing to Lose* 1997; *Blue Streak* 1999; *Life* 1999; *Big Momma's House* 2000; *Black Knight* 2001; *What's the Worst That Could Happen?* 2001; *National Security* 2002; *Bad Boys II* 2003
Lawrence, Matthew (1980–) *Pulse* 1988; *Danielle Steel's Daddy* 1991; *Tales from the Darkside: the Movie* 1991; *Mrs Doubtfire* 1993; *The Hot Chick* 2002
Lawrence, Peter Lee (1943–1973) *Killer Calibre 32* 1967; *Black Beauty* 1971
Lawrence, Rosina (1912–1997) *General Spanky* 1936; *Pick a Star* 1937; *Way Out West* 1937
Lawrence, Sharon (1963–) *Stolen Youth* 1996; *The Only Thrill* 1997; *Gossip* 1999
Lawrence, Sheldon *The Crooked Sky* 1957; *The Man without a Body* 1957; *Mark of the Phoenix* 1957; *The Pursuers* 1961
Lawrence, Stephanie (1949–2000) *Buster* 1988; *The Phantom of the Opera* 1989
Lawrence, Steve (1935–) *The Lonely Guy* 1984; *The Yards* 2000
Laws, Sam (1924–1990) *Hit Man* 1972; *Truck Turner* 1974; *White Line Fever* 1975
Lawson, Bianca (1979–) *Save the Last Dance* 2000; *Bones* 2001; *Breakin' All the Rules* 2004
Lawson, Denis (1947–) *Providence* 1977; *Local Hero* 1983; *The Chain* 1984
Lawson, Leigh (1945–) *Brother Sun, Sister Moon* 1972; *Ghost Story* 1974; *Percy's Progress* 1974; *Love among the Ruins* 1975; *The Devil's Advocate* 1977; *Tess* 1979; *Sword of the Valiant* 1984; *Madame Sousatzka* 1988; *Out of Depth* 1998
Lawson, Linda (1936–) *Night Tide* 1961; *Apache Rifles* 1964; *Sometimes a Great Notion* 1971
Lawson, Mary (1911–1941) *D'Ye Ken John Peel?* 1934; *A Fire Has Been Arranged* 1935; *Cotton Queen* 1937
Lawson, Priscilla (1914–1958) *Flash Gordon* 1936; *The Girl of the Golden West* 1938
Lawson, Richard (1947–) *Scream Blacula Scream* 1973; *Sugar Hill* 1974; *The Jericho Mile* 1979; *The Main Event* 1979; *Stick* 1985; *How Stella Got Her Groove Back* 1998
Lawson, Sarah (1928–) *You Know What Sailors Are* 1954; *The Blue Peter* 1955; *It's Never Too Late* 1956; *The World Ten Times Over* 1963; *Night of the Big Heat* 1967; *The Devil Rides Out* 1968
Lawson, Shannon *Butterbox Babies* 1995; *The War between Us* 1995; *Forever Mine* 1999
Lawson, Wilfrid (1900–1966) *Pygmalion* 1938; *The First Rebel* 1939; *Stolen Life* 1939; *The Long Voyage Home* 1940; *Pastor Hall* 1940; *Danny Boy* 1941; *Jeannie* 1941; *The Great Mr Handel* 1942; *The Night Has Eyes* 1942; *Fanny by Gaslight* 1944; *The Prisoner* 1955; *Hell Drivers* 1957; *Postman's Knock* 1961; *The Wrong Box* 1966; *The Viking Queen* 1967
Lawton, Frank (1904–1969) *The Skin Game* 1931; *Friday the Thirteenth* 1933; *One More River* 1934; *David Copperfield* 1935; *The Devil-Doll* 1936; *The Invisible Ray* 1936; *The Mill on the Floss* 1937; *The Four Just Men* 1939; *Went the Day Well?* 1942; *The Winslow Boy* 1948; *Rough Shoot* 1952; *Double Cross* 1955
Laydu, Claude (1927–) *Diary of a Country Priest* 1950; *Nous Sommes Tous des Assassins* 1952
Laye, Dilys (1934–) *Please Turn Over* 1960; *Carry On Cruising* 1962; *Carry On Spying* 1964
Laye, Evelyn (1900–1996) *One Heavenly Night* 1931; *Evensong* 1934; *Theatre of Death* 1966; *Say Hello to Yesterday* 1971
Layton, George (1943–) *Confessions of a Driving Instructor* 1976; *Stand Up Virgin Soldiers* 1977
Lazar, Veronica *aka* **Lazare, Veronica** *La Luna* 1979; *Identification of a Woman* 1982; *Berlin Jerusalem* 1989
Lazard, Justin (1967–) *Born to Ride* 1991; *Species II* 1998; *The Brutal Truth* 1999; *Universal Soldier – the Return* 1999
Lazenby, George (1939–) *On Her Majesty's Secret Service* 1969; *The Man from Hong Kong* 1975; *The Kentucky Fried Movie* 1977; *Saint Jack* 1979; *Gettysburg* 1993; *Four Dogs Playing Poker* 1999
Le Beau, Bettine (1936–) *Village of Daughters* 1961; *The Best of Benny Hill* 1974
Le Besco, Isild *Girls Can't Swim* 1999; *Roberto Succo* 2000
Le Bihan, Samuel *aka* **LeBihan, Samuel** (1965–) *Three Colours Red* 1994; *Venus Beauty Institute* 1998; *Brotherhood of the Wolf* 2001; *He Loves Me... He Loves Me Not* 2002; *La Mentale* 2002
Le Clezio, Odile *Young Einstein* 1988; *Backsliding* 1991
Le Coq, Bernard (1950–) *Burnt Barns* 1973; *Van Gogh* 1991; *The School of Flesh* 1998; *The Flower of Evil* 2002; *The Bridesmaid* 2004
Le Mat, Paul (1952–) *American Graffiti* 1973; *Aloha, Bobby and Rose* 1975; *Citizens Band* 1977; *More American Graffiti* 1979; *Melvin and Howard* 1980; *Death Valley* 1982; *Jimmy the Kid* 1982; *PK and the Kid* 1982; *Strange Invaders* 1983; *The Burning Bed* 1984; *Hanoi Hilton* 1987; *Private Investigations* 1987; *Easy Wheels* 1989; *Puppet Master* 1989; *Wishman* 1991
Le Mesurier, John (1912–1983) *The Blue Parrot* 1953; *Police Dog* 1955; *Brothers in Law* 1956; *Happy Is the Bride* 1957; *High Flight* 1957; *The Moonraker* 1957; *Blood of the Vampire* 1958; *Carlton-Browne of the FO* 1958; *I Was Monty's Double* 1958; *Jack the Ripper* 1958; *Law and Disorder* 1958; *Too Many Crooks* 1958; *Follow a Star* 1959; *The Hound of the Baskervilles* 1959; *I'm All Right Jack* 1959; *The Bulldog Breed* 1960; *The Day They Robbed the Bank of England* 1960; *Let's Get Married* 1960; *Never Let Go* 1960; *The Night We Got the Bird* 1960; *The Rebel* 1960; *School for Scoundrels* 1960; *Don't Bother to Knock* 1961; *Invasion Quartet* 1961; *Only Two Can Play* 1961; *Village of Daughters* 1961; *Jigsaw* 1962; *The Main Attraction* 1962; *The Punch and Judy Man* 1962; *Waltz of the Toreadors* 1962; *We Joined the Navy* 1962; *The Wrong Arm of the Law* 1962; *Hot Enough for June* 1963; *In the Cool of the Day* 1963; *The Mouse on the Moon* 1963; *The Pink Panther* 1963; *The Moon-Spinners* 1964; *City under the Sea* 1965; *The Early Bird* 1965; *Masquerade* 1965; *Where the Spies Are* 1965; *Eye of the Devil* 1966; *Finders Keepers* 1966; *Our Man in Marrakesh* 1966; *The Sandwich Man* 1966; *Mister Ten Per Cent* 1967; *The 25th Hour* 1967; *Salt & Pepper* 1968; *The Italian Job* 1969; *Midas Run* 1969; *Doctor in Trouble* 1970; *On a Clear Day You Can See Forever* 1970; *Dad's Army* 1971; *Barry McKenzie Holds His Own* 1974; *Brief Encounter* 1974; *Confessions of a Window Cleaner* 1974; *The Adventure of Sherlock Holmes' Smarter Brother* 1975; *Jabberwocky* 1977; *Stand Up Virgin Soldiers* 1977; *Rosie Dixon: Night Nurse* 1978; *The Spaceman and King Arthur* 1979; *The Fiendish Plot of Dr Fu Manchu* 1980
Le Poulain, Jean (1924–1988) *Le Bossu* 1959; *The Sign of Leo* 1959
Le Prevost, Nicholas *The Girl in a Swing* 1988; *Letters from the East* 1995
Le Saché, Bernadette *Le Cheval d'Orgeuil* 1980; *The Vanishing* 1988
Le Vaillant, Nigel (1958–) *Seven Minutes* 1989; *Tom's Midnight Garden* 1998
Lea, Nicholas (1962–) *The Raffle* 1994; *Kiss Tomorrow Goodbye* 2000
Lea, Ron *The Gunrunner* 1984; *Criminal Law* 1988; *Clearcut* 1992
Leach, Rosemary (1925–) *That'll Be the Day* 1973; *Brief Encounter* 1974; *A Room with a View* 1985; *Turtle Diary* 1985; *The Children* 1990; *The Hawk* 1992; *The Mystery of Edwin Drood* 1993
Leachman, Cloris (1926–) *Kiss Me Deadly* 1955; *The Rack* 1956; *Butch Cassidy and the Sundance Kid* 1969; *The People Next Door* 1970; *WUSA* 1970; *The Last Picture Show* 1971; *Charley and the Angel* 1973; *Dillinger* 1973; *Happy Mother's Day... Love, George* 1973; *Daisy Miller* 1974; *Young Frankenstein* 1974; *Crazy Mama* 1975; *High Anxiety* 1977; *The Mouse and His Child* 1977; *Hill's Angels* 1979; *SOS Titanic* 1979; *Scavenger Hunt* 1979; *Foolin' Around* 1980; *Herbie Goes Bananas* 1980; *History of the World Part 1* 1981; *My Little Pony* 1986; *Shadow Play* 1986; *Walk like a Man* 1987; *Prancer* 1989; *Danielle Steel's Fine Things* 1990; *Love Hurts* 1990; *Texasville* 1990; *The Beverly Hillbillies* 1993; *Stanley's Magic Garden* 1994; *Beavis and Butt-head Do America* 1996; *Never Too Late* 1996; *The Iron Giant* 1999; *Music of the Heart* 1999; *Alex & Emma* 2003; *Spanglish* 2004
Leadbitter, Bill *Knights and Emeralds* 1986; *Tai-Pan* 1986
Leak, Jennifer *Yours, Mine and Ours* 1968; *Eye of the Cat* 1969
Learned, Michael (1939–) *Touched by Love* 1979; *The Parade* 1984; *Power* 1986; *Murder in New Hampshire* 1991; *Dragon: the Bruce Lee Story* 1993
Leary, Denis (1957–) *Demolition Man* 1993; *Judgment Night* 1993; *The Sandlot* 1993; *Who's the Man?* 1993; *Gunmen* 1994; *Hostile Hostages* 1994; *The Neon Bible* 1995; *Operation Dumbo Drop* 1995; *Stolen Hearts* 1996; *Underworld* 1996; *Love Walked In* 1997; *The Matchmaker* 1997; *Noose* 1997; *The Real Blonde* 1997; *Subway Stories: Tales from the Underground* 1997; *Suicide Kings* 1997; *Wag the Dog* 1997; *A Bug's Life* 1998; *Small Soldiers* 1998; *Wide Awake* 1998; *Jesus' Son* 1999; *The Thomas Crown Affair* 1999; *True Crime* 1999; *Company Man* 2000; *Dawg* 2001; *Double Whammy* 2001; *Ice Age* 2002; *The Secret Lives of Dentists* 2002
Leary, Timothy (1920–1996) *Ted & Venus* 1991; *Roadside Prophets* 1992
Lease, Rex (1901–1966) *The Younger Generation* 1929; *Aces and Eights* 1936; *Law and Order* 1936
Léaud, Jean-Pierre (1944–) *The 400 Blows* 1959; *Le Testament d'Orphée* 1960; *Love at Twenty* 1962; *Pierrot le Fou* 1965; *Made in USA* 1966; *Masculine Feminine* 1966; *La Chinoise* 1967; *The Oldest Profession* 1967; *Weekend* 1967; *Le Gai Savoir* 1968; *Stolen Kisses* 1968; *Pigsty* 1969; *Bed and Board* 1970; *Anne and Muriel* 1971; *Last Tango in Paris* 1972; *Day for Night* 1973; *La Maman et la Putain* 1973; *Out 1: Spectre* 1973; *Love on the Run* 1979; *Detective* 1985; *Grandeur et Décadence d'un Petit Commerce de Cinéma* 1986; *Treasure Island* 1986; *I Hired a Contract Killer* 1990; *Irma Vep* 1996; *Mon Homme* 1996; *Pour Rire!* 1996; *The Pornographer* 2001; *What Time Is It There?* 2001
Leaver, Philip (1904–) *Dr Morelle – the Case of the Missing Heiress* 1949; *Spaceways* 1953
Lebeau, Madeleine (1921–) *Casablanca* 1942; *Paris after Dark* 1943; *Cage of Gold* 1950; *Une Parisienne* 1957
Lebedeff, Ivan (1899–1953) *Bachelor Apartment* 1931; *Blonde Bombshell* 1933; *Goin' to Town* 1935; *Love on the Run* 1936; *Angel* 1937; *History Is Made at Night* 1937
LeBlanc, Matt (1967–) *Killing Box* 1993; *Lookin' Italian* 1994; *Reform School Girl* 1994; *Ed* 1996; *Lost in Space* 1998; *Charlie's Angels* 2000; *Charlie's Angels: Full Throttle* 2003
LeBrock, Kelly (1960–) *The Woman in Red* 1984; *Weird Science* 1985; *Hard to Kill* 1989; *Wrongfully Accused* 1998
Leclerc, Ginette (1912–1992) *The Baker's Wife* 1938; *The Raven* 1943; *Goto, l'Ile d'Amour* 1968; *Popsy-Pop* 1970

Ledebur, Friedrich (1900–1986) *Moby Dick* 1956; *The 27th Day* 1957; *The Christmas Tree* 1969
Leder, Erwin *Das Boot* 1981; *Underworld* 2003
Lederer, Francis *aka* **Lederer, Franz** (1899–2000) *Pandora's Box* 1929; *The Wonderful Lie of Nina Petrovna* 1929; *Romance in Manhattan* 1934; *The Gay Deception* 1935; *One Rainy Afternoon* 1936; *Confessions of a Nazi Spy* 1939; *Midnight* 1939; *The Man I Married* 1940; *Diary of a Chambermaid* 1946; *A Woman of Distinction* 1950; *The Ambassador's Daughter* 1956; *Lisbon* 1956; *Maracaibo* 1958; *The Return of Dracula* 1958; *Terror Is a Man* 1959
Lederman, Caz (1952–) *Tail of a Tiger* 1984; *Malpractice* 1989; *Deadly* 1991; *Fatal Bond* 1991
Ledger, Heath (1979–) *Blackrock* 1997; *10 Things I Hate about You* 1999; *Two Hands* 1999; *The Patriot* 2000; *A Knight's Tale* 2001; *Monster's Ball* 2001; *The Four Feathers* 2002; *The Sin Eater* 2002; *Ned Kelly* 2003; *Lords of Dogtown* 2005
Ledoux, Fernand (1897–1993) *La Bête Humaine* 1938; *Volpone* 1941; *Les Visiteurs du Soir* 1942; *Les Misérables* 1957; *The Magic Donkey* 1970; *To Each His Own Hell* 1977
Ledoyen, Virginie (1976–) *L'Eau Froide* 1994; *La Cérémonie* 1995; *En Plein Coeur* 1998; *Late August, Early September* 1998; *The Beach* 2000; *8 Women* 2001; *Bon Voyage* 2003
Lee, Anna (1913–2004) *The Camels Are Coming* 1934; *First a Girl* 1935; *The Passing of the Third Floor Back* 1935; *The Man Who Changed His Mind* 1936; *You're In the Army Now* 1936; *King Solomon's Mines* 1937; *The Four Just Men* 1939; *Return to Yesterday* 1940; *Seven Sinners* 1940; *How Green Was My Valley* 1941; *My Life with Caroline* 1941; *The Commandos Strike at Dawn* 1942; *Flying Tigers* 1942; *Hangmen Also Die* 1943; *Summer Storm* 1944; *Bedlam* 1946; *The Ghost and Mrs Muir* 1947; *Gideon's Day* 1958; *The Crimson Kimono* 1959; *The Horse Soldiers* 1959; *Jet over the Atlantic* 1960; *What Ever Happened to Baby Jane?* 1962; *7 Women* 1966; *In like Flint* 1967
Lee, Belinda (1935–1961) *No Smoking* 1954; *The Runaway Bus* 1954; *Footsteps in the Fog* 1955; *Man of the Moment* 1955; *The Big Money* 1956; *Eyewitness* 1956; *The Feminine Touch* 1956; *Who Done It?* 1956; *Dangerous Exile* 1957; *Miracle in Soho* 1957; *Nor the Moon by Night* 1958; *Constantine and the Cross* 1961
Lee, Bernard (1908–1981) *Rhodes of Africa* 1936; *Let George Do It* 1940; *Spare a Copper* 1940; *Elizabeth of Ladymead* 1948; *The Fallen Idol* 1948; *The Blue Lamp* 1949; *The Third Man* 1949; *The Adventurers* 1950; *Cage of Gold* 1950; *Last Holiday* 1950; *Odette* 1950; *Appointment with Venus* 1951; *The Gift Horse* 1951; *Mr Denning Drives North* 1951; *The Yellow Balloon* 1952; *Beat the Devil* 1953; *Sailor of the King* 1953; *Father Brown* 1954; *The Purple Plain* 1954; *Seagulls over Sorrento* 1954; *The Ship That Died of Shame* 1955; *The Battle of the River Plate* 1956; *The Spanish Gardener* 1956; *Across the Bridge* 1957; *High Flight* 1957; *Danger Within* 1958; *Dunkirk* 1958; *The Key* 1958; *The Man Upstairs* 1958; *Nowhere to Go* 1958; *Beyond This Place* 1959; *The Angry Silence* 1960; *Cone of Silence* 1960; *Kidnapped* 1960; *Fury at Smugglers Bay* 1961; *The Secret Partner* 1961; *Whistle down the Wind* 1961; *The Brain* 1962; *Dr No* 1962; *The L-Shaped Room* 1962; *From Russia with Love* 1963; *A Place to Go* 1963; *Ring of Spies* 1963; *Saturday Night Out* 1963; *Two Left Feet* 1963; *Goldfinger* 1964; *The Legend of Young Dick Turpin* 1965; *Thunderball* 1965; *Operation Kid Brother* 1967; *You Only Live Twice* 1967; *Crossplot* 1969; *On Her Majesty's Secret Service* 1969; *The Raging Moon* 1970; *Diamonds Are Forever* 1971; *Dulcima* 1971; *Frankenstein and the Monster from Hell* 1973; *Live and Let Die* 1973; *The Man with the Golden Gun* 1974; *The Spy Who Loved Me* 1977; *Moonraker* 1979
Lee, Brandon (1965–1993) *Showdown in Little Tokyo* 1991; *Rapid Fire* 1992; *The Crow* 1994
Lee, Bruce (1940–1973) *Marlowe* 1969; *The Big Boss* 1971; *Fist of Fury* 1972; *Enter the Dragon* 1973; *The Way of the Dragon* 1973; *Game of Death* 1978
Lee, Canada (1907–1952) *Lifeboat* 1944; *Body and Soul* 1947; *Cry, the Beloved Country* 1951
Lee, Carl (1926–1986) *The Connection* 1961; *The Cool World* 1963; *Superfly* 1972; *Gordon's War* 1973
Lee, Christopher (1922–) *Captain Horatio Hornblower RN* 1951; *Valley of Eagles* 1951; *The Crimson Pirate* 1952; *Storm over the Nile* 1955; *That Lady* 1955; *Fortune Is a Woman* 1956; *Beyond Mombasa* 1957; *Bitter Victory* 1957; *The Curse of Frankenstein* 1957; *A Tale of Two Cities* 1957; *The Traitor* 1957; *The Battle of the V1* 1958; *Horror of Dracula* 1958; *The Hound of the Baskervilles* 1959; *The Man Who Could Cheat Death* 1959; *The Mummy* 1959; *The Treasure of San Teresa* 1959; *Beat Girl* 1960; *The City of the Dead* 1960; *The Hands of Orlac* 1960; *Too Hot to Handle* 1960; *The Two Faces of Dr Jekyll* 1960; *The Pirates of Blood River* 1961; *Taste of Fear* 1961; *Corridors of Blood* 1962; *The Longest Day* 1962; *Sherlock Holmes and the Deadly Necklace* 1962; *The Devil-Ship Pirates* 1964; *Dr Terror's House of Horrors* 1964; *The Gorgon* 1964; *Dracula – Prince of Darkness* 1965; *The Face of Fu Manchu* 1965; *Rasputin, the Mad Monk* 1965; *She* 1965; *The Skull* 1965; *The Brides of Fu Manchu* 1966; *Theatre of Death* 1966; *The Blood Demon* 1967; *Circus of Fear* 1967; *Five Golden Dragons* 1967; *Night of the Big Heat* 1967; *The Vengeance of Fu Manchu* 1967; *The Blood of Fu Manchu* 1968; *The Castle of Fu Manchu* 1968; *Curse of the Crimson Altar* 1968; *The Devil Rides Out* 1968; *Dracula Has Risen from the Grave* 1968; *The Bloody Judge* 1969; *The Magic Christian* 1969; *The Oblong Box* 1969; *Scream and Scream Again* 1969; *Taste the Blood of Dracula* 1969; *Count Dracula* 1970; *One More Time* 1970; *The Private Life of Sherlock Holmes* 1970; *The Scars of Dracula* 1970; *Hannie Caulder* 1971; *The House That Dripped Blood* 1971; *I, Monster* 1971; *The Creeping Flesh* 1972; *Death Line* 1972; *Dracula AD 1972* 1972; *Horror Express* 1972; *Nothing but the Night* 1972; *Dark Places* 1973; *The Satanic Rites of Dracula* 1973; *The Three Musketeers* 1973; *The Wicker Man* 1973; *Diagnosis: Murder* 1974; *The Four Musketeers* 1974; *The Man with the Golden Gun* 1974; *Death in the Sun* 1975; *Killer Force* 1975; *The Keeper* 1976; *To the Devil a Daughter* 1976; *Airport '77* 1977; *End of the World* 1977; *Caravans* 1978; *The Passage* 1978; *Return from Witch Mountain* 1978; *The Silent Flute* 1978; *Arabian Adventure* 1979; *Bear Island* 1979; *Jaguar Lives!* 1979; *1941* 1979; *The Last Unicorn* 1980; *Serial* 1980; *An Eye for an Eye* 1981; *The Salamander* 1981; *House of the Long Shadows* 1983; *The Return of Captain Invincible* 1983; *Howling II: Your Sister Is a Werewolf* 1984; *The Girl* 1986; *Jocks* 1986; *Mio in the Land of Faraway* 1987; *The Return of the Musketeers* 1989; *For Better or for Worse* 1990; *Gremlins 2: the New Batch* 1990; *The Rainbow Thief* 1990; *Treasure Island* 1990; *Curse III: Blood Sacrifice* 1991; *Shogun Warrior* 1991; *Death Train* 1993; *A Feast at Midnight* 1994; *The Funny Man* 1994; *Police Academy: Mission to Moscow* 1994; *The Stupids* 1995; *Talos the Mummy* 1997; *Jinnah* 1998; *The Lord of the Rings: The Fellowship of the Ring* 2001; *The Lord of the Rings: The Two Towers* 2002; *Star Wars Episode II: Attack of the Clones* 2002; *Star Wars Episode III: Revenge of the Sith* 2005
Lee, Cinqué (1968–) *Mystery Train* 1989; *Coffee and Cigarettes* 2003
Lee, Conan *Gymkata* 1985; *New York Cop* 1995
Lee, Cosette (1910–1976) *The First Time* 1969; *Deranged* 1974
Lee, Danny *aka* **Lee Sau Yin** *City on Fire* 1987; *The Killer* 1989
Lee, Davey (1925–) *The Singing Fool* 1928; *Say It with Songs* 1929
Lee, Dorothy (1911–1999) *Rio Rita* 1929; *Laugh and Get Rich* 1931
Lee Eun-joo (1979–2005) *Take Care of My Cat* 2002; *Brotherhood* 2004
Lee, Gwen (1904–1961) *Laugh, Clown, Laugh* 1928; *Free and Easy* 1930
Lee, Gypsy Rose *aka* **Hovick, Louise** (1914–1970) *You Can't Have Everything* 1937; *My Lucky Star* 1938; *Sally, Irene and Mary* 1938; *Stage Door Canteen* 1943; *Belle of the Yukon* 1944; *Screaming Mimi* 1958; *Wind across the Everglades* 1958; *The Stripper* 1963; *The Trouble with Angels* 1966
Lee, Jason (1970–) *Mallrats* 1995; *Chasing Amy* 1996; *Enemy of the State* 1998; *Kissing a Fool* 1998; *Dogma* 1999; *Mumford* 1999; *Almost Famous* 2000; *Heartbreakers* 2001; *Vanilla Sky* 2001; *A Guy Thing* 2002; *Stealing Harvard* 2002; *Dreamcatcher* 2003; *Jersey Girl* 2003; *The Incredibles* 2004
Lee, Jason Scott (1966–) *Map of the Human Heart* 1992; *Dragon: the Bruce Lee Story* 1993; *The Jungle Book* 1994; *Rapa Nui* 1994; *Murder in Mind* 1996; *Talos the Mummy* 1997; *Soldier* 1998; *Lilo & Stitch* 2002
Lee (1), Jennifer *Act of Vengeance* 1974; *The Duchess and the Dirtwater Fox* 1976
Lee, Jesse (1984–) *Matinee* 1993; *The Brady Bunch Movie* 1995; *A Very Brady Sequel* 1996
Lee, Joie (1962–) *She's Gotta Have It* 1986; *Mo' Better Blues* 1990; *Coffee and Cigarettes* 2003
Lee, Kaaren *Roadhouse 66* 1984; *Remote Control* 1988
Lee, Kaiulani *Zelly and Me* 1988; *Hush* 1998
Lee Kang-sheng *Rebels of the Neon God* 1992; *Vive L'Amour* 1994; *Goodbye, Dragon Inn* 2003
Lee, Lila (1901–1973) *Male and Female* 1919; *Blood and Sand* 1922; *Drag* 1929; *Flight* 1929; *The Unholy Three* 1930; *Stand Up and Cheer!* 1934; *The Ex-Mrs Bradford* 1936
Lee, Margaret (1943–) *The Theft of the Mona Lisa* 1965; *Circus of Fear* 1967; *Five Golden Dragons* 1967; *Ghosts – Italian Style* 1967; *The Bloody Judge* 1969
Lee, Mark (1958–) *Gallipoli* 1981; *Emma's War* 1985; *Blackwater Trail* 1995
Lee Mi-sook (1960–) *Untold Scandal* 2003; *3-iron* 2004
Lee, Michele (1942–) *How to Succeed in Business without Really Trying* 1967; *The Comic* 1969; *The Love Bug* 1969; *Dark Victory* 1976; *Broadway Bound* 1991
Lee, Peggy (1920–2002) *Stage Door Canteen* 1943; *The Jazz Singer* 1952; *Lady and the Tramp* 1955; *Pete Kelly's Blues* 1955
Lee, Robbie *Big Bad Mama* 1974; *Switchblade Sisters* 1975
Lee, Robinne (1974–) *Hav Plenty* 1998; *National Security* 2002
Lee, Ruta (1936–) *Gaby* 1956; *Sergeants 3* 1962; *Bullet for a Badman* 1964
Lee, Sam *aka* **Lee Chan-Sam, Sam** (1891–1980) *Made in Hong Kong* 1997; *Beast Cops* 1998; *Gen-X Cops* 1999; *Ping Pong* 2002
Lee, Shannon (1969–) *And Now You're Dead* 1998; *High Voltage* 1998
Lee, Sheryl (1967–) *Jersey Girl* 1992; *Twin Peaks: Fire Walk with Me* 1992; *Backbeat* 1993; *Fall Time* 1994; *Homage* 1995; *Mother Night* 1996; *This World, Then the Fireworks* 1996; *Bliss* 1997; *The Blood Oranges* 1997; *Vampires* 1998; *Angel's Dance* 1999
Lee, Sophie (1968–) *The Castle* 1997; *Holy Smoke* 1999; *Bootmen* 2000
Lee, Spike (1957–) *She's Gotta Have It* 1986; *School Daze* 1988; *Do the Right Thing* 1989; *Mo' Better Blues* 1990; *Jungle Fever* 1991; *Malcolm X* 1992; *Crooklyn* 1994; *Girl 6* 1996; *Summer of Sam* 1999
Lee, Stan (1922–) *The Ambulance* 1990; *Mallrats* 1995; *Daredevil* 2003; *Hulk* 2003
Lee, Stephen (1951–) *Purple Hearts* 1984; *Dolls* 1987; *RoboCop 2* 1990; *Me and the Mob* 1992; *Prehysteria!* 1993
Lee Waise *A Better Tomorrow* 1986; *Bullet in the Head* 1990; *The Actress* 1992
Lee, Will Yun (1975–) *Die Another Day* 2002; *Torque* 2003; *Elektra* 2005
Lee-Potts, Andrew (1979–) *New Year's Day* 1999; *The Bunker* 2001
Leech, Richard (1922–2004) *Dublin Nightmare* 1958; *Ice Cold in Alex* 1958; *A Lady Mislaid* 1958
Leeds, Andrea (1914–1984) *Come and Get It* 1936; *Stage Door* 1937; *The Goldwyn Follies* 1938; *Letter of Introduction* 1938; *The Real Glory* 1939; *Swanee River* 1939; *They Shall Have Music* 1939
Leeds, Peter (1917–1996) *The Lady Gambles* 1949; *Tight Spot* 1955; *The Facts of Life* 1960
Leeds, Thelma (1912–) *New Faces of 1937* 1937; *The Toast of New York* 1937
Leegant, Dan *Signal 7* 1983; *Ernest Goes to Jail* 1990
Leerhsen, Erica (1977–) *Book of Shadows: Blair Witch 2* 2000; *Anything Else* 2003; *The Texas Chainsaw Massacre* 2003
Leeves, Jane (1963–) *Miracle on 34th Street* 1994; *James and the Giant Peach* 1996; *Don't Go Breaking My Heart* 1999; *Music of the Heart* 1999; *The Adventures of Tom Thumb and Thumbelina* 2002
Lefebvre, Jean (1919–2004) *Gigot* 1962; *The Gendarme of St Tropez* 1964; *The Gendarme in New York* 1965; *The Theft of the Mona Lisa* 1965; *Man in the Trunk* 1973; *No Problem!* 1975
LeFevre, Adam (1950–) *Return of the Secaucus Seven* 1980; *Only You* 1994; *Tadpole* 2002
Lefèvre, René (1898–1991) *Le Million* 1931; *Le Crime de Monsieur Lange* 1935; *Le Doulos* 1962
Leggatt, Alison (1904–1990) *This Happy Breed* 1944; *Waterloo Road* 1944; *Encore* 1951; *Touch and Go* 1955; *Never Take Sweets from a Stranger* 1960; *The Day of the Triffids* 1962; *Nothing but the Best* 1963; *One Way Pendulum* 1965; *Far from the Madding Crowd* 1967
Legge, Michael (1978–) *Angela's Ashes* 1999; *Whatever Happened to Harold Smith?* 1999
LeGros, James *aka* **Le Gros, James** (1962–) *Solarbabies* 1986; *Phantasm II* 1988; *Drugstore Cowboy* 1989; *Leather Jackets* 1991; *Point Break* 1991; *Guncrazy* 1992; *My New Gun* 1992; *Singles* 1992; *Where the Day Takes You* 1992; *Bad Girls* 1994; *Floundering* 1994; *Boys* 1995; *Destiny Turns on the Radio* 1995; *Living in Oblivion* 1995; *The Low Life* 1995; *[Safe]* 1995; *Countdown* 1996; *Marshal Law* 1996; *The Myth of Fingerprints* 1996; *Wishful Thinking* 1997; *Thursday* 1998; *Lovely & Amazing* 2001; *Catch That Kid* 2004
Leguizamo, John (1964–) *Casualties of War* 1989; *Hangin' with the Homeboys* 1991; *Whispers in the Dark* 1992; *Carlito's Way* 1993; *Super Mario Bros* 1993; *A Pyromaniac's Love Story* 1995; *To Wong Foo, Thanks for Everything, Julie Newmar* 1995; *Executive Decision* 1996; *The Fan* 1996; *William Shakespeare's Romeo + Juliet* 1996; *Body Count* 1997; *The Pest* 1997; *Spawn* 1997; *Joe the King* 1999; *Summer of Sam* 1999; *Titan AE* 2000; *Collateral Damage* 2001; *Moulin Rouge!* 2001; *What's the Worst That Could Happen?* 2001; *Empire* 2002; *Ice Age* 2002; *Spun* 2002; *Assault on Precinct 13* 2005; *The Honeymooners* 2005
Lehman, Kristin *Hemoglobin* 1997; *Dog Park* 1998
Lehmann, Beatrix (1903–1979) *The Key* 1958; *Psyche '59* 1964; *Wonderwall* 1968; *Staircase* 1969; *The Cat and the Canary* 1979
Lehmann, Carla (1917–1990) *Sailors Three* 1940; *Cottage to Let* 1941; *Secret Mission* 1942; *Candlelight in Algeria* 1943; *29 Acacia Avenue* 1945
Lehne, Fredric *aka* **Lehne, Frederic** *aka* **Lehne, Fredrick** *Ordinary People* 1980; *Amityville: the Evil Escapes* 1989; *Dream Lover* 1993; *Man's Best Friend* 1993
Lehne, John *Who?* 1974; *Bound for Glory* 1976; *The Disappearance of Aimee* 1976; *American Hot Wax* 1977; *Brothers* 1977; *Carny* 1980; *Ladies and Gentlemen, the Fabulous Stains* 1981
Lei, Lydia *Hammett* 1982; *Doctor Detroit* 1983
Leiber, Fritz (1882–1949) *The Story of Louis Pasteur* 1936; *Pack Up Your Troubles* 1939; *All This, and Heaven Too* 1940; *The Web* 1947
Leibman, Ron (1937–) *Where's Poppa?* 1970; *The Hot Rock* 1972; *Slaughterhouse-Five* 1972; *The Super Cops* 1973; *Your Three Minutes Are Up* 1973; *Won Ton Ton, the Dog Who Saved Hollywood* 1976; *Norma Rae* 1979; *Up the Academy* 1980; *Zorro, the Gay Blade* 1981; *Phar Lap* 1983; *Romantic Comedy* 1983; *Rhinestone* 1984; *Seven Hours to Judgment* 1988; *Just the Ticket* 1998; *Auto Focus* 2002; *Dummy* 2002; *Garden State* 2003
Leigh, Barbara (1946–) *Junior Bonner* 1972; *Seven* 1979
Leigh, Janet (1927–2004) *If Winter Comes* 1947; *Hills of Home* 1948; *Words and Music* 1948; *Act of Violence* 1949; *The Doctor and the Girl* 1949; *The Forsyte Saga* 1949; *Holiday Affair* 1949; *Little Women* 1949; *The Red Danube* 1949; *Angels in the Outfield* 1951; *It's a Big Country* 1951; *Two Tickets to Broadway* 1951; *Scaramouche* 1952; *Confidentially Connie* 1953; *Houdini* 1953; *The Naked Spur* 1953; *The Black Shield of Falworth* 1954; *Living It Up* 1954; *Prince Valiant* 1954; *Rogue Cop* 1954; *My Sister Eileen* 1955; *Pete Kelly's Blues* 1955; *Safari* 1956; *Jet Pilot* 1957; *The Perfect Furlough* 1958; *Touch of Evil* 1958; *The Vikings* 1958; *Pepe* 1960; *Psycho* 1960; *Who Was That Lady?* 1960; *The Manchurian Candidate* 1962; *Bye Bye Birdie* 1963; *Wives and Lovers* 1963; *An American Dream* 1966; *Harper* 1966; *Kid Rodelo* 1966; *The Spy*

in the Green Hat 1966; Three on a Couch 1966; Grand Slam 1967; Hello Down There 1969; Night of the Lepus 1972; One Is a Lonely Number 1972; Boardwalk 1979; The Fog 1980; Halloween H20: 20 Years Later 1998
Leigh, Jennifer Jason (1962–) Eyes of a Stranger 1980; Fast Times at Ridgemont High 1982; Easy Money 1983; Grandview, USA 1984; Flesh + Blood 1985; The Hitcher 1986; The Men's Club 1986; Heart of Midnight 1988; The Big Picture 1989; Last Exit to Brooklyn 1989; Buried Alive 1990; Miami Blues 1990; Backdraft 1991; Crooked Hearts 1991; Rush 1991; Single White Female 1992; Short Cuts 1993; The Hudsucker Proxy 1994; Mrs Parker and the Vicious Circle 1994; Dolores Claiborne 1995; Georgia 1995; Kansas City 1995; A Thousand Acres 1997; Washington Square 1997; eXistenZ 1999; The King Is Alive 2000; The Anniversary Party 2001; Hey Arnold! the Movie 2002; Road to Perdition 2002; In the Cut 2003; The Machinist 2003; Palindromes 2004; The Jacket 2005
Leigh, Nelson (1905–1985) Thief of Damascus 1952; World without End 1955
Leigh, Spencer Caravaggio 1986; The Garden 1990
Leigh, Suzanna (1945–) Boeing Boeing 1965; Deadlier than the Male 1966; Paradise, Hawaiian Style 1966; The Deadly Bees 1967; The Lost Continent 1968; Subterfuge 1968; Lust for a Vampire 1970; The Fiend 1971
Leigh, Vivien (1913–1967) Look Up and Laugh 1935; Dark Journey 1937; Fire over England 1937; Storm in a Teacup 1937; 21 Days 1937; St Martin's Lane 1938; A Yank at Oxford 1938; Gone with the Wind 1939; Waterloo Bridge 1940; That Hamilton Woman 1941; Caesar and Cleopatra 1945; Anna Karenina 1947; A Streetcar Named Desire 1951; The Deep Blue Sea 1955; The Roman Spring of Mrs Stone 1961; Ship of Fools 1965
Leigh-Hunt, Barbara (1935–) A Midsummer Night's Dream 1961; Bequest to the Nation 1972; Frenzy 1972; Henry VIII and His Six Wives 1972; Oh, Heavenly Dog! 1980; Paper Mask 1990; Keep the Aspidistra Flying 1997; The Martins 2001
Leigh-Hunt, Ronald (1916–) Where the Bullets Fly 1966; Le Mans 1971
Leighton, Margaret (1922–1976) Bonnie Prince Charlie 1948; The Winslow Boy 1948; The Astonished Heart 1949; Under Capricorn 1949; The Elusive Pimpernel 1950; Calling Bulldog Drummond 1951; The Holly and the Ivy 1952; Home at Seven 1952; Carrington VC 1954; The Good Die Young 1954; The Teckman Mystery 1954; The Constant Husband 1955; The Passionate Stranger 1957; The Sound and the Fury 1959; Waltz of the Toreadors 1962; The Best Man 1964; 7 Women 1966; The Madwoman of Chaillot 1969; The Go-Between 1971; Zee and Co 1971; Bequest to the Nation 1972; Lady Caroline Lamb 1972; From beyond the Grave 1973; Galileo 1974; Great Expectations 1974; Trial by Combat 1976
Leister, Frederick (1885–1970) Next of Kin 1942; We'll Meet Again 1942; The Captive Heart 1946; The Rossiter Case 1950; Green Grow the Rushes 1951; Footsteps in the Fog 1955; The Time of His Life 1955
Leisure, David (1950–) You Can't Hurry Love 1988; Dogmatic 1996
Leitch, Donovan (1968–) And God Created Woman 1988; The Blob 1988; The In Crowd 1988; Cutting Class 1989; Glory 1989; Love Kills 1998
Leith, Virginia (1932–) Fear and Desire 1953; Black Widow 1954; Violent Saturday 1955; White Feather 1955; A Kiss before Dying 1956; Toward the Unknown 1956; The Brain That Wouldn't Die 1959
Leitso, Tyron (1976–) Snow White 2001; House of the Dead 2003
Leland, David (1947–) Nothing but Trouble 1944; Gawain and the Green Knight 1973
Lemaire, Philippe (1927–2004) The Bad Liaisons 1955; Cartouche 1961; Arsène Lupin 2004
Lembeck, Harvey (1923–1982) Stalag 17 1953; The Command 1954; Beach Party 1963; Love with the Proper Stranger 1963; Bikini Beach 1964; Pajama Party 1964; The Unsinkable Molly Brown 1964; Beach Blanket Bingo 1965; How to Fill a Wild Bikini 1965; Sergeant Deadhead 1965; Fireball 500 1966; The Ghost in the Invisible Bikini 1966; Hello Down There 1969
Lembeck, Michael (1948–) The Boys in Company C 1978; GORP 1980; On the Right Track 1981; Danielle Steel's Heartbeat 1992
Lemche, Kris (1978–) Ginger Snaps 2000; My Little Eye 2002
Lemercier, Valérie (1964–) Les Visiteurs 1993; Vendredi Soir 2002
Lemkow, Tutte (1918–1991) The Captain's Paradise 1953; The Boy Who Stole a Million 1960
Lemme, Steve (1973–) Super Troopers 2001; Broken Lizard's Club Dread 2004
Lemmeke, Ole (1959–) A Day in October 1991; The Magnetist's Fifth Winter 1999; Possessed 1999
Lemmertz, Julia (1963–) The Color of Destiny 1986; The Three Marias 2002
Lemmon, Chris (1954–) Just before Dawn 1980; Yellow Pages 1984; That's Life 1986; Weekend Warriors 1986; Lena's Holiday 1990; Firehead 1991
Lemmon, Jack (1925–2001) It Should Happen to You 1954; Phffft! 1954; Mister Roberts 1955; My Sister Eileen 1955; Three for the Show 1955; You Can't Run Away from It 1956; Fire Down Below 1957; Operation Mad Ball 1957; Bell, Book and Candle 1958; Cowboy 1958; It Happened to Jane 1959; Some Like It Hot 1959; The Apartment 1960; Pepe 1960; The Wackiest Ship in the Army 1961; Days of Wine and Roses 1962; The Notorious Landlady 1962; Irma la Douce 1963; Under the Yum Yum Tree 1963; Good Neighbor Sam 1964; The Great Race 1965; How to Murder Your Wife 1965; The Fortune Cookie 1966; Luv 1967; The Odd Couple 1968; The April Fools 1969; The Out of Towners 1970; Avanti! 1972; The War between Men and Women 1972; Save the Tiger 1973; The Front Page 1974; The Prisoner of Second Avenue 1974; The Entertainer 1975; Alex and the Gypsy 1976; Airport '77 1977; The China Syndrome 1979; Tribute 1980; Buddy Buddy 1981; Missing 1981; Mass Appeal 1984; Macaroni 1985; That's Life 1986; Dad 1989; JFK 1991; Glengarry Glen Ross 1992; Grumpy Old Men 1993; A Life in the Theater 1993; Short Cuts 1993; The Grass Harp 1995; Getting Away with Murder 1996; Grumpier Old Men 1996; Hamlet 1996; My Fellow Americans 1996; Out to Sea 1997; 12 Angry Men 1997; The Long Way Home 1998; The Odd Couple II 1998; Inherit the Wind 1999; Tuesdays with Morrie 1999
Lemmons, Kasi (1961–) Vampire's Kiss 1988; The Court-Martial of Jackie Robinson 1990; The Silence of the Lambs 1991; Candyman 1992; Fear of a Black Hat 1992; Hard Target 1993
Lemmy (1945–) Eat the Rich 1987; Tromeo & Juliet 1996
Lemon, Geneviève Sweetie 1989; The Piano 1993; Soft Fruit 1999
Lenard, Mark (1928–1996) Star Trek III: the Search for Spock 1984; Star Trek IV: the Voyage Home 1986; Star Trek VI: the Undiscovered Country 1991
Lennix, Harry aka **Lennix, Harry J** (1965–) The Five Heartbeats 1991; Bob Roberts 1992; Mo' Money 1992; Get on the Bus 1996; Titus 1999; Love & Basketball 2000; The Human Stain 2003; Barbershop 2: Back in Business 2004; Ray 2004; Suspect Zero 2004
Lennon, John (1940–1980) A Hard Day's Night 1964; Help! 1965; How I Won the War 1967; Dynamite Chicken 1971; Imagine: John Lennon 1988
Leno, Jay (1950–) American Hot Wax 1977; Silver Bears 1977; Americathon 1979; Collision Course 1987; We're Back! A Dinosaur's Story 1993; In & Out 1997
Lenska, Rula (1947–) Alfie Darling 1975; Paradise Grove 2003; Fakers 2004
Lenya, Lotte (1898–1981) The Threepenny Opera 1931; The Roman Spring of Mrs Stone 1961; From Russia with Love 1963; The Appointment 1968; Semi-Tough 1977
Lenz, Kay (1953–) Breezy 1973; White Line Fever 1975; The Great Scout & Cathouse Thursday 1976; Mean Dog Blues 1978; The Passage 1978; Fast-Walking 1982; House 1986; Death Wish 4: the Crackdown 1987; Fear 1988; Physical Evidence 1988; Falling from Grace 1992
Lenz, Rick (1939–) Cactus Flower 1969; Scandalous John 1971; Where Does It Hurt? 1971
Leo, Melissa (1960–) Always 1985; A Time of Destiny 1988; Immaculate Conception 1991; Last Summer in the Hamptons 1995; 21 Grams 2003; Hide and Seek 2005
Leon aka **Robinson, Leon** (1962–) The Five Heartbeats 1991; Cliffhanger 1993; Cool Runnings 1993; Above the Rim 1994; Runaway Car 1997; Side Streets 1998; Bats 1999; Little Richard 2000; Buffalo Soldiers 2001
Leon, Joseph (1918–2001) Sweet Smell of Success 1957; Act One 1963; Daniel 1983
Leon, Loles (1950–) Tie Me Up! Tie Me Down! 1990; The Girl of Your Dreams 1998
Leon, Valerie (1945–) Blood from the Mummy's Tomb 1971; Ups and Downs of a Handyman 1975
Leonard, Joshua (1975–) The Blair Witch Project 1998; Cubbyhouse 2001
Leonard, Lu (1932–2004) The Princess Academy 1987; Circuitry Man 1990; Shadowzone 1990; Without You I'm Nothing 1990
Leonard, Queenie (1905–2002) Moonlight Sonata 1937; The Lodger 1944; Molly and Me 1945; The Narrow Margin 1952
Leonard, Robert Sean (1969–) Dead Poets Society 1989; Mr and Mrs Bridge 1990; Married to It 1991; The Age of Innocence 1993; Much Ado about Nothing 1993; Swing Kids 1993; Safe Passage 1994; Killer: a Journal of Murder 1995; In the Gloaming 1997; The Last Days of Disco 1998; Tape 2001; The I Inside 2003
Leonard, Sheldon (1907–1997) Tall, Dark and Handsome 1941; Weekend in Havana 1941; Tortilla Flat 1942; Hit the Ice 1943; The Falcon in Hollywood 1944; To Have and Have Not 1944; Frontier Gal 1945; Abbott and Costello Meet the Invisible Man 1951; The Diamond Queen 1953; Guys and Dolls 1955; The Brink's Job 1978
Leonardi, Marco (1971–) Cinema Paradiso 1988; Like Water for Chocolate 1993; Desperate Measures 1995; The Stendhal Syndrome 1996; The Five Senses 1999; From Dusk till Dawn 3: the Hangman's Daughter 2000
Leong, Al Bill & Ted's Excellent Adventure 1988; Cage 1989
Leoni, Téa (1966–) Bad Boys 1995; Flirting with Disaster 1996; Deep Impact 1998; The Family Man 2000; Jurassic Park III 2001; Hollywood Ending 2002; People I Know 2002; Spanglish 2004
Leonidas, Stephanie Fogbound 2002; Yes 2004
Leontovich, Eugenie (1894–1993) Four Sons 1940; The Men in Her Life 1941; Anything Can Happen 1952; The World in His Arms 1952; The Rains of Ranchipur 1955; Homicidal 1961
Leopardi, Chauncey (1981–) Huck and the King of Hearts 1993; The Sandlot 1993; The Big Green 1995; Houseguest 1995; Sticks and Stones 1996
Léotard, Philippe (1940–2001) Anne and Muriel 1971; Une Belle Fille Comme Moi 1973; Kamouraska 1973; The Mouth Agape 1974; La Balance 1982; Le Choc 1982; Tangos, Exilo de Gardel 1985; Le Paltoquet 1986; Sur 1987; Death of a Schoolboy 1990; Elisa 1994; Les Misérables 1995
Lepage, Robert (1957–) Jesus of Montreal 1989; Stardom 2000
Lepvrier, Diana The Long Absence 1961; Fire and Ice 1962
Lerner, Ken Relentless 1989; Unlawful Entry 1992
Lerner, Michael (1941–) Alex in Wonderland 1970; The Candidate 1972; Hangup 1973; Newman's Law 1974; Dark Victory 1976; The Other Side of Midnight 1977; Outlaw Blues 1977; The Baltimore Bullet 1980; Borderline 1980; Coast to Coast 1980; The Postman Always Rings Twice 1981; Threshold 1981; National Lampoon's Class Reunion 1982; Strange Invaders 1983; Movers and Shakers 1985; Anguish 1986; Vibes 1988; Harlem Nights 1989; Any Man's Death 1990; Maniac Cop 2 1990; Barton Fink 1991; Omen IV: the Awakening 1991; Amos & Andrew 1993; Blank Check 1994; The Road to Wellville 1994; A Pyromaniac's Love Story 1995; No Way Back 1996; The Beautician and the Beast 1997; For Richer or Poorer 1997; Godzilla 1997; Talos the Mummy 1997; Safe Men 1998; My Favorite Martian 1999; 29 Palms 2002; The Calcium Kid 2003; Elf 2003
Leroux, Maxime Romuald et Juliette 1989; Tango 1993
LeRoy, Baby (1932–) Tillie and Gus 1933; It's a Gift 1934; The Lemon Drop Kid 1934; The Old-Fashioned Way 1934
LeRoy, Gloria Welcome to Arrow Beach 1974; Barfly 1987; Cool Blue 1988
Leroy, Philippe (1930–) Le Trou 1959; The Married Woman 1964; The Night Porter 1973
Leroy-Beaulieu, Philippine (1963–) 3 Men and a Cradle 1985; Nine Months 1994; Two Brothers 2004
Lesaffre, Roland (1927–) Thérèse Raquin 1953; Les Tricheurs 1958; Trois Chambres à Manhattan 1965
Lesley, Carole (1935–1974) Woman in a Dressing Gown 1957; Operation Bullshine 1959; Doctor in Love 1960; Three on a Spree 1961; What a Whopper! 1961; The Pot Carriers 1962
Lesley, Lorna (1956–) The Settlement 1982; The Shiralee 1986
Leslie, Bethel (1929–1999) Captain Newman, MD 1963; A Rage to Live 1965; The Molly Maguires 1970; Old Boyfriends 1979
Leslie, Joan (1925–) High Sierra 1941; Sergeant York 1941; The Wagons Roll at Night 1941; The Hard Way 1942; The Male Animal 1942; Yankee Doodle Dandy 1942; The Sky's the Limit 1943; Thank Your Lucky Stars 1943; This Is the Army 1943; Hollywood Canteen 1944; Rhapsody in Blue 1945; Where Do We Go from Here? 1945; Cinderella Jones 1946; Two Guys from Milwaukee 1946; Northwest Stampede 1948; Born to Be Bad 1950; Man in the Saddle 1951; Hellgate 1952; The Woman They Almost Lynched 1953; The Revolt of Mamie Stover 1956
Leslie, Nan (1926–2000) The Devil Thumbs a Ride 1947; The Woman on the Beach 1947; The Arizona Ranger 1948; Guns of Hate 1948
Leslie, William (1928–) Bring Your Smile Along 1955; The Long Gray Line 1955; Hellcats of the Navy 1957; The Lineup 1958; Up Periscope 1959
Lespert, Jalil (1976–) Human Resources 1999; Pas sur la Bouche 2003; The Last Mitterrand 2005
Lesser, Anton (1952–) The Assam Garden 1985; Esther Kahn 2000; Charlotte Gray 2001; Otherworld 2003
Lessey, George (1879–1947) Sky Murder 1940; Strike Up the Band 1940; Blossoms in the Dust 1941
Lester, Adrian (1970–) Up on the Roof 1997; Primary Colors 1998; Love's Labour's Lost 1999; Maybe Baby 1999; Born Romantic 2000; Dust 2001; The Final Curtain 2002; The Day after Tomorrow 2004
Lester, Bruce aka **Lister, Bruce** (1912–) Boy Meets Girl 1938; The Letter 1940; My Son, My Son! 1940; Pride and Prejudice 1940; Shadows on the Stairs 1941; Golden Earrings 1947; Celia 1949
Lester, Buddy (1917–) Sergeants 3 1962; Three on a Couch 1966; The Big Mouth 1967; The Party 1968; Smorgasbord 1983
Lester (2), Mark (1958–) Our Mother's House 1967; Oliver! 1968; Run Wild, Run Free 1969; Eyewitness 1970; Black Beauty 1971; Melody 1971; Who Slew Auntie Roo? 1971; Scalawag 1973; The Prince and the Pauper 1977
Lester, Ron (1975–) Good Burger 1997; Varsity Blues 1999
Lester, Vicki The Mad Miss Manton 1938; Tom, Dick and Harry 1941
Letch, David Sylvia 1984; Mr Wrong 1985
Leto, Jared (1971–) Last of the High Kings 1996; Prefontaine 1997; Switchback 1997; Basil 1998; Urban Legend 1998; Black and White 1999; Fight Club 1999; Girl, Interrupted 1999; American Psycho 2000; Requiem for a Dream 2000; Sunset Strip 2000; Panic Room 2002; Alexander 2004
Letondal, Henri (1901–1955) On the Riviera 1951; Monkey Business 1952
Lett, Dan Paris France 1993; Under the Piano 1995; No One Could Protect Her 1996; The Secret Laughter of Women 1998
Lettieri, Al aka **Lettieri, Alfredo** (1928–1975) The Bobo 1967; The Getaway 1972; Pulp 1972; The Deadly Trackers 1973; The Don Is Dead 1973; Mr Majestyk 1974
Lettinger, Rudolf aka **Lettinger, Rudolph** (1879–) The Cabinet of Dr Caligari 1919; The Spiders 1919
Leung (1), Tony aka **Leung, Tony Kar-Fai** aka **Leung Kar-Fai, Tony** aka **Leung Kar-Fai, Tony** aka **Leung Ka-fai** aka **Leung Ka-fai, Tony** (1958–) The Laserman 1988; A Better Tomorrow III 1989; The Actress 1992; The Lover 1992; Ashes of Time 1994; To Live and Die in Tsimshatsui 1994; Love Will Tear Us Apart 1999; Double Vision 2002
Leung (2), Tony aka **Leung, Tony Chiu-Wai** aka **Leung Chiu-Wai, Tony** aka **Tony Leung Chiu-Wai** (1962–) A City of Sadness 1989; Bullet in the Head 1990; Days of Being Wild 1990; Hard-Boiled 1992; Ashes of Time 1994; Chung King Express 1994; Cyclo 1995; Happy Together 1997; Flowers of Shanghai 1998; Gorgeous 1999; In the Mood for Love 2000; Tokyo Raiders 2000; Chinese Odyssey 2002 2002; Hero 2002; Infernal Affairs 2002; Infernal Affairs 3 2003; 2046 2004

Levant, Oscar (1906–1972) *Rhythm on the River* 1940; *Kiss the Boys Goodbye* 1941; *Humoresque* 1946; *Romance on the High Seas* 1948; *You Were Meant for Me* 1948; *The Barkleys of Broadway* 1949; *An American in Paris* 1951; *The I Don't Care Girl* 1952; *O Henry's Full House* 1952; *The Band Wagon* 1953

Levels, Calvin (1954–) *A Night on the Town* 1987; *Johnny Suede* 1991

Levene, Sam (1905–1980) *Three Men on a Horse* 1936; *The Mad Miss Manton* 1938; *Golden Boy* 1939; *Shadow of the Thin Man* 1941; *The Big Street* 1942; *Grand Central Murder* 1942; *Action in the North Atlantic* 1943; *I Dood It* 1943; *Whistling in Brooklyn* 1943; *The Killers* 1946; *Boomerang!* 1947; *Brute Force* 1947; *Crossfire* 1947; *Killer McCoy* 1947; *The Babe Ruth Story* 1948; *Guilty Bystander* 1950; *Three Sailors and a Girl* 1953; *Designing Woman* 1957; *Sweet Smell of Success* 1957; *Act One* 1963; *A Dream of Kings* 1969; *God Told Me to* 1976; *...And Justice for All* 1979; *Last Embrace* 1979

Lever, Johnny *aka* **Lever, Johny** *Baazigar* 1993; *Raja Hindustani* 1996; *Jab Pyaar Kisise Hota Hai* 1998; *Khushi* 2002; *Koi... Mil Gaya* 2003; *Main Prem Ki Diwani Hoon* 2003

Levesque, Marcel (1877–1962) *Judex* 1916; *Le Crime de Monsieur Lange* 1935

Levine, Anna *aka* **Thomson, Anna** (1957–) *Unforgiven* 1992; *Hand Gun* 1994; *Angus* 1995; *Other Voices, Other Rooms* 1995; *Water Drops on Burning Rocks* 1999

Levine, Floyd *Bloodbrothers* 1978; *Ice* 1994

Levine, Jerry (1957–) *Teen Wolf* 1985; *Casual Sex?* 1988

Levine, Ted (1958–) *Betrayed* 1988; *The Silence of the Lambs* 1991; *Nowhere to Run* 1992; *Death Train* 1993; *The Last Outlaw* 1993; *The Mangler* 1994; *Bullet* 1995; *Georgia* 1995; *Flubber* 1997; *Mad City* 1997; *Switchback* 1997; *You Can Thank Me Later* 1998; *Wild Wild West* 1999; *Evolution* 2001; *The Truth about Charlie* 2002; *Wonderland* 2003; *The Manchurian Candidate* 2004

Levy, Eugene (1946–) *Cannibal Girls* 1973; *Running* 1979; *Going Berserk* 1983; *Splash* 1984; *Armed and Dangerous* 1986; *Club Paradise* 1986; *Stay Tuned* 1992; *Dogmatic* 1996; *Multiplicity* 1996; *Waiting for Guffman* 1996; *Almost Heroes* 1998; *American Pie* 1999; *Best in Show* 2000; *American Pie 2* 2001; *Down to Earth* 2001; *Serendipity* 2001; *American Pie: the Wedding* 2003; *Bringing Down the House* 2003; *Dumb and Dumberer: When Harry Met Lloyd* 2003; *A Mighty Wind* 2003; *New York Minute* 2004

Levy, Ori *Before Winter Comes* 1968; *The Chairman* 1969; *Moon Zero Two* 1969; *The Sellout* 1975

Lewgoy, José (1920–2003) *Fitzcarraldo* 1982; *Blame It on Rio* 1984; *Kiss of the Spider Woman* 1985; *The Lady from the Shanghai Cinema* 1987; *Cobra Verde* 1988

Lewis, Al (1919–) *Munster, Go Home!* 1966; *They Shoot Horses, Don't They?* 1969; *Car 54 Where Are You?* 1991

Lewis, Charlotte (1967–) *The Golden Child* 1986; *Pirates* 1986; *Storyville* 1992; *Excessive Force* 1993; *Embrace of the Vampire* 1994; *Men of War* 1995; *The Glass Cage* 1996

Lewis, Damian (1971–) *Daniel Defoe's Robinson Crusoe* 1996; *Dreamcatcher* 2003

Lewis (1), David (1916–2000) *That Certain Feeling* 1956; *The Apartment* 1960; *Generation* 1969

Lewis, Diana (1919–1997) *Bitter Sweet* 1940; *Go West* 1940; *The People vs Dr Kildare* 1941; *Whistling in Dixie* 1942; *Cry Havoc* 1943

Lewis, Fiona (1946–) *Otley* 1968; *Where's Jack?* 1969; *Villain* 1971; *Blue Blood* 1973; *Dracula* 1974; *Lisztomania* 1975; *Drum* 1976; *Stunts* 1977; *The Fury* 1978; *Wanda Nevada* 1979; *Strange Invaders* 1983; *Innerspace* 1987

Lewis, Forrest (1899–1977) *Take Me to Town* 1953; *Man's Favorite Sport?* 1964

Lewis, Gary (1946–) *Carla's Song* 1996; *My Name Is Joe* 1998; *Orphans* 1998; *Postmortem* 1999; *Billy Elliot* 2000; *The Escapist* 2002; *Gangs of New York* 2002; *Pure* 2002; *Skagerrak* 2003; *Yes* 2004

Lewis, Geoffrey (1935–) *The Culpepper Cattle Co* 1972; *Dillinger* 1973; *Macon County Line* 1973; *Thunderbolt and Lightfoot* 1974; *The Great Waldo Pepper* 1975; *Lucky Lady* 1975; *Smile* 1975; *The Wind and the Lion* 1975; *The Return of a Man Called Horse* 1976; *Every Which Way but Loose* 1978; *Salem's Lot* 1979; *Any Which Way You Can* 1980; *Bronco Billy* 1980; *I, the Jury* 1982; *10 to Midnight* 1983; *Lust in the Dust* 1984; *Night of the Comet* 1984; *Pink Cadillac* 1989; *Tango & Cash* 1989; *Disturbed* 1990; *Double Impact* 1991; *Wishman* 1991; *The Lawnmower Man* 1992; *Army of One* 1993; *The Man without a Face* 1993; *Only the Strong* 1993; *Maverick* 1994; *National Lampoon's Scuba School* 1994; *White Fang 2: Myth of the White Wolf* 1994; *American Perfekt* 1997

Lewis, Harry (1920–) *Key Largo* 1948; *Gun Crazy* 1949

Lewis, Huey (1950–) *Shadow of Doubt* 1998; *Duets* 2000

Lewis, Jarma (1931–1985) *It's a Dog's Life* 1955; *The Marauders* 1955; *The Tender Trap* 1955

Lewis, Jenifer (1957–) *Tina: What's Love Got to Do with It* 1993; *Corrina, Corrina* 1994; *Girl 6* 1996; *The Preacher's Wife* 1996; *Little Richard* 2000; *Partners* 2000; *Juwanna Mann* 2002

Lewis, Jenny (1977–) *Trading Hearts* 1988; *Shannon's Deal* 1989; *Danielle Steel's Daddy* 1991; *Foxfire* 1996

Lewis, Jerry (1926–) *My Friend Irma* 1949; *At War with the Army* 1950; *My Friend Irma Goes West* 1950; *Sailor Beware* 1951; *The Stooge* 1951; *That's My Boy* 1951; *Jumping Jacks* 1952; *The Caddy* 1953; *Money from Home* 1953; *Scared Stiff* 1953; *Living It Up* 1954; *Three Ring Circus* 1954; *Artists and Models* 1955; *You're Never Too Young* 1955; *Hollywood or Bust* 1956; *Pardners* 1956; *The Delicate Delinquent* 1957; *The Sad Sack* 1957; *The Geisha Boy* 1958; *Rock-a-Bye Baby* 1958; *Don't Give Up the Ship* 1959; *Li'l Abner* 1959; *The Bellboy* 1960; *Cinderfella* 1960; *Visit to a Small Planet* 1960; *The Errand Boy* 1961; *The Ladies' Man* 1961; *It'$ Only Money* 1962; *The Nutty Professor* 1963; *Who's Minding the Store?* 1963; *The Disorderly Orderly* 1964; *The Patsy* 1964; *Boeing Boeing* 1965; *The Family Jewels* 1965; *Three on a Couch* 1966; *Way... Way Out* 1966; *The Big Mouth* 1967; *Don't Raise the Bridge, Lower the River* 1968; *Hook, Line and Sinker* 1969; *Which Way to the Front?* 1970; *Hardly Working* 1981; *Slapstick of Another Kind* 1982; *The King of Comedy* 1983; *Smorgasbord* 1983; *Cookie* 1989; *Arizona Dream* 1991; *Mr Saturday Night* 1992; *Funny Bones* 1994

Lewis, Juliette (1973–) *National Lampoon's Christmas Vacation* 1989; *Cape Fear* 1991; *Crooked Hearts* 1991; *Husbands and Wives* 1992; *Romeo Is Bleeding* 1992; *That Night* 1992; *Kalifornia* 1993; *What's Eating Gilbert Grape* 1993; *Mixed Nuts* 1994; *Natural Born Killers* 1994; *The Basketball Diaries* 1995; *From Dusk till Dawn* 1995; *Strange Days* 1995; *The Evening Star* 1996; *Some Girls* 1998; *The Other Sister* 1999; *Room to Rent* 2000; *The Way of the Gun* 2000; *Enough* 2002; *Hysterical Blindness* 2002; *Cold Creek Manor* 2003; *Old School* 2003; *Blueberry* 2004; *Starsky & Hutch* 2004

Lewis, Mitchell (1880–1956) *Salome* 1922; *Beau Sabreur* 1928; *The Docks of New York* 1928; *The Black Watch* 1929; *Ann Vickers* 1933

Lewis, Monica (1925–) *Everything I Have Is Yours* 1952; *Affair with a Stranger* 1953

Lewis, Ralph (1872–1937) *The Birth of a Nation* 1915; *Somewhere in Sonora* 1933; *Dillinger* 1945

Lewis, Richard (1947–) *Once upon a Crime* 1992; *Robin Hood: Men in Tights* 1993; *Wagons East!* 1994; *Leaving Las Vegas* 1995; *Pool Girl* 1997

Lewis, Robert Q (1921–1991) *An Affair to Remember* 1957; *Ski Party* 1965

Lewis, Ronald (1928–1982) *The Square Ring* 1953; *The Prisoner* 1955; *Storm over the Nile* 1955; *A Hill in Korea* 1956; *Sailor Beware!* 1956; *Robbery under Arms* 1957; *Bachelor of Hearts* 1958; *The Wind Cannot Read* 1958; *Conspiracy of Hearts* 1960; *The Full Treatment* 1961; *Mr Sardonicus* 1961; *Taste of Fear* 1961; *Billy Budd* 1962; *Jigsaw* 1962; *Twice round the Daffodils* 1962; *Nurse on Wheels* 1963; *The Siege of the Saxons* 1963; *Friends* 1971; *Paul and Michelle* 1974

Lewis, Stephen (1936–) *Staircase* 1969; *On the Buses* 1971; *Mutiny on the Buses* 1972; *Holiday on the Buses* 1973

Lewis, Tommy (1957–) *The Chant of Jimmie Blacksmith* 1978; *We of the Never Never* 1982; *The Naked Country* 1985; *Slate, Wyn & Me* 1987

Lewis, Vera (1873–1956) *Stella Dallas* 1925; *The Iron Mask* 1929; *The Man on the Flying Trapeze* 1935

Lexy, Edward (1897–1970) *The Mark of Cain* 1947; *Blanche Fury* 1948; *Night Was Our Friend* 1951

Ley, John (1951–) *BMX Bandits* 1983; *Out of the Body* 1988

Leysen, Johan (1950–) *The Girl with Red Hair* 1981; *Je Vous Salue, Marie* 1984; *The Music Teacher* 1988; *True Blue* 1996; *The Gambler* 1997; *Le Roi Danse* 2000; *Tattoo* 2002

Leyton, John (1939–) *The Great Escape* 1963; *Every Day's a Holiday* 1964; *Guns at Batasi* 1964; *Von Ryan's Express* 1965; *The Idol* 1966; *Krakatoa, East of Java* 1969; *Schizo* 1976

Leza, Conchita *Valentina* 1982; *1919* 1983

Lhermitte, Thierry (1957–) *Until September* 1984; *Le Cop* 1985; *Le Cop II* 1989; *Tango* 1993; *Love in the Strangest Way* 1994; *An American Werewolf in Paris* 1997; *Marquise* 1997; *Le Dîner de Cons* 1998; *The Closet* 2001; *Le Divorce* 2003; *Strange Gardens* 2003

Li Baotian *Ju Dou* 1990; *Shanghai Triad* 1995; *Keep Cool* 1997

Li, Gong (1966–) *Red Sorghum* 1987; *Ju Dou* 1990; *Raise the Red Lantern* 1991; *The Story of Qiu Ju* 1992; *Farewell My Concubine* 1993; *To Live* 1994; *Shanghai Triad* 1995; *Temptress Moon* 1996; *Chinese Box* 1997; *The Emperor and the Assassin* 1999; *2046* 2004

Li Jai-Xing *The Legend* 1993; *The Legend II* 1993

Li, Jet (1963–) *The Master* 1989; *Once upon a Time in China* 1991; *Once upon a Time in China II* 1992; *The Legend* 1993; *The Legend II* 1993; *Twin Warriors* 1993; *The Defender* 1994; *Fist of Legend* 1994; *The Enforcer* 1995; *Black Mask* 1996; *Lethal Weapon 4* 1998; *Romeo Must Die* 2000; *Kiss of the Dragon* 2001; *The One* 2001; *Hero* 2002; *Cradle 2 the Grave* 2003; *Unleashed* 2005

Li Kangsheng *The River* 1997; *The Hole* 1998; *What Time Is It There?* 2001

Li Tianlu (?–1998) *Dust in the Wind* 1987; *A City of Sadness* 1989; *The Puppetmaster* 1993

Li Xuejian *Shanghai Triad* 1995; *The Emperor and the Assassin* 1999; *Happy Times* 2001

Libaire, Dorothy *Baby, Take a Bow* 1934; *Murder on a Honeymoon* 1935

Liberace (1919–1987) *Sincerely Yours* 1955; *The Loved One* 1965

Libertini, Richard (1933–) *Don't Drink the Water* 1969; *I Wonder Who's Killing Her Now?* 1975; *The In-Laws* 1979; *Popeye* 1980; *Sharky's Machine* 1981; *Unfaithfully Yours* 1983; *All of Me* 1984; *Big Trouble* 1985; *Animal Behavior* 1989; *Fletch Lives* 1989; *The Lemon Sisters* 1989; *Duck Tales: the Movie – Treasure of the Lost Lamp* 1990; *And You Thought Your Parents Were Weird* 1991; *Nell* 1994; *Telling You* 1998

Liberty, Richard (1932–2000) *The Crazies* 1973; *Day of the Dead* 1985

Libman, Andrea (1984–) *Andre* 1994; *Madeline: Lost in Paris* 1999

Libolt, Alain *The Wanderer* 1967; *L'Armée des Ombres* 1969; *An Autumn Tale* 1998; *The Lady & the Duke* 2001

Lichtenstein, Mitchell (1956–) *Streamers* 1983; *The Wedding Banquet* 1993

Licudi, Gabriella *Unearthly Stranger* 1963; *The Last Safari* 1967

Liden, Anki *Father to Be* 1979; *My Life as a Dog* 1985

Lien, Jennifer (1974–) *American History X* 1998; *SLC Punk!* 1999

Lieven, Albert (1906–1971) *Jeannie* 1941; *Yellow Canary* 1943; *The Seventh Veil* 1945; *Beware of Pity* 1946; *Frieda* 1947; *Sleeping Car to Trieste* 1948; *The Dark Light* 1951; *Hotel Sahara* 1951; *Desperate Moment* 1953; *The Devil's General* 1955; *Subway in the Sky* 1958; *Conspiracy of Hearts* 1960; *Foxhole in Cairo* 1960; *City of Fear* 1965

Lifford, Tina *Grand Canyon* 1991; *Paris Trout* 1991; *Mandela and de Klerk* 1997; *Blood Work* 2002

Light, Judith (1949–) *My Boyfriend's Back* 1989; *Murder at My Door* 1996; *Carriers* 1998; *Joseph: King of Dreams* 2000

Lightner, Winnie (1899–1971) *Gold Diggers of Broadway* 1929; *Dancing Lady* 1933

Lightning, Cody *Smoke Signals* 1998; *Manic* 2001

Lightstone, Marilyn (1941–) *Lies My Father Told Me* 1975; *In Praise of Older Women* 1978; *Heavy Metal* 1981; *GoBots: Battle of the Rocklords* 1986

Ligon, Tom (1945–) *Paint Your Wagon* 1969; *Joyride* 1977

Lil' Bow Wow *aka* **Bow Wow** (1987–) *Like Mike* 2002; *Johnson Family Vacation* 2004

Lillard, Matthew (1970–) *Serial Mom* 1994; *Hackers* 1995; *Mad Love* 1995; *Scream* 1996; *Dead Man's Curve* 1997; *Devil's Child* 1997; *Senseless* 1998; *Telling You* 1998; *Without Limits* 1998; *Love's Labour's Lost* 1999; *SLC Punk!* 1999; *She's All That* 1999; *Wing Commander* 1999; *Summer Catch* 2001; *Thir13en Ghosts* 2001; *Scooby-Doo* 2002; *The Perfect Score* 2004; *Scooby-Doo 2: Monsters Unleashed* 2004; *Wicker Park* 2004; *Without a Paddle* 2004

Lillie, Beatrice (1894–1989) *Doctor Rhythm* 1938; *Thoroughly Modern Millie* 1967

Lillis, Rachael (1978–) *Pokémon the Movie 2000* 1999; *Pokémon 3: Spell of the Unown* 2001

Lim Kay Siu *Night Watch* 1995; *Anna and the King* 1999

Lim Kay Tong *Shanghai Surprise* 1986; *Saigon* 1988; *Fifty/Fifty* 1991; *Dragon: the Bruce Lee Story* 1993

Lime, Yvonne (1938–) *I Was a Teenage Werewolf* 1957; *Untamed Youth* 1957

Limos, Tiffany (1980–) *Teenage Caveman* 2001; *Ken Park* 2002

Lin, Brigitte *aka* **Lin Ching Hsia** *aka* **Lin Ching Hsia, Brigitte** *aka* **Lin, Qingxia** (1954–) *Zu Warriors* 1983; *Police Story* 1985; *Peking Opera Blues* 1986; *Peking Opera Blues* 1986; *The Bride with White Hair* 1993; *Ashes of Time* 1994; *Chung King Express* 1994

Lin Xiuling *A Summer at Grandpa's* 1984; *Taipei Story* 1984

Linaker, Kay (1913–) *Crack-Up* 1936; *Charlie Chan at Monte Carlo* 1937

Lincoln, Abbey (1930–) *Nothing but a Man* 1964; *For Love of Ivy* 1968

Lincoln, Andrew (1973–) *Boston Kickout* 1995; *Gangster No 1* 2000; *Offending Angels* 2000; *Enduring Love* 2004

Lincoln, Elmo (1889–1952) *Tarzan of the Apes* 1918; *Wyoming Outlaw* 1939

Lind, Gillian (1904–1983) *Open All Night* 1934; *The Oracle* 1952; *Don't Talk to Strange Men* 1962

Lind, Traci *aka* **Lin, Traci** (1966–) *Fright Night Part 2* 1988; *Class of 1999* 1990; *The Handmaid's Tale* 1990; *Voyager* 1991; *My Boyfriend's Back* 1993; *The Road to Wellville* 1994; *The End of Violence* 1997

Lindberg, Chad (1976–) *The Velocity of Gary* 1998; *October Sky* 1999; *The Fast and the Furious* 2001; *The Rookie* 2002

Lindberg, Sven (1918–) *Dreams* 1955; *Face to Face* 1976

Lindblom, Gunnel (1935–) *The Virgin Spring* 1960; *Winter Light* 1962; *The Silence* 1963; *Hunger* 1966

Linden, Eric (1909–1994) *The Age of Consent* 1932; *The Crowd Roars* 1932; *Life Begins* 1932; *The Roadhouse Murder* 1932; *The Silver Cord* 1933; *Ah, Wilderness!* 1935; *Let 'Em Have It* 1935; *A Family Affair* 1937; *Girl Loves Boy* 1937

Linden, Hal (1931–) *When You Comin' Back, Red Ryder?* 1979; *Starflight One* 1983; *A New Life* 1988; *Out to Sea* 1997

Linden, Jennie (1939–) *Nightmare* 1963; *Doctor Who and the Daleks* 1965; *Women in Love* 1969; *A Severed Head* 1970; *Hedda* 1975; *Vampira* 1975

Linden, Marta (1903–1990) *A Yank at Eton* 1942; *The Youngest Profession* 1943; *Keep Your Powder Dry* 1945

Linder, Cec (1921–1992) *Subway in the Sky* 1958; *Goldfinger* 1964; *A Touch of Class* 1973; *Sunday in the Country* 1975

Lindfors, Viveca (1920–1995) *Adventures of Don Juan* 1948; *Night unto Night* 1949; *Backfire* 1950; *No Sad Songs for Me* 1950; *Moonfleet* 1955; *Run for Cover* 1955; *The Halliday Brand* 1957; *I Accuse!* 1958; *Tempest* 1959; *The Story of Ruth* 1960; *The Damned* 1961; *King of Kings* 1961; *Sylvia* 1964; *Brainstorm* 1965; *Cauldron of Blood* 1967; *Puzzle of a Downfall Child* 1970; *The Bell of Hell* 1973; *The Way We Were* 1973; *Welcome to LA* 1976; *The Hand* 1981; *Yellow Pages* 1984; *The Sure Thing* 1985; *Unfinished Business...* 1987; *Misplaced* 1989; *The Linguini Incident* 1991; *Zandalee* 1991; *Stargate* 1994; *Last Summer in the Hamptons* 1995

Lindley, Audra (1918–1997) *Taking Off* 1971; *The Heartbreak Kid* 1972; *Best Friends* 1982; *Cannery Row* 1982; *Desert Hearts* 1985; *Spellbinder* 1988; *Troop Beverly Hills* 1989

Lindo, Delroy (1952–) *Mountains of the Moon* 1989; *The Salute of the Jugger* 1989; *Bright Angel* 1990; *The Hard Way* 1991; *Blood In Blood Out* 1992; *Malcolm X* 1992; *Mr Jones* 1993; *Crooklyn* 1994; *Clockers* 1995; *Get Shorty* 1995; *Broken Arrow* 1996; *Feeling Minnesota* 1996; *Ransom* 1996;

Soul of the Game 1996; *The Winner* 1996; *First Time Felon* 1997; *A Life Less Ordinary* 1997; *Glory & Honor* 1998; *The Cider House Rules* 1999; *Strange Justice* 1999; *Gone in Sixty Seconds* 2000; *Romeo Must Die* 2000; *Heist* 2001; *The Last Castle* 2001; *The One* 2001; *The Core* 2002; *Wondrous Oblivion* 2003; *Sahara* 2004
Lindo, Olga (1899–1968) *The Last Journey* 1936; *Return to Yesterday* 1940; *Time Flies* 1944; *Obsession* 1948; *Train of Events* 1949; *An Inspector Calls* 1954; *Raising a Riot* 1955; *Yield to the Night* 1956; *Make Mine a Million* 1959; *Sapphire* 1959
Lindon, Vincent (1959–) *A Man in Love* 1987; *La Crise* 1992; *The School of Flesh* 1998; *Vendredi Soir* 2002
Lindsay, Helen *Dublin Nightmare* 1958; *Playing Away* 1986
Lindsay, Margaret (1910–1981) *Baby Face* 1933; *Lady Killer* 1933; *The World Changes* 1933; *Fog over Frisco* 1934; *Bordertown* 1935; *Dangerous* 1935; *Devil Dogs of the Air* 1935; *The Florentine Dagger* 1935; *Frisco Kid* 1935; *"G" Men* 1935; *Isle of Fury* 1936; *Green Light* 1937; *Slim* 1937; *Garden of the Moon* 1938; *Gold Is Where You Find It* 1938; *Jezebel* 1938; *Hell's Kitchen* 1939; *Ellery Queen Master Detective* 1940; *The House of the Seven Gables* 1940; *The Spoilers* 1942; *Crime Doctor* 1943; *Scarlet Street* 1945; *Seven Keys to Baldpate* 1947; *The Vigilantes Return* 1947; *BF's Daughter* 1948; *The Restless Years* 1958; *Tammy and the Doctor* 1963
Lindsay, Robert (1949–) *That'll Be the Day* 1973; *Adventures of a Taxi Driver* 1975; *Bert Rigby, You're a Fool* 1989; *Loser Takes All* 1990; *Remember Me?* 1996; *Fierce Creatures* 1997; *Divorcing Jack* 1998; *Wimbledon* 2004
Lindström, Jörgen (1951–) *The Silence* 1963; *Persona* 1966
Liné, Helga (1932–) *Spartacus and the Ten Gladiators* 1964; *The Spartan Gladiators* 1964; *Labyrinth of Passion* 1982
Lineback, Richard *Speed* 1994; *The Jackal* 1997; *Varsity Blues* 1999
Linehan, Rosaleen (1937–) *A Portrait of the Artist as a Young Man* 1977; *About Adam* 2000
Linklater, Richard (1961–) *Slacker* 1989; *Beavis and Butt-head Do America* 1996
Linn, Rex *Cliffhanger* 1993; *CutThroat Island* 1995; *Tin Cup* 1996; *Breakdown* 1997; *Blast from the Past* 1998; *Rush Hour* 1998
Linn-Baker, Mark (1954–) *My Favorite Year* 1982; *Noises Off* 1992; *Laughter on the 23rd Floor* 2000
Linnane, Joe (1910–1981) *The Woman in Question* 1950; *Hunted* 1952; *The Angel Who Pawned Her Harp* 1954
Linnestad, Eli Anne *aka* **Linnestad, Eli-Anne** (1944–) *Junk Mail* 1997; *Elling* 2001
Linney, Laura (1964–) *Lorenzo's Oil* 1992; *Class of '61* 1993; *A Simple Twist of Fate* 1994; *Congo* 1995; *Absolute Power* 1996; *Primal Fear* 1996; *The Truman Show* 1998; *You Can Count on Me* 1999; *The House of Mirth* 2000; *The Mothman Prophecies* 2001; *The Laramie Project* 2002; *The Life of David Gale* 2003; *Love Actually* 2003; *Mystic River* 2003; *Kinsey* 2004
Linow, Ivan (1888–1940) *The Red Dance* 1928; *The Unholy Three* 1930; *Scarlet Dawn* 1932
Linville, Joanne (1928–) *Gable and Lombard* 1976; *James Dean* 2001
Linville, Larry (1939–2000) *School Spirit* 1985; *No Dessert Dad, Till You Mow the Lawn* 1994
Linz, Alex D (1989–) *Danielle Steel's Vanished* 1995; *One Fine Day* 1996; *Home Alone 3* 1997; *My Brother the Pig* 1999; *Bounce* 2000; *Titan AE* 2000; *Max Keeble's Big Move* 2001
Lio (1962–) *Golden Eighties* 1986; *Après l'Amour* 1992; *La Madre Muerta* 1993; *Carnages* 2002
Lion, Leon M (1879–1947) *Number Seventeen* 1932; *The Amazing Quest of Ernest Bliss* 1936; *Crackerjack* 1938; *Strange Boarders* 1938
Liotard, Thérèse *One Sings, the Other Doesn't* 1976; *Deathwatch* 1980; *Full Moon in Paris* 1984; *Le Château de Ma Mère* 1990; *La Gloire de Mon Père* 1990
Liotta, Ray (1955–) *The Lonely Lady* 1983; *Something Wild* 1986; *Dominick and Eugene* 1988; *Field of Dreams* 1989; *GoodFellas* 1990; *Article 99* 1992; *Unlawful Entry* 1992; *Corrina, Corrina* 1994; *No Escape* 1994; *Operation Dumbo Drop* 1995; *Unforgettable* 1996; *Cop Land* 1997; *Turbulence* 1997; *Phoenix* 1998; *The Rat Pack* 1998; *Forever Mine* 1999; *Muppets from Space* 1999; *A Rumor of Angels* 2000; *Blow* 2001; *Hannibal* 2001; *Heartbreakers* 2001; *John Q* 2001; *Narc* 2001; *Identity* 2003
Lipinski, Eugene (1956–) *Moonlighting* 1982; *Riders of the Storm* 1986; *Perfectly Normal* 1990; *Never Talk to Strangers* 1995; *Aldrich Ames: Traitor Within* 1998; *The Recruit* 2002
Lipman, Maureen (1946–) *Up the Junction* 1967; *The Smashing Bird I Used to Know* 1969; *Gumshoe* 1971; *The Wildcats of St Trinian's* 1980; *Educating Rita* 1983; *National Lampoon's European Vacation* 1985; *Water* 1985; *Carry On Columbus* 1992; *Captain Jack* 1998; *Solomon and Gaenor* 1998; *The Pianist* 2002
Lipnicki, Jonathan (1990–) *Jerry Maguire* 1996; *Stuart Little* 1999; *The Little Vampire* 2000; *Like Mike* 2002; *Stuart Little 2* 2002
Lipper, David *Swearing Allegiance* 1997; *Federal Protection* 2002
Lipscomb, Dennis *Union City* 1980; *Love Child* 1982; *WarGames* 1983; *A Soldier's Story* 1984; *Crossroads* 1986; *Amazing Grace and Chuck* 1987
Lipton, Peggy (1947–) *Blue* 1968; *The Purple People Eater* 1988; *Kinjite: Forbidden Subjects* 1989; *Deadly Vows* 1994; *Jackpot* 2001
Lisi, Virna (1937–) *Duel of the Titans* 1961; *Eva* 1962; *The Black Tulip* 1963; *Le Bambole* 1965; *The Birds, the Bees, and the Italians* 1965; *Casanova '70* 1965; *How to Murder Your Wife* 1965; *Assault on a Queen* 1966; *Not with My Wife, You Don't!* 1966; *Arabella* 1967; *The Girl and the General* 1967; *The 25th Hour* 1967; *The Christmas Tree* 1969; *The Last Shot* 1969; *The Secret of Santa Vittoria* 1969; *Bluebeard* 1972; *The Serpent* 1972; *La Reine Margot* 1994; *The Best Day of My Life* 2002
Lister, Francis (1899–1951) *Cardinal Richelieu* 1935; *Clive of India* 1935; *The Return of the Scarlet Pimpernel* 1937; *Home to Danger* 1951
Lister, Moira (1923–) *Love Story* 1944; *Another Shore* 1948; *A Run for Your Money* 1949; *Pool of London* 1950; *White Corridors* 1951; *Something Money Can't Buy* 1952; *Grand National Night* 1953; *The Limping Man* 1953; *Trouble in Store* 1953; *The Deep Blue Sea* 1955; *John and Julie* 1955; *Seven Waves Away* 1957; *The Double Man* 1967; *Stranger in the House* 1967; *Not Now Darling* 1972
Lister Jr, Tom "Tiny" *aka* **Lister, Tom "Tiny"** *aka* **Lister Jr, "Tiny"** *aka* **Lister, Tiny** *aka* **Lister Jr, Tiny "Zeus"** *aka* **Lister, Tiny "Zeus"** *aka* **Lister Jr, Tommy "Tiny"** *No Holds Barred* 1989; *Talkin' Dirty after Dark* 1991; *Trespass* 1992; *Posse* 1993; *Friday* 1995; *Men of War* 1995; *The Set Up* 1995; *Jackie Brown* 1997; *I Got the Hook Up* 1998; *Circus* 1999; *Judgment Day* 1999; *Supreme Sanction* 1999; *Little Nicky* 2000; *The Wash* 2001
Liston, Sonny (1932–1970) *Harlow* 1965; *Head* 1968
Litefoot *The Indian in the Cupboard* 1995; *Kull the Conqueror* 1997
Litel, John (1892–1972) *Gold Is Where You Find It* 1938; *Nancy Drew – Detective* 1938; *A Slight Case of Murder* 1938; *Dodge City* 1939; *The Return of Dr X* 1939; *You Can't Get Away with Murder* 1939; *It All Came True* 1940; *Virginia City* 1940; *They Died with Their Boots On* 1941; *The Trial of Mary Dugan* 1941; *Crime Doctor* 1943; *Swell Guy* 1946; *Heaven Only Knows* 1947; *Pitfall* 1948; *Outpost in Morocco* 1949; *The Sundowners* 1950; *Flight to Mars* 1951; *Sitting Bull* 1954; *Comanche* 1956; *Runaway Daughters* 1956; *The Hired Gun* 1957
Lithgow, John (1945–) *Dealing: or the Berkeley-to-Boston Forty-Brick Lost-Bag Blues* 1971; *Obsession* 1976; *The Big Fix* 1978; *Rich Kids* 1979; *Blow Out* 1981; *I'm Dancing as Fast as I Can* 1982; *The World According to Garp* 1982; *Terms of Endearment* 1983; *The Adventures of Buckaroo Banzai across the 8th Dimension* 1984; *Footloose* 1984; *Mesmerized* 1984; *2010* 1984; *Santa Claus* 1985; *The Deadly Game* 1986; *Resting Place* 1986; *Bigfoot and the Hendersons* 1987; *Distant Thunder* 1988; *Out Cold* 1989; *Memphis Belle* 1990; *At Play in the Fields of the Lord* 1991; *The Boys* 1991; *Ricochet* 1991; *Raising Cain* 1992; *Cliffhanger* 1993; *A Good Man in Africa* 1993; *The Pelican Brief* 1993; *Love, Cheat & Steal* 1994; *Princess Caraboo* 1994; *Silent Fall* 1994; *The Tuskegee Airmen* 1995; *Hollow Point* 1996; *A Civil Action* 1998; *Homegrown* 1998; *Don Quixote* 2000; *Orange County* 2001; *Shrek* 2001; *The Life and Death of Peter Sellers* 2003; *Kinsey* 2004
Little, Cleavon (1939–1992) *What's So Bad About Feeling Good?* 1968; *Cotton Comes to Harlem* 1970; *Vanishing Point* 1971; *Blazing Saddles* 1974; *FM* 1977; *Greased Lightning* 1977; *Scavenger Hunt* 1979; *High Risk* 1981; *The Salamander* 1981; *The Gig* 1985; *Once Bitten* 1985
Little, Michelle *aka* **Little, Michele** *Radioactive Dreams* 1986; *My Demon Lover* 1987
Little, Natasha (1970–) *The Clandestine Marriage* 1999; *The Criminal* 1999; *Another Life* 2000; *Greenfingers* 2000
Little, Rich (1938–) *The Curse of the Pink Panther* 1983; *Happy Hour* 1987
Little Richard (1932–) *Don't Knock the Rock* 1956; *Down and Out in Beverly Hills* 1986; *The Purple People Eater* 1988; *The Pickle* 1993; *Chairman of the Board* 1998; *Why Do Fools Fall in Love?* 1998; *Mystery, Alaska* 1999
Little Sky, Eddie *aka* **Little, Eddie** (1926–1997) *Ride a Crooked Trail* 1958; *Journey through Rosebud* 1972
Littlefield, Lucien (1895–1960) *The Sheik* 1921; *Tumbleweeds* 1925; *My Best Girl* 1927; *Drag* 1929; *Tom Sawyer* 1930; *It Pays to Advertise* 1931; *Shopworn* 1932; *The Bitter Tea of General Yen* 1933; *Kiss and Make-Up* 1934; *I Dream Too Much* 1935; *The Man on the Flying Trapeze* 1935; *Ruggles of Red Gap* 1935; *Rose Marie* 1936; *The Gladiator* 1938
Littler, Craig *More Dead than Alive* 1969; *Barquero* 1970
Littler, Susan (1949–1982) *The Lovers!* 1972; *Rough Cut* 1980
Littman, Julian *Evita* 1996; *Mad about Mambo* 1999
Liu, Harrison *Bethune: the Making of a Hero* 1990; *Black Robe* 1991
Liu, Lucy (1968–) *Guy* 1996; *The Mating Habits of the Earthbound Human* 1999; *Charlie's Angels* 2000; *Play It to the Bone* 2000; *Shanghai Noon* 2000; *Hotel* 2001; *Ballistic: Ecks vs Sever* 2002; *Chicago* 2002; *Cypher* 2002; *Charlie's Angels: Full Throttle* 2003; *Kill Bill Vol 1* 2003
Liu Peiqi *The Story of Qiu Ju* 1992; *Ermo* 1994; *Shadow Magic* 2000; *Together with You* 2002
Lively, Robyn (1906–1976) *Wildcats* 1986; *The Karate Kid III* 1989; *Teen Witch* 1989; *Crazy from the Heart* 1991; *Santa Who?* 2000
Livesey, Jack (1901–1961) *The Wandering Jew* 1933; *It's Never Too Late to Mend* 1937; *Old Bones of the River* 1938; *Penny Paradise* 1938; *Murder at the Windmill* 1949
Livesey, Roger (1906–1976) *Lorna Doone* 1934; *Rembrandt* 1936; *The Drum* 1938; *The Girl in the News* 1940; *The Life and Death of Colonel Blimp* 1943; *I Know Where I'm Going!* 1945; *A Matter of Life and Death* 1946; *Vice Versa* 1947; *That Dangerous Age* 1949; *Green Grow the Rushes* 1951; *The Master of Ballantrae* 1953; *The Intimate Stranger* 1956; *The Entertainer* 1960; *The League of Gentlemen* 1960; *No My Darling Daughter* 1961; *Of Human Bondage* 1964; *Oedipus the King* 1967; *Hamlet* 1969
Livesey, Sam (1873–1936) *Dreyfus* 1931; *The Shadow* 1936
Livingston, John (1970–) *Mr Wrong* 1996; *The Stickup* 2001
Livingston, Margaret (1895–1984) *Sunrise* 1927; *The Last Warning* 1928; *What a Widow!* 1930; *Smart Money* 1931
Livingston, Robert (1904–1988) *Buried Loot* 1934; *Speed* 1936; *Hit the Saddle* 1937; *Brazil* 1944; *Bells of Rosarita* 1945; *The Cheaters* 1945; *Riders in the Sky* 1949; *Mule Train* 1950; *Winning of the West* 1953
Livingston, Ron (1968–) *The Low Life* 1995; *Swingers* 1996; *Body Shots* 1999; *Office Space* 1999; *A Rumor of Angels* 2000; *The Cooler* 2002; *King of the Ants* 2003; *Little Black Book* 2004
Lizaran, Anna *aka* **Lizaran, Ana** *High Heels* 1991; *Actresses* 1996
Llewellyn, Suzette *Playing Away* 1986; *Sammy and Rosie Get Laid* 1987; *Welcome II the Terrordome* 1994
Llewelyn, Desmond (1914–1999) *From Russia with Love* 1963; *Goldfinger* 1964; *Thunderball* 1965; *You Only Live Twice* 1967; *On Her Majesty's Secret Service* 1969; *Diamonds Are Forever* 1971; *The Man with the Golden Gun* 1974; *The Spy Who Loved Me* 1977; *Moonraker* 1979; *For Your Eyes Only* 1981; *Octopussy* 1983; *A View to a Kill* 1985; *The Living Daylights* 1987; *Prisoner of Rio* 1988; *Licence to Kill* 1989; *GoldenEye* 1995; *Tomorrow Never Dies* 1997; *The World Is Not Enough* 1999
Lloyd, Christopher *aka* **Lloyd, Chris** (1938–) *One Flew over the Cuckoo's Nest* 1975; *Goin' South* 1978; *Butch and Sundance: the Early Days* 1979; *The Lady in Red* 1979; *The Onion Field* 1979; *The Legend of the Lone Ranger* 1981; *National Lampoon's Movie Madness* 1981; *The Postman Always Rings Twice* 1981; *Mr Mom* 1983; *To Be or Not to Be* 1983; *The Adventures of Buckaroo Banzai across the 8th Dimension* 1984; *Star Trek III: the Search for Spock* 1984; *Back to the Future* 1985; *Clue* 1985; *Legend of the White Horse* 1985; *Miracles* 1985; *Walk like a Man* 1987; *Track 29* 1988; *Who Framed Roger Rabbit* 1988; *Back to the Future Part II* 1989; *The Dream Team* 1989; *Back to the Future Part III* 1990; *Duck Tales: the Movie – Treasure of the Lost Lamp* 1990; *Why Me?* 1990; *The Addams Family* 1991; *Suburban Commando* 1991; *Rent-a-Kid* 1992; *Addams Family Values* 1993; *Dennis* 1993; *Twenty Bucks* 1993; *Angels in the Outfield* 1994; *Camp Nowhere* 1994; *The Pagemaster* 1994; *Radioland Murders* 1994; *Things to Do in Denver When You're Dead* 1995; *Cadillac Ranch* 1996; *Anastasia* 1997; *Changing Habits* 1997; *The Real Blonde* 1997; *Baby Geniuses* 1999; *My Favorite Martian* 1999; *Kids World* 2001; *Wit* 2001; *Hey Arnold! the Movie* 2002
Lloyd, Doris (1896–1968) *The Black Bird* 1926; *Charley's Aunt* 1930; *Sarah and Son* 1930; *Waterloo Bridge* 1931; *Back Street* 1932; *Tarzan, the Ape Man* 1932; *Secrets* 1933; *Glamour* 1934; *Kind Lady* 1935; *The Letter* 1940; *Molly and Me* 1945; *My Name Is Julia Ross* 1945; *Kind Lady* 1951; *The Time Machine* 1960
Lloyd, Emily (1970–) *Wish You Were Here* 1987; *Chicago Joe and the Showgirl* 1989; *Cookie* 1989; *In Country* 1989; *Scorchers* 1991; *A River Runs through It* 1992; *Under the Hula Moon* 1995; *When Saturday Comes* 1995; *Welcome to Sarajevo* 1997
Lloyd, Emily Ann (1989–) *Annie: a Royal Adventure* 1995; *Apollo 13* 1995
Lloyd, Eric (1986–) *The Santa Clause* 1994; *Dunston Checks In* 1996; *The Santa Clause 2* 2002
Lloyd, George *aka* **Lloyd, George H** (1897–1967) *Singapore* 1947; *Under California Stars* 1948
Lloyd, Harold (1893–1971) *A Sailor-Made Man* 1921; *Safety Last* 1923; *Girl Shy* 1924; *Hot Water* 1924; *The Freshman* 1925; *For Heaven's Sake* 1926; *The Kid Brother* 1927; *Speedy* 1928; *Feet First* 1930; *Movie Crazy* 1932; *The Cat's Paw* 1934; *The Milky Way* 1936; *Mad Wednesday* 1950
Lloyd Jr, Harold (1931–1971) *A Yank in Ermine* 1955; *Girls' Town* 1959; *Platinum High School* 1960
Lloyd, Hugh (1923–) *The Punch and Judy Man* 1962; *White Cargo* 1973; *August* 1995
Lloyd, Jake (1989–) *Jingle All the Way* 1996; *Unhook the Stars* 1996; *Star Wars Episode I: the Phantom Menace* 1999
Lloyd, Jeremy (1932–) *We Joined the Navy* 1962; *Death Drums along the River* 1963; *The Liquidator* 1966; *Smashing Time* 1967
Lloyd, John Bedford *Tough Guys Don't Dance* 1987; *The Abyss* 1989; *Waiting for the Light* 1989
Lloyd, Kathleen (1949–) *The Missouri Breaks* 1976; *The Car* 1977; *It Lives Again* 1978; *Skateboard* 1978; *Take Down* 1978
Lloyd, Norman (1914–) *Saboteur* 1942; *The Southerner* 1945; *The Unseen* 1945; *A Walk in the Sun* 1945; *No Minor Vices* 1948; *Calamity Jane and Sam Bass* 1949; *Reign of Terror* 1949; *Scene of the Crime* 1949; *He Ran All the Way* 1951; *Limelight* 1952; *Audrey Rose* 1977; *FM* 1977; *Jaws of Satan* 1979; *Amityville: the Evil Escapes* 1989; *Dead Poets Society* 1989; *Shogun Warrior* 1991
Lloyd, Rollo (1883–1938) *Today We Live* 1933; *Anthony Adverse* 1936; *Girl Loves Boy* 1937
Lloyd, Sue (1939–) *Hysteria* 1964; *The Ipcress File* 1965; *Attack on the Iron Coast* 1968; *Corruption* 1968; *Where's Jack?* 1969; *Go for a Take* 1972; *Innocent Bystanders* 1972; *That's Your Funeral* 1972; *Penny Gold* 1973; *Ups and Downs of a Handyman* 1975; *Revenge of the Pink Panther* 1978; *The Stud* 1978; *The Bitch* 1979; *UFO* 1993; *Bullet to Beijing* 1995
Lloyd, Suzanne *Seven Ways from Sundown* 1960; *The Return of Mr Moto* 1965; *The Champagne Murders* 1966; *That Riviera Touch* 1966
Lloyd Pack, Charles (1902–1983) *River Beat* 1954; *Quatermass II* 1957; *The Revenge of Frankenstein* 1958; *Cover Girl Killer* 1959; *The Three Worlds of*

Gulliver 1959; *The Siege of the Saxons* 1963; *The Reptile* 1966
Lloyd Pack, Roger (1944–) *Nineteen Eighty-Four* 1984; *Wilt* 1989; *American Friends* 1991; *UFO* 1993; *The Young Poisoner's Handbook* 1994
Lo, Candy *Time and Tide* 2000; *The Eye* 2002
Lo Cascio, Luigi (1967–) *The Hundred Steps* 2000; *The Best Day of My Life* 2002; *The Best of Youth* 2003; *Good Morning, Night* 2003
Lo Lieh (1939–2002) *Blood Money* 1974; *Sex and Zen* 1992
Lo Verso, Enrico (1964–) *The Stolen Children* 1992; *La Scorta* 1993; *Farinelli il Castrato* 1994; *Lamerica* 1994; *Il Cielo è Sempre Più Blu* 1995
LoBlanco, Tony (1935–) *The Honeymoon Killers* 1969; *The French Connection* 1971; *The Seven-Ups* 1973; *God Told Me to* 1976; *Bloodbrothers* 1978; *FIST* 1978; *Separate Ways* 1981; *City Heat* 1984; *City of Hope* 1991; *Boiling Point* 1993; *The Ascent* 1994; *The Juror* 1996; *Mary Higgins Clark's Let Me Call You Sweetheart* 1997
Lobre, Jane *A Gentle Creature* 1969; *The Green Room* 1978
Loc, Tone (1966–) *Bebe's Kids* 1992; *Ace Ventura: Pet Detective* 1993; *Whispers: an Elephant's Tale* 2000; *They Crawl* 2001
Locane, Amy (1971–) *Cry-Baby* 1989; *The Road Home* 1989; *Blue Sky* 1991; *School Ties* 1992; *Airheads* 1994; *Acts of Love* 1995; *Going All the Way* 1997; *Love to Kill* 1997; *Bram Stoker's Legend of the Mummy* 1998; *Route 9* 1998; *Bad Karma* 2001; *Secretary* 2001
Lochary, David (1944–1977) *Mondo Trasho* 1970; *Multiple Maniacs* 1970; *Pink Flamingos* 1972; *Female Trouble* 1974
Locke, Harry (1913–1987) *Judgement Deferred* 1951; *A Yank in Ermine* 1955; *Light Up the Sky* 1960; *The Man in the Back Seat* 1961; *The Creeping Flesh* 1972
Locke, Katherine (1910–1995) *The Sound of Fury* 1950; *Flesh and Fury* 1952
Locke, Philip (1928–2004) *The Girl on the Boat* 1962; *Tom & Viv* 1994
Locke, Sondra (1947–) *The Heart Is a Lonely Hunter* 1968; *Willard* 1971; *A Reflection of Fear* 1973; *The Second Coming of Suzanne* 1974; *Death Game* 1976; *The Outlaw Josey Wales* 1976; *The Gauntlet* 1977; *Every Which Way but Loose* 1978; *Any Which Way You Can* 1980; *Bronco Billy* 1980; *Sudden Impact* 1983; *Ratboy* 1986; *The Prophet's Game* 1999
Lockhart, Anne (1953–) *Joyride* 1977; *Young Warriors* 1983; *Hambone and Hillie* 1984; *Dark Tower* 1989
Lockhart, Calvin (1934–) *Joanna* 1969; *Cotton Comes to Harlem* 1970; *Halls of Anger* 1970; *Leo the Last* 1970; *The Beast Must Die* 1974; *Let's Do It Again* 1975; *The Baltimore Bullet* 1980; *Coming to America* 1988
Lockhart, Gene (1891–1957) *Captain Hurricane* 1935; *Star of Midnight* 1935; *The Devil Is a Sissy* 1936; *Wedding Present* 1936; *Something to Sing About* 1937; *Algiers* 1938; *Blondie!* 1938; *A Christmas Carol* 1938; *Listen, Darling* 1938; *Sinners in Paradise* 1938; *Blackmail* 1939; *Geronimo* 1939; *His Girl Friday* 1939; *The Story of Alexander Graham Bell* 1939; *Tell No Tales* 1939; *A Dispatch from Reuters* 1940; *Dr Kildare Goes Home* 1940; *Edison, the Man* 1940; *South of Pago Pago* 1940; *Spirit of the People* 1940; *Billy the Kid* 1941; *Daniel and the Devil* 1941; *International Lady* 1941; *Meet John Doe* 1941; *One Foot in Heaven* 1941; *The Sea Wolf* 1941; *They Died with Their Boots On* 1941; *The Gay Sisters* 1942; *You Can't Escape Forever* 1942; *Forever and a Day* 1943; *Hangmen Also Die* 1943; *Mission to Moscow* 1943; *Northern Pursuit* 1943; *Action in Arabia* 1944; *The Desert Song* 1944; *Going My Way* 1944; *The House on 92nd Street* 1945; *Leave Her to Heaven* 1945; *The Strange Woman* 1946; *Thieves' Holiday* 1946; *Cynthia* 1947; *The Foxes of Harrow* 1947; *Her Husband's Affairs* 1947; *Miracle on 34th Street* 1947; *The Shocking Miss Pilgrim* 1947; *Apartment for Peggy* 1948; *Joan of Arc* 1948; *That Wonderful Urge* 1948; *Down to the Sea in Ships* 1949; *The Inspector General* 1949; *Madame Bovary* 1949; *Red Light* 1949; *I'd Climb the Highest Mountain* 1951; *Rhubarb* 1951; *Androcles and the Lion* 1952; *Apache War Smoke* 1952; *Face to Face* 1952; *A Girl in Every Port* 1952; *Hoodlum Empire* 1952; *Confidentially Connie* 1953; *Francis Covers the Big Town* 1953; *The Lady Wants Mink* 1953; *World for Ransom* 1953; *Carousel* 1956; *The Man in the Gray Flannel Suit* 1956; *Jeanne Eagels* 1957
Lockhart, June (1925–) *Adam Had Four Sons* 1941; *Meet Me in St Louis* 1944; *Son of Lassie* 1945; *Easy to Wed* 1946; *T-Men* 1947; *Time Limit* 1957; *Lassie's Great Adventure* 1963
Lockhart, Kathleen (1894–1978) *Blondie!* 1938; *A Christmas Carol* 1938; *Love Crazy* 1941; *Bewitched* 1945; *I'd Climb the Highest Mountain* 1951
Locklear, Heather (1962–) *Firestarter* 1984; *The Return of Swamp Thing* 1989; *Wayne's World 2* 1993; *The Terror Inside* 1996; *Double Tap* 1997; *Money Talks* 1997; *Uptown Girls* 2003; *Looney Tunes: Back in Action* 2004
Locklin, Loryn *Taking Care of Business* 1990; *Fortress* 1992; *Fugitive from Justice* 1996
Lockwood, Gary (1937–) *Wild in the Country* 1961; *It Happened at the World's Fair* 1962; *The Magic Sword* 1962; *Firecreek* 1968; *They Came to Rob Las Vegas* 1968; *2001: a Space Odyssey* 1968; *Model Shop* 1969; *RPM – Revolutions per Minute* 1970; *Project: Kill* 1976; *The Wild Pair* 1987
Lockwood, Julia (1941–) *The Flying Eye* 1955; *My Teenage Daughter* 1956; *No Kidding* 1960; *Please Turn Over* 1960
Lockwood, Margaret (1916–1990) *Lorna Doone* 1934; *Dr Syn* 1937; *Bank Holiday* 1938; *The Lady Vanishes* 1938; *Owd Bob* 1938; *Rulers of the Sea* 1939; *The Stars Look Down* 1939; *Susannah of the Mounties* 1939; *The Girl in the News* 1940; *Night Train to Munich* 1940; *Quiet Wedding* 1940; *The Man in Grey* 1943; *Give Us the Moon* 1944; *Love Story* 1944; *A Place of One's Own* 1944; *I'll Be Your Sweetheart* 1945; *The Wicked Lady* 1945; *Bedelia* 1946; *Hungry Hill* 1946; *Jassy* 1947; *Cardboard Cavalier* 1949; *Madness of the Heart* 1949; *Highly Dangerous* 1950; *Trent's Last Case* 1952; *Trouble in the Glen* 1954; *Cast a Dark Shadow* 1957; *The Slipper and the Rose* 1976
Loden, Barbara (1932–1980) *Splendor in the Grass* 1961; *Wanda* 1971
Loder, John (1898–1988) *Wedding Rehearsal* 1932; *The Battle* 1934; *Lorna Doone* 1934; *Love, Life and Laughter* 1934; *Sing as We Go* 1934; *Java Head* 1935; *The Man Who Changed His Mind* 1936; *Sabotage* 1936; *Dr Syn* 1937; *King Solomon's Mines* 1937; *Owd Bob* 1938; *Tin Pan Alley* 1940; *Confirm or Deny* 1941; *How Green Was My Valley* 1941; *Gentleman Jim* 1942; *Now, Voyager* 1942; *Murder on the Waterfront* 1943; *Old Acquaintance* 1943; *Abroad with Two Yanks* 1944; *The Hairy Ape* 1944; *Passage to Marseille* 1944; *The Brighton Strangler* 1945; *A Game of Death* 1945; *Dishonored Lady* 1947; *Small Hotel* 1957; *The Story of Esther Costello* 1957; *The Woman and the Hunter* 1957
Lodge, David (1921–2003) *The Cockleshell Heroes* 1955; *Stranger's Meeting* 1957; *The Running, Jumping and Standing Still Film* 1959; *The Bulldog Breed* 1960; *Two Way Stretch* 1960; *Watch Your Stern* 1960; *The Hellfire Club* 1961; *On the Beat* 1962; *Trial and Error* 1962; *The Long Ships* 1963; *Saturday Night Out* 1963; *Two Left Feet* 1963; *Catch Us If You Can* 1965; *Corruption* 1968; *Scream and Scream Again* 1969; *What's Good for the Goose* 1969; *Hoffman* 1970; *Incense for the Damned* 1970; *The Fiend* 1971; *Go for a Take* 1972; *The Return of the Pink Panther* 1974; *Edge of Sanity* 1989
Lodge, Jean *Dr Morelle – the Case of the Missing Heiress* 1949; *Brandy for the Parson* 1951; *Death of an Angel* 1951; *Final Appointment* 1954
Lodge, John *aka* **Lodge, John Davis** (1903–1985) *Little Women* 1933; *Murders in the Zoo* 1933; *The Scarlet Empress* 1934; *Königsmark* 1935; *The Little Colonel* 1935; *Bank Holiday* 1938
Loff, Jeanette (1906–1942) *The King of Jazz* 1930; *Party Girl* 1930
Löfgren, Marianne (1910–1957) *June Night* 1940; *Crisis* 1945
Loft, Arthur (1897–1947) *I Am the Law* 1938; *Dr Broadway* 1942; *The Man in the Trunk* 1942; *My Friend Flicka* 1943; *Charlie Chan in the Secret Service* 1944; *Along Came Jones* 1945; *Scarlet Street* 1945; *The Shanghai Cobra* 1945; *The Woman in the Window* 1945
Loftus, Cecilia (1876–1943) *East Lynne* 1931; *It's a Date* 1940; *Lucky Partners* 1940
Logan, Jimmy (1928–2001) *Floodtide* 1949; *The Wild Affair* 1963; *Carry On Abroad* 1972
Logan, Phyllis (1956–) *Another Time, Another Place* 1983; *The Chain* 1984; *Every Picture Tells a Story* 1984; *Nineteen Eighty-Four* 1984; *The Doctor and the Devils* 1985; *The Kitchen Toto* 1987; *Freddie as FRO7* 1992; *Soft Top, Hard Shoulder* 1992; *Secrets & Lies* 1995
Logan, Robert *aka* **Logan, Robert F** (1941–) *The Adventures of the Wilderness Family* 1975; *Across the Great Divide* 1977; *The Sea Gypsies* 1978; *Mountain Family Robinson* 1979; *A Night in Heaven* 1983
Loggia, Robert (1930–) *Somebody Up There Likes Me* 1956; *The Garment Jungle* 1957; *Cattle King* 1963; *The Greatest Story Ever Told* 1965; *The Three Sisters* 1966; *Che!* 1969; *First Love* 1977; *Revenge of the Pink Panther* 1978; *The Ninth Configuration* 1979; *SOB* 1981; *An Officer and a Gentleman* 1982; *Trail of the Pink Panther* 1982; *The Curse of the Pink Panther* 1983; *Psycho II* 1983; *Scarface* 1983; *Jagged Edge* 1985; *Prizzi's Honor* 1985; *Armed and Dangerous* 1986; *That's Life* 1986; *The Believers* 1987; *Gaby: a True Story* 1987; *Hot Pursuit* 1987; *Over the Top* 1987; *Big* 1988; *Oliver & Company* 1988; *Relentless* 1989; *Triumph of the Spirit* 1989; *Opportunity Knocks* 1990; *Necessary Roughness* 1991; *Too Hot to Handle* 1991; *Gladiator* 1992; *Innocent Blood* 1992; *Bad Girls* 1994; *I Love Trouble* 1994; *Coldblooded* 1995; *Independence Day* 1996; *Lost Highway* 1996; *Smilla's Feeling for Snow* 1996; *Hard Time* 1998; *Holy Man* 1998; *The Proposition* 1998; *Wide Awake* 1998; *Live Virgin* 2000; *Return to Me* 2000
Logue, Donal (1966–) *Blade* 1998; *The Big Tease* 1999; *Deception* 2000; *The Opportunists* 2000; *The Tao of Steve* 2000; *Confidence* 2002
Lohan, Lindsay (1986–) *The Parent Trap* 1998; *Life-Size* 2000; *Freaky Friday* 2003; *Confessions of a Teenage Drama Queen* 2004; *Mean Girls* 2004
Lohman, Alison (1979–) *Fortune Hunters* 1999; *White Oleander* 2002; *Big Fish* 2003; *Matchstick Men* 2003
Lohr, Marie (1890–1975) *Fighting Stock* 1935; *Foreign Affaires* 1935; *Oh, Daddy!* 1935; *Pygmalion* 1938; *South Riding* 1938; *Went the Day Well?* 1942; *Anna Karenina* 1947; *The Winslow Boy* 1948; *A Town like Alice* 1956; *Seven Waves Away* 1957; *Small Hotel* 1957; *Great Catherine* 1968
Loiret Caille, Florence *Le Chignon d'Olga* 2002; *Vendredi Soir* 2002
Loken, Kristanna (1979–) *Terminator 3: Rise of the Machines* 2003; *Sword of Xanten* 2004
Lollobrigida, Gina (1927–) *Pagliacci* 1948; *Fanfan la Tulipe* 1951; *Les Belles de Nuit* 1952; *Beat the Devil* 1953; *Bread, Love and Dreams* 1953; *Crossed Swords* 1954; *Beautiful but Dangerous* 1955; *The Hunchback of Notre Dame* 1956; *Trapeze* 1956; *Never So Few* 1959; *Solomon and Sheba* 1959; *Where the Hot Wind Blows!* 1959; *Come September* 1961; *Go Naked in the World* 1961; *Imperial Venus* 1963; *Woman of Straw* 1964; *Le Bambole* 1965; *Strange Bedfellows* 1965; *Hotel Paradiso* 1966; *Buona Sera, Mrs Campbell* 1968; *Cervantes* 1968; *The Private Navy of Sgt O'Farrell* 1968; *Bad Man's River* 1971; *King, Queen, Knave* 1972
Lom, Herbert (1917–) *Secret Mission* 1942; *Tomorrow We Live* 1942; *Hotel Reserve* 1944; *The Seventh Veil* 1945; *Night Boat to Dublin* 1946; *The Brass Monkey* 1948; *Good Time Girl* 1948; *Portrait from Life* 1948; *Snowbound* 1948; *Golden Salamander* 1949; *The Black Rose* 1950; *Cage of Gold* 1950; *Night and the City* 1950; *State Secret* 1950; *Mr Denning Drives North* 1951; *The Man Who Watched Trains Go By* 1952; *Rough Shoot* 1952; *The Love Lottery* 1953; *The Net* 1953; *Beautiful Stranger* 1954; *Star of India* 1954; *The Ladykillers* 1955; *War and Peace* 1956; *Action of the Tiger* 1957; *Chase a Crooked Shadow* 1957; *Fire Down Below* 1957; *Hell Drivers* 1957; *I Accuse!* 1958; *Intent to Kill* 1958; *No Trees in the Street* 1958; *Passport to Shame* 1958; *The Roots of Heaven* 1958; *The Big Fisherman* 1959; *North West Frontier* 1959; *Third Man on the Mountain* 1959; *I Aim at the Stars* 1960; *El Cid* 1961; *The Frightened City* 1961; *Mr Topaze* 1961; *Mysterious Island* 1961; *The Phantom of the Opera* 1962; *Tiara Tahiti* 1962; *A Shot in the Dark* 1964; *Return from the Ashes* 1965; *Gambit* 1966; *Our Man in Marrakesh* 1966; *The Karate Killers* 1967; *Assignment to Kill* 1968; *Villa Rides* 1968; *Journey to the Far Side of the Sun* 1969; *Mister Jerico* 1969; *Count Dracula* 1970; *Mark of the Devil* 1970; *Murders in the Rue Morgue* 1971; *Asylum* 1972; *And Now the Screaming Starts!* 1973; *Dark Places* 1973; *And Then There Were None* 1974; *The Return of the Pink Panther* 1974; *The Pink Panther Strikes Again* 1976; *Revenge of the Pink Panther* 1978; *The Lady Vanishes* 1979; *Hopscotch* 1980; *The Man with Bogart's Face* 1980; *Trail of the Pink Panther* 1982; *The Curse of the Pink Panther* 1983; *The Dead Zone* 1983; *King Solomon's Mines* 1985; *Whoops Apocalypse* 1986; *River of Death* 1989; *The Pope Must Die* 1991; *The Sect* 1991; *Son of the Pink Panther* 1993
Lomas, Herbert (1887–1961) *When London Sleeps* 1932; *Java Head* 1935; *Knight without Armour* 1937; *Ask a Policeman* 1938
Lombard, Carole *aka* **Lombard, Carol** (1908–1942) *Big News* 1929; *High Voltage* 1929; *Fast and Loose* 1930; *It Pays to Advertise* 1931; *Ladies' Man* 1931; *Man of the World* 1931; *No Man of Her Own* 1932; *No One Man* 1932; *Sinners in the Sun* 1932; *The Eagle and the Hawk* 1933; *Supernatural* 1933; *White Woman* 1933; *Bolero* 1934; *The Gay Bride* 1934; *Lady by Choice* 1934; *Now and Forever* 1934; *Twentieth Century* 1934; *We're Not Dressing* 1934; *Hands across the Table* 1935; *Rumba* 1935; *Love before Breakfast* 1936; *My Man Godfrey* 1936; *The Princess Comes Across* 1936; *Nothing Sacred* 1937; *Swing High, Swing Low* 1937; *True Confession* 1937; *Fools for Scandal* 1938; *In Name Only* 1939; *Made for Each Other* 1939; *They Knew What They Wanted* 1940; *Vigil in the Night* 1940; *Mr and Mrs Smith* 1941; *To Be or Not to Be* 1942
Lombard, Karina (1964–) *Wide Sargasso Sea* 1992; *Legends of the Fall* 1994; *Last Man Standing* 1996; *Kull the Conqueror* 1997
Lombard, Louise (1970–) *Gold in the Streets* 1996; *Talos the Mummy* 1997; *My Kingdom* 2001; *Hidalgo* 2003
Lombard, Michael (1934–) *Fatso* 1979; *"Crocodile" Dundee* 1986; *Pet Sematary* 1989
Lombardi, Louis *Amongst Friends* 1993; *The Animal* 2001
Lombardi, Paolo *A Month by the Lake* 1994; *A Pure Formality* 1994
Lommel, Ulli (1944–) *Fanny Hill: Memoirs of a Woman of Pleasure* 1964; *Love Is Colder Than Death* 1969; *The American Soldier* 1970; *Whity* 1970; *Effi Briest* 1974; *Chinese Roulette* 1976; *Satan's Brew* 1976; *Orbit* 1996
Lomnicki, Tadeusz (1927–1992) *A Generation* 1954; *Man of Marble* 1977; *The Contract* 1980; *Blind Chance* 1987
Loncar, Beba (1943–) *The Long Ships* 1963; *The Birds, the Bees, and the Italians* 1965; *Some Girls Do* 1969
Londez, Guilaine *Night and Day* 1991; *Skin of Man, Heart of Beast* 1999
London, Alexandra *Van Gogh* 1991; *Pourquoi Pas Moi?* 1999; *Les Destinées Sentimentales* 2000
London, Daniel *Patch Adams* 1998; *Four Dogs Playing Poker* 1999
London, Jason (1972–) *December* 1991; *The Man in the Moon* 1991; *Dazed and Confused* 1993; *Fall Time* 1994; *Safe Passage* 1994; *To Wong Foo, Thanks for Everything, Julie Newmar* 1995; *Countdown* 1996; *If These Walls Could Talk* 1996; *Broken Vessels* 1998; *The Rage: Carrie 2* 1999; *Poor White Trash* 2000
London, Jeremy (1972–) *The Babysitter* 1995; *Mallrats* 1995
London, Julie (1926–2000) *The Red House* 1947; *Task Force* 1949; *The Great Man* 1956; *Drango* 1957; *Man of the West* 1958; *Saddle the Wind* 1958; *Voice in the Mirror* 1958; *The Wonderful Country* 1959; *The Third Voice* 1960; *The George Raft Story* 1961
London, Tony (1963–) *Sid and Nancy* 1986; *24 Hours in London* 1999
Lone, John (1952–) *Iceman* 1984; *Year of the Dragon* 1985; *The Last Emperor* 1987; *Shadows of the Peacock* 1987; *The Moderns* 1988; *M Butterfly* 1993; *The Shadow* 1994; *The Hunted* 1995; *Rush Hour 2* 2001
Long, Audrey (1922–) *Tall in the Saddle* 1944; *A Game of Death* 1945; *Pan-Americana* 1945; *Desperate* 1947; *Lady of Deceit* 1947; *The Petty Girl* 1950; *Cavalry Scout* 1951; *Indian Uprising* 1951
Long, Howie (1960–) *Broken Arrow* 1996; *Dollar for the Dead* 1998; *Firestorm* 1998; *3000 Miles to Graceland* 2000
Long, Jodi *Patty Hearst* 1988; *Soursweet* 1988

Long, Joseph *Queen of Hearts* 1989; *The Unexpected Mrs Pollifax* 1999

Long, Justin (1978–) *Jeepers Creepers* 2001; *Crossroads* 2002; *Dodgeball: a True Underdog Story* 2004

Long, Mark *Stormy Monday* 1987; *Ten Minutes Older: the Cello* 2002

Long, Nia (1970–) *Buried Alive* 1990; *Boyz N the Hood* 1991; *Made in America* 1993; *Friday* 1995; *Love Jones* 1997; *Soul Food* 1997; *The Secret Laughter of Women* 1998; *The Best Man* 1999; *Held Up* 1999; *In Too Deep* 1999; *Stigmata* 1999; *Big Momma's House* 2000; *Boiler Room* 2000; *Baadasssss!* 2003; *Alfie* 2004; *Are We There Yet?* 2005

Long, Richard aka **Long, Dick** (1927–1974) *Tomorrow Is Forever* 1945; *The Dark Mirror* 1946; *The Stranger* 1946; *The Egg and I* 1947; *Criss Cross* 1949; *Ma and Pa Kettle* 1949; *Kansas Raiders* 1950; *Air Cadet* 1951; *The All American* 1953; *All I Desire* 1953; *Playgirl* 1954; *Cult of the Cobra* 1955; *He Laughed Last* 1956; *House on Haunted Hill* 1958

Long, Shelley (1949–) *The Cracker Factory* 1979; *A Small Circle of Friends* 1980; *Caveman* 1981; *Night Shift* 1982; *Losin' It* 1983; *Irreconcilable Differences* 1984; *The Money Pit* 1985; *Hello Again* 1987; *Outrageous Fortune* 1987; *Troop Beverly Hills* 1989; *The Boyfriend School* 1990; *Frozen Assets* 1992; *The Brady Bunch Movie* 1995; *A Very Brady Sequel* 1996; *Dr T & the Women* 2000

Long, Tom *Strange Planet* 1999; *The Dish* 2000; *Risk* 2000

Long, Walter (1879–1952) *The Birth of a Nation* 1915; *A Romance of the Redwoods* 1917; *The Sheik* 1921; *Blood and Sand* 1922; *Moby Dick* 1930; *Other Men's Women* 1931; *Pardon Us* 1931

Longden, John (1900–1971) *Blackmail* 1929; *Juno and the Paycock* 1930; *The Skin Game* 1931; *Young and Innocent* 1937; *Quatermass II* 1957

Longden, Terence aka **Longdon, Terence** (1922–) *Carry On Nurse* 1959; *Carry On Regardless* 1960; *Clash by Night* 1963

Longley, Victoria (1962–) *The More Things Change* 1985; *Celia* 1988; *Turtle Beach* 1992; *Dallas Doll* 1994

Longo, Tony (1962–) *Bloodhounds of Broadway* 1989; *Prehysteria!* 1993

Longstreth, Emily *Private Resort* 1985; *The Big Picture* 1989; *Confessions of a Hit Man* 1994

Lonsdale, Michel aka **Lonsdale, Michael** (1931–) *The Trial* 1962; *The Bride Wore Black* 1967; *Stolen Kisses* 1968; *There Was Once a Cop* 1969; *Le Souffle au Coeur* 1971; *The Day of the Jackal* 1973; *Out 1: Spectre* 1973; *Caravan to Vaccares* 1974; *Le Fantôme de la Liberté* 1974; *Galileo* 1974; *Stavisky* 1974; *The Evil Trap* 1975; *The Pink Telephone* 1975; *The Romantic Englishwoman* 1975; *Mr Klein* 1976; *The Passage* 1978; *Moonraker* 1979; *Enigma* 1982; *Erendira* 1982; *The Holcroft Covenant* 1985; *The Name of the Rose* 1986; *Operation Madonna* 1987; *Souvenir* 1987; *The Remains of the Day* 1993; *Jefferson in Paris* 1995; *Ronin* 1998; *5x2* 2004

Loo, Richard (1903–1983) *The Bitter Tea of General Yen* 1933; *Back to Bataan* 1945; *Betrayal from the East* 1945; *China Sky* 1945; *First Yank into Tokyo* 1945; *The Clay Pigeon* 1949; *The Steel Helmet* 1951; *Love Is a Many-Splendored Thing* 1955; *Confessions of an Opium Eater* 1962; *The Man with the Golden Gun* 1974

Loomis, Rod *The Beastmaster* 1982; *Bill & Ted's Excellent Adventure* 1988; *Jack's Back* 1988

Loos, Theodor aka **Loos, Theodore** (1883–1954) *The Nibelungen* 1924; *Metropolis* 1926; *Ariane* 1931; *M* 1931

Lopert, Tanya *Navajo Joe* 1966; *Once in Paris* 1978; *Tales of Ordinary Madness* 1981

Lopez, George (1961–) *Real Women Have Curves* 2002; *The Adventures of Sharkboy and Lavagirl in 3-D* 2005

Lopez, Gerry *Conan the Barbarian* 1982; *North Shore* 1987

Lopez, Jennifer (1970–) *Money Train* 1995; *Blood and Wine* 1996; *Jack* 1996; *Anaconda* 1997; *Selena* 1997; *U Turn* 1997; *Antz* 1998; *Out of Sight* 1998; *The Cell* 2000; *Angel Eyes* 2001; *The Wedding Planner* 2001; *Enough* 2002; *Maid in Manhattan* 2002; *Gigli* 2003; *Jersey Girl* 2003; *Shall We Dance* 2004; *Monster-in-Law* 2005

López, Mónica (1969–) *A Bench in the Park* 1998; *Intacto* 2001

Lopez, Perry (1931–) *Hell on Frisco Bay* 1955; *I Died a Thousand Times* 1955; *The Lone Ranger* 1956; *Violent Road* 1958; *Taras Bulba* 1962; *Chinatown* 1974; *Death Wish 4: the Crackdown* 1987; *Kinjite: Forbidden Subjects* 1989

Lopez, Sal (1954–) *Pucker Up and Bark like a Dog* 1989; *Blue Tiger* 1994

Lopez, Seidy *Mi Vida Loca* 1993; *The Stray* 1999

Lopez, Sergi (1965–) *Western* 1997; *Une Liaison Pornographique* 1999; *Lisboa* 1999; *La Nouvelle Eve* 1999; *Rien à Faire* 1999; *Harry, He's Here to Help* 2000; *Dirty Pretty Things* 2002

Lopez, Trini (1937–) *Marriage on the Rocks* 1965; *The Dirty Dozen* 1967

Lopez Moctezuma, Carlos (1909–1980) *The Proud Ones* 1953; *Viva Maria!* 1965

Lorain, Sophie (1957–) *In Her Defense* 1998; *Mambo Italiano* 2003

Lorca, Isabel *Lightning the White Stallion* 1986; *She's Having a Baby* 1988

Lord, Jack (1920–1998) *The Court-Martial of Billy Mitchell* 1955; *The Vagabond King* 1956; *Tip on a Dead Jockey* 1957; *The True Story of Lynn Stuart* 1957; *God's Little Acre* 1958; *Man of the West* 1958; *The Hangman* 1959; *Walk like a Dragon* 1960; *Dr No* 1962; *The Doomsday Flight* 1966; *The Ride to Hangman's Tree* 1967; *The Counterfeit Killer* 1968

Lord, Marion aka **Lord, Marian** (1883–1942) *Broadway* 1929; *One Heavenly Night* 1931

Lord, Marjorie (1922–) *Johnny Come Lately* 1943; *Sherlock Holmes in Washington* 1943; *Boy, Did I Get a Wrong Number* 1966

Lordan, John *Going All the Way* 1997; *The Company* 2003

Lords, Traci (1968–) *Not of This Earth* 1988; *Cry-Baby* 1989; *Fast Food* 1989; *Raw Nerve* 1991; *A Time to Die* 1991; *Intent to Kill* 1992; *Ice* 1994; *Plughead Rewired: Circuitry Man II* 1994; *Serial Mom* 1994; *Underworld* 1996; *Blade* 1998

Loren, Sophia (1934–) *Gold of Naples* 1954; *Lucky to Be a Woman* 1955; *The Miller's Wife* 1955; *Too Bad She's Bad* 1955; *Woman of the River* 1955; *Boy on a Dolphin* 1957; *Legend of the Lost* 1957; *The Pride and the Passion* 1957; *Desire under the Elms* 1958; *Houseboat* 1958; *The Key* 1958; *The Black Orchid* 1959; *That Kind of Woman* 1959; *A Breath of Scandal* 1960; *Heller in Pink Tights* 1960; *It Started in Naples* 1960; *The Millionairess* 1960; *Two Women* 1960; *Boccaccio '70* 1961; *El Cid* 1961; *Madame* 1961; *The Condemned of Altona* 1962; *Five Miles to Midnight* 1963; *Yesterday, Today and Tomorrow* 1963; *The Fall of the Roman Empire* 1964; *Marriage – Italian Style* 1964; *Lady L* 1965; *Operation Crossbow* 1965; *Arabesque* 1966; *Judith* 1966; *A Countess from Hong Kong* 1967; *Ghosts – Italian Style* 1967; *More than a Miracle* 1967; *Sunflower* 1969; *The Priest's Wife* 1970; *Lady Liberty* 1971; *Man of La Mancha* 1972; *Brief Encounter* 1974; *Verdict* 1974; *The Voyage* 1974; *The Cassandra Crossing* 1976; *A Special Day* 1977; *Brass Target* 1978; *Blood Feud* 1979; *Firepower* 1979; *Pret-a-Porter* 1994; *Grumpier Old Men* 1996; *Francesca and Nunziata* 2001

Lorenzon, Livio (1923–1971) *Goliath and the Barbarians* 1959; *Pontius Pilate* 1961; *The Spartan Gladiators* 1964

Lorimer, Glennis (1913–) *Alf's Button Afloat* 1938; *Ask a Policeman* 1938

Lorimer, Louise (1898–1995) *Japanese War Bride* 1952; *–30–* 1959

Loring, Teala (1924–) *Bluebeard* 1944; *Dark Alibi* 1946

Lorinz, James *Frankenhooker* 1990; *Me and the Mob* 1992; *The Jerky Boys* 1995

Lorit, Jean-Pierre *Jeanne la Pucelle* 1994; *Three Colours Red* 1994; *Alice et Martin* 1998

Lorne, Marion (1888–1968) *Strangers on a Train* 1951; *The Girl Rush* 1955

Lorre, Peter (1904–1964) *M* 1931; *The Man Who Knew Too Much* 1934; *Crime and Punishment* 1935; *Mad Love* 1935; *Crack-Up* 1936; *Secret Agent* 1936; *Lancer Spy* 1937; *Nancy Steele Is Missing* 1937; *Thank You, Mr Moto* 1937; *Think Fast, Mr Moto* 1937; *Mr Moto Takes a Chance* 1938; *Mr Moto's Gamble* 1938; *Mysterious Mr Moto* 1938; *Mr Moto in Danger Island* 1939; *Mr Moto Takes a Vacation* 1939; *Mr Moto's Last Warning* 1939; *I Was an Adventuress* 1940; *Strange Cargo* 1940; *Stranger on the Third Floor* 1940; *You'll Find Out* 1940; *The Face behind the Mask* 1941; *The Maltese Falcon* 1941; *They Met in Bombay* 1941; *All through the Night* 1942; *The Boogie Man Will Get You* 1942; *Casablanca* 1942; *The Invisible Agent* 1942; *Background to Danger* 1943; *The Constant Nymph* 1943; *The Cross of Lorraine* 1943; *Arsenic and Old Lace* 1944; *The Conspirators* 1944; *Hollywood Canteen* 1944; *The Mask of Dimitrios* 1944; *Passage to Marseille* 1944; *Confidential Agent* 1945; *Hotel Berlin* 1945; *The Beast with Five Fingers* 1946; *Black Angel* 1946; *The Chase* 1946; *Three Strangers* 1946; *The Verdict* 1946; *My Favorite Brunette* 1947; *Casbah* 1948; *Rope of Sand* 1949; *Quicksand* 1950; *The Lost One* 1951; *Beat the Devil* 1953; *20,000 Leagues under the Sea* 1954; *Around the World in 80 Days* 1956; *Congo Crossing* 1956; *The Buster Keaton Story* 1957; *Hell Ship Mutiny* 1957; *The Sad Sack* 1957; *Silk Stockings* 1957; *The Big Circus* 1959; *Scent of Mystery* 1960; *Voyage to the Bottom of the Sea* 1961; *Five Weeks in a Balloon* 1962; *Tales of Terror* 1962; *The Raven* 1963; *The Comedy of Terrors* 1964; *Muscle Beach Party* 1964; *The Patsy* 1964

Lorring, Joan (1926–) *The Corn Is Green* 1945; *Three Strangers* 1946; *The Verdict* 1946; *The Gangster* 1947; *The Lost Moment* 1947; *The Other Love* 1947; *Good Sam* 1948; *The Big Night* 1951; *The Midnight Man* 1974

Lorys, Diana (1940–) *The Awful Dr Orloff* 1962; *Bad Man's River* 1971

Losch, Tilly (1904–1975) *The Garden of Allah* 1936; *The Good Earth* 1937

Lothar, Susanne (1960–) *Funny Games* 1997; *The Piano Teacher* 2001

Lotis, Dennis (1928–) *The City of the Dead* 1960; *She'll Have to Go* 1961

Lottimer, Eb *Streets* 1990; *The Finest Hour* 1991; *Quake!* 1992

Louanne (1970–) *Oh God! Book II* 1980; *A Night in the Life of Jimmy Reardon* 1988

Loughlin, Lori (1965–) *Amityville III: the Demon* 1983; *Secret Admirer* 1985; *Brotherhood of Justice* 1986; *Back to the Beach* 1987; *The Night Before* 1988; *One of Her Own* 1994

Louie, "Ducky" *Back to Bataan* 1945; *China Sky* 1945; *Black Gold* 1947

Louie, John (1970–) *Oh God! Book II* 1980; *Gremlins* 1984

Louis, Joe (1914–1981) *This Is the Army* 1943; *The Square Jungle* 1955

Louis, Justin (1967–) *Jack Reed: One of Our Own* 1995; *Everything Put Together* 2000

Louis, Willard (1886–1926) *Robin Hood* 1922; *Kiss Me Again* 1925; *Don Juan* 1926

Louis-Dreyfus, Julia (1961–) *Troll* 1986; *North* 1994; *Deconstructing Harry* 1997; *Fathers' Day* 1997; *A Bug's Life* 1998; *Animal Farm* 1999; *Geppetto* 2000

Louise, Anita (1915–1970) *Our Betters* 1933; *Judge Priest* 1934; *Madame Du Barry* 1934; *A Midsummer Night's Dream* 1935; *Anthony Adverse* 1936; *The Story of Louis Pasteur* 1936; *First Lady* 1937; *Green Light* 1937; *That Certain Woman* 1937; *Tovarich* 1937; *Going Places* 1938; *Marie Antoinette* 1938; *The Sisters* 1938; *The Little Princess* 1939; *The Villain Still Pursued Her* 1940; *Casanova Brown* 1944; *Love Letters* 1945; *The Bandit of Sherwood Forest* 1946; *Personality Kid* 1946; *Retreat, Hell!* 1952

Louise, Tina (1934–) *God's Little Acre* 1958; *The Baited Trap* 1959; *Day of the Outlaw* 1959; *The Hangman* 1959; *The Siege of Syracuse* 1959; *Armored Command* 1961; *For Those Who Think Young* 1964; *The Good Guys and the Bad Guys* 1969; *The Happy Ending* 1969; *The Wrecking Crew* 1969; *The Stepford Wives* 1975; *Mean Dog Blues* 1978; *Hellriders* 1983

Louiso, Todd (1970–) *Jerry Maguire* 1996; *8 Heads in a Duffel Bag* 1997; *High Fidelity* 2000

Louvigny, Jacques (1880–1951) *On Purge Bébé* 1931; *La Symphonie Pastorale* 1946

Love, Alan *That Sinking Feeling* 1979; *The Apple* 1980

Love, Bessie (1898–1986) *The Lost World* 1925; *The Matinee Idol* 1928; *The Broadway Melody* 1929; *Hollywood Revue* 1929; *Next to No Time* 1958; *Nowhere to Go* 1958; *Isadora* 1968; *Catlow* 1971; *Lady Chatterley's Lover* 1981; *Reds* 1981

Love, Courtney (1964–) *Sid and Nancy* 1986; *Straight to Hell* 1987; *Basquiat* 1996; *Feeling Minnesota* 1996; *The People vs Larry Flynt* 1996; *Man on the Moon* 1999; *200 Cigarettes* 1999; *Trapped* 2002

Love, Darlene (1938–) *Lethal Weapon* 1987; *Lethal Weapon 2* 1989; *Lethal Weapon 3* 1992; *Lethal Weapon 4* 1998

Love, David *Teenagers from Outer Space* 1959; *The House of Yes* 1997

Love, Faizon (1968–) *Bebe's Kids* 1992; *3 Strikes* 2000; *Wonderland* 2003

Love, Montagu aka **Love, Montague** (1877–1943) *Hands Up!* 1926; *The Son of the Sheik* 1926; *The Last Warning* 1928; *The Wind* 1928; *Bulldog Drummond* 1929; *The Mysterious Island* 1929; *Outward Bound* 1930; *His Double Life* 1933; *The Man Who Broke the Bank at Monte Carlo* 1935; *Lloyd's of London* 1936; *One in a Million* 1936; *Sing, Baby, Sing* 1936; *A Damsel in Distress* 1937; *London by Night* 1937; *Parnell* 1937; *Gunga Din* 1939; *Rulers of the Sea* 1939; *We Are Not Alone* 1939; *Dr Ehrlich's Magic Bullet* 1940; *The Mark of Zorro* 1940; *Son of Monte Cristo* 1940; *The Devil and Miss Jones* 1941; *Shining Victory* 1941; *Sherlock Holmes and the Voice of Terror* 1942; *Forever and a Day* 1943

Love, Patti *Terror* 1979; *Steaming* 1985

Love, Victor (1957–) *Native Son* 1986; *Heaven Is a Playground* 1991

Lovegrove, Arthur (1913–1981) *The Steel Key* 1953; *Naked Fury* 1959

Lovejoy, Frank (1914–1982) *Home of the Brave* 1949; *Breakthrough* 1950; *In a Lonely Place* 1950; *The Sound of Fury* 1950; *Three Secrets* 1950; *Force of Arms* 1951; *Goodbye, My Fancy* 1951; *I Was a Communist for the FBI* 1951; *I'll See You in My Dreams* 1951; *Retreat, Hell!* 1952; *The Charge at Feather River* 1953; *The Hitch-Hiker* 1953; *House of Wax* 1953; *Beachhead* 1954; *Men of the Fighting Lady* 1954; *The Americano* 1955; *Shack Out on 101* 1955; *Strategic Air Command* 1955; *Julie* 1956; *Three Brave Men* 1956

Lovelace, Linda (1952–2002) *Deep Throat* 1972; *Linda Lovelace for President* 1975

Lovell, Raymond (1900–1953) *Contraband* 1940; *The Common Touch* 1941; *Uncensored* 1942; *The Young Mr Pitt* 1942; *Candlelight in Algeria* 1943; *The Man in Grey* 1943; *Hotel Reserve* 1944; *Caesar and Cleopatra* 1945; *Night Boat to Dublin* 1946; *The End of the River* 1947; *The Blind Goddess* 1948; *The Calendar* 1948; *My Brother's Keeper* 1948; *The Three Weird Sisters* 1948; *The Bad Lord Byron* 1949; *Fools Rush In* 1949; *Madness of the Heart* 1949; *The Romantic Age* 1949; *The Mudlark* 1950; *Time Gentlemen Please!* 1952; *The Steel Key* 1953

Lovelock, Raymond (1950–) *Django Kill* 1967; *Fiddler on the Roof* 1971; *The Living Dead at the Manchester Morgue* 1974

Lovett, Dorothy (1915–1998) *Meet Dr Christian* 1939; *Call Out the Marines* 1941; *Look Who's Laughing* 1941

Lovett, Lyle (1957–) *Pret-a-Porter* 1994; *Breast Men* 1997; *Fear and Loathing in Las Vegas* 1998; *The Opposite of Sex* 1998; *The New Guy* 2002

Lovgren, David *Live Bait* 1995; *Rollercoaster* 1999

Lovitz, Jon (1957–) *The Brave Little Toaster* 1987; *Big* 1988; *My Stepmother Is an Alien* 1988; *Mr Destiny* 1990; *An American Tail: Fievel Goes West* 1991; *Mom and Dad Save the World* 1992; *Coneheads* 1993; *National Lampoon's Loaded Weapon 1* 1993; *City Slickers II: the Legend of Curly's Gold* 1994; *North* 1994; *Trapped in Paradise* 1994; *The Great White Hype* 1996; *High School High* 1996; *Happiness* 1998; *Lost & Found* 1999; *Small Time Crooks* 2000; *3000 Miles to Graceland* 2000; *Good Advice* 2001; *Rat Race* 2001; *Adam Sandler's Eight Crazy Nights* 2003; *Dickie Roberts: Former Child Star* 2003; *The Stepford Wives* 2004

Lovsky, Celia (1897–1979) *Captain Carey, USA* 1950; *Man of a Thousand Faces* 1957; *The Mobster* 1958; *The Gene Krupa Story* 1959; *36 Hours* 1964; *Harlow* 1965

Löw, Victor (1962–) *House Call* 1996; *Character* 1997

Lowe, Alex *Peter's Friends* 1992; *Haunted* 1995

Lowe, Arthur (1915–1982) *Final Appointment* 1954; *One Way Out* 1955; *This Sporting Life* 1963; *if....* 1968; *The Bed Sitting Room* 1969; *A Hole Lot of Trouble* 1969; *The Rise and Rise of Michael Rimmer* 1970; *Dad's Army* 1971; *Adolf Hitler – My Part in His Downfall* 1972; *The Ruling Class* 1972; *No Sex Please – We're British* 1973; *O Lucky Man!* 1973; *Theatre of Blood* 1973;

Man about the House 1974; *The Bawdy Adventures of Tom Jones* 1976; *The Lady Vanishes* 1979
Lowe, Barry *Cash on Demand* 1961; *Sands of the Kalahari* 1965
Lowe, Chad (1968–) *Apprentice to Murder* 1988; *Highway to Hell* 1992; *Take Me Home: the John Denver Story* 2000; *Unfaithful* 2002
Lowe, Edmund (1890–1971) *What Price Glory* 1926; *The Cock-Eyed World* 1929; *In Old Arizona* 1929; *Born Reckless* 1930; *The Cisco Kid* 1931; *Chandu the Magician* 1932; *Dinner at Eight* 1933; *Black Sheep* 1935; *Seven Sinners* 1936; *Espionage* 1937; *Every Day's a Holiday* 1937; *The Squeaker* 1937; *I Love You Again* 1940; *Call Out the Marines* 1941; *Dillinger* 1945; *Good Sam* 1948; *The Wings of Eagles* 1957; *Heller in Pink Tights* 1960
Lowe, Rob (1964–) *Class* 1983; *The Outsiders* 1983; *The Hotel New Hampshire* 1984; *Oxford Blues* 1984; *St Elmo's Fire* 1985; *About Last Night...* 1986; *Youngblood* 1986; *Square Dance* 1987; *Illegally Yours* 1988; *Masquerade* 1988; *Bad Influence* 1990; *The Dark Backward* 1991; *The Finest Hour* 1991; *Wayne's World* 1992; *Frank and Jesse* 1995; *Tommy Boy* 1995; *Contact* 1997; *For Hire* 1997; *Atomic Train* 1999; *Austin Powers: the Spy Who Shagged Me* 1999; *Dead Silent* 1999; *Escape under Pressure* 2000; *The Specials* 2000; *Framed* 2002; *View from the Top* 2003
Lowell, Carey (1961–) *Dangerously Close* 1986; *Down Twisted* 1987; *Licence to Kill* 1989; *The Guardian* 1990; *Road to Ruin* 1992; *Fierce Creatures* 1997
Lowell, Helen (1866–1937) *Isn't Life Wonderful* 1924; *Devil Dogs of the Air* 1935; *Strike Me Pink* 1936
Lowenadler, Holger (1904–1977) *A Ship to India* 1947; *Lacombe Lucien* 1974
Lowensohn, Elina (1967–) *Simple Men* 1992; *Amateur* 1994; *Nadja* 1995; *I'm Not Rappaport* 1996; *In the Presence of Mine Enemies* 1997; *Six Ways to Sunday* 1997; *The Wisdom of Crocodiles* 1998
Lowery, Andrew (1970–) *School Ties* 1992; *My Boyfriend's Back* 1993; *Color of Night* 1994
Lowery, Robert (1913–1971) *Four Sons* 1940; *The Mummy's Ghost* 1944; *Jalopy* 1953; *The Parson and the Outlaw* 1957; *The Rise and Fall of Legs Diamond* 1960
Löwitsch, Klaus *aka* **Lowitsch, Klaus** *aka* **Loewitsch, Klaus** (1936–2002) *The Odessa File* 1974; *Cross of Iron* 1977; *Breakthrough* 1978; *Despair* 1978; *The Marriage of Maria Braun* 1978; *Gotcha!* 1985; *Extreme Ops* 2003
Lowry, Lynn (1947–) *The Crazies* 1973; *Shivers* 1975; *Fighting Mad* 1976
Lowry, Morton (1908–1987) *The Dawn Patrol* 1938; *A Yank in the RAF* 1941; *Pursuit to Algiers* 1945; *The Verdict* 1946
Lowther, T J (1986–) *A Home of Our Own* 1993; *A Perfect World* 1993
Loy, Myrna (1905–1993) *Don Juan* 1926; *The Exquisite Sinner* 1926; *So This Is Paris* 1926; *The Jazz Singer* 1927; *Noah's Ark* 1928; *The Black Watch* 1929; *The Desert Song* 1929; *The Show of Shows* 1929; *The Devil to Pay* 1930; *Renegades* 1930; *Under a Texas Moon* 1930; *Arrowsmith* 1931; *Body and Soul* 1931; *A Connecticut Yankee* 1931; *Consolation Marriage* 1931; *The Animal Kingdom* 1932; *Emma* 1932; *Love Me Tonight* 1932; *The Mask of Fu Manchu* 1932; *The Wet Parade* 1932; *The Barbarian* 1933; *Night Flight* 1933; *Penthouse* 1933; *The Prizefighter and the Lady* 1933; *Topaze* 1933; *When Ladies Meet* 1933; *Broadway Bill* 1934; *Evelyn Prentice* 1934; *Manhattan Melodrama* 1934; *Men in White* 1934; *Stamboul Quest* 1934; *The Thin Man* 1934; *Whipsaw* 1935; *Wings in the Dark* 1935; *After the Thin Man* 1936; *The Great Ziegfeld* 1936; *Libeled Lady* 1936; *Wife vs Secretary* 1936; *Double Wedding* 1937; *Man-Proof* 1937; *Parnell* 1937; *Test Pilot* 1938; *Too Hot to Handle* 1938; *Another Thin Man* 1939; *The Rains Came* 1939; *I Love You Again* 1940; *Third Finger, Left Hand* 1940; *Love Crazy* 1941; *Shadow of the Thin Man* 1941; *The Thin Man Goes Home* 1944; *The Best Years of Our Lives* 1946; *So Goes My Love* 1946; *The Bachelor and the Bobby-Soxer* 1947; *The Senator Was Indiscreet* 1947; *Song of the Thin Man* 1947; *Mr Blandings Builds His Dream House* 1948; *The Red Pony* 1949; *That Dangerous Age* 1949; *Cheaper by the Dozen* 1950; *Belles on Their Toes* 1952; *The Ambassador's Daughter* 1956; *Lonelyhearts* 1958; *From the Terrace* 1960; *Midnight Lace* 1960; *The April Fools* 1969; *Airport 1975* 1974; *The End* 1978; *Just Tell Me What You Want* 1980
Lozano, Manuel *Butterfly's Tongue* 1999; *You're My Hero* 2003
Lozano, Margarita (1931–) *Viridiana* 1961; *A Fistful of Dollars* 1964; *The Night of San Lorenzo* 1981; *Kaos* 1984; *Manon des Sources* 1986; *Night Sun* 1990
Lu Liping *The Blue Kite* 1992; *Love Will Tear Us Apart* 1999; *Shadow Magic* 2000
Lu, Lisa (1931–) *The Mountain Road* 1960; *Demon Seed* 1977; *Don't Cry, It's Only Thunder* 1982; *The Joy Luck Club* 1993
Lualdi, Antonella (1931–) *Le Rouge et le Noir* 1954; *Young Husbands* 1958; *Web of Passion* 1959; *The Mongols* 1961; *Let's Talk About Women* 1964; *Ragan* 1967; *Vincent, François, Paul and the Others* 1974
Luca, Loes *The Girl with Red Hair* 1981; *Abel* 1986
Lucas, Josh *aka* **Lucas, Joshua** (1971–) *Class of '61* 1993; *True Blue* 1996; *The Weight of Water* 2000; *A Beautiful Mind* 2001; *The Deep End* 2001; *Session 9* 2001; *Sweet Home Alabama* 2002; *Hulk* 2003; *Wonderland* 2003; *Around the Bend* 2004; *Undertow* 2004
Lucas, Laurent (1965–) *Rien sur Robert* 1998; *La Nouvelle Eve* 1999; *Pola X* 1999; *Harry, He's Here to Help* 2000; *In My Skin* 2002; *Who Killed Bambi?* 2003; *The Ordeal* 2004
Lucas, Lisa (1961–) *An Unmarried Woman* 1978; *Hadley's Rebellion* 1984
Lucas, Wilfred (1871–1940) *Dishonored* 1931; *Pardon Us* 1931; *Criminal Lawyer* 1937
Lucas, William (1925–) *X the Unknown* 1956; *Crack in the Mirror* 1960; *Sons and Lovers* 1960; *Payroll* 1961; *The Shadow of the Cat* 1961; *The Break* 1962; *Calculated Risk* 1963; *The Marked One* 1963; *Night of the Big Heat* 1967
Luce, Angela (1938–) *The Decameron* 1970; *L'Amore Molesto* 1995
Luce, Claire (1903–1989) *Up the River* 1930; *Lazybones* 1935; *Vintage Wine* 1935; *Over She Goes* 1937
Lucero, Enrique (1920–1989) *Villa!* 1958; *Macario* 1960; *Tarzan and the Valley of Gold* 1966; *Shark!* 1969; *Two Mules for Sister Sara* 1970; *The Return of a Man Called Horse* 1976; *Green Ice* 1981
Luchini, Fabrice (1951–) *Immoral Tales* 1974; *Perceval le Gallois* 1978; *Full Moon in Paris* 1984; *Hôtel du Paradis* 1986; *Uranus* 1990; *Le Colonel Chabert* 1994; *Beaumarchais l'Insolent* 1996; *Men, Women: a User's Manual* 1996; *Le Bossu* 1997; *Rien sur Robert* 1998; *Confidences Trop Intimes* 2004
Luckham, Cyril (1907–1989) *Stranger from Venus* 1954; *The Naked Runner* 1967; *Providence* 1977
Luckinbill, Laurence (1934–) *The Boys in the Band* 1970; *Such Good Friends* 1971; *Corky* 1972; *Face of a Stranger* 1978; *Not for Publication* 1984; *Cocktail* 1988; *Messenger of Death* 1988; *Star Trek V: the Final Frontier* 1989
Lucking, William *aka* **Lucking, Bill** (1942–) *The Magnificent Seven Ride!* 1972; *Oklahoma Crude* 1973; *Doc Savage: the Man of Bronze* 1975; *Birch Interval* 1976; *The Return of a Man Called Horse* 1976; *Rescue Me* 1991; *The River Wild* 1994; *Welcome to the Jungle* 2003
Luddy, Barbara (1908–1979) *Lady and the Tramp* 1955; *Sleeping Beauty* 1959
Ludlow, Patrick (1903–1996) *Evergreen* 1934; *Gangway* 1937; *Old Mother Riley* 1937
Ludwig, Pamela *Over the Edge* 1979; *Death of an Angel* 1985; *Race for Glory* 1989
Ludwig, Salem (1915–) *Never Love a Stranger* 1958; *America, America* 1963
Lugagne, Françoise (1918–) *The Witches of Salem* 1957; *The Diary of a Chambermaid* 1964
Lugosi, Bela (1882–1956) *Renegades* 1930; *Dracula* 1931; *Chandu the Magician* 1932; *Island of Lost Souls* 1932; *Murders in the Rue Morgue* 1932; *White Zombie* 1932; *The Death Kiss* 1933; *The Devil's in Love* 1933; *International House* 1933; *The Black Cat* 1934; *Mark of the Vampire* 1935; *The Raven* 1935; *The Invisible Ray* 1936; *Dark Eyes of London* 1939; *Ninotchka* 1939; *Son of Frankenstein* 1939; *Devil Bat* 1940; *The Saint's Double Trouble* 1940; *You'll Find Out* 1940; *The Black Cat* 1941; *Invisible Ghost* 1941; *Spooks Run Wild* 1941; *The Wolf Man* 1941; *The Ghost of Frankenstein* 1942; *Frankenstein Meets the Wolf Man* 1943; *Ghosts in the Night* 1943; *The Return of the Vampire* 1943; *Voodoo Man* 1944; *The Body Snatcher* 1945; *Scared to Death* 1947; *Abbott and Costello Meet Frankenstein* 1948; *Bela Lugosi Meets a Brooklyn Gorilla* 1952; *Glen or Glenda* 1953; *Bride of the Monster* 1955; *The Black Sleep* 1956; *Plan 9 from Outer Space* 1959
Luguet, André (1892–1979) *The Mad Genius* 1931; *Jewel Robbery* 1932; *The Man Who Played God* 1932; *Madame du Barry* 1954; *Une Parisienne* 1957
Luisi, James (1928–) *Stunts* 1977; *Feds* 1988
Lukas, Paul (1887–1971) *The Shopworn Angel* 1928; *Anybody's Woman* 1930; *The Devil's Holiday* 1930; *Grumpy* 1930; *City Streets* 1931; *No One Man* 1932; *Rockabye* 1932; *The Kiss before the Mirror* 1933; *Little Women* 1933; *By Candlelight* 1934; *The Fountain* 1934; *Glamour* 1934; *The Casino Murder Case* 1935; *I Found Stella Parish* 1935; *The Three Musketeers* 1935; *Dodsworth* 1936; *Ladies in Love* 1936; *Dinner at the Ritz* 1937; *Espionage* 1937; *The Lady Vanishes* 1938; *Confessions of a Nazi Spy* 1939; *A Window in London* 1939; *The Ghost Breakers* 1940; *Strange Cargo* 1940; *They Dare Not Love* 1941; *Hostages* 1943; *Watch on the Rhine* 1943; *Address Unknown* 1944; *Experiment Perilous* 1944; *Uncertain Glory* 1944; *Deadline at Dawn* 1946; *Temptation* 1946; *Berlin Express* 1948; *Kim* 1950; *20,000 Leagues under the Sea* 1954; *The Roots of Heaven* 1958; *Scent of Mystery* 1960; *Tender Is the Night* 1961; *Fun in Acapulco* 1963; *Lord Jim* 1965; *Sol Madrid* 1968
Lukaszewicz, Olgierd *The Story of Sin* 1975; *Interrogation* 1982
Luke, Benny *La Cage aux Folles* 1978; *La Cage aux Folles II* 1980; *La Cage aux Folles III: "Elles" Se Marient* 1985
Luke, Derek (1974–) *Antwone Fisher* 2002; *Pieces of April* 2002; *Biker Boyz* 2003; *Friday Night Lights* 2004; *Spartan* 2004
Luke, Jorge *The Revengers* 1972; *Ulzana's Raid* 1972; *The Return of a Man Called Horse* 1976; *Eagle's Wing* 1978
Luke, Keye (1904–1991) *Charlie Chan in Paris* 1935; *Charlie Chan in Shanghai* 1935; *Charlie Chan at the Circus* 1936; *Charlie Chan at the Opera* 1936; *Charlie Chan at Monte Carlo* 1937; *Charlie Chan at the Olympics* 1937; *Charlie Chan on Broadway* 1937; *The Good Earth* 1937; *International Settlement* 1938; *Mr Moto's Gamble* 1938; *Dr Gillespie's New Assistant* 1942; *Dr Gillespie's Criminal Case* 1943; *Salute to the Marines* 1943; *Andy Hardy's Blonde Trouble* 1944; *Three Men in White* 1944; *First Yank into Tokyo* 1945; *Sleep, My Love* 1948; *Hell's Half Acre* 1954; *Yangtse Incident* 1956; *The Amsterdam Kill* 1978; *Just You and Me, Kid* 1979; *Gremlins* 1984; *Dead Heat* 1988
Lukschy, Wolfgang (1905–1983) *Sherlock Holmes and the Deadly Necklace* 1962; *A Fistful of Dollars* 1964; *Inside Out* 1975
Lulli, Folco (1912–1970) *Lights of Variety* 1950; *The Wages of Fear* 1953; *The Sign of the Gladiator* 1958; *The Great War* 1959
Lulli, Piero (1923–1991) *Hero of Babylon* 1963; *Django Kill* 1967; *My Name Is Nobody* 1973
Lulu (1948–) *Gonks Go Beat* 1965; *To Sir, with Love* 1967; *Whatever Happened to Harold Smith?* 1999
Lumbly, Carl (1952–) *The Bedroom Window* 1987; *Everybody's All-American* 1988; *Judgment in Berlin* 1988; *Pacific Heights* 1990; *To Sleep with Anger* 1990; *South Central* 1992; *Buffalo Soldiers* 1997; *Little Richard* 2000
Lumet, Baruch (1898–1992) *The Killer Shrews* 1959; *The Pawnbroker* 1965
Lumley, Joanna (1946–) *Don't Just Lie There, Say Something!* 1973; *The Satanic Rites of Dracula* 1973; *Trail of the Pink Panther* 1982; *The Curse of the Pink Panther* 1983; *Shirley Valentine* 1989; *A Ghost in Monte Carlo* 1990; *Innocent Lies* 1995; *James and the Giant Peach* 1996; *Prince Valiant* 1997; *Parting Shots* 1998; *Mad Cows* 1999; *Maybe Baby* 1999; *Whispers: an Elephant's Tale* 2000; *The Cat's Meow* 2001; *Ella Enchanted* 2004; *The Magic Roundabout* 2005
Lummis, Dayton (1903–1988) *Man in the Dark* 1953; *The Flight That Disappeared* 1961; *Beauty and the Beast* 1962
Luna, Barbara (1939–) *The Devil at Four o'Clock* 1961; *Mail Order Bride* 1963; *Get off My Back* 1965; *Che!* 1969; *The Concrete Jungle* 1982
Luna, Diego (1979–) *Y Tu Mamá También* 2001; *Dirty Dancing 2* 2003; *Open Range* 2003; *Criminal* 2004; *The Terminal* 2004
Lund, Art (1915–1990) *The Molly Maguires* 1970; *Black Caesar* 1973; *The Last American Hero* 1973
Lund, Deanna (1937–) *Hardly Working* 1981; *Elves* 1989
Lund, John (1913–1992) *To Each His Own* 1946; *The Perils of Pauline* 1947; *A Foreign Affair* 1948; *Miss Tatlock's Millions* 1948; *Night Has a Thousand Eyes* 1948; *Bride of Vengeance* 1949; *My Friend Irma* 1949; *My Friend Irma Goes West* 1950; *No Man of Her Own* 1950; *Darling, How Could You!* 1951; *The Mating Season* 1951; *The Battle at Apache Pass* 1952; *Bronco Buster* 1952; *Latin Lovers* 1953; *The Woman They Almost Lynched* 1953; *Chief Crazy Horse* 1955; *Five Guns West* 1955; *White Feather* 1955; *Dakota Incident* 1956; *High Society* 1956; *The Wackiest Ship in the Army* 1961; *If a Man Answers* 1962
Lundgren, Dolph (1959–) *Rocky IV* 1985; *Masters of the Universe* 1987; *Dark Angel* 1989; *The Punisher* 1989; *Red Scorpion* 1989; *Cover-Up* 1991; *Showdown in Little Tokyo* 1991; *Universal Soldier* 1992; *Army of One* 1993; *Pentathlon* 1994; *The Shooter* 1994; *Johnny Mnemonic* 1995; *Men of War* 1995; *Silent Trigger* 1996; *The Peacekeeper* 1997; *The Minion* 1998; *Bridge of Dragons* 1999; *Storm Catcher* 1999; *Sweepers* 1999; *Agent Red* 2000; *Jill Rips* 2000; *Hidden Agenda* 2001; *Fat Slags* 2004
Lundigan, William (1914–1975) *Wives under Suspicion* 1938; *Three Smart Girls Grow Up* 1939; *East of the River* 1940; *The Case of the Black Parrot* 1941; *Andy Hardy's Double Life* 1942; *Apache Trail* 1942; *The Courtship of Andy Hardy* 1942; *Dishonored Lady* 1947; *The Fabulous Dorseys* 1947; *Mystery in Mexico* 1948; *Pinky* 1949; *The House on Telegraph Hill* 1951; *I'd Climb the Highest Mountain* 1951; *Love Nest* 1951; *Inferno* 1953; *Serpent of the Nile* 1953
Lundy, Jessica (1966–) *Vampire's Kiss* 1988; *Madhouse* 1990; *The Stupids* 1995; *Rocketman* 1997
Lung Sihung (1930–2002) *Pushing Hands* 1991; *The Wedding Banquet* 1993; *Eat Drink Man Woman* 1994
Lunge, Romilly *Königsmark* 1935; *His Lordship* 1936
Lunghi, Cherie (1953–) *Excalibur* 1981; *Oliver Twist* 1982; *The Sign of Four* 1983; *Parker* 1984; *King David* 1985; *Letters to an Unknown Lover* 1985; *The Mission* 1986; *To Kill a Priest* 1988; *Jack & Sarah* 1995; *Burn Hollywood Burn* 1997
Lunsford, Beverly (1945–) *That Night* 1957; *The Intruder* 1961
Lunt, Alfred (1892–1977) *Sally of the Sawdust* 1925; *The Guardsman* 1931
Luong Ham Chau *The Game Is Over* 1966; *The Chinese Connection* 1988
Lupi, Roldano (1908–1989) *Crossed Swords* 1954; *The Mongols* 1961
Lupien, Tabitha (1990–) *Rent-a-Kid* 1992; *Look Who's Talking Now!* 1993
Lupino, Ida (1914–1995) *The Ghost Camera* 1933; *I Lived with You* 1933; *Peter Ibbetson* 1935; *Anything Goes* 1936; *The Gay Desperado* 1936; *One Rainy Afternoon* 1936; *Artists and Models* 1937; *Sea Devils* 1937; *The Adventures of Sherlock Holmes* 1939; *The Light That Failed* 1939; *The Lone Wolf Spy Hunt* 1939; *They Drive by Night* 1940; *High Sierra* 1941; *Ladies in Retirement* 1941; *Out of the Fog* 1941; *The Sea Wolf* 1941; *The Hard Way* 1942; *Life Begins at 8.30* 1942; *Moontide* 1942; *Forever and a Day* 1943; *In Our Time* 1944; *Devotion* 1946; *The Man I Love* 1946; *Deep Valley* 1947; *Escape Me Never* 1947; *Road House* 1948; *On Dangerous Ground* 1951; *Beware, My Lovely* 1952; *The Bigamist* 1953; *Jennifer* 1953; *Private Hell 36* 1954; *The Big Knife* 1955; *Women's Prison* 1955; *While the City Sleeps* 1956; *Backtrack* 1969; *Deadhead Miles* 1972; *Junior Bonner* 1972; *The Devil's Rain* 1975; *The Food of the Gods* 1975
Lupino, Stanley (1893–1942) *Happy* 1933; *Cheer Up!* 1936; *Over She Goes* 1937; *Hold My Hand* 1938
Lupo, Alberto (1924–1984) *The Bacchantes* 1960; *The Giant of Marathon* 1960; *The Agony and the Ecstasy* 1965
LuPone, Patti (1949–) *Death Vengeance* 1982; *Witness* 1985; *Wise Guys* 1986; *Driving Miss Daisy* 1989; *Family Prayers* 1991; *The 24 Hour Woman* 1999; *State*

and Main 2000; *Heist* 2001; *City by the Sea* 2002
Luppi, Federico (1934–) *Funny Dirty Little War* 1983; *La Amiga* 1988; *Cronos* 1992; *A Place in the World* 1992; *Men with Guns* 1997; *Lisboa* 1999; *The Devil's Backbone* 2001; *Machuca* 2004
Lupton, John (1926–1993) *Man with the Gun* 1955; *The Great Locomotive Chase* 1956; *Drango* 1957; *The Man in the Net* 1959; *The Rebel Set* 1959; *Jesse James Meets Frankenstein's Daughter* 1966
Lurie, John (1952–) *Permanent Vacation* 1982; *Stranger than Paradise* 1984; *Down by Law* 1986
Lutes, Eric (1962–) *Distant Justice* 1992; *Danielle Steel's Full Circle* 1996; *Bram Stoker's Legend of the Mummy* 1998
Luttazzi, Lello (1923–) *L'Avventura* 1960; *Snow Job* 1972
Lutter, Alfred *aka* **Lutter, Alfred W** (1962–) *Alice Doesn't Live Here Anymore* 1974; *The Bad News Bears* 1976
Lutz, Adelle *Beyond Rangoon* 1995; *Dead Funny* 1995
Lyby, Troels (1966–) *The Idiots* 1998; *Okay* 2002
Lycan, Georges *Gold for the Caesars* 1964; *Triple Cross* 1966
Lydon, Gary *Ailsa* 1994; *Nothing Personal* 1995
Lydon, James *aka* **Lydon, Jimmy** (1923–) *Back Door to Heaven* 1939; *Tom Brown's Schooldays* 1940; *Cynthia* 1947; *Life with Father* 1947; *September Affair* 1950; *When Willie Comes Marching Home* 1950; *The Last Time I Saw Archie* 1961
Lydon, John *aka* **Rotten, Johnny** (1956–) *The Great Rock 'n' Roll Swindle* 1979; *Order of Death* 1983
Lye, Reg (1912–1988) *Smiley Gets a Gun* 1959; *The Amorous Prawn* 1962; *Sunday Too Far Away* 1974; *Tarka the Otter* 1978; *The Killing of Angel Street* 1981
Lynas, Jeffrey *aka* **Lynas, Jeff** *Lies My Father Told Me* 1975; *Something for Joey* 1977
Lynch, Alfred (1933–2003) *On the Fiddle* 1961; *Two and Two Make Six* 1961; *The Password Is Courage* 1962; *West 11* 1963; *The Hill* 1965; *The Taming of the Shrew* 1967; *The Blockhouse* 1973; *Loophole* 1980
Lynch, Barry *Pentathlon* 1994; *A Midsummer Night's Dream* 1996
Lynch, Jane (1960–) *Best in Show* 2000; *A Mighty Wind* 2003; *Sleepover* 2004
Lynch, Joe (1925–2001) *Loot* 1970; *Never Too Young to Rock* 1975; *Eat the Peach* 1986; *Thumbelina* 1994
Lynch, John (1961–) *Cal* 1984; *1871* 1989; *Hardware* 1990; *Edward II* 1991; *In the Name of the Father* 1993; *The Secret Garden* 1993; *The Secret of Roan Inish* 1993; *Angel Baby* 1995; *Moll Flanders* 1995; *Nothing Personal* 1995; *Some Mother's Son* 1996; *This Is the Sea* 1996; *Sliding Doors* 1997; *Best* 1999; *Puckoon* 2002; *Re-inventing Eddie* 2002
Lynch, John Carroll (1963–) *Dead Men Can't Dance* 1997; *Bubble Boy* 2001; *Gothika* 2003; *Catch That Kid* 2004
Lynch, Kate *Meatballs* 1979; *Def-Con 4* 1984
Lynch, Kelly (1959–) *Cocktail* 1988; *Drugstore Cowboy* 1989; *Road House* 1989; *Desperate Hours* 1990; *Curly Sue* 1991; *Three of Hearts* 1992; *For Better and for Worse* 1993; *The Beans of Egypt, Maine* 1994; *Imaginary Crimes* 1994; *Virtuosity* 1995; *White Man's Burden* 1995; *Heaven's Prisoners* 1996; *Persons Unknown* 1996; *Mr Magoo* 1997; *Homegrown* 1998; *Charlie's Angels* 2000; *Joe Somebody* 2001; *Homeless to Harvard: the Liz Murray Story* 2003; *The Jacket* 2005
Lynch, Ken (1910–1990) *The Bonnie Parker Story* 1958; *I Married a Monster from Outer Space* 1958; *The Legend of Tom Dooley* 1959; *Seven Ways from Sundown* 1960; *Apache Rifles* 1964
Lynch, Richard (1940–) *Scarecrow* 1973; *The Seven-Ups* 1973; *Open Season* 1974; *The Happy Hooker* 1975; *The Premonition* 1975; *Stunts* 1977; *Deathsport* 1978; *The Sword and the Sorcerer* 1982; *Invasion USA* 1985; *Savage Dawn* 1985; *Little Nikita* 1988; *High Stakes* 1989; *Lambada! The Forbidden Dance* 1990; *Alligator II: the Mutation* 1991; *Double Threat* 1992; *Inside Edge* 1992; *Necronomicon* 1993; *Branwen* 1994; *Cyborg 3: The Recycler* 1994; *Scanner Cop* 1994; *Darklands* 1996; *The Proposition* 1996
Lynch, Sean *One Plus One* 1968; *At the Earth's Core* 1976
Lynch, Susan (1971–) *The Secret of Roan Inish* 1993; *Downtime* 1997; *Waking Ned* 1998; *Nora* 1999; *Beautiful Creatures* 2000; *Casa de los Babys* 2003; *16 Years of Alcohol* 2003; *Enduring Love* 2004
Lynde, Paul (1926–1982) *New Faces* 1954; *Son of Flubber* 1962; *Bye Bye Birdie* 1963; *Under the Yum Yum Tree* 1963; *For Those Who Think Young* 1964; *Send Me No Flowers* 1964; *Beach Blanket Bingo* 1965; *The Glass Bottom Boat* 1966; *How Sweet It Is!* 1968; *Charlotte's Web* 1973; *Cactus Jack* 1979
Lyndon, Simon *Blackrock* 1997; *Chopper* 2000
Lynley, Carol (1942–) *The Light in the Forest* 1958; *Blue Denim* 1959; *Holiday for Lovers* 1959; *Hound Dog Man* 1959; *The Last Sunset* 1961; *Return to Peyton Place* 1961; *The Cardinal* 1963; *The Stripper* 1963; *Under the Yum Yum Tree* 1963; *The Pleasure Seekers* 1964; *Shock Treatment* 1964; *Bunny Lake Is Missing* 1965; *Harlow* 1965; *Danger Route* 1967; *The Shuttered Room* 1967; *The Helicopter Spies* 1968; *The Maltese Bippy* 1969; *Once You Kiss a Stranger* 1969; *Beware! The Blob* 1971; *The Poseidon Adventure* 1972; *The Four Deuces* 1976; *The Cat and the Canary* 1979; *Balboa* 1982; *Dark Tower* 1989
Lynn, Ann (1934–) *Strongroom* 1961; *The Wind of Change* 1961; *The Black Torment* 1964; *The System* 1964; *The Uncle* 1964; *Four in the Morning* 1965; *The Party's Over* 1965
Lynn, Betty (1926–) *June Bride* 1948; *Father Was a Fullback* 1949; *Mother Is a Freshman* 1949; *Cheaper by the Dozen* 1950; *Payment on Demand* 1951; *Meet Me in Las Vegas* 1956; *Gun for a Coward* 1957
Lynn, Diana *aka* **Loehr, Dolly** (1926–1971) *They Shall Have Music* 1939; *The Major and the Minor* 1942; *And the Angels Sing* 1944; *The Miracle of Morgan's Creek* 1944; *Out of This World* 1945; *The Bride Wore Boots* 1946; *Every Girl Should Be Married* 1948; *Ruthless* 1948; *My Friend Irma* 1949; *My Friend Irma Goes West* 1950; *Paid in Full* 1950; *Rogues of Sherwood Forest* 1950; *Bedtime for Bonzo* 1951; *The People against O'Hara* 1951; *Meet Me at the Fair* 1952; *Track of the Cat* 1954; *An Annapolis Story* 1955; *The Kentuckian* 1955; *You're Never Too Young* 1955
Lynn, George (1906–1967) *The Werewolf* 1956; *I Was a Teenage Frankenstein* 1957
Lynn, Jeffrey (1909–1995) *Daughters Courageous* 1939; *The Roaring Twenties* 1939; *All This, and Heaven Too* 1940; *The Fighting 69th* 1940; *It All Came True* 1940; *The Body Disappears* 1941; *Four Mothers* 1941; *Million Dollar Baby* 1941; *Underground* 1941; *Black Bart* 1948; *For the Love of Mary* 1948; *A Letter to Three Wives* 1949; *Home Town Story* 1951; *Butterfield 8* 1960; *Tony Rome* 1967
Lynn, Ralph (1882–1964) *Rookery Nook* 1930; *A Cuckoo in the Nest* 1933; *Fighting Stock* 1935; *Foreign Affaires* 1935; *In the Soup* 1936; *For Valour* 1937
Lynn, Vera (1917–) *We'll Meet Again* 1942; *Rhythm Serenade* 1943
Lynn, William *Harvey* 1950; *Mr Belvedere Rings the Bell* 1951
Lynne, Sharon *aka* **Lynn, Sharon** (1901–1963) *Fox Movietone Follies of 1929* 1929; *Sunny Side Up* 1929; *Up the River* 1930; *The Big Broadcast* 1932; *Enter Madame!* 1933; *Go into Your Dance* 1935; *Way Out West* 1937
Lynskey, Melanie (1977–) *Heavenly Creatures* 1994; *Ever After: a Cinderella Story* 1998; *But I'm a Cheerleader* 1999; *Shattered Glass* 2003
Lyon, Barbara (1931–1995) *Life with the Lyons* 1953; *The Lyons in Paris* 1955
Lyon, Ben (1901–1979) *For the Love of Mike* 1927; *Hell's Angels* 1930; *Her Majesty Love* 1931; *Indiscreet* 1931; *Night Nurse* 1931; *Lady with a Past* 1932; *I Cover the Waterfront* 1933; *Hi, Gang!* 1941; *Life with the Lyons* 1953; *The Lyons in Paris* 1955
Lyon, Richard (1934–) *The Unseen* 1945; *Anna and the King of Siam* 1946; *The Tender Years* 1947; *The Boy with Green Hair* 1948; *The Great Lover* 1949; *Life with the Lyons* 1953; *The Lyons in Paris* 1955
Lyon, Sue (1946–) *Lolita* 1961; *The Night of the Iguana* 1964; *7 Women* 1966; *One Born Every Minute* 1967; *Evel Knievel* 1971; *Invisible Strangler* 1976; *Crash!* 1977; *End of the World* 1977
Lyonne, Natasha (1979–) *Dennis* 1993; *Everyone Says I Love You* 1996; *Krippendorf's Tribe* 1998; *Slums of Beverly Hills* 1998; *American Pie* 1999; *But I'm a Cheerleader* 1999; *Confessions of a Trickbaby* 1999; *American Pie 2* 2001; *Kate & Leopold* 2002; *Party Monster* 2003; *Blade: Trinity* 2004
Lyons, James *Postcards from America* 1994; *Frisk* 1995
Lyons, Phyllis (1960–) *The Bridges of Madison County* 1995; *Thirst* 1998
Lyons, Robert F (1940–) *Pendulum* 1969; *Getting Straight* 1970; *Dealing: or the Berkeley-to-Boston Forty-Brick Lost-Bag Blues* 1971; *Shoot Out* 1971; *The Todd Killings* 1971; *10 to Midnight* 1983; *Avenging Angel* 1985; *Murphy's Law* 1986; *Exit in Red* 1996
Lyons, Susan (1957–) *The Winds of Jarrah* 1983; *Almost* 1990
Lys, Lya (1908–1986) *L'Age d'Or* 1930; *Confessions of a Nazi Spy* 1939; *The Return of Dr X* 1939

M

Ma Jingwu *Raise the Red Lantern* 1991; *The Day the Sun Turned Cold* 1994
Ma Tzi *Rapid Fire* 1992; *Golden Gate* 1994; *The Quiet American* 2002; *The Ladykillers* 2004
Maaskri, Moussa *Vidocq* 2001; *Two Brothers* 2004
Mabius, Eric (1971–) *The Journey of August King* 1995; *Lawn Dogs* 1997; *The Minus Man* 1999; *Splendor* 1999; *Resident Evil* 2002
Mably, Luke (1976–) *The Prince & Me* 2004; *Spirit Trap* 2005
Mac, Bernie (1958–) *Above the Rim* 1994; *Get on the Bus* 1996; *The Players Club* 1998; *Life* 1999; *Ocean's Eleven* 2001; *What's the Worst That Could Happen?* 2001; *Bad Santa* 2003; *Charlie's Angels: Full Throttle* 2003; *Head of State* 2003; *Ocean's Twelve* 2004; *Guess Who* 2005
McAdams, Rachel (1976–) *The Hot Chick* 2002; *The Notebook* 2003; *Mean Girls* 2004; *Wedding Crashers* 2005
McAleer, Des *Anne Devlin* 1984; *Butterfly Kiss* 1994
McAllister, Paul *The Winning of Barbara Worth* 1926; *Noah's Ark* 1928
McAnally, Ray (1926–1989) *Sea of Sand* 1958; *The Naked Edge* 1961; *Billy Budd* 1962; *He Who Rides a Tiger* 1965; *The Looking Glass War* 1969; *Quest for Love* 1971; *Fear Is the Key* 1972; *Angel* 1982; *Cal* 1984; *The Mission* 1986; *No Surrender* 1986; *The Fourth Protocol* 1987; *The Sicilian* 1987; *White Mischief* 1987; *High Spirits* 1988; *Taffin* 1988; *My Left Foot* 1989; *Venus Peter* 1989; *We're No Angels* 1989
McAndrew, Marianne (1938–) *Hello, Dolly!* 1969; *The Seven Minutes* 1971
MacAninch, Cal (1982–) *The Woodlanders* 1997; *Best* 1999; *The Point Men* 2000
McArthur, Alex (1957–) *Rampage* 1987; *Race for Glory* 1989; *Perfect Alibi* 1994; *Ed McBain's 87th Precinct* 1995; *Conspiracy Theory* 1997; *Kiss the Girls* 1997
MacArthur, James (1937–) *The Young Stranger* 1957; *The Light in the Forest* 1958; *Third Man on the Mountain* 1959; *Kidnapped* 1960; *Swiss Family Robinson* 1960; *The Interns* 1962; *Spencer's Mountain* 1963; *The Truth about Spring* 1964; *The Bedford Incident* 1965; *Ride beyond Vengeance* 1966; *Hang 'Em High* 1968
Macaulay, Marc *Hidden Fears* 1993; *Palmetto* 1998
Macauley, Tom *The Chiltern Hundreds* 1949; *The Planter's Wife* 1952
McAvoy, James (1979–) *Bollywood Queen* 2002; *Bright Young Things* 2003; *Inside I'm Dancing* 2004; *Strings* 2004; *Wimbledon* 2004
McAvoy, May (1901–1984) *Ben-Hur: a Tale of the Christ* 1925; *Lady Windermere's Fan* 1925; *The Jazz Singer* 1927
McBain, Diane (1941–) *Ice Palace* 1960; *Claudelle Inglish* 1961; *Parrish* 1961; *Black Gold* 1963; *Mary, Mary* 1963; *A Distant Trumpet* 1964; *Spinout* 1966; *Thunder Alley* 1967; *The Delta Factor* 1970
McBride, Chi (1961–) *Mercury Rising* 1998; *Disney's The Kid* 2000; *Gone in Sixty Seconds* 2000; *Narc* 2001; *Undercover Brother* 2002; *I, Robot* 2004; *The Terminal* 2004
MacBride, Donald (1889–1957) *Annabel Takes a Tour* 1938; *The Amazing Mr Williams* 1939; *The Girl from Mexico* 1939; *The Great Man Votes* 1939; *Michael Shayne, Private Detective* 1940; *My Favorite Wife* 1940; *Northwest Passage* 1940; *Hold That Blonde* 1945; *Out of This World* 1945; *The Killers* 1946; *Good News* 1947; *The Story of Seabiscuit* 1949; *Meet Danny Wilson* 1952
McBurney, Simon (1957–) *Mesmer* 1994; *The Reckoning* 2001; *Skagerrak* 2003
McCabe, Ruth *My Left Foot* 1989; *The Field* 1990; *The Snapper* 1993; *Talk of Angels* 1998; *The Closer You Get* 2000
McCaffrey, James (1960–) *Nick and Jane* 1996; *The Truth about Cats and Dogs* 1996; *Mistaken Identity* 1999; *American Splendor* 2003
McCain, Frances Lee (1944–) *Tex* 1982; *Gremlins* 1984; *The Rape of Richard Beck* 1985; *Patch Adams* 1998
McCallany, Holt (1964–) *Alien^3* 1992; *The Search for One-Eye Jimmy* 1996; *Kiss Tomorrow Goodbye* 2000; *Below* 2002
McCallin, Clement (1913–1977) *The Rossiter Case* 1950; *Murder in the Cathedral* 1952
McCallister, Lon (1923–2005) *Stage Door Canteen* 1943; *Home in Indiana* 1944; *Winged Victory* 1944; *Bob, Son of Battle* 1947; *The Red House* 1947; *The Story of Seabiscuit* 1949
McCallum, David (1933–) *Hell Drivers* 1957; *Robbery under Arms* 1957; *A Night to Remember* 1958; *Violent Playground* 1958; *The Long and the Short and the Tall* 1960; *Billy Budd* 1962; *The Great Escape* 1963; *Around the World under the Sea* 1965; *The Greatest Story Ever Told* 1965; *One of Our Spies Is Missing* 1966; *One Spy Too Many* 1966; *The Spy in the Green Hat* 1966; *The Spy with My Face* 1966; *To Trap a Spy* 1966; *The Karate Killers* 1967; *Three Bites of the Apple* 1967; *The Helicopter Spies* 1968; *How to Steal the World* 1968; *Mosquito Squadron* 1968; *Sol Madrid* 1968; *Frankenstein: the True Story* 1973; *Dogs* 1976; *King Solomon's Treasure* 1977; *The Watcher in the Woods* 1982; *Terminal Choice* 1983; *The Haunting of Morella* 1990; *Hear My Song* 1991; *Dirty Weekend* 1992
McCallum, John (1917–) *The Root of All Evil* 1946; *Bush Christmas* 1947; *It Always Rains on Sunday* 1947; *The Loves of Joanna Godden* 1947; *Miranda* 1947; *The Calendar* 1948; *A Boy, a Girl and a Bike* 1949; *Traveller's Joy* 1949; *The Woman in Question* 1950; *Lady Godiva Rides Again* 1951; *Valley of Eagles* 1951; *Derby Day* 1952; *The Long Memory* 1952; *Trent's Last Case* 1952; *Devil on Horseback* 1954; *Trouble in the Glen* 1954; *Port of Escape* 1956; *Smiley* 1956
McCallum, Neil (1929–1976) *The Siege of Pinchgut* 1959; *Dr Terror's House of Horrors* 1964; *The Lost Continent* 1968
McCalman, Macon *Rollover* 1981; *Valentino Returns* 1987
McCambridge, Mercedes (1916–2004) *All the King's Men* 1949; *Inside Straight* 1951; *Lightning Strikes Twice* 1951; *The Scarf* 1951; *Johnny Guitar* 1954; *Giant* 1956; *A Farewell to Arms* 1957; *Touch of Evil* 1958; *Suddenly, Last Summer* 1959; *Cimarron* 1960; *Angel Baby* 1961; *The Exorcist* 1973; *Thieves* 1977; *Airport '79: the Concorde* 1979; *Echoes* 1983
McCamus, Tom *I Love a Man in Uniform* 1993; *Long Day's Journey into Night* 1996; *The Sweet Hereafter* 1997; *Possible Worlds* 2000
McCann, Chuck (1934–) *The Heart Is a Lonely Hunter* 1968; *The Projectionist* 1970; *The Comeback Trail* 1972; *CHOMPS* 1979; *Cameron's Closet* 1988; *Duck Tales: the Movie – Treasure of the Lost Lamp* 1990; *Storyville* 1992
McCann, Donal (1943–1999) *Philadelphia, Here I Come* 1975; *Cal* 1984; *The Dead* 1987; *December Bride* 1990; *The Miracle* 1990; *Stealing Beauty* 1995; *The Nephew* 1997
McCann, Sean (1935–) *Hockey Night* 1984; *Bordertown Cafe* 1991; *Run* 1991; *The Air Up There* 1993; *Swann* 1996; *A House Divided* 2000; *Possible Worlds* 2000; *Miracle* 2004
McCardie, Brian (1965–) *Rob Roy* 1995; *Speed 2: Cruise Control* 1997
McCarren, Fred (1952–) *Xanadu* 1980; *National Lampoon's Class Reunion* 1982
McCarthy, Andrew (1963–) *Class* 1983; *Catholic Boys* 1985; *St Elmo's Fire* 1985; *Pretty in Pink* 1986; *Less than Zero* 1987; *Mannequin* 1987; *Waiting for the Moon* 1987; *Fresh Horses* 1988; *Kansas* 1988; *Weekend at Bernie's* 1989; *Year of the Gun* 1991; *Only You* 1992; *Weekend at Bernie's II* 1992; *Getting In* 1994; *Mrs Parker and the Vicious Circle* 1994; *Dead Funny* 1995; *Stag* 1996; *I Woke Up Early the Day I Died* 1998; *I'm Losing You* 1998; *New World Disorder* 1999; *Nowhere in Sight* 2000; *A Storm in Summer* 2000
McCarthy, Henry (1882–1954) *Part-Time Wife* 1961; *French Dressing* 1964

McCarthy, Jenny (1972–) *BASEketball* 1998; *Diamonds* 1999; *Scream 3* 1999
McCarthy, Kevin (1914–) *Death of a Salesman* 1951; *Drive a Crooked Road* 1954; *An Annapolis Story* 1955; *Stranger on Horseback* 1955; *Invasion of the Body Snatchers* 1956; *Nightmare* 1956; *The Misfits* 1961; *A Gathering of Eagles* 1963; *The Best Man* 1964; *Mirage* 1965; *A Big Hand for a Little Lady* 1966; *The Three Sisters* 1966; *Hotel* 1967; *Ace High* 1968; *The Hell with Heroes* 1968; *Kansas City Bomber* 1972; *Dan Candy's Law* 1973; *Buffalo Bill and the Indians, or Sitting Bull's History Lesson* 1976; *Invasion of the Body Snatchers* 1978; *Piranha* 1978; *Hero at Large* 1980; *The Howling* 1981; *My Tutor* 1983; *Innerspace* 1987; *Dark Tower* 1989; *UHF* 1989; *Love or Money* 1990; *Final Approach* 1991; *The Distinguished Gentleman* 1992; *Addams Family Reunion* 1998
McCarthy, Neil (1935–) *Offbeat* 1960; *Sands of the Desert* 1960; *Zulu* 1964; *Steptoe and Son Ride Again* 1973
McCarthy, Nobu *aka* **McCarthy, Nobu Atsumi** (1934–2002) *The Geisha Boy* 1958; *Five Gates to Hell* 1959; *Wake Me When It's Over* 1960; *Walk like a Dragon* 1960; *Two Loves* 1961; *The Karate Kid Part II* 1986; *Pacific Heights* 1990
McCarthy, Sheila (1956–) *I've Heard the Mermaids Singing* 1987; *Beautiful Dreamers* 1990; *White Room* 1990; *George's Island* 1991; *Paradise* 1991; *Stepping Out* 1991; *A Private Matter* 1992; *Being Julia* 2004; *Confessions of a Teenage Drama Queen* 2004
McCartney, Paul (1942–) *A Hard Day's Night* 1964; *Help!* 1965; *Breaking Glass* 1980; *Give My Regards to Broad Street* 1984; *Eat the Rich* 1987
McCarty, Mary (1923–1980) *The French Line* 1954; *Somebody Killed Her Husband* 1978
McCary, Rod *No Drums, No Bugles* 1971; *Night of the Demons 2* 1994
Macchio, Ralph (1961–) *Up the Academy* 1980; *The Outsiders* 1983; *The Karate Kid* 1984; *Teachers* 1984; *Crossroads* 1986; *The Karate Kid Part II* 1986; *Distant Thunder* 1988; *The Karate Kid III* 1989; *Too Much Sun* 1990; *My Cousin Vinny* 1992; *Naked in New York* 1994; *The Secret of NIMH II: Timmy to the Rescue* 1998
Maccione, Aldo (1935–) *The Loves and Times of Scaramouche* 1976; *The Chambermaid on the Titanic* 1997
McClanahan, Rue (1935–) *The People Next Door* 1970; *They Might Be Giants* 1971; *Modern Love* 1990; *Dear God* 1996; *This World, Then the Fireworks* 1996
McCleery, Gary *Hard Choices* 1984; *Matewan* 1987
McClements, Catherine (1965–) *Just Us* 1986; *Struck by Lightning* 1990; *Redheads* 1992; *Better than Sex* 2000
McClory, Belinda (1968–) *Hotel de Love* 1996; *Cubbyhouse* 2001; *Mullet* 2001
McClory, Sean (1924–2003) *The Daughter of Rosie O'Grady* 1950; *Anne of the Indies* 1951; *Lorna Doone* 1951; *The King's Thief* 1955; *The Gnome-Mobile* 1967; *My Chauffeur* 1986
McCloskey, Leigh (1955–) *Inferno* 1980; *Fraternity Vacation* 1985; *Cameron's Closet* 1988
McClure, Doug (1934–1995) *Because They're Young* 1960; *Shenandoah* 1965; *Beau Geste* 1966; *The King's Pirate* 1967; *Nobody's Perfect* 1968; *Backtrack* 1969; *The Birdmen* 1971; *The Land That Time Forgot* 1974; *What Changed Charley Farthing?* 1974; *At the Earth's Core* 1976; *The People That Time Forgot* 1977; *Warlords of Atlantis* 1978; *Firebird 2015 AD* 1980; *Monster* 1980; *The House Where Evil Dwells* 1982; *52 Pick-Up* 1986; *Tapeheads* 1988
McClure, Greg (1918–) *The Great John L* 1945; *Lulu Belle* 1948; *Breakthrough* 1950
McClure, Marc (1957–) *I Wanna Hold Your Hand* 1978; *Pandemonium* 1982; *Back to the Future* 1985; *Perfect Match* 1987; *Superman IV: the Quest for Peace* 1987; *After Midnight* 1989; *Grim Prairie Tales* 1990; *The Vagrant* 1992; *Storm* 1999
McClure, Molly *Daddy's Dyin'... Who's Got the Will?* 1990; *Pure Country* 1992; *The Patriot* 1998
McClurg, Edie (1950–) *Ferris Bueller's Day Off* 1986; *Elvira, Mistress of the Dark* 1988; *The Little Mermaid* 1989; *A River Runs through It* 1992; *Airborne* 1993; *Flubber* 1997; *The Master of Disguise* 2002; *Dickie Roberts: Former Child Star* 2003
McCole, Stephen *The Acid House* 1998; *Orphans* 1998; *Postmortem* 1999
McComb, Heather (1977–) *New York Stories* 1989; *Stay Tuned* 1992; *The Joyriders* 1999
McConaughey, Matthew (1969–) *Dazed and Confused* 1993; *Angels in the Outfield* 1994; *Texas Chainsaw Massacre: the Next Generation* 1994; *Boys on the Side* 1995; *Glory Daze* 1995; *Lone Star* 1995; *Scorpion Spring* 1995; *Larger than Life* 1996; *A Time to Kill* 1996; *Amistad* 1997; *Contact* 1997; *The Newton Boys* 1998; *Edtv* 1999; *U-571* 2000; *Frailty* 2001; *Reign of Fire* 2001; *13 Conversations about One Thing* 2001; *The Wedding Planner* 2001; *How to Lose a Guy in 10 Days* 2003; *Sahara* 2004
McConnohie, Michael *Fist of the North Star* 1986; *The Little Polar Bear* 2001
MacCorkindale, Simon (1952–) *Death on the Nile* 1978; *The Riddle of the Sands* 1978; *The Quatermass Conclusion* 1979; *Caboblanco* 1980; *The Sword and the Sorcerer* 1982; *Jaws III* 1983; *Danielle Steel's No Greater Love* 1996
McCormack, Catherine (1972–) *Loaded* 1994; *Braveheart* 1995; *North Star* 1996; *Dangerous Beauty* 1997; *The Land Girls* 1997; *Dancing at Lughnasa* 1998; *This Year's Love* 1999; *Born Romantic* 2000; *A Rumor of Angels* 2000; *Shadow of the Vampire* 2000; *The Tailor of Panama* 2000; *The Weight of Water* 2000; *Spy Game* 2001; *Strings* 2004
McCormack, Eric (1973–) *Free Enterprise* 1998; *Holy Man* 1998; *The Audrey Hepburn Story* 2000
McCormack, Mary (1969–) *The Alarmist* 1997; *Private Parts* 1997; *The Big Tease* 1999; *Mystery, Alaska* 1999; *The Broken Hearts Club: a Romantic Comedy* 2000; *Gun Shy* 2000; *High Heels and Low Lifes* 2001; *K-PAX* 2001; *Full Frontal* 2002; *Dickie Roberts: Former Child Star* 2003
McCormack, Patty (1945–) *The Bad Seed* 1956; *The Day They Gave Babies Away* 1957; *The Snow Queen* 1959; *The Adventures of Huckleberry Finn* 1960; *The Explosive Generation* 1961; *Saturday the 14th Strikes Back* 1988; *Shallow Ground* 2004
McCormick, F J (1891–1947) *The Plough and the Stars* 1936; *Hungry Hill* 1946; *Odd Man Out* 1946
McCormick, Gilmer (1947–) *Godspell* 1973; *Silent Night, Deadly Night* 1984
McCormick, Maureen (1956–) *Moonshine County Express* 1977; *Take Down* 1978; *The Idolmaker* 1980; *Fortune Hunters* 1999
McCormick, Myron (1908–1962) *One Third of a Nation* 1939; *China Girl* 1942; *Jigsaw* 1949; *Jolson Sings Again* 1949; *Not as a Stranger* 1955; *Three for the Show* 1955; *No Time for Sergeants* 1958; *The Man Who Understood Women* 1959; *The Hustler* 1961
McCormick, Pat (1934–) *Smokey and the Bandit* 1977; *Smokey and the Bandit III* 1983; *Broadway Bound* 1991
McCourt, Emer *London Kills Me* 1991; *Riff-Raff* 1991; *Boston Kickout* 1995
McCourt, Malachy *Kick!* 1979; *Q – the Winged Serpent* 1982; *Ash Wednesday* 2002; *The Guru* 2002
McCowen, Alec (1925–) *The Cruel Sea* 1953; *The Deep Blue Sea* 1955; *The Good Companions* 1956; *The Long Arm* 1956; *Town on Trial* 1956; *The One That Got Away* 1957; *Time without Pity* 1957; *The Silent Enemy* 1958; *A Midsummer Night's Dream* 1961; *The Witches* 1966; *The Hawaiians* 1970; *Frenzy* 1972; *Travels with My Aunt* 1972; *Stevie* 1978; *Hanover Street* 1979; *Never Say Never Again* 1983; *Forever Young* 1984; *The Assam Garden* 1985; *Cry Freedom* 1987; *Personal Services* 1987; *Henry V* 1989; *The Age of Innocence* 1993; *Gangs of New York* 2002
McCoy, Matt (1958–) *Police Academy 5: Assignment Miami Beach* 1988; *DeepStar Six* 1989; *Police Academy 6: City under Siege* 1989; *Wind Dancer* 1991; *The Hand That Rocks the Cradle* 1992; *Rent-a-Kid* 1992; *The Cool Surface* 1993; *Snapdragon* 1993; *Desperate Measures* 1995; *Fast Money* 1995; *Little Bigfoot* 1995; *Memory Run* 1995; *LA Confidential* 1997; *Beethoven's 4th* 2001; *National Security* 2002
McCracken, Jeff *One Man Jury* 1978; *Waiting for the Light* 1989
McCrackin, Daisy *A Crack in the Floor* 2000; *Halloween: Resurrection* 2002
McCrea, Jody (1934–) *The First Texan* 1956; *The Broken Land* 1962; *Young Guns of Texas* 1962; *Beach Party* 1963; *Muscle Beach Party* 1964; *Beach Blanket Bingo* 1965; *The Glory Stompers* 1967
McCrea, Joel (1905–1990) *Dynamite* 1929; *Girls about Town* 1931; *Kept Husbands* 1931; *Bird of Paradise* 1932; *The Lost Squadron* 1932; *The Most Dangerous Game* 1932; *Rockabye* 1932; *The Silver Cord* 1933; *Gambling Lady* 1934; *The Richest Girl in the World* 1934; *Barbary Coast* 1935; *Our Little Girl* 1935; *Private Worlds* 1935; *Splendor* 1935; *Woman Wanted* 1935; *Banjo on My Knee* 1936; *Come and Get It* 1936; *These Three* 1936; *Dead End* 1937; *Internes Can't Take Money* 1937; *Wells Fargo* 1937; *Woman Chases Man* 1937; *Three Blind Mice* 1938; *They Shall Have Music* 1939; *Union Pacific* 1939; *Foreign Correspondent* 1940; *Primrose Path* 1940; *Sullivan's Travels* 1941; *The Great Man's Lady* 1942; *The Palm Beach Story* 1942; *The More the Merrier* 1943; *Buffalo Bill* 1944; *The Great Moment* 1944; *The Unseen* 1945; *The Virginian* 1946; *Ramrod* 1947; *They Passed This Way* 1948; *Colorado Territory* 1949; *South of St Louis* 1949; *Frenchie* 1950; *The Outriders* 1950; *Saddle Tramp* 1950; *Cattle Drive* 1951; *Rough Shoot* 1952; *The San Francisco Story* 1952; *The Lone Hand* 1953; *Black Horse Canyon* 1954; *Border River* 1954; *Stranger on Horseback* 1955; *Wichita* 1955; *The First Texan* 1956; *Gunsight Ridge* 1957; *The Oklahoman* 1957; *The Tall Stranger* 1957; *Trooper Hook* 1957; *Cattle Empire* 1958; *Fort Massacre* 1958; *The Gunfight at Dodge City* 1959; *Ride the High Country* 1962; *The Great American Cowboy* 1973; *Mustang Country* 1976
McCrory, Helen *Dad Savage* 1997; *The James Gang* 1997; *Hotel Splendide* 1999; *The Count of Monte Cristo* 2001; *Enduring Love* 2004
McCulloch, Bruce (1961–) *Kids in the Hall: Brain Candy* 1996; *Dog Park* 1998; *Dick* 1999
McCulloch, Ian (1939–) *The Ghoul* 1975; *Zombie Flesh Eaters* 1979; *Zombie Holocaust* 1979
McCullough, David (1933–) *Huey Long* 1985; *Seabiscuit* 2003
McCullough, Julie (1965–) *Big Bad Mama II* 1987; *Round Trip to Heaven* 1992
McCullough, Rohan *Strapless* 1988; *War Requiem* 1988
McCullough, Suli (1968–) *Terminal Velocity* 1994; *Don't Be a Menace to South Central while Drinking Your Juice in the Hood* 1996
McCurley, Mathew *North* 1994; *The Secret Agent Club* 1995
McCurry, John *Fritz the Cat* 1972; *Deathmask* 1984
McCutcheon, Bill (1924–2002) *Family Business* 1989; *Aunt Julia and the Scriptwriter* 1990; *Mr Destiny* 1990
McCutcheon, Martine (1976–) *Kiss Kiss (Bang Bang)* 2001; *Love Actually* 2003
McDaniel, Hattie *aka* **McDaniels, Hattie** (1895–1952) *Blonde Venus* 1932; *Hello Sister!* 1933; *Judge Priest* 1934; *Alice Adams* 1935; *The Little Colonel* 1935; *The Bride Walks Out* 1936; *Nothing Sacred* 1937; *True Confession* 1937; *The Mad Miss Manton* 1938; *The Shining Hour* 1938; *The Shopworn Angel* 1938; *Vivacious Lady* 1938; *Gone with the Wind* 1939; *Zenobia* 1939; *Maryland* 1940; *Affectionately Yours* 1941; *The Great Lie* 1941; *They Died with Their Boots On* 1941; *George Washington Slept Here* 1942; *In This Our Life* 1942; *The Male Animal* 1942; *Johnny Come Lately* 1943; *Since You Went Away* 1944; *Margie* 1946; *Never Say Goodbye* 1946; *Song of the South* 1946
McDermott, Dylan (1962–) *Hamburger Hill* 1987; *The Blue Iguana* 1988; *Steel Magnolias* 1989; *Twister* 1989; *Hardware* 1990; *Where Sleeping Dogs Lie* 1991; *Jersey Girl* 1992; *In the Line of Fire* 1993; *The Cowboy Way* 1994; *Miracle on 34th Street* 1994; *Destiny Turns on the Radio* 1995; *Home for the Holidays* 1995; *'Til There Was You* 1997; *Three to Tango* 1999; *Party Monster* 2003; *Wonderland* 2003
McDermott, Hugh (1908–1972) *Where's That Fire?* 1939; *Neutral Port* 1940; *Pimpernel Smith* 1941; *The Seventh Veil* 1945; *No Orchids for Miss Blandish* 1948; *The Huggetts Abroad* 1949; *Trent's Last Case* 1952; *Devil Girl from Mars* 1954; *Malaga* 1954; *The Man Who Wouldn't Talk* 1957; *You Pay Your Money* 1957; *The Adding Machine* 1969; *Guns in the Heather* 1969
MacDermott, John *My Hustler* 1965; *Vinyl* 1965
McDermott, Keith *Tourist Trap* 1979; *Without a Trace* 1983
MacDermott, Marc (1881–1929) *He Who Gets Slapped* 1924; *The Sea Hawk* 1924; *The Lucky Lady* 1926; *The Temptress* 1926
McDevitt, Ruth (1895–1976) *The Birds* 1963; *Love Is a Ball* 1963; *The Shakiest Gun in the West* 1967
McDiarmid, Ian (1947–) *Dragonslayer* 1981; *Star Wars Episode VI: Return of the Jedi* 1983; *Dirty Rotten Scoundrels* 1988; *Annie: a Royal Adventure* 1995; *Restoration* 1995; *Star Wars Episode I: the Phantom Menace* 1999; *Star Wars Episode II: Attack of the Clones* 2002; *Star Wars Episode III: Revenge of the Sith* 2005
MacDonald, Aimi *Take a Girl like You* 1970; *Keep It Up Downstairs* 1976
McDonald, Audra (1970–) *Annie* 1999; *The Last Debate* 2000; *Wit* 2001
McDonald, Christopher (1955–) *Grease 2* 1982; *Breakdance* 1984; *Chattanooga Choo Choo* 1984; *The Boys Next Door* 1985; *Chances Are* 1989; *Driving Me Crazy* 1991; *Thelma & Louise* 1991; *Wild Orchid 2: Two Shades of Blue* 1992; *Benefit of the Doubt* 1993; *Fatal Instinct* 1993; *Monkey Trouble* 1994; *Roadflower* 1994; *Terminal Velocity* 1994; *Fair Game* 1995; *Happy Gilmore* 1996; *The Rich Man's Wife* 1996; *Unforgettable* 1996; *The Eighteenth Angel* 1997; *Flubber* 1997; *Lawn Dogs* 1997; *Leave It to Beaver* 1997; *A Smile like Yours* 1997; *Dirty Work* 1998; *The Iron Giant* 1999; *SLC Punk!* 1999; *Requiem for a Dream* 2000; *The Skulls* 2000
MacDonald, Donald *The Kentuckian* 1955; *The Brass Legend* 1956; *Constance* 1984
MacDonald, Edmund (1908–1951) *The Gay Caballero* 1940; *Great Guns* 1941; *Detour* 1945
McDonald, Francis (1891–1968) *Battling Butler* 1926; *The Dragnet* 1928; *A Girl in Every Port* 1928; *Morocco* 1930
McDonald, Garry (1948–) *The Pirate Movie* 1982; *The Rage in Placid Lake* 2002
McDonald, Grace (1918–1999) *Gung Ho!* 1943; *It Ain't Hay* 1943; *Follow the Boys* 1944
MacDonald, Ian (1914–1978) *Ramrod* 1947; *Colt .45* 1950; *Comanche Territory* 1950; *Montana* 1950; *This Woman Is Dangerous* 1952; *Blowing Wild* 1953; *Apache* 1954
MacDonald, J Farrell (1875–1952) *3 Bad Men* 1926; *Sunrise* 1927; *Abie's Irish Rose* 1928; *In Old Arizona* 1929; *Dangerous Female* 1931; *Other Men's Women* 1931; *The Painted Desert* 1931; *Sporting Blood* 1931; *Me and My Gal* 1932; *The Thirteenth Guest* 1932; *Vanishing Frontier* 1932; *Peg o' My Heart* 1933; *Star of Midnight* 1935; *Stormy* 1935; *Riffraff* 1936; *Slim* 1937; *White Banners* 1938; *Susannah of the Mounties* 1939; *Clancy Street Boys* 1943
MacDonald, Jeanette (1901–1965) *The Love Parade* 1929; *Monte Carlo* 1930; *Love Me Tonight* 1932; *One Hour with You* 1932; *The Cat and the Fiddle* 1934; *The Merry Widow* 1934; *Naughty Marietta* 1935; *Rose Marie* 1936; *San Francisco* 1936; *The Firefly* 1937; *Maytime* 1937; *The Girl of the Golden West* 1938; *Sweethearts* 1938; *Broadway Serenade* 1939; *Bitter Sweet* 1940; *New Moon* 1940; *Smilin' Through* 1941; *I Married an Angel* 1942; *Follow the Boys* 1944; *Three Daring Daughters* 1948
Macdonald, Kelly (1976–) *Trainspotting* 1995; *Cousin Bette* 1997; *Stella Does Tricks* 1997; *The Loss of Sexual Innocence* 1999; *My Life So Far* 1999; *Splendor* 1999; *House!* 2000; *Some Voices* 2000; *Strictly Sinatra* 2000; *Gosford Park* 2001; *interMission* 2003; *Finding Neverland* 2004
McDonald, Kevin (1961–) *Kids in the Hall: Brain Candy* 1996; *Lilo & Stitch* 2002
McDonald, Marie (1923–1965) *Guest in the House* 1944; *Getting Gertie's Garter* 1945; *It's a Pleasure* 1945; *Living in a Big Way* 1947; *Tell It to the Judge* 1949; *The Geisha Boy* 1958
MacDonald, Norm (1963–) *Billy Madison* 1995; *Dirty Work* 1998; *Screwed* 2000
McDonald, Peter (1972–) *I Went Down* 1997; *Captain Jack* 1998; *Felicia's Journey* 1999; *Nora* 1999; *Saltwater* 1999; *The Opportunists* 2000; *Some Voices* 2000; *When Brendan Met Trudy* 2000
McDonald, Ray (1920–1959) *Babes on Broadway* 1941; *Life Begins for Andy Hardy* 1941; *Good News* 1947; *All Ashore* 1953
MacDonald, Shauna *Daybreak* 2000; *Late Night Shopping* 2001; *The Descent* 2005
MacDonald, Wallace (1891–1978) *The Sea Hawk* 1924; *Vanishing Frontier* 1932
McDonnell, Mary (1952–) *Tiger Warsaw* 1988; *Dances with Wolves* 1990; *Grand Canyon* 1991; *Passion Fish* 1992;

Sneakers 1992; Blue Chips 1994; Independence Day 1996; Behind the Mask 1999; Mumford 1999; A Father's Choice 2000; Donnie Darko 2001

McDonough, Neal (1966–) Grace and Glorie 1998; Timeline 2003; Walking Tall 2004

McDormand, Frances (1957–) Blood Simple 1983; Raising Arizona 1987; Mississippi Burning 1988; Chattahoochee 1989; Darkman 1990; Hidden Agenda 1990; The Butcher's Wife 1991; Crazy in Love 1992; Passed Away 1992; Short Cuts 1993; Beyond Rangoon 1995; Fargo 1995; Lone Star 1995; Palookaville 1995; Primal Fear 1996; Paradise Road 1997; Madeline 1998; Talk of Angels 1998; Almost Famous 2000; Wonder Boys 2000; The Man Who Wasn't There 2001; City by the Sea 2002; Laurel Canyon 2002; Something's Gotta Give 2003

McDowall, Betty Time Lock 1957; Jack the Ripper 1958; Spare the Rod 1961; Echo of Diana 1963; Ballad in Blue 1964; First Men in the Moon 1964

McDowall, Roddy (1928–1998) Just William 1939; Confirm or Deny 1941; How Green Was My Valley 1941; Man Hunt 1941; The Pied Piper 1942; Son of Fury 1942; Lassie Come Home 1943; My Friend Flicka 1943; The Keys of the Kingdom 1944; The White Cliffs of Dover 1944; Molly and Me 1945; Thunderhead – Son of Flicka 1945; Holiday in Mexico 1946; Kidnapped 1948; Macbeth 1948; Tuna Clipper 1949; Midnight Lace 1960; The Subterraneans 1960; The Longest Day 1962; Cleopatra 1963; Shock Treatment 1964; The Greatest Story Ever Told 1965; Inside Daisy Clover 1965; That Darn Cat! 1965; The Third Day 1965; The Defector 1966; It! 1966; Lord Love a Duck 1966; The Adventures of Bullwhip Griffin 1967; The Cool Ones 1967; Planet of the Apes 1967; 5 Card Stud 1968; Angel, Angel Down We Go 1969; Beneath the Planet of the Apes 1969; Hello Down There 1969; Midas Run 1969; Bedknobs and Broomsticks 1971; Escape from the Planet of the Apes 1971; Pretty Maids All in a Row 1971; Conquest of the Planet of the Apes 1972; The Life and Times of Judge Roy Bean 1972; The Poseidon Adventure 1972; Arnold 1973; Battle for the Planet of the Apes 1973; The Legend of Hell House 1973; Dirty Mary Crazy Larry 1974; Funny Lady 1975; Embryo 1976; Sixth and Main 1977; The Cat from Outer Space 1978; Laserblast 1978; The Silent Flute 1978; The Thief of Baghdad 1978; Scavenger Hunt 1979; Charlie Chan and the Curse of the Dragon Queen 1981; Class of 1984 1982; Evil under the Sun 1982; Fright Night 1985; GoBots: Battle of the Rocklords 1986; Dead of Winter 1987; Overboard 1987; Fright Night Part 2 1988; Cutting Class 1989; Going Under 1990; Double Trouble 1992; Last Summer in the Hamptons 1995; It's My Party 1996; The Second Jungle Book 1997; Something to Believe In 1997; A Bug's Life 1998

MacDowell, Andie (1958–) Greystoke: the Legend of Tarzan, Lord of the Apes 1984; St Elmo's Fire 1985; sex, lies, and videotape 1989; Green Card 1990; Hudson Hawk 1991; The Object of Beauty 1991; Ruby Cairo 1992; Groundhog Day 1993; Short Cuts 1993; Bad Girls 1994; Four Weddings and a Funeral 1994; Unstrung Heroes 1995; Michael 1996; Multiplicity 1996; The End of Violence 1997; Just the Ticket 1998; Muppets from Space 1999; The Muse 1999; Harrison's Flowers 2000; Crush 2001; Dinner with Friends 2001; Town & Country 2001; Beauty Shop 2005

McDowell, Claire (1877–1966) The Mark of Zorro 1920; Ben-Hur: a Tale of the Christ 1925; The Big Parade 1925; An American Tragedy 1931

McDowell, Malcolm (1943–) Poor Cow 1967; if.... 1968; Figures in a Landscape 1970; The Raging Moon 1970; A Clockwork Orange 1971; O Lucky Man! 1973; Royal Flash 1975; Aces High 1976; Voyage of the Damned 1976; The Passage 1978; Caligula 1979; Time after Time 1979; Britannia Hospital 1982; Cat People 1982; The Compleat Beatles 1982; Blue Thunder 1983; Cross Creek 1983; Get Crazy 1983; The Caller 1987; Buy & Cell 1988; Sunset 1988; Il Maestro 1989; Class of 1999 1990; Disturbed 1990; Happily Ever After 1990; Moon 44 1990; Out of Darkness 1990; Assassin of the Tsar 1991; Chain of Desire 1992; Bopha! 1993; Night Train to Venice 1993; Cyborg 3: The Recycler 1994; Milk Money 1994; Star Trek: Generations 1994; Exquisite Tenderness 1995; Fist of the North Star 1995; Tank Girl 1995; Mr Magoo 1997; Pool Girl 1997; My Life So Far 1999; Gangster No 1 2000; St Patrick: the Irish Legend 2000; Just Visiting 2001; I Spy 2002; The Company 2003; I'll Sleep When I'm Dead 2003; Bobby Jones: Stroke of Genius 2004

McEachin, James (1930–) Play Misty for Me 1971; Buck and the Preacher 1972; Fuzz 1972; The Groundstar Conspiracy 1972

Macedo, Rita (1928–1993) The Criminal Life of Archibaldo de la Cruz 1955; Nazarín 1958

McElduff, Ellen Dead End Kids 1986; Maximum Overdrive 1986; Working Girls 1986

McElhatton, Michael I Went Down 1997; Crush Proof 1998; The Actors 2003; interMission 2003

McElhone, Jack Dear Frankie 2003; Young Adam 2003

McElhone, Natascha (1971–) Surviving Picasso 1996; The Devil's Own 1997; Mrs Dalloway 1997; Ronin 1998; The Truman Show 1998; What Rats Won't Do 1998; Love's Labour's Lost 1999; Contagion 2000; Killing Me Softly 2001; City of Ghosts 2002; FearDotCom 2002; Laurel Canyon 2002; Solaris 2003; Ladies in Lavender 2004

McEnery, John (1945–) Romeo and Juliet 1968; The Lady in the Car with Glasses and a Gun 1970; Bartleby 1971; Nicholas and Alexandra 1971; The Land That Time Forgot 1974; Little Malcolm and His Struggle Against the Eunuchs 1974; Hamlet 1990; Prince of Shadows 1991; Black Beauty 1994; When Saturday Comes 1995

McEnery, Peter (1940–) Beat Girl 1960; Victim 1961; The Moon-Spinners 1964; The Fighting Prince of Donegal 1966; The Game Is Over 1966; Entertaining Mr Sloane 1969; The Adventures of Gerard 1970; Tales That Witness Madness 1973; The Cat and the Canary 1979

McEnnan, Jaime And God Created Woman 1988; Munchie 1992

McEnroe, Annie The Hand 1981; Battletruck 1982; The Survivors 1983; Howling II: Your Sister Is a Werewolf 1984; True Stories 1986

McEntire, Reba (1955–) Tremors 1989; One Night at McCool's 2001

McErlean, Keith Goldfish Memory 2003; The Blackwater Lightship 2004

McEvoy, Barry Gloria 1998; An Everlasting Piece 2000

McEwan, Geraldine (1932–) No Kidding 1960; The Dance of Death 1969; The Bawdy Adventures of Tom Jones 1976; The Littlest Horse Thieves 1976; Foreign Body 1986; Robin Hood: Prince of Thieves 1991; The Love Letter 1999; Love's Labour's Lost 1999; Contagion 2000; Food of Love 2002; The Magdalene Sisters 2002; Pure 2002; Vanity Fair 2004

McFadden, Gates (1949–) Star Trek: Generations 1994; Star Trek: First Contact 1996; Star Trek: Insurrection 1998; Star Trek: Nemesis 2002

McFadden, Joseph (1975–) Small Faces 1995; Dad Savage 1997

MacFadyen, Angus (1964–) Braveheart 1995; The Brylcreem Boys 1996; Warriors of Virtue 1996; The Rat Pack 1998; Cradle Will Rock 1999; Titus 1999; Styx 2000; Divine Secrets of the Ya-Ya Sisterhood 2002; Equilibrium 2002

McFarland, Spanky (1928–1993) General Spanky 1936; The Aurora Encounter 1985

McFerran, Douglas Sliding Doors 1997; Antitrust 2001; Charlie 2003

McGann, Joe (1958–) The Brylcreem Boys 1996; Food of Love 1997

McGann, Mark (1961–) Business as Usual 1987; Let Him Have It 1991

McGann, Paul (1959–) Withnail & I 1986; Empire of the Sun 1987; The Rainbow 1988; Tree of Hands 1988; Dealers 1989; The Monk 1990; Paper Mask 1990; Afraid of the Dark 1991; Alien³ 1992; The Three Musketeers 1993; Downtime 1997; FairyTale: a True Story 1997; My Kingdom 2001; Queen of the Damned 2002; Otherworld 2003

McGavin, Darren (1922–) The Court-Martial of Billy Mitchell 1955; The Man with the Golden Arm 1955; Summertime 1955; Beau James 1957; The Delicate Delinquent 1957; Bullet for a Badman 1964; The Great Sioux Massacre 1965; Mrs Pollifax – Spy 1970; Smash-Up Alley 1972; The Six Million Dollar Man 1973; No Deposit No Return 1976; Airport '77 1977; Hot Lead and Cold Feet 1978; Zero to Sixty 1978; Firebird 2015 AD 1980; Hangar 18 1980; A Christmas Story 1983; Turk 182! 1985; From the Hip 1987; Dead Heat 1988; Captain America 1990; Danielle Steel's A Perfect Stranger 1994; Billy Madison 1995

McGaw, Patrick Amongst Friends 1993; The Beans of Egypt, Maine 1994; The Basketball Diaries 1995; Scorpion Spring 1995; Dream with the Fishes 1996

McGee, Henry (1929–) The Best of Benny Hill 1974; Adventures of a Taxi Driver 1975; Asterix Conquers America 1994

McGee, Jack Across the Tracks 1990; Star Kid 1997; Bread and Roses 2000

McGee, Vonetta (1948–) The Great Silence 1967; Blacula 1972; Hammer 1972; Detroit 9000 1973; Shaft in Africa 1973; The Eiger Sanction 1975; Brothers 1977; To Sleep with Anger 1990; The Man Next Door 1996

McGhee, Johnny Ray White Line Fever 1975; Project X 1987

McGill, Bruce (1950–) Citizens Band 1977; The Hand 1981; Tough Enough 1982; The Ballad of Gregorio Cortez 1983; Into the Night 1985; Waiting for the Moon 1987; Out Cold 1989; Little Vegas 1990; The Last Boy Scout 1991; My Cousin Vinny 1992; Timecop 1994; Black Sheep 1996; Lawn Dogs 1997; Rosewood 1997; Everything That Rises 1998; A Dog of Flanders 1999; The Legend of Bagger Vance 2000; The Ballad of Lucy Whipple 2001; Shallow Hal 2001; 61* 2001; Live from Baghdad 2002; Path to War 2002; The Sum of All Fears 2002; Legally Blonde 2: Red, White & Blonde 2003; Matchstick Men 2003; Runaway Jury 2003; Collateral 2004; Cinderella Man 2005

McGill, Everett (1945–) Union City 1980; Quest for Fire 1981; Silver Bullet 1985; Heartbreak Ridge 1986; Licence to Kill 1989; The People under the Stairs 1991; Under Siege 2 1995; The Straight Story 1999

MacGill, Moyna (1895–1975) The Strange Affair of Uncle Harry 1945; Black Beauty 1946

McGillis, Kelly (1957–) Reuben, Reuben 1983; Witness 1985; Top Gun 1986; The House on Carroll Street 1987; Made in Heaven 1987; The Accused 1988; Winter People 1988; Cat Chaser 1989; The Babe 1992; Painted Angels 1997; At First Sight 1998; When the Bough Breaks 2: Perfect Prey 1998; The Monkey's Mask 2000

McGillivray, David (1947–) House of Whipcord 1974; Satan's Slave 1976

McGinley, John C (1959–) Platoon 1986; Talk Radio 1988; Shadow Makers 1989; Suffering Bastards 1989; Highlander II: the Quickening 1990; Car 54 Where Are You? 1991; A Midnight Clear 1991; Point Break 1991; Article 99 1992; Little Noises 1992; Hear No Evil 1993; The Last Outlaw 1993; On Deadly Ground 1994; Surviving the Game 1994; Wagons East! 1994; Born to Be Wild 1995; Se7en 1995; Mother 1996; The Rock 1996; Set It Off 1996; Nothing to Lose 1997; The Pentagon Wars 1998; The Jack Bull 1999; Office Space 1999; Three to Tango 1999; The Animal 2001; Stealing Harvard 2002; Identity 2003

McGinley, Sean The Disappearance of Finbar 1996; Trojan Eddie 1996; Bogwoman 1997; Resurrection Man 1997; The General 1998; Simon Magus 1998; The Closer You Get 2000; Freeze Frame 2003; On a Clear Day 2005

McGinley, Ted (1958–) Revenge of the Nerds 1984; Physical Evidence 1988; Major League: Back to the Minors 1998

McGinn, Walter (1936–1977) The Parallax View 1974; Three Days of the Condor 1975; Bobby Deerfield 1977

MacGinnis, Niall (1913–1978) The Edge of the World 1937; The Last Adventurers 1937; East of Piccadilly 1940; 49th Parallel 1941; The Day Will Dawn 1942; Undercover 1943; We Dive at Dawn 1943; Tawny Pipit 1944; Anna Karenina 1947; Captain Boycott 1947; Diamond City 1949; Chance of a Lifetime 1950; Conflict of Wings 1953; Betrayed 1954; Hell below Zero 1954; Helen of Troy 1955; Special Delivery 1955; Lust for Life 1956; Night of the Demon 1957; Behind the Mask 1958; Tarzan's Greatest Adventure 1959; This Other Eden 1959; Foxhole in Cairo 1960; Kidnapped 1960; Never Take Sweets from a Stranger 1960; Sword of Sherwood Forest 1960; A Terrible Beauty 1960; The Man Who Finally Died 1962; The Playboy of the Western World 1962; The Prince and the Pauper 1962; A Face in the Rain 1963; Jason and the Argonauts 1963; The Truth about Spring 1964; The War Lord 1965; The Viking Queen 1967

McGinnis, Scott Wacko 1981; Gunbus 1986; Odd Jobs 1986; 3:15 1986; You Can't Hurry Love 1988

McGiver, John (1912–1975) Love in the Afternoon 1957; I Married a Woman 1958; The Gazebo 1959; Breakfast at Tiffany's 1961; Love in a Goldfish Bowl 1961; The Manchurian Candidate 1962; Mr Hobbs Takes a Vacation 1962; My Six Loves 1962; Period of Adjustment 1962; Take Her, She's Mine 1963; Who's Minding the Store? 1963; Man's Favorite Sport? 1964; Marriage on the Rocks 1965; The Glass Bottom Boat 1966; Made in Paris 1966; Fitzwilly 1967; Midnight Cowboy 1969; Arnold 1973

McGlone, Mike (1972–) The Brothers McMullen 1995; She's the One 1996; One Tough Cop 1998; The Bone Collector 1999; Dinner Rush 2000; Hardball 2001

McGlynn Sr, Frank (1866–1951) Riders of the Purple Sage 1931; The Littlest Rebel 1935; The Plainsman 1936

McGlynn Jr, Frank (1904–1939) Hopalong Cassidy 1935; Westward Ho 1935

McGoohan, Patrick (1928–) Passage Home 1955; Zarak 1956; Hell Drivers 1957; High Tide at Noon 1957; The Gypsy and the Gentleman 1958; Nor the Moon by Night 1958; All Night Long 1961; Two Living, One Dead 1961; Life for Ruth 1962; The Quare Fellow 1962; Dr Syn, Alias the Scarecrow 1963; The Three Lives of Thomasina 1963; Ice Station Zebra 1968; Mary, Queen of Scots 1971; Silver Streak 1976; The Man in the Iron Mask 1977; Brass Target 1978; Escape from Alcatraz 1979; Scanners 1980; Kings and Desperate Men 1981; Baby: Secret of the Lost Legend 1985; Braveheart 1995; Treasure Planet 2002

McGovern, Elizabeth (1961–) Ordinary People 1980; Ragtime 1981; Lovesick 1983; Once upon a Time in America 1984; Racing with the Moon 1984; Native Son 1986; The Bedroom Window 1987; She's Having a Baby 1988; Johnny Handsome 1989; Aunt Julia and the Scriptwriter 1990; The Handmaid's Tale 1990; A Shock to the System 1990; King of the Hill 1993; The Favor 1994; The Summer of Ben Tyler 1996; The Wings of the Dove 1997; If Only 1998; The Misadventures of Margaret 1998; The House of Mirth 2000; Buffalo Soldiers 2001

McGowan, J P (1880–1952) Somewhere in Sonora 1933; Hit the Saddle 1937

McGowan, Rose (1975–) California Man 1992; Doom Generation 1995; Lewis & Clark & George 1996; Scream 1996; Going All the Way 1997; Phantoms 1998; Jawbreaker 1999; Ready to Rumble 2000

McGowan, Tom (1958–) Mrs Parker and the Vicious Circle 1994; Heavyweights 1995

MacGowran, Jack (1918–1973) No Resting Place 1950; Sailor Beware! 1956; Manuela 1957; The Rising of the Moon 1957; Rooney 1958; The Giant Behemoth 1959; Cul-de-Sac 1966; The Fearless Vampire Killers 1967; How I Won the War 1967; Wonderwall 1968; Age of Consent 1969; King Lear 1970; Start the Revolution without Me 1970; The Exorcist 1973

MacGowran, Tara (1964–) Secret Places 1984; The Dawning 1988

McGrail, Walter (1888–1970) Men without Women 1930; In Old Montana 1939

McGrath, Doug Twilight Zone: the Movie 1983; Pale Rider 1985

McGrath, Frank (1903–1967) Riders of the Purple Sage 1941; The Reluctant Astronaut 1967; The Shakiest Gun in the West 1967

MacGrath, Leueen (1914–1992) The Saint's Vacation 1941; Edward, My Son 1949

McGrath, Matt (1969–) Boys Don't Cry 1999; The Broken Hearts Club: a Romantic Comedy 2000

McGrath, Pat Somewhere on Leave 1942; Confession 1955

MacGraw, Ali (1938–) A Lovely Way to Go 1968; Goodbye, Columbus 1969; Love Story 1970; The Getaway 1972; Convoy 1978; Players 1979; Just Tell Me What You Want 1980

McGraw, Charles (1914–1980) The Killers 1946; T-Men 1947; Reign of Terror 1949; Armored Car Robbery 1950; Side Street 1950; Double Crossbones 1951; His Kind of Woman 1951; Roadblock 1951; The Narrow Margin 1952; One Minute to Zero 1952; Thunder over the Plains 1953; War Paint 1953; The Bridges at Toko-Ri 1954; Toward the Unknown 1956; Slaughter on Tenth Avenue 1957; The Defiant Ones 1958; Saddle the Wind 1958; Twilight for the Gods 1958; The Man in the Net 1959; The

Wonderful Country 1959; *The Horizontal Lieutenant* 1962; *The Birds* 1963; *In Cold Blood* 1967; *Nightmare in Chicago* 1968; *Pendulum* 1969; *Tell Them Willie Boy Is Here* 1969; *Johnny Got His Gun* 1971; *A Boy and His Dog* 1975; *The Killer inside Me* 1975
McGreevey, Michael (1948–) *Sammy, the Way Out Seal* 1962; *The Way West* 1967; *Now You See Him, Now You Don't* 1972; *Snowball Express* 1972
McGregor, Angela Punch *aka* **Punch, Angela** (1953–) *The Chant of Jimmie Blacksmith* 1978; *Newsfront* 1978; *The Island* 1980; *Double Deal* 1981; *The Survivor* 1981; *We of the Never Never* 1982; *Annie's Coming Out* 1984; *The Delinquents* 1989
McGregor, Charles (?–1996) *Superfly* 1972; *Three the Hard Way* 1974
McGregor, Ewan (1971–) *Being Human* 1994; *Shallow Grave* 1994; *Blue Juice* 1995; *The Pillow Book* 1995; *Trainspotting* 1995; *Brassed Off* 1996; *Emma* 1996; *A Life Less Ordinary* 1997; *Nightwatch* 1997; *The Serpent's Kiss* 1997; *Little Voice* 1998; *Rogue Trader* 1998; *Velvet Goldmine* 1998; *Eye of the Beholder* 1999; *Nora* 1999; *Star Wars Episode I: the Phantom Menace* 1999; *Black Hawk Down* 2001; *Moulin Rouge!* 2001; *Star Wars Episode II: Attack of the Clones* 2002; *Big Fish* 2003; *Down with Love* 2003; *Young Adam* 2003; *Robots* 2005; *Star Wars Episode III: Revenge of the Sith* 2005; *Valiant* 2005
McGregor-Stewart, Kate *[Safe]* 1995; *The Maker* 1997
McGuire, Biff (1926–) *The Phenix City Story* 1955; *Station Six-Sahara* 1962; *The Heart Is a Lonely Hunter* 1968; *The Thomas Crown Affair* 1968; *Serpico* 1973
McGuire, Don (1919–1999) *The Fuller Brush Man* 1948; *Armored Car Robbery* 1950; *Double Dynamite* 1951
McGuire, Dorothy (1916–2001) *Claudia* 1943; *The Enchanted Cottage* 1945; *A Tree Grows in Brooklyn* 1945; *Claudia and David* 1946; *The Spiral Staircase* 1946; *Till the End of Time* 1946; *Gentleman's Agreement* 1947; *Mister 880* 1950; *Callaway Went Thataway* 1951; *I Want You* 1951; *Make Haste to Live* 1954; *Three Coins in the Fountain* 1954; *Trial* 1955; *Friendly Persuasion* 1956; *Old Yeller* 1957; *The Remarkable Mr Pennypacker* 1959; *A Summer Place* 1959; *This Earth Is Mine* 1959; *The Dark at the Top of the Stairs* 1960; *Swiss Family Robinson* 1960; *Susan Slade* 1961; *Summer Magic* 1963; *The Greatest Story Ever Told* 1965; *Flight of the Doves* 1971; *Caroline?* 1990
McGuire, John (1910–1980) *Steamboat round the Bend* 1935; *Stranger on the Third Floor* 1940; *Invisible Ghost* 1941; *Bells of San Angelo* 1947
McGuire, Kathryn (1903–1978) *The Navigator* 1924; *Sherlock Junior* 1924
McGuire, Marcy (1926–) *Seven Days' Leave* 1942; *Higher and Higher* 1943
McGuire, Michael (1934–) *Larry* 1974; *Hard Times* 1975; *Report to the Commissioner* 1975; *Jekyll and Hyde... Together Again* 1982; *Bird* 1988
McGuire, Tucker *Shipyard Sally* 1939; *The Night Has Eyes* 1942
McHattie, Stephen (1947–) *The People Next Door* 1970; *Von Richthofen and Brown* 1971; *The Ultimate Warrior* 1975; *Tomorrow Never Comes* 1977; *Gray Lady Down* 1978; *Death Valley* 1982; *Best Revenge* 1983; *Belizaire the Cajun* 1985; *Salvation! Have You Said Your Prayers Today?* 1987; *Call Me* 1988; *Sticky Fingers* 1988; *Bloodhounds of Broadway* 1989; *Art Deco Detective* 1994; *Beverly Hills Cop III* 1994; *Theodore Rex* 1995; *Visitors of the Night* 1995; *My Friend Joe* 1996; *The Highwayman* 1999; *Secretary* 2001; *A History of Violence* 2005
Machiavelli, Nicoletta (1945–) *Navajo Joe* 1966; *Someone Is Bleeding* 1974
Machowski, Ignacy (1919–2001) *The Shadow* 1956; *Eroica* 1958
Macht, Gabriel (1972–) *The Audrey Hepburn Story* 2000; *American Outlaws* 2001; *Behind Enemy Lines* 2001; *Bad Company* 2002; *The Recruit* 2002; *A Love Song for Bobby Long* 2004
Macht, Stephen (1942–) *The Choirboys* 1977; *Nightwing* 1979; *Galaxina* 1980; *The Mountain Men* 1980; *Agatha Christie's A Caribbean Mystery* 1983; *The Monster Squad* 1987; *My Boyfriend's Back* 1989; *Graveyard Shift* 1990
McHugh, Frank (1898–1981) *Bad Company* 1931; *The Crowd Roars* 1932; *High Pressure* 1932; *One Way Passage* 1932; *The Strange Love of Molly Louvain* 1932; *Union Depot* 1932; *Ex-Lady* 1933; *Mystery of the Wax Museum* 1933; *The Telegraph Trail* 1933; *Fashions of 1934* 1934; *Here Comes the Navy* 1934; *Devil Dogs of the Air* 1935; *The Irish in Us* 1935; *A Midsummer Night's Dream* 1935; *Page Miss Glory* 1935; *Bullets or Ballots* 1936; *Stage Struck* 1936; *Three Men on a Horse* 1936; *Swing Your Lady* 1937; *Boy Meets Girl* 1938; *Daughters Courageous* 1939; *Dodge City* 1939; *Dust Be My Destiny* 1939; *Indianapolis Speedway* 1939; *On Your Toes* 1939; *The Roaring Twenties* 1939; *The Fighting 69th* 1940; *I Love You Again* 1940; *'Til We Meet Again* 1940; *Virginia City* 1940; *Back Street* 1941; *Manpower* 1941; *All through the Night* 1942; *Her Cardboard Lover* 1942; *Going My Way* 1944; *Marine Raiders* 1944; *A Medal for Benny* 1945; *State Fair* 1945; *Carnegie Hall* 1947; *The Velvet Touch* 1948; *Mighty Joe Young* 1949; *Miss Grant Takes Richmond* 1949; *Paid in Full* 1950; *My Son John* 1952; *A Lion Is in the Streets* 1953; *Career* 1959; *Say One for Me* 1959; *Easy Come, Easy Go* 1967
McHugh, Matt (1894–1971) *Street Scene* 1931; *Taxi!* 1932
McIlwraith, David *Outrageous!* 1977; *Too Outrageous!* 1987; *On My Own* 1992
McInnerny, Lizzy (1961–) *Rowing with the Wind* 1987; *Being Human* 1994
McInnerny, Tim (1956–) *Wetherby* 1985; *Erik the Viking* 1989; *101 Dalmatians* 1996; *Rogue Trader* 1998; *Notting Hill* 1999; *102 Dalmatians* 2000; *The Emperor's New Clothes* 2001
MacInnes, Angus (1947–) *Force 10 from Navarone* 1978; *Strange Brew* 1983
McInnes, William (1963–) *The Heartbreak Kid* 1993; *Dirty Deeds* 2002
McIntire, John *aka* **McIntyre, John** (1907–1991) *The Street with No Name* 1948; *Down to the Sea in Ships* 1949; *Francis* 1949; *Johnny Stool Pigeon* 1949; *Red Canyon* 1949; *Scene of the Crime* 1949; *The Asphalt Jungle* 1950; *No Sad Songs for Me* 1950; *Saddle Tramp* 1950; *Winchester '73* 1950; *That's My Boy* 1951; *Westward the Women* 1951; *You're in the Navy Now* 1951; *Glory Alley* 1952; *Horizons West* 1952; *The Lawless Breed* 1952; *The World in His Arms* 1952; *A Lion Is in the Streets* 1953; *The Mississippi Gambler* 1953; *The President's Lady* 1953; *War Arrow* 1953; *Apache* 1954; *The Far Country* 1954; *Four Guns to the Border* 1954; *The Yellow Mountain* 1954; *The Kentuckian* 1955; *The Phenix City Story* 1955; *The Scarlet Coat* 1955; *The Spoilers* 1955; *Stranger on Horseback* 1955; *Backlash* 1956; *The Mark of the Hawk* 1957; *The Tin Star* 1957; *The Light in the Forest* 1958; *Sing, Boy, Sing* 1958; *The Gunfight at Dodge City* 1959; *Elmer Gantry* 1960; *Flaming Star* 1960; *Psycho* 1960; *Seven Ways from Sundown* 1960; *Who Was That Lady?* 1960; *Summer and Smoke* 1961; *Two Rode Together* 1961; *Rough Night in Jericho* 1967; *Challenge to Be Free* 1972; *Herbie Rides Again* 1974; *Rooster Cogburn* 1975; *Honkytonk Man* 1982; *Cloak and Dagger* 1984; *Turner & Hooch* 1989
McIntire, Tim (1943–1986) *The Sterile Cuckoo* 1969; *Aloha, Bobby and Rose* 1975; *The Gumball Rally* 1976; *American Hot Wax* 1977; *The Choirboys* 1977; *Brubaker* 1980; *Fast-Walking* 1982; *Sacred Ground* 1983
McIntosh, Burr (1862–1942) *Way Down East* 1920; *The Last Warning* 1928; *Lilac Time* 1928
McIntyre, Marvin J *The Running Man* 1987; *Wilder Napalm* 1993; *Born to Be Wild* 1995
MacIvor, Daniel (1962–) *I Love a Man in Uniform* 1993; *Beefcake* 1998
Mack, Allison (1982–) *Desperate Justice* 1993; *Honey, We Shrunk Ourselves* 1997
Mack, Charles Emmett (1900–1927) *Dream Street* 1921; *America* 1924
Mack, Helen (1913–1986) *Blind Adventure* 1933; *Melody Cruise* 1933; *Son of Kong* 1933; *Kiss and Make-Up* 1934; *The Lemon Drop Kid* 1934; *Captain Hurricane* 1935; *The Return of Peter Grimm* 1935; *She* 1935; *The Milky Way* 1936; *The Last Train from Madrid* 1937
Mack, James *aka* **Mack, James T** (1871–1948) *Anna Christie* 1930; *Bonnie Scotland* 1935
Mackaill, Dorothy (1903–1990) *Love Affair* 1932; *No Man of Her Own* 1932
McKamy, Kim *aka* **Patton, Kimberly** (1959–) *Creepozoids* 1987; *Willard* 2003
Mackay, Barry (1906–1985) *Evergreen* 1934; *Forever England* 1935; *Oh, Daddy!* 1935; *The Private Secretary* 1935; *Gangway* 1937; *The Great Barrier* 1937; *A Christmas Carol* 1938; *Sailing Along* 1938
McKay, David *The Girl in the Picture* 1985; *My Name Is Joe* 1998
Mackay, Fulton (1922–1987) *The Brave Don't Cry* 1952; *Laxdale Hall* 1953; *Gumshoe* 1971; *Nothing but the Night* 1972; *Porridge* 1979; *Britannia Hospital* 1982; *Local Hero* 1983; *Defence of the Realm* 1985; *Water* 1985
McKay, George (1884–1945) *Girls Can Play* 1937; *The Boogie Man Will Get You* 1942
MacKay, John *Trust* 1990; *Niagara Niagara* 1997
Mackay, Mathew *The Peanut Butter Solution* 1985; *Lapse of Memory* 1992
McKay, Scott (1922–1987) *Guest in the House* 1944; *Thirty Seconds over Tokyo* 1944; *You Better Watch Out* 1980
McKay, Wanda (1916–1996) *The Monster Maker* 1944; *Voodoo Man* 1944
McKean, Michael (1947–) *Used Cars* 1980; *Young Doctors in Love* 1982; *This Is Spinal Tap* 1984; *Clue* 1985; *DARYL* 1985; *Light of Day* 1987; *Planes, Trains and Automobiles* 1987; *Earth Girls Are Easy* 1988; *Short Circuit 2* 1988; *The Big Picture* 1989; *Hider in the House* 1989; *Flashback* 1990; *True Identity* 1991; *Man Trouble* 1992; *Memoirs of an Invisible Man* 1992; *Coneheads* 1993; *Airheads* 1994; *Radioland Murders* 1994; *The Brady Bunch Movie* 1995; *Jack* 1996; *Casper: a Spirited Beginning* 1997; *Nothing to Lose* 1997; *The Sunshine Boys* 1997; *That Darn Cat* 1997; *Teaching Mrs Tingle* 1999; *True Crime* 1999; *Best in Show* 2000; *Slap Her, She's French!* 2001; *The Guru* 2002; *A Mighty Wind* 2003
McKechnie, James (1911–1964) *The Life and Death of Colonel Blimp* 1943; *The Years Between* 1946
McKee, Gina (1964–) *The Lair of the White Worm* 1988; *The Life of Stuff* 1997; *Croupier* 1998; *Joan of Arc* 1999; *The Loss of Sexual Innocence* 1999; *Notting Hill* 1999; *Women Talking Dirty* 1999; *Wonderland* 1999; *There's Only One Jimmy Grimble* 2000; *The Reckoning* 2001; *Divine Secrets of the Ya-Ya Sisterhood* 2002; *The Blackwater Lightship* 2004
McKee, John *That Touch of Mink* 1962; *Monte Walsh* 1970
McKee, Lafe (1872–1959) *Riders of Destiny* 1933; *The Man from Utah* 1934; *The Desert Trail* 1935
McKee, Lonette (1954–) *Which Way Is Up?* 1977; *The Cotton Club* 1984; *Brewster's Millions* 1985; *'Round Midnight* 1986; *Jungle Fever* 1991; *Malcolm X* 1992; *He Got Game* 1998; *Honey* 2003
McKegg, Dorothy *Carry Me Back* 1982; *Footrot Flats: the Dog's Tale* 1986
McKellar, Don (1963–) *Roadkill* 1989; *Highway 61* 1992; *Exotica* 1994; *When Night Is Falling* 1995; *Last Night* 1998; *eXistenZ* 1999; *waydowntown* 2000; *Clean* 2004
McKellen, Ian (1939–) *Alfred the Great* 1969; *A Touch of Love* 1969; *Priest of Love* 1981; *The Scarlet Pimpernel* 1982; *The Keep* 1983; *Plenty* 1985; *Zina* 1985; *Scandal* 1988; *And the Band Played On* 1993; *The Ballad of Little Jo* 1993; *Last Action Hero* 1993; *Six Degrees of Separation* 1993; *I'll Do Anything* 1994; *The Shadow* 1994; *Thin Ice* 1994; *To Die For* 1994; *Jack & Sarah* 1995; *Restoration* 1995; *Richard III* 1995; *Bent* 1996; *A Bit of Scarlet* 1996; *Rasputin* 1996; *Amy Foster* 1997; *Apt Pupil* 1997; *Gods and Monsters* 1998; *X-Men* 2000; *The Lord of the Rings: The Fellowship of the Ring* 2001; *The Lord of the Rings: The Two Towers* 2002; *Emile* 2003; *The Lord of the Rings: The Return of the King* 2003; *X2* 2003; *The Magic Roundabout* 2005
McKenna, Bernard *My Childhood* 1972; *My Ain Folk* 1973
MacKenna, Kenneth (1899–1962) *Men without Women* 1930; *The Virtuous Sin* 1930; *13 West Street* 1962
McKenna, Siobhan (1923–1986) *Daughter of Darkness* 1948; *The Lost People* 1949; *The Adventurers* 1950; *King of Kings* 1961; *The Playboy of the Western World* 1962; *Of Human Bondage* 1964; *Doctor Zhivago* 1965; *Philadelphia, Here I Come* 1975
McKenna, T P (1929–) *The Siege of Sidney Street* 1960; *Girl with Green Eyes* 1963; *Ulysses* 1967; *The Beast in the Cellar* 1970; *Perfect Friday* 1970; *Straw Dogs* 1971; *Villain* 1971; *All Creatures Great and Small* 1974; *A Portrait of the Artist as a Young Man* 1977; *The Outsider* 1979; *Pascali's Island* 1988; *Red Scorpion* 1989; *Valmont* 1989
McKenna, Virginia (1931–) *Father's Doing Fine* 1952; *The Oracle* 1952; *The Cruel Sea* 1953; *The Ship That Died of Shame* 1955; *Simba* 1955; *The Barretts of Wimpole Street* 1956; *A Town like Alice* 1956; *The Smallest Show on Earth* 1957; *Carve Her Name with Pride* 1958; *Passionate Summer* 1958; *The Wreck of the Mary Deare* 1959; *Two Living, One Dead* 1961; *Born Free* 1966; *An Elephant Called Slowly* 1969; *Ring of Bright Water* 1969; *Waterloo* 1970; *Swallows and Amazons* 1974; *The Disappearance* 1977; *Holocaust 2000* 1977; *Sliding Doors* 1997
Mackenzie, Alex (1885–1965) *The Maggie* 1953; *The Bridal Path* 1959; *The Battle of the Sexes* 1960; *Greyfriars Bobby* 1961
McKenzie, Fay (1918–) *Down Mexico Way* 1941; *The Singing Sheriff* 1944
McKenzie, Jacqueline (1967–) *Romper Stomper* 1992; *Traps* 1994; *Angel Baby* 1995; *Mr Reliable* 1996; *Deep Blue Sea* 1999; *Kiss Kiss (Bang Bang)* 2001
MacKenzie, Joyce (1929–) *Broken Arrow* 1950; *Destination Murder* 1950; *The Racket* 1951; *Wait 'til the Sun Shines, Nellie* 1952; *Tarzan and the She-Devil* 1953; *The French Line* 1954; *Rails into Laramie* 1954
McKenzie, Julia (1941–) *The Wildcats of St Trinian's* 1980; *Those Glory, Glory Days* 1983; *Shirley Valentine* 1989; *Bright Young Things* 2003
Mackenzie, Mary (1922–1966) *Stolen Face* 1952; *The Master Plan* 1954; *Cloak without Dagger* 1955; *Yield to the Night* 1956
McKenzie, Tim *Gallipoli* 1981; *The Lighthorsemen* 1987
McKeon, Doug (1966–) *Night Crossing* 1981; *On Golden Pond* 1981; *Mischief* 1985
McKern, Leo (1920–2002) *Murder in the Cathedral* 1952; *All for Mary* 1955; *X the Unknown* 1956; *Time without Pity* 1957; *Beyond This Place* 1959; *The Mouse That Roared* 1959; *The Running, Jumping and Standing Still Film* 1959; *Yesterday's Enemy* 1959; *The Day the Earth Caught Fire* 1961; *Mr Topaze* 1961; *The Inspector* 1962; *Doctor in Distress* 1963; *Hot Enough for June* 1963; *A Jolly Bad Fellow* 1964; *King and Country* 1964; *The Amorous Adventures of Moll Flanders* 1965; *Help!* 1965; *A Man for All Seasons* 1966; *Assignment K* 1968; *Decline and Fall... of a Birdwatcher* 1968; *The Shoes of the Fisherman* 1968; *Ryan's Daughter* 1970; *Massacre in Rome* 1973; *The Adventure of Sherlock Holmes' Smarter Brother* 1975; *The Omen* 1976; *Candleshoe* 1977; *The Blue Lagoon* 1980; *The French Lieutenant's Woman* 1981; *The Chain* 1984; *Agatha Christie's Murder with Mirrors* 1985; *Ladyhawke* 1985; *Travelling North* 1986; *Dad and Dave: on Our Selection* 1995
Mackey, Brendan *9 Dead Gay Guys* 2001; *Touching the Void* 2003
McKidd, Kevin (1973–) *Small Faces* 1995; *Trainspotting* 1995; *Dad Savage* 1997; *The Acid House* 1998; *Bedrooms and Hallways* 1998; *Topsy-Turvy* 1999; *Dog Soldiers* 2001; *AfterLife* 2003; *One Last Chance* 2003; *16 Years of Alcohol* 2003; *De-Lovely* 2004; *Kingdom of Heaven* 2005
Mackie, Anthony *Million Dollar Baby* 2004; *She Hate Me* 2004
McKim, Robert (1886–1927) *The Mark of Zorro* 1920; *The Strong Man* 1926
McKinnel, Norman (1870–1932) *Hindle Wakes* 1927; *Hindle Wakes* 1931
McKinney, Bill (1931–) *She Freak* 1967; *Deliverance* 1972; *Junior Bonner* 1972; *Cleopatra Jones* 1973; *Cannonball* 1976; *The Outlaw Josey Wales* 1976; *The Shootist* 1976; *The Gauntlet* 1977; *Bronco Billy* 1980; *Tex* 1982; *Heart like a Wheel* 1983; *Kinjite: Forbidden Subjects* 1989; *City Slickers II: the Legend of Curly's Gold* 1994; *Undertow* 2004
McKinney, Florine (1909–1975) *Cynara* 1932; *Strangers All* 1935
McKinney, Mark (1959–) *Kids in the Hall: Brain Candy* 1996; *Jacob Two Two Meets the Hooded Fang* 1999; *The Out-of-Towners* 1999; *Superstar* 1999; *The Saddest Music in the World* 2003
McKinney, Nina Mae (1913–1967) *Hallelujah* 1929; *Sanders of the River* 1935
McKinnon, Ray (1961–) *Paris Trout* 1991; *The Gun in Betty Lou's Handbag* 1992; *Needful Things* 1993; *The Net* 1995; *Goodbye Lover* 1997; *Old Man* 1997; *The Missing* 2003
Mackintosh, Kenneth *Othello* 1965; *Three Sisters* 1970
Mackintosh, Louise (1864–1933) *The Phantom President* 1932; *The Little Giant* 1933

Mackintosh, Steven (1967–) London Kills Me 1991; Blue Juice 1995; The Grotesque 1995; Different for Girls 1996; House of America 1996; Twelfth Night 1996; The Land Girls 1997; Lock, Stock and Two Smoking Barrels 1998; The Criminal 1999; The Mother 2003; The Jacket 2005

McKnight, David Pizza Man 1991; Under Siege 1992

MacKrell, James aka **MacKrell, Jim** Teen Wolf 1985; The Dream Machine 1990

McKuen, Rod (1933–) Rock, Pretty Baby 1956; Wild Heritage 1958

MacLachlan, Janet Uptight 1968; tick... tick... tick... 1969; Halls of Anger 1970; The Man 1972; Dark Victory 1976; The Boy Who Could Fly 1986

MacLachlan, Kyle (1959–) Dune 1984; Blue Velvet 1986; The Hidden 1987; The Boyfriend School 1990; The Doors 1991; Rich in Love 1992; Twin Peaks: Fire Walk with Me 1992; Where the Day Takes You 1992; The Trial 1993; Against the Wall 1994; The Flintstones 1994; Roswell 1994; Showgirls 1995; The Trigger Effect 1996; Trigger Happy 1996; One Night Stand 1997; Route 9 1998; Timecode 1999; Hamlet 2000; XChange 2000; Me without You 2001; Miranda 2001; Northfork 2002

McLaglen, Victor (1886–1959) The Unholy Three 1925; Beau Geste 1926; What Price Glory 1926; A Girl in Every Port 1928; Hangman's House 1928; The Black Watch 1929; The Cock-Eyed World 1929; Dishonored 1931; Laughing at Life 1933; The Captain Hates the Sea 1934; The Lost Patrol 1934; Murder at the Vanities 1934; The Informer 1935; Klondike Annie 1936; Under Two Flags 1936; Nancy Steele Is Missing 1937; Sea Devils 1937; This Is My Affair 1937; Wee Willie Winkie 1937; We're Going to Be Rich 1938; Full Confession 1939; Gunga Din 1939; South of Pago Pago 1940; Broadway Limited 1941; Call Out the Marines 1941; China Girl 1942; The Princess and the Pirate 1944; Whistle Stop 1946; The Foxes of Harrow 1947; Fort Apache 1948; She Wore a Yellow Ribbon 1949; Rio Grande 1950; The Quiet Man 1952; Fair Wind to Java 1953; Prince Valiant 1954; Trouble in the Glen 1954; Bengazi 1955; Lady Godiva 1955; Many Rivers to Cross 1955; Sea Fury 1958

MacLaine, Shirley (1934–) The Trouble with Harry 1954; Artists and Models 1955; Around the World in 80 Days 1956; Hot Spell 1958; The Matchmaker 1958; The Sheepman 1958; Some Came Running 1958; Ask Any Girl 1959; Career 1959; All in a Night's Work 1960; The Apartment 1960; Can-Can 1960; The Children's Hour 1961; Two Loves 1961; My Geisha 1962; Two for the Seesaw 1962; Irma la Douce 1963; John Goldfarb, Please Come Home 1964; What a Way to Go! 1964; The Yellow Rolls-Royce 1964; Gambit 1966; Woman Times Seven 1967; The Bliss of Mrs Blossom 1968; Sweet Charity 1968; Two Mules for Sister Sara 1970; Desperate Characters 1971; The Possession of Joel Delaney 1971; The Turning Point 1977; Being There 1979; A Change of Seasons 1980; Loving Couples 1980; Cannonball Run II 1983; Terms of Endearment 1983; Madame Sousatzka 1988; Steel Magnolias 1989; Waiting for the Light 1989; Postcards from the Edge 1990; Used People 1992; Wrestling Ernest Hemingway 1993; Guarding Tess 1994; The West Side Waltz 1995; The Evening Star 1996; Mrs Winterbourne 1996; A Smile like Yours 1997; These Old Broads 2001; The Battle of Mary Kay 2002

MacLane, Barton (1900–1969) Tillie and Gus 1933; Black Fury 1935; The Case of the Lucky Legs 1935; Ceiling Zero 1935; Dr Socrates 1935; Frisco Kid 1935; "G" Men 1935; Go into Your Dance 1935; Bullets or Ballots 1936; Smart Blonde 1936; The Walking Dead 1936; Born Reckless 1937; God's Country and the Woman 1937; The Prince and the Pauper 1937; San Quentin 1937; You Only Live Once 1937; Gold Is Where You Find It 1938; The Storm 1938; You and Me 1938; Come Live with Me 1941; Dr Jekyll and Mr Hyde 1941; High Sierra 1941; The Maltese Falcon 1941; Manpower 1941; Western Union 1941; Wild Geese Calling 1941; All through the Night 1942; The Big Street 1942; Bombardier 1943; Song of Texas 1943; Cry of the Werewolf 1944; Marine Raiders 1944; The Mummy's Ghost 1944; Secret Command 1944; The Spanish Main 1945; Tarzan and the Amazons 1945; San Quentin 1946; Tarzan and the Huntress 1947; Angel in Exile 1948; Relentless 1948; Silver River 1948; The Treasure of the Sierra Madre 1948; Red Light 1949; Let's Dance 1950; Best of the Badmen 1951; Bugles in the Afternoon 1952; The Half-Breed 1952; Thunderbirds 1952; Rails into Laramie 1954; Foxfire 1955; Jail Busters 1955; Backlash 1956; Three Violent People 1956; The Geisha Boy 1958; Girl on the Run 1958; The Rounders 1965; Arizona Bushwhackers 1968

McLaren, Hollis Sunday in the Country 1975; Partners 1976; Outrageous! 1977; Welcome to Blood City 1977; Lost and Found 1979; Atlantic City, USA 1980; Too Outrageous! 1987

MacLaren, Ian (1875–1952) Journey's End 1930; Body and Soul 1931; Cleopatra 1934

McLaughlin, Gibb (1884–1960) The Farmer's Wife 1928; Congress Dances 1931; Bulldog Jack 1934; The Old Curiosity Shop 1934; Broken Blossoms 1936; Where There's a Will 1936; The Lavender Hill Mob 1951; The Man Who Watched Trains Go By 1952; The Brain Machine 1954

McLean, David (1922–1995) X-15 1961; The Strangler 1964; Kingdom of the Spiders 1977; Deathsport 1978

MacLean, Ian The Arsenal Stadium Mystery 1939; Dreaming 1944

McLeod, Catherine (1921–1997) I've Always Loved You 1946; That's My Man 1947; The Outcast 1954

Macleod, Gavin (1930–) War Hunt 1962; Deathwatch 1966; The Party 1968; A Man Called Gannon 1969; The 1,000 Plane Raid 1969

McLeod, Gordon (1890–1961) The Saint in London 1939; Crooks' Tour 1940; The Saint's Vacation 1941; We'll Smile Again 1942; The Saint Meets the Tiger 1943; A Case for PC 49 1950

McLerie, Allyn Ann aka **McLerie, Allyn** (1926–) Calamity Jane 1953; The Desert Song 1953; Phantom of the Rue Morgue 1954; Jeremiah Johnson 1972; Cinderella Liberty 1973; The Way We Were 1973

MacLiam, Eanna My Left Foot 1989; The Snapper 1993; The General 1998; Angela's Ashes 1999

McLiam, John (1918–1994) Showdown 1973; The Dove 1974; The Food of the Gods 1975; The Missouri Breaks 1976; Walk like a Man 1987

MacLiammoir, Michael (1899–1978) Othello 1952; What's the Matter with Helen? 1971

McLynn, Pauline (1962–) My Friend Joe 1996; Angela's Ashes 1999; The Most Fertile Man in Ireland 1999; An Everlasting Piece 2000; When Brendan Met Trudy 2000

MacMahon, Aline (1899–1991) Life Begins 1932; One Way Passage 1932; Gold Diggers of 1933 1933; Heroes for Sale 1933; The World Changes 1933; Ah, Wilderness! 1935; I Live My Life 1935; Kind Lady 1935; When You're in Love 1937; Back Door to Heaven 1939; Out of the Fog 1941; The Lady Is Willing 1942; Dragon Seed 1944; Guest in the House 1944; The Search 1948; The Flame and the Arrow 1950; The Eddie Cantor Story 1953; The Man from Laramie 1955; Diamond Head 1962; All the Way Home 1963; I Could Go On Singing 1963

McMahon, Ed (1923–) Slaughter's Big Rip-Off 1973; Fun with Dick and Jane 1977; Butterfly 1982; Full Moon High 1982

McMahon, Horace (1906–1971) Detective Story 1951; Abbott and Costello Go to Mars 1953; Man in the Dark 1953; Susan Slept Here 1954; Beau James 1957; The Delicate Delinquent 1957; Never Steal Anything Small 1959; The Detective 1968

McMartin, John Sweet Charity 1968; What's So Bad About Feeling Good? 1968; Thieves 1977; Blow Out 1981; Pennies from Heaven 1981; Dream Lover 1986; Legal Eagles 1986; Native Son 1986; Who's That Girl 1987; Day One 1989

McMenamin, Ciaran (1975–) Titanic Town 1998; To End All Wars 2001; Bollywood Queen 2002

McMillan, Kenneth (1932–1989) Bloodbrothers 1978; Oliver's Story 1978; Chilly Scenes of Winter 1979; Salem's Lot 1979; Borderline 1980; Carny 1980; Hide in Plain Sight 1980; Little Miss Marker 1980; Eyewitness 1981; Heartbeeps 1981; Ragtime 1981; True Confessions 1981; Whose Life Is It Anyway? 1981; Partners 1982; Cat's Eye 1984; Dune 1984; The Pope of Greenwich Village 1984; Runaway Train 1985; Armed and Dangerous 1986; Malone 1987; Three Fugitives 1989

McMillan, Roddy (1923–1979) The Gorbals Story 1949; The Bridal Path 1959; Ring of Bright Water 1969

McMillan, Ross The Twilight of the Ice Nymphs 1997; The Saddest Music in the World 2003

McMullan, Jim aka **McMullan, James** (1938–) The Raiders 1964; Downhill Racer 1969; Extreme Close-Up 1973

MacMurray, Fred (1908–1991) Alice Adams 1935; The Bride Comes Home 1935; The Gilded Lily 1935; Hands across the Table 1935; The Princess Comes Across 1936; The Texas Rangers 1936; The Trail of the Lonesome Pine 1936; Swing High, Swing Low 1937; True Confession 1937; Men with Wings 1938; Invitation to Happiness 1939; Little Old New York 1940; Remember the Night 1940; Too Many Husbands 1940; Dive Bomber 1941; The Forest Rangers 1942; The Lady Is Willing 1942; Star Spangled Rhythm 1942; Take a Letter, Darling 1942; Above Suspicion 1943; Flight for Freedom 1943; No Time for Love 1943; And the Angels Sing 1944; Double Indemnity 1944; Practically Yours 1944; Standing Room Only 1944; Captain Eddie 1945; Murder, He Says 1945; Pardon My Past 1945; Where Do We Go from Here? 1945; Smoky 1946; The Egg and I 1947; Singapore 1947; Suddenly It's Spring 1947; The Miracle of the Bells 1948; On Our Merry Way 1948; Father Was a Fullback 1949; Never a Dull Moment 1950; Callaway Went Thataway 1951; A Millionaire for Christy 1951; Fair Wind to Java 1953; The Moonlighter 1953; The Caine Mutiny 1954; Pushover 1954; Woman's World 1954; At Gunpoint 1955; The Far Horizons 1955; The Rains of Ranchipur 1955; There's Always Tomorrow 1956; Gun for a Coward 1957; Quantez 1957; Day of the Bad Man 1958; Good Day for a Hanging 1958; Face of a Fugitive 1959; The Oregon Trail 1959; The Shaggy Dog 1959; The Apartment 1960; The Absent-Minded Professor 1961; Bon Voyage! 1962; Son of Flubber 1962; Kisses for My President 1964; Follow Me, Boys! 1966; The Happiest Millionaire 1967; Charley and the Angel 1973; The Swarm 1978

McMurray, Sam (1941–) Union City 1980; LA Story 1991; Stone Cold 1991; Getting Even with Dad 1994; The Adventures of Slappy the Sea Lion 1998; Drop Dead Gorgeous 1999; Soccer Dog: the Movie 1999

McMurtrey, Joan The Betty Ford Story 1987; Welcome Home, Roxy Carmichael 1990

McNair, Barbara (1939–) Change of Habit 1969; They Call Me Mister Tibbs! 1970; The Organization 1971

McNally, Kevin aka **McNally, Kevin R** (1956–) Enigma 1982; Not Quite Jerusalem 1985; Cry Freedom 1987; Entrapment 1999; When the Sky Falls 2000; High Heels and Low Lifes 2001; Johnny English 2003; Pirates of the Caribbean: the Curse of the Black Pearl 2003; De-Lovely 2004

McNally, Stephen aka **McNally, Horace** (1913–1994) Dr Gillespie's New Assistant 1942; Eyes in the Night 1942; For Me and My Gal 1942; Keeper of the Flame 1942; The Man from Down Under 1943; Magnificent Doll 1946; Johnny Belinda 1948; City across the River 1949; Criss Cross 1949; The Lady Gambles 1949; No Way Out 1950; Winchester '73 1950; Wyoming Mail 1950; Air Cadet 1951; Apache Drums 1951; Iron Man 1951; The Lady Pays Off 1951; The Black Castle 1952; Diplomatic Courier 1952; The Duel at Silver Creek 1952; Devil's Canyon 1953; Split Second 1953; The Stand at Apache River 1953; A Bullet Is Waiting 1954; Make Haste to Live 1954; The Man from Bitter Ridge 1955; Violent Saturday 1955; Tribute to a Bad Man 1956; The Fiend Who Walked the West 1958; Hell Bent for Leather 1960; Panic in the City 1968; Once You Kiss a Stranger 1969

McNamara, Brian The Flamingo Kid 1984; Short Circuit 1986; Arachnophobia 1990; Mystery Date 1991; When the Party's Over 1992

McNamara, J Patrick Obsession 1976; Close Encounters of the Third Kind 1977

McNamara, John (1925–1968) From Hell It Came 1957; The Return of Dracula 1958

McNamara, Maggie (1928–1978) The Moon Is Blue 1953; Three Coins in the Fountain 1954; Prince of Players 1955

McNamara, Pat The Last Time I Committed Suicide 1996; The Daytrippers 1998; Ash Wednesday 2002

McNamara, William (1965–) Stealing Home 1988; Texasville 1990; Wildflower 1991; Chasers 1994; Surviving the Game 1994; Copycat 1995; Storybook 1995; The Brylcreem Boys 1996; Stag 1996; Something to Believe In 1997; Ringmaster 1998; Time Lapse 2001

MacNaughtan, Alan (1920–) Frankenstein Created Woman 1966; Family Life 1971

McNaughton, Gus (1881–1969) Happy 1933; Keep Your Seats, Please 1936; Keep Fit 1937; Storm in a Teacup 1937; The Divorce of Lady X 1938; St Martin's Lane 1938; We're Going to Be Rich 1938; Trouble Brewing 1939; Old Bill and Son 1940; Jeannie 1941

McNaughton, Jack (1905–1990) Cardboard Cavalier 1949; Trent's Last Case 1952; The Purple Plain 1954

MacNaughton, Robert (1966–) ET the Extra-Terrestrial 1982; I Am the Cheese 1983

McNear, Howard (1905–1969) Bachelor Flat 1961; Blue Hawaii 1961; The Errand Boy 1961

Macnee, Patrick (1922–) Scrooge 1951; The Battle of the River Plate 1956; Les Girls 1957; Mister Jerico 1969; Incense for the Damned 1970; Sherlock Holmes in New York 1976; King Solomon's Treasure 1977; The Sea Wolves 1980; The Howling 1981; The Hot Touch 1982; Young Doctors in Love 1982; This Is Spinal Tap 1984; Shadey 1985; A View to a Kill 1985; Waxwork 1988; Waxwork II: Lost in Time 1992; The Avengers 1998

McNeice, Ian (1950–) The Lonely Passion of Judith Hearne 1987; The Raggedy Rawney 1987; 1871 1989; The Russia House 1990; Year of the Comet 1992; No Escape 1994; Ace Ventura: When Nature Calls 1995; The Englishman Who Went up a Hill, but Came down a Mountain 1995; The Beautician and the Beast 1997; A Life Less Ordinary 1997; A Christmas Carol 1999; The Nine Lives of Tomas Katz 1999; Anazapta 2001; Conspiracy 2001; The Fourth Angel 2001; The Final Curtain 2002; Blackball 2003; Freeze Frame 2003; I'll Be There 2003; White Noise 2004

McNeil, Claudia (1917–1993) A Raisin in the Sun 1961; Black Girl 1972

McNeil, Kate Monkey Shines 1988; One Kill 2000

McNeil, Scott The Adventures of Mowgli 1967; Rudolph the Red-Nosed Reindeer and the Island of the Misfit Toys 2001

MacNeill, Peter aka **MacNeil, Peter** Whispers 1990; Butterbox Babies 1995; Crash 1996; The Hanging Garden 1997; Blessed Stranger: after Flight 111 2000; A History of Violence 2005

MacNeille, Tress (1951–) Rugrats in Paris: the Movie 2000; Cinderella II: Dreams Come True 2002; Hey Arnold! the Movie 2002

McNichol, Kristy (1962–) Summer of My German Soldier 1978; Little Darlings 1980; The Night the Lights Went Out in Georgia 1981; Only When I Laugh 1981; White Dog 1981; The Pirate Movie 1982; Just the Way You Are 1984; Dream Lover 1986; Two Moon Junction 1988; You Can't Hurry Love 1988

MacNicol, Peter (1954–) Dragonslayer 1981; Sophie's Choice 1982; Heat 1987; American Blue Note 1989; Ghostbusters II 1989; Hard Promises 1991; HouseSitter 1992; Addams Family Values 1993; Roswell 1994; Dracula: Dead and Loving It 1995; Fugitive from Justice 1996; Bean 1997; The Secret of NIMH II: Timmy to the Rescue 1998; Baby Geniuses 1999; Recess: School's Out 2001; Breakin' All the Rules 2004

Macowan, Norman (1877–1961) The Dark Light 1951; The City of the Dead 1960

Macpherson, Elle (1964–) Sirens 1994; If Lucy Fell 1996; Jane Eyre 1996; The Mirror Has Two Faces 1996; The Edge 1997

McQuade, Kris (1952–) The Coca-Cola Kid 1985; Better than Sex 2000

McQuarrie, Stuart (1963–) The Life of Stuff 1997; Young Adam 2003

McQueen, Butterfly (1911–1995) Gone with the Wind 1939; Affectionately Yours 1941; Mildred Pierce 1945; Duel in the Sun 1946

McQueen, Chad (1960–) Hadley's Rebellion 1984; New York Cop 1995

McQueen, Steve aka **McQueen, Steven** (1930–1980) Somebody Up There Likes Me 1956; The Blob 1958; Never Love a Stranger 1958; The Great St Louis Bank Robbery 1959; Never So Few 1959; The Magnificent Seven

1960; *The Honeymoon Machine* 1961; *Hell Is for Heroes* 1962; *The War Lover* 1962; *The Great Escape* 1963; *Love with the Proper Stranger* 1963; *Soldier in the Rain* 1963; *Baby the Rain Must Fall* 1965; *The Cincinnati Kid* 1965; *Nevada Smith* 1966; *The Sand Pebbles* 1966; *Bullitt* 1968; *The Thomas Crown Affair* 1968; *The Reivers* 1969; *Le Mans* 1971; *The Getaway* 1972; *Junior Bonner* 1972; *Papillon* 1973; *The Towering Inferno* 1974; *An Enemy of the People* 1977; *The Hunter* 1980; *Tom Horn* 1980
McQueeney, Robert *aka* **McQueeny, Robert** *The World Was His Jury* 1957; *The Glory Guys* 1965
McRae, Alan *3 Ninjas* 1992; *3 Ninjas Kick Back* 1994
McRae, Carmen (1922–1994) *Hotel* 1967; *Jo Jo Dancer, Your Life Is Calling* 1986
Macrae, Duncan (1905–1967) *The Brothers* 1947; *The Woman in Question* 1950; *You're Only Young Twice* 1952; *The Kidnappers* 1953; *Rockets Galore* 1958; *The Best of Enemies* 1961; *Greyfriars Bobby* 1961; *A Jolly Bad Fellow* 1964; *30 Is a Dangerous Age, Cynthia* 1968
McRae, Frank (1952–) *Paradise Alley* 1978; *Used Cars* 1980; *Cannery Row* 1982; *48 HRS* 1982; **batteries not included* 1987; *Farewell to the King* 1988; *Licence to Kill* 1989; *Lock Up* 1989; *Last Action Hero* 1993; *National Lampoon's Loaded Weapon 1* 1993; *Lightning Jack* 1994
MacRae, Gordon (1921–1986) *Look for the Silver Lining* 1949; *Backfire* 1950; *The Daughter of Rosie O'Grady* 1950; *Tea for Two* 1950; *The West Point Story* 1950; *On Moonlight Bay* 1951; *By the Light of the Silvery Moon* 1953; *The Desert Song* 1953; *Three Sailors and a Girl* 1953; *Oklahoma!* 1955; *The Best Things in Life Are Free* 1956; *Carousel* 1956; *The Pilot* 1979
McRae, Hilton *The French Lieutenant's Woman* 1981; *The Secret Rapture* 1993
MacRae, Meredith (1944–2000) *Grand Jury* 1976; *Earthbound* 1981
McRaney, Gerald (1948–) *The NeverEnding Story* 1984; *Deadly Vows* 1994; *Take Me Home: the John Denver Story* 2000; *Danger beneath the Sea* 2001
Macready, George (1908–1973) *The Conspirators* 1944; *Follow the Boys* 1944; *Counter-Attack* 1945; *My Name Is Julia Ross* 1945; *A Song to Remember* 1945; *The Bandit of Sherwood Forest* 1946; *Gilda* 1946; *Down to Earth* 1947; *The Big Clock* 1948; *The Black Arrow* 1948; *The Gallant Blade* 1948; *Alias Nick Beal* 1949; *The Doolins of Oklahoma* 1949; *Johnny Allegro* 1949; *Knock on Any Door* 1949; *A Lady without Passport* 1950; *Rogues of Sherwood Forest* 1950; *The Desert Fox* 1951; *Detective Story* 1951; *Tarzan's Peril* 1951; *The Golden Blade* 1953; *Julius Caesar* 1953; *The Stranger Wore a Gun* 1953; *Treasure of the Golden Condor* 1953; *Vera Cruz* 1954; *A Kiss before Dying* 1956; *Thunder over Arizona* 1956; *Paths of Glory* 1957; *The Alligator People* 1959; *Jet over the Atlantic* 1960; *Taras Bulba* 1962; *Dead Ringer* 1964; *Seven Days in May* 1964; *Where Love Has Gone* 1964
McShane, Ian (1942–) *The Wild and the Willing* 1962; *The Pleasure Girls* 1965; *Sky West and Crooked* 1965; *Battle of Britain* 1969; *If It's Tuesday, This Must Be Belgium* 1969; *Villain* 1971; *Sitting Target* 1972; *The Last of Sheila* 1973; *Ransom* 1975; *The Fifth Musketeer* 1979; *Yesterday's Hero* 1979; *Too Scared to Scream* 1982; *Exposed* 1983; *Ordeal by Innocence* 1984; *Torchlight* 1984; *Sexy Beast* 2000; *Bollywood Queen* 2002; *Agent Cody Banks* 2003
McShane, Micheal *aka* **McShane, Michael** *aka* **McShane, Mike** (1957–) *Robin Hood: Prince of Thieves* 1991; *Richie Rich* 1994; *Tom and Huck* 1995; *A Bug's Life* 1998
McSharry, Carmel *Life in Danger* 1959; *All Coppers Are...* 1972
McSorley, Gerard *The Boxer* 1997; *Felicia's Journey* 1999; *Bloody Sunday* 2001; *Veronica Guerin* 2003; *Inside I'm Dancing* 2004
McTeer, Janet (1962–) *Hawks* 1988; *Wuthering Heights* 1992; *Carrington* 1995; *Velvet Goldmine* 1998; *Songcatcher* 1999; *Tumbleweeds* 1999; *The King Is Alive* 2000; *Waking the Dead* 2000
McVey, Patrick *aka* **McVey, Pat** (1910–1973) *The Big Caper* 1957; *The Visitors* 1972; *Bang the Drum Slowly* 1973
McVey, Paul (1898–1973) *Force of Evil* 1948; *Bwana Devil* 1952
McVey, Tyler (1912–2003) *The Come On* 1956; *Attack of the Giant Leeches* 1960; *Lt Robin Crusoe, USN* 1966
MacVittie, Bruce *Stonewall* 1995; *Where the Money Is* 2000
McWade, Margaret (1872–1956) *The Lost World* 1925; *Theodora Goes Wild* 1936
McWade, Robert (1872–1938) *Feet First* 1930; *Kept Husbands* 1931; *The First Year* 1932; *The Lemon Drop Kid* 1934; *Anything Goes* 1936; *Next Time We Love* 1936; *California Straight Ahead* 1937
McWhirter, Jillian *After Midnight* 1989; *The Dentist II* 1998; *Progeny* 1998
McWilliams, Caroline (1945–) *White Water Summer* 1987; *Mermaids* 1990
Macy, Bill (1922–) *The Late Show* 1977; *The Jerk* 1979; *Serial* 1980; *My Favorite Year* 1982; *Bad Medicine* 1985; *Movers and Shakers* 1985; *Analyze This* 1999; *Surviving Christmas* 2004
Macy, William H *aka* **Macy, Bill** (1950–) *Homicide* 1991; *The Heart of Justice* 1992; *A Murderous Affair* 1992; *Benny and Joon* 1993; *Twenty Bucks* 1993; *Being Human* 1994; *Dead on Sight* 1994; *Murder in the First* 1994; *Oleanna* 1994; *Fargo* 1995; *Mr Holland's Opus* 1995; *Down Periscope* 1996; *Ghosts of Mississippi* 1996; *Air Force One* 1997; *Boogie Nights* 1997; *Wag the Dog* 1997; *A Civil Action* 1998; *Jerry and Tom* 1998; *Pleasantville* 1998; *Psycho* 1998; *Happy, Texas* 1999; *Magnolia* 1999; *Mystery Men* 1999; *A Slight Case of Murder* 1999; *Panic* 2000; *State and Main* 2000; *Focus* 2001; *Jurassic Park III* 2001; *The Cooler* 2002; *It's a Very Merry Muppet Christmas Movie* 2002; *Welcome to Collinwood* 2002; *Seabiscuit* 2003; *Cellular* 2004; *Sahara* 2004; *Spartan* 2004
Madden, Ciaran (1945–) *Gawain and the Green Knight* 1973; *The Beast Must Die* 1974
Madden, Dave (1931–) *Charlotte's Web* 1973; *Eat My Dust!* 1976
Madden, Peter (1905–1976) *The Loneliness of the Long Distance Runner* 1962; *The Road to Hong Kong* 1962; *He Who Rides a Tiger* 1965
Maddern, Victor (1926–1993) *Sailor of the King* 1953; *Street of Shadows* 1953; *Terror on a Train* 1953; *Carrington VC* 1954; *The Cockleshell Heroes* 1955; *Child in the House* 1956; *The Man in the Sky* 1956; *Barnacle Bill* 1957; *Seven Waves Away* 1957; *Blood of the Vampire* 1958; *Cat and Mouse* 1958; *I Was Monty's Double* 1958; *The Safecracker* 1958; *The Siege of Pinchgut* 1959; *Let's Get Married* 1960; *Light Up the Sky* 1960; *Petticoat Pirates* 1961; *HMS Defiant* 1962; *Rotten to the Core* 1965; *A Hole Lot of Trouble* 1969; *Steptoe and Son* 1972
Madhubala (1933–1969) *Tarana* 1951; *Mr and Mrs '55* 1955; *Mughal-e-Azam* 1960; *Roja* 1992
Madigan, Amy (1950–) *Love Child* 1982; *Love Letters* 1983; *Places in the Heart* 1984; *Streets of Fire* 1984; *Alamo Bay* 1985; *Twice in a Lifetime* 1985; *Nowhere to Hide* 1987; *The Prince of Pennsylvania* 1988; *Field of Dreams* 1989; *Roe vs Wade* 1989; *Uncle Buck* 1989; *The Dark Half* 1991; *Female Perversions* 1996; *Loved* 1996; *Pollock* 2000
Madison, Guy (1922–1996) *Till the End of Time* 1946; *The Charge at Feather River* 1953; *The Command* 1954; *Five against the House* 1955; *The Last Frontier* 1955; *The Beast of Hollow Mountain* 1956; *Hilda Crane* 1956; *Bullwhip* 1958; *Jet over the Atlantic* 1960; *The Executioner of Venice* 1963; *Kidnapped to Mystery Island* 1964; *Sandokan against the Leopard of Sarawak* 1964; *Sandokan Fights Back* 1964; *This Man Can't Die* 1967; *Where's Willie?* 1977
Madison, Leigh *The Giant Behemoth* 1959; *Naked Fury* 1959
Madison, Mae (1914–2004) *The Big Stampede* 1932; *So Big* 1932
Madison, Noel (1897–1975) *Doorway to Hell* 1931; *Me and My Gal* 1932; *The Cocaine Fiends* 1935; *Gangway* 1937; *Climbing High* 1938; *Crackerjack* 1938; *Sailing Along* 1938
Madoc, Philip (1934–) *Dr Jekyll and Sister Hyde* 1971; *Zina* 1985; *Otherworld* 2003
Madonna (1958–) *Desperately Seeking Susan* 1985; *Shanghai Surprise* 1986; *Who's That Girl* 1987; *Bloodhounds of Broadway* 1989; *Dick Tracy* 1990; *Shadows and Fog* 1991; *Body of Evidence* 1992; *A League of Their Own* 1992; *Dangerous Game* 1993; *Blue in the Face* 1995; *Four Rooms* 1995; *Evita* 1996; *Girl 6* 1996; *The Next Best Thing* 2000; *Die Another Day* 2002; *Swept Away* 2002
Madsen, Michael (1958–) *The Killing Time* 1987; *Blood Red* 1988; *Kill Me Again* 1989; *The End of Innocence* 1990; *The Doors* 1991; *Reservoir Dogs* 1991; *Thelma & Louise* 1991; *Inside Edge* 1992; *Straight Talk* 1992; *Final Combination* 1993; *Free Willy* 1993; *Money for Nothing* 1993; *Trouble Bound* 1993; *Fixing the Shadow* 1994; *The Getaway* 1994; *Wyatt Earp* 1994; *Free Willy 2: the Adventure Home* 1995; *Species* 1995; *Executive Target* 1996; *The Last Days of Frankie the Fly* 1996; *Mulholland Falls* 1996; *The Winner* 1996; *Diary of a Serial Killer* 1997; *Donnie Brasco* 1997; *Love to Kill* 1997; *The Maker* 1997; *Species II* 1998; *Too Hard to Die* 1998; *The Stray* 1999; *Supreme Sanction* 1999; *The Ghost* 2000; *Luck of the Draw* 2000; *Die Another Day* 2002; *Kill Bill Vol 1* 2003; *Kill Bill Vol 2* 2003; *My Boss's Daughter* 2003; *Blueberry* 2004; *Sin City* 2005
Madsen, Virginia (1963–) *Dune* 1984; *Electric Dreams* 1984; *Creator* 1985; *Fire with Fire* 1986; *Slam Dance* 1987; *Zombie High* 1987; *The Dead Can't Lie* 1988; *Hot to Trot* 1988; *Mr North* 1988; *Heart of Dixie* 1989; *Highlander II: the Quickening* 1990; *The Hot Spot* 1990; *Becoming Colette* 1991; *Victim of Love* 1991; *Candyman* 1992; *A Murderous Affair* 1992; *Blue Tiger* 1994; *The Prophecy* 1994; *Just Your Luck* 1996; *John Grisham's The Rainmaker* 1997; *The Haunting* 1999; *American Gun* 2002; *Sideways* 2004
Maelen, Christian *I Think I Do* 1997; *Wisegirls* 2001
Maestro, Mia *Tango* 1998; *For Love or Country: the Arturo Sandoval Story* 2000; *Frida* 2002; *The Motorcycle Diaries* 2004
Maffia, Roma (1958–) *Disclosure* 1994; *Nick of Time* 1995; *Route 9* 1998
Magee, Patrick (1922–1982) *The Criminal* 1960; *Rag Doll* 1960; *Dementia 13* 1963; *The Masque of the Red Death* 1964; *Seance on a Wet Afternoon* 1964; *The Skull* 1965; *Marat/Sade* 1966; *The Birthday Party* 1968; *Hard Contract* 1969; *Cromwell* 1970; *King Lear* 1970; *You Can't Win 'em All* 1970; *A Clockwork Orange* 1971; *Demons of the Mind* 1971; *The Fiend* 1971; *The Trojan Women* 1971; *Asylum* 1972; *Tales from the Crypt* 1972; *And Now the Screaming Starts!* 1973; *The Final Programme* 1973; *Lady Ice* 1973; *Luther* 1974; *Barry Lyndon* 1975; *Telefon* 1977; *The Brontë Sisters* 1979; *Rough Cut* 1980; *Sir Henry at Rawlinson End* 1980; *The Black Cat* 1981; *Chariots of Fire* 1981
Magimel, Benoît (1974–) *Life Is a Long Quiet River* 1988; *Les Voleurs* 1996; *Les Enfants du Siècle* 1999; *Le Roi Danse* 2000; *The Piano Teacher* 2001; *The Flower of Evil* 2002; *Strange Gardens* 2003; *The Bridesmaid* 2004
Maglietta, Licia (1954–) *L'Amore Molesto* 1995; *Bread and Tulips* 2000
Magnan, Philippe (1948–) *Le Parfum d'Yvonne* 1994; *La Veuve de Saint-Pierre* 2000; *Arsène Lupin* 2004
Magnani, Anna (1907–1973) *Rome, Open City* 1945; *L'Amore* 1948; *Volcano* 1950; *Bellissima* 1951; *The Golden Coach* 1953; *The Rose Tattoo* 1955; *Wild Is the Wind* 1957; *The Fugitive Kind* 1960; *Mamma Roma* 1962; *The Secret of Santa Vittoria* 1969; *Fellini's Roma* 1972
Magnuson, Ann (1956–) *Blind Alley* 1984; *Making Mr Right* 1987; *Checking Out* 1988; *A Night in the Life of Jimmy Reardon* 1988; *Tequila Sunrise* 1988; *Before and After* 1996; *Small Soldiers* 1998; *Love & Sex* 2000; *Glitter* 2001; *Panic Room* 2002
Magre, Judith (1926–) *Les Amants* 1958; *Nathalie...* 2003
Maguelon, Pierre *Garde à Vue* 1981; *Cyrano de Bergerac* 1990; *Alice et Martin* 1998
Maguire, Kathleen (1925–1989) *Edge of the City* 1957; *Flipper* 1963; *Bill* 1981
Maguire, Mary (1917–) *Confession* 1937; *Mysterious Mr Moto* 1938; *Black Eyes* 1939
Maguire, Tobey (1975–) *This Boy's Life* 1993; *The Ice Storm* 1997; *Fear and Loathing in Las Vegas* 1998; *Pleasantville* 1998; *The Cider House Rules* 1999; *Ride with the Devil* 1999; *Wonder Boys* 2000; *Cats & Dogs* 2001; *Spider-Man* 2002; *Seabiscuit* 2003; *Spider-Man 2* 2004
Mahaffey, Valerie *National Lampoon's Senior Trip* 1995; *Jungle 2 Jungle* 1997
Mahal, Taj (1942–) *Sounder* 1972; *Part 2, Sounder* 1976
Maharis, George (1928–) *Sylvia* 1964; *Quick, before It Melts* 1965; *The Satan Bug* 1965; *A Covenant with Death* 1967; *The Happening* 1967; *The Desperados* 1969; *Land Raiders* 1969; *The Sword and the Sorcerer* 1982; *Doppelganger* 1993
Maher, Bill (1956–) *House II: the Second Story* 1987; *Cannibal Women in the Avocado Jungle of Death* 1989; *Pizza Man* 1991; *Tomcats* 2000
Maher, Joseph (1934–1998) *Under the Rainbow* 1981; *The Evil That Men Do* 1984; *Funny Farm* 1988; *My Stepmother Is an Alien* 1988; *IQ* 1994; *Killer* 1994; *Surviving Picasso* 1996
Mahler, Bruce (1950–) *Police Academy 2: Their First Assignment* 1985; *Police Academy 6: City under Siege* 1989
Mahoney, Jock (1919–1989) *A Day of Fury* 1956; *Showdown at Abilene* 1956; *Battle Hymn* 1957; *The Land Unknown* 1957; *The Last of the Fast Guns* 1958; *Money, Women and Guns* 1958; *A Time to Love and a Time to Die* 1958; *Tarzan the Magnificent* 1960; *Tarzan Goes to India* 1962; *Tarzan's Three Challenges* 1963; *The Glory Stompers* 1967; *Tarzan's Deadly Silence* 1970
Mahoney, John (1940–) *The Deadly Game* 1986; *Moonstruck* 1987; *Suspect* 1987; *Tin Men* 1987; *Betrayed* 1988; *Eight Men Out* 1988; *Frantic* 1988; *Say Anything...* 1989; *The Image* 1990; *Love Hurts* 1990; *The Russia House* 1990; *Barton Fink* 1991; *Article 99* 1992; *In the Line of Fire* 1993; *Striking Distance* 1993; *The Hudsucker Proxy* 1994; *The American President* 1995; *Primal Fear* 1996; *She's the One* 1996; *Antz* 1998; *The Iron Giant* 1999; *The Broken Hearts Club: a Romantic Comedy* 2000; *Atlantis: the Lost Empire* 2001
Maiden, Rita *The Married Woman* 1964; *Playtime* 1967
Mailer, Norman (1923–) *Beyond the Law* 1968; *Ragtime* 1981; *King Lear – Fear and Loathing* 1987; *Cremaster 2* 1999
Mailer, Stephen (1966–) *Reversal of Fortune* 1990; *Getting In* 1994
Mailes, Charles Hill *aka* **Mailes, Charles H** (1870–1937) *The Battle of Elderbush* 1914; *The Mark of Zorro* 1920
Mailman, Deborah (1973–) *Radiance* 1998; *Rabbit-Proof Fence* 2002
Main, Laurie (1929–) *The Master Plan* 1954; *Time after Time* 1979
Main, Marjorie (1890–1975) *Dead End* 1937; *The Man Who Cried Wolf* 1937; *Stella Dallas* 1937; *Too Hot to Handle* 1938; *The Women* 1939; *I Take This Woman* 1940; *Honky Tonk* 1941; *The Shepherd of the Hills* 1941; *A Woman's Face* 1941; *The Affairs of Martha* 1942; *Tennessee Johnson* 1942; *Heaven Can Wait* 1943; *Johnny Come Lately* 1943; *Meet Me in St Louis* 1944; *Murder, He Says* 1945; *Bad Bascomb* 1946; *The Harvey Girls* 1946; *The Egg and I* 1947; *Big Jack* 1949; *Ma and Pa Kettle* 1949; *Mrs O'Malley and Mr Malone* 1950; *Summer Stock* 1950; *The Law and the Lady* 1951; *Mr Imperium* 1951; *The Belle of New York* 1952; *The Long, Long Trailer* 1954; *Rose Marie* 1954; *Friendly Persuasion* 1956
Mairesse, Valérie (1955–) *One Sings, the Other Doesn't* 1976; *[Three] Après la Vie* 2002; *[Two] Un Couple Epatant* 2002
Maistre, François (1925–) *Paris Nous Appartient* 1960; *Les Innocents aux Mains Sales* 1975
Maitland, Lorna *Lorna* 1964; *Mudhoney* 1965
Maitland, Marne (1920–1991) *Bhowani Junction* 1956; *The Mark of the Hawk* 1957; *The Wind Cannot Read* 1958; *Sands of the Desert* 1960; *The Return of Mr Moto* 1965; *The Reptile* 1966; *The Bobo* 1967
Majorino, Tina (1985–) *Andre* 1994; *Corrina, Corrina* 1994; *When a Man Loves a Woman* 1994; *Waterworld* 1995; *Before Women Had Wings* 1997; *Alice in Wonderland* 1999; *Napoleon Dynamite* 2004
Majors, Lee (1940–) *Will Penny* 1967; *The Liberation of LB Jones* 1970; *The Six Million Dollar Man* 1973; *Killer Fish* 1978; *The Norseman* 1978; *Steel* 1980; *Agency* 1981; *The Last Chase* 1981; *Starflight One* 1983; *Keaton's Cop* 1990; *Primary Suspect* 2000; *Big Fat Liar* 2002
Majumdar, Sreela *And Quiet Rolls the Dawn* 1979; *In Search of Famine* 1980
Makatsch, Heike (1971–) *Aimée and Jaguar* 1999; *Late Night Shopping* 2001
Makeham, Eliot (1882–1956) *Rome Express* 1932; *Friday the Thirteenth* 1933; *I Lived with You* 1933; *Dark Journey* 1937; *Head over Heels in Love* 1937; *Bell-Bottom George* 1943; *Daybreak* 1946; *Children of Chance* 1949; *Murder at the Windmill* 1949; *Green Grow the Rushes* 1951;

The Scarlet Thread 1951; *The Yellow Balloon* 1952
Makepeace, Chris (1964–) *My Bodyguard* 1980; *The Last Chase* 1981; *Vamp* 1986; *Aloha Summer* 1988; *Captive Hearts* 1988; *Memory Run* 1995
Makhmalbaf, Mohsen (1952–) *Close-Up* 1989; *A Moment of Innocence* 1996
Makkena, Wendy *Sister Act* 1992; *Sister Act 2: Back in the Habit* 1993; *Air Bud* 1997; *Finding North* 1997
Mako (1933–) *The Sand Pebbles* 1966; *The Ugly Dachshund* 1966; *The Private Navy of Sgt O'Farrell* 1968; *The Great Bank Robbery* 1969; *The Hawaiians* 1970; *The Island at the Top of the World* 1974; *The Killer Elite* 1975; *The Big Brawl* 1980; *The Bushido Blade* 1981; *An Eye for an Eye* 1981; *Under the Rainbow* 1981; *Conan the Barbarian* 1982; *Conan the Destroyer* 1984; *Armed Response* 1986; *POW the Escape* 1986; *Silent Assassins* 1988; *Tucker: the Man and His Dream* 1988; *An Unremarkable Life* 1989; *Fatal Mission* 1990; *Pacific Heights* 1990; *Rising Sun* 1993; *RoboCop 3* 1993; *Sidekicks* 1993; *Red Sun Rising* 1994; *Crying Freeman* 1995; *Highlander III: the Sorcerer* 1995; *Seven Years in Tibet* 1997; *Bulletproof Monk* 2002
Makovetsky, Sergei (1958–) *Rothschild's Violin* 1996; *Of Freaks and Men* 1998
Maksimovic, Dragan (1949–2001) *Meetings with Remarkable Men* 1979; *Time of Miracles* 1990; *Pretty Village Pretty Flame* 1996
Malahide, Patrick (1945–) *Comfort and Joy* 1984; *A Month in the Country* 1987; *Smack and Thistle* 1989; *December Bride* 1990; *A Man of No Importance* 1994; *Two Deaths* 1994; *CutThroat Island* 1995; *The Long Kiss Goodnight* 1996; *The Beautician and the Beast* 1997; *Captain Jack* 1998; *Heaven* 1998; *Fortress 2: Re-entry* 1999; *Ordinary Decent Criminal* 1999; *Quills* 2000; *The Abduction Club* 2002; *The Final Curtain* 2002; *Sahara* 2004
Malavoy, Christophe (1952–) *La Balance* 1982; *Death in a French Garden* 1985; *Le Cri du Hibou* 1987; *Madame Bovary* 1991
Malcolm, Christopher *Figures in a Landscape* 1970; *Labyrinth* 1986
Malden, Karl (1914–) *They Knew What They Wanted* 1940; *Kiss of Death* 1947; *The Gunfighter* 1950; *Halls of Montezuma* 1950; *Where the Sidewalk Ends* 1950; *The Sellout* 1951; *A Streetcar Named Desire* 1951; *Diplomatic Courier* 1952; *Ruby Gentry* 1952; *I Confess* 1953; *Take the High Ground* 1953; *On the Waterfront* 1954; *Phantom of the Rue Morgue* 1954; *Baby Doll* 1956; *Bombers B-52* 1957; *Fear Strikes Out* 1957; *The Hanging Tree* 1959; *Pollyanna* 1960; *One-Eyed Jacks* 1961; *Parrish* 1961; *All Fall Down* 1962; *Birdman of Alcatraz* 1962; *Come Fly with Me* 1962; *Gypsy* 1962; *How the West Was Won* 1962; *Cheyenne Autumn* 1964; *Dead Ringer* 1964; *The Cincinnati Kid* 1965; *Murderers' Row* 1966; *Nevada Smith* 1966; *The Adventures of Bullwhip Griffin* 1967; *Billion Dollar Brain* 1967; *Hotel* 1967; *Blue* 1968; *Hot Millions* 1968; *Patton* 1970; *Cat o'Nine Tails* 1971; *Wild Rovers* 1971; *Beyond the Poseidon Adventure* 1979; *Meteor* 1979; *The Sting II* 1983; *Billy Galvin* 1986; *Nuts* 1987; *Vanished without a Trace* 1993
Malet, Arthur (1927–) *Lt Robin Crusoe, USN* 1966; *Halloween* 1978; *Savage Harvest* 1981; *The Secret of NIMH* 1982; *The Black Cauldron* 1985; *Toys* 1992; *A Little Princess* 1995
Malet, Laurent (1955–) *Blood Relatives* 1977; *Roads to the South* 1978; *Querelle* 1982
Maley, Peggy (1926–) *The Wild One* 1953; *Human Desire* 1954; *Live Fast, Die Young* 1958
Malfatti, Marina (1940–) *More than a Miracle* 1967; *Without Warning* 1973
Malherbe, Annet *Abel* 1986; *The Northerners* 1992
Malhotra, Pavan *Bagh Bahadur* 1989; *Brothers in Trouble* 1995
Mali, Antara *Company* 2001; *Road* 2002; *Gayab* 2004; *Naach* 2004
Malick, Wendie (1950–) *The Emperor's New Groove* 2000; *Racing Stripes* 2004
Malik, Art *aka* **Malik, Athar** (1952–) *Arabian Adventure* 1979; *A Passage to India* 1984; *The Living Daylights* 1987; *City of Joy* 1992; *Hostage* 1992; *Turtle Beach* 1992; *Year of the Comet* 1992; *Clockwork Mice* 1994; *True Lies* 1994; *Booty Call* 1997; *Side Streets* 1998; *Fakers* 2004
Malikyan, Kevork *The Man Who Haunted Himself* 1970; *Flight of the Phoenix* 2004
Malin, Eddie (1894–1977) *A Hard Day's Night* 1964; *Nearest and Dearest* 1972
Malina, Judith (1926–) *Enemies, a Love Story* 1989; *Awakenings* 1990; *The Addams Family* 1991; *Household Saints* 1993
Malinger, Ross (1984–) *Sleepless in Seattle* 1993; *Little Bigfoot* 1995; *Sudden Death* 1995
Malkovich, John (1953–) *The Killing Fields* 1984; *Places in the Heart* 1984; *Death of a Salesman* 1985; *Eleni* 1985; *Empire of the Sun* 1987; *The Glass Menagerie* 1987; *Making Mr Right* 1987; *Dangerous Liaisons* 1988; *Miles from Home* 1988; *The Sheltering Sky* 1990; *The Object of Beauty* 1991; *Queens Logic* 1991; *Shadows and Fog* 1991; *Jennifer Eight* 1992; *Of Mice and Men* 1992; *In the Line of Fire* 1993; *Beyond the Clouds* 1995; *The Convent* 1995; *Mary Reilly* 1995; *Mulholland Falls* 1996; *The Portrait of a Lady* 1996; *Con Air* 1997; *The Man in the Iron Mask* 1997; *Rounders* 1998; *Being John Malkovich* 1999; *Joan of Arc* 1999; *RKO 281* 1999; *Time Regained* 1999; *Shadow of the Vampire* 2000; *Hotel* 2001; *I'm Going Home* 2001; *Knockaround Guys* 2001; *Ripley's Game* 2002; *Un Filme Falado* 2003; *Johnny English* 2003; *The Libertine* 2004; *The Hitchhiker's Guide to the Galaxy* 2005
Mallalieu, Aubrey (1873–1948) *Music Hath Charms* 1935; *The Face at the Window* 1939; *Gert and Daisy's Weekend* 1941; *My Learned Friend* 1943
Malle, Louis (1932–1995) *Phantom India* 1968; *God's Country* 1985
Malleson, Miles (1888–1969) *Nell Gwyn* 1934; *Vintage Wine* 1935; *The Thief of Bagdad* 1940; *Unpublished Story* 1942; *While the Sun Shines* 1946; *Golden Salamander* 1949; *Kind Hearts and Coronets* 1949; *The Perfect Woman* 1949; *Stage Fright* 1949; *The Man in the White Suit* 1951; *Folly to Be Wise* 1952; *Treasure Hunt* 1952; *Trent's Last Case* 1952; *The Captain's Paradise* 1953; *Brothers in Law* 1956; *The Silken Affair* 1957; *Horror of Dracula* 1958; *The Hound of the Baskervilles* 1959; *And the Same to You* 1960; *The Brides of Dracula* 1960; *Kidnapped* 1960; *Double Bunk* 1961; *Fury at Smugglers Bay* 1961; *Go to Blazes* 1961; *The Hellfire Club* 1961; *Postman's Knock* 1961; *A Jolly Bad Fellow* 1964; *Murder Ahoy* 1964
Mallinson, Rory (1903–1976) *Deep Valley* 1947; *Cavalry Scout* 1951
Malloy, Matt *Boys* 1995; *In the Company of Men* 1997; *Everything Put Together* 2000
Malm, Mona (1935–) *Fanny and Alexander* 1982; *Best Intentions* 1992
Malmsjö, Jan (1932–) *Scenes from a Marriage* 1973; *Fanny and Alexander* 1982
Malmsten, Birger (1920–1991) *It Rains on Our Love* 1946; *A Ship to India* 1947; *Night Is My Future* 1948; *The Devil's Wanton* 1949; *Three Strange Loves* 1949; *Summer Interlude* 1950; *Waiting Women* 1952
Malo, Gina (1909–1963) *Southern Roses* 1936; *Where There's a Will* 1936; *Over She Goes* 1937
Malone, Bonz *Slam* 1998; *Whiteboys* 1999
Malone, Dorothy (1925–) *The Big Sleep* 1946; *Night and Day* 1946; *Colorado Territory* 1949; *South of St Louis* 1949; *Convicted* 1950; *Mrs O'Malley and Mr Malone* 1950; *Law and Order* 1953; *Scared Stiff* 1953; *Private Hell 36* 1954; *Pushover* 1954; *Security Risk* 1954; *Artists and Models* 1955; *At Gunpoint* 1955; *Five Guns West* 1955; *Sincerely Yours* 1955; *Tall Man Riding* 1955; *Young at Heart* 1955; *Pillars of the Sky* 1956; *Tension at Table Rock* 1956; *Written on the Wind* 1956; *Man of a Thousand Faces* 1957; *Quantez* 1957; *The Tarnished Angels* 1957; *Tip on a Dead Jockey* 1957; *Too Much, Too Soon* 1958; *Warlock* 1959; *The Last Voyage* 1960; *The Last Sunset* 1961; *Beach Party* 1963; *Fate Is the Hunter* 1964; *Abduction* 1975; *The Man Who Would Not Die* 1975; *Golden Rendezvous* 1977; *Good Luck, Miss Wyckoff* 1979; *Winter Kills* 1979; *The Day Time Ended* 1980
Malone, Jena (1984–) *Stepmom* 1998; *For Love of the Game* 1999; *The Ballad of Lucy Whipple* 2001; *The Dangerous Lives of Altar Boys* 2001; *Donnie Darko* 2001; *The United States of Leland* 2001; *Saved!* 2004
Malone, Mark *Dead of Winter* 1987; *Straight out of Brooklyn* 1991
Maloney, Michael (1957–) *La Maschera* 1988; *Henry V* 1989; *Hamlet* 1990; *Truly Madly Deeply* 1990; *In the Bleak Midwinter* 1995; *Othello* 1995; *Hamlet* 1996; *Kisna – the Warrior Poet* 2004
Maloney, Peter *The Thing* 1982; *Washington Square* 1997; *Thicker than Blood* 1998
Maltby, H F (1880–1963) *Where There's a Will* 1936; *Under Your Hat* 1940; *Home Sweet Home* 1945
Man, Alex (1957–) *Rouge* 1987; *As Tears Go By* 1988
Manahan, Anna (1924–) *A Business Affair* 1993; *A Man of No Importance* 1994
Manahan, Sheila (1924–1988) *Another Shore* 1948; *Seven Days to Noon* 1950; *Only Two Can Play* 1961
Mancini, Al *Miller's Crossing* 1990; *It Runs in the Family* 1994
Mancini, Ray *aka* **Mancini, Ray "Boom Boom"** (1961–) *Wishful Thinking* 1990; *Time Bomb* 1991; *Aces: Iron Eagle III* 1992; *The Search for One-Eye Jimmy* 1996
Mancuso, Nick (1948–) *Nightwing* 1979; *Ticket to Heaven* 1981; *Maria Chapdelaine* 1982; *Mother Lode* 1982; *Blame It on the Night* 1984; *Heartbreakers* 1984; *Love Songs* 1984; *Death of an Angel* 1985; *Lena's Holiday* 1990; *Milena* 1990; *Rapid Fire* 1992; *Young Ivanhoe* 1994; *Under Siege 2* 1995; *Young Connecticut Yankee in King Arthur's Court* 1995; *Mary Higgins Clark's Let Me Call You Sweetheart* 1997; *Captured* 1998
Mandalis, Elena *Only the Brave* 1994; *Head On* 1997
Mandan, Robert (1932–) *The Best Little Whorehouse in Texas* 1982; *Zapped!* 1982; *National Lampoon's Scuba School* 1994
Mandel, Howie (1955–) *A Fine Mess* 1986; *Walk like a Man* 1987; *Little Monsters* 1989; *Gremlins 2: the New Batch* 1990; *Shake, Rattle and Rock* 1994
Mander, Miles (1888–1946) *The Pleasure Garden* 1925; *Murder* 1930; *Don Quixote* 1932; *Bitter Sweet* 1933; *The Battle* 1934; *Kidnapped* 1938; *The Man in the Iron Mask* 1939; *The Three Musketeers* 1939; *Primrose Path* 1940; *Shadows on the Stairs* 1941; *Apache Trail* 1942; *Fingers at the Window* 1942; *Five Graves to Cairo* 1943; *The Return of the Vampire* 1943; *Enter Arsene Lupin* 1944; *Farewell My Lovely* 1944; *The Pearl of Death* 1944; *The Brighton Strangler* 1945
Mandvi, Aasif *ABCD* 1999; *The Mystic Masseur* 2001
Mandylor, Costas (1965–) *Triumph of the Spirit* 1989; *Mobsters* 1991; *Delta of Venus* 1995; *Fist of the North Star* 1995; *Double Take* 1997; *Shelter* 1997; *Stealth Fighter* 1999
Mandylor, Louis (1966–) *The Heartbreak Kid* 1993; *The Set Up* 1995; *My Big Fat Greek Wedding* 2002
Manfredi, Nino (1921–2004) *Le Bambole* 1965; *We All Loved Each Other So Much* 1974; *Down and Dirty* 1976; *In the Name of the Pope King* 1977
Mangano, Silvana (1930–1989) *Bitter Rice* 1949; *Gold of Naples* 1954; *Mambo* 1954; *Ulysses* 1954; *This Angry Age* 1957; *The Great War* 1959; *Tempest* 1959; *Five Branded Women* 1960; *Barabbas* 1961; *The Witches* 1966; *Oedipus Rex* 1967; *Theorem* 1968; *Death in Venice* 1971; *Ludwig* 1973; *Conversation Piece* 1974; *Dune* 1984; *Dark Eyes* 1987
Mango, Alec *They Who Dare* 1953; *Mask of Dust* 1954; *Interpol* 1957; *The Strange World of Planet X* 1957; *The 7th Voyage of Sinbad* 1958; *Gothic* 1986
Mangold, Erni (1927–) *I Only Want You to Love Me* 1976; *Before Sunrise* 1995
Manheim, Camryn (1961–) *Joe the King* 1999; *Scary Movie 3* 2003; *Twisted* 2003
Manion, Cindy *Preppies* 1984; *The Toxic Avenger* 1985
Mankuma, Blu *Stockade* 1991; *Whale Music* 1994; *Bliss* 1997; *Bone Daddy* 1998
Mann, Alakina *The Others* 2001; *Girl with a Pearl Earring* 2003
Mann, Byron (1967–) *Crying Freeman* 1995; *Red Corner* 1997; *The Corruptor* 1999
Mann, Claude (1940–) *Bay of the Angels* 1963; *L'Armée des Ombres* 1969
Mann, Danny *Little Nemo: Adventures in Slumberland* 1992; *Babe* 1995
Mann, Gabriel *High Art* 1998; *Cherry Falls* 1999; *Live Virgin* 2000; *Josie and the Pussycats* 2001; *The Life of David Gale* 2003; *The Bourne Supremacy* 2004; *A Lot like Love* 2005
Mann, Leonard (1947–) *The Humanoid* 1979; *Order of Death* 1983
Mann, Leslie (1972–) *The Cable Guy* 1996; *George of the Jungle* 1997; *Big Daddy* 1999; *Stealing Harvard* 2002
Mann, Terrence *aka* **Mann, Terrence V** (1951–) *A Chorus Line* 1985; *Critters* 1986; *Big Top Pee-wee* 1988; *Critters 2: the Main Course* 1988; *Critters 4* 1992
Mann, Tracy *Hard Knocks* 1980; *The Scarecrow* 1982
Manners, David (1901–1998) *Journey's End* 1930; *Dracula* 1931; *The Last Flight* 1931; *The Miracle Woman* 1931; *A Bill of Divorcement* 1932; *Lady with a Past* 1932; *The Mummy* 1932; *The Death Kiss* 1933; *The Devil's in Love* 1933; *Roman Scandals* 1933; *Torch Singer* 1933; *The Black Cat* 1934; *The Moonstone* 1934; *The Mystery of Edwin Drood* 1935; *A Woman Rebels* 1936
Mannhardt, Renate (1923–) *The Lost One* 1951; *Fear* 1954
Mannheim, Lucie (1899–1976) *The 39 Steps* 1935; *Yellow Canary* 1943; *Hotel Reserve* 1944; *Tawny Pipit* 1944; *Beyond the Curtain* 1960
Manni, Ettore (1927–1979) *Le Amiche* 1955; *Gold for the Caesars* 1964; *Mademoiselle* 1966; *Ringo and His Golden Pistol* 1966; *City of Women* 1980
Manning, Irene (1912–2004) *The Big Shot* 1942; *Yankee Doodle Dandy* 1942; *The Desert Song* 1944; *Make Your Own Bed* 1944; *Shine On, Harvest Moon* 1944
Manning, Taryn (1978–) *Crossroads* 2002; *A Lot like Love* 2005
Mannion, Tom *That Sinking Feeling* 1979; *Beautiful Creatures* 2000
Manoff, Dinah (1958–) *Ordinary People* 1980; *I Ought to Be in Pictures* 1982; *Child's Play* 1988; *Staying Together* 1989
Manojlovic, Miki *aka* **Manojlovic, Predrag Miki** *aka* **Manojlovic, Pedrag** (1950–) *When Father Was Away on Business* 1985; *Time of Miracles* 1990; *Tito and Me* 1992; *Someone Else's America* 1995; *Underground* 1995; *Artemisia* 1997; *Cabaret Balkan* 1998; *Criminal Lovers* 1999
Manookian, Roland *Goodbye Charlie Bright* 2000; *The Football Factory* 2004
Mansard, Claude *A Bout de Souffle* 1959; *Shoot the Pianist* 1960
Mansfield, Jayne (1933–1967) *The Female Jungle* 1955; *Hell on Frisco Bay* 1955; *Illegal* 1955; *The Burglar* 1956; *The Girl Can't Help It* 1956; *Kiss Them for Me* 1957; *The Wayward Bus* 1957; *Will Success Spoil Rock Hunter?* 1957; *The Sheriff of Fractured Jaw* 1958; *The Challenge* 1960; *Too Hot to Handle* 1960; *The George Raft Story* 1961; *Panic Button* 1964; *Single Room Furnished* 1968
Manson, Alan (1918–2002) *Let's Scare Jessica to Death* 1971; *Whiffs* 1975; *Leadbelly* 1976
Mantee, Paul (1931–) *Robinson Crusoe on Mars* 1964; *Breakout* 1975; *Wolf Lake* 1979
Mantegna, Joe (1947–) *Second Thoughts* 1982; *Compromising Positions* 1985; *The Money Pit* 1985; *Off Beat* 1986; *Critical Condition* 1987; *House of Games* 1987; *Suspect* 1987; *Weeds* 1987; *Things Change* 1988; *Wait until Spring, Bandini* 1989; *Alice* 1990; *The Godfather Part III* 1990; *Bugsy* 1991; *Family Prayers* 1991; *Homicide* 1991; *Queens Logic* 1991; *Body of Evidence* 1992; *Innocent Moves* 1993; *Airheads* 1994; *Baby's Day Out* 1994; *The Bomber Boys* 1995; *Eye for an Eye* 1995; *For Better or Worse* 1995; *Forget Paris* 1995; *Albino Alligator* 1996; *Persons Unknown* 1996; *Stephen King's Thinner* 1996; *Underworld* 1996; *Up Close & Personal* 1996; *Airspeed* 1997; *For Hire* 1997; *Celebrity* 1998; *Jerry and Tom* 1998; *The Rat Pack* 1998; *Liberty Heights* 1999; *The Runner* 1999
Mantel, Bronwen *Barnum* 1986; *Pin* 1988
Mantel, Henriette *The Brady Bunch Movie* 1995; *A Very Brady Sequel* 1996
Mantell, Joe (1920–) *Marty* 1955; *Storm Center* 1956; *Beau James* 1957; *The Sad Sack* 1957; *Onionhead* 1958; *The Murder Men* 1961
Mantell, Michael *Out of the Rain* 1991; *The Night We Never Met* 1993
Manuel, Robert (1916–1995) *Rififi* 1955; *The Black Tulip* 1963
Manukov, Grigori *aka* **Manoukov, Grigori** *East-West* 1999; *Triple Agent* 2003
Manver, Kiti (1953–) *Women on the Verge of a Nervous Breakdown* 1988; *Take My Eyes* 2003
Manville, Lesley (1956–) *Dance with a Stranger* 1984; *High Season* 1987; *High Hopes* 1988; *Secrets & Lies* 1995; *Milk* 1999; *Topsy-Turvy* 1999; *All or Nothing* 2002

Manz, Linda (1961–) *Days of Heaven* 1978; *The Wanderers* 1979; *Out of the Blue* 1980
Manza, Ralph (1921–2000) *Gang War* 1958; *Too Soon to Love* 1960; *Lookin' Italian* 1994
Maples, Marla (1963–) *Happiness* 1998; *Black and White* 1999
Mapother, William (1965–) *In the Bedroom* 2001; *The Grudge* 2004
Mara, Adele (1923–) *You Were Never Lovelier* 1942; *Reveille with Beverly* 1943; *Atlantic City* 1944; *Bells of Rosarita* 1945; *Angel in Exile* 1948; *Sands of Iwo Jima* 1949; *Wake of the Red Witch* 1949
Mara, Mary *Empire City* 1991; *The Hard Way* 1991; *Love Potion No 9* 1992; *Mr Saturday Night* 1992; *Bound* 1996; *Mistaken Identity* 1999; *Stranger Inside* 2001
Marachuk, Steve *Piranha II: the Spawning* 1981; *Hot Target* 1985
Marais, Jean (1913–1998) *Drôle de Drame* 1937; *Eternal Love* 1943; *La Belle et la Bête* 1946; *The Eagle Has Two Heads* 1948; *Les Parents Terribles* 1948; *Orphée* 1950; *Royal Affairs in Versailles* 1953; *Napoléon* 1955; *Elena et les Hommes* 1956; *White Nights* 1957; *Le Bossu* 1959; *The Battle of Austerlitz* 1960; *The Captain* 1960; *Le Testament d'Orphée* 1960; *Pontius Pilate* 1961; *Le Masque de Fer* 1962; *The Mysteries of Paris* 1962; *The Magic Donkey* 1970; *Stealing Beauty* 1995
Marangosoff, Janna *In the Belly of the Whale* 1984; *Men…* 1985
Maranne, André *Darling Lili* 1970; *The Return of the Pink Panther* 1974; *The Pink Panther Strikes Again* 1976; *Revenge of the Pink Panther* 1978; *Plenty* 1985
Marceau, Marcel (1923–) *Barbarella* 1967; *Shanks* 1974
Marceau, Sophie (1966–) *Fort Saganne* 1984; *Police* 1985; *Descent into Hell* 1986; *D'Artagnan's Daughter* 1994; *Beyond the Clouds* 1995; *Braveheart* 1995; *Anna Karenina* 1997; *Firelight* 1997; *Marquise* 1997; *Lost & Found* 1999; *A Midsummer Night's Dream* 1999; *The World Is Not Enough* 1999; *La Fidélité* 2000; *Alex & Emma* 2003
March, Elspeth (1911–1999) *The Playboy of the Western World* 1962; *Psyche '59* 1964
March, Eve (1910–1974) *The Curse of the Cat People* 1944; *Adam's Rib* 1949
March, Fredric (1897–1975) *The Marriage Playground* 1929; *The Wild Party* 1929; *Laughter* 1930; *Manslaughter* 1930; *Paramount on Parade* 1930; *The Royal Family of Broadway* 1930; *Sarah and Son* 1930; *Dr Jekyll and Mr Hyde* 1931; *Honor among Lovers* 1931; *My Sin* 1931; *Merrily We Go to Hell* 1932; *The Sign of the Cross* 1932; *Smilin' Through* 1932; *Design for Living* 1933; *The Eagle and the Hawk* 1933; *The Affairs of Cellini* 1934; *The Barretts of Wimpole Street* 1934; *Death Takes a Holiday* 1934; *We Live Again* 1934; *Anna Karenina* 1935; *The Dark Angel* 1935; *Les Misérables* 1935; *Anthony Adverse* 1936; *Mary of Scotland* 1936; *The Road to Glory* 1936; *Nothing Sacred* 1937; *A Star Is Born* 1937; *The Buccaneer* 1938; *There Goes My Heart* 1938; *Trade Winds* 1938; *Susan and God* 1940; *Victory* 1940; *One Foot in Heaven* 1941; *So Ends Our Night* 1941; *Bedtime Story* 1942; *I Married a Witch* 1942; *The Adventures of Mark Twain* 1944; *Tomorrow the World!* 1944; *The Best Years of Our Lives* 1946; *Another Part of the Forest* 1948; *Christopher Columbus* 1949; *Death of a Salesman* 1951; *It's a Big Country* 1951; *Man on a Tightrope* 1953; *The Bridges at Toko-Ri* 1954; *Executive Suite* 1954; *The Desperate Hours* 1955; *Alexander the Great* 1956; *The Man in the Gray Flannel Suit* 1956; *Middle of the Night* 1959; *Inherit the Wind* 1960; *The Young Doctors* 1961; *The Condemned of Altona* 1962; *Seven Days in May* 1964; *Hombre* 1967; *tick… tick… tick…* 1969; *The Iceman Cometh* 1973
March, Jane (1973–) *The Lover* 1992; *Color of Night* 1994; *Circle of Passion* 1996; *Tarzan and the Lost City* 1998; *Dark Prince – the Legend of Dracula* 2000
March, Philippe (1924–1980) *Two People* 1973; *Once in Paris* 1978
Marchal, Georges (1920–1997) *Celà S'Appelle l'Aurore* 1956; *Death in the Garden* 1956; *The Sign of the Gladiator* 1958; *The Colossus of Rhodes* 1961; *The Secret Mark of D'Artagnan* 1962; *The Milky Way* 1968
Marchand, Corinne (1937–) *Cleo from 5 to 7* 1961; *Borsalino* 1970; *Rider on the Rain* 1970; *Le Parfum d'Yvonne* 1994
Marchand, Guy (1937–) *Une Belle Fille Comme Moi* 1973; *Cousin, Cousine* 1975; *Loulou* 1980; *Clean Slate* 1981; *Garde à Vue* 1981; *Entre Nous* 1983; *Petit Con* 1984; *Hold-Up* 1985; *Le Cop II* 1989; *May Wine* 1990
Marchand, Nancy (1928–2000) *The Bachelor Party* 1957; *The Hospital* 1971; *Agatha Christie's Sparkling Cyanide* 1983; *The Bostonians* 1984; *The Naked Gun* 1988; *Brain Donors* 1992; *Sabrina* 1995
Marcon, André (1948–) *Jeanne la Pucelle* 1994; *Requiem* 1998; *Les Destinées Sentimentales* 2000; *The Pornographer* 2001
Marcovicci, Andrea (1948–) *The Front* 1976; *The Hand* 1981; *Kings and Desperate Men* 1981; *Spacehunter: Adventures in the Forbidden Zone* 1983; *The Stuff* 1985; *Someone to Love* 1987
Marcus, James A (1867–1937) *Regeneration* 1915; *Little Lord Fauntleroy* 1921; *The Iron Horse* 1924; *The Eagle* 1925; *The Texan* 1930
Marcus, Richard *Enemy Mine* 1985; *Deadly Friend* 1986; *Tremors* 1989
Marcus, Stephen (1962–) *Lock, Stock and Two Smoking Barrels* 1998; *Londinium* 1999
Marcuse, Theo (1920–1967) *Harum Scarum* 1965; *The Picasso Summer* 1969
Marescotti, Ivano (1946–) *Johnny Stecchino* 1991; *Il Cielo è Sempre Più Blu* 1995
Margaritis, Gilles (1912–1965) *Les Affaires Publiques* 1934; *L'Atalante* 1934
Margetson, Arthur (1887–1951) *Music Hath Charms* 1935; *Broken Blossoms* 1936; *Pagliacci* 1936; *Smash and Grab* 1937; *Sherlock Holmes Faces Death* 1943
Margheriti, Antonio *aka* **Dawson, Anthony** (1930–2002) *Death Rides a Horse* 1967; *Operation Kid Brother* 1967; *The Battle of Neretva* 1969
Margo (1917–1985) *Crime without Passion* 1934; *Rumba* 1935; *The Robin Hood of El Dorado* 1936; *Winterset* 1936; *Lost Horizon* 1937; *Miracle on Main Street* 1940; *Behind the Rising Sun* 1943; *The Leopard Man* 1943; *Viva Zapata!* 1952; *I'll Cry Tomorrow* 1955; *Who's Got the Action?* 1962
Margo, George (1915–2002) *Who Done It?* 1956; *Mark of the Phoenix* 1957
Margolin, Janet (1943–1993) *David and Lisa* 1962; *Bus Riley's Back in Town* 1965; *The Saboteur, Code Name Morituri* 1965; *Nevada Smith* 1966; *Enter Laughing* 1967; *Buona Sera, Mrs Campbell* 1968; *Take the Money and Run* 1969; *Your Three Minutes Are Up* 1973; *Annie Hall* 1977; *Last Embrace* 1979; *Distant Thunder* 1988
Margolin, Stuart (1940–) *The Gamblers* 1969; *Kelly's Heroes* 1970; *Limbo* 1972; *Death Wish* 1974; *Futureworld* 1976; *Days of Heaven* 1978; *SOB* 1981; *Class* 1983; *Running Hot* 1983; *A Fine Mess* 1986; *Iron Eagle II* 1988; *Bye Bye Blues* 1989
Margolis, Mark (1939–) *Delta Force 2* 1990; *Pi* 1997
Margolyes, Miriam (1941–) *Stand Up Virgin Soldiers* 1977; *The Apple* 1980; *The Awakening* 1980; *Electric Dreams* 1984; *The Good Father* 1986; *Little Dorrit* 1987; *I Love You to Death* 1990; *The Butcher's Wife* 1991; *As You Like It* 1992; *The Age of Innocence* 1993; *Motherhood* 1993; *Immortal Beloved* 1994; *Babe* 1995; *Different for Girls* 1996; *James and the Giant Peach* 1996; *William Shakespeare's Romeo + Juliet* 1996; *Babe: Pig in the City* 1998; *Dreaming of Joseph Lees* 1998; *Mulan* 1998; *End of Days* 1999; *House!* 2000; *Cats & Dogs* 2001; *Harry Potter and the Chamber of Secrets* 2002; *The Life and Death of Peter Sellers* 2003; *Being Julia* 2004; *Ladies in Lavender* 2004
Margotta, Michael (1946–) *Drive, He Said* 1971; *Partners* 1976; *Can She Bake a Cherry Pie?* 1983
Margulies, David *Dressed to Kill* 1980; *Times Square* 1980; *Nine ½ Weeks* 1985; *Out on a Limb* 1992
Margulies, Julianna (1966–) *Paradise Road* 1997; *A Price above Rubies* 1997; *Traveller* 1997; *The Newton Boys* 1998; *Dinosaur* 2000; *What's Cooking?* 2000; *Evelyn* 2002; *Ghost Ship* 2002
Maricle, Leona (1905–1988) *Woman Chases Man* 1937; *Beauty for the Asking* 1939
Marie, Constance (1969–) *Selena* 1997; *The Last Marshal* 1999; *Tortilla Soup* 2001
Marielle, Jean-Pierre (1932–) *Banana Peel* 1964; *Without Apparent Motive* 1972; *Man in the Trunk* 1973; *Un Moment d'Egarement* 1977; *Clean Slate* 1981; *Hold-Up* 1985; *Tenue de Soirée* 1986; *Uranus* 1990; *Tous les Matins du Monde* 1991; *Le Parfum d'Yvonne* 1994
Marienthal, Eli (1986–) *Slums of Beverly Hills* 1998; *The Iron Giant* 1999; *The Country Bears* 2002; *Confessions of a Teenage Drama Queen* 2004
Marietto (1951–) *It Started in Naples* 1960; *The Pigeon That Took Rome* 1962
Marihugh, Tammy *The Last Voyage* 1960; *Back Street* 1961
Marin, Jacques (1919–2001) *Jeux Interdits* 1953; *Gigot* 1962; *Tiara Tahiti* 1962; *Charade* 1963; *How to Steal a Million* 1966; *Darling Lili* 1970; *The Island at the Top of the World* 1974; *Herbie Goes to Monte Carlo* 1977
Marin, Richard "Cheech" *aka* **Marin, Cheech** (1946–) *Cheech & Chong's Up in Smoke* 1978; *Cheech and Chong's Next Movie* 1980; *Cheech and Chong's Nice Dreams* 1981; *Things Are Tough All Over* 1982; *Cheech & Chong's Still Smokin'* 1983; *Yellowbeard* 1983; *Cheech & Chong's The Corsican Brothers* 1984; *After Hours* 1985; *Echo Park* 1985; *Born in East LA* 1987; *Fatal Beauty* 1987; *Oliver & Company* 1988; *Rude Awakening* 1989; *The Shrimp on the Barbie* 1990; *Charlie's Ghost Story* 1994; *The Lion King* 1994; *Ring of the Musketeers* 1994; *Desperado* 1995; *From Dusk till Dawn* 1995; *The Great White Hype* 1996; *Tin Cup* 1996; *Paulie* 1998; *Picking Up the Pieces* 2000; *SPYkids* 2001; *SPYkids 2: the Island of Lost Dreams* 2002; *Once upon a Time in Mexico* 2003; *SPYkids 3-D: Game Over* 2003; *Christmas with the Kranks* 2004
Marin, Rikki *Cheech and Chong's Next Movie* 1980; *Things Are Tough All Over* 1982; *Cheech & Chong's The Corsican Brothers* 1984
Marion, George F (1860–1945) *Anna Christie* 1930; *The Big House* 1930
Marion, Joan (1908–2001) *For Valour* 1937; *Ten Days in Paris* 1939
Marion, Paul (1915–) *Scared Stiff* 1953; *Shotgun* 1955
Marion-Crawford, Howard *aka* **Marion-Crawford, H** (1914–1969) *Forever England* 1935; *Freedom Radio* 1940; *The Hasty Heart* 1949; *Mr Drake's Duck* 1950; *The Man in the White Suit* 1951; *The Birthday Present* 1957; *The Silken Affair* 1957; *Nowhere to Go* 1958; *Virgin Island* 1958; *Life in Danger* 1959; *The Face of Fu Manchu* 1965; *The Brides of Fu Manchu* 1966; *The Vengeance of Fu Manchu* 1967; *The Blood of Fu Manchu* 1968; *The Castle of Fu Manchu* 1968
Maris, Mona (1903–1991) *Kiss and Make-Up* 1934; *A Date with the Falcon* 1941; *Underground* 1941; *Berlin Correspondent* 1942; *The Falcon in Mexico* 1944
Mark, Michael (1886–1975) *Frankenstein* 1931; *Search for Danger* 1949; *Attack of the Puppet People* 1958; *The Wasp Woman* 1959
Marken, Jane *aka* **Marken, Jeanne** (1895–1976) *Abel Gance's Beethoven* 1936; *Une Partie de Campagne* 1936; *Hôtel du Nord* 1938; *Eternal Love* 1943; *And God Created Woman* 1956
Markey, Enid (1896–1981) *Civilization* 1916; *Tarzan of the Apes* 1918
Markham, David (1913–1983) *Blood from the Mummy's Tomb* 1971; *ZPG: Zero Population Growth* 1971; *Tess* 1979
Markham, Kika *Anne and Muriel* 1971; *Outland* 1981; *The Innocent* 1984; *Wonderland* 1999; *Killing Me Softly* 2001
Markham, Monte (1935–) *Project X* 1968; *Guns of the Magnificent Seven* 1969; *One Is a Lonely Number* 1972; *Ginger in the Morning* 1973; *Hot Pursuit* 1987; *…At First Sight* 1995; *Piranhas* 1996
Markinson, Brian *Forgotten Sins* 1996; *Sweet and Lowdown* 1999; *Take Me Home: the John Denver Story* 2000; *The Curse of the Jade Scorpion* 2001
Markland, Ted *The Hired Hand* 1971; *Wanda Nevada* 1979; *Fatal Mission* 1990
Markov, Margaret *Black Mama, White Mama* 1972; *The Hot Box* 1972
Marks, Alfred (1921–1996) *Desert Mice* 1959; *There Was a Crooked Man* 1960; *The Frightened City* 1961; *She'll Have to Go* 1961; *Scream and Scream Again* 1969; *Our Miss Fred* 1972; *Fanny Hill* 1983
Marks, George Harrison (1926–1997) *9 Ages of Nakedness* 1969; *Come Play with Me* 1977
Marlé, Arnold (1887–1970) *Men of Two Worlds* 1946; *Portrait from Life* 1948; *Break in the Circle* 1955; *Little Red Monkey* 1955
Marleau, Louise (1944–) *Anne Trister* 1986; *Une Histoire Inventée* 1990
Marley, John (1907–1984) *The Joe Louis Story* 1953; *Cat Ballou* 1965; *Faces* 1968; *Love Story* 1970; *Dead of Night* 1972; *The Godfather* 1972; *Jory* 1972; *Framed* 1975; *WC Fields and Me* 1976; *The Car* 1977; *The Greatest* 1977; *Kid Vengeance* 1977; *Hooper* 1978; *It Lives Again* 1978; *Tribute* 1980; *The Amateur* 1981; *Threshold* 1981; *Utilities* 1981; *Mother Lode* 1982; *On the Edge* 1985
Marlier, Carla *Zazie dans le Métro* 1960; *Any Number Can Win* 1963
Marlon, Ged *Frankenstein 90* 1984; *Laissez-passer* 2001
Marlow, Lucy (1932–) *A Star Is Born* 1954; *Bring Your Smile Along* 1955; *My Sister Eileen* 1955; *He Laughed Last* 1956
Marlowe, Faye (1926–) *Junior Miss* 1945; *Rendezvous with Annie* 1946
Marlowe, Hugh (1911–1982) *Marriage Is a Private Affair* 1944; *Come to the Stable* 1949; *Twelve O'Clock High* 1949; *All about Eve* 1950; *Night and the City* 1950; *The Day the Earth Stood Still* 1951; *Mr Belvedere Rings the Bell* 1951; *Rawhide* 1951; *Bugles in the Afternoon* 1952; *Monkey Business* 1952; *Wait 'til the Sun Shines, Nellie* 1952; *Way of a Gaucho* 1952; *The Stand at Apache River* 1953; *Garden of Evil* 1954; *Illegal* 1955; *World without End* 1955; *Earth vs the Flying Saucers* 1956; *Birdman of Alcatraz* 1962; *Seven Days in May* 1964; *Castle of Evil* 1966
Marlowe, Jo Ann (1935–1991) *Mildred Pierce* 1945; *Thieves' Holiday* 1946
Marlowe, Linda *Impact* 1963; *The World Ten Times Over* 1963; *Mr Love* 1985
Marlowe, Scott (1932–2001) *Gaby* 1956; *The Young Guns* 1956; *The Cool and the Crazy* 1958; *A Cold Wind in August* 1961
Marlowe, William (1932–) *The Uncle* 1964; *Robbery* 1967; *Where's Jack?* 1969
Marly, Florence (1919–1978) *Tokyo Joe* 1949; *Planet of Blood* 1966
Marmont, Percy (1883–1977) *Mantrap* 1926; *Rich and Strange* 1932; *Secret Agent* 1936; *Young and Innocent* 1937; *Four Sided Triangle* 1953; *Knave of Hearts* 1954; *Lisbon* 1956
Marner, Richard (1922–2004) *The Password Is Courage* 1962; *Where the Spies Are* 1965; *Tiffany Jones* 1973
Maro, Akaji *The Most Terrible Time in My Life* 1993; *Kikujiro* 1999
Maross, Joe *Elmer Gantry* 1960; *Zigzag* 1970; *The Salzburg Connection* 1972; *Sixth and Main* 1977
Marquand, Christian (1927–2000) *And God Created Woman* 1956; *Behold a Pale Horse* 1964; *The Corrupt Ones* 1966; *The Road to Corinth* 1967; *Ciao! Manhattan* 1973; *The Other Side of Midnight* 1977; *Apocalypse Now* 1979; *Je Vous Aime* 1980; *Choice of Arms* 1981
Marquand, Serge (1930–2004) *The Last Train* 1972; *The Big Red One* 1980; *Frankenstein 90* 1984
Marques, Maria Elena (1926–) *Across the Wide Missouri* 1951; *Ambush at Tomahawk Gap* 1953
Marquet, Mary (1895–1979) *Bluebeard* 1962; *La Vie de Château* 1965
Marquette, Christopher George *aka* **Marquette, Chris** (1984–) *The Tic Code* 1998; *Freddy vs Jason* 2003; *The Girl Next Door* 2004
Marr, Eddie *aka* **Marr, Edward** (1900–1987) *The Steel Trap* 1952; *The Night Holds Terror* 1955
Marriott, Moore (1885–1949) *Windbag the Sailor* 1936; *Oh, Mr Porter!* 1937; *Ask a Policeman* 1938; *Convict 99* 1938; *Old Bones of the River* 1938; *Owd Bob* 1938; *Band Waggon* 1939; *Cheer Boys Cheer* 1939; *Where's That Fire?* 1939; *Charley's (Big Hearted) Aunt* 1940; *Gasbags* 1940; *Hi, Gang!* 1941; *I Thank You* 1941; *Back Room Boy* 1942; *Time Flies* 1944; *I'll Be Your Sweetheart* 1945; *Green for Danger* 1946; *The Hills of Donegal* 1947; *The History of Mr Polly* 1948
Marriott, Steven *Live It Up* 1963; *Be My Guest* 1965
Marriott, Sylvia *Return of a Stranger* 1937; *Crimes at the Dark House* 1939; *Anne and Muriel* 1971; *The Story of Adèle H* 1975
Mars, Kenneth (1936–) *The Producers* 1968; *The April Fools* 1969; *Viva Max!* 1969; *Desperate Characters* 1971; *What's Up, Doc?* 1972; *Young Frankenstein* 1974; *Night Moves* 1975; *Goin' Coconuts* 1978; *The Apple Dumpling Gang Rides Again* 1979; *Full Moon High* 1982; *Prince Jack* 1984; *Beer* 1985; *For Keeps* 1987; *Illegally Yours* 1988; *The Little Mermaid* 1989; *Thumbelina* 1994; *Rough Magic* 1995; *Citizen Ruth* 1996; *The Little Mermaid II: Return to the Sea* 2000

Marsalis, Branford (1960–) *Throw Momma from the Train* 1987; *School Daze* 1988; *Eve's Bayou* 1997

Marsan, Eddie *The Emperor's New Clothes* 2001; *21 Grams* 2003; *Vera Drake* 2004

Marsden, Betty (1919–1998) *The Young Lovers* 1954; *Let's Get Married* 1960; *The Leather Boys* 1963; *The Wild Affair* 1963; *Eyewitness* 1970; *The Dresser* 1983

Marsden, James (1973–) *Taken Away* 1996; *Disturbing Behaviour* 1998; *Gossip* 1999; *X-Men* 2000; *Sugar & Spice* 2001; *The Notebook* 2003; *X2* 2003

Marsden, Jason (1975–) *A Goofy Movie* 1995; *Trojan War* 1997; *Spirited Away* 2001

Marsden, Roy (1941–) *Toomorrow* 1970; *The Squeeze* 1977

Marsh, Carol (1929–) *Brighton Rock* 1947; *Marry Me!* 1949; *The Romantic Age* 1949; *Scrooge* 1951; *Horror of Dracula* 1958

Marsh, Garry (1902–1981) *Dreyfus* 1931; *Number Seventeen* 1932; *Death on the Set* 1935; *Scrooge* 1935; *The Man in the Mirror* 1936; *When Knights Were Bold* 1936; *The Vicar of Bray* 1937; *Bank Holiday* 1938; *Convict 99* 1938; *I See Ice* 1938; *It's in the Air* 1938; *Trouble Brewing* 1939; *Let George Do It* 1940; *Pink String and Sealing Wax* 1945; *Dancing with Crime* 1946; *The Shop at Sly Corner* 1946; *Just William's Luck* 1947; *William at the Circus* 1948; *Murder at the Windmill* 1949; *Someone at the Door* 1950; *Something in the City* 1950; *The Lost Hours* 1952; *Double Exposure* 1954; *Man of the Moment* 1955; *Who Done It?* 1956; *Trouble with Eve* 1959

Marsh, Jamie *Montenegro* 1981; *Brainscan* 1994; *Best Laid Plans* 1999; *Beethoven's 3rd* 2000

Marsh, Jean (1934–) *Unearthly Stranger* 1963; *Frenzy* 1972; *The Eagle Has Landed* 1976; *The Changeling* 1980; *Return to Oz* 1985; *Willow* 1988

Marsh, Joan (1913–2000) *You're Telling Me!* 1934; *Charlie Chan on Broadway* 1937; *Follow the Leader* 1944

Marsh, Linda *Hamlet* 1964; *Freebie and the Bean* 1974

Marsh, Mae (1895–1968) *The Battle of Elderbush* 1914; *The Birth of a Nation* 1915; *Intolerance* 1916; *Three Godfathers* 1948; *Impact* 1949

Marsh, Marian (1913–) *Five Star Final* 1931; *The Mad Genius* 1931; *Svengali* 1931; *The Black Room* 1935; *Crime and Punishment* 1935; *The Man Who Lived Twice* 1936

Marsh, Matthew *Diamond Skulls* 1989; *Miranda* 2001; *Bad Company* 2002

Marsh, Reginald (1926–2001) *Shadow of Fear* 1963; *The Sicilians* 1964

Marsh, Sally Ann *The Princess and the Goblin* 1992; *A Monkey's Tale* 1999

Marsh, William *Proteus* 1995; *Dead Babies* 2000

Marshal, Alan (1909–1961) *After the Thin Man* 1936; *Conquest* 1937; *Night Must Fall* 1937; *Parnell* 1937; *Dramatic School* 1938; *I Met My Love Again* 1938; *The Adventures of Sherlock Holmes* 1939; *Four Girls in White* 1939; *The Hunchback of Notre Dame* 1939; *The Howards of Virginia* 1940; *Irene* 1940; *Lydia* 1941; *Tom, Dick and Harry* 1941; *Bride by Mistake* 1944; *The White Cliffs of Dover* 1944; *House on Haunted Hill* 1958; *Day of the Outlaw* 1959

Marshall, Brenda (1915–1992) *East of the River* 1940; *The Sea Hawk* 1940; *Footsteps in the Dark* 1941; *Captains of the Clouds* 1942; *You Can't Escape Forever* 1942; *Background to Danger* 1943; *The Constant Nymph* 1943; *Paris after Dark* 1943; *Strange Impersonation* 1946; *Whispering Smith* 1948

Marshall, Bryan (1938–) *I Start Counting* 1970; *The Spy Who Loved Me* 1977; *The Long Good Friday* 1979; *BMX Bandits* 1983; *Bliss* 1985; *Hot Target* 1985; *Return to Snowy River* 1988; *The Punisher* 1989

Marshall, Connie (1938–) *Sunday Dinner for a Soldier* 1944; *Home Sweet Homicide* 1946; *Mother Wore Tights* 1947; *Mr Blandings Builds His Dream House* 1948

Marshall, David Anthony *Across the Tracks* 1990; *Another 48 HRS* 1990; *Roadside Prophets* 1992

Marshall, Dodie *Spinout* 1966; *Easy Come, Easy Go* 1967

Marshall, Don (1936–) *The Thing with Two Heads* 1972; *Terminal Island* 1973

Marshall, E G (1910–1998) *Broken Lance* 1954; *The Caine Mutiny* 1954; *Pushover* 1954; *The Left Hand of God* 1955; *The Mountain* 1956; *The Bachelor Party* 1957; *12 Angry Men* 1957; *The Buccaneer* 1958; *Compulsion* 1959; *The Journey* 1959; *Cash McCall* 1960; *Town without Pity* 1961; *The Chase* 1966; *The Poppy Is Also a Flower* 1966; *The Bridge at Remagen* 1969; *Tora! Tora! Tora!* 1970; *The Pursuit of Happiness* 1971; *Billy Jack Goes to Washington* 1977; *Interiors* 1978; *Superman II* 1980; *Creepshow* 1982; *My Chauffeur* 1986; *National Lampoon's Christmas Vacation* 1989; *Two Evil Eyes* 1990; *Consenting Adults* 1992; *Nixon* 1995; *Absolute Power* 1996; *Miss Evers' Boys* 1997

Marshall, Herbert (1890–1966) *The Letter* 1929; *Murder* 1930; *Blonde Venus* 1932; *Trouble in Paradise* 1932; *Four Frightened People* 1934; *I Was a Spy* 1934; *The Painted Veil* 1934; *Riptide* 1934; *Accent on Youth* 1935; *The Dark Angel* 1935; *The Good Fairy* 1935; *If You Could Only Cook* 1935; *Till We Meet Again* 1936; *A Woman Rebels* 1936; *Angel* 1937; *Breakfast for Two* 1937; *Always Goodbye* 1938; *Mad about Music* 1938; *Zaza* 1939; *A Bill of Divorcement* 1940; *Foreign Correspondent* 1940; *The Letter* 1940; *The Little Foxes* 1941; *When Ladies Meet* 1941; *The Moon and Sixpence* 1942; *Flight for Freedom* 1943; *Young Ideas* 1943; *Andy Hardy's Blonde Trouble* 1944; *The Enchanted Cottage* 1945; *The Unseen* 1945; *Crack-Up* 1946; *Duel in the Sun* 1946; *The Razor's Edge* 1946; *High Wall* 1947; *Ivy* 1947; *The Secret Garden* 1949; *The Underworld Story* 1950; *Anne of the Indies* 1951; *Black Jack* 1952; *Angel Face* 1953; *The Black Shield of Falworth* 1954; *Gog* 1954; *The Virgin Queen* 1955; *The Fly* 1958; *Stage Struck* 1958; *Midnight Lace* 1960; *A Fever in the Blood* 1961; *The Caretakers* 1963; *The List of Adrian Messenger* 1963; *The Third Day* 1965

Marshall, James (1967–) *Stockade* 1991; *A Few Good Men* 1992; *Gladiator* 1992; *The Unspoken Truth* 1995; *Doomsday Man* 1998; *Soccer Dog: the Movie* 1999; *Luck of the Draw* 2000

Marshall, Ken (1950–) *Tilt* 1978; *La Pelle* 1981; *Krull* 1983; *Feds* 1988

Marshall, Kris (1974–) *The Most Fertile Man in Ireland* 1999; *The Four Feathers* 2002; *William Shakespeare's The Merchant of Venice* 2004

Marshall, Marion *aka* **Marshall, M T** *I Was a Male War Bride* 1949; *Stella* 1950; *Sailor Beware* 1951; *The Stooge* 1951; *That's My Boy* 1951; *Gunn* 1967

Marshall, Paula (1964–) *Hellraiser III: Hell on Earth* 1992; *Warlock: the Armageddon* 1993; *The New Age* 1994; *That Old Feeling* 1997; *Thursday* 1998

Marshall, Penny (1942–) *Evil Roy Slade* 1971; *Movers and Shakers* 1985; *The Hard Way* 1991

Marshall, Trudy (1922–2004) *The Dancing Masters* 1943; *The Fighting Sullivans* 1944; *Circumstantial Evidence* 1945; *The Fuller Brush Man* 1948

Marshall, Tully (1864–1943) *A Romance of the Redwoods* 1917; *The Fall of Babylon* 1919; *The Covered Wagon* 1923; *The Hunchback of Notre Dame* 1923; *He Who Gets Slapped* 1924; *The Merry Widow* 1925; *The Cat and the Canary* 1927; *Thunderbolt* 1929; *The Trail of '98* 1929; *The Big Trail* 1930; *Mammy* 1930; *Tom Sawyer* 1930; *Fighting Caravans* 1931; *The Unholy Garden* 1931; *Arsene Lupin* 1932; *The Beast of the City* 1932; *The Hatchet Man* 1932; *The Hurricane Express* 1932; *Red Dust* 1932; *Murder on the Blackboard* 1934; *California Straight Ahead* 1937; *Ball of Fire* 1941; *This Gun for Hire* 1942

Marshall (2), William (1924–2003) *Lydia Bailey* 1952; *Something of Value* 1957; *To Trap a Spy* 1966; *The Hell with Heroes* 1968; *Zigzag* 1970; *Blacula* 1972; *Scream Blacula Scream* 1973; *Abby* 1974

Marshall, Zena (1927–) *The Lost People* 1949; *Marry Me!* 1949; *Meet Simon Cherry* 1949; *Deadly Nightshade* 1953; *Dr No* 1962; *The Marked One* 1963

Marshe, Vera (1905–1984) *Getting Gertie's Garter* 1945; *Where There's Life* 1947

Marsillach, Cristina (1963–) *1919* 1983; *Every Time We Say Goodbye* 1986; *Opera* 1987

Marson, Ania *Puppet on a Chain* 1970; *Nicholas and Alexandra* 1971; *The Abdication* 1974

Marstini, Rosita (1887–1948) *Blood and Sand* 1922; *The Big Parade* 1925

Marston, Nathaniel (1975–) *The Craft* 1996; *Love Is All There Is* 1996

Martel, K C *The Amityville Horror* 1979; *ET the Extra-Terrestrial* 1982; *White Water Summer* 1987

Martell, Chris *The Gruesome Twosome* 1967; *Flesh Feast* 1970

Martell, Donna (1827–) *Last Train from Bombay* 1952; *Project Moonbase* 1953

Martell, Gregg *I Was a Shoplifter* 1950; *Dinosaurus!* 1960

Martelli, Norma *The Night of San Lorenzo* 1981; *Everybody's Fine* 1990

Marthouret, François (1943–) *Hit List* 1984; *Marquis* 1989; *Annabelle Partagée* 1990; *Sitcom* 1997; *The Lady & the Duke* 2001

Martial, Jacques *Broken English* 1981; *Noir et Blanc* 1986

Martin, Andra (1935–) *The Lady Takes a Flyer* 1958; *Up Periscope* 1959

Martin, Andrea (1947–) *Cannibal Girls* 1973; *Black Christmas* 1974; *Too Much Sun* 1990; *Bogus* 1996; *Wag the Dog* 1997; *Bartok the Magnificent* 1999; *Hedwig and the Angry Inch* 2001; *Jimmy Neutron: Boy Genius* 2001; *My Big Fat Greek Wedding* 2002; *New York Minute* 2004

Martin, Anne-Marie *aka* **Benton, Eddie** *Prom Night* 1980; *Savage Harvest* 1981

Martin, Chris-Pin (1893–1953) *The Cisco Kid and the Lady* 1939; *Stagecoach* 1939; *The Gay Caballero* 1940

Martin, Christopher (1963–) *House Party* 1990; *House Party 2* 1991; *Class Act* 1992; *House Party 3* 1994

Martin, Damon *Pee-wee's Big Adventure* 1985; *Kid* 1990

Martin, Dean (1917–1995) *My Friend Irma* 1949; *At War with the Army* 1950; *My Friend Irma Goes West* 1950; *Sailor Beware* 1951; *The Stooge* 1951; *That's My Boy* 1951; *Jumping Jacks* 1952; *The Caddy* 1953; *Money from Home* 1953; *Scared Stiff* 1953; *Living It Up* 1954; *Three Ring Circus* 1954; *Artists and Models* 1955; *You're Never Too Young* 1955; *Hollywood or Bust* 1956; *Pardners* 1956; *Ten Thousand Bedrooms* 1957; *Some Came Running* 1958; *The Young Lions* 1958; *Career* 1959; *Rio Bravo* 1959; *All in a Night's Work* 1960; *Bells Are Ringing* 1960; *Ocean's Eleven* 1960; *Pepe* 1960; *Who Was That Lady?* 1960; *Ada* 1961; *The Road to Hong Kong* 1962; *Sergeants 3* 1962; *Who's Got the Action?* 1962; *Come Blow Your Horn* 1963; *4 for Texas* 1963; *Toys in the Attic* 1963; *Who's Been Sleeping in My Bed?* 1963; *Kiss Me, Stupid* 1964; *Robin and the 7 Hoods* 1964; *What a Way to Go!* 1964; *Marriage on the Rocks* 1965; *The Sons of Katie Elder* 1965; *Murderers' Row* 1966; *The Silencers* 1966; *Texas across the River* 1966; *The Ambushers* 1967; *Rough Night in Jericho* 1967; *Bandolero!* 1968; *5 Card Stud* 1968; *How to Save a Marriage and Ruin Your Life* 1968; *The Wrecking Crew* 1969; *Airport* 1970; *something big* 1971; *Showdown* 1973; *Mr Ricco* 1975; *The Cannonball Run* 1981; *Cannonball Run II* 1983

Martin, Dean Paul (1951–1987) *Players* 1979; *Heart like a Wheel* 1983; *Backfire* 1987

Martin, Dewey (1923–) *Kansas Raiders* 1950; *The Thing from Another World* 1951; *The Big Sky* 1952; *Men of the Fighting Lady* 1954; *Prisoner of War* 1954; *Tennessee Champ* 1954; *The Desperate Hours* 1955; *Land of the Pharaohs* 1955; *The Proud and Profane* 1956; *Ten Thousand Bedrooms* 1957; *Savage Sam* 1963; *Flight to Fury* 1966; *Seven Alone* 1974

Martin, Dick (1923–) *The Maltese Bippy* 1969; *Zero to Sixty* 1978; *Carbon Copy* 1981; *Bartleby* 2000

Martin, Duane *Above the Rim* 1994; *Woo* 1998; *Mutiny* 1999

Martin, D'Urville (1939–1984) *Watermelon Man* 1970; *The Final Comedown* 1972; *Black Caesar* 1973; *Hell Up in Harlem* 1973

Martin, Edie (1880–1964) *The Demi-Paradise* 1943; *The Lavender Hill Mob* 1951; *The Ladykillers* 1955

Martin, Eugene *Terror in a Texas Town* 1958; *This Rebel Breed* 1960; *Tower of London* 1962

Martin (1), George *CHUD* 1984; *Falling in Love* 1984; *The Associate* 1996

Martin, Helen (1909–2000) *A Hero Ain't Nothin' but a Sandwich* 1978; *Hollywood Shuffle* 1987; *Don't Be a Menace to South Central while Drinking Your Juice in the Hood* 1996

Martin, Jared (1943–) *Murder à la Mod* 1968; *The Second Coming of Suzanne* 1974; *The Lonely Lady* 1983; *Quiet Cool* 1986

Martin, Jean *Jamboree* 1957; *The Battle of Algiers* 1965; *My Name Is Nobody* 1973; *Lucie Aubrac* 1997

Martin, José Manuel (1924–) *A Bullet for the General* 1966; *A Bullet for Sandoval* 1970

Martin, Kellie (1975–) *Matinee* 1993; *Death of a Cheerleader* 1994; *A Goofy Movie* 1995; *About Sarah* 1998

Martin, Lewis *Ace in the Hole* 1951; *The War of the Worlds* 1953; *Witness to Murder* 1954; *Diary of a Madman* 1963

Martin, Marion (1908–1985) *Sinners in Paradise* 1938; *Sergeant Madden* 1939; *The Big Street* 1942; *They Got Me Covered* 1943

Martin, Mary (1913–1990) *Rhythm on the River* 1940; *The Birth of the Blues* 1941; *Kiss the Boys Goodbye* 1941; *Star Spangled Rhythm* 1942; *Happy Go Lucky* 1943; *True to Life* 1943

Martin, Millicent (1934–) *Libel* 1959; *Invasion Quartet* 1961; *The Girl on the Boat* 1962; *Nothing but the Best* 1963; *Alfie* 1966; *Stop the World, I Want to Get Off* 1966

Martin, Nan (1927–) *Toys in the Attic* 1963; *For Love of Ivy* 1968; *Three in the Attic* 1968; *Goodbye, Columbus* 1969; *The Other Side of the Mountain* 1975; *Jackson County Jail* 1976; *The Other Side of the Mountain – Part 2* 1978; *Loving Couples* 1980; *A Small Circle of Friends* 1980; *Animal Behavior* 1989; *Big Eden* 2000

Martin, Pamela Sue (1953–) *The Poseidon Adventure* 1972; *Buster and Billie* 1974; *The Lady in Red* 1979; *Torchlight* 1984

Martin (1), Richard (1919–1994) *Tender Comrade* 1943; *Marine Raiders* 1944; *Nevada* 1944; *The Bamboo Blonde* 1946; *Thunder Mountain* 1947; *The Arizona Ranger* 1948; *Guns of Hate* 1948; *Stagecoach Kid* 1949; *Rider from Tucson* 1950; *Storm over Wyoming* 1950; *Desert Passage* 1952

Martin, Rosemary (1936–1998) *Tess* 1979; *Laughterhouse* 1984; *The Dressmaker* 1988; *The Object of Beauty* 1991

Martin, Ross (1920–1981) *Conquest of Space* 1955; *The Colossus of New York* 1958; *Experiment in Terror* 1962; *Geronimo* 1962

Martin, Rudolf (1967–) *Fall* 1997; *Dark Prince – the Legend of Dracula* 2000

Martin, Sandy (1950–) *Extremities* 1986; *Barfly* 1987

Martin, Steve (1945–) *Sgt Pepper's Lonely Hearts Club Band* 1978; *The Jerk* 1979; *Pennies from Heaven* 1981; *Dead Men Don't Wear Plaid* 1982; *The Man with Two Brains* 1983; *All of Me* 1984; *The Lonely Guy* 1984; *Movers and Shakers* 1985; *Little Shop of Horrors* 1986; *Three Amigos!* 1986; *Planes, Trains and Automobiles* 1987; *Roxanne* 1987; *Dirty Rotten Scoundrels* 1988; *Parenthood* 1989; *My Blue Heaven* 1990; *Father of the Bride* 1991; *Grand Canyon* 1991; *LA Story* 1991; *HouseSitter* 1992; *Leap of Faith* 1992; *And the Band Played On* 1993; *Mixed Nuts* 1994; *A Simple Twist of Fate* 1994; *Father of the Bride Part 2* 1995; *Sgt Bilko* 1996; *The Spanish Prisoner* 1997; *The Prince of Egypt* 1998; *Bowfinger* 1999; *Fantasia 2000* 1999; *The Out-of-Towners* 1999; *Novocaine* 2001; *Bringing Down the House* 2003; *Cheaper by the Dozen* 2003; *Looney Tunes: Back in Action* 2004

Martin, Strother (1919–1980) *The Deadly Companions* 1961; *Showdown* 1963; *Invitation to a Gunfighter* 1964; *An Eye for an Eye* 1966; *Cool Hand Luke* 1967; *Butch Cassidy and the Sundance Kid* 1969; *The Ballad of Cable Hogue* 1970; *Brotherhood of Satan* 1970; *Dynamite Man from Glory Jail* 1971; *Hannie Caulder* 1971; *Pocket Money* 1972; *Sssssss* 1973; *Hard Times* 1975; *Rooster Cogburn* 1975; *The Great Scout & Cathouse Thursday* 1976; *Slap Shot* 1977; *Cheech & Chong's Up in Smoke* 1978; *The End* 1978; *Love and Bullets* 1978; *Cactus Jack* 1979; *The Champ* 1979; *Nightwing* 1979

Martin, Todd (1927–) *The Thomas Crown Affair* 1968; *Jory* 1972; *Alex and the Gypsy* 1976

Martin, Tony *aka* **Martin, Anthony** (1913–) *Banjo on My Knee* 1936; *Pigskin Parade* 1936; *Life Begins in College* 1937; *You Can't Have Everything* 1937; *Kentucky Moonshine* 1938; *Sally, Irene and Mary* 1938; *Music in My Heart* 1940; *The Big Store* 1941; *Ziegfeld Girl* 1941; *Casbah* 1948; *Two Tickets to Broadway* 1951; *Easy to Love* 1953; *Here Come the Girls* 1953; *Deep in My Heart* 1954; *Hit the Deck* 1955

Martindale, Margo (1951–) *Lorenzo's Oil* 1992; *Critical Care* 1997; *Eye of God* 1997; *First Do No Harm* 1997; *It's All about Love* 2002

Martindel, Edward (1873–1955) *Lady Windermere's Fan* 1925; *The Singing Fool* 1928; *The Desert Song* 1929; *Check and Double Check* 1930

Martinelli, Elsa (1932–) *The Indian Fighter* 1955; *Manuela* 1957; *Blood and Roses* 1960; *The Captain* 1960; *Hatari!* 1962; *The Pigeon That Took Rome*

The Trial 1962; *Rampage* 1963; *The VIPs* 1963; *The Tenth Victim* 1965; *Maroc 7* 1966; *Madigan's Millions* 1967; *The Oldest Profession* 1967

Martinelli, Jean (1910–1983) *Le Rouge et le Noir* 1954; *To Catch a Thief* 1955; *Heroines of Evil* 1979

Martines, Alessandra (1963–) *Les Misérables* 1995; *Men, Women: a User's Manual* 1996; *Chance or Coincidence* 1999

Martinez, A (1948–) *Once upon a Scoundrel* 1973; *The Take* 1974; *The Honorary Consul* 1983; *Powwow Highway* 1988; *One Night Stand* 1994; *Before the Night* 1995; *Last Rites* 1998; *Wind River* 1999

Martinez, Alma *Barbarosa* 1982; *Under Fire* 1983

Martínez, Fele (1976–) *Tesis* 1996; *Open Your Eyes* 1997; *The Lovers of the Arctic Circle* 1998; *Captains of April* 2000; *Darkness* 2002; *Bad Education* 2004

Martinez, Joaquin *Jeremiah Johnson* 1972; *Ulzana's Raid* 1972; *Flashpoint* 1984; *Revenge* 1990

Martinez, Olivier (1966–) *IP5* 1992; *The Horseman on the Roof* 1995; *Mon Homme* 1996; *The Chambermaid on the Titanic* 1997; *Before Night Falls* 2000; *Unfaithful* 2002; *SWAT* 2003; *Taking Lives* 2004

Martinez, Vanessa (1979–) *Limbo* 1999; *Casa de los Babys* 2003

Martinez, Vincent *The School of Flesh* 1998; *Le Clan* 2004

Martini, Nino (1904–1976) *Paramount on Parade* 1930; *The Gay Desperado* 1936; *One Night with You* 1948

Martins, Orlando (1899–1985) *Men of Two Worlds* 1946; *The End of the River* 1947; *West of Zanzibar* 1954; *Safari* 1956; *Mister Moses* 1965

Martyn, Peter (1928–1955) *Child's Play* 1954; *Mad about Men* 1954; *No Smoking* 1954

Marull, Laia (1973–) *Lisboa* 1999; *Take My Eyes* 2003

Marvin, Hank (1941–) *The Young Ones* 1961; *Summer Holiday* 1962; *Wonderful Life* 1964; *Finders Keepers* 1966

Marvin, Lee (1924–1987) *The Duel at Silver Creek* 1952; *Eight Iron Men* 1952; *Hangman's Knot* 1952; *We're Not Married* 1952; *The Big Heat* 1953; *The Glory Brigade* 1953; *Gun Fury* 1953; *Seminole* 1953; *The Stranger Wore a Gun* 1953; *The Wild One* 1953; *The Caine Mutiny* 1954; *Gorilla at Large* 1954; *The Raid* 1954; *Bad Day at Black Rock* 1955; *I Died a Thousand Times* 1955; *A Life in the Balance* 1955; *Not as a Stranger* 1955; *Pete Kelly's Blues* 1955; *Shack Out on 101* 1955; *Violent Saturday* 1955; *Attack!* 1956; *Pillars of the Sky* 1956; *The Rack* 1956; *Seven Men from Now* 1956; *Raintree County* 1957; *The Missouri Traveler* 1958; *The Comancheros* 1961; *The Man Who Shot Liberty Valance* 1962; *Donovan's Reef* 1963; *The Killers* 1964; *Cat Ballou* 1965; *Ship of Fools* 1965; *The Professionals* 1966; *The Dirty Dozen* 1967; *Point Blank* 1967; *Hell in the Pacific* 1968; *Sergeant Ryker* 1968; *Paint Your Wagon* 1969; *Monte Walsh* 1970; *Pocket Money* 1972; *Prime Cut* 1972; *Emperor of the North* 1973; *The Iceman Cometh* 1973; *The Klansman* 1974; *The Spikes Gang* 1974; *The Great Scout & Cathouse Thursday* 1976; *Shout at the Devil* 1976; *Avalanche Express* 1979; *The Big Red One* 1980; *Death Hunt* 1981; *Gorky Park* 1983; *The Delta Force* 1986

Marx, Brett (1964–) *The Bad News Bears Go to Japan* 1978; *The Lucky Star* 1980; *Thrashin'* 1986

Marx, Chico (1886–1961) *The Cocoanuts* 1929; *Animal Crackers* 1930; *Monkey Business* 1931; *Horse Feathers* 1932; *Duck Soup* 1933; *A Night at the Opera* 1935; *A Day at the Races* 1937; *Room Service* 1938; *At the Circus* 1939; *Go West* 1940; *The Big Store* 1941; *A Night in Casablanca* 1946; *Love Happy* 1949; *The Story of Mankind* 1957

Marx, Groucho (1890–1977) *The Cocoanuts* 1929; *Animal Crackers* 1930; *Monkey Business* 1931; *Horse Feathers* 1932; *Duck Soup* 1933; *A Night at the Opera* 1935; *A Day at the Races* 1937; *Room Service* 1938; *At the Circus* 1939; *Go West* 1940; *The Big Store* 1941; *A Night in Casablanca* 1946; *Copacabana* 1947; *Love Happy* 1949; *Double Dynamite* 1951; *A Girl in Every Port* 1952; *The Story of Mankind* 1957; *Will Success Spoil Rock Hunter?* 1957; *Skidoo* 1968

Marx, Harpo (1888–1964) *The Cocoanuts* 1929; *Animal Crackers* 1930; *Monkey Business* 1931; *Horse Feathers* 1932; *Duck Soup* 1933; *A Night at the Opera* 1935; *A Day at the Races* 1937; *Room Service* 1938; *At the Circus* 1939; *Go West* 1940; *The Big Store* 1941; *Stage Door Canteen* 1943; *A Night in Casablanca* 1946; *Love Happy* 1949; *The Story of Mankind* 1957

Marx, Zeppo (1901–1979) *The Cocoanuts* 1929; *Animal Crackers* 1930; *Monkey Business* 1931; *Horse Feathers* 1932; *Duck Soup* 1933

Mascolo, Joseph (1935–) *Shaft's Big Score!* 1972; *Happy Mother's Day... Love, George* 1973; *Jaws 2* 1978; *Heat* 1987; *The Trial of the Incredible Hulk* 1989

Mase, Marino (1939–) *Les Carabiniers* 1963; *Fists in the Pocket* 1965

Mashkov, Vladimir (1963–) *Katia Ismailova* 1994; *The Thief* 1997

Masina, Giulietta (1920–1994) *Lights of Variety* 1950; *The White Sheik* 1951; *Europa '51* 1952; *La Strada* 1954; *The Swindle* 1955; *Nights of Cabiria* 1957; *Juliet of the Spirits* 1965; *The Madwoman of Chaillot* 1969; *Ginger & Fred* 1986

Masini, Galliano *Pagliacci* 1948; *La Forza del Destino* 1949

Mask, Ace (1948–) *Not of This Earth* 1988; *The Return of Swamp Thing* 1989; *Transylvania Twist* 1989

Maskell, Virginia (1936–1968) *The Man Upstairs* 1958; *Virgin Island* 1958; *Jet Storm* 1959; *Doctor in Love* 1960; *Suspect* 1960; *Only Two Can Play* 1961; *The Wild and the Willing* 1962; *Interlude* 1968

Maslow, Walter *The Cosmic Man* 1959; *Atlas* 1960

Mason, Brewster (1922–1987) *Private Potter* 1963; *The Quatermass Conclusion* 1979

Mason, Connie (1937–) *Blood Feast* 1963; *Two Thousand Maniacs!* 1964

Mason, Elliot (1897–1949) *The Ghost of St Michael's* 1941; *It's Turned Out Nice Again* 1941

Mason, Hilary (1917–) *Don't Look Now* 1973; *I Don't Want to Be Born* 1975; *Dolls* 1987; *Robot Jox* 1989

Mason, James (1909–1984) *Fire over England* 1937; *The Mill on the Floss* 1937; *The Return of the Scarlet Pimpernel* 1937; *Hatter's Castle* 1941; *The Night Has Eyes* 1942; *Secret Mission* 1942; *Thunder Rock* 1942; *The Bells Go Down* 1943; *Candlelight in Algeria* 1943; *The Man in Grey* 1943; *They Met in the Dark* 1943; *Fanny by Gaslight* 1944; *Hotel Reserve* 1944; *A Place of One's Own* 1944; *The Seventh Veil* 1945; *They Were Sisters* 1945; *The Wicked Lady* 1945; *Odd Man Out* 1946; *The Upturned Glass* 1947; *Caught* 1949; *East Side, West Side* 1949; *Madame Bovary* 1949; *The Reckless Moment* 1949; *One Way Street* 1950; *Pandora and the Flying Dutchman* 1950; *The Desert Fox* 1951; *Botany Bay* 1952; *Face to Face* 1952; *5 Fingers* 1952; *The Prisoner of Zenda* 1952; *The Desert Rats* 1953; *Julius Caesar* 1953; *The Man Between* 1953; *The Story of Three Loves* 1953; *Prince Valiant* 1954; *A Star Is Born* 1954; *20,000 Leagues under the Sea* 1954; *Bigger than Life* 1956; *Forever, Darling* 1956; *Island in the Sun* 1957; *Cry Terror* 1958; *The Decks Ran Red* 1958; *Journey to the Center of the Earth* 1959; *North by Northwest* 1959; *A Touch of Larceny* 1959; *The Marriage-Go-Round* 1960; *The Trials of Oscar Wilde* 1960; *Lolita* 1961; *Escape from Zahrain* 1962; *Hero's Island* 1962; *Tiara Tahiti* 1962; *The Fall of the Roman Empire* 1964; *Genghis Khan* 1964; *The Pumpkin Eater* 1964; *Lord Jim* 1965; *The Blue Max* 1966; *The Deadly Affair* 1966; *Georgy Girl* 1966; *Stranger in the House* 1967; *Duffy* 1968; *Mayerling* 1968; *The Sea Gull* 1968; *Age of Consent* 1969; *Spring and Port Wine* 1969; *Bad Man's River* 1971; *Cold Sweat* 1971; *Child's Play* 1972; *Kill!* 1972; *Frankenstein: the True Story* 1973; *The Last of Sheila* 1973; *The Mackintosh Man* 1973; *11 Harrowhouse* 1974; *Great Expectations* 1974; *The Marseille Contract* 1974; *Autobiography of a Princess* 1975; *Inside Out* 1975; *Mandingo* 1975; *The Masters* 1975; *Voyage of the Damned* 1976; *Cross of Iron* 1977; *The Boys from Brazil* 1978; *Heaven Can Wait* 1978; *Murder by Decree* 1978; *The Passage* 1978; *The Water Babies* 1978; *Bloodline* 1979; *North Sea Hijack* 1979; *Salem's Lot* 1979; *A Dangerous Summer* 1981; *Evil under the Sun* 1982; *The Verdict* 1982; *Yellowbeard* 1983; *The Shooting Party* 1984; *The Assisi Underground* 1985

Mason, LeRoy (1903–1947) *Texas Terror* 1935; *Santa Fe Stampede* 1938; *Wyoming Outlaw* 1939; *Riders of the Purple Sage* 1941; *My Pal Trigger* 1946

Mason, Lola *The Brain That Wouldn't Die* 1959; *The End of Innocence* 1990

Mason, Madison (1942–) *Dangerously Close* 1986; *Omen IV: the Awakening* 1991

Mason, Marsha (1942–) *Blume in Love* 1973; *Cinderella Liberty* 1973; *Audrey Rose* 1977; *The Goodbye Girl* 1977; *The Cheap Detective* 1978; *Chapter Two* 1979; *Promises in the Dark* 1979; *Only When I Laugh* 1981; *Max Dugan Returns* 1983; *Surviving* 1985; *Heartbreak Ridge* 1986; *The Image* 1990; *Stella* 1990; *Drop Dead Fred* 1991; *I Love Trouble* 1994; *Nick of Time* 1995; *2 Days in the Valley* 1996

Mason, Reginald *Shanghai Madness* 1933; *Topaze* 1933

Mason, Tom *Men Don't Leave* 1990; *A Murderous Affair* 1992; *Flashfire* 1993; *The Puppet Masters* 1994

Massari, Lea (1933–) *L'Avventura* 1960; *The Colossus of Rhodes* 1961; *Captive City* 1962; *The Four Days of Naples* 1962; *The Things of Life* 1969; *Le Souffle au Coeur* 1971; *And Hope to Die* 1972; *The Silent One* 1973; *Story of a Love Story* 1973; *Les Rendez-vous d'Anna* 1978; *Christ Stopped at Eboli* 1979

Massee, Michael *Tales from the Hood* 1995; *Guy* 1996; *Lost Highway* 1996; *Playing God* 1997

Massen, Osa (1916–) *A Woman's Face* 1941; *You'll Never Get Rich* 1941; *Background to Danger* 1943; *Cry of the Werewolf* 1944; *Jack London* 1944; *The Master Race* 1944; *Deadline at Dawn* 1946; *Night unto Night* 1949

Massey, Anna (1937–) *Gideon's Day* 1958; *Peeping Tom* 1960; *Bunny Lake Is Missing* 1965; *De Sade* 1969; *Frenzy* 1972; *A Doll's House* 1973; *Vault of Horror* 1973; *Sweet William* 1980; *Five Days One Summer* 1982; *Another Country* 1984; *The Chain* 1984; *The Little Drummer Girl* 1984; *Foreign Body* 1986; *Killing Dad* 1989; *The Tall Guy* 1989; *Impromptu* 1991; *The Grotesque* 1995; *Haunted* 1995; *Driftwood* 1996; *Sweet Angel Mine* 1996; *The Slab Boys* 1997; *Captain Jack* 1998; *Mad Cows* 1999; *Room to Rent* 2000; *The Importance of Being Earnest* 2002; *Possession* 2002; *The Machinist* 2003

Massey, Daniel (1933–1998) *In Which We Serve* 1942; *Operation Bullshine* 1959; *Upstairs and Downstairs* 1959; *The Entertainer* 1960; *The Queen's Guards* 1960; *Go to Blazes* 1961; *The Jokers* 1967; *Star!* 1968; *Fragment of Fear* 1970; *Mary, Queen of Scots* 1971; *Vault of Horror* 1973; *The Incredible Sarah* 1976; *The Devil's Advocate* 1977; *Warlords of Atlantis* 1978; *The Cat and the Canary* 1979; *Bad Timing* 1980; *Escape to Victory* 1981; *Scandal* 1988

Massey, Edith (1918–1984) *Pink Flamingos* 1972; *Female Trouble* 1974; *Desperate Living* 1977; *Polyester* 1981

Massey, Ilona (1910–1974) *Rosalie* 1937; *Balalaika* 1939; *International Lady* 1941; *The Invisible Agent* 1942; *Frankenstein Meets the Wolf Man* 1943; *Holiday in Mexico* 1946; *Northwest Outpost* 1947; *The Plunderers* 1948; *Love Happy* 1949; *Jet over the Atlantic* 1960

Massey, Raymond (1896–1983) *The Old Dark House* 1932; *The Scarlet Pimpernel* 1934; *Things to Come* 1936; *Fire over England* 1937; *The Hurricane* 1937; *The Prisoner of Zenda* 1937; *Under the Red Robe* 1937; *The Drum* 1938; *Santa Fe Trail* 1940; *Spirit of the People* 1940; *49th Parallel* 1941; *Dangerously They Live* 1942; *Desperate Journey* 1942; *Reap the Wild Wind* 1942; *Action in the North Atlantic* 1943; *Arsenic and Old Lace* 1944; *God Is My Co-Pilot* 1945; *Hotel Berlin* 1945; *The Woman in the Window* 1945; *A Matter of Life and Death* 1946; *Mourning Becomes Electra* 1947; *Possessed* 1947; *The Fountainhead* 1949; *Roseanna McCoy* 1949; *Barricade* 1950; *Chain Lightning* 1950; *Dallas* 1950; *Come Fill the Cup* 1951; *David and Bathsheba* 1951; *Sugarfoot* 1951; *Carson City* 1952; *The Desert Song* 1953; *Battle Cry* 1955; *East of Eden* 1955; *Prince of Players* 1955; *Seven Angry Men* 1955; *Omar Khayyam* 1957; *The Naked and the Dead* 1958; *The Queen's Guards* 1960; *The Fiercest Heart* 1961; *How the West Was Won* 1962; *Mackenna's Gold* 1969

Massey, Walter *Blood Relatives* 1977; *The Boy in Blue* 1986

Massie, Paul (1932–) *Orders to Kill* 1958; *Libel* 1959; *Sapphire* 1959; *The Rebel* 1960; *The Two Faces of Dr Jekyll* 1960; *Raising the Wind* 1961; *The Pot Carriers* 1962

Massine, Léonide (1896–1979) *The Red Shoes* 1948; *The Tales of Hoffmann* 1951; *Honeymoon* 1959

Master P (1969–) *I Got the Hook Up* 1998; *Gang Law* 1999; *Hollywood Homicide* 2003

Masters, Ben (1947–) *Key Exchange* 1985; *Dream Lover* 1986; *Making Mr Right* 1987

Masterson, Chris (1980–) *Dragonheart: a New Beginning* 1999; *Scary Movie 2* 2001

Masterson, Danny (1976–) *Beethoven's 2nd* 1993; *Trojan War* 1997

Masterson, Fay (1974–) *The Power of One* 1991; *The Man without a Face* 1993; *Cops and Robbersons* 1994; *Sorted* 2000

Masterson, Mary Stuart (1966–) *At Close Range* 1985; *Catholic Boys* 1985; *My Little Girl* 1986; *Gardens of Stone* 1987; *Some Kind of Wonderful* 1987; *Mr North* 1988; *Chances Are* 1989; *Immediate Family* 1989; *Funny about Love* 1990; *Fried Green Tomatoes at the Whistle Stop Cafe* 1991; *Married to It* 1991; *Mad at the Moon* 1992; *Benny and Joon* 1993; *Bad Girls* 1994; *Radioland Murders* 1994; *Bed of Roses* 1995; *Heaven's Prisoners* 1996; *Digging to China* 1998; *Leo* 2002

Masterson, Peter (1934–) *Ambush Bay* 1966; *Tomorrow* 1972; *The Stepford Wives* 1975

Masterson, Ronnie *The Dawning* 1988; *Angela's Ashes* 1999

Mastrantonio, Mary Elizabeth (1958–) *Scarface* 1983; *The Color of Money* 1986; *Slam Dance* 1987; *The Abyss* 1989; *The January Man* 1989; *Fools of Fortune* 1990; *Class Action* 1991; *Robin Hood: Prince of Thieves* 1991; *Consenting Adults* 1992; *White Sands* 1992; *Three Wishes* 1995; *Two Bits* 1995; *Limbo* 1999; *My Life So Far* 1999; *Witness Protection* 1999; *The Perfect Storm* 2000

Mastroianni, Chiara (1972–) *Ma Saison Préferée* 1993; *All Men Are Mortal* 1995; *Don't Forget You're Going to Die* 1995; *Ma Vie Sexuelle* 1996; *Three Lives and Only One Death* 1996; *Nowhere* 1997; *Time Regained* 1999; *Hotel* 2001; *Carnages* 2002

Mastroianni, Marcello (1923–1996) *Sunday in August* 1949; *Lucky to Be a Woman* 1955; *The Miller's Wife* 1955; *Too Bad She's Bad* 1955; *White Nights* 1957; *Big Deal on Madonna Street* 1958; *Where the Hot Wind Blows!* 1959; *La Dolce Vita* 1960; *Divorce – Italian Style* 1961; *La Notte* 1961; *A Very Private Affair* 1962; *8½* 1963; *The Organizer* 1963; *Yesterday, Today and Tomorrow* 1963; *Marriage – Italian Style* 1964; *Casanova '70* 1965; *The Tenth Victim* 1965; *The Poppy Is Also a Flower* 1966; *Shout Loud, Louder... I Don't Understand* 1966; *Ghosts – Italian Style* 1967; *The Stranger* 1967; *Diamonds for Breakfast* 1968; *A Place for Lovers* 1968; *Sunflower* 1969; *Jealousy, Italian Style* 1970; *Leo the Last* 1970; *The Priest's Wife* 1970; *Fellini's Roma* 1972; *The Bit Player* 1973; *La Grande Bouffe* 1973; *Massacre in Rome* 1973; *What?* 1973; *A Special Day* 1977; *Bye Bye Monkey* 1978; *Blood Feud* 1979; *City of Women* 1980; *La Pelle* 1981; *Gabriela* 1983; *La Nuit de Varennes* 1983; *Storia di Piera* 1983; *Macaroni* 1985; *The Bee Keeper* 1986; *Ginger & Fred* 1986; *Dark Eyes* 1987; *Intervista* 1987; *Everybody's Fine* 1990; *A Touch of Adultery* 1991; *Used People* 1992; *We Don't Want to Talk about It* 1993; *Pret-a-Porter* 1994; *Beyond the Clouds* 1995; *Les Cent et Une Nuits* 1995; *Three Lives and Only One Death* 1996; *Journey to the Beginning of the World* 1997

Masur, Richard (1948–) *Semi-Tough* 1977; *Who'll Stop the Rain?* 1978; *Hanover Street* 1979; *Heaven's Gate* 1980; *The Thing* 1982; *Adam* 1983; *Risky Business* 1983; *The Burning Bed* 1984; *The Mean Season* 1985; *My Science Project* 1985; *Heartburn* 1986; *The Believers* 1987; *Walker* 1987; *Deadly Pursuit* 1988; *License to Drive* 1988; *Rent-a-Cop* 1988; *Far from Home* 1989; *Flashback* 1990; *My Girl* 1991; *California Man* 1992; *The Man without a Face* 1993; *Six Degrees of Separation* 1993; *My Girl 2* 1994; *Patriots* 1994; *Forget Paris* 1995; *Multiplicity* 1996; *Play It to the Bone* 2000; *61** 2001; *Palindromes* 2004

Matania, Clelia (1918–1981) *The Monte Carlo Story* 1957; *Seven Hills of Rome* 1957; *Don't Look Now* 1973

Matarazzo, Heather (1982–) *Welcome to the Dollhouse* 1995; *Our Guys: Outrage in Glen Ridge* 1999; *The Princess Diaries* 2001; *Sorority Boys* 2002; *The Princess Diaries 2: Royal Engagement* 2004; *Saved!* 2004

Mateos, Julian (1938–1996) *Return of the Seven* 1966; *10:30 PM Summer* 1966; *Catlow* 1971

Mather, Aubrey (1885–1958) *The Man Who Changed His Name* 1934; *The Man in the Mirror* 1936; *When Knights Were Bold*

1936; *Careful, Soft Shoulder* 1942; *The Undying Monster* 1942; *The House of Fear* 1944; *The Lodger* 1944; *Temptation* 1946; *The Hucksters* 1947; *South of Algiers* 1952
Matheron, Marie *Le Grand Chemin* 1987; *Western* 1997; *Presque Rien* 2000
Mathers, Jerry (1948–) *The Trouble with Harry* 1954; *That Certain Feeling* 1956
Matheson, Hans (1975–) *Les Misérables* 1997; *Stella Does Tricks* 1997; *Mojo* 1998; *Bodywork* 1999
Matheson, Murray (1912–1985) *Botany Bay* 1952; *Love Is a Many-Splendored Thing* 1955; *How to Succeed in Business without Really Trying* 1967
Matheson, Tim (1947–) *How to Commit Marriage* 1969; *Magnum Force* 1973; *Almost Summer* 1977; *National Lampoon's Animal House* 1978; *The Apple Dumpling Gang Rides Again* 1979; *Dreamer* 1979; *1941* 1979; *A Little Sex* 1981; *To Be or Not to Be* 1983; *Impulse* 1984; *Fletch* 1985; *Cannonball Fever* 1989; *Buried Alive* 1990; *Solar Crisis* 1990; *Drop Dead Fred* 1991; *Sometimes They Come Back* 1991; *Quicksand: No Escape* 1992; *Black Sheep* 1996; *The Story of Us* 1999; *Van Wilder: Party Liaison* 2002
Mathews, Carole (1920–) *The Great Gatsby* 1949; *Meet Me at the Fair* 1952; *Port of Hell* 1954; *Assignment Redhead* 1956; *Showdown at Boot Hill* 1958; *Look in Any Window* 1961; *Tender Is the Night* 1961
Mathews, Dorothy (1912–1977) *A Girl in Every Port* 1928; *Doorway to Hell* 1931
Mathews, George (1911–1984) *Up in Arms* 1944; *The Great John L* 1945; *Last of the Comanches* 1952; *City beneath the Sea* 1953; *The Great Diamond Robbery* 1953; *The Man with the Golden Arm* 1955; *Heller in Pink Tights* 1960
Mathews, Kerwin (1926–) *Five against the House* 1955; *The Garment Jungle* 1957; *The Last Blitzkrieg* 1958; *The 7th Voyage of Sinbad* 1958; *The Three Worlds of Gulliver* 1959; *The Devil at Four o'Clock* 1961; *The Pirates of Blood River* 1961; *Jack the Giant Killer* 1962; *Maniac* 1962; *Shadow of Evil* 1964; *Battle beneath the Earth* 1968; *Barquero* 1970
Mathews, Thom (1965–) *Return of the Living Dead* 1984; *Dangerously Close* 1986; *Friday the 13th Part VI: Jason Lives* 1986; *Down Twisted* 1987; *Return of the Living Dead Part II* 1988; *Born to Ride* 1991
Mathias, Bob (1930–) *The Bob Mathias Story* 1954; *China Doll* 1958
Mathis, Milly (1901–1965) *César* 1936; *Un Carnet de Bal* 1937; *Topaze* 1951
Mathis, Samantha (1970–) *Pump Up the Volume* 1990; *FernGully: the Last Rainforest* 1992; *This Is My Life* 1992; *The Music of Chance* 1993; *Super Mario Bros* 1993; *The Thing Called Love* 1993; *Little Women* 1994; *The American President* 1995; *How to Make an American Quilt* 1995; *Jack & Sarah* 1995; *Broken Arrow* 1996; *American Psycho* 2000; *Attraction* 2000; *The Simian Line* 2000; *The Punisher* 2004
Mathou, Jacques *Betty Blue* 1986; *Delicatessen* 1990; *The Hairdresser's Husband* 1990
Mativo, Kyalo *Roar* 1981; *Baby: Secret of the Lost Legend* 1985
Matlin, Marlee (1965–) *Children of a Lesser God* 1986; *Walker* 1987; *The Linguini Incident* 1991; *Hear No Evil* 1993; *It's My Party* 1996; *In Her Defense* 1998; *What the #$*! Do We Know!?* 2004
Matondkar, Urmila (1973–) *Rangeela* 1995; *Bhoot* 2003; *Tehzeeb* 2003
Matshikiza, John *Dust* 1985; *Dust Devil* 1992
Matsubara, Chieko *Tokyo Drifter* 1966; *Dolls* 2002
Matsuo, Kayo (1943–) *Gate of Flesh* 1964; *Baby Cart at the River Styx* 1972
Matsuoka, Shunsuke (1972–) *Freezer* 2000; *A Tender Place* 2001
Matsushima, Nanako *Ring* 1997; *Ring 2* 1998
Mattei, Danilo *aka* **Redford, Bryan** *In the Name of the Pope King* 1977; *Cannibal Ferox* 1981
Mattes, Eva (1954–) *The Bitter Tears of Petra von Kant* 1972; *Jail Bait* 1972; *Stroszek* 1977; *In a Year of 13 Moons* 1978; *Woyzeck* 1978; *David* 1979; *Now or Never* 1986; *The Promise* 1994; *Enemy at the Gates* 2001
Matthau, Walter *aka* **Matuschanskavasky, Walter** (1920–2000) *The Indian Fighter* 1955; *The Kentuckian* 1955; *Bigger than Life* 1956; *A Face in the Crowd* 1957; *Slaughter on Tenth Avenue* 1957; *King Creole* 1958; *Onionhead* 1958; *Ride a Crooked Trail* 1958; *Voice in the Mirror* 1958; *Gangster Story* 1959; *Strangers When We Meet* 1960; *Lonely Are the Brave* 1962; *Who's Got the Action?* 1962; *Charade* 1963; *Island of Love* 1963; *Ensign Pulver* 1964; *Fail-Safe* 1964; *Goodbye Charlie* 1964; *Mirage* 1965; *The Fortune Cookie* 1966; *A Guide for the Married Man* 1967; *Candy* 1968; *The Odd Couple* 1968; *The Secret Life of an American Wife* 1968; *Cactus Flower* 1969; *Hello, Dolly!* 1969; *Kotch* 1971; *A New Leaf* 1971; *Plaza Suite* 1971; *Pete 'n' Tillie* 1972; *Charley Varrick* 1973; *The Laughing Policeman* 1973; *Earthquake* 1974; *The Front Page* 1974; *The Taking of Pelham One Two Three* 1974; *The Sunshine Boys* 1975; *The Bad News Bears* 1976; *California Suite* 1978; *Casey's Shadow* 1978; *House Calls* 1978; *Hopscotch* 1980; *Little Miss Marker* 1980; *Buddy Buddy* 1981; *First Monday in October* 1981; *I Ought to Be in Pictures* 1982; *The Survivors* 1983; *Movers and Shakers* 1985; *Pirates* 1986; *The Couch Trip* 1988; *JFK* 1991; *Dennis* 1993; *Grumpy Old Men* 1993; *IQ* 1994; *The Grass Harp* 1995; *Grumpier Old Men* 1996; *I'm Not Rappaport* 1996; *Out to Sea* 1997; *The Marriage Fool* 1998; *The Odd Couple II* 1998; *Hanging Up* 2000
Matthes, Ulrich (1959–) *Wintersleepers* 1997; *Downfall* 2004
Matthews, A E (1869–1960) *Men Are Not Gods* 1936; *Quiet Wedding* 1940; *The Life and Death of Colonel Blimp* 1943; *Just William's Luck* 1947; *William at the Circus* 1948; *The Chiltern Hundreds* 1949; *Laughter in Paradise* 1951; *Made in Heaven* 1952; *Something Money Can't Buy* 1952; *The Weak and the Wicked* 1953; *Happy Ever After* 1954; *Jumping for Joy* 1955; *Carry On Admiral* 1957; *Inn for Trouble* 1960
Matthews, Al *Rough Cut* 1980; *Aliens* 1986; *Riders of the Storm* 1986
Matthews, Christopher *The Scars of Dracula* 1970; *Blind Terror* 1971
Matthews, Dakin *The Fabulous Baker Boys* 1989; *Formula for Death* 1995
Matthews, Francis (1927–) *Bhowani Junction* 1956; *The Revenge of Frankenstein* 1958; *The Pursuers* 1961; *Dracula – Prince of Darkness* 1965; *Rasputin, the Mad Monk* 1965; *Just like a Woman* 1966; *Crossplot* 1969
Matthews, Jessie (1907–1981) *Friday the Thirteenth* 1933; *The Good Companions* 1933; *Waltzes from Vienna* 1933; *Evergreen* 1934; *First a Girl* 1935; *It's Love Again* 1936; *Gangway* 1937; *Head over Heels in Love* 1937; *Climbing High* 1938; *Sailing Along* 1938; *Forever and a Day* 1943; *tom thumb* 1958
Matthews, Lester (1900–1975) *The Raven* 1935; *Crack-Up* 1936; *Thank You, Jeeves* 1936; *Rulers of the Sea* 1939; *The Biscuit Eater* 1940; *The Pied Piper* 1942; *Two O'Clock Courage* 1945; *Rogues of Sherwood Forest* 1950; *Lorna Doone* 1951
Matthews, Liesel (1984–) *A Little Princess* 1995; *Air Force One* 1997
Mattox, Matt (1921–) *Seven Brides for Seven Brothers* 1954; *Pepe* 1960
Mattson, Robin (1956–) *Namu, the Killer Whale* 1966; *Return to Macon County* 1975; *Wolf Lake* 1979
Mature, Victor (1915–1999) *The Housekeeper's Daughter* 1939; *No, No, Nanette* 1940; *One Million BC* 1940; *I Wake Up Screaming* 1941; *The Shanghai Gesture* 1941; *Footlight Serenade* 1942; *My Gal Sal* 1942; *Seven Days' Leave* 1942; *Song of the Islands* 1942; *My Darling Clementine* 1946; *Kiss of Death* 1947; *Moss Rose* 1947; *Cry of the City* 1948; *Fury at Furnace Creek* 1948; *Easy Living* 1949; *Samson and Delilah* 1949; *Stella* 1950; *Wabash Avenue* 1950; *Androcles and the Lion* 1952; *The Las Vegas Story* 1952; *Million Dollar Mermaid* 1952; *Affair with a Stranger* 1953; *The Glory Brigade* 1953; *The Robe* 1953; *Betrayed* 1954; *Dangerous Mission* 1954; *Demetrius and the Gladiators* 1954; *The Egyptian* 1954; *Chief Crazy Horse* 1955; *The Last Frontier* 1955; *Violent Saturday* 1955; *Safari* 1956; *Zarak* 1956; *Interpol* 1957; *China Doll* 1958; *No Time to Die* 1958; *The Bandit of Zhobe* 1959; *The Big Circus* 1959; *Escort West* 1959; *Hannibal* 1959; *Timbuktu* 1959; *After the Fox* 1966; *Head* 1968; *Every Little Crook and Nanny* 1972; *Firepower* 1979
Matuszak, John (1950–1989) *Caveman* 1981; *The Ice Pirates* 1984; *The Goonies* 1985; *One Man Force* 1989
Mauban, Maria (1924–) *Cage of Gold* 1950; *Cairo Road* 1950; *Journey to Italy* 1953; *The Spacemen of St Tropez* 1978
Mauch, Billy (1924–) *Anthony Adverse* 1936; *The Prince and the Pauper* 1937
Maude-Roxby, Roddy (1930–) *The Aristocats* 1970; *Shadowlands* 1993
Maughan, Monica (1938–) *Annie's Coming Out* 1984; *Cactus* 1986; *Golden Braid* 1991; *Road to Nhill* 1997
Maur-Thorp, Sarah *Edge of Sanity* 1989; *River of Death* 1989
Maura, Carmen (1945–) *Pepi, Luci, Bom…* 1980; *Dark Habits* 1983; *What Have I Done to Deserve This?* 1984; *Matador* 1986; *The Law of Desire* 1987; *Women on the Verge of a Nervous Breakdown* 1988; *Ay, Carmela!* 1990; *How to Be a Woman and Not Die in the Attempt* 1991; *Le Bonheur Est dans le Pré* 1995; *Alice et Martin* 1998; *Lisboa* 1999; *La Comunidad* 2000; *Valentín* 2002
Maurey, Nicole (1925–) *Diary of a Country Priest* 1950; *Little Boy Lost* 1953; *Secret of the Incas* 1954; *The Constant Husband* 1955; *The Bold and the Brave* 1956; *Rogue's Yarn* 1956; *Me and the Colonel* 1958; *The House of the Seven Hawks* 1959; *The Jayhawkers* 1959; *The Scapegoat* 1959; *High Time* 1960; *His and Hers* 1960; *Don't Bother to Knock* 1961; *The Day of the Triffids* 1962; *The Very Edge* 1962
Maurier, Claire (1929–) *The 400 Blows* 1959; *La Cage aux Folles* 1978; *Un Air de Famille* 1996
Maurus, Gerda (1903–1968) *Spies* 1928; *The Woman in the Moon* 1929
Maury, Jean-Louis *Ophélia* 1962; *Madame Bovary* 1991
Maximova, Antonina (1916–1986) *Othello* 1955; *Ballad of a Soldier* 1959
Maxwell Conover, Theresa (1884–1968) *The Age of Innocence* 1934; *Chained* 1934
Maxwell, Edwin (1886–1948) *The Taming of the Shrew* 1929; *Inspiration* 1931; *Tiger Shark* 1932; *Mystery of the Wax Museum* 1933; *The Blue Bird* 1940; *The Great Moment* 1944
Maxwell, Frank (1916–2004) *Lonelyhearts* 1958; *Ada* 1961; *The Intruder* 1961; *The Haunted Palace* 1963; *Mr Majestyk* 1974
Maxwell, James (1929–1995) *Girl on Approval* 1962; *Private Potter* 1963; *One Day in the Life of Ivan Denisovich* 1971
Maxwell, John *The Prowler* 1951; *The Bigamist* 1953
Maxwell, Lois (1927–) *The Dark Past* 1948; *Mantrap* 1952; *Women of Twilight* 1952; *Passport to Treason* 1956; *Satellite in the Sky* 1956; *Kill Me Tomorrow* 1957; *Time without Pity* 1957; *Come Fly with Me* 1962; *Dr No* 1962; *From Russia with Love* 1963; *The Haunting* 1963; *Goldfinger* 1964; *Thunderball* 1965; *Operation Kid Brother* 1967; *You Only Live Twice* 1967; *On Her Majesty's Secret Service* 1969; *The Adventurers* 1970; *Diamonds Are Forever* 1971; *Endless Night* 1971; *Live and Let Die* 1973; *The Man with the Golden Gun* 1974; *The Spy Who Loved Me* 1977; *Moonraker* 1979; *For Your Eyes Only* 1981; *Octopussy* 1983; *A View to a Kill* 1985
Maxwell, Marilyn (1921–1972) *Stand by for Action* 1942; *Salute to the Marines* 1943; *Swing Fever* 1943; *Lost in a Harem* 1944; *Three Men in White* 1944; *High Barbaree* 1947; *Summer Holiday* 1948; *Champion* 1949; *Key to the City* 1950; *The Lemon Drop Kid* 1951; *East of Sumatra* 1953; *Military Policeman* 1953; *New York Confidential* 1955; *Rock-a-Bye Baby* 1958; *Critic's Choice* 1963; *Arizona Bushwhackers* 1968
Maxwell, Paul (1921–1991) *Submarine Seahawk* 1959; *Shadow of Fear* 1963; *City of Fear* 1965; *It!* 1966; *Madame Sin* 1972; *Baxter* 1973
Maxwell, Roberta (1944–) *Rich Kids* 1979; *Popeye* 1980; *Psycho III* 1986; *Last Night* 1998
May, Anthony (1946–) *No Blade of Grass* 1970; *The Triple Echo* 1972
May, Elaine (1932–) *Enter Laughing* 1967; *Luv* 1967; *A New Leaf* 1971; *California Suite* 1978; *In the Spirit* 1990; *Small Time Crooks* 2000
May, Jack (1922–1997) *Trog* 1970; *The Man Who Would Be King* 1975
May, Jodhi (1975–) *A World Apart* 1987; *Eminent Domain* 1991; *The Last of the Mohicans* 1992; *Sister My Sister* 1994; *The Scarlet Letter* 1995; *The Gambler* 1997; *The Woodlanders* 1997; *The House of Mirth* 2000; *The Escapist* 2002; *On a Clear Day* 2005
May, Mathilda (1965–) *Letters to an Unknown Lover* 1985; *Lifeforce* 1985; *Le Cri du Hibou* 1987; *Naked Tango* 1990; *Becoming Colette* 1991; *Scream of Stone* 1991; *The Tit and the Moon* 1994; *The Jackal* 1997
Mayall, Rik (1958–) *An American Werewolf in London* 1981; *Shock Treatment* 1981; *Whoops Apocalypse* 1986; *Eat the Rich* 1987; *Drop Dead Fred* 1991; *Carry On Columbus* 1992; *Little Noises* 1992; *The Princess and the Goblin* 1992; *Remember Me?* 1996; *Bring Me the Head of Mavis Davis* 1997; *Guest House Paradiso* 1999; *A Monkey's Tale* 1999; *Merlin the Return* 2000; *Churchill: the Hollywood Years* 2004; *Valiant* 2005
Mayama, Miko *Impasse* 1969; *That Man Bolt* 1973
Mayehoff, Eddie (1911–1992) *The Stooge* 1951; *That's My Boy* 1951; *Military Policeman* 1953; *Artists and Models* 1955; *How to Murder Your Wife* 1965; *Luv* 1967
Mayhew, Peter (1944–) *Star Wars Episode IV: a New Hope* 1977; *Star Wars Episode V: the Empire Strikes Back* 1980; *Star Wars Episode VI: Return of the Jedi* 1983; *Star Wars Episode III: Revenge of the Sith* 2005
Maynard, Bill (1928–) *Till Death Us Do Part* 1968; *A Hole Lot of Trouble* 1969; *Carry On Loving* 1970; *Carry On at Your Convenience* 1971; *Carry On Henry* 1971; *Adolf Hitler – My Part in His Downfall* 1972; *Bless This House* 1972; *Carry On Matron* 1972; *Steptoe and Son Ride Again* 1973; *Confessions of a Window Cleaner* 1974; *Confessions of a Pop Performer* 1975; *Confessions of a Driving Instructor* 1976; *Robin and Marian* 1976; *Confessions from a Holiday Camp* 1977; *It Shouldn't Happen to a Vet* 1979; *Oddball Hall* 1990
Maynard, Mimi *Hawmps* 1976; *False Identity* 1990
Mayne, Ferdy *aka* **Mayne, Ferdinand** (1916–1998) *The Blue Parrot* 1953; *Beautiful Stranger* 1954; *Gentlemen Marry Brunettes* 1955; *The Big Chance* 1957; *The Fearless Vampire Killers* 1967; *The Vampire Lovers* 1970; *The Walking Stick* 1970; *Eagle in a Cage* 1971; *When Eight Bells Toll* 1971; *Frightmare* 1981; *The Black Stallion Returns* 1983; *The Secret Diary of Sigmund Freud* 1984; *Pirates* 1986; *Knight Moves* 1992; *Benefit of the Doubt* 1993
Mayniel, Juliette (1936–) *Les Cousins* 1959; *Eyes without a Face* 1959; *The Trojan War* 1961; *Bluebeard* 1962; *Ophélia* 1962
Mayo, Alfredo (1911–1985) *The Hunt* 1966; *Peppermint Frappé* 1967; *The Bell of Hell* 1973
Mayo, Virginia (1920–2005) *Jack London* 1944; *The Princess and the Pirate* 1944; *Wonder Man* 1945; *The Best Years of Our Lives* 1946; *The Kid from Brooklyn* 1946; *Out of the Blue* 1947; *The Secret Life of Walter Mitty* 1947; *A Song Is Born* 1948; *Always Leave Them Laughing* 1949; *Colorado Territory* 1949; *Red Light* 1949; *White Heat* 1949; *Backfire* 1950; *The Flame and the Arrow* 1950; *The West Point Story* 1950; *Along the Great Divide* 1951; *Captain Horatio Hornblower RN* 1951; *Painting the Clouds with Sunshine* 1951; *The Iron Mistress* 1952; *She's Working Her Way through College* 1952; *Devil's Canyon* 1953; *South Sea Woman* 1953; *King Richard and the Crusaders* 1954; *The Silver Chalice* 1954; *Pearl of the South Pacific* 1955; *Congo Crossing* 1956; *Great Day in the Morning* 1956; *The Proud Ones* 1956; *The Big Land* 1957; *The Story of Mankind* 1957; *The Tall Stranger* 1957; *Westbound* 1959; *Jet over the Atlantic* 1960; *Castle of Evil* 1966; *Evil Spirits* 1991; *The Man Next Door* 1998
Mayron, Gale *Heart of Midnight* 1988; *The Feud* 1989
Mayron, Melanie (1952–) *Harry and Tonto* 1974; *Gable and Lombard* 1976; *The Great Smokey Roadblock* 1977; *You Light Up My Life* 1977; *Girlfriends* 1978; *Heartbeeps* 1981; *Missing* 1981; *Checking Out* 1988; *Sticky Fingers* 1988; *My Blue Heaven* 1990
Maza, Bob (1939–2000) *The Fringe Dwellers* 1985; *Ground Zero* 1987; *Reckless Kelly* 1993; *Back of Beyond* 1995
Mazar, Debi (1964–) *Little Man Tate* 1991; *Beethoven's 2nd* 1993; *Money for Nothing* 1993; *So I Married an Axe Murderer* 1993; *Batman Forever* 1995; *Empire Records* 1995; *Girl 6* 1996; *Space Truckers* 1996; *Nowhere* 1997; *She's So Lovely* 1997; *David and Lisa* 1998; *Hush* 1998; *The Insider* 1999; *The Tuxedo* 2002
Mazur, Monet (1976–) *Just Married* 2003; *Torque* 2003; *Monster-in-Law* 2005

Mazurki, Mike (1907–1990) *The Shanghai Gesture* 1941; *Farewell My Lovely* 1944; *Abbott and Costello in Hollywood* 1945; *Dick Tracy* 1945; *Nightmare Alley* 1947; *Sinbad the Sailor* 1947; *The Noose Hangs High* 1948; *Relentless* 1948; *Neptune's Daughter* 1949; *Dark City* 1950; *Night and the City* 1950; *Ten Tall Men* 1951; *Blood Alley* 1955; *Kismet* 1955; *Hell Ship Mutiny* 1957; *Pocketful of Miracles* 1961; *Donovan's Reef* 1963; *7 Women* 1966; *Challenge to Be Free* 1972
Mazurowna, Ernestine *Jean de Florette* 1986; *Manon des Sources* 1986
Mazursky, Paul (1930–) *Fear and Desire* 1953; *Deathwatch* 1966; *Alex in Wonderland* 1970; *Blume in Love* 1973; *A Star Is Born* 1976; *A Man, a Woman and a Bank* 1979; *Punchline* 1988; *Scenes from the Class Struggle In Beverly Hills* 1989; *Scenes from a Mall* 1991; *Love Affair* 1994; *Miami Rhapsody* 1995; *Faithful* 1996; *Touch* 1996; *2 Days in the Valley* 1996; *Antz* 1998; *Why Do Fools Fall in Love?* 1998; *Big Shot's Funeral* 2001
Mazzarella, Marcello *Time Regained* 1999; *Christie Malry's Own Double-Entry* 2000
Mazzello, Joseph (1983–) *Jersey Girl* 1992; *Radio Flyer* 1992; *Jurassic Park* 1993; *Shadowlands* 1993; *The River Wild* 1994; *The Cure* 1995; *Three Wishes* 1995; *Star Kid* 1997; *Simon Birch* 1998
Meacham, Anne (1925–) *Lilith* 1964; *Seizure* 1974
Mead, Courtland (1987–) *Lake Consequence* 1992; *Dragonworld* 1994; *Recess: School's Out* 2001
Mead, Taylor *Lonesome Cowboys* 1968; *Coffee and Cigarettes* 2003
Meade, Julia (1928–) *Pillow Talk* 1959; *Tammy Tell Me True* 1961; *Zotz* 1962
Meadows, Audrey (1922–1996) *That Touch of Mink* 1962; *Take Her, She's Mine* 1963; *Rosie!* 1967
Meadows, Jayne (1920–) *Lady in the Lake* 1947; *Enchantment* 1948; *David and Bathsheba* 1951
Meadows, Shane (1972–) *Smalltime* 1996; *A Room for Romeo Brass* 1999; *Once upon a Time in the Midlands* 2002
Meadows, Stephen *The End of Innocence* 1990; *Night Eyes* 1990
Meadows, Tim (1961–) *The Ladies Man* 2000; *Mean Girls* 2004
Meaney, Colm (1953–) *Far and Away* 1992; *Under Siege* 1992; *The Snapper* 1993; *War of the Buttons* 1993; *The Road to Wellville* 1994; *The Englishman Who Went up a Hill, but Came down a Mountain* 1995; *Last of the High Kings* 1996; *The Van* 1996; *Con Air* 1997; *Noose* 1997; *Claire Dolan* 1998; *Four Days* 1999; *Mystery, Alaska* 1999; *This Is My Father* 1999; *interMission* 2003; *Blueberry* 2004; *Layer Cake* 2004
Means, Russell (1939–) *The Last of the Mohicans* 1992; *Pocahontas II: Journey to a New World* 1998; *Wind River* 1999; *Thomas and the Magic Railroad* 2000; *29 Palms* 2002
Meara, Anne (1929–) *The Out of Towners* 1970; *Nasty Habits* 1976; *The Longshot* 1986; *My Little Girl* 1986; *The Search for One-Eye Jimmy* 1996; *The Daytrippers* 1998; *Judy Berlin* 1999; *Get Well Soon* 2001; *Zoolander* 2001; *Like Mike* 2002
Meat Loaf aka **Aday, Meat Loaf** (1948–) *The Rocky Horror Picture Show* 1975; *Americathon* 1979; *Roadie* 1980; *Motorama* 1991; *Leap of Faith* 1992; *Black Dog* 1998; *Everything That Rises* 1998; *The Mighty* 1998; *Crazy in Alabama* 1999; *Fight Club* 1999; *The Ballad of Lucy Whipple* 2001; *The 51st State* 2001; *Focus* 2001
Mechlowicz, Scott (1981–) *EuroTrip* 2004; *Mean Creek* 2004
Mechoso, Julio Oscar *Virus* 1998; *Assassination Tango* 2002
Medford, Kay (1914–1980) *Guilty Bystander* 1950; *Jamboree* 1957; *Girl of the Night* 1960; *The Rat Race* 1960; *Ensign Pulver* 1964; *The Busy Body* 1967; *Angel in My Pocket* 1968; *Funny Girl* 1968
Medin, Harriet aka **White, Harriet** *Paisà* 1946; *The Horrible Dr Hichcock* 1962; *The Spectre* 1963
Medina, Ofelia (1950–) *The Big Fix* 1978; *Wall of Silence* 1993
Medina, Patricia (1920–) *Don't Take It to Heart* 1944; *The Foxes of Harrow* 1947; *Moss Rose* 1947; *The Fighting O'Flynn* 1948; *Children of Chance* 1949; *Francis* 1949; *Abbott and Costello in the Foreign Legion* 1950; *The Jackpot* 1950; *Valentino* 1951; *Botany Bay* 1952; *Desperate Search* 1952; *The Black Knight* 1954; *Phantom of the Rue Morgue* 1954; *Confidential Report* 1955; *The Beast of Hollow Mountain* 1956; *Stranger at My Door* 1956; *The Battle of the V1* 1958; *The Killing of Sister George* 1968; *Latitude Zero* 1969
Medrano, Frank *Amongst Friends* 1993; *Telling You* 1998
Medvedev, Vadim (1929–1988) *Hamlet* 1964; *Vassa* 1983
Medwin, Michael (1923–) *The Courtneys of Curzon Street* 1947; *Another Shore* 1948; *Night Beat* 1948; *Trottie True* 1949; *Someone at the Door* 1950; *Miss Robin Hood* 1952; *The Oracle* 1952; *The Intruder* 1953; *Spaceways* 1953; *Bang! You're Dead* 1954; *The Teckman Mystery* 1954; *Above Us the Waves* 1955; *Doctor at Sea* 1955; *A Man on the Beach* 1955; *Charley Moon* 1956; *Checkpoint* 1956; *A Hill in Korea* 1956; *Doctor at Large* 1957; *The Steel Bayonet* 1957; *The Duke Wore Jeans* 1958; *The Heart of a Man* 1959; *Crooks Anonymous* 1962; *It's All Happening* 1963; *Night Must Fall* 1964; *Rattle of a Simple Man* 1964; *I've Gotta Horse* 1965; *The Sandwich Man* 1966; *A Countess from Hong Kong* 1967; *Scrooge* 1970; *The Jigsaw Man* 1984; *Hôtel du Paradis* 1986
Meehan, Tony (1942–) *The Young Ones* 1961; *Summer Holiday* 1962
Meek, Donald (1880–1946) *Mrs Wiggs of the Cabbage Patch* 1934; *Accent on Youth* 1935; *The Bride Comes Home* 1935; *The Gilded Lily* 1935; *Mark of the Vampire* 1935; *The Return of Peter Grimm* 1935; *Top Hat* 1935; *Village Tale* 1935; *The Whole Town's Talking* 1935; *And So They Were Married* 1936; *One Rainy Afternoon* 1936; *Pennies from Heaven* 1936; *Artists and Models* 1937; *Behind the Headlines* 1937; *Breakfast for Two* 1937; *Parnell* 1937; *The Toast of New York* 1937; *You're a Sweetheart* 1937; *The Adventures of Tom Sawyer* 1938; *Hold That Co-Ed* 1938; *The Housekeeper's Daughter* 1939; *Nick Carter, Master Detective* 1939; *Stagecoach* 1939; *The Ghost Comes Home* 1940; *The Man from Dakota* 1940; *My Little Chickadee* 1940; *Phantom Raiders* 1940; *The Return of Frank James* 1940; *Sky Murder* 1940; *Star Dust* 1940; *Babes on Broadway* 1941; *Come Live with Me* 1941; *Design for Scandal* 1941; *The Feminine Touch* 1941; *A Woman's Face* 1941; *Keeper of the Flame* 1942; *Tortilla Flat* 1942; *DuBarry Was a Lady* 1943; *They Got Me Covered* 1943; *Bathing Beauty* 1944; *State Fair* 1945; *Because of Him* 1946; *Magic Town* 1947
Meek, Jeffrey aka **Meek, Jeff** (1959–) *Perfume of the Cyclone* 1989; *Heart Condition* 1990
Meeker, George (1904–1984) *Four Sons* 1928; *Back Street* 1932; *The First Year* 1932; *Tess of the Storm Country* 1932; *Only Yesterday* 1933; *The Richest Girl in the World* 1934; *Murder on a Honeymoon* 1935; *Remember Last Night?* 1935; *History Is Made at Night* 1937; *Tarzan's Revenge* 1938; *Rough Riders' Roundup* 1939; *Come Out Fighting* 1945; *Docks of New York* 1945; *Mr Muggs Rides Again* 1945; *Twilight in the Sierras* 1950
Meeker, Ralph (1920–1988) *Teresa* 1951; *Glory Alley* 1952; *Somebody Loves Me* 1952; *Jeopardy* 1953; *The Naked Spur* 1953; *Big House, USA* 1955; *Kiss Me Deadly* 1955; *Battle Shock* 1956; *The Fuzzy Pink Nightgown* 1957; *Paths of Glory* 1957; *Run of the Arrow* 1957; *Ada* 1961; *The Dirty Dozen* 1967; *Gentle Giant* 1967; *The St Valentine's Day Massacre* 1967; *The Detective* 1968; *I Walk the Line* 1970; *The Anderson Tapes* 1971; *The Mind Snatchers* 1972; *The Food of the Gods* 1975; *The Alpha Incident* 1977; *Winter Kills* 1979
Megowan, Don (1922–1981) *The Creature Walks among Us* 1956; *The Werewolf* 1956; *Tarzan and the Valley of Gold* 1966
Meier, Armin *Mother Küsters Goes to Heaven* 1975; *Fear of Fear* 1976
Meier, Shane (1977–) *Andre* 1994; *Taken Away* 1996
Meighan, Thomas (1879–1936) *Male and Female* 1919; *Why Change Your Wife?* 1920; *The Racket* 1928
Meillon, John (1934–1989) *The Long and the Short and the Tall* 1960; *Offbeat* 1960; *Watch It, Sailor!* 1961; *Cairo* 1962; *Walkabout* 1970; *Sunstruck* 1972; *The Cars That Ate Paris* 1974; *The Picture Show Man* 1977; *Heatwave* 1981; *The Wild Duck* 1983; *"Crocodile" Dundee* 1986; *"Crocodile" Dundee II* 1988
Meineke, Eva-Maria aka **Meineke, Eva Maria** *Yesterday Girl* 1966; *Something for Everyone* 1970
Meintjes, Tertius *Jobman* 1990; *Friends* 1993
Meisel, Kurt (1912–1994) *The Odessa File* 1974; *Please Let the Flowers Live* 1986
Meiser, Edith (1898–1993) *It Grows on Trees* 1952; *Middle of the Night* 1959
Meisner, Günter (1928–1994) *Inside Out* 1975; *Roselyne and the Lions* 1989
Mejias, Isabelle *Unfinished Business* 1983; *Bay Boy* 1984; *Meatballs III: Summer Job* 1987; *Scanners II: The New Order* 1991
Melato, Mariangela (1941–) *The Working Class Goes to Heaven* 1971; *The Seduction of Mimi* 1972; *Swept Away... by an Unusual Destiny in the Blue Sea of August* 1974; *Moses* 1975; *So Fine* 1981
Melchior, Lauritz (1890–1973) *Thrill of a Romance* 1945; *Two Sisters from Boston* 1946; *This Time for Keeps* 1947
Meldrum, Wendel (1958–) *Beautiful Dreamers* 1990; *Sodbusters* 1994
Melford, Jack (1899–1972) *Command Performance* 1937; *Jump for Glory* 1937; *Hold My Hand* 1938
Melford, Jill (1934–) *A Stitch in Time* 1963; *The Vengeance of She* 1968
Melia, Joe (1935–) *Too Many Crooks* 1958; *Four in the Morning* 1965; *Modesty Blaise* 1966; *Oh! What a Lovely War* 1969; *The Wildcats of St Trinian's* 1980; *The Sign of Four* 1983
Melki, Gilbert *Would I Lie to You?* 1997; *[One] Cavale* 2002; *[Three] Après la Vie* 2002; *[Two] Un Couple Epatant* 2002; *Monsieur Ibrahim and the Flowers of the Koran* 2003; *Confidences Trop Intimes* 2004
Mell, Marisa (1939–1992) *French Dressing* 1964; *Casanova '70* 1965; *City of Fear* 1965; *Masquerade* 1965; *Danger: Diabolik* 1967; *Mahogany* 1975; *Casanova & Co* 1976; *Mad Dog Murderer* 1977
Mellish Jr, Fuller (1895–1930) *Applause* 1929; *Sarah and Son* 1930
Melly, Andrée (1932–) *Nowhere to Go* 1958; *Beyond the Curtain* 1960
Meloni, Christopher (1961–) *Bound* 1996; *Runaway Bride* 1999; *Harold & Kumar Get the Munchies* 2004
Melton, Frank (1907–1951) *Stand Up and Cheer!* 1934; *Second Chorus* 1940; *Pot o' Gold* 1941
Melton, Sid (1920–) *The Steel Helmet* 1951; *Lady Sings the Blues* 1972; *Sheila Levine Is Dead and Living in New York* 1975
Melville, Jean-Pierre (1917–1973) *A Bout de Souffle* 1959; *Two Men in Manhattan* 1959
Melville, Sam (1936–1989) *The Thomas Crown Affair* 1968; *Big Wednesday* 1978; *Twice Dead* 1988
Melvin, Murray (1932–) *A Taste of Honey* 1961; *HMS Defiant* 1962; *Kaleidoscope* 1966; *A Day in the Death of Joe Egg* 1971; *The Devils* 1971; *Gawain and the Green Knight* 1973; *Ghost Story* 1974; *The Emperor's New Clothes* 2001
Memmoli, George (1938–1985) *Phantom of the Paradise* 1974; *New York, New York* 1977; *Blue Collar* 1978
Mendelsohn, Ben (1969–) *The Year My Voice Broke* 1987; *Return Home* 1989; *The Big Steal* 1990; *Nirvana Street Murder* 1990; *Spotswood* 1991; *Cosi* 1996; *Idiot Box* 1996; *Mullet* 2001; *Black and White* 2002
Mendenhall, David (1971–) *Space Raiders* 1983; *Over the Top* 1987; *Streets* 1990
Mendes, Eva (1974–) *My Brother the Pig* 1999; *Once upon a Time in Mexico* 2003; *Out of Time* 2003; *Stuck on You* 2003; *2 Fast 2 Furious* 2003; *Hitch* 2005
Mendillo, Stephen *Lianna* 1983; *City of Hope* 1991; *Ethan Frome* 1993; *Lone Star* 1995
Mendonca, Maria Luisa (1970–) *The Three Marias* 2002; *Carandiru* 2003
Mendoza, Natalie *South Pacific* 2001; *The Descent* 2005
Mendoza, Victor Manuel aka **Mendoza, Victor** *Susana* 1951; *The Proud Ones* 1953; *Garden of Evil* 1954; *Cowboy* 1958; *The Wonderful Country* 1959
Menez, Bernard (1944–) *Day for Night* 1973; *Day for Night* 1973; *No Problem!* 1975
Menglet, Alex (1956–) *Georgia* 1988; *Holidays on the River Yarra* 1991
Menjou, Adolphe (1890–1963) *The Sheik* 1921; *The Three Musketeers* 1921; *A Woman of Paris* 1923; *The Marriage Circle* 1924; *Sinners in Silk* 1924; *Morocco* 1930; *Friends and Lovers* 1931; *The Front Page* 1931; *A Farewell to Arms* 1932; *Forbidden* 1932; *Morning Glory* 1933; *The Worst Woman in Paris?* 1933; *Easy to Love* 1934; *Little Miss Marker* 1934; *The Mighty Barnum* 1934; *Gold Diggers of 1935* 1935; *The Milky Way* 1936; *One in a Million* 1936; *Sing, Baby, Sing* 1936; *Café Metropole* 1937; *One Hundred Men and a Girl* 1937; *Stage Door* 1937; *A Star Is Born* 1937; *The Goldwyn Follies* 1938; *Letter of Introduction* 1938; *Thanks for Everything* 1938; *Golden Boy* 1939; *The Housekeeper's Daughter* 1939; *King of the Turf* 1939; *That's Right – You're Wrong* 1939; *A Bill of Divorcement* 1940; *Turnabout* 1940; *Road Show* 1941; *Roxie Hart* 1942; *Syncopation* 1942; *You Were Never Lovelier* 1942; *Sweet Rosie O'Grady* 1943; *Step Lively* 1944; *Heartbeat* 1946; *The Hucksters* 1947; *I'll Be Yours* 1947; *State of the Union* 1948; *Dancing in the Dark* 1949; *My Dream Is Yours* 1949; *To Please a Lady* 1950; *Across the Wide Missouri* 1951; *The Tall Target* 1951; *The Sniper* 1952; *Man on a Tightrope* 1953; *Timberjack* 1955; *The Ambassador's Daughter* 1956; *Bundle of Joy* 1956; *The Fuzzy Pink Nightgown* 1957; *Paths of Glory* 1957; *I Married a Woman* 1958; *Pollyanna* 1960
Menshikov, Oleg (1960–) *Dream Flights* 1983; *Burnt by the Sun* 1995; *Prisoner of the Mountains* 1996; *The Barber of Siberia* 1999; *East-West* 1999
Mensik, Vladimir (1924–1988) *A Blonde in Love* 1965; *All My Good Countrymen* 1968
Menzel, Jirí (1938–) *Capricious Summer* 1968; *The Cremator* 1968; *Elementary School* 1991
Menzer, Ernest *Bande à Part* 1964; *Made in USA* 1966
Menzies, Heather (1949–) *The Sound of Music* 1965; *Hawaii* 1966; *Ssssss* 1973; *Piranha* 1978
Menzies, Robert (1955–) *Cactus* 1986; *Tender Hooks* 1988; *Golden Braid* 1991; *Innocence* 2000
Merande, Doro (1892–1975) *Mr Belvedere Rings the Bell* 1951; *The Gazebo* 1959
Mercadier, Marthe (1928–) *Act of Love* 1953; *Obsession* 1954
Mercado, Hector (1949–) *Nomads* 1985; *Delta Force 2* 1990
Mercer, Beryl (1882–1939) *All Quiet on the Western Front* 1930; *Outward Bound* 1930; *East Lynne* 1931; *Inspiration* 1931; *The Miracle Woman* 1931; *The Public Enemy* 1931; *Smilin' Through* 1932; *Berkeley Square* 1933; *Cavalcade* 1933; *Supernatural* 1933; *Change of Heart* 1934; *The Little Minister* 1934; *The Richest Girl in the World* 1934; *The Hound of the Baskervilles* 1939
Mercer, Frances (1915–2000) *Annabel Takes a Tour* 1938; *The Mad Miss Manton* 1938; *Smashing the Rackets* 1938; *Vivacious Lady* 1938; *Beauty for the Asking* 1939; *Piccadilly Incident* 1946
Mercer, Mae *The Beguiled* 1971; *Dirty Harry* 1971
Mercer, Marian (1935–) *Sammy Stops the World* 1978; *The Cracker Factory* 1979; *Out on a Limb* 1992
Merchant, Veronica *'Til Death* 1993; *Deep Crimson* 1996
Merchant, Vivien (1929–1983) *Alfie* 1966; *Accident* 1967; *Alfred the Great* 1969; *Under Milk Wood* 1971; *Frenzy* 1972; *The Offence* 1972; *A War of Children* 1972; *The Homecoming* 1973; *The Maids* 1974; *The Man in the Iron Mask* 1977
Mercier, Michèle (1939–) *Shoot the Pianist* 1960; *Fury at Smugglers Bay* 1961; *Goodbye Again* 1961; *L'Ainé des Ferchaux* 1963; *Black Sabbath* 1963; *A Global Affair* 1964; *Casanova '70* 1965; *The Oldest Profession* 1967; *You Can't Win 'em All* 1970; *Call of the Wild* 1972
Mercouri, Melina (1925–1994) *Stella* 1955; *The Gypsy and the Gentleman* 1958; *Where the Hot Wind Blows!* 1959; *Never on Sunday* 1960; *Phaedra* 1962; *The Victors* 1963; *Topkapi* 1964; *A Man Could Get Killed* 1966; *10:30 PM Summer* 1966; *Gaily, Gaily* 1969; *Once Is Not Enough* 1975; *Nasty Habits* 1976; *A Dream of Passion* 1978
Mercure, Jean (1909–1998) *Le Rouge et le Noir* 1954; *The Battle of Austerlitz* 1960
Mercure, Monique (1930–) *My Uncle Antoine* 1971; *Naked Lunch* 1991
Mercurio, Gus (1928–) *The Blue Lagoon* 1980; *Dead Man's Float* 1980; *Harlequin* 1980; *Turkey Shoot* 1981; *The Man from Snowy River* 1982; *"Crocodile" Dundee II* 1988; *Doing Time for Patsy Cline* 1997
Mercurio, Micole *Mask* 1985; *Gleaming the Cube* 1988; *Roe vs Wade* 1989; *Wrestling Ernest Hemingway* 1993; *While You Were Sleeping* 1995
Mercurio, Paul (1963–) *Strictly Ballroom* 1992; *Exit to Eden* 1994; *Back of Beyond* 1995; *Welcome to Woop Woop* 1997; *Kick* 1999
Meredith, Burgess (1908–1997) *The Scoundrel* 1935; *Winterset* 1936; *There Goes the Groom*

1937; *Idiot's Delight* 1939; *Of Mice and Men* 1939; *Castle on the Hudson* 1940; *Second Chorus* 1940; *That Uncertain Feeling* 1941; *Tom, Dick and Harry* 1941; *The Story of GI Joe* 1945; *Diary of a Chambermaid* 1946; *Magnificent Doll* 1946; *Mine Own Executioner* 1947; *On Our Merry Way* 1948; *The Gay Adventure* 1949; *The Man on the Eiffel Tower* 1949; *Joe Butterfly* 1957; *Advise and Consent* 1962; *The Cardinal* 1963; *Batman* 1966; *A Big Hand for a Little Lady* 1966; *Madame X* 1966; *Hurry Sundown* 1967; *Torture Garden* 1967; *Skidoo* 1968; *Stay Away, Joe* 1968; *Hard Contract* 1969; *Mackenna's Gold* 1969; *The Reivers* 1969; *There Was a Crooked Man...* 1970; *Such Good Friends* 1971; *The Man* 1972; *Golden Needles* 1974; *The Day of the Locust* 1975; *The Hindenburg* 1975; *92 in the Shade* 1975; *Burnt Offerings* 1976; *Rocky* 1976; *Golden Rendezvous* 1977; *The Great Georgia Bank Hoax* 1977; *The Sentinel* 1977; *The Amazing Captain Nemo* 1978; *Foul Play* 1978; *Magic* 1978; *Rocky II* 1979; *When Time Ran Out* 1980; *Clash of the Titans* 1981; *The Last Chase* 1981; *True Confessions* 1981; *Rocky III* 1982; *Twilight Zone: the Movie* 1983; *Santa Claus* 1985; *King Lear – Fear and Loathing* 1987; *Full Moon in Blue Water* 1988; *Oddball Hall* 1990; *Rocky V* 1990; *State of Grace* 1990; *Grumpy Old Men* 1993; *Camp Nowhere* 1994; *Grumpier Old Men* 1996

Meredith, Judi *aka* **Meredith, Judy** *aka* **Meredith, Judith** (1936–) *Wild Heritage* 1958; *Jack the Giant Killer* 1962; *The Night Walker* 1964; *The Raiders* 1964; *Dark Intruder* 1965; *Planet of Blood* 1966

Meredith, Lee (1947–) *The Producers* 1968; *The Sunshine Boys* 1975

Meredith, Madge (1921–) *Child of Divorce* 1946; *The Falcon's Adventure* 1946; *Trail Street* 1947

Merhar, Stanislas (1971–) *Dry Cleaning* 1997; *The Captive* 2000; *Almost Peaceful* 2002; *Merci Docteur Rey* 2002

Merhi, Jalal *TC 2000* 1993; *Expect No Mercy* 1995

Méril, Macha (1940–) *Who's Been Sleeping in My Bed?* 1963; *The Married Woman* 1964; *The Defector* 1966; *Belle de Jour* 1967; *Deep Red* 1975; *Chinese Roulette* 1976; *Robert et Robert* 1978; *Vagabond* 1985

Meritz, Michèle *Le Beau Serge* 1958; *Les Cousins* 1959

Merivale, John (1917–1990) *Caltiki, the Immortal Monster* 1959; *The List of Adrian Messenger* 1963; *Arabesque* 1966

Merivale, Philip (1886–1946) *Mr and Mrs Smith* 1941; *Lady for a Night* 1942; *This above All* 1942; *Lost Angel* 1943; *The Hour before the Dawn* 1944; *Nothing but Trouble* 1944; *Sister Kenny* 1946; *The Stranger* 1946

Meriwether, Lee (1935–) *Batman* 1966; *Namu, the Killer Whale* 1966; *Angel in My Pocket* 1968; *The Undefeated* 1969

Merkel, Una (1903–1986) *Abraham Lincoln* 1930; *Daddy Long Legs* 1931; *Dangerous Female* 1931; *Private Lives* 1931; *The Impatient Maiden* 1932; *Red-Headed Woman* 1932; *Blonde Bombshell* 1933; *42nd Street* 1933; *Reunion in Vienna* 1933; *The Secret of Madame Blanche* 1933; *Bulldog Drummond Strikes Back* 1934; *The Cat's Paw* 1934; *Evelyn Prentice* 1934; *The Merry Widow* 1934; *This Side of Heaven* 1934; *Broadway Melody of 1936* 1935; *Born to Dance* 1936; *Riffraff* 1936; *Speed* 1936; *Checkers* 1937; *Saratoga* 1937; *True Confession* 1937; *Destry Rides Again* 1939; *Four Girls in White* 1939; *Some Like It Hot* 1939; *The Bank Dick* 1940; *Road to Zanzibar* 1941; *The Mad Doctor of Market Street* 1942; *Twin Beds* 1942; *My Blue Heaven* 1950; *Golden Girl* 1951; *A Millionaire for Christy* 1951; *Rich, Young and Pretty* 1951; *The Merry Widow* 1952; *With a Song in My Heart* 1952; *I Love Melvin* 1953; *The Kentuckian* 1955; *Bundle of Joy* 1956; *The Girl Most Likely* 1957; *The Mating Game* 1959; *The Parent Trap* 1961; *Summer and Smoke* 1961; *Summer Magic* 1963

Merkerson, S Epatha *aka* **Merkinson, Epatha** (1952–) *She's Gotta Have It* 1986; *Terminator 2: Judgment Day* 1991; *A Place for Annie* 1994; *Radio* 2003

Merli, Adalberto Maria (1938–) *The Lady with Red Boots* 1974; *The Card Player* 2004

Merlin, Jan (1925–) *Running Wild* 1955; *Hell Bent for Leather* 1960; *Gunfight at Comanche Creek* 1964; *Take the Money and Run* 1969

Merlin, Joanna (1931–) *Love Child* 1982; *Baby It's You* 1983; *Mystic Pizza* 1988; *Class Action* 1991

Merlini, Marisa (1923–) *Bread, Love and Dreams* 1953; *Jealousy, Italian Style* 1970

Merman, Ethel (1908–1984) *Kid Millions* 1934; *We're Not Dressing* 1934; *The Big Broadcast of 1936* 1935; *Anything Goes* 1936; *Strike Me Pink* 1936; *Alexander's Ragtime Band* 1938; *Happy Landing* 1938; *Stage Door Canteen* 1943; *Call Me Madam* 1953; *There's No Business like Show Business* 1954; *It's a Mad Mad Mad Mad World* 1963; *Journey back to Oz* 1964; *Art of Love* 1965

Merr, Juliano (1957–) *Yom Yom* 1998; *Kippur* 2000

Merrall, Mary (1890–1976) *Love on the Dole* 1941; *Dead of Night* 1945; *Pink String and Sealing Wax* 1945; *Nicholas Nickleby* 1947; *They Made Me a Fugitive* 1947; *The Three Weird Sisters* 1948; *The Late Edwina Black* 1951; *It's Great to Be Young* 1956

Merrick, Doris *The Big Noise* 1944; *Child of Divorce* 1946; *The Counterfeiters* 1948

Merrill, Dina (1925–) *Desk Set* 1957; *A Nice Little Bank That Should Be Robbed* 1958; *Don't Give Up the Ship* 1959; *Operation Petticoat* 1959; *Butterfield 8* 1960; *The Sundowners* 1960; *The Young Savages* 1961; *The Courtship of Eddie's Father* 1963; *I'll Take Sweden* 1965; *Running Wild* 1973; *Caddyshack II* 1988; *True Colors* 1991; *Shattering the Silence* 1992; *Suture* 1993; *Open Season* 1995

Merrill, Gary (1915–1990) *Slattery's Hurricane* 1949; *Twelve O'Clock High* 1949; *All about Eve* 1950; *Where the Sidewalk Ends* 1950; *Another Man's Poison* 1951; *Decision before Dawn* 1951; *The Frogmen* 1951; *The Girl in White* 1952; *Phone Call from a Stranger* 1952; *The Human Jungle* 1954; *Witness to Murder* 1954; *Crash Landing* 1958; *The Missouri Traveler* 1958; *The Savage Eye* 1959; *The Wonderful Country* 1959; *The Great Impostor* 1960; *Mysterious Island* 1961; *The Pleasure of His Company* 1961; *A Girl Named Tamiko* 1962; *Cast a Giant Shadow* 1966; *Destination Inner Space* 1966; *Ride beyond Vengeance* 1966; *Clambake* 1967; *The Last Challenge* 1967; *The Power* 1968; *Huckleberry Finn* 1974; *Thieves* 1977

Merriman, Ryan (1983–) *Everything That Rises* 1998; *The Deep End of the Ocean* 1999; *Night Ride Home* 1999; *A Ring of Endless Light* 2002; *The Ring Two* 2004

Merrison, Clive (1945–) *The Sign of Four* 1983; *Rebecca's Daughters* 1991; *Heavenly Creatures* 1994

Merritt, George (1890–1977) *Dreyfus* 1931; *FP1* 1932; *The Ghost Camera* 1933; *Dr Syn* 1937; *Q Planes* 1939; *Spare a Copper* 1940; *I, Monster* 1971

Merritt, Theresa (1922–1998) *The Goodbye Girl* 1977; *The Wiz* 1978; *The Great Santini* 1979; *The Serpent and the Rainbow* 1987

Merrow, Jane (1941–) *The System* 1964; *Night of the Big Heat* 1967; *Assignment K* 1968; *The Lion in Winter* 1968; *Adam's Woman* 1970; *Hands of the Ripper* 1971; *Diagnosis: Murder* 1974; *The Appointment* 1981; *The Patricia Neal Story: an Act of Love* 1981

Merton, John (1901–1959) *In Old Montana* 1939; *Knight of the Plains* 1939

Mervyn, William (1912–1976) *Murder Ahoy* 1964; *The Railway Children* 1970; *The Ruling Class* 1972; *Up the Front* 1972

Mesquida, Roxane (1981–) *A Ma Soeur!* 2001; *Sex Is Comedy* 2002

Messemer, Hannes (1924–) *General Della Rovere* 1959; *The Defector* 1966

Messick, Don (1926–1997) *Charlotte's Web* 1973; *Jetsons: the Movie* 1990

Messier, Marc (1947–) *Portion d'Eternité* 1989; *Une Histoire Inventée* 1990

Messing, Debra (1968–) *A Walk in the Clouds* 1995; *McHale's Navy* 1997; *The Mothman Prophecies* 2001; *Hollywood Ending* 2002; *Along Came Polly* 2004; *Garfield* 2004; *The Wedding Date* 2004

Messinger, Jack *Stereo* 1969; *Crimes of the Future* 1970

Messner, Johnny (1970–) *Anacondas: the Hunt for the Blood Orchid* 2004; *The Whole Ten Yards* 2004

Mestral, Armand (1917–2000) *Gervaise* 1956; *Morgan the Pirate* 1960; *That Riviera Touch* 1966; *Uncle Benjamin* 1969

Metcalf, Laurie (1955–) *Desperately Seeking Susan* 1985; *Candy Mountain* 1987; *Making Mr Right* 1987; *Miles from Home* 1988; *Stars and Bars* 1988; *Uncle Buck* 1989; *Internal Affairs* 1990; *Pacific Heights* 1990; *JFK* 1991; *Mistress* 1992; *A Dangerous Woman* 1993; *Blink* 1994; *Leaving Las Vegas* 1995; *Dear God* 1996; *Scream 2* 1997; *Chicago Cab* 1998; *Runaway Bride* 1999; *Toy Story 2* 1999; *Treasure Planet* 2002

Metcalf, Mark (1946–) *The Heavenly Kid* 1985; *One Crazy Summer* 1986; *Hijacking Hollywood* 1997; *Drive Me Crazy* 1999

Method Man *aka* **Method Man** (1971–) *Belly* 1998; *Garden State* 2003; *Soul Plane* 2004

Methot, Mayo (1904–1951) *The Mind Reader* 1933; *Marked Woman* 1937

Methven, Eleanor *The Boxer* 1997; *Disco Pigs* 2001

Metrano, Art (1936–) *The All-American Boy* 1973; *Seven* 1979; *Going Ape!* 1981; *Breathless* 1983; *Police Academy 2: Their First Assignment* 1985; *Police Academy 3: Back in Training* 1986

Metzler, Jim (1955–) *Tex* 1982; *Do You Remember Love* 1985; *Hot to Trot* 1988; *976-EVIL* 1988; *Old Gringo* 1989; *Circuitry Man* 1990; *Delusion* 1991; *One False Move* 1992; *Plughead Rewired: Circuitry Man II* 1994; *Children of the Corn III: Urban Harvest* 1995; *Cadillac Ranch* 1996

Meurisse, Paul (1912–1979) *Les Diaboliques* 1954; *Lunch on the Grass* 1959; *La Vérité* 1960; *Le Deuxième Souffle* 1966; *L'Armée des Ombres* 1969; *Take It Easy* 1971

Meury, Anne-Laure *The Aviator's Wife* 1980; *My Girlfriend's Boyfriend* 1987

Mewes, Jason (1974–) *Clerks* 1994; *Mallrats* 1995; *Chasing Amy* 1996; *Dogma* 1999; *Jay and Silent Bob Strike Back* 2001

Meyer, Breckin (1974–) *Freddy's Dead: the Final Nightmare* 1991; *The Craft* 1996; *Prefontaine* 1997; *Dancer, Texas Pop 81* 1998; *54* 1998; *Road Trip* 2000; *Kate & Leopold* 2002; *Garfield* 2004

Meyer, David (1947–) *The Tempest* 1979; *Octopussy* 1983

Meyer, Dina (1968–) *Johnny Mnemonic* 1995; *DragonHeart* 1996; *Starship Troopers* 1997; *Poodle Springs* 1998; *Bats* 1999; *Stranger than Fiction* 1999; *Time Lapse* 2001; *Federal Protection* 2002; *Saw* 2004

Meyer, Emile *aka* **Meyer, Emil** (1910–1987) *The Big Night* 1951; *Shane* 1953; *The Human Jungle* 1954; *Riot in Cell Block 11* 1954; *Shield for Murder* 1954; *Silver Lode* 1954; *The Blackboard Jungle* 1955; *Man with the Gun* 1955; *Stranger on Horseback* 1955; *The Tall Men* 1955; *White Feather* 1955; *Baby Face Nelson* 1957; *The Lineup* 1958; *The Blue Knight* 1973

Meyer, Russ (1922–2004) *Cherry, Harry & Raquel* 1969; *Amazon Women on the Moon* 1987

Meyers, Ari (1969–) *Driving Me Crazy* 1991; *Dark Horse* 1992

Meylan, Gérard *Marius et Jeannette* 1997; *A la Place du Coeur* 1998; *A l'Attaque!* 2000; *La Ville Est Tranquille* 2000

Meyrink, Michelle (1962–) *Valley Girl* 1983; *Joy of Sex* 1984; *Revenge of the Nerds* 1984; *Real Genius* 1985; *Nice Girls Don't Explode* 1987; *Permanent Record* 1988

Mézières, Myriam (1947–) *Jonah Who Will Be 25 in the Year 2000* 1976; *Blueberry Hill* 1989; *The Diary of Lady M* 1992; *Mouth to Mouth* 1995; *Krámpack* 2000

Mezzogiorno, Giovanna (1974–) *The Last Kiss* 2001; *Facing Window* 2003

Mezzogiorno, Vittorio (1941–1994) *Three Brothers* 1980; *The Moon in the Gutter* 1983; *La Garce* 1984; *Scream of Stone* 1991; *Golem, the Spirit of Exile* 1992

Miano, Robert (1942–) *A Time to Die* 1991; *Storm Catcher* 1999; *The Stickup* 2001

Miao, Cora *Dim Sum: a Little Bit of Heart* 1985; *The Terroriser* 1986; *Eat a Bowl of Tea* 1989; *Life Is Cheap... but Toilet Paper Is Expensive* 1990

Miao, Nora *The Big Boss* 1971; *Fist of Fury* 1972; *The Way of the Dragon* 1973

Miao Tien (1925–2005) *The River* 1997; *The Hole* 1998; *What Time Is It There?* 2001; *Goodbye, Dragon Inn* 2003

Michael, Gertrude (1911–1964) *Ann Vickers* 1933; *I'm No Angel* 1933; *Bolero* 1934; *Cleopatra* 1934; *Murder at the Vanities* 1934; *Murder on the Blackboard* 1934; *The Last Outpost* 1935; *Till We Meet Again* 1936

Michael, Ralph (1907–1994) *For Those in Peril* 1943; *San Demetrio London* 1943; *Dead of Night* 1945; *Johnny Frenchman* 1945; *The Astonished Heart* 1949; *The Hasty Heart* 1949; *The Sound Barrier* 1952; *Private Potter* 1963; *Murder Most Foul* 1964; *House of Cards* 1968

Michaels, Beverly (1928–) *Crashout* 1955; *Women without Men* 1956

Michaels, Dolores (1933–2001) *April Love* 1957; *Time Limit* 1957; *The Wayward Bus* 1957; *The Fiend Who Walked the West* 1958; *Five Gates to Hell* 1959; *Warlock* 1959; *One Foot in Hell* 1960; *Battle at Bloody Beach* 1961; *Wizards of the Lost Kingdom* 1985

Michel, Marc *Le Trou* 1959; *Lola* 1960; *The Umbrellas of Cherbourg* 1964

Michele, Michael (1966–) *New Jack City* 1991; *The 6th Man* 1997; *The Substitute 2: School's Out* 1997; *Dark Blue* 2002; *How to Lose a Guy in 10 Days* 2003

Michell, Keith (1928–) *True as a Turtle* 1956; *Dangerous Exile* 1957; *The Gypsy and the Gentleman* 1958; *All Night Long* 1961; *The Hellfire Club* 1961; *Seven Seas to Calais* 1962; *House of Cards* 1968; *Prudence and the Pill* 1968; *Henry VIII and His Six Wives* 1972; *Grendel, Grendel, Grendel* 1981; *The Deceivers* 1988

Michelle, Ann (1952–) *House of Whipcord* 1974; *Young Lady Chatterley* 1976

Michie, John *Monk Dawson* 1997; *To Walk with Lions* 1999

Middlemass, Frank (1919–) *The Island* 1980; *Mrs Caldicot's Cabbage War* 2000

Middleton, Charles *aka* **Middleton, Charles B** (1879–1949) *The Miracle Woman* 1931; *Duck Soup* 1933; *White Woman* 1933; *Mrs Wiggs of the Cabbage Patch* 1934; *Murder at the Vanities* 1934; *Hopalong Cassidy* 1935; *Flash Gordon* 1936; *Blackmail* 1939; *The Flying Deuces* 1939; *The Oklahoma Kid* 1939; *Wyoming Outlaw* 1939

Middleton, Guy (1906–1973) *Keep Fit* 1937; *French without Tears* 1939; *Night Boat to Dublin* 1946; *A Man about the House* 1947; *Once upon a Dream* 1948; *One Night with You* 1948; *Snowbound* 1948; *Marry Me!* 1949; *No Place for Jennifer* 1949; *The Happiest Days of Your Life* 1950; *Laughter in Paradise* 1951; *Young Wives' Tale* 1951; *Albert, RN* 1953; *Conflict of Wings* 1953; *Malaga* 1954; *Break in the Circle* 1955; *Gentlemen Marry Brunettes* 1955; *A Yank in Ermine* 1955; *Passionate Summer* 1958

Middleton, Noelle (1926–) *Carrington VC* 1954; *Happy Ever After* 1954; *John and Julie* 1955; *A Yank in Ermine* 1955; *The Vicious Circle* 1957

Middleton, Ray (1907–1984) *Lady from Louisiana* 1941; *Lady for a Night* 1942; *I Dream of Jeanie* 1952; *The Road to Denver* 1955

Middleton, Robert (1911–1977) *The Big Combo* 1955; *Trial* 1955; *The Court Jester* 1956; *Friendly Persuasion* 1956; *Love Me Tender* 1956; *The Proud Ones* 1956; *Red Sundown* 1956; *The Lonely Man* 1957; *The Tarnished Angels* 1957; *Day of the Bad Man* 1958; *The Law and Jake Wade* 1958; *Career* 1959; *Don't Give Up the Ship* 1959; *The Great Impostor* 1960; *Hell Bent for Leather* 1960; *Gold of the Seven Saints* 1961; *Cattle King* 1963; *A Big Hand for a Little Lady* 1966; *The Cheyenne Social Club* 1970; *Which Way to the Front?* 1970

Midkiff, Dale (1959–) *Pet Sematary* 1989; *Love Potion No 9* 1992; *Visitors of the Night* 1995

Midler, Bette (1945–) *The Rose* 1979; *Jinxed!* 1982; *Down and Out in Beverly Hills* 1986; *Ruthless People* 1986; *Outrageous Fortune* 1987; *Beaches* 1988; *Big Business* 1988; *Oliver & Company* 1988; *Stella* 1990; *For the Boys* 1991; *Scenes from a Mall* 1991; *Gypsy* 1993; *Hocus Pocus* 1993; *The First Wives Club* 1996; *That Old Feeling* 1997; *Fantasia 2000* 1999; *Isn't She Great* 1999; *Drowning Mona* 2000; *What Women Want* 2001; *The Stepford Wives* 2004

Midwinter, Danny *Fast Food* 1998; *Out of Depth* 1998

Mifune, Toshiro (1920–1997) *Drunken Angel* 1948; *Stray Dog* 1949; *Rashomon* 1950; *The Idiot* 1951; *The Life of Oharu* 1952; *Samurai* 1954; *Seven Samurai* 1954; *I Live in Fear* 1955; *The Lower Depths* 1956; *Throne of Blood* 1957; *The Hidden Fortress* 1958; *The Bad Sleep Well* 1960; *The Important Man* 1961; *Yojimbo* 1961; *Sanjuro* 1962; *High and Low* 1963; *Red Beard* 1965; *Grand Prix* 1966; *Rebellion* 1967; *Hell in the Pacific* 1968; *Zatoichi Meets Yojimbo* 1970; *Red Sun* 1971; *Paper Tiger* 1974; *Battle of Midway* 1976; *1941* 1979; *Winter Kills* 1979; *The Bushido Blade* 1981; *The Challenge* 1982; *Shogun Warrior* 1991; *Shadow of the Wolf* 1992; *Picture Bride* 1994

Migenes-Johnson, Julia (1949–) *Carmen* 1984; *Mack the Knife* 1989
Migicovsky, Allan *Shivers* 1975; *A Man, a Woman and a Bank* 1979
Mihashi, Tatsuya (1923–2004) *The Burmese Harp* 1956; *High and Low* 1963; *None but the Brave* 1965; *What's Up, Tiger Lily?* 1966; *Tora! Tora! Tora!* 1970; *Dolls* 2002
Mihok, Dash (1974–) *William Shakespeare's Romeo + Juliet* 1996; *Telling You* 1998; *Whiteboys* 1999; *Dark Blue* 2002; *The Day after Tomorrow* 2004
Mikael, Ludmila (1947–) *The Sergeant* 1968; *Noce Blanche* 1989
Mikami, Hiroshi (1962–) *Tokyo Pop* 1988; *Circus Boys* 1989
Mikell, George *Beyond the Curtain* 1960; *The Primitives* 1962
Mikhalkov, Nikita (1945–) *Sibiriada* 1979; *A Station for Two* 1983; *Burnt by the Sun* 1995
Mikhelson, André *Desperate Moment* 1953; *The Intimate Stranger* 1956
Mikkelsen, Mads (1965–) *Bleeder* 1999; *Open Hearts* 2002; *Wilbur (Wants to Kill Himself)* 2002; *The Green Butchers* 2003; *Torremolinos 73* 2003
Miko, Izabella (1981–) *Coyote Ugly* 2000; *The Forsaken* 2001
Mikuni, Rentaro (1923–) *Samurai* 1954; *The Burmese Harp* 1956; *Harakiri* 1962; *Kwaidan* 1964; *Kwaidan* 1964; *The Profound Desire of the Gods* 1968; *Vengeance Is Mine* 1979; *Rikyu* 1989
Milan, Lita *The Left Handed Gun* 1958; *The Mobster* 1958; *Never Love a Stranger* 1958
Milano, Alyssa (1972–) *Commando* 1985; *Where the Day Takes You* 1992; *Double Dragon* 1994; *Embrace of the Vampire* 1994; *Glory Daze* 1995; *Poison Ivy 2* 1995; *Fear* 1996; *Pool Girl* 1997; *Buying the Cow* 2000; *Lady and the Tramp II: Scamp's Adventure* 2000; *Dickie Roberts: Former Child Star* 2003
Milburn, Oliver (1973–) *Loaded* 1994; *Sweet Angel Mine* 1996; *Me without You* 2001
Miles, Bernard (1907–1991) *The Love Test* 1935; *Midnight at Madame Tussaud's* 1936; *The Big Blockade* 1942; *In Which We Serve* 1942; *One of Our Aircraft Is Missing* 1942; *Tawny Pipit* 1944; *Carnival* 1946; *Great Expectations* 1946; *Fame Is the Spur* 1947; *Nicholas Nickleby* 1947; *The Guinea Pig* 1948; *Chance of a Lifetime* 1950; *Never Let Me Go* 1953; *The Man Who Knew Too Much* 1956; *Moby Dick* 1956; *Tiger in the Smoke* 1956; *Zarak* 1956; *Saint Joan* 1957; *The Smallest Show on Earth* 1957; *tom thumb* 1958; *Sapphire* 1959; *Heavens Above!* 1963; *Run Wild, Run Free* 1969
Miles, Joanna (1940–) *Bug* 1975; *The Ultimate Warrior* 1975; *Rosencrantz and Guildenstern Are Dead* 1990; *The Heart of Justice* 1992; *Barbara Taylor Bradford's Everything to Gain* 1996
Miles, Kevin (1920–) *The Cars That Ate Paris* 1974; *Boulevard of Broken Dreams* 1988
Miles, Peter (1938–2002) *Heaven Only Knows* 1947; *The Red Pony* 1949
Miles, Sarah (1941–) *Term of Trial* 1962; *The Ceremony* 1963; *The Servant* 1963; *Those Magnificent Men in Their Flying Machines* 1965; *Blowup* 1966; *I Was Happy Here* 1966; *Ryan's Daughter* 1970; *Lady Caroline Lamb* 1972; *The Hireling* 1973; *The Man Who Loved Cat Dancing* 1973; *Great Expectations* 1974; *The Sailor Who Fell from Grace with the Sea* 1976; *The Big Sleep* 1978; *Priest of Love* 1981; *Venom* 1981; *Ordeal by Innocence* 1984; *Steaming* 1985; *Hope and Glory* 1987; *White Mischief* 1987; *A Ghost in Monte Carlo* 1990; *The Silent Touch* 1992
Miles, Sherry *The Todd Killings* 1971; *The Velvet Vampire* 1971
Miles, Sylvia (1932–) *Psychomania* 1964; *Midnight Cowboy* 1969; *Who Killed Mary Whats'ername?* 1971; *Heat* 1972; *Farewell, My Lovely* 1975; *92 in the Shade* 1975; *The Great Scout & Cathouse Thursday* 1976; *Zero to Sixty* 1978; *Evil under the Sun* 1982; *No Big Deal* 1983; *Critical Condition* 1987; *Wall Street* 1987; *Crossing Delancey* 1988; *Spike of Bensonhurst* 1988; *She-Devil* 1989
Miles, Vera (1929–) *The Charge at Feather River* 1953; *Pride of the Blue Grass* 1954; *Tarzan's Hidden Jungle* 1955; *Wichita* 1955; *Autumn Leaves* 1956; *The Searchers* 1956; *23 Paces to Baker Street* 1956; *The Wrong Man* 1956; *Beau James* 1957; *Beyond This Place* 1959; *The FBI Story* 1959; *A Touch of Larceny* 1959; *Five Branded Women* 1960; *Psycho* 1960; *Back Street* 1961; *The Man Who Shot Liberty Valance* 1962; *Those Calloways* 1964; *A Tiger Walks* 1964; *Follow Me, Boys!* 1966; *One of Our Spies Is Missing* 1966; *Gentle Giant* 1967; *Kona Coast* 1968; *Sergeant Ryker* 1968; *Hellfighters* 1969; *The Wild Country* 1971; *Molly and Lawless John* 1972; *One Little Indian* 1973; *Runaway!* 1973; *The Castaway Cowboy* 1974; *Run for the Roses* 1978; *Brainwaves* 1982; *Psycho II* 1983; *The Initiation* 1984; *Separate Lives* 1995
Milford, Kim (1951–1988) *Corvette Summer* 1978; *Laserblast* 1978
Milford, Penelope (1948–) *Coming Home* 1978; *Take This Job and Shove It* 1981; *The Golden Seal* 1983; *The Burning Bed* 1984; *Heathers* 1989; *Cold Justice* 1991; *Henry: Portrait of a Serial Killer, Part II* 1996
Milian, Christina (1981–) *Love Don't Cost a Thing* 2003; *Man of the House* 2005
Milian, Tomas (1937–) *Boccaccio '70* 1961; *Time of Indifference* 1964; *Django Kill* 1967; *Face to Face* 1967; *A Fine Pair* 1968; *Beatrice Cenci* 1969; *The Last Movie* 1971; *The Evil Trap* 1975; *La Luna* 1979; *Winter Kills* 1979; *Identification of a Woman* 1982; *Cat Chaser* 1989; *Havana* 1990; *Revenge* 1990; *Fools Rush In* 1997
Military, Frank *Dead-Bang* 1989; *Everybody Wins* 1990
Miljan, John (1892–1960) *Free and Easy* 1930; *The Unholy Three* 1930; *Inspiration* 1931; *The Iron Man* 1931; *Susan Lenox: Her Fall and Rise* 1931; *Arsene Lupin* 1932; *The Beast of the City* 1932; *Emma* 1932; *Flesh* 1932; *The Kid from Spain* 1932; *The Rich Are Always with Us* 1932; *Blind Adventure* 1933; *The Mad Game* 1933; *What – No Beer?* 1933; *Belle of the Nineties* 1934; *The Plainsman* 1936; *Fast and Furious* 1939; *The Merry Monahans* 1944; *Mrs Mike* 1949
Millais, Hugh *Images* 1972; *The Dogs of War* 1980
Millan, Victor (1920–) *Terror in a Texas Town* 1958; *Boulevard Nights* 1979
Milland, Ray *aka* **Milland, Raymond** (1905–1986) *Piccadilly* 1929; *The Bachelor Father* 1931; *Blonde Crazy* 1931; *Payment Deferred* 1932; *Polly of the Circus* 1932; *Bolero* 1934; *Charlie Chan in London* 1934; *We're Not Dressing* 1934; *The Gilded Lily* 1935; *The Glass Key* 1935; *The Big Broadcast of 1937* 1936; *Next Time We Love* 1936; *Bulldog Drummond Escapes* 1937; *Easy Living* 1937; *Three Smart Girls* 1937; *Men with Wings* 1938; *Beau Geste* 1939; *French without Tears* 1939; *Arise, My Love* 1940; *The Doctor Takes a Wife* 1940; *Irene* 1940; *I Wanted Wings* 1941; *Skylark* 1941; *The Major and the Minor* 1942; *Reap the Wild Wind* 1942; *Star Spangled Rhythm* 1942; *The Crystal Ball* 1943; *Forever and a Day* 1943; *Lady in the Dark* 1944; *Till We Meet Again* 1944; *The Uninvited* 1944; *Kitty* 1945; *The Lost Weekend* 1945; *Ministry of Fear* 1945; *California* 1946; *The Well Groomed Bride* 1946; *Golden Earrings* 1947; *The Imperfect Lady* 1947; *Variety Girl* 1947; *The Big Clock* 1948; *Miss Tatlock's Millions* 1948; *Alias Nick Beal* 1949; *It Happens Every Spring* 1949; *Circle of Danger* 1950; *Copper Canyon* 1950; *A Life of Her Own* 1950; *A Woman of Distinction* 1950; *Close to My Heart* 1951; *Rhubarb* 1951; *Bugles in the Afternoon* 1952; *Something to Live For* 1952; *The Thief* 1952; *Jamaica Run* 1953; *Let's Do It Again* 1953; *Dial M for Murder* 1954; *The Girl in the Red Velvet Swing* 1955; *A Man Alone* 1955; *Lisbon* 1956; *Three Brave Men* 1956; *High Flight* 1957; *The River's Edge* 1957; *The Safecracker* 1958; *Panic in Year Zero* 1962; *The Premature Burial* 1962; *The Man with the X-Ray Eyes* 1963; *Quick, Let's Get Married* 1964; *Hostile Witness* 1968; *Company of Killers* 1970; *Love Story* 1970; *Embassy* 1972; *Frogs* 1972; *The Thing with Two Heads* 1972; *The House in Nightmare Park* 1973; *Terror in the Wax Museum* 1973; *Gold* 1974; *Escape to Witch Mountain* 1975; *The Swiss Conspiracy* 1975; *Aces High* 1976; *The Last Tycoon* 1976; *Slavers* 1977; *The Uncanny* 1977; *Oliver's Story* 1978; *A Game for Vultures* 1979; *Survival Run* 1979; *Starflight One* 1983
Millar, Marjie (1930–1970) *Money from Home* 1953; *About Mrs Leslie* 1954
Millard, Helene (1906–) *The Divorcee* 1930; *Break of Hearts* 1935; *The Biscuit Eater* 1940
Millay, Diana *Tarzan and the Great River* 1967; *Night of Dark Shadows* 1971
Miller, Andrew *Last of the Dogmen* 1995; *Cube* 1997
Miller, Ann (1919–2004) *New Faces of 1937* 1937; *Stage Door* 1937; *Radio City Revels* 1938; *Room Service* 1938; *You Can't Take It with You* 1938; *Too Many Girls* 1940; *Time Out for Rhythm* 1941; *Reveille with Beverly* 1943; *Easter Parade* 1948; *The Kissing Bandit* 1949; *On the Town* 1949; *Watch the Birdie* 1950; *Texas Carnival* 1951; *Two Tickets to Broadway* 1951; *Lovely to Look At* 1952; *Kiss Me Kate* 1953; *Deep in My Heart* 1954; *Hit the Deck* 1955; *The Opposite Sex* 1956; *Mulholland Drive* 2001
Miller, Barry (1958–) *Saturday Night Fever* 1977; *Voices* 1979; *The Chosen* 1981; *The Roommate* 1984; *The Journey of Natty Gann* 1985; *Peggy Sue Got Married* 1986; *The Pickle* 1993; *Flawless* 1999
Miller, Ben (1966–) *The Parole Officer* 2001; *Johnny English* 2003; *The Prince & Me* 2004
Miller, Carl (1893–1979) *The Kid* 1921; *A Woman of Paris* 1923
Miller, Colleen (1932–) *Four Guns to the Border* 1954; *Playgirl* 1954; *The Purple Mask* 1955; *The Rawhide Years* 1956; *Hot Summer Night* 1957; *Man in the Shadow* 1957; *The Night Runner* 1957; *Gunfight at Comanche Creek* 1964
Miller, David (1909–1992) *Attack of the Killer Tomatoes* 1978; *Gunpowder* 1985
Miller, Dean (1924–2004) *Because You're Mine* 1952; *Everything I Have Is Yours* 1952; *Skirts Ahoy!* 1952
Miller, Dennis (1953–) *Heatwave* 1981; *Frog Dreaming* 1985; *Madhouse* 1990; *Disclosure* 1994; *The Net* 1995; *Never Talk to Strangers* 1995; *Tales from the Crypt Presents: Bordello of Blood* 1996; *Murder at 1600* 1997; *Joe Dirt* 2001
Miller, Denny (1934–) *Tarzan, the Ape Man* 1959; *The Party* 1968; *Buck and the Preacher* 1972; *The Gravy Train* 1974
Miller, Dick *aka* **Miller, Richard** (1928–) *The Gunslinger* 1956; *Not of This Earth* 1956; *Rock All Night* 1957; *Sorority Girl* 1957; *War of the Satellites* 1958; *A Bucket of Blood* 1959; *The Terror* 1963; *The Trip* 1967; *Hollywood Boulevard* 1976; *Mr Billion* 1977; *Piranha* 1978; *Rock 'n' Roll High School* 1979; *Heartbeeps* 1981; *The Howling* 1981; *Get Crazy* 1983; *Gremlins* 1984; *The Terminator* 1984; *Explorers* 1985; *Armed Response* 1986; *Gremlins 2: the New Batch* 1990; *Batman: Mask of the Phantasm* 1993; *Shake, Rattle and Rock* 1994; *Tales from the Crypt: Demon Knight* 1995
Miller, Eve (1923–1973) *April in Paris* 1952; *The Big Trees* 1952
Miller, Glenn (1904–1944) *Sun Valley Serenade* 1941; *Orchestra Wives* 1942
Miller, Jason (1939–2001) *The Exorcist* 1973; *The Devil's Advocate* 1977; *The Ninth Configuration* 1979; *Monsignor* 1982; *Light of Day* 1987; *The Exorcist III* 1990
Miller, Joan (1910–1988) *Yield to the Night* 1956; *No Trees in the Street* 1958
Miller, John *The Girl in the Picture* 1956; *Ratcatcher* 1999
Miller, Jonny Lee (1972–) *Hackers* 1995; *Trainspotting* 1995; *Afterglow* 1997; *Regeneration* 1997; *Complicity* 1999; *Mansfield Park* 1999; *Plunkett & Macleane* 1999; *Dracula 2001* 2000; *Love, Honour and Obey* 2000; *The Escapist* 2002; *Mindhunters* 2003; *Melinda and Melinda* 2004
Miller, Joshua *Near Dark* 1987; *River's Edge* 1987; *Teen Witch* 1989
Miller, Ken *aka* **Miller, Kenny** (1931–) *I Was a Teenage Werewolf* 1957; *Attack of the Puppet People* 1958
Miller, Kristine (1929–) *Desert Fury* 1947; *I Walk Alone* 1947; *High Lonesome* 1950; *Thunder over Arizona* 1956
Miller, Larry (1953–) *Necessary Roughness* 1991; *Suburban Commando* 1991; *Frozen Assets* 1992; *Dream Lover* 1993; *Undercover Blues* 1993; *Corrina, Corrina* 1994; *The Favor* 1994; *The Nutty Professor* 1996; *Chairman of the Board* 1998; *The Big Tease* 1999; *Carnival of Souls* 1999; *Nutty Professor 2: the Klumps* 2000; *Max Keeble's Big Move* 2001; *What's the Worst That Could Happen?* 2001
Miller, Linda (1942–) *One Summer Love* 1975; *Alice, Sweet Alice* 1977; *An Unmarried Woman* 1978
Miller, Lydia *Backlash* 1986; *Deadly* 1991
Miller, Mandy (1944–) *Mandy* 1952; *Background* 1953; *Dance Little Lady* 1954; *Raising a Riot* 1955; *Child in the House* 1956
Miller, Marilyn (1898–1936) *Sunny* 1930; *Her Majesty Love* 1931
Miller, Mark *Ginger in the Morning* 1973; *Savannah Smiles* 1982
Miller, Martin (1899–1969) *Hotel Reserve* 1944; *Night Boat to Dublin* 1946; *Mark of the Phoenix* 1957; *Libel* 1959; *The Phantom of the Opera* 1962
Miller, Marvin (1913–1985) *Johnny Angel* 1945; *Deadline at Dawn* 1946; *Dead Reckoning* 1947; *Intrigue* 1947; *Peking Express* 1951; *Red Planet Mars* 1952; *Forbidden* 1953; *The Shanghai Story* 1954; *Forbidden Planet* 1956; *Senior Prom* 1958; *Fantastic Planet* 1973
Miller, Omar Benson *aka* **Miller, Omar** *8 Mile* 2002; *Shall We Dance* 2004
Miller, Patsy Ruth (1904–1995) *The Hunchback of Notre Dame* 1923; *So This Is Paris* 1926
Miller, Penelope Ann (1964–) *A Night on the Town* 1987; *Big Top Pee-wee* 1988; *Biloxi Blues* 1988; *Dead-Bang* 1989; *Awakenings* 1990; *Downtown* 1990; *The Freshman* 1990; *Kindergarten Cop* 1990; *Other People's Money* 1991; *Chaplin* 1992; *The Gun in Betty Lou's Handbag* 1992; *Year of the Comet* 1992; *Carlito's Way* 1993; *The Shadow* 1994; *The Relic* 1996; *Little City* 1997; *Break Up* 1998; *Along Came a Spider* 2001
Miller, Rebecca (1962–) *Seven Minutes* 1989; *Regarding Henry* 1991; *Consenting Adults* 1992; *Wind* 1992
Miller, Sienna (1981–) *Alfie* 2004; *Layer Cake* 2004
Miller, Stephen E *Home Is Where the Hart Is* 1987; *Stranded* 1989
Miller, Walter *aka* **Miller, W Chrystie** (1892–1940) *The Musketeers of Pig Alley* 1912; *The Battle of Elderbush* 1914; *Stormy* 1935
Milli, Robert (1933–) *The Curse of the Living Corpse* 1964; *Hamlet* 1964
Millican, James (1910–1955) *The Tender Years* 1947; *The Man from Colorado* 1948; *Mister 880* 1950; *Cavalry Scout* 1951; *I Was a Communist for the FBI* 1951; *Warpath* 1951; *Bugles in the Afternoon* 1952; *Carson City* 1952; *Diplomatic Courier* 1952; *Springfield Rifle* 1952; *Riding Shotgun* 1954; *The Big Tip Off* 1955; *Red Sundown* 1956
Milligan, Deanna (1972–) *Avalanche* 1994; *Suspicious River* 2000
Milligan, Spike (1918–2002) *Down among the Z-Men* 1952; *The Case of the Mukkinese Battle Horn* 1955; *The Running, Jumping and Standing Still Film* 1959; *Suspect* 1960; *Watch Your Stern* 1960; *Invasion Quartet* 1961; *Postman's Knock* 1961; *What a Whopper!* 1961; *The Bed Sitting Room* 1969; *The Magic Christian* 1969; *The Magnificent Seven Deadly Sins* 1971; *Adolf Hitler – My Part in His Downfall* 1972; *The Adventures of Barry McKenzie* 1972; *Alice's Adventures in Wonderland* 1972; *Rentadick* 1972; *Digby, the Biggest Dog in the World* 1973; *Ghost in the Noonday Sun* 1973; *The Three Musketeers* 1973; *The Great McGonagall* 1974; *Man about the House* 1974; *The Hound of the Baskervilles* 1977; *The Last Remake of Beau Geste* 1977; *Yellowbeard* 1983
Milliken, Angie *Act of Necessity* 1991; *Rough Diamonds* 1994; *Dead Heart* 1996; *Paperback Hero* 1998
Millot, Charles (1921–) *Trans-Europ-Express* 1966; *French Connection II* 1975
Mills, Donna (1942–) *The Incident* 1967; *Play Misty for Me* 1971; *Live a Little, Steal a Lot* 1974; *Dangerous Intentions* 1995
Mills, Freddie (1919–1965) *Emergency Call* 1952; *Kill Me Tomorrow* 1957; *Saturday Night Out* 1963
Mills, Hayley (1946–) *Tiger Bay* 1959; *Pollyanna* 1960; *In Search of the Castaways* 1961; *The Parent Trap* 1961; *Whistle down the Wind* 1961; *Summer Magic* 1963; *The Chalk Garden* 1964; *The Moon-Spinners* 1964; *The Truth about Spring* 1964; *Sky West and Crooked* 1965; *That Darn Cat!* 1965; *The Family Way* 1966; *The Trouble with Angels* 1966; *Africa – Texas Style!* 1967; *Pretty Polly* 1967; *Twisted Nerve* 1968; *Take a Girl like You* 1970; *Endless Night* 1971; *What Changed Charley Farthing?* 1974; *Appointment with Death* 1988; *After Midnight* 1990; *Stanley's Magic Garden* 1994
Mills, John *aka* **Mills, Sir John** (1908–2005) *The Ghost Camera* 1933; *Doctor's Orders* 1934; *Those Were the Days* 1934; *Car of Dreams* 1935; *Forever England* 1935; *Tudor Rose* 1936; *You're In the Army Now* 1936; *The Green Cockatoo* 1937; *Goodbye, Mr Chips* 1939; *Old Bill and Son* 1940; *The Black Sheep of Whitehall* 1941; *Cottage to Let*

1941; *The Big Blockade* 1942; *In Which We Serve* 1942; *We Dive at Dawn* 1943; *This Happy Breed* 1944; *Waterloo Road* 1944; *The Way to the Stars* 1945; *Great Expectations* 1946; *The October Man* 1947; *So Well Remembered* 1947; *The History of Mr Polly* 1948; *Scott of the Antarctic* 1948; *The Rocking Horse Winner* 1949; *Morning Departure* 1950; *Mr Denning Drives North* 1951; *The Gentle Gunman* 1952; *The Long Memory* 1952; *Hobson's Choice* 1953; *The Colditz Story* 1954; *The End of the Affair* 1954; *Above Us the Waves* 1955; *Around the World in 80 Days* 1956; *The Baby and the Battleship* 1956; *It's Great to Be Young* 1956; *Town on Trial* 1956; *War and Peace* 1956; *The Vicious Circle* 1957; *Dunkirk* 1958; *I Was Monty's Double* 1958; *Ice Cold in Alex* 1958; *Tiger Bay* 1959; *Season of Passion* 1960; *The Singer Not the Song* 1960; *Swiss Family Robinson* 1960; *Tunes of Glory* 1960; *Flame in the Streets* 1961; *Tiara Tahiti* 1962; *The Chalk Garden* 1964; *The Truth about Spring* 1964; *King Rat* 1965; *Operation Crossbow* 1965; *The Family Way* 1966; *The Wrong Box* 1966; *Africa – Texas Style!* 1967; *Chuka* 1967; *A Black Veil for Lisa* 1969; *Oh! What a Lovely War* 1969; *Run Wild, Run Free* 1969; *Adam's Woman* 1970; *Ryan's Daughter* 1970; *Dulcima* 1971; *Lady Caroline Lamb* 1972; *Young Winston* 1972; *Oklahoma Crude* 1973; *The Human Factor* 1975; *Trial by Combat* 1976; *The Devil's Advocate* 1977; *The Big Sleep* 1978; *The Thirty-Nine Steps* 1978; *The Quatermass Conclusion* 1979; *Zulu Dawn* 1979; *Gandhi* 1982; *Sahara* 1983; *Agatha Christie's Murder with Mirrors* 1985; *When the Wind Blows* 1986; *Who's That Girl* 1987; *Deadly Advice* 1993; *Bright Young Things* 2003

Mills, Juliet (1941–) *The October Man* 1947; *So Well Remembered* 1947; *No My Darling Daughter* 1961; *Twice round the Daffodils* 1962; *Carry On Jack* 1963; *Nurse on Wheels* 1963; *The Rare Breed* 1966; *Avanti!* 1972; *Jonathan Livingston Seagull* 1973; *The Cracker Factory* 1979; *The Other Sister* 1999

Mills, Mort (1919–1993) *Davy Crockett and the River Pirates* 1956; *Ride a Crooked Trail* 1958; *The Outlaws Is Coming* 1965

Milner, Martin *aka* **Milner, Marty** (1927–) *Life with Father* 1947; *Operation Pacific* 1951; *Springfield Rifle* 1952; *Destination Gobi* 1953; *Francis in the Navy* 1955; *Sweet Smell of Success* 1957; *Marjorie Morningstar* 1958; *Too Much, Too Soon* 1958; *Compulsion* 1959; *The Private Lives of Adam and Eve* 1959; *13 Ghosts* 1959; *Sex Kittens Go to College* 1960; *Valley of the Dolls* 1967; *Three Guns for Texas* 1968; *Runaway!* 1973

Milo, Jean-Roger (1957–) *Sarraouina* 1986; *L.627* 1992; *Germinal* 1993; *Lucie Aubrac* 1997; *Bent Keltoum* 2001

Milo, Sandra (1935–) *General Della Rovere* 1959; *The Big Risk* 1960; *8½* 1963; *Juliet of the Spirits* 1965

Milton, Billy (1905–1989) *Aunt Sally* 1933; *Music Hath Charms* 1935; *Someone at the Door* 1936

Milton, Ernest (1890–1974) *It's Love Again* 1936; *The Foreman Went to France* 1941

Mimieux, Yvette (1942–) *Platinum High School* 1960; *The Time Machine* 1960; *Where the Boys Are* 1960; *Light in the Piazza* 1961; *Diamond Head* 1962; *The Wonderful World of the Brothers Grimm* 1962; *Toys in the Attic* 1963; *Joy in the Morning* 1965; *The Reward* 1965; *Monkeys, Go Home!* 1966; *Dark of the Sun* 1967; *Three in the Attic* 1968; *The Picasso Summer* 1969; *The Delta Factor* 1970; *Skyjacked* 1972; *The Neptune Factor* 1973; *Jackson County Jail* 1976; *The Black Hole* 1979

Minardos, Nico (1930–) *Samar* 1962; *Daring Game* 1968; *Day of the Evil Gun* 1968

Minazzoli, Christiane (1931–) *The Story of O* 1975; *L'Enfer* 1994

Minchenberg, Richard *Wisdom* 1986; *One Good Turn* 1996

Minciotti, Esther (1888–1962) *Shockproof* 1949; *Marty* 1955; *Full of Life* 1956; *The Wrong Man* 1956

Mineo, Sal (1939–1976) *The Private War of Major Benson* 1955; *Rebel without a Cause* 1955; *Six Bridges to Cross* 1955; *Crime in the Streets* 1956; *Giant* 1956; *Rock, Pretty Baby* 1956; *Somebody Up There Likes Me* 1956; *Dino* 1957; *Tonka* 1958; *The Gene Krupa Story* 1959; *A Private's Affair* 1959; *Exodus* 1960; *Escape from Zahrain* 1962; *The Longest Day* 1962; *Cheyenne Autumn* 1964; *The Greatest Story Ever Told* 1965; *Who Killed Teddy Bear?* 1965; *Stranger on the Run* 1967; *Eighty Steps to Jonah* 1969; *Krakatoa, East of Java* 1969; *Escape from the Planet of the Apes* 1971

Miner, Jan (1917–2004) *Lenny* 1974; *Willie and Phil* 1980; *Mermaids* 1990

Ming-Na *aka* **Wen Ming-Na** (1963–) *The Joy Luck Club* 1993; *Street Fighter* 1994; *One Night Stand* 1997; *Mulan* 1998; *Final Fantasy: the Spirits Within* 2001

Minguez, Elvira *The Reckoning* 2001; *The Dancer Upstairs* 2002

Minnelli, Liza (1946–) *In the Good Old Summertime* 1949; *Journey back to Oz* 1964; *Charlie Bubbles* 1967; *The Sterile Cuckoo* 1969; *Tell Me That You Love Me, Junie Moon* 1970; *Cabaret* 1972; *Lucky Lady* 1975; *A Matter of Time* 1976; *New York, New York* 1977; *Arthur* 1981; *The King of Comedy* 1983; *Arthur 2: On the Rocks* 1988; *Rent-a-Cop* 1988; *Stepping Out* 1991; *The West Side Waltz* 1995

Minogue, Kylie (1968–) *The Delinquents* 1989; *Street Fighter* 1994; *Bio-Dome* 1996; *Diana & Me* 1997; *Cut* 2000; *Moulin Rouge!* 2001; *The Magic Roundabout* 2005

Minotis, Alexis (1898–1990) *Land of the Pharaohs* 1955; *Boy on a Dolphin* 1957

Minter, Kelly Jo *aka* **Minter, Kelly** *Miracle Mile* 1989; *A Nightmare on Elm Street 5: The Dream Child* 1989

Minter, Kristin *Cool as Ice* 1991; *Flashfire* 1993; *There Goes My Baby* 1994

Minty, Emil (1972–) *Mad Max 2* 1981; *The Winds of Jarrah* 1983

Mioni, Fabrizio (1930–) *Hercules* 1957; *The Blue Angel* 1959; *Get Yourself a College Girl* 1964; *Girl Happy* 1965; *The Spy with My Face* 1966

Miou-Miou (1950–) *Burnt Barns* 1973; *Les Valseuses* 1974; *No Problem!* 1975; *Jonah Who Will Be 25 in the Year 2000* 1976; *Roads to the South* 1978; *The Lady Cop* 1979; *Double Dare* 1981; *Entre Nous* 1983; *Tenue de Soirée* 1986; *La Lectrice* 1988; *The Revolving Doors* 1988; *Milou en Mai* 1989; *Germinal* 1993; *Tango* 1993; *The Eighth Day* 1996; *Dry Cleaning* 1997

Mira, Brigitte (1910–2005) *Fear Eats the Soul* 1973; *The Enigma of Kaspar Hauser* 1974; *Mother Küsters Goes to Heaven* 1975; *Chinese Roulette* 1976; *Fear of Fear* 1976; *Berlin Alexanderplatz* 1980; *Kamikaze 1989* 1983

Miracle, Irene (1954–) *Midnight Express* 1978; *Inferno* 1980; *Puppet Master* 1989

Miranda, Aurora (1915–) *Brazil* 1944; *Phantom Lady* 1944

Miranda, Carmen (1909–1955) *Down Argentine Way* 1940; *That Night in Rio* 1941; *Weekend in Havana* 1941; *Springtime in the Rockies* 1942; *The Gang's All Here* 1943; *Greenwich Village* 1944; *Something for the Boys* 1944; *Copacabana* 1947; *A Date with Judy* 1948; *Nancy Goes to Rio* 1950; *Scared Stiff* 1953

Miranda, Isa (1905–1982) *La Signora di Tutti* 1934; *Summertime* 1955; *The Empty Canvas* 1963; *The Great British Train Robbery* 1966; *The Night Porter* 1973

Miranda, Robert *Sons* 1989; *Sister Act* 1992; *Judge & Jury* 1995; *Blue Streak* 1999

Miranda, Soledad (1943–1970) *Count Dracula* 1970; *Vampyros Lesbos* 1970

Mirel, Nicole *Léon Morin, Priest* 1961; *The Seven Deadly Sins* 1961

Mironov, Yevgeni *aka* **Mironov, Yevgeni F** *aka* **Mironov, Yevgeny** (1966–) *Lost in Siberia* 1991; *House of Fools* 2002

Miroslava (1925–1955) *The Brave Bulls* 1951; *The Criminal Life of Archibaldo de la Cruz* 1955; *Stranger on Horseback* 1955

Mirren, Helen (1945–) *Age of Consent* 1969; *A Midsummer Night's Dream* 1969; *Savage Messiah* 1972; *O Lucky Man!* 1973; *Caligula* 1979; *Hussy* 1979; *The Long Good Friday* 1979; *SOS Titanic* 1979; *The Fiendish Plot of Dr Fu Manchu* 1980; *Excalibur* 1981; *Cal* 1984; *2010* 1984; *White Nights* 1985; *Heavenly Pursuits* 1986; *The Mosquito Coast* 1986; *Pascali's Island* 1988; *The Cook, the Thief, His Wife and Her Lover* 1989; *When the Whales Came* 1989; *Bethune: the Making of a Hero* 1990; *The Comfort of Strangers* 1991; *Where Angels Fear to Tread* 1991; *The Hawk* 1992; *Prince of Jutland* 1994; *The Madness of King George* 1995; *Some Mother's Son* 1996; *Critical Care* 1997; *The Prince of Egypt* 1998; *Teaching Mrs Tingle* 1999; *Greenfingers* 2000; *The Pledge* 2000; *Gosford Park* 2001; *Last Orders* 2001; *Calendar Girls* 2003; *The Clearing* 2004; *Raising Helen* 2004; *The Hitchhiker's Guide to the Galaxy* 2005

Mirza, Diya *aka* **Mirza, Dia** (1981–) *Tehzeeb* 2003; *Dum* 2002; *Parineeta* 2005

Mishra, Smriti *Jaya Ganga* 1996; *Train to Pakistan* 1997

Mistal, Karen *Return of the Killer Tomatoes* 1988; *Cannibal Women in the Avocado Jungle of Death* 1989

Mr T (1952–) *Rocky III* 1982; *DC Cab* 1983; *Freaked* 1993; *Not Another Teen Movie* 2001

Mistral, Jorge (1920–1972) *Wuthering Heights* 1953; *Boy on a Dolphin* 1957; *The Sword and the Cross* 1958

Mistry, Jimi (1973–) *East Is East* 1999; *Born Romantic* 2000; *My Kingdom* 2001; *The Guru* 2002; *Ella Enchanted* 2004

Mitchel, Mary *Panic in Year Zero* 1962; *Dementia 13* 1963; *Spider Baby* 1964

Mitchell, Ann *Lady Chatterley's Lover* 1981; *Paper Marriage* 1991

Mitchell, Brian Stokes (1958–) *Double Platinum* 1999; *Call Me Claus* 2001

Mitchell, Cameron (1918–1994) *High Barbaree* 1947; *Command Decision* 1948; *Homecoming* 1948; *Death of a Salesman* 1951; *Flight to Mars* 1951; *The Sellout* 1951; *Japanese War Bride* 1952; *Les Misérables* 1952; *Pony Soldier* 1952; *How to Marry a Millionaire* 1953; *Man on a Tightrope* 1953; *Powder River* 1953; *Desiree* 1954; *Garden of Evil* 1954; *Gorilla at Large* 1954; *Hell and High Water* 1954; *House of Bamboo* 1955; *Love Me or Leave Me* 1955; *Strange Lady in Town* 1955; *The Tall Men* 1955; *The View from Pompey's Head* 1955; *Carousel* 1956; *Tension at Table Rock* 1956; *The Day They Gave Babies Away* 1957; *Escapade in Japan* 1957; *No Down Payment* 1957; *Face of Fire* 1959; *Blood and Black Lace* 1964; *Ride in the Whirlwind* 1966; *Hombre* 1967; *Rebel Rousers* 1967; *Buck and the Preacher* 1972; *Slaughter* 1972; *The Klansman* 1974; *The Midnight Man* 1974; *Viva Knievel!* 1977; *The Toolbox Murders* 1978; *Without Warning* 1980; *Prince Jack* 1984; *Rage to Kill* 1988

Mitchell, Charlotte *Curtain Up* 1952; *Blood on Satan's Claw* 1970; *The French Lieutenant's Woman* 1981

Mitchell, Chuck (1927–1992) *Porky's* 1981; *Porky's Revenge* 1985

Mitchell, Daryl *aka* **Mitchell, Daryl "Chill"** *Sgt Bilko* 1996; *A Thin Line between Love and Hate* 1996; *Galaxy Quest* 1999; *The Country Bears* 2002

Mitchell, Donna *The Bell Jar* 1979; *Less than Zero* 1987; *Psycho IV: the Beginning* 1990; *Party Girl* 1994; *Two Bits* 1995

Mitchell, Eddy (1942–) *Clean Slate* 1981; *Frankenstein 90* 1984; *Le Bonheur Est dans le Pré* 1995

Mitchell, Elizabeth (1970–) *Gia* 1998; *Molly* 1999; *Frequency* 2000; *The Santa Clause 2* 2002

Mitchell, Frank (1905–1991) *Stand Up and Cheer!* 1934; *The Singing Kid* 1936

Mitchell, George (1905–1972) *The Wild and the Innocent* 1959; *Ride in the Whirlwind* 1966; *The Andromeda Strain* 1970

Mitchell (1), Gordon (1923–2003) *Achilles* 1962; *Brennus – Enemy of Rome* 1963; *The Good Die First* 1967; *Reflections in a Golden Eye* 1967

Mitchell, Grant (1874–1957) *No Man of Her Own* 1932; *A Successful Calamity* 1932; *Central Airport* 1933; *Our Betters* 1933; *20,000 Years in Sing Sing* 1933; *The Case of the Howling Dog* 1934; *The Cat's Paw* 1934; *The Secret Bride* 1934; *Gold Diggers of 1935* 1935; *In Person* 1935; *A Midsummer Night's Dream* 1935; *The Ex-Mrs Bradford* 1936; *Next Time We Love* 1936; *Hell's Kitchen* 1939; *The Great Lie* 1941; *One Foot in Heaven* 1941; *Skylark* 1941; *Dixie* 1943; *Arsenic and Old Lace* 1944; *Laura* 1944; *Bedside Manner* 1945; *Bring on the Girls* 1945; *Conflict* 1945; *Guest Wife* 1945

Mitchell, James (1920–) *Border Incident* 1949; *Colorado Territory* 1949; *Devil's Doorway* 1950; *Stars in My Crown* 1950; *The Toast of New Orleans* 1950; *The Band Wagon* 1953; *The Prodigal* 1955

Mitchell, John Cameron (1963–) *Misplaced* 1989; *Hedwig and the Angry Inch* 2001

Mitchell, Julien (1884–1954) *The Last Journey* 1936; *It's in the Air* 1938; *Vigil in the Night* 1940; *The Goose Steps Out* 1942; *Rhythm Serenade* 1943; *Hotel Reserve* 1944; *Chance of a Lifetime* 1950

Mitchell, Justine *Citizen Verdict* 2003; *Goldfish Memory* 2003; *The Honeymooners* 2003

Mitchell, Kel (1978–) *Good Burger* 1997; *Mystery Men* 1999; *Clifford's Really Big Movie* 2004

Mitchell, Kirsty (1974–) *The Pilot's Wife* 2001; *Butterfly Man* 2002

Mitchell, Laurie *Calypso Joe* 1957; *Queen of Outer Space* 1958

Mitchell, Millard (1900–1953) *Swell Guy* 1946; *A Double Life* 1947; *A Foreign Affair* 1948; *Everybody Does It* 1949; *Thieves' Highway* 1949; *Twelve O'Clock High* 1949; *Convicted* 1950; *The Gunfighter* 1950; *Mister 880* 1950; *Winchester '73* 1950; *You're in the Navy Now* 1951; *My Six Convicts* 1952; *Singin' in the Rain* 1952; *Here Come the Girls* 1953; *The Naked Spur* 1953

Mitchell, Norman (1918–2001) *Dick Turpin – Highwayman* 1956; *Nearest and Dearest* 1972; *Frankenstein and the Monster from Hell* 1973; *Revenge of Billy the Kid* 1991

Mitchell, Radha (1973–) *Love and Other Catastrophes* 1996; *High Art* 1998; *Kick* 1999; *Pitch Black* 1999; *Everything Put Together* 2000; *Dead Heat* 2002; *Phone Booth* 2002; *Finding Neverland* 2004; *Man on Fire* 2004; *Melinda and Melinda* 2004

Mitchell, Sasha (1967–) *Death before Dishonor* 1987; *Spike of Bensonhurst* 1988; *Kickboxer 2: the Road Back* 1990; *Kickboxer III: the Art of War* 1992

Mitchell, Silas Weir *The Patriot* 1998; *The Whole Ten Yards* 2004

Mitchell, Thomas (1892–1962) *Theodora Goes Wild* 1936; *The Hurricane* 1937; *Lost Horizon* 1937; *Make Way for Tomorrow* 1937; *When You're in Love* 1937; *Trade Winds* 1938; *Gone with the Wind* 1939; *The Hunchback of Notre Dame* 1939; *Mr Smith Goes to Washington* 1939; *Only Angels Have Wings* 1939; *Stagecoach* 1939; *Angels over Broadway* 1940; *The Long Voyage Home* 1940; *Our Town* 1940; *Swiss Family Robinson* 1940; *Out of the Fog* 1941; *The Black Swan* 1942; *Joan of Paris* 1942; *Moontide* 1942; *Song of the Islands* 1942; *This above All* 1942; *Bataan* 1943; *The Immortal Sergeant* 1943; *The Outlaw* 1943; *Buffalo Bill* 1944; *Dark Waters* 1944; *The Fighting Sullivans* 1944; *The Keys of the Kingdom* 1944; *Wilson* 1944; *Adventure* 1945; *Captain Eddie* 1945; *The Dark Mirror* 1946; *It's a Wonderful Life* 1946; *High Barbaree* 1947; *Silver River* 1948; *Alias Nick Beal* 1949; *The Big Wheel* 1949; *High Noon* 1952; *Destry* 1954; *Secret of the Incas* 1954; *While the City Sleeps* 1956; *Handle with Care* 1958; *By Love Possessed* 1961; *Pocketful of Miracles* 1961

Mitchell, Warren (1926–) *Barnacle Bill* 1957; *Manuela* 1957; *The Trollenberg Terror* 1958; *Tommy the Toreador* 1959; *The Boy Who Stole a Million* 1960; *Surprise Package* 1960; *Don't Bother to Knock* 1961; *Postman's Knock* 1961; *The Main Attraction* 1962; *Calculated Risk* 1963; *The Small World of Sammy Lee* 1963; *Unearthly Stranger* 1963; *Carry On Cleo* 1964; *The Sicilians* 1964; *The Intelligence Men* 1965; *The Night Caller* 1965; *Drop Dead Darling* 1966; *The Sandwich Man* 1966; *The Jokers* 1967; *The Best House in London* 1968; *Diamonds for Breakfast* 1968; *Till Death Us Do Part* 1968; *The Assassination Bureau* 1969; *Moon Zero Two* 1969; *Innocent Bystanders* 1972; *What Changed Charley Farthing?* 1974; *Jabberwocky* 1977; *Stand Up Virgin Soldiers* 1977; *Meetings with Remarkable Men* 1979; *Norman Loves Rose* 1982; *The Plague Dogs* 1982; *The Chain* 1984; *Foreign Body* 1986; *Knights and Emeralds* 1986; *Kokoda Crescent* 1989

Mitchell, Yvonne (1925–1979) *The Queen of Spades* 1948; *Children of Chance* 1949; *Turn the Key Softly* 1953; *The Divided Heart* 1954; *Yield to the Night* 1956; *Woman in a Dressing Gown* 1957; *Passionate Summer* 1958; *Sapphire* 1959; *Tiger Bay* 1959; *Conspiracy of Hearts* 1960; *The Trials of Oscar Wilde* 1960; *The Main Attraction* 1962; *Genghis Khan* 1964; *The Corpse* 1969; *Demons of the Mind* 1971; *The Great Waltz* 1972; *The Incredible Sarah* 1976

Mitchell-Smith, Ilan (1969–) *The Wild Life* 1984; *Weird Science* 1985; *The Chocolate War* 1988; *Journey to the Center of the Earth* 1989

Mitchum, Bentley (1967–) *The Man in the Moon* 1991; *Ruby in Paradise* 1993; *Orbit* 1996; *Shark Attack* 1999; *A Crack in the Floor* 2000

Mitchum, Christopher *aka* **Mitchum, Chris** (1943–) *Rio Lobo* 1970; *Big Jake* 1971; *One Man Jury* 1978; *The Day Time Ended* 1980; *Orbit* 1996

Mitchum, James *aka* **Mitchum, Jim** (1941–) *Thunder Road* 1958; *The Beat Generation* 1959; *Young Guns of Texas* 1962; *Ambush Bay* 1966; *The Money Trap* 1966; *The*

Heroes 1968; *Trackdown* 1976; *Maniac* 1977; *Fatal Mission* 1990

Mitchum, John (1919–2001) *Hitler* 1962; *Dirty Harry* 1971; *The Enforcer* 1976

Mitchum, Robert aka **Mitchum, Bob** (1917–1997) *Corvette K-225* 1943; *The Dancing Masters* 1943; *Gung Ho!* 1943; *Betrayed* 1944; *Girl Rush* 1944; *Johnny Doesn't Live Here Anymore* 1944; *Mr Winkle Goes to War* 1944; *Nevada* 1944; *Thirty Seconds over Tokyo* 1944; *The Story of GI Joe* 1945; *The Locket* 1946; *Till the End of Time* 1946; *Undercurrent* 1946; *Build My Gallows High* 1947; *Crossfire* 1947; *Desire Me* 1947; *Pursued* 1947; *Blood on the Moon* 1948; *Rachel and the Stranger* 1948; *The Big Steal* 1949; *Holiday Affair* 1949; *The Red Pony* 1949; *Where Danger Lives* 1950; *His Kind of Woman* 1951; *My Forbidden Past* 1951; *The Racket* 1951; *The Lusty Men* 1952; *Macao* 1952; *One Minute to Zero* 1952; *Angel Face* 1953; *Second Chance* 1953; *White Witch Doctor* 1953; *Beautiful but Dangerous* 1954; *River of No Return* 1954; *Track of the Cat* 1954; *Man with the Gun* 1955; *The Night of the Hunter* 1955; *Not as a Stranger* 1955; *Bandido* 1956; *Foreign Intrigue* 1956; *The Enemy Below* 1957; *Fire Down Below* 1957; *Heaven Knows, Mr Allison* 1957; *The Hunters* 1958; *Thunder Road* 1958; *The Angry Hills* 1959; *The Wonderful Country* 1959; *The Grass Is Greener* 1960; *Home from the Hill* 1960; *The Sundowners* 1960; *A Terrible Beauty* 1960; *The Last Time I Saw Archie* 1961; *Cape Fear* 1962; *The Longest Day* 1962; *Two for the Seesaw* 1962; *The List of Adrian Messenger* 1963; *Rampage* 1963; *The Man in the Middle* 1964; *What a Way to Go!* 1964; *Mister Moses* 1965; *El Dorado* 1967; *The Way West* 1967; *Anzio* 1968; *5 Card Stud* 1968; *Secret Ceremony* 1968; *Villa Rides* 1968; *The Good Guys and the Bad Guys* 1969; *Young Billy Young* 1969; *Ryan's Daughter* 1970; *Going Home* 1971; *The Wrath of God* 1972; *The Friends of Eddie Coyle* 1973; *Farewell, My Lovely* 1975; *The Yakuza* 1975; *Battle of Midway* 1976; *The Last Tycoon* 1976; *The Amsterdam Kill* 1978; *The Big Sleep* 1978; *Breakthrough* 1978; *Matilda* 1978; *Agency* 1981; *That Championship Season* 1982; *The Ambassador* 1984; *Maria's Lovers* 1984; *Reunion at Fairborough* 1985; *Mr North* 1988; *Scrooged* 1988; *Cape Fear* 1991; *Tombstone* 1993; *Woman of Desire* 1994; *Dead Man* 1995

Mitevska, Labina (1975–) *Before the Rain* 1994; *I Want You* 1998

Mito, Mitsuko (1919–1981) *There Was a Father* 1942; *My Love Has Been Burning* 1949; *Ugetsu Monogatari* 1953

Mitra, Rhona (1976–) *A Kid in Aladdin's Palace* 1997; *Get Carter* 2000; *Ali G indahouse* 2002; *Highwaymen* 2003; *The Life of David Gale* 2003

Mitsuishi, Ken (1961–) *The Pillow Book* 1995; *Chaos* 1999; *Eureka* 2000

Miura, Mitsuko *The Loyal 47 Ronin* 1941; *The Victory of Women* 1946

Miura, Tomokazu (1958–) *M/Other* 1999; *A Tender Place* 2001

Miyaguchi, Seiji (1913–1985) *Seven Samurai* 1954; *The Ballad of Narayama* 1958; *Twin Sisters of Kyoto* 1963

Miyake, Kuniko *Poppy* 1935; *Hen in the Wind* 1948; *My Love Has Been Burning* 1949; *Early Summer* 1951; *The Flavour of Green Tea over Rice* 1952; *Tokyo Story* 1953; *Early Spring* 1956; *Escapade in Japan* 1957; *Ohayo* 1959; *An Autumn Afternoon* 1962

Miyamoto, Nobuko (1945–) *Death Japanese Style* 1984; *Tampopo* 1986; *A Taxing Woman* 1987; *Minbo – or the Gentle Art of Japanese Extortion* 1992

Miyori, Kim *The Big Picture* 1989; *The Punisher* 1989; *Body Shot* 1994; *Metro* 1997

Miyoshi, Eiko *No Regrets for Our Youth* 1946; *I Live in Fear* 1955

Mizuno, Kumi (1937–) *Frankenstein Conquers the World* 1964; *Invasion of the Astro-Monster* 1965; *Ebirah, Horror of the Deep* 1966; *War of the Gargantuas* 1970

Mlodzik, Ronald *Stereo* 1969; *Crimes of the Future* 1970

Mobley, Mary Ann (1939–) *Get Yourself a College Girl* 1964; *Girl Happy* 1965; *Harum Scarum* 1965; *Three on a Couch* 1966; *The King's Pirate* 1967

Mobley, Roger (1949–) *A Dog's Best Friend* 1960; *The Boy Who Caught a Crook* 1961; *Jack the Giant Killer* 1962; *Emil and the Detectives* 1964

Mochrie, Peter (1959–) *The Winter of Our Dreams* 1981; *Frauds* 1992

Mocky, Jean-Pierre (1929–) *The Vanquished* 1953; *Grandeur et Décadence d'un Petit Commerce de Cinéma* 1986

Modine, Matthew (1959–) *Baby It's You* 1983; *Private School* 1983; *Streamers* 1983; *Birdy* 1984; *The Hotel New Hampshire* 1984; *Mrs Soffel* 1984; *Vision Quest* 1985; *Full Metal Jacket* 1987; *Orphans* 1987; *The Gamble* 1988; *Married to the Mob* 1988; *A Cut Above* 1989; *Memphis Belle* 1990; *Pacific Heights* 1990; *Equinox* 1992; *Wind* 1992; *And the Band Played On* 1993; *Short Cuts* 1993; *The Browning Version* 1994; *Jacob* 1994; *Bye Bye Love* 1995; *CutThroat Island* 1995; *Fluke* 1995; *The Blackout* 1997; *The Maker* 1997; *The Real Blonde* 1997; *What the Deaf Man Heard* 1997; *Any Given Sunday* 1999; *Le Divorce* 2003

Modot, Gaston (1887–1970) *The Ship of Lost Men* 1929; *L'Age d'Or* 1930; *Sous les Toits de Paris* 1930; *La Grande Illusion* 1937; *La Règle du Jeu* 1939; *Casque d'Or* 1952

Moeller, Ralph (1959–) *Best of the Best II* 1992; *Universal Soldier* 1992; *The Viking Sagas* 1995

Moffat, Donald (1930–) *Rachel, Rachel* 1968; *The Great Northfield Minnesota Raid* 1972; *Showdown* 1973; *The Terminal Man* 1974; *On the Nickel* 1979; *Promises in the Dark* 1979; *Popeye* 1980; *The White Lions* 1980; *Monster in the Closet* 1983; *The Right Stuff* 1983; *Alamo Bay* 1985; *The Best of Times* 1986; *Far North* 1988; *The Unbearable Lightness of Being* 1988; *Music Box* 1989; *Danielle Steel's Kaleidoscope* 1990; *Class Action* 1991; *Regarding Henry* 1991; *HouseSitter* 1992; *Clear and Present Danger* 1994; *Love, Cheat & Steal* 1994; *Trapped in Paradise* 1994

Moffatt, Graham (1919–1965) *Where There's a Will* 1936; *Windbag the Sailor* 1936; *Dr Syn* 1937; *Good Morning, Boys* 1937; *Oh, Mr Porter!* 1937; *Ask a Policeman* 1938; *Convict 99* 1938; *Old Bones of the River* 1938; *Owd Bob* 1938; *Cheer Boys Cheer* 1939; *Where's That Fire?* 1939; *Charley's (Big Hearted) Aunt* 1940; *Hi, Gang!* 1941; *I Thank You* 1941; *Back Room Boy* 1942; *Time Flies* 1944

Moffett, D W (1954–) *An Early Frost* 1985; *Danielle Steel's Fine Things* 1990; *In the Deep Woods* 1992; *Rough Magic* 1995; *Stealing Beauty* 1995; *When the Bough Breaks 2: Perfect Prey* 1998; *Molly* 1999; *Kill Me Later* 2001; *Thirteen* 2003; *Twisted* 2003

Moffett, Gregory *Let's Dance* 1950; *Robot Monster* 1953

Moffett, Michelle *Hired to Kill* 1990; *Indecent Behavior* 1993

Moffett, Sharyn (1936–) *The Body Snatcher* 1945; *The Falcon in San Francisco* 1945; *Child of Divorce* 1946; *The Locket* 1946; *Mr Blandings Builds His Dream House* 1948; *The Judge Steps Out* 1949

Mohner, Carl (1921–2005) *The Last Bridge* 1954; *Rififi* 1955; *Celui Qui Doit Mourir* 1957; *Behind the Mask* 1958; *The Camp on Blood Island* 1958; *Passionate Summer* 1958; *The Challenge* 1960; *Sink the Bismarck!* 1960; *The Kitchen* 1961; *Callan* 1974

Mohr, Gerald (1914–1968) *Gilda* 1946; *Undercover Girl* 1950; *Sirocco* 1951; *The Duel at Silver Creek* 1952; *Invasion USA* 1952; *The Ring* 1952; *The Sniper* 1952; *The Eddie Cantor Story* 1953; *Raiders of the Seven Seas* 1953; *The Angry Red Planet* 1959; *This Rebel Breed* 1960

Mohr, Jay (1970–) *For Better or Worse* 1995; *Jerry Maguire* 1996; *Picture Perfect* 1997; *Suicide Kings* 1997; *Jane Austen's Mafia* 1998; *Paulie* 1998; *Cherry Falls* 1999; *Go* 1999; *200 Cigarettes* 1999; *Pay It Forward* 2000; *Pluto Nash* 2001; *S1MØNE* 2002; *Are We There Yet?* 2005

Mohyeddin, Zia (1933–) *Sammy Going South* 1963; *Khartoum* 1966; *The Sailor from Gibraltar* 1967; *They Came from beyond Space* 1967; *Work Is a Four Letter Word* 1968; *Bombay Talkie* 1970; *The Assam Garden* 1985

Moir, Richard (1950–) *The Odd Angry Shot* 1979; *Heatwave* 1981; *Remember Me* 1985; *Welcome to Woop Woop* 1997

Mok, Karen (1970–) *Fallen Angels* 1995; *Black Mask* 1996; *Kitchen* 1997; *So Close* 2002

Mokae, Zakes (1935–) *Agatha Christie's A Caribbean Mystery* 1983; *Cry Freedom* 1987; *The Serpent and the Rainbow* 1987; *Dad* 1989; *A Dry White Season* 1989; *Body Parts* 1991; *A Rage in Harlem* 1991; *Dust Devil* 1992; *Vampire in Brooklyn* 1995

Mol, Gretchen (1973–) *The Funeral* 1996; *Girl 6* 1996; *The Last Time I Committed Suicide* 1996; *Subway Stories: Tales from the Underground* 1997; *Music from Another Room* 1998; *Rounders* 1998; *Finding Graceland* 1999; *Forever Mine* 1999; *Sweet and Lowdown* 1999; *The Thirteenth Floor* 1999; *Attraction* 2000; *Get Carter* 2000; *The Shape of Things* 2003

Molander, Karin (1889–1978) *Thomas Graal's Best Film* 1917; *Erotikon* 1920

Molina, Alfred (1953–) *Raiders of the Lost Ark* 1981; *Number One* 1984; *Eleni* 1985; *Ladyhawke* 1985; *Letter to Brezhnev* 1985; *Prick Up Your Ears* 1987; *Not without My Daughter* 1990; *American Friends* 1991; *Enchanted April* 1991; *The Trial* 1993; *Maverick* 1994; *The Steal* 1994; *White Fang 2: Myth of the White Wolf* 1994; *Hideaway* 1995; *The Perez Family* 1995; *Scorpion Spring* 1995; *Species* 1995; *Before and After* 1996; *A Further Gesture* 1996; *Mojave Moon* 1996; *Anna Karenina* 1997; *The Man Who Knew Too Little* 1997; *The Impostors* 1998; *Dudley Do-Right* 1999; *Magnolia* 1999; *Chocolat* 2000; *Murder on the Orient Express* 2001; *Frida* 2002; *My Life without Me* 2002; *Coffee and Cigarettes* 2003; *Identity* 2003; *Spider-Man 2* 2004

Molina, Angela (1955–) *That Obscure Object of Desire* 1977; *Camorra* 1985; *Lola* 1986; *Streets of Gold* 1986; *1492: Conquest of Paradise* 1992; *Live Flesh* 1997; *Wind with the Gone* 1998; *El Mar* 1999; *One of the Hollywood Ten* 2000; *Carnages* 2002

Molina, Miguel (1963–) *1919* 1983; *The Law of Desire* 1987

Moll, Giorgia aka **Moll, Georgia** (1938–) *The Quiet American* 1958; *The Cossacks* 1959; *The White Warrior* 1959; *Island of Love* 1963; *Le Mépris* 1963

Moll, Richard (1943–) *The Sword and the Sorcerer* 1982; *House* 1986; *Wicked Stepmother* 1989; *No Dessert Dad, Till You Mow the Lawn* 1994; *The Secret Agent Club* 1995; *Storybook* 1995; *The Glass Cage* 1996

Mollà, Jordi (1968–) *Jamon Jamon* 1992; *Dollar for the Dead* 1998; *Second Skin* 2000; *Blow* 2001

Mollison, Clifford (1897–1986) *Mister Cinders* 1934; *The Baby and the Battleship* 1956

Mollison, Henry (1905–1985) *The Lone Wolf Returns* 1936; *The Loves of Joanna Godden* 1947; *What the Butler Saw* 1950; *The Man in the White Suit* 1951

Molloy, Dearbhla *Taffin* 1988; *The Run of the Country* 1995; *This Is the Sea* 1996

Molnar, Tibor *The Round-Up* 1966; *The Red and the White* 1967

Monaghan, Dominic (1976–) *The Lord of the Rings: The Fellowship of the Ring* 2001; *The Lord of the Rings: The Two Towers* 2002; *The Lord of the Rings: The Return of the King* 2003; *Spivs* 2003

Monaghan, Michelle (1977–) *It Runs in the Family* 2002; *Mr & Mrs Smith* 2005

Monahan, Dan *Porky's* 1981; *Porky's II: The Next Day* 1983; *Porky's Revenge* 1985; *Stephen King's The Night Flier* 1997

Mondy, Pierre (1925–) *The Battle of Austerlitz* 1960; *The Mysteries of Paris* 1962; *The Sleeping Car Murders* 1965; *The Pink Telephone* 1975

Monette, Richard (1944–) *Dancing in the Dark* 1986; *I've Heard the Mermaids Singing* 1987

Monfort, Sylvia (1925–1991) *The Eagle Has Two Heads* 1948; *The Case of Dr Laurent* 1957

Mong, William V (1875–1940) *The Strong Man* 1926; *What Price Glory* 1926; *Treasure Island* 1934

Monk, Debra (1949–) *Center Stage* 2000; *Milwaukee, Minnesota* 2002; *Palindromes* 2004

Monkhouse, Bob (1928–2003) *The Secret People* 1951; *Carry On Sergeant* 1958; *Dentist in the Chair* 1960; *Dentist on the Job* 1961; *She'll Have to Go* 1961; *Thunderbirds Are Go!* 1966; *The Bliss of Mrs Blossom* 1968; *Simon, Simon* 1970

Monlaur, Yvonne *The Brides of Dracula* 1960; *Circus of Horrors* 1960; *Inn for Trouble* 1960

Monroe, Marilyn (1926–1962) *Dangerous Years* 1947; *Ladies of the Chorus* 1949; *Love Happy* 1949; *All about Eve* 1950; *The Asphalt Jungle* 1950; *The Fireball* 1950; *Right Cross* 1950; *A Ticket to Tomahawk* 1950; *As Young as You Feel* 1951; *Home Town Story* 1951; *Let's Make It Legal* 1951; *Love Nest* 1951; *Clash by Night* 1952; *Don't Bother to Knock* 1952; *Monkey Business* 1952; *O Henry's Full House* 1952; *We're Not Married* 1952; *Gentlemen Prefer Blondes* 1953; *How to Marry a Millionaire* 1953; *Niagara* 1953; *River of No Return* 1954; *There's No Business like Show Business* 1954; *The Seven Year Itch* 1955; *Bus Stop* 1956; *The Prince and the Showgirl* 1957; *Some Like It Hot* 1959; *Let's Make Love* 1960; *The Misfits* 1961

Montague, Lee (1927–) *The Secret Partner* 1961; *Operation Snatch* 1962; *The Secret of Blood Island* 1964; *How I Won the War* 1967; *Nobody Runs Forever* 1968; *Eagle in a Cage* 1971; *The Best Pair of Legs in the Business* 1972; *Brother Sun, Sister Moon* 1972; *Mahler* 1974; *The Legacy* 1978; *Silver Dream Racer* 1980; *Kim* 1984; *Madame Sousatzka* 1988

Montaigu, Sandra *L'Amour par Terre* 1984; *Polar* 1984

Montalban, Carlos (1903–1991) *The Harder They Fall* 1956; *Pepe* 1960; *Bananas* 1971

Montalban, Ricardo (1920–) *Fiesta* 1947; *On an Island with You* 1948; *Battleground* 1949; *Border Incident* 1949; *The Kissing Bandit* 1949; *Neptune's Daughter* 1949; *Mystery Street* 1950; *Right Cross* 1950; *Across the Wide Missouri* 1951; *Sombrero* 1952; *Latin Lovers* 1953; *A Life in the Balance* 1955; *Sayonara* 1957; *Let No Man Write My Epitaph* 1960; *Gordon the Black Pirate* 1961; *Hemingway's Adventures of a Young Man* 1962; *The Reluctant Saint* 1962; *Love Is a Ball* 1963; *Cheyenne Autumn* 1964; *Madame X* 1966; *The Money Trap* 1966; *The Singing Nun* 1966; *Blue* 1968; *Sol Madrid* 1968; *Sweet Charity* 1968; *The Deserter* 1971; *The Face of Fear* 1971; *Conquest of the Planet of the Apes* 1972; *The Train Robbers* 1973; *Joe Panther* 1976; *Star Trek II: the Wrath of Khan* 1982; *The Naked Gun* 1988; *SPYkids 2: the Island of Lost Dreams* 2002; *SPYkids 3-D: Game Over* 2003

Montand, Yves (1921–1991) *Les Portes de la Nuit* 1946; *The Wages of Fear* 1953; *Marguerite de la Nuit* 1955; *Napoléon* 1955; *The Witches of Salem* 1957; *Where the Hot Wind Blows!* 1959; *Let's Make Love* 1960; *Goodbye Again* 1961; *Sanctuary* 1961; *Le Joli Mai* 1962; *My Geisha* 1962; *The Sleeping Car Murders* 1965; *Grand Prix* 1966; *La Guerre Est Finie* 1966; *Is Paris Burning?* 1966; *Vivre pour Vivre* 1967; *Z* 1968; *The Confession* 1970; *On a Clear Day You Can See Forever* 1970; *The Red Circle* 1970; *Delusions of Grandeur* 1971; *César and Rosalie* 1972; *State of Siege* 1972; *Tout Va Bien* 1972; *Vincent, François, Paul and the Others* 1974; *Call Him Savage* 1975; *Roads to the South* 1978; *Choice of Arms* 1981; *Jean de Florette* 1986; *Manon des Sources* 1986; *IP5* 1992

Montejo, Carmen *The Vampire* 1957; *The Children of Sanchez* 1978

Montell, Lisa (1933–) *Escape to Burma* 1955; *Ten Thousand Bedrooms* 1957; *The Lone Ranger and the Lost City of Gold* 1958

Montenegro, Conchita (1912–) *The Cisco Kid* 1931; *Laughing at Life* 1933; *Caravan* 1934

Montenegro, Fernanda (1929–) *Hour of the Star* 1985; *Central Station* 1998

Montero, Germaine (1909–2000) *Knave of Hearts* 1954; *Le Masque de Fer* 1962; *Any Number Can Win* 1963; *Robert et Robert* 1978

Monteros, Rosenda (1935–) *Battle Shock* 1956; *Villa!* 1958; *The Magnificent Seven* 1960; *Tiara Tahiti* 1962; *She* 1965; *Cauldron of Blood* 1967

Montés, Elisa (1936–) *As If It Were Raining* 1963; *Return of the Seven* 1966; *Texas Adios* 1966; *Captain Apache* 1971

Montevecchi, Liliane (1932–) *The Living Idol* 1955; *Moonfleet* 1955; *Meet Me in Las Vegas* 1956; *King Creole* 1958

Montez, Maria (1918–1951) *That Night in Rio* 1941; *Arabian Nights* 1942; *White Savage* 1943; *Ali Baba and the Forty Thieves* 1944; *Cobra Woman* 1944; *Follow the Boys* 1944; *Sudan* 1945; *The Exile* 1947; *Siren of Atlantis* 1948

Montgomery, Belinda J aka **Montgomery, Belinda** (1950–) *The Todd Killings* 1971; *The Other Side of the Mountain* 1975; *Breaking Point* 1976; *The Other Side of the Mountain – Part 2* 1978

Montgomery, Douglass aka **Douglass, Kent** (1907–1966) *Waterloo Bridge* 1931; *Little Women* 1933; *Little Man, What Now?* 1934; *The Mystery of Edwin Drood* 1935; *Everything Is Thunder* 1936; *The Cat and the Canary* 1939; *The Way to the Stars* 1945

Montgomery, Elizabeth (1933–1995) *The Court-Martial of Billy Mitchell* 1955; *Johnny Cool* 1963; *Who's Been Sleeping in My Bed?* 1963; *How to Fill a Wild Bikini* 1965; *Dark Victory* 1976

Montgomery, Flora (1974–) *When Brendan Met Trudy* 2000; *Goldfish Memory* 2003

Montgomery, George (1916–2000) *The Cisco Kid and the Lady* 1939; *Young People*

1940; *Riders of the Purple Sage* 1941; *China Girl* 1942; *Orchestra Wives* 1942; *Roxie Hart* 1942; *Ten Gentlemen from West Point* 1942; *Bomber's Moon* 1943; *Coney Island* 1943; *Three Little Girls in Blue* 1946; *Belle Starr's Daughter* 1948; *The Girl from Manhattan* 1948; *Lulu Belle* 1948; *Indian Uprising* 1951; *The Sword of Monte Cristo* 1951; *Gun Duel in Durango* 1957; *Last of the Badmen* 1957; *Samar* 1962; *Battle of the Bulge* 1965; *Satan's Harvest* 1965; *Hostile Guns* 1967
Montgomery, Lee *aka* **Montgomery, Lee H** *aka* **Montgomery, Lee Harcourt** (1961–) *The Harness* 1971; *The Million Dollar Duck* 1971; *Ben* 1972; *Pete 'n' Tillie* 1972; *Runaway!* 1973; *The Savage Is Loose* 1974; *Baker's Hawk* 1976; *Burnt Offerings* 1976; *Mutant* 1984; *Girls Just Want to Have Fun* 1985; *Prime Risk* 1985
Montgomery, Poppy (1975–) *Dead Man on Campus* 1998; *The Other Sister* 1999
Montgomery, Robert (1904–1981) *The Big House* 1930; *The Divorcee* 1930; *Free and Easy* 1930; *Inspiration* 1931; *Private Lives* 1931; *Strangers May Kiss* 1931; *Blondie of the Follies* 1932; *Faithless* 1932; *Night Flight* 1933; *When Ladies Meet* 1933; *Forsaking All Others* 1934; *Riptide* 1934; *Vanessa, Her Love Story* 1935; *Piccadilly Jim* 1936; *Trouble for Two* 1936; *The Last of Mrs Cheyney* 1937; *Live, Love and Learn* 1937; *Night Must Fall* 1937; *Three Loves Has Nancy* 1938; *Yellow Jack* 1938; *Fast and Loose* 1939; *Busman's Honeymoon* 1940; *The Earl of Chicago* 1940; *Here Comes Mr Jordan* 1941; *Mr and Mrs Smith* 1941; *Rage in Heaven* 1941; *Unfinished Business* 1941; *They Were Expendable* 1945; *Lady in the Lake* 1947; *June Bride* 1948; *The Saxon Charm* 1948; *Eye Witness* 1949; *Once More, My Darling* 1949
Montiel, Sarita (1928–) *Vera Cruz* 1954; *Serenade* 1956; *Run of the Arrow* 1957
Montoute, Edouard *La Haine* 1995; *Port Djema* 1997; *Femme Fatale* 2002
Montoya, Alex *Southwest to Sonora* 1966; *Daring Game* 1968
Moody, Jim (1932–) *Personal Best* 1982; *Bad Boys* 1983; *Who's the Man?* 1993
Moody, King *Teenagers from Outer Space* 1959; *The Dark Backward* 1991
Moody, Lynne *Scream Blacula Scream* 1973; *The Evil* 1978; *White Dog* 1981; *Some Kind of Hero* 1982; *Last Light* 1993
Moody, Ralph (1887–1971) *Road to Bali* 1952; *The Lone Ranger and the Lost City of Gold* 1958; *The Legend of Tom Dooley* 1959
Moody, Ron (1924–) *A Pair of Briefs* 1961; *Ladies Who Do* 1963; *The Mouse on the Moon* 1963; *Every Day's a Holiday* 1964; *Murder Most Foul* 1964; *The Sandwich Man* 1966; *Oliver!* 1968; *The Twelve Chairs* 1970; *Flight of the Doves* 1971; *Dogpound Shuffle* 1974; *Legend of the Werewolf* 1974; *Dominique* 1978; *The Spaceman and King Arthur* 1979; *Where Is Parsifal?* 1983; *Asterix and the Big Fight* 1989; *A Ghost in Monte Carlo* 1990; *Revelation* 2001; *Paradise Grove* 2003
Moog, Heinz (1908–1989) *Senso* 1954; *The Secret Ways* 1961
Moon, Keith (1947–1978) *200 Motels* 1971; *That'll Be the Day* 1973; *Stardust* 1974; *Tommy* 1975; *Sextette* 1978
Moon, Sheri *House of 1000 Corpses* 2001; *The Devil's Rejects* 2005
Mooney, Laura *She's Out of Control* 1989; *Little Nemo: Adventures in Slumberland* 1992
Mooney, Paul *Dance with a Stranger* 1984; *Bamboozled* 2000
Moore, Alvy (1921–1997) *The Glory Brigade* 1953; *Riot in Cell Block 11* 1954; *Susan Slept Here* 1954; *An Annapolis Story* 1955; *Five against the House* 1955; *Brotherhood of Satan* 1970; *A Boy and His Dog* 1975
Moore Jr, Carlyle (1909–1977) *The Case of the Black Cat* 1936; *Arizona Legion* 1939
Moore, Clayton (1908–1999) *The Far Frontier* 1949; *The Lone Ranger* 1956; *The Lone Ranger and the Lost City of Gold* 1958
Moore, Colleen (1900–1988) *Lilac Time* 1928; *The Power and the Glory* 1933; *Success at Any Price* 1934
Moore, Constance (1919–) *Wives under Suspicion* 1938; *You Can't Cheat an Honest Man* 1939; *Argentine Nights* 1940; *I Wanted Wings* 1941; *Take a Letter, Darling* 1942; *Atlantic City* 1944; *Show Business* 1944; *Earl Carroll Vanities* 1945
Moore, Del (1916–1970) *The Last Time I Saw Archie* 1961; *Stagecoach to Dancer's Rock* 1962; *The Nutty Professor* 1963; *The Disorderly Orderly* 1964; *The Big Mouth* 1967
Moore, Demi (1962–) *Touchdown* 1981; *Parasite* 1982; *Young Doctors in Love* 1982; *Blame It on Rio* 1984; *No Small Affair* 1984; *St Elmo's Fire* 1985; *About Last Night…* 1986; *One Crazy Summer* 1986; *Wisdom* 1986; *The Seventh Sign* 1988; *We're No Angels* 1989; *Ghost* 1990; *The Butcher's Wife* 1991; *Mortal Thoughts* 1991; *Nothing but Trouble* 1991; *A Few Good Men* 1992; *Indecent Proposal* 1993; *Disclosure* 1994; *Now and Then* 1995; *The Scarlet Letter* 1995; *Beavis and Butt-head Do America* 1996; *The Hunchback of Notre Dame* 1996; *If These Walls Could Talk* 1996; *The Juror* 1996; *Striptease* 1996; *Deconstructing Harry* 1997; *GI Jane* 1997; *Passion of Mind* 2000; *Charlie's Angels: Full Throttle* 2003
Moore, Dennie (1907–1978) *Sylvia Scarlett* 1936; *Saturday's Children* 1940
Moore, Dennis *aka* **Meadows, Denny** (1908–1964) *The Dawn Rider* 1935; *The Mummy's Curse* 1944
Moore, Dickie (1925–) *Blonde Venus* 1932; *So Big* 1932; *Union Depot* 1932; *Gabriel over the White House* 1933; *Man's Castle* 1933; *Gallant Lady* 1934; *Upper World* 1934; *Peter Ibbetson* 1935; *So Red the Rose* 1935; *The Gladiator* 1938; *Miss Annie Rooney* 1942; *Sweet and Lowdown* 1944; *Tuna Clipper* 1949
Moore, Dudley (1935–2002) *The Wrong Box* 1966; *Bedazzled* 1967; *30 Is a Dangerous Age, Cynthia* 1968; *The Bed Sitting Room* 1969; *Monte Carlo or Bust* 1969; *Alice's Adventures in Wonderland* 1972; *Pleasure at Her Majesty's* 1976; *The Hound of the Baskervilles* 1977; *Foul Play* 1978; *10* 1979; *Wholly Moses!* 1980; *Arthur* 1981; *Six Weeks* 1982; *Lovesick* 1983; *Romantic Comedy* 1983; *Unfaithfully Yours* 1983; *Best Defense* 1984; *Micki & Maude* 1984; *Santa Claus* 1985; *The Adventures of Milo and Otis* 1986; *Like Father, like Son* 1987; *Arthur 2: On the Rocks* 1988; *Crazy People* 1990; *Blame It on the Bellboy* 1992; *The Pickle* 1993; *The Disappearance of Kevin Johnson* 1995
Moore, Duke *aka* **Moore, James "Duke"** (1913–1976) *Plan 9 from Outer Space* 1959; *Hellborn* 1961
Moore, Eileen (1932–) *Mr Denning Drives North* 1951; *The Happy Family* 1952; *An Inspector Calls* 1954; *Men of Sherwood Forest* 1954; *Devil's Bait* 1959
Moore, Eva (1870–1955) *The Old Dark House* 1932; *Vintage Wine* 1935
Moore, Frank *Rabid* 1976; *Food of the Gods II* 1989
Moore, Gar (1920–1985) *Abbott and Costello Meet the Killer, Boris Karloff* 1949; *Johnny Stool Pigeon* 1949; *The Underworld Story* 1950
Moore, Grace *aka* **Moore, Miss Grace** (1898–1947) *A Lady's Morals* 1930; *One Night of Love* 1934; *The King Steps Out* 1936; *I'll Take Romance* 1937; *When You're in Love* 1937
Moore, Joanna (1934–1997) *Monster on the Campus* 1958; *Ride a Crooked Trail* 1958; *Touch of Evil* 1958; *The Last Angry Man* 1959; *Follow That Dream* 1962; *Son of Flubber* 1962; *Walk on the Wild Side* 1962; *Countdown* 1968; *Never a Dull Moment* 1968
Moore, Juanita (1922–) *The Girl Can't Help It* 1956; *Imitation of Life* 1959; *Walk on the Wild Side* 1962; *The Singing Nun* 1966; *Abby* 1974; *Paternity* 1981
Moore, Julianne (1961–) *Tales from the Darkside: the Movie* 1991; *Body of Evidence* 1992; *The Gun in Betty Lou's Handbag* 1992; *The Hand That Rocks the Cradle* 1992; *Benny and Joon* 1993; *The Fugitive* 1993; *Short Cuts* 1993; *Vanya on 42nd Street* 1994; *Assassins* 1995; *Nine Months* 1995; *Roommates* 1995; *[Safe]* 1995; *The Myth of Fingerprints* 1996; *Surviving Picasso* 1996; *The Big Lebowski* 1997; *Boogie Nights* 1997; *The Lost World: Jurassic Park* 1997; *Chicago Cab* 1998; *Psycho* 1998; *Cookie's Fortune* 1999; *The End of the Affair* 1999; *An Ideal Husband* 1999; *Magnolia* 1999; *A Map of the World* 1999; *Evolution* 2001; *Hannibal* 2001; *The Shipping News* 2001; *Far from Heaven* 2002; *The Hours* 2002; *Laws of Attraction* 2003; *The Forgotten* 2004
Moore, Kieron (1925–) *Anna Karenina* 1947; *A Man about the House* 1947; *Mine Own Executioner* 1947; *David and Bathsheba* 1951; *Ten Tall Men* 1951; *Mantrap* 1952; *Conflict of Wings* 1953; *The Green Scarf* 1954; *The Blue Peter* 1955; *Satellite in the Sky* 1956; *The Steel Bayonet* 1957; *The Key* 1958; *Darby O'Gill and the Little People* 1959; *The Day They Robbed the Bank of England* 1960; *Doctor Blood's Coffin* 1960; *The League of Gentlemen* 1960; *The Siege of Sidney Street* 1960; *The Day of the Triffids* 1962; *I Thank a Fool* 1962; *The Main Attraction* 1962; *Girl in the Headlines* 1963; *Hide and Seek* 1963; *Crack in the World* 1964; *Son of a Gunfighter* 1964; *Arabesque* 1966
Moore, Lisa (1940–1989) *Hit Man* 1972; *Act of Vengeance* 1974
Moore, Mandy (1984–) *The Princess Diaries* 2001; *A Walk to Remember* 2002; *Chasing Liberty* 2004; *Racing Stripes* 2004; *Saved!* 2004
Moore, Margo (1931–2000) *Wake Me When It's Over* 1960; *The George Raft Story* 1961
Moore, Mary Tyler (1936–) *X-15* 1961; *Thoroughly Modern Millie* 1967; *Don't Just Stand There* 1968; *What's So Bad About Feeling Good?* 1968; *Change of Habit* 1969; *Ordinary People* 1980; *Six Weeks* 1982; *Just between Friends* 1986; *Flirting with Disaster* 1996; *Keys to Tulsa* 1996; *Payback* 1997
Moore, Matt (1888–1960) *Traffic in Souls* 1913; *20,000 Leagues under the Sea* 1916; *The Pride of the Clan* 1917; *The Unholy Three* 1925; *Coquette* 1929; *Consolation Marriage* 1931; *Deluge* 1933
Moore, Melba (1945–) *Lost in the Stars* 1974; *All Dogs Go to Heaven* 1989; *Def by Temptation* 1990; *The Fighting Temptations* 2003
Moore (2), Michael (1954–) *The Big One* 1997; *Edtv* 1999
Moore, Owen (1886–1939) *The Battle of the Sexes* 1914; *The Black Bird* 1926; *The Road to Mandalay* 1926; *High Voltage* 1929; *What a Widow!* 1930; *As You Desire Me* 1932; *She Done Him Wrong* 1933; *A Star Is Born* 1937
Moore, Pauline (1914–2001) *Born Reckless* 1937; *Charlie Chan at the Olympics* 1937; *Heidi* 1937; *Love Is News* 1937; *Three Blind Mice* 1938; *Charlie Chan at Treasure Island* 1939; *Charlie Chan in Reno* 1939; *The Three Musketeers* 1939; *Young Mr Lincoln* 1939
Moore, Roger (1927–) *Piccadilly Incident* 1946; *The Last Time I Saw Paris* 1954; *Diane* 1955; *Interrupted Melody* 1955; *The King's Thief* 1955; *The Miracle* 1959; *The Sins of Rachel Cade* 1960; *Gold of the Seven Saints* 1961; *Crossplot* 1969; *The Man Who Haunted Himself* 1970; *Live and Let Die* 1973; *Gold* 1974; *The Man with the Golden Gun* 1974; *That Lucky Touch* 1975; *Sherlock Holmes in New York* 1976; *Shout at the Devil* 1976; *The Sicilian Cross* 1976; *The Spy Who Loved Me* 1977; *The Wild Geese* 1978; *Escape to Athena* 1979; *Moonraker* 1979; *North Sea Hijack* 1979; *The Sea Wolves* 1980; *The Cannonball Run* 1981; *For Your Eyes Only* 1981; *The Curse of the Pink Panther* 1983; *Octopussy* 1983; *The Naked Face* 1984; *A View to a Kill* 1985; *Bullseye!* 1990; *Fire, Ice and Dynamite* 1990; *Bed & Breakfast* 1992; *The Quest* 1996; *The Enemy* 2000; *Boat Trip* 2002
Moore, Sheila (1938–) *Bye Bye Blues* 1989; *The Reflecting Skin* 1990
Moore, Stephen (1937–) *A Midsummer Night's Dream* 1961; *Laughterhouse* 1984; *Clockwise* 1986
Moore, Terry (1929–) *The Return of October* 1948; *Mighty Joe Young* 1949; *Come Back, Little Sheba* 1952; *Beneath the 12-Mile Reef* 1953; *King of the Khyber Rifles* 1953; *Man on a Tightrope* 1953; *Daddy Long Legs* 1955; *Postmark for Danger* 1955; *Shack Out on 101* 1955; *Between Heaven and Hell* 1956; *Cast a Long Shadow* 1959; *A Private's Affair* 1959; *Platinum High School* 1960; *Black Spurs* 1965; *City of Fear* 1965; *Waco* 1966; *Beverly Hills Brats* 1989
Moore, Victor (1876–1962) *Gold Diggers of 1937* 1936; *Swing Time* 1936; *Make Way for Tomorrow* 1937; *Radio City Revels* 1938; *Louisiana Purchase* 1941; *Star Spangled Rhythm* 1942; *The Heat's On* 1943; *Riding High* 1943; *True to Life* 1943; *It Happened on Fifth Avenue* 1947; *On Our Merry Way* 1948; *A Kiss in the Dark* 1949; *We're Not Married* 1952; *The Seven Year Itch* 1955
Moorehead, Agnes (1906–1974) *Citizen Kane* 1941; *The Big Street* 1942; *Journey into Fear* 1942; *The Magnificent Ambersons* 1942; *Government Girl* 1943; *Jane Eyre* 1943; *The Youngest Profession* 1943; *Dragon Seed* 1944; *Mrs Parkington* 1944; *The Seventh Cross* 1944; *Since You Went Away* 1944; *Tomorrow the World!* 1944; *Keep Your Powder Dry* 1945; *Our Vines Have Tender Grapes* 1945; *Dark Passage* 1947; *The Lost Moment* 1947; *Johnny Belinda* 1948; *Station West* 1948; *Summer Holiday* 1948; *The Woman in White* 1948; *The Great Sinner* 1949; *The Stratton Story* 1949; *Caged* 1950; *Adventures of Captain Fabian* 1951; *The Blue Veil* 1951; *Fourteen Hours* 1951; *Show Boat* 1951; *Black Jack* 1952; *Main Street to Broadway* 1953; *Scandal at Scourie* 1953; *The Story of Three Loves* 1953; *Magnificent Obsession* 1954; *All That Heaven Allows* 1955; *The Left Hand of God* 1955; *Untamed* 1955; *The Conqueror* 1956; *Meet Me in Las Vegas* 1956; *The Opposite Sex* 1956; *Pardners* 1956; *The Revolt of Mamie Stover* 1956; *The Swan* 1956; *Jeanne Eagels* 1957; *Raintree County* 1957; *The Story of Mankind* 1957; *The True Story of Jesse James* 1957; *The Bat* 1959; *Tempest* 1959; *Pollyanna* 1960; *How the West Was Won* 1962; *Jessica* 1962; *Who's Minding the Store?* 1963; *Hush… Hush, Sweet Charlotte* 1964; *The Singing Nun* 1966; *What's the Matter with Helen?* 1971; *Charlotte's Web* 1973
Moorhead, Natalie (1901–1992) *Manslaughter* 1930; *Illicit* 1931; *Three Wise Girls* 1932; *The Mind Reader* 1933; *Lady of the Tropics* 1939
Mooy, Genevieve *Thank God He Met Lizzie* 1997; *The Dish* 2000
Morales, Esai (1962–) *Bad Boys* 1983; *La Bamba* 1987; *The Principal* 1987; *Naked Tango* 1990; *The Burning Season* 1994; *In the Army Now* 1994; *My Family* 1994; *Rapa Nui* 1994; *Scorpion Spring* 1995; *The Disappearance of Garcia Lorca* 1997; *Dogwatch* 1997; *Doomsday Man* 1998; *Atomic Train* 1999; *The Adventures of Tom Thumb and Thumbelina* 2002
Morales, Jacobo (1934–) *Bananas* 1971; *Up the Sandbox* 1972; *What Happened to Santiago* 1989
Moran, Dolores (1924–1982) *Old Acquaintance* 1943; *To Have and Have Not* 1944; *The Horn Blows at Midnight* 1945; *The Man I Love* 1946; *Christmas Eve* 1947; *Count the Hours* 1953; *Silver Lode* 1954
Moran, Dylan (1971–) *The Actors* 2003; *Shaun of the Dead* 2004
Moran, Erin (1961–) *Eighty Steps to Jonah* 1969; *Watermelon Man* 1970
Moran, Jackie (1923–1990) *And So They Were Married* 1936; *The Adventures of Tom Sawyer* 1938; *Mad about Music* 1938; *Song of the Open Road* 1944
Moran, Lois (1909–1990) *Stella Dallas* 1925; *The Road to Mandalay* 1926; *Mammy* 1930; *Alice in the Cities* 1974
Morán, Mercedes (1955–) *La Cienaga* 2001; *The Motorcycle Diaries* 2004; *La Niña Santa* 2004
Moran, Nick (1969–) *Buddy's Song* 1990; *Lock, Stock and Two Smoking Barrels* 1998; *Another Life* 2000; *Christie Malry's Own Double-Entry* 2000; *The Proposal* 2000; *The Musketeer* 2001; *Spivs* 2003
Moran, Peggy (1918–2002) *Argentine Nights* 1940; *The Mummy's Hand* 1940; *Trail of the Vigilantes* 1940; *There's One Born Every Minute* 1942
Moran, Polly (1884–1952) *The Divine Woman* 1928; *Guilty Hands* 1931; *The Passionate Plumber* 1932; *Red River Range* 1938; *Adam's Rib* 1949
Moranis, Rick (1954–) *Strange Brew* 1983; *Ghostbusters* 1984; *Hockey Night* 1984; *Streets of Fire* 1984; *The Wild Life* 1984; *Brewster's Millions* 1985; *Club Paradise* 1986; *Head Office* 1986; *Little Shop of Horrors* 1986; *Spaceballs* 1987; *Ghostbusters II* 1989; *Honey, I Shrunk the Kids* 1989; *Parenthood* 1989; *My Blue Heaven* 1990; *Honey, I Blew Up the Kid* 1992; *Splitting Heirs* 1993; *The Flintstones* 1994; *Little Giants* 1994; *Big Bully* 1996; *Honey, We Shrunk Ourselves* 1997; *Rudolph the Red-Nosed Reindeer and the Island of the Misfit Toys* 2001; *Brother Bear* 2003
Morante, Laura (1956–) *The Tragedy of a Ridiculous Man* 1981; *Man on Fire* 1987; *Marianna Ucria* 1997; *The Son's Room* 2001; *The Dancer Upstairs* 2002
Mordyukova, Nonna (1925–) *The Commissar* 1967; *A Station for Two* 1983
More, Kenneth (1914–1982) *Look Up and Laugh* 1935; *Scott of the Antarctic* 1948; *Now Barabbas Was a Robber* 1949; *Chance of a Lifetime* 1950; *The Clouded Yellow* 1950; *Appointment with Venus* 1951; *Brandy for the Parson* 1951; *The Yellow Balloon* 1952; *Genevieve* 1953; *Never Let Me Go* 1953; *Our Girl Friday* 1953; *Doctor in the House* 1954; *The Deep Blue Sea* 1955; *Raising*

a Riot 1955; Reach for the Sky 1956; The Admirable Crichton 1957; Next to No Time 1958; A Night to Remember 1958; The Sheriff of Fractured Jaw 1958; North West Frontier 1959; The Thirty-Nine Steps 1959; Man in the Moon 1960; Sink the Bismarck! 1960; The Greengage Summer 1961; The Longest Day 1962; Some People 1962; We Joined the Navy 1962; The Comedy Man 1964; Dark of the Sun 1967; Fraulein Doktor 1968; Battle of Britain 1969; Oh! What a Lovely War 1969; Scrooge 1970; The Slipper and the Rose 1976; The Spaceman and King Arthur 1979

Moreau, Jeanne (1928–) Honour among Thieves 1954; La Reine Margot 1954; Secrets d'Alcove 1954; Lift to the Scaffold 1957; Les Amants 1958; Les Liaisons Dangereuses 1959; Five Branded Women 1960; Une Femme Est une Femme 1961; Jules et Jim 1961; La Notte 1961; Eva 1962; The Trial 1962; Bay of the Angels 1963; Le Feu Follet 1963; The Victors 1963; Banana Peel 1964; The Diary of a Chambermaid 1964; The Train 1964; The Yellow Rolls-Royce 1964; Viva Maria! 1965; Chimes at Midnight 1966; Mademoiselle 1966; The Bride Wore Black 1967; The Oldest Profession 1967; The Sailor from Gibraltar 1967; Great Catherine 1968; The Immortal Story 1968; The Little Theatre of Jean Renoir 1969; Alex in Wonderland 1970; Monte Walsh 1970; Les Valseuses 1974; The Last Tycoon 1976; Mr Klein 1976; Querelle 1982; Le Paltoquet 1986; Hotel Terminus: the Life and Times of Klaus Barbie 1987; Nikita 1990; The Old Lady Who Walked in the Sea 1991; Until the End of the World 1991; Map of the Human Heart 1992; Beyond the Clouds 1995; The Proprietor 1996; I Love You, I Love You Not 1997

Moreau, Nathaniel (1978–) The Last Winter 1989; George's Island 1991

Moreau, Yolande Vagabond 1985; Amélie 2001

Morecambe, Eric (1926–1984) The Intelligence Men 1965; That Riviera Touch 1966; The Magnificent Two 1967; Simon, Simon 1970

Morel, François (1959–) Le Bonheur Est dans le Pré 1995; [Three] Après la Vie 2002; [Two] Un Couple Epatant 2002

Morel, Jacques (1922–) Topaze 1951; Marie Antoinette 1956; One Night at the Music Hall 1956

Moreland, Mantan (1902–1973) Footlight Serenade 1942; Charlie Chan in The Chinese Cat 1944; Charlie Chan in the Secret Service 1944; Meeting at Midnight 1944; The Jade Mask 1945; The Scarlet Clue 1945; The Shanghai Cobra 1945; Dark Alibi 1946; The Trap 1947; Spider Baby 1964; Watermelon Man 1970

Morell, André (1909–1978) Madeleine 1949; Stage Fright 1949; The Clouded Yellow 1950; Seven Days to Noon 1950; Stolen Face 1952; His Majesty O'Keefe 1953; The Black Knight 1954; The Man Who Never Was 1955; They Can't Hang Me 1955; The Black Tent 1956; The Bridge on the River Kwai 1957; The Camp on Blood Island 1958; Paris Holiday 1958; The Giant Behemoth 1959; The Hound of the Baskervilles 1959; Cone of Silence 1960; Cash on Demand 1961; The Shadow of the Cat 1961; The Plague of the Zombies 1965; The Mummy's Shroud 1966

Morelli, Rina (1908–1976) Senso 1954; The Leopard 1962; L'Innocente 1976

Moreno, Antonio (1887–1967) Mare Nostrum 1926; The Temptress 1926; It 1927; The Bohemian Girl 1936; Valley of the Sun 1942; Captain from Castile 1947; Dallas 1950; Creature from the Black Lagoon 1954

Moreno, Rita (1931–) The Ring 1952; Singin' in the Rain 1952; Garden of Evil 1954; Jivaro 1954; The Yellow Tomahawk 1954; Seven Cities of Gold 1955; Untamed 1955; The King and I 1956; The Lieutenant Wore Skirts 1956; The Vagabond King 1956; The Deerslayer 1957; This Rebel Breed 1960; Summer and Smoke 1961; West Side Story 1961; The Night of the Following Day 1968; Marlowe 1969; Popi 1969; Carnal Knowledge 1971; The Ritz 1976; Happy Birthday, Gemini 1980; The Four Seasons 1981; Age Isn't Everything 1991; Italian Movie 1994; Angus 1995; Slums of Beverly Hills 1998; Resurrection 1999; Piñero 2001; Casa de los Babys 2003

Moreno, Rosita (1907–1993) Her Wedding Night 1930; The Scoundrel 1935

Moretti, Michèle Les Roseaux Sauvages 1994; Who Killed Bambi? 2003; Look at Me 2004

Moretti, Nanni (1953–) Dear Diary 1994; Aprile 1998; The Son's Room 2001

Morfogen, George (1933–) The Thief Who Came to Dinner 1973; Those Lips, Those Eyes 1980

Morgan, Cindy (1954–) Caddyshack 1980; Tron 1982

Morgan, Debbi (1956–) Eve's Bayou 1997; The Hurricane 1999; Love & Basketball 2000; Coach Carter 2005

Morgan, Dennis (1910–1994) The Return of Dr X 1939; Kitty Foyle 1940; Affectionately Yours 1941; Captains of the Clouds 1942; The Hard Way 1942; In This Our Life 1942; Thank Your Lucky Stars 1943; The Desert Song 1944; Shine On, Harvest Moon 1944; The Very Thought of You 1944; Christmas in Connecticut 1945; God Is My Co-Pilot 1945; Two Guys from Milwaukee 1946; My Wild Irish Rose 1947; It's a Great Feeling 1949; Perfect Strangers 1950; Pretty Baby 1950; Painting the Clouds with Sunshine 1951; This Woman Is Dangerous 1952; Pearl of the South Pacific 1955

Morgan, Frank (1890–1949) Fast and Loose 1930; Laughter 1930; The Half Naked Truth 1932; Blonde Bombshell 1933; Broadway to Hollywood 1933; Hallelujah, I'm a Bum 1933; The Kiss before the Mirror 1933; Reunion in Vienna 1933; When Ladies Meet 1933; The Affairs of Cellini 1934; The Cat and the Fiddle 1934; Success at Any Price 1934; Escapade 1935; The Good Fairy 1935; I Live My Life 1935; Naughty Marietta 1935; The Perfect Gentleman 1935; Dimples 1936; The Great Ziegfeld 1936; Piccadilly Jim 1936; Trouble for Two 1936; The Emperor's Candlesticks 1937; The Last of Mrs Cheyney 1937; Rosalie 1937; Saratoga 1937; The Crowd Roars 1938; Paradise for Three 1938; Port of Seven Seas 1938; Sweethearts 1938; Balalaika 1939; Broadway Serenade 1939; The Wizard of Oz 1939; Boom Town 1940; Broadway Melody of 1940 1940; The Ghost Comes Home 1940; The Mortal Storm 1940; The Shop around the Corner 1940; Honky Tonk 1941; The Vanishing Virginian 1941; Tortilla Flat 1942; White Cargo 1942; The Human Comedy 1943; Casanova Brown 1944; The White Cliffs of Dover 1944; Yolanda and the Thief 1945; Courage of Lassie 1946; Lady Luck 1946; Green Dolphin Street 1947; Summer Holiday 1948; The Three Musketeers 1948; Any Number Can Play 1949; The Great Sinner 1949; The Stratton Story 1949; Key to the City 1950

Morgan, Gary Logan's Run 1976; Matilda 1978; Storybook 1995

Morgan, Gene (1893–1940) Blonde Venus 1932; If You Could Only Cook 1935

Morgan, Harry aka **Morgan, Henry** (1915–) To the Shores of Tripoli 1942; Happy Land 1943; The Ox-Bow Incident 1943; The Eve of St Mark 1944; A Bell for Adano 1945; From This Day Forward 1946; It Shouldn't Happen to a Dog 1946; The Gangster 1947; Moonrise 1948; The Saxon Charm 1948; Yellow Sky 1948; Down to the Sea in Ships 1949; Holiday Affair 1949; Appointment with Danger 1950; Dark City 1950; The Well 1951; Apache War Smoke 1952; High Noon 1952; My Six Convicts 1952; Arena 1953; The Glenn Miller Story 1953; Torch Song 1953; The Far Country 1954; The Teahouse of the August Moon 1956; Inherit the Wind 1960; The Mountain Road 1960; Frankie & Johnny 1966; What Did You Do in the War, Daddy? 1966; One Born Every Minute 1967; Support Your Local Sheriff! 1969; Viva Max! 1969; The Barefoot Executive 1971; Scandalous John 1971; Support Your Local Gunfighter 1971; Snowball Express 1972; Charley and the Angel 1973; The Apple Dumpling Gang 1974; The Shootist 1976; The Cat from Outer Space 1978; The Apple Dumpling Gang Rides Again 1979; Dragnet 1987

Morgan (1), Helen (1900–1941) Applause 1929; Marie Galante 1934; Go into Your Dance 1935; Show Boat 1936

Morgan, Henry (1915–1994) So This Is New York 1948; Murder, Inc 1960

Morgan, Horace aka **Morgan, Horace "Cupid"** aka **Morgan, H A** The Three Ages 1923; Beggars of Life 1928

Morgan, Michèle (1920–) Gribouille 1937; Le Quai des Brumes 1938; Stormy Waters 1941; Joan of Paris 1942; Higher and Higher 1943; Passage to Marseille 1944; The Chase 1946; La Symphonie Pastorale 1946; The Fallen Idol 1948; The Seven Deadly Sins 1952; The Proud Ones 1953; Obsession 1954; Les Grandes Manoeuvres 1955; Marguerite de la Nuit 1955; Napoléon 1955; Marie Antoinette 1956; Bluebeard 1962; Lost Command 1966; Everybody's Fine 1990

Morgan, Nancy (1949–) Fraternity Row 1977; Grand Theft Auto 1977; Americathon 1979; Danielle Steel's Heartbeat 1992

Morgan, Ralph (1882–1956) Rasputin and the Empress 1932; Strange Interlude 1932; The Kennel Murder Case 1933; The Mad Game 1933; The Power and the Glory 1933; Shanghai Madness 1933; The Last Gentleman 1934; Stand Up and Cheer! 1934; Magnificent Obsession 1935; Star of Midnight 1935; Crack-Up 1936; General Spanky 1936; Human Cargo 1936; Speed 1936; Mannequin 1937; Wells Fargo 1937; Wives under Suspicion 1938; Fast and Loose 1939; Geronimo 1939; The Lone Wolf Spy Hunt 1939; Hitler's Madman 1943; The Impostor 1944; Jack London 1944; The Monster Maker 1944; Weird Woman 1944; Sleep, My Love 1948

Morgan, Robbi What's the Matter with Helen? 1971; Friday the 13th 1980

Morgan, Russ (1904–1969) The Great Man 1956; Mister Cory 1957

Morgan, Stafford Cleopatra Jones 1973; The Alpha Incident 1977

Morgan, Terence (1921–) Hamlet 1948; Captain Horatio Hornblower RN 1951; Encore 1951; It Started in Paradise 1952; Mandy 1952; The Steel Key 1953; Turn the Key Softly 1953; Dance Little Lady 1954; Forbidden Cargo 1954; Svengali 1954; They Can't Hang Me 1955; It's a Wonderful World 1956; The March Hare 1956; The Scamp 1957; Tread Softly Stranger 1958; The Shakedown 1959; Piccadilly Third Stop 1960; The Curse of the Mummy's Tomb 1964; The Penthouse 1967

Morgan, Trevor (1986–) Barney's Great Adventure 1998; I'll Remember April 1999; The Sixth Sense 1999; A Rumor of Angels 2000; The Glass House 2001; Jurassic Park III 2001; Mean Creek 2004

Morgan, Wendy Yanks 1979; 84 Charing Cross Road 1986

Morgenstern, Maia (1962–) Ulysses' Gaze 1995; The Passion of the Christ 2004

Mori, Masayuki (1911–1973) Rashomon 1950; The Idiot 1951; The Lady of Musashino 1951; Ugetsu Monogatari 1953; The Princess Yang Kwei Fei 1955; The Bad Sleep Well 1960; Alone on the Pacific 1963

Mori, Paola (1930–1986) Crossed Swords 1954; Confidential Report 1955

Moriarty, Cathy aka **Moriarty-Gentile, Cathy** (1960–) Raging Bull 1980; Neighbors 1981; White of the Eye 1986; Kindergarten Cop 1990; Soapdish 1991; The Gun in Betty Lou's Handbag 1992; The Mambo Kings 1992; Another Stakeout 1993; Matinee 1993; Me and the Kid 1993; Pontiac Moon 1994; Casper 1995; Dream with the Fishes 1996; Cop Land 1997; Pool Girl 1997; Casper Meets Wendy 1998; Digging to China 1998; Gloria 1998; But I'm a Cheerleader 1999; Crazy in Alabama 1999; Red Team 1999; Analyze That 2002

Moriarty, Michael (1941–) Glory Boy 1971; The Last Detail 1973; Report to the Commissioner 1975; Who'll Stop the Rain? 1978; Q – the Winged Serpent 1982; Odd Birds 1985; Pale Rider 1985; The Stuff 1985; Troll 1986; Hanoi Hilton 1987; It's Alive III: Island of the Alive 1987; A Return to Salem's Lot 1987; Dark Tower 1989; Full Fathom Five 1990; Courage under Fire 1996; Crime of the Century 1996; Shiloh 1996; The Art of Murder 1999; Along Came a Spider 2001; James Dean 2001

Moriarty, P H Jaws III 1983; Number One 1984; Lock, Stock and Two Smoking Barrels 1998

Morice, Tara (1964–) Strictly Ballroom 1992; Hotel Sorrento 1994

Morier-Genoud, Philippe Au Revoir les Enfants 1987; Cyrano de Bergerac 1990; Laissez-passer 2001

Morison, Patricia (1914–) The Roundup 1941; Beyond the Blue Horizon 1942; Calling Dr Death 1943; The Fallen Sparrow 1943; Hitler's Madman 1943; Without Love 1945; Sherlock Holmes and the Secret Code 1946; Song of the Thin Man 1947; Tarzan and the Huntress 1947; The Prince of Thieves 1948; Song without End 1960

Morissette, Alanis (1974–) Dogma 1999; Jay and Silent Bob Strike Back 2001

Morita, Pat aka **Morita, Noriyuki "Pat"** (1932–) Evil Roy Slade 1971; Full Moon High 1982; Slapstick of Another Kind 1982; The Karate Kid 1984; Night Patrol 1984; The Karate Kid Part II 1986; Collision Course 1987; Captive Hearts 1988; The Karate Kid III 1989; Lena's Holiday 1990; Auntie Lee's Meat Pies 1991; Honeymoon in Vegas 1992; Even Cowgirls Get the Blues 1993; The Next Karate Kid 1994; Bloodsport II: The Next Kumite 1996; Mulan 1998; I'll Remember April 1999; King Cobra 1999; The Center of the World 2001

Moritzen, Henning (1928–) Cries and Whispers 1972; Waltzing Regitze 1989

Morley, Karen (1905–2003) Mata Hari 1931; Arsene Lupin 1932; Flesh 1932; The Mask of Fu Manchu 1932; Scarface 1932; Gabriel over the White House 1933; Our Daily Bread 1934; Black Fury 1935; The Littlest Rebel 1935; Beloved Enemy 1936; The Last Train from Madrid 1937; Kentucky 1938; Pride and Prejudice 1940; Framed 1947; M 1951

Morley, Robert (1908–1992) Marie Antoinette 1938; The Foreman Went to France 1941; Major Barbara 1941; The Big Blockade 1942; The Young Mr Pitt 1942; I Live in Grosvenor Square 1945; The Ghosts of Berkeley Square 1947; The Small Back Room 1949; The African Queen 1951; Outcast of the Islands 1951; Curtain Up 1952; Beat the Devil 1953; The Final Test 1953; The Story of Gilbert and Sullivan 1953; Beau Brummell 1954; The Good Die Young 1954; Quentin Durward 1955; Around the World in 80 Days 1956; Loser Takes All 1956; The Doctor's Dilemma 1958; Law and Disorder 1958; The Rainbow Jacket 1958; The Sheriff of Fractured Jaw 1958; The Journey 1959; Libel 1959; Oscar Wilde 1959; The Battle of the Sexes 1960; The Boys 1961; Go to Blazes 1961; The Young Ones 1961; The Road to Hong Kong 1962; Hot Enough for June 1963; Ladies Who Do 1963; Murder at the Gallop 1963; Nine Hours to Rama 1963; The Old Dark House 1963; Take Her, She's Mine 1963; Genghis Khan 1964; Of Human Bondage 1964; Topkapi 1964; The Dot and the Line 1965; Life at the Top 1965; A Study in Terror 1965; Those Magnificent Men in Their Flying Machines 1965; The Alphabet Murders 1966; Finders Keepers 1966; Hotel Paradiso 1966; Way... Way Out 1966; The Trygon Factor 1967; Woman Times Seven 1967; Hot Millions 1968; Sinful Davey 1969; Some Girls Do 1969; Twinky 1969; Cromwell 1970; Doctor in Trouble 1970; Song of Norway 1970; When Eight Bells Toll 1971; Theatre of Blood 1973; Great Expectations 1974; The Blue Bird 1976; Who Is Killing the Great Chefs of Europe? 1978; The Human Factor 1979; Scavenger Hunt 1979; Loophole 1980; Oh, Heavenly Dog! 1980; The Great Muppet Caper 1981; High Road to China 1983; The Trouble with Spies 1987

Morris, Anita (1944–1994) Maria's Lovers 1984; Blue City 1986; Ruthless People 1986; Aria 1987; 18 Again! 1988; A Sinful Life 1989; Martians Go Home 1990; Me and the Kid 1993

Morris, Aubrey Blood from the Mummy's Tomb 1971; A Clockwork Orange 1971; The Wicker Man 1973; Oxford Blues 1984; The Rachel Papers 1989; Tales from the Crypt Presents: Bordello of Blood 1996; Bram Stoker's Legend of the Mummy 1998

Morris, Barboura aka **O'Neill, Barboura** (1932–1975) Sorority Girl 1957; A Bucket of Blood 1959; The Wasp Woman 1959; Atlas 1960; The Trip 1967

Morris, Beth (1949–) Crucible of Terror 1971; Old Scores 1991

Morris, Chester (1901–1970) Alibi 1929; The Bat Whispers 1930; The Big House 1930; The Divorcee 1930; Red-Headed Woman 1932; Sinners in the Sun 1932; The Gay Bride 1934; Princess O'Hara 1935; Public Hero No 1 1935; Flight from Glory 1937; Law of the Underworld 1938; Smashing the Rackets 1938; Blind Alley 1939; Five Came Back 1939; Thunder Afloat 1939; Meet Boston Blackie 1941; Secret Command 1944; Unchained 1955; The She-Creature 1956; The Great White Hope 1970

Morris, Dorothy (1922–) Young Ideas 1943; None Shall Escape 1944

Morris, Garrett (1944–) The Stuff 1985; Santa with Muscles 1996; Little Richard 2000; Jackpot 2001

Morris, Haviland (1959–) Sixteen Candles 1984; Who's That Girl 1987; Love or Money 1990; Home Alone 3 1997

Morris, Howard (1919–2005) Forty Pounds of Trouble 1962; Fluffy 1965; Way... Way Out

1966; *High Anxiety* 1977; *Life Stinks* 1991

Morris, Jeff (1936–2004) *Goin' South* 1978; *The Border* 1981

Morris, Judy (1947–) *The Plumber* 1979; *Phar Lap* 1983; *The More Things Change* 1985

Morris, Kathryn (1969–) *Sleepstalker* 1995; *Mindhunters* 2003

Morris, Lana (1930–1998) *The Weaker Sex* 1948; *The Chiltern Hundreds* 1949; *Trottie True* 1949; *Morning Departure* 1950; *The Woman in Question* 1950; *Trouble in Store* 1953; *Man of the Moment* 1955; *Home and Away* 1956; *I Start Counting* 1970

Morris, Libby *Tiara Tahiti* 1962; *The Adding Machine* 1969

Morris, Mary (1915–1988) *Victoria the Great* 1937; *The Thief of Bagdad* 1940; *Pimpernel Smith* 1941; *Undercover* 1943; *The Man from Morocco* 1944; *Train of Events* 1949

Morris, Phyllis (1893–1982) *The Adventures of Tartu* 1943; *The Silver Darlings* 1947; *Three Came Home* 1950

Morris, Wayne (1914–1959) *Kid Galahad* 1937; *The Return of Dr X* 1939; *I Wanted Wings* 1941; *Deep Valley* 1947; *Voice of the Turtle* 1947; *The Time of Your Life* 1948; *A Kiss in the Dark* 1949; *Task Force* 1949; *The Younger Brothers* 1949; *The Master Plan* 1954; *Port of Hell* 1954; *Riding Shotgun* 1954; *The Crooked Sky* 1957; *Paths of Glory* 1957; *Plunder Road* 1957

Morrison, James (1954–) *Unfinished Business…* 1987; *The One* 2001

Morrison, Jennifer *aka* **Morrison, Jenny** (1979–) *Intersection* 1994; *Stir of Echoes* 1999; *Urban Legends: Final Cut* 2000; *Surviving Christmas* 2004

Morrison, Shelley (1936–) *Castle of Evil* 1966; *Man and Boy* 1971

Morrison, "Sunshine Sammy" *aka* **Morrison, Sunshine** *aka* **Morrison, Sammy** (1912–1989) *Boys of the City* 1940; *That Gang of Mine* 1940; *Pride of the Bowery* 1941; *Spooks Run Wild* 1941; *Ghosts in the Night* 1943

Morrison, Temuera *aka* **Morrison, Temuera Derek** (1961–) *Once Were Warriors* 1994; *Barb Wire* 1995; *The Island of Dr Moreau* 1996; *Speed 2: Cruise Control* 1997; *Six Days Seven Nights* 1998; *What Becomes of the Broken Hearted?* 1999; *From Dusk till Dawn 3: the Hangman's Daughter* 2000; *Star Wars Episode II: Attack of the Clones* 2002; *The Beautiful Country* 2004; *Blueberry* 2004

Morrissey, Betty (1908–1944) *A Woman of Paris* 1923; *The Gold Rush* 1925

Morrissey, David (1963–) *Drowning by Numbers* 1988; *Robin Hood* 1990; *Waterland* 1992; *Hilary and Jackie* 1998; *Fanny & Elvis* 1999; *Born Romantic* 2000; *Some Voices* 2000; *Captain Corelli's Mandolin* 2001

Morrissey, Neil (1962–) *I Bought a Vampire Motorcycle* 1989; *Up 'n' Under* 1997; *Triggermen* 2002

Morrow, Jeff (1913–1993) *The Siege at Red River* 1954; *Sign of the Pagan* 1954; *Tanganyika* 1954; *Captain Lightfoot* 1955; *This Island Earth* 1955; *The Creature Walks among Us* 1956; *The First Texan* 1956; *Pardners* 1956; *The Hour of Decision* 1957; *Kronos* 1957; *The Story of Ruth* 1960

Morrow, Jo (1940–) *Juke Box Rhythm* 1959; *The Legend of Tom Dooley* 1959; *Our Man in Havana* 1959; *13 Ghosts* 1959; *The Three Worlds of Gulliver* 1959; *Brushfire!* 1962; *Sunday in New York* 1963; *He Rides Tall* 1964

Morrow, Max (1991–) *Jacob Two Two Meets the Hooded Fang* 1999; *Santa Who?* 2000

Morrow, Rob (1962–) *Private Resort* 1985; *Quiz Show* 1994; *Last Dance* 1996; *Mother* 1996; *The Emperor's Club* 2002; *The Guru* 2002

Morrow, Susan (1931–) *The Savage* 1953; *Macabre* 1958

Morrow, Vic (1932–1982) *Tribute to a Bad Man* 1956; *Men in War* 1957; *God's Little Acre* 1958; *King Creole* 1958; *Posse from Hell* 1961; *The Glass House* 1972; *Dirty Mary Crazy Larry* 1974; *The Take* 1974; *The Bad News Bears* 1976; *Treasure of Matecumbe* 1976; *The Evictors* 1979; *Monster* 1980; *Twilight Zone: the Movie* 1983

Morse, Barry (1918–) *Daughter of Darkness* 1948; *No Trace* 1950; *Kings of the Sun* 1963; *Puzzle of a Downfall Child* 1970; *Asylum* 1972; *Welcome to Blood City* 1977; *Power Play* 1978; *The Changeling* 1980; *Murder by Phone* 1982; *Reunion at Fairborough* 1985

Morse, David (1953–) *Inside Moves: the Guys from Max's Bar* 1980; *Personal Foul* 1987; *The Indian Runner* 1991; *The Good Son* 1993; *The Getaway* 1994; *The Crossing Guard* 1995; *Twelve Monkeys* 1995; *Extreme Measures* 1996; *The Long Kiss Goodnight* 1996; *The Rock* 1996; *Contact* 1997; *The Negotiator* 1998; *Crazy in Alabama* 1999; *The Green Mile* 1999; *Dancer in the Dark* 2000; *Proof of Life* 2000; *Diary of a City Priest* 2001; *Hearts in Atlantis* 2001; *Double Vision* 2002

Morse, Helen (1947–) *Petersen* 1974; *Picnic at Hanging Rock* 1975; *Caddie* 1976; *Agatha* 1978; *Far East* 1982

Morse, Natalie *Anchoress* 1993; *My Mother's Courage* 1995

Morse, Robert (1931–) *The Matchmaker* 1958; *Honeymoon Hotel* 1964; *The Loved One* 1965; *Quick, before It Melts* 1965; *A Guide for the Married Man* 1967; *How to Succeed in Business without Really Trying* 1967; *Oh Dad, Poor Dad, Mama's Hung You in the Closet and I'm Feelin' So Sad* 1967; *Where Were You When the Lights Went Out?* 1968; *The Boatniks* 1970; *The Emperor's New Clothes* 1987; *Hunk* 1987

Mortensen, Viggo (1958–) *Witness* 1985; *Prison* 1987; *Salvation! Have You Said Your Prayers Today?* 1987; *Leatherface: the Texas Chainsaw Massacre III* 1990; *The Reflecting Skin* 1990; *The Indian Runner* 1991; *Ruby Cairo* 1992; *Boiling Point* 1993; *Carlito's Way* 1993; *The Young Americans* 1993; *American Yakuza* 1994; *The Prophecy* 1994; *Crimson Tide* 1995; *The Passion of Darkly Noon* 1995; *Albino Alligator* 1996; *Daylight* 1996; *The Portrait of a Lady* 1996; *GI Jane* 1997; *A Perfect Murder* 1998; *Psycho* 1998; *A Walk on the Moon* 1999; *28 Days* 2000; *The Lord of the Rings: The Fellowship of the Ring* 2001; *The Lord of the Rings: The Two Towers* 2002; *Hidalgo* 2003; *The Lord of the Rings: The Return of the King* 2003; *A History of Violence* 2005

Mortimer, Bob (1959–) *Once upon a Time in the Midlands* 2002; *Churchill: the Hollywood Years* 2004

Mortimer, Caroline (1942–) *A Place for Lovers* 1968; *The Hireling* 1973

Mortimer, Charles (1885–1964) *The Return of Bulldog Drummond* 1934; *Someone at the Door* 1936

Mortimer, Emily (1971–) *The Ghost and the Darkness* 1996; *Last of the High Kings* 1996; *Love's Labour's Lost* 1999; *Disney's The Kid* 2000; *The 51st State* 2001; *Lovely & Amazing* 2001; *Bright Young Things* 2003; *Dear Frankie* 2003; *Young Adam* 2003

Morton, Clive (1904–1975) *Kind Hearts and Coronets* 1949; *A Run for Your Money* 1949; *The Lavender Hill Mob* 1951; *Carrington VC* 1954; *Orders Are Orders* 1954; *Lucky Jim* 1957; *The Moonraker* 1957; *Seven Waves Away* 1957; *The Duke Wore Jeans* 1958; *A Matter of WHO* 1961; *Stranger in the House* 1967

Morton, James C (1884–1942) *Tit for Tat* 1934; *Wild Geese Calling* 1941

Morton, Joe (1947–) *The Brother from Another Planet* 1984; *Trouble in Mind* 1985; *Crossroads* 1986; *Stranded* 1987; *The Price of Passion* 1988; *Zelly and Me* 1988; *Tap* 1989; *City of Hope* 1991; *Terminator 2: Judgment Day* 1991; *Forever Young* 1992; *Of Mice and Men* 1992; *No Ordinary Summer* 1994; *Speed* 1994; *The Walking Dead* 1995; *Executive Decision* 1996; *Miss Evers' Boys* 1997; *The Pest* 1997; *Blues Brothers 2000* 1998; *The Astronaut's Wife* 1999; *Mutiny* 1999; *Ali: an American Hero* 2000; *Bounce* 2000; *What Lies Beneath* 2000; *Dragonfly* 2002; *Paycheck* 2003

Morton, Samantha (1977–) *This Is the Sea* 1996; *Under the Skin* 1997; *Dreaming of Joseph Lees* 1998; *Jesus' Son* 1999; *The Last Yellow* 1999; *Sweet and Lowdown* 1999; *Pandaemonium* 2000; *Morvern Callar* 2001; *Minority Report* 2002; *Code 46* 2003; *In America* 2003; *Enduring Love* 2004; *The Libertine* 2004

Morton, Tom *aka* **Morton, Tommy** *Wait 'til the Sun Shines, Nellie* 1952; *Main Street to Broadway* 1953

Mos Def (1973–) *Monster's Ball* 2001; *Brown Sugar* 2002; *The Italian Job* 2003; *The Woodsman* 2004; *The Hitchhiker's Guide to the Galaxy* 2005

Moschin, Gastone (1929–) *The Birds, the Bees, and the Italians* 1965; *Spy in Your Eye* 1965; *The Conformist* 1969

Moscovich, Maurice *aka* **Moscovitch, Maurice** (1871–1940) *Winterset* 1936; *Lancer Spy* 1937; *Make Way for Tomorrow* 1937; *Suez* 1938; *In Name Only* 1939; *Love Affair* 1939; *Susannah of the Mounties* 1939

Moscow, David (1974–) *Big* 1988; *Restaurant* 1998; *Honey* 2003; *Just Married* 2003

Moseley, Bill *aka* **Mosley, Bill** (1953–) *The Texas Chainsaw Massacre Part 2* 1986; *Night of the Living Dead* 1990; *White Fang* 1991; *House of 1000 Corpses* 2001; *The Devil's Rejects* 2005

Moses, David (1962–) *The Daring Dobermans* 1973; *Storm* 1999

Moses, William R (1959–) *Mystic Pizza* 1988; *Fun* 1994; *Wicked* 1998; *Alone with a Stranger* 2000; *Living in Fear* 2001; *Her Best Friend's Husband* 2002

Moshesh, Nthati *Kini and Adams* 1997; *The Long Run* 2000

Mosley, Roger E (1944–) *The Mack* 1973; *Leadbelly* 1976; *The River Niger* 1976; *Stay Hungry* 1976; *Semi-Tough* 1977; *The Jericho Mile* 1979; *Magnum: Don't Eat the Snow in Hawaii* 1980; *Steel* 1980; *Heart Condition* 1990; *Unlawful Entry* 1992; *Pentathlon* 1994; *A Thin Line between Love and Hate* 1996

Moss, Arnold (1910–1989) *Temptation* 1946; *The Loves of Carmen* 1948; *Border Incident* 1949; *Reign of Terror* 1949; *Kim* 1950; *My Favorite Spy* 1951; *Viva Zapata!* 1952; *Bengal Brigade* 1954; *Hell's Island* 1955; *The 27th Day* 1957; *The Fool Killer* 1965; *Gambit* 1966

Moss, Carrie-Anne (1970–) *Lethal Tender* 1996; *The Matrix* 1999; *Chocolat* 2000; *Memento* 2000; *Red Planet* 2000; *The Matrix Reloaded* 2002; *The Matrix Revolutions* 2003; *Suspect Zero* 2004

Moss, Elisabeth (1983–) *Once upon a Forest* 1992; *Separate Lives* 1995; *Earthly Possessions* 1999; *The Joyriders* 1999

Mossé, Mireille *The City of Lost Children* 1995; *Swimming Pool* 2003

Mostel, Josh (1946–) *Going Home* 1971; *Sophie's Choice* 1982; *Star 80* 1983; *Almost You* 1984; *Windy City* 1984; *The Money Pit* 1985; *Radio Days* 1987; *Animal Behavior* 1989; *Naked Tango* 1990; *The Chase* 1994; *Billy Madison* 1995; *The Maddening* 1995; *Great Expectations* 1997; *Rounders* 1998; *Thicker than Blood* 1998; *Big Daddy* 1999

Mostel, Zero (1915–1977) *DuBarry Was a Lady* 1943; *Panic in the Streets* 1950; *The Enforcer* 1951; *Mr Belvedere Rings the Bell* 1951; *The Model and the Marriage Broker* 1951; *Sirocco* 1951; *A Funny Thing Happened on the Way to the Forum* 1966; *Great Catherine* 1968; *The Producers* 1968; *The Great Bank Robbery* 1969; *The Angel Levine* 1970; *The Hot Rock* 1972; *Marco* 1973; *Once upon a Scoundrel* 1973; *Rhinoceros* 1974; *The Front* 1976; *Mastermind* 1976; *Watership Down* 1978

Motta, Bess *The Terminator* 1984; *You Talkin' to Me?* 1987

Mottet, Alain (1928–) *Ho!* 1968; *The Last Known Address* 1969

Mouchet, Catherine (1959–) *Thérèse* 1986; *Extension du Domaine de la Lutte* 1999; *The Pornographer* 2001

Mouglalis, Anna (1978–) *Merci pour le Chocolat* 2000; *Novo* 2002

Moulder-Brown, John (1953–) *Deep End* 1970; *First Love* 1970; *Vampire Circus* 1971; *King, Queen, Knave* 1972; *Rumpelstiltskin* 1986

Mouloudji, Marcel *aka* **Mouloudji** (1922–1994) *Nous Sommes Tous des Assassins* 1952; *Secrets d'Alcove* 1954

Mount, Anson (1973–) *Urban Legends: Final Cut* 2000; *City by the Sea* 2002; *Crossroads* 2002

Mount, Peggy (1916–2001) *Dry Rot* 1956; *Sailor Beware!* 1956; *The Naked Truth* 1957; *Inn for Trouble* 1960; *Ladies Who Do* 1963; *One Way Pendulum* 1965; *Hotel Paradiso* 1966; *Oliver!* 1968; *The Princess and the Goblin* 1992

Mouton, Benjamin *And God Created Woman* 1988; *Whore* 1991; *The Whole Wide World* 1996; *All the Real Girls* 2003

Mowbray, Alan (1896–1969) *God's Gift to Women* 1931; *Guilty Hands* 1931; *The Man from Yesterday* 1932; *Sherlock Holmes* 1932; *Berkeley Square* 1933; *Our Betters* 1933; *Peg o' My Heart* 1933; *Roman Scandals* 1933; *Charlie Chan in London* 1934; *The Girl from Missouri* 1934; *Long Lost Father* 1934; *One More River* 1934; *The Gay Deception* 1935; *In Person* 1935; *Desire* 1936; *My Man Godfrey* 1936; *Rainbow on the River* 1936; *The King and the Chorus Girl* 1937; *On the Avenue* 1937; *Stand-In* 1937; *Topper* 1937; *Vogues of 1938* 1937; *Merrily We Live* 1938; *There Goes My Heart* 1938; *The Llano Kid* 1939; *Never Say Die* 1939; *Topper Takes a Trip* 1939; *The Boys from Syracuse* 1940; *Music in My Heart* 1940; *The Villain Still Pursued Her* 1940; *I Wake Up Screaming* 1941; *That Hamilton Woman* 1941; *That Uncertain Feeling* 1941; *Holy Matrimony* 1943; *Slightly Dangerous* 1943; *Earl Carroll Vanities* 1945; *Where Do We Go from Here?* 1945; *Terror by Night* 1946; *Lured* 1947; *Merton of the Movies* 1947; *Every Girl Should Be Married* 1948; *The Prince of Thieves* 1948; *The Lovable Cheat* 1949; *The Jackpot* 1950; *Wagonmaster* 1950; *Androcles and the Lion* 1952; *Blackbeard the Pirate* 1952; *The King and I* 1956; *The Man Who Knew Too Much* 1956

Mower, Patrick (1940–) *The Devil Rides Out* 1968; *The Smashing Bird I Used to Know* 1969; *Cry of the Banshee* 1970; *Incense for the Damned* 1970; *Black Beauty* 1971; *Catch Me a Spy* 1971; *Carry On England* 1976; *The Devil's Advocate* 1977

Moxey, Hugh (1909–1991) *Meet Simon Cherry* 1949; *You Pay Your Money* 1957

Moxley, Gina *The Sun, the Moon and the Stars* 1995; *Snakes & Ladders* 1996

Moya, Antoinette *Pétain* 1992; *Son Frère* 2003

Moynahan, Bridget (1972–) *Serendipity* 2001; *The Recruit* 2002; *The Sum of All Fears* 2002; *I, Robot* 2004

Mrozowska, Zofla (1922–1983) *The Constant Factor* 1980; *The Contract* 1980

Mudie, Leonard (1883–1965) *The Magnetic Monster* 1953; *Timbuktu* 1959

Mueller, Cookie (1949–1989) *Multiple Maniacs* 1970; *Pink Flamingos* 1972; *Female Trouble* 1974; *Desperate Living* 1977; *Polyester* 1981

Mueller, Elisabeth (1926–) *The Power and the Prize* 1956; *The Angry Hills* 1959

Mueller, Maureen *In a Shallow Grave* 1988; *Over Her Dead Body* 1990

Mueller-Stahl, Armin (1930–) *Jacob the Liar* 1974; *Lola* 1982; *Colonel Redl* 1984; *Thousand Eyes* 1984; *Forget Mozart* 1985; *Midnight Cop* 1988; *Music Box* 1989; *Avalon* 1990; *Kafka* 1991; *The Power of One* 1991; *Night on Earth* 1992; *Utz* 1992; *The House of the Spirits* 1993; *Holy Matrimony* 1994; *The Last Good Time* 1994; *A Pyromaniac's Love Story* 1995; *Theodore Rex* 1995; *Shine* 1996; *The Game* 1997; *In the Presence of Mine Enemies* 1997; *The Peacemaker* 1997; *12 Angry Men* 1997; *The X-Files* 1998; *Jakob the Liar* 1999; *Mission to Mars* 1999; *The Thirteenth Floor* 1999; *The Long Run* 2000

Mühe, Ulrich (1953–) *Benny's Video* 1992; *Funny Games* 1997; *Amen.* 2002

Muhich, Donald F *Bob & Carol & Ted & Alice* 1969; *Blume in Love* 1973; *Down and Out in Beverly Hills* 1986

Mui, Anita *aka* **Mui Yim-Fong** (1963–2003) *Rouge* 1987; *A Better Tomorrow III* 1989; *The Heroic Trio* 1992; *The Enforcer* 1995; *Rumble in the Bronx* 1996; *Eighteen Springs* 1997

Muir, Gavin (1900–1972) *Mary of Scotland* 1936; *Fair Warning* 1937; *Sherlock Holmes in Washington* 1943; *The Merry Monahans* 1944; *Calcutta* 1947; *Abbott and Costello Meet the Invisible Man* 1951; *Night Tide* 1961

Muir, Jean (1911–1996) *The World Changes* 1933; *A Midsummer Night's Dream* 1935; *Oil for the Lamps of China* 1935; *White Fang* 1936; *The Lone Wolf Meets a Lady* 1940

Mukherjee, Arun *Kangchenjunga* 1962; *And Quiet Rolls the Dawn* 1979

Mukherjee, Madhabi (1943–) *The Big City* 1963; *Charulata* 1964

Mukherji, Rani *aka* **Mukerji, Rani** *aka* **Mukherjee, Rani** (1978–) *Kuch Kuch Hota Hai* 1998; *Mujhse Dosti Karoge!* 2002; *Saathiya* 2002; *Black* 2004; *Hum Tum* 2004; *Veer-Zaara* 2004; *Bunty Aur Babli* 2005

Mulay, Suhasini *Lagaan: Once upon a Time in India* 2001; *Kuch Naa Kaho* 2003

Muldaur, Diana (1938–) *The Lawyer* 1969; *Number One* 1969; *One More Train to Rob* 1971; *The Other* 1972; *Chosen Survivors* 1974; *McQ* 1974

Muldoon, Patrick (1968–) *Wicked* 1998; *Red Team* 1999; *Chain of Command* 2000; *Bad Karma* 2001

Mulgrew, Kate (1955–) *Lovespell* 1979; *Remo – Unarmed and Dangerous* 1985; *Throw Momma from the Train* 1987; *Danielle Steel's Daddy* 1991; *Camp Nowhere* 1994; *The Bomber Boys* 1995; *Star Trek: Nemesis* 2002

Mulhare, Edward (1923–1997) *Signpost to Murder* 1964; *Von Ryan's Express* 1965; *Eye of the*

Devil 1966; *Our Man Flint* 1966; *Caprice* 1967
Mulhern, Matt (1960–) *Extreme Prejudice* 1987; *Biloxi Blues* 1988; *Sunchaser* 1996
Mulkey, Chris (1948–) *Runaway* 1984; *Patti Rocks* 1987; *Heartbreak Hotel* 1988; *From Hollywood to Deadwood* 1989; *Roe vs Wade* 1989; *Bound and Gagged: a Love Story* 1992; *Gas, Food, Lodging* 1992; *Ghost in the Machine* 1993; *The Switch* 1993; *Twist of Fate* 1997; *Radio* 2003
Mull, Martin (1943–) *FM* 1977; *Serial* 1980; *Take This Job and Shove It* 1981; *Mr Mom* 1983; *Clue* 1985; *Home Is Where the Hart Is* 1987; *Cutting Class* 1989; *Ski Patrol* 1989; *Think Big* 1990; *Jingle All the Way* 1996
Mullally, Megan (1958–) *Everything Put Together* 2000; *Stealing Harvard* 2002
Mullan, Peter (1959–) *Trainspotting* 1995; *Bogwoman* 1997; *My Name Is Joe* 1998; *Miss Julie* 1999; *Ordinary Decent Criminal* 1999; *The Claim* 2000; *Session 9* 2001; *Kiss of Life* 2003; *Young Adam* 2003; *Criminal* 2004; *On a Clear Day* 2005
Mullaney, Jack (1932–1982) *The Young Stranger* 1957; *All the Fine Young Cannibals* 1960; *Dr Goldfoot and the Bikini Machine* 1965; *Tickle Me* 1965; *Spinout* 1966
Mullard, Arthur (1912–1995) *The Bank Raiders* 1958; *It's Trad, Dad* 1961; *Smashing Time* 1967; *Crooks and Coronets* 1969; *Holiday on the Buses* 1973; *Adventures of a Plumber's Mate* 1978
Mullen, Barbara (1914–1979) *Jeannie* 1941; *Thunder Rock* 1942; *A Place of One's Own* 1944; *The Gentle Gunman* 1952; *Innocent Sinners* 1957; *The Siege of Pinchgut* 1959; *The Very Edge* 1962
Mullen, Conor *Saltwater* 1999; *Silent Grace* 2001; *The Honeymooners* 2003
Mullen, Marie *The Disappearance of Finbar* 1996; *When Brendan Met Trudy* 2000
Mullen, Patty *Doom Asylum* 1987; *Frankenhooker* 1990
Muller, Paul (1923–) *Journey to Italy* 1953; *Checkpoint* 1956; *Lust of the Vampire* 1956; *Queen of the Pirates* 1960; *Count Dracula* 1970; *Vampyros Lesbos* 1970; *Treasure Island* 1972
Mulligan, Richard (1932–2000) *One Potato, Two Potato* 1964; *The Group* 1966; *Little Big Man* 1970; *The Hideaways* 1973; *Scavenger Hunt* 1979; *SOB* 1981; *Trail of the Pink Panther* 1982; *Meatballs 2* 1984; *Micki & Maude* 1984; *Teachers* 1984; *The Heavenly Kid* 1985; *A Fine Mess* 1986; *Oliver & Company* 1988
Mullinar, Rod (1942–) *Patrick* 1978; *Thirst* 1979; *Dead Calm* 1988
Mulock, Al (1925–1970) *High Hell* 1957; *Tarzan's Greatest Adventure* 1959; *Battle beneath the Earth* 1968
Mulroney, Dermot (1963–) *Young Guns* 1988; *Staying Together* 1989; *Unconquered* 1989; *Bright Angel* 1990; *Career Opportunities* 1991; *The Heart of Justice* 1992; *Where the Day Takes You* 1992; *The Assassin* 1993; *The Last Outlaw* 1993; *Point of No Return* 1993; *Silent Tongue* 1993; *The Thing Called Love* 1993; *Angels in the Outfield* 1994; *Bad Girls* 1994; *There Goes My Baby* 1994; *Copycat* 1995; *How to Make an American Quilt* 1995; *Kansas City* 1995; *Living in Oblivion* 1995; *The Trigger Effect* 1996; *Goodbye Lover* 1997; *My Best Friend's Wedding* 1997; *Trixie* 2000; *Where the Money Is* 2000; *Lovely & Amazing* 2001; *The Safety of Objects* 2001; *About Schmidt* 2002; *Undertow* 2004; *The Wedding Date* 2004
Mulroney, Kieran (1965–) *Career Opportunities* 1991; *The Spitfire Grill* 1996
Mumba, Samantha (1983–) *The Time Machine* 2002; *Boy Eats Girl* 2005
Mumy, Bill *aka* **Mumy, Billy** (1954–) *Sammy, the Way Out Seal* 1962; *Palm Springs Weekend* 1963; *A Ticklish Affair* 1963; *Dear Brigitte* 1966; *Bless the Beasts and Children* 1971; *Papillon* 1973; *Double Trouble* 1992
Mumy, Liliana (1995–) *The Santa Clause 2* 2002; *Cheaper by the Dozen* 2003
Mundin, Herbert (1898–1939) *Chandu the Magician* 1932; *Cavalcade* 1933; *The Devil's in Love* 1933; *Shanghai Madness* 1933; *Mutiny on the Bounty* 1935; *The Perfect Gentleman* 1935; *A Message to Garcia* 1936; *Tarzan Escapes* 1936; *Under Two Flags* 1936; *Angel* 1937; *Another Dawn* 1937
Muni, Paul (1895–1967) *The Valiant* 1929; *I Am a Fugitive from a Chain Gang* 1932; *Scarface* 1932; *The World Changes* 1933; *Hi, Nellie!* 1934; *Black Fury* 1935; *Bordertown* 1935; *Dr Socrates* 1935; *The Story of Louis Pasteur* 1936; *The Good Earth* 1937; *The Life of Emile Zola* 1937; *The Woman I Love* 1937; *Juarez* 1939; *We Are Not Alone* 1939; *Hudson's Bay* 1940; *The Commandos Strike at Dawn* 1942; *Stage Door Canteen* 1943; *Counter-Attack* 1945; *A Song to Remember* 1945; *Angel on My Shoulder* 1946; *The Last Angry Man* 1959
Muniz, Frankie (1985–) *My Dog Skip* 1999; *Big Fat Liar* 2002; *Agent Cody Banks* 2003; *Agent Cody Banks 2: Destination London* 2003; *Racing Stripes* 2004
Muñiz, Tommy *What Happened to Santiago* 1989; *Crazy from the Heart* 1991
Munks, Sheryl (1965–) *The Big Steal* 1990; *Holidays on the River Yarra* 1991
Munro, Caroline (1950–) *Captain Kronos: Vampire Hunter* 1972; *Dracula AD 1972* 1972; *The Golden Voyage of Sinbad* 1973; *I Don't Want to Be Born* 1975; *At the Earth's Core* 1976; *The Spy Who Loved Me* 1977; *To Die For* 1994
Munro, Janet (1934–1972) *Small Hotel* 1957; *The Trollenberg Terror* 1958; *Darby O'Gill and the Little People* 1959; *Third Man on the Mountain* 1959; *Tommy the Toreador* 1959; *Swiss Family Robinson* 1960; *The Day the Earth Caught Fire* 1961; *Life for Ruth* 1962; *Bitter Harvest* 1963; *Hide and Seek* 1963; *A Jolly Bad Fellow* 1964; *Sebastian* 1968
Munro, Lochlyn (1966–) *Dead Man on Campus* 1998; *High Voltage* 1998; *Scary Movie* 2000; *Kill Me Later* 2001; *A Guy Thing* 2002; *White Chicks* 2004
Munro, Neil *Confidential* 1986; *Dancing in the Dark* 1986; *Gate II* 1992
Munshin, Jules (1915–1970) *Easter Parade* 1948; *On the Town* 1949; *Take Me Out to the Ball Game* 1949; *That Midnight Kiss* 1949; *Silk Stockings* 1957; *Mastermind* 1976
Munson, Ona (1906–1956) *Five Star Final* 1931; *Gone with the Wind* 1939; *Lady from Louisiana* 1941; *The Shanghai Gesture* 1941; *Wild Geese Calling* 1941; *The Cheaters* 1945; *Dakota* 1945
Murat, Jean (1888–1968) *Carnival in Flanders* 1935; *Eternal Love* 1943; *On the Riviera* 1951
Murata, Takehiro (1960–) *Godzilla vs Mothra* 1992; *Okoge* 1992; *When the Last Sword Is Drawn* 2003
Murcell, George (1925–1998) *The Pursuers* 1961; *Pascali's Island* 1988; *Year of the Gun* 1991
Murdoch, Richard (1907–1990) *Band Waggon* 1939; *Charley's (Big Hearted) Aunt* 1940; *The Ghost Train* 1941; *I Thank You* 1941; *The Gay Adventure* 1949
Murdock, Jack (1922–2001) *Big Top Pee-wee* 1988; *Rain Man* 1988
Murgia, Tiberio (1929–) *Big Deal on Madonna Street* 1958; *That Man George* 1965
Murney, Christopher *The Last Dragon* 1985; *The Secret of My Success* 1987
Murnik, Peter (1965–) *Body Parts* 1991; *Pastime* 1991; *Golden Gate* 1994
Murphy, Audie (1924–1971) *Kansas Raiders* 1950; *The Kid from Texas* 1950; *Sierra* 1950; *The Cimarron Kid* 1951; *The Red Badge of Courage* 1951; *The Duel at Silver Creek* 1952; *Column South* 1953; *Gunsmoke* 1953; *Tumbleweed* 1953; *Destry* 1954; *Drums across the River* 1954; *Ride Clear of Diablo* 1954; *To Hell and Back* 1955; *Walk the Proud Land* 1956; *Guns of Fort Petticoat* 1957; *Joe Butterfly* 1957; *Night Passage* 1957; *The Gun Runners* 1958; *The Quiet American* 1958; *Ride a Crooked Trail* 1958; *Cast a Long Shadow* 1959; *No Name on the Bullet* 1959; *The Wild and the Innocent* 1959; *Hell Bent for Leather* 1960; *Seven Ways from Sundown* 1960; *The Unforgiven* 1960; *Battle at Bloody Beach* 1961; *Posse from Hell* 1961; *Six Black Horses* 1962; *Showdown* 1963; *Apache Rifles* 1964; *Bullet for a Badman* 1964; *Gunfight at Comanche Creek* 1964; *Arizona Raiders* 1965; *40 Guns to Apache Pass* 1966; *Gunpoint* 1966; *A Time for Dying* 1971
Murphy, Ben (1942–) *Yours, Mine and Ours* 1968; *The 1,000 Plane Raid* 1969; *Runaway!* 1973
Murphy, Bill *The Story of GI Joe* 1945; *A Foreign Affair* 1948
Murphy, Brian (1933–) *Sparrows Can't Sing* 1962; *The Ragman's Daughter* 1972; *Man about the House* 1974; *George and Mildred* 1980
Murphy, Brittany (1977–) *Clueless* 1995; *Drive* 1997; *The Prophecy II* 1997; *David and Lisa* 1998; *Cherry Falls* 1999; *The Devil's Arithmetic* 1999; *Girl, Interrupted* 1999; *Sidewalks of New York* 2000; *Trixie* 2000; *Don't Say a Word* 2001; *Riding in Cars with Boys* 2001; *Summer Catch* 2001; *8 Mile* 2002; *Spun* 2002; *Just Married* 2003; *Uptown Girls* 2003; *Little Black Book* 2004; *Sin City* 2005
Murphy, Cillian (1974–) *Disco Pigs* 2001; *28 Days Later...* 2002; *Girl with a Pearl Earring* 2003; *interMission* 2003; *Batman Begins* 2005
Murphy, Donna (1958–) *Jade* 1995; *Passion* 1996; *Star Trek: Insurrection* 1998; *The Astronaut's Wife* 1999; *Center Stage* 2000; *The Last Debate* 2000; *Spider-Man 2* 2004
Murphy, Eddie (1961–) *48 HRS* 1982; *Trading Places* 1983; *Best Defense* 1984; *Beverly Hills Cop* 1984; *The Golden Child* 1986; *Beverly Hills Cop II* 1987; *Eddie Murphy Raw* 1987; *Coming to America* 1988; *Harlem Nights* 1989; *Another 48 HRS* 1990; *Boomerang* 1992; *The Distinguished Gentleman* 1992; *Beverly Hills Cop III* 1994; *Vampire in Brooklyn* 1995; *The Nutty Professor* 1996; *Metro* 1997; *Doctor Dolittle* 1998; *Holy Man* 1998; *Mulan* 1998; *Bowfinger* 1999; *Life* 1999; *Nutty Professor 2: the Klumps* 2000; *Dr Dolittle 2* 2001; *Pluto Nash* 2001; *Shrek* 2001; *I Spy* 2002; *Showtime* 2002; *Daddy Day Care* 2003; *The Haunted Mansion* 2003; *Shrek 2* 2004
Murphy, George (1902–1992) *Kid Millions* 1934; *Broadway Melody of 1938* 1937; *London by Night* 1937; *You're a Sweetheart* 1937; *Hold That Co-Ed* 1938; *Letter of Introduction* 1938; *Little Miss Broadway* 1938; *Broadway Melody of 1940* 1940; *Little Nellie Kelly* 1940; *The Navy Steps Out* 1941; *Tom, Dick and Harry* 1941; *For Me and My Gal* 1942; *The Navy Comes Through* 1942; *Bataan* 1943; *This Is the Army* 1943; *Broadway Rhythm* 1944; *Show Business* 1944; *Step Lively* 1944; *The Arnelo Affair* 1947; *Cynthia* 1947; *Battleground* 1949; *Border Incident* 1949; *Walk East on Beacon* 1952
Murphy, Gerard (1956–) *The Brink's Job* 1978; *Waterworld* 1995
Murphy, Johnny *The Commitments* 1991; *Into the West* 1992
Murphy, Mary (1931–) *Main Street to Broadway* 1953; *The Wild One* 1953; *Beachhead* 1954; *The Mad Magician* 1954; *Make Haste to Live* 1954; *Sitting Bull* 1954; *The Desperate Hours* 1955; *Hell's Island* 1955; *A Man Alone* 1955; *The Maverick Queen* 1955; *The Intimate Stranger* 1956; *Escapement* 1958; *Live Fast, Die Young* 1958; *Crime and Punishment, USA* 1959; *Junior Bonner* 1972
Murphy, Maurice (1913–1978) *Faithless* 1932; *Pilgrimage* 1933; *Curly Top* 1935; *Tovarich* 1937
Murphy, Michael (1938–) *Countdown* 1968; *Brewster McCloud* 1970; *The Loves of Count Iorga, Vampire* 1970; *What's Up, Doc?* 1972; *Phase IV* 1973; *The Thief Who Came to Dinner* 1973; *The Autobiography of Miss Jane Pittman* 1974; *The Front* 1976; *The Great Georgia Bank Hoax* 1977; *The Class of Miss MacMichael* 1978; *An Unmarried Woman* 1978; *Hot Money* 1979; *Manhattan* 1979; *The Year of Living Dangerously* 1982; *Cloak and Dagger* 1984; *Mesmerized* 1984; *Salvador* 1986; *Shocker* 1989; *Batman Returns* 1992; *Clean Slate* 1994; *Kansas City* 1995; *Silver City* 2004
Murphy, Reilly *Body Snatchers* 1993; *Dangerous Game* 1993
Murphy, Rosemary (1927–) *To Kill a Mockingbird* 1962; *Any Wednesday* 1966; *Ben* 1972; *You'll Like My Mother* 1972; *Ace Eli and Rodger of the Skies* 1973; *Julia* 1977; *The Hand* 1981; *For the Boys* 1991; *Dust* 2001
Murphy, Timothy Patrick (1959–1988) *Sam's Son* 1984; *Doin' Time on Planet Earth* 1988
Murphy, Tom *The General* 1998; *Adam & Paul* 2004
Murray, Barbara (1929–) *Boys in Brown* 1949; *Passport to Pimlico* 1949; *Tony Draws a Horse* 1950; *Another Man's Poison* 1951; *The Frightened Man* 1952; *Meet Mr Lucifer* 1953; *Campbell's Kingdom* 1957; *A Cry from the Streets* 1957; *Operation Bullshine* 1959; *The Punch and Judy Man* 1962; *Doctor in Distress* 1963; *A Dandy in Aspic* 1968; *Some Will, Some Won't* 1969; *Up Pompeii* 1971
Murray, Bill (1950–) *Meatballs* 1979; *Caddyshack* 1980; *Where the Buffalo Roam* 1980; *Stripes* 1981; *Tootsie* 1982; *Ghostbusters* 1984; *Nothing Lasts Forever* 1984; *The Razor's Edge* 1984; *Little Shop of Horrors* 1986; *Scrooged* 1988; *Ghostbusters II* 1989; *Quick Change* 1990; *What about Bob?* 1991; *Mad Dog and Glory* 1992; *Groundhog Day* 1993; *Ed Wood* 1994; *Kingpin* 1996; *Larger than Life* 1996; *The Man Who Knew Too Little* 1997; *Space Jam* 1997; *Rushmore* 1998; *Wild Things* 1998; *Cradle Will Rock* 1999; *Charlie's Angels* 2000; *Hamlet* 2000; *Osmosis Jones* 2001; *The Royal Tenenbaums* 2001; *Coffee and Cigarettes* 2003; *Lost in Translation* 2003; *Garfield* 2004; *The Life Aquatic with Steve Zissou* 2004
Murray, Billy (1941–) *Poor Cow* 1967; *McVicar* 1980; *Essex Boys* 1999
Murray, Chad Michael (1981–) *Freaky Friday* 2003; *A Cinderella Story* 2004; *House of Wax* 2004
Murray, Chic (1919–1985) *Ups and Downs of a Handyman* 1975; *Gregory's Girl* 1980
Murray, Don (1929–) *Bus Stop* 1956; *The Bachelor Party* 1957; *A Hatful of Rain* 1957; *From Hell to Texas* 1958; *Shake Hands with the Devil* 1959; *These Thousand Hills* 1959; *One Foot in Hell* 1960; *The Hoodlum Priest* 1961; *Advise and Consent* 1962; *One Man's Way* 1964; *Baby the Rain Must Fall* 1965; *Kid Rodelo* 1966; *The Plainsman* 1966; *The Viking Queen* 1967; *Happy Birthday, Wanda June* 1971; *Conquest of the Planet of the Apes* 1972; *Deadly Hero* 1976; *Endless Love* 1981; *I Am the Cheese* 1983; *Peggy Sue Got Married* 1986; *Radioactive Dreams* 1986; *Made in Heaven* 1987; *Ghosts Can't Do It* 1990
Murray, James (1901–1936) *The Crowd* 1928; *Central Airport* 1933; *Teenage Mutant Ninja Turtles III* 1992
Murray, Jan (1917–) *Who Killed Teddy Bear?* 1965; *The Busy Body* 1967; *Tarzan and the Great River* 1967; *Thunder Alley* 1967; *Which Way to the Front?* 1970; *Day of the Wolves* 1973
Murray, Ken (1903–1988) *You're a Sweetheart* 1937; *The Man Who Shot Liberty Valance* 1962; *Son of Flubber* 1962
Murray, Mae (1889–1965) *The Merry Widow* 1925; *Bachelor Apartment* 1931
Murray, Mary *The Magdalene Sisters* 2002; *Adam & Paul* 2004
Murray, Stephen (1912–1983) *The Prime Minister* 1940; *The Master of Bankdam* 1947; *My Brother Jonathan* 1947; *London Belongs to Me* 1948; *Silent Dust* 1948; *Now Barabbas Was a Robber* 1949; *The Magnet* 1950; *Four Sided Triangle* 1953; *The End of the Affair* 1954; *Guilty?* 1956; *A Tale of Two Cities* 1957; *Master Spy* 1964
Murray Hill, Peter (1908–1957) *The Ghost Train* 1941; *Bell-Bottom George* 1943; *Rhythm Serenade* 1943; *Madonna of the Seven Moons* 1944; *They Were Sisters* 1945
Murton, Lionel (1915–) *The Pickwick Papers* 1952; *The Battle of the River Plate* 1956; *Surprise Package* 1960; *The Truth about Spring* 1964; *Zeta One* 1969; *The Revolutionary* 1970
Murua, Lautaro (1926–1995) *Triumphs of a Man Called Horse* 1983; *I, the Worst of All* 1990; *The Plague* 1992
Musante, Tony (1936–) *The Incident* 1967; *A Professional Gun* 1968; *The Bird with the Crystal Plumage* 1969; *The Grissom Gang* 1971; *The Last Run* 1971; *The Pope of Greenwich Village* 1984
Muse, Clarence (1889–1979) *Dirigible* 1931; *Huckleberry Finn* 1931; *Washington Merry-Go-Round* 1932; *White Zombie* 1932; *The Mind Reader* 1933; *Broadway Bill* 1934; *That Gang of Mine* 1940; *Invisible Ghost* 1941; *Riding High* 1950; *Apache Drums* 1951; *The Black Stallion* 1979
Musick, Pat *An American Tail: the Treasure of Manhattan Island* 1998; *An American Tail: the Mystery of the Night Monster* 2000
Mutambirwa, Garikayi *aka* **Mutambirwa, Garikayi "G K"** *Clockstoppers* 2002; *Jeepers Creepers 2* 2003
Muti, Ornella (1955–) *To Kill a Rat* 1977; *Viva Italia!* 1978; *Flash Gordon* 1980; *Tales of Ordinary Madness* 1981; *Love and Money* 1982; *Swann in Love* 1984; *Chronicle of a Death Foretold* 1987; *Wait until Spring, Bandini* 1989; *Oscar* 1991; *Once upon a Crime* 1992; *Pour Rire!* 1996; *[One] Cavale* 2002; *[Three] Après la Vie* 2002; *[Two] Un Couple Epatant* 2002; *The Heart Is Deceitful above All Things* 2004
Muzquiz, Carlos (1906–1960) *Captain Scarlett* 1953; *The Black Scorpion* 1957; *Villa!* 1958
Myers, Bruce *Henry & June* 1990; *Fausto* 1992
Myers, Cynthia (1950–) *Beyond the Valley of the Dolls* 1970; *Molly and Lawless John* 1972
Myers, Mike (1963–) *Wayne's World* 1992; *So I Married an Axe Murderer* 1993; *Wayne's World 2* 1993; *Austin Powers: International Man of Mystery* 1997; *54* 1998;

Austin Powers: the Spy Who Shagged Me 1999; *Mystery, Alaska* 1999; *Shrek* 2001; *Austin Powers in Goldmember* 2002; *Dr Seuss' The Cat in the Hat* 2003; *View from the Top* 2003; *Shrek 2* 2004
Myers, Peter *Bachelor of Hearts* 1958; *The Reluctant Debutante* 1958; *Hello – Goodbye* 1970
Myhers, John (1921–1992) *The Private Navy of Sgt O'Farrell* 1968; *The Billion Dollar Hobo* 1978
Myles, Sophia (1980–) *The Abduction Club* 2002; *Underworld* 2003; *Thunderbirds* 2004
Mynster, Karen-Lise (1952–) *Sofie* 1992; *Minor Mishaps* 2002

N

Nabors, Jim (1930–) *The Best Little Whorehouse in Texas* 1982; *Stroker Ace* 1983
Naceri, Samy (1961–) *Taxi* 1998; *Taxi 2* 2000; *La Mentale* 2002
Nachtergaele, Matheus (1969–) *Four Days in September* 1997; *City of God* 2002
Nader, George (1921–2002) *Robot Monster* 1953; *Carnival Story* 1954; *Four Guns to the Border* 1954; *Lady Godiva* 1955; *Six Bridges to Cross* 1955; *Away All Boats* 1956; *Congo Crossing* 1956; *Joe Butterfly* 1957; *The Female Animal* 1958; *Nowhere to Go* 1958; *The Secret Mark of D'Artagnan* 1962; *House of a Thousand Dolls* 1967; *Sumuru* 1967
Nag, Anant (1948–) *Ankur* 1974; *Nishant* 1975
Nagase, Masatoshi (1966–) *Mystery Train* 1989; *Autumn Moon* 1992; *The Most Terrible Time in My Life* 1993; *Cold Fever* 1994; *The Sea Is Watching* 2002
Nagel, Anne (1912–1966) *The Case of the Stuttering Bishop* 1937; *Argentine Nights* 1940; *Man Made Monster* 1941; *Never Give a Sucker an Even Break* 1941; *Road Agent* 1941
Nagel, Conrad (1897–1970) *Sinners in Silk* 1924; *The Exquisite Sinner* 1926; *London after Midnight* 1927; *The Mysterious Lady* 1928; *Dynamite* 1929; *Hollywood Revue* 1929; *The Kiss* 1929; *The Divorcee* 1930; *One Romantic Night* 1930; *Bad Sister* 1931; *East Lynne* 1931; *Hell Divers* 1932; *Ann Vickers* 1933; *Dangerous Corner* 1934; *Wedding Present* 1936; *One Million BC* 1940; *All That Heaven Allows* 1955; *Hidden Fear* 1957; *The Man Who Understood Women* 1959; *A Stranger in My Arms* 1959
Nagy, Bill (1900–1973) *The Brain Machine* 1954; *Shadow of a Man* 1954; *Across the Bridge* 1957; *First Man into Space* 1958; *The Boy Who Stole a Million* 1960; *Never Take Sweets from a Stranger* 1960; *Surprise Package* 1960; *Danger by My Side* 1962; *Night of the Prowler* 1962
Nahon, Philippe (1938–) *Seul contre Tous* 1998; *Irreversible* 2002; *La Mentale* 2002; *Switchblade Romance* 2003; *The Ordeal* 2004
Naidu, Ajay (1972–) *Touch and Go* 1986; *Where the River Runs Black* 1986; *subUrbia* 1996; *Office Space* 1999
Naidu, Leela *The Householder* 1963; *Electric Moon* 1992
Nail, Jimmy (1954–) *Morons from Outer Space* 1985; *Crusoe* 1988; *Dream Demon* 1988; *Just Ask for Diamond* 1988; *Evita* 1996; *Still Crazy* 1998
Nail, Joanne *Switchblade Sisters* 1975; *The Visitor* 1980; *Full Moon High* 1982
Naish, J Carrol *aka* **Naish, J Carroll** (1900–1973) *The Hatchet Man* 1932; *The Kid from Spain* 1932; *Tiger Shark* 1932; *Two Seconds* 1932; *The Devil's in Love* 1933; *The Mad Game* 1933; *British Agent* 1934; *Upper World* 1934; *Black Fury* 1935; *Confidential* 1935; *The Lives of a Bengal Lancer* 1935; *The Robin Hood of El Dorado* 1936; *Bulldog Drummond Comes Back* 1937; *Bulldog Drummond in Africa* 1938; *King of Alcatraz* 1938; *Beau Geste* 1939; *Down Argentine Way* 1940; *Typhoon* 1940; *The Birth of the Blues* 1941; *Blood and Sand* 1941; *The Corsican Brothers* 1941; *That Night in Rio* 1941; *Dr Broadway* 1942; *A Gentleman at Heart* 1942; *The Man in the Trunk* 1942; *The Pied Piper* 1942; *Behind the Rising Sun* 1943; *Calling Dr Death* 1943; *Gung Ho!* 1943; *Sahara* 1943; *Enter Arsene Lupin* 1944; *House of Frankenstein* 1944; *The Monster Maker* 1944; *The Whistler* 1944; *Getting Gertie's Garter* 1945; *A Medal for Benny* 1945; *The Southerner* 1945; *Strange Confession* 1945; *Bad Bascomb* 1946; *The Beast with Five Fingers* 1946; *Humoresque* 1946; *The Fugitive* 1947; *Joan of Arc* 1948; *Canadian Pacific* 1949; *The Kissing Bandit* 1949; *That Midnight Kiss* 1949; *Annie Get Your Gun* 1950; *The Black Hand* 1950; *Please Believe Me* 1950; *Rio Grande* 1950; *The Toast of New Orleans* 1950; *Across the Wide Missouri* 1951; *Clash by Night* 1952; *Denver & Rio Grande* 1952; *Ride the Man Down* 1952; *Beneath the 12-Mile Reef* 1953; *Saskatchewan* 1954; *Sitting Bull* 1954; *The Last Command* 1955; *New York Confidential* 1955; *Rage at Dawn* 1955; *Violent Saturday* 1955; *Rebel in Town* 1956; *Dracula vs Frankenstein* 1970
Naismith, Laurence (1908–1992) *Train of Events* 1949; *Mogambo* 1953; *The Black Knight* 1954; *Carrington VC* 1954; *The Man Who Never Was* 1955; *The Extra Day* 1956; *Tiger in the Smoke* 1956; *Boy on a Dolphin* 1957; *Robbery under Arms* 1957; *Seven Waves Away* 1957; *The Naked Earth* 1958; *Solomon and Sheba* 1959; *Third Man on the Mountain* 1959; *The Angry Silence* 1960; *The Singer Not the Song* 1960; *Sink the Bismarck!* 1960; *Village of the Damned* 1960; *The World of Suzie Wong* 1960; *Greyfriars Bobby* 1961; *The Prince and the Pauper* 1962; *We Joined the Navy* 1962; *Jason and the Argonauts* 1963; *The Three Lives of Thomasina* 1963; *Sky West and Crooked* 1965; *The Long Duel* 1966; *Camelot* 1967; *Eye of the Cat* 1969; *The Valley of Gwangi* 1969; *Scrooge* 1970; *Quest for Love* 1971; *The Amazing Mr Blunden* 1972
Naito, Takashi (1955–) *Maborosi* 1995; *After Life* 1998
Najimy, Kathy (1957–) *Soapdish* 1991; *Sister Act* 1992; *Hocus Pocus* 1993; *Sister Act 2: Back in the Habit* 1993; *Cats Don't Dance* 1998; *Hope Floats* 1998; *Rat Race* 2001
Nakadai, Tatsuya (1932–) *Conflagration* 1958; *The Human Condition* 1958; *The Key* 1959; *Harakiri* 1962; *Sanjuro* 1962; *High and Low* 1963; *Kwaidan* 1964; *Illusion of Blood* 1965; *The Face of Another* 1966; *Today It's Me... Tomorrow You!* 1968; *Portrait of Hell* 1969; *The Wolves* 1971; *Kagemusha* 1980; *The Empty Table* 1985; *Ran* 1985
Nakai, Kiichi (1961–) *The Burmese Harp* 1985; *The Empty Table* 1985; *When the Last Sword Is Drawn* 2003
Nakamura, Ganjiro (1902–1983) *The Lower Depths* 1956; *Conflagration* 1958; *Floating Weeds* 1959; *The Key* 1959; *The End of Summer* 1961; *An Actor's Revenge* 1963
Nakamura, Kanemon (1901–1982) *The Loyal 47 Ronin* 1941; *Musashi Miyamoto* 1944
Nakamura, Satoshi *Red Sun* 1971; *That Man Bolt* 1973
Nakamura, Toru (1965–) *Blue Tiger* 1994; *New York Cop* 1995; *Gen-X Cops* 1999; *Tokyo Raiders* 2000
Nakatani, Miki (1976–) *Ring* 1997; *Ring 2* 1998; *Chaos* 1999; *When the Last Sword Is Drawn* 2003
Nalder, Reggie (1911–1991) *The Man Who Knew Too Much* 1956; *Mark of the Devil* 1970; *Zoltan... Hound of Dracula* 1977; *Salem's Lot* 1979
Naldi, Nita (1897–1961) *Dr Jekyll and Mr Hyde* 1920; *Blood and Sand* 1922; *The Pleasure Garden* 1925
Namath, Joe (1943–) *The Last Rebel* 1971; *Avalanche Express* 1979; *Chattanooga Choo Choo* 1984
Namdeo, Govind *Bandit Queen* 1994; *Virasat* 1997; *Dum* 2002
Nance, Jack *aka* **Nance, John** (1943–1996) *Eraserhead* 1976; *Ghoulies* 1985; *Blue Velvet* 1986; *Barfly* 1987; *Motorama* 1991; *The Secret Agent Club* 1995; *Lost Highway* 1996
Nanty, Isabelle (1962–) *Tatie Danielle* 1990; *Pas sur la Bouche* 2003
Napier, Alan (1903–1988) *The Four Just Men* 1939; *We Are Not Alone* 1939; *The Invisible Man Returns* 1940; *Cat People* 1942; *Lost Angel* 1943; *The Silent Bell* 1944; *The Uninvited* 1944; *Ministry of Fear* 1945; *Macbeth* 1948; *Tarzan's Magic Fountain* 1949; *Across the Wide Missouri* 1951; *Double Crossbones* 1951; *Big Jim McLain* 1952; *Julius Caesar* 1953; *The Mole People* 1956; *Until They Sail* 1957; *The Premature Burial* 1962; *The Sword in the Stone* 1963; *Marnie* 1964; *36 Hours* 1964; *Batman* 1966
Napier, Charles (1936–) *Cherry, Harry & Raquel* 1969; *Beyond the Valley of the Dolls* 1970; *Supervixens* 1975; *Citizens Band* 1977; *Last Embrace* 1979; *The Night Stalker* 1985; *Rambo: First Blood, Part II* 1985; *Hit List* 1988; *One Man Force* 1989; *Ernest Goes to Jail* 1990; *Miami Blues* 1990; *Good Cop, Bad Cop* 1993; *Philadelphia* 1993; *Jury Duty* 1995; *3 Ninjas Knuckle Up* 1995; *Jailbreak* 1997; *Steel* 1997; *The Big Tease* 1999
Napier, Diana (1905–1982) *Heart's Desire* 1935; *Land without Music* 1936; *Pagliacci* 1936
Napier, Jessica *Love Serenade* 1996; *Cut* 2000
Napier, Marshall *Bad Blood* 1982; *Starlight Hotel* 1987; *Georgia* 1988; *The Navigator – a Medieval Odyssey* 1988; *The Big Steal* 1990; *Paperback Romance* 1994
Napier, Russell (1910–1974) *Death of an Angel* 1951; *The Brain Machine* 1954; *The Stranger Came Home* 1954; *The Blue Peter* 1955; *Little Red Monkey* 1955
Nardini, Daniela (1968–) *Elephant Juice* 1999; *Festival* 2005
Nardini, Tom (1945–) *Cat Ballou* 1965; *Africa – Texas Style!* 1967
Nargis (1929–1981) *Andaz* 1949; *Barsaat* 1949; *Babul* 1950; *Chori Chori* 1956; *Mother India* 1957
Nascarella, Arthur *aka* **Nascarella, Arthur J** *After the Storm* 2001; *Wisegirls* 2001; *The Cooler* 2002
Nash, Johnny (1940–) *Take a Giant Step* 1959; *Key Witness* 1960
Nash, Mary (1885–1976) *Easy Living* 1937; *Heidi* 1937; *The King and the Chorus Girl* 1937; *Wells Fargo* 1937; *The Little Princess* 1939; *The Philadelphia Story* 1940; *Cobra Woman* 1944; *In the Meantime, Darling* 1944; *The Lady and the Monster* 1944; *Yolanda and the Thief* 1945; *Swell Guy* 1946; *Till the Clouds Roll By* 1946
Nash, Noreen (1924–) *The Tender Years* 1947; *Storm over Wyoming* 1950; *The Lone Ranger and the Lost City of Gold* 1958
Nat, Marie-José (1940–) *La Vérité* 1960; *The Seven Deadly Sins* 1961; *Embassy* 1972
Nath, Alok (1956–) *Pardes* 1997; *Taal* 1999; *Hum Tumhare Hain Sanam* 2000
Nathan, Vivian (1921–) *The Outsider* 1961; *The Young Savages* 1961; *Klute* 1971
Nathenson, Zoe *Those Glory, Glory Days* 1983; *Mona Lisa* 1986; *The Raggedy Rawney* 1987
Natividad, Kitten *aka* **Natividad, Francesca "Kitten"** (1948–) *Beneath the Valley of the Ultra Vixens* 1979; *My Tutor* 1983
Natsukawa, Daijiro *The Downfall of Osen* 1935; *Poppy* 1935
Natsukawa, Yui (1968–) *Distance* 2001; *When the Last Sword Is Drawn* 2003; *Zatoichi* 2003
Natwick, Mildred (1905–1994) *The Long Voyage Home* 1940; *The Enchanted Cottage* 1945; *Yolanda and the Thief* 1945; *The Late George Apley* 1947; *Three Godfathers* 1948; *The Kissing Bandit* 1949; *She Wore a Yellow Ribbon* 1949; *Cheaper by the Dozen* 1950; *Against All Flags* 1952; *The Trouble with Harry* 1954; *The Court Jester* 1956; *Teenage Rebel* 1956; *Tammy and the Bachelor* 1957; *Barefoot in the Park* 1967; *If It's Tuesday, This Must Be Belgium* 1969; *The Maltese Bippy* 1969; *Trilogy* 1969; *Daisy Miller* 1974; *At Long Last Love* 1975; *Kiss Me Goodbye* 1982; *Dangerous Liaisons* 1988
Naughton, Charlie (1887–1976) *O-Kay for Sound* 1937; *Alf's Button Afloat* 1938; *Gasbags* 1940; *Life Is a Circus* 1958
Naughton, David (1951–) *Midnight Madness* 1980; *An American Werewolf in London* 1981; *Separate Ways* 1981; *Hot Dog – The Movie* 1984; *Not for Publication* 1984; *The Boy in Blue* 1986; *Separate Vacations* 1986; *Amityville: a New Generation* 1993; *Sky Blue* 2003
Naughton, James (1945–) *Cat's Eye* 1984; *The Glass Menagerie* 1987; *The Price of Passion* 1988; *Danielle Steel's Mixed Blessings* 1995; *First Kid* 1996; *Oxygen* 1999
Navarre, Elodie (1979–) *Love etc* 1997; *He Loves Me... He Loves Me Not* 2002; *Love Me If You Dare* 2003
Nayar, Nisha K *aka* **Nayar, Nisha** *Bhaji on the Beach* 1993; *The Darkest Light* 1999
Nazimova, Alla *aka* **Nazimova** (1879–1945) *Camille* 1921; *Salome* 1922; *Escape* 1940; *Blood and Sand* 1941
Nazzari, Amedeo (1907–1979) *Nights of Cabiria* 1957; *The Naked Maja* 1959; *The Best of Enemies* 1961; *Nefertite, Queen of the Nile* 1961; *The Sicilian Clan* 1969; *The Valachi Papers* 1972
Neagle, Anna (1904–1986) *Bitter Sweet* 1933; *Nell Gwyn* 1934; *Limelight* 1936; *London Melody* 1937; *Victoria the Great* 1937; *Sixty Glorious Years* 1938; *Nurse Edith Cavell* 1939; *Irene* 1940; *No, No, Nanette* 1940; *Sunny* 1941; *They Flew Alone* 1941; *Forever and a Day* 1943; *Yellow Canary* 1943; *I Live in Grosvenor Square* 1945; *Piccadilly Incident* 1946; *The Courtneys of Curzon Street* 1947; *Elizabeth of Ladymead* 1948; *Spring in Park Lane* 1948; *Maytime in Mayfair* 1949; *Odette* 1950; *The Lady with the Lamp* 1951; *Derby Day* 1952; *King's Rhapsody* 1955; *Lilacs in the Spring* 1955; *My Teenage Daughter* 1956; *The Man Who Wouldn't Talk* 1957; *No Time for Tears* 1957
Neal, Billie (1955–1999) *Down by Law* 1986; *Mortal Thoughts* 1991; *Sweet Nothing* 1995
Neal, Elise (1970–) *Rosewood* 1997; *Scream 2* 1997; *Restaurant* 1998
Neal, Patricia (1926–) *The Fountainhead* 1949; *The Hasty Heart* 1949; *It's a Great Feeling* 1949; *The Breaking Point* 1950; *Bright Leaf* 1950; *Three Secrets* 1950; *The Day the Earth Stood Still* 1951; *Operation Pacific* 1951; *Weekend with Father* 1951; *Diplomatic Courier* 1952; *Washington Story* 1952; *Stranger from Venus* 1954; *A Face in the Crowd* 1957; *Breakfast at Tiffany's* 1961; *Hud* 1963; *Psyche '59* 1964; *In Harm's Way* 1965; *The Subject Was Roses* 1968; *The Road Builder* 1971; *Baxter* 1973; *Happy Mother's Day... Love, George* 1973; *The Passage* 1978; *All Quiet on the Western Front* 1979; *Ghost Story* 1981; *An Unremarkable Life* 1989; *Caroline?* 1990; *Cookie's Fortune* 1999
Neal, Tom (1914–1972) *Andy Hardy Meets Debutante* 1940; *Behind the Rising Sun* 1943; *Detour* 1945; *First Yank into Tokyo* 1945
Nealon, Kevin (1953–) *All I Want for Christmas* 1991; *Adam Sandler's Eight Crazy Nights* 2003; *Daddy Day Care* 2003; *Good Boy!* 2003
Neame, Christopher (1947–) *Dracula AD 1972* 1972; *DOA* 1988; *Diplomatic Immunity* 1991
Near, Holly *Angel, Angel Down We Go* 1969; *The Magic Garden of Stanley Sweetheart* 1970; *The Todd Killings* 1971; *FTA* 1972; *Dogfight* 1991
Neckar, Vaclav (1943–) *Closely Observed Trains* 1966; *Larks on a String* 1969
Nedell, Bernard (1898–1972) *Lazybones* 1935; *Some Like It Hot* 1939
Nedjari, Al *Frantz Fanon: Black Skin White Mask* 1996; *Strong Language* 1998
Needham, Tracey (1967–) *Lush Life* 1993; *Prophet of Evil* 1993; *Last Stand at Saber River* 1997
Needles, Nique (1964–) *The Boy Who Had Everything* 1984; *Dogs in Space* 1986; *Tender Hooks* 1988
Neeson, Liam (1952–) *Excalibur* 1981; *Krull* 1983; *The Bounty* 1984; *The Innocent* 1984; *Lamb* 1985; *The Mission* 1986; *A Prayer for the Dying* 1987; *Suspect* 1987; *The Dead Pool* 1988; *High Spirits* 1988; *The Price of Passion* 1988; *Satisfaction* 1988; *Next of Kin* 1989; *The Big Man* 1990; *Darkman* 1990; *Under Suspicion* 1991; *Husbands and Wives* 1992; *Leap of Faith* 1992; *Ruby Cairo* 1992; *Shining Through* 1992; *Ethan Frome* 1993; *Schindler's List* 1993; *Nell* 1994; *Rob Roy* 1995; *Before and After* 1996; *Michael Collins* 1996; *Les Misérables* 1997; *The Haunting* 1999; *Star Wars Episode I: the Phantom Menace* 1999; *The Endurance: Shackelton's Legendary Antarctic Expedition* 2000; *Gun Shy* 2000; *Gangs of New York* 2002; *K-19: the Widowmaker* 2002; *Love Actually* 2003; *Kinsey* 2004; *Batman Begins* 2005; *Kingdom of Heaven* 2005
Neff, Hildegarde *aka* **Knef, Hildegarde** (1925–2002) *The Murderers Are amongst Us* 1946; *Decision before Dawn* 1951; *Diplomatic Courier* 1952; *The Snows of Kilimanjaro* 1952; *The Man Between* 1953; *Svengali* 1954; *Subway in the Sky* 1958; *Bluebeard* 1962; *The Lost Continent* 1968; *Fedora* 1978; *Witchcraft* 1989
Negishi, Toshie *Akira Kurosawa's Dreams* 1990; *Rhapsody in August* 1990
Negoda, Natalya (1964–) *Little Vera* 1988; *Back in the USSR* 1992
Négret, François *Noce Blanche* 1989; *Mister Frost* 1990; *Night and Day* 1991
Negri, Pola (1894–1987) *Hotel Imperial* 1927; *The Moon-Spinners* 1964
Negron, Taylor (1958–) *Easy Money* 1983; *The Last Boy Scout* 1991; *Nothing but Trouble* 1991; *A Kid in Aladdin's Palace* 1997; *Call Me Claus* 2001; *The Fluffer* 2001
Neil, Christopher *Adventures of a Private Eye* 1977; *Adventures of a Plumber's Mate* 1978; *Train of Dreams* 1987
Neil, Hildegard (1939–) *The Man Who Haunted Himself* 1970; *Antony and Cleopatra* 1972; *England Made Me* 1973; *A Touch of Class* 1973; *The Legacy* 1978; *Macbeth* 1997

Neill, James (1860–1931) *The Cheat* 1915; *The Ten Commandments* 1923; *The King of Kings* 1927

Neill, Noel (1920–) *Here Come the Waves* 1944; *Music Man* 1948

Neill, Sam (1947–) *My Brilliant Career* 1979; *Omen III: the Final Conflict* 1980; *Attack Force Z* 1981; *Possession* 1981; *Enigma* 1982; *The Country Girls* 1983; *The Blood of Others* 1984; *Plenty* 1985; *The Good Wife* 1986; *A Cry in the Dark* 1988; *Dead Calm* 1988; *Death in Brunswick* 1990; *The Hunt for Red October* 1990; *One against the Wind* 1991; *Until the End of the World* 1991; *Hostage* 1992; *Memoirs of an Invisible Man* 1992; *Jurassic Park* 1993; *The Piano* 1993; *Country Life* 1994; *In the Mouth of Madness* 1994; *The Jungle Book* 1994; *Sirens* 1994; *Restoration* 1995; *Victory* 1995; *Children of the Revolution* 1996; *Snow White: a Tale of Terror* 1996; *Event Horizon* 1997; *The Revengers' Comedies* 1997; *The Horse Whisperer* 1998; *Bicentennial Man* 1999; *The Dish* 2000; *The Magic Pudding* 2000; *My Mother Frank* 2000; *Jurassic Park III* 2001; *Dirty Deeds* 2002; *Framed* 2002; *Wimbledon* 2004; *Yes* 2004

Neise, George N *aka* **Neise, George** (1916–1996) *The Tall Stranger* 1957; *The Three Stooges in Orbit* 1962

Nell, Nathalie (1950–) *Echoes* 1983; *Man, Woman and Child* 1983

Nelligan, Kate (1951–) *The Count of Monte Cristo* 1974; *The Romantic Englishwoman* 1975; *Dracula* 1979; *Eye of the Needle* 1981; *Without a Trace* 1983; *Eleni* 1985; *White Room* 1990; *Frankie & Johnny* 1991; *The Prince of Tides* 1991; *Fatal Instinct* 1993; *Shattered Trust* 1993; *Wolf* 1994; *How to Make an American Quilt* 1995; *Margaret's Museum* 1995; *Up Close & Personal* 1996; *US Marshals* 1998; *The Cider House Rules* 1999; *Blessed Stranger: after Flight 111* 2000

Nelson, Barry (1920–) *Shadow of the Thin Man* 1941; *The Affairs of Martha* 1942; *A Guy Named Joe* 1944; *The First Travelling Saleslady* 1956; *Mary, Mary* 1963; *Pete 'n' Tillie* 1972; *The Shining* 1980

Nelson, Billy (1903–1979) *Look Up and Laugh* 1935; *The Penny Pool* 1937

Nelson, Bob *Brain Donors* 1992; *This Is My Life* 1992

Nelson, Charlie *aka* **Nelson, Charles** *Wild Target* 1993; *Le Bossu* 1997; *L'Homme du Train* 2002

Nelson, Craig T (1945–) *Stir Crazy* 1980; *Poltergeist* 1982; *All the Right Moves* 1983; *Man, Woman and Child* 1983; *The Osterman Weekend* 1983; *Silkwood* 1983; *The Killing Fields* 1984; *Poltergeist II: the Other Side* 1986; *Red Riding Hood* 1987; *Action Jackson* 1988; *Troop Beverly Hills* 1989; *Turner & Hooch* 1989; *The Switch* 1993; *The Lies Boys Tell* 1994; *Ghosts of Mississippi* 1996; *I'm Not Rappaport* 1996; *The Devil's Advocate* 1997; *Wag the Dog* 1997; *Dirty Pictures* 2000; *The Skulls* 2000; *The Incredibles* 2004

Nelson, David (1936–) *The Big Circus* 1959; *The Remarkable Mr Pennypacker* 1959; *–30–* 1959; *The Big Show* 1961

Nelson, Ed (1928–) *The Young Captives* 1958; *A Bucket of Blood* 1959; *Runaway!* 1973; *Acapulco Gold* 1976; *For the Love of Benji* 1977; *Jackie Chan's Who Am I?* 1998

Nelson, Gene (1920–1996) *I Wonder Who's Kissing Her Now* 1947; *The Daughter of Rosie O'Grady* 1950; *Tea for Two* 1950; *The West Point Story* 1950; *Lullaby of Broadway* 1951; *Painting the Clouds with Sunshine* 1951; *She's Working Her Way through College* 1952; *Three Sailors and a Girl* 1953; *The City Is Dark* 1954; *So This Is Paris* 1954; *Oklahoma!* 1955; *Timeslip* 1955; *Thunder Island* 1963

Nelson, Gwen (1901–1990) *Don't Talk to Strange Men* 1962; *A Kind of Loving* 1962; *Say Hello to Yesterday* 1971

Nelson, Harriet *aka* **Hilliard, Harriet** (1909–1994) *Follow the Fleet* 1936; *New Faces of 1937* 1937; *Sweetheart of the Campus* 1941; *The Falcon Strikes Back* 1943

Nelson, Jerry (1934–) *The Muppet Movie* 1979; *The Muppet Christmas Carol* 1992

Nelson, John Allen (1959–) *Hunk* 1987; *Killer Klowns from Outer Space* 1988; *Shelter* 1997

Nelson, Judd (1959–) *The Breakfast Club* 1985; *Fandango* 1985; *St Elmo's Fire* 1985; *Blue City* 1986; *Transformers – The Movie* 1986; *From the Hip* 1987; *Never on Tuesday* 1988; *Relentless* 1989; *The Dark Backward* 1991; *New Jack City* 1991; *Primary Motive* 1992; *Every Breath* 1993; *Airheads* 1994; *Hail Caesar* 1994; *Blackwater Trail* 1995; *Steel* 1997; *Light It Up* 1999; *Cabin by the Lake* 2000

Nelson, Lori (1933–) *Bend of the River* 1952; *Francis Goes to West Point* 1952; *The All American* 1953; *All I Desire* 1953; *Tumbleweed* 1953; *Destry* 1954; *I Died a Thousand Times* 1955; *Revenge of the Creature* 1955; *Sincerely Yours* 1955; *Underwater!* 1955; *The Day the World Ended* 1956; *Mohawk* 1956; *Pardners* 1956; *Untamed Youth* 1957

Nelson, Mimi (1922–1999) *Port of Call* 1948; *Three Strange Loves* 1949

Nelson, Novella (1939–) *Orphans* 1987; *Dear Wendy* 2005

Nelson, Ricky (1940–1985) *The Story of Three Loves* 1953; *Rio Bravo* 1959; *The Wackiest Ship in the Army* 1961

Nelson, Ruth (1905–1992) *The Eve of St Mark* 1944; *Wilson* 1944; *A Tree Grows in Brooklyn* 1945; *Humoresque* 1946; *Mother Wore Tights* 1947; *The Sea of Grass* 1947; *Arch of Triumph* 1948; *3 Women* 1977; *Awakenings* 1990

Nelson, Sean *Fresh* 1994; *American Buffalo* 1995; *The Wood* 1999

Nelson, Tim Blake (1965–) *O Brother, Where Art Thou?* 2000; *The Good Girl* 2001; *Cherish* 2002; *Minority Report* 2002; *Holes* 2003; *Wonderland* 2003; *Meet the Fockers* 2004; *Scooby-Doo 2: Monsters Unleashed* 2004

Nelson, Tracy (1963–) *Down and Out in Beverly Hills* 1986; *The Night Caller* 1998

Nelson, Willie (1933–) *The Electric Horseman* 1979; *Honeysuckle Rose* 1980; *Thief* 1981; *Barbarosa* 1982; *Songwriter* 1984; *Once upon a Texas Train* 1988; *Gone Fishin'* 1997; *Wag the Dog* 1997; *Half-Baked* 1998; *The Big Bounce* 2004

Nemec, Corin *aka* **Nemec, Corin "Corky"** (1971–) *Solar Crisis* 1990; *Drop Zone* 1994; *Operation Dumbo Drop* 1995; *The War at Home* 1996; *Shadow Hours* 2000

Neri, Francesca (1964–) *The Ages of Lulu* 1990; *Flight of the Innocent* 1993; *Outrage* 1993; *Live Flesh* 1997; *Strong Hands* 1997; *Collateral Damage* 2001; *Hannibal* 2001

Nero, Franco (1941–) *The Wild, Wild Planet* 1965; *The Bible...in the Beginning* 1966; *Django* 1966; *Texas Adios* 1966; *Camelot* 1967; *A Professional Gun* 1968; *The Battle of Neretva* 1969; *Tristana* 1970; *The Virgin and the Gypsy* 1970; *The Monk* 1972; *The Last Days of Mussolini* 1974; *The Masters* 1975; *Keoma* 1976; *Force 10 from Navarone* 1978; *The Man with Bogart's Face* 1980; *Enter the Ninja* 1981; *The Salamander* 1981; *Querelle* 1982; *Kamikaze 1989* 1983; *The Girl* 1986; *Die Hard 2: Die Harder* 1990; *Fratelli e Sorelle* 1992; *The Innocent Sleep* 1995; *Talk of Angels* 1998

Nervo, Jimmy (1890–1975) *O-Kay for Sound* 1937; *Alf's Button Afloat* 1938; *Gasbags* 1940; *Life Is a Circus* 1958

Nesbitt, Cathleen (1888–1982) *The Passing of the Third Floor Back* 1935; *The Lamp Still Burns* 1943; *Fanny by Gaslight* 1944; *Men of Two Worlds* 1946; *So Long at the Fair* 1950; *Desiree* 1954; *Three Coins in the Fountain* 1954; *An Affair to Remember* 1957; *Separate Tables* 1958; *The Parent Trap* 1961; *The Trygon Factor* 1967; *Staircase* 1969; *French Connection II* 1975; *Family Plot* 1976; *Full Circle* 1977

Nesbitt, Derren (1935–) *Life in Danger* 1959; *The Man in the Back Seat* 1961; *Strongroom* 1961; *The Informers* 1963; *The Naked Runner* 1967; *Innocent Bystanders* 1972; *Not Now Darling* 1972; *Ooh... You Are Awful* 1972; *Give Us Tomorrow* 1978; *Bullseye!* 1990; *Double X: the Name of the Game* 1991

Nesbitt, James (1966–) *Hear My Song* 1991; *Go Now* 1995; *Resurrection Man* 1997; *Welcome to Sarajevo* 1997; *Waking Ned* 1998; *The Most Fertile Man in Ireland* 1999; *Women Talking Dirty* 1999; *Wild about Harry* 2000; *Bloody Sunday* 2001; *Lucky Break* 2001; *Millions* 2004

Nettleton, John (1929–) *And Soon the Darkness* 1970; *Black Beauty* 1971; *Burning Secret* 1988

Nettleton, Lois (1929–) *Come Fly with Me* 1962; *Period of Adjustment* 1962; *Mail Order Bride* 1963; *Valley of Mystery* 1967; *The Good Guys and the Bad Guys* 1969; *Dirty Dingus Magee* 1970; *The Sidelong Glances of a Pigeon Kicker* 1970; *The Honkers* 1971; *The Man in the Glass Booth* 1975; *Echoes of a Summer* 1976; *Deadly Blessing* 1981; *The Best Little Whorehouse in Texas* 1982; *Butterfly* 1982

Neumann, Birthe *Open Hearts* 2002; *Someone like Hodder* 2003

Neutze, Günther (1921–1991) *The Great British Train Robbery* 1966; *The Last Escape* 1970

Neuwirth, Bebe (1958–) *Say Anything...* 1989; *Green Card* 1990; *Bugsy* 1991; *Painted Heart* 1992; *Malice* 1993; *Jumanji* 1995; *The Adventures of Pinocchio* 1996; *All Dogs Go to Heaven 2* 1996; *The Associate* 1996; *Celebrity* 1998; *Liberty Heights* 1999; *The Adventures of Tom Thumb and Thumbelina* 2002; *Tadpole* 2002; *Le Divorce* 2003; *How to Lose a Guy in 10 Days* 2003; *The Big Bounce* 2004

Neve, Suzanne *Mosquito Squadron* 1968; *Scrooge* 1970

Neville, John (1925–) *Oscar Wilde* 1959; *Mr Topaze* 1961; *Billy Budd* 1962; *Unearthly Stranger* 1963; *A Study in Terror* 1965; *The Adventures of Gerard* 1970; *The Adventures of Baron Munchausen* 1988; *The Road to Wellville* 1994; *Swann* 1996; *Regeneration* 1997; *The X-Files* 1998; *Spider* 2002

Nevin, Robyn (1942–) *The Irishman* 1978; *Careful, He Might Hear You* 1983; *The Gold and Glory* 1984; *Paperback Romance* 1994

Nevins, Claudette *The Mask* 1961; *Tuff Turf* 1984; *Sleeping with the Enemy* 1991

New, Barbara *Thin Ice* 1994; *Ali G indahouse* 2002

Newark, Derek (1933–1998) *City under the Sea* 1965; *The Blue Max* 1966; *Dad's Army* 1971; *The Offence* 1972; *Diamonds on Wheels* 1973; *Bellman & True* 1987

Newbern, George (1964–) *Switching Channels* 1987; *Father of the Bride* 1991; *Doppelganger* 1993; *I Spy Returns* 1994; *Father of the Bride Part 2* 1995; *Theodore Rex* 1995; *The Evening Star* 1996; *The Simple Life of Noah Dearborn* 1999

Newell, Patrick (1932–1988) *Unearthly Stranger* 1963; *Go for a Take* 1972; *Man about the House* 1974

Newhart, Bob (1929–) *Hell Is for Heroes* 1962; *Hot Millions* 1968; *Cold Turkey* 1969; *Catch-22* 1970; *On a Clear Day You Can See Forever* 1970; *The Rescuers* 1977; *First Family* 1980; *Little Miss Marker* 1980; *The Rescuers Down Under* 1990; *Rudolph the Red-Nosed Reindeer* 1998; *Elf* 2003; *Legally Blonde 2: Red, White & Blonde* 2003

Newlands, Anthony (1926–) *Solo for Sparrow* 1962; *Hysteria* 1964; *Kaleidoscope* 1966; *Circus of Fear* 1967; *Scream and Scream Again* 1969

Newley, Anthony (1931–1999) *Vice Versa* 1947; *Oliver Twist* 1948; *A Boy, a Girl and a Bike* 1949; *Don't Ever Leave Me* 1949; *Top of the Form* 1953; *Above Us the Waves* 1955; *The Blue Peter* 1955; *The Cockleshell Heroes* 1955; *The Good Companions* 1956; *Fire Down Below* 1957; *High Flight* 1957; *How to Murder a Rich Uncle* 1957; *The Man Inside* 1958; *No Time to Die* 1958; *The Bandit of Zhobe* 1959; *The Heart of a Man* 1959; *Killers of Kilimanjaro* 1960; *Let's Get Married* 1960; *The Small World of Sammy Lee* 1963; *Doctor Dolittle* 1967; *Sweet November* 1968; *Can Heironymus Merkin Ever Forget Mercy Humppe and Find True Happiness?* 1969; *Mister Quilp* 1975; *The Garbage Pail Kids Movie* 1987

Newman, Alec (1974–) *GMT Greenwich Mean Time* 1998; *Long Time Dead* 2001; *The Principles of Lust* 2002

Newman, Barry (1938–) *Pretty Boy Floyd* 1960; *The Lawyer* 1969; *Vanishing Point* 1971; *Fear Is the Key* 1972; *The Salzburg Connection* 1972; *City on Fire* 1979; *Amy* 1981; *Bowfinger* 1999; *The Limey* 1999; *G-Men from Hell* 2000; *Good Advice* 2001; *What the #$*! Do We Know!?* 2004

Newman, Laraine (1952–) *Tunnelvision* 1976; *American Hot Wax* 1977; *Wholly Moses!* 1980; *Perfect* 1985; *Invaders from Mars* 1986; *Problem Child 2* 1991; *Coneheads* 1993

Newman, Nanette (1934–) *Faces in the Dark* 1960; *House of Mystery* 1961; *The Painted Smile* 1961; *Pit of Darkness* 1961; *Twice round the Daffodils* 1962; *The Wrong Arm of the Law* 1962; *Of Human Bondage* 1964; *Seance on a Wet Afternoon* 1964; *The Wrong Box* 1966; *The Whisperers* 1967; *Deadfall* 1968; *Captain Nemo and the Underwater City* 1969; *The Madwoman of Chaillot* 1969; *The Raging Moon* 1970; *The Stepford Wives* 1975; *International Velvet* 1978; *Restless Natives* 1985; *The Mystery of Edwin Drood* 1993

Newman, Paul (1925–) *The Silver Chalice* 1954; *The Rack* 1956; *Somebody Up There Likes Me* 1956; *The Helen Morgan Story* 1957; *Until They Sail* 1957; *Cat on a Hot Tin Roof* 1958; *The Left Handed Gun* 1958; *The Long Hot Summer* 1958; *Rally 'round the Flag, Boys!* 1958; *The Young Philadelphians* 1959; *Exodus* 1960; *From the Terrace* 1960; *The Hustler* 1961; *Paris Blues* 1961; *Hemingway's Adventures of a Young Man* 1962; *Sweet Bird of Youth* 1962; *Hud* 1963; *A New Kind of Love* 1963; *The Prize* 1963; *The Outrage* 1964; *What a Way to Go!* 1964; *Lady L* 1965; *Harper* 1966; *Torn Curtain* 1966; *Cool Hand Luke* 1967; *Hombre* 1967; *The Secret War of Harry Frigg* 1967; *Butch Cassidy and the Sundance Kid* 1969; *Winning* 1969; *King: a Filmed Record... Montgomery to Memphis* 1970; *WUSA* 1970; *Sometimes a Great Notion* 1971; *The Life and Times of Judge Roy Bean* 1972; *Pocket Money* 1972; *The Mackintosh Man* 1973; *The Sting* 1973; *The Towering Inferno* 1974; *The Drowning Pool* 1975; *Buffalo Bill and the Indians, or Sitting Bull's History Lesson* 1976; *Slap Shot* 1977; *Quintet* 1979; *When Time Ran Out* 1980; *Absence of Malice* 1981; *Fort Apache, the Bronx* 1981; *The Verdict* 1982; *Harry and Son* 1984; *The Color of Money* 1986; *Blaze* 1989; *Shadow Makers* 1989; *Mr and Mrs Bridge* 1990; *The Hudsucker Proxy* 1994; *Nobody's Fool* 1994; *Message in a Bottle* 1998; *Twilight* 1998; *Where the Money Is* 2000; *Road to Perdition* 2002

Newman, Phyllis (1935–) *Bye Bye Braverman* 1968; *The Beautician and the Beast* 1997

Newmar, Julie (1935–) *Li'l Abner* 1959; *The Marriage-Go-Round* 1960; *For Love or Money* 1963; *Mackenna's Gold* 1969; *The Maltese Bippy* 1969; *Dance Academy* 1988; *Ghosts Can't Do It* 1990; *Oblivion* 1993

Newton, Robert (1905–1956) *The Green Cockatoo* 1937; *The Squeaker* 1937; *21 Days* 1937; *Vessel of Wrath* 1938; *Jamaica Inn* 1939; *Poison Pen* 1939; *Busman's Honeymoon* 1940; *Gaslight* 1940; *Hatter's Castle* 1941; *Major Barbara* 1941; *They Flew Alone* 1941; *Henry V* 1944; *This Happy Breed* 1944; *Night Boat to Dublin* 1946; *Odd Man Out* 1946; *Blood on My Hands* 1948; *Obsession* 1948; *Oliver Twist* 1948; *Snowbound* 1948; *Treasure Island* 1950; *Waterfront* 1950; *Soldiers Three* 1951; *Tom Brown's Schooldays* 1951; *Androcles and the Lion* 1952; *Blackbeard the Pirate* 1952; *Les Misérables* 1952; *The Desert Rats* 1953; *The Beachcomber* 1954; *The High and the Mighty* 1954; *Long John Silver* 1954; *Around the World in 80 Days* 1956

Newton, Thandie (1972–) *Flirting* 1989; *The Young Americans* 1993; *Loaded* 1994; *Jefferson in Paris* 1995; *The Journey of August King* 1995; *Gridlock'd* 1996; *The Leading Man* 1996; *Beloved* 1998; *Besieged* 1998; *Mission: Impossible 2* 1999; *It Was an Accident* 2000; *The Truth about Charlie* 2002; *The Chronicles of Riddick* 2004; *Crash* 2004

Newton, Theodore (1904–1963) *Ace of Aces* 1933; *The Sphinx* 1933; *Upper World* 1934; *The Come On* 1956

Newton, Wayne (1942–) *Eighty Steps to Jonah* 1969; *Licence to Kill* 1989; *The Adventures of Ford Fairlane* 1990; *The Dark Backward* 1991; *Best of the Best II* 1992; *Vegas Vacation* 1997

Newton-John, Olivia (1948–) *Toomorrow* 1970; *Grease* 1978; *Xanadu* 1980; *Two of a Kind* 1983; *A Christmas Romance* 1994; *It's My Party* 1996

Ney, Marie (1895–1981) *The Wandering Jew* 1933; *Scrooge* 1935; *Night Was Our Friend* 1951; *Simba* 1955

Ney, Richard (1915–2004) *Mrs Miniver* 1942; *The War against Mrs Hadley* 1942; *Ivy* 1947; *The Late George Apley* 1947; *The Lovable Cheat* 1949; *The Premature Burial* 1962

Neyland, Anne *Hidden Fear* 1957; *Jailhouse Rock* 1957; *Motorcycle Gang* 1957

Ng, Carrie (1963–) *City on Fire* 1987; *Rock 'n' Roll Cop* 1994

Ng, Francis *aka* **Ng Chun-yu** (1961–) *The Bride with White Hair* 1993; *Full Alert* 1997; *Infernal Affairs II* 2003

Ng, Irene (1974–) *Night Watch* 1995; *Hard Men* 1996; *Rogue Trader* 1998

Ng, Lawrence *The Actress* 1992; *Sex and Zen* 1992

Ngoombujarra, David *Black and White* 2002; *Kangaroo Jack* 2003

Ngor, Haing S (1940–1996) *The Killing Fields* 1984; *The Iron Triangle* 1988; *Ambition* 1991; *Heaven and Earth* 1993; *My Life* 1993

Nguyen, Dustin (1962–) 3 Ninjas Kick Back 1994; Doom Generation 1995
Nguyen Nhu Quynh Cyclo 1995; At the Height of Summer 1999
Niblo, Fred (1874–1948) Free and Easy 1930; Ellery Queen Master Detective 1940
Nicastro, Michelle (1960–) Bad Guys 1986; The Swan Princess 1994
Nichetti, Maurizio (1948–) The Icicle Thief 1989; Volere, Volare 1991
Nicholas, Denise aka **Nicholas-Hill, Denise** (1944–) Blacula 1972; Let's Do It Again 1975; Mr Ricco 1975; A Piece of the Action 1977; Marvin and Tige 1983; Ghost Dad 1990
Nicholas, Paul (1945–) Blind Terror 1971; Stardust 1974; Lisztomania 1975; Tommy 1975; Sgt Pepper's Lonely Hearts Club Band 1978; The World Is Full of Married Men 1979; Yesterday's Hero 1979; The Jazz Singer 1980; Nutcracker 1982; Invitation to the Wedding 1983
Nicholas, Thomas Ian (1980–) Rookie of the Year 1993; Judge & Jury 1995; A Kid in Aladdin's Palace 1997; American Pie 1999; American Pie 2 2001; The Rules of Attraction 2002; American Pie: the Wedding 2003
Nicholls, Allan Buffalo Bill and the Indians, or Sitting Bull's History Lesson 1976; Threshold 1981; Home Free All 1983
Nicholls, Anthony (1902–1977) The Dancing Years 1949; The Hasty Heart 1949; No Place for Jennifer 1949; The Franchise Affair 1950; The Weak and the Wicked 1953; Dunkirk 1958; Night of the Eagle 1961; Victim 1961; Othello 1965; Mister Ten Per Cent 1967; A Walk with Love and Death 1969
Nicholls, Paul (1979–) The Clandestine Marriage 1999; The Trench 1999; Goodbye Charlie Bright 2000
Nicholls, Phoebe aka **Nicholls, Sarah** (1958–) Our Mother's House 1967; Women in Love 1969; The Missionary 1982; Party Party 1983; Persuasion 1995; FairyTale: a True Story 1997
Nichols, Austin (1980–) Holiday in the Sun 2001; The Day after Tomorrow 2004; Wimbledon 2004
Nichols, Barbara (1929–1976) The King and Four Queens 1956; Miracle in the Rain 1956; The Pajama Game 1957; Pal Joey 1957; Sweet Smell of Success 1957; The Naked and the Dead 1958; That Kind of Woman 1959; Woman Obsessed 1959; Where the Boys Are 1960; Who Was That Lady? 1960; The George Raft Story 1961; House of Women 1962; Dear Heart 1964
Nichols, Dandy (1907–1986) The Fallen Idol 1948; Dance Hall 1950; The Happy Family 1952; The Deep Blue Sea 1955; Where There's a Will 1955; Don't Talk to Strange Men 1962; Ladies Who Do 1963; The Birthday Party 1968; Till Death Us Do Part 1968; O Lucky Man! 1973; Confessions of a Window Cleaner 1974; Britannia Hospital 1982
Nichols, George (1864–1927) The Eagle 1925; The Wedding March 1928
Nichols, Nichelle (1933–) Tarzan's Deadly Silence 1970; Truck Turner 1974; Star Trek: the Motion Picture 1979; Star Trek II: the Wrath of Khan 1982; Star Trek III: the Search for Spock 1984; Star Trek IV: the Voyage Home 1986; Star Trek V: the Final Frontier 1989; Star Trek VI: the Undiscovered Country 1991; Snow Dogs 2002; Are We There Yet? 2005
Nichols, Rachel (1980–) Dumb and Dumberer: When Harry Met Lloyd 2003; The Amityville Horror 2005
Nichols, Robert (1924–) Jennifer 1953; The Out of Towners 1970
Nichols, Stephen (1951–) Witchboard 1987; The Glass Cage 1996
Nichols, Taylor Metropolitan 1990; Barcelona 1994; Norma Jean & Marilyn 1996
Nicholson, Jack (1937–) The Cry Baby Killer 1958; The Little Shop of Horrors 1960; Studs Lonigan 1960; Too Soon to Love 1960; The Wild Ride 1960; The Broken Land 1962; The Raven 1963; The Terror 1963; Back Door to Hell 1964; Ensign Pulver 1964; Flight to Fury 1966; Ride in the Whirlwind 1966; Hell's Angels on Wheels 1967; Rebel Rousers 1967; The St Valentine's Day Massacre 1967; The Shooting 1967; Psych-Out 1968; Easy Rider 1969; Five Easy Pieces 1970; On a Clear Day You Can See Forever 1970; Carnal Knowledge 1971; A Safe Place 1971; The King of Marvin Gardens 1972; The Last Detail 1973; Chinatown 1974; The Fortune 1975; One Flew over the Cuckoo's Nest 1975; The Passenger 1975; Tommy 1975; The Last Tycoon 1976; The Missouri Breaks 1976; Goin' South 1978; The Shining 1980; The Border 1981; The Postman Always Rings Twice 1981; Reds 1981; Terms of Endearment 1983; Prizzi's Honor 1985; Heartburn 1986; Broadcast News 1987; Ironweed 1987; The Witches of Eastwick 1987; Batman 1989; The Two Jakes 1990; A Few Good Men 1992; Hoffa 1992; Man Trouble 1992; Wolf 1994; The Crossing Guard 1995; Blood and Wine 1996; The Evening Star 1996; Mars Attacks! 1996; As Good as It Gets 1997; The Pledge 2000; About Schmidt 2002; Anger Management 2003; Something's Gotta Give 2003
Nicholson, Julianne (1971–) The Love Letter 1999; I'm with Lucy 2002; Kinsey 2004; Little Black Book 2004
Nicholson, Nora (1892–1973) The Blue Lagoon 1949; Tread Softly 1952; Upstairs and Downstairs 1959; Dangerous Afternoon 1961; Devil Doll 1964
Nickerson, Denise (1959–) Willy Wonka and the Chocolate Factory 1971; Zero to Sixty 1978
Nickson-Soul, Julia aka **Nickson, Julia** (1959–) Rambo: First Blood, Part II 1985; China Cry 1990; K2 1991; Amityville: a New Generation 1993; Sidekicks 1993; Double Dragon 1994
Nicol, Alex (1916–2001) The Sleeping City 1950; Air Cadet 1951; Target Unknown 1951; Tomahawk 1951; Meet Danny Wilson 1952; Red Ball Express 1952; Law and Order 1953; The Lone Hand 1953; The Redhead from Wyoming 1953; About Mrs Leslie 1954; Dawn at Socorro 1954; Face the Music 1954; The Gilded Cage 1954; The Man from Laramie 1955; Sincerely Yours 1955; Strategic Air Command 1955; Great Day in the Morning 1956; Under Ten Flags 1960; Look in Any Window 1961; A Matter of WHO 1961; Bloody Mama 1970; Homer 1970
Nicolodi, Daria (1950–) Deep Red 1975; Inferno 1980; Macaroni 1985; Opera 1987
Nielsen, Brigitte (1963–) Red Sonja 1985; Rocky IV 1985; Cobra 1986; Beverly Hills Cop II 1987; Mission of Justice 1992; 976-EVIL 2 1992
Nielsen, Connie (1964–) Voyage 1993; The Devil's Advocate 1997; Soldier 1998; Mission to Mars 1999; Gladiator 2000; One Hour Photo 2001; Demonlover 2002; The Hunted 2002; Basic 2003; Brothers 2004
Nielsen, Hans (1911–1965) The Door with Seven Locks 1962; Sherlock Holmes and the Deadly Necklace 1962
Nielsen, Leslie (1926–) Forbidden Planet 1956; The Opposite Sex 1956; Ransom! 1956; The Vagabond King 1956; Hot Summer Night 1957; Tammy and the Bachelor 1957; The Sheepman 1958; Dark Intruder 1965; Harlow 1965; Beau Geste 1966; The Plainsman 1966; Counterpoint 1967; Gunfight in Abilene 1967; The Reluctant Astronaut 1967; Rosie! 1967; Dayton's Devils 1968; How to Steal the World 1968; How to Commit Marriage 1969; The Resurrection of Zachary Wheeler 1971; The Poseidon Adventure 1972; And Millions Will Die! 1973; Grand Jury 1976; Project: Kill 1976; Day of the Animals 1977; Sixth and Main 1977; Viva Knievel! 1977; The Amsterdam Kill 1978; City on Fire 1979; Airplane! 1980; Prom Night 1980; Creepshow 1982; The Man with the Deadly Lens 1982; The Patriot 1986; Soul Man 1986; Home Is Where the Hart Is 1987; The Naked Gun 1988; Repossessed 1990; All I Want for Christmas 1991; The Naked Gun $2\frac{1}{2}$: the Smell of Fear 1991; Rent-a-Kid 1992; Surf Ninjas 1993; Naked Gun $33\frac{1}{3}$: the Final Insult 1994; Dracula: Dead and Loving It 1995; Spy Hard 1996; Family Plan 1997; Mr Magoo 1997; Wrongfully Accused 1998; Santa Who? 2000; Scary Movie 3 2003
Niemczyk, Leon (1923–) Eroica 1958; Knife in the Water 1962
Nieto, José aka **Nieto, Pepe** (1903–1982) Contraband Spain 1955; Les Bijoutiers du Clair de Lune 1957; The Pride and the Passion 1957; Solomon and Sheba 1959; The Son of Captain Blood 1962; Kid Rodelo 1966
Nigh, Jane (1925–1993) Give My Regards to Broadway 1948; Fighting Man of the Plains 1949
Nighy, Bill (1949–) The Little Drummer Girl 1984; Thirteen at Dinner 1985; The Phantom of the Opera 1989; Alive and Kicking 1996; FairyTale: a True Story 1997; Still Crazy 1998; Guest House Paradiso 1999; Blow Dry 2000; The Lawless Heart 2001; Lucky Break 2001; AKA 2002; I Capture the Castle 2002; Love Actually 2003; Underworld 2003; Enduring Love 2004; Shaun of the Dead 2004; The Hitchhiker's Guide to the Galaxy 2005; The Magic Roundabout 2005
Nihill, Julie (1957–) Careful, He Might Hear You 1983; Rebel 1985; Kangaroo 1986; Boundaries of the Heart 1988
Nikaido, Miho Tokyo Decadence 1992; Flirt 1995; The Book of Life 1998; Side Streets 1998
Nikkari, Esko (1938–) Crime and Punishment 1983; Hamlet Goes Business 1987; The Match Factory Girl 1990; A Summer by the River 1998
Niklas, Jan Colonel Redl 1984; Dr M 1989; The Rose Garden 1989
Nikolaev, Valery (1963–) Aberration 1997; The Saint 1997
Nilsson, Maj-Britt (1924–) Summer Interlude 1950; To Joy 1950; Waiting Women 1952
Nimmo, Derek (1931–1999) It's Trad, Dad 1961; The Amorous Prawn 1962; Tamahine 1963; The Bargee 1964; Murder Ahoy 1964; The Liquidator 1966; Casino Royale 1967; Mister Ten Per Cent 1967; One of Our Dinosaurs Is Missing 1975
Nimoy, Leonard (1931–) Them! 1954; The Brain Eaters 1958; The Balcony 1963; Deathwatch 1966; Catlow 1971; Invasion of the Body Snatchers 1978; Star Trek: the Motion Picture 1979; Star Trek II: the Wrath of Khan 1982; Star Trek IV: the Voyage Home 1986; Transformers – The Movie 1986; Star Trek V: the Final Frontier 1989; Star Trek VI: the Undiscovered Country 1991; The Halloween Tree 1993; The Pagemaster 1994; Atlantis: the Lost Empire 2001
Nimri, Najwa (1972–) Open Your Eyes 1997; The Lovers of the Arctic Circle 1998; Fausto 5.0 2001; Sex and Lucia 2001
Ninchi, Carlo (1897–1974) La Beauté du Diable 1949; Two Women 1960
Ning Jing Red Firecracker, Green Firecracker 1993; The Missing Gun 2002
Ninidze, Merab (1965–) Repentance 1984; Nowhere in Africa 2001
Nischol, Navin Bollywood Calling 2000; Khushi 2002
Nishijima, Hidetoshi License to Live 1999; Dolls 2002
Nissen, Aud Egede (1893–1974) Anna Boleyn 1920; Dr Mabuse, the Gambler 1922
Nissen, Greta (1906–1988) The Lucky Lady 1926; Fazil 1928; Melody Cruise 1933
Niven, David (1909–1983) Mutiny on the Bounty 1935; Splendor 1935; Beloved Enemy 1936; The Charge of the Light Brigade 1936; Dodsworth 1936; Rose Marie 1936; Thank You, Jeeves 1936; Dinner at the Ritz 1937; The Prisoner of Zenda 1937; Bluebeard's Eighth Wife 1938; The Dawn Patrol 1938; Four Men and a Prayer 1938; Three Blind Mice 1938; Bachelor Mother 1939; Eternally Yours 1939; Raffles 1939; The Real Glory 1939; Wuthering Heights 1939; The First of the Few 1942; The Way Ahead 1944; Magnificent Doll 1946; A Matter of Life and Death 1946; The Bishop's Wife 1947; The Other Love 1947; Bonnie Prince Charlie 1948; Enchantment 1948; A Kiss for Corliss 1949; A Kiss in the Dark 1949; The Elusive Pimpernel 1950; Happy Go Lovely 1950; The Toast of New Orleans 1950; Appointment with Venus 1951; Soldiers Three 1951; The Love Lottery 1953; The Moon Is Blue 1953; Carrington VC 1954; Happy Ever After 1954; The King's Thief 1955; Around the World in 80 Days 1956; The Birds and the Bees 1956; The Little Hut 1957; My Man Godfrey 1957; Oh, Men! Oh, Women! 1957; The Silken Affair 1957; Bonjour Tristesse 1958; Separate Tables 1958; Ask Any Girl 1959; Happy Anniversary 1959; Please Don't Eat the Daisies 1960; The Best of Enemies 1961; The Guns of Navarone 1961; Captive City 1962; Guns of Darkness 1962; The Road to Hong Kong 1962; 55 Days at Peking 1963; The Pink Panther 1963; Bedtime Story 1964; Lady L 1965; Where the Spies Are 1965; Eye of the Devil 1966; Casino Royale 1967; Before Winter Comes 1968; Prudence and the Pill 1968; The Brain 1969; The Extraordinary Seaman 1969; King, Queen, Knave 1972; Paper Tiger 1974; Vampira 1975; Murder by Death 1976; No Deposit No Return 1976; Candleshoe 1977; Death on the Nile 1978; Escape to Athena 1979; A Nightingale Sang in Berkeley Square 1979; Rough Cut 1980; The Sea Wolves 1980; Trail of the Pink Panther 1982; Better Late Than Never 1983; The Curse of the Pink Panther 1983
Nivola, Alessandro (1972–) Face/Off 1997; I Want You 1998; Best Laid Plans 1999; Love's Labour's Lost 1999; Mansfield Park 1999; Jurassic Park III 2001; Laurel Canyon 2002; The Clearing 2004
Nixon, Cynthia (1966–) Tattoo 1980; I Am the Cheese 1983; The Deadly Game 1986; Baby's Day Out 1994; Igby Goes Down 2002
Nixon, Marian aka **Nixon, Marion** (1904–1983) Hands Up! 1926; Say It with Songs 1929; Dr Bull 1933; Pilgrimage 1933
Noble, James (1922–) Who? 1974; One Summer Love 1975; Summer of My German Soldier 1978; You Talkin' to Me? 1987
Noble, John (1948–) Virtual Nightmare 2000; The Lord of the Rings: The Return of the King 2003
Noel, Chris (1941–) Get Yourself a College Girl 1964; The Glory Stompers 1967
Noël, Hubert aka **Noel, Hubert** (1924–1987) Le Bossu 1959; Devils of Darkness 1964
Noël, Magali (1932–) Les Possédées 1955; Razzia sur la Chnouf 1955; Rififi 1955; Elena et les Hommes 1956; La Dolce Vita 1960; The Secret Mark of D'Artagnan 1962; Amarcord 1973; Les Rendez-vous d'Anna 1978; The Death of Mario Ricci 1983; La Fidélité 2000
Noël-Noël A Cage of Nightingales 1945; The Seven Deadly Sins 1952; The Diary of Major Thompson 1955; Jessica 1962
Noguera, Hector Archipelago 1991; La Frontera 1991
Nogulich, Natalija aka **Nogulich, Natalia** The Guardian 1990; Homicide 1991
Noiret, Philippe (1930–) Zazie dans le Métro 1960; Thérèse Desqueyroux 1962; Lady L 1965; La Vie de Château 1965; The Night of the Generals 1966; Woman Times Seven 1967; The Assassination Bureau 1969; Justine 1969; Topaz 1969; Murphy's War 1971; Sweet Torture 1971; A Time for Loving 1971; The Serpent 1972; La Grande Bouffe 1973; The Watchmaker of St Paul 1973; The Purple Taxi 1977; Who Is Killing the Great Chefs of Europe? 1978; Three Brothers 1980; Clean Slate 1981; L'Etoile du Nord 1982; Fort Saganne 1984; Le Cop 1985; Let's Hope It's a Girl 1985; Masques 1987; Cinema Paradiso 1988; Young Toscanini 1988; Le Cop II 1989; Life and Nothing But 1989; The Return of the Musketeers 1989; Uranus 1990; J'Embrasse Pas 1991; Tango 1993; D'Artagnan's Daughter 1994; Il Postino 1994; The King of Paris 1995; Le Bossu 1997; Marianna Ucria 1997
Nolan, Jeanette (1911–1998) Macbeth 1948; No Sad Songs for Me 1950; Saddle Tramp 1950; The Big Heat 1953; Seventh Cavalry 1956; April Love 1957; Guns of Fort Petticoat 1957; The Halliday Brand 1957; The Deep Six 1958; Twilight of Honor 1963; My Blood Runs Cold 1965; The Reluctant Astronaut 1967; Did You Hear the One about the Traveling Saleslady? 1968; Avalanche 1978; The Fox and the Hound 1981; Cloak and Dagger 1984
Nolan, Jim Dick Tracy Meets Gruesome 1947; The Miracle of the Bells 1948
Nolan, John (1938–) Terror 1979; Following 1998
Nolan, Kathleen (1933–) Limbo 1972; Amy 1981; The Switch 1993
Nolan, Lloyd (1902–1985) Atlantic Adventure 1935; "G" Men 1935; Big Brown Eyes 1936; The Texas Rangers 1936; Every Day's a Holiday 1937; Internes Can't Take Money 1937; Wells Fargo 1937; King of Alcatraz 1938; The House across the Bay 1940; Johnny Apollo 1940; The Man I Married 1940; The Man Who Wouldn't Talk 1940; Michael Shayne, Private Detective 1940; Blues in the Night 1941; Apache Trail 1942; Bataan 1943; Guadalcanal Diary 1943; Captain Eddie 1945; Circumstantial Evidence 1945; The House on 92nd Street 1945; A Tree Grows in Brooklyn 1945; Somewhere in the Night 1946; Lady in the Lake 1947; Green Grass of Wyoming 1948; The Street with No Name 1948; Easy Living 1949; The Lemon Drop Kid 1951; Island in the Sky 1953; The Last Hunt 1956; Santiago 1956; Toward the Unknown 1956; A Hatful of Rain 1957; Peyton Place 1957; Seven Waves Away 1957; Girl of the Night 1960; Portrait in Black 1960; Susan Slade 1961; We Joined the Navy 1962; The Girl Hunters 1963; The Magnificent Showman 1964; An American Dream 1966; The Double Man 1967; Ice Station Zebra 1968; Sergeant Ryker 1968; Earthquake 1974; Prince Jack 1984; Hannah and Her Sisters 1986
Nolan, Tom Chastity 1969; School Spirit 1985
Nollier, Claude (1923–) Les Mains Sales 1951; Moulin Rouge

1952; *The Greengage Summer* 1961
Nolot, Jacques *Les Roseaux Sauvages* 1994; *Under the Sand* 2000
Nolte, Nick (1941–) *Return to Macon County* 1975; *The Deep* 1977; *Who'll Stop the Rain?* 1978; *Heart Beat* 1979; *North Dallas Forty* 1979; *Cannery Row* 1982; *48 HRS* 1982; *Under Fire* 1983; *Grace Quigley* 1984; *Teachers* 1984; *Down and Out in Beverly Hills* 1986; *Extreme Prejudice* 1987; *Weeds* 1987; *Farewell to the King* 1988; *New York Stories* 1989; *Three Fugitives* 1989; *Another 48 HRS* 1990; *Everybody Wins* 1990; *Q & A* 1990; *Cape Fear* 1991; *The Prince of Tides* 1991; *Lorenzo's Oil* 1992; *Blue Chips* 1994; *I Love Trouble* 1994; *I'll Do Anything* 1994; *Jefferson in Paris* 1995; *Mother Night* 1996; *Mulholland Falls* 1996; *Affliction* 1997; *Afterglow* 1997; *Nightwatch* 1997; *U Turn* 1997; *The Thin Red Line* 1998; *Breakfast of Champions* 1999; *Simpatico* 1999; *The Golden Bowl* 2000; *Trixie* 2000; *The Good Thief* 2002; *Northfork* 2002; *Hulk* 2003; *The Beautiful Country* 2004; *Clean* 2004; *Hotel Rwanda* 2004
Nono, Clare *Fire and Ice* 1983; *Nightmares* 1983
Nonyela, Valentine *Young Soul Rebels* 1991; *Welcome II the Terrordome* 1994
Noonan, Tom (1951–) *Gloria* 1980; *Wolfen* 1981; *Eddie Macon's Run* 1983; *Manhunter* 1986; *Collision Course* 1987; *The Monster Squad* 1987; *RoboCop 2* 1990; *Last Action Hero* 1993; *What Happened Was...* 1994; *Phoenix* 1998; *Knockaround Guys* 2001
Noonan, Tommy (1921–1968) *Gentlemen Prefer Blondes* 1953; *A Star Is Born* 1954; *How to Be Very, Very Popular* 1955; *Violent Saturday* 1955; *The Ambassador's Daughter* 1956; *The Best Things in Life Are Free* 1956; *Bundle of Joy* 1956; *The Girl Most Likely* 1957
Noone, Nora-Jane (1984–) *The Magdalene Sisters* 2002; *The Descent* 2005
Norby, Ghita (1935–) *Waltzing Regitze* 1989; *Best Intentions* 1992; *Sofie* 1992; *The Kingdom* 1994; *Hamsun* 1996; *The Inheritance* 2003
Norden, Christine (1924–1988) *An Ideal Husband* 1947; *Mine Own Executioner* 1947; *Night Beat* 1948; *The Interrupted Journey* 1949; *A Case for PC 49* 1950
Nordling, Jeffrey (1962–) *Ruby* 1992; *D3: the Mighty Ducks* 1996; *Danielle Steel's Remembrance* 1996
Noriega (1), Eduardo (1916–) *Captain Scarlett* 1953; *The Far Horizons* 1955; *Hell's Island* 1955; *The Living Idol* 1955; *The Magnificent Matador* 1955; *Seven Cities of Gold* 1955; *The Beast of Hollow Mountain* 1956; *Of Love and Desire* 1963; *Tarzan and the Valley of Gold* 1966
Noriega (2), Eduardo (1973–) *Tesis* 1996; *Open Your Eyes* 1997; *Cha-Cha-Cha* 1998; *The Devil's Backbone* 2001; *Novo* 2002
Norman, Lucille (1921–1998) *Painting the Clouds with Sunshine* 1951; *Carson City* 1952
Norman, Maidie (1913–1998) *The Well* 1951; *Bright Road* 1953; *What Ever Happened to Baby Jane?* 1962
Norman, Zack *Sitting Ducks* 1979; *Romancing the Stone* 1984; *America* 1986; *Cadillac Man* 1990; *Babyfever* 1994
Noro, Line (1900–1985) *Pépé le Moko* 1937; *J'Accuse* 1938; *La Symphonie Pastorale* 1946
Norris, Chuck (1940–) *The Wrecking Crew* 1969; *The Way of the Dragon* 1973; *Good Guys Wear Black* 1977; *Game of Death* 1978; *A Force of One* 1979; *The Octagon* 1980; *An Eye for an Eye* 1981; *Forced Vengeance* 1982; *Silent Rage* 1982; *Lone Wolf McQuade* 1983; *Missing in Action* 1984; *Code of Silence* 1985; *Invasion USA* 1985; *Missing in Action 2: the Beginning* 1985; *The Delta Force* 1986; *Firewalker* 1986; *Braddock: Missing in Action III* 1988; *Hero and the Terror* 1988; *Delta Force 2* 1990; *The Hitman* 1991; *Sidekicks* 1993; *Top Dog* 1995; *Logan's War: Bound by Honor* 1998; *The President's Man* 2000
Norris, Daran *The Little Polar Bear* 2001; *Team America: World Police* 2004
Norris, Dean *Hard to Kill* 1989; *The Lawnmower Man* 1992; *The Last Seduction* 1993; *Forgotten Sins* 1996
Norris, Edward (1911–2002) *They Won't Forget* 1937; *Boys Town* 1938; *Frontier Marshal* 1939; *The Singing Sheriff* 1944
North, Alan (1920–2000) *Billy Galvin* 1986; *Highlander* 1986; *Lean on Me* 1989; *See No Evil, Hear No Evil* 1989; *Crazy People* 1990; *The Jerky Boys* 1995
North, Sheree (1933–) *Living It Up* 1954; *How to Be Very, Very Popular* 1955; *The Best Things in Life Are Free* 1956; *The Lieutenant Wore Skirts* 1956; *No Down Payment* 1957; *The Way to the Gold* 1957; *In Love and War* 1958; *Mardi Gras* 1958; *Destination Inner Space* 1966; *Madigan* 1968; *The Gypsy Moths* 1969; *The Trouble with Girls* 1969; *Lawman* 1971; *The Organization* 1971; *Charley Varrick* 1973; *The Outfit* 1973; *Breakout* 1975; *The Shootist* 1976; *Telefon* 1977; *Cold Dog Soup* 1989
North, Ted *aka* **North, Michael** (1916–) *Chad Hanna* 1940; *Charlie Chan in Rio* 1941; *Syncopation* 1942; *The Devil Thumbs a Ride* 1947; *The Unsuspected* 1947
North, Virginia *The Long Duel* 1966; *The Abominable Dr Phibes* 1971
Northam, Jeremy (1961–) *Soft Top, Hard Shoulder* 1992; *Wuthering Heights* 1992; *Carrington* 1995; *The Net* 1995; *Emma* 1996; *Amistad* 1997; *Mimic* 1997; *Gloria* 1998; *The Misadventures of Margaret* 1998; *Happy, Texas* 1999; *An Ideal Husband* 1999; *The Winslow Boy* 1999; *The Golden Bowl* 2000; *Enigma* 2001; *Gosford Park* 2001; *Cypher* 2002; *Possession* 2002; *The Singing Detective* 2003; *The Statement* 2003; *Bobby Jones: Stroke of Genius* 2004
Northup, Harry (1940–) *Over the Edge* 1979; *Kansas* 1988
Norton, Alex (1950–) *Gregory's Girl* 1980; *Comfort and Joy* 1984; *Every Picture Tells a Story* 1984; *Comrades: a Lanternist's Account of the Tolpuddle Martyrs and What Became of Them* 1986; *Hidden City* 1987; *Robin Hood* 1990; *Orphans* 1998; *Beautiful Creatures* 2000
Norton, Barry (1905–1956) *Dishonored* 1931; *Lady for a Day* 1933
Norton, DeeDee *Confessions of a Serial Killer* 1987; *Dakota* 1987
Norton, Edgar (1868–1953) *The Love Parade* 1929; *One Romantic Night* 1930; *Dr Jekyll and Mr Hyde* 1931
Norton, Edward (1969–) *Everyone Says I Love You* 1996; *The People vs Larry Flynt* 1996; *Primal Fear* 1996; *American History X* 1998; *Rounders* 1998; *Fight Club* 1999; *Keeping the Faith* 2000; *The Score* 2001; *Death to Smoochy* 2002; *Frida* 2002; *Red Dragon* 2002; *25th Hour* 2002; *The Italian Job* 2003; *Kingdom of Heaven* 2005
Norton, Jack *The Big Noise* 1944; *The Scarlet Clue* 1945
Norton, Jim (1938–) *Straw Dogs* 1971; *Adolf Hitler – My Part in His Downfall* 1972; *Hidden Agenda* 1990; *Memoirs of an Invisible Man* 1992; *Sunset Heights* 1996; *A Love Divided* 1999
Norton, Ken (1945–) *Mandingo* 1975; *Drum* 1976
Norton, Richard (1950–) *Gymkata* 1985; *China O'Brien* 1988; *Mr Nice Guy* 1996
Noseworthy, Jack (1969–) *A Place for Annie* 1994; *Barb Wire* 1995; *Mojave Moon* 1996; *Breakdown* 1997; *Idle Hands* 1999; *Murder at Devil's Glen* 1999; *Cecil B Demented* 2000
Noth, Christopher *aka* **Noth, Chris** (1956–) *Fugitive from Justice* 1996; *Double Whammy* 2001; *The Glass House* 2001
Nouri, Michael (1945–) *Flashdance* 1983; *GoBots: Battle of the Rocklords* 1986; *The Imagemaker* 1986; *The Hidden* 1987; *Little Vegas* 1990; *Project: Alien* 1990; *Danielle Steel's Changes* 1991; *A Passion for Murder* 1992; *The Hidden II* 1993; *American Yakuza* 1994; *Finding Forrester* 2000; *Lovely & Amazing* 2001
Novak, Kim (1933–) *Phffft!* 1954; *Pushover* 1954; *Five against the House* 1955; *The Man with the Golden Arm* 1955; *Picnic* 1955; *Son of Sinbad* 1955; *The Eddy Duchin Story* 1956; *Jeanne Eagels* 1957; *Pal Joey* 1957; *Bell, Book and Candle* 1958; *Vertigo* 1958; *Middle of the Night* 1959; *Pepe* 1960; *Strangers When We Meet* 1960; *Boys' Night Out* 1962; *The Notorious Landlady* 1962; *Kiss Me, Stupid* 1964; *Of Human Bondage* 1964; *The Amorous Adventures of Moll Flanders* 1965; *The Legend of Lylah Clare* 1968; *The Great Bank Robbery* 1969; *Tales That Witness Madness* 1973; *The White Buffalo* 1977; *Just a Gigolo* 1978; *The Mirror Crack'd* 1980; *The Children* 1990; *Liebestraum* 1991
Novarro, Ramon *aka* **Samaniegos, Ramon** (1899–1968) *The Prisoner of Zenda* 1922; *Scaramouche* 1923; *The Arab* 1924; *Ben-Hur: a Tale of the Christ* 1925; *The Student Prince in Old Heidelberg* 1927; *Daybreak* 1931; *Mata Hari* 1931; *The Barbarian* 1933; *The Cat and the Fiddle* 1934; *The Big Steal* 1949; *We Were Strangers* 1949; *Crisis* 1950; *The Outriders* 1950; *Heller in Pink Tights* 1960
Novello, Don (1943–) *Head Office* 1986; *One Night Stand* 1994; *Before the Night* 1995; *Atlantis: the Lost Empire* 2001
Novello, Ivor (1893–1951) *The Lodger* 1926; *Downhill* 1927; *The Constant Nymph* 1928; *I Lived with You* 1933
Novello, Jay (1904–1982) *Blood on My Hands* 1948; *The Miracle of Our Lady of Fatima* 1952; *The Diamond Queen* 1953; *The City Is Dark* 1954; *Bengazi* 1955; *Son of Sinbad* 1955; *Lisbon* 1956; *The Pride and the Passion* 1957; *The Perfect Furlough* 1958; *This Rebel Breed* 1960; *Harum Scarum* 1965
Novo, Nancho (1958–) *The Red Squirrel* 1993; *Tierra* 1995; *The Lovers of the Arctic Circle* 1998
Novotna, Jarmila (1908–1994) *The Search* 1948; *The Great Caruso* 1951
Novy, Pavel (1948–) *Conspirators of Pleasure* 1996; *Little Otik* 2000
Nowak, Jerzy (1923–) *Camera Buff* 1979; *Three Colours White* 1993
Nowicki, Jan (1939–) *Diary for My Children* 1982; *Diary for My Loves* 1987; *Diary for My Father and Mother* 1990
Noy, Zachi (1953–) *Lemon Popsicle* 1978; *Enter the Ninja* 1981
Nozick, Bruce *Hit the Dutchman* 1992; *And the Beat Goes On: the Sonny and Cher Story* 1999
Ntshona, Winston *The Wild Geese* 1978; *A Dry White Season* 1989; *The Air Up There* 1993; *Tarzan and the Lost City* 1998
Nucci, Danny (1968–) *Rescue Me* 1991; *Roosters* 1993; *Homage* 1995; *The Big Squeeze* 1996; *Eraser* 1996; *That Old Feeling* 1997; *American Cousins* 2003
Nugent, Edward *aka* **Nugent, Eddie** (1904–1995) *Our Dancing Daughters* 1928; *Our Modern Maidens* 1929; *Night Nurse* 1931; *This Day and Age* 1933; *She Loves Me Not* 1934
Nugent, Elliott (1899–1980) *Romance* 1930; *The Unholy Three* 1930; *The Last Flight* 1931
Nunez Jr, Miguel A *aka* **Nunez, Miguel A** (1964–) *Shadowzone* 1990; *Why Do Fools Fall in Love?* 1998; *Life* 1999; *Juwanna Mann* 2002; *Scooby-Doo* 2002
Nunn, Bill (1953–) *School Daze* 1988; *Do the Right Thing* 1989; *Def by Temptation* 1990; *New Jack City* 1991; *Regarding Henry* 1991; *Sister Act* 1992; *The Last Seduction* 1993; *Canadian Bacon* 1995; *Candyman: Farewell to the Flesh* 1995; *Things to Do in Denver When You're Dead* 1995; *True Crime* 1995; *Extreme Measures* 1996; *Kiss the Girls* 1997; *Carriers* 1998; *He Got Game* 1998; *The Legend of 1900* 1999
Nunn, Larry (1925–1974) *Strike Up the Band* 1940; *Men of Boys Town* 1941
Nureyev, Rudolf (1938–1993) *Romeo and Juliet* 1966; *Don Quixote* 1973; *Valentino* 1977; *Exposed* 1983
Nussbaum, Danny *TwentyFourSeven* 1997; *One More Kiss* 1999; *Chunky Monkey* 2001; *Club le Monde* 2001
Nussbaum, Mike *House of Games* 1987; *Things Change* 1988; *Desperate Hours* 1990
Nutan (1936–1991) *Anari* 1959; *Sujata* 1959; *Bandini* 1963; *Tere Ghar Ke Saamne* 1963
Nuttall, Jeff (1933–2004) *Robin Hood* 1990; *The Baby of Macon* 1993; *Captives* 1994; *Anazapta* 2001
Nutter, Tarah *Chilly Scenes of Winter* 1979; *Without Warning* 1980
Nuyen, France (1939–) *In Love and War* 1958; *South Pacific* 1958; *The Last Time I Saw Archie* 1961; *Diamond Head* 1962; *A Girl Named Tamiko* 1962; *Satan Never Sleeps* 1962; *The Man in the Middle* 1964; *One More Train to Rob* 1971; *China Cry* 1990; *The Joy Luck Club* 1993
N!xau (1944–2003) *The Gods Must Be Crazy* 1980; *The Gods Must Be Crazy II* 1989
Nye, Carrie (1937–) *The Seduction of Joe Tynan* 1979; *Too Scared to Scream* 1982
Nye, Louis (1922–) *The Facts of Life* 1960; *Sex Kittens Go to College* 1960; *The Last Time I Saw Archie* 1961; *The Stripper* 1963; *Who's Been Sleeping in My Bed?* 1963; *Harper Valley PTA* 1978; *Full Moon High* 1982
Nyman, Lena (1944–) *I Am Curious – Yellow* 1967; *Autumn Sonata* 1978

O, Henry *Dragonheart: a New Beginning* 1999; *Romeo Must Die* 2000
Oakes, Lee *DragonHeart* 1996; *Large* 2000; *Club le Monde* 2001
Oakie, Jack (1903–1978) *Paramount on Parade* 1930; *If I Had a Million* 1932; *Million Dollar Legs* 1932; *The Eagle and the Hawk* 1933; *Sitting Pretty* 1933; *Looking for Trouble* 1934; *Murder at the Vanities* 1934; *The Big Broadcast of 1936* 1935; *The Call of the Wild* 1935; *Colleen* 1936; *King of Burlesque* 1936; *The Texas Rangers* 1936; *Super-Sleuth* 1937; *The Toast of New York* 1937; *The Affairs of Annabel* 1938; *Annabel Takes a Tour* 1938; *Radio City Revels* 1938; *Thanks for Everything* 1938; *The Great Dictator* 1940; *Tin Pan Alley* 1940; *Young People* 1940; *The Great American Broadcast* 1941; *Song of the Islands* 1942; *Hello, Frisco, Hello* 1943; *Wintertime* 1943; *It Happened Tomorrow* 1944; *The Merry Monahans* 1944; *Sweet and Lowdown* 1944; *Northwest Stampede* 1948; *When My Baby Smiles at Me* 1948; *Thieves' Highway* 1949; *Tomahawk* 1951; *The Wonderful Country* 1959; *The Rat Race* 1960; *Lover Come Back* 1961
Oakland, Simon (1922–1983) *I Want to Live!* 1958; *Murder, Inc* 1960; *Psycho* 1960; *The Rise and Fall of Legs Diamond* 1960; *West Side Story* 1961; *The Raiders* 1964; *Chubasco* 1967; *Tony Rome* 1967; *Bullitt* 1968; *On a Clear Day You Can See Forever* 1970; *Chato's Land* 1971; *The Hunting Party* 1971; *Scandalous John* 1971; *Emperor of the North* 1973; *Happy Mother's Day... Love, George* 1973
Oakman, Wheeler (1890–1949) *Lights of New York* 1928; *Aces and Eights* 1936
Oates, Cicely (1934–) *The Wandering Jew* 1933; *The Man Who Knew Too Much* 1934
Oates, Warren (1928–1982) *Yellowstone Kelly* 1959; *The Rise and Fall of Legs Diamond* 1960; *Hero's Island* 1962; *Ride the High Country* 1962; *Mail Order Bride* 1963; *Return of the Seven* 1966; *In the Heat of the Night* 1967; *The Shooting* 1967; *Welcome to Hard Times* 1967; *The Split* 1968; *Crooks and Coronets* 1969; *Smith!* 1969; *The Wild Bunch* 1969; *Barquero* 1970; *There Was a Crooked Man...* 1970; *The Hired Hand* 1971; *Kid Blue* 1971; *Two-Lane Blacktop* 1971; *Badlands* 1973; *Dillinger* 1973; *The Thief Who Came to Dinner* 1973; *Tom Sawyer* 1973; *Bring Me the Head of Alfredo Garcia* 1974; *The White Dawn* 1974; *92 in the Shade* 1975; *Race with the Devil* 1975; *Dixie Dynamite* 1976; *Drum* 1976; *The Brink's Job* 1978; *China 9, Liberty 37* 1978; *1941* 1979; *The Border* 1981; *Stripes* 1981; *Tough Enough* 1982; *Blue Thunder* 1983
Obata, Toshishiro *Showdown in Little Tokyo* 1991; *Teenage Mutant Ninja Turtles II: the Secret of the Ooze* 1991
Ober, Philip (1902–1982) *The Magnificent Yankee* 1950; *Never a Dull Moment* 1950; *The Clown* 1952; *Come Back, Little Sheba* 1952; *Washington Story* 1952; *From Here to Eternity* 1953; *The High Cost of Loving* 1958; *Ten North Frederick* 1958; *Torpedo Run* 1958; *Beloved Infidel* 1959; *North by Northwest* 1959; *The Facts of Life* 1960; *Go Naked in the World* 1961; *The Brass Bottle* 1964; *The Ghost and Mr Chicken* 1966
Oberman, Claire (1956–) *Goodbye Pork Pie* 1981; *The Beautiful End of This World* 1983
Oberoi, Suresh *Mirch Masala* 1987; *Raja Hindustani* 1996
Oberoi, Vivek (1976–) *Company* 2001; *Dum* 2002; *Road* 2002; *Saathiya* 2002; *Kisna – the Warrior Poet* 2004; *Kyun! Ho Gaya Na ...* 2004; *Masti* 2004; *Kaal* 2005
Oberon, Merle (1911–1979) *Wedding Rehearsal* 1932; *The Private Life of Henry VIII* 1933; *The Battle* 1934; *The Private Life of Don Juan* 1934; *The Scarlet Pimpernel* 1934; *The Dark Angel* 1935; *Folies Bergère* 1935; *Beloved Enemy* 1936; *These Three* 1936; *Over the Moon* 1937; *The Cowboy and the Lady* 1938; *The Divorce of Lady X* 1938; *The Lion Has Wings* 1939; *Wuthering Heights* 1939; *'Til We Meet Again* 1940; *Affectionately Yours* 1941; *Lydia* 1941; *That Uncertain Feeling* 1941; *Forever and a Day* 1943; *Stage Door Canteen* 1943; *Dark Waters* 1944; *The Lodger* 1944; *A Song to Remember* 1945; *This Love of Ours* 1945; *Temptation* 1946; *Night Song* 1947; *Berlin Express* 1948; *Deep in My Heart* 1954; *Desiree* 1954; *Of Love and Desire* 1963; *The Oscar* 1966; *Hotel* 1967; *Interval* 1973
Obradors, Jacqueline (1967–) *Six Days Seven Nights* 1998; *Atlantis: the Lost Empire* 2001; *Tortilla Soup* 2001; *A Man Apart* 2003
O'Brady, Frédéric *aka* **O'Brady** *aka* **O'Brady, Frederick** (1903–)

La Vie Est à Nous 1936; Foreign Intrigue 1956

O'Brian, Hugh (1925–) Cave of Outlaws 1951; Vengeance Valley 1951; The Lawless Breed 1952; Meet Me at the Fair 1952; Red Ball Express 1952; Son of Ali Baba 1952; Back to God's Country 1953; The Man from the Alamo 1953; Seminole 1953; The Stand at Apache River 1953; Broken Lance 1954; Drums across the River 1954; Fireman Save My Child 1954; Saskatchewan 1954; There's No Business like Show Business 1954; The Twinkle in God's Eye 1955; The Brass Legend 1956; The Fiend Who Walked the West 1958; Alias Jesse James 1959; Come Fly with Me 1962; Love Has Many Faces 1965; Ten Little Indians 1965; Ambush Bay 1966; Africa – Texas Style! 1967; Killer Force 1975; The Shootist 1976; Game of Death 1978

O'Brien, Austin (1981–) Last Action Hero 1993; Prehysteria! 1993; My Girl 2 1994; Lawnmower Man 2: Beyond Cyberspace 1995

O'Brien, Clay (1961–) Cahill, United States Marshal 1973; One Little Indian 1973

O'Brien, Dave aka **O'Brien, David** (1912–1969) The Little Colonel 1935; Reefer Madness 1936; Boys of the City 1940; Devil Bat 1940; That Gang of Mine 1940; Tennessee Champ 1954

O'Brien, Edmond (1915–1985) The Hunchback of Notre Dame 1939; The Navy Steps Out 1941; The Amazing Mrs Holliday 1943; Winged Victory 1944; The Killers 1946; A Double Life 1947; The Web 1947; Another Part of the Forest 1948; Fighter Squadron 1948; For the Love of Mary 1948; DOA 1949; White Heat 1949; The Admiral Was a Lady 1950; Backfire 1950; The Redhead and the Cowboy 1950; 711 Ocean Drive 1950; Warpath 1951; Denver & Rio Grande 1952; The Turning Point 1952; The Bigamist 1953; The Hitch-Hiker 1953; Julius Caesar 1953; Man in the Dark 1953; The Barefoot Contessa 1954; The Shanghai Story 1954; Shield for Murder 1954; 1984 1955; Pete Kelly's Blues 1955; A Cry in the Night 1956; D-Day the Sixth of June 1956; The Girl Can't Help It 1956; The Rack 1956; The Big Land 1957; Stopover Tokyo 1957; The World Was His Jury 1957; Sing, Boy, Sing 1958; Up Periscope 1959; The Great Impostor 1960; The Last Voyage 1960; The Third Voice 1960; Birdman of Alcatraz 1962; The Longest Day 1962; The Man Who Shot Liberty Valance 1962; Moon Pilot 1962; Rio Conchos 1964; Seven Days in May 1964; Sylvia 1964; Get off My Back 1965; The Doomsday Flight 1966; Fantastic Voyage 1966; The Love God? 1969; The Wild Bunch 1969; Isn't It Shocking? 1973; 99 and 44/100% Dead 1974

O'Brien, Eileen Runners 1983; Between Two Women 2000

O'Brien, Erin (1935–) Girl on the Run 1958; Onionhead 1958; John Paul Jones 1959

O'Brien, George (1900–1985) The Iron Horse 1924; 3 Bad Men 1926; Sunrise 1927; Noah's Ark 1928; Riders of the Purple Sage 1931; Painted Desert 1938; Arizona Legion 1939; My Wild Irish Rose 1947; Fort Apache 1948

O'Brien, Joan (1936–) Handle with Care 1958; Operation Petticoat 1959; The Alamo 1960; It Happened at the World's Fair 1962; It$ Only Money 1962; Samar 1962; Six Black Horses 1962; We Joined the Navy 1962; Get Yourself a College Girl 1964

O'Brien, Kieran (1973–) Bellman & True 1987; Virtual Sexuality 1999

O'Brien, Leo The Last Dragon 1985; Rappin' 1985

O'Brien, Margaret (1937–) Journey for Margaret 1942; Dr Gillespie's Criminal Case 1943; Jane Eyre 1943; Lost Angel 1943; The Canterville Ghost 1944; Meet Me in St Louis 1944; Music for Millions 1944; Our Vines Have Tender Grapes 1945; Bad Bascomb 1946; The Unfinished Dance 1947; Little Women 1949; The Secret Garden 1949; Heller in Pink Tights 1960; Amy 1981

O'Brien, Mariah (1971–) Halloween 6: the Curse of Michael Myers 1995; Diamonds 1999

O'Brien, Maureen (1943–) She'll Be Wearing Pink Pyjamas 1984; The Land Girls 1997

O'Brien, Niall The Outsider 1979; Half Moon Street 1986; Rawhead Rex 1986; Broken Harvest 1994; The Legend of 1900 1999

O'Brien, Pat (1899–1983) Consolation Marriage 1931; The Front Page 1931; Honor among Lovers 1931; Air Mail 1932; American Madness 1932; Hell's House 1932; Blonde Bombshell 1933; Bureau of Missing Persons 1933; Flirtation Walk 1934; Gambling Lady 1934; Here Comes the Navy 1934; Ceiling Zero 1935; Devil Dogs of the Air 1935; In Caliente 1935; The Irish in Us 1935; Oil for the Lamps of China 1935; Page Miss Glory 1935; China Clipper 1936; The Great O'Malley 1937; San Quentin 1937; Slim 1937; Angels with Dirty Faces 1938; Boy Meets Girl 1938; Garden of the Moon 1938; Indianapolis Speedway 1939; Slightly Honorable 1939; Castle on the Hudson 1940; The Fighting 69th 1940; Knute Rockne – All American 1940; 'Til We Meet Again 1940; Torrid Zone 1940; Broadway 1942; The Navy Comes Through 1942; Bombardier 1943; His Butler's Sister 1943; The Iron Major 1943; Marine Raiders 1944; Secret Command 1944; Crack-Up 1946; Riff-Raff 1947; The Boy with Green Hair 1948; Fighting Father Dunne 1948; A Dangerous Profession 1949; The Fireball 1950; The People against O'Hara 1951; Kill Me Tomorrow 1957; The Last Hurrah 1958; Some Like It Hot 1959; Ragtime 1981

O'Brien, Richard (1942–) The Andromeda Strain 1970; Pieces of Dreams 1970; The Rocky Horror Picture Show 1975; The Pack 1977; Jubilee 1978; Flash Gordon 1980; Shock Treatment 1981; Revolution 1985; The Wolves of Willoughby Chase 1988; Dark City 1998; Dungeons & Dragons 2000

O'Brien, Tom (1890–1947) The Big Parade 1925; Moby Dick 1930; The Accused 1988; Physical Evidence 1988

O'Brien, Trever (1984–) Lawnmower Man 2: Beyond Cyberspace 1995; Homecoming 1996

O'Brien, Virginia (1921–) Lady Be Good 1941; Ship Ahoy 1942; Meet the People 1944; Ziegfeld Follies 1944; The Harvey Girls 1946; Merton of the Movies 1947

O'Brien-Moore, Erin (1902–1979) Dangerous Corner 1934; Our Little Girl 1935; Seven Keys to Baldpate 1935; Streamline Express 1935; The Black Legion 1937; Green Light 1937; The Life of Emile Zola 1937; Destination Moon 1950

O'Bryan, Patrick 976-EVIL 1988; Relentless 1989; 976-EVIL 2 1992

O'Byrne, Brian F The Last Bus Home 1997; An Everlasting Piece 2000; Bandits 2001; Disco Pigs 2001; interMission 2003

O'Callaghan, Richard (1940–) The Bofors Gun 1968; Butley 1973

O'Casey, Ronan Tiger by the Tail 1955; Inn for Trouble 1960

Occhini, Ilaria (1936–) Carthage in Flames 1960; The Man Who Laughs 1966; Two against the Law 1973

Occhipinti, Andrea (1957–) Bolero 1984; The Family 1987

Ochsenknecht, Uwe (1956–) Forget Mozart 1985; Men... 1985; Fire, Ice and Dynamite 1990; Schtonk! 1992; Kaspar Hauser 1993

O'Connell, Arthur (1908–1981) Bus Stop 1956; The Proud Ones 1956; The Solid Gold Cadillac 1956; April Love 1957; The Monte Carlo Story 1957; Operation Mad Ball 1957; Man of the West 1958; Voice in the Mirror 1958; Anatomy of a Murder 1959; Gidget 1959; Hound Dog Man 1959; Operation Petticoat 1959; Cimarron 1960; The Great Impostor 1960; Pocketful of Miracles 1961; A Thunder of Drums 1961; Follow That Dream 1962; 7 Faces of Dr Lao 1963; Kissin' Cousins 1964; Nightmare in the Sun 1964; Your Cheatin' Heart 1964; The Great Race 1965; The Monkey's Uncle 1965; The Third Day 1965; Fantastic Voyage 1966; Ride beyond Vengeance 1966; The Silencers 1966; A Covenant with Death 1967; There Was a Crooked Man... 1970; The Last Valley 1971; Ben 1972; Huckleberry Finn 1974; The Hiding Place 1975

O'Connell, Deirdre Misplaced 1989; Straight Talk 1992; Fearless 1993; Lifeform 1996; Imaginary Heroes 2004

O'Connell, Hugh (1898–1943) The Smiling Lieutenant 1931; Broadway through a Keyhole 1933; That Certain Woman 1937

O'Connell, Jerry (1974–) Stand by Me 1986; Calendar Girl 1993; Jerry Maguire 1996; Joe's Apartment 1996; Scream 2 1997; What the Deaf Man Heard 1997; Body Shots 1999; Mission to Mars 1999; Buying the Cow 2000; Tomcats 2000; Kangaroo Jack 2003; Fat Slags 2004

O'Connell, Patrick (1934–) The McKenzie Break 1970; The Ragman's Daughter 1972

O'Connell, Raoul Frisk 1995; Lifeform 1996

O'Connell, William Paint Your Wagon 1969; Big Bad Mama 1974

O'Connor, Carroll (1924–2001) By Love Possessed 1961; Lonely Are the Brave 1962; Hawaii 1966; Not with My Wife, You Don't! 1966; What Did You Do in the War, Daddy? 1966; Point Blank 1967; Warning Shot 1967; Waterhole #3 1967; For Love of Ivy 1968; Death of a Gunfighter 1969; Marlowe 1969; Doctors' Wives 1970; Kelly's Heroes 1970; Law and Disorder 1974; Gideon 1999; 36 Hours to Die 1999; Return to Me 2000

O'Connor, Derrick Sweeney 2 1978; Dealers 1989; Lethal Weapon 2 1989; Deep Rising 1998

O'Connor, Donald (1925–2003) Men with Wings 1938; Million Dollar Legs 1939; On Your Toes 1939; Private Buckaroo 1942; Follow the Boys 1944; The Merry Monahans 1944; Patrick the Great 1944; Something in the Wind 1947; Are You with It? 1948; Francis 1949; Double Crossbones 1951; Francis Goes to the Races 1951; Francis Goes to West Point 1952; Singin' in the Rain 1952; Call Me Madam 1953; Francis Covers the Big Town 1953; I Love Melvin 1953; Francis Joins the WACS 1954; There's No Business like Show Business 1954; Francis in the Navy 1955; Anything Goes 1956; The Buster Keaton Story 1957; Cry for Happy 1961; That Funny Feeling 1965; Pandemonium 1982; Toys 1992; Out to Sea 1997

O'Connor, Frances (1969–) Love and Other Catastrophes 1996; Kiss or Kill 1997; Thank God He Met Lizzie 1997; Mansfield Park 1999; About Adam 2000; Bedazzled 2000; AI: Artificial Intelligence 2001; The Importance of Being Earnest 2002; Timeline 2003; Iron Jawed Angels 2004

O'Connor, Glynnis (1956–) Jeremy 1973; The Boy in the Plastic Bubble 1976; Ode to Billy Joe 1976; Kid Vengeance 1977; California Dreaming 1979; Those Lips, Those Eyes 1980; The White Lions 1980; Night Crossing 1981; Johnny Dangerously 1984; A Conspiracy of Love 1987; Death in Small Doses 1995

O'Connor, Hazel (1955–) Breaking Glass 1980; Car Trouble 1985

O'Connor, Kevin (1938–1991) Let's Scare Jessica to Death 1971; Welcome to the Club 1971

O'Connor, Kevin J (1964–) Peggy Sue Got Married 1986; Candy Mountain 1987; The Moderns 1988; FX 2 1991; Accidental Hero 1992; Equinox 1992; Color of Night 1994; No Escape 1994; Canadian Bacon 1995; Lord of Illusions 1995; Chicago Cab 1998; Deep Rising 1998; Gods and Monsters 1998; The Mummy 1999; Van Helsing 2004

O'Connor, Raymond (1955–) Life Stinks 1991; Mr Nanny 1992

O'Connor, Renee (1971–) Danielle Steel's Changes 1991; Darkman II: the Return of Durant 1995

O'Connor, Robert Emmett (1885–1962) The Public Enemy 1931; Blonde Venus 1932

O'Connor, Sinead (1966–) Wuthering Heights 1992; The Butcher Boy 1997

O'Connor, Tim (1927–) Black Jack 1972; The Groundstar Conspiracy 1972; Sssssss 1973; Buck Rogers in the 25th Century 1979; The Naked Gun 2½: the Smell of Fear 1991

O'Connor, Una (1880–1959) Cavalcade 1933; The Invisible Man 1933; The Barretts of Wimpole Street 1934; Chained 1934; Bride of Frankenstein 1935; David Copperfield 1935; The Perfect Gentleman 1935; Lloyd's of London 1936; Rose Marie 1936; Personal Property 1937; The Adventures of Robin Hood 1938; We Are Not Alone 1939; It All Came True 1940; Lillian Russell 1940; The Sea Hawk 1940; The Strawberry Blonde 1941; Always in My Heart 1942; My Favorite Spy 1942; Holy Matrimony 1943; Christmas in Connecticut 1945; Child of Divorce 1946; Fighting Father Dunne 1948; Witness for the Prosecution 1957

O'Conor, Hugh (1975–) Lamb 1985; Da 1988; My Left Foot 1989; The Three Musketeers 1993; The Young Poisoner's Handbook 1994; The Boy from Mercury 1996; Hotel Splendide 1999; bl,.m 2003

O'Conor, Joseph (1916–2001) Gorgo 1961; Oliver! 1968; Doomwatch 1972; Penny Gold 1973; The Black Windmill 1974

Odaka, Megumi (1972–) Godzilla vs King Ghidorah 1991; Godzilla vs Mothra 1992

O'Dea, Denis (1905–1978) The Plough and the Stars 1936; The Mark of Cain 1947; The Fallen Idol 1948; Under Capricorn 1949; Treasure Island 1950; The Long Dark Hall 1951; Never Take No for an Answer 1951; Sea Devils 1952; Niagara 1953; The Rising of the Moon 1957; The Story of Esther Costello 1957; Esther and the King 1960

O'Dea, Jimmy (1899–1965) Penny Paradise 1938; Cheer Boys Cheer 1939; Let's Be Famous 1939; The Rising of the Moon 1957; Darby O'Gill and the Little People 1959

Odent, Christophe First Name: Carmen 1983; Port Djema 1997

Odetta (1930–) Sanctuary 1961; The Autobiography of Miss Jane Pittman 1974

O'Donnell, Cathy (1925–1970) The Best Years of Our Lives 1946; They Live by Night 1948; The Miniver Story 1950; Side Street 1950; Detective Story 1951; Eight O'Clock Walk 1953; The Loves of Three Queens 1954; The Man from Laramie 1955; The Deerslayer 1957; Ben-Hur 1959

O'Donnell, Chris aka **O'Donnell, Christopher** (1970–) Men Don't Leave 1990; Blue Sky 1991; Scent of a Woman 1992; School Ties 1992; The Three Musketeers 1993; Batman Forever 1995; Circle of Friends 1995; Mad Love 1995; The Chamber 1996; In Love and War 1996; Batman and Robin 1997; The Bachelor 1999; Cookie's Fortune 1999; Vertical Limit 2000; 29 Palms 2002; Kinsey 2004

O'Donnell, Rosie (1962–) Car 54 Where Are You? 1991; A League of Their Own 1992; Another Stakeout 1993; Sleepless in Seattle 1993; Exit to Eden 1994; The Flintstones 1994; Now and Then 1995; Beautiful Girls 1996; Harriet the Spy 1996; Wide Awake 1998

O'Driscoll, Martha (1922–1998) The Lady Eve 1941; Young and Willing 1942; The Fallen Sparrow 1943; Ghost Catchers 1944; The Daltons Ride Again 1945; Here Come the Co-Eds 1945; House of Dracula 1945; Under Western Skies 1945; Criminal Court 1946; Carnegie Hall 1947

O'Farrell, Bernadette (1924–1999) The Happiest Days of Your Life 1950; Lady Godiva Rides Again 1951

O'Farrell, Peter Hawk the Slayer 1980; Legend 1985

O'Flynn, Damian (1907–1982) The Gay Falcon 1941; Crack-Up 1946; The Half-Breed 1952; Daniel Boone, Trail Blazer 1957; Gunfight at Comanche Creek 1964

Ogata, Ken (1937–) Vengeance Is Mine 1979; Virus 1980; The Ballad of Narayama 1983; Mishima: a Life in Four Chapters 1985; The Pillow Book 1995

Ogier, Bulle (1939–) L'Amour Fou 1968; The Discreet Charm of the Bourgeoisie 1972; The Valley 1972; Out 1: Spectre 1973; Celine and Julie Go Boating 1974; Maîtresse 1976; The Third Generation 1979; Candy Mountain 1987; See How They Fall 1993; Don't Forget You're Going to Die 1995; Irma Vep 1996; Shattered Image 1998; Venus Beauty Institute 1998; The Colour of Lies 1999; Merci Docteur Rey 2002

Ogilvy, Ian (1943–) The She Beast 1965; The Day the Fish Came Out 1967; The Sorcerers 1967; Stranger in the House 1967; The Heroes 1968; Witchfinder General 1968; And Now the Screaming Starts! 1973; From beyond the Grave 1973; No Sex Please – We're British 1973; Death Becomes Her 1992; The Disappearance of Kevin Johnson 1995

Ogle, Charles (1865–1940) Rebecca of Sunnybrook Farm 1917; A Romance of the Redwoods 1917; The Covered Wagon 1923; Ruggles of Red Gap 1923

O'Grady, Gail (1963–) Celtic Pride 1996; That Old Feeling 1997; Deuce Bigalow: Male Gigolo 1999; Walking across Egypt 1999

Oh, Sandra (1971–) Last Night 1998; Dancing at the Blue Iguana 2000; Waking the Dead 2000; Under the Tuscan Sun 2003; Sideways 2004

Oh, Soon-Teck aka **Oh, Soon Taik** aka **Oh, Soon-Tek** (1943–) One More Train to Rob 1971; The Man with the Golden Gun 1974; Missing in Action 2: the Beginning 1985; Death Wish 4: the Crackdown 1987; Soursweet 1988; A Home of Our Own 1993; Beverly Hills Ninja 1997

O'Halloran, Jack (1943–) Farewell, My Lovely 1975; March or Die 1977; The Baltimore Bullet 1980; Superman II 1980; Dragnet 1987; Hero and the Terror 1988

Ohana, Claudia (1962–) Erendira 1982; Opera do Malandro 1986

O'Hanlon, George (1912–1989) The Counterfeiters 1948; Park Row 1952; Kronos 1957; Jetsons: the Movie 1990

O'Hara, Catherine (1954–) Heartburn 1986; Beetle Juice 1988; Betsy's Wedding 1990; Home Alone 1990; Little Vegas 1990; Home Alone 2: Lost in New

York 1992; Paydirt 1992; The Nightmare before Christmas 1993; The Paper 1994; A Simple Twist of Fate 1994; Tall Tale 1994; Wyatt Earp 1994; Last of the High Kings 1996; Waiting for Guffman 1996; Pippi Longstocking 1997; Home Fries 1998; Bartok the Magnificent 1999; The Life before This 1999; Best in Show 2000; Orange County 2001; A Mighty Wind 2003; Surviving Christmas 2004

O'Hara, David aka **O'Hara, David Patrick** (1965–) Link 1986; The Bridge 1990; Braveheart 1995; The Near Room 1995; Some Mother's Son 1996; The Devil's Own 1997; The Matchmaker 1997; Janice Beard 45 WPM 1999; Stander 2003; Hotel Rwanda 2004

O'Hara, Jenny (1942–) Career Opportunities 1991; Angie 1994

O'Hara, Maureen (1920–) The Hunchback of Notre Dame 1939; Jamaica Inn 1939; A Bill of Divorcement 1940; Dance, Girl, Dance 1940; How Green Was My Valley 1941; The Black Swan 1942; Ten Gentlemen from West Point 1942; To the Shores of Tripoli 1942; The Fallen Sparrow 1943; The Immortal Sergeant 1943; This Land Is Mine 1943; Buffalo Bill 1944; The Spanish Main 1945; Do You Love Me? 1946; Sentimental Journey 1946; The Foxes of Harrow 1947; Miracle on 34th Street 1947; Sinbad the Sailor 1947; Sitting Pretty 1948; Britannia Mews 1949; Father Was a Fullback 1949; A Woman's Secret 1949; Comanche Territory 1950; Rio Grande 1950; Sons of the Musketeers 1951; Against All Flags 1952; Kangaroo 1952; The Quiet Man 1952; The Redhead from Wyoming 1953; War Arrow 1953; Malaga 1954; Lady Godiva 1955; The Long Gray Line 1955; The Magnificent Matador 1955; Lisbon 1956; The Wings of Eagles 1957; Our Man in Havana 1959; The Deadly Companions 1961; The Parent Trap 1961; Mr Hobbs Takes a Vacation 1962; McLintock! 1963; Spencer's Mountain 1963; The Battle of the Villa Fiorita 1965; The Rare Breed 1966; How Do I Love Thee? 1970; Big Jake 1971; Only the Lonely 1991

O'Hara, Paige (1961–) Beauty and the Beast 1991; Beauty and the Beast: the Enchanted Christmas 1997

O'Herlihy, Dan aka **O'Herlihy, Daniel** (1919–2005) Kidnapped 1948; Macbeth 1948; Soldiers Three 1951; Sons of the Musketeers 1951; Actors and Sin 1952; The Adventures of Robinson Crusoe 1952; Invasion USA 1952; Bengal Brigade 1954; The Black Shield of Falworth 1954; The Purple Mask 1955; The Virgin Queen 1955; That Woman Opposite 1957; Home before Dark 1958; Imitation of Life 1959; The Young Land 1959; One Foot in Hell 1960; A Terrible Beauty 1960; King of the Roaring 20s – the Story of Arnold Rothstein 1961; The Cabinet of Caligari 1962; Fail-Safe 1964; The Big Cube 1969; 100 Rifles 1969; Waterloo 1970; The Carey Treatment 1972; The Tamarind Seed 1974; MacArthur 1977; Halloween III: Season of the Witch 1982; The Last Starfighter 1984; The Dead 1987; RoboCop 1987; RoboCop 2 1990; Love, Cheat & Steal 1994

O'Herlihy, Gavan (1954–) Death Wish 3 1985; The Shooter 1994; Butterfly Man 2002

Ohmart, Carol (1927–) House on Haunted Hill 1958; Born Reckless 1959; Spider Baby 1964

Ojeda, Manuel Eagle's Wing 1978; Romancing the Stone 1984

Okada, Eiji (1920–1995) Hiroshima, Mon Amour 1959; The Ugly American 1963; Woman of the Dunes 1963

Okada, Mariko (1933–) Late Autumn 1960; An Autumn Afternoon 1962; Illusion of Blood 1965

O'Kane, Deirdre interMission 2003; Boy Eats Girl 2005

Okawa, Henry The Wind Cannot Read 1958; One of Those Things 1970

O'Keefe, Dennis (1908–1968) Bad Man of Brimstone 1938; That's Right – You're Wrong 1939; Arise, My Love 1940; You'll Find Out 1940; Broadway Limited 1941; Topper Returns 1941; Hangmen Also Die 1943; The Leopard Man 1943; Abroad with Two Yanks 1944; The Fighting Seabees 1944; Sensations 1944; The Story of Dr Wassell 1944; Up in Mabel's Room 1944; The Affairs of Susan 1945; Brewster's Millions 1945; Earl Carroll Vanities 1945; Getting Gertie's Garter 1945; Dishonored Lady 1947; T-Men 1947; Raw Deal 1948; Siren of Atlantis 1948; Walk a Crooked Mile 1948; The Company She Keeps 1950; Follow the Sun: the Ben Hogan Story 1951; Everything I Have Is Yours 1952; The Lady Wants Mink 1953; The Diamond 1954; Angela 1955; Las Vegas Shakedown 1955; Dragoon Wells Massacre 1957; All Hands on Deck 1961

O'Keefe, Jodi Lyn (1978–) Halloween H20: 20 Years Later 1998; She's All That 1999; Whatever It Takes 2000

O'Keefe, Michael (1955–) The Great Santini 1979; Caddyshack 1980; Split Image 1982; Savage Islands 1983; Finders Keepers 1984; The Slugger's Wife 1985; The Whoopee Boys 1986; Ironweed 1987; Out of the Rain 1991; Nina Takes a Lover 1993; Three Wishes 1995; The Pledge 2000; Prancer Returns 2001

O'Keeffe, Miles (1954–) Tarzan, the Ape Man 1981; Sword of the Valiant 1984; The Drifter 1988; Waxwork 1988; Relentless 2: Dead On 1991

O'Kelly, Don aka **Kelly, Don** (1924–1966) Bombers B-52 1957; The Hostage 1966

O'Kelly, Donal The Van 1996; The Last Bus Home 1997

Okhlopkov, Nikolai P aka **Okhlopkov, N P** (1900–1967) Lenin in October 1937; Alexander Nevsky 1938

Okiyama, Hideko The Profound Desire of the Gods 1968; Dodes'ka-Den 1970

Okking, Jens (1939–) The Kingdom 1994; The Beast Within 1995

Okochi, Denjiro (1898–1962) Sanshiro Sugata 1943; No Regrets for Our Youth 1946

Okonedo, Sophie (1969–) Young Soul Rebels 1991; Ace Ventura: When Nature Calls 1995; Go Now 1995; This Year's Love 1999; Dirty Pretty Things 2002; Hotel Rwanda 2004

Okuma, Enuka (1976–) The Hunted 1998; House of the Dead 2003

Okumoto, Yuji (1960–) The Karate Kid Part II 1986; Aloha Summer 1988; True Believer 1989; Blue Tiger 1994; Mean Guns 1996; I'll Remember April 1999

Okura, Chiyoko Poppy 1935; Osaka Elegy 1936

Olaf, Pierre (1928–1995) Wild and Wonderful 1964; Art of Love 1965; Camelot 1967; The Gamblers 1969; The Little Theatre of Jean Renoir 1969

Oland, Warner (1880–1938) Don Q, Son of Zorro 1925; Riders of the Purple Sage 1925; Don Juan 1926; When a Man Loves 1926; The Jazz Singer 1927; The Return of Dr Fu Manchu 1930; Dishonored 1931; Shanghai Express 1932; Bulldog Drummond Strikes Back 1934; Charlie Chan in London 1934; Mandalay 1934; The Painted Veil 1934; Charlie Chan in Egypt 1935; Charlie Chan in Paris 1935; Charlie Chan in Shanghai 1935; Charlie Chan at the Circus 1936; Charlie Chan at the Opera 1936; Charlie Chan at Monte Carlo 1937; Charlie Chan at the Olympics 1937; Charlie Chan on Broadway 1937

Olandt, Ken (1958–) April Fool's Day 1986; Leprechaun 1992; Velocity Trap 1997

Olbrychski, Daniel (1945–) Landscape after Battle 1970; The Young Ladies of Wilko 1979; Les Uns et les Autres 1981; Dangerous Moves 1984; Rosa Luxemburg 1986; The Barber of Siberia 1999

Oldham, Will Matewan 1987; Everybody's Baby: the Rescue of Jessica McClure 1989

Oldman, Gary (1958–) Sid and Nancy 1986; Prick Up Your Ears 1987; Criminal Law 1988; Track 29 1988; We Think the World of You 1988; Chattahoochee 1989; Rosencrantz and Guildenstern Are Dead 1990; State of Grace 1990; JFK 1991; Bram Stoker's Dracula 1992; Romeo Is Bleeding 1992; True Romance 1993; Immortal Beloved 1994; Leon 1994; Murder in the First 1994; The Scarlet Letter 1995; Basquiat 1996; Air Force One 1997; The Fifth Element 1997; The Magic Sword: Quest for Camelot 1997; Lost in Space 1998; The Contender 2000; Hannibal 2001; Harry Potter and the Prisoner of Azkaban 2004; Batman Begins 2005

O'Leary, Jack Inside Moves: the Guys from Max's Bar 1980; Death Valley 1982

O'Leary, Matt (1987–) Domestic Disturbance 2001; Frailty 2001

O'Leary, William Nice Girls Don't Explode 1987; Bull Durham 1988; Hot Shots! 1991; Candyman: Farewell to the Flesh 1995

Oleynik, Larisa (1981–) The Baby-Sitter's Club 1995; 10 Things I Hate about You 1999

Olin, Lena (1956–) After the Rehearsal 1984; The Unbearable Lightness of Being 1988; Enemies, a Love Story 1989; Havana 1990; Romeo Is Bleeding 1992; Mr Jones 1993; Night Falls on Manhattan 1997; Hamilton 1998; Polish Wedding 1998; The Ninth Gate 1999; Chocolat 2000; Darkness 2002; Queen of the Damned 2002; The United States of Leland 2002; Hollywood Homicide 2003

Olin, Stig (1920–) Crisis 1945; The Devil's Wanton 1949; To Joy 1950

Olliver, Anthony (1923–1995) Lost 1955; They Can't Hang Me 1955; Danger by My Side 1962

Oliver, Barret (1973–) The NeverEnding Story 1984; Cocoon 1985; DARYL 1985

Oliver, Charles The Avenging Hand 1936; Midnight at Madame Tussaud's 1936; The Green Cockatoo 1937; Ask a Policeman 1938; Sexton Blake and the Hooded Terror 1938; Crooks' Tour 1940; Under Your Hat 1940

Oliver, Edna May (1883–1942) The Saturday Night Kid 1929; Half Shot at Sunrise 1930; Laugh and Get Rich 1931; The Penguin Pool Murder 1932; Alice in Wonderland 1933; Ann Vickers 1933; Little Women 1933; Meet the Baron 1933; Only Yesterday 1933; The Last Gentleman 1934; Murder on the Blackboard 1934; David Copperfield 1935; Murder on a Honeymoon 1935; A Tale of Two Cities 1935; Romeo and Juliet 1936; Parnell 1937; Rosalie 1937; Little Miss Broadway 1938; Paradise for Three 1938; Drums along the Mohawk 1939; Nurse Edith Cavell 1939; Second Fiddle 1939; The Story of Vernon and Irene Castle 1939; Pride and Prejudice 1940; Lydia 1941

Oliver, Gordon (1911–1995) Blondie! 1938; Sweetheart of the Campus 1941; The Spiral Staircase 1946; Station West 1948; My Forbidden Past 1951; The Las Vegas Story 1952

Oliver, Guy (1878–1932) The Covered Wagon 1923; The Docks of New York 1928

Oliver, Michael (1982–) Problem Child 1990; Problem Child 2 1991; Dillinger and Capone 1995

Oliver, Susan (1937–1990) The Gene Krupa Story 1959; The Disorderly Orderly 1964; Your Cheatin' Heart 1964; A Man Called Gannon 1969; Ginger in the Morning 1973; Hardly Working 1981

Oliver, Vic (1898–1964) Hi, Gang! 1941; Give Us the Moon 1944; I'll Be Your Sweetheart 1945

Olivier, Laurence (1907–1989) Friends and Lovers 1931; Westward Passage 1932; Moscow Nights 1935; As You Like It 1936; Conquest of the Air 1936; Fire over England 1937; 21 Days 1937; The Divorce of Lady X 1938; Q Planes 1939; Wuthering Heights 1939; Pride and Prejudice 1940; Rebecca 1940; 49th Parallel 1941; That Hamilton Woman 1941; The Demi-Paradise 1943; Henry V 1944; This Happy Breed 1944; Hamlet 1948; The Magic Box 1951; Carrie 1952; The Beggar's Opera 1953; Richard III 1955; The Prince and the Showgirl 1957; The Devil's Disciple 1959; The Entertainer 1960; Spartacus 1960; Term of Trial 1962; Bunny Lake Is Missing 1965; Othello 1965; Khartoum 1966; Romeo and Juliet 1968; The Shoes of the Fisherman 1968; Battle of Britain 1969; The Dance of Death 1969; Oh! What a Lovely War 1969; Three Sisters 1970; Lady Caroline Lamb 1972; Sleuth 1972; Love among the Ruins 1975; Marathon Man 1976; The Seven-Per-Cent Solution 1976; A Bridge Too Far 1977; The Betsy 1978; The Boys from Brazil 1978; Dracula 1979; A Little Romance 1979; The Jazz Singer 1980; Clash of the Titans 1981; Inchon 1981; Wagner 1983; The Bounty 1984; The Jigsaw Man 1984; Wild Geese II 1985; War Requiem 1988

Olivier, Paul (1877–1948) A Nous la Liberté 1931; Le Million 1931

Olivieri, Enrico Woman of the River 1955; The Mask of Satan 1960

Olmos, Edward James aka **Olmos, Eddie** (1947–) Aloha, Bobby and Rose 1975; Virus 1980; Wolfen 1981; Zoot Suit 1981; Blade Runner 1982; The Ballad of Gregorio Cortez 1983; Saving Grace 1985; Stand and Deliver 1988; Triumph of the Spirit 1989; Talent for the Game 1991; American Me 1992; Roosters 1993; The Burning Season 1994; A Million to Juan 1994; My Family 1994; Caught 1996; The Disappearance of Garcia Lorca 1997; Selena 1997; 12 Angry Men 1997; Gossip 1999; The Road to El Dorado 2000

Olmsted, Gertrude (1897–1975) The Monster 1925; The Torrent 1926

O'Loughlin, Gerald S aka **O'Loughlin, Gerald** (1921–) A Hatful of Rain 1957; Ensign Pulver 1964; In Cold Blood 1967; Riot 1969; Desperate Characters 1971; The Organization 1971; The Valachi Papers 1972; Something for Joey 1977; Frances 1982

Olsen, Ashley (1986–) It Takes Two 1995; Our Lips Are Sealed 2000; Holiday in the Sun 2001; Winning London 2001; New York Minute 2004

Olsen, Christopher aka **Olsen, Chris** (1947–) Bigger than Life 1956; The Tarnished Angels 1957

Olsen, Eric Christian (1976–) Not Another Teen Movie 2001; The Hot Chick 2002; Dumb and Dumberer: When Harry Met Lloyd 2003; Cellular 2004

Olsen, Gary (1957–2000) Party Party 1983; The Cook, the Thief, His Wife and Her Lover 1989; Up 'n' Under 1997; 24 Hours in London 1999

Olsen, Mary-Kate (1986–) It Takes Two 1995; Our Lips Are Sealed 2000; Holiday in the Sun 2001; Winning London 2001; New York Minute 2004

Olsen, Moroni (1889–1954) Annie Oakley 1935; Seven Keys to Baldpate 1935; The Three Musketeers 1935; Snow White and the Seven Dwarfs 1937; Kentucky 1938; Rose of Washington Square 1939; East of the River 1940; One Foot in Heaven 1941; Dangerously They Live 1942; Ali Baba and the Forty Thieves 1944; Buffalo Bill 1944; Cobra Woman 1944; Mildred Pierce 1945; High Wall 1947; The Long Night 1947; Possessed 1947; Father of the Bride 1950; Father's Little Dividend 1951; Washington Story 1952; The Long, Long Trailer 1954

Olsen, Ole (1892–1963) All over Town 1937; Hellzapoppin' 1941; Ghost Catchers 1944

Olson, James (1930–) The Strange One 1957; The Three Sisters 1966; Rachel, Rachel 1968; Moon Zero Two 1969; The Andromeda Strain 1970; Crescendo 1970; Wild Rovers 1971; The Groundstar Conspiracy 1972; Amityville II: the Possession 1982; The Parade 1984; Commando 1985

Olson, Nancy (1928–) Canadian Pacific 1949; Mr Music 1950; Sunset Blvd 1950; Union Station 1950; Force of Arms 1951; Big Jim McLain 1952; So Big 1953; The Boy from Oklahoma 1954; Battle Cry 1955; Pollyanna 1960; The Absent-Minded Professor 1961; Son of Flubber 1962; Smith! 1969; Snowball Express 1972; Making Love 1982

Olyphant, Timothy (1968–) Go 1999; Auggie Rose 2000; The Broken Hearts Club: a Romantic Comedy 2000; Rock Star 2001; The Safety of Objects 2001; Dreamcatcher 2003; A Man Apart 2003; The Girl Next Door 2004

O'Malley, Daragh (1954–) Withnail & I 1986; Puckoon 2002

O'Malley, J Pat (1904–1985) Alice in Wonderland 1951; Courage of Black Beauty 1957; One Hundred and One Dalmatians 1960; Apache Rifles 1964; Gunn 1967; The Jungle Book 1967

O'Malley, Leonard Every Picture Tells a Story 1984; Conquest of the South Pole 1989

O'Malley, Rex (1901–1976) Camille 1937; Midnight 1939; Taxi 1953

O'Mara, Kate (1939–) Corruption 1968; The Desperados 1969; The Horror of Frankenstein 1970; The Vampire Lovers 1970

Omen, Judd Howling II: Your Sister Is a Werewolf 1984; Pee-wee's Big Adventure 1985

O'Moore, Patrick aka **O'Moore, Pat** (1909–1983) Evensong 1934; Smilin' Through 1941; Conflict 1945; The Two Mrs Carrolls 1945; Bulldog Drummond Strikes Back 1947; Jungle Gents 1954; Khyber Patrol 1954

Ondine (1937–1989) Vinyl 1965; The Chelsea Girls 1967; Dynamite Chicken 1971

Ondra, Anny (1903–1987) Blackmail 1929; The Manxman 1929

O'Neal, Frederick (1905–1992) Anna Lucasta 1958; Take a Giant Step 1959

O'Neal, Griffin (1964–) The Escape Artist 1982; Hadley's Rebellion 1984; April Fool's Day 1986; The Wraith 1986

O'Neal, Patrick (1927–1994) The Mad Magician 1954; In Harm's Way 1965; King Rat 1965; Alvarez Kelly 1966; Chamber of Horrors 1966; A Fine Madness 1966; Assignment to Kill 1968; The Secret Life of an American Wife 1968; Where Were You When the Lights Went Out? 1968; Castle Keep 1969; El Condor 1970; The Kremlin Letter 1970; Corky 1972; Silent Night, Bloody Night 1972; The Way We Were 1973; The Stepford Wives 1975; The Stuff 1985; Like Father, like Son 1987; Alice 1990; Q & A 1990; For the Boys 1991; Under Siege 1992

O'Neal, Ron (1937–2004) The Organization 1971; Superfly 1972; The Master Gunfighter 1975; Brothers 1977; A Force of One 1979; Freedom Road 1979; When a Stranger Calls 1979; The Final Countdown 1980; Hero and the

Terror 1988; *Original Gangstas* 1996

O'Neal, Ryan (1941–) *The Big Bounce* 1969; *The Games* 1970; *Love Story* 1970; *Wild Rovers* 1971; *What's Up, Doc?* 1972; *Paper Moon* 1973; *The Thief Who Came to Dinner* 1973; *Barry Lyndon* 1975; *Nickelodeon* 1976; *A Bridge Too Far* 1977; *The Driver* 1978; *Oliver's Story* 1978; *The Main Event* 1979; *Green Ice* 1981; *So Fine* 1981; *Partners* 1982; *Irreconcilable Differences* 1984; *Fever Pitch* 1985; *Tough Guys Don't Dance* 1987; *Chances Are* 1989; *Faithful* 1996; *Burn Hollywood Burn* 1997; *Zero Effect* 1997; *The List* 2000; *People I Know* 2002; *Malibu's Most Wanted* 2003

O'Neal, Shaquille (1972–) *CB4* 1993; *Blue Chips* 1994; *Kazaam* 1996; *Steel* 1997

O'Neal, Tatum (1963–) *Paper Moon* 1973; *The Bad News Bears* 1976; *Nickelodeon* 1976; *International Velvet* 1978; *Circle of Two* 1980; *Little Darlings* 1980; *Certain Fury* 1985; *Little Noises* 1992; *Basquiat* 1996

O'Neil, Barbara (1910–1980) *Stella Dallas* 1937; *I Am the Law* 1938; *The Toy Wife* 1938; *Gone with the Wind* 1939; *Tower of London* 1939; *When Tomorrow Comes* 1939; *All This, and Heaven Too* 1940; *Shining Victory* 1941; *Secret beyond the Door* 1948; *Whirlpool* 1949; *Angel Face* 1953

O'Neil, Nance (1874–1965) *Ladies of Leisure* 1930; *The Rogue Song* 1930; *Cimarron* 1931

O'Neil, Sally *Sally, Irene and Mary* 1925; *Battling Butler* 1926

O'Neill, Chris (1946–1997) *Backbeat* 1993; *2by4* 1998

O'Neill, Con *Dancin' thru the Dark* 1989; *The Last Seduction 2* 1998

O'Neill, Dick (1928–1998) *Gamera the Invincible* 1965; *The Taking of Pelham One Two Three* 1974; *House Calls* 1978; *The Jerk* 1979; *Wolfen* 1981; *Chiller* 1985; *She's Out of Control* 1989; *The Unspoken Truth* 1995

O'Neill, Ed (1946–) *Disorganized Crime* 1989; *K-9* 1989; *Sibling Rivalry* 1990; *Driving Me Crazy* 1991; *Blue Chips* 1994; *Little Giants* 1994; *Prefontaine* 1997; *The Bone Collector* 1999; *Spartan* 2004

O'Neill, Henry (1891–1961) *Lady Killer* 1933; *Fashions of 1934* 1934; *Flirtation Walk* 1934; *The Key* 1934; *Madame Du Barry* 1934; *The Secret Bride* 1934; *Black Fury* 1935; *The Florentine Dagger* 1935; *Oil for the Lamps of China* 1935; *Special Agent* 1935; *The Story of Louis Pasteur* 1936; *The Walking Dead* 1936; *The White Angel* 1936; *The Great O'Malley* 1937; *Green Light* 1937; *Wells Fargo* 1937; *Jezebel* 1938; *Racket Busters* 1938; *White Banners* 1938; *Angels Wash Their Faces* 1939; *Confessions of a Nazi Spy* 1939; *Castle on the Hudson* 1940; *Billy the Kid* 1941; *Men of Boys Town* 1941; *The Trial of Mary Dugan* 1941; *Whistling in the Dark* 1941; *White Cargo* 1942; *The Heavenly Body* 1943; *Whistling in Brooklyn* 1943; *Nothing but Trouble* 1944; *Two Girls and a Sailor* 1944; *Anchors Aweigh* 1945; *The Virginian* 1946; *The Return of October* 1948; *Holiday Affair* 1949; *The Reckless Moment* 1949; *No Man of Her Own* 1950; *The Second Woman* 1951; *Scarlet Angel* 1952

O'Neill, Jennifer (1948–) *Rio Lobo* 1970; *Such Good Friends* 1971; *Summer of '42* 1971; *The Carey Treatment* 1972; *Glass Houses* 1972; *Lady Ice* 1973; *The Masters* 1975; *The Reincarnation of Peter Proud* 1975; *Whiffs* 1975; *L'Innocente* 1976; *Caravans* 1978; *Cloud Dancer* 1979; *A Force of One* 1979; *Scanners* 1980; *Steel* 1980

O'Neill, Maggie (1967–) *Seven Minutes* 1989; *Under Suspicion* 1991; *All Men Are Mortal* 1995

Ongg, Judy *Zu Warriors* 1983; *The Pillow Book* 1995

Onorati, Peter (1954–) *Wings of the Apache* 1990; *Shelter* 1997; *The Art of Murder* 1999

Ontiveros, Lupe *Born in East LA* 1987; *As Good as It Gets* 1997; *Chuck & Buck* 2000; *Real Women Have Curves* 2002

Ontkean, Michael (1950–) *Slap Shot* 1977; *Voices* 1979; *Willie and Phil* 1980; *Making Love* 1982; *The Blood of Others* 1984; *Just the Way You Are* 1984; *The Allnighter* 1987; *Maid to Order* 1987; *Clara's Heart* 1988; *Bye Bye Blues* 1989; *Cold Front* 1989; *The Man Next Door* 1996; *Swann* 1996; *Nico the Unicorn* 1998

Opatoshu, David (1918–1996) *The Best of Enemies* 1961; *Guns of Darkness* 1962; *The Defector* 1966; *Tarzan and the Valley of Gold* 1966; *Enter Laughing* 1967; *Death of a Gunfighter* 1969; *Romance of a Horse Thief* 1971; *Beyond Evil* 1980; *Forced Vengeance* 1982

Ophir, Shai K *Diamonds* 1975; *America 3000* 1986

Oppenheimer, Alan (1930–) *The Groundstar Conspiracy* 1972; *Westworld* 1973; *Little Nemo: Adventures in Slumberland* 1992

Opper, Don *aka* **Opper, Don Keith** (1949–) *Android* 1982; *Critters* 1986; *Slam Dance* 1987; *Critters 2: the Main Course* 1988; *Critters 3* 1991; *Critters 4* 1992

O'Quinn, Terry *aka* **O'Quinn, Terrance** (1952–) *Heaven's Gate* 1980; *Silver Bullet* 1985; *The Stepfather* 1986; *Black Widow* 1987; *Pin* 1988; *Roe vs Wade* 1989; *Stepfather II* 1989; *Blind Fury* 1990; *Blood Oath* 1990; *Company Business* 1991; *Rocketeer* 1991; *The Cutting Edge* 1992; *Amityville: a New Generation* 1993; *Death of a Cheerleader* 1994; *Hard Evidence* 1994; *Heart of a Child* 1994; *Primal Fear* 1996; *Breast Men* 1997; *Rated X* 2000

O'Rawe, Geraldine *Circle of Friends* 1995; *Resurrection Man* 1997; *Disco Pigs* 2001; *Mr In-Between* 2001

Orbach, Jerry (1935–2004) *Mad Dog Coll* 1961; *The Gang That Couldn't Shoot Straight* 1971; *The Sentinel* 1977; *Prince of the City* 1981; *Brewster's Millions* 1985; *FX: Murder by Illusion* 1985; *The Imagemaker* 1986; *Dirty Dancing* 1987; *Someone to Watch over Me* 1987; *Last Exit to Brooklyn* 1989; *Dead Women in Lingerie* 1990; *Beauty and the Beast* 1991; *Broadway Bound* 1991; *Delirious* 1991; *Delusion* 1991; *Out for Justice* 1991; *Mr Saturday Night* 1992; *Straight Talk* 1992; *Universal Soldier* 1992; *Upworld* 1992; *Aladdin and the King of Thieves* 1996; *Beauty and the Beast: the Enchanted Christmas* 1997

Orbach, Ron *Love Crimes* 1991; *Erotique* 1994

Orbison, Roy (1936–1988) *The Fastest Guitar Alive* 1966; *Hail! Hail! Rock 'n' Roll!* 1987

O'Reilly, Cyril *Porky's* 1981; *Porky's II: The Next Day* 1983; *Purple Hearts* 1984; *Across the Tracks* 1990; *The Philadelphia Experiment 2* 1993; *Shattered Family* 1993

Orfei, Liana (1937–) *Gordon the Black Pirate* 1961; *Nefertite, Queen of the Nile* 1961; *Hercules, Samson and Ulysses* 1963

Orfei, Moira (1931–) *Hero of Babylon* 1963; *Scent of a Woman* 1974

Orgolini, Lisa *Trick or Treat* 1986; *Two Deaths* 1994

Oriel, Ray *Stones for Ibarra* 1988; *Ticks* 1993

O'Riordan, Shaun *The Man Who Liked Funerals* 1959; *Inn for Trouble* 1960

Orlamond, William (1867–1957) *Flesh and the Devil* 1926; *Mantrap* 1926; *The Wind* 1928

Orlandi, Felice (1925–2003) *Killer's Kiss* 1955; *The Outside Man* 1973; *The Driver* 1978

Orlando, Orazio (?–1990) *Le Bambole* 1965; *The Masters* 1975; *Tigers in Lipstick* 1979

Orlando, Silvio (1957–) *Il Cielo è Sempre Più Blu* 1995; *Aprile* 1998; *Children of Hannibal* 1998; *Not of This World* 1998; *The Son's Room* 2001

Ormond, Julia (1965–) *The Baby of Macon* 1993; *Nostradamus* 1993; *Captives* 1994; *Legends of the Fall* 1994; *First Knight* 1995; *Sabrina* 1995; *Smilla's Feeling for Snow* 1996; *Animal Farm* 1999; *The Barber of Siberia* 1999; *The Prime Gig* 2000; *Varian's War* 2000; *Iron Jawed Angels* 2004

O'Rorke, Brefni (1889–1946) *Unpublished Story* 1942; *Don't Take It to Heart* 1944; *The Root of All Evil* 1946

O'Ross, Ed (1949–) *The Hidden* 1987; *Red Heat* 1988; *Another 48 HRS* 1990; *Universal Soldier* 1992

O'Rourke, Heather (1975–1988) *Poltergeist* 1982; *Surviving* 1985; *Poltergeist II: the Other Side* 1986; *Poltergeist III* 1988

Orr, William T (1917–2002) *The Mortal Storm* 1940; *Unholy Partners* 1941

Orser, Leland (1960–) *Very Bad Things* 1998; *The Bone Collector* 1999; *Resurrection* 1999

Orsi, Leigh Ann (1981–) *The Favor* 1994; *Pet Shop* 1995

Orsini, Umberto (1934–) *Mademoiselle* 1966; *The Girl and the General* 1967; *The Sailor from Gibraltar* 1967; *Violent City* 1970; *César and Rosalie* 1972; *Ludwig* 1973; *Emmanuelle 2* 1975; *Goodbye Emmanuelle* 1977; *Love in the Strangest Way* 1994

Orth, Frank (1880–1962) *Nancy Drew – Detective* 1938; *Footlight Serenade* 1942; *The Magnificent Dope* 1942; *Rings on Her Fingers* 1942

Orth, Zak (1970–) *Spanking the Monkey* 1994; *When Trumpets Fade* 1998; *Down to You* 2000; *Loser* 2000

Osborn, Lyn (1926–1958) *The Amazing Colossal Man* 1957; *The Cosmic Man* 1959

Osborne, Holmes (1952–) *Bring It On* 2000; *Donnie Darko* 2001; *The Quiet American* 2002

Osborne, John (1929–1994) *First Love* 1970; *Get Carter* 1971; *Tomorrow Never Comes* 1977; *Flash Gordon* 1980

Osborne, Vivienne (1896–1961) *Two Seconds* 1932; *The Devil's in Love* 1933; *Supernatural* 1933

Osbourne, Ozzy (1948–) *Riders of the Storm* 1986; *Trick or Treat* 1986; *Private Parts* 1997

Oscar, Henry (1891–1969) *The Tunnel* 1935; *Seven Sinners* 1936; *The Return of the Scarlet Pimpernel* 1937; *The Saint in London* 1939; *Hatter's Castle* 1941; *The Greed of William Hart* 1948; *The Spaniard's Curse* 1958; *The Brides of Dracula* 1960; *Murder Ahoy* 1964; *City under the Sea* 1965

Oscarsson, Per (1927–) *Hunger* 1966; *My Sister, My Love* 1966; *A Dandy in Aspic* 1968; *Doctor Glas* 1968; *The Night Visitor* 1970; *Endless Night* 1971; *The Last Valley* 1971; *Secrets* 1971; *The Blockhouse* 1973; *Victor Frankenstein* 1977; *Montenegro* 1981; *House of Angels* 1992

O'Shaughnessy, Brian *Satan's Harvest* 1965; *Mr Kingstreet's War* 1970; *Creatures the World Forgot* 1971

O'Shea, Kevin (1952–) *The Purple Heart* 1944; *Wing and a Prayer* 1944

O'Shea, Michael (1906–1973) *Lady of Burlesque* 1943; *The Eve of St Mark* 1944; *Jack London* 1944; *Something for the Boys* 1944; *Circumstantial Evidence* 1945; *It's a Pleasure* 1945; *Smart Woman* 1948; *The Big Wheel* 1949; *The Underworld Story* 1950; *Fixed Bayonets* 1951; *The Model and the Marriage Broker* 1951; *Bloodhounds of Broadway* 1952; *It Should Happen to You* 1954

O'Shea, Milo (1925–) *This Other Eden* 1959; *Carry On Cabby* 1963; *Barbarella* 1967; *Ulysses* 1967; *Romeo and Juliet* 1968; *The Adding Machine* 1969; *The Angel Levine* 1970; *Loot* 1970; *Digby, the Biggest Dog in the World* 1973; *Steptoe and Son Ride Again* 1973; *Arabian Adventure* 1979; *The Pilot* 1979; *The Verdict* 1982; *The Purple Rose of Cairo* 1985; *The Dream Team* 1989; *Opportunity Knocks* 1990; *Only the Lonely* 1991; *The Playboys* 1992; *The Butcher Boy* 1997; *The Matchmaker* 1997

O'Shea, Oscar (1881–1960) *Big City* 1937; *Captains Courageous* 1937; *Mannequin* 1937; *Riders of the Purple Sage* 1941

O'Shea, Tessie (1917–1995) *The Shiralee* 1957; *Bedknobs and Broomsticks* 1971

Oshinari, Shugo (1981–) *All about Lily Chou-Chou* 2001; *Battle Royale 2: Requiem* 2003

Osment, Haley Joel (1988–) *Bogus* 1996; *Beauty and the Beast: the Enchanted Christmas* 1997; *Last Stand at Saber River* 1997; *I'll Remember April* 1999; *The Sixth Sense* 1999; *Pay It Forward* 2000; *AI: Artificial Intelligence* 2001; *The Country Bears* 2002; *The Jungle Book 2* 2003; *Secondhand Lions* 2003

Osmond, Cliff (1937–) *Kiss Me, Stupid* 1964; *The Fortune Cookie* 1966; *Shark's Treasure* 1975; *Joe Panther* 1976

Osmond, Donny (1957–) *Goin' Coconuts* 1978; *Mulan* 1998

Osmond, Hal (1919–1959) *To Dorothy, a Son* 1954; *Dick Turpin – Highwayman* 1956; *Blood of the Vampire* 1958

Osterloh, Robert (1918–2001) *The Dark Past* 1948; *The Ring* 1952; *Riot in Cell Block 11* 1954

Ostrander, William *Fire and Ice* 1983; *Stryker* 1983; *Red Heat* 1985

Osugi, Ren (1951–) *Hana-Bi* 1997; *Eyes of the Spider* 1999; *The Twilight Samurai* 2002

O'Sullivan, Aisling *The Butcher Boy* 1997; *The One and Only* 2001; *The Actors* 2003

O'Sullivan, Arthur (1912–1981) *Girl with Green Eyes* 1963; *Ryan's Daughter* 1970

O'Sullivan, Maureen (1911–1998) *Just Imagine* 1930; *Song o' My Heart* 1930; *A Connecticut Yankee* 1931; *Payment Deferred* 1932; *Skyscraper Souls* 1932; *Strange Interlude* 1932; *Tarzan, the Ape Man* 1932; *Tugboat Annie* 1933; *The Barretts of Wimpole Street* 1934; *Tarzan and His Mate* 1934; *The Thin Man* 1934; *Anna Karenina* 1935; *Cardinal Richelieu* 1935; *David Copperfield* 1935; *Woman Wanted* 1935; *The Devil-Doll* 1936; *Tarzan Escapes* 1936; *A Day at the Races* 1937; *The Emperor's Candlesticks* 1937; *The Crowd Roars* 1938; *Port of Seven Seas* 1938; *A Yank at Oxford* 1938; *Tarzan Finds a Son!* 1939; *Pride and Prejudice* 1940; *Tarzan's Secret Treasure* 1941; *Tarzan's New York Adventure* 1942; *The Big Clock* 1948; *No Resting Place* 1950; *Where Danger Lives* 1950; *All I Desire* 1953; *The Tall T* 1957; *Wild Heritage* 1958; *Never Too Late* 1965; *Too Scared to Scream* 1982; *Hannah and Her Sisters* 1986; *Peggy Sue Got Married* 1986; *Stranded* 1987

O'Sullivan, Richard (1944–) *The Stranger's Hand* 1953; *Dance Little Lady* 1954; *The Green Scarf* 1954; *Dangerous Exile* 1957; *Witness in the Dark* 1959; *And Women Shall Weep* 1960; *Spare the Rod* 1961; *The Young Ones* 1961; *Wonderful Life* 1964; *A Dandy in Aspic* 1968; *The Haunted House of Horror* 1969; *Father Dear Father* 1972; *Man about the House* 1974

Otaki, Hideji *Kagemusha* 1980; *Minbo – or the Gentle Art of Japanese Extortion* 1992

Oteri, Cheri (1965–) *Lured Innocence* 1999; *Love & Sex* 2000; *Dumb and Dumberer: When Harry Met Lloyd* 2003

Otis, Carré (1968–) *Wild Orchid* 1990; *Exit in Red* 1996

Otis, James *One Summer Love* 1975; *Another Day in Paradise* 1998

O'Toole, Annette (1953–) *The Entertainer* 1975; *Smile* 1975; *One on One* 1977; *Foolin' Around* 1980; *Cat People* 1982; *48 HRS* 1982; *Superman III* 1983; *Cross My Heart* 1987; *Love at Large* 1990; *Desperate Justice* 1993; *The Man Next Door* 1996; *Here on Earth* 2000

O'Toole, Peter (1932–) *The Day They Robbed the Bank of England* 1960; *Kidnapped* 1960; *The Savage Innocents* 1960; *Lawrence of Arabia* 1962; *Becket* 1964; *Lord Jim* 1965; *The Sandpiper* 1965; *What's New, Pussycat?* 1965; *The Bible...in the Beginning* 1966; *How to Steal a Million* 1966; *The Night of the Generals* 1966; *Casino Royale* 1967; *Great Catherine* 1968; *The Lion in Winter* 1968; *Goodbye, Mr Chips* 1969; *Country Dance* 1970; *Murphy's War* 1971; *Under Milk Wood* 1971; *Man of La Mancha* 1972; *The Ruling Class* 1972; *Man Friday* 1975; *Rosebud* 1975; *Power Play* 1978; *Caligula* 1979; *Zulu Dawn* 1979; *The Stunt Man* 1980; *My Favorite Year* 1982; *Kim* 1984; *Supergirl* 1984; *Creator* 1985; *Club Paradise* 1986; *The Last Emperor* 1987; *High Spirits* 1988; *The Nutcracker Prince* 1990; *The Rainbow Thief* 1990; *Wings of Fame* 1990; *King Ralph* 1991; *Rebecca's Daughters* 1991; *The Seventh Coin* 1993; *FairyTale: a True Story* 1997; *Phantoms* 1998; *The Final Curtain* 2002; *Bright Young Things* 2003; *Troy* 2004

Otowa, Nobuko (1925–1994) *Miss Oyu* 1951; *The Island* 1961; *Onibaba* 1964

Ottiano, Rafaela (1888–1942) *As You Desire Me* 1932; *The Last Gentleman* 1934; *Curly Top* 1935; *Maytime* 1937

Otto, Barry (1941–) *Undercover* 1983; *Bliss* 1985; *The More Things Change* 1985; *The Howling III* 1987; *The Punisher* 1989; *Strictly Ballroom* 1992; *The Custodian* 1993; *Cosi* 1996; *Kiss or Kill* 1997; *Dead Letter Office* 1998

Otto, Miranda (1967–) *Emma's War* 1985; *Daydream Believer* 1991; *The Last Days of Chez Nous* 1992; *Love Serenade* 1996; *Doing Time for Patsy Cline* 1997; *Dead Letter Office* 1998; *The Jack Bull* 1999; *Kin* 2000; *What Lies Beneath* 2000; *Human Nature* 2001; *Doctor Sleep* 2002; *The Lord of the Rings: The Two Towers* 2002; *The Lord of the Rings: The Return of the King* 2003; *Flight of the Phoenix* 2004; *In My Father's Den* 2004; *War of the Worlds* 2005

Oudrey, Pierre *Tout Va Bien* 1972; *Number Two* 1975

Ouedraogo, Assita *Yam Daabo* 1986; *La Promesse* 1996

Ouedraogo, Rasmane *Tilaï* 1990; *La Promesse* 1996

Oulton, Brian (1908–1992) *The Million Pound Note* 1953; *The Damned* 1961

Oumansky, André (1933–) *Sundays and Cybèle* 1962; *The Love Cage* 1964; *The Marseille Contract* 1974; *Othello* 1995

Oury, Gérard (1919–) *Sea Devils* 1952; *The Heart of the Matter* 1953; *They Who Dare* 1953; *Father Brown* 1954; *The Loves of Three Queens* 1954; *Woman of the River* 1955; *House of Secrets* 1956; *The Prize* 1963

Ousdal, Sverre Anker (1944–) *Orion's Belt* 1985; *The Dive* 1989; *Kristin Lavransdatter* 1995; *Hamsun* 1996; *Insomnia* 1997

Ouspenskaya, Maria (1876–1949) *Dodsworth* 1936; *Conquest* 1937; *Love Affair* 1939; *Dance, Girl, Dance* 1940; *Dr Ehrlich's Magic Bullet* 1940; *The Man I Married* 1940; *Waterloo Bridge* 1940; *The Shanghai Gesture* 1941; *The Wolf*

Man 1941; *Frankenstein Meets the Wolf Man* 1943; *Tarzan and the Amazons* 1945; *I've Always Loved You* 1946; *A Kiss in the Dark* 1949
Outerbridge, Peter (1966–) *Cool Runnings* 1993; *Paris France* 1993; *For the Moment* 1994; *Kissed* 1996
Outinen, Kati (1961–) *Hamlet Goes Business* 1987; *The Match Factory Girl* 1990; *Take Care of Your Scarf, Tatjana* 1994; *Drifting Clouds* 1996; *Juha* 1999; *The Man without a Past* 2002; *Ten Minutes Older: the Trumpet* 2002
Overall, Park (1967–) *Biloxi Blues* 1988; *The Vanishing* 1993; *Taming Andrew* 2000
Overman, Lynne (1887–1943) *Enter Madame!* 1933; *Broadway Bill* 1934; *Little Miss Marker* 1934; *Midnight* 1934; *She Loves Me Not* 1934; *Rumba* 1935; *Men with Wings* 1938; *Spawn of the North* 1938; *Union Pacific* 1939; *Edison, the Man* 1940; *North West Mounted Police* 1940; *Typhoon* 1940; *The Forest Rangers* 1942; *Reap the Wild Wind* 1942; *Roxie Hart* 1942; *Dixie* 1943; *The Desert Song* 1944
Overton, Frank (1918–1967) *Desire under the Elms* 1958; *The Last Mile* 1959; *Claudelle Inglish* 1961; *To Kill a Mockingbird* 1962; *Fail-Safe* 1964
Overton, Rick (1954–) *Odd Jobs* 1986; *Money Mania* 1987; *A Sinful Life* 1989; *Eight Legged Freaks* 2001
Owen, Bill (1914–1999) *Dancing with Crime* 1946; *Daybreak* 1946; *Easy Money* 1947; *When the Bough Breaks* 1947; *My Brother's Keeper* 1948; *Once a Jolly Swagman* 1948; *Trottie True* 1949; *Hotel Sahara* 1951; *The Story of Robin Hood and His Merrie Men* 1952; *A Day to Remember* 1953; *The Square Ring* 1953; *The Ship That Died of Shame* 1955; *Carry On Sergeant* 1958; *Carve Her Name with Pride* 1958; *The Rainbow Jacket* 1958; *Carry On Nurse* 1959; *The Shakedown* 1959; *Carry On Regardless* 1960; *The Hellfire Club* 1961; *Carry On Cabby* 1963; *The Secret of Blood Island* 1964; *Georgy Girl* 1966; *In Celebration* 1974; *The Comeback* 1977; *Laughterhouse* 1984
Owen, Catherine Dale (1900–1965) *Born Reckless* 1930; *The Rogue Song* 1930
Owen, Chris (1980–) *Angus* 1995; *October Sky* 1999; *Dear Wendy* 2005
Owen, Clare *Echo of Diana* 1963; *Shadow of Fear* 1963
Owen, Clive (1965–) *Vroom* 1988; *Close My Eyes* 1991; *Century* 1993; *Class of '61* 1993; *Bent* 1996; *The Rich Man's Wife* 1996; *Croupier* 1998; *Greenfingers* 2000; *Gosford Park* 2001; *The Bourne Identity* 2002; *Beyond Borders* 2003; *I'll Sleep When I'm Dead* 2003; *Closer* 2004; *King Arthur* 2004; *Sin City* 2005
Owen, Garry (1902–1951) *Hold Your Man* 1933; *Arsenic and Old Lace* 1944
Owen, Glyn (1928–2004) *Life in Emergency Ward 10* 1959; *Inn for Trouble* 1960; *Attack on the Iron Coast* 1968
Owen, Reginald (1887–1972) *The Letter* 1929; *Platinum Blonde* 1931; *Sherlock Holmes* 1932; *Fashions of 1934* 1934; *The House of Rothschild* 1934; *Madame Du Barry* 1934; *Mandalay* 1934; *Of Human Bondage* 1934; *Anna Karenina* 1935; *The Call of the Wild* 1935; *Escapade* 1935; *The Good Fairy* 1935; *A Tale of Two Cities* 1935; *The Great Ziegfeld* 1936; *Love on the Run* 1936; *Rose Marie* 1936; *Trouble for Two* 1936; *The Bride Wore Red* 1937; *Conquest* 1937; *Madame X* 1937; *Personal Property* 1937; *Rosalie* 1937; *A Christmas Carol* 1938; *Everybody Sing* 1938; *Kidnapped* 1938; *Paradise for Three* 1938; *Three Loves Has Nancy* 1938; *Fast and Loose* 1939; *The Real Glory* 1939; *Remember?* 1939; *The Earl of Chicago* 1940; *Florian* 1940; *The Ghost Comes Home* 1940; *Charley's Aunt* 1941; *Tarzan's Secret Treasure* 1941; *They Met in Bombay* 1941; *A Woman's Face* 1941; *Crossroads* 1942; *I Married an Angel* 1942; *Mrs Miniver* 1942; *Random Harvest* 1942; *Reunion in France* 1942; *Somewhere I'll Find You* 1942; *White Cargo* 1942; *Woman of the Year* 1942; *Above Suspicion* 1943; *Forever and a Day* 1943; *Salute to the Marines* 1943; *The Canterville Ghost* 1944; *National Velvet* 1944; *Captain Kidd* 1945; *Kitty* 1945; *The Sailor Takes a Wife* 1945; *The Valley of Decision* 1945; *Cluny Brown* 1946; *Monsieur Beaucaire* 1946; *Piccadilly Incident* 1946; *Bob, Son of Battle* 1947; *Green Dolphin Street* 1947; *The Imperfect Lady* 1947; *Hills of Home* 1948; *The Pirate* 1948; *Challenge to Lassie* 1949; *The Secret Garden* 1949; *Kim* 1950; *The Miniver Story* 1950; *Tammy and the Doctor* 1963; *The Thrill of It All* 1963; *Mary Poppins* 1964; *Bedknobs and Broomsticks* 1971
Owen, Rena (1960–) *Once Were Warriors* 1994; *When Love Comes* 1998
Owen, Seena (1894–1966) *Intolerance* 1916; *The Fall of Babylon* 1919; *Queen Kelly* 1928
Owen, Tudor (1898–1979) *My Cousin Rachel* 1952; *Back to God's Country* 1953; *Arrow in the Dust* 1954; *The King's Thief* 1955; *Congo Crossing* 1956; *The Oklahoma Woman* 1956
Owen, Yvonne (1923–1990) *The Seventh Veil* 1945; *Easy Money* 1947; *Holiday Camp* 1947; *Miranda* 1947; *My Brother's Keeper* 1948; *Third Time Lucky* 1949; *Someone at the Door* 1950
Owens, Ciaran *Agnes Browne* 1999; *Angela's Ashes* 1999
Owens, Patricia (1925–2000) *No Down Payment* 1957; *Sayonara* 1957; *The Fly* 1958; *The Gun Runners* 1958; *The Law and Jake Wade* 1958; *Five Gates to Hell* 1959; *These Thousand Hills* 1959; *Hell to Eternity* 1960; *Black Spurs* 1965; *The Destructors* 1968
Owsley, Monroe (1900–1937) *Holiday* 1930; *Honor among Lovers* 1931; *Indiscreet* 1931; *This Modern Age* 1931; *Ex-Lady* 1933; *Goin' to Town* 1935; *Remember Last Night?* 1935
Oxenberg, Catherine (1961–) *Still Crazy like a Fox* 1987; *The Lair of the White Worm* 1988; *Sanctimony* 2000
Oxley, David (1920–1985) *Ill Met by Moonlight* 1956; *Sea Fury* 1958; *The Hound of the Baskervilles* 1959; *Yesterday's Enemy* 1959
Oz, Frank (1944–) *The Muppet Movie* 1979; *Star Wars Episode V: the Empire Strikes Back* 1980; *The Great Muppet Caper* 1981; *Star Wars Episode VI: Return of the Jedi* 1983; *The Muppets Take Manhattan* 1984; *Sesame Street Presents: Follow That Bird* 1985; *The Muppet Christmas Carol* 1992; *Muppet Treasure Island* 1996; *Muppets from Space* 1999; *Star Wars Episode I: the Phantom Menace* 1999; *Monsters, Inc* 2001; *Star Wars Episode II: Attack of the Clones* 2002; *Star Wars Episode III: Revenge of the Sith* 2005
Ozawa, Eitaro *aka* **Ozawa, Sakae** (1909–1988) *Record of a Tenement Gentleman* 1947; *My Love Has Been Burning* 1949; *The Thick-Walled Room* 1953; *Ugetsu Monogatari* 1953; *The Crucified Lovers* 1954; *The H-Man* 1954; *The Princess Yang Kwei Fei* 1955; *The Human Condition* 1958; *The Return of Godzilla* 1984; *A Taxing Woman* 1987
Ozawa, Shoichi (1929–) *The Ballad of Narayama* 1983; *Black Rain* 1988
Ozeki, Yuya *The Grudge 2* 2003; *The Grudge: Ju-On* 2003
Ozeray, Madeleine (1908–1989) *Crime and Punishment* 1935; *The End of the Day* 1939

P

Paar, Jack (1918–2004) *Variety Time* 1948; *Easy Living* 1949; *Walk Softly, Stranger* 1949; *Love Nest* 1951
Pace, Judy (1946–) *Three in the Attic* 1968; *Cotton Comes to Harlem* 1970; *Up in the Cellar* 1970; *Brian's Song* 1971; *Frogs* 1972; *The Slams* 1973
Pacino, Al (1940–) *The Panic in Needle Park* 1971; *The Godfather* 1972; *Scarecrow* 1973; *Serpico* 1973; *The Godfather, Part II* 1974; *Dog Day Afternoon* 1975; *Bobby Deerfield* 1977; *...And Justice for All* 1979; *Cruising* 1980; *Author! Author!* 1982; *Scarface* 1983; *Revolution* 1985; *Sea of Love* 1989; *Dick Tracy* 1990; *The Godfather Part III* 1990; *Frankie & Johnny* 1991; *Glengarry Glen Ross* 1992; *Scent of a Woman* 1992; *Carlito's Way* 1993; *Heat* 1995; *Two Bits* 1995; *City Hall* 1996; *Looking for Richard* 1996; *The Devil's Advocate* 1997; *Donnie Brasco* 1997; *Any Given Sunday* 1999; *The Insider* 1999; *Insomnia* 2002; *People I Know* 2002; *The Recruit* 2002; *S1MØNE* 2002; *Gigli* 2003; *William Shakespeare's The Merchant of Venice* 2004
Packer, David (1962–) *You Can't Hurry Love* 1988; *Trust Me* 1989; *Almost Heroes* 1998
Pacôme, Maria (1923–) *Up to His Ears* 1965; *La Crise* 1992
Pacula, Joanna (1957–) *Gorky Park* 1983; *Not Quite Jerusalem* 1985; *Death before Dishonor* 1987; *Escape from Sobibor* 1987; *The Kiss* 1988; *Marked for Death* 1990; *A Passion for Murder* 1992; *Every Breath* 1993; *The Silence of the Hams* 1993; *Warlock: the Armageddon* 1993; *The Bomber Boys* 1995; *Last Gasp* 1995; *My Giant* 1998; *Virus* 1998; *The Art of Murder* 1999
Padalecki, Jared (1982–) *A Ring of Endless Light* 2002; *House of Wax* 2004; *New York Minute* 2004
Padden, Sarah (1881–1967) *He Was Her Man* 1934; *Girl Rush* 1944; *House by the River* 1950
Paddick, Hugh (1915–2000) *The Killing of Sister George* 1968; *Up the Chastity Belt* 1971
Padilla Jr, Manuel (1956–) *Tarzan and the Valley of Gold* 1966; *Tarzan and the Great River* 1967; *Tarzan's Deadly Silence* 1970; *American Graffiti* 1973
Padovani, Lea (1920–1991) *Give Us This Day* 1949; *Montparnasse 19* 1958; *The Naked Maja* 1959; *The Reluctant Saint* 1962; *The Empty Canvas* 1963
Padrão, Ana (1968–) *1871* 1989; *The Edge of the Horizon* 1993
Padula, Vincent *aka* **Padula, Vincente** (1898–1967) *The Cyclops* 1957; *The Flame Barrier* 1958
Page, Anita (1910–) *Our Dancing Daughters* 1928; *The Broadway Melody* 1929; *Our Modern Maidens* 1929; *Free and Easy* 1930; *Skyscraper Souls* 1932
Page, Bradley (1901–1985) *Love Affair* 1932; *This Day and Age* 1933; *Super-Sleuth* 1937; *The Affairs of Annabel* 1938; *Annabel Takes a Tour* 1938; *The Law West of Tombstone* 1938
Page, Diamond Dallas (1956–) *First Daughter* 1999; *Ready to Rumble* 2000
Page, Gale (1913–1983) *The Amazing Dr Clitterhouse* 1938; *Four Daughters* 1938; *Four Wives* 1939; *Indianapolis Speedway* 1939; *Naughty but Nice* 1939; *You Can't Get Away with Murder* 1939; *Knute Rockne – All American* 1940; *They Drive by Night* 1940; *Four Mothers* 1941; *Anna Lucasta* 1949
Page, Genevieve *aka* **Page, Geneviève** (1930–) *Foreign Intrigue* 1956; *The Silken Affair* 1957; *Song without End* 1960; *El Cid* 1961; *Youngblood Hawke* 1964; *Trois Chambres à Manhattan* 1965; *Belle de Jour* 1967; *Decline and Fall... of a Birdwatcher* 1968; *Mayerling* 1968; *The Private Life of Sherlock Holmes* 1970; *Buffet Froid* 1979; *Aria* 1987; *Beyond Therapy* 1987; *Lovers* 1999
Page, Geraldine (1924–1987) *Hondo* 1953; *Taxi* 1953; *Summer and Smoke* 1961; *Sweet Bird of Youth* 1962; *Toys in the Attic* 1963; *Dear Heart* 1964; *The Three Sisters* 1966; *You're a Big Boy Now* 1966; *The Happiest Millionaire* 1967; *Trilogy* 1969; *Whatever Happened to Aunt Alice?* 1969; *The Beguiled* 1971; *JW Coop* 1971; *Pete 'n' Tillie* 1972; *The Day of the Locust* 1975; *Nasty Habits* 1976; *The Rescuers* 1977; *Something for Joey* 1977; *Interiors* 1978; *Harry's War* 1981; *Honky Tonk Freeway* 1981; *I'm Dancing as Fast as I Can* 1982; *The Dollmaker* 1984; *The Parade* 1984; *The Pope of Greenwich Village* 1984; *The Bride* 1985; *The Trip to Bountiful* 1985; *Walls of Glass* 1985; *White Nights* 1985; *My Little Girl* 1986; *Native Son* 1986; *Nazi Hunter: the Beate Klarsfeld Story* 1986
Page, Harrison *Vixen!* 1968; *AWOL* 1990; *Carnosaur* 1993
Page, Joy *aka* **Page, Joy Ann** (1921–) *Kismet* 1944; *The Bullfighter and the Lady* 1951; *The Shrike* 1955; *Tonka* 1958
Page, Ken *Torch Song Trilogy* 1988; *The Nightmare before Christmas* 1993
Page, Patti (1927–) *Elmer Gantry* 1960; *Boys' Night Out* 1962
Page, Paul (1903–1974) *Men without Women* 1930; *Palmy Days* 1931
Page, Rita (1905–1954) *Little Nellie Kelly* 1940; *Vigil in the Night* 1940
Paget, Alfred (1880–1925) *The Battle of Elderbush* 1914; *Intolerance* 1916; *The Fall of Babylon* 1919
Paget, Debra (1933–) *Cry of the City* 1948; *Broken Arrow* 1950; *Anne of the Indies* 1951; *Bird of Paradise* 1951; *Fourteen Hours* 1951; *Belles on Their Toes* 1952; *Les Misérables* 1952; *Stars and Stripes Forever* 1952; *Demetrius and the Gladiators* 1954; *Prince Valiant* 1954; *Princess of the Nile* 1954; *Seven Angry Men* 1955; *White Feather* 1955; *The Last Hunt* 1956; *Love Me Tender* 1956; *The Ten Commandments* 1956; *Omar Khayyam* 1957; *The River's Edge* 1957; *From the Earth to the Moon* 1958; *The Indian Tomb* 1959; *The Tiger of Eschnapur* 1959; *The Most Dangerous Man Alive* 1961; *Tales of Terror* 1962; *The Haunted Palace* 1963
Pagett, Nicola (1945–) *The Viking Queen* 1967; *There's a Girl in My Soup* 1970; *Frankenstein: the True Story* 1973; *Operation Daybreak* 1975; *Oliver's Story* 1978; *Privates on Parade* 1982; *An Awfully Big Adventure* 1994
Paglia, Camille (1947–) *The Watermelon Woman* 1996; *Henry Fool* 1997
Pagnol, Jacqueline *Topaze* 1951; *Manon des Sources* 1952
Paige, Janis (1922–) *Hollywood Canteen* 1944; *Of Human Bondage* 1946; *Two Guys from Milwaukee* 1946; *Romance on the High Seas* 1948; *Winter Meeting* 1948; *The Younger Brothers* 1949; *Silk Stockings* 1957; *Please Don't Eat the Daisies* 1960; *Bachelor in Paradise* 1961; *The Caretakers* 1963; *Follow the Boys* 1963
Paige, Mabel (1879–1954) *Young and Willing* 1942; *Happy Go Lucky* 1943; *True to Life* 1943
Paige, Robert *aka* **Carlyle, David** (1910–1987) *Cain and Mabel* 1936; *Smart Blonde* 1936; *Who Killed Gail Preston?* 1938; *Hellzapoppin'* 1941; *Pardon My Sarong* 1942; *Frontier Badmen* 1943; *Son of Dracula* 1943; *Can't Help Singing* 1944; *Abbott and Costello Go to Mars* 1953; *Split Second* 1953; *The Marriage-Go-Round* 1960
Pailhas, Géraldine (1971–) *IP5* 1992; *Suite 16* 1994; *Don Juan DeMarco* 1995; *5x2* 2004
Pain, Didier *Le Château de Ma Mère* 1990; *La Gloire de Mon Père* 1990; *Le Bossu* 1997
Pais, Josh (1964–) *Teenage Mutant Ninja Turtles* 1990; *Safe Men* 1998; *The Station Agent* 2003
Paiva, Nestor (1905–1966) *Meet Boston Blackie* 1941; *Fly by Night* 1942; *The Falcon in Mexico* 1944; *The Southerner* 1945; *Badman's Territory* 1946; *Road to Rio* 1947; *Double Dynamite* 1951; *A Millionaire for Christy* 1951; *Prisoners of the Casbah* 1953; *Creature from the Black Lagoon* 1954; *Hell on Frisco Bay* 1955; *Revenge of the Creature* 1955; *Tarantula* 1955; *Comanche* 1956; *The Mole People* 1956
Pajala, Turo *Hamlet Goes Business* 1987; *Ariel* 1988
Palance, Holly (1950–) *The Comeback* 1977; *Under Fire* 1983; *The Best of Times* 1986
Palance, Jack *aka* **Palance, Walter (Jack)** (1919–) *Halls of Montezuma* 1950; *Panic in the Streets* 1950; *Sudden Fear* 1952; *Arrowhead* 1953; *Flight to Tangier* 1953; *Man in the Attic* 1953; *Second Chance* 1953; *Shane* 1953; *Sign of the Pagan* 1954; *The Silver Chalice* 1954; *The Big Knife* 1955; *I Died a Thousand Times* 1955; *Kiss of Fire* 1955; *Attack!* 1956; *House of Numbers* 1957; *The Lonely Man* 1957; *The Man Inside* 1958; *Ten Seconds to Hell* 1959; *The Battle of Austerlitz* 1960; *Barabbas* 1961; *The Mongols* 1961; *Le Mépris* 1963; *Once a Thief* 1965; *The Professionals* 1966; *The Spy in the Green Hat* 1966; *Kill a Dragon* 1967; *Torture Garden* 1967; *A Professional Gun* 1968; *They Came to Rob Las Vegas* 1968; *Che!* 1969; *The Desperados* 1969; *The McMasters* 1970; *Monte Walsh* 1970; *Chato's Land* 1971; *The Horsemen* 1971; *Craze* 1973; *Oklahoma Crude* 1973; *Dracula* 1974; *The Four Deuces* 1976; *God's Gun* 1977; *Portrait of a Hitman* 1977; *Welcome to Blood City* 1977; *One Man Jury* 1978; *Hawk the Slayer* 1980; *Without Warning* 1980; *Alone in the Dark* 1982; *Bagdad Café* 1987; *Gor* 1987; *Young Guns* 1988; *Batman* 1989; *Tango & Cash* 1989; *Solar Crisis* 1990; *City Slickers* 1991; *Cyborg 2: Glass Shadow* 1993; *City Slickers II: the Legend of Curly's Gold* 1994; *Cops and Robbersons* 1994; *The Swan Princess* 1994; *Treasure Island* 1998; *Prancer Returns* 2001
Palau, Pierre (1885–1966) *Devil in the Flesh* 1947; *Marguerite de la Nuit* 1955
Palfrey, Lisa *House of America* 1996; *Otherworld* 2003
Palin, Michael (1943–) *And Now for Something Completely Different* 1971; *Monty Python and the Holy Grail* 1975; *Pleasure at Her Majesty's* 1976; *Jabberwocky* 1977; *The Rutles – All You Need Is Cash* 1978; *Monty Python's Life of Brian* 1979; *Time Bandits* 1981; *The Missionary* 1982; *Monty Python Live at the Hollywood Bowl* 1982; *Monty Python's The Meaning of Life* 1983; *A Private Function* 1984; *Brazil* 1985; *A Fish Called Wanda* 1988; *American Friends* 1991; *The Wind in the Willows* 1996; *Fierce Creatures* 1997
Palk, Anna (1941–1990) *Play It Cool* 1962; *The Frozen Dead* 1966; *Tower of Evil* 1972
Palladino, Aleksa (1981–) *The Adventures of Sebastian Cole* 1998; *Wrestling with Alligators* 1998

Pallenberg, Anita (1944–) Barbarella 1967; Candy 1968; Performance 1970
Pallette, Eugene (1889–1954) The Three Musketeers 1921; Mantrap 1926; Lights of New York 1928; The Virginian 1929; Paramount on Parade 1930; Girls about Town 1931; Gun Smoke 1931; It Pays to Advertise 1931; The Half Naked Truth 1932; Shanghai Express 1932; The Kennel Murder Case 1933; Shanghai Madness 1933; All the King's Horses 1935; Black Sheep 1935; Bordertown 1935; The Ghost Goes West 1935; Steamboat round the Bend 1935; My Man Godfrey 1936; Stowaway 1936; One Hundred Men and a Girl 1937; Topper 1937; The Adventures of Robin Hood 1938; First Love 1939; Mr Smith Goes to Washington 1939; Wife, Husband and Friend 1939; It's a Date 1940; The Mark of Zorro 1940; Young Tom Edison 1940; Appointment for Love 1941; The Bride Came COD 1941; The Lady Eve 1941; Swamp Water 1941; Unfinished Business 1941; The Big Street 1942; The Forest Rangers 1942; Lady in a Jam 1942; The Male Animal 1942; The Gang's All Here 1943; It Ain't Hay 1943; Slightly Dangerous 1943; In the Meantime, Darling 1944; Pin Up Girl 1944; Sensations 1944; Step Lively 1944; The Cheaters 1945
Palma, Andrea (1903–1987) Tarzan and the Mermaids 1948; The Criminal Life of Archibaldo de la Cruz 1955
Palme, Ulf (1920–1993) Miss Julie 1951; Dreams 1955; The Counterfeit Traitor 1962; Doctor Glas 1968
Palmer, Betsy (1929–) The Long Gray Line 1955; Mister Roberts 1955; Queen Bee 1955; The Tin Star 1957; The True Story of Lynn Stuart 1957; The Last Angry Man 1959; Friday the 13th 1980
Palmer, Geoffrey (1927–) A Fish Called Wanda 1988; Smack and Thistle 1989; The Madness of King George 1995; Mrs Brown 1997; Tomorrow Never Dies 1997; Rat 2000; Peter Pan 2003
Palmer, Gregg aka **Lee, Palmer** (1927–) Francis Goes to West Point 1952; The All American 1953; Magnificent Obsession 1954; Playgirl 1954; Taza, Son of Cochise 1954; To Hell and Back 1955; The Creature Walks among Us 1956; Hilda Crane 1956; From Hell It Came 1957; The Rebel Set 1959; The Sad Horse 1959; The Most Dangerous Man Alive 1961
Palmer, Lilli (1914–1986) Secret Agent 1936; Command Performance 1937; Good Morning, Boys 1937; The Great Barrier 1937; Crackerjack 1938; Thunder Rock 1942; The Gentle Sex 1943; English without Tears 1944; The Rake's Progress 1945; Beware of Pity 1946; Cloak and Dagger 1946; Body and Soul 1947; My Girl Tisa 1948; No Minor Vices 1948; The Long Dark Hall 1951; The Four Poster 1953; Is Anna Anderson Anastasia? 1956; Montparnasse 19 1958; But Not for Me 1959; Conspiracy of Hearts 1960; The Pleasure of His Company 1961; The Counterfeit Traitor 1962; Miracle of the White Stallions 1963; The Amorous Adventures of Moll Flanders 1965; Operation Crossbow 1965; Jack of Diamonds 1967; Oedipus the King 1967; Nobody Runs Forever 1968; Sebastian 1968; De Sade 1969; Hard Contract 1969; Murders in the Rue Morgue 1971; The Boys from Brazil 1978; The Holcroft Covenant 1985
Palmer, Maria (1917–1981) Days of Glory 1944; The Web 1947; By the Light of the Silvery Moon 1953
Palminteri, Chazz (1952–) Home Free All 1983; Oscar 1991; Innocent Blood 1992; A Bronx Tale 1993; Bullets over Broadway 1994; Jade 1995; The Perez Family 1995; The Usual Suspects 1995; Diabolique 1996; Faithful 1996; Mulholland Falls 1996; Hurlyburly 1998; Scarred City 1998; Analyze This 1999; Stuart Little 1999; Lady and the Tramp II: Scamp's Adventure 2000; Down to Earth 2001
Palomino, Carlos (1949–) Strangers Kiss 1983; Die Watching 1993
Paltrow, Gwyneth (1973–) Hook 1991; Flesh and Bone 1993; Malice 1993; Jefferson in Paris 1995; Moonlight and Valentino 1995; Se7en 1995; Emma 1996; Hard Eight 1996; The Pallbearer 1996; Great Expectations 1997; Sliding Doors 1997; Hush 1998; A Perfect Murder 1998; Shakespeare in Love 1998; The Talented Mr Ripley 1999; Bounce 2000; Duets 2000; The Anniversary Party 2001; The Royal Tenenbaums 2001; Shallow Hal 2001; Possession 2002; Sylvia 2003; View from the Top 2003; Sky Captain and the World of Tomorrow 2004
Paluzzi, Luciana (1937–) Carlton-Browne of the FO 1958; No Time to Die 1958; Sea Fury 1958; Return to Peyton Place 1961; Muscle Beach Party 1964; Thunderball 1965; To Trap a Spy 1966; The Venetian Affair 1966; Chuka 1967; The Green Slime 1968; Sharaz 1968; A Black Veil for Lisa 1969; Captain Nemo and the Underwater City 1969; The Italian Connection 1973; The Klansman 1974
Panaro, Alessandra aka **Panaro, Sandra** (1939–) The Bacchantes 1960; The Secret Mark of D'Artagnan 1962; The Son of Captain Blood 1962; The Executioner of Venice 1963
Pandey, Nirmal Bandit Queen 1994; The Square Circle 1996; Train to Pakistan 1997
Panebianco, Richard (1971–) China Girl 1987; Dogfight 1991
Panettiere, Hayden (1989–) A Bug's Life 1998; Joe Somebody 2001; Normal 2002; Racing Stripes 2004; Raising Helen 2004
Pang, Adrian Peggy Su! 1997; Second Generation 1999
Pangborn, Franklin (1893–1958) Her Man 1930; The Half Naked Truth 1932; Design for Living 1933; My Man Godfrey 1936; All over Town 1937; All over Town 1937; Easy Living 1937; Stage Door 1937; Three Smart Girls 1937; Bluebeard's Eighth Wife 1938; Just around the Corner 1938; Vivacious Lady 1938; Topper Takes a Trip 1939; The Bank Dick 1940; Christmas in July 1940; Call Out the Marines 1941; The Navy Steps Out 1941; Never Give a Sucker an Even Break 1941; Sullivan's Travels 1941; Reveille with Beverly 1943; The Horn Blows at Midnight 1945; I'll Be Yours 1947; Mad Wednesday 1950
Panjabi, Archie East Is East 1999; Bend It like Beckham 2001
Pankin, Stuart (1946–) The Dirt Bike Kid 1986; Fatal Attraction 1987; Love at Stake 1987; Second Sight 1989; Arachnophobia 1990; Life Stinks 1991; Mannequin on the Move 1991; Congo 1995
Pankow, John (1954–) To Live and Die in LA 1985; The Secret of My Success 1987; Monkey Shines 1988; Talk Radio 1988; Mortal Thoughts 1991; Year of the Gun 1991; A Stranger among Us 1992; The Object of My Affection 1998
Pantoliano, Joe (1951–) The Idolmaker 1980; Eddie and the Cruisers 1983; Risky Business 1983; The Goonies 1985; The Mean Season 1985; Running Scared 1986; La Bamba 1987; Empire of the Sun 1987; The In Crowd 1988; Midnight Run 1988; Nightbreaker 1989; Blue Heat 1990; Downtown 1990; Short Time 1990; Zandalee 1991; Three of Hearts 1992; Calendar Girl 1993; The Fugitive 1993; Me and the Kid 1993; Baby's Day Out 1994; Steal Big, Steal Little 1995; Bound 1996; Tinseltown 1997; Top of the World 1997; Taxman 1998; US Marshals 1998; The Life before This 1999; The Matrix 1999; A Better Way to Die 2000; Memento 2000; Cats & Dogs 2001; Pluto Nash 2001; Bad Boys II 2003; Daredevil 2003; Racing Stripes 2004
Paoli, Cécile Near Mrs 1990; Kaspar Hauser 1993
Papas, Irene (1926–) The Man from Cairo 1953; Tribute to a Bad Man 1956; The Guns of Navarone 1961; Elektra 1962; The Moon-Spinners 1964; Zorba the Greek 1964; The Desperate Ones 1967; We Still Kill the Old Way 1967; The Brotherhood 1968; Z 1968; Anne of the Thousand Days 1969; A Dream of Kings 1969; The Trojan Women 1971; Moses 1975; Iphigenia 1976; The Message 1976; Bloodline 1979; Christ Stopped at Eboli 1979; Lion of the Desert 1981; Erendira 1982; The Assisi Underground 1985; Chronicle of a Death Foretold 1987; High Season 1987; Island 1989; Jacob 1994; The Odyssey 1997; Captain Corelli's Mandolin 2001; Un Filme Falado 2003
Pape, Lionel (1877–1944) The Big Broadcast of 1938 1937; Raffles 1939
Paquin, Anna (1982–) The Piano 1993; Fly Away Home 1996; Jane Eyre 1996; Amistad 1997; Hurlyburly 1998; She's All That 1999; A Walk on the Moon 1999; Almost Famous 2000; Finding Forrester 2000; X-Men 2000; Buffalo Soldiers 2001; Darkness 2002; 25th Hour 2002; X2 2003
Paradis, Vanessa (1972–) Noce Blanche 1989; Elisa 1994; The Girl on the Bridge 1999
Paramore, Kiri The Last Days of Chez Nous 1992; Doing Time for Patsy Cline 1997; Ned Kelly 2003
Paratene, Rawiri Footrot Flats: the Dog's Tale 1986; What Becomes of the Broken Hearted? 1999; Whale Rider 2002
Pardue, Kip (1976–) Driven 2001; The Rules of Attraction 2002; Thirteen 2003; The Heart Is Deceitful above All Things 2004; Imaginary Heroes 2004
Paré, Jessica (1982–) Stardom 2000; Bollywood/Hollywood 2002; Wicker Park 2004
Paré, Michael (1959–) Eddie and the Cruisers 1983; Undercover 1983; The Philadelphia Experiment 1984; Streets of Fire 1984; World Gone Wild 1988; Eddie and the Cruisers II: Eddie Lives! 1989; The Closer 1990; Moon 44 1990; Empire City 1991; Into the Sun 1992; Village of the Damned 1995; Bad Moon 1996; Men of Means 1997; Hope Floats 1998
Parédès, Jean (1918–1998) La Nuit Fantastique 1942; Fanfan la Tulipe 1951
Paredes, Marisa (1946–) Dark Habits 1983; High Heels 1991; The Flower of My Secret 1995; Deep Crimson 1996; Three Lives and Only One Death 1996; Life Is Beautiful 1997; Talk of Angels 1998; All about My Mother 1999; No One Writes to the Colonel 1999; The Devil's Backbone 2001
Parely, Mila (1917–) La Règle du Jeu 1939; Les Anges du Péché 1943; La Belle et la Bête 1946; Blood Orange 1953
Parfitt, Judy (1935–) Hide and Seek 1963; Hamlet 1969; The Mind of Mr Soames 1970; Champions 1983; The Chain 1984; Maurice 1987; Diamond Skulls 1989; Dolores Claiborne 1995; Wilde 1997; Ever After: a Cinderella Story 1998; Girl with a Pearl Earring 2003
Parillaud, Anne (1960–) Ecoute Voir... 1978; Nikita 1990; Innocent Blood 1992; Map of the Human Heart 1992; Six Days, Six Nights 1994; Frankie Starlight 1995; The Man in the Iron Mask 1997; Shattered Image 1998; Sex Is Comedy 2002
Paris, Jerry (1925–1986) The Glass Wall 1953; Drive a Crooked Road 1954; Good Morning, Miss Dove 1955; Marty 1955; The Naked Street 1955; Unchained 1955; D-Day the Sixth of June 1956; Zero Hour! 1957; The Female Animal 1958; Sing, Boy, Sing 1958
Park Joong-Hoon (1964–) American Dragons 1997; Nowhere to Hide 1999; The Truth about Charlie 2002
Park, Ray (1975–) Star Wars Episode I: the Phantom Menace 1999; X-Men 2000; Ballistic: Ecks vs Sever 2002
Park-Lincoln, Lar The Princess Academy 1987; Friday the 13th Part VII: the New Blood 1988
Parke, MacDonald (1891–1960) Summertime 1955; Beyond Mombasa 1957; The Mouse That Roared 1959
Parker, Barnett (1886–1941) Listen, Darling 1938; Tall, Dark and Handsome 1941
Parker, Cecil (1897–1971) The Man Who Changed His Mind 1936; Storm in a Teacup 1937; The Citadel 1938; Housemaster 1938; The Lady Vanishes 1938; Sons of the Sea 1939; Under Your Hat 1940; The Saint's Vacation 1941; Caesar and Cleopatra 1945; Hungry Hill 1946; The Magic Bow 1946; Captain Boycott 1947; Quartet 1948; The Weaker Sex 1948; The Chiltern Hundreds 1949; Dear Mr Prohack 1949; Under Capricorn 1949; Tony Draws a Horse 1950; The Man in the White Suit 1951; I Believe in You 1952; Isn't Life Wonderful! 1952; Father Brown 1954; For Better, for Worse 1954; The Constant Husband 1955; The Ladykillers 1955; The Court Jester 1956; It's Great to Be Young 1956; True as a Turtle 1956; 23 Paces to Baker Street 1956; The Admirable Crichton 1957; Happy Is the Bride 1957; A Tale of Two Cities 1957; I Was Monty's Double 1958; Indiscreet 1958; The Navy Lark 1959; The Night We Dropped a Clanger 1959; The Wreck of the Mary Deare 1959; A French Mistress 1960; The Pure Hell of St Trinian's 1960; Swiss Family Robinson 1960; Under Ten Flags 1960; On the Fiddle 1961; Petticoat Pirates 1961; The Amorous Prawn 1962; The Brain 1962; Heavens Above! 1963; The Comedy Man 1964; Lady L 1965; A Man Could Get Killed 1966; The Magnificent Two 1967
Parker, Cecilia (1905–1993) Enter Madame! 1933; Riders of Destiny 1933; The Painted Veil 1934; Ah, Wilderness! 1935; A Family Affair 1937; Girl Loves Boy 1937; Judge Hardy's Children 1938; Love Finds Andy Hardy 1938; Out West with the Hardys 1938; You're Only Young Once 1938; Andy Hardy Gets Spring Fever 1939; The Hardys Ride High 1939; Judge Hardy and Son 1939; Andy Hardy Meets Debutante 1940; Andy Hardy's Double Life 1942; The Courtship of Andy Hardy 1942; Grand Central Murder 1942; Andy Hardy Comes Home 1958
Parker, Corey (1965–) Biloxi Blues 1988; Big Man on Campus 1989; How I Got Into College 1989; White Palace 1990; Broadway Bound 1991
Parker, Eddie aka **Parker, Ed** (1900–1960) The Star Packer 1934; The Trail Beyond 1934; Abbott and Costello Meet the Mummy 1955
Parker, Eleanor (1922–) Mission to Moscow 1943; Between Two Worlds 1944; The Very Thought of You 1944; Pride of the Marines 1945; Never Say Goodbye 1946; Of Human Bondage 1946; Escape Me Never 1947; Voice of the Turtle 1947; The Woman in White 1948; It's a Great Feeling 1949; Caged 1950; Chain Lightning 1950; Three Secrets 1950; Detective Story 1951; A Millionaire for Christy 1951; Valentino 1951; Above and Beyond 1952; Scaramouche 1952; Escape from Fort Bravo 1953; The Naked Jungle 1953; Valley of the Kings 1954; Interrupted Melody 1955; The Man with the Golden Arm 1955; Many Rivers to Cross 1955; The King and Four Queens 1956; Lizzie 1957; A Hole in the Head 1959; Home from the Hill 1960; Return to Peyton Place 1961; Madison Avenue 1962; Panic Button 1964; The Sound of Music 1965; An American Dream 1966; The Oscar 1966; The Tiger and the Pussycat 1967; Warning Shot 1967; How to Steal the World 1968; Eye of the Cat 1969; Sunburn 1979
Parker, F William Personal Foul 1987; Hard Eight 1996
Parker, Fess (1926–) Thunder over the Plains 1953; Davy Crockett, King of the Wild Frontier 1955; Davy Crockett and the River Pirates 1956; The Great Locomotive Chase 1956; Westward Ho the Wagons! 1956; Old Yeller 1957; The Light in the Forest 1958; Alias Jesse James 1959; The Hangman 1959; The Jayhawkers 1959; Hell Is for Heroes 1962
Parker, Jameson (1947–) A Small Circle of Friends 1980; White Dog 1981; Agatha Christie's A Caribbean Mystery 1983; Prince of Darkness 1987; Dead before Dawn 1993
Parker, Jean (1915–) Gabriel over the White House 1933; Lady for a Day 1933; Little Women 1933; Caravan 1934; Operator 13 1934; The Ghost Goes West 1935; Princess O'Hara 1935; The Texas Rangers 1936; The Flying Deuces 1939; Zenobia 1939; Bluebeard 1944; Dead Man's Eyes 1944; The Gunfighter 1950; A Lawless Street 1955; The Parson and the Outlaw 1957; Apache Uprising 1965
Parker, Lara (1942–) Hi, Mom! 1970; Night of Dark Shadows 1971; Race with the Devil 1975
Parker, Mary-Louise aka **Parker, Mary Louise** (1964–) Longtime Companion 1990; Fried Green Tomatoes at the Whistle Stop Cafe 1991; Grand Canyon 1991; Mr Wonderful 1992; Bullets over Broadway 1994; The Client 1994; Naked in New York 1994; A Place for Annie 1994; Boys on the Side 1995; Reckless 1995; Murder in Mind 1996; The Portrait of a Lady 1996; Goodbye Lover 1997; The Maker 1997; Legalese 1998; The Five Senses 1999; Let the Devil Wear Black 1999; The Simple Life of Noah Dearborn 1999; Red Dragon 2002; Saved! 2004
Parker, Molly (1972–) Kissed 1996; The Five Senses 1999; Sunshine 1999; Wonderland 1999; Suspicious River 2000; Waking the Dead 2000; The Center of the World 2001; The War Bride 2001; Max 2002; Pure 2002; Iron Jawed Angels 2004
Parker, Nathaniel (1963–) War Requiem 1988; Hamlet 1990; Wide Sargasso Sea 1992; Squanto: the Last Great Warrior 1994; Othello 1995; Beverly Hills Ninja 1997; The Haunted Mansion 2003
Parker, Nicole Ari aka **Parker, Nicole** (1970–) The Incredibly True Adventures of Two Girls in Love 1995; Subway Stories: Tales from the Underground 1997; Blue Streak 1999; Brown Sugar 2002
Parker, Noelle (1969–) Ernest Saves Christmas 1988; Leave of Absence 1994
Parker, Paula Jai Friday 1995; Woo 1998
Parker, Sarah Jessica (1965–) Somewhere Tomorrow 1983; Firstborn 1984; Footloose 1984; Girls Just Want to Have Fun 1985; Flight of the Navigator 1986; LA Story 1991; Honeymoon in Vegas 1992; Hocus Pocus 1993; Striking Distance 1993; Ed Wood 1994; Miami Rhapsody 1995; Extreme Measures 1996; The First Wives Club 1996; If Lucy Fell 1996; Mars Attacks! 1996; The Substance of Fire 1996; The Sunshine Boys 1997; 'Til There

Was You 1997; Dudley Do-Right 1999; Isn't She Great 1999; State and Main 2000

Parker, Suzy (1932–2003) Kiss Them for Me 1957; Ten North Frederick 1958; The Best of Everything 1959; Circle of Deception 1960; The Interns 1962; Flight from Ashiya 1964; Chamber of Horrors 1966

Parker, Trey aka **Schwartz, Juan** (1969–) Cannibal! the Musical 1993; Orgazmo 1997; BASEketball 1998; South Park: Bigger, Longer & Uncut 1999; Team America: World Police 2004

Parker, Willard (1912–1996) A Slight Case of Murder 1938; What a Woman! 1943; Relentless 1948; You Gotta Stay Happy 1948; Calamity Jane and Sam Bass 1949; Slightly French 1949; Apache Drums 1951; The Earth Dies Screaming 1964

Parkes, Gerard The First Time 1969; The Gunrunner 1984; The Last Winter 1989

Parkes, Shaun Human Traffic 1999; Rage 1999; Offending Angels 2000

Parkin, Dean aka **Parkin, Duncan "Dean"** aka **Parkin, Dean** (1930–) The Cyclops 1957; War of the Colossal Beast 1958

Parkins, Barbara (1942–) Valley of the Dolls 1967; The Kremlin Letter 1970; Puppet on a Chain 1970; The Deadly Trap 1971; The Mephisto Waltz 1971; Asylum 1972; Shout at the Devil 1976; Bear Island 1979

Parks, Catherine Friday the 13th Part III 1982; Weekend at Bernie's 1989

Parks, Larry (1914–1975) The Boogie Man Will Get You 1942; Reveille with Beverly 1943; Stars on Parade 1944; Counter-Attack 1945; The Jolson Story 1946; Down to Earth 1947; The Gallant Blade 1948; Jolson Sings Again 1949; Love Is Better Than Ever 1951; Tiger by the Tail 1955; Freud 1962

Parks, Michael (1938–) Bus Riley's Back in Town 1965; Wild Seed 1965; The Bible...in the Beginning 1966; The Idol 1966; The Happening 1967; Stranger on the Run 1967; The Last Hard Men 1976; Love and the Midnight Auto Supply 1977; The Private Files of J Edgar Hoover 1977; Sidewinder One 1977; Breakthrough 1978; The Evictors 1979; North Sea Hijack 1979; Hard Country 1981; Savannah Smiles 1982; The Return of Josey Wales 1986; The Hitman 1991; Storyville 1992; Death Wish V: the Face of Death 1994; Julian Po 1997; Liar 1997; Niagara Niagara 1997; Wicked 1998; From Dusk till Dawn 3: the Hangman's Daughter 2000; Kill Bill Vol 1 2003

Parkyakarkus (1904–1958) New Faces of 1937 1937; Out of This World 1945

Parlavecchio, Steve Amongst Friends 1993; Bandwagon 1995

Parlo, Dita (1906–1971) Heimkehr 1928; L'Atalante 1934; Mademoiselle Docteur 1936; La Grande Illusion 1937

Parnell, Emory (1892–1979) Two O'Clock Courage 1945; Abie's Irish Rose 1946; The Falcon's Alibi 1946; Lost in Alaska 1952; The Rocket Man 1954

Parr, Antony Agency 1981; Confidential 1986

Parrish, Helen (1924–1959) Mad about Music 1938; First Love 1939; Three Smart Girls Grow Up 1939; Winter Carnival 1939; You'll Find Out 1940; In Old California 1942

Parrish, Julie (1940–2003) Fireball 500 1966; The Doberman Gang 1972

Parrish, Leslie (1935–) Li'l Abner 1959; The Manchurian Candidate 1962; Sex and the Single Girl 1964; Three on a Couch 1966; The Candy Man 1969; The Giant Spider Invasion 1975; Invisible Strangler 1976; Crash! 1977

Parrish, Steve Midnight 1989; Scanners III: the Takeover 1992

Parry, Natasha (1930–) Dance Hall 1950; Knave of Hearts 1954; Windom's Way 1957; The Rough and the Smooth 1959; Midnight Lace 1960; Girl in the Headlines 1963; Romeo and Juliet 1968; Meetings with Remarkable Men 1979

Parsons, Estelle (1927–) Bonnie and Clyde 1967; Rachel, Rachel 1968; Don't Drink the Water 1969; I Never Sang for My Father 1969; I Walk the Line 1970; Watermelon Man 1970; Two People 1973; For Pete's Sake 1974; The Lemon Sisters 1989; Dick Tracy 1990; A Private Matter 1992; Boys on the Side 1995; Looking for Richard 1996; That Darn Cat 1997

Parsons, Karyn (1968–) Mixing Nia 1998; The Ladies Man 2000

Parsons, Nancy (1942–2001) Motel Hell 1980; Porky's 1981; Porky's II: The Next Day 1983; Porky's Revenge 1985; Wishman 1991

Parsons, Nicholas (1928–) Brothers in Law 1956; The Long Arm 1956; Happy Is the Bride 1957; Too Many Crooks 1958; Doctor in Love 1960; Murder Ahoy 1964; Don't Raise the Bridge, Lower the River 1968; The Best of Benny Hill 1974

Parsons, Percy (1878–1944) The Good Companions 1933; Dangerous Moonlight 1941

Parton, Dolly (1946–) Nine to Five 1980; The Best Little Whorehouse in Texas 1982; Rhinestone 1984; Steel Magnolias 1989; Straight Talk 1992; The Beverly Hillbillies 1993; Blue Valley Songbird 1999

Partridge, Ross Amityville: a New Generation 1993; Black and White 1998

Pas, Michael (1966–) Blueberry Hill 1989; Daens 1992

Pascal, Christine (1953–1996) The Watchmaker of St Paul 1973; The Young Ladies of Wilko 1979; 'Round Midnight 1986; Le Grand Chemin 1987; See How They Fall 1993; Patriots 1994

Pascal, Jean-Claude (1927–1992) The Crimson Curtain 1952; The Bad Liaisons 1955

Pasco, Isabelle (1966–) Roselyne and the Lions 1989; Prospero's Books 1991

Pasco, Richard (1926–) Yesterday's Enemy 1959; Sword of Sherwood Forest 1960; The Gorgon 1964; Rasputin, the Mad Monk 1965; The Watcher in the Woods 1982; Mrs Brown 1997

Pasdar, Adrian (1965–) Solarbabies 1986; Streets of Gold 1986; Near Dark 1987; Cookie 1989; Torn Apart 1990; Vital Signs 1990; Just like a Woman 1992; Killing Box 1993; The Last Good Time 1994; The Pompatus of Love 1995; Mutiny 1999

Pasolini, Pier Paolo (1922–1975) Kill and Pray 1967; Oedipus Rex 1967; The Decameron 1970; The Canterbury Tales 1971

Pass, Cyndi Mission of Justice 1992; The Night Caller 1998

Passante, Mario Gold of Naples 1954; The Mask of Satan 1960

Passgård, Lars (1941–) Through a Glass Darkly 1961; The Pram 1963

Pastell, George Maniac 1962; Impact 1963; The Curse of the Mummy's Tomb 1964

Pastor, Rosana The Ages of Lulu 1990; Land and Freedom 1995; A Further Gesture 1996

Pastore, Vincent aka **Pastore, Vinny** (1946–) Me and the Mob 1992; Serving Sara 2002; American Cousins 2003

Pastorelli, Robert (1954–2004) Dances with Wolves 1990; FernGully: the Last Rainforest 1992; Folks! 1992; Painted Heart 1992; Striking Distance 1993; The West Side Waltz 1995; Eraser 1996; Michael 1996; A Simple Wish 1997; South Pacific 2001

Patachou Wild Target 1993; Drôle de Félix 2000

Pataki, Michael (1938–) Spider-Man 1977; Zoltan... Hound of Dracula 1977; The Glove 1978; Rocky IV 1985; Halloween 4: the Return of Michael Myers 1988

Patch, Wally (1888–1970) Death on the Set 1935; Street Song 1935; Alf's Button Afloat 1938; Bank Holiday 1938; Band Waggon 1939; Gasbags 1940; Gert and Daisy's Weekend 1941; Get Cracking 1943; George in Civvy Street 1946; A Date with a Dream 1948

Pate, Michael (1920–) Bitter Springs 1950; The Strange Door 1951; The Black Castle 1952; Face to Face 1952; Hondo 1953; Houdini 1953; Julius Caesar 1953; The Maze 1953; Congo Crossing 1956; The Revolt of Mamie Stover 1956; Seventh Cavalry 1956; The Oklahoman 1957; Green Mansions 1959; Westbound 1959; Beauty and the Beast 1962; Tower of London 1962; PT 109 1963; The Great Sioux Massacre 1965; Mad Dog 1976; The Return of Captain Invincible 1983; The Wild Duck 1983

Patekar, Nana (1951–) Salaam Bombay! 1988; Disha 1990; Shakti – the Power 2002; Bhoot 2003

Paterson, Bill (1945–) The Odd Job 1978; Comfort and Joy 1984; The Killing Fields 1984; A Private Function 1984; Defence of the Realm 1985; Hidden City 1987; The Adventures of Baron Munchausen 1988; Just Ask for Diamond 1988; The Rachel Papers 1989; The Witches 1989; Truly Madly Deeply 1990; The Object of Beauty 1991; Victory 1995; Heart 1997; Hilary and Jackie 1998; Complicity 1999; Crush 2001; Bright Young Things 2003

Paterson, Caroline Venus Peter 1989; The Hawk 1992

Paterson, Pat (1911–1978) Bitter Sweet 1933; Charlie Chan in Egypt 1935; Spendthrift 1936

Patil, Smita aka **Smita** (1955–1986) Nishant 1975; In Search of Famine 1980; Sadgati 1981; Mandi 1983; Tarang 1983; Mirch Masala 1987

Patinkin, Mandy (1952–) The Big Fix 1978; French Postcards 1979; Last Embrace 1979; Night of the Juggler 1980; Ragtime 1981; Daniel 1983; Yentl 1983; Maxie 1985; The House on Carroll Street 1987; The Princess Bride 1987; Alien Nation 1988; Dick Tracy 1990; The Doctor 1991; Impromptu 1991; True Colors 1991; The Music of Chance 1993; Squanto: the Last Great Warrior 1994; Men with Guns 1997; Lulu on the Bridge 1998; The Adventures of Elmo in Grouchland 1999; Strange Justice 1999; Piñero 2001

Paton, Charles (1874–1970) Blackmail 1929; The Adventurers 1950

Patric, Jason (1966–) Solarbabies 1986; The Lost Boys 1987; The Beast of War 1988; After Dark, My Sweet 1990; Frankenstein Unbound 1990; Rush 1991; Geronimo: an American Legend 1993; The Journey of August King 1995; Sleepers 1996; Incognito 1997; Speed 2: Cruise Control 1997; Your Friends & Neighbours 1998; Narc 2001; The Alamo 2004

Patrick, Butch (1953–) The Two Little Bears 1961; Munster, Go Home! 1966; The Phantom Tollbooth 1969; The Defiant 1972

Patrick, Dennis (1918–2002) Joe 1970; Touchdown 1981; The Air Up There 1993

Patrick, Dorothy (1922–1987) Till the Clouds Roll By 1946; High Wall 1947; Come to the Stable 1949; House by the River 1950; 711 Ocean Drive 1950; Desert Passage 1952; Torch Song 1953; Thunder Pass 1954

Patrick, Gail (1911–1980) Murders in the Zoo 1933; Death Takes a Holiday 1934; Murder at the Vanities 1934; Mississippi 1935; Rumba 1935; The Lone Wolf Returns 1936; My Man Godfrey 1936; Artists and Models 1937; Stage Door 1937; King of Alcatraz 1938; Mad about Music 1938; Wives under Suspicion 1938; Man of Conquest 1939; The Doctor Takes a Wife 1940; My Favorite Wife 1940; Love Crazy 1941; Quiet Please, Murder 1942; Change of Heart 1943; Up in Mabel's Room 1944; Brewster's Millions 1945; Claudia and David 1946; Rendezvous with Annie 1946

Patrick, Lee (1901–1982) Condemned Women 1938; Law of the Underworld 1938; Invisible Stripes 1939; Saturday's Children 1940; Footsteps in the Dark 1941; The Maltese Falcon 1941; Million Dollar Baby 1941; Dangerously They Live 1942; George Washington Slept Here 1942; A Night to Remember 1942; Somewhere I'll Find You 1942; Mrs Parkington 1944; Keep Your Powder Dry 1945; Mildred Pierce 1945; Caged 1950; The Lawless 1950; Take Me to Town 1953; Visit to a Small Planet 1960; A Girl Named Tamiko 1962; 7 Faces of Dr Lao 1963; Wives and Lovers 1963; The Black Bird 1975

Patrick, Nigel (1913–1981) Noose 1948; Silent Dust 1948; The Perfect Woman 1949; Morning Departure 1950; Pandora and the Flying Dutchman 1950; Trio 1950; The Browning Version 1951; Encore 1951; Young Wives' Tale 1951; Meet Me Tonight 1952; The Pickwick Papers 1952; The Sound Barrier 1952; Grand National Night 1953; Forbidden Cargo 1954; The Sea Shall Not Have Them 1954; All for Mary 1955; A Prize of Gold 1955; Count Five and Die 1957; How to Murder a Rich Uncle 1957; Raintree County 1957; The Man Inside 1958; Sapphire 1959; The League of Gentlemen 1960; The Trials of Oscar Wilde 1960; The Informers 1963; The Virgin Soldiers 1969; The Executioner 1970; The Great Waltz 1972; Tales from the Crypt 1972; The Mackintosh Man 1973

Patrick, Robert (1959–) Terminator 2: Judgment Day 1991; The Cool Surface 1993; Fire in the Sky 1993; Body Shot 1994; Double Dragon 1994; Last Gasp 1995; Striptease 1996; Cop Land 1997; The Only Thrill 1997; The Faculty 1998; Tactical Assault 1998; The Vivero Letter 1998; From Dusk till Dawn II: Texas Blood Money 1999; All the Pretty Horses 2000; SPYkids 2001; Charlie's Angels: Full Throttle 2003; Ladder 49 2004

Patten, Luana (1938–1996) Song of the South 1946; Fun and Fancy Free 1947; Rock, Pretty Baby 1956; Johnny Tremain 1957; The Restless Years 1958; The Young Captives 1958; Home from the Hill 1960; Go Naked in the World 1961; A Thunder of Drums 1961

Patterson, Elizabeth (1875–1966) A Bill of Divorcement 1932; No Man of Her Own 1932; So Red the Rose 1935; Go West, Young Man 1936; Small Town Girl 1936; High, Wide and Handsome 1937; Bluebeard's Eighth Wife 1938; Bulldog Drummond's Peril 1938; Bulldog Drummond's Bride 1939; The Cat and the Canary 1939; Anne of Windy Poplars 1940; Michael Shayne, Private Detective 1940; Remember the Night 1940; Belle Starr 1941; Kiss the Boys Goodbye 1941; Tobacco Road 1941; Beyond the Blue Horizon 1942; Her Cardboard Lover 1942; I Married a Witch 1942; The Sky's the Limit 1943; Together Again 1944; Colonel Effingham's Raid 1945; The Secret Heart 1946; The Shocking Miss Pilgrim 1947; Welcome Stranger 1947; Little Women 1949; Bright Leaf 1950; Washington Story 1952; Pal Joey 1957

Patterson, James (1932–1972) Lilith 1964; In the Heat of the Night 1967; Silent Night, Bloody Night 1972

Patterson, Jay (1954–) Nadine 1987; Street Smart 1987; Teenage Mutant Ninja Turtles 1990; McBain 1991; American Perfekt 1997

Patterson, Lee (1929–) Above Us the Waves 1955; Dry Rot 1956; Reach for the Sky 1956; The Flying Scot 1957; The Story of Esther Costello 1957; Time Lock 1957; Cat and Mouse 1958; The Golden Disc 1958; Jack the Ripper 1958; The Spaniard's Curse 1958; The Three Worlds of Gulliver 1959; Bullseye! 1990

Patterson, Neva (1922–) Taxi 1953; The Solid Gold Cadillac 1956; An Affair to Remember 1957; Desk Set 1957; Too Much, Too Soon 1958; David and Lisa 1962; The Spiral Road 1962

Patterson, Sarah (1972–) The Company of Wolves 1984; Do I Love You? 2003

Patton, Mark (1964–) Come Back to the Five and Dime, Jimmy Dean, Jimmy Dean 1982; A Nightmare on Elm Street 2: Freddy's Revenge 1985

Patton, Mary (1914–1982) The Search 1948; The Marriage-Go-Round 1960

Patton, Will (1954–) Chinese Boxes 1984; Belizaire the Cajun 1985; Desperately Seeking Susan 1985; No Way Out 1986; Everybody Wins 1990; A Shock to the System 1990; The Rapture 1991; Cold Heaven 1992; In the Deep Woods 1992; In the Soup 1992; Painted Heart 1992; Romeo Is Bleeding 1992; The Client 1994; The Puppet Masters 1994; Tollbooth 1994; Copycat 1995; Judicial Consent 1995; Fled 1996; The Spitfire Grill 1996; This World, Then the Fireworks 1996; Inventing the Abbotts 1997; The Postman 1997; Armageddon 1998; I Woke Up Early the Day I Died 1998; Entrapment 1999; Jesus' Son 1999; Gone in Sixty Seconds 2000; Remember the Titans 2000; Trixie 2000; The Mothman Prophecies 2001; The Punisher 2004

Paul, Adrian (1959–) Dead Men Can't Dance 1997; Susan's Plan 1998; Highlander: Endgame 2000; Merlin the Return 2000; The Breed 2001

Paul, Alexandra (1963–) Christine 1983; Just the Way You Are 1984; American Flyers 1985; 8 Million Ways to Die 1986; Dragnet 1987; Sunset Grill 1992; Death Train 1993; Baywatch the Movie: Forbidden Paradise 1995; Danielle Steel's Mixed Blessings 1995; Night Watch 1995; Piranhas 1996; Eternal Revenge 1999; Exposure 2000; Diary of a Sex Addict 2001; Facing the Enemy 2001

Paul, David Think Big 1990; Double Trouble 1992

Paul, Don Michael (1963–) Dangerously Close 1986; Aloha Summer 1988; Heart of Dixie 1989; Robot Wars 1993

Paul, John (1921–1995) The Steel Bayonet 1957; The Curse of the Mummy's Tomb 1964; Doomwatch 1972

Paul, Peter Think Big 1990; Double Trouble 1992

Paul, Richard (1940–1998) Uphill All the Way 1985; The Princess Academy 1987

Paul, Richard Joseph Under the Boardwalk 1988; Oblivion 1993

Paul, Steven Happy Birthday, Wanda June 1971; Falling in Love Again 1980

Paulin, Scott From Hollywood to Deadwood 1989; Turner & Hooch 1989; Captain America 1990; Grim Prairie Tales 1990; Pump Up the Volume 1990

Paull, Morgan Cahill, United States Marshal 1973; Norma Rae 1979; Fade to Black 1980; GoBots: Battle of the Rocklords 1986

Paulsen, Albert (1929–2004) The Three Sisters 1966; Gunn 1967; Mrs Pollifax – Spy 1970; The Laughing Policeman 1973; The Next Man 1976

Paulsen, Pat (1927–1997) *Harper Valley PTA* 1978; *Ellie* 1984; *Night Patrol* 1984; *Auntie Lee's Meat Pies* 1991
Paulsen, Rob (1956–) *A Goofy Movie* 1995; *Cinderella II: Dreams Come True* 2002
Paulson, Sarah (1975–) *The Long Way Home* 1998; *The Other Sister* 1999; *Down with Love* 2003
Pauly, Rebecca *Near Mrs* 1990; *Road to Ruin* 1992
Pauly, Rodolphe *Merci pour le Chocolat* 2000; *Nathalie...* 2003; *Before Sunset* 2004
Pavan, Marisa (1932–) *Down Three Dark Streets* 1954; *Drum Beat* 1954; *Diane* 1955; *The Rose Tattoo* 1955; *The Man in the Gray Flannel Suit* 1956; *The Midnight Story* 1957; *John Paul Jones* 1959; *Solomon and Sheba* 1959
Pávez, Terele (1939–) *Los Santos Inocentes* 1984; *The Day of the Beast* 1995; *La Comunidad* 2000
Pavlow, Muriel (1921–) *Night Boat to Dublin* 1946; *The Shop at Sly Corner* 1946; *It Started in Paradise* 1952; *Conflict of Wings* 1953; *Malta Story* 1953; *The Net* 1953; *Doctor in the House* 1954; *Simon and Laura* 1955; *Eyewitness* 1956; *Reach for the Sky* 1956; *Tiger in the Smoke* 1956; *Doctor at Large* 1957; *Rooney* 1958; *Murder She Said* 1961
Pawar, Lalita (1916–1998) *Mr and Mrs '55* 1955; *Anari* 1959
Pawle, Lennox (1872–1936) *David Copperfield* 1935; *The Gay Deception* 1935
Pawley, Edward (1901–1988) *"G" Men* 1935; *Smashing the Rackets* 1938
Pawley, William (1905–1952) *Bad Girl* 1931; *Speak Easily* 1932; *Gabriel over the White House* 1933; *Born Reckless* 1937; *Rough Riders' Roundup* 1939
Pax, James *Kinjite: Forbidden Subjects* 1989; *Bethune: the Making of a Hero* 1990
Paxinou, Katina (1900–1973) *For Whom the Bell Tolls* 1943; *Hostages* 1943; *Confidential Agent* 1945; *Mourning Becomes Electra* 1947; *Uncle Silas* 1947; *Confidential Report* 1955; *The Miracle* 1959; *Rocco and His Brothers* 1960
Paxton, Bill (1955–) *The Lords of Discipline* 1983; *Impulse* 1984; *Streets of Fire* 1984; *Weird Science* 1985; *Aliens* 1986; *Near Dark* 1987; *Pass the Ammo* 1988; *Next of Kin* 1989; *Slipstream* 1989; *Blue Heat* 1990; *Brain Dead* 1990; *Navy SEALS* 1990; *Predator 2* 1990; *The Dark Backward* 1991; *One False Move* 1992; *Trespass* 1992; *The Vagrant* 1992; *Boxing Helena* 1993; *Indian Summer* 1993; *Tombstone* 1993; *True Lies* 1994; *Apollo 13* 1995; *Frank and Jesse* 1995; *The Last Supper* 1995; *The Evening Star* 1996; *Twister* 1996; *Titanic* 1997; *Traveller* 1997; *Mighty Joe Young* 1998; *A Simple Plan* 1998; *U-571* 2000; *Vertical Limit* 2000; *Frailty* 2001; *Broken Lizard's Club Dread* 2004; *Thunderbirds* 2004
Paymer, David (1954–) *Crazy People* 1990; *Mr Saturday Night* 1992; *Heart and Souls* 1993; *Innocent Moves* 1993; *Quiz Show* 1994; *The American President* 1995; *Nixon* 1995; *Carpool* 1996; *City Hall* 1996; *Unforgettable* 1996; *Amistad* 1997; *Gang Related* 1997; *The 6th Man* 1997; *Mighty Joe Young* 1998; *Payback* 1998; *Chill Factor* 1999; *Bartleby* 2000; *For Love or Country: the Arturo Sandoval Story* 2000; *Partners* 2000; *Focus* 2001; *Alex & Emma* 2003; *In Good Company* 2004
Payne, Allen (1968–) *Rooftops* 1989; *New Jack City* 1991; *CB4* 1993; *Jason's Lyric* 1994; *The Tuskegee Airmen* 1995; *Vampire in Brooklyn* 1995; *The Walking Dead* 1995; *A Price above Rubies* 1997; *Double Platinum* 1999
Payne, Bruce *aka* **Payne, Bruce Martyn** (1960–) *For Queen and Country* 1988; *Silence like Glass* 1989; *Pyrates* 1991; *Switch* 1991; *Passenger 57* 1992; *Full Eclipse* 1993; *Necronomicon* 1993; *Sweepers* 1999; *Warlock III: the End of Innocence* 1999; *Britannic* 2000; *Highlander: Endgame* 2000; *Steal* 2002
Payne, Eric *aka* **Payne, Eric A** *DROP Squad* 1994; *Gridlock'd* 1996
Payne, Freda (1945–) *Book of Numbers* 1972; *Nutty Professor 2: the Klumps* 2000
Payne, John *aka* **Payne, John Howard** (1912–1989) *Fair Warning* 1937; *College Swing* 1938; *Garden of the Moon* 1938; *Indianapolis Speedway* 1939; *Kid Nightingale* 1939; *Maryland* 1940; *Star Dust* 1940; *Tin Pan Alley* 1940; *The Great American Broadcast* 1941; *Remember the Day* 1941; *Sun Valley Serenade* 1941; *Weekend in Havana* 1941; *Footlight Serenade* 1942; *Springtime in the Rockies* 1942; *To the Shores of Tripoli* 1942; *Hello, Frisco, Hello* 1943; *The Dolly Sisters* 1945; *The Razor's Edge* 1946; *Sentimental Journey* 1946; *Miracle on 34th Street* 1947; *The Saxon Charm* 1948; *Kansas City Confidential* 1952; *99 River Street* 1953; *Raiders of the Seven Seas* 1953; *Rails into Laramie* 1954; *Silver Lode* 1954; *Hell's Island* 1955; *The Road to Denver* 1955; *Santa Fe Passage* 1955; *Tennessee's Partner* 1955; *Rebel in Town* 1956; *Slightly Scarlet* 1956; *Hidden Fear* 1957
Payne, Laurence (1919–) *Train of Events* 1949; *Ill Met by Moonlight* 1956; *The Trollenberg Terror* 1958; *The Third Alibi* 1961; *Vampire Circus* 1971
Pays, Amanda (1959–) *Oxford Blues* 1984; *The Kindred* 1986; *Saigon* 1988; *Leviathan* 1989; *Solitaire for 2* 1994
Payton, Barbara (1927–1967) *Dallas* 1950; *Kiss Tomorrow Goodbye* 1950; *Only the Valiant* 1950; *Four Sided Triangle* 1953
Payton-Wright, Pamela (1941–) *Corky* 1972; *Going in Style* 1979; *Resurrection* 1980; *My Little Girl* 1986; *Starlight* 1989
Peach, Mary (1934–) *Room at the Top* 1958; *No Love for Johnnie* 1960; *A Pair of Briefs* 1961; *A Gathering of Eagles* 1963; *Ballad in Blue* 1964; *The Projected Man* 1966
Peacock, Daniel *Party Party* 1983; *I Bought a Vampire Motorcycle* 1989
Peacock, Trevor (1931–) *Hamlet* 1990; *Roseanna's Grave* 1996
Peake, Michael *Mark of the Phoenix* 1957; *The Bay of Saint Michel* 1963
Peaker, E J (1944–) *Hello, Dolly!* 1969; *The All-American Boy* 1973; *The Four Deuces* 1976
Pearce, Alice (1913–1966) *On the Town* 1949; *The Belle of New York* 1952; *The Disorderly Orderly* 1964
Pearce, Guy (1967–) *Heaven Tonight* 1990; *Hunting* 1992; *The Adventures of Priscilla, Queen of the Desert* 1994; *Flynn* 1995; *LA Confidential* 1997; *Ravenous* 1999; *Memento* 2000; *Rules of Engagement* 2000; *The Count of Monte Cristo* 2001; *The Hard Word* 2002; *The Time Machine* 2002; *Two Brothers* 2004
Pearce, Jacqueline *The Plague of the Zombies* 1965; *The Reptile* 1966; *Don't Raise the Bridge, Lower the River* 1968; *Guru in Seven* 1997
Pearce, John (1927–2000) *The Great Northfield Minnesota Raid* 1972; *Billy Two Hats* 1973; *Little Treasure* 1985
Pearce, Mary Vivian *Mondo Trasho* 1970; *Multiple Maniacs* 1970; *Pink Flamingos* 1972; *Female Trouble* 1974; *Desperate Living* 1977; *Cry-Baby* 1989; *Serial Mom* 1994
Pearce, Vera (1896–1966) *Southern Roses* 1936; *Please Teacher* 1937
Pearl, Barry (1950–) *Grease* 1978; *Avenging Angel* 1985
Pearlman, Stephen (1935–1998) *Rollercoaster* 1977; *Pi* 1997
Pearlstein, Randy (1971–) *Revenge of the Radioactive Reporter* 1990; *Dead Man on Campus* 1998
Pearson, Neil (1959–) *The Secret Rapture* 1993; *Fever Pitch* 1996; *Bridget Jones: the Edge of Reason* 2004
Pearson, Richard (1918–) *The Blue Parrot* 1953; *Guns of Darkness* 1962; *Charlie Bubbles* 1967; *The Rise and Rise of Michael Rimmer* 1970; *It Shouldn't Happen to a Vet* 1979; *Tess* 1979
Peary, Harold (1908–1985) *Look Who's Laughing* 1941; *Here We Go Again* 1942; *Seven Days' Leave* 1942; *Port of Hell* 1954
Pease, Patsy (1956–) *He Knows You're Alone* 1981; *Space Raiders* 1983
Pecheur, Bruce (1942–1973) *Road to Salina* 1969; *Trash* 1970
Pecheur, Sierra *3 Women* 1977; *Bronco Billy* 1980; *Kalifornia* 1993
Peck, Anthony (1947–1996) *Pirates* 1986; *Die Hard with a Vengeance* 1995
Peck, Bob (1945–1999) *Parker* 1984; *The Kitchen Toto* 1987; *On the Black Hill* 1987; *Ladder of Swords* 1988; *Slipstream* 1989; *Jurassic Park* 1993; *Smilla's Feeling for Snow* 1996; *Surviving Picasso* 1996; *FairyTale: a True Story* 1997; *The Miracle Maker* 1999
Peck, Cecilia (1958–) *Torn Apart* 1990; *Ambition* 1991
Peck, Ed (1917–1992) *The Ride to Hangman's Tree* 1967; *The Comic* 1969
Peck, Gregory (1916–2003) *Days of Glory* 1944; *The Keys of the Kingdom* 1944; *Spellbound* 1945; *The Valley of Decision* 1945; *Duel in the Sun* 1946; *The Yearling* 1946; *Gentleman's Agreement* 1947; *The Macomber Affair* 1947; *The Paradine Case* 1947; *Yellow Sky* 1948; *The Great Sinner* 1949; *Twelve O'Clock High* 1949; *The Gunfighter* 1950; *Only the Valiant* 1950; *Captain Horatio Hornblower RN* 1951; *David and Bathsheba* 1951; *The Snows of Kilimanjaro* 1952; *The World in His Arms* 1952; *The Million Pound Note* 1953; *Roman Holiday* 1953; *Night People* 1954; *The Purple Plain* 1954; *The Man in the Gray Flannel Suit* 1956; *Moby Dick* 1956; *Designing Woman* 1957; *The Big Country* 1958; *The Bravados* 1958; *Beloved Infidel* 1959; *On the Beach* 1959; *Pork Chop Hill* 1959; *The Guns of Navarone* 1961; *Cape Fear* 1962; *How the West Was Won* 1962; *To Kill a Mockingbird* 1962; *Captain Newman, MD* 1963; *Behold a Pale Horse* 1964; *Mirage* 1965; *Arabesque* 1966; *The Stalking Moon* 1968; *The Chairman* 1969; *Mackenna's Gold* 1969; *Marooned* 1969; *I Walk the Line* 1970; *Shoot Out* 1971; *Billy Two Hats* 1973; *The Omen* 1976; *MacArthur* 1977; *The Boys from Brazil* 1978; *The Sea Wolves* 1980; *The Scarlet and the Black* 1983; *Amazing Grace and Chuck* 1987; *Old Gringo* 1989; *Cape Fear* 1991; *Other People's Money* 1991
Peck, J Eddie (1958–) *Dangerously Close* 1986; *Curse II: The Bite* 1989; *Lambada* 1990
Peck, Josh (1986–) *Max Keeble's Big Move* 2001; *Mean Creek* 2004
Peck, Tony (1956–) *Brenda Starr* 1989; *Inside Edge* 1992
Peckinpah, Sam (1925–1984) *China 9, Liberty 37* 1978; *The Visitor* 1980
Pecoraro, Susu (1953–) *Camila* 1984; *Sur* 1987
Peeples, Nia (1961–) *North Shore* 1987; *DeepStar Six* 1989; *I Don't Buy Kisses Anymore* 1992; *Improper Conduct* 1994; *Poodle Springs* 1998; *Alone with a Stranger* 2000; *Half Past Dead* 2002
Peers, Joan (1909–1975) *Applause* 1929; *Rain or Shine* 1930; *Tol'able David* 1930; *Parlor, Bedroom and Bath* 1931
Peet, Amanda (1972–) *Touch Me* 1997; *Body Shots* 1999; *Whipped* 1999; *Evil Woman* 2001; *Changing Lanes* 2002; *High Crimes* 2002; *Igby Goes Down* 2002; *Identity* 2003; *Something's Gotta Give* 2003; *Melinda and Melinda* 2004; *The Whole Ten Yards* 2004; *A Lot like Love* 2005
Pegg, Simon (1970–) *Guest House Paradiso* 1999; *Shaun of the Dead* 2004
Peil Sr, Edward *aka* **Peil, Edward** *aka* **Peil Sr, Ed** (1882–1958) *Broken Blossoms* 1919; *Dream Street* 1921; *Blue Steel* 1934; *The Man from Utah* 1934; *The Lone Rider in Ghost Town* 1941
Peirse, Sarah *Heavenly Creatures* 1994; *Rain* 2001
Peldon, Ashley (1984–) *Deceived* 1991; *Drop Dead Fred* 1991; *Waking Up Horton* 1997; *Cats Don't Dance* 1998
Pelé (1940–) *Escape to Victory* 1981; *Hot Shot* 1986; *Mike Bassett: England Manager* 2001
Pelikan, Lisa *Jennifer* 1978; *Ghoulies* 1985; *AWOL* 1990; *Return to the Blue Lagoon* 1991
Pelka, Valentine *Nanou* 1986; *Rowing with the Wind* 1987
Pellegrin, Raymond (1925–) *Manon des Sources* 1952; *Nous Sommes Tous des Assassins* 1952; *Napoléon* 1955; *The Light across the Street* 1956; *Bitter Victory* 1957; *The Mysteries of Paris* 1962; *Imperial Venus* 1963; *Behold a Pale Horse* 1964; *Le Deuxième Souffle* 1966; *Beatrice Cenci* 1969
Pellegrino, Mark *No Holds Barred* 1989; *Prayer of the Rollerboys* 1990; *Mulholland Drive* 2001; *The Hunted* 2002; *Twisted* 2003
Pelletier, Andrée *Outrageous!* 1977; *Walls* 1984; *Bach and Broccoli* 1986
Pelletier, Yves (1960–) *Karmina* 1996; *2 Seconds* 1998
Pellicer, Pina (1935–1964) *Macario* 1960; *One-Eyed Jacks* 1961
Pellonpaa, Matti (1951–1995) *Ariel* 1988; *Leningrad Cowboys Go America* 1989; *Leningrad Cowboys Meet Moses* 1993; *Take Care of Your Scarf, Tatjana* 1994
Peltola, Markku (1956–) *Drifting Clouds* 1996; *Juha* 1999; *The Man without a Past* 2002; *Ten Minutes Older: the Trumpet* 2002
Pempeit, Lilo (1922–1993) *Effi Briest* 1974; *Fear of Fear* 1976
Peña, Candela (1973–) *All about My Mother* 1999; *Take My Eyes* 2003; *Torremolinos 73* 2003
Peña, Elizabeth (1961–) *Crossover Dreams* 1985; *Down and Out in Beverly Hills* 1986; *La Bamba* 1987; **batteries not included* 1987; *Vibes* 1988; *Shannon's Deal* 1989; *Blue Steel* 1990; *Jacob's Ladder* 1990; *The Waterdance* 1991; *Dead Funny* 1995; *Lone Star* 1995; *Aldrich Ames: Traitor Within* 1998; *Dee Snider's Strangeland* 1998; *Rush Hour* 1998; *Impostor* 2001; *Tortilla Soup* 2001; *The Incredibles* 2004
Peña, Pasqual Garcia *The Big Steal* 1949; *The Black Scorpion* 1957
Peña, Vicky (1954–) *The House of Bernarda Alba* 1987; *Secrets of the Heart* 1997
Pendleton, Austin (1940–) *Petulia* 1968; *Catch-22* 1970; *Every Little Crook and Nanny* 1972; *What's Up, Doc?* 1972; *The Thief Who Came to Dinner* 1973; *The Great Smokey Roadblock* 1977; *Starting Over* 1979; *Simon* 1980; *Short Circuit* 1986; *Hello Again* 1987; *The Ballad of the Sad Café* 1991; *Mr Nanny* 1992; *My Cousin Vinny* 1992; *Guarding Tess* 1994; *The Associate* 1996; *The Mirror Has Two Faces* 1996; *The Proprietor* 1996; *Men of Means* 1997; *Trial and Error* 1997; *Joe the King* 1999; *Finding Nemo* 2003; *Uptown Girls* 2003
Pendleton, Nat (1895–1967) *The Big Pond* 1930; *Horse Feathers* 1932; *Lady for a Day* 1933; *Penthouse* 1933; *The Cat's Paw* 1934; *The Gay Bride* 1934; *Manhattan Melodrama* 1934; *The Thin Man* 1934; *Reckless* 1935; *The Great Ziegfeld* 1936; *Gangway* 1937; *Life Begins in College* 1937; *Swing Your Lady* 1937; *Arsene Lupin Returns* 1938; *The Crowd Roars* 1938; *Fast Company* 1938; *The Shopworn Angel* 1938; *Young Dr Kildare* 1938; *Another Thin Man* 1939; *At the Circus* 1939; *Calling Dr Kildare* 1939; *It's a Wonderful World* 1939; *The Secret of Dr Kildare* 1939; *Dr Kildare Goes Home* 1940; *Dr Kildare's Crisis* 1940; *Dr Kildare's Strange Case* 1940; *Northwest Passage* 1940; *Phantom Raiders* 1940; *Calling Dr Gillespie* 1942; *Dr Gillespie's New Assistant* 1942; *The Mad Doctor of Market Street* 1942; *Dr Gillespie's Criminal Case* 1943; *Swing Fever* 1943; *Buck Privates Come Home* 1947; *Scared to Death* 1947
Pendleton, Steve *aka* **Pendleton, Gaylord** (1908–1984) *Internes Can't Take Money* 1937; *The Duke of West Point* 1938
Pendrell, Tony *aka* **Pendrell, Anthony** *Home Sweet Home* 1945; *Blue Scar* 1947
Penella, Emma (1930–) *Padre Nuestro* 1985; *El Amor Brujo* 1986
Penghlis, Thaao (1945–) *Slow Dancing in the Big City* 1978; *Altered States* 1980; *Les Patterson Saves the World* 1987
Penhaligon, Susan (1949–) *No Sex Please – We're British* 1973; *The Land That Time Forgot* 1974; *House of Mortal Sin* 1975; *Nasty Habits* 1976; *Soldier of Orange* 1977; *The Uncanny* 1977; *Patrick* 1978
Penn, Chris *aka* **Penn, Christopher** (1962–) *All the Right Moves* 1983; *Rumble Fish* 1983; *Footloose* 1984; *The Wild Life* 1984; *At Close Range* 1985; *Pale Rider* 1985; *Return from the River Kwai* 1988; *Best of the Best* 1989; *Leather Jackets* 1991; *Reservoir Dogs* 1991; *Best of the Best II* 1992; *Beethoven's 2nd* 1993; *Josh and SAM* 1993; *The Music of Chance* 1993; *The Pickle* 1993; *Short Cuts* 1993; *True Romance* 1993; *Imaginary Crimes* 1994; *Fist of the North Star* 1995; *To Wong Foo, Thanks for Everything, Julie Newmar* 1995; *Under the Hula Moon* 1995; *The Boys Club* 1996; *The Funeral* 1996; *Mulholland Falls* 1996; *Liar* 1997; *One Tough Cop* 1998; *Rush Hour* 1998; *Corky Romano* 2001; *Kiss Kiss (Bang Bang)* 2001; *Murder by Numbers* 2002; *Stealing Harvard* 2002; *After the Sunset* 2004; *Starsky & Hutch* 2004
Penn, Kal (1977–) *American Desi* 2001; *Van Wilder: Party Liaison* 2002; *Love Don't Cost a Thing* 2003; *Harold & Kumar Get the Munchies* 2004; *A Lot like Love* 2005
Penn, Leo (1921–1998) *The Undercover Man* 1949; *Sixth and Main* 1977
Penn, Leonard (1907–1975) *Man-Proof* 1937; *The Girl of the Golden West* 1938; *The Dead Don't Dream* 1948
Penn, Sean (1960–) *Taps* 1981; *Fast Times at Ridgemont High* 1982; *Bad Boys* 1983; *Crackers* 1984; *Racing with the Moon* 1984; *At Close Range* 1985; *The Falcon and the Snowman* 1985; *Shanghai Surprise* 1986; *Colors* 1988; *Cool Blue* 1988; *Judgment in Berlin* 1988; *Casualties of War* 1989; *We're No Angels* 1989; *State of Grace* 1990; *Carlito's Way* 1993; *Dead Man Walking* 1995; *Loved* 1996; *The Game* 1997; *Pool Girl* 1997; *She's So Lovely* 1997; *U Turn* 1997; *Hurlyburly* 1998; *The Thin Red Line* 1998; *Up at the Villa* 1998; *Being John Malkovich* 1999;

Sweet and Lowdown 1999; *Before Night Falls* 2000; *The Weight of Water* 2000; *Dogtown and Z-Boys* 2001; *I Am Sam* 2001; *It's All about Love* 2002; *Mystic River* 2003; *21 Grams* 2003; *The Assassination of Richard Nixon* 2004; *The Interpreter* 2005

Pennell, Jon *aka* **Pennell, John** *Two Came Back* 1997; *Storm Catcher* 1999

Pennell, Larry *Seven Angry Men* 1955; *The Devil's Hairpin* 1957; *The FBI Story* 1959; *The Borrower* 1989

Penner, Joe (1904–1941) *New Faces of 1937* 1937; *Go Chase Yourself* 1938; *The Boys from Syracuse* 1940

Penner, Jonathan *The Last Supper* 1995; *Wedding Bell Blues* 1996; *Let the Devil Wear Black* 1999

Pennick, Jack (1895–1964) *Lady from Louisiana* 1941; *Operation Pacific* 1951; *The Beast from 20,000 Fathoms* 1953

Pennock, Christopher *aka* **Pennock, Chris** *Night of Dark Shadows* 1971; *The Great Texas Dynamite Chase* 1976; *Frances* 1982

Penny, Joe (1956–) *The Little Unicorn* 1998; *The Prophet's Game* 1999

Penot, Jacques (1959–) *Le Cri du Hibou* 1987; *The Revolving Doors* 1988

Penrose, John (1914–1983) *Freedom Radio* 1940; *Kind Hearts and Coronets* 1949; *Street of Shadows* 1953

Penry-Jones, Rupert (1970–) *Hilary and Jackie* 1998; *Virtual Sexuality* 1999; *Charlotte Gray* 2001; *The Four Feathers* 2002

Peppard, George (1928–1994) *The Strange One* 1957; *Pork Chop Hill* 1959; *Home from the Hill* 1960; *The Subterraneans* 1960; *Breakfast at Tiffany's* 1961; *How the West Was Won* 1962; *The Victors* 1963; *The Carpetbaggers* 1964; *Operation Crossbow* 1965; *The Third Day* 1965; *The Blue Max* 1966; *Tobruk* 1966; *Rough Night in Jericho* 1967; *House of Cards* 1968; *New Face in Hell* 1968; *What's So Bad About Feeling Good?* 1968; *Pendulum* 1969; *Cannon for Cordoba* 1970; *The Executioner* 1970; *One More Train to Rob* 1971; *The Groundstar Conspiracy* 1972; *Newman's Law* 1974; *Damnation Alley* 1977; *Five Days from Home* 1978; *From Hell to Victory* 1979; *Torn between Two Lovers* 1979; *Battle beyond the Stars* 1980; *Treasure of the Yankee Zephyr* 1981; *Target Eagle* 1982; *Silence like Glass* 1989

Pepper, Barbara (1915–1969) *Our Daily Bread* 1934; *Kiss Me, Stupid* 1964

Pepper, Barry (1970–) *Saving Private Ryan* 1998; *Battlefield Earth* 2000; *Knockaround Guys* 2001; *61** 2001; *25th Hour* 2002; *We Were Soldiers* 2002

Pêra, Marília (1943–) *Pixote* 1981; *Mixed Blood* 1984; *Central Station* 1998

Perabo, Piper (1977–) *The Adventures of Rocky & Bullwinkle* 1999; *Whiteboys* 1999; *Coyote Ugly* 2000; *Slap Her, She's French!* 2001; *Cheaper by the Dozen* 2003; *The I Inside* 2003

Percival, Lance (1933–) *Carry On Cruising* 1962; *Twice round the Daffodils* 1962; *The Big Job* 1965; *Joey Boy* 1965; *Yellow Submarine* 1968; *Darling Lili* 1970; *Too Late the Hero* 1970; *Up Pompeii* 1971; *Up the Chastity Belt* 1971; *Our Miss Fred* 1972; *Up the Front* 1972

Percy, Esme (1887–1957) *Murder* 1930; *Bitter Sweet* 1933; *Lord Edgware Dies* 1934; *Love, Life and Laughter* 1934; *Nell Gwyn* 1934; *An Old Spanish Custom* 1935; *Accused* 1936; *Land without Music* 1936; *Song of Freedom* 1936; *21 Days* 1937

Perego, Didi *aka* **Sullivan, Didi** (1937–1993) *Caltiki, the Immortal Monster* 1959; *Kapo* 1959; *The Appointment* 1968

Perez, Rosie (1964–) *Do the Right Thing* 1989; *Night on Earth* 1992; *White Men Can't Jump* 1992; *Fearless* 1993; *Untamed Heart* 1993; *It Could Happen to You* 1994; *Somebody to Love* 1994; *Perdita Durango* 1997; *Subway Stories: Tales from the Underground* 1997; *The 24 Hour Woman* 1999; *The Road to El Dorado* 2000; *Human Nature* 2001; *Riding in Cars with Boys* 2001

Perez, Vincent (1965–) *Cyrano de Bergerac* 1990; *Indochine* 1991; *La Reine Margot* 1994; *Beyond the Clouds* 1995; *The Crow: City of Angels* 1996; *Amy Foster* 1997; *Le Bossu* 1997; *Talk of Angels* 1998; *Those Who Love Me Can Take the Train* 1998; *Time Regained* 1999; *I Dreamed of Africa* 2000; *Le Libertin* 2000; *Bride of the Wind* 2001; *Queen of the Damned* 2002

Périer, François (1919–2002) *Man about Town* 1947; *Orphée* 1950; *Secrets d'Alcove* 1954; *Gervaise* 1956; *Nights of Cabiria* 1957; *Too Many Lovers* 1957; *Le Samouraï* 1967; *Z* 1968; *The Red Circle* 1970; *Juste avant la Nuit* 1971; *Stavisky* 1974; *Doctor Françoise Gailland* 1975; *The Police War* 1979; *Soigne Ta Droite* 1986

Perkins, Anthony (1932–1992) *The Actress* 1953; *Friendly Persuasion* 1956; *Fear Strikes Out* 1957; *The Lonely Man* 1957; *This Angry Age* 1957; *The Tin Star* 1957; *Desire under the Elms* 1958; *The Matchmaker* 1958; *Green Mansions* 1959; *On the Beach* 1959; *Psycho* 1960; *Goodbye Again* 1961; *Phaedra* 1962; *The Trial* 1962; *Five Miles to Midnight* 1963; *The Fool Killer* 1965; *The Champagne Murders* 1966; *Is Paris Burning?* 1966; *Pretty Poison* 1968; *Catch-22* 1970; *WUSA* 1970; *Someone behind the Door* 1971; *Ten Days' Wonder* 1971; *The Life and Times of Judge Roy Bean* 1972; *Play It As It Lays* 1972; *Lovin' Molly* 1974; *Murder on the Orient Express* 1974; *Mahogany* 1975; *Les Misérables* 1978; *Remember My Name* 1978; *The Black Hole* 1979; *North Sea Hijack* 1979; *Winter Kills* 1979; *Psycho II* 1983; *Crimes of Passion* 1984; *Psycho III* 1986; *Destroyer* 1988; *Edge of Sanity* 1989; *Psycho IV: the Beginning* 1990; *In the Deep Woods* 1992

Perkins, Clare *Ladybird Ladybird* 1994; *Bullet Boy* 2004

Perkins, Elizabeth (1960–) *About Last Night...* 1986; *From the Hip* 1987; *Big* 1988; *Sweet Hearts Dance* 1988; *Avalon* 1990; *Love at Large* 1990; *Over Her Dead Body* 1990; *The Doctor* 1991; *He Said, She Said* 1991; *For Their Own Good* 1993; *Indian Summer* 1993; *The Flintstones* 1994; *Miracle on 34th Street* 1994; *Moonlight and Valentino* 1995; *I'm Losing You* 1998; *Crazy in Alabama* 1999; *28 Days* 2000; *Cats & Dogs* 2001; *The Ring Two* 2004

Perkins, Millie (1938–) *The Diary of Anne Frank* 1959; *Wild in the Country* 1961; *Ensign Pulver* 1964; *Ride in the Whirlwind* 1966; *The Shooting* 1967; *Wild in the Streets* 1968; *Table for Five* 1983; *At Close Range* 1985; *Slam Dance* 1987; *Two Moon Junction* 1988; *Murder of Innocence* 1993

Perkins, Osgood (1892–1937) *Tarnished Lady* 1931; *Scarface* 1932; *Madame Du Barry* 1934; *I Dream Too Much* 1935; *Gold Diggers of 1937* 1936

Perle, Rebecca *Tightrope* 1984; *Not of This Earth* 1988

Perlich, Max (1968–) *Drugstore Cowboy* 1989; *Knife Edge* 1990; *The Butcher's Wife* 1991; *Rush* 1991; *Born Yesterday* 1993; *Dead Beat* 1994; *Shake, Rattle and Rock* 1994; *Georgia* 1995; *The Brave* 1997; *Sometimes They Come Back... for More* 1998

Perlman, Itzhak (1945–) *Fantasia 2000* 1999; *Music of the Heart* 1999

Perlman, Rhea (1948–) *My Little Pony* 1986; *Over Her Dead Body* 1990; *Ted & Venus* 1991; *Paydirt* 1992; *Shattered Family* 1993; *We're Back! A Dinosaur's Story* 1993; *Canadian Bacon* 1995; *Carpool* 1996; *Matilda* 1996; *Sunset Park* 1996

Perlman, Ron (1950–) *Quest for Fire* 1981; *The Ice Pirates* 1984; *The Name of the Rose* 1986; *Cronos* 1992; *Romeo Is Bleeding* 1992; *Sleepwalkers* 1992; *The Adventures of Huck Finn* 1993; *When the Bough Breaks* 1993; *Police Academy: Mission to Moscow* 1994; *The City of Lost Children* 1995; *Body Armor* 1996; *The Island of Dr Moreau* 1996; *Alien: Resurrection* 1997; *Prince Valiant* 1997; *Tinseltown* 1997; *An American Tail: the Treasure of Manhattan Island* 1998; *I Woke Up Early the Day I Died* 1998; *Happy, Texas* 1999; *Primal Force* 1999; *Supreme Sanction* 1999; *Price of Glory* 2000; *Titan AE* 2000; *Enemy at the Gates* 2001; *Blade II* 2002; *Star Trek: Nemesis* 2002; *Hellboy* 2004

Pernel, Florence (1966–) *Three Colours Blue* 1993; *The Cow and the President* 2000

Perreau, Gigi (1941–) *For Heaven's Sake* 1950; *Never a Dull Moment* 1950; *The Lady Pays Off* 1951; *Weekend with Father* 1951; *Has Anybody Seen My Gal?* 1952; *Dance with Me Henry* 1956; *There's Always Tomorrow* 1956; *The Cool and the Crazy* 1958; *Wild Heritage* 1958; *Girls' Town* 1959; *Look in Any Window* 1961

Perrey, Mireille *Madame de...* 1953; *The Umbrellas of Cherbourg* 1964

Perri, Paul *Delta Force 2* 1990; *Memoirs of an Invisible Man* 1992

Perrier, Mireille (1959–) *Chocolat* 1988; *A World without Pity* 1989; *Toto Le Héros* 1991; *A Shadow of Doubt* 1992

Perrier, Olivier (1940–) *Les Destinées Sentimentales* 2000; *Read My Lips* 2001

Perrin, Jacques (1941–) *Z* 1968; *The Magic Donkey* 1970; *Blanche* 1971; *Love Songs* 1984; *Cinema Paradiso* 1988; *Flight of the Innocent* 1993; *Love in Ambush* 1997; *Winged Migration* 2001; *Eugenio* 2002

Perrine, Valerie (1944–) *Slaughterhouse-Five* 1972; *The Last American Hero* 1973; *Lenny* 1974; *WC Fields and Me* 1976; *Mr Billion* 1977; *The Electric Horseman* 1979; *The Magician of Lublin* 1979; *Can't Stop the Music* 1980; *Superman II* 1980; *Agency* 1981; *The Border* 1981; *Water* 1985; *Maid to Order* 1987; *Bright Angel* 1990; *Boiling Point* 1993; *Curtain Call* 1998

Perrineau, Harold *aka* **Perrineau Jr, Harold** *Smoke* 1995; *Blood and Wine* 1996; *William Shakespeare's Romeo + Juliet* 1996; *The Edge* 1997; *The Best Man* 1999; *Woman on Top* 2000

Perrins, Leslie (1902–1962) *Scotland Yard Mystery* 1933; *D'Ye Ken John Peel?* 1934; *Lord Edgware Dies* 1934; *The Man Who Changed His Name* 1934; *Open All Night* 1934; *Tudor Rose* 1936; *A Run for Your Money* 1949

Perrot, François (1924–) *Les Innocents aux Mains Sales* 1975; *Le Choc* 1982; *Life and Nothing But* 1989; *Merci la Vie* 1991

Perry, Felton (1955–) *Magnum Force* 1973; *Mean Dog Blues* 1978

Perry, Joan (1911–1996) *Meet Nero Wolfe* 1936; *Start Cheering* 1938; *Blind Alley* 1939; *Strange Alibi* 1941

Perry, John Bennett (1941–) *Lipstick* 1976; *Danielle Steel's Secrets* 1992; *Fools Rush In* 1997

Perry, Linda (1912–2001) *The Case of the Stuttering Bishop* 1937; *They Won't Forget* 1937

Perry, Luke (1966–) *Terminal Bliss* 1990; *Scorchers* 1991; *Buffy the Vampire Slayer* 1992; *8 Seconds* 1994; *Normal Life* 1995; *American Strays* 1996; *The Fifth Element* 1997; *Storm* 1999; *The Enemy* 2000; *Fogbound* 2002

Perry, Matthew *aka* **Perry, Matthew L** (1969–) *A Night in the Life of Jimmy Reardon* 1988; *Getting In* 1994; *Fools Rush In* 1997; *Almost Heroes* 1998; *Three to Tango* 1999; *The Whole Nine Yards* 2000; *Serving Sara* 2002; *The Whole Ten Yards* 2004

Perry, Roger *The Loves of Count Iorga, Vampire* 1970; *The Return of Count Yorga* 1971; *The Thing with Two Heads* 1972; *Roller Boogie* 1979

Persbrandt, Mikael *The Last Contract* 1998; *Dragonflies* 2001

Perschy, Maria (1938–2004) *The Password Is Courage* 1962; *Man's Favorite Sport?* 1964; *633 Squadron* 1964; *The Desperate Ones* 1967; *Murders in the Rue Morgue* 1971

Persky, Lisa Jane *aka* **Persky, Lisa** (1955–) *The Great Santini* 1979; *Breathless* 1983; *The Sure Thing* 1985; *The Big Easy* 1986; *When Harry Met Sally...* 1989; *Coneheads* 1993; *Pontiac Moon* 1994; *Dead Funny* 1995

Persoff, Nehemiah (1920–) *The Wrong Man* 1956; *Men in War* 1957; *This Angry Age* 1957; *The Badlanders* 1958; *Al Capone* 1959; *Day of the Outlaw* 1959; *Green Mansions* 1959; *Never Steal Anything Small* 1959; *Some Like It Hot* 1959; *The Big Show* 1961; *The Comancheros* 1961; *The Hook* 1962; *A Global Affair* 1964; *Panic in the City* 1968; *The Girl Who Knew Too Much* 1969; *Mrs Pollifax – Spy* 1970; *Psychic Killer* 1975; *Yentl* 1983; *An American Tail* 1986; *An American Tail: Fievel Goes West* 1991; *An American Tail: the Treasure of Manhattan Island* 1998; *An American Tail: the Mystery of the Night Monster* 2000

Pertwee, Jon (1919–1996) *Murder at the Windmill* 1949; *Mr Drake's Duck* 1950; *Will Any Gentleman...?* 1953; *A Yank in Ermine* 1955; *Nearly a Nasty Accident* 1961; *Ladies Who Do* 1963; *Carry On Cowboy* 1965; *I've Gotta Horse* 1965; *Carry On Screaming* 1966; *The House That Dripped Blood* 1971; *Adventures of a Private Eye* 1977; *Wombling Free* 1977; *The Boys in Blue* 1983; *Carry On Columbus* 1992

Pertwee, Sean (1964–) *Dirty Weekend* 1992; *Leon the Pig Farmer* 1992; *Shopping* 1993; *ID* 1994; *Blue Juice* 1995; *Event Horizon* 1997; *Stiff Upper Lips* 1997; *Talos the Mummy* 1997; *Soldier* 1998; *Love, Honour and Obey* 2000; *7 Days to Live* 2000; *Dog Soldiers* 2001; *The 51st State* 2001; *Equilibrium* 2002

Perugorría, Jorge (1965–) *Strawberry and Chocolate* 1993; *Guantanamera* 1995

Pesci, Joe (1943–) *Death Collector* 1976; *Raging Bull* 1980; *Eureka* 1982; *I'm Dancing as Fast as I Can* 1982; *Easy Money* 1983; *Once upon a Time in America* 1984; *Man on Fire* 1987; *Moonwalker* 1988; *Catchfire* 1989; *Lethal Weapon 2* 1989; *Betsy's Wedding* 1990; *GoodFellas* 1990; *Home Alone* 1990; *JFK* 1991; *The Super* 1991; *Home Alone 2: Lost in New York* 1992; *Lethal Weapon 3* 1992; *My Cousin Vinny* 1992; *The Public Eye* 1992; *A Bronx Tale* 1993; *Jimmy Hollywood* 1994; *With Honors* 1994; *Casino* 1995; *8 Heads in a Duffel Bag* 1997; *Gone Fishin'* 1997; *Lethal Weapon 4* 1998

Pescia, Lisa *Body Chemistry* 1990; *Body Chemistry 2: Voice of a Stranger* 1992

Petelius, Pirkka-Pekka (1953–) *The Unknown Soldier* 1983; *Hamlet Goes Business* 1987

Peters, Bernadette (1948–) *Ace Eli and Rodger of the Skies* 1973; *Vigilante Force* 1975; *Silent Movie* 1976; *WC Fields and Me* 1976; *The Jerk* 1979; *Heartbeeps* 1981; *Pennies from Heaven* 1981; *Annie* 1982; *Pink Cadillac* 1989; *Slaves of New York* 1989; *Alice* 1990; *Impromptu* 1991; *Anastasia* 1997; *Beauty and the Beast: the Enchanted Christmas* 1997; *The Odyssey* 1997; *Rodgers & Hammerstein's Cinderella* 1997; *What the Deaf Man Heard* 1997; *It Runs in the Family* 2002

Peters, Brock (1927–) *Carmen Jones* 1954; *Porgy and Bess* 1959; *The L-Shaped Room* 1962; *To Kill a Mockingbird* 1962; *Heavens Above!* 1963; *Major Dundee* 1965; *The Pawnbroker* 1965; *The Incident* 1967; *Ace High* 1968; *New Face in Hell* 1968; *The McMasters* 1970; *Black Girl* 1972; *Slaughter's Big Rip-Off* 1973; *Soylent Green* 1973; *Lost in the Stars* 1974; *Alligator II: the Mutation* 1991; *The Importance of Being Earnest* 1992

Peters, Clarke *Silver Dream Racer* 1980; *Outland* 1981; *Mona Lisa* 1986; *Death Train* 1993

Peters Jr, House (1916–) *Under California Stars* 1948; *Winning of the West* 1953

Peters, Jean (1926–2000) *Captain from Castile* 1947; *It Happens Every Spring* 1949; *Love That Brute* 1950; *Anne of the Indies* 1951; *As Young as You Feel* 1951; *O Henry's Full House* 1952; *Viva Zapata!* 1952; *Wait 'til the Sun Shines, Nellie* 1952; *Niagara* 1953; *Pickup on South Street* 1953; *Apache* 1954; *Broken Lance* 1954; *Three Coins in the Fountain* 1954; *A Man Called Peter* 1955

Peters, Kelly Jean *Any Wednesday* 1966; *Little Big Man* 1970; *Pocket Money* 1972; *Ace Eli and Rodger of the Skies* 1973; *Witches' Brew* 1979

Peters, Lauri *Mr Hobbs Takes a Vacation* 1962; *Summer Holiday* 1962; *For Love of Ivy* 1968

Peters, Ralph (1902–1959) *You Belong to Me* 1941; *Meeting at Midnight* 1944

Peters, Scott (1930–1994) *Suicide Battalion* 1958; *The Girl Hunters* 1963

Peters, Susan (1921–1952) *The Big Shot* 1942; *Dr Gillespie's New Assistant* 1942; *Random Harvest* 1942; *Young Ideas* 1943; *Keep Your Powder Dry* 1945

Peters, Werner (1918–1971) *The Thousand Eyes of Dr Mabuse* 1960; *The Door with Seven Locks* 1962; *36 Hours* 1964; *Dead Run* 1967

Petersen, Colin (1946–) *Smiley* 1956; *A Cry from the Streets* 1957; *The Scamp* 1957

Petersen, Stewart *Seven Alone* 1974; *Where the Red Fern Grows* 1974; *Against a Crooked Sky* 1975

Petersen, William L *aka* **Petersen, William** (1953–) *To Live and Die in LA* 1985; *Manhunter* 1986; *Amazing Grace and Chuck* 1987; *Cousins* 1989; *Young Guns II* 1990; *Hard Promises* 1991; *Passed Away* 1992; *Fear* 1996; *12 Angry Men* 1997; *The Rat Pack* 1998; *The Contender* 2000; *The Skulls* 2000

Peterson, Amanda (1971–) *Explorers* 1985; *Can't Buy Me Love* 1987; *Listen to Me* 1989

Peterson, Cassandra (1951–) *Allan Quatermain and the Lost City of Gold* 1987; *Elvira, Mistress of the Dark* 1988

Peterson, Dorothy (1900–1979) *The Beast of the City* 1932; *Forbidden* 1932; *Payment Deferred* 1932; *The Country Doctor* 1936; *Confession* 1937; *Girl Loves Boy* 1937; *Lillian Russell* 1940; *Too Many Husbands* 1940; *The Man in the Trunk* 1942

Peterson, Kimberlee (1980–) *Homecoming* 1996; *Primal Force* 1999

Peterson, Lenka (1925–) *The Phenix City Story* 1955; *Black like Me* 1964; *Homer* 1970; *Pals* 1986

Peterson, Marion *Lapse of Memory* 1992; *For Better and for Worse* 1993

Peterson, Paul (1945–) *The Happiest Millionaire* 1967; *Journey to Shiloh* 1967; *A Time for Killing* 1967

Peterson, Vidal *Something Wicked This Way Comes* 1983; *Wizards of the Lost Kingdom* 1985

Petit-Jacques, Isabelle *The Girl on the Bridge* 1999; *L'Homme du Train* 2002

Petrenko, Alexei (1938–) *Agony* 1975; *The Barber of Siberia* 1999

Petri, Mario (1922–1985) *Achilles* 1962; *The Secret Mark of D'Artagnan* 1962; *The Executioner of Venice* 1963; *Sandokan against the Leopard of Sarawak* 1964

Petrie, Hay (1895–1948) *The Wandering Jew* 1933; *The Old Curiosity Shop* 1934; *Conquest of the Air* 1936; *21 Days* 1937; *Crimes at the Dark House* 1939; *Contraband* 1940; *Pastor Hall* 1940; *The Thief of Bagdad* 1940; *The Ghost of St Michael's* 1941; *The Great Mr Handel* 1942; *A Canterbury Tale* 1944

Petrie, Howard (1906–1968) *Walk Softly, Stranger* 1949; *Rocky Mountain* 1950; *Cattle Drive* 1951; *Pony Soldier* 1952; *The Wild North* 1952; *The Bob Mathias Story* 1954; *Border River* 1954; *The Bounty Hunter* 1954; *Seven Brides for Seven Brothers* 1954; *The Maverick Queen* 1955

Petrovich, Ivan (1894–1962) *Alraune* 1927; *The Garden of Allah* 1927

Petrovitch, Michael *Neither the Sea nor the Sand* 1972; *Tales That Witness Madness* 1973; *Turkey Shoot* 1981

Petruzzi, Joe *Dingo* 1991; *Paws* 1997

Pettet, Joanna (1944–) *The Group* 1966; *The Night of the Generals* 1966; *Casino Royale* 1967; *Robbery* 1967; *The Best House in London* 1968; *Blue* 1968; *Welcome to Arrow Beach* 1974; *The Evil* 1978

Pettiet, Christopher (1976–2000) *Horses and Champions* 1994; *Acts of Love* 1995

Pettingell, Frank (1891–1966) *Sing as We Go* 1934; *Sailing Along* 1938; *Busman's Honeymoon* 1940; *Gaslight* 1940; *The Goose Steps Out* 1942; *Get Cracking* 1943; *Gaiety George* 1946; *Value for Money* 1955; *Trial and Error* 1962

Petty, Lori (1963–) *Cadillac Man* 1990; *Point Break* 1991; *A League of Their Own* 1992; *Free Willy* 1993; *Poetic Justice* 1993; *In the Army Now* 1994; *The Glass Shield* 1995; *Tank Girl* 1995; *Countdown* 1996; *Relax... It's Just Sex* 1998; *Firetrap* 2001

Petty, Tom (1950–) *FM* 1977; *The Postman* 1997

Pevney, Joseph (1911–) *Nocturne* 1946; *Body and Soul* 1947; *The Street with No Name* 1948; *Thieves' Highway* 1949

Peyser, Penny (1951–) *The Frisco Kid* 1979; *The In-Laws* 1979; *Still Crazy like a Fox* 1987

Pfeiffer, Dedee (1965–) *Dangerously Close* 1986; *Vamp* 1986; *The Allnighter* 1987; *Brothers in Arms* 1988; *House III: The Horror Show* 1989; *Red Surf* 1990; *A Row of Crows* 1991; *Running Cool* 1993; *Up Close & Personal* 1996

Pfeiffer, Michelle (1957–) *Falling in Love Again* 1980; *Charlie Chan and the Curse of the Dragon Queen* 1981; *Grease 2* 1982; *Scarface* 1983; *Into the Night* 1985; *Ladyhawke* 1985; *Sweet Liberty* 1986; *Amazon Women on the Moon* 1987; *The Witches of Eastwick* 1987; *Dangerous Liaisons* 1988; *Married to the Mob* 1988; *Tequila Sunrise* 1988; *The Fabulous Baker Boys* 1989; *The Russia House* 1990; *Frankie & Johnny* 1991; *Batman Returns* 1992; *Love Field* 1992; *The Age of Innocence* 1993; *Wolf* 1994; *Dangerous Minds* 1995; *One Fine Day* 1996; *To Gillian on Her 37th Birthday* 1996; *Up Close & Personal* 1996; *A Thousand Acres* 1997; *The Prince of Egypt* 1998; *The Deep End of the Ocean* 1999; *A Midsummer Night's Dream* 1999; *The Story of Us* 1999; *What Lies Beneath* 2000; *I Am Sam* 2001; *White Oleander* 2002; *Sinbad: Legend of the Seven Seas* 2003

Pflug, Jo Ann (1947–) *MASH* 1969; *Catlow* 1971; *Where Does It Hurt?* 1971

Phelan, Brian *The Kitchen* 1961; *Four in the Morning* 1965

Phelan, Shawn (1975–1998) *Caroline?* 1990; *Breaking the Rules* 1992

Phelps, Lee (1893–1953) *Anna Christie* 1930; *Chained* 1934

Phelps, Peter (1960–) *Undercover* 1983; *The Lighthorsemen* 1987; *Starlight Hotel* 1987; *Rough Diamonds* 1994; *Blackwater Trail* 1995

Phifer, Mekhi (1975–) *Clockers* 1995; *High School High* 1996; *Soul Food* 1997; *I Still Know What You Did Last Summer* 1998; *A Lesson Before Dying* 1999; *O* 2001; *8 Mile* 2002; *Honey* 2003; *Dawn of the Dead* 2004

Philbin, John (1965–) *Children of the Corn* 1984; *Return of the Living Dead* 1984; *North Shore* 1987; *Shy People* 1987; *Point Break* 1991

Philbin, Mary (1903–1993) *The Phantom of the Opera* 1925; *The Man Who Laughs* 1928

Philbrook, James (1924–1982) *Son of a Gunfighter* 1964; *The Thin Red Line* 1964

Philipe, Gérard (1922–1959) *Devil in the Flesh* 1947; *La Beauté du Diable* 1949; *Fanfan la Tulipe* 1951; *Les Belles de Nuit* 1952; *The Seven Deadly Sins* 1952; *The Proud Ones* 1953; *Royal Affairs in Versailles* 1953; *Knave of Hearts* 1954; *Le Rouge et le Noir* 1954; *Les Grandes Manoeuvres* 1955; *Montparnasse 19* 1958; *La Fièvre Monte à el Pao* 1959; *Les Liaisons Dangereuses* 1959

Philippe, Andre *Alex in Wonderland* 1970; *Black Belt Jones* 1974; *Goodbye, Norma Jean* 1976

Philips, Gina *aka* **Phillips, Gina** (1975–) *Unforgivable* 1995; *Jeepers Creepers* 2001

Philips, Lee (1927–1999) *Peyton Place* 1957; *The Hunters* 1958; *Middle of the Night* 1959; *Tess of the Storm Country* 1960; *Psychomania* 1964

Philips, Mary *aka* **Phillips, Mary** (1901–1975) *A Farewell to Arms* 1932; *The Bride Wore Red* 1937; *Mannequin* 1937; *Captain Eddie* 1945; *Leave Her to Heaven* 1945; *Dear Ruth* 1947; *A Woman's Secret* 1949

Philliber, John (1872–1944) *It Happened Tomorrow* 1944; *Summer Storm* 1944

Phillippe, Ryan (1974–) *Lifeform* 1996; *White Squall* 1996; *I Know What You Did Last Summer* 1997; *54* 1998; *Homegrown* 1998; *Playing by Heart* 1998; *Cruel Intentions* 1999; *Company Man* 2000; *The Way of the Gun* 2000; *Antitrust* 2001; *Gosford Park* 2001; *Igby Goes Down* 2002; *The I Inside* 2003; *Crash* 2004

Phillips, Barney (1913–1982) *I Was a Teenage Werewolf* 1957; *Gang War* 1958

Phillips, Bijou (1980–) *Bully* 2001; *Octane* 2003; *The Door in the Floor* 2004

Phillips, Bobbie (1972–) *Back in Action* 1993; *TC 2000* 1993; *Carnival of Souls* 1999

Phillips, Chris *Felix the Cat: the Movie* 1989; *Doug's 1st Movie* 1999

Phillips, Chynna (1968–) *Some Kind of Wonderful* 1987; *The Invisible Kid* 1988

Phillips, Conrad (1930–) *The Last Page* 1952; *Stranger's Meeting* 1957; *Witness in the Dark* 1959; *Circus of Horrors* 1960; *Sons and Lovers* 1960; *The Shadow of the Cat* 1961; *Dead Man's Evidence* 1962; *Don't Talk to Strange Men* 1962; *Impact* 1963; *Stopover Forever* 1964

Phillips, Eddie (1899–1969) *The Thirteenth Guest* 1932; *Champagne Charlie* 1944

Phillips, Ethan (1955–) *Lean on Me* 1989; *Green Card* 1990

Phillips, Grace *All the Vermeers in New York* 1990; *Truth or Consequences, NM* 1997

Phillips, Gregory *I Could Go On Singing* 1963; *I Start Counting* 1970

Phillips, Greigh *The Brain Eaters* 1958; *Forbidden Island* 1959

Phillips, Jean (?–1970) *Among the Living* 1941; *Dr Broadway* 1942

Phillips (1), John (1915–1995) *Floods of Fear* 1958; *Man in the Moon* 1960; *Offbeat* 1960; *Romanoff and Juliet* 1961; *The Mummy's Shroud* 1966

Phillips, Jonathan *aka* **Phillips, Johnny** (1963–) *Killing Dad* 1989; *One for the Road* 2003

Phillips, Julianne (1960–) *Odd Jobs* 1986; *Seven Hours to Judgment* 1988; *Fletch Lives* 1989; *Skin Deep* 1989; *Big Bully* 1996

Phillips, Leslie (1924–) *The Sound Barrier* 1952; *The Limping Man* 1953; *The Big Money* 1956; *Les Girls* 1957; *High Flight* 1957; *Just My Luck* 1957; *The Smallest Show on Earth* 1957; *I Was Monty's Double* 1958; *The Angry Hills* 1959; *Carry On Nurse* 1959; *Carry On Teacher* 1959; *The Man Who Liked Funerals* 1959; *The Navy Lark* 1959; *The Night We Dropped a Clanger* 1959; *This Other Eden* 1959; *Carry On Constable* 1960; *Doctor in Love* 1960; *Inn for Trouble* 1960; *No Kidding* 1960; *Please Turn Over* 1960; *Watch Your Stern* 1960; *In the Doghouse* 1961; *Raising the Wind* 1961; *Very Important Person* 1961; *Crooks Anonymous* 1962; *The Fast Lady* 1963; *Father Came Too* 1963; *You Must Be Joking!* 1965; *Doctor in Clover* 1966; *Maroc 7* 1966; *Some Will, Some Won't* 1969; *Doctor in Trouble* 1970; *The Magnificent Seven Deadly Sins* 1971; *Not Now Darling* 1972; *Don't Just Lie There, Say Something!* 1973; *Not Now, Comrade* 1976; *Empire of the Sun* 1987; *Scandal* 1988; *King Ralph* 1991; *Carry On Columbus* 1992; *August* 1995; *Caught in the Act* 1996; *The Jackal* 1997; *Saving Grace* 2000; *Harry Potter and the Philosopher's Stone* 2001; *Lara Croft: Tomb Raider* 2001; *Thunderpants* 2002; *Churchill: the Hollywood Years* 2004

Phillips, Lou Diamond (1962–) *La Bamba* 1987; *Dakota* 1987; *Stand and Deliver* 1988; *Young Guns* 1988; *Disorganized Crime* 1989; *Renegades* 1989; *The First Power* 1990; *A Show of Force* 1990; *Young Guns II* 1990; *Ambition* 1991; *The Dark Wind* 1991; *Shadow of the Wolf* 1992; *Boulevard* 1994; *Sioux City* 1994; *Courage under Fire* 1996; *Another Day in Paradise* 1998; *The Big Hit* 1998; *Bats* 1999; *Brokedown Palace* 1999; *A Better Way to Die* 2000; *Hangman* 2000; *Picking Up the Pieces* 2000; *Supernova* 2000; *Stark Raving Mad* 2002; *Hollywood Homicide* 2003

Phillips, Mackenzie (1959–) *American Graffiti* 1973; *Rafferty and the Gold Dust Twins* 1974; *More American Graffiti* 1979; *Love Child* 1982

Phillips, Michelle (1944–) *The Last Movie* 1971; *Dillinger* 1973; *Valentino* 1977; *Bloodline* 1979; *The Man with Bogart's Face* 1980; *Savage Harvest* 1981; *Scissors* 1991; *Army of One* 1993

Phillips, Robin (1942–) *Decline and Fall... of a Birdwatcher* 1968; *Two Gentlemen Sharing* 1969

Phillips, Sally (1970–) *Birthday Girl* 2001; *Bridget Jones's Diary* 2001; *Tooth* 2003; *Bridget Jones: the Edge of Reason* 2004

Phillips, Sian (1934–) *Becket* 1964; *Young Cassidy* 1965; *Goodbye, Mr Chips* 1969; *Laughter in the Dark* 1969; *Murphy's War* 1971; *Under Milk Wood* 1971; *Clash of the Titans* 1981; *Valmont* 1989; *The Age of Innocence* 1993; *House of America* 1996

Phillips, William "Bill" *aka* **Phillips, William** (1908–1957) *The Hidden Eye* 1945; *Red Light* 1949; *Cavalry Scout* 1951; *Hellcats of the Navy* 1957

Philpotts, Ambrosine (1912–1980) *Up in the World* 1956; *The Duke Wore Jeans* 1958; *Room at the Top* 1958; *Expresso Bongo* 1959; *Two and Two Make Six* 1961

Phipps, Max (1939–) *Thirst* 1979; *Savage Islands* 1983; *Sky Pirates* 1986

Phipps, Nicholas (1913–1980) *Elizabeth of Ladymead* 1948; *Spring in Park Lane* 1948; *Maytime in Mayfair* 1949; *Mad about Men* 1954; *All for Mary* 1955; *The Navy Lark* 1959

Phipps, William (1922–) *Crossfire* 1947; *Belle Starr's Daughter* 1948; *Cinderella* 1950; *Five* 1951; *Rose of Cimarron* 1952; *Cat-women of the Moon* 1953; *The War of the Worlds* 1953; *Black Gold* 1963

Phoenix, Joaquin *aka* **Phoenix, Leaf** (1974–) *SpaceCamp* 1986; *Russkies* 1987; *Parenthood* 1989; *To Die For* 1995; *Inventing the Abbotts* 1997; *U Turn* 1997; *Clay Pigeons* 1998; *Return to Paradise* 1998; *8mm* 1999; *Gladiator* 2000; *Quills* 2000; *The Yards* 2000; *Buffalo Soldiers* 2001; *It's All about Love* 2002; *Signs* 2002; *Brother Bear* 2003; *Hotel Rwanda* 2004; *Ladder 49* 2004; *The Village* 2004

Phoenix, Rain (1973–) *Even Cowgirls Get the Blues* 1993; *O* 2001; *Stranger Inside* 2001

Phoenix, River (1970–1993) *Explorers* 1985; *Surviving* 1985; *The Mosquito Coast* 1986; *Stand by Me* 1986; *Little Nikita* 1988; *A Night in the Life of Jimmy Reardon* 1988; *Running on Empty* 1988; *Indiana Jones and the Last Crusade* 1989; *I Love You to Death* 1990; *Dogfight* 1991; *My Own Private Idaho* 1991; *Sneakers* 1992; *Silent Tongue* 1993; *The Thing Called Love* 1993

Phoenix, Summer (1978–) *Russkies* 1987; *Girl* 1998; *SLC Punk!* 1999; *Dinner Rush* 2000; *Esther Kahn* 2000; *The Believer* 2001; *The Laramie Project* 2002; *Suzie Gold* 2003

Pholdee, Jesdaporn (1977–) *The Iron Ladies* 2000; *The Eye 2* 2004

Pialat, Maurice (1925–2003) *Que la Bête Meure* 1969; *To Our Loves* 1984; *Sous le Soleil de Satan* 1987

Piazza, Ben (1934–1991) *The Hanging Tree* 1959; *Tell Me That You Love Me, Junie Moon* 1970; *The Bad News Bears* 1976; *I Never Promised You a Rose Garden* 1977; *Guilty by Suspicion* 1990

Pica, Tina (1884–1968) *Bread, Love and Dreams* 1953; *Yesterday, Today and Tomorrow* 1963

Picardo, Robert (1953–) *The Howling* 1981; *Legend* 1985; *Munchies* 1987; *Jack's Back* 1988; *Gremlins 2: the New Batch* 1990; *Motorama* 1991; *A Murderous Affair* 1992; *Wagons East!* 1994; *Star Trek: First Contact* 1996

Piccoli, Michel (1925–) *Death in the Garden* 1956; *Le Doulos* 1962; *Le Mépris* 1963; *The Diary of a Chambermaid* 1964; *Lady L* 1965; *Masquerade* 1965; *The Sleeping Car Murders* 1965; *Les Créatures* 1966; *The Game Is Over* 1966; *La Guerre Est Finie* 1966; *Belle de Jour* 1967; *Danger: Diabolik* 1967; *La Chamade* 1968; *The Things of Life* 1969; *Topaz* 1969; *Ten Days' Wonder* 1971; *The Discreet Charm of the Bourgeoisie* 1972; *La Grande Bouffe* 1973; *Les Noces Rouges* 1973; *Le Fantôme de la Liberté* 1974; *Vincent, François, Paul and the Others* 1974; *Mado* 1976; *Atlantic City, USA* 1980; *A Strange Affair* 1981; *Passion* 1982; *La Nuit de Varennes* 1983; *Dangerous Moves* 1984; *Long Live Life* 1984; *Success Is the Best Revenge* 1984; *Death in a French Garden* 1985; *The Night Is Young* 1986; *Le Paltoquet* 1986; *The Chinese Connection* 1988; *Milou en Mai* 1989; *Martha and I* 1990; *La Belle Noiseuse* 1991; *Les Cent et Une Nuits* 1995; *Beaumarchais l'Insolent* 1996; *Généalogies d'un Crime* 1997; *Passion in the Desert* 1998; *Rien sur Robert* 1998; *I'm Going Home* 2001

Piccolo, Ottavia (1949–) *The Widow Couderc* 1971; *Zorro* 1975; *Mado* 1976

Picerni, Paul (1922–) *Breakthrough* 1950; *Force of Arms* 1951; *Operation Pacific* 1951; *Mara Maru* 1952; *House of Wax* 1953; *The Adventures of Hajji Baba* 1954; *Drive a Crooked Road* 1954; *To Hell and Back* 1955; *The Big Caper* 1957

Pichel, Irving (1891–1954) *An American Tragedy* 1931; *Madame Butterfly* 1932; *Westward Passage* 1932; *British Agent* 1934; *Special Agent* 1935; *Dracula's Daughter* 1936; *General Spanky* 1936; *The Battle of Midway* 1942; *The Moon Is Down* 1943

Pichette, Jean-François *Une Histoire Inventée* 1990; *Being at Home with Claude* 1992

Pichler, Joe (1987–) *Beethoven's 3rd* 2000; *Beethoven's 4th* 2001

Pickard, Helena (1900–1959) *Nell Gwyn* 1934; *The Lady with the Lamp* 1951

Pickard, John (1913–1993) *Hellgate* 1952; *Black Horse Canyon* 1954; *The Lone Ranger* 1956; *Rage* 1999

Pickens Jr, James *Dead Presidents* 1995; *Rocketman* 1997

Pickens, Slim (1919–1983) *Rocky Mountain* 1950; *The Outcast* 1954; *Santa Fe Passage* 1955; *The Great Locomotive Chase* 1956; *Stranger at My Door* 1956; *Gunsight Ridge* 1957; *The Sheepman* 1958; *Escort West* 1959; *One-Eyed Jacks* 1961; *A Thunder of Drums* 1961; *Dr Strangelove, or How I Learned to Stop Worrying and Love the Bomb* 1963; *The Glory Guys* 1965; *In Harm's Way* 1965; *Up from the Beach* 1965; *An Eye for an Eye* 1966; *Stagecoach* 1966; *One Born Every Minute* 1967; *Rough Night in Jericho* 1967; *Will Penny* 1967; *Never a Dull Moment* 1968; *Eighty Steps to Jonah* 1969; *The Ballad of Cable Hogue* 1970; *The Deserter* 1971; *The Honkers* 1971; *The Cowboys* 1972; *The Getaway* 1972; *Ginger in the Morning* 1973; *Pat Garrett and Billy the Kid* 1973; *The Apple Dumpling Gang* 1974; *Blazing Saddles* 1974; *Rancho Deluxe* 1975; *White Line Fever* 1975; *Hawmps* 1976; *Mr Billion* 1977; *The White Buffalo* 1977; *Smokey and the Good Time Outlaws* 1978; *Beyond the Poseidon Adventure* 1979; *1941* 1979; *Honeysuckle Rose* 1980; *Tom Horn* 1980; *The Howling* 1981

Pickett, Cindy (1947–) *Night Games* 1979; *Ferris Bueller's Day Off* 1986; *Hot to Trot* 1988; *DeepStar Six* 1989; *Crooked Hearts* 1991; *Sleepwalkers* 1992; *Son in Law* 1993; *Shadow of the Past* 1995

Pickford, Mary (1893–1979) *The Pride of the Clan* 1917; *Rebecca of Sunnybrook Farm* 1917; *A Romance of the Redwoods* 1917; *Stella Maris* 1918; *Daddy Long Legs* 1919; *Pollyanna* 1920; *Little Lord Fauntleroy* 1921; *Tess of the Storm Country* 1922; *Hollywood* 1923; *Rosita* 1923; *Little Annie Rooney* 1925; *Sparrows* 1926; *The Gaucho* 1927; *My Best Girl* 1927; *Coquette* 1929; *The Taming of the Shrew* 1929; *Secrets* 1933

Pickles, Christina (1935–) *Seizure* 1974; *Legends of the Fall* 1994

Pickles, Vivian (1933–) Play Dirty 1969; Sunday, Bloody Sunday 1971; Harold and Maude 1972

Pickles, Wilfred (1904–1978) Billy Liar 1963; The Family Way 1966; For the Love of Ada 1972

Pickup, Ronald (1941–) Three Sisters 1970; The Thirty-Nine Steps 1978; Nijinsky 1980; Eleni 1985; The Mission 1986; Testimony 1987; Bethune: the Making of a Hero 1990; Shogun Warrior 1991; Bring Me the Head of Mavis Davis 1997

Picon, Molly (1898–1992) Come Blow Your Horn 1963; Fiddler on the Roof 1971; For Pete's Sake 1974

Picot, Genevieve (1956–) Undercover 1983; Proof 1991

Pidgeon, Rebecca (1963–) The Dawning 1988; Homicide 1991; The Spanish Prisoner 1997; The Winslow Boy 1999; State and Main 2000; Heist 2001

Pidgeon, Walter (1897–1984) Rockabye 1932; The Kiss before the Mirror 1933; Big Brown Eyes 1936; Fatal Lady 1936; Man-Proof 1937; Saratoga 1937; The Girl of the Golden West 1938; Listen, Darling 1938; The Shopworn Angel 1938; Too Hot to Handle 1938; Nick Carter, Master Detective 1939; Dark Command 1940; Flight Command 1940; The House across the Bay 1940; It's a Date 1940; Phantom Raiders 1940; Sky Murder 1940; Blossoms in the Dust 1941; Design for Scandal 1941; How Green Was My Valley 1941; Man Hunt 1941; Mrs Miniver 1942; White Cargo 1942; Madame Curie 1943; Mrs Parkington 1944; Week-End at the Waldorf 1945; Holiday in Mexico 1946; The Secret Heart 1946; If Winter Comes 1947; Command Decision 1948; Julia Misbehaves 1948; The Forsyte Saga 1949; The Red Danube 1949; The Miniver Story 1950; Calling Bulldog Drummond 1951; The Sellout 1951; Soldiers Three 1951; The Bad and the Beautiful 1952; Million Dollar Mermaid 1952; Dream Wife 1953; Scandal at Scourie 1953; Deep in My Heart 1954; Executive Suite 1954; The Last Time I Saw Paris 1954; Men of the Fighting Lady 1954; Hit the Deck 1955; Forbidden Planet 1956; The Rack 1956; These Wilder Years 1956; Voyage to the Bottom of the Sea 1961; Advise and Consent 1962; Big Red 1962; How I Spent My Summer Vacation 1967; Warning Shot 1967; Funny Girl 1968; Skyjacked 1972; Harry in Your Pocket 1973; The Neptune Factor 1973; The Lindbergh Kidnapping Case 1976; Two-Minute Warning 1976

Pieiller, Jacques A l'Attaque! 2000; La Ville Est Tranquille 2000

Piéplu, Claude (1923–) The Discreet Charm of the Bourgeoisie 1972; Les Noces Rouges 1973; Le Paltoquet 1986; Asterix and Obelix Take On Caesar 1999

Piéral, Pierre aka **Piéral** (1923–2003) Eternal Love 1943; That Obscure Object of Desire 1977

Pierce, Bradley aka **Pierce, Bradley Michael** (1982–) Beauty and the Beast 1991; Jumanji 1995; The Borrowers 1997

Pierce, Charles B Grayeagle 1977; The Aurora Encounter 1985

Pierce, David Hyde aka **Pierce, David** (1959–) The Fisher King 1991; Little Man Tate 1991; Sleepless in Seattle 1993; Wolf 1994; Nixon 1995; A Bug's Life 1998; Isn't She Great 1999; The Mating Habits of the Earthbound Human 1999; Osmosis Jones 2001; Full Frontal 2002; Treasure Planet 2002; Down with Love 2003

Pierce, Justin (1975–2000) kids 1995; First Time Felon 1997; Next Friday 1999

Pierce, Linda Black Rainbow 1989; Victim of Beauty 1991

Pierce, Maggie Tales of Terror 1962; The Fastest Guitar Alive 1966

Pierce, Norman The Crimes of Stephen Hawke 1936; Saloon Bar 1940

Pierce, Stack Psychic Killer 1975; The Patriot 1986

Pierce, Wendell (1962–) It Could Happen to You 1994; Hackers 1995; The 24 Hour Woman 1999

Pierlot, Francis (1875–1955) The Affairs of Susan 1945; Bewitched 1945; Anne of the Indies 1951

Pieroni, Ania House by the Cemetery 1981; Tenebrae 1982

Pierro, Marina (1960–) Behind Convent Walls 1977; Heroines of Evil 1979; The Art of Love 1983

Pierrot, Frédéric (1960–) Land and Freedom 1995; For Ever Mozart 1996; Artemisia 1997; Port Djema 1997; Captains of April 2000; The Girl from Paris 2001; Monsieur N 2003

Pigaut, Roger (1919–1989) The Light across the Street 1956; Une Histoire Simple 1978

Pigg, Alexandra Letter to Brezhnev 1985; A Chorus of Disapproval 1988

Pigott, Tempe (1884–1962) The Black Pirate 1926; Dr Jekyll and Mr Hyde 1931; The Devil Is a Woman 1935

Pigott-Smith, Tim (1946–) Sweet William 1980; Clash of the Titans 1981; Escape to Victory 1981; The Hunchback of Notre Dame 1982; Dead Man's Folly 1986; The Remains of the Day 1993; Bloody Sunday 2001; The Four Feathers 2002; Johnny English 2003

Pike, John (1945–) The Cat Gang 1959; Live It Up 1963; Be My Guest 1965

Pike, Rosamund (1979–) Die Another Day 2002; The Libertine 2004

Pilavin, Barbara (1923–2005) The Voyage 1974; Frightmare 1981

Pilbeam, Nova (1919–) The Man Who Knew Too Much 1934; Young and Innocent 1937; Cheer Boys Cheer 1939; Pastor Hall 1940; Banana Ridge 1941; Yellow Canary 1943; Counterblast 1948; The Three Weird Sisters 1948

Pileggi, Mitch (1952–) Brothers in Arms 1988; Shocker 1989; The X-Files 1998

Pilkington, Lorraine (1975–) The Miracle 1990; The Disappearance of Finbar 1996; Gold in the Streets 1996; Last of the High Kings 1996; Human Traffic 1999; My Kingdom 2001

Pill, Alison (1985–) No Higher Love 1999; The Pilot's Wife 2001; Pieces of April 2002; Confessions of a Teenage Drama Queen 2004; Dear Wendy 2005

Pilmark, Soren (1955–) The Kingdom 1994; The Beast Within 1995

Pilon, Daniel (1940–) Malpertuis 1971; Brannigan 1975; Malarek 1989; Obsessed 1989

Pinal, Silvia (1931–) Viridiana 1961; The Exterminating Angel 1962; Simon of the Desert 1965; Guns for San Sebastian 1968; Shark! 1969

Pinchot, Bronson (1959–) Risky Business 1983; Beverly Hills Cop 1984; Hot Resort 1985; Second Sight 1989; Blame It on the Bellboy 1992; True Romance 1993; Beverly Hills Cop III 1994; Napoleon 1995; Courage under Fire 1996; The Adventures of Slappy the Sea Lion 1998

Pine, Larry Anna 1987; Plain Clothes 1988; Vanya on 42nd Street 1994; Sunday 1997; The Clearing 2004

Pine, Phillip aka **Pine, Phillip E** (1920–) Men in War 1957; Murder by Contract 1958; Project X 1968; Glass Houses 1972

Pine, Robert (1941–) Munster, Go Home! 1966; The Young Warriors 1967; One Little Indian 1973; The Bears and I 1974; Empire of the Ants 1977; The Apple Dumpling Gang Rides Again 1979

Pinette, John Reckless Kelly 1993; Simon Sez 1999

Pinkett Smith, Jada aka **Pinkett, Jada** (1971–) Menace II Society 1993; Jason's Lyric 1994; A Low Down Dirty Shame 1994; Tales from the Crypt: Demon Knight 1995; If These Walls Could Talk 1996; The Nutty Professor 1996; Set It Off 1996; Scream 2 1997; Return to Paradise 1998; Woo 1998; Bamboozled 2000; Ali 2001; The Matrix Reloaded 2002; The Matrix Revolutions 2003; Collateral 2004; Madagascar 2005

Pinon, Dominique (1955–) The Moon in the Gutter 1983; The Legend of the Holy Drinker 1988; 1871 1989; Delicatessen 1990; The City of Lost Children 1995; Alien: Resurrection 1997; Amélie 2001

Pinsent, Gordon (1930–) Colossus: the Forbin Project 1969; Blacula 1972; Newman's Law 1974; Who Has Seen the Wind 1977; Silence of the North 1981; Pippi Longstocking 1997

Pinsent, Leah aka **Pinsent, Leah King** (1968–) Bay Boy 1984; April Fool's Day 1986

Pinter, Harold (1930–) The Servant 1963; Accident 1967; The Rise and Rise of Michael Rimmer 1970; Mojo 1998; Mansfield Park 1999; The Tailor of Panama 2000; Wit 2001

Pinza, Ezio (1893–1957) Mr Imperium 1951; Tonight We Sing 1953

Piper, Billie (1982–) The Calcium Kid 2003; Spirit Trap 2005

Piper, Frederick (1902–1979) In Which We Serve 1942; San Demetrio London 1943; Johnny Frenchman 1945; Hue and Cry 1947; The October Man 1947; Brandy for the Parson 1951; Escape Route 1952; Home at Seven 1952; Hunted 1952; The Monster of Highgate Ponds 1961; Only Two Can Play 1961

Piper, Roddy aka **Piper, "Rowdy" Roddy** (1951–) Hell Comes to Frogtown 1988; They Live 1988; Back in Action 1993

Piro, Grant Love in Ambush 1997; Darkness Falls 2003

Pirri, Jim Ring of Steel 1994; And the Beat Goes On: the Sonny and Cher Story 1999

Piscopo, Joe (1951–) Johnny Dangerously 1984; Wise Guys 1986; Dead Heat 1988; Huck and the King of Hearts 1993; Sidekicks 1993; The Bomber Boys 1995; Two-Bits and Pepper 1995; Bartleby 2000

Pisier, Marie-France (1944–) Love at Twenty 1962; Trans-Europ-Express 1966; Celine and Julie Go Boating 1974; Cousin, Cousine 1975; The Other Side of Midnight 1977; The Brontë Sisters 1979; French Postcards 1979; Love on the Run 1979; Chanel Solitaire 1981; The Hot Touch 1982; Time Regained 1999

Pistilli, Luigi (1930–1996) Death Rides a Horse 1967; We Still Kill the Old Way 1967; Bay of Blood 1971

Pisu, Mario (1910–1976) $8\frac{1}{2}$ 1963; Juliet of the Spirits 1965; The Looters 1966; Without Warning 1973

Pitagora, Paola (1942–) Fists in the Pocket 1965; The Devil's Advocate 1977

Pitarresi, Maria Ca Commence Aujourd'hui 1999; Laissez-passer 2001

Pithey, Wensley (1914–1993) Kill Me Tomorrow 1957; The Boys 1961; The Knack... and How to Get It 1965

Pitillo, Maria (1965–1993) Spike of Bensonhurst 1988; Bye Bye Love 1995; Frank and Jesse 1995; Dear God 1996; Godzilla 1997; Something to Believe In 1997

Pitoeff, Sacha (1920–1990) Anastasia 1956; Last Year at Marienbad 1961

Pitoniak, Anne aka **Pitoniak, Ann** (1922–) The Survivors 1983; Agnes of God 1985; Best Seller 1987; Housekeeping 1987; The Wizard of Loneliness 1988; Where the Money Is 2000

Pitt, Brad (1963–) Cutting Class 1989; Happy Together 1989; Across the Tracks 1990; The Image 1990; He Said, She Said 1991; Johnny Suede 1991; Thelma & Louise 1991; Cool World 1992; A River Runs through It 1992; Kalifornia 1993; True Romance 1993; The Favor 1994; Interview with the Vampire: the Vampire Chronicles 1994; Legends of the Fall 1994; Se7en 1995; Twelve Monkeys 1995; Sleepers 1996; The Devil's Own 1997; Seven Years in Tibet 1997; Meet Joe Black 1998; Being John Malkovich 1999; Fight Club 1999; Snatch 2000; The Mexican 2001; Ocean's Eleven 2001; Spy Game 2001; Sinbad: Legend of the Seven Seas 2003; Ocean's Twelve 2004; Troy 2004; Mr & Mrs Smith 2005

Pitt, Chris Lionheart 1986; The Lair of the White Worm 1988

Pitt, Ingrid (1937–) Countess Dracula 1970; The Vampire Lovers 1970; The House That Dripped Blood 1971; The Wicker Man 1973; Parker 1984

Pitt, Michael (1981–) Finding Forrester 2000; Bully 2001; Hedwig and the Angry Inch 2001; Murder by Numbers 2002; The Dreamers 2003; The Heart Is Deceitful above All Things 2004; Last Days 2005

Pitts, ZaSu (1898–1963) Rebecca of Sunnybrook Farm 1917; Hollywood 1923; Greed 1925; The Wedding March 1928; Monte Carlo 1930; Bad Sister 1931; The Guardsman 1931; Back Street 1932; Blondie of the Follies 1932; Make Me a Star 1932; The Man I Killed 1932; Shopworn 1932; Vanishing Frontier 1932; Westward Passage 1932; Hello Sister! 1933; Meet the Baron 1933; Dames 1934; The Gay Bride 1934; Mrs Wiggs of the Cabbage Patch 1934; Ruggles of Red Gap 1935; The Plot Thickens 1936; Eternally Yours 1939; Naughty but Nice 1939; Nurse Edith Cavell 1939; It All Came True 1940; No, No, Nanette 1940; Broadway Limited 1941; Let's Face It 1943; Life with Father 1947; Francis 1949; Denver & Rio Grande 1952; Francis Joins the WACS 1954; The Gazebo 1959; The Thrill of It All 1963

Piven, Jeremy (1965–) Car 54 Where Are You? 1991; Judgment Night 1993; 12:01 1993; PCU 1994; Twogether 1994; Dr Jekyll and Ms Hyde 1995; Music from Another Room 1998; Phoenix 1998; Very Bad Things 1998; The Family Man 2000; Serendipity 2001; Old School 2003; Runaway Jury 2003; Chasing Liberty 2004

Place, Mary Kay (1947–) New York, New York 1977; Starting Over 1979; Modern Problems 1981; The Big Chill 1983; Explorers 1985; Smooth Talk 1985; A New Life 1988; Bright Angel 1990; Crazy from the Heart 1991; Captain Ron 1992; The Price of Vengeance 1994; Citizen Ruth 1996; Eye of God 1997; John Grisham's The Rainmaker 1997; Pecker 1998; Being John Malkovich 1999; Human Nature 2001; My First Mister 2001; The Safety of Objects 2001; Sweet Home Alabama 2002; Silver City 2004

Placido, Michele (1946–) Tigers in Lipstick 1979; Three Brothers 1980; The Art of Love 1983; Big Business 1988; Lamerica 1994

Plana, Tony (1953–) Latino 1985; Salvador 1986; Disorderlies 1987; Break of Dawn 1988; Romero 1989; Havana 1990; Why Me? 1990; One Good Cop 1991; Live Wire 1992; Half Past Dead 2002

Planer, Nigel (1955–) The Supergrass 1985; Eat the Rich 1987; Carry On Columbus 1992; Clockwork Mice 1994; The Wind in the Willows 1996

Platt, Edward aka **Platt, Edward C** (1916–1974) The Shrike 1955; Backlash 1956; Rock, Pretty Baby 1956; House of Numbers 1957; Damn Citizen 1958; The Gift of Love 1958; The High Cost of Loving 1958; The Rebel Set 1959; Atlantis, the Lost Continent 1960

Platt, Howard TR Baskin 1971; Three the Hard Way 1974

Platt, Louise (1915–2003) I Met My Love Again 1938; Spawn of the North 1938; Stagecoach 1939; Tell No Tales 1939

Platt, Marc (1913–) Tonight and Every Night 1945; Down to Earth 1947; Seven Brides for Seven Brothers 1954

Platt, Oliver (1960–) Working Girl 1988; Flatliners 1990; Beethoven 1992; Midnight Sting 1992; Benny and Joon 1993; Indecent Proposal 1993; The Temp 1993; The Three Musketeers 1993; Funny Bones 1994; Tall Tale 1994; The Infiltrator 1995; Executive Decision 1996; A Time to Kill 1996; Dangerous Beauty 1997; Doctor Dolittle 1998; The Impostors 1998; Simon Birch 1998; Bicentennial Man 1999; Lake Placid 1999; Three to Tango 1999; Gun Shy 2000; Ready to Rumble 2000; Don't Say a Word 2001; Ash Wednesday 2002; Hope Springs 2002; Liberty Stands Still 2002; Pieces of April 2002; Kinsey 2004

Playfair, Nigel (1874–1934) Lady Windermere's Fan 1916; Crime on the Hill 1933

Playten, Alice (1947–) Who Killed Mary Whats'ername? 1971; Legend 1985; Felix the Cat: the Movie 1989

Plaza, Begona (1966–) Maid to Order 1987; Delta Force 2 1990

Pleasence, Angela From beyond the Grave 1973; The Godsend 1980; The Favour, the Watch and the Very Big Fish 1991

Pleasence, Donald (1919–1995) The Beachcomber 1954; Orders Are Orders 1954; 1984 1955; Value for Money 1955; The Black Tent 1956; The Man in the Sky 1956; Barnacle Bill 1957; Manuela 1957; A Tale of Two Cities 1957; The Man Inside 1958; The Two-Headed Spy 1958; The Flesh and the Fiends 1959; Hell Is a City 1959; Look Back in Anger 1959; The Shakedown 1959; Circus of Horrors 1960; The Hands of Orlac 1960; Killers of Kilimanjaro 1960; No Love for Johnnie 1960; Sons and Lovers 1960; Suspect 1960; Spare the Rod 1961; What a Carve Up! 1961; The Wind of Change 1961; Dr Crippen 1962; The Inspector 1962; The Caretaker 1963; The Great Escape 1963; The Greatest Story Ever Told 1965; The Hallelujah Trail 1965; Cul-de-Sac 1966; Eye of the Devil 1966; Fantastic Voyage 1966; The Night of the Generals 1966; Will Penny 1967; You Only Live Twice 1967; The Madwoman of Chaillot 1969; Soldier Blue 1970; Kidnapped 1971; The Pied Piper 1971; THX 1138 1971; Death Line 1972; Henry VIII and His Six Wives 1972; Innocent Bystanders 1972; The Jerusalem File 1972; From beyond the Grave 1973; Malachi's Cove 1973; The Mutations 1973; Tales That Witness Madness 1973; Barry McKenzie Holds His Own 1974; The Black Windmill 1974; The Count of Monte Cristo 1974; Escape to Witch Mountain 1975; Hearts of the West 1975; I Don't Want to Be Born 1975; The Eagle Has Landed 1976; The Last Tycoon 1976; The Passover Plot 1976; Trial by Combat 1976; Blood Relatives 1977; Oh, God! 1977; Telefon 1977; Tomorrow Never Comes 1977; The Uncanny 1977; Halloween 1978; Power Play 1978; Sgt Pepper's Lonely Hearts Club Band 1978; All Quiet on the Western Front 1979; Dracula 1979; Good Luck, Miss Wyckoff 1979; Jaguar Lives! 1979; The Monster Club 1980; Escape from New York 1981; Halloween II 1981; Treasure of the Yankee Zephyr 1981; Where Is Parsifal? 1983; The Ambassador 1984; A Breed Apart 1984; Warrior Queen 1986; Ground Zero 1987; Prince of

Darkness 1987; *Vampire in Venice* 1987; *Halloween 4: the Return of Michael Myers* 1988; *Hanna's War* 1988; *Phantom of Death* 1988; *Halloween 5: the Revenge of Michael Myers* 1989; *River of Death* 1989; *Buried Alive* 1990; *Shadows and Fog* 1991; *The Hour of the Pig* 1993; *Arabian Knight* 1995; *Halloween 6: the Curse of Michael Myers* 1995

Pleshette, John (1942–) *Micki & Maude* 1984; *Eye of the Stranger* 1993

Pleshette, Suzanne (1937–) *The Geisha Boy* 1958; *Forty Pounds of Trouble* 1962; *Rome Adventure* 1962; *The Birds* 1963; *A Distant Trumpet* 1964; *Fate Is the Hunter* 1964; *Youngblood Hawke* 1964; *Mister Buddwing* 1965; *A Rage to Live* 1965; *Nevada Smith* 1966; *The Ugly Dachshund* 1966; *The Adventures of Bullwhip Griffin* 1967; *Blackbeard's Ghost* 1967; *The Power* 1968; *If It's Tuesday, This Must Be Belgium* 1969; *Suppose They Gave a War and Nobody Came?* 1970; *Support Your Local Gunfighter* 1971; *The Shaggy DA* 1976; *Hot Stuff* 1979; *Oh God! Book II* 1980; *Spirited Away* 2001

Plimpton, George (1927–2003) *Beyond the Law* 1968; *Volunteers* 1985; *Easy Wheels* 1989; *Little Man Tate* 1991; *Just Visiting* 2001

Plimpton, Martha (1970–) *The River Rat* 1984; *The Goonies* 1985; *The Mosquito Coast* 1986; *Shy People* 1987; *Another Woman* 1988; *Running on Empty* 1988; *Stars and Bars* 1988; *Parenthood* 1989; *Silence like Glass* 1989; *Stanley & Iris* 1989; *Josh and SAM* 1993; *The Beans of Egypt, Maine* 1994; *I Shot Andy Warhol* 1995; *Last Summer in the Hamptons* 1995; *Beautiful Girls* 1996; *I'm Not Rappaport* 1996; *Eye of God* 1997; *Music from Another Room* 1998; *Pecker* 1998; *200 Cigarettes* 1999

Plotnick, Jack *Say It Isn't So* 2001; *Down with Love* 2003

Plowman, Melinda *Home Town Story* 1951; *Billy the Kid vs Dracula* 1966

Plowright, Joan (1929–) *The Entertainer* 1960; *Three Sisters* 1970; *Equus* 1977; *Brimstone and Treacle* 1982; *Britannia Hospital* 1982; *Revolution* 1985; *The Dressmaker* 1988; *Drowning by Numbers* 1988; *Avalon* 1990; *I Love You to Death* 1990; *Enchanted April* 1991; *Dennis* 1993; *Widows' Peak* 1993; *Hotel Sorrento* 1994; *A Pin for the Butterfly* 1994; *A Place for Annie* 1994; *A Pyromaniac's Love Story* 1995; *The Scarlet Letter* 1995; *Jane Eyre* 1996; *Mr Wrong* 1996; *101 Dalmatians* 1996; *Surviving Picasso* 1996; *Aldrich Ames: Traitor Within* 1998; *Dance with Me* 1998; *Tea with Mussolini* 1998; *Tom's Midnight Garden* 1998; *Dinosaur* 2000; *Callas Forever* 2002; *Bringing Down the House* 2003; *I Am David* 2003

Plummer, Amanda (1957–) *Cattle Annie and Little Britches* 1980; *Daniel* 1983; *The Dollmaker* 1984; *The Hotel New Hampshire* 1984; *Static* 1985; *Joe versus the Volcano* 1990; *The Fisher King* 1991; *Freejack* 1992; *Miss Rose White* 1992; *Last Light* 1993; *Needful Things* 1993; *Nostradamus* 1993; *So I Married an Axe Murderer* 1993; *Butterfly Kiss* 1994; *The Prophecy* 1994; *Pulp Fiction* 1994; *The Final Cut* 1995; *Under the Piano* 1995; *Freeway* 1996; *American Perfekt* 1997; *A Simple Wish* 1997; *You Can Thank Me Later* 1998; *8½ Women* 1999; *The Million Dollar Hotel* 1999; *7 Days to Live* 2000; *Ken Park* 2002; *My Life without Me* 2002; *Triggermen* 2002

Plummer, Christopher (1927–) *Stage Struck* 1958; *Wind across the Everglades* 1958; *The Fall of the Roman Empire* 1964; *Inside Daisy Clover* 1965; *The Sound of Music* 1965; *Triple Cross* 1966; *Oedipus the King* 1967; *Nobody Runs Forever* 1968; *Battle of Britain* 1969; *Lock Up Your Daughters!* 1969; *The Royal Hunt of the Sun* 1969; *Waterloo* 1970; *The Return of the Pink Panther* 1974; *Conduct Unbecoming* 1975; *The Man Who Would Be King* 1975; *Aces High* 1976; *The Disappearance* 1977; *International Velvet* 1978; *Murder by Decree* 1978; *The Silent Partner* 1978; *Hanover Street* 1979; *Highpoint* 1979; *Somewhere in Time* 1980; *The Amateur* 1981; *Eyewitness* 1981; *The Scarlet and the Black* 1983; *Dreamscape* 1984; *Ordeal by Innocence* 1984; *Lily in Love* 1985; *An American Tail* 1986; *The Boy in Blue* 1986; *Dragnet* 1987; *Souvenir* 1987; *Vampire in Venice* 1987; *Light Years* 1988; *A Ghost in Monte Carlo* 1990; *Rock-a-Doodle* 1990; *Where the Heart Is* 1990; *Firehead* 1991; *Star Trek VI: the Undiscovered Country* 1991; *Danielle Steel's Secrets* 1992; *Wolf* 1994; *Dolores Claiborne* 1995; *Twelve Monkeys* 1995; *Skeletons* 1996; *The Insider* 1999; *Madeline: Lost in Paris* 1999; *Dracula 2001* 2000; *Possessed* 2000; *A Beautiful Mind* 2001; *Lucky Break* 2001; *Ararat* 2002; *Nicholas Nickleby* 2002; *Cold Creek Manor* 2003; *Alexander* 2004; *National Treasure* 2004

Plummer, Glenn (1966–) *Pastime* 1991; *South Central* 1992; *Trespass* 1992; *Speed* 1994; *Showgirls* 1995; *Strange Days* 1995; *The Substitute* 1996; *Up Close & Personal* 1996; *Thursday* 1998; *History Is Made at Night* 1999; *The Salton Sea* 2002; *The Day after Tomorrow* 2004

Plunkett, Patricia (1928–) *It Always Rains on Sunday* 1947; *Bond Street* 1948; *Landfall* 1949; *Murder without Crime* 1950

Pochath, Werner (1939–1993) *Vengeance* 1968; *Sky Riders* 1976

Podalydès, Denis (1963–) *En Plein Coeur* 1998; *A l'Attaque!* 2000; *Laissez-passer* 2001; *The Officers' Ward* 2001; *Almost Peaceful* 2002; *Summer Things* 2002

Podesta, Rossana (1934–) *Ulysses* 1954; *Helen of Troy* 1955; *Santiago* 1956; *Raw Wind in Eden* 1958; *The Sword and the Cross* 1958; *Sodom and Gomorrah* 1962

Podewell, Cathy (1964–) *Night of the Demons* 1988; *Beverly Hills Brats* 1989

Poehler, Amy (1971–) *Envy* 2003; *Mean Girls* 2004

Poelvoorde, Benoît (1964–) *Man Bites Dog* 1992; *Les Convoyeurs Attendent* 1999; *Aaltra* 2004

Pogue, Ken *The Silent Partner* 1978; *The Grey Fox* 1982; *Crazy Moon* 1986; *Keeping Track* 1986; *Dead of Winter* 1987; *Welcome Home* 1989; *The Hitman* 1991; *Run* 1991; *Dangerous Intentions* 1995; *The 6th Day* 2000

Pohlmann, Eric aka **Pohlman, Eric** (1913–1979) *Children of Chance* 1949; *Blackout* 1950; *Emergency Call* 1952; *The Gambler and the Lady* 1952; *Blood Orange* 1953; *Mogambo* 1953; *They Who Dare* 1953; *The Belles of St Trinian's* 1954; *Break in the Circle* 1955; *Gentlemen Marry Brunettes* 1955; *The Glass Cage* 1955; *Across the Bridge* 1957; *Mark of the Phoenix* 1957; *Alive and Kicking* 1958; *The Duke Wore Jeans* 1958; *Nor the Moon by Night* 1958; *Expresso Bongo* 1959; *The Singer Not the Song* 1960; *Surprise Package* 1960; *The Kitchen* 1961; *Cairo* 1962; *Shadow of Fear* 1963; *The Sicilians* 1964; *Where the Spies Are* 1965; *Tiffany Jones* 1973; *The Return of the Pink Panther* 1974

Pointer, Priscilla (1924–) *Carrie* 1976; *The Onion Field* 1979; *Honeysuckle Rose* 1980; *The Falcon and the Snowman* 1985; *Rumpelstiltskin* 1986; *A Nightmare on Elm Street 3: Dream Warriors* 1987; *Disturbed* 1990; *The Magic Bubble* 1992; *Acts of Love* 1995

Poiret, Jean (1926–1992) *The Last Metro* 1980; *Cop au Vin* 1984; *Inspecteur Lavardin* 1986

Poitier, Sidney (1924–) *No Way Out* 1950; *Cry, the Beloved Country* 1951; *Red Ball Express* 1952; *Go, Man, Go!* 1953; *Good-bye, My Lady* 1956; *Band of Angels* 1957; *Edge of the City* 1957; *The Mark of the Hawk* 1957; *Something of Value* 1957; *The Defiant Ones* 1958; *Virgin Island* 1958; *Porgy and Bess* 1959; *All the Young Men* 1960; *Paris Blues* 1961; *A Raisin in the Sun* 1961; *Pressure Point* 1962; *Lilies of the Field* 1963; *The Long Ships* 1963; *The Bedford Incident* 1965; *The Greatest Story Ever Told* 1965; *A Patch of Blue* 1965; *The Slender Thread* 1965; *Duel at Diablo* 1966; *Guess Who's Coming to Dinner* 1967; *In the Heat of the Night* 1967; *To Sir, with Love* 1967; *For Love of Ivy* 1968; *The Lost Man* 1969; *Brother John* 1970; *King: a Filmed Record... Montgomery to Memphis* 1970; *They Call Me Mister Tibbs!* 1970; *The Organization* 1971; *Buck and the Preacher* 1972; *A Warm December* 1973; *Uptown Saturday Night* 1974; *Let's Do It Again* 1975; *The Wilby Conspiracy* 1975; *A Piece of the Action* 1977; *Deadly Pursuit* 1988; *Little Nikita* 1988; *Sneakers* 1992; *The Jackal* 1997; *Mandela and de Klerk* 1997; *David and Lisa* 1998; *The Simple Life of Noah Dearborn* 1999

Pol, Talitha (1940–1971) *Village of Daughters* 1961; *Return from the Ashes* 1965

Polanski, Roman (1933–) *A Generation* 1954; *Repulsion* 1965; *The Fearless Vampire Killers* 1967; *The Magic Christian* 1969; *What?* 1973; *Blood for Dracula* 1974; *Chinatown* 1974; *The Tenant* 1976; *Back in the USSR* 1992; *A Pure Formality* 1994

Poletti, Victor *And the Ship Sails On* 1983; *Meeting Venus* 1990

Polish, Mark (1972–) *Twin Falls Idaho* 1999; *Northfork* 2002

Polito, Jon (1950–) *Fire with Fire* 1986; *Homeboy* 1988; *The Freshman* 1990; *Miller's Crossing* 1990; *Barton Fink* 1991; *Leather Jackets* 1991; *Blankman* 1994; *Bushwhacked* 1995; *Just Your Luck* 1996; *Angel's Dance* 1999; *The Man Who Wasn't There* 2001; *29 Palms* 2002; *The Singing Detective* 2003; *The Honeymooners* 2005

Politoff, Haydée (1949–) *La Collectionneuse* 1967; *The Human Factor* 1975

Polk, Brigid aka **Berlin, Brigid** *Bike Boy* 1967; *The Chelsea Girls* 1967; *Bad* 1976; *Pecker* 1998

Pollack, Sydney (1934–) *War Hunt* 1962; *Tootsie* 1982; *Husbands and Wives* 1992; *The Player* 1992; *A Civil Action* 1998; *Eyes Wide Shut* 1999; *Random Hearts* 1999; *Changing Lanes* 2002; *Charlie: the Life and Art of Charles Chaplin* 2003

Pollak, Kevin (1958–) *Avalon* 1990; *Another You* 1991; *LA Story* 1991; *Ricochet* 1991; *A Few Good Men* 1992; *Grumpy Old Men* 1993; *Indian Summer* 1993; *The Opposite Sex and How to Live with Them* 1993; *Clean Slate* 1994; *Canadian Bacon* 1995; *Casino* 1995; *Miami Rhapsody* 1995; *The Usual Suspects* 1995; *Grumpier Old Men* 1996; *House Arrest* 1996; *That Thing You Do!* 1996; *Truth or Consequences, NM* 1997; *Deterrence* 1999; *End of Days* 1999; *She's All That* 1999; *3000 Miles to Graceland* 2000; *Dr Dolittle 2* 2001; *Juwanna Mann* 2002; *The Santa Clause 2* 2002; *Stolen Summer* 2002; *Hostage* 2004; *The Whole Ten Yards* 2004

Pollan, Tracy (1960–) *Bright Lights, Big City* 1988; *Promised Land* 1988; *Danielle Steel's Fine Things* 1990; *A Stranger among Us* 1992

Pollard, Daphne (1891–1978) *Thicker than Water* 1935; *Our Relations* 1936

Pollard, Michael J (1939–) *Summer Magic* 1963; *The Wild Angels* 1966; *Bonnie and Clyde* 1967; *Caprice* 1967; *Enter Laughing* 1967; *Hannibal Brooks* 1968; *Little Fauss and Big Halsy* 1970; *Dirty Little Billy* 1972; *Sunday in the Country* 1975; *Between the Lines* 1977; *Melvin and Howard* 1980; *America* 1986; *The Patriot* 1986; *Riders of the Storm* 1986; *American Gothic* 1987; *Roxanne* 1987; *Fast Food* 1989; *Night Visitor* 1989; *Season of Fear* 1989; *Tango & Cash* 1989; *Over Her Dead Body* 1990; *Why Me?* 1990; *Arizona Dream* 1991; *Motorama* 1991; *Split Second* 1991; *Tumbleweeds* 1999

Polley, Sarah (1979–) *The Adventures of Baron Munchausen* 1988; *Exotica* 1994; *The Hanging Garden* 1997; *The Sweet Hereafter* 1997; *Last Night* 1998; *eXistenZ* 1999; *Go* 1999; *Guinevere* 1999; *The Life before This* 1999; *The Claim* 2000; *The Weight of Water* 2000; *My Life without Me* 2002; *The I Inside* 2003; *Dawn of the Dead* 2004

Pollock, Ellen (1903–1997) *Sons of the Sea* 1939; *Something in the City* 1950; *To Have and to Hold* 1951; *The Time of His Life* 1955; *The Hypnotist* 1957; *Horror Hospital* 1973

Pollock, Nancy R (1902–1979) *The Last Angry Man* 1959; *Go Naked in the World* 1961

Polo, Teri (1969–) *Born to Ride* 1991; *Mystery Date* 1991; *Aspen Extreme* 1993; *Quick* 1993; *Golden Gate* 1994; *The Arrival* 1996; *Danielle Steel's Full Circle* 1996; *The Marriage Fool* 1998; *Meet the Parents* 2000; *Domestic Disturbance* 2001; *Beyond Borders* 2003; *Meet the Fockers* 2004

Polony, Anna (1939–) *Diary for My Children* 1982; *Diary for My Loves* 1987; *Diary for My Father and Mother* 1990

Polson, John (1965–) *Tender Hooks* 1988; *Back of Beyond* 1995; *The Sum of Us* 1995; *Idiot Box* 1996; *The Boys* 1998; *Mission: Impossible 2* 1999

Polycarpou, Peter *Julie and the Cadillacs* 1997; *De-Lovely* 2004

Pomares, Raul (1934–) *Plaff!* 1988; *The Elephant and the Bicycle* 1995

Pomeranc, Max (1984–) *Innocent Moves* 1993; *Fluke* 1995

Pompeo, Ellen (1969–) *Moonlight Mile* 2002; *Old School* 2003

Poncela, Eusebio (1947–) *The Law of Desire* 1987; *El Dorado* 1988; *Intacto* 2001

Poncin, Marcel (1953–) *So Long at the Fair* 1950; *Saadia* 1953

Ponton, Yvan (1945–) *Cold Front* 1989; *Scanners II: The New Order* 1991

Poole, Roy (1924–1986) *Experiment in Terror* 1962; *The Face of Fear* 1971

Pooley, Olaf *Highly Dangerous* 1950; *The Corpse* 1969

Pop, Iggy (1947–) *Cry-Baby* 1989; *Hardware* 1990; *Dead Man* 1995; *The Crow: City of Angels* 1996; *The Rugrats Movie* 1998; *Snow Day* 2000; *Coffee and Cigarettes* 2003

Poppe, Nils (1908–2000) *The Seventh Seal* 1957; *The Devil's Eye* 1960

Poppel, Marc *The Boost* 1988; *Damned River* 1989; *Separate Lives* 1995

Popwell, Albert (1926–1999) *Cleopatra Jones and the Casino of Gold* 1975; *The Buddy Holly Story* 1978

Porcasi, Paul (1879–1946) *Broadway* 1929; *Devil and the Deep* 1932; *Enter Madame!* 1933

Porizkova, Paulina (1965–) *Anna* 1987; *Her Alibi* 1989; *Arizona Dream* 1991; *Female Perversions* 1996; *Wedding Bell Blues* 1996; *Thursday* 1998

Porter, Don aka **Porter, Donald** (1912–1996) *Wild Beauty* 1946; *Buck Privates Come Home* 1947; *711 Ocean Drive* 1950; *Bachelor in Paradise* 1961; *Live a Little, Love a Little* 1968; *The Candidate* 1972; *Mame* 1974; *White Line Fever* 1975

Porter, Eric (1928–1995) *The Fall of the Roman Empire* 1964; *The Pumpkin Eater* 1964; *The Heroes of Telemark* 1965; *Kaleidoscope* 1966; *The Lost Continent* 1968; *Hands of the Ripper* 1971; *Antony and Cleopatra* 1972; *The Belstone Fox* 1973; *The Day of the Jackal* 1973; *Hitler: the Last Ten Days* 1973; *Callan* 1974; *Hennessy* 1975; *The Thirty-Nine Steps* 1978

Porter, Jean (1925–) *Andy Hardy's Blonde Trouble* 1944; *Bathing Beauty* 1944; *Abbott and Costello in Hollywood* 1945; *Till the End of Time* 1946; *Cry Danger* 1951; *The Left Hand of God* 1955

Porter, Nyree Dawn (1936–2001) *Part-Time Wife* 1961; *Live Now – Pay Later* 1962; *The Cracksman* 1963; *Two Left Feet* 1963; *The House That Dripped Blood* 1971

Porter, Susie *Welcome to Woop Woop* 1997; *Feeling Sexy* 1999; *Two Hands* 1999; *Better than Sex* 2000; *Bootmen* 2000; *The Monkey's Mask* 2000; *Mullet* 2001

Portman, Eric (1903–1969) *Maria Marten, or the Murder in the Red Barn* 1935; *The Crimes of Stephen Hawke* 1936; *Moonlight Sonata* 1937; *The Prince and the Pauper* 1937; *49th Parallel* 1941; *One of Our Aircraft Is Missing* 1942; *Uncensored* 1942; *Millions like Us* 1943; *We Dive at Dawn* 1943; *A Canterbury Tale* 1944; *Great Day* 1944; *Daybreak* 1946; *Men of Two Worlds* 1946; *Wanted for Murder* 1946; *Dear Murderer* 1947; *The Mark of Cain* 1947; *The Blind Goddess* 1948; *The Spider and the Fly* 1949; *Cairo Road* 1950; *The Magic Box* 1951; *South of Algiers* 1952; *The Colditz Story* 1954; *The Deep Blue Sea* 1955; *Child in the House* 1956; *The Good Companions* 1956; *The Naked Edge* 1961; *Freud* 1962; *The Man Who Finally Died* 1962; *West 11* 1963; *The Bedford Incident* 1965; *The Spy with a Cold Nose* 1966; *The Whisperers* 1967; *Assignment to Kill* 1968; *Deadfall* 1968

Portman, Natalie (1981–) *Leon* 1994; *Heat* 1995; *Beautiful Girls* 1996; *Everyone Says I Love You* 1996; *Anywhere but Here* 1999; *Star Wars Episode I: the Phantom Menace* 1999; *Where the Heart Is* 2000; *Star Wars Episode II: Attack of the Clones* 2002; *Cold Mountain* 2003; *Garden State* 2003; *Closer* 2004; *Star Wars Episode III: Revenge of the Sith* 2005

Portnow, Richard (1953–) *Aunt Julia and the Scriptwriter* 1990; *Trial by Jury* 1994; *Guy* 1996; *Laughter on the 23rd Floor* 2000

Posey, Parker (1968–) *Party Girl* 1994; *Flirt* 1995; *Kicking and Screaming* 1995; *Basquiat* 1996; *subUrbia* 1996; *Waiting for Guffman* 1996; *Clockwatchers* 1997; *Henry Fool* 1997; *The House of Yes* 1997; *The Daytrippers* 1998; *The Misadventures of Margaret* 1998; *What Rats Won't Do* 1998; *You've Got Mail* 1998; *Scream 3* 1999; *Best in Show* 2000; *The Anniversary Party* 2001; *Josie and the Pussycats* 2001; *Personal Velocity* 2001; *The Battle of Mary Kay* 2002; *The Sweetest Thing* 2002; *Laws of Attraction* 2003; *A Mighty Wind* 2003; *Blade: Trinity* 2004

Post, Markie (1950–) *Visitors of the Night* 1995; *There's Something about Mary* 1998

Post, Saskia (1961–) *One Night Stand* 1984; *Dogs in Space* 1986

Post Jr, William (1901–1989) *Mr and Mrs North* 1941; *Sherlock Holmes and the Secret Weapon* 1942; *Ship Ahoy* 1942; *Bride by Mistake* 1944

Posta, Adrienne (1948–) *Here We Go round the Mulberry Bush* 1967; *Up the Junction* 1967; *Up Pompeii* 1971; *Percy's Progress*

1974; *Adventures of a Taxi Driver* 1975; *Adventures of a Private Eye* 1977

Postlethwaite, Pete *aka* **Postlethwaite, Peter** (1945–) *A Private Function* 1984; *Distant Voices, Still Lives* 1988; *The Dressmaker* 1988; *To Kill a Priest* 1988; *Split Second* 1991; *Anchoress* 1993; *In the Name of the Father* 1993; *Suite 16* 1994; *The Usual Suspects* 1995; *When Saturday Comes* 1995; *Brassed Off* 1996; *DragonHeart* 1996; *James and the Giant Peach* 1996; *William Shakespeare's Romeo + Juliet* 1996; *Amistad* 1997; *The Lost World: Jurassic Park* 1997; *The Serpent's Kiss* 1997; *Among Giants* 1998; *Animal Farm* 1999; *Rat* 2000; *When the Sky Falls* 2000; *The Shipping News* 2001; *Triggermen* 2002

Poston, Tom (1921–) *Zotz* 1962; *The Old Dark House* 1963; *Soldier in the Rain* 1963; *Cold Turkey* 1969; *The Happy Hooker* 1975; *Up the Academy* 1980

Potel, Victor (1889–1947) *The Virginian* 1929; *Doughboys* 1930

Potente, Franka (1974–) *Run Lola Run* 1998; *Anatomy* 2000; *The Princess & the Warrior* 2000; *Blow* 2001; *The Bourne Identity* 2002; *The Bourne Supremacy* 2004; *Creep* 2004

Potter, Chris (1960–) *Arachnid* 2001; *The Pacifier* 2005

Potter, Madeleine (1963–) *The Bostonians* 1984; *Slaves of New York* 1989; *Two Evil Eyes* 1990; *The Golden Bowl* 2000

Potter, Martin (1944–) *Satyricon* 1969; *All Coppers Are…* 1972; *Satan's Slave* 1976; *Gunpowder* 1985

Potter, Monica (1971–) *Martha – Meet Frank, Daniel and Laurence* 1997; *A Cool, Dry Place* 1998; *Patch Adams* 1998; *Without Limits* 1998; *Head over Heels* 2000; *Along Came a Spider* 2001; *I'm with Lucy* 2002; *Saw* 2004

Potts, Annie (1952–) *Corvette Summer* 1978; *Heartaches* 1981; *Crimes of Passion* 1984; *Ghostbusters* 1984; *Jumpin' Jack Flash* 1986; *Pretty in Pink* 1986; *Pass the Ammo* 1988; *Ghostbusters II* 1989; *Who's Harry Crumb?* 1989; *Texasville* 1990; *Breaking the Rules* 1992; *Toy Story* 1995; *Toy Story 2* 1999

Potts, Cliff (1942–) *Silent Running* 1971; *Cry for Me Billy* 1972; *The Groundstar Conspiracy* 1972; *Snow Job* 1972; *Hangup* 1973; *Sahara* 1983

Potts, Nell (1959–) *Rachel, Rachel* 1968; *The Effect of Gamma Rays on Man-in-the-Moon Marigolds* 1972

Pou, José Maria *aka* **Pou, Josep Maria** *The Butterfly Effect* 1995; *Beloved/Friend* 1998; *Goya in Bordeaux* 1999

Pouget, Ely (1961–) *Cool Blue* 1988; *Death Machine* 1994; *Lawnmower Man 2: Beyond Cyberspace* 1995

Poujouly, Georges (1940–2000) *Jeux Interdits* 1953; *And God Created Woman* 1956; *Lift to the Scaffold* 1957

Poulton, Mabel (1901–1994) *The Constant Nymph* 1928; *Escape* 1930

Pounder, C C H (1952–) *Go Tell It on the Mountain* 1984; *Resting Place* 1986; *Bagdad Café* 1987; *Murder in Mississippi* 1990; *Psycho IV: the Beginning* 1990; *The Importance of Being Earnest* 1992; *Benny and Joon* 1993; *For Their Own Good* 1993; *RoboCop 3* 1993; *Sliver* 1993; *Jack Reed: One of Our Own* 1995; *Tales from the Crypt: Demon Knight* 1995; *If These Walls Could Talk* 1996; *End of Days* 1999; *Disappearing Acts* 2000; *Boycott* 2001; *Redemption* 2004

Poupaud, Melvil (1973–) *Treasure Island* 1986; *The Lover* 1992; *A Summer's Tale* 1996; *Three Lives and Only One Death* 1996; *Généalogies d'un Crime* 1997; *Le Divorce* 2003

Poupon, Henri (1882–1953) *Jofroi* 1933; *Angèle* 1934; *Manon des Sources* 1952

Pousse, André (1919–) *Un Flic* 1972; *Police Story* 1975

Povah, Phyllis (1902–1975) *The Women* 1939; *Let's Face It* 1943; *The Marrying Kind* 1952; *Happy Anniversary* 1959

Powell, Addison *In the French Style* 1963; *Three Days of the Condor* 1975

Powell, Brittney *Airborne* 1993; *Dragonworld* 1994

Powell, Charles (1963–) *Screamers* 1995; *The Call of the Wild* 1996; *For Hire* 1997

Powell, Clifton *The Pentagon Wars* 1998; *Phantoms* 1998; *Bones* 2001; *Never Die Alone* 2004; *Ray* 2004

Powell, Dick (1904–1963) *Blessed Event* 1932; *Footlight Parade* 1933; *42nd Street* 1933; *Gold Diggers of 1933* 1933; *The King's Vacation* 1933; *Dames* 1934; *Flirtation Walk* 1934; *Wonder Bar* 1934; *Gold Diggers of 1935* 1935; *A Midsummer Night's Dream* 1935; *Page Miss Glory* 1935; *Shipmates Forever* 1935; *Thanks a Million* 1935; *Colleen* 1936; *Gold Diggers of 1937* 1936; *Stage Struck* 1936; *Hollywood Hotel* 1937; *On the Avenue* 1937; *Going Places* 1938; *Hard to Get* 1938; *Naughty but Nice* 1939; *Christmas in July* 1940; *In the Navy* 1941; *Star Spangled Rhythm* 1942; *Happy Go Lucky* 1943; *Riding High* 1943; *True to Life* 1943; *Farewell My Lovely* 1944; *It Happened Tomorrow* 1944; *Meet the People* 1944; *Cornered* 1945; *Johnny O'Clock* 1947; *Pitfall* 1948; *Station West* 1948; *To the Ends of the Earth* 1948; *Mrs Mike* 1949; *Right Cross* 1950; *Cry Danger* 1951; *The Tall Target* 1951; *The Bad and the Beautiful* 1952; *Susan Slept Here* 1954

Powell, Eleanor (1912–1982) *Broadway Melody of 1936* 1935; *George White's 1935 Scandals* 1935; *Born to Dance* 1936; *Broadway Melody of 1938* 1937; *Rosalie* 1937; *Honolulu* 1939; *Broadway Melody of 1940* 1940; *Lady Be Good* 1941; *Ship Ahoy* 1942; *I Dood It* 1943; *Sensations* 1944

Powell, Esteban (1977–) *Late Bloomers* 1995; *Hitman's Run* 1999

Powell, Jane (1929–) *Song of the Open Road* 1944; *Holiday in Mexico* 1946; *A Date with Judy* 1948; *Three Daring Daughters* 1948; *Nancy Goes to Rio* 1950; *Rich, Young and Pretty* 1951; *Royal Wedding* 1951; *Three Sailors and a Girl* 1953; *Athena* 1954; *Deep in My Heart* 1954; *Seven Brides for Seven Brothers* 1954; *Hit the Deck* 1955; *The Girl Most Likely* 1957; *The Female Animal* 1958

Powell, Lovelady *I Never Sang for My Father* 1969; *The Happy Hooker* 1975

Powell, Michael (1905–1990) *The Edge of the World* 1937; *Boxcar Bertha* 1972

Powell, Robert (1944–) *Secrets* 1971; *The Asphyx* 1972; *Asylum* 1972; *Mahler* 1974; *Tommy* 1975; *The Thirty-Nine Steps* 1978; *Harlequin* 1980; *Jane Austen in Manhattan* 1980; *The Survivor* 1981; *The Hunchback of Notre Dame* 1982; *Imperative* 1982; *The Jigsaw Man* 1984; *Secrets of the Phantom Caverns* 1984; *The Mystery of Edwin Drood* 1993

Powell, William (1892–1984) *Beau Geste* 1926; *Beau Sabreur* 1928; *The Dragnet* 1928; *The Last Command* 1928; *The Canary Murder Case* 1929; *The Four Feathers* 1929; *Paramount on Parade* 1930; *Ladies' Man* 1931; *Man of the World* 1931; *High Pressure* 1932; *Jewel Robbery* 1932; *Lawyer Man* 1932; *One Way Passage* 1932; *The Kennel Murder Case* 1933; *Evelyn Prentice* 1934; *Fashions of 1934* 1934; *The Key* 1934; *Manhattan Melodrama* 1934; *The Thin Man* 1934; *Escapade* 1935; *Reckless* 1935; *Rendezvous* 1935; *Star of Midnight* 1935; *After the Thin Man* 1936; *The Ex-Mrs Bradford* 1936; *The Great Ziegfeld* 1936; *Libeled Lady* 1936; *My Man Godfrey* 1936; *Double Wedding* 1937; *The Emperor's Candlesticks* 1937; *The Last of Mrs Cheyney* 1937; *The Baroness and the Butler* 1938; *Another Thin Man* 1939; *I Love You Again* 1940; *Love Crazy* 1941; *Shadow of the Thin Man* 1941; *Crossroads* 1942; *The Heavenly Body* 1943; *The Thin Man Goes Home* 1944; *Ziegfeld Follies* 1944; *The Hoodlum Saint* 1946; *Life with Father* 1947; *The Senator Was Indiscreet* 1947; *Song of the Thin Man* 1947; *Mr Peabody and the Mermaid* 1948; *Dancing in the Dark* 1949; *Treasure of Lost Canyon* 1952; *The Girl Who Had Everything* 1953; *How to Marry a Millionaire* 1953; *Mister Roberts* 1955

Power, Chad (1984–) *Ruby Cairo* 1992; *3 Ninjas* 1992; *3 Ninjas Knuckle Up* 1995

Power, Hartley (1894–1966) *Aunt Sally* 1933; *The Camels Are Coming* 1934; *Evergreen* 1934; *Where There's a Will* 1936; *A Window in London* 1939; *Return to Yesterday* 1940; *The Man from Morocco* 1944; *The Million Pound Note* 1953; *Roman Holiday* 1953; *To Dorothy, a Son* 1954

Power, Taryn (1953–) *Sinbad and the Eye of the Tiger* 1977; *Tracks* 1977

Power, Tyrone *aka* **Power Jr, Tyrone** *aka* **Power USMCR, Tyrone** (1913–1958) *Fury* 1923; *Ladies in Love* 1936; *Lloyd's of London* 1936; *Café Metropole* 1937; *In Old Chicago* 1937; *Love Is News* 1937; *Thin Ice* 1937; *Alexander's Ragtime Band* 1938; *Marie Antoinette* 1938; *Suez* 1938; *Jesse James* 1939; *The Rains Came* 1939; *Rose of Washington Square* 1939; *Second Fiddle* 1939; *Brigham Young* 1940; *Johnny Apollo* 1940; *The Mark of Zorro* 1940; *Blood and Sand* 1941; *A Yank in the RAF* 1941; *The Black Swan* 1942; *Son of Fury* 1942; *This above All* 1942; *Crash Dive* 1943; *The Razor's Edge* 1946; *Captain from Castile* 1947; *Nightmare Alley* 1947; *That Wonderful Urge* 1948; *Prince of Foxes* 1949; *An American Guerrilla in the Philippines* 1950; *The Black Rose* 1950; *Rawhide* 1951; *Diplomatic Courier* 1952; *Pony Soldier* 1952; *King of the Khyber Rifles* 1953; *The Mississippi Gambler* 1953; *The Long Gray Line* 1955; *Untamed* 1955; *The Eddy Duchin Story* 1956; *The Rising of the Moon* 1957; *Seven Waves Away* 1957; *The Sun Also Rises* 1957; *Witness for the Prosecution* 1957

Powers, Alexandra (1967–) *The Seventh Coin* 1993; *Last Man Standing* 1996

Powers, Mala (1931–) *Cyrano de Bergerac* 1950; *Edge of Doom* 1950; *Outrage* 1950; *Rose of Cimarron* 1952; *City beneath the Sea* 1953; *City That Never Sleeps* 1953; *The Yellow Mountain* 1954; *Bengazi* 1955; *Rage at Dawn* 1955; *Tammy and the Bachelor* 1957; *The Colossus of New York* 1958; *Sierra Baron* 1958; *Daddy's Gone A-Hunting* 1969

Powers, Stefanie (1942–) *Experiment in Terror* 1962; *If a Man Answers* 1962; *The Interns* 1962; *McLintock!* 1963; *Palm Springs Weekend* 1963; *Die! Die! My Darling* 1964; *The New Interns* 1964; *Love Has Many Faces* 1965; *Stagecoach* 1966; *Warning Shot* 1967; *The Boatniks* 1970; *Crescendo* 1970; *The Magnificent Seven Ride!* 1972; *Herbie Rides Again* 1974; *Invisible Strangler* 1976; *Little Moon & Jud McGraw* 1978; *Escape to Athena* 1979

Powers, Tom (1890–1955) *Double Indemnity* 1944; *The Blue Dahlia* 1946; *Angel and the Badman* 1947; *They Won't Believe Me* 1947; *Station West* 1948; *Up in Central Park* 1948; *Destination Moon* 1950; *Right Cross* 1950; *The Strip* 1951; *The Well* 1951

Powley, Bryan (1871–1962) *Conquest of the Air* 1936; *Love from a Stranger* 1936

Pownall, Leon *Bye Bye Blues* 1989; *Angel Square* 1990; *Dirty Pictures* 2000

Prada, José Maria (1925–1978) *The Hunt* 1966; *Pancho Villa* 1971

Prado, Lilia (1929–) *Mexican Bus Ride* 1951; *Wuthering Heights* 1953

Praed, Michael (1960–) *Nightflyers* 1987; *Staggered* 1993; *Darkness Falls* 1998; *9 Dead Gay Guys* 2001

Prager, Stanley *aka* **Praeger, Stanley** (1917–1972) *The Eve of St Mark* 1944; *In the Meantime, Darling* 1944; *A Bell for Adano* 1945; *Do You Love Me?* 1946; *A Foreign Affair* 1948; *Gun Crazy* 1949

Pran (1920–) *Munimji* 1955; *Upkaar* 1967; *Bobby* 1973; *Dharam Veer* 1977

Prat, Gloria *Blood of the Virgins* 1967; *Curious Dr Humpp* 1967

Prather, Joan (1950–) *Big Bad Mama* 1974; *The Devil's Rain* 1975

Pratt, Judson (1916–) *Monster on the Campus* 1958; *The Rise and Fall of Legs Diamond* 1960; *Sergeant Rutledge* 1960; *Vigilante Force* 1975

Pratt, Kyla (1988–) *Barney's Great Adventure* 1998; *Doctor Dolittle* 1998; *Dr Dolittle 2* 2001; *Fat Albert* 2004

Pratt, Mike (1931–1976) *This Is My Street* 1963; *Assassin* 1973

Pratt, Purnell (1885–1941) *The Trespasser* 1929; *I Cover the Waterfront* 1933

Pratt, Susan May (1974–) *Drive Me Crazy* 1999; *10 Things I Hate about You* 1999; *Center Stage* 2000

Preboist, Paul (1927–1997) *The Two of Us* 1967; *Take It Easy* 1971; *An Adventure for Two* 1979

Prechtel, Volker *Heart of Glass* 1976; *Waller's Last Walk* 1989

Preiss, Wolfgang (1910–2002) *The Thousand Eyes of Dr Mabuse* 1960; *The Return of Dr Mabuse* 1961; *The Train* 1964; *Von Ryan's Express* 1965; *Hannibal Brooks* 1968; *Raid on Rommel* 1971; *A Man to Respect* 1972; *The Salzburg Connection* 1972; *Forget Mozart* 1985

Preisser, June (1920–1984) *Babes in Arms* 1939; *Strike Up the Band* 1940; *Music Man* 1948

Préjean, Albert (1893–1979) *Paris Qui Dort* 1923; *An Italian Straw Hat* 1927; *Sous les Toits de Paris* 1930

Preminger, Otto (1906–1986) *The Pied Piper* 1942; *Margin for Error* 1943; *They Got Me Covered* 1943; *Where Do We Go from Here?* 1945; *Stalag 17* 1953

Premnath *Barsaat* 1949; *Bobby* 1973

Prentiss, Ann (1941–) *Any Wednesday* 1966; *The Out of Towners* 1970; *California Split* 1974

Prentiss, Paula (1939–) *Where the Boys Are* 1960; *Bachelor in Paradise* 1961; *The Honeymoon Machine* 1961; *The Horizontal Lieutenant* 1962; *Follow the Boys* 1963; *Man's Favorite Sport?* 1964; *The World of Henry Orient* 1964; *In Harm's Way* 1965; *What's New, Pussycat?* 1965; *Catch-22* 1970; *Born to Win* 1971; *The Last of the Red Hot Lovers* 1972; *The Parallax View* 1974; *The Stepford Wives* 1975; *The Black Marble* 1980; *Buddy Buddy* 1981; *Saturday the 14th* 1981

Presle, Micheline (1922–) *La Nuit Fantastique* 1942; *Devil in the Flesh* 1947; *An American Guerrilla in the Philippines* 1950; *Adventures of Captain Fabian* 1951; *Royal Affairs in Versailles* 1953; *The Bride Is Too Beautiful* 1956; *Blind Date* 1959; *The Seven Deadly Sins* 1961; *If a Man Answers* 1962; *Imperial Venus* 1963; *The Prize* 1963; *Male Hunt* 1964; *La Religieuse* 1965; *The Magic Donkey* 1970; *The Blood of Others* 1984; *I Want to Go Home* 1989

Presley, Elvis (1935–1977) *Love Me Tender* 1956; *Jailhouse Rock* 1957; *Loving You* 1957; *King Creole* 1958; *Flaming Star* 1960; *GI Blues* 1960; *Blue Hawaii* 1961; *Wild in the Country* 1961; *Follow That Dream* 1962; *Girls! Girls! Girls!* 1962; *It Happened at the World's Fair* 1962; *Kid Galahad* 1962; *Fun in Acapulco* 1963; *Kissin' Cousins* 1964; *Roustabout* 1964; *Viva Las Vegas* 1964; *Girl Happy* 1965; *Harum Scarum* 1965; *Tickle Me* 1965; *Frankie & Johnny* 1966; *Paradise, Hawaiian Style* 1966; *Spinout* 1966; *Clambake* 1967; *Double Trouble* 1967; *Easy Come, Easy Go* 1967; *Live a Little, Love a Little* 1968; *Speedway* 1968; *Stay Away, Joe* 1968; *Change of Habit* 1969; *Charro!* 1969; *The Trouble with Girls* 1969

Presley, Priscilla (1945–) *The Naked Gun* 1988; *The Adventures of Ford Fairlane* 1990; *The Naked Gun $2\frac{1}{2}$: the Smell of Fear* 1991; *Naked Gun $33\frac{1}{3}$: the Final Insult* 1994

Presnell, Harve (1933–) *The Unsinkable Molly Brown* 1964; *The Glory Guys* 1965; *When the Boys Meet the Girls* 1965; *Paint Your Wagon* 1969; *Fargo* 1995; *The Whole Wide World* 1996; *Face/Off* 1997; *Julian Po* 1997; *Everything That Rises* 1998

Pressly, Jaime (1977–) *Ringmaster* 1998; *Tomcats* 2000; *Joe Dirt* 2001; *Not Another Teen Movie* 2001; *Ticker* 2001; *Torque* 2003

Pressman, Lawrence (1939–) *The Hellstrom Chronicle* 1971; *Shaft* 1971; *The Man in the Glass Booth* 1975; *Hanoi Hilton* 1987; *Angus* 1995; *Freshman Fall* 1996; *The Maker* 1997; *Very Bad Things* 1998

Presson, Jason (1971–) *The Stone Boy* 1984; *Explorers* 1985; *Lady in White* 1988; *Saturday the 14th Strikes Back* 1988

Prestia, Jo (1960–) *The Dream Life of Angels* 1998; *Irreversible* 2002; *The Ordeal* 2004

Preston, Billy (1946–) *Sgt Pepper's Lonely Hearts Club Band* 1978; *Blame It on the Night* 1984

Preston, Carrie *The Journey* 1997; *My Best Friend's Wedding* 1997; *Grace and Glorie* 1998

Preston, Cyndy *Pin* 1988; *Whale Music* 1994

Preston, J A *Real Life* 1979; *Body Heat* 1981; *Remo – Unarmed and Dangerous* 1985; *Wings of the Apache* 1990; *Captain Ron* 1992

Preston, Kelly (1962–) *Mischief* 1985; *Secret Admirer* 1985; *52 Pick-Up* 1986; *SpaceCamp* 1986; *Love at Stake* 1987; *A Tiger's Tale* 1987; *Spellbinder* 1988; *Twins* 1988; *The Experts* 1989; *Run* 1991; *Only You* 1992; *Cheyenne Warrior* 1994; *Love Is a Gun* 1994; *Citizen Ruth* 1996; *Jerry Maguire* 1996; *Addicted to Love* 1997; *Nothing to Lose* 1997; *Holy Man* 1998; *Jack Frost* 1998; *For Love of the Game* 1999; *Dr Seuss' The Cat in the Hat* 2003; *View from the Top* 2003; *What a Girl Wants* 2003

Preston, Robert (1918–1987) *King of Alcatraz* 1938; *Beau Geste* 1939; *Union Pacific* 1939; *North West Mounted Police* 1940; *Typhoon* 1940; *Reap the Wild Wind* 1942; *This Gun for Hire* 1942; *Wake Island* 1942; *The Macomber Affair* 1947; *Blood on the Moon* 1948; *Whispering Smith* 1948; *The Lady Gambles* 1949; *Tulsa* 1949; *The Sundowners* 1950; *Best of the Badmen* 1951; *Cloudburst* 1951; *Face to Face* 1952; *The Last Frontier* 1955; *The Dark at the Top of the Stairs* 1960; *How the West Was Won* 1962; *The Music Man* 1962; *All the Way Home* 1963; *Island of Love* 1963; *Child's Play* 1972; *Junior Bonner* 1972; *Mame* 1974; *Semi-Tough* 1977; *SOB* 1981;

Victor/Victoria 1982; *The Last Starfighter* 1984
Preu, Dana *Gal Young Un* 1979; *Something Wild* 1986
Préville, Gisèle *Against the Wind* 1947; *The Dancing Years* 1949
Prévost, Daniel (1939–) *Uranus* 1990; *Le Colonel Chabert* 1994; *Le Dîner de Cons* 1998; *Pas sur la Bouche* 2003
Prévost, Françoise (1930–1997) *Paris Nous Appartient* 1960; *Payroll* 1961; *The Condemned of Altona* 1962; *The Pink Telephone* 1975
Prevost, Marie (1898–1937) *The Marriage Circle* 1924; *Kiss Me Again* 1925; *The Racket* 1928; *Ladies of Leisure* 1930; *Party Girl* 1930; *The Sin of Madelon Claudet* 1931; *Sporting Blood* 1931; *Hell Divers* 1932; *Three Wise Girls* 1932; *Only Yesterday* 1933; *Hands across the Table* 1935
Price, Dennis (1915–1973) *A Canterbury Tale* 1944; *A Place of One's Own* 1944; *Caravan* 1946; *Hungry Hill* 1946; *The Magic Bow* 1946; *Dear Murderer* 1947; *Easy Money* 1947; *Holiday Camp* 1947; *Jassy* 1947; *The Master of Bankdam* 1947; *Good Time Girl* 1948; *Snowbound* 1948; *The Bad Lord Byron* 1949; *The Dancing Years* 1949; *Kind Hearts and Coronets* 1949; *The Lost People* 1949; *The Adventurers* 1950; *Murder without Crime* 1950; *Lady Godiva Rides Again* 1951; *The Intruder* 1953; *For Better, for Worse* 1954; *Oh, Rosalinda!!* 1955; *That Lady* 1955; *Charley Moon* 1956; *Fortune Is a Woman* 1956; *Private's Progress* 1956; *A Touch of the Sun* 1956; *The Naked Truth* 1957; *Danger Within* 1958; *I'm All Right Jack* 1959; *Oscar Wilde* 1959; *The Millionairess* 1960; *No Love for Johnnie* 1960; *Piccadilly Third Stop* 1960; *The Pure Hell of St Trinian's* 1960; *The Rebel* 1960; *School for Scoundrels* 1960; *Tunes of Glory* 1960; *Double Bunk* 1961; *Go to Blazes* 1961; *Victim* 1961; *Watch It, Sailor!* 1961; *What a Carve Up!* 1961; *The Amorous Prawn* 1962; *Kill or Cure* 1962; *Play It Cool* 1962; *The Pot Carriers* 1962; *The Cracksman* 1963; *Doctor in Distress* 1963; *Tamahine* 1963; *The VIPs* 1963; *The Comedy Man* 1964; *The Earth Dies Screaming* 1964; *A Jolly Bad Fellow* 1964; *Ten Little Indians* 1965; *Just like a Woman* 1966; *Some Will, Some Won't* 1969; *The Horror of Frankenstein* 1970; *The Rise and Rise of Michael Rimmer* 1970; *Vampyros Lesbos* 1970; *Twins of Evil* 1971; *The Adventures of Barry McKenzie* 1972; *Dracula, Prisoner of Frankenstein* 1972; *Go for a Take* 1972; *Pulp* 1972; *That's Your Funeral* 1972; *Horror Hospital* 1973; *Theatre of Blood* 1973
Price, Marc (1968–) *Trick or Treat* 1986; *The Rescue* 1988
Price, Molly (1966–) *Jersey Girl* 1992; *Risk* 1993; *Kiss Me, Guido* 1997
Price, Nancy (1880–1970) *The Stars Look Down* 1939; *Secret Mission* 1942; *Madonna of the Seven Moons* 1944; *I Know Where I'm Going!* 1945; *I Live in Grosvenor Square* 1945; *The Master of Bankdam* 1947; *The Three Weird Sisters* 1948; *Mandy* 1952
Price, Vincent (1911–1993) *Green Hell* 1939; *The Private Lives of Elizabeth and Essex* 1939; *Tower of London* 1939; *Brigham Young* 1940; *The House of the Seven Gables* 1940; *Hudson's Bay* 1940; *The Invisible Man Returns* 1940; *The Song of Bernadette* 1943; *The Eve of St Mark* 1944; *The Keys of the Kingdom* 1944; *Laura* 1944; *Wilson* 1944; *Leave Her to Heaven* 1945; *A Royal Scandal* 1945; *Dragonwyck* 1946; *The Long Night* 1947; *Moss Rose* 1947; *The Web* 1947; *The Three Musketeers* 1948; *Up in Central Park* 1948; *The Bribe* 1949; *The Baron of Arizona* 1950; *Champagne for Caesar* 1950; *Adventures of Captain Fabian* 1951; *His Kind of Woman* 1951; *The Las Vegas Story* 1952; *House of Wax* 1953; *Casanova's Big Night* 1954; *Dangerous Mission* 1954; *The Mad Magician* 1954; *Son of Sinbad* 1955; *Serenade* 1956; *The Ten Commandments* 1956; *While the City Sleeps* 1956; *The Story of Mankind* 1957; *The Fly* 1958; *House on Haunted Hill* 1958; *The Bat* 1959; *The Big Circus* 1959; *Return of the Fly* 1959; *The Tingler* 1959; *The Fall of the House of Usher* 1960; *Gordon the Black Pirate* 1961; *Master of the World* 1961; *Nefertite, Queen of the Nile* 1961; *The Pit and the Pendulum* 1961; *Confessions of an Opium Eater* 1962; *Convicts Four* 1962; *Tales of Terror* 1962; *Tower of London* 1962; *Diary of a Madman* 1963; *The Haunted Palace* 1963; *The Raven* 1963; *Twice Told Tales* 1963; *The Comedy of Terrors* 1964; *The Last Man on Earth* 1964; *The Masque of the Red Death* 1964; *The Tomb of Ligeia* 1964; *City under the Sea* 1965; *Dr Goldfoot and the Bikini Machine* 1965; *Dr Goldfoot and the Girl Bombs* 1966; *Histoires Extraordinaires* 1967; *House of a Thousand Dolls* 1967; *Witchfinder General* 1968; *More Dead than Alive* 1969; *The Oblong Box* 1969; *Scream and Scream Again* 1969; *The Trouble with Girls* 1969; *Cry of the Banshee* 1970; *The Abominable Dr Phibes* 1971; *Dr Phibes Rises Again* 1972; *Theatre of Blood* 1973; *Madhouse* 1974; *Percy's Progress* 1974; *Scavenger Hunt* 1979; *The Monster Club* 1980; *Bloodbath at the House of Death* 1983; *House of the Long Shadows* 1983; *Basil the Great Mouse Detective* 1986; *The Whales of August* 1987; *Dead Heat* 1988; *Catchfire* 1989; *Edward Scissorhands* 1990; *The Heart of Justice* 1992; *Arabian Knight* 1995
Prichard, Robert *The Toxic Avenger* 1985; *Class of Nuke 'em High* 1986; *Alien Space Avenger* 1989
Priest, Pat (1936–) *Easy Come, Easy Go* 1967; *The Incredible Two-Headed Transplant* 1971
Priestley, Jason (1969–) *Calendar Girl* 1993; *Tombstone* 1993; *Coldblooded* 1995; *Love and Death on Long Island* 1998; *Eye of the Beholder* 1999; *The Highwayman* 1999; *Kiss Tomorrow Goodbye* 2000; *Lion of Oz* 2000; *The Fourth Angel* 2001; *Cherish* 2002
Prieto, Aurore *Thérèse* 1986; *Docteur Petiot* 1990
Prim, Suzy (1895–1991) *The Lower Depths* 1936; *Mayerling* 1936
Prima, Louis (1910–1978) *Senior Prom* 1958; *Hey Boy! Hey Girl!* 1959; *The Jungle Book* 1967
Primus, Barry (1938–) *Puzzle of a Downfall Child* 1970; *Von Richthofen and Brown* 1971; *Boxcar Bertha* 1972; *The Gravy Train* 1974; *New York, New York* 1977; *Avalanche* 1978; *Heartland* 1979; *Night Games* 1979; *The Rose* 1979; *Absence of Malice* 1981; *The River* 1984; *SpaceCamp* 1986; *The Stranger* 1987; *Big Business* 1988; *Torn Apart* 1990; *Night and the City* 1992; *Flipping* 1996; *James Dean* 2001
Prince (1958–) *Purple Rain* 1984; *Under the Cherry Moon* 1986; *Graffiti Bridge* 1990
Prince, Faith (1957–) *The Last Dragon* 1985; *Dave* 1993; *My Father the Hero* 1994; *Big Bully* 1996; *Picture Perfect* 1997
Prince, William (1913–1996) *Destination Tokyo* 1943; *Objective, Burma!* 1945; *Cinderella Jones* 1946; *Carnegie Hall* 1947; *Dead Reckoning* 1947; *Cyrano de Bergerac* 1950; *Secret of Treasure Mountain* 1956; *The Vagabond King* 1956; *Macabre* 1958; *The Heartbreak Kid* 1972; *The Gauntlet* 1977; *Face of a Stranger* 1978; *Gideon's Trumpet* 1980; *Kiss Me Goodbye* 1982; *Spies like Us* 1985; *Vice Versa* 1988
Principal, Victoria (1950–) *The Life and Times of Judge Roy Bean* 1972; *Earthquake* 1974; *Vigilante Force* 1975; *I Will... I Will... for Now* 1976
Prine, Andrew (1936–) *The Miracle Worker* 1962; *Bandolero!* 1968; *The Devil's Brigade* 1968; *Generation* 1969; *Grizzly* 1976; *The Evil* 1978; *Amityville II: the Possession* 1982; *They're Playing With Fire* 1984; *Serial Killer* 1996; *Possums* 1998
Pringle, Bryan (1935–2002) *Saturday Night and Sunday Morning* 1960; *French Dressing* 1964; *The Early Bird* 1965; *The Boy Friend* 1971; *Haunted Honeymoon* 1986; *Drowning by Numbers* 1988; *The Steal* 1994; *Darkness Falls* 1998
Prinsloo, Sandra *The Gods Must Be Crazy* 1980; *Quest for Love* 1988
Prinze Jr, Freddie (1976–) *The House of Yes* 1997; *I Know What You Did Last Summer* 1997; *I Still Know What You Did Last Summer* 1998; *She's All That* 1999; *Wing Commander* 1999; *Boys and Girls* 2000; *Down to You* 2000; *Head over Heels* 2000; *Summer Catch* 2001; *Scooby-Doo* 2002; *Scooby-Doo 2: Monsters Unleashed* 2004
Prip, Henrik (1960–) *The Idiots* 1998; *Minor Mishaps* 2002; *In Your Hands* 2004
Pritchard, Hilary *Under the Doctor* 1976; *A Touch of the Sun* 1979
Pritchett, Paula (1947–) *Chappaqua* 1966; *The Wrath of God* 1972
Prival, Lucien (1900–1994) *Hell's Angels* 1930; *Party Girl* 1930
Privat, Gilles *Romuald et Juliette* 1989; *La Crise* 1992
Prochnow, Jürgen (1941–) *The Lost Honour of Katharina Blum* 1975; *Das Boot* 1981; *The Keep* 1983; *Killing Cars* 1986; *Beverly Hills Cop II* 1987; *The Seventh Sign* 1988; *A Dry White Season* 1989; *The Fourth War* 1990; *The Man Inside* 1990; *Robin Hood* 1990; *Body of Evidence* 1992; *In the Mouth of Madness* 1994; *Judge Dredd* 1995; *DNA* 1996; *The English Patient* 1996; *Air Force One* 1997; *The Replacement Killers* 1998; *Wing Commander* 1999; *House of the Dead* 2003
Procopio, Lou (1938–1995) *The Wild Angels* 1966; *Gas-s-s-s, or It Became Necessary to Destroy the World in Order to Save It* 1970
Procter, Emily (1968–) *Breast Men* 1997; *Family Plan* 1997; *Body Shots* 1999
Proctor, Philip aka **Proctor, Phil** (1940–) *A Safe Place* 1971; *Tunnelvision* 1976; *The Rugrats Movie* 1998
Proctor, Rupert aka **Procter, Rupert** *The Low Down* 2000; *One for the Road* 2003
Proietti, Luigi (1940–) *Lady Liberty* 1971; *The Inheritance* 1976
Prophet, Melissa *Players* 1979; *Van Nuys Blvd* 1979; *Better Late Than Never* 1983; *Invasion USA* 1985
Prosky, Robert (1930–) *Thief* 1981; *Hanky Panky* 1982; *Christine* 1983; *The Keep* 1983; *The Lords of Discipline* 1983; *The Natural* 1984; *Outrageous Fortune* 1987; *Things Change* 1988; *Funny about Love* 1990; *Green Card* 1990; *Gremlins 2: the New Batch* 1990; *Loose Cannons* 1990; *Age Isn't Everything* 1991; *Far and Away* 1992; *Last Action Hero* 1993; *Dead Man Walking* 1995; *The Scarlet Letter* 1995; *The Chamber* 1996; *Mad City* 1997; *Dudley Do-Right* 1999
Prouty, Jed (1879–1956) *The Broadway Melody* 1929; *The Devil's Holiday* 1930; *The Duke of West Point* 1938; *The Gracie Allen Murder Case* 1939; *Hollywood Cavalcade* 1939; *Pot o' Gold* 1941; *Guilty Bystander* 1950
Proval, David (1942–) *Mean Streets* 1973; *Wizards* 1977; *Vice Versa* 1988; *Innocent Blood* 1992; *Romeo Is Bleeding* 1992; *Flipping* 1996
Provine, Dorothy (1937–) *The Bonnie Parker Story* 1958; *Good Neighbor Sam* 1964; *The Great Race* 1965; *That Darn Cat!* 1965; *One Spy Too Many* 1966; *Who's Minding the Mint?* 1967; *Never a Dull Moment* 1968
Provost, Jon (1950–) *Escapade in Japan* 1957; *Lassie's Great Adventure* 1963
Prowse, Dave aka **Prowse, David** (1935–) *The Horror of Frankenstein* 1970; *A Clockwork Orange* 1971; *Frankenstein and the Monster from Hell* 1973; *White Cargo* 1973; *The Best of Benny Hill* 1974; *Callan* 1974; *The People That Time Forgot* 1977; *Star Wars Episode IV: a New Hope* 1977; *Star Wars Episode V: the Empire Strikes Back* 1980; *Star Wars Episode VI: Return of the Jedi* 1983
Prowse, Juliet (1937–1996) *Can-Can* 1960; *GI Blues* 1960; *The Fiercest Heart* 1961; *The Second Time Around* 1961; *Who Killed Teddy Bear?* 1965
Pruner, Karl *One True Love* 2000; *The Recruit* 2002
Pryce, Jonathan (1947–) *Breaking Glass* 1980; *Loophole* 1980; *The Ploughman's Lunch* 1983; *Something Wicked This Way Comes* 1983; *Brazil* 1985; *The Doctor and the Devils* 1985; *Haunted Honeymoon* 1986; *Man on Fire* 1987; *The Adventures of Baron Munchausen* 1988; *Consuming Passions* 1988; *The Rachel Papers* 1989; *Freddie as FRO7* 1992; *Glengarry Glen Ross* 1992; *Barbarians at the Gate* 1993; *A Business Affair* 1993; *Deadly Advice* 1993; *Shades of Fear* 1993; *Shopping* 1993; *Stanley's Magic Garden* 1994; *Carrington* 1995; *Evita* 1996; *Regeneration* 1997; *Tomorrow Never Dies* 1997; *Ronin* 1998; *Stigmata* 1999; *Very Annie-Mary* 2000; *The Affair of the Necklace* 2001; *Bride of the Wind* 2001; *Unconditional Love* 2001; *Pirates of the Caribbean: the Curse of the Black Pearl* 2003; *What a Girl Wants* 2003; *De-Lovely* 2004
Pryor, Nicholas (1935–) *The Happy Hooker* 1975; *Smile* 1975; *Damien – Omen II* 1978; *Gideon's Trumpet* 1980; *Risky Business* 1983; *On Dangerous Ground* 1986; *Home Front* 1987; *Less than Zero* 1987; *Nightbreaker* 1989; *Brain Dead* 1990; *Hail Caesar* 1994; *Carriers* 1998
Pryor, Richard (1940–) *The Busy Body* 1967; *Wild in the Streets* 1968; *Dynamite Chicken* 1971; *Lady Sings the Blues* 1972; *Hit!* 1973; *The Mack* 1973; *Uptown Saturday Night* 1974; *Adios Amigo* 1975; *The Bingo Long Travelling All-Stars and Motor Kings* 1976; *Car Wash* 1976; *Silver Streak* 1976; *Greased Lightning* 1977; *Which Way Is Up?* 1977; *Blue Collar* 1978; *California Suite* 1978; *The Wiz* 1978; *In God We Trust* 1980; *Stir Crazy* 1980; *Wholly Moses!* 1980; *Bustin' Loose* 1981; *Richard Pryor: Live on the Sunset Strip* 1982; *Some Kind of Hero* 1982; *The Toy* 1982; *Superman III* 1983; *Brewster's Millions* 1985; *Jo Jo Dancer, Your Life Is Calling* 1986; *Critical Condition* 1987; *Moving* 1988; *Harlem Nights* 1989; *See No Evil, Hear No Evil* 1989; *Another You* 1991; *Lost Highway* 1996
Pryor, Roger (1901–1974) *Belle of the Nineties* 1934; *Lady by Choice* 1934; *The Man They Could Not Hang* 1939; *The Lone Wolf Meets a Lady* 1940
Pryse, Hugh (1910–1955) *Three Cases of Murder* 1953; *Valley of Song* 1953
Pszoniak, Wojciech aka **Pszoniak, Wojtek** (1942–) *Danton* 1982; *Korczak* 1990
Pu Quanxin *The Blue Kite* 1992; *Shower* 1999
Puente, Jesus (1930–2000) *Adios Gringo* 1965; *Hatchet for the Honeymoon* 1969
Pugh, Robert *Old Scores* 1991; *Priest* 1994; *The Englishman Who Went up a Hill, but Came down a Mountain* 1995; *The Tichborne Claimant* 1998
Pugh, Willard *The Color Purple* 1985; *RoboCop 2* 1990; *Ambition* 1991
Puglia, Frank (1892–1975) *Isn't Life Wonderful* 1924; *Bulldog Drummond's Revenge* 1937; *Arise, My Love* 1940; *That Night in Rio* 1941; *The Boogie Man Will Get You* 1942; *Jungle Book* 1942; *Ali Baba and the Forty Thieves* 1944; *Blood on the Sun* 1945; *Without Reservations* 1946; *Road to Rio* 1947; *Colorado Territory* 1949; *Walk Softly, Stranger* 1949; *The Black Hand* 1950; *The Bandits of Corsica* 1953; *20 Million Miles to Earth* 1957; *The Black Orchid* 1959; *Girls! Girls! Girls!* 1962
Puglisi, Aldo *Marriage – Italian Style* 1964; *Seduced and Abandoned* 1964
Pullman, Bill (1953–) *Ruthless People* 1986; *The Serpent and the Rainbow* 1987; *Spaceballs* 1987; *The Accidental Tourist* 1988; *Rocket Gibraltar* 1988; *Cold Feet* 1989; *Brain Dead* 1990; *Bright Angel* 1990; *Going Under* 1990; *Sibling Rivalry* 1990; *Liebestraum* 1991; *Crazy in Love* 1992; *The News Boys* 1992; *Singles* 1992; *The Last Seduction* 1993; *Malice* 1993; *Mr Jones* 1993; *Sleepless in Seattle* 1993; *Sommersby* 1993; *The Favor* 1994; *Wyatt Earp* 1994; *Casper* 1995; *While You Were Sleeping* 1995; *Independence Day* 1996; *Lost Highway* 1996; *Mr Wrong* 1996; *The End of Violence* 1997; *Zero Effect* 1997; *Brokedown Palace* 1999; *History Is Made at Night* 1999; *Lake Placid* 1999; *The Guilty* 2000; *Titan AE* 2000; *Igby Goes Down* 2002; *The Grudge* 2004; *Dear Wendy* 2005
Pully, B S (1910–1972) *Greenwich Village* 1944; *Nob Hill* 1945; *Do You Love Me?* 1946; *Guys and Dolls* 1955
Pulver, Liselotte aka **Pulver, Lilo** (1929–) *Arms and the Man* 1958; *A Time to Love and a Time to Die* 1958; *One, Two, Three* 1961; *A Global Affair* 1964; *La Religieuse* 1965
Punsley, Bernard (1923–2004) *Dead End* 1937; *Angels Wash Their Faces* 1939
Purcell, Dick aka **Purcell, Richard** (1908–1944) *Bullets or Ballots* 1936; *Arise, My Love* 1940; *The Bank Dick* 1940; *New Moon* 1940; *Reveille with Beverly* 1943
Purcell, Dominic (1970–) *Equilibrium* 2002; *Blade: Trinity* 2004
Purcell, Irene (1902–1972) *The Passionate Plumber* 1932; *Westward Passage* 1932
Purcell, Lee (1957–) *Adam at 6 AM* 1970; *Kid Blue* 1971; *Dirty Little Billy* 1972; *Mr Majestyk* 1974; *Almost Summer* 1977; *Big Wednesday* 1978; *Eddie Macon's Run* 1983; *The Incredible Hulk Returns* 1988
Purcell, Noel (1900–1985) *The Blue Lagoon* 1949; *No Resting Place* 1950; *Appointment with Venus* 1951; *Encore* 1951; *Father's Doing Fine* 1952; *Grand National Night* 1953; *Mad about Men* 1954; *The Seekers* 1954; *Jacqueline* 1956; *Lust for Life* 1956; *The Rising of the Moon* 1957; *Ferry to Hong Kong* 1958; *The Key* 1958; *Merry Andrew* 1958; *Rockets Galore* 1958; *Rooney* 1958; *No Kidding* 1960; *Double Bunk* 1961; *The Iron Maiden* 1962; *The Violent Enemy* 1969; *Where's Jack?* 1969
Purdell, Reginald (1896–1963) *Congress Dances* 1931; *The Old Curiosity Shop* 1934; *Variety Jubilee* 1942; *Bell-Bottom George* 1943; *We Dive at Dawn* 1943; *Love Story* 1944; *Two Thousand Women* 1944

Purdom, Edmund (1924–) *Athena* 1954; *The Egyptian* 1954; *The Student Prince* 1954; *The King's Thief* 1955; *The Prodigal* 1955; *The Cossacks* 1959; *Moment of Danger* 1960; *Nefertite, Queen of the Nile* 1961; *The Beauty Jungle* 1964; *The Comedy Man* 1964; *The Yellow Rolls-Royce* 1964; *The Man Who Laughs* 1966; *Pieces* 1982

Purefoy, James (1964–) *Feast of July* 1995; *Bedrooms and Hallways* 1998; *Lighthouse* 1999; *Mansfield Park* 1999; *Maybe Baby* 1999; *Women Talking Dirty* 1999; *Don Quixote* 2000; *The Wedding Tackle* 2000; *Resident Evil* 2002; *Vanity Fair* 2004

Puri, Amrish (1937–2005) *Nishant* 1975; *Indiana Jones and the Temple of Doom* 1984; *Mr India* 1986; *Dilwale Dulhania Le Jayenge* 1995; *Chachi 420* 1997; *Pardes* 1997; *Virasat* 1997; *Taal* 1999; *Zubeidaa* 2000; *Khushi* 2002; *Aitraaz* 2004; *Dev* 2004; *Garv: Pride & Honour* 2004; *Hulchul* 2004; *Kisna – the Warrior Poet* 2004; *Mujhse Shaadi Karogi* 2004

Puri, Om (1950–) *Sadgati* 1981; *Mirch Masala* 1987; *Disha* 1990; *City of Joy* 1992; *In Custody* 1993; *Wolf* 1994; *Brothers in Trouble* 1995; *The Ghost and the Darkness* 1996; *Maachis* 1996; *Chachi 420* 1997; *My Son the Fanatic* 1997; *Such a Long Journey* 1998; *East Is East* 1999; *Bollywood Calling* 2000; *The Mystic Masseur* 2001; *The Parole Officer* 2001; *Awara Paagal Deewana* 2002; *Code 46* 2003; *Dev* 2004; *Kisna – the Warrior Poet* 2004; *Kyun! Ho Gaya Na ...* 2004; *Lakshya* 2004

Puri, Linda (1955–) *Crazy Mama* 1975; *The High Country* 1981; *Visiting Hours* 1982; *Danielle Steel's Secrets* 1992

Purviance, Edna (1894–1958) *The Tramp* 1915; *Work* 1915; *Behind the Screen* 1916; *The Floorwalker* 1916; *The Pawnshop* 1916; *The Rink* 1916; *The Vagabond* 1916; *The Cure* 1917; *The Immigrant* 1917; *Shoulder Arms* 1918; *A Day's Pleasure* 1919; *Sunnyside* 1919; *The Idle Class* 1921; *The Kid* 1921; *Pay Day* 1922; *The Pilgrim* 1923; *A Woman of Paris* 1923

Putzulu, Bruno (1967–) *The Bait* 1995; *Pourquoi Pas Moi?* 1999; *Eloge de l'Amour* 2001; *Monsieur N* 2003

Pyle, Denver (1920–1997) *The Flying Saucer* 1949; *Rage at Dawn* 1955; *Seventh Cavalry* 1956; *Gun Duel in Durango* 1957; *The Lonely Man* 1957; *Fort Massacre* 1958; *Cast a Long Shadow* 1959; *Geronimo* 1962; *Mail Order Bride* 1963; *The Rounders* 1965; *Gunpoint* 1966; *Bonnie and Clyde* 1967; *Welcome to Hard Times* 1967; *Bandolero!* 1968; *something big* 1971; *Who Fears the Devil?* 1972; *Winterhawk* 1975; *Hawmps* 1976; *Welcome to LA* 1976; *Delta Fever* 1988

Pyne, Natasha (1946–) *The Idol* 1966; *The Taming of the Shrew* 1967; *Father Dear Father* 1972; *Madhouse* 1974; *One of Our Dinosaurs Is Missing* 1975

Pyper-Ferguson, John *Ski School* 1991; *Space Marines* 1996; *Drive* 1997

Q

Qi Shu (1976–) *Gorgeous* 1999; *A Man Called Hero* 1999; *The Transporter* 2002; *The Eye 2* 2004

Qin Shaobo (1982–) *Ocean's Eleven* 2001; *Ocean's Twelve* 2004

Qissi, Michel *AWOL* 1990; *Kickboxer 2: the Road Back* 1990

Quaid, Dennis (1954–) *Crazy Mama* 1975; *September 30, 1955* 1977; *The Seniors* 1978; *Breaking Away* 1979; *GORP* 1980; *The Long Riders* 1980; *All Night Long* 1981; *Bill* 1981; *Caveman* 1981; *The Night the Lights Went Out in Georgia* 1981; *Tough Enough* 1982; *Jaws III* 1983; *The Right Stuff* 1983; *Dreamscape* 1984; *Enemy Mine* 1985; *The Big Easy* 1986; *Innerspace* 1987; *Suspect* 1987; *DOA* 1988; *Everybody's All-American* 1988; *Great Balls of Fire!* 1989; *Come See the Paradise* 1990; *Postcards from the Edge* 1990; *Flesh and Bone* 1993; *Undercover Blues* 1993; *Wilder Napalm* 1993; *Wyatt Earp* 1994; *Something to Talk About* 1995; *DragonHeart* 1996; *Gang Related* 1997; *Savior* 1997; *Switchback* 1997; *Everything That Rises* 1998; *The Parent Trap* 1998; *Playing by Heart* 1998; *Any Given Sunday* 1999; *Frequency* 2000; *Traffic* 2000; *Dinner with Friends* 2001; *Far from Heaven* 2002; *The Rookie* 2002; *Cold Creek Manor* 2003; *The Alamo* 2004; *The Day after Tomorrow* 2004; *Flight of the Phoenix* 2004; *In Good Company* 2004

Quaid, Randy *aka* **Quaid, Randall R "Randy"** (1950–) *The Last Picture Show* 1971; *What's Up, Doc?* 1972; *The Last Detail* 1973; *The Lolly-Madonna War* 1973; *Paper Moon* 1973; *The Apprenticeship of Duddy Kravitz* 1974; *Breakout* 1975; *Bound for Glory* 1976; *The Missouri Breaks* 1976; *The Choirboys* 1977; *Midnight Express* 1978; *Foxes* 1980; *The Long Riders* 1980; *Heartbeeps* 1981; *National Lampoon's Vacation* 1983; *The Wild Life* 1984; *Fool for Love* 1985; *The Slugger's Wife* 1985; *The Wraith* 1986; *No Man's Land* 1987; *Caddyshack II* 1988; *Moving* 1988; *Parents* 1988; *Bloodhounds of Broadway* 1989; *Cold Dog Soup* 1989; *National Lampoon's Christmas Vacation* 1989; *Out Cold* 1989; *Days of Thunder* 1990; *Martians Go Home* 1990; *Quick Change* 1990; *Texasville* 1990; *Freaked* 1993; *The Paper* 1994; *Bye Bye Love* 1995; *Ed McBain's 87th Precinct* 1995; *Independence Day* 1996; *Kingpin* 1996; *Last Dance* 1996; *Hard Rain* 1997; *Vegas Vacation* 1997; *Last Rites* 1998; *The Adventures of Rocky & Bullwinkle* 1999; *Purgatory* 1999; *The Day the World Ended* 2001; *Not Another Teen Movie* 2001; *Pluto Nash* 2001; *Milwaukee, Minnesota* 2002; *Home on the Range* 2004

Qualen, John (1899–1987) *Counsellor-at-Law* 1933; *Our Daily Bread* 1934; *Black Fury* 1935; *The Road to Glory* 1936; *Thunder Afloat* 1939; *Angels over Broadway* 1940; *The Grapes of Wrath* 1940; *The Long Voyage Home* 1940; *Daniel and the Devil* 1941; *Out of the Fog* 1941; *Arabian Nights* 1942; *Jungle Book* 1942; *Tortilla Flat* 1942; *An American Romance* 1944; *Dark Waters* 1944; *Adventure* 1945; *Captain Kidd* 1945; *Hollow Triumph* 1948; *The Big Steal* 1949; *Hans Christian Andersen* 1952; *Ambush at Tomahawk Gap* 1953; *Passion* 1954; *At Gunpoint* 1955; *Unchained* 1955; *The Searchers* 1956; *The Big Land* 1957

Qualls, D J *Road Trip* 2000; *The Core* 2002; *The New Guy* 2002

Quan, Ke Huy (1971–) *Indiana Jones and the Temple of Doom* 1984; *The Goonies* 1985

Quarrier, Iain *Cul-de-Sac* 1966; *The Fearless Vampire Killers* 1967; *One Plus One* 1968; *Wonderwall* 1968

Quarry, Robert (1925–) *The Loves of Count Iorga, Vampire* 1970; *The Return of Count Yorga* 1971; *Dr Phibes Rises Again* 1972; *Madhouse* 1974; *Sugar Hill* 1974; *Haunting Fear* 1990

Quarshie, Hugh (1954–) *Baby: Secret of the Lost Legend* 1985; *The Church* 1988; *Nightbreed* 1990; *To Walk with Lions* 1999; *It Was an Accident* 2000

Quartermaine, Leon (1876–1967) *Escape Me Never* 1935; *As You Like It* 1936

Quayle, Anna (1936–) *A Hard Day's Night* 1964; *Drop Dead Darling* 1966; *The Sandwich Man* 1966; *Smashing Time* 1967; *Chitty Chitty Bang Bang* 1968; *Up the Chastity Belt* 1971; *Adventures of a Private Eye* 1977; *Adventures of a Plumber's Mate* 1978

Quayle, Anthony (1913–1989) *Hamlet* 1948; *Saraband for Dead Lovers* 1948; *Oh, Rosalinda!!* 1955; *The Battle of the River Plate* 1956; *The Wrong Man* 1956; *The Man Who Wouldn't Talk* 1957; *No Time for Tears* 1957; *Woman in a Dressing Gown* 1957; *Ice Cold in Alex* 1958; *Serious Charge* 1959; *Tarzan's Greatest Adventure* 1959; *The Challenge* 1960; *The Guns of Navarone* 1961; *HMS Defiant* 1962; *Lawrence of Arabia* 1962; *East of Sudan* 1964; *The Fall of the Roman Empire* 1964; *Operation Crossbow* 1965; *A Study in Terror* 1965; *The Poppy Is Also a Flower* 1966; *Before Winter Comes* 1968; *Anne of the Thousand Days* 1969; *Mackenna's Gold* 1969; *Bequest to the Nation* 1972; *Everything You Always Wanted to Know about Sex ... but Were Afraid to Ask* 1972; *Great Expectations* 1974; *The Tamarind Seed* 1974; *Moses* 1975; *The Eagle Has Landed* 1976; *Holocaust 2000* 1977; *Murder by Decree* 1978; *The Legend of the Holy Drinker* 1988; *King of the Wind* 1989

Quéant, Gilles *Odette* 1950; *Night without Stars* 1951

Queen Latifah (1970–) *House Party 2* 1991; *My Life* 1993; *Set It Off* 1996; *Living Out Loud* 1998; *Sphere* 1998; *The Bone Collector* 1999; *Brown Sugar* 2002; *Chicago* 2002; *Bringing Down the House* 2003; *Scary Movie 3* 2003; *Barbershop 2: Back in Business* 2004; *Taxi* 2004; *Beauty Shop* 2005

Quennessen, Valérie (1957–1989) *French Postcards* 1979; *Summer Lovers* 1982

Quentin, John *Blue* 1993; *Wittgenstein* 1993

Questel, Mae (1908–1998) *A Majority of One* 1961; *It'$ Only Money* 1962; *Funny Girl* 1968; *New York Stories* 1989

Quester, Hugues (1948–) *The Flesh of the Orchid* 1974; *Anne Trister* 1986; *Hôtel du Paradis* 1986; *A Tale of Springtime* 1989

Quick, Diana (1946–) *The Duellists* 1977; *The Odd Job* 1978; *Nineteen Nineteen* 1984; *Ordeal by Innocence* 1984; *Vroom* 1988; *Wilt* 1989; *Nostradamus* 1993; *The Leading Man* 1996; *Vigo: Passion for Life* 1997; *Saving Grace* 2000; *AKA* 2002; *Revengers Tragedy* 2002

Quigley, Godfrey (1923–1994) *The Siege of Sidney Street* 1960; *Nothing but the Best* 1963; *Daleks – Invasion Earth 2150 AD* 1966; *Barry Lyndon* 1975; *Educating Rita* 1983

Quigley, Juanita *aka* **Quigley, Baby Jane "Juanita"** (1931–) *Riffraff* 1936; *A Yank at Eton* 1942; *National Velvet* 1944

Quigley, Linnea (1958–) *Creepozoids* 1987; *Night of the Demons* 1988

Quigley, Pearce *Ladder of Swords* 1988; *Millions* 2004

Quill, Tim *Listen to Me* 1989; *Staying Together* 1989; *The Closer* 1990

Quillan, Eddie (1907–1990) *Broadway to Hollywood* 1933; *Mutiny on the Bounty* 1935; *Big City* 1937; *The Grapes of Wrath* 1940; *Kid Glove Killer* 1942; *Twilight on the Prairie* 1944

Quilley, Denis (1927–2003) *Evil under the Sun* 1982; *Privates on Parade* 1982; *King David* 1985; *Foreign Body* 1986; *Mister Johnson* 1991

Quilligan, Veronica *Malachi's Cove* 1973; *Lisztomania* 1975; *Candleshoe* 1977; *Angel* 1982

Quine, Richard (1920–1989) *Babes on Broadway* 1941; *Dr Gillespie's New Assistant* 1942; *For Me and My Gal* 1942; *My Sister Eileen* 1942; *The Clay Pigeon* 1949; *No Sad Songs for Me* 1950

Quinlan, Kathleen (1954–) *Lifeguard* 1976; *I Never Promised You a Rose Garden* 1977; *Face of a Stranger* 1978; *The Runner Stumbles* 1979; *Hanky Panky* 1982; *Independence Day* 1983; *Warning Sign* 1985; *Wild Thing* 1987; *Clara's Heart* 1988; *Sunset* 1988; *The Doors* 1991; *Last Light* 1993; *Perfect Alibi* 1994; *Trial by Jury* 1994; *Apollo 13* 1995; *Breakdown* 1997; *Event Horizon* 1997; *Lawn Dogs* 1997; *Zeus and Roxanne* 1997; *A Civil Action* 1998; *My Giant* 1998

Quinn, Aidan (1959–) *Desperately Seeking Susan* 1985; *An Early Frost* 1985; *The Mission* 1986; *Stakeout* 1987; *Crusoe* 1988; *The Lemon Sisters* 1989; *Avalon* 1990; *The Handmaid's Tale* 1990; *At Play in the Fields of the Lord* 1991; *The Playboys* 1992; *A Private Matter* 1992; *Benny and Joon* 1993; *Blink* 1994; *Legends of the Fall* 1994; *Mary Shelley's Frankenstein* 1994; *Haunted* 1995; *The Stars Fell on Henrietta* 1995; *Commandments* 1996; *Looking for Richard* 1996; *Michael Collins* 1996; *The Assignment* 1997; *In Dreams* 1998; *Practical Magic* 1998; *Music of the Heart* 1999; *Songcatcher* 1999; *This Is My Father* 1999; *Evelyn* 2002; *Song for a Raggy Boy* 2002; *Stolen Summer* 2002

Quinn, Anthony (1915–2001) *The Plainsman* 1936; *Swing High, Swing Low* 1937; *Waikiki Wedding* 1937; *The Buccaneer* 1938; *Bulldog Drummond in Africa* 1938; *King of Alcatraz* 1938; *City for Conquest* 1940; *The Ghost Breakers* 1940; *Road to Singapore* 1940; *Texas Rangers Ride Again* 1940; *Blood and Sand* 1941; *They Died with Their Boots On* 1941; *The Black Swan* 1942; *Larceny, Inc* 1942; *Road to Morocco* 1942; *Guadalcanal Diary* 1943; *The Ox-Bow Incident* 1943; *Buffalo Bill* 1944; *Irish Eyes Are Smiling* 1944; *Back to Bataan* 1945; *China Sky* 1945; *Where Do We Go from Here?* 1945; *California* 1946; *Black Gold* 1947; *The Imperfect Lady* 1947; *Sinbad the Sailor* 1947; *Tycoon* 1947; *The Brave Bulls* 1951; *Against All Flags* 1952; *Viva Zapata!* 1952; *The World in His Arms* 1952; *Blowing Wild* 1953; *City beneath the Sea* 1953; *East of Sumatra* 1953; *Ride, Vaquero!* 1953; *Seminole* 1953; *The Long Wait* 1954; *La Strada* 1954; *Ulysses* 1954; *The Magnificent Matador* 1955; *The Naked Street* 1955; *Seven Cities of Gold* 1955; *The Hunchback of Notre Dame* 1956; *Lust for Life* 1956; *The River's Edge* 1957; *Wild Is the Wind* 1957; *Hot Spell* 1958; *The Black Orchid* 1959; *Last Train from Gun Hill* 1959; *Warlock* 1959; *Heller in Pink Tights* 1960; *Portrait in Black* 1960; *The Savage Innocents* 1960; *Barabbas* 1961; *The Guns of Navarone* 1961; *Lawrence of Arabia* 1962; *Requiem for a Heavyweight* 1962; *Behold a Pale Horse* 1964; *The Visit* 1964; *Zorba the Greek* 1964; *A High Wind in Jamaica* 1965; *Lost Command* 1966; *The Happening* 1967; *The Rover* 1967; *The 25th Hour* 1967; *Guns for San Sebastian* 1968; *The Magus* 1968; *The Shoes of the Fisherman* 1968; *A Dream of Kings* 1969; *The Secret of Santa Vittoria* 1969; *Flap* 1970; *RPM – Revolutions per Minute* 1970; *A Walk in the Spring Rain* 1970; *Across 110th Street* 1972; *The Don Is Dead* 1973; *The Marseille Contract* 1974; *The Con Artists* 1976; *The Inheritance* 1976; *The Message* 1976; *Caravans* 1978; *The Children of Sanchez* 1978; *The Greek Tycoon* 1978; *The Passage* 1978; *High Risk* 1981; *Lion of the Desert* 1981; *The Salamander* 1981; *Regina* 1982; *Valentina* 1982; *1919* 1983; *Ghosts Can't Do It* 1990; *Revenge* 1990; *Jungle Fever* 1991; *Mobsters* 1991; *Only the Lonely* 1991; *Last Action Hero* 1993; *Somebody to Love* 1994; *A Walk in the Clouds* 1995; *Avenging Angelo* 2002

Quinn, Daniel *Scanner Cop* 1994; *Living in Fear* 2001

Quinn, J C (1940–2004) *Vision Quest* 1985; *Barfly* 1987; *The Chinese Connection* 1988; *The Abyss* 1989; *Turner & Hooch* 1989; *Days of Thunder* 1990; *Prayer of the Rollerboys* 1990; *CrissCross* 1992

Quinn, Marian *Broken Harvest* 1994; *Heavy* 1995

Quinn, Martha (1961–) *Eddie and the Cruisers II: Eddie Lives!* 1989; *Chopper Chicks in Zombietown* 1990; *Motorama* 1991

Quinn, Patricia *aka* **Quinn, Pat** (1944–) *Alice's Restaurant* 1969; *Zachariah* 1970; *Shoot Out* 1971; *The Rocky Horror Picture Show* 1975; *An Unmarried Woman* 1978; *The Outsider* 1979; *Shock Treatment* 1981

Quinn, Thomas *Odd Jobs* 1986; *Homeboy* 1988

Quinn, Tony (1899–1967) *Shadow of a Man* 1954; *Booby Trap* 1957; *The Rising of the Moon* 1957; *Trouble with Eve* 1959

Quinones, Adolfo "Shabba-Doo" *Breakdance* 1984; *Breakdance 2 – Electric Boogaloo* 1984

Quinteros, Lorenzo *Hombre Mirando al Sudeste* 1986; *Last Images of the Shipwreck* 1989; *After the Storm* 1990

Quirke, Pauline (1959–) *The Return of the Soldier* 1982; *Getting It Right* 1989; *Arthur's Dyke* 2001

Quiroz, Walter (1972–) *The Voyage* 1991; *Foolish Heart* 1998

Quitak, Oscar *The Traitor* 1957; *The Revenge of Frankenstein* 1958

Quo, Beulah (1923–2002) *The 7th Dawn* 1964; *Yes, Giorgio* 1982

Quon, Marianne *China* 1943; *Charlie Chan in the Secret Service* 1944

Raab, Ellie (1977–) *The Fabulous Baker Boys* 1989; *Eyes of an Angel* 1991

Raab, Kurt (1941–1988) *The American Soldier* 1970; *Why Does Herr R Run Amok?* 1970; *Fear of Fear* 1976; *Satan's Brew* 1976; *Bolwieser* 1977; *Parker* 1984; *Escape from Sobibor* 1987

Raaz, Vijay *Monsoon Wedding* 2001; *Mumbai Matinee* 2003

Rabagliati, Alberto (1906–1974) *Street Angel* 1928; *Crossed Swords* 1954; *The Monte Carlo Story* 1957

Rabal, Francisco (1926–2001) *Nazarín* 1958; *Viridiana* 1961; *The Eclipse* 1962; *La Religieuse* 1965; *The Witches* 1966; *Belle de Jour* 1967; *Sorcerer* 1977; *Los Santos Inocentes* 1984; *Camorra* 1985; *Padre Nuestro* 1985; *A Time of Destiny* 1988; *Tie Me Up! Tie Me Down!* 1990; *Goya in Bordeaux* 1999

Rabe, Pamela (1959–) *Sirens* 1994; *Cosi* 1996

Racette, Francine (1947–) *The Disappearance* 1977; *Au Revoir les Enfants* 1987

Rachins, Alan (1947–) *Always* 1985; *Heart Condition* 1990; *Showgirls* 1995

Racimo, Victoria (1950–) *The Magic Garden of Stanley Sweetheart* 1970; *Journey through Rosebud* 1972; *Prophecy* 1979; *The Mountain Men* 1980; *On Dangerous Ground* 1986; *Ernest Goes to Camp* 1987; *White Fang 2: Myth of the White Wolf* 1994

Radcliffe, Daniel (1989–) *Harry Potter and the Philosopher's Stone* 2001; *Harry Potter and the Chamber of Secrets* 2002; *Harry Potter and the Prisoner of Azkaban* 2004

Radd, Ronald (1929–1976) *The Sea Gull* 1968; *The Kremlin Letter* 1970
Radford, Basil (1897–1952) *Young and Innocent* 1937; *Convict 99* 1938; *The Lady Vanishes* 1938; *Just William* 1939; *Let's Be Famous* 1939; *Crooks' Tour* 1940; *Night Train to Munich* 1940; *Unpublished Story* 1942; *Millions like Us* 1943; *A Girl in a Million* 1946; *It's Not Cricket* 1948; *Quartet* 1948; *The Winslow Boy* 1948; *Passport to Pimlico* 1949; *Whisky Galore!* 1949; *Chance of a Lifetime* 1950
Radley, Ken *Sniper* 1992; *The Adventures of Priscilla, Queen of the Desert* 1994
Radner, Gilda (1946–1989) *Animalympics* 1979; *First Family* 1980; *Hanky Panky* 1982; *The Woman in Red* 1984; *Movers and Shakers* 1985; *Haunted Honeymoon* 1986
Radzin, Elsa *aka* **Radzinya, Elsa** (1917–) *Hamlet* 1964; *King Lear* 1970
Radziwilowicz, Jerzy (1950–) *Man of Marble* 1977; *Man of Iron* 1981; *Passion* 1982; *No End* 1984; *Secret Defense* 1997; *Histoire de Marie et Julien* 2003
Rae, Charlotte (1926–) *Jenny* 1969; *Sidewinder One* 1977; *Tom and Jerry: the Movie* 1992
Rae, John *The Brave Don't Cry* 1952; *The Kidnappers* 1953; *The Big Chance* 1957; *The Bridal Path* 1959
Rafferty, Chips (1909–1971) *Forty Thousand Horsemen* 1941; *The Overlanders* 1946; *Bush Christmas* 1947; *The Loves of Joanna Godden* 1947; *Eureka Stockade* 1949; *Bitter Springs* 1950; *Kangaroo* 1952; *The Desert Rats* 1953; *Smiley* 1956; *Smiley Gets a Gun* 1959; *The Sundowners* 1960; *The Wackiest Ship in the Army* 1961; *They're a Weird Mob* 1966; *Double Trouble* 1967; *Kona Coast* 1968; *Skullduggery* 1969
Rafferty, Frances (1922–2004) *Young Ideas* 1943; *Barbary Coast Gent* 1944; *Dragon Seed* 1944; *Mrs Parkington* 1944; *Abbott and Costello in Hollywood* 1945; *The Hidden Eye* 1945; *Bad Bascomb* 1946
Raffin, Deborah (1953–) *40 Carats* 1973; *The Dove* 1974; *Once Is Not Enough* 1975; *God Told Me to* 1976; *Maniac* 1977; *Touched by Love* 1979; *Agatha Christie's Sparkling Cyanide* 1983; *Dance of the Dwarfs* 1983; *Death Wish 3* 1985; *Scanners II: The New Order* 1991
Raft, George (1895–1980) *Palmy Days* 1931; *Quick Millions* 1931; *If I Had a Million* 1932; *Love Is a Racket* 1932; *Night after Night* 1932; *Scarface* 1932; *Taxi!* 1932; *The Bowery* 1933; *Bolero* 1934; *The Glass Key* 1935; *Rumba* 1935; *Souls at Sea* 1937; *Spawn of the North* 1938; *You and Me* 1938; *Each Dawn I Die* 1939; *Invisible Stripes* 1939; *The House across the Bay* 1940; *They Drive by Night* 1940; *Manpower* 1941; *Broadway* 1942; *Background to Danger* 1943; *Stage Door Canteen* 1943; *Follow the Boys* 1944; *Johnny Angel* 1945; *Nob Hill* 1945; *Nocturne* 1946; *Whistle Stop* 1946; *Christmas Eve* 1947; *Intrigue* 1947; *A Dangerous Profession* 1949; *Johnny Allegro* 1949; *Outpost in Morocco* 1949; *Red Light* 1949; *I'll Get You for This* 1950; *Escape Route* 1952; *The Man from Cairo* 1953; *Black Widow* 1954; *Rogue Cop* 1954; *A Bullet for Joey* 1955; *Around the World in 80 Days* 1956; *Some Like It Hot* 1959; *Jet over the Atlantic* 1960; *The Ladies' Man* 1961; *Casino Royale* 1967; *Five Golden Dragons* 1967; *Skidoo* 1968; *Deadhead Miles* 1972; *Hammersmith Is Out* 1972; *Sextette* 1978; *The Man with Bogart's Face* 1980
Raglan, Robert (1906–1985) *Man from Tangier* 1957; *Hidden Homicide* 1958; *Information Received* 1962
Ragland, Rags *aka* **Ragland, "Rags"** (1905–1946) *Whistling in the Dark* 1941; *Whistling in Dixie* 1942; *DuBarry Was a Lady* 1943; *Girl Crazy* 1943; *Whistling in Brooklyn* 1943; *Meet the People* 1944; *Anchors Aweigh* 1945
Ragsdale, William (1961–) *Fright Night* 1985; *Fright Night Part 2* 1988; *Mannequin on the Move* 1991
Raho, Umberto *aka* **Newman, Raoul H** *The Spectre* 1963; *Aladdin* 1986
Rai, Aishwarya (1973–) *Hum Dil De Chuke Sanam* 1999; *Taal* 1999; *Mohabbatein* 2000; *Devdas* 2002; *Shakti – the Power* 2002; *Chokher Bali* 2003; *Khakee* 2003; *Kuch Naa Kaho* 2003; *Bride & Prejudice* 2004; *Kyun! Ho Gaya Na ...* 2004; *Raincoat* 2004; *Bunty Aur Babli* 2005
Railsback, Steve (1948–) *The Visitors* 1972; *The Stunt Man* 1980; *Turkey Shoot* 1981; *The Golden Seal* 1983; *Torchlight* 1984; *Lifeforce* 1985; *Blue Monkey* 1987; *Distortions* 1987; *Alligator II: the Mutation* 1991; *Scissors* 1991; *Nukie* 1992; *Quake!* 1992; *Final Mission* 1993; *Barb Wire* 1995; *Disturbing Behaviour* 1998; *Made Men* 1999; *Ed Gein* 2000
Raimi, Ted *aka* **Raimi, Theodore** (1965–) *Evil Dead II* 1987; *Easy Wheels* 1989; *Darkman* 1990; *Lunatics: a Love Story* 1991; *Candyman* 1992; *The Shot* 1996
Raimondi, Ruggero (1941–) *Don Giovanni* 1979; *Life Is a Bed of Roses* 1983; *Carmen* 1984; *Tosca* 2001
Raimu (1883–1946) *Marius* 1931; *Fanny* 1932; *César* 1936; *Un Carnet de Bal* 1937; *Gribouille* 1937; *The Baker's Wife* 1938
Rain, Douglas (1928–) *2001: a Space Odyssey* 1968; *2010* 1984
Rainer, Luise (1910–) *Escapade* 1935; *The Great Ziegfeld* 1936; *Big City* 1937; *The Emperor's Candlesticks* 1937; *The Good Earth* 1937; *Dramatic School* 1938; *The Great Waltz* 1938; *The Toy Wife* 1938; *Hostages* 1943; *The Gambler* 1997
Raines, Cristina (1952–) *The Duellists* 1977; *The Sentinel* 1977; *Touched by Love* 1979; *Silver Dream Racer* 1980; *Nightmares* 1983; *Real Life* 1983
Raines, Ella (1921–1988) *Corvette K-225* 1943; *Cry Havoc* 1943; *Enter Arsene Lupin* 1944; *Hail the Conquering Hero* 1944; *Phantom Lady* 1944; *The Suspect* 1944; *Tall in the Saddle* 1944; *The Strange Affair of Uncle Harry* 1945; *Brute Force* 1947; *The Senator Was Indiscreet* 1947; *Time Out of Mind* 1947; *The Web* 1947; *A Dangerous Profession* 1949; *Impact* 1949; *The Walking Hills* 1949; *Ride the Man Down* 1952; *The Man in the Road* 1957
Rainey, Ford (1908–) *The Last Mile* 1959; *Ada* 1961; *Glory Boy* 1971; *Bed & Breakfast* 1992
Rains, Claude (1889–1967) *The Invisible Man* 1933; *The Clairvoyant* 1934; *Crime without Passion* 1934; *The Last Outpost* 1935; *The Mystery of Edwin Drood* 1935; *Anthony Adverse* 1936; *The Prince and the Pauper* 1937; *They Won't Forget* 1937; *The Adventures of Robin Hood* 1938; *Four Daughters* 1938; *Gold Is Where You Find It* 1938; *White Banners* 1938; *Daughters Courageous* 1939; *Four Wives* 1939; *Juarez* 1939; *Mr Smith Goes to Washington* 1939; *They Made Me a Criminal* 1939; *Saturday's Children* 1940; *The Sea Hawk* 1940; *Four Mothers* 1941; *Here Comes Mr Jordan* 1941; *The Wolf Man* 1941; *Casablanca* 1942; *Kings Row* 1942; *Moontide* 1942; *Now, Voyager* 1942; *Strange Holiday* 1942; *Forever and a Day* 1943; *Phantom of the Opera* 1943; *Mr Skeffington* 1944; *Passage to Marseille* 1944; *Caesar and Cleopatra* 1945; *This Love of Ours* 1945; *Angel on My Shoulder* 1946; *Deception* 1946; *Notorious* 1946; *The Unsuspected* 1947; *The Passionate Friends* 1948; *Rope of Sand* 1949; *Where Danger Lives* 1950; *The White Tower* 1950; *Sealed Cargo* 1951; *The Man Who Watched Trains Go By* 1952; *Lisbon* 1956; *This Earth Is Mine* 1959; *The Lost World* 1960; *Lawrence of Arabia* 1962; *Twilight of Honor* 1963; *The Greatest Story Ever Told* 1965
Rajot, Pierre-Loup (1958–) *La Nouvelle Eve* 1999; *Drôle de Félix* 2000
Rajskub, Mary Lynn *Punch-Drunk Love* 2002; *Mysterious Skin* 2004
Raki, Laya (1927–) *The Seekers* 1954; *Up to His Neck* 1954
Rall, Tommy *aka* **Rall, Thomas** (1929–) *Kiss Me Kate* 1953; *Seven Brides for Seven Brothers* 1954; *My Sister Eileen* 1955; *Invitation to the Dance* 1956; *Walk the Proud Land* 1956; *Merry Andrew* 1958; *Dancers* 1987
Ralli, Giovanna (1935–) *General Della Rovere* 1959; *What Did You Do in the War, Daddy?* 1966; *Deadfall* 1968; *A Professional Gun* 1968; *Cannon for Cordoba* 1970; *We All Loved Each Other So Much* 1974
Ralph, Hanna (1885–1978) *The Nibelungen* 1924; *Faust* 1926
Ralph, Jessie (1864–1944) *The Affairs of Cellini* 1934; *Murder at the Vanities* 1934; *One Night of Love* 1934; *David Copperfield* 1935; *I Found Stella Parish* 1935; *Les Misérables* 1935; *After the Thin Man* 1936; *San Francisco* 1936; *Camille* 1937; *Double Wedding* 1937; *The Good Earth* 1937; *The Last of Mrs Cheyney* 1937; *Port of Seven Seas* 1938; *Drums along the Mohawk* 1939; *The Bank Dick* 1940; *They Met in Bombay* 1941
Ralph, Michael *DROP Squad* 1994; *Woo* 1998
Ralph, Sheryl Lee (1956–) *Oliver & Company* 1988; *The Mighty Quinn* 1989; *The Distinguished Gentleman* 1992; *Bogus* 1996; *Deterrence* 1999
Ralston, Esther (1902–1994) *The Case of Lena Smith* 1929; *Rome Express* 1932; *Black Beauty* 1933; *By Candlelight* 1934; *Sadie McKee* 1934; *Streamline Express* 1935; *Tin Pan Alley* 1940
Ralston, Jobyna (1900–1967) *Girl Shy* 1924; *Hot Water* 1924; *The Freshman* 1925; *For Heaven's Sake* 1926; *The Kid Brother* 1927; *Wings* 1927
Ralston, Vera *aka* **Hruba Ralston, Vera** (1921–2003) *The Lady and the Monster* 1944; *Dakota* 1945; *Murder in the Music Hall* 1946; *The Fighting Kentuckian* 1949; *Hoodlum Empire* 1952; *Fair Wind to Java* 1953; *Timberjack* 1955; *Accused of Murder* 1956
Ramage, Cecil (1895–1988) *King of the Damned* 1935; *Return of a Stranger* 1937; *Kind Hearts and Coronets* 1949
Ramallo, Fernando (1980–) *Krámpack* 2000; *Only Human* 2004
Rambeau, Marjorie (1889–1970) *Her Man* 1930; *Min and Bill* 1930; *Inspiration* 1931; *Laughing Sinners* 1931; *The Secret Six* 1931; *Strangers May Kiss* 1931; *Hell Divers* 1932; *Man's Castle* 1933; *Palooka* 1934; *East of the River* 1940; *Primrose Path* 1940; *Tobacco Road* 1941; *Broadway* 1942; *War of the Wildcats* 1943; *Salome, Where She Danced* 1945; *The Lucky Stiff* 1949; *Forever Female* 1953; *Torch Song* 1953; *A Man Called Peter* 1955; *The View from Pompey's Head* 1955; *Man of a Thousand Faces* 1957
Ramel, Jacqueline (1964–) *The Last Contract* 1998; *Fear X* 2002
Ramer, Henry *The Apprenticeship of Duddy Kravitz* 1974; *Welcome to Blood City* 1977; *Between Friends* 1983; *Hockey Night* 1984
Ramirez, Carlos (1914–1986) *Bathing Beauty* 1944; *Where Do We Go from Here?* 1945
Ramirez, Frank *Smith!* 1969; *The Snail's Strategy* 1993
Ramis, Harold (1944–) *Heavy Metal* 1981; *Stripes* 1981; *Ghostbusters* 1984; *Baby Boom* 1987; *Stealing Home* 1988; *Ghostbusters II* 1989; *Orange County* 2001; *I'm with Lucy* 2002
Ramón, Eulalia (1959–) *Outrage* 1993; *Goya in Bordeaux* 1999
Ramos, Rudy (1950–) *The Driver* 1978; *Defiance* 1979; *Quicksilver* 1986
Rampling, Charlotte (1945–) *Rotten to the Core* 1965; *Georgy Girl* 1966; *The Long Duel* 1966; *The Damned* 1969; *Three* 1969; *Asylum* 1972; *Corky* 1972; *Henry VIII and His Six Wives* 1972; *The Night Porter* 1973; *Zardoz* 1973; *Caravan to Vaccares* 1974; *The Flesh of the Orchid* 1974; *Farewell, My Lovely* 1975; *Sherlock Holmes in New York* 1976; *Orca ... Killer Whale* 1977; *The Purple Taxi* 1977; *Stardust Memories* 1980; *The Verdict* 1982; *Long Live Life* 1984; *Max Mon Amour* 1986; *Angel Heart* 1987; *Mascara* 1987; *DOA* 1988; *Paris by Night* 1988; *Hammers over the Anvil* 1992; *The Wings of the Dove* 1997; *The Cherry Orchard* 1998; *Aberdeen* 2000; *Under the Sand* 2000; *The Fourth Angel* 2001; *Spy Game* 2001; *Superstition* 2001; *Summer Things* 2002; *I'll Sleep When I'm Dead* 2003; *The Statement* 2003; *Swimming Pool* 2003; *The Keys to the House* 2004
Ramsay, Anne (1960–) *The Final Cut* 1995; *Woman on Top* 2000
Ramsay, Bruce (1968–) *Alive* 1992; *Killing Zoe* 1993; *Dead Beat* 1994; *Curdled* 1995; *Hellraiser: Bloodline* 1996
Ramsay, Remak (1937–) *The House on Carroll Street* 1987; *Addicted to Love* 1997
Ramsey, Anne (1929–1988) *When You Comin' Back, Red Ryder?* 1979; *The Goonies* 1985; *Deadly Friend* 1986; *Throw Momma from the Train* 1987; *Homer and Eddie* 1989
Ramsey, David *Mutiny* 1999; *Ali: an American Hero* 2000
Ramsey, Logan (1921–2000) *The Hoodlum Priest* 1961; *Head* 1968; *Busting* 1974
Ramsey, Marion *Police Academy 2: Their First Assignment* 1985; *Police Academy 3: Back in Training* 1986; *Police Academy 6: City under Siege* 1989
Ramsey, Ward *Dinosaurus!* 1960; *Posse from Hell* 1961
Rand, Edwin (1911–1993) *The Capture* 1950; *Tarantula* 1955
Rand, John (1871–1940) *The Pawnshop* 1916; *The Cure* 1917; *The Idle Class* 1921
Randall, Anne (1944–) *The Christian Licorice Store* 1971; *A Time for Dying* 1971
Randall, Lexi *aka* **Randall, Lexi Faith** (1980–) *The Long Walk Home* 1990; *The War* 1994; *The Stars Fell on Henrietta* 1995
Randall, Meg (1926–) *Ma and Pa Kettle* 1949; *Last of the Badmen* 1957
Randall, Tony (1920–2004) *No Down Payment* 1957; *Oh, Men! Oh, Women!* 1957; *Will Success Spoil Rock Hunter?* 1957; *The Mating Game* 1959; *Pillow Talk* 1959; *The Adventures of Huckleberry Finn* 1960; *Let's Make Love* 1960; *Lover Come Back* 1961; *Boys' Night Out* 1962; *Island of Love* 1963; *7 Faces of Dr Lao* 1963; *The Brass Bottle* 1964; *Send Me No Flowers* 1964; *Fluffy* 1965; *The Alphabet Murders* 1966; *Our Man in Marrakesh* 1966; *Hello Down There* 1969; *Everything You Always Wanted to Know about Sex ... but Were Afraid to Ask* 1972; *Scavenger Hunt* 1979; *Foolin' Around* 1980; *The King of Comedy* 1983; *Gremlins 2: the New Batch* 1990; *Down with Love* 2003
Randell, Ron (1918–2005) *Bulldog Drummond Strikes Back* 1947; *It Had to Be You* 1947; *The Loves of Carmen* 1948; *China Corsair* 1951; *Lorna Doone* 1951; *Kiss Me Kate* 1953; *I Am a Camera* 1955; *Beyond Mombasa* 1957; *The Girl in Black Stockings* 1957; *The Story of Esther Costello* 1957; *King of Kings* 1961; *The Most Dangerous Man Alive* 1961; *Follow the Boys* 1963; *Gold for the Caesars* 1964; *Whity* 1970; *Exposed* 1983
Randle, Frank (1901–1957) *Somewhere on Leave* 1942; *Home Sweet Home* 1945; *When You Come Home* 1947; *It's a Grand Life* 1953
Randle, Theresa (1967–) *Malcolm X* 1992; *Sugar Hill* 1993; *Beverly Hills Cop III* 1994; *Bad Boys* 1995; *Girl 6* 1996; *Space Jam* 1997; *Spawn* 1997; *Bad Boys II* 2003
Randolf, Anders (1870–1930) *The Black Pirate* 1926; *The Kiss* 1929
Randolph, Donald (1906–1993) *Bride of Vengeance* 1949; *Assignment – Paris* 1952; *Khyber Patrol* 1954; *The Mad Magician* 1954; *Phffft!* 1954; *The Deadly Mantis* 1957
Randolph, Jane (1919–) *Cat People* 1942; *The Falcon's Brother* 1942; *The Falcon Strikes Back* 1943; *The Curse of the Cat People* 1944; *Fool's Gold* 1946; *Railroaded* 1947; *T-Men* 1947; *Abbott and Costello Meet Frankenstein* 1948
Randolph, John (1915–2004) *Seconds* 1966; *Pretty Poison* 1968; *Number One* 1969; *Smith!* 1969; *There Was a Crooked Man...* 1970; *Escape from the Planet of the Apes* 1971; *Little Murders* 1971; *Conquest of the Planet of the Apes* 1972; *Serpico* 1973; *King Kong* 1976; *Prizzi's Honor* 1985; *The Wizard of Loneliness* 1988; *National Lampoon's Christmas Vacation* 1989; *Iron Maze* 1991; *A Price above Rubies* 1997
Randolph, Lillian (1898–1980) *The Bachelor and the Bobby-Soxer* 1947; *Once More, My Darling* 1949; *Magic* 1978
Randone, Salvo (1906–1991) *Salvatore Giuliano* 1961; *Hands over the City* 1963; *The Tenth Victim* 1965; *We Still Kill the Old Way* 1967; *Satyricon* 1969; *Investigation of a Citizen above Suspicion* 1970; *The Working Class Goes to Heaven* 1971; *In the Name of the Pope King* 1977
Ransom, Kenneth *aka* **Ransom, Kenny** *There Goes My Baby* 1994; *The Crocodile Hunter: Collision Course* 2002
Ransom, Tim (1963–) *The Dressmaker* 1988; *Vital Signs* 1990; *Vanished without a Trace* 1993
Ransome, Prunella (1943–) *Far from the Madding Crowd* 1967; *Alfred the Great* 1969; *Man in the Wilderness* 1971
Rao, Amrita (1981–) *Deewaar: Let's Bring Our Heroes Home* 2004; *Main Hoon Na* 2004; *Masti* 2004
Rapaport, Michael (1970–) *Zebrahead* 1992; *Money for Nothing* 1993; *True Romance* 1993; *Hand Gun* 1994; *Kiss of Death* 1994; *The Scout* 1994; *Higher Learning* 1995; *Mighty Aphrodite* 1995; *Beautiful Girls* 1996; *illtown* 1996; *The Pallbearer* 1996; *Cop Land* 1997; *Kicked in the Head* 1997; *Metro* 1997; *Subway Stories: Tales from the Underground* 1997; *The Naked Man* 1998; *Palmetto* 1998; *Some Girls* 1998; *Deep Blue Sea* 1999; *Bamboozled* 2000; *Men of Honor* 2000; *The 6th Day* 2000; *Small Time Crooks* 2000; *Triggermen* 2002; *29 Palms* 2002; *Hitch* 2005
Rapp, Anthony (1971–) *A Night on the Town* 1987; *Far from Home* 1989; *School Ties* 1992; *Dazed and Confused* 1993; *A Beautiful Mind* 2001
Rasche, David (1944–) *Death Vengeance* 1982; *An Innocent Man* 1989; *Wicked Stepmother* 1989; *Masters of Menace* 1990; *Bingo* 1991; *Delirious* 1991; *That Old Feeling* 1997; *Just Married* 2003
Rasp, Fritz (1891–1976) *Metropolis* 1926; *The Love of*

Jeanne Ney 1927; Diary of a Lost Girl 1929; The Woman in the Moon 1929; The Threepenny Opera 1931; The Red Circle 1960

Rasuk, Victor (1984–) Raising Victor Vargas 2002; Lords of Dogtown 2005

Rasulala, Thalmus (1939–1991) Blacula 1972; The Autobiography of Miss Jane Pittman 1974; Adios Amigo 1975; Friday Foster 1975; Mr Ricco 1975; Bulletproof 1987; Mom and Dad Save the World 1992

Rasumny, Mikhail (1890–1956) Road to Morocco 1942; Wake Island 1942; For Whom the Bell Tolls 1943; A Medal for Benny 1945; Anna and the King of Siam 1946; Heartbeat 1946; Her Husband's Affairs 1947; Anything Can Happen 1952; Hot Blood 1956

Ratcliff, Sandy (1950–) Family Life 1971; Radio On 1979; Yesterday's Hero 1979

Rathbone, Basil (1892–1967) The Last of Mrs Cheyney 1929; Anna Karenina 1935; Captain Blood 1935; David Copperfield 1935; Kind Lady 1935; The Last Days of Pompeii 1935; A Tale of Two Cities 1935; The Garden of Allah 1936; Love from a Stranger 1936; Romeo and Juliet 1936; Confession 1937; Tovarich 1937; The Adventures of Marco Polo 1938; The Adventures of Robin Hood 1938; The Dawn Patrol 1938; If I Were King 1938; The Adventures of Sherlock Holmes 1939; The Hound of the Baskervilles 1939; Son of Frankenstein 1939; Tower of London 1939; The Mark of Zorro 1940; Rhythm on the River 1940; The Black Cat 1941; International Lady 1941; Paris Calling 1941; Crossroads 1942; Fingers at the Window 1942; Sherlock Holmes and the Secret Weapon 1942; Sherlock Holmes and the Voice of Terror 1942; Above Suspicion 1943; Sherlock Holmes Faces Death 1943; Sherlock Holmes in Washington 1943; Bathing Beauty 1944; Frenchman's Creek 1944; The House of Fear 1944; The Pearl of Death 1944; The Scarlet Claw 1944; Sherlock Holmes and the Spider Woman 1944; Pursuit to Algiers 1945; The Woman in Green 1945; Heartbeat 1946; Sherlock Holmes and the Secret Code 1946; Terror by Night 1946; The Adventures of Ichabod and Mr Toad 1949; Casanova's Big Night 1954; We're No Angels 1955; The Black Sleep 1956; The Court Jester 1956; The Last Hurrah 1958; Pontius Pilate 1961; The Magic Sword 1962; Tales of Terror 1962; The Comedy of Terrors 1964; Voyage to the Prehistoric Planet 1965; The Ghost in the Invisible Bikini 1966; Planet of Blood 1966

Rathebe, Dolly (1928–2004) Mapantsula 1988; Friends 1993; Cry, the Beloved Country 1995

Ratoff, Gregory (1897–1960) Skyscraper Souls 1932; Symphony of Six Million 1932; What Price Hollywood? 1932; Broadway through a Keyhole 1933; I'm No Angel 1933; Sitting Pretty 1933; George White's Scandals 1934; Remember Last Night? 1935; The Road to Glory 1936; Sing, Baby, Sing 1936; Under Two Flags 1936; Café Metropole 1937; Seventh Heaven 1937; Sally, Irene and Mary 1938; All about Eve 1950; O Henry's Full House 1952; The Sun Also Rises 1957; Once More, with Feeling 1959; Exodus 1960; The Big Gamble 1961

Ratray, Peter (1941–) Young Lady Chatterley 1976; Stonewall 1995

Rattray, Heather (1966–) Across the Great Divide 1977; The Sea Gypsies 1978; Mountain Family Robinson 1979; Basket Case 2 1990

Ratzenberger, John (1947–) Warlords of Atlantis 1978; Arabian Adventure 1979; The Bitch 1979; Hanover Street 1979; Outland 1981; Battletruck 1982; House II: the Second Story 1987; Toy Story 1995; That Darn Cat 1997; Under Pressure 1997; Toy Story 2 1999; Determination of Death 2001; Monsters, Inc 2001; Spirited Away 2001; Finding Nemo 2003; The Incredibles 2004

Rauch, Siegfried (1932–) Le Mans 1971; The Big Red One 1980

Raven, Mike (1924–1997) Crucible of Terror 1971; I, Monster 1971

Ravenscroft, Thurl (1914–2005) The Aristocats 1970; The Brave Little Toaster 1987

Rawal, Paresh (1950–) Sardar 1993; Tamanna 1997; Awara Paagal Deewana 2002; Baghban 2003; Aitraaz 2004; Hulchul 2004

Rawlings, Margaret (1906–1996) Roman Holiday 1953; Beautiful Stranger 1954; No Road Back 1957; Follow Me 1971

Rawlins, Adrian Mountains of the Moon 1989; Breaking the Waves 1996; My Brother Tom 2001; Wilbur (Wants to Kill Himself) 2002

Rawlinson, Herbert (1885–1953) Confidential 1935; The Counterfeiters 1948; Jail Bait 1954

Rawls, Lou (1936–) Angel, Angel Down We Go 1969; Lookin' Italian 1994; Wildly Available 1996

Ray, Aldo (1926–1991) The Marrying Kind 1952; Pat and Mike 1952; Let's Do It Again 1953; Miss Sadie Thompson 1953; Battle Cry 1955; We're No Angels 1955; Nightfall 1956; Men in War 1957; God's Little Acre 1958; The Naked and the Dead 1958; The Siege of Pinchgut 1959; The Day They Robbed the Bank of England 1960; Nightmare in the Sun 1964; Sylvia 1964; Dead Heat on a Merry-Go-Round 1966; What Did You Do in the War, Daddy? 1966; Kill a Dragon 1967; The Violent Ones 1967; Welcome to Hard Times 1967; The Green Berets 1968; And Hope to Die 1972; Seven Alone 1974; Inside Out 1975; The Man Who Would Not Die 1975; Psychic Killer 1975; The Glove 1978; Little Moon & Jud McGraw 1978

Ray, Andrew (1939–2003) The Mudlark 1950; The Yellow Balloon 1952; Escape by Night 1953; Woman in a Dressing Gown 1957; Gideon's Day 1958; Serious Charge 1959; Twice round the Daffodils 1962; Paris by Night 1988

Ray, Michel (1944–) The Divided Heart 1954; The Brave One 1956; The Tin Star 1957

Ray, Nicholas (1911–1979) The American Friend 1977; Hair 1979

Ray, René (1911–1993) When London Sleeps 1932; The Passing of the Third Floor Back 1935; Street Song 1935; His Lordship 1936; The Green Cockatoo 1937; Please Teacher 1937; Bank Holiday 1938; Housemaster 1938; Old Bill and Son 1940; They Made Me a Fugitive 1947; Women of Twilight 1952; The Good Die Young 1954; The Vicious Circle 1957

Ray, Ted (1906–1977) Meet Me Tonight 1952; Escape by Night 1953; Carry On Teacher 1959; Please Turn Over 1960

Raye, Carol (1923–) While I Live 1947; Remember Me 1985

Raye, Martha (1916–1994) The Big Broadcast of 1937 1936; Rhythm on the Range 1936; Artists and Models 1937; The Big Broadcast of 1938 1937; Waikiki Wedding 1937; College Swing 1938; Never Say Die 1939; The Boys from Syracuse 1940; Hellzapoppin' 1941; Keep 'em Flying 1941; Pin Up Girl 1944; Monsieur Verdoux 1947; Jumbo 1962; Pufnstuf 1970

Raymond, Bill My New Gun 1992; Where the Rivers Flow North 1993

Raymond, Candy (1950–) The Plumber 1979; Monkey Grip 1983; A Case of Honor 1988

Raymond, Cyril (1897–1973) The Ghost Train 1931; Accused 1936; The Shadow 1936; Come On George 1939; Saloon Bar 1940; Brief Encounter 1945; This Was a Woman 1947; Angels One Five 1952; Lease of Life 1954; The Safecracker 1958; Don't Talk to Strange Men 1962

Raymond, Gary (1935–) The Moonraker 1957; Look Back in Anger 1959; Suddenly, Last Summer 1959; The Millionairess 1960; El Cid 1961; The Playboy of the Western World 1962; Jason and the Argonauts 1963

Raymond, Gene (1908–1998) If I Had a Million 1932; Red Dust 1932; Ex-Lady 1933; Flying down to Rio 1933; Zoo in Budapest 1933; Sadie McKee 1934; Hooray for Love 1935; Seven Keys to Baldpate 1935; The Woman in Red 1935; The Bride Walks Out 1936; Mr and Mrs Smith 1941; Smilin' Through 1941; The Locket 1946; Hit the Deck 1955; Plunder Road 1957; The Best Man 1964; I'd Rather Be Rich 1964

Raymond, Paula (1924–2003) Crisis 1950; Devil's Doorway 1950; The Sellout 1951; The Tall Target 1951; Texas Carnival 1951; The Bandits of Corsica 1953; The Beast from 20,000 Fathoms 1953; City That Never Sleeps 1953; The Human Jungle 1954; The Flight That Disappeared 1961; Blood of Dracula's Castle 1967

Rayner, Minnie (1869–1941) I Lived with You 1933; Gaslight 1940

Rea, Peggy (1921–) Love Field 1992; Made in America 1993

Rea, Stephen (1946–) Angel 1982; Loose Connections 1983; The Company of Wolves 1984; The Doctor and the Devils 1985; Life Is Sweet 1990; Bad Behaviour 1992; The Crying Game 1992; Angie 1994; Interview with the Vampire: the Vampire Chronicles 1994; Pret-a-Porter 1994; Princess Caraboo 1994; All Men Are Mortal 1995; Between the Devil and the Deep Blue Sea 1995; Citizen X 1995; Crime of the Century 1996; Fever Pitch 1996; A Further Gesture 1996; Last of the High Kings 1996; Michael Collins 1996; Trojan Eddie 1996; The Butcher Boy 1997; Double Tap 1997; In Dreams 1998; Still Crazy 1998; The End of the Affair 1999; Guinevere 1999; I Could Read the Sky 1999; The Life before This 1999; This Is My Father 1999; The Musketeer 2001; FearDotCom 2002; bl,.m 2003; The I Inside 2003

Read, Barbara (1917–1963) Make Way for Tomorrow 1937; The Man Who Cried Wolf 1937; Three Smart Girls 1937; The Spellbinder 1939

Read, James (1953–) The Initiation 1984; Beaches 1988; Love Crimes 1991; The Other Woman 1994

Reagan, Ronald (1911–2004) Hollywood Hotel 1937; Swing Your Lady 1937; Boy Meets Girl 1938; Going Places 1938; Angels Wash Their Faces 1939; Dark Victory 1939; Hell's Kitchen 1939; Naughty but Nice 1939; Knute Rockne – All American 1940; Santa Fe Trail 1940; Million Dollar Baby 1941; Desperate Journey 1942; Kings Row 1942; This Is the Army 1943; Voice of the Turtle 1947; The Hasty Heart 1949; It's a Great Feeling 1949; Night unto Night 1949; Storm Warning 1950; Bedtime for Bonzo 1951; She's Working Her Way through College 1952; Law and Order 1953; Cattle Queen of Montana 1954; Prisoner of War 1954; Tennessee's Partner 1955; Hellcats of the Navy 1957; The Killers 1964

Reason, Rex aka **Roberts, Bart** (1928–) Taza, Son of Cochise 1954; Yankee Pasha 1954; Kiss of Fire 1955; Smoke Signal 1955; This Island Earth 1955; The Creature Walks among Us 1956; Raw Edge 1956; Band of Angels 1957; The Sad Horse 1959

Rebhorn, James (1948–) He Knows You're Alone 1981; Scent of a Woman 1992; Carlito's Way 1993; Blank Check 1994; 8 Seconds 1994; Guarding Tess 1994; I Love Trouble 1994; If Lucy Fell 1996; Up Close & Personal 1996; The Game 1997; Snow Falling on Cedars 1999; The Talented Mr Ripley 1999; Meet the Parents 2000; Pluto Nash 2001; Far from Heaven 2002; Head of State 2003

Reddin, Keith The Heart of Justice 1992; Lolita 1997

Reddy, Helen (1942–) Airport 1975 1974; Pete's Dragon 1977

Redeker, Quinn (1936–) The Three Stooges Meet Hercules 1962; Spider Baby 1964; The Candidate 1972; At Long Last Love 1975; Coast to Coast 1980

Redfield, William (1927–1976) Conquest of Space 1955; The Proud and Profane 1956; I Married a Woman 1958; The Connection 1961; Hamlet 1964; Duel at Diablo 1966; Fantastic Voyage 1966; The Sidelong Glances of a Pigeon Kicker 1970; A New Leaf 1971; Death Wish 1974; For Pete's Sake 1974; Fear on Trial 1975; One Flew over the Cuckoo's Nest 1975; Mr Billion 1977

Redford, Robert (1937–) War Hunt 1962; Inside Daisy Clover 1965; Situation Hopeless – but Not Serious 1965; The Chase 1966; This Property Is Condemned 1966; Barefoot in the Park 1967; Butch Cassidy and the Sundance Kid 1969; Downhill Racer 1969; Tell Them Willie Boy Is Here 1969; Little Fauss and Big Halsy 1970; The Candidate 1972; The Hot Rock 1972; Jeremiah Johnson 1972; The Sting 1973; The Way We Were 1973; The Great Gatsby 1974; The Great Waldo Pepper 1975; Three Days of the Condor 1975; All the President's Men 1976; A Bridge Too Far 1977; The Electric Horseman 1979; Brubaker 1980; The Natural 1984; Out of Africa 1985; Legal Eagles 1986; Havana 1990; Sneakers 1992; Indecent Proposal 1993; Up Close & Personal 1996; The Horse Whisperer 1998; The Last Castle 2001; Spy Game 2001; The Clearing 2004

Redgrave, Corin (1939–) Crooks in Cloisters 1963; A Man for All Seasons 1966; The Charge of the Light Brigade 1968; Oh! What a Lovely War 1969; Von Richthofen and Brown 1971; When Eight Bells Toll 1971; Excalibur 1981; Eureka 1982; In the Name of the Father 1993; Four Weddings and a Funeral 1994; Persuasion 1995; Honest 2000; Enigma 2001; Doctor Sleep 2002; To Kill a King 2003; Enduring Love 2004

Redgrave, Jemma (1965–) Dream Demon 1988; Howards End 1992; I'll Be There 2003

Redgrave, Lynn (1943–) Girl with Green Eyes 1963; Tom Jones 1963; The Deadly Affair 1966; Georgy Girl 1966; Smashing Time 1967; The Virgin Soldiers 1969; Last of the Mobile Hot-Shots 1970; Every Little Crook and Nanny 1972; Everything You Always Wanted to Know about Sex ... but Were Afraid to Ask 1972; The National Health 1973; The Happy Hooker 1975; Home Front 1987; Getting It Right 1989; Midnight 1989; Shine 1996; A Father's Betrayal 1997; Gods and Monsters 1998; Strike! 1998; Lion of Oz 2000; The Next Best Thing 2000; The Simian Line 2000; Varian's War 2000; My Kingdom 2001; Unconditional Love 2001; Anita & Me 2002; Spider 2002; Peter Pan 2003; The Wild Thornberrys Movie 2003

Redgrave, Michael (1908–1985) Climbing High 1938; The Lady Vanishes 1938; The Stars Look Down 1939; Stolen Life 1939; A Window in London 1939; Jeannie 1941; Kipps 1941; The Big Blockade 1942; Thunder Rock 1942; Dead of Night 1945; The Way to the Stars 1945; The Captive Heart 1946; The Years Between 1946; Fame Is the Spur 1947; The Man Within 1947; Mourning Becomes Electra 1947; Secret beyond the Door 1948; The Browning Version 1951; The Magic Box 1951; The Importance of Being Earnest 1952; The Dam Busters 1954; The Green Scarf 1954; The Sea Shall Not Have Them 1954; Confidential Report 1955; The Night My Number Came Up 1955; 1984 1955; Oh, Rosalinda!! 1955; The Happy Road 1956; Time without Pity 1957; Behind the Mask 1958; Law and Disorder 1958; The Quiet American 1958; Shake Hands with the Devil 1959; The Wreck of the Mary Deare 1959; The Innocents 1961; No My Darling Daughter 1961; The Loneliness of the Long Distance Runner 1962; The Heroes of Telemark 1965; The Hill 1965; Young Cassidy 1965; The 25th Hour 1967; Assignment K 1968; Battle of Britain 1969; Connecting Rooms 1969; Goodbye, Mr Chips 1969; Oh! What a Lovely War 1969; The Go-Between 1971

Redgrave, Vanessa (1937–) Behind the Mask 1958; Blowup 1966; A Man for All Seasons 1966; Morgan – a Suitable Case for Treatment 1966; Camelot 1967; The Sailor from Gibraltar 1967; The Charge of the Light Brigade 1968; Isadora 1968; The Sea Gull 1968; Oh! What a Lovely War 1969; The Devils 1971; Mary, Queen of Scots 1971; The Trojan Women 1971; Murder on the Orient Express 1974; Out of Season 1975; The Seven-Per-Cent Solution 1976; Julia 1977; Agatha 1978; Bear Island 1979; Yanks 1979; Playing for Time 1980; Wagner 1983; The Bostonians 1984; Steaming 1985; Wetherby 1985; Comrades: a Lanternist's Account of the Tolpuddle Martyrs and What Became of Them 1986; Second Serve 1986; Prick Up Your Ears 1987; Consuming Passions 1988; The Ballad of the Sad Café 1991; Howards End 1992; The House of the Spirits 1993; Mother's Boys 1993; Shades of Fear 1993; Sparrow 1993; Wall of Silence 1993; Little Odessa 1994; A Month by the Lake 1994; Mission: Impossible 1996; Smilla's Feeling for Snow 1996; Déjà Vu 1997; Mrs Dalloway 1997; Wilde 1997; Deep Impact 1998; Lulu on the Bridge 1998; Cradle Will Rock 1999; Girl, Interrupted 1999; If These Walls Could Talk 2 2000; The Pledge 2000; A Rumor of Angels 2000; Merci Docteur Rey 2002; Good Boy! 2003

Reding, Nick (1962–) Captive 1986; Mister Johnson 1991

Redman, Amanda (1959–) For Queen and Country 1988; Sexy Beast 2000; The Wedding Tackle 2000; Mike Bassett: England Manager 2001

Redman, Joyce (1918–) Othello 1965; Prudence and the Pill 1968

Redmond, Liam (1913–1989) I See a Dark Stranger 1946; Daughter of Darkness 1948; Devil on Horseback 1954; The Divided Heart 1954; Final Appointment 1954; The Glass Cage 1955; Jacqueline 1956; 23 Paces to Baker Street 1956; Night of the Demon 1957; Alive and Kicking 1958; Rooney 1958; Scent of Mystery 1960; Under Ten Flags 1960; The Playboy of the Western World 1962; The Luck of Ginger Coffey 1964; The Ghost and Mr Chicken 1966; The Adventures of Bullwhip Griffin 1967; The Last Safari 1967; Till Death Us Do Part 1968; Philadelphia, Here I Come 1975

Redmond, Moira Pit of Darkness 1961; Jigsaw 1962; Kill or Cure 1962; Nightmare 1963; The Winter's Tale 1966

Redmond, Siobhan (1959–) Captives 1994; Beautiful People 1999

Reece, Brian (1913–1962) *A Case for PC 49* 1950; *Orders Are Orders* 1954; *Carry On Admiral* 1957
Reed, Alan *aka* **Openshaw, Falstaff** (1907–1977) *Days of Glory* 1944; *Nob Hill* 1945; *Perfect Strangers* 1950; *The Redhead and the Cowboy* 1950; *Viva Zapata!* 1952; *I, the Jury* 1953; *The Far Horizons* 1955; *Kiss of Fire* 1955; *He Laughed Last* 1956; *Timetable* 1956; *The Tarnished Angels* 1957; *The Man Called Flintstone* 1966; *Shinbone Alley* 1971; *The Seniors* 1978
Reed, Alyson *A Chorus Line* 1985; *Skin Deep* 1989
Reed, Donna (1921–1986) *Shadow of the Thin Man* 1941; *Apache Trail* 1942; *Calling Dr Gillespie* 1942; *The Courtship of Andy Hardy* 1942; *Eyes in the Night* 1942; *Dr Gillespie's Criminal Case* 1943; *The Human Comedy* 1943; *The Man from Down Under* 1943; *See Here, Private Hargrove* 1944; *The Picture of Dorian Gray* 1945; *They Were Expendable* 1945; *It's a Wonderful Life* 1946; *Green Dolphin Street* 1947; *Hangman's Knot* 1952; *The Caddy* 1953; *From Here to Eternity* 1953; *Gun Fury* 1953; *Raiders of the Seven Seas* 1953; *Trouble along the Way* 1953; *The Last Time I Saw Paris* 1954; *They Rode West* 1954; *Three Hours to Kill* 1954; *The Benny Goodman Story* 1955; *The Far Horizons* 1955; *Backlash* 1956; *Ransom!* 1956; *Beyond Mombasa* 1957; *The Whole Truth* 1958
Reed, George (1866–1952) *The Green Pastures* 1936; *Swanee River* 1939
Reed, Jerry (1937–) *WW and the Dixie Dancekings* 1975; *Gator* 1976; *Smokey and the Bandit* 1977; *High-ballin'* 1978; *Hot Stuff* 1979; *Smokey and the Bandit II* 1980; *Smokey and the Bandit III* 1983; *The Survivors* 1983; *BAT-21* 1988; *The Waterboy* 1998
Reed, Lou (1942–) *One-Trick Pony* 1980; *Get Crazy* 1983; *Faraway, So Close* 1993; *Blue in the Face* 1995
Reed, Marshall (1917–1980) *The Lineup* 1958; *The Hard Ride* 1971
Reed, Maxwell (1919–1974) *Daybreak* 1946; *The Brothers* 1947; *Dear Murderer* 1947; *Daughter of Darkness* 1948; *Night Beat* 1948; *The Lost People* 1949; *Madness of the Heart* 1949; *Blackout* 1950; *The Clouded Yellow* 1950; *There Is Another Sun* 1951; *Sea Devils* 1952; *The Square Ring* 1953; *The Brain Machine* 1954; *The Notorious Landlady* 1962; *Picture Mommy Dead* 1966
Reed, Nikki (1988–) *Thirteen* 2003; *Lords of Dogtown* 2005
Reed, Oliver (1938–1999) *The Angry Silence* 1960; *Beat Girl* 1960; *The Bulldog Breed* 1960; *His and Hers* 1960; *Sword of Sherwood Forest* 1960; *The Two Faces of Dr Jekyll* 1960; *The Curse of the Werewolf* 1961; *The Damned* 1961; *The Pirates of Blood River* 1961; *Paranoiac* 1963; *The Scarlet Blade* 1963; *The System* 1964; *The Party's Over* 1965; *The Trap* 1966; *I'll Never Forget What's 'Is Name* 1967; *The Jokers* 1967; *The Shuttered Room* 1967; *Hannibal Brooks* 1968; *Oliver!* 1968; *The Assassination Bureau* 1969; *Women in Love* 1969; *The Lady in the Car with Glasses and a Gun* 1970; *Take a Girl like You* 1970; *The Devils* 1971; *The Hunting Party* 1971; *ZPG: Zero Population Growth* 1971; *Sitting Target* 1972; *The Triple Echo* 1972; *Blue Blood* 1973; *The Three Musketeers* 1973; *And Then There Were None* 1974; *The Four Musketeers* 1974; *Royal Flash* 1975; *The Sellout* 1975; *Tommy* 1975; *Burnt Offerings* 1976; *The Great Scout & Cathouse Thursday* 1976; *Maniac* 1977; *The Prince and the Pauper* 1977; *Tomorrow Never Comes* 1977; *The Big Sleep* 1978; *The Class of Miss MacMichael* 1978; *The Brood* 1979; *A Touch of the Sun* 1979; *Dr Heckyl & Mr Hype* 1980; *Condorman* 1981; *Lion of the Desert* 1981; *Venom* 1981; *Fanny Hill* 1983; *The Sting II* 1983; *Two of a Kind* 1983; *Captive* 1986; *Castaway* 1986; *Dragonard* 1987; *Gor* 1987; *The Adventures of Baron Munchausen* 1988; *Captive Rage* 1988; *The House of Usher* 1988; *Rage to Kill* 1988; *The Return of the Musketeers* 1989; *A Ghost in Monte Carlo* 1990; *Hired to Kill* 1990; *Treasure Island* 1990; *The Pit and the Pendulum* 1991; *Prisoner of Honor* 1991; *Funny Bones* 1994; *The Bruce* 1996; *Parting Shots* 1998; *Gladiator* 2000
Reed, Pamela (1949–) *Eyewitness* 1981; *The Right Stuff* 1983; *The Goodbye People* 1984; *The Best of Times* 1986; *The Clan of the Cave Bear* 1986; *Chattahoochee* 1989; *Cadillac Man* 1990; *Caroline?* 1990; *Kindergarten Cop* 1990; *Passed Away* 1992; *Junior* 1994; *Deadly Whispers* 1995; *The Man Next Door* 1996; *Bean* 1997; *Carriers* 1998; *Proof of Life* 2000
Reed, Paul *The Ride to Hangman's Tree* 1967; *Did You Hear the One about the Traveling Saleslady?* 1968
Reed, Philip *aka* **Reed, Phillip** (1908–1996) *British Agent* 1934; *Fashions of 1934* 1934; *Gambling Lady* 1934; *Glamour* 1934; *Jimmy the Gent* 1934; *Accent on Youth* 1935; *The Girl from 10th Avenue* 1935; *The Woman in Red* 1935; *Klondike Annie* 1936; *A Gentleman after Dark* 1942; *Old Acquaintance* 1943; *Rendezvous with Annie* 1946; *Song of Scheherazade* 1947; *Song of the Thin Man* 1947; *Bodyguard* 1948; *Take Me to Town* 1953; *Harum Scarum* 1965
Reed, Ralph *Reform School Girl* 1957; *The Cry Baby Killer* 1958
Reed, Robert (1932–1992) *Star!* 1968; *The Maltese Bippy* 1969; *The Boy in the Plastic Bubble* 1976; *Prime Target* 1991
Reed, Tracy (1949–) *Dr Strangelove, or How I Learned to Stop Worrying and Love the Bomb* 1963; *Devils of Darkness* 1964; *A Shot in the Dark* 1964; *Adam's Woman* 1970; *The Take* 1974; *A Piece of the Action* 1977; *The California Dolls* 1981
Reed, Walter (1916–) *Seven Days' Leave* 1942; *Bombardier* 1943; *Child of Divorce* 1946; *Mystery in Mexico* 1948; *Return of the Bad Men* 1948; *The Clown* 1952; *Desert Passage* 1952; *The Yellow Tomahawk* 1954; *Hell's Island* 1955; *Seven Men from Now* 1956; *Moment to Moment* 1966
Reedus, Norman (1969–) *Six Ways to Sunday* 1997; *Dark Harbor* 1998; *The Boondock Saints* 1999; *Gossip* 1999; *Blade II* 2002; *Octane* 2003
Reems, Harry (1947–) *Deep Throat* 1972; *Deadly Weapons* 1974
Reenberg, Jørgen (1927–) *The Wolf at the Door* 1986; *Europa* 1991
Rees, Betty Anne *The Unholy Rollers* 1972; *Sugar Hill* 1974
Rees, Donogh *Constance* 1984; *Lorca and the Outlaws* 1985; *Crush* 1992
Rees, John *The Long and the Short and the Tall* 1960; *Passenger* 1963
Rees, Roger (1944–) *Star 80* 1983; *Teen Agent* 1991; *Stop! or My Mom Will Shoot* 1992; *Robin Hood: Men in Tights* 1993; *The Substance of Fire* 1996; *Double Platinum* 1999; *The Crossing* 2000; *Frida* 2002; *Return to Never Land* 2002
Reese, Della (1932–) *Psychic Killer* 1975; *Harlem Nights* 1989; *A Thin Line between Love and Hate* 1996; *Dinosaur* 2000
Reese, Tom (1939–) *The Money Trap* 1966; *Stranger on the Run* 1967
Reeve, Christopher (1952–2004) *Superman* 1978; *Somewhere in Time* 1980; *Superman II* 1980; *Deathtrap* 1982; *Monsignor* 1982; *Superman III* 1983; *The Bostonians* 1984; *The Aviator* 1985; *Street Smart* 1987; *Superman IV: the Quest for Peace* 1987; *Switching Channels* 1987; *Noises Off* 1992; *The Remains of the Day* 1993; *Speechless* 1994; *Village of the Damned* 1995; *Rear Window* 1998
Reeves, George (1914–1959) *Argentine Nights* 1940; *Lydia* 1941; *So Proudly We Hail* 1943; *Jungle Jim* 1948; *The Sainted Sisters* 1948; *Bugles in the Afternoon* 1952; *Rancho Notorious* 1952; *The Blue Gardenia* 1953; *Westward Ho the Wagons!* 1956
Reeves, Keanu (1964–) *Brotherhood of Justice* 1986; *Youngblood* 1986; *River's Edge* 1987; *Bill & Ted's Excellent Adventure* 1988; *Dangerous Liaisons* 1988; *The Night Before* 1988; *Permanent Record* 1988; *The Prince of Pennsylvania* 1988; *Parenthood* 1989; *Aunt Julia and the Scriptwriter* 1990; *I Love You to Death* 1990; *Bill & Ted's Bogus Journey* 1991; *My Own Private Idaho* 1991; *Point Break* 1991; *Bram Stoker's Dracula* 1992; *Even Cowgirls Get the Blues* 1993; *Freaked* 1993; *Little Buddha* 1993; *Much Ado about Nothing* 1993; *Speed* 1994; *Johnny Mnemonic* 1995; *A Walk in the Clouds* 1995; *Chain Reaction* 1996; *Feeling Minnesota* 1996; *The Last Time I Committed Suicide* 1996; *The Devil's Advocate* 1997; *The Matrix* 1999; *The Gift* 2000; *The Replacements* 2000; *The Watcher* 2000; *Hardball* 2001; *Sweet November* 2001; *The Matrix Reloaded* 2002; *The Matrix Revolutions* 2003; *Something's Gotta Give* 2003; *Constantine* 2005
Reeves, Kynaston (1893–1971) *Vintage Wine* 1935; *Sons of the Sea* 1939; *Penny Princess* 1952; *Eight O'Clock Walk* 1953; *Fiend without a Face* 1957
Reeves, Phil *Election* 1999; *13 Going on 30* 2004
Reeves, Saskia (1962–) *The Bridge* 1990; *December Bride* 1990; *Close My Eyes* 1991; *Butterfly Kiss* 1994; *ID* 1994; *Traps* 1994; *Different for Girls* 1996; *Heart* 1997; *LA without a Map* 1998; *A Christmas Carol* 1999
Reeves, Steve (1926–2000) *Athena* 1954; *Jail Bait* 1954; *Hercules* 1957; *Goliath and the Barbarians* 1959; *Hercules Unchained* 1959; *The White Warrior* 1959; *The Giant of Marathon* 1960; *The Last Days of Pompeii* 1960; *Morgan the Pirate* 1960; *Duel of the Titans* 1961; *The Trojan War* 1961; *Sandokan the Great* 1963; *The Pirates of Malaysia* 1964
Reeves, Vic (1959–) *Once upon a Time in the Midlands* 2002; *Churchill: the Hollywood Years* 2004
Reevis, Steve *Geronimo: an American Legend* 1993; *Last of the Dogmen* 1995; *The Missing* 2003
Regalbuto, Joe (1949–) *Six Weeks* 1982; *The Star Chamber* 1983; *Lassiter* 1984
Regan, Jayne (1909–2000) *Thank You, Mr Moto* 1937; *Mr Moto's Gamble* 1938
Regan, Laura *My Little Eye* 2002; *They* 2002
Regan, Mary *Sylvia* 1984; *Fever* 1988
Regan, Phil (1906–1996) *Dames* 1934; *In Caliente* 1935; *Sweet Rosie O'Grady* 1943
Regan, Vincent (1966–) *Hard Men* 1996; *The Point Men* 2000; *Black Knight* 2001
Regas, George (1890–1940) *Bulldog Drummond Strikes Back* 1934; *Rose Marie* 1936; *Mr Moto Takes a Chance* 1938
Regehr, Duncan (1952–) *The Monster Squad* 1987; *Danielle Steel's Once in a Lifetime* 1994; *Blood Surf* 2000
Régent, Benoît (1953–1994) *Dr M* 1989; *Three Colours Blue* 1993
Reggiani, Serge (1922–2004) *Les Portes de la Nuit* 1946; *La Ronde* 1950; *The Secret People* 1951; *Casque d'Or* 1952; *Napoléon* 1955; *Paris Blues* 1961; *Le Doulos* 1962; *The Leopard* 1962; *The 25th Hour* 1967; *L'Armée des Ombres* 1969; *Vincent, François, Paul and the Others* 1974; *The Bee Keeper* 1986; *The Night Is Young* 1986
Regin, Nadja (1931–) *The Man without a Body* 1957; *Solo for Sparrow* 1962
Regina, Paul (1956–) *A Change of Seasons* 1980; *Adam* 1983
Régine (1929–) *Marry Me! Marry Me!* 1968; *The Last Train* 1972; *Robert et Robert* 1978; *Le Cop* 1985
Regnier, Carola *Seduction: the Cruel Woman* 1985; *Hôtel du Paradis* 1986; *Walk on Water* 2004
Régnier, Natacha (1974–) *The Dream Life of Angels* 1998; *Criminal Lovers* 1999; *Comment J'ai Tué Mon Père* 2001
Rehak, Frantisek *Capricious Summer* 1968; *Cutting It Short* 1980
Rehman, Waheeda (1936–) *Kaagaz Ke Phool* 1959; *Abhijaan* 1962; *Teesri Kasam* 1966; *Kabhi Kabhie* 1976
Reicher, Frank (1875–1965) *Beau Sabreur* 1928; *King Kong* 1933; *Son of Kong* 1933; *Topaze* 1933; *Espionage* 1937; *Westbound Limited* 1937; *Dr Cyclops* 1940; *The Mummy's Ghost* 1944; *The Jade Mask* 1945
Reichmann, Wolfgang (1932–1991) *Signs of Life* 1968; *Woyzeck* 1978; *The Second Victory* 1986
Reid, Alex *Arachnid* 2001; *The Honeymooners* 2003; *The Descent* 2005
Reid, Anne (1935–) *Liam* 2000; *The Mother* 2003
Reid, Audrey *Dancehall Queen* 1996; *Third World Cop* 1999
Reid, Beryl (1920–1996) *Two Way Stretch* 1960; *Trial and Error* 1962; *Inspector Clouseau* 1968; *The Killing of Sister George* 1968; *Star!* 1968; *The Assassination Bureau* 1969; *Entertaining Mr Sloane* 1969; *The Beast in the Cellar* 1970; *Father Dear Father* 1972; *Psychomania* 1972; *No Sex Please – We're British* 1973; *Joseph Andrews* 1977; *Carry On Emmannuelle* 1978; *Rosie Dixon: Night Nurse* 1978; *Yellowbeard* 1983
Reid, Carl Benton (1893–1973) *The Little Foxes* 1941; *Convicted* 1950; *The Fuller Brush Girl* 1950; *In a Lonely Place* 1950; *Boots Malone* 1951; *The Great Caruso* 1951; *Indian Uprising* 1951; *Lorna Doone* 1951; *Carbine Williams* 1952; *Escape from Fort Bravo* 1953; *The Command* 1954; *One Desire* 1955; *The Spoilers* 1955; *Wichita* 1955; *A Day of Fury* 1956; *The Last Wagon* 1956; *Time Limit* 1957; *The Last of the Fast Guns* 1958; *Tarzan's Fight for Life* 1958; *The Baited Trap* 1959; *Pressure Point* 1962
Reid, Christopher *House Party* 1990; *House Party 2* 1991; *Class Act* 1992; *House Party 3* 1994
Reid, Elliott (1920–) *Young Ideas* 1943; *The Whip Hand* 1951; *Gentlemen Prefer Blondes* 1953; *Inherit the Wind* 1960; *The Absent-Minded Professor* 1961; *Son of Flubber* 1962; *Move Over, Darling* 1963; *The Thrill of It All* 1963; *Follow Me, Boys!* 1966; *Blackbeard's Ghost* 1967
Reid, Kate (1930–1993) *This Property Is Condemned* 1966; *The Andromeda Strain* 1970; *The Sidelong Glances of a Pigeon Kicker* 1970; *A Delicate Balance* 1973; *Equus* 1977; *Highpoint* 1979; *Atlantic City, USA* 1980; *Circle of Two* 1980; *Catholic Boys* 1985; *Death of a Salesman* 1985; *Fire with Fire* 1986; *Sweet Hearts Dance* 1988; *Deceived* 1991
Reid, Sheila *Othello* 1965; *Three Sisters* 1970; *The Touch* 1971; *Sir Henry at Rawlinson End* 1980; *The Dresser* 1983; *American Friends* 1991; *The Winter Guest* 1996; *Mrs Caldicot's Cabbage War* 2000
Reid, Tara (1975–) *The Big Lebowski* 1997; *Girl* 1998; *American Pie* 1999; *Body Shots* 1999; *Murder at Devil's Glen* 1999; *Dr T & the Women* 2000; *American Pie 2* 2001; *Josie and the Pussycats* 2001; *Just Visiting* 2001; *Van Wilder: Party Liaison* 2002; *My Boss's Daughter* 2003
Reilly, Charles Nelson (1931–) *All Dogs Go to Heaven* 1989; *Rock-a-Doodle* 1990
Reilly, John (1936–) *The Patricia Neal Story: an Act of Love* 1981; *Touch and Go* 1986
Reilly, John C (1965–) *Casualties of War* 1989; *Days of Thunder* 1990; *State of Grace* 1990; *Hoffa* 1992; *Out on a Limb* 1992; *What's Eating Gilbert Grape* 1993; *The River Wild* 1994; *Boys* 1995; *Dolores Claiborne* 1995; *Georgia* 1995; *Hard Eight* 1996; *Boogie Nights* 1997; *Chicago Cab* 1998; *For Love of the Game* 1999; *Magnolia* 1999; *Never Been Kissed* 1999; *The Perfect Storm* 2000; *The Anniversary Party* 2001; *The Good Girl* 2001; *Chicago* 2002; *Gangs of New York* 2002; *The Hours* 2002; *The Aviator* 2004; *Criminal* 2004
Reilly, Kelly *Peaches* 2000; *Pot Luck* 2002
Reiman, Eric *Forty Thousand Horsemen* 1941; *Long John Silver* 1954
Reina, Lucy *The Penitent* 1988; *Romero* 1989
Reineke, Gary *Why Shoot the Teacher* 1976; *The Grey Fox* 1982; *Murder by Phone* 1982; *George's Island* 1991; *Spider* 2002
Reiner, Carl (1922–) *The Gazebo* 1959; *Happy Anniversary* 1959; *Gidget Goes Hawaiian* 1961; *The Thrill of It All* 1963; *Art of Love* 1965; *The Russians Are Coming, the Russians Are Coming* 1966; *Generation* 1969; *The Jerk* 1979; *Skokie* 1981; *Dead Men Don't Wear Plaid* 1982; *Slums of Beverly Hills* 1998; *Ocean's Eleven* 2001; *Good Boy!* 2003; *Ocean's Twelve* 2004
Reiner, Rob (1945–) *Halls of Anger* 1970; *Where's Poppa?* 1970; *Fire Sale* 1977; *This Is Spinal Tap* 1984; *Throw Momma from the Train* 1987; *Postcards from the Edge* 1990; *Sleepless in Seattle* 1993; *Bullets over Broadway* 1994; *Mixed Nuts* 1994; *Bye Bye Love* 1995; *For Better or Worse* 1995; *Primary Colors* 1998; *Edtv* 1999; *Alex & Emma* 2003; *Dickie Roberts: Former Child Star* 2003
Reinheart, Alice (1910–1993) *The Lieutenant Wore Skirts* 1956; *Grand Jury* 1976
Reinhold, Judge (1957–) *Stripes* 1981; *Fast Times at Ridgemont High* 1982; *Pandemonium* 1982; *The Lords of Discipline* 1983; *Beverly Hills Cop* 1984; *Roadhouse 66* 1984; *Head Office* 1986; *Off Beat* 1986; *Ruthless People* 1986; *Beverly Hills Cop II* 1987; *Promised a Miracle* 1988; *A Soldier's Tale* 1988; *Vice Versa* 1988; *Rosalie Goes Shopping* 1989; *Daddy's Dyin'... Who's Got the Will?* 1990; *Near Mrs* 1990; *Over Her Dead Body* 1990; *Zandalee* 1991; *Baby on Board* 1993; *Bank Robber* 1993; *Beverly Hills Cop III* 1994; *The Santa Clause* 1994; *Family Plan* 1997; *Runaway Car* 1997; *Homegrown* 1998; *My Brother the Pig* 1999; *Walking across Egypt* 1999; *Beethoven's 3rd* 2000; *Beethoven's 4th* 2001; *The Santa Clause 2* 2002; *Clifford's Really Big Movie* 2004
Reinking, Ann (1979–) *All That Jazz* 1979; *Annie* 1982; *Micki & Maude* 1984

Reis, Michelle (1970–) *A Chinese Ghost Story II* 1990; *Fallen Angels* 1995; *Flowers of Shanghai* 1998

Reiser, Paul (1957–) *Diner* 1982; *Aliens* 1986; *Odd Jobs* 1986; *Cross My Heart* 1987; *Crazy People* 1990; *Family Prayers* 1991; *Too Hot to Handle* 1991; *Bye Bye Love* 1995; *The Story of Us* 1999; *One Night at McCool's* 2001

Rekert, Winston (1949–) *Heartaches* 1981; *Dead Wrong* 1983; *Walls* 1984; *Agnes of God* 1985; *Silhouette* 1994; *A Cooler Climate* 1999

Rekha (1954–) *Kama Sutra: a Tale of Love* 1996; *Zubeidaa* 2000; *Bhoot* 2003; *Koi... Mil Gaya* 2003

Relph, George (1888–1960) *I Believe in You* 1952; *The Titfield Thunderbolt* 1952; *The Final Test* 1953

Remar, James (1953–) *The Warriors* 1979; *Windwalker* 1980; *48 HRS* 1982; *The Cotton Club* 1984; *The Clan of the Cave Bear* 1986; *Quiet Cool* 1986; *Rent-a-Cop* 1988; *Drugstore Cowboy* 1989; *Tales from the Darkside: the Movie* 1991; *White Fang* 1991; *Fatal Instinct* 1993; *Blink* 1994; *Confessions of a Hit Man* 1994; *Miracle on 34th Street* 1994; *Renaissance Man* 1994; *Boys on the Side* 1995; *Exquisite Tenderness* 1995; *One Good Turn* 1996; *The Phantom* 1996; *The Quest* 1996; *Mortal Kombat: Annihilation* 1997; *Blowback* 1999; *Rites of Passage* 1999; *Guardian* 2000; *What Lies Beneath* 2000; *Fear X* 2002; *Our House* 2003; *2 Fast 2 Furious* 2003; *The Girl Next Door* 2004

Remberg, Erika (1932–) *Circus of Horrors* 1960; *Saturday Night Out* 1963

Remick, Lee (1935–1991) *A Face in the Crowd* 1957; *The Long Hot Summer* 1958; *Anatomy of a Murder* 1959; *These Thousand Hills* 1959; *Wild River* 1960; *Sanctuary* 1961; *Days of Wine and Roses* 1962; *Experiment in Terror* 1962; *The Running Man* 1963; *The Wheeler Dealers* 1963; *Baby the Rain Must Fall* 1965; *The Hallelujah Trail* 1965; *The Detective* 1968; *No Way to Treat a Lady* 1968; *Hard Contract* 1969; *Loot* 1970; *A Severed Head* 1970; *Sometimes a Great Notion* 1971; *The Blue Knight* 1973; *A Delicate Balance* 1973; *Hennessy* 1975; *The Omen* 1976; *Telefon* 1977; *The Medusa Touch* 1978; *The Europeans* 1979; *Torn between Two Lovers* 1979; *The Competition* 1980; *Tribute* 1980; *Emma's War* 1985

Remsen, Bert (1925–1999) *Tess of the Storm Country* 1960; *McCabe and Mrs Miller* 1971; *Thieves like Us* 1974; *Borderline* 1980; *Lookin' to Get Out* 1982; *Code of Silence* 1985; *Stand Alone* 1985; *Eye of the Tiger* 1986; *TerrorVision* 1986; *Three for the Road* 1987; *Remote Control* 1988; *Daddy's Dyin'... Who's Got the Will?* 1990; *Peacemaker* 1990; *Evil Spirits* 1991; *Only the Lonely* 1991

Rémy, Albert (1911–1967) *Razzia sur la Chnouf* 1955; *The 400 Blows* 1959; *Shoot the Pianist* 1960; *Gigot* 1962

Renaldo, Duncan (1904–1980) *Trader Horn* 1931; *Down Mexico Way* 1941; *The Capture* 1950

Renaldo, Tito *Anna and the King of Siam* 1946; *The Bribe* 1949; *One Way Street* 1950

Renant, Simone (1911–2004) *Quai des Orfèvres* 1947; *Bedevilled* 1955; *Les Liaisons Dangereuses* 1959; *That Man from Rio* 1964

Renaud *Germinal* 1993; *Crime Spree* 2002

Renaud, Madeleine (1900–1994) *Stormy Waters* 1941; *Le Plaisir* 1951

Renavent, Georges (1894–1969) *Rio Rita* 1929; *Whipsaw* 1935

Renfro, Brad (1982–) *The Client* 1994; *The Cure* 1995; *Tom and Huck* 1995; *Apt Pupil* 1997; *Telling Lies in America* 1997; *Bully* 2001; *Ghost World* 2001; *The Jacket* 2005

Rénier, Jérémie (1982–) *La Promesse* 1996; *Criminal Lovers* 1999; *Brotherhood of the Wolf* 2001; *The Pornographer* 2001

Renko, Serge *Les Rendez-vous de Paris* 1995; *Triple Agent* 2003

Renna, Patrick (1979–) *The Sandlot* 1993; *Son in Law* 1993; *The Big Green* 1995

Renner, Jeremy (1971–) *National Lampoon's Senior Trip* 1995; *Dahmer* 2002; *SWAT* 2003; *The Heart Is Deceitful above All Things* 2004

Rennie, Callum Keith (1960–) *Last Night* 1998; *eXistenZ* 1999; *The Life before This* 1999; *Memento* 2000; *Suspicious River* 2000; *The Butterfly Effect* 2003

Rennie, Michael (1909–1971) *Pimpernel Smith* 1941; *The Big Blockade* 1942; *I'll Be Your Sweetheart* 1945; *The Wicked Lady* 1945; *The Root of All Evil* 1946; *The Black Rose* 1950; *The 13th Letter* 1950; *Trio* 1950; *The Day the Earth Stood Still* 1951; *5 Fingers* 1952; *Les Misérables* 1952; *Phone Call from a Stranger* 1952; *King of the Khyber Rifles* 1953; *The Robe* 1953; *Sailor of the King* 1953; *Demetrius and the Gladiators* 1954; *Desiree* 1954; *Mambo* 1954; *Princess of the Nile* 1954; *The Rains of Ranchipur* 1955; *Seven Cities of Gold* 1955; *Soldier of Fortune* 1955; *Teenage Rebel* 1956; *Omar Khayyam* 1957; *The Battle of the V1* 1958; *Third Man on the Mountain* 1959; *The Lost World* 1960; *Mary, Mary* 1963; *Ride beyond Vengeance* 1966; *Hotel* 1967; *The Battle of El Alamein* 1968; *The Devil's Brigade* 1968; *The Power* 1968; *Subterfuge* 1968

Reno, Ginette (1946–) *Léolo* 1992; *Mambo Italiano* 2003

Reno, Jean (1948–) *The Last Battle* 1983; *Subway* 1985; *The Big Blue* 1988; *Nikita* 1990; *Les Visiteurs* 1993; *Leon* 1994; *Beyond the Clouds* 1995; *French Kiss* 1995; *Mission: Impossible* 1996; *Roseanna's Grave* 1996; *Godzilla* 1997; *Ronin* 1998; *Les Visiteurs 2: Les Couloirs du Temps* 1998; *The Crimson Rivers* 2000; *Just Visiting* 2001; *Rollerball* 2001

Reno, Kelly (1966–) *The Black Stallion* 1979; *The Black Stallion Returns* 1983; *The Long Ride* 1984

Renoir, Jean (1894–1979) *Une Partie de Campagne* 1936; *La Vie Est à Nous* 1936; *La Bête Humaine* 1938; *La Règle du Jeu* 1939; *The Testament of Dr Cordelier* 1959; *The Little Theatre of Jean Renoir* 1969; *The Christian Licorice Store* 1971

Renoir, Pierre (1885–1952) *La Nuit du Carrefour* 1932; *Madame Bovary* 1933; *La Marseillaise* 1938; *Pièges* 1939; *Les Enfants du Paradis* 1945

Renoir, Sophie *Le Beau Mariage* 1982; *My Girlfriend's Boyfriend* 1987

Renucci, Robin (1956–) *Entre Nous* 1983; *Masques* 1987; *The Chinese Connection* 1988; *The King's Whore* 1990; *Les Enfants du Siècle* 1999; *The Dreamers* 2003; *Arsène Lupin* 2004

Renzi, Eva (1944–) *Funeral in Berlin* 1966; *The Pink Jungle* 1968; *The Bird with the Crystal Plumage* 1969

Renzulli, Frank (1958–) *Broadway Danny Rose* 1984; *Wild Hearts Can't Be Broken* 1991

Repp, Stafford (1918–1974) *Plunder Road* 1957; *Batman* 1966

Resines, Antonio (1954–) *How to Be a Woman and Not Die in the Attempt* 1991; *Acción Mutante* 1993; *The Girl of Your Dreams* 1998

Ressel, Franco (1925–1985) *Blood and Black Lace* 1964; *Sabata* 1969

Restorick, Hughie *My Childhood* 1972; *My Ain Folk* 1973

Rettig, Tommy (1941–1996) *For Heaven's Sake* 1950; *The Jackpot* 1950; *The Strip* 1951; *Weekend with Father* 1951; *The 5,000 Fingers of Dr T* 1953; *The Raid* 1954; *River of No Return* 1954; *At Gunpoint* 1955; *The Last Wagon* 1956

Reuben, Gloria (1964–) *Timecop* 1994; *Nick of Time* 1995

Reubens, Paul aka **Mall, Paul** aka **Herman, Pee-wee** (1952–) *The Blues Brothers* 1980; *Cheech and Chong's Next Movie* 1980; *Cheech and Chong's Nice Dreams* 1981; *Pandemonium* 1982; *Meatballs 2* 1984; *Pee-wee's Big Adventure* 1985; *Flight of the Navigator* 1986; *Back to the Beach* 1987; *Big Top Pee-wee* 1988; *Buffy the Vampire Slayer* 1992; *The Nightmare before Christmas* 1993; *Dunston Checks In* 1996; *Matilda* 1996; *Beauty and the Beast: the Enchanted Christmas* 1997; *Buddy* 1997; *Mystery Men* 1999; *South of Heaven, West of Hell* 2000; *Blow* 2001

Revere, Anne (1903–1990) *The Devil Commands* 1941; *Star Spangled Rhythm* 1942; *The Meanest Man in the World* 1943; *The Song of Bernadette* 1943; *National Velvet* 1944; *Sunday Dinner for a Soldier* 1944; *The Thin Man Goes Home* 1944; *Fallen Angel* 1945; *Dragonwyck* 1946; *Body and Soul* 1947; *Forever Amber* 1947; *Gentleman's Agreement* 1947; *The Shocking Miss Pilgrim* 1947; *Secret beyond the Door* 1948; *You're My Everything* 1949; *A Place in the Sun* 1951; *Macho Callahan* 1970; *Birch Interval* 1976

Revier, Dorothy (1904–1993) *The Red Dance* 1928; *The Iron Mask* 1929; *By Candlelight* 1934

Revill, Clive (1930–) *Bunny Lake Is Missing* 1965; *A Fine Madness* 1966; *Kaleidoscope* 1966; *Modesty Blaise* 1966; *The Double Man* 1967; *Nobody Runs Forever* 1968; *The Shoes of the Fisherman* 1968; *The Assassination Bureau* 1969; *The Buttercup Chain* 1970; *The Private Life of Sherlock Holmes* 1970; *A Severed Head* 1970; *Avanti!* 1972; *Ghost in the Noonday Sun* 1973; *The Legend of Hell House* 1973; *The Black Windmill* 1974; *Galileo* 1974; *The Little Prince* 1974; *One of Our Dinosaurs Is Missing* 1975; *Matilda* 1978; *Zorro, the Gay Blade* 1981; *Rumpelstiltskin* 1986; *The Emperor's New Clothes* 1987; *Mack the Knife* 1989; *Arabian Knight* 1995

Rex, Simon (1974–) *The Forsaken* 2001; *Scary Movie 3* 2003

Rey, Alejandro (1930–1987) *Solomon and Sheba* 1959; *Battle at Bloody Beach* 1961; *Get off My Back* 1965; *Blindfold* 1966; *The Defiant* 1972; *Mr Majestyk* 1974; *Breakout* 1975; *High Velocity* 1977; *Moscow on the Hudson* 1984; *TerrorVision* 1986

Rey, Fernando (1917–1994) *The Last Days of Pompeii* 1960; *Viridiana* 1961; *The Castilian* 1963; *Son of a Gunfighter* 1964; *Chimes at Midnight* 1966; *Navajo Joe* 1966; *Return of the Seven* 1966; *The Desperate Ones* 1967; *Cervantes* 1968; *The Immortal Story* 1968; *Villa Rides* 1968; *Guns of the Magnificent Seven* 1969; *The Adventurers* 1970; *Tristana* 1970; *The French Connection* 1971; *The Light at the Edge of the World* 1971; *A Town Called Hell* 1971; *Antony and Cleopatra* 1972; *The Discreet Charm of the Bourgeoisie* 1972; *The Lady with Red Boots* 1974; *French Connection II* 1975; *Illustrious Corpses* 1976; *Seven Beauties* 1976; *That Obscure Object of Desire* 1977; *Quintet* 1979; *Caboblanco* 1980; *Monsignor* 1982; *The Hit* 1984; *Padre Nuestro* 1985; *Rustler's Rhapsody* 1985; *Saving Grace* 1985; *Hôtel du Paradis* 1986; *Moon over Parador* 1988; *Naked Tango* 1990; *1492: Conquest of Paradise* 1992

Reyer, Walter (1922–1999) *The Indian Tomb* 1959; *The Tiger of Eschnapur* 1959

Reyes Jr, Ernie (1972–) *Red Sonja* 1985; *Teenage Mutant Ninja Turtles II: the Secret of the Ooze* 1991; *Surf Ninjas* 1993; *Welcome to the Jungle* 2003

Reymond, Dominique aka ' *Will It Snow for Christmas?* 1996; *The Bridge* 1999; *Les Destinées Sentimentales* 2000; *Presque Rien* 2000; *Demonlover* 2002; *Ma Mère* 2004

Reynolds, Adeline De Walt (1862–1961) *The Tuttles of Tahiti* 1942; *Lydia Bailey* 1952; *Pony Soldier* 1952

Reynolds, Burt (1936–) *Angel Baby* 1961; *Armored Command* 1961; *Operation CIA* 1965; *Navajo Joe* 1966; *Impasse* 1969; *100 Rifles* 1969; *Sam Whiskey* 1969; *Shark!* 1969; *Skullduggery* 1969; *Deliverance* 1972; *Everything You Always Wanted to Know about Sex ... but Were Afraid to Ask* 1972; *Fuzz* 1972; *The Man Who Loved Cat Dancing* 1973; *Shamus* 1973; *White Lightning* 1973; *The Mean Machine* 1974; *At Long Last Love* 1975; *Hustle* 1975; *Lucky Lady* 1975; *WW and the Dixie Dancekings* 1975; *Gator* 1976; *Nickelodeon* 1976; *Semi-Tough* 1977; *Smokey and the Bandit* 1977; *The End* 1978; *Hooper* 1978; *Starting Over* 1979; *Rough Cut* 1980; *Smokey and the Bandit II* 1980; *The Cannonball Run* 1981; *Paternity* 1981; *Sharky's Machine* 1981; *Best Friends* 1982; *The Best Little Whorehouse in Texas* 1982; *Cannonball Run II* 1983; *The Man Who Loved Women* 1983; *Smokey and the Bandit III* 1983; *Stroker Ace* 1983; *City Heat* 1984; *Stick* 1985; *Uphill All the Way* 1985; *Heat* 1987; *Malone* 1987; *Switching Channels* 1987; *Physical Evidence* 1988; *Rent-a-Cop* 1988; *All Dogs Go to Heaven* 1989; *Breaking In* 1989; *Modern Love* 1990; *Cop and a Half* 1993; *The Maddening* 1995; *Citizen Ruth* 1996; *Striptease* 1996; *Trigger Happy* 1996; *Bean* 1997; *Boogie Nights* 1997; *Hard Time* 1998; *Universal Soldier 2: Brothers in Arms* 1998; *Universal Soldier 3: Unfinished Business* 1998; *Mystery, Alaska* 1999; *The Last Producer* 2000; *Driven* 2001; *Hotel* 2001; *Tempted* 2001; *Gumball 3000: the Movie* 2003; *Without a Paddle* 2004; *The Longest Yard* 2005

Reynolds, Craig (1907–1949) *The Case of the Black Cat* 1936; *Smart Blonde* 1936; *Stage Struck* 1936; *The Case of the Stuttering Bishop* 1937; *Nevada* 1944

Reynolds, Debbie (1932–) *June Bride* 1948; *The Daughter of Rosie O'Grady* 1950; *Three Little Words* 1950; *Mr Imperium* 1951; *Singin' in the Rain* 1952; *Skirts Ahoy!* 1952; *The Affairs of Dobie Gillis* 1953; *Give a Girl a Break* 1953; *I Love Melvin* 1953; *Athena* 1954; *Susan Slept Here* 1954; *Hit the Deck* 1955; *The Tender Trap* 1955; *Bundle of Joy* 1956; *The Catered Affair* 1956; *Tammy and the Bachelor* 1957; *This Happy Feeling* 1958; *The Gazebo* 1959; *It Started with a Kiss* 1959; *The Mating Game* 1959; *Say One for Me* 1959; *Pepe* 1960; *The Rat Race* 1960; *The Pleasure of His Company* 1961; *The Second Time Around* 1961; *How the West Was Won* 1962; *My Six Loves* 1962; *Mary, Mary* 1963; *Goodbye Charlie* 1964; *The Unsinkable Molly Brown* 1964; *The Singing Nun* 1966; *Divorce American Style* 1967; *How Sweet It Is!* 1968; *What's the Matter with Helen?* 1971; *Charlotte's Web* 1973; *Heaven and Earth* 1993; *Mother* 1996; *Wedding Bell Blues* 1996; *In & Out* 1997; *Rudolph the Red-Nosed Reindeer* 1998; *Rugrats in Paris: the Movie* 2000; *These Old Broads* 2001; *Connie and Carla* 2004

Reynolds, Gene (1925–) *Boys Town* 1938; *They Shall Have Music* 1939; *The Penalty* 1941; *The Tuttles of Tahiti* 1942; *The Country Girl* 1954; *Down Three Dark Streets* 1954

Reynolds, Helene (1914–1990) *Confirm or Deny* 1941; *Moontide* 1942; *The Bermuda Mystery* 1944

Reynolds, Joyce (1925–) *George Washington Slept Here* 1942; *The Constant Nymph* 1943

Reynolds, Marjorie (1917–1997) *Holiday Inn* 1942; *Dixie* 1943; *Up in Mabel's Room* 1944; *Bring on the Girls* 1945; *Ministry of Fear* 1945; *Monsieur Beaucaire* 1946; *The Time of Their Lives* 1946; *Heaven Only Knows* 1947; *The Great Jewel Robber* 1950; *Home Town Story* 1951

Reynolds, Michael J *Why Shoot the Teacher* 1976; *Too Outrageous!* 1987

Reynolds, Peter (1926–1975) *The Guinea Pig* 1948; *The Last Page* 1952; *The Vanquished* 1953; *Devil Girl from Mars* 1954; *The Bank Raiders* 1958; *The Challenge* 1960; *Your Money or Your Wife* 1960; *The Breaking Point* 1961; *The Painted Smile* 1961; *Spare the Rod* 1961; *Gaolbreak* 1962

Reynolds, Robert *Traps* 1994; *Tunnel Vision* 1994

Reynolds, Ryan (1976–) *Ordinary Magic* 1993; *The Alarmist* 1997; *Buying the Cow* 2000; *Van Wilder: Party Liaison* 2002; *The In-Laws* 2003; *Blade: Trinity* 2004; *The Amityville Horror* 2005

Reynolds, William (1931–) *Francis Goes to West Point* 1952; *Has Anybody Seen My Gal?* 1952; *Son of Ali Baba* 1952; *Gunsmoke* 1953; *The Mississippi Gambler* 1953; *All That Heaven Allows* 1955; *Away All Boats* 1956; *There's Always Tomorrow* 1956; *The Land Unknown* 1957; *Mister Cory* 1957; *A Distant Trumpet* 1964

Rhames, Ving (1961–) *Go Tell It on the Mountain* 1984; *Patty Hearst* 1988; *Casualties of War* 1989; *The Long Walk Home* 1990; *Homicide* 1991; *The People under the Stairs* 1991; *Dave* 1993; *The Saint of Fort Washington* 1993; *DROP Squad* 1994; *Kiss of Death* 1994; *Pulp Fiction* 1994; *Deadly Whispers* 1995; *Ed McBain's 87th Precinct* 1995; *Dangerous Ground* 1996; *Mission: Impossible* 1996; *Striptease* 1996; *Body Count* 1997; *Con Air* 1997; *Rosewood* 1997; *Out of Sight* 1998; *Bringing out the Dead* 1999; *Entrapment* 1999; *Mission: Impossible 2* 1999; *Baby Boy* 2001; *Final Fantasy: the Spirits Within* 2001; *Dark Blue* 2002; *Lilo & Stitch* 2002; *Undisputed* 2002; *Dawn of the Dead* 2004

Rhee, Phillip (1960–) *Silent Assassins* 1988; *Best of the Best* 1989; *Best of the Best II* 1992

Rhind-Tutt, Julian (1968–) *The Madness of King George* 1995; *The Trench* 1999; *Miranda* 2001

Rhoades, Barbara (1947–) *The Shakiest Gun in the West* 1967; *Don't Just Stand There* 1968; *The Goodbye Girl* 1977

Rhodes, Christopher (1914–1964) *The Colditz Story* 1954; *Tiger in the Smoke* 1956; *Operation Amsterdam* 1958; *Gorgo* 1961

Rhodes, Cynthia (1957–) *Staying Alive* 1983; *Runaway* 1984; *Dirty Dancing* 1987

Rhodes, Donnelly (1937–) *Gunfight in Abilene* 1967; *Oh, Heavenly Dog!* 1980

Rhodes, Erik (1906–1990) *The Gay Divorce* 1934; *Charlie Chan in Paris* 1935; *Top Hat* 1935; *Chatterbox* 1936; *One Rainy Afternoon* 1936; *Criminal Lawyer* 1937; *Woman Chases Man* 1937; *Mysterious Mr Moto* 1938

Rhodes, Grandon (1904–1987) *Magnificent Doll* 1946; *Born Yesterday* 1950; *On Top of Old Smoky* 1953; *Revenge of the Creature* 1955; *Earth vs the Flying Saucers* 1956

Rhodes, Hari aka **Rhodes, Harry** (1932–1992) *Blindfold* 1966; *Conquest of the Planet of the*

Apes 1972; *Detroit 9000* 1973; *Coma* 1977
Rhodes, Marjorie (1902–1979) *Great Day* 1944; *This Was a Woman* 1947; *The Cure for Love* 1949; *The Yellow Balloon* 1952; *Children Galore* 1954; *Just My Luck* 1957; *Alive and Kicking* 1958; *Watch It, Sailor!* 1961; *I've Gotta Horse* 1965; *The Family Way* 1966; *Hands of the Ripper* 1971
Rhue, Madlyn (1934–2003) *A Majority of One* 1961; *Escape from Zahrain* 1962; *He Rides Tall* 1964
Rhys, Matthew (1974–) *House of America* 1996; *Heart* 1997; *Titus* 1999; *Peaches* 2000; *Shooters* 2000; *Sorted* 2000; *Very Annie-Mary* 2000; *The Abduction Club* 2002; *Deathwatch* 2002; *Otherworld* 2003; *Fakers* 2004
Rhys, Paul (1963–) *Vincent and Theo* 1990; *Becoming Colette* 1991; *Rebecca's Daughters* 1991; *Chaplin* 1992; *Nina Takes a Lover* 1993; *The Haunting of Helen Walker* 1995; *Food of Love* 2002
Rhys-Davies, John (1944–) *Sphinx* 1980; *Raiders of the Lost Ark* 1981; *Victor/Victoria* 1982; *Best Revenge* 1983; *Sahara* 1983; *Kim* 1984; *King Solomon's Mines* 1985; *Firewalker* 1986; *The Living Daylights* 1987; *Waxwork* 1988; *Young Toscanini* 1988; *Indiana Jones and the Last Crusade* 1989; *The Trial of the Incredible Hulk* 1989; *Shogun Warrior* 1991; *Sunset Grill* 1992; *The Unnamable Returns* 1992; *Cyborg Cop* 1993; *The Seventh Coin* 1993; *Ring of the Musketeers* 1994; *Aladdin and the King of Thieves* 1996; *Body Armor* 1996; *Cats Don't Dance* 1998; *Britannic* 2000; *The Lord of the Rings: The Fellowship of the Ring* 2001; *The Lord of the Rings: The Two Towers* 2002; *The Jungle Book 2* 2003; *The Lord of the Rings: The Return of the King* 2003; *The Medallion* 2003; *The Princess Diaries 2: Royal Engagement* 2004
Rhys Jones, Griff (1953–) *Morons from Outer Space* 1985; *Wilt* 1989; *As You Like It* 1992; *Staggered* 1993; *The Adventures of Pinocchio* 1996; *Up 'n' Under* 1997; *Puckoon* 2002
Rhys Meyers, Jonathan (1977–) *B Monkey* 1996; *The Disappearance of Finbar* 1996; *The Governess* 1997; *The Maker* 1997; *Velvet Goldmine* 1998; *The Loss of Sexual Innocence* 1999; *Ride with the Devil* 1999; *Titus* 1999; *Bend It like Beckham* 2001; *I'll Sleep When I'm Dead* 2003; *Octane* 2003; *Vanity Fair* 2004
Riaboukine, Serge *Wild Target* 1993; *Skin of Man, Heart of Beast* 1999; *Grégoire Moulin* 2001; *Le Chignon d'Olga* 2002; *Look at Me* 2004
Rialson, Candice (1952–) *Mama's Dirty Girls* 1974; *Hollywood Boulevard* 1976
Ribisi, Giovanni *aka* **Ribisi, Vonni** (1976–) *Promised a Miracle* 1988; *Lost Highway* 1996; *subUrbia* 1996; *Saving Private Ryan* 1998; *Some Girls* 1998; *The Mod Squad* 1999; *The Other Sister* 1999; *Boiler Room* 2000; *The Gift* 2000; *Gone in Sixty Seconds* 2000; *Heaven* 2002; *Basic* 2003; *Cold Mountain* 2003; *Lost in Translation* 2003; *Flight of the Phoenix* 2004; *Sky Captain and the World of Tomorrow* 2004
Ricca, Marco *Four Days in September* 1997; *The Trespasser* 2001
Ricci, Christina (1980–) *Mermaids* 1990; *The Addams Family* 1991; *The Hard Way* 1991; *Addams Family Values* 1993; *The Cemetery Club* 1993; *Casper* 1995; *Gold Diggers: the Secret of Bear Mountain* 1995; *Now and Then* 1995; *Last of the High Kings* 1996; *The Ice Storm* 1997; *That Darn Cat* 1997; *Buffalo '66* 1998; *Desert Blue* 1998; *Fear and Loathing in Las Vegas* 1998; *The Opposite of Sex* 1998; *Pecker* 1998; *Small Soldiers* 1998; *Sleepy Hollow* 1999; *200 Cigarettes* 1999; *Bless the Child* 2000; *The Man Who Cried* 2000; *All over the Guy* 2001; *Miranda* 2001; *The Laramie Project* 2002; *Anything Else* 2003; *Monster* 2003; *Cursed* 2005
Ricci, Renzo (1898–1978) *L'Avventura* 1960; *Of a Thousand Delights* 1965
Rice, Florence (1907–1974) *Double Wedding* 1937; *Navy Blue and Gold* 1937; *Fast Company* 1938; *Paradise for Three* 1938; *Sweethearts* 1938; *At the Circus* 1939; *Four Girls in White* 1939; *Miracles for Sale* 1939; *Broadway Melody of 1940* 1940; *Cherokee Strip* 1940; *Phantom Raiders* 1940
Rice, Joan (1930–1997) *The Gift Horse* 1951; *Curtain Up* 1952; *The Story of Robin Hood and His Merrie Men* 1952; *A Day to Remember* 1953; *His Majesty O'Keefe* 1953; *The Steel Key* 1953; *One Good Turn* 1954; *Police Dog* 1955; *Women without Men* 1956; *Operation Bullshine* 1959; *The Horror of Frankenstein* 1970
Rich, Claude (1929–) *Mitsou* 1957; *The Vanishing Corporal* 1962; *Male Hunt* 1964; *The Bride Wore Black* 1967; *Je T'Aime, Je T'Aime* 1968; *Stavisky* 1974; *The Police War* 1979; *Maria Chapdelaine* 1982; *L'Accompagnatrice* 1992; *D'Artagnan's Daughter* 1994; *Lautrec* 1998; *La Bûche* 1999; *Asterix & Obelix: Mission Cleopatra* 2001
Rich, Irene (1891–1988) *Rosita* 1923; *Lady Windermere's Fan* 1925; *They Had to See Paris* 1929; *Beau Ideal* 1931; *The Champ* 1931; *Strangers May Kiss* 1931; *That Certain Age* 1938; *The Lady in Question* 1940; *The Mortal Storm* 1940; *Angel and the Badman* 1947
Richard, Cliff (1940–) *Expresso Bongo* 1959; *Serious Charge* 1959; *The Young Ones* 1961; *Summer Holiday* 1962; *Wonderful Life* 1964; *Finders Keepers* 1966; *Two a Penny* 1968; *Take Me High* 1973
Richard, Firmine *Romuald et Juliette* 1989; *8 Women* 2001
Richard, Frida (1873–1946) *Faust* 1926; *The Holy Mountain* 1926; *Three Loves* 1929
Richard, Jean-Louis (1927–) *The Last Metro* 1980; *Jeanne la Pucelle* 1994; *The Bait* 1995; *Don't Forget You're Going to Die* 1995; *Skin of Man, Heart of Beast* 1999
Richard, Nathalie (1962–) *Irma Vep* 1996; *Novo* 2002
Richard, Pierre (1934–) *The Tall Blond Man with One Black Shoe* 1972; *Les Compères* 1983
Ri'chard, Robert (1983–) *Light It Up* 1999; *House of Wax* 2004; *Coach Carter* 2005
Richard, Wendy (1946–) *No Blade of Grass* 1970; *Gumshoe* 1971; *Bless This House* 1972; *Carry On Girls* 1973; *Are You Being Served?* 1977
Richards, Addison (1887–1964) *Our Daily Bread* 1934; *Smart Blonde* 1936; *The Black Legion* 1937; *Boys Town* 1938; *Bad Lands* 1939; *The Man from Dakota* 1940; *Betrayal from the East* 1945; *Bewitched* 1945; *Come Out Fighting* 1945; *The Shanghai Cobra* 1945; *Criminal Court* 1946; *Gunsight Ridge* 1957
Richards, Ann (1917–) *An American Romance* 1944; *Love Letters* 1945; *Badman's Territory* 1946; *The Searching Wind* 1946; *Love from a Stranger* 1947; *Sorry, Wrong Number* 1948
Richards, Ariana (1979–) *Tremors* 1989; *Jurassic Park* 1993; *Angus* 1995; *Tremors 3: Back to Perfection* 2001
Richards, Aubrey (1920–2000) *The Ipcress File* 1965; *It!* 1966
Richards, Beah (1926–2000) *The Miracle Worker* 1962; *Gone Are the Days* 1963; *Guess Who's Coming to Dinner* 1967; *Hurry Sundown* 1967; *The Biscuit Eater* 1972; *Mahogany* 1975; *Drugstore Cowboy* 1989; *Homer and Eddie* 1989; *Beloved* 1998
Richards, Denise (1971–) *Starship Troopers* 1997; *Wild Things* 1998; *Drop Dead Gorgeous* 1999; *The World Is Not Enough* 1999; *Good Advice* 2001; *Valentine* 2001; *Empire* 2002; *Undercover Brother* 2002
Richards, Evan *Down and Out in Beverly Hills* 1986; *Society* 1989; *The Dream Machine* 1990; *Mute Witness* 1995
Richards, Jeff (1922–1989) *Big Leaguer* 1953; *Seagulls over Sorrento* 1954; *Seven Brides for Seven Brothers* 1954; *It's a Dog's Life* 1955; *Many Rivers to Cross* 1955; *The Marauders* 1955; *The Opposite Sex* 1956; *Born Reckless* 1959; *The Secret of the Purple Reef* 1960
Richards, Kim (1964–) *Escape to Witch Mountain* 1975; *Assault on Precinct 13* 1976; *No Deposit No Return* 1976; *Return from Witch Mountain* 1978; *Meatballs 2* 1984; *Tuff Turf* 1984
Richards, Kyle (1964–) *Halloween* 1978; *The Watcher in the Woods* 1982
Richards, Lisa *Rolling Thunder* 1977; *Return* 1985; *Eating* 1990
Richards, Michael (1948–) *Transylvania 6-5000* 1985; *Whoops Apocalypse* 1986; *UHF* 1989; *Unstrung Heroes* 1995; *Trial and Error* 1997
Richards, Michele Lamar *The Bodyguard* 1992; *Top Dog* 1995
Richards (1), Paul (1924–1974) *Hot Summer Night* 1957; *The Strange One* 1957; *Beneath the Planet of the Apes* 1969
Richardson, Ian (1934–) *Marat/Sade* 1966; *A Midsummer Night's Dream* 1969; *The Darwin Adventure* 1972; *The Hound of the Baskervilles* 1983; *The Sign of Four* 1983; *Brazil* 1985; *Whoops Apocalypse* 1986; *Cry Freedom* 1987; *Burning Secret* 1988; *King of the Wind* 1989; *Rosencrantz and Guildenstern Are Dead* 1990; *Dirty Weekend* 1992; *Year of the Comet* 1992; *M Butterfly* 1993; *BAPS* 1997; *Incognito* 1997; *Dark City* 1998; *A Knight in Camelot* 1998; *The King and I* 1999; *102 Dalmatians* 2000; *From Hell* 2001
Richardson, Jake (1985–) *Honey, We Shrunk Ourselves* 1997; *The Dangerous Lives of Altar Boys* 2001
Richardson, Joely (1965–) *The Hotel New Hampshire* 1984; *Wetherby* 1985; *Drowning by Numbers* 1988; *King Ralph* 1991; *Rebecca's Daughters* 1991; *Shining Through* 1992; *I'll Do Anything* 1994; *Loch Ness* 1994; *Sister My Sister* 1994; *Hollow Reed* 1995; *101 Dalmatians* 1996; *Event Horizon* 1997; *Wrestling with Alligators* 1998; *Maybe Baby* 1999; *The Patriot* 2000; *Return to Me* 2000; *The Affair of the Necklace* 2001; *Shoreditch* 2002
Richardson, John (1936–) *The Mask of Satan* 1960; *She* 1965; *One Million Years BC* 1966; *On My Way to the Crusades, I Met a Girl Who...* 1967; *The Vengeance of She* 1968; *On a Clear Day You Can See Forever* 1970
Richardson, LaTanya (1941–) *US Marshals* 1998; *The Fighting Temptations* 2003
Richardson, Lee (1926–1999) *Prizzi's Honor* 1985; *Amazing Grace and Chuck* 1987; *The Believers* 1987; *Tiger Warsaw* 1988; *The Fly II* 1989; *Q & A* 1990; *A Stranger among Us* 1992
Richardson, Marie (1959–) *Eyes Wide Shut* 1999; *Daybreak* 2003; *Evil* 2003
Richardson, Miranda (1958–) *Dance with a Stranger* 1984; *The Innocent* 1984; *Eat the Rich* 1987; *Empire of the Sun* 1987; *The Bachelor* 1990; *Enchanted April* 1991; *The Crying Game* 1992; *Damage* 1992; *Century* 1993; *Tom & Viv* 1994; *Kansas City* 1995; *The Evening Star* 1996; *Swann* 1996; *The Apostle* 1997; *The Designated Mourner* 1997; *Alice in Wonderland* 1999; *All for Love* 1999; *Jacob Two Two Meets the Hooded Fang* 1999; *The King and I* 1999; *The Miracle Maker* 1999; *Sleepy Hollow* 1999; *Chicken Run* 2000; *Get Carter* 2000; *Snow White* 2001; *The Hours* 2002; *The Rage in Placid Lake* 2002; *Spider* 2002; *The Actors* 2003; *Churchill: the Hollywood Years* 2004; *The Phantom of the Opera* 2004; *The Prince & Me* 2004
Richardson, Natasha (1963–) *Every Picture Tells a Story* 1984; *Gothic* 1986; *A Month in the Country* 1987; *Patty Hearst* 1988; *Shadow Makers* 1989; *The Handmaid's Tale* 1990; *The Comfort of Strangers* 1991; *The Favour, the Watch and the Very Big Fish* 1991; *Hostages* 1993; *Widows' Peak* 1993; *Nell* 1994; *The Parent Trap* 1998; *Blow Dry* 2000; *Maid in Manhattan* 2002
Richardson, Patricia (1951–) *The Road Home* 1989; *Ulee's Gold* 1997
Richardson, Peter (1952–) *The Supergrass* 1985; *Carry On Columbus* 1992
Richardson, Ralph (1902–1982) *Friday the Thirteenth* 1933; *The Ghoul* 1933; *Bulldog Jack* 1934; *The Return of Bulldog Drummond* 1934; *Java Head* 1935; *The Man Who Could Work Miracles* 1936; *Things to Come* 1936; *Thunder in the City* 1937; *The Citadel* 1938; *The Divorce of Lady X* 1938; *South Riding* 1938; *The Four Feathers* 1939; *The Lion Has Wings* 1939; *Q Planes* 1939; *The Day Will Dawn* 1942; *The Silver Fleet* 1943; *School for Secrets* 1946; *Anna Karenina* 1947; *The Fallen Idol* 1948; *The Heiress* 1949; *Outcast of the Islands* 1951; *The Holly and the Ivy* 1952; *Home at Seven* 1952; *The Sound Barrier* 1952; *Richard III* 1955; *Smiley* 1956; *The Passionate Stranger* 1957; *Oscar Wilde* 1959; *Our Man in Havana* 1959; *Exodus* 1960; *Long Day's Journey into Night* 1962; *The 300 Spartans* 1962; *Woman of Straw* 1964; *Doctor Zhivago* 1965; *Chimes at Midnight* 1966; *Khartoum* 1966; *The Wrong Box* 1966; *Battle of Britain* 1969; *The Bed Sitting Room* 1969; *The Looking Glass War* 1969; *Midas Run* 1969; *Oh! What a Lovely War* 1969; *Eagle in a Cage* 1971; *Who Slew Auntie Roo?* 1971; *Alice's Adventures in Wonderland* 1972; *Lady Caroline Lamb* 1972; *Tales from the Crypt* 1972; *A Doll's House* 1973; *Frankenstein: the True Story* 1973; *O Lucky Man!* 1973; *Rollerball* 1975; *The Man in the Iron Mask* 1977; *Watership Down* 1978; *Dragonslayer* 1981; *Time Bandits* 1981; *Invitation to the Wedding* 1983; *Wagner* 1983; *Give My Regards to Broad Street* 1984; *Greystoke: the Legend of Tarzan, Lord of the Apes* 1984
Richardson, Salli *aka* **Richardson-Whitfield, Salli** (1967–) *How U Like Me Now* 1992; *I Spy Returns* 1994; *A Low Down Dirty Shame* 1994; *Sioux City* 1994; *Antwone Fisher* 2002; *Anacondas: the Hunt for the Blood Orchid* 2004
Richardson, Sy *Repo Man* 1984; *Cold Steel* 1987; *Straight to Hell* 1987; *Walker* 1987; *Kinjite: Forbidden Subjects* 1989; *Eye of the Stranger* 1993
Richert, William *My Own Private Idaho* 1991; *The Man in the Iron Mask* 1997
Richfield, Edwin (1922–1990) *The Brain Machine* 1954; *The Break* 1962
Richings, Julian *Cube* 1997; *My Life without Me* 2002; *Wrong Turn* 2003
Richman, Josh *Thrashin'* 1986; *River's Edge* 1987
Richman, Peter Mark *aka* **Richman, Mark** (1927–) *The Strange One* 1957; *The Black Orchid* 1959; *The Murder Men* 1961; *Dark Intruder* 1965; *Agent for HARM* 1966; *Friday the 13th Part VIII: Jason Takes Manhattan* 1989
Richmond, Branscombe *The Chicken Chronicles* 1977; *Cage* 1989; *The Taking of Beverly Hills* 1991
Richmond, Deon (1978–) *Enemy Territory* 1987; *Trippin'* 1999; *Not Another Teen Movie* 2001
Richmond, Fiona *Exposé* 1975; *Hardcore* 1977; *Let's Get Laid* 1977; *Eat the Rich* 1987
Richmond, Kane (1906–1973) *Charlie Chan in Reno* 1939; *The Return of the Cisco Kid* 1939; *Great Guns* 1941; *Riders of the Purple Sage* 1941; *Black Gold* 1947
Richmond, Warner (1886–1948) *Big News* 1929; *Hell's Highway* 1932
Richter, Andy (1966–) *My Boss's Daughter* 2003; *New York Minute* 2004; *Madagascar* 2005
Richter, Deborah (1961–) *Square Dance* 1987; *Promised Land* 1988; *Cyborg* 1989
Richter, Jason James (1980–) *Free Willy* 1993; *Cops and Robbersons* 1994; *The NeverEnding Story III* 1994; *Free Willy 2: the Adventure Home* 1995; *Free Willy 3: the Rescue* 1997; *Laserhawk* 1997
Richter, Paul (1887–1961) *Dr Mabuse, the Gambler* 1922; *The Nibelungen* 1924
Richter, Sonja (1974–) *Open Hearts* 2002; *In Your Hands* 2004
Rickles, Don (1926–) *Run Silent, Run Deep* 1958; *The Rat Race* 1960; *The Man with the X-Ray Eyes* 1963; *Bikini Beach* 1964; *Muscle Beach Party* 1964; *Pajama Party* 1964; *Beach Blanket Bingo* 1965; *Where It's At* 1969; *Kelly's Heroes* 1970; *Keaton's Cop* 1990; *Innocent Blood* 1992; *Casino* 1995; *Toy Story* 1995; *The Magic Sword: Quest for Camelot* 1997; *Dennis the Menace Strikes Again* 1998; *Dirty Work* 1998; *Toy Story 2* 1999
Rickman, Alan (1946–) *Die Hard* 1988; *The January Man* 1989; *Quigley Down Under* 1990; *Truly Madly Deeply* 1990; *Close My Eyes* 1991; *Closet Land* 1991; *Robin Hood: Prince of Thieves* 1991; *Bob Roberts* 1992; *An Awfully Big Adventure* 1994; *Mesmer* 1994; *Sense and Sensibility* 1995; *Michael Collins* 1996; *Rasputin* 1996; *Dark Harbor* 1998; *Judas Kiss* 1998; *Dogma* 1999; *Galaxy Quest* 1999; *Blow Dry* 2000; *Help, I'm a Fish!* 2000; *Harry Potter and the Philosopher's Stone* 2001; *The Search for John Gissing* 2001; *Harry Potter and the Chamber of Secrets* 2002; *Love Actually* 2003; *Harry Potter and the Prisoner of Azkaban* 2004; *The Hitchhiker's Guide to the Galaxy* 2005
Ricotta, Vincenzo *aka* **Riotta, Vincent** *Car Trouble* 1985; *Leon the Pig Farmer* 1992; *Under the Tuscan Sun* 2003
Rideau, Stéphane (1976–) *Les Roseaux Sauvages* 1994; *A Toute Vitesse* 1996; *Sitcom* 1997; *Presque Rien* 2000; *Far Away* 2001; *Le Clan* 2004
Ridgely, John (1909–1968) *Strange Alibi* 1941; *Dangerously They Live* 1942; *Air Force* 1943; *Destination Tokyo* 1943; *Northern Pursuit* 1943; *The Doughgirls* 1944; *God Is My Co-Pilot* 1945; *Pride of the Marines* 1945; *The Big Sleep* 1946; *My Reputation* 1946; *Cry Wolf* 1947; *Nora Prentiss* 1947; *Possessed* 1947; *Half Angel* 1951; *Room for One More* 1952
Ridgely, Robert (1931–1996) *Nightmare in Chicago* 1968; *Philadelphia* 1993; *Boogie Nights* 1997
Ridges, Stanley *aka* **Ridges, Stanley C** (1891–1951) *Crime without Passion* 1934; *The Scoundrel* 1935; *Internes Can't Take Money* 1937; *The Mad Miss Manton* 1938; *Each Dawn I Die* 1939; *Nick Carter, Master Detective* 1939; *The Sea Wolf*

1941; *Sergeant York* 1941; *They Died with Their Boots On* 1941; *The Big Shot* 1942; *The Lady Is Willing* 1942; *To Be or Not to Be* 1942; *Tarzan Triumphs* 1943; *The Master Race* 1944; *The Suspect* 1944; *God Is My Co-Pilot* 1945; *Because of Him* 1946; *Possessed* 1947; *The File on Thelma Jordon* 1949; *Streets of Laredo* 1949; *You're My Everything* 1949

Ridley, Arnold (1896–1984) *The Interrupted Journey* 1949; *Stolen Face* 1952; *Dad's Army* 1971

Riefenstahl, Leni (1902–2003) *The Holy Mountain* 1926; *The Blue Light* 1932; *SOS Iceberg* 1933; *The Wonderful, Horrible Life of Leni Riefenstahl* 1993

Riegert, Peter (1947–) *National Lampoon's Animal House* 1978; *Americathon* 1979; *Chilly Scenes of Winter* 1979; *National Lampoon's Movie Madness* 1981; *Local Hero* 1983; *The City Girl* 1984; *A Man in Love* 1987; *The Stranger* 1987; *Crossing Delancey* 1988; *A Shock to the System* 1990; *The Object of Beauty* 1991; *Oscar* 1991; *The Runestone* 1991; *Passed Away* 1992; *Utz* 1992; *Barbarians at the Gate* 1993; *Gypsy* 1993; *The Mask* 1994; *Coldblooded* 1995; *The Infiltrator* 1995; *Pie in the Sky* 1995; *Infinity* 1996; *Hi-Life* 1998; *Jerry and Tom* 1998; *Passion of Mind* 2000

Riehle, Richard (1948–) *Of Mice and Men* 1992; *The Public Eye* 1992; *Lightning Jack* 1994; *The Odd Couple II* 1998; *Deuce Bigalow: Male Gigolo* 1999; *Home on the Range* 2004

Riemann, Katja (1963–) *Making Up* 1992; *The Most Desired Man* 1994

Rietty, Robert (1923–) *Stock Car* 1955; *The Crooked Road* 1964; *The Hiding Place* 1975

Rifkin, Ron (1939–) *Flareup* 1969; *Silent Running* 1971; *Do You Remember Love* 1985; *Manhattan Murder Mystery* 1993; *Wolf* 1994; *Last Summer in the Hamptons* 1995; *I'm Not Rappaport* 1996; *Norma Jean & Marilyn* 1996; *The Substance of Fire* 1996; *LA Confidential* 1997; *The Negotiator* 1998; *Boiler Room* 2000; *Keeping the Faith* 2000; *Dragonfly* 2002; *The Sum of All Fears* 2002; *Tadpole* 2002

Rigaud, Georges aka **Rigaud, Jorge** aka **Rigaud, George** (1905–1984) *Divine* 1935; *The Castilian* 1963; *Grand Slam* 1967

Rigby, Edward (1879–1951) *Lorna Doone* 1934; *Accused* 1936; *The Show Goes On* 1937; *Young and Innocent* 1937; *A Yank at Oxford* 1938; *Poison Pen* 1939; *The Stars Look Down* 1939; *Convoy* 1940; *The Proud Valley* 1940; *The Common Touch* 1941; *Went the Day Well?* 1942; *Get Cracking* 1943; *They Met in the Dark* 1943; *Daybreak* 1946; *The Happiest Days of Your Life* 1950; *Tony Draws a Horse* 1950; *What the Butler Saw* 1950

Rigby, Terence (1937–) *The Homecoming* 1973; *Watership Down* 1978; *The Sign of Four* 1983; *Testimony* 1987; *The Children* 1990; *Elizabeth* 1998; *Essex Boys* 1999

Rigg, Carl *The Oblong Box* 1969; *Cry of the Banshee* 1970

Rigg, Diana (1938–) *The Assassination Bureau* 1969; *A Midsummer Night's Dream* 1969; *On Her Majesty's Secret Service* 1969; *Julius Caesar* 1970; *The Hospital* 1971; *Theatre of Blood* 1973; *A Little Night Music* 1977; *The Great Muppet Caper* 1981; *Evil under the Sun* 1982; *Mrs 'arris Goes to Paris* 1992; *A Good Man in Africa* 1993; *The Haunting of Helen Walker* 1995; *Parting Shots* 1998

Rigg, Rebecca (1967–) *Spotswood* 1991; *Hunting* 1992; *Tunnel Vision* 1994

Rignault, Alexandre (1901–1985) *Crime and Punishment* 1935; *Volpone* 1941; *Number Two* 1975

Riker, Robin *Alligator* 1980; *Body Chemistry 2: Voice of a Stranger* 1992

Riley, Elaine (1923–) *The Devil's Playground* 1946; *Rider from Tucson* 1950

Riley, Gary *Stand by Me* 1986; *Summer School* 1987

Riley, Jack (1935–) *High Anxiety* 1977; *Attack of the Killer Tomatoes* 1978; *Night Patrol* 1984

Riley, Jeannine (1940–) *The Big Mouth* 1967; *Electra Glide in Blue* 1973

Riley, Larry (1953–1992) *Crackers* 1984; *A Soldier's Story* 1984; *Unconquered* 1989

Riley, Michael (1962–) *Perfectly Normal* 1990; *...And God Spoke* 1993; *Butterbox Babies* 1995; *Dogmatic* 1996; *The Grace of God* 1998; *Homeless to Harvard: the Liz Murray Story* 2003

Rilla, Walter (1895–1980) *The Scarlet Pimpernel* 1934; *Victoria the Great* 1937; *Sixty Glorious Years* 1938; *Black Eyes* 1939; *The Gang's All Here* 1939; *The Adventures of Tartu* 1943; *Candlelight in Algeria* 1943; *Golden Salamander* 1949; *I'll Get You for This* 1950; *Shadow of the Eagle* 1950; *State Secret* 1950; *Venetian Bird* 1952; *Star of India* 1954; *The Secret Ways* 1961; *Cairo* 1962; *Death Drums along the River* 1963; *The Face of Fu Manchu* 1965

Rimkus, Stevan *Cal* 1984; *Conquest of the South Pole* 1989; *London Kills Me* 1991; *American Cousins* 2003

Rimmer, Shane (1932–) *Thunderbirds Are Go!* 1966; *Thunderbird 6* 1968; *The People That Time Forgot* 1977; *The Spy Who Loved Me* 1977; *Warlords of Atlantis* 1978; *Hanover Street* 1979; *Reunion at Fairborough* 1985; *A Kiss before Dying* 1991; *Space Truckers* 1996

Rinaldi, Gérard *Descent into Hell* 1986; *For Better and for Worse* 1993

Ringwald, Molly (1968–) *PK and the Kid* 1982; *Tempest* 1982; *Spacehunter: Adventures in the Forbidden Zone* 1983; *Sixteen Candles* 1984; *The Breakfast Club* 1985; *Surviving* 1985; *Pretty in Pink* 1986; *For Keeps* 1987; *King Lear – Fear and Loathing* 1987; *The Pick-Up Artist* 1987; *Fresh Horses* 1988; *Betsy's Wedding* 1990; *Loser Takes All* 1990; *The Brutal Truth* 1999; *Teaching Mrs Tingle* 1999; *Cut* 2000; *Not Another Teen Movie* 2001

Riordan, Marjorie (1921–1984) *Stage Door Canteen* 1943; *Mr Skeffington* 1944; *Pursuit to Algiers* 1945; *Three Strangers* 1946

Rios, Lalo (1927–1973) *The Lawless* 1950; *The Ring* 1952; *City beneath the Sea* 1953

Ripley, Fay (1967–) *Mute Witness* 1995; *Roseanna's Grave* 1996

Ripper, Michael (1913–2000) *Eye Witness* 1949; *A Man on the Beach* 1955; *Quatermass II* 1957; *The Steel Bayonet* 1957; *Woman in a Dressing Gown* 1957; *The Scarlet Blade* 1963; *What a Crazy World* 1963; *The Devil-Ship Pirates* 1964; *The Plague of the Zombies* 1965; *The Mummy's Shroud* 1966; *The Reptile* 1966; *Where the Bullets Fly* 1966; *The Deadly Bees* 1967; *Dracula Has Risen from the Grave* 1968; *Mumsy, Nanny, Sonny & Girly* 1970; *The Creeping Flesh* 1972; *Legend of the Werewolf* 1974

Rippy, Leon *Track 29* 1988; *Eye of the Storm* 1991; *Universal Soldier* 1992; *Stargate* 1994; *Eight Legged Freaks* 2001; *The Life of David Gale* 2003; *The Alamo* 2004

Risch, Maurice (1943–) *The Spacemen of St Tropez* 1978; *The Gendarme Wore Skirts* 1982

Risdon, Elisabeth (1887–1958) *Crime and Punishment* 1935; *The King Steps Out* 1936; *Theodora Goes Wild* 1936; *Make Way for Tomorrow* 1937; *Mannequin* 1937; *The Woman I Love* 1937; *The Affairs of Annabel* 1938; *The Adventures of Huckleberry Finn* 1939; *Full Confession* 1939; *The Girl from Mexico* 1939; *The Great Man Votes* 1939; *The Howards of Virginia* 1940; *Let's Make Music* 1940; *Mexican Spitfire* 1940; *Higher and Higher* 1943; *Tall in the Saddle* 1944; *Weird Woman* 1944; *Lover Come Back* 1946; *Bodyguard* 1948; *Every Girl Should Be Married* 1948; *Bunco Squad* 1950

Rispoli, Michael *Household Saints* 1993; *Angie* 1994; *While You Were Sleeping* 1995; *Volcano* 1997; *Scarred City* 1998; *Summer of Sam* 1999

Riss, Dan (1910–1970) *Panic in the Streets* 1950; *Wyoming Mail* 1950

Risso, Roberto (1925–) *Bread, Love and Dreams* 1953; *A Breath of Scandal* 1960

Rissone, Checco (1909–1985) *Bitter Rice* 1949; *Eva* 1962

Ristovski, Lazar (1952–) *Tito and Me* 1992; *Underground* 1995; *Cabaret Balkan* 1998

Ritch, Steven (1921–1995) *The Werewolf* 1956; *Plunder Road* 1957; *City of Fear* 1959

Ritchard, Cyril (1897–1977) *Blackmail* 1929; *Piccadilly* 1929; *I See Ice* 1938; *Half a Sixpence* 1967

Ritchie, Clint (1938–) *The St Valentine's Day Massacre* 1967; *Bandolero!* 1968; *A Force of One* 1979

Ritchie, June (1939–) *A Kind of Loving* 1962; *Live Now – Pay Later* 1962; *The Mouse on the Moon* 1963; *This Is My Street* 1963; *The World Ten Times Over* 1963

Ritt, Martin (1914–1990) *End of the Game* 1976; *The Slugger's Wife* 1985

Ritter, Jason (1980–) *Swimfan* 2002; *Freddy vs Jason* 2003

Ritter, John (1948–2003) *The Barefoot Executive* 1971; *Evil Roy Slade* 1971; *Scandalous John* 1971; *The Other* 1972; *Nickelodeon* 1976; *Americathon* 1979; *Hero at Large* 1980; *Wholly Moses!* 1980; *They All Laughed* 1981; *Real Men* 1987; *Skin Deep* 1989; *Problem Child* 1990; *Problem Child 2* 1991; *Danielle Steel's Heartbeat* 1992; *Noises Off* 1992; *Stay Tuned* 1992; *Sling Blade* 1995; *Unforgivable* 1995; *Montana* 1997; *Bride of Chucky* 1998; *Panic* 2000; *Tadpole* 2002; *Bad Santa* 2003; *Clifford's Really Big Movie* 2004

Ritter, Thelma (1905–1969) *City across the River* 1949; *Father Was a Fullback* 1949; *All about Eve* 1950; *Perfect Strangers* 1950; *As Young as You Feel* 1951; *The Mating Season* 1951; *The Model and the Marriage Broker* 1951; *With a Song in My Heart* 1952; *The Farmer Takes a Wife* 1953; *Pickup on South Street* 1953; *Titanic* 1953; *Rear Window* 1954; *Daddy Long Legs* 1955; *Lucy Gallant* 1955; *The Proud and Profane* 1956; *Pillow Talk* 1959; *The Misfits* 1961; *The Second Time Around* 1961; *Birdman of Alcatraz* 1962; *How the West Was Won* 1962; *For Love or Money* 1963; *Move Over, Darling* 1963; *A New Kind of Love* 1963; *Boeing Boeing* 1965; *The Incident* 1967; *What's So Bad About Feeling Good?* 1968

Ritz, Al aka **The Ritz Brothers** (1901–1965) *One in a Million* 1936; *Sing, Baby, Sing* 1936; *Life Begins in College* 1937; *On the Avenue* 1937; *You Can't Have Everything* 1937; *The Goldwyn Follies* 1938; *Kentucky Moonshine* 1938; *Pack Up Your Troubles* 1939; *The Three Musketeers* 1939; *Argentine Nights* 1940

Ritz, Harry aka **The Ritz Brothers** (1906–1986) *One in a Million* 1936; *Sing, Baby, Sing* 1936; *Life Begins in College* 1937; *On the Avenue* 1937; *You Can't Have Everything* 1937; *The Goldwyn Follies* 1938; *Kentucky Moonshine* 1938; *Pack Up Your Troubles* 1939; *The Three Musketeers* 1939; *Argentine Nights* 1940

Ritz, Jimmy aka **The Ritz Brothers** (1903–1985) *One in a Million* 1936; *Sing, Baby, Sing* 1936; *Life Begins in College* 1937; *On the Avenue* 1937; *You Can't Have Everything* 1937; *The Goldwyn Follies* 1938; *Kentucky Moonshine* 1938; *Pack Up Your Troubles* 1939; *The Three Musketeers* 1939; *Argentine Nights* 1940

Riva, Emmanuelle (1927–) *Hiroshima, Mon Amour* 1959; *Kapo* 1959; *Léon Morin, Priest* 1961; *Thérèse Desqueyroux* 1962; *Thomas the Imposter* 1964; *A Shadow of Doubt* 1992

Rivas, Carlos (1928–2003) *The Beast of Hollow Mountain* 1956; *The King and I* 1956; *The Black Scorpion* 1957; *The Deerslayer* 1957

Rivault, Pascale *La Bête* 1975; *Lady Chatterley's Lover* 1981

Rivera, Marika *Hussy* 1979; *Hôtel du Paradis* 1986

Rivero, Jorge aka **Rivero, George** (1938–) *Rio Lobo* 1970; *Soldier Blue* 1970; *The Last Hard Men* 1976; *Priest of Love* 1981; *Target Eagle* 1982

Rivers, Joan (1933–) *Spaceballs* 1987; *Napoleon* 1995; *Whispers: an Elephant's Tale* 2000

Rivers, Victor *Blood In Blood Out* 1992; *A Million to Juan* 1994; *Two for Texas* 1998; *What's Cooking?* 2000

Rivière, Marie (1956–) *The Aviator's Wife* 1980; *Four Adventures of Reinette and Mirabelle* 1986; *The Green Ray* 1986; *An Autumn Tale* 1998; *Girls Can't Swim* 1999

Rix, Brian (1924–) *Up to His Neck* 1954; *Dry Rot* 1956; *Not Wanted on Voyage* 1957; *The Night We Dropped a Clanger* 1959; *And the Same to You* 1960; *The Night We Got the Bird* 1960; *Don't Just Lie There, Say Something!* 1973

Rizzo, Gianni (1925–1992) *Spartacus and the Ten Gladiators* 1964; *Face to Face* 1967; *Adios, Sabata* 1970; *The Decameron* 1970

Roach, Bert (1891–1971) *The Crowd* 1928; *Bird of Paradise* 1932; *Murders in the Rue Morgue* 1932; *The Man in the Iron Mask* 1939

Roach, Pat (1937–2004) *Clash of the Titans* 1981; *Willow* 1988

Roache, Linus (1964–) *Priest* 1994; *The Wings of the Dove* 1997; *Best* 1999; *Siam Sunset* 1999; *Pandaemonium* 2000; *Hart's War* 2002; *Beyond Borders* 2003; *Blind Flight* 2003; *The Chronicles of Riddick* 2004; *The Forgotten* 2004

Roarke, Adam (1938–1996) *Hell's Angels on Wheels* 1967; *Psych-Out* 1968; *Frogs* 1972; *Play It As It Lays* 1972; *This Is a Hijack* 1973; *Dirty Mary Crazy Larry* 1974; *The Four Deuces* 1976; *Sioux City* 1994

Robards Sr, Jason aka **Robards, Jason** (1892–1963) *Hills of Kentucky* 1927; *The Silent Bell* 1944; *A Game of Death* 1945; *Isle of the Dead* 1945; *Bedlam* 1946; *Desperate* 1947; *Riff-Raff* 1947; *Thunder Mountain* 1947; *Trail Street* 1947; *Guns of Hate* 1948

Robards, Jason aka **Robards Jr, Jason** (1922–2000) *The Journey* 1959; *By Love Possessed* 1961; *Tender Is the Night* 1961; *Wild in the Country* 1961; *Long Day's Journey into Night* 1962; *Act One* 1963; *A Thousand Clowns* 1965; *Any Wednesday* 1966; *A Big Hand for a Little Lady* 1966; *Divorce American Style* 1967; *Hour of the Gun* 1967; *The St Valentine's Day Massacre* 1967; *Isadora* 1968; *The Night They Raided Minsky's* 1968; *Once upon a Time in the West* 1968; *The Ballad of Cable Hogue* 1970; *Fools* 1970; *Julius Caesar* 1970; *Tora! Tora! Tora!* 1970; *Johnny Got His Gun* 1971; *Murders in the Rue Morgue* 1971; *The War between Men and Women* 1972; *Pat Garrett and Billy the Kid* 1973; *Mr Sycamore* 1974; *A Boy and His Dog* 1975; *All the President's Men* 1976; *Julia* 1977; *Comes a Horseman* 1978; *Hurricane* 1979; *Caboblanco* 1980; *Melvin and Howard* 1980; *Raise the Titanic* 1980; *The Legend of the Lone Ranger* 1981; *Max Dugan Returns* 1983; *Something Wicked This Way Comes* 1983; *Square Dance* 1987; *Bright Lights, Big City* 1988; *The Price of Passion* 1988; *Black Rainbow* 1989; *Dream a Little Dream* 1989; *Parenthood* 1989; *Reunion* 1989; *Quick Change* 1990; *Storyville* 1992; *The Adventures of Huck Finn* 1993; *Philadelphia* 1993; *The Trial* 1993; *The Enemy Within* 1994; *Little Big League* 1994; *The Paper* 1994; *A Thousand Acres* 1997; *Enemy of the State* 1998; *Magnolia* 1999

Robards, Sam (1961–) *Tempest* 1982; *Fandango* 1985; *Not Quite Jerusalem* 1985; *The Ballad of Little Jo* 1993; *American Beauty* 1999; *AI: Artificial Intelligence* 2001; *Life as a House* 2001; *Catch That Kid* 2004

Robb, David (1947–) *The Deceivers* 1988; *Treasure Island* 1998

Robb, R D (1972–) *A Christmas Story* 1983; *Eight Days a Week* 1996

Robbins, Amy (1971–) *Up on the Roof* 1997; *All the Little Animals* 1998

Robbins, Gale (1921–1980) *My Girl Tisa* 1948; *Oh, You Beautiful Doll* 1949; *The Fuller Brush Girl* 1950; *Three Little Words* 1950; *The Belle of New York* 1952; *Calamity Jane* 1953; *Quantrill's Raiders* 1958

Robbins, James *San Quentin* 1937; *The Barbarian and the Geisha* 1958

Robbins, Michael (1930–1992) *Lunch Hour* 1962; *On the Buses* 1971; *Mutiny on the Buses* 1972; *Holiday on the Buses* 1973; *Just Ask for Diamond* 1988

Robbins, Peter (1956–) *A Ticklish Affair* 1963; *And Now Miguel* 1966; *Moment to Moment* 1966; *A Boy Named Charlie Brown* 1969

Robbins, Tim (1958–) *No Small Affair* 1984; *Fraternity Vacation* 1985; *The Sure Thing* 1985; *Howard, a New Breed of Hero* 1986; *Top Gun* 1986; *Five Corners* 1987; *Bull Durham* 1988; *Tapeheads* 1988; *Erik the Viking* 1989; *Miss Firecracker* 1989; *Cadillac Man* 1990; *Jacob's Ladder* 1990; *Jungle Fever* 1991; *Bob Roberts* 1992; *The Player* 1992; *Short Cuts* 1993; *The Hudsucker Proxy* 1994; *IQ* 1994; *Pret-a-Porter* 1994; *The Shawshank Redemption* 1994; *Nothing to Lose* 1997; *Arlington Road* 1998; *Mission to Mars* 1999; *High Fidelity* 2000; *Antitrust* 2001; *Human Nature* 2001; *The Truth about Charlie* 2002; *Code 46* 2003; *Mystic River* 2003; *War of the Worlds* 2005

Rober, Richard (1910–1952) *The File on Thelma Jordon* 1949; *Port of New York* 1949; *The Woman on Pier 13* 1949; *Sierra* 1950; *Watch the Birdie* 1950; *Man in the Saddle* 1951; *The Tall Target* 1951; *The Well* 1951; *The Devil Makes Three* 1952; *The Savage* 1953; *Jet Pilot* 1957

Robert, Yves (1920–2002) *The Bad Liaisons* 1955; *Les Grandes Manoeuvres* 1955; *One Night at the Music Hall* 1956; *Cleo from 5 to 7* 1961; *La Crise* 1992

Roberti, Lyda (1906–1938) *The Kid from Spain* 1932; *Million Dollar Legs* 1932; *Torch Singer* 1933; *George White's 1935 Scandals* 1935

Roberts, Aled *A Feast at Midnight* 1994; *The Haunting of Helen Walker* 1995

Roberts, Allene (1928–) *The Red House* 1947; *Knock on Any Door* 1949; *Union Station* 1950

Roberts, Beverly (1914–) *China Clipper* 1936; *God's Country and*

the Woman 1937; *The Perfect Specimen* 1937
Roberts, Christian (1944–) *To Sir, with Love* 1967; *The Anniversary* 1968; *The Desperados* 1969; *The Mind of Mr Soames* 1970; *The Last Valley* 1971
Roberts, Doris (1930–) *A Lovely Way to Go* 1968; *The Honeymoon Killers* 1969; *Little Murders* 1971; *A New Leaf* 1971; *Hester Street* 1975; *Good Luck, Miss Wyckoff* 1979; *Number One with a Bullet* 1986; *National Lampoon's Christmas Vacation* 1989; *One True Love* 2000
Roberts, Eric (1956–) *The North Star* 1943; *King of the Gypsies* 1978; *The Alternative Miss World* 1980; *Raggedy Man* 1981; *Star 80* 1983; *The Pope of Greenwich Village* 1984; *The Coca-Cola Kid* 1985; *Runaway Train* 1985; *Nobody's Fool* 1986; *Blood Red* 1988; *Best of the Best* 1989; *Rude Awakening* 1989; *The Ambulance* 1990; *Best of the Best II* 1992; *By the Sword* 1992; *Final Analysis* 1992; *Voyage* 1993; *Babyfever* 1994; *Bad Company* 1994; *Freefall* 1994; *Love, Cheat & Steal* 1994; *Love Is a Gun* 1994; *The Specialist* 1994; *American Strays* 1996; *The Cable Guy* 1996; *The Glass Cage* 1996; *Heaven's Prisoners* 1996; *It's My Party* 1996; *The Odyssey* 1997; *The Prophecy II* 1997; *Hitman's Run* 1999; *Lansky* 1999; *Purgatory* 1999; *Luck of the Draw* 2000; *Race against Time* 2000; *Sanctimony* 2000; *National Security* 2002; *Spun* 2002
Roberts, Evelyn (1886–1962) *Keep Fit* 1937; *Man of the Moment* 1955
Roberts, Ewan (1914–1983) *Colonel March Investigates* 1953; *River Beat* 1954; *Night of the Demon* 1957
Roberts, Florence (1861–1940) *Kept Husbands* 1931; *Make Me a Star* 1932; *Babes in Toyland* 1934; *Top Hat* 1935
Roberts, Ian *Jane and the Lost City* 1987; *Tarzan and the Lost City* 1998; *Sweepers* 1999
Roberts, Ivor (1925–1999) *The Sailor's Return* 1978; *We Think the World of You* 1988
Roberts, J H (1884–1961) *The Divorce of Lady X* 1938; *Charley's (Big Hearted) Aunt* 1940
Roberts, Joe (1871–1923) *Neighbors* 1920; *One Week* 1920; *The Scarecrow* 1920; *The Paleface* 1921; *The Three Ages* 1923
Roberts, Julia (1967–) *Blood Red* 1988; *Mystic Pizza* 1988; *Satisfaction* 1988; *Steel Magnolias* 1989; *Flatliners* 1990; *Pretty Woman* 1990; *Dying Young* 1991; *Hook* 1991; *Sleeping with the Enemy* 1991; *The Pelican Brief* 1993; *I Love Trouble* 1994; *Pret-a-Porter* 1994; *Mary Reilly* 1995; *Something to Talk About* 1995; *Everyone Says I Love You* 1996; *Michael Collins* 1996; *Conspiracy Theory* 1997; *My Best Friend's Wedding* 1997; *Stepmom* 1998; *Notting Hill* 1999; *Runaway Bride* 1999; *Erin Brockovich* 2000; *America's Sweethearts* 2001; *The Mexican* 2001; *Ocean's Eleven* 2001; *Confessions of a Dangerous Mind* 2002; *Full Frontal* 2002; *Mona Lisa Smile* 2003; *Closer* 2004; *Ocean's Twelve* 2004
Roberts, Lynne *aka* **Hart, Mary** (1919–1978) *Billy the Kid Returns* 1938; *Shine On, Harvest Moon* 1938; *Rough Riders' Roundup* 1939; *Riders of the Purple Sage* 1941; *The Man in the Trunk* 1942; *Quiet Please, Murder* 1942
Roberts, Michael D *The Ice Pirates* 1984; *Rain Man* 1988; *Sleepstalker* 1995
Roberts, Nancy (1882–1962) *Cosh Boy* 1952; *It's a Great Day* 1955
Roberts, Pascale *The Sleeping Car Murders* 1965; *Three* 1969; *Le Grand Chemin* 1987; *Marius et Jeannette* 1997; *La Ville Est Tranquille* 2000
Roberts, Pernell (1928–) *Desire under the Elms* 1958; *The Sheepman* 1958; *Ride Lonesome* 1959; *The Magic of Lassie* 1978
Roberts (1), Rachel (1927–1980) *Valley of Song* 1953; *The Good Companions* 1956; *Saturday Night and Sunday Morning* 1960; *Girl on Approval* 1962; *This Sporting Life* 1963; *A Flea in Her Ear* 1968; *Doctors' Wives* 1970; *Alpha Beta* 1973; *The Belstone Fox* 1973; *O Lucky Man!* 1973; *Murder on the Orient Express* 1974; *Picnic at Hanging Rock* 1975; *Foul Play* 1978; *When a Stranger Calls* 1979; *Yanks* 1979; *Charlie Chan and the Curse of the Dragon Queen* 1981
Roberts, Rick (1965–) *Love and Human Remains* 1993; *Waiting for Michelangelo* 1995
Roberts, Roy (1900–1975) *Guadalcanal Diary* 1943; *Circumstantial Evidence* 1945; *Smoky* 1946; *Force of Evil* 1948; *He Walked by Night* 1948; *Wyoming Mail* 1950; *The Enforcer* 1951; *The Glory Brigade* 1953; *House of Wax* 1953; *The Lone Hand* 1953; *Tumbleweed* 1953
Roberts, Stephen (1917–1999) *Gog* 1954; *Diary of a Madman* 1963
Roberts, Tanya (1954–) *California Dreaming* 1979; *Tourist Trap* 1979; *The Beastmaster* 1982; *Sheena* 1984; *A View to a Kill* 1985; *Purgatory* 1988; *Night Eyes* 1990
Roberts, Theodore (1861–1928) *Male and Female* 1919; *The Ten Commandments* 1923
Roberts, Tony (1939–) *The Million Dollar Duck* 1971; *Play It Again, Sam* 1972; *Serpico* 1973; *Call Him Savage* 1975; *Annie Hall* 1977; *Just Tell Me What You Want* 1980; *Stardust Memories* 1980; *A Midsummer Night's Sex Comedy* 1982; *Amityville III: the Demon* 1983; *Key Exchange* 1985; *Hannah and Her Sisters* 1986; *18 Again!* 1988; *Switch* 1991
Robertson, Cliff (1925–) *Picnic* 1955; *Autumn Leaves* 1956; *The Girl Most Likely* 1957; *The Naked and the Dead* 1958; *Battle of the Coral Sea* 1959; *Gidget* 1959; *All in a Night's Work* 1960; *The Big Show* 1961; *Underworld USA* 1961; *The Interns* 1962; *My Six Loves* 1962; *PT 109* 1963; *Sunday in New York* 1963; *The Best Man* 1964; *633 Squadron* 1964; *Love Has Many Faces* 1965; *Masquerade* 1965; *Up from the Beach* 1965; *The Honey Pot* 1967; *Charly* 1968; *The Devil's Brigade* 1968; *Too Late the Hero* 1970; *JW Coop* 1971; *The Great Northfield Minnesota Raid* 1972; *Ace Eli and Rodger of the Skies* 1973; *Out of Season* 1975; *Three Days of the Condor* 1975; *Battle of Midway* 1976; *Obsession* 1976; *Shoot* 1976; *Fraternity Row* 1977; *Dominique* 1978; *The Pilot* 1979; *Brainstorm* 1983; *Class* 1983; *Star 80* 1983; *Shaker Run* 1985; *Malone* 1987; *Wild Hearts Can't Be Broken* 1991; *Wind* 1992; *Renaissance Man* 1994; *Escape from LA* 1996; *Spider-Man* 2002
Robertson, Dale (1923–) *Fighting Man of the Plains* 1949; *The Cariboo Trail* 1950; *Two Flags West* 1950; *Call Me Mister* 1951; *Golden Girl* 1951; *Lydia Bailey* 1952; *O Henry's Full House* 1952; *Devil's Canyon* 1953; *The Farmer Takes a Wife* 1953; *Sitting Bull* 1954; *Son of Sinbad* 1955; *Dakota Incident* 1956; *A Day of Fury* 1956; *The Man from Button Willow* 1965
Robertson, Iain (1981–) *Small Faces* 1995; *The Debt Collector* 1999; *One Last Chance* 2003
Robertson, Kathleen (1973–) *Lapse of Memory* 1992; *Nowhere* 1997; *Dog Park* 1998; *Splendor* 1999; *Beautiful* 2000; *Scary Movie 2* 2001; *XX/XY* 2001
Robertson, Robbie (1943–) *Carny* 1980; *The Crossing Guard* 1995
Robertson, Tim (1944–) *Bliss* 1985; *The Time Guardian* 1987; *The Big Steal* 1990; *Holy Smoke* 1999
Robertson, Willard (1886–1948) *Skippy* 1931; *Lady Killer* 1933; *Tugboat Annie* 1933; *Kentucky* 1938; *Background to Danger* 1943; *Deep Valley* 1947
Robertson-Justice, James *aka* **Robertson Justice, James** (1905–1975) *For Those in Peril* 1943; *Against the Wind* 1947; *My Brother Jonathan* 1947; *Vice Versa* 1947; *Scott of the Antarctic* 1948; *Whisky Galore!* 1949; *Pool of London* 1950; *Anne of the Indies* 1951; *Captain Horatio Hornblower RN* 1951; *David and Bathsheba* 1951; *Les Misérables* 1952; *Miss Robin Hood* 1952; *The Story of Robin Hood and His Merrie Men* 1952; *The Sword and the Rose* 1952; *Voice of Merrill* 1952; *Rob Roy, the Highland Rogue* 1953; *Doctor in the House* 1954; *Out of the Clouds* 1954; *Above Us the Waves* 1955; *An Alligator Named Daisy* 1955; *Doctor at Sea* 1955; *Land of the Pharaohs* 1955; *The Living Idol* 1955; *Storm over the Nile* 1955; *Checkpoint* 1956; *The Iron Petticoat* 1956; *Moby Dick* 1956; *Campbell's Kingdom* 1957; *Doctor at Large* 1957; *Seven Thunders* 1957; *Orders to Kill* 1958; *Upstairs and Downstairs* 1959; *Doctor in Love* 1960; *Foxhole in Cairo* 1960; *A French Mistress* 1960; *The Guns of Navarone* 1961; *Murder She Said* 1961; *A Pair of Briefs* 1961; *Raising the Wind* 1961; *Very Important Person* 1961; *Crooks Anonymous* 1962; *Dr Crippen* 1962; *Guns of Darkness* 1962; *Doctor in Distress* 1963; *The Fast Lady* 1963; *Father Came Too* 1963; *The Face of Fu Manchu* 1965; *Up from the Beach* 1965; *You Must Be Joking!* 1965; *Doctor in Clover* 1966; *The Trygon Factor* 1967; *Chitty Chitty Bang Bang* 1968; *Mayerling* 1968; *Some Will, Some Won't* 1969; *Zeta One* 1969; *Doctor in Trouble* 1970
Robeson, Paul (1898–1976) *The Emperor Jones* 1933; *Sanders of the River* 1935; *Show Boat* 1936; *Song of Freedom* 1936; *Big Fella* 1937; *King Solomon's Mines* 1937; *The Proud Valley* 1940; *Native Land* 1942; *Tales of Manhattan* 1942
Robey, George (1869–1954) *Don Quixote* 1932; *Chu Chin Chow* 1934; *Southern Roses* 1936
Roble, Wendy (1953–) *The People under the Stairs* 1991; *The Dentist II* 1998
Robin, Dany *aka* **Robin, Mme Dany** (1927–1995) *Man about Town* 1947; *Act of Love* 1953; *The Mysteries of Paris* 1962; *Waltz of the Toreadors* 1962; *Follow the Boys* 1963; *The Best House in London* 1968; *Topaz* 1969
Robin, Michel (1930–) *Harem* 1985; *Marquis* 1989; *Merci pour le Chocolat* 2000
Robins, Laila (1959–) *An Innocent Man* 1989; *Welcome Home, Roxy Carmichael* 1990; *Live Nude Girls* 1995; *Female Perversions* 1996; *The Blood Oranges* 1997
Robinson, Andrew *aka* **Robinson, Andy** (1942–) *Dirty Harry* 1971; *Charley Varrick* 1973; *Cobra* 1986; *Hellraiser* 1987; *Prime Target* 1991; *The Revenge of Pumpkinhead – Blood Wings* 1994
Robinson, Ann (1935–) *The Glass Wall* 1953; *The War of the Worlds* 1953; *Dragnet* 1954; *Gun Duel in Durango* 1957; *Damn Citizen* 1958; *Midnight Movie Massacre* 1987
Robinson, Bartlett (1912–1986) *The Spirit of St Louis* 1957; *All Hands on Deck* 1961; *Sleeper* 1973
Robinson, Bill (1878–1949) *The Big Broadcast of 1936* 1935; *Hooray for Love* 1935; *In Old Kentucky* 1935; *The Littlest Rebel* 1935; *Just around the Corner* 1938; *Rebecca of Sunnybrook Farm* 1938; *Stormy Weather* 1943
Robinson, Bruce (1946–) *The Story of Adèle H* 1975; *Still Crazy* 1998
Robinson, Cardew (1917–1992) *The Navy Lark* 1959; *Let's Get Married* 1960; *Light Up the Sky* 1960; *I Was Happy Here* 1966; *Come Play with Me* 1977
Robinson, Charles (1945–) *Shenandoah* 1965; *The Sand Pebbles* 1966; *Brotherhood of Satan* 1970
Robinson, Chris (1938–) *Amy* 1981; *Savannah Smiles* 1982
Robinson, Edward G (1893–1973) *Five Star Final* 1931; *Little Caesar* 1931; *Smart Money* 1931; *The Hatchet Man* 1932; *Tiger Shark* 1932; *Two Seconds* 1932; *The Little Giant* 1933; *Barbary Coast* 1935; *The Whole Town's Talking* 1935; *Bullets or Ballots* 1936; *Kid Galahad* 1937; *The Last Gangster* 1937; *Thunder in the City* 1937; *The Amazing Dr Clitterhouse* 1938; *I Am the Law* 1938; *A Slight Case of Murder* 1938; *Blackmail* 1939; *Confessions of a Nazi Spy* 1939; *Brother Orchid* 1940; *A Dispatch from Reuters* 1940; *Dr Ehrlich's Magic Bullet* 1940; *Manpower* 1941; *The Sea Wolf* 1941; *Unholy Partners* 1941; *Larceny, Inc* 1942; *Tales of Manhattan* 1942; *Flesh and Fantasy* 1943; *Double Indemnity* 1944; *Journey Together* 1944; *Mr Winkle Goes to War* 1944; *Our Vines Have Tender Grapes* 1945; *Scarlet Street* 1945; *The Woman in the Window* 1945; *The Stranger* 1946; *The Red House* 1947; *All My Sons* 1948; *Key Largo* 1948; *Night Has a Thousand Eyes* 1948; *House of Strangers* 1949; *It's a Great Feeling* 1949; *Actors and Sin* 1952; *Big Leaguer* 1953; *The Glass Web* 1953; *Vice Squad* 1953; *A Bullet for Joey* 1955; *Hell on Frisco Bay* 1955; *Illegal* 1955; *Tight Spot* 1955; *The Violent Men* 1955; *Nightmare* 1956; *The Ten Commandments* 1956; *A Hole in the Head* 1959; *Pepe* 1960; *Seven Thieves* 1960; *My Geisha* 1962; *Two Weeks in Another Town* 1962; *The Prize* 1963; *Sammy Going South* 1963; *Cheyenne Autumn* 1964; *Good Neighbor Sam* 1964; *The Outrage* 1964; *Robin and the 7 Hoods* 1964; *The Cincinnati Kid* 1965; *Grand Slam* 1967; *The Biggest Bundle of Them All* 1968; *Never a Dull Moment* 1968; *Mackenna's Gold* 1969; *Song of Norway* 1970; *Soylent Green* 1973
Robinson, Forrest (1858–1924) *Tol'able David* 1921; *Tess of the Storm Country* 1922
Robinson, Frances (1916–1971) *Forbidden Valley* 1938; *Smilin' Through* 1941
Robinson, Jay (1930–) *The Robe* 1953; *Demetrius and the Gladiators* 1954; *The Virgin Queen* 1955; *My Man Godfrey* 1957; *Bunny O'Hare* 1971; *This Is a Hijack* 1973; *Three the Hard Way* 1974; *Shampoo* 1975; *Born Again* 1978; *Partners* 1982
Robinson (1), John (1908–1979) *Emergency Call* 1952; *Ghost Ship* 1952; *The Doctor's Dilemma* 1958; *Nothing but the Night* 1972
Robinson (3), John (1985–) *Elephant* 2003; *Lords of Dogtown* 2005
Robinson, Madeleine (1916–2004) *Dieu A Besoin des Hommes* 1950; *Les Possédées* 1955; *Web of Passion* 1959; *Une Histoire Simple* 1978; *I Married a Dead Man* 1983; *Camille Claudel* 1988
Robinson, Roger (1940–) *Believe in Me* 1971; *Newman's Law* 1974
Robinson, Wendy Raquel *Ringmaster* 1998; *Two Can Play That Game* 2001
Robinson, Zuleikha (1977–) *Hidalgo* 2003; *William Shakespeare's The Merchant of Venice* 2004
Robson, Flora (1902–1984) *The Rise of Catherine the Great* 1934; *Fire over England* 1937; *Invisible Stripes* 1939; *Poison Pen* 1939; *We Are Not Alone* 1939; *Wuthering Heights* 1939; *The Sea Hawk* 1940; *Great Day* 1944; *Two Thousand Women* 1944; *Caesar and Cleopatra* 1945; *Saratoga Trunk* 1945; *Black Narcissus* 1946; *The Years Between* 1946; *Frieda* 1947; *Holiday Camp* 1947; *Good Time Girl* 1948; *Saraband for Dead Lovers* 1948; *Malta Story* 1953; *Romeo and Juliet* 1954; *High Tide at Noon* 1957; *Innocent Sinners* 1957; *No Time for Tears* 1957; *The Gypsy and the Gentleman* 1958; *55 Days at Peking* 1963; *Murder at the Gallop* 1963; *Guns at Batasi* 1964; *Those Magnificent Men in Their Flying Machines* 1965; *Young Cassidy* 1965; *Eye of the Devil* 1966; *7 Women* 1966; *The Shuttered Room* 1967; *The Beast in the Cellar* 1970; *Fragment of Fear* 1970; *Alice's Adventures in Wonderland* 1972; *Sin* 1972; *Dominique* 1978; *Les Misérables* 1978
Robson, Greer (1971–) *Smash Palace* 1981; *Starlight Hotel* 1987
Robson, May (1858–1942) *If I Had a Million* 1932; *Red-Headed Woman* 1932; *Strange Interlude* 1932; *Dancing Lady* 1933; *Lady for a Day* 1933; *Reunion in Vienna* 1933; *The White Sister* 1933; *Lady by Choice* 1934; *Anna Karenina* 1935; *Reckless* 1935; *Strangers All* 1935; *Vanessa, Her Love Story* 1935; *Rainbow on the River* 1936; *Wife vs Secretary* 1936; *The Perfect Specimen* 1937; *A Star Is Born* 1937; *The Adventures of Tom Sawyer* 1938; *Bringing Up Baby* 1938; *Four Daughters* 1938; *The Texans* 1938; *Daughters Courageous* 1939; *Nurse Edith Cavell* 1939; *That's Right – You're Wrong* 1939; *They Made Me a Criminal* 1939; *Texas Rangers Ride Again* 1940; *Four Mothers* 1941; *Million Dollar Baby* 1941; *Playmates* 1941; *Joan of Paris* 1942
Robson, Wayne *The Grey Fox* 1982; *One Magic Christmas* 1985; *Dead of Winter* 1987; *Housekeeping* 1987; *Bye Bye Blues* 1989; *Stolen Hearts* 1996; *Cube* 1997; *Pippi Longstocking* 1997
Roc, Patricia (1915–2003) *A Window in London* 1939; *We'll Meet Again* 1942; *Millions like Us* 1943; *Love Story* 1944; *Madonna of the Seven Moons* 1944; *Two Thousand Women* 1944; *Johnny Frenchman* 1945; *The Wicked Lady* 1945; *Canyon Passage* 1946; *The Brothers* 1947; *Jassy* 1947; *So Well Remembered* 1947; *When the Bough Breaks* 1947; *One Night with You* 1948; *The Man on the Eiffel Tower* 1949; *The Perfect Woman* 1949; *Circle of Danger* 1950; *Black Jack* 1952; *Something Money Can't Buy* 1952; *Cartouche* 1954; *House in the Woods* 1957; *The Hypnotist* 1957
Rocca, Daniela (1938–1995) *Caltiki, the Immortal Monster* 1959; *The Giant of Marathon* 1960; *Divorce – Italian Style* 1961; *Captive City* 1962; *The Empty Canvas* 1963; *Behold a Pale Horse* 1964
Rocca, Stefania (1971–) *Nirvana* 1996; *Heaven* 2002; *The Card Player* 2004
Rocco, Alex (1936–) *Motor Psycho* 1965; *Detroit 9000* 1973; *The Friends of Eddie Coyle* 1973; *Rafferty and the Gold Dust Twins* 1974; *Hearts of the West* 1975; *Voices* 1979; *Herbie Goes Bananas* 1980; *The Stunt Man* 1980; *PK and the Kid* 1982; *Gotcha!* 1985; *Lady in White* 1988; *Wired* 1989; *The Pope Must Die* 1991; *Dead of Night* 1997; *Goodbye Lover* 1997; *Dudley Do-Right* 1999
Roche, Eugene (1928–2004) *Slaughterhouse-Five* 1972; *Newman's Law* 1974; *W* 1974; *Mr Ricco* 1975; *The Late Show* 1977; *Corvette Summer* 1978; *Oh, God! You Devil* 1984

Roche, John (1893–1952) *Kiss Me Again* 1925; *Don Juan* 1926
Rochefort, Jean (1930–) *Le Masque de Fer* 1962; *Up to His Ears* 1965; *The Tall Blond Man with One Black Shoe* 1972; *The Bit Player* 1973; *The Inheritor* 1973; *The Watchmaker of St Paul* 1973; *Les Innocents aux Mains Sales* 1975; *Pardon Mon Affaire* 1976; *French Postcards* 1979; *Frankenstein 90* 1984; *The Hairdresser's Husband* 1990; *Tango* 1993; *Wild Target* 1993; *Circle of Passion* 1996; *Ridicule* 1996; *Wind with the Gone* 1998; *The Closet* 2001; *L'Homme du Train* 2002
Rochfort, Spencer (1966–) *Ski School* 1991; *Operation Delta Force II: Mayday* 1998
Rochon, Lela *aka* **Fuqua, Lela Rochon** (1966–) *The Wild Pair* 1987; *Boomerang* 1992; *Waiting to Exhale* 1995; *The Chamber* 1996; *Gang Related* 1997; *Knock Off* 1998; *Why Do Fools Fall in Love?* 1998; *First Daughter* 2004
Rock, Chris (1966–) *New Jack City* 1991; *Boomerang* 1992; *CB4* 1993; *Beverly Hills Ninja* 1997; *Lethal Weapon 4* 1998; *Dogma* 1999; *Nurse Betty* 2000; *Down to Earth* 2001; *Jay and Silent Bob Strike Back* 2001; *Osmosis Jones* 2001; *Bad Company* 2002; *Head of State* 2003; *The Longest Yard* 2005; *Madagascar* 2005
Rock, The (1972–) *The Mummy Returns* 2001; *The Scorpion King* 2002; *Welcome to the Jungle* 2003; *Walking Tall* 2004; *Be Cool* 2005
Rocket, Charles (1949–) *Down Twisted* 1987; *Earth Girls Are Easy* 1988; *How I Got into College* 1989; *Dances with Wolves* 1990; *Delirious* 1991; *Brain Smasher… a Love Story* 1993; *Charlie's Ghost Story* 1994; *Dumb and Dumber* 1994; *Tom and Huck* 1995; *The Killing Grounds* 1997
Rockwell, Sam (1968–) *Clownhouse* 1988; *Glory Daze* 1995; *Box of Moonlight* 1996; *Lawn Dogs* 1997; *Jerry and Tom* 1998; *Safe Men* 1998; *Galaxy Quest* 1999; *The Green Mile* 1999; *Charlie's Angels* 2000; *Heist* 2001; *Confessions of a Dangerous Mind* 2002; *Welcome to Collinwood* 2002; *Matchstick Men* 2003; *The Hitchhiker's Guide to the Galaxy* 2005
Rodan, Jay *The Triumph of Love* 2001; *Callas Forever* 2002; *Monsieur N* 2003
Rodann, Ziva (1935–) *Last Train from Gun Hill* 1959; *Samar* 1962
Rodd, Marcia (1940–) *Little Murders* 1971; *TR Baskin* 1971; *Citizens Band* 1977
Roden, Karel (1962–) *15 Minutes* 2001; *Bulletproof Monk* 2002; *Hellboy* 2004
Roderick, Sue *Rebecca's Daughters* 1991; *Hedd Wyn* 1992
Rodgers, Anton (1933–) *Part-Time Wife* 1961; *Rotten to the Core* 1965; *The Man Who Haunted Himself* 1970; *Scrooge* 1970; *East of Elephant Rock* 1976; *Agatha Christie's Murder with Mirrors* 1985; *Dirty Rotten Scoundrels* 1988; *Impromptu* 1991
Rodgers, Ilona (1942–) *Salt & Pepper* 1968; *Utu* 1983
Rodman, Dennis (1961–) *Double Team* 1997; *Simon Sez* 1999; *Cutaway* 2000
Rodney, John (1916–) *Pursued* 1947; *Fighter Squadron* 1948; *Key Largo* 1948
Rodriguez, Freddy (1975–) *Dead Presidents* 1995; *A Walk in the Clouds* 1995; *The Pest* 1997
Rodriguez, José Antonio *The Last Supper* 1976; *Knocks at My Door* 1991
Rodriguez, Marco *Disorderlies* 1987; *Serial Killer* 1996; *Toolbox Murders* 2003
Rodriguez, Michelle (1978–) *Girlfight* 2000; *The Fast and the Furious* 2001; *Blue Crush* 2002; *Resident Evil* 2002; *SWAT* 2003
Rodriguez, Paul (1955–) *Miracles* 1985; *Quicksilver* 1986; *The Whoopee Boys* 1986; *Born in East LA* 1987; *Made in America* 1993; *A Million to Juan* 1994; *Rough Magic* 1995; *Tortilla Soup* 2001; *Blood Work* 2002; *Baadasssss!* 2003
Rodriguez, Valente *Roosters* 1993; *The Big Squeeze* 1996; *Guy* 1996
Rodway, Norman (1929–2001) *This Other Eden* 1959; *Four in the Morning* 1965; *Chimes at Midnight* 1966; *The Penthouse* 1967
Roe, Raymond *The Major and the Minor* 1942; *The West Point Story* 1950
Roebuck, Daniel (1963–) *Dudes* 1987; *River's Edge* 1987; *The Late Shift* 1996; *US Marshals* 1998; *Double Take* 2001; *Agent Cody Banks 2: Destination London* 2003
Roel, Gabriela *El Dorado* 1988; *Old Gringo* 1989
Roëves, Maurice (1937–) *Ulysses* 1967; *Oh! What a Lovely War* 1969; *When Eight Bells Toll* 1971; *The Big Man* 1990; *The Last of the Mohicans* 1992; *The Acid House* 1998; *Beautiful Creatures* 2000
Rogers, Charles "Buddy" (1904–1999) *My Best Girl* 1927; *Wings* 1927; *This Reckless Age* 1932; *Old Man Rhythm* 1935; *The Parson and the Outlaw* 1957
Rogers, Ginger (1911–1995) *Honor among Lovers* 1931; *The Thirteenth Guest* 1932; *Flying down to Rio* 1933; *42nd Street* 1933; *Gold Diggers of 1933* 1933; *Sitting Pretty* 1933; *Change of Heart* 1934; *Finishing School* 1934; *The Gay Divorce* 1934; *Romance in Manhattan* 1934; *Upper World* 1934; *In Person* 1935; *Roberta* 1935; *Star of Midnight* 1935; *Top Hat* 1935; *Follow the Fleet* 1936; *Swing Time* 1936; *Shall We Dance* 1937; *Stage Door* 1937; *Carefree* 1938; *Having Wonderful Time* 1938; *Vivacious Lady* 1938; *Bachelor Mother* 1939; *Fifth Avenue Girl* 1939; *The Story of Vernon and Irene Castle* 1939; *Kitty Foyle* 1940; *Lucky Partners* 1940; *Primrose Path* 1940; *Tom, Dick and Harry* 1941; *The Major and the Minor* 1942; *Once upon a Honeymoon* 1942; *Roxie Hart* 1942; *Tales of Manhattan* 1942; *Tender Comrade* 1943; *I'll Be Seeing You* 1944; *Lady in the Dark* 1944; *Week-End at the Waldorf* 1945; *Heartbeat* 1946; *Magnificent Doll* 1946; *It Had to Be You* 1947; *The Barkleys of Broadway* 1949; *Perfect Strangers* 1950; *Storm Warning* 1950; *Dreamboat* 1952; *Monkey Business* 1952; *We're Not Married* 1952; *Forever Female* 1953; *Beautiful Stranger* 1954; *Black Widow* 1954; *Tight Spot* 1955; *The First Travelling Saleslady* 1956; *Teenage Rebel* 1956; *Oh, Men! Oh, Women!* 1957; *Quick, Let's Get Married* 1964; *Harlow* 1965
Rogers, Jean (1916–1991) *Stormy* 1935; *Flash Gordon* 1936; *Brigham Young* 1940; *Let's Make Music* 1940; *The Man Who Wouldn't Talk* 1940; *Design for Scandal* 1941; *Dr Kildare's Victory* 1941; *The War against Mrs Hadley* 1942; *Whistling in Brooklyn* 1943
Rogers, John (1888–1963) *Think Fast, Mr Moto* 1937; *Bob, Son of Battle* 1947
Rogers, Mimi (1956–) *Gung Ho* 1986; *Someone to Watch over Me* 1987; *Street Smart* 1987; *Hider in the House* 1989; *The Mighty Quinn* 1989; *Desperate Hours* 1990; *The Rapture* 1991; *Dark Horse* 1992; *Shooting Elizabeth* 1992; *White Sands* 1992; *Far from Home: the Adventures of Yellow Dog* 1994; *Killer* 1994; *Monkey Trouble* 1994; *Reflections on a Crime* 1994; *In the Blink of an Eye* 1996; *The Mirror Has Two Faces* 1996; *Austin Powers: International Man of Mystery* 1997; *Lost in Space* 1998; *The Devil's Arithmetic* 1999; *Cruel Intentions 2* 2000; *Ginger Snaps* 2000; *Dumb and Dumberer: When Harry Met Lloyd* 2003; *The Door in the Floor* 2004
Rogers, Paul (1917–) *The Beachcomber* 1954; *Beau Brummell* 1954; *Svengali* 1954; *Circle of Deception* 1960; *Life for Ruth* 1962; *The Pot Carriers* 1962; *The Wild and the Willing* 1962; *Stolen Hours* 1963; *The Third Secret* 1964; *He Who Rides a Tiger* 1965; *The Looking Glass War* 1969; *Three into Two Won't Go* 1969; *I Want What I Want* 1971; *The Homecoming* 1973; *Lost in the Stars* 1974; *Mister Quilp* 1975
Rogers, Reg (1962–) *Runaway Bride* 1999; *Analyze That* 2002
Rogers, Roy (1912–1998) *Billy the Kid Returns* 1938; *Shine On, Harvest Moon* 1938; *The Arizona Kid* 1939; *Rough Riders' Roundup* 1939; *Dark Command* 1940; *Song of Texas* 1943; *Brazil* 1944; *Hollywood Canteen* 1944; *The Yellow Rose of Texas* 1944; *Bells of Rosarita* 1945; *My Pal Trigger* 1946; *Bells of San Angelo* 1947; *Springtime in the Sierras* 1947; *Under California Stars* 1948; *The Far Frontier* 1949; *North of the Great Divide* 1950; *Trail of Robin Hood* 1950; *Son of Paleface* 1952; *Alias Jesse James* 1959
Rogers, Wayne (1933–) *Pocket Money* 1972; *Once in Paris* 1978; *The Hot Touch* 1982; *The Gig* 1985; *The Killing Time* 1987
Rogers, Will (1879–1935) *Hollywood* 1923; *They Had to See Paris* 1929; *A Connecticut Yankee* 1931; *Dr Bull* 1933; *State Fair* 1933; *Judge Priest* 1934; *In Old Kentucky* 1935; *Life Begins at 40* 1935; *Steamboat round the Bend* 1935
Rogers Jr, Will (1911–1993) *Look for the Silver Lining* 1949; *The Boy from Oklahoma* 1954; *Wild Heritage* 1958
Rohde, Armin (1955–) *Life Is All You Get* 1998; *Run Lola Run* 1998; *Taking Sides* 2001
Rohm, Maria (1949–) *The Blood of Fu Manchu* 1968; *The Bloody Judge* 1969; *Count Dracula* 1970; *Black Beauty* 1971; *Treasure Island* 1972
Rohner, Clayton (1961–) *Just One of the Guys* 1985; *Private Investigations* 1987; *BAT-21* 1988; *Destroyer* 1988; *The Relic* 1996; *Sometimes They Come Back… for More* 1998
Rojas, Eduardo Lopez (1937–1999) *Reed: Insurgent Mexico* 1971; *My Family* 1994
Rojas, Manuel *The Magnificent Matador* 1955; *Buchanan Rides Alone* 1958
Rojo, Gustavo (1926–) *Action of the Tiger* 1957; *It Started with a Kiss* 1959; *The Miracle* 1959; *El Condor* 1970
Rojo, Maria (1943–) *Break of Dawn* 1988; *Danzón* 1991; *Midaq Alley* 1995; *Perfume de Violetas* 2001
Rojo, Ruben *La Hija del Engaño* 1951; *Cauldron of Blood* 1967
Roland, Gilbert (1905–1994) *Camille* 1927; *Life Begins* 1932; *The Passionate Plumber* 1932; *Our Betters* 1933; *She Done Him Wrong* 1933; *The Last Train from Madrid* 1937; *My Life with Caroline* 1941; *Captain Kidd* 1945; *The Other Love* 1947; *Malaya* 1949; *We Were Strangers* 1949; *Crisis* 1950; *The Furies* 1950; *The Bullfighter and the Lady* 1951; *Ten Tall Men* 1951; *Apache War Smoke* 1952; *Glory Alley* 1952; *The Miracle of Our Lady of Fatima* 1952; *My Six Convicts* 1952; *Beneath the 12-Mile Reef* 1953; *The Diamond Queen* 1953; *Thunder Bay* 1953; *The French Line* 1954; *The Racers* 1955; *That Lady* 1955; *The Treasure of Pancho Villa* 1955; *Underwater!* 1955; *Bandido* 1956; *Three Violent People* 1956; *The Midnight Story* 1957; *The Last of the Fast Guns* 1958; *The Big Circus* 1959; *The Wild and the Innocent* 1959; *Guns of the Timberland* 1960; *Samar* 1962; *Cheyenne Autumn* 1964; *The Reward* 1965; *The Poppy Is Also a Flower* 1966; *The Christian Licorice Store* 1971; *Running Wild* 1973; *Islands in the Stream* 1976; *Caboblanco* 1980; *Barbarosa* 1982
Roland, Jeanne *The Curse of the Mummy's Tomb* 1964; *Salt & Pepper* 1968
Rolf, Tutta (1907–1994) *Swedenhielms* 1935; *Dollar* 1938
Rolfe, Guy (1915–2003) *Broken Journey* 1948; *Portrait from Life* 1948; *Fools Rush In* 1949; *The Spider and the Fly* 1949; *Prelude to Fame* 1950; *The Reluctant Widow* 1950; *Home to Danger* 1951; *King of the Khyber Rifles* 1953; *Young Bess* 1953; *Dance Little Lady* 1954; *It's Never Too Late* 1956; *Girls at Sea* 1958; *Yesterday's Enemy* 1959; *Mr Sardonicus* 1961; *Taras Bulba* 1962; *The Alphabet Murders* 1966; *And Now the Screaming Starts!* 1973; *Dolls* 1987
Rolffes, Kirsten (1928–2000) *Buster's World* 1984; *The Kingdom* 1994
Rolle, Esther (1920–1998) *Summer of My German Soldier* 1978; *PK and the Kid* 1982; *Driving Miss Daisy* 1989; *The Mighty Quinn* 1989; *House of Cards* 1993; *Down in the Delta* 1997; *Rosewood* 1997
Rollett, Raymond (1907–1961) *Dick Turpin – Highwayman* 1956; *Blue Murder at St Trinian's* 1957
Rollins, David (1907–1997) *The Black Watch* 1929; *The Big Trail* 1930
Rollins, Henry (1961–) *The Chase* 1994; *Johnny Mnemonic* 1995; *Lost Highway* 1996; *Jack Frost* 1998; *Time Lapse* 2001
Rolston, Mark (1956–) *Lethal Weapon 2* 1989; *A Sinful Life* 1989; *The Shawshank Redemption* 1994; *The Set Up* 1995
Romain, Yvonne *aka* **Warren, Yvonne** (1938–) *Action of the Tiger* 1957; *The Curse of the Werewolf* 1961; *Village of Daughters* 1961; *Devil Doll* 1964; *Smokescreen* 1964; *The Swinger* 1966; *Double Trouble* 1967
Roman, Candice *The Big Bird Cage* 1972; *The Unholy Rollers* 1972
Roman, Leticia *aka* **Roman, Letitia** (1941–) *GI Blues* 1960; *Gold of the Seven Saints* 1961; *Pontius Pilate* 1961; *Fanny Hill: Memoirs of a Woman of Pleasure* 1964; *The Spy in the Green Hat* 1966
Roman, Ric *Appointment in Honduras* 1953; *Lizzie* 1957
Roman, Ruth (1924–1999) *Belle Starr's Daughter* 1948; *Always Leave Them Laughing* 1949; *Beyond the Forest* 1949; *Champion* 1949; *The Window* 1949; *Barricade* 1950; *Colt .45* 1950; *Dallas* 1950; *Three Secrets* 1950; *Lightning Strikes Twice* 1951; *Strangers on a Train* 1951; *Mara Maru* 1952; *Young Man with Ideas* 1952; *Blowing Wild* 1953; *Down Three Dark Streets* 1954; *The Far Country* 1954; *The Shanghai Story* 1954; *Tanganyika* 1954; *Joe Macbeth* 1955; *Beyond the River* 1956; *Great Day in the Morning* 1956; *Rebel in Town* 1956; *Bitter Victory* 1957; *Five Steps to Danger* 1957; *Look in Any Window* 1961; *Love Has Many Faces* 1965; *The Baby* 1973; *The Killing Kind* 1973; *Impulse* 1975; *Echoes* 1983
Roman, Susan (1957–) *Rabid* 1976; *Heavy Metal* 1981
Romance, Viviane (1912–1991) *La Belle Equipe* 1936; *Mademoiselle Docteur* 1936; *Any Number Can Win* 1963
Romand, Béatrice (1952–) *Claire's Knee* 1970; *Soft Beds, Hard Battles* 1973; *The Romantic Englishwoman* 1975; *Le Beau Mariage* 1982; *Four Adventures of Reinette and Mirabelle* 1986; *The Green Ray* 1986; *An Autumn Tale* 1998
Romano, Andy *Over the Edge* 1979; *Pump Up the Volume* 1990; *Pizza Man* 1991; *The Gun in Betty Lou's Handbag* 1992; *Death of a Cheerleader* 1994; *Two Bits* 1995; *Under Siege 2* 1995; *Eraser* 1996; *Getting Away with Murder* 1996; *Listen* 1996
Romano, Larry *Lock Up* 1989; *No Way Home* 1996
Romano, Ray (1957–) *Ice Age* 2002; *Welcome to Mooseport* 2004
Romano, Renato *The Bird with the Crystal Plumage* 1969; *The Last Rebel* 1971
Romanus, Richard (1943–) *Mean Streets* 1973; *The Gravy Train* 1974; *Wizards* 1977; *Sitting Ducks* 1979; *Heavy Metal* 1981; *Strangers Kiss* 1983; *Protocol* 1984; *Murphy's Law* 1986; *The Couch Trip* 1988; *The Resurrected* 1992; *To Protect and Serve* 1992; *The Assassin* 1993; *Point of No Return* 1993
Romay, Lina (1954–) *The Big Wheel* 1949; *The Female Vampire* 1973
Rome, Stewart (1886–1965) *Dinner at the Ritz* 1937; *Wings of the Morning* 1937
Rome, Sydne (1947–) *Some Girls Do* 1969; *What?* 1973; *That Lucky Touch* 1975; *The Twist* 1976; *Just a Gigolo* 1978
Rome, Tina (1923–1998) *The Baron of Arizona* 1950; *Park Row* 1952
Romer, Piet (1928–) *Business Is Business* 1971; *The Lift* 1983
Romero, Cesar (1907–1994) *British Agent* 1934; *Cardinal Richelieu* 1935; *The Devil Is a Woman* 1935; *The Good Fairy* 1935; *Rendezvous* 1935; *Love before Breakfast* 1936; *Wee Willie Winkie* 1937; *Always Goodbye* 1938; *Happy Landing* 1938; *My Lucky Star* 1938; *Charlie Chan at Treasure Island* 1939; *The Cisco Kid and the Lady* 1939; *Frontier Marshal* 1939; *The Little Princess* 1939; *The Return of the Cisco Kid* 1939; *Wife, Husband and Friend* 1939; *The Gay Caballero* 1940; *The Great American Broadcast* 1941; *Tall, Dark and Handsome* 1941; *Weekend in Havana* 1941; *A Gentleman at Heart* 1942; *Orchestra Wives* 1942; *Springtime in the Rockies* 1942; *Tales of Manhattan* 1942; *Coney Island* 1943; *Wintertime* 1943; *Captain from Castile* 1947; *Julia Misbehaves* 1948; *That Lady in Ermine* 1948; *The Beautiful Blonde from Bashful Bend* 1949; *Happy Go Lovely* 1950; *Love That Brute* 1950; *Prisoners of the Casbah* 1953; *Street of Shadows* 1953; *Vera Cruz* 1954; *The Americano* 1955; *Villa!* 1958; *Ocean's Eleven* 1960; *Pepe* 1960; *If a Man Answers* 1962; *The Castilian* 1963; *Donovan's Reef* 1963; *Two on a Guillotine* 1964; *Marriage on the Rocks* 1965; *Sergeant Deadhead* 1965; *Batman* 1966; *Madigan's Millions* 1967; *Hot Millions* 1968; *The Computer Wore Tennis Shoes* 1969; *Crooks and Coronets* 1969; *Latitude Zero* 1969; *Midas Run* 1969; *Now You See Him, Now You Don't* 1972; *The Proud and the Damned* 1972; *The Strongest Man in the World* 1975; *Lust in the Dust* 1984
Romero, George A (1940–) *Dawn of the Dead* 1978; *Martin* 1978
Romijn-Stamos, Rebecca (1972–) *X-Men* 2000; *Rollerball* 2001; *Femme Fatale* 2002; *Godsend* 2003; *X2* 2003; *The Punisher* 2004
Ron, Tiny *aka* **Taylor, Tiny Ron** *Seven Hours to Judgment* 1988; *Rocketeer* 1991; *Ace Ventura: Pet Detective* 1993
Ronane, John (1933–) *Doctor Blood's Coffin* 1960; *That's Your Funeral* 1972; *A War of Children* 1972
Ronay, Edina (1945–) *The Black Torment* 1964; *The Big Job* 1965; *Praise Marx and Pass the Ammunition* 1968; *Three* 1969
Ronet, Maurice (1927–1983) *Lift to the Scaffold* 1957; *Carve Her Name with Pride* 1958; *Plein Soleil* 1960; *Le Feu Follet* 1963; *The Victors* 1963; *La Ronde*

1964; *Trois Chambres à Manhattan* 1965; *The Champagne Murders* 1966; *Lost Command* 1966; *The Road to Corinth* 1967; *La Femme Infidèle* 1968; *How Sweet It Is!* 1968; *The Swimming Pool* 1968; *Don Juan 73, or If Don Juan Were a Woman* 1973; *Without Warning* 1973; *The Marseille Contract* 1974; *To Kill a Rat* 1977; *Bloodline* 1979; *Sphinx* 1980; *La Balance* 1982
Ronstadt, Linda (1946–) *FM* 1977; *The Pirates of Penzance* 1983
Rooke, Irene (1878–1958) *Lady Windermere's Fan* 1916; *Hindle Wakes* 1927
Rooker, Michael (1955–) *Henry: Portrait of a Serial Killer* 1986; *Mississippi Burning* 1988; *Sea of Love* 1989; *Days of Thunder* 1990; *The Dark Half* 1991; *JFK* 1991; *Cliffhanger* 1993; *American Yakuza 2: Back to Back* 1996; *The Trigger Effect* 1996; *Bram Stoker's Shadowbuilder* 1997; *Liar* 1997; *Brown's Requiem* 1998; *The Replacement Killers* 1998; *The Bone Collector* 1999; *Here on Earth* 2000; *The 6th Day* 2000; *Replicant* 2001; *Undisputed* 2002
Rooney, Mickey (1920–) *The Beast of the City* 1932; *Broadway to Hollywood* 1933; *Manhattan Melodrama* 1934; *Upper World* 1934; *Ah, Wilderness!* 1935; *A Midsummer Night's Dream* 1935; *The Devil Is a Sissy* 1936; *Little Lord Fauntleroy* 1936; *Riffraff* 1936; *Captains Courageous* 1937; *A Family Affair* 1937; *Live, Love and Learn* 1937; *Slave Ship* 1937; *Thoroughbreds Don't Cry* 1937; *Boys Town* 1938; *Judge Hardy's Children* 1938; *Love Finds Andy Hardy* 1938; *Out West with the Hardys* 1938; *You're Only Young Once* 1938; *The Adventures of Huckleberry Finn* 1939; *Andy Hardy Gets Spring Fever* 1939; *Babes in Arms* 1939; *The Hardys Ride High* 1939; *Judge Hardy and Son* 1939; *Andy Hardy Meets Debutante* 1940; *Strike Up the Band* 1940; *Young Tom Edison* 1940; *Andy Hardy's Private Secretary* 1941; *Babes on Broadway* 1941; *Life Begins for Andy Hardy* 1941; *Men of Boys Town* 1941; *Andy Hardy's Double Life* 1942; *The Courtship of Andy Hardy* 1942; *A Yank at Eton* 1942; *Girl Crazy* 1943; *The Human Comedy* 1943; *Andy Hardy's Blonde Trouble* 1944; *National Velvet* 1944; *Love Laughs at Andy Hardy* 1946; *Killer McCoy* 1947; *Summer Holiday* 1948; *Words and Music* 1948; *The Big Wheel* 1949; *The Fireball* 1950; *Quicksand* 1950; *The Strip* 1951; *All Ashore* 1953; *Military Policeman* 1953; *The Atomic Kid* 1954; *The Bridges at Toko-Ri* 1954; *Drive a Crooked Road* 1954; *The Twinkle in God's Eye* 1955; *The Bold and the Brave* 1956; *Francis in the Haunted House* 1956; *Baby Face Nelson* 1957; *Operation Mad Ball* 1957; *Andy Hardy Comes Home* 1958; *A Nice Little Bank That Should Be Robbed* 1958; *The Big Operator* 1959; *The Last Mile* 1959; *The Private Lives of Adam and Eve* 1959; *Platinum High School* 1960; *Breakfast at Tiffany's* 1961; *King of the Roaring 20s – the Story of Arnold Rothstein* 1961; *Requiem for a Heavyweight* 1962; *It's a Mad Mad Mad Mad World* 1963; *Journey back to Oz* 1964; *The Secret Invasion* 1964; *How to Fill a Wild Bikini* 1965; *Ambush Bay* 1966; *Skidoo* 1968; *The Comic* 1969; *Eighty Steps to Jonah* 1969; *The Extraordinary Seaman* 1969; *The Cockeyed Cowboys of Calico County* 1970; *Evil Roy Slade* 1971; *Pulp* 1972; *Rachel's Man* 1975; *Find the Lady* 1976; *The Domino Principle* 1977; *Pete's Dragon* 1977; *The Magic of Lassie* 1978; *Arabian Adventure* 1979; *The Black Stallion* 1979; *Bill* 1981; *The Fox and the Hound* 1981; *Leave 'em Laughing* 1981; *The Care Bears Movie* 1985; *Lightning the White Stallion* 1986; *Erik the Viking* 1989; *My Heroes Have Always Been Cowboys* 1991; *Little Nemo: Adventures in Slumberland* 1992; *The Magic Voyage* 1992; *The Road Home* 1995; *Babe: Pig in the City* 1998; *The First of May* 2000
Rooney, Teddy (1950–) *Andy Hardy Comes Home* 1958; *It Happened to Jane* 1959
Roope, Fay (1893–1961) *Callaway Went Thataway* 1951; *The Clown* 1952; *All Ashore* 1953
Roos, Joanna (1901–1989) *Patterns* 1956; *Two Weeks in Another Town* 1962
Root, Amanda (1963–) *Persuasion* 1995; *Whatever Happened to Harold Smith?* 1999
Root, Stephen (1951–) *Monkey Shines* 1988; *Bed & Breakfast* 1992; *Bicentennial Man* 1999; *Jersey Girl* 2003; *Dodgeball: a True Underdog Story* 2004
Roper, Brian (1933–) *Just William's Luck* 1947; *William at the Circus* 1948; *The Secret Garden* 1949
Roquevert, Noël (1892–1973) *Fanfan la Tulipe* 1951; *Les Diaboliques* 1954; *Nana* 1955; *Une Parisienne* 1957; *Cartouche* 1961; *A Monkey in Winter* 1962
Rorke, Hayden (1910–1987) *The Law and the Lady* 1951; *Room for One More* 1952; *Confidentially Connie* 1953; *The Girl Next Door* 1953; *Project Moonbase* 1953; *South Sea Woman* 1953; *Lucky Me* 1954; *A Stranger in My Arms* 1959; *The Night Walker* 1964; *The Barefoot Executive* 1971
Rory, Rossana (1940–) *The Angel Wore Red* 1960; *Come September* 1961; *The Eclipse* 1962
Rosanova, Rosa (1869–1944) *Blood and Sand* 1922; *The Younger Generation* 1929
Rosario, Bert *Cold Justice* 1991; *A Million to Juan* 1994
Rosato, Tony (1954–) *Mystery Date* 1991; *Rent-a-Kid* 1992
Rosay, Françoise (1891–1974) *Le Grand Jeu* 1933; *Carnival in Flanders* 1935; *Un Carnet de Bal* 1937; *Drôle de Drame* 1937; *The Halfway House* 1943; *Johnny Frenchman* 1945; *Saraband for Dead Lovers* 1948; *September Affair* 1950; *The 13th Letter* 1950; *La Reine Margot* 1954; *That Lady* 1955; *Interlude* 1957; *Me and the Colonel* 1958; *The Sound and the Fury* 1959; *The Full Treatment* 1961; *Up from the Beach* 1965; *The Pedestrian* 1974
Roscoe, Alan (1888–1933) *Long Pants* 1927; *Flight* 1929
Rose, Clifford (1929–) *Marat/Sade* 1966; *The Girl* 1986
Rose, Gabrielle *Family Viewing* 1987; *Speaking Parts* 1989; *The Adjuster* 1991; *The Sweet Hereafter* 1997
Rose, George (1920–1988) *The Square Ring* 1953; *Barnacle Bill* 1957; *The Shiralee* 1957; *Cat and Mouse* 1958; *Jack the Ripper* 1958; *The Flesh and the Fiends* 1959; *A New Leaf* 1971; *The Hideaways* 1973; *The Pirates of Penzance* 1983; *Pound Puppies and the Legend of Big Paw* 1988
Rose, Jamie (1960–) *Heartbreakers* 1984; *Chopper Chicks in Zombietown* 1990
Rose, Jane (1913–1979) *Summertime* 1955; *The Monte Carlo Story* 1957; *Flipper* 1963
Rose Marie (1925–) *Top Banana* 1953; *Dead Heat on a Merry-Go-Round* 1966
Rose, Reva (1940–) *Bunny O'Hare* 1971; *The Nine Lives of Fritz the Cat* 1974
Rose, Veronica (1911–1968) *A Cuckoo in the Nest* 1933; *Fighting Stock* 1935; *For Valour* 1937
Rosenbaum, Michael (1972–) *Urban Legend* 1998; *Sorority Boys* 2002
Rosenberg, Alan (1950–) *The Wanderers* 1979; *Happy Birthday, Gemini* 1980; *Promise* 1986; *White of the Eye* 1986; *Impulse* 1990; *The Boys* 1991
Rosenberg, Arthur *Cutter's Way* 1981; *Second Thoughts* 1982
Rosenbloom, Maxie (1903–1976) *Nothing Sacred* 1937; *Louisiana Purchase* 1941; *The Boogie Man Will Get You* 1942; *To the Shores of Tripoli* 1942; *Abbott and Costello Meet the Keystone Cops* 1955; *Hollywood or Bust* 1956
Roshan, Hrithik (1974–) *Fiza* 2000; *Kabhi Khushi Kabhie Gham...* 2001; *Yaadein* 2001; *Mujhse Dosti Karoge!* 2002; *Na Tum Jaano Na Hum* 2002; *Armaan* 2003; *Koi... Mil Gaya* 2003; *Main Prem Ki Diwani Hoon* 2003; *Lakshya* 2004
Rosing, Bodil (1878–1942) *Sunrise* 1927; *The Big Noise* 1928; *Eternal Love* 1929
Rosmer, Milton (1881–1971) *Lady Windermere's Fan* 1916; *The Phantom Light* 1934; *South Riding* 1938; *Goodbye, Mr Chips* 1939; *Return to Yesterday* 1940
Ross, Annie (1930–) *Alfie Darling* 1975; *Superman III* 1983; *Witchcraft* 1989; *Basket Case 2* 1990; *Basket Case 3: the Progeny* 1992; *Short Cuts* 1993
Ross, Anthony (1909–1955) *Kiss of Death* 1947; *The Window* 1949; *The Gunfighter* 1950; *Perfect Strangers* 1950; *On Dangerous Ground* 1951; *The Country Girl* 1954
Ross, Beverly *SOS Titanic* 1979; *Broken English* 1981
Ross, Charlotte (1968–) *Foreign Student* 1994; *Fall into Darkness* 1996
Ross, Chelcie (1942–) *The Package* 1989; *The Last Boy Scout* 1991; *Amos & Andrew* 1993; *Chain Reaction* 1996; *A Simple Plan* 1998
Ross, Diana (1944–) *Lady Sings the Blues* 1972; *Mahogany* 1975; *The Wiz* 1978; *Double Platinum* 1999
Ross, Hector (1914–1980) *Deadly Nightshade* 1953; *The Steel Key* 1953
Ross, Hugh *Zero Effect* 1997; *Before You Go* 2002
Ross, Joe E (1914–1982) *Teaserama* 1955; *Maracaibo* 1958; *All Hands on Deck* 1961
Ross, Katharine (1942–) *Mister Buddwing* 1965; *Shenandoah* 1965; *The Singing Nun* 1966; *Games* 1967; *The Graduate* 1967; *Butch Cassidy and the Sundance Kid* 1969; *Hellfighters* 1969; *Tell Them Willie Boy Is Here* 1969; *Fools* 1970; *Get to Know Your Rabbit* 1972; *They Only Kill Their Masters* 1972; *The Stepford Wives* 1975; *Voyage of the Damned* 1976; *The Betsy* 1978; *The Legacy* 1978; *The Swarm* 1978; *The Final Countdown* 1980; *The Man with the Deadly Lens* 1982; *A Row of Crows* 1991; *Donnie Darko* 2001
Ross, Lee *Buddy's Song* 1990; *Secrets & Lies* 1995; *Hard Men* 1996; *The Island on Bird Street* 1997; *Metroland* 1997; *Vigo: Passion for Life* 1997; *Dreaming of Joseph Lees* 1998
Ross, Marion (1928–) *The Glenn Miller Story* 1953; *The Proud and Profane* 1956; *Lizzie* 1957; *Grand Theft Auto* 1977; *Danielle Steel's A Perfect Stranger* 1994; *The Evening Star* 1996; *About Sarah* 1998
Ross, Matt *Ed's Next Move* 1996; *Just Visiting* 2001
Ross, Shirley (1913–1975) *The Big Broadcast of 1937* 1936; *San Francisco* 1936; *The Big Broadcast of 1938* 1937; *Waikiki Wedding* 1937; *Paris Honeymoon* 1939; *Some Like It Hot* 1939
Ross, Ted (1934–2002) *The Wiz* 1978; *Arthur* 1981
Ross, Terry Ann *The Three Faces of Eve* 1957; *Cry Terror* 1958
Rossellini, Isabella (1952–) *A Matter of Time* 1976; *White Nights* 1985; *Blue Velvet* 1986; *Red Riding Hood* 1987; *Siesta* 1987; *Tough Guys Don't Dance* 1987; *Zelly and Me* 1988; *Cousins* 1989; *Wild at Heart* 1990; *Death Becomes Her* 1992; *Fearless* 1993; *The Innocent* 1993; *Immortal Beloved* 1994; *Wyatt Earp* 1994; *Big Night* 1996; *Crime of the Century* 1996; *The Funeral* 1996; *Left Luggage* 1997; *The Odyssey* 1997; *The Impostors* 1998; *Don Quixote* 2000; *Empire* 2002; *Roger Dodger* 2002; *The Saddest Music in the World* 2003
Rossi, George *Comfort and Joy* 1984; *I Bought a Vampire Motorcycle* 1989
Rossi, Leo (1959–) *Heart like a Wheel* 1983; *The Accused* 1988; *Hit List* 1988; *Relentless* 1989; *Too Much Sun* 1990; *Relentless 2: Dead On* 1991; *Good Cop, Bad Cop* 1993
Rossi-Drago, Eleonora (1925–) *Le Amiche* 1955; *Love at Twenty* 1962; *Let's Talk About Women* 1964
Rossi Stuart, Giacomo *aka* **Rossi-Stuart, Giacomo** (1931–) *Kidnapped to Mystery Island* 1964; *The Last Man on Earth* 1964; *Hornet's Nest* 1970
Rossi Stuart, Kim (1969–) *Beyond the Clouds* 1995; *The Keys to the House* 2004
Rossington, Norman (1928–1999) *Saturday Night and Sunday Morning* 1960; *Go to Blazes* 1961; *Nurse on Wheels* 1963; *The Comedy Man* 1964; *A Hard Day's Night* 1964; *Tobruk* 1966; *Double Trouble* 1967; *Two Gentlemen Sharing* 1969; *The Adventures of Gerard* 1970; *Simon, Simon* 1970; *Man in the Wilderness* 1971; *Death Line* 1972; *Go for a Take* 1972; *Digby, the Biggest Dog in the World* 1973
Rossiter, Leonard (1926–1984) *Billy Liar* 1963; *A Jolly Bad Fellow* 1964; *King Rat* 1965; *The Witches* 1966; *The Whisperers* 1967; *Deadfall* 1968; *Diamonds for Breakfast* 1968; *Oliver!* 1968; *Otley* 1968; *2001: a Space Odyssey* 1968; *Luther* 1974; *Barry Lyndon* 1975; *The Pink Panther Strikes Again* 1976; *Rising Damp* 1980; *Britannia Hospital* 1982; *Water* 1985
Rossitto, Angelo (1908–1991) *Scared to Death* 1947; *Mad Max beyond Thunderdome* 1985
Rossovich, Rick (1957–) *The Lords of Discipline* 1983; *The Terminator* 1984; *Let's Get Harry* 1986; *Top Gun* 1986; *Roxanne* 1987; *Spellbinder* 1988; *Paint It Black* 1989; *Navy SEALS* 1990
Rossum, Emmy (1986–) *Mystic River* 2003; *The Day after Tomorrow* 2004; *The Phantom of the Opera* 2004
Rostill, John (1942–1973) *Wonderful Life* 1964; *Finders Keepers* 1966
Roswell, Maggie *Midnight Madness* 1980; *Fire and Ice* 1983; *Lost in America* 1985
Roth, Andrea *Crossworlds* 1996; *Highwaymen* 2003
Roth, Cecilia (1958–) *Pepi, Luci, Bom...* 1980; *Labyrinth of Passion* 1982; *The Stranger* 1987; *A Place in the World* 1992; *All about My Mother* 1999; *Second Skin* 2000
Roth, Gene *aka* **Stutenroth, Gene** (1903–1976) *A Game of Death* 1945; *Earth vs the Spider* 1958; *She Demons* 1958; *Attack of the Giant Leeches* 1960
Roth, Lillian (1910–1980) *The Love Parade* 1929; *Animal Crackers* 1930; *Madam Satan* 1930; *Paramount on Parade* 1930; *Ladies They Talk About* 1933
Roth, Sandy (1891–1943) *The Beast of the City* 1932; *Hell's Highway* 1932
Roth, Tim (1961–) *The Hit* 1984; *Agatha Christie's Murder with Mirrors* 1985; *A World Apart* 1987; *To Kill a Priest* 1988; *The Cook, the Thief, His Wife and Her Lover* 1989; *Rosencrantz and Guildenstern Are Dead* 1990; *Vincent and Theo* 1990; *Backsliding* 1991; *Jumpin' at the Boneyard* 1991; *Reservoir Dogs* 1991; *Bodies, Rest and Motion* 1993; *Captives* 1994; *Little Odessa* 1994; *Pulp Fiction* 1994; *Four Rooms* 1995; *Rob Roy* 1995; *Everyone Says I Love You* 1996; *Gridlock'd* 1996; *No Way Home* 1996; *Hoodlum* 1997; *Liar* 1997; *The Legend of 1900* 1999; *The Million Dollar Hotel* 1999; *Vatel* 2000; *Invincible* 2001; *The Musketeer* 2001; *Planet of the Apes* 2001; *To Kill a King* 2003; *The Beautiful Country* 2004; *Silver City* 2004
Rotha, Wanda (1910–1982) *Saadia* 1953; *The Magnificent Showman* 1964
Rothman, John (1949–) *Stardust Memories* 1980; *The Boost* 1988; *Copycat* 1995; *Say It Isn't So* 2001
Rothrock, Cynthia (1957–) *China O'Brien* 1988; *Angel of Fury* 1991
Rotondo, Paolo *The Ugly* 1996; *Stickmen* 2000
Rouffe, Alida (1874–1949) *Marius* 1931; *Fanny* 1932
Roulien, Raul (1905–2000) *Delicious* 1931; *Flying down to Rio* 1933; *The World Moves On* 1934
Rounds, David (1930–1983) *Child's Play* 1972; *So Fine* 1981
Roundtree, Richard (1942–) *Shaft* 1971; *Embassy* 1972; *Shaft's Big Score!* 1972; *Shaft in Africa* 1973; *Earthquake* 1974; *Diamonds* 1975; *Man Friday* 1975; *Escape to Athena* 1979; *A Game for Vultures* 1979; *An Eye for an Eye* 1981; *Q – the Winged Serpent* 1982; *Young Warriors* 1983; *City Heat* 1984; *Hell Camp* 1986; *Jocks* 1986; *Maniac Cop* 1988; *Party Line* 1988; *Bad Jim* 1989; *Crack House* 1989; *Night Visitor* 1989; *A Time to Die* 1991; *Amityville: a New Generation* 1993; *Body of Influence* 1993; *Se7en* 1995; *Theodore Rex* 1995; *Original Gangstas* 1996; *George of the Jungle* 1997; *Steel* 1997; *Shaft* 2000; *Antitrust* 2001; *Corky Romano* 2001; *Boat Trip* 2002
Rounseville, Robert (1914–1974) *The Tales of Hoffmann* 1951; *Carousel* 1956
Rourke, Mickey (1953–) *1941* 1979; *Fade to Black* 1980; *Heaven's Gate* 1980; *Body Heat* 1981; *Diner* 1982; *Eureka* 1982; *Rumble Fish* 1983; *The Pope of Greenwich Village* 1984; *Nine ½ Weeks* 1985; *Year of the Dragon* 1985; *Angel Heart* 1987; *Barfly* 1987; *A Prayer for the Dying* 1987; *Homeboy* 1988
Rourke, Mickey (1953–) *Johnny Handsome* 1989; *Desperate Hours* 1990; *Wild Orchid* 1990; *Harley Davidson and the Marlboro Man* 1991; *White Sands* 1992; *The Last Outlaw* 1993; *FTW* 1994; *Fall Time* 1994; *Bullet* 1995; *Exit in Red* 1996; *Another 9½ Weeks* 1997; *Double Team* 1997; *John Grisham's The Rainmaker* 1997; *Point Blank* 1997; *Buffalo '66* 1998; *Thicker than Blood* 1998; *Thursday* 1998; *Animal Factory* 2000; *Get Carter* 2000; *The Pledge* 2000; *They Crawl* 2001; *Spun* 2002; *Once upon a Time in Mexico* 2003; *Man on Fire* 2004; *Sin City* 2005
Rouse, Graham (1934–) *Ride a Wild Pony* 1976; *Weekend of Shadows* 1978
Roussel, Myriem (1962–) *First Name: Carmen* 1983; *Je Vous Salue, Marie* 1984
Roussel, Nathalie *Le Château de Ma Mère* 1990; *La Gloire de Mon Père* 1990
Roussillon, Jean-Paul (1831–) *The Girl from Paris* 2001; *Kings & Queen* 2004
Routledge, Patricia (1929–) *Pretty Polly* 1967; *To Sir, with Love* 1967; *The Bliss of Mrs Blossom* 1968; *Don't Raise the Bridge, Lower the River* 1968; *30 Is a Dangerous Age, Cynthia* 1968; *If It's Tuesday, This Must Be Belgium* 1969
Rouvel, Catherine (1939–) *Lunch on the Grass* 1959; *Borsalino* 1970; *Borsalino and Co* 1974; *The Marseille Contract* 1974; *Black and White in Color* 1976
Rouverol, Jean *It's a Gift* 1934; *The Law West of Tombstone* 1938
Rovena, Marcella (1908–1998) *Friends for Life* 1955; *White Nights* 1957
Rovère, Liliane *Voyages* 1999; *The Captive* 2000; *Harry, He's Here to Help* 2000

Rowan, Diana *Beyond Reasonable Doubt* 1980; *Battletruck* 1982
Rowan, Kelly (1967–) *The Gate* 1987; *Assassins* 1995; *Candyman: Farewell to the Flesh* 1995; *One Eight Seven* 1997
Rowe, Brad (1970–) *Billy's Hollywood Screen Kiss* 1998; *Body Shots* 1999; *Purgatory* 1999; *Web of Lies* 1999
Rowe, Greg (1964–) *Storm Boy* 1976; *Dead Man's Float* 1980
Rowe, Nicholas (1966–) *Young Sherlock Holmes* 1985; *Lock, Stock and Two Smoking Barrels* 1998
Rowell, Victoria (1960–) *Leonard, Part 6* 1987; *Full Eclipse* 1993; *Dumb and Dumber* 1994; *Barb Wire* 1995
Rowland, Henry (1913–1984) *Return to Treasure Island* 1954; *Supervixens* 1975
Rowlands, Gena (1934–) *The High Cost of Loving* 1958; *A Child Is Waiting* 1962; *Lonely Are the Brave* 1962; *The Spiral Road* 1962; *Tony Rome* 1967; *Faces* 1968; *Minnie and Moskowitz* 1971; *A Woman under the Influence* 1974; *Two-Minute Warning* 1976; *Opening Night* 1977; *The Brink's Job* 1978; *Gloria* 1980; *Tempest* 1982; *Love Streams* 1984; *An Early Frost* 1985; *The Betty Ford Story* 1987; *Light of Day* 1987; *Another Woman* 1988; *Once Around* 1991; *Crazy in Love* 1992; *Night on Earth* 1992; *The Neon Bible* 1995; *Something to Talk About* 1995; *Unhook the Stars* 1996; *She's So Lovely* 1997; *Grace and Glorie* 1998; *Hope Floats* 1998; *The Mighty* 1998; *Paulie* 1998; *Playing by Heart* 1998; *The Color of Love: Jacey's Story* 2000; *Hysterical Blindness* 2002; *The Notebook* 2003; *Taking Lives* 2004; *The Skeleton Key* 2005
Rowlands, Lady (1904–1999) *Minnie and Moskowitz* 1971; *A Woman under the Influence* 1974
Rowlands, Patsy (1934–2005) *Carry On Again Doctor* 1969; *Carry On Loving* 1970; *Carry On at Your Convenience* 1971; *Carry On Abroad* 1972; *Carry On Matron* 1972; *Carry On Girls* 1973
Rowley, Peter *Savage Islands* 1983; *Footrot Flats: the Dog's Tale* 1986
Roxburgh, Richard (1962–) *Children of the Revolution* 1996; *Doing Time for Patsy Cline* 1997; *Oscar and Lucinda* 1997; *Thank God He Met Lizzie* 1997; *The Last September* 1999; *Mission: Impossible 2* 1999; *Passion* 1999; *Moulin Rouge!* 2001; *The One and Only* 2001; *Van Helsing* 2004
Roy, Nirupa (1931–2004) *Do Bigha Zameen* 1953; *Munimji* 1955
Royal, Allan *Title Shot* 1979; *Visitors of the Night* 1995
Royce, Lionel (1886–1946) *Four Sons* 1940; *Son of Monte Cristo* 1940; *My Favorite Blonde* 1942
Roye, Phillip *The Sergeant* 1968; *Black Caesar* 1973
Royer, Régis *La Lectrice* 1988; *Lautrec* 1998
Royle, Selena (1904–1983) *The Fighting Sullivans* 1944; *Mrs Parkington* 1944; *This Man's Navy* 1945; *Courage of Lassie* 1946; *The Green Years* 1946; *You Were Meant for Me* 1948; *The Heiress* 1949; *My Dream Is Yours* 1949; *The Big Hangover* 1950; *Branded* 1950; *The Damned Don't Cry* 1950; *Come Fill the Cup* 1951; *He Ran All the Way* 1951; *Robot Monster* 1953
Rozakis, Gregory (1943–1989) *America, America* 1963; *Abduction* 1975
Rubes, Jan (1920–) *The Amateur* 1981; *One Magic Christmas* 1985; *Witness* 1985; *Dead of Winter* 1987; *Something about Love* 1987; *The Kiss* 1988; *Courage Mountain* 1989; *The Amityville Curse* 1990; *Class Action* 1991; *On My Own* 1992; *D2: the Mighty Ducks* 1994; *Mesmer* 1994; *Roommates* 1995; *Never Too Late* 1996
Rubin, Andrew *aka* **Rubin, Andrew A** (1946–) *Casey's Shadow* 1978; *Police Academy* 1984
Rubin, Jennifer (1964–) *Blueberry Hill* 1988; *Permanent Record* 1988; *Delusion* 1991; *A Woman, Her Men and Her Futon* 1992; *Bitter Harvest* 1993; *The Crush* 1993; *Playmaker* 1994; *Screamers* 1995; *Loved* 1996; *Sanctimony* 2000
Rubin-Vega, Daphne (1969–) *Wild Things* 1998; *Flawless* 1999
Rubinek, Saul (1949–) *Highpoint* 1979; *Nothing Personal* 1980; *Agency* 1981; *Ticket to Heaven* 1981; *Against All Odds* 1984; *Sweet Liberty* 1986; *Wall Street* 1987; *Obsessed* 1989; *The Bonfire of the Vanities* 1990; *Man Trouble* 1992; *Unforgiven* 1992; *And the Band Played On* 1993; *True Romance* 1993; *Death Wish V: the Face of Death* 1994; *Getting Even with Dad* 1994; *I Love Trouble* 1994; *Memory Run* 1995; *Open Season* 1995; *Rainbow* 1995; *Bad Manners* 1998; *36 Hours to Die* 1999; *The Contender* 2000; *The Family Man* 2000; *Laughter on the 23rd Floor* 2000; *Triggermen* 2002; *Baadasssss!* 2003
Rubini, Giulia (1935–) *Goliath and the Barbarians* 1959; *Gordon the Black Pirate* 1961; *The Magnificent Rebel* 1961; *Kidnapped to Mystery Island* 1964; *Ringo and His Golden Pistol* 1966
Rubini, Sergio (1959–) *Intervista* 1987; *A Pure Formality* 1994; *Nirvana* 1996; *Shooting the Moon* 1998; *The Passion of the Christ* 2004
Rubinoff, David (1897–1986) *Thanks a Million* 1935; *You Can't Have Everything* 1937
Rubinstein, Artur (1887–1982) *Follow the Boys* 1944; *Night Song* 1947
Rubinstein, John (1946–) *Zachariah* 1970; *The Defiant* 1972; *The Car* 1977; *The Boys from Brazil* 1978; *Skokie* 1981; *Someone to Watch over Me* 1987; *Still Crazy like a Fox* 1987; *Norma Jean & Marilyn* 1996
Rubinstein, Zelda (1936–) *Poltergeist* 1982; *Anguish* 1986; *Poltergeist II: the Other Side* 1986; *Poltergeist III* 1988; *Teen Witch* 1989
Ruby, Thelma (1925–) *Where There's a Will* 1955; *Invasion Quartet* 1961
Ruck, Alan (1960–) *Ferris Bueller's Day Off* 1986; *Three for the Road* 1987; *Three Fugitives* 1989; *Young Guns II* 1990; *Speed* 1994; *Twister* 1996; *Everything Put Together* 2000
Rudd, Paul (1969–) *Clueless* 1995; *Halloween 6: the Curse of Michael Myers* 1995; *William Shakespeare's Romeo + Juliet* 1996; *Overnight Delivery* 1997; *A Secret Sin* 1997; *The Object of My Affection* 1998; *The Cider House Rules* 1999; *200 Cigarettes* 1999; *The Shape of Things* 2003; *Anchorman: the Legend of Ron Burgundy* 2004
Rudley, Herbert (1911–) *The Seventh Cross* 1944; *Rhapsody in Blue* 1945; *A Walk in the Sun* 1945; *The Black Sleep* 1956; *Raw Edge* 1956; *Beloved Infidel* 1959; *The Jayhawkers* 1959
Rudolph, Lars (1966–) *The Inheritors* 1997; *The Princess & the Warrior* 2000; *Werckmeister Harmonies* 2000
Rudoy, Joshua (1975–) *Bigfoot and the Hendersons* 1987; *Flatliners* 1990
Ruehl, Mercedes (1948–) *The Warriors* 1979; *84 Charing Cross Road* 1986; *The Secret of My Success* 1987; *Big* 1988; *Married to the Mob* 1988; *Slaves of New York* 1989; *Crazy People* 1990; *Another You* 1991; *The Fisher King* 1991; *Last Action Hero* 1993; *Lost in Yonkers* 1993; *Indictment: the McMartin Trial* 1995; *Roseanna's Grave* 1996; *Subway Stories: Tales from the Underground* 1997; *Gia* 1998; *The Minus Man* 1999; *Spooky House* 1999; *What's Cooking?* 2000
Ruffalo, Mark (1967–) *The Last Big Thing* 1996; *Safe Men* 1998; *You Can Count on Me* 1999; *Committed* 2000; *The Last Castle* 2001; *Windtalkers* 2001; *XX/XY* 2001; *My Life without Me* 2002; *Eternal Sunshine of the Spotless Mind* 2003; *In the Cut* 2003; *View from the Top* 2003; *We Don't Live Here Anymore* 2003; *Collateral* 2004; *13 Going on 30* 2004
Rufus (1942–) *Jonah Who Will Be 25 in the Year 2000* 1976; *The Police War* 1979; *Delicatessen* 1990; *Metroland* 1997; *Train of Life* 1999; *Amélie* 2001
Ruggles, Charles *aka* **Ruggles, Charlie** (1886–1970) *Charley's Aunt* 1930; *Her Wedding Night* 1930; *Honor among Lovers* 1931; *The Smiling Lieutenant* 1931; *If I Had a Million* 1932; *Love Me Tonight* 1932; *Madame Butterfly* 1932; *One Hour with You* 1932; *This Is the Night* 1932; *This Reckless Age* 1932; *Trouble in Paradise* 1932; *Alice in Wonderland* 1933; *Melody Cruise* 1933; *Murders in the Zoo* 1933; *Six of a Kind* 1934; *Ruggles of Red Gap* 1935; *Anything Goes* 1936; *Bringing Up Baby* 1938; *Balalaika* 1939; *Invitation to Happiness* 1939; *The Invisible Woman* 1940; *Maryland* 1940; *No Time for Comedy* 1940; *Friendly Enemies* 1942; *The Doughgirls* 1944; *Bedside Manner* 1945; *Incendiary Blonde* 1945; *My Brother Talks to Horses* 1946; *A Stolen Life* 1946; *It Happened on Fifth Avenue* 1947; *Ramrod* 1947; *Give My Regards to Broadway* 1948; *Look for the Silver Lining* 1949; *The Lovable Cheat* 1949; *All in a Night's Work* 1960; *The Parent Trap* 1961; *The Pleasure of His Company* 1961; *Son of Flubber* 1962; *Papa's Delicate Condition* 1963; *I'd Rather Be Rich* 1964; *Follow Me, Boys!* 1966; *The Ugly Dachshund* 1966
Ruginis, Vyto *Clean Slate* 1994; *Last Gasp* 1995
Ruick, Barbara (1930–1974) *Apache War Smoke* 1952; *The Affairs of Dobie Gillis* 1953; *Carousel* 1956
Rule, Janice (1931–2003) *Goodbye, My Fancy* 1951; *Battle Shock* 1956; *Gun for a Coward* 1957; *The Subterraneans* 1960; *Invitation to a Gunfighter* 1964; *Alvarez Kelly* 1966; *The Chase* 1966; *The Ambushers* 1967; *Welcome to Hard Times* 1967; *The Swimmer* 1968; *Doctors' Wives* 1970; *Gumshoe* 1971; *Kid Blue* 1971; *3 Women* 1977; *American Flyers* 1985
Ruman, Sig *aka* **Rumann, Sig** *aka* **Rumann, Siegfried** *aka* **Rumann, Siegfried "Sig"** (1884–1967) *Marie Galante* 1934; *The World Moves On* 1934; *The Farmer Takes a Wife* 1935; *A Night at the Opera* 1935; *The Wedding Night* 1935; *Heidi* 1937; *Lancer Spy* 1937; *Nothing Sacred* 1937; *Thank You, Mr Moto* 1937; *Think Fast, Mr Moto* 1937; *The Saint in New York* 1938; *Suez* 1938; *Never Say Die* 1939; *Ninotchka* 1939; *Only Angels Have Wings* 1939; *Comrade X* 1940; *Dr Ehrlich's Magic Bullet* 1940; *I Was an Adventuress* 1940; *Victory* 1940; *Shining Victory* 1941; *The Wagons Roll at Night* 1941; *Berlin Correspondent* 1942; *China Girl* 1942; *Desperate Journey* 1942; *To Be or Not to Be* 1942; *Sweet Rosie O'Grady* 1943; *Tarzan Triumphs* 1943; *Summer Storm* 1944; *A Royal Scandal* 1945; *A Night in Casablanca* 1946; *The Emperor Waltz* 1948; *Give My Regards to Broadway* 1948; *On the Riviera* 1951; *O Henry's Full House* 1952; *The World in His Arms* 1952; *Houdini* 1953; *Stalag 17* 1953; *Three Ring Circus* 1954; *White Christmas* 1954; *The Errand Boy* 1961
Runacre, Jenny (1943–) *Husbands* 1970; *The Final Programme* 1973; *The Passenger* 1975; *Jubilee* 1978; *Hussy* 1979
Runyon, Jennifer (1960–) *18 Again!* 1988; *The In Crowd* 1988; *Carnosaur* 1993
RuPaul *aka* **Charles, RuPaul** (1960–) *But I'm a Cheerleader* 1999; *The Eyes of Tammy Faye* 2000
Rupé, Katja *Germany in Autumn* 1978; *Les Favoris de la Lune* 1984
Rupp, Sieghardt *A Fistful of Dollars* 1964; *Dead Pigeon on Beethoven Street* 1972
Rush, Barbara (1927–) *The First Legion* 1951; *When Worlds Collide* 1951; *It Came from Outer Space* 1953; *Prince of Pirates* 1953; *The Black Shield of Falworth* 1954; *Magnificent Obsession* 1954; *Taza, Son of Cochise* 1954; *Captain Lightfoot* 1955; *Kiss of Fire* 1955; *Bigger than Life* 1956; *No Down Payment* 1957; *Oh, Men! Oh, Women!* 1957; *Harry Black and the Tiger* 1958; *The Young Lions* 1958; *The Young Philadelphians* 1959; *The Bramble Bush* 1960; *Strangers When We Meet* 1960; *Come Blow Your Horn* 1963; *Robin and the 7 Hoods* 1964; *Hombre* 1967; *The Man* 1972; *Superdad* 1974; *Can't Stop the Music* 1980; *Summer Lovers* 1982
Rush, Deborah *A Night in Heaven* 1983; *Big Business* 1988; *Parents* 1988; *Family Business* 1989; *My Blue Heaven* 1990; *Three to Tango* 1999
Rush, Geoffrey (1951–) *Dad and Dave: on Our Selection* 1995; *Children of the Revolution* 1996; *Shine* 1996; *Les Misérables* 1997; *Elizabeth* 1998; *Shakespeare in Love* 1998; *House on Haunted Hill* 1999; *The Magic Pudding* 2000; *Quills* 2000; *The Tailor of Panama* 2000; *Lantana* 2001; *The Banger Sisters* 2002; *Frida* 2002; *Finding Nemo* 2003; *Intolerable Cruelty* 2003; *The Life and Death of Peter Sellers* 2003; *Ned Kelly* 2003; *Pirates of the Caribbean: the Curse of the Black Pearl* 2003; *Swimming Upstream* 2003
Rushbrook, Claire (1970–) *Secrets & Lies* 1995; *Under the Skin* 1997; *Shiner* 2000; *Doctor Sleep* 2002
Rushton, Jared (1974–) *Overboard* 1987; *Big* 1988; *Lady in White* 1988; *Honey, I Shrunk the Kids* 1989; *Pet Sematary II* 1992
Rushton, William (1937–1996) *The Best House in London* 1968; *The Bliss of Mrs Blossom* 1968; *Flight of the Doves* 1971; *Keep It Up Downstairs* 1976; *Adventures of a Private Eye* 1977; *Consuming Passions* 1988
Rusler, Robert (1965–) *A Nightmare on Elm Street 2: Freddy's Revenge* 1985; *Weird Science* 1985; *Thrashin'* 1986; *Vamp* 1986; *Shag* 1988; *Sometimes They Come Back* 1991
Ruspoli, Esmeralda *L'Avventura* 1960; *A Place for Lovers* 1968
Russ, William (1950–) *Beer* 1985; *Second Serve* 1986; *Wanted Dead or Alive* 1986; *Dead of Winter* 1987; *The Unholy* 1988; *Crazy from the Heart* 1991; *Pastime* 1991; *Traces of Red* 1992; *Aspen Extreme* 1993; *Breach of Trust* 1999
Russek, Jorge (1932–1998) *The Return of a Man Called Horse* 1976; *Miracles* 1985; *Pure Luck* 1991
Russel, Tony (1925–) *The Spartan Gladiators* 1964; *The Wild, Wild Planet* 1965; *The Hard Ride* 1971
Russell, Andy (1919–1992) *Make Mine Music* 1946; *Copacabana* 1947
Russell, Betsy (1964–) *Private School* 1983; *Avenging Angel* 1985; *Tomboy* 1985
Russell, Bing (1928–) *Cattle Empire* 1958; *Suicide Battalion* 1958; *Elvis – the Movie* 1979
Russell, Bryan *Safe at Home* 1962; *A Ticklish Affair* 1963; *Emil and the Detectives* 1964; *The Adventures of Bullwhip Griffin* 1967
Russell, Catherine (1966–) *Soft Top, Hard Shoulder* 1992; *Clockwork Mice* 1994
Russell, Charles (1918–1985) *The Late George Apley* 1947; *Give My Regards to Broadway* 1948
Russell, Clive (1945–) *The Hawk* 1992; *Margaret's Museum* 1995; *Oscar and Lucinda* 1997; *Out of Depth* 1998; *Bodywork* 1999; *The Emperor's New Clothes* 2001; *Mr In-Between* 2001; *Ladies in Lavender* 2004; *Festival* 2005
Russell, Connie (1923–1990) *This Is My Love* 1954; *Nightmare* 1956
Russell, Craig (1948–1990) *Outrageous!* 1977; *Too Outrageous!* 1987
Russell, Elizabeth (1916–) *Cat People* 1942; *The Curse of the Cat People* 1944
Russell, Gail (1924–1961) *The Uninvited* 1944; *Salty O'Rourke* 1945; *The Unseen* 1945; *Angel and the Badman* 1947; *Calcutta* 1947; *Moonrise* 1948; *Night Has a Thousand Eyes* 1948; *Wake of the Red Witch* 1949; *The Lawless* 1950; *Air Cadet* 1951; *Seven Men from Now* 1956
Russell, Jane (1921–) *The Outlaw* 1943; *The Paleface* 1948; *Double Dynamite* 1951; *His Kind of Woman* 1951; *The Las Vegas Story* 1952; *Macao* 1952; *Son of Paleface* 1952; *Gentlemen Prefer Blondes* 1953; *The French Line* 1954; *Foxfire* 1955; *Gentlemen Marry Brunettes* 1955; *The Tall Men* 1955; *Underwater!* 1955; *Hot Blood* 1956; *The Revolt of Mamie Stover* 1956; *The Fuzzy Pink Nightgown* 1957; *Fate Is the Hunter* 1964; *Johnny Reno* 1966; *Waco* 1966; *Born Losers* 1967; *Darker than Amber* 1970
Russell, John (1921–1991) *Yellow Sky* 1948; *The Gal Who Took the West* 1949; *Slattery's Hurricane* 1949; *Undertow* 1949; *Frenchie* 1950; *Saddle Tramp* 1950; *Man in the Saddle* 1951; *Hoodlum Empire* 1952; *Fair Wind to Java* 1953; *The Sun Shines Bright* 1953; *Untamed Youth* 1957; *Fort Massacre* 1958; *Rio Bravo* 1959; *Yellowstone Kelly* 1959; *Apache Uprising* 1965; *Hostile Guns* 1967
Russell, Ken (1927–) *Valentino* 1977; *Salome's Last Dance* 1988; *The Russia House* 1990
Russell, Keri (1976–) *Honey, I Blew Up the Kid* 1992; *Eight Days a Week* 1996; *Dead Man's Curve* 1997; *Mad about Mambo* 1999; *We Were Soldiers* 2002
Russell, Kimberly *Ghost Dad* 1990; *Hangin' with the Homeboys* 1991
Russell, Kurt (1951–) *It Happened at the World's Fair* 1962; *Follow Me, Boys!* 1966; *The Horse in the Gray Flannel Suit* 1968; *The One and Only, Genuine, Original Family Band* 1968; *The Computer Wore Tennis Shoes* 1969; *Guns in the Heather* 1969; *The Barefoot Executive* 1971; *Dynamite Man from Glory Jail* 1971; *Now You See Him, Now You Don't* 1972; *Charley and the Angel* 1973; *Superdad* 1974; *The Strongest Man in the World* 1975; *Elvis – the Movie* 1979; *Used Cars* 1980; *Escape from New York* 1981; *The Fox and the Hound* 1981; *The Thing* 1982; *Silkwood* 1983; *Swing Shift* 1984; *The Mean Season* 1985; *The Best of Times* 1986; *Big Trouble in Little China* 1986; *Overboard* 1987; *Tequila Sunrise* 1988; *Winter People* 1988; *Tango & Cash* 1989; *Backdraft* 1991; *Captain Ron* 1992; *Unlawful Entry* 1992; *Tombstone* 1993; *Stargate* 1994; *Escape from LA* 1996; *Executive Decision* 1996; *Breakdown* 1997; *Soldier* 1998; *3000 Miles to Graceland* 2000; *Vanilla Sky* 2001; *Dark Blue* 2002; *Miracle* 2004
Russell, Lucy *Following* 1998; *The Lady & the Duke* 2001
Russell, Nipsey (1924–) *The Wiz* 1978; *Wildcats* 1986; *Car 54 Where Are You?* 1991

Russell, Rebel (1905–1978) *Emma's War* 1985; *Frauds* 1992

Russell, Robert *Bedazzled* 1967; *Witchfinder General* 1968

Russell, Rosalind (1908–1976) *Evelyn Prentice* 1934; *Forsaking All Others* 1934; *The Casino Murder Case* 1935; *China Seas* 1935; *Reckless* 1935; *Rendezvous* 1935; *Craig's Wife* 1936; *Trouble for Two* 1936; *Under Two Flags* 1936; *Live, Love and Learn* 1937; *Man-Proof* 1937; *Night Must Fall* 1937; *The Citadel* 1938; *Four's a Crowd* 1938; *Fast and Loose* 1939; *His Girl Friday* 1939; *The Women* 1939; *Hired Wife* 1940; *No Time for Comedy* 1940; *This Thing Called Love* 1940; *Design for Scandal* 1941; *The Feminine Touch* 1941; *They Met in Bombay* 1941; *My Sister Eileen* 1942; *Take a Letter, Darling* 1942; *Flight for Freedom* 1943; *What a Woman!* 1943; *Roughly Speaking* 1945; *Sister Kenny* 1946; *The Guilt of Janet Ames* 1947; *Mourning Becomes Electra* 1947; *The Velvet Touch* 1948; *Tell It to the Judge* 1949; *A Woman of Distinction* 1950; *Never Wave at a WAC* 1952; *The Girl Rush* 1955; *Picnic* 1955; *Auntie Mame* 1958; *A Majority of One* 1961; *Five Finger Exercise* 1962; *Gypsy* 1962; *The Trouble with Angels* 1966; *Oh Dad, Poor Dad, Mama's Hung You in the Closet and I'm Feelin' So Sad* 1967; *Rosie!* 1967; *Where Angels Go...Trouble Follows* 1968; *Mrs Pollifax – Spy* 1970

Russell, T E *Trespass* 1992; *Swimming with Sharks* 1994

Russell, Theresa (1957–) *The Last Tycoon* 1976; *Straight Time* 1978; *Bad Timing* 1980; *Eureka* 1982; *The Razor's Edge* 1984; *Insignificance* 1985; *Aria* 1987; *Black Widow* 1987; *Physical Evidence* 1988; *Track 29* 1988; *Impulse* 1990; *Kafka* 1991; *Whore* 1991; *Cold Heaven* 1992; *Being Human* 1994; *The Grotesque* 1995; *Young Connecticut Yankee in King Arthur's Court* 1995; *The Proposition* 1996; *Wild Things* 1998; *The Believer* 2001

Russell, William (1924–) *One Good Turn* 1954; *Above Us the Waves* 1955; *The Big Chance* 1957

Russo, Gianni *Lepke* 1975; *Laserblast* 1978

Russo, James (1953–) *Exposed* 1983; *Beverly Hills Cop* 1984; *Extremities* 1986; *China Girl* 1987; *The Blue Iguana* 1988; *We're No Angels* 1989; *A Kiss before Dying* 1991; *My Own Private Idaho* 1991; *Cold Heaven* 1992; *Dangerous Game* 1993; *Trauma* 1993; *Bad Girls* 1994; *The Set Up* 1995; *American Strays* 1996; *No Way Home* 1996; *Donnie Brasco* 1997; *Love to Kill* 1997; *The Postman* 1997; *Too Hard to Die* 1998; *The Ninth Gate* 1999; *Open Range* 2003

Russo, Rene (1954–) *Major League* 1989; *Mr Destiny* 1990; *One Good Cop* 1991; *Freejack* 1992; *Lethal Weapon 3* 1992; *In the Line of Fire* 1993; *Get Shorty* 1995; *Outbreak* 1995; *Ransom* 1996; *Tin Cup* 1996; *Buddy* 1997; *Lethal Weapon 4* 1998; *The Adventures of Rocky & Bullwinkle* 1999; *The Thomas Crown Affair* 1999; *Big Trouble* 2002; *Showtime* 2002

Rust, Richard (1938–) *The Legend of Tom Dooley* 1959; *Comanche Station* 1960; *Homicidal* 1961; *Underworld USA* 1961; *Walk on the Wild Side* 1962; *I Escaped from Devil's Island* 1973

Ruth, Babe *aka* **Ruth, George Herman "Babe"** (1895–1948) *Speedy* 1928; *The Pride of the Yankees* 1942

Rutherford, Ann (1917–) *Dramatic School* 1938; *Judge Hardy's Children* 1938; *Love Finds Andy Hardy* 1938; *Of Human Hearts* 1938; *Out West with the Hardys* 1938; *You're Only Young Once* 1938; *Andy Hardy Gets Spring Fever* 1939; *Dancing Co-Ed* 1939; *Four Girls in White* 1939; *The Hardys Ride High* 1939; *Judge Hardy and Son* 1939; *Andy Hardy Meets Debutante* 1940; *The Ghost Comes Home* 1940; *Pride and Prejudice* 1940; *Andy Hardy's Private Secretary* 1941; *Life Begins for Andy Hardy* 1941; *Whistling in the Dark* 1941; *Andy Hardy's Double Life* 1942; *The Courtship of Andy Hardy* 1942; *Orchestra Wives* 1942; *Whistling in Dixie* 1942; *Happy Land* 1943; *Whistling in Brooklyn* 1943; *The Bermuda Mystery* 1944; *Bedside Manner* 1945; *Two O'Clock Courage* 1945; *Murder in the Music Hall* 1946; *The Secret Life of Walter Mitty* 1947; *Adventures of Don Juan* 1948; *They Only Kill Their Masters* 1972

Rutherford, John (1893–1982) *Half Shot at Sunrise* 1930; *Whoopee!* 1930

Rutherford, Kelly (1968–) *I Love Trouble* 1994; *Danielle Steel's No Greater Love* 1996

Rutherford, Margaret (1892–1972) *Dusty Ermine* 1936; *The Demi-Paradise* 1943; *Yellow Canary* 1943; *English without Tears* 1944; *Blithe Spirit* 1945; *Meet Me at Dawn* 1946; *While the Sun Shines* 1946; *Miranda* 1947; *Passport to Pimlico* 1949; *The Happiest Days of Your Life* 1950; *The Magic Box* 1951; *Curtain Up* 1952; *The Importance of Being Earnest* 1952; *Miss Robin Hood* 1952; *Innocents in Paris* 1953; *Trouble in Store* 1953; *Mad about Men* 1954; *The Runaway Bus* 1954; *An Alligator Named Daisy* 1955; *Just My Luck* 1957; *The Smallest Show on Earth* 1957; *I'm All Right Jack* 1959; *Murder She Said* 1961; *On the Double* 1961; *The Mouse on the Moon* 1963; *Murder at the Gallop* 1963; *The VIPs* 1963; *Murder Ahoy* 1964; *Murder Most Foul* 1964; *The Alphabet Murders* 1966; *Chimes at Midnight* 1966; *Arabella* 1967; *A Countess from Hong Kong* 1967

Ruttan, Susan (1950–) *Do You Remember Love* 1985; *Jack Reed: Badge of Honor* 1993; *Jack Reed: a Search for Justice* 1994; *Jack Reed: One of Our Own* 1995; *Jack Reed: Death and Vengeance* 1996

Ruysdael, Basil (1888–1960) *Colorado Territory* 1949; *Come to the Stable* 1949; *Pinky* 1949; *Broken Arrow* 1950; *High Lonesome* 1950; *Boots Malone* 1951; *Half Angel* 1951; *Carrie* 1952; *The Shanghai Story* 1954; *Davy Crockett, King of the Wild Frontier* 1955; *Jubal* 1956; *These Wilder Years* 1956

Ryall, David (1935–) *Wilt* 1989; *Truly Madly Deeply* 1990; *Blackball* 2003

Ryan, Amanda *Elizabeth* 1998; *Britannic* 2000

Ryan, Edmon *aka* **Ryan, Edmond** (1905–1984) *Dark Eyes of London* 1939; *The Breaking Point* 1950; *Side Street* 1950; *Undercover Girl* 1950; *Go, Man, Go!* 1953; *Good Day for a Hanging* 1958; *Two for the Seesaw* 1962

Ryan, Eileen *At Close Range* 1985; *Winter People* 1988; *Anywhere but Here* 1999

Ryan, Ger *The Van* 1996; *interMission* 2003

Ryan, Irene (1902–1973) *Diary of a Chambermaid* 1946; *The Woman on the Beach* 1947; *Half Angel* 1951; *Blackbeard the Pirate* 1952

Ryan, James *Kill and Kill Again* 1981; *Rage to Kill* 1988; *Any Man's Death* 1990

Ryan, Jeri *aka* **Ryan, Jeri Lynn** (1968–) *Victim of Beauty* 1991; *Down with Love* 2003

Ryan, John P *aka* **Ryan, John** (1938–) *Cops and Robbers* 1973; *Dillinger* 1973; *Shamus* 1973; *It's Alive* 1974; *Futureworld* 1976; *It Lives Again* 1978; *The Postman Always Rings Twice* 1981; *The Escape Artist* 1982; *Breathless* 1983; *Runaway Train* 1985; *Avenging Force* 1986; *Death Wish 4: the Crackdown* 1987; *Three O'Clock High* 1987; *Class of 1999* 1990; *Delta Force 2* 1990; *Bound* 1996

Ryan, Kathleen (1922–1985) *Odd Man Out* 1946; *Captain Boycott* 1947; *Esther Waters* 1948; *Christopher Columbus* 1949; *Give Us This Day* 1949; *Prelude to Fame* 1950; *The Sound of Fury* 1950; *The Yellow Balloon* 1952; *Laxdale Hall* 1953; *Captain Lightfoot* 1955; *Jacqueline* 1956

Ryan, Madge (1919–1994) *Witness in the Dark* 1959; *Tiara Tahiti* 1962; *This Is My Street* 1963; *Kokoda Crescent* 1989

Ryan, Meg (1961–) *Rich and Famous* 1981; *Amityville III: the Demon* 1983; *Armed and Dangerous* 1986; *Top Gun* 1986; *Innerspace* 1987; *DOA* 1988; *The Presidio* 1988; *Promised Land* 1988; *When Harry Met Sally...* 1989; *Joe versus the Volcano* 1990; *The Doors* 1991; *Prelude to a Kiss* 1992; *Flesh and Bone* 1993; *Sleepless in Seattle* 1993; *IQ* 1994; *When a Man Loves a Woman* 1994; *French Kiss* 1995; *Restoration* 1995; *Courage under Fire* 1996; *Addicted to Love* 1997; *Anastasia* 1997; *City of Angels* 1998; *Hurlyburly* 1998; *You've Got Mail* 1998; *Hanging Up* 2000; *Proof of Life* 2000; *Kate & Leopold* 2002; *Against the Ropes* 2003; *In the Cut* 2003

Ryan, Mitchell *aka* **Ryan, Mitch** (1928–) *Monte Walsh* 1970; *Glory Boy* 1971; *The Hunting Party* 1971; *Electra Glide in Blue* 1973; *The Friends of Eddie Coyle* 1973; *High Plains Drifter* 1973; *Magnum Force* 1973; *A Reflection of Fear* 1973; *The Entertainer* 1975; *Lethal Weapon* 1987; *Winter People* 1988; *Blue Sky* 1991; *The Opposite Sex and How to Live with Them* 1993; *Halloween 6: the Curse of Michael Myers* 1995; *The Devil's Own* 1997; *Grosse Pointe Blank* 1997; *Liar Liar* 1997

Ryan, Natasha (1970–) *The Amityville Horror* 1979; *The Day Time Ended* 1980

Ryan, Peggy (1924–2004) *Miss Annie Rooney* 1942; *Private Buckaroo* 1942; *The Merry Monahans* 1944; *Patrick the Great* 1944; *Here Come the Co-Eds* 1945; *All Ashore* 1953

Ryan, R L *Class of Nuke 'em High* 1986; *Eat and Run* 1986

Ryan, Robert (1909–1973) *Behind the Rising Sun* 1943; *Bombardier* 1943; *The Iron Major* 1943; *The Sky's the Limit* 1943; *Tender Comrade* 1943; *Marine Raiders* 1944; *Crossfire* 1947; *Trail Street* 1947; *The Woman on the Beach* 1947; *Berlin Express* 1948; *The Boy with Green Hair* 1948; *Return of the Bad Men* 1948; *Act of Violence* 1949; *Caught* 1949; *The Set-Up* 1949; *The Woman on Pier 13* 1949; *Born to Be Bad* 1950; *Best of the Badmen* 1951; *Flying Leathernecks* 1951; *On Dangerous Ground* 1951; *The Racket* 1951; *Beware, My Lovely* 1952; *Clash by Night* 1952; *Horizons West* 1952; *City beneath the Sea* 1953; *Inferno* 1953; *The Naked Spur* 1953; *About Mrs Leslie* 1954; *Alaska Seas* 1954; *Her Twelve Men* 1954; *Bad Day at Black Rock* 1955; *Escape to Burma* 1955; *House of Bamboo* 1955; *The Tall Men* 1955; *Back from Eternity* 1956; *The Proud Ones* 1956; *Men in War* 1957; *God's Little Acre* 1958; *Lonelyhearts* 1958; *Day of the Outlaw* 1959; *Odds against Tomorrow* 1959; *Ice Palace* 1960; *The Canadians* 1961; *King of Kings* 1961; *Billy Budd* 1962; *The Longest Day* 1962; *The Crooked Road* 1964; *Battle of the Bulge* 1965; *The Dirty Game* 1965; *The Professionals* 1966; *The Busy Body* 1967; *The Dirty Dozen* 1967; *Hour of the Gun* 1967; *Anzio* 1968; *Custer of the West* 1968; *Captain Nemo and the Underwater City* 1969; *The Wild Bunch* 1969; *Lawman* 1971; *The Love Machine* 1971; *And Hope to Die* 1972; *Executive Action* 1973; *The Iceman Cometh* 1973; *The Lolly-Madonna War* 1973; *The Outfit* 1973

Ryan, Sheila (1921–1975) *The Gay Caballero* 1940; *Great Guns* 1941; *A-Haunting We Will Go* 1942; *Careful, Soft Shoulder* 1942; *Song of Texas* 1943; *Something for the Boys* 1944; *Getting Gertie's Garter* 1945; *Railroaded* 1947; *Mule Train* 1950; *On Top of Old Smoky* 1953

Ryan, Thomas Jay (1962–) *Henry Fool* 1997; *The Book of Life* 1998

Ryan, Tim (1899–1956) *Bedtime Story* 1942; *Reveille with Beverly* 1943; *Detour* 1945; *Force of Evil* 1948; *The Runestone* 1991

Rydall, Derek *Night Visitor* 1989; *Popcorn* 1991

Rydeberg, Georg (1907–1983) *Dollar* 1938; *A Woman's Face* 1938

Rydell, Christopher *aka* **Rydell, Chris** *On Golden Pond* 1981; *Gotcha!* 1985; *Blood and Sand* 1989; *How I Got Into College* 1989; *Side Out* 1990; *For the Boys* 1991; *By the Sword* 1992; *In the Deep Woods* 1992; *Flesh and Bone* 1993; *Trauma* 1993

Rydell, Mark (1934–) *Crime in the Streets* 1956; *The Long Goodbye* 1973; *Punchline* 1988; *Havana* 1990; *Hollywood Ending* 2002

Ryder, Alfred (1919–1995) *T-Men* 1947; *Invitation to a Gunfighter* 1964; *The Raiders* 1964

Ryder, Eddie (1923–1997) *The Country Girl* 1954; *Not with My Wife, You Don't!* 1966

Ryder, Winona (1971–) *Lucas* 1986; *Square Dance* 1987; *Beetle Juice* 1988; *1969* 1988; *Great Balls of Fire!* 1989; *Heathers* 1989; *Edward Scissorhands* 1990; *Mermaids* 1990; *Welcome Home, Roxy Carmichael* 1990; *Bram Stoker's Dracula* 1992; *Night on Earth* 1992; *The Age of Innocence* 1993; *The House of the Spirits* 1993; *Little Women* 1994; *Reality Bites* 1994; *Boys* 1995; *How to Make an American Quilt* 1995; *The Crucible* 1996; *Looking for Richard* 1996; *Alien: Resurrection* 1997; *Celebrity* 1998; *Girl, Interrupted* 1999; *Autumn in New York* 2000; *Lost Souls* 2000; *Mr Deeds* 2002; *S1MØNE* 2002; *The Heart Is Deceitful above All Things* 2004

Rye, Preben Lerdorff (1917–1995) *Day of Wrath* 1943; *Ordet* 1955

Rylance, Mark (1960–) *Prospero's Books* 1991; *Angels and Insects* 1995; *Institute Benjamenta, or This Dream People Call Human Life* 1995; *Intimacy* 2000

Ryon, Rex *You Talkin' to Me?* 1987; *Jack's Back* 1988; *The Man in the Iron Mask* 1997

Ryu, Chishu (1904–1993) *The Brothers and Sisters of the Toda Family* 1941; *There Was a Father* 1942; *Record of a Tenement Gentleman* 1947; *Hen in the Wind* 1948; *Late Spring* 1949; *Early Summer* 1951; *The Flavour of Green Tea over Rice* 1952; *Tokyo Story* 1953; *Early Spring* 1956; *Tokyo Twilight* 1957; *Floating Weeds* 1959; *Ohayo* 1959; *Late Autumn* 1960; *An Autumn Afternoon* 1962; *Akira Kurosawa's Dreams* 1990

S

S, Bruno *The Enigma of Kaspar Hauser* 1974; *Stroszek* 1977

Saad, Margit (1929–) *The Criminal* 1960; *The Rebel* 1960; *The Magnificent Two* 1967; *The Last Escape* 1970

Sabara, Daryl (1992–) *SPYkids* 2001; *SPYkids 2: the Island of Lost Dreams* 2002; *SPYkids 3-D: Game Over* 2003; *The Polar Express* 2004

Sabatier, William *Casque d'Or* 1952; *The Trap* 1975

Sabato, Antonio (1943–) *Grand Prix* 1966; *The Good Die First* 1967

Sabato Jr, Antonio (1972–) *The Big Hit* 1998; *High Voltage* 1998

Sabela, Simon *Gold* 1974; *E' Lollipop* 1975

Sabourin, Marcel (1934–) *The Hitman* 1991; *Lilies* 1996

Sabri, Hend *The Silences of the Palace* 1994; *La Saison des Hommes* 2000

Sabrina (1) (1933–) *Blue Murder at St Trinian's* 1957; *Satan in High Heels* 1962

Sabu (1924–1963) *Elephant Boy* 1937; *The Drum* 1938; *The Thief of Bagdad* 1940; *Arabian Nights* 1942; *Jungle Book* 1942; *White Savage* 1943; *Cobra Woman* 1944; *Black Narcissus* 1946; *The End of the River* 1947; *Rampage* 1963; *A Tiger Walks* 1964

Saburi, Shin (1909–1982) *The Brothers and Sisters of the Toda Family* 1941; *There Was a Father* 1942; *The Flavour of Green Tea over Rice* 1952; *Equinox Flower* 1958

Sachs, Andrew (1930–) *Are You Being Served?* 1977; *Asterix and the Big Fight* 1989; *Faust* 1994

Sachs, Leonard (1909–1990) *Men of Sherwood Forest* 1954; *Man from Tangier* 1957; *The Giant Behemoth* 1959; *The Siege of Sidney Street* 1960; *Pit of Darkness* 1961; *Taste of Fear* 1961

Sack, Graham (1981–) *A Pig's Tale* 1994; *Dunston Checks In* 1996

Sacks, Michael (1948–) *Slaughterhouse-Five* 1972; *The Sugarland Express* 1974; *The Private Files of J Edgar Hoover* 1977; *The Amityville Horror* 1979; *Hanover Street* 1979

Sada, Keiji (1926–1964) *Ohayo* 1959; *Late Autumn* 1960; *An Autumn Afternoon* 1962

Sadler, William *aka* **Sadler, Bill** (1950–) *Project X* 1987; *Hard to Kill* 1989; *Die Hard 2: Die Harder* 1990; *The Hot Spot* 1990; *Bill & Ted's Bogus Journey* 1991; *Rush* 1991; *Trespass* 1992; *Freaked* 1993; *Jack Reed: Badge of Honor* 1993; *Roadracers* 1994; *The Shawshank Redemption* 1994; *Tales from the Crypt: Demon Knight* 1995; *Solo* 1996; *Rocketman* 1997; *Disturbing Behaviour* 1998; *Stealth Fighter* 1999; *Witness Protection* 1999

Sadoyan, Isabelle *The Return of Martin Guerre* 1982; *The Eighth Day* 1996

Safrankova, Libuse (1953–) *Elementary School* 1991; *Kolya* 1996

Sage, Bill *aka* **Sage, William** *Simple Men* 1992; *Boys* 1995; *Flirt* 1995; *High Art* 1998; *Boiler Room* 2000; *Mysterious Skin* 2004

Sage, Willard (1922–1974) *It's a Dog's Life* 1955; *The Brass Legend* 1956; *Dirty Little Billy* 1972

Sägebrecht, Marianne (1945–) *Sugarbaby* 1985; *Bagdad Café* 1987; *Rosalie Goes Shopping* 1989; *The War of the Roses* 1989; *Martha and I* 1990; *Dust Devil* 1992; *Erotique* 1994; *All Men Are Mortal* 1995; *Left Luggage* 1997; *Asterix and Obelix Take On Caesar* 1999

Sagemiller, Melissa (1974–) *Get over It* 2001; *Soul Survivors* 2001; *Sorority Boys* 2002; *The Clearing* 2004

Sagnier, Ludivine (1979–) *Water Drops on Burning Rocks* 1999; *8 Women* 2001; *Ma Femme Est une Actrice* 2001; *Petites Coupures* 2002; *Peter Pan* 2003; *Swimming Pool* 2003

Sahara, Kenji (1932–) *The H-Man* 1954; *Rodan* 1956; *Matango* 1963; *Godzilla's Revenge* 1969

Sahl, Mort (1927–) *All the Young Men* 1960; *Don't Make Waves* 1967; *Nothing Lasts Forever* 1984

Sahni, Balraj (1913–1973) *Do Bigha Zameen* 1953; *Garam Hawa* 1973

Saint, Eva Marie (1924–) *On the Waterfront* 1954; *That Certain Feeling* 1956; *A Hatful of Rain* 1957; *Raintree County* 1957; *North by Northwest* 1959; *Exodus*

1960; *All Fall Down* 1962; *36 Hours* 1964; *The Sandpiper* 1965; *Grand Prix* 1966; *The Russians Are Coming, the Russians Are Coming* 1966; *The Stalking Moon* 1968; *Loving* 1970; *Cancel My Reservation* 1972; *Nothing in Common* 1986; *Danielle Steel's Palomino* 1991; *I Dreamed of Africa* 2000; *Because of Winn-Dixie* 2004

St Angel, Michael (1916–1984) *Bride by Mistake* 1944; *The Brighton Strangler* 1945

St Clement, Pam (1942–) *Hedda* 1975; *Scrubbers* 1982

St Cyr, Lili (1918–1999) *Son of Sinbad* 1955; *The Mobster* 1958; *The Naked and the Dead* 1958

Saint-Cyr, Renée (1904–2004) *Strange Boarders* 1938; *Double Dare* 1981

St Helier, Ivy (1886–1971) *Bitter Sweet* 1933; *London Belongs to Me* 1948; *The Gold Express* 1955

St Jacques, Raymond (1930–1990) *Mister Moses* 1965; *The Green Berets* 1968; *Uptight* 1968; *Cotton Comes to Harlem* 1970; *Book of Numbers* 1972; *The Final Comedown* 1972; *Lost in the Stars* 1974; *Born Again* 1978; *Cuba Crossing* 1980; *The Evil That Men Do* 1984; *The Wild Pair* 1987; *They Live* 1988

Saint James, Susan (1946–) *Jigsaw* 1968; *New Face in Hell* 1968; *Where Angels Go...Trouble Follows* 1968; *Outlaw Blues* 1977; *Love at First Bite* 1979; *SOS Titanic* 1979; *How to Beat the High Cost of Living* 1980; *Carbon Copy* 1981; *Don't Cry, It's Only Thunder* 1982

St John, Al (1893–1963) *The Butcher Boy* 1917; *Knight of the Plains* 1939; *The Lone Rider in Ghost Town* 1941; *Sheriff of Sage Valley* 1942; *Frontier Outlaws* 1944

St John, Betta (1929–) *All the Brothers Were Valiant* 1953; *Dream Wife* 1953; *The Robe* 1953; *Dangerous Mission* 1954; *The Student Prince* 1954; *The Naked Dawn* 1955; *Tarzan and the Lost Safari* 1956; *High Tide at Noon* 1957; *The City of the Dead* 1960; *Tarzan the Magnificent* 1960; *Corridors of Blood* 1962

St John, Howard (1905–1974) *Shockproof* 1949; *The Undercover Man* 1949; *Born Yesterday* 1950; *Mister 880* 1950; *The Big Night* 1951; *Close to My Heart* 1951; *Goodbye, My Fancy* 1951; *Stop, You're Killing Me* 1952; *Three Coins in the Fountain* 1954; *Illegal* 1955; *The Tender Trap* 1955; *Li'l Abner* 1959; *Cry for Happy* 1961; *One, Two, Three* 1961; *Sanctuary* 1961; *Madison Avenue* 1962; *Strait-Jacket* 1963; *Strange Bedfellows* 1965; *Don't Drink the Water* 1969

St John, Jill (1940–) *Holiday for Lovers* 1959; *The Remarkable Mr Pennypacker* 1959; *The Lost World* 1960; *The Roman Spring of Mrs Stone* 1961; *Tender Is the Night* 1961; *Come Blow Your Horn* 1963; *Who's Been Sleeping in My Bed?* 1963; *Who's Minding the Store?* 1963; *Honeymoon Hotel* 1964; *The Liquidator* 1966; *The Oscar* 1966; *Banning* 1967; *Eight on the Lam* 1967; *How I Spent My Summer Vacation* 1967; *The King's Pirate* 1967; *Tony Rome* 1967; *Diamonds Are Forever* 1971; *Sitting Target* 1972; *The Concrete Jungle* 1982; *Something to Believe In* 1997

St John, Marco (1939–) *The Mind Snatchers* 1972; *The Next Man* 1976; *Tightrope* 1984; *Friday the 13th: a New Beginning* 1985; *Monster* 2003

St Polis, John (1873–1946) *Coquette* 1929; *Party Girl* 1930

Saint-Simon, Lucile *Les Bonnes Femmes* 1960; *The Hands of Orlac* 1960

Saito, James *Hot Dog – The Movie* 1984; *Mortal Sins* 1989; *Henry Fool* 1997

Saito, Tatsuo *Tokyo Chorus* 1931; *The Brothers and Sisters of the Toda Family* 1941

Sakai, Sachio *Godzilla* 1954; *Godzilla's Revenge* 1969

Sakai, Seth *The Golden Seal* 1983; *Captive Hearts* 1988

Sakall, S Z *aka* **Sakall, S Z "Cuddles"** (1884–1955) *It's a Date* 1940; *Ball of Fire* 1941; *The Devil and Miss Jones* 1941; *That Night in Rio* 1941; *Broadway* 1942; *Casablanca* 1942; *Yankee Doodle Dandy* 1942; *Thank Your Lucky Stars* 1943; *Wintertime* 1943; *Shine On, Harvest Moon* 1944; *Christmas in Connecticut* 1945; *The Dolly Sisters* 1945; *San Antonio* 1945; *Wonder Man* 1945; *Cinderella Jones* 1946; *Never Say Goodbye* 1946; *Two Guys from Milwaukee* 1946; *Cynthia* 1947; *In the Good Old Summertime* 1949; *My Dream Is Yours* 1949; *Oh, You Beautiful Doll* 1949; *The Daughter of Rosie O'Grady* 1950; *Montana* 1950; *Tea for Two* 1950; *Lullaby of Broadway* 1951; *Sugarfoot* 1951; *The Student Prince* 1954

Sakamoto, Ryuichi (1952–) *Merry Christmas Mr Lawrence* 1982; *The Last Emperor* 1987

Sakamoto, Takeshi *I Was Born, but...* 1932; *There Was a Father* 1942; *Record of a Tenement Gentleman* 1947; *Hen in the Wind* 1948

Sakasitz, Amy *Dennis* 1993; *A Home of Our Own* 1993; *Mad Love* 1995; *House Arrest* 1996

Sakata, Harold (1920–1982) *Goldfinger* 1964; *The Poppy Is Also a Flower* 1966; *Impulse* 1975; *Goin' Coconuts* 1978

Saks, Gene (1921–) *A Thousand Clowns* 1965; *The Prisoner of Second Avenue* 1974; *The One and Only* 1978; *Lovesick* 1983; *The Goodbye People* 1984; *IQ* 1994; *Nobody's Fool* 1994

Saldana, Theresa (1954–) *I Wanna Hold Your Hand* 1978; *Defiance* 1979; *Raging Bull* 1980; *The Evil That Men Do* 1984; *The Night Before* 1988

Saldana, Zoë *aka* **Saldana, Zoe** (1978–) *Center Stage* 2000; *Crossroads* 2002; *Drumline* 2002; *Pirates of the Caribbean: the Curse of the Black Pearl* 2003; *The Terminal* 2004; *Guess Who* 2005

Sale, Charles "Chic" (1885–1936) *Treasure Island* 1934; *You Only Live Once* 1937

Salem, Kario *Starlight* 1989; *Triumph of the Spirit* 1989; *Killing Zoe* 1993

Salem, Pamela *Never Say Never Again* 1983; *After Darkness* 1985; *Gods and Monsters* 1998

Salen, Jesper (1978–) *The Slingshot* 1993; *Evil* 2003

Salenger, Meredith (1970–) *The Journey of Natty Gann* 1985; *The Kiss* 1988; *A Night in the Life of Jimmy Reardon* 1988; *Dream a Little Dream* 1989; *Dead Beat* 1994; *Village of the Damned* 1995; *No Code of Conduct* 1998

Salerno, Enrico Maria (1926–1994) *The Siege of Syracuse* 1959; *The Oldest Profession* 1967; *The Battle of El Alamein* 1968; *The Bird with the Crystal Plumage* 1969

Sales, Soupy (1926–) *The Two Little Bears* 1961; *...And God Spoke* 1993

Salew, John (1897–1961) *Time Flies* 1944; *Caravan* 1946; *Green Grow the Rushes* 1951; *The Lavender Hill Mob* 1951; *Three Cases of Murder* 1953; *Face the Music* 1954; *It's Great to Be Young* 1956; *Alive and Kicking* 1958; *Three on a Spree* 1961; *The Impersonator* 1962

Salinas, Jorge (1968–) *Sex, Shame and Tears* 1999; *Amores Perros* 2000

Salinger, Diane *Pee-wee's Big Adventure* 1985; *The Morning After* 1986; *The Magic Bubble* 1992; *One Night Stand* 1994; *Before the Night* 1995; *Guy* 1996

Salinger, Emmanuel *Les Cent et Une Nuits* 1995; *Don't Forget You're Going to Die* 1995; *Ma Vie Sexuelle* 1996

Salinger, Matt (1960–) *Captain America* 1990; *Babyfever* 1994

Sall, Sekkou *IP5* 1992; *Elisa* 1994

Sallis, Peter (1921–) *The Doctor's Dilemma* 1958; *I Thank a Fool* 1962; *Clash by Night* 1963; *The Third Secret* 1964; *Inadmissible Evidence* 1968; *Scream and Scream Again* 1969; *Taste the Blood of Dracula* 1969; *The Road Builder* 1971

Salmi, Albert (1928–1990) *The Bravados* 1958; *The Brothers Karamazov* 1958; *The Unforgiven* 1960; *Wild River* 1960; *The Outrage* 1964; *The Ambushers* 1967; *Hour of the Gun* 1967; *One Born Every Minute* 1967; *Three Guns for Texas* 1968; *The Deserter* 1971; *Escape from the Planet of the Apes* 1971; *Lawman* 1971; *something big* 1971; *The Take* 1974; *Empire of the Ants* 1977; *Cloud Dancer* 1979; *Steel* 1980; *Dragonslayer* 1981; *Love Child* 1982; *Hard to Hold* 1984; *Breaking In* 1989

Salminen, Esko (1940–) *Flame Top* 1980; *Hamlet Goes Business* 1987

Salmon, Colin (1966–) *Captives* 1994; *All Men Are Mortal* 1995; *Frantz Fanon: Black Skin White Mask* 1996; *Tomorrow Never Dies* 1997; *The Wisdom of Crocodiles* 1998; *Fanny & Elvis* 1999; *Resident Evil* 2002; *Freeze Frame* 2003; *AVP: Alien vs Predator* 2004

Salo, Elina (1936–) *Hamlet Goes Business* 1987; *The Match Factory Girl* 1990; *Take Care of Your Scarf, Tatjana* 1994; *Drifting Clouds* 1996

Salonga, Lea (1971–) *Aladdin* 1992; *Mulan* 1998

Salsedo, Frank *aka* **Salsedo, Frank S** *aka* **Salsedo, Frank Sotonoma** *Creepshow 2* 1987; *Magic in the Water* 1995

Salt, Jennifer (1944–) *The Wedding Party* 1966; *Midnight Cowboy* 1969; *Hi, Mom!* 1970; *The Revolutionary* 1970; *Play It Again, Sam* 1972; *Sisters* 1973; *Out of the Darkness* 1985

Salter, Ivor *Be My Guest* 1965; *Tiffany Jones* 1973

Salvatori, Renato (1933–1988) *Big Deal on Madonna Street* 1958; *Rocco and His Brothers* 1960; *Two Women* 1960; *The Organizer* 1963; *Burn!* 1970; *The Burglars* 1971; *State of Siege* 1972; *Burnt Barns* 1973; *Police Story* 1975; *Armaguedon* 1976; *La Luna* 1979

Salviat, Catherine *Just the Way You Are* 1984; *Romuald et Juliette* 1989; *The Last Mitterrand* 2005

Sambrell, Aldo (1937–) *Navajo Joe* 1966; *Sea Devils* 1982

Samel, Udo (1953–) *Knife in the Head* 1978; *The Seventh Continent* 1989; *Kaspar Hauser* 1993; *71 Fragments of a Chronology of Chance* 1994; *The Piano Teacher* 2001

Samms, Emma (1960–) *Arabian Adventure* 1979; *Agatha Christie's Murder in Three Acts* 1986; *The Shrimp on the Barbie* 1990; *Delirious* 1991; *The Little Unicorn* 1998

Sampson, Robert *Look in Any Window* 1961; *The Broken Land* 1962; *Hero's Island* 1962; *Re-Animator* 1985; *Robot Jox* 1989

Sampson, Will (1934–1987) *One Flew over the Cuckoo's Nest* 1975; *Orca ... Killer Whale* 1977; *The White Buffalo* 1977; *Insignificance* 1985; *Firewalker* 1986; *Poltergeist II: the Other Side* 1986

Samuel, Joanne (1957–) *Alison's Birthday* 1979; *Mad Max* 1979; *Nightmaster* 1987

San Giacomo, Laura (1962–) *sex, lies, and videotape* 1989; *Pretty Woman* 1990; *Quigley Down Under* 1990; *Vital Signs* 1990; *Once Around* 1991; *Under Suspicion* 1991; *For Their Own Good* 1993; *Nina Takes a Lover* 1993; *Stuart Saves His Family* 1995; *Jenifer* 2001

San Juan, Alberto (1968–) *The Other Side of the Bed* 2002; *Football Days* 2003

San Juan, Olga (1927–) *Blue Skies* 1946; *Variety Girl* 1947; *Are You with It?* 1948; *The Countess of Monte Cristo* 1948; *One Touch of Venus* 1948; *The Beautiful Blonde from Bashful Bend* 1949

San Martin, Conrado (1921–) *The Colossus of Rhodes* 1961; *The Awful Dr Orloff* 1962

Sanada, Hiroyuki (1960–) *Ring* 1997; *Ring 2* 1998; *The Twilight Samurai* 2002; *The Last Samurai* 2003

Sanchez, Jaime *The Pawnbroker* 1965; *The Wild Bunch* 1969; *Bobby Deerfield* 1977; *Piñero* 2001

Sanchez, Roselyn (1970–) *Rush Hour 2* 2001; *Boat Trip* 2002

Sanchez-Gijon, Aitana (1968–) *Jarrapellejos* 1987; *The Monk* 1990; *Mouth to Mouth* 1995; *A Walk in the Clouds* 1995; *The Chambermaid on the Titanic* 1997; *Love Walked In* 1997; *I'm Not Scared* 2003; *The Machinist* 2003

Sancho, José (1944–) *El Dorado* 1988; *Ay, Carmela!* 1990; *Live Flesh* 1997; *Arachnid* 2001

Sand, Paul (1935–) *Every Little Crook and Nanny* 1972; *The Hot Rock* 1972; *The Second Coming of Suzanne* 1974; *The Great Georgia Bank Hoax* 1977; *The Main Event* 1979; *Can't Stop the Music* 1980; *Wholly Moses!* 1980

Sanda, Dominique (1948–) *The Conformist* 1969; *A Gentle Creature* 1969; *First Love* 1970; *The Garden of the Finzi-Continis* 1971; *Without Apparent Motive* 1972; *The Mackintosh Man* 1973; *Story of a Love Story* 1973; *Steppenwolf* 1974; *The Inheritance* 1976; *1900* 1976; *Damnation Alley* 1977; *Caboblanco* 1980; *I, the Worst of All* 1990; *Garage Olimpo* 1999

Sande, Walter (1906–1971) *Corvette K-225* 1943; *I Love a Soldier* 1944; *Killer McCoy* 1947; *The Woman on the Beach* 1947; *The Duel at Silver Creek* 1952; *Red Planet Mars* 1952; *Apache* 1954; *Texas Lady* 1955; *Johnny Tremain* 1957

Sander, Otto (1941–) *The Marquise of O* 1976; *Palermo oder Wolfsburg* 1980; *Rosa Luxemburg* 1986; *Wings of Desire* 1987; *Faraway, So Close* 1993

Sanderford, John *The Alchemist* 1981; *My Boyfriend's Back* 1989; *Leprechaun* 1992

Sanders, George (1906–1972) *Lloyd's of London* 1936; *Things to Come* 1936; *Lancer Spy* 1937; *Love Is News* 1937; *Slave Ship* 1937; *Four Men and a Prayer* 1938; *International Settlement* 1938; *Confessions of a Nazi Spy* 1939; *The First Rebel* 1939; *Green Hell* 1939; *Mr Moto's Last Warning* 1939; *Nurse Edith Cavell* 1939; *The Saint in London* 1939; *The Saint Strikes Back* 1939; *Bitter Sweet* 1940; *Foreign Correspondent* 1940; *The House of the Seven Gables* 1940; *Rebecca* 1940; *The Saint Takes Over* 1940; *The Saint's Double Trouble* 1940; *Son of Monte Cristo* 1940; *A Date with the Falcon* 1941; *The Gay Falcon* 1941; *Man Hunt* 1941; *Rage in Heaven* 1941; *The Saint in Palm Springs* 1941; *Sundown* 1941; *The Black Swan* 1942; *The Falcon Takes Over* 1942; *The Falcon's Brother* 1942; *Her Cardboard Lover* 1942; *The Moon and Sixpence* 1942; *Quiet Please, Murder* 1942; *Son of Fury* 1942; *Tales of Manhattan* 1942; *Paris after Dark* 1943; *This Land Is Mine* 1943; *Action in Arabia* 1944; *The Lodger* 1944; *Summer Storm* 1944; *Hangover Square* 1945; *The Picture of Dorian Gray* 1945; *The Strange Affair of Uncle Harry* 1945; *The Strange Woman* 1946; *Thieves' Holiday* 1946; *Forever Amber* 1947; *The Ghost and Mrs Muir* 1947; *Lured* 1947; *The Private Affairs of Bel Ami* 1947; *The Fan* 1949; *Samson and Delilah* 1949; *All about Eve* 1950; *I Can Get It for You Wholesale* 1951; *The Light Touch* 1951; *Assignment – Paris* 1952; *Black Jack* 1952; *Ivanhoe* 1952; *Call Me Madam* 1953; *Journey to Italy* 1953; *King Richard and the Crusaders* 1954; *Witness to Murder* 1954; *The Big Tip Off* 1955; *Jupiter's Darling* 1955; *The King's Thief* 1955; *Moonfleet* 1955; *Never Say Goodbye* 1955; *The Scarlet Coat* 1955; *Death of a Scoundrel* 1956; *That Certain Feeling* 1956; *While the City Sleeps* 1956; *From the Earth to the Moon* 1958; *The Whole Truth* 1958; *Solomon and Sheba* 1959; *That Kind of Woman* 1959; *A Touch of Larceny* 1959; *Cone of Silence* 1960; *The Last Voyage* 1960; *The Rebel* 1960; *Village of the Damned* 1960; *In Search of the Castaways* 1961; *Cairo* 1962; *Operation Snatch* 1962; *The Cracksman* 1963; *A Shot in the Dark* 1964; *The Amorous Adventures of Moll Flanders* 1965; *The Quiller Memorandum* 1966; *Good Times* 1967; *The Jungle Book* 1967; *Warning Shot* 1967; *The Best House in London* 1968; *The Body Stealers* 1969; *The Candy Man* 1969; *The Kremlin Letter* 1970; *Endless Night* 1971; *Doomwatch* 1972; *Psychomania* 1972

Sanders, Hugh (1911–1966) *The Damned Don't Cry* 1950; *Mister 880* 1950; *Storm Warning* 1950; *Along the Great Divide* 1951; *Boots Malone* 1951; *Sugarfoot* 1951; *That's My Boy* 1951; *The Fighter* 1952; *The Pride of St Louis* 1952; *The Glass Web* 1953; *The Wild One* 1953; *Voice in the Mirror* 1958

Sanders, Jay O (1953–) *Starting Over* 1979; *The Prince of Pennsylvania* 1988; *Meeting Venus* 1990; *Mr Destiny* 1990; *Defenseless* 1991; *JFK* 1991; *VI Warshawski* 1991; *Hostages* 1993; *My Boyfriend's Back* 1993; *Angels in the Outfield* 1994; *The Big Green* 1995; *Three Wishes* 1995; *Daylight* 1996; *For Richer or Poorer* 1997; *Kiss the Girls* 1997; *The Matchmaker* 1997; *Wrestling with Alligators* 1998; *Earthly Possessions* 1999; *Tumbleweeds* 1999; *The Day after Tomorrow* 2004

Sanderson, Martyn *Beyond Reasonable Doubt* 1980; *Bad Blood* 1982; *Sylvia* 1984

Sanderson, William (1948–) *Coal Miner's Daughter* 1980; *Death Hunt* 1981; *Raggedy Man* 1981; *Blade Runner* 1982; *Black Moon Rising* 1985; *Sometimes They Come Back* 1991; *Wagons East!* 1994; *Last Man Standing* 1996

Sandford, Christopher (1939–) *Deep End* 1970; *Die Screaming Marianne* 1970

Sandler, Adam (1966–) *Shakes the Clown* 1991; *Airheads* 1994; *Mixed Nuts* 1994; *Billy Madison* 1995; *Bulletproof* 1996; *Happy Gilmore* 1996; *Dirty Work* 1998; *The Waterboy* 1998; *The Wedding Singer* 1998; *Big Daddy* 1999; *Fortune Hunters* 1999; *Little Nicky* 2000; *The Animal* 2001; *The Hot Chick* 2002; *Mr Deeds* 2002; *Punch-Drunk Love* 2002; *Adam Sandler's Eight Crazy Nights* 2003; *Anger Management* 2003; *50 First Dates* 2004; *Spanglish* 2004; *The Longest Yard* 2005

Sandor, Steve (1937–) *One More Train to Rob* 1971; *Stryker* 1983

Sandoval, Miguel (1951–) *Clear and Present Danger* 1994; *Fair Game* 1995; *Mrs Winterbourne* 1996; *Flight of Fancy* 2000; *Things You Can Tell Just by Looking at Her* 2000; *Black Point* 2001; *Ballistic: Ecks vs Sever* 2002

Sandow, Nick *No Looking Back* 1998; *Return to Paradise* 1998

Sandre, Didier *The Lie* 1992; *An Autumn Tale* 1998

Sandrelli, Stefania (1946–) *Divorce – Italian Style* 1961; *L'Ainé des Ferchaux* 1963; *Seduced and Abandoned* 1964; *Partner* 1968; *The Conformist* 1969; *Alfredo Alfredo* 1971; *Somewhere beyond Love* 1974; *We All Loved Each Other So Much*

1974; *1900* 1976; *The Family* 1987; *Mignon Has Left* 1988; *Jamon Jamon* 1992; *Of Love and Shadows* 1994; *Stealing Beauty* 1995; *The Last Kiss* 2001; *Un Filme Falado* 2003

Sandri, Anna-Maria (1936–) *Le Rouge et le Noir* 1954; *The Black Tent* 1956

Sands, Diana (1934–1973) *A Raisin in the Sun* 1961; *Doctors' Wives* 1970; *The Landlord* 1970; *Georgia, Georgia* 1972

Sands, Johnny *aka* **Sands, John** (1927–2003) *Till the End of Time* 1946; *The Bachelor and the Bobby-Soxer* 1947; *Blaze of Noon* 1947; *Adventure in Baltimore* 1949; *The Admiral Was a Lady* 1950; *The Lawless* 1950

Sands, Julian (1957–) *The Killing Fields* 1984; *After Darkness* 1985; *The Doctor and the Devils* 1985; *A Room with a View* 1985; *Gothic* 1986; *Siesta* 1987; *Vibes* 1988; *Warlock* 1989; *Arachnophobia* 1990; *Night Sun* 1990; *Impromptu* 1991; *Naked Lunch* 1991; *Crazy in Love* 1992; *Tale of a Vampire* 1992; *The Turn of the Screw* 1992; *Boxing Helena* 1993; *Warlock: the Armageddon* 1993; *The Browning Version* 1994; *Leaving Las Vegas* 1995; *Circle of Passion* 1996; *The Autumn Heart* 1998; *The Phantom of the Opera* 1998; *The Loss of Sexual Innocence* 1999; *The Million Dollar Hotel* 1999; *Timecode* 1999; *Mercy* 2000; *Vatel* 2000; *Hotel* 2001; *The Medallion* 2003; *Sword of Xanten* 2004

Sands, Leslie (1921–2001) *One More Time* 1970; *The Ragman's Daughter* 1972

Sands, Tommy (1937–) *Mardi Gras* 1958; *Sing, Boy, Sing* 1958; *Babes in Toyland* 1961; *Love in a Goldfish Bowl* 1961; *Ensign Pulver* 1964; *None but the Brave* 1965; *The Violent Ones* 1967

Sanford, Erskine (1885–1969) *Citizen Kane* 1941; *The Magnificent Ambersons* 1942; *Ministry of Fear* 1945; *Angel on My Shoulder* 1946; *Crack-Up* 1946; *The Lady from Shanghai* 1948; *Macbeth* 1948

Sanford, Garwin (1955–) *Quarantine* 1989; *Max* 1994; *The Long Way Home* 1998; *Life-Size* 2000

Sanford, Isabel *aka* **Sanford, Isabell** (1917–2004) *Guess Who's Coming to Dinner* 1967; *Hickey and Boggs* 1972; *Love at First Bite* 1979; *Original Gangstas* 1996

Sanford, Ralph (1899–1963) *Thunderhead – Son of Flicka* 1945; *Copacabana* 1947; *The Glass Menagerie* 1950

Sanford, Tiny *aka* **Stanford, Stanley J** *aka* **Sanford, Stanley** (1894–1961) *The Immigrant* 1917; *The Circus* 1928; *Modern Times* 1936

Sano, Shiro (1955–) *Violent Cop* 1989; *The Most Terrible Time in My Life* 1993

Sano, Shuji (1912–1978) *There Was a Father* 1942; *Hen in the Wind* 1948

Sansa, Maya (1975–) *Benzina* 2001; *The Best of Youth* 2003; *Good Morning, Night* 2003

Sansom, Ken *Winnie the Pooh's Most Grand Adventure* 1997; *The Tigger Movie* 2000; *Piglet's Big Movie* 2003; *Pooh's Heffalump Movie* 2005

Santamaria, Claudio (1974–) *Besieged* 1998; *The Last Kiss* 2001; *The Card Player* 2004

Santiago, Renoly *Dangerous Minds* 1995; *Hackers* 1995

Santiago-Hudson, Ruben (1957–) *Rear Window* 1998; *Domestic Disturbance* 2001

Santini, Pierre (1938–) *Les Innocents aux Mains Sales* 1975; *American Dreamer* 1984; *Polar* 1984

Santoni, Reni (1939–) *Enter Laughing* 1967; *Anzio* 1968; *Dirty Harry* 1971; *I Never Promised You a Rose Garden* 1977; *Dead Men Don't Wear Plaid* 1982; *Bad Boys* 1983; *Brewster's Millions* 1985; *Cobra* 1986

Santos, Joe (1931–) *The Blue Knight* 1973; *The Friends of Eddie Coyle* 1973; *Shamus* 1973; *Zandy's Bride* 1974; *Fear City* 1984; *Mo' Money* 1992; *Art Deco Detective* 1994; *Auggie Rose* 2000

Santschi, Tom (1878–1931) *3 Bad Men* 1926; *Hills of Kentucky* 1927

Sanz, Jorge (1969–) *Valentina* 1982; *Lovers* 1991; *Belle Epoque* 1992; *A Further Gesture* 1996; *Cha-Cha-Cha* 1998; *The Girl of Your Dreams* 1998

Sara, Mia (1967–) *Legend* 1985; *Ferris Bueller's Day Off* 1986; *Apprentice to Murder* 1988; *Any Man's Death* 1990; *A Row of Crows* 1991; *By the Sword* 1992; *A Stranger among Us* 1992; *Timecop* 1994; *Bullet to Beijing* 1995; *The Maddening* 1995; *The Pompatus of Love* 1995; *The Set Up* 1995; *Hard Time* 1998

Sarafian, Richard C *aka* **Sarafian, Richard** (1925–) *Bugsy* 1991; *Bound* 1996; *Dr Dolittle 2* 2001

Sarandon, Chris (1942–) *Dog Day Afternoon* 1975; *Lipstick* 1976; *The Sentinel* 1977; *Cuba* 1979; *The Osterman Weekend* 1983; *Protocol* 1984; *Fright Night* 1985; *Collision Course* 1987; *The Princess Bride* 1987; *Child's Play* 1988; *Forced March* 1989; *Slaves of New York* 1989; *Whispers* 1990; *A Murderous Affair* 1992; *The Resurrected* 1992; *The Nightmare before Christmas* 1993; *David's Mother* 1994; *Temptress* 1995; *Danielle Steel's No Greater Love* 1996; *Tales from the Crypt Presents: Bordello of Blood* 1996; *American Perfekt* 1997; *Race against Time* 2000

Sarandon, Susan (1946–) *Joe* 1970; *Lady Liberty* 1971; *The Front Page* 1974; *Lovin' Molly* 1974; *The Great Waldo Pepper* 1975; *One Summer Love* 1975; *The Rocky Horror Picture Show* 1975; *The Great Smokey Roadblock* 1977; *The Other Side of Midnight* 1977; *King of the Gypsies* 1978; *Pretty Baby* 1978; *Something Short of Paradise* 1979; *Atlantic City, USA* 1980; *Loving Couples* 1980; *Tempest* 1982; *The Hunger* 1983; *The Buddy System* 1984; *Compromising Positions* 1985; *The Witches of Eastwick* 1987; *Bull Durham* 1988; *Sweet Hearts Dance* 1988; *A Dry White Season* 1989; *The January Man* 1989; *White Palace* 1990; *Light Sleeper* 1991; *Thelma & Louise* 1991; *Bob Roberts* 1992; *Lorenzo's Oil* 1992; *The Client* 1994; *Little Women* 1994; *Safe Passage* 1994; *Dead Man Walking* 1995; *James and the Giant Peach* 1996; *Stepmom* 1998; *Twilight* 1998; *Anywhere but Here* 1999; *Cradle Will Rock* 1999; *Earthly Possessions* 1999; *Cats & Dogs* 2001; *The Banger Sisters* 2002; *Igby Goes Down* 2002; *Moonlight Mile* 2002; *Ice Bound* 2003; *Alfie* 2004; *Shall We Dance* 2004

Sarda, Rosa Maria (1941–) *The Butterfly Effect* 1995; *Actresses* 1996; *Beloved/Friend* 1998; *All about My Mother* 1999; *Take My Eyes* 2003

Sardou, Fernand (1910–1976) *Marguerite de la Nuit* 1955; *Une Parisienne* 1957; *Lunch on the Grass* 1959; *The Little Theatre of Jean Renoir* 1969

Sargent, Dick *aka* **Sargent, Richard** (1933–1994) *The Beast with a Million Eyes* 1955; *Mardi Gras* 1958; *Operation Petticoat* 1959; *Billie* 1965; *The Ghost and Mr Chicken* 1966; *Live a Little, Love a Little* 1968; *The Private Navy of Sgt O'Farrell* 1968; *Hardcore* 1979; *Teen Witch* 1989

Sarkisyan, Rose *Family Viewing* 1987; *The Adjuster* 1991

Sarne, Michael *aka* **Sarne, Mike** (1939–) *A Place to Go* 1963; *Every Day's a Holiday* 1964

Sarrazin, Michael (1940–) *The Doomsday Flight* 1966; *Gunfight in Abilene* 1967; *Journey to Shiloh* 1967; *One Born Every Minute* 1967; *The Sweet Ride* 1967; *Eye of the Cat* 1969; *A Man Called Gannon* 1969; *They Shoot Horses, Don't They?* 1969; *In Search of Gregory* 1970; *Believe in Me* 1971; *The Pursuit of Happiness* 1971; *Sometimes a Great Notion* 1971; *The Groundstar Conspiracy* 1972; *Frankenstein: the True Story* 1973; *Harry in Your Pocket* 1973; *For Pete's Sake* 1974; *The Reincarnation of Peter Proud* 1975; *The Gumball Rally* 1976; *The Loves and Times of Scaramouche* 1976; *Caravans* 1978; *Death Vengeance* 1982; *Joshua Then and Now* 1985; *Keeping Track* 1986; *Mascara* 1987; *Captive Hearts* 1988; *Malarek* 1989; *Lena's Holiday* 1990; *Bullet to Beijing* 1995; *Midnight in St Petersburg* 1995; *The Peacekeeper* 1997

Sarsgaard, Peter (1971–) *Another Day in Paradise* 1998; *Boys Don't Cry* 1999; *The Center of the World* 2001; *Unconditional Love* 2001; *Empire* 2002; *K-19: the Widowmaker* 2002; *Garden State* 2003; *Shattered Glass* 2003; *Kinsey* 2004; *The Skeleton Key* 2005

Sartain, Gailard (1946–) *Roadie* 1980; *Hard Country* 1981; *Endangered Species* 1982; *Ernest Saves Christmas* 1988; *Mississippi Burning* 1988; *Blaze* 1989; *Ernest Goes to Jail* 1990; *Fried Green Tomatoes at the Whistle Stop Cafe* 1991; *Stop! or My Mom Will Shoot* 1992; *The Real McCoy* 1993; *Getting Even with Dad* 1994; *Open Season* 1995; *Murder in Mind* 1996; *The Patriot* 1998

Sartor, Fabio (1954–) *Phantom of Death* 1988; *The Luzhin Defence* 2000

Sassard, Jacqueline (1940–) *The Pirates of Malaysia* 1964; *Accident* 1967; *Les Biches* 1968

Sastre, Inés (1973–) *Beyond the Clouds* 1995; *The Best Man* 1998; *Druids* 2001; *Vidocq* 2001

Sato, Hitomi *Ring* 1997; *Ring 2* 1998

Sato, Kei *Onibaba* 1964; *Death by Hanging* 1968

Satoransky, Jaroslav *End of a Priest* 1969; *Larks on a String* 1969

Satton, Lon *The Heroes* 1968; *Hello – Goodbye* 1970

Sauer, Gary *The Unbelievable Truth* 1989; *Trust* 1990

Saunders, Jennifer (1958–) *The Supergrass* 1985; *Eat the Rich* 1987; *In the Bleak Midwinter* 1995; *Muppet Treasure Island* 1996; *Fanny & Elvis* 1999; *Shrek 2* 2004

Saunders, Mary Jane (1943–) *Sorrowful Jones* 1949; *A Woman of Distinction* 1950

Sauvegrain, Didier *Sarraouina* 1986; *Jeanne la Pucelle* 1994

Savage, Ann (1921–) *What a Woman!* 1943; *Detour* 1945

Savage, Brad (1965–) *The Apple Dumpling Gang* 1974; *Echoes of a Summer* 1976; *No Deposit No Return* 1976; *Return from Witch Mountain* 1978; *Red Dawn* 1984

Savage, Fred (1976–) *The Boy Who Could Fly* 1986; *The Princess Bride* 1987; *Vice Versa* 1988; *Little Monsters* 1989; *Austin Powers in Goldmember* 2002; *The Rules of Attraction* 2002; *Welcome to Mooseport* 2004

Savage, John (1949–) *Bad Company* 1972; *The Killing Kind* 1973; *Steelyard Blues* 1973; *The Deer Hunter* 1978; *Hair* 1979; *The Onion Field* 1979; *Cattle Annie and Little Britches* 1980; *Inside Moves: the Guys from Max's Bar* 1980; *The Amateur* 1981; *The Long Ride* 1984; *Maria's Lovers* 1984; *Salvador* 1986; *Beauty and the Beast* 1987; *Hotel Colonial* 1987; *Do the Right Thing* 1989; *Any Man's Death* 1990; *Hunting* 1992; *Primary Motive* 1992; *Killing Obsession* 1994; *Flynn* 1995; *American Strays* 1996; *One Good Turn* 1996; *White Squall* 1996; *Before Women Had Wings* 1997; *Message in a Bottle* 1998; *The Jack Bull* 1999

Saval, Dany (1942–) *Moon Pilot* 1962; *Boeing Boeing* 1965

Savalas, Telly (1924–1994) *Mad Dog Coll* 1961; *The Young Savages* 1961; *Birdman of Alcatraz* 1962; *Cape Fear* 1962; *The Interns* 1962; *Johnny Cool* 1963; *Love Is a Ball* 1963; *The Man from the Diner's Club* 1963; *Genghis Khan* 1964; *The New Interns* 1964; *The Greatest Story Ever Told* 1965; *The Slender Thread* 1965; *Beau Geste* 1966; *The Dirty Dozen* 1967; *The Karate Killers* 1967; *Buona Sera, Mrs Campbell* 1968; *The Scalphunters* 1968; *Sol Madrid* 1968; *The Assassination Bureau* 1969; *Crooks and Coronets* 1969; *Land Raiders* 1969; *Mackenna's Gold* 1969; *On Her Majesty's Secret Service* 1969; *Kelly's Heroes* 1970; *Violent City* 1970; *Pancho Villa* 1971; *Pretty Maids All in a Row* 1971; *A Town Called Hell* 1971; *Horror Express* 1972; *Inside Out* 1975; *Killer Force* 1975; *Lisa and the Devil* 1976; *Capricorn One* 1978; *Beyond the Poseidon Adventure* 1979; *Escape to Athena* 1979; *Cannonball Run II* 1983; *GoBots: Battle of the Rocklords* 1986

Savant, Doug (1964–) *Trick or Treat* 1986; *Masquerade* 1988; *Paint It Black* 1989; *Red Surf* 1990; *Shaking the Tree* 1990; *First Daughter* 1999

Savelyeva, Lyudmila (1942–) *War and Peace* 1966; *Sunflower* 1969

Savident, John (1938–) *Mountains of the Moon* 1989; *Brain Donors* 1992; *Mrs 'arris Goes to Paris* 1992

Savin, Eric *The Beating of the Butterfly's Wings* 2000; *He Loves Me... He Loves Me Not* 2002

Savini, Tom (1946–) *Martin* 1978; *Knightriders* 1981; *Creepshow 2* 1987

Savoy, Teresa Ann *aka* **Savoy, Theresa Ann** (1955–) *Salon Kitty* 1976; *Caligula* 1979

Savvina, Iya (1936–) *The Lady with the Little Dog* 1960; *Asya's Happiness* 1967; *Private Life* 1982

Sawa, Devon (1978–) *Little Giants* 1994; *The Boys Club* 1996; *Wild America* 1997; *A Cool, Dry Place* 1998; *Idle Hands* 1999; *SLC Punk!* 1999; *Final Destination* 2000; *The Guilty* 2000; *Slackers* 2001; *Extreme Ops* 2003

Sawalha, Julia (1968–) *In the Bleak Midwinter* 1995; *The Wind in the Willows* 1996; *Chicken Run* 2000; *The Final Curtain* 2002

Sawalha, Nadim (1935–) *The Wind and the Lion* 1975; *Sinbad and the Eye of the Tiger* 1977; *The Awakening* 1980; *Sphinx* 1980; *Misunderstood* 1984; *Half Moon Street* 1986; *Knights and Emeralds* 1986; *Pascali's Island* 1988; *The Hawk* 1992

Sawyer, Joe *aka* **Sawyer, Joseph** (1906–1982) *I Found Stella Parish* 1935; *Special Agent* 1935; *The Petrified Forest* 1936; *The Black Legion* 1937; *San Quentin* 1937; *Down Mexico Way* 1941; *Hit the Ice* 1943; *The Outlaw* 1943; *Tarzan's Desert Mystery* 1943; *Gilda* 1946; *Stagecoach Kid* 1949; *Red Skies of Montana* 1952; *Riding Shotgun* 1954

Saxena, Sharat *Tan-Badan* 1986; *Saathiya* 2002

Saxon, John (1935–) *Running Wild* 1955; *Rock, Pretty Baby* 1956; *The Reluctant Debutante* 1958; *The Restless Years* 1958; *This Happy Feeling* 1958; *The Big Fisherman* 1959; *Portrait in Black* 1960; *The Unforgiven* 1960; *Posse from Hell* 1961; *Mr Hobbs Takes a Vacation* 1962; *War Hunt* 1962; *The Night Caller* 1965; *The Doomsday Flight* 1966; *Planet of Blood* 1966; *Southwest to Sonora* 1966; *Company of Killers* 1970; *Mr Kingstreet's War* 1970; *Joe Kidd* 1972; *Enter the Dragon* 1973; *Black Christmas* 1974; *Mitchell* 1975; *The Swiss Conspiracy* 1975; *Moonshine County Express* 1977; *Raid on Entebbe* 1977; *The Glove* 1978; *The Electric Horseman* 1979; *Battle beyond the Stars* 1980; *Beyond Evil* 1980; *Blood Beach* 1981; *The Man with the Deadly Lens* 1982; *Tenebrae* 1982; *A Nightmare on Elm Street* 1984; *Fever Pitch* 1985; *Beverly Hills Cop III* 1994; *Killing Obsession* 1994; *Living in Fear* 2001

Sayer, Diane (1938–2001) *Kitten with a Whip* 1964; *The Strangler* 1964

Sayer, Philip (?–1991) *The Green Horizon* 1981; *Slayground* 1983; *Xtro* 1983; *Shanghai Surprise* 1986

Sayers, Jo Ann (1918–) *Young Dr Kildare* 1938; *The Adventures of Huckleberry Finn* 1939; *Honolulu* 1939

Sayle, Alexei (1952–) *Gorky Park* 1983; *The Bride* 1985; *Solarbabies* 1986; *Whoops Apocalypse* 1986; *Siesta* 1987; *Indiana Jones and the Last Crusade* 1989; *Carry On Columbus* 1992; *Reckless Kelly* 1993; *Swing* 1998

Sayles, John (1950–) *Return of the Secaucus Seven* 1980; *Lianna* 1983; *Hard Choices* 1984; *Eight Men Out* 1988; *Little Vegas* 1990; *Straight Talk* 1992; *Gridlock'd* 1996

Saylor, Syd (1895–1962) *Hell Town* 1937; *The Prince of Thieves* 1948; *Mule Train* 1950

Sbaraglia, Leonardo (1970–) *Intacto* 2001; *The City of No Limits* 2002; *Carmen* 2003

Sbarge, Raphael (1964–) *Risky Business* 1983; *My Man Adam* 1985; *My Science Project* 1985; *Carnosaur* 1993; *The Hidden II* 1993

Sbragia, Mattia *Year of the Gun* 1991; *Christie Malry's Own Double-Entry* 2000; *Heaven* 2002; *The Sin Eater* 2002; *The Passion of the Christ* 2004

Scacchi, Greta (1960–) *Heat and Dust* 1982; *Burke and Wills* 1985; *The Coca-Cola Kid* 1985; *Defence of the Realm* 1985; *Good Morning, Babylon* 1987; *A Man in Love* 1987; *White Mischief* 1987; *Three Sisters* 1988; *Presumed Innocent* 1990; *Fires Within* 1991; *Shattered* 1991; *The Player* 1992; *Salt on Our Skin* 1992; *Turtle Beach* 1992; *The Browning Version* 1994; *Country Life* 1994; *Jefferson in Paris* 1995; *Emma* 1996; *Rasputin* 1996; *The Odyssey* 1997; *The Serpent's Kiss* 1997; *The Red Violin* 1998; *Tom's Midnight Garden* 1998; *Cotton Mary* 1999; *One of the Hollywood Ten* 2000; *Festival in Cannes* 2001; *Beyond the Sea* 2004

Scala, Gia (1934–1972) *Don't Go Near the Water* 1957; *The Garment Jungle* 1957; *Tip on a Dead Jockey* 1957; *Ride a Crooked Trail* 1958; *The Tunnel of Love* 1958; *The Two-Headed Spy* 1958; *The Angry Hills* 1959; *Battle of the Coral Sea* 1959; *I Aim at the Stars* 1960; *The Guns of Navarone* 1961

Scales, Prunella (1932–) *Hobson's Choice* 1953; *Laxdale Hall* 1953; *Waltz of the Toreadors* 1962; *The Littlest Horse Thieves* 1976; *The Hound of the Baskervilles* 1977; *The Boys from Brazil* 1978; *The Wicked Lady* 1983; *The Lonely Passion of Judith Hearne* 1987; *A Chorus of Disapproval* 1988; *Consuming Passions* 1988; *Howards End* 1992; *Second Best* 1993; *An Awfully Big Adventure* 1994; *Wolf* 1994; *Stiff Upper Lips* 1997; *Mad Cows* 1999; *The Ghost of Greville Lodge* 2000

Scalia, Jack (1951–) *Fear City* 1984; *Amore!* 1993; *T-Force* 1995; *Barbara Taylor Bradford's Everything to Gain* 1996; *Darkbreed* 1996

Scarano, Tecla (1894–1965) *Marriage – Italian Style* 1964; *Shout Loud, Louder... I Don't Understand* 1966

Scarborough, Adrian *Love Is the Devil: Study for a Portrait of*

Francis Bacon 1998; *Vera Drake* 2004
Scardino, Don (1949–) *Homer* 1970; *The People Next Door* 1970; *Squirm* 1976; *Cruising* 1980; *He Knows You're Alone* 1981
Scardino, Hal (1984–) *The Indian in the Cupboard* 1995; *Marvin's Room* 1996
Scarfe, Alan (1946–) *Bay Boy* 1984; *Walls* 1984; *Joshua Then and Now* 1985; *Keeping Track* 1986; *Iron Eagle II* 1988; *Double Impact* 1991; *Sanctuary* 1997
Scarpa, Renato (1939–) *Don't Look Now* 1973; *The Icicle Thief* 1989; *Il Postino* 1994
Scarpitta, Carmen (1933–) *Casanova* 1976; *In the Name of the Pope King* 1977; *La Cage aux Folles* 1978
Scarwid, Diana (1955–) *Inside Moves: the Guys from Max's Bar* 1980; *Mommie Dearest* 1981; *Rumble Fish* 1983; *Silkwood* 1983; *Strange Invaders* 1983; *Extremities* 1986; *The Ladies Club* 1986; *Psycho III* 1986; *Heat* 1987; *Brenda Starr* 1989; *The Cure* 1995; *Gold Diggers: the Secret of Bear Mountain* 1995; *The Neon Bible* 1995; *Truman* 1995; *Dirty Pictures* 2000; *What Lies Beneath* 2000; *A Guy Thing* 2002; *Party Monster* 2003; *The Clearing* 2004
Schaake, Katrin *Love Is Colder Than Death* 1969; *Whity* 1970; *The Bitter Tears of Petra von Kant* 1972
Schade, Doris (1924–) *The German Sisters* 1981; *Veronika Voss* 1982
Schaech, Johnathon (1969–) *Sparrow* 1993; *Doom Generation* 1995; *Poison Ivy 2* 1995; *That Thing You Do!* 1996; *Welcome to Woop Woop* 1997; *Hush* 1998; *The Brutal Truth* 1999; *Finding Graceland* 1999; *Splendor* 1999; *The Forsaken* 2001
Schaefer, Joshua *aka* **Schaefer, Josh** *The Bomber Boys* 1995; *Johns* 1995; *True Crime* 1995; *Eight Days a Week* 1996
Schaeffer, Eric (1962–) *If Lucy Fell* 1996; *Fall* 1997
Schafer, Natalie (1900–1991) *Keep Your Powder Dry* 1945; *Molly and Me* 1945; *Secret beyond the Door* 1948; *Caught* 1949; *Callaway Went Thataway* 1951; *The Girl Next Door* 1953; *Female on the Beach* 1955; *Anastasia* 1956; *Forever, Darling* 1956
Schallert, William (1922–) *The Man from Planet X* 1951; *The Incredible Shrinking Man* 1957; *Lonely Are the Brave* 1962; *In the Heat of the Night* 1967; *Speedway* 1968; *Colossus: the Forbin Project* 1969; *The Computer Wore Tennis Shoes* 1969
Schanz, Heidi *Mixing Nia* 1998; *Universal Soldier – the Return* 1999
Schanzer, Karl *Tonight for Sure!* 1961; *Dementia 13* 1963
Schedeen, Anne (1949–) *Embryo* 1976; *Second Thoughts* 1982
Scheider, Roy *aka* **Scheider, Roy R** (1932–) *The Curse of the Living Corpse* 1964; *Puzzle of a Downfall Child* 1970; *The French Connection* 1971; *Klute* 1971; *The Outside Man* 1973; *The Seven-Ups* 1973; *Jaws* 1975; *Sheila Levine Is Dead and Living in New York* 1975; *Marathon Man* 1976; *Sorcerer* 1977; *Jaws 2* 1978; *All That Jazz* 1979; *Last Embrace* 1979; *Still of the Night* 1982; *Blue Thunder* 1983; *2010* 1984; *52 Pick-Up* 1986; *The Men's Club* 1986; *Cohen and Tate* 1988; *Listen to Me* 1989; *Night Game* 1989; *The Fourth War* 1990; *The Russia House* 1990; *Naked Lunch* 1991; *Romeo Is Bleeding* 1992; *Executive Target* 1996; *The Myth of Fingerprints* 1996; *John Grisham's The Rainmaker* 1997; *The Peacekeeper* 1997; *RKO 281* 1999; *Chain of Command* 2000; *Time Lapse* 2001; *Citizen Verdict* 2003; *The Punisher* 2004
Scheine, Raynor (1942–) *Ace Ventura: Pet Detective* 1993; *The Real McCoy* 1993
Scheitz, Clemens *Heart of Glass* 1976; *Stroszek* 1977
Schell, Catherine *aka* **von Schell, Catherina** (1946–) *Moon Zero Two* 1969; *Madame Sin* 1972; *Callan* 1974; *The Return of the Pink Panther* 1974; *Gulliver's Travels* 1977
Schell, Maria (1926–2005) *The Magic Box* 1951; *The Heart of the Matter* 1953; *The Last Bridge* 1954; *Napoléon* 1955; *The Rats* 1955; *Gervaise* 1956; *White Nights* 1957; *The Brothers Karamazov* 1958; *The Hanging Tree* 1959; *Cimarron* 1960; *The Mark* 1961; *The Bloody Judge* 1969; *The Odessa File* 1974; *Just a Gigolo* 1978; *Nineteen Nineteen* 1984
Schell, Maximilian (1930–) *The Young Lions* 1958; *Judgment at Nuremberg* 1961; *The Condemned of Altona* 1962; *Five Finger Exercise* 1962; *The Reluctant Saint* 1962; *Topkapi* 1964; *Return from the Ashes* 1965; *The Deadly Affair* 1966; *Counterpoint* 1967; *The Desperate Ones* 1967; *Krakatoa, East of Java* 1969; *First Love* 1970; *Pope Joan* 1972; *The Odessa File* 1974; *The Pedestrian* 1974; *The Man in the Glass Booth* 1975; *St Ives* 1976; *A Bridge Too Far* 1977; *Cross of Iron* 1977; *Julia* 1977; *Avalanche Express* 1979; *The Black Hole* 1979; *Players* 1979; *The Chosen* 1981; *Marlene* 1984; *The Assisi Underground* 1985; *The Rose Garden* 1989; *Labyrinth* 1991; *Miss Rose White* 1992; *A Far Off Place* 1993; *Little Odessa* 1994; *The Eighteenth Angel* 1997; *Left Luggage* 1997; *Telling Lies in America* 1997; *Deep Impact* 1998; *Vampires* 1998; *Festival in Cannes* 2001
Schellenberg, August *Kings and Desperate Men* 1981; *Confidential* 1986; *Black Robe* 1991; *Free Willy* 1993; *Getting Gotti* 1994; *Iron Will* 1994; *Free Willy 2: the Adventure Home* 1995; *The West Side Waltz* 1995; *What Love Sees* 1996; *Free Willy 3: the Rescue* 1997
Schellhardt, Mary Kate (1978–) *What's Eating Gilbert Grape* 1993; *Apollo 13* 1995; *Free Willy 2: the Adventure Home* 1995
Scherrer, Paul (1968–) *Children of the Corn II: the Final Sacrifice* 1993; *Fall into Darkness* 1996
Scheydt, Karl *The American Soldier* 1970; *Fear Eats the Soul* 1973
Schiaffino, Rosanna (1938–) *RoGoPaG* 1962; *Two Weeks in Another Town* 1962; *The Long Ships* 1963; *The Victors* 1963; *Drop Dead Darling* 1966; *The Rover* 1967; *The Heroes* 1972
Schiavelli, Vincent (1948–) *Waiting for the Light* 1989; *American Yakuza 2: Back to Back* 1996; *The People vs Larry Flynt* 1996; *Tomorrow Never Dies* 1997; *Man on the Moon* 1999; *Snow White* 2001; *Hey Arnold! the Movie* 2002
Schiff, Richard (1955–) *The Arrival* 1996; *Doctor Dolittle* 1998; *Heaven* 1998; *Living Out Loud* 1998; *The Pentagon Wars* 1998; *Gun Shy* 2000; *I Am Sam* 2001; *People I Know* 2002
Schiffer, Claudia (1970–) *The Blackout* 1997; *Black and White* 1999; *In Pursuit* 2000
Schildkraut, Joseph (1895–1964) *Orphans of the Storm* 1921; *The Road to Yesterday* 1925; *The King of Kings* 1927; *Cleopatra* 1934; *Viva Villa!* 1934; *The Crusades* 1935; *The Garden of Allah* 1936; *Lancer Spy* 1937; *The Life of Emile Zola* 1937; *Slave Ship* 1937; *The Baroness and the Butler* 1938; *Marie Antoinette* 1938; *Suez* 1938; *Idiot's Delight* 1939; *Lady of the Tropics* 1939; *The Man in the Iron Mask* 1939; *Mr Moto Takes a Vacation* 1939; *Pack Up Your Troubles* 1939; *The Three Musketeers* 1939; *Phantom Raiders* 1940; *The Shop around the Corner* 1940; *The Cheaters* 1945; *Flame of the Barbary Coast* 1945; *Monsieur Beaucaire* 1946; *Northwest Outpost* 1947; *The Diary of Anne Frank* 1959
Schilling, Gus (1908–1957) *Citizen Kane* 1941; *Hers to Hold* 1943; *It's a Pleasure* 1945; *The Lady from Shanghai* 1948; *Bride for Sale* 1949; *Our Very Own* 1950
Schilling, William G *Ruthless People* 1986; *White of the Eye* 1986
Schlatter, Charlie (1966–) *Bright Lights, Big City* 1988; *18 Again!* 1988; *Heartbreak Hotel* 1988; *The Delinquents* 1989
Schmid, Helmut (1925–1992) *A Prize of Arms* 1961; *The Salzburg Connection* 1972
Schmidtmer, Christiane (1940–2003) *Boeing Boeing* 1965; *The Big Doll House* 1971; *The Giant Spider Invasion* 1975
Schmolzer, August *Requiem for Dominic* 1990; *Bride of the Wind* 2001
Schnabel, Stefan (1912–1999) *The Iron Curtain* 1948; *Diplomatic Courier* 1952; *Houdini* 1953; *The 27th Day* 1957; *Rampage* 1963; *Dracula's Widow* 1988
Schnarre, Monika (1971–) *Waxwork II: Lost in Time* 1992; *Killer* 1994; *Sanctuary* 1997
Schneider, Betty *Mon Oncle* 1958; *Paris Nous Appartient* 1960
Schneider, Dan (1966–) *Hot Resort* 1985; *Happy Together* 1989; *Good Burger* 1997
Schneider, Gary *The Toxic Avenger* 1985; *Class of Nuke 'em High* 1986
Schneider, John (1960–) *Eddie Macon's Run* 1983; *The Curse* 1987; *Snow Day* 2000
Schneider, Maria (1952–) *Last Tango in Paris* 1972; *The Passenger* 1975; *A Song for Europe* 1985; *Les Nuits Fauves* 1992; *Jane Eyre* 1996; *Something to Believe In* 1997
Schneider, Michael *Beauty and the Beast* 1987; *Double Edge* 1992
Schneider, Rob (1963–) *The Beverly Hillbillies* 1993; *Surf Ninjas* 1993; *Judge Dredd* 1995; *The Adventures of Pinocchio* 1996; *Down Periscope* 1996; *Knock Off* 1998; *Susan's Plan* 1998; *Big Daddy* 1999; *Deuce Bigalow: Male Gigolo* 1999; *The Animal* 2001; *The Hot Chick* 2002; *Adam Sandler's Eight Crazy Nights* 2003; *50 First Dates* 2004
Schneider, Romy (1938–1982) *Boccaccio '70* 1961; *Fire and Ice* 1962; *The Trial* 1962; *The Cardinal* 1963; *The Victors* 1963; *Good Neighbor Sam* 1964; *What's New, Pussycat?* 1965; *10:30 PM Summer* 1966; *Triple Cross* 1966; *Otley* 1968; *The Swimming Pool* 1968; *Bloomfield* 1969; *The Things of Life* 1969; *The Assassination of Trotsky* 1972; *César and Rosalie* 1972; *The Last Train* 1972; *Ludwig* 1973; *Loving in the Rain* 1974; *Les Innocents aux Mains Sales* 1975; *Mado* 1976; *Une Histoire Simple* 1978; *Bloodline* 1979; *Deathwatch* 1980; *Garde à Vue* 1981
Schober, Andrea *The Merchant of Four Seasons* 1971; *Chinese Roulette* 1976
Schoeffling, Michael (1960–) *Sixteen Candles* 1984; *Belizaire the Cajun* 1985; *Sylvester* 1985; *Vision Quest* 1985; *Let's Get Harry* 1986; *Mermaids* 1990; *Wild Hearts Can't Be Broken* 1991
Schoelen, Jill (1970–) *Chiller* 1985; *That Was Then... This Is Now* 1985; *The Stepfather* 1986; *Curse II: The Bite* 1989; *Cutting Class* 1989; *The Phantom of the Opera* 1989; *Popcorn* 1991; *There Goes My Baby* 1994
Schofield, Andrew *Sid and Nancy* 1986; *Revengers Tragedy* 2002
Schofield, Annabel (1963–) *Dragonard* 1987; *Solar Crisis* 1990; *Body Armor* 1996; *Exit in Red* 1996
Schofield, David *An American Werewolf in London* 1981; *Tree of Hands* 1988; *Gladiator* 2000; *Chunky Monkey* 2001
Schollin, Christina (1937–) *Dear John* 1964; *Song of Norway* 1970; *Fanny and Alexander* 1982
Scholz, Eva-Ingeborg (1926–) *The Lost One* 1951; *The Devil's General* 1955; *The American Soldier* 1970
Schöner, Ingeborg (1935–) *It Happened in Rome* 1956; *Kidnapped to Mystery Island* 1964
Schorm, Evald (1931–1988) *The Party and the Guests* 1966; *The Joke* 1968
Schrader, Maria (1965–) *I Was on Mars* 1991; *Aimée and Jaguar* 1999
Schram, Bitty *A League of Their Own* 1992; *Caught* 1996; *The Pallbearer* 1996
Schrecker, Frederick (1893–1976) *Counterspy* 1953; *The Master Plan* 1954
Schreiber, Avery (1934–2002) *Swashbuckler* 1976; *Galaxina* 1980; *Caveman* 1981; *Saturday the 14th Strikes Back* 1988
Schreiber, Liev (1967–) *Mixed Nuts* 1994; *Party Girl* 1994; *Denise Calls Up* 1995; *Ransom* 1996; *Scream* 1996; *Walking and Talking* 1996; *Scream 2* 1997; *The Sunshine Boys* 1997; *The Daytrippers* 1998; *Phantoms* 1998; *Sphere* 1998; *Twilight* 1998; *The Hurricane* 1999; *Jakob the Liar* 1999; *RKO 281* 1999; *Scream 3* 1999; *A Walk on the Moon* 1999; *Hamlet* 2000; *Kate & Leopold* 2002; *The Sum of All Fears* 2002; *The Manchurian Candidate* 2004
Schrier, Paul (1970–) *Mighty Morphin Power Rangers: the Movie* 1995; *Turbo: a Power Rangers Adventure* 1997
Schröder, Ernst *aka* **Schroeder, Ernst** (1915–1994) *The Man Between* 1953; *The Counterfeit Traitor* 1962; *Heidi* 1965
Schroder, Rick *aka* **Schroder, Ricky** (1970–) *The Champ* 1979; *The Earthling* 1980; *The Last Flight of Noah's Ark* 1980; *Across the Tracks* 1990; *There Goes My Baby* 1994; *Murder at Devil's Glen* 1999
Schroeder, Barbet (1941–) *The Boulangère de Monceau* 1962; *Les Carabiniers* 1963; *Paris Vu Par...* 1965; *Celine and Julie Go Boating* 1974
Schub, Steven *Little Noises* 1992; *Caught* 1996; *The Thirteenth Floor* 1999
Schubert, Karin (1944–) *Delusions of Grandeur* 1971; *Bluebeard* 1972
Schuck, John (1940–) *Brewster McCloud* 1970; *McCabe and Mrs Miller* 1971; *Thieves like Us* 1974; *Butch and Sundance: the Early Days* 1979; *Outrageous Fortune* 1987; *Second Sight* 1989; *Holy Matrimony* 1994
Schull, Rebecca *My Life* 1993; *Mortal Fear* 1994
Schultz, Dwight (1947–) *Alone in the Dark* 1982; *Shadow Makers* 1989; *The Long Walk Home* 1990; *The Temp* 1993; *Star Trek: First Contact* 1996
Schulze, Matt *The Transporter* 2002; *Torque* 2003
Schulze, Paul *Laws of Gravity* 1992; *Hand Gun* 1994
Schumann, Erik (1925–) *The Two-Headed Spy* 1958; *Lili Marleen* 1980; *Veronika Voss* 1982
Schündler, Rudolf (1906–1988) *Kings of the Road* 1976; *Suspiria* 1976
Schünzel, Reinhold (1886–1954) *The Threepenny Opera* 1931; *Notorious* 1946; *Golden Earrings* 1947
Schuurman, Betty *Character* 1997; *Twin Sisters* 2002
Schwartz, Scott (1968–) *The Toy* 1982; *A Christmas Story* 1983; *Fear* 1988
Schwartzman, Jason (1980–) *Rushmore* 1998; *Slackers* 2001; *S1MØNE* 2002; *Spun* 2002; *I ❤ Huckabees* 2004
Schwarzenegger, Arnold *aka* **Strong, Arnold** (1947–) *Hercules in New York* 1969; *Stay Hungry* 1976; *Cactus Jack* 1979; *Scavenger Hunt* 1979; *Conan the Barbarian* 1982; *Conan the Destroyer* 1984; *The Terminator* 1984; *Commando* 1985; *Red Sonja* 1985; *Raw Deal* 1986; *Predator* 1987; *The Running Man* 1987; *Red Heat* 1988; *Twins* 1988; *Kindergarten Cop* 1990; *Total Recall* 1990; *Terminator 2: Judgment Day* 1991; *Last Action Hero* 1993; *Junior* 1994; *True Lies* 1994; *Eraser* 1996; *Jingle All the Way* 1996; *Batman and Robin* 1997; *End of Days* 1999; *The 6th Day* 2000; *Collateral Damage* 2001; *Terminator 3: Rise of the Machines* 2003; *Around the World in 80 Days* 2004
Schweig, Eric (1967–) *The Last of the Mohicans* 1992; *Pontiac Moon* 1994; *Squanto: the Last Great Warrior* 1994; *Tom and Huck* 1995; *Big Eden* 2000; *The Missing* 2003
Schweiger, Heinrich (1933–) *Echo Park* 1985; *Operation Madonna* 1987
Schweiger, Til (1963–) *The Most Desired Man* 1994; *A Girl Called Rosemarie* 1996; *Knockin' on Heaven's Door* 1997; *Judas Kiss* 1998; *The Replacement Killers* 1998; *Driven* 2001; *King Arthur* 2004
Schwiers, Ellen (1929–) *Is Anna Anderson Anastasia?* 1956; *Arms and the Man* 1958; *The Brain* 1962
Schwimmer, David (1966–) *The Pallbearer* 1996; *Apt Pupil* 1997; *Breast Men* 1997; *Kissing a Fool* 1998; *Six Days Seven Nights* 1998; *Picking Up the Pieces* 2000; *Hotel* 2001; *Madagascar* 2005
Schwimmer, Rusty *Jason Goes to Hell: the Final Friday* 1993; *A Little Princess* 1995; *Los Locos* 1997
Schygulla, Hanna (1943–) *Gods of the Plague* 1969; *Love Is Colder Than Death* 1969; *Beware of a Holy Whore* 1970; *Whity* 1970; *Why Does Herr R Run Amok?* 1970; *The Merchant of Four Seasons* 1971; *The Bitter Tears of Petra von Kant* 1972; *Effi Briest* 1974; *The Marriage of Maria Braun* 1978; *The Third Generation* 1979; *Berlin Alexanderplatz* 1980; *Lili Marleen* 1980; *Circle of Deceit* 1981; *Passion* 1982; *La Nuit de Varennes* 1983; *Storia di Piera* 1983; *Barnum* 1986; *The Delta Force* 1986; *Forever Lulu* 1987; *Dead Again* 1991; *Golem, the Spirit of Exile* 1992; *The Girl of Your Dreams* 1998; *Werckmeister Harmonies* 2000
Sciorra, Annabella (1964–) *True Love* 1989; *Cadillac Man* 1990; *Reversal of Fortune* 1990; *The Hard Way* 1991; *Jungle Fever* 1991; *The Hand That Rocks the Cradle* 1992; *Mr Wonderful* 1992; *Romeo Is Bleeding* 1992; *Whispers in the Dark* 1992; *The Night We Never Met* 1993; *The Addiction* 1994; *The Cure* 1995; *The Innocent Sleep* 1995; *The Funeral* 1996; *Underworld* 1996; *Cop Land* 1997; *Little City* 1997; *Mr Jealousy* 1997; *New Rose Hotel* 1998; *What Dreams May Come* 1998; *Jenifer* 2001; *Chasing Liberty* 2004
Scob, Edith (1937–) *Eyes without a Face* 1959; *Thérèse Desqueyroux* 1962; *Judex* 1963; *The Milky Way* 1968; *Comédie de l'Innocence* 2000; *Vidocq* 2001
Scofield, Paul (1922–) *That Lady* 1955; *Carve Her Name with Pride* 1958; *The Train* 1964; *A Man for All Seasons* 1966; *Tell Me Lies* 1967; *King Lear* 1970; *Bartleby* 1971; *A Delicate Balance* 1973; *Scorpio* 1973; *Nineteen Nineteen* 1984; *The Attic: the Hiding of Anne Frank* 1988; *Henry V* 1989; *When the Whales Came* 1989; *Hamlet* 1990; *Utz* 1992; *London* 1994; *Quiz Show* 1994; *The Crucible* 1996; *Robinson in Space* 1997; *Animal Farm* 1999; *Kurosawa* 2001
Scoggins, Tracy (1959–) *The Gumshoe Kid* 1990; *Time Bomb* 1991; *A Crack in the Floor* 2000

Scolari, Peter (1954–) *Ticks* 1993; *The Polar Express* 2004
Scorsese, Martin (1942–) *Cannonball* 1976; *Taxi Driver* 1976; *The King of Comedy* 1983; *Akira Kurosawa's Dreams* 1990; *The Grifters* 1990; *Guilty by Suspicion* 1990; *Search and Destroy* 1995; *Bringing out the Dead* 1999; *Gangs of New York* 2002; *Shark Tale* 2004
Scorupco, Izabella (1970–) *GoldenEye* 1995; *Vertical Limit* 2000; *Reign of Fire* 2001; *Exorcist: the Beginning* 2004
Scott, Adam (1973–) *High Crimes* 2002; *Torque* 2003; *Monster-in-Law* 2005
Scott (1), Alex *The Sicilians* 1964; *Darling* 1965; *Fahrenheit 451* 1966; *The Abominable Dr Phibes* 1971; *The Asphyx* 1972
Scott (2), Alex *Sky Pirates* 1986; *Romper Stomper* 1992
Scott, Andrew *Korea* 1995; *Nora* 1999
Scott, Avis *Waterfront* 1950; *To Have and to Hold* 1951
Scott, Brenda *Johnny Tiger* 1966; *Journey to Shiloh* 1967
Scott, Campbell (1962–) *From Hollywood to Deadwood* 1989; *Longtime Companion* 1990; *The Sheltering Sky* 1990; *Dead Again* 1991; *Dying Young* 1991; *Singles* 1992; *The Innocent* 1993; *Mrs Parker and the Vicious Circle* 1994; *Let It Be Me* 1995; *Big Night* 1996; *The Spanish Prisoner* 1997; *The Daytrippers* 1998; *Hi-Life* 1998; *The Impostors* 1998; *The Pilot's Wife* 2001; *Roger Dodger* 2002; *The Secret Lives of Dentists* 2002; *Duma* 2005
Scott, Debralee (1953–2005) *Pandemonium* 1982; *Misplaced* 1989
Scott, Donovan (1946–) *Zorro, the Gay Blade* 1981; *Savannah Smiles* 1982; *Police Academy* 1984; *Sheena* 1984; *The Best of Times* 1986
Scott, Douglas (1925–1988) *And So They Were Married* 1936; *The Last Gangster* 1937; *Intermezzo* 1939
Scott, Dougray (1965–) *Another 9½ Weeks* 1997; *Regeneration* 1997; *Twin Town* 1997; *Ever After: a Cinderella Story* 1998; *Gregory's Two Girls* 1999; *Mission: Impossible 2* 1999; *This Year's Love* 1999; *Enigma* 2001; *The Boy David Story* 2002; *Ripley's Game* 2002; *One Last Chance* 2003; *To Kill a King* 2003
Scott, Fred (1902–1991) *In Old Montana* 1939; *Knight of the Plains* 1939
Scott, George C (1927–1999) *Anatomy of a Murder* 1959; *The Hanging Tree* 1959; *The Hustler* 1961; *Dr Strangelove, or How I Learned to Stop Worrying and Love the Bomb* 1963; *The List of Adrian Messenger* 1963; *The Yellow Rolls-Royce* 1964; *The Bible...in the Beginning* 1966; *Not with My Wife, You Don't!* 1966; *One Born Every Minute* 1967; *Petulia* 1968; *Patton* 1970; *The Hospital* 1971; *The Last Run* 1971; *They Might Be Giants* 1971; *The New Centurions* 1972; *Rage* 1972; *The Day of the Dolphin* 1973; *Oklahoma Crude* 1973; *Bank Shot* 1974; *The Savage Is Loose* 1974; *Fear on Trial* 1975; *The Hindenburg* 1975; *Islands in the Stream* 1976; *The Prince and the Pauper* 1977; *Movie Movie* 1978; *Hardcore* 1979; *The Changeling* 1980; *The Formula* 1980; *Taps* 1981; *Oliver Twist* 1982; *Firestarter* 1984; *Pals* 1986; *The Exorcist III* 1990; *The Rescuers Down Under* 1990; *Malice* 1993; *Angus* 1995; *12 Angry Men* 1997; *Gloria* 1998; *Inherit the Wind* 1999
Scott, Gordon (1927–) *Tarzan's Hidden Jungle* 1955; *Tarzan and the Lost Safari* 1956; *Tarzan and the Trappers* 1958; *Tarzan's Fight for Life* 1958; *Tarzan's Greatest Adventure* 1959; *Tarzan the Magnificent* 1960; *Duel of the Titans* 1961; *Hero of Babylon* 1963
Scott, Jacqueline *Macabre* 1958; *Duel* 1971; *Charley Varrick* 1973; *Empire of the Ants* 1977
Scott, Janette (1938–) *No Place for Jennifer* 1949; *No Highway* 1951; *Background* 1953; *As Long as They're Happy* 1955; *The Good Companions* 1956; *Happy Is the Bride* 1957; *The Devil's Disciple* 1959; *His and Hers* 1960; *School for Scoundrels* 1960; *Double Bunk* 1961; *Two and Two Make Six* 1961; *The Day of the Triffids* 1962; *The Old Dark House* 1963; *Paranoiac* 1963; *The Siege of the Saxons* 1963; *The Beauty Jungle* 1964; *Crack in the World* 1964
Scott, Judith *Boulevard* 1994; *My Brother Tom* 2001; *Guess Who* 2005
Scott, Kathryn Leigh (1933–) *House of Dark Shadows* 1970; *Witches' Brew* 1979
Scott, Ken (1928–1986) *Stopover Tokyo* 1957; *Beloved Infidel* 1959; *Five Gates to Hell* 1959; *Woman Obsessed* 1959; *Desire in the Dust* 1960; *The Fiercest Heart* 1961; *The Second Time Around* 1961
Scott, Kimberly *The Abyss* 1989; *Downtown* 1990; *Flatliners* 1990
Scott, Larry B (1961–) *A Hero Ain't Nothin' but a Sandwich* 1978; *Revenge of the Nerds* 1984; *My Man Adam* 1985; *That Was Then... This Is Now* 1985; *SpaceCamp* 1986; *Fear of a Black Hat* 1992
Scott, Lizabeth (1922–) *The Strange Love of Martha Ivers* 1946; *Dead Reckoning* 1947; *Desert Fury* 1947; *I Walk Alone* 1947; *Pitfall* 1948; *Easy Living* 1949; *The Company She Keeps* 1950; *Dark City* 1950; *Paid in Full* 1950; *The Racket* 1951; *Red Mountain* 1951; *Stolen Face* 1952; *Scared Stiff* 1953; *Bad for Each Other* 1954; *Silver Lode* 1954; *Loving You* 1957; *Pulp* 1972
Scott, Margaretta (1912–2005) *Things to Come* 1936; *The Return of the Scarlet Pimpernel* 1937; *The Girl in the News* 1940; *Fanny by Gaslight* 1944; *The Man from Morocco* 1944; *Counterblast* 1948; *The Scamp* 1957; *Crescendo* 1970
Scott, Martha (1914–2003) *The Howards of Virginia* 1940; *Our Town* 1940; *Cheers for Miss Bishop* 1941; *One Foot in Heaven* 1941; *They Dare Not Love* 1941; *War of the Wildcats* 1943; *So Well Remembered* 1947; *The Desperate Hours* 1955; *Sayonara* 1957; *Ben-Hur* 1959; *Charlotte's Web* 1973; *The Turning Point* 1977; *Adam* 1983; *Doin' Time on Planet Earth* 1988
Scott, Pippa (1935–) *My Six Loves* 1962; *Petulia* 1968; *Cold Turkey* 1969
Scott, Randolph (1898–1987) *Island of Lost Souls* 1932; *Murders in the Zoo* 1933; *Supernatural* 1933; *Roberta* 1935; *She* 1935; *So Red the Rose* 1935; *Village Tale* 1935; *Follow the Fleet* 1936; *Go West, Young Man* 1936; *The Last of the Mohicans* 1936; *High, Wide and Handsome* 1937; *Rebecca of Sunnybrook Farm* 1938; *The Texans* 1938; *Frontier Marshal* 1939; *Jesse James* 1939; *Susannah of the Mounties* 1939; *My Favorite Wife* 1940; *Virginia City* 1940; *When the Daltons Rode* 1940; *Belle Starr* 1941; *Paris Calling* 1941; *Western Union* 1941; *Pittsburgh* 1942; *The Spoilers* 1942; *To the Shores of Tripoli* 1942; *Bombardier* 1943; *Corvette K-225* 1943; *The Desperadoes* 1943; *Gung Ho!* 1943; *Belle of the Yukon* 1944; *Follow the Boys* 1944; *Abilene Town* 1945; *Captain Kidd* 1945; *China Sky* 1945; *Badman's Territory* 1946; *Home Sweet Homicide* 1946; *Christmas Eve* 1947; *Trail Street* 1947; *Return of the Bad Men* 1948; *Canadian Pacific* 1949; *The Doolins of Oklahoma* 1949; *Fighting Man of the Plains* 1949; *The Walking Hills* 1949; *The Cariboo Trail* 1950; *Colt .45* 1950; *Fort Worth* 1951; *Man in the Saddle* 1951; *Santa Fe* 1951; *Sugarfoot* 1951; *Carson City* 1952; *Hangman's Knot* 1952; *The Stranger Wore a Gun* 1953; *Thunder over the Plains* 1953; *The Bounty Hunter* 1954; *Riding Shotgun* 1954; *A Lawless Street* 1955; *Rage at Dawn* 1955; *Tall Man Riding* 1955; *Seven Men from Now* 1956; *Seventh Cavalry* 1956; *Decision at Sundown* 1957; *Shoot-Out at Medicine Bend* 1957; *The Tall T* 1957; *Buchanan Rides Alone* 1958; *Ride Lonesome* 1959; *Westbound* 1959; *Comanche Station* 1960; *Ride the High Country* 1962
Scott, Seann William *aka* **Scott, Seann W** (1977–) *American Pie* 1999; *Dude, Where's My Car?* 2000; *Final Destination* 2000; *Road Trip* 2000; *American Pie 2* 2001; *Evolution* 2001; *Jay and Silent Bob Strike Back* 2001; *Bulletproof Monk* 2002; *Stark Raving Mad* 2002; *American Pie: the Wedding* 2003; *Old School* 2003; *Welcome to the Jungle* 2003
Scott, Terry (1927–1994) *The Night We Got the Bird* 1960; *What a Whopper!* 1961; *Gonks Go Beat* 1965; *Carry On Up the Khyber* 1968; *Carry On Camping* 1969; *Carry On Loving* 1970; *Carry On Up the Jungle* 1970; *Carry On Henry* 1971; *Bless This House* 1972; *Carry On Matron* 1972
Scott, Tom Everett (1970–) *That Thing You Do!* 1996; *An American Werewolf in Paris* 1997; *Dead Man on Campus* 1998; *One True Thing* 1998; *The Love Letter* 1999; *Attraction* 2000; *Boiler Room* 2000
Scott, William Lee (1973–) *Before Women Had Wings* 1997; *The Opposite of Sex* 1998; *October Sky* 1999; *The Butterfly Effect* 2003; *Identity* 2003
Scott, Zachary (1914–1965) *The Mask of Dimitrios* 1944; *Mildred Pierce* 1945; *The Southerner* 1945; *Cass Timberlane* 1947; *The Unfaithful* 1947; *Ruthless* 1948; *Flamingo Road* 1949; *South of St Louis* 1949; *Born to Be Bad* 1950; *Colt .45* 1950; *Guilty Bystander* 1950; *Pretty Baby* 1950; *Let's Make It Legal* 1951; *Lightning Strikes Twice* 1951; *The Secret of Convict Lake* 1951; *Wings of Danger* 1952; *Appointment in Honduras* 1953; *Shotgun* 1955; *Bandido* 1956; *The Young One* 1960; *It'$ Only Money* 1962
Scott Thomas, Kristin (1960–) *Under the Cherry Moon* 1986; *A Handful of Dust* 1987; *Force Majeure* 1989; *The Bachelor* 1990; *Autobus* 1991; *Bitter Moon* 1992; *Four Weddings and a Funeral* 1994; *An Unforgettable Summer* 1994; *Angels and Insects* 1995; *The Confessional* 1995; *The Pompatus of Love* 1995; *Richard III* 1995; *The English Patient* 1996; *Microcosmos* 1996; *Mission: Impossible* 1996; *The Revengers' Comedies* 1997; *The Horse Whisperer* 1998; *Up at the Villa* 1998; *Random Hearts* 1999; *Gosford Park* 2001; *Life as a House* 2001; *Petites Coupures* 2002; *Arsène Lupin* 2004
Scott Thomas, Serena (1961–) *Let Him Have It* 1991; *Relax... It's Just Sex* 1998; *Hostage* 2004
Scotti, Vito (1918–1996) *Master of the World* 1961; *Cactus Flower* 1969; *The Aristocats* 1970; *When the Legends Die* 1972; *I Wonder Who's Killing Her Now?* 1975
Scoular, Angela (1945–) *Here We Go round the Mulberry Bush* 1967; *Doctor in Trouble* 1970
Scourby, Alexander (1913–1985) *Affair in Trinidad* 1952; *The Big Heat* 1953; *The Glory Brigade* 1953; *The Redhead from Wyoming* 1953; *The Silver Chalice* 1954; *Me and the Colonel* 1958; *The Shaggy Dog* 1959; *Seven Thieves* 1960; *The Devil at Four o'Clock* 1961; *Jesus* 1979
Scrimm, Angus (1926–) *Phantasm* 1978; *Phantasm II* 1988; *Transylvania Twist* 1989; *Subspecies* 1991; *Deadfall* 1993; *Munchie Strikes Back* 1994; *Phantasm III – Lord of the Dead* 1994; *Wishmaster* 1997
Seacat, Sandra *The Golden Seal* 1983; *Country* 1984
Seaforth, Susan *aka* **Seaforth Hayes, Susan** (1943–) *Gunfight at Comanche Creek* 1964; *Billie* 1965; *The Dream Machine* 1990
Seagal, Steven (1951–) *Nico* 1988; *Hard to Kill* 1989; *Marked for Death* 1990; *Out for Justice* 1991; *Under Siege* 1992; *On Deadly Ground* 1994; *Under Siege 2* 1995; *Executive Decision* 1996; *The Glimmer Man* 1996; *Fire Down Below* 1997; *The Patriot* 1998; *Exit Wounds* 2001; *Ticker* 2001; *Half Past Dead* 2002
Seagrove, Jenny (1958–) *Local Hero* 1983; *Savage Islands* 1983; *Appointment with Death* 1988; *A Chorus of Disapproval* 1988; *The Guardian* 1990; *Don't Go Breaking My Heart* 1999
Seal, Elizabeth (1933–) *Town on Trial* 1956; *Cone of Silence* 1960
Seale, Douglas (1913–1999) *Ernest Saves Christmas* 1988; *Almost an Angel* 1990; *Aladdin* 1992
Seales, Franklyn (1952–1990) *The Onion Field* 1979; *Southern Comfort* 1981
Searcy, Nick *Nell* 1994; *Stolen Innocence* 1995; *About Sarah* 1998; *Cast Away* 2000; *Head of State* 2003; *Runaway Jury* 2003
Searle, Jackie *aka* **Searl, Jackie** (1920–) *Huckleberry Finn* 1931; *Skippy* 1931; *Topaze* 1933; *Murder on the Blackboard* 1934; *No Greater Glory* 1934; *That Certain Age* 1938; *The Paleface* 1948
Sears, Ann *Cat and Mouse* 1958; *The Brain* 1962
Sears, Heather (1935–1994) *Dry Rot* 1956; *The Story of Esther Costello* 1957; *Room at the Top* 1958; *The Siege of Pinchgut* 1959; *Sons and Lovers* 1960; *The Phantom of the Opera* 1962; *Saturday Night Out* 1963; *The Black Torment* 1964
Seay, James (1914–1992) *The Face behind the Mask* 1941; *Miracle on 34th Street* 1947; *Close to My Heart* 1951; *Return to Treasure Island* 1954; *The Amazing Colossal Man* 1957; *Beginning of the End* 1957
Sebanek, Josef *A Blonde in Love* 1965; *The Fireman's Ball* 1967
Sebastian, Dorothy (1906–1957) *Our Dancing Daughters* 1928; *The Single Standard* 1929; *Spite Marriage* 1929; *The Arizona Kid* 1939; *Rough Riders' Roundup* 1939
Sebastian, Tracy *On the Air Live with Captain Midnight* 1979; *Running Cool* 1993
Seberg, Jean (1938–1979) *Saint Joan* 1957; *Bonjour Tristesse* 1958; *A Bout de Souffle* 1959; *The Mouse That Roared* 1959; *Let No Man Write My Epitaph* 1960; *In the French Style* 1963; *Lilith* 1964; *A Fine Madness* 1966; *The Looters* 1966; *Moment to Moment* 1966; *The Road to Corinth* 1967; *Paint Your Wagon* 1969; *Pendulum* 1969; *Airport* 1970; *Macho Callahan* 1970; *Kill!* 1972
Secombe, Harry (1921–2001) *Down among the Z-Men* 1952; *Forces' Sweetheart* 1953; *Svengali* 1954; *Jet Storm* 1959; *Oliver!* 1968; *The Bed Sitting Room* 1969; *Doctor in Trouble* 1970; *Song of Norway* 1970; *The Magnificent Seven Deadly Sins* 1971; *Sunstruck* 1972
Secor, Kyle (1958–) *Heart of Dixie* 1989; *Delusion* 1991; *Late for Dinner* 1991; *Sleeping with the Enemy* 1991; *Untamed Heart* 1993; *Drop Zone* 1994
Seda, Jon (1970–) *Gladiator* 1992; *I Like It like That* 1994; *Twelve Monkeys* 1995; *Dear God* 1996; *Sunchaser* 1996; *Selena* 1997; *Price of Glory* 2000; *Undisputed* 2002
Sedan, Rolfe (1896–1982) *The Iron Mask* 1929; *The Story of Vernon and Irene Castle* 1939
Sedaris, Amy (1961–) *Commandments* 1996; *Six Days Seven Nights* 1998
Seddon, Margaret (1872–1968) *Smilin' Through* 1932; *The Worst Woman in Paris?* 1933; *The Meanest Man in the World* 1943
Sedgwick, Edie (1943–1971) *Vinyl* 1965; *The Chelsea Girls* 1967; *Ciao! Manhattan* 1973
Sedgwick, Kyra (1965–) *Tai-Pan* 1986; *Kansas* 1988; *Born on the Fourth of July* 1989; *Mr and Mrs Bridge* 1990; *Pyrates* 1991; *Miss Rose White* 1992; *Singles* 1992; *Heart and Souls* 1993; *The Low Life* 1995; *Something to Talk About* 1995; *Phenomenon* 1996; *Critical Care* 1997; *Montana* 1997; *What's Cooking?* 2000; *Personal Velocity* 2001; *Just a Kiss* 2002; *Secondhand Lions* 2003; *The Woodsman* 2004
Seely, Tim *Please Turn Over* 1960; *Mutiny on the Bounty* 1962
Segado, Alberto *I, the Worst of All* 1990; *We Don't Want to Talk about It* 1993
Segal, George (1934–) *The Young Doctors* 1961; *Act One* 1963; *Invitation to a Gunfighter* 1964; *The New Interns* 1964; *King Rat* 1965; *Ship of Fools* 1965; *Lost Command* 1966; *The Quiller Memorandum* 1966; *Who's Afraid of Virginia Woolf?* 1966; *The St Valentine's Day Massacre* 1967; *Bye Bye Braverman* 1968; *No Way to Treat a Lady* 1968; *The Bridge at Remagen* 1969; *The Southern Star* 1969; *Loving* 1970; *The Owl and the Pussycat* 1970; *Where's Poppa?* 1970; *Born to Win* 1971; *The Hot Rock* 1972; *Blume in Love* 1973; *A Touch of Class* 1973; *California Split* 1974; *The Terminal Man* 1974; *The Black Bird* 1975; *The Duchess and the Dirtwater Fox* 1976; *Fun with Dick and Jane* 1977; *Rollercoaster* 1977; *Who Is Killing the Great Chefs of Europe?* 1978; *Lost and Found* 1979; *The Last Married Couple in America* 1980; *Carbon Copy* 1981; *Killing 'em Softly* 1982; *Stick* 1985; *All's Fair* 1989; *Look Who's Talking* 1989; *For the Boys* 1991; *Army of One* 1993; *Look Who's Talking Now!* 1993; *The Babysitter* 1995; *The November Conspiracy* 1995; *The Cable Guy* 1996; *Flirting with Disaster* 1996; *It's My Party* 1996; *The Mirror Has Two Faces* 1996
Ségal, Gilles *Topkapi* 1964; *Without Apparent Motive* 1972; *Lumière Noire* 1994
Segal, Zohra (1912–) *Harem* 1985; *Masala* 1991; *Bhaji on the Beach* 1993; *Chicken Tikka Masala* 2005
Segall, Pamela *aka* **Segall Adlon, Pamela** (1968–) *Willy/Milly* 1986; *After Midnight* 1989; *Say Anything...* 1989; *Gate II* 1992; *...At First Sight* 1995; *Bed of Roses* 1995; *Some Girls* 1998; *Recess: School's Out* 2001
Segel, Jason (1980–) *SLC Punk!* 1999; *Slackers* 2001
Segura, Santiago (1965–) *The Day of the Beast* 1995; *Perdita Durango* 1997; *Dying of Laughter* 1999; *Girl from Rio* 2001
Seigner, Emmanuelle (1966–) *Detective* 1985; *Frantic* 1988; *Bitter Moon* 1992; *Nirvana* 1996; *Place Vendôme* 1998; *Buddy Boy* 1999; *The Ninth Gate* 1999
Seigner, Françoise *L'Enfant Sauvage* 1970; *Les Misérables* 1982
Seigner, Mathilde (1968–) *Dry Cleaning* 1997; *Harry, He's Here to Help* 2000; *Betty Fisher and Other Stories* 2001; *The Girl from Paris* 2001
Seiphemo, Rapulana *Jump the Gun* 1996; *Tarzan and the Lost City* 1998; *Hijack Stories* 2000
Seitz, John *Hard Choices* 1984; *Call Me* 1988; *Forced March* 1989; *Out of the Rain* 1991; *Blood and Wine* 1996
Sekka, Johnny (1939–) *Flame in the Streets* 1961; *East of Sudan* 1964; *Woman of Straw* 1964; *Khartoum* 1966; *The Last Safari* 1967; *Incense for the Damned*

1970; *A Warm December* 1973; *The Message* 1976
Selby, David (1941–) *Night of Dark Shadows* 1971; *Up the Sandbox* 1972; *The Super Cops* 1973; *Rich Kids* 1979; *Raise the Titanic* 1980; *Rich and Famous* 1981; *Dying Young* 1991; *D3: the Mighty Ducks* 1996
Selby, Nicholas (1925–) *A Midsummer Night's Dream* 1969; *Macbeth* 1971
Selby, Sarah aka **Selby, Sara** (1905–1980) *Beyond the Forest* 1949; *Tower of London* 1962
Selby, Tony (1938–) *In Search of Gregory* 1970; *Adolf Hitler – My Part in His Downfall* 1972
Seldes, Marian (1928–) *Crime and Punishment, USA* 1959; *Fingers* 1978; *Tom and Huck* 1995; *Digging to China* 1998; *The Haunting* 1999; *Town & Country* 2001
Sellars, Elizabeth (1923–) *Floodtide* 1949; *Cloudburst* 1951; *Night Was Our Friend* 1951; *The Gentle Gunman* 1952; *Hunted* 1952; *The Long Memory* 1952; *Three Cases of Murder* 1953; *The Barefoot Contessa* 1954; *Desiree* 1954; *Forbidden Cargo* 1954; *Prince of Players* 1955; *The Man in the Sky* 1956; *The Shiralee* 1957; *Law and Disorder* 1958; *The Day They Robbed the Bank of England* 1960; *Never Let Go* 1960; *The Chalk Garden* 1964; *The Mummy's Shroud* 1966; *The Hireling* 1973
Selleck, Tom (1945–) *Myra Breckinridge* 1970; *The Seven Minutes* 1971; *Daughters of Satan* 1972; *Terminal Island* 1973; *Coma* 1977; *Magnum: Don't Eat the Snow in Hawaii* 1980; *Divorce Wars* 1982; *High Road to China* 1983; *Lassiter* 1984; *Runaway* 1984; *Three Men and a Baby* 1987; *Her Alibi* 1989; *An Innocent Man* 1989; *Quigley Down Under* 1990; *Three Men and a Little Lady* 1990; *Christopher Columbus: the Discovery* 1992; *Folks!* 1992; *Mr Baseball* 1992; *In & Out* 1997; *Last Stand at Saber River* 1997; *The Love Letter* 1999
Sellers, Peter (1925–1980) *Down among the Z-Men* 1952; *Orders Are Orders* 1954; *The Case of the Mukkinese Battle Horn* 1955; *John and Julie* 1955; *The Ladykillers* 1955; *The Naked Truth* 1957; *The Smallest Show on Earth* 1957; *Carlton-Browne of the FO* 1958; *tom thumb* 1958; *Up the Creek* 1958; *I'm All Right Jack* 1959; *The Mouse That Roared* 1959; *The Running, Jumping and Standing Still Film* 1959; *The Battle of the Sexes* 1960; *The Millionairess* 1960; *Never Let Go* 1960; *Two Way Stretch* 1960; *Lolita* 1961; *Mr Topaze* 1961; *Only Two Can Play* 1961; *The Road to Hong Kong* 1962; *Trial and Error* 1962; *Waltz of the Toreadors* 1962; *The Wrong Arm of the Law* 1962; *Dr Strangelove, or How I Learned to Stop Worrying and Love the Bomb* 1963; *Heavens Above!* 1963; *The Pink Panther* 1963; *A Shot in the Dark* 1964; *The World of Henry Orient* 1964; *What's New, Pussycat?* 1965; *After the Fox* 1966; *The Wrong Box* 1966; *The Bobo* 1967; *Casino Royale* 1967; *Woman Times Seven* 1967; *I Love You, Alice B Toklas* 1968; *The Party* 1968; *The Magic Christian* 1969; *Hoffman* 1970; *Simon, Simon* 1970; *There's a Girl in My Soup* 1970; *Where Does It Hurt?* 1971; *Alice's Adventures in Wonderland* 1972; *The Blockhouse* 1973; *Ghost in the Noonday Sun* 1973; *The Optimists of Nine Elms* 1973; *Soft Beds, Hard Battles* 1973; *The Great McGonagall* 1974; *The Return of the Pink Panther* 1974; *Murder by Death* 1976; *The Pink Panther Strikes Again* 1976; *Revenge of the Pink Panther* 1978; *Being There* 1979; *The Prisoner of Zenda* 1979; *The Fiendish Plot of Dr Fu Manchu* 1980; *Trail of the Pink Panther* 1982
Sellon, Charles aka **Sellon, Charles A** (1870–1937) *The Monster* 1925; *The Saturday Night Kid* 1929; *Make Me a Star* 1932; *Bright Eyes* 1934; *It's a Gift* 1934; *In Old Kentucky* 1935
Selten, Morton (1860–1939) *Moscow Nights* 1935; *In the Soup* 1936; *Fire over England* 1937; *The Divorce of Lady X* 1938; *Shipyard Sally* 1939; *The Thief of Bagdad* 1940
Selwyn, Ruth (1905–1954) *Polly of the Circus* 1932; *Speak Easily* 1932
Selzer, Milton (1918–) *Marnie* 1964; *The Legend of Lylah Clare* 1968; *Miss Rose White* 1992
Semmelrogge, Willy (1923–1984) *The Enigma of Kaspar Hauser* 1974; *Woyzeck* 1978
Semon, Larry (1889–1928) *The Wizard of Oz* 1925; *Underworld* 1927
Sen, Aparna (1945–) *The Guru* 1969; *Bombay Talkie* 1970; *The Middleman* 1975; *Hullabaloo over Georgie and Bonnie's Pictures* 1979
Sen, Gita (1930–) *And Quiet Rolls the Dawn* 1979; *In Search of Famine* 1980
Senda, Koreya (1904–1994) *Gate of Hell* 1953; *The H-Man* 1954
Seneca, Joe (1914–1996) *Crossroads* 1986; *School Daze* 1988; *Mississippi Masala* 1991; *The Saint of Fort Washington* 1993
Sentier, Jean-Pierre (1940–1995) *Angel Dust* 1987; *A Strange Place to Meet* 1988
Serato, Massimo (1916–1989) *The Man from Cairo* 1953; *Cartouche* 1954; *The Loves of Three Queens* 1954; *Queen of the Pirates* 1960; *El Cid* 1961; *Constantine and the Cross* 1961; *Pontius Pilate* 1961; *The Secret Mark of D'Artagnan* 1962; *Brennus – Enemy of Rome* 1963; *The Spartan Gladiators* 1964; *The Tenth Victim* 1965; *The Wild, Wild Planet* 1965; *The Gamblers* 1969; *Don't Look Now* 1973
Serbedzija, Rade aka **Sherbedgia, Rade** (1946–) *Before the Rain* 1994; *Broken English* 1996; *The Saint* 1997; *The Truce* 1997; *Mighty Joe Young* 1998; *Polish Wedding* 1998; *Eyes Wide Shut* 1999; *Stigmata* 1999; *Snatch* 2000; *South Pacific* 2001; *The Quiet American* 2002
Serious, Yahoo (1954–) *Young Einstein* 1988; *Reckless Kelly* 1993
Serkis, Andy (1964–) *Career Girls* 1997; *Stella Does Tricks* 1997; *Among Giants* 1998; *Mojo* 1998; *Pandaemonium* 2000; *Shiner* 2000; *The Lord of the Rings: The Fellowship of the Ring* 2001; *24 Hour Party People* 2001; *Deathwatch* 2002; *The Escapist* 2002; *The Lord of the Rings: The Two Towers* 2002; *The Lord of the Rings: The Return of the King* 2003; *13 Going on 30* 2004
Serna, Assumpta (1957–) *Lola* 1986; *Matador* 1986; *I, the Worst of All* 1990; *Wild Orchid* 1990; *Nostradamus* 1993; *The Shooter* 1994
Serna, Pepe (1944–) *Shoot Out* 1971; *Walk Proud* 1979; *Vice Squad* 1982; *Break of Dawn* 1988; *Bad Jim* 1989; *The Rookie* 1990; *American Me* 1992; *A Million to Juan* 1994
Sernas, Jacques (1925–) *Golden Salamander* 1949; *Helen of Troy* 1955; *The Sign of the Gladiator* 1958; *Duel of Champions* 1961; *Duel of the Titans* 1961; *Hornet's Nest* 1970
Serra, Raymond aka **Serra, Ray** (1931–2003) *Alphabet City* 1984; *Forever Lulu* 1987; *Men of Means* 1997; *Safe Men* 1998
Serrano, Diego (1973–) *Mixing Nia* 1998; *The 24 Hour Woman* 1999
Serrano, Julieta (1933–) *Dark Habits* 1983; *Matador* 1986; *Women on the Verge of a Nervous Breakdown* 1988; *Tie Me Up! Tie Me Down!* 1990
Serrano, Nestor (1957–) *Brenda Starr* 1989; *Hangin' with the Homeboys* 1991; *Bad Boys* 1995; *After the Storm* 2001; *Empire* 2002
Serrault, Michel (1928–) *Les Diaboliques* 1954; *King of Hearts* 1966; *Get out Your Handkerchiefs* 1977; *La Cage aux Folles* 1978; *Buffet Froid* 1979; *La Cage aux Folles II* 1980; *Garde à Vue* 1981; *La Cage aux Folles III: "Elles" Se Marient* 1985; *En Toute Innocence* 1987; *Docteur Petiot* 1990; *The Old Lady Who Walked in the Sea* 1991; *Le Bonheur Est dans le Pré* 1995; *Nelly & Monsieur Arnaud* 1995; *Beaumarchais l'Insolent* 1996; *Artemisia* 1997; *Rien Ne Va Plus* 1997; *The Children of the Marshland* 1998; *Le Libertin* 2000; *The Girl from Paris* 2001
Serre, Henri (1931–) *Jules et Jim* 1961; *Fire and Ice* 1962
Serret, John *The Gold Express* 1955; *Rogue's Yarn* 1956; *Taste of Fear* 1961
Servais, Jean (1910–1976) *Angèle* 1934; *Rififi* 1955; *Celui Qui Doit Mourir* 1957; *La Fièvre Monte à el Pao* 1959; *That Man from Rio* 1964; *Thomas the Imposter* 1964; *Lost Command* 1966; *They Came to Rob Las Vegas* 1968
Sesay, Mo *Young Soul Rebels* 1991; *Bhaji on the Beach* 1993
Sesselman, Sabina aka **Selman, Sabina** (1936–1998) *Le Bossu* 1959; *Information Received* 1962
Sessions, John (1953–) *The Bounty* 1984; *The Pope Must Die* 1991; *Freddie as FRO7* 1992; *Princess Caraboo* 1994; *In the Bleak Midwinter* 1995; *The Adventures of Pinocchio* 1996; *The Scarlet Tunic* 1997; *A Midsummer Night's Dream* 1999; *One of the Hollywood Ten* 2000; *High Heels and Low Lifes* 2001; *Five Children and It* 2004; *William Shakespeare's The Merchant of Venice* 2004
Seth, Roshan (1942–) *Gandhi* 1982; *Indiana Jones and the Temple of Doom* 1984; *My Beautiful Laundrette* 1985; *Little Dorrit* 1987; *1871* 1989; *Not without My Daughter* 1990; *London Kills Me* 1991; *Mississippi Masala* 1991; *Electric Moon* 1992; *Solitaire for 2* 1994; *Street Fighter* 1994; *The Journey* 1997; *Bombay Boys* 1998; *Such a Long Journey* 1998
Seth, Sushma *Chal Mere Bhai* 2000; *Kal Ho Naa Ho* 2003
Seton, Bruce (1909–1969) *Love from a Stranger* 1936; *Sweeney Todd, the Demon Barber of Fleet Street* 1936; *The Green Cockatoo* 1937; *The Curse of the Wraydons* 1946; *The Blue Lamp* 1949; *Whisky Galore!* 1949; *Eight O'Clock Walk* 1953; *Delayed Action* 1954; *The Crooked Sky* 1957; *Undercover Girl* 1957; *Hidden Homicide* 1958; *Life in Danger* 1959; *Gorgo* 1961
Settle, Matthew (1969–) *Attraction* 2000; *The In Crowd* 2000
Séty, Gérard (1922–1998) *Les Espions* 1957; *Montparnasse 19* 1958; *Van Gogh* 1991
Severance, Joan (1958–) *No Holds Barred* 1989; *See No Evil, Hear No Evil* 1989; *Bird on a Wire* 1990; *The Runestone* 1991; *Lake Consequence* 1992; *The Last Seduction 2* 1998
Severn, Christopher (1935–) *Mrs Miniver* 1942; *The Man from Down Under* 1943
Severn, Raymond (1932–1994) *We Are Not Alone* 1939; *The Suspect* 1944
Severn, William (1938–1983) *Journey for Margaret* 1942; *Son of Lassie* 1945
Severne, Mary Anne *The Adventures of Barry McKenzie* 1972; *Run, Rebecca, Run* 1981
Sevigny, Chloë aka **Sevigny, Chloe** (1974–) *kids* 1995; *Trees Lounge* 1996; *Gummo* 1997; *The Last Days of Disco* 1998; *Palmetto* 1998; *Boys Don't Cry* 1999; *julien donkey-boy* 1999; *A Map of the World* 1999; *American Psycho* 2000; *If These Walls Could Talk 2* 2000; *Demonlover* 2002; *Ten Minutes Older: the Trumpet* 2002; *The Brown Bunny* 2003; *Dogville* 2003; *Party Monster* 2003; *Shattered Glass* 2003; *Melinda and Melinda* 2004
Sevilla, Carmen (1930–) *King of Kings* 1961; *Antony and Cleopatra* 1972
Sewell, George (1924–) *Sparrows Can't Sing* 1962; *Kaleidoscope* 1966; *The Vengeance of She* 1968; *Diamonds on Wheels* 1973
Sewell, Rufus (1967–) *Twenty-One* 1991; *Dirty Weekend* 1992; *A Man of No Importance* 1994; *Carrington* 1995; *Victory* 1995; *Hamlet* 1996; *Dangerous Beauty* 1997; *Martha – Meet Frank, Daniel and Laurence* 1997; *The Woodlanders* 1997; *Dark City* 1998; *Bless the Child* 2000; *A Knight's Tale* 2001; *She Creature* 2001; *Extreme Ops* 2003
Seweryn, Andrzej (1946–) *The Conductor* 1980; *Schindler's List* 1993; *Généalogies d'un Crime* 1997; *Lucie Aubrac* 1997
Sexton III, Brendan aka **Sexton Jr, Brendan** (1980–) *Welcome to the Dollhouse* 1995; *Hurricane Streets* 1997; *Desert Blue* 1998; *Pecker* 1998; *Boys Don't Cry* 1999; *Session 9* 2001
Seyferth, Wilfried aka **Seyfert, Wilfried** (1908–1954) *Decision before Dawn* 1951; *The Devil Makes Three* 1952
Seyler, Athene (1889–1990) *Blossom Time* 1934; *Moscow Nights* 1935; *Southern Roses* 1936; *Quiet Wedding* 1940; *The Franchise Affair* 1950; *Young Wives' Tale* 1951; *Made in Heaven* 1952; *Treasure Hunt* 1952; *The Beggar's Opera* 1953; *Campbell's Kingdom* 1957; *Happy Is the Bride* 1957; *How to Murder a Rich Uncle* 1957; *Night of the Demon* 1957; *A Tale of Two Cities* 1957; *The Inn of the Sixth Happiness* 1958; *Make Mine Mink* 1960; *Two and Two Make Six* 1961; *The Girl on the Boat* 1962; *I Thank a Fool* 1962; *Satan Never Sleeps* 1962; *Nurse on Wheels* 1963
Seymour, Anne (1909–1988) *All the King's Men* 1949; *The Gift of Love* 1958; *All the Fine Young Cannibals* 1960; *The Subterraneans* 1960; *Good Neighbor Sam* 1964; *Where Love Has Gone* 1964; *Blindfold* 1966; *Triumphs of a Man Called Horse* 1983; *Trancers* 1985
Seymour, Cara *Silent Grace* 2001; *Adaptation.* 2002; *Hotel Rwanda* 2004
Seymour, Carolyn *Gumshoe* 1971; *Unman, Wittering and Zigo* 1971; *The Ruling Class* 1972; *Steptoe and Son* 1972; *The Bitch* 1979; *Reform School Girl* 1994
Seymour, Dan (1915–1993) *A Night in Casablanca* 1946; *The Searching Wind* 1946; *Intrigue* 1947; *Johnny Belinda* 1948; *Face to Face* 1952; *Abbott and Costello Meet the Mummy* 1955; *Return of the Fly* 1959
Seymour (1), Jane (1898–1956) *Back Door to Heaven* 1939; *Remember the Day* 1941; *Tom, Dick and Harry* 1941
Seymour (2), Jane (1951–) *Frankenstein: the True Story* 1973; *Live and Let Die* 1973; *Sinbad and the Eye of the Tiger* 1977; *Battlestar Galactica* 1978; *Oh, Heavenly Dog!* 1980; *Somewhere in Time* 1980; *The Scarlet Pimpernel* 1982; *Lassiter* 1984; *Head Office* 1986; *Wedding Crashers* 2005
Seymour, Ralph *Just before Dawn* 1980; *Meatballs 2* 1984; *Killer Party* 1986
Seyrig, Delphine (1932–1990) *Pull My Daisy* 1959; *Last Year at Marienbad* 1961; *Muriel* 1963; *Accident* 1967; *The Milky Way* 1968; *Stolen Kisses* 1968; *Daughters of Darkness* 1970; *The Magic Donkey* 1970; *The Discreet Charm of the Bourgeoisie* 1972; *The Day of the Jackal* 1973; *A Doll's House* 1973; *The Black Windmill* 1974; *Jeanne Dielman, 23 Quai du Commerce, 1080 Bruxelles* 1975; *Golden Eighties* 1986
Shaban, Nabil (1953–) *Born of Fire* 1987; *Wittgenstein* 1993
Shadix, Glenn (1952–) *Heathers* 1989; *Bingo* 1991; *Meet the Applegates* 1991; *Demolition Man* 1993; *The Nightmare before Christmas* 1993; *Dunston Checks In* 1996
Shah, Naseeruddin (1950–) *Nishant* 1975; *Junoon* 1978; *Mandi* 1983; *Mirch Masala* 1987; *The Perfect Murder* 1988; *Electric Moon* 1992; *Bombay Boys* 1998; *Such a Long Journey* 1998; *Monsoon Wedding* 2001; *The League of Extraordinary Gentlemen* 2003; *Main Hoon Na* 2004
Shah, Satish *Mujhse Dosti Karoge!* 2002; *Saathiya* 2002; *Kuch Naa Kaho* 2003; *Mujhse Shaadi Karogi* 2004
Shakur, Tupac (1971–1996) *Juice* 1991; *Poetic Justice* 1993; *Above the Rim* 1994; *Bullet* 1995; *Gridlock'd* 1996; *Gang Related* 1997
Shalhoub, Tony (1953–) *Barton Fink* 1991; *IQ* 1994; *Big Night* 1996; *Men in Black* 1997; *A Civil Action* 1998; *Paulie* 1998; *The Siege* 1998; *Galaxy Quest* 1999; *Impostor* 2001; *The Man Who Wasn't There* 2001; *SPYkids* 2001; *Thir13en Ghosts* 2001; *Life or Something like It* 2002; *Men in Black 2* 2002; *Against the Ropes* 2003
Shamata, Chuck aka **Shamata, Charles** *Running* 1979; *Scanners* 1980; *The Devil and Max Devlin* 1981; *Between Friends* 1983; *Unfinished Business* 1983
Shandling, Garry (1949–) *Love Affair* 1994; *Mixed Nuts* 1994; *Hurlyburly* 1998; *What Planet Are You From?* 2000; *Town & Country* 2001
Shane, Gene *Run, Angel, Run* 1969; *The Velvet Vampire* 1971
Shane, Paul (1940–) *La Passione* 1996; *Between Two Women* 2000; *Heartlands* 2002
Shane, Sara (1926–) *The King and Four Queens* 1956; *Affair in Havana* 1957; *Tarzan's Greatest Adventure* 1959
Shaner, Michael *Bloodfist* 1989; *The Expert* 1994
Shankar, Mamata *And Quiet Rolls the Dawn* 1979; *An Enemy of the People* 1989; *Branches of the Tree* 1990; *The Stranger* 1991
Shanks, Don aka **Shanks, Donald L** (1950–) *The Life and Times of Grizzly Adams* 1974; *Halloween 5: the Revenge of Michael Myers* 1989; *Spirit of the Eagle* 1991; *Wind Dancer* 1991; *3 Ninjas Knuckle Up* 1995
Shannon, Al *The Drifter* 1988; *Out of the Rain* 1991
Shannon, Frank (1874–1959) *Flash Gordon* 1936; *The Texas Rangers* 1936
Shannon, Harry (1890–1964) *Once upon a Honeymoon* 1942; *Song of Texas* 1943; *The Yellow Rose of Texas* 1944; *San Quentin* 1946; *The Devil Thumbs a Ride* 1947; *Mr Blandings Builds His Dream House* 1948; *Tulsa* 1949; *Cry of the Hunted* 1953; *Witness to Murder* 1954; *The Marauders* 1955; *The Tall Men* 1955; *Written on the Wind* 1956; *Gypsy* 1962
Shannon, Michael aka **Shannon, Mike** *Cecil B Demented* 2000; *Grand Theft Parsons* 2003; *Kangaroo Jack* 2003; *The Woodsman* 2004
Shannon, Molly (1964–) *Analyze This* 1999; *Never Been Kissed* 1999; *Superstar* 1999; *The Grinch* 2000; *Serendipity* 2001; *Good Boy!* 2003
Shannon, Peggy (1910–1941) *This Reckless Age* 1932; *Deluge* 1933; *Turn Back the Clock* 1933; *The Case of the Lucky Legs* 1935; *The House across the Bay* 1940
Shannon, Richard *Arrowhead* 1953; *Alaska Seas* 1954; *The Bridges at Toko-Ri* 1954; *Beau James* 1957
Shannon, Vicellous Reon (1981–) *The Hurricane* 1999; *Freedom Song* 2000

Shaps, Cyril (1923–2003) *Passport to Shame* 1958; *The Pursuers* 1961; *Operation Daybreak* 1975; *The Lost Son* 1998; *The Clandestine Marriage* 1999
Sharian, John *Death Machine* 1994; *The Machinist* 2003
Sharif, Omar (1932–) *Lawrence of Arabia* 1962; *Behold a Pale Horse* 1964; *The Fall of the Roman Empire* 1964; *Genghis Khan* 1964; *The Yellow Rolls-Royce* 1964; *Doctor Zhivago* 1965; *The Night of the Generals* 1966; *The Poppy Is Also a Flower* 1966; *More than a Miracle* 1967; *The Appointment* 1968; *Funny Girl* 1968; *Mayerling* 1968; *Che!* 1969; *Mackenna's Gold* 1969; *The Burglars* 1971; *The Horsemen* 1971; *The Last Valley* 1971; *Juggernaut* 1974; *The Tamarind Seed* 1974; *Funny Lady* 1975; *Crime and Passion* 1976; *Ashanti* 1979; *Bloodline* 1979; *The Baltimore Bullet* 1980; *Oh, Heavenly Dog!* 1980; *Green Ice* 1981; *Top Secret!* 1984; *The Rainbow Thief* 1990; *Mrs 'arris Goes to Paris* 1992; *The 13th Warrior* 1999; *Hidalgo* 2003; *Monsieur Ibrahim and the Flowers of the Koran* 2003
Sharkey, Billy Ray *Dudes* 1987; *After Midnight* 1989
Sharkey, Ray (1953–1993) *The Lords of Flatbush* 1974; *Who'll Stop the Rain?* 1978; *Heart Beat* 1979; *The Idolmaker* 1980; *Willie and Phil* 1980; *Love and Money* 1982; *Regina* 1982; *Some Kind of Hero* 1982; *No Mercy* 1986; *Wise Guys* 1986; *Private Investigations* 1987; *Scenes from the Class Struggle In Beverly Hills* 1989; *Wired* 1989; *Act of Piracy* 1990; *Relentless 2: Dead On* 1991; *Round Trip to Heaven* 1992; *Zebrahead* 1992; *Cop and a Half* 1993
Sharma, Romesh *Siddhartha* 1972; *Hum* 1991
Sharp, Anthony (1915–1984) *Die Screaming Marianne* 1970; *Gawain and the Green Knight* 1973; *House of Mortal Sin* 1975
Sharp, Lesley *Rita, Sue and Bob Too* 1987; *Close My Eyes* 1991; *Naked* 1993; *Priest* 1994; *The Full Monty* 1997
Sharp, Timm *Stark Raving Mad* 2002; *King of the Ants* 2003
Sharpe, Albert (1885–1970) *Portrait of Jennie* 1948; *The Return of October* 1948; *Up in Central Park* 1948; *Adventure in Baltimore* 1949; *Royal Wedding* 1951; *Face to Face* 1952; *Brigadoon* 1954; *Darby O'Gill and the Little People* 1959; *The Day They Robbed the Bank of England* 1960
Sharpe, Cornelia (1947–) *Serpico* 1973; *Open Season* 1974; *The Reincarnation of Peter Proud* 1975; *The Next Man* 1976; *Venom* 1981
Sharpe, Edith (1870–1968) *Old Mother Riley* 1937; *The Guinea Pig* 1948; *Landfall* 1949; *Happy Is the Bride* 1957; *A French Mistress* 1960; *Satan Never Sleeps* 1962
Sharpe, Karen (1934–) *Man with the Gun* 1955; *The Disorderly Orderly* 1964
Sharrett, Michael (1965–) *The Magic of Lassie* 1978; *Deadly Friend* 1986
Sharron, Nitzan *That Summer of White Roses* 1989; *The Devil's Arithmetic* 1999
Shatner, William (1931–) *The Brothers Karamazov* 1958; *The Explosive Generation* 1961; *The Intruder* 1961; *Judgment at Nuremberg* 1961; *The Outrage* 1964; *Incubus* 1965; *Big Bad Mama* 1974; *The Devil's Rain* 1975; *Impulse* 1975; *Kingdom of the Spiders* 1977; *Star Trek: the Motion Picture* 1979; *The Kidnapping of the President* 1980; *Airplane II: the Sequel* 1982; *Star Trek II: the Wrath of Khan* 1982; *Visiting Hours* 1982; *Star Trek III: the Search for Spock* 1984; *Star Trek IV: the Voyage Home* 1986; *Star Trek V: the Final Frontier* 1989; *Star Trek VI: the Undiscovered Country* 1991; *National Lampoon's Loaded Weapon 1* 1993; *Star Trek: Generations* 1994; *Free Enterprise* 1998; *Miss Congeniality* 2000; *Osmosis Jones* 2001; *American Psycho II: All American Girl* 2002; *Showtime* 2002; *Miss Congeniality 2: Armed & Fabulous* 2005
Shaughnessy, Mickey (1920–1985) *Last of the Comanches* 1952; *Conquest of Space* 1955; *The Burglar* 1956; *Designing Woman* 1957; *Jailhouse Rock* 1957; *Gunman's Walk* 1958; *A Nice Little Bank That Should Be Robbed* 1958; *The Sheepman* 1958; *Don't Give Up the Ship* 1959; *Edge of Eternity* 1959; *The Adventures of Huckleberry Finn* 1960; *North to Alaska* 1960; *Sex Kittens Go to College* 1960; *The Boatniks* 1970
Shaver, Helen (1951–) *Shoot* 1976; *Outrageous!* 1977; *High-ballin'* 1978; *In Praise of Older Women* 1978; *The Amityville Horror* 1979; *The Osterman Weekend* 1983; *Best Defense* 1984; *Desert Hearts* 1985; *The Color of Money* 1986; *The Believers* 1987; *The Land before Time* 1988; *Tree of Hands* 1988; *Bethune: the Making of a Hero* 1990; *That Night* 1992; *Born to Be Wild* 1995; *Open Season* 1995; *Tremors II: Aftershocks* 1995
Shaw, Alonna *Double Impact* 1991; *Cyborg Cop* 1993
Shaw, Anabel *aka* **Shaw, Annabel** (1923–) *Bulldog Drummond Strikes Back* 1947; *Dangerous Years* 1947; *Gun Crazy* 1949
Shaw, Denis *aka* **Shaw, Dennis** (1921–1971) *House of Blackmail* 1953; *Who Done It?* 1956; *Passport to Shame* 1958; *Trouble with Eve* 1959; *Beyond the Curtain* 1960
Shaw, Fiona (1958–) *Mountains of the Moon* 1989; *My Left Foot* 1989; *Three Men and a Little Lady* 1990; *London Kills Me* 1991; *Super Mario Bros* 1993; *Undercover Blues* 1993; *Persuasion* 1995; *Jane Eyre* 1996; *Anna Karenina* 1997; *The Butcher Boy* 1997; *The Avengers* 1998; *The Last September* 1999; *RKO 281* 1999; *Harry Potter and the Philosopher's Stone* 2001; *The Triumph of Love* 2001; *Doctor Sleep* 2002; *Harry Potter and the Chamber of Secrets* 2002
Shaw, Lewis (1910–1987) *Open All Night* 1934; *Death on the Set* 1935
Shaw, Martin (1945–) *Macbeth* 1971; *The Golden Voyage of Sinbad* 1973; *Operation Daybreak* 1975; *The Hound of the Baskervilles* 1983; *Ladder of Swords* 1988
Shaw, Maxwell (1929–1985) *Once More, with Feeling* 1959; *The Oblong Box* 1969
Shaw, Oscar (1887–1967) *The Cocoanuts* 1929; *Rhythm on the River* 1940
Shaw (1), Peter (1918–2003) *Clive of India* 1935; *Sons of the Sea* 1939
Shaw, Reta (1912–1982) *The Pajama Game* 1957; *The Lady Takes a Flyer* 1958; *Mary Poppins* 1964; *The Ghost and Mr Chicken* 1966
Shaw, Richard *Booby Trap* 1957; *Man from Tangier* 1957; *Hidden Homicide* 1958
Shaw, Robert (1927–1978) *The Dam Busters* 1954; *A Hill in Korea* 1956; *Sea Fury* 1958; *Tomorrow at Ten* 1962; *The Caretaker* 1963; *From Russia with Love* 1963; *The Luck of Ginger Coffey* 1964; *Battle of the Bulge* 1965; *A Man for All Seasons* 1966; *The Birthday Party* 1968; *Custer of the West* 1968; *Battle of Britain* 1969; *The Royal Hunt of the Sun* 1969; *Figures in a Landscape* 1970; *A Town Called Hell* 1971; *Young Winston* 1972; *The Hireling* 1973; *A Reflection of Fear* 1973; *The Sting* 1973; *The Taking of Pelham One Two Three* 1974; *Diamonds* 1975; *Jaws* 1975; *Black Sunday* 1976; *End of the Game* 1976; *Robin and Marian* 1976; *Swashbuckler* 1976; *The Deep* 1977; *Force 10 from Navarone* 1978; *Avalanche Express* 1979
Shaw, Sebastian (1905–1994) *Men Are Not Gods* 1936; *The Squeaker* 1937; *The Spy in Black* 1939; *East of Piccadilly* 1940; *The Glass Mountain* 1949; *Landfall* 1949; *Laxdale Hall* 1953; *It Happened Here* 1963; *Star Wars Episode VI: Return of the Jedi* 1983; *High Season* 1987
Shaw, Stan (1952–) *The Boys in Company C* 1978; *The Great Santini* 1979; *Tough Enough* 1982; *Runaway* 1984; *Harlem Nights* 1989; *The Court-Martial of Jackie Robinson* 1990; *Fried Green Tomatoes at the Whistle Stop Cafe* 1991; *Body of Evidence* 1992; *Rising Sun* 1993; *CutThroat Island* 1995; *Snake Eyes* 1998
Shaw, Susan *aka* **Damante Shaw, Susan** (1929–1978) *It Always Rains on Sunday* 1947; *Here Come the Huggetts* 1948; *It's Not Cricket* 1948; *London Belongs to Me* 1948; *Quartet* 1948; *Vote for Huggett* 1948; *The Huggetts Abroad* 1949; *Marry Me!* 1949; *Train of Events* 1949; *Pool of London* 1950; *Waterfront* 1950; *The Woman in Question* 1950; *There Is Another Sun* 1951; *Stock Car* 1955; *Fire Maidens from Outer Space* 1956; *The Adventures of the Wilderness Family* 1975; *Mountain Family Robinson* 1979
Shaw, Victoria (1935–1988) *The Eddy Duchin Story* 1956; *The Crimson Kimono* 1959; *Edge of Eternity* 1959; *Because They're Young* 1960; *I Aim at the Stars* 1960; *Alvarez Kelly* 1966; *Westworld* 1973
Shaw, Vinessa (1976–) *Ladybugs* 1992; *Hocus Pocus* 1993; *LA without a Map* 1998; *Eyes Wide Shut* 1999; *Corky Romano* 2001; *40 Days and 40 Nights* 2002
Shaw, Winifred (1910–1982) *Front Page Woman* 1935; *Gold Diggers of 1935* 1935; *The Case of the Velvet Claws* 1936; *Satan Met a Lady* 1936; *Smart Blonde* 1936
Shawlee, Joan (1929–1987) *Francis Joins the WACS* 1954; *Some Like It Hot* 1959; *The Apartment* 1960; *Buddy Buddy* 1981
Shawn, Dick (1929–) *Wake Me When It's Over* 1960; *The Wizard of Baghdad* 1960; *It's a Mad Mad Mad Mad World* 1963; *A Very Special Favor* 1965; *Penelope* 1966; *Way... Way Out* 1966; *What Did You Do in the War, Daddy?* 1966; *The Producers* 1968; *The Happy Ending* 1969; *Evil Roy Slade* 1971; *Love at First Bite* 1979; *Angel* 1984; *The Secret Diary of Sigmund Freud* 1984; *Beer* 1985; *Water* 1985; *Maid to Order* 1987
Shawn, Wallace (1943–) *Manhattan* 1979; *Simon* 1980; *My Dinner with Andre* 1981; *Strange Invaders* 1983; *Crackers* 1984; *The Hotel New Hampshire* 1984; *Micki & Maude* 1984; *Catholic Boys* 1985; *Head Office* 1986; *The Bedroom Window* 1987; *Nice Girls Don't Explode* 1987; *Prick Up Your Ears* 1987; *The Princess Bride* 1987; *The Moderns* 1988; *Scenes from the Class Struggle In Beverly Hills* 1989; *She's Out of Control* 1989; *We're No Angels* 1989; *Nickel & Dime* 1991; *The Magic Bubble* 1992; *Mom and Dad Save the World* 1992; *The Cemetery Club* 1993; *Vanya on 42nd Street* 1994; *Clueless* 1995; *A Goofy Movie* 1995; *Toy Story* 1995; *House Arrest* 1996; *Critical Care* 1997; *My Favorite Martian* 1999; *Toy Story 2* 1999; *The Prime Gig* 2000; *The Curse of the Jade Scorpion* 2001; *Personal Velocity* 2001; *The Haunted Mansion* 2003; *Our House* 2003; *The Incredibles* 2004; *Melinda and Melinda* 2004
Shay, John *The Cry Baby Killer* 1958; *Roadracers* 1958
Shaye, Lin (1944–) *There's Something about Mary* 1998; *Boat Trip* 2002; *Dead End* 2003; *A Cinderella Story* 2004; *The Hillside Strangler* 2004
Shayne, Konstantin (1888–1974) *Till We Meet Again* 1944; *The Secret Life of Walter Mitty* 1947; *Vertigo* 1958
Shayne, Robert (1900–1992) *Mr Skeffington* 1944; *Christmas in Connecticut* 1945; *Three Strangers* 1946; *Let's Live a Little* 1948; *Rider from Tucson* 1950; *Indestructible Man* 1956
Shayne, Tamara (1902–1983) *The Jolson Story* 1946; *Romanoff and Juliet* 1961
Shea, Eric (1960–) *Ace Eli and Rodger of the Skies* 1973; *The Castaway Cowboy* 1974
Shea, John (1948–) *Hussy* 1979; *Missing* 1981; *Windy City* 1984; *Light Years* 1988; *A New Life* 1988; *Stealing Home* 1988; *Honey, I Blew Up the Kid* 1992; *Hard Evidence* 1994; *Forgotten Sins* 1996; *The Adventures of Sebastian Cole* 1998
Sheard, Michael *England Made Me* 1973; *The Riddle of the Sands* 1978; *All Quiet on the Western Front* 1979; *Green Ice* 1981
Shearer, Harry (1943–) *Animalympics* 1979; *This Is Spinal Tap* 1984; *Pure Luck* 1991; *Godzilla* 1997; *Dick* 1999; *A Mighty Wind* 2003
Shearer, Moira (1926–) *The Red Shoes* 1948; *The Tales of Hoffmann* 1951; *The Story of Three Loves* 1953; *The Man Who Loved Redheads* 1954; *Peeping Tom* 1960
Shearer, Norma (1900–1983) *Way Down East* 1920; *He Who Gets Slapped* 1924; *The Student Prince in Old Heidelberg* 1927; *Hollywood Revue* 1929; *The Last of Mrs Cheyney* 1929; *The Divorcee* 1930; *A Free Soul* 1931; *Private Lives* 1931; *Strangers May Kiss* 1931; *Smilin' Through* 1932; *Strange Interlude* 1932; *The Barretts of Wimpole Street* 1934; *Riptide* 1934; *Romeo and Juliet* 1936; *Marie Antoinette* 1938; *Idiot's Delight* 1939; *The Women* 1939; *Escape* 1940; *Her Cardboard Lover* 1942
Sheedy, Ally (1962–) *Bad Boys* 1983; *WarGames* 1983; *Oxford Blues* 1984; *The Breakfast Club* 1985; *St Elmo's Fire* 1985; *Twice in a Lifetime* 1985; *Blue City* 1986; *Short Circuit* 1986; *Maid to Order* 1987; *Heart of Dixie* 1989; *Betsy's Wedding* 1990; *Only the Lonely* 1991; *Man's Best Friend* 1993; *One Night Stand* 1994; *Ultimate Betrayal* 1994; *Before the Night* 1995; *Jailbreak* 1997; *The Autumn Heart* 1998; *High Art* 1998; *Our Guys: Outrage in Glen Ridge* 1999; *Sugar Town* 1999
Sheen, Charlie *aka* **Sheen, Charles** (1965–) *Red Dawn* 1984; *The Boys Next Door* 1985; *Out of the Darkness* 1985; *Ferris Bueller's Day Off* 1986; *Lucas* 1986; *Platoon* 1986; *The Wraith* 1986; *No Man's Land* 1987; *Three for the Road* 1987; *Wall Street* 1987; *Eight Men Out* 1988; *Never on Tuesday* 1988; *Young Guns* 1988; *Catchfire* 1989; *Courage Mountain* 1989; *Major League* 1989; *Men at Work* 1990; *Navy SEALS* 1990; *The Rookie* 1990; *Hot Shots!* 1991; *Stockade* 1991; *Deadfall* 1993; *Hot Shots! Part Deux* 1993; *The Three Musketeers* 1993; *The Chase* 1994; *Fixing the Shadow* 1994; *Major League II* 1994; *Terminal Velocity* 1994; *All Dogs Go to Heaven 2* 1996; *The Arrival* 1996; *Shadow Conspiracy* 1996; *Money Talks* 1997; *Under Pressure* 1997; *Free Money* 1998; *No Code of Conduct* 1998; *Being John Malkovich* 1999; *Postmortem* 1999; *Rated X* 2000; *Good Advice* 2001; *Scary Movie 3* 2003; *The Big Bounce* 2004
Sheen, Martin (1940–) *The Incident* 1967; *The Subject Was Roses* 1968; *Catch-22* 1970; *No Drums, No Bugles* 1971; *Rage* 1972; *Badlands* 1973; *The Cassandra Crossing* 1976; *The Little Girl Who Lives Down the Lane* 1976; *Eagle's Wing* 1978; *Apocalypse Now* 1979; *The Final Countdown* 1980; *Loophole* 1980; *Enigma* 1982; *Gandhi* 1982; *That Championship Season* 1982; *The Dead Zone* 1983; *Man, Woman and Child* 1983; *Firestarter* 1984; *Out of the Darkness* 1985; *The Believers* 1987; *Siesta* 1987; *Wall Street* 1987; *Beyond the Stars* 1988; *Da* 1988; *Judgment in Berlin* 1988; *Beverly Hills Brats* 1989; *Cold Front* 1989; *Nightbreaker* 1989; *The Maid* 1991; *Stockade* 1991; *Running Wild* 1992; *Gettysburg* 1993; *Hear No Evil* 1993; *Killing Box* 1993; *When the Bough Breaks* 1993; *One of Her Own* 1994; *Roswell* 1994; *The American President* 1995; *The Bomber Boys* 1995; *Dillinger and Capone* 1995; *Gospa* 1995; *Entertaining Angels: the Dorothy Day Story* 1996; *Hostile Waters* 1996; *The War at Home* 1996; *Noose* 1997; *Spawn* 1997; *Truth or Consequences, NM* 1997; *No Code of Conduct* 1998; *Forget Me Never* 1999; *Lost & Found* 1999; *Storm* 1999; *O* 2001; *Catch Me If You Can* 2002
Sheen, Michael (1969–) *Mary Reilly* 1995; *Othello* 1995; *Wilde* 1997; *The Four Feathers* 2002; *Heartlands* 2002; *Bright Young Things* 2003; *Laws of Attraction* 2003; *Timeline* 2003; *Underworld* 2003; *Kingdom of Heaven* 2005; *The League of Gentlemen's Apocalypse* 2005
Sheen, Ruth *High Hopes* 1988; *The Young Poisoner's Handbook* 1994; *All or Nothing* 2002; *Vera Drake* 2004
Sheffer, Craig (1960–) *That Was Then... This Is Now* 1985; *Fire with Fire* 1986; *Some Kind of Wonderful* 1987; *Nightbreed* 1990; *Eye of the Storm* 1991; *A River Runs through It* 1992; *Fire in the Sky* 1993; *The Program* 1993; *Roadflower* 1994; *Sleep with Me* 1994; *Head above Water* 1996; *Bliss* 1997; *Double Take* 1997; *Miss Evers' Boys* 1997; *Executive Power* 1998; *Merlin the Return* 2000; *Without Malice* 2000
Sheffield, Jeremy (1966–) *Her Own Rules* 1998; *Creep* 2004; *The Wedding Date* 2004
Sheffield, Johnny *aka* **Sheffield, John** (1931–) *Tarzan Finds a Son!* 1939; *Tarzan's Secret Treasure* 1941; *Tarzan's New York Adventure* 1942; *Tarzan Triumphs* 1943; *Tarzan's Desert Mystery* 1943; *Tarzan and the Amazons* 1945; *Tarzan and the Leopard Woman* 1946; *Tarzan and the Huntress* 1947
Sheffield, Reginald (1901–1957) *The Green Goddess* 1930; *Of Human Bondage* 1934
Sheiner, David *The Odd Couple* 1968; *A Man Called Gannon* 1969; *Winning* 1969; *They Call Me Mister Tibbs!* 1970; *The Stone Killer* 1973; *The Big Brawl* 1980; *Blue Thunder* 1983
Sheldon, Gene (1908–1982) *Where Do We Go from Here?* 1945; *Golden Girl* 1951; *Three Ring Circus* 1954; *Toby Tyler, or Ten Weeks with a Circus* 1960
Shellen, Stephen (1957–) *The Stepfather* 1986; *Casual Sex?* 1988; *Damned River* 1989; *A River Runs through It* 1992
Shelley, Barbara (1933–) *Blood of the Vampire* 1958; *The Camp on Blood Island* 1958; *Bobbikins* 1959; *Village of the Damned* 1960; *Postman's Knock* 1961; *The Shadow of the Cat* 1961; *The Gorgon* 1964; *The Secret of Blood Island* 1964; *Dracula – Prince of Darkness* 1965; *Rasputin, the Mad Monk* 1965; *Quatermass and the Pit* 1967
Shelley, Carole (1939–) *The Odd Couple* 1968; *The Whoopee Boys* 1986; *Little Noises* 1992
Shelley, Norman (1903–1980) *The Silver Darlings* 1947; *The*

Great Adventure 1953; *Gulliver's Travels* 1977
Shelley, Paul (1942–) *Macbeth* 1971; *It Shouldn't Happen to a Vet* 1979; *Caught in the Act* 1996
Shelley, Rachel *Lighthouse* 1999; *Lagaan: Once upon a Time in India* 2001
Shelly, Adrienne (1966–) *The Unbelievable Truth* 1989; *Trust* 1990; *Hold Me, Thrill Me, Kiss Me* 1992; *Stepkids* 1992; *Hexed* 1993; *Roadflower* 1994; *Sleep with Me* 1994; *Wrestling with Alligators* 1998
Shelton, Anne (1923–1994) *King Arthur Was a Gentleman* 1942; *Bees in Paradise* 1943; *Miss London Ltd* 1943
Shelton, Deborah (1952–) *Body Double* 1984; *Hunk* 1987; *Blind Vision* 1992; *Nemesis* 1993; *Plughead Rewired: Circuitry Man II* 1994
Shelton, John (1915–1972) *Dr Kildare Goes Home* 1940; *The Ghost Comes Home* 1940; *A-Haunting We Will Go* 1942; *The Time of Their Lives* 1946
Shelton, Joy (1922–2000) *Bees in Paradise* 1943; *Millions like Us* 1943; *Waterloo Road* 1944; *Send for Paul Temple* 1946; *No Room at the Inn* 1948; *A Case for PC 49* 1950; *Emergency Call* 1952; *Park Plaza 605* 1953; *Impulse* 1955
Shelton, Marley (1974–) *Warriors of Virtue* 1996; *Trojan War* 1997; *The Bachelor* 1999; *Lured Innocence* 1999; *Bubble Boy* 2001; *Sugar & Spice* 2001; *Valentine* 2001; *Just a Kiss* 2002; *Grand Theft Parsons* 2003; *Uptown Girls* 2003
Shenar, Paul (1936–1989) *The Secret of NIMH* 1982; *Deadly Force* 1983; *Dream Lover* 1986; *Raw Deal* 1986; *The Bedroom Window* 1987; *Best Seller* 1987; *Man on Fire* 1987; *The Big Blue* 1988
Shenkman, Ben *Pi* 1997; *Roger Dodger* 2002
Shepard, Hilary aka **Shepard Turner, Hilary** *Peacemaker* 1990; *Scanner Cop* 1994; *Turbo: a Power Rangers Adventure* 1997
Shepard, Jan *King Creole* 1958; *Attack of the Giant Leeches* 1960
Shepard, Jewel (1962–) *Hollywood Hot Tubs* 1984; *Return of the Living Dead* 1984
Shepard, Sam (1943–) *Days of Heaven* 1978; *Resurrection* 1980; *Raggedy Man* 1981; *Frances* 1982; *The Right Stuff* 1983; *Country* 1984; *Fool for Love* 1985; *Crimes of the Heart* 1986; *Baby Boom* 1987; *Steel Magnolias* 1989; *Bright Angel* 1990; *Defenseless* 1991; *Voyager* 1991; *Thunderheart* 1992; *The Pelican Brief* 1993; *Safe Passage* 1994; *The Only Thrill* 1997; *Curtain Call* 1998; *Purgatory* 1999; *Snow Falling on Cedars* 1999; *Hamlet* 2000; *One Kill* 2000; *The Pledge* 2000; *Black Hawk Down* 2001; *Kurosawa* 2001; *Swordfish* 2001; *Leo* 2002; *The Notebook* 2003
Shepherd, Cybill (1950–) *The Last Picture Show* 1971; *The Heartbreak Kid* 1972; *Daisy Miller* 1974; *At Long Last Love* 1975; *Special Delivery* 1976; *Taxi Driver* 1976; *Silver Bears* 1977; *The Lady Vanishes* 1979; *Seduced* 1985; *Chances Are* 1989; *Alice* 1990; *Texasville* 1990; *Married to It* 1991; *Once upon a Crime* 1992
Shepherd, Elizabeth (1936–) *The Tomb of Ligeia* 1964; *Hell Boats* 1970
Shepherd, Jack (1940–) *All Neat in Black Stockings* 1969; *The Virgin Soldiers* 1969; *Escape from Sobibor* 1987; *The Object of Beauty* 1991; *Twenty-One* 1991; *Blue Black Permanent* 1992; *Blue Ice* 1992; *No Escape* 1994; *The Scarlet Tunic* 1997; *Wonderland* 1999
Shepherd, Jean (1921–1999) *Fame Is the Spur* 1947; *The Silver Darlings* 1947
Shepherd, John *Friday the 13th: a New Beginning* 1985; *Thunder Run* 1986
Shepherd, Simon (1956–) *Fire, Ice and Dynamite* 1990; *Wuthering Heights* 1992
Shepherd, Steve John *GMT Greenwich Mean Time* 1998; *Virtual Sexuality* 1999
Shepherd, Suzanne *The Jerky Boys* 1995; *Lolita* 1997; *Living Out Loud* 1998; *A Dirty Shame* 2004
Shepley, Michael (1907–1961) *A Shot in the Dark* 1933; *Lord Edgware Dies* 1934; *Lazybones* 1935; *Squibs* 1935; *The Great Mr Handel* 1942; *A Place of One's Own* 1944; *Mine Own Executioner* 1947; *Maytime in Mayfair* 1949; *Home at Seven* 1952; *Happy Ever After* 1954; *Where There's a Will* 1955
Sheppard, Mark *In the Name of the Father* 1993; *Lover's Knot* 1995
Sheppard, Morgan aka **Sheppard, W Morgan** *Hawk the Slayer* 1980; *The Keep* 1983; *Elvira, Mistress of the Dark* 1988
Sheppard, Paula (1957–) *Alice, Sweet Alice* 1977; *Liquid Sky* 1982
Sher, Antony (1949–) *Shadey* 1985; *Erik the Viking* 1989; *The Young Poisoner's Handbook* 1994; *Alive and Kicking* 1996; *The Wind in the Willows* 1996; *Mrs Brown* 1997; *The Miracle Maker* 1999; *Churchill: the Hollywood Years* 2004
Shergill, Jimmy (1970–) *Mohabbatein* 2000; *Hum Tum* 2004
Sheridan, Ann aka **Sheridan, Clara Lou** (1915–1967) *Kiss and Make-Up* 1934; *Ladies Should Listen* 1934; *Mrs Wiggs of the Cabbage Patch* 1934; *Murder at the Vanities* 1934; *Rumba* 1935; *The Black Legion* 1937; *San Quentin* 1937; *Angels with Dirty Faces* 1938; *Letter of Introduction* 1938; *Angels Wash Their Faces* 1939; *Dodge City* 1939; *Indianapolis Speedway* 1939; *Naughty but Nice* 1939; *They Made Me a Criminal* 1939; *Winter Carnival* 1939; *Castle on the Hudson* 1940; *City for Conquest* 1940; *It All Came True* 1940; *They Drive by Night* 1940; *Torrid Zone* 1940; *The Man Who Came to Dinner* 1941; *George Washington Slept Here* 1942; *Kings Row* 1942; *Edge of Darkness* 1943; *The Doughgirls* 1944; *Shine On, Harvest Moon* 1944; *Nora Prentiss* 1947; *The Unfaithful* 1947; *Good Sam* 1948; *Silver River* 1948; *I Was a Male War Bride* 1949; *Stella* 1950; *Appointment in Honduras* 1953; *Take Me to Town* 1953; *Come Next Spring* 1956; *The Opposite Sex* 1956; *The Woman and the Hunter* 1957
Sheridan, Dan (1916–1963) *Bullwhip* 1958; *The Young Captives* 1958
Sheridan, Dinah (1920–) *Get Cracking* 1943; *29 Acacia Avenue* 1945; *The Hills of Donegal* 1947; *The Huggetts Abroad* 1949; *Blackout* 1950; *No Trace* 1950; *Where No Vultures Fly* 1951; *Appointment in London* 1952; *The Sound Barrier* 1952; *Genevieve* 1953; *The Story of Gilbert and Sullivan* 1953; *The Railway Children* 1970
Sheridan, Frank (1869–1943) *Danger Lights* 1930; *Washington Merry-Go-Round* 1932
Sheridan, Jamey (1951–) *Distant Thunder* 1988; *Shannon's Deal* 1989; *Stanley & Iris* 1989; *All I Want for Christmas* 1991; *Talent for the Game* 1991; *A Stranger among Us* 1992; *Whispers in the Dark* 1992; *Wild America* 1997; *Let the Devil Wear Black* 1999; *The Simian Line* 2000; *Life as a House* 2001
Sheridan, Margaret (1926–1982) *The Thing from Another World* 1951; *One Minute to Zero* 1952; *I, the Jury* 1953; *The Diamond* 1954; *Pride of the Blue Grass* 1954
Sheridan, Nicollette (1963–) *The Sure Thing* 1985; *Formula for Death* 1995; *Spy Hard* 1996; *Beverly Hills Ninja* 1997
Sherman, Geraldine (1944–) *Poor Cow* 1967; *Take a Girl like You* 1970; *There's a Girl in My Soup* 1970
Sherman, Hiram (1908–1989) *One Third of a Nation* 1939; *The Solid Gold Cadillac* 1956; *Mary, Mary* 1963
Sherman, Lowell (1885–1934) *Way Down East* 1920; *The Divine Woman* 1928; *Ladies of Leisure* 1930; *Mammy* 1930; *Bachelor Apartment* 1931; *What Price Hollywood?* 1932
Sherrill, David (1962–) *The Wraith* 1986; *Unhook the Stars* 1996
Sherwood, Madeleine (1922–) *Cat on a Hot Tin Roof* 1958; *Sweet Bird of Youth* 1962; *Pendulum* 1969
Sherwood, Robin *Tourist Trap* 1979; *Death Wish II* 1981
Shetty, Shefali aka **Shah, Shefali** *Monsoon Wedding* 2001; *WAQT: the Race Against Time* 2005
Shetty, Shilpa (1975–) *Baazigar* 1993; *Garv: Pride & Honour* 2004
Shetty, Sunil aka **Shetty, Suniel** (1961–) *Awara Paagal Deewana* 2002; *Hulchul* 2004; *Main Hoon Na* 2004
Sheybal, Vladek aka **Sheybal, Wladyslaw** (1923–1992) *Kanal* 1957; *Billion Dollar Brain* 1967; *Women in Love* 1969; *Puppet on a Chain* 1970; *The Boy Friend* 1971; *Innocent Bystanders* 1972; *The Sellout* 1975; *The Wind and the Lion* 1975; *After Midnight* 1990
Shields, Arthur (1896–1970) *The Plough and the Stars* 1936; *Little Nellie Kelly* 1940; *Confirm or Deny* 1941; *The Gay Falcon* 1941; *The Man from Down Under* 1943; *Youth Runs Wild* 1944; *The Corn Is Green* 1945; *Three Strangers* 1946; *The Verdict* 1946; *The Fabulous Dorseys* 1947; *Seven Keys to Baldpate* 1947; *The Fighting O'Flynn* 1948; *She Wore a Yellow Ribbon* 1949; *Tarzan and the Slave Girl* 1950; *Apache Drums* 1951; *The River* 1951; *Scandal at Scourie* 1953; *World for Ransom* 1953; *Pride of the Blue Grass* 1954; *Daughter of Dr Jekyll* 1957; *For the Love of Mike* 1960
Shields, Brooke (1965–) *Alice, Sweet Alice* 1977; *King of the Gypsies* 1978; *Pretty Baby* 1978; *Tilt* 1978; *Just You and Me, Kid* 1979; *Wanda Nevada* 1979; *The Blue Lagoon* 1980; *Endless Love* 1981; *Sahara* 1983; *Brenda Starr* 1989; *Backstreet Dreams* 1990; *Running Wild* 1992; *Freaked* 1993; *Stalking Laura* 1993; *Freeway* 1996; *The Misadventures of Margaret* 1998; *The Bachelor* 1999; *Black and White* 1999
Shiganoya, Benkei *Osaka Elegy* 1936; *Sisters of the Gion* 1936; *Story of the Late Chrysanthemums* 1939
Shigeta, James (1933–) *The Crimson Kimono* 1959; *Walk like a Dragon* 1960; *Bridge to the Sun* 1961; *Cry for Happy* 1961; *Flower Drum Song* 1961; *Paradise, Hawaiian Style* 1966; *Nobody's Perfect* 1968; *Lost Horizon* 1973; *The Yakuza* 1975; *Die Hard* 1988; *Cage* 1989; *China Cry* 1990; *Drive* 1997
Shillo, Michael *Dunkirk* 1958; *The Whole Truth* 1958
Shiloh, Shmuel *Goodbye New York* 1984; *Double Edge* 1992
Shimada, Teru (1905–1988) *Tokyo Joe* 1949; *Battle of the Coral Sea* 1959; *You Only Live Twice* 1967
Shimizu, Masao (1908–1975) *The Straits of Love and Hate* 1937; *The Life of Oharu* 1952; *Sansho the Bailiff* 1954; *Sanjuro* 1962
Shimizu, Misa (1970–) *Okoge* 1992; *The Eel* 1997; *Warm Water under a Red Bridge* 2001; *The Sea Is Watching* 2002
Shimkus, Joanna (1943–) *Paris Vu Par…* 1965; *The Adventurers* 1968; *Boom* 1968; *Ho!* 1968; *The Lost Man* 1969; *The Virgin and the Gypsy* 1970; *The Marriage of a Young Stockbroker* 1971; *A Time for Loving* 1971
Shimono, Sab (1943–) *Come See the Paradise* 1990; *Teenage Mutant Ninja Turtles III* 1992; *Suture* 1993; *The Shadow* 1994; *The Big Hit* 1998
Shimura, Takashi (1905–1982) *Sanshiro Sugata* 1943; *Drunken Angel* 1948; *Stray Dog* 1949; *Rashomon* 1950; *The Idiot* 1951; *Ikiru* 1952; *Godzilla* 1954; *Seven Samurai* 1954; *I Live in Fear* 1955; *Throne of Blood* 1957; *The Hidden Fortress* 1958; *The Bad Sleep Well* 1960; *Sanjuro* 1962; *High and Low* 1963; *Ghidrah, the Three-Headed Monster* 1965
Shin Ha-gyun (1974–) *Sympathy for Mr Vengeance* 2002; *Save the Green Planet!* 2003
Shindo, Eitaro (1899–1977) *Osaka Elegy* 1936; *Sisters of the Gion* 1936; *The Crucified Lovers* 1954; *Sansho the Bailiff* 1954; *Street of Shame* 1955
Shiner, Ronald (1903–1966) *Doctor's Orders* 1934; *Old Bill and Son* 1940; *South American George* 1941; *Bees in Paradise* 1943; *Get Cracking* 1943; *George in Civvy Street* 1946; *The Man Within* 1947; *Innocents in Paris* 1953; *Top of the Form* 1953; *Up to His Neck* 1954; *Dry Rot* 1956; *Not Wanted on Voyage* 1957; *Girls at Sea* 1958; *The Navy Lark* 1959; *Operation Bullshine* 1959; *The Night We Got the Bird* 1960
Shingler, Helen *Quiet Weekend* 1946; *The Silver Darlings* 1947; *The Rossiter Case* 1950; *Judgement Deferred* 1951; *The Lady with the Lamp* 1951
Shioya, Toshi *Blood Oath* 1990; *Mr Baseball* 1992
Shipman, Nina *Blue Denim* 1959; *The Oregon Trail* 1959
Shipp, John Wesley (1956–) *The NeverEnding Story II: the Next Chapter* 1991; *Soft Deceit* 1994
Shirakawa, Yumi (1936–) *The H-Man* 1954; *Rodan* 1956; *The End of Summer* 1961
Shire, Talia aka **Coppola, Talia** (1946–) *The Wild Racers* 1968; *The Dunwich Horror* 1970; *Gas-s-s-s, or It Became Necessary to Destroy the World in Order to Save It* 1970; *The Outside Man* 1973; *The Godfather, Part II* 1974; *Rocky* 1976; *Kill Me If You Can* 1977; *Old Boyfriends* 1979; *Prophecy* 1979; *Rocky II* 1979; *Rocky III* 1982; *Rocky IV* 1985; *New York Stories* 1989; *The Godfather Part III* 1990; *Rocky V* 1990; *Bed & Breakfast* 1992; *Cold Heaven* 1992; *Deadfall* 1993; *Lured Innocence* 1999
Shirley, Anne aka **O'Day, Dawn** (1918–1993) *Anne of Green Gables* 1934; *Steamboat round the Bend* 1935; *Chatterbox* 1936; *Stella Dallas* 1937; *Boy Slaves* 1938; *Condemned Women* 1938; *Law of the Underworld* 1938; *Anne of Windy Poplars* 1940; *Saturday's Children* 1940; *Vigil in the Night* 1940; *Bombardier* 1943; *Government Girl* 1943; *Farewell My Lovely* 1944; *Music in Manhattan* 1944
Shirley, Bill (1921–1989) *Abbott and Costello Meet Captain Kidd* 1952; *I Dream of Jeanie* 1952; *Sleeping Beauty* 1959
Shishido, Jo (1933–) *Gate of Flesh* 1964; *Branded to Kill* 1967
Shivdasani, Aftab (1978–) *Koi Mere Dil Se Pooche* 2001; *Awara Paagal Deewana* 2002; *Masti* 2004
Shoemaker, Ann (1891–1978) *Alice Adams* 1935; *My Favorite Wife* 1940; *Strike Up the Band* 1940; *Above Suspicion* 1943; *Conflict* 1945; *House by the River* 1950; *Sunrise at Campobello* 1960
Shoop, Pamela aka **Shoop, Pamela Susan** (1948–) *Empire of the Ants* 1977; *One Man Jury* 1978; *Magnum: Don't Eat the Snow in Hawaii* 1980; *Halloween II* 1981
Shor, Dan aka **Shor, Daniel** *Wise Blood* 1979; *Back Roads* 1981; *Tron* 1982; *Strangers Kiss* 1983; *Mesmerized* 1984; *Black Moon Rising* 1985; *Bill & Ted's Excellent Adventure* 1988
Shor, Miriam (1971–) *Bedazzled* 2000; *Hedwig and the Angry Inch* 2001
Shore, Dinah (1917–1994) *Thank Your Lucky Stars* 1943; *Belle of the Yukon* 1944; *Follow the Boys* 1944; *Up in Arms* 1944; *Make Mine Music* 1946; *Till the Clouds Roll By* 1946; *Fun and Fancy Free* 1947
Shore, Pauly (1968–) *California Man* 1992; *Son in Law* 1993; *In the Army Now* 1994; *Jury Duty* 1995; *Bio-Dome* 1996; *Casper: a Spirited Beginning* 1997
Short, Martin (1950–) *Lost and Found* 1979; *Three Amigos!* 1986; *Cross My Heart* 1987; *Innerspace* 1987; *The Big Picture* 1989; *Three Fugitives* 1989; *Father of the Bride* 1991; *Pure Luck* 1991; *Captain Ron* 1992; *We're Back! A Dinosaur's Story* 1993; *Father of the Bride Part 2* 1995; *The Pebble and the Penguin* 1995; *Mars Attacks!* 1996; *Jungle 2 Jungle* 1997; *A Simple Wish* 1997; *The Prince of Egypt* 1998; *Alice in Wonderland* 1999; *Mumford* 1999; *Get over It* 2001; *Jimmy Neutron: Boy Genius* 2001; *Treasure Planet* 2002
Shotter, Winifred (1904–1996) *Rookery Nook* 1930; *D'Ye Ken John Peel?* 1934
Shou, Robin (1960–) *Beverly Hills Ninja* 1997; *Mortal Kombat: Annihilation* 1997
Showalter, Max aka **Adams, Casey** (1917–2000) *Destination Gobi* 1953; *Niagara* 1953; *Down Three Dark Streets* 1954; *Naked Alibi* 1954; *Bus Stop* 1956; *Dragoon Wells Massacre* 1957; *The Monster That Challenged the World* 1957; *How to Murder Your Wife* 1965; *Racing with the Moon* 1984
Shrapnel, John (1942–) *Testimony* 1987; *How to Get Ahead in Advertising* 1989; *101 Dalmatians* 1996; *The Body* 2000; *Gladiator* 2000; *K-19: the Widowmaker* 2002
Shroff, Jackie (1958–) *Rangeela* 1995; *Yaadein* 2001; *Devdas* 2002; *Ek Aur Ek Gyarah* 2003; *Hulchul* 2004
Shue, Elisabeth (1963–) *The Karate Kid* 1984; *Link* 1986; *A Night on the Town* 1987; *Cocktail* 1988; *Back to the Future Part II* 1989; *Back to the Future Part III* 1990; *Soapdish* 1991; *Too Hot to Handle* 1991; *Heart and Souls* 1993; *Twenty Bucks* 1993; *Leaving Las Vegas* 1995; *The Underneath* 1995; *The Trigger Effect* 1996; *Cousin Bette* 1997; *Deconstructing Harry* 1997; *The Saint* 1997; *Palmetto* 1998; *Molly* 1999; *Hollow Man* 2000; *Leo* 2002; *Tuck Everlasting* 2002; *Mysterious Skin* 2004; *Hide and Seek* 2005
Shukla, Saurabh *Bandit Queen* 1994; *Mumbai Matinee* 2003
Shull, Richard B (1929–1999) *Slither* 1973; *Ssssss* 1973; *The Fortune* 1975; *Hearts of the West* 1975; *The Pack* 1977; *Dreamer* 1979; *Unfaithfully Yours* 1983; *Splash* 1984; *HouseSitter* 1992
Shvorin, Aleksandr aka **Stewart, Andy** *The Cranes Are Flying* 1957; *Battle beyond the Sun* 1959
Shyamalan, M Night (1970–) *The Sixth Sense* 1999; *Signs* 2002
Siao, Josephine (1947–) *The Legend* 1993; *The Legend II* 1993
Siberry, Michael *Biggles* 1986; *Boundaries of the Heart* 1988; *Teen Agent* 1991
Siddig, Alexander (1965–) *Reign of Fire* 2001; *Kingdom of Heaven* 2005
Siddons, Harold *Genevieve* 1953; *The Purple Plain* 1954; *The Baby and the Battleship* 1956
Sidney (1), George (1876–1945) *For the Love of Mike* 1927; *High Pressure* 1932; *Manhattan Melodrama* 1934
Sidney, Sylvia (1910–1999) *An American Tragedy* 1931; *City Streets* 1931; *Street Scene* 1931; *Madame Butterfly* 1932; *Merrily We Go to Hell* 1932; *Jennie*

Gerhardt 1933; *Thirty-Day Princess* 1934; *Accent on Youth* 1935; *Fury* 1936; *Sabotage* 1936; *The Trail of the Lonesome Pine* 1936; *Dead End* 1937; *You Only Live Once* 1937; *You and Me* 1938; *One Third of a Nation* 1939; *The Wagons Roll at Night* 1941; *Blood on the Sun* 1945; *The Searching Wind* 1946; *Love from a Stranger* 1947; *Les Misérables* 1952; *Violent Saturday* 1955; *Summer Wishes, Winter Dreams* 1973; *God Told Me to* 1976; *Raid on Entebbe* 1977; *Damien – Omen II* 1978; *Order of Death* 1983; *An Early Frost* 1985; *Pals* 1986; *Beetle Juice* 1988; *Used People* 1992

Siebert, Charles (1938–) *Blue Sunshine* 1976; *Deadly Hero* 1976; *White Water Summer* 1987

Sledow, Jim (1920–2003) *The Texas Chain Saw Massacre* 1974; *The Texas Chainsaw Massacre Part 2* 1986

Siegel, Bernard *Laugh, Clown, Laugh* 1928; *Beau Ideal* 1931

Siegel, Don (1912–1991) *Play Misty for Me* 1971; *Invasion of the Body Snatchers* 1978

Siegmann, George (1882–1928) *The Birth of a Nation* 1915; *The Three Musketeers* 1921; *Oliver Twist* 1922; *Hotel Imperial* 1927

Siemaszko, Casey (1961–) *Secret Admirer* 1985; *Stand by Me* 1986; *Three O'Clock High* 1987; *Biloxi Blues* 1988; *Young Guns* 1988; *Breaking In* 1989; *Near Mrs* 1990; *Of Mice and Men* 1992; *Painted Heart* 1992; *Milk Money* 1994; *Bliss* 1997; *Limbo* 1999

Siemaszko, Nina (1970–) *Bed & Breakfast* 1992; *Little Noises* 1992; *Wild Orchid 2: Two Shades of Blue* 1992; *The Saint of Fort Washington* 1993; *Airheads* 1994; *Runaway Car* 1997; *Jakob the Liar* 1999

Sierra, Gregory (1941–) *The Thief Who Came to Dinner* 1973; *The Castaway Cowboy* 1974; *Mean Dog Blues* 1978; *The Trouble with Spies* 1987; *A Low Down Dirty Shame* 1994; *Vampires* 1998

Siffredi, Rocco (1964–) *Romance* 1998; *Anatomy of Hell* 2003

Signorelli, Tom *Thief* 1981; *Crossover Dreams* 1985

Signoret, Simone (1921–1985) *Les Visiteurs du Soir* 1942; *Against the Wind* 1947; *La Ronde* 1950; *Casque d'Or* 1952; *Thérèse Raquin* 1953; *Les Diaboliques* 1954; *Death in the Garden* 1956; *The Witches of Salem* 1957; *Room at the Top* 1958; *Le Joli Mai* 1962; *Term of Trial* 1962; *Ship of Fools* 1965; *The Sleeping Car Murders* 1965; *The Deadly Affair* 1966; *Is Paris Burning?* 1966; *Games* 1967; *The Sea Gull* 1968; *L'Armée des Ombres* 1969; *The Confession* 1970; *The Widow Couderc* 1971; *Burnt Barns* 1973; *The Flesh of the Orchid* 1974; *Madame Rosa* 1977; *L'Etoile du Nord* 1982

Sihol, Caroline *Confidentially Yours* 1983; *Tenue de Soirée* 1986; *Tous les Matins du Monde* 1991

Sikes, Cynthia (1951–) *Ladies and Gentlemen, the Fabulous Stains* 1981; *The Man Who Loved Women* 1983; *Love Hurts* 1990; *Possums* 1998

Sikking, James B *aka* **Sikking, James** (1934–) *Point Blank* 1967; *Charro!* 1969; *Daddy's Gone A-Hunting* 1969; *The New Centurions* 1972; *Ordinary People* 1980; *Outland* 1981; *The Star Chamber* 1983; *Star Trek III: the Search for Spock* 1984; *Morons from Outer Space* 1985; *Soul Man* 1986; *Narrow Margin* 1990; *Final Approach* 1991; *The Pelican Brief* 1993; *Dead Badge* 1995; *Mutiny* 1999; *The Perfect Catch* 2005

Siletti, Mario (1897–1977) *The Black Hand* 1950; *Kansas City Confidential* 1952; *Bring Your Smile Along* 1955

Silla, Felix (1937–) *She Freak* 1967; *The Black Bird* 1975; *Buck Rogers in the 25th Century* 1979

Sillas, Karen (1965–) *Simple Men* 1992; *Risk* 1993; *What Happened Was…* 1994; *Female Perversions* 1996; *Sour Grapes* 1998

Sills, Milton (1882–1930) *The Sea Hawk* 1924; *The Barker* 1928

Silva, David (1917–1976) *El Topo* 1971; *Alucarda* 1975

Silva, Franco (1920–) *Hannibal* 1959; *The Mongols* 1961

Silva, Henry (1928–) *A Hatful of Rain* 1957; *The Tall T* 1957; *The Bravados* 1958; *The Law and Jake Wade* 1958; *Ride a Crooked Trail* 1958; *Green Mansions* 1959; *Cinderfella* 1960; *The Manchurian Candidate* 1962; *Sergeants 3* 1962; *A Gathering of Eagles* 1963; *Johnny Cool* 1963; *The Secret Invasion* 1964; *The Return of Mr Moto* 1965; *The Reward* 1965; *The Plainsman* 1966; *Never a Dull Moment* 1968; *The Italian Connection* 1973; *Shoot* 1976; *Love and Bullets* 1978; *Buck Rogers in the 25th Century* 1979; *Thirst* 1979; *Alligator* 1980; *Virus* 1980; *Sharky's Machine* 1981; *The Man with the Deadly Lens* 1982; *Chained Heat* 1983; *The Outsider* 1983; *Lust in the Dust* 1984; *Code of Silence* 1985; *Allan Quatermain and the Lost City of Gold* 1987; *Bulletproof* 1987; *Nico* 1988; *The Harvest* 1993; *Ghost Dog: the Way of the Samurai* 1999

Silva, Maria *The Awful Dr Orloff* 1962; *As If It Were Raining* 1963

Silva, Simone (1928–1957) *Escape by Night* 1953; *Street of Shadows* 1953

Silva, Trinidad (1950–1988) *Walk Proud* 1979; *Crackers* 1984; *The Night Before* 1988; *Stones for Ibarra* 1988; *UHF* 1989

Silvani, Aldo (1891–1964) *Four Steps in the Clouds* 1942; *La Strada* 1954; *Nights of Cabiria* 1957

Silveira, Leonor (1970–) *The Divine Comedy* 1992; *Abraham Valley* 1993; *The Convent* 1995; *Journey to the Beginning of the World* 1997; *I'm Going Home* 2001; *Un Filme Falado* 2003

Silver, Joe (1922–) *The Apprenticeship of Duddy Kravitz* 1974; *Rhinoceros* 1974; *Shivers* 1975; *Rabid* 1976; *You Light Up My Life* 1977; *Boardwalk* 1979; *The Gig* 1985

Silver, Ron (1946–) *Semi-Tough* 1977; *The Entity* 1981; *Best Friends* 1982; *Silent Rage* 1982; *Lovesick* 1983; *Silkwood* 1983; *Garbo Talks* 1984; *The Goodbye People* 1984; *Oh, God! You Devil* 1984; *Eat and Run* 1986; *Enemies, a Love Story* 1989; *Fellow Traveller* 1989; *Blue Steel* 1990; *Reversal of Fortune* 1990; *Married to It* 1991; *Live Wire* 1992; *Mr Saturday Night* 1992; *Timecop* 1994; *The Arrival* 1996; *Danger Zone* 1996; *Skeletons* 1996; *Black and White* 1998; *In the Company of Spies* 1999; *Mistaken Identity* 1999; *Cutaway* 2000; *Exposure* 2000; *Ali* 2001; *Festival in Cannes* 2001

Silver, Véronique *The Woman Next Door* 1981; *Noce Blanche* 1989

Silvera, Frank (1914–1970) *The Fighter* 1952; *The Miracle of Our Lady of Fatima* 1952; *White Mane* 1952; *Fear and Desire* 1953; *Killer's Kiss* 1955; *Crime and Punishment, USA* 1959; *Key Witness* 1960; *The Mountain Road* 1960; *The St Valentine's Day Massacre* 1967; *The Stalking Moon* 1968; *Uptight* 1968; *Valdez Is Coming* 1971

Silverheels, Jay (1919–1980) *Broken Arrow* 1950; *The Battle at Apache Pass* 1952; *Drums across the River* 1954; *Saskatchewan* 1954; *The Lone Ranger* 1956; *Walk the Proud Land* 1956; *The Lone Ranger and the Lost City of Gold* 1958; *Alias Jesse James* 1959; *The Man Who Loved Cat Dancing* 1973; *Santee* 1973

Silverman, Jonathan (1966–) *Girls Just Want to Have Fun* 1985; *Brighton Beach Memoirs* 1986; *Caddyshack II* 1988; *Stealing Home* 1988; *Weekend at Bernie's* 1989; *Age Isn't Everything* 1991; *Broadway Bound* 1991; *Class Action* 1991; *Breaking the Rules* 1992; *Weekend at Bernie's II* 1992; *12:01* 1993; *Little Big League* 1994; *…At First Sight* 1995; *The Odd Couple II* 1998; *Something about Sex* 1998; *These Old Broads* 2001

Silverman, Robert *Head On* 1980; *Prom Night* 1980

Silverman, Sarah *The Bachelor* 1999; *The School of Rock* 2003

Silvers, Phil (1912–1985) *Strike Up the Band* 1940; *Lady Be Good* 1941; *The Penalty* 1941; *Tom, Dick and Harry* 1941; *All through the Night* 1942; *Footlight Serenade* 1942; *My Gal Sal* 1942; *Roxie Hart* 1942; *Coney Island* 1943; *A Lady Takes a Chance* 1943; *Cover Girl* 1944; *Something for the Boys* 1944; *Billy Rose's Diamond Horseshoe* 1945; *A Thousand and One Nights* 1945; *Summer Stock* 1950; *Top Banana* 1953; *Lucky Me* 1954; *Forty Pounds of Trouble* 1962; *It's a Mad Mad Mad Mad World* 1963; *A Funny Thing Happened on the Way to the Forum* 1966; *Carry On Follow That Camel* 1967; *Buona Sera, Mrs Campbell* 1968; *The Boatniks* 1970; *The Strongest Man in the World* 1975; *The Chicken Chronicles* 1977; *The Cheap Detective* 1978; *There Goes the Bride* 1979; *The Happy Hooker Goes to Hollywood* 1980

Silvers, Sid (1901–1976) *Broadway Melody of 1936* 1935; *Born to Dance* 1936

Silverstone, Alicia (1976–) *The Crush* 1993; *The Babysitter* 1995; *Clueless* 1995; *Hideaway* 1995; *True Crime* 1995; *Batman and Robin* 1997; *Excess Baggage* 1997; *Blast from the Past* 1998; *Love's Labour's Lost* 1999; *Scooby-Doo 2: Monsters Unleashed* 2004; *Beauty Shop* 2005

Silverstone, Ben (1979–) *The Browning Version* 1994; *Get Real* 1998

Silvestre, Armando *Apache Drums* 1951; *For the Love of Mike* 1960; *Kings of the Sun* 1963; *Rage* 1966; *The Scalphunters* 1968; *Two Mules for Sister Sara* 1970

Sim, Alastair (1900–1976) *A Fire Has Been Arranged* 1935; *Keep Your Seats, Please* 1936; *The Man in the Mirror* 1936; *Gangway* 1937; *The Squeaker* 1937; *Alf's Button Afloat* 1938; *Climbing High* 1938; *Sailing Along* 1938; *Cottage to Let* 1941; *Waterloo Road* 1944; *Green for Danger* 1946; *Captain Boycott* 1947; *Hue and Cry* 1947; *London Belongs to Me* 1948; *Stage Fright* 1949; *The Happiest Days of Your Life* 1950; *Lady Godiva Rides Again* 1951; *Laughter in Paradise* 1951; *Scrooge* 1951; *Folly to Be Wise* 1952; *Innocents in Paris* 1953; *The Belles of St Trinian's* 1954; *An Inspector Calls* 1954; *Geordie* 1955; *The Green Man* 1956; *Blue Murder at St Trinian's* 1957; *The Doctor's Dilemma* 1958; *Left, Right and Centre* 1959; *The Millionairess* 1960; *School for Scoundrels* 1960; *The Ruling Class* 1972; *Royal Flash* 1975; *The Littlest Horse Thieves* 1976

Sim, Gerald (1925–) *Seance on a Wet Afternoon* 1964; *King Rat* 1965; *The Whisperers* 1967; *The Raging Moon* 1970; *Dr Jekyll and Sister Hyde* 1971

Sim, Sheila (1922–) *A Canterbury Tale* 1944; *Great Day* 1944; *Dancing with Crime* 1946; *The Guinea Pig* 1948; *Dear Mr Prohack* 1949; *Pandora and the Flying Dutchman* 1950; *West of Zanzibar* 1954; *The Night My Number Came Up* 1955

Simm, John (1971–) *Boston Kickout* 1995; *Diana & Me* 1997; *Human Traffic* 1999; *Wonderland* 1999; *Miranda* 2001

Simmons, Dick *aka* **Simmons, Richard** (1913–2003) *Pilot #5* 1943; *Thousands Cheer* 1943; *Lady in the Lake* 1947; *On an Island with You* 1948; *I Dream of Jeanie* 1952

Simmons, Gene (1949–) *Runaway* 1984; *Trick or Treat* 1986; *Wanted Dead or Alive* 1986; *Red Surf* 1990; *Detroit Rock City* 1999

Simmons, J K (1955–) *The Jackal* 1997; *For Love of the Game* 1999; *Spider-Man* 2002; *The Ladykillers* 2004; *Spider-Man 2* 2004

Simmons, Jean (1929–) *Give Us the Moon* 1944; *Black Narcissus* 1946; *Great Expectations* 1946; *Hungry Hill* 1946; *Uncle Silas* 1947; *Hamlet* 1948; *Adam and Evelyne* 1949; *The Blue Lagoon* 1949; *Cage of Gold* 1950; *The Clouded Yellow* 1950; *So Long at the Fair* 1950; *Trio* 1950; *Androcles and the Lion* 1952; *The Actress* 1953; *Affair with a Stranger* 1953; *Angel Face* 1953; *The Robe* 1953; *Young Bess* 1953; *Beautiful but Dangerous* 1954; *A Bullet Is Waiting* 1954; *Desiree* 1954; *The Egyptian* 1954; *Footsteps in the Fog* 1955; *Guys and Dolls* 1955; *Hilda Crane* 1956; *This Could Be the Night* 1957; *Until They Sail* 1957; *The Big Country* 1958; *Home before Dark* 1958; *This Earth Is Mine* 1959; *Elmer Gantry* 1960; *The Grass Is Greener* 1960; *Spartacus* 1960; *All the Way Home* 1963; *Life at the Top* 1965; *Mister Buddwing* 1965; *Divorce American Style* 1967; *Rough Night in Jericho* 1967; *The Happy Ending* 1969; *Say Hello to Yesterday* 1971; *Mr Sycamore* 1974; *Dominique* 1978; *Yellow Pages* 1984; *The Dawning* 1988; *How to Make an American Quilt* 1995; *Her Own Rules* 1998; *Final Fantasy: the Spirits Within* 2001

Simms, Ginny (1913–1994) *Playmates* 1941; *Here We Go Again* 1942; *Seven Days' Leave* 1942; *Hit the Ice* 1943; *Broadway Rhythm* 1944; *Night and Day* 1946

Simms, Larry (1934–) *Blondie!* 1938; *The Gay Sisters* 1942

Simon, Carly (1945–) *Taking Off* 1971; *Perfect* 1985

Simon, Michel (1895–1975) *The Passion of Joan of Arc* 1928; *La Chienne* 1931; *On Purge Bébé* 1931; *Boudu, Saved from Drowning* 1932; *L'Atalante* 1934; *Drôle de Drame* 1937; *Le Quai des Brumes* 1938; *The End of the Day* 1939; *La Beauté du Diable* 1949; *Saadia* 1953; *The Train* 1964; *The Two of Us* 1967; *Blanche* 1971

Simon, Paul (1941–) *Annie Hall* 1977; *One-Trick Pony* 1980

Simon, Robert F *aka* **Simon, Robert** (1908–1992) *The Benny Goodman Story* 1955; *Foxfire* 1955; *Bigger than Life* 1956; *The Catered Affair* 1956; *Edge of the City* 1957; *Spring Reunion* 1957; *Gunman's Walk* 1958; *Face of Fire* 1959; *Pay or Die* 1960; *The Wizard of Baghdad* 1960

Simon, Simone (1910–2005) *Ladies in Love* 1936; *Seventh Heaven* 1937; *La Bête Humaine* 1938; *Josette* 1938; *Daniel and the Devil* 1941; *Cat People* 1942; *The Curse of the Cat People* 1944; *Johnny Doesn't Live Here Anymore* 1944; *The Silent Bell* 1944; *Olivia* 1950; *La Ronde* 1950; *Le Plaisir* 1951; *The Extra Day* 1956

Simonds, David *Amateur* 1994; *The Book of Life* 1998

Simons, William *Where No Vultures Fly* 1951; *West of Zanzibar* 1954

Simpson, Ivan (1875–1951) *The Man Who Played God* 1932; *British Agent* 1934; *Trouble for Two* 1936; *The Male Animal* 1942

Simpson, O J (1947–) *The Klansman* 1974; *The Towering Inferno* 1974; *Killer Force* 1975; *The Cassandra Crossing* 1976; *Capricorn One* 1978; *Firepower* 1979; *Hambone and Hillie* 1984; *The Naked Gun* 1988; *The Naked Gun $2\frac{1}{2}$: the Smell of Fear* 1991; *CIA – Codename Alexa* 1992; *No Place to Hide* 1992; *Naked Gun $33\frac{1}{3}$: the Final Insult* 1994

Simpson, Russell (1880–1959) *Annie Laurie* 1927; *Billy the Kid* 1930; *Susan Lenox: Her Fall and Rise* 1931; *Law and Order* 1932; *Way Down East* 1935; *The Grapes of Wrath* 1940; *Wild Geese Calling* 1941; *Along Came Jones* 1945; *Bad Bascomb* 1946; *Tuna Clipper* 1949; *Saddle Tramp* 1950; *The Sun Shines Bright* 1953

Sims, Joan (1930–2001) *Colonel March Investigates* 1953; *The Square Ring* 1953; *Trouble in Store* 1953; *Will Any Gentleman…?* 1953; *The Young Lovers* 1954; *As Long as They're Happy* 1955; *Dry Rot* 1956; *Carry On Admiral* 1957; *Just My Luck* 1957; *The Naked Truth* 1957; *No Time for Tears* 1957; *The Captain's Table* 1958; *Passport to Shame* 1958; *Carry On Nurse* 1959; *Carry On Teacher* 1959; *Life in Emergency Ward 10* 1959; *Upstairs and Downstairs* 1959; *Carry On Constable* 1960; *Carry On Regardless* 1960; *Doctor in Love* 1960; *His and Hers* 1960; *Please Turn Over* 1960; *Watch Your Stern* 1960; *Mr Topaze* 1961; *No My Darling Daughter* 1961; *Twice round the Daffodils* 1962; *Nurse on Wheels* 1963; *Carry On Cleo* 1964; *The Big Job* 1965; *Carry On Cowboy* 1965; *Carry On – Don't Lose Your Head* 1966; *Carry On Screaming* 1966; *Doctor in Clover* 1966; *Carry On Follow That Camel* 1967; *Carry On Doctor* 1968; *Carry On Up the Khyber* 1968; *Carry On Again Doctor* 1969; *Carry On Camping* 1969; *Carry On Loving* 1970; *Carry On Up the Jungle* 1970; *Doctor in Trouble* 1970; *Carry On at Your Convenience* 1971; *Carry On Henry* 1971; *The Magnificent Seven Deadly Sins* 1971; *Carry On Abroad* 1972; *Carry On Matron* 1972; *Not Now Darling* 1972; *Carry On Girls* 1973; *Don't Just Lie There, Say Something!* 1973; *Carry On Dick* 1974; *Carry On Behind* 1975; *Love among the Ruins* 1975; *One of Our Dinosaurs Is Missing* 1975; *Carry On England* 1976; *Carry On Emmannuelle* 1978

Sims, Warwick *He's My Girl* 1987; *Night Eyes* 1990

Sinatra, Frank (1915–1998) *Ship Ahoy* 1942; *Higher and Higher* 1943; *Reveille with Beverly* 1943; *Step Lively* 1944; *Anchors Aweigh* 1945; *Till the Clouds Roll By* 1946; *It Happened in Brooklyn* 1947; *The Miracle of the Bells* 1948; *The Kissing Bandit* 1949; *On the Town* 1949; *Take Me Out to the Ball Game* 1949; *Double Dynamite* 1951; *Meet Danny Wilson* 1952; *From Here to Eternity* 1953; *Suddenly* 1954; *Guys and Dolls* 1955; *The Man with the Golden Arm* 1955; *Not as a Stranger* 1955; *The Tender Trap* 1955; *Young at Heart* 1955; *Around the World in 80 Days* 1956; *High Society* 1956; *Johnny Concho* 1956; *The Joker Is Wild* 1957; *Pal Joey* 1957; *The Pride and the Passion* 1957; *Kings Go Forth* 1958; *Some Came Running* 1958; *A Hole in the Head* 1959; *Never So Few* 1959; *Can-Can* 1960; *Ocean's Eleven* 1960; *Pepe* 1960; *The Devil at Four o'Clock* 1961; *The Manchurian Candidate* 1962; *The Road to Hong Kong* 1962; *Sergeants 3* 1962; *Come Blow Your Horn* 1963; *4 for Texas* 1963; *The List of Adrian Messenger* 1963; *Paris When It Sizzles* 1964; *Robin and the 7 Hoods* 1964; *Marriage on the Rocks* 1965; *None but the Brave* 1965; *Von Ryan's Express* 1965; *Assault on a Queen* 1966; *Cast a Giant Shadow* 1966; *The Oscar* 1966; *The Naked Runner* 1967; *Tony Rome* 1967; *The Detective* 1968; *Lady in Cement* 1968; *Dirty Dingus Magee* 1970; *The First Deadly Sin* 1980; *Cannonball Run II* 1983

Sinatra, Nancy (1940–) *For Those Who Think Young* 1964; *Get Yourself a College Girl* 1964; *Marriage on the Rocks* 1965; *The Ghost in the Invisible Bikini* 1966; *The Last of the Secret Agents*

1966; *The Oscar* 1966; *The Wild Angels* 1966; *Speedway* 1968
Sinbad (1956–) *Necessary Roughness* 1991; *Coneheads* 1993; *Houseguest* 1995; *First Kid* 1996; *Jingle All the Way* 1996; *Good Burger* 1997
Sinclair, Betty (1907–1983) *City Streets* 1931; *Something in the City* 1950
Sinclair, Hugh (1903–1962) *Our Betters* 1933; *Escape Me Never* 1935; *The Four Just Men* 1939; *The Saint's Vacation* 1941; *Tomorrow We Live* 1942; *The Saint Meets the Tiger* 1943; *They Were Sisters* 1945; *Don't Ever Leave Me* 1949; *The Rocking Horse Winner* 1949; *Trottie True* 1949; *Circle of Danger* 1950; *No Trace* 1950; *Judgement Deferred* 1951; *Mantrap* 1952
Sinclair, Madge (1938–1995) *Conrack* 1974; *Leadbelly* 1976; *Convoy* 1978; *Coming to America* 1988; *The Lion King* 1994
Sinclair, Peter (1900–1994) *The Man from Morocco* 1944; *The Time of His Life* 1955; *The Heart of a Man* 1959
Sinclair Blyth, Stuart *Hold Back the Night* 1999; *16 Years of Alcohol* 2003
Sinclaire, Crystin *Ruby* 1977; *Goin' Coconuts* 1978
Sinden, Donald (1923–) *The Cruel Sea* 1953; *A Day to Remember* 1953; *Mogambo* 1953; *The Beachcomber* 1954; *Doctor in the House* 1954; *Mad about Men* 1954; *You Know What Sailors Are* 1954; *Above Us the Waves* 1955; *An Alligator Named Daisy* 1955; *Josephine and Men* 1955; *Simba* 1955; *The Black Tent* 1956; *Eyewitness* 1956; *Tiger in the Smoke* 1956; *Doctor at Large* 1957; *The Captain's Table* 1958; *Rockets Galore* 1958; *Operation Bullshine* 1959; *The Siege of Sidney Street* 1960; *Your Money or Your Wife* 1960; *Mix Me a Person* 1962; *Twice round the Daffodils* 1962; *Decline and Fall... of a Birdwatcher* 1968; *Villain* 1971; *Father Dear Father* 1972; *Rentadick* 1972; *The Day of the Jackal* 1973; *The National Health* 1973; *The Island at the Top of the World* 1974; *That Lucky Touch* 1975; *The Children* 1990
Singer, Campbell (1909–1976) *Blackout* 1950; *A Case for PC 49* 1950; *Someone at the Door* 1950; *Conflict of Wings* 1953; *The Square Peg* 1958
Singer, Johnny (1923–1987) *Street Song* 1935; *It's Never Too Late to Mend* 1937
Singer, Lori (1962–) *Footloose* 1984; *The Falcon and the Snowman* 1985; *The Man with One Red Shoe* 1985; *Trouble in Mind* 1985; *Warlock* 1989; *Equinox* 1992; *Sunset Grill* 1992; *Short Cuts* 1993; *FTW* 1994
Singer, Marc (1948–) *Go Tell the Spartans* 1977; *Something for Joey* 1977; *The Beastmaster* 1982; *Body Chemistry* 1990; *Beastmaster 2: through the Portal of Time* 1991; *Determination of Death* 2001
Singer, Ritchie *"Crocodile" Dundee* 1986; *Encounter at Raven's Gate* 1988; *Cappuccino* 1989
Singh, Gracy *Lagaan: Once upon a Time in India* 2001; *Armaan* 2003
Singleton, Penny (1908–2003) *Swing Your Lady* 1937; *Blondie!* 1938; *Garden of the Moon* 1938; *Hard to Get* 1938; *Racket Busters* 1938; *Jetsons: the Movie* 1990
Sini, Linda (1926–) *The Easy Life* 1962; *The Man Who Laughs* 1966
Sinise, Gary (1955–) *My Name Is Bill W* 1989; *A Midnight Clear* 1991; *Of Mice and Men* 1992; *Jack the Bear* 1993; *Forrest Gump* 1994; *Apollo 13* 1995; *The Quick and the Dead* 1995; *Truman* 1995; *Albino Alligator* 1996; *Ransom* 1996; *Snake Eyes* 1998; *Mission to Mars* 1999; *Deception* 2000; *Impostor* 2001; *The Human Stain* 2003; *The Big Bounce* 2004; *The Forgotten* 2004
Sirico, Tony (1942–) *Innocent Blood* 1992; *New York Cop* 1995; *The Search for One-Eye Jimmy* 1996
Sirola, Joseph aka **Sirola, Joe** *The Super Cops* 1973; *Seizure* 1974; *Love Is a Gun* 1994
Sirtis, Marina (1960–) *Blind Date* 1984; *Waxwork II: Lost in Time* 1992; *Star Trek: Generations* 1994; *Star Trek: First Contact* 1996; *Star Trek: Insurrection* 1998; *Star Trek: Nemesis* 2002
Sisqo aka **SisQo** (1978–) *Get over It* 2001; *Pieces of April* 2002; *Snow Dogs* 2002
Sisti, Michelan *Teenage Mutant Ninja Turtles* 1990; *Teenage Mutant Ninja Turtles II: the Secret of the Ooze* 1991
Sisto, Jeremy (1974–) *Grand Canyon* 1991; *Hideaway* 1995; *White Squall* 1996; *Suicide Kings* 1997; *Some Girls* 1998; *Without Limits* 1998; *Angel Eyes* 2001; *Thirteen* 2003; *Wrong Turn* 2003; *A Lot like Love* 2005
Sisto, Rocco *Red Riding Hood* 1987; *Innocent Blood* 1992
Sivero, Frank *The Billion Dollar Hobo* 1978; *Going Ape!* 1981; *GoodFellas* 1990; *Cop and a Half* 1993
Sives, Jamie *Wilbur (Wants to Kill Himself)* 2002; *One Last Chance* 2003; *On a Clear Day* 2005
Sizemore, Tom (1964–) *Lock Up* 1989; *Blue Steel* 1990; *Where Sleeping Dogs Lie* 1991; *Passenger 57* 1992; *Heart and Souls* 1993; *Striking Distance* 1993; *True Romance* 1993; *Natural Born Killers* 1994; *Devil in a Blue Dress* 1995; *Heat* 1995; *Strange Days* 1995; *The Relic* 1996; *Enemy of the State* 1998; *Saving Private Ryan* 1998; *Bringing out the Dead* 1999; *The Match* 1999; *Witness Protection* 1999; *Play It to the Bone* 2000; *Red Planet* 2000; *Black Hawk Down* 2001; *Pearl Harbor* 2001; *Ticker* 2001; *Big Trouble* 2002; *Dreamcatcher* 2003; *Paparazzi* 2004
Sjöberg, Emma (1968–) *Taxi* 1998; *Taxi 2* 2000
Sjöberg, Gunnar (1909–1977) *The Great Adventure* 1953; *So Close to Life* 1957
Sjöström, Victor aka **Seastrom, Victor** (1879–1960) *The Outlaw and His Wife* 1917; *Thomas Graal's Best Film* 1917; *A Dangerous Pledge* 1920; *The Phantom Carriage* 1920; *Walpurgis Night* 1935; *To Joy* 1950; *Wild Strawberries* 1957
Skaggs, Jimmie F aka **Skaggs, Jimmie** (1944–2004) *Ghost Town* 1988; *Oblivion* 1993; *Underworld* 1996
Skala, Lilia (1896–1994) *Lilies of the Field* 1963; *Caprice* 1967; *Charly* 1968; *Deadly Hero* 1976; *Roseland* 1977; *Heartland* 1979; *Flashdance* 1983; *Testament* 1983; *House of Games* 1987
Skarsgård, Stellan (1951–) *Anita* 1973; *The Simple-Minded Murderer* 1982; *Ake and His World* 1984; *The Perfect Murder* 1988; *The Hunt for Red October* 1990; *The Ox* 1991; *The Democratic Terrorist* 1992; *Wind* 1992; *The Slingshot* 1993; *Zero Kelvin* 1995; *Breaking the Waves* 1996; *Amistad* 1997; *Good Will Hunting* 1997; *Insomnia* 1997; *My Son the Fanatic* 1997; *Savior* 1997; *Ronin* 1998; *Deep Blue Sea* 1999; *Timecode* 1999; *Aberdeen* 2000; *Passion of Mind* 2000; *The Glass House* 2001; *Kiss Kiss (Bang Bang)* 2001; *Taking Sides* 2001; *City of Ghosts* 2002; *No Good Deed* 2002; *Dogville* 2003; *Exorcist: the Beginning* 2004; *King Arthur* 2004
Skarstedt, Georg (1900–1976) *To Joy* 1950; *Summer with Monika* 1952
Skelton, Red aka **Skelton, Richard** (1913–1997) *Having Wonderful Time* 1938; *Flight Command* 1940; *Dr Kildare's Wedding Day* 1941; *Lady Be Good* 1941; *The People vs Dr Kildare* 1941; *Whistling in the Dark* 1941; *Ship Ahoy* 1942; *Whistling in Dixie* 1942; *DuBarry Was a Lady* 1943; *I Dood It* 1943; *Whistling in Brooklyn* 1943; *Bathing Beauty* 1944; *Merton of the Movies* 1947; *The Fuller Brush Man* 1948; *A Southern Yankee* 1948; *Neptune's Daughter* 1949; *The Fuller Brush Girl* 1950; *Three Little Words* 1950; *Watch the Birdie* 1950; *The Yellow Cab Man* 1950; *Texas Carnival* 1951; *The Clown* 1952; *Lovely to Look At* 1952; *The Great Diamond Robbery* 1953
Skerritt, Tom (1933–) *War Hunt* 1962; *Those Calloways* 1964; *MASH* 1969; *The Birdmen* 1971; *Wild Rovers* 1971; *Fuzz* 1972; *Big Bad Mama* 1974; *Thieves like Us* 1974; *The Devil's Rain* 1975; *The Turning Point* 1977; *Cheech & Chong's Up in Smoke* 1978; *Ice Castles* 1978; *Alien* 1979; *A Dangerous Summer* 1981; *Savage Harvest* 1981; *Silence of the North* 1981; *Death Vengeance* 1982; *The Dead Zone* 1983; *Hell Camp* 1986; *SpaceCamp* 1986; *Top Gun* 1986; *Wisdom* 1986; *The Big Town* 1987; *Maid to Order* 1987; *Poltergeist III* 1988; *Big Man on Campus* 1989; *Steel Magnolias* 1989; *The Rookie* 1990; *Knight Moves* 1992; *Poison Ivy* 1992; *A River Runs through It* 1992; *Wild Orchid 2: Two Shades of Blue* 1992; *Contact* 1997; *What the Deaf Man Heard* 1997; *Two for Texas* 1998; *The Other Sister* 1999; *Path to War* 2002; *Tears of the Sun* 2003
Skilton, Gerry *"Crocodile" Dundee II* 1988; *Crocodile Dundee in Los Angeles* 2001
Skinner, Claire (1965–) *Life Is Sweet* 1990; *Naked* 1993; *Clockwork Mice* 1994; *ID* 1994; *The Escort* 1999; *You're Dead* 1999; *Strings* 2004
Skinner, Cornelia Otis (1901–1979) *The Uninvited* 1944; *The Girl in the Red Velvet Swing* 1955
Skipper, Pat *Demonstone* 1989; *Femme Fatale* 1991; *Memoirs of an Invisible Man* 1992; *Ed Gein* 2000
Skipworth, Alison (1863–1952) *Outward Bound* 1930; *Raffles* 1930; *If I Had a Million* 1932; *Night after Night* 1932; *Sinners in the Sun* 1932; *The Song of Songs* 1933; *Tillie and Gus* 1933; *The Captain Hates the Sea* 1934; *Six of a Kind* 1934; *Becky Sharp* 1935; *The Casino Murder Case* 1935; *Dangerous* 1935; *The Devil Is a Woman* 1935; *The Girl from 10th Avenue* 1935; *The Gorgeous Hussy* 1936; *The Princess Comes Across* 1936; *Satan Met a Lady* 1936
Skolimowski, Jerzy (1938–) *Circle of Deceit* 1981; *White Nights* 1985
Skotnicki, Jan *Illumination* 1972; *The Scar* 1976
Skvorecka, Zdena aka **Skvorecka, Zdenka** *The Party and the Guests* 1966; *End of a Priest* 1969
Sky, Jennifer (1977–) *My Little Eye* 2002; *Never Die Alone* 2004
Skye, Ione (1971–) *River's Edge* 1987; *Stranded* 1987; *A Night in the Life of Jimmy Reardon* 1988; *The Rachel Papers* 1989; *Say Anything...* 1989; *Mindwalk* 1990; *Gas, Food, Lodging* 1992; *Guncrazy* 1992; *Dream for an Insomniac* 1996; *The Perfect Catch* 2005
Slade, Demian *Better Off Dead* 1985; *Back to the Beach* 1987
Slade, Max Elliott (1980–) *3 Ninjas* 1992; *3 Ninjas Kick Back* 1994; *3 Ninjas Knuckle Up* 1995
Slate, Henry (1910–1996) *Bloodhounds of Broadway* 1952; *Somebody Loves Me* 1952; *Hey Boy! Hey Girl!* 1959
Slate, Jeremy (1926–) *Girls! Girls! Girls!* 1962; *Wives and Lovers* 1963; *I'll Take Sweden* 1965; *Born Losers* 1967; *True Grit* 1969; *The Dream Machine* 1990; *The Lawnmower Man* 1992
Slater, Christian (1969–) *The Legend of Billie Jean* 1985; *The Name of the Rose* 1986; *Beyond the Stars* 1988; *Gleaming the Cube* 1988; *Tucker: the Man and His Dream* 1988; *Heathers* 1989; *Pump Up the Volume* 1990; *Young Guns II* 1990; *Kuffs* 1991; *Mobsters* 1991; *Robin Hood: Prince of Thieves* 1991; *Star Trek VI: the Undiscovered Country* 1991; *Tales from the Darkside: the Movie* 1991; *FernGully: the Last Rainforest* 1992; *Where the Day Takes You* 1992; *True Romance* 1993; *Untamed Heart* 1993; *Interview with the Vampire: the Vampire Chronicles* 1994; *Jimmy Hollywood* 1994; *Murder in the First* 1994; *Bed of Roses* 1995; *Broken Arrow* 1996; *Hard Rain* 1997; *Julian Po* 1997; *Basil* 1998; *Very Bad Things* 1998; *The Contender* 2000; *3000 Miles to Graceland* 2000; *Windtalkers* 2001; *Mindhunters* 2003; *Churchill: the Hollywood Years* 2004
Slater, Helen (1963–) *Supergirl* 1984; *The Legend of Billie Jean* 1985; *Ruthless People* 1986; *The Secret of My Success* 1987; *Sticky Fingers* 1988; *Happy Together* 1989; *City Slickers* 1991; *12:01* 1993; *Lassie: a New Generation* 1994; *The Steal* 1994; *No Way Back* 1996; *Nowhere in Sight* 2000
Slater, John (1916–1975) *Gert and Daisy's Weekend* 1941; *For Those in Peril* 1943; *Against the Wind* 1947; *Conspiracy in Teheran* 1947; *It Always Rains on Sunday* 1947; *Passport to Pimlico* 1949; *The Long Memory* 1952; *Star of India* 1954; *Violent Playground* 1958; *The Night We Got the Bird* 1960; *Three on a Spree* 1961; *A Place to Go* 1963
Slater, Ryan (1983–) *The Amazing Panda Adventure* 1995; *Home Team* 1998
Slattery, John (1963–) *The Naked Man* 1998; *Bad Company* 2002; *Dirty Dancing 2* 2003; *Mona Lisa Smile* 2003
Slattery, Tony (1959–) *Carry On Columbus* 1992; *The Crying Game* 1992; *Peter's Friends* 1992; *To Die For* 1994; *Up 'n' Under* 1997; *The Wedding Tackle* 2000
Slaughter, Tod (1885–1956) *Maria Marten, or the Murder in the Red Barn* 1935; *The Crimes of Stephen Hawke* 1936; *Sweeney Todd, the Demon Barber of Fleet Street* 1936; *It's Never Too Late to Mend* 1937; *Song of the Road* 1937; *The Ticket of Leave Man* 1937; *Sexton Blake and the Hooded Terror* 1938; *Crimes at the Dark House* 1939; *The Face at the Window* 1939; *The Curse of the Wraydons* 1946; *The Greed of William Hart* 1948
Sleep, Wayne (1948–) *The Tales of Beatrix Potter* 1971; *The First Great Train Robbery* 1978; *Elizabeth* 1998
Sleeper, Martha (1907–1983) *Penthouse* 1933; *Spitfire* 1934; *The Scoundrel* 1935; *The Bells of St Mary's* 1945
Slezak, Victor *Beyond Rangoon* 1995; *The Bridges of Madison County* 1995
Slezak, Walter (1902–1983) *Once upon a Honeymoon* 1942; *The Fallen Sparrow* 1943; *This Land Is Mine* 1943; *Lifeboat* 1944; *The Princess and the Pirate* 1944; *Step Lively* 1944; *Till We Meet Again* 1944; *Cornered* 1945; *Salome, Where She Danced* 1945; *The Spanish Main* 1945; *Lady of Deceit* 1947; *Riff-Raff* 1947; *Sinbad the Sailor* 1947; *The Pirate* 1948; *The Inspector General* 1949; *Abbott and Costello in the Foreign Legion* 1950; *The Yellow Cab Man* 1950; *Bedtime for Bonzo* 1951; *People Will Talk* 1951; *Call Me Madam* 1953; *Confidentially Connie* 1953; *White Witch Doctor* 1953; *Ten Thousand Bedrooms* 1957; *The Miracle* 1959; *Come September* 1961; *The Wonderful World of the Brothers Grimm* 1962; *Emil and the Detectives* 1964; *Wonderful Life* 1964; *A Very Special Favor* 1965; *Black Beauty* 1971; *Treasure Island* 1972
Sloane, Everett (1909–1965) *Citizen Kane* 1941; *Journey into Fear* 1942; *The Lady from Shanghai* 1948; *Prince of Foxes* 1949; *The Men* 1950; *Bird of Paradise* 1951; *The Desert Fox* 1951; *The Enforcer* 1951; *The Prince Who Was a Thief* 1951; *The Sellout* 1951; *Sirocco* 1951; *Way of a Gaucho* 1952; *Lust for Life* 1956; *Patterns* 1956; *Somebody Up There Likes Me* 1956; *The Gun Runners* 1958; *Marjorie Morningstar* 1958; *Home from the Hill* 1960; *By Love Possessed* 1961; *Brushfire!* 1962; *The Man from the Diner's Club* 1963; *The Disorderly Orderly* 1964; *The Patsy* 1964
Sloane, Olive (1896–1963) *Seven Days to Noon* 1950; *Curtain Up* 1952; *The Man in the Road* 1957
Sloatman, Lala (1970–) *Watchers* 1988; *Amityville: a New Generation* 1993
Slotnick, Joey (1966–) *Blast from the Past* 1998; *Hollow Man* 2000
Sloyan, James aka **Sloyan, James J** (1940–) *The Traveling Executioner* 1970; *The Disappearance of Aimee* 1976; *Xanadu* 1980
Small, Marya aka **Small, Merrya** *Sleeper* 1973; *The Great Smokey Roadblock* 1977; *Dreamer* 1979; *Fade to Black* 1980; *National Lampoon's Class Reunion* 1982; *Puppet Master* 1989
Small, Neva *Fiddler on the Roof* 1971; *The Laserman* 1988
Small, Sharon (1967–) *About a Boy* 2002; *Dear Frankie* 2003
Smalley, Phillips (1875–1939) *High Voltage* 1929; *Charley's Aunt* 1930
Smallhorne, Jimmy *2by4* 1998; *When the Sky Falls* 2000
Smart, Amy (1976–) *Dee Snider's Strangeland* 1998; *High Voltage* 1998; *Road Trip* 2000; *Rat Race* 2001; *The Butterfly Effect* 2003; *Starsky & Hutch* 2004; *Win a Date with Tad Hamilton!* 2004
Smart, Dee *Back of Beyond* 1995; *Blackwater Trail* 1995; *Welcome to Woop Woop* 1997
Smart, Jean (1959–) *Fire with Fire* 1986; *The Odd Couple II* 1998; *Guinevere* 1999; *Disney's The Kid* 2000; *Snow Day* 2000; *Sweet Home Alabama* 2002; *Bringing Down the House* 2003; *Garden State* 2003
Smart, Rebecca (1976–) *The Shiralee* 1986; *Celia* 1988; *Blackrock* 1997
Smerczak, Ron aka **Smerczac, Ron** *Cyborg Cop* 1993; *Freefall* 1994; *Dangerous Ground* 1996; *Jackie Chan's Who Am I?* 1998
Smethurst, Jack (1932–) *A Kind of Loving* 1962; *For the Love of Ada* 1972; *Love Thy Neighbour* 1973
Smith, Alexis (1921–1993) *Affectionately Yours* 1941; *Dive Bomber* 1941; *Gentleman Jim* 1942; *The Constant Nymph* 1943; *The Adventures of Mark Twain* 1944; *The Doughgirls* 1944; *Conflict* 1945; *The Horn Blows at Midnight* 1945; *Rhapsody in Blue* 1945; *San Antonio* 1945; *The Two Mrs Carrolls* 1945; *Night and Day* 1946; *Of Human Bondage* 1946; *The Woman in White* 1948; *Any Number Can Play* 1949; *South of St Louis* 1949; *Montana* 1950; *Undercover Girl* 1950; *Wyoming Mail* 1950; *Cave of Outlaws* 1951; *Here Comes the Groom* 1951; *The Turning Point* 1952; *Split Second* 1953; *The Sleeping Tiger* 1954; *Beau James* 1957; *This Happy Feeling* 1958; *The Young Philadelphians* 1959; *Once Is Not Enough* 1975; *The Little Girl Who Lives Down the Lane* 1976; *Casey's Shadow* 1978; *Tough Guys* 1986; *The Age of Innocence* 1993
Smith, Allison (1969–) *...At First Sight* 1995; *Danielle Steel's Full Circle* 1996
Smith, Amber (1972–) *Faithful* 1996; *Sleeping Together* 1997; *Dead End* 2003

Smith, Anjela Lauren *Babymother* 1998; *GMT Greenwich Mean Time* 1998; *24 Hours in London* 1999
Smith, Anna Deavere (1950–) *Unfinished Business...* 1987; *The American President* 1995
Smith, Anne *The Time of His Life* 1955; *Backlash* 1986
Smith, Art (1899–1973) *T-Men* 1947; *Angel in Exile* 1948; *Letter from an Unknown Woman* 1948; *Mr Peabody and the Mermaid* 1948; *Caught* 1949; *In a Lonely Place* 1950; *The Next Voice You Hear* 1950; *Quicksand* 1950
Smith, Billy *Underground* 1998; *The Ghost of Greville Lodge* 2000
Smith, Brandon (1949–) *Blaze* 1989; *Powder* 1995; *Jeepers Creepers* 2001; *Slap Her, She's French!* 2001
Smith, Britta *The Country Girls* 1983; *In the Name of the Father* 1993; *Her Own Rules* 1998; *The Magdalene Sisters* 2002
Smith, Brooke (1967–) *Vanya on 42nd Street* 1994; *Kansas City* 1995; *Series 7: the Contenders* 2001
Smith, Bubba (1945–) *Stroker Ace* 1983; *Police Academy* 1984; *Black Moon Rising* 1985; *Police Academy 2: Their First Assignment* 1985; *Police Academy 3: Back in Training* 1986; *Police Academy 4: Citizens on Patrol* 1987; *The Wild Pair* 1987; *Police Academy 5: Assignment Miami Beach* 1988; *Police Academy 6: City under Siege* 1989
Smith, C Aubrey (1863–1948) *The Bachelor Father* 1931; *Daybreak* 1931; *Guilty Hands* 1931; *Trader Horn* 1931; *Love Me Tonight* 1932; *Polly of the Circus* 1932; *Tarzan, the Ape Man* 1932; *Trouble in Paradise* 1932; *The Barbarian* 1933; *Blonde Bombshell* 1933; *Morning Glory* 1933; *Secrets* 1933; *Bulldog Drummond Strikes Back* 1934; *Caravan* 1934; *Cleopatra* 1934; *Gambling Lady* 1934; *The House of Rothschild* 1934; *One More River* 1934; *The Scarlet Empress* 1934; *We Live Again* 1934; *China Seas* 1935; *The Crusades* 1935; *The Florentine Dagger* 1935; *The Gilded Lily* 1935; *The Lives of a Bengal Lancer* 1935; *The Tunnel* 1935; *The Garden of Allah* 1936; *Little Lord Fauntleroy* 1936; *Lloyd's of London* 1936; *Romeo and Juliet* 1936; *The Hurricane* 1937; *The Prisoner of Zenda* 1937; *Thoroughbreds Don't Cry* 1937; *Wee Willie Winkie* 1937; *Four Men and a Prayer* 1938; *Kidnapped* 1938; *Sixty Glorious Years* 1938; *Another Thin Man* 1939; *Balalaika* 1939; *East Side of Heaven* 1939; *Eternally Yours* 1939; *Five Came Back* 1939; *The Four Feathers* 1939; *A Bill of Divorcement* 1940; *Rebecca* 1940; *Waterloo Bridge* 1940; *Dr Jekyll and Mr Hyde* 1941; *Forever and a Day* 1943; *Madame Curie* 1943; *The Adventures of Mark Twain* 1944; *Sensations* 1944; *The White Cliffs of Dover* 1944; *And Then There Were None* 1945; *Cluny Brown* 1946; *Rendezvous with Annie* 1946; *An Ideal Husband* 1947; *Unconquered* 1947; *Little Women* 1949
Smith, Charles (1920–1988) *The General* 1927; *Three Little Girls in Blue* 1946
Smith, Charles Martin *aka* **Smith, Charlie Martin** (1953–) *The Culpepper Cattle Co* 1972; *American Graffiti* 1973; *Rafferty and the Gold Dust Twins* 1974; *The Spikes Gang* 1974; *The Hazing* 1977; *The Buddy Holly Story* 1978; *More American Graffiti* 1979; *Herbie Goes Bananas* 1980; *Never Cry Wolf* 1983; *Starman* 1984; *The Untouchables* 1987; *The Experts* 1989; *The Hot Spot* 1990; *Fifty/Fifty* 1991; *Deep Cover* 1992; *And the Band Played On* 1993; *Speechless* 1994; *The Final Cut* 1995; *Wedding Bell Blues* 1996
Smith, Cheryl (1955–2002) *Slumber Party '57* 1976; *Laserblast* 1978
Smith, Constance (1928–) *Room to Let* 1949; *The 13th Letter* 1950; *Red Skies of Montana* 1952; *Man in the Attic* 1953; *Taxi* 1953; *Treasure of the Golden Condor* 1953; *The Big Tip Off* 1955; *Impulse* 1955; *Tiger by the Tail* 1955
Smith, Cotter (1949–) *The Rape of Richard Beck* 1985; *Lady Beware* 1987; *Cameron's Closet* 1988; *K-9* 1989; *Shattered Family* 1993; *Lifeform* 1996
Smith, Cynthia *Benji* 1974; *For the Love of Benji* 1977
Smith, Cyril (1892–1963) *Friday the Thirteenth* 1933; *The Black Abbot* 1934; *The Rocking Horse Winner* 1949; *Green Grow the Rushes* 1951; *Sailor Beware!* 1956; *Light Up the Sky* 1960; *Watch It, Sailor!* 1961
Smith, Dean (1933–) *The Autobiography of Miss Jane Pittman* 1974; *Seven Alone* 1974
Smith, Desirée *The Delinquents* 1989; *Almost* 1990
Smith, Ethel (1910–1996) *Bathing Beauty* 1944; *George White's Scandals* 1945
Smith, Gerald Oliver (1892–1974) *When You're in Love* 1937; *The Sailor Takes a Wife* 1945
Smith, Geraldine *Flesh* 1968; *Mixed Blood* 1984; *Spike of Bensonhurst* 1988
Smith, Gregory (1983–) *Harriet the Spy* 1996; *Krippendorf's Tribe* 1998; *Small Soldiers* 1998
Smith, Howard *aka* **Smith, Howard I** (1893–1968) *Kiss of Death* 1947; *Death of a Salesman* 1951; *The Caddy* 1953; *No Time for Sergeants* 1958; *Wind across the Everglades* 1958; *Murder, Inc* 1960
Smith, Jaclyn (1947–) *The Adventurers* 1970; *Déjà Vu* 1984; *Danielle Steel's Kaleidoscope* 1990; *Victim of Rage* 1994
Smith, John (1931–1995) *Seven Angry Men* 1955; *Wichita* 1955; *The Bold and the Brave* 1956; *Rebel in Town* 1956; *Fury at Showdown* 1957; *Handle with Care* 1958; *The Magnificent Showman* 1964; *Waco* 1966
Smith, Keely (1932–) *Senior Prom* 1958; *Thunder Road* 1958; *Hey Boy! Hey Girl!* 1959
Smith, Kent (1907–1985) *Cat People* 1942; *Hitler's Children* 1943; *This Land Is Mine* 1943; *The Curse of the Cat People* 1944; *Youth Runs Wild* 1944; *The Spiral Staircase* 1946; *Magic Town* 1947; *Nora Prentiss* 1947; *Voice of the Turtle* 1947; *The Fountainhead* 1949; *My Foolish Heart* 1949; *The Damned Don't Cry* 1950; *Comanche* 1956; *The Badlanders* 1958; *Imitation General* 1958; *Party Girl* 1958; *This Earth Is Mine* 1959; *Strangers When We Meet* 1960; *Games* 1967; *Kona Coast* 1968; *Death of a Gunfighter* 1969
Smith, Kerr (1972–) *Final Destination* 2000; *The Forsaken* 2001
Smith (2), Kevin (1970–) *Clerks* 1994; *Mallrats* 1995; *Chasing Amy* 1996; *Dogma* 1999; *Scream 3* 1999; *Jay and Silent Bob Strike Back* 2001; *Daredevil* 2003
Smith, Kurtwood (1943–) *RoboCop* 1987; *Rambo III* 1988; *Dead Poets Society* 1989; *True Believer* 1989; *Company Business* 1991; *Fortress* 1992; *Boxing Helena* 1993; *The Crush* 1993; *Dead on Sight* 1994; *Last of the Dogmen* 1995; *Under Siege 2* 1995; *Citizen Ruth* 1996
Smith, Lane (1936–2005) *On the Yard* 1978; *Purple Hearts* 1984; *Prison* 1987; *Weeds* 1987; *The Final Days* 1989; *Air America* 1990; *The Distinguished Gentleman* 1992; *The Mighty Ducks* 1992; *My Cousin Vinny* 1992; *Son in Law* 1993; *The Scout* 1994; *Inherit the Wind* 1999
Smith, Lewis (1958–) *Southern Comfort* 1981; *I Ought to Be in Pictures* 1982; *Love Child* 1982; *The Adventures of Buckaroo Banzai across the 8th Dimension* 1984; *The Heavenly Kid* 1985; *Diary of a Hitman* 1992
Smith, Liz (1925–) *Bleak Moments* 1971; *It Shouldn't Happen to a Vet* 1979; *A Private Function* 1984; *Apartment Zero* 1988; *High Spirits* 1988; *We Think the World of You* 1988; *Bert Rigby, You're a Fool* 1989; *The Cook, the Thief, His Wife and Her Lover* 1989; *Son of the Pink Panther* 1993; *Haunted* 1995; *Keep the Aspidistra Flying* 1997; *The Revengers' Comedies* 1997; *Tom's Midnight Garden* 1998
Smith, Lois (1930–) *East of Eden* 1955; *Strange Lady in Town* 1955; *Five Easy Pieces* 1970; *Next Stop, Greenwich Village* 1976; *Foxes* 1980; *Reuben, Reuben* 1983; *Falling Down* 1992; *Holy Matrimony* 1994; *Dead Man Walking* 1995; *Twister* 1996; *The Eternal* 1998; *Minority Report* 2002
Smith, Loring (1891–1981) *The Clown* 1952; *Happy Anniversary* 1959
Smith, Madeline (1949–) *The Vampire Lovers* 1970; *The Amazing Mr Blunden* 1972; *Up the Front* 1972; *Frankenstein and the Monster from Hell* 1973; *Take Me High* 1973
Smith, Madolyn *aka* **Smith Osborne, Madolyn** (1957–) *Urban Cowboy* 1980; *All of Me* 1984; *2010* 1984; *The Caller* 1987; *Funny Farm* 1988; *Final Approach* 1991; *The Super* 1991
Smith, Maggie (1934–) *Nowhere to Go* 1958; *Go to Blazes* 1961; *The VIPs* 1963; *The Pumpkin Eater* 1964; *Othello* 1965; *Young Cassidy* 1965; *The Honey Pot* 1967; *Hot Millions* 1968; *Oh! What a Lovely War* 1969; *The Prime of Miss Jean Brodie* 1969; *Travels with My Aunt* 1972; *Love and Pain and the Whole Damn Thing* 1973; *Murder by Death* 1976; *California Suite* 1978; *Death on the Nile* 1978; *Clash of the Titans* 1981; *Quartet* 1981; *Evil under the Sun* 1982; *The Missionary* 1982; *Better Late Than Never* 1983; *A Private Function* 1984; *Lily in Love* 1985; *A Room with a View* 1985; *The Lonely Passion of Judith Hearne* 1987; *Hook* 1991; *Sister Act* 1992; *The Secret Garden* 1993; *Sister Act 2: Back in the Habit* 1993; *Richard III* 1995; *The First Wives Club* 1996; *Washington Square* 1997; *Curtain Call* 1998; *Tea with Mussolini* 1998; *The Last September* 1999; *Gosford Park* 2001; *Harry Potter and the Philosopher's Stone* 2001; *Divine Secrets of the Ya-Ya Sisterhood* 2002; *Harry Potter and the Chamber of Secrets* 2002; *My House in Umbria* 2002; *Harry Potter and the Prisoner of Azkaban* 2004; *Ladies in Lavender* 2004
Smith, Mel (1952–) *Babylon* 1980; *Bullshot* 1983; *Slayground* 1983; *Number One* 1984; *Morons from Outer Space* 1985; *National Lampoon's European Vacation* 1985; *Restless Natives* 1985; *The Princess Bride* 1987; *The Wolves of Willoughby Chase* 1988; *Wilt* 1989; *Brain Donors* 1992; *Twelfth Night* 1996
Smith, Michael Bailey *Cyborg 3: The Recycler* 1994; *Ice* 1994; *Monster Man* 2003
Smith, Oliver *Hellraiser* 1987; *Hellbound: Hellraiser II* 1988
Smith, Patricia (1930–) *The Bachelor Party* 1957; *The Spirit of St Louis* 1957; *The Girl Who Knew Too Much* 1969; *Save the Tiger* 1973
Smith, Paul *aka* **Smith, Paul L** (1939–) *Madron* 1970; *Midnight Express* 1978; *Popeye* 1980; *Pieces* 1982; *Crimewave* 1985; *Red Sonja* 1985; *Haunted Honeymoon* 1986; *Gor* 1987; *Outlaw Force* 1988
Smith, Pete *The Quiet Earth* 1985; *Crush* 1992; *Flight of the Albatross* 1995; *The Boys* 1998; *What Becomes of the Broken Hearted?* 1999
Smith, Queenie (1898–1978) *Mississippi* 1935; *Show Boat* 1936; *The Long Night* 1947; *Sleep, My Love* 1948
Smith, Ray (1936–1991) *The Painted Smile* 1961; *Operation Daybreak* 1975; *The Sailor's Return* 1978
Smith, Rex (1956–) *The Pirates of Penzance* 1983; *The Trial of the Incredible Hulk* 1989; *Danielle Steel's Once in a Lifetime* 1994
Smith, Riley (1978–) *Radio* 2003; *New York Minute* 2004
Smith, Roger (1932–) *Auntie Mame* 1958; *Crash Landing* 1958; *Never Steal Anything Small* 1959
Smith, Sally (1942–) *Trouble with Eve* 1959; *Father Came Too* 1963
Smith, Shawn (1922–1995) *The Long Wait* 1954; *The Land Unknown* 1957; *It! The Terror from beyond Space* 1958; *The River Rat* 1984
Smith, Shawnee (1970–) *Summer School* 1987; *The Blob* 1988; *Who's Harry Crumb?* 1989; *Dead Men Can't Dance* 1997; *Carnival of Souls* 1999
Smith, Will (1968–) *Where the Day Takes You* 1992; *Made in America* 1993; *Six Degrees of Separation* 1993; *Bad Boys* 1995; *Independence Day* 1996; *Men in Black* 1997; *Enemy of the State* 1998; *Wild Wild West* 1999; *The Legend of Bagger Vance* 2000; *Ali* 2001; *Men in Black 2* 2002; *Bad Boys II* 2003; *Jersey Girl* 2003; *I, Robot* 2004; *Shark Tale* 2004; *Hitch* 2005
Smith, William *aka* **Smith, Bill** *aka* **Smith II, William** (1934–) *Atlantis, the Lost Continent* 1960; *Three Guns for Texas* 1968; *Backtrack* 1969; *Run, Angel, Run* 1969; *Hammer* 1972; *The Deadly Trackers* 1973; *The Last American Hero* 1973; *The Rockford Files* 1974; *The Ultimate Warrior* 1975; *Scorchy* 1976; *The Frisco Kid* 1979; *Seven* 1979; *Any Which Way You Can* 1980; *Eye of the Tiger* 1986; *Hell Comes to Frogtown* 1988; *Maniac Cop* 1988; *East LA Warriors* 1989; *Spirit of the Eagle* 1991
Smith, Yeardley (1964–) *The Legend of Billie Jean* 1985; *Maximum Overdrive* 1986; *As Good as It Gets* 1997
Smith Boucher, Savannah *Odd Jobs* 1986; *Everybody's All-American* 1988
Smith-Cameron, J *That Night* 1992; *Harriet the Spy* 1996; *The Rage: Carrie 2* 1999; *You Can Count on Me* 1999
Smith-Jackson, Jamie *The Affair* 1973; *Breezy* 1973; *Bug* 1975
Smithers, William (1927–) *Attack!* 1956; *Trouble Man* 1972; *Deathsport* 1978
Smitrovich, Bill (1947–) *A Killing Affair* 1985; *Renegades* 1989; *Crazy People* 1990; *The Phantom* 1996; *The Trigger Effect* 1996; *Futuresport* 1998; *Mr Murder* 1998
Smits, Jimmy (1956–) *Hot Shot* 1986; *Running Scared* 1986; *Old Gringo* 1989; *Vital Signs* 1990; *Fires Within* 1991; *Switch* 1991; *My Family* 1994; *Marshal Law* 1996; *Murder in Mind* 1996; *The Million Dollar Hotel* 1999; *Bless the Child* 2000; *Price of Glory* 2000; *Star Wars Episode II: Attack of the Clones* 2002
Smits, Sonja (1958–) *Videodrome* 1982; *Owning Mahowny* 2002
Smollett, Jurnee (1986–) *Eve's Bayou* 1997; *Beautiful Joe* 2000
Smothers, Tom (1937–) *Get to Know Your Rabbit* 1972; *Silver Bears* 1977; *There Goes the Bride* 1979; *Pandemonium* 1982
Smurfit, Victoria (1974–) *The Run of the Country* 1995; *The Wedding Tackle* 2000; *About a Boy* 2002; *Bulletproof Monk* 2002; *The Last Great Wilderness* 2002
Smuts Kennedy, Sarah *An Angel at My Table* 1990; *Jack Be Nimble* 1992
Smyrner, Ann (1934–) *The Good Die First* 1967; *House of a Thousand Dolls* 1967
Snipes, Wesley (1962–) *Streets of Gold* 1986; *Wildcats* 1986; *King of New York* 1989; *Major League* 1989; *Mo' Better Blues* 1990; *Jungle Fever* 1991; *New Jack City* 1991; *The Waterdance* 1991; *Passenger 57* 1992; *White Men Can't Jump* 1992; *Boiling Point* 1993; *Demolition Man* 1993; *Rising Sun* 1993; *Sugar Hill* 1993; *Drop Zone* 1994; *Money Train* 1995; *To Wong Foo, Thanks for Everything, Julie Newmar* 1995; *The Fan* 1996; *Down in the Delta* 1997; *Murder at 1600* 1997; *One Night Stand* 1997; *Blade* 1998; *Futuresport* 1998; *US Marshals* 1998; *The Art of War* 2000; *Disappearing Acts* 2000; *Play It to the Bone* 2000; *Blade II* 2002; *Liberty Stands Still* 2002; *Undisputed* 2002; *Blade: Trinity* 2004
Snodgress, Carrie (1946–2004) *Diary of a Mad Housewife* 1970; *Rabbit, Run* 1970; *The Fury* 1978; *Trick or Treats* 1982; *A Night in Heaven* 1983; *Pale Rider* 1985; *Murphy's Law* 1986; *Blueberry Hill* 1988; *Across the Tracks* 1990; *Blue Sky* 1991; *The Ballad of Little Jo* 1993; *8 Seconds* 1994; *White Man's Burden* 1995; *Bartleby* 2000; *Ed Gein* 2000; *The Forsaken* 2001
Snoop Dogg *aka* **Snoop Doggy Dogg** (1971–) *Half-Baked* 1998; *I Got the Hook Up* 1998; *Ride* 1998; *Gang Law* 1999; *Whiteboys* 1999; *Baby Boy* 2001; *Bones* 2001; *Training Day* 2001; *The Wash* 2001; *Malibu's Most Wanted* 2003; *Old School* 2003; *Racing Stripes* 2004; *Soul Plane* 2004; *Starsky & Hutch* 2004
Snowden, Leigh (1929–1982) *The Square Jungle* 1955; *The Creature Walks among Us* 1956
Snyder, Arlen Dean (1933–) *The Night the Lights Went Out in Georgia* 1981; *Deadly Force* 1983; *Heartbreak Ridge* 1986; *Kansas* 1988; *Running Cool* 1993
Snyder, Drew *Space Raiders* 1983; *Misplaced* 1989; *Separate Lives* 1995
Snyder, John *Hard Choices* 1984; *K-9* 1989
Snyder, Suzanne *Weird Science* 1985; *PrettyKill* 1987; *Killer Klowns from Outer Space* 1988; *The Night Before* 1988; *Return of the Living Dead Part II* 1988; *Femme Fatale* 1991
Soans, Robin *Comrades: a Lanternist's Account of the Tolpuddle Martyrs and What Became of Them* 1986; *Clockwork Mice* 1994
Sobieski, Leelee (1982–) *Jungle 2 Jungle* 1997; *A Soldier's Daughter Never Cries* 1998; *Never Been Kissed* 1999; *Here on Earth* 2000; *The Glass House* 2001; *My First Mister* 2001; *Roadkill* 2001; *Max* 2002
Socas, Maria *The Warrior and the Sorceress* 1983; *Wizards of the Lost Kingdom* 1985
Soderbergh, Steven (1963–) *Schizopolis* 1996; *Waking Life* 2001
Soeberg, Camilla (1966–) *Twist and Shout* 1985; *Erotique* 1994
Sofaer, Abraham (1896–1988) *Crooks' Tour* 1940; *Christopher Columbus* 1949; *Judgement Deferred* 1951; *Quo Vadis* 1951; *His Majesty O'Keefe* 1953; *Elephant Walk* 1954; *Bhowani Junction* 1956; *The First Texan* 1956; *Captain Sindbad* 1963; *Twice Told Tales* 1963; *Head* 1968
Söhnker, Hans *aka* **Sohnker, Hans** (1903–1981) *For the First Time* 1959; *Sherlock Holmes and the Deadly Necklace* 1962
Sokol, Marilyn *Something Short of Paradise* 1979; *The Last Married Couple in America* 1980
Sokoloff, Marla (1980–) *True Crime* 1995; *Dude, Where's My Car?* 2000; *Whatever It Takes* 2000; *Sugar & Spice* 2001
Sokoloff, Vladimir *aka* **Sokoloff, Wladimir** (1889–1962) *The Love of Jeanne Ney* 1927; *The Ship of Lost Men* 1929; *The Lower Depths* 1936; *Blockade* 1938;

Comrade X 1940; *Love Crazy* 1941; *Road to Morocco* 1942; *For Whom the Bell Tolls* 1943; *The Conspirators* 1944; *Till We Meet Again* 1944; *Cloak and Dagger* 1946; *To the Ends of the Earth* 1948; *The Baron of Arizona* 1950; *Monster from Green Hell* 1958; *Beyond the Time Barrier* 1960; *The Magnificent Seven* 1960; *Mr Sardonicus* 1961
Sola, Miguel Angel (1950–) *Funny Dirty Little War* 1983; *Tangos, Exilo de Gardel* 1985; *Sur* 1987; *Foolish Heart* 1998; *Tango* 1998; *Fausto 5.0* 2001
Soler, Andres (1898–1969) *The Great Madcap* 1949; *El Bruto* 1952; *La Fièvre Monte à el Pao* 1959
Soler, Fernando (1896–1979) *The Great Madcap* 1949; *La Hija del Engaño* 1951; *Susana* 1951
Soles, P J (1955–) *Halloween* 1978; *Rock 'n' Roll High School* 1979; *Stripes* 1981; *Sweet Dreams* 1985; *Shake, Rattle and Rock* 1994; *Little Bigfoot* 1995
Soles, Paul *The Gunrunner* 1984; *The Score* 2001
Solon, Ewen (1917–1985) *Behind the Headlines* 1956; *Account Rendered* 1957; *Jack the Ripper* 1958; *The Hound of the Baskervilles* 1959; *The Sundowners* 1960
Solonitsyn, Anatoli *aka* **Solonitsin, Anatoly** *aka* **Solonitsin, Anatoli** (1934–1982) *Andrei Rublev* 1966; *Trial on the Road* 1971; *Solaris* 1972; *Stalker* 1979
Solovei, Elena (1947–) *A Slave of Love* 1976; *An Unfinished Piece for Mechanical Piano* 1976; *Oblomov* 1980
Somack, Jack (1918–1983) *Desperate Characters* 1971; *Portnoy's Complaint* 1972
Somers, Julian (1903–1976) *The Gambler and the Lady* 1952; *Hunted* 1952
Somers, Kristi *Tomboy* 1985; *Hell Comes to Frogtown* 1988
Somers, Suzanne (1946–) *Yesterday's Hero* 1979; *Nothing Personal* 1980; *Serial Mom* 1994
Somerville, Geraldine *Haunted* 1995; *True Blue* 1996; *Re-inventing Eddie* 2002
Sommars, Julie (1942–) *The Great Sioux Massacre* 1965; *The Pad (and How to Use It)* 1966; *The Harness* 1971; *Herbie Goes to Monte Carlo* 1977
Sommer, Elke (1940–) *Don't Bother to Knock* 1961; *The Prize* 1963; *The Victors* 1963; *A Shot in the Dark* 1964; *Art of Love* 1965; *Le Bambole* 1965; *Boy, Did I Get a Wrong Number* 1966; *The Corrupt Ones* 1966; *Deadlier than the Male* 1966; *The Money Trap* 1966; *The Oscar* 1966; *The Venetian Affair* 1966; *The Heroes* 1968; *They Came to Rob Las Vegas* 1968; *The Wicked Dreams of Paula Schultz* 1968; *The Wrecking Crew* 1969; *Percy* 1971; *Zeppelin* 1971; *Baron Blood* 1972; *And Then There Were None* 1974; *Percy's Progress* 1974; *Carry On Behind* 1975; *The Swiss Conspiracy* 1975; *Invisible Strangler* 1976; *Lisa and the Devil* 1976; *The Treasure Seekers* 1977; *The Double McGuffin* 1979; *A Nightingale Sang in Berkeley Square* 1979; *The Prisoner of Zenda* 1979; *Lily in Love* 1985
Sommer, Josef (1934–) *Oliver's Story* 1978; *Hide in Plain Sight* 1980; *Absence of Malice* 1981; *Rollover* 1981; *Hanky Panky* 1982; *Still of the Night* 1982; *Agatha Christie's Sparkling Cyanide* 1983; *Independence Day* 1983; *Iceman* 1984; *DARYL* 1985; *Target* 1985; *Witness* 1985; *The Betty Ford Story* 1987; *The Rosary Murders* 1987; *Dracula's Widow* 1988; *Bloodhounds of Broadway* 1989; *Chances Are* 1989; *Forced March* 1989; *The Mighty Ducks* 1992; *Hostages* 1993; *The Enemy Within* 1994; *Nobody's Fool* 1994; *The Chamber* 1996; *Patch Adams* 1998; *The Proposition* 1998; *The Family Man* 2000; *The Next Best Thing* 2000
Somr, Josef (1934–) *Closely Observed Trains* 1966; *The Joke* 1968; *Funeral Ceremony* 1969
Sondergaard, Gale (1899–1985) *Anthony Adverse* 1936; *The Life of Emile Zola* 1937; *Seventh Heaven* 1937; *Dramatic School* 1938; *The Cat and the Canary* 1939; *Juarez* 1939; *The Llano Kid* 1939; *Never Say Die* 1939; *The Blue Bird* 1940; *The Letter* 1940; *The Mark of Zorro* 1940; *The Black Cat* 1941; *Paris Calling* 1941; *My Favorite Blonde* 1942; *A Night to Remember* 1942; *Christmas Holiday* 1944; *Enter Arsene Lupin* 1944; *The Invisible Man's Revenge* 1944; *Sherlock Holmes and the Spider Woman* 1944; *Anna and the King of Siam* 1946; *The Time of Their Lives* 1946; *Road to Rio* 1947; *East Side, West Side* 1949; *Slaves* 1969; *The Return of a Man Called Horse* 1976; *Echoes* 1983
Song Kang-ho (1967–) *The Quiet Family* 1998; *Shiri* 1999; *Sympathy for Mr Vengeance* 2002; *Memories of Murder* 2003
Sonkkila, Paul *That Eye, the Sky* 1994; *Mr Reliable* 1996
Soo, Jack (1916–1979) *Flower Drum Song* 1961; *Return from Witch Mountain* 1978
Soral, Agnes (1960–) *Un Moment d'Egarement* 1977; *Killing Cars* 1986; *Three Sisters* 1988; *Australia* 1989
Sordi, Alberto (1920–2003) *The White Sheik* 1951; *I Vitelloni* 1953; *A Farewell to Arms* 1957; *The Great War* 1959; *The Best of Enemies* 1961; *Those Magnificent Men in Their Flying Machines* 1965; *The Witches* 1966
Sorel, Jean (1934–) *The Four Days of Naples* 1962; *Le Bambole* 1965; *Of a Thousand Delights* 1965; *The Man Who Laughs* 1966; *Belle de Jour* 1967; *The Short Night of the Glass Dolls* 1971
Sorel, Louise (1940–) *The Party's Over* 1965; *Plaza Suite* 1971; *Every Little Crook and Nanny* 1972
Sorel, Ted (1936–) *From Beyond* 1986; *Basket Case 2* 1990
Sorensen, Rickie (1946–1994) *Tarzan and the Trappers* 1958; *Tarzan's Fight for Life* 1958; *The Sword in the Stone* 1963
Sorenson, Linda *Breaking Point* 1976; *Heavenly Bodies* 1985; *Joshua Then and Now* 1985; *Whispers* 1990
Sorvino, Mira (1967–) *Amongst Friends* 1993; *Barcelona* 1994; *Erotic Tales* 1994; *Mighty Aphrodite* 1995; *New York Cop* 1995; *Sweet Nothing* 1995; *Beautiful Girls* 1996; *Norma Jean & Marilyn* 1996; *Mimic* 1997; *Romy and Michele's High School Reunion* 1997; *At First Sight* 1998; *Free Money* 1998; *Lulu on the Bridge* 1998; *The Replacement Killers* 1998; *Summer of Sam* 1999; *The Triumph of Love* 2001; *Wisegirls* 2001; *Gods and Generals* 2002; *The Final Cut* 2004
Sorvino, Paul (1939–) *Where's Poppa?* 1970; *The Panic in Needle Park* 1971; *The Day of the Dolphin* 1973; *A Touch of Class* 1973; *The Gambler* 1974; *I Will... I Will... for Now* 1976; *Bloodbrothers* 1978; *The Brink's Job* 1978; *Slow Dancing in the Big City* 1978; *Lost and Found* 1979; *Cruising* 1980; *Reds* 1981; *I, the Jury* 1982; *That Championship Season* 1982; *Chiller* 1985; *The Stuff* 1985; *Surviving* 1985; *Turk 182!* 1985; *A Fine Mess* 1986; *Dick Tracy* 1990; *GoodFellas* 1990; *Age Isn't Everything* 1991; *Rocketeer* 1991; *Nixon* 1995; *Love Is All There Is* 1996; *William Shakespeare's Romeo + Juliet* 1996; *American Perfekt* 1997; *Dogwatch* 1997; *Money Talks* 1997; *Most Wanted* 1997; *Bulworth* 1998; *Knock Off* 1998; *See Spot Run* 2001; *The Cooler* 2002; *Hey Arnold! the Movie* 2002; *Mambo Italiano* 2003
Sosa, Roberto *Cabeza de Vaca* 1990; *Highway Patrolman* 1991; *Dollar Mambo* 1993
Sossamon, Shannyn (1979–) *A Knight's Tale* 2001; *40 Days and 40 Nights* 2002; *The Rules of Attraction* 2002; *The Sin Eater* 2002
Soter, Paul (1972–) *Super Troopers* 2001; *Broken Lizard's Club Dread* 2004
Sothern, Ann (1909–2001) *Kid Millions* 1934; *Folies Bergère* 1935; *Hooray for Love* 1935; *Danger – Love at Work* 1937; *Super-Sleuth* 1937; *There Goes the Groom* 1937; *Trade Winds* 1938; *Fast and Furious* 1939; *Maisie* 1939; *Brother Orchid* 1940; *Lady Be Good* 1941; *Cry Havoc* 1943; *Words and Music* 1948; *The Judge Steps Out* 1949; *A Letter to Three Wives* 1949; *Nancy Goes to Rio* 1950; *The Blue Gardenia* 1953; *The Best Man* 1964; *Lady in a Cage* 1964; *Sylvia* 1964; *Chubasco* 1967; *The Killing Kind* 1973; *Golden Needles* 1974; *Crazy Mama* 1975; *The Manitou* 1978; *The Whales of August* 1987
Sothern, Hugh (1881–1947) *The Buccaneer* 1938; *The Oklahoma Kid* 1939
Soto, Hugo (1954–1994) *Hombre Mirando al Sudeste* 1986; *Last Images of the Shipwreck* 1989
Soto, Talisa (1967–) *Spike of Bensonhurst* 1988; *Licence to Kill* 1989; *Hostage* 1992; *Don Juan DeMarco* 1995; *Mortal Kombat* 1995; *Sunchaser* 1996; *Mortal Kombat: Annihilation* 1997; *Flight of Fancy* 2000; *Piñero* 2001; *Ballistic: Ecks vs Sever* 2002
Souchon, Alain (1944–) *Je Vous Aime* 1980; *One Deadly Summer* 1983
Soucie, Kath *A Christmas Carol* 1997; *The Rugrats Movie* 1998; *Rugrats in Paris: the Movie* 2000; *The Tigger Movie* 2000; *Return to Never Land* 2002; *Piglet's Big Movie* 2003; *Rugrats Go Wild* 2003; *Pooh's Heffalump Movie* 2005
Soul, David (1943–) *Magnum Force* 1973; *Dogpound Shuffle* 1974; *Starsky and Hutch* 1975; *Salem's Lot* 1979; *Hanoi Hilton* 1987; *Appointment with Death* 1988; *Pentathlon* 1994
Soutendijk, Renée (1957–) *Spetters* 1980; *The Girl with Red Hair* 1981; *The Fourth Man* 1983; *Out of Order* 1984; *The Second Victory* 1986; *Operation Madonna* 1987; *Forced March* 1989; *Eve of Destruction* 1991; *House Call* 1996
Souther, J D *aka* **Souther, John David** *My Girl 2* 1994; *Purgatory* 1999
Spaak, Catherine (1945–) *The Easy Life* 1962; *The Empty Canvas* 1963; *La Ronde* 1964; *Hotel* 1967; *Cat o'Nine Tails* 1971; *Take a Hard Ride* 1975
Space, Arthur (1908–1983) *The Big Noise* 1944; *A Man Alone* 1955
Spacek, Sissy (1949–) *Prime Cut* 1972; *Badlands* 1973; *Ginger in the Morning* 1973; *Carrie* 1976; *Welcome to LA* 1976; *3 Women* 1977; *Heart Beat* 1979; *Coal Miner's Daughter* 1980; *Missing* 1981; *Raggedy Man* 1981; *The Man with Two Brains* 1983; *The River* 1984; *Marie: a True Story* 1985; *Crimes of the Heart* 1986; *'Night, Mother* 1986; *Violets Are Blue* 1986; *The Long Walk Home* 1990; *Hard Promises* 1991; *JFK* 1991; *A Private Matter* 1992; *The Mommy Market* 1994; *A Place for Annie* 1994; *The Grass Harp* 1995; *Beyond the Call* 1996; *If These Walls Could Talk* 1996; *Affliction* 1997; *Blast from the Past* 1998; *The Straight Story* 1999; *Songs in Ordinary Time* 2000; *In the Bedroom* 2001; *Tuck Everlasting* 2002; *A Home at the End of the World* 2004; *The Ring Two* 2004
Spacey, Kevin (1959–) *Rocket Gibraltar* 1988; *Working Girl* 1988; *Dad* 1989; *See No Evil, Hear No Evil* 1989; *Henry & June* 1990; *A Show of Force* 1990; *Consenting Adults* 1992; *Glengarry Glen Ross* 1992; *Hostile Hostages* 1994; *Iron Will* 1994; *Swimming with Sharks* 1994; *Outbreak* 1995; *Se7en* 1995; *The Usual Suspects* 1995; *Looking for Richard* 1996; *A Time to Kill* 1996; *LA Confidential* 1997; *Midnight in the Garden of Good and Evil* 1997; *A Bug's Life* 1998; *Hurlyburly* 1998; *The Negotiator* 1998; *American Beauty* 1999; *The Big Kahuna* 1999; *Ordinary Decent Criminal* 1999; *Pay It Forward* 2000; *K-PAX* 2001; *The Shipping News* 2001; *The United States of Leland* 2001; *The Life of David Gale* 2003; *Beyond the Sea* 2004
Spadaro, Odoardo (1895–1965) *The Golden Coach* 1953; *Divorce – Italian Style* 1961
Spade, David (1964–) *Coneheads* 1993; *PCU* 1994; *Tommy Boy* 1995; *Black Sheep* 1996; *8 Heads in a Duffel Bag* 1997; *The Rugrats Movie* 1998; *Senseless* 1998; *Lost & Found* 1999; *The Emperor's New Groove* 2000; *Joe Dirt* 2001; *Dickie Roberts: Former Child Star* 2003
Spader, James (1960–) *Endless Love* 1981; *Tuff Turf* 1984; *Pretty in Pink* 1986; *Baby Boom* 1987; *Less than Zero* 1987; *Mannequin* 1987; *Wall Street* 1987; *Jack's Back* 1988; *The Rachel Papers* 1989; *sex, lies, and videotape* 1989; *Bad Influence* 1990; *White Palace* 1990; *True Colors* 1991; *Bob Roberts* 1992; *Storyville* 1992; *Dream Lover* 1993; *The Music of Chance* 1993; *Stargate* 1994; *Wolf* 1994; *Crash* 1996; *Driftwood* 1996; *Keys to Tulsa* 1996; *2 Days in the Valley* 1996; *Critical Care* 1997; *Curtain Call* 1998; *Supernova* 2000; *The Watcher* 2000; *Secretary* 2001; *The Stickup* 2001
Spain, Douglas *Star Maps* 1997; *Cherry Falls* 1999
Spain, Fay (1932–1983) *Dragstrip Girl* 1957; *God's Little Acre* 1958; *Al Capone* 1959; *The Beat Generation* 1959; *The Private Lives of Adam and Eve* 1959; *Black Gold* 1963; *Thunder Island* 1963; *Flight to Fury* 1966; *The Gentle Rain* 1966; *Welcome to Hard Times* 1967; *The Todd Killings* 1971
Spain, Mark *Harlequin* 1980; *Bush Christmas* 1983
Spalding, Kim *The True Story of Lynn Stuart* 1957; *It! The Terror from beyond Space* 1958
Spall, Timothy (1957–) *Gothic* 1986; *Crusoe* 1988; *Dream Demon* 1988; *To Kill a Priest* 1988; *1871* 1989; *Life Is Sweet* 1990; *The Sheltering Sky* 1990; *White Hunter, Black Heart* 1990; *Secrets & Lies* 1995; *Hamlet* 1996; *Still Crazy* 1998; *The Wisdom of Crocodiles* 1998; *The Clandestine Marriage* 1999; *Love's Labour's Lost* 1999; *Topsy-Turvy* 1999; *Chicken Run* 2000; *Intimacy* 2000; *The Old Man Who Read Love Stories* 2000; *Vatel* 2000; *Lucky Break* 2001; *Rock Star* 2001; *Vacuuming Completely Nude in Paradise* 2001; *Vanilla Sky* 2001; *All or Nothing* 2002; *My House in Umbria* 2002; *Nicholas Nickleby* 2002; *The Last Samurai* 2003; *Harry Potter and the Prisoner of Azkaban* 2004; *Lemony Snicket's A Series of Unfortunate Events* 2004
Spalla, Ignazio *aka* **Sanchez, Pedro** (1924–1995) *Beatrice Cenci* 1969; *Sabata* 1969; *Adios, Sabata* 1970; *Night and the City* 1992
Spano, Joe (1946–) *Roadie* 1980; *Terminal Choice* 1983; *Brotherhood of Justice* 1986; *Apollo 13* 1995; *Logan's War: Bound by Honor* 1998
Spano, Vincent (1962–) *Baby It's You* 1983; *The Black Stallion Returns* 1983; *Rumble Fish* 1983; *Alphabet City* 1984; *Creator* 1985; *Good Morning, Babylon* 1987; *And God Created Woman* 1988; *City of Hope* 1991; *Oscar* 1991; *Alive* 1992; *The Ascent* 1994; *The Tie That Binds* 1995; *The Prophecy 3: the Ascent* 2000
Sparks, Adrian *Apprentice to Murder* 1988; *My Stepmother Is an Alien* 1988
Sparks, Ned (1883–1957) *The Big Noise* 1928; *The Devil's Holiday* 1930; *Kept Husbands* 1931; *Blessed Event* 1932; *Gold Diggers of 1933* 1933; *Lady for a Day* 1933; *Secrets* 1933; *Hi, Nellie!* 1934; *Imitation of Life* 1934; *Marie Galante* 1934; *George White's 1935 Scandals* 1935; *Sweet Adeline* 1935; *The Bride Walks Out* 1936; *One in a Million* 1936; *Wake Up and Live* 1937; *The Star Maker* 1939; *Magic Town* 1947
Sparrow, Walter (1927–2000) *The Secret Garden* 1993; *The Woodlanders* 1997; *Prometheus* 1998; *Treasure Island* 1998
Sparv, Camilla (1943–) *Dead Heat on a Merry-Go-Round* 1966; *Murderers' Row* 1966; *The Trouble with Angels* 1966; *Assignment K* 1968; *Nobody Runs Forever* 1968; *Downhill Racer* 1969; *Mackenna's Gold* 1969; *Caboblanco* 1980; *America 3000* 1986
Speakman, Jeff (1958–) *The Expert* 1994; *Gang Law* 1999
Spearritt, Hannah (1981–) *Agent Cody Banks 2: Destination London* 2003; *Seeing Double* 2003; *Seed of Chucky* 2004
Spears, Aries (1975–) *Out of Sync* 1995; *The Pest* 1997
Speed, Carol (1945–) *The Big Bird Cage* 1972; *The Mack* 1973; *Abby* 1974
Speedman, Scott (1975–) *Duets* 2000; *Dark Blue* 2002; *My Life without Me* 2002; *Underworld* 2003; *xXx: the Next Level* 2005
Speer, Hugo (1969–) *The Full Monty* 1997; *Swing* 1998; *Deathwatch* 2002
Spell, George (1958–) *Man and Boy* 1971; *The Biscuit Eater* 1972
Spelling, Tori (1973–) *Death of a Cheerleader* 1994; *The House of Yes* 1997; *Trick* 1999
Spence, Bruce (1945–) *Double Deal* 1981; *Mad Max 2* 1981; *Where the Green Ants Dream* 1984; *Mad Max beyond Thunderdome* 1985; *Rikky and Pete* 1988; *Almost* 1990; *The Shrimp on the Barbie* 1990; *Hercules Returns* 1993
Spence, Paul J *Fubar* 2002; *It's All Gone Pete Tong* 2004
Spence, Peter *Unfinished Business* 1983; *Crazy Moon* 1986
Spencer, Bud (1929–) *Ace High* 1968; *Today It's Me... Tomorrow You!* 1968; *Boot Hill* 1969; *They Call Me Trinity* 1970; *Aladdin* 1986; *Extralarge: Moving Target* 1990
Spencer, Douglas (1910–1960) *The Thing from Another World* 1951; *The Glass Wall* 1953; *Shane* 1953; *River of No Return* 1954; *Smoke Signal* 1955; *This Island Earth* 1955; *The Three Faces of Eve* 1957
Spencer, Jesse (1979–) *Winning London* 2001; *Swimming Upstream* 2003; *Uptown Girls* 2003
Spencer, John (1946–) *Black Rain* 1989; *Albino Alligator* 1996; *The Rock* 1996; *The Negotiator* 1998; *Ravenous* 1999
Spengler, Volker *Satan's Brew* 1976; *Bolwieser* 1977; *Despair* 1978; *In a Year of 13 Moons* 1978; *The Third Generation* 1979
Spenser, Jeremy (1937–) *Portrait of Clare* 1950; *Prelude to Fame* 1950; *The Planter's Wife* 1952; *Background* 1953; *Devil on Horseback* 1954; *It's Great to Be Young* 1956; *The Prince and the Showgirl* 1957; *Ferry to Hong Kong* 1958; *The Roman Spring of Mrs Stone* 1961; *The Brain* 1962; *He Who Rides a Tiger* 1965; *Fahrenheit 451* 1966
Sperandeo, Tony (1953–) *La Scorta* 1993; *The Hundred Steps* 2000
Sperber, Wendie Jo (1962–) *I Wanna Hold Your Hand* 1978; *Back to the Future* 1985; *Delta Fever* 1988

Spielberg, David (1939–) *Law and Disorder* 1974; *The Stranger* 1987; *A Place for Annie* 1994

Spijkers, Jaap *The Polish Bride* 1998; *Twin Sisters* 2002

Spinell, Joe (1938–1989) *Rocky* 1976; *One Man Jury* 1978; *Rocky II* 1979; *Hollywood Harry* 1985

Spinella, Stephen *Virtuosity* 1995; *Love! Valour! Compassion!* 1997; *Connie and Carla* 2004

Spiner, Brent (1949–) *Star Trek: Generations* 1994; *Independence Day* 1996; *Star Trek: First Contact* 1996; *Out to Sea* 1997; *Star Trek: Insurrection* 1998; *Introducing Dorothy Dandridge* 1999; *South Park: Bigger, Longer & Uncut* 1999; *Geppetto* 2000; *The Master of Disguise* 2002; *Star Trek: Nemesis* 2002

Spinetti, Victor (1933–) *The Wild Affair* 1963; *A Hard Day's Night* 1964; *Help!* 1965; *The Taming of the Shrew* 1967; *The Biggest Bundle of Them All* 1968; *Can Heironymus Merkin Ever Forget Mercy Humppe and Find True Happiness?* 1969; *Start the Revolution without Me* 1970; *Under Milk Wood* 1971; *Digby, the Biggest Dog in the World* 1973; *The Little Prince* 1974; *Hardcore* 1977; *The Attic: the Hiding of Anne Frank* 1988; *The Krays* 1990; *The Princess and the Goblin* 1992; *Julie and the Cadillacs* 1997

Spirtas, Kevin *aka* **Blair, Kevin** (1962–) *The Hills Have Eyes Part II* 1985; *Friday the 13th Part VII: the New Blood* 1988

Sporleder, Gregory *Clay Pigeons* 1998; *G-Men from Hell* 2000

Spradlin, G D (1920–) *Number One* 1969; *Zabriskie Point* 1970; *The Hunting Party* 1971; *One on One* 1977; *Apocalypse Now* 1979; *The Formula* 1980; *The Man with the Deadly Lens* 1982; *The Lords of Discipline* 1983; *Tank* 1984; *Resting Place* 1986; *The War of the Roses* 1989; *Ed Wood* 1994

Spriggs, Elizabeth (1929–) *Work Is a Four Letter Word* 1968; *Three into Two Won't Go* 1969; *Lady Chatterley's Lover* 1981; *An Unsuitable Job for a Woman* 1981; *Those Glory, Glory Days* 1983; *Sense and Sensibility* 1995; *The Secret Agent* 1996; *Paradise Road* 1997

Springer, Gary *Hometown USA* 1979; *A Small Circle of Friends* 1980

Springer, Jerry (1944–) *Ringmaster* 1998; *Citizen Verdict* 2003

Sprouse, Cole (1992–) *Big Daddy* 1999; *The Heart Is Deceitful above All Things* 2004

Sprouse, Dylan (1992–) *Big Daddy* 1999; *The Heart Is Deceitful above All Things* 2004

Squibb, June (1935–) *About Schmidt* 2002; *Welcome to Mooseport* 2004

Squire, Katherine (1903–1995) *Ride in the Whirlwind* 1966; *The Lolly-Madonna War* 1973

Squire, Ronald (1886–1958) *The Unfinished Symphony* 1934; *Dusty Ermine* 1936; *While the Sun Shines* 1946; *Woman Hater* 1948; *The Rocking Horse Winner* 1949; *Encore* 1951; *No Highway* 1951; *It Started in Paradise* 1952; *My Cousin Rachel* 1952; *Laxdale Hall* 1953; *The Million Pound Note* 1953; *Footsteps in the Fog* 1955; *Josephine and Men* 1955; *Raising a Riot* 1955; *Sea Wife* 1957; *The Silken Affair* 1957; *The Inn of the Sixth Happiness* 1958; *Law and Disorder* 1958; *The Sheriff of Fractured Jaw* 1958

Squire, William (1916–1989) *Anne of the Thousand Days* 1969; *The Lord of the Rings* 1978

Staats, Robert *The Projectionist* 1970; *The Comeback Trail* 1972

Stack, Robert (1919–2003) *First Love* 1939; *The Mortal Storm* 1940; *Nice Girl?* 1941; *Men of Texas* 1942; *To Be or Not to Be* 1942; *A Date with Judy* 1948; *Fighter Squadron* 1948; *Miss Tatlock's Millions* 1948; *Mr Music* 1950; *The Bullfighter and the Lady* 1951; *Bwana Devil* 1952; *War Paint* 1953; *The High and the Mighty* 1954; *The Iron Glove* 1954; *Good Morning, Miss Dove* 1955; *House of Bamboo* 1955; *Great Day in the Morning* 1956; *Written on the Wind* 1956; *The Tarnished Angels* 1957; *The Gift of Love* 1958; *John Paul Jones* 1959; *The Last Voyage* 1960; *The Caretakers* 1963; *The Corrupt Ones* 1966; *Is Paris Burning?* 1966; *1941* 1979; *Airplane!* 1980; *Uncommon Valor* 1983; *Big Trouble* 1985; *Transformers – The Movie* 1986; *Caddyshack II* 1988; *Plain Clothes* 1988; *Joe versus the Volcano* 1990; *Beavis and Butt-head Do America* 1996; *Mumford* 1999; *Recess: School's Out* 2001

Stack, William (1882–1949) *Sarah and Son* 1930; *Tarzan and His Mate* 1934

Stacy, James (1936–) *Flareup* 1969; *Posse* 1975

Stacy, John *The Cat Gang* 1959; *The Agony and the Ecstasy* 1965

Stadvec, Michael *The Dentist* 1996; *Sometimes They Come Back... for More* 1998

Stafford, Frederick (1928–1979) *The Looters* 1966; *The Battle of El Alamein* 1968; *Topaz* 1969; *Naked Werewolf Woman* 1976

Stafford, Hanley (1899–1968) *A Girl in Every Port* 1952; *The Affairs of Dobie Gillis* 1953

Stahl, Nick (1979–) *The Man without a Face* 1993; *Safe Passage* 1994; *Tall Tale* 1994; *Eye of God* 1997; *Disturbing Behaviour* 1998; *Sunset Strip* 2000; *Bully* 2001; *In the Bedroom* 2001; *Terminator 3: Rise of the Machines* 2003; *Sin City* 2005

Stainton, Philip (1908–1961) *Mogambo* 1953; *The Ladykillers* 1955

Staiola, Enzo (1939–) *Bicycle Thieves* 1948; *I'll Get You for This* 1950

Staley, James *American Dreamer* 1984; *Sweet Dreams* 1985; *Robot Wars* 1993

Staley, Joan (1940–) *Roustabout* 1964; *The Ghost and Mr Chicken* 1966

Stallone, Frank (1950–) *Barfly* 1987; *Fear* 1988; *Heart of Midnight* 1988; *Midnight Cop* 1988; *Outlaw Force* 1988

Stallone, Sage (1976–) *Rocky V* 1990; *Daylight* 1996

Stallone, Sylvester *aka* **Stallone, Sylvester E** (1946–) *Bananas* 1971; *Rebel* 1973; *The Lords of Flatbush* 1974; *The Prisoner of Second Avenue* 1974; *Capone* 1975; *Death Race 2000* 1975; *Farewell, My Lovely* 1975; *Cannonball* 1976; *Rocky* 1976; *FIST* 1978; *Paradise Alley* 1978; *Rocky II* 1979; *Escape to Victory* 1981; *Nighthawks* 1981; *First Blood* 1982; *Rocky III* 1982; *Rhinestone* 1984; *Rambo: First Blood, Part II* 1985; *Rocky IV* 1985; *Cobra* 1986; *Over the Top* 1987; *Rambo III* 1988; *Lock Up* 1989; *Tango & Cash* 1989; *Rocky V* 1990; *Oscar* 1991; *Stop! or My Mom Will Shoot* 1992; *Cliffhanger* 1993; *Demolition Man* 1993; *The Specialist* 1994; *Assassins* 1995; *Judge Dredd* 1995; *Daylight* 1996; *Burn Hollywood Burn* 1997; *Cop Land* 1997; *Antz* 1998; *Get Carter* 2000; *D-Tox* 2001; *Driven* 2001; *Avenging Angelo* 2002; *SPYkids 3-D: Game Over* 2003

Stalnaker, Charles *Custer of the West* 1968; *Captain Apache* 1971

Stamos, John (1963–) *Born to Ride* 1991; *The Marriage Fool* 1998

Stamp, Terence (1939–) *Billy Budd* 1962; *Term of Trial* 1962; *The Collector* 1965; *Modesty Blaise* 1966; *Far from the Madding Crowd* 1967; *Histoires Extraordinaires* 1967; *Poor Cow* 1967; *Blue* 1968; *Theorem* 1968; *The Mind of Mr Soames* 1970; *Superman* 1978; *The Thief of Baghdad* 1978; *Meetings with Remarkable Men* 1979; *Superman II* 1980; *The Hit* 1984; *Legal Eagles* 1986; *Link* 1986; *The Sicilian* 1987; *Wall Street* 1987; *Alien Nation* 1988; *Young Guns* 1988; *Genuine Risk* 1990; *Prince of Shadows* 1991; *The Real McCoy* 1993; *The Adventures of Priscilla, Queen of the Desert* 1994; *Bliss* 1997; *Love Walked In* 1997; *Bowfinger* 1999; *The Limey* 1999; *Star Wars Episode I: the Phantom Menace* 1999; *Red Planet* 2000; *Ma Femme Est une Actrice* 2001; *Revelation* 2001; *The Haunted Mansion* 2003; *My Boss's Daughter* 2003; *Elektra* 2005

Stamp-Taylor, Enid (1904–1946) *Easy Virtue* 1927; *Climbing High* 1938; *Hatter's Castle* 1941; *South American George* 1941; *Candlelight in Algeria* 1943; *The Wicked Lady* 1945

Stanczak, Wadeck *Rendez-vous* 1985; *The Scene of the Crime* 1986

Stander, Lionel (1908–1994) *Hooray for Love* 1935; *If You Could Only Cook* 1935; *Meet Nero Wolfe* 1936; *The Milky Way* 1936; *Mr Deeds Goes to Town* 1936; *The Last Gangster* 1937; *The League of Frightened Men* 1937; *A Star Is Born* 1937; *The Crowd Roars* 1938; *The Ice Follies of 1939* 1939; *Guadalcanal Diary* 1943; *The Kid from Brooklyn* 1946; *Specter of the Rose* 1946; *Unfaithfully Yours* 1948; *Mad Wednesday* 1950; *The Loved One* 1965; *Cul-de-Sac* 1966; *Promise Her Anything* 1966; *The Good Die First* 1967; *A Dandy in Aspic* 1968; *The Gang That Couldn't Shoot Straight* 1971; *Pulp* 1972; *Treasure Island* 1972; *The Black Bird* 1975; *New York, New York* 1977; *Matilda* 1978; *Transformers – The Movie* 1986; *Cookie* 1989; *Wicked Stepmother* 1989; *The Last Good Time* 1994

Standing, Guy *aka* **Standing, Sir Guy** (1873–1937) *The Eagle and the Hawk* 1933; *Death Takes a Holiday* 1934; *Now and Forever* 1934; *The Lives of a Bengal Lancer* 1935; *Lloyd's of London* 1936; *Bulldog Drummond Escapes* 1937

Standing, John (1934–) *King Rat* 1965; *The Psychopath* 1966; *Walk, Don't Run* 1966; *Torture Garden* 1967; *A Touch of Love* 1969; *Zee and Co* 1971; *The Eagle Has Landed* 1976; *The Class of Miss MacMichael* 1978; *The Legacy* 1978; *Nightflyers* 1987; *The Man Who Knew Too Little* 1997; *Mrs Dalloway* 1997; *8½ Women* 1999; *Mad Cows* 1999; *Shoreditch* 2002; *A Good Woman* 2004

Stang, Arnold (1925–) *The Man with the Golden Arm* 1955; *The Wonderful World of the Brothers Grimm* 1962; *Hercules in New York* 1969

Stanley, Florence (1924–2003) *The Prisoner of Second Avenue* 1974; *The Fortune* 1975; *Trouble Bound* 1993; *Trapped in Paradise* 1994; *A Goofy Movie* 1995; *The Brainiacs.com* 2000

Stanley, Helene (1929–1990) *The Snows of Kilimanjaro* 1952; *Wait 'til the Sun Shines, Nellie* 1952; *Carnival Story* 1954; *Davy Crockett, King of the Wild Frontier* 1955

Stanley, Kim (1925–2001) *The Goddess* 1958; *Seance on a Wet Afternoon* 1964; *The Three Sisters* 1966; *Frances* 1982; *The Right Stuff* 1983

Stanley, Margo *Career Girls* 1997; *Girls' Night* 1997

Stanley, Paul (1952–) *I Heard the Owl Call My Name* 1973; *Detroit Rock City* 1999

Stanley, Phyllis (1914–) *We'll Smile Again* 1942; *They Met in the Dark* 1943; *Take Me to Town* 1953

Stansfield, Claire *Wes Craven's Mind Ripper* 1995; *Sweepers* 1999

Stanton, Harry Dean *aka* **Stanton, Dean** *aka* **Stanton, H D** (1926–) *The Proud Rebel* 1958; *Pork Chop Hill* 1959; *The Adventures of Huckleberry Finn* 1960; *A Dog's Best Friend* 1960; *Hero's Island* 1962; *The Man from the Diner's Club* 1963; *The Hostage* 1966; *Ride in the Whirlwind* 1966; *Rebel Rousers* 1967; *Day of the Evil Gun* 1968; *Cisco Pike* 1971; *Two-Lane Blacktop* 1971; *Cry for Me Billy* 1972; *Dillinger* 1973; *Pat Garrett and Billy the Kid* 1973; *Rafferty and the Gold Dust Twins* 1974; *Where the Lilies Bloom* 1974; *Zandy's Bride* 1974; *Farewell, My Lovely* 1975; *92 in the Shade* 1975; *Rancho Deluxe* 1975; *The Missouri Breaks* 1976; *Straight Time* 1978; *Alien* 1979; *The Rose* 1979; *Wise Blood* 1979; *The Black Marble* 1980; *Deathwatch* 1980; *Private Benjamin* 1980; *UFOria* 1980; *Escape from New York* 1981; *One from the Heart* 1982; *Young Doctors in Love* 1982; *Christine* 1983; *Paris, Texas* 1984; *Red Dawn* 1984; *Repo Man* 1984; *The Care Bears Movie* 1985; *Fool for Love* 1985; *One Magic Christmas* 1985; *Pretty in Pink* 1986; *Slam Dance* 1987; *The Last Temptation of Christ* 1988; *Mr North* 1988; *Stars and Bars* 1988; *Dream a Little Dream* 1989; *Twister* 1989; *The Fourth War* 1990; *Wild at Heart* 1990; *Man Trouble* 1992; *Twin Peaks: Fire Walk with Me* 1992; *Hostages* 1993; *Against the Wall* 1994; *Blue Tiger* 1994; *Never Talk to Strangers* 1995; *Down Periscope* 1996; *Fire Down Below* 1997; *She's So Lovely* 1997; *The Mighty* 1998; *The Green Mile* 1999; *The Straight Story* 1999; *The Man Who Cried* 2000; *The Pledge* 2000; *Sonny* 2002; *The Big Bounce* 2004

Stanton, John (1944–) *Run, Rebecca, Run* 1981; *Dusty* 1982; *Kitty and the Bagman* 1982; *The Naked Country* 1985; *Tai-Pan* 1986; *Rent-a-Cop* 1988

Stanton, Paul (1884–1955) *Red Salute* 1935; *The Road to Glory* 1936; *The People vs Dr Kildare* 1941

Stanton, Robert *Bob Roberts* 1992; *Dennis* 1993; *Red Corner* 1997; *Washington Square* 1997; *Mercury Rising* 1998; *The Quiet American* 2002

Stanton, Will (1885–1969) *Sadie Thompson* 1928; *Devil's Island* 1940

Stanwyck, Barbara (1907–1990) *Ladies of Leisure* 1930; *Illicit* 1931; *The Miracle Woman* 1931; *Night Nurse* 1931; *Forbidden* 1932; *The Purchase Price* 1932; *Shopworn* 1932; *So Big* 1932; *Baby Face* 1933; *The Bitter Tea of General Yen* 1933; *Ever in My Heart* 1933; *Ladies They Talk About* 1933; *Gambling Lady* 1934; *The Secret Bride* 1934; *Annie Oakley* 1935; *Red Salute* 1935; *The Woman in Red* 1935; *Banjo on My Knee* 1936; *The Bride Walks Out* 1936; *His Brother's Wife* 1936; *A Message to Garcia* 1936; *The Plough and the Stars* 1936; *Breakfast for Two* 1937; *Internes Can't Take Money* 1937; *Stella Dallas* 1937; *This Is My Affair* 1937; *Always Goodbye* 1938; *The Mad Miss Manton* 1938; *Golden Boy* 1939; *Union Pacific* 1939; *Remember the Night* 1940; *Ball of Fire* 1941; *The Lady Eve* 1941; *Meet John Doe* 1941; *You Belong to Me* 1941; *The Gay Sisters* 1942; *The Great Man's Lady* 1942; *Flesh and Fantasy* 1943; *Lady of Burlesque* 1943; *Double Indemnity* 1944; *Hollywood Canteen* 1944; *Christmas in Connecticut* 1945; *The Two Mrs Carrolls* 1945; *The Bride Wore Boots* 1946; *California* 1946; *My Reputation* 1946; *The Strange Love of Martha Ivers* 1946; *Cry Wolf* 1947; *The Other Love* 1947; *Variety Girl* 1947; *BF's Daughter* 1948; *Sorry, Wrong Number* 1948; *East Side, West Side* 1949; *The File on Thelma Jordon* 1949; *The Lady Gambles* 1949; *The Furies* 1950; *No Man of Her Own* 1950; *To Please a Lady* 1950; *The Man with a Cloak* 1951; *Clash by Night* 1952; *All I Desire* 1953; *Blowing Wild* 1953; *Jeopardy* 1953; *The Moonlighter* 1953; *Titanic* 1953; *Cattle Queen of Montana* 1954; *Executive Suite* 1954; *Witness to Murder* 1954; *Escape to Burma* 1955; *The Maverick Queen* 1955; *The Violent Men* 1955; *There's Always Tomorrow* 1956; *These Wilder Years* 1956; *Crime of Passion* 1957; *Forty Guns* 1957; *Trooper Hook* 1957; *Walk on the Wild Side* 1962; *The Night Walker* 1964; *Roustabout* 1964

Stapel, Huub (1954–) *The Lift* 1983; *Amsterdamned* 1988

Stapleton, Jean (1923–) *Damn Yankees* 1958; *Bells Are Ringing* 1960; *Up the Down Staircase* 1967; *Cold Turkey* 1969; *The Buddy System* 1984; *Dead Man's Folly* 1986; *The Trial* 1993; *Michael* 1996; *Pocahontas II: Journey to a New World* 1998

Stapleton, Maureen (1925–) *Lonelyhearts* 1958; *The Fugitive Kind* 1960; *Bye Bye Birdie* 1963; *Trilogy* 1969; *Airport* 1970; *Plaza Suite* 1971; *Interiors* 1978; *Lost and Found* 1979; *The Runner Stumbles* 1979; *The Fan* 1981; *On the Right Track* 1981; *Reds* 1981; *Johnny Dangerously* 1984; *Cocoon* 1985; *The Money Pit* 1985; *Heartburn* 1986; *Made in Heaven* 1987; *Nuts* 1987; *Cocoon: the Return* 1988; *Miss Rose White* 1992; *Passed Away* 1992; *The Last Good Time* 1994; *The Mommy Market* 1994; *Addicted to Love* 1997

Stapleton, Nicola *Courage Mountain* 1989; *A Fistful of Fingers* 1995; *Urban Ghost Story* 1998; *It Was an Accident* 2000; *Lava* 2000; *Chunky Monkey* 2001

Stapleton, Sullivan *River Street* 1996; *Bored Olives* 2000; *Darkness Falls* 2003

Stapley, Richard (1922–) *King of the Khyber Rifles* 1953; *Charge of the Lancers* 1954; *The Iron Glove* 1954; *D-Day the Sixth of June* 1956

Stark, Don *Santa with Muscles* 1996; *American Dragons* 1997

Stark, Graham (1922–) *The Running, Jumping and Standing Still Film* 1959; *Dentist on the Job* 1961; *Only Two Can Play* 1961; *She'll Have to Go* 1961; *Watch It, Sailor!* 1961; *Ladies Who Do* 1963; *A Shot in the Dark* 1964; *The Plank* 1967; *Salt & Pepper* 1968; *Simon, Simon* 1970; *The Return of the Pink Panther* 1974; *Hardcore* 1977; *Let's Get Laid* 1977; *Revenge of the Pink Panther* 1978; *Trail of the Pink Panther* 1982; *Victor/Victoria* 1982; *Jane and the Lost City* 1987; *Son of the Pink Panther* 1993

Stark, Jonathan (1952–) *Fright Night* 1985; *House II: the Second Story* 1987; *Project X* 1987

Stark, Koo (1956–) *Electric Dreams* 1984; *Eat the Rich* 1987

Starke, Anthony (1963–) *Return of the Killer Tomatoes* 1988; *Repossessed* 1990; *Nowhere to Run* 1992

Starr, Beau (1944–) *Halloween 5: the Revenge of Michael Myers* 1989; *Relentless* 1989; *Empire City* 1991; *The November Men* 1993; *Mercy* 2000

Starr, Frances (1886–1973) *Five Star Final* 1931; *This Reckless Age* 1932

Starr, Fredro *The Addiction* 1994; *Sunset Park* 1996; *Ride* 1998; *Light It Up* 1999; *Save the Last Dance* 2000

Starr, Mike (1950–) *The Last Dragon* 1985; *GoodFellas* 1990; *Miller's Crossing* 1990; *The Bodyguard* 1992; *Mad Dog and Glory* 1992; *Dumb and Dumber* 1994; *Ed Wood* 1994; *Blood and Wine* 1996; *Flipping* 1996; *Stolen Hearts* 1996; *Gloria* 1998; *The Lady in Question* 1999; *Murder in a Small Town* 1999; *Tempted* 2001; *Jersey Girl* 2003

Starr, Ringo (1940–) *A Hard Day's Night* 1964; *Help!* 1965; *Candy* 1968; *The Magic Christian* 1969; *200 Motels* 1971; *That'll Be the Day* 1973; *Lisztomania* 1975; *Sextette* 1978; *Caveman* 1981; *Give My Regards to Broad Street* 1984

Starrett, Charles (1903–1986) *Fast and Loose* 1930; *The Royal Family of Broadway* 1930; *The Mask of Fu Manchu* 1932; *Our Betters* 1933; *This Man Is Mine* 1934; *So Red the Rose* 1935; *Start Cheering* 1938
Starrett, Jack (1936–1989) *The Gravy Train* 1974; *First Blood* 1982; *The River* 1984; *Brothers in Arms* 1988
Stassino, Paul *Moment of Danger* 1960; *Sammy Going South* 1963; *Where the Spies Are* 1965; *That Riviera Touch* 1966
Statham, Jason (1972–) *Lock, Stock and Two Smoking Barrels* 1998; *Snatch* 2000; *John Carpenter's Ghosts of Mars* 2001; *Mean Machine* 2001; *The One* 2001; *The Transporter* 2002; *The Italian Job* 2003; *Cellular* 2004
Staunton, Imelda (1956–) *Peter's Friends* 1992; *Deadly Advice* 1993; *Much Ado about Nothing* 1993; *Sense and Sensibility* 1995; *Remember Me?* 1996; *Twelfth Night* 1996; *Shakespeare in Love* 1998; *Another Life* 2000; *Chicken Run* 2000; *Rat* 2000; *Crush* 2001; *Blackball* 2003; *I'll Be There* 2003; *Vera Drake* 2004
Staunton, Kim *Glory & Honor* 1998; *Changing Lanes* 2002
Steadman, Alison (1946–) *P'Tang, Yang, Kipperbang* 1982; *Champions* 1983; *Number One* 1984; *A Private Function* 1984; *Clockwise* 1986; *The Adventures of Baron Munchausen* 1988; *Shirley Valentine* 1989; *Wilt* 1989; *Life Is Sweet* 1990; *Blame It on the Bellboy* 1992; *Topsy-Turvy* 1999; *Chunky Monkey* 2001
Steadman, John (1909–1993) *The Mean Machine* 1974; *The Hills Have Eyes* 1977; *Things Are Tough All Over* 1982
Steafel, Sheila (1935–) *The Smashing Bird I Used to Know* 1969; *Never Too Young to Rock* 1975; *Bloodbath at the House of Death* 1983
Steel, Amy (1963–) *Friday the 13th Part 2* 1981; *Walk like a Man* 1987
Steel, Anthony (1920–2001) *The Mudlark* 1950; *The Wooden Horse* 1950; *Another Man's Poison* 1951; *Laughter in Paradise* 1951; *Where No Vultures Fly* 1951; *Emergency Call* 1952; *The Planter's Wife* 1952; *Albert, RN* 1953; *Malta Story* 1953; *The Master of Ballantrae* 1953; *Out of the Clouds* 1954; *The Sea Shall Not Have Them* 1954; *West of Zanzibar* 1954; *Passage Home* 1955; *Storm over the Nile* 1955; *The Black Tent* 1956; *Checkpoint* 1956; *Valerie* 1957; *Harry Black and the Tiger* 1958; *Honeymoon* 1959; *Tiger of the Seven Seas* 1962; *Anzio* 1968; *The Story of O* 1975; *Hardcore* 1977; *Let's Get Laid* 1977; *The World Is Full of Married Men* 1979
Steele, Barbara (1937–) *The Mask of Satan* 1960; *The Pit and the Pendulum* 1961; *The Horrible Dr Hichcock* 1962; *8½* 1963; *The Spectre* 1963; *The She Beast* 1965; *Curse of the Crimson Altar* 1968; *Caged Heat* 1974; *Shivers* 1975; *Piranha* 1978; *Pretty Baby* 1978
Steele, Bob aka **Steele, Robert** (1907–1988) *Of Mice and Men* 1939; *The Big Sleep* 1946; *Cattle Drive* 1951; *The Enforcer* 1951; *Rose of Cimarron* 1952; *Pork Chop Hill* 1959; *The Atomic Submarine* 1960; *Hell Bent for Leather* 1960; *The Bounty Killer* 1965
Steele, Freddie (1912–1984) *The Story of GI Joe* 1945; *Black Angel* 1946; *Desperate* 1947
Steele, Karen (1931–) *Marty* 1955; *Decision at Sundown* 1957; *Ride Lonesome* 1959; *Westbound* 1959; *The Rise and Fall of Legs Diamond* 1960
Steele, Mary *Girls at Sea* 1958; *The Golden Disc* 1958
Steele, Tommy (1936–) *Kill Me Tomorrow* 1957; *The Tommy Steele Story* 1957; *The Duke Wore Jeans* 1958; *Tommy the Toreador* 1959; *Light Up the Sky* 1960; *It's All Happening* 1963; *Half a Sixpence* 1967; *The Happiest Millionaire* 1967; *Finian's Rainbow* 1968; *Where's Jack?* 1969
Steen, Jessica (1965–) *Threshold* 1981; *A Judgement in Stone* 1986; *Sing* 1989; *Trial and Error* 1997
Steen, Paprika (1964–) *Festen* 1998; *Okay* 2002; *Open Hearts* 2002
Steenburgen, Mary (1953–) *Goin' South* 1978; *Time after Time* 1979; *Melvin and Howard* 1980; *A Midsummer Night's Sex Comedy* 1982; *Cross Creek* 1983; *Romantic Comedy* 1983; *One Magic Christmas* 1985; *Dead of Winter* 1987; *End of the Line* 1987; *The Attic: the Hiding of Anne Frank* 1988; *Miss Firecracker* 1989; *Parenthood* 1989; *Back to the Future Part III* 1990; *The Butcher's Wife* 1991; *Philadelphia* 1993; *What's Eating Gilbert Grape* 1993; *It Runs in the Family* 1994; *Pontiac Moon* 1994; *The Grass Harp* 1995; *Nixon* 1995; *Powder* 1995; *About Sarah* 1998; *I Am Sam* 2001; *Life as a House* 2001; *Hope Springs* 2002; *Sunshine State* 2002; *Casa de los Babys* 2003; *Elf* 2003
Stefanson, Leslie (1971–) *Burn Hollywood Burn* 1997; *The General's Daughter* 1999; *Beautiful* 2000; *The Stickup* 2001; *The Hunted* 2002
Stegers, Bernice *City of Women* 1980; *Light Years Away* 1981; *Xtro* 1983; *The Girl* 1986
Steiger, Rod (1925–2002) *Teresa* 1951; *On the Waterfront* 1954; *The Big Knife* 1955; *The Court-Martial of Billy Mitchell* 1955; *Oklahoma!* 1955; *Back from Eternity* 1956; *The Harder They Fall* 1956; *Jubal* 1956; *Across the Bridge* 1957; *Run of the Arrow* 1957; *The Unholy Wife* 1957; *Cry Terror* 1958; *Al Capone* 1959; *Seven Thieves* 1960; *The Mark* 1961; *Convicts Four* 1962; *The Longest Day* 1962; *13 West Street* 1962; *Hands over the City* 1963; *Time of Indifference* 1964; *Doctor Zhivago* 1965; *The Loved One* 1965; *The Pawnbroker* 1965; *The Girl and the General* 1967; *In the Heat of the Night* 1967; *No Way to Treat a Lady* 1968; *The Sergeant* 1968; *The Illustrated Man* 1969; *Three into Two Won't Go* 1969; *Waterloo* 1970; *A Fistful of Dynamite* 1971; *Happy Birthday, Wanda June* 1971; *The Heroes* 1972; *The Lolly-Madonna War* 1973; *Lucky Luciano* 1973; *The Last Days of Mussolini* 1974; *Hennessy* 1975; *Les Innocents aux Mains Sales* 1975; *WC Fields and Me* 1976; *Portrait of a Hitman* 1977; *Breakthrough* 1978; *FIST* 1978; *Love and Bullets* 1978; *The Amityville Horror* 1979; *Wolf Lake* 1979; *Cattle Annie and Little Britches* 1980; *The Lucky Star* 1980; *The Chosen* 1981; *Lion of the Desert* 1981; *The Naked Face* 1984; *The Kindred* 1986; *American Gothic* 1987; *The January Man* 1989; *That Summer of White Roses* 1989; *Men of Respect* 1990; *The Ballad of the Sad Café* 1991; *Guilty as Charged* 1991; *The Specialist* 1994; *The Bomber Boys* 1995; *Carpool* 1996; *Mars Attacks!* 1996; *Shiloh* 1996; *Incognito* 1997; *Truth or Consequences, NM* 1997; *Crazy in Alabama* 1999; *End of Days* 1999; *The Hurricane* 1999; *The Last Producer* 2000
Stein, Saul *Beer* 1985; *New Jersey Drive* 1995; *illtown* 1996; *Wisegirls* 2001; *Open Water* 2004
Steinberg, David (1942–) *The End* 1978; *Something Short of Paradise* 1979
Steiner, John (1941–) *Massacre in Rome* 1973; *Yor, the Hunter from the Future* 1983
Steiner, Sigfrit (1906–1988) *Imperative* 1982; *Fatherland* 1986
Steinmiller Jr, Robert J (1978–) *Bingo* 1991; *Jack the Bear* 1993; *Hostile Hostages* 1994
Steinrück, Albert (1872–1929) *The Golem* 1920; *Asphalt* 1928
Sten, Anna (1908–1993) *Nana* 1934; *We Live Again* 1934; *The Wedding Night* 1935; *The Man I Married* 1940; *So Ends Our Night* 1941; *Let's Live a Little* 1948; *Runaway Daughters* 1956
Stensgaard, Yutte (1946–) *Zeta One* 1969; *Lust for a Vampire* 1970
Stepanek, Karel (1899–1980) *Tomorrow We Live* 1942; *State Secret* 1950; *Walk East on Beacon* 1952; *City beneath the Sea* 1953; *Never Let Me Go* 1953; *Man of the Moment* 1955; *Anastasia* 1956; *The Man in the Road* 1957; *Sink the Bismarck!* 1960; *Devil Doll* 1964; *Licensed to Kill* 1965; *The Frozen Dead* 1966; *Before Winter Comes* 1968
Stéphane, Idwig (1948–) *Le Roi Danse* 2000; *Pauline & Paulette* 2001
Stéphane, Nicole (1928–) *Le Silence de la Mer* 1947; *Les Enfants Terribles* 1949; *Le Défroqué* 1953
Stephen, Susan (1931–2000) *Father's Doing Fine* 1952; *Stolen Face* 1952; *Treasure Hunt* 1952; *The Red Beret* 1953; *For Better, for Worse* 1954; *As Long as They're Happy* 1955; *Value for Money* 1955; *The Barretts of Wimpole Street* 1956; *It's Never Too Late* 1956
Stephens, Ann (1931–) *The Upturned Glass* 1947; *No Room at the Inn* 1948; *The Franchise Affair* 1950
Stephens, Harvey (1901–1986) *The Worst Woman in Paris?* 1933; *Evelyn Prentice* 1934; *After Office Hours* 1935; *Let 'Em Have It* 1935; *Murder Man* 1935; *Whipsaw* 1935; *Swing High, Swing Low* 1937; *The Oklahoma Kid* 1939; *You Can't Get Away with Murder* 1939; *Spirit of the People* 1940; *Our Wife* 1941; *Joe Smith, American* 1942
Stephens, James (1951–) *First Monday in October* 1981; *The Getaway* 1994
Stephens, Laraine (1942–) *40 Guns to Apache Pass* 1966; *The 1,000 Plane Raid* 1969
Stephens, Martin (1949–) *Harry Black and the Tiger* 1958; *Count Your Blessings* 1959; *Village of the Damned* 1960; *The Innocents* 1961; *The Battle of the Villa Fiorita* 1965
Stephens, Perry *Two-Bits and Pepper* 1995; *Grizzly Mountain* 1997
Stephens, Robert (1931–1995) *Circle of Deception* 1960; *The Queen's Guards* 1960; *A Taste of Honey* 1961; *The Inspector* 1962; *Lunch Hour* 1962; *The Small World of Sammy Lee* 1963; *Morgan – a Suitable Case for Treatment* 1966; *The Prime of Miss Jean Brodie* 1969; *The Private Life of Sherlock Holmes* 1970; *The Asphyx* 1972; *Travels with My Aunt* 1972; *Luther* 1974; *The Duellists* 1977; *The Shout* 1978; *Empire of the Sun* 1987; *High Season* 1987; *Henry V* 1989; *The Children* 1990; *Afraid of the Dark* 1991; *The Pope Must Die* 1991; *Century* 1993; *Innocent Moves* 1993; *The Secret Rapture* 1993
Stephens, Toby (1969–) *Sunset Heights* 1996; *Twelfth Night* 1996; *Cousin Bette* 1997; *Photographing Fairies* 1997; *Onegin* 1999; *Die Another Day* 2002; *Possession* 2002
Stephenson, Henry (1871–1956) *The Animal Kingdom* 1932; *A Bill of Divorcement* 1932; *Cynara* 1932; *Red-Headed Woman* 1932; *If I Were Free* 1933; *Little Women* 1933; *One More River* 1934; *The Richest Girl in the World* 1934; *She Loves Me Not* 1934; *Thirty-Day Princess* 1934; *Mutiny on the Bounty* 1935; *Reckless* 1935; *Vanessa, Her Love Story* 1935; *The Charge of the Light Brigade* 1936; *Little Lord Fauntleroy* 1936; *Conquest* 1937; *The Emperor's Candlesticks* 1937; *The Prince and the Pauper* 1937; *When You're in Love* 1937; *The Baroness and the Butler* 1938; *Dramatic School* 1938; *Marie Antoinette* 1938; *Suez* 1938; *The Adventures of Sherlock Holmes* 1939; *Tarzan Finds a Son!* 1939; *Down Argentine Way* 1940; *It's a Date* 1940; *Little Old New York* 1940; *Lady from Louisiana* 1941; *Rings on Her Fingers* 1942; *This above All* 1942; *Mr Lucky* 1943; *The Hour before the Dawn* 1944; *Two Girls and a Sailor* 1944; *Tarzan and the Amazons* 1945; *The Locket* 1946; *Of Human Bondage* 1946; *Oliver Twist* 1948
Stephenson, James (1889–1941) *Nancy Drew – Detective* 1938; *White Banners* 1938; *King of the Underworld* 1939; *We Are Not Alone* 1939; *Devil's Island* 1940; *The Letter* 1940; *Shining Victory* 1941
Stephenson, Mark Kinsey *The Unnamable* 1988; *The Unnamable Returns* 1992
Stephenson, Pamela (1950–) *The Comeback* 1977; *Stand Up Virgin Soldiers* 1977; *History of the World Part 1* 1981; *Bloodbath at the House of Death* 1983; *Scandalous* 1983; *Superman III* 1983; *Finders Keepers* 1984; *Les Patterson Saves the World* 1987
Sterke, Jeannette *The Prisoner* 1955; *The Safecracker* 1958; *Live Now – Pay Later* 1962; *A Stitch in Time* 1963
Sterling, Ford (1883–1939) *He Who Gets Slapped* 1924; *Stage Struck* 1925; *For the Love of Mike* 1927; *Her Majesty Love* 1931
Sterling, Jan (1923–2004) *Johnny Belinda* 1948; *Appointment with Danger* 1950; *Caged* 1950; *Mystery Street* 1950; *Union Station* 1950; *Ace in the Hole* 1951; *The Mating Season* 1951; *Rhubarb* 1951; *Flesh and Fury* 1952; *Pony Express* 1953; *Split Second* 1953; *Alaska Seas* 1954; *The High and the Mighty* 1954; *The Human Jungle* 1954; *Female on the Beach* 1955; *Man with the Gun* 1955; *1984* 1955; *Women's Prison* 1955; *The Harder They Fall* 1956; *Slaughter on Tenth Avenue* 1957; *The Female Animal* 1958; *High School Confidential* 1958; *Love in a Goldfish Bowl* 1961; *First Monday in October* 1981
Sterling, Mindy (1953–) *Austin Powers: International Man of Mystery* 1997; *Austin Powers: the Spy Who Shagged Me* 1999; *Drop Dead Gorgeous* 1999; *Austin Powers in Goldmember* 2002
Sterling, Robert (1917–) *The Gay Caballero* 1940; *Dr Kildare's Victory* 1941; *Johnny Eager* 1941; *The Penalty* 1941; *Two-Faced Woman* 1941; *Somewhere I'll Find You* 1942; *The Secret Heart* 1946; *Roughshod* 1949; *Bunco Squad* 1950; *The Sundowners* 1950; *Show Boat* 1951; *Column South* 1953; *Return to Peyton Place* 1961; *Voyage to the Bottom of the Sea* 1961; *A Global Affair* 1964
Sterling, Tisha (1944–) *Village of the Giants* 1965; *Coogan's Bluff* 1968; *The Defiant* 1972; *The Killer inside Me* 1975
Stern, Daniel (1957–) *Breaking Away* 1979; *It's My Turn* 1980; *Diner* 1982; *I'm Dancing as Fast as I Can* 1982; *Blue Thunder* 1983; *Get Crazy* 1983; *CHUD* 1984; *Key Exchange* 1985; *Hannah and Her Sisters* 1986; *Born in East LA* 1987; *DOA* 1988; *Leviathan* 1989; *Little Monsters* 1989; *Coupe de Ville* 1990; *The Court-Martial of Jackie Robinson* 1990; *Home Alone* 1990; *My Blue Heaven* 1990; *City Slickers* 1991; *Home Alone 2: Lost in New York* 1992; *City Slickers II: the Legend of Curly's Gold* 1994; *Bushwhacked* 1995; *Celtic Pride* 1996; *Very Bad Things* 1998
Stern, Isaac (1920–2001) *Tonight We Sing* 1953; *Music of the Heart* 1999
Stern, Wes (1947–) *The First Time* 1969; *Up in the Cellar* 1970
Sternhagen, Frances (1930–) *Two People* 1973; *Fedora* 1978; *Starting Over* 1979; *Outland* 1981; *Independence Day* 1983; *Romantic Comedy* 1983; *Resting Place* 1986; *Bright Lights, Big City* 1988; *Communion* 1989; *See You in the Morning* 1989; *Misery* 1990; *Sibling Rivalry* 1990; *Doc Hollywood* 1991; *Raising Cain* 1992
Stevan, Robyn *The Stepfather* 1986; *Bye Bye Blues* 1989; *Stepping Out* 1991
Stévenin, Jean-François (1944–) *Small Change* 1976; *Olivier Olivier* 1991; *Le Bossu* 1997; *L'Homme du Train* 2002
Stevens, Andrew (1955–) *The Boys in Company C* 1978; *The Fury* 1978; *Death Hunt* 1981; *10 to Midnight* 1983; *The Terror Within* 1988; *Night Eyes* 1990; *Double Threat* 1992; *Munchie* 1992; *Munchie Strikes Back* 1994
Stevens, Charles aka **Stevens, Charlie** (1893–) *The Three Musketeers* 1921; *The Black Pirate* 1926; *Mantrap* 1926; *Aces and Eights* 1936; *Warpath* 1951
Stevens, Connie (1938–) *Rock-a-Bye Baby* 1958; *Parrish* 1961; *Susan Slade* 1961; *Palm Springs Weekend* 1963; *Two on a Guillotine* 1964; *Never Too Late* 1965; *Way... Way Out* 1966; *Mister Jerico* 1969; *Scorchy* 1976; *Back to the Beach* 1987; *Tapeheads* 1988; *Love Is All There Is* 1996
Stevens, Craig (1918–2000) *The Doughgirls* 1944; *God Is My Co-Pilot* 1945; *Night unto Night* 1949; *Abbott and Costello Meet Dr Jekyll and Mr Hyde* 1953; *The Deadly Mantis* 1957; *Buchanan Rides Alone* 1958; *Gunn* 1967; *SOB* 1981
Stevens, Dodie (1946–) *Hound Dog Man* 1959; *Convicts Four* 1962
Stevens, Fisher (1963–) *The Burning* 1981; *The Flamingo Kid* 1984; *My Science Project* 1985; *Short Circuit* 1986; *Short Circuit 2* 1988; *Reversal of Fortune* 1990; *Mystery Date* 1991; *Too Hot to Handle* 1991; *When the Party's Over* 1992; *Nina Takes a Lover* 1993; *Super Mario Bros* 1993; *Cold Fever* 1994; *Only You* 1994; *Hackers* 1995; *Undisputed* 2002
Stevens, Inger (1934–1970) *The Buccaneer* 1958; *Cry Terror* 1958; *The World, the Flesh and the Devil* 1959; *The New Interns* 1964; *A Guide for the Married Man* 1967; *A Time for Killing* 1967; *Firecreek* 1968; *5 Card Stud* 1968; *Hang 'Em High* 1968; *House of Cards* 1968; *Madigan* 1968; *A Dream of Kings* 1969
Stevens, Joe *Texas Chainsaw Massacre: the Next Generation* 1994; *Lone Star* 1995
Stevens, K T aka **Stevens, Katharine** (1919–1994) *The Great Man's Lady* 1942; *Address Unknown* 1944; *Port of New York* 1949; *Harriet Craig* 1950; *Tumbleweed* 1953; *Vice Squad* 1953; *Bob & Carol & Ted & Alice* 1969; *They're Playing With Fire* 1984
Stevens, Kay *The Man from the Diner's Club* 1963; *The New Interns* 1964
Stevens, Mark (1915–1994) *The Dark Corner* 1946; *From This Day Forward* 1946; *I Wonder Who's Kissing Her Now* 1947; *The Snake Pit* 1948; *The Street with No Name* 1948; *Dancing in the Dark* 1949; *Oh, You Beautiful Doll* 1949; *Please Believe Me* 1950; *Target Unknown* 1951; *The Lost Hours* 1952; *Mutiny* 1952; *Cry Vengeance* 1954; *Timetable* 1956; *Gunsight Ridge* 1957; *White Angel* 1993
Stevens, Onslow (1902–1977) *Counsellor-at-Law* 1933; *Peg o' My Heart* 1933; *The Three Musketeers* 1935; *Flight from Glory* 1937; *There Goes the Groom* 1937; *When Tomorrow Comes* 1939; *The Man Who Wouldn't Talk* 1940; *House of Dracula* 1945; *Angel on My Shoulder* 1946; *Walk a Crooked Mile* 1948; *Lorna Doone* 1951; *Sealed Cargo* 1951; *The San Francisco Story* 1952; *Them!* 1954; *They Rode West* 1954; *All the Fine Young Cannibals* 1960

Stevens, Paul (1921–1986) *The Mask* 1961; *Corky* 1972
Stevens, Risë (1913–) *The Chocolate Soldier* 1941; *Going My Way* 1944
Stevens, Ronnie (1925–) *Dentist in the Chair* 1960; *Dentist on the Job* 1961; *Nearly a Nasty Accident* 1961; *Some Girls Do* 1969
Stevens, Stella (1936–) *Li'l Abner* 1959; *Man-Trap* 1961; *Too Late Blues* 1961; *Girls! Girls! Girls!* 1962; *The Courtship of Eddie's Father* 1963; *The Nutty Professor* 1963; *Advance to the Rear* 1964; *Get off My Back* 1965; *The Secret of My Success* 1965; *Rage* 1966; *The Silencers* 1966; *How to Save a Marriage and Ruin Your Life* 1968; *Sol Madrid* 1968; *Where Angels Go...Trouble Follows* 1968; *The Mad Room* 1969; *The Ballad of Cable Hogue* 1970; *A Town Called Hell* 1971; *The Poseidon Adventure* 1972; *Slaughter* 1972; *Arnold* 1973; *Cleopatra Jones and the Casino of Gold* 1975; *Nickelodeon* 1976; *The Manitou* 1978; *Wacko* 1981; *Chained Heat* 1983; *Monster in the Closet* 1983; *Eye of the Stranger* 1993
Stevens, Warren (1919–) *The Frogmen* 1951; *Deadline – USA* 1952; *Phone Call from a Stranger* 1952; *Red Skies of Montana* 1952; *Gorilla at Large* 1954; *Women's Prison* 1955; *Accused of Murder* 1956; *Forbidden Planet* 1956; *Hot Spell* 1958; *Intent to Kill* 1958; *No Name on the Bullet* 1959; *Forty Pounds of Trouble* 1962; *Stagecoach to Dancer's Rock* 1962; *Gunpoint* 1966
Stevenson, Charles (1887–1943) *Hot Water* 1924; *The Freshman* 1925
Stevenson, Cynthia (1963–) *The Player* 1992; *Forget Paris* 1995; *Live Nude Girls* 1995; *Air Bud: Golden Receiver* 1998; *Agent Cody Banks* 2003; *Agent Cody Banks 2: Destination London* 2003
Stevenson, Houseley *aka* **Stevenson, Housley** (1879–1953) *Kidnapped* 1948; *The Lady Gambles* 1949; *The Wild North* 1952
Stevenson, Jessica (1973–) *Bridget Jones: the Edge of Reason* 2004; *Shaun of the Dead* 2004
Stevenson, Juliet (1956–) *Drowning by Numbers* 1988; *Ladder of Swords* 1988; *Truly Madly Deeply* 1990; *The Secret Rapture* 1993; *The Trial* 1993; *Paris Was a Woman* 1995; *Emma* 1996; *Bend It like Beckham* 2001; *Christmas Carol: the Movie* 2001; *The Search for John Gissing* 2001; *Food of Love* 2002; *Nicholas Nickleby* 2002; *Mona Lisa Smile* 2003; *Being Julia* 2004
Stevenson, Parker (1952–) *Lifeguard* 1976; *Stroker Ace* 1983
Stevenson, Venetia (1938–) *Darby's Rangers* 1958; *Day of the Outlaw* 1959; *The City of the Dead* 1960; *Seven Ways from Sundown* 1960; *Studs Lonigan* 1960
Stewart, Alexandra (1939–) *Tarzan the Magnificent* 1960; *RoGoPaG* 1962; *Mickey One* 1965; *Maroc 7* 1966; *Only When I Larf* 1968; *The Man Who Had Power over Women* 1970; *Zeppelin* 1971; *Day for Night* 1973; *Black Moon* 1974; *The Marseille Contract* 1974; *The Uncanny* 1977; *In Praise of Older Women* 1978; *Phobia* 1980; *Agency* 1981; *The Last Chase* 1981; *Sans Soleil* 1982; *Under the Cherry Moon* 1986; *Under the Sand* 2000
Stewart, Athole (1879–1940) *The Clairvoyant* 1934; *Accused* 1936; *Dusty Ermine* 1936; *Return of a Stranger* 1937; *The Spy in Black* 1939
Stewart, Catherine Mary (1959–) *The Apple* 1980; *The Last Starfighter* 1984; *Night of the Comet* 1984; *Mischief* 1985; *Nightflyers* 1987; *World Gone Wild* 1988; *Weekend at Bernie's* 1989; *Dead Silent* 1999
Stewart, Charlotte (1941–) *Eraserhead* 1976; *Human Highway* 1982; *Tremors* 1989; *Tremors 3: Back to Perfection* 2001
Stewart, Elaine (1929–) *Everything I Have Is Yours* 1952; *Take the High Ground* 1953; *The Adventures of Hajji Baba* 1954; *Brigadoon* 1954; *High Hell* 1957; *Night Passage* 1957; *Escort West* 1959; *The Rise and Fall of Legs Diamond* 1960; *The Most Dangerous Man Alive* 1961
Stewart, Ewan *Resurrected* 1989; *Stella Does Tricks* 1997; *The Closer You Get* 2000; *The Last Great Wilderness* 2002; *One Last Chance* 2003; *Young Adam* 2003
Stewart, French (1964–) *Glory Daze* 1995; *Love Stinks* 1999; *Clockstoppers* 2002
Stewart, Jack (1913–1966) *The Gorbals Story* 1949; *A Case for PC 49* 1950; *The Dark Light* 1951; *Hunted* 1952; *Ragan* 1967
Stewart, James (1908–1997) *Murder Man* 1935; *After the Thin Man* 1936; *Born to Dance* 1936; *The Gorgeous Hussy* 1936; *Next Time We Love* 1936; *Rose Marie* 1936; *Small Town Girl* 1936; *Speed* 1936; *Wife vs Secretary* 1936; *The Last Gangster* 1937; *Navy Blue and Gold* 1937; *Seventh Heaven* 1937; *Of Human Hearts* 1938; *The Shopworn Angel* 1938; *Vivacious Lady* 1938; *You Can't Take It with You* 1938; *Destry Rides Again* 1939; *The Ice Follies of 1939* 1939; *It's a Wonderful World* 1939; *Made for Each Other* 1939; *Mr Smith Goes to Washington* 1939; *The Mortal Storm* 1940; *No Time for Comedy* 1940; *The Philadelphia Story* 1940; *The Shop around the Corner* 1940; *Come Live with Me* 1941; *Pot o' Gold* 1941; *Ziegfeld Girl* 1941; *It's a Wonderful Life* 1946; *Magic Town* 1947; *Call Northside 777* 1948; *On Our Merry Way* 1948; *Rope* 1948; *You Gotta Stay Happy* 1948; *Malaya* 1949; *The Stratton Story* 1949; *Broken Arrow* 1950; *Harvey* 1950; *The Jackpot* 1950; *Winchester '73* 1950; *No Highway* 1951; *Bend of the River* 1952; *Carbine Williams* 1952; *The Greatest Show on Earth* 1952; *The Glenn Miller Story* 1953; *The Naked Spur* 1953; *Thunder Bay* 1953; *The Far Country* 1954; *Rear Window* 1954; *The Man from Laramie* 1955; *Strategic Air Command* 1955; *The Man Who Knew Too Much* 1956; *Night Passage* 1957; *The Spirit of St Louis* 1957; *Bell, Book and Candle* 1958; *Vertigo* 1958; *Anatomy of a Murder* 1959; *The FBI Story* 1959; *The Mountain Road* 1960; *Two Rode Together* 1961; *X-15* 1961; *How the West Was Won* 1962; *The Man Who Shot Liberty Valance* 1962; *Mr Hobbs Takes a Vacation* 1962; *Take Her, She's Mine* 1963; *Cheyenne Autumn* 1964; *The Flight of the Phoenix* 1965; *Shenandoah* 1965; *Dear Brigitte* 1966; *The Rare Breed* 1966; *Bandolero!* 1968; *Firecreek* 1968; *The Cheyenne Social Club* 1970; *Dynamite Man from Glory Jail* 1971; *The Shootist* 1976; *Airport '77* 1977; *The Big Sleep* 1978; *The Magic of Lassie* 1978; *The Green Horizon* 1981; *An American Tail: Fievel Goes West* 1991
Stewart, Johnny *Boots Malone* 1951; *Last of the Comanches* 1952
Stewart, Jon (1962–) *Wishful Thinking* 1997; *Big Daddy* 1999; *Death to Smoochy* 2002
Stewart, Kristen (1990–) *The Safety of Objects* 2001; *Panic Room* 2002; *Cold Creek Manor* 2003; *Catch That Kid* 2004
Stewart, Marianne *Timetable* 1956; *The Facts of Life* 1960
Stewart, Martha (1922–) *Daisy Kenyon* 1947; *I Wonder Who's Kissing Her Now* 1947; *Are You with It?* 1948; *In a Lonely Place* 1950
Stewart, Patrick (1940–) *Hedda* 1975; *Excalibur* 1981; *Dune* 1984; *Code Name: Emerald* 1985; *Lady Jane* 1985; *Lifeforce* 1985; *LA Story* 1991; *Death Train* 1993; *Robin Hood: Men in Tights* 1993; *Gunmen* 1994; *The Pagemaster* 1994; *Star Trek: Generations* 1994; *Jeffrey* 1995; *Let It Be Me* 1995; *Star Trek: First Contact* 1996; *Conspiracy Theory* 1997; *Dad Savage* 1997; *Masterminds* 1997; *The Prince of Egypt* 1998; *Star Trek: Insurrection* 1998; *Animal Farm* 1999; *A Christmas Carol* 1999; *X-Men* 2000; *Jimmy Neutron: Boy Genius* 2001; *Star Trek: Nemesis* 2002; *X2* 2003; *Boo, Zino and the Snurks* 2004
Stewart, Paul (1908–1986) *Citizen Kane* 1941; *Government Girl* 1943; *Mr Lucky* 1943; *Champion* 1949; *Easy Living* 1949; *Twelve O'Clock High* 1949; *Walk Softly, Stranger* 1949; *The Window* 1949; *Appointment with Danger* 1950; *Edge of Doom* 1950; *Carbine Williams* 1952; *Deadline – USA* 1952; *The Joe Louis Story* 1953; *The Juggler* 1953; *Deep in My Heart* 1954; *Hell on Frisco Bay* 1955; *Kiss Me Deadly* 1955; *Top Secret Affair* 1957; *King Creole* 1958; *A Child Is Waiting* 1962; *In Cold Blood* 1967; *Jigsaw* 1968; *Live a Little, Steal a Lot* 1974; *WC Fields and Me* 1976; *Opening Night* 1977; *Revenge of the Pink Panther* 1978
Stewart, Peggy (1923–) *That Certain Age* 1938; *Back Street* 1941
Stewart, Penelope *Vigil* 1984; *Boulevard of Broken Dreams* 1988
Stewart, Robin *The Haunted House of Horror* 1969; *The Legend of the 7 Golden Vampires* 1974
Stewart, Rod (1945–) *Breaking Glass* 1980; *Play It to the Bone* 2000
Stewart, Roy (1883–1933) *Sparrows* 1926; *Zoo in Budapest* 1933
Stewart, Sophie (1908–1977) *Maria Marten, or the Murder in the Red Barn* 1935; *As You Like It* 1936; *The Man Who Could Work Miracles* 1936; *Things to Come* 1936; *The Return of the Scarlet Pimpernel* 1937; *Under the Red Robe* 1937; *Nurse Edith Cavell* 1939; *My Son, My Son!* 1940; *The Lamp Still Burns* 1943; *Uncle Silas* 1947; *Made in Heaven* 1952; *Yangtse Incident* 1956
Stich, Patricia *aka* **Stich, Pat** *Halls of Anger* 1970; *The Loners* 1971
Stickney, Dorothy (1900–1998) *And So They Were Married* 1936; *The Uninvited* 1944; *The Great Diamond Robbery* 1953; *I Never Sang for My Father* 1969
Stickney, Phyllis Yvonne *Talkin' Dirty after Dark* 1991; *Tina: What's Love Got to Do with It* 1993
Stiers, David Ogden (1942–) *Magic* 1978; *Harry's War* 1981; *Better Off Dead* 1985; *Creator* 1985; *Mrs Delafield Wants to Marry* 1986; *The Accidental Tourist* 1988; *Another Woman* 1988; *The Final Days* 1989; *Beauty and the Beast* 1991; *Doc Hollywood* 1991; *Iron Will* 1994; *Mighty Aphrodite* 1995; *Napoleon* 1995; *Pocahontas* 1995; *Steal Big, Steal Little* 1995; *Beauty and the Beast: the Enchanted Christmas* 1997; *Krippendorf's Tribe* 1998; *Pocahontas II: Journey to a New World* 1998; *Tomcats* 2000; *Atlantis: the Lost Empire* 2001; *The Curse of the Jade Scorpion* 2001; *The Majestic* 2001; *Spirited Away* 2001; *Lilo & Stitch* 2002; *Pooh's Heffalump Movie* 2005
Stiglitz, Hugo (1940–) *Tintorera* 1977; *Naked Lies* 1997
Stiles, Julia (1981–) *Before Women Had Wings* 1997; *Wicked* 1998; *10 Things I Hate about You* 1999; *Down to You* 2000; *Hamlet* 2000; *Save the Last Dance* 2000; *State and Main* 2000; *The Business of Strangers* 2001; *O* 2001; *A Guy Thing* 2002; *Mona Lisa Smile* 2003; *The Bourne Supremacy* 2004; *The Prince & Me* 2004
Still, Aline *A World without Pity* 1989; *Autobus* 1991
Stiller, Ben (1965–) *Hot Pursuit* 1987; *Fresh Horses* 1988; *Next of Kin* 1989; *Stella* 1990; *Highway to Hell* 1992; *Reality Bites* 1994; *The Cable Guy* 1996; *Flirting with Disaster* 1996; *If Lucy Fell* 1996; *Zero Effect* 1997; *Permanent Midnight* 1998; *There's Something about Mary* 1998; *Your Friends & Neighbours* 1998; *Mystery Men* 1999; *The Suburbans* 1999; *Keeping the Faith* 2000; *Meet the Parents* 2000; *Orange County* 2001; *The Royal Tenenbaums* 2001; *Zoolander* 2001; *Envy* 2003; *Our House* 2003; *Along Came Polly* 2004; *Dodgeball: a True Underdog Story* 2004; *Meet the Fockers* 2004; *Starsky & Hutch* 2004; *Madagascar* 2005
Stiller, Jerry (1927–) *The Taking of Pelham One Two Three* 1974; *The Ritz* 1976; *Those Lips, Those Eyes* 1980; *Hot Pursuit* 1987; *Nadine* 1987; *Hairspray* 1988; *Little Vegas* 1990; *The Pickle* 1993; *Stag* 1996; *Subway Stories: Tales from the Underground* 1997; *A Rat's Tale* 1998; *On the Line* 2001; *Zoolander* 2001; *Serving Sara* 2002
Stimac, Slavko (1960–) *Underground* 1995; *Life Is a Miracle* 2004
Sting (1951–) *Quadrophenia* 1979; *Radio On* 1979; *Brimstone and Treacle* 1982; *Dune* 1984; *The Bride* 1985; *Plenty* 1985; *Julia and Julia* 1987; *Stormy Monday* 1987; *The Adventures of Baron Munchausen* 1988; *The Grotesque* 1995; *Lock, Stock and Two Smoking Barrels* 1998
Stirling, Pamela *Candlelight in Algeria* 1943; *Conspiracy in Teheran* 1947; *Nor the Moon by Night* 1958
Stirling, Rachael (1977–) *Complicity* 1999; *Another Life* 2000; *The Triumph of Love* 2001; *Freeze Frame* 2003
Stirner, Brian *All Creatures Great and Small* 1974; *Overlord* 1975
Stock, Nigel (1919–1986) *Sons of the Sea* 1939; *Brighton Rock* 1947; *Eyewitness* 1956; *The Silent Enemy* 1958; *HMS Defiant* 1962; *The Password Is Courage* 1962; *The Lion in Winter* 1968; *The Lost Continent* 1968; *Cromwell* 1970; *Bequest to the Nation* 1972; *Young Sherlock Holmes* 1985
Stockbridge, Sara *UFO* 1993; *24 Hours in London* 1999; *The Wedding Tackle* 2000
Stockdale, Carl (1874–1953) *The Fall of Babylon* 1919; *Oliver Twist* 1922; *Along the Rio Grande* 1941
Stockfeld, Betty (1905–1956) *The Battle* 1934; *The Man Who Changed His Name* 1934; *The Lad* 1935; *I See Ice* 1938; *Guilty?* 1956
Stockwell, Dean (1936–) *Anchors Aweigh* 1945; *The Green Years* 1946; *Home Sweet Homicide* 1946; *The Arnelo Affair* 1947; *Song of the Thin Man* 1947; *The Boy with Green Hair* 1948; *Down to the Sea in Ships* 1949; *The Secret Garden* 1949; *The Happy Years* 1950; *Kim* 1950; *Stars in My Crown* 1950; *Cattle Drive* 1951; *The Careless Years* 1957; *Gun for a Coward* 1957; *Compulsion* 1959; *Sons and Lovers* 1960; *Long Day's Journey into Night* 1962; *Psych-Out* 1968; *The Dunwich Horror* 1970; *The Last Movie* 1971; *The Loners* 1971; *Tracks* 1977; *Alsino and the Condor* 1982; *Human Highway* 1982; *Dune* 1984; *Paris, Texas* 1984; *The Legend of Billie Jean* 1985; *To Live and Die in LA* 1985; *Blue Velvet* 1986; *Beverly Hills Cop II* 1987; *Gardens of Stone* 1987; *The Time Guardian* 1987; *Married to the Mob* 1988; *Palais Royale* 1988; *Tucker: the Man and His Dream* 1988; *Catchfire* 1989; *Limit Up* 1989; *The Player* 1992; *Chasers* 1994; *Hard Evidence* 1994; *The Price of Vengeance* 1994; *Naked Souls* 1995; *Mr Wrong* 1996; *Air Force One* 1997; *John Grisham's The Rainmaker* 1997; *McHale's Navy* 1997; *Rites of Passage* 1999; *In Pursuit* 2000; *Buffalo Soldiers* 2001; *The Manchurian Candidate* 2004
Stockwell, Guy (1934–2002) *The War Lord* 1965; *And Now Miguel* 1966; *Beau Geste* 1966; *Blindfold* 1966; *The Plainsman* 1966; *Tobruk* 1966; *Banning* 1967; *The King's Pirate* 1967; *In Enemy Country* 1968; *It's Alive* 1974; *Santa Sangre* 1989
Stockwell, Harry (1902–1984) *All over Town* 1937; *Snow White and the Seven Dwarfs* 1937
Stockwell, John (1961–) *Christine* 1983; *Losin' It* 1983; *City Limits* 1985; *My Science Project* 1985; *Dangerously Close* 1986; *Radioactive Dreams* 1986; *Top Gun* 1986; *Born to Ride* 1991; *Stag* 1996; *Breast Men* 1997
Stoddard, Malcolm (1948–) *The Godsend* 1980; *Tree of Hands* 1988
Stojka, Andre *Winnie the Pooh's Most Grand Adventure* 1997; *The Tigger Movie* 2000; *Piglet's Big Movie* 2003
Stoker, Austin (1948–) *Battle for the Planet of the Apes* 1973; *Abby* 1974; *Assault on Precinct 13* 1976
Stokes, Barry *Ups and Downs of a Handyman* 1975; *Prey* 1977
Stokowski, Leopold (1882–1977) *The Big Broadcast of 1937* 1936; *One Hundred Men and a Girl* 1937
Stole, Mink *Mondo Trasho* 1970; *Multiple Maniacs* 1970; *Pink Flamingos* 1972; *Female Trouble* 1974; *Desperate Living* 1977; *Polyester* 1981; *Cry-Baby* 1989; *Serial Mom* 1994; *Lost Highway* 1996; *Pecker* 1998; *But I'm a Cheerleader* 1999; *A Dirty Shame* 2004
Stoler, Shirley (1929–1999) *The Honeymoon Killers* 1969; *Seven Beauties* 1976; *The Deer Hunter* 1978; *Frankenhooker* 1990
Stoleru, Josiane *Cyrano de Bergerac* 1990; *Wild Side* 2004
Stolhanske, Erik *Super Troopers* 2001; *Broken Lizard's Club Dread* 2004
Stoll, Günther (1924–1977) *The Castle of Fu Manchu* 1968; *Cold Blood* 1975
Stollery, David (1941–) *Darling, How Could You!* 1951; *Jack and the Beanstalk* 1952; *Westward Ho the Wagons!* 1956
Stoltz, Eric (1961–) *Fast Times at Ridgemont High* 1982; *Running Hot* 1983; *The Wild Life* 1984; *Code Name: Emerald* 1985; *Mask* 1985; *Lionheart* 1986; *Some Kind of Wonderful* 1987; *Haunted Summer* 1988; *The Fly II* 1989; *Say Anything...* 1989; *Memphis Belle* 1990; *The Waterdance* 1991; *The Heart of Justice* 1992; *Bodies, Rest and Motion* 1993; *Killing Zoe* 1993; *Little Women* 1994; *Naked in New York* 1994; *The Prophecy* 1994; *Pulp Fiction* 1994; *Sleep with Me* 1994; *Fluke* 1995; *Kicking and Screaming* 1995; *Rob Roy* 1995; *Grace of My Heart* 1996; *Jerry Maguire* 1996; *Keys to Tulsa* 1996; *Anaconda* 1997; *Mr Jealousy* 1997; *Hi-Life* 1998; *A Murder of Crows* 1998; *Our Guys: Outrage in Glen Ridge* 1999; *The House of Mirth* 2000; *One Kill* 2000; *The Simian Line* 2000; *The Rules of Attraction* 2002; *The Butterfly Effect* 2003; *The Honeymooners* 2005
Stolze, Lena (1956–) *Swing* 1983; *The Nasty Girl* 1990
Stona, Winston *The Harder They Come* 1972; *The Lunatic* 1992
Stone, Bobby (1922–1977) *Ghosts in the Night* 1943; *Follow the Leader* 1944
Stone, Christopher (1940–1995) *The Grasshopper* 1970; *The Howling* 1981; *Cujo* 1983
Stone, Fred (1873–1959) *Alice Adams* 1935; *The Trail of the Lonesome Pine* 1936; *Life Begins*

in College 1937; *The Westerner* 1940

Stone, George E *aka* **Stone, George** (1903–1967) *The Racket* 1928; *Five Star Final* 1931; *Little Caesar* 1931; *Taxi!* 1932; *The Vampire Bat* 1933; *Viva Villa!* 1934; *Frisco Kid* 1935; *The Housekeeper's Daughter* 1939; *Cherokee Strip* 1940; *The Face behind the Mask* 1941; *Road Show* 1941; *Abie's Irish Rose* 1946; *Bloodhounds of Broadway* 1952

Stone, Harold J (1913–) *The Harder They Fall* 1956; *Somebody Up There Likes Me* 1956; *The Wrong Man* 1956; *The Garment Jungle* 1957; *House of Numbers* 1957; *The Invisible Boy* 1957; *These Thousand Hills* 1959; *The Man with the X-Ray Eyes* 1963; *Showdown* 1963; *Girl Happy* 1965; *The Big Mouth* 1967; *The Seven Minutes* 1971; *Hardly Working* 1981

Stone, James (1898–1969) *Five Guns West* 1955; *Barefoot in the Park* 1967

Stone, Leonard *The Big Mouth* 1967; *Getting Straight* 1970; *Willy Wonka and the Chocolate Factory* 1971

Stone, Lewis (1879–1953) *The Prisoner of Zenda* 1922; *Scaramouche* 1923; *The Lost World* 1925; *The Private Life of Helen of Troy* 1927; *The Patriot* 1928; *A Woman of Affairs* 1928; *Madame X* 1929; *Wild Orchids* 1929; *The Big House* 1930; *Romance* 1930; *Inspiration* 1931; *Mata Hari* 1931; *The Secret Six* 1931; *The Sin of Madelon Claudet* 1931; *The Mask of Fu Manchu* 1932; *Red-Headed Woman* 1932; *The Wet Parade* 1932; *Bureau of Missing Persons* 1933; *Queen Christina* 1933; *The White Sister* 1933; *The Girl from Missouri* 1934; *Treasure Island* 1934; *China Seas* 1935; *David Copperfield* 1935; *Public Hero No 1* 1935; *Shipmates Forever* 1935; *Vanessa, Her Love Story* 1935; *Woman Wanted* 1935; *Small Town Girl* 1936; *Suzy* 1936; *The Man Who Cried Wolf* 1937; *Bad Man of Brimstone* 1938; *Judge Hardy's Children* 1938; *Love Finds Andy Hardy* 1938; *Out West with the Hardys* 1938; *Yellow Jack* 1938; *You're Only Young Once* 1938; *Andy Hardy Gets Spring Fever* 1939; *The Hardys Ride High* 1939; *The Ice Follies of 1939* 1939; *Judge Hardy and Son* 1939; *Andy Hardy Meets Debutante* 1940; *Andy Hardy's Private Secretary* 1941; *Life Begins for Andy Hardy* 1941; *Andy Hardy's Double Life* 1942; *The Courtship of Andy Hardy* 1942; *Andy Hardy's Blonde Trouble* 1944; *The Hoodlum Saint* 1946; *Love Laughs at Andy Hardy* 1946; *State of the Union* 1948; *Any Number Can Play* 1949; *Key to the City* 1950; *Stars in My Crown* 1950; *Angels in the Outfield* 1951; *The Prisoner of Zenda* 1952; *All the Brothers Were Valiant* 1953

Stone, Marianne (1924–) *Passport to Treason* 1956; *Lolita* 1961; *Night of the Prowler* 1962; *Vault of Horror* 1973

Stone, Matt *aka* **Stone, Matthew** (1971–) *Cannibal! the Musical* 1993; *Orgazmo* 1997; *BASEketball* 1998; *South Park: Bigger, Longer & Uncut* 1999; *Team America: World Police* 2004

Stone, Milburn (1904–1980) *The Frozen Ghost* 1944; *Strange Confession* 1945; *Branded* 1950; *Roadblock* 1951; *Arrowhead* 1953; *The Siege at Red River* 1954; *Smoke Signal* 1955

Stone, Philip (1924–2003) *Unearthly Stranger* 1963; *The Shining* 1980; *Green Ice* 1981; *Indiana Jones and the Temple of Doom* 1984; *The Baby of Macon* 1993

Stone, Sharon (1958–) *Deadly Blessing* 1981; *Irreconcilable Differences* 1984; *King Solomon's Mines* 1985; *Allan Quatermain and the Lost City of Gold* 1987; *Cold Steel* 1987; *Police Academy 4: Citizens on Patrol* 1987; *Action Jackson* 1988; *Beyond the Stars* 1988; *Nico* 1988; *Blood and Sand* 1989; *Total Recall* 1990; *He Said, She Said* 1991; *Scissors* 1991; *Where Sleeping Dogs Lie* 1991; *Year of the Gun* 1991; *Basic Instinct* 1992; *Diary of a Hitman* 1992; *Sliver* 1993; *Intersection* 1994; *The Specialist* 1994; *Casino* 1995; *The Quick and the Dead* 1995; *Diabolique* 1996; *Last Dance* 1996; *Antz* 1998; *Gloria* 1998; *The Mighty* 1998; *Sphere* 1998; *The Muse* 1999; *Simpatico* 1999; *Beautiful Joe* 2000; *If These Walls Could Talk 2* 2000; *Picking Up the Pieces* 2000; *Cold Creek Manor* 2003; *Catwoman* 2004

Stone, Stuart *Heavenly Bodies* 1985; *The Boys Club* 1996; *Roadkill* 2001

Stoney, Kevin (1921–) *Cash on Demand* 1961; *The Blood Beast Terror* 1967

Stoppa, Paolo (1906–1988) *La Beauté du Diable* 1949; *Miracle in Milan* 1950; *The Miller's Wife* 1955; *Rocco and His Brothers* 1960; *The Leopard* 1962; *Becket* 1964; *Behold a Pale Horse* 1964; *The Visit* 1964; *After the Fox* 1966

Storch, Arthur (1925–) *The Strange One* 1957; *Girl of the Night* 1960

Storch, Larry (1923–) *The Last Blitzkrieg* 1958; *Who Was That Lady?* 1960; *Forty Pounds of Trouble* 1962; *Captain Newman, MD* 1963; *Sex and the Single Girl* 1964; *Wild and Wonderful* 1964; *Bus Riley's Back in Town* 1965; *That Funny Feeling* 1965; *A Very Special Favor* 1965; *The Great Bank Robbery* 1969

Storey, Ruth (1913–1997) *The Blue Gardenia* 1953; *Bells Are Ringing* 1960; *The Subterraneans* 1960

Storke, Adam (1962–) *Mystic Pizza* 1988; *Death Becomes Her* 1992; *Highway to Hell* 1992

Storm, Gale (1922–) *It Happened on Fifth Avenue* 1947; *The Kid from Texas* 1950; *The Underworld Story* 1950

Stormare, Peter (1953–) *Damage* 1992; *Fargo* 1995; *Le Polygraphe* 1996; *Playing God* 1997; *Hamilton* 1998; *Circus* 1999; *8mm* 1999; *The Million Dollar Hotel* 1999; *Purgatory* 1999; *Chocolat* 2000; *Dancer in the Dark* 2000; *Windtalkers* 2001; *Bad Company* 2002; *Minority Report* 2002; *Spun* 2002; *The Tuxedo* 2002; *Bad Boys II* 2003; *Birth* 2004; *Constantine* 2005

Stossel, Ludwig (1883–1973) *The Man I Married* 1940; *Great Guns* 1941; *Man Hunt* 1941; *Hers to Hold* 1943; *Hitler's Madman* 1943; *Bluebeard* 1944; *Dillinger* 1945; *House of Dracula* 1945; *The Beginning or the End* 1947; *Escape Me Never* 1947; *The Great Sinner* 1949; *Somebody Loves Me* 1952; *The Sun Shines Bright* 1953; *The Blue Angel* 1959

Stott, Ken (1955–) *Shallow Grave* 1994; *Fever Pitch* 1996; *The Boxer* 1997; *The Debt Collector* 1999; *Plunkett & Macleane* 1999; *I'll Sleep When I'm Dead* 2003; *Spivs* 2003

Stovin, Jerry *Lolita* 1961; *Solo for Sparrow* 1962

Stowe, Madeleine (1958–) *Stakeout* 1987; *Revenge* 1990; *The Two Jakes* 1990; *Closet Land* 1991; *The Last of the Mohicans* 1992; *Unlawful Entry* 1992; *Another Stakeout* 1993; *Short Cuts* 1993; *Bad Girls* 1994; *Blink* 1994; *China Moon* 1994; *Twelve Monkeys* 1995; *Playing by Heart* 1998; *The Proposition* 1998; *The General's Daughter* 1999; *Impostor* 2001; *Avenging Angelo* 2002; *We Were Soldiers* 2002; *Octane* 2003

Strachan, Antony *The Trench* 1999; *Sylvia* 2003

Stradner, Rose (1913–1958) *The Last Gangster* 1937; *Blind Alley* 1939; *The Keys of the Kingdom* 1944

Straight, Beatrice (1918–2001) *Patterns* 1956; *The Silken Affair* 1957; *The Nun's Story* 1959; *The Young Lovers* 1964; *Network* 1976; *Face of a Stranger* 1978; *Bloodline* 1979; *Endless Love* 1981; *Poltergeist* 1982; *Two of a Kind* 1983; *Chiller* 1985

Strait, Ralph (1936–1992) *The Beastmaster* 1982; *Halloween III: Season of the Witch* 1982

Strand, Jimmy *Block Busters* 1944; *Bowery Champs* 1944; *Follow the Leader* 1944

Strange, Glenn (1899–1973) *Rough Riders' Roundup* 1939; *House of Frankenstein* 1944; *Knickerbocker Holiday* 1944; *The Monster Maker* 1944; *House of Dracula* 1945; *Abbott and Costello Meet Frankenstein* 1948

Strange, Robert (1881–1952) *The Walking Dead* 1936; *The Far Frontier* 1949

Strasberg, Lee (1901–1982) *The Godfather, Part II* 1974; *The Cassandra Crossing* 1976; *...And Justice for All* 1979; *Boardwalk* 1979; *Going in Style* 1979; *Skokie* 1981

Strasberg, Susan (1938–1999) *The Cobweb* 1955; *Picnic* 1955; *Stage Struck* 1958; *Kapo* 1959; *Taste of Fear* 1961; *Hemingway's Adventures of a Young Man* 1962; *The High Bright Sun* 1965; *Chubasco* 1967; *The Trip* 1967; *The Brotherhood* 1968; *Psych-Out* 1968; *Sweet Hunters* 1969; *And Millions Will Die!* 1973; *Rollercoaster* 1977; *In Praise of Older Women* 1978; *The Manitou* 1978; *The Delta Force* 1986; *Out of Darkness* 1990

Strassman, Marcia (1948–) *The Aviator* 1985; *Honey, I Shrunk the Kids* 1989; *And You Thought Your Parents Were Weird* 1991; *Honey, I Blew Up the Kid* 1992; *Another Stakeout* 1993

Stratas, Teresa (1938–) *La Traviata* 1982; *Under the Piano* 1995

Strathairn, David (1949–) *Return of the Secaucus Seven* 1980; *Enormous Changes at the Last Minute* 1983; *Lovesick* 1983; *Iceman* 1984; *Call Me* 1988; *Dominick and Eugene* 1988; *Eight Men Out* 1988; *The Feud* 1989; *Without Warning: the James Brady Story* 1991; *Passion Fish* 1992; *Sneakers* 1992; *Stepkids* 1992; *A Dangerous Woman* 1993; *The Firm* 1993; *Lost in Yonkers* 1993; *The River Wild* 1994; *Dolores Claiborne* 1995; *Losing Isaiah* 1995; *Beyond the Call* 1996; *In the Gloaming* 1997; *LA Confidential* 1997; *Bad Manners* 1998; *Simon Birch* 1998; *Limbo* 1999; *A Map of the World* 1999; *Harrison's Flowers* 2000; *Blue Car* 2001; *Twisted* 2003

Stratten, Dorothy (1960–1980) *Skatetown, USA* 1979; *Galaxina* 1980; *They All Laughed* 1981

Stratton, Gil *aka* **Stratton Jr, Gil** *Girl Crazy* 1943; *Stalag 17* 1953

Stratton, John (1925–) *The Cure for Love* 1949; *The Happy Family* 1952; *The Cruel Sea* 1953; *The Long Arm* 1956; *The Man in the Sky* 1956; *Seven Waves Away* 1957; *Terror from the Year 5,000* 1958

Strauss, Peter (1947–) *Hail, Hero!* 1969; *Soldier Blue* 1970; *The Last Tycoon* 1976; *The Jericho Mile* 1979; *The Secret of NIMH* 1982; *Spacehunter: Adventures in the Forbidden Zone* 1983; *Thicker than Blood* 1993; *Nick of Time* 1995; *Keys to Tulsa* 1996; *Death in the Shadows* 1998; *A Father's Choice* 2000; *Murder on the Orient Express* 2001; *xXx: the Next Level* 2005

Strauss, Robert (1913–1975) *Sailor Beware* 1951; *Jumping Jacks* 1952; *Act of Love* 1953; *Here Come the Girls* 1953; *Money from Home* 1953; *The Redhead from Wyoming* 1953; *Stalag 17* 1953; *The Atomic Kid* 1954; *The Bridges at Toko-Ri* 1954; *The Man with the Golden Arm* 1955; *The Seven Year Itch* 1955; *Attack!* 1956; *The Mobster* 1958; *Girls! Girls! Girls!* 1962; *Harlow* 1965

Streep, Meryl (1949–) *Julia* 1977; *The Deer Hunter* 1978; *Kramer vs Kramer* 1979; *Manhattan* 1979; *The Seduction of Joe Tynan* 1979; *The French Lieutenant's Woman* 1981; *Sophie's Choice* 1982; *Still of the Night* 1982; *Silkwood* 1983; *Falling in Love* 1984; *Out of Africa* 1985; *Plenty* 1985; *Heartburn* 1986; *Ironweed* 1987; *A Cry in the Dark* 1988; *She-Devil* 1989; *Postcards from the Edge* 1990; *Defending Your Life* 1991; *Death Becomes Her* 1992; *The House of the Spirits* 1993; *The River Wild* 1994; *The Bridges of Madison County* 1995; *Before and After* 1996; *Marvin's Room* 1996; *First Do No Harm* 1997; *Dancing at Lughnasa* 1998; *One True Thing* 1998; *Music of the Heart* 1999; *AI: Artificial Intelligence* 2001; *Adaptation.* 2002; *The Hours* 2002; *Lemony Snicket's A Series of Unfortunate Events* 2004; *The Manchurian Candidate* 2004

Streisand, Barbra (1942–) *Funny Girl* 1968; *Hello, Dolly!* 1969; *On a Clear Day You Can See Forever* 1970; *The Owl and the Pussycat* 1970; *Up the Sandbox* 1972; *What's Up, Doc?* 1972; *The Way We Were* 1973; *For Pete's Sake* 1974; *Funny Lady* 1975; *A Star Is Born* 1976; *The Main Event* 1979; *All Night Long* 1981; *Yentl* 1983; *Nuts* 1987; *The Prince of Tides* 1991; *The Mirror Has Two Faces* 1996; *Meet the Fockers* 2004

Stretch, Gary (1968–) *Final Combination* 1993; *Dead Man's Shoes* 2004

Stribling, Melissa (1927–1992) *Horror of Dracula* 1958; *The Safecracker* 1958; *Only When I Larf* 1968

Strickland, Gail (1947–) *The Drowning Pool* 1975; *Bittersweet Love* 1976; *Bound for Glory* 1976; *One on One* 1977; *Who'll Stop the Rain?* 1978; *Norma Rae* 1979; *Starflight One* 1983; *Oxford Blues* 1984; *Protocol* 1984; *The Man in the Moon* 1991; *Three of Hearts* 1993

Strickland, KaDee (1977–) *Anything Else* 2003; *Anacondas: the Hunt for the Blood Orchid* 2004; *The Grudge* 2004; *The Perfect Catch* 2005

Strickland, Robert E *aka* **Strickland, Robert** *Girl Crazy* 1943; *Good News* 1947

Stricklyn, Ray (1928–2002) *The Last Wagon* 1956; *The Return of Dracula* 1958; *Ten North Frederick* 1958; *The Big Fisherman* 1959; *The Remarkable Mr Pennypacker* 1959; *The Lost World* 1960; *Arizona Raiders* 1965

Stride, John (1936–) *Bitter Harvest* 1963; *Macbeth* 1971; *Something to Hide* 1971; *Brannigan* 1975; *The Omen* 1976; *Thirteen at Dinner* 1985

Striker, Joseph (1898–1974) *Annie Laurie* 1927; *The King of Kings* 1927

Strimpell, Stephen *Jenny* 1969; *Hester Street* 1975

Stringfield, Sherry (1967–) *54* 1998; *Autumn in New York* 2000

Stritch, Elaine (1925–) *Three Violent People* 1956; *A Farewell to Arms* 1957; *The Perfect Furlough* 1958; *Who Killed Teddy Bear?* 1965; *The Sidelong Glances of a Pigeon Kicker* 1970; *Providence* 1977; *September* 1987; *Cocoon: the Return* 1988; *Out to Sea* 1997; *Autumn in New York* 2000; *Screwed* 2000; *Small Time Crooks* 2000; *Monster-in-Law* 2005

Strode, Woody (1914–1994) *City beneath the Sea* 1953; *Pork Chop Hill* 1959; *The Last Voyage* 1960; *Sergeant Rutledge* 1960; *The Sins of Rachel Cade* 1960; *The Man Who Shot Liberty Valance* 1962; *Tarzan's Three Challenges* 1963; *Genghis Khan* 1964; *The Professionals* 1966; *7 Women* 1966; *Shalako* 1968; *Boot Hill* 1969; *Che!* 1969; *Tarzan's Deadly Silence* 1970; *The Deserter* 1971; *The Last Rebel* 1971; *The Revengers* 1972; *The Italian Connection* 1973; *Winterhawk* 1975; *Keoma* 1976; *Kingdom of the Spiders* 1977; *Jaguar Lives!* 1979; *Cuba Crossing* 1980; *The Black Stallion Returns* 1983; *Lust in the Dust* 1984; *Storyville* 1992; *Posse* 1993

Strohmeier, Tara (1908–1980) *The Great Texas Dynamite Chase* 1976; *Van Nuys Blvd* 1979

Strong, Danny (1974–) *The Prophecy II* 1997; *Shriek If You Know What I Did Last Friday the 13th* 2000

Strong, Leonard (1908–1980) *Blood on the Sun* 1945; *First Yank into Tokyo* 1945; *The Naked Jungle* 1953; *Hell's Half Acre* 1954; *Jet Attack* 1958

Strong, Mark (1963–) *Captives* 1994; *Fever Pitch* 1996; *If Only* 1998; *Elephant Juice* 1999; *Superstition* 2001; *To End All Wars* 2001; *Heartlands* 2002; *It's All about Love* 2002

Strong, Michael (1924–1980) *Point Blank* 1967; *Secret Ceremony* 1968; *Patton* 1970

Strong, Rider (1979–) *Benefit of the Doubt* 1993; *Cabin Fever* 2002

Stroud, Don (1937–) *Games* 1967; *Journey to Shiloh* 1967; *Coogan's Bluff* 1968; *tick... tick... tick...* 1969; *Bloody Mama* 1970; *Von Richthofen and Brown* 1971; *Joe Kidd* 1972; *Scalawag* 1973; *Slaughter's Big Rip-Off* 1973; *Live a Little, Steal a Lot* 1974; *The Killer inside Me* 1975; *The Choirboys* 1977; *The Buddy Holly Story* 1978; *Search and Destroy* 1978; *The Amityville Horror* 1979; *The Night the Lights Went Out in Georgia* 1981; *Armed and Dangerous* 1986; *Dillinger and Capone* 1995

Strudwick, Shepperd *aka* **Shepperd, John** (1907–1983) *Fast Company* 1938; *Dr Kildare's Strange Case* 1940; *Flight Command* 1940; *Belle Starr* 1941; *The Men in Her Life* 1941; *Remember the Day* 1941; *Rings on Her Fingers* 1942; *Ten Gentlemen from West Point* 1942; *Joan of Arc* 1948; *All the King's Men* 1949; *The Reckless Moment* 1949; *The Red Pony* 1949; *The Kid from Texas* 1950; *Let's Dance* 1950; *Autumn Leaves* 1956; *Beyond a Reasonable Doubt* 1956; *The Eddy Duchin Story* 1956; *That Night* 1957; *Girl on the Run* 1958; *Psychomania* 1964; *Daring Game* 1968; *Cops and Robbers* 1973

Strummer, Joe (1952–2002) *Candy Mountain* 1987; *Straight to Hell* 1987; *Mystery Train* 1989

Struycken, Carel (1949–) *The Witches of Eastwick* 1987; *The Addams Family* 1991; *Addams Family Values* 1993; *I Woke Up Early the Day I Died* 1998

Stryker, Amy *A Wedding* 1978; *Impulse* 1984

Stuart, Barbara *Dreamer* 1979; *Bachelor Party* 1984

Stuart, Cassie *Secret Places* 1984; *Dolls* 1987; *Hidden City* 1987

Stuart, Eric (1967–) *Pokémon the Movie 2000* 1999; *Pokémon 3: Spell of the Unown* 2001; *Yu-Gi-Oh! The Movie* 2004

Stuart, Gloria (1910–) *Air Mail* 1932; *The Old Dark House* 1932; *The Invisible Man* 1933; *The Kiss before the Mirror* 1933; *Roman Scandals* 1933; *Here Comes the Navy* 1934; *Gold Diggers of 1935* 1935; *Poor Little Rich Girl* 1936; *The Prisoner of Shark Island* 1936; *Life Begins in College* 1937; *Rebecca of Sunnybrook Farm* 1938; *The Three Musketeers* 1939; *The Whistler* 1944; *Titanic* 1997; *The Love Letter* 1999

Stuart, Jeanne (1908–2003) *Death on the Set* 1935; *Forget-Me-Not* 1936; *The Shadow* 1936

Stuart, John (1898–1979) *The Pleasure Garden* 1925; *Hindle Wakes* 1927; *Kitty* 1928; *Hindle Wakes* 1931; *Number Seventeen* 1932; *The Black Abbot* 1934; *D'Ye Ken John Peel?* 1934; *The Show Goes On* 1937; *The Big*

Blockade 1942; Madonna of the Seven Moons 1944; The Gilded Cage 1954
Stuart, Kathleen (1925–) Just William's Luck 1947; William at the Circus 1948
Stuart, Maxine The Prisoner of Second Avenue 1974; Coast to Coast 1980
Stuart, Randy (1924–1996) Apartment for Peggy 1948; Sitting Pretty 1948; Dancing in the Dark 1949; I Was a Male War Bride 1949; Stella 1950; I Can Get It for You Wholesale 1951; Room for One More 1952; Star in the Dust 1956; The Incredible Shrinking Man 1957
Stubbs, Harry (1874–1950) Alibi 1929; Her Majesty Love 1931
Stubbs, Imogen (1961–) Nanou 1986; A Summer Story 1987; Erik the Viking 1989; Fellow Traveller 1989; True Colors 1991; A Pin for the Butterfly 1994; Jack & Sarah 1995; Sense and Sensibility 1995; Twelfth Night 1996
Stubbs, Una (1937–) Summer Holiday 1962; Wonderful Life 1964; Three Hats for Lisa 1965; Till Death Us Do Part 1968; Penny Gold 1973
Studer, Carl Le Doulos 1962; The Love Cage 1964
Studi, Wes (1947–) The Last of the Mohicans 1992; Geronimo: an American Legend 1993; Street Fighter 1994; Heat 1995; Deep Rising 1998; Mystery Men 1999; Wind River 1999; Undisputed 2002
Stuhr, Jerzy (1947–) The Scar 1976; Camera Buff 1979; Three Colours White 1993
Stuke, Neil Dead Bolt Dead 1999; Christie Malry's Own Double-Entry 2000; The Wedding Tackle 2000; School for Seduction 2004
Sturges, Preston (1898–1959) Sullivan's Travels 1941; Star Spangled Rhythm 1942; Paris Holiday 1958
Sturges, Shannon (1968–) Desire & Hell at Sunset Motel 1991; Tornado! 1996
Styles, Edwin (1899–1960) Adam and Evelyne 1949; The Lady with the Lamp 1951; Penny Princess 1952
Suarez, Emma (1964–) 1919 1983; Vacas 1991; The Red Squirrel 1993; Tierra 1995
Suarez, José (1919–1981) Calle Mayor 1956; Texas Adios 1966
Suarez, Miguel Angel aka **Suarez, Miguel** Bananas 1971; Stir Crazy 1980; Under Suspicion 2000
Subkoff, Tara (1973–) When the Bough Breaks 1993; All over Me 1996; Teenage Caveman 2001
Subor, Michel (1935–) Le Petit Soldat 1960; Topaz 1969; Beau Travail 1999
Suchet, David (1946–) The Hunchback of Notre Dame 1982; Trenchcoat 1983; The Little Drummer Girl 1984; The Falcon and the Snowman 1985; Iron Eagle 1985; A Song for Europe 1985; Thirteen at Dinner 1985; Bigfoot and the Hendersons 1987; A World Apart 1987; To Kill a Priest 1988; When the Whales Came 1989; Executive Decision 1996; Sunday 1997; A Perfect Murder 1998; RKO 281 1999; Wing Commander 1999; Live from Baghdad 2002; The In-Laws 2003
Sugai, Ichiro (1907–1973) My Love Has Been Burning 1949; Early Summer 1951; The Life of Oharu 1952; The Crucified Lovers 1954
Sugai, Kin (1926–) Dodes'ka-Den 1970; Death Japanese Style 1984
Sugarman, Sara Those Glory, Glory Days 1983; Dealers 1989
Sugata, Shun (1955–) Eyes of the Spider 1999; License to Live 1999; Marebito 2004
Sugawara, Bunta (1933–) The Yakuza Papers 1973; The Burmese Harp 1985; Distant Justice 1992
Sugawara, Hideo Tokyo Chorus 1931; I Was Born, but... 1932
Sugimura, Haruko (1905–1997) Late Spring 1949; Early Summer 1951; Tokyo Story 1953; Early Spring 1956; Floating Weeds 1959; Ohayo 1959
Sukhorukov, Viktor (1951–) Brother 1997; Of Freaks and Men 1998
Sukowa, Barbara (1950–) Berlin Alexanderplatz 1980; The German Sisters 1981; Deadly Game 1982; Lola 1982; Rosa Luxemburg 1986; Europa 1991; Voyager 1991; M Butterfly 1993; The Lady in Question 1999; 13 Conversations about One Thing 2001
Suli, Ania Hold Me, Thrill Me, Kiss Me 1992; Fun 1994
Sullavan, Margaret (1911–1960) Only Yesterday 1933; Little Man, What Now? 1934; The Good Fairy 1935; So Red the Rose 1935; The Moon's Our Home 1936; Next Time We Love 1936; The Shining Hour 1938; The Shopworn Angel 1938; Three Comrades 1938; The Mortal Storm 1940; The Shop around the Corner 1940; Appointment for Love 1941; Back Street 1941; So Ends Our Night 1941; Cry Havoc 1943; No Sad Songs for Me 1950
Sullivan, Barry (1912–1994) And Now Tomorrow 1944; Lady in the Dark 1944; Getting Gertie's Garter 1945; Framed 1947; The Gangster 1947; Smart Woman 1948; Any Number Can Play 1949; The Great Gatsby 1949; Tension 1949; A Life of Her Own 1950; Nancy Goes to Rio 1950; The Outriders 1950; Cause for Alarm 1951; Inside Straight 1951; Mr Imperium 1951; Payment on Demand 1951; The Bad and the Beautiful 1952; Skirts Ahoy! 1952; Cry of the Hunted 1953; Jeopardy 1953; Her Twelve Men 1954; Playgirl 1954; The Maverick Queen 1955; Queen Bee 1955; Strategic Air Command 1955; Texas Lady 1955; Julie 1956; Dragoon Wells Massacre 1957; Forty Guns 1957; The Way to the Gold 1957; Another Time, Another Place 1958; Wolf Larsen 1958; Seven Ways from Sundown 1960; Light in the Piazza 1961; A Gathering of Eagles 1963; The Man in the Middle 1964; Harlow 1965; My Blood Runs Cold 1965; Planet of the Vampires 1965; An American Dream 1966; How to Steal the World 1968; Shark! 1969; Tell Them Willie Boy Is Here 1969; Earthquake 1974; The Human Factor 1975; Take a Hard Ride 1975
Sullivan, Billy L aka **Sullivan, Billy** (1980–) Light of Day 1987; Little Big League 1994; The Big Green 1995
Sullivan, Brad (1931–) The Untouchables 1987; Funny Farm 1988; The Prince of Tides 1991; Bushwhacked 1995; The Fantasticks 1995; The Jerky Boys 1995
Sullivan, Don (1938–) The Giant Gila Monster 1959; The Rebel Set 1959
Sullivan, Ed (1902–1974) Senior Prom 1958; Bye Bye Birdie 1963; The Singing Nun 1966
Sullivan, Elliott (1907–1974) The Lady Gambles 1949; The Sergeant 1968
Sullivan, Erik Per (1991–) Wendigo 2001; Christmas with the Kranks 2004
Sullivan, Francis L aka **Sullivan, Francis** (1903–1956) When London Sleeps 1932; The Return of Bulldog Drummond 1934; The Mystery of Edwin Drood 1935; Dinner at the Ritz 1937; 21 Days 1937; The Citadel 1938; Climbing High 1938; The Drum 1938; The Four Just Men 1939; Pimpernel Smith 1941; The Day Will Dawn 1942; Fiddlers Three 1944; Caesar and Cleopatra 1945; Great Expectations 1946; The Man Within 1947; Take My Life 1947; Broken Journey 1948; Joan of Arc 1948; Oliver Twist 1948; The Winslow Boy 1948; Christopher Columbus 1949; The Red Danube 1949; Night and the City 1950; My Favorite Spy 1951; Hell's Island 1955
Sullivan, Jean (1923–2003) Uncertain Glory 1944; Roughly Speaking 1945; Squirm 1976
Sullivan, Peter The Butterfly Effect 1995; Christie Malry's Own Double-Entry 2000
Sullivan, Sean During One Night 1961; 2001: a Space Odyssey 1968; The Boy in Blue 1986
Sullivan, Sean Gregory The In Crowd 1988; Ski Patrol 1989
Sullivan, Susan (1942–) The Incredible Hulk 1977; Danielle Steel's A Perfect Stranger 1994; Two Came Back 1997
Sully, Frank (1908–1975) The Doctor Takes a Wife 1940; The Grapes of Wrath 1940; The More the Merrier 1943; Along Came Jones 1945; The Naked Street 1955
Summer, Cree (1969–) The Rugrats Movie 1998; Atlantis: the Lost Empire 2001
Summerfield, Eleanor (1921–2001) Isn't Life Wonderful! 1952; The Last Page 1952; Face the Music 1954; Final Appointment 1954; Lost 1955; Don't Bother to Knock 1961; On the Fiddle 1961; Petticoat Pirates 1961; Spare the Rod 1961; Guns of Darkness 1962; The Running Man 1963
Summerville, Slim aka **Summerville, George "Slim"** (1892–1946) All Quiet on the Western Front 1930; Bad Sister 1931; Air Mail 1932; The Farmer Takes a Wife 1935; Life Begins at 40 1935; Way Down East 1935; Captain January 1936; The Country Doctor 1936; White Fang 1936; Love Is News 1937; Kentucky Moonshine 1938; Rebecca of Sunnybrook Farm 1938; Submarine Patrol 1938; Charlie Chan in Reno 1939; Anne of Windy Poplars 1940
Sumner, Geoffrey (1908–1989) Traveller's Joy 1949; The Flying Eye 1955; Cul-de-Sac 1966
Sumner, Peter (1942–) Ned Kelly 1970; The Survivor 1981; Bush Christmas 1983
Sumpter, Donald (1943–) Rosencrantz and Guildenstern Are Dead 1990; K-19: the Widowmaker 2002
Sumpter, Jeremy (1989–) Frailty 2001; Peter Pan 2003
Sundberg, Clinton (1906–1987) Easter Parade 1948; Good Sam 1948; Mr Peabody and the Mermaid 1948; Big Jack 1949; In the Good Old Summertime 1949; Annie Get Your Gun 1950; On the Riviera 1951; The Belle of New York 1952; The Caddy 1953; The Girl Next Door 1953; Main Street to Broadway 1953
Sundquist, Bjorn (1948–) The Dive 1989; Shipwrecked 1990; Zero Kelvin 1995; The Other Side of Sunday 1996
Superstar, Ingrid Bike Boy 1967; The Chelsea Girls 1967
Suplee, Ethan (1969–) Chasing Amy 1996; American History X 1998; Desert Blue 1998; Remember the Titans 2000; Evolution 2001; The Butterfly Effect 2003; Without a Paddle 2004
Surgère, Hélène (1928–) Salo, or the 120 Days of Sodom 1975; The Brontë Sisters 1979; Australia 1989; Ma Vraie Vie à Rouen 2002; Confidences Trop Intimes 2004
Surovy, Nicolas aka **Surovy, Nicholas** (1944–) 12:01 1993; The Man Who Captured Eichmann 1996
Susman, Todd (1947–) The Loners 1971; Only the Strong 1993
Sutera, Paul (1979–) The Brady Bunch Movie 1995; A Very Brady Sequel 1996
Sutherland, Claudette A Little Romance 1979; Man of the Year 1995
Sutherland, Donald (1934–) Die! Die! My Darling 1964; Dr Terror's House of Horrors 1964; The Bedford Incident 1965; Promise Her Anything 1966; The Dirty Dozen 1967; Oedipus the King 1967; Interlude 1968; Sebastian 1968; The Split 1968; Joanna 1969; MASH 1969; Act of the Heart 1970; Alex in Wonderland 1970; Kelly's Heroes 1970; Start the Revolution without Me 1970; Klute 1971; Little Murders 1971; FTA 1972; Dan Candy's Law 1973; Don't Look Now 1973; Lady Ice 1973; Steelyard Blues 1973; SPYS 1974; The Day of the Locust 1975; Casanova 1976; The Eagle Has Landed 1976; End of the Game 1976; 1900 1976; Blood Relatives 1977; The Disappearance 1977; The Kentucky Fried Movie 1977; The First Great Train Robbery 1978; Invasion of the Body Snatchers 1978; Murder by Decree 1978; Bear Island 1979; A Man, a Woman and a Bank 1979; Nothing Personal 1980; Ordinary People 1980; Eye of the Needle 1981; Threshold 1981; Max Dugan Returns 1983; Crackers 1984; Ordeal by Innocence 1984; Catholic Boys 1985; Revolution 1985; The Wolf at the Door 1986; The Rosary Murders 1987; The Trouble with Spies 1987; Apprentice to Murder 1988; A Dry White Season 1989; Lock Up 1989; The Road Home 1989; Bethune: the Making of a Hero 1990; Backdraft 1991; Eminent Domain 1991; JFK 1991; Scream of Stone 1991; Buffy the Vampire Slayer 1992; Quicksand: No Escape 1992; Shadow of the Wolf 1992; Benefit of the Doubt 1993; Six Degrees of Separation 1993; Younger and Younger 1993; Disclosure 1994; The Puppet Masters 1994; Citizen X 1995; Outbreak 1995; Hollow Point 1996; Shadow Conspiracy 1996; A Time to Kill 1996; The Assignment 1997; Fallen 1998; Free Money 1998; Virus 1998; Without Limits 1998; Behind the Mask 1999; The Hunley 1999; Instinct 1999; The Art of War 2000; Panic 2000; Space Cowboys 2000; Big Shot's Funeral 2001; Final Fantasy: the Spirits Within 2001; Path to War 2002; Cold Mountain 2003; The Italian Job 2003
Sutherland, Kiefer (1967–) Max Dugan Returns 1983; Bay Boy 1984; At Close Range 1985; Brotherhood of Justice 1986; Crazy Moon 1986; Stand by Me 1986; The Killing Time 1987; The Lost Boys 1987; Bright Lights, Big City 1988; 1969 1988; Promised Land 1988; Young Guns 1988; Chicago Joe and the Showgirl 1989; Renegades 1989; Flashback 1990; Flatliners 1990; The Nutcracker Prince 1990; Young Guns II 1990; Article 99 1992; A Few Good Men 1992; Last Light 1993; The Three Musketeers 1993; The Vanishing 1993; The Cowboy Way 1994; Eye for an Eye 1995; Freeway 1996; The Last Days of Frankie the Fly 1996; A Time to Kill 1996; Truth or Consequences, NM 1997; Break Up 1998; Dark City 1998; Eye of the Killer 1999; Picking Up the Pieces 2000; To End All Wars 2001; Dead Heat 2002; Phone Booth 2002; Taking Lives 2004
Sutton, Dudley (1933–) The Boys 1961; The Leather Boys 1963; Rotten to the Core 1965; The Devils 1971; A Town Called Hell 1971; Madame Sin 1972; Diamonds on Wheels 1973; The Island 1980; The Rainbow 1988; Edward II 1991; Orlando 1992; Up at the Villa 1998; This Filthy Earth 2001; Song for a Raggy Boy 2002; The Football Factory 2004
Sutton, Frank (1923–1974) Marty 1955; Town without Pity 1961; The Satan Bug 1965
Sutton, Grady (1908–1995) Pack Up Your Troubles 1932; Bachelor Bait 1934; Alice Adams 1935; The Man on the Flying Trapeze 1935; Hard to Get 1938; Vivacious Lady 1938; The Bank Dick 1940; A Lady Takes a Chance 1943; Support Your Local Gunfighter 1971
Sutton, John (1908–1963) Tower of London 1939; Hudson's Bay 1940; The Invisible Man Returns 1940; A Yank in the RAF 1941; My Gal Sal 1942; Ten Gentlemen from West Point 1942; Jane Eyre 1943; The Hour before the Dawn 1944; Claudia and David 1946; Captain from Castile 1947; The Counterfeiters 1948; Bride of Vengeance 1949; The Second Woman 1951; My Cousin Rachel 1952; Thief of Damascus 1952; East of Sumatra 1953; The Bat 1959; Beloved Infidel 1959; Return of the Fly 1959; The Canadians 1961
Sutton, Kay (1915–1988) Carefree 1938; The Saint in New York 1938
Sutton, Michael (1970–) Inventing the Abbotts 1997; Dark Prince – the Legend of Dracula 2000
Sutton, Nick Gummo 1997; Underground 1998
Suvari, Mena (1979–) Nowhere 1997; Slums of Beverly Hills 1998; American Beauty 1999; American Pie 1999; Atomic Train 1999; Live Virgin 2000; Loser 2000; American Pie 2 2001; The Musketeer 2001; Sugar & Spice 2001; Sonny 2002; Spun 2002; Trauma 2004; Beauty Shop 2005
Suzman, Janet (1939–) A Day in the Death of Joe Egg 1971; Nicholas and Alexandra 1971; The Black Windmill 1974; Priest of Love 1981; The Draughtsman's Contract 1982; And the Ship Sails On 1983; A Dry White Season 1989; Nuns on the Run 1990; Leon the Pig Farmer 1992; Max 2002
Svennberg, Tore (1858–1941) The Phantom Carriage 1920; A Woman's Face 1938
Svenson, Bo (1941–) The Great Waldo Pepper 1975; Part 2 Walking Tall 1975; Breaking Point 1976; Special Delivery 1976; Final Chapter – Walking Tall 1977; Portrait of a Hitman 1977; North Dallas Forty 1979; Night Warning 1981; Wizards of the Lost Kingdom 1985; The Delta Force 1986; Heartbreak Ridge 1986; On Dangerous Ground 1986; Curse II: The Bite 1989; Death Train 1989; Kill Bill Vol 2 2003
Sverak, Zdenek (1936–) Elementary School 1991; Kolya 1996
Swain, Dominique (1980–) Face/Off 1997; Lolita 1997; Girl 1998
Swain, Mack (1876–1935) Tillie's Punctured Romance 1914; The Idle Class 1921; Pay Day 1922; The Pilgrim 1923; The Gold Rush 1925; Hands Up! 1926
Swamy, Arvind Roja 1992; Bombay 1995; Sapnay 1997
Swan, Bob The Dollmaker 1984; Going All the Way 1997
Swank, Hilary (1974–) Buffy the Vampire Slayer 1992; The Next Karate Kid 1994; Victim of Rage 1994; Sometimes They Come Back... Again 1996; Boys Don't Cry 1999; The Gift 2000; The Affair of the Necklace 2001; The Core 2002; Insomnia 2002; Iron Jawed Angels 2004; Million Dollar Baby 2004
Swann, Robert if.... 1968; Mumsy, Nanny, Sonny & Girly 1970
Swanson, Gary Vice Squad 1982; Convicts 1991
Swanson, Gloria (1897–1983) His New Job 1915; Male and Female 1919; Why Change Your Wife? 1920; Hollywood 1923; Stage Struck 1925; Queen Kelly 1928; Sadie Thompson 1928; The Trespasser 1929; What a Widow! 1930; Indiscreet 1931; Sunset Blvd 1950; Airport 1975 1974
Swanson, Jackie (1968–) Lethal Weapon 1987; Oblivion 1993
Swanson, Kristy (1969–) Deadly Friend 1986; Flowers in the Attic 1987; Hot Shots! 1991; Mannequin on the Move 1991; Buffy the Vampire Slayer 1992; Highway to Hell 1992; The Program 1993; The Chase 1994; Getting In 1994; Higher Learning 1995; Marshal Law 1996; The Phantom 1996; 8 Heads in a Duffel Bag 1997; Tinseltown 1997; Big Daddy 1999; Supreme

Sanction 1999; *Dude, Where's My Car?* 2000
Swanson, Maureen (1932–) *Knights of the Round Table* 1953; *Valley of Song* 1953; *Jacqueline* 1956; *The Spanish Gardener* 1956; *A Town like Alice* 1956; *Up in the World* 1956; *Robbery under Arms* 1957
Swanson, Rochelle *Hungry for You* 1996; *Walnut Creek* 1996
Swart, Rufus *The House of Usher* 1988; *Purgatory* 1988; *Dust Devil* 1992; *Cyborg Cop* 1993
Swayze, Don (1958–) *Shy People* 1987; *Driving Force* 1988; *Body of Influence* 1993; *Eye of the Stranger* 1993
Swayze, Patrick (1952–) *Skatetown, USA* 1979; *The Outsiders* 1983; *Uncommon Valor* 1983; *Grandview, USA* 1984; *Red Dawn* 1984; *Youngblood* 1986; *Dirty Dancing* 1987; *Tiger Warsaw* 1988; *Next of Kin* 1989; *Road House* 1989; *Ghost* 1990; *Point Break* 1991; *City of Joy* 1992; *Father Hood* 1993; *Tall Tale* 1994; *Three Wishes* 1995; *To Wong Foo, Thanks for Everything, Julie Newmar* 1995; *Black Dog* 1998; *Donnie Darko* 2001; *Dirty Dancing 2* 2003
Sweeney, Bob *Toby Tyler, or Ten Weeks with a Circus* 1960; *Moon Pilot* 1962; *Marnie* 1964
Sweeney, D B (1961–) *Gardens of Stone* 1987; *No Man's Land* 1987; *Eight Men Out* 1988; *Sons* 1989; *Memphis Belle* 1990; *A Day in October* 1991; *Heaven Is a Playground* 1991; *Leather Jackets* 1991; *The Cutting Edge* 1992; *Miss Rose White* 1992; *Fire in the Sky* 1993; *Hear No Evil* 1993; *Roommates* 1995; *Spawn* 1997; *Dinosaur* 2000; *Hardball* 2001; *Brother Bear* 2003
Sweeney, Garry *Small Faces* 1995; *The Acid House* 1998
Sweeney, Julia (1961–) *God Said, "Ha!"* 1998; *Beethoven's 3rd* 2000; *Whatever It Takes* 2000; *Beethoven's 4th* 2001; *Clockstoppers* 2002
Sweet, Gary (1957–) *The Lighthorsemen* 1987; *Fever* 1988; *Love in Ambush* 1997
Sweet, Sheila *Conflict of Wings* 1953; *The Angel Who Pawned Her Harp* 1954; *It's a Great Day* 1955
Sweet, Vonte *The Walking Dead* 1995; *American Strays* 1996; *Marshal Law* 1996
Swenson, Karl (1908–1978) *Kings Go Forth* 1958; *The Hanging Tree* 1959; *No Name on the Bullet* 1959; *Ice Palace* 1960; *One Foot in Hell* 1960; *Lonely Are the Brave* 1962; *Walk on the Wild Side* 1962; *The Sword in the Stone* 1963; *Ulzana's Raid* 1972
Swerdlow, Tommy *Blueberry Hill* 1988; *Child's Play* 1988
Swift, Clive (1936–) *The National Health* 1973; *The Sailor's Return* 1978
Swift, David (1919–2001) *No Sex Please – We're British* 1973; *Arthur's Hallowed Ground* 1985; *Jack & Sarah* 1995
Swift, Susan (1964–) *Audrey Rose* 1977; *Harper Valley PTA* 1978
Swinburne, Nora (1902–2000) *They Flew Alone* 1941; *The Man in Grey* 1943; *Fanny by Gaslight* 1944; *They Knew Mr Knight* 1945; *Jassy* 1947; *The Blind Goddess* 1948; *Quartet* 1948; *Christopher Columbus* 1949; *Fools Rush In* 1949; *The River* 1951; *Betrayed* 1954; *Helen of Troy* 1955; *Conspiracy of Hearts* 1960; *Interlude* 1968
Swinton, Tilda (1961–) *Caravaggio* 1986; *Aria* 1987; *The Last of England* 1987; *War Requiem* 1988; *Play Me Something* 1989; *The Garden* 1990; *Edward II* 1991; *Orlando* 1992; *Blue* 1993; *Wittgenstein* 1993; *Female Perversions* 1996; *Love Is the Devil: Study for a Portrait of Francis Bacon* 1998; *The War Zone* 1999; *The Beach* 2000; *Possible Worlds* 2000; *The Deep End* 2001; *Vanilla Sky* 2001; *Adaptation.* 2002; *The Statement* 2003; *Young Adam* 2003; *Constantine* 2005
Swit, Loretta (1937–) *Deadhead Miles* 1972; *Freebie and the Bean* 1974; *Race with the Devil* 1975; *Cagney & Lacey* 1981; *SOB* 1981; *Beer* 1985; *Whoops Apocalypse* 1986
Switzer, Carl "Alfalfa" aka **Switzer, Carl** (1926–1959) *General Spanky* 1936; *There's One Born Every Minute* 1942; *Track of the Cat* 1954; *Motorcycle Gang* 1957
Swofford, Ken (1932–) *Common-Law Cabin* 1967; *The Domino Principle* 1977; *Thelma & Louise* 1991
Swope, Topo *Glory Boy* 1971; *Tracks* 1977
Swope, Tracy Brooks (1952–) *Happy New Year* 1987; *Terminal Entry* 1988; *Keaton's Cop* 1990
Syal, Meera (1962–) *Sammy and Rosie Get Laid* 1987; *Beautiful Thing* 1995; *Girls' Night* 1997; *Anita & Me* 2002
Sydney, Basil (1894–1968) *The Tunnel* 1935; *Accused* 1936; *Rhodes of Africa* 1936; *The Black Sheep of Whitehall* 1941; *Ships with Wings* 1942; *Went the Day Well?* 1942; *Caesar and Cleopatra* 1945; *Meet Me at Dawn* 1946; *Jassy* 1947; *The Man Within* 1947; *Hamlet* 1948; *Treasure Island* 1950; *Salome* 1953; *The Dam Busters* 1954; *Hell below Zero* 1954; *Star of India* 1954; *Simba* 1955; *Sea Wife* 1957; *The Three Worlds of Gulliver* 1959; *The Hands of Orlac* 1960
Sykes, Brenda (1949–) *Skin Game* 1971; *Cleopatra Jones* 1973; *Mandingo* 1975
Sykes, Eric (1923–) *Orders Are Orders* 1954; *Tommy the Toreador* 1959; *Watch Your Stern* 1960; *Invasion Quartet* 1961; *Very Important Person* 1961; *Village of Daughters* 1961; *Kill or Cure* 1962; *Heavens Above!* 1963; *The Bargee* 1964; *One Way Pendulum* 1965; *Rotten to the Core* 1965; *Those Magnificent Men in Their Flying Machines* 1965; *The Liquidator* 1966; *The Spy with a Cold Nose* 1966; *The Plank* 1967; *Shalako* 1968; *Monte Carlo or Bust* 1969; *The Boys in Blue* 1983; *Splitting Heirs* 1993; *The Others* 2001
Sylvester, Harold *Part 2, Sounder* 1976; *Fast Break* 1979; *Uncommon Valor* 1983; *Vision Quest* 1985; *Corrina, Corrina* 1994; *Trippin'* 1999
Sylvester, William (1922–1995) *Give Us This Day* 1949; *Appointment in London* 1952; *The Yellow Balloon* 1952; *Albert, RN* 1953; *House of Blackmail* 1953; *The Stranger Came Home* 1954; *Postmark for Danger* 1955; *High Tide at Noon* 1957; *Dublin Nightmare* 1958; *Offbeat* 1960; *Gorgo* 1961; *Information Received* 1962; *Ring of Spies* 1963; *Devil Doll* 1964; *Devils of Darkness* 1964; *The Hand of Night* 1966; *2001: a Space Odyssey* 1968; *Busting* 1974
Sylvie (1883–1970) *Un Carnet de Bal* 1937; *The End of the Day* 1939; *Les Anges du Péché* 1943; *The Little World of Don Camillo* 1951; *Thérèse Raquin* 1953; *Ulysses* 1954
Sylwan, Kari *Cries and Whispers* 1972; *Face to Face* 1976
Symonds, Amanda *Scrubbers* 1982; *UFO* 1993
Syms, Sylvia (1934–) *My Teenage Daughter* 1956; *The Birthday Present* 1957; *The Moonraker* 1957; *No Time for Tears* 1957; *Woman in a Dressing Gown* 1957; *Bachelor of Hearts* 1958; *Ferry to Hong Kong* 1958; *Ice Cold in Alex* 1958; *No Trees in the Street* 1958; *Expresso Bongo* 1959; *Conspiracy of Hearts* 1960; *The World of Suzie Wong* 1960; *Flame in the Streets* 1961; *Victim* 1961; *The Punch and Judy Man* 1962; *The Quare Fellow* 1962; *The World Ten Times Over* 1963; *East of Sudan* 1964; *The Big Job* 1965; *Danger Route* 1967; *Hostile Witness* 1968; *The Desperados* 1969; *Run Wild, Run Free* 1969; *Born to Win* 1971; *Asylum* 1972; *The Tamarind Seed* 1974; *Give Us Tomorrow* 1978; *There Goes the Bride* 1979; *A Chorus of Disapproval* 1988; *Shirley Valentine* 1989; *Dirty Weekend* 1992; *Shining Through* 1992; *Staggered* 1993; *Food of Love* 1997; *I'll Sleep When I'm Dead* 2003; *What a Girl Wants* 2003
Szabo, Laszlo *Le Petit Soldat* 1960; *Alphaville* 1965; *Pierrot le Fou* 1965; *Made in USA* 1966; *The Confession* 1970; *Passion* 1982; *L'Amour par Terre* 1984; *L'Eau Froide* 1994
Szapolowska, Grazyna (1953–) *No End* 1984; *Hanussen* 1988; *A Short Film about Love* 1988
Szarabajka, Keith (1952–) *Marie: a True Story* 1985; *Billy Galvin* 1986; *A Perfect World* 1993; *One Woman's Courage* 1994
Szekely, Miklos B *Damnation* 1988; *Rothschild's Violin* 1996
Szemes, Mari (1932–1988) *Diary for My Children* 1982; *Diary for My Loves* 1987
Szeps, Henri (1943–) *Run, Rebecca, Run* 1981; *Warming Up* 1983; *Travelling North* 1986; *Les Patterson Saves the World* 1987
Szubanski, Magda (1961–) *Babe* 1995; *Babe: Pig in the City* 1998; *The Crocodile Hunter: Collision Course* 2002

T

Tabakov, Oleg (1935–) *War and Peace* 1966; *Oblomov* 1980; *Dream Flights* 1983; *Taking Sides* 2001
Tablian, Vic *Sphinx* 1980; *Raiders of the Lost Ark* 1981
Tabori, Kristoffer (1952–) *The Glass House* 1972; *Journey through Rosebud* 1972; *Wildly Available* 1996
Tabu *Maachis* 1996; *Chachi 420* 1997; *Virasat* 1997; *Hawa* 2003
Taeger, Ralph (1936–) *X-15* 1961; *The Delta Factor* 1970
Tafler, Sydney aka **Tafler, Sidney** (1916–1979) *It Always Rains on Sunday* 1947; *Dance Hall* 1950; *Assassin for Hire* 1951; *Hotel Sahara* 1951; *The Scarlet Thread* 1951; *Emergency Call* 1952; *The Glass Cage* 1955; *The Woman for Joe* 1955; *Fire Maidens from Outer Space* 1956; *Booby Trap* 1957; *The Bank Raiders* 1958; *Bottoms Up* 1959; *Let's Get Married* 1960; *Light Up the Sky* 1960; *The Birthday Party* 1968; *The Adventurers* 1970
Tagawa, Cary-Hiroyuki (1950–) *Spellbinder* 1988; *Kickboxer 2: the Road Back* 1990; *Showdown in Little Tokyo* 1991; *American Me* 1992; *Nemesis* 1993; *Rising Sun* 1993; *Picture Bride* 1994; *Mortal Kombat* 1995; *Danger Zone* 1996; *The Phantom* 1996; *American Dragons* 1997; *Top of the World* 1997; *Bridge of Dragons* 1999; *The Art of War* 2000; *The Ghost* 2000; *Planet of the Apes* 2001; *Elektra* 2005
Taggart, Ben (1889–1947) *Before I Hang* 1940; *Man Made Monster* 1941
Taggart, Rita *Die Laughing* 1980; *Torchlight* 1984; *Weeds* 1987; *House III: The Horror Show* 1989; *Coupe de Ville* 1990
Taghmaoui, Saïd (1973–) *La Haine* 1995; *Hideous Kinky* 1998; *Ali Zaoua* 2000; *Room to Rent* 2000; *Crime Spree* 2002; *The Good Thief* 2002; *Hidalgo* 2003; *Spartan* 2004
Tagore, Sharmila (1936–) *The World of Apu* 1959; *Devi* 1960; *Waqt* 1965; *Company Limited* 1971; *Mississippi Masala* 1991
Taguchi, Tomoroh (1957–) *Tetsuo: the Iron Man* 1989; *Tetsuo II: Body Hammer* 1991
Tahil, Dalip aka **Tahil, Dilip** *The Perfect Murder* 1988; *Baazigar* 1993; *Chal Mere Bhai* 2000
Tahir, Faran (1963–) *ABCD* 1999; *Anywhere but Here* 1999
Taka, Miiko (1932–) *Hell to Eternity* 1960; *Cry for Happy* 1961; *A Global Affair* 1964; *Walk, Don't Run* 1966; *The Challenge* 1982
Takakura, Ken (1931–) *Too Late the Hero* 1970; *The Yakuza* 1975; *Black Rain* 1989; *Mr Baseball* 1992
Takamine, Hideko (1924–) *Tokyo Chorus* 1931; *Somewhere under the Broad Sky* 1954
Takarada, Akira (1934–) *Godzilla* 1954; *Godzilla vs Mothra* 1964; *Invasion of the Astro-Monster* 1965; *Ebirah, Horror of the Deep* 1966; *Latitude Zero* 1969; *Minbo – or the Gentle Art of Japanese Extortion* 1992
Takashima, Tadao (1930–) *King Kong vs Godzilla* 1962; *Frankenstein Conquers the World* 1964; *Son of Godzilla* 1967
Takeda, Shinji (1972–) *Gohatto* 1999; *The Happiness of the Katakuris* 2001
Takei, George (1940–) *Hell to Eternity* 1960; *Ice Palace* 1960; *Red Line 7000* 1965; *Walk, Don't Run* 1966; *The Green Berets* 1968; *Star Trek: the Motion Picture* 1979; *Star Trek II: the Wrath of Khan* 1982; *Star Trek III: the Search for Spock* 1984; *Star Trek IV: the Voyage Home* 1986; *Return from the River Kwai* 1988; *Star Trek V: the Final Frontier* 1989; *Blood Oath* 1990; *Star Trek VI: the Undiscovered Country* 1991; *The Curse of the Dragon* 1993; *Oblivion* 1993; *Mulan* 1998
Takenaka, Naoto (1956–) *Shall We Dance?* 1995; *Tokyo Fist* 1995; *Freezer* 2000; *The Happiness of the Katakuris* 2001
Taktarov, Oleg (1968–) *15 Minutes* 2001; *Rollerball* 2001
Talbot, Lyle (1902–1996) *Love Is a Racket* 1932; *The Purchase Price* 1932; *The Thirteenth Guest* 1932; *Three on a Match* 1932; *Havana Widows* 1933; *Ladies They Talk About* 1933; *20,000 Years in Sing Sing* 1933; *Fog over Frisco* 1934; *Mandalay* 1934; *One Night of Love* 1934; *The Case of the Lucky Legs* 1935; *Oil for the Lamps of China* 1935; *Our Little Girl* 1935; *Go West, Young Man* 1936; *The Singing Kid* 1936; *Westbound Limited* 1937; *Second Fiddle* 1939; *Miracle on Main Street* 1940; *Sensations* 1944; *Appointment with Murder* 1948; *Devil's Cargo* 1948; *Glen or Glenda* 1953; *Jail Bait* 1954; *City of Fear* 1959; *Plan 9 from Outer Space* 1959
Talbot, Nita (1930–) *Bundle of Joy* 1956; *I Married a Woman* 1958; *Who's Got the Action?* 1962; *Girl Happy* 1965; *That Funny Feeling* 1965; *The Cool Ones* 1967; *Buck and the Preacher* 1972; *Serial* 1980; *Frightmare* 1981; *The Check Is in the Mail* 1986
Talbott, Gloria (1931–2000) *All That Heaven Allows* 1955; *Crashout* 1955; *Lucy Gallant* 1955; *We're No Angels* 1955; *The Young Guns* 1956; *The Cyclops* 1957; *Daughter of Dr Jekyll* 1957; *The Oklahoman* 1957; *Cattle Empire* 1958; *I Married a Monster from Outer Space* 1958; *Alias Jesse James* 1959; *The Oregon Trail* 1959; *The Leech Woman* 1960; *Arizona Raiders* 1965; *An Eye for an Eye* 1966
Talbott, Michael (1955–) *Foolin' Around* 1980; *Jack Reed: One of Our Own* 1995
Taliferro, Michael "Bear" *Half Past Dead* 2002; *You Got Served* 2004
Tallichet, Margaret (1919–1919) *Stranger on the Third Floor* 1940; *It Started with Eve* 1941
Tallier, Nadine *Girls at Sea* 1958; *The Treasure of San Teresa* 1959
Tallman, Patricia (1957–) *Knightriders* 1981; *Night of the Living Dead* 1990
Talmadge, Constance (1897–1973) *Intolerance* 1916; *The Fall of Babylon* 1919
Talman, William (1915–1968) *The Woman on Pier 13* 1949; *Armored Car Robbery* 1950; *The Racket* 1951; *One Minute to Zero* 1952; *City That Never Sleeps* 1953; *The Hitch-Hiker* 1953; *Big House, USA* 1955; *Crashout* 1955; *Smoke Signal* 1955; *The Ballad of Josie* 1968
Talton, Alix aka **Talton, Alice** (1919–1992) *The Great Jewel Robber* 1950; *Rock around the Clock* 1956; *The Deadly Mantis* 1957; *Romanoff and Juliet* 1961
Tamba, Tetsuro aka **Tanba, Tetsuro** (1922–) *Bridge to the Sun* 1961; *The 7th Dawn* 1964; *You Only Live Twice* 1967; *Tokyo Pop* 1988; *The Happiness of the Katakuris* 2001
Tamblyn, Amber (1983–) *Ten Minutes Older: the Trumpet* 2002; *The Sisterhood of the Traveling Pants* 2005
Tamblyn, Russ aka **Tamblyn, Russell** aka **Tamblyn, Rusty** (1934–) *Samson and Delilah* 1949; *Retreat, Hell!* 1952; *Take the High Ground* 1953; *Seven Brides for Seven Brothers* 1954; *Hit the Deck* 1955; *Many Rivers to Cross* 1955; *The Fastest Gun Alive* 1956; *The Last Hunt* 1956; *The Young Guns* 1956; *Don't Go Near the Water* 1957; *Peyton Place* 1957; *High School Confidential* 1958; *tom thumb* 1958; *Cimarron* 1960; *West Side Story* 1961; *The Wonderful World of the Brothers Grimm* 1962; *Follow the Boys* 1963; *The Haunting* 1963; *The Long Ships* 1963; *Son of a Gunfighter* 1964; *The Female Bunch* 1969; *Dracula vs Frankenstein* 1970; *War of the Gargantuas* 1970; *The Last Movie* 1971; *Human Highway* 1982
Tambor, Jeffrey (1944–) *...And Justice for All* 1979; *Saturday the 14th* 1981; *No Small Affair* 1984; *Three O'Clock High* 1987; *Brenda Starr* 1989; *Life Stinks* 1991; *Big Bully* 1996; *The Man Who Captured Eichmann* 1996; *Doctor Dolittle* 1998; *Meet Joe Black* 1998; *There's Something about Mary* 1998; *Girl, Interrupted* 1999; *Teaching Mrs Tingle* 1999; *The Grinch* 2000; *Pollock* 2000; *Get Well Soon* 2001; *Malibu's Most Wanted* 2003; *My Boss's Daughter* 2003; *Hellboy* 2004; *The SpongeBob SquarePants Movie* 2004
Tamiroff, Akim (1899–1972) *The Big Broadcast of 1936* 1935; *The Gay Deception* 1935; *The Last Outpost* 1935; *The Lives of a Bengal Lancer* 1935; *Anthony Adverse* 1936; *Desire* 1936; *The General Died at Dawn* 1936; *The Adventures of Michael Strogoff* 1937; *High, Wide and Handsome* 1937; *The Buccaneer* 1938; *Spawn of the North* 1938; *Paris Honeymoon* 1939; *Union Pacific* 1939; *The Great McGinty* 1940; *North West Mounted Police* 1940; *Texas Rangers Ride Again* 1940; *The Way of All Flesh* 1940; *The Corsican Brothers* 1941; *Tortilla Flat* 1942; *Five Graves to Cairo* 1943; *For Whom the Bell Tolls* 1943; *His Butler's Sister* 1943; *Can't Help Singing* 1944; *Dragon Seed* 1944; *The Miracle of Morgan's Creek* 1944; *Pardon My Past* 1945; *Thieves' Holiday* 1946; *Fiesta* 1947; *The Gangster* 1947; *My Girl Tisa* 1948; *Relentless* 1948; *Black Magic* 1949; *Outpost in Morocco* 1949; *Desert Legion* 1953; *They Who Dare* 1953; *Cartouche* 1954; *You Know What Sailors Are* 1954; *Confidential Report* 1955; *Anastasia* 1956; *The Black Sleep* 1956; *Yangtse Incident* 1956; *Me and the Colonel* 1958; *Touch of Evil* 1958; *The Bacchantes* 1960; *Ocean's Eleven* 1960; *Romanoff and Juliet* 1961; *The Reluctant Saint* 1962; *The Trial* 1962; *The Black Tulip* 1963; *Panic Button* 1964; *Topkapi* 1964; *Alphaville* 1965; *Le Bambole* 1965; *Lord Jim* 1965; *After the Fox* 1966; *Hotel Paradiso* 1966; *Lt Robin Crusoe, USN* 1966; *The Liquidator* 1966; *The Vulture* 1966; *Great Catherine* 1968; *The Great Bank Robbery* 1969

Tamm, Mary (1950–) *Tales That Witness Madness* 1973; *The Odessa File* 1974; *The Likely Lads* 1976; *Sorted* 2000
Tamura, Takahiro (1928–) *Tora! Tora! Tora!* 1970; *Muddy River* 1981
Tan, Philip (1942–) *Vroom* 1988; *China Cry* 1990; *Showdown in Little Tokyo* 1991; *Bloodsport II: The Next Kumite* 1996
Tanaka, Haruo *The Straits of Love and Hate* 1937; *The Crucified Lovers* 1954; *Ohayo* 1959
Tanaka, Kinuyo (1910–1977) *Musashi Miyamoto* 1944; *Five Women around Utamaro* 1946; *The Victory of Women* 1946; *The Love of Sumako the Actress* 1947; *Hen in the Wind* 1948; *Women of the Night* 1948; *My Love Has Been Burning* 1949; *The Lady of Musashino* 1951; *Miss Oyu* 1951; *The Life of Oharu* 1952; *Ugetsu Monogatari* 1953; *Sansho the Bailiff* 1954; *The Ballad of Narayama* 1958; *Equinox Flower* 1958; *Alone on the Pacific* 1963
Tanaka, Yoshiko (1956–) *Black Rain* 1988; *Ring 0* 2000
Tandon, Raveena (1972–) *Anari No 1* 1999; *Aks* 2001
Tandy, Jessica (1909–1994) *The Seventh Cross* 1944; *The Green Years* 1946; *Forever Amber* 1947; *September Affair* 1950; *The Desert Fox* 1951; *The Light in the Forest* 1958; *Hemingway's Adventures of a Young Man* 1962; *The Birds* 1963; *Butley* 1973; *Honky Tonk Freeway* 1981; *Best Friends* 1982; *Still of the Night* 1982; *The World According to Garp* 1982; *The Bostonians* 1984; *Cocoon* 1985; **batteries not included* 1987; *The House on Carroll Street* 1987; *Cocoon: the Return* 1988; *Driving Miss Daisy* 1989; *Fried Green Tomatoes at the Whistle Stop Cafe* 1991; *Used People* 1992; *Camilla* 1993; *Nobody's Fool* 1994
Tani, Yoko (1932–1999) *The Wind Cannot Read* 1958; *Piccadilly Third Stop* 1960; *The Savage Innocents* 1960; *Invasion* 1965
Tannen, Charles (1915–1980) *The Return of Frank James* 1940; *Careful, Soft Shoulder* 1942
Tanner, Antwon *Never Die Alone* 2004; *Coach Carter* 2005
Tanner, Mary *A Billion for Boris* 1984; *Willy/Milly* 1986
Tanner, Tony (1932–) *The Pleasure Girls* 1965; *Stop the World, I Want to Get Off* 1966
Tanuja (1943–) *Saathiya* 2002; *Bhoot* 2003; *Deewaar: Let's Bring Our Heroes Home* 2004
Tapley, Colin (1907–1995) *The Last Outpost* 1935; *Thank You, Jeeves* 1936; *Cloudburst* 1951; *Wings of Danger* 1952; *The Steel Key* 1953; *The Dam Busters* 1954; *Emergency* 1962
Tarantino, Quentin (1963–) *Reservoir Dogs* 1991; *Pulp Fiction* 1994; *Sleep with Me* 1994; *Somebody to Love* 1994; *Desperado* 1995; *Destiny Turns on the Radio* 1995; *Four Rooms* 1995; *From Dusk till Dawn* 1995; *Little Nicky* 2000
Tarbuck, Barbara *The Tie That Binds* 1995; *Walking Tall* 2004
Tarbuck, Jimmy (1940–) *The Plank* 1967; *Strictly Sinatra* 2000
Tarso, Ignacio Lopez (1925–) *Nazarín* 1958; *Macario* 1960; *Under the Volcano* 1984
Tashman, Lilyan (1899–1934) *So This Is Paris* 1926; *Camille* 1927; *Bulldog Drummond* 1929; *Gold Diggers of Broadway* 1929; *The Marriage Playground* 1929; *Girls about Town* 1931; *One Heavenly Night* 1931; *Scarlet Dawn* 1932; *The Wiser Sex* 1932; *Riptide* 1934
Tate, Harry (1872–1940) *Happy* 1933; *Look Up and Laugh* 1935; *Keep Your Seats, Please* 1936; *Wings of the Morning* 1937
Tate, Larenz (1975–) *Menace II Society* 1993; *No Ordinary Summer* 1994; *Dead Presidents* 1995; *Love Jones* 1997; *The Postman* 1997; *Why Do Fools Fall in Love?* 1998; *Biker Boyz* 2003; *A Man Apart* 2003; *Ray* 2004
Tate, Nick (1942–) *The Devil's Playground* 1976; *Summerfield* 1977; *The Gold and Glory* 1984; *The Empty Beach* 1985; *A Cry in the Dark* 1988
Tate, Reginald *aka* **Tate, Sqn/Ldr Reginald** (1896–1955) *The Phantom Light* 1934; *Poison Pen* 1939; *Next of Kin* 1942; *The Man from Morocco* 1944; *So Well Remembered* 1947; *Uncle Silas* 1947; *The Secret People* 1951; *Escape Route* 1952; *The Story of Robin Hood and His Merrie Men* 1952; *Malta Story* 1953
Tate, Sharon (1943–1969) *Eye of the Devil* 1966; *Don't Make Waves* 1967; *The Fearless Vampire Killers* 1967; *Valley of the Dolls* 1967; *Twelve plus One* 1969; *The Wrecking Crew* 1969
Tati, Jacques (1908–1982) *Devil in the Flesh* 1947; *Jour de Fête* 1947; *School for Postmen* 1947; *Monsieur Hulot's Holiday* 1953; *Mon Oncle* 1958; *Cours du Soir* 1967; *Playtime* 1967; *Traffic* 1970; *Parade* 1974
Taube, Aino *aka* **Taube-Henrikson, Aino** (1912–1990) *One Single Night* 1939; *Face to Face* 1976
Taube, Sven-Bertil (1934–) *Hugs and Kisses* 1967; *The Buttercup Chain* 1970; *Puppet on a Chain* 1970; *A Game for Vultures* 1979; *Jerusalem* 1996
Tauber, Richard (1891–1948) *Blossom Time* 1934; *Heart's Desire* 1935; *Land without Music* 1936; *Pagliacci* 1936
Tautou, Audrey (1978–) *The Beating of the Butterfly's Wings* 2000; *Amélie* 2001; *Dirty Pretty Things* 2002; *He Loves Me... He Loves Me Not* 2002; *Pot Luck* 2002; *Pas sur la Bouche* 2003; *A Very Long Engagement* 2004
Tavarone, Dino (1942–) *2 Seconds* 1998; *Mambo Italiano* 2003
Tavernier, Nils (1965–) *Une Affaire de Femmes* 1988; *L.627* 1992; *Mina Tannenbaum* 1993; *D'Artagnan's Daughter* 1994
Tayback, Vic (1930–1990) *Door-to-Door Maniac* 1961; *The Blue Knight* 1973; *Alice Doesn't Live Here Anymore* 1974; *The Gambler* 1974; *Lepke* 1975; *Dark Victory* 1976; *Treasure Island* 1986; *Weekend Warriors* 1986; *All Dogs Go to Heaven* 1989; *Knife Edge* 1990
Taylor, Benedict (1960–) *Thirteen at Dinner* 1985; *Every Time We Say Goodbye* 1986
Taylor, Buck (1938–) *The Wild Angels* 1966; *Triumphs of a Man Called Horse* 1983
Taylor, Chip *The Catamount Killing* 1974; *Melvin and Howard* 1980
Taylor, Christine (1971–) *The Brady Bunch Movie* 1995; *The Craft* 1996; *A Very Brady Sequel* 1996; *Overnight Delivery* 1997; *Something about Sex* 1998; *The Wedding Singer* 1998; *Zoolander* 2001; *Dodgeball: a True Underdog Story* 2004
Taylor, Delores (1939–) *Billy Jack* 1971; *The Trial of Billy Jack* 1974; *Billy Jack Goes to Washington* 1977
Taylor, Don (1920–1998) *For the Love of Mary* 1948; *The Naked City* 1948; *Ambush* 1949; *Battleground* 1949; *Father of the Bride* 1950; *The Blue Veil* 1951; *Father's Little Dividend* 1951; *Flying Leathernecks* 1951; *Target Unknown* 1951; *Japanese War Bride* 1952; *Destination Gobi* 1953; *Stalag 17* 1953; *Johnny Dark* 1954; *Men of Sherwood Forest* 1954; *I'll Cry Tomorrow* 1955; *The Bold and the Brave* 1956
Taylor, Dub (1907–1994) *The Bounty Hunter* 1954; *Black Gold* 1963; *Bonnie and Clyde* 1967; *The Reivers* 1969; *A Man Called Horse* 1970; *Evel Knievel* 1971; *The Wild Country* 1971; *This Is a Hijack* 1973; *Burnt Offerings* 1976; *Gator* 1976; *Moonshine County Express* 1977; *Back to the Future Part III* 1990; *My Heroes Have Always Been Cowboys* 1991; *Falling from Grace* 1992; *Maverick* 1994
Taylor, Elaine *Half a Sixpence* 1967; *The Anniversary* 1968; *Diamonds for Breakfast* 1968; *Lock Up Your Daughters!* 1969; *The Games* 1970
Taylor, Elizabeth (1932–) *There's One Born Every Minute* 1942; *Jane Eyre* 1943; *Lassie Come Home* 1943; *National Velvet* 1944; *The White Cliffs of Dover* 1944; *Courage of Lassie* 1946; *Cynthia* 1947; *Life with Father* 1947; *A Date with Judy* 1948; *Julia Misbehaves* 1948; *Conspirator* 1949; *Little Women* 1949; *The Big Hangover* 1950; *Father of the Bride* 1950; *Callaway Went Thataway* 1951; *Father's Little Dividend* 1951; *Love Is Better Than Ever* 1951; *A Place in the Sun* 1951; *Quo Vadis* 1951; *Ivanhoe* 1952; *The Girl Who Had Everything* 1953; *Beau Brummell* 1954; *Elephant Walk* 1954; *The Last Time I Saw Paris* 1954; *Rhapsody* 1954; *Giant* 1956; *Raintree County* 1957; *Cat on a Hot Tin Roof* 1958; *Suddenly, Last Summer* 1959; *Butterfield 8* 1960; *Scent of Mystery* 1960; *Cleopatra* 1963; *The VIPs* 1963; *The Sandpiper* 1965; *Who's Afraid of Virginia Woolf?* 1966; *The Comedians* 1967; *Doctor Faustus* 1967; *Reflections in a Golden Eye* 1967; *The Taming of the Shrew* 1967; *Boom* 1968; *Secret Ceremony* 1968; *Anne of the Thousand Days* 1969; *The Only Game in Town* 1970; *Under Milk Wood* 1971; *Zee and Co* 1971; *Hammersmith Is Out* 1972; *Ash Wednesday* 1973; *Night Watch* 1973; *The Driver's Seat* 1975; *The Blue Bird* 1976; *Victory at Entebbe* 1976; *A Little Night Music* 1977; *Winter Kills* 1979; *The Mirror Crack'd* 1980; *Genocide* 1981; *Between Friends* 1983; *Young Toscanini* 1988; *And the Band Played On* 1993; *The Flintstones* 1994; *These Old Broads* 2001
Taylor, Estelle (1899–1958) *The Ten Commandments* 1923; *Don Juan* 1926; *Cimarron* 1931; *Street Scene* 1931; *The Unholy Garden* 1931; *The Southerner* 1945
Taylor, Holland (1943–) *Romancing the Stone* 1984; *Cop and a Half* 1993; *Last Summer in the Hamptons* 1995; *Steal Big, Steal Little* 1995; *George of the Jungle* 1997; *The Truman Show* 1998; *Keeping the Faith* 2000; *Legally Blonde* 2001; *Cinderella II: Dreams Come True* 2002; *SPYkids 2: the Island of Lost Dreams* 2002; *SPYkids 3-D: Game Over* 2003; *The Wedding Date* 2004
Taylor, Howard *Boom* 1968; *Big Meat Eater* 1982
Taylor, Jack (1936–) *Count Dracula* 1970; *The Female Vampire* 1973; *Gulliver's Travels* 1983; *The Ninth Gate* 1999
Taylor, Joan (1925–) *Fighting Man of the Plains* 1949; *The Savage* 1953; *War Paint* 1953; *Rose Marie* 1954; *Apache Woman* 1955; *Earth vs the Flying Saucers* 1956; *20 Million Miles to Earth* 1957
Taylor, Joyce (1932–) *The FBI Story* 1959; *Atlantis, the Lost Continent* 1960; *Ring of Fire* 1961; *Beauty and the Beast* 1962; *Twice Told Tales* 1963
Taylor, Kent (1907–1987) *I'm No Angel* 1933; *White Woman* 1933; *Death Takes a Holiday* 1934; *Mrs Wiggs of the Cabbage Patch* 1934; *The Gracie Allen Murder Case* 1939; *I Take This Woman* 1940; *Bomber's Moon* 1943; *The Daltons Ride Again* 1945; *Payment on Demand* 1951; *Playgirl* 1954; *Slightly Scarlet* 1956; *The Iron Sheriff* 1957; *Gang War* 1958; *The Broken Land* 1962; *The Crawling Hand* 1963
Taylor, Kit (1942–) *Long John Silver* 1954; *Early Frost* 1981; *Rough Diamonds* 1994
Taylor, Lili (1967–) *Mystic Pizza* 1988; *Say Anything...* 1989; *Bright Angel* 1990; *Arizona Dream* 1991; *Dogfight* 1991; *Household Saints* 1993; *Rudy* 1993; *The Addiction* 1994; *Cold Fever* 1994; *Pret-a-Porter* 1994; *I Shot Andy Warhol* 1995; *Girls Town* 1996; *illtown* 1996; *Ransom* 1996; *Kicked in the Head* 1997; *Subway Stories: Tales from the Underground* 1997; *The Impostors* 1998; *Pecker* 1998; *The Haunting* 1999; *High Fidelity* 2000; *Live from Baghdad* 2002; *Casa de los Babys* 2003
Taylor, Marjorie *The Crimes of Stephen Hawke* 1936; *It's Never Too Late to Mend* 1937; *The Ticket of Leave Man* 1937; *The Face at the Window* 1939
Taylor, Meshach (1947–) *Mannequin* 1987; *Mannequin on the Move* 1991; *Class Act* 1992
Taylor, Noah (1969–) *The Year My Voice Broke* 1987; *Flirting* 1989; *Dad and Dave: on Our Selection* 1995; *Shine* 1996; *Simon Magus* 1998; *The Escort* 1999; *Almost Famous* 2000; *Lara Croft: Tomb Raider* 2001; *Vanilla Sky* 2001; *Max* 2002; *Lara Croft Tomb Raider: the Cradle of Life* 2003; *The Life Aquatic with Steve Zissou* 2004
Taylor, Regina *Clockers* 1995; *The Keeper* 1995; *Courage under Fire* 1996; *A Family Thing* 1996; *Hostile Waters* 1996; *Strange Justice* 1999
Taylor, Renee (1935–) *The Producers* 1968; *A New Leaf* 1971; *The Last of the Red Hot Lovers* 1972; *Lovesick* 1983; *Love Is All There Is* 1996
Taylor, Rip (1934–) *Things Are Tough All Over* 1982; *Alex & Emma* 2003
Taylor (1), Robert (1911–1969) *Buried Loot* 1934; *Broadway Melody of 1936* 1935; *Magnificent Obsession* 1935; *The Gorgeous Hussy* 1936; *His Brother's Wife* 1936; *Small Town Girl* 1936; *Broadway Melody of 1938* 1937; *Camille* 1937; *Personal Property* 1937; *This Is My Affair* 1937; *The Crowd Roars* 1938; *Three Comrades* 1938; *A Yank at Oxford* 1938; *Lady of the Tropics* 1939; *Remember?* 1939; *Escape* 1940; *Flight Command* 1940; *Waterloo Bridge* 1940; *Billy the Kid* 1941; *Johnny Eager* 1941; *When Ladies Meet* 1941; *Her Cardboard Lover* 1942; *Stand by for Action* 1942; *Bataan* 1943; *Undercurrent* 1946; *High Wall* 1947; *Ambush* 1949; *The Bribe* 1949; *Conspirator* 1949; *Devil's Doorway* 1950; *Quo Vadis* 1951; *Westward the Women* 1951; *Above and Beyond* 1952; *Ivanhoe* 1952; *All the Brothers Were Valiant* 1953; *Knights of the Round Table* 1953; *Ride, Vaquero!* 1953; *Rogue Cop* 1954; *Valley of the Kings* 1954; *Many Rivers to Cross* 1955; *Quentin Durward* 1955; *D-Day the Sixth of June* 1956; *The Last Hunt* 1956; *The Power and the Prize* 1956; *Tip on a Dead Jockey* 1957; *The Law and Jake Wade* 1958; *Party Girl* 1958; *Saddle the Wind* 1958; *The Hangman* 1959; *The House of the Seven Hawks* 1959; *Killers of Kilimanjaro* 1960; *Cattle King* 1963; *Miracle of the White Stallions* 1963; *The Night Walker* 1964; *Johnny Tiger* 1966; *Where Angels Go...Trouble Follows* 1968
Taylor, Rod *aka* **Taylor, Rodney** (1929–) *Hell on Frisco Bay* 1955; *World without End* 1955; *The Catered Affair* 1956; *Raintree County* 1957; *Separate Tables* 1958; *Ask Any Girl* 1959; *One Hundred and One Dalmatians* 1960; *The Time Machine* 1960; *Seven Seas to Calais* 1962; *The Birds* 1963; *A Gathering of Eagles* 1963; *Sunday in New York* 1963; *The VIPs* 1963; *Fate Is the Hunter* 1964; *36 Hours* 1964; *Do Not Disturb* 1965; *Young Cassidy* 1965; *The Glass Bottom Boat* 1966; *The Liquidator* 1966; *Chuka* 1967; *Dark of the Sun* 1967; *Hotel* 1967; *The Hell with Heroes* 1968; *Nobody Runs Forever* 1968; *Darker than Amber* 1970; *The Man Who Had Power over Women* 1970; *Zabriskie Point* 1970; *The Heroes* 1972; *The Deadly Trackers* 1973; *The Train Robbers* 1973; *The Picture Show Man* 1977; *The Treasure Seekers* 1977; *On the Run* 1983; *Danielle Steel's Palomino* 1991; *Open Season* 1995; *Welcome to Woop Woop* 1997
Taylor (1), Ron *The Bloody Brood* 1959; *Long Shot* 1978
Taylor, Russi *Duck Tales: the Movie – Treasure of the Lost Lamp* 1990; *Cinderella II: Dreams Come True* 2002
Taylor, Valerie (1902–1988) *Berkeley Square* 1933; *Went the Day Well?* 1942; *Faces in the Dark* 1960; *What a Carve Up!* 1961
Taylor, Vaughn (1910–1983) *Meet Danny Wilson* 1952; *It Should Happen to You* 1954; *Jailhouse Rock* 1957; *Cat on a Hot Tin Roof* 1958; *The Wizard of Baghdad* 1960
Taylor, Veronica (1978–) *Pokémon the Movie 2000* 1999; *Pokémon 3: Spell of the Unown* 2001
Taylor, Wally *Shaft's Big Score!* 1972; *Hangup* 1973; *Peacemaker* 1990
Taylor-Smith, Jean (1900–1990) *Rob Roy, the Highland Rogue* 1953; *It's Never Too Late* 1956; *Ring of Bright Water* 1969; *My Childhood* 1972; *My Ain Folk* 1973
Taylor-Young, Leigh (1944–) *I Love You, Alice B Toklas* 1968; *The Big Bounce* 1969; *The Adventurers* 1970; *The Buttercup Chain* 1970; *The Gang That Couldn't Shoot Straight* 1971; *The Horsemen* 1971; *Soylent Green* 1973; *Looker* 1981; *Jagged Edge* 1985; *Secret Admirer* 1985; *For Better or for Worse* 1990; *Slackers* 2001
Tazaki, Jun (1910–1985) *Gate of Hell* 1953; *Ebirah, Horror of the Deep* 1966; *Destroy All Monsters* 1968
Tcherina, Ludmilla (1924–2004) *The Red Shoes* 1948; *The Tales of Hoffmann* 1951; *Sign of the Pagan* 1954; *Oh, Rosalinda!!* 1955; *Honeymoon* 1959
Te Wiata, Inia *The Seekers* 1954; *Man of the Moment* 1955
Teagarden, Jack (1905–1964) *The Birth of the Blues* 1941; *Glory Alley* 1952
Teakle, Spencer *Cover Girl Killer* 1959; *The Gentle Trap* 1960
Teal, Ray (1902–1976) *The Bandit of Sherwood Forest* 1946; *Ace in the Hole* 1951; *Along the Great Divide* 1951; *Distant Drums* 1951; *The Captive City* 1952; *Carrie* 1952; *Ambush at Tomahawk Gap* 1953; *The Wild One* 1953; *The Command* 1954; *Run for Cover* 1955; *The Burning Hills* 1956; *Girl on the Run* 1958
Teale, Owen (1961–) *War Requiem* 1988; *Robin Hood* 1990; *The Hawk* 1992; *The Cherry Orchard* 1998; *Conspiracy* 2001
Tearle, Conway (1878–1938) *Stella Maris* 1918; *Gold Diggers of Broadway* 1929; *The Hurricane Express* 1932
Tearle, Godfrey (1884–1953) *The 39 Steps* 1935; *The Last Journey* 1936; *One of Our Aircraft Is Missing* 1942; *Tomorrow We Live* 1942; *The Lamp Still Burns* 1943; *Undercover* 1943; *The Rake's Progress* 1945; *The Beginning or the End* 1947; *White Corridors* 1951; *I Believe in You* 1952; *Mandy* 1952; *The Titfield Thunderbolt* 1952; *Decameron Nights* 1953
Teasdale, Verree (1904–1987) *Payment Deferred* 1932; *Skyscraper Souls* 1932; *Roman Scandals* 1933; *Fashions of 1934* 1934; *Madame Du Barry* 1934; *A Midsummer Night's Dream* 1935; *The Milky Way* 1936; *First Lady* 1937; *Fifth Avenue Girl* 1939; *Topper Takes a Trip* 1939; *I Take This Woman* 1940; *Turnabout* 1940; *Come Live with Me* 1941
Teer, Barbara Ann (1937–) *Slaves* 1969; *The Angel Levine* 1970

Tefkin, Blair *Three for the Road* 1987; *A Sinful Life* 1989
Teixeira, Virgilio aka **Texera, Virgilio** (1917–) *The Boy Who Stole a Million* 1960; *Return of the Seven* 1966; *The Magnificent Two* 1967
Tejero, Fernando (1967–) *Football Days* 2003; *Torremolinos 73* 2003
Telezynska, Isabella *The Music Lovers* 1970; *Ludwig* 1973
Tell, Olive (1894–1951) *Delicious* 1931; *Ladies' Man* 1931
Teller (1948–) *My Chauffeur* 1986; *Penn & Teller Get Killed* 1989; *Fantasia 2000* 1999
Temple, Shirley (1928–) *Baby, Take a Bow* 1934; *Bright Eyes* 1934; *Change of Heart* 1934; *Little Miss Marker* 1934; *Mandalay* 1934; *Now and Forever* 1934; *Stand Up and Cheer!* 1934; *Curly Top* 1935; *The Little Colonel* 1935; *The Littlest Rebel* 1935; *Our Little Girl* 1935; *Captain January* 1936; *Dimples* 1936; *Poor Little Rich Girl* 1936; *Stowaway* 1936; *Heidi* 1937; *Wee Willie Winkie* 1937; *Just around the Corner* 1938; *Little Miss Broadway* 1938; *Rebecca of Sunnybrook Farm* 1938; *The Little Princess* 1939; *Susannah of the Mounties* 1939; *The Blue Bird* 1940; *Young People* 1940; *Miss Annie Rooney* 1942; *I'll Be Seeing You* 1944; *Since You Went Away* 1944; *Kiss and Tell* 1945; *The Bachelor and the Bobby-Soxer* 1947; *Fort Apache* 1948; *Adventure in Baltimore* 1949; *A Kiss for Corliss* 1949; *Mr Belvedere Goes to College* 1949; *The Story of Seabiscuit* 1949
Tengroth, Birgit (1915–1983) *Dollar* 1938; *Three Strange Loves* 1949
Tennant, David *LA without a Map* 1998; *The Last September* 1999; *Bright Young Things* 2003
Tennant, Victoria (1950–) *The Ragman's Daughter* 1972; *Strangers Kiss* 1983; *All of Me* 1984; *The Holcroft Covenant* 1985; *Best Seller* 1987; *Flowers in the Attic* 1987; *The Handmaid's Tale* 1990; *Whispers* 1990; *LA Story* 1991; *The Plague* 1992
Tenney, Jon (1961–) *Lassie: a New Generation* 1994; *Fools Rush In* 1997; *Music from Another Room* 1998; *Buying the Cow* 2000
Tepper, William *Drive, He Said* 1971; *Breathless* 1983; *Bachelor Party* 1984
Ter Steege, Johanna (1961–) *The Vanishing* 1988; *Sweet Emma Dear Böbe* 1992; *Immortal Beloved* 1994
Terajima, Susumu (1963–) *Hana-Bi* 1997; *After Life* 1998; *Eyes of the Spider* 1999; *Brother* 2000; *Ichi the Killer* 2001
Terao, Akira (1947–) *Ran* 1985; *Akira Kurosawa's Dreams* 1990; *Casshern* 2004
Terhune, Max (1891–1973) *Hit the Saddle* 1937; *Overland Stage Raiders* 1938; *Red River Range* 1938; *Santa Fe Stampede* 1938; *Three Texas Steers* 1939
Terlesky, John *The Allnighter* 1987; *Damned River* 1989
Terof, Georges *La Roue* 1923; *La Nuit du Carrefour* 1932
Terra, Scott (1987–) *Eight Legged Freaks* 2001; *Dickie Roberts: Former Child Star* 2003
Terranova, Dan *Baby Face Nelson* 1957; *Young Dillinger* 1965
Terrell, Ken (1904–1966) *Attack of the 50 Foot Woman* 1958; *The Brain from Planet Arous* 1958
Terrell, Steven *Dragstrip Girl* 1957; *Invasion of the Saucer Men* 1957; *Motorcycle Gang* 1957
Terry, Alice (1899–1987) *The Four Horsemen of the Apocalypse* 1921; *The Prisoner of Zenda* 1922; *Scaramouche* 1923; *The Arab* 1924; *Mare Nostrum* 1926; *The Garden of Allah* 1927
Terry, Don (1902–1988) *Who Killed Gail Preston?* 1938; *White Savage* 1943
Terry, John *Hawk the Slayer* 1980; *Evidence of Love* 1990; *Of Mice and Men* 1992; *The Resurrected* 1992; *A Dangerous Woman* 1993; *Reflections on a Crime* 1994; *The Big Green* 1995; *Blue Valley Songbird* 1999
Terry, Nigel (1945–) *The Lion in Winter* 1968; *Excalibur* 1981; *Déjà Vu* 1984; *Sylvia* 1984; *Caravaggio* 1986; *The Last of England* 1987; *War Requiem* 1988; *Edward II* 1991; *Blue* 1993; *The Emperor's New Clothes* 2001; *FearDotCom* 2002
Terry, Phillip (1909–1993) *Music in Manhattan* 1944; *George White's Scandals* 1945; *The Lost Weekend* 1945; *Pan-Americana* 1945; *To Each His Own* 1946; *Lady of Deceit* 1947; *Seven Keys to Baldpate* 1947; *The Leech Woman* 1960
Terry, Ruth (1920–) *Hold That Co-Ed* 1938; *Slightly Honorable* 1939; *Appointment for Love* 1941; *The Cheaters* 1945
Terry, Sheila (1910–1957) *Lawyer Man* 1932; *Scarlet Dawn* 1932; *The Mayor of Hell* 1933; *The Sphinx* 1933; *'Neath the Arizona Skies* 1934; *The Lawless Frontier* 1935
Terry, William (1914–1962) *Stage Door Canteen* 1943; *Johnny Doesn't Live Here Anymore* 1944
Terry-Thomas (1911–1989) *A Date with a Dream* 1948; *Brothers in Law* 1956; *The Green Man* 1956; *Private's Progress* 1956; *Blue Murder at St Trinian's* 1957; *Happy Is the Bride* 1957; *Lucky Jim* 1957; *The Naked Truth* 1957; *Carlton-Browne of the FO* 1958; *tom thumb* 1958; *Too Many Crooks* 1958; *I'm All Right Jack* 1959; *His and Hers* 1960; *Make Mine Mink* 1960; *School for Scoundrels* 1960; *Bachelor Flat* 1961; *A Matter of WHO* 1961; *Kill or Cure* 1962; *Operation Snatch* 1962; *The Wonderful World of the Brothers Grimm* 1962; *It's a Mad Mad Mad Mad World* 1963; *The Mouse on the Moon* 1963; *The Wild Affair* 1963; *How to Murder Your Wife* 1965; *Strange Bedfellows* 1965; *Those Magnificent Men in Their Flying Machines* 1965; *You Must Be Joking!* 1965; *Don't Look Now... We're Being Shot At* 1966; *Munster, Go Home!* 1966; *Our Man in Marrakesh* 1966; *The Sandwich Man* 1966; *Arabella* 1967; *Danger: Diabolik* 1967; *Jules Verne's Rocket to the Moon* 1967; *The Karate Killers* 1967; *The Perils of Pauline* 1967; *Don't Raise the Bridge, Lower the River* 1968; *How Sweet It Is!* 1968; *Where Were You When the Lights Went Out?* 1968; *Monte Carlo or Bust* 1969; *Twelve plus One* 1969; *The Abominable Dr Phibes* 1971; *The Heroes* 1972; *Robin Hood* 1973; *Vault of Horror* 1973; *Side by Side* 1975; *The Bawdy Adventures of Tom Jones* 1976; *The Hound of the Baskervilles* 1977; *The Last Remake of Beau Geste* 1977
Terzieff, Laurent (1935–) *Les Tricheurs* 1958; *Kapo* 1959; *Thou Shalt Not Kill* 1961; *The Milky Way* 1968; *Medea* 1970; *Detective* 1985; *Rouge Baiser* 1985; *Germinal* 1993
Tesco, Nicky *Leningrad Cowboys Go America* 1989; *I Hired a Contract Killer* 1990
Tessier, Robert (1934–1990) *Born Losers* 1967; *The Glory Stompers* 1967; *Hard Times* 1975; *The Deep* 1977; *One Man Force* 1989
Tester, Desmond (1919–2002) *Sabotage* 1936; *Tudor Rose* 1936; *The Drum* 1938
Testi, Fabio (1941–) *The Garden of the Finzi-Continis* 1971; *Nada* 1974; *The Inheritance* 1976; *China 9, Liberty 37* 1978; *The Ambassador* 1984
Testud, Sylvie (1971–) *Beyond Silence* 1996; *Karnaval* 1998; *The Captive* 2000; *Fear and Trembling* 2003
Tetzel, Joan (1921–1977) *The File on Thelma Jordon* 1949; *Hell below Zero* 1954; *Joy in the Morning* 1965
Tewes, Lauren (1954–) *Eyes of a Stranger* 1980; *Doom Generation* 1995
Texada, Tia *Nurse Betty* 2000; *Glitter* 2001; *13 Conversations about One Thing* 2001; *Spartan* 2004
Teynac, Maurice (1915–1992) *Night without Stars* 1951; *Bedevilled* 1955; *Paris Holiday* 1958; *Crack in the Mirror* 1960; *In the French Style* 1963; *Ash Wednesday* 1973
Thal, Eric (1965–) *The Gun in Betty Lou's Handbag* 1992; *A Stranger among Us* 1992; *The Puppet Masters* 1994; *Wishful Thinking* 1997; *Mixing Nia* 1998
Thalbach, Katharina (1954–) *The Tin Drum* 1979; *Kaspar Hauser* 1993
Thames, Byron (1969–) *Blame It on the Night* 1984; *Johnny Dangerously* 1984
Thatcher, Heather (1896–1987) *It's a Boy* 1933; *If I Were King* 1938; *Man Hunt* 1941; *The Undying Monster* 1942; *Dear Mr Prohack* 1949; *Father's Doing Fine* 1952; *Will Any Gentleman...?* 1953
Thatcher, Torin (1905–1981) *Next of Kin* 1942; *The End of the River* 1947; *Affair in Trinidad* 1952; *Blackbeard the Pirate* 1952; *The Crimson Pirate* 1952; *The Snows of Kilimanjaro* 1952; *The Desert Rats* 1953; *Houdini* 1953; *The Robe* 1953; *Bengal Brigade* 1954; *The Black Shield of Falworth* 1954; *Knock on Wood* 1954; *Diane* 1955; *Lady Godiva* 1955; *Love Is a Many-Splendored Thing* 1955; *Band of Angels* 1957; *Istanbul* 1957; *Witness for the Prosecution* 1957; *Darby's Rangers* 1958; *The 7th Voyage of Sinbad* 1958; *The Canadians* 1961; *Jack the Giant Killer* 1962; *Hawaii* 1966
Thaw, John (1942–2002) *The Bofors Gun* 1968; *Praise Marx and Pass the Ammunition* 1968; *The Last Grenade* 1970; *Dr Phibes Rises Again* 1972; *Sweeney!* 1976; *Sweeney 2* 1978; *Business as Usual* 1987; *Cry Freedom* 1987; *Chaplin* 1992
Thaxter, Phyllis (1921–) *Thirty Seconds over Tokyo* 1944; *Bewitched* 1945; *Week-End at the Waldorf* 1945; *Living in a Big Way* 1947; *The Sea of Grass* 1947; *Blood on the Moon* 1948; *Act of Violence* 1949; *The Breaking Point* 1950; *No Man of Her Own* 1950; *Come Fill the Cup* 1951; *Fort Worth* 1951; *Jim Thorpe – All-American* 1951; *She's Working Her Way through College* 1952; *Springfield Rifle* 1952; *Women's Prison* 1955; *The World of Henry Orient* 1964
Thayer, Lorna (1919–2005) *Jennifer* 1953; *The Beast with a Million Eyes* 1955
Theron, Charlize (1975–) *That Thing You Do!* 1996; *2 Days in the Valley* 1996; *The Devil's Advocate* 1997; *Trial and Error* 1997; *Celebrity* 1998; *Mighty Joe Young* 1998; *The Astronaut's Wife* 1999; *The Cider House Rules* 1999; *Deception* 2000; *The Legend of Bagger Vance* 2000; *Men of Honor* 2000; *The Yards* 2000; *The Curse of the Jade Scorpion* 2001; *15 Minutes* 2001; *Sweet November* 2001; *Trapped* 2002; *The Italian Job* 2003; *The Life and Death of Peter Sellers* 2003; *Monster* 2003
Theroux, Justin (1971–) *Romy and Michele's High School Reunion* 1997; *American Psycho* 2000; *The Broken Hearts Club: a Romantic Comedy* 2000; *Mulholland Drive* 2001; *Charlie's Angels: Full Throttle* 2003; *Our House* 2003
Thesiger, Ernest (1879–1961) *The Old Dark House* 1932; *The Ghoul* 1933; *Night of the Party* 1934; *Bride of Frankenstein* 1935; *The Man Who Could Work Miracles* 1936; *Caesar and Cleopatra* 1945; *Beware of Pity* 1946; *The Ghosts of Berkeley Square* 1947; *The Man Within* 1947; *The Brass Monkey* 1948; *The Man in the White Suit* 1951; *The Robe* 1953; *Father Brown* 1954; *Quentin Durward* 1955; *Value for Money* 1955; *Who Done It?* 1956; *The Battle of the Sexes* 1960; *Sons and Lovers* 1960
Thévenet, Virginie *Full Moon in Paris* 1984; *Le Cri du Hibou* 1987
Thewlis, David (1963–) *Vroom* 1988; *Resurrected* 1989; *Life Is Sweet* 1990; *Naked* 1993; *Black Beauty* 1994; *Restoration* 1995; *Total Eclipse* 1995; *DragonHeart* 1996; *The Island of Dr Moreau* 1996; *James and the Giant Peach* 1996; *American Perfekt* 1997; *Seven Years in Tibet* 1997; *Besieged* 1998; *Divorcing Jack* 1998; *The Miracle Maker* 1999; *Whatever Happened to Harold Smith?* 1999; *Gangster No 1* 2000; *Goodbye Charlie Bright* 2000; *Timeline* 2003; *Harry Potter and the Prisoner of Azkaban* 2004; *Kingdom of Heaven* 2005
Thibeau, Jack *Escape from Alcatraz* 1979; *Action Jackson* 1988
Thiele, Hertha (1908–1984) *Girls in Uniform* 1931; *Kühle Wampe* 1931
Thieriot, Max (1988–) *Catch That Kid* 2004; *The Pacifier* 2005
Thiess, Ursula (1924–) *Bengal Brigade* 1954; *The Iron Glove* 1954; *The Americano* 1955; *Bandido* 1956
Thiessen, Tiffani-Amber aka **Thiessen, Tiffani** (1974–) *Son in Law* 1993; *From Dusk till Dawn II: Texas Blood Money* 1999; *ivansxtc.* 1999; *Love Stinks* 1999; *The Ladies Man* 2000; *Shriek If You Know What I Did Last Friday the 13th* 2000; *Hollywood Ending* 2002
Thigpen, Lynne (1948–2003) *Godspell* 1973; *Lean on Me* 1989; *Blankman* 1994; *The Paper* 1994; *Night Ride Home* 1999; *Novocaine* 2001; *Anger Management* 2003
Thimig, Hermann (1890–1982) *The Threepenny Opera* 1931; *Viktor und Viktoria* 1933
Thinnes, Roy (1936–) *Journey to the Far Side of the Sun* 1969; *The Hindenburg* 1975
Thomas, Ben aka **Thomas, Benny** *Toomorrow* 1970; *Hotel Sorrento* 1994
Thomas, Damien (1942–) *Twins of Evil* 1971; *Tiffany Jones* 1973; *The Message* 1976; *Pirates* 1986
Thomas, Danny (1914–1991) *The Unfinished Dance* 1947; *Call Me Mister* 1951; *I'll See You in My Dreams* 1951; *The Jazz Singer* 1952; *Journey back to Oz* 1964
Thomas, Dave (1949–) *Strange Brew* 1983; *My Man Adam* 1985; *Love at Stake* 1987; *Moving* 1988; *Cold Sweat* 1993; *Pippi Longstocking* 1997; *Brother Bear* 2003
Thomas, Eddie Kaye (1980–) *American Pie* 1999; *Freddy Got Fingered* 2001; *Stolen Summer* 2002; *American Pie: the Wedding* 2003; *Harold & Kumar Get the Munchies* 2004
Thomas, Frank M (1889–1989) *Behind the Headlines* 1937; *Criminal Lawyer* 1937; *Danger Patrol* 1937; *Law of the Underworld* 1938; *Smashing the Rackets* 1938; *Among the Living* 1941; *The Great Man's Lady* 1942
Thomas, Frankie (1921–) *Nancy Drew – Detective* 1938; *Angels Wash Their Faces* 1939; *One Foot in Heaven* 1941; *Always in My Heart* 1942; *The Major and the Minor* 1942
Thomas, Henry (1971–) *Raggedy Man* 1981; *ET the Extra-Terrestrial* 1982; *Cloak and Dagger* 1984; *Misunderstood* 1984; *Frog Dreaming* 1985; *Valmont* 1989; *Psycho IV: the Beginning* 1990; *Fire in the Sky* 1993; *Legends of the Fall* 1994; *Indictment: the McMartin Trial* 1995; *Hijacking Hollywood* 1997; *Niagara Niagara* 1997; *Happy Face Murders* 1999; *All the Pretty Horses* 2000; *Gangs of New York* 2002; *I Capture the Castle* 2002; *I'm with Lucy* 2002
Thomas, Jake (1990–) *AI: Artificial Intelligence* 2001; *The Lizzie McGuire Movie* 2003
Thomas, Jameson (1888–1939) *The Farmer's Wife* 1928; *Piccadilly* 1929; *Three Wise Girls* 1932; *It Happened One Night* 1934; *The Moonstone* 1934; *Charlie Chan in Egypt* 1935; *The Last Outpost* 1935
Thomas, Jay (1948–) *The Gig* 1985; *Mr Holland's Opus* 1995; *A Smile like Yours* 1997
Thomas, Jonathan Taylor (1981–) *The Lion King* 1994; *Man of the House* 1994; *Tom and Huck* 1995; *The Adventures of Pinocchio* 1996; *Wild America* 1997; *I'll Be Home for Christmas* 1998; *Walking across Egypt* 1999
Thomas, Khleo (1989–) *Holes* 2003; *Walking Tall* 2004
Thomas, Leonard *Bad Lieutenant* 1992; *Dangerous Game* 1993; *DROP Squad* 1994
Thomas, Marlo (1938–) *Jenny* 1969; *Thieves* 1977; *Nobody's Child* 1986; *In the Spirit* 1990; *Ultimate Betrayal* 1994
Thomas, Philip Michael aka **Thomas, Philip** (1949–) *Book of Numbers* 1972; *Mr Ricco* 1975; *The Wizard of Speed and Time* 1988; *Extralarge: Moving Target* 1990
Thomas, Rachel (1905–1995) *The Proud Valley* 1940; *Undercover* 1943; *The Captive Heart* 1946; *Blue Scar* 1947; *Valley of Song* 1953
Thomas, Richard (1951–) *Last Summer* 1969; *Winning* 1969; *Red Sky at Morning* 1971; *The Todd Killings* 1971; *You'll Like My Mother* 1972; *September 30, 1955* 1977; *All Quiet on the Western Front* 1979; *Battle beyond the Stars* 1980; *Stalking Laura* 1993; *Death in Small Doses* 1995; *What Love Sees* 1996; *Fortune Hunters* 1999; *Wonder Boys* 2000
Thomas, Robin (1961–) *About Last Night...* 1986; *Summer School* 1987; *Amityville Dollhouse* 1996; *Star Maps* 1997; *Clockstoppers* 2002
Thomas, Sean Patrick (1970–) *Dracula 2001* 2000; *Save the Last Dance* 2000; *Barbershop* 2002; *Halloween: Resurrection* 2002; *Barbershop 2: Back in Business* 2004
Thomas, Trevor *Black Joy* 1977; *Sheena* 1984
Thomason, Marsha (1976–) *Black Knight* 2001; *Pure* 2002; *The Haunted Mansion* 2003
Thomassin, Florence *Mina Tannenbaum* 1993; *Elisa* 1994; *Rien à Faire* 1999
Thomerson, Tim aka **Thomerson, Timothy** (1945–) *Remember My Name* 1978; *Carny* 1980; *Fade to Black* 1980; *Take This Job and Shove It* 1981; *Jekyll and Hyde... Together Again* 1982; *Uncommon Valor* 1983; *Rhinestone* 1984; *Iron Eagle* 1985; *Trancers* 1985; *Volunteers* 1985; *Near Dark* 1987; *Cherry 2000* 1988; *The Incredible Hulk Returns* 1988; *Who's Harry Crumb?* 1989; *Trancers II: The Return of Jack Deth* 1991; *Brain Smasher... a Love Story* 1993; *Die Watching* 1993; *The Harvest* 1993; *Nemesis* 1993; *Fleshtone* 1994; *American Yakuza 2: Back to Back* 1996; *Too Hard to Die* 1998; *Red Team* 1999; *They Crawl* 2001
Thompson, Al *A Walk to Remember* 2002; *Love Don't Cost a Thing* 2003
Thompson, Beatrix *Dreyfus* 1931; *The Old Curiosity Shop* 1934
Thompson, Bill (1913–1971) *Here We Go Again* 1942; *Alice in Wonderland* 1951; *Peter Pan* 1953; *Toot, Whistle, Plunk and Boom* 1953; *Lady and the Tramp* 1955; *Sleeping Beauty* 1959
Thompson, Brian (1962–) *You Talkin' to Me?* 1987; *AWOL* 1990; *Hired to Kill* 1990; *Moon 44* 1990; *Life Stinks* 1991; *Ted & Venus* 1991; *DragonHeart* 1996; *The Order* 2001
Thompson, Carlos (1923–1990) *Fort Algiers* 1953; *Valley of the*

Kings 1954; *Magic Fire* 1956; *Raw Wind in Eden* 1958; *La Vie de Château* 1965
Thompson, Christopher *La Bûche* 1999; *The Luzhin Defence* 2000
Thompson, Derek (1948–) *The Long Good Friday* 1979; *Resurrection Man* 1997
Thompson, Emma (1959–) *Henry V* 1989; *The Tall Guy* 1989; *Dead Again* 1991; *Impromptu* 1991; *Howards End* 1992; *Peter's Friends* 1992; *In the Name of the Father* 1993; *Much Ado about Nothing* 1993; *The Remains of the Day* 1993; *Junior* 1994; *Carrington* 1995; *Sense and Sensibility* 1995; *The Winter Guest* 1996; *Judas Kiss* 1998; *Primary Colors* 1998; *Maybe Baby* 1999; *Wit* 2001; *Treasure Planet* 2002; *Imagining Argentina* 2003; *Love Actually* 2003; *Harry Potter and the Prisoner of Azkaban* 2004
Thompson, Eric (1929–1982) *Private Potter* 1963; *Dougal and the Blue Cat* 1970; *One Day in the Life of Ivan Denisovich* 1971
Thompson, Fred Dalton (1942–) *No Way Out* 1986; *Feds* 1988; *Days of Thunder* 1990; *Curly Sue* 1991; *Thunderheart* 1992; *Barbarians at the Gate* 1993; *In the Line of Fire* 1993; *Baby's Day Out* 1994
Thompson, Jack (1940–) *Petersen* 1974; *Sunday Too Far Away* 1974; *Caddie* 1976; *Mad Dog* 1976; *The Chant of Jimmie Blacksmith* 1978; *Breaker Morant* 1979; *The Club* 1980; *The Earthling* 1980; *Bad Blood* 1982; *The Man from Snowy River* 1982; *Merry Christmas Mr Lawrence* 1982; *Burke and Wills* 1985; *Flesh + Blood* 1985; *Ground Zero* 1987; *Ruby Cairo* 1992; *Turtle Beach* 1992; *Wind* 1992; *A Far Off Place* 1993; *Flight of the Albatross* 1995; *The Sum of Us* 1995; *Broken Arrow* 1996; *Last Dance* 1996; *Excess Baggage* 1997; *Midnight in the Garden of Good and Evil* 1997; *The Magic Pudding* 2000; *Original Sin* 2001; *The Assassination of Richard Nixon* 2004
Thompson, Kay (1902–1998) *Funny Face* 1957; *Tell Me That You Love Me, Junie Moon* 1970
Thompson, Kenan (1978–) *Heavyweights* 1995; *Good Burger* 1997; *Love Don't Cost a Thing* 2003; *Fat Albert* 2004
Thompson, Lea (1961–) *All the Right Moves* 1983; *Jaws III* 1983; *Red Dawn* 1984; *The Wild Life* 1984; *Yellow Pages* 1984; *Back to the Future* 1985; *Howard, a New Breed of Hero* 1986; *SpaceCamp* 1986; *Some Kind of Wonderful* 1987; *Casual Sex?* 1988; *The Wizard of Loneliness* 1988; *Back to the Future Part II* 1989; *Nightbreaker* 1989; *Back to the Future Part III* 1990; *Article 99* 1992; *The Beverly Hillbillies* 1993; *Dennis* 1993; *The Unspoken Truth* 1995
Thompson, Marshall (1925–1992) *The Clock* 1945; *They Were Expendable* 1945; *Bad Bascomb* 1946; *The Secret Heart* 1946; *Words and Music* 1948; *Battleground* 1949; *Devil's Doorway* 1950; *Mystery Street* 1950; *The Tall Target* 1951; *My Six Convicts* 1952; *The Caddy* 1953; *Port of Hell* 1954; *Battle Taxi* 1955; *Crashout* 1955; *Cult of the Cobra* 1955; *Good Morning, Miss Dove* 1955; *To Hell and Back* 1955; *Fiend without a Face* 1957; *First Man into Space* 1958; *It! The Terror from beyond Space* 1958; *Around the World under the Sea* 1965; *Clarence, the Cross-Eyed Lion* 1965; *White Dog* 1981
Thompson, Peter M (1920–2001) *Santa Fe* 1951; *A Yank in Ermine* 1955
Thompson, Rex (1942–) *Her Twelve Men* 1954; *The Eddy Duchin Story* 1956; *The King and I* 1956; *The Day They Gave Babies Away* 1957
Thompson, Robert *Patrick* 1978; *Thirst* 1979
Thompson, Ross (1946–) *The Chain Reaction* 1980; *Boulevard of Broken Dreams* 1988
Thompson, Sada (1929–) *Desperate Characters* 1971; *The Entertainer* 1975; *Indictment: the McMartin Trial* 1995
Thompson, Scott (1959–) *Kids in the Hall: Brain Candy* 1996; *Hijacking Hollywood* 1997; *The Pacifier* 2005
Thompson, Sophie (1962–) *Twenty-One* 1991; *Persuasion* 1995; *Emma* 1996; *Dancing at Lughnasa* 1998; *Relative Values* 2000; *Fat Slags* 2004
Thompson, Susanna (1958–) *Little Giants* 1994; *Ghosts of Mississippi* 1996; *Dragonfly* 2002
Thomsen, Ulrich (1963–) *Festen* 1998; *The Weight of Water* 2000; *Killing Me Softly* 2001; *Mostly Martha* 2001; *Max* 2002; *The Inheritance* 2003; *Brothers* 2004
Thomsett, Sally (1950–) *The Railway Children* 1970; *Baxter* 1973; *Man about the House* 1974
Thomson, John *The Girl with Brains in Her Feet* 1997; *Re-inventing Eddie* 2002
Thomson, Kenneth (1899–1967) *The Broadway Melody* 1929; *Just Imagine* 1930; *Lawyer Man* 1932; *Movie Crazy* 1932; *The Little Giant* 1933
Thomson, Kim (1960–) *Stealing Heaven* 1988; *The Tall Guy* 1989
Thomson, Pat (1930–1992) *Malpractice* 1989; *Strictly Ballroom* 1992
Thomson, R H (1947–) *Ticket to Heaven* 1981; *Max* 1994; *Murder at My Door* 1996; *The Twilight of the Ice Nymphs* 1997; *Bone Daddy* 1998
Thor, Larry (1916–1976) *Five Guns West* 1955; *The Amazing Colossal Man* 1957
Thorburn, June (1931–1967) *Children Galore* 1954; *Delayed Action* 1954; *Orders Are Orders* 1954; *The Hornet's Nest* 1955; *Touch and Go* 1955; *True as a Turtle* 1956; *Rooney* 1958; *tom thumb* 1958; *The Three Worlds of Gulliver* 1959; *Don't Bother to Knock* 1961; *Fury at Smugglers Bay* 1961; *The Scarlet Blade* 1963; *Master Spy* 1964
Thordsen, Kelly (1917–1978) *The Fearmakers* 1958; *Boy, Did I Get a Wrong Number* 1966; *The Ugly Dachshund* 1966; *The Parallax View* 1974
Thornbury, Bill *Phantasm* 1978; *Phantasm III – Lord of the Dead* 1994
Thorndike, Sybil (1882–1976) *Hindle Wakes* 1931; *Tudor Rose* 1936; *Major Barbara* 1941; *Nicholas Nickleby* 1947; *Britannia Mews* 1949; *Stage Fright* 1949; *Gone to Earth* 1950; *The Prince and the Showgirl* 1957; *Alive and Kicking* 1958; *Shake Hands with the Devil* 1959; *Smiley Gets a Gun* 1959; *The Big Gamble* 1961
Thorne-Smith, Courtney (1967–) *Lucas* 1986; *Summer School* 1987; *Side Out* 1990; *Chairman of the Board* 1998
Thornton, Billy Bob (1955–) *One False Move* 1992; *Killing Box* 1993; *Trouble Bound* 1993; *Floundering* 1994; *On Deadly Ground* 1994; *Sling Blade* 1995; *The Stars Fell on Henrietta* 1995; *The Winner* 1996; *The Apostle* 1997; *U Turn* 1997; *Armageddon* 1998; *Homegrown* 1998; *Primary Colors* 1998; *A Simple Plan* 1998; *Pushing Tin* 1999; *South of Heaven, West of Hell* 2000; *Bandits* 2001; *The Man Who Wasn't There* 2001; *Monster's Ball* 2001; *Levity* 2002; *Bad Santa* 2003; *Intolerable Cruelty* 2003; *Love Actually* 2003; *The Alamo* 2004; *Friday Night Lights* 2004
Thornton, David *Off and Running* 1991; *Home Alone 3* 1997; *High Art* 1998; *Hush* 1998; *XX/XY* 2001; *Swept Away* 2002; *The Notebook* 2003
Thornton, Frank (1921–) *Gonks Go Beat* 1965; *Side by Side* 1975; *Are You Being Served?* 1977
Thornton, Sigrid (1959–) *The Man from Snowy River* 1982; *The Lighthorsemen* 1987; *Slate, Wyn & Me* 1987; *Return to Snowy River* 1988; *Over the Hill* 1992; *Love in Ambush* 1997
Thorpe, George (1891–1961) *Meet Me at Dawn* 1946; *Quiet Weekend* 1946; *Daughter of Darkness* 1948; *The Man on the Eiffel Tower* 1949; *Father's Doing Fine* 1952
Thorsen, Sven-Ole (1944–) *Abraxas* 1991; *Relentless 2: Dead On* 1991; *The Viking Sagas* 1995
Thorson, Linda (1947–) *Joey* 1985; *Walls of Glass* 1985; *The Other Sister* 1999
Threlfall, David (1953–) *When the Whales Came* 1989; *The Russia House* 1990; *Chunky Monkey* 2001; *Conspiracy* 2001
Thring, Frank (1926–1994) *The Vikings* 1958; *Ben-Hur* 1959; *El Cid* 1961; *King of Kings* 1961; *The Man from Hong Kong* 1975; *Mad Dog* 1976; *Mad Max beyond Thunderdome* 1985; *The Howling III* 1987
Thuillier, Luc *Monsieur Hire* 1989; *The Old Lady Who Walked in the Sea* 1991
Thulin, Ingrid *aka* **Tulean, Ingrid** (1926–2004) *Foreign Intrigue* 1956; *So Close to Life* 1957; *Wild Strawberries* 1957; *The Magician* 1958; *The Four Horsemen of the Apocalypse* 1962; *Winter Light* 1962; *The Silence* 1963; *Return from the Ashes* 1965; *La Guerre Est Finie* 1966; *The Hour of the Wolf* 1967; *The Damned* 1969; *The Rite* 1969; *The Short Night of the Glass Dolls* 1971; *Cries and Whispers* 1972; *Moses* 1975; *The Trap* 1975; *The Cassandra Crossing* 1976; *Salon Kitty* 1976; *After the Rehearsal* 1984
Thundercloud, Chief (1899–1955) *Annie Oakley* 1935; *Geronimo* 1939; *Colt .45* 1950
Thurman, Bill (1920–1995) *The Evictors* 1979; *Alamo Bay* 1985; *Hawken's Breed* 1989
Thurman, Uma (1970–) *Kiss Daddy Good Night* 1987; *The Adventures of Baron Munchausen* 1988; *Dangerous Liaisons* 1988; *Johnny Be Good* 1988; *Henry & June* 1990; *Robin Hood* 1990; *Where the Heart Is* 1990; *Final Analysis* 1992; *Jennifer Eight* 1992; *Mad Dog and Glory* 1992; *Even Cowgirls Get the Blues* 1993; *A Month by the Lake* 1994; *Pulp Fiction* 1994; *Beautiful Girls* 1996; *The Truth about Cats and Dogs* 1996; *Batman and Robin* 1997; *Gattaca* 1997; *Les Misérables* 1997; *The Avengers* 1998; *Sweet and Lowdown* 1999; *The Golden Bowl* 2000; *Vatel* 2000; *Tape* 2001; *Hysterical Blindness* 2002; *Kill Bill Vol 1* 2003; *Kill Bill Vol 2* 2003; *Paycheck* 2003; *Be Cool* 2005
Thursfield, Sophie *The Girl in a Swing* 1988; *Sister My Sister* 1994
Thurston, Carol (1923–1969) *The Conspirators* 1944; *The Story of Dr Wassell* 1944; *China Sky* 1945
Ti Lung (1946–) *Shatter* 1974; *A Better Tomorrow* 1986; *A Better Tomorrow II* 1987
Tibbs, Casey (1929–1990) *Bronco Buster* 1952; *Wild Heritage* 1958
Ticotin, Rachel (1958–) *Fort Apache, the Bronx* 1981; *Critical Condition* 1987; *Total Recall* 1990; *FX 2* 1991; *One Good Cop* 1991; *Falling Down* 1992; *Thicker than Blood* 1993; *Don Juan DeMarco* 1995; *Steal Big, Steal Little* 1995; *Con Air* 1997; *First Time Felon* 1997; *Turbulence* 1997; *Something's Gotta Give* 2003; *Man on Fire* 2004; *The Sisterhood of the Traveling Pants* 2005
Tidblad, Inga (1901–1975) *Intermezzo* 1936; *Foreign Intrigue* 1956
Tidof, Max (1960–) *Forget Mozart* 1985; *Who's Afraid of Red Yellow Blue?* 1990; *Making Up* 1992
Tien, James *The Big Boss* 1971; *Fist of Fury* 1972
Tiernan, Andrew *Edward II* 1991; *As You Like It* 1992; *Playing God* 1997; *The Criminal* 1999; *Mr In-Between* 2001
Tiernan, Tommy *Hold Back the Night* 1999; *About Adam* 2000
Tierney, Gene (1920–1991) *Hudson's Bay* 1940; *The Return of Frank James* 1940; *Belle Starr* 1941; *The Shanghai Gesture* 1941; *Sundown* 1941; *Tobacco Road* 1941; *China Girl* 1942; *Rings on Her Fingers* 1942; *Son of Fury* 1942; *Heaven Can Wait* 1943; *Laura* 1944; *A Bell for Adano* 1945; *Leave Her to Heaven* 1945; *Dragonwyck* 1946; *The Razor's Edge* 1946; *The Ghost and Mrs Muir* 1947; *The Iron Curtain* 1948; *That Wonderful Urge* 1948; *Whirlpool* 1949; *Night and the City* 1950; *Where the Sidewalk Ends* 1950; *Close to My Heart* 1951; *The Mating Season* 1951; *On the Riviera* 1951; *The Secret of Convict Lake* 1951; *Plymouth Adventure* 1952; *Way of a Gaucho* 1952; *Never Let Me Go* 1953; *Personal Affair* 1953; *Black Widow* 1954; *The Egyptian* 1954; *The Left Hand of God* 1955; *Advise and Consent* 1962; *Toys in the Attic* 1963; *The Pleasure Seekers* 1964
Tierney, Jacob (1979–) *Josh and SAM* 1993; *The Neon Bible* 1995; *This Is My Father* 1999; *Poor White Trash* 2000
Tierney, Lawrence (1919–2002) *Youth Runs Wild* 1944; *Dillinger* 1945; *Badman's Territory* 1946; *San Quentin* 1946; *The Devil Thumbs a Ride* 1947; *Lady of Deceit* 1947; *Bodyguard* 1948; *Shakedown* 1950; *Best of the Badmen* 1951; *The Greatest Show on Earth* 1952; *The Female Jungle* 1955; *Custer of the West* 1968; *Abduction* 1975; *The Kirlian Witness* 1978; *Midnight* 1980; *Silver Bullet* 1985; *Tough Guys Don't Dance* 1987; *Reservoir Dogs* 1991; *The Runestone* 1991
Tierney, Maura (1965–) *Dead Women in Lingerie* 1990; *Liar Liar* 1997; *Forces of Nature* 1998; *Primary Colors* 1998; *Instinct* 1999; *Oxygen* 1999; *Insomnia* 2002; *Welcome to Mooseport* 2004
Tiffin, Pamela (1942–) *One, Two, Three* 1961; *Come Fly with Me* 1962; *State Fair* 1962; *For Those Who Think Young* 1964; *The Pleasure Seekers* 1964; *The Hallelujah Trail* 1965; *Harper* 1966; *Viva Max!* 1969
Tigar, Kenneth *Creator* 1985; *The Betty Ford Story* 1987; *Snapdragon* 1993; *Little Bigfoot* 1995
Tighe, Kevin (1944–) *Matewan* 1987; *K-9* 1989; *Road House* 1989; *Another 48 HRS* 1990; *School Ties* 1992; *Geronimo: an American Legend* 1993; *I Love a Man in Uniform* 1993; *What's Eating Gilbert Grape* 1993; *Men of War* 1995; *Scorpion Spring* 1995; *Race the Sun* 1996
Tikhonov, Vyacheslav (1928–) *War and Peace* 1966; *Burnt by the Sun* 1995
Tilden, Leif (1964–) *Teenage Mutant Ninja Turtles* 1990; *Teenage Mutant Ninja Turtles II: the Secret of the Ooze* 1991
Till, Jenny *Theatre of Death* 1966; *A Challenge for Robin Hood* 1967
Tiller, Nadja (1929–) *The Rough and the Smooth* 1959; *The Monk* 1972
Tilly, Grant *Beyond Reasonable Doubt* 1980; *Treasure of the Yankee Zephyr* 1981; *Carry Me Back* 1982; *Savage Islands* 1983; *Warm Nights on a Slow Moving Train* 1986
Tilly, Jennifer (1958–) *No Small Affair* 1984; *Moving Violations* 1985; *He's My Girl* 1987; *High Spirits* 1988; *Johnny Be Good* 1988; *Remote Control* 1988; *The Fabulous Baker Boys* 1989; *Far from Home* 1989; *Let It Ride* 1989; *Scorchers* 1991; *Shadow of the Wolf* 1992; *Made in America* 1993; *Bullets over Broadway* 1994; *Embrace of the Vampire* 1994; *The Getaway* 1994; *The Pompatus of Love* 1995; *American Strays* 1996; *Bound* 1996; *House Arrest* 1996; *Liar Liar* 1997; *The Wrong Guy* 1997; *Bride of Chucky* 1998; *Music from Another Room* 1998; *Relax... It's Just Sex* 1998; *Bartok the Magnificent* 1999; *Stuart Little* 1999; *Dancing at the Blue Iguana* 2000; *Hide and Seek* 2000; *Play It to the Bone* 2000; *The Cat's Meow* 2001; *Monsters, Inc* 2001; *The Haunted Mansion* 2003; *Home on the Range* 2004; *Seed of Chucky* 2004
Tilly, Meg (1960–) *One Dark Night* 1982; *Tex* 1982; *The Big Chill* 1983; *Psycho II* 1983; *Impulse* 1984; *Agnes of God* 1985; *Off Beat* 1986; *The Girl in a Swing* 1988; *Masquerade* 1988; *Valmont* 1989; *The Two Jakes* 1990; *Leaving Normal* 1992; *Body Snatchers* 1993; *Sleep with Me* 1994
Tilton, Charlene (1958–) *Border Shootout* 1990; *Problem Child 2* 1991; *The Silence of the Hams* 1993
Tilvern, Alan (1920–2003) *The Bespoke Overcoat* 1955; *Chase a Crooked Shadow* 1957; *The Siege of Pinchgut* 1959; *Danger by My Side* 1962; *Shadow of Fear* 1963; *Who Framed Roger Rabbit* 1988
Timothy, Christopher (1940–) *Here We Go round the Mulberry Bush* 1967; *Alfred the Great* 1969; *The Virgin Soldiers* 1969
Timsit, Patrick (1959–) *La Crise* 1992; *Marquise* 1997
Tingwell, Charles *aka* **Tingwell, Charles "Bud"** (1923–) *Bitter Springs* 1950; *Kangaroo* 1952; *The Desert Rats* 1953; *Bobbikins* 1959; *Life in Emergency Ward 10* 1959; *Murder She Said* 1961; *Murder at the Gallop* 1963; *Murder Ahoy* 1964; *Murder Most Foul* 1964; *The Secret of Blood Island* 1964; *Dracula – Prince of Darkness* 1965; *Summerfield* 1977; *Breaker Morant* 1979; *Windrider* 1986; *A Cry in the Dark* 1988; *Innocence* 2000
Tinti, Gabriele (1932–1991) *The Legend of Lylah Clare* 1968; *Delusions of Grandeur* 1971
Tirelli, Jaime *Rooftops* 1989; *Girlfight* 2000
Tissier, Jean (1896–1973) *And God Created Woman* 1956; *The Hunchback of Notre Dame* 1956; *Dead Run* 1967; *The Widow Couderc* 1971
Tissot, Alice (1895–1971) *An Italian Straw Hat* 1927; *Madame Bovary* 1933
To, Chapman *Infernal Affairs* 2002; *Infernal Affairs II* 2003
Tobey, Kenneth (1919–2002) *The Thing from Another World* 1951; *Angel Face* 1953; *The Beast from 20,000 Fathoms* 1953; *The Bigamist* 1953; *Down Three Dark Streets* 1954; *Davy Crockett, King of the Wild Frontier* 1955; *It Came from beneath the Sea* 1955; *Davy Crockett and the River Pirates* 1956; *The Great Locomotive Chase* 1956; *The Wings of Eagles* 1957; *Cry Terror* 1958; *Seven Ways from Sundown* 1960; *X-15* 1961; *40 Guns to Apache Pass* 1966; *Billy Jack* 1971; *Dirty Mary Crazy Larry* 1974; *Strange Invaders* 1983; *Desire & Hell at Sunset Motel* 1991
Tobias, George (1901–1980) *Maisie* 1939; *East of the River* 1940; *Music in My Heart* 1940; *Saturday's Children* 1940; *Torrid Zone* 1940; *Affectionately Yours* 1941; *The Bride Came COD* 1941; *Out of the Fog* 1941; *Sergeant York* 1941; *The Strawberry Blonde* 1941; *Captains of the Clouds* 1942; *My Sister Eileen* 1942; *Yankee Doodle Dandy* 1942; *Air Force* 1943; *Mission to Moscow* 1943; *This Is the Army* 1943; *Between Two Worlds* 1944; *Make Your Own Bed* 1944; *The Mask of Dimitrios* 1944; *Passage to Marseille* 1944; *Objective, Burma!* 1945; *Nobody Lives Forever* 1946; *My Wild Irish Rose* 1947; *Sinbad the Sailor* 1947; *The Judge Steps Out* 1949; *The Set-Up* 1949; *Rawhide* 1951; *Ten Tall Men* 1951; *The Glenn Miller Story* 1953; *Seven Little*

Foys 1955; *Silk Stockings* 1957; *A New Kind of Love* 1963; *Bullet for a Badman* 1964
Tobias, Oliver (1947–) *Romance of a Horse Thief* 1971; *The Stud* 1978; *Arabian Adventure* 1979; *A Nightingale Sang in Berkeley Square* 1979; *The Wicked Lady* 1983; *Mata Hari* 1985; *The Brylcreem Boys* 1996; *Darkness Falls* 1998; *Grizzly Falls* 1999
Tobin, Dan (1910–1982) *The Big Clock* 1948; *The Velvet Touch* 1948
Tobin, Genevieve (1899–1995) *One Hour with You* 1932; *Easy to Love* 1934; *Kiss and Make-Up* 1934; *Success at Any Price* 1934; *The Case of the Lucky Legs* 1935; *The Woman in Red* 1935; *The Man in the Mirror* 1936; *The Petrified Forest* 1936; *Dramatic School* 1938; *Zaza* 1939; *No Time for Comedy* 1940
Tobin, Vivian (1904–2002) *The Sign of the Cross* 1932; *If I Were Free* 1933
Tobolowsky, Stephen (1951–) *Nobody's Fool* 1986; *Mississippi Burning* 1988; *Breaking In* 1989; *Great Balls of Fire!* 1989; *Roe vs Wade* 1989; *Bird on a Wire* 1990; *Funny about Love* 1990; *Thelma & Louise* 1991; *Accidental Hero* 1992; *Memoirs of an Invisible Man* 1992; *Single White Female* 1992; *Calendar Girl* 1993; *Groundhog Day* 1993; *Josh and SAM* 1993; *Murder in the First* 1994; *My Father the Hero* 1994; *Dr Jekyll and Ms Hyde* 1995; *The Glimmer Man* 1996; *Mr Magoo* 1997; *The Insider* 1999; *Memento* 2000; *The Prime Gig* 2000; *The Day the World Ended* 2001; *Freddy Got Fingered* 2001; *Love Liza* 2001; *The Country Bears* 2002; *Freaky Friday* 2003; *Garfield* 2004; *Little Black Book* 2004
Todd, Ann (1909–1993) *The Ghost Train* 1931; *The Return of Bulldog Drummond* 1934; *Things to Come* 1936; *The Squeaker* 1937; *South Riding* 1938; *Poison Pen* 1939; *Danny Boy* 1941; *Ships with Wings* 1942; *Perfect Strangers* 1945; *The Seventh Veil* 1945; *Daybreak* 1946; *Gaiety George* 1946; *The Paradine Case* 1947; *The Passionate Friends* 1948; *Madeleine* 1949; *The Sound Barrier* 1952; *The Green Scarf* 1954; *Time without Pity* 1957; *Taste of Fear* 1961; *The Son of Captain Blood* 1962; *The Fiend* 1971; *The Human Factor* 1979
Todd, Ann E *aka* **Todd, Ann** (1931–) *Intermezzo* 1939; *Zaza* 1939; *The Men in Her Life* 1941; *Remember the Day* 1941; *Dangerous Years* 1947; *Three Daring Daughters* 1948
Todd, Beverly (1946–) *Brother John* 1970; *Vice Squad* 1982; *The Ladies Club* 1986; *Clara's Heart* 1988; *Moving* 1988; *Lean on Me* 1989
Todd, Bob (1921–1992) *The Best of Benny Hill* 1974; *Confessions of a Pop Performer* 1975; *Ups and Downs of a Handyman* 1975
Todd, Hallie (1962–) *Sam's Son* 1984; *The Check Is in the Mail* 1986; *The Lizzie McGuire Movie* 2003
Todd, James (1908–1968) *Riders of the Purple Sage* 1931; *Torch Song* 1953; *The Wings of Eagles* 1957
Todd, Mabel (1907–1977) *The Cowboy and the Lady* 1938; *Garden of the Moon* 1938; *Gold Diggers in Paris* 1938
Todd, Richard (1919–) *The Hasty Heart* 1949; *The Interrupted Journey* 1949; *Stage Fright* 1949; *Portrait of Clare* 1950; *Lightning Strikes Twice* 1951; *The Story of Robin Hood and His Merrie Men* 1952; *The Sword and the Rose* 1952; *Venetian Bird* 1952; *Rob Roy, the Highland Rogue* 1953; *The Dam Busters* 1954; *Secrets d'Alcove* 1954; *A Man Called Peter* 1955; *The Virgin Queen* 1955; *D-Day the Sixth of June* 1956; *Marie Antoinette* 1956; *Yangtse Incident* 1956; *Chase a Crooked Shadow* 1957; *Saint Joan* 1957; *Danger Within* 1958; *Intent to Kill* 1958; *The Naked Earth* 1958; *The Long and the Short and the Tall* 1960; *Never Let Go* 1960; *The Boys* 1961; *Don't Bother to Knock* 1961; *The Longest Day* 1962; *The Very Edge* 1962; *Death Drums along the River* 1963; *The Battle of the Villa Fiorita* 1965; *Subterfuge* 1968; *Asylum* 1972; *House of the Long Shadows* 1983
Todd, Thelma (1905–1935) *Monkey Business* 1931; *Horse Feathers* 1932; *Speak Easily* 1932; *This Is the Night* 1932; *Bogus Bandits* 1933; *Counsellor-at-Law* 1933; *Sitting Pretty* 1933; *Palooka* 1934; *The Bohemian Girl* 1936
Todd, Tony (1952–) *Enemy Territory* 1987; *Night of the Living Dead* 1990; *Candyman* 1992; *Excessive Force* 1993; *Candyman: Farewell to the Flesh* 1995; *Bram Stoker's Shadowbuilder* 1997; *Wishmaster* 1997; *Candyman: Day of the Dead* 1999; *Le Secret* 2000
Todeschini, Bruno (1962–) *Those Who Love Me Can Take the Train* 1998; *Va Savoir* 2001; *Son Frère* 2003
Todoroki, Yukiko (1917–1967) *Sanshiro Sugata* 1943; *The Lady of Musashino* 1951
Todorovic, Bora (1930–) *Montenegro* 1981; *Time of the Gypsies* 1988
Todorovic, Srdjan (1965–) *Hey Babu Riba* 1986; *Underground* 1995; *Black Cat, White Cat* 1998
Tognazzi, Ugo (1922–1990) *RoGoPaG* 1962; *Barbarella* 1967; *Pigsty* 1969; *La Grande Bouffe* 1973; *La Cage aux Folles* 1978; *Viva Italia!* 1978; *La Cage aux Folles II* 1980; *The Tragedy of a Ridiculous Man* 1981; *La Cage aux Folles III: "Elles" Se Marient* 1985
Tolbin, Niall (1929–) *Eat the Peach* 1986; *Rawhead Rex* 1986; *Fools of Fortune* 1990; *The Nephew* 1997
Tokos, Lubor (1923–2003) *Invention of Destruction* 1958; *The Ear* 1969
Tokuda, Marilyn *Farewell to the King* 1988; *Cage* 1989
Tolan, Michael (1925–) *John and Mary* 1969; *The Lost Man* 1969; *All That Jazz* 1979
Toledo, Guillermo (1970–) *The Other Side of the Bed* 2002; *Only Human* 2004
Toler, Sidney (1874–1947) *Blonde Venus* 1932; *Blondie of the Follies* 1932; *The Phantom President* 1932; *Speak Easily* 1932; *The Call of the Wild* 1935; *Our Relations* 1936; *Double Wedding* 1937; *Charlie Chan at Treasure Island* 1939; *Charlie Chan in Reno* 1939; *Charlie Chan in Rio* 1941; *A Night to Remember* 1942; *White Savage* 1943; *Charlie Chan in The Chinese Cat* 1944; *Charlie Chan in the Secret Service* 1944; *Meeting at Midnight* 1944; *The Jade Mask* 1945; *The Red Dragon* 1945; *The Scarlet Clue* 1945; *The Shanghai Cobra* 1945; *Dangerous Money* 1946; *Dark Alibi* 1946; *The Trap* 1947
Toles-Bey, John *Weeds* 1987; *A Rage in Harlem* 1991; *Stockade* 1991; *Love Is a Gun* 1994; *Extreme Measures* 1996
Tolkan, James (1931–) *The River* 1984; *Opportunity Knocks* 1990; *Hangfire* 1991; *Boiling Point* 1993; *Love in Ambush* 1997
Tolo, Marilu (1944–) *Marriage – Italian Style* 1964; *Django Kill* 1967; *Bluebeard* 1972
Tolubeyev, Yuri (1905–1979) *Don Quixote* 1957; *Hamlet* 1964
Tom, David (1978–) *Stay Tuned* 1992; *Swing Kids* 1993
Tom, Lauren (1961–) *Nothing Lasts Forever* 1984; *The Joy Luck Club* 1993; *When a Man Loves a Woman* 1994; *Kidnapped* 1995; *Bad Santa* 2003
Tom, Nicholle (1978–) *Beethoven* 1992; *Beethoven's 2nd* 1993
Tombes, Andrew (1885–1976) *Checkers* 1937; *Down Mexico Way* 1941; *They All Kissed the Bride* 1942; *Can't Help Singing* 1944; *Frontier Gal* 1945; *The Devil Thumbs a Ride* 1947; *Oh, You Beautiful Doll* 1949
Tomei, Concetta (1945–) *The Betty Ford Story* 1987; *Don't Tell Mom the Babysitter's Dead* 1991
Tomei, Marisa (1964–) *The Toxic Avenger* 1985; *Playing for Keeps* 1986; *Oscar* 1991; *Zandalee* 1991; *Chaplin* 1992; *Equinox* 1992; *My Cousin Vinny* 1992; *Untamed Heart* 1993; *Only You* 1994; *The Paper* 1994; *Four Rooms* 1995; *The Perez Family* 1995; *Unhook the Stars* 1996; *Welcome to Sarajevo* 1997; *Slums of Beverly Hills* 1998; *The Watcher* 2000; *Animal Attraction* 2001; *In the Bedroom* 2001; *What Women Want* 2001; *The Guru* 2002; *Just a Kiss* 2002; *Anger Management* 2003; *The Wild Thornberrys Movie* 2003; *Alfie* 2004
Tomelty, Frances *Bullshot* 1983; *Lamb* 1985; *Bellman & True* 1987; *The Field* 1990; *High Boot Benny* 1993; *Monk Dawson* 1997
Tomelty, Joseph (1911–1995) *The Gentle Gunman* 1952; *The Oracle* 1952; *The Sound Barrier* 1952; *You're Only Young Twice* 1952; *Hobson's Choice* 1953; *Meet Mr Lucifer* 1953; *Devil Girl from Mars* 1954; *Happy Ever After* 1954; *Hell below Zero* 1954; *The Young Lovers* 1954; *Bedevilled* 1955; *Simba* 1955; *Timeslip* 1955; *Hell Is a City* 1959; *Upstairs and Downstairs* 1959; *The Day They Robbed the Bank of England* 1960; *The Black Torment* 1964
Tomikawa, Akihiro *Baby Cart at the River Styx* 1972; *Sword of Vengeance* 1972
Tomita, Tamlyn (1966–) *The Karate Kid Part II* 1986; *Come See the Paradise* 1990; *The Joy Luck Club* 1993; *Picture Bride* 1994; *The Day after Tomorrow* 2004
Tomlin, Lily (1939–) *Nashville* 1975; *The Late Show* 1977; *Moment by Moment* 1978; *Nine to Five* 1980; *The Incredible Shrinking Woman* 1981; *All of Me* 1984; *Big Business* 1988; *The Search for Signs of Intelligent Life in the Universe* 1991; *Shadows and Fog* 1991; *And the Band Played On* 1993; *The Beverly Hillbillies* 1993; *Short Cuts* 1993; *Blue in the Face* 1995; *The Celluloid Closet* 1995; *Flirting with Disaster* 1996; *Getting Away with Murder* 1996; *Krippendorf's Tribe* 1998; *Tea with Mussolini* 1998; *Disney's The Kid* 2000; *Orange County* 2001; *I ❤ Huckabees* 2004
Tomlinson, David (1917–2000) *Journey Together* 1944; *School for Secrets* 1946; *The Master of Bankdam* 1947; *Miranda* 1947; *Here Come the Huggetts* 1948; *My Brother's Keeper* 1948; *Sleeping Car to Trieste* 1948; *Vote for Huggett* 1948; *The Chiltern Hundreds* 1949; *Marry Me!* 1949; *So Long at the Fair* 1950; *The Wooden Horse* 1950; *Calling Bulldog Drummond* 1951; *Hotel Sahara* 1951; *Made in Heaven* 1952; *All for Mary* 1955; *Three Men in a Boat* 1956; *Carry On Admiral* 1957; *Further up the Creek* 1958; *Up the Creek* 1958; *Mary Poppins* 1964; *The Truth about Spring* 1964; *City under the Sea* 1965; *The Liquidator* 1966; *The Love Bug* 1969; *Bedknobs and Broomsticks* 1971; *Wombling Free* 1977; *Dominique* 1978; *The Water Babies* 1978; *The Fiendish Plot of Dr Fu Manchu* 1980
Tomlinson, Ricky (1939–) *Riff-Raff* 1991; *Raining Stones* 1993; *Butterfly Kiss* 1994; *Bob's Weekend* 1996; *Preaching to the Perverted* 1997; *Life Is All You Get* 1998; *Mojo* 1998; *Nasty Neighbours* 2000; *The 51st State* 2001; *Mike Bassett: England Manager* 2001; *Once upon a Time in the Midlands* 2002
Tompkins, Angel (1943–) *I Love My... Wife* 1970; *Prime Cut* 1972; *One Man Jury* 1978; *Crack House* 1989; *Relentless* 1989
Tompkins, Joan *Popi* 1969; *I Love My... Wife* 1970; *The Harness* 1971
Tompkinson, Stephen (1966–) *Brassed Off* 1996; *Hotel Splendide* 1999
Tone, Franchot (1905–1968) *The Wiser Sex* 1932; *Blonde Bombshell* 1933; *Dancing Lady* 1933; *Gabriel over the White House* 1933; *The Stranger's Return* 1933; *Today We Live* 1933; *The Girl from Missouri* 1934; *Sadie McKee* 1934; *The World Moves On* 1934; *Dangerous* 1935; *The Lives of a Bengal Lancer* 1935; *Mutiny on the Bounty* 1935; *Reckless* 1935; *The Gorgeous Hussy* 1936; *The King Steps Out* 1936; *Love on the Run* 1936; *Suzy* 1936; *The Bride Wore Red* 1937; *Man-Proof* 1937; *Quality Street* 1937; *They Gave Him a Gun* 1937; *Three Comrades* 1938; *Three Loves Has Nancy* 1938; *Fast and Furious* 1939; *Trail of the Vigilantes* 1940; *Nice Girl?* 1941; *Star Spangled Rhythm* 1942; *Five Graves to Cairo* 1943; *His Butler's Sister* 1943; *Pilot #5* 1943; *True to Life* 1943; *Dark Waters* 1944; *The Hour before the Dawn* 1944; *Phantom Lady* 1944; *Because of Him* 1946; *Her Husband's Affairs* 1947; *Every Girl Should Be Married* 1948; *Jigsaw* 1949; *The Man on the Eiffel Tower* 1949; *Here Comes the Groom* 1951; *Advise and Consent* 1962; *La Bonne Soupe* 1963; *Mickey One* 1965; *Nobody Runs Forever* 1968
Tonge, Philip (1897–1959) *Miracle on 34th Street* 1947; *Hans Christian Andersen* 1952; *Khyber Patrol* 1954; *Track of the Cat* 1954; *Macabre* 1958
Tono, Eijiro (1907–1994) *The Love of Sumako the Actress* 1947; *Hen in the Wind* 1948; *Early Spring* 1956; *Yojimbo* 1961
Tonoyama, Taiji (1915–1989) *The Island* 1961; *In the Realm of the Senses* 1976; *Tokyo Pop* 1988
Toomey, Regis (1898–1991) *Alibi* 1929; *The Finger Points* 1931; *Other Men's Women* 1931; *The Crowd Roars* 1932; *Shopworn* 1932; *Laughing at Life* 1933; *Murder on the Blackboard* 1934; *The Invisible Menace* 1938; *Thunder Afloat* 1939; *Arizona* 1940; *Dive Bomber* 1941; *They Died with Their Boots On* 1941; *The Forest Rangers* 1942; *Tennessee Johnson* 1942; *Betrayal from the East* 1945; *The Big Sleep* 1946; *Child of Divorce* 1946; *Magic Town* 1947; *The Boy with Green Hair* 1948; *Station West* 1948; *Beyond the Forest* 1949; *Frenchie* 1950; *Cry Danger* 1951; *My Pal Gus* 1952; *My Six Convicts* 1952; *Drums across the River* 1954; *The Human Jungle* 1954; *Guys and Dolls* 1955; *Warlock* 1959; *The Last Sunset* 1961; *Voyage to the Bottom of the Sea* 1961; *Gunn* 1967
Toone, Geoffrey (1910–2005) *Poison Pen* 1939; *The Man Between* 1953; *The King and I* 1956; *Zero Hour!* 1957; *Once More, with Feeling* 1959; *Dr Crippen* 1962; *Echo of Diana* 1963; *Doctor Who and the Daleks* 1965
Tootoosis, Gordon *Dan Candy's Law* 1973; *Legends of the Fall* 1994; *Alaska* 1996; *Black Point* 2001
Topart, Jean (1927–) *The Testament of Dr Cordelier* 1959; *Cop au Vin* 1984
Topol *aka* **Topol, Chaim** *aka* **Topol, Haym** (1935–) *Sallah* 1964; *Cast a Giant Shadow* 1966; *Before Winter Comes* 1968; *Fiddler on the Roof* 1971; *Follow Me* 1971; *Galileo* 1974; *Flash Gordon* 1980; *For Your Eyes Only* 1981; *Left Luggage* 1997
Toren, Marta (1926–1957) *Casbah* 1948; *Mystery Submarine* 1950; *One Way Street* 1950; *Sirocco* 1951; *Assignment – Paris* 1952; *The Man Who Watched Trains Go By* 1952
Torena, Juan (1898–1983) *A Message to Garcia* 1936; *An American Guerrilla in the Philippines* 1950
Torgov, Sarah *Meatballs* 1979; *American Gothic* 1987
Tormé, Mel (1925–1999) *Higher and Higher* 1943; *Good News* 1947; *Words and Music* 1948; *The Fearmakers* 1958; *The Big Operator* 1959; *Girls' Town* 1959; *The Private Lives of Adam and Eve* 1959; *Walk like a Dragon* 1960; *A Man Called Adam* 1966
Torn, Rip (1931–) *Time Limit* 1957; *Pork Chop Hill* 1959; *King of Kings* 1961; *Hero's Island* 1962; *Sweet Bird of Youth* 1962; *Critic's Choice* 1963; *The Cincinnati Kid* 1965; *One Spy Too Many* 1966; *You're a Big Boy Now* 1966; *Beach Red* 1967; *Beyond the Law* 1968; *Sol Madrid* 1968; *Payday* 1972; *Slaughter* 1972; *Birch Interval* 1976; *The Man Who Fell to Earth* 1976; *Coma* 1977; *The Private Files of J Edgar Hoover* 1977; *Heartland* 1979; *The Seduction of Joe Tynan* 1979; *One-Trick Pony* 1980; *The Beastmaster* 1982; *Jinxed!* 1982; *Cross Creek* 1983; *City Heat* 1984; *Flashpoint* 1984; *Misunderstood* 1984; *Songwriter* 1984; *Beer* 1985; *Summer Rental* 1985; *Extreme Prejudice* 1987; *Nadine* 1987; *Hit List* 1988; *Cold Feet* 1989; *Silence like Glass* 1989; *Beautiful Dreamers* 1990; *Defending Your Life* 1991; *Hard Promises* 1991; *RoboCop 3* 1993; *Where the Rivers Flow North* 1993; *Fixing the Shadow* 1994; *Heart of a Child* 1994; *Canadian Bacon* 1995; *For Better or Worse* 1995; *How to Make an American Quilt* 1995; *Down Periscope* 1996; *Hercules* 1997; *Men in Black* 1997; *Trial and Error* 1997; *Senseless* 1998; *The Insider* 1999; *Wonder Boys* 2000; *Freddy Got Fingered* 2001; *Men in Black 2* 2002; *Dodgeball: a True Underdog Story* 2004; *Welcome to Mooseport* 2004
Torocsik, Mari (1935–) *Merry-Go-Round* 1956; *The Boys of Paul Street* 1968; *Love* 1971; *Diary for My Father and Mother* 1990; *Rothschild's Violin* 1996
Torrence, David (1864–1951) *Tess of the Storm Country* 1922; *The Big Noise* 1928; *The Black Watch* 1929; *Disraeli* 1929; *The Devil to Pay* 1930; *Raffles* 1930; *The Bachelor Father* 1931; *A Successful Calamity* 1932; *The Masquerader* 1933; *What Every Woman Knows* 1934; *Bonnie Scotland* 1935; *Rulers of the Sea* 1939
Torrence, Ernest (1878–1933) *Tol'able David* 1921; *The Covered Wagon* 1923; *The Hunchback of Notre Dame* 1923; *Ruggles of Red Gap* 1923; *The Pony Express* 1925; *Mantrap* 1926; *The King of Kings* 1927; *Steamboat Bill, Jr* 1928; *Fighting Caravans* 1931; *Sporting Blood* 1931; *Sherlock Holmes* 1932; *I Cover the Waterfront* 1933
Torrens, Pip *Eminent Domain* 1991; *Valiant* 2005
Torrent, Ana (1966–) *The Spirit of the Beehive* 1973; *Cría Cuervos* 1975; *Blood and Sand* 1989; *Vacas* 1991; *Tesis* 1996
Torres, Fernanda (1965–) *Eu Sei Que Vou Te Amar* 1986; *Four Days in September* 1997; *Midnight* 1998
Torres, Liz (1947–) *America* 1986; *Rescue Me* 1991
Torres, Raquel (1908–1987) *White Shadows in the South Seas* 1928; *Under a Texas Moon* 1930; *Duck Soup* 1933
Torreton, Philippe (1965–) *L.627* 1992; *Ca Commence Aujourd'hui* 1999; *Monsieur N* 2003
Torry, Guy *Ride* 1998; *Trippin'* 1999; *The Animal* 2001; *Don't Say a Word* 2001
Torry, Joe *Poetic Justice* 1993; *Tales from the Hood* 1995
Tortosa, Silvia (1947–) *Horror Express* 1972; *La Señora* 1987
Torvay, José *aka* **Torvay, José I** (?–1973) *The Treasure of the*

Sierra Madre 1948; *The Brave Bulls* 1951; *The Hitch-Hiker* 1953; *Green Fire* 1954; *Bandido* 1956; *Battle Shock* 1956
Tosar, Luis (1971–) *Mondays in the Sun* 2002; *Take My Eyes* 2003
Toto (1898–1967) *Gold of Naples* 1954; *Big Deal on Madonna Street* 1958; *Hawks and Sparrows* 1966
Tottenham, Merle (1901–1959) *Night Must Fall* 1937; *Bank Holiday* 1938; *Room to Let* 1949
Totter, Audrey (1918–) *The Sailor Takes a Wife* 1945; *The Postman Always Rings Twice* 1946; *The Beginning or the End* 1947; *High Wall* 1947; *Lady in the Lake* 1947; *The Unsuspected* 1947; *The Saxon Charm* 1948; *Alias Nick Beal* 1949; *Any Number Can Play* 1949; *The Set-Up* 1949; *Tension* 1949; *The Blue Veil* 1951; *The Sellout* 1951; *Assignment – Paris* 1952; *My Pal Gus* 1952; *Man in the Dark* 1953; *The Woman They Almost Lynched* 1953; *A Bullet for Joey* 1955; *Women's Prison* 1955; *Jet Attack* 1958; *Harlow* 1965; *Chubasco* 1967
Toullatos, George *Firebird 2015 AD* 1980; *Heavy Metal* 1981; *Lena: My 100 Children* 1987; *Avenging Angelo* 2002
Toumanova, Tamara (1919–1996) *Days of Glory* 1944; *Tonight We Sing* 1953; *Deep in My Heart* 1954; *Invitation to the Dance* 1956; *Torn Curtain* 1966; *The Private Life of Sherlock Holmes* 1970
Tousey, Sheila *Thunderheart* 1992; *Silent Tongue* 1993
Toutain, Roland (1905–1977) *La Règle du Jeu* 1939; *Eternal Love* 1943
Tovey, Roberta (1953–) *The Piper's Tune* 1962; *Doctor Who and the Daleks* 1965; *A High Wind in Jamaica* 1965; *Daleks – Invasion Earth 2150 AD* 1966
Towb, Harry (1925–) *The Sleeping Tiger* 1954; *The Blue Max* 1966; *All Neat in Black Stockings* 1969; *Lamb* 1985
Towers, Constance (1933–) *Bring Your Smile Along* 1955; *The Horse Soldiers* 1959; *Sergeant Rutledge* 1960; *Shock Corridor* 1963; *The Naked Kiss* 1964; *Sylvester* 1985; *The Next Karate Kid* 1994
Towles, Tom (1950–) *Henry: Portrait of a Serial Killer* 1986; *The Borrower* 1989; *Night of the Living Dead* 1990; *Blood In Blood Out* 1992; *Mad Dog and Glory* 1992; *Normal Life* 1995; *Warriors of Virtue* 1996
Towne, Robert *aka* **Wain, Edward** (1936–) *The Last Woman on Earth* 1960; *Drive, He Said* 1971
Townes, Harry (1914–2001) *Screaming Mimi* 1958; *Sanctuary* 1961; *Fitzwilly* 1967; *Santee* 1973; *The Warrior and the Sorceress* 1983
Townsend, Colleen (1928–) *Chicken Every Sunday* 1948; *When Willie Comes Marching Home* 1950
Townsend, Jill (1945–) *Sitting Target* 1972; *Alfie Darling* 1975; *The Awakening* 1980
Townsend, Patrice *Sitting Ducks* 1979; *Always* 1985
Townsend, Robert (1957–) *A Soldier's Story* 1984; *Streets of Fire* 1984; *American Flyers* 1985; *Odd Jobs* 1986; *Ratboy* 1986; *Hollywood Shuffle* 1987; *The Mighty Quinn* 1989; *The Five Heartbeats* 1991; *The Meteor Man* 1993; *Taxman* 1998
Townsend, Stanley *My Friend Joe* 1996; *Suzie Gold* 2003; *Wondrous Oblivion* 2003
Townsend, Stuart (1972–) *Trojan Eddie* 1996; *Resurrection Man* 1997; *Shooting Fish* 1997; *Under the Skin* 1997; *Simon Magus* 1998; *The Escort* 1999; *Wonderland* 1999; *About Adam* 2000; *Queen of the Damned* 2002; *Trapped* 2002; *The League of Extraordinary Gentlemen* 2003
Toyohara, Kosuke *Godzilla vs King Ghidorah* 1991; *Mr Baseball* 1992
Tozzi, Fausto (1921–1978) *Constantine and the Cross* 1961; *The Return of Dr Mabuse* 1961; *The Appointment* 1968; *The Valachi Papers* 1972; *The Valdez Horses* 1973; *The Sicilian Cross* 1976
Trabaud, Pierre (1922–2005) *Le Défroqué* 1953; *War of the Buttons* 1962
Tracey, Ian (1964–) *The Keeper* 1976; *Stakeout* 1987; *The Last Island* 1990; *The War between Us* 1995; *Owning Mahowny* 2002; *Emile* 2003
Trachtenberg, Michelle (1985–) *Harriet the Spy* 1996; *Inspector Gadget* 1999; *A Father's Choice* 2000; *EuroTrip* 2004; *Mysterious Skin* 2004
Tracy, Arthur (1899–1997) *Limelight* 1936; *Command Performance* 1937
Tracy, Lee (1898–1968) *Born Reckless* 1930; *Blessed Event* 1932; *Doctor X* 1932; *The Half Naked Truth* 1932; *Love Is a Racket* 1932; *The Strange Love of Molly Louvain* 1932; *Washington Merry-Go-Round* 1932; *Advice to the Lovelorn* 1933; *Blonde Bombshell* 1933; *Dinner at Eight* 1933; *Turn Back the Clock* 1933; *The Lemon Drop Kid* 1934; *Behind the Headlines* 1937; *Criminal Lawyer* 1937; *The Spellbinder* 1939; *Betrayal from the East* 1945; *The Best Man* 1964
Tracy, Spencer (1900–1967) *Up the River* 1930; *Quick Millions* 1931; *Six Cylinder Love* 1931; *Me and My Gal* 1932; *The Mad Game* 1933; *Man's Castle* 1933; *The Power and the Glory* 1933; *Shanghai Madness* 1933; *20,000 Years in Sing Sing* 1933; *Looking for Trouble* 1934; *Marie Galante* 1934; *Dante's Inferno* 1935; *Murder Man* 1935; *Whipsaw* 1935; *Fury* 1936; *Libeled Lady* 1936; *Riffraff* 1936; *San Francisco* 1936; *Big City* 1937; *Captains Courageous* 1937; *Mannequin* 1937; *They Gave Him a Gun* 1937; *Boys Town* 1938; *Test Pilot* 1938; *Stanley and Livingstone* 1939; *Boom Town* 1940; *Edison, the Man* 1940; *I Take This Woman* 1940; *Northwest Passage* 1940; *Dr Jekyll and Mr Hyde* 1941; *Men of Boys Town* 1941; *Keeper of the Flame* 1942; *Tortilla Flat* 1942; *Woman of the Year* 1942; *A Guy Named Joe* 1944; *The Seventh Cross* 1944; *Thirty Seconds over Tokyo* 1944; *Without Love* 1945; *Cass Timberlane* 1947; *The Sea of Grass* 1947; *State of the Union* 1948; *Adam's Rib* 1949; *Edward, My Son* 1949; *Malaya* 1949; *Father of the Bride* 1950; *Father's Little Dividend* 1951; *The People against O'Hara* 1951; *Pat and Mike* 1952; *Plymouth Adventure* 1952; *The Actress* 1953; *Broken Lance* 1954; *Bad Day at Black Rock* 1955; *The Mountain* 1956; *Desk Set* 1957; *The Last Hurrah* 1958; *The Old Man and the Sea* 1958; *Inherit the Wind* 1960; *The Devil at Four o'Clock* 1961; *Judgment at Nuremberg* 1961; *How the West Was Won* 1962; *It's a Mad Mad Mad Mad World* 1963; *Guess Who's Coming to Dinner* 1967
Tracy, William (1917–1967) *The Shop around the Corner* 1940; *Strike Up the Band* 1940; *Mr and Mrs Smith* 1941; *Tobacco Road* 1941; *George Washington Slept Here* 1942; *To the Shores of Tripoli* 1942
Train, Jack (1902–1966) *It's That Man Again* 1942; *King Arthur Was a Gentleman* 1942; *Miss London Ltd* 1943
Trainor, Mary Ellen (1950–) *Romancing the Stone* 1984; *Wings of the Apache* 1990; *Little Giants* 1994; *Congo* 1995
Tran Nu Yen-Khe (1965–) *The Scent of Green Papaya* 1993; *Cyclo* 1995; *At the Height of Summer* 1999
Traubel, Helen (1899–1972) *Deep in My Heart* 1954; *The Ladies' Man* 1961; *Gunn* 1967
Travanti, Daniel J *aka* **Travanty, Dan** (1940–) *Who Killed Teddy Bear?* 1965; *St Ives* 1976; *Adam* 1983; *Midnight Crossing* 1988; *Fellow Traveller* 1989; *Millennium* 1989; *Just Cause* 1995
Travers, Bill (1922–1994) *The Browning Version* 1951; *Hindle Wakes* 1952; *Counterspy* 1953; *The Square Ring* 1953; *Street of Shadows* 1953; *Romeo and Juliet* 1954; *Footsteps in the Fog* 1955; *Geordie* 1955; *The Barretts of Wimpole Street* 1956; *Bhowani Junction* 1956; *The Smallest Show on Earth* 1957; *Passionate Summer* 1958; *The Bridal Path* 1959; *The Green Helmet* 1960; *Gorgo* 1961; *Invasion Quartet* 1961; *Two Living, One Dead* 1961; *Born Free* 1966; *Duel at Diablo* 1966; *An Elephant Called Slowly* 1969; *Ring of Bright Water* 1969; *The Belstone Fox* 1973
Travers, Henry (1874–1965) *The Invisible Man* 1933; *Reunion in Vienna* 1933; *After Office Hours* 1935; *Captain Hurricane* 1935; *The Sisters* 1938; *Dark Victory* 1939; *Dodge City* 1939; *Remember?* 1939; *Stanley and Livingstone* 1939; *You Can't Get Away with Murder* 1939; *Anne of Windy Poplars* 1940; *Edison, the Man* 1940; *Primrose Path* 1940; *Ball of Fire* 1941; *High Sierra* 1941; *The Navy Steps Out* 1941; *Mrs Miniver* 1942; *Random Harvest* 1942; *Shadow of a Doubt* 1942; *Madame Curie* 1943; *The Moon Is Down* 1943; *None Shall Escape* 1944; *The Bells of St Mary's* 1945; *The Naughty Nineties* 1945; *Thrill of a Romance* 1945; *It's a Wonderful Life* 1946; *The Yearling* 1946
Travers, Linden (1913–2001) *The Last Adventurers* 1937; *Bank Holiday* 1938; *The Lady Vanishes* 1938; *The Ghost Train* 1941; *South American George* 1941; *Beware of Pity* 1946; *The Master of Bankdam* 1947; *No Orchids for Miss Blandish* 1948; *The Bad Lord Byron* 1949; *Christopher Columbus* 1949; *Don't Ever Leave Me* 1949
Travis, June (1914–) *Ceiling Zero* 1935; *The Case of the Black Cat* 1936; *The Gladiator* 1938; *Go Chase Yourself* 1938; *The Star* 1953
Travis, Kylie (1970–) *Sanctuary* 1997; *Gia* 1998
Travis, Nancy (1961–) *Three Men and a Baby* 1987; *Air America* 1990; *Internal Affairs* 1990; *Loose Cannons* 1990; *Three Men and a Little Lady* 1990; *Passed Away* 1992; *So I Married an Axe Murderer* 1993; *The Vanishing* 1993; *Greedy* 1994; *Destiny Turns on the Radio* 1995; *Fluke* 1995; *Bogus* 1996; *Auggie Rose* 2000; *The Sisterhood of the Traveling Pants* 2005
Travis, Randy (1959–) *Frank and Jesse* 1995; *Black Dog* 1998; *Fortune Hunters* 1999
Travis, Richard *aka* **Travis, Richard "Dick"** (1913–1989) *The Man Who Came to Dinner* 1941; *The Big Shot* 1942; *Mission to Moscow* 1943; *Women without Men* 1956
Travis, Stacey *Hardware* 1990; *The Super* 1991; *Only the Strong* 1993; *Bandits* 2001
Travolta, Joey (1952–) *The Prodigal* 1983; *Hollywood Vice Squad* 1986; *Amazon Women on the Moon* 1987; *Round Trip to Heaven* 1992
Travolta, John (1954–) *The Devil's Rain* 1975; *The Boy in the Plastic Bubble* 1976; *Carrie* 1976; *Saturday Night Fever* 1977; *Grease* 1978; *Moment by Moment* 1978; *Urban Cowboy* 1980; *Blow Out* 1981; *Staying Alive* 1983; *Two of a Kind* 1983; *Perfect* 1985; *Chains of Gold* 1989; *The Experts* 1989; *Look Who's Talking* 1989; *Look Who's Talking Too* 1990; *Eyes of an Angel* 1991; *Shout* 1991; *Look Who's Talking Now!* 1993; *Pulp Fiction* 1994; *Get Shorty* 1995; *White Man's Burden* 1995; *Broken Arrow* 1996; *Michael* 1996; *Phenomenon* 1996; *Face/Off* 1997; *Mad City* 1997; *She's So Lovely* 1997; *A Civil Action* 1998; *Primary Colors* 1998; *The Thin Red Line* 1998; *The General's Daughter* 1999; *Battlefield Earth* 2000; *Domestic Disturbance* 2001; *Swordfish* 2001; *Basic* 2003; *Ladder 49* 2004; *A Love Song for Bobby Long* 2004; *The Punisher* 2004; *Be Cool* 2005
Traylor, Susan *Sleep with Me* 1994; *Broken Vessels* 1998
Treacher, Arthur (1894–1975) *Anything Goes* 1936; *Satan Met a Lady* 1936; *Stowaway* 1936; *Thank You, Jeeves* 1936; *Heidi* 1937; *Step Lively, Jeeves* 1937; *Thin Ice* 1937; *You Can't Have Everything* 1937; *Mad about Music* 1938; *My Lucky Star* 1938; *The Little Princess* 1939; *Irene* 1940; *The Amazing Mrs Holliday* 1943; *Abbott and Costello in Society* 1944; *National Velvet* 1944; *Slave Girl* 1947; *The Countess of Monte Cristo* 1948; *Love That Brute* 1950; *Mary Poppins* 1964
Treacy, Emerson (1900–1967) *California Straight Ahead* 1937; *The Prowler* 1951
Treanor, Michael (1979–) *3 Ninjas* 1992; *3 Ninjas Knuckle Up* 1995
Trebor, Robert *GORP* 1980; *Out of the Darkness* 1985; *52 Pick-Up* 1986; *My Demon Lover* 1987
Tree, David (1915–) *Knight without Armour* 1937; *The Return of the Scarlet Pimpernel* 1937; *The Drum* 1938; *Pygmalion* 1938; *French without Tears* 1939; *Just William* 1939; *Return to Yesterday* 1940; *Major Barbara* 1941; *Don't Look Now* 1973
Tree, Dorothy (1906–1992) *Here Comes the Navy* 1934; *The Woman in Red* 1935; *Sky Murder* 1940; *Spirit of the People* 1940
Treen, Mary *aka* **Treen, Mary Lou** (1907–1989) *They Gave Him a Gun* 1937; *Change of Heart* 1943; *I Love a Soldier* 1944; *Let's Live a Little* 1948; *Room for One More* 1952
Tréjan, Guy (1921–2001) *Marie Antoinette* 1956; *Piaf: the Sparrow of Pigalle* 1974; *La Bête* 1975; *I Married a Dead Man* 1983
Trejo, Danny (1944–) *From Dusk till Dawn* 1995; *Anaconda* 1997; *Los Locos* 1997; *Point Blank* 1997; *The Replacement Killers* 1998; *From Dusk till Dawn II: Texas Blood Money* 1999; *Animal Factory* 2000; *From Dusk till Dawn 3: the Hangman's Daughter* 2000; *Bubble Boy* 2001; *SPYkids* 2001; *SPYkids 2: the Island of Lost Dreams* 2002; *xXx* 2002; *Once upon a Time in Mexico* 2003
Tremarco, Christine *Under the Skin* 1997; *Hold Back the Night* 1999
Tremayne, Les (1913–2003) *Francis Goes to West Point* 1952; *Dream Wife* 1953; *I Love Melvin* 1953; *The War of the Worlds* 1953; *A Man Called Peter* 1955; *The Lieutenant Wore Skirts* 1956; *The Monolith Monsters* 1957; *The Perfect Furlough* 1958; *The Angry Red Planet* 1959; *Say One for Me* 1959; *The Gallant Hours* 1960; *Daffy Duck's Movie: Fantastic Island* 1983
Tremblay, Johanne-Marie *Jesus of Montreal* 1989; *Being at Home with Claude* 1992; *The Barbarian Invasions* 2003
Trenker, Luis (1892–1990) *The Holy Mountain* 1926; *The Challenge* 1938
Trent, Philip *aka* **Jones, Clifford** (1907–2001) *The Power and the Glory* 1933; *Tillie and Gus* 1933; *Strangers All* 1935
Trese, Adam (1969–) *Laws of Gravity* 1992; *Palookaville* 1995; *The Underneath* 1995; *illtown* 1996; *Polish Wedding* 1998
Treves, Frederick (1925–) *Paper Mask* 1990; *Mad Dogs and Englishmen* 1994
Trevino, George *Captain Scarlett* 1953; *The Brave One* 1956
Trevor, Austin (1897–1978) *Lord Edgware Dies* 1934; *As You Like It* 1936; *Dark Journey* 1937; *Knight without Armour* 1937; *Under Your Hat* 1940; *Champagne Charlie* 1944; *To Paris with Love* 1954; *Horrors of the Black Museum* 1959; *Konga* 1960; *The Day the Earth Caught Fire* 1961
Trevor, Claire (1909–2000) *The Mad Game* 1933; *Baby, Take a Bow* 1934; *Black Sheep* 1935; *Dante's Inferno* 1935; *Human Cargo* 1936; *Dead End* 1937; *The Amazing Dr Clitterhouse* 1938; *The First Rebel* 1939; *Stagecoach* 1939; *Dark Command* 1940; *Honky Tonk* 1941; *Texas* 1941; *Crossroads* 1942; *The Desperadoes* 1943; *Farewell My Lovely* 1944; *Johnny Angel* 1945; *Crack-Up* 1946; *Lady of Deceit* 1947; *The Babe Ruth Story* 1948; *Key Largo* 1948; *Raw Deal* 1948; *The Velvet Touch* 1948; *The Lucky Stiff* 1949; *Best of the Badmen* 1951; *Hard, Fast and Beautiful* 1951; *Hoodlum Empire* 1952; *Stop, You're Killing Me* 1952; *The Stranger Wore a Gun* 1953; *The High and the Mighty* 1954; *Lucy Gallant* 1955; *Man without a Star* 1955; *The Mountain* 1956; *Marjorie Morningstar* 1958; *Two Weeks in Another Town* 1962; *The Stripper* 1963; *How to Murder Your Wife* 1965; *Kiss Me Goodbye* 1982
Trevor, Jack (1893–1976) *Secrets of a Soul* 1926; *Champagne* 1928; *Crisis* 1928
Trevor, Spencer (1875–1945) *The Return of Bulldog Drummond* 1934; *The Life and Death of Colonel Blimp* 1943
Trickett, Vicki (1938–) *Pepe* 1960; *Gidget Goes Hawaiian* 1961; *The Three Stooges Meet Hercules* 1962
Triesault, Ivan (1898–1980) *Border River* 1954; *The Amazing Transparent Man* 1960
Trieste, Leopoldo (1917–2003) *The White Sheik* 1951; *I Vitelloni* 1953; *Divorce – Italian Style* 1961; *Seduced and Abandoned* 1964; *The Starmaker* 1994
Trifunovic, Sergej (1972–) *Cabaret Balkan* 1998; *Lovers* 1999
Trigger, Sarah *Kid* 1990; *Bill & Ted's Bogus Journey* 1991; *Deadfall* 1993; *PCU* 1994
Trinder, Tommy (1909–1989) *Sailors Three* 1940; *The Foreman Went to France* 1941; *The Bells Go Down* 1943; *Champagne Charlie* 1944; *Fiddlers Three* 1944; *Bitter Springs* 1950; *The Beauty Jungle* 1964; *Barry McKenzie Holds His Own* 1974
Trintignant, Jean-Louis (1930–) *And God Created Woman* 1956; *Les Liaisons Dangereuses* 1959; *The Seven Deadly Sins* 1961; *The Easy Life* 1962; *Fire and Ice* 1962; *The Sleeping Car Murders* 1965; *Un Homme et une Femme* 1966; *Trans-Europ-Express* 1966; *The Great Silence* 1967; *Les Biches* 1968; *Z* 1968; *The Conformist* 1969; *My Night with Maud* 1969; *And Hope to Die* 1972; *The Last Train* 1972; *Without Apparent Motive* 1972; *The Outside Man* 1973; *Police Story* 1975; *Je Vous Aime* 1980; *Le Grand Pardon* 1981; *Confidentially Yours* 1983; *La Nuit de Varennes* 1983; *Under Fire* 1983; *Long Live Life* 1984; *Rendez-vous* 1985; *A Man and a Woman: 20 Years Later* 1986; *Merci la Vie* 1991; *See How They Fall* 1993; *Three Colours Red* 1994; *A Self-Made Hero* 1995; *Those Who Love Me Can Take the Train* 1998
Trintignant, Marie (1962–2003) *Une Affaire de Femmes* 1988; *Wings of Fame* 1990; *Wild Target* 1993; *Les Apprentis* 1995; *News from the Good Lord* 1996; *Ponette* 1996; *Portraits Chinois* 1996
Tripp, Louis (1974–) *The Gate* 1987; *Gate II* 1992
Tripplehorn, Jeanne (1963–) *Basic Instinct* 1992; *The Firm* 1993; *The Night We Never Met* 1993; *Waterworld* 1995; *Noose* 1997; *Old Man* 1997; *Sliding Doors* 1997; *'Til There Was You*

1997; *Very Bad Things* 1998; *Mickey Blue Eyes* 1999; *Timecode* 1999; *Relative Values* 2000; *Swept Away* 2002

Triska, Jan (1936–) *Elementary School* 1991; *Ronin* 1998

Trissenaar, Elisabeth (1944–) *Bolwieser* 1977; *In a Year of 13 Moons* 1978; *Berlin Alexanderplatz* 1980

Tristan, Dorothy *End of the Road* 1970; *Klute* 1971; *Isn't It Shocking?* 1973; *Scarecrow* 1973; *Fear on Trial* 1975; *Rollercoaster* 1977; *California Dreaming* 1979

Troisi, Massimo (1953–1994) *Hotel Colonial* 1987; *Il Postino* 1994

Trooger, Margot (1923–1994) *Heidi* 1965; *Pippi Longstocking* 1968

Troughton, David (1950–) *The Chain* 1984; *Dance with a Stranger* 1984; *Captain Jack* 1998

Troughton, Patrick (1920–1987) *Chance of a Lifetime* 1950; *The Black Knight* 1954; *The Moonraker* 1957; *The Black Torment* 1964; *The Gorgon* 1964; *The Viking Queen* 1967; *The Scars of Dracula* 1970; *Frankenstein and the Monster from Hell* 1973; *The Omen* 1976; *Sinbad and the Eye of the Tiger* 1977

Troughton, Sam *Sylvia* 2003; *Spirit Trap* 2005

Troup, Bobby (1918–1999) *The High Cost of Loving* 1958; *First to Fight* 1967

Trowbridge, Charles (1882–1967) *Nancy Drew – Detective* 1938; *Great Guns* 1941; *The Great Lie* 1941; *Strange Alibi* 1941; *Tarzan and the Huntress* 1947; *The Paleface* 1948

Troyer, Verne *Austin Powers: the Spy Who Shagged Me* 1999; *Austin Powers in Goldmember* 2002

Trubshawe, Michael (1905–1985) *They Were Not Divided* 1950; *Brandy for the Parson* 1951; *Something Money Can't Buy* 1952; *Operation Snatch* 1962

True, Jim *Singles* 1992; *The Hudsucker Proxy* 1994; *Normal Life* 1995; *Affliction* 1997

True, Rachel (1966–) *The Craft* 1996; *Nowhere* 1997; *Half-Baked* 1998; *Groove* 2000

Trueman, Paula (1900–1994) *Crime without Passion* 1934; *The Outlaw Josey Wales* 1976

Truex, Ernest (1890–1973) *The Adventures of Marco Polo* 1938; *His Girl Friday* 1939; *Christmas in July* 1940; *Twin Beds* 1942; *The Crystal Ball* 1943; *Pan-Americana* 1945; *The Girl from Manhattan* 1948; *Twilight for the Gods* 1958; *Fluffy* 1965

Truffaut, François (1932–1984) *L'Enfant Sauvage* 1970; *Anne and Muriel* 1971; *Day for Night* 1973; *Close Encounters of the Third Kind* 1977; *The Green Room* 1978

Trujillo, Raoul *Scanners II: The New Order* 1991; *Paris France* 1993; *Highlander III: the Sorcerer* 1995; *Waking Up Horton* 1997

Truman, Ralph (1900–1977) *The Saint in London* 1939; *Henry V* 1944; *Mr Perrin and Mr Traill* 1948; *Oliver Twist* 1948; *Eureka Stockade* 1949; *Treasure Island* 1950; *The Golden Coach* 1953; *Malta Story* 1953; *The Night My Number Came Up* 1955; *The Ship That Died of Shame* 1955; *The Black Tent* 1956; *The Long Arm* 1956; *The Man Who Knew Too Much* 1956; *The Spaniard's Curse* 1958; *El Cid* 1961

Trump, Donald (1946–) *The Pickle* 1993; *The Little Rascals* 1994

Trundy, Natalie (1940–) *The Careless Years* 1957; *Escape from the Planet of the Apes* 1971; *Conquest of the Planet of the Apes* 1972; *Battle for the Planet of the Apes* 1973; *Huckleberry Finn* 1974

Tryon, Glenn (1894–1970) *Broadway* 1929; *George White's Scandals* 1945

Tryon, Tom (1926–1991) *Three Violent People* 1956; *The Unholy Wife* 1957; *I Married a Monster from Outer Space* 1958; *The Story of Ruth* 1960; *The Longest Day* 1962; *Moon Pilot* 1962; *The Cardinal* 1963; *The Glory Guys* 1965; *In Harm's Way* 1965; *Color Me Dead* 1969

Tsai Chin (1937–) *The Face of Fu Manchu* 1965; *Invasion* 1965; *The Vengeance of Fu Manchu* 1967; *The Blood of Fu Manchu* 1968; *The Castle of Fu Manchu* 1968; *The Virgin Soldiers* 1969; *The Joy Luck Club* 1993

Tsang, Eric *aka* **Tsang, Eric Chi Wai** (1953–) *Eat a Bowl of Tea* 1989; *Gen-X Cops* 1999; *The Accidental Spy* 2001; *Infernal Affairs* 2002; *Infernal Affairs II* 2003; *Infernal Affairs 3* 2003

Tsang, Kenneth (1938–) *The Killer* 1989; *The Replacement Killers* 1998; *Die Another Day* 2002

Tschechowa, Olga (1897–1980) *Moulin Rouge* 1928; *Liebelei* 1932

Tschechowa, Vera (1940–) *Cold Blood* 1975; *Thousand Eyes* 1984

Tse, Nicholas (1980–) *Gen-X Cops* 1999; *A Man Called Hero* 1999; *Time and Tide* 2000

Tsu, Irene (1910–1989) *Paradise, Hawaiian Style* 1966; *Paper Tiger* 1974; *Snapdragon* 1993

Tsubouchi, Yoshiko *The Only Son* 1936; *The Brothers and Sisters of the Toda Family* 1941

Tsuchiya, Yoshio (1927–) *Matango* 1963; *Red Beard* 1965; *Destroy All Monsters* 1968

Tsukamoto, Shinya (1960–) *Tetsuo: the Iron Man* 1989; *Tetsuo II: Body Hammer* 1991; *The Most Terrible Time in My Life* 1993; *Tokyo Fist* 1995; *Ichi the Killer* 2001; *A Snake of June* 2002; *Marebito* 2004

Tsukasa, Yoko (1934–) *Late Autumn* 1960; *The End of Summer* 1961; *Rebellion* 1967

Tu, Francisca *aka* **Tu, Francesca** *Diamonds for Breakfast* 1968; *Welcome to the Club* 1971

Tubb, Barry (1963–) *The Legend of Billie Jean* 1985; *Top Gun* 1986; *Valentino Returns* 1987

Tubbs, William (1909–1953) *Paisà* 1946; *The Wages of Fear* 1953

Tucci, Maria (1941–) *Enormous Changes at the Last Minute* 1983; *Touch and Go* 1986

Tucci, Stanley (1960–) *Monkey Shines* 1988; *Fear, Anxiety, and Depression* 1989; *Slaves of New York* 1989; *Men of Respect* 1990; *Beethoven* 1992; *The Public Eye* 1992; *The Pelican Brief* 1993; *Undercover Blues* 1993; *Kiss of Death* 1994; *Somebody to Love* 1994; *Jury Duty* 1995; *Sex and the Other Man* 1995; *Big Night* 1996; *A Modern Affair* 1996; *The Alarmist* 1997; *Deconstructing Harry* 1997; *The Eighteenth Angel* 1997; *Montana* 1997; *The Daytrippers* 1998; *The Impostors* 1998; *In Too Deep* 1999; *A Midsummer Night's Dream* 1999; *Sidewalks of New York* 2000; *America's Sweethearts* 2001; *Conspiracy* 2001; *Big Trouble* 2002; *The Core* 2002; *Maid in Manhattan* 2002; *Road to Perdition* 2002; *The Life and Death of Peter Sellers* 2003; *Shall We Dance* 2004; *The Terminal* 2004; *Robots* 2005

Tucker, Chris (1972–) *House Party 3* 1994; *Dead Presidents* 1995; *Friday* 1995; *The Fifth Element* 1997; *Money Talks* 1997; *Rush Hour* 1998; *Rush Hour 2* 2001

Tucker, Forrest (1919–1986) *The Westerner* 1940; *Keeper of the Flame* 1942; *Never Say Goodbye* 1946; *The Yearling* 1946; *The Plunderers* 1948; *Sands of Iwo Jima* 1949; *Warpath* 1951; *Bugles in the Afternoon* 1952; *Hoodlum Empire* 1952; *Ride the Man Down* 1952; *Pony Express* 1953; *Trouble in the Glen* 1954; *Break in the Circle* 1955; *Rage at Dawn* 1955; *Three Violent People* 1956; *The Abominable Snowman* 1957; *The Deerslayer* 1957; *The Strange World of Planet X* 1957; *Auntie Mame* 1958; *Fort Massacre* 1958; *The Trollenberg Terror* 1958; *The Night They Raided Minsky's* 1968; *Barquero* 1970; *Chisum* 1970; *Cancel My Reservation* 1972; *Final Chapter – Walking Tall* 1977; *A Rare Breed* 1981; *Thunder Run* 1986

Tucker, Joe *Career Girls* 1997; *Lava* 2000

Tucker, Jonathan (1982–) *Stolen Hearts* 1996; *The Deep End* 2001; *The Texas Chainsaw Massacre* 2003; *Criminal* 2004; *Hostage* 2004

Tucker, Michael (1944–) *Eyes of Laura Mars* 1978; *The Goodbye People* 1984; *Radio Days* 1987; *Checking Out* 1988; *Day One* 1989; *For Love or Money* 1993; *D2: the Mighty Ducks* 1994; *Taken Away* 1996

Tucker, Richard (1884–1942) *The Jazz Singer* 1927; *The Bat Whispers* 1930; *Manslaughter* 1930; *The Plot Thickens* 1936

Tucker, Sophie (1884–1966) *Broadway Melody of 1938* 1937; *Thoroughbreds Don't Cry* 1937; *Follow the Boys* 1944; *The Joker Is Wild* 1957

Tudyk, Alan (1971–) *28 Days* 2000; *A Knight's Tale* 2001; *I, Robot* 2004

Tufts, Sonny (1911–1970) *Government Girl* 1943; *So Proudly We Hail* 1943; *Here Come the Waves* 1944; *I Love a Soldier* 1944; *Bring on the Girls* 1945; *Duffy's Tavern* 1945; *Miss Susie Slagle's* 1945; *Swell Guy* 1946; *The Virginian* 1946; *The Well Groomed Bride* 1946; *Blaze of Noon* 1947; *Variety Girl* 1947; *Easy Living* 1949; *The Gift Horse* 1951; *Cat-women of the Moon* 1953; *The Seven Year Itch* 1955; *Come Next Spring* 1956; *The Parson and the Outlaw* 1957

Tukur, Ulrich (1957–) *The Democratic Terrorist* 1992; *My Mother's Courage* 1995; *Taking Sides* 2001; *Amen.* 2002; *Solaris* 2003

Tully, Tom (1908–1982) *Destination Tokyo* 1943; *Northern Pursuit* 1943; *I'll Be Seeing You* 1944; *Secret Command* 1944; *Adventure* 1945; *Kiss and Tell* 1945; *Till the End of Time* 1946; *Intrigue* 1947; *Killer McCoy* 1947; *Lady in the Lake* 1947; *Blood on the Moon* 1948; *June Bride* 1948; *Rachel and the Stranger* 1948; *A Kiss for Corliss* 1949; *Branded* 1950; *Where the Sidewalk Ends* 1950; *Love Is Better Than Ever* 1951; *Tomahawk* 1951; *The Jazz Singer* 1952; *Ruby Gentry* 1952; *The Turning Point* 1952; *The Moon Is Blue* 1953; *Trouble along the Way* 1953; *Arrow in the Dust* 1954; *The Caine Mutiny* 1954; *Love Me or Leave Me* 1955; *Ten North Frederick* 1958; *The Wackiest Ship in the Army* 1961; *The Carpetbaggers* 1964; *Coogan's Bluff* 1968

Tunc, Irène (1938–1972) *Léon Morin, Priest* 1961; *Vivre pour Vivre* 1967; *La Chamade* 1968

Tung, Bill *Police Story* 1985; *Police Story 2* 1986; *Jackie Chan's First Strike* 1996; *Rumble in the Bronx* 1996

Tunney, Robin (1972–) *California Man* 1992; *Empire Records* 1995; *The Craft* 1996; *Julian Po* 1997; *Montana* 1997; *Niagara Niagara* 1997; *End of Days* 1999; *Supernova* 2000; *Vertical Limit* 2000; *Cherish* 2002; *The Secret Lives of Dentists* 2002; *The In-Laws* 2003; *Paparazzi* 2004

Tupou, Manu (1935–2004) *The Extraordinary Seaman* 1969; *A Man Called Horse* 1970; *The Castaway Cowboy* 1974

Turco, Paige (1965–) *Teenage Mutant Ninja Turtles II: the Secret of the Ooze* 1991; *Teenage Mutant Ninja Turtles III* 1992; *Dead Funny* 1995; *The November Conspiracy* 1995

Turgeon, Peter (1919–2000) *Muscle Beach Party* 1964; *Last Summer* 1969

Turkel, Ann (1942–) *Paper Lion* 1968; *99 and 44/100% Dead* 1974; *The Cassandra Crossing* 1976; *Golden Rendezvous* 1977; *Portrait of a Hitman* 1977; *Monster* 1980; *The Fear* 1995

Turkel, Joe *aka* **Turkel, Joseph** (1927–) *Paths of Glory* 1957; *The Bonnie Parker Story* 1958; *The Shining* 1980

Turman, Glynn (1946–) *JD's Revenge* 1976; *The River Niger* 1976; *A Hero Ain't Nothin' but a Sandwich* 1978; *No Ordinary Summer* 1994; *Buffalo Soldiers* 1997; *Sahara* 2004

Turnbull, John (1880–1956) *The Black Abbot* 1934; *Lord Edgware Dies* 1934; *The Lad* 1935; *The Passing of the Third Floor Back* 1935; *The Amazing Quest of Ernest Bliss* 1936; *The Shadow* 1936; *Song of the Road* 1937; *Spare a Copper* 1940; *Daybreak* 1946

Turner, Geraldine (1950–) *Summerfield* 1977; *Careful, He Might Hear You* 1983

Turner, Guinevere (1968–) *Go Fish* 1994; *Chasing Amy* 1996; *The Watermelon Woman* 1996; *Preaching to the Perverted* 1997

Turner, Janine (1963–) *Monkey Shines* 1988; *The Ambulance* 1990; *Cliffhanger* 1993; *Leave It to Beaver* 1997; *A Secret Affair* 1999

Turner, Jim *Destroyer* 1988; *Shelf Life* 1993; *Joe's Apartment* 1996

Turner, John (1932–) *The Giant Behemoth* 1959; *Petticoat Pirates* 1961; *The Black Torment* 1964; *Captain Nemo and the Underwater City* 1969

Turner, Kathleen (1954–) *Body Heat* 1981; *The Man with Two Brains* 1983; *A Breed Apart* 1984; *Crimes of Passion* 1984; *Romancing the Stone* 1984; *The Jewel of the Nile* 1985; *Prizzi's Honor* 1985; *Peggy Sue Got Married* 1986; *Julia and Julia* 1987; *Switching Channels* 1987; *The Accidental Tourist* 1988; *Who Framed Roger Rabbit* 1988; *The War of the Roses* 1989; *VI Warshawski* 1991; *House of Cards* 1993; *Undercover Blues* 1993; *Naked in New York* 1994; *Serial Mom* 1994; *Moonlight and Valentino* 1995; *The Real Blonde* 1997; *A Simple Wish* 1997; *Legalese* 1998; *Baby Geniuses* 1999; *The Virgin Suicides* 1999; *Beautiful* 2000

Turner, Lana (1920–1995) *The Great Garrick* 1937; *They Won't Forget* 1937; *The Adventures of Marco Polo* 1938; *Dramatic School* 1938; *Love Finds Andy Hardy* 1938; *Calling Dr Kildare* 1939; *Dancing Co-Ed* 1939; *Dr Jekyll and Mr Hyde* 1941; *Honky Tonk* 1941; *Johnny Eager* 1941; *Ziegfeld Girl* 1941; *Somewhere I'll Find You* 1942; *Slightly Dangerous* 1943; *Marriage Is a Private Affair* 1944; *Keep Your Powder Dry* 1945; *Week-End at the Waldorf* 1945; *The Postman Always Rings Twice* 1946; *Cass Timberlane* 1947; *Green Dolphin Street* 1947; *Homecoming* 1948; *The Three Musketeers* 1948; *A Life of Her Own* 1950; *Mr Imperium* 1951; *The Bad and the Beautiful* 1952; *The Merry Widow* 1952; *Latin Lovers* 1953; *Betrayed* 1954; *Diane* 1955; *The Prodigal* 1955; *The Rains of Ranchipur* 1955; *The Sea Chase* 1955; *Peyton Place* 1957; *Another Time, Another Place* 1958; *The Lady Takes a Flyer* 1958; *Imitation of Life* 1959; *Portrait in Black* 1960; *Bachelor in Paradise* 1961; *By Love Possessed* 1961; *Who's Got the Action?* 1962; *Love Has Many Faces* 1965; *Madame X* 1966; *The Big Cube* 1969; *Persecution* 1974; *Bittersweet Love* 1976; *Witches' Brew* 1979

Turner, Tim *Police Dog* 1955; *Grip of the Strangler* 1958

Turner, Tina (1939–) *Taking Off* 1971; *Tommy* 1975; *Mad Max beyond Thunderdome* 1985

Turner, Tyrin *Menace II Society* 1993; *Panther* 1995; *Belly* 1998

Turpin, Ben (1874–1940) *His New Job* 1915; *Make Me a Star* 1932; *Saps at Sea* 1940

Turturro, Aida (1962–) *True Love* 1989; *Jersey Girl* 1992; *Angie* 1994; *Denise Calls Up* 1995; *Woo* 1998

Turturro, John (1957–) *Exterminator 2* 1980; *Desperately Seeking Susan* 1985; *To Live and Die in LA* 1985; *The Color of Money* 1986; *Gung Ho* 1986; *Off Beat* 1986; *Five Corners* 1987; *The Sicilian* 1987; *Catchfire* 1989; *Do the Right Thing* 1989; *Men of Respect* 1990; *Miller's Crossing* 1990; *State of Grace* 1990; *Barton Fink* 1991; *Jungle Fever* 1991; *Brain Donors* 1992; *Mac* 1992; *Fearless* 1993; *Being Human* 1994; *Erotic Tales* 1994; *Quiz Show* 1994; *Clockers* 1995; *Search and Destroy* 1995; *Unstrung Heroes* 1995; *Box of Moonlight* 1996; *Girl 6* 1996; *Grace of My Heart* 1996; *The Search for One-Eye Jimmy* 1996; *The Big Lebowski* 1997; *The Truce* 1997; *He Got Game* 1998; *Rounders* 1998; *Cradle Will Rock* 1999; *Summer of Sam* 1999; *Company Man* 2000; *The Luzhin Defence* 2000; *The Man Who Cried* 2000; *Monkeybone* 2000; *O Brother, Where Art Thou?* 2000; *Collateral Damage* 2001; *13 Conversations about One Thing* 2001; *Fear X* 2002; *Mr Deeds* 2002; *Anger Management* 2003; *Secret Window* 2004; *She Hate Me* 2004

Turturro, Nicholas *aka* **Turturro, Nick** (1962–) *Federal Hill* 1994; *Freefall: Flight 174* 1995; *The Search for One-Eye Jimmy* 1996; *Shadow Conspiracy* 1996; *Excess Baggage* 1997; *The Hillside Strangler* 2004

Tushingham, Rita (1940–) *A Taste of Honey* 1961; *Girl with Green Eyes* 1963; *The Leather Boys* 1963; *A Place to Go* 1963; *Doctor Zhivago* 1965; *The Knack... and How to Get It* 1965; *The Trap* 1966; *Smashing Time* 1967; *Diamonds for Breakfast* 1968; *The Bed Sitting Room* 1969; *The Guru* 1969; *The Human Factor* 1975; *Rachel's Man* 1975; *A Judgement in Stone* 1986; *Resurrected* 1989; *Paper Marriage* 1991; *An Awfully Big Adventure* 1994; *The Boy from Mercury* 1996; *Under the Skin* 1997; *Out of Depth* 1998; *Swing* 1998; *Being Julia* 2004

Tutin, Dorothy (1930–2001) *The Importance of Being Earnest* 1952; *The Beggar's Opera* 1953; *A Tale of Two Cities* 1957; *Cromwell* 1970; *Savage Messiah* 1972; *The Shooting Party* 1984; *Agatha Christie's Murder with Mirrors* 1985; *Shades of Fear* 1993; *Alive and Kicking* 1996

Tuttle, Lurene (1906–1986) *Goodbye, My Fancy* 1951; *The Whip Hand* 1951; *Don't Bother to Knock* 1952; *Never Wave at a WAC* 1952; *Room for One More* 1952; *The Affairs of Dobie Gillis* 1953; *Niagara* 1953; *Sincerely Yours* 1955; *Untamed Youth* 1957; *The Fortune Cookie* 1966; *The Ghost and Mr Chicken* 1966; *Final Chapter – Walking Tall* 1977

Tweed, Shannon (1957–) *Of Unknown Origin* 1983; *Hot Dog – The Movie* 1984; *Meatballs III: Summer Job* 1987; *Cannibal Women in the Avocado Jungle of Death* 1989; *Night Visitor* 1989; *Cold Sweat* 1993; *Indecent Behavior* 1993; *Naked Lies* 1997; *Forbidden Sins* 1998; *Power Play* 1998; *Detroit Rock City* 1999; *Dead Sexy* 2001

Twelvetrees, Helen (1907–1958) *Her Man* 1930; *Bad Company* 1931; *The Painted Desert* 1931

Twiggy (1949–) *The Boy Friend* 1971; *W* 1974; *There Goes the Bride* 1979; *The Blues Brothers* 1980; *The Doctor and the Devils* 1985; *Club Paradise* 1986; *Madame Sousatzka* 1988

Twitty, Conway (1933–1993) *Platinum High School* 1960; *Sex Kittens Go to College* 1960

Twomey, Anne (1951–) *Deadly Friend* 1986; *The Imagemaker* 1986; *Last Rites* 1988; *The Scout* 1994; *Picture Perfect* 1997

Tykkyiainen, Kirsi *Leningrad Cowboys Meet Moses* 1993; *Take Care of Your Scarf, Tatjana* 1994

Tyler, Beverly (1928–) *The Green Years* 1946; *My Brother Talks to Horses* 1946; *The Beginning or the End* 1947; *The Fireball* 1950; *The Cimarron Kid* 1951; *The Battle at Apache Pass* 1952; *Chicago Confidential* 1957

Tyler, Liv (1977–) *Silent Fall* 1994; *Empire Records* 1995; *Heavy* 1995; *Stealing Beauty* 1995; *That Thing You Do!* 1996; *Inventing the Abbotts* 1997; *U Turn* 1997; *Armageddon* 1998; *Cookie's Fortune* 1999; *Onegin* 1999; *Plunkett & Macleane* 1999; *Dr T & the Women* 2000; *The Lord of the Rings: The Fellowship of the Ring* 2001; *One Night at McCool's* 2001; *The Lord of the Rings: The Two Towers* 2002; *Jersey Girl* 2003; *The Lord of the Rings: The Return of the King* 2003

Tyler, Steven (1948–) *The Polar Express* 2004; *Be Cool* 2005

Tyler, Tom (1903–1954) *The Last Outlaw* 1936; *Law and Order* 1936; *The Mummy's Hand* 1940; *Valley of the Sun* 1942; *Badman's Territory* 1946; *Trail of Robin Hood* 1950

Tyne, George (1911–) *A Walk in the Sun* 1945; *They Won't Believe Me* 1947; *Not with My Wife, You Don't!* 1966

Tyner, Charles (1925–) *Harold and Maude* 1972; *Jeremiah Johnson* 1972; *Emperor of the North* 1973; *The Mean Machine* 1974; *Pulse* 1988; *Over Her Dead Body* 1990

Tyrrell, Ann *Bride for Sale* 1949; *The Glass Menagerie* 1950

Tyrrell, Susan (1946–) *Shoot Out* 1971; *Fat City* 1972; *Catch My Soul* 1973; *The Killer inside Me* 1975; *Bad* 1976; *Islands in the Stream* 1976; *Another Man, Another Chance* 1977; *I Never Promised You a Rose Garden* 1977; *September 30, 1955* 1977; *Night Warning* 1981; *Tales of Ordinary Madness* 1981; *Fast-Walking* 1982; *Liar's Moon* 1982; *Fire and Ice* 1983; *Angel* 1984; *Avenging Angel* 1985; *Flesh + Blood* 1985; *Big Top Pee-wee* 1988; *Cry-Baby* 1989; *Far from Home* 1989; *Rockula* 1989; *Motorama* 1991; *Powder* 1995; *Relax... It's Just Sex* 1998; *Buddy Boy* 1999

Tyson, Barbara aka **Bush, Barbara** *Between Friends* 1983; *Ernest Goes to Jail* 1990

Tyson, Cathy (1965–) *Mona Lisa* 1986; *Business as Usual* 1987; *The Serpent and the Rainbow* 1987; *Priest* 1994; *The Old Man Who Read Love Stories* 2000

Tyson, Cicely (1933–) *A Man Called Adam* 1966; *The Heart Is a Lonely Hunter* 1968; *Sounder* 1972; *The Autobiography of Miss Jane Pittman* 1974; *The Blue Bird* 1976; *The River Niger* 1976; *A Hero Ain't Nothin' but a Sandwich* 1978; *Airport '79: the Concorde* 1979; *Bustin' Loose* 1981; *Heat Wave* 1990; *Fried Green Tomatoes at the Whistle Stop Cafe* 1991; *Hoodlum* 1997; *A Lesson Before Dying* 1999; *Because of Winn-Dixie* 2004

Tyson, Richard (1961–) *Three O'Clock High* 1987; *Two Moon Junction* 1988; *Kindergarten Cop* 1990; *The Glass Cage* 1996; *Kingpin* 1996; *Desert Thunder* 1998; *The Pandora Project* 1998; *Battlefield Earth* 2000; *Firetrap* 2001

Tyzack, Margaret (1933–) *Ring of Spies* 1963; *2001: a Space Odyssey* 1968; *A Touch of Love* 1969; *The Legacy* 1978; *The Quatermass Conclusion* 1979; *Mr Love* 1985; *The King's Whore* 1990; *Bright Young Things* 2003

Ubach, Alanna (1977–) *Denise Calls Up* 1995; *Just Your Luck* 1996; *Clockwatchers* 1997

Udenio, Fabiana (1964–) *Bride of Re-Animator* 1991; *Diplomatic Immunity* 1991; *Austin Powers: International Man of Mystery* 1997

Udy, Claudia (1960–) *Savage Dawn* 1985; *Dragonard* 1987; *Captive Rage* 1988

Uhl, Nadja *The Legends of Rita* 2000; *Twin Sisters* 2002

Uhlen, Gisela (1919–) *The Door with Seven Locks* 1962; *Toto Le Héros* 1991

Ullman, Tracey (1959–) *Give My Regards to Broad Street* 1984; *Plenty* 1985; *Jumpin' Jack Flash* 1986; *Happily Ever After* 1990; *I Love You to Death* 1990; *Household Saints* 1993; *Robin Hood: Men in Tights* 1993; *I'll Do Anything* 1994; *Pret-a-Porter* 1994; *Panic* 2000; *Small Time Crooks* 2000; *A Dirty Shame* 2004

Ullmann, Liv (1939–) *Persona* 1966; *The Hour of the Wolf* 1967; *Shame* 1968; *A Passion* 1969; *The Night Visitor* 1970; *Cold Sweat* 1971; *The Emigrants* 1971; *Cries and Whispers* 1972; *The New Land* 1972; *Pope Joan* 1972; *40 Carats* 1973; *Lost Horizon* 1973; *Scenes from a Marriage* 1973; *The Abdication* 1974; *Zandy's Bride* 1974; *Face to Face* 1976; *The Serpent's Egg* 1977; *Autumn Sonata* 1978; *The Wild Duck* 1983; *Bay Boy* 1984; *Dangerous Moves* 1984; *Let's Hope It's a Girl* 1985; *Gaby: a True Story* 1987; *La Amiga* 1988; *The Rose Garden* 1989; *Mindwalk* 1990; *The Ox* 1991; *The Long Shadow* 1992; *Saraband* 2003

Ulric, Lenore (1892–1970) *Camille* 1937; *Temptation* 1946

Ulrich, Skeet (1969–) *Boys* 1995; *Albino Alligator* 1996; *The Craft* 1996; *Last Dance* 1996; *Scream* 1996; *Touch* 1996; *As Good as It Gets* 1997; *The Newton Boys* 1998; *Chill Factor* 1999; *Ride with the Devil* 1999

Ulyanov, Mikhail (1927–) *The Theme* 1979; *Private Life* 1982; *A Private Conversation* 1983

Umbach, Martin (1956–) *Witness in the War Zone* 1986; *The NeverEnding Story II: the Next Chapter* 1991

Umeki, Miyoshi (1929–) *Sayonara* 1957; *Cry for Happy* 1961; *Flower Drum Song* 1961; *A Girl Named Tamiko* 1962; *The Horizontal Lieutenant* 1962

Umemura, Yoko *Osaka Elegy* 1936; *Sisters of the Gion* 1936; *Story of the Late Chrysanthemums* 1939

Underdown, Edward (1908–1989) *The Brass Monkey* 1948; *They Were Not Divided* 1950; *Voice of Merrill* 1952; *Beat the Devil* 1953; *Street of Shadows* 1953; *The Camp on Blood Island* 1958; *The Rainbow Jacket* 1958; *The Third Alibi* 1961; *Information Received* 1962; *The Bay of Saint Michel* 1963; *Dr Terror's House of Horrors* 1964; *The Hand of Night* 1966; *Tarka the Otter* 1978

Underwood, Betty *A Dangerous Profession* 1949; *Storm over Wyoming* 1950

Underwood, Blair (1964–) *Heat Wave* 1990; *Murder in Mississippi* 1990; *Posse* 1993; *Just Cause* 1995; *Set It Off* 1996; *Soul of the Game* 1996; *Rules of Engagement* 2000; *Full Frontal* 2002; *Malibu's Most Wanted* 2003

Underwood, Jay (1968–) *Desert Bloom* 1985; *The Boy Who Could Fly* 1986; *The Invisible Kid* 1988; *Promised Land* 1988; *Uncle Buck* 1989; *The Gumshoe Kid* 1990; *Sleepstalker* 1995; *Afterglow* 1997; *And the Beat Goes On: the Sonny and Cher Story* 1999

Underwood, Loyal (1893–1966) *Shoulder Arms* 1918; *The Pilgrim* 1923

Unger, Deborah Kara aka **Unger, Deborah** (1966–) *Blood Oath* 1990; *Till There Was You* 1990; *Whispers in the Dark* 1992; *Highlander III: the Sorcerer* 1995; *Crash* 1996; *Keys to Tulsa* 1996; *No Way Home* 1996; *The Game* 1997; *Payback* 1998; *The Hurricane* 1999; *Sunshine* 1999; *Fear X* 2002; *Leo* 2002; *Emile* 2003; *Stander* 2003; *Thirteen* 2003; *A Love Song for Bobby Long* 2004; *White Noise* 2004

Unger, Joe *Go Tell the Spartans* 1977; *Barfly* 1987; *Leatherface: the Texas Chainsaw Massacre III* 1990

Union, Gabrielle (1973–) *Bring It On* 2000; *Two Can Play That Game* 2001; *Welcome to Collinwood* 2002; *Bad Boys II* 2003; *Cradle 2 the Grave* 2003; *Breakin' All the Rules* 2004; *The Honeymooners* 2005

Urabe, Kumeko (1902–1989) *The Straits of Love and Hate* 1937; *Ikiru* 1952; *Street of Shame* 1955

Uranga, Kandido *Vacas* 1991; *Dollar Mambo* 1993

Urban, Karl (1972–) *Heaven* 1998; *The Price of Milk* 2000; *The Truth about Demons* 2000; *The Bourne Supremacy* 2004; *The Chronicles of Riddick* 2004

Urbaniak, James (1963–) *Henry Fool* 1997; *The Sticky Fingers of Time* 1997; *American Splendor* 2003

Ure, Mary (1933–1975) *Storm over the Nile* 1955; *Windom's Way* 1957; *Look Back in Anger* 1959; *Sons and Lovers* 1960; *The Mind Benders* 1963; *The Luck of Ginger Coffey* 1964; *Custer of the West* 1968; *Where Eagles Dare* 1969; *A Reflection of Fear* 1973

Urecal, Minerva (1894–1966) *Block Busters* 1944; *Mr Muggs Rides Again* 1945; *Good Sam* 1948

Urich, Robert (1946–2002) *Magnum Force* 1973; *Endangered Species* 1982; *The Ice Pirates* 1984; *Turk 182!* 1985; *Danielle Steel's A Perfect Stranger* 1994; *Death at Clover Bend* 2001

Urquhart, Molly (1906–1977) *Geordie* 1955; *Devil's Bait* 1959; *House of Mystery* 1961

Urquhart, Robert (1922–1995) *You're Only Young Twice* 1952; *Knights of the Round Table* 1953; *Happy Ever After* 1954; *The Dark Avenger* 1955; *Yangtse Incident* 1956; *The Curse of Frankenstein* 1957; *Dunkirk* 1958; *Trouble with Eve* 1959; *The Bulldog Breed* 1960; *The Break* 1962; *Murder at the Gallop* 1963; *The Looking Glass War* 1969; *Country Dance* 1970; *P'Tang, Yang, Kipperbang* 1982; *Restless Natives* 1985; *Playing Away* 1986; *The Kitchen Toto* 1987

Urzi, Saro (1913–1979) *Seduced and Abandoned* 1964; *Alfredo Alfredo* 1971

Ustinov, Peter (1921–2004) *Odette* 1950; *Hotel Sahara* 1951; *The Magic Box* 1951; *Le Plaisir* 1951; *Quo Vadis* 1951; *Beau Brummell* 1954; *The Egyptian* 1954; *Lola Montès* 1955; *We're No Angels* 1955; *Les Espions* 1957; *Spartacus* 1960; *The Sundowners* 1960; *Romanoff and Juliet* 1961; *Billy Budd* 1962; *John Goldfarb, Please Come Home* 1964; *Topkapi* 1964; *Lady L* 1965; *Blackbeard's Ghost* 1967; *The Comedians* 1967; *Hot Millions* 1968; *Viva Max!* 1969; *Hammersmith Is Out* 1972; *Robin Hood* 1973; *One of Our Dinosaurs Is Missing* 1975; *Logan's Run* 1976; *Treasure of Matecumbe* 1976; *The Last Remake of Beau Geste* 1977; *The Mouse and His Child* 1977; *The Purple Taxi* 1977; *Death on the Nile* 1978; *Tarka the Otter* 1978; *The Thief of Baghdad* 1978; *Ashanti* 1979; *Charlie Chan and the Curse of the Dragon Queen* 1981; *The Great Muppet Caper* 1981; *Grendel, Grendel, Grendel* 1981; *Evil under the Sun* 1982; *Thirteen at Dinner* 1985; *Agatha Christie's Murder in Three Acts* 1986; *Dead Man's Folly* 1986; *Appointment with Death* 1988; *Lorenzo's Oil* 1992; *Stiff Upper Lips* 1997; *Animal Farm* 1999; *The Bachelor* 1999

Vaananen, Kari (1953–) *Hamlet Goes Business* 1987; *Leningrad Cowboys Go America* 1989; *Leningrad Cowboys Meet Moses* 1993; *Drifting Clouds* 1996

Vaccaro, Brenda (1939–) *Midnight Cowboy* 1969; *Where It's At* 1969; *I Love My... Wife* 1970; *Going Home* 1971; *Once Is Not Enough* 1975; *Airport '77* 1977; *Capricorn One* 1978; *Fast Charlie: the Moonbeam Rider* 1978; *The First Deadly Sin* 1980; *Zorro, the Gay Blade* 1981; *Supergirl* 1984; *Water* 1985; *Heart of Midnight* 1988; *Cookie* 1989; *Love Affair* 1994; *The Mirror Has Two Faces* 1996; *Sonny* 2002

Vadim, Annette (1936–) *Les Liaisons Dangereuses* 1959; *Blood and Roses* 1960

Vadim, Roger (1928–2000) *Le Testament d'Orphée* 1960; *Ciao! Manhattan* 1973; *Into the Night* 1985

Vadis, Dan (1938–1987) *Spartacus and the Ten Gladiators* 1964; *The Scalphunters* 1968; *Cahill, United States Marshal* 1973; *Bronco Billy* 1980

Vail, Lester (1900–1959) *Beau Ideal* 1931; *Consolation Marriage* 1931; *Dance, Fools, Dance* 1931

Valandrey, Charlotte (1968–) *Rouge Baiser* 1985; *Orlando* 1992

Valberg, Birgitta (1916–) *Smiles of a Summer Night* 1955; *The Virgin Spring* 1960; *Shame* 1968

Valcke, Serge-Henri (1946–) *Amsterdamned* 1988; *Il Maestro* 1989; *No Man's Land* 2001

Valenska, Paula (1922–) *Bond Street* 1948; *The Gay Adventure* 1949

Valenta, Vladimir (1923–2001) *Closely Observed Trains* 1966; *Sunday in the Country* 1975

Valentin, Barbara (1940–2002) *Fear Eats the Soul* 1973; *Martha* 1973

Valentine, Anthony (1939–) *Performance* 1970; *Tower of Evil* 1972; *To the Devil a Daughter* 1976; *Les Enfants de Lumière* 1995; *Two Men Went to War* 2002

Valentine, Karen (1947–) *E' Lollipop* 1975; *Hot Lead and Cold Feet* 1978; *Hill's Angels* 1979

Valentine, Nancy *-30-* 1959; *Tess of the Storm Country* 1960

Valentine, Paul (1919–) *Build My Gallows High* 1947; *House of Strangers* 1949; *Love Happy* 1949; *Something to Live For* 1952

Valentini, Mariella *Volere, Volare* 1991; *Benzina* 2001

Valentino, Rudolph (1895–1926) *Camille* 1921; *The Four Horsemen of the Apocalypse* 1921; *The Sheik* 1921; *Blood and Sand* 1922; *The Eagle* 1925; *The Son of the Sheik* 1926

Valenty, Lili (1900–1987) *Wild Is the Wind* 1957; *The Baby Maker* 1970; *Tell Me a Riddle* 1980

Valère, Simone (1923–) *La Beauté du Diable* 1949; *The Game Is Over* 1966; *The Assassination of Trotsky* 1972

Valerie, Joan (1911–1983) *Submarine Patrol* 1938; *Michael Shayne, Private Detective* 1940

Valk, Frederick (1895–1956) *Thunder Rock* 1942; *Hotel Reserve* 1944; *Saraband for Dead Lovers* 1948; *Never Let Me Go* 1953; *Magic Fire* 1956; *Zarak* 1956

Vallée, Marcel (1885–1957) *Paris Qui Dort* 1923; *Caravan* 1934; *Topaze* 1951

Vallee, Rudy (1901–1986) *International House* 1933; *George White's Scandals* 1934; *Gold Diggers in Paris* 1938; *Second Fiddle* 1939; *Time Out for Rhythm* 1941; *The Palm Beach Story* 1942; *Happy Go Lucky* 1943; *The Bachelor and the Bobby-Soxer* 1947; *I Remember Mama* 1948; *My Dear Secretary* 1948; *So This Is New York* 1948; *Unfaithfully Yours* 1948; *The Beautiful Blonde from Bashful Bend* 1949; *Father Was a Fullback* 1949; *Mother Is a Freshman* 1949; *The Admiral Was a Lady* 1950; *Gentlemen Marry Brunettes* 1955; *How to Succeed in Business without Really Trying* 1967; *Live a Little, Love a Little* 1968

Valletta, Amber (1974–) *What Lies Beneath* 2000; *Hitch* 2005

Valli, Alida aka **Valli** (1921–) *We the Living* 1942; *The Paradine Case* 1947; *The Miracle of the Bells* 1948; *The Third Man* 1949; *Walk Softly, Stranger* 1949; *The White Tower* 1950; *The Stranger's Hand* 1953; *Senso* 1954; *Les Bijoutiers du Clair de Lune* 1957; *Il Grido* 1957; *This Angry Age* 1957; *Eyes without a Face* 1959; *The Long Absence* 1961; *The Happy Thieves* 1962; *Ophélia* 1962; *The Castilian* 1963; *The Spider's Stratagem* 1970; *The Flesh of the Orchid* 1974; *Lisa and the Devil* 1976; *1900* 1976; *Suspiria* 1976; *Killer Nun* 1978; *La Luna* 1979; *A Month by the Lake* 1994

Valli, Romolo (1925–1980) *The Great War* 1959; *Boccaccio '70* 1961; *The Leopard* 1962; *The Visit* 1964; *Boom* 1968; *A Fistful of Dynamite* 1971; *The Garden of the Finzi-Continis* 1971; *What?* 1973; *Bobby Deerfield* 1977

Vallin, Rick (1919–1977) *Clancy Street Boys* 1943; *Ghosts in the Night* 1943; *Dangerous Money* 1946; *Tuna Clipper* 1949; *Comanche Territory* 1950

Vallone, Raf (1916–2002) *Bitter Rice* 1949; *Thérèse Raquin* 1953; *Obsession* 1954; *Les Possédées* 1955; *Two Women* 1960; *El Cid* 1961; *Phaedra* 1962; *The Cardinal* 1963; *The Secret Invasion* 1964; *Nevada Smith* 1966; *The Desperate Ones* 1967; *Sharaz* 1968; *The Italian Job* 1969; *Cannon for Cordoba* 1970; *A Gunfight* 1971; *The Human Factor* 1975; *Rosebud* 1975; *That Lucky Touch* 1975; *The Devil's Advocate* 1977; *The Other Side of Midnight* 1977; *The Greek Tycoon* 1978; *An Almost Perfect Affair* 1979; *Lion of the Desert* 1981; *The Scarlet and the Black* 1983

Vampira aka **Nurmi, Maila** (1921–) *The Beat Generation* 1959; *Night of the Ghouls* 1959; *Plan 9 from Outer Space* 1959; *Sex Kittens Go to College* 1960

Van, Bobby (1930–1980) *Skirts Ahoy!* 1952; *The Affairs of Dobie Gillis* 1953; *Kiss Me Kate* 1953; *The Navy vs the Night Monsters* 1966; *Lost Horizon* 1973

Van Cleef, Lee (1925–1989) *High Noon* 1952; *Kansas City Confidential* 1952; *The Lawless Breed* 1952; *Untamed Frontier* 1952; *Arena* 1953; *The Bandits of Corsica* 1953; *The Beast from 20,000 Fathoms* 1953; *Tumbleweed* 1953; *Vice Squad* 1953; *Arrow in the Dust* 1954; *Dawn at Socorro* 1954; *Gypsy Colt* 1954; *Rails into Laramie* 1954; *The Yellow Tomahawk* 1954; *The Big Combo* 1955; *A Man Alone* 1955; *The Road to Denver* 1955; *Accused of Murder* 1956; *The Conqueror* 1956; *It Conquered the World* 1956; *Pardners* 1956; *Tribute to a Bad Man* 1956; *China Gate* 1957; *Gunfight at the OK Corral* 1957; *The Lonely Man* 1957; *The Tin Star* 1957; *The Bravados* 1958; *Day of the Bad Man* 1958; *The Young Lions* 1958; *Ride Lonesome* 1959; *Posse from Hell* 1961; *For a Few Dollars More* 1965; *The Good, the Bad and the Ugly* 1966; *Death Rides a Horse* 1967; *The Good Die First* 1967; *Sabata* 1969; *Barquero* 1970; *El Condor* 1970; *Bad Man's River* 1971; *Captain Apache* 1971; *The Big Showdown* 1972; *The Magnificent Seven Ride!* 1972; *Blood Money* 1974; *Take a Hard Ride* 1975; *God's Gun* 1977; *Kid Vengeance* 1977; *The Octagon* 1980; *Escape from New York* 1981; *Codename*

Wildgeese 1984; *Armed Response* 1986; *Cannonball Fever* 1989
Van Dam, José *Don Giovanni* 1979; *The Music Teacher* 1988
Van Damme, Jean-Claude (1961–) *No Retreat, No Surrender* 1985; *Bloodsport* 1987; *Black Eagle* 1988; *Cyborg* 1989; *Kickboxer* 1989; *AWOL* 1990; *Death Warrant* 1990; *Double Impact* 1991; *Nowhere to Run* 1992; *Universal Soldier* 1992; *Hard Target* 1993; *Street Fighter* 1994; *Timecop* 1994; *Sudden Death* 1995; *Maximum Risk* 1996; *The Quest* 1996; *Double Team* 1997; *Knock Off* 1998; *Legionnaire* 1998; *Desert Heat* 1999; *Universal Soldier – the Return* 1999; *The Order* 2001; *Replicant* 2001
van de Ven, Monique (1952–) *Turkish Delight* 1973; *Keetje Tippel* 1975; *The Assault* 1986; *Amsterdamned* 1988; *The Man Inside* 1990
Van Der Beek, James (1977–) *I Love You, I Love You Not* 1997; *Varsity Blues* 1999; *The Rules of Attraction* 2002
Van Der Velde, Nadine *Critters* 1986; *Munchies* 1987; *After Midnight* 1989
Van Der Vlis, Diana *aka* **Vandervlis, Diana** (1935–2001) *The Girl in Black Stockings* 1957; *The Man with the X-Ray Eyes* 1963
Van Der Wal, Frederique (1967–) *Two Girls and a Guy* 1997; *Wild Wild West* 1999
Van Devere, Trish (1943–) *Where's Poppa?* 1970; *One Is a Lonely Number* 1972; *The Day of the Dolphin* 1973; *Harry in Your Pocket* 1973; *The Savage Is Loose* 1974; *Movie Movie* 1978; *The Changeling* 1980; *The Hearse* 1980; *Uphill All the Way* 1985; *Hollywood Vice Squad* 1986; *Messenger of Death* 1988
Van Dien, Casper (1968–) *Orbit* 1996; *Starship Troopers* 1997; *Tarzan and the Lost City* 1998; *Shark Attack* 1999; *Sleepy Hollow* 1999; *Partners* 2000; *Python* 2000; *Sanctimony* 2000; *Danger beneath the Sea* 2001
Van Doren, Mamie (1931–) *The All American* 1953; *Francis Joins the WACS* 1954; *Yankee Pasha* 1954; *Ain't Misbehavin'* 1955; *Running Wild* 1955; *Star in the Dust* 1956; *The Girl in Black Stockings* 1957; *Untamed Youth* 1957; *High School Confidential* 1958; *Teacher's Pet* 1958; *The Beat Generation* 1959; *The Big Operator* 1959; *Born Reckless* 1959; *Girls' Town* 1959; *The Private Lives of Adam and Eve* 1959; *Sex Kittens Go to College* 1960; *The Navy vs the Night Monsters* 1966; *Voyage to the Planet of Prehistoric Women* 1966; *Slackers* 2001
Van Doude *Love in the Afternoon* 1957; *A Bout de Souffle* 1959; *The Sign of Leo* 1959
Van Dreelen, John (1922–1992) *The Leech Woman* 1960; *The Wizard of Baghdad* 1960; *Becoming Colette* 1991
Van Dyke, Conny (1945–) *Framed* 1975; *WW and the Dixie Dancekings* 1975
Van Dyke, Dick (1925–) *Bye Bye Birdie* 1963; *Mary Poppins* 1964; *What a Way to Go!* 1964; *Art of Love* 1965; *Lt Robin Crusoe, USN* 1966; *Divorce American Style* 1967; *Fitzwilly* 1967; *Chitty Chitty Bang Bang* 1968; *Never a Dull Moment* 1968; *Cold Turkey* 1969; *The Comic* 1969; *The Runner Stumbles* 1979; *Dick Tracy* 1990
Van Dyke, Jerry (1932–) *The Courtship of Eddie's Father* 1963; *Angel in My Pocket* 1968
Van Eyck, Peter (1911–1969) *Five Graves to Cairo* 1943; *The Moon Is Down* 1943; *Address Unknown* 1944; *The Impostor* 1944; *Sailor of the King* 1953; *The Wages of Fear* 1953; *A Bullet for Joey* 1955; *Tarzan's Hidden Jungle* 1955; *The Rawhide Years* 1956; *Run for the Sun* 1956; *Foxhole in Cairo* 1960; *The Thousand Eyes of Dr Mabuse* 1960; *The Brain* 1962; *Station Six-Sahara* 1962; *Kidnapped to Mystery Island* 1964; *The Dirty Game* 1965; *The Spy Who Came in from the Cold* 1965; *Assignment to Kill* 1968; *Shalako* 1968; *The Bridge at Remagen* 1969
Van Eyssen, John (1922–1995) *Four Sided Triangle* 1953; *Men of Sherwood Forest* 1954; *The Traitor* 1957; *Horror of Dracula* 1958; *Blind Date* 1959
Van Fleet, Jo (1919–1996) *East of Eden* 1955; *I'll Cry Tomorrow* 1955; *The Rose Tattoo* 1955; *The King and Four Queens* 1956; *Gunfight at the OK Corral* 1957; *This Angry Age* 1957; *Wild River* 1960; *Cool Hand Luke* 1967; *I Love You, Alice B Toklas* 1968; *Eighty Steps to Jonah* 1969; *The Gang That Couldn't Shoot Straight* 1971; *The Tenant* 1976
Van Gorkum, Harry *Dragonheart: a New Beginning* 1999; *Escape under Pressure* 2000; *Avenging Angelo* 2002
Van Heerden, Marcel *Mapantsula* 1988; *Jobman* 1990
Van Hentenryck, Kevin *Basket Case* 1982; *Basket Case 2* 1990; *Basket Case 3: the Progeny* 1992
Van Holt, Brian (1969–) *Whipped* 1999; *Confidence* 2002; *Basic* 2003; *SWAT* 2003; *House of Wax* 2004; *Man of the House* 2005
Van Horn, Patrick *California Man* 1992; *Swingers* 1996; *Free Enterprise* 1998
Van Huet, Fedja (1973–) *Character* 1997; *The Delivery* 1998
Van Lidth, Erland (1953–1987) *Alone in the Dark* 1982; *The Running Man* 1987
van Lyck, Henry (1941–) *Signs of Life* 1968; *The Enigma of Kaspar Hauser* 1974
Van Nutter, Rik (1930–) *Thunderball* 1965; *Pacific Inferno* 1979
Van Pallandt, Nina (1932–) *The Long Goodbye* 1973; *A Wedding* 1978; *Quintet* 1979; *American Gigolo* 1980; *Cutter's Way* 1981
Van Patten, Dick *aka* **Van Patten, Richard** (1928–) *Psychomania* 1964; *Charly* 1968; *Zachariah* 1970; *Westworld* 1973; *Superdad* 1974; *The Strongest Man in the World* 1975; *Freaky Friday* 1976; *Gus* 1976; *The Shaggy DA* 1976; *High Anxiety* 1977; *Spaceballs* 1987; *Love Is All There Is* 1996
Van Patten, James *aka* **Van Patten, Jimmy** (1956–) *Roller Boogie* 1979; *Young Warriors* 1983
Van Patten, Joyce (1934–) *I Love You, Alice B Toklas* 1968; *something big* 1971; *Bone* 1972; *Thumb Tripping* 1972; *Mame* 1974; *The Bad News Bears* 1976; *Billy Galvin* 1986; *Monkey Shines* 1988; *Trust Me* 1989
Van Patten, Timothy (1959–) *Class of 1984* 1982; *Catacombs* 1988
Van Patten, Vincent (1957–) *The Valdez Horses* 1973; *Rock 'n' Roll High School* 1979; *Survival Run* 1979; *Hell Night* 1981
Van Peebles, Mario (1958–) *Exterminator 2* 1980; *Rappin'* 1985; *Heartbreak Ridge* 1986; *Hot Shot* 1986; *3:15* 1986; *Jaws the Revenge* 1987; *New Jack City* 1991; *Full Eclipse* 1993; *Posse* 1993; *Gunmen* 1994; *Highlander III: the Sorcerer* 1995; *Solo* 1996; *Stag* 1996; *Los Locos* 1997; *Love Kills* 1998; *Blowback* 1999; *Judgment Day* 1999; *Guardian* 2000; *Ali* 2001; *Baadasssss!* 2003
Van Peebles, Melvin (1932–) *Sweet Sweetback's Baad Asssss Song* 1971; *Posse* 1993; *Terminal Velocity* 1994; *Fist of the North Star* 1995; *Love Kills* 1998
Van Rooten, Luis (1906–1973) *City across the River* 1949; *My Favorite Spy* 1951; *Lydia Bailey* 1952; *The Unholy Wife* 1957
Van Sloan, Edward (1881–1964) *Dracula* 1931; *Frankenstein* 1931; *The Mummy* 1932; *The Death Kiss* 1933; *Deluge* 1933; *Dracula's Daughter* 1936; *Before I Hang* 1940
Van Tongeren, Hans (1955–1982) *Spetters* 1980; *Summer Lovers* 1982
Van Valkenburgh, Deborah (1952–) *King of the Mountain* 1981; *Streets of Fire* 1984; *Rampage* 1987; *Phantom of the Ritz* 1988; *Brain Smasher... a Love Story* 1993; *Mean Guns* 1996
Van Vooren, Monique (1933–) *Tarzan and the She-Devil* 1953; *Happy Anniversary* 1959; *Frank's Greatest Adventure* 1967; *Flesh for Frankenstein* 1974
van Wageningen, Yorick (1964–) *Beyond Borders* 2003; *The Chronicles of Riddick* 2004
Van Warmerdam, Alex (1952–) *Abel* 1986; *The Northerners* 1992
Van Wormer, Steve *Meet the Deedles* 1998; *Groove* 2000
Van Zandt, Philip (1904–1958) *A Thousand and One Nights* 1945; *Thief of Damascus* 1952; *Gog* 1954; *Playgirl* 1954
Vanbrugh, Irene (1872–1949) *The Rise of Catherine the Great* 1934; *Escape Me Never* 1935; *Knight without Armour* 1937; *Wings of the Morning* 1937
Vance, Courtney B (1960–) *The Hunt for Red October* 1990; *The Adventures of Huck Finn* 1993; *Fixing the Shadow* 1994; *Holy Matrimony* 1994; *Dangerous Minds* 1995; *The Last Supper* 1995; *Panther* 1995; *The Tuskegee Airmen* 1995; *The Preacher's Wife* 1996; *12 Angry Men* 1997; *Space Cowboys* 2000
Vance, Danitra (1959–1994) *Limit Up* 1989; *Jumpin' at the Boneyard* 1991
Vance, Vivian (1909–1979) *Goodbye, My Lady* 1956; *The Great Race* 1965
Vander, Musetta (1969–) *Under the Hula Moon* 1995; *Wild Wild West* 1999; *Kicking & Screaming* 2005
Vandernoot, Alexandra (1965–) *Le Dîner de Cons* 1998; *The Closet* 2001; *The Five Obstructions* 2003
Vandis, Titos *aka* **Wandis, Titos** (1917–2003) *Never on Sunday* 1960; *Topkapi* 1964; *Once upon a Scoundrel* 1973; *A Piece of the Action* 1977; *A Perfect Couple* 1979
Vanel, Charles (1892–1989) *Le Grand Jeu* 1933; *Les Misérables* 1934; *La Belle Equipe* 1936; *The Wages of Fear* 1953; *Les Diaboliques* 1954; *To Catch a Thief* 1955; *Death in the Garden* 1956; *La Vérité* 1960; *L'Aîné des Ferchaux* 1963; *Boomerang* 1976; *Three Brothers* 1980
Vanity (1959–) *The Last Dragon* 1985; *52 Pick-Up* 1986; *Deadly Illusion* 1987; *Action Jackson* 1988
Vanni, Renata (1910–2004) *Pay or Die* 1960; *Lady in White* 1988; *Wait until Spring, Bandini* 1989
Vannicola, Joanne (1968–) *Love and Human Remains* 1993; *Iron Eagle IV* 1995
Vannucchi, Luigi (1930–1978) *The Red Tent* 1969; *The Assassination of Trotsky* 1972; *Call Him Savage* 1975
Varconi, Victor (1891–1976) *The Divine Lady* 1928; *Eternal Love* 1929; *Roberta* 1935; *The Plainsman* 1936; *Big City* 1937; *The Atomic Submarine* 1960
Vardalos, Nia (1962–) *My Big Fat Greek Wedding* 2002; *Connie and Carla* 2004
Varden, Evelyn (1893–1958) *Stella* 1950; *When Willie Comes Marching Home* 1950; *Phone Call from a Stranger* 1952; *Desiree* 1954; *The Night of the Hunter* 1955; *The Bad Seed* 1956; *Hilda Crane* 1956
Varden, Norma (1898–1989) *Boys Will Be Boys* 1935; *Foreign Affaires* 1935; *Where There's a Will* 1936; *Windbag the Sailor* 1936; *Shipyard Sally* 1939; *The Earl of Chicago* 1940; *National Velvet* 1944; *Witness for the Prosecution* 1957; *Doctor Dolittle* 1967
Varela, Leonor (1972–) *The Tailor of Panama* 2000; *Blade II* 2002
Varennes, Jacques (1895–1958) *The Eagle Has Two Heads* 1948; *Orphée* 1950
Vargas, Jacob (1971–) *Mi Vida Loca* 1993; *Selena* 1997; *Flight of the Phoenix* 2004
Vargas, Valentina (1964–) *Street of No Return* 1989; *Hellraiser: Bloodline* 1996
Varley, Beatrice (1896–1964) *Hatter's Castle* 1941; *Waterloo Road* 1944; *Send for Paul Temple* 1946; *Adam and Evelyne* 1949; *Gone to Earth* 1950; *The Black Rider* 1954; *Horrors of the Black Museum* 1959
Varma, Indira *Kama Sutra: a Tale of Love* 1996; *Bride & Prejudice* 2004
Varney, Jim (1949–2000) *Ernest Goes to Camp* 1987; *Ernest Saves Christmas* 1988; *Fast Food* 1989; *Ernest Goes to Jail* 1990; *Ernest Scared Stupid* 1991; *The Beverly Hillbillies* 1993; *Ernest Rides Again* 1993; *Wilder Napalm* 1993; *The Expert* 1994; *Slam Dunk Ernest* 1995; *Toy Story* 1995; *3 Ninjas: High Noon at Mega Mountain* 1998; *Toy Story 2* 1999; *Atlantis: the Lost Empire* 2001
Varney, Reg (1916–) *Joey Boy* 1965; *The Great St Trinian's Train Robbery* 1966; *On the Buses* 1971; *The Best Pair of Legs in the Business* 1972; *Go for a Take* 1972; *Mutiny on the Buses* 1972; *Holiday on the Buses* 1973
Varno, Roland (1908–1996) *Three Faces West* 1940; *Hostages* 1943; *The Return of the Vampire* 1943; *My Name Is Julia Ross* 1945; *Scared to Death* 1947
Varsi, Diane (1938–1992) *Peyton Place* 1957; *From Hell to Texas* 1958; *Ten North Frederick* 1958; *Compulsion* 1959; *Wild in the Streets* 1968; *Bloody Mama* 1970; *Johnny Got His Gun* 1971
Vartan, Michael (1968–) *Fiorile* 1993; *Dead Man's Curve* 1997; *Touch Me* 1997; *Never Been Kissed* 1999; *The Next Best Thing* 2000; *One Hour Photo* 2001; *Monster-in-Law* 2005
Varte, Rosy (1927–) *Thomas the Imposter* 1964; *Uncle Benjamin* 1969
Vasconcelos, Luiz Carlos *Midnight* 1998; *Me, You, Them* 2000; *Carandiru* 2003
Vassar, Queenie (1870–1960) *Primrose Path* 1940; *Lady in a Jam* 1942
Vattier, Robert (1906–1982) *Fanny* 1932; *The Baker's Wife* 1938; *Manon des Sources* 1952
Vaughan, Frankie (1928–1999) *The Heart of a Man* 1959; *Let's Make Love* 1960
Vaughan, Martin (1931–) *Alison's Birthday* 1979; *We of the Never Never* 1982; *Phar Lap* 1983; *The Winds of Jarrah* 1983; *Constance* 1984; *Kokoda Crescent* 1989
Vaughan, Peter (1923–) *Die! Die! My Darling* 1964; *Smokescreen* 1964; *The Naked Runner* 1967; *A Twist of Sand* 1967; *The Bofors Gun* 1968; *Alfred the Great* 1969; *Eyewitness* 1970; *Straw Dogs* 1971; *Savage Messiah* 1972; *The Blockhouse* 1973; *The Mackintosh Man* 1973; *Malachi's Cove* 1973; *11 Harrowhouse* 1974; *Valentino* 1977; *Porridge* 1979; *The Razor's Edge* 1984; *Brazil* 1985; *Haunted Honeymoon* 1986; *King of the Wind* 1989; *Mountains of the Moon* 1989; *Prisoner of Honor* 1991; *The Remains of the Day* 1993; *The Crucible* 1996; *The Secret Agent* 1996; *Face* 1997; *Les Misérables* 1997; *An Ideal Husband* 1999; *The Legend of 1900* 1999; *Kiss Kiss (Bang Bang)* 2001; *The Life and Death of Peter Sellers* 2003; *The Mother* 2003
Vaughn, Hilda (1898–1957) *Manslaughter* 1930; *Susan Lenox: Her Fall and Rise* 1931; *Today We Live* 1933; *Anne of Green Gables* 1934
Vaughn, Ned (1964–) *The Rescue* 1988; *Wind* 1992; *Max Q: Emergency Landing* 1998
Vaughn, Robert (1932–) *Good Day for a Hanging* 1958; *Teenage Caveman* 1958; *The Young Philadelphians* 1959; *The Magnificent Seven* 1960; *The Big Show* 1961; *The Caretakers* 1963; *The Glass Bottom Boat* 1966; *One of Our Spies Is Missing* 1966; *One Spy Too Many* 1966; *The Spy in the Green Hat* 1966; *The Spy with My Face* 1966; *To Trap a Spy* 1966; *The Venetian Affair* 1966; *The Karate Killers* 1967; *Bullitt* 1968; *The Helicopter Spies* 1968; *How to Steal the World* 1968; *The Bridge at Remagen* 1969; *If It's Tuesday, This Must Be Belgium* 1969; *Julius Caesar* 1970; *The Mind of Mr Soames* 1970; *The Towering Inferno* 1974; *Demon Seed* 1977; *Brass Target* 1978; *Good Luck, Miss Wyckoff* 1979; *Battle beyond the Stars* 1980; *Cuba Crossing* 1980; *Hangar 18* 1980; *SOB* 1981; *Superman III* 1983; *Black Moon Rising* 1985; *The Delta Force* 1986; *Hour of the Assassin* 1987; *Renegade* 1987; *Captive Rage* 1988; *CHUD II: Bud the Chud* 1989; *River of Death* 1989; *Transylvania Twist* 1989; *Buried Alive* 1990; *Going Under* 1990; *Blind Vision* 1992; *Joe's Apartment* 1996; *Motel Blue* 1997; *BASEketball* 1998
Vaughn, Vince (1970–) *Just Your Luck* 1996; *Swingers* 1996; *The Lost World: Jurassic Park* 1997; *A Secret Sin* 1997; *Clay Pigeons* 1998; *A Cool, Dry Place* 1998; *Psycho* 1998; *Return to Paradise* 1998; *The Cell* 2000; *The Prime Gig* 2000; *South of Heaven, West of Hell* 2000; *Domestic Disturbance* 2001; *Made* 2001; *Blackball* 2003; *Old School* 2003; *Dodgeball: a True Underdog Story* 2004; *Starsky & Hutch* 2004; *Be Cool* 2005; *Mr & Mrs Smith* 2005; *Wedding Crashers* 2005
Vavasseur, Sophie (1992–) *Evelyn* 2002; *Resident Evil: Apocalypse* 2004
Vavitch, Michael (1885–1930) *Hotel Imperial* 1927; *Two Arabian Knights* 1927
Vawter, Ron (1949–1994) *sex, lies, and videotape* 1989; *Empire City* 1991; *Swoon* 1992; *Philadelphia* 1993
Veazie, Carol (1895–1984) *A Cry in the Night* 1956; *Baby the Rain Must Fall* 1965
Vedey, Julian *Command Performance* 1937; *The Green Cockatoo* 1937
Vega, Alexa (1988–) *SPYkids* 2001; *SPYkids 2: the Island of Lost Dreams* 2002; *SPYkids 3-D: Game Over* 2003; *Sleepover* 2004
Vega, Isela (1940–) *Bring Me the Head of Alfredo Garcia* 1974; *Drum* 1976; *Barbarosa* 1982
Vega, Paz (1976–) *Sex and Lucia* 2001; *Novo* 2002; *The Other Side of the Bed* 2002; *Carmen* 2003; *Spanglish* 2004
Vegas, Johnny (1971–) *Blackball* 2003; *Sex Lives of the Potato Men* 2003
Veidt, Conrad (1893–1943) *The Cabinet of Dr Caligari* 1919; *Hands of Orlac* 1924; *Waxworks* 1924; *The Man Who Laughs* 1928; *Congress Dances* 1931; *FP1* 1932; *Rome Express* 1932; *The Wandering Jew* 1933; *I Was a Spy* 1934; *Jew Süss* 1934; *King of the Damned* 1935; *The Passing of the Third Floor Back* 1935; *Dark Journey* 1937; *Under the Red Robe* 1937; *The Spy in Black* 1939; *Contraband* 1940; *Escape* 1940; *The Thief of Bagdad* 1940; *The Men in Her Life* 1941; *Whistling in the Dark* 1941; *A Woman's Face* 1941; *All through the Night* 1942; *Casablanca* 1942; *Above Suspicion* 1943
Velasquez, Patricia (1971–) *Committed* 2000; *The Mummy Returns* 2001; *Mindhunters* 2003
Velez, Eddie (1958–) *Repo Man* 1984; *Extremities* 1986; *Romero* 1989; *Rooftops* 1989; *A Father's Choice* 2000

Velez, Lauren *I Like It like That* 1994; *I Think I Do* 1997; *Thicker than Blood* 1998
Velez, Lupe (1908–1944) *The Gaucho* 1927; *The Squaw Man* 1931; *The Half Naked Truth* 1932; *Hollywood Party* 1934; *Palooka* 1934; *The Girl from Mexico* 1939; *Mexican Spitfire* 1940; *Playmates* 1941; *Ladies' Day* 1943
VelJohnson, Reginald (1952–) *Die Hard* 1988; *Turner & Hooch* 1989; *Die Hard 2: Die Harder* 1990; *One of Her Own* 1994
Venable, Evelyn (1913–1993) *Death Takes a Holiday* 1934; *Mrs Wiggs of the Cabbage Patch* 1934; *Alice Adams* 1935; *The Little Colonel* 1935; *Streamline Express* 1935; *Pinocchio* 1940
Venables, Bruce *Mortgage* 1989; *Daydream Believer* 1991; *Paperback Hero* 1998
Venantini, Venantino (1930–) *The Agony and the Ecstasy* 1965; *The Priest's Wife* 1970
Veness, Amy (1876–1960) *The Show Goes On* 1937; *Just William* 1939; *This Happy Breed* 1944; *Vote for Huggett* 1948; *The Astonished Heart* 1949
Vennera, Chick (1952–) *Thank God It's Friday* 1978; *Yanks* 1979; *High Risk* 1981; *Last Rites* 1988; *Double Threat* 1992; *Alone in the Woods* 1996
Venocur, Johnny *Savage Streets* 1984; *Exit in Red* 1996
Venora, Diane (1952–) *Wolfen* 1981; *Terminal Choice* 1983; *FX: Murder by Illusion* 1985; *Ironweed* 1987; *Bird* 1988; *Heat* 1995; *The Substitute* 1996; *Surviving Picasso* 1996; *William Shakespeare's Romeo + Juliet* 1996; *The Jackal* 1997; *The Insider* 1999; *The Joyriders* 1999; *The 13th Warrior* 1999; *True Crime* 1999; *Hamlet* 2000; *Race against Time* 2000
Ventham, Wanda (1939–) *The Blood Beast Terror* 1967; *Mister Ten Per Cent* 1967; *Captain Kronos: Vampire Hunter* 1972
Ventimiglia, John *The Funeral* 1996; *Girls Town* 1996; *Personal Velocity* 2001
Ventura, Jesse (1951–) *Predator* 1987; *The Running Man* 1987; *Abraxas* 1991
Ventura, Lino (1919–1987) *Honour among Thieves* 1954; *Razzia sur la Chnouf* 1955; *The Big Risk* 1960; *Le Deuxième Souffle* 1966; *The Adventurers* 1968; *L'Armée des Ombres* 1969; *The Last Known Address* 1969; *The Sicilian Clan* 1969; *The Valachi Papers* 1972; *A Pain in the A...!* 1973; *The Silent One* 1973; *Happy New Year* 1974; *Three Tough Guys* 1974; *The Trap* 1975; *Illustrious Corpses* 1976; *The Medusa Touch* 1978; *Garde à Vue* 1981; *Les Misérables* 1982
Ventura, Viviane *A High Wind in Jamaica* 1965; *Battle beneath the Earth* 1968
Venture, Richard (1923–) *The Effect of Gamma Rays on Man-in-the-Moon Marigolds* 1972; *The Hunter* 1980; *Missing* 1981; *Scent of a Woman* 1992; *Series 7: the Contenders* 2001
Venuta, Benay *Annie Get Your Gun* 1950; *Call Me Mister* 1951; *Stars and Stripes Forever* 1952
Vera-Ellen (1920–1981) *Wonder Man* 1945; *The Kid from Brooklyn* 1946; *Three Little Girls in Blue* 1946; *Words and Music* 1948; *Love Happy* 1949; *On the Town* 1949; *Happy Go Lovely* 1950; *Three Little Words* 1950; *The Belle of New York* 1952; *Big Leaguer* 1953; *Call Me Madam* 1953; *White Christmas* 1954
Verbeke, Natalia (1975–) *Jump Tomorrow* 2001; *Son of the Bride* 2001; *The Other Side of the Bed* 2002; *Dot the i* 2003; *Football Days* 2003
Verdon, Gwen aka **Verdon, Gwyneth** (1925–2000) *On the Riviera* 1951; *Damn Yankees* 1958; *The Cotton Club* 1984; *Cocoon* 1985; *Nadine* 1987; *Cocoon: the Return* 1988; *Alice* 1990; *Marvin's Room* 1996
Verdú, Maribel (1970–) *Lovers* 1991; *Belle Epoque* 1992; *Golden Balls* 1993; *Goya in Bordeaux* 1999; *Y Tu Mamá También* 2001
Verdugo, Elena (1926–) *The Frozen Ghost* 1944; *Little Giant* 1946; *Tuna Clipper* 1949; *Thief of Damascus* 1952
Vereen, Ben (1946–) *Gas-s-s-s, or It Became Necessary to Destroy the World in Order to Save It* 1970; *Funny Lady* 1975; *All That Jazz* 1979; *Buy & Cell* 1988; *Once upon a Forest* 1992; *Why Do Fools Fall in Love?* 1998
Vereza, Carlos (1939–) *Midnight* 1998; *The Three Marias* 2002
Verhoeven, Simon (1972–) *My Mother's Courage* 1995; *Bride of the Wind* 2001
Verley, Bernard (1939–) *The Milky Way* 1968; *Love in the Afternoon* 1972; *L'Accompagnatrice* 1992; *Hélas pour Moi* 1993; *Six Days, Six Nights* 1994
Vermilyea, Harold (1889–1958) *The Big Clock* 1948; *The Emperor Waltz* 1948; *Born to Be Bad* 1950
Verne, Kaaren aka **Verne, Karen** (1918–1967) *Ten Days in Paris* 1939; *Sky Murder* 1940; *Underground* 1941; *All through the Night* 1942; *Sherlock Holmes and the Secret Weapon* 1942
Vernier, Pierre (1931–) *Piaf: the Sparrow of Pigalle* 1974; *Les Chiens* 1978; *The Outsider* 1983; *Romuald et Juliette* 1989; *Under the Sand* 2000
Verno, Jerry (1895–1975) *Broken Blossoms* 1936; *Sweeney Todd, the Demon Barber of Fleet Street* 1936
Vernoff, Kaili *No Looking Back* 1998; *Jump Tomorrow* 2001
Vernon, Anne (1924–) *Shakedown* 1950; *The Love Lottery* 1953; *Terror on a Train* 1953; *Beautiful but Dangerous* 1955; *General Della Rovere* 1959; *The Umbrellas of Cherbourg* 1964
Vernon, Glenn (1923–1999) *Youth Runs Wild* 1944; *Bedlam* 1946; *The Devil Thumbs a Ride* 1947
Vernon, Howard (1914–1996) *Le Silence de la Mer* 1947; *Bob Le Flambeur* 1955; *The Thousand Eyes of Dr Mabuse* 1960; *The Secret Ways* 1961; *The Awful Dr Orloff* 1962; *Alphaville* 1965; *Dracula, Prisoner of Frankenstein* 1972
Vernon, John (1932–2005) *Point Blank* 1967; *Tell Them Willie Boy Is Here* 1969; *Topaz* 1969; *Dirty Harry* 1971; *One More Train to Rob* 1971; *Fear Is the Key* 1972; *Charley Varrick* 1973; *The Black Windmill* 1974; *W* 1974; *Brannigan* 1975; *The Outlaw Josey Wales* 1976; *Golden Rendezvous* 1977; *A Special Day* 1977; *National Lampoon's Animal House* 1978; *Herbie Goes Bananas* 1980; *Chained Heat* 1983; *Savage Streets* 1984; *Blue Monkey* 1987; *Ernest Goes to Camp* 1987; *Killer Klowns from Outer Space* 1988; *Sodbusters* 1994
Vernon, Kate (1961–) *Alphabet City* 1984; *Roadhouse 66* 1984; *Malcolm X* 1992; *Soft Deceit* 1994
Vernon, Richard (1925–1997) *Cash on Demand* 1961; *Hot Enough for June* 1963; *The Servant* 1963; *A Hard Day's Night* 1964; *The Tomb of Ligeia* 1964; *The Early Bird* 1965; *The Intelligence Men* 1965; *The Satanic Rites of Dracula* 1973; *A Month in the Country* 1987
Vernon, Valerie *Gog* 1954; *The Glass Cage* 1955
Vernon, Wally (1905–1970) *Happy Landing* 1938; *Kentucky Moonshine* 1938; *Broadway Serenade* 1939; *Bloodhounds of Broadway* 1952; *Affair with a Stranger* 1953
Verrell, Cec *Hell Comes to Frogtown* 1988; *Mad at the Moon* 1992; *Three of Hearts* 1992
Versois, Odile (1930–1980) *A Day to Remember* 1953; *To Paris with Love* 1954; *The Young Lovers* 1954; *Checkpoint* 1956; *Passport to Shame* 1958; *Cartouche* 1961
Verveen, Arie *Caught* 1996; *Running Free* 1999; *Cabin Fever* 2002
VeSota, Bruno (1922–1976) *The Gunslinger* 1956; *Rock All Night* 1957; *Daddy-O* 1959; *Attack of the Giant Leeches* 1960
Vessey, Tricia (1972–) *The Alarmist* 1997; *Ghost Dog: the Way of the Samurai* 1999; *Trouble Every Day* 2000
Vetchy, Ondrej (1962–) *Martha and I* 1990; *Kolya* 1996; *Dark Blue World* 2001
Vetri, Victoria aka **Dorian, Angela** (1944–) *Kings of the Sun* 1963; *Chuka* 1967; *When Dinosaurs Ruled the Earth* 1969
Viana, Henrique (1936–2003) *Recollections of the Yellow House* 1989; *Here on Earth* 1993
Viard, Karin (1966–) *Delicatessen* 1990; *La Séparation* 1994; *Les Enfants du Siècle* 1999; *La Nouvelle Eve* 1999; *Time Out* 2001; *Summer Things* 2002
Vickers, Martha (1925–1971) *The Big Sleep* 1946; *The Man I Love* 1946; *Ruthless* 1948; *The Burglar* 1956
Vickers, Yvette (1936–) *Reform School Girl* 1957; *Short Cut to Hell* 1957; *Attack of the 50 Foot Woman* 1958; *The Mobster* 1958; *Attack of the Giant Leeches* 1960
Victor, Charles (1896–1965) *My Learned Friend* 1943; *Rhythm Serenade* 1943; *The Silver Fleet* 1943; *Fear in the Night* 1947; *The Calendar* 1948; *The Cure for Love* 1949; *The Woman in Question* 1950; *Calling Bulldog Drummond* 1951; *The Frightened Man* 1952; *Made in Heaven* 1952; *The Love Lottery* 1953; *Police Dog* 1955; *Value for Money* 1955; *The Extra Day* 1956; *Home and Away* 1956
Victor, Henry (1898–1945) *Freaks* 1932; *Conquest of the Air* 1936
Vidal, Christina (1981–) *Life with Mikey* 1993; *Welcome to the Dollhouse* 1995; *Freaky Friday* 2003
Vidal, Gil (1931–) *Marianne de Ma Jeunesse* 1955; *Too Many Lovers* 1957
Vidal, Gore (1925–) *Fellini's Roma* 1972; *Bob Roberts* 1992; *With Honors* 1994; *Shadow Conspiracy* 1996; *Gattaca* 1997
Vidal, Henri (1919–1959) *The House on the Waterfront* 1955; *Gates of Paris* 1957; *Une Parisienne* 1957; *Too Many Lovers* 1957
Vidal, Lisa (1965–) *Fall* 1997; *Hit and Run* 1999
Vidarte, Walter (1931–) *1919* 1983; *Outrage* 1993
Vidler, Steven (1960–) *The Good Wife* 1986; *Encounter at Raven's Gate* 1988; *Two Hands* 1999
Vidler, Susan *Naked* 1993; *Trainspotting* 1995; *The Wedding Tackle* 2000; *Wilbur (Wants to Kill Himself)* 2002
Vidor, Florence (1895–1977) *The Marriage Circle* 1924; *The Patriot* 1928
Vidor, King (1894–1982) *It's a Great Feeling* 1949; *Love and Money* 1982
Vieira, Asia (1982–) *The Price of Passion* 1988; *Omen IV: the Awakening* 1991
Vigoda, Abe (1921–) *Newman's Law* 1974; *Plain Clothes* 1988; *Look Who's Talking* 1989; *Joe versus the Volcano* 1990; *Keaton's Cop* 1990; *Batman: Mask of the Phantasm* 1993; *Sugar Hill* 1993; *Jury Duty* 1995; *Love Is All There Is* 1996; *Underworld* 1996; *Good Burger* 1997
Vigran, Herb (1911–1986) *Bedtime for Bonzo* 1951; *Go, Johnny, Go!* 1959; *Charlotte's Web* 1973
Viharo, Robert (1939–) *Villa Rides* 1968; *Return to Macon County* 1975; *Happy Birthday, Gemini* 1980; *Hide in Plain Sight* 1980; *The Night Stalker* 1985
Villagra, Nelson (1937–) *The Last Supper* 1976; *Amnesia* 1994
Villalonga, Marthe (1932–) *Ma Saison Préferée* 1993; *Alice et Martin* 1998
Villard, Frank (1917–1980) *The Seven Deadly Sins* 1952; *No Exit* 1954; *Guilty?* 1956
Villard, Tom (1954–1994) *Parasite* 1982; *Popcorn* 1991
Villechaize, Herve (1943–1993) *The Gang That Couldn't Shoot Straight* 1971; *The Man with the Golden Gun* 1974; *Seizure* 1974; *The One and Only* 1978
Villeret, Jacques (1951–2005) *Robert et Robert* 1978; *An Adventure for Two* 1979; *Les Uns et les Autres* 1981; *Edith and Marcel* 1983; *Hold-Up* 1985; *Soigne Ta Droite* 1986; *The Favour, the Watch and the Very Big Fish* 1991; *The Children of the Marshland* 1998; *Le Dîner de Cons* 1998; *Strange Gardens* 2003
Villiers, James (1933–1998) *Eva* 1962; *Operation Snatch* 1962; *Father Came Too* 1963; *Murder at the Gallop* 1963; *King and Country* 1964; *The Nanny* 1965; *Otley* 1968; *A Nice Girl like Me* 1969; *Some Girls Do* 1969; *Blood from the Mummy's Tomb* 1971; *The Amazing Mr Blunden* 1972; *The Ruling Class* 1972; *Ghost in the Noonday Sun* 1973; *Seven Nights in Japan* 1976; *Saint Jack* 1979; *The Scarlet Pimpernel* 1982; *Under the Volcano* 1984; *Mountains of the Moon* 1989; *King Ralph* 1991
Villiers, Mavis (1915–1976) *Suddenly, Last Summer* 1959; *Philadelphia, Here I Come* 1975
Vince, Pruitt Taylor (1960–) *Shy People* 1987; *Mississippi Burning* 1988; *Jacob's Ladder* 1990; *City Slickers II: the Legend of Curly's Gold* 1994; *Nobody's Fool* 1994; *Heavy* 1995; *Under the Hula Moon* 1995; *A Further Gesture* 1996; *The Legend of 1900* 1999; *Mumford* 1999; *Nurse Betty* 2000; *S1MØNE* 2002; *Trapped* 2002; *Identity* 2003; *Monster* 2003; *Constantine* 2005
Vincent, Alex (1981–) *Child's Play* 1988; *Child's Play 2* 1990
Vincent, Frank (1940–) *Death Collector* 1976; *Raging Bull* 1980; *Jungle Fever* 1991; *Mortal Thoughts* 1991; *Hand Gun* 1994
Vincent, Hélène (1943–) *J'Embrasse Pas* 1991; *Three Colours Blue* 1993; *Ma Vie en Rose* 1997
Vincent, Jan-Michael aka **Vincent, Michael** (1944–) *The Undefeated* 1969; *Going Home* 1971; *The Mechanic* 1972; *The World's Greatest Athlete* 1973; *Buster and Billie* 1974; *Bite the Bullet* 1975; *Vigilante Force* 1975; *White Line Fever* 1975; *Damnation Alley* 1977; *Big Wednesday* 1978; *Hooper* 1978; *Defiance* 1979; *Hard Country* 1981; *Last Plane Out* 1983; *Born in East LA* 1987; *Enemy Territory* 1987; *Hit List* 1988; *Demonstone* 1989; *Haunting Fear* 1990; *Hangfire* 1991; *Raw Nerve* 1991; *Indecent Behavior* 1993; *Orbit* 1996; *Buffalo '66* 1998
Vincent, June (1924–) *Can't Help Singing* 1944; *Here Come the Co-Eds* 1945; *Black Angel* 1946; *Marry Me Again* 1953
Vincent, Virginia (1924–) *I Want to Live!* 1958; *The Return of Dracula* 1958; *The Black Orchid* 1959; *The Hills Have Eyes* 1977
Vines, Margaret (1910–1997) *Open All Night* 1934; *The Vicar of Bray* 1937
Ving, Lee aka **Ving James, Lee** *Streets of Fire* 1984; *Black Moon Rising* 1985; *Dudes* 1987; *The Taking of Beverly Hills* 1991
Vinovich, Steve aka **Vinovich, Stephen** *Jennifer on My Mind* 1971; *Mannequin* 1987
Vinson, Helen (1907–1999) *I Am a Fugitive from a Chain Gang* 1932; *Lawyer Man* 1932; *The Kennel Murder Case* 1933; *The Little Giant* 1933; *The Power and the Glory* 1933; *Broadway Bill* 1934; *The Captain Hates the Sea* 1934; *King of the Damned* 1935; *Private Worlds* 1935; *The Tunnel* 1935; *The Wedding Night* 1935; *Live, Love and Learn* 1937; *Vogues of 1938* 1937; *In Name Only* 1939; *Torrid Zone* 1940; *Nothing but the Truth* 1941; *The Lady and the Monster* 1944; *The Thin Man Goes Home* 1944
Vint, Alan *The Panic in Needle Park* 1971; *Welcome Home, Soldier Boys* 1971; *The Unholy Rollers* 1972; *Badlands* 1973; *Macon County Line* 1973; *The Ballad of Gregorio Cortez* 1983
Vint, Jesse *Silent Running* 1971; *Macon County Line* 1973; *Bug* 1975; *Deathsport* 1978; *Fast Charlie: the Moonbeam Rider* 1978
Vintas, Gustav *Silent Assassins* 1988; *Midnight* 1989
Vinton, Arthur *Washington Merry-Go-Round* 1932; *Dames* 1934
Vinton, Bobby *Big Jake* 1971; *The Train Robbers* 1973
Visnjic, Goran (1972–) *Welcome to Sarajevo* 1997; *Practical Magic* 1998; *Committed* 2000; *The Deep End* 2001; *Doctor Sleep* 2002; *Ice Age* 2002; *Elektra* 2005
Vitale, Joseph (1901–1994) *Road to Rio* 1947; *The Paleface* 1948; *Apache Rifles* 1964
Vitale, Milly (1932–) *The Juggler* 1953; *Seven Little Foys* 1955; *The Flesh Is Weak* 1957; *The Battle of the V1* 1958; *Hannibal* 1959; *A Breath of Scandal* 1960
Viterelli, Joe (1941–2004) *Bullets over Broadway* 1994; *American Strays* 1996; *Heaven's Prisoners* 1996; *Analyze This* 1999; *Mickey Blue Eyes* 1999; *See Spot Run* 2001; *Shallow Hal* 2001; *Analyze That* 2002
Vitez, Antoine (1930–1990) *My Night with Maud* 1969; *Ecoute Voir...* 1978; *The Green Room* 1978
Vitold, Michel (1915–1994) *La Nuit Fantastique* 1942; *The Testament of Dr Cordelier* 1959; *Judex* 1963; *Thomas the Imposter* 1964; *The Confession* 1970
Vitti, Monica (1931–) *L'Avventura* 1960; *La Notte* 1961; *The Eclipse* 1962; *The Red Desert* 1964; *Le Bambole* 1965; *Modesty Blaise* 1966; *On My Way to the Crusades, I Met a Girl Who...* 1967; *Jealousy, Italian Style* 1970; *Le Fantôme de la Liberté* 1974; *An Almost Perfect Affair* 1979; *Tigers in Lipstick* 1979; *Immortal Bachelor* 1980; *The Oberwald Mystery* 1980
Viva (1941–) *Bike Boy* 1967; *Lonesome Cowboys* 1968; *Lions Love* 1969; *Sam's Song* 1969; *Cisco Pike* 1971; *Play It Again, Sam* 1972; *Ciao! Manhattan* 1973
Vlady, Marina (1938–) *The Theft of the Mona Lisa* 1965; *Chimes at Midnight* 1966; *Two or Three Things I Know about Her* 1966; *The Thief of Baghdad* 1978; *Tangos, Exilo de Gardel* 1985
Vlahos, Sam *Powwow Highway* 1988; *The Big Squeeze* 1996
Voe, Sandra *Breaking the Waves* 1996; *The Winter Guest* 1996; *Janice Beard 45 WPM* 1999
Vogler, Karl Michael (1928–) *The Blue Max* 1966; *How I Won the War* 1967; *Deep End* 1970
Vogler, Rüdiger (1942–) *Alice in the Cities* 1974; *Kings of the Road* 1976; *The German Sisters* 1981; *Until the End of the World* 1991; *Faraway, So Close* 1993; *Lisbon Story* 1994
Vohs, Joan (1927–2001) *Cry Vengeance* 1954; *Sabrina* 1954
Voight, Jon (1938–) *Frank's Greatest Adventure* 1967; *Hour of the Gun* 1967; *Midnight Cowboy* 1969; *Catch-22* 1970; *The Revolutionary* 1970; *Deliverance* 1972; *The All-American Boy* 1973; *Conrack* 1974; *The Odessa File* 1974; *End of the Game* 1976; *Coming Home* 1978; *The Champ* 1979; *Lookin' to Get Out* 1982; *Table for Five* 1983; *Desert Bloom* 1985; *Runaway Train* 1985; *Eternity* 1990; *Heat* 1995; *Mission: Impossible* 1996; *Anaconda* 1997; *John Grisham's The Rainmaker* 1997; *Most Wanted* 1997; *Rosewood* 1997; *U Turn* 1997; *Enemy of the State* 1998; *The General* 1998; *A Dog*

of Flanders 1999; *Varsity Blues* 1999; *Ali* 2001; *Lara Croft: Tomb Raider* 2001; *Pearl Harbor* 2001; *Zoolander* 2001; *Holes* 2003; *The Manchurian Candidate* 2004; *National Treasure* 2004

Voit, Mieczyslaw *The Devil and the Nun* 1960; *The Story of Sin* 1975

Volchek, Galina (1957–) *King Lear* 1970; *The Little Mermaid* 1976

Volonté, Gian Maria aka **Wels, John** (1933–1994) *The Four Days of Naples* 1962; *A Fistful of Dollars* 1964; *For a Few Dollars More* 1965; *A Bullet for the General* 1966; *Face to Face* 1967; *We Still Kill the Old Way* 1967; *Vent d'Est* 1969; *Investigation of a Citizen above Suspicion* 1970; *The Red Circle* 1970; *Sacco and Vanzetti* 1971; *The Working Class Goes to Heaven* 1971; *The Mattei Affair* 1972; *Lucky Luciano* 1973; *Christ Stopped at Eboli* 1979; *The Death of Mario Ricci* 1983; *Chronicle of a Death Foretold* 1987; *Open Doors* 1990

Volter, Philippe (1959–2005) *The Music Teacher* 1988; *The Double Life of Véronique* 1991; *Three Colours Blue* 1993

Von Bargen, Daniel (1950–) *Company Business* 1991; *Lord of Illusions* 1995; *Before and After* 1996; *GI Jane* 1997; *The Postman* 1997; *The General's Daughter* 1999; *Universal Soldier – the Return* 1999; *Super Troopers* 2001

von Borsody, Suzanne (1957–) *Flight of the Albatross* 1995; *Run Lola Run* 1998

von Brömssen, Tomas (1943–) *My Life as a Dog* 1985; *All Things Fair* 1995

Von Detten, Erik (1982–) *Top Dog* 1995; *Leave It to Beaver* 1997

Von Dohlen, Lenny (1958–) *Tender Mercies* 1982; *Electric Dreams* 1984; *Billy Galvin* 1986; *Dracula's Widow* 1988; *Blind Vision* 1992; *Leaving Normal* 1992; *Tollbooth* 1994; *Entertaining Angels: the Dorothy Day Story* 1996; *One Good Turn* 1996; *Home Alone 3* 1997

von Eltz, Theodore (1894–1964) *The Four Feathers* 1929; *Confidential* 1935; *Beloved Enemy* 1936; *California Straight Ahead* 1937; *Devil's Cargo* 1948

von Fürstenberg, Ira aka **Furstenberg, Ira** aka **Fürstenberg, Ira** (1940–) *Dead Run* 1967; *The Battle of El Alamein* 1968; *Hello – Goodbye* 1970

Von Leer, Hunter (1944–) *Halloween II* 1981; *Under the Boardwalk* 1988

Von Lehndorff, Veruschka aka **Verushka** aka **Veruschka** *Blowup* 1966; *The Bride* 1985

von Rezzori, Gregor (1914–1998) *A Very Private Affair* 1962; *Viva Maria!* 1965

von Schlettow, Hans Adalbert (1887–1945) *Dr Mabuse, the Gambler* 1922; *Asphalt* 1928

von Seyffertitz, Gustav (1863–1943) *Sparrows* 1926; *The Gaucho* 1927; *The Student Prince in Old Heidelberg* 1927; *The Docks of New York* 1928; *The Mysterious Lady* 1928; *The Canary Murder Case* 1929; *The Case of Lena Smith* 1929; *Dishonored* 1931; *Shanghai Express* 1932; *Change of Heart* 1934; *The Moonstone* 1934; *She* 1935

von Stroheim, Erich (1885–1957) *Hearts of the World* 1918; *Blind Husbands* 1919; *Foolish Wives* 1920; *The Wedding March* 1928; *The Great Gabbo* 1929; *Friends and Lovers* 1931; *As You Desire Me* 1932; *The Lost Squadron* 1932; *La Grande Illusion* 1937; *Pièges* 1939; *I Was an Adventuress* 1940; *So Ends Our Night* 1941; *Five Graves to Cairo* 1943; *The North Star* 1943; *The Lady and the Monster* 1944; *The Great Flamarion* 1945; *Sunset Blvd* 1950; *Napoléon* 1955

von Sydow, Max (1929–) *The Seventh Seal* 1957; *So Close to Life* 1957; *The Magician* 1958; *The Virgin Spring* 1960; *Through a Glass Darkly* 1961; *Winter Light* 1962; *The Greatest Story Ever Told* 1965; *The Reward* 1965; *Hawaii* 1966; *The Quiller Memorandum* 1966; *The Hour of the Wolf* 1967; *Shame* 1968; *A Passion* 1969; *The Kremlin Letter* 1970; *The Night Visitor* 1970; *The Emigrants* 1971; *The Touch* 1971; *Embassy* 1972; *The New Land* 1972; *The Exorcist* 1973; *Steppenwolf* 1974; *Three Days of the Condor* 1975; *The Ultimate Warrior* 1975; *Illustrious Corpses* 1976; *Voyage of the Damned* 1976; *Exorcist II: The Heretic* 1977; *March or Die* 1977; *Brass Target* 1978; *Hurricane* 1979; *Deathwatch* 1980; *Flash Gordon* 1980; *Escape to Victory* 1981; *She Dances Alone* 1981; *Conan the Barbarian* 1982; *Target Eagle* 1982; *Never Say Never Again* 1983; *Strange Brew* 1983; *Dreamscape* 1984; *Dune* 1984; *Code Name: Emerald* 1985; *Duet for One* 1986; *Hannah and Her Sisters* 1986; *The Second Victory* 1986; *The Wolf at the Door* 1986; *Pelle the Conqueror* 1987; *Awakenings* 1990; *The Bachelor* 1990; *Father* 1990; *Europa* 1991; *A Kiss before Dying* 1991; *The Ox* 1991; *Until the End of the World* 1991; *Best Intentions* 1992; *The Silent Touch* 1992; *Needful Things* 1993; *Citizen X* 1995; *Judge Dredd* 1995; *Hamsun* 1996; *Hostile Waters* 1996; *Jerusalem* 1996; *Private Confessions* 1996; *What Dreams May Come* 1998; *Snow Falling on Cedars* 1999; *Druids* 2001; *Intacto* 2001; *Minority Report* 2002; *Sword of Xanten* 2004

von Trotta, Margarethe (1942–) *Gods of the Plague* 1969; *The American Soldier* 1970; *Beware of a Holy Whore* 1970

von Twardowski, Hans (1898–1958) *The Cabinet of Dr Caligari* 1919; *The Scarlet Empress* 1934

von Walther, Hertha (1903–1987) *The Love of Jeanne Ney* 1927; *Crisis* 1928

von Wangenheim, Gustav (1895–1975) *Nosferatu, a Symphony of Horrors* 1922; *The Woman in the Moon* 1929

Von Weitershausen, Gila (1944–) *The Pedestrian* 1974; *Circle of Deceit* 1981; *Trenchcoat* 1983

von Wernherr, Otto *Liquid Sky* 1982; *Blind Alley* 1984

Von Zell, Harry (1906–1981) *The Guilt of Janet Ames* 1947; *The Saxon Charm* 1948; *For Heaven's Sake* 1950; *Two Flags West* 1950; *I Can Get It for You Wholesale* 1951; *Son of Paleface* 1952

Von Zerneck, Danielle (1966–) *My Science Project* 1985; *La Bamba* 1987; *Under the Boardwalk* 1988; *Living in Oblivion* 1995

Vonn, Veola (1918–1995) *Phantom of the Rue Morgue* 1954; *Hell Bent for Glory* 1957

Voskovec, George (1905–1981) *12 Angry Men* 1957; *The 27th Day* 1957; *Wind across the Everglades* 1958; *Barbarosa* 1982

Vosloo, Arnold (1962–) *Hard Target* 1993; *Darkman II: the Return of Durant* 1995; *Darkman III: Die Darkman Die* 1996; *Diary of a Serial Killer* 1997; *Zeus and Roxanne* 1997; *Progeny* 1998; *The Mummy* 1999; *The Mummy Returns* 2001; *Agent Cody Banks* 2003

Vosper, Frank (1899–1937) *Waltzes from Vienna* 1933; *Jew Süss* 1934; *The Man Who Knew Too Much* 1934; *Open All Night* 1934; *Heart's Desire* 1935; *Königsmark* 1935

Vosselli, Judith (1895–1966) *The Rogue Song* 1930; *Inspiration* 1931

Votrian, Peter *Big House, USA* 1955; *Crime in the Streets* 1956; *Fear Strikes Out* 1957

Voutsinas, Andreas *The Producers* 1968; *A Dream of Passion* 1978

Voyagis, Yorgo *The Last Valley* 1971; *Chronicle of the Burning Years* 1975; *The Little Drummer Girl* 1984; *Vampire in Venice* 1987; *Frantic* 1988; *Courage Mountain* 1989; *Swept Away* 2002

Vrana, Vlasta *Scanners II: The New Order* 1991; *Brainscan* 1994; *The Assignment* 1997; *Grey Owl* 1999

Vriends, Brian *Mortgage* 1989; *Struck by Lightning* 1990

Vroom, Frederick (1857–1942) *The Navigator* 1924; *The General* 1927

Vuco, Olivera (1940–) *I Even Met Happy Gypsies* 1967; *Mark of the Devil* 1970

Vukotic, Milena (1930–) *Blood for Dracula* 1974; *The Art of Love* 1983; *A Good Woman* 2004

Vye, Murvyn (1913–1976) *Golden Earrings* 1947; *Whispering Smith* 1948; *A Connecticut Yankee in King Arthur's Court* 1949; *Road to Bali* 1952; *Destination Gobi* 1953; *Pickup on South Street* 1953; *Black Horse Canyon* 1954; *Green Fire* 1954; *River of No Return* 1954; *Escape to Burma* 1955; *Pearl of the South Pacific* 1955; *The Best Things in Life Are Free* 1956; *Short Cut to Hell* 1957; *Al Capone* 1959

Vyjayanthimala (1936–) *Sadhna* 1958; *Sangam* 1964

Vyner, Margaret (1914–1993) *Climbing High* 1938; *The Lamp Still Burns* 1943

W

Waddell, Justine (1976–) *The Misadventures of Margaret* 1998; *Dracula 2001* 2000; *The One and Only* 2001

Waddington, Steven (1968–) *Edward II* 1991; *The Last of the Mohicans* 1992; *Don't Get Me Started* 1994; *Prince of Jutland* 1994; *Carrington* 1995; *Face* 1997; *Tarzan and the Lost City* 1998; *The Hole* 2001; *The Parole Officer* 2001

Wade, Adam (1935–) *Gordon's War* 1973; *Claudine* 1974

Wade, Russell (1917–) *The Ghost Ship* 1943; *The Iron Major* 1943; *The Body Snatcher* 1945; *A Game of Death* 1945; *The Bamboo Blonde* 1946

Wadham, Julian (1958–) *The Madness of King George* 1995; *The English Patient* 1996; *Keep the Aspidistra Flying* 1997; *Preaching to the Perverted* 1997; *Exorcist: the Beginning* 2004

Wadsworth, Henry (1902–1974) *Applause* 1929; *Fast and Loose* 1930; *The Thin Man* 1934; *Ceiling Zero* 1935

Wager, Anthony (1932–) *Great Expectations* 1946; *The Hi-Jackers* 1963

Wagner, David *Thrashin'* 1986; *Pet Shop* 1995

Wagner, Fernando (1973–) *Tarzan and the Mermaids* 1948; *Garden of Evil* 1954

Wagner, Lindsay (1949–) *The Paper Chase* 1973; *Two People* 1973; *The Rockford Files* 1974; *High Risk* 1981; *Nighthawks* 1981; *Martin's Day* 1984; *Ricochet* 1991; *Danielle Steel's Once in a Lifetime* 1994

Wagner, Lou (1948–) *Planet of the Apes* 1967; *Conquest of the Planet of the Apes* 1972; *GORP* 1980

Wagner, Robert (1930–) *Halls of Montezuma* 1950; *The Happy Years* 1950; *The Frogmen* 1951; *Let's Make It Legal* 1951; *Stars and Stripes Forever* 1952; *What Price Glory?* 1952; *With a Song in My Heart* 1952; *Beneath the 12-Mile Reef* 1953; *Titanic* 1953; *Broken Lance* 1954; *Prince Valiant* 1954; *White Feather* 1955; *Between Heaven and Hell* 1956; *A Kiss before Dying* 1956; *The Mountain* 1956; *Stopover Tokyo* 1957; *The True Story of Jesse James* 1957; *The Hunters* 1958; *In Love and War* 1958; *Say One for Me* 1959; *All the Fine Young Cannibals* 1960; *Sail a Crooked Ship* 1961; *The Condemned of Altona* 1962; *The Longest Day* 1962; *The War Lover* 1962; *The Pink Panther* 1963; *Harper* 1966; *Banning* 1967; *How I Spent My Summer Vacation* 1967; *The Biggest Bundle of Them All* 1968; *Don't Just Stand There* 1968; *Winning* 1969; *City beneath the Sea* 1971; *Madame Sin* 1972; *The Affair* 1973; *The Towering Inferno* 1974; *Battle of Midway* 1976; *Airport '79: the Concorde* 1979; *The Curse of the Pink Panther* 1983; *I Am the Cheese* 1983; *Delirious* 1991; *Dragon: the Bruce Lee Story* 1993; *Austin Powers: International Man of Mystery* 1997; *Something to Believe In* 1997; *Wild Things* 1998; *Austin Powers: the Spy Who Shagged Me* 1999; *Crazy in Alabama* 1999; *Play It to the Bone* 2000; *Austin Powers in Goldmember* 2002

Wagner, Wende (1941–1997) *Rio Conchos* 1964; *Destination Inner Space* 1966

Wahl, Ken (1957–) *The Wanderers* 1979; *Fort Apache, the Bronx* 1981; *Treasure of the Yankee Zephyr* 1981; *Jinxed!* 1982; *Purple Hearts* 1984; *The Taking of Beverly Hills* 1991; *The Favor* 1994

Wahlberg, Donnie (1969–) *Bullet* 1995; *Body Count* 1997; *Purgatory* 1999; *The Sixth Sense* 1999; *Triggermen* 2002; *Dreamcatcher* 2003

Wahlberg, Mark aka **Mark, Marky** (1971–) *Renaissance Man* 1994; *The Basketball Diaries* 1995; *Fear* 1996; *Boogie Nights* 1997; *Traveller* 1997; *The Big Hit* 1998; *The Corruptor* 1999; *Three Kings* 1999; *The Perfect Storm* 2000; *The Yards* 2000; *Planet of the Apes* 2001; *Rock Star* 2001; *The Truth about Charlie* 2002; *The Italian Job* 2003; *I ❤ Huckabees* 2004

Wainwright, James (1938–1999) *Joe Kidd* 1972; *Mean Dog Blues* 1978; *Battletruck* 1982; *The Survivors* 1983

Wainwright III, Loudon (1946–) *The Slugger's Wife* 1985; *Jacknife* 1988

Waite, Ralph (1928–) *A Lovely Way to Go* 1968; *Last Summer* 1969; *Five Easy Pieces* 1970; *Chato's Land* 1971; *Kid Blue* 1971; *The Magnificent Seven Ride!* 1972; *Trouble Man* 1972; *The Stone Killer* 1973; *On the Nickel* 1979; *The Bodyguard* 1992; *Sioux City* 1994; *Homeward Bound II: Lost in San Francisco* 1996; *The President's Man* 2000; *Sunshine State* 2002

Waites, Thomas G aka **Waites, Thomas** aka **Waites, Tom** *On the Yard* 1978; *The Warriors* 1979; *The Clan of the Cave Bear* 1986; *Light of Day* 1987; *Blue Jean Cop* 1988

Waits, Tom (1949–) *The Outsiders* 1983; *Rumble Fish* 1983; *Down by Law* 1986; *Candy Mountain* 1987; *Ironweed* 1987; *Cold Feet* 1989; *Mystery Train* 1989; *At Play in the Fields of the Lord* 1991; *Queens Logic* 1991; *Bram Stoker's Dracula* 1992; *Short Cuts* 1993; *Coffee and Cigarettes* 2003

Wakabayashi, Akiko (1941–) *What's Up, Tiger Lily?* 1966; *You Only Live Twice* 1967

Wakao, Ayako (1933–) *Street of Shame* 1955; *Floating Weeds* 1959; *An Actor's Revenge* 1963

Wakayama, Tomisaburo (1929–1992) *Baby Cart at the River Styx* 1972; *Sword of Vengeance* 1972; *Black Rain* 1989

Wakefield, Douglas aka **Wakefield, Duggie** (1899–1951) *Look Up and Laugh* 1935; *The Penny Pool* 1937

Wakefield, Hugh (1888–1971) *The Man Who Knew Too Much* 1934; *Forget-Me-Not* 1936; *Journey Together* 1944; *Blithe Spirit* 1945; *One Night with You* 1948

Wakeham, Deborah (1955–) *Middle Age Crazy* 1980; *Stranded* 1989

Walbrook, Anton aka **Wohlbruck, Adolf** (1900–1967) *Viktor und Viktoria* 1933; *The Adventures of Michael Strogoff* 1937; *Victoria the Great* 1937; *Sixty Glorious Years* 1938; *Gaslight* 1940; *Dangerous Moonlight* 1941; *49th Parallel* 1941; *The Life and Death of Colonel Blimp* 1943; *The Man from Morocco* 1944; *The Queen of Spades* 1948; *The Red Shoes* 1948; *La Ronde* 1950; *Lola Montès* 1955; *Oh, Rosalinda!!* 1955; *Saint Joan* 1957; *I Accuse!* 1958

Walburn, Raymond (1887–1969) *Broadway Bill* 1934; *The Count of Monte Cristo* 1934; *Lady by Choice* 1934; *She Married Her Boss* 1935; *Thanks a Million* 1935; *Born to Dance* 1936; *The King Steps Out* 1936; *The Lone Wolf Returns* 1936; *Mr Deeds Goes to Town* 1936; *High, Wide and Handsome* 1937; *Thin Ice* 1937; *Start Cheering* 1938; *Christmas in July* 1940; *Third Finger, Left Hand* 1940; *Confirm or Deny* 1941; *Kiss the Boys Goodbye* 1941; *Louisiana Purchase* 1941; *The Man in the Trunk* 1942; *The Desperadoes* 1943; *Dixie* 1943; *And the Angels Sing* 1944; *Hail the Conquering Hero* 1944; *Music in Manhattan* 1944; *The Cheaters* 1945; *Lover Come Back* 1946; *Rendezvous with Annie* 1946; *Key to the City* 1950; *Mad Wednesday* 1950; *Riding High* 1950; *Golden Girl* 1951; *Beautiful but Dangerous* 1954

Walcott, Gregory (1928–) *Texas Lady* 1955; *The Lieutenant Wore Skirts* 1956; *Thunder over Arizona* 1956; *Jet Attack* 1958; *Plan 9 from Outer Space* 1959; *The Outsider* 1961; *Prime Cut* 1972; *The Sugarland Express* 1974; *House II: the Second Story* 1987

Walden, Robert (1943–) *Bloody Mama* 1970; *The Sidelong Glances of a Pigeon Kicker* 1970; *Larry* 1974; *Blue Sunshine* 1976

Waldis, Otto (1901–1974) *The Exile* 1947; *Bird of Paradise* 1951; *Unknown World* 1951; *The Whip Hand* 1951

Waldman, Marian (1924–) *Black Christmas* 1974; *Deranged* 1974

Waldo, Janet *Waterloo Bridge* 1940; *Fantastic Planet* 1973

Waldron, Charles (1874–1946) *Kentucky* 1938; *Remember the Night* 1940; *Stranger on the Third Floor* 1940; *The Big Sleep* 1946

Waldron, Shawna (1982–) *Little Giants* 1994; *The American President* 1995

Wales, Ethel (1898–1952) *The Covered Wagon* 1923; *The Saturday Night Kid* 1929; *Tom Sawyer* 1930; *The Gladiator* 1938

Walken, Christopher (1943–) *The Anderson Tapes* 1971; *The Mind Snatchers* 1972; *Next Stop, Greenwich Village* 1976; *Annie Hall* 1977; *Roseland* 1977; *The Sentinel* 1977; *The Deer Hunter* 1978; *Last Embrace* 1979; *The Dogs of War* 1980; *Heaven's Gate* 1980; *Pennies from Heaven* 1981; *Brainstorm* 1983; *The Dead Zone* 1983; *At Close Range* 1985; *A View to a Kill* 1985; *Witness in the War Zone* 1986; *Biloxi Blues* 1988; *Homeboy* 1988; *The Milagro Beanfield War* 1988; *Communion* 1989; *King of New York* 1989; *The Comfort of Strangers* 1991; *McBain* 1991; *Batman Returns* 1992; *Day of Atonement* 1992; *Mistress* 1992; *A Business Affair* 1993; *True Romance* 1993; *Wayne's World 2* 1993; *The Addiction* 1994; *The Prophecy* 1994; *Pulp Fiction* 1994; *Nick of Time* 1995; *Search and Destroy* 1995; *Things to Do in Denver When You're Dead* 1995; *Wild Side* 1995; *Basquiat* 1996; *The Funeral* 1996; *Last Man Standing* 1996; *Touch* 1996; *Excess Baggage* 1997; *Mousehunt* 1997; *The Prophecy II*

1997; *Suicide Kings* 1997; *Antz* 1998; *Blast from the Past* 1998; *The Eternal* 1998; *New Rose Hotel* 1998; *Sleepy Hollow* 1999; *The Opportunists* 2000; *The Prophecy 3: the Ascent* 2000; *The Affair of the Necklace* 2001; *America's Sweethearts* 2001; *Joe Dirt* 2001; *Catch Me If You Can* 2002; *The Country Bears* 2002; *Envy* 2003; *Gigli* 2003; *Kangaroo Jack* 2003; *Welcome to the Jungle* 2003; *Around the Bend* 2004; *Man on Fire* 2004; *The Stepford Wives* 2004; *Wedding Crashers* 2005

Walker, Ally (1961–) *Universal Soldier* 1992; *The Seventh Coin* 1993; *When the Bough Breaks* 1993; *Bed of Roses* 1995; *Steal Big, Steal Little* 1995; *Kazaam* 1996; *Happy, Texas* 1999

Walker, Amanda (1961–) *Heat and Dust* 1982; *7 Days to Live* 2000

Walker, Arnetia (1961–) *Scenes from the Class Struggle in Beverly Hills* 1989; *Love Crimes* 1991

Walker, Chris *The Funny Man* 1994; *When Saturday Comes* 1995

Walker, Clint (1927–) *Yellowstone Kelly* 1959; *Gold of the Seven Saints* 1961; *Send Me No Flowers* 1964; *None but the Brave* 1965; *The Night of the Grizzly* 1966; *The Dirty Dozen* 1967; *The Great Bank Robbery* 1969; *More Dead than Alive* 1969; *Sam Whiskey* 1969; *Pancho Villa* 1971; *Baker's Hawk* 1976; *The White Buffalo* 1977; *Small Soldiers* 1998

Walker, Eamonn (1970–) *Tears of the Sun* 2003; *Duma* 2005

Walker, Fiona (1944–) *Far from the Madding Crowd* 1967; *The Asphyx* 1972

Walker, Helen (1920–1968) *Abroad with Two Yanks* 1944; *Brewster's Millions* 1945; *Murder, He Says* 1945; *Cluny Brown* 1946; *Murder in the Music Hall* 1946; *Nightmare Alley* 1947; *Call Northside 777* 1948; *My Dear Secretary* 1948; *Impact* 1949; *The Big Combo* 1955

Walker, Jimmie (1947–) *Water* 1985; *The Guyver* 1991

Walker, Johnny (1923–2003) *Aar Paar* 1954; *Mr and Mrs '55* 1955; *Chori Chori* 1956; *Kaagaz Ke Phool* 1959

Walker, Kathryn (1943–) *Rich Kids* 1979; *Neighbors* 1981; *DARYL* 1985

Walker, Kerry (1948–) *Almost* 1990; *The Piano* 1993

Walker, Martin (1901–1955) *Sanders of the River* 1935; *The Vicar of Bray* 1937; *The Drum* 1938; *Love on the Dole* 1941

Walker, Matthew (1942–) *Little Women* 1994; *Intimate Relations* 1995

Walker, Nancy (1922–1992) *Best Foot Forward* 1943; *Girl Crazy* 1943; *Broadway Rhythm* 1944; *Lucky Me* 1954; *The World's Greatest Athlete* 1973

Walker, Nella (1886–1971) *The Woman in Red* 1935; *In Name Only* 1939; *Three Smart Girls Grow Up* 1939; *When Tomorrow Comes* 1939; *I Love You Again* 1940; *Hers to Hold* 1943; *Sabrina* 1954

Walker, Paul (1973–) *Meet the Deedles* 1998; *She's All That* 1999; *Varsity Blues* 1999; *The Skulls* 2000; *The Fast and the Furious* 2001; *Roadkill* 2001; *Timeline* 2003; *2 Fast 2 Furious* 2003

Walker, Polly (1966–) *Enchanted April* 1991; *Shogun Warrior* 1991; *Patriot Games* 1992; *Sliver* 1993; *The Trial* 1993; *Restoration* 1995; *Daniel Defoe's Robinson Crusoe* 1996; *Emma* 1996; *Roseanna's Grave* 1996; *The Gambler* 1997; *The Woodlanders* 1997; *Curtain Call* 1998; *Dark Harbor* 1998; *Talk of Angels* 1998; *8½ Women* 1999; *Eye of the Killer* 1999; *D-Tox* 2001

Walker, Ray (1904–1980) *Baby, Take a Bow* 1934; *Stars on Parade* 1944; *Marry Me Again* 1953

Walker, Robert (1918–1951) *Madame Curie* 1943; *See Here, Private Hargrove* 1944; *Since You Went Away* 1944; *Thirty Seconds over Tokyo* 1944; *The Clock* 1945; *The Sailor Takes a Wife* 1945; *Till the Clouds Roll By* 1946; *The Beginning or the End* 1947; *The Sea of Grass* 1947; *Song of Love* 1947; *One Touch of Venus* 1948; *Please Believe Me* 1950; *Strangers on a Train* 1951; *Vengeance Valley* 1951; *My Son John* 1952

Walker Jr, Robert *aka* **Walker, Robert** (1940–) *The Hook* 1962; *The Ceremony* 1963; *Ensign Pulver* 1964; *The Happening* 1967; *The War Wagon* 1967; *Easy Rider* 1969; *Road to Salina* 1969; *Young Billy Young* 1969; *Beware! The Blob* 1971; *Don Juan 73, or If Don Juan Were a Woman* 1973; *Hambone and Hillie* 1984

Walker, Scott (1944–) *Cahill, United States Marshal* 1973; *Orca ... Killer Whale* 1977

Walker, Syd (1886–1945) *Over She Goes* 1937; *The Gang's All Here* 1939

Walker, Sydney (1921–1994) *Love Story* 1970; *Prelude to a Kiss* 1992; *Getting Even with Dad* 1994

Walker, Tippy (1947–) *The World of Henry Orient* 1964; *Jennifer on My Mind* 1971

Walker, William (1917–1992) *The Girl Who Had Everything* 1953; *The Boy Who Caught a Crook* 1961

Walker, Zena (1934–2003) *Emergency* 1962; *Sammy Going South* 1963; *One of Those Things* 1970; *The Likely Lads* 1976; *The Dresser* 1983

Wall, Max (1908–1990) *The Hound of the Baskervilles* 1977; *Jabberwocky* 1977; *Hanover Street* 1979; *Little Dorrit* 1987; *We Think the World of You* 1988; *Loser Takes All* 1990

Wall, Robert *aka* **Wall, Bob** (1939–) *Enter the Dragon* 1973; *The Way of the Dragon* 1973; *Game of Death* 1978

Wallace, Anzac (1943–) *Utu* 1983; *The Silent One* 1984; *The Quiet Earth* 1985

Wallace, Basil *Marked for Death* 1990; *Return of the Living Dead III* 1993; *Roadkill* 2001

Wallace, Bill *A Force of One* 1979; *Avenging Force* 1986

Wallace, George (1952–) *3 Strikes* 2000; *The Wash* 2001

Wallace, Ian (1919–) *Assassin for Hire* 1951; *tom thumb* 1958

Wallace, Jean (1923–1990) *Blaze of Noon* 1947; *Jigsaw* 1949; *The Man on the Eiffel Tower* 1949; *Native Son* 1951; *Star of India* 1954; *The Big Combo* 1955; *The Devil's Hairpin* 1957; *Maracaibo* 1958; *Lancelot and Guinevere* 1963; *Beach Red* 1967; *No Blade of Grass* 1970

Wallace, Julie T (1961–) *Hawks* 1988; *The Lunatic* 1992

Wallace, Morgan (1881–1953) *Blonde Venus* 1932; *Hell's House* 1932; *Confidential* 1935; *Billy the Kid Returns* 1938; *Dick Tracy* 1945

Wallace, Paul *Johnny Trouble* 1957; *Gypsy* 1962

Wallace, Rowena (1948–) *Relatives* 1985; *Cappuccino* 1989; *Blackwater Trail* 1995

Wallace Stone, Dee *aka* **Wallace, Dee** (1948–) *The Hills Have Eyes* 1977; *10* 1979; *The Howling* 1981; *ET the Extra-Terrestrial* 1982; *Jimmy the Kid* 1982; *Cujo* 1983; *Legend of the White Horse* 1985; *Secret Admirer* 1985; *Critters* 1986; *Shadow Play* 1986; *Alligator II: the Mutation* 1991; *Popcorn* 1991; *Rescue Me* 1991; *Huck and the King of Hearts* 1993; *Prophet of Evil* 1993; *The Road Home* 1995; *Temptress* 1995; *The Frighteners* 1996; *Skeletons* 1996; *Swearing Allegiance* 1997

Wallach, Eli (1915–) *Baby Doll* 1956; *The Lineup* 1958; *The Magnificent Seven* 1960; *Seven Thieves* 1960; *The Misfits* 1961; *Hemingway's Adventures of a Young Man* 1962; *How the West Was Won* 1962; *Act One* 1963; *The Victors* 1963; *Genghis Khan* 1964; *Kisses for My President* 1964; *The Moon-Spinners* 1964; *Lord Jim* 1965; *The Good, the Bad and the Ugly* 1966; *How to Steal a Million* 1966; *The Poppy Is Also a Flower* 1966; *The Tiger Makes Out* 1967; *Ace High* 1968; *How to Save a Marriage and Ruin Your Life* 1968; *A Lovely Way to Go* 1968; *The Brain* 1969; *Mackenna's Gold* 1969; *The Adventures of Gerard* 1970; *The Angel Levine* 1970; *The People Next Door* 1970; *Zigzag* 1970; *Romance of a Horse Thief* 1971; *Cinderella Liberty* 1973; *The Deep* 1977; *The Domino Principle* 1977; *The Sentinel* 1977; *Girlfriends* 1978; *The Silent Flute* 1978; *Firepower* 1979; *Winter Kills* 1979; *The Hunter* 1980; *The Salamander* 1981; *Skokie* 1981; *Sam's Son* 1984; *Tough Guys* 1986; *Nuts* 1987; *The Godfather Part III* 1990; *The Two Jakes* 1990; *Article 99* 1992; *Mistress* 1992; *Night and the City* 1992; *Two Much* 1995; *The Associate* 1996; *Keeping the Faith* 2000

Waller, Eddy *aka* **Waller, Eddy C** (1889–1977) *Indian Uprising* 1951; *Man without a Star* 1955

Waller, Fats (1904–1943) *King of Burlesque* 1936; *Stormy Weather* 1943

Walley, Deborah (1943–2001) *Gidget Goes Hawaiian* 1961; *Bon Voyage!* 1962; *Summer Magic* 1963; *The Young Lovers* 1964; *Beach Blanket Bingo* 1965; *Sergeant Deadhead* 1965; *Ski Party* 1965; *The Bubble* 1966; *The Ghost in the Invisible Bikini* 1966; *Spinout* 1966

Wallis, Shani (1941–) *Oliver!* 1968; *Arnold* 1973; *Terror in the Wax Museum* 1973; *The Pebble and the Penguin* 1995

Wallraff, Diego (1962–) *Of Love and Shadows* 1994; *The Perez Family* 1995; *Deadlocked* 2000

Walls, Tom (1883–1949) *Rookery Nook* 1930; *A Cuckoo in the Nest* 1933; *Fighting Stock* 1935; *Foreign Affaires* 1935; *For Valour* 1937; *Crackerjack* 1938; *Strange Boarders* 1938; *The Halfway House* 1943; *They Met in the Dark* 1943; *Undercover* 1943; *Love Story* 1944; *Johnny Frenchman* 1945; *The Master of Bankdam* 1947; *While I Live* 1947; *Spring in Park Lane* 1948; *The Interrupted Journey* 1949; *Maytime in Mayfair* 1949

Walsh, Dermot (1924–) *Hungry Hill* 1946; *Jassy* 1947; *The Mark of Cain* 1947; *Third Time Lucky* 1949; *The Frightened Man* 1952; *Ghost Ship* 1952; *The Blue Parrot* 1953; *Counterspy* 1953; *Sea Fury* 1958; *The Bandit of Zhobe* 1959; *The Flesh and the Fiends* 1959; *Make Mine a Million* 1959; *The Breaking Point* 1961; *Emergency* 1962

Walsh, Dylan (1963–) *Nobody's Fool* 1994; *Congo* 1995; *Changing Habits* 1997; *Blood Work* 2002

Walsh, Edward *aka* **Walsh, Ed** (1928–1997) *California Split* 1974; *Let It Ride* 1989

Walsh, Eileen (1978–) *Janice Beard 45 WPM* 1999; *The Magdalene Sisters* 2002

Walsh, George (1889–1981) *Rosita* 1923; *Me and My Gal* 1932; *Black Beauty* 1933; *The Bowery* 1933

Walsh, Gwynyth *Blue Monkey* 1987; *The Crush* 1993

Walsh, J T (1943–1998) *Hard Choices* 1984; *Power* 1986; *Good Morning, Vietnam* 1987; *House of Games* 1987; *Tin Men* 1987; *Tequila Sunrise* 1988; *The Big Picture* 1989; *Dad* 1989; *Wired* 1989; *Crazy People* 1990; *The Grifters* 1990; *Narrow Margin* 1990; *The Russia House* 1990; *Why Me?* 1990; *Backdraft* 1991; *Defenseless* 1991; *Iron Maze* 1991; *True Identity* 1991; *A Few Good Men* 1992; *Hoffa* 1992; *Red Rock West* 1992; *Sniper* 1992; *The Last Seduction* 1993; *Needful Things* 1993; *Blue Chips* 1994; *Charlie's Ghost Story* 1994; *The Client* 1994; *Miracle on 34th Street* 1994; *Silent Fall* 1994; *The Babysitter* 1995; *The Low Life* 1995; *Nixon* 1995; *Sling Blade* 1995; *Crime of the Century* 1996; *Persons Unknown* 1996; *Breakdown* 1997; *The Negotiator* 1998; *Pleasantville* 1998

Walsh, John (1945–) *The Wild Women of Wongo* 1958; *Body Parts* 1991

Walsh, Joseph *aka* **Walsh, Joey** (1937–) *Hans Christian Andersen* 1952; *The Juggler* 1953; *Anzio* 1968; *California Split* 1974; *The Driver* 1978

Walsh, Kate (1967–) *Henry: Portrait of a Serial Killer, Part II* 1996; *Kicking & Screaming* 2005

Walsh, Kay (1914–2005) *Keep Fit* 1937; *The Last Adventurers* 1937; *I See Ice* 1938; *Sons of the Sea* 1939; *In Which We Serve* 1942; *This Happy Breed* 1944; *The October Man* 1947; *Vice Versa* 1947; *Oliver Twist* 1948; *Stage Fright* 1949; *Last Holiday* 1950; *The Magnet* 1950; *Encore* 1951; *Hunted* 1952; *Meet Me Tonight* 1952; *Young Bess* 1953; *Lease of Life* 1954; *Cast a Dark Shadow* 1957; *The Horse's Mouth* 1958; *The Rainbow Jacket* 1958; *Tunes of Glory* 1960; *Greyfriars Bobby* 1961; *Lunch Hour* 1962; *Reach for Glory* 1962; *Dr Syn, Alias the Scarecrow* 1963; *80,000 Suspects* 1963; *The Beauty Jungle* 1964; *He Who Rides a Tiger* 1965; *The Witches* 1966; *Connecting Rooms* 1969; *The Virgin and the Gypsy* 1970; *The Ruling Class* 1972

Walsh, M Emmet (1935–) *Alice's Restaurant* 1969; *The Traveling Executioner* 1970; *The Prisoner of Second Avenue* 1974; *At Long Last Love* 1975; *Mikey and Nicky* 1976; *Straight Time* 1978; *The Fish That Saved Pittsburgh* 1979; *The Jerk* 1979; *Ordinary People* 1980; *Raise the Titanic* 1980; *Back Roads* 1981; *Reds* 1981; *Blade Runner* 1982; *Cannery Row* 1982; *The Escape Artist* 1982; *Fast-Walking* 1982; *Blood Simple* 1983; *Scandalous* 1983; *Grandview, USA* 1984; *Missing in Action* 1984; *The Pope of Greenwich Village* 1984; *Raw Courage* 1984; *Fletch* 1985; *Back to School* 1986; *The Best of Times* 1986; *Critters* 1986; *Resting Place* 1986; *Wildcats* 1986; *Bigfoot and the Hendersons* 1987; *No Man's Land* 1987; *Clean and Sober* 1988; *Sunset* 1988; *Chattahoochee* 1989; *The Mighty Quinn* 1989; *Red Scorpion* 1989; *Narrow Margin* 1990; *Equinox* 1992; *White Sands* 1992; *Bitter Harvest* 1993; *The Music of Chance* 1993; *Wilder Napalm* 1993; *Camp Nowhere* 1994; *Dead Badge* 1995; *Free Willy 2: the Adventure Home* 1995; *Albino Alligator* 1996; *My Best Friend's Wedding* 1997; *Chairman of the Board* 1998; *Erasable You* 1998; *The Iron Giant* 1999; *Random Hearts* 1999; *Wild Wild West* 1999; *Poor White Trash* 2000; *Snow Dogs* 2002; *Christmas with the Kranks* 2004; *Racing Stripes* 2004

Walsh, Percy (1888–1952) *Boys Will Be Boys* 1935; *King of the Damned* 1935; *Pastor Hall* 1940

Walsh, Raoul (1887–1980) *Sadie Thompson* 1928; *It's a Great Feeling* 1949

Walston, Ray (1918–2001) *Kiss Them for Me* 1957; *Damn Yankees* 1958; *South Pacific* 1958; *Say One for Me* 1959; *The Apartment* 1960; *Portrait in Black* 1960; *Convicts Four* 1962; *Who's Minding the Store?* 1963; *Wives and Lovers* 1963; *Kiss Me, Stupid* 1964; *Caprice* 1967; *Paint Your Wagon* 1969; *The Sting* 1973; *Silver Streak* 1976; *The Happy Hooker Goes to Washington* 1977; *Popeye* 1980; *Private School* 1983; *Johnny Dangerously* 1984; *Saturday the 14th Strikes Back* 1988; *Ski Patrol* 1989; *Of Mice and Men* 1992; *Addams Family Reunion* 1998; *My Favorite Martian* 1999

Walter, Harriet (1950–) *Turtle Diary* 1985; *The Good Father* 1986; *Milou en Mai* 1989; *The Hour of the Pig* 1993; *Sense and Sensibility* 1995; *The Governess* 1997; *Keep the Aspidistra Flying* 1997; *Bedrooms and Hallways* 1998; *Onegin* 1999; *Villa des Roses* 2002; *Bright Young Things* 2003

Walter, Jessica (1940–) *Lilith* 1964; *Grand Prix* 1966; *The Group* 1966; *Bye Bye Braverman* 1968; *Number One* 1969; *Play Misty for Me* 1971; *Going Ape!* 1981; *The Flamingo Kid* 1984; *Tapeheads* 1988; *Ghost in the Machine* 1993; *Leave of Absence* 1994; *Temptress* 1995; *Slums of Beverly Hills* 1998; *Dummy* 2002

Walter, Lisa Ann (1963–) *Eddie* 1996; *The Parent Trap* 1998; *Bruce Almighty* 2003; *Shall We Dance* 2004

Walter, Tracey (1942–) *The Hunter* 1980; *Raggedy Man* 1981; *Conan the Destroyer* 1984; *Repo Man* 1984; *Something Wild* 1986; *City Slickers* 1991; *Kidnapped* 1995; *Devil's Child* 1997; *Drive* 1997; *Wild America* 1997; *Face Value* 2001

Walters, Jamie *aka* **Walters, James** (1969–) *Shout* 1991; *Bed & Breakfast* 1992

Walters, Julie (1950–) *Educating Rita* 1983; *She'll Be Wearing Pink Pyjamas* 1984; *Car Trouble* 1985; *Personal Services* 1987; *Prick Up Your Ears* 1987; *Buster* 1988; *Killing Dad* 1989; *Mack the Knife* 1989; *Stepping Out* 1991; *Just like a Woman* 1992; *Sister My Sister* 1994; *Intimate Relations* 1995; *Girls' Night* 1997; *Titanic Town* 1998; *Billy Elliot* 2000; *Harry Potter and the Philosopher's Stone* 2001; *Before You Go* 2002; *Harry Potter and the Chamber of Secrets* 2002; *Calendar Girls* 2003; *Harry Potter and the Prisoner of Azkaban* 2004

Walters, Laurie (1947–) *The Harrad Experiment* 1973; *The Harrad Summer* 1974

Walters, Melora (1968–) *Twenty Bucks* 1993; *Boogie Nights* 1997; *Los Locos* 1997; *Magnolia* 1999; *Wisegirls* 2001; *The Butterfly Effect* 2003

Walters, Nancy *Monster on the Campus* 1958; *The Green Helmet* 1960; *Blue Hawaii* 1961

Walters, Susan (1963–) *Russkies* 1987; *...At First Sight* 1995; *Two Came Back* 1997

Walters, Thorley (1913–1991) *Carlton-Browne of the FO* 1958; *A Lady Mislaid* 1958; *The Pure Hell of St Trinian's* 1960; *Suspect* 1960; *Invasion Quartet* 1961; *Murder She Said* 1961; *Petticoat Pirates* 1961; *The Phantom of the Opera* 1962; *Sherlock Holmes and the Deadly Necklace* 1962; *Ring of Spies* 1963; *Dracula – Prince of Darkness* 1965; *Frankenstein Created Woman* 1966; *Frankenstein Must Be Destroyed* 1969; *The Man Who Haunted Himself* 1970; *Trog* 1970; *Bartleby* 1971; *Vampire Circus* 1971; *The Adventure of Sherlock Holmes' Smarter Brother* 1975; *The People That Time Forgot* 1977; *The Wildcats of St Trinian's* 1980; *The Sign of Four* 1983

Walthall, Henry B (1878–1936) *Home, Sweet Home* 1914; *The Birth of a Nation* 1915; *The Road to Mandalay* 1926; *The Scarlet Letter* 1926; *London after Midnight* 1927; *The Trespasser* 1929; *Abraham Lincoln* 1930; *Tol'able David* 1930; *Chandu the Magician* 1932; *Me and My Gal* 1932; *Ride Him, Cowboy* 1932; *Strange Interlude* 1932; *Laughing at Life* 1933; *Somewhere in Sonora* 1933; *Judge Priest* 1934; *The Lemon Drop Kid* 1934; *Dante's Inferno* 1935; *A Tale of Two Cities* 1935; *China Clipper* 1936; *The Devil-Doll* 1936; *The Last Outlaw* 1936

Walton, Douglas (1910–1961) *The Secret of Madame Blanche*

1933; *Charlie Chan in London* 1934; *Bride of Frankenstein* 1935; *Captain Hurricane* 1935; *Mary of Scotland* 1936; *Bad Lands* 1939; *Raffles* 1939; *Farewell My Lovely* 1944; *The Picture of Dorian Gray* 1945; *Dick Tracy vs Cueball* 1946

Walton, John (1953–) *Undercover* 1983; *Kangaroo* 1986; *The Lighthorsemen* 1987

Waltz, Lisa *Brighton Beach Memoirs* 1986; *The Odd Couple II* 1998

Wanamaker, Sam (1919–1993) *My Girl Tisa* 1948; *Give Us This Day* 1949; *Mr Denning Drives North* 1951; *The Criminal* 1960; *Taras Bulba* 1962; *The Man in the Middle* 1964; *The Spy Who Came in from the Cold* 1965; *Danger Route* 1967; *The Day the Fish Came Out* 1967; *Warning Shot* 1967; *The Sellout* 1975; *Voyage of the Damned* 1976; *Billy Jack Goes to Washington* 1977; *Death on the Nile* 1978; *From Hell to Victory* 1979; *The Competition* 1980; *Private Benjamin* 1980; *Irreconcilable Differences* 1984; *The Aviator* 1985; *Raw Deal* 1986; *Baby Boom* 1987; *Superman IV: the Quest for Peace* 1987; *Judgment in Berlin* 1988; *Guilty by Suspicion* 1990; *Pure Luck* 1991

Wanamaker, Zoë (1949–) *The Raggedy Rawney* 1987; *Amy Foster* 1997; *Wilde* 1997; *Harry Potter and the Philosopher's Stone* 2001; *Five Children and It* 2004

Wang Hong Wei *Xiao Wu* 1997; *Unknown Pleasures* 2002

Wang, Peter *Chan Is Missing* 1982; *A Great Wall* 1985; *The Laserman* 1988

Wang Shuangbao *Balzac and the Little Chinese Seamstress* 2002; *Blind Shaft* 2003

Wang Xueqi *Yellow Earth* 1984; *The Big Parade* 1986

Wang Yu-wen *Rebels of the Neon God* 1992; *Eat Drink Man Woman* 1994

Wang Zhiwen *The Emperor and the Assassin* 1999; *Together with You* 2002

Wanninger, Ashley *Europa, Europa* 1991; *Romance* 1998; *Sex Is Comedy* 2002

War Eagle, John *The Wild North* 1952; *The Great Sioux Uprising* 1953; *When the Legends Die* 1972

Waram, Percy (1881–1961) *Ministry of Fear* 1945; *It Had to Be You* 1947; *The Late George Apley* 1947; *The Big Hangover* 1950; *A Face in the Crowd* 1957

Warbeck, David (1941–1997) *Twins of Evil* 1971; *The Black Cat* 1981

Warburton, John (1887–1981) *Nothing but Trouble* 1944; *Confidential Agent* 1945; *Saratoga Trunk* 1945; *Tarzan and the Huntress* 1947

Warburton, Patrick (1964–) *Dragonard* 1987; *The Dish* 2000; *The Emperor's New Groove* 2000; *Joe Somebody* 2001; *Men in Black 2* 2002

Ward, Amelita *Clancy Street Boys* 1943; *The Falcon and the Co-Eds* 1943; *The Falcon in Danger* 1943; *Come Out Fighting* 1945

Ward, B J *Daffy Duck's Quackbusters* 1988; *Pound Puppies and the Legend of Big Paw* 1988; *Scooby-Doo and the Alien Invaders* 2000

Ward, Fred (1942–) *Escape from Alcatraz* 1979; *UFOria* 1980; *Southern Comfort* 1981; *The Right Stuff* 1983; *Silkwood* 1983; *Uncommon Valor* 1983; *Swing Shift* 1984; *Remo – Unarmed and Dangerous* 1985; *Secret Admirer* 1985; *Train of Dreams* 1987; *Big Business* 1988; *The Prince of Pennsylvania* 1988; *Saigon* 1988; *Catchfire* 1989; *Tremors* 1989; *Henry & June* 1990; *Miami Blues* 1990; *The Dark Wind* 1991; *Equinox* 1992; *The Player* 1992; *Thunderheart* 1992; *Short Cuts* 1993; *Two Small Bodies* 1993; *The Blue Villa* 1994; *Naked Gun 33⅓: the Final Insult* 1994; *Tremors II: Aftershocks* 1995; *Chain Reaction* 1996; *Best Men* 1997; *Dangerous Beauty* 1997; *First Do No Harm* 1997; *The Vivero Letter* 1998; *Circus* 1999; *Red Team* 1999; *Corky Romano* 2001; *Summer Catch* 2001; *Enough* 2002; *Sweet Home Alabama* 2002

Ward, James *Kitten with a Whip* 1964; *The Night of the Iguana* 1964; *Red Line 7000* 1965; *Casper: a Spirited Beginning* 1997

Ward, Jonathan (1970–) *White Water Summer* 1987; *Mac and Me* 1988; *FernGully: the Last Rainforest* 1992

Ward, Kelly (1956–) *Grease* 1978; *The Big Red One* 1980

Ward, Lyman (1941–) *Ferris Bueller's Day Off* 1986; *Guilty as Charged* 1991; *No Dessert Dad, Till You Mow the Lawn* 1994; *The Secret Agent Club* 1995

Ward, Mackenzie *Sunny* 1930; *As You Like It* 1936; *Sons of the Sea* 1939

Ward, Mary B *Playing for Keeps* 1986; *Hangin' with the Homeboys* 1991

Ward, Megan (1969–) *Trancers II: The Return of Jack Deth* 1991; *California Man* 1992; *Freaked* 1993; *PCU* 1994; *Glory Daze* 1995; *Joe's Apartment* 1996; *Wes Craven's Don't Look Down* 1998; *Rated X* 2000

Ward, Michael (1909–1997) *What the Butler Saw* 1950; *The Frightened Man* 1952

Ward, Polly (1909–1987) *The Old Curiosity Shop* 1934; *Hold My Hand* 1938; *It's in the Air* 1938

Ward, Rachel (1957–) *Sharky's Machine* 1981; *Dead Men Don't Wear Plaid* 1982; *Against All Odds* 1984; *The Good Wife* 1986; *Hotel Colonial* 1987; *How to Get Ahead in Advertising* 1989; *After Dark, My Sweet* 1990; *Christopher Columbus: the Discovery* 1992; *Double Jeopardy* 1992; *Wide Sargasso Sea* 1992; *The Ascent* 1994

Ward, Richard *aka* **Ward, Dick** (1915–1979) *The Learning Tree* 1969; *Across 110th Street* 1972; *Cops and Robbers* 1973; *Mandingo* 1975; *Starsky and Hutch* 1975; *The Jerk* 1979; *Brubaker* 1980

Ward, Roger (1936–) *Mad Max* 1979; *Turkey Shoot* 1981; *Fatal Bond* 1991

Ward, Ronald (1901–1978) *We'll Meet Again* 1942; *They Met in the Dark* 1943

Ward, Sandy (?–2005) *The Velvet Vampire* 1971; *Tank* 1984

Ward, Sela (1957–) *The Man Who Loved Women* 1983; *Nothing in Common* 1986; *Hello Again* 1987; *Double Jeopardy* 1992; *The Fugitive* 1993; *My Fellow Americans* 1996; *54* 1998; *Dirty Dancing 2* 2003; *The Day after Tomorrow* 2004

Ward, Simon (1941–) *Frankenstein Must Be Destroyed* 1969; *I Start Counting* 1970; *Young Winston* 1972; *Hitler: the Last Ten Days* 1973; *All Creatures Great and Small* 1974; *Dracula* 1974; *The Four Musketeers* 1974; *Aces High* 1976; *Holocaust 2000* 1977; *Dominique* 1978; *Zulu Dawn* 1979; *The Monster Club* 1980; *Supergirl* 1984; *Leave All Fair* 1985; *Double X: the Name of the Game* 1991

Ward, Skip (1932–2003) *Roadracers* 1958; *Easy Come, Easy Go* 1967; *The Mad Room* 1969

Ward, Sophie (1965–) *Young Sherlock Holmes* 1985; *Aria* 1987; *A Summer Story* 1987; *Young Toscanini* 1988; *The Monk* 1990; *Waxwork II: Lost in Time* 1992; *Wuthering Heights* 1992; *Class of '61* 1993

Ward, Tony *Color Me Dead* 1969; *Hustler White* 1996

Ward, Wally *aka* **Langham, Wallace** (1965–) *Thunder Run* 1986; *The Chocolate War* 1988; *The Invisible Kid* 1988

Ward, Warwick (1891–1967) *Vaudeville* 1925; *The Wonderful Lie of Nina Petrovna* 1929; *FP1* 1932

Warde, Harlan (1917–1980) *Julie* 1956; *The Monster That Challenged the World* 1957

Warden, Jack (1920–) *From Here to Eternity* 1953; *The Bachelor Party* 1957; *Edge of the City* 1957; *12 Angry Men* 1957; *Darby's Rangers* 1958; *Run Silent, Run Deep* 1958; *The Sound and the Fury* 1959; *That Kind of Woman* 1959; *Wake Me When It's Over* 1960; *Escape from Zahrain* 1962; *Donovan's Reef* 1963; *The Thin Red Line* 1964; *Blindfold* 1966; *Bye Bye Braverman* 1968; *Brian's Song* 1971; *The Face of Fear* 1971; *Welcome to the Club* 1971; *Who Is Harry Kellerman, and Why Is He Saying Those Terrible Things about Me?* 1971; *Billy Two Hats* 1973; *The Man Who Loved Cat Dancing* 1973; *The Apprenticeship of Duddy Kravitz* 1974; *Shampoo* 1975; *All the President's Men* 1976; *Raid on Entebbe* 1977; *The White Buffalo* 1977; *Death on the Nile* 1978; *Heaven Can Wait* 1978; *...And Justice for All* 1979; *Being There* 1979; *Beyond the Poseidon Adventure* 1979; *The Champ* 1979; *Dreamer* 1979; *Used Cars* 1980; *Carbon Copy* 1981; *Chu Chu and the Philly Flash* 1981; *The Great Muppet Caper* 1981; *So Fine* 1981; *The Verdict* 1982; *Crackers* 1984; *The Aviator* 1985; *September* 1987; *Still Crazy like a Fox* 1987; *The Presidio* 1988; *Everybody Wins* 1990; *Problem Child* 1990; *Problem Child 2* 1991; *Night and the City* 1992; *Passed Away* 1992; *Toys* 1992; *Guilty as Sin* 1993; *Bullets over Broadway* 1994; *Things to Do in Denver When You're Dead* 1995; *While You Were Sleeping* 1995; *Ed* 1996; *The Island on Bird Street* 1997; *Chairman of the Board* 1998; *Dirty Work* 1998; *A Dog of Flanders* 1999; *The Replacements* 2000

Wardwell, Geoffrey (1900–1955) *The Challenge* 1938; *Crimes at the Dark House* 1939

Ware, Helen (1877–1939) *The Virginian* 1929; *Tol'able David* 1930

Ware, Herta *Cocoon* 1985; *Crazy in Love* 1992

Ware, Irene (1911–1993) *Chandu the Magician* 1932; *The Raven* 1935

Warhol, Andy (1928–1987) *Dynamite Chicken* 1971; *The Driver's Seat* 1975

Waring, Richard (1925–1994) *The Perfect Gentleman* 1935; *Mr Skeffington* 1944

Warlock, Billy (1961–) *Hot Shot* 1986; *Society* 1989

Warnecke, Gordon *My Beautiful Laundrette* 1985; *The Pleasure Principle* 1991

Warner, Amelia (1982–) *Don Quixote* 2000; *Quills* 2000

Warner, David (1941–) *Tom Jones* 1963; *Morgan – a Suitable Case for Treatment* 1966; *The Bofors Gun* 1968; *The Fixer* 1968; *The Sea Gull* 1968; *Work Is a Four Letter Word* 1968; *A Midsummer Night's Dream* 1969; *The Ballad of Cable Hogue* 1970; *Perfect Friday* 1970; *A Doll's House* 1973; *From beyond the Grave* 1973; *Little Malcolm and His Struggle Against the Eunuchs* 1974; *Mister Quilp* 1975; *The Omen* 1976; *Cross of Iron* 1977; *The Disappearance* 1977; *Providence* 1977; *Silver Bears* 1977; *The Thirty-Nine Steps* 1978; *Airport '79: the Concorde* 1979; *Nightwing* 1979; *SOS Titanic* 1979; *Time after Time* 1979; *The Island* 1980; *Tron* 1982; *The Man with Two Brains* 1983; *The Company of Wolves* 1984; *Hanna's War* 1988; *Mr North* 1988; *Waxwork* 1988; *Mortal Passions* 1989; *Star Trek V: the Final Frontier* 1989; *Star Trek VI: the Undiscovered Country* 1991; *Teenage Mutant Ninja Turtles II: the Secret of the Ooze* 1991; *The Unnamable Returns* 1992; *Necronomicon* 1993; *Quest of the Delta Knights* 1993; *In the Mouth of Madness* 1994; *Naked Souls* 1995; *The Leading Man* 1996; *Rasputin* 1996; *Money Talks* 1997; *Scream 2* 1997; *Winnie the Pooh's Most Grand Adventure* 1997; *The Little Unicorn* 1998; *Wing Commander* 1999; *Superstition* 2001; *Kiss of Life* 2003; *Ladies in Lavender* 2004; *The League of Gentlemen's Apocalypse* 2005

Warner, H B (1876–1958) *The King of Kings* 1927; *The Divine Lady* 1928; *The Show of Shows* 1929; *The Green Goddess* 1930; *Five Star Final* 1931; *Jennie Gerhardt* 1933; *Supernatural* 1933; *Mr Deeds Goes to Town* 1936; *Lost Horizon* 1937; *Victoria the Great* 1937; *Bulldog Drummond in Africa* 1938; *Kidnapped* 1938; *The Toy Wife* 1938; *Bulldog Drummond's Bride* 1939; *Mr Smith Goes to Washington* 1939; *New Moon* 1940; *The Corsican Brothers* 1941; *Topper Returns* 1941; *Hitler's Children* 1943; *Action in Arabia* 1944; *It's a Wonderful Life* 1946; *Strange Impersonation* 1946; *High Wall* 1947; *The Prince of Thieves* 1948

Warner, Jack (1894–1981) *The Captive Heart* 1946; *Against the Wind* 1947; *Dear Murderer* 1947; *Easy Money* 1947; *Holiday Camp* 1947; *Hue and Cry* 1947; *Here Come the Huggetts* 1948; *My Brother's Keeper* 1948; *Vote for Huggett* 1948; *The Blue Lamp* 1949; *Boys in Brown* 1949; *The Huggetts Abroad* 1949; *Train of Events* 1949; *Scrooge* 1951; *Valley of Eagles* 1951; *Emergency Call* 1952; *Meet Me Tonight* 1952; *Albert, RN* 1953; *The Final Test* 1953; *The Square Ring* 1953; *Bang! You're Dead* 1954; *Forbidden Cargo* 1954; *The Ladykillers* 1955; *The Quatermass Xperiment* 1955; *Home and Away* 1956; *Carve Her Name with Pride* 1958; *Jigsaw* 1962; *Dominique* 1978

Warner, Julie (1965–) *Doc Hollywood* 1991; *Mr Saturday Night* 1992; *The Puppet Masters* 1994; *Tommy Boy* 1995; *Wedding Bell Blues* 1996; *Mr Murder* 1998

Warner, Malcolm-Jamal (1970–) *Drop Zone* 1994; *The Tuskegee Airmen* 1995; *Restaurant* 1998

Warner, Richard *To Have and to Hold* 1951; *Village of the Damned* 1960

Warren, Barry (1933–) *The Devil-Ship Pirates* 1964; *Frankenstein Created Woman* 1966

Warren, Betty (1905–1990) *Variety Jubilee* 1942; *Champagne Charlie* 1944; *Passport to Pimlico* 1949; *So Long at the Fair* 1950; *Tread Softly Stranger* 1958

Warren, C Denier (1889–1971) *Good Morning, Boys* 1937; *Keep Fit* 1937; *It's in the Air* 1938; *Strange Boarders* 1938

Warren, E Alyn (1874–1940) *Abraham Lincoln* 1930; *Tarzan the Fearless* 1933

Warren, Estella (1978–) *Planet of the Apes* 2001; *The Cooler* 2002; *Kangaroo Jack* 2003

Warren, Gloria (1926–) *Always in My Heart* 1942; *Dangerous Money* 1946

Warren, Jennifer (1941–) *Sam's Song* 1969; *Night Moves* 1975; *Another Man, Another Chance* 1977; *Slap Shot* 1977; *Ice Castles* 1978; *Mutant* 1984

Warren, Katherine *aka* **Warren, Katharine** (1905–1965) *All the King's Men* 1949; *Tell It to the Judge* 1949; *Force of Arms* 1951; *The Prowler* 1951; *The Star* 1953

Warren, Kenneth J (1929–1973) *Doctor Blood's Coffin* 1960; *Part-Time Wife* 1961; *I, Monster* 1971; *The Creeping Flesh* 1972

Warren, Lesley Ann (1946–) *The Happiest Millionaire* 1967; *The One and Only, Genuine, Original Family Band* 1968; *Harry and Walter Go to New York* 1976; *Treasure of the Yankee Zephyr* 1981; *Victor/Victoria* 1982; *A Night in Heaven* 1983; *Choose Me* 1984; *Songwriter* 1984; *Clue* 1985; *Burglar* 1987; *Cop* 1988; *Life Stinks* 1991; *Pure Country* 1992; *Desperate Justice* 1993; *Color of Night* 1994; *Going All the Way* 1997; *Love Kills* 1998; *The Limey* 1999; *Twin Falls Idaho* 1999; *Trixie* 2000; *Secretary* 2001

Warren, Marc (1967–) *Boston Kickout* 1995; *Dad Savage* 1997; *The Principles of Lust* 2002; *Song for a Raggy Boy* 2002

Warren, Marcia *Don't Get Me Started* 1994; *Unconditional Love* 2001

Warren, Michael *aka* **Warren, Mike** (1946–) *Butterflies Are Free* 1972; *Norman... Is That You?* 1976; *Fast Break* 1979; *Heaven Is a Playground* 1991; *Storyville* 1992

Warren, Ruth *Zoo in Budapest* 1933; *Bring Your Smile Along* 1955

Warrender, Harold (1903–1953) *Scott of the Antarctic* 1948; *Conspirator* 1949; *Pandora and the Flying Dutchman* 1950; *Where No Vultures Fly* 1951

Warrick, Ruth (1915–2005) *Citizen Kane* 1941; *The Corsican Brothers* 1941; *Journey into Fear* 1942; *The Iron Major* 1943; *Guest in the House* 1944; *Mr Winkle Goes to War* 1944; *Secret Command* 1944; *China Sky* 1945; *Driftwood* 1946; *Song of the South* 1946; *Swell Guy* 1946; *Daisy Kenyon* 1947; *Arch of Triumph* 1948; *Let's Dance* 1950; *Ride beyond Vengeance* 1966; *The Great Bank Robbery* 1969

Warrington, Don (1952–) *Rising Damp* 1980; *Bloodbath at the House of Death* 1983; *Babymother* 1998; *Lighthouse* 1999

Warshofsky, David *Suffering Bastards* 1989; *Personal Velocity* 2001

Warwick, Dionne (1940–) *Slaves* 1969; *Rent-a-Cop* 1988

Warwick, John (1905–1972) *The Ticket of Leave Man* 1937; *The Face at the Window* 1939; *Flying 55* 1939; *Spare a Copper* 1940; *Danny Boy* 1941; *The Saint's Vacation* 1941; *Dancing with Crime* 1946; *Conspiracy in Teheran* 1947; *While I Live* 1947; *Escape Route* 1952; *Contraband Spain* 1955; *The Square Peg* 1958; *Horrors of the Black Museum* 1959

Warwick, Richard (1945–1997) *if....* 1968; *Sebastiane* 1976; *The Tempest* 1979

Warwick, Robert (1878–1964) *Hopalong Cassidy* 1935; *Whipsaw* 1935; *The Bride Walks Out* 1936; *Blockade* 1938; *Devil's Island* 1940; *Sullivan's Travels* 1941; *I Married a Witch* 1942; *The Falcon's Adventure* 1946; *Adventures of Don Juan* 1948; *A Woman's Secret* 1949; *In a Lonely Place* 1950; *Sugarfoot* 1951; *The Sword of Monte Cristo* 1951; *Against All Flags* 1952; *Silver Lode* 1954; *Chief Crazy Horse* 1955; *Escape to Burma* 1955; *Walk the Proud Land* 1956

Washbourne, Mona (1903–1988) *Once upon a Dream* 1948; *Child's Play* 1954; *To Dorothy, a Son* 1954; *John and Julie* 1955; *It's Great to Be Young* 1956; *Cast a Dark Shadow* 1957; *A Cry from the Streets* 1957; *The Brides of Dracula* 1960; *Billy Liar* 1963; *My Fair Lady* 1964; *Night Must Fall* 1964; *The Collector* 1965; *One Way Pendulum* 1965; *The Third Day* 1965; *if....* 1968; *The Bed Sitting Room* 1969; *The Driver's Seat* 1975; *Mister Quilp* 1975; *The Blue Bird* 1976; *Stevie* 1978

Washburn, Beverly (1943–) *The Juggler* 1953; *The Lone Ranger* 1956; *Old Yeller* 1957; *Spider Baby* 1964

Washington, Denzel (1954–) *Carbon Copy* 1981; *A Soldier's Story* 1984; *Power* 1986; *Cry Freedom* 1987; *For Queen and Country* 1988; *Glory* 1989; *The Mighty Quinn* 1989; *Heart Condition* 1990; *Mo' Better Blues* 1990; *Mississippi Masala* 1991;

Ricochet 1991; *Malcolm X* 1992; *Much Ado about Nothing* 1993; *The Pelican Brief* 1993; *Philadelphia* 1993; *Crimson Tide* 1995; *Devil in a Blue Dress* 1995; *Virtuosity* 1995; *Courage under Fire* 1996; *The Preacher's Wife* 1996; *Fallen* 1998; *He Got Game* 1998; *The Siege* 1998; *The Bone Collector* 1999; *The Hurricane* 1999; *Remember the Titans* 2000; *John Q* 2001; *Training Day* 2001; *Antwone Fisher* 2002; *Out of Time* 2003; *Man on Fire* 2004; *The Manchurian Candidate* 2004
Washington, Fredi (1903–1994) *The Emperor Jones* 1933; *Imitation of Life* 1934
Washington, Isaiah (1963–) *Clockers* 1995; *Girl 6* 1996; *Love Jones* 1997; *Mixing Nia* 1998; *True Crime* 1999; *Kin* 2000; *Romeo Must Die* 2000; *Exit Wounds* 2001; *Ghost Ship* 2002; *Welcome to Collinwood* 2002; *Hollywood Homicide* 2003
Washington, Kerry (1977–) *Save the Last Dance* 2000; *Bad Company* 2002; *Against the Ropes* 2003; *Ray* 2004; *She Hate Me* 2004; *Mr & Mrs Smith* 2005
Wass, Ted (1952–) *The Curse of the Pink Panther* 1983; *Oh, God! You Devil* 1984; *Sheena* 1984; *The Longshot* 1986; *Danielle Steel's Star* 1993
Wasserman, Jerry (1945–) *Quarantine* 1989; *A Cooler Climate* 1999; *I, Robot* 2004
Wasson, Craig (1954–) *Go Tell the Spartans* 1977; *The Boys in Company C* 1978; *The Outsider* 1979; *Ghost Story* 1981; *Second Thoughts* 1982; *Body Double* 1984; *The Men's Club* 1986; *A Nightmare on Elm Street 3: Dream Warriors* 1987; *Escape under Pressure* 2000
Watanabe, Gedde (1955–) *Sixteen Candles* 1984; *Volunteers* 1985; *Gung Ho* 1986; *Vamp* 1986; *Nick and Jane* 1996
Watanabe, Ken (1959–) *Tampopo* 1986; *The Last Samurai* 2003; *Batman Begins* 2005
Watanabe, Tetsu *Sonatine* 1993; *Hana-Bi* 1997
Waterman, Dennis (1948–) *The Pirates of Blood River* 1961; *Up the Junction* 1967; *The Smashing Bird I Used to Know* 1969; *The Scars of Dracula* 1970; *Fright* 1971; *Man in the Wilderness* 1971; *The Belstone Fox* 1973; *Sweeney!* 1976; *Sweeney 2* 1978; *Cold Justice* 1991; *Arthur's Dyke* 2001
Waterman, Felicity *Lena's Holiday* 1990; *Unlawful Passage* 1994
Waters, Ethel (1896–1977) *Tales of Manhattan* 1942; *Cabin in the Sky* 1943; *Stage Door Canteen* 1943; *Pinky* 1949; *The Member of the Wedding* 1952; *The Sound and the Fury* 1959
Waters (3), John (1948–) *The Getting of Wisdom* 1977; *Summerfield* 1977; *Weekend of Shadows* 1978; *Breaker Morant* 1979; *Attack Force Z* 1981; *Grievous Bodily Harm* 1987; *Boulevard of Broken Dreams* 1988; *Heaven Tonight* 1990
Waters, Russell (1908–1982) *Death of an Angel* 1951; *Mr Denning Drives North* 1951; *Yesterday's Enemy* 1959; *The Wicker Man* 1973; *Black Jack* 1979
Waterston, Sam (1940–) *Fitzwilly* 1967; *Generation* 1969; *Three* 1969; *Who Killed Mary Whats'ername?* 1971; *The Great Gatsby* 1974; *Rancho Deluxe* 1975; *Capricorn One* 1978; *Eagle's Wing* 1978; *Interiors* 1978; *Friendly Fire* 1979; *Heaven's Gate* 1980; *Hopscotch* 1980; *Sweet William* 1980; *The Killing Fields* 1984; *Warning Sign* 1985; *Hannah and Her Sisters* 1986; *Just between Friends* 1986; *September* 1987; *Swimming to Cambodia* 1987; *Crimes and Misdemeanors* 1989; *Welcome Home* 1989; *Mindwalk* 1990; *A Captive in the Land* 1991; *The Man in the Moon* 1991; *David's Mother* 1994; *The Enemy Within* 1994; *Serial Mom* 1994; *The Journey of August King* 1995; *The Proprietor* 1996; *Shadow Conspiracy* 1996; *A House Divided* 2000; *Le Divorce* 2003
Watford, Gwen (1927–1994) *Never Take Sweets from a Stranger* 1960; *Taste the Blood of Dracula* 1969; *The Ghoul* 1975
Watkin, Pierre (1889–1960) *Dangerous* 1935; *The Bank Dick* 1940; *Road to Singapore* 1940; *Little Giant* 1946; *The Story of Seabiscuit* 1949
Watkins, Linda (1908–1976) *From Hell It Came* 1957; *Because They're Young* 1960
Watling, Dilys (1946–) *Calculated Risk* 1963; *Two Left Feet* 1963
Watling, Jack (1923–) *Journey Together* 1944; *The Courtneys of Curzon Street* 1947; *Easy Money* 1947; *Quartet* 1948; *The Winslow Boy* 1948; *Under Capricorn* 1949; *White Corridors* 1951; *Meet Mr Lucifer* 1953; *The Sea Shall Not Have Them* 1954; *The Admirable Crichton* 1957; *The Birthday Present* 1957; *That Woman Opposite* 1957; *Three on a Spree* 1961; *The Nanny* 1965; *Father Dear Father* 1972; *11 Harrowhouse* 1974
Watling, Leonor (1975–) *Talk to Her* 2001; *My Life without Me* 2002
Watson, Alberta (1955–) *In Praise of Older Women* 1978; *Best Revenge* 1983; *The Keep* 1983; *White of the Eye* 1986; *The Hitman* 1991; *Spanking the Monkey* 1994; *Seeds of Doubt* 1996; *Sweet Angel Mine* 1996; *The Sweet Hereafter* 1997; *Hedwig and the Angry Inch* 2001; *The Prince & Me* 2004
Watson, Barry (1974–) *Teaching Mrs Tingle* 1999; *Sorority Boys* 2002; *Boogeyman* 2005
Watson, Bobby *aka* **Watson, Robert** (1888–1965) *Going Hollywood* 1933; *The Paleface* 1948
Watson, Bobs (1930–1999) *Blackmail* 1939; *Dr Kildare's Crisis* 1940; *Men of Boys Town* 1941
Watson, Debbie (1949–) *Munster, Go Home!* 1966; *The Cool Ones* 1967
Watson, Emily (1967–) *Breaking the Waves* 1996; *The Boxer* 1997; *Metroland* 1997; *Hilary and Jackie* 1998; *Angela's Ashes* 1999; *Cradle Will Rock* 1999; *The Luzhin Defence* 2000; *Trixie* 2000; *Gosford Park* 2001; *Equilibrium* 2002; *Punch-Drunk Love* 2002; *Red Dragon* 2002; *The Life and Death of Peter Sellers* 2003; *Boo, Zino and the Snurks* 2004
Watson, Emma (1990–) *Harry Potter and the Philosopher's Stone* 2001; *Harry Potter and the Chamber of Secrets* 2002; *Harry Potter and the Prisoner of Azkaban* 2004
Watson, Jack (1915–1999) *Konga* 1960; *This Sporting Life* 1963; *The Gorgon* 1964; *Master Spy* 1964; *The Hill* 1965; *The Night Caller* 1965; *Tobruk* 1966; *The Strange Affair* 1968; *Every Home Should Have One* 1970; *The McKenzie Break* 1970; *Tower of Evil* 1972; *11 Harrowhouse* 1974; *Schizo* 1976; *The Purple Taxi* 1977; *The Wild Geese* 1978; *North Sea Hijack* 1979
Watson Jr, James A *Halls of Anger* 1970; *The Organization* 1971; *Extreme Close-Up* 1973; *Goldengirl* 1979
Watson, Lucile (1879–1962) *What Every Woman Knows* 1934; *Made for Each Other* 1939; *The Women* 1939; *Florian* 1940; *Waterloo Bridge* 1940; *Footsteps in the Dark* 1941; *The Great Lie* 1941; *Mr and Mrs Smith* 1941; *Rage in Heaven* 1941; *Watch on the Rhine* 1943; *The Thin Man Goes Home* 1944; *Till We Meet Again* 1944; *Uncertain Glory* 1944; *Tomorrow Is Forever* 1945; *My Reputation* 1946; *Never Say Goodbye* 1946; *Song of the South* 1946; *The Emperor Waltz* 1948; *Julia Misbehaves* 1948; *That Wonderful Urge* 1948; *Everybody Does It* 1949; *Little Women* 1949; *Harriet Craig* 1950; *Let's Dance* 1950; *My Forbidden Past* 1951
Watson, Mills (1940–) *Dirty Little Billy* 1972; *Yellow Pages* 1984
Watson, Minor (1889–1965) *The Woman I Love* 1937; *Boys Town* 1938; *The Adventures of Huckleberry Finn* 1939; *The Llano Kid* 1939; *Spirit of the People* 1940; *The Big Shot* 1942; *Gentleman Jim* 1942; *Woman of the Year* 1942; *Christmas Holiday* 1944; *The Falcon Out West* 1944; *A Southern Yankee* 1948; *Beyond the Forest* 1949; *Mister 880* 1950; *Bright Victory* 1951; *Face to Face* 1952; *My Son John* 1952; *Untamed Frontier* 1952; *The Star* 1953; *Trapeze* 1956
Watson, Muse (1948–) *Assassins* 1995; *I Know What You Did Last Summer* 1997; *I Still Know What You Did Last Summer* 1998; *From Dusk till Dawn II: Texas Blood Money* 1999
Watson, Tom (1932–2001) *Another Time, Another Place* 1983; *The Slab Boys* 1997
Watson, Wylie (1889–1966) *The 39 Steps* 1935; *Please Teacher* 1937; *Jamaica Inn* 1939; *The Saint Meets the Tiger* 1943; *Don't Take It to Heart* 1944; *A Girl in a Million* 1946; *Brighton Rock* 1947; *London Belongs to Me* 1948; *Eye Witness* 1949; *Whisky Galore!* 1949; *The Magnet* 1950
Wattis, Richard (1912–1975) *The Happiest Days of Your Life* 1950; *Appointment with Venus* 1951; *Made in Heaven* 1952; *Blood Orange* 1953; *Colonel March Investigates* 1953; *Hobson's Choice* 1953; *The Intruder* 1953; *Park Plaza 605* 1953; *Top of the Form* 1953; *The Colditz Story* 1954; *An Alligator Named Daisy* 1955; *Simon and Laura* 1955; *The Time of His Life* 1955; *A Yank in Ermine* 1955; *The Abominable Snowman* 1957; *The Prince and the Showgirl* 1957; *Follow a Star* 1959; *Left, Right and Centre* 1959; *Libel* 1959; *Ten Seconds to Hell* 1959; *Your Money or Your Wife* 1960; *Dentist on the Job* 1961; *Nearly a Nasty Accident* 1961; *Very Important Person* 1961; *Come Fly with Me* 1962; *I Thank a Fool* 1962; *Play It Cool* 1962; *Bunny Lake Is Missing* 1965; *The Great St Trinian's Train Robbery* 1966; *Wonderwall* 1968; *Take Me High* 1973
Watts, Charles (1912–1966) *An Affair to Remember* 1957; *The High Cost of Loving* 1958; *The Lone Ranger and the Lost City of Gold* 1958; *Ada* 1961; *Jumbo* 1962; *The Wheeler Dealers* 1963; *Baby the Rain Must Fall* 1965
Watts, Naomi (1968–) *Tank Girl* 1995; *Persons Unknown* 1996; *Strange Planet* 1999; *Mulholland Drive* 2001; *The Ring* 2002; *Le Divorce* 2003; *Ned Kelly* 2003; *21 Grams* 2003; *We Don't Live Here Anymore* 2003; *The Assassination of Richard Nixon* 2004; *I ❤ Huckabees* 2004; *The Ring Two* 2004
Watts, Queenie (1926–1980) *Poor Cow* 1967; *All Coppers Are...* 1972; *Schizo* 1976
Wauthion, Claire *Je, Tu, Il, Elle* 1974; *Port Djema* 1997
Wax, Ruby (1953–) *Chariots of Fire* 1981; *Shock Treatment* 1981; *Water* 1985; *Eat the Rich* 1987; *The Borrowers* 1997
Waxman, Al (1935–2001) *Sunday in the Country* 1975; *Atlantic City, USA* 1980; *Cagney & Lacey* 1981; *Class of 1984* 1982; *Collision Course* 1987; *Meatballs III: Summer Job* 1987; *Switching Channels* 1987; *Malarek* 1989; *The Hitman* 1991; *Live Wire* 1992; *Iron Eagle IV* 1995; *Holiday Affair* 1996
Way, Ann (1915–1993) *Clockwise* 1986; *Killing Dad* 1989
Way, Eileen (1911–1994) *Blood Orange* 1953; *Queen of Hearts* 1989
Wayans, Damon (1960–) *Earth Girls Are Easy* 1988; *Look Who's Talking Too* 1990; *The Last Boy Scout* 1991; *Mo' Money* 1992; *Blankman* 1994; *Bulletproof* 1996; *Celtic Pride* 1996; *The Great White Hype* 1996; *Bamboozled* 2000; *Marci X* 2003
Wayans, Keenen Ivory (1958–) *Hollywood Shuffle* 1987; *I'm Gonna Git You Sucka* 1988; *A Low Down Dirty Shame* 1994; *Don't Be a Menace to South Central while Drinking Your Juice in the Hood* 1996; *The Glimmer Man* 1996; *Most Wanted* 1997
Wayans, Kim (1961–) *A Low Down Dirty Shame* 1994; *Juwanna Mann* 2002
Wayans, Marlon (1972–) *Mo' Money* 1992; *Above the Rim* 1994; *Don't Be a Menace to South Central while Drinking Your Juice in the Hood* 1996; *The 6th Man* 1997; *Senseless* 1998; *Dungeons & Dragons* 2000; *Requiem for a Dream* 2000; *Scary Movie* 2000; *Scary Movie 2* 2001; *The Ladykillers* 2004; *White Chicks* 2004
Wayans, Shawn (1971–) *Don't Be a Menace to South Central while Drinking Your Juice in the Hood* 1996; *Scary Movie* 2000; *Scary Movie 2* 2001; *White Chicks* 2004
Wayne, David (1914–1995) *Portrait of Jennie* 1948; *Adam's Rib* 1949; *My Blue Heaven* 1950; *Stella* 1950; *As Young as You Feel* 1951; *M* 1951; *The I Don't Care Girl* 1952; *Wait 'til the Sun Shines, Nellie* 1952; *We're Not Married* 1952; *With a Song in My Heart* 1952; *How to Marry a Millionaire* 1953; *Tonight We Sing* 1953; *Hell and High Water* 1954; *The Tender Trap* 1955; *The Sad Sack* 1957; *The Three Faces of Eve* 1957; *The Last Angry Man* 1959; *The Big Gamble* 1961; *The Andromeda Strain* 1970; *The Apple Dumpling Gang* 1974; *The Front Page* 1974; *Huckleberry Finn* 1974; *The Prize Fighter* 1979
Wayne, John (1907–1979) *Hangman's House* 1928; *The Big Trail* 1930; *Men without Women* 1930; *The Big Stampede* 1932; *The Hurricane Express* 1932; *Ride Him, Cowboy* 1932; *Baby Face* 1933; *Riders of Destiny* 1933; *Somewhere in Sonora* 1933; *The Telegraph Trail* 1933; *Blue Steel* 1934; *The Lucky Texan* 1934; *The Man from Utah* 1934; *'Neath the Arizona Skies* 1934; *Randy Rides Alone* 1934; *Sagebrush Trail* 1934; *The Star Packer* 1934; *The Trail Beyond* 1934; *West of the Divide* 1934; *The Dawn Rider* 1935; *The Desert Trail* 1935; *The Lawless Frontier* 1935; *Paradise Canyon* 1935; *Texas Terror* 1935; *Westward Ho* 1935; *Winds of the Wasteland* 1936; *California Straight Ahead* 1937; *Hell Town* 1937; *Overland Stage Raiders* 1938; *Red River Range* 1938; *Santa Fe Stampede* 1938; *The First Rebel* 1939; *Frontier Horizon* 1939; *Stagecoach* 1939; *Three Texas Steers* 1939; *Wyoming Outlaw* 1939; *Dark Command* 1940; *The Long Voyage Home* 1940; *Seven Sinners* 1940; *Three Faces West* 1940; *Lady from Louisiana* 1941; *A Man Betrayed* 1941; *The Shepherd of the Hills* 1941; *Flying Tigers* 1942; *In Old California* 1942; *Lady for a Night* 1942; *Pittsburgh* 1942; *Reap the Wild Wind* 1942; *Reunion in France* 1942; *The Spoilers* 1942; *A Lady Takes a Chance* 1943; *War of the Wildcats* 1943; *The Fighting Seabees* 1944; *Tall in the Saddle* 1944; *Back to Bataan* 1945; *Dakota* 1945; *Flame of the Barbary Coast* 1945; *They Were Expendable* 1945; *Without Reservations* 1946; *Angel and the Badman* 1947; *Tycoon* 1947; *Fort Apache* 1948; *Red River* 1948; *Three Godfathers* 1948; *The Fighting Kentuckian* 1949; *Sands of Iwo Jima* 1949; *She Wore a Yellow Ribbon* 1949; *Wake of the Red Witch* 1949; *Rio Grande* 1950; *Flying Leathernecks* 1951; *Operation Pacific* 1951; *Big Jim McLain* 1952; *The Quiet Man* 1952; *Hondo* 1953; *Island in the Sky* 1953; *Trouble along the Way* 1953; *The High and the Mighty* 1954; *Blood Alley* 1955; *The Sea Chase* 1955; *The Conqueror* 1956; *The Searchers* 1956; *Jet Pilot* 1957; *Legend of the Lost* 1957; *The Wings of Eagles* 1957; *The Barbarian and the Geisha* 1958; *I Married a Woman* 1958; *The Horse Soldiers* 1959; *Rio Bravo* 1959; *The Alamo* 1960; *North to Alaska* 1960; *The Comancheros* 1961; *Hatari!* 1962; *How the West Was Won* 1962; *The Longest Day* 1962; *The Man Who Shot Liberty Valance* 1962; *Donovan's Reef* 1963; *McLintock!* 1963; *The Magnificent Showman* 1964; *The Greatest Story Ever Told* 1965; *In Harm's Way* 1965; *The Sons of Katie Elder* 1965; *Cast a Giant Shadow* 1966; *El Dorado* 1967; *The War Wagon* 1967; *The Green Berets* 1968; *Hellfighters* 1969; *True Grit* 1969; *The Undefeated* 1969; *Chisum* 1970; *Rio Lobo* 1970; *Big Jake* 1971; *The Cowboys* 1972; *Cahill, United States Marshal* 1973; *The Train Robbers* 1973; *McQ* 1974; *Brannigan* 1975; *Rooster Cogburn* 1975; *The Shootist* 1976
Wayne, Naunton (1901–1970) *The Lady Vanishes* 1938; *Crooks' Tour* 1940; *Night Train to Munich* 1940; *Millions like Us* 1943; *A Girl in a Million* 1946; *It's Not Cricket* 1948; *Obsession* 1948; *Passport to Pimlico* 1949; *Circle of Danger* 1950; *Highly Dangerous* 1950; *The Happy Family* 1952; *The Titfield Thunderbolt* 1952; *Treasure Hunt* 1952; *You Know What Sailors Are* 1954; *Operation Bullshine* 1959
Wayne, Nina *Dead Heat on a Merry-Go-Round* 1966; *Luv* 1967; *The Comic* 1969
Wayne, Patrick *aka* **Wayne, Pat** (1939–) *The Long Gray Line* 1955; *The Young Land* 1959; *The Alamo* 1960; *The Comancheros* 1961; *McLintock!* 1963; *Shenandoah* 1965; *An Eye for an Eye* 1966; *Big Jake* 1971; *The Deserter* 1971; *The Bears and I* 1974; *Mustang Country* 1976; *The People That Time Forgot* 1977; *Sinbad and the Eye of the Tiger* 1977; *Her Alibi* 1989
Weatherly, Shawn (1960–) *Party Line* 1988; *Shadowzone* 1990
Weathers, Carl (1948–) *Rocky* 1976; *Semi-Tough* 1977; *Force 10 from Navarone* 1978; *Rocky II* 1979; *Death Hunt* 1981; *Rocky III* 1982; *Rocky IV* 1985; *Predator* 1987; *Action Jackson* 1988; *Happy Gilmore* 1996
Weaver, Dennis (1924–) *Horizons West* 1952; *The Lawless Breed* 1952; *Column South* 1953; *Law and Order* 1953; *War Arrow* 1953; *Seven Angry Men* 1955; *Touch of Evil* 1958; *The Gallant Hours* 1960; *Duel at Diablo* 1966; *Way... Way Out* 1966; *Gentle Giant* 1967; *Duel* 1971; *What's the Matter with Helen?* 1971; *Two-Bits and Pepper* 1995
Weaver, Fritz (1926–) *Fail-Safe* 1964; *The Guns of August* 1964; *To Trap a Spy* 1966; *The Maltese Bippy* 1969; *Company of Killers* 1970; *A Walk in the Spring Rain* 1970; *The Day of the Dolphin* 1973; *Black Sunday* 1976; *Marathon Man* 1976; *Demon Seed* 1977; *The Big Fix* 1978; *Jaws of Satan* 1979; *Magnum: Don't Eat the Snow in Hawaii* 1980; *Creepshow* 1982; *My Name Is Bill W* 1989; *The Thomas Crown Affair* 1999
Weaver, Jacki (1947–) *Petersen* 1974; *Picnic at Hanging Rock* 1975; *Caddie* 1976
Weaver, Jason (1979–) *The Long Walk Home* 1990; *Drumline* 2002
Weaver, Marjorie (1913–1994) *Hold That Co-Ed* 1938; *Kentucky Moonshine* 1938; *Sally, Irene and Mary* 1938; *Three Blind Mice* 1938; *The Cisco Kid and the Lady* 1939; *Young Mr Lincoln* 1939; *Maryland* 1940; *Michael Shayne, Private Detective* 1940
Weaver, Sigourney (1949–) *Alien* 1979; *Eyewitness* 1981; *The Year*

of Living Dangerously 1982; Deal of the Century 1983; Ghostbusters 1984; Aliens 1986; Half Moon Street 1986; Gorillas in the Mist 1988; Working Girl 1988; Ghostbusters II 1989; Alien³ 1992; 1492: Conquest of Paradise 1992; Dave 1993; Death and the Maiden 1994; Copycat 1995; Jeffrey 1995; Snow White: a Tale of Terror 1996; Alien: Resurrection 1997; The Ice Storm 1997; Galaxy Quest 1999; A Map of the World 1999; Company Man 2000; Heartbreakers 2001; Tadpole 2002; Holes 2003; Imaginary Heroes 2004; The Village 2004

Weaving, Hugo (1959–) Almost 1990; Proof 1991; Frauds 1992; The Custodian 1993; Reckless Kelly 1993; The Adventures of Priscilla, Queen of the Desert 1994; Babe 1995; Babe: Pig in the City 1998; Bedrooms and Hallways 1998; The Matrix 1999; Strange Planet 1999; The Magic Pudding 2000; The Old Man Who Read Love Stories 2000; The Lord of the Rings: The Fellowship of the Ring 2001; The Lord of the Rings: The Two Towers 2002; The Matrix Reloaded 2002; The Lord of the Rings: The Return of the King 2003; The Matrix Revolutions 2003

Webb, Alan (1906–1982) Challenge to Lassie 1949; The Third Secret 1964; King Rat 1965; The Taming of the Shrew 1967; Interlude 1968; Entertaining Mr Sloane 1969; Women in Love 1969; King Lear 1970; The First Great Train Robbery 1978

Webb, Chloe (1960–) Sid and Nancy 1986; The Belly of an Architect 1987; Twins 1988; Heart Condition 1990; Queens Logic 1991; A Dangerous Woman 1993; Love Affair 1994; The Ballad of Lucy Whipple 2001

Webb, Clifton (1891–1966) Laura 1944; The Dark Corner 1946; The Razor's Edge 1946; Sitting Pretty 1948; Mr Belvedere Goes to College 1949; Cheaper by the Dozen 1950; For Heaven's Sake 1950; Mr Belvedere Rings the Bell 1951; Dreamboat 1952; Stars and Stripes Forever 1952; Titanic 1953; Three Coins in the Fountain 1954; Woman's World 1954; The Man Who Never Was 1955; Boy on a Dolphin 1957; Holiday for Lovers 1959; The Remarkable Mr Pennypacker 1959; Satan Never Sleeps 1962

Webb, Daniel aka **Webb, Danny** A Year of the Quiet Sun 1984; Alien³ 1992; Shiner 2000

Webb, Jack (1920–1982) Appointment with Danger 1950; Dark City 1950; Halls of Montezuma 1950; The Men 1950; Sunset Blvd 1950; Dragnet 1954; Pete Kelly's Blues 1955; -30- 1959; The Last Time I Saw Archie 1961

Webb, Richard (1915–1993) Build My Gallows High 1947; Night Has a Thousand Eyes 1948; A Connecticut Yankee in King Arthur's Court 1949; Sands of Iwo Jima 1949; Distant Drums 1951; Carson City 1952; Mara Maru 1952; This Woman Is Dangerous 1952; Beware! The Blob 1971

Webb, Rita Stranger in the House 1967; Frenzy 1972

Webber, Mark (1980–) Whiteboys 1999; Snow Day 2000; Storytelling 2001; Dear Wendy 2005

Webber, Robert (1924–1989) 12 Angry Men 1957; The Stripper 1963; Hysteria 1964; Dead Heat on a Merry-Go-Round 1966; Harper 1966; The Silencers 1966; The Dirty Dozen 1967; Don't Make Waves 1967; The Big Bounce 1969; The Great White Hope 1970; Dollars 1971; Bring Me the Head of Alfredo Garcia 1974; The Choirboys 1977; Casey's Shadow 1978; Revenge of the Pink Panther 1978; 10 1979; Private Benjamin 1980; SOB 1981; Who Dares Wins 1982; Wild Geese II 1985; Nuts 1987

Webber, Timothy The Grey Fox 1982; Cypher 2002

Weber, André (1928–1996) The Loser 1971; That Obscure Object of Desire 1977

Weber, Jacques (1949–) State of Siege 1972; The Lady with Red Boots 1974; Cyrano de Bergerac 1990; Beaumarchais l'Insolent 1996

Weber, Jake (1964–) Meet Joe Black 1998; Pushing Tin 1999; Wendigo 2001; Leo 2002; Dawn of the Dead 2004

Weber, Sharon (1943–) Lifeguard 1976; The Billion Dollar Hobo 1978

Weber, Steven (1961–) Walls of Glass 1985; Single White Female 1992; The Temp 1993; Dracula: Dead and Loving It 1995; Jeffrey 1995; Leaving Las Vegas 1995; At First Sight 1998; Break Up 1998; Sour Grapes 1998; Joseph: King of Dreams 2000

Webster, Ben Downhill 1927; The Old Curiosity Shop 1934

Webster, Hugh (1927–1986) King of the Grizzlies 1969; Never Cry Wolf 1983

Webster, Joy Sailor Beware! 1956; The Woman Eater 1957; The Two Faces of Dr Jekyll 1960; During One Night 1961

Webster, Mary The Delicate Delinquent 1957; The Tin Star 1957; Master of the World 1961

Wedgeworth, Ann (1935–) Bang the Drum Slowly 1973; Scarecrow 1973; The Catamount Killing 1974; Law and Disorder 1974; Birch Interval 1976; Citizens Band 1977; No Small Affair 1984; Sweet Dreams 1985; Made in Heaven 1987; A Tiger's Tale 1987; Far North 1988; Miss Firecracker 1989; Love and a .45 1994; The Whole Wide World 1996

Weeks, Alan Black Belt Jones 1974; Truck Turner 1974

Weeks, Jimmie Ray aka **Weeks, Jimmy Ray** Frantic 1988; War Party 1988

Wegener, Paul (1874–1948) The Golem 1920; Alraune 1927; The Living Dead 1932

Wei Heling (1907–1979) Street Angel 1937; Crows and Sparrows 1949

Weidler, Virginia (1926–1968) Peter Ibbetson 1935; Souls at Sea 1937; Men with Wings 1938; Out West with the Hardys 1938; Too Hot to Handle 1938; The Great Man Votes 1939; The Lone Wolf Spy Hunt 1939; The Women 1939; All This, and Heaven Too 1940; The Philadelphia Story 1940; Young Tom Edison 1940; Babes on Broadway 1941; The Affairs of Martha 1942; Best Foot Forward 1943; The Youngest Profession 1943

Weil, Liza (1980–) Whatever 1998; Stir of Echoes 1999

Weingarten, Isabelle Four Nights of a Dreamer 1971; La Maman et la Putain 1973; The State of Things 1982

Weinger, Scott (1975–) Aladdin 1992; Aladdin and the King of Thieves 1996; Metropolis 2001

Weiss, Michael T (1962–) Howling IV 1988; Jeffrey 1995; Bones 2001

Weiss, Shaun (1978–) The Mighty Ducks 1992; Heavyweights 1995

Weisser, Norbert (1946–) Midnight Express 1978; Android 1982; Radioactive Dreams 1986; Down Twisted 1987; Adrenalin: Fear the Rush 1995; Omega Doom 1996; Around the Bend 2004

Weissmuller, Johnny (1904–1984) Tarzan, the Ape Man 1932; Tarzan and His Mate 1934; Tarzan Escapes 1936; Tarzan Finds a Son! 1939; Tarzan's Secret Treasure 1941; Tarzan's New York Adventure 1942; Stage Door Canteen 1943; Tarzan Triumphs 1943; Tarzan's Desert Mystery 1943; Tarzan and the Amazons 1945; Tarzan and the Leopard Woman 1946; Tarzan and the Huntress 1947; Jungle Jim 1948; Tarzan and the Mermaids 1948

Weisz, Rachel (1971–) Death Machine 1994; Stealing Beauty 1995; Chain Reaction 1996; Amy Foster 1997; Going All the Way 1997; The Land Girls 1997; I Want You 1998; The Mummy 1999; Sunshine 1999; Beautiful Creatures 2000; Enemy at the Gates 2001; The Mummy Returns 2001; About a Boy 2002; Confidence 2002; Envy 2003; Runaway Jury 2003; The Shape of Things 2003; Constantine 2005

Weitz, Bruce (1943–) No Place to Hide 1992; Danielle Steel's Mixed Blessings 1995; Velocity Trap 1997; Facing the Enemy 2001

Weitz, Chris (1970–) Chuck & Buck 2000; Mr & Mrs Smith 2005

Welch, Bruce (1941–) The Young Ones 1961; Summer Holiday 1962; Wonderful Life 1964; Finders Keepers 1966

Welch, Elisabeth aka **Welch, Elizabeth** (1904–2003) Song of Freedom 1936; Big Fella 1937; Over the Moon 1937; Fiddlers Three 1944; The Tempest 1979

Welch, Raquel (1940–) Roustabout 1964; Fantastic Voyage 1966; One Million Years BC 1966; Shout Loud, Louder... I Don't Understand 1966; Bedazzled 1967; Fathom 1967; The Oldest Profession 1967; Bandolero! 1968; The Biggest Bundle of Them All 1968; Lady in Cement 1968; Flareup 1969; The Magic Christian 1969; 100 Rifles 1969; Myra Breckinridge 1970; Hannie Caulder 1971; Bluebeard 1972; Fuzz 1972; Kansas City Bomber 1972; Sin 1972; The Last of Sheila 1973; The Three Musketeers 1973; The Four Musketeers 1974; The Wild Party 1975; Mother, Jugs & Speed 1976; The Prince and the Pauper 1977; Chairman of the Board 1998; Legally Blonde 2001; Tortilla Soup 2001

Welch, Sandy Chasing the Deer 1994; The Bruce 1996

Welch, Tahnee (1961–) Cocoon 1985; Night Train to Venice 1993; Improper Conduct 1994; The Criminal Mind 1995; I Shot Andy Warhol 1995

Welchman, Harry (1886–1966) The Common Touch 1941; Eight O'Clock Walk 1953

Weld, Tuesday (1943–) Rock, Rock, Rock! 1956; Rally 'round the Flag, Boys! 1958; The Five Pennies 1959; The Private Lives of Adam and Eve 1959; Because They're Young 1960; High Time 1960; Sex Kittens Go to College 1960; Bachelor Flat 1961; Return to Peyton Place 1961; Wild in the Country 1961; Soldier in the Rain 1963; The Cincinnati Kid 1965; I'll Take Sweden 1965; Lord Love a Duck 1966; Pretty Poison 1968; I Walk the Line 1970; A Safe Place 1971; Play It As It Lays 1972; Looking for Mr Goodbar 1977; Who'll Stop the Rain? 1978; Serial 1980; Thief 1981; Author! Author! 1982; Once upon a Time in America 1984; Heartbreak Hotel 1988; Falling Down 1992; Feeling Minnesota 1996

Welden, Ben (1901–1997) The Black Abbot 1934; The Man Who Changed His Name 1934; The Avenging Hand 1936; Smashing the Rackets 1938; Search for Danger 1949

Weldon, Charles Stir Crazy 1980; Fast-Walking 1982

Weldon, Joan (1933–) So This Is Love 1953; The Stranger Wore a Gun 1953; The Command 1954; Riding Shotgun 1954; Them! 1954; Gunsight Ridge 1957; Day of the Bad Man 1958; Home before Dark 1958

Welker, Frank (1945–) How to Frame a Figg 1971; Aladdin 1992; The Pagemaster 1994; A Goofy Movie 1995; Aladdin and the King of Thieves 1996; A Christmas Carol 1997; Doug's 1st Movie 1999; The Road to El Dorado 2000; Scooby-Doo and the Alien Invaders 2000

Welland, Colin (1934–) Kes 1969; Straw Dogs 1971; Sweeney! 1976; Dancin' thru the Dark 1989

Weller, Frederick Stonewall 1995; The Business of Strangers 2001; The Shape of Things 2003

Weller, Mary Louise The Bell Jar 1979; Forced Vengeance 1982

Weller, Peter (1947–) Butch and Sundance: the Early Days 1979; Just Tell Me What You Want 1980; Shoot the Moon 1982; Of Unknown Origin 1983; The Adventures of Buckaroo Banzai across the 8th Dimension 1984; Firstborn 1984; A Killing Affair 1985; RoboCop 1987; Blue Jean Cop 1988; Cat Chaser 1989; Leviathan 1989; RoboCop 2 1990; Fifty/Fifty 1991; Naked Lunch 1991; Road to Ruin 1992; Sunset Grill 1992; The New Age 1994; Beyond the Clouds 1995; Screamers 1995; Top of the World 1997; Diplomatic Siege 1999; ivansxtc. 1999; Contagion 2000; Dark Prince – the Legend of Dracula 2000; Shadow Hours 2000; Styx 2000; The Sin Eater 2002

Welles, Gwen (1951–1993) A Safe Place 1971; Hit! 1973; California Split 1974; Between the Lines 1977; Desert Hearts 1985; Nobody's Fool 1986; Eating 1990

Welles, Mel Attack of the Crab Monsters 1957; The Undead 1957; The Little Shop of Horrors 1960; Dr Heckyl & Mr Hype 1980

Welles, Orson (1915–1985) Swiss Family Robinson 1940; Citizen Kane 1941; Journey into Fear 1942; The Magnificent Ambersons 1942; Jane Eyre 1943; Follow the Boys 1944; Tomorrow Is Forever 1945; Duel in the Sun 1946; The Stranger 1946; The Lady from Shanghai 1948; Macbeth 1948; Black Magic 1949; Prince of Foxes 1949; The Third Man 1949; The Black Rose 1950; The Little World of Don Camillo 1951; Return to Glennascaul 1951; Othello 1952; Trent's Last Case 1952; Royal Affairs in Versailles 1953; Three Cases of Murder 1953; Trouble in the Glen 1954; Confidential Report 1955; Napoléon 1955; Moby Dick 1956; Man in the Shadow 1957; Ferry to Hong Kong 1958; The Long Hot Summer 1958; The Roots of Heaven 1958; Touch of Evil 1958; Compulsion 1959; The Battle of Austerlitz 1960; Crack in the Mirror 1960; King of Kings 1961; RoGoPaG 1962; The Trial 1962; The VIPs 1963; Chimes at Midnight 1966; Is Paris Burning? 1966; A Man for All Seasons 1966; Casino Royale 1967; I'll Never Forget What's 'Is Name 1967; Oedipus the King 1967; The Sailor from Gibraltar 1967; House of Cards 1968; The Immortal Story 1968; The Battle of Neretva 1969; The Southern Star 1969; Twelve plus One 1969; Catch-22 1970; The Kremlin Letter 1970; Start the Revolution without Me 1970; Waterloo 1970; Malpertuis 1971; A Safe Place 1971; Ten Days' Wonder 1971; Get to Know Your Rabbit 1972; Treasure Island 1972; F for Fake 1973; And Then There Were None 1974; Voyage of the Damned 1976; The Double McGuffin 1979; Hot Money 1979; Genocide 1981; History of the World Part 1 1981; Butterfly 1982; Slapstick of Another Kind 1982; Where Is Parsifal? 1983; Transformers – The Movie 1986; Someone to Love 1987; It's All True 1993

Welles, Virginia (1925–) Kiss and Tell 1945; To Each His Own 1946; Dear Ruth 1947; A Kiss for Corliss 1949; Francis in the Haunted House 1956

Wellman Jr, William aka **Wellman Jr, Bill** (1937–) Hell Bent for Glory 1957; Born Losers 1967; The Trial of Billy Jack 1974

Wells, Carole (1942–) The House of Seven Corpses 1973; Funny Lady 1975

Wells, Ingeborg (1917–) House of Blackmail 1953; Child's Play 1954

Wells, Jerold (1908–1999) High Hell 1957; The Element of Crime 1984

Wells, John (1936–1998) 30 Is a Dangerous Age, Cynthia 1968; Rentadick 1972; For Your Eyes Only 1981; Greystoke: the Legend of Tarzan, Lord of the Apes 1984; Revolution 1985

Wells, Tico Misplaced 1989; The Five Heartbeats 1991; Universal Soldier 1992

Wells, Vernon (1945–) Mad Max 2 1981; Commando 1985; Innerspace 1987; Circuitry Man 1990; The Shrimp on the Barbie 1990; Plughead Rewired: Circuitry Man II 1994; T-Force 1995

Welsh, Jane (1905–2001) Just William's Luck 1947; William at the Circus 1948

Welsh, John (1904–1985) Confession 1955; The Birthday Present 1957; The Revenge of Frankenstein 1958; The Night We Dropped a Clanger 1959; Beyond the Curtain 1960; Circle of Deception 1960; Krull 1983

Welsh, Kenneth (1942–) Of Unknown Origin 1983; Physical Evidence 1988; Perfectly Normal 1990; Getting Gotti 1994; Margaret's Museum 1995; The Day after Tomorrow 2004; Miracle 2004

Welsh, Margaret Smooth Talk 1985; Mr and Mrs Bridge 1990

Welter, Ariadna The Criminal Life of Archibaldo de la Cruz 1955; The Vampire 1957; Rage 1966

Wenders, Wim (1945–) Long Shot 1978; Notebook on Cities and Clothes 1989

Wendt, George (1948–) Dreamscape 1984; No Small Affair 1984; Thief of Hearts 1984; Fletch 1985; Gung Ho 1986; House 1986; Plain Clothes 1988; Guilty by Suspicion 1990; Forever Young 1992; The Little Rascals 1994; Man of the House 1994; Space Truckers 1996; Spice World: the Movie 1997; Dennis the Menace Strikes Again 1998; Alice in Wonderland 1999; Outside Providence 1999; The Prime Gig 2000; Wild about Harry 2000; King of the Ants 2003

Wengraf, John (1897–1974) The Lovable Cheat 1949; 5 Fingers 1952; Gog 1954; The Pride and the Passion 1957; Valerie 1957; The Return of Dracula 1958; Hitler 1962

Wenham, David (1965–) The Boys 1998; Better than Sex 2000; The Bank 2001; Dust 2001; The Crocodile Hunter: Collision Course 2002; Pure 2002; The Lord of the Rings: The Return of the King 2003; Van Helsing 2004

Wentworth, Martha (1889–1974) Clancy Street Boys 1943; Daughter of Dr Jekyll 1957; One Hundred and One Dalmatians 1960; The Sword in the Stone 1963

Wepper, Fritz (1941–) The Bridge 1959; The Games 1970; Cabaret 1972; The Last Battle 1983

Werle, Barbara Battle of the Bulge 1965; Gunfight in Abilene 1967; Charro! 1969; Krakatoa, East of Java 1969

Werner, Oskar (1922–1984) Decision before Dawn 1951; Lola Montès 1955; Jules et Jim 1961; Ship of Fools 1965; The Spy Who Came in from the Cold 1965; Fahrenheit 451 1966; Interlude 1968; The Shoes of the Fisherman 1968; Voyage of the Damned 1976

Wernicke, Otto (1893–1965) M 1931; The Testament of Dr Mabuse 1932

Wert, Doug By the Sword 1992; A Murder of Crows 1998

Wesson, Dick (1919–1979) Destination Moon 1950; Force of Arms 1951; Jim Thorpe – All-American 1951; Calamity Jane 1953; The Charge at Feather River 1953; The Desert Song 1953; The Errand Boy 1961

West, Adam (1928–) *Geronimo* 1962; *Soldier in the Rain* 1963; *Tammy and the Doctor* 1963; *Robinson Crusoe on Mars* 1964; *The Outlaws Is Coming* 1965; *Batman* 1966; *The Girl Who Knew Too Much* 1969; *The Marriage of a Young Stockbroker* 1971; *Hooper* 1978; *The Happy Hooker Goes to Hollywood* 1980; *One Dark Night* 1982; *Hellriders* 1983; *Doin' Time on Planet Earth* 1988; *The New Age* 1994; *Drop Dead Gorgeous* 1999; *Baadasssss!* 2003

West, Chandra (1970–) *Universal Soldier 2: Brothers in Arms* 1998; *Universal Soldier 3: Unfinished Business* 1998; *White Noise* 2004

West, Dominic (1970–) *True Blue* 1996; *Diana & Me* 1997; *The Gambler* 1997; *A Midsummer Night's Dream* 1999; *28 Days* 2000; *Rock Star* 2001; *Chicago* 2002; *Ten Minutes Older: the Cello* 2002; *Mona Lisa Smile* 2003; *The Forgotten* 2004

West, Judi *The Fortune Cookie* 1966; *A Man Called Gannon* 1969

West, Lockwood (1905–1989) *The Birthday Present* 1957; *The Leather Boys* 1963

West, Mae (1892–1980) *Night after Night* 1932; *I'm No Angel* 1933; *She Done Him Wrong* 1933; *Belle of the Nineties* 1934; *Goin' to Town* 1935; *Go West, Young Man* 1936; *Klondike Annie* 1936; *Every Day's a Holiday* 1937; *My Little Chickadee* 1940; *The Heat's On* 1943; *Myra Breckinridge* 1970; *Sextette* 1978

West, Martin *Lord Love a Duck* 1966; *Sweet November* 1968; *Assault on Precinct 13* 1976; *Mac and Me* 1988

West, Red (1936–) *Road House* 1989; *The Legend of Grizzly Adams* 1990

West, Samuel aka **West, Sam** (1966–) *Reunion* 1989; *Howards End* 1992; *A Feast at Midnight* 1994; *Carrington* 1995; *Persuasion* 1995; *Stiff Upper Lips* 1997; *Pandaemonium* 2000; *Iris* 2001; *Sword of Xanten* 2004; *Van Helsing* 2004

West, Shane (1978–) *Whatever It Takes* 2000; *Get over It* 2001; *A Walk to Remember* 2002; *The League of Extraordinary Gentlemen* 2003

West, Tamsin (1974–) *Jenny Kissed Me* 1984; *Frog Dreaming* 1985

West, Timothy (1934–) *Twisted Nerve* 1968; *The Day of the Jackal* 1973; *Hedda* 1975; *Operation Daybreak* 1975; *The Devil's Advocate* 1977; *Agatha* 1978; *The Thirty-Nine Steps* 1978; *Rough Cut* 1980; *Oliver Twist* 1982; *Cry Freedom* 1987; *Ever After: a Cinderella Story* 1998; *Joan of Arc* 1999; *Iris* 2001; *Villa des Roses* 2002; *Beyond Borders* 2003; *Sinbad: Legend of the Seven Seas* 2003

Westbrook, John (1922–1989) *Room at the Top* 1958; *The Tomb of Ligeia* 1964

Westcott, Helen (1928–1998) *The Gunfighter* 1950; *With a Song in My Heart* 1952; *Abbott and Costello Meet Dr Jekyll and Mr Hyde* 1953; *The Charge at Feather River* 1953; *Hot Blood* 1956; *God's Little Acre* 1958; *Monster on the Campus* 1958

Westerfield, James (1913–1971) *On the Waterfront* 1954; *Three Hours to Kill* 1954; *The Proud Rebel* 1958; *The Gunfight at Dodge City* 1959; *Wild River* 1960; *That Funny Feeling* 1965; *Blue* 1968; *Hang 'Em High* 1968; *A Man Called Gannon* 1969

Westergren, Håkan (1899–1991) *Swedenhielms* 1935; *Dollar* 1938

Westerman, Floyd Red Crow aka **Westerman, Floyd** (1935–) *Renegades* 1989; *Dances with Wolves* 1990; *Clearcut* 1992

Westley, Helen (1875–1942) *The Age of Innocence* 1934; *Anne of Green Gables* 1934; *Death Takes a Holiday* 1934; *Captain Hurricane* 1935; *Roberta* 1935; *Splendor* 1935; *Banjo on My Knee* 1936; *Dimples* 1936; *Show Boat* 1936; *Stowaway* 1936; *Café Metropole* 1937; *Heidi* 1937; *I'll Take Romance* 1937; *Alexander's Ragtime Band* 1938; *The Baroness and the Butler* 1938; *Rebecca of Sunnybrook Farm* 1938; *Zaza* 1939; *Lillian Russell* 1940; *Adam Had Four Sons* 1941; *Lady from Louisiana* 1941; *Million Dollar Baby* 1941; *Bedtime Story* 1942; *My Favorite Spy* 1942

Westman, Nydia (1902–1970) *Ladies Should Listen* 1934; *Success at Any Price* 1934; *When Tomorrow Comes* 1939; *The Chocolate Soldier* 1941; *The Swinger* 1966

Weston, Brad *Rough Night in Jericho* 1967; *Barquero* 1970

Weston, Celia *The Road Home* 1989; *Dead Man Walking* 1995; *In the Bedroom* 2001; *Far from Heaven* 2002

Weston, David (1938–) *The Beauty Jungle* 1964; *The Masque of the Red Death* 1964; *The Heroes of Telemark* 1965; *The Legend of Young Dick Turpin* 1965

Weston, Jack (1924–1996) *All in a Night's Work* 1960; *The Honeymoon Machine* 1961; *It'$ Only Money* 1962; *Palm Springs Weekend* 1963; *The Incredible Mr Limpet* 1964; *The Cincinnati Kid* 1965; *Mirage* 1965; *Wait until Dark* 1967; *The Counterfeit Killer* 1968; *The Thomas Crown Affair* 1968; *The April Fools* 1969; *Cactus Flower* 1969; *A New Leaf* 1971; *Fuzz* 1972; *Marco* 1973; *Gator* 1976; *The Ritz* 1976; *Cuba* 1979; *The Four Seasons* 1981; *High Road to China* 1983; *The Longshot* 1986; *Dirty Dancing* 1987; *Ishtar* 1987; *Short Circuit 2* 1988

Westwood, Patrick *The Tommy Steele Story* 1957; *Guns in the Heather* 1969

Wettig, Patricia (1951–) *Guilty by Suspicion* 1990; *City Slickers* 1991; *City Slickers II: the Legend of Curly's Gold* 1994; *Dancer, Texas Pop 81* 1998

Wexler, Paul (1929–1979) *Timbuktu* 1959; *Doc Savage: the Man of Bronze* 1975

Weyers, Marius (1945–) *The Gods Must Be Crazy* 1980; *Farewell to the King* 1988; *DeepStar Six* 1989; *Happy Together* 1989; *Windprints* 1989; *Bopha!* 1993; *Friends* 1993; *Charlie* 2003; *Stander* 2003

Whalen, Michael (1902–1974) *The Country Doctor* 1936; *Poor Little Rich Girl* 1936; *White Fang* 1936; *Wee Willie Winkie* 1937; *Ellery Queen Master Detective* 1940

Whaley, Frank (1963–) *Cold Dog Soup* 1989; *Field of Dreams* 1989; *Unconquered* 1989; *The Freshman* 1990; *Career Opportunities* 1991; *The Doors* 1991; *A Midnight Clear* 1991; *Back in the USSR* 1992; *Hoffa* 1992; *Swing Kids* 1993; *Swimming with Sharks* 1994; *Homage* 1995; *Broken Arrow* 1996; *The Winner* 1996; *Curtain Call* 1998; *When Trumpets Fade* 1998

Whalin, Justin (1974–) *Child's Play 3* 1991; *Serial Mom* 1994; *Dungeons & Dragons* 2000

Whalley, Joanne aka **Whalley-Kilmer, Joanne** (1964–) *Dance with a Stranger* 1984; *The Good Father* 1986; *No Surrender* 1986; *Scandal* 1988; *To Kill a Priest* 1988; *Willow* 1988; *Kill Me Again* 1989; *The Big Man* 1990; *Navy SEALS* 1990; *Shattered* 1991; *Storyville* 1992; *A Good Man in Africa* 1993; *Mother's Boys* 1993; *The Secret Rapture* 1993; *Trial by Jury* 1994; *The Man Who Knew Too Little* 1997; *The Guilty* 2000; *Before You Go* 2002

Whately, Kevin (1951–) *The Return of the Soldier* 1982; *The English Patient* 1996; *Purely Belter* 2000

Wheatley, Alan (1907–1991) *Conquest of the Air* 1936; *Brighton Rock* 1947; *It's Not Cricket* 1948; *Home to Danger* 1951; *The Limping Man* 1953; *Spaceways* 1953; *Delayed Action* 1954; *The Diamond* 1954; *The Duke Wore Jeans* 1958; *Tomorrow at Ten* 1962; *Clash by Night* 1963; *Master Spy* 1964

Wheatley, Thomas *The Living Daylights* 1987; *Where Angels Fear to Tread* 1991

Wheaton, Wil (1972–) *The Buddy System* 1984; *Stand by Me* 1986; *The Curse* 1987; *December* 1991; *Toy Soldiers* 1991; *Pie in the Sky* 1995; *Flubber* 1997; *Python* 2000; *Star Trek: Nemesis* 2002

Wheeler, Bert (1895–1968) *Rio Rita* 1929; *Half Shot at Sunrise* 1930

Wheeler, Ira *September* 1987; *Swimming to Cambodia* 1987

Wheeler-Nicholson, Dana *Fletch* 1985; *Circuitry Man* 1990; *Denise Calls Up* 1995; *Frank and Jesse* 1995; *Nick and Jane* 1996

Whelan, Arleen (1916–1993) *Kidnapped* 1938; *Thanks for Everything* 1938; *Young Mr Lincoln* 1939; *Young People* 1940; *Ramrod* 1947; *The Senator Was Indiscreet* 1947; *Suddenly It's Spring* 1947; *That Wonderful Urge* 1948; *Never Wave at a WAC* 1952; *The Sun Shines Bright* 1953

Whigham, Shea *Tigerland* 2000; *All the Real Girls* 2003

Whiley, Manning (1915–1975) *Pimpernel Smith* 1941; *The Saint's Vacation* 1941; *Bell-Bottom George* 1943; *The Shop at Sly Corner* 1946; *Conspiracy in Teheran* 1947; *Uncle Silas* 1947; *Children of Chance* 1949

Whirry, Shannon (1964–) *Body of Influence* 1993; *Omega Doom* 1996; *The Prophet's Game* 1999

Whishaw, Ben (1980–) *My Brother Tom* 2001; *Layer Cake* 2004

Whitaker, Damon (1970–) *Bird* 1988; *Mr Holland's Opus* 1995

Whitaker, Forest (1961–) *Fast Times at Ridgemont High* 1982; *Vision Quest* 1985; *The Color of Money* 1986; *Platoon* 1986; *Bloodsport* 1987; *Good Morning, Vietnam* 1987; *Stakeout* 1987; *Bird* 1988; *Johnny Handsome* 1989; *Downtown* 1990; *A Rage in Harlem* 1991; *Article 99* 1992; *Consenting Adults* 1992; *The Crying Game* 1992; *Diary of a Hitman* 1992; *Bank Robber* 1993; *Body Snatchers* 1993; *Last Light* 1993; *Lush Life* 1993; *Blown Away* 1994; *The Enemy Within* 1994; *Jason's Lyric* 1994; *Prêt-a-Porter* 1994; *Smoke* 1995; *Species* 1995; *Phenomenon* 1996; *Body Count* 1997; *Four Dogs Playing Poker* 1999; *Ghost Dog: the Way of the Samurai* 1999; *Light It Up* 1999; *Witness Protection* 1999; *Battlefield Earth* 2000; *The Fourth Angel* 2001; *Panic Room* 2002; *Phone Booth* 2002; *First Daughter* 2004

Whitaker, Johnny (1959–) *The Biscuit Eater* 1972; *Napoleon and Samantha* 1972; *Snowball Express* 1972; *Tom Sawyer* 1973

White, Alan (1949–) *No Time for Tears* 1957; *Girls at Sea* 1958; *A Lady Mislaid* 1958

White, Alice (1904–1983) *The Big Noise* 1928; *Employees' Entrance* 1933; *Picture Snatcher* 1933; *Jimmy the Gent* 1934

White, Barbara (1923–) *Quiet Weekend* 1946; *While the Sun Shines* 1946; *Mine Own Executioner* 1947; *This Was a Woman* 1947

White, Betty (1922–) *Hard Rain* 1997; *Dennis the Menace Strikes Again* 1998; *Lake Placid* 1999; *Whispers: an Elephant's Tale* 2000; *Bringing Down the House* 2003

White, Carol (1942–1991) *Circus Friends* 1956; *Never Let Go* 1960; *The Man in the Back Seat* 1961; *Village of Daughters* 1961; *Gaolbreak* 1962; *I'll Never Forget What's 'Is Name* 1967; *Poor Cow* 1967; *The Fixer* 1968; *Daddy's Gone A-Hunting* 1969; *The Man Who Had Power over Women* 1970; *Dulcima* 1971; *something big* 1971; *The Squeeze* 1977; *Nutcracker* 1982

White, David (1916–1990) *Madison Avenue* 1962; *Spider-Man* 1977

White, De'Voreaux *Die Hard* 1988; *Trespass* 1992

White, Jacqueline (1922–) *Crossfire* 1947; *Night Song* 1947; *Seven Keys to Baldpate* 1947; *Mystery in Mexico* 1948; *Return of the Bad Men* 1948; *The Capture* 1950; *The Narrow Margin* 1952

White, Jesse (1917–1997) *Harvey* 1950; *Bedtime for Bonzo* 1951; *Callaway Went Thataway* 1951; *Francis Goes to the Races* 1951; *The Girl in White* 1952; *Million Dollar Mermaid* 1952; *Forever Female* 1953; *Gunsmoke* 1953; *Hell's Half Acre* 1954; *Witness to Murder* 1954; *The Bad Seed* 1956; *The Come On* 1956; *Designing Woman* 1957; *Johnny Trouble* 1957; *The Rise and Fall of Legs Diamond* 1960; *Tomboy and the Champ* 1961; *It'$ Only Money* 1962; *The Yellow Canary* 1963; *Pajama Party* 1964; *The Ghost in the Invisible Bikini* 1966; *The Reluctant Astronaut* 1967; *Bless the Beasts and Children* 1971; *The Cat from Outer Space* 1978

White, Leo (1882–1948) *His New Job* 1915; *The Tramp* 1915; *Work* 1915; *The Vagabond* 1916

White, Marjorie (1908–1935) *Sunny Side Up* 1929; *Just Imagine* 1930; *Possessed* 1931

White, Michael Jai *City of Industry* 1996; *Spawn* 1997; *Ringmaster* 1998; *Mutiny* 1999; *Universal Soldier – the Return* 1999; *Freedom Song* 2000; *Exit Wounds* 2001

White, Mike (1970–) *Chuck & Buck* 2000; *The Good Girl* 2001; *The School of Rock* 2003

White, Ron *Too Outrageous!* 1987; *Guilty as Sin* 1993; *Screamers* 1995; *Danger beneath the Sea* 2001

White, Ruth (1914–1969) *Edge of the City* 1957; *To Kill a Mockingbird* 1962; *Baby the Rain Must Fall* 1965; *The Tiger Makes Out* 1967; *Up the Down Staircase* 1967; *Hang 'Em High* 1968; *Midnight Cowboy* 1969; *The Reivers* 1969; *The Pursuit of Happiness* 1971

White, Sammy (1894–1960) *Show Boat* 1936; *711 Ocean Drive* 1950; *Pat and Mike* 1952; *About Mrs Leslie* 1954

White, Sheila (1950–) *Here We Go round the Mulberry Bush* 1967; *Oliver!* 1968; *Confessions of a Window Cleaner* 1974; *Alfie Darling* 1975; *Confessions of a Pop Performer* 1975; *Confessions of a Driving Instructor* 1976; *Confessions from a Holiday Camp* 1977; *The Spaceman and King Arthur* 1979

White, Valerie (1915–1975) *Hue and Cry* 1947; *The Blue Parrot* 1953; *Travels with My Aunt* 1972

Whitehead, O Z (1911–1998) *The Grapes of Wrath* 1940; *Road House* 1948; *Beware, My Lovely* 1952

Whitehead, Paxton (1937–) *Back to School* 1986; *The Adventures of Huck Finn* 1993

Whitehouse, Paul (1958–) *Kevin & Perry Go Large* 2000; *Finding Neverland* 2004

Whitelaw, Billie (1932–) *The Sleeping Tiger* 1954; *Small Hotel* 1957; *Carve Her Name with Pride* 1958; *Bobbikins* 1959; *The Flesh and the Fiends* 1959; *Hell Is a City* 1959; *Make Mine Mink* 1960; *No Love for Johnnie* 1960; *Mr Topaze* 1961; *Payroll* 1961; *The Comedy Man* 1964; *Charlie Bubbles* 1967; *Twisted Nerve* 1968; *The Adding Machine* 1969; *Leo the Last* 1970; *Start the Revolution without Me* 1970; *Eagle in a Cage* 1971; *Gumshoe* 1971; *Frenzy* 1972; *Night Watch* 1973; *The Omen* 1976; *The Water Babies* 1978; *An Unsuitable Job for a Woman* 1981; *The Dark Crystal* 1982; *Tangier* 1982; *Slayground* 1983; *The Chain* 1984; *Shadey* 1985; *Maurice* 1987; *The Dressmaker* 1988; *Joyriders* 1988; *The Krays* 1990; *Freddie as FRO7* 1992; *Deadly Advice* 1993; *Jane Eyre* 1996; *The Lost Son* 1998; *Quills* 2000

Whiteley, Jon (1945–) *Hunted* 1952; *The Kidnappers* 1953; *The Spanish Gardener* 1956

Whiteman, Paul (1890–1967) *Atlantic City* 1944; *The Fabulous Dorseys* 1947

Whitfield, June (1925–) *Bless This House* 1972; *Carry On Abroad* 1972; *Carry On Girls* 1973; *Not Now, Comrade* 1976; *Carry On Columbus* 1992; *Jude* 1996

Whitfield, Lynn (1953–) *Doctor Detroit* 1983; *Thicker than Blood* 1993; *A Thin Line between Love and Hate* 1996; *Eve's Bayou* 1997; *Gone Fishin'* 1997; *Stepmom* 1998; *Head of State* 2003; *Redemption* 2004

Whitfield, Mitchell (1968–) *Dogfight* 1991; *My Cousin Vinny* 1992; *Best Men* 1997; *Lost & Found* 1999

Whitford, Bradley aka **Whitford, Brad** (1959–) *Scent of a Woman* 1992; *My Life* 1993; *A Perfect World* 1993; *Billy Madison* 1995; *Masterminds* 1997; *Red Corner* 1997; *Behind the Mask* 1999; *Kate & Leopold* 2002; *The Sisterhood of the Traveling Pants* 2005

Whitford, Peter (1939–) *Careful, He Might Hear You* 1983; *Strictly Ballroom* 1992

Whiting, Barbara (1931–2004) *Beware, My Lovely* 1952; *Dangerous When Wet* 1953

Whiting, Leonard (1950–) *Romeo and Juliet* 1968; *The Royal Hunt of the Sun* 1969; *Say Hello to Yesterday* 1971; *Frankenstein: the True Story* 1973; *Rachel's Man* 1975

Whiting, Margaret (1924–) *The Informers* 1963; *Sinbad and the Eye of the Tiger* 1977

Whitley, Ray (1901–1979) *Painted Desert* 1938; *Along the Rio Grande* 1941

Whitlow, Jill *Thunder Run* 1986; *Twice Dead* 1988

Whitman, Mae (1988–) *When a Man Loves a Woman* 1994; *One Fine Day* 1996; *Hope Floats* 1998; *An American Rhapsody* 2001; *The Jungle Book 2* 2003

Whitman, Stuart (1926–) *The All American* 1953; *Rhapsody* 1954; *Johnny Trouble* 1957; *Darby's Rangers* 1958; *The Decks Ran Red* 1958; *Ten North Frederick* 1958; *Hound Dog Man* 1959; *The Sound and the Fury* 1959; *These Thousand Hills* 1959; *Murder, Inc* 1960; *The Story of Ruth* 1960; *The Comancheros* 1961; *The Fiercest Heart* 1961; *Francis of Assisi* 1961; *The Mark* 1961; *Convicts Four* 1962; *The Longest Day* 1962; *Rio Conchos* 1964; *Shock Treatment* 1964; *Signpost to Murder* 1964; *Sands of the Kalahari* 1965; *Those Magnificent Men in Their Flying Machines* 1965; *An American Dream* 1966; *The Heroes* 1968; *Sweet Hunters* 1969; *The Last Escape* 1970; *Captain Apache* 1971; *City beneath the Sea* 1971; *Night of the Lepus* 1972; *Shatter* 1974; *Welcome to Arrow Beach* 1974; *Crazy Mama* 1975; *Eaten Alive* 1976; *Maniac* 1977; *Ruby* 1977; *The Treasure Seekers* 1977; *The White Buffalo* 1977; *Run for the Roses* 1978; *Cuba Crossing* 1980; *Butterfly* 1982; *Once upon a Texas Train* 1988; *Improper Conduct* 1994

Whitmire, Steve (1959–) *The Muppets Take Manhattan* 1984; *The Muppet Christmas Carol* 1992; *Muppet Treasure Island* 1996; *Muppets from Space* 1999; *It's a Very Merry Muppet Christmas Movie* 2002

Whitmore, James (1921–) *Battleground* 1949; *The Undercover Man* 1949; *The Asphalt Jungle* 1950; *Mrs O'Malley and Mr Malone* 1950; *The Next Voice You Hear* 1950; *The Outriders* 1950; *Please Believe Me* 1950; *The Red Badge of Courage* 1951; *Above and Beyond* 1952; *Because You're*

Mine 1952; *All the Brothers Were Valiant* 1953; *The Girl Who Had Everything* 1953; *The Great Diamond Robbery* 1953; *Kiss Me Kate* 1953; *The Command* 1954; *Them!* 1954; *Battle Cry* 1955; *The Last Frontier* 1955; *The McConnell Story* 1955; *Oklahoma!* 1955; *Crime in the Streets* 1956; *The Eddy Duchin Story* 1956; *The Deep Six* 1958; *The Restless Years* 1958; *Face of Fire* 1959; *Who Was That Lady?* 1960; *Black like Me* 1964; *Chuka* 1967; *Planet of the Apes* 1967; *Waterhole #3* 1967; *Madigan* 1968; *Nobody's Perfect* 1968; *Guns of the Magnificent Seven* 1969; *Tora! Tora! Tora!* 1970; *Chato's Land* 1971; *The Harrad Experiment* 1973; *Where the Red Fern Grows* 1974; *Give 'em Hell, Harry!* 1975; *The Serpent's Egg* 1977; *The Shawshank Redemption* 1994; *The Relic* 1996; *The Majestic* 2001; *A Ring of Endless Light* 2002
Whitmore Jr, James (1948–) *The Boys in Company C* 1978; *A Force of One* 1979; *Don't Cry, It's Only Thunder* 1982
Whitney, Claire (1890–1969) *A Free Soul* 1931; *Betrayed* 1944
Whitney, Peter (1916–1972) *Underground* 1941; *Whistling in Dixie* 1942; *Bring on the Girls* 1945; *Murder, He Says* 1945; *The Big Heat* 1953; *Gorilla at Large* 1954; *The Last Frontier* 1955; *Buchanan Rides Alone* 1958; *Chubasco* 1967; *The Ballad of Cable Hogue* 1970
Whitsun-Jones, Paul (1923–1974) *Stock Car* 1955; *The Wild Affair* 1963; *Dr Jekyll and Sister Hyde* 1971
Whittaker (1), Stephen (1947–2003) *Chastity* 1969; *Bury Me an Angel* 1972
Whitten, Frank *Vigil* 1984; *Waiting* 1990
Whitton, Margaret (1950–) *Love Child* 1982; *Nine ½ Weeks* 1985; *The Best of Times* 1986; *The Secret of My Success* 1987; *Little Monsters* 1989; *Major League* 1989; *Stepkids* 1992; *The Man without a Face* 1993; *Major League II* 1994; *Trial by Jury* 1994
Whitty, Dame May aka **Whitty, May** (1865–1948) *Conquest* 1937; *Night Must Fall* 1937; *I Met My Love Again* 1938; *The Lady Vanishes* 1938; *Raffles* 1939; *A Bill of Divorcement* 1940; *Return to Yesterday* 1940; *Suspicion* 1941; *Mrs Miniver* 1942; *The Constant Nymph* 1943; *Crash Dive* 1943; *Forever and a Day* 1943; *Lassie Come Home* 1943; *Madame Curie* 1943; *Slightly Dangerous* 1943; *Gaslight* 1944; *My Name Is Julia Ross* 1945; *Devotion* 1946; *Green Dolphin Street* 1947; *If Winter Comes* 1947; *The Return of October* 1948
Whorf, Richard (1906–1966) *Midnight* 1934; *Blues in the Night* 1941; *Keeper of the Flame* 1942; *Yankee Doodle Dandy* 1942; *The Cross of Lorraine* 1943; *Christmas Holiday* 1944; *The Impostor* 1944; *Chain Lightning* 1950
Whyte, Patrick (1907–1984) *Hideous Sun Demon* 1959; *Kitten with a Whip* 1964
Wiazemsky, Anne (1947–) *Au Hasard, Balthazar* 1966; *La Chinoise* 1967; *One Plus One* 1968; *Theorem* 1968; *The Seed of Man* 1969; *Vent d'Est* 1969; *Vladimir et Rosa* 1970
Wickes, Mary (1916–1995) *The Man Who Came to Dinner* 1941; *Now, Voyager* 1942; *Private Buckaroo* 1942; *Who Done It?* 1942; *Higher and Higher* 1943; *Anna Lucasta* 1949; *The Petty Girl* 1950; *I'll See You in My Dreams* 1951; *On Moonlight Bay* 1951; *Young Man with Ideas* 1952; *The Actress* 1953; *By the Light of the Silvery Moon* 1953; *White Christmas* 1954; *Fate Is the Hunter* 1964; *Where Angels Go...Trouble Follows* 1968; *Touched by Love* 1979; *Postcards from the Edge* 1990; *Sister Act* 1992; *Sister Act 2: Back in the Habit* 1993; *Little Women* 1994
Wicki, Bernhard (1919–2000) *The Last Bridge* 1954; *La Notte* 1961; *Crime and Passion* 1976; *Despair* 1978; *Paris, Texas* 1984
Widdoes, Kathleen (1939–) *Petulia* 1968; *The Sea Gull* 1968; *The Mephisto Waltz* 1971; *Without a Trace* 1983
Widerberg, Johan (1974–) *All Things Fair* 1995; *Under the Sun* 1998
Widmark, Richard (1914–) *Kiss of Death* 1947; *Road House* 1948; *The Street with No Name* 1948; *Yellow Sky* 1948; *Down to the Sea in Ships* 1949; *Slattery's Hurricane* 1949; *Halls of Montezuma* 1950; *Night and the City* 1950; *No Way Out* 1950; *Panic in the Streets* 1950; *The Frogmen* 1951; *Don't Bother to Knock* 1952; *My Pal Gus* 1952; *O Henry's Full House* 1952; *Red Skies of Montana* 1952; *Destination Gobi* 1953; *Pickup on South Street* 1953; *Take the High Ground* 1953; *Broken Lance* 1954; *Garden of Evil* 1954; *Hell and High Water* 1954; *The Cobweb* 1955; *A Prize of Gold* 1955; *Backlash* 1956; *The Last Wagon* 1956; *Run for the Sun* 1956; *Saint Joan* 1957; *Time Limit* 1957; *The Law and Jake Wade* 1958; *The Tunnel of Love* 1958; *The Baited Trap* 1959; *Warlock* 1959; *The Alamo* 1960; *Judgment at Nuremberg* 1961; *The Secret Ways* 1961; *Two Rode Together* 1961; *How the West Was Won* 1962; *The Long Ships* 1963; *Cheyenne Autumn* 1964; *Flight from Ashiya* 1964; *The Bedford Incident* 1965; *Alvarez Kelly* 1966; *The Way West* 1967; *Madigan* 1968; *Death of a Gunfighter* 1969; *When the Legends Die* 1972; *Murder on the Orient Express* 1974; *The Sellout* 1975; *To the Devil a Daughter* 1976; *Coma* 1977; *The Domino Principle* 1977; *Rollercoaster* 1977; *Twilight's Last Gleaming* 1977; *The Swarm* 1978; *Bear Island* 1979; *National Lampoon's Movie Madness* 1981; *Hanky Panky* 1982; *Who Dares Wins* 1982; *Against All Odds* 1984; *Once upon a Texas Train* 1988; *True Colors* 1991
Wieman, Mathias (1902–1969) *Paracelsus* 1943; *Fear* 1954
Wiener, Elisabeth (1946–) *Marry Me! Marry Me!* 1968; *The Monk* 1972
Wiest, Dianne (1948–) *It's My Turn* 1980; *I'm Dancing as Fast as I Can* 1982; *Independence Day* 1983; *Falling in Love* 1984; *Footloose* 1984; *The Purple Rose of Cairo* 1985; *Hannah and Her Sisters* 1986; *The Lost Boys* 1987; *Radio Days* 1987; *September* 1987; *Bright Lights, Big City* 1988; *Cookie* 1989; *Parenthood* 1989; *Edward Scissorhands* 1990; *Little Man Tate* 1991; *Bullets over Broadway* 1994; *Cops and Robbersons* 1994; *The Scout* 1994; *The Associate* 1996; *The Birdcage* 1996; *The Horse Whisperer* 1998; *Practical Magic* 1998; *The Simple Life of Noah Dearborn* 1999; *I Am Sam* 2001; *Merci Docteur Rey* 2002; *The Blackwater Lightship* 2004; *Robots* 2005
Wieth, Mogens (1919–1962) *The Man Who Knew Too Much* 1956; *Private Potter* 1963
Wifstrand, Naima (1890–1968) *Dreams* 1955; *The Magician* 1958
Wiggins, Chris (1931–) *King of the Grizzlies* 1969; *The Neptune Factor* 1973; *Why Shoot the Teacher* 1976; *Welcome to Blood City* 1977; *High-ballin'* 1978; *Bay Boy* 1984
Wiggins, Wiley (1976–) *Dazed and Confused* 1993; *Boys* 1995; *Waking Life* 2001
Wight, Peter *Naked* 1993; *Vera Drake* 2004
Wightman, Natasha *Revelation* 2001; *Shoreditch* 2002
Wightman, Robert *Impulse* 1984; *Hell Camp* 1986
Wilbanks, Don *Stagecoach to Dancer's Rock* 1962; *Cry for Me Billy* 1972
Wilborn, Carlton *Grief* 1993; *Made Men* 1999
Wilbur, George P *Halloween 4: the Return of Michael Myers* 1988; *Halloween 6: the Curse of Michael Myers* 1995
Wilby, James (1958–) *A Handful of Dust* 1987; *Maurice* 1987; *A Summer Story* 1987; *Immaculate Conception* 1991; *Howards End* 1992; *Regeneration* 1997; *Tom's Midnight Garden* 1998; *Cotton Mary* 1999; *Jump Tomorrow* 2001; *De-Lovely* 2004
Wilcox, Claire *Forty Pounds of Trouble* 1962; *Wives and Lovers* 1963
Wilcox, Frank (1907–1974) *Conflict* 1945; *Abbott and Costello Meet the Keystone Cops* 1955; *Go, Johnny, Go!* 1959
Wilcox, Lisa (1964–) *A Nightmare on Elm Street 4: The Dream Master* 1988; *A Nightmare on Elm Street 5: The Dream Child* 1989
Wilcox, Paula (1949–) *The Lovers!* 1972; *Man about the House* 1974
Wilcox, Robert (1910–1955) *The Man They Could Not Hang* 1939; *Wild Beauty* 1946; *The Vigilantes Return* 1947
Wilcox, Shannon *The Border* 1981; *Six Weeks* 1982; *Hollywood Harry* 1985
Wilcox-Horne, Collin (1937–) *The Baby Maker* 1970; *The Revolutionary* 1970
Wilcoxon, Henry (1905–1984) *Cleopatra* 1934; *The Crusades* 1935; *The Last of the Mohicans* 1936; *Souls at Sea* 1937; *If I Were King* 1938; *Mysterious Mr Moto* 1938; *Tarzan Finds a Son!* 1939; *The Corsican Brothers* 1941; *That Hamilton Woman* 1941; *Mrs Miniver* 1942; *Unconquered* 1947; *A Connecticut Yankee in King Arthur's Court* 1949; *Samson and Delilah* 1949; *The Greatest Show on Earth* 1952; *Scaramouche* 1952; *The Private Navy of Sgt O'Farrell* 1968; *Man in the Wilderness* 1971; *Against a Crooked Sky* 1975
Wild, Jack (1952–) *Oliver!* 1968; *Pufnstuf* 1970; *Flight of the Doves* 1971; *Melody* 1971; *The Pied Piper* 1971; *Keep It Up Downstairs* 1976; *Basil* 1998
Wild, Katy *Evil of Frankenstein* 1964; *The Settlement* 1982
Wilde, Brian (1924–) *We Joined the Navy* 1962; *Rattle of a Simple Man* 1964; *Porridge* 1979
Wilde, Cornel (1915–1989) *Life Begins at 8.30* 1942; *Wintertime* 1943; *Leave Her to Heaven* 1945; *A Song to Remember* 1945; *A Thousand and One Nights* 1945; *The Bandit of Sherwood Forest* 1946; *Centennial Summer* 1946; *Forever Amber* 1947; *It Had to Be You* 1947; *Road House* 1948; *Shockproof* 1949; *Two Flags West* 1950; *Sons of the Musketeers* 1951; *The Greatest Show on Earth* 1952; *Saadia* 1953; *Treasure of the Golden Condor* 1953; *Passion* 1954; *Star of India* 1954; *Woman's World* 1954; *The Big Combo* 1955; *The Scarlet Coat* 1955; *Hot Blood* 1956; *Beyond Mombasa* 1957; *The Devil's Hairpin* 1957; *Omar Khayyam* 1957; *Maracaibo* 1958; *Edge of Eternity* 1959; *Constantine and the Cross* 1961; *Lancelot and Guinevere* 1963; *The Naked Prey* 1966; *Beach Red* 1967; *The Comic* 1969; *Shark's Treasure* 1975; *The Norseman* 1978; *The Fifth Musketeer* 1979
Wilde, Marty (1939–) *What a Crazy World* 1963; *Stardust* 1974
Wilder, Gene (1935–) *Bonnie and Clyde* 1967; *The Producers* 1968; *Quackser Fortune Has a Cousin in the Bronx* 1970; *Start the Revolution without Me* 1970; *Willy Wonka and the Chocolate Factory* 1971; *Everything You Always Wanted to Know about Sex ... but Were Afraid to Ask* 1972; *Blazing Saddles* 1974; *The Little Prince* 1974; *Rhinoceros* 1974; *Young Frankenstein* 1974; *The Adventure of Sherlock Holmes' Smarter Brother* 1975; *Silver Streak* 1976; *The World's Greatest Lover* 1977; *The Frisco Kid* 1979; *Stir Crazy* 1980; *Hanky Panky* 1982; *The Woman in Red* 1984; *Haunted Honeymoon* 1986; *See No Evil, Hear No Evil* 1989; *Funny about Love* 1990; *Another You* 1991; *Alice in Wonderland* 1999; *The Lady in Question* 1999; *Murder in a Small Town* 1999
Wilder, James (1963–) *Zombie High* 1987; *Scorchers* 1991; *Tollbooth* 1994; *The Face* 1996; *Face Value* 2001
Wilder, Yvonne *The Return of Count Yorga* 1971; *Bloodbrothers* 1978; *Seems like Old Times* 1980
Wildgruber, Ulrich (1937–1999) *Melancholia* 1989; *The Inheritors* 1997
Wilding, Michael (1912–1979) *Convoy* 1940; *Sailors Three* 1940; *Cottage to Let* 1941; *Kipps* 1941; *The Big Blockade* 1942; *In Which We Serve* 1942; *Secret Mission* 1942; *Ships with Wings* 1942; *Undercover* 1943; *English without Tears* 1944; *Carnival* 1946; *Piccadilly Incident* 1946; *The Courtneys of Curzon Street* 1947; *An Ideal Husband* 1947; *Spring in Park Lane* 1948; *Maytime in Mayfair* 1949; *Stage Fright* 1949; *Under Capricorn* 1949; *The Lady with the Lamp* 1951; *The Law and the Lady* 1951; *Derby Day* 1952; *Trent's Last Case* 1952; *Torch Song* 1953; *The Egyptian* 1954; *The Glass Slipper* 1955; *The Scarlet Coat* 1955; *Zarak* 1956; *Danger Within* 1958; *The World of Suzie Wong* 1960; *The Best of Enemies* 1961; *The Naked Edge* 1961; *A Girl Named Tamiko* 1962; *The Sweet Ride* 1967; *Waterloo* 1970
Wilding Jr, Michael aka **Wilding, Michael** (1953–) *Blame It on the Night* 1984; *Deadly Illusion* 1987
Wildman, John (1961–) *My American Cousin* 1985; *American Boyfriends* 1989
Wiles, Jason (1970–) *Roadracers* 1994; *Kicking and Screaming* 1995
Wilhoite, Kathleen (1964–) *Private School* 1983; *Murphy's Law* 1986; *Witchboard* 1987; *Dream Demon* 1988; *Bad Influence* 1990; *Everybody Wins* 1990; *Lorenzo's Oil* 1992; *Breast Men* 1997; *The Edge* 1997
Wilke, Robert J aka **Wilke, Robert** (1914–1989) *20,000 Leagues under the Sea* 1954; *Shotgun* 1955; *The Lone Ranger* 1956; *Written on the Wind* 1956; *Hot Summer Night* 1957; *The Tarnished Angels* 1957; *Man of the West* 1958; *Tony Rome* 1967; *The Resurrection of Zachary Wheeler* 1971; *Santee* 1973; *Days of Heaven* 1978
Wilker, José (1945–) *Dona Flor and Her Two Husbands* 1977; *Bye Bye Brazil* 1979; *Prisoner of Rio* 1988; *Medicine Man* 1992; *The Man of the Year* 2002
Wilkin, Jeremy *Curse of the Fly* 1965; *Thunderbirds Are Go!* 1966; *Thunderbird 6* 1968
Wilkinson, Tom (1948–) *Parker* 1984; *Sylvia* 1984; *Wetherby* 1985; *Paper Mask* 1990; *A Business Affair* 1993; *Priest* 1994; *Sense and Sensibility* 1995; *The Ghost and the Darkness* 1996; *The Full Monty* 1997; *The Governess* 1997; *Oscar and Lucinda* 1997; *Wilde* 1997; *Rush Hour* 1998; *Shakespeare in Love* 1998; *Essex Boys* 1999; *Ride with the Devil* 1999; *The Patriot* 2000; *Black Knight* 2001; *In the Bedroom* 2001; *Before You Go* 2002; *The Importance of Being Earnest* 2002; *Normal* 2002; *Eternal Sunshine of the Spotless Mind* 2003; *Girl with a Pearl Earring* 2003; *A Good Woman* 2004; *Stage Beauty* 2004; *Batman Begins* 2005
Wilkof, Lee (1951–) *Chattahoochee* 1989; *Addicted to Love* 1997
Willard, Fred (1939–) *Jenny* 1969; *Americathon* 1979; *Roxanne* 1987; *Sodbusters* 1994; *Waiting for Guffman* 1996; *Best in Show* 2000; *American Pie: the Wedding* 2003; *A Mighty Wind* 2003; *Anchorman: the Legend of Ron Burgundy* 2004
Willcox, Toyah (1958–) *Jubilee* 1978; *Quadrophenia* 1979; *The Tempest* 1979; *Anchoress* 1993; *Julie and the Cadillacs* 1997; *The Most Fertile Man in Ireland* 1999
Willes, Jean (1923–1989) *Invasion of the Body Snatchers* 1956; *The King and Four Queens* 1956; *Desire under the Elms* 1958; *The FBI Story* 1959
William, Warren (1895–1948) *Skyscraper Souls* 1932; *Three on a Match* 1932; *Employees' Entrance* 1933; *Gold Diggers of 1933* 1933; *Lady for a Day* 1933; *The Mind Reader* 1933; *The Case of the Howling Dog* 1934; *Cleopatra* 1934; *Imitation of Life* 1934; *The Secret Bride* 1934; *Upper World* 1934; *The Case of the Lucky Legs* 1935; *The Case of the Velvet Claws* 1936; *Go West, Young Man* 1936; *Satan Met a Lady* 1936; *Stage Struck* 1936; *The Firefly* 1937; *Madame X* 1937; *Arsene Lupin Returns* 1938; *Wives under Suspicion* 1938; *The Gracie Allen Murder Case* 1939; *The Lone Wolf Spy Hunt* 1939; *The Man in the Iron Mask* 1939; *Arizona* 1940; *Lillian Russell* 1940; *The Lone Wolf Meets a Lady* 1940; *Trail of the Vigilantes* 1940; *Wild Geese Calling* 1941; *The Wolf Man* 1941
Williams, Adam (1929–) *Vice Squad* 1953; *The Proud and Profane* 1956; *Fear Strikes Out* 1957; *The Badlanders* 1958; *North by Northwest* 1959
Williams (2), Barbara *Thief of Hearts* 1984; *Jo Jo Dancer, Your Life Is Calling* 1986; *Tiger Warsaw* 1988; *Watchers* 1988; *City of Hope* 1991; *Oh, What a Night* 1992; *Kidnapped* 1995; *Bone Daddy* 1998
Williams, Bert (1922–2001) *From Noon till Three* 1976; *10 to Midnight* 1983
Williams, Bill (1916–1992) *Deadline at Dawn* 1946; *Till the End of Time* 1946; *The Clay Pigeon* 1949; *A Dangerous Profession* 1949; *Fighting Man of the Plains* 1949; *The Stratton Story* 1949; *A Woman's Secret* 1949; *The Cariboo Trail* 1950; *Rose of Cimarron* 1952; *Son of Paleface* 1952; *The Halliday Brand* 1957; *Space Master X 7* 1958; *A Dog's Best Friend* 1960; *Tickle Me* 1965; *Scandalous John* 1971
Williams, Billy Dee (1937–) *The Last Angry Man* 1959; *Brian's Song* 1971; *The Final Comedown* 1972; *The Glass House* 1972; *Lady Sings the Blues* 1972; *Hit!* 1973; *The Take* 1974; *Mahogany* 1975; *The Bingo Long Travelling All-Stars and Motor Kings* 1976; *Scott Joplin* 1977; *Star Wars Episode V: the Empire Strikes Back* 1980; *Nighthawks* 1981; *Marvin and Tige* 1983; *Star Wars Episode VI: Return of the Jedi* 1983; *Fear City* 1984; *Number One with a Bullet* 1986; *Deadly Illusion* 1987; *Batman* 1989; *Hard Time* 1998; *The Ladies Man* 2000; *Undercover Brother* 2002
Williams, Brook *The Plague of the Zombies* 1965; *Absolution* 1978
Williams, Cara (1925–) *Happy Land* 1943; *Boomerang!* 1947; *The Saxon Charm* 1948; *Knock on Any Door* 1949; *The Girl Next Door* 1953; *The Great Diamond Robbery* 1953; *The Helen Morgan Story* 1957; *Never Steal Anything Small* 1959; *The Man from the Diner's Club* 1963; *One Man Jury* 1978
Williams, Caroline *Getting Even* 1986; *The Texas Chainsaw Massacre Part 2* 1986; *Stepfather II* 1989; *Flashfire* 1993
Williams, Charles (1898–1958) *Faithless* 1932; *Convoy* 1940
Williams, Cindy (1947–) *Gas-s-s-s, or It Became Necessary to Destroy the World in Order to*

Save It 1970; *Travels with My Aunt* 1972; *American Graffiti* 1973; *The Killing Kind* 1973; *The Conversation* 1974; *Mr Ricco* 1975; *More American Graffiti* 1979; *UFOria* 1980; *Big Man on Campus* 1989; *Rude Awakening* 1989; *Bingo* 1991

Williams III, Clarence (1939–) *The Cool World* 1963; *King: a Filmed Record… Montgomery to Memphis* 1970; *Purple Rain* 1984; *Tough Guys Don't Dance* 1987; *Maniac Cop 2* 1990; *My Heroes Have Always Been Cowboys* 1991; *Deep Cover* 1992; *Sugar Hill* 1993; *Against the Wall* 1994; *Tales from the Hood* 1995; *The Brave* 1997; *Hoodlum* 1997; *Half-Baked* 1998; *Last Rites* 1998; *The General's Daughter* 1999; *Life* 1999; *Ali: an American Hero* 2000; *Deception* 2000

Williams, Cynda (1966–) *Mo' Better Blues* 1990; *One False Move* 1992; *Killing Box* 1993; *Erotic Tales* 1994; *Relax… It's Just Sex* 1998; *Introducing Dorothy Dandridge* 1999

Williams, D J *Maria Marten, or the Murder in the Red Barn* 1935; *The Crimes of Stephen Hawke* 1936; *Sweeney Todd, the Demon Barber of Fleet Street* 1936; *Elephant Boy* 1937; *It's Never Too Late to Mend* 1937

Williams, Darnell (1955–) *Sidewalk Stories* 1989; *How U Like Me Now* 1992

Williams, Dick Anthony aka **Williams, Dick** (1938–) *The Anderson Tapes* 1971; *Who Killed Mary Whats'ername?* 1971; *The Mack* 1973; *An Almost Perfect Affair* 1979; *The Jerk* 1979; *Gardens of Stone* 1987; *Tap* 1989; *Mo' Better Blues* 1990

Williams, Edy (1942–) *The Pad (and How to Use It)* 1966; *The Secret Life of an American Wife* 1968; *Where It's At* 1969; *Beyond the Valley of the Dolls* 1970; *The Seven Minutes* 1971; *Chained Heat* 1983; *Hollywood Hot Tubs* 1984

Williams, Emlyn (1905–1987) *Friday the Thirteenth* 1933; *Evensong* 1934; *The Dictator* 1935; *Broken Blossoms* 1936; *The Citadel* 1938; *Jamaica Inn* 1939; *The Stars Look Down* 1939; *The Girl in the News* 1940; *Hatter's Castle* 1941; *Major Barbara* 1941; *The Last Days of Dolwyn* 1949; *Another Man's Poison* 1951; *The Scarf* 1951; *Ivanhoe* 1952; *The Deep Blue Sea* 1955; *I Accuse!* 1958; *Beyond This Place* 1959; *The Wreck of the Mary Deare* 1959; *The L-Shaped Room* 1962; *Eye of the Devil* 1966; *The Walking Stick* 1970

Williams, Esther (1923–) *Andy Hardy's Double Life* 1942; *Bathing Beauty* 1944; *A Guy Named Joe* 1944; *Ziegfeld Follies* 1944; *Thrill of a Romance* 1945; *Easy to Wed* 1946; *The Hoodlum Saint* 1946; *Fiesta* 1947; *This Time for Keeps* 1947; *On an Island with You* 1948; *Neptune's Daughter* 1949; *Take Me Out to the Ball Game* 1949; *Callaway Went Thataway* 1951; *Texas Carnival* 1951; *Million Dollar Mermaid* 1952; *Skirts Ahoy!* 1952; *Dangerous When Wet* 1953; *Easy to Love* 1953; *Jupiter's Darling* 1955; *Raw Wind in Eden* 1958; *The Big Show* 1961

Williams, Grant (1930–1985) *Red Sundown* 1956; *Showdown at Abilene* 1956; *Written on the Wind* 1956; *The Incredible Shrinking Man* 1957; *The Monolith Monsters* 1957; *The Leech Woman* 1960; *Susan Slade* 1961; *PT 109* 1963

Williams, Guinn "Big Boy" aka **Williams, Guinn** (1899–1962) *Noah's Ark* 1928; *The Bachelor Father* 1931; *The Glass Key* 1935; *The Littlest Rebel* 1935; *Village Tale* 1935; *Girls Can Play* 1937; *Bad Lands* 1939; *Blackmail* 1939; *Castle on the Hudson* 1940; *Santa Fe Trail* 1940; *Virginia City* 1940; *Billy the Kid* 1941; *Hoppity Goes to Town* 1941; *You'll Never Get Rich* 1941; *The Desperadoes* 1943; *Belle of the Yukon* 1944; *Nevada* 1944; *Station West* 1948; *Rocky Mountain* 1950; *Southwest Passage* 1954

Williams, Guy (1924–1989) *Seven Angry Men* 1955; *Captain Sindbad* 1963; *Thin Ice* 1994

Williams, Hal (1938–) *On the Nickel* 1979; *Guess Who* 2005

Williams, Harcourt (1880–1957) *Henry V* 1944; *Brighton Rock* 1947; *No Room at the Inn* 1948; *Eye Witness* 1949; *Third Time Lucky* 1949; *Trottie True* 1949; *The Late Edwina Black* 1951; *Roman Holiday* 1953; *Terror on a Train* 1953; *The Flying Eye* 1955

Williams, Harland (1967–) *Rocketman* 1997; *Half-Baked* 1998; *Superstar* 1999; *Sorority Boys* 2002

Williams, Heathcote (1941–) *The Tempest* 1979; *Orlando* 1992; *The Steal* 1994; *Blue Juice* 1995

Williams, Hugh (1904–1969) *Charley's Aunt* 1930; *Rome Express* 1932; *The Last Journey* 1936; *Bank Holiday* 1938; *Dark Eyes of London* 1939; *Wuthering Heights* 1939; *The Day Will Dawn* 1942; *One of Our Aircraft Is Missing* 1942; *Secret Mission* 1942; *A Girl in a Million* 1946; *An Ideal Husband* 1947; *Take My Life* 1947; *The Blind Goddess* 1948; *Elizabeth of Ladymead* 1948; *The Romantic Age* 1949; *The Gift Horse* 1951; *The Holly and the Ivy* 1952; *The Intruder* 1953

Williams, Jamie (1985–) *The Second Jungle Book* 1997; *Erasable You* 1998

Williams, JoBeth (1953–) *Kramer vs Kramer* 1979; *The Dogs of War* 1980; *Stir Crazy* 1980; *Endangered Species* 1982; *Poltergeist* 1982; *Adam* 1983; *The Big Chill* 1983; *American Dreamer* 1984; *Teachers* 1984; *Desert Bloom* 1985; *Poltergeist II: the Other Side* 1986; *Memories of Me* 1988; *My Name Is Bill W* 1989; *Welcome Home* 1989; *Driving Me Crazy* 1991; *Switch* 1991; *Victim of Love* 1991; *Stop! or My Mom Will Shoot* 1992; *Silhouette* 1994; *Jungle 2 Jungle* 1997; *Little City* 1997; *The Perfect Catch* 2005

Williams, John (1903–1983) *Kind Lady* 1951; *Dial M for Murder* 1954; *Sabrina* 1954; *The Student Prince* 1954; *To Catch a Thief* 1955; *D-Day the Sixth of June* 1956; *The Solid Gold Cadillac* 1956; *Will Success Spoil Rock Hunter?* 1957; *Witness for the Prosecution* 1957; *Midnight Lace* 1960; *Harlow* 1965; *Dear Brigitte* 1966; *The Last of the Secret Agents* 1966; *Double Trouble* 1967; *A Flea in Her Ear* 1968; *Hot Lead and Cold Feet* 1978

Williams, Kate *Poor Cow* 1967; *Love Thy Neighbour* 1973

Williams, Kathlyn (1888–1960) *Our Dancing Daughters* 1928; *Daddy Long Legs* 1931

Williams, Kelli (1970–) *For Their Own Good* 1993; *There Goes My Baby* 1994

Williams, Kenneth (1926–1988) *Valley of Song* 1953; *The Seekers* 1954; *Carry On Sergeant* 1958; *Carry On Nurse* 1959; *Carry On Teacher* 1959; *Tommy the Toreador* 1959; *Carry On Constable* 1960; *Carry On Regardless* 1960; *His and Hers* 1960; *Make Mine Mink* 1960; *Raising the Wind* 1961; *Carry On Cruising* 1962; *Twice round the Daffodils* 1962; *Carry On Jack* 1963; *Carry On Cleo* 1964; *Carry On Spying* 1964; *Carry On Cowboy* 1965; *Carry On – Don't Lose Your Head* 1966; *Carry On Screaming* 1966; *Carry On Follow That Camel* 1967; *Carry On Doctor* 1968; *Carry On Up the Khyber* 1968; *Carry On Again Doctor* 1969; *Carry On Camping* 1969; *Carry On Loving* 1970; *Carry On at Your Convenience* 1971; *Carry On Henry* 1971; *Carry On Abroad* 1972; *Carry On Matron* 1972; *Carry On Dick* 1974; *Carry On Behind* 1975; *The Hound of the Baskervilles* 1977; *That's Carry On* 1977; *Carry On Emmannuelle* 1978

Williams, Kimberly (1971–) *Father of the Bride* 1991; *Coldblooded* 1995; *Father of the Bride Part 2* 1995; *The War at Home* 1996; *Elephant Juice* 1999

Williams, Lia *Dirty Weekend* 1992; *Firelight* 1997; *The King Is Alive* 2000; *Girl from Rio* 2001

Williams, Malinda (1975–) *High School High* 1996; *A Thin Line between Love and Hate* 1996; *The Wood* 1999

Williams, Mark (1959–) *101 Dalmatians* 1996; *The Borrowers* 1997; *High Heels and Low Lifes* 2001; *Anita & Me* 2002; *Harry Potter and the Chamber of Secrets* 2002

Williams, Michael (1935–2001) *Marat/Sade* 1966; *Dead Cert* 1974; *Educating Rita* 1983; *The Blair Witch Project* 1998

Williams, Michelle (1980–) *Halloween H20: 20 Years Later* 1998; *Dick* 1999; *Me without You* 2001; *The United States of Leland* 2002; *The Station Agent* 2003; *Imaginary Heroes* 2004

Williams, Olivia (1968–) *The Postman* 1997; *Rushmore* 1998; *Four Dogs Playing Poker* 1999; *The Sixth Sense* 1999; *The Body* 2000; *Born Romantic* 2000; *Dead Babies* 2000; *Lucky Break* 2001; *Below* 2002; *The Heart of Me* 2002; *Peter Pan* 2003; *To Kill a King* 2003; *Valiant* 2005

Williams, Paul (1940–) *Battle for the Planet of the Apes* 1973; *Phantom of the Paradise* 1974; *Smokey and the Bandit* 1977; *Smokey and the Bandit II* 1980; *Smokey and the Bandit III* 1983; *The November Men* 1993; *A Kind of Hush* 1998

Williams, Rex (1914–) *Tarzan Triumphs* 1943; *Salty O'Rourke* 1945; *The Marrying Kind* 1952

Williams, Rhoda (1937–) *Cinderella* 1950; *Space Master X 7* 1958

Williams, Rhys (1897–1969) *The Corn Is Green* 1945; *The Farmer's Daughter* 1946; *So Goes My Love* 1946; *The Strange Woman* 1946; *Hills of Home* 1948; *Devil's Doorway* 1950; *Lightning Strikes Twice* 1951; *The Sword of Monte Cristo* 1951; *Carbine Williams* 1952; *Meet Me at the Fair* 1952; *Mutiny* 1952; *Man in the Attic* 1953; *The Black Shield of Falworth* 1954; *The Scarlet Coat* 1955; *Nightmare* 1956; *The Restless Breed* 1957

Williams, Richard (1933–) *The Greengage Summer* 1961; *Slaughter's Big Rip-Off* 1973

Williams, Robert B (1904–1978) *Stars on Parade* 1944; *Stagecoach Kid* 1949; *The Great Jewel Robber* 1950; *Revenge of the Creature* 1955; *Viva Las Vegas* 1964

Williams, Robin aka **Fromage, Marty** (1952–) *Popeye* 1980; *The World According to Garp* 1982; *The Survivors* 1983; *Moscow on the Hudson* 1984; *The Best of Times* 1986; *Club Paradise* 1986; *Good Morning, Vietnam* 1987; *The Adventures of Baron Munchausen* 1988; *Dead Poets Society* 1989; *Awakenings* 1990; *Cadillac Man* 1990; *The Fisher King* 1991; *Hook* 1991; *Shakes the Clown* 1991; *Aladdin* 1992; *FernGully: the Last Rainforest* 1992; *Toys* 1992; *Mrs Doubtfire* 1993; *Being Human* 1994; *Jumanji* 1995; *Nine Months* 1995; *Aladdin and the King of Thieves* 1996; *The Birdcage* 1996; *Jack* 1996; *The Secret Agent* 1996; *Deconstructing Harry* 1997; *Fathers' Day* 1997; *Flubber* 1997; *Good Will Hunting* 1997; *Patch Adams* 1998; *What Dreams May Come* 1998; *Bicentennial Man* 1999; *Jakob the Liar* 1999; *AI: Artificial Intelligence* 2001; *One Hour Photo* 2001; *Death to Smoochy* 2002; *Insomnia* 2002; *The Final Cut* 2004; *Robots* 2005

Williams, Samm-Art (1946–) *Blood Simple* 1983; *Hot Resort* 1985

Williams, Saul (1972–) *Downtown 81* 1981; *Slam* 1998; *K-PAX* 2001

Williams, Simon (1946–) *The Incredible Sarah* 1976; *The Odd Job* 1978; *The Prisoner of Zenda* 1979

Williams, Steven (1949–) *Missing in Action 2: the Beginning* 1985; *Jason Goes to Hell: the Final Friday* 1993

Williams, Treat (1952–) *Deadly Hero* 1976; *The Ritz* 1976; *Hair* 1979; *1941* 1979; *Why Would I Lie?* 1980; *Prince of the City* 1981; *The Pursuit of DB Cooper* 1981; *Flashpoint* 1984; *Once upon a Time in America* 1984; *Smooth Talk* 1985; *The Men's Club* 1986; *Dead Heat* 1988; *Heart of Dixie* 1989; *Where the Rivers Flow North* 1993; *Hand Gun* 1994; *Things to Do in Denver When You're Dead* 1995; *Mulholland Falls* 1996; *The Phantom* 1996; *The Devil's Own* 1997; *The Substitute 2: School's Out* 1997; *Deep Rising* 1998; *The Deep End of the Ocean* 1999; *36 Hours to Die* 1999; *Hollywood Ending* 2002; *Miss Congeniality 2: Armed & Fabulous* 2005

Williams, Vanessa (1963–) *Candyman* 1992; *DROP Squad* 1994

Williams, Vanessa L aka **Williams, Vanessa** (1963–) *The Pick-Up Artist* 1987; *Another You* 1991; *Harley Davidson and the Marlboro Man* 1991; *Eraser* 1996; *Hoodlum* 1997; *Soul Food* 1997; *Dance with Me* 1998; *Futuresport* 1998; *The Adventures of Elmo in Grouchland* 1999; *Don Quixote* 2000; *Shaft* 2000; *Johnson Family Vacation* 2004

Williams, Wade Andrew *Candyman: Day of the Dead* 1999; *K-911* 1999; *Ken Park* 2002

Williams, Wendy O (1949–1998) *Reform School Girls* 1986; *Pucker Up and Bark like a Dog* 1989

Williamson, Felix *Me Myself I* 1999; *Strange Planet* 1999; *Dirty Deeds* 2002

Williamson, Fred (1938–) *Hammer* 1972; *Black Caesar* 1973; *Hell Up in Harlem* 1973; *That Man Bolt* 1973; *Three the Hard Way* 1974; *Three Tough Guys* 1974; *Adios Amigo* 1975; *Take a Hard Ride* 1975; *From Dusk till Dawn* 1995; *Original Gangstas* 1996; *Starsky & Hutch* 2004

Williamson, Kate *Dream Lover* 1993; *The Last Time I Committed Suicide* 1996; *Dahmer* 2002

Williamson, Mykelti aka **Williamson, Mykel T** (1960–) *You Talkin' to Me?* 1987; *Miracle Mile* 1989; *The First Power* 1990; *Forrest Gump* 1994; *Heat* 1995; *Waiting to Exhale* 1995; *Soul of the Game* 1996; *Buffalo Soldiers* 1997; *Double Tap* 1997; *Truth or Consequences, NM* 1997; *12 Angry Men* 1997; *Species II* 1998; *Three Kings* 1999; *Ali* 2001; *After the Sunset* 2004; *The Assassination of Richard Nixon* 2004

Williamson, Nicol (1938–) *The Bofors Gun* 1968; *Inadmissible Evidence* 1968; *Hamlet* 1969; *Laughter in the Dark* 1969; *The Reckoning* 1969; *The Jerusalem File* 1972; *The Monk* 1972; *The Wilby Conspiracy* 1975; *Robin and Marian* 1976; *The Seven-Per-Cent Solution* 1976; *The Cheap Detective* 1978; *The Human Factor* 1979; *Excalibur* 1981; *Venom* 1981; *I'm Dancing as Fast as I Can* 1982; *Return to Oz* 1985; *Black Widow* 1987; *The Exorcist III* 1990; *The Hour of the Pig* 1993; *The Wind in the Willows* 1996; *Spawn* 1997

Willingham, Noble (1930–2004) *Big Bad Mama* 1974; *Aloha, Bobby and Rose* 1975; *Sheila Levine Is Dead and Living in New York* 1975; *The Boys in Company C* 1978; *Unconquered* 1989; *Blind Fury* 1990; *City Slickers* 1991; *The Last Boy Scout* 1991; *The Distinguished Gentleman* 1992; *Of Mice and Men* 1992; *Ace Ventura: Pet Detective* 1993

Willis, Bruce (1955–) *Blind Date* 1987; *Die Hard* 1988; *Sunset* 1988; *In Country* 1989; *Look Who's Talking* 1989; *The Bonfire of the Vanities* 1990; *Die Hard 2: Die Harder* 1990; *Look Who's Talking Too* 1990; *Billy Bathgate* 1991; *Hudson Hawk* 1991; *The Last Boy Scout* 1991; *Mortal Thoughts* 1991; *Death Becomes Her* 1992; *Striking Distance* 1993; *Color of Night* 1994; *Nobody's Fool* 1994; *North* 1994; *Pulp Fiction* 1994; *Die Hard with a Vengeance* 1995; *Four Rooms* 1995; *Twelve Monkeys* 1995; *Beavis and Butt-head Do America* 1996; *Last Man Standing* 1996; *The Fifth Element* 1997; *The Jackal* 1997; *Armageddon* 1998; *Mercury Rising* 1998; *The Siege* 1998; *Breakfast of Champions* 1999; *The Sixth Sense* 1999; *The Story of Us* 1999; *Disney's The Kid* 2000; *Unbreakable* 2000; *The Whole Nine Yards* 2000; *Bandits* 2001; *Hart's War* 2002; *Rugrats Go Wild* 2003; *Tears of the Sun* 2003; *Hostage* 2004; *The Whole Ten Yards* 2004; *Sin City* 2005

Willis, Jerome *The Siege of the Saxons* 1963; *Winstanley* 1975

Willman, Noel (1917–1988) *The Net* 1953; *Across the Bridge* 1957; *Seven Waves Away* 1957; *Two Living, One Dead* 1961; *The Girl on the Boat* 1962; *The Reptile* 1966

Willmer, Catherine *Women in Love* 1969; *The Boy Friend* 1971

Willock, Dave (1909–1990) *Let's Face It* 1943; *Revenge of the Creature* 1955; *The Buster Keaton Story* 1957; *Ten Seconds to Hell* 1959

Wills, Chill (1903–1978) *Arizona Legion* 1939; *Boom Town* 1940; *The Westerner* 1940; *Belle Starr* 1941; *Honky Tonk* 1941; *Western Union* 1941; *Apache Trail* 1942; *Her Cardboard Lover* 1942; *Tarzan's New York Adventure* 1942; *Barbary Coast Gent* 1944; *See Here, Private Hargrove* 1944; *Sunday Dinner for a Soldier* 1944; *The Harvey Girls* 1946; *The Yearling* 1946; *Northwest Stampede* 1948; *The Sainted Sisters* 1948; *The Saxon Charm* 1948; *Francis* 1949; *Red Canyon* 1949; *Tulsa* 1949; *High Lonesome* 1950; *Rio Grande* 1950; *The Sundowners* 1950; *Cattle Drive* 1951; *Francis Goes to the Races* 1951; *Bronco Buster* 1952; *Francis Goes to West Point* 1952; *Ride the Man Down* 1952; *City That Never Sleeps* 1953; *Francis Covers the Big Town* 1953; *The Man from the Alamo* 1953; *Tumbleweed* 1953; *Francis Joins the WACS* 1954; *Francis Joins the WACS* 1954; *Francis in the Navy* 1955; *Timberjack* 1955; *Giant* 1956; *Santiago* 1956; *Gun for a Coward* 1957; *Gun Glory* 1957; *From Hell to Texas* 1958; *The Sad Horse* 1959; *The Alamo* 1960; *Where the Boys Are* 1960; *The Deadly Companions* 1961; *Gold of the Seven Saints* 1961; *Young Guns of Texas* 1962; *McLintock!* 1963; *The Wheeler Dealers* 1963; *The Rounders* 1965; *Fireball 500* 1966; *The Liberation of LB Jones* 1970; *Pat Garrett and Billy the Kid* 1973; *Mr Billion* 1977

Wilmer, Douglas (1920–) *The Battle of the River Plate* 1956; *El Cid* 1961; *The Brides of Fu Manchu* 1966; *The Vengeance of Fu Manchu* 1967; *The Vampire Lovers* 1970; *Unman, Wittering and Zigo* 1971; *The Golden Voyage of Sinbad* 1973; *The Adventure of Sherlock Holmes' Smarter Brother* 1975; *The Incredible Sarah* 1976

Wilmot, David *I Went Down* 1997; *Rat* 2000; *interMission* 2003

Wilmot, Ronan *Lamb* 1985; *Rawhead Rex* 1986

Wilms, André *A Strange Place to Meet* 1988; *Monsieur Hire* 1989; *Europa, Europa* 1991; *L'Enfer* 1994; *Juha* 1999

Wilson, Andrew (1964–) *Bottle Rocket* 1996; *Freeze Frame* 2003; *The Big Bounce* 2004

Wilson, Bridgette aka **Wilson, Bridgette L** aka **Wilson-Sampras, Bridgette** (1973–) *Billy Madison* 1995; *Mortal Kombat* 1995; *I Know What You Did Last Summer* 1997; *House on Haunted Hill* 1999; *Love Stinks* 1999; *Beautiful* 2000; *Buying the Cow* 2000; *The Wedding Planner* 2001; *Extreme Ops* 2003

Wilson, Clarence aka **Wilson, Clarence H** (1876–1941) *The Penguin Pool Murder* 1932; *Son of Kong* 1933; *Tillie and Gus* 1933; *Bachelor Bait* 1934; *The Lemon Drop Kid* 1934

Wilson, Dale *Mother Lode* 1982; *Dead Wrong* 1983

Wilson, Dana (1949–) *A Cry from the Streets* 1957; *The Shiralee* 1957

Wilson, David *Hometown USA* 1979; *Eddie and the Cruisers* 1983; *The Inside Man* 1984

Wilson, Don (1900–1982) *The Roundup* 1941; *Niagara* 1953

Wilson, Don "The Dragon" (1955–) *Bloodfist* 1989; *Ring of Fire* 1991; *Red Sun Rising* 1994

Wilson, Dooley (1894–1953) *Casablanca* 1942; *Stormy Weather* 1943; *Come to the Stable* 1949

Wilson, Dorothy (1909–1998) *The Age of Consent* 1932; *Lucky Devils* 1933; *The White Parade* 1934; *In Old Kentucky* 1935; *Craig's Wife* 1936; *The Milky Way* 1936

Wilson, Elizabeth (1921–) *Patterns* 1956; *The Tunnel of Love* 1958; *The Graduate* 1967; *Jenny* 1969; *Little Murders* 1971; *The Prisoner of Second Avenue* 1974; *The Happy Hooker* 1975; *Nine to Five* 1980; *Grace Quigley* 1984; *Where Are the Children?* 1986; *The Believers* 1987; *A Conspiracy of Love* 1987; *The Addams Family* 1991; *Regarding Henry* 1991; *It's All True* 1993

Wilson, Flip (1933–1998) *Uptown Saturday Night* 1974; *Skatetown, USA* 1979

Wilson, Frank (1885–1956) *The Emperor Jones* 1933; *The Green Pastures* 1936; *The Club* 1980

Wilson, Georges (1921–) *The Long Absence* 1961; *The Seven Deadly Sins* 1961; *The Empty Canvas* 1963; *More than a Miracle* 1967; *The Stranger* 1967; *Beatrice Cenci* 1969; *Blanche* 1971

Wilson, Josephine *We Dive at Dawn* 1943; *Chance of a Lifetime* 1950

Wilson, Julie *The Strange One* 1957; *This Could Be the Night* 1957

Wilson, Kristen (1969–) *Bulletproof* 1996; *Doctor Dolittle* 1998; *Dungeons & Dragons* 2000; *Dr Dolittle 2* 2001; *Confessions of a Dangerous Mind* 2002; *Walking Tall* 2004

Wilson, Lambert (1958–) *Five Days One Summer* 1982; *Sahara* 1983; *The Blood of Others* 1984; *La Femme Publique* 1984; *Rendez-vous* 1985; *Rouge Baiser* 1985; *The Belly of an Architect* 1987; *El Dorado* 1988; *Shuttlecock* 1991; *The Leading Man* 1996; *Marquise* 1997; *On Connaît la Chanson* 1997; *The Last September* 1999; *Don Quixote* 2000; *Pas sur la Bouche* 2003; *Catwoman* 2004; *Sahara* 2004

Wilson, Lisle (1943–) *Sisters* 1973; *The Incredible Melting Man* 1977

Wilson, Lois (1894–1988) *The Covered Wagon* 1923; *Ruggles of Red Gap* 1923; *Deluge* 1933; *Female* 1933; *Laughing at Life* 1933; *Bright Eyes* 1934

Wilson, Luke (1971–) *Bottle Rocket* 1996; *Best Men* 1997; *Telling Lies in America* 1997; *Dog Park* 1998; *Home Fries* 1998; *Blue Streak* 1999; *My Dog Skip* 1999; *Committed* 2000; *Legally Blonde* 2001; *The Royal Tenenbaums* 2001; *Soul Survivors* 2001; *Alex & Emma* 2003; *Legally Blonde 2: Red, White & Blonde* 2003; *Masked and Anonymous* 2003; *Old School* 2003; *Around the World in 80 Days* 2004

Wilson, Mara (1987–) *Mrs Doubtfire* 1993; *Miracle on 34th Street* 1994; *Matilda* 1996; *A Simple Wish* 1997; *Thomas and the Magic Railroad* 2000

Wilson, Marie (1916–1972) *China Clipper* 1936; *Satan Met a Lady* 1936; *The Great Garrick* 1937; *Boy Meets Girl* 1938; *Fools for Scandal* 1938; *The Invisible Menace* 1938; *My Friend Irma* 1949; *My Friend Irma Goes West* 1950; *A Girl in Every Port* 1952; *Never Wave at a WAC* 1952; *Marry Me Again* 1953; *Mr Hobbs Takes a Vacation* 1962; *And the Beat Goes On: the Sonny and Cher Story* 1999

Wilson, Neil (1916–) *Dr Jekyll and Sister Hyde* 1971; *Dulcima* 1971

Wilson, Owen aka **Wilson, Owen C** (1968–) *Bottle Rocket* 1996; *Anaconda* 1997; *Permanent Midnight* 1998; *Rushmore* 1998; *The Haunting* 1999; *The Minus Man* 1999; *Meet the Parents* 2000; *Shanghai Noon* 2000; *Behind Enemy Lines* 2001; *The Royal Tenenbaums* 2001; *Zoolander* 2001; *I Spy* 2002; *Shanghai Knights* 2002; *Around the World in 80 Days* 2004; *The Big Bounce* 2004; *The Life Aquatic with Steve Zissou* 2004; *Meet the Fockers* 2004; *Starsky & Hutch* 2004; *Wedding Crashers* 2005

Wilson, Patrick (1973–) *The Alamo* 2004; *The Phantom of the Opera* 2004

Wilson, Perry *Fear Strikes Out* 1957; *The Matchmaker* 1958

Wilson, Peta (1970–) *Mercy* 2000; *The League of Extraordinary Gentlemen* 2003

Wilson, Rainn (1968–) *House of 1000 Corpses* 2001; *Sahara* 2004

Wilson, Reno *Diary of a Serial Killer* 1997; *She Creature* 2001

Wilson, Richard (1915–1991) *A Passage to India* 1984; *Fellow Traveller* 1989; *How to Get Ahead in Advertising* 1989; *Carry On Columbus* 1992; *Soft Top, Hard Shoulder* 1992; *It's All True* 1993; *The Man Who Knew Too Little* 1997; *Women Talking Dirty* 1999

Wilson, Rita (1958–) *Volunteers* 1985; *Sleepless in Seattle* 1993; *Mixed Nuts* 1994; *Now and Then* 1995; *Jingle All the Way* 1996; *Runaway Bride* 1999; *The Story of Us* 1999; *Auto Focus* 2002; *Raise Your Voice* 2004

Wilson, Roger (1958–) *Porky's* 1981; *Porky's II: The Next Day* 1983

Wilson, Scott (1942–) *In Cold Blood* 1967; *The Gypsy Moths* 1969; *The Grissom Gang* 1971; *The New Centurions* 1972; *The Lolly-Madonna War* 1973; *The Great Gatsby* 1974; *The Passover Plot* 1976; *The Ninth Configuration* 1979; *A Year of the Quiet Sun* 1984; *The Aviator* 1985; *Blue City* 1986; *Malone* 1987; *Johnny Handsome* 1989; *Femme Fatale* 1991; *Pure Luck* 1991; *Flesh and Bone* 1993; *Shiloh* 1996; *GI Jane* 1997; *Clay Pigeons* 1998; *The Way of the Gun* 2000; *Monster* 2003

Wilson, Sheree J (1958–) *Crimewave* 1985; *Fraternity Vacation* 1985

Wilson (1), Stuart (1946–) *Dulcima* 1971; *Lethal Weapon 3* 1992; *Teenage Mutant Ninja Turtles III* 1992; *Death and the Maiden* 1994; *Exit to Eden* 1994; *No Escape* 1994; *Crossworlds* 1996; *The Mask of Zorro* 1998; *The Luzhin Defence* 2000

Wilson, Teddy aka **Wilson, Theodore** (1943–1991) *Run for the Roses* 1978; *Carny* 1980; *Genuine Risk* 1990; *Life Stinks* 1991

Wilson, Thomas F aka **Wilson, Tom** (1959–) *Back to the Future* 1985; *Let's Get Harry* 1986; *Action Jackson* 1988; *Back to the Future Part II* 1989; *Back to the Future Part III* 1990

Wilson, Tom (1880–1965) *A Day's Pleasure* 1919; *Sunnyside* 1919; *The Kid* 1921; *Battling Butler* 1926

Wilson, Trey (1948–1989) *Raising Arizona* 1987; *Bull Durham* 1988; *Twins* 1988; *Great Balls of Fire!* 1989; *Welcome Home* 1989

Wilson-Jones, Anna *Mrs Caldicot's Cabbage War* 2000; *The Mother* 2003

Wilton, Penelope (1946–) *Laughterhouse* 1984; *Clockwise* 1986; *Cry Freedom* 1987; *Blame It on the Bellboy* 1992; *The Secret Rapture* 1993; *Carrington* 1995; *Tom's Midnight Garden* 1998; *Iris* 2001; *Calendar Girls* 2003; *Shaun of the Dead* 2004

Wilton, Robb (1882–1957) *A Fire Has Been Arranged* 1935; *It's Love Again* 1936; *The Love Match* 1955

Wimmer, Brian (1959–) *Late for Dinner* 1991; *Dead Badge* 1995; *The Maddening* 1995; *The Evil beneath Loch Ness* 2001

Winchell, Paul (1922–) *The Aristocats* 1970; *Which Way to the Front?* 1970; *Winnie the Pooh's Most Grand Adventure* 1997

Wincott, Jeff (1957–) *Mission of Justice* 1992; *The Donor* 1994; *Universal Soldier 2: Brothers in Arms* 1998; *Universal Soldier 3: Unfinished Business* 1998

Wincott, Michael (1959–) *Circle of Two* 1980; *Talk Radio* 1988; *Suffering Bastards* 1989; *Robin Hood: Prince of Thieves* 1991; *1492: Conquest of Paradise* 1992; *Romeo Is Bleeding* 1992; *The Three Musketeers* 1993; *The Crow* 1994; *Strange Days* 1995; *Basquiat* 1996; *Alien: Resurrection* 1997; *Metro* 1997; *Before Night Falls* 2000; *Along Came a Spider* 2001; *The Count of Monte Cristo* 2001; *Treasure Planet* 2002; *The Assassination of Richard Nixon* 2004

Windom, William (1923–) *The Americanization of Emily* 1964; *One Man's Way* 1964; *The Detective* 1968; *Prescription: Murder* 1968; *The Gypsy Moths* 1969; *Brewster McCloud* 1970; *Dynamite Man from Glory Jail* 1971; *Escape from the Planet of the Apes* 1971; *The Mephisto Waltz* 1971; *The Man* 1972; *Now You See Him, Now You Don't* 1972; *Echoes of a Summer* 1976; *Leave 'em Laughing* 1981; *Separate Ways* 1981; *Last Plane Out* 1983; *Grandview, USA* 1984; *She's Having a Baby* 1988; *Attack of the 50 Ft Woman* 1993; *Sommersby* 1993

Windsor, Barbara (1937–) *Too Hot to Handle* 1960; *Sparrows Can't Sing* 1962; *Crooks in Cloisters* 1963; *Carry On Spying* 1964; *A Study in Terror* 1965; *Carry On Doctor* 1968; *Carry On Again Doctor* 1969; *Carry On Camping* 1969; *The Boy Friend* 1971; *Carry On Henry* 1971; *Carry On Abroad* 1972; *Carry On Matron* 1972; *Not Now Darling* 1972; *Carry On Girls* 1973; *Carry On Dick* 1974; *That's Carry On* 1977

Windsor, Frank (1927–) *Sunday, Bloody Sunday* 1971; *Assassin* 1973; *Between Two Women* 2000

Windsor, Marie (1922–2000) *Force of Evil* 1948; *The Fighting Kentuckian* 1949; *Outpost in Morocco* 1949; *Frenchie* 1950; *Japanese War Bride* 1952; *The Narrow Margin* 1952; *The Sniper* 1952; *Cat-women of the Moon* 1953; *City That Never Sleeps* 1953; *Trouble along the Way* 1953; *The Bounty Hunter* 1954; *Hell's Half Acre* 1954; *Abbott and Costello Meet the Mummy* 1955; *The Killing* 1956; *The Girl in Black Stockings* 1957; *The Parson and the Outlaw* 1957; *The Unholy Wife* 1957; *Day of the Bad Man* 1958; *Mail Order Bride* 1963; *Bedtime Story* 1964; *Support Your Local Gunfighter* 1971; *Cahill, United States Marshal* 1973; *The Outfit* 1973

Windsor, Romy aka **Walthall, Romy** *The House of Usher* 1988; *Howling IV* 1988; *My Brother the Pig* 1999

Winfield, Paul (1941–2004) *RPM – Revolutions per Minute* 1970; *Sounder* 1972; *Trouble Man* 1972; *Gordon's War* 1973; *Conrack* 1974; *Huckleberry Finn* 1974; *Hustle* 1975; *Damnation Alley* 1977; *High Velocity* 1977; *Twilight's Last Gleaming* 1977; *A Hero Ain't Nothin' but a Sandwich* 1978; *Carbon Copy* 1981; *White Dog* 1981; *Star Trek II: the Wrath of Khan* 1982; *On the Run* 1983; *Go Tell It on the Mountain* 1984; *Mike's Murder* 1984; *The Terminator* 1984; *Blue City* 1986; *Death before Dishonor* 1987; *The Serpent and the Rainbow* 1987; *Presumed Innocent* 1990; *Cliffhanger* 1993; *Dennis* 1993; *Desperate Measures* 1995; *Original Gangstas* 1996; *Dead of Night* 1997; *Relax… It's Just Sex* 1998

Winfrey, Oprah (1954–) *The Color Purple* 1985; *Native Son* 1986; *Throw Momma from the Train* 1987; *Before Women Had Wings* 1997; *Beloved* 1998

Wing, Anna (1914–) *A Doll's House* 1973; *Full Circle* 1977

Winger, Debra (1955–) *Slumber Party '57* 1976; *Thank God It's Friday* 1978; *French Postcards* 1979; *Urban Cowboy* 1980; *Cannery Row* 1982; *An Officer and a Gentleman* 1982; *Terms of Endearment* 1983; *Mike's Murder* 1984; *Legal Eagles* 1986; *Black Widow* 1987; *Betrayed* 1988; *Everybody Wins* 1990; *The Sheltering Sky* 1990; *Leap of Faith* 1992; *A Dangerous Woman* 1993; *Shadowlands* 1993; *Wilder Napalm* 1993; *Forget Paris* 1995; *Radio* 2003

Wingett, Mark (1961–) *Quadrophenia* 1979; *Breaking Glass* 1980

Winkler, Angela (1944–) *The Lost Honour of Katharina Blum* 1975; *Germany in Autumn* 1978; *Knife in the Head* 1978; *The Tin Drum* 1979; *Danton* 1982; *Benny's Video* 1992

Winkler, Henry (1945–) *The Lords of Flatbush* 1974; *Heroes* 1977; *The One and Only* 1978; *Night Shift* 1982; *Scream* 1996; *The Waterboy* 1998; *Down to You* 2000; *Holes* 2003

Winkler, Mel *Convicts* 1991; *Doc Hollywood* 1991; *Untamed Love* 1994; *Devil in a Blue Dress* 1995; *A Life Less Ordinary* 1997

Winn, Kitty (1944–) *The Panic in Needle Park* 1971; *The Exorcist* 1973; *Peeper* 1975; *Exorcist II: The Heretic* 1977

Winninger, Charles (1884–1969) *Bad Sister* 1931; *God's Gift to Women* 1931; *Gun Smoke* 1931; *Night Nurse* 1931; *Show Boat* 1936; *White Fang* 1936; *Café Metropole* 1937; *Every Day's a Holiday* 1937; *Nothing Sacred* 1937; *Three Smart Girls* 1937; *Woman Chases Man* 1937; *You Can't Have Everything* 1937; *You're a Sweetheart* 1937; *Hard to Get* 1938; *Babes in Arms* 1939; *Destry Rides Again* 1939; *Three Smart Girls Grow Up* 1939; *Little Nellie Kelly* 1940; *My Life with Caroline* 1941; *Pot o' Gold* 1941; *Ziegfeld Girl* 1941; *Friendly Enemies* 1942; *Coney Island* 1943; *Hers to Hold* 1943; *Belle of the Yukon* 1944; *Broadway Rhythm* 1944; *Sunday Dinner for a Soldier* 1944; *State Fair* 1945; *Lover Come Back* 1946; *Living in a Big Way* 1947; *Something in the Wind* 1947; *Give My Regards to Broadway* 1948; *The Sun Shines Bright* 1953; *Las Vegas Shakedown* 1955

Winningham, Mare (1959–) *One-Trick Pony* 1980; *Threshold* 1981; *St Elmo's Fire* 1985; *Nobody's Fool* 1986; *Made in Heaven* 1987; *Shy People* 1987; *Miracle Mile* 1989; *Turner & Hooch* 1989; *Hard Promises* 1991; *The War* 1994; *Georgia* 1995; *Under Pressure* 1997; *Everything That Rises* 1998

Winslet, Kate (1975–) *Heavenly Creatures* 1994; *Sense and Sensibility* 1995; *Hamlet* 1996; *Jude* 1996; *Titanic* 1997; *Hideous Kinky* 1998; *Holy Smoke* 1999; *Quills* 2000; *Christmas Carol: the Movie* 2001; *Enigma* 2001; *Iris* 2001; *Eternal Sunshine of the Spotless Mind* 2003; *The Life of David Gale* 2003; *Finding Neverland* 2004

Winslow, George aka **Winslow, George "Foghorn"** (1946–) *My Pal Gus* 1952; *Room for One More* 1952; *Gentlemen Prefer Blondes* 1953; *The Rocket Man* 1954; *Artists and Models* 1955; *Wild Heritage* 1958

Winslow, Michael (1960–) *Cheech and Chong's Next Movie* 1980; *Alphabet City* 1984; *Police Academy 2: Their First Assignment* 1985; *Police Academy 3: Back in Training* 1986; *Police Academy 4: Citizens on Patrol* 1987; *Spaceballs* 1987; *Buy & Cell* 1988; *Police Academy 5: Assignment Miami Beach* 1988; *Police Academy 6: City under Siege* 1989; *Police Academy: Mission to Moscow* 1994

Winston, Hattie (1945–) *Clara's Heart* 1988; *Jackie Brown* 1997

Winston, Helene (?–2004) *What's the Matter with Helen?* 1971; *A Boy and His Dog* 1975

Winstone, Ray aka **Winstone, Raymond** (1957–) *Quadrophenia* 1979; *Scum* 1979; *Ladies and Gentlemen, the Fabulous Stains* 1981; *Ladybird Ladybird* 1994; *Face* 1997; *Martha – Meet Frank, Daniel and Laurence* 1997; *Nil by Mouth* 1997; *Darkness Falls* 1998; *Final Cut* 1998; *Agnes Browne* 1999; *Fanny & Elvis* 1999; *The War Zone* 1999; *Love, Honour and Obey* 2000; *Sexy Beast* 2000; *There's Only One Jimmy Grimble* 2000; *Last Orders* 2001; *The Martins* 2001; *Ripley's Game* 2002; *Cold Mountain* 2003; *King Arthur* 2004; *The Magic Roundabout* 2005

Wint, Maurice Dean *Rude* 1995; *Cube* 1997; *Hedwig and the Angry Inch* 2001

Winter, Alex (1965–) *Death Wish 3* 1985; *Bill & Ted's Excellent Adventure* 1988; *Haunted Summer* 1988; *Bill & Ted's Bogus Journey* 1991; *Freaked* 1993

Winter, Claude *Sunday in the Country* 1984; *Les Nuits Fauves* 1992

Winter, Edward aka **Winter, Ed** (1938–2001) *A Change of Seasons* 1980; *The Buddy System* 1984

Winter, Vincent (1947–1998) *The Kidnappers* 1953; *Time Lock* 1957; *Beyond This Place* 1959; *Gorgo* 1961

Winters, Bernie (1932–1991) *Let's Get Married* 1960; *Simon, Simon* 1970

Winters, Deborah (1955–) *The People Next Door* 1970; *Kotch* 1971; *Class of '44* 1973; *Blue Sunshine* 1976; *The Lamp* 1987

Winters, Jonathan (1925–) *It's a Mad Mad Mad Mad World* 1963; *The Loved One* 1965; *Penelope* 1966; *The Russians Are Coming, the Russians Are Coming* 1966; *Eight on the Lam* 1967; *Oh Dad, Poor Dad, Mama's Hung You in the Closet and I'm Feelin' So Sad* 1967; *Viva Max!* 1969; *The Fish That Saved Pittsburgh* 1979; *The Longshot* 1986; *Moon over Parador* 1988; *The Shadow* 1994; *Arabian Knight* 1995

Winters, Roland (1904–1989) *Cry of the City* 1948; *Kidnapped* 1948; *A Dangerous Profession* 1949; *Tuna Clipper* 1949; *To Please a Lady* 1950; *The West Point Story* 1950; *Follow the Sun: the Ben Hogan Story* 1951; *She's Working Her Way through College* 1952; *Bigger than Life* 1956; *Jet Pilot* 1957; *Blue Hawaii* 1961

Winters, Shelley aka **Winter, Shelley** (1922–) *What a Woman!* 1943; *Knickerbocker Holiday* 1944; *A Thousand and One Nights* 1945; *Tonight and Every Night* 1945; *A Double Life* 1947; *Cry of the City* 1948; *Red River*

1948; *The Great Gatsby* 1949; *Johnny Stool Pigeon* 1949; *Frenchie* 1950; *Winchester '73* 1950; *He Ran All the Way* 1951; *A Place in the Sun* 1951; *Meet Danny Wilson* 1952; *Phone Call from a Stranger* 1952; *Untamed Frontier* 1952; *Executive Suite* 1954; *Mambo* 1954; *Playgirl* 1954; *Saskatchewan* 1954; *Tennessee Champ* 1954; *To Dorothy, a Son* 1954; *The Big Knife* 1955; *I Am a Camera* 1955; *I Died a Thousand Times* 1955; *The Night of the Hunter* 1955; *The Treasure of Pancho Villa* 1955; *The Diary of Anne Frank* 1959; *Odds against Tomorrow* 1959; *Let No Man Write My Epitaph* 1960; *Lolita* 1961; *The Young Savages* 1961; *The Chapman Report* 1962; *The Balcony* 1963; *Wives and Lovers* 1963; *Time of Indifference* 1964; *The Greatest Story Ever Told* 1965; *A Patch of Blue* 1965; *Alfie* 1966; *Harper* 1966; *The Three Sisters* 1966; *Enter Laughing* 1967; *Buona Sera, Mrs Campbell* 1968; *The Scalphunters* 1968; *Wild in the Streets* 1968; *The Mad Room* 1969; *Bloody Mama* 1970; *Flap* 1970; *How Do I Love Thee?* 1970; *Something to Hide* 1971; *What's the Matter with Helen?* 1971; *Who Slew Auntie Roo?* 1971; *The Poseidon Adventure* 1972; *Blume in Love* 1973; *Cleopatra Jones* 1973; *Diamonds* 1975; *That Lucky Touch* 1975; *Next Stop, Greenwich Village* 1976; *The Tenant* 1976; *Pete's Dragon* 1977; *Tentacles* 1977; *King of the Gypsies* 1978; *City on Fire* 1979; *Elvis – the Movie* 1979; *The Magician of Lublin* 1979; *The Visitor* 1980; *SOB* 1981; *Fanny Hill* 1983; *Over the Brooklyn Bridge* 1983; *Déjà Vu* 1984; *Ellie* 1984; *The Delta Force* 1986; *The Purple People Eater* 1988; *An Unremarkable Life* 1989; *Stepping Out* 1991; *The Pickle* 1993; *The Silence of the Hams* 1993; *Heavy* 1995; *The Portrait of a Lady* 1996; *Gideon* 1999

Winton, Jane (1905–1959) *Don Juan* 1926; *The Patsy* 1928; *Limelight* 1936

Winwood, Estelle (1883–1984) *The Glass Slipper* 1955; *The Swan* 1956; *23 Paces to Baker Street* 1956; *Alive and Kicking* 1958; *Darby O'Gill and the Little People* 1959; *The Misfits* 1961; *The Magic Sword* 1962; *The Notorious Landlady* 1962; *Dead Ringer* 1964; *Camelot* 1967; *Games* 1967; *The Producers* 1968; *Jenny* 1969

Wirth, Billy (1962–) *War Party* 1988; *Body Snatchers* 1993; *Final Mission* 1993; *Boys on the Side* 1995; *Judicial Consent* 1995; *Space Marines* 1996

Wisden, Robert *The War between Us* 1995; *Taken Away* 1996; *Excess Baggage* 1997

Wisdom, Norman (1920–) *A Date with a Dream* 1948; *Trouble in Store* 1953; *One Good Turn* 1954; *Man of the Moment* 1955; *Up in the World* 1956; *Just My Luck* 1957; *The Square Peg* 1958; *Follow a Star* 1959; *The Bulldog Breed* 1960; *There Was a Crooked Man* 1960; *The Girl on the Boat* 1962; *On the Beat* 1962; *A Stitch in Time* 1963; *The Early Bird* 1965; *Press for Time* 1966; *The Sandwich Man* 1966; *The Night They Raided Minsky's* 1968; *What's Good for the Goose* 1969; *Double X: the Name of the Game* 1991; *Five Children and It* 2004

Wisdom, Robert *Mighty Joe Young* 1998; *Live from Baghdad* 2002; *Our House* 2003; *Barbershop 2: Back in Business* 2004; *The Forgotten* 2004

Wise, Ernie (1925–1999) *The Intelligence Men* 1965; *That Riviera Touch* 1966; *The Magnificent Two* 1967; *Simon, Simon* 1970

Wise, Greg (1966–) *Feast of July* 1995; *Sense and Sensibility* 1995; *Judas Kiss* 1998; *Mad Cows* 1999; *Johnny English* 2003

Wise, Ray (1947–) *Swamp Thing* 1982; *The Journey of Natty Gann* 1985; *Seduced* 1985; *RoboCop* 1987; *Race for Glory* 1989; *Season of Fear* 1989; *Bob Roberts* 1992; *Twin Peaks: Fire Walk with Me* 1992; *Killing Box* 1993; *Rising Sun* 1993; *Body Shot* 1994; *Two Can Play That Game* 2001; *Dead End* 2003; *Jeepers Creepers 2* 2003

Wise, William *TR Baskin* 1971; *In the Bedroom* 2001; *13 Conversations about One Thing* 2001

Wiseman, Joseph (1918–) *Detective Story* 1951; *Viva Zapata!* 1952; *The Silver Chalice* 1954; *Dr No* 1962; *The Happy Thieves* 1962; *Bye Bye Braverman* 1968; *The Counterfeit Killer* 1968; *The Night They Raided Minsky's* 1968; *Lawman* 1971; *The Valachi Papers* 1972; *The Apprenticeship of Duddy Kravitz* 1974; *The Betsy* 1978; *Buck Rogers in the 25th Century* 1979; *Jaguar Lives!* 1979

Wisniewski, Andreas (1959–) *Gothic* 1986; *Aria* 1987; *The Living Daylights* 1987

Withers, Googie (1917–) *The Love Test* 1935; *Accused* 1936; *Convict 99* 1938; *The Lady Vanishes* 1938; *Strange Boarders* 1938; *The Gang's All Here* 1939; *Trouble Brewing* 1939; *Busman's Honeymoon* 1940; *Jeannie* 1941; *Back Room Boy* 1942; *One of Our Aircraft Is Missing* 1942; *The Silver Fleet* 1943; *Dead of Night* 1945; *Pink String and Sealing Wax* 1945; *It Always Rains on Sunday* 1947; *The Loves of Joanna Godden* 1947; *Miranda* 1947; *Once upon a Dream* 1948; *Traveller's Joy* 1949; *Night and the City* 1950; *White Corridors* 1951; *Derby Day* 1952; *Devil on Horseback* 1954; *Port of Escape* 1956; *Country Life* 1994; *Shine* 1996

Withers, Grant (1904–1959) *College* 1927; *Other Men's Women* 1931; *Tennessee Johnson* 1942; *A Lady Takes a Chance* 1943; *War of the Wildcats* 1943; *The Yellow Rose of Texas* 1944; *Tycoon* 1947; *Angel in Exile* 1948; *The Plunderers* 1948; *Hoodlum Empire* 1952; *Fair Wind to Java* 1953; *Run for Cover* 1955; *The Mobster* 1958

Withers, Jane (1926–) *Bright Eyes* 1934; *The Farmer Takes a Wife* 1935; *Checkers* 1937; *Pack Up Your Troubles* 1939; *The North Star* 1943; *Giant* 1956; *Captain Newman, MD* 1963

Withers, Margaret *Car of Dreams* 1935; *Daybreak* 1946; *Home at Seven* 1952; *The Flying Scot* 1957; *Ferry to Hong Kong* 1958

Witherspoon, Cora (1890–1957) *Libeled Lady* 1936; *Piccadilly Jim* 1936; *On the Avenue* 1937; *Personal Property* 1937; *Quality Street* 1937; *Just around the Corner* 1938; *Port of Seven Seas* 1938; *Three Loves Has Nancy* 1938; *Dark Victory* 1939; *The Bank Dick* 1940; *I Was an Adventuress* 1940; *Just for You* 1952

Witherspoon, John *Talkin' Dirty after Dark* 1991; *Friday* 1995; *Vampire in Brooklyn* 1995; *Ride* 1998; *Next Friday* 1999

Witherspoon, Reese (1976–) *The Man in the Moon* 1991; *Wildflower* 1991; *A Far Off Place* 1993; *SFW* 1994; *Fear* 1996; *Freeway* 1996; *Overnight Delivery* 1997; *Pleasantville* 1998; *Twilight* 1998; *Best Laid Plans* 1999; *Cruel Intentions* 1999; *Election* 1999; *American Psycho* 2000; *Legally Blonde* 2001; *The Importance of Being Earnest* 2002; *Sweet Home Alabama* 2002; *Legally Blonde 2: Red, White & Blonde* 2003; *Vanity Fair* 2004

Withrow, Glenn *The Lady in Red* 1979; *The Outsiders* 1983; *Dudes* 1987; *Pass the Ammo* 1988

Witney, Michael *aka* **Witney, Mike** (1983–) *The Way West* 1967; *Darling Lili* 1970; *Doc* 1971; *W* 1974; *There Goes the Bride* 1979

Witt, Alicia (1975–) *Bodies, Rest and Motion* 1993; *Fun* 1994; *Mr Holland's Opus* 1995; *Urban Legend* 1998; *Cecil B Demented* 2000; *Vanilla Sky* 2001; *Two Weeks Notice* 2002; *Sword of Xanten* 2004

Witter, Karen (1961–) *Out of the Dark* 1988; *Midnight* 1989; *Buried Alive* 1990

Witty, Christopher (1950–) *Life in Danger* 1959; *No Kidding* 1960

Wodoslawsky, Stefan *The Masculine Mystique* 1984; *90 Days* 1986; *Something about Love* 1987

Wolders, Robert (1936–) *Beau Geste* 1966; *Interval* 1973

Wolf, Hillary (1977–) *Waiting for the Light* 1989; *Home Alone 2: Lost in New York* 1992; *Stepkids* 1992

Wolf, Kelly *Triumph of the Spirit* 1989; *Graveyard Shift* 1990; *A Day in October* 1991

Wolf, Lawrence *Putney Swope* 1969; *Deadhead Miles* 1972

Wolf, Scott (1968–) *Double Dragon* 1994; *The Evening Star* 1996; *White Squall* 1996; *Go* 1999; *Lady and the Tramp II: Scamp's Adventure* 2000

Wolfe, David (1915–1994) *The Undercover Man* 1949; *Appointment with Danger* 1950; *Salt of the Earth* 1954

Wolfe, Ian (1896–1992) *Clive of India* 1935; *Bedlam* 1946; *The Falcon's Adventure* 1946; *The Marauders* 1947; *They Live by Night* 1948; *The Magnificent Yankee* 1950; *The Actress* 1953; *Houdini* 1953; *Gaby* 1956; *Witness for the Prosecution* 1957; *Diary of a Madman* 1963; *Games* 1967; *THX 1138* 1971; *The Seniors* 1978; *Up the Academy* 1980; *Reds* 1981; *Checking Out* 1988

Wolfe, Traci (1961–) *Lethal Weapon* 1987; *Lethal Weapon 2* 1989; *Lethal Weapon 3* 1992; *Lethal Weapon 4* 1998

Wolff, Frank (1928–1971) *Beast from Haunted Cave* 1959; *Atlas* 1960; *Salvatore Giuliano* 1961; *The Four Days of Naples* 1962; *America, America* 1963; *Situation Hopeless – but Not Serious* 1965; *Once upon a Time in the West* 1968; *Villa Rides* 1968; *Sartana, Angel of Death* 1969; *Sin* 1972

Wolff, Rikard (1958–) *House of Angels* 1992; *House of Angels II: The Second Summer* 1994

Wolfit, Donald (1902–1968) *Isn't Life Wonderful!* 1952; *The Pickwick Papers* 1952; *Svengali* 1954; *A Man on the Beach* 1955; *A Prize of Gold* 1955; *Guilty?* 1956; *Satellite in the Sky* 1956; *The Man in the Road* 1957; *The Traitor* 1957; *Blood of the Vampire* 1958; *I Accuse!* 1958; *Room at the Top* 1958; *The House of the Seven Hawks* 1959; *The Rough and the Smooth* 1959; *The Hands of Orlac* 1960; *The Mark* 1961; *Dr Crippen* 1962; *Lawrence of Arabia* 1962; *Becket* 1964; *Life at the Top* 1965; *Decline and Fall... of a Birdwatcher* 1968

Wolfman Jack (1938–1995) *American Graffiti* 1973; *Motel Hell* 1980

Wolheim, Louis (1880–1931) *Dr Jekyll and Mr Hyde* 1920; *Two Arabian Knights* 1927; *The Racket* 1928; *Condemned* 1929; *All Quiet on the Western Front* 1930; *Danger Lights* 1930; *The Sin Ship* 1931

Wolk, Emil *Escape from Sobibor* 1987; *The Tall Guy* 1989

Wollter, Sven (1934–) *The Sacrifice* 1986; *House of Angels* 1992; *House of Angels II: The Second Summer* 1994

Wolter, Ralf (1926–) *One, Two, Three* 1961; *The Desperado Trail* 1965

Womack, Mark *Dancin' thru the Dark* 1989; *Letters from the East* 1995; *Under the Skin* 1997

Wong, Anna May (1907–1961) *The Thief of Bagdad* 1924; *Piccadilly* 1929; *Shanghai Express* 1932; *Chu Chin Chow* 1934; *Java Head* 1935; *Impact* 1949; *Portrait in Black* 1960

Wong (1), Anthony *aka* **Wong Chau-Sang, Anthony** (1961–) *Full Contact* 1992; *Hard-Boiled* 1992; *The Heroic Trio* 1992; *Rock 'n' Roll Cop* 1994; *Beast Cops* 1998; *Time and Tide* 2000; *Infernal Affairs* 2002; *Infernal Affairs II* 2003; *Infernal Affairs 3* 2003; *The Medallion* 2003

Wong, B D (1962–) *Father of the Bride* 1991; *Mystery Date* 1991; *Jurassic Park* 1993; *Men of War* 1995; *Executive Decision* 1996; *Seven Years in Tibet* 1997; *The Substitute 2: School's Out* 1997; *The Adventures of Slappy the Sea Lion* 1998; *Mulan* 1998

Wong, Benedict *Dirty Pretty Things* 2002; *On a Clear Day* 2005

Wong, Faye *Chung King Express* 1994; *Chinese Odyssey 2002* 2002; *2046* 2004

Wong, Michael *aka* **Wong Man-Tak, Michael** *Thunderbolt* 1995; *And Now You're Dead* 1998; *Beast Cops* 1998

Wong, Pauline (1962–) *Mr Vampire* 1986; *Spiritual Love* 1987

Wong, Russell (1963–) *Tai-Pan* 1986; *Eat a Bowl of Tea* 1989; *China Cry* 1990; *The Prophecy II* 1997; *Romeo Must Die* 2000; *Twisted* 2003

Wong (2), Victor (1927–2001) *Dim Sum: a Little Bit of Heart* 1985; *Big Trouble in Little China* 1986; *The Golden Child* 1986; *The Last Emperor* 1987; *Prince of Darkness* 1987; *Eat a Bowl of Tea* 1989; *Life Is Cheap... but Toilet Paper Is Expensive* 1990; *3 Ninjas* 1992; *3 Ninjas Kick Back* 1994; *3 Ninjas Knuckle Up* 1995; *Seven Years in Tibet* 1997; *3 Ninjas: High Noon at Mega Mountain* 1998

Wontner, Arthur (1875–1960) *Lady Windermere's Fan* 1916; *The Sign of Four* 1932; *Thunder in the City* 1937

Wood, David (1944–) *if...* 1968; *Sweet William* 1980

Wood, Elijah (1981–) *Avalon* 1990; *Paradise* 1991; *Forever Young* 1992; *Radio Flyer* 1992; *The Adventures of Huck Finn* 1993; *The Good Son* 1993; *North* 1994; *The War* 1994; *Flipper* 1996; *The Ice Storm* 1997; *Deep Impact* 1998; *The Faculty* 1998; *The Lord of the Rings: The Fellowship of the Ring* 2001; *The Adventures of Tom Thumb and Thumbelina* 2002; *Ash Wednesday* 2002; *The Lord of the Rings: The Two Towers* 2002; *Eternal Sunshine of the Spotless Mind* 2003; *The Lord of the Rings: The Return of the King* 2003; *Sin City* 2005

Wood, Evan Rachel (1987–) *Digging to China* 1998; *The Missing* 2003; *Thirteen* 2003

Wood, G (1920–2000) *Harold and Maude* 1972; *Bank Shot* 1974

Wood, Gary *The Glory Stompers* 1967; *Hungry for You* 1996

Wood, Helen (1917–1988) *Crack-Up* 1936; *Give a Girl a Break* 1953

Wood, Janet *Slumber Party '57* 1976; *Up* 1976

Wood, John (1937–) *The Last Days of Pompeii* 1935; *Over She Goes* 1937; *Hold My Hand* 1938; *Black Eyes* 1939; *Stolen Face* 1952; *Invasion Quartet* 1961; *Postman's Knock* 1961; *Just like a Woman* 1966; *One More Time* 1970; *Which Way to the Front?* 1970; *Somebody Killed Her Husband* 1978; *WarGames* 1983; *The Empty Beach* 1985; *Lady Jane* 1985; *Ladyhawke* 1985; *The Purple Rose of Cairo* 1985; *Jumpin' Jack Flash* 1986; *Orlando* 1992; *Shadowlands* 1993; *Citizen X* 1995; *Sabrina* 1995; *Rasputin* 1996; *The Gambler* 1997; *The Revengers' Comedies* 1997; *An Ideal Husband* 1999; *The Body* 2000; *The Little Vampire* 2000; *Imagining Argentina* 2003

Wood, Lana (1946–) *Diamonds Are Forever* 1971; *Grayeagle* 1977

Wood, Mary Laura *Valley of Eagles* 1951; *The Hour of Decision* 1957

Wood, Natalie (1938–1981) *Tomorrow Is Forever* 1945; *The Bride Wore Boots* 1946; *Driftwood* 1946; *The Ghost and Mrs Muir* 1947; *Miracle on 34th Street* 1947; *Chicken Every Sunday* 1948; *Father Was a Fullback* 1949; *The Jackpot* 1950; *Never a Dull Moment* 1950; *No Sad Songs for Me* 1950; *Our Very Own* 1950; *The Blue Veil* 1951; *Just for You* 1952; *The Star* 1953; *The Silver Chalice* 1954; *One Desire* 1955; *Rebel without a Cause* 1955; *The Burning Hills* 1956; *A Cry in the Night* 1956; *The Girl He Left Behind* 1956; *The Searchers* 1956; *Bombers B-52* 1957; *Kings Go Forth* 1958; *Marjorie Morningstar* 1958; *All the Fine Young Cannibals* 1960; *Cash McCall* 1960; *Splendor in the Grass* 1961; *West Side Story* 1961; *Gypsy* 1962; *Love with the Proper Stranger* 1963; *Sex and the Single Girl* 1964; *The Great Race* 1965; *Inside Daisy Clover* 1965; *Penelope* 1966; *This Property Is Condemned* 1966; *Bob & Carol & Ted & Alice* 1969; *The Affair* 1973; *Peeper* 1975; *The Cracker Factory* 1979; *Meteor* 1979; *The Last Married Couple in America* 1980; *Brainstorm* 1983

Wood, Peggy (1892–1978) *A Star Is Born* 1937; *The Housekeeper's Daughter* 1939; *The Bride Wore Boots* 1946; *Magnificent Doll* 1946; *Dream Girl* 1948; *The Story of Ruth* 1960; *The Sound of Music* 1965

Wood, Tom (1963–) *Bushwhacked* 1995; *Tinseltown* 1997; *US Marshals* 1998

Wood, Victoria (1953–) *The Wind in the Willows* 1996; *The League of Gentlemen's Apocalypse* 2005

Wood, Ward *Air Force* 1943; *The Loners* 1971

Woodard, Alfre (1953–) *Remember My Name* 1978; *Freedom Road* 1979; *HEALTH* 1980; *Cross Creek* 1983; *Go Tell It on the Mountain* 1984; *The Killing Floor* 1984; *Extremities* 1986; *Scrooged* 1988; *Miss Firecracker* 1989; *Grand Canyon* 1991; *The Gun in Betty Lou's Handbag* 1992; *Passion Fish* 1992; *Rich in Love* 1992; *Bopha!* 1993; *Heart and Souls* 1993; *Blue Chips* 1994; *Crooklyn* 1994; *How to Make an American Quilt* 1995; *Primal Fear* 1996; *Star Trek: First Contact* 1996; *Down in the Delta* 1997; *Miss Evers' Boys* 1997; *Mumford* 1999; *Dinosaur* 2000; *Love & Basketball* 2000; *What's Cooking?* 2000; *K-PAX* 2001; *The Core* 2002; *Radio* 2003; *The Forgotten* 2004; *Beauty Shop* 2005

Woodard, Charlayne *aka* **Woodard, Charlaine** (1955–) *Hard Feelings* 1981; *Unbreakable* 2000

Woodbine, Bokeem (1973–) *Jason's Lyric* 1994; *Panther* 1995; *Almost Heroes* 1998; *The Big Hit* 1998; *Life* 1999; *The Runner* 1999; *The Breed* 2001; *Ray* 2004

Woodbridge, George (1907–1973) *Children of Chance* 1949; *Murder in the Cathedral* 1952; *Son of Robin Hood* 1958

Woodburn, Eric *The Bridal Path* 1959; *Trial and Error* 1962

Woodbury, Joan (1915–1989) *Super-Sleuth* 1937; *Dr Broadway* 1942; *Charlie Chan in The Chinese Cat* 1944; *The Whistler* 1944

Woode, Margo *It Shouldn't Happen to a Dog* 1946; *Moss Rose* 1947

Woodell, Barbara (1910–1997) *Westward Ho the Wagons!* 1956; *Go, Johnny, Go!* 1959

Woodell, Pat (1944–) *The Big Doll House* 1971; *Twilight People* 1973

Woodlawn, Holly (1947–) *Trash* 1970; *Is There Sex after Death?* 1971; *Women in Revolt* 1971; *Milwaukee, Minnesota* 2002

Woodruff, Largo *Bill* 1981; *The Funhouse* 1981

Woods, Aubrey (1928–) *Loot* 1970; *The Abominable Dr Phibes* 1971; *ZPG: Zero Population Growth* 1971
Woods, Carol *Stepping Out* 1991; *The Honeymooners* 2005
Woods, Donald (1904–1998) *The Florentine Dagger* 1935; *Frisco Kid* 1935; *Sweet Adeline* 1935; *A Tale of Two Cities* 1935; *Anthony Adverse* 1936; *Isle of Fury* 1936; *The Story of Louis Pasteur* 1936; *The White Angel* 1936; *The Case of the Stuttering Bishop* 1937; *Charlie Chan on Broadway* 1937; *Sea Devils* 1937; *Beauty for the Asking* 1939; *The Girl from Mexico* 1939; *Mexican Spitfire* 1940; *Watch on the Rhine* 1943; *Roughly Speaking* 1945; *Wonder Man* 1945; *Never Say Goodbye* 1946; *Scene of the Crime* 1949; *The Beast from 20,000 Fathoms* 1953; *13 Ghosts* 1959; *Door-to-Door Maniac* 1961; *Moment to Moment* 1966
Woods, Edward (1903–1989) *The Public Enemy* 1931; *Tarzan the Fearless* 1933
Woods, Harry (1889–1968) *Palmy Days* 1931; *Law and Order* 1932; *Thunder Mountain* 1947; *She Wore a Yellow Ribbon* 1949
Woods, James (1947–) *Hickey and Boggs* 1972; *The Visitors* 1972; *The Way We Were* 1973; *Night Moves* 1975; *Alex and the Gypsy* 1976; *The Disappearance of Aimee* 1976; *The Choirboys* 1977; *The Onion Field* 1979; *The Black Marble* 1980; *Eyewitness* 1981; *Fast-Walking* 1982; *Split Image* 1982; *Videodrome* 1982; *Against All Odds* 1984; *Cat's Eye* 1984; *Once upon a Time in America* 1984; *Joshua Then and Now* 1985; *Promise* 1986; *Salvador* 1986; *Best Seller* 1987; *The Boost* 1988; *Cop* 1988; *Immediate Family* 1989; *My Name Is Bill W* 1989; *True Believer* 1989; *The Boys* 1991; *The Hard Way* 1991; *Chaplin* 1992; *Midnight Sting* 1992; *Straight Talk* 1992; *The Getaway* 1994; *The Specialist* 1994; *Casino* 1995; *For Better or Worse* 1995; *Indictment: the McMartin Trial* 1995; *Killer: a Journal of Murder* 1995; *Nixon* 1995; *Ghosts of Mississippi* 1996; *The Summer of Ben Tyler* 1996; *Contact* 1997; *Hercules* 1997; *Kicked in the Head* 1997; *Another Day in Paradise* 1998; *Vampires* 1998; *Any Given Sunday* 1999; *The General's Daughter* 1999; *True Crime* 1999; *The Virgin Suicides* 1999; *Dirty Pictures* 2000; *Play It to the Bone* 2000; *Final Fantasy: the Spirits Within* 2001; *John Q* 2001; *Recess: School's Out* 2001; *Riding in Cars with Boys* 2001; *Scary Movie 2* 2001; *Northfork* 2002; *Stuart Little 2* 2002
Woods, Kevin Jamal *The Little Rascals* 1994; *The Brainiacs.com* 2000
Woods, Michael (1957–) *Lady Beware* 1987; *Omen IV: the Awakening* 1991
Woodthorpe, Peter (1931–2004) *Evil of Frankenstein* 1964; *The Blue Max* 1966
Woodville, Catherine (1938–) *The Wild and the Willing* 1962; *The Informers* 1963; *The Crooked Road* 1964; *The Party's Over* 1965
Woodville, Kate (1938–) *Extreme Close-Up* 1973; *Where's Willie?* 1977
Woodvine, John (1929–) *An American Werewolf in London* 1981; *Leon the Pig Farmer* 1992; *Dragonworld* 1994; *Persuasion* 1995
Woodward, Edward (1930–) *Where There's a Will* 1955; *The File of the Golden Goose* 1969; *Incense for the Damned* 1970; *Sitting Target* 1972; *The Wicker Man* 1973; *Callan* 1974; *Stand Up Virgin Soldiers* 1977; *Breaker Morant* 1979; *The Appointment* 1981; *Who Dares Wins* 1982; *Champions* 1983; *King David* 1985; *Mister Johnson* 1991; *Deadly Advice* 1993; *The Abduction Club* 2002
Woodward, Joanne (1930–) *Count Three and Pray* 1955; *A Kiss before Dying* 1956; *No Down Payment* 1957; *The Three Faces of Eve* 1957; *The Long Hot Summer* 1958; *Rally 'round the Flag, Boys!* 1958; *The Sound and the Fury* 1959; *From the Terrace* 1960; *The Fugitive Kind* 1960; *Paris Blues* 1961; *A New Kind of Love* 1963; *The Stripper* 1963; *Signpost to Murder* 1964; *A Big Hand for a Little Lady* 1966; *A Fine Madness* 1966; *Rachel, Rachel* 1968; *Winning* 1969; *King: a Filmed Record… Montgomery to Memphis* 1970; *WUSA* 1970; *They Might Be Giants* 1971; *The Effect of Gamma Rays on Man-in-the-Moon Marigolds* 1972; *Summer Wishes, Winter Dreams* 1973; *The Drowning Pool* 1975; *The End* 1978; *Harry and Son* 1984; *Do You Remember Love* 1985; *The Glass Menagerie* 1987; *Mr and Mrs Bridge* 1990; *The Age of Innocence* 1993; *Philadelphia* 1993
Woodward, Morgan (1925–) *The Wild Country* 1971; *One Little Indian* 1973; *Running Wild* 1973; *The Midnight Man* 1974; *The Killing of a Chinese Bookie* 1976; *A Small Town in Texas* 1976; *Final Chapter – Walking Tall* 1977; *Moonshine County Express* 1977; *Which Way Is Up?* 1977; *Battle beyond the Stars* 1980; *Girls Just Want to Have Fun* 1985
Woodward, Tim (1953–) *Personal Services* 1987; *B Monkey* 1996; *Some Mother's Son* 1996; *K-19: the Widowmaker* 2002
Woof, Emily (1970–) *The Full Monty* 1997; *Photographing Fairies* 1997; *The Woodlanders* 1997; *Fast Food* 1998; *Velvet Goldmine* 1998; *Passion* 1999; *This Year's Love* 1999; *Pandaemonium* 2000; *Wondrous Oblivion* 2003; *School for Seduction* 2004
Wooland, Norman (1910–1989) *Hamlet* 1948; *Madeleine* 1949; *Background* 1953; *The Master Plan* 1954; *Guilty?* 1956; *My Teenage Daughter* 1956; *The Flesh Is Weak* 1957; *No Road Back* 1957; *The Bandit of Zhobe* 1959; *The Rough and the Smooth* 1959; *The Fighting Prince of Donegal* 1966; *The Projected Man* 1966
Wooldridge, Susan *Dead Man's Folly* 1986; *Hope and Glory* 1987; *How to Get Ahead in Advertising* 1989; *Twenty-One* 1991; *Just like a Woman* 1992
Woolf, Henry *Figures in a Landscape* 1970; *The Love Pill* 1971
Woolf King, Walter (1899–1984) *Swiss Miss* 1938; *Go West* 1940
Woolgar, Jack (1914–1978) *Say Hello to Yesterday* 1971; *Swallows and Amazons* 1974
Woolley, Monty (1888–1963) *Live, Love and Learn* 1937; *Arsene Lupin Returns* 1938; *Everybody Sing* 1938; *Young Dr Kildare* 1938; *Dancing Co-Ed* 1939; *Midnight* 1939; *The Man Who Came to Dinner* 1941; *Life Begins at 8.30* 1942; *The Pied Piper* 1942; *Holy Matrimony* 1943; *Irish Eyes Are Smiling* 1944; *Since You Went Away* 1944; *Molly and Me* 1945; *Night and Day* 1946; *The Bishop's Wife* 1947; *Miss Tatlock's Millions* 1948; *As Young as You Feel* 1951; *Kismet* 1955
Woolsey, Robert (1889–1938) *Rio Rita* 1929; *Half Shot at Sunrise* 1930
Woolvett, Gordon Michael (1970–) *Bordertown Cafe* 1991; *Bride of Chucky* 1998; *The Highwayman* 1999
Woolvett, Jaimz (1967–) *Unforgiven* 1992; *Sanctuary* 1997; *Rites of Passage* 1999; *The Guilty* 2000
Worden, Hank (1901–1992) *The Big Sky* 1952; *UFOria* 1980
Wordsworth, Richard (1915–1993) *The Quatermass Xperiment* 1955; *The Revenge of Frankenstein* 1958; *The Curse of the Werewolf* 1961
Workman, Jimmy (1980–) *The Addams Family* 1991; *Addams Family Values* 1993
Worlock, Frederick aka **Worlock, Frederic** (1886–1973) *Man Hunt* 1941; *Pursuit to Algiers* 1945; *Sherlock Holmes and the Secret Code* 1946; *One Hundred and One Dalmatians* 1960
Woronov, Mary aka **Might, Mary** (1943–) *The Chelsea Girls* 1967; *Silent Night, Bloody Night* 1972; *Death Race 2000* 1975; *Hollywood Boulevard* 1976; *Jackson County Jail* 1976; *Rock 'n' Roll High School* 1979; *Eating Raoul* 1982; *Get Crazy* 1983; *Night of the Comet* 1984; *TerrorVision* 1986; *Scenes from the Class Struggle In Beverly Hills* 1989; *Warlock* 1989; *Motorama* 1991; *The Living End* 1992; *Shake, Rattle and Rock* 1994
Worth, Brian (1914–1978) *The Arsenal Stadium Mystery* 1939; *Pastor Hall* 1940; *Cardboard Cavalier* 1949; *Scrooge* 1951; *Hindle Wakes* 1952; *It Started in Paradise* 1952; *An Inspector Calls* 1954; *Assignment Redhead* 1956; *The Square Peg* 1958; *The Boy Who Turned Yellow* 1972
Worth, Constance (1912–1963) *Meet Boston Blackie* 1941; *Crime Doctor* 1943
Worth, Irene (1916–2002) *The Secret People* 1951; *Orders to Kill* 1958; *The Scapegoat* 1959; *Seven Seas to Calais* 1962; *To Die in Madrid* 1963; *King Lear* 1970; *Eyewitness* 1981; *Deathtrap* 1982; *Lost in Yonkers* 1993; *Onegin* 1999
Worth, Nicholas (1942–) *Swamp Thing* 1982; *Hell Comes to Frogtown* 1988; *Plughead Rewired: Circuitry Man II* 1994
Worthington, Sam (1976–) *Bootmen* 2000; *Dirty Deeds* 2002; *Somersault* 2004
Wouassi, Félicité (1961–) *The Diary of Lady M* 1992; *Le Cri du Coeur* 1994
Wray, Fay (1907–2004) *The Wedding March* 1928; *The Four Feathers* 1929; *Thunderbolt* 1929; *Paramount on Parade* 1930; *The Texan* 1930; *Dirigible* 1931; *The Finger Points* 1931; *The Unholy Garden* 1931; *Doctor X* 1932; *The Most Dangerous Game* 1932; *The Bowery* 1933; *King Kong* 1933; *Mystery of the Wax Museum* 1933; *Shanghai Madness* 1933; *The Vampire Bat* 1933; *The Affairs of Cellini* 1934; *Bulldog Jack* 1934; *The Clairvoyant* 1934; *The Richest Girl in the World* 1934; *Viva Villa!* 1934; *When Knights Were Bold* 1936; *Adam Had Four Sons* 1941; *Treasure of the Golden Condor* 1953; *Hell on Frisco Bay* 1955; *Queen Bee* 1955; *Rock, Pretty Baby* 1956; *Crime of Passion* 1957; *Tammy and the Bachelor* 1957; *Gideon's Trumpet* 1980
Wray, John (1887–1940) *All Quiet on the Western Front* 1930; *Quick Millions* 1931; *Doctor X* 1932; *The Death Kiss* 1933; *Atlantic Adventure* 1935; *Blackmail* 1939
Wright, Amy (1950–) *Girlfriends* 1978; *Breaking Away* 1979; *Heartland* 1979; *Wise Blood* 1979; *Inside Moves: the Guys from Max's Bar* 1980; *Off Beat* 1986; *The Accidental Tourist* 1988; *The Telephone* 1988; *Daddy's Dyin'… Who's Got the Will?* 1990; *Love Hurts* 1990; *Deceived* 1991; *Where the Rivers Flow North* 1993; *Tom and Huck* 1995
Wright (1), Ben (1915–1989) *One Hundred and One Dalmatians* 1960; *The Jungle Book* 1967; *The Little Mermaid* 1989
Wright Jr, Cobina (1921–) *Charlie Chan in Rio* 1941; *Moon over Miami* 1941; *Weekend in Havana* 1941; *Footlight Serenade* 1942
Wright, Dorsey *Hair* 1979; *The Warriors* 1979
Wright, Howard (1896–1990) *Stranger at My Door* 1956; *The Legend of Tom Dooley* 1959
Wright, Janet *Bordertown Cafe* 1991; *Beyond the Call* 1996; *Emile* 2003
Wright, Jeffrey (1965–) *Jumpin' at the Boneyard* 1991; *Basquiat* 1996; *Ride with the Devil* 1999; *Crime + Punishment in Suburbia* 2000; *Shaft* 2000; *Ali* 2001; *Boycott* 2001; *The Manchurian Candidate* 2004
Wright, Jenny (1962–) *Pink Floyd – The Wall* 1982; *The Wild Life* 1984; *Near Dark* 1987; *Valentino Returns* 1987; *Twister* 1989; *A Shock to the System* 1990; *The Lawnmower Man* 1992
Wright, Jenny Lee (1947–) *Husbands* 1970; *The Triple Echo* 1972; *The Best of Benny Hill* 1974
Wright, Marie (1862–1949) *Sexton Blake and the Hooded Terror* 1938; *Black Eyes* 1939
Wright, Michael *Streamers* 1983; *The Principal* 1987; *The Five Heartbeats* 1991; *Sugar Hill* 1993; *Confessions of a Hit Man* 1994; *Point Blank* 1997; *Piñero* 2001; *The Interpreter* 2005
Wright, N'Bushe (1970–) *Zebrahead* 1992; *Fresh* 1994; *Dead Presidents* 1995; *Blade* 1998; *3 Strikes* 2000
Wright, Samuel E (1946–) *Bird* 1988; *Thelonious Monk: Straight No Chaser* 1988; *The Little Mermaid* 1989; *Dinosaur* 2000; *The Little Mermaid II: Return to the Sea* 2000
Wright, Steven (1955–) *Desperately Seeking Susan* 1985; *The Swan Princess* 1994; *Canadian Bacon* 1995; *Babe: Pig in the City* 1998; *The Muse* 1999; *Coffee and Cigarettes* 2003
Wright, Teresa (1918–2005) *The Little Foxes* 1941; *Mrs Miniver* 1942; *The Pride of the Yankees* 1942; *Shadow of a Doubt* 1942; *Casanova Brown* 1944; *The Best Years of Our Lives* 1946; *The Imperfect Lady* 1947; *Pursued* 1947; *Enchantment* 1948; *The Capture* 1950; *The Men* 1950; *Something to Live For* 1952; *The Steel Trap* 1952; *The Actress* 1953; *Count the Hours* 1953; *Track of the Cat* 1954; *Escapade in Japan* 1957; *The Restless Years* 1958; *Hail, Hero!* 1969; *The Happy Ending* 1969; *Roseland* 1977; *Somewhere in Time* 1980; *The Price of Passion* 1988; *John Grisham's The Rainmaker* 1997
Wright, Tom *The Brother from Another Planet* 1984; *Marked for Death* 1990; *Weekend at Bernie's II* 1992; *Tales from the Hood* 1995; *Palmetto* 1998; *The Pentagon Wars* 1998
Wright, Tony (1925–1986) *Jumping for Joy* 1955; *Jacqueline* 1956; *Tiger in the Smoke* 1956; *Seven Thunders* 1957; *The Spaniard's Curse* 1958; *The Rough and the Smooth* 1959; *Faces in the Dark* 1960
Wright, Tracy *When Night Is Falling* 1995; *Last Night* 1998
Wright, Whittni (1987–) *I'll Do Anything* 1994; *Sudden Death* 1995
Wright, Will (1894–1962) *Green Grass of Wyoming* 1948; *They Live by Night* 1948; *Mrs Mike* 1949; *A Ticket to Tomahawk* 1950; *Quantrill's Raiders* 1958; *Alias Jesse James* 1959; *The Deadly Companions* 1961
Wright, William (1911–1949) *A Night to Remember* 1942; *Reveille with Beverly* 1943
Wright Penn, Robin aka **Wright, Robin** (1966–) *Hollywood Vice Squad* 1986; *The Princess Bride* 1987; *State of Grace* 1990; *The Playboys* 1992; *Toys* 1992; *Forrest Gump* 1994; *The Crossing Guard* 1995; *Moll Flanders* 1995; *Loved* 1996; *She's So Lovely* 1997; *Hurlyburly* 1998; *Message in a Bottle* 1998; *The Pledge* 2000; *Unbreakable* 2000; *White Oleander* 2002; *The Singing Detective* 2003; *A Home at the End of the World* 2004
Wrixon, Maris (1916–1999) *The Ape* 1940; *The Case of the Black Parrot* 1941
Wu Chien-lien (1968–) *Eat Drink Man Woman* 1994; *To Live and Die in Tsimshatsui* 1994; *Eighteen Springs* 1997
Wu Jiang *To Live* 1994; *Shower* 1999
Wu Ma *A Chinese Ghost Story* 1987; *A Chinese Ghost Story II* 1990
Wu Nianzhen (1952–) *Taipei Story* 1984; *A One and a Two* 1999
Wu, Vivian (1966–) *Iron and Silk* 1990; *The Guyver* 1991; *Teenage Mutant Ninja Turtles III* 1992; *The Pillow Book* 1995; *8½ Women* 1999; *Dinner Rush* 2000
Wu Yin (1909–1991) *Spring River Flows East* 1947; *Crows and Sparrows* 1949
Wuhl, Robert (1951–) *Good Morning, Vietnam* 1987; *Bull Durham* 1988; *Batman* 1989; *Missing Pieces* 1991; *Mistress* 1992; *Cobb* 1994; *Open Season* 1995
Wuhrer, Kari (1967–) *Beastmaster 2: through the Portal of Time* 1991; *Boulevard* 1994; *Sex and the Other Man* 1995; *Anaconda* 1997; *Touch Me* 1997; *Kissing a Fool* 1998; *G-Men from Hell* 2000; *Kiss Tomorrow Goodbye* 2000; *Eight Legged Freaks* 2001; *King of the Ants* 2003
Wussow, Klaus-Jürgen (1929–) *The Red Circle* 1960; *Please Let the Flowers Live* 1986
Wyatt, Jane (1911–) *One More River* 1934; *Lost Horizon* 1937; *The Navy Comes Through* 1942; *None but the Lonely Heart* 1944; *Boomerang!* 1947; *Gentleman's Agreement* 1947; *No Minor Vices* 1948; *Pitfall* 1948; *Canadian Pacific* 1949; *Task Force* 1949; *House by the River* 1950; *My Blue Heaven* 1950; *Our Very Own* 1950; *The Two Little Bears* 1961; *Never Too Late* 1965; *Treasure of Matecumbe* 1976; *Star Trek IV: the Voyage Home* 1986; *Amityville: the Evil Escapes* 1989
Wyatt, Tessa (1948–) *The Beast in the Cellar* 1970; *England Made Me* 1973
Wycherly, Margaret (1881–1956) *Midnight* 1934; *Victory* 1940; *Sergeant York* 1941; *Crossroads* 1942; *Keeper of the Flame* 1942; *Random Harvest* 1942; *Hangmen Also Die* 1943; *The Moon Is Down* 1943; *Johnny Angel* 1945; *The Yearling* 1946; *Something in the Wind* 1947; *White Heat* 1949; *The Man with a Cloak* 1951
Wyldeck, Martin (1913–1988) *The Hypnotist* 1957; *The Return of Mr Moto* 1965; *Die Screaming Marianne* 1970
Wyle, Noah (1971–) *Crooked Hearts* 1991; *There Goes My Baby* 1994; *The Myth of Fingerprints* 1996; *Fail Safe* 2000; *Donnie Darko* 2001; *Enough* 2002; *White Oleander* 2002
Wyllie, Dan aka **Wyllie, Daniel** *Spotswood* 1991; *Romper Stomper* 1992; *Holy Smoke* 1999; *Chopper* 2000
Wyman, Jane (1914–) *Smart Blonde* 1936; *The King and the Chorus Girl* 1937; *Slim* 1937; *The Crowd Roars* 1938; *Kid Nightingale* 1939; *The Body Disappears* 1941; *Footlight Serenade* 1942; *Larceny, Inc* 1942; *My Favorite Spy* 1942; *Princess O'Rourke* 1943; *The Doughgirls* 1944; *Hollywood Canteen* 1944; *Make Your Own Bed* 1944; *The Lost Weekend* 1945; *Night and Day* 1946; *The Yearling* 1946; *Magic Town* 1947; *Johnny Belinda* 1948; *It's a Great Feeling* 1949; *A Kiss in the Dark* 1949; *Stage Fright* 1949; *The Glass Menagerie* 1950; *The Blue Veil* 1951; *Here Comes the Groom* 1951; *Just for You* 1952; *Let's Do It Again* 1953; *So Big* 1953; *Magnificent Obsession* 1954; *All That Heaven Allows* 1955; *Lucy Gallant* 1955; *Miracle in the Rain* 1956; *Holiday for Lovers* 1959; *Pollyanna* 1960; *Bon Voyage!* 1962; *How to Commit Marriage* 1969

Wymark, Patrick (1926–1970) *West 11* 1963; *Repulsion* 1965; *The Skull* 1965; *The Psychopath* 1966; *Tell Me Lies* 1967; *Witchfinder General* 1968; *Journey to the Far Side of the Sun* 1969; *Where Eagles Dare* 1969; *Blood on Satan's Claw* 1970; *Cromwell* 1970
Wymore, Patrice (1926–) *Rocky Mountain* 1950; *Tea for Two* 1950; *I'll See You in My Dreams* 1951; *The Big Trees* 1952; *She's Working Her Way through College* 1952; *King's Rhapsody* 1955; *The Sad Horse* 1959; *Ocean's Eleven* 1960; *Chamber of Horrors* 1966
Wyn Davies, Geraint (1957–) *One of the Hollywood Ten* 2000; *American Psycho II: All American Girl* 2002
Wynant, H M (1927–) *Tonka* 1958; *Marlowe* 1969
Wyner, George (1945–) *Dogs* 1976; *Spaceballs* 1987; *Listen to Me* 1989
Wyngarde, Peter (1933–) *The Siege of Sidney Street* 1960; *The Innocents* 1961; *Night of the Eagle* 1961
Wynn, Ed (1886–1966) *Alice in Wonderland* 1951; *The Great Man* 1956; *Marjorie Morningstar* 1958; *The Diary of Anne Frank* 1959; *Cinderfella* 1960; *Babes in Toyland* 1961; *Son of Flubber* 1962; *Mary Poppins* 1964; *Those Calloways* 1964; *Dear Brigitte* 1966; *The Gnome-Mobile* 1967
Wynn, Keenan (1916–1986) *For Me and My Gal* 1942; *Somewhere I'll Find You* 1942; *Lost Angel* 1943; *Marriage Is a Private Affair* 1944; *See Here, Private Hargrove* 1944; *The Clock* 1945; *Week-End at the Waldorf* 1945; *Without Love* 1945; *Easy to Wed* 1946; *The Hucksters* 1947; *Song of the Thin Man* 1947; *BF's Daughter* 1948; *My Dear Secretary* 1948; *Neptune's Daughter* 1949; *That Midnight Kiss* 1949; *Annie Get Your Gun* 1950; *Love That Brute* 1950; *Three Little Words* 1950; *Angels in the Outfield* 1951; *Kind Lady* 1951; *Mr Imperium* 1951; *Royal Wedding* 1951; *Texas Carnival* 1951; *The Belle of New York* 1952; *Desperate Search* 1952; *Phone Call from a Stranger* 1952; *All the Brothers Were Valiant* 1953; *Battle Circus* 1953; *Kiss Me Kate* 1953; *The Long, Long Trailer* 1954; *Men of the Fighting Lady* 1954; *Tennessee Champ* 1954; *The Glass Slipper* 1955; *The Marauders* 1955; *Running Wild* 1955; *Shack Out on 101* 1955; *The Great Man* 1956; *Johnny Concho* 1956; *The Man in the Gray Flannel Suit* 1956; *Don't Go Near the Water* 1957; *The Fuzzy Pink Nightgown* 1957; *Joe Butterfly* 1957; *The Deep Six* 1958; *The Perfect Furlough* 1958; *A Time to Love and a Time to Die* 1958; *Touch of Evil* 1958; *The Crowded Sky* 1960; *The Absent-Minded Professor* 1961; *King of the Roaring 20s – the Story of Arnold Rothstein* 1961; *Son of Flubber* 1962; *The Bay of Saint Michel* 1963; *Dr Strangelove, or How I Learned to Stop Worrying and Love the Bomb* 1963; *The Americanization of Emily* 1964; *Bikini Beach* 1964; *Honeymoon Hotel* 1964; *The Man in the Middle* 1964; *Nightmare in the Sun* 1964; *The Patsy* 1964; *Around the World under the Sea* 1965; *The Great Race* 1965; *The Night of the Grizzly* 1966; *Promise Her Anything* 1966; *Stagecoach* 1966; *Point Blank* 1967; *The War Wagon* 1967; *Warning Shot* 1967; *Welcome to Hard Times* 1967; *Finian's Rainbow* 1968; *Once upon a Time in the West* 1968; *Eighty Steps to Jonah* 1969; *Mackenna's Gold* 1969; *Smith!* 1969; *Viva Max!* 1969; *Loving* 1970; *Pretty Maids All in a Row* 1971; *Black Jack* 1972; *Cancel My Reservation* 1972; *The Mechanic* 1972; *Panhandle Calibre 38* 1972; *Snowball Express* 1972; *Herbie Rides Again* 1974; *The Internecine Project* 1974; *The Devil's Rain* 1975; *The Killer inside Me* 1975; *The Man Who Would Not Die* 1975; *The Lindbergh Kidnapping Case* 1976; *The Shaggy DA* 1976; *High Velocity* 1977; *Orca ... Killer Whale* 1977; *The Treasure Seekers* 1977; *The Glove* 1978; *Laserblast* 1978; *Piranha* 1978; *Sunburn* 1979; *A Touch of the Sun* 1979; *Just Tell Me What You Want* 1980; *The Last Unicorn* 1980; *Best Friends* 1982; *A Piano for Mrs Cimino* 1982; *Wavelength* 1983; *Black Moon Rising* 1985; *Prime Risk* 1985
Wynn, May (1930–) *They Rode West* 1954; *The Violent Men* 1955
Wynne, Christopher *Cop* 1988; *Remote Control* 1988
Wynter, Dana (1931–) *The View from Pompey's Head* 1955; *D-Day the Sixth of June* 1956; *Invasion of the Body Snatchers* 1956; *Something of Value* 1957; *In Love and War* 1958; *Shake Hands with the Devil* 1959; *Sink the Bismarck!* 1960; *On the Double* 1961; *The List of Adrian Messenger* 1963; *Santee* 1973; *Call Him Savage* 1975
Wynter, Sarah (1973–) *Lost Souls* 2000; *Race against Time* 2000; *The 6th Day* 2000; *Bride of the Wind* 2001
Wynters, Charlotte (1899–1991) *The Struggle* 1931; *Sinners in Paradise* 1938; *Lulu Belle* 1948
Wynyard, Diana (1906–1964) *Rasputin and the Empress* 1932; *Cavalcade* 1933; *Reunion in Vienna* 1933; *One More River* 1934; *Freedom Radio* 1940; *Gaslight* 1940; *The Prime Minister* 1940; *Kipps* 1941; *An Ideal Husband* 1947; *Tom Brown's Schooldays* 1951; *The Feminine Touch* 1956
Wyss, Amanda (1960–) *A Nightmare on Elm Street* 1984; *Powwow Highway* 1988

X

Xavier, Nelson (1941–) *Dona Flor and Her Two Husbands* 1977; *Girl from Rio* 2001
Xin Shufen *Dust in the Wind* 1987; *A City of Sadness* 1989
Xu Qing *Life on a String* 1991; *The Emperor's Shadow* 1996
Xuereb, Salvator (1965–) *Born to Ride* 1991; *Killing Zoe* 1993; *Lewis & Clark & George* 1996

Y

Yadav, Raghuvir *aka* **Yadav, Raghubir** *aka* **Yadav, Raghuveer** *Salaam Bombay!* 1988; *Disha* 1990; *Electric Moon* 1992; *Bandit Queen* 1994; *Lagaan: Once upon a Time in India* 2001; *Deewaar: Let's Bring Our Heroes Home* 2004; *Gayab* 2004
Yadav, Rajpal *Road* 2002; *Mujhse Shaadi Karogi* 2004
Yadin, Yossi (1920–2001) *Bloomfield* 1969; *Lies My Father Told Me* 1975
Yagher, Jeff (1962–) *Dead Man's Folly* 1986; *Big Bad Mama II* 1987
Yagi, James *Bridge to the Sun* 1961; *King Kong vs Godzilla* 1962
Yakusho, Koji (1956–) *Tampopo* 1986; *Shall We Dance?* 1995; *The Eel* 1997; *Lost Paradise* 1997; *License to Live* 1999; *Eureka* 2000; *Warm Water under a Red Bridge* 2001
Yam, Simon (1955–) *Bullet in the Head* 1990; *Full Contact* 1992; *Fulltime Killer* 2002
Yamada, Isuzu (1917–) *The Downfall of Osen* 1935; *Osaka Elegy* 1936; *Sisters of the Gion* 1936; *The Famous Sword* 1945; *The Lower Depths* 1956; *Throne of Blood* 1957; *Tokyo Twilight* 1957; *Yojimbo* 1961
Yamaguchi, Shirley (1920–) *Japanese War Bride* 1952; *House of Bamboo* 1955
Yamamoto, Reisaburo *Drunken Angel* 1948; *Stray Dog* 1949
Yamamura, So *aka* **Yamamura, Soh** (1910–2000) *The Love of Sumako the Actress* 1947; *The Lady of Musashino* 1951; *Tokyo Story* 1953; *The Princess Yang Kwei Fei* 1955; *Early Spring* 1956; *The Barbarian and the Geisha* 1958; *The Human Condition* 1958; *Tora! Tora! Tora!* 1970; *Gung Ho* 1986
Yamazaki, Tsutomu (1936–) *Kagemusha* 1980; *Death Japanese Style* 1984; *Tampopo* 1986; *A Taxing Woman* 1987; *Rikyu* 1989
Yang Kuei-Mei *Eat Drink Man Woman* 1994; *Vive L'Amour* 1994; *The Hole* 1998; *Double Vision* 2002
Yankovsky, Oleg (1944–) *Mirror* 1974; *Dream Flights* 1983; *Nostalgia* 1983; *The Kreutzer Sonata* 1987; *Assassin of the Tsar* 1991
Yanne, Jean (1933–2003) *Life Upside Down* 1964; *Weekend* 1967; *Le Boucher* 1969; *Que la Bête Meure* 1969; *Armaguedon* 1976; *Quicker than the Eye* 1989; *Indochine* 1991; *Madame Bovary* 1991; *Fausto* 1992; *Pétain* 1992; *See How They Fall* 1993; *The Horseman on the Roof* 1995; *Victory* 1995; *News from the Good Lord* 1996; *Brotherhood of the Wolf* 2001; *Petites Coupures* 2002
Yarde, Margaret (1878–1944) *Squibs* 1935; *Crimes at the Dark House* 1939
Yasbeck, Amy (1963–) *House II: the Second Story* 1987; *Problem Child* 1990; *Problem Child 2* 1991; *Robin Hood: Men in Tights* 1993; *The Mask* 1994; *Dracula: Dead and Loving It* 1995; *Something about Sex* 1998
Yates, Cassie (1951–) *FM* 1977; *Rolling Thunder* 1977; *The Evil* 1978; *Agatha Christie's A Caribbean Mystery* 1983; *Unfaithfully Yours* 1983
Yates, Marjorie (1941–) *The Optimists of Nine Elms* 1973; *Legend of the Werewolf* 1974; *Wetherby* 1985; *The Long Day Closes* 1992
Yeh, Sally (1961–) *Peking Opera Blues* 1986; *The Laserman* 1988; *The Killer* 1989
Yen, Donnie *aka* **Yen, Donnie Chi-Tan** (1963–) *Once upon a Time in China II* 1992; *Iron Monkey* 1993; *Highlander: Endgame* 2000; *Hero* 2002; *Shanghai Knights* 2002
Yeoh, Michelle (1962–) *Drunken Master* 1978; *The Heroic Trio* 1992; *Police Story III: Supercop* 1992; *Twin Warriors* 1993; *Tomorrow Never Dies* 1997; *Crouching Tiger, Hidden Dragon* 2000
Yerles, Bernard *Les Apprentis* 1995; *The Cow and the President* 2000
Yeung, Bolo *Double Impact* 1991; *TC 2000* 1993
Yi Ding *The Amazing Panda Adventure* 1995; *Pavilion of Women* 2000
Yiasoumi, George *Gold Diggers* 1983; *King Kong Lives* 1986
Yilmaz, Cem *Vizontele* 2001; *GORA* 2004
Yilmaz, Serra *Harem Suare* 1999; *Le Fate Ignoranti* 2001; *Facing Window* 2003
Ying Da *Farewell My Concubine* 1993; *Big Shot's Funeral* 2001
Ying Ruocheng (1929–2003) *The Last Emperor* 1987; *Little Buddha* 1993
Yip, David (1951–) *Indiana Jones and the Temple of Doom* 1984; *A View to a Kill* 1985
Yip, Françoise (1972–) *Black Mask* 1996; *Rumble in the Bronx* 1996
Yniguez, Richard *Boulevard Nights* 1979; *Stalking Laura* 1993
Yoakam, Dwight (1956–) *Roswell* 1994; *Shadow of the Past* 1995; *Sling Blade* 1995; *The Newton Boys* 1998; *When Trumpets Fade* 1998; *The Minus Man* 1999; *South of Heaven, West of Hell* 2000; *Panic Room* 2002; *Hollywood Homicide* 2003
Yoba, Malik (1967–) *Cool Runnings* 1993; *Ride* 1998
Yohn, Erica *An American Tail* 1986; *An American Tail: Fievel Goes West* 1991; *Jack the Bear* 1993; *Corrina, Corrina* 1994; *An American Tail: the Treasure of Manhattan Island* 1998
Yordanoff, Wladimir *Vincent and Theo* 1990; *Wild Target* 1993; *Un Air de Famille* 1996; *Nathalie...* 2003
York, Daniel *Peggy Su!* 1997; *The Beach* 2000
York, Dick *aka* **York, Richard** (1928–1992) *My Sister Eileen* 1955; *Operation Mad Ball* 1957; *Cowboy* 1958; *The Last Blitzkrieg* 1958; *Inherit the Wind* 1960
York, Jeff (1912–1995) *Fear in the Night* 1947; *Davy Crockett and the River Pirates* 1956; *The Great Locomotive Chase* 1956; *Westward Ho the Wagons!* 1956; *Johnny Tremain* 1957; *Old Yeller* 1957; *Savage Sam* 1963
York, Kathleen *Checking Out* 1988; *Cold Feet* 1989; *Wild Hearts Can't Be Broken* 1991; *Dream Lover* 1993; *Dead Men Can't Dance* 1997
York, Michael (1942–) *Accident* 1967; *Smashing Time* 1967; *The Taming of the Shrew* 1967; *Romeo and Juliet* 1968; *The Strange Affair* 1968; *Alfred the Great* 1969; *The Guru* 1969; *Justine* 1969; *Something for Everyone* 1970; *Zeppelin* 1971; *Cabaret* 1972; *England Made Me* 1973; *Lost Horizon* 1973; *The Three Musketeers* 1973; *The Four Musketeers* 1974; *Great Expectations* 1974; *Murder on the Orient Express* 1974; *Conduct Unbecoming* 1975; *Logan's Run* 1976; *Seven Nights in Japan* 1976; *The Island of Dr Moreau* 1977; *The Last Remake of Beau Geste* 1977; *Fedora* 1978; *The Riddle of the Sands* 1978; *The White Lions* 1980; *Success Is the Best Revenge* 1984; *Midnight Cop* 1988; *Phantom of Death* 1988; *The Return of the Musketeers* 1989; *The Long Shadow* 1992; *Wide Sargasso Sea* 1992; *Gospa* 1995; *Young Connecticut Yankee in King Arthur's Court* 1995; *Austin Powers: International Man of Mystery* 1997; *A Christmas Carol* 1997; *A Knight in Camelot* 1998; *Wrongfully Accused* 1998; *Austin Powers: the Spy Who Shagged Me* 1999; *A Monkey's Tale* 1999; *Austin Powers in Goldmember* 2002
York, Morgan (1993–) *Cheaper by the Dozen* 2003; *The Pacifier* 2005
York, Susannah (1941–) *There Was a Crooked Man* 1960; *Tunes of Glory* 1960; *The Greengage Summer* 1961; *Freud* 1962; *Tom Jones* 1963; *The 7th Dawn* 1964; *Sands of the Kalahari* 1965; *Kaleidoscope* 1966; *A Man for All Seasons* 1966; *Duffy* 1968; *The Killing of Sister George* 1968; *Sebastian* 1968; *Battle of Britain* 1969; *Lock Up Your Daughters!* 1969; *Oh! What a Lovely War* 1969; *They Shoot Horses, Don't They?* 1969; *Country Dance* 1970; *Happy Birthday, Wanda June* 1971; *Zee and Co* 1971; *Images* 1972; *Gold* 1974; *The Maids* 1974; *Conduct Unbecoming* 1975; *That Lucky Touch* 1975; *Sky Riders* 1976; *Long Shot* 1978; *The Shout* 1978; *The Silent Partner* 1978; *Superman* 1978; *The Awakening* 1980; *Falling in Love Again* 1980; *Loophole* 1980; *Superman II* 1980; *Yellowbeard* 1983; *Mio in the Land of Faraway* 1987; *PrettyKill* 1987; *A Summer Story* 1987; *Just Ask for Diamond* 1988; *Melancholia* 1989; *St Patrick: the Irish Legend* 2000
Yoshida, Teruo *Twin Sisters of Kyoto* 1963; *Goke, Bodysnatcher from Hell* 1968
Yoshikawa, Mitsuko *I Was Born, but...* 1932; *The Brothers and Sisters of the Toda Family* 1941
Yost, Herbert (1880–1945) *Fast and Loose* 1930; *The Age of Innocence* 1934
Younane, Doris *Mortgage* 1989; *The Heartbreak Kid* 1993
Young, Aden (1972–) *Black Robe* 1991; *Sniper* 1992; *Cosi* 1996; *Hotel de Love* 1996; *River Street* 1996; *The War Bride* 2001; *The Crocodile Hunter: Collision Course* 2002
Young, Alan (1919–) *Margie* 1946; *Chicken Every Sunday* 1948; *Mr Belvedere Goes to College* 1949; *Androcles and the Lion* 1952; *Gentlemen Marry Brunettes* 1955; *tom thumb* 1958; *The Time Machine* 1960; *Baker's Hawk* 1976; *The Cat from Outer Space* 1978; *Duck Tales: the Movie – Treasure of the Lost Lamp* 1990
Young, Arthur (1898–1959) *The Root of All Evil* 1946; *The Lady with the Lamp* 1951; *John of the Fair* 1952; *An Inspector Calls* 1954; *Stranger from Venus* 1954
Young, Bill *Chopper* 2000; *Japanese Story* 2003
Young, Bruce A *aka* **Young, Bruce** *Trespass* 1992; *Blink* 1994; *Normal Life* 1995; *Jurassic Park III* 2001
Young, Burt (1940–) *Cinderella Liberty* 1973; *The Gambler* 1974; *Live a Little, Steal a Lot* 1974; *The Killer Elite* 1975; *Rocky* 1976; *The Choirboys* 1977; *Twilight's Last Gleaming* 1977; *Convoy* 1978; *Rocky II* 1979; *Blood Beach* 1981; *The California Dolls* 1981; *Amityville II: the Possession* 1982; *Lookin' to Get Out* 1982; *Rocky III* 1982; *Over the Brooklyn Bridge* 1983; *Once upon a Time in America* 1984; *The Pope of Greenwich Village* 1984; *Rocky IV* 1985; *Back to School* 1986; *Blood Red* 1988; *Beverly Hills Brats* 1989; *Last Exit to Brooklyn* 1989; *Wait until Spring, Bandini* 1989; *Backstreet Dreams* 1990; *Bright Angel* 1990; *Rocky V* 1990; *Excessive Force* 1993; *Before Women Had Wings* 1997; *Kicked in the Head* 1997; *Mickey Blue Eyes* 1999
Young, Carleton (1907–1971) *Reefer Madness* 1936; *Pride of the Bowery* 1941; *Thunderhead – Son of Flicka* 1945; *Smash Up – the Story of a Woman* 1947; *An American Guerrilla in the Philippines* 1950; *Hard, Fast and Beautiful* 1951; *20,000 Leagues under the Sea* 1954; *Sergeant Rutledge* 1960; *Armored Command* 1961
Young, Chris (1971–) *The Great Outdoors* 1988; *December* 1991; *Warlock: the Armageddon* 1993; *PCU* 1994
Young, Dan *Off the Dole* 1935; *Somewhere on Leave* 1942; *Demobbed* 1944; *It's a Grand Life* 1953
Young, Dey (1955–) *Rock 'n' Roll High School* 1979; *Back in the USSR* 1992; *No Place to Hide* 1992; *Pie in the Sky* 1995; *Tactical Assault* 1998
Young, Felicity *Cover Girl Killer* 1959; *The Gentle Trap* 1960
Young, Gig *aka* **Barr, Byron** (1913–1978) *The Gay Sisters* 1942; *Air Force* 1943; *Old Acquaintance* 1943; *Escape Me Never* 1947; *The Woman in White* 1948; *Tell It to the Judge* 1949; *Wake of the Red Witch* 1949; *Only the Valiant* 1950; *Come Fill the Cup* 1951; *Slaughter Trail* 1951; *Target Unknown* 1951; *Arena* 1953; *City That Never Sleeps* 1953; *The Girl Who Had Everything* 1953; *Torch Song* 1953; *The Desperate Hours* 1955; *Young at Heart* 1955; *Desk Set* 1957; *Teacher's Pet* 1958; *The Tunnel of Love* 1958; *Ask Any Girl* 1959; *The Story on Page One* 1959; *Kid Galahad* 1962; *That Touch of Mink* 1962; *Five Miles to Midnight* 1963; *For Love or Money* 1963; *A Ticklish Affair* 1963; *Strange Bedfellows* 1965; *The Shuttered Room* 1967; *They Shoot Horses, Don't They?* 1969; *Lovers and Other Strangers* 1970; *Bring Me the Head of Alfredo Garcia* 1974; *The Hindenburg* 1975; *The Killer Elite* 1975; *Sherlock Holmes in New York* 1976; *Game of Death* 1978

Young, Gladys (1905–1975) The Courtneys of Curzon Street 1947; The Lady with the Lamp 1951

Young, James The Thing from Another World 1951; My Son John 1952

Young, Joan (1903–1984) Easy Money 1947; Vice Versa 1947; The Small Voice 1948; Child's Play 1954; Suddenly, Last Summer 1959

Young, John (1916–1996) Hollywood High 1976; Black Jack 1979

Young, Karen (1958–) Handgun 1983; Almost You 1984; Birdy 1984; Maria's Lovers 1984; Nine ½ Weeks 1985; Heat 1987; Jaws the Revenge 1987; Criminal Law 1988; Torch Song Trilogy 1988; Night Game 1989; The Boy Who Cried Bitch 1991; Daylight 1996; Joe the King 1999; Mercy 2000

Young, Lee Thompson (1984–) Friday Night Lights 2004; Redemption 2004

Young, Loretta (1913–2000) Laugh, Clown, Laugh 1928; The Devil to Pay 1930; Beau Ideal 1931; Platinum Blonde 1931; The Hatchet Man 1932; Life Begins 1932; Taxi! 1932; The Devil's in Love 1933; Employees' Entrance 1933; Heroes for Sale 1933; Man's Castle 1933; Zoo in Budapest 1933; Bulldog Drummond Strikes Back 1934; Caravan 1934; The House of Rothschild 1934; The White Parade 1934; The Call of the Wild 1935; Clive of India 1935; The Crusades 1935; Ladies in Love 1936; Café Metropole 1937; Love Is News 1937; Wife, Doctor and Nurse 1937; Four Men and a Prayer 1938; Kentucky 1938; Suez 1938; Three Blind Mice 1938; Eternally Yours 1939; The Story of Alexander Graham Bell 1939; Wife, Husband and Friend 1939; The Doctor Takes a Wife 1940; The Men in Her Life 1941; Bedtime Story 1942; A Night to Remember 1942; China 1943; And Now Tomorrow 1944; Along Came Jones 1945; The Farmer's Daughter 1946; The Stranger 1946; The Bishop's Wife 1947; Rachel and the Stranger 1948; The Accused 1949; Come to the Stable 1949; Mother Is a Freshman 1949; Key to the City 1950; Cause for Alarm 1951; Half Angel 1951

Young, Nedrick aka **Young, Ned** (1914–1968) Gun Crazy 1949; Captain Scarlett 1953; Terror in a Texas Town 1958

Young, Noah (1887–1958) A Sailor-Made Man 1921; Safety Last 1923; For Heaven's Sake 1926; Feet First 1930

Young, Oliver The Killing Zone 1998; Small Time Obsession 2000

Young, Otis (1932–2001) The Last Detail 1973; Blood Beach 1981

Young, Paul (1944–) Another Time, Another Place 1983; The Girl in the Picture 1985

Young, Polly Ann (1908–1997) The Man from Utah 1934; Invisible Ghost 1941

Young, Raymond (1918–) Adam and Evelyne 1949; Death of an Angel 1951

Young, Ric The Last Emperor 1987; Dragon: the Bruce Lee Story 1993; Booty Call 1997; The Corruptor 1999; Chain of Command 2000; Kiss of the Dragon 2001; The Transporter 2002

Young, Richard Friday the 13th: a New Beginning 1985; An Innocent Man 1989

Young (1), Robert (1907–1998) The Sin of Madelon Claudet 1931; Hell Divers 1932; The Kid from Spain 1932; Strange Interlude 1932; The Wet Parade 1932; Today We Live 1933; Tugboat Annie 1933; The House of Rothschild 1934; Spitfire 1934; The Bride Comes Home 1935; Red Salute 1935; Remember Last Night? 1935; The Bride Walks Out 1936; It's Love Again 1936; Secret Agent 1936; Stowaway 1936; The Bride Wore Red 1937; The Emperor's Candlesticks 1937; I Met Him in Paris 1937; Navy Blue and Gold 1937; Josette 1938; Paradise for Three 1938; The Shining Hour 1938; Three Comrades 1938; The Toy Wife 1938; Honolulu 1939; Maisie 1939; Miracles for Sale 1939; Dr Kildare's Crisis 1940; Florian 1940; The Mortal Storm 1940; Northwest Passage 1940; HM Pulham Esq 1941; Lady Be Good 1941; The Trial of Mary Dugan 1941; Western Union 1941; Joe Smith, American 1942; Journey for Margaret 1942; Claudia 1943; Slightly Dangerous 1943; Sweet Rosie O'Grady 1943; The Canterville Ghost 1944; The Enchanted Cottage 1945; Those Endearing Young Charms 1945; Claudia and David 1946; Lady Luck 1946; The Searching Wind 1946; Crossfire 1947; They Won't Believe Me 1947; Relentless 1948; Sitting Pretty 1948; Adventure in Baltimore 1949; And Baby Makes Three 1949; Bride for Sale 1949; The Forsyte Saga 1949; Goodbye, My Fancy 1951; The Second Woman 1951; The Half-Breed 1952; Secret of the Incas 1954; A Conspiracy of Love 1987

Young, Roland (1887–1953) Madam Satan 1930; The Guardsman 1931; The Squaw Man 1931; One Hour with You 1932; This Is the Night 1932; Wedding Rehearsal 1932; Blind Adventure 1933; His Double Life 1933; David Copperfield 1935; Ruggles of Red Gap 1935; The Man Who Could Work Miracles 1936; One Rainy Afternoon 1936; King Solomon's Mines 1937; Topper 1937; Sailing Along 1938; The Young in Heart 1938; Topper Takes a Trip 1939; Irene 1940; No, No, Nanette 1940; The Philadelphia Story 1940; Star Dust 1940; The Flame of New Orleans 1941; Topper Returns 1941; Two-Faced Woman 1941; They All Kissed the Bride 1942; Standing Room Only 1944; And Then There Were None 1945; Bond Street 1948; You Gotta Stay Happy 1948; The Great Lover 1949; Let's Dance 1950

Young, Sean (1959–) Jane Austen in Manhattan 1980; Stripes 1981; Blade Runner 1982; Young Doctors in Love 1982; Dune 1984; Baby: Secret of the Lost Legend 1985; No Way Out 1986; Wall Street 1987; The Boost 1988; Cousins 1989; Wings of the Apache 1990; A Kiss before Dying 1991; Love Crimes 1991; Blue Ice 1992; Hold Me, Thrill Me, Kiss Me 1992; Once upon a Crime 1992; Ace Ventura: Pet Detective 1993; Even Cowgirls Get the Blues 1993; Fatal Instinct 1993; Forever 1993; Dr Jekyll and Ms Hyde 1995; Barbara Taylor Bradford's Everything to Gain 1996; The Proprietor 1996; Motel Blue 1997; Poor White Trash 2000; Sugar & Spice 2001

Young, Stephen (1931–) Patton 1970; Breaking Point 1976; Lifeguard 1976; Strange Justice 1999

Young, Tammany (1886–1936) Tugboat Annie 1933; The Mighty Barnum 1934; The Old-Fashioned Way 1934; The Glass Key 1935

Young, Tony (1938–2002) He Rides Tall 1964; Taggart 1964

Young, William Allen (1953–) Wisdom 1986; The Waterdance 1991; Stalking Laura 1993; Fear X 2002

Youngman, Henny (1906–1998) The Gore-Gore Girls 1972; National Lampoon's Movie Madness 1981

Youngs, Gail (1953–) Hockey Night 1984; The Stone Boy 1984; Belizaire the Cajun 1985

Youngs, Jim (1956–) The Wanderers 1979; Hot Shot 1986; Nobody's Fool 1986; You Talkin' to Me? 1987

Yu Ji-tae (1976–) Into the Mirror 2003; Oldboy 2003

Yu Rong Guang Iron Monkey 1993; The Enforcer 1995

Yue, Shawn (1981–) Infernal Affairs 2002; Infernal Affairs II 2003; Infernal Affairs 3 2003

Yuen, Anita aka **Yuen Wing-Yee, Anita** (1971–) I've Got You, Babe 1994; Thunderbolt 1995; And Now You're Dead 1998

Yuen Biao (1957–) The Prodigal Son 1983; Project A 1983; Zu Warriors 1983; Wheels on Meals 1984; Once upon a Time in China 1991; A Man Called Hero 1999

Yuen Wah The Master 1989; Kung Fu Hustle 2004

Yui, Masayuki (1947–) Ran 1985; To End All Wars 2001

Yulin, Harris (1937–) End of the Road 1970; Doc 1971; The Midnight Man 1974; Watched 1974; Night Moves 1975; Victory at Entebbe 1976; Steel 1980; Good to Go 1986; The Believers 1987; Candy Mountain 1987; Fatal Beauty 1987; Ghostbusters II 1989; The Heart of Justice 1992; Clear and Present Danger 1994; Loch Ness 1994; Stuart Saves His Family 1995; Hostile Waters 1996; Multiplicity 1996; Bean 1997; American Outlaws 2001; Training Day 2001

Yune, Rick (1971–) Snow Falling on Cedars 1999; The Fast and the Furious 2001; Die Another Day 2002

Yung, Victor Sen (1915–1980) Charlie Chan at Treasure Island 1939; Charlie Chan in Reno 1939; The Letter 1940; Charlie Chan in Rio 1941; Across the Pacific 1942; China 1943; Dangerous Money 1946; The Trap 1947; Forbidden 1953; She Demons 1958

Yurka, Blanche (1887–1974) A Tale of Two Cities 1935; Lady for a Night 1942; Cry of the Werewolf 1944; The Southerner 1945; Sons of the Musketeers 1951; Taxi 1953; Thunder in the Sun 1959

Yuro, Robert (1932–) Satan in High Heels 1962; The Ride to Hangman's Tree 1967

Z

Z'Dar, Robert (1950–) The Night Stalker 1985; Maniac Cop 1988; Tango & Cash 1989; Maniac Cop 2 1990; Beastmaster 2: through the Portal of Time 1991; Upworld 1992

Zabka, William (1965–) The Karate Kid 1984; Just One of the Guys 1985; A Tiger's Tale 1987; Unlawful Passage 1994; High Voltage 1998

Zabou aka **Breitman, Zabou** (1959–) Dandin 1988; C'est la Vie 1990; La Crise 1992; Almost Peaceful 2002

Zabriskie, Grace (1938–) The Private Eyes 1980; An Officer and a Gentleman 1982; The Burning Bed 1984; Leonard, Part 6 1987; The Boost 1988; Drugstore Cowboy 1989; Child's Play 2 1990; Wild at Heart 1990; Ambition 1991; My Own Private Idaho 1991; Chain of Desire 1992; FernGully: the Last Rainforest 1992; Even Cowgirls Get the Blues 1993; The Passion of Darkly Noon 1995; A Family Thing 1996; Dead Men Can't Dance 1997; Devil's Child 1997; They Crawl 2001; No Good Deed 2002; The Grudge 2004

Zadok, Arnon (1949–) Beyond the Walls 1984; Witness in the War Zone 1986; Torn Apart 1990

Zadora, Pia (1954–) Santa Claus Conquers the Martians 1964; Butterfly 1982; The Lonely Lady 1983; Hairspray 1988

Zagarino, Frank Operation Delta Force 1996; The Stray 1999

Zahn, Steve (1968–) Reality Bites 1994; Race the Sun 1996; subUrbia 1996; That Thing You Do! 1996; Subway Stories: Tales from the Underground 1997; Forces of Nature 1998; Safe Men 1998; You've Got Mail 1998; Happy, Texas 1999; Stuart Little 1999; Hamlet 2000; Dr Dolittle 2 2001; Evil Woman 2001; Riding in Cars with Boys 2001; Roadkill 2001; National Security 2002; Stuart Little 2 2002; Daddy Day Care 2003; Shattered Glass 2003; Sahara 2004

Zal, Roxana (1969–) Table for Five 1983; Testament 1983; Under the Boardwalk 1988; Everybody's Baby: the Rescue of Jessica McClure 1989; Broken Vessels 1998; Primal Force 1999

Zamansky, Vladimir aka **Zamansky, V** (1928–) Katok i Skrypka 1961; Trial on the Road 1971; 100 Days before the Command 1990

Zamora, Del Repo Man 1984; Straight to Hell 1987

Zane, Billy (1966–) Brotherhood of Justice 1986; Critters 1986; Dead Calm 1988; Memphis Belle 1990; Femme Fatale 1991; Lake Consequence 1992; Orlando 1992; Sniper 1992; Flashfire 1993; Poetic Justice 1993; Posse 1993; The Silence of the Hams 1993; Only You 1994; Reflections on a Crime 1994; The Set Up 1995; Tales from the Crypt: Demon Knight 1995; Danger Zone 1996; Head above Water 1996; The Phantom 1996; This World, Then the Fireworks 1996; Titanic 1997; I Woke Up Early the Day I Died 1998; Pocahontas II: Journey to a New World 1998; Susan's Plan 1998; The Believer 2001

Zane, Lisa (1967–) Pucker Up and Bark like a Dog 1989; Bad Influence 1990; Femme Fatale 1991; Freddy's Dead: the Final Nightmare 1991; Monkeybone 2000

Zann, Lenore Visiting Hours 1982; Def-Con 4 1984; Return 1985; Cold Sweat 1993

Zapasiewicz, Zbigniew (1934–) Camouflage 1977; Blind Chance 1987

Zappa, Frank (1940–1993) Head 1968; 200 Motels 1971

Zappa, Moon (1967–) Pterodactyl Woman from Beverly Hills 1996; The Brutal Truth 1999

Zappa, William (1948–) Crush 1992; Bootmen 2000

Zardi, Dominique (1930–) Les Biches 1968; Juste avant la Nuit 1971; The Trap 1975

Zaremba, John (1908–1986) Earth vs the Flying Saucers 1956; 20 Million Miles to Earth 1957

Zbruev, Aleksandr (1938–) Lonely Woman Seeks Lifetime Companion 1987; The Inner Circle 1991

Zech, Rosel (1942–) Veronika Voss 1982; Salmonberries 1991

Zegers, Kevin (1984–) Air Bud 1997; Bram Stoker's Shadowbuilder 1997; Air Bud: Golden Receiver 1998; Nico the Unicorn 1998; Treasure Island 1998; Four Days 1999; Komodo 1999; Bitter Suite 2000; Wrong Turn 2003; Dawn of the Dead 2004

Zellweger, Renee aka **Zellweger, Renée** (1969–) Love and a .45 1994; Reality Bites 1994; Shake, Rattle and Rock 1994; Texas Chainsaw Massacre: the Next Generation 1994; Empire Records 1995; The Low Life 1995; Jerry Maguire 1996; The Whole Wide World 1996; Liar 1997; A Price above Rubies 1997; One True Thing 1998; The Bachelor 1999; Me, Myself & Irene 2000; Nurse Betty 2000; Bridget Jones's Diary 2001; Chicago 2002; White Oleander 2002; Cold Mountain 2003; Down with Love 2003; Bridget Jones: the Edge of Reason 2004; Shark Tale 2004; Cinderella Man 2005

Zelniker, Michael Bird 1988; Naked Lunch 1991

Zem, Roschdy (1965–) Don't Forget You're Going to Die 1995; Clubbed to Death 1996; Monsieur N 2003

Zenor, Suzanne Get to Know Your Rabbit 1972; The Baby 1973

Zeplichal, Vitus I Only Want You to Love Me 1976; The Third Generation 1979

Zerbe, Anthony (1936–) The Liberation of LB Jones 1970; The Molly Maguires 1970; They Call Me Mister Tibbs! 1970; The Omega Man 1971; The Strange Vengeance of Rosalie 1972; The Laughing Policeman 1973; Papillon 1973; Rooster Cogburn 1975; Who'll Stop the Rain? 1978; The Dead Zone 1983; Hell Camp 1986; Licence to Kill 1989; Listen to Me 1989; See No Evil, Hear No Evil 1989; Star Trek: Insurrection 1998

Zeta-Jones, Catherine (1969–) Christopher Columbus: the Discovery 1992; Splitting Heirs 1993; Blue Juice 1995; The Phantom 1996; The Mask of Zorro 1998; Entrapment 1999; The Haunting 1999; High Fidelity 2000; Traffic 2000; America's Sweethearts 2001; Chicago 2002; Intolerable Cruelty 2003; Sinbad: Legend of the Seven Seas 2003; Ocean's Twelve 2004; The Terminal 2004

Zetterling, Mai (1925–1994) Torment 1944; Frieda 1947; Night Is My Future 1948; Portrait from Life 1948; Quartet 1948; The Bad Lord Byron 1949; The Lost People 1949; The Romantic Age 1949; Desperate Moment 1953; Dance Little Lady 1954; Knock on Wood 1954; A Prize of Gold 1955; Seven Waves Away 1957; The Truth about Women 1958; Faces in the Dark 1960; Offbeat 1960; Piccadilly Third Stop 1960; Only Two Can Play 1961; The Main Attraction 1962; The Man Who Finally Died 1962; The Bay of Saint Michel 1963; The Witches 1989; Hidden Agenda 1990

Zhang Fengyi (1956–) Farewell My Concubine 1993; The Emperor and the Assassin 1999

Zhang Guozhu The Butterfly Murders 1979; A Brighter Summer Day 1991

Zhang Ziyi (1980–) The Road Home 1999; Crouching Tiger, Hidden Dragon 2000; Rush Hour 2 2001; Hero 2002; House of Flying Daggers 2004; 2046 2004

Zhao Dan (1915–1980) Street Angel 1937; Crows and Sparrows 1949

Zhao Tao Platform 2000; Unknown Pleasures 2002

Zhao Wei aka **Zhao, Vicki** aka **Zhao Wei, Vicky** (1976–) Shaolin Soccer 2001; Chinese Odyssey 2002 2002; So Close 2002

Zhao Wei Wei Unknown Pleasures 2002; All Tomorrow's Parties 2003

Zharov, Mikhail (1900–1981) Ivan the Terrible, Part I 1944; Ivan the Terrible, Part II 1946

Zhou Xun Suzhou River 2000; Beijing Bicycle 2001; Balzac and the Little Chinese Seamstress 2002

Ziemann, Sonja (1925–) Made in Heaven 1952; A Matter of WHO 1961; The Secret Ways 1961

Zima, Madeline (1985–) The Hand That Rocks the Cradle 1992; Mr Nanny 1992; A Cinderella Story 2004

Zima, Vanessa (1986–) The Baby-Sitter's Club 1995; Wicked 1998; The Brainiacs.com 2000

Zima, Yvonne (1989–) The Long Kiss Goodnight 1996; Storm Catcher 1999; A Father's Choice 2000

Zimbalist Jr, Efrem (1918–) House of Strangers 1949; Band of Angels 1957; Bombers B-52 1957; The Deep Six 1958; Girl on the Run 1958; Home before Dark 1958; Too Much, Too Soon 1958; Violent Road 1958; The Crowded Sky 1960; By Love Possessed 1961; A Fever in the Blood 1961; The Chapman Report 1962; Harlow 1965; The Reward 1965; Wait until Dark 1967; Airport 1975 1974; Hot Shots! 1991

Zimbalist, Stephanie (1956–) The Magic of Lassie 1978; The Awakening 1980; Caroline? 1990; Silhouette 1994; The Prophet's Game 1999

Zimmerman, Matt Thunderbirds Are Go! 1966; Thunderbird 6 1968

Zingg, Delphine *Annabelle Partagée* 1990; *L'Afrance* 2001
Zinny, Victoria *Viridiana* 1961; *Death Train* 1989
Zinta, Preity (1975–) *Armaan* 2003; *Kal Ho Naa Ho* 2003; *Koi... Mil Gaya* 2003; *Lakshya* 2004; *Veer-Zaara* 2004
Zirner, August (1959–) *Now or Never* 1986; *Voyager* 1991; *The Promise* 1994; *Mostly Martha* 2001; *Taking Sides* 2001
Zischler, Hanns (1947–) *Kings of the Road* 1976; *Dr M* 1989; *Francesco* 1989; *The Cement Garden* 1992; *Taking Sides* 2001; *Walk on Water* 2004
Zivojinovic, Bata *aka* **Zivojinovic, Velimir Bata** (1933–) *Three* 1965; *I Even Met Happy Gypsies* 1967; *Pretty Village Pretty Flame* 1996
Zmed, Adrian (1954–) *Grease 2* 1982; *Bachelor Party* 1984
Znaimer, Moses *Atlantic City, USA* 1980; *Best Revenge* 1983
Zolnay, Pal (1928–1995) *Diary for My Children* 1982; *Diary for My Loves* 1987
Zolotin, Adam *Jack* 1996; *Leave It to Beaver* 1997
Zorich, Louis (1924–) *For Pete's Sake* 1974; *Newman's Law* 1974; *Sunday in the Country* 1975; *Death of a Salesman* 1985
Zorina, Vera *aka* **Zorina** (1917–2003) *The Goldwyn Follies* 1938; *On Your Toes* 1939; *I Was an Adventuress* 1940; *Louisiana Purchase* 1941; *Star Spangled Rhythm* 1942; *Follow the Boys* 1944; *Lover Come Back* 1946
Zouzou *Love in the Afternoon* 1972; *SPYS* 1974; *Sky Riders* 1976
Zucco, George (1886–1960) *The Bride Wore Red* 1937; *London by Night* 1937; *Arsene Lupin Returns* 1938; *Three Comrades* 1938; *The Adventures of Sherlock Holmes* 1939; *The Cat and the Canary* 1939; *Arise, My Love* 1940; *The Mummy's Hand* 1940; *New Moon* 1940; *The Black Swan* 1942; *The Mummy's Tomb* 1942; *My Favorite Blonde* 1942; *Sherlock Holmes in Washington* 1943; *The Mummy's Ghost* 1944; *Voodoo Man* 1944; *Fog Island* 1945; *Hold That Blonde* 1945; *Sudan* 1945; *Desire Me* 1947; *Lured* 1947; *Moss Rose* 1947; *Scared to Death* 1947; *Where There's Life* 1947; *The Pirate* 1948; *Tarzan and the Mermaids* 1948
Zuniga, Daphne (1963–) *The Initiation* 1984; *The Sure Thing* 1985; *Vision Quest* 1985; *Spaceballs* 1987; *Last Rites* 1988; *A Cut Above* 1989; *The Fly II* 1989; *Mad at the Moon* 1992; *800 Leagues down the Amazon* 1993; *Charlie's Ghost Story* 1994
Zuniga, José *Fresh* 1994; *Smoke* 1995; *Hurricane Streets* 1997; *Gun Shy* 2000; *The Opportunists* 2000; *Snow White* 2001; *The Hunted* 2002
Zushi, Yoshitaka (1955–) *Dodes'ka-Den* 1970; *Akira Kurosawa's Dreams* 1990
Zwerling, Darrell *Chinatown* 1974; *Doc Savage: the Man of Bronze* 1975; *The Ultimate Warrior* 1975

Alternative titles

A Chacun Son Enfer To Each His Own Hell
A la Folie Six Days, Six Nights
A la Folie... Pas du Tout He Loves Me... He Loves Me Not
A La Mode Fausto
A la Verticale de l'Eté At the Height of Summer
A Mezzanotte Va la Ronda del Piacere Immortal Bachelor
A Nos Amours To Our Loves
A Nous Deux An Adventure for Two
Aakaler Sandhane In Search of Famine
Abandon Ship! Seven Waves Away
Abbott and Costello Lost in Alaska Lost in Alaska
The ABC Murders The Alphabet Murders
Abducted: A Father's Love Fugitive from Justice
Abe Lincoln in Illinois Spirit of the People
Abendland Abendland
The Aberdeen Experiment Scared to Death
Abgeschminkt Making Up
Able Seaman Brown Sailor of the King
Above the Law Nico
Abraxas, Guardian of the Universe Abraxas
El Abrazo Partido Lost Embrace
Abre Los Ojos Open Your Eyes
Abril Despedaçado Behind the Sun
Abschied – Brecht's Letzer Sommer The Farewell – Brecht's Last Summer
Absinthe Madame X
Absinthe Man on Fire
Abwärts Out of Order
Abwege Crisis
The Accompanist L'Accompagnatrice
The Accursed The Traitor
Accused The Mark of the Hawk
The Ace The Great Santini
Acque di Primavera Torrents of Spring
Across the Brooklyn Bridge Over the Brooklyn Bridge
Across the Heart Aar Paar
Actors Blood and Woman of Sin Actors and Sin
Actrius Actresses
Ad ogni Costo Grand Slam
Adalen Riots Adalen 31
Adam and Evalyn Adam and Evelyne
Adamson of Africa Killers of Kilimanjaro
Addict Born to Win
Addio Kira! We the Living
Adieu, Plancher des Vaches! Farewell, Home Sweet Home
Adios Caballero One after the Other
Adios Ohio He's My Girl
Admissions How I Got Into College
Adorables Mentiras Adorable Lies
The Adulteress Thérèse Raquin
Advance to Ground Zero Nightbreaker
Adventure for Two The Demi-Paradise
The Adventurer The Rover
Adventures in Babysitting A Night on the Town
Adventures in Music: Toot, Whistle, Plunk and Boom Toot, Whistle, Plunk and Boom
The Adventures of a Gnome Named Gnorm Upworld
Adventures of a Young Man Hemingway's Adventures of a Young Man
The Adventures of Baron Munchhausen Baron Münchhausen
The Adventures of Don Quixote Don Quixote
The Adventures of Heidi Courage Mountain
The Adventures of Hercules Hercules II
The Adventures of Mike S Blueberry Blueberry
The Adventures of Pico and Columbus The Magic Voyage
The Adventures of Pluto Nash Pluto Nash
The Adventures of Quentin Durward Quentin Durward
The Adventures of Robin Hood Robin Hood
Adventures of Rugby Tom Brown's Schooldays
The Adventures of Sadie Our Girl Friday
The Adventures of St Francis Francis, God's Jester
The Adventures of the Flying Pickle The Pickle
The Adventures of Tintin: Lake of the Sharks Tintin and the Lake of Sharks
The Adventures of Young Brave Waking Up Horton
The Adventuress I See a Dark Stranger
The Advocate The Hour of the Pig
Aelita: Queen of Mars Aelita
Aelita: the Revolt of the Robots Aelita
The Affair at the Villa Florita The Battle of the Villa Fiorita
An Affair of Love Une Liaison Pornographique
The Affair of Villa Florita The Battle of the Villa Fiorita
L'Affaire Wallraff The Man Inside
Affairs in Versailles Royal Affairs in Versailles
Affairs of Adelaide Britannia Mews
The Affairs of Sally The Fuller Brush Girl
As a Man L'Afrance
Africa Story The Green Horizon
Cowboy in Africa Africa – Texas Style!
African Fury Cry, the Beloved Country
The African Story Hatari!
After Alice Eye of the Killer
After Jenny Died Revenge
After Love Après l'Amour
After Midnight Captain Carey, USA
After the Hole The Hole
After the Silence Shattering the Silence
Aftershock Marshal Law
Agaguk Shadow of the Wolf
Agantuk The Stranger
Agatha Christie's Endless Night Endless Night
Agatha Christie's Thirteen at Dinner Thirteen at Dinner
Age of Infidelity Death of a Cyclist
Agent Double 007 Operation Kid Brother
Agent 8¾ Hot Enough for June
Agi Murad il Diavolo Bianco The White Warrior
L'Aigle à Deux Têtes The Eagle Has Two Heads
Aimez-Moi Ce Soir! Love Me Tonight
Aiqing Wansui Vive L'Amour
Air Speed Airspeed
Airport '80: the Concorde Airport '79: the Concorde
Airport: the Concorde Airport '79: the Concorde
Akahige Red Beard
Akaler Sandhaney In Search of Famine
An Alan Smithee Film: Burn, Hollywood, Burn Burn Hollywood Burn
L'Albero degli Zoccoli The Tree of Wooden Clogs
L'Albero delle pere Shooting the Moon
Albino Death in the Sun
The Aldrich Ames Story – The Last Spy Aldrich Ames: Traitor Within
Alexandre Dumas' The Count of Monte Cristo The Count of Monte Cristo
Alexis Zorbas Zorba the Greek
Alferd Packer: the Musical Cannibal! the Musical
Alfred Hitchcock's Aventure Malgache Aventure Malgache
The Algonquin Silent Trigger
Algonquin Goodbye Silent Trigger
Ali: Fear Eats the Soul Fear Eats the Soul
Alias Bulldog Drummond Bulldog Jack
Alice in den Städten Alice in the Cities
Alien Orders Malaya
Alien Prey Prey
Alien Thunder Dan Candy's Law
Alien vs Predator AVP: Alien vs Predator
Alien Warning Without Warning
Alistair MacLean's Death Train Death Train
Alistair MacLean's Night Watch Night Watch
Alistair MacLean's Puppet on a Chain Puppet on a Chain
Alistair MacLean's River of Death River of Death
All at Sea Barnacle Bill
All Is Well Tout Va Bien
All Mine to Give The Day They Gave Babies Away
All Monsters Attack Godzilla's Revenge
All That Money Can Buy Daniel and the Devil
All the Children Are In Roadkill
...All the Marbles The California Dolls
All the Mornings of the World Tous les Matins du Monde
All the Way The Joker Is Wild
All Things Bright and Beautiful It Shouldn't Happen to a Vet
All This and Glamour Too Vogues of 1938
All This and Money Too Love Is a Ball
All Tied Up Jill Rips
Allegheny Uprising The First Rebel
Alley of Nightmares She Freak
All's Fair Weekend Warriors All's Fair
Almost Human Shock Waves
Almost Nothing Presque Rien
Alone Solas
Along Came Sally Aunt Sally
Alsino y el Cóndor Alsino and the Condor
Amado Beloved/Friend
L'Amante Milena
L'Amante di Paride The Loves of Three Queens
L'Amante Perduto The Lost Lover
Amantes Lovers
Los Amantes del Circolo Polar The Lovers of the Arctic Circle
Amanti A Place for Lovers
The Lovers Les Amants
Les Amants Criminels Criminal Lovers
The Amazing Dr G Dr Goldfoot and the Girl Bombs
The Amazing Mr Beecham The Chiltern Hundreds
The Amazing Mr Forrest The Gang's All Here
Amazing Adventure The Amazing Quest of Ernest Bliss
The Amazing Spider-Man Spider-Man
Los Ambiciosos La Fièvre Monte à el Pao
American Cannibale Snuff
An American Murder Season of Fear
American Pie 3 American Pie: the Wedding
American Virgin Live Virgin
The American Way Riders of the Storm
American Wedding American Pie: the Wedding
Der Amerikanische Soldat The American Soldier
L'Ami de Mon Amie My Girlfriend's Boyfriend
L'Ami Retrouvé Reunion
Amici per la Pelle Friends for Life
Amigo Beloved/Friend
Amityville 3-D Amityville III: the Demon
Amok 71 Fragments of a Chronology of Chance
Amok Schizo
Amor Indio Tizoc
The Amorous Adventures of Uncle Benjamin Uncle Benjamin
The Amorous General Waltz of the Toreadors
The Amorous Mr Prawn The Amorous Prawn
L'Amour de Banquier The Maid
Un Amour de Pluie Loving in the Rain
Un Amour de Swann Swann in Love
L'Amour en Embuscade Love in Ambush
L'Amour en Fuite Love on the Run
L'Amour l'Apres-Midi Love in the Afternoon
Les Amours de Toni Toni
Anastasia – die Letzte Zarentochter Is Anna Anderson Anastasia?
Anatahan The Saga of Anatahan
The Anatolian Smile America, America
Anatomie Anatomy
Anatomie de l'Enfer Anatomy of Hell
Anatomy of a Syndicate The Big Operator
Anchor Man Anchorman: the Legend of Ron Burgundy
And Nothing but the Truth Giro City
And Quiet Rolls the Day And Quiet Rolls the Dawn
And So They Were Married Johnny Doesn't Live Here Anymore
And Then There Were None Ten Little Indians
And Your Mother, Too Y Tu Mamá También
An Andalusian Dog Un Chien Andalou
Andrews' Raiders The Great Locomotive Chase
Andy Warhol's Bad Bad
Andy Warhol's Dracula Blood for Dracula
Andy Warhol's Flesh Flesh
Andy Warhol's Frankenstein Flesh for Frankenstein
Andy Warhol's Trash Trash
Andy Warhol's Women in Revolt Women in Revolt
Angel Cast a Dark Shadow
El Angel de la Muerte Snuff
Angel Farm House of Angels
Angel Farm 2 House of Angels II: The Second Summer
Angel of Vengeance Ms 45
Angel on the Right Shoulder Angel on the Right
Angel Street Gaslight
Los Angeles without a Map LA without a Map
Angels Angels in the Outfield
Angels and Pirates Angels in the Outfield
Angels of the Streets Les Anges du Péché
Les Anges Gardiens Guardian Angels
L'Anglaise et le Duc The Lady & the Duke
Die Angst Fear
Die Angst des Tormanns beim Elfmeter The Goalkeeper's Fear of the Penalty Kick
Angst Essen Seele Auf Fear Eats the Soul
Angst vor der Angst Fear of Fear
Angustia Anguish
Aniki, Mon Frère Brother
Animas Trujano The Important Man
Anne Boleyn Anna Boleyn
Anne of Windy Willows Anne of Windy Poplars
L'Année Dernière à Marienbad Last Year at Marienbad
Les Années du Mur The Promise
Les Années Lumières Light Years Away
Annibale Hannibal
Annie II Annie: a Royal Adventure
Ansiktet The Magician
Antefatto Bay of Blood
The Anti-Extortion Woman Minbo – or the Gentle Art of Japanese Extortion
Antonia Antonia's Line
The Anxious Years Dark Journey
Any Special Way Business Is Business
Anyone for Venice? The Honey Pot
Apocalypse Now Redux Apocalypse Now
The Appaloosa Southwest to Sonora
L'Appât The Bait
The Applegates Meet the Applegates
Appointment with a Shadow The Midnight Story
Apprenticeship of a Mahatma The Making of the Mahatma
L'Approche Finale Final Approach
April Blossoms Blossom Time
April Captains Captains of April
April Romance Blossom Time
Aquarius Stage Fright – Aquarius
Aqui na Terra Here on Earth
The Arab The Barbarian
Arabian Night Arabian Knight
Aranyer Din Ratri Days and Nights in the Forest
L'Arbre de Noël The Christmas Tree
Archy and Mehitabel Shinbone Alley
La Ardilla Roja The Red Squirrel
Are These Our Children? The Age of Consent
Are We All Murderers? Nous Sommes Tous des Assassins
L'Argent de poche Small Change
The Arm The Big Town
Armageddon Armagueđon
The Armour of God II Operation Condor: the Armour of God II
Armoured Command Armored Command
Arms and the Woman Mr Winkle Goes to War
The Army in the Shadows L'Armée des Ombres
Army of Shadows L'Armée des Ombres
Arouse and Beware The Man from Dakota
Arrivederci, Baby! Drop Dead Darling
Arthur Conan Doyle's Sign of Four The Sign of Four
Arven The Inheritance
L'Ascenseur pour l'Échafaud Lift to the Scaffold
Ascent to Heaven Mexican Bus Ride
Ashoka the Great Asoka
The Assassin Venetian Bird
The Assassin Point of No Return
The Assassin The Emperor and the Assassin
Assassins The Emperor and the Assassin
Assault on Paradise Maniac
L'Assedio Besieged
Assignment: Istanbul The Castle of Fu Manchu
Assignment: Kill Castro Cuba Crossing
Assignment Redhead Undercover Girl
Asterix and Obelix vs Caesar Asterix and Obelix Take On Caesar
Asterix and the Stone's Blow Asterix and the Big Fight
Astérix chez les Bretons Asterix in Britain
Astérix et la Surprise de César Asterix vs Caesar
Astérix et Obéix contre César Asterix and Obelix Take On Caesar
Asterix le Gaulois Asterix the Gaul
The Astral Factor Invisible Strangler
Asylum of Horror The Living Dead
At Dawn We Die Tomorrow We Live
At First Sight Entre Nous
At Sword's Point Sons of the Musketeers
Atame Tie Me Up! Tie Me Down!
Atlantis Siren of Atlantis
Atoll K Utopia
Atomic Man Timeslip
The Atomic Man Timeslip
The Atomic Monster Man Made Monster
Atomic Rocketship Flash Gordon
The Atonement of Gösta Berling Gösta Berlings Saga
Attack All Monsters Godzilla's Revenge
Attack from Mars Midnight Movie Massacre
Attack of the Giant Crabs Attack of the Crab Monsters
Attack of the Mushroom People Matango
Au Coeur du Mensonge The Colour of Lies
Au Loin s'en Vont les Nuages Drifting Clouds
Au Travers des Oliviers Through the Olive Trees
L'Auberge Espagnole Pot Luck
Auch Zwerge Haben Klein Angefangen Even Dwarfs Started Small
Aufzeichnungen zu Kleidern und Städten Notebook on Cities and Clothes
Auntie Danielle Tatie Danielle
Aus dem Leben der Marionetten From the Life of the Marionettes
Une Aussi Longue Absence The Long Absence
Austerlitz The Battle of Austerlitz
Die Austernprinzessin The Oyster Princess
Austria 1700 Mark of the Devil
Autofocus Auto Focus
Un Autre Homme, Une Autre Chance Another Man, Another Chance
The Autumn of the Kohayagawa Family The End of Summer

Aux Yeux du Monde Autobus
L'Avare Dandin
Ave Maria Twilight Avengers
The Avenger Texas Adios
The Avengers The Day Will Dawn
Avenging Angels Messenger of Death
Les Aventures Extraordinaires de Cervantes Cervantes
L'Aveu The Confession
Les Aveux les plus doux Sweet Torture
L'Avventuriero The Rover

B

Bab el Hadid Cairo Station
Babettes Gaestebud Babette's Feast
The Baby I Don't Want to Be Born
Baby Bump A Sinful Life
The Baby Carriage The Pram
The Baby Vanishes Broadway Limited
Le Baccanti The Bacchantes
Bach et Bottine Bach and Broccoli
Bachelor Bait Adventure in Baltimore
Bachelor Girl Apartment Any Wednesday
Bachelor Knight The Bachelor and the Bobby-Soxer
Back Streets Back Street
Back to Back: American Yakuza 2 American Yakuza 2: Back to Back
Back to Gaya Boo, Zino and the Snurks
Backlash of the Hunter The Rockford Files
Backstage Limelight
Backtrack Catchfire
Backwoods Massacre Midnight
Bacon Bits Slaughterhouse
Bad Blood The Night Is Young
Bad Boy Dawg
Bad Day on the Block Under Pressure
The Bad One Sorority Girl
La Baie des Anges Bay of the Angels
Baiju the Poet Baiju Bawra
The Bailiff Sansho the Bailiff
Baisers Volés Stolen Kisses
The Baker of Monceau The Boulangère de Monceau
The Ballad of Joe Hill Joe Hill
Ballad of the Soldier Ballad of a Soldier
Le Ballon Rouge Red Balloon
Balthazar Au Hasard, Balthazar
Balzac et la Petite Tailleuse Chinoise Balzac and the Little Chinese Seamstress
I Bambini ci Guardano The Children Are Watching Us
Bamboo Dolls House The Big Doll House
The Banana Monster Schlock
The Bananas Boat What Changed Charley Farthing?
Un Banco en el Parque A Bench in the Park
Band of Gold How to Save a Marriage and Ruin Your Life
Banditi a Orgosolo Bandits of Orgosolo
Bang Bang! Our Man in Marrakesh
Bang, Bang, Bang! Marrakesh Our Man in Marrakesh
Bang! Bang! You're Dead! Our Man in Marrakesh
The Bank Breakers Kaleidoscope
The Bank Detective The Bank Dick
Banner in the Sky Third Man on the Mountain
Barbara Taylor Bradford's Her Own Rules Her Own Rules
Barbara Taylor Bradford's Secret Affair A Secret Affair
The Barber Movie The Man Who Wasn't There
Barber Shop Barbershop
Bare Breasted Countess The Female Vampire
Barnabo delle Montagne Barnabo of the Mountains
Barney Who Says I Can't Ride a Rainbow?
Barnvagnen The Pram
Baron Vampire Baron Blood
Les Bas-Fonds The Lower Depths
The Bat Masterson Story The Gunfight at Dodge City
La Bataille The Battle
La Bataille de San Sebastian Guns for San Sebastian
Batalla en el Cielo Battle in Heaven
Le Battement d'Ailes du Papillon The Beating of the Butterfly's Wings
The Battle at Elderbush The Battle of Elderbush
Battle Creek The Big Brawl
Battle Creek Brawl The Big Brawl
The Battle for Anzio Anzio
Battle Hell Yangtse Incident
Battle of Powder River Tomahawk
Battle of the Astros Invasion of the Astro-Monster
Battle of the Giants One Million BC
Battle of the Valiant Brennus – Enemy of Rome
The Battle on the River Neretva The Battle of Neretva
Battle Rage Missing in Action
Battlefront Attack! Attack!
Battles without Honour and Humanity The Yakuza Papers
The Battling Bellhop Kid Galahad
Battling Hooper Something to Sing About
Baywatch: Forbidden Paradise Baywatch the Movie: Forbidden Paradise
Be Prepared Troop Beverly Hills
The Beachcomber Vessel of Wrath
Bearboy Grizzly Falls
The Beast in Heat La Bête
The Beast of Babylon Against the Son of Hercules Hero of Babylon
The Beast of Morocco The Hand of Night
The Beast The Beast of War
Beastly Christmas The Naked Jungle
The Beasts of Marseilles Seven Thunders
The Beate Klarsfeld Story Nazi Hunter: the Beate Klarsfeld Story
A Beating Heart Your Beating Heart
Beatsville The Rebel Set
Beaumarchais Beaumarchais l'Insolent
Beaumarchais: the Scoundrel Beaumarchais l'Insolent
Beautiful but Deadly The Don Is Dead
The Beautiful Game The Match
The Beautiful Stranger Beautiful Stranger
Beautiful Women and the Hydrogen Man The H-Man
Beauty and the Devil La Beauté du Diable
Beby Inauguré Les Affaires Publiques
The Bed Secrets d'Alcove
Beethoven Abel Gance's Beethoven
Beethoven's Great Love Abel Gance's Beethoven
Before the Fact – Ecology of a Crime Bay of Blood
The Beginners The First Time
The Beginners Three The First Time
Behemoth, the Sea Monster The Giant Behemoth
Behind the Cellar Door Revenge
Behind the Iron Curtain The Iron Curtain
Behind the Iron Mask The Fifth Musketeer
Behold We Live If I Were Free
La Bella Mugnaia The Miller's Wife
Bells Murder by Phone
The Beloved Sin
Beloved Milena Milena
La Belva col mitra Mad Dog Murderer
Beneath Loch Ness The Evil beneath Loch Ness
Bengal Rifles Bengal Brigade
Berg-Ejvind och Hans Hustru The Outlaw and His Wife
Berlin, Appointment for the Spies Spy in Your Eye
Berlin Blue Midnight Cop
Berlino Appuntamento per le Spie Spy in Your Eye
Berry Gordy's The Last Dragon The Last Dragon
Best Shot Hoosiers
La Bestia de la Montana The Beast of Hollow Mountain
The Beast La Bête
Betty Fisher et Autres Histoires Betty Fisher and Other Stories
Between Two Worlds Destiny
Beverly Hills Nightmare Bone
Beware My Brethren The Fiend
Beware of Children No Kidding
Beware the Holy Whore Beware of a Holy Whore
Beyond Suspicion Auggie Rose
Beyond the Door III Death Train
Beyond the Fog Tower of Evil
Beyond the Law Beyond the Walls
Beyond the Law Fixing the Shadow
Beyond the Limit The Honorary Consul
Beyond the Mountains The Desperate Ones
Beyond the Wall Destiny
The Bicycle Thief Bicycle Thieves
Il Bidone The Swindle
The Big Bang Theory Bang
The Big Bankroll King of the Roaring 20s – the Story of Arnold Rothstein
The Big Carnival Ace in the Hole
Big Deal at Dodge City A Big Hand for a Little Lady
The Big Feast La Grande Bouffe
The Big Frame The Lost Hours
Big Girls Don't Cry... They Get Even Stepkids
The Big Grab Any Number Can Win
The Big Heart Miracle on 34th Street
The Big Parade of Comedy MGM's Big Parade of Comedy
The Big Pardon Le Grand Pardon
Big Shots The Boys Next Door
The Big Silence The Great Silence
Big Six Common-Law Cabin
The Big Snatch Any Number Can Win
Big Time Operators The Smallest Show on Earth
The Biggest Bank Robbery A Nightingale Sang in Berkeley Square
The Bill Wilson Story My Name Is Bill W
Billy Rose's Jumbo Jumbo
Billy the Kid, Sheriff of Sage Valley Sheriff of Sage Valley
Bird with the Glass Feathers The Bird with the Crystal Plumage
The Birds Three Daring Daughters
Birds of a Feather La Cage aux Folles
Birthmark The Omen
The Bitch La Garce
The Bitch Drôle de Drame
The Bite Curse II: The Bite
Bits and Pieces Il Cielo è Sempre Più Blu
The Bitter End Love Walked In
Bitter Reunion Le Beau Serge
Die Bitteren Tränen der Petra von Kant The Bitter Tears of Petra von Kant
Bizarre, Bizarre Drôle de Drame
Bizet's Carmen Carmen
Black Arrow Strikes The Black Arrow
Black Bart Highwayman Black Bart
The Black Book Reign of Terror
The Black Buccaneer The Black Pirate
The Black Buccaneer Gordon the Black Pirate
The Black Countess The Female Vampire
Black Dice No Orchids for Miss Blandish
Black Eyes Dark Eyes
Black Flowers Wall of Silence
Black Flowers for the Bride Something for Everyone
Black Glove Face the Music
Black Ice A Passion for Murder
Black Magic Meeting at Midnight
Black Peter Peter and Pavla
Black Rock Blackrock
Black Shack Alley Rue Cases Nègres
Black Sunday The Mask of Satan
Black Victory Black and White in Color
Blackout Contraband
Blacula 2 Scream Blacula Scream
Blade af Satans Bog Leaves from Satan's Book
Blair Witch 2 Book of Shadows: Blair Witch 2
Blake Edwards' Son of the Pink Panther Son of the Pink Panther
Blake Edwards' That's Life! That's Life
Blanc de Chine The Chinese Connection
Blank Cheque Blank Check
Blast The Final Comedown
Blast Off Jules Verne's Rocket to the Moon
Der Blaue Engel The Blue Angel
Das Blaue Licht The Blue Light
Blazing Arrows Fighting Caravans
Le Blé en Herbe The Ripening Seed
Die Blechtrommel The Tin Drum
Bleeders Hemoglobin
Die Bleierne Zeit The German Sisters
Blind Man's Bluff Cauldron of Blood
Blind Rage The Boys Next Door
Blind Spot Death in the Sun
Block Party Marshal Law
Blokpost Checkpoint
Blonde Bait Women without Men
Blonde Sinner Yield to the Night
Blood and Guts Patton
Blood Bath Bay of Blood
Blood Beast from Outer Space The Night Caller
Blood Brides Hatchet for the Honeymoon
Blood Couple Ganja and Hess
Blood Creature Terror Is a Man
Blood Fiend Theatre of Death
Blood Is My Heritage Blood of Dracula
Blood Kin Last of the Mobile Hot-Shots
Blood Mad The Glove
Blood Money Requiem for a Heavyweight
Blood Moon Bats
Blood of Frankenstein Dracula vs Frankenstein
The Blood of Heroes The Salute of the Jugger
Blood of the Demon Blood of Dracula
Blood of the Undead Schizo
Blood on His Lips Hideous Sun Demon
Blood on the Streets Borsalino and Co
Blood Orgy The Gore-Gore Girls
Blood Ransom Captive Rage
Blood Related Wildflower
The Blood Seekers Dracula vs Frankenstein
Blood Sisters Sisters
Blood Snow Lady Snowblood
Blood Splash Nightmares in a Damaged Brain
Blood Wedding Les Noces Rouges
Bloodbath Bay of Blood
Bloodstone Maximum Risk
Bloodsuckers Incense for the Damned
Bloodwings: Pumpkinhead's Revenge The Revenge of Pumpkinhead – Blood Wings
Bloodwork Blood Work
Bloody Bird ALA Stage Fright – Aquarius
The Bloody Bushido Blade The Bushido Blade
Bloom bl,.m
Blow Up Blowup
Blue Three Colours Blue
The Blue and the Gold An Annapolis Story
Blue Jeans Blue Denim
Blue Manhattan Hi, Mom!
Blue Sierra Courage of Lassie
Bluebird – die Geschichte von Eva Norvind Didn't Do It for Love
The Blues – A Musical Journey – Feel Like Going Home Martin Scorsese Presents The Blues: Feel Like Going Home
The Blues – A Musical Journey – Godfathers and Sons Martin Scorsese Presents the Blues: Godfathers and Sons
The Blues – A Musical Journey – Piano Blues Martin Scorsese Presents The Blues: Piano Blues
The Blues – A Musical Journey – Red, White & Blues Martin Scorsese Presents The Blues: Red, White & Blues
The Blues – A Musical Journey – The Road to Memphis Martin Scorsese Presents the Blues: The Road to Memphis
The Blues – A Musical Journey – The Soul of a Man Martin Scorsese Presents the Blues: The Soul of a Man
The Blues – A Musical Journey – Warming by the Devil's Fire Martin Scorsese Presents The Blues: Warming by the Devil's Fire
Blues for a Junkman The Murder Men
Blues for Lovers Ballad in Blue
Bluff storia di truffe e di imbroglioni The Con Artists
Blutige Seide Blood and Black Lace
Bob Marley: Time Will Tell Time Will Tell
Boca a Boca Mouth to Mouth
Boda Secreta Secret Wedding
Bodas de Sangre Blood Wedding
Body Beat Dance Academy
Body of a Woman The Big Squeeze
Body Snatcher from Hell Goke, Bodysnatcher from Hell
Bodycount Body Count
The Bodyguard Yojimbo
The Bodyguard from Beijing The Defender
Bolero Les Uns et les Autres
Bombshell Blonde Bombshell
Bombsight Stolen Cottage to Let
Bon Appetit, Mama Motherhood
Bonaventure Thunder on the Hill
La Bonne Année Happy New Year
Bop The Thief
Bordello of Blood Tales from the Crypt Presents: Bordello of Blood
Borderlines The Caretakers
Boredom L'Ennui
Born for Glory Forever England
Born to Be Kissed The Girl from Missouri
Born to Kill Lady of Deceit
Born to Lose Born to Win
Born Wild Running Wild
Bosambo Sanders of the River
Boston Blackie Meet Boston Blackie
Both Ends of the Candle The Helen Morgan Story
The Bottom of the Bottle Beyond the River
Boudu Sauvé des Eaux Boudu, Saved from Drowning
Bound by Honor Blood In Blood Out
The Bounty Hunters Adios, Sabata
Boy of Two Worlds Paw
A Boy Ten Feet Tall Sammy Going South
The Boyfriend from Hell The Shrimp on the Barbie
Boyfriends and Girlfriends My Girlfriend's Boyfriend
The Boys from Brooklyn Bela Lugosi Meets a Brooklyn Gorilla
Brady's Escape The Long Ride
Brain Candy Kids in the Hall: Brain Candy
The Brainsnatcher The Man Who Changed His Mind
Bram Stoker's The Mummy Bram Stoker's Legend of the Mummy
Brandy Ashore Green Grow the Rushes
Brat Brother
The Brave and the Beautiful The Magnificent Matador
The Brave Young Men of Weinberg Up the Academy
Bread and Flower A Moment of Innocence
Bread and Plant A Moment of Innocence
The Break A Further Gesture
Break for Freedom Albert, RN
The Break Up La Rupture
Breakers Heartbreakers
Breakfast at Manchester Morgue The Living Dead at the Manchester Morgue
Breakin' Breakdance
Breakin' 2: Electric Boogaloo Breakdance 2 – Electric Boogaloo
Breaking the Silence Shattering the Silence
Breaking the Silence The Unspoken Truth
Breaking the Sound Barrier The Sound Barrier
Breakout Danger Within
The Breakup La Rupture
Breathless A Bout de Souffle

Brenn, Hexe, Brenn Mark of the Devil
Brenno il Nemico di Roma Brennus – Enemy of Rome
The Bride Comes to Yellow Sky Face to Face
The Bride Is Much Too Beautiful The Bride Is Too Beautiful
Bride of Dragons Bridge of Dragons
Bride of the Atom Bride of the Monster
The Bride Wasn't Willing Frontier Gal
The Bridge Between Two Banks The Bridge
Bring on the Dancing Girls Who's That Knocking at My Door
Brink of Hell Toward the Unknown
Brink of Life So Close to Life
Broadway Singer Torch Singer
Brodeuses A Common Thread
Broken Hearts and Noses Crimewave
The Broken Hearts League The Broken Hearts Club: a Romantic Comedy
Broken Lullaby The Man I Killed
Bronco Busters Little Moon & Jud McGraw
The Brothaz The Brothers
The Brotherhood I've Been Watching You
Brotherhood of the Yakuza The Yakuza
Brotherly Love Country Dance
Brothers and Sisters Fratelli e Sorelle
Brothers' Destiny The Road Home
Brown on Resolution Forever England
Bruce Lee: Curse of the Dragon The Curse of the Dragon
Bruce Lee's Game of Death Game of Death
Die Brücke The Bridge
Un Bruit Qui Rend Fou The Blue Villa
The Brute El Bruto
Brute Force The Expert
Brutti, Sporchi e Cattivi Down and Dirty
Die Büchse der Pandora Pandora's Box
Bucket of Blood The Tell-Tale Heart
Bud the Chud CHUD II: Bud the Chud
The Buddy Factor Swimming with Sharks
Bugs Bunny The Bugs Bunny/Road Runner Movie
A Bullet from God God's Gun
Bullet Proof Bulletproof
Bulletproof Heart Killer
Buongiorno, Notte Good Morning, Night
Il Buono, il Brutto, il Cattivo The Good, the Bad and the Ugly
Bure Baruta Cabaret Balkan
Buried Alive: the Chowchilla Kidnapping Vanished without a Trace
Burn Burn!
Burn, Baby, Burn Heat Wave
Burn, Witch, Burn Night of the Eagle
Burn, Witch, Burn Mark of the Devil
Burnin' Love Love at Stake
The Burning Cross The Klansman
The Burning Man A Dangerous Summer
The Burning Question Reefer Madness
The Butcher Le Boucher
Butcher Baker, Nightmare Maker Night Warning
Butter Cream Gang II Secret of Treasure Mountain
The Butterfly Affair Popsy-Pop
The Button-Pinchers Buttoners
The Button-Pushers Buttoners
By Hook or by Crook I Dood It
By Hook or by Crook Ek Aur Ek Gyarah
By Rocket to the Moon The Woman in the Moon
By Whose Hand Guilty?

CSS Hunley The Hunley
Cabal Nightbreed
Cabiria Nights of Cabiria
Caccia al Maschio Male Hunt
Les Cachetonneurs The Music Freelancers
Cadaveri Eccellenti Illustrious Corpses
Cadence Stockade
La Caduta degli Dei The Damned
Cafe of the Seven Sinners Seven Sinners
La Cage The Trap
The Cage The Trap
La Cage aux Folles III: The Wedding La Cage aux Folles III: "Elles" Se Marient
La Cage aux Rossignols A Cage of Nightingales
Caged Females Caged Heat
Cajun Louisiana Story
California Gold The Ballad of Lucy Whipple
California Holiday Spinout
Call Harry Crown 99 and 44/100% Dead
Call Him Mr Shatter Shatter
Call It Murder Midnight
Call Me a Cab Carry On Cabby
Call Me Genius The Rebel
Call the Cops! Find the Lady
El Callejon de los Milagros Midaq Alley
The Calling Murder by Phone
Calling All Cats 6.5 Special
Calvaire The Ordeal
Les Camarades The Organizer
Camels West Southwest Passage
Camille without Camellias La Signora senza Camelie
La Campana del Infierno The Bell of Hell
Candyman II Candyman: Farewell to the Flesh
Cannibal Orgy, or the Maddest Story Ever Told Spider Baby
Cannon Movie Tales: Red Riding Hood Red Riding Hood
Capitães de Abril Captains of April
Le Caporal Epinglé The Vanishing Corporal
Captain Blood The Captain
Captain Midnight On the Air Live with Captain Midnight
Captain Moonlight D'Ye Ken John Peel?
Captain Nuke and the Bomber Boys The Bomber Boys
Captured Agent Red
Caravan Himalaya
Caravane Caravan
Care of the Spitfire Grill The Spitfire Grill
Careless Love La Bonne Soupe
Carelessly We Love I Met My Love Again
Carnage Bay of Blood
Carnage Corruption
Carnage Carnages
The Carnal Prayer Mat Sex and Zen
Carne Trémula Live Flesh
Carne y Demonio Susana
Les Carnets du Major Thompson The Diary of Major Thompson
Carnival of Terror The Funhouse
Caro Diario Dear Diary
The Carolyn Warmus Story A Murderous Affair
Le Carosse d'Or The Golden Coach
Carquake Cannonball
Carrie 2 The Rage: Carrie 2
Carried Away Acts of Love
The Carriers Are Waiting Les Convoyeurs Attendent
Carrot Top Poil de Carotte
Carry On Venus Carry On Jack
The Cars That Eat People The Cars That Ate Paris
Cartagine in Fiamme Carthage in Flames
Il Cartaio The Card Player
La Carte du Tendre Map of the Human Heart
Le Cas du Docteur Laurent The Case of Dr Laurent
La Casa de Bernarda Alba The House of Bernarda Alba
La Casa dell'Exorcismo Lisa and the Devil
The Case against Paul Ryker Sergeant Ryker
The Case of Jonathan Drew The Lodger
Case of the Red Monkey Little Red Monkey
CASH Whiffs
Cash on Delivery To Dorothy, a Son
Il Caso Mattei The Mattei Affair
Casper and Wendy Casper Meets Wendy
Le Casse The Burglars
Cast Iron The Virtuous Sin
The Castaway The Cheaters
Castle of Doom Vampyr
The Castle of the Spider's Web Throne of Blood
The Cat in the Hat Dr Seuss' The Cat in the Hat
The Cathedral The Church
Cathedral of Demons The Church
Catherine the Great The Rise of Catherine the Great
Cathy Tippel Keetje Tippel
Caught in the Act Cosi
I Cavalieri dell'Illusione The Loves of Three Queens
Un Cave The Loser
The Cave Dwellers One Million BC
Cave Man One Million BC
La Caza The Hunt
Ce Cher Intrus Once Around
The Celebration Festen
Celebrity 15 Minutes
Celine et Julie Vont en Bateau Celine and Julie Go Boating
Cemetery Girls The Velvet Vampire
I Cento Passi The Hundred Steps
Central do Brasil Central Station
Centre Stage The Actress
C'Era una Volta More than a Miracle
C'Eravamo Tanto Amati We All Loved Each Other So Much
Le Cercle Rouge The Red Circle
Le Cerveau The Brain
César et Rosalie César and Rosalie
C'est Arrivé près de Chez Vous Man Bites Dog
Cesta do Praveku Voyage into Prehistory
Cet Obscur Objet du Désir That Obscure Object of Desire
Ceux Qui M'Aiment Prendront le Train Those Who Love Me Can Take the Train
Chacun Cherche Son Chat When the Cat's Away…
Chagrin and Pity The Sorrow and the Pity
Le Chagrin et la Pitié The Sorrow and the Pity
Chained to Yesterday Limbo
Chains of Hate Black Mama, White Mama
La Chair de l'Orchidée The Flesh of the Orchid
Le Chaland Qui Passe L'Atalante
Chamber of Horrors Bedlam
Chamber of Tortures Baron Blood
The Chambermaid The Chambermaid on the Titanic
La Chambre des Officiers The Officers' Ward
La Chambre Verte The Green Room
Champion for the King The Captain
Champions The Mighty Ducks
Chance Meeting Blind Date
Chance Meeting The Young Lovers
A Change of Heart Two and Two Make Six
Changes Danielle Steel's Changes
Chantons et Choeur Grandeur et Décadence d'un Petit Commerce de Cinéma
Chaos Kaos
Un Chapeau de Paille d'Italie An Italian Straw Hat
Chapter 24 in the Complete Adventures of Indiana Jones: Indiana Jones and the Raiders of the Lost Ark Raiders of the Lost Ark
The Charge Is Murder Twilight of Honor
Charley's American Aunt Charley's Aunt
Charlie at Work Work
Charlie Chan and the Red Dragon The Red Dragon
Charlie Chan in Black Magic Meeting at Midnight
Charlie Chan in Dangerous Money Dangerous Money
Charlie Chan in Dark Alibi Dark Alibi
Charlie Chan in Meeting at Midnight Meeting at Midnight
Charlie Chan in The Jade Mask The Jade Mask
Charlie Chan in The Scarlet Clue The Scarlet Clue
Charlie Chan in The Shanghai Cobra The Shanghai Cobra
Charlie Chan in the Trap The Trap
Charlie on the Farm The Tramp
Charlie the Decorator Work
Charlie the Hobo The Tramp
Charlie the Tramp The Tramp
Charlie's Family The Manson Family
Charlie's Kids Listen to Me
Charlotte and Lulu An Impudent Girl
Charlotte Bronte's Jane Eyre Jane Eyre
Le Charme Discret de la Bourgeoisie The Discreet Charm of the Bourgeoisie
The Charmer Moonlight Sonata
The Chase for the Golden Needles Golden Needles
La Chasse à l'Homme Male Hunt
The Chastity Belt On My Way to the Crusades, I Met a Girl Who…
Che? What?
Che Ho Fatto Per Meritare Questo? What Have I Done to Deserve This?
The Cheaters Les Tricheurs
Cheatin' Hearts Paper Hearts
Checkpoint Trial on the Road
The Cheque Is in the Post The Check Is in the Mail
Cherished Memories Yaadein
Chetnik Undercover
Cheval Sauvage White Mane
Chicago, Chicago Gaily, Gaily
La Chiesa The Church
Child of the Night Les Voleurs
Children's Faces Faces of Children
China Blue Crimes of Passion
China Mountain Big Brother The Big Boss
Chinchero The Last Movie
Chinese Adventures in China Up to His Ears
The Chinese Cat Charlie Chan in The Chinese Cat
The Chinese Connection Fist of Fury
The Chinese Portrait Portraits Chinois
Chinese White The Chinese Connection
Chino The Valdez Horses
Chloë in the Afternoon Love in the Afternoon
The Chocolate Cobweb Merci pour le Chocolat
The Choice Yam Daabo
Choice of Arms Trial by Combat
The Choice of Weapons Choice of Arms
Le Choix des Armes Choice of Arms
Choke Canyon On Dangerous Ground
Les Choristes The Chorus
The Chosen Holocaust 2000
Les Choses de la Vie The Things of Life
Choses Secrètes Secret Things
Christine Un Carnet de Bal
A Christmas Carol Scrooge
Christmas Evil You Better Watch Out
Christopher Pike's Fall into Darkness Fall into Darkness
Chronicle of the Years of Embers Chronicle of the Burning Years
Chronicle of the Years of Fire Chronicle of the Burning Years
Chronik der Anna Magdalena Bach Chronicle of Anna Magdalena Bach
Chubby Goes Down Under Chubby Down Under and Other Sticky Regions
Chuck Berry: Hail! Hail! Rock'n'Roll! Hail! Hail! Rock 'n' Roll!
CHUD Cannibalistic Humanoid Underground Dwellers CHUD
Ciao Maschio Bye Bye Monkey
A Ciascuno il Suo We Still Kill the Old Way
Cible Emouvante Wild Target
Le Ciel et la Boue The Sky above, the Mud below
Le Ciel, les Oiseaux et… Ta Mère! Boys on the Beach
Cien The Shadow
Cinderella Rodgers & Hammerstein's Cinderella
Cinderella – Italian Style More than a Miracle
5x2 Cinq fois deux 5x2
La Ciociara Two Women
The Circle The Vicious Circle
Circle of Iron The Silent Flute
Circle of Love La Ronde
Circus World The Magnificent Showman
Citadel of Crime A Man Betrayed
La Cité des enfants perdus The City of Lost Children
Citizen's Band FM
La Citta delle Donne City of Women
La Città Prigioniera Captive City
The City Jungle The Young Philadelphians
City Loop Bored Olives
City Unplugged Darkness in Tallinn
La Ciudad y los Perros The City and the Dogs
Le Clan des Siciliens The Sicilian Clan
The Clansman The Birth of a Nation
Class Trip La Classe de Neige
La Classe Operaia Va in Paradiso The Working Class Goes to Heaven
Classe Tous Risques The Big Risk
Claude The Two of Us
Cleo de 5 à 7 Cleo from 5 to 7
The Cleopatra Arms A Kiss in the Dark
Clickety-Clack Dodes'ka-Den
Clive Barker's Hellraiser Hellraiser
Clive Barker's Lord of Illusions Lord of Illusions
The Clockmaker The Watchmaker of St Paul
Close to Eden A Stranger among Us
Close to Eden Urga
Close Your Eyes Doctor Sleep
Closely Watched Trains Closely Observed Trains
The Closer You Come The Closer You Get
Clouds over Europe Q Planes
Clover Bend Death at Clover Bend
Clown House Clownhouse
A Clown Must Laugh Pagliacci
Club Dread Broken Lizard's Club Dread
Club Extinction Dr M
Coach Sunset Park
Cobweb Castle Throne of Blood
Cocaine Mixed Blood
Cocaine Kids illtown
Cocktails in the Kitchen For Better, for Worse
The Code La Mentale
Code Inconnu Récit Incomplet de Divers Voyages Code Unknown
Code Name: Trixie The Crazies
Code of Scotland Yard The Shop at Sly Corner
Code of the Dragon The Ghost
Un Coeur Qui Bat Your Beating Heart
Coffee Jikou Cafe Lumière
Cold Cash Top of the World
Cold Cuts Buffet Froid
Cold Water L'Eau Froide
Colder than Death Love Is Colder Than Death
Colette Becoming Colette
Colin Nutley's House of Angels House of Angels
La Collina Degli Stavali Boot Hill
Colonel Blimp The Life and Death of Colonel Blimp
Colonization of the Planet of the Apes Battle for the Planet of the Apes
The Colony Double Team
The Color of a Hero A Better Tomorrow
Colossus 1980 Colossus: the Forbin Project
The Colour of Love Zebrahead
The Colour of Paradise The Color of Paradise
Columbo: Prescription Murder Prescription: Murder
Columbo: Ransom for a Dead Man Ransom for a Dead Man
Le Combat dans l'Ile Fire and Ice
Come Undone Presque Rien

The Comedy of Innocence Comédie de l'Innocence
Comes a Time Silence of the North
Coming Down to Earth Doin' Time on Planet Earth
A Coming-Out Party Very Important Person
Commander Hamilton Hamilton
Comme un Boomerang Boomerang
Comme une Image Look at Me
Comment Je Me Suis Dispute... Ma Vie Sexuelle Ma Vie Sexuelle
Comment le Désir Vient aux Filles I Am Frigid... Why?
Common Wealth La Comunidad
The Communicants Winter Light
Communion Alice, Sweet Alice
Como Agua para Chocolate Like Water for Chocolate
Como Ser Mujer y no Morir en el Intento How to Be a Woman and Not Die in the Attempt
Company of Cowards? Advance to the Rear
Compartiment Tueurs The Sleeping Car Murders
A Complex Plot about Woman, Alleys and Crimes Camorra
Un Complicato Intrigo di Donne, Vicoli e Delitti Camorra
Computer Kid Where's Willie?
Computer Killers Horror Hospital
Computer Wizard Where's Willie?
Comrades of 1918 Westfront 1918
Comradeship Kameradschaft
Comstock and Rosemary Keep the Aspidistra Flying
The Con Men The Con Artists
Concerto I've Always Loved You
The Concierge For Love or Money
The Concorde – Airport '79 Airport '79: the Concorde
The Concrete Jungle The Criminal
Un Condamné à Mort S'Est Echappé A Man Escaped
Condemned to Death Death by Hanging
The Conductor Il Maestro
The Confession Quick, Let's Get Married
The Confessional House of Mortal Sin
Confessions Private Confessions
Confessions of a Sorority Girl Sorority Girl
Confessions of an Odd Job Man Ups and Downs of a Handyman
The Confluence Sangam
Conjugal Cabin Common-Law Cabin
The Connecticut Look The Secret Life of an American Wife
A Connecticut Yankee in King Arthur's Court A Knight in Camelot
Conquered City Captive City
Conqueror Worm Witchfinder General
Le Conseguenze Dell'amore The Consequences of Love
Consider All Risks The Big Risk
Conspiracy of Silence: The Shari Karney Story Shattered Trust
Constancy The Constant Factor
Constans The Constant Factor
Constantine the Great Constantine and the Cross
The Contact Man Alias Nick Beal
The Contaminated Man Contagion
Conte d'Automne An Autumn Tale
Conte d'Eté A Summer's Tale
Contes Immoraux Immoral Tales
Contest Girl The Beauty Jungle
The Context Illustrious Corpses
Contract in Blood Le Choc
Control Kontroll
Convention City Sons of the Desert
Conway Body Armor
Cool Baby, Cool! The Cool Ones
Coolangatta Gold The Gold and Glory
Cop Killers Order of Death
Cop-Out Stranger in the House
Cop Story Police Story
Copkiller Order of Death
Copland Cop Land
La Coquille et le Clergman The Seashell and the Clergyman
A Cor do seu Destino The Color of Destiny
Corazon Iluminado Foolish Heart
Le Corbeau The Raven
Cord Hide and Seek
Cordillera Flight to Fury
El Coronel no Tiene Quien le Escriba No One Writes to the Colonel
The Corpse Collectors Cauldron of Blood
Corrupt Order of Death
La Corsa dell'Innocente Flight of the Innocent
The Corsican Brothers Cheech & Chong's The Corsican Brothers
Corte notte delle bambole di vetro The Short Night of the Glass Dolls
I Cosacchi The Cossacks
Cosmic Monsters The Strange World of Planet X
Cosmonauts on Venus Planeta Burg
Costa Brava Family Album
Count Dracula and His Vampire Bride The Satanic Rites of Dracula
Count Iorga, Vampire The Loves of Count Iorga, Vampire
The Count of Monk's Bridge The Count of the Old Town
Count Yorga, Vampire The Loves of Count Iorga, Vampire
Count Your Bullets Cry for Me Billy
Counted Moments Nick of Time
Coup de Foudre Entre Nous
Le Coup de Menhir Asterix and the Big Fight
Coup de Torchon Clean Slate
Un Coupable Idéal Murder on a Sunday Morning
Courage Raw Courage
La Course du Lièvre à travers les Champs And Hope to Die
Court Martial Carrington VC
The Courtney Affair The Courtneys of Curzon Street
Le Couvent The Convent
Cover Up Frightmare
Cows Vacas
Coyote Moon Desert Heat
Crack Shot The Counterfeit Killer
Cracking Up Smorgasbord
Crackshot The Counterfeit Killer
The Crash of Silence Mandy
Crawlers They Crawl
The Crawling Eye The Trollenberg Terror
Crazed I Dismember Mama
Crazy For You Vision Quest
The Crazy Ray Paris Qui Dort
Crazy Streets Forever Lulu
Crazy to Kill Dr Gillespie's Criminal Case
The Crazysitter Two Much Trouble
Creative Detour Cool Blue
Creatures From beyond the Grave
The Creatures from beyond the Grave From beyond the Grave
The Creeping Unknown The Quatermass Xperiment
Crest of the Wave Seagulls over Sorrento
Cries in the Night The Awful Dr Orloff
Cries Unheard: the Donna Yaklich Story Victim of Rage
Crime et Châtiment Crime and Punishment
Crime in the Museum of Horrors Horrors of the Black Museum
The Crime of Father Amaro El Crimen del Padre Amaro
Crime of Honor A Song for Europe
The Crime of the Century Walk East on Beacon
Crime Squad The Man from Cairo
Crime Wave The City Is Dark
The Crimes of Dr Mabuse The Testament of Dr Mabuse
Criminal Story The Road to Corinth
I Criminali della Galassia The Wild, Wild Planet
The Criminals of the Galaxy The Wild, Wild Planet
The Crimson Blade The Scarlet Blade
Crimson Circle The Red Circle
Crimson Code Red Team
The Crimson Cult Curse of the Crimson Altar
Crin-Blanc White Mane
Cristo si è Fermato a Eboli Christ Stopped at Eboli
Critical Decision Executive Decision
Critical List Terminal Choice
Crocodile Blood Surf
Cronaca di un Amore Chronicle of a Love
Cronaca di una Morte Annunciata Chronicle of a Death Foretold
Crooks in Clover Penthouse
Cross-Up Tiger by the Tail
Crossed Swords The Prince and the Pauper
Crossfire Quick
Crossing the Line The Big Man
Crosspoint The November Men
Crossroads of Destiny Jailbreak
The Crown Caper The Thomas Crown Affair
The Crucible The Witches of Salem
Crucible of Horror The Corpse
The Cruel Deep Escape under Pressure
Cry Devil Night Visitor
A Cry for Justice A Song for Europe
The Cry of the Owl Le Cri du Hibou
Crying Out Loud Cotton Queen
Cult of the Damned Angel, Angel Down We Go
La Curée The Game Is Over
The Curious Case of the Campus Corpse The Hazing
The Curse Xala
Curse IV: the Ultimate Sacrifice Catacombs
The Curse of San Michel The Bay of Saint Michel
Curse of the Demon Night of the Demon
Curse of the Golem It!
Curse of the Mushroom People Matango
The Curve Dead Man's Curve
Cutter and Bone Cutter's Way
Cybèle ou les Dimanches de Ville d'Avray Sundays and Cybèle
Cyber Space Lawnmower Man 2: Beyond Cyberspace
Czarina A Royal Scandal

Da Uomo a Uomo Death Rides a Horse
Daan Don
Daayraa The Square Circle
Daddy Danielle Steel's Daddy
Daddy Nostalgia These Foolish Things
Daddy's Little Girl She's Out of Control
Daft Punk & Leiji Matsumoto's Interstella 5555 Interstella 5555
Dal Polo all'Equatore From the Pole to the Equator
Daleka Cesta The Long Journey
La Dame dans l'Auto avec des Lunettes et un Fusil The Lady in the Car with Glasses and a Gun
Damn the Defiant! HMS Defiant
Dance of Death House of Evil
Dance of Life Un Carnet de Bal
Dance of the Vampires or Pardon Me, but Your Teeth Are in My Neck The Fearless Vampire Killers
Dance Program Un Carnet de Bal
Dancer Billy Elliot
Dancing in the Dark Original Sin
Dancing with the Devil Perdita Durango
Danger Grows Wild The Poppy Is Also a Flower
Danger in the Skies The Pilot
Danger Island Mr Moto in Danger Island
Danger Rides the Range Three Texas Steers
Dangerous Business Party Girl
A Dangerous Friend The Todd Killings
Dangerous Kiss True Crime
Dangerous Love Affairs Les Liaisons Dangereuses
Dangerous Obsession Mortal Sins
Danny Boy Angel
Danny the Dog Unleashed
Dans la Ville Blanche In the White City
Dans Ma Peau In My Skin
Un Danseur: Rudolph Nureyev I Am a Dancer
Daria in Is It Fall Yet? Daria the Movie: Is It Fall Yet?
Dario Argento's Inferno Inferno
Dario Argento's The Phantom of the Opera The Phantom of the Opera
Dario Argento's Trauma Trauma
Dark Breed Darkbreed
Dark Empire Dark City
Dark End They Met in the Dark
Dark Fortress A Nymphoid Barbarian in Dinosaur Hell
Dark Goddess Temptress
Dark Hunger Dead of Night
Dark Matters Normal Life
Dark Obsession Diamond Skulls
Dark of the Night Mr Wrong
Dark Prince – the True Story of Dracula Dark Prince – the Legend of Dracula
Dark World Dark City
The Darkest Hour Hell on Frisco Bay
Darkman 3 Darkman III: Die Darkman Die
Die Darkman Die Darkman III: Die Darkman Die
A Date with a Lonely Girl TR Baskin
A Date with Death The High Bright Sun
A Date with Destiny The Return of October
Daughter of Deceit La Hija del Engaño
Daughter of Destiny Alraune
The Daughter of Keltoum Bent Keltoum
David Sullivan's Come Play with Me Come Play with Me
Dawandeh The Runner
Dawn Streets
The Day After Up from the Beach
Day after Day Yom Yom
The Day after Tomorrow Strange Holiday
A Day in the Country Une Partie de Campagne
Day of the Landgrabbers Land Raiders
The Day the Screaming Stopped The Comeback
A Day to Remember Two Bits
Dayereh The Circle
Days of Hope Man's Hope
Dead Ahead 36 Hours to Die
Dead Alive Braindead
Dead Connection Final Combination
Dead End Dogwatch
Dead End: Cradle of Crime Dead End
Dead Giveaway Murder at My Door
Dead Heat Thunderbolt
Dead Image Dead Ringer
A Dead Man Seeks His Murderer The Brain
Dead of Night Lighthouse
Dead on Course Wings of Danger
Dead On: Relentless 2 Relentless 2: Dead On
Dead Simple Alone with a Stranger
Dead Suzy The Terror Inside
Dead Waters Dark Waters
The Deadliest Sin Confession
Deadline Witness in the War Zone
Deadline Midnight -30-
Deadly Current Lethal Tender
Deadly Is the Female Gun Crazy
Deadly Justice Jack Reed: One of Our Own
Deadly Measures Desperate Measures
The Deadly Mr Frost Mister Frost
Deadly Roulette How I Spent My Summer Vacation
Deadly Seduction Blind Date
The Deadly Silence Tarzan's Deadly Silence
The Deadly Trap The Deadly Trap
Dean Koontz's Mr Murder Mr Murder
Dear Emma, Sweet Böbe Sweet Emma Dear Böbe
Dear Mr Grasler The Bachelor
Dearest Love Le Souffle au Coeur
Death and Vengeance Jack Reed: Death and Vengeance
Death Angel Dark Angel
Death Bed Terminal Choice
Death Comes from the Dark Cauldron of Blood
Death Corps Shock Waves
Death Has No Sex A Black Veil for Lisa
Death House Silent Night, Bloody Night
Death in Full View Deathwatch
Death in Granada The Disappearance of Garcia Lorca
Death List Terminal Choice
Death of a Corrupt Man To Kill a Rat
Death of a Hooker Who Killed Mary Whats'ername?
Death of a Yankee Hostile Waters
Death Trap Eaten Alive
Death Watch Deathwatch
Deathbed Terminal Choice
Deathdream Dead of Night
Death's Ecstasy La Bête
The Debt Véronico Cruz
The Debutantes Los Debutantes
La Décade Prodigieuse Ten Days' Wonder
Deceiver Liar
Deception Ruby Cairo
Deception Anna Boleyn
La Decima Vittima The Tenth Victim
Decision against Time The Man in the Sky
Le Declin de l'Empire Americain The Decline of the American Empire
Dedication Sadhna
Deep Desire of Gods The Profound Desire of the Gods
Deep in the Heart Handgun
Deep Red Hatchet Murders Deep Red
Def Jam's How to Be a Player How to Be a Player
The Defeated The Vanquished
Le Déjeuner sur l'Herbe Lunch on the Grass
Deliria Stage Fright – Aquarius
Deliverance Sadgati
Dellamorte Dellamore Cemetery Man
Demasiado Miedo a la Vida, o Plaff Plaff!
La Demoiselle d'Honneur The Bridesmaid
Les Demoiselles de Rochefort The Young Girls of Rochefort
Demolition Day The Bomber Boys
The Demon Onibaba
Demon God Told Me to
The Demon Barber of Fleet Street Sweeney Todd, the Demon Barber of Fleet Street
Demon Cathedral The Church
The Demon Doctor The Awful Dr Orloff
Demon Knight Tales from the Crypt: Demon Knight
Demons 3 The Church
Demons of the Swamp Attack of the Giant Leeches
Denial Something about Sex
Dennis Strikes Again Dennis the Menace Strikes Again
Dennis the Menace Dennis
La Dentellière The Lacemaker
Depuis qu'Otar est Parti... Since Otar Left
Le Dernier Combat The Last Battle
Dernier Domicile Connu The Last Known Address
Le Dernier Métro The Last Metro
Le Dernier Mitterrand The Last Mitterrand
The Descendant of Genghis-Khan Storm over Asia
Descente aux Enfers Descent into Hell
Desert Attack Ice Cold in Alex
Desert Patrol Sea of Sand
Desert Tanks The Battle of El Alamein
Il Deserto Rosso Red Desert
Desire Salt on Our Skin
Los Desperados A Bullet for Sandoval
The Desperate Men Cat and Mouse
Desperate Prey Redheads
Después de la Tormenta After the Storm
The Destructors The Marseille Contract
The Detective Father Brown
The Detective Kid The Gumshoe Kid

Detonator Death Train
Detour Too Hard to Die
La Deuda Interna Véronico Cruz
Deus e o Diabo Na Terra do Sol Black God, White Devil
Deutschland im Herbst Germany in Autumn
Deutschland im Jahre Null Germany, Year Zero
Les Deux Anglaises et le Continent Anne and Muriel
Deux Billets pour Mexico Dead Run
Deux Frères Two Brothers
Deux Hommes dans la Ville Two against the Law
Deux Hommes dans Manhattan Two Men in Manhattan
Deux ou Trois Choses Que Je Sais d'Elle Two or Three Things I Know about Her
Les Deux Rivales Time of Indifference
2 Secondes 2 Seconds
The Devil and Daniel Webster Daniel and the Devil
The Devil and the Dead Lisa and the Devil
The Devil and the Flesh Susana
The Devil in the House of Exorcism Lisa and the Devil
The Devil Inside Offbeat
The Devil Never Sleeps Satan Never Sleeps
Devil on Wheels Indianapolis Speedway
The Devil Takes the Count The Devil Is a Sissy
The Devil within Her I Don't Want to Be Born
The Devil Woman Onibaba
The Devils Les Diables
The Devil's Bride The Devil Rides Out
The Devil's Brother Bogus Bandits
The Devil's Commandment Lust of the Vampire
The Devil's Daughter The Sect
The Devil's Envoys Les Visiteurs du Soir
Devil's Odds The Wild Pair
Devil's Odds Damned River
The Devil's Own The Witches
The Devil's Plot Counterblast
Devil's Treasure Treasure Island
The Devious Path Crisis
El Dia de la Bestia The Day of the Beast
Le Diable au Corps Devil in the Flesh
Le Diable Probablement The Devil, Probably
The Diabolic Invention Invention of Destruction
The Diabolical Dr Satan The Awful Dr Orloff
Diabolik Danger: Diabolik
Diaboliquement Vôtre Diabolically Yours
La Diagonale du Fou Dangerous Moves
Dial Rat for Terror Bone
Diamante Lobo God's Gun
Diamantes a Go-Go Grand Slam
The Diamond Earrings Madame de...
Diamond Horseshoe Billy Rose's Diamond Horseshoe
The Diamond Mercenaries Killer Force
The Diamond Wizard The Diamond
Diamond's Edge Just Ask for Diamond
Diarios de Motocicleta The Motorcycle Diaries
Diary for My Loved Ones Diary for My Loves
Diary for My Loves Diary for My Father and Mother
Diary of a Hooker Business Is Business
Diary of Forbidden Dreams What?
Días de Fútbol Football Days
Dick Tracy Meets Karloff Dick Tracy Meets Gruesome
Dick Tracy's Amazing Adventure Dick Tracy Meets Gruesome
Die Unberührbare No Place to Go
Diggstown Midnight Sting
Un Dimanche à la Campagne Sunday in the Country
Les Dimanches de Ville d'Avray Sundays and Cybèle
Dime Box Kid Blue
The Dinner Game Le Dîner de Cons
The Dion Brothers: the Gravy Train The Gravy Train
Dionysus Dionysus in '69
Dip Bin The Butterfly Murders
Dirty Dancing: Havana Nights Dirty Dancing 2
Dirty Hands Les Innocents aux Mains Sales
Dirty Hands Les Mains Sales
Dirty Knight's Work Trial by Combat
Dirty Money Un Flic
Disc Jockey Jamboree Jamboree
Disney's First Kid First Kid
Disney's That Darn Cat That Darn Cat
Dispara Outrage
Distant Uzak
Distant Journey The Long Journey
The Dividing Line The Lawless
A Divina Comedia The Divine Comedy
Divorzio all'Italiana Divorce – Italian Style
Dizzy Gillespie in Cuba A Night in Havana: Dizzy Gillespie in Cuba

The Dock Brief Trial and Error
Dr Rey Merci Docteur Rey
Dr Bethune Bethune: the Making of a Hero
Dr Butcher MD Zombie Holocaust
Dr Cadmem's Secret The Black Sleep
The Doctor from Seven Dials Corridors of Blood
Dr G and the Bikini Machine Dr Goldfoot and the Bikini Machine
Doctor in the Nude Shock Treatment
Dr Jekyll and Mr Hyde Edge of Sanity
Dr Laurent's Case The Case of Dr Laurent
Doctor Maniac The Man Who Changed His Mind
Doctor Maniac Who Lived Again The Man Who Changed His Mind
Dr Seuss's How the Grinch Stole Christmas The Grinch
The Doctor's Horrible Experiment The Testament of Dr Cordelier
The Does Les Biches
Dog Show Best in Show
Dog Soldiers Who'll Stop the Rain?
The Dog That Stopped the War The Dog Who Stopped the War
Dog Watch Dogwatch
Dogma 2: "The Idiots" The Idiots
Dogma 5: "Lovers" Lovers
Dogma 95 – Idioterne The Idiots
Dogme 12: Italiensk for Begyndere Italian for Beginners
The Dogs Les Chiens
A Dog's Life Mondo Cane
Dogtanian and the Three Muskehounds Dogtanian – the Movie
Doktor Glas Doctor Glas
Un Dollaro a Testa Navajo Joe
The Dolls Le Bambole
Una Domenica d'Agosto Sunday in August
Domicile Conjugal Bed and Board
The Domino Killings The Domino Principle
Don Bluth's Thumbelina Thumbelina
Doña Flor e Seus Dois Maridos Dona Flor and Her Two Husbands
Donald Cammell's Wild Side Wild Side
Dong The Hole
Donkey Skin The Magic Donkey
La Donna del Fiume Woman of the River
La Donna Piu Bella del Mondo Beautiful but Dangerous
Don't Look Down Wes Craven's Don't Look Down
Don't Open the Window The Living Dead at the Manchester Morgue
Don't Tell Her It's Me The Boyfriend School
Don't Touch the Loot Honour among Thieves
Doomed Ikiru
Doomed Cargo Seven Sinners
The Doorman Too Scared to Scream
Dope Addict Reefer Madness
Doped Youth Reefer Madness
Doppelgänger Journey to the Far Side of the Sun
The Double Kagemusha
Double Agenda Hidden Agenda
Double Edge American Dragons
00's Enemy Public Enemy
Double Play Lily in Love
A Double Tour Web of Passion
Double Trouble No Deposit No Return
Double Twist Web of Passion
La Double Vie de Véronique The Double Life of Véronique
Doucement les Basses Take It Easy
Doulos – the Finger Man Le Doulos
Les Douze Travaux d'Asterix The 12 Tasks of Asterix
Down and Under Kangaroo Jack
Down Home Something about Love
Down on the Farm On Our Selection
Down to Earth Flame Top
Down to the Sea in Ships The Last Adventurers
Down Went McGinty The Great McGinty
The Downfall The Downfall of Osen
Dracula Horror of Dracula
Dracula 2000 Dracula 2001
Dracula and the Seven Golden Vampires The Legend of the 7 Golden Vampires
Dracula contra Frankenstein Dracula, Prisoner of Frankenstein
Dracula Is Dead and Well and Living in London The Satanic Rites of Dracula
Dracula versus Frankenstein Dracula, Prisoner of Frankenstein
Dracula's Castle Blood of Dracula's Castle
Dracula's Dog Zoltan... Hound of Dracula
Dragon Dragon: the Bruce Lee Story
The Dragon Flies The Man from Hong Kong
Dragonfly One Summer Love
Dragonheart II Dragonheart: a New Beginning
Drama of Jealousy Jealousy, Italian Style
The Dream Maker It's All Happening
Dream of Life Life Begins
The Dream of Light The Quince Tree Sun
The Dream of Olwen While I Live

The Dreamlife of Angels The Dream Life of Angels
Dreams Akira Kurosawa's Dreams
Die Dreigroschenoper The Threepenny Opera
Dressed to Kill Sherlock Holmes and the Secret Code
The Dreyfus Case Dreyfus
Drifting Weeds Floating Weeds
Dripping Deep Red Deep Red
Die Dritte Generation The Third Generation
The Drug Kids in the Hall: Brain Candy
Drum Crazy The Gene Krupa Story
Drums The Drum
Drunk Monkey in the Tiger's Eyes Drunken Master
Drunk on Women and Poetry Chihwaseon (Drunk on Women and Poetry)
The Dubious Patriots You Can't Win 'em All
Duck, You Sucker! A Fistful of Dynamite
The Duckweed Story Floating Weeds
Due Contro La Citta Two against the Law
Due Marines e un Generale War Italian Style
Due Soldi di Speranza Two Pennyworth of Hope
Duel – Enemy at the Gates Enemy at the Gates
Dulcimer Street London Belongs to Me
The Dungeon The Scarf
Duplex Our House
Dura Lex By the Law
Durango Drango
Dutch Driving Me Crazy
Dynamite Women The Great Texas Dynamite Chase

E

E la Nave Va And the Ship Sails On
Eagle with Two Heads The Eagle Has Two Heads
Early Autumn The End of Summer
The Earrings of Madame de... Madame de...
The Earth Will Tremble La Terra Trema
East LA My Family
East of Shanghai Rich and Strange
East of the Rising Sun Malaya
East Palace, West Palace Behind the Forbidden City
The East Side Kids Meet Bela Lugosi Ghosts in the Night
East Wind Vent d'Est
Eastern Three Heroes The Heroic Trio
Easy Go Free and Easy
The Easy Way Room for One More
Eboli Christ Stopped at Eboli
Echoes of Paradise Shadows of the Peacock
L'Eclisse The Eclipse
L'Ecole Innocence
Ecole de la Chair The School of Flesh
L'Ecole des Facteurs School for Postmen
Ecologia del Delitto Bay of Blood
Ed and His Dead Mother Motherhood
Ed McBain's 87th Precinct: Lightning Ed McBain's 87th Precinct
Las Edades de Lulú The Ages of Lulu
Edgar Allan Poe's Conqueror Worm Witchfinder General
Edgar Allan Poe's The Haunting of Morella The Haunting of Morella
Edgar Allen Poe's The Oblong Box The Oblong Box
Edipo Re Oedipus Rex
Edith et Marcel Edith and Marcel
Edna Ferber's Glamour Glamour
Edwards and Hunt Almost Heroes
El Efecto Mariposa The Butterfly Effect
The Efficiency Expert Spotswood
L'Effrontée An Impudent Girl
Effroyable Jardins Strange Gardens
Die Ehe der Maria Braun The Marriage of Maria Braun
Ehi, Amico... C'è Sabata, Hai Chiuso Adios, Sabata
Eight on the Run Eight on the Lam
87th Precinct: Lightning Ed McBain's 87th Precinct
Eisenstein's Mexican Film Time in the Sun
Ek Din Pratidin And Quiet Rolls the Dawn
Electra Elektra
The Electric Man Man Made Monster
The Electronic Monster Escapement
El Elefante y la Bicicleta The Elephant and the Bicycle
Elena and Her Men Elena et les Hommes
Un Eléphant Ca Trompe Enormément Pardon Mon Affaire
An Elephant Can Be Extremely Deceptive Pardon Mon Affaire
Elephant Gun Nor the Moon by Night
Elephants Never Forget Zenobia
Elevator to the Gallows Lift to the Scaffold
11 September 11'09''01 – September 11

Elizabeth the Queen The Private Lives of Elizabeth and Essex
Ella Monkey Shines
Ellen The Second Woman
Elles N'Oublient Jamais Love in the Strangest Way
Elles N'Oublient Pas Love in the Strangest Way
Elmo in Grouchland The Adventures of Elmo in Grouchland
The Elusive Corporal The Vanishing Corporal
Elvira Elvira, Mistress of the Dark
Elvis Elvis – the Movie
Embers Sholay
Embrassez Qui Vous Voudrez Summer Things
Emergency Ward The Carey Treatment
Emily Brontë's Wuthering Heights Wuthering Heights
Emmanuelle the Joys of a Woman Emmanuelle 2
Emmanuelle's 7th Heaven Emmanuelle 2
L'Emmerdeur A Pain in the A...!
Emperor of the North Pole Emperor of the North
L'Empire d'Alexandre Stavisky
Empire of the Senses In the Realm of the Senses
The Empire Strikes Back Star Wars Episode V: the Empire Strikes Back
L'Emploi du Temps Time Out
The Empress Yang Kwei Fei The Princess Yang Kwei Fei
Empty Days Rien à Faire
En Attendant le Bonheur Waiting for Happiness
En Chair et en Os Live Flesh
En la Ciudad sin Limites The City of No Limits
Encino Man California Man
End as a Man The Strange One
End of Innocence Out of the Rain
The End of Old Times The Last of the Good Old Days
The End of the Good Old Days The Last of the Good Old Days
End of the Rainbow Northwest Outpost
Endstation 13 Sahara Station Six-Sahara
Enemies of the Public The Public Enemy
Enemy Fatal Mission
Enemy from Space Quatermass II
Les Enfants du Marais The Children of the Marshland
Enid Is Sleeping Over Her Dead Body
Enter the Street Fighter The Street Fighter
Entity Force One Dark Night
Entrapment Dead Wrong
Entre Tinieblas Dark Habits
Envoyé Spécial Cover-Up
The Epic Hero & the Beast Ilya Muromets
Episoda del Mare La Terra Trema
Ercole, Sfida e Sansone Hercules, Samson and Ulysses
Ernest Bliss The Amazing Quest of Ernest Bliss
Ernest Hemingway's The Killers The Killers
Erotikill The Female Vampire
Erste Liebe First Love
The Ervil LeBaron Story Prophet of Evil
Escapade Utopia
Escape The McKenzie Break
Escape by Night Clash by Night
Escape from the Dark The Littlest Horse Thieves
Escape of the Amethyst Yangtse Incident
Escape of the Birdmen The Birdmen
Escape to Freedom Judgment in Berlin
Escape to Happiness Intermezzo
Escape to Nowhere The Silent One
Escape 2000 Turkey Shoot
La Esclava del Paraíso Sharaz
Esh Tzoleveth Crossfire
Eskimo Limon Lemon Popsicle
El Espinazo del Diablo The Devil's Backbone
El Espiritu de la Colmena The Spirit of the Beehive
Espoir – Sierra de Teruel Man's Hope
Est-Ce Bien Raisonnable? Double Dare
Estouffade à la Caraïbe The Looters
La Estrategia del Caracol The Snail's Strategy
Et Dieu... Créa la Femme And God Created Woman
Et Là-bas, Quelle Heure Est-il? What Time Is It There?
Et Mourir de Plaisir Blood and Roses
Etat de Siege State of Siege
Une Eté Inoubliable An Unforgettable Summer
L'Eté Meurtrier One Deadly Summer
Eterna Femmina The Loves of Three Queens
Eternal Woman The Loves of Three Queens
L'Eternel Retour Eternal Love
Une Etrange Affaire A Strange Affair
L'Etranger The Stranger
Eugenio, I Love You Eugenio

Euro Pudding Pot Luck
Eva, the Devil's Woman Eva
Eve Eva
Evening Dress Tenue de Soirée
Every Man for Himself Slow Motion
Every Man for Himself and God against All The Enigma of Kaspar Hauser
Every Minute Counts Count the Hours
Every Nightmare Has a Zipcode – What's Yours? Bloody Angels
Every Other Inch a Lady Dancing Co-Ed
Every Woman's Man The Prizefighter and the Lady
Everybody's Cheering Take Me Out to the Ball Game
Everything to Gain Barbara Taylor Bradford's Everything to Gain
Everytime We Say Goodbye Every Time We Say Goodbye
Evil Angels A Cry in the Dark
Evil Dead 3 Army of Darkness
Evil Eden Death in the Garden
Evil Gun Day of the Evil Gun
Evil Heritage Satan's Slave
Evil Mind The Clairvoyant
Evils of Chinatown Confessions of an Opium Eater
The Executors The Sicilian Cross
Exils Exiles
Experiment in Evil The Testament of Dr Cordelier
The Extraordinary Adventures of Baron Muenchhausen Baron Münchhausen
Eye of Evil The Thousand Eyes of Dr Mabuse
Eyes from Hell The Mask
Eyes of Hell The Mask
Eyes of the Storm Eye of the Storm

F

FP1 Doesn't Answer FP1
FP1 Antwortet Nicht FP1
F/X FX: Murder by Illusion
Le Fabuleux Destin d'Amélie Poulain Amélie
The Fabulous Baron Munchausen Baron Munchhausen
The Fabulous World of Jules Verne Invention of Destruction
Faccia a Faccia Face to Face
The Face The Magician
Face behind the Scar Return of a Stranger
Face of an Angel Introducing Dorothy Dandridge
Face of Fear Peeping Tom
Face of Fire The Mask
The Face That Launched a Thousand Ships The Loves of Three Queens
A Face to Die For The Face
Face to the Wind Cry for Me Billy
Facing En Face
Facing Fear Flight of Fancy
Facing Windows Facing Window
The Facts of Love 29 Acacia Avenue
Fair Trade Captive Rage
The Falcon's Malteser Just Ask for Diamond
The Fall of Lola Montès Lola Montès
The Fall of the House of Usher The House of Usher
Fallen Angel Eternal Revenge
Fallen Angels Confessions of a Hit Man
Fallen Knight The Minion
Falling from the Sky! Flight 174 Freefall: Flight 174
Die Fälschung Circle of Deceit
False Faces Let 'Em Have It
False Witness Zigzag
False Witness Circle of Deceit
Falstaff Chimes at Midnight
La Famiglia The Family
The Family Violent City
Family Affair Life with the Lyons
A Family Divided Family Prayers
Family Enforcer Death Collector
Family Resemblances Un Air de Famille
A Family Torn Apart Sudden Fury
Family without a Dinner Table The Empty Table
The Famous Sword Bijomaru The Famous Sword
Fanatic Die! Die! My Darling
Fanny Hawthorne Hindle Wakes
Il Fantasma dell'Opera The Phantom of the Opera
The Fantastic Disappearing Man The Return of Dracula
The Fantastic Invasion of Planet Earth The Bubble
The Fantastic Invention Invention of Destruction
The Fantastic Puppet People Attack of the Puppet People
Faraon Pharaoh
Fararuv Konec End of a Priest
Fargo Wild Seed
The Farm The Curse
Fashions Fashions of 1934
The Fast and the Furious 2 2 Fast 2 Furious
Fast Bullets Law and Order
Fat Chance Peeper
Fat Girl A Ma Soeur!
Fat Man and Little Boy Shadow Makers
Fatal Attraction Head On
Fatal Chase Nowhere to Hide
Fatal Confinement Della
The Fatal Passions Dr Mabuse, the Gambler
Fatal Sky Project: Alien
Fate of a Hunter Captive Hearts
Fate of a Man Destiny of a Man
Father Apa
Father Master Padre Padrone
Father's Arcane Daughter Caroline?
Father's on a Business Trip When Father Was Away on Business
Fatto di Sangue fra Due Uomini per Causa di una Vedova – Si Sospettano Moventi Politici Blood Feud
Favourites of the Moon Les Favoris de la Lune
Fearless Frank Frank's Greatest Adventure
Feast of Flesh Blood Feast
Federico Fellini's Intervista Intervista
Feiying Gaiwak Operation Condor: the Armour of God II
Les Félins The Love Cage
Fellini Satyricon Satyricon
Fellini's Casanova Casanova
The Female and the Flesh The Light across the Street
The Feminine Touch The November Conspiracy
La Femme d'à Côté The Woman Next Door
La Femme de Chambre du Titanic The Chambermaid on the Titanic
La Femme de l'Aviateur The Aviator's Wife
Une Femme Douce A Gentle Creature
La Femme du Boulanger The Baker's Wife
La Femme Flic The Lady Cop
La Femme Mariée The Married Woman
La Femme Nikita Nikita
La Femme aux Bottes Rouges The Lady with Red Boots
Feroce Mad Dog Murderer
Die Fetten Jahre Sind Vorbei The Edukators
Feux Rouges Red Lights
Fever over Anatahan The Saga of Anatahan
Fever Pitch The Perfect Catch
Ffolkes North Sea Hijack
Fidelity La Fidélité
Field of Honour Soul of the Game
Fielder's Field Girls Can Play
The Fiends Les Diaboliques
The Fifth Chair It's in the Bag
50 First Kisses 50 First Dates
Fight without Honour The Yakuza Papers
Fighting Back Death Vengeance
Fighting Justice True Believer
The Fighting Pimpernel The Elusive Pimpernel
Figli di Annibale Children of Hannibal
La Fille de D'Artagnan D'Artagnan's Daughter
La Fille de Keltoum Bent Keltoum
La Fille sur le Pont The Girl on the Bridge
Les Filles Ne Savent Pas Nager Girls Can't Swim
Un Film Parlé Un Filme Falado
Filofax Taking Care of Business
Le Fils The Son
Fils de Deux Mères ou Comédie de l'Innocence Comédie de l'Innocence
Fin Août, Début Septembre Late August, Early September
Fin de Semana para los Muertos The Living Dead at the Manchester Morgue
La Fin du Jour The End of the Day
The Final Conflict Omen III: the Final Conflict
The Final Crash Steelyard Blues
The Final Lie A Matter of Dignity
The Final Option Who Dares Wins
Finally, Sunday Confidentially Yours
Fine and Dandy The West Point Story
A Fine Romance A Touch of Adultery
Fine Snow The Makioka Sisters
Fine Things Danielle Steel's Fine Things
La Finestra di Fronte Facing Window
Finger of Guilt The Intimate Stranger
The Fingerman Le Doulos
Fiona Hardcore
Fire and Ice II Fire, Ice and Dynamite
Fire Birds Wings of the Apache
The Fire Monster Godzilla Raids Again
Fire over Africa Malaga
Fire with Fire Captive Rage
The Fire Within Le Feu Follet
The First and the Last 21 Days
The First Emperor The Emperor and the Assassin
The First Hello The High Country
The First Letter Abjad
First Strike Jackie Chan's First Strike
Fist in His Pocket Fists in the Pocket
Fist-Right of Freedom Fox and His Friends
A Fistful of Chopsticks They Call Me Bruce
A Fistful of Revolution A Fistful of Dynamite
Fists of Fury The Big Boss
Fists of Fury Fist of Fury
Fitzwilly Strikes Back Fitzwilly
Five Angles on Murder The Woman in Question
Five Days Home Welcome Home, Soldier Boys
Five Dedicated to Ozu Five
Five Million Years to Earth Quatermass and the Pit
Five Minutes to Live Door-to-Door Maniac
Five Sinister Stories The Living Dead
Flame Slade in Flame
Flame of My Love My Love Has Been Burning
The Flame of Torment Conflagration
Flame over India North West Frontier
Flames of the Sun Sholay
The Flaming Torch The Bob Mathias Story
Flanagan Walls of Glass
Flesh Gordon 2 Flesh Gordon Meets the Cosmic Cheerleaders
La Fleur de Mon Secret The Flower of My Secret
La Fleur du Mal The Flower of Evil
Flic Story Police Story
The Flight Flight of Fancy
Flight from Terror Satan Never Sleeps
The Flight of the White Stallions Miracle of the White Stallions
The Flight That Vanished The Flight That Disappeared
Flights of Fancy Dream Flights
The Flim-Flam Man One Born Every Minute
Flip Out Get Crazy
Flipper and the Pirates Flipper's New Adventure
La Flor de Mi Secreto The Flower of My Secret
Flower and Fire Hana-Bi
The Flower in His Mouth The Masters
The Flowers of St Francis Francis, God's Jester
Flucht aus Laos Little Dieter Needs to Fly
FM Citizens Band
Fog A Study in Terror
Folies Bergère One Night at the Music Hall
Folle à Tuer The Evil Trap
La Folle des Grandeurs Delusions of Grandeur
Follow That Bird Sesame Street Presents: Follow That Bird
Follow That Camel Carry On Follow That Camel
Follow That Guy with the One Black Shoe The Tall Blond Man with One Black Shoe
Follow Your Dreams Independence Day
Fong Sai Yuk The Legend
Fong Sai Yuk II The Legend II
Fontane Effi Briest Effi Briest
Fools' Parade Dynamite Man from Glory Jail
For Love of a Queen The Dictator
For Love or Money Love or Money
For My Sister A Ma Soeur!
For Roseanna Roseanna's Grave
For You Alone When You're in Love
Forbidden Choices The Beans of Egypt, Maine
The Forbidden Dance Lambada! The Forbidden Dance
Forbidden Games Jeux Interdits
Forbidden Love Freaks
Forbidden Love Torn Apart
Forbidden Music Land without Music
Forbidden Paradise The Hurricane
Forbidden Paradise Hurricane
Forbidden Passions I Am a Nymphomaniac
The Forbidden Street Britannia Mews
Forbidden Subjects Kinjite: Forbidden Subjects
The Forbin Project Colossus: the Forbin Project
Forever in Love Pride of the Marines
Forever Mozart For Ever Mozart
Forever Young, Forever Free E' Lollipop
Forever Yours Forget-Me-Not
The Forgiven Sinner Léon Morin, Priest
Forgotten City The Vivero Letter
Forgotten Faces Till We Meet Again
Fork at Devil's Glen Murder at Devil's Glen
Formula 51 The 51st State
La Fortuna di Essere Donna Lucky to Be a Woman
The Fortune Hunter The Outcast
Fortune in Diamonds The Adventurers
48 Hours Went the Day Well?
43, the Petty Story Smash-Up Alley
Forward March Doughboys
Fountains of Home Eaux d'Artifice
Four against Fate Derby Day
Four Bags Full La Traversée de Paris
Four Dark Hours The Green Cockatoo
Four Desperate Men The Siege of Pinchgut
Four Faces West They Passed This Way
Four Gunmen of Ave Maria Ace High
Four Kinds of Love Le Bambole
Fox Fox and His Friends
La Fracture du Myocarde Cross My Heart
Francesco, Guillare di Dio Francis, God's Jester
Francis, God's Fool Francis, God's Jester
Francis the Talking Mule Francis
Frank Miller's Sin City Sin City
Frankenstein Mary Shelley's Frankenstein
Frankenstein vs Baragon Frankenstein Conquers the World
Frankenstein versus the Giant Devil Fish Frankenstein Conquers the World
Frankie the Fly The Last Days of Frankie the Fly
Frantic Lift to the Scaffold
Frasier the Lovable Lion Frasier, the Sensuous Lion
Fraternally Yours Sons of the Desert
Frau im Mond The Woman in the Moon
Die Frau, nach der Man sich Sehnt Three Loves
Freddie the Frog Freddie as FRO7
Freedom for Us A Nous la Liberté
Freefall: the Fate of Flight 174 Freefall: Flight 174
The Freelancers The Music Freelancers
Freeway II: Confessions of a Trickbaby Confessions of a Trickbaby
Freeze-Die-Come to Life Don't Move, Die and Rise Again
Freeze Me Freezer
French Lesson The Frog Prince
The French They Are a Funny Race The Diary of Major Thompson
French Twist Gazon Maudit
French Vampire in America Innocent Blood
A French Woman Une Femme Française
Fresa y Chocolate Strawberry and Chocolate
Fresh Bait The Bait
Freud – the Secret Passion Freud
Die Freudlose Gasse The Joyless Street
Frevel Mischief
Friday Night Vendredi Soir
Friday the 13th Part X Jason X
A Friend to Die For Death of a Cheerleader
A Friend's Betrayal Stolen Youth
Le Frisson des Vampires Shiver of the Vampires
Frissons Shivers
From beyond the Grave Judge & Jury
From One Side to the Other Aar Paar
From the Heart Dil Se...
From the Mixed-Up Files of Mrs Basil E Frankweiler The Hideaways
From the Murky Depths Dark Water
Frou-Frou The Toy Wife
Frozen Sometimes They Come Back... for More
Full Circle Danielle Steel's Full Circle
Full House O Henry's Full House
Full Speed A Toute Vitesse
Fun Loving Quackser Fortune Has a Cousin in the Bronx
The Funeral Death Japanese Style
Funeral Rites Death Japanese Style
Fungus of Terror Matango
Funny Place for a Meeting A Strange Place to Meet
Funnyman The Funny Man
Fuori dal Mondo Not of This World
The Fury of the Dragon The Way of the Dragon
Fuss over Feathers Conflict of Wings
Der Fussgänger The Pedestrian
Future Cop Trancers

GI Joe The Story of GI Joe
La Gabbianella e il Gatto Lucky and Zorba
Gadael Lenin Leaving Lenin
Galileo Galilei Galileo
The Gallery Murders The Bird with the Crystal Plumage
Game of Danger Bang! You're Dead
The Game of Love The Ripening Seed
Game Pass Jail Bait
Gandahar Light Years
Ganesh Ordinary Magic
Gang Walk Proud
Gang War Odd Man Out
The Gangster's Moll Minbo – or the Gentle Art of Japanese Extortion
The Gargon Terror Teenagers from Outer Space
Garm Hava Garam Hawa
Gas Benzina
Gasoline Benzina
Gaston Leroux's The Wax Mask Wax Mask
Gates of the Night Les Portes de la Nuit
Il Gatto a Nove Code Cat o'Nine Tails
Il Gatto Nero The Black Cat
Il Gattopardo The Leopard

Gauguin, le Loup dans le Soleil The Wolf at the Door
Gay Confessions The Alternative Miss World
The Gay Divorcee The Gay Divorce
The Gay Duellist Meet Me at Dawn
Gay Impostors Gold Diggers in Paris
The Gay Knowledge Le Gai Savoir
The Gay Mrs Trexel Susan and God
Gegen die Wand Head-On
Geheimnisse einer Seele Secrets of a Soul
Geliebte Milena Milena
Gemar Gavia Cup Final
Le Gendarme à New York The Gendarme in New York
Le Gendarme de Saint-Tropez The Gendarme of St Tropez
Le Gendarme et les Extra-Terrestres The Spacemen of St Tropez
Genealogies of a Crime Généalogies d'un Crime
A Genius in the Family So Goes My Love
Le Genou de Claire Claire's Knee
Les Gens de la Rizière Rice People
Gente di Rispetto The Masters
The Gentle Touch The Feminine Touch
A Gentle Woman A Gentle Creature
Gentleman for a Day Union Depot
Die Gentlemen Bitten zur Kasse The Great British Train Robbery
Gentlemen Don't Eat Poets The Grotesque
Georges Dandin Dandin
Georges et Georgette Viktor und Viktoria
Get Charlie Tully Ooh... You Are Awful
Get On with It Dentist on the Job
Get Your Handkerchiefs Ready Get out Your Handkerchiefs
Gettin' the Man's Foot Outta Your Baadasssss! Baadasssss!
Getting Away with Murder End of the Game
Getting Even Utilities
Gharbar The Householder
Ghare Baire The Home and the World
Ghastly Tales The Living Dead
Ghidora, the Three-Headed Monster Ghidrah, the Three-Headed Monster
Ghidrah: the Greatest Battle on Earth Ghidrah, the Three-Headed Monster
The Ghost The Spectre
Ghost at Noon Le Mépris
The Ghost Brigade Killing Box
The Ghost Creeps Boys of the City
Ghost of Rashmon Hall Night Comes Too Soon
The Ghost Steps Out The Time of Their Lives
Ghosts Spooks Run Wild
Ghosts from the Past Ghosts of Mississippi
Ghosts of Mars John Carpenter's Ghosts of Mars
Ghosts on the Loose Ghosts in the Night
Giant Killer Jack the Giant Killer
The Giant Leeches Attack of the Giant Leeches
Il Giardino dei Finzi-Contini The Garden of the Finzi-Continis
Gideon of Scotland Yard Gideon's Day
Gift from a Red Planet The Alpha Incident
Gigantis, the Fire Monster Godzilla Raids Again
Gill Women of Venus Voyage to the Planet of Prehistoric Women
Gina Death in the Garden
Gingerbread House Who Slew Auntie Roo?
Il Giovane Toscanini Young Toscanini
Giovani Mariti Young Husbands
A Girl, a Guy and a Gob The Navy Steps Out
The Girl – an Erotic Thriller The Girl
The Girl at the Monceau Bakery The Boulangère de Monceau
A Girl Called Katy Tippel Keetje Tippel
A Girl for Joe Force of Arms
The Girl Friends Le Amiche
The Girl from Hanoi Little Girl from Hanoi
The Girl Gets Moe Love to Kill
The Girl-Getters The System
Girl in Distress Jeannie
Girl in Pawn Little Miss Marker
The Girl in Room 17 Vice Squad
Girl in the Moon The Woman in the Moon
The Girl in the Painting Portrait from Life
Girl in the Street London Melody
The Girl in the Trunk Man in the Trunk
Girl of the Year The Petty Girl
The Girl Swappers Two and Two Make Six
Girl Talk Some Girls
The Girl with the Red Hair The Girl with Red Hair
Girlfriends Les Biches
The Girlfriends Le Amiche
The Girls Les Bonnes Femmes
Girls' Club Club de Femmes
Girls Gang Easy Wheels
The Girls He Left Behind The Gang's All Here
Girls on the Moon Nude on the Moon
Girly Mumsy, Nanny, Sonny & Girly

Giulia e Giulia Julia and Julia
Giulietta degli Spiriti Juliet of the Spirits
Give Me a Break Life with Mikey
The Giver The Donor
The Giving Tree The Brutal Truth
Gladiatorerna The Peace Game
The Gladiators The Peace Game
Les Glaneurs et la Glaneuse The Gleaners and I
The Glass Tomb The Glass Cage
Glenn O'Brien's New York Beat Movie Downtown 81
Glenorky Magic in the Water
Gli Indifferenti Time of Indifference
Gli Orrori del Castello di Norimberga Baron Blood
Glitter I Live My Life
Glory at Sea The Gift Horse
Gnaw: Food of the Goods II Food of the Gods II
A Gnome Named Gnorm Upworld
The Goalie's Anxiety at the Penalty Kick The Goalkeeper's Fear of the Penalty Kick
The God Game The Magus
God Gave Him a Dog The Biscuit Eater
God Needs Men Dieu A Besoin des Hommes
The Godfather of Harlem Black Caesar
God's Army The Prophecy
God's New Plan No Higher Love
God's Payroll Mortal Sins
Godzilla and Mothra: the Battle for Earth Godzilla vs Mothra
Godzilla, King of the Monsters Godzilla
Godzilla 1985 The Return of Godzilla
Godzilla on Monster Island Godzilla vs Gigan
Godzilla vs Monster Zero Invasion of the Astro-Monster
Godzilla versus the Bionic Monster Godzilla vs Mechagodzilla
Godzilla vs the Cosmic Monster Godzilla vs Mechagodzilla
Godzilla versus the Sea Monster Ebirah, Horror of the Deep
Godzilla vs the Thing Godzilla vs Mothra
Godzilla's Leverage Godzilla's Revenge
Going Places Les Valseuses
Going Undercover Yellow Pages
Gojira Godzilla
Gojira no Gyakushu Godzilla Raids Again
Goke the Vampire Goke, Bodysnatcher from Hell
Gold Rush! The Highwayman
Gold Town Barbary Coast Gent
Golden Arrow The Gay Adventure
Golden Girl Goldengirl
The Golden Heist Inside Out
The Golden Hour Pot o' Gold
Golden Marie Casque d'Or
The Golden Mask South of Algiers
The Golden Virgin The Story of Esther Costello
Das Goldene Bäumchen The Singing, Ringing Tree
Golem, l'Esprit de l'Exil Golem, the Spirit of Exile
Der Golem, Wie Er in die Welt Kam The Golem
Goliath Hero of Babylon
Goliath, King of the Slaves Hero of Babylon
Golpes a Mi Puerta Knocks at My Door
Gone in a Heartbeat Taken Away
Gone with the West Little Moon & Jud McGraw
Good Deed Upkaar
Good Luck Bonne Chance
A Good Marriage Le Beau Mariage
Good Morning Ohayo
Good Morning, Boys Where There's a Will
The Good Mother The Price of Passion
The Good-Time Outlaws Smokey and the Good Time Outlaws
The Good Year Happy New Year
Goodbye Bruce Lee: His Last Game of Death Game of Death
Goodbye Children Au Revoir les Enfants
Goodbye Texas Texas Adios
A Gorgeous Bird Like Me Une Belle Fille Comme Moi
Gorilla The Ape
The Gospel According to Vic Heavenly Pursuits
Gotham The Dead Can't Lie
Götter der Pest Gods of the Plague
Götterdämmerung The Damned
Gouttes d'Eau sur Pierres Brûlantes Water Drops on Burning Rocks
Goya Goya in Bordeaux
Le Graal Lancelot du Lac
The Grace Moore Story So This Is Love
Graceland Finding Graceland
The Graduate of Malibu High Young Warriors
The Grail Lancelot du Lac
El Gran Calavera The Great Madcap
La Gran Vida Living It Up

Un Grand Amour de Beethoven Abel Gance's Beethoven
Le Grand Blond avec une Chaussure Noire The Tall Blond Man with One Black Shoe
The Grand Duel The Big Showdown
The Grand Maneuver Les Grandes Manoeuvres
Le Grand Meaulnes The Wanderer
Le Grand Pardon II Day of Atonement
Il Grande Bluff The Con Artists
La Grande Guerra The Great War
Il Grande Silenzio The Great Silence
La Grande Vadrouille Don't Look Now... We're Being Shot At
The Grandeur and Decadence of a Small Time Filmmaker Grandeur et Décadence d'un Petit Commerce de Cinéma
Les Granges Brulées Burnt Barns
Grave Indiscretions The Grotesque
Grave Robbers from Outer Space Plan 9 from Outer Space
The Graveyard Persecution
The Great Adventure The Adventurers
The Great American Bugs Bunny–Road Runner Chase The Bugs Bunny/Road Runner Movie
Gt Am Movie Book 5 Fingers
The Great Armored Car Swindle The Breaking Point
The Great Bank Hoax The Great Georgia Bank Hoax
Great Charge of All Monsters Godzilla's Revenge
The Great City Skyscraper Wilderness The Big City
The Great Feed La Grande Bouffe
The Great Gilbert and Sullivan The Story of Gilbert and Sullivan
The Great Manhunt The Doolins of Oklahoma
The Great Manhunt State Secret
Great Moments in Aviation Shades of Fear
The Great Mouse Detective Basil the Great Mouse Detective
The Great Mughal Mughal-e-Azam
The Great Rat Swarm Gamera the Invincible
The Great Schnozzle Palooka
The Great Train Robbery The First Great Train Robbery
The Great Wall Is a Great Wall A Great Wall
The Greatest Love Europa '51
Greedy Guts Little Otik
Green-Eyed Woman Take a Letter, Darling
Green Monkey Blue Monkey
Greetings From Nantucket One Crazy Summer
Gregoire Moulin contre L'Humanité Grégoire Moulin
Grey Knight Killing Box
The Grey Zone Strong Hands
Grimm's Snow White Snow White: a Tale of Terror
Grine Felder Green Fields
The Grip of Fear Experiment in Terror
Grisbi Honour among Thieves
Gross Anatomy A Cut Above
G's Trippin Trippin'
La Guerra Segreta The Dirty Game
La Guerre des Boutons War of the Buttons
La Guerre des Polices The Police War
La Guerre du Feu Quest for Fire
La Guerre sans Nom The Undeclared War
Guerre Secrète The Dirty Game
The Guest The Caretaker
La Gueule Ouverte The Mouth Agape
A Guide for the Married Woman The Secret Life of an American Wife
Gumby 1 Gumby: the Movie
Gun Moll Jigsaw
Gun Point At Gunpoint
The Gun Runners Santiago
Gunfire China 9, Liberty 37
Gunnar Hedes Saga Gunnar Hede's Saga
Guns A' Blazing Law and Order
Guns in the Afternoon Ride the High Country
Guns of Wrath Guns of Hate
Guns of Wyoming Cattle King
Guns, Sin and Bathtub Gin The Lady in Red
Gunshy Gun Shy
Gunslinger The Gunslinger
A Guy and a Gal A Lover and His Lass
Guy with a Grin No Time for Comedy
The Guys The Boys
Gypsy Blood Wild at Heart
Gypsy Blood Gone to Earth
Gypsy Girl Sky West and Crooked

HP Lovecraft's Necronomicon Necronomicon
HP Lovecraft's The Resurrected The Resurrected
HR Pufnstuf Pufnstuf

Ha-Hesder Time of Favor
Hable con Ella Talk to Her
Un Hacha para la Luna de Miel Hatchet for the Honeymoon
Haendeligt Uheld One of Those Things
Hail the Artist The Bit Player
Halcyon Days Innocent Lies
Half Life Fate Eighteen Springs
Hallelujah, I'm a Tramp! Hallelujah, I'm a Bum
Hamam Il bagno turco Hamam: the Turkish Bath
Hamlet Liikemaailmassa Hamlet Goes Business
Hamnstad Port of Call
A Handful of Clouds Doorway to Hell
A Handful of Grain Mother India
Handle with Care Citizens Band
Der Händler der vier Jahreszeiten The Merchant of Four Seasons
Hands across the City Hands over the City
Hands of a Strangler The Hands of Orlac
The Hands of Orlac Mad Love
Hang Tough Hard Feelings
Hanging Death by Hanging
The Hangover The Female Jungle
The Hank Williams Story Your Cheatin' Heart
Hannibal's Children Children of Hannibal
Hannibal's Sons Children of Hannibal
Hans Christian Andersen's Thumbelina Thumbelina
Happenstance The Beating of the Butterfly's Wings
Happiness Le Bonheur
The Happiness Cage The Mind Snatchers
Happy Go Lucky Hallelujah, I'm a Bum
Happy Gypsies I Even Met Happy Gypsies
Happy Times The Inspector General
Harbour of Desire The House on the Waterfront
Hard City Tales from a Hard City
Hard Cover Best Seller
Hard Driver The Last American Hero
The Hardcore Life Hardcore
Harem Holiday Harum Scarum
Harmony Parade Pigskin Parade
Harold and Kumar Go to White Castle Harold & Kumar Get the Munchies
Harp of Burma The Burmese Harp
Harry, a Friend Who Wishes You Well Harry, He's Here to Help
Harry and the Hendersons Bigfoot and the Hendersons
Harry Potter and the Sorcerer's Stone Harry Potter and the Philosopher's Stone
Harry, un Ami Qui Vous Veut du Bien Harry, He's Here to Help
Harry's Machine Hollywood Harry
Hartbreak Hotel Home Is Where the Hart Is
Hartbreak Motel Home Is Where the Hart Is
Hasards ou Coïncidences Chance or Coincidence
Hasta Morir 'Til Death
Hatchet Man Bad Company
The Hatchet Murders Deep Red
The Haunted and the Hunted Dementia 13
Haunted Honeymoon Busman's Honeymoon
The Haunted Strangler Grip of the Strangler
The Haunting of Julia Full Circle
The Haunting of Maurella The Haunting of Morella
Haute Tension Switchblade Romance
Havana Nights: Dirty Dancing 2 Dirty Dancing 2
Have Gun Will Travel Ace High
Having a Wild Weekend Catch Us If You Can
The Hawk Ride Him, Cowboy
Hawken Hawken's Breed
He Who Must Die Celui Qui Doit Mourir
Head over Heels Chilly Scenes of Winter
Head over Heels Head over Heels in Love
The Head That Wouldn't Die The Brain That Wouldn't Die
The Headline Story Home Town Story
A Heart in Winter Un Coeur en Hiver
The Heart of New York Hallelujah, I'm a Bum
Heart of Paris Gribouille
Heartbeat Danielle Steel's Heartbeat
Heartfarm Middle Age Crazy
Hearts and Minds A Man to Respect
The Heart's Dark Side The Dark Side of the Heart
Heartstone Demonstone
Heaven Fell That Night Les Bijoutiers du Clair de Lune
Heaven Help Us Catholic Boys
Heaven's a Drag To Die For
The Heavens Call Battle beyond the Sun
A Heidi Adventure Courage Mountain
Der Heilige Berg The Holy Mountain
Heimat 3: Chronik Einer Zeitenwende Heimat 3: a Chronicle of Endings and Beginnings

Heinrich von Kleist's The Prince of Homburg The Prince of Homburg
The Heir to Genghis Khan Storm over Asia
The Heiress of Dracula Vampyros Lesbos
The Heist Dollars
Heksen Häxan
Helden Arms and the Man
Helen of Troy The Private Life of Helen of Troy
Hell Bent The Peacekeeper
Hell Fighters Hellfighters
Hell, Heaven and Hoboken I Was Monty's Double
Hell in Korea A Hill in Korea
Hell on Heels: the Battle of Mary Kay The Battle of Mary Kay
Hell Riders Hellriders
Hell to Macao The Corrupt Ones
Hellbent The Peacekeeper
Hellcab Chicago Cab
Hell's Bells Murder by Phone
Hell's Crossroads Our Daily Bread
Hell's Gate Gate of Hell
Hell's Highway Violent Road
Heloise et Abelard Stealing Heaven
Her Bridal Night The Bride Is Too Beautiful
Her Enlisted Man Red Salute
Her Favourite Patient Bedside Manner
Her Majesty, Mrs Brown Mrs Brown
Her Man Gilbey English without Tears
Hercules: the Movie Hercules in New York
Here Come the Tigers Kick!
Here Lies Love The Second Woman
Here We Go Again Pride of the Bowery
Heremakono Waiting for Happiness
Here's the Knife Dear, Now Use It Nightmare
The Heritage of Dracula Vampyros Lesbos
L'Héritier The Inheritor
Hero Accidental Hero
The Hero Bloomfield
Hero: The Official Film of the 1986 Fifa World Cup Hero
Heroes Die Hard Mr Kingstreet's War
Heroes of the Regiment Bonnie Scotland
The Heroin Gang Sol Madrid
Les Héroïnes du Mal Heroines of Evil
Heroines of Pain Heroines of Evil
Heroism Eroica
Un Héros Très Discret A Self-Made Hero
Herr Tartüff Tartuffe
Herz aus Glas Heart of Glass
Hexen bis aufs Blut Gequält Mark of the Devil
Die Hexen von Salem The Witches of Salem
Hey Cousin! Salut Cousin!
Hey Sailor Here Comes the Navy
Hidden Assassin The Shooter
Hidden Face Jail Bait
The Hidden Room Obsession
Hidden Vision Night Eyes
Hide and Shriek American Gothic
Hideo Nakata's Chaos Chaos
Hideout The Small Voice
Hideout in the Alps Dusty Ermine
High and Dry The Maggie
The High Commissioner Nobody Runs Forever
High Encounters (of the Ultimate Kind) Cheech and Chong's Next Movie
High Heels and Lowlifes High Heels and Low Lifes
High School Honeymoon Too Soon to Love
High Tension Switchblade Romance
Highball Mr Jealousy
Highlander: the Final Dimension Highlander III: the Sorcerer
Highlander: the Magician Highlander III: the Sorcerer
Highway to Hell Running Hot
Hijinks Tigers in Lipstick
El Hijo de la Novia Son of the Bride
Der Himmel über Berlin Wings of Desire
Une Hirondelle A Fait le Printemps The Girl from Paris
His Affair This Is My Affair
His Brother Son Frère
His, Hers and Theirs Yours, Mine and Ours
His Lady When a Man Loves
His Other Woman Desk Set
His Secret Life Le Fate Ignoranti
L'Histoire d'Adèle H The Story of Adèle H
Histoire d'O The Story of O
Une Histoire Immortelle The Immortal Story
La Historia Oficial The Official Version
Historias del Subdesarrollo Memories of Underdevelopment
Hit Parade of 1943 Change of Heart
The Hit Team Company of Killers
Hitler's Gold Inside Out
Hitler's Hangman Hitler's Madman
Höhenfeuer Alpine Fire
Hold That Girl Hold That Co-Ed
The Hole Onibaba
Holiday in Spain Scent of Mystery
Holiday Week Hindle Wakes
Hollywood Cowboy Hearts of the West
Holy Blood Santa Sangre
The Holy Girl La Niña Santa
The Holy Innocents Los Santos Inocentes
Holy Terror Alice, Sweet Alice
Hombres Armados Men with Guns
Home Fires Burning The Turning
Home Town Girl Home Town Story
Homeboys at the Beach Boys on the Beach
Homecoming Heimkehr
Homefront Home Front
O Homem do Ano The Man of the Year
Hometown Story Home Town Story
Un Homme Amoureux A Man in Love
L'Homme de Rio That Man from Rio
Un Homme Est Mort The Outside Man
L'Homme est une Femme comme les Autres Man Is a Woman
Un Homme et une Femme: Vingt Ans Déjà A Man and a Woman: 20 Years Later
L'Homme Qui Aimait les Femmes The Man Who Loved Women
L'Homme sans Visage Shadowman
Hommes, Femmes, Mode d'Emploi Men, Women: a User's Manual
Homo Faber Voyager
The Honest Courtesan Dangerous Beauty
The Honest Thief Barbary Coast Gent
The Honest Thief The Good Thief
Honeymoon Academy For Better or for Worse
Honor Guard Wolf Lake
The Honourable Mr Wong The Hatchet Man
Hoofbeats Running Free
A Hora da Estrela Hour of the Star
Las Horas del Dia The Hours of the Day
L'Horloger de Saint-Paul The Watchmaker of St Paul
The Horror Chamber of Dr Faustus Eyes without a Face
Horror Hotel The City of the Dead
Horror Hotel Eaten Alive
Horror House The Haunted House of Horror
Horror Maniacs The Greed of William Hart
The Horror of Death The Asphyx
Horror on Snape Island Tower of Evil
Horror Planet Inseminoid
The Horror Star Frightmare
Horrors of the Black Zoo Black Zoo
HorrorScope 976-EVIL
A Horse Called Comanche Tonka
The Horse of Pride Le Cheval d'Orgeuil
Horseplayer Knife Edge
The Horse's Mouth The Oracle
Hostage: Dallas Getting Even
Hot Boyz Gang Law
Hot City Original Gangstas
Hot Dogs: Wau – Wir Sind Reich! Millionaire Dogs
Hot Money Girl The Treasure of San Teresa
The Hot One Corvette Summer
Hot Shots 2 Hot Shots! Part Deux
Hot Spot I Wake Up Screaming
Hot Sweat Keetje Tippel
Hotspot I Wake Up Screaming
Hounded Johnny Allegro
The Hounds of Zaroff The Most Dangerous Game
Hour of Glory The Small Back Room
Hour of Judgment The Hour of the Pig
The House at the End of the World Die, Monster, Die!
The House in Trubnoi Street The House on Trubnaya Square
The House Keys The Keys to the House
House of a Thousand Pleasures House of a Thousand Dolls
House of Crazies Asylum
House of Doom The Black Cat
The House of Exorcism Lisa and the Devil
House of Fright The Two Faces of Dr Jekyll
House of Menace Kind Lady
House of Pleasure Le Plaisir
House of 7 Joys The Wrecking Crew
House of Unclaimed Women The Smashing Bird I Used to Know
House of Usher The Fall of the House of Usher
The House on Chimney Square The House on Trubnaya Square
House on Rubens St Phantom of Death
The House on Sorority Row House of Evil
The House on Straw Hill Exposé
The House on Turk Street No Good Deed
The House outside the Cemetery House by the Cemetery
The House under the Trees The Deadly Trap
House without Windows Seven Alone
The Housekeeper A Judgement in Stone
Housewife Bone
How Much Loving Does a Normal Couple Need? Common-Law Cabin
How Often... That Night Four Times That Night
How to Be a Woman and Survive How to Be a Woman and Not Die in the Attempt
How to Get the Man's Foot Outta Your Asss! Baadasssss!
How to Rob a Bank A Nice Little Bank That Should Be Robbed
How to Steal a Diamond in Four Uneasy Lessons The Hot Rock
How to Stuff a Wild Bikini How to Fill a Wild Bikini
How Understanding Comes to Young Girls Mitsou
How You Like Me Now How U Like Me Now
Howard the Duck Howard, a New Breed of Hero
Huayang Nianhua In the Mood for Love
Huckleberry Finn The Adventures of Huckleberry Finn
Huevos de oro Golden Balls
Hugo Pool Pool Girl
Huis-Clos No Exit
8 Femmes 8 Women
Le Huitième Jour The Eighth Day
The Human Beast Mad Dog Murderer
The Human Monster Dark Eyes of London
Humanity L'Humanité
Humanoids from the Deep Monster
The Hunchback Le Bossu
The Hunchback Hairball of UCLA Big Man on Campus
Hundred Hour Hunt Emergency Call
Hungry Heart Life Is a Miracle
Hungry Wives Season of the Witch
Hunt to Kill The White Buffalo
The Hunted Benji the Hunted
Hunted Hunting
Las Hurdes Land without Bread
Hurly Burly Hurlyburly
Le Hussard sur le Toit The Horseman on the Roof
Hyperspace Gremloids
Hypnotic Doctor Sleep
The Hypnotist London after Midnight

I Accuse J'Accuse
I Am a Fugitive I Am a Fugitive from a Chain Gang
I Became a Criminal They Made Me a Fugitive
I Call First Who's That Knocking at My Door
I Can Make You Love Me: the Stalking of Laura Black Stalking Laura
I Can Read The Sky I Could Read the Sky
I Come in Peace Dark Angel
I Dance Alone Stealing Beauty
I Don't Know What It Means to Say Phoenix, Arizona Smoke Signals
I Don't Want to Talk about It We Don't Want to Talk about It
I Fought the Law Dead Heat
I Hate Your Guts The Intruder
I Like Money Mr Topaze
I Love You All Je Vous Aime
I Love You Eugenio Eugenio
I Love You to Death Stalking Laura
I Married a Communist The Woman on Pier 13
I Married a Nazi The Man I Married
I, Mobster The Mobster
I-95 Ride
I See Ice! I See Ice
I Shall Return An American Guerrilla in the Philippines
I Spy, You Spy Our Man in Marrakesh
I Stand Alone Seul contre Tous
I Stand Condemned Moscow Nights
I Want Her Dead W
I Was a Fireman Fires Were Started
I Was a Teenage Boy Willy/Milly
I Was a Teenage Gorilla Konga
I Was Faithless Cynara
Ice Station Erebus Sometimes They Come Back... for More
Ich Will Doch Nur, Dass Ihr Mich Liebt I Only Want You to Love Me
Icy Breasts Someone Is Bleeding
Icy Flesh Someone Is Bleeding
Identificazione di una Donna Identification of a Woman
Identikit The Driver's Seat
The Idiot Returns Return of the Idiot
Idioterne The Idiots
Ieri, Oggi, Domani Yesterday, Today and Tomorrow
If Looks Could Kill Teen Agent
If This Be Sin That Dangerous Age
If You Feel Like Singing Summer Stock
If You Love Me I Live My Life
Ignorant Fairies Le Fate Ignoranti
Il Etait une Fois un Flic There Was Once a Cop
Il Etait une Fois un Pays Underground
L'Ile des Chèvres Les Possédées
I'll Be You Whatever It Takes
I'll Dig Your Grave Sartana, Angel of Death
I'll Get You Escape Route
Ill Town illtown
Illicit Interlude Summer Interlude
I'm Here Now! Main Hoon Na
Im Lauf der Zeit Kings of the Road
Im Stahlnetz des Dr Mabuse The Return of Dr Mabuse
Imaginando Argentina Imagining Argentina
An Imaginary Tale Une Histoire Inventée
The Immaculate Conception of Baby Bump A Sinful Life
The Immaculate Sword The Famous Sword
Immediate Disaster Stranger from Venus
Immoral Charge Serious Charge
Immortal Battalion The Way Ahead
The Imperfect Lady The Perfect Gentleman
Impossible Object Story of a Love Story
Les Impures Anita
In a Wild Moment Un Moment d'Egarement
In a Year with 13 Moons In a Year of 13 Moons
In All Innocence En Plein Coeur
In Einem Jahr mit 13 Monden In a Year of 13 Moons
In Front of Your House Tere Ghar Ke Saamne
In Nome del Papa Re In the Name of the Pope King
In Old Oklahoma War of the Wildcats
In Praise of Love Eloge de l'Amour
In Rosie's Room Rosie the Riveter
In Search of Our Roots Asa Nu Maan Watna Da
In Self Defense In Her Defense
In the Body of the Whale In the Belly of the Whale
In the Devil's Garden Assault
In the Flesh Desperate Measures
In the Light of the Moon Ed Gein
In the Line of Duty: Kidnapped Kidnapped
In the Line of Duty: the Price of Vengeance The Price of Vengeance
In the Mood The Woo Woo Kid
In the Shadow of the Past Shadows of Our Forgotten Ancestors
In the Woods Rashomon
Im Toten Winkel – Hitlers Sekretärin Blind Spot: Hitler's Secretary
In Weiter Ferne, So Nah! Faraway, So Close
The Inbetween Age The Golden Disc
An Inch over the Horizon Captain Jack
Incident at Raven's Gate Encounter at Raven's Gate
The Incredible Invasion Alien Terror
The Incredible Praying Mantis The Deadly Mantis
Indagine su un Cittadino al di Sopra di ogni Sospetto Investigation of a Citizen above Suspicion
L'Inde Fantôme: Réflexions sur un Voyage Phantom India
Indefensible: the Truth about Edward Brannigan A Father's Betrayal
India Indien
Indian Summer Alive and Kicking
Indian Summer The Judge Steps Out
Indiana Jones and the Raiders of the Lost Ark Raiders of the Lost Ark
Das Indische Grabmal The Indian Tomb
Indiscretion Christmas in Connecticut
Indiscretion Indiscretion of an American Wife
The Infernal Idol Craze
Inferno Desert Heat
Infested Ticks
Informant Primary Suspect
The Inheritance Uncle Silas
The Inkwell No Ordinary Summer
Inn of the Frightened People Revenge
Innocence Is Bliss Miss Grant Takes Richmond
The Innocent L'Innocente
The Innocent and the Damned Girls' Town
Innocent Victim Tree of Hands
An Innocent War December
Innocents from Hell Alucarda
Innocents with Dirty Hands Les Innocents aux Mains Sales
L'Inondation The Flood
The Ins and the Outs Les Uns et les Autres
Insatiable Lust The Female Vampire
Inside Out Life Upside Down
L'Inspecteur Lavardin ou la Justice Inspecteur Lavardin
Inspector Maigret Maigret Sets a Trap
Insurgent Mexico Reed: Insurgent Mexico
Intermission Entr'Acte
L'Interno di un Convento Behind Convent Walls
Interval Entr'Acte
The Interview Intervista
Interview with a Serial Killer White Angel
Intimate Strangers Confidences Trop Intimes
Intruder Moon 44
Invader Lifeform
The Invader An Old Spanish Custom
The Invaders 49th Parallel
Invasion Earth 2150 AD Daleks – Invasion Earth 2150 AD

Invasion Force Hangar 18
Invasion of Planet X Invasion of the Astro-Monster
Invasion of the Astros Invasion of the Astro-Monster
Invasion of the Body Stealers The Body Stealers
Invasion of the Flying Saucers Earth vs the Flying Saucers
Les Invasions Barbares The Barbarian Invasions
O Invasor The Trespasser
Invention Diabolique Invention of Destruction
An Invention for Destruction Invention of Destruction
An Investigation of Murder The Laughing Policeman
Invictus Unconquered
The Invincible Six The Heroes
Invisible Power Washington Merry-Go-Round
Io Non Ho Paura I'm Not Scared
Iron Eagle 3 Aces: Iron Eagle III
The Iron Hand Fist of Fury
The Iron Kiss The Naked Kiss
The (Irrefutable) Truth about Demons The Truth about Demons
Irrgarten der Leidenschaft The Pleasure Garden
Island of Shame The Young One
Island of the Alive It's Alive III: Island of the Alive
Island of the Burning Damned Night of the Big Heat
Island of the Last Zombies Zombie Holocaust
Island Rescue Appointment with Venus
Islands Doctors Dear Diary
Isle of Sinners Dieu A Besoin des Hommes
L'Isola delle Donne Sole Les Possédées
Istanbul Tales Anlat Istanbul
It All Starts Today Ca Commence Aujourd'hui
It Came without Warning Without Warning
It Comes Up Murder The Honey Pot
It Fell From the Sky The Alien Dead
It Happened in Paris The Lady in Question
It Happened in Your Neighbourhood Man Bites Dog
It Happened One Summer State Fair
It Hurts Only When I Laugh Only When I Laugh
It Lives within Her I Don't Want to Be Born
It Only Happens With You Let It Be Me
It Takes a Thief The Challenge
It! the Vampire from beyond Space It! The Terror from beyond Space
Italiensk for Begyndere Italian for Beginners
It's Alive 2 It Lives Again
It's Growing inside Her I Don't Want to Be Born
It's Hot in Hell A Monkey in Winter
It's Magic Romance on the High Seas
It's My Life Vivre Sa Vie
It's Not the Size That Counts Percy's Progress
It's Only Money Double Dynamite
It's Raining Money As If It Were Raining
Ivan's Xtc ivansxtc.
Ivory Hunter Where No Vultures Fly

J

JR Who's That Knocking at My Door
Jack London's The Call of the Wild The Call of the Wild
Jack Reed: a Killer amongst Us Jack Reed: One of Our Own
Jack Reed: an Honest Cop Jack Reed: Badge of Honor
Jack Reed: the Ridges Case Jack Reed: One of Our Own
Jackie Chan's Police Story Police Story
Jack's Wife Season of the Witch
Jacqueline Susann's Once Is Not Enough Once Is Not Enough
Jacula The Female Vampire
J'ai Epousé une Ombre I Married a Dead Man
Jailbird Sweet Hunters
Jakob der Lügner Jacob the Liar
Jakob the Liar Jacob the Liar
Jalsaghar The Music Room
James Kick
The James Brady Story Without Warning: the James Brady Story
The James Brothers The True Story of Jesse James
James Dean: an Invented Life James Dean
Jana Aranya The Middleman
The Janitor Eyewitness
Japan Japón
Jason and the Golden Fleece Jason and the Argonauts
Jason Lives: Friday the 13th Part VI Friday the 13th Part VI: Jason Lives
Jaws 4 Jaws the Revenge
Jaws 3-D Jaws III
Jaya, Fille du Gange Jaya Ganga
Jazz '34 Robert Altman's Jazz '34: Remembrances of Kansas City Swing
Je Rentre à la Maison I'm Going Home
Je Suis Frigide...Pourquoi? I Am Frigid... Why?
Je Suis une Nymphomane I Am a Nymphomaniac
Je Veux Rentrer à la Maison I Want to Go Home
Jean Taris, Swimming Champion Taris
Jeder für Sich und Gott Gegen Alle The Enigma of Kaspar Hauser
The Jenifer Estess Story Jenifer
Jennie Portrait of Jennie
Jenny Lamour Quai des Orfèvres
Jenny Lind A Lady's Morals
Jenseits der Stille Beyond Silence
Jerrico, the Wonder Clown Three Ring Circus
Jerry Springer: Ringmaster Ringmaster
The Jessica McClure Story Everybody's Baby: the Rescue of Jessica McClure
Jessie Shattered Image
Jésus de Montréal Jesus of Montreal
Jet Li's The Enforcer The Enforcer
Jet Li's The Legend The Legend
Jet Li's The Legend 2 The Legend II
Jet Li's The One The One
Jetstream Jet Storm
Jeux d'Enfants Love Me If You Dare
Jew Suess Jew Süss
The Jezebelles Switchblade Sisters
Jigokumon Gate of Hell
Jihad Warrior The Order
Jill the Ripper Jill Rips
Jimmy Reardon A Night in the Life of Jimmy Reardon
Jimmy Spud Gabriel & Me
Joan of Arc Jeanne la Pucelle
"Jock" Petersen Petersen
Joco Invoco Dio... e Muori Vengeance
Joe Cocker: Mad Dogs and Englishmen Mad Dogs and Englishmen
Joe Palooka Palooka
Joey Making Contact
John Carpenter's Escape from LA Escape from LA
John Carpenter's Vampires Vampires
John Osborne's Luther Luther
Johnny Cien Pesos Johnny 100 Pesos
Johnny in the Clouds The Way to the Stars
Johnny Toothpick Johnny Stecchino
Joligud Hollywood
Jon Jost's Frameup Frameup
Jonas Qui Aura 25 Ans en l'An 2000 Jonah Who Will Be 25 in the Year 2000
Joseph Conrad's The Secret Agent The Secret Agent
Joshua Tree Army of One
Le Joueur d'Échecs The Chess Player
Le Journal de Lady M The Diary of Lady M
Le Journal d'un Curé de Campagne Diary of a Country Priest
Le Journal d'une Femme de Chambre The Diary of a Chambermaid
Une Journée Bien Remplie A Full Day's Work
The Journey The Voyage
Journey into Autumn Dreams
Journey into Primeval Times Voyage into Prehistory
Journey of Honor Shogun Warrior
The Journey that Shook the World Jules Verne's Rocket to the Moon
Journey to the Beginning of Time Voyage into Prehistory
Journey to the Lost City The Tiger of Eschnapur
Journey to the Lost City The Indian Tomb
Joy House The Love Cage
The Joy of Knowledge Le Gai Savoir
The Joy Parade Life Begins in College
Joyful Wisdom Le Gai Savoir
Joyride Roadkill
Ju-On The Grudge: Ju-On
Ju-On 2 The Grudge 2
Ju-On: The Grudge 2 The Grudge 2
Judas Was a Beast La Bête Humaine
The Judgement Gunnar Hede's Saga
A Judgement in Stone La Cérémonie
Judo Saga Sanshiro Sugata
Judou Ju Dou
Die Jungfrauenmaschine Virgin Machine
The Jungle Book The Adventures of Mowgli
Jungle Fighters The Long and the Short and the Tall
Jungle Heat Dance of the Dwarfs
Jungle Queen Tarzan's Peril
Jurassic Park 2 The Lost World: Jurassic Park
Jury of One Verdict
Just a Kiss Ae Fond Kiss...
Just before Nightfall Juste avant la Nuit
Just for Laughs Pour Rire!
Just Great Tout Va Bien
Just Like a Man Erotikon
Justice in a Small Town Hard Evidence

K

KKK The Klansman
Das Kabinett des Dr Caligari The Cabinet of Dr Caligari
Kain of Dark Planet The Warrior and the Sorceress
Kaleidoscope Danielle Steel's Kaleidoscope
Kälter als der Tod Love Is Colder Than Death
Karakter Character
Karate Tiger No Retreat, No Surrender
Katie Tippel Keetje Tippel
Katie's Passion Keetje Tippel
Keep Up Your Right Soigne Ta Droite
Keep Your Right Up Soigne Ta Droite
La Kermesse Héroïque Carnival in Flanders
Key West Crossing Cuba Crossing
The Keys of the House The Keys to the House
Khrustalyov, My Car! Khrustaliov, My Car!
The Kick Boxer Bloodsport
Kick Start Afraid to Dance
The Kid Disney's The Kid
Kigusi Story Man of Africa
Kikujiro's Summer Kikujiro
Kill and Say Your Prayers Kill and Pray
Kill Castro Cuba Crossing
Kill! Kill! Kill! Kill!
Killer! Que la Bête Meure
A Killer amongst Us Jack Reed: One of Our Own
Killer Dino Dino
Killer Grizzly Grizzly
Killer of Killers The Mechanic
Killers from Kilimanjaro Killers of Kilimanjaro
Killing Games The Driver's Seat
A Killing in a Small Town Evidence of Love
Killing Urge Jet Storm
The King Avenger Le Bossu
King Cobra Jaws of Satan
The King Is Dancing Le Roi Danse
King Lear King Lear – Fear and Loathing
King of Slaves Hero of Babylon
King of the World Muhammad Ali: King of the World
Kingu Kongu Tai Gojira King Kong vs Godzilla
Kipperbang P'Tang, Yang, Kipperbang
Kippour Kippur
Kirikou et la Sorcière Kirikou and the Sorceress
Kirina The Hunted
Kisenga, Man of Africa Men of Two Worlds
Kiss and Kill The Blood of Fu Manchu
A Kiss from Eddie The Arousers
Kiss My Butterfly I Love You, Alice B Toklas
Kiss the Blood off My Hands Blood on My Hands
Kisses for the President Kisses for My President
Kitten on the Keys Do You Love Me?
Knight of the Apocalypse The Minion
Knuckle-Men Terminal Island
Koktebel Roads to Koktebel
Der Kongress Tanzt Congress Dances
Kopek and Broom Find the Lady
Körkarlen The Phantom Carriage
Korol Lir King Lear
Kransen Kristin Lavransdatter
Krasnaya Palatka The Red Tent
Kreitzerova Sonata The Kreutzer Sonata
Der Krieger und die Kaiserin The Princess & the Warrior
Kris Crisis
Krocodylus Blood Surf
Krug and Company Last House on the Left
Kung Fu Soccer Shaolin Soccer
Kuragejima – Legends from a Southern Island The Profound Desire of the Gods

L

LOC LOC Kargil
Laberinto de Pasiones Labyrinth of Passion
Labyrinth A Reflection of Fear
The Lace-Maker The Lacemaker
Ladies of the Mob House of Women
Ladies of the Park Les Dames du Bois de Boulogne
El Lado Oscuro del Corazon The Dark Side of the Heart
Ladri di Biciclette Bicycle Thieves
Ladri di Saponette The Icicle Thief
Il Ladro di Bambini The Stolen Children
The Lady and the Outlaw Billy Two Hats
Lady Beware The Thirteenth Guest
The Lady Dances The Merry Widow
The Lady from Musashino The Lady of Musashino
Lady from New Orleans Lady from Louisiana
Lady Hamilton That Hamilton Woman
Lady in Distress A Window in London
Lady Musashino The Lady of Musashino
Lady of the Shadows The Terror
Lady Snowblood: Blizzard from the Netherworld Lady Snowblood
A Lady Surrenders Love Story
Lady Windermere's Fan The Fan
The Lady with a Lamp The Lady with the Lamp
The Lady with the Dog The Lady with the Little Dog
The Lady without Camellias La Signora senza Camelie
Lafayette Escadrille Hell Bent for Glory
Il Lago di Satana The She Beast
Lame Ducks Brain Donors
The Land of Faraway Mio in the Land of Faraway
The Land We Love Hero's Island
Landru Bluebeard
Lara Croft: Tomb Raider 2 Lara Croft Tomb Raider: the Cradle of Life
Larceny Street Smash and Grab
Larks on a Thread Larks on a String
Larry Flynt: The Naked Truth The People vs Larry Flynt
Larsen, Wolf of the Seven Seas Wolf Larsen
Laser Killer Corruption
Lassie Lassie: a New Generation
The Last Adventure The Adventurers
The Last American The Patriot
Last Assassins Dusting Cliff 7
The Last Castle Echoes of a Summer
The Last Combat The Last Battle
Last Cry Sexual Predator
Last Dance The Hole
The Last Days of Man on Earth The Final Programme
The Last Days of Sodom and Gomorrah Sodom and Gomorrah
The Last Four Days The Last Days of Mussolini
The Last Great Treasure Mother Lode
The Last Great Warrior Squanto: the Last Great Warrior
The Last Man The Last Laugh
Last Message from Saigon Operation CIA
Last of Summer The End of Summer
The Last of the Cowboys The Great Smokey Roadblock
Last of the Finest Blue Heat
The Last Patriot The Patriot
Last Resort National Lampoon's Scuba School
The Last Ride FTW
The Last Semester Twice Dead
The Last Stop The Last Stage
The Last Thrill The Female Vampire
Last Train to Wonderland Next Stop Wonderland
The Last Warrior Flap
The Last Will of Dr Mabuse The Testament of Dr Mabuse
Last Year in Marienbad Last Year at Marienbad
Laura The Raven
The Laura Black Story Stalking Laura
Lauras Stern Laura's Star
Laurel and Hardy in Toyland Babes in Toyland
Laviamoci il Cervello RoGoPaG
The Law Where the Hot Wind Blows!
The Law Kanoon
Lazy Bones Hallelujah, I'm a Bum
Leader of the Pack The Unholy Rollers
Learn, Baby, Learn The Learning Tree
Das Leben Ist eine Baustelle Life Is All You Get
Lebenszeichen Signs of Life
Leda Web of Passion
The Legacy of Maggie Walsh The Legacy
Legend in Leotards The Return of Captain Invincible
The Legend Lives Madman
The Legend of Fong Sai-Yuk I The Legend
The Legend of Fong Sai-Yuk II The Legend II
The Legend of Gösta Berling Gösta Berlings Saga
Legend of Hero A Man Called Hero
The Legend of Hillbilly John Who Fears the Devil?
The Legend of Musashi Samurai
The Legend of Prague The Golem
Legend of the Bayou Eaten Alive
Legend of the Lawman Part 2 Walking Tall
Legend of the Mummy Bram Stoker's Legend of the Mummy
Legend of the Overfiend Urotsukidoji: Legend of the Overfiend
Legend of the Sea Wolf Wolf Larsen
Legend of the Wolf Woman, '76 Naked Werewolf Woman
La Legge Where the Hot Wind Blows!
Len Deighton's Bullet to Beijing Bullet to Beijing
La Lengua de las Mariposas Butterfly's Tongue

Leo Tolstoy's Anna Karenina Anna Karenina
Lesbian Vampires Vampyros Lesbos
Lesbian Vampires: The Heiress of Dracula Vampyros Lesbos
Lest We Forget Hangmen Also Die
Let Me Call You Sweetheart Mary Higgins Clark's Let Me Call You Sweetheart
Let Sleeping Corpses Lie The Living Dead at the Manchester Morgue
Let Them Rest Kill and Pray
Lethal Contact Dark Angel
Lethal Orbit Orbit
Lethal Terminator The Glove
Let's Be Friends! Mujhse Dosti Karoge!
Let's Make Up Lilacs in the Spring
Let's Wash Our Brains RoGoPaG
Letter to Daddy The Enforcer
Letti Selvaggi Tigers in Lipstick
Der Letze Mann The Last Laugh
Die Letzte Bruecke The Last Bridge
Lèvres de Sang Lips of Blood
La Ley del Deseo The Law of Desire
Liberty for Us A Nous la Liberté
Libido I Am a Nymphomaniac
Die Liebe der Jeanne Ney The Love of Jeanne Ney
Liebe Ist Kälter als der Tod Love Is Colder Than Death
Liebeswalzer The Love Waltz
Das Lied der Gefangene Heimkehr
Les Liens de Sang Blood Relatives
Le Lieu du crime The Scene of the Crime
Life Jiyan
A Life Ahead Madame Rosa
The Life and Death of Chico Mendes The Burning Season
The Life and Loves of Beethoven Abel Gance's Beethoven
Life and Nothing More And Life Goes On...
Life before Him Madame Rosa
Life Begins at College Life Begins in College
Life Dances On Un Carnet de Bal
Life during Wartime The Alarmist
Life in the Food Chain Age Isn't Everything
Life of Brian Monty Python's Life of Brian
The Life of Jesus La Vie de Jésus
Lifetimes To Live
The Light Fantastic Love Is Better Than Ever
Light in the Darkness A Generation
The Light in the Jungle Out of Darkness
Lighthouse Stranded
Lights Out Bright Victory
Like a House on Fire The Fireman's Ball
Lili Marlene Lili Marleen
Line of Control LOC Kargil
Line of Fire Sam's Song
The Line of the Horizon The Edge of the Horizon
A Linha do Horizonte The Edge of the Horizon
The Lion of Oz and the Badge of Courage Lion of Oz
Lion of Sparta The 300 Spartans
Lionheart AWOL
Lionheart: the Children's Crusade Lionheart
Lisa The Inspector
Lisbon Lisboa
Liste Noire Hit List
Little Fairground Swing Merry-Go-Round
The Little Girl of Hanoi Little Girl from Hanoi
The Little Kidnappers The Kidnappers
Little Malcolm Little Malcolm and His Struggle Against the Eunuchs
The Little Martyr The Children Are Watching Us
Little Orphan Annie Annie: a Royal Adventure
Little Red Riding Hood Red Riding Hood
The Little Soldier Le Petit Soldat
Live Bait The Bait
Live for Life Vivre pour Vivre
The Liver Eaters Spider Baby
Living Ikiru
The Living Dead Scotland Yard Mystery
Living Russia or the Man with the Camera Man with a Movie Camera
Living the Lie The Unspoken Truth
Lo Que Le Páso a Santiago What Happened to Santiago
Lock Up Walls
Loco de Amor Two Much
The Locusts A Secret Sin
Loin Far Away
Loin du Viêtnam Far from Vietnam
Lola Clubbed to Death
Lola Twinky
Lola Rennt Run Lola Run
Lola und Bilidikid Lola and Bilidikid
Lola's Mistake This Rebel Breed
Lollipop E' Lollipop
The London Scene Tonite Let's All Make Love in London
Lone Wolf and Cub: Baby Cart at the River Styx Baby Cart at the River Styx
Lone Wolf and Cub: Sword of Vengeance Sword of Vengeance
The Lonely Hearts Killers The Honeymoon Killers
The Lonely Wife Charulata
The Lonely Woman Journey to Italy
Lonesome Gun Stranger on the Run
Long Ago Tomorrow The Raging Moon
Long Corridor Shock Corridor
The Long Dark Night The Pack
Un Long Dimanche de Fiançailles A Very Long Engagement
Long Island Expressway LIE
Long John Silver's Return to Treasure Island Long John Silver
The Long Lost Friend Apprentice to Murder
The Long Ride Home A Time for Killing
Long Road Home The Road Home
Long Way Home Raising Victor Vargas
The Longest Yard The Mean Machine
Look Before You Laugh Make Mine a Million
Look Down and Die Steel
Look See Ecoute Voir...
Lookin' Good Corky
Looking for Eternity Portion d'Eternité
Lorca The Disappearance of Garcia Lorca
Loss of Innocence The Greengage Summer
Lost Angels The Road Home
The Lost Illusion The Fallen Idol
Lost Lady The Lady Vanishes
Lost Treasure of the Amazon Jivaro
The Loudest Whisper The Children's Hour
Louis Pasteur The Story of Louis Pasteur
Louisiana Gal Old Louisiana
Les Louves Letters to an Unknown Lover
Love after Death The Marriage Fool
Love and Death in Saigon A Better Tomorrow III
Love and Money Love or Money
Love and Sacrifice America
A Love Bewitched El Amor Brujo
Love Eternal Eternal Love
The Love Factor Zeta One
Love in Las Vegas Viva Las Vegas
Love in Paris Another 9½ Weeks
Love Is a Weapon Hell's Island
Love Is Strange The Mysterious Island
Love Lessons All Things Fair
Love Madness Reefer Madness
The Love Maker Calle Mayor
Love Match Une Partie de Plaisir
Love Me for Ever or Never Eu Sei Que Vou Te Amar
Love of a Clown Pagliacci
Love on the Ground L'Amour par Terre
Love Stinks Only You
Love Stories Mohabbatein
Love Sucks Telling You
Love, the Magician El Amor Brujo
Love: the Only Law The Outlaw and His Wife
Love Trap Let's Get Laid
Love with a Proper Stranger Love with the Proper Stranger
Love You to Death Deadly Illusion
Lovely to Look At Thin Ice
A Lovely Way to Die A Lovely Way to Go
The Lover Milena
Lover Boy Knave of Hearts
Lover Divine The Unfinished Symphony
A Lover in Pawn A Dangerous Pledge
Lovers and Liars Travels with Anita
Lovers, Happy Lovers! Knave of Hearts
Lovers like Us Call Him Savage
Lovers Must Learn Rome Adventure
Lovers of Deceit A Murderous Affair
The Lovers of Montparnasse Montparnasse 19
Love's a Bitch Amores Perros
Love's Deadly Triangle: The Texas Cadet Murder Swearing Allegiance
Loves of a Blonde A Blonde in Love
The Loves of a Dictator The Dictator
The Loves of Ariane Ariane
The Loves of Count Yorga, Vampire The Loves of Count Iorga, Vampire
The Loves of Irina The Female Vampire
The Loves of Isadora Isadora
The Loves of Jeanne Ney The Love of Jeanne Ney
Luci del Varietà Lights of Variety
Lucia y el Sexo Sex and Lucia
Lucky Break Paperback Romance
The Lucky Mascot The Brass Monkey
Lucky Nick Cain I'll Get You for This
Lucky Ralston Law and Order
Lucky 13 Running Hot
Un Lugar en el Mundo A Place in the World
Lugosi Meets a Brooklyn Gorilla Bela Lugosi Meets a Brooklyn Gorilla
The Lullaby The Sin of Madelon Claudet
Lulu, the Tool The Working Class Goes to Heaven
La Lumière d'en Face The Light across the Street
Lunatic The Night Visitor
Lundi Matin Monday Morning
La Lune dans le Caniveau The Moon in the Gutter
Los Lunes al Sol Mondays in the Sun
Lunga Vita Alla Signora Long Live the Lady!
La Lunga Vita di Marianna Ucria Marianna Ucria
I Lunghi Capelli della Morte The Long Hair of Death
Lunghi Giorni dell'Odio This Man Can't Die
La Lupa Mannara Naked Werewolf Woman
The Lure of the Jungle Paw
Lust For Evil Plein Soleil
The Lust Seekers Good Morning... and Goodbye
Lusts of the Flesh The Love of Jeanne Ney

M

MDC Maschera di Cera Wax Mask
M1187511 In This World
M:I 2 Mission: Impossible 2
MST3K: the Movie Mystery Science Theater 3000: the Movie
Ma Nuit chez Maud My Night with Maud
Ma Vie Ma Vraie Vie à Rouen
Macabre Serenade House of Evil
Maccheroni Macaroni
MacDonald of the Canadian Mounties Pony Soldier
McGuire, Go Home! The High Bright Sun
The Machine La Machine
Die Macht der Biler: Leni Riefenstahl The Wonderful, Horrible Life of Leni Riefenstahl
McKlusky White Lightning
Macon County Jail Jailbreak
Macu, la Mujer del Policia Macu, the Policeman's Wife
Mad Cage La Cage aux Folles
The Mad Dog Killer Mad Dog Murderer
Mad Dog Morgan Mad Dog
Mad Dog Time Trigger Happy
Mad Enough to Kill The Evil Trap
Mad Magazine's Up the Academy Up the Academy
The Mad Monk Rasputin and the Empress
Mad Trapper of the Yukon Challenge to Be Free
Madadayo No, Not Yet
Madagascar Landing Aventure Malgache
Madame Sans-Gêne Madame
Madame Satan Madam Satan
Mädchen in Uniform Girls in Uniform
Das Mädchen Rosemarie A Girl Called Rosemarie
Made in New York Maid in Manhattan
Mademoiselle Fifi The Silent Bell
Mademoiselle France Reunion in France
Madhouse Mansion Ghost Story
Madman Marz Madman
Mafia! Jane Austen's Mafia
Mafia Kid Spike of Bensonhurst
Magnet of Doom L'Ainé des Ferchaux
The Magnetician's Fifth Winter The Magnetist's Fifth Winter
Magnum PI Magnum: Don't Eat the Snow in Hawaii
Mahanagar The Big City
Maid for Murder She'll Have to Go
The Maids of Wilko The Young Ladies of Wilko
Maigret Tend un Piège Maigret Sets a Trap
Mailbag Robbery The Flying Scot
Main Street Calle Mayor
La Maison sous les Arbres The Deadly Trap
Le Maître de Musique The Music Teacher
Major League 3 Major League: Back to the Minors
Make Me Over But I'm a Cheerleader
Make Mine a Double The Night We Dropped a Clanger
Make Them Die Slowly Cannibal Ferox
Makica Sisters The Makioka Sisters
Makin' Up! Making Up
Making It Les Valseuses
La Mala Educación Bad Education
La Mala Ordina The Italian Connection
Maladie Contagieuse The Raven
Malaga Moment of Danger
Malastrana The Short Night of the Glass Dolls
The Maltese Falcon Dangerous Female
Mama Turns a Hundred Mamá Cumple 100 Años
A Man and a Woman Un Homme et une Femme
Man and His Mate One Million BC
Man Bait The Last Page
A Man Called Sullivan The Great John L
The Man from C.O.T.T.O.N. Gone Are the Days
Man from Marrakesh That Man George
The Man from Tokyo Tokyo Drifter
The Man He Found The Whip Hand
Man Hunt Male Hunt
Man in a Cocked Hat Carlton-Browne of the FO
Man in Hiding Man-Trap
A Man in Mommy's Bed With Six You Get Eggroll
A Man Is Ten Feet Tall Edge of the City
Man Looking Southeast Hombre Mirando al Sudeste
Man o' War Men o' War
Man of Affairs His Lordship
Man of Bronze Jim Thorpe – All-American
Man of Evil Fanny by Gaslight
Man of the Hour Colonel Effingham's Raid
Man of the Nile The Barbarian
Man of the Year The Man of the Year
The Man on America's Conscience Tennessee Johnson
The Man Who Came Back Swamp Water
The Man Who Lived Again The Man Who Changed His Mind
The Man Who Lost His Way Crossroads
Man with a Camera Man with a Movie Camera
Man with a Million The Million Pound Note
The Man with My Name The Man Who Wasn't There
The Man with 100 Faces Crackerjack
The Man with Rain in His Shoes If Only
The Man with the Flower in his Mouth The Masters
The Man with the Green Carnation The Trials of Oscar Wilde
Man with the Movie Camera Man with a Movie Camera
The Man with Thirty Sons The Magnificent Yankee
The Man with Three Arms The Dark Backward
The Man without a Face Shadowman
Man without a Gun Man with the Gun
Mandela: Son of Africa, Father of a Nation Mandela
Mandrake Alraune
Maneater Shark!
The Manhattan Project The Deadly Game
Manhunt From Hell to Texas
Manhunt The Italian Connection
Le Mani Forti Strong Hands
Le Mani Sulla Città Hands over the City
Mania The Flesh and the Fiends
Maniacs on Wheels Once a Jolly Swagman
Mannequin Two: On the Move Mannequin on the Move
Männer Men...
Manon of the Springs Manon des Sources
Mao to Mozart: Isaac Stern in China From Mao to Mozart: Isaac Stern in China
Y Mapiwr The Making of Maps
Mar Adentro The Sea Inside
March of the Wooden Soldiers Babes in Toyland
Marching Along Stars and Stripes Forever
La Marge The Streetwalker
The Margin The Streetwalker
Le Marginal The Outsider
Le Mari de la Coiffeuse The Hairdresser's Husband
Maria Candelaria Portrait of Maria
Maria, Llena Eres de Gracia Maria Full of Grace
Marianne Marianne de Ma Jeunesse
Marianne and Julianne The German Sisters
Marie Baie des Anges Angel Sharks
Marie et Julien Histoire de Marie et Julien
Marie s'en Va-t-en Ville Marie in the City
Marie Walewska Conquest
La Mariée Est Trop Belle The Bride Is Too Beautiful
La Mariée Etait en Noir The Bride Wore Black
Les Mariés de l'An Deux Sink or Swim
Marius and Jeanette Marius et Jeannette
Mark of the Beast Fear No Evil
Mark of the Claw Dick Tracy's Dilemma
Mark of the Devil 3 Alucarda
The Market Place Mandi
Marquis de Sade Marquis
Die Marquise von O... The Marquise of O
Married but Single This Thing Called Love
Married in Haste Consolation Marriage
The Marrying Man Too Hot to Handle
Mars Project Conquest of Space
The Marsupials: the Howling III The Howling III
Martha und Ich Martha and I
Martial Law III Mission of Justice
Marx Brothers Go West Go West
La Maschera del Demonio The Mask of Satan
Maschera Di Cera Wax Mask
Masculin Féminin Masculine Feminine
Mashq-e-Shab Homework
The Mask of the Demon The Mask of Satan
Masks Persona
The Massacre at the Rosebud The Great Sioux Massacre
Massacre Hill Eureka Stockade
Master of Dragonard Hill Dragonard
Master of Lassie Hills of Home
Master of the Islands The Hawaiians
Master Swordsman Samurai

The Master Touch A Man to Respect
Mästerman A Dangerous Pledge
Masters of the Universe II: The Cyborg Cyborg
Matango: Fungus of Terror Matango
The Match The Gamble
Mathilda Matilda
Matrimonio all'Italiana Marriage – Italian Style
A Matter of Conviction The Young Savages
A Matter of Honour The Reckoning
A Matter of Innocence Pretty Polly
A Matter of Resistance La Vie de Château
A Matter of Style Andaz
Maurice Sendak's The Nutcracker Nutcracker
Mausoleum One Dark Night
Mauvais Sang The Night Is Young
Mauvaise Passe The Escort
Les Mauvaises Rencontres The Bad Liaisons
Maxwell Smart and the Nude Bomb The Nude Bomb
Maybe Baby For Keeps
Maybe, Maybe Not The Most Desired Man
Mazel Tov ou le Mariage Marry Me! Marry Me!
Me L'Enfance Nue
Me and My Gal For Me and My Gal
The Mechanical Piano An Unfinished Piece for Mechanical Piano
Meet Whiplash Willie The Fortune Cookie
La Meglio Gioventù The Best of Youth
Meia Noite Midnight
Mein Liebster Feind – Klaus Kinski My Best Fiend
Mein Stern Be My Star
Melencolia Melancholia
Mélodie en Sous-Sol Any Number Can Win
Melody Inn Riding High
Melody of Life Symphony of Six Million
The Melody of Life Sur
Melody of Youth They Shall Have Music
Mémoire Traquée Lapse of Memory
Memorias del Subdesarrollo Memories of Underdevelopment
Memories Yaadein
Memories of a Marriage Waltzing Regitze
Memory Lapse of Memory
The Memory Expert The Man on the Flying Trapeze
Memory of Evil Forgotten Sins
Men Some Girls
Men Are Children Twice Valley of Song
Men of Destiny Men of Texas
Men of Steel Steel
Men on Her Mind The Girl from 10th Avenue
Menage Tenue de Soirée
Ménage à Trois Better Late Than Never
Menschen am Sonntag People on Sunday
Mensonge The Lie
The Mercado Family Debut The Debut
The Mercenaries Cuba Crossing
The Mercenaries Dark of the Sun
Il Mercenario The Swordsman of Siena
The Mercenary A Professional Gun
The Merchant of Venice William Shakespeare's The Merchant of Venice
Meredith Willson's The Music Man The Music Man
Mermaid Chronicles Part 1: She Creature She Creature
Merrily We Go to... Merrily We Go to Hell
A Merry War Keep the Aspidistra Flying
The Messenger: the Story of Joan of Arc Joan of Arc
The Metal Years The Decline of Western Civilization Part II: the Metal Years
Meteor Monster Teenage Monster
The Metropolis The Big City
Mi Buenos Aires Querido The Tango Lesson
Mi Vida sin Mí My Life without Me
Michael Allred's G-Men from Hell G-Men from Hell
Michael Jackson's Moonwalker Moonwalker
Michael's Fright The Peanut Butter Solution
Midnight at the Wax Museum Midnight at Madame Tussaud's
Midnight Auto Supply Love and the Midnight Auto Supply
Midnight Lovers Immortal Bachelor
Midnight Pleasures Immortal Bachelor
Midway Battle of Midway
A Midwinter's Tale In the Bleak Midwinter
The Mighty Warrior The Trojan War
Mignon è Partita Mignon Has Left
Mil Nove Cientos Diecinueve Crónica del Alba 1919
Mille Mois A Thousand Months
Mille di Garibaldi 1860
The Miller's Beautiful Wife The Miller's Wife
Millie the Non-Stop Variety Girl Friday the Thirteenth
The Million Dollar Kid Fortune Hunters
Million Dollar Manhunt Assignment Redhead
Million Dollar Mystery Money Mania
The Million Eyes of Su-Muru Sumuru
A Million to One A Million to Juan
The Millstone A Touch of Love
Mimi Metallurgico Ferito Nell'Onore The Seduction of Mimi
Mimi, the Metalworker The Seduction of Mimi
Mind Games Agency
Mind Games Brainwaves
Mind Ripper Wes Craven's Mind Ripper
Minimal Stories Historias Mínimas
Minuit Midnight
Minya, Son of Godzilla Godzilla's Revenge
Mio min Mio Mio in the Land of Faraway
Il Mio Nome è Nessuno My Name Is Nobody
Il Mio Viaggio in Italia My Voyage to Italy
A Miracle Can Happen On Our Merry Way
The Miracle of Fatima The Miracle of Our Lady of Fatima
Miracle of Life Our Daily Bread
Miracolo a Milano Miracle in Milan
The Misadventures of Mr Wilt Wilt
Les Misérables du Vingtième Siècle Les Misérables
Miss Europe Prix de Beauté
Miss Jude The Truth about Spring
Miss Sherri A Private Matter
Miss Shumway Jette un Sort Rough Magic
Missile from Hell The Battle of the V1
Missing Action 3 Braddock: Missing in Action III
The Missing Head Strange Confession
Missing Ten Days Ten Days in Paris
Mission without Permission Catch That Kid
Mississippi Summer Murder in Mississippi
Mr Arkadin Confidential Report
Mr Bug Goes to Town Hoppity Goes to Town
Mr Fox of Venice The Honey Pot
Mr Hulot's Holiday Monsieur Hulot's Holiday
Mr Jim – American, Soldier and a Gentleman Dolina Mira
Mr Lord Says No The Happy Family
Mr Mum Mr Mom
Mr Prohack Dear Mr Prohack
Mr Teas and His Playthings Immoral Mr Teas
Mr Toad's Wild Ride The Wind in the Willows
Mister V Pimpernel Smith
I Misteri della Giungla Nera Kidnapped to Mystery Island
Il Mistero di Oberwald The Oberwald Mystery
Mixed Blessings Danielle Steel's Mixed Blessings
Miyazaki's Spirited Away Spirited Away
Mockery of Justice: The True Story of the Sheppard Murder Case Death in the Shadows
The Model Shop Model Shop
Modern Day Houdini The Escapist
The Modern Miracle The Story of Alexander Graham Bell
Modigliani of Montparnasse Montparnasse 19
La Moglie del Prete The Priest's Wife
Mohammed, Messenger of God The Message
The Mole El Topo
The Molester Never Take Sweets from a Stranger
Molly Louvain The Strange Love of Molly Louvain
El Momento de la Verdad The Moment of Truth
Il Momento della Verità The Moment of Truth
Momma's Boy Night Warning
Mom's 100 Years Old Mamá Cumple 100 Años
Mon Oncle Antoine My Uncle Antoine
Mon Oncle Benjamin Uncle Benjamin
The Mona Lisa Is Missing The Theft of the Mona Lisa
Monday, Tuesday, Wednesday A Killing Affair
Un Monde Presque Paisible Almost Peaceful
Un Monde sans Pitié A World without Pity
Le Monde sans Soleil World without Sun
Mondes Possibles Possible Worlds
Mondo Cane Numero 1 Mondo Cane
Money for Jam It Ain't Hay
Money Talks Loser Takes All
Mongkok Carmen As Tears Go By
Monika Summer with Monika
Monsieur Ibrahim et les Fleurs du Coran Monsieur Ibrahim and the Flowers of the Koran
Monsieur Klein Mr Klein
The Monsoons Barsaat
The Monster I Don't Want to Be Born
The Monster and the Woman Four Sided Triangle
The Monster Horror Show Freaks
The Monster of Fate The Golem
Monster of Monsters Ghidrah, the Three-Headed Monster
Monster of Terror Die, Monster, Die!
Monster Zero Invasion of the Astro-Monster
Monsters from the Moon Robot Monster
El Monstruo de la Montana Hueca The Beast of Hollow Mountain
Montana Mike Heaven Only Knows
Montecarlo The Monte Carlo Story
Monty Python meets Beyond the Fringe Pleasure at Her Majesty's
Monty Python's Holy Grail Monty Python and the Holy Grail
Monument Ave Noose
Moon over Miami Off and Running
The Moondolls Nude on the Moon
Moonshot Countdown
Die Mörder Sind Unter Uns The Murderers Are amongst Us
Morder Unter Uns M
Morgan Stewart's Coming Home Home Front
Morituri The Saboteur, Code Name Morituri
Morris West's The Naked Country The Naked Country
La Mort de Mario Ricci The Death of Mario Ricci
Mort d'un Pourri To Kill a Rat
La Mort en Ce Jardin Death in the Garden
La Mort en Direct Deathwatch
La Mortadella Lady Liberty
Mortal Kombat 2 Mortal Kombat: Annihilation
Moscow Does Not Believe in Tears Moscow Distrusts Tears
Moscow Today Man with a Movie Camera
Moses the Lawgiver Moses
The Most Dangerous Man in the World The Chairman
Mosura Mothra
Mother The Haunted Heart
Mother M/Other
The Mother and the Whore La Maman et la Putain
Mother Goose a Go-Go The Unkissed Bride
Mother Joan of the Angels The Devil and the Nun
Mother Knows Best Mother Is a Freshman
Mother Küsters' Trip to Heaven Mother Küsters Goes to Heaven
A Mother's Revenge Desperate Justice
Mothers and Daughters The Other Woman
A Mother's Justice Desperate Justice
Mothra vs Godzilla Godzilla vs Mothra
Mothra vs Gojira Godzilla vs Mothra
Motor Mods and Rockers Motor Psycho
Mourir à Madrid To Die in Madrid
Mouse Hunt Mousehunt
Movie Struck Pick a Star
Movietone Follies of 1929 Fox Movietone Follies of 1929
Moving In Firstborn
The Moving Target Harper
Mowgli and Baloo: Jungle Book II The Second Jungle Book
Mrs Loring's Secret The Imperfect Lady
Mud Honey Mudhoney
Der Müde Tod Destiny
La Muerte de un Burocrata Death of a Bureaucrat
Muerte de un Ciclista Death of a Cyclist
La Muerte en este Jardín Death in the Garden
Muertos de Risa Dying of Laughter
Mugsy's Girls Delta Pi
Una Mujer sin Amor A Woman without Love
Mujeres al Borde de un Ataque de Nervios Women on the Verge of a Nervous Breakdown
Münchhausen Baron Münchhausen
Mur Wall
Muraya (L'Expérience Secrète de Mike Blueberry Blueberry
Murder at Malibu Beach The Trap
Murder at the Burlesque Murder at the Windmill
Murder by Confession Absolution
Murder Can Be Deadly The Painted Smile
Murder in the Old Red Barn Maria Marten, or the Murder in the Red Barn
The Murder in Thornton Square Gaslight
Murder in Three Acts Agatha Christie's Murder in Three Acts
Murder, Inc The Enforcer
Murder, My Sweet Farewell My Lovely
Murder on Danger Island Mr Moto in Danger Island
Murder on Monday Home at Seven
Murder on the Set Death on the Set
Murder Will Out Voice of Merrill
Murder with Mirrors Agatha Christie's Murder with Mirrors
Murderer in the Motel Motel
Murderers Among Us The Murderers Are amongst Us
Muriel, or the Time of Return Muriel
Muriel, Ou le Temps d'un Retour Muriel
Un Muro de Silencio Wall of Silence
Murph the Surf Live a Little, Steal a Lot
Musashi Miyamoto Samurai
The Muse Concert: No Nukes No Nukes
Music in Darkness Night Is My Future
Musical May Il Maestro
Musime si Pomahat Divided We Fall
Mutronics The Guyver
Mutter Küsters Fahrt Zum Himmel Mother Küsters Goes to Heaven
Mutters Courage My Mother's Courage
My Crazy Life Mi Vida Loca
My Darling Shiksa Over the Brooklyn Bridge
My Enemy the Sea Alone on the Pacific
My Father Is a Hero The Enforcer
My Father, My Master Padre Padrone
My Father's Glory La Gloire de Mon Père
My Father's Shadow: The Sam Sheppard Story Death in the Shadows
My Favorite Season Ma Saison Préferée
My Forgotten Man Flynn
My Good Fiend My Best Fiend
My Heart Goes Crazy London Town
My Hero A Southern Yankee
My Life Is Yours The People vs Dr Kildare
My Life to Live Vivre Sa Vie
My Love Burns My Love Has Been Burning
My Love Letters Love Letters
My Love, My Honor Judicial Consent
My Man Mon Homme
My Mother Ma Mère
My Name Is Ivan Ivan's Childhood
My Name Is John Who Fears the Devil?
My Name Is Trinity They Call Me Trinity
My New Partner Le Cop
My New Partner II Le Cop II
My Night at Maud's My Night with Maud
My Old Man's Place Glory Boy
My Sex Life ... or How I got into an Argument Ma Vie Sexuelle
My Summer Story It Runs in the Family
My Summer Vacation One Crazy Summer
My Two Husbands Too Many Husbands
My Uncle Mon Oncle
My Wife Is an Actress Ma Femme Est une Actrice
Les Mystères de Paris The Mysteries of Paris
Mysteries of the Organism WR – Mysteries of the Organism
Mysterious Invader The Astounding She-Monster
Mystery at the Burlesque Murder at the Windmill
The Mystery of Kaspar Hauser The Enigma of Kaspar Hauser
The Mystery of Picasso Le Mystère Picasso
The Mystery of Thug Island Kidnapped to Mystery Island

N

Nachtgestalten Night Shapes
La Nación Clandestina The Secret Nation
The Nada Gang Nada
Naked Childhood L'Enfance Nue
Naked Island The Island
The Naked Night Sawdust and Tinsel
Naked Revenge Cry for Me Billy
Naked under Leather The Girl on a Motorcycle
Nakter Tango Naked Tango
The Nanny The Guardian
Napoléon Bonaparte Napoléon
Napoléon vu par Abel Gance Napoléon
Nate and Hayes Savage Islands
Nathaniel Hawthorne's "Twice Told Tales" Twice Told Tales
National Lampoon Goes to the Movies National Lampoon's Movie Madness
National Lampoon's Last Resort National Lampoon's Scuba School
National Lampoon's Van Wilder Van Wilder: Party Liaison
National Lampoon's Vegas Vacation Vegas Vacation
Nature Girls on the Moon Nude on the Moon
The Nature of the Beast Bad Company
Nature's Mistakes Freaks
Naughty Arlette The Romantic Age
Navy Heroes The Blue Peter
Ne Me Demandez Pas Pourquoi Le Testament d'Orphée
Near Misses Near Mrs
Nefertiti, Regina del Nilo Nefertite, Queen of the Nile
Neil Simon's Broadway Bound Broadway Bound
Neil Simon's Laughter on the 23rd Floor Laughter on the 23rd Floor
Neil Simon's Lost in Yonkers Lost in Yonkers
Neil Simon's The Odd Couple II The Odd Couple II

Neil Simon's The Slugger's Wife The Slugger's Wife
Neil Simon's The Sunshine Boys The Sunshine Boys
The Nelson Affair Bequest to the Nation
The Nelson Touch Corvette K-225
The Neptune Disaster The Neptune Factor
Nettoyage à Sec Dry Cleaning
Neuf Mois Nine Months
Neuve Reinas Nine Queens
Never Cry Devil Night Visitor
Never Ever Circle of Passion
Never Give an Inch Sometimes a Great Notion
Never Take Candy from a Stranger Never Take Sweets from a Stranger
Never to Love A Bill of Divorcement
Neverever Circle of Passion
Neverland: the Rise and Fall of the Symbionese Liberation Army Guerrilla: the Taking of Patty Hearst
The New Adventures of Dr Fu Manchu The Return of Dr Fu Manchu
The New Adventures of Don Juan Adventures of Don Juan
The New China Woman The Actress
The New Enchantment L'Inhumaine
The New Eve La Nouvelle Eve
New Frontier Frontier Horizon
The New Monsters Viva Italia!
New Tales of the Taira Clan Tales of the Taira Clan
New Wave Nouvelle Vague
New York Hallelujah, I'm a Bum
New York Beat Movie Downtown 81
A New York Fiasco I Was on Mars
New York the Magnificent Manhatta
The Newcomers The Wild Country
Newlyweds Young Husbands
Newsboys The News Boys
Newsies The News Boys
Next Time We Live Next Time We Love
Ni Neibian Jidian What Time Is It There?
Nice Dreams Cheech and Chong's Nice Dreams
A Nice Guy Mr Nice Guy
Nicht Versöhnt oder "Es Hilft Nur Gewalt, Wo Gewalt Herrscht " Not Reconciled, or Only Violence Helps Where Violence Rules
Nick Carter in Panama Phantom Raiders
Nick's Movie Lightning over Water
Nicky and Gino Dominick and Eugene
Nico and Dani Krámpack
Nico and Dani – Krampáck Krámpack
Das Niebelungenlied Sword of Xanten
The Night La Notte
Night Ambush Ill Met by Moonlight
Night and Fog Nuit et Brouillard
The Night Andy Came Home Dead of Night
Night at the Crossroads La Nuit du Carrefour
Night Breed Nightbreed
The Night Comers The Nightcomers
The Night Crawlers The Navy vs the Night Monsters
Night Demons Night of the Demons
The Night Digger The Road Builder
The Night Fighters A Terrible Beauty
The Night Flier Stephen King's The Night Flier
Night Flight from Moscow The Serpent
Night Full of Rain The End of the World (in Our Usual Bed in a Night Full of Rain)
The Night Heaven Fell Les Bijoutiers du Clair de Lune
A Night in Cairo The Barbarian
Night in the Crypt One Dark Night
The Night Is Ending Paris after Dark
Night Legs Fright
The Night of St Lawrence The Night of San Lorenzo
A Night of Terror Love from a Stranger
Night of the Blood Monster The Bloody Judge
Night of the Cyclone Perfume of the Cyclone
Night of the Dark Full Moon Silent Night, Bloody Night
Night of the Demons 3 Demon House
Night of the Demons: Angela's Revenge Night of the Demons 2
Night of the Flesh Eaters Night of the Living Dead
Night of the Laughing Dead The House in Nightmare Park
The Night of the Shooting Stars The Night of San Lorenzo
Night of the Tiger Ride beyond Vengeance
Night Shadows Mutant
The Night the Sun Came Out Watermelon Man
The Night They Invented Striptease The Night They Raided Minsky's
Night Train Night Train to Munich
Night Walk Dead of Night
The Night Watch Le Trou
Night Watch Nightwatch
Night Wind Le Vent de la Nuit
Night's End Nishant
Nightcap Merci pour le Chocolat
Nightfall Abendland
Nightfliers Nightflyers
Nightmare Nightmares in a Damaged Brain
Nightmare in Columbia County Victim of Beauty
Nightmare Maker Night Warning
Nightmare on Elm Street 7 Wes Craven's New Nightmare
Nights in a Harem Son of Sinbad
Nightshapes Night Shapes
Nina A Matter of Time
La Niña de Tus Ojos The Girl of Your Dreams
Nine Days a Queen Tudor Rose
Nine Hours to Live Nine Hours to Rama
1947: Earth Earth
Ninja I Enter the Ninja
9/30/55 September 30, 1955
Nirgendwo in Afrika Nowhere in Africa
Nite Vision Hotel
No Cause for Alarm Project: Alien
No Greater Love Danielle Steel's No Greater Love
No Habra Mas Penas Ni Olvido Funny Dirty Little War
No Harm Intended En Toute Innocence
No Highway in the Sky No Highway
No Knife The Frisco Kid
No Looking Back Out of the Blue
No Man Walks Alone Black like Me
No More Mr Nice Guy Mr Nice Guy
No Place Like Homicide What a Carve Up!
No Place to Hide Rebel
No Regrets for My Youth No Regrets for Our Youth
No Secrets A Touch of the Sun
No Sleep Till Dawn Bombers B-52
No Time for Breakfast Doctor Françoise Gailland
No Toys for Christmas Once Before I Die
No Tree in the Street No Trees in the Street
No Trespassing The Red House
Noah's Ark: The Story of the Deluge Noah's Ark
Nobody Loves a Drunken Indian Flap
Nobody Loves Flapping Eagle Flap
Nobody Makes Me Cry Between Friends
Nobody Someday Robbie Williams: Nobody Someday
Nobody's Nervous A Better Way to Die
Les Noces de Papier A Paper Wedding
Noi the Albino Noi Albinoi
Noi vivi We the Living
Noirs et Blancs en Couleurs Black and White in Color
Non Si Seve Profanare Ol Sonne Die Morte The Living Dead at the Manchester Morgue
Non ti muovere Don't Move
None but the Brave For the Love of Mike
De Noorderlingen The Northerners
Norman Conquest Park Plaza 605
Norman Mailer's Tough Guys Don't Dance Tough Guys Don't Dance
The North El Norte
The North Avenue Irregulars Hill's Angels
The North Star L'Etoile du Nord
Northwest Mounted Police North West Mounted Police
Un Nos ola Leuad One Full Moon
Nosferatu, a Symphony of Terror Nosferatu, a Symphony of Horrors
Nosferatu a Venezia Vampire in Venice
Nosferatu, eine Symphonie des Grauens Nosferatu, a Symphony of Horrors
Nosferatu, Phantom der Nacht Nosferatu, the Vampire
Nosferatu, Phantom of the Night Nosferatu, the Vampire
Nosferatu, the Vampire Nosferatu, a Symphony of Horrors
Not a Route 66 The Delivery
Not in My Family Shattering the Silence
Not Mine to Love Three Days and a Child
Not on the Lips Pas sur la Bouche
Not on Your Life Island of Love
Not Quite Paradise Not Quite Jerusalem
Not So Quiet Days Quiet Days in Clichy
Not Yet No, Not Yet
A Notebook on Clothes and Cities Notebook on Cities and Clothes
The Noted Sword The Famous Sword
Notorious Gentleman The Rake's Progress
Notre Dame de Paris The Hunchback of Notre Dame
La Notte di San Lorenzo The Night of San Lorenzo
Le Notti Bianche White Nights
Le Notti di Cabiria Nights of Cabiria
N'Oublie Pas Que Tu Vas Mourir Don't Forget You're Going to Die
Des Nouvelles du Bon Dieu News from the Good Lord
Novecento 1900
A Novel Affair The Passionate Stranger
Now about These Women All These Women
Nowhere to Hide Dangerous Intentions
Nuclear Run The Chain Reaction
Nuclear Terror Golden Rendezvous
Nudes on the Moon Nude on the Moon
La Nuit Américaine Day for Night
Nuit et Jour Night and Day
Nuits Blanches White Nights
Les Nuits de la Pleine Lune Full Moon in Paris
Nuits Rouges Shadowman
Nuke Nukie
Nuke 'em High Class of Nuke 'em High
Numéro Deux Number Two
The Nun La Religieuse
I Nuovi Mostri Viva Italia!
Nuovo Cinema Paradiso Cinema Paradiso
The Nurse The Guardian

O

OHMS You're In the Army Now
OK Connery Operation Kid Brother
O Que E Isso, Companheiro? Four Days in September
Obsessed The Late Edwina Black
Obsession Circle of Two
Occi Ciornie Dark Eyes
Odd Obsession The Key
Off Balance Phantom of Death
Off Limits Military Policeman
Off Limits Saigon
The Official Story The Official Version
Offret The Sacrifice
The O'Flynn The Fighting O'Flynn
Oh, Charlie Hold That Ghost
Oh Doctor Hit the Ice
Oh! For a Man Will Success Spoil Rock Hunter?
Oh, Woe Is Me Hélas pour Moi
Oil Town Lucy Gallant
Old and the New The General Line
Old Boy Oldboy
The Old Capital Twin Sisters of Kyoto
The Old Curiosity Shop Mister Quilp
Old Drac Vampira
Old Dracula Vampira
Old New Borrowed Blue With or without You
O'Leary Night Happy Ever After
Olga's Chignon Le Chignon d'Olga
Olly, Olly, Oxen Free The Great Balloon Adventure
Olympia Olympiad
Olympiad Berlin 1936 Olympiad
Olympic Visions Visions of Eight
Olympische Spiele 1936 Olympiad
Ombre Blanche The Savage Innocents
L'Ombre du Doute A Shadow of Doubt
On a Volé la Joconde The Theft of the Mona Lisa
On Guard Le Bossu
On My Vespa Dear Diary
On Our Little Place On Our Selection
On the Carpet Little Giant
On the Road Again Honeysuckle Rose
On Wings of Fear Dangerous Intentions
Once a Thief The Happy Thieves
Once in a Lifetime Danielle Steel's Once in a Lifetime
Once Upon a Frightmare Frightmare
Once upon a Savage Night Nightmare in Chicago
Once upon a Thursday The Affairs of Martha
Once upon a Time in India Lagaan: Once upon a Time in India
One against All Seul contre Tous
One Against Seven Counter-Attack
One Child Untamed Love
One Cup of Coffee Pastime
187 One Eight Seven
One Final Hour Five Star Final
One for the Book Voice of the Turtle
One Horse Town Small Town Girl
One Hour to Doomsday City beneath the Sea
100% Pure The Girl from Missouri
One Last Kiss The Last Kiss
One Man Mutiny The Court-Martial of Billy Mitchell
One-Piece Bathing Suit Million Dollar Mermaid
One Swallow Brought Spring The Girl from Paris
One Way Out Convicted
One Wild Moment Un Moment d'Egarement
One Wild Night Career Opportunities
One Woman's Story The Passionate Friends
Only One Night One Single Night
Only the Best I Can Get It for You Wholesale
Only the French Can French Cancan
The Only Woman on Earth The Saga of Anatahan
Open City Rome, Open City
Operation Braindrain Codename Chessboard The Birdmen
Operation Cicero 5 Fingers
Operation Conspiracy Cloak without Dagger
Operation Disaster Morning Departure
Operation Madball Operation Mad Ball
Operation Masquerade Masquerade
Operation Mermaid The Bay of Saint Michel
Operation Monsterland Destroy All Monsters
Operation Snafu On the Fiddle
Operation Undercover Report to the Commissioner
Operation War Head On the Fiddle
Opposing Force Hell Camp
Opposing Forces Hell Camp
The Opposite Sex The Opposite Sex and How to Live with Them
Oprah Winfrey Presents: Before Women Had Wings Before Women Had Wings
Oprah Winfrey Presents: David and Lisa David and Lisa
Oprah Winfrey Presents: Tuesdays with Morrie Tuesdays with Morrie
The Optimist Hallelujah, I'm a Bum
The Optimists The Optimists of Nine Elms
Orazi e Curiazi Duel of Champions
Orca: The Killer Whale Orca ... Killer Whale
The Orchestra Conductor The Conductor
The Order The Sin Eater
Ordinary Heroes: the Sandra Prine Story Hard Evidence
Orfeu Negro Black Orpheus
Les Orgueilleux The Proud Ones
Oriental Dream Kismet
The Original Fabulous Adventure of Baron Munchausen Baron Munchhausen
The Original Old Mother Riley Old Mother Riley
Orlacs Hände Hands of Orlac
L'Oro di Napoli Gold of Naples
Oro per i Cesari Gold for the Caesars
O'Rourke of the Royal Mounted Saskatchewan
Orson Welles' Macbeth Macbeth
Orson Welles's Ghost Story Return to Glennascaul
Oscar Wilde Wilde
Ostatni Etap The Last Stage
Otesanke Little Otik
Othello Otello
Otoshiana Pitfall
El Otro Lado de la Cama The Other Side of the Bed
Our Father Padre Nuestro
Our Little Angel Think Big
Our Man in Marrakesh That Man George
Our Music Notre Musique
Our Sea Mare Nostrum
L'Ours The Bear
Out of Control Runaway Car
Out of Present Out of the Present
Out of Rosenheim Bagdad Café
Out of the Darkness Teenage Caveman
Out of the Past Build My Gallows High
The Outcast Man in the Saddle
The Outcry Il Grido
The Outing The Lamp
The Outpost Wes Craven's Mind Ripper
Outpost in Malaya The Planter's Wife
The Outsider The Guinea Pig
The Outsiders Bande à Part
Over My Dead Body The Brain
Over the Bridge Over the Brooklyn Bridge
Ovirl The Wolf at the Door
Oxen The Ox

P

PI Private Investigations Private Investigations
PJ New Face in Hell
PJ Waters Holy Smoke
PT Barnum's Rocket to the Moon Jules Verne's Rocket to the Moon
PT Raiders The Ship That Died of Shame
The Pace That Kills The Cocaine Fiends
Le Pacte des Loups Brotherhood of the Wolf
The Pad The Pad (and How to Use It)
O Pagador de Promessas The Given Word
Pain in the Neck A Pain in the A...!
The Paint Job Painted Heart
Painted Black Paint It Black
Painted Fire Chihwaseon (Drunk on Women and Poetry)
Painted Hero Shadow of the Past
Paisan Paisà
Palermo or Wolfsburg Palermo oder Wolfsburg
Palle D'Acciaio Head Office
Palomino Danielle Steel's Palomino
Pane, Amore e Fantasia Bread, Love and Dreams
Pane e Tulipani Bread and Tulips
Panga Curse III: Blood Sacrifice
Panic in Bangkok for Agent OSS 117 Shadow of Evil

Panic in the Parlour Sailor Beware!
Panny and Wilka The Young Ladies of Wilko
The Paper Cranes of Osen The Downfall of Osen
Paper Flowers Kaagaz Ke Phool
The Paperhanger Work
Par-delà les Nuages Beyond the Clouds
Paradise Lagoon The Admirable Crichton
Paradise Lost Lost Paradise
Paralyzed The Short Night of the Glass Dolls
Paranoia Brain Dead
Les Parapluies de Cherbourg The Umbrellas of Cherbourg
The Parasite Murders Shivers
Parasites Drag
Paratrooper The Red Beret
Paris Belongs to Us Paris Nous Appartient
Paris Brûle-t-il? Is Paris Burning?
Paris Does Strange Things Elena et les Hommes
The Paris Express The Man Who Watched Trains Go By
Paris Was Made for Lovers A Time for Loving
Parisian Belle New Moon
Parisian Encounters Les Rendez-vous de Paris
Paroles et Musique Love Songs
Parting at Dusk Floating Weeds
La Partita The Gamble
Partyline Party Line
Pas de Problème No Problem!
Pasolini's 120 Days of Sodom Salo, or the 120 Days of Sodom
Pasqualino Settebellezze Seven Beauties
Pasqualino: Seven Beauties Seven Beauties
Pass the Ammunition Pass the Ammo
Le Passager de la Pluie Rider on the Rain
Passe-Passe Quicker than the Eye
Passenger Faber Voyager
Passenger of the Rain Rider on the Rain
La Passion de Jeanne d'Arc The Passion of Joan of Arc
A Passion Play – Chokher Bali Chokher Bali
The Passion of Anna A Passion
Passion: the Story of Percy Grainger Passion
A Passion to Kill Rules of Obsession
Passionate Summer Les Possédées
Passport to Fame The Whole Town's Talking
Past Tense Time Lapse
Les Patriotes Patriots
El Patrullero Highway Patrolman
Pattern for Plunder The Bay of Saint Michel
Patterns of Power Patterns
Paul et Michelle Paul and Michelle
Paula Framed
Pauline à la Plage Pauline at the Beach
La Paura Fear
Paura e Amore Three Sisters
Pay the Devil Man in the Shadow
The Pear Tree Shooting the Moon
The Pearl Necklace Desire
Peau d'Âne The Magic Donkey
Peau de Banane Banana Peel
Peau d'Homme Coeur de Bête Skin of Man, Heart of Beast
Peccato Che Sia una Canaglia Too Bad She's Bad
Peccatori in Blue Jeans Les Tricheurs
The Peddler of Four Seasons The Merchant of Four Seasons
Uma Pedra No Bolso Tall Stories
The Peking Medallion The Corrupt Ones
La Pelota Vasca, la Piel Contra la Piedra The Basque Ball: Skin against Stone
The Penance Sadhna
The Penguin Pool Mystery The Penguin Pool Murder
Pensioner The Long Way Home
Pentagram The First Power
The People of France La Vie Est à Nous
Peppermint Soda Diabolo Menthe
Per Qualche Dollaro in Più For a Few Dollars More
Perceval Perceval le Gallois
The Perfect Alibi Alibi
Perfect Prey When the Bough Breaks 2: Perfect Prey
Perfect Stranger Danielle Steel's A Perfect Stranger
Perfect Strangers Blind Alley
Péril Death in a French Garden
Péril en la Demeure Death in a French Garden
El Perro Bombón – El Perro
The Persecution and Assassination of Jean Paul Marat as Performed by the Inmates of the Asylum of Charenton under the Direction of the Marquis de Sade Marat/Sade
Personal Choice Beyond the Stars
Personal Column Lured
Personal Column Pièges
Personal Velocity: Three Portraits Personal Velocity
Persons Unknown Big Deal on Madonna Street
Pervyj Uchitel The First Teacher
La Peste The Plague
Peter Rabbit and Tales of Beatrix Potter The Tales of Beatrix Potter
Le Petit Amour Kung-Fu Master
Le Petit Théâtre de Jean Renoir The Little Theatre of Jean Renoir
La Petite Lola Clubbed to Death
Le Peuple Migrateur Winged Migration
Peversion Story Beatrice Cenci
The Phantom Fiend The Lodger
Phantom Fiend The Return of Dr Mabuse
The Phantom Menace Star Wars Episode I: the Phantom Menace
The Phantom of Liberty Le Fantôme de la Liberté
Phantom of Terror The Bird with the Crystal Plumage
Philip Run Wild, Run Free
Philly Private Lessons
Der Philosoph Three Women in Love
Piaf: the Early Years Piaf: the Sparrow of Pigalle
La Pianiste The Piano Teacher
Pickup Alley Interpol
Picnic on the Grass Lunch on the Grass
Pie in the Sky Terror in the City
The Pied Piper of Hamelin The Pied Piper
Piera's Story Storia di Piera
A Pig aross Paris La Traversée de Paris
Pigeons The Sidelong Glances of a Pigeon Kicker
Pigpen Pigsty
Pink Triangle Paragraph 175
Piranha Piranhas
Piranha Women in the Avocado Jungle of Death Cannibal Women in the Avocado Jungle of Death
La Piscine The Swimming Pool
The Pistolero of Red River The Last Challenge
The Pit of Loneliness Olivia
Pitch Black 2: The Chronicles of Riddick The Chronicles of Riddick
Pittsville – ein Safe Voll Blut The Catamount Killing
Il Piu Bel Giorno della Mia Vita The Best Day of My Life
Pixote: a Lei Do Mais Fraco Pixote
The Pizza Triangle Jealousy, Italian Style
Le Placard The Closet
A Place to Be Loved Shattered Family
Planet of Blood Planet of the Vampires
Planet of Incredible Creatures Fantastic Planet
Planet of Storms Planeta Burg
La Planète Sauvage Fantastic Planet
The Plants Are Watching The Kirlian Witness
Platonov An Unfinished Piece for Mechanical Piano
Playgirl after Dark Too Hot to Handle
The Playgirl and the War Minister The Amorous Prawn
Playgirl Gang Switchblade Sisters
Playing for Keeps Lily in Love
Playing with Death Target Eagle
The Pleasure Lovers Naked Fury
Pleasure Party Une Partie de Plaisir
The Plot to Kill Roosevelt Conspiracy in Teheran
The Plough that Broke the Plains The Plow That Broke the Plains
Pluck of the Irish Great Guy
Les Plus Belles Escroqueries du Monde The Beautiful Swindlers
Le Plus Vieux Métier du Monde The Oldest Profession
Pocket Money Small Change
Poe's Tales of Terror Tales of Terror
Point of No Return The Assassin
A Poke in the Eye with a Sharp Stick Pleasure at Her Majesty's
Pokémon 2 Pokémon the Movie 2000
Pokémon 3: the Movie Pokémon 3: Spell of the Unown
Pokémon: the Power of One Pokémon the Movie 2000
Police Academy 7: Mission to Moscow Police Academy: Mission to Moscow
Police Force Police Story
Police Story 4: First Strike Jackie Chan's First Strike
Polissons et Galipettes The Good Old Naughty Days
Politically Correct Party Animals PCU
Polly Fulton BF's Daughter
The Polygraph Le Polygraphe
La Pomme The Apple
Un Pont entre Deux Rives The Bridge
Le Pont vers le Soleil Bridge to the Sun
Pooh's Grand Adventure: the Search for Christopher Robin Winnie the Pooh's Most Grand Adventure
Pookie The Sterile Cuckoo
Poor Albert and Little Annie I Dismember Mama
The Pope Must Diet The Pope Must Die
Porcile Pigsty
Le Pornographe The Pornographer
Pornographic Affair Une Liaison Pornographique
Port Chicago Mutiny Mutiny
Le Port du Désir The House on the Waterfront
Port of Shadows Le Quai des Brumes
Porte Aperte Open Doors
Porte des Lilas Gates of Paris
Portrait of a Sinner The Rough and the Smooth
Portrait of Alison Postmark for Danger
Posse 2 – Los Locos Los Locos
The Possessed Les Possédées
Possessed Junoon
The Postman Il Postino
Potato Fritz Montana Trap
Poulet au Vinaigre Cop au Vin
Les Poupées Le Bambole
Poussière d'Ange Angel Dust
Poussières de Vie Dust of Life
The Powder Keg Cabaret Balkan
Power Jew Süss
Power Rangers 2 Turbo: a Power Rangers Adventure
Pratidwandi The Adversary
Precinct 45: Los Angeles Police The New Centurions
Precious Citizen Ruth
Prehistoric Adventure Voyage into Prehistory
Prehistoric World Teenage Caveman
Prénom Carmen First Name: Carmen
Préparez Vos Mouchoirs Get out Your Handkerchiefs
Prescription Revolution The Hot Box
Pretty Kill PrettyKill
Prey for Us All Love, Cheat & Steal
Price of Freedom Operation Daybreak
The Pride of Hollywood Behind the Screen
Pride of Kentucky The Story of Seabiscuit
Prima della Rivoluzione Before the Revolution
O Primeiro Dia Midnight
Prince and the Great Race Bush Christmas
Prince of the Blue Grass Pride of the Blue Grass
Il Principe di Homburg The Prince of Homburg
La Prise de Pouvoir par Louis XIV The Rise to Power of Louis XIV
Prison The Devil's Wanton
Prison Release Celebration The Wolves
Prisoners of the Sun Blood Oath
The Prisoners' Song Heimkehr
The Private Life of Oliver the Eighth Oliver the Eighth
The Private Wore Skirts Never Wave at a WAC
Prize of Gold A Prize of Gold
The Pro Number One
The Proceedings against Hamsun Hamsun
Le Procès de Jeanne d'Arc The Passion of Joan of Arc
Profession: Reporter The Passenger
The Professional Leon
Professione: Reporter The Passenger
Profile of Terror The Sadist
Profondo Rosso Deep Red
A Profound Longing for the Gods The Profound Desire of the Gods
Profumo di Donna Scent of a Woman
Profundo Carmesi Deep Crimson
The Programme The Program
Il Proiezionista The Inner Circle
Project A II Project A: Part II
Project M7 The Net
Le Promeneur du Champ de Mars The Last Mitterrand
The Promise Face of a Stranger
The Promise La Promesse
The Promoter The Card
La Propriétaire The Proprietor
The Protector Body Armor
The Proud and the Beautiful The Proud Ones
Proud, Damned and Dead The Proud and the Damned
The Proud Ones Le Cheval d'Orgeuil
Prova d'Orchestra Orchestra Rehearsal
Psycho-Circus Circus of Fear
Psychopath Twist of Fate
Psychotherapy Don't Get Me Started
Psychotic The Driver's Seat
P'tit Con Petit Con
Public Affairs Les Affaires Publiques
The Public Eye Follow Me
I Pugni in Tasca Fists in the Pocket
Pull No Punches The Prodigal Son
Pulling It Off He's My Girl
Pumpkinhead 2: Blood Wings The Revenge of Pumpkinhead – Blood Wings
Punto de mira One of the Hollywood Ten
Una Pura Formalità A Pure Formality
The Pure Pakeezah
Pure Heart Pakeezah
The Pure One Pakeezah
Pure Vamp Razor Blade Smile
Purgatory West of the Pecos Purgatory
The Purging On Purge Bébé
Purlie Victorious Gone Are the Days
Purple Haze More American Graffiti
Purple Noon Plein Soleil
Pursuit The Pursuit of DB Cooper
Pursuit of the Graf Spee The Battle of the River Plate
Puss och Kram Hugs and Kisses
Pussycat Alley WUSA
Pussycat Alley The World Ten Times Over

Q

Quatermass The Quatermass Conclusion
The Quatermass Experiment The Quatermass Xperiment
Les Quatre Cents Coups The 400 Blows
Quatre Nuits d'un Rêveur Four Nights of a Dreamer
Le Quattro Giornate di Napoli The Four Days of Naples
Quattro Passi fra le Nuvole Four Steps in the Clouds
Que Viva Mexico! Time in the Sun
The Queen Margot La Reine Margot
Queen Margot La Reine Margot
Queen of Atlantis Siren of Atlantis
Queen of Blood Planet of Blood
Queen of Destiny Sixty Glorious Years
Queen of Diamonds Popsy-Pop
Queen of the Cannibals Zombie Holocaust
Queen of the Gorillas The Bride and the Beast
Queen of the Nile Nefertite, Queen of the Nile
The Queen's Diamonds The Three Musketeers
Queimada! Burn!
Quella Villa Accanto al Cimitero House by the Cemetery
The Quest Frog Dreaming
Quest for Camelot The Magic Sword: Quest for Camelot
Questi Fantasmi Ghosts – Italian Style
Qui a Tué Bambi? Who Killed Bambi?
Qui Veut Tuer Carlos? Dead Run
15 Moments Stardom
Quirky Gate Pool Girl

R

RPM RPM – Revolutions per Minute
RSVP For Better and for Worse
RX: Revolution The Hot Box
Raba Lubvi A Slave of Love
A Race for Life Mask of Dust
Race for the Yankee Zephyr Treasure of the Yankee Zephyr
Race Gang The Green Cockatoo
Race to the Yankee Zephyr Treasure of the Yankee Zephyr
Rachel Cade The Sins of Rachel Cade
Rafferty and the Highway Hustlers Rafferty and the Gold Dust Twins
La Ragazza e il Generale The Girl and the General
Ragazzi Shoeshine
Rage Paris Trout
Rage of the Buccaneers The Black Pirate
Rage of the Buccaneers Gordon the Black Pirate
Ragged Angels They Shall Have Music
Raghs-e-Khak Dance of Dust
Raid Razzia sur la Chnouf
Rain Barsaat
The Rainmaker John Grisham's The Rainmaker
Raise Ravens Cría Cuervos
Ramatou Hyènes
Rambo: First Blood First Blood
Ranghe Khoda The Color of Paradise
Ransom Maniac
Rape Me Baise-Moi
The Rape of Malaya A Town like Alice
Rape Squad Act of Vengeance
Rappresaglia Massacre in Rome
Rasputin Agony
Le Rat des Villes et le Rat des Champs Town Rat, Country Rat
Die Ratten The Rats
Raw Eddie Murphy Raw
Raw Deal Good Cop, Bad Cop
Raw Justice Good Cop, Bad Cop
Raw Meat Death Line
The Rawney The Raggedy Rawney
Raye Makhfi Secret Ballot
Le Rayon Diabolique Paris Qui Dort
Le Rayon Invisible Paris Qui Dort
Le Rayon Vert The Green Ray
Re: Lucky Luciano Lucky Luciano
Ready to Wear Pret-a-Porter
Re-Animator 2 Bride of Re-Animator

Reasonable Doubt Shadow of Doubt
Reazione a Catena Bay of Blood
The Rebel Rebel
Rebel Highway Shake, Rattle and Rock
The Rebel Priest Le Défroqué
Rebel with a Cause The Loneliness of the Long Distance Runner
Recollected Memory Forgotten Sins
Record of a Living Being I Live in Fear
Red Three Colours Red
The Red and the Black Le Rouge et le Noir
The Red Baron Von Richthofen and Brown
The Red Head Poil de Carotte
Red Hot Wheels To Please a Lady
Red Light District Street of Shame
The Red Mark of Madness Hatchet for the Honeymoon
Red Neck Zombies Redneck Zombies
Red Wedding Les Noces Rouges
Red Zone The Peacekeeper
Redneck County Rape Redneck Zombies
Reed: Mexico Insurgente Reed: Insurgent Mexico
The Ref Hostile Hostages
Reflections in the Dark Reflections on a Crime
The Refugee Three Faces West
Regalo di Natale Christmas Present
Le Regard d'Ulysse Ulysses' Gaze
Regarde les Hommes Tomber See How They Fall
Regina Reflections on a Crime
La Regina dei Cannibali Zombie Holocaust
Regina Roma Regina
Rehearsal for a Crime The Criminal Life of Archibaldo de la Cruz
Reindeer Games Deception
Reise der Hoffnung Journey of Hope
Rejuvenatrix The Rejuvenator
La Religieuse de Diderot La Religieuse
The Remarkable Mr Kipps Kipps
Remembering Satan Forgotten Sins
Remembrance Danielle Steel's Remembrance
Remembrance of Things Past Swann in Love
Remo Williams: the Adventure Begins... Remo – Unarmed and Dangerous
Remorques Stormy Waters
Renegade Girls Caged Heat
Repo Zero to Sixty
A Report on the Party and the Guests The Party and the Guests
Reprieve Convicts Four
Republic of Sin La Fièvre Monte à el Pao
Reputation Lady with a Past
Requiescant Kill and Pray
Rescue Me Trojan War
Ressources Humaines Human Resources
Rest in Peace One Dark Night
Restless Sin
The Resurrection Syndicate Nothing but the Night
Le Retour de Martin Guerre The Return of Martin Guerre
The Return of Godzilla Godzilla Raids Again
The Return of I Spy I Spy Returns
The Return of Maxwell Smart The Nude Bomb
The Return of Old Mother Riler Old Mother Riley
The Return of Sandokan Sandokan against the Leopard of Sarawak
The Return of She The Vengeance of She
Return of the Badmen Return of the Bad Men
Return of the Boomerang Adam's Woman
Return of the Corsican Brothers The Bandits of Corsica
The Return of the Dragon The Way of the Dragon
Return of the Magnificent Seven Return of the Seven
The Return of the Texas Chainsaw Massacre Texas Chainsaw Massacre: the Next Generation
The Return of the Vigilantes The Vigilantes Return
Return to the Land of the Demons The Church
Reunion Reunion in France
The Reunion Eternal Revenge
Rêve de Singe Bye Bye Monkey
Revenge Blood Feud
Revenge Eternal Revenge
Revenge at El Paso Ace High
Revenge Is Sweet Babes in Toyland
Revenge of Dracula Dracula – Prince of Darkness
The Revenge of the Blood Beast The She Beast
Revenge of the Dead Night of the Ghouls
The Revenge of the Musketeers D'Artagnan's Daughter
Revenge of the Vampire The Mask of Satan
The Revenge of Yuki-No-Jo An Actor's Revenge
The Revolt of the Seven The Spartan Gladiators
Revolution The Love of Jeanne Ney
Rhodes Rhodes of Africa
Rhythm Romance Some Like It Hot
Riata The Deadly Trackers
Rice Paddy People Rice People
The Rich, Full Life Cynthia
Rich, Young and Deadly Platinum High School
Riches and Romance The Amazing Quest of Ernest Bliss
Ride a Dark Horse Man and Boy
Ride the Whirlwind Ride in the Whirlwind
Ride to Glory The Deserter
Le Rideau Cramoisi The Crimson Curtain
Du Rififi chez les Hommes Rififi
Riget The Kingdom
Ring 0: Birthday Ring 0
Ring-a-Ding Rhythm It's Trad, Dad
The Ring of the Nibelungs Sword of Xanten
Ring of Treason Ring of Spies
Ring up the Curtain Broadway to Hollywood
Ringu Ring
Rio Vengeance Motor Psycho
El Rio y la Muerte The River and Death
Rip Tide Riptide
Les Ripoux Le Cop
Ripoux contre Ripoux Le Cop II
Rise and Fall of a Little Film Company from a Novel by James Hadley Chase Grandeur et Décadence d'un Petit Commerce de Cinéma
The Rise of Helga Susan Lenox: Her Fall and Rise
Rising to Fame Susan Lenox: Her Fall and Rise
Riso Amaro Bitter Rice
Rites of Spring White Water Summer
Rites of Summer White Water Summer
The Ritual The Rite
Rive Droite, Rive Gauche Right Bank, Left Bank
The River of Death The River and Death
Les Rivières Pourpres The Crimson Rivers
La Rivolta dei Sette The Spartan Gladiators
Road Check Trial on the Road
Road Gangs, Adventures in the Creep Zone Spacehunter: Adventures in the Forbidden Zone
The Road Home The Long Way Home
Road Kill Roadkill
The Road Killers Roadflower
Road of Shame Street of Shame
The Road Racers Roadracers
The Road to Graceland Finding Graceland
Road Trip Jocks
The Road Warrior Mad Max 2
Roadgames Road Games
Roads of the South Roads to the South
Roald Dahl's Matilda Matilda
Roaring Timber Come and Get It
Rob Roy Rob Roy, the Highland Rogue
Robert A Heinlein's The Puppet Masters The Puppet Masters
Robert and Robert Robert et Robert
Robert Louis Stevenson's St Ives All for Love
Robin Cook's Formula for Death Formula for Death
Robin Cook's Mortal Fear Mortal Fear
Robin Cook's Virus Formula for Death
Robinson Crusoe Daniel Defoe's Robinson Crusoe
Robinson Crusoe The Adventures of Robinson Crusoe
Robinson Crusoeland Utopia
Robinsonada anu Chemi Inglesi Papa My English Grandfather
Robo Man Who?
Roboman Who?
Rock and Roll High School Rock 'n' Roll High School
Rock around the World The Tommy Steele Story
The Rocket Boys October Sky
Rocket Man Rocketman
Rocket Ship Flash Gordon
Rocket to the Moon Jules Verne's Rocket to the Moon
Rocket to the Moon Cat-women of the Moon
Rod Serling's The Doomsday Flight The Doomsday Flight
The Rodgers Sisters Story Ultimate Betrayal
Rodon the Flying Monster Rodan
Roger Corman's Frankenstein Unbound Frankenstein Unbound
Le Roi de Coeur King of Hearts
Le Roi de Paris The King of Paris
Rois et Reine Kings & Queen
Rojin Z Roujin Z
Roller and Violin Katok i Skrypka
Rolling Family Familia Rodante
Roma Fellini's Roma
Roma, Città Aperta Rome, Open City
Roma Regina Regina
Le Roman de Renard The Tale of the Fox
Le Roman d'un Tricheur The Story of a Cheat
Romance and Riches The Amazing Quest of Ernest Bliss
Romance for Three Paradise for Three
Romance Is Sacred The King and the Chorus Girl
Romeo and Juliet William Shakespeare's Romeo + Juliet
Romeo in Pyjamas Parlor, Bedroom and Bath
Rommel – Desert Fox The Desert Fox
Romolo e Remo Duel of the Titans
Romp of Fanny Hill Fanny Hill: Memoirs of a Woman of Pleasure
Romuald and Juliette Romuald et Juliette
The Rook Something for Everyone
Rookies Buck Privates
Rookies Come Home Buck Privates Come Home
Room 43 Passport to Shame
The Room Upstairs Martin Roumagnac
Room with Thick Walls The Thick-Walled Room
Roommates Raising the Wind
Rope Mudhoney
Rope of Flesh Mudhoney
La Rose du Rail La Roue
The Rosegarden The Rose Garden
Roselyne et les Lions Roselyne and the Lions
Der Rosengarten The Rose Garden
Rosie the Riveter The Life and Times of Rosie the Riveter
Il Rosso Segno della Follia Hatchet for the Honeymoon
Der Rote Kreis The Red Circle
La Roue du Rail La Roue
Le Rouge aux Lèvres Daughters of Darkness
Rough Company The Violent Men
Roughriding Dance of the Dwarfs
La Route de Corinthe The Road to Corinth
Les Routes du Sud Roads to the South
Royal Bay Della
Royal Deceit Prince of Jutland
Royal Flush Two Guys from Milwaukee
Rozmarné Léto Capricious Summer
Ruba al Prossimo Tuo A Fine Pair
The Ruby Virgin Hell's Island
Rude Boy Featuring The Clash Rude Boy
Rudyard Kipling's Jungle Book Adventure Jungle Book
Rudyard Kipling's The Jungle Book The Jungle Book
Rudyard Kipling's The Jungle Book The Adventures of Mowgli
Rudyard Kipling's The Second Jungle Book: Mowgli and Baloo The Second Jungle Book
Rue Saint-Sulpice The Favour, the Watch and the Very Big Fish
Rules of Attraction Attraction
Rumplestiltskin Rumpelstiltskin
A Run on Gold Midas Run
Run Rabbit Run Double X: the Name of the Game
Run, Stranger, Run Happy Mother's Day... Love, George
Runaway Daughter Red Salute
The Runaway Train Runaway!
The Rundown Welcome to the Jungle
Running Home The Long Way Home
Russ Meyer's Super Vixens Supervixens
Russ Meyer's Common Law Cabin Common-Law Cabin
Russ Meyer's Up! Up
Russ Meyer's Vixen Vixen!
Russell Mulcahy's Tale of the Mummy Talos the Mummy

SF Shinseiki Lensman Lensman
SOS Spaceship The Invisible Boy
S.W.A.L.K. Melody
SW9 South West Nine
The Sabre and the Arrow Last of the Comanches
Sabrina Fair Sabrina
Sacco e Vanzetti Sacco and Vanzetti
The Sacred Mountain The Holy Mountain
Sacrificatio The Sacrifice
Sacrifice of Youth Sacrificed Youth
The Sacrilegious Hero Tales of the Taira Clan
A Sad Comedy Autumn Marathon
Sadhana Sadhna
Safe Conduct Laissez-passer
La Sage-Femme, le Curé et le Bon Dieu Jessica
St Francis of Assisi Francesco
St George and the Seven Curses The Magic Sword
St Ives All for Love
Le Salaire de la Peur The Wages of Fear
Salem Come to Supper The Night Visitor
Sallah Shabati Sallah
Salò, o le 120 Giornate di Sodoma Salo, or the 120 Days of Sodom
Salonique, Nid d'Espions Mademoiselle Docteur
Salt to the Devil Give Us This Day
Salut l'Artiste The Bit Player
Salvation! Salvation! Have You Said Your Prayers Today?
Sam Marlow, Private Eye The Man with Bogart's Face
Samantha A New Kind of Love
Samaria Samaritan Girl
Same Old Song On Connaît la Chanson
Samurai Force Red Sun
Samurai Musashi Miyamoto Samurai
Samurai Rebellion Rebellion
Sand in the Eye Chokher Bali
Sanders Death Drums along the River
The Sandlot Kids The Sandlot
The Sandpit Generals The Defiant
Sandra Of a Thousand Delights
The Sandra Prine Story Hard Evidence
Le Sang des Autres The Blood of Others
Le Sang d'un Poète The Blood of a Poet
Sangre de Vírgenes Blood of the Virgins
Sangre y Arena Blood and Sand
Il Sangue e la Rosa Blood and Roses
Sans Douleur The Case of Dr Laurent
Sans Espoir de Retour Street of No Return
Sans Mobile Apparent Without Apparent Motive
Sans Sommation Without Warning
Sans Toit Ni Loi Vagabond
Sansho Dayu Sansho the Bailiff
Santa Claus Conquers Mars Santa Claus Conquers the Martians
Santa Claus Defeats the Aliens Santa Claus Conquers the Martians
Santa Fe Satan Catch My Soul
Santiago, the Story of His New Life What Happened to Santiago
Saraband Saraband for Dead Lovers
Sardonicus Mr Sardonicus
Sartana the Gravedigger Sartana, Angel of Death
Satan Mark of the Devil
Satan's Claw Blood on Satan's Claw
Satan's Dog Play Dead
Satan's Skin Blood on Satan's Claw
Satansbraten Satan's Brew
Satellite of Blood First Man into Space
Saturday Island Island of Desire
Le Sauvage Call Him Savage
Sauve Qui Peut – la Vie Slow Motion
The Savage Call Him Savage
Savage Attraction Hostage: the Christine Maresch Story
Savage Nights Les Nuits Fauves
Savage Wilderness The Last Frontier
Saving Grace One Woman's Courage
Saving Silverman Evil Woman
The Scandal Untold Scandal
Scandal in Paris Thieves' Holiday
Le Scandale The Champagne Murders
Scandals George White's Scandals
Scandals of Clochemerle Clochemerle
Scanner Force Scanners III: the Takeover
The Scar Hollow Triumph
SCAR Scarred City
Scar City Scarred City
Scaramouche The Loves and Times of Scaramouche
The Scarlet Buccaneer Swashbuckler
The Scarlet Pen The 13th Letter
The Scarlet Riders North West Mounted Police
Lo Sceicco Bianco The White Sheik
Scènes Intimes Sex Is Comedy
Die Schaukel Swing
Das Schiff der Verlorenen Menschen The Ship of Lost Men
Schizo Nightmares in a Damaged Brain
Das Schlangenei The Serpent's Egg
Die Schlangengrube und das Pendel The Blood Demon
Das Schöne Ende dieser Welt The Beautiful End of This World
School for Unclaimed Girls The Smashing Bird I Used to Know
The School That Stole My Brain Zombie High
The Schoolmistress and the Devil The Masters
Das Schreckliche Mädchen The Nasty Girl
Schrei aus Stein Scream of Stone
Schweitzer and Lambarene Out of Darkness
Schwestern oder die Balance des Glücks Sisters, or the Balance of Happiness
Sciuscia Shoeshine
Scorching Winds Garam Hawa
Scorpion Rising Scorpion Spring
Scotch on the Rocks Laxdale Hall
Scotland Yard Dragnet The Hypnotist
Scream: The Sequel Scream 2
Screen Kiss Billy's Hollywood Screen Kiss
Screwface Marked for Death
Screwloose Screw Loose
Se Permettete Let's Talk About Women
The Sea El Mar
The Sea Wall This Angry Age
The Sea Watches The Sea Is Watching

Sea Wyf and Biscuit Sea Wife
Search for the Mother Lode Mother Lode
Searching for Bobby Fischer Innocent Moves
Seaside Swingers Every Day's a Holiday
The Season of Men La Saison des Hommes
Season's Beatings La Bûche
The Seaweed Children Malachi's Cove
The Second Best Secret Agent in the Whole Wide World Licensed to Kill
Second Breath Le Deuxième Souffle
Second Family Affair You're Only Young Once
The Second Heimat Heimat 2
Secret Raaz
Secret Abduction Visitors of the Night
The Secret Agents The Dirty Game
Le Secret de D'Artagnan The Secret Mark of D'Artagnan
Secret Flight School for Secrets
The Secret Four The Four Just Men
The Secret Four Kansas City Confidential
Secret Interlude The View from Pompey's Head
A Secret Life Breach of Trust
The Secret of Boyne Castle Guns in the Heather
The Secret of Monte Cristo The Treasure of Monte Cristo
The Secret Passion Freud
The Secret Sharer Face to Face
Secret Yearnings Good Luck, Miss Wyckoff
Secretos del Corazón Secrets of the Heart
Secrets Danielle Steel's Secrets
Secrets of FP1 FP1
Secrets of G32 Fly by Night
Secrets of Women Waiting Women
Sedotta e Abbandonata Seduced and Abandoned
Seduction of a Priest The Monk
See How They Run Summer Things
See No Evil Blind Terror
See You in Hell, Darling An American Dream
Seeds of Evil The Gardener
Seeing Stars The Decline of Western Civilization Part II: the Metal Years
Seemabaddha Company Limited
Segunda Piel Second Skin
Die Sehnsucht der Veronika Voss Veronika Voss
Sei Donne per l'Assassino Blood and Black Lace
Les Seins de glace Someone Is Bleeding
Sélect Amour Sélect Hôtel
Self Storage Tinseltown
The Sell Out The Sellout
Il Seme dell'Uomo The Seed of Man
Sensations of 1945 Sensations
The Sensuous Teenager I Am a Nymphomaniac
La Senyora La Señora
Separate Beds The Wheeler Dealers
The Separation La Séparation
Seppuku Harakiri
Sept Fois Femme Woman Times Seven
Les Sept Péchés Capitaux The Seven Deadly Sins
I Sequestrati di Altona The Condemned of Altona
Seres Queridos Only Human
Sergeant Jim Dolina Mira
Sergeant Steiner Breakthrough
Serial Bomber Countdown
A Series of Unfortunate Events Lemony Snicket's A Series of Unfortunate Events
Le Serpent The Serpent
The Servile Vidheyan
The Set-Up The Sellout
La Setta The Sect
Sette volte donna Woman Times Seven
The Settlers The New Land
Seven Se7en
Seven Bad Men Rage at Dawn
Seven Cities to Atlantis Warlords of Atlantis
Seven Days Brown Sugar
The Seven Descents of Myrtle Last of the Mobile Hot-Shots
Seven Different Ways Quick, Let's Get Married
Seven Sisters House of Evil
Seventeen Anita
71 Fragmente einer Chronologie des Zufalls 71 Fragments of a Chronology of Chance
Sex Academy Not Another Teen Movie
Sex and the Vampire Shiver of the Vampires
Sex Crime of the Century Last House on the Left
Sex Life in a Convent Behind Convent Walls
Sex Mad I Am Frigid... Why?
Sex on the Run Casanova & Co
Sex through a Window Extreme Close-Up
Sexo, Pudor y Lagrimas Sex, Shame and Tears
The Shabby Tiger Masquerade
Shades of Doubt A Shadow of Doubt
The Shadow Army L'Armée des Ombres
Shadow Builder Bram Stoker's Shadowbuilder
Shadow Man Street of Shadows
The Shadow versus the Thousand Eyes of Dr Mabuse The Thousand Eyes of Dr Mabuse
The Shadow Warrior Kagemusha
Shadowbuilder Bram Stoker's Shadowbuilder
Shadows of Forgotten Ancestors Shadows of Our Forgotten Ancestors
Shadows of Our Ancestors Shadows of Our Forgotten Ancestors
Shakedown Blue Jean Cop
Shakespeare's Hamlet Hamlet
Shame The Intruder
The Shame of Mary Boyle Juno and the Paycock
Shameless Mad Dogs and Englishmen
The Shaming Good Luck, Miss Wyckoff
Shatterbrain The Resurrected
Shattered Mind The Terror Inside
She Couldn't Say No Beautiful but Dangerous
She Cried No Freshman Fall
She Demons of the Swamp Attack of the Giant Leeches
She Let Him Continue Pretty Poison
She Played with Fire Fortune Is a Woman
She Should Have Stayed in Bed I Am Frigid... Why?
Sheba Persecution
Sheena, Queen of the Jungle Sheena
Sheka Zulu The Mark of the Hawk
Sheltered Lady Lady in a Jam
The Sheltered Side Lady in a Jam
Shenanigans The Great Georgia Bank Hoax
Sherlock Holmes and the Pearl of Death The Pearl of Death
Sherlock Holmes and the Scarlet Claw The Scarlet Claw
Sherlock Holmes in Dressed to Kill Sherlock Holmes and the Secret Code
The Sherri Finkbine Story A Private Matter
A Ship Bound for India A Ship to India
The Ship of Lost Souls The Ship of Lost Men
The Ship Was Loaded Carry On Admiral
Shipwreck! The Sea Gypsies
Shiqi Sui de Dan Che Beijing Bicycle
Shlosha Yamim Veyeled Three Days and a Child
Shock Le Choc
Shocked Mesmerized
Shocker Town without Pity
Shocker: No More Mr Nice Guy Shocker
Shockwave The Arrival
Shockwave Stranded
Shoe Shine Shoeshine
Shoeshine Boys Shoeshine
Shogun Assassin Baby Cart at the River Styx
Shoot! Outrage
Shoot First Rough Shoot
Shoot the Piano Player Shoot the Pianist
Shoot to Kill Deadly Pursuit
Shootout Shoot Out
The Shop on Main Street The Shop on the High Street
Short Fuse Good to Go
The Shot Title Shot
Show and Tell The Adjuster
Showdown Top of the World
Showtime Gaiety George
The Shrinking Corpse Cauldron of Blood
Si Versailles M'Etait Conté Royal Affairs in Versailles
Siberiade Sibiriada
Sicarius – the Midnight Party The Female Vampire
Sicilia 1860 1860
Siddharta and the City The Adversary
Sidewalks of London St Martin's Lane
Sidney Sheldon's Bloodline Bloodline
Der Siebente Kontinent The Seventh Continent
Die Siebtelbauern The Inheritors
The Siege of Hell Street The Siege of Sidney Street
The Siege of Red River The Siege at Red River
Sierra de Teruel Man's Hope
The Sign of the Vampire Vampyros Lesbos
Le Signe du Lion The Sign of Leo
El Signo del Vampiro Vampyros Lesbos
Signore & Signori The Birds, the Bees, and the Italians
The Silence Sokhout
Le Silence Est d'Or Man about Town
Silence Is Golden Man about Town
Les Silences du Palais The Silences of the Palace
Les Silencieux The Silent One
Silent Barriers The Great Barrier
Silent Voice Amazing Grace and Chuck
The Silent Voice The Man Who Played God
The Silent World Le Monde du Silence
The Silk Noose Noose
Silken Skin La Peau Douce
Silver Stallion: King of the Wild Brumbies The Silver Brumby
Simone S1MØNE
Simoom: A Passion in the Desert Passion in the Desert
A Simple Story Une Histoire Simple
The Sin Good Luck, Miss Wyckoff
Sin compasión No Mercy
The Sin of Harold Diddlebock Mad Wednesday
La Sindrome di Stendhal The Stendhal Syndrome
Sing and Swing Live It Up
Un Singe en Hiver A Monkey in Winter
Das Singende, Klingende Bäumchen The Singing, Ringing Tree
The Singing Musketeer The Three Musketeers
Single-Handed Sailor of the King
The Single Standard The Battle of the Sexes
Singleton's Pluck Laughterhouse
The Sinister Invasion Alien Terror
The Sinister Urge Hellborn
Sinner's Holiday Christmas Eve
The Sins of Lola Montès Lola Montès
Sir Arthur Conan Doyle's Sign of Four The Sign of Four
Sir Gawain and the Green Knight Gawain and the Green Knight
La Sirène du Mississippi Mississippi Mermaid
Sisters Some Girls
Sisters of Satan Alucarda
Situation Normal All Fed Up The Pentagon Wars
Six Femmes pour l'Assassin Blood and Black Lace
Six in Paris Paris Vu Par...
Six Inches Tall Attack of the Puppet People
The Skating Rink and the Violin Katok i Skrypka
The Ski Raiders Snow Job
Skip-Tracer Good Cop, Bad Cop
Skipper The Todd Killings
Skirmish All's Fair
Skrivánci na niti Larks on a String
Sky Above and Mud Beneath The Sky above, the Mud below
Sky Bandits Gunbus
The Sky Calls Battle beyond the Sun
The Sky Is Calling Battle beyond the Sun
Skylarks on a String Larks on a String
Skyscraper Wilderness Big City
Slappy and the Stinkers The Adventures of Slappy the Sea Lion
Slapstick Slapstick of Another Kind
Slapstick of a Different Kind Slapstick of Another Kind
Slate & Wyn and Blanche McBride Slate, Wyn & Me
Slaughter Snuff
Slave Coast Cobra Verde
The Slaves of Sumuru Sumuru
O Slavnosti a Hostech The Party and the Guests
Slayride Silent Night, Deadly Night
Sleep Stalker: The Sandman's Last Rites Sleepstalker
The Sleepers Little Nikita
Slithis Spawn of the Slithis
Slow Burn Wilder
Small Cuts Petites Coupures
The Small Miracle Never Take No for an Answer
Small Time Smalltime
Smart Alec Masterminds
The Smell of Green Papaya The Scent of Green Papaya
Smilla's Sense of Snow Smilla's Feeling for Snow
Smoke Physical Evidence
Smoke Jumpers Red Skies of Montana
Smoke Jumpers In the Line of Duty: Smoke Jumpers
Smoke Screen Palais Royale
Smokey and the Bandit Ride Again Smokey and the Bandit II
The Smugglers The Man Within
SNAFU The Pentagon Wars
Snake Eyes Dangerous Game
The Snake Goddess Jennifer
The Snake Pit The Blood Demon
Snap Dragon Snapdragon
Snares Pièges
Sneakers Hard Feelings
Snitch Noose
The Snout The Informers
Snow White in Happily Ever After Happily Ever After
Snow White in the Black Forest Snow White: a Tale of Terror
Snowbound Avalanche
Snuff Tesis
So Bright the Flame The Girl in White
Soccor Days Football Days
Les Soeurs Brontë The Brontë Sisters
Soft Skin La Peau Douce
Soil Earth
Un Soir au Music Hall One Night at the Music Hall
Un Soir sur la Plage Violent Summer
El Sol del Membrillo The Quince Tree Sun
Solar Babies Solarbabies
Solarwarriors Solarbabies
The Soldier and the Lady The Adventures of Michael Strogoff
Soldier in Love Fanfan la Tulipe
The Soldiers Les Carabiniers
Soldiers of Fortune You Can't Win 'em All
Il Sole Anche di Notte Night Sun
Soleil Rouge Red Sun
I Soliti Ignoti Big Deal on Madonna Street
Solomon a Gaenor Solomon and Gaenor
Some Girl Some Girls
Some Like It Cool Casanova & Co
Someone Like You Animal Attraction
Something Like the Truth The Offence
Something Special Willy/Milly
Somewhere Beneath the Wide Sky Somewhere under the Broad Sky
Somewhere in France The Foreman Went to France
Sommaren med Monika Summer with Monika
Sommarlek Summer Interlude
Les Somnambules Mon Oncle d'Amérique
Son of Blob Beware! The Blob
Sondagsbarn Sunday's Children
Song of Exile Song of the Exile
A Song of Love Un Chant d'Amour
Song of New Life Earth
Song of the Little Road Pather Panchali
Song of the Road Pather Panchali
Sono Sartana, il Vostro Becchino Sartana, Angel of Death
Sons of the Legion Sons of the Desert
Sophie Sofie
Sophie's Place Crooks and Coronets
Les Sorcières The Witches
Les Sorcières de Salem The Witches of Salem
La Sorella di Satana The She Beast
Il Sorpasso The Easy Life
Sorrento Beach Hotel Sorrento
The Sorrow and the Shame The Sorrow and the Pity
Sotto gli Occhi dell'assassino Tenebrae
Souls for Sale Confessions of an Opium Eater
The Sound of Trumpets Il Posto
Sounder, Part 2 Part 2, Sounder
Sour Grapes Happy Hour
Sous le Sable Under the Sand
The South Sur
The South El Sur
South: Ernest Shackelton and the Endurance Expedition South
South Sea Fury Hell's Island
South: Sir Ernest Shackleton's Glorious Epic of the Antarctic South
Southern Blade A Time for Killing
Southward on the Quest South
Soy Cuba I Am Cuba
Space Avenger Alien Space Avenger
Space Camp SpaceCamp
Space Soldiers Flash Gordon
Spacemaster X 7 Space Master X 7
Spaceship to the Unknown Flash Gordon
Lo Spadaccino di Siena The Swordsman of Siena
Spara Forte, Più Forte... Non Capisco Shout Loud, Louder... I Don't Understand
Spectre Out 1: Spectre
Speed Zone Cannonball Fever
Spellbinders The Spellbinder
Spending Money Small Change
Speriamo Che Sia Femmina Let's Hope It's a Girl
Lo Spettro The Spectre
Spices Mirch Masala
The Spider Earth vs the Spider
Spider Woman Sherlock Holmes and the Spider Woman
The Spies Les Espions
Spies from Salonika Mademoiselle Docteur
Die Spinnen The Spiders
Spinster Two Loves
Spione unter Sich The Dirty Game
Spirit of the Dead The Asphyx
Spirits of the Dead Histoires Extraordinaires
Spitfire The First of the Few
The Spivs I Vitelloni
The Split Body Count
The Spooky Movie Show The Mask
Spoorloos The Vanishing
Spot See Spot Run
Spree Survival Run
Sprung! The Magic Roundabout The Magic Roundabout
The Spy Spies
Spy Busters Guns in the Heather
Spy in the Pantry Ten Days in Paris
Spy Kids SPYkids
Spy Kids 3 SPYkids 3-D: Game Over
Spy 13 Operator 13
Spylarks The Intelligence Men

Squadron 633 633 Squadron
Squanto: a Warrior's Tale Squanto: the Last Great Warrior
Squelch Roadkill
Ssssnake Sssssss
Stacking Season of Dreams
Stage Sisters Two Stage Sisters
Stagefright Stage Fright – Aquarius
Stairway to Heaven A Matter of Life and Death
The Stalking of Laura Black Stalking Laura
Stampede The Big Land
Stampede Guns of the Timberland
Der Stand der Dinge The State of Things
Stand-Up Tragedy Thicker than Blood
Stanno Tutti Bene Everybody's Fine
La Stanza del Figlio The Son's Room
Star Danielle Steel's Star
Star-Rock The Apple
The Star Said No Callaway Went Thataway
Starflight: the Plane That Couldn't Land Starflight One
Starlight Slaughter Eaten Alive
Staroye I Novoye The General Line
Starship Lorca and the Outlaws
The Stationmaster's Wife Bolwieser
Steam Heat Immoral Mr Teas
Steamboat Steamboat round the Bend
The Steamroller and the Violin Katok i Skrypka
Steel Force Legion of Iron
The Steel Highway Other Men's Women
Step Mom Stepmom
Stephen King's Graveyard Shift Graveyard Shift
Stephen King's Silver Bullet Silver Bullet
Stephen King's Sleepwalkers Sleepwalkers
Stephen King's Sometimes They Come Back Sometimes They Come Back
Sterne Stars
Stiffs Out Cold
Stiletto Cold Steel
Still Smokin Cheech & Chong's Still Smokin'
Stille Dage i Clichy Quiet Days in Clichy
Die Stille nach dem Schuss The Legends of Rita
Stillwater Almost Famous
Sto dnej do prikaza 100 Days before the Command
Stonebrook Web of Lies
Stop Me Before I Kill! The Full Treatment
Stop the World – I Want to Get Off Sammy Stops the World
Stories of American Communists Seeing Red
Storm Planet Planeta Burg
Storm Rider The Big Showdown
Storm Tracker Storm
The Storm Within Les Parents Terribles
A Story from Chikamatsu The Crucified Lovers
The Story of a Divorce Payment on Demand
Story of a Love Affair Chronicle of a Love
Story of a Marriage Part 3 1918
The Story of a Sin The Story of Sin
The Story of Asya Klyachinka Asya's Happiness
The Story of Benjamin Blake Son of Fury
The Story of Dr Ehrlich's Magic Bullet Dr Ehrlich's Magic Bullet
The Story of Gosta Berling Gösta Berlings Saga
The Story of HMS Amethyst Yangtse Incident
The Story of Marie and Julien Histoire de Marie et Julien
The Story of Mary Lindell One against the Wind
The Story of Piera Storia di Piera
Story of Women Une Affaire de Femmes
Stowaway Girl Manuela
Straight from the Heart Hum Dil De Chuke Sanam
Straight Shootin' Straight Shooting
Stranded Valley of Mystery
Stranded in Paris Artists and Models Abroad
The Strange Adventure of Jonathan Harker Vampyros Lesbos
Strange Confession The Impostor
Strange Deception The Accused
Strange Incident The Ox-Bow Incident
Strange Interval Strange Interlude
The Strange Ones Les Enfants Terribles
A Strange Place for an Encounter A Strange Place to Meet
Strange Skirts When Ladies Meet
Strange Things Happen at Night Shiver of the Vampires
The Stranger The Intruder
The Stranger and the Gunfighter Blood Money
The Stranger from Afar Marebito
The Stranger in Between Hunted
Stranger Things For Better or Worse
A Stranger Walked In Love from a Stranger
Strangers Journey to Italy
The Stranger's Gundown Django the Bastard
Strangers in Good Company The Company of Strangers
The Strangler East of Piccadilly
Lo Straniero The Stranger
La Strategia del Ragno The Spider's Stratagem
The Strategy of the Snail The Snail's Strategy
Strauss's Great Waltz Waltzes from Vienna
Street Fighters Only the Strong
Street Killers Mad Dog Murderer
Street Legal Blue Heat
The Street of Sorrow The Joyless Street
Street People The Sicilian Cross
The Streetfighter Hard Times
The Streetfighter The Street Fighter
Streets of Sorrow The Joyless Street
Le Streghe The Witches
Strictly Confidential Broadway Bill
Strictly for Pleasure The Perfect Furlough
Strike It Rich Loser Takes All
Strike Me Deadly The Crawling Hand
Striker The Night Stalker
The Strikers The Organizer
Striking Back Search and Destroy
Striptease Lady Lady of Burlesque
The Stroke of Midnight The Phantom Carriage
Strokes of Fire Chihwaseon (Drunk on Women and Poetry)
Strong Boys Goodbye Charlie Bright
Strong City Dark City
Stronger than Fear Edge of Doom
Stryker Savage Dawn
The Student Prince The Student Prince in Old Heidelberg
Stupeur et Tremblements Fear and Trembling
Stützen der Gesellschaft Pillars of Society
Sub-a-Dub-Dub Hello Down There
Subida al Cielo Mexican Bus Ride
The Success The American Success Company
Such a Gorgeous Kid Like Me Une Belle Fille Comme Moi
Such a Lovely Kid Like Me Une Belle Fille Comme Moi
Such Men Are Dangerous The Racers
Such Things Happen Love Is a Racket
Sudba Cheloveka Destiny of a Man
Sudden Attack: the Killing Fist The Street Fighter
Sudden Terror Eyewitness
Sugar Cane Alley Rue Cases Nègres
Sugata Sanshiro Sanshiro Sugata
The Suicide Club Trouble for Two
Suicide Squadron Dangerous Moonlight
A Suitable Case for Treatment Morgan – a Suitable Case for Treatment
The Sullivans The Fighting Sullivans
Suit Hunger
Summer The Green Ray
A Summer Affair Un Moment d'Egarement
Summer Fever Delta Fever
Summer Flight Stolen Hours
Summer Fling Last of the High Kings
The Summer Hurricane Senso
Summer Lightning I Met My Love Again
Summer Madness Summertime
Summer Manoeuvres Les Grandes Manoeuvres
Summer of the Seventeenth Doll Season of Passion
The Sun behind the Moon Kandahar
The Sun Demon Hideous Sun Demon
Sunless Sans Soleil
Sunset of a Clown Sawdust and Tinsel
Sunshine Club Ikinai
Sunshine Even by Night Night Sun
Suor Omicidio Killer Nun
Super Dude Hangup
SuperChef Mr Nice Guy
Supercop Police Story III: Supercop
SuperFantaGenio Aladdin
Sur Mes Lèvres Read My Lips
Surface Is Illusion But So Is Depth A Day on the Grand Canal with the Emperor of China
The Surgeon Exquisite Tenderness
Survival Run Damnation Alley
Survival Run Soldier of Orange
Suzanne The Second Coming of Suzanne
Suzanne Simonin La Religieuse
Suzanne's Career La Carrière de Suzanne
Svält Hunger
Svitati Screw Loose
The Swamp La Cienaga
Swamp of the Blood Leeches The Alien Dead
Swann's Way Swann in Love
The Swap Sam's Song
The Swashbuckler Sink or Swim
Swedish Nymphet Anita
Sweeper Sweepers
Sweet Baby Charlie The Sadist
Sweet Kill The Arousers
Sweet Revenge The Revengers' Comedies
Sweet Violent Tony Cuba Crossing
Swept from the Sea Amy Foster
The Swindle Rien Ne Va Plus
The Swindlers The Swindle
Swing, Teacher, Swing College Swing
Swinger's Paradise Wonderful Life
The Swingin' Maiden The Iron Maiden
The Swinging Pearl Mystery The Plot Thickens
Swirl of Glory Sugarfoot
Switched at Birth Mistaken Identity
The Sword and the Dragon Ilya Muromets
Sword of Lancelot Lancelot and Guinevere
Swords of Blood Cartouche
The Swordsman Musashi Miyamoto
Sympathy for the Devil One Plus One
Symphony of Love Ecstasy
Synanon Get off My Back
Synapse Memory Run
Szczesliwy Czlowiek Happy Man

T

Ta'ame-Gilas A Taste of Cherry
Taboo Gohatto
Tacones Lejanos High Heels
Tae Guk Gi: The Brotherhood of War Brotherhood
Taegukgi Brotherhood
Das Tagebuch einer Verlorenen Diary of a Lost Girl
The Tai Chi Master Twin Warriors
The Taira Clan Tales of the Taira Clan
The Taira Clan Saga Tales of the Taira Clan
Take Me Home Again The Lies Boys Tell
Tale for All Summer of the Colt
A Tale from Chikamatsu The Crucified Lovers
A Tale of Africa The Green Horizon
A Tale of Summer A Summer's Tale
Tale of the Mummy Talos the Mummy
Tale of the Pale and Silvery Moon after the Rain Ugetsu Monogatari
Tale of the Tiger Tail of a Tiger
The Tale of Zatoichi Zatoichi
Tales for All (Part 7) Tommy Tricker and the Stamp Traveller
Tales of a Pale and Mysterious Moon after the Rain Ugetsu Monogatari
Tales of Erotica Erotic Tales
Tales of Mystery and Imagination Histoires Extraordinaires
Tales of the Dead Histoires Extraordinaires
Talion An Eye for an Eye
Talking Back Listen to Me
Talking Dirty after Dark Talkin' Dirty after Dark
A Talking Picture Un Filme Falado
Tall Tale: the Incredible Adventure Tall Tale
Tall Tale: the Unbelievable Adventures of Pecos Bill Tall Tale
Tammy Tammy and the Bachelor
Tan de Repente Suddenly
Tangos, the Exile of Gardel Tangos, Exilo de Gardel
Tank Force No Time to Die
Target for Scandal Washington Story
Target in the Sun The Man Who Would Not Die
Tarnished Code of the Yakuza The Yakuza Papers
Tartu The Adventures of Tartu
Tarzan and the Jungle Queen Tarzan and the Slave Girl
Tarzan and the Jungle Queen Tarzan's Peril
Tarzan and the Lost Goddess The New Adventures of Tarzan
Tarzan in Guatemala The New Adventures of Tarzan
Tarzan Meets the Vampire Tarzan and the She-Devil
Tarzan the Invincible Tarzan the Fearless
Tashunga North Star
The Taste of Others Le Goût des Autres
The Taste of Sunshine Sunshine
Tausend Augen Thousand Eyes
Die Tausend Augen des Dr Mabuse The Thousand Eyes of Dr Mabuse
Un Taxi Mauve The Purple Taxi
Taxidi Sta Kithira Voyage to Cythera
Tchin Tchin A Touch of Adultery
Te Doy Mis Ojos Take My Eyes
Tea and Rice The Flavour of Green Tea over Rice
Team Riders Steal
Tears for Simon Lost
Tears of Rapture The Game Is Over
Tears of the Yangtse Spring River Flows East
Ted Bundy Bundy
The Ted Bundy Story Bundy
Teenage Dracula Dracula vs Frankenstein
Teenage Lovers Too Soon to Love
Teenage Psycho Meets Bloody Mary The Incredibly Strange Creatures Who Stopped Living and Became Mixed-up Zombies
Teenage Slumber Party Slumber Party '57
Le Téléphone Rose The Pink Telephone
Tell Me Lies about London Tell Me Lies
Tell Your Children Reefer Madness
La Tempesta Tempest
Temporada de Patos Duck Season
Le Temps Waati
Le Temps des Amants A Place for Lovers
Le Temps des Loups The Last Shot
Le Temps du Loup Time of the Wolf
Le Temps d'un Retour Muriel
Le Temps Retrouvé Time Regained
Temptation Asphalt
Ten Days That Shook the World October
Ten Little Indians And Then There Were None
Ten Little Niggers And Then There Were None
Tender Flesh Welcome to Arrow Beach
The Tenderfoot Bushwhacked
Tenebre Tenebrae
Tentacoli Tentacles
La Tentation de Vénus Meeting Venus
Teorema Theorem
Terminal Station Indiscretion of an American Wife
Terminus des Anges Far Away
Terminus Paradis Last Stop Paradise
Terror at the Opera Opera
Terror en el Espacio Planet of the Vampires
The Terror Factor Scared to Death
Terror from under the House Revenge
Terror House The Night Has Eyes
Terror in Toyland You Better Watch Out
The Terror of Dr Chaney Mansion of the Doomed
The Terror of Dr Hichcock The Horrible Dr Hichcock
Terror of Frankenstein Victor Frankenstein
Terror of Sheba Persecution
The Terror of the Vampires Shiver of the Vampires
Il Terrore dei Barbari Goliath and the Barbarians
Terrore nello Spazio Planet of the Vampires
The Terrorists Ransom
A Test of Love Annie's Coming Out
Das Testament des Dr Mabuse The Testament of Dr Mabuse
Le Testament du Docteur Cordelier The Testament of Dr Cordelier
The Testament of Orpheus Le Testament d'Orphée
Il Testimone dello Sposo The Best Man
La Teta y la Luna The Tit and the Moon
Des Teufels General The Devil's General
Texas Chainsaw Massacre 4 Texas Chainsaw Massacre: the Next Generation
Texas Guns Once upon a Texas Train
Texas Kid, Outlaw The Kid from Texas
Texas Road Agent Road Agent
Thank You All Very Much A Touch of Love
That Forsyte Woman The Forsyte Saga
That Girl from Rio Girl from Rio
That Is the Dawn Celà S'Appelle l'Aurore
That Mad Mr Jones The Fuller Brush Man
That Man Flintstone The Man Called Flintstone
That They May Live J'Accuse
Theatre Royal The Royal Family of Broadway
Their Secret Affair Top Secret Affair
There Goes the Neighborhood Paydirt
Thérèse Thérèse Desqueyroux
These Are the Damned The Damned
Thesis Tesis
They All Died Laughing A Jolly Bad Fellow
They Came From Within Shivers
They Don't Wear Pajamas at Rosie's The First Time
They Loved Life Kanal
They Met at Midnight Piccadilly Incident
They Were Five La Belle Equipe
They're Coming to Get You Dracula vs Frankenstein
They've Taken Our Children: the Chowchilla Kidnapping Story Vanished without a Trace
Thicker than Water: the Larry McLinden Story Thicker than Blood
The Thief of Bagdad An Arabian Fantasy The Thief of Bagdad
Thieves Les Voleurs
The Thing The Thing from Another World
Think Dirty Every Home Should Have One
Thinner Stephen King's Thinner
The Third Circle Cubbyhouse
The Third Key The Long Arm
Thirst Three Strange Loves
The Thirst of Baron Blood Baron Blood
The Thirteen Chairs Twelve plus One
32 Calibre Killer Killer Calibre 32
This Air The Body Stealers
This Is My Affair I Can Get It for You Wholesale
This Is What It Means to Say Phoenix, Arizona Smoke Signals
This Man Must Die Que la Bête Meure

This Man Reuter A Dispatch from Reuters
This Rebel Age The Beat Generation
This Strange Passion El
This Strange Passion Torments El
Thomas Crown and Company The Thomas Crown Affair
Thomas Graals Bästa Film Thomas Graal's Best Film
Thomas l'Imposteur Thomas the Imposter
Thomas the Tank Engine and Friends Thomas and the Magic Railroad
Thomas the Tank Engine: the Movie Thomas and the Magic Railroad
Thoroughbred Run for the Roses
Those Daring Young Men in Their Jaunty Jalopies Monte Carlo or Bust
Those Desperate Men Who Smell of Dirt and Death A Bullet for Sandoval
Those Fantastic Flying Fools Jules Verne's Rocket to the Moon
Those Were the Happy Times Star!
Thou Shalt Honour Thy Wife Master of the House
Though the Sky Falls When the Sky Falls
A Thousand and One Nights Sharaz
A Thousand and One Nights The Arabian Nights
Threat over the City Racket Busters
Three Cockeyed Sailors Sailors Three
Three Dancing Slaves Le Clan
Three Daughters Teen Kanya
The Three Faces of Fear Black Sabbath
The Three Faces of Terror Black Sabbath
Three Ifs and a Maybe The Big Squeeze
Three Immoral Women Heroines of Evil
Three in the Cellar Up in the Cellar
Three Lives and One Death Three Lives and Only One Death
Three Men and a Girl Kentucky Moonshine
Three Men to Kill Three Men to Destroy
The Three Musketeers Meet the Man in the Iron Mask The Man in the Iron Mask
3 Ninja Kids 3 Ninjas
Three on a Weekend Bank Holiday
Three Rooms in Manhattan Trois Chambres à Manhattan
Three Shades of Love This Rebel Breed
Three Stooges Meet the Gunslinger The Outlaws Is Coming
Three Stops to Murder Blood Orange
Three Ways to Love Cherry, Harry & Raquel
The Threepenny Opera Mack the Knife
Through the Looking Glass The Velvet Vampire
Thumbs Up Without Warning: the James Brady Story
Thunder in the Dust The Sundowners
Thunder in the East The Battle
Thunder in the Valley Bob, Son of Battle
Thunder over Mexico Time in the Sun
Thunder over Tangier Man from Tangier
Thunderbolt That Man Bolt
Thundercloud Colt .45
Thursday the 12th Pandemonium
Thy Soul Shall Bear Witness The Phantom Carriage
Ti voglio bene Eugenio Eugenio
Tidal Wave Portrait of Jennie
Tierra Sin Pan Land without Bread
The Tiger Dancer Bagh Bahadur
Tiger in the Sky The McConnell Story
The Tiger Man The Lady and the Monster
Tiger of Bengal The Tiger of Eschnapur
Tiger of Bengal The Indian Tomb
Tiger of Terror Sandokan Fights Back
Tigerman Bagh Bahadur
Tight Little Island Whisky Galore!
Il Tigre The Tiger and the Pussycat
La Tigre dei Sette Mari Tiger of the Seven Seas
Le Tigre des mers Tiger of the Seven Seas
Tikhij Don And Quiet Flows the Don
Til There Was You Till There Was You
Till Death Do Us Part Buried Alive
Till Glädje To Joy
Tillsammans Together
Tim Burton's The Nightmare before Christmas The Nightmare before Christmas
Time Bomb Terror on a Train
Time for Action Tip on a Dead Jockey
A Time for Caring Generation
A Time for Giving Generation
Time for Terror Flesh Feast
Time Is on Our Side Let's Spend the Night Together
Time Lost and Time Remembered I Was Happy Here
The Time of Return Muriel
Time Share Bitter Suite
A Time to Live and a Time to Die Le Feu Follet
A Time to Run The Female Bunch
The Time Travellers The Time Travelers
Time Warp The Day Time Ended
Timecode 2000 Timecode
Tintin et le Lac aux Requins Tintin and the Lake of Sharks
Tintorera... Bloody Waters Tintorera
Tintorera... Tiger Shark Tintorera
Tirez sur le Pianiste Shoot the Pianist
Tito and I Tito and Me
Titus Andronicus Titus
Tmavomodry Svet Dark Blue World
To Be and to Have Etre et Avoir
To Catch a Spy Catch Me a Spy
To Catch a Spy Catch My Soul
To Each His Own We Still Kill the Old Way
To Elvis, With Love Touched by Love
To Kill a Dragon That Man Bolt
To Live Ikiru
To Love a Vampire Lust for a Vampire
To Telefteo Psemma A Matter of Dignity
To The Limit Six Days, Six Nights
To the Victor Owd Bob
The Toda Brothers and Sisters The Brothers and Sisters of the Toda Family
Todo Sobre Mi Madre All about My Mother
Together Together with You
Tom and Jerry Jerry and Tom
Tom & Jerry Jerry and Tom
Tom Waits: Big Time Big Time
The Tomahawk and the Cross Pillars of the Sky
Tomato Pummaro
Tomb of the Cat The Tomb of Ligeia
Tomb Raider Lara Croft: Tomb Raider
The Tongue of the Butterfly Butterfly's Tongue
Tonight at 8:30 Meet Me Tonight
Tonight Let's All Make Love in London Tonite Let's All Make Love in London
Tonight's the Night Happy Ever After
Too Afraid of Life or Splat Plaff!
Too Dangerous to Love Perfect Strangers
Too Many Chefs Who Is Killing the Great Chefs of Europe?
Too Many Women God's Gift to Women
Top Job Grand Slam
Top Secret The Salzburg Connection
Topaz Tokyo Decadence
Topio stin Omichli Landscape in the Mist
Tops Is the Limit Anything Goes
Toronto the Good Palais Royale
Torst Three Strange Loves
The Torture Chamber of Baron Blood Baron Blood
The Torture Chamber of Dr Sadism The Blood Demon
Tosca de Giacomo Puccini Tosca
Total Defense In Her Defense
Toto the Hero Toto Le Héros
A Touch of Hell Serious Charge
Touch White, Touch Black The Violent Ones
Touchez Pas au Grisbi Honour among Thieves
Toujours les Femmes Near Mrs
Tout Sur Ma Mère All about My Mother
Toute une Vie And Now My Love
The Tower The Last Castle
A Town Called Bastard A Town Called Hell
The Town Is Quiet La Ville Est Tranquille
The Town Rat and the Country Rat Town Rat, Country Rat
The Town that Cried Terror Maniac
The Townsend Harris Story The Barbarian and the Geisha
Tracks Voyages
Trading Mom The Mommy Market
Trafic Traffic
La Tragedia di un Uomo Ridicolo The Tragedy of a Ridiculous Man
La Tragédie de la Mine Kameradschaft
Train de Vie Train of Life
Train of Terror Terror Train
Trained to Kill White Dog
Traitement de Choc Shock Treatment
Trance The Eternal
Transatlantic Tunnel The Tunnel
A Transistor Love Story Monrak Transistor
Transit The First Power
The Trap The Baited Trap
Trauma Terminal Choice
Trauma Exposé
The Travelling Birds Winged Migration
A Travesty A Slight Case of Murder
Travolti da un Insolito Destino Nell'Azzurro Mare d'Agosto Swept Away... by an Unusual Destiny in the Blue Sea of August
I Tre Fratelli Three Brothers
I Tre Volti della Paura Black Sabbath
Treason Old Louisiana
The Treasure of San Lucas Down Twisted
Treasure of the Piranha Killer Fish
Tree of Liberty The Howards of Virginia
37'2 le Matin Betty Blue
Tri Three
The Trial of Joan of Arc Le Procès de Jeanne d'Arc
The Trial of Sergeant Rutledge Sergeant Rutledge
Triangle on Safari The Woman and the Hunter
Les Tribulations d'un Chinois en Chine Up to His Ears
La Trilogie 1: Cavale [One] Cavale
La Trilogie 3: Après la Vie [Three] Après la Vie
La Trilogie 2: un Couple Epatant [Two] Un Couple Epatant
Trilogy One [One] Cavale
Trilogy I: The Weeping Meadow Trilogy: the Weeping Meadow
Trilogy Part I: the Weeping Meadow Trilogy: the Weeping Meadow
Trilogy Two [Two] Un Couple Epatant
Trilogy Three [Three] Après la Vie
Trip to the Moon Le Voyage dans la Lune
A Trip with Anita Travels with Anita
Triple Cross Angel of Fury
Triple Deception House of Secrets
The Triplets of Belleville Belleville Rendez-vous
Les Triplettes de Belleville Belleville Rendez-vous
Tristan and Isolde Lovespell
Triumph des Willens Triumph of the Will
Trois Hommes à Abattre Three Men to Destroy
3 Hommes et un Couffin 3 Men and a Cradle
Trois Huit Nightshift
Trois Vies et une Seule Mort Three Lives and Only One Death
The Trojan Horse The Trojan War
A Troll in Central Park Stanley's Magic Garden
Trolösa Faithless
Il Trono di fuoco The Bloody Judge
Tropicana The Heat's On
Trouble at 16 Platinum High School
Trouble at the Royal Rose The Trouble with Spies
Trouble in the Sky Cone of Silence
The Trouble with Stevenson Curtain Call
The Troubleshooter Man with the Gun
The True and the Brave Betrayed
True Colors of Hero A Better Tomorrow
True Detective True Crime
The True Story of My Life in Rouen Ma Vraie Vie à Rouen
Le Truffe Più Belle del Mondo The Beautiful Swindlers
Truman Capote's The Glass House The Glass House
Truman Capote's Trilogy Trilogy
Trumps Enormous Changes at the Last Minute
Trust Nobody Partners
The Truth La Vérité
Truth or Dare In Bed with Madonna
Try and Get Me The Sound of Fury
Tu Ne Tueras Point Thou Shalt Not Kill
Tulipää Flame Top
La Tulipe Noire The Black Tulip
Tune in Tomorrow Aunt Julia and the Scriptwriter
The Turbulent Man The Most Desired Man
The Turkish Bath Hamam: the Turkish Bath
Turks Fruit Turkish Delight
The Turn of the Screw The Haunting of Helen Walker
Turned Out Nice Again It's Turned Out Nice Again
Tutti Pazzi Meno Io King of Hearts
Twelve Miles Out The Second Woman
2084 Lorca and the Outlaws
24/7 TwentyFourSeven
Twenty Four Seven TwentyFourSeven
The 21 Carat Snatch Popsy-Pop
Twenty-One Days Together 21 Days
Twice upon a Yesterday If Only
Twilight in Tokyo Tokyo Twilight
Twilight Women Women of Twilight
Twinkle and Shine It Happened to Jane
Twinkle, Twinkle, "Killer" Kane The Ninth Configuration
Twist of Fate Beautiful Stranger
The Twisted Road They Live by Night
Twitch of the Death Nerve Bay of Blood
Two Acres of Land Do Bigha Zameen
Two Actresses Two Stage Sisters
Two Babies: Switched at Birth Mistaken Identity
Two Cents Worth of Hope Two Pennyworth of Hope
Two Daughters Teen Kanya
Two English Girls Anne and Muriel
Two Guys Talkin' about Girls ...At First Sight
Two If by Sea Stolen Hearts
Two Men in Town Two against the Law
Two Minds for Murder Someone behind the Door

U-Boat 29 The Spy in Black
USS Teakettle You're in the Navy Now
Uccellacci e Uccellini Hawks and Sparrows
L'Uccello dalle piume di cristallo The Bird with the Crystal Plumage
Ugly, Dirty and Bad Down and Dirty
Ugly, Dirty and Mean Down and Dirty
La Ultima Cena The Last Supper
Ultimas Imagenes Del Naufragio Last Images of the Shipwreck
Ultimate Revenge Sioux City
The Ultimate Solution of Grace Quigley Grace Quigley
The Ultimate Versus Versus
Gli Ultimi Giorni di Pompeii The Last Days of Pompeii
L'Ultimo Bacio The Last Kiss
L'Ultimo Uomo della Terra The Last Man on Earth
L'Umanoide The Humanoid
Unbecoming Age The Magic Bubble
Uncle Harry The Strange Affair of Uncle Harry
Under California Skies Under California Stars
Under Pressure Escape under Pressure
Under Satan's Sun Sous le Soleil de Satan
Under Solen Under the Sun
Under the Clock The Clock
Under the Olive Trees Through the Olive Trees
Under the Roofs of Paris Sous les Toits de Paris
Under the Sun of Satan Sous le Soleil de Satan
Undercovers Hero Soft Beds, Hard Battles
Undercurrent Desperate Measures
Underground Guerrillas Undercover
An Undersea Odyssey The Neptune Factor
Underworld The Lower Depths
Underworld Informers The Informers
L'Une Chante l'Autre Pas One Sings, the Other Doesn't
Uneasy Riders Nationale 7
The Unfrocked One Le Défroqué
Unheimliche Geschichten The Living Dead
The Unholy Four The Stranger Came Home
Unholy Love Alraune
Unidentified Flying Oddball The Spaceman and King Arthur
Unknown Deathmask
The Unnamable II The Unnamable Returns
Uno Dopo l'Altro One after the Other
Unpromised Land Land without Bread
Unreconciled Not Reconciled, or Only Violence Helps Where Violence Rules
Unsane Tenebrae
Unseen Heroes The Battle of the V1
The Untamed West The Far Horizons
Der Untergang Downfall
Unto a Good Land The New Land
An Unusual Crime Phantom of Death
Unzere Kinder Our Children
Uomini Duri Three Tough Guys
L'Uomo Che Ride The Man Who Laughs
Un Uomo da Rispettare A Man to Respect
L'Uomo delle Stelle The Starmaker
Up and Under Up 'n' Under
Up in Smoke Cheech & Chong's Up in Smoke
Up Tight! Uptight
The Uprooted Disha
Urs Al-Jalil Wedding in Galilee
Us Begins with You Don't Go Breaking My Heart
Us Two An Adventure for Two
The Usual Unidentified Thieves Big Deal on Madonna Street
Utamaro and His Five Women Five Women around Utamaro

Les Vacances de Monsieur Hulot Monsieur Hulot's Holiday
Vacation from Marriage Perfect Strangers
La Vache et le Président The Cow and the President
La Vagabonde Vagabond
Vaghe Stelle dell'Orsa Of a Thousand Delights
Valdez the Halfbreed The Valdez Horses
Vale Abraao Abraham Valley
La Valise Man in the Trunk
La Vallée The Valley
The Valley Obscured by Clouds The Valley
The Valley of Abraham Abraham Valley
Valley of Fear Sherlock Holmes and the Deadly Necklace
Valley of the Swords The Castilian
The Vampire-Beast Craves Blood The Blood Beast Terror
Vampire Kiss Vampire's Kiss
Vampire of Venice Vampire in Venice
Vampire Thrills Shiver of the Vampires
The Vampire Women Vampyros Lesbos
The Vampires Lust of the Vampire
The Vampire's Thrill Shiver of the Vampires
I Vampiri Lust of the Vampire
El Vampiro The Vampire
Vampiros en La Habana Vampires in Havana

Il Vangelo Secondo Matteo The Gospel According to St Matthew
Vanished Danielle Steel's Vanished
Variété Vaudeville
Variety Lights Lights of Variety
The Velvet House The Corpse
Venere Imperiale Imperial Venus
La Venganza del Saxo Curious Dr Humpp
Vengeance The Brain
Vengeance Is Mine A Bullet for Sandoval
Vengeance the Demon Pumpkinhead
Vénus Beauté (Institut) Venus Beauty Institute
Venus Beauty (Salon) Venus Beauty Institute
Venus Impériale Imperial Venus
The Venusian Stranger from Venus
El Verano del Potro Summer of the Colt
Verbrechen am Seelenleben eines Menschen Kaspar Hauser
Vercingetorix Druids
Verführung: die Grausame Frau Seduction: the Cruel Woman
Vergesst Mozart Forget Mozart
The Verification Trial on the Road
La Verité Si Je Mens! Would I Lie to You?
Der Verlorene The Lost One
Die Verlorene Ehre Der Katharina Blum The Lost Honour of Katharina Blum
Veronica Guerin When the Sky Falls
Versailles Royal Affairs in Versailles
Das Versprechen The Promise
The Vertical Ray of the Sun At the Height of Summer
A Very Big Weekend A Man, a Woman and a Bank
A Very Discreet Hero A Self-Made Hero
A Very Shy Hero A Self-Made Hero
The Very Thought of You Martha – Meet Frank, Daniel and Laurence
The Veteran Dead of Night
La Veuve Couderc The Widow Couderc
Viagem a Lisboa Lisbon Story
Viagem ao principio do mundo Journey to the Beginning of the World
Viaggio con Anita Travels with Anita
Viaggio in Italia Journey to Italy
La Victoire en Chantant Black and White in Color
Victory Escape to Victory
La Vida Criminal de Archibaldo de la Cruz The Criminal Life of Archibaldo de la Cruz
La Vie à L'Envers Life Upside Down
La Vie devant Soi Madame Rosa
La Vie Est un Long Fleuve Tranquille Life Is a Long Quiet River
La Vie Est un Roman Life Is a Bed of Roses
La Vie Privée A Very Private Affair
La Vie Rêvée des Anges The Dream Life of Angels
La Vie Sexuelle des Belges 1950-1978 The Sexual Life of the Belgians 1950-1978
Le Vieil Homme et l'Enfant The Two of Us
La Vieille Qui Marchait dans la Mer The Old Lady Who Walked in the Sea
El Viento se Llevó lo Qué Wind with the Gone
Vier von der Infanterie Westfront 1918
De Vierde Man The Fourth Man
Vigo Vigo: Passion for Life
Vigo: Histoire d'une Passion Vigo: Passion for Life
The Villain Cactus Jack
The Vilna Town Cantor Overture to Glory
Der Vilner Shtot Khazn Overture to Glory
Vincent Vincent: the Life and Death of Vincent Van Gogh
Vincent, François, Paul ... et les autres Vincent, François, Paul and the Others
La Vingt-Cinquième Heure The 25th Hour
I Vinti The Vanquished
The Violator Act of Vengeance
The Violent Breed Keoma
Violent Journey The Fool Killer
Violent Midnight Psychomania
Violent Stranger Wetherby
Violent Streets Thief
Violet Perfume: No One Hears You Perfume de Violetas
Violette Violette Nozière
Violin and Roller Katok i Skrypka
Il Violino Rosso The Red Violin
Le Violon de Rothschild Rothschild's Violin
La Virgen de los Sicarios Our Lady of the Assassins
Virgin Nights Wildflower
The Virtuous Tramps Bogus Bandits
Virus Formula for Death
Visages d'Enfants Faces of Children
The Visitors Les Visiteurs
The Visitors 2: the Corridors of Time Les Visiteurs 2: Les Couloirs du Temps
La Vita E Bella Life Is Beautiful
Vital Contact Orbit
Viva la Vie! Long Live Life
Vivement Dimanche! Confidentially Yours
Vladimir and Rosa Vladimir et Rosa
Voice from the Grave The Sin of Nora Moran
A Voice in the Night Freedom Radio
A Voice in the Night Wanted for Murder
Voices from Within Silhouette
Void Votes Secret Ballot
La Voie Lactée The Milky Way
The Volcano Monster Godzilla Raids Again
Le Voleur The Thief of Paris
Vol 2 Kill Bill Vol 2
Voodoo Girl Sugar Hill
Vortex The Day Time Ended
Voyage au Début du Monde Journey to the Beginning of the World
The Voyage Home – Star Trek IV Star Trek IV: the Voyage Home
Voyage to a Prehistoric Planet Voyage to the Prehistoric Planet
Voyage to Italy Journey to Italy
Voyage to the Beginning of the World Journey to the Beginning of the World
Vulcano Volcano

W

Das Wachsfigurenkabinett Waxworks
Wages and Profit Tarang
Wages of Fear Sorcerer
The Waking Hour The Velvet Vampire
Waking Ned Devine Waking Ned
Walk in the Shadow Life for Ruth
Walking Down Broadway Hello Sister!
Walking Tall, Part II Part 2 Walking Tall
Wall of Death There Is Another Sun
Waller's Last Trip Waller's Last Walk
Wallers Letzter Gang Waller's Last Walk
Walter Wanger's Vogues of 1938 Vogues of 1938
Want a Ride, Little Girl? Impulse
Wanted Crime Spree
Wanted High Voltage
The Wanton Contessa Senso
War Bride The War Bride
War Correspondent The Story of GI Joe
War Games Suppose They Gave a War and Nobody Came?
War-Gods of the Deep City under the Sea
War Head On the Fiddle
War of the Monsters Godzilla vs Gigan
War Shock Battle Shock
Warlock II Warlock: the Armageddon
Warlords of the 21st Century Battletruck
Warnung vor einer Heiligen Nutte Beware of a Holy Whore
The Warriors The Dark Avenger
Warum Läuft Herr R Amok? Why Does Herr R Run Amok?
Wat Zien Ik? Business Is Business
Watch the Shadows Dance Nightmaster
The Water Boy The Waterboy
The Water Cure The Cure
Water Drops on Raining Rocks Water Drops on Burning Rocks
The Water Melon Woman The Watermelon Woman
Water Works Eaux d'Artifice
Waterfront Women Waterfront
The Wave Tarang
The Way I Killed My Father Comment J'ai Tué Mon Père
Ways of Love L'Amore
Ways of Love: A Day in the Country Une Partie de Campagne
Ways of Love: Jofroi Jofroi
We Are All Murderers Nous Sommes Tous des Assassins
We Are in the Navy Now We Joined the Navy
We Know the Song On Connaît la Chanson
The Weary Death Destiny
Weather Girl Weather Woman
A Weatherwoman Weather Woman
Web of Evidence Beyond This Place
Wedding Bells Royal Wedding
Wedding Breakfast The Catered Affair
Wedding in Blood Les Noces Rouges
Wednesday's Child Family Life
Wee Geordie Geordie
The Weeping Meadow Trilogy: the Weeping Meadow
Welcome Mr Marshall Bienvenido Mr Marshall
The Well-Made Marriage Le Beau Mariage
Wendy Cracked a Walnut Almost
We're in the Army Now Pack Up Your Troubles
Werewolf Woman Naked Werewolf Woman
Wernher von Braun I Aim at the Stars
Wes Craven Presents: Dracula 2000 Dracula 2001
Wes Craven Presents Mind Ripper Wes Craven's Mind Ripper
Wes Craven's Chiller Chiller
Wes Craven's Dracula Dracula 2001
Wes Craven's Wishmaster Wishmaster
West Beyrouth West Beirut
West of Montana Mail Order Bride
West of the Great Divide North of the Great Divide
Western Front 1918 Westfront 1918
What a Man Never Give a Sucker an Even Break
What about Me? Pourquoi Pas Moi?
What Ever Happened to Aunt Alice? Whatever Happened to Aunt Alice?
What Lola Wants Damn Yankees
What the Birds Knew I Live in Fear
What the Bleep Do We Know!? What the #$*! We Know!?
What the F* Do We Know!?** What the #$*! Do We Know!?
What Waits Below Secrets of the Phantom Caverns
What We Did That Night Murder at Devil's Glen
Whatever Extension du Domaine de la Lutte
What's Good for the Gander What's Good for the Goose
What's Love Got to Do with It Tina: What's Love Got to Do with It
Wheel of Fortune A Man Betrayed
When Andrew Came Home Taming Andrew
When Boys Leave Home Downhill
When Harry Met Lloyd: Dumb and Dumberer Dumb and Dumberer: When Harry Met Lloyd
When I Fall in Love Everybody's All-American
When Knighthood Was in Flower The Sword and the Rose
When Love Comes Along When Love Comes
When Lovers Meet Lover Come Back
When Strangers Marry Betrayed
When the Door Opened Escape
When the Heavens Fall When the Sky Falls
When Thief Meets Thief Jump for Glory
When Wolves Cry The Christmas Tree
Where the Hart Is Home Is Where the Hart Is
Where the River Bends Bend of the River
Where There's a Will Good Morning, Boys
Where's Mommy Now? Perfect Alibi
Which Witch Is Which? Witches' Brew
The Whipped The Underworld Story
Whiskey Down Just Your Luck
Whispering Death Death in the Sun
Whispers Dead of Night
White Three Colours White
White Captive White Savage
The White Man The Squaw Man
The White People's Fountain The Autobiography of Miss Jane Pittman
A White, White Boy... Mirror
A White, White Day... Mirror
Whiteboyz Whiteboys
Whiz Kid Zapped!
Who Am I? Jackie Chan's Who Am I?
Who Do I Gotta Kill? Me and the Mob
Who Is Killing the Stuntmen? Stunts
Who Knows Va Savoir
Who Shot Pat? Who Shot Patakango?
Whoever Slew Auntie Roo? Who Slew Auntie Roo?
Who's Got the Black Box? The Road to Corinth
Whose Little Girl Are You? Better Late Than Never
Why Bother to Knock Don't Bother to Knock
Why Did Bodhi-Dharma Leave for the East? Why Has Bhodi-Dharma Left for the East?
Why Not! Pourquoi Pas!
Why We Fight, 1 Prelude to War
Wicked Wife Grand National Night
The Widow of Saint-Pierre La Veuve de Saint-Pierre
The Widower Love and Pain and the Whole Damn Thing
The Widower An Autumn Afternoon
Wild Beasts with Machine Guns Mad Dog Murderer
Wild Beds Tigers in Lipstick
The Wild Child L'Enfant Sauvage
Wild Flower Wildflower
Wild for Kicks Beat Girl
The Wild Game Jail Bait
The Wild Heart Gone to Earth
Wild in the Sky Black Jack
Wild Orchid 2: Blue Movie Blue Wild Orchid 2: Two Shades of Blue
The Wild Pack The Defiant
The Wild Reeds Les Roseaux Sauvages
Wild Stallion White Mane
Wildcat The Great Scout & Cathouse Thursday
Wildstyle Wild Style
Wildwechsel Jail Bait
The Will of Doctor Cordelier The Testament of Dr Cordelier
Will Tomorrow Ever Come? That's My Man
William Comes to Town William at the Circus
William Faulkner's Old Man Old Man
William Peter Blatty's The Exorcist The Exorcist III
William Shakespeare's A Midsummer Night's Dream A Midsummer Night's Dream
The Wind Bloweth Where It Listeth A Man Escaped
Wind from the East Vent d'Est
The Windfall Mr Billion
The Window in Front Facing Window
Window Shopping Golden Eighties
A Window to the Sky The Other Side of the Mountain
The Winged Serpent Q – the Winged Serpent
Wings and the Woman They Flew Alone
Wings over the World Rockshow
Winning Streak Stacy's Knights
The Winning Way The All American
The Winston Affair The Man in the Middle
Winter Hawk Winterhawk
Winter Rates Out of Season
Winter Sleepers Wintersleepers
Winterschläfer Wintersleepers
Wise Girls Wisegirls
Witch Doctor Men of Two Worlds
Witchcraft Curse III: Blood Sacrifice
Witchcraft through the Ages Häxan
Witchery Witchcraft
With a Friend like Harry... Harry, He's Here to Help
With All My Heart The Intimate Stranger
Within a Cloister Behind Convent Walls
Without Witnesses A Private Conversation
Wo die Grünen Ameisen Traümen Where the Green Ants Dream
Woman L'Amore
A Woman Alone Sabotage
Woman-Bait Maigret Sets a Trap
A Woman Destroyed Smash Up – the Story of a Woman
Woman from Deep River Cannibal Ferox
The Woman Between The Woman I Love
Woman in Hiding Mantrap
The Woman in His House The Animal Kingdom
Woman in the Dunes Woman of the Dunes
Woman of Summer The Stripper
The Woman on the Moon The Woman in the Moon
The Woman One Longs for Three Loves
The Woman That Men Long for Three Loves
The Woman That Men Yearn for Three Loves
Woman with a Whip Forty Guns
The Woman with Red Boots The Lady with Red Boots
Woman without a Face Mister Buddwing
A Woman's Devotion Battle Shock
The Women Two Women
Women in Chains Black Mama, White Mama
Women in Limbo Limbo
Women of Nazi Germany Hitler
Women on Wheels Easy Wheels
Women's Penitentiary 1 The Big Doll House
Women's Penitentiary III Women in Cages
Women's Victory The Victory of Women
Wonderful Day I've Gotta Horse
Wonderful Days Sky Blue
Wonderful to be Young! The Young Ones
The Wonderful Years The Restless Years
Wooden Crosses The Road to Glory
The Word Ordet
The World and His Wife State of the Union
The World of Silence Le Monde du Silence
The World of Yor Yor, the Hunter from the Future
Worlds Apart The Seventh Coin
World's Greatest Swindles The Beautiful Swindlers
The World's Most Beautiful Woman Beautiful but Dangerous
The Worlds of Gulliver The Three Worlds of Gulliver
Wrecking Crew illtown
Written on the Sand Play Dirty
Wrong Bet AWOL
The Wrong Blonde The Escort
Wrong Is Right The Man with the Deadly Lens
The Wrong Kind of Girl Bus Stop
The Wrong Side of Bed The Other Side of the Bed
Das Wunder von Bern The Miracle of Bern
Die Wunderbare Lüge der Nina Petrowna The Wonderful Lie of Nina Petrovna

X The Man with the X-Ray Eyes
X Change XChange
The X Files Movie The X-Files
X Men 2 X2
X-Rated Rated X

X: the Man with the X-Ray Eyes The Man with the X-Ray Eyes
xXx: State of the Union xXx: the Next Level
X, Y and Zee Zee and Co
Xochimilco Portrait of Maria

Y Aura-t-il de la Neige à Noël? Will It Snow for Christmas?
Ya-Cuba I Am Cuba
Yacula The Female Vampire
Yang Kwei The Princess Yang Kwei Fei
A Yank in London I Live in Grosvenor Square
A Yankee in King Arthur's Court A Connecticut Yankee in King Arthur's Court
Yash Chopra's Veer-Zaara Veer-Zaara
Year Punk Broke 1991: The Year Punk Broke
Years without Days Castle on the Hudson
The Yellow Winton Flyer The Reivers
Les Yeux sans Visage Eyes without a Face
Yo, la Peor de Todas I, the Worst of All
Yo Yo Yoyo
The Yokel The Captain
Yolande and the Thief Yolanda and the Thief
The Yotsuya Ghost Story Illusion of Blood
You and I The Outlaw and His Wife
You Belong to My Heart Mr Imperium
You Can't Sleep Here I Was a Male War Bride
You Can't Steal Love Live a Little, Steal a Lot
You Can't Take Money Internes Can't Take Money
You Don't Know What Love Is Heaven's Burning
You Don't Need Pajamas at Rosie's The First Time
Young and Eager Claudelle Inglish
The Young and the Damned Los Olvidados
The Young and the Immoral Hellborn
The Young and the Passionate I Vitelloni
The Young and the Willing The Wild and the Willing
The Young Flynn Flynn
The Young Girls of Wilko The Young Ladies of Wilko
Young Hearts Promised Land
The Young Hellions High School Confidential
The Young Invaders Darby's Rangers
Young Man of Music Young Man with a Horn
The Young Rebel Cervantes
Young Scarface Brighton Rock
Young Sherlock Holmes and the Pyramid of Fear Young Sherlock Holmes
Young, Willing and Eager Rag Doll
The Youngest Spy Ivan's Childhood
Your Past Is Showing The Naked Truth
Your Red Wagon They Live by Night
Your Witness Eye Witness
Youth and Perversion The Vanquished
Youthful Sinners Les Tricheurs
Yukinojo's Revenge An Actor's Revenge

Z

Zamani Barayé Masti Asbha A Time for Drunken Horses
Zap – Invocation of My Demon Brother Invocation of My Demon Brother
Zatoichi 1 Zatoichi
Der Zauber der Venus Meeting Venus
Zazie in the Metro Zazie dans le Métro
Zendegi Va Digar Hich And Life Goes On…
Zentropa Europa
Zero Degrees Kelvin Zero Kelvin
Zero Hour The Road to Glory
Zero Population ZPG: Zero Population Growth
Zimiya Earth
Zombie Zombie Flesh Eaters
Zombie 2 Zombie Flesh Eaters
Zombies Dawn of the Dead
The Zombies of Sugar Hill Sugar Hill
Zoo A Zed & Two Noughts
The Zoo The Bubble
Un Zoo la Nuit Night Zoo
Zora Silent Night, Bloody Night
Zormba Zorba the Greek
Zu Time Warrior Zu Warriors
Zuckerbaby Sugarbaby
Zwei gegen Tod und Teufel Montana Trap
Die Zweite Heimat Heimat 2
Zwischengleis Yesterday's Tomorrow

Awards

1927/28

Academy Awards

OUTSTANDING PICTURE: ***Wings*** • *The Last Command* • *The Racket* • *7th Heaven* • *The Way of All Flesh*
UNIQUE AND ARTISTIC PICTURE: ***Sunrise*** • *Chang* • *The Crowd*
DIRECTING (DRAMATIC PICTURE): **Frank Borzage** *7th Heaven* • Herbert Brenon *Sorrell and Son* • King Vidor *The Crowd*
DIRECTING (COMEDY PICTURE): **Lewis Milestone** *Two Arabian Knights* • Charles Chaplin *The Circus* • Ted Wilde *Speedy*
ACTOR: **Emil Jannings** *The Last Command* • **Emil Jannings** *The Way of All Flesh* • Richard Barthelmess *The Noose* • Richard Barthelmess *The Patent Leather Kid* • Charles Chaplin *The Circus*
ACTRESS: **Janet Gaynor** *7th Heaven* • **Janet Gaynor** *Street Angel* • **Janet Gaynor** *Sunrise* • Louise Dresser *A Ship Comes In* • Gloria Swanson *Sadie Thompson*
WRITING (ORIGINAL STORY): **Ben Hecht** *Underworld* • Lajos Biró *The Last Command* • Rupert Hughes *The Patent Leather Kid*
WRITING (ADAPTATION): **Benjamin Glazer** *7th Heaven* • Anthony Coldeway *Glorious Betsy* • Al Cohn *The Jazz Singer*
WRITING (TITLE WRITING): **Joseph Farnham** *Telling the World* • Joseph Farnham *The Fair Co-Ed* • Joseph Farnham *Laugh, Clown, Laugh* • George Marion Jr *Oh Kay!* • Gerald Duffy *The Private Life of Helen of Troy*

1928/29

Academy Awards

OUTSTANDING PICTURE: ***The Broadway Melody*** • *Alibi* • *Hollywood Revue* • *In Old Arizona* • *The Patriot*
DIRECTING: **Frank Lloyd** *The Divine Lady* • Lionel Barrymore *Madame X* • Harry Beaumont *The Broadway Melody* • Irving Cummings *In Old Arizona* • Frank Lloyd *Drag* • Frank Lloyd *Weary River* • Ernst Lubitsch *The Patriot*
ACTOR: **Warner Baxter** *In Old Arizona* • George Bancroft *Thunderbolt* • Chester Morris *Alibi* • Paul Muni *The Valiant* • Lewis Stone *The Patriot*
ACTRESS: **Mary Pickford** *Coquette* • Ruth Chatterton *Madame X* • Betty Compson *The Barker* • Jeanne Eagels *The Letter* • Corinne Griffith *The Divine Lady* • Bessie Love *The Broadway Melody*
WRITING: **Hans Kräly** *The Patriot* • Elliott Clawson *The Cop* • Tom Barry *In Old Arizona* • Hans Kräly *The Last of Mrs Cheyney* • Elliott Clawson *The Leatherneck* • Josephine Lovett *Our Dancing Daughters* • Elliott Clawson *Sal of Singapore* • Elliott Clawson *Skyscraper* • Bess Meredyth *A Woman of Affairs* • Bess Meredyth *Wonder of Women*

1929/30

Academy Awards

OUTSTANDING PRODUCTION: ***All Quiet on the Western Front*** • *The Big House* • *Disraeli* • *The Divorcee* • *The Love Parade*
DIRECTING: **Lewis Milestone** *All Quiet on the Western Front* • Clarence Brown *Anna Christie* • Clarence Brown *Romance* • Ernst Lubitsch *The Love Parade* • King Vidor *Hallelujah*
ACTOR: **George Arliss** *Disraeli* • George Arliss *The Green Goddess* • Wallace Beery *The Big House* • Maurice Chevalier *The Big Pond* • Maurice Chevalier *The Love Parade* • Ronald Colman *Bulldog Drummond* • Ronald Colman *Condemned* • Lawrence Tibbett *The Rogue Song*
ACTRESS: **Norma Shearer** *The Divorcee* • Nancy Carroll *The Devil's Holiday* • Ruth Chatterton *Sarah and Son* • Greta Garbo *Anna Christie* • Greta Garbo *Romance* • Norma Shearer *Their Own Desire* • Gloria Swanson *The Trespasser*
WRITING: **Frances Marion** *The Big House* • Maxwell Anderson, George Abbott, Del Andrews *All Quiet on the Western Front* • Julien Josephson *Disraeli*
DIRECTING: Robert Z Leonard *The Divorcee*
WRITING: John Meehan *The Divorcee* • Howard Estabrook *Street of Chance*

1930/31

Academy Awards

OUTSTANDING PRODUCTION: ***Cimarron*** • *East Lynne* • *The Front Page* • *Skippy* • *Trader Horn*
DIRECTING: **Norman Taurog** *Skippy* • Clarence Brown *A Free Soul* • Lewis Milestone *The Front Page* • Wesley Ruggles *Cimarron* • Josef von Sternberg *Morocco*
ACTOR: **Lionel Barrymore** *A Free Soul* • Jackie Cooper *Skippy* • Richard Dix *Cimarron* • Fredric March *The Royal Family of Broadway* • Adolphe Menjou *The Front Page*
ACTRESS: **Marie Dressler** *Min and Bill* • Marlene Dietrich *Morocco* • Irene Dunne *Cimarron* • Ann Harding *Holiday* • Norma Shearer *A Free Soul*
WRITING (ORIGINAL STORY): **John Monk Saunders** *The Dawn Patrol* • Rowland Brown *Doorway to Hell* • Harry d'Abbadie D'Arrast, Douglas Doty, Donald Ogden Stewart *Laughter* • Kubec Glasmon, John Bright *The Public Enemy* • Lucien Hubbard, Joseph Jackson *Smart Money*
WRITING (ADAPTATION): **Howard Estabrook** *Cimarron* • Fred Niblo Jr, Seton I Miller *The Criminal Code* • Horace Jackson *Holiday* • Robert N Lee, Francis Edward Faragoh *Little Caesar* • Joseph L Mankiewicz, Sam Mintz *Skippy*

1931/32

Academy Awards

OUTSTANDING PRODUCTION: ***Grand Hotel*** • *Arrowsmith* • *Bad Girl* • *The Champ* • *Five Star Final* • *One Hour with You* • *Shanghai Express* • *The Smiling Lieutenant*
DIRECTING: **Frank Borzage** *Bad Girl* • King Vidor *The Champ* • Josef von Sternberg *Shanghai Express*
ACTOR: **Wallace Beery** *The Champ* • **Fredric March** *Dr Jekyll and Mr Hyde* • Alfred Lunt *The Guardsman*
ACTRESS: **Helen Hayes** *The Sin of Madelon Claudet* • Marie Dressler *Emma* • Lynn Fontanne *The Guardsman*
WRITING (ORIGINAL STORY): **Frances Marion** *The Champ* • Grover Jones, William Slavens McNutt *Lady and Gent* • Lucien Hubbard *The Star Witness* • Jane Murfin, Adela Rogers St John *What Price Hollywood?*
WRITING (ADAPTATION): **Edwin Burke** *Bad Girl* • Sidney Howard *Arrowsmith* • Percy Heath, Samuel Hoffenstein *Dr Jekyll and Mr Hyde*

1932/33

Academy Awards

OUTSTANDING PRODUCTION: ***Cavalcade*** • *A Farewell to Arms* • *42nd Street* • *I Am a Fugitive from a Chain Gang* • *Lady for a Day* • *Little Women* • *The Private Life of Henry VIII* • *She Done Him Wrong* • *Smilin' Through* • *State Fair*
DIRECTING: **Frank Lloyd** *Cavalcade* • Frank Capra *Lady for a Day* • George Cukor *Little Women*
ACTOR: **Charles Laughton** *The Private Life of Henry VIII* • Leslie Howard *Berkeley Square* • Paul Muni *I Am a Fugitive from a Chain Gang*
ACTRESS: **Katharine Hepburn** *Morning Glory* • May Robson *Lady for a Day* • Diana Wynyard *Cavalcade*
WRITING (ORIGINAL STORY): **Robert Lord** *One Way Passage* • Frances Marion *The Prizefighter and the Lady* • Charles MacArthur *Rasputin and the Empress*
WRITING (ADAPTATION): **Sarah Y Mason, Victor Heerman** *Little Women* • Robert Riskin *Lady for a Day* • Paul Green, Sonya Levien *State Fair*

1934

Academy Awards

OUTSTANDING PRODUCTION: ***It Happened One Night*** • *The Barretts of Wimpole Street* • *Cleopatra* • *Flirtation Walk* • *The Gay Divorcee* • *Here Comes the Navy* • *The House of Rothschild* • *Imitation of Life* • *One Night of Love* • *The Thin Man* • *Viva Villa!* • *The White Parade*
DIRECTING: **Frank Capra** *It Happened One Night* • Victor Schertzinger *One Night of Love* • W S Van Dyke *The Thin Man*
ACTOR: **Clark Gable** *It Happened One Night* • Frank Morgan *The Affairs of Cellini* • William Powell *The Thin Man*
ACTRESS: **Claudette Colbert** *It Happened One Night* • Bette Davis *Of Human Bondage* • Grace Moore *One Night of Love* • Norma Shearer *The Barretts of Wimpole Street*
WRITING (ORIGINAL STORY): **Arthur Caesar** *Manhattan Melodrama* • Mauri Grashin *Hide-Out* • Norman Krasna *The Richest Girl in the World*
WRITING (ADAPTATION): **Robert Riskin** *It Happened One Night* • Albert Hackett, Frances Goodrich *The Thin Man* • Ben Hecht *Viva Villa!*

1935

Academy Awards

OUTSTANDING PRODUCTION: ***Mutiny on the Bounty*** • *Alice Adams* • *Broadway Melody of 1936* • *Captain Blood* • *David Copperfield* • *The Informer* • *The Lives of a Bengal Lancer* • *A Midsummer Night's Dream* • *Les Misérables* • *Naughty Marietta* • *Ruggles of Red Gap* • *Top Hat*
DIRECTING: **John Ford** *The Informer* • Michael Curtiz *Captain Blood* • Henry Hathaway *The Lives of a Bengal Lancer* • Frank Lloyd *Mutiny on the Bounty*
ACTOR: **Victor McLaglen** *The Informer* • Clark Gable, Charles Laughton *Mutiny on the Bounty* • Paul Muni *Black Fury* • Franchot Tone *Mutiny on the Bounty*
ACTRESS: **Bette Davis** *Dangerous* • Elisabeth Bergner *Escape Me Never* • Claudette Colbert *Private Worlds* • Katharine Hepburn *Alice Adams* • Miriam Hopkins *Becky Sharp* • Merle Oberon *The Dark Angel*
WRITING (SCREENPLAY): **Dudley Nichols** *The Informer* • Casey Robinson *Captain Blood* • Achmed Abdullah, John L Balderston, Grover Jones, William Slavens McNutt, Waldemar Young *The Lives of a Bengal Lancer* • Jules Furthman, Talbot Jennings, Carey Wilson *Mutiny on the Bounty*
WRITING (ORIGINAL STORY): **Ben Hecht, Charles MacArthur** *The Scoundrel* • Moss Hart *Broadway Melody of 1936* • Gregory Rogers *"G" Men* • Stephen Morehouse Avery, Don Hartman *The Gay Deception*

1936

Academy Awards

OUTSTANDING PRODUCTION: ***The Great Ziegfeld*** • *Anthony Adverse* • *Dodsworth* • *Libeled Lady* • *Mr Deeds Goes to Town* • *Romeo and Juliet* • *San Francisco* • *The Story of Louis Pasteur* • *A Tale of Two Cities* • *Three Smart Girls*
DIRECTING: **Frank Capra** *Mr Deeds Goes to Town* • Gregory La Cava *My Man Godfrey* • Robert Z Leonard *The Great Ziegfeld* • W S Van Dyke *San Francisco* • William Wyler *Dodsworth*
ACTOR: **Paul Muni** *The Story of Louis Pasteur* • Gary Cooper *Mr Deeds Goes to Town* • Walter Huston *Dodsworth* • William Powell *My Man Godfrey* • Spencer Tracy *San Francisco*
ACTRESS: **Luise Rainer** *The Great Ziegfeld* • Irene Dunne *Theodora Goes Wild* • Gladys George *Valiant Is the Word for Carrie* • Carole Lombard *My Man Godfrey* • Norma Shearer *Romeo and Juliet*
ACTOR IN A SUPPORTING ROLE: **Walter Brennan** *Come and Get It* • Mischa Auer *My Man Godfrey* • Stuart Erwin *Pigskin Parade* • Basil Rathbone *Romeo and Juliet* • Akim Tamiroff *The General Died at Dawn*
ACTRESS IN A SUPPORTING ROLE: **Gale Sondergaard** *Anthony Adverse* • Beulah Bondi *The Gorgeous Hussy* • Alice Brady *My Man Godfrey* • Bonita Granville *These Three* • Maria Ouspenskaya *Dodsworth*
WRITING (SCREENPLAY): **Sheridan Gibney, Pierre Collings** *The Story of Louis Pasteur* • Frances Goodrich, Albert Hackett *After the Thin Man* • Sidney Howard *Dodsworth* • Robert Riskin *Mr Deeds Goes to Town* • Morrie Ryskind, Eric Hatch *My Man Godfrey*
WRITING (ORIGINAL STORY): **Sheridan Gibney, Pierre Collings** *The Story of Louis Pasteur* • Norman Krasna *Fury* • William Anthony McGuire *The Great Ziegfeld* • Robert Hopkins *San Francisco* • Adele Comandini *Three Smart Girls*

1937

Academy Awards

OUTSTANDING PRODUCTION: ***The Life of Emile Zola*** • *The Awful Truth* • *Captains Courageous* • *Dead End* • *The Good Earth* • *In Old Chicago* • *Lost Horizon* • *One Hundred Men and a Girl* • *Stage Door* • *A Star Is Born*
DIRECTING: **Leo McCarey** *The Awful Truth* • William Dieterle *The Life of Emile Zola* • Sidney Franklin *The Good Earth* • Gregory La Cava *Stage Door* • William A Wellman *A Star Is Born*
ACTOR: **Spencer Tracy** *Captains Courageous* • Charles Boyer *Conquest* • Fredric March *A Star Is Born* • Robert Montgomery *Night Must Fall* • Paul Muni *The Life of Emile Zola*
ACTRESS: **Luise Rainer** *The Good Earth* • Irene Dunne *The Awful Truth* • Greta Garbo *Camille* • Janet Gaynor *A Star Is Born* • Barbara Stanwyck *Stella Dallas*
ACTOR IN A SUPPORTING ROLE: **Joseph Schildkraut** *The Life of Emile Zola* • Ralph Bellamy *The Awful Truth* • Thomas Mitchell *The Hurricane* • H B Warner *Lost Horizon* • Roland Young *Topper*
ACTRESS IN A SUPPORTING ROLE: **Alice Brady** *In Old Chicago* • Andrea Leeds *Stage Door* • Anne Shirley *Stella Dallas* • Claire Trevor *Dead End* • Dame May Whitty *Night Must Fall*
WRITING (SCREENPLAY): **Norman Reilly Raine, Heinz Herald, Geza Herczeg** *The Life of Emile Zola* • Viña Delmar *The Awful Truth* • Marc Connelly, Dale Van Every, John Lee Mahin *Captains Courageous* • Morrie Ryskind, Anthony Veiller *Stage Door* • Alan Campbell, Robert Carson, Dorothy Parker *A Star Is Born*
WRITING (ORIGINAL STORY): **William A Wellman, Robert Carson** *A Star Is Born* • Robert Lord *The Black Legion* • Niven Busch *In Old Chicago* • Heinz Herald, Geza Herczeg *The Life of Emile Zola* • Hans Kräly *One Hundred Men and a Girl*

1938

Academy Awards

OUTSTANDING PRODUCTION: ***You Can't Take It with You*** • *The Adventures of Robin Hood* • *Alexander's Ragtime Band* • *Boys Town* • *The Citadel* • *Four Daughters* • *La Grande Illusion* • *Jezebel* • *Pygmalion* • *Test Pilot*
DIRECTING: **Frank Capra** *You Can't Take It with You* • Michael Curtiz *Angels with Dirty Faces* • Michael Curtiz *Four Daughters* • Norman Taurog *Boys Town* • King Vidor *The Citadel*
ACTOR: **Spencer Tracy** *Boys Town* • Charles Boyer *Algiers* • James Cagney *Angels with Dirty Faces* • Robert Donat *The Citadel* • Leslie Howard *Pygmalion*
ACTRESS: **Bette Davis** *Jezebel* • Fay Bainter *White Banners* • Wendy Hiller *Pygmalion* • Norma Shearer *Marie Antoinette* • Margaret Sullavan *Three Comrades*

Actor in a Supporting Role: **Walter Brennan** *Kentucky* • John Garfield *Four Daughters* • Gene Lockhart *Algiers* • Robert Morley *Marie Antoinette* • Basil Rathbone *If I Were King*
Actress in a Supporting Role: **Fay Bainter** *Jezebel* • Beulah Bondi *Of Human Hearts* • Billie Burke *Merrily We Live* • Spring Byington *You Can't Take It with You* • Miliza Korjus *The Great Waltz*
Writing (Screenplay): **Ian Dalrymple**, **Cecil Lewis**, **W P Lipscomb**, **George Bernard Shaw** *Pygmalion* • John Meehan, Dore Schary *Boys Town* • Ian Dalrymple, Elizabeth Hill, Frank Wead *The Citadel* • Julius J Epstein, Lenore Coffee *Four Daughters* • Robert Riskin *You Can't Take It with You*
Writing (Original Story): **Dore Schary**, **Eleanore Griffin** *Boys Town* • Irving Berlin *Alexander's Ragtime Band* • Rowland Brown *Angels with Dirty Faces* • John Howard Lawson *Blockade* • Marcella Burke, Frederick Kohner *Mad about Music* • Frank Wead *Test Pilot*

1939

Academy Awards

Outstanding Production: ***Gone with the Wind*** • *Dark Victory* • *Goodbye, Mr Chips* • *Love Affair* • *Mr Smith Goes to Washington* • *Ninotchka* • *Of Mice and Men* • *Stagecoach* • *The Wizard of Oz* • *Wuthering Heights*
Directing: **Victor Fleming** *Gone with the Wind* • Frank Capra *Mr Smith Goes to Washington* • John Ford *Stagecoach* • Sam Wood *Goodbye, Mr Chips* • William Wyler *Wuthering Heights*
Actor: **Robert Donat** *Goodbye, Mr Chips* • Clark Gable *Gone with the Wind* • Laurence Olivier *Wuthering Heights* • Mickey Rooney *Babes in Arms* • James Stewart *Mr Smith Goes to Washington*
Actress: **Vivien Leigh** *Gone with the Wind* • Bette Davis *Dark Victory* • Irene Dunne *Love Affair* • Greta Garbo *Ninotchka* • Greer Garson *Goodbye, Mr Chips*
Actor in a Supporting Role: **Thomas Mitchell** *Stagecoach* • Brian Aherne *Juarez* • Harry Carey *Mr Smith Goes to Washington* • Brian Donlevy *Beau Geste* • Claude Rains *Mr Smith Goes to Washington*
Actress in a Supporting Role: **Hattie McDaniel**, Olivia de Havilland *Gone with the Wind* • Geraldine Fitzgerald *Wuthering Heights* • Edna May Oliver *Drums along the Mohawk* • Maria Ouspenskaya *Love Affair*
Writing (Screenplay): **Sidney Howard** *Gone with the Wind* • R C Sherriff, Claudine West, Eric Maschwitz *Goodbye, Mr Chips* • Sidney Buchman *Mr Smith Goes to Washington* • Charles Brackett, Walter Reisch, Billy Wilder *Ninotchka* • Ben Hecht, Charles MacArthur *Wuthering Heights*
Writing (Original Story): **Sidney Buchman** *Mr Smith Goes to Washington* • Felix Jackson *Bachelor Mother* • Mildred Cram, Leo McCarey *Love Affair* • Melchior Lengyel *Ninotchka* • Lamar Trotti *Young Mr Lincoln*

1940

Academy Awards

Outstanding Production: ***Rebecca*** • *All This, and Heaven Too* • *Foreign Correspondent* • *The Grapes of Wrath* • *The Great Dictator* • *Kitty Foyle* • *The Letter* • *The Long Voyage Home* • *Our Town* • *The Philadelphia Story*
Directing: **John Ford** *The Grapes of Wrath* • George Cukor *The Philadelphia Story* • Alfred Hitchcock *Rebecca* • Sam Wood *Kitty Foyle* • William Wyler *The Letter*
Actor: **James Stewart** *The Philadelphia Story* • Charles Chaplin *The Great Dictator* • Henry Fonda *The Grapes of Wrath* • Raymond Massey *Spirit of the People* • Laurence Olivier *Rebecca*
Actress: **Ginger Rogers** *Kitty Foyle* • Bette Davis *The Letter* • Joan Fontaine *Rebecca* • Katharine Hepburn *The Philadelphia Story* • Martha Scott *Our Town*
Actor in a Supporting Role: **Walter Brennan** *The Westerner* • Albert Basserman *Foreign Correspondent* • William Gargan *They Knew What They Wanted* • Jack Oakie *The Great Dictator* • James Stephenson *The Letter*
Actress in a Supporting Role: **Jane Darwell** *The Grapes of Wrath* • Judith Anderson *Rebecca* • Ruth Hussey *The Philadelphia Story* • Barbara O'Neil *All This, and Heaven Too* • Marjorie Rambeau *Primrose Path*
Writing (Original Screenplay): **Preston Sturges** *The Great McGinty* • Ben Hecht *Angels over Broadway* • Norman Burnside, Heinz Herald, John Huston *Dr Ehrlich's Magic Bullet* • Charles Bennett, Joan Harrison *Foreign Correspondent* • Charles Chaplin *The Great Dictator*
Writing (Original Story): **Benjamin Glazer**, **John S Toldy** *Arise, My Love* • Walter Reisch *Comrade X* • Dore Schary, Hugo Butler *Edison, the Man* • Leo McCarey, Bella Spewack, Sam Spewack *My Favorite Wife* • Stuart N Lake *The Westerner*
Writing (Screenplay): **Donald Ogden Stewart** *The Philadelphia Story* • Nunnally Johnson *The Grapes of Wrath* • Dalton Trumbo *Kitty Foyle* • Dudley Nichols *The Long Voyage Home* • Robert E Sherwood, Joan Harrison *Rebecca*

1941

Academy Awards

Outstanding Motion Picture: ***How Green Was My Valley*** • *Blossoms in the Dust* • *Citizen Kane* • *Here Comes Mr Jordan* • *Hold Back the Dawn* • *The Little Foxes* • *The Maltese Falcon* • *One Foot in Heaven* • *Sergeant York* • *Suspicion*
Directing: **John Ford** *How Green Was My Valley* • Alexander Hall *Here Comes Mr Jordan* • Howard Hawks *Sergeant York* • Orson Welles *Citizen Kane* • William Wyler *The Little Foxes*
Actor: **Gary Cooper** *Sergeant York* • Cary Grant *Penny Serenade* • Walter Huston *Daniel and the Devil* • Robert Montgomery *Here Comes Mr Jordan* • Orson Welles *Citizen Kane*
Actress: **Joan Fontaine** *Suspicion* • Bette Davis *The Little Foxes* • Olivia de Havilland *Hold Back the Dawn* • Greer Garson *Blossoms in the Dust* • Barbara Stanwyck *Ball of Fire*
Actor in a Supporting Role: **Donald Crisp** *How Green Was My Valley* • Walter Brennan *Sergeant York* • Charles Coburn *The Devil and Miss Jones* • James Gleason *Here Comes Mr Jordan* • Sydney Greenstreet *The Maltese Falcon*
Actress in a Supporting Role: **Mary Astor** *The Great Lie* • Sara Allgood *How Green Was My Valley* • Patricia Collinge, Teresa Wright *The Little Foxes* • Margaret Wycherly *Sergeant York*
Writing (Original Screenplay): **Herman J Mankiewicz**, **Orson Welles** *Citizen Kane* • Norman Krasna *The Devil and Miss Jones* • Abem Finkel, Harry Chandlee, Howard Koch, John Huston *Sergeant York* • Karl Tunberg, Darrell Ware *Tall, Dark and Handsome* • Paul Jarrico *Tom, Dick and Harry*
Writing (Original Story): **Harry Segall** *Here Comes Mr Jordan* • Thomas Monroe, Billy Wilder *Ball of Fire* • Monckton Hoffe *The Lady Eve* • Robert Presnell, Richard Connell *Meet John Doe* • Gordon Wellesley *Night Train to Munich*
Writing (Screenplay): **Sidney Buchman**, **Seton I Miller** *Here Comes Mr Jordan* • Charles Brackett, Billy Wilder *Hold Back the Dawn* • Philip Dunne *How Green Was My Valley* • Lillian Hellman *The Little Foxes* • John Huston *The Maltese Falcon*

1942

Academy Awards

Outstanding Motion Picture: ***Mrs Miniver*** • *49th Parallel* • *Kings Row* • *The Magnificent Ambersons* • *The Pied Piper* • *The Pride of the Yankees* • *Random Harvest* • *The Talk of the Town* • *Wake Island* • *Yankee Doodle Dandy*
Directing: **William Wyler** *Mrs Miniver* • Michael Curtiz *Yankee Doodle Dandy* • John Farrow *Wake Island* • Mervyn LeRoy *Random Harvest* • Sam Wood *Kings Row*
Actor: **James Cagney** *Yankee Doodle Dandy* • Ronald Colman *Random Harvest* • Gary Cooper *The Pride of the Yankees* • Walter Pidgeon *Mrs Miniver* • Monty Woolley *The Pied Piper*
Actress: **Greer Garson** *Mrs Miniver* • Bette Davis *Now, Voyager* • Katharine Hepburn *Woman of the Year* • Rosalind Russell *My Sister Eileen* • Teresa Wright *The Pride of the Yankees*
Actor in a Supporting Role: **Van Heflin** *Johnny Eager* • William Bendix *Wake Island* • Walter Huston *Yankee Doodle Dandy* • Frank Morgan *Tortilla Flat* • Henry Travers *Mrs Miniver*
Actress in a Supporting Role: **Teresa Wright** *Mrs Miniver* • Gladys Cooper *Now, Voyager* • Agnes Moorehead *The Magnificent Ambersons* • Susan Peters *Random Harvest* • Dame May Whitty *Mrs Miniver*
Writing (Original Screenplay): **Michael Kanin**, **Ring Lardner Jr** *Woman of the Year* • Michael Powell, Emeric Pressburger *One of Our Aircraft Is Missing* • Don Hartman, Frank Butler *Road to Morocco* • W R Burnett, Frank Butler *Wake Island* • George Oppenheimer *The War against Mrs Hadley*
Writing (Screenplay): **Arthur Wimperis**, **George Froeschel**, **James Hilton**, **Claudine West** *Mrs Miniver* • Emeric Pressburger, Rodney Ackland *49th Parallel* • Herman J Mankiewicz, Jo Swerling *The Pride of the Yankees* • George Froeschel, Claudine West, Arthur Wimperis *Random Harvest* • Irwin Shaw, Sidney Buchman *The Talk of the Town*
Writing (Original Motion Picture Story): **Emeric Pressburger** *49th Parallel* • Irving Berlin *Holiday Inn* • Paul Gallico *The Pride of the Yankees* • Sidney Harmon *The Talk of the Town* • Robert Buckner *Yankee Doodle Dandy*

1943

Academy Awards

Outstanding Motion Picture: ***Casablanca*** • *Disraeli* • *Heaven Can Wait* • *The Human Comedy* • *In Which We Serve* • *Madame Curie* • *The More the Merrier* • *The Ox-Bow Incident* • *The Song of Bernadette* • *Watch on the Rhine*
Directing: **Michael Curtiz** *Casablanca* • Clarence Brown *The Human Comedy* • Henry King *The Song of Bernadette* • Ernst Lubitsch *Heaven Can Wait* • George Stevens *The More the Merrier*
Actor: **Paul Lukas** *Watch on the Rhine* • Humphrey Bogart *Casablanca* • Gary Cooper *For Whom the Bell Tolls* • Walter Pidgeon *Madame Curie* • Mickey Rooney *The Human Comedy*
Actress: **Jennifer Jones** *The Song of Bernadette* • Jean Arthur *The More the Merrier* • Ingrid Bergman *For Whom the Bell Tolls* • Joan Fontaine *The Constant Nymph* • Greer Garson *Madame Curie*
Actor in a Supporting Role: **Charles Coburn** *The More the Merrier* • Charles Bickford *The Song of Bernadette* • J Carrol Naish *Sahara* • Claude Rains *Casablanca* • Akim Tamiroff *For Whom the Bell Tolls*
Actress in a Supporting Role: **Katina Paxinou** *For Whom the Bell Tolls* • Gladys Cooper *The Song of Bernadette* • Paulette Goddard *So Proudly We Hail* • Anne Revere *The Song of Bernadette* • Lucile Watson *Watch on the Rhine*
Writing (Original Screenplay): **Norman Krasna** *Princess O'Rourke* • Dudley Nichols *Air Force* • Noël Coward *In Which We Serve* • Lillian Hellman *The North Star* • Allan Scott *So Proudly We Hail*
Writing (Screenplay): **Philip G Epstein**, **Julius J Epstein**, **Howard Koch** *Casablanca* • Nunnally Johnson *Holy Matrimony* • Robert Russell, Frank Ross, Richard Flournoy, Lewis R Foster *The More the Merrier* • George Seaton *The Song of Bernadette* • Dashiell Hammett *Watch on the Rhine*
Writing (Original Motion Picture Story): **William Saroyan** *The Human Comedy* • Guy Gilpatric *Action in the North Atlantic* • Delmer Daves *Destination Tokyo* • Robert Russell, Frank Ross *The More the Merrier* • Gordon McDonell *Shadow of a Doubt*

Golden Globe Awards

Best Motion Picture – Drama: ***The Song of Bernadette***
Best Performance by an Actor in a Motion Picture – Drama: **Paul Lukas** *Watch on the Rhine*
Best Performance by an Actress in a Motion Picture – Drama: **Jennifer Jones** *The Song of Bernadette*
Best Performance by an Actor in a Supporting Role – Motion Picture: **Akim Tamiroff** *For Whom the Bell Tolls*
Best Performance by an Actress in a Supporting Role – Motion Picture: **Katina Paxinou** *For Whom the Bell Tolls*

1944

Academy Awards

Best Motion Picture: ***Going My Way*** • *Double Indemnity* • *Gaslight* • *Since You Went Away* • *Wilson*
Directing: **Leo McCarey** *Going My Way* • Alfred Hitchcock *Lifeboat* • Henry King *Wilson* • Otto Preminger *Laura* • Billy Wilder *Double Indemnity*
Actor: **Bing Crosby** *Going My Way* • Charles Boyer *Gaslight* • Barry Fitzgerald *Going My Way* • Cary Grant *None but the Lonely Heart* • Alexander Knox *Wilson*
Actress: **Ingrid Bergman** *Gaslight* • Claudette Colbert *Since You Went Away* • Bette Davis *Mr Skeffington* • Greer Garson *Mrs Parkington* • Barbara Stanwyck *Double Indemnity*
Actor in a Supporting Role: **Barry Fitzgerald** *Going My Way* • Hume Cronyn *The Seventh Cross* • Claude Rains *Mr Skeffington* • Clifton Webb *Laura* • Monty Woolley *Since You Went Away*
Actress in a Supporting Role: **Ethel Barrymore** *None but the Lonely Heart* • Jennifer Jones *Since You Went Away* • Angela Lansbury *Gaslight* • Aline MacMahon *Dragon Seed* • Agnes Moorehead *Mrs Parkington*
Writing (Original Screenplay): **Lamar Trotti** *Wilson* • Preston Sturges *Hail the Conquering Hero* • Preston Sturges *The Miracle of Morgan's Creek* • Richard Connell, Gladys Lehman *Two Girls and a Sailor* • Jerome Cady *Wing and a Prayer*
Writing (Screenplay): **Frank Butler**, **Frank Cavett** *Going My Way* • Billy Wilder, Raymond Chandler *Double Indemnity* • Walter Reisch, John L Balderston, John Van Druten *Gaslight* • Jay Dratler, Betty Reinhardt, Samuel Hoffenstein *Laura* • Irving Brecher, Fred F Finklehoffe *Meet Me in St Louis*
Writing (Original Motion Picture Story): **Leo McCarey** *Going My Way* • Chandler Sprague, David Boehm *A Guy Named Joe* • John Steinbeck *Lifeboat* • Alfred Neumann, Joseph Than *None Shall Escape* • Edward Doherty, Jules Schermer *The Fighting Sullivans*

Golden Globe Awards

Best Motion Picture – Drama: ***Going My Way***
Best Director – Motion Picture: **Leo McCarey** *Going My Way*
Best Performance by an Actor in a Motion Picture – Drama: **Alexander Knox** *Wilson*
Best Performance by an Actress in a Motion Picture – Drama: **Ingrid Bergman** *Gaslight*
Best Performance by an Actor in a Supporting Role – Motion Picture: **Barry Fitzgerald** *Going My Way*
Best Performance by an Actress in a Supporting Role – Motion Picture: **Agnes Moorehead** *Mrs Parkington*

1945

Academy Awards

BEST MOTION PICTURE: ***The Lost Weekend*** • *Anchors Aweigh* • *The Bells of St Mary's* • *Mildred Pierce* • *Spellbound*
DIRECTING: **Billy Wilder** *The Lost Weekend* • Clarence Brown *National Velvet* • Alfred Hitchcock *Spellbound* • Leo McCarey *The Bells of St Mary's* • Jean Renoir *The Southerner*
ACTOR: **Ray Milland** *The Lost Weekend* • Bing Crosby *The Bells of St Mary's* • Gene Kelly *Anchors Aweigh* • Gregory Peck *The Keys of the Kingdom* • Cornel Wilde *A Song to Remember*
ACTRESS: **Joan Crawford** *Mildred Pierce* • Ingrid Bergman *The Bells of St Mary's* • Greer Garson *The Valley of Decision* • Jennifer Jones *Love Letters* • Gene Tierney *Leave Her to Heaven*
ACTOR IN A SUPPORTING ROLE: **James Dunn** *A Tree Grows in Brooklyn* • Michael Chekhov *Spellbound* • John Dall *The Corn Is Green* • Robert Mitchum *The Story of GI Joe* • J Carrol Naish *A Medal for Benny*
ACTRESS IN A SUPPORTING ROLE: **Anne Revere** *National Velvet* • Eve Arden, Ann Blyth *Mildred Pierce* • Angela Lansbury *The Picture of Dorian Gray* • Joan Lorring *The Corn Is Green*
WRITING (ORIGINAL SCREENPLAY): **Richard Schweizer** *Marie-Louise* • Phil Yordan *Dillinger* • Myles Connolly *Music for Millions* • Milton Holmes *Salty O'Rourke* • Harry Kurnitz *See Here, Private Hargrove*
WRITING (SCREENPLAY): **Charles Brackett**, **Billy Wilder** *The Lost Weekend* • Leopold Atlas, Guy Endore, Philip Stevenson *The Story of GI Joe* • Ranald MacDougall *Mildred Pierce* • Albert Maltz *Pride of the Marines* • Frank Davis (1), Tess Slesinger *A Tree Grows in Brooklyn*
WRITING (ORIGINAL MOTION PICTURE STORY): **Charles G Booth** *The House on 92nd Street* • Thomas Monroe, Laszlo Gorog *The Affairs of Susan* • John Steinbeck, Jack Wagner *A Medal for Benny* • Alvah Bessie *Objective, Burma!* • Ernst Marischka *A Song to Remember*

Golden Globe Awards

BEST MOTION PICTURE – DRAMA: ***The Lost Weekend***
BEST DIRECTOR – MOTION PICTURE: **Billy Wilder** *The Lost Weekend*
BEST PERFORMANCE BY AN ACTOR IN A MOTION PICTURE – DRAMA: **Ray Milland** *The Lost Weekend*
BEST PERFORMANCE BY AN ACTRESS IN A MOTION PICTURE – DRAMA: **Ingrid Bergman** *The Bells of St Mary's*
BEST PERFORMANCE BY AN ACTOR IN A SUPPORTING ROLE – MOTION PICTURE: **J Carrol Naish** *A Medal for Benny*
BEST PERFORMANCE BY AN ACTRESS IN A SUPPORTING ROLE – MOTION PICTURE: **Angela Lansbury** *The Picture of Dorian Gray*

1946

Academy Awards

BEST MOTION PICTURE: ***The Best Years of Our Lives*** • *Henry V* • *It's a Wonderful Life* • *The Razor's Edge* • *The Yearling*
DIRECTING: **William Wyler** *The Best Years of Our Lives* • Clarence Brown *The Yearling* • Frank Capra *It's a Wonderful Life* • David Lean *Brief Encounter* • Robert Siodmak *The Killers*
ACTOR: **Fredric March** *The Best Years of Our Lives* • Laurence Olivier *Henry V* • Larry Parks *The Jolson Story* • Gregory Peck *The Yearling* • James Stewart *It's a Wonderful Life*
ACTRESS: **Olivia de Havilland** *To Each His Own* • Celia Johnson *Brief Encounter* • Jennifer Jones *Duel in the Sun* • Rosalind Russell *Sister Kenny* • Jane Wyman *The Yearling*
ACTOR IN A SUPPORTING ROLE: **Harold Russell** *The Best Years of Our Lives* • Charles Coburn *The Green Years* • William Demarest *The Jolson Story* • Claude Rains *Notorious* • Clifton Webb *The Razor's Edge*
ACTRESS IN A SUPPORTING ROLE: **Anne Baxter** *The Razor's Edge* • Ethel Barrymore *The Spiral Staircase* • Lillian Gish *Duel in the Sun* • Flora Robson *Saratoga Trunk* • Gale Sondergaard *Anna and the King of Siam*
WRITING (ORIGINAL SCREENPLAY): **Sydney Box**, **Muriel Box** *The Seventh Veil* • Raymond Chandler *The Blue Dahlia* • Jacques Prévert *Les Enfants du Paradis* • Ben Hecht *Notorious* • Melvin Frank, Norman Panama *Road to Utopia*
WRITING (SCREENPLAY): **Robert E Sherwood** *The Best Years of Our Lives* • Talbot Jennings, Sally Benson *Anna and the King of Siam* • David Lean, Anthony Havelock-Allan, Ronald Neame *Brief Encounter* • Anthony Veiller *The Killers* • Sergio Amidei, Federico Fellini *Rome, Open City*
WRITING (ORIGINAL MOTION PICTURE STORY): **Clemence Dane** *Perfect Strangers* • Vladimir Pozner *The Dark Mirror* • Jack Patrick *The Strange Love of Martha Ivers* • Victor Trivas *The Stranger* • Charles Brackett *To Each His Own*

Golden Globe Awards

BEST MOTION PICTURE – DRAMA: ***The Best Years of Our Lives***
BEST DIRECTOR – MOTION PICTURE: **Frank Capra** *It's a Wonderful Life*
BEST PERFORMANCE BY AN ACTOR IN A MOTION PICTURE – DRAMA: **Gregory Peck** *The Yearling*
BEST PERFORMANCE BY AN ACTRESS IN A MOTION PICTURE – DRAMA: **Rosalind Russell** *Sister Kenny*
BEST PERFORMANCE BY AN ACTOR IN A SUPPORTING ROLE – MOTION PICTURE: **Clifton Webb** *The Razor's Edge*
BEST PERFORMANCE BY AN ACTRESS IN A SUPPORTING ROLE – MOTION PICTURE: **Anne Baxter** *The Razor's Edge*

Cannes International Film Festival

INTERNATIONAL JURY PRIZE: ***La Bataille du Rail***
DIRECTOR: **René Clément** *La Bataille du Rail*
ACTOR: **Ray Milland** *The Lost Weekend*
ACTRESS: **Michèle Morgan** *La Symphonie Pastorale*
SCREENPLAY: **Boris Tchirkov** *The Turning Point*

1947

British Film Academy Awards

BEST FILM FROM ANY SOURCE, BRITISH OR FOREIGN: ***The Best Years of Our Lives***
BEST BRITISH FILM: ***Odd Man Out***

Academy Awards

BEST MOTION PICTURE: ***Gentleman's Agreement*** • *The Bishop's Wife* • *Crossfire* • *Great Expectations* • *Miracle on 34th Street*
DIRECTING: **Elia Kazan** *Gentleman's Agreement* • George Cukor *A Double Life* • Edward Dmytryk *Crossfire* • Henry Koster *The Bishop's Wife* • David Lean *Great Expectations*
ACTOR: **Ronald Colman** *A Double Life* • John Garfield *Body and Soul* • Gregory Peck *Gentleman's Agreement* • William Powell *Life with Father* • Michael Redgrave *Mourning Becomes Electra*
ACTRESS: **Loretta Young** *The Farmer's Daughter* • Joan Crawford *Possessed* • Susan Hayward *Smash Up – the Story of a Woman* • Dorothy McGuire *Gentleman's Agreement* • Rosalind Russell *Mourning Becomes Electra*
ACTOR IN A SUPPORTING ROLE: **Edmund Gwenn** *Miracle on 34th Street* • Charles Bickford *The Farmer's Daughter* • Thomas Gomez *Ride the Pink Horse* • Robert Ryan *Crossfire* • Richard Widmark *Kiss of Death*
ACTRESS IN A SUPPORTING ROLE: **Celeste Holm** *Gentleman's Agreement* • Ethel Barrymore *The Paradine Case* • Gloria Grahame *Crossfire* • Marjorie Main *The Egg and I* • Anne Revere *Gentleman's Agreement*
WRITING (ORIGINAL SCREENPLAY): **Sidney Sheldon** *The Bachelor and the Bobby-Soxer* • Abraham Polonsky *Body and Soul* • Ruth Gordon, Garson Kanin *A Double Life* • Charles Chaplin *Monsieur Verdoux* • Cesare Zavattini, Adolfo Franci, Sergio Amidei, Cesare Giulio Viola *Shoeshine*
WRITING (SCREENPLAY): **George Seaton** *Miracle on 34th Street* • Richard Murphy *Boomerang!* • John Paxton *Crossfire* • Moss Hart *Gentleman's Agreement* • Ronald Neame, Anthony Havelock-Allan, David Lean *Great Expectations*
WRITING (MOTION PICTURE STORY): **Valentine Davies** *Miracle on 34th Street* • Georges Chaperot, René Wheeler *A Cage of Nightingales* • Herbert Clyde Lewis, Frederick Stephani *It Happened on Fifth Avenue* • Eleazar Lipsky *Kiss of Death* • Frank Cavett, Dorothy Parker *Smash Up – the Story of a Woman*

Golden Globe Awards

BEST MOTION PICTURE – DRAMA: ***Gentleman's Agreement***
BEST DIRECTOR – MOTION PICTURE: **Elia Kazan** *Gentleman's Agreement*
BEST PERFORMANCE BY AN ACTOR IN A MOTION PICTURE – DRAMA: **Ronald Colman** *A Double Life*
BEST PERFORMANCE BY AN ACTRESS IN A MOTION PICTURE – DRAMA: **Rosalind Russell** *Mourning Becomes Electra*
BEST PERFORMANCE BY AN ACTOR IN A SUPPORTING ROLE – MOTION PICTURE: **Edmund Gwenn** *Miracle on 34th Street*
BEST PERFORMANCE BY AN ACTRESS IN A SUPPORTING ROLE – MOTION PICTURE: **Celeste Holm** *Gentleman's Agreement*
BEST SCREENPLAY – MOTION PICTURE: **George Seaton** *Miracle on 34th Street*

Cannes International Film Festival

GRAND PRIX – PSYCHOLOGICAL AND ROMANTIC FILMS: ***Antoine et Antoinette***
GRAND PRIX – ADVENTURE AND CRIME FILMS: ***Les Maudits***
GRAND PRIX – SOCIAL FILMS: ***Crossfire***
GRAND PRIX – MUSICAL COMEDIES: ***Ziegfeld Follies***
GRAND PRIX – ANIMATED FILMS: ***Dumbo***
GRAND PRIX – DOCUMENTARIES: ***Inondations en Pologne***

1948

British Film Academy Awards

BEST FILM FROM ANY SOURCE, BRITISH OR FOREIGN: ***Hamlet*** • *Crossfire* • *The Fallen Idol* • *Four Steps in the Clouds* • *Monsieur Vincent* • *The Naked City* • *Paisà*
BEST BRITISH FILM: ***The Fallen Idol*** • *Hamlet* • *Oliver Twist* • *Once a Jolly Swagman* • *The Red Shoes* • *Scott of the Antarctic* • *The Small Voice*

Academy Awards

BEST MOTION PICTURE: ***Hamlet*** • *Johnny Belinda* • *The Red Shoes* • *The Snake Pit* • *The Treasure of the Sierra Madre*
SPECIAL FOREIGN LANGUAGE FILM AWARD: ***Monsieur Vincent***
DIRECTING: **John Huston** *The Treasure of the Sierra Madre* • Anatole Litvak *The Snake Pit* • Jean Negulesco *Johnny Belinda* • Laurence Olivier *Hamlet* • Fred Zinnemann *The Search*
ACTOR: **Laurence Olivier** *Hamlet* • Lew Ayres *Johnny Belinda* • Montgomery Clift *The Search* • Dan Dailey *When My Baby Smiles at Me* • Clifton Webb *Sitting Pretty*
ACTRESS: **Jane Wyman** *Johnny Belinda* • Ingrid Bergman *Joan of Arc* • Olivia de Havilland *The Snake Pit* • Irene Dunne *I Remember Mama* • Barbara Stanwyck *Sorry, Wrong Number*
ACTOR IN A SUPPORTING ROLE: **Walter Huston** *The Treasure of the Sierra Madre* • Charles Bickford *Johnny Belinda* • José Ferrer *Joan of Arc* • Oscar Homolka *I Remember Mama* • Cecil Kellaway *The Luck of the Irish*
ACTRESS IN A SUPPORTING ROLE: **Claire Trevor** *Key Largo* • Barbara Bel Geddes, Ellen Corby *I Remember Mama* • Agnes Moorehead *Johnny Belinda* • Jean Simmons *Hamlet*
WRITING (SCREENPLAY): **John Huston** *The Treasure of the Sierra Madre* • Charles Brackett, Billy Wilder, Richard L Breen *A Foreign Affair* • Allen Vincent, Irmgard von Cube *Johnny Belinda* • Richard Schweizer, David Wechsler *The Search* • Frank Partos, Millen Brand *The Snake Pit*
WRITING (MOTION PICTURE STORY): **Richard Schweizer**, **David Wechsler** *The Search* • Robert Flaherty, Frances Flaherty *Louisiana Story* • Malvin Wald *The Naked City* • Borden Chase *Red River* • Emeric Pressburger *The Red Shoes*

Golden Globe Awards

BEST MOTION PICTURE – DRAMA: ***Johnny Belinda*** • ***The Treasure of the Sierra Madre***
BEST DIRECTOR – MOTION PICTURE: **John Huston** *The Treasure of the Sierra Madre*
BEST PERFORMANCE BY AN ACTOR IN A MOTION PICTURE – DRAMA: **Laurence Olivier** *Hamlet*
BEST PERFORMANCE BY AN ACTRESS IN A MOTION PICTURE – DRAMA: **Jane Wyman** *Johnny Belinda*
BEST PERFORMANCE BY AN ACTOR IN A SUPPORTING ROLE – MOTION PICTURE: **Walter Huston** *The Treasure of the Sierra Madre*
BEST PERFORMANCE BY AN ACTRESS IN A SUPPORTING ROLE – MOTION PICTURE: **Ellen Corby** *I Remember Mama*
BEST SCREENPLAY – MOTION PICTURE: **Richard Schweizer** *The Search*

1949

British Film Academy Awards

BEST FILM FROM ANY SOURCE: ***Bicycle Thieves*** • *Berliner Ballade* • *The Last Stage* • *The Set-Up* • *The Third Man* • *The Treasure of the Sierra Madre* • *The Window*
BEST BRITISH FILM: ***The Third Man*** • *Kind Hearts and Coronets* • *Passport to Pimlico* • *The Queen of Spades* • *A Run for Your Money* • *The Small Back Room* • *Whisky Galore!*

Academy Awards

BEST MOTION PICTURE: ***All the King's Men*** • *Battleground* • *The Heiress* • *A Letter to Three Wives* • *Twelve O'Clock High*
SPECIAL FOREIGN LANGUAGE FILM AWARD: ***Bicycle Thieves***
DIRECTING: **Joseph L Mankiewicz** *A Letter to Three Wives* • Carol Reed *The Fallen Idol* • Robert Rossen *All the King's Men* • William A Wellman *Battleground* • William Wyler *The Heiress*
ACTOR: **Broderick Crawford** *All the King's Men* • Kirk Douglas *Champion* • Gregory Peck *Twelve O'Clock High* • Richard Todd *The Hasty Heart* • John Wayne *Sands of Iwo Jima*
ACTRESS: **Olivia de Havilland** *The Heiress* • Jeanne Crain *Pinky* • Susan Hayward *My Foolish Heart* • Deborah Kerr *Edward, My Son* • Loretta Young *Come to the Stable*
ACTOR IN A SUPPORTING ROLE: **Dean Jagger** *Twelve O'Clock High* • John Ireland *All the King's Men* • Arthur Kennedy *Champion* • Ralph Richardson *The Heiress* • James Whitmore *Battleground*
ACTRESS IN A SUPPORTING ROLE: **Mercedes McCambridge** *All the King's Men* • Ethel Barrymore *Pinky* • Celeste Holm, Elsa Lanchester *Come to the Stable* • Ethel Waters *Pinky*
WRITING (STORY AND SCREENPLAY): **Robert Pirosh** *Battleground* • Sidney Buchman *Jolson Sings Again* • Sergio Amidei, Federico Fellini, Roberto Rossellini, Marcello Pagliero, Alfred Hayes *Paisà* • TEB Clarke *Passport to Pimlico* • Helen Levitt, Janice Loeb, Sidney Meyers *The Quiet One*
WRITING (SCREENPLAY): **Joseph L Mankiewicz** *A Letter to Three Wives* • Robert Rossen *All the King's Men* • Cesare Zavattini *Bicycle Thieves* • Carl Foreman *Champion* • Graham Greene *The Fallen Idol*
WRITING (MOTION PICTURE STORY): **Douglas Morrow** *The Stratton Story* • Clare Boothe Luce *Come to the Stable* • Valentine Davies, Shirley W Smith *It Happens Every Spring* • Harry Brown *Sands of Iwo Jima* • Virginia Kellogg *White Heat*

Golden Globe Awards

BEST MOTION PICTURE – DRAMA: ***All the King's Men***
BEST FOREIGN LANGUAGE FILM: ***Bicycle Thieves***
BEST DIRECTOR – MOTION PICTURE: **Robert Rossen** *All the King's Men*
BEST PERFORMANCE BY AN ACTOR IN A MOTION PICTURE – DRAMA: **Broderick Crawford** *All the King's Men*
BEST PERFORMANCE BY AN ACTRESS IN A MOTION PICTURE – DRAMA: **Olivia de Havilland** *The Heiress*
BEST PERFORMANCE BY AN ACTOR IN A SUPPORTING ROLE – MOTION PICTURE: **James Whitmore** *Battleground*

Best Performance by an Actress in a Supporting Role – Motion Picture: **Mercedes McCambridge** *All the King's Men*
Best Screenplay – Motion Picture: **Robert Pirosh** *Battleground*

Cannes International Film Festival

Grand Prix: ***The Third Man***
Director: **René Clément** *The Walls of Malapaga*
Actor: **Edward G Robinson** *House of Strangers*
Actress: **Isa Miranda** *The Walls of Malapaga*
Screenplay: **Alfred Werker** *Lost Boundaries*

1950

British Film Academy Awards

Best Film From any Source: ***All about Eve*** • *The Asphalt Jungle* • *La Beauté du Diable* • *Intruder in the Dust* • *The Men* • *On the Town* • *Orphée*
Best British Film: ***The Blue Lamp*** • *Chance of a Lifetime* • *Morning Departure* • *Seven Days to Noon* • *State Secret* • *The Wooden Horse*

Academy Awards

Best Motion Picture: ***All about Eve*** • *Born Yesterday* • *Father of the Bride* • *King Solomon's Mines* • *Sunset Blvd*
Honorary Foreign Language Film Award: ***The Walls of Malapaga***
Directing: **Joseph L Mankiewicz** *All about Eve* • George Cukor *Born Yesterday* • John Huston *The Asphalt Jungle* • Carol Reed *The Third Man* • Billy Wilder *Sunset Blvd*
Actor: **José Ferrer** *Cyrano de Bergerac* • Louis Calhern *The Magnificent Yankee* • William Holden (2) *Sunset Blvd* • James Stewart *Harvey* • Spencer Tracy *Father of the Bride*
Actress: **Judy Holliday** *Born Yesterday* • Anne Baxter, Bette Davis *All about Eve* • Eleanor Parker *Caged* • Gloria Swanson *Sunset Blvd*
Actor in a Supporting Role: **George Sanders** *All about Eve* • Jeff Chandler *Broken Arrow* • Edmund Gwenn *Mister 880* • Sam Jaffe *The Asphalt Jungle* • Erich von Stroheim *Sunset Blvd*
Actress in a Supporting Role: **Josephine Hull** *Harvey* • Hope Emerson *Caged* • Celeste Holm *All about Eve* • Nancy Olson *Sunset Blvd* • Thelma Ritter *All about Eve*
Writing (Story and Screenplay): **Billy Wilder, Charles Brackett, D M Marshman Jr** *Sunset Blvd* • Ruth Gordon, Garson Kanin *Adam's Rib* • Virginia Kellogg, Bernard C Schoenfeld *Caged* • Carl Foreman *The Men* • Joseph L Mankiewicz, Lesser Samuels *No Way Out*
Writing (Screenplay): **Joseph L Mankiewicz** *All about Eve* • Ben Maddow, John Huston *The Asphalt Jungle* • Albert Mannheimer *Born Yesterday* • Albert Maltz *Broken Arrow* • Albert Hackett, Francis Goodrich *Father of the Bride*
Writing (Motion Picture Story): **Edna Anhalt, Edward Anhalt** *Panic in the Streets* • Carlo Lizzani, Giuseppe De Santis *Bitter Rice* • William Bowers, Andre De Toth *The Gunfighter* • Leonard Spiegelgass *Mystery Street* • Sy Gomberg *When Willie Comes Marching Home*

Golden Globe Awards

Best Motion Picture – Drama: ***Sunset Blvd***
Best Director – Motion Picture: **Billy Wilder** *Sunset Blvd*
Best Performance by an Actor in a Motion Picture – Drama: **José Ferrer** *Cyrano de Bergerac*
Best Performance by an Actress in a Motion Picture – Drama: **Gloria Swanson** *Sunset Blvd*
Best Performance by an Actor in a Motion Picture – Comedy or Musical: **Fred Astaire** *Three Little Words*
Best Performance by an Actress in a Motion Picture – Comedy or Musical: **Judy Holliday** *Born Yesterday*
Best Performance by an Actor in a Supporting Role – Motion Picture: **Edmund Gwenn** *Mister 880*
Best Performance by an Actress in a Supporting Role – Motion Picture: **Josephine Hull** *Harvey*
Best Screenplay – Motion Picture: **Joseph L Mankiewicz** *All about Eve*

1951

British Film Academy Awards

Best Film From any Source: ***La Ronde*** • *An American in Paris* • *The Browning Version* • *Detective Story* • *Edouard et Caroline* • *Fourteen Hours* • *The Lavender Hill Mob* • *The Magic Box* • *The Magic Garden* • *The Man in the White Suit* • *Miss Julie* • *Never Take No for an Answer* • *No Resting Place* • *The Red Badge of Courage* • *The Sound of Fury* • *Sunday in August* • *A Walk in the Sun* • *White Corridors*
Best British Film: ***The Lavender Hill Mob*** • *The Browning Version* • *The Magic Box* • *The Magic Garden* • *The Man in the White Suit* • *Never Take No for an Answer* • *White Corridors*

Academy Awards

Best Motion Picture: ***An American in Paris*** • *Decision before Dawn* • *A Place in the Sun* • *Quo Vadis* • *A Streetcar Named Desire*
Honorary Foreign Language Film Award: ***Rashomon***
Directing: **George Stevens** *A Place in the Sun* • John Huston *The African Queen* • Elia Kazan *A Streetcar Named Desire* • Vincente Minnelli *An American in Paris* • William Wyler *Detective Story*
Actor: **Humphrey Bogart** *The African Queen* • Marlon Brando *A Streetcar Named Desire* • Montgomery Clift *A Place in the Sun* • Arthur Kennedy *Bright Victory* • Fredric March *Death of a Salesman*
Actress: **Vivien Leigh** *A Streetcar Named Desire* • Katharine Hepburn *The African Queen* • Eleanor Parker *Detective Story* • Shelley Winters *A Place in the Sun* • Jane Wyman *The Blue Veil*
Actor in a Supporting Role: **Karl Malden** *A Streetcar Named Desire* • Leo Genn *Quo Vadis* • Kevin McCarthy *Death of a Salesman* • Peter Ustinov *Quo Vadis* • Gig Young *Come Fill the Cup*
Actress in a Supporting Role: **Kim Hunter** *A Streetcar Named Desire* • Joan Blondell *The Blue Veil* • Mildred Dunnock *Death of a Salesman* • Lee Grant *Detective Story* • Thelma Ritter *The Mating Season*
Writing (Story and Screenplay): **Alan Jay Lerner** *An American in Paris* • Billy Wilder, Lesser Samuels, Walter Newman *Ace in the Hole* • Philip Dunne *David and Bathsheba* • Robert Pirosh *Go for Broke!* • Clarence Greene, Russell Rouse *The Well*
Writing (Screenplay): **Michael Wilson, Harry Brown** *A Place in the Sun* • John Huston, James Agee *The African Queen* • Philip Yordan, Robert Wyler *Detective Story* • Max Ophüls, Jacques Natanson *La Ronde* • Tennessee Williams *A Streetcar Named Desire*
Writing (Motion Picture Story): **James Bernard, Paul Dehn** *Seven Days to Noon* • Budd Boetticher, Ray Nazarro *The Bullfighter and the Lady* • Oscar Millard *The Frogmen* • Liam O'Brien, Robert Riskin *Here Comes the Groom* • Alfred Hayes, Stewart Stern *Teresa*

Golden Globe Awards

Best Motion Picture – Drama: ***A Place in the Sun***
Best Motion Picture – Comedy or Musical: ***An American in Paris***
Best Director – Motion Picture: **Laslo Benedek** *Death of a Salesman*
Best Performance by an Actor in a Motion Picture – Drama: **Fredric March** *Death of a Salesman*
Best Performance by an Actress in a Motion Picture – Drama: **Jane Wyman** *The Blue Veil*
Best Performance by an Actor in a Motion Picture – Comedy or Musical: **Danny Kaye** *On the Riviera*
Best Performance by an Actress in a Motion Picture – Comedy or Musical: **June Allyson** *Too Young to Kiss*
Best Performance by an Actor in a Supporting Role – Motion Picture: **Peter Ustinov** *Quo Vadis*
Best Performance by an Actress in a Supporting Role – Motion Picture: **Kim Hunter** *A Streetcar Named Desire*
Best Screenplay – Motion Picture: **Robert Buckner** *Bright Victory*

Cannes International Film Festival

Grand Prix: ***Miracle in Milan* • *Miss Julie***
Director: **Luis Buñuel** *Los Olvidados*
Actor: **Michael Redgrave** *The Browning Version*
Actress: **Bette Davis** *All about Eve*
Screenplay: **Terence Rattigan** *The Browning Version*

Berlin International Film Festival

Golden Berlin Bear (Dramatic Films): ***Four in a Jeep***
Golden Berlin Bear (Crime and Adventure Films): ***Justice Est Faite***
Golden Berlin Bear (Comedies): ***Sans Laisser d'Adresse***
Golden Berlin Bear (Musicals): ***Cinderella***

1952

British Film Academy Awards

Best Film From any Source: ***The Sound Barrier*** • *The African Queen* • *Angels One Five* • *The Boy Kumasenu* • *Carrie* • *Casque d'Or* • *Cry, the Beloved Country* • *Death of a Salesman* • *Limelight* • *Los Olvidados* • *Mandy* • *Miracle in Milan* • *Outcast of the Islands* • *Rashomon* • *The River* • *Singin' in the Rain* • *A Streetcar Named Desire* • *Viva Zapata!*
Best British Film: ***The Sound Barrier*** • *Angels One Five* • *Cry, the Beloved Country* • *Mandy* • *Outcast of the Islands* • *The River*
Best Foreign Actor: **Marlon Brando** *Viva Zapata!* • Jean Aurenche *Dieu A Besoin des Hommes* • Humphrey Bogart *The African Queen* • Francesco Golisano *Miracle in Milan* • Fredric March *Death of a Salesman*
Best Foreign Actress: **Simone Signoret** *Casque d'Or* • Colette Audry *Olivia* • Katharine Hepburn *Pat and Mike* • Judy Holliday *The Marrying Kind* • Nicole Stéphane *Les Enfants Terribles*
Best British Actor: **Ralph Richardson** *The Sound Barrier* • Jack Hawkins *Mandy* • James Hayter *The Pickwick Papers* • Laurence Olivier *Carrie* • Nigel Patrick *The Sound Barrier* • Alastair Sim *Folly to Be Wise*
Best British Actress: **Vivien Leigh** *A Streetcar Named Desire* • Phyllis Calvert *Mandy* • Celia Johnson *I Believe in You* • Ann Todd *The Sound Barrier*

Academy Awards

Best Motion Picture: ***The Greatest Show on Earth*** • *High Noon* • *Ivanhoe* • *Moulin Rouge* • *The Quiet Man*
Honorary Foreign Language Film Award: ***Jeux Interdits***
Directing: **John Ford** *The Quiet Man* • Cecil B DeMille *The Greatest Show on Earth* • John Huston *Moulin Rouge* • Joseph L Mankiewicz *5 Fingers* • Fred Zinnemann *High Noon*
Actor: **Gary Cooper** *High Noon* • Marlon Brando *Viva Zapata!* • Kirk Douglas *The Bad and the Beautiful* • José Ferrer *Moulin Rouge* • Alec Guinness *The Lavender Hill Mob*
Actress: **Shirley Booth** *Come Back, Little Sheba* • Joan Crawford *Sudden Fear* • Bette Davis *The Star* • Julie Harris *The Member of the Wedding* • Susan Hayward *With a Song in My Heart*
Actor in a Supporting Role: **Anthony Quinn** *Viva Zapata!* • Richard Burton *My Cousin Rachel* • Arthur Hunnicutt *The Big Sky* • Victor McLaglen *The Quiet Man* • Jack Palance *Sudden Fear*
Actress in a Supporting Role: **Gloria Grahame** *The Bad and the Beautiful* • Jean Hagen *Singin' in the Rain* • Colette Marchand *Moulin Rouge* • Terry Moore *Come Back, Little Sheba* • Thelma Ritter *With a Song in My Heart*
Writing (Story and Screenplay): **TEB Clarke** *The Lavender Hill Mob* • Sydney Boehm *The Atomic City* • Terence Rattigan *The Sound Barrier* • Ruth Gordon, Garson Kanin *Pat and Mike* • John Steinbeck *Viva Zapata!*
Writing (Screenplay): **Charles Schnee** *The Bad and the Beautiful* • Michael Wilson *5 Fingers* • Carl Foreman *High Noon* • Roger MacDougall, John Dighton, Alexander Mackendrick *The Man in the White Suit* • Frank S Nugent *The Quiet Man*
Writing (Motion Picture Story): **Frank Cavett, Fredric M Frank, Theodore St John** *The Greatest Show on Earth* • Leo McCarey *My Son John* • Martin Goldsmith, Jack Leonard *The Narrow Margin* • Guy Trosper *The Pride of St Louis* • Edward Anhalt, Edna Anhalt *The Sniper*

Golden Globe Awards

Best Motion Picture – Drama: ***The Greatest Show on Earth***
Best Motion Picture – Comedy or Musical: ***With a Song in My Heart***
Best Director – Motion Picture: **Cecil B DeMille** *The Greatest Show on Earth*
Best Performance by an Actor in a Motion Picture – Drama: **Gary Cooper** *High Noon*
Best Performance by an Actress in a Motion Picture – Drama: **Shirley Booth** *Come Back, Little Sheba*
Best Performance by an Actor in a Motion Picture – Comedy or Musical: **Donald O'Connor** *Singin' in the Rain*
Best Performance by an Actress in a Motion Picture – Comedy or Musical: **Susan Hayward** *With a Song in My Heart*
Best Performance by an Actor in a Supporting Role – Motion Picture: **Millard Mitchell** *My Six Convicts*
Best Performance by an Actress in a Supporting Role – Motion Picture: **Katy Jurado** *High Noon*
Best Screenplay – Motion Picture: **Michael Wilson** *5 Fingers*

Cannes International Film Festival

Grand Prix: ***Two Pennyworth of Hope* • *Othello***
Director: **Christian-Jaque** *Fanfan la Tulipe*
Actor: **Marlon Brando** *Viva Zapata!*
Actress: **Lee Grant** *Detective Story*
Screenplay: **Piero Tellini** *Guardie e Ladri*

Berlin International Film Festival

Golden Berlin Bear: ***One Summer of Happiness***

1953

British Film Academy Awards

Best Film From any Source: ***Jeux Interdits*** • *The Bad and the Beautiful* • *Come Back, Little Sheba* • *The Cruel Sea* • *From Here to Eternity* • *Genevieve* • *The Heart of the Matter* • *Julius Caesar* • *The Kidnappers* • *Lili* • *The Little World of Don Camillo* • *The Medium* • *Mogambo* • *Moulin Rouge* • *Nous Sommes Tous des Assassins* • *Roman Holiday* • *Shane* • *The Sun Shines Bright* • *Two Pennyworth of Hope*
Best British Film: ***Genevieve*** • *The Cruel Sea* • *The Heart of the Matter* • *The Kidnappers* • *Moulin Rouge*
Best Foreign Actor: **Marlon Brando** *Julius Caesar* • Eddie Albert *Roman Holiday* • Van Heflin *Shane* • Claude Laydu *Diary of a Country Priest* • Marcel Mouloudji *Nous Sommes Tous des Assassins* • Gregory Peck *Roman Holiday* • Spencer Tracy *The Actress*
Best Foreign Actress: **Leslie Caron** *Lili* • Shirley Booth *Come Back, Little Sheba* • Marie Powers *The Medium* • Maria Schell *The Heart of the Matter*
Best British Actor: **John Gielgud** *Julius Caesar* • Jack Hawkins *The Cruel Sea* • Trevor Howard *The Heart of the Matter* • Duncan Macrae *The Kidnappers* • Kenneth More *Genevieve*
Best British Actress: **Audrey Hepburn** *Roman Holiday* • Celia Johnson *The Captain's Paradise*

Academy Awards

Best Motion Picture: ***From Here to Eternity*** • *Julius Caesar* • *The Robe* • *Roman Holiday* • *Shane*
Directing: **Fred Zinnemann** *From Here to Eternity* • George Stevens *Shane* • Charles Walters *Lili* • Billy Wilder *Stalag 17* • William Wyler *Roman Holiday*
Actor: **William Holden (2)** *Stalag 17* • Marlon Brando *Julius Caesar* • Richard Burton *The Robe* • Montgomery Clift, Burt Lancaster *From Here to Eternity*
Actress: **Audrey Hepburn** *Roman Holiday* • Leslie Caron *Lili* • Ava Gardner *Mogambo* • Deborah Kerr *From Here to Eternity* • Maggie McNamara *The Moon Is Blue*
Actor in a Supporting Role: **Frank Sinatra** *From Here to Eternity* • Eddie Albert *Roman Holiday* • Brandon de Wilde, Jack Palance *Shane* • Robert Strauss *Stalag 17*

Actress in a Supporting Role: **Donna Reed** *From Here to Eternity* • Grace Kelly *Mogambo* • Geraldine Page *Hondo* • Marjorie Rambeau *Torch Song* • Thelma Ritter *Pickup on South Street*
Writing (Story and Screenplay): **Charles Brackett, Walter Reisch, Richard L Breen** *Titanic* • Betty Comden, Adolph Green *The Band Wagon* • Richard Murphy *The Desert Rats* • Harold Jack Bloom, Sam Rolfe *The Naked Spur* • Millard Kaufman *Take the High Ground*
Writing (Screenplay): **Daniel Taradash** *From Here to Eternity* • Eric Ambler *The Cruel Sea* • Helen Deutsch *Lili* • John Dighton, Ian McLellan Hunter *Roman Holiday* • A B Guthrie Jr *Shane*
Writing (Motion Picture Story): **Ian McLellan Hunter, Dalton Trumbo** *Roman Holiday* • Beirne Lay Jr *Above and Beyond* • Alec Coppel *The Captain's Paradise* • Louis L'Amour *Hondo* • Ray Ashley, Morris Engel, Ruth Orkin *The Little Fugitive*

Golden Globe Awards

Best Motion Picture – Drama: ***The Robe***
Best Director – Motion Picture: **Fred Zinnemann** *From Here to Eternity*
Best Performance by an Actor in a Motion Picture – Drama: **Spencer Tracy** *The Actress*
Best Performance by an Actress in a Motion Picture – Drama: **Audrey Hepburn** *Roman Holiday*
Best Performance by an Actor in a Motion Picture – Comedy or Musical: **David Niven** *The Moon Is Blue*
Best Performance by an Actress in a Motion Picture – Comedy or Musical: **Ethel Merman** *Call Me Madam*
Best Performance by an Actor in a Supporting Role – Motion Picture: **Frank Sinatra** *From Here to Eternity*
Best Performance by an Actress in a Supporting Role – Motion Picture: **Grace Kelly** *Mogambo*
Best Screenplay – Motion Picture: **Helen Deutsch** *Lili*

Cannes International Film Festival

Grand Prix: ***The Wages of Fear***

Berlin International Film Festival

Golden Berlin Bear: ***The Wages of Fear***

1954

British Film Academy Awards

Best Film from any Source: ***The Wages of Fear*** • *The Adventures of Robinson Crusoe* • *Bread, Love and Dreams* • *The Caine Mutiny* • *Carrington VC* • *The Divided Heart* • *Doctor in the House* • *Executive Suite* • *For Better, for Worse* • *Gate of Hell* • *Hobson's Choice* • *How to Marry a Millionaire* • *The Maggie* • *The Moon Is Blue* • *On the Waterfront* • *The Purple Plain* • *Rear Window* • *Riot in Cell Block 11* • *Romeo and Juliet* • *Seven Brides for Seven Brothers*
Best British Film: ***Hobson's Choice*** • *Carrington VC* • *The Divided Heart* • *Doctor in the House* • *For Better, for Worse* • *The Maggie* • *The Purple Plain*
Best Foreign Actor: **Marlon Brando** *On the Waterfront* • Neville Brand *Riot in Cell Block 11* • José Ferrer *The Caine Mutiny* • Fredric March *Executive Suite* • James Stewart *The Glenn Miller Story*
Best Foreign Actress: **Cornell Borchers** *The Divided Heart* • Shirley Booth *About Mrs Leslie* • Judy Holliday *Phffft!* • Grace Kelly *Dial M for Murder* • Gina Lollobrigida *Bread, Love and Dreams*
Best British Actor: **Kenneth More** *Doctor in the House* • Maurice Denham *The Purple Plain* • Robert Donat *Lease of Life* • John Mills *Hobson's Choice* • David Niven *Carrington VC* • Donald Wolfit *Svengali*
Best British Actress: **Yvonne Mitchell** *The Divided Heart* • Brenda de Banzie *Hobson's Choice* • Audrey Hepburn *Sabrina* • Margaret Leighton, Noelle Middleton *Carrington VC*
Best British Screenplay: **Robin Estridge, George Tabori** *The Young Lovers* • Jack Whittingham *The Divided Heart* • Nicholas Phipps *Doctor in the House* • David Lean, Norman Spencer, Wynyard Browne *Hobson's Choice* • Hugh Mills, René Clément *Knave of Hearts* • William Rose *The Maggie* • Eric Ambler *The Purple Plain* • Renato Castellani *Romeo and Juliet*
Best British Film: *Romeo and Juliet*

Academy Awards

Best Motion Picture: ***On the Waterfront*** • *The Caine Mutiny* • *The Country Girl* • *Seven Brides for Seven Brothers* • *Three Coins in the Fountain*
Honorary Foreign Language Film Award: ***Gate of Hell***
Directing: **Elia Kazan** *On the Waterfront* • Alfred Hitchcock *Rear Window* • George Seaton *The Country Girl* • William A Wellman *The High and the Mighty* • Billy Wilder *Sabrina*
Actor: **Marlon Brando** *On the Waterfront* • Humphrey Bogart *The Caine Mutiny* • Bing Crosby *The Country Girl* • James Mason *A Star Is Born* • Dan O'Herlihy *The Adventures of Robinson Crusoe*
Actress: **Grace Kelly** *The Country Girl* • Dorothy Dandridge *Carmen Jones* • Judy Garland *A Star Is Born* • Audrey Hepburn *Sabrina* • Jane Wyman *Magnificent Obsession*
Actor in a Supporting Role: **Edmond O'Brien** *The Barefoot Contessa* • Lee J Cobb, Karl Malden, Rod Steiger *On the Waterfront* • Tom Tully *The Caine Mutiny*
Actress in a Supporting Role: **Eva Marie Saint** *On the Waterfront* • Nina Foch *Executive Suite* • Katy Jurado *Broken Lance* • Jan Sterling, Claire Trevor *The High and the Mighty*
Writing (Story and Screenplay): **Budd Schulberg** *On the Waterfront* • Joseph L Mankiewicz *The Barefoot Contessa* • William Rose *Genevieve* • Oscar Brodney, Valentine Davies *The Glenn Miller Story* • Melvin Frank, Norman Panama *Knock on Wood*
Writing (Screenplay): **George Seaton** *The Country Girl* • Stanley Roberts *The Caine Mutiny* • John Michael Hayes *Rear Window* • Billy Wilder, Ernest Lehman, Samuel Taylor *Sabrina* • Albert Hackett, Frances Goodrich, Dorothy Kingsley *Seven Brides for Seven Brothers*
Writing (Motion Picture Story): **Philip Yordan** *Broken Lance* • Ettore Maria Margadonna *Bread, Love and Dreams* • Francois Boyer *Jeux Interdits* • Jed Harris, Thomas Reed *Night People* • Lamar Trotti *There's No Business like Show Business*

Golden Globe Awards

Best Motion Picture – Drama: ***On the Waterfront***
Best Motion Picture – Comedy or Musical: ***Carmen Jones***
Best Foreign Language Film: ***Genevieve*** • ***La Mujer de las Camelias*** • ***No Way Back*** • ***Twenty-Four Eyes***
Best Director – Motion Picture: **Elia Kazan** *On the Waterfront*
Best Performance by an Actor in a Motion Picture – Drama: **Marlon Brando** *On the Waterfront*
Best Performance by an Actress in a Motion Picture – Drama: **Grace Kelly** *The Country Girl*
Best Performance by an Actor in a Motion Picture – Comedy or Musical: **James Mason** *A Star Is Born*
Best Performance by an Actress in a Motion Picture – Comedy or Musical: **Judy Garland** *A Star Is Born*
Best Performance by an Actor in a Supporting Role – Motion Picture: **Edmond O'Brien** *The Barefoot Contessa*
Best Performance by an Actress in a Supporting Role – Motion Picture: **Jan Sterling** *The High and the Mighty*
Best Screenplay – Motion Picture: **Billy Wilder, Samuel Taylor, Ernest Lehman** *Sabrina*

Cannes International Film Festival

Grand Prix: ***Gate of Hell***

Berlin International Film Festival

Golden Berlin Bear: ***Hobson's Choice***

1955

British Film Academy Awards

Best Film from any Source: ***Richard III*** • *Bad Day at Black Rock* • *Carmen Jones* • *The Colditz Story* • *The Dam Busters* • *East of Eden* • *The Ladykillers* • *Marty* • *The Night My Number Came Up* • *The Prisoner* • *Seven Samurai* • *Simba* • *La Strada* • *Summertime*
Best British Film: ***Richard III*** • *The Colditz Story* • *The Dam Busters* • *The Ladykillers* • *The Night My Number Came Up* • *The Prisoner* • *Simba*
Best Foreign Actor: **Ernest Borgnine** *Marty* • James Dean *East of Eden* • Jack Lemmon *Mister Roberts* • Toshiro Mifune, Takashi Shimura *Seven Samurai* • Frank Sinatra *Not as a Stranger*
Best Foreign Actress: **Betsy Blair** *Marty* • Dorothy Dandridge *Carmen Jones* • Judy Garland *A Star Is Born* • Julie Harris *I Am a Camera* • Katharine Hepburn *Summertime* • Grace Kelly *The Country Girl* • Giulietta Masina *La Strada* • Marilyn Monroe *The Seven Year Itch*
Best British Actor: **Laurence Olivier** *Richard III* • Alfie Bass *The Bespoke Overcoat* • Jack Hawkins, Alec Guinness *The Prisoner* • David Kossoff *A Kid for Two Farthings* • Kenneth More *The Deep Blue Sea* • Michael Redgrave *The Night My Number Came Up*
Best British Actress: **Katie Johnson** *The Ladykillers* • Margaret Johnston *Touch and Go* • Deborah Kerr *The End of the Affair* • Margaret Lockwood *Cast a Dark Shadow*
Best British Screenplay: **William Rose** *The Ladykillers* • Sidney Gilliat, Val Valentine *The Constant Husband* • R C Sherriff *The Dam Busters* • Terence Rattigan *The Deep Blue Sea* • Nicholas Phipps, Jack Davies *Doctor at Sea* • R C Sherriff *The Night My Number Came Up* • Bridget Boland *The Prisoner* • John Baines *Simba* • William Rose *Touch and Go*

Academy Awards

Best Motion Picture: ***Marty*** • *Love Is a Many-Splendored Thing* • *Mister Roberts* • *Picnic* • *The Rose Tattoo*
Honorary Foreign Language Film Award: ***Samurai***
Directing: **Delbert Mann** *Marty* • Elia Kazan *East of Eden* • David Lean *Summertime* • Joshua Logan *Picnic* • John Sturges *Bad Day at Black Rock*
Actor: **Ernest Borgnine** *Marty* • James Cagney *Love Me or Leave Me* • James Dean *East of Eden* • Frank Sinatra *The Man with the Golden Arm* • Spencer Tracy *Bad Day at Black Rock*
Actress: **Anna Magnani** *The Rose Tattoo* • Susan Hayward *I'll Cry Tomorrow* • Katharine Hepburn *Summertime* • Jennifer Jones *Love Is a Many-Splendored Thing* • Eleanor Parker *Interrupted Melody*
Actor in a Supporting Role: **Jack Lemmon** *Mister Roberts* • Arthur Kennedy *Trial* • Joe Mantell *Marty* • Sal Mineo *Rebel without a Cause* • Arthur O'Connell *Picnic*
Actress in a Supporting Role: **Jo Van Fleet** *East of Eden* • Betsy Blair *Marty* • Peggy Lee *Pete Kelly's Blues* • Marisa Pavan *The Rose Tattoo* • Natalie Wood *Rebel without a Cause*
Writing (Story and Screenplay): **William Ludwig, Sonya Levien** *Interrupted Melody* • Milton Sperling, Emmet Lavery *The Court-Martial of Billy Mitchell* • Betty Comden, Adolph Green *It's Always Fair Weather* • Jacques Tati, Henri Marquet *Monsieur Hulot's Holiday* • Jack Rose, Melville Shavelson *Seven Little Foys*
Writing (Screenplay): **Paddy Chayefsky** *Marty* • Millard Kaufman *Bad Day at Black Rock* • Richard Brooks *The Blackboard Jungle* • Paul Osborn *East of Eden* • Daniel Fuchs, Isobel Lennart *Love Me or Leave Me*
Writing (Motion Picture Story): **Daniel Fuchs** *Love Me or Leave Me* • Joe Connelly, Bob Mosher *The Private War of Major Benson* • Nicholas Ray *Rebel without a Cause* • Jean Marsan, Jacques Perret, Raoul Ploquin, Henry Troyat, Henri Verneuil *The Sheep Has Five Legs* • Beirne Lay Jr *Strategic Air Command*

Golden Globe Awards

Best Motion Picture – Drama: ***East of Eden*** • ***Wichita***
Best Motion Picture – Comedy or Musical: ***Guys and Dolls***
Best Foreign Language Film: ***Dangerous Curves*** • ***Eyes of Children*** • ***Ordet*** • ***Sons, Mothers and a General*** • ***Stella***
Best Director – Motion Picture: **Joshua Logan** *Picnic*
Best Performance by an Actor in a Motion Picture – Drama: **Ernest Borgnine** *Marty*
Best Performance by an Actress in a Motion Picture – Drama: **Anna Magnani** *The Rose Tattoo*
Best Performance by an Actor in a Motion Picture – Comedy or Musical: **Tom Ewell** *The Seven Year Itch*
Best Performance by an Actress in a Motion Picture – Comedy or Musical: **Jean Simmons** *Guys and Dolls*
Best Performance by an Actor in a Supporting Role – Motion Picture: **Arthur Kennedy** *Trial*
Best Performance by an Actress in a Supporting Role – Motion Picture: **Marisa Pavan** *The Rose Tattoo*

Cannes International Film Festival

Palme d'Or: ***Marty***
Director: **Sergei Vasiliev** *Heroes of Shipka* • **Jules Dassin** *Rififi*
Actor: **Spencer Tracy** *Bad Day at Black Rock*
Actress: **Female Cast** *A Big Family*
Actor: **Male Cast** *A Big Family*

Berlin International Film Festival

Golden Berlin Bear: ***The Rats***

1956

British Film Academy Awards

Best Film from any Source: ***Gervaise*** • *Baby Doll* • *The Battle of the River Plate* • *Le Défroqué* • *Friends for Life* • *The Grasshopper* • *Guys and Dolls* • *The Killing* • *The Man with the Golden Arm* • *The Man Who Never Was* • *Picnic* • *Reach for the Sky* • *Rebel without a Cause* • *The Shadow* • *Smiles of a Summer Night* • *A Town like Alice* • *The Trouble with Harry* • *War and Peace* • *Yield to the Night*
Best British Film: ***Reach for the Sky*** • *The Battle of the River Plate* • *The Man Who Never Was* • *A Town like Alice* • *Yield to the Night*
Best Foreign Actor: **François Périer** *Gervaise* • James Dean *Rebel without a Cause* • Gunnar Björnstrand *Smiles of a Summer Night* • Pierre Fresnay *Le Défroqué* • William Holden (2) *Picnic* • Karl Malden *Baby Doll* • Frank Sinatra *The Man with the Golden Arm* • Spencer Tracy *The Mountain*
Best Foreign Actress: **Anna Magnani** *The Rose Tattoo* • Carroll Baker *Baby Doll* • Eva Dahlbeck *Smiles of a Summer Night* • Ava Gardner *Bhowani Junction* • Susan Hayward *I'll Cry Tomorrow* • Shirley MacLaine *The Trouble with Harry* • Kim Novak *Picnic* • Marisa Pavan *The Rose Tattoo* • Maria Schell *Gervaise* • Jean Simmons *Guys and Dolls*
Best British Actor: **Peter Finch** *A Town like Alice* • Jack Hawkins *The Long Arm* • Kenneth More *Reach for the Sky*
Best British Actress: **Virginia McKenna** *A Town like Alice* • Dorothy Alison *Reach for the Sky* • Audrey Hepburn *War and Peace*
Best British Screenplay: **Nigel Balchin** *The Man Who Never Was* • Michael Powell, Emeric Pressburger *The Battle of the River Plate* • Sidney Gilliat, Frank Launder *The Green Man* • John Boulting, Frank Harvey *Private's Progress* • Lewis Gilbert *Reach for the Sky* • Moore Raymond, Anthony Kimmins *Smiley* • Hubert Gregg, Vernon Harris *Three Men in a Boat* • WP Lipscomb, Richard Mason *A Town like Alice* • Joan Henry, John Cresswell *Yield to the Night*

Academy Awards

Best Motion Picture: ***Around the World in 80 Days*** • *Friendly Persuasion* • *Giant* • *The King and I* • *The Ten Commandments*
Foreign Language Film: ***La Strada*** • *The Captain from Kopenick* • *Gervaise* • *The Burmese Harp* • *Qivitoq*
Directing: **George Stevens** *Giant* • Michael Anderson *Around the World in 80 Days* • Walter Lang *The King and I* • King Vidor *War and Peace* • William Wyler *Friendly Persuasion*
Actor: **Yul Brynner** *The King and I* • James Dean *Giant* • Kirk Douglas *Lust for Life* • Rock Hudson *Giant* • Laurence Olivier *Richard III*
Actress: **Ingrid Bergman** *Anastasia* • Carroll Baker *Baby Doll* • Katharine Hepburn *The Rainmaker* • Nancy Kelly *The Bad Seed* • Deborah Kerr *The King and I*
Actor in a Supporting Role: **Anthony Quinn** *Lust for Life* • Don Murray *Bus Stop* • Anthony Perkins *Friendly*

Persuasion • Mickey Rooney *The Bold and the Brave* • Robert Stack *Written on the Wind*
ACTRESS IN A SUPPORTING ROLE: **Dorothy Malone** *Written on the Wind* • Mildred Dunnock *Baby Doll* • Eileen Heckart *The Bad Seed* • Mercedes McCambridge *Giant* • Patty McCormack *The Bad Seed*
WRITING (SCREENPLAY ORIGINAL): **Albert Lamorisse** *Red Balloon* • Robert Lewin *The Bold and the Brave* • Andrew L Stone *Julie* • Federico Fellini, Tullio Pinelli *La Strada* • William Rose *The Ladykillers*
WRITING (SCREENPLAY ADAPTED): **S J Perelman**, **James Poe**, **John Farrow** *Around the World in 80 Days* • Tennessee Williams *Baby Doll* • Michael Wilson *Friendly Persuasion* • Fred Guiol, Ivan Moffat *Giant* • Norman Corwin *Lust for Life*
WRITING (MOTION PICTURE STORY): **Dalton Trumbo** *The Brave One* • Leo Katcher *The Eddy Duchin Story* • Edward Bernds, Elwood Ullman *High Society* • Jean-Paul Sartre *The Proud Ones* • Cesare Zavattini *Umberto D*

Golden Globe Awards

BEST MOTION PICTURE – DRAMA: ***Around the World in 80 Days***
BEST MOTION PICTURE – COMEDY OR MUSICAL: ***The King and I***
BEST FOREIGN LANGUAGE FILM: ***Before Sundown* • *The Girl in Black* • *Richard III* • *Roses on the Arm* • *War and Peace* • *The White Reindeer***
BEST DIRECTOR – MOTION PICTURE: **Elia Kazan** *Baby Doll*
BEST PERFORMANCE BY AN ACTOR IN A MOTION PICTURE – DRAMA: **Kirk Douglas** *Lust for Life*
BEST PERFORMANCE BY AN ACTRESS IN A MOTION PICTURE – DRAMA: **Ingrid Bergman** *Anastasia*
BEST PERFORMANCE BY AN ACTOR IN A MOTION PICTURE – COMEDY OR MUSICAL: **Cantinflas** *Around the World in 80 Days*
BEST PERFORMANCE BY AN ACTRESS IN A MOTION PICTURE – COMEDY OR MUSICAL: **Deborah Kerr** *The King and I*
BEST PERFORMANCE BY AN ACTOR IN A SUPPORTING ROLE – MOTION PICTURE: **Earl Holliman** *The Rainmaker*
BEST PERFORMANCE BY AN ACTRESS IN A SUPPORTING ROLE – MOTION PICTURE: **Eileen Heckart** *The Bad Seed*

Cannes International Film Festival

PALME D'OR: ***Le Monde du Silence***
DIRECTOR: **Sergei Yutkevitch** *Othello*
ACTRESS: **Susan Hayward** *I'll Cry Tomorrow*

Berlin International Film Festival

GOLDEN BERLIN BEAR: ***Invitation to the Dance***
SILVER BERLIN BEAR FOR THE BEST DIRECTOR: **Robert Aldrich** *Autumn Leaves*
SILVER BERLIN BEAR FOR THE BEST ACTOR: **Burt Lancaster** *Trapeze*
SILVER BERLIN BEAR FOR THE BEST ACTRESS: **Elsa Martinelli** *Donatella*

1957

British Film Academy Awards

BEST FILM FROM ANY SOURCE: ***The Bridge on the River Kwai*** • *The Bachelor Party* • *Celui Qui Doit Mourir* • *Edge of the City* • *Heaven Knows, Mr Allison* • *A Man Escaped* • *Paths of Glory* • *Pather Panchali* • *The Prince and the Showgirl* • *The Shiralee* • *The Tin Star* • *That Night* • *3:10 to Yuma* • *12 Angry Men* • *Windom's Way*
BEST BRITISH FILM: ***The Bridge on the River Kwai*** • *The Prince and the Showgirl* • *The Shiralee* • *Windom's Way*
BEST FOREIGN ACTOR: **Henry Fonda** *12 Angry Men* • Richard Basehart *Time Limit* • Pierre Brasseur *Gates of Paris* • Tony Curtis *Sweet Smell of Success* • Jean Gabin *La Traversée de Paris* • Robert Mitchum *Heaven Knows, Mr Allison* • Sidney Poitier *Edge of the City* • Ed Wynn *The Great Man*
BEST FOREIGN ACTRESS: **Simone Signoret** *The Witches of Salem* • Augusta Dabney *That Night* • Katharine Hepburn *The Rainmaker* • Marilyn Monroe *The Prince and the Showgirl* • Lilli Palmer *Is Anna Anderson Anastasia?* • Eva Marie Saint *A Hatful of Rain* • Joanne Woodward *The Three Faces of Eve*
BEST BRITISH ACTOR: **Alec Guinness** *The Bridge on the River Kwai* • Peter Finch *Windom's Way* • Trevor Howard *Manuela* • Laurence Olivier *The Prince and the Showgirl* • Michael Redgrave *Time without Pity*
BEST BRITISH ACTRESS: **Heather Sears** *The Story of Esther Costello* • Deborah Kerr *Tea and Sympathy* • Sylvia Syms *Woman in a Dressing Gown*
BEST BRITISH SCREENPLAY: **Pierre Boulle** *The Bridge on the River Kwai* • Arthur Laurents *Anastasia* • Jack Whittingham *The Birthday Present* • John Kruse, Cy Endfield *Hell Drivers* • William Rose, John Eldridge *The Man in the Sky* • Terence Rattigan *The Prince and the Showgirl* • William Rose, John Eldridge *The Smallest Show on Earth* • Charles Kaufman *The Story of Esther Costello* • Jill Craigie *Windom's Way* • Ted Willis *Woman in a Dressing Gown*

Academy Awards

BEST MOTION PICTURE: ***The Bridge on the River Kwai*** • *Peyton Place* • *Sayonara* • *12 Angry Men* • *Witness for the Prosecution*
FOREIGN LANGUAGE FILM: ***Nights of Cabiria*** • *The Devil Came at Night* • *Gates of Paris* • *Mother India* • *Nine Lives*
DIRECTING: **David Lean** *The Bridge on the River Kwai* • Joshua Logan *Sayonara* • Sidney Lumet *12 Angry Men* • Mark Robson *Peyton Place* • Billy Wilder *Witness for the Prosecution*
ACTOR: **Alec Guinness** *The Bridge on the River Kwai* • Marlon Brando *Sayonara* • Anthony Franciosa *A Hatful of Rain* • Charles Laughton *Witness for the Prosecution* • Anthony Quinn *Wild Is the Wind*
ACTRESS: **Joanne Woodward** *The Three Faces of Eve* • Deborah Kerr *Heaven Knows, Mr Allison* • Anna Magnani *Wild Is the Wind* • Elizabeth Taylor *Raintree County* • Lana Turner *Peyton Place*
ACTOR IN A SUPPORTING ROLE: **Red Buttons** *Sayonara* • Vittorio De Sica *A Farewell to Arms* • Sessue Hayakawa *The Bridge on the River Kwai* • Arthur Kennedy, Russ Tamblyn *Peyton Place*
ACTRESS IN A SUPPORTING ROLE: **Miyoshi Umeki** *Sayonara* • Carolyn Jones *The Bachelor Party* • Elsa Lanchester *Witness for the Prosecution* • Hope Lange, Diane Varsi *Peyton Place*
WRITING (STORY AND SCREENPLAY WRITTEN DIRECTLY FOR THE SCREEN): **George Wells** *Designing Woman* • Leonard Gershe *Funny Face* • R Wright Campbell, Ivan Goff, Ben Roberts, Ralph Wheelwright *Man of a Thousand Faces* • Joel Kane, Dudley Nichols, Barney Slater *The Tin Star* • Federico Fellini, Ennio Flaiano, Tullio Pinelli *I Vitelloni*
WRITING (SCREENPLAY BASED ON MATERIAL FROM ANOTHER MEDIUM): **Pierre Boulle**, **Carl Foreman**, **Michael Wilson** *The Bridge on the River Kwai* • Reginald Rose *12 Angry Men* • John Huston, John Lee Mahin *Heaven Knows, Mr Allison* • John Michael Hayes *Peyton Place* • Paul Osborn *Sayonara*

Golden Globe Awards

BEST MOTION PICTURE – DRAMA: ***The Bridge on the River Kwai***
BEST MOTION PICTURE – COMEDY OR MUSICAL: ***Les Girls***
BEST FOREIGN LANGUAGE FILM: ***The Confessions of Felix Krull* • *Tizoc* • *Woman in a Dressing Gown* • *Yellow Crow***
BEST DIRECTOR – MOTION PICTURE: **David Lean** *The Bridge on the River Kwai*
BEST PERFORMANCE BY AN ACTOR IN A MOTION PICTURE – DRAMA: **Alec Guinness** *The Bridge on the River Kwai*
BEST PERFORMANCE BY AN ACTRESS IN A MOTION PICTURE – DRAMA: **Joanne Woodward** *The Three Faces of Eve*
BEST PERFORMANCE BY AN ACTOR IN A MOTION PICTURE – COMEDY OR MUSICAL: **Frank Sinatra** *Pal Joey*
BEST PERFORMANCE BY AN ACTRESS IN A MOTION PICTURE – COMEDY OR MUSICAL: **Kay Kendall** *Les Girls*
BEST PERFORMANCE BY AN ACTOR IN A SUPPORTING ROLE – MOTION PICTURE: **Red Buttons** *Sayonara*
BEST PERFORMANCE BY AN ACTRESS IN A SUPPORTING ROLE – MOTION PICTURE: **Elsa Lanchester** *Witness for the Prosecution*

Cannes International Film Festival

PALME D'OR: ***Friendly Persuasion***
DIRECTOR: **Robert Bresson** *A Man Escaped*
ACTOR: **John Kitzmiller** *Dolina Mira*
ACTRESS: **Giulietta Masina** *Nights of Cabiria*

Berlin International Film Festival

GOLDEN BERLIN BEAR: ***12 Angry Men***
SILVER BERLIN BEAR FOR THE BEST DIRECTOR: **Mario Monicelli** *Padri e Figli*
SILVER BERLIN BEAR FOR THE BEST ACTOR: **Pedro Infante** *Tizoc*
SILVER BERLIN BEAR FOR THE BEST ACTRESS: **Yvonne Mitchell** *Woman in a Dressing Gown*

1958

British Film Academy Awards

BEST FILM FROM ANY SOURCE: ***Room at the Top*** • *Aparajito* • *Cat on a Hot Tin Roof* • *The Cranes Are Flying* • *The Defiant Ones* • *Ice Cold in Alex* • *Indiscreet* • *Nights of Cabiria* • *No Down Payment* • *Orders to Kill* • *Sea of Sand* • *The Sheepman* • *Wild Strawberries* • *The Young Lions*
BEST BRITISH FILM: ***Room at the Top*** • *Ice Cold in Alex* • *Indiscreet* • *Orders to Kill* • *Sea of Sand*
BEST FOREIGN ACTOR: **Sidney Poitier** *The Defiant Ones* • Marlon Brando *The Young Lions* • Tony Curtis *The Defiant Ones* • Glenn Ford *The Sheepman* • Curt Jurgens *The Enemy Below* • Curt Jurgens *The Inn of the Sixth Happiness* • Charles Laughton *Witness for the Prosecution* • Paul Newman *Cat on a Hot Tin Roof* • Spencer Tracy *The Last Hurrah* • Victor Sjöström *Wild Strawberries*
BEST FOREIGN ACTRESS: **Simone Signoret** *Room at the Top* • Karuna Bannerjee *Aparajito* • Ingrid Bergman *The Inn of the Sixth Happiness* • Anna Magnani *Wild Is the Wind* • Giulietta Masina *Nights of Cabiria* • Tatyana Samoilova *The Cranes Are Flying* • Elizabeth Taylor *Cat on a Hot Tin Roof* • Joanne Woodward *No Down Payment*
BEST BRITISH ACTOR: **Trevor Howard** *The Key* • Sydney Boehm *Harry Black and the Tiger* • Michael Craig *Sea of Sand* • Laurence Harvey *Room at the Top* • Anthony Quayle *Ice Cold in Alex* • Terry-Thomas *tom thumb* • Donald Wolfit *Room at the Top*
BEST BRITISH ACTRESS: **Irene Worth** *Orders to Kill* • Hermione Baddeley *Room at the Top* • Virginia McKenna *Carve Her Name with Pride*
BEST BRITISH SCREENPLAY: **Paul Dehn** *Orders to Kill*

Academy Awards

BEST MOTION PICTURE: ***Gigi*** • *Auntie Mame* • *Cat on a Hot Tin Roof* • *The Defiant Ones* • *Separate Tables*
FOREIGN LANGUAGE FILM: ***Mon Oncle*** • *Arms and the Man* • *Big Deal on Madonna Street* • *The Road a Year Long* • *La Venganza*
DIRECTING: **Vincente Minnelli** *Gigi* • Richard Brooks *Cat on a Hot Tin Roof* • Stanley Kramer *The Defiant Ones* • Mark Robson *The Inn of the Sixth Happiness* • Robert Wise *I Want to Live!*
ACTOR: **David Niven** *Separate Tables* • Tony Curtis *The Defiant Ones* • Paul Newman *Cat on a Hot Tin Roof* • Sidney Poitier *The Defiant Ones* • Spencer Tracy *The Old Man and the Sea*
ACTRESS: **Susan Hayward** *I Want to Live!* • Deborah Kerr *Separate Tables* • Shirley MacLaine *Some Came Running* • Rosalind Russell *Auntie Mame* • Elizabeth Taylor *Cat on a Hot Tin Roof*
ACTOR IN A SUPPORTING ROLE: **Burl Ives** *The Big Country* • Theodore Bikel *The Defiant Ones* • Lee J Cobb *The Brothers Karamazov* • Arthur Kennedy *Some Came Running* • Gig Young *Teacher's Pet*
ACTRESS IN A SUPPORTING ROLE: **Wendy Hiller** *Separate Tables* • Peggy Cass *Auntie Mame* • Martha Hyer *Some Came Running* • Maureen Stapleton *Lonelyhearts* • Cara Williams *The Defiant Ones*
WRITING (STORY AND SCREENPLAY WRITTEN DIRECTLY FOR THE SCREEN): **Nedrick Young**, **Harold Jacob Smith** *The Defiant Ones* • Paddy Chayefsky *The Goddess* • Melville Shavelson, Jack Rose *Houseboat* • William Bowers, James Edward Grant *The Sheepman* • Fay Kanin, Michael Kanin *Teacher's Pet*
WRITING (SCREENPLAY BASED ON MATERIAL FROM ANOTHER MEDIUM): **Alan Jay Lerner** *Gigi* • Richard Brooks, James Poe *Cat on a Hot Tin Roof* • Alec Guinness *The Horse's Mouth* • Nelson Gidding, Don Mankiewicz *I Want to Live!* • John Gay, Terence Rattigan *Separate Tables*

Golden Globe Awards

BEST MOTION PICTURE – DRAMA: ***The Defiant Ones***
BEST MOTION PICTURE – COMEDY: ***Auntie Mame***
BEST MOTION PICTURE – MUSICAL: ***Gigi***
BEST FOREIGN LANGUAGE FILM: ***The Girl and the River* • *A Night to Remember* • *The Road a Year Long***
BEST DIRECTOR – MOTION PICTURE: **Vincente Minnelli** *Gigi*
BEST PERFORMANCE BY AN ACTOR IN A MOTION PICTURE – DRAMA: **David Niven** *Separate Tables*
BEST PERFORMANCE BY AN ACTRESS IN A MOTION PICTURE – DRAMA: **Susan Hayward** *I Want to Live!*
BEST PERFORMANCE BY AN ACTOR IN A MOTION PICTURE – COMEDY OR MUSICAL: **Danny Kaye** *Me and the Colonel*
BEST PERFORMANCE BY AN ACTRESS IN A MOTION PICTURE – COMEDY OR MUSICAL: **Rosalind Russell** *Auntie Mame*
BEST PERFORMANCE BY AN ACTOR IN A SUPPORTING ROLE – MOTION PICTURE: **Burl Ives** *The Big Country*
BEST PERFORMANCE BY AN ACTRESS IN A SUPPORTING ROLE – MOTION PICTURE: **Hermione Gingold** *Gigi*

Cannes International Film Festival

PALME D'OR: ***The Cranes Are Flying***
DIRECTOR: **Ingmar Bergman** *So Close to Life*
ACTOR: **Paul Newman** *The Long Hot Summer*
ACTRESS: **Bibi Andersson**, **Barbro Hiort Af Ornas**, **Ingrid Thulin**, **Eva Dahlbeck** *So Close to Life*
ORIGINAL SCREENPLAY: **Pier Paolo Pasolini**, **Massimo Franciosa**, **Pasquale Festa Campanile** *Young Husbands*

Berlin International Film Festival

GOLDEN BERLIN BEAR: ***Wild Strawberries***
SILVER BERLIN BEAR FOR THE BEST DIRECTOR: **Tadashi Imai** *Jun-Ai Monogatari*
SILVER BERLIN BEAR FOR THE BEST ACTOR: **Sidney Poitier** *The Defiant Ones*
SILVER BERLIN BEAR FOR THE BEST ACTRESS: **Anna Magnani** *Wild Is the Wind*

1959

British Film Academy Awards

BEST FILM FROM ANY SOURCE: ***Ben-Hur*** • *Anatomy of a Murder* • *Ashes and Diamonds* • *The Big Country* • *Compulsion* • *The Magician* • *Gigi* • *Look Back in Anger* • *Maigret Sets a Trap* • *North West Frontier* • *The Nun's Story* • *Sapphire* • *Some Like It Hot* • *Tiger Bay* • *Yesterday's Enemy*
BEST BRITISH FILM: ***Sapphire*** • *Look Back in Anger* • *North West Frontier* • *Tiger Bay* • *Yesterday's Enemy*
BEST FOREIGN ACTOR: **Jack Lemmon** *Some Like It Hot* • Zbigniew Cybulski *Ashes and Diamonds* • Jean Desailly, Jean Gabin *Maigret Sets a Trap* • Takashi Shimura *Ikiru* • James Stewart *Anatomy of a Murder*
BEST FOREIGN ACTRESS: **Shirley MacLaine** *Ask Any Girl* • Ava Gardner *On the Beach* • Susan Hayward *I Want to Live!* • **Ellie Lambetti** *A Matter of Dignity* • Rosalind Russell *Auntie Mame*
BEST BRITISH ACTOR: **Peter Sellers** *I'm All Right Jack* • Stanley Baker *Yesterday's Enemy* • Richard Burton *Look Back in Anger* • Peter Finch *The Nun's Story* • Laurence Harvey *Expresso Bongo* • Gordon Jackson *Yesterday's Enemy* • Laurence Olivier *The Devil's Disciple*
BEST BRITISH ACTRESS: **Audrey Hepburn**, Peggy Ashcroft *The Nun's Story* • Wendy Hiller *Separate Tables* • Yvonne Mitchell *Sapphire* • Sylvia Syms *No Trees in the Street* • Kay Walsh *The Horse's Mouth*
BEST BRITISH SCREENPLAY: **Frank Harvey**, **Alan Hackney**, **John Boulting** *I'm All Right Jack* • Ben Barzman, Millard

Lampbell *Blind Date* • Wolf Mankowitz *Expresso Bongo* • Alec Guinness *The Horse's Mouth* • Nigel Kneale *Look Back in Anger* • Robin Estridge *North West Frontier* • Ted Willis *No Trees in the Street* • Janet Green *Sapphire* • John Hawkesworth, Shelley Smith *Tiger Bay*

Academy Awards

BEST MOTION PICTURE: ***Ben-Hur*** • *Anatomy of a Murder* • *The Diary of Anne Frank* • *The Nun's Story* • *Room at the Top*

FOREIGN LANGUAGE FILM: ***Black Orpheus*** • *The Bridge* • *The Great War* • *Paw* • *The Village on the River*

DIRECTING: **William Wyler** *Ben-Hur* • Jack Clayton *Room at the Top* • George Stevens *The Diary of Anne Frank* • Billy Wilder *Some Like It Hot* • Fred Zinnemann *The Nun's Story*

ACTOR: **Charlton Heston** *Ben-Hur* • Laurence Harvey *Room at the Top* • Jack Lemmon *Some Like It Hot* • Paul Muni *The Last Angry Man* • James Stewart *Anatomy of a Murder*

ACTRESS: **Simone Signoret** *Room at the Top* • Doris Day *Pillow Talk* • Audrey Hepburn *The Nun's Story* • Katharine Hepburn, Elizabeth Taylor *Suddenly, Last Summer*

ACTOR IN A SUPPORTING ROLE: **Hugh Griffith** *Ben-Hur* • Arthur O'Connell, George C Scott *Anatomy of a Murder* • Robert Vaughn *The Young Philadelphians* • Ed Wynn *The Diary of Anne Frank*

ACTRESS IN A SUPPORTING ROLE: **Shelley Winters** *The Diary of Anne Frank* • Hermione Baddeley *Room at the Top* • Susan Kohner, Juanita Moore *Imitation of Life* • Thelma Ritter *Pillow Talk*

WRITING (STORY AND SCREENPLAY WRITTEN DIRECTLY FOR THE SCREEN): **Stanley Shapiro**, **Maurice Richlin**, **Russell Rouse**, **Clarence Greene** *Pillow Talk* • François Truffaut, Marcel Moussy *The 400 Blows* • Ernest Lehman *North by Northwest* • Stanley Shapiro, Maurice Richlin, Paul King, Joseph Stone *Operation Petticoat* • Ingmar Bergman *Wild Strawberries*

WRITING (SCREENPLAY BASED ON MATERIAL FROM ANOTHER MEDIUM): **Neil Paterson** *Room at the Top* • Wendell Mayes *Anatomy of a Murder* • Karl Tunberg *Ben-Hur* • Robert Anderson *The Nun's Story* • Billy Wilder, IAL Diamond *Some Like It Hot*

Golden Globe Awards

BEST MOTION PICTURE – DRAMA: ***Ben-Hur***

BEST MOTION PICTURE – COMEDY: ***Some Like It Hot***

BEST MOTION PICTURE – MUSICAL: ***Porgy and Bess***

BEST FOREIGN LANGUAGE FILM: ***Aren't We Wonderful* • *Black Orpheus* • *The Bridge* • *The Key* • *Wild Strawberries***

BEST DIRECTOR – MOTION PICTURE: **William Wyler** *Ben-Hur*

BEST PERFORMANCE BY AN ACTOR IN A MOTION PICTURE – DRAMA: **Anthony Franciosa** *Career*

BEST PERFORMANCE BY AN ACTRESS IN A MOTION PICTURE – DRAMA: **Elizabeth Taylor** *Suddenly, Last Summer*

BEST PERFORMANCE BY AN ACTOR IN A MOTION PICTURE – COMEDY OR MUSICAL: **Jack Lemmon** *Some Like It Hot*

BEST PERFORMANCE BY AN ACTRESS IN A MOTION PICTURE – COMEDY OR MUSICAL: **Marilyn Monroe** *Some Like It Hot*

BEST PERFORMANCE BY AN ACTOR IN A SUPPORTING ROLE – MOTION PICTURE: **Stephen Boyd** *Ben-Hur*

BEST PERFORMANCE BY AN ACTRESS IN A SUPPORTING ROLE – MOTION PICTURE: **Susan Kohner** *Imitation of Life*

Cannes International Film Festival

PALME D'OR: ***Black Orpheus***

DIRECTOR: **François Truffaut** *The 400 Blows*

ACTOR: **Dean Stockwell**, **Bradford Dillman**, **Orson Welles** *Compulsion*

ACTRESS: **Simone Signoret** *Room at the Top*

Berlin International Film Festival

GOLDEN BERLIN BEAR: ***Les Cousins***

SILVER BERLIN BEAR FOR THE BEST DIRECTOR: **Akira Kurosawa** *The Hidden Fortress*

SILVER BERLIN BEAR FOR THE BEST ACTOR: **Jean Gabin** *Archimède the Tramp*

SILVER BERLIN BEAR FOR THE BEST ACTRESS: **Shirley MacLaine** *Ask Any Girl*

1960

British Film Academy Awards

BEST FILM FROM ANY SOURCE: ***The Apartment*** • *The Angry Silence* • *L'Avventura* • *Black Orpheus* • *La Dolce Vita* • *Elmer Gantry* • *The 400 Blows* • *Hiroshima, Mon Amour* • *Inherit the Wind* • *Let's Make Love* • *Never on Sunday* • *Saturday Night and Sunday Morning* • *Shadows* • *Spartacus* • *Le Testament d'Orphée* • *The Trials of Oscar Wilde* • *Tunes of Glory*

BEST BRITISH FILM: ***Saturday Night and Sunday Morning*** • *The Angry Silence* • *The Trials of Oscar Wilde* • *Tunes of Glory*

BEST FOREIGN ACTOR: **Jack Lemmon** *The Apartment* • George Hamilton *Crime and Punishment, USA* • Burt Lancaster *Elmer Gantry* • Fredric March *Inherit the Wind* • Yves Montand *Let's Make Love* • Spencer Tracy *Inherit the Wind*

BEST FOREIGN ACTRESS: **Shirley MacLaine** *The Apartment* • Pier Angeli *The Angry Silence* • Melina Mercouri *Never on Sunday* • Emmanuelle Riva *Hiroshima, Mon Amour* • Jean Simmons *Elmer Gantry* • Monica Vitti *L'Avventura*

BEST BRITISH ACTOR: **Peter Finch** *The Trials of Oscar Wilde* • Richard Attenborough *The Angry Silence* • Albert Finney *Saturday Night and Sunday Morning* • John Fraser *The Trials of Oscar Wilde* • Alec Guinness, John Mills *Tunes of Glory* • Laurence Olivier *The Entertainer*

BEST BRITISH ACTRESS: **Rachel Roberts (1)** *Saturday Night and Sunday Morning* • Wendy Hiller *Sons and Lovers* • Hayley Mills *Pollyanna*

BEST BRITISH SCREENPLAY: **Bryan Forbes** *The Angry Silence* • Howard Clewes *The Day They Robbed the Bank of England* • John Osborne, Nigel Kneale *The Entertainer* • Val Guest *Hell Is a City* • Bryan Forbes *The League of Gentlemen* • Wolf Mankowitz *The Millionairess* • Alan Sillitoe *Saturday Night and Sunday Morning* • Roger MacDougall, Guy Hamilton, Ivan Foxwell *A Touch of Larceny* • Ken Hughes *The Trials of Oscar Wilde* • James Kennaway *Tunes of Glory*

Academy Awards

BEST MOTION PICTURE: ***The Apartment*** • *The Alamo* • *Elmer Gantry* • *Sons and Lovers* • *The Sundowners*

FOREIGN LANGUAGE FILM: ***The Virgin Spring*** • *Kapo* • *Macario* • *The Ninth Circle* • *La Vérité*

DIRECTING: **Billy Wilder** *The Apartment* • Jack Cardiff *Sons and Lovers* • Jules Dassin *Never on Sunday* • Alfred Hitchcock *Psycho* • Fred Zinnemann *The Sundowners*

ACTOR: **Burt Lancaster** *Elmer Gantry* • Trevor Howard *Sons and Lovers* • Jack Lemmon *The Apartment* • Laurence Olivier *The Entertainer* • Spencer Tracy *Inherit the Wind*

ACTRESS: **Elizabeth Taylor** *Butterfield 8* • Greer Garson *Sunrise at Campobello* • Deborah Kerr *The Sundowners* • Shirley MacLaine *The Apartment* • Melina Mercouri *Never on Sunday*

ACTOR IN A SUPPORTING ROLE: **Peter Ustinov** *Spartacus* • Peter Falk *Murder, Inc* • Jack Kruschen *The Apartment* • Sal Mineo *Exodus* • Chill Wills *The Alamo*

ACTRESS IN A SUPPORTING ROLE: **Shirley Jones** *Elmer Gantry* • Glynis Johns *The Sundowners* • Shirley Knight *The Dark at the Top of the Stairs* • Janet Leigh *Psycho* • Mary Ure *Sons and Lovers*

WRITING (STORY AND SCREENPLAY WRITTEN DIRECTLY FOR THE SCREEN): **Billy Wilder**, **IAL Diamond** *The Apartment* • Bryan Forbes, Michael Craig, Richard Gregson *The Angry Silence* • Norman Panama, Melvin Frank *The Facts of Life* • Marguerite Duras *Hiroshima, Mon Amour* • Jules Dassin *Never on Sunday*

WRITING (SCREENPLAY BASED ON MATERIAL FROM ANOTHER MEDIUM): **Richard Brooks** *Elmer Gantry* • Nedrick Young, Harold Jacob Smith *Inherit the Wind* • TEB Clarke, Gavin Lambert *Sons and Lovers* • Isobel Lennart *The Sundowners* • James Kennaway *Tunes of Glory*

Golden Globe Awards

BEST MOTION PICTURE – DRAMA: ***Spartacus***

BEST MOTION PICTURE – COMEDY: ***The Apartment***

BEST MOTION PICTURE – MUSICAL: ***Song without End***

BEST FOREIGN LANGUAGE FILM: ***The Trials of Oscar Wilde* • *La Vérité* • *The Virgin Spring***

BEST DIRECTOR – MOTION PICTURE: **Jack Cardiff** *Sons and Lovers*

BEST PERFORMANCE BY AN ACTOR IN A MOTION PICTURE – DRAMA: **Burt Lancaster** *Elmer Gantry*

BEST PERFORMANCE BY AN ACTRESS IN A MOTION PICTURE – DRAMA: **Greer Garson** *Sunrise at Campobello*

BEST PERFORMANCE BY AN ACTOR IN A MOTION PICTURE – COMEDY OR MUSICAL: **Jack Lemmon** *The Apartment*

BEST PERFORMANCE BY AN ACTRESS IN A MOTION PICTURE – COMEDY OR MUSICAL: **Shirley MacLaine** *The Apartment*

BEST PERFORMANCE BY AN ACTOR IN A SUPPORTING ROLE – MOTION PICTURE: **Sal Mineo** *Exodus*

BEST PERFORMANCE BY AN ACTRESS IN A SUPPORTING ROLE – MOTION PICTURE: **Janet Leigh** *Psycho*

Cannes International Film Festival

PALME D'OR: ***La Dolce Vita***

ACTRESS: **Melina Mercouri** *Never on Sunday* • **Jeanne Moreau** *Moderato Cantabile*

Berlin International Film Festival

GOLDEN BERLIN BEAR: ***Lazarillo***

SILVER BERLIN BEAR FOR THE BEST DIRECTOR: **Jean-Luc Godard** *A Bout de Souffle*

SILVER BERLIN BEAR FOR THE BEST ACTOR: **Fredric March** *Inherit the Wind*

SILVER BERLIN BEAR FOR THE BEST ACTRESS: **Juliette Mayniel** *Kirmes*

1961

British Film Academy Awards

BEST FILM FROM ANY SOURCE: ***Ballad of a Soldier* • *The Hustler*** • *The Innocents* • *Judgment at Nuremberg* • *The Long and the Short and the Tall* • *Rocco and His Brothers* • *A Taste of Honey* • *The Sundowners* • *Le Trou* • *Whistle down the Wind* • *The World of Apu*

BEST BRITISH FILM: ***A Taste of Honey*** • *The Innocents* • *The Long and the Short and the Tall* • *The Sundowners* • *Whistle down the Wind*

BEST FOREIGN ACTOR: **Paul Newman** *The Hustler* • Montgomery Clift *Judgment at Nuremberg* • Vladimir Ivashov *Ballad of a Soldier* • Philippe Leroy *Le Trou* • Sidney Poitier *A Raisin in the Sun* • Maximilian Schell *Judgment at Nuremberg* • Alberto Sordi *The Best of Enemies*

BEST FOREIGN ACTRESS: **Sophia Loren** *Two Women* • Annie Girardot *Rocco and His Brothers* • Piper Laurie *The Hustler* • Claudia McNeil *A Raisin in the Sun* • Jean Seberg *A Bout de Souffle*

BEST BRITISH ACTOR: **Peter Finch** *No Love for Johnnie* • Dirk Bogarde *Victim*

BEST BRITISH ACTRESS: **Dora Bryan** *A Taste of Honey* • Deborah Kerr *The Sundowners* • Hayley Mills *Whistle down the Wind*

BEST BRITISH SCREENPLAY: **Wolf Mankowitz**, **Val Guest** *The Day the Earth Caught Fire* • **Tony Richardson**, **Shelagh Delaney** *A Taste of Honey* • Ted Willis *Flame in the Streets* • Carl Foreman *The Guns of Navarone* • Janet Green, John McCormick *Victim* • Keith Waterhouse, Willis Hall *Whistle down the Wind*

Academy Awards

BEST MOTION PICTURE: ***West Side Story*** • *Fanny* • *The Guns of Navarone* • *The Hustler* • *Judgment at Nuremberg*

FOREIGN LANGUAGE FILM: ***Through a Glass Darkly*** • *Harry and the Butler* • *Immortal Love* • *The Important Man* • *Placido*

DIRECTING: **Jerome Robbins**, **Robert Wise** *West Side Story* • Federico Fellini *La Dolce Vita* • Stanley Kramer *Judgment at Nuremberg* • J Lee Thompson *The Guns of Navarone* • Robert Rossen *The Hustler*

ACTOR: **Maximilian Schell** *Judgment at Nuremberg* • Charles Boyer *Fanny* • Paul Newman *The Hustler* • Spencer Tracy *Judgment at Nuremberg* • Stuart Whitman *The Mark*

ACTRESS: **Sophia Loren** *Two Women* • Audrey Hepburn *Breakfast at Tiffany's* • Piper Laurie *The Hustler* • Geraldine Page *Summer and Smoke* • Natalie Wood *Splendor in the Grass*

ACTOR IN A SUPPORTING ROLE: **George Chakiris** *West Side Story* • Montgomery Clift *Judgment at Nuremberg* • Peter Falk *Pocketful of Miracles* • Jackie Gleason, George C Scott *The Hustler*

ACTRESS IN A SUPPORTING ROLE: **Rita Moreno** *West Side Story* • Fay Bainter *The Children's Hour* • Judy Garland *Judgment at Nuremberg* • Una Merkel *Summer and Smoke* • Jill St John *The Roman Spring of Mrs Stone*

WRITING (STORY AND SCREENPLAY WRITTEN DIRECTLY FOR THE SCREEN): **William Inge** *Splendor in the Grass* • Grigori Chukhrai, Valentin Yezhov *Ballad of a Soldier* • Federico Fellini, Ennio Flaiano, Tullio Pinelli, Brunello Rondi *La Dolce Vita* • Indro Montanelli, Sergio Amidei, Diego Fabbri *General Della Rovere* • Stanley Shapiro, Paul Henning *Lover Come Back*

WRITING (SCREENPLAY BASED ON MATERIAL FROM ANOTHER MEDIUM): **Abby Mann** *Judgment at Nuremberg* • George Axelrod *Breakfast at Tiffany's* • Carl Foreman *The Guns of Navarone* • Sidney Carroll, Robert Rossen *The Hustler* • Ernest Lehman *West Side Story*

Golden Globe Awards

BEST MOTION PICTURE – DRAMA: ***The Guns of Navarone***

BEST MOTION PICTURE – COMEDY: ***A Majority of One***

BEST MOTION PICTURE – MUSICAL: ***West Side Story***

BEST FOREIGN LANGUAGE FILM: ***Two Women***

BEST DIRECTOR – MOTION PICTURE: **Stanley Kramer** *Judgment at Nuremberg*

BEST PERFORMANCE BY AN ACTOR IN A MOTION PICTURE – DRAMA: **Maximilian Schell** *Judgment at Nuremberg*

BEST PERFORMANCE BY AN ACTRESS IN A MOTION PICTURE – DRAMA: **Geraldine Page** *Summer and Smoke*

BEST PERFORMANCE BY AN ACTOR IN A MOTION PICTURE – COMEDY OR MUSICAL: **Glenn Ford** *Pocketful of Miracles*

BEST PERFORMANCE BY AN ACTRESS IN A MOTION PICTURE – COMEDY OR MUSICAL: **Rosalind Russell** *A Majority of One*

BEST PERFORMANCE BY AN ACTOR IN A SUPPORTING ROLE – MOTION PICTURE: **George Chakiris** *West Side Story*

BEST PERFORMANCE BY AN ACTRESS IN A SUPPORTING ROLE – MOTION PICTURE: **Rita Moreno** *West Side Story*

Cannes International Film Festival

PALME D'OR: ***Viridiana* • *The Long Absence***

DIRECTOR: **Yulia Solntseva** *The Flaming Years*

ACTOR: **Anthony Perkins** *Goodbye Again*

ACTRESS: **Sophia Loren** *Two Women*

Berlin International Film Festival

GOLDEN BERLIN BEAR: ***La Notte***

SILVER BERLIN BEAR FOR THE BEST DIRECTOR: **Bernhard Wicki** *The Miracle of Malachias*

SILVER BERLIN BEAR FOR THE BEST ACTOR: **Peter Finch** *No Love for Johnnie*

SILVER BERLIN BEAR FOR THE BEST ACTRESS: **Anna Karina** *Une Femme Est une Femme*

1962

British Film Academy Awards

BEST FILM FROM ANY SOURCE: ***Lawrence of Arabia*** • *Billy Budd* • *The Island* • *Jules et Jim* • *A Kind of Loving* • *The L-Shaped Room* • *The Lady with the Little Dog* • *Last Year at Marienbad* • *The Long Absence* • *Lola* • *The Manchurian Candidate* • *The Miracle Worker* • *Only Two Can Play* • *Phaedra* • *Thou Shalt Not Kill* • *Through a Glass Darkly* • *The Vanishing Corporal* • *West Side Story*

BEST BRITISH FILM: ***Lawrence of Arabia*** • *Billy Budd* • *A Kind of Loving* • *The L-Shaped Room* • *Only Two Can Play*

BEST FOREIGN ACTOR: **Burt Lancaster** *Birdman of Alcatraz* • Jean-Paul Belmondo *Léon Morin, Priest* • Franco Citti *Accattone* • Kirk Douglas *Lonely Are the Brave* • George Hamilton *Light in the Piazza* • Charles Laughton *Advise and Consent* • Anthony Quinn *Lawrence of Arabia* • Robert Ryan *Billy Budd* • Georges Wilson *The Long Absence*

BEST FOREIGN ACTRESS: **Anne Bancroft** *The Miracle Worker* • Harriet Andersson *Through a Glass Darkly* • Anouk Aimée *Lola* • Melina Mercouri *Phaedra* • Jeanne Moreau *Jules et Jim* • Geraldine Page *Sweet Bird of Youth* • Natalie Wood *Splendor in the Grass*
BEST BRITISH ACTOR: **Peter O'Toole** *Lawrence of Arabia* • Richard Attenborough *Trial and Error* • Alan Bates *A Kind of Loving* • James Mason *Lolita* • Laurence Olivier *Term of Trial* • Peter Sellers *Only Two Can Play*
BEST BRITISH ACTRESS: **Leslie Caron** *The L-Shaped Room* • Virginia Maskell *The Wild and the Willing* • Janet Munro *Life for Ruth*
BEST BRITISH SCREENPLAY: **Robert Bolt** *Lawrence of Arabia* • Peter Ustinov, DeWitt Bodeen *Billy Budd* • Willis Hall, Keith Waterhouse *A Kind of Loving* • Bryan Forbes *Only Two Can Play* • Geoffrey Cotterell, Ivan Foxwell *Tiara Tahiti* • Wolf Mankowitz *Waltz of the Toreadors*

Academy Awards

BEST PICTURE: ***Lawrence of Arabia*** • *The Longest Day* • *The Music Man* • *Mutiny on the Bounty* • *To Kill a Mockingbird*
FOREIGN LANGUAGE FILM: ***Sundays and Cybèle*** • *Elektra* • *The Four Days of Naples* • *The Given Word* • *Tlayucan*
DIRECTING: **David Lean** *Lawrence of Arabia* • Pietro Germi *Divorce – Italian Style* • Robert Mulligan *To Kill a Mockingbird* • Arthur Penn *The Miracle Worker* • Frank Perry *David and Lisa*
ACTOR: **Gregory Peck** *To Kill a Mockingbird* • Burt Lancaster *Birdman of Alcatraz* • Jack Lemmon *Days of Wine and Roses* • Marcello Mastroianni *Divorce – Italian Style* • Peter O'Toole *Lawrence of Arabia*
ACTRESS: **Anne Bancroft** *The Miracle Worker* • Bette Davis *What Ever Happened to Baby Jane?* • Katharine Hepburn *Long Day's Journey into Night* • Geraldine Page *Sweet Bird of Youth* • Lee Remick *Days of Wine and Roses*
ACTOR IN A SUPPORTING ROLE: **Ed Begley** *Sweet Bird of Youth* • Victor Buono *What Ever Happened to Baby Jane?* • Telly Savalas *Birdman of Alcatraz* • Omar Sharif *Lawrence of Arabia* • Terence Stamp *Billy Budd*
ACTRESS IN A SUPPORTING ROLE: **Patty Duke** *The Miracle Worker* • Mary Badham *To Kill a Mockingbird* • Shirley Knight *Sweet Bird of Youth* • Angela Lansbury *The Manchurian Candidate* • Thelma Ritter *Birdman of Alcatraz*
WRITING (STORY AND SCREENPLAY WRITTEN DIRECTLY FOR THE SCREEN): **Pietro Germi, Ennio De Concini, Alfredo Giannetti** *Divorce – Italian Style* • Charles Kaufman, Wolfgang Reinhardt *Freud* • Alain Robbe-Grillet *Last Year at Marienbad* • Stanley Shapiro, Nate Monaster *That Touch of Mink* • Ingmar Bergman *Through a Glass Darkly*
WRITING (SCREENPLAY BASED ON MATERIAL FROM ANOTHER MEDIUM): **Horton Foote** *To Kill a Mockingbird* • Eleanor Perry *David and Lisa* • Robert Bolt, Michael Wilson *Lawrence of Arabia* • Vladimir Nabokov *Lolita* • William Gibson *The Miracle Worker*

Golden Globe Awards

BEST MOTION PICTURE – DRAMA: ***Lawrence of Arabia***
BEST MOTION PICTURE – COMEDY: ***That Touch of Mink***
BEST MOTION PICTURE – MUSICAL: ***The Music Man***
BEST FOREIGN LANGUAGE FILM: ***The Best of Enemies* • *Divorce – Italian Style***
BEST DIRECTOR – MOTION PICTURE: **David Lean** *Lawrence of Arabia*
BEST PERFORMANCE BY AN ACTOR IN A MOTION PICTURE – DRAMA: **Gregory Peck** *To Kill a Mockingbird*
BEST PERFORMANCE BY AN ACTRESS IN A MOTION PICTURE – DRAMA: **Geraldine Page** *Sweet Bird of Youth*
BEST PERFORMANCE BY AN ACTOR IN A MOTION PICTURE – COMEDY OR MUSICAL: **Marcello Mastroianni** *Divorce – Italian Style*
BEST PERFORMANCE BY AN ACTRESS IN A MOTION PICTURE – COMEDY OR MUSICAL: **Rosalind Russell** *Gypsy*
BEST PERFORMANCE BY AN ACTOR IN A SUPPORTING ROLE – MOTION PICTURE: **Omar Sharif** *Lawrence of Arabia*
BEST PERFORMANCE BY AN ACTRESS IN A SUPPORTING ROLE – MOTION PICTURE: **Angela Lansbury** *The Manchurian Candidate*

Cannes International Film Festival

PALME D'OR: ***The Given Word***
ACTOR: **Ralph Richardson, Jason Robards, Dean Stockwell** *Long Day's Journey into Night* • **Murray Melvin** *A Taste of Honey*
ACTRESS: **Katharine Hepburn** *Long Day's Journey into Night* • **Rita Tushingham** *A Taste of Honey*

Berlin International Film Festival

GOLDEN BERLIN BEAR: ***A Kind of Loving***
SILVER BERLIN BEAR FOR THE BEST DIRECTOR: **Francesco Rosi** *Salvatore Giuliano*
SILVER BERLIN BEAR FOR THE BEST ACTOR: **James Stewart** *Mr Hobbs Takes a Vacation*
SILVER BERLIN BEAR FOR THE BEST ACTRESS: **Rita Gam, Viveca Lindfors** *No Exit*

1963

British Film Academy Awards

BEST FILM FROM ANY SOURCE: ***Tom Jones*** • *Billy Liar* • *David and Lisa* • *Days of Wine and Roses* • *Divorce – Italian Style* • *8½* • *The Four Days of Naples* • *Hud* • *Knife in the Water* • *The Servant* • *This Sporting Life* • *To Kill a Mockingbird*
BEST BRITISH FILM: ***The Servant*** • *Billy Liar* • *This Sporting Life* • *Tom Jones*
BEST FOREIGN ACTOR: **Marcello Mastroianni** *Divorce – Italian Style* • Howard Da Silva *David and Lisa* • Jack Lemmon *Days of Wine and Roses* • Paul Newman *Hud* • Gregory Peck *To Kill a Mockingbird*
BEST FOREIGN ACTRESS: **Patricia Neal** *Hud* • Joan Crawford, Bette Davis *What Ever Happened to Baby Jane?* • Lee Remick *Days of Wine and Roses* • Daniela Rocca *Divorce – Italian Style*
BEST BRITISH ACTOR: **Dirk Bogarde** *The Servant* • Tom Courtenay *Billy Liar* • Albert Finney, Hugh Griffith *Tom Jones* • Richard Harris *This Sporting Life*
BEST BRITISH ACTRESS: **Rachel Roberts (1)** *This Sporting Life* • Julie Christie *Billy Liar* • Edith Evans *Tom Jones* • Sarah Miles *The Servant* • Barbara Windsor *Sparrows Can't Sing*
BEST BRITISH SCREENPLAY: **John Osborne** *Tom Jones* • Keith Waterhouse, Willis Hall *Billy Liar* • Harold Pinter *The Servant* • David Storey *This Sporting Life*

Academy Awards

BEST PICTURE: ***Tom Jones*** • *America, America* • *Cleopatra* • *How the West Was Won* • *Lilies of the Field*
FOREIGN LANGUAGE FILM: ***8½*** • *Knife in the Water* • *The Red Lanterns* • *Los Tarantos* • *Twin Sisters of Kyoto*
DIRECTING: **Tony Richardson** *Tom Jones* • Federico Fellini *8½* • Elia Kazan *America, America* • Otto Preminger *The Cardinal* • Martin Ritt *Hud*
ACTOR: **Sidney Poitier** *Lilies of the Field* • Albert Finney *Tom Jones* • Richard Harris *This Sporting Life* • Rex Harrison *Cleopatra* • Paul Newman *Hud*
ACTRESS: **Patricia Neal** *Hud* • Leslie Caron *The L-Shaped Room* • Shirley MacLaine *Irma la Douce* • Rachel Roberts (1) *This Sporting Life* • Natalie Wood *Love with the Proper Stranger*
ACTOR IN A SUPPORTING ROLE: **Melvyn Douglas** *Hud* • Nick Adams *Twilight of Honor* • Bobby Darin *Captain Newman, MD* • Hugh Griffith *Tom Jones* • John Huston *The Cardinal*
ACTRESS IN A SUPPORTING ROLE: **Margaret Rutherford** *The VIPs* • Diane Cilento, Edith Evans, Joyce Redman *Tom Jones* • Lilia Skala *Lilies of the Field*
WRITING (STORY AND SCREENPLAY WRITTEN DIRECTLY FOR THE SCREEN): **James R Webb** *How the West Was Won* • Elia Kazan *America, America* • Federico Fellini, Tullio Pinelli, Ennio Flajano, Brunello Rondi *8½* • Pasquale Festa Campanile, Massimo Franciosa, Nanni Loy, Carlo Benari, Vasco Pratolini *The Four Days of Naples* • Arnold Schulman *Love with the Proper Stranger*
WRITING (SCREENPLAY BASED ON MATERIAL FROM ANOTHER MEDIUM): **John Osborne** *Tom Jones* • Richard L Breen, Phoebe Ephron, Henry Ephron *Captain Newman, MD* • Irving Ravetch, Harriet Frank Jr *Hud* • James Poe *Lilies of the Field* • Serge Bourguignon, Antoine Tudal *Sundays and Cybèle*

Golden Globe Awards

BEST MOTION PICTURE – DRAMA: ***The Cardinal***
BEST MOTION PICTURE – COMEDY OR MUSICAL: ***Tom Jones***
BEST FOREIGN LANGUAGE FILM: ***Any Number Can Win***
BEST DIRECTOR – MOTION PICTURE: **Elia Kazan** *America, America*
BEST PERFORMANCE BY AN ACTOR IN A MOTION PICTURE – DRAMA: **Sidney Poitier** *Lilies of the Field*
BEST PERFORMANCE BY AN ACTRESS IN A MOTION PICTURE – DRAMA: **Leslie Caron** *The L-Shaped Room*
BEST PERFORMANCE BY AN ACTOR IN A MOTION PICTURE – COMEDY OR MUSICAL: **Alberto Sordi** *The Devil*
BEST PERFORMANCE BY AN ACTRESS IN A MOTION PICTURE – COMEDY OR MUSICAL: **Shirley MacLaine** *Irma la Douce*
BEST PERFORMANCE BY AN ACTOR IN A SUPPORTING ROLE – MOTION PICTURE: **John Huston** *The Cardinal*
BEST PERFORMANCE BY AN ACTRESS IN A SUPPORTING ROLE – MOTION PICTURE: **Margaret Rutherford** *The VIPs*

Cannes International Film Festival

PALME D'OR: ***The Leopard***
ACTOR: **Richard Harris** *This Sporting Life*
ACTRESS: **Marina Vlady** *The Conjugal Bed*
SCREENPLAY: **Henri Colpi** *Codine*

Berlin International Film Festival

GOLDEN BERLIN BEAR: ***The Devil* • *Bushido Zankoku Monogatari***
SILVER BERLIN BEAR FOR THE BEST DIRECTOR: **Nikos Koundouros** *Mikres Aphrodites*
SILVER BERLIN BEAR FOR THE BEST ACTOR: **Sidney Poitier** *Lilies of the Field*
SILVER BERLIN BEAR FOR THE BEST ACTRESS: **Bibi Andersson** *The Swedish Mistress*

1964

British Film Academy Awards

BEST FILM FROM ANY SOURCE: ***Dr Strangelove, or How I Learned to Stop Worrying and Love the Bomb*** • *Becket* • *The Pumpkin Eater* • *The Train*
BEST BRITISH FILM: ***Dr Strangelove, or How I Learned to Stop Worrying and Love the Bomb*** • *Becket* • *King and Country* • *The Pumpkin Eater*
BEST FOREIGN ACTOR: **Marcello Mastroianni** *Yesterday, Today and Tomorrow* • Cary Grant *Charade* • Sterling Hayden *Dr Strangelove, or How I Learned to Stop Worrying and Love the Bomb* • Sidney Poitier *Lilies of the Field*
BEST FOREIGN ACTRESS: **Anne Bancroft** *The Pumpkin Eater* • Ava Gardner *The Night of the Iguana* • Shirley MacLaine *Irma la Douce* • Shirley MacLaine *What a Way to Go!* • Kim Stanley *Seance on a Wet Afternoon*
BEST BRITISH ACTOR: **Richard Attenborough** *Guns at Batasi* • **Richard Attenborough** *Seance on a Wet Afternoon* • Tom Courtenay *King and Country* • Peter O'Toole *Becket* • Peter Sellers *Dr Strangelove, or How I Learned to Stop Worrying and Love the Bomb* • Peter Sellers *The Pink Panther*
BEST BRITISH ACTRESS: **Audrey Hepburn** *Charade* • Edith Evans, Deborah Kerr *The Chalk Garden* • Rita Tushingham *Girl with Green Eyes*
BEST SCREENPLAY FOR A BRITISH FILM: **Harold Pinter** *The Pumpkin Eater* • Edward Anhalt *Becket* • Stanley Kubrick, Terry Southern, Peter George *Dr Strangelove, or How I Learned to Stop Worrying and Love the Bomb* • Bryan Forbes *Seance on a Wet Afternoon*

Academy Awards

BEST PICTURE: ***My Fair Lady*** • *Becket* • *Dr Strangelove, or How I Learned to Stop Worrying and Love the Bomb* • *Mary Poppins* • *Zorba the Greek*
FOREIGN LANGUAGE FILM: ***Yesterday, Today and Tomorrow*** • *Raven's End* • *Sallah* • *The Umbrellas of Cherbourg* • *Woman in the Dunes*
DIRECTING: **George Cukor** *My Fair Lady* • Michael Cacoyannis *Zorba the Greek* • Peter Glenville *Becket* • Stanley Kubrick *Dr Strangelove, or How I Learned to Stop Worrying and Love the Bomb* • Robert Stevenson *Mary Poppins*
ACTOR: **Rex Harrison** *My Fair Lady* • Richard Burton, Peter O'Toole *Becket* • Anthony Quinn *Zorba the Greek* • Peter Sellers *Dr Strangelove, or How I Learned to Stop Worrying and Love the Bomb*
ACTRESS: **Julie Andrews** *Mary Poppins* • Anne Bancroft *The Pumpkin Eater* • Sophia Loren *Marriage – Italian Style* • Debbie Reynolds *The Unsinkable Molly Brown* • Kim Stanley *Seance on a Wet Afternoon*
ACTOR IN A SUPPORTING ROLE: **Peter Ustinov** *Topkapi* • John Gielgud *Becket* • Stanley Holloway *My Fair Lady* • Edmond O'Brien *Seven Days in May* • Lee Tracy *The Best Man*
ACTRESS IN A SUPPORTING ROLE: **Lila Kedrova** *Zorba the Greek* • Gladys Cooper *My Fair Lady* • Edith Evans *The Chalk Garden* • Grayson Hall *The Night of the Iguana* • Agnes Moorehead *Hush... Hush, Sweet Charlotte*
WRITING (STORY AND SCREENPLAY WRITTEN DIRECTLY FOR THE SCREEN): **Frank Tarloff, Peter Stone, S H Barnett** *Father Goose* • Alun Owen *A Hard Day's Night* • Raphael Hayes, Orville H Hampton *One Potato, Two Potato* • Mario Monicelli, Scarpelli, Age *The Organizer* • Daniel Boulanger, Ariane Mnouchkine, Jean-Paul Rappeneau, Philippe de Broca *That Man from Rio*
WRITING (SCREENPLAY BASED ON MATERIAL FROM ANOTHER MEDIUM): **Edward Anhalt** *Becket* • Stanley Kubrick, Terry Southern, Peter George *Dr Strangelove, or How I Learned to Stop Worrying and Love the Bomb* • Bill Walsh, Don DaGradi *Mary Poppins* • Alan Jay Lerner *My Fair Lady* • Michael Cacoyannis *Zorba the Greek*

Golden Globe Awards

BEST MOTION PICTURE – DRAMA: ***Becket***
BEST MOTION PICTURE – COMEDY OR MUSICAL: ***My Fair Lady***
BEST FOREIGN LANGUAGE FILM: ***Girl with Green Eyes* • *Marriage – Italian Style* • *Sallah***
BEST DIRECTOR – MOTION PICTURE: **George Cukor** *My Fair Lady*
BEST PERFORMANCE BY AN ACTOR IN A MOTION PICTURE – DRAMA: **Peter O'Toole** *Becket*
BEST PERFORMANCE BY AN ACTRESS IN A MOTION PICTURE – DRAMA: **Anne Bancroft** *The Pumpkin Eater*
BEST PERFORMANCE BY AN ACTOR IN A MOTION PICTURE – COMEDY OR MUSICAL: **Rex Harrison** *My Fair Lady*
BEST PERFORMANCE BY AN ACTRESS IN A MOTION PICTURE – COMEDY OR MUSICAL: **Julie Andrews** *Mary Poppins*
BEST PERFORMANCE BY AN ACTOR IN A SUPPORTING ROLE – MOTION PICTURE: **Edmond O'Brien** *Seven Days in May*
BEST PERFORMANCE BY AN ACTRESS IN A SUPPORTING ROLE – MOTION PICTURE: **Agnes Moorehead** *Hush... Hush, Sweet Charlotte*

Cannes International Film Festival

GRAND PRIX: ***The Umbrellas of Cherbourg***
ACTOR: **Antal Pager** *Pacsirta*
ACTRESS: **Anne Bancroft** *The Pumpkin Eater*

Berlin International Film Festival

GOLDEN BERLIN BEAR: ***Susuz Yaz***
SILVER BERLIN BEAR FOR THE BEST DIRECTOR: **Satyajit Ray** *The Big City*
SILVER BERLIN BEAR FOR THE BEST ACTOR: **Rod Steiger** *The Pawnbroker*
SILVER BERLIN BEAR FOR THE BEST ACTRESS: **Sachiko Hidari** *The Insect Woman* • **Sachiko Hidari** *Kanajo To Kare*

1965

British Film Academy Awards

BEST FILM FROM ANY SOURCE: ***My Fair Lady*** • *Hamlet* • *The Hill* • *The Knack... and How to Get It* • *Zorba the Greek*
BEST BRITISH FILM: ***The Ipcress File*** • *Darling* • *The Hill* • *The Knack... and How to Get It*
BEST FOREIGN ACTOR: **Lee Marvin** *The Killers* • **Lee Marvin** *Cat Ballou* • Jack Lemmon *Good Neighbor Sam* • Jack Lemmon *How to Murder Your Wife* • Anthony Quinn

Zorba the Greek • Innokenti Smoktunovsky *Hamlet* • Oskar Werner *Ship of Fools*
BEST FOREIGN ACTRESS: **Patricia Neal** *In Harm's Way* • Jane Fonda *Cat Ballou* • Lila Kedrova *Zorba the Greek* • Simone Signoret *Ship of Fools*
BEST BRITISH ACTOR: **Dirk Bogarde** *Darling* • Harry Andrews *The Hill* • Michael Caine *The Ipcress File* • Rex Harrison *My Fair Lady*
BEST BRITISH ACTRESS: **Julie Christie** *Darling* • Julie Andrews *The Americanization of Emily* • Julie Andrews *The Sound of Music* • Maggie Smith *Young Cassidy* • Rita Tushingham *The Knack... and How to Get It*
BEST BRITISH SCREENPLAY: **Frederic Raphael** *Darling* • Ray Rigby *The Hill* • Bill Canaway, James Doran *The Ipcress File* • Charles Wood *The Knack... and How to Get It*

Academy Awards

BEST PICTURE: ***The Sound of Music*** • *Darling* • *Doctor Zhivago* • *Ship of Fools* • *A Thousand Clowns*
FOREIGN LANGUAGE FILM: ***The Shop on the High Street*** • *Blood on the Land* • *Dear John* • *Kwaidan* • *Marriage – Italian Style*
DIRECTING: **Robert Wise** *The Sound of Music* • David Lean *Doctor Zhivago* • John Schlesinger *Darling* • Hiroshi Teshigahara *Woman in the Dunes* • William Wyler *The Collector*
ACTOR: **Lee Marvin** *Cat Ballou* • Richard Burton *The Spy Who Came in from the Cold* • Laurence Olivier *Othello* • Rod Steiger *The Pawnbroker* • Oskar Werner *Ship of Fools*
ACTRESS: **Julie Christie** *Darling* • Julie Andrews *The Sound of Music* • Samantha Eggar *The Collector* • Elizabeth Hartman *A Patch of Blue* • Simone Signoret *Ship of Fools*
ACTOR IN A SUPPORTING ROLE: **Martin Balsam** *A Thousand Clowns* • Ian Bannen *The Flight of the Phoenix* • Tom Courtenay *Doctor Zhivago* • Michael Dunn *Ship of Fools* • Frank Finlay *Othello*
ACTRESS IN A SUPPORTING ROLE: **Shelley Winters** *A Patch of Blue* • Ruth Gordon *Inside Daisy Clover* • Joyce Redman, Maggie Smith *Othello* • Peggy Wood *The Sound of Music*
WRITING (STORY AND SCREENPLAY WRITTEN DIRECTLY FOR THE SCREEN): **Frederic Raphael** *Darling* • Agenore Incrocci, Furio Scarpelli, Suso Cecchi D'Amico, Mario Monicelli, Tonino Guerra, Giorgio Salvioni *Casanova '70* • Jack Davies, Ken Annakin *Those Magnificent Men in Their Flying Machines* • Franklin Coen, Frank Davis (1) *The Train* • Jacques Demy *The Umbrellas of Cherbourg*
WRITING (SCREENPLAY BASED ON MATERIAL FROM ANOTHER MEDIUM): **Robert Bolt** *Doctor Zhivago* • Frank Pierson, Walter Newman *Cat Ballou* • Stanley Mann, John Kohn *The Collector* • Abby Mann *Ship of Fools* • Herb Gardner *A Thousand Clowns*

Golden Globe Awards

BEST MOTION PICTURE – DRAMA: ***Doctor Zhivago***
BEST MOTION PICTURE – COMEDY OR MUSICAL: ***The Sound of Music***
BEST FOREIGN LANGUAGE FILM: ***Darling* • *Juliet of the Spirits***
BEST DIRECTOR – MOTION PICTURE: **David Lean** *Doctor Zhivago*
BEST PERFORMANCE BY AN ACTOR IN A MOTION PICTURE – DRAMA: **Omar Sharif** *Doctor Zhivago*
BEST PERFORMANCE BY AN ACTRESS IN A MOTION PICTURE – DRAMA: **Samantha Eggar** *The Collector*
BEST PERFORMANCE BY AN ACTOR IN A MOTION PICTURE – COMEDY OR MUSICAL: **Lee Marvin** *Cat Ballou*
BEST PERFORMANCE BY AN ACTRESS IN A MOTION PICTURE – COMEDY OR MUSICAL: **Julie Andrews** *The Sound of Music*
BEST PERFORMANCE BY AN ACTOR IN A SUPPORTING ROLE – MOTION PICTURE: **Oskar Werner** *The Spy Who Came in from the Cold*
BEST PERFORMANCE BY AN ACTRESS IN A SUPPORTING ROLE – MOTION PICTURE: **Ruth Gordon** *Inside Daisy Clover*
BEST SCREENPLAY – MOTION PICTURE: **Robert Bolt** *Doctor Zhivago*

Cannes International Film Festival

GRAND PRIX: ***The Knack... and How to Get It***
DIRECTOR: **Liviu Ciulei** *The Lost Forest*
ACTOR: **Terence Stamp** *The Collector*
ACTRESS: **Samantha Eggar** *The Collector*
SCREENPLAY: **R S Allen, Ray Rigby** *The Hill* • **Pierre Schoendoerffer** *La 317eme Section*

Berlin International Film Festival

GOLDEN BERLIN BEAR: ***Alphaville***
SILVER BERLIN BEAR FOR THE BEST DIRECTOR: **Satyajit Ray** *Charulata*
SILVER BERLIN BEAR FOR THE BEST ACTOR: **Lee Marvin** *Cat Ballou*
SILVER BERLIN BEAR FOR THE BEST ACTRESS: **Madhur Jaffrey** *Shakespeare Wallah*

1966

British Film Academy Awards

BEST FILM FROM ANY SOURCE: ***Who's Afraid of Virginia Woolf?*** • *Doctor Zhivago* • *Morgan – a Suitable Case for Treatment* • *The Spy Who Came in from the Cold*
BEST BRITISH FILM: ***The Spy Who Came In from the Cold*** • *Alfie* • *Georgy Girl* • *Morgan – a Suitable Case for Treatment*
BEST FOREIGN ACTOR: **Rod Steiger** *The Pawnbroker* • Jean-Paul Belmondo *Pierrot le Fou* • Sidney Poitier *A Patch of Blue* • Oskar Werner *The Spy Who Came in from the Cold*
BEST FOREIGN ACTRESS: **Jeanne Moreau**, Brigitte Bardot *Viva Maria!* • Joan Hackett *The Group*
BEST BRITISH ACTOR: **Richard Burton** *The Spy Who Came in from the Cold* • **Richard Burton** *Who's Afraid of Virginia Woolf?* • Michael Caine *Alfie* • Ralph Richardson *The Wrong Box* • Ralph Richardson *Doctor Zhivago* • Ralph Richardson *Khartoum* • David Warner *Morgan – a Suitable Case for Treatment*
BEST BRITISH ACTRESS: **Elizabeth Taylor** *Who's Afraid of Virginia Woolf?* • Julie Christie *Doctor Zhivago* • Julie Christie *Fahrenheit 451* • Lynn Redgrave *Georgy Girl* • Vanessa Redgrave *Morgan – a Suitable Case for Treatment*
BEST BRITISH SCREENPLAY: **David Mercer** *Morgan – a Suitable Case for Treatment* • Bill Naughton *Alfie* • Kevin Brownlow, Andrew Mollo *It Happened Here* • Harold Pinter *The Quiller Memorandum*

Academy Awards

BEST PICTURE: ***A Man for All Seasons*** • *Alfie* • *The Russians Are Coming, the Russians Are Coming* • *The Sand Pebbles* • *Who's Afraid of Virginia Woolf?*
FOREIGN LANGUAGE FILM: ***Un Homme et une Femme*** • *The Battle of Algiers* • *A Blonde in Love* • *Pharaoh* • *Three*
DIRECTING: **Fred Zinnemann** *A Man for All Seasons* • Michelangelo Antonioni *Blowup* • Richard Brooks *The Professionals* • Claude Lelouch *Un Homme et une Femme* • Mike Nichols *Who's Afraid of Virginia Woolf?*
ACTOR: **Paul Scofield** *A Man for All Seasons* • Alan Arkin *The Russians Are Coming, the Russians Are Coming* • Richard Burton *Who's Afraid of Virginia Woolf?* • Michael Caine *Alfie* • Steve McQueen *The Sand Pebbles*
ACTRESS: **Elizabeth Taylor** *Who's Afraid of Virginia Woolf?* • Anouk Aimée *Un Homme et une Femme* • Ida Kaminska *The Shop on the High Street* • Lynn Redgrave *Georgy Girl* • Vanessa Redgrave *Morgan – a Suitable Case for Treatment*
ACTOR IN A SUPPORTING ROLE: **Walter Matthau** *The Fortune Cookie* • Mako *The Sand Pebbles* • James Mason *Georgy Girl* • George Segal *Who's Afraid of Virginia Woolf?* • Robert Shaw *A Man for All Seasons*
ACTRESS IN A SUPPORTING ROLE: **Sandy Dennis** *Who's Afraid of Virginia Woolf?* • Wendy Hiller *A Man for All Seasons* • Jocelyn La Garde *Hawaii* • Vivien Merchant *Alfie* • Geraldine Page *You're a Big Boy Now*
WRITING (STORY AND SCREENPLAY WRITTEN DIRECTLY FOR THE SCREEN): **Claude Lelouch, Pierre Uytterhoeven** *Un Homme et une Femme* • Michelangelo Antonioni, Tonino Guerra, Edward Bond *Blowup* • Billy Wilder, IAL Diamond *The Fortune Cookie* • Robert Ardrey *Khartoum* • Clint Johnston, Don Peters *The Naked Prey*
WRITING (SCREENPLAY BASED ON MATERIAL FROM ANOTHER MEDIUM): **Robert Bolt** *A Man for All Seasons* • Bill Naughton *Alfie* • Richard Brooks *The Professionals* • William Rose *The Russians Are Coming, the Russians Are Coming* • Ernest Lehman *Who's Afraid of Virginia Woolf?*

Golden Globe Awards

BEST MOTION PICTURE – DRAMA: ***A Man for All Seasons***
BEST MOTION PICTURE – COMEDY OR MUSICAL: ***The Russians Are Coming, the Russians Are Coming***
BEST FOREIGN LANGUAGE FILM: ***Alfie* • *Un Homme et une Femme***
BEST DIRECTOR – MOTION PICTURE: **Fred Zinnemann** *A Man for All Seasons*
BEST PERFORMANCE BY AN ACTOR IN A MOTION PICTURE – DRAMA: **Paul Scofield** *A Man for All Seasons*
BEST PERFORMANCE BY AN ACTRESS IN A MOTION PICTURE – DRAMA: **Anouk Aimée** *Un Homme et une Femme*
BEST PERFORMANCE BY AN ACTOR IN A MOTION PICTURE – COMEDY OR MUSICAL: **Alan Arkin** *The Russians Are Coming, the Russians Are Coming*
BEST PERFORMANCE BY AN ACTRESS IN A MOTION PICTURE – COMEDY OR MUSICAL: **Lynn Redgrave** *Georgy Girl*
BEST PERFORMANCE BY AN ACTOR IN A SUPPORTING ROLE – MOTION PICTURE: **Richard Attenborough** *The Sand Pebbles*
BEST PERFORMANCE BY AN ACTRESS IN A SUPPORTING ROLE – MOTION PICTURE: **Jocelyn La Garde** *Hawaii*
BEST SCREENPLAY – MOTION PICTURE: **Robert Bolt** *A Man for All Seasons*

Cannes International Film Festival

GRAND PRIX: ***Un Homme et une Femme* • *The Birds, the Bees, and the Italians***
DIRECTOR: **Sergei Yutkevitch** *Lenin in Poland*
ACTOR: **Per Oscarsson** *Hunger*
ACTRESS: **Vanessa Redgrave** *Morgan – a Suitable Case for Treatment*

Berlin International Film Festival

GOLDEN BERLIN BEAR: ***Cul-de-Sac***
SILVER BERLIN BEAR FOR THE BEST DIRECTOR: **Carlos Saura** *The Hunt*
SILVER BERLIN BEAR FOR THE BEST ACTOR: **Jean-Pierre Léaud** *Masculine Feminine*
SILVER BERLIN BEAR FOR THE BEST ACTRESS: **Lola Albright** *Lord Love a Duck*

1967

British Film Academy Awards

BEST FILM FROM ANY SOURCE: ***A Man for All Seasons*** • *Bonnie and Clyde* • *Un Homme et une Femme* • *In the Heat of the Night*
BEST BRITISH FILM: ***A Man for All Seasons*** • *Accident* • *Blowup* • *The Deadly Affair*
BEST FOREIGN ACTOR: **Rod Steiger** *In the Heat of the Night* • Warren Beatty *Bonnie and Clyde* • Sidney Poitier *In the Heat of the Night* • Orson Welles *Chimes at Midnight*
BEST FOREIGN ACTRESS: **Anouk Aimée** *Un Homme et une Femme* • Bibi Andersson *My Sister, My Love* • Bibi Andersson *Persona* • Jane Fonda *Barefoot in the Park* • Simone Signoret *The Deadly Affair*
BEST BRITISH ACTOR: **Paul Scofield** *A Man for All Seasons* • Dirk Bogarde *Accident* • Dirk Bogarde *Our Mother's House* • Richard Burton *The Taming of the Shrew* • James Mason *The Deadly Affair*
BEST BRITISH ACTRESS: **Edith Evans** *The Whisperers* • Barbara Jefford *Ulysses* • Elizabeth Taylor *The Taming of the Shrew*
BEST BRITISH SCREENPLAY: **Robert Bolt** *A Man for All Seasons* • Harold Pinter *Accident* • Paul Dehn *The Deadly Affair* • Frederic Raphael *Two for the Road*

Academy Awards

BEST PICTURE: ***In the Heat of the Night*** • *Bonnie and Clyde* • *Doctor Dolittle* • *The Graduate* • *Guess Who's Coming to Dinner*
FOREIGN LANGUAGE FILM: ***Closely Observed Trains*** • *El Amor Brujo* • *I Even Met Happy Gypsies* • *Portrait of Chieko* • *Vivre pour Vivre*
DIRECTING: **Mike Nichols** *The Graduate* • Richard Brooks *In Cold Blood* • Norman Jewison *In the Heat of the Night* • Stanley Kramer *Guess Who's Coming to Dinner* • Arthur Penn *Bonnie and Clyde*
ACTOR: **Rod Steiger** *In the Heat of the Night* • Warren Beatty *Bonnie and Clyde* • Dustin Hoffman *The Graduate* • Paul Newman *Cool Hand Luke* • Spencer Tracy *Guess Who's Coming to Dinner*
ACTRESS: **Katharine Hepburn** *Guess Who's Coming to Dinner* • Anne Bancroft *The Graduate* • Faye Dunaway *Bonnie and Clyde* • Edith Evans *The Whisperers* • Audrey Hepburn *Wait until Dark*
ACTOR IN A SUPPORTING ROLE: **George Kennedy** *Cool Hand Luke* • John Cassavetes *The Dirty Dozen* • Gene Hackman *Bonnie and Clyde* • Cecil Kellaway *Guess Who's Coming to Dinner* • Michael J Pollard *Bonnie and Clyde*
ACTRESS IN A SUPPORTING ROLE: **Estelle Parsons** *Bonnie and Clyde* • Carol Channing *Thoroughly Modern Millie* • Mildred Natwick *Barefoot in the Park* • Beah Richards *Guess Who's Coming to Dinner* • Katharine Ross *The Graduate*
WRITING (STORY AND SCREENPLAY WRITTEN DIRECTLY FOR THE SCREEN): **William Rose** *Guess Who's Coming to Dinner* • David Newman, Robert Benton *Bonnie and Clyde* • Norman Lear, Robert Kaufman *Divorce American Style* • Jorge Semprun *La Guerre Est Finie* • Frederic Raphael *Two for the Road*
WRITING (SCREENPLAY BASED ON MATERIAL FROM ANOTHER MEDIUM): **Stirling Silliphant** *In the Heat of the Night* • Donn Pearce, Frank Pierson *Cool Hand Luke* • Calder Willingham, Buck Henry *The Graduate* • Richard Brooks *In Cold Blood* • Joseph Strick, Fred Haines *Ulysses*

Golden Globe Awards

BEST MOTION PICTURE – DRAMA: ***In the Heat of the Night***
BEST MOTION PICTURE – COMEDY OR MUSICAL: ***The Graduate***
BEST FOREIGN LANGUAGE FILM: ***The Fox* • *Vivre pour Vivre***
BEST DIRECTOR – MOTION PICTURE: **Mike Nichols** *The Graduate*
BEST PERFORMANCE BY AN ACTOR IN A MOTION PICTURE – DRAMA: **Rod Steiger** *In the Heat of the Night*
BEST PERFORMANCE BY AN ACTRESS IN A MOTION PICTURE – DRAMA: **Edith Evans** *The Whisperers*
BEST PERFORMANCE BY AN ACTOR IN A MOTION PICTURE – COMEDY OR MUSICAL: **Richard Harris** *Camelot*
BEST PERFORMANCE BY AN ACTRESS IN A MOTION PICTURE – COMEDY OR MUSICAL: **Anne Bancroft** *The Graduate*
BEST PERFORMANCE BY AN ACTOR IN A SUPPORTING ROLE – MOTION PICTURE: **Richard Attenborough** *Doctor Dolittle*
BEST PERFORMANCE BY AN ACTRESS IN A SUPPORTING ROLE – MOTION PICTURE: **Carol Channing** *Thoroughly Modern Millie*
BEST SCREENPLAY – MOTION PICTURE: **Stirling Silliphant** *In the Heat of the Night*

Cannes International Film Festival

GRAND PRIX: ***Blowup***
DIRECTOR: **Ferenc Kosa** *Tizezer Nap*
ACTOR: **Uri Zohar** *Three Days and a Child*
ACTRESS: **Pia Degermark** *Elvira Madigan*
SCREENPLAY: **Alain Jessua** *Jeu de Massacre* • **Elio Petri, Ugo Pirro** *We Still Kill the Old Way*

Berlin International Film Festival

GOLDEN BERLIN BEAR: ***Le Départ***
SILVER BERLIN BEAR FOR THE BEST DIRECTOR: **Zivojin Pavlovic** *Budjenje Pacova*
SILVER BERLIN BEAR FOR THE BEST ACTOR: **Michel Simon** *The Two of Us*
SILVER BERLIN BEAR FOR THE BEST ACTRESS: **Edith Evans** *The Whisperers*

1968

British Film Academy Awards

BEST FILM: ***The Graduate*** • *Closely Observed Trains* • *Oliver!* • *2001: a Space Odyssey*
BEST DIRECTOR: **Mike Nichols** *The Graduate* • Lindsay Anderson *if...* • Carol Reed *Oliver!* • Franco Zeffirelli *Romeo and Juliet*
BEST ACTOR: **Spencer Tracy** *Guess Who's Coming to Dinner* • Trevor Howard *The Charge of the Light Brigade* • Ron Moody *Oliver!* • Nicol Williamson *The Bofors Gun*
BEST ACTRESS: **Katharine Hepburn** *The Lion in Winter* • **Katharine Hepburn** *Guess Who's Coming to Dinner* • Anne Bancroft *The Graduate* • Catherine Deneuve *Belle de Jour* • Joanne Woodward *Rachel, Rachel*
BEST SUPPORTING ACTOR: **Ian Holm** *The Bofors Gun* • Anthony Hopkins *The Lion in Winter* • John McEnery *Romeo and Juliet* • George Segal *No Way to Treat a Lady*
BEST SUPPORTING ACTRESS: **Billie Whitelaw** *Charlie Bubbles* • **Billie Whitelaw** *Twisted Nerve* • Pat Heywood *Romeo and Juliet* • Virginia Maskell *Interlude* • Simone Signoret *Games*
BEST SCREENPLAY: **Calder Willingham**, **Buck Henry** *The Graduate* • William Rose *Guess Who's Coming to Dinner* • David Sherwin *if...* • James Goldman *The Lion in Winter*

Academy Awards

BEST PICTURE: ***Oliver!*** • *Funny Girl* • *The Lion in Winter* • *Rachel, Rachel* • *Romeo and Juliet*
FOREIGN LANGUAGE FILM: ***War and Peace*** • *The Boys of Paul Street* • *The Fireman's Ball* • *The Girl with the Pistol* • *Stolen Kisses*
DIRECTING: **Carol Reed** *Oliver!* • Anthony Harvey *The Lion in Winter* • Stanley Kubrick *2001: a Space Odyssey* • Gillo Pontecorvo *The Battle of Algiers* • Franco Zeffirelli *Romeo and Juliet*
ACTOR: **Cliff Robertson** *Charly* • Alan Arkin *The Heart Is a Lonely Hunter* • Alan Bates *The Fixer* • Ron Moody *Oliver!* • Peter O'Toole *The Lion in Winter*
ACTRESS: **Katharine Hepburn** *The Lion in Winter* • **Barbra Streisand** *Funny Girl* • Patricia Neal *The Subject Was Roses* • Vanessa Redgrave *Isadora* • Joanne Woodward *Rachel, Rachel*
ACTOR IN A SUPPORTING ROLE: **Jack Albertson** *The Subject Was Roses* • Seymour Cassel *Faces* • Daniel Massey *Star!* • Jack Wild *Oliver!* • Gene Wilder *The Producers*
ACTRESS IN A SUPPORTING ROLE: **Ruth Gordon** *Rosemary's Baby* • Lynn Carlin *Faces* • Sondra Locke *The Heart Is a Lonely Hunter* • Kay Medford *Funny Girl* • Estelle Parsons *Rachel, Rachel*
WRITING (STORY AND SCREENPLAY WRITTEN DIRECTLY FOR THE SCREEN): **Mel Brooks** *The Producers* • Stanley Kubrick, Arthur C Clarke *2001: a Space Odyssey* • Franco Solinas, Gillo Pontecorvo *The Battle of Algiers* • John Cassavetes *Faces* • Ira Wallach, Peter Ustinov *Hot Millions*
WRITING (SCREENPLAY BASED ON MATERIAL FROM ANOTHER MEDIUM): **James Goldman** *The Lion in Winter* • Neil Simon *The Odd Couple* • Vernon Harris *Oliver!* • Stewart Stern *Rachel, Rachel* • Roman Polanski *Rosemary's Baby*

Golden Globe Awards

BEST MOTION PICTURE – DRAMA: ***The Lion in Winter***
BEST MOTION PICTURE – COMEDY OR MUSICAL: ***Funny Girl***
BEST FOREIGN LANGUAGE FILM: ***Romeo and Juliet*** • ***War and Peace***
BEST DIRECTOR – MOTION PICTURE: **Paul Newman** *Rachel, Rachel*
BEST PERFORMANCE BY AN ACTOR IN A MOTION PICTURE – DRAMA: **Peter O'Toole** *The Lion in Winter*
BEST PERFORMANCE BY AN ACTRESS IN A MOTION PICTURE – DRAMA: **Joanne Woodward** *Rachel, Rachel*
BEST PERFORMANCE BY AN ACTOR IN A MOTION PICTURE – COMEDY OR MUSICAL: **Ron Moody** *Oliver!*
BEST PERFORMANCE BY AN ACTRESS IN A MOTION PICTURE – COMEDY OR MUSICAL: **Barbra Streisand** *Funny Girl*
BEST PERFORMANCE BY AN ACTOR IN A SUPPORTING ROLE – MOTION PICTURE: **Daniel Massey** *Star!*
BEST PERFORMANCE BY AN ACTRESS IN A SUPPORTING ROLE – MOTION PICTURE: **Ruth Gordon** *Rosemary's Baby*
BEST SCREENPLAY – MOTION PICTURE: **Stirling Silliphant** *Charly*

Berlin International Film Festival

GOLDEN BERLIN BEAR: ***Who Saw Him Die?***
SILVER BERLIN BEAR FOR THE BEST DIRECTOR: **Carlos Saura** *Peppermint Frappé*
SILVER BERLIN BEAR FOR THE BEST ACTOR: **Jean-Louis Trintignant** *L'Homme Qui Ment*
SILVER BERLIN BEAR FOR THE BEST ACTRESS: **Stéphane Audran** *Les Biches*

1969

British Film Academy Awards

BEST FILM: ***Midnight Cowboy*** • *Oh! What a Lovely War* • *Women in Love* • *Z*
BEST DIRECTOR: **John Schlesinger** *Midnight Cowboy* • Richard Attenborough *Oh! What a Lovely War* • Ken Russell *Women in Love* • Peter Yates *Bullitt*
BEST ACTOR: **Dustin Hoffman** *Midnight Cowboy* • **Dustin Hoffman** *John and Mary* • Alan Bates *Women in Love* • Walter Matthau *Hello, Dolly!* • Walter Matthau *The Secret Life of an American Wife* • Nicol Williamson *Inadmissible Evidence*
BEST ACTRESS: **Maggie Smith** *The Prime of Miss Jean Brodie* • Mia Farrow *John and Mary* • Mia Farrow *Rosemary's Baby* • Mia Farrow *Secret Ceremony* • Glenda Jackson *Women in Love* • Barbra Streisand *Funny Girl* • Barbra Streisand *Hello, Dolly!*
BEST SUPPORTING ACTOR: **Laurence Olivier** *Oh! What a Lovely War* • Jack Klugman *Goodbye, Columbus* • Jack Nicholson *Easy Rider* • Robert Vaughn *Bullitt*
BEST SUPPORTING ACTRESS: **Celia Johnson** *The Prime of Miss Jean Brodie* • Peggy Ashcroft *Three into Two Won't Go* • Pamela Franklin *The Prime of Miss Jean Brodie* • Mary Wimbush *Oh! What a Lovely War*
BEST SCREENPLAY: **Waldo Salt** *Midnight Cowboy* • Arnold Schulman *Goodbye, Columbus* • Larry Kramer *Women in Love* • Costa-Gavras, Jorge Semprun *Z*

Academy Awards

BEST PICTURE: ***Midnight Cowboy*** • *Anne of the Thousand Days* • *Butch Cassidy and the Sundance Kid* • *Hello, Dolly!* • *Z*
FOREIGN LANGUAGE FILM: ***Z*** • *Adalen 31* • *The Battle of Neretva* • *The Brothers Karamazov* • *My Night with Maud*
DIRECTING: **John Schlesinger** *Midnight Cowboy* • Costa-Gavras *Z* • George Roy Hill *Butch Cassidy and the Sundance Kid* • Arthur Penn *Alice's Restaurant* • Sydney Pollack *They Shoot Horses, Don't They?*
ACTOR: **John Wayne** *True Grit* • Richard Burton *Anne of the Thousand Days* • Dustin Hoffman *Midnight Cowboy* • Peter O'Toole *Goodbye, Mr Chips* • Jon Voight *Midnight Cowboy*
ACTRESS: **Maggie Smith** *The Prime of Miss Jean Brodie* • Geneviève Bujold *Anne of the Thousand Days* • Jane Fonda *They Shoot Horses, Don't They?* • Liza Minnelli *The Sterile Cuckoo* • Jean Simmons *The Happy Ending*
ACTOR IN A SUPPORTING ROLE: **Gig Young** *They Shoot Horses, Don't They?* • Rupert Crosse *The Reivers* • Elliott Gould *Bob & Carol & Ted & Alice* • Jack Nicholson *Easy Rider* • Anthony Quayle *Anne of the Thousand Days*
ACTRESS IN A SUPPORTING ROLE: **Goldie Hawn** *Cactus Flower* • Catherine Burns *Last Summer* • Dyan Cannon *Bob & Carol & Ted & Alice* • Sylvia Miles *Midnight Cowboy* • Susannah York *They Shoot Horses, Don't They?*
WRITING (STORY AND SCREENPLAY BASED ON MATERIAL NOT PREVIOUSLY PUBLISHED OR PRODUCED): **William Goldman** *Butch Cassidy and the Sundance Kid* • Paul Mazursky, Larry Tucker *Bob & Carol & Ted & Alice* • Nicola Badalucco, Enrico Medioli, Luchino Visconti *The Damned* • Peter Fonda, Dennis Hopper, Terry Southern *Easy Rider* • Walon Green, Sam Peckinpah, Roy N Sickner *The Wild Bunch*
WRITING (SCREENPLAY BASED ON MATERIAL FROM ANOTHER MEDIUM): **Waldo Salt** *Midnight Cowboy* • Bridget Boland, John Hale, Richard Sokolove *Anne of the Thousand Days* • Arnold Schulman *Goodbye, Columbus* • James Poe, Robert E Thompson *They Shoot Horses, Don't They?* • Costa-Gavras, Jorge Semprun *Z*

Golden Globe Awards

BEST MOTION PICTURE – DRAMA: ***Anne of the Thousand Days***
BEST MOTION PICTURE – COMEDY OR MUSICAL: ***The Secret of Santa Vittoria***
BEST FOREIGN LANGUAGE FILM: ***Oh! What a Lovely War*** • ***Z***
BEST DIRECTOR – MOTION PICTURE: **Charles Jarrott** *Anne of the Thousand Days*
BEST PERFORMANCE BY AN ACTOR IN A MOTION PICTURE – DRAMA: **John Wayne** *True Grit*
BEST PERFORMANCE BY AN ACTRESS IN A MOTION PICTURE – DRAMA: **Geneviève Bujold** *Anne of the Thousand Days*
BEST PERFORMANCE BY AN ACTOR IN A MOTION PICTURE – COMEDY OR MUSICAL: **Peter O'Toole** *Goodbye, Mr Chips*
BEST PERFORMANCE BY AN ACTRESS IN A MOTION PICTURE – COMEDY OR MUSICAL: **Patty Duke** *Me, Natalie*
BEST PERFORMANCE BY AN ACTOR IN A SUPPORTING ROLE – MOTION PICTURE: **Gig Young** *They Shoot Horses, Don't They?*
BEST PERFORMANCE BY AN ACTRESS IN A SUPPORTING ROLE – MOTION PICTURE: **Goldie Hawn** *Cactus Flower*
BEST SCREENPLAY – MOTION PICTURE: **John Hale**, **Bridget Boland** *Anne of the Thousand Days*

Cannes International Film Festival

GRAND PRIX: ***If...***
DIRECTOR: **Glauber Rocha** *Antonio das Mortes* • **Vojtech Jasny** *All My Good Countrymen*
ACTOR: **Jean-Louis Trintignant** *Z*
ACTRESS: **Vanessa Redgrave** *Isadora*

Berlin International Film Festival

GOLDEN BERLIN BEAR: ***Rani Radovi***

1970

British Film Academy Awards

BEST FILM: ***Butch Cassidy and the Sundance Kid*** • *Kes* • *MASH* • *Ryan's Daughter*
BEST DIRECTOR: **George Roy Hill** *Butch Cassidy and the Sundance Kid* • Robert Altman *MASH* • David Lean *Ryan's Daughter* • Ken Loach *Kes*
BEST ACTOR: **Robert Redford** *Butch Cassidy and the Sundance Kid* • **Robert Redford** *Downhill Racer* • **Robert Redford** *Tell Them Willie Boy Is Here* • Elliott Gould *Bob & Carol & Ted & Alice* • Elliott Gould *MASH* • Paul Newman *Butch Cassidy and the Sundance Kid* • George C Scott *Patton*
BEST ACTRESS: **Katharine Ross** *Butch Cassidy and the Sundance Kid* • **Katharine Ross** *Tell Them Willie Boy Is Here* • Jane Fonda *They Shoot Horses, Don't They?* • Goldie Hawn *Cactus Flower* • Goldie Hawn *There's a Girl in My Soup* • Sarah Miles *Ryan's Daughter*
BEST SUPPORTING ACTOR: **Colin Welland** *Kes* • Bernard Cribbins *The Railway Children* • John Mills *Ryan's Daughter* • Gig Young *They Shoot Horses, Don't They?*
BEST SUPPORTING ACTRESS: **Susannah York** *They Shoot Horses, Don't They?* • Evin Crowley *Ryan's Daughter* • Estelle Parsons *Watermelon Man* • Maureen Stapleton *Airport*
BEST SCREENPLAY: **William Goldman** *Butch Cassidy and the Sundance Kid* • Paul Mazursky, Larry Tucker *Bob & Carol & Ted & Alice* • Ken Loach, Tony Garnett, Barry Hines *Kes* • James Poe, Robert E Thompson *They Shoot Horses, Don't They?*

Academy Awards

BEST PICTURE: ***Patton*** • *Airport* • *Five Easy Pieces* • *Love Story* • *MASH*
FOREIGN LANGUAGE FILM: ***Investigation of a Citizen above Suspicion*** • *First Love* • *Hoa-Binh* • *Paix sur les Champs* • *Tristana*
DIRECTING: **Franklin J Schaffner** *Patton* • Robert Altman *MASH* • Federico Fellini *Satyricon* • Arthur Hiller *Love Story* • Ken Russell *Women in Love*
ACTOR: **George C Scott** *Patton* • Melvyn Douglas *I Never Sang for My Father* • James Earl Jones *The Great White Hope* • Jack Nicholson *Five Easy Pieces* • Ryan O'Neal *Love Story*
ACTRESS: **Glenda Jackson** *Women in Love* • Jane Alexander *The Great White Hope* • Ali MacGraw *Love Story* • Sarah Miles *Ryan's Daughter* • Carrie Snodgress *Diary of a Mad Housewife*
ACTOR IN A SUPPORTING ROLE: **John Mills** *Ryan's Daughter* • Richard Castellano *Lovers and Other Strangers* • Chief Dan George *Little Big Man* • Gene Hackman *I Never Sang for My Father* • John Marley *Love Story*
ACTRESS IN A SUPPORTING ROLE: **Helen Hayes** *Airport* • Karen Black *Five Easy Pieces* • Lee Grant *The Landlord* • Sally Kellerman *MASH* • Maureen Stapleton *Airport*
WRITING (STORY AND SCREENPLAY BASED ON FACTUAL MATERIAL OR MATERIAL NOT PREVIOUSLY PUBLISHED OR PRODUCED): **Francis Ford Coppola**, **Edmund H North** *Patton* • Carole Eastman, Bob Rafelson *Five Easy Pieces* • Norman Wexler *Joe* • Erich Segal *Love Story* • Eric Rohmer *My Night with Maud*
WRITING (SCREENPLAY BASED ON MATERIAL FROM ANOTHER MEDIUM): **Ring Lardner Jr** *MASH* • George Seaton *Airport* • Robert W Anderson *I Never Sang for My Father* • Renee Taylor, Joseph Bologna, David Zelag Goodman *Lovers and Other Strangers* • Larry Kramer *Women in Love*

Golden Globe Awards

BEST MOTION PICTURE – DRAMA: ***Love Story***
BEST MOTION PICTURE – COMEDY OR MUSICAL: ***MASH***
BEST FOREIGN LANGUAGE FILM: ***Women in Love*** • ***Rider on the Rain***
BEST DIRECTOR – MOTION PICTURE: **Arthur Hiller** *Love Story*
BEST PERFORMANCE BY AN ACTOR IN A MOTION PICTURE – DRAMA: **George C Scott** *Patton*
BEST PERFORMANCE BY AN ACTRESS IN A MOTION PICTURE – DRAMA: **Ali MacGraw** *Love Story*
BEST PERFORMANCE BY AN ACTOR IN A MOTION PICTURE – COMEDY OR MUSICAL: **Albert Finney** *Scrooge*
BEST PERFORMANCE BY AN ACTRESS IN A MOTION PICTURE – COMEDY OR MUSICAL: **Carrie Snodgress** *Diary of a Mad Housewife*
BEST PERFORMANCE BY AN ACTOR IN A SUPPORTING ROLE – MOTION PICTURE: **John Mills** *Ryan's Daughter*
BEST PERFORMANCE BY AN ACTRESS IN A SUPPORTING ROLE – MOTION PICTURE: **Karen Black** *Five Easy Pieces* • **Maureen Stapleton** *Airport*
BEST SCREENPLAY – MOTION PICTURE: **Erich Segal** *Love Story*

Cannes International Film Festival

GRAND PRIX: ***MASH***
DIRECTOR: **John Boorman** *Leo the Last*
ACTOR: **Marcello Mastroianni** *Jealousy, Italian Style*
ACTRESS: **Ottavia Piccolo** *Metello*

1971

British Film Academy Awards

BEST FILM: ***Sunday, Bloody Sunday*** • *Death in Venice* • *The Go-Between* • *Taking Off*
BEST DIRECTOR: **John Schlesinger** *Sunday, Bloody Sunday* • Milos Forman *Taking Off* • Joseph Losey *The Go-Between* • Luchino Visconti *Death in Venice*
BEST ACTOR: **Peter Finch** *Sunday, Bloody Sunday* • Dirk Bogarde *Death in Venice* • Albert Finney *Gumshoe* • Dustin Hoffman *Little Big Man*
BEST ACTRESS: **Glenda Jackson** *Sunday, Bloody Sunday* • Lynn Carlin *Taking Off* • Julie Christie *The Go-Between* • Jane Fonda *Klute* • Nanette Newman *The Raging Moon*
BEST SUPPORTING ACTOR: **Edward Fox**, Michael Gough *The Go-Between* • Ian Hendry *Get Carter* • John Hurt *10 Rillington Place*

BEST SUPPORTING ACTRESS: **Margaret Leighton** *The Go-Between* • Jane Asher *Deep End* • Georgia Brown *The Raging Moon* • Georgia Engel *Taking Off*
BEST SCREENPLAY: **Harold Pinter** *The Go-Between* • Neville Smith *Gumshoe* • Penelope Gilliatt *Sunday, Bloody Sunday* • Milos Forman, John Guare, Jean-Claude Carrière, John Klein *Taking Off*

Academy Awards

BEST PICTURE: ***The French Connection*** • *A Clockwork Orange* • *Fiddler on the Roof* • *The Last Picture Show* • *Nicholas and Alexandra*
FOREIGN LANGUAGE FILM: ***The Garden of the Finzi-Contini*s** • *Dodes'ka-Den* • *The Emigrants* • *The Policeman* • *Tchaikovsky*
DIRECTING: **William Friedkin** *The French Connection* • Peter Bogdanovich *The Last Picture Show* • Norman Jewison *Fiddler on the Roof* • Stanley Kubrick *A Clockwork Orange* • John Schlesinger *Sunday, Bloody Sunday*
ACTOR: **Gene Hackman** *The French Connection* • Peter Finch *Sunday, Bloody Sunday* • Walter Matthau *Kotch* • George C Scott *The Hospital* • Topol *Fiddler on the Roof*
ACTRESS: **Jane Fonda** *Klute* • Julie Christie *McCabe and Mrs Miller* • Glenda Jackson *Sunday, Bloody Sunday* • Vanessa Redgrave *Mary, Queen of Scots* • Janet Suzman *Nicholas and Alexandra*
ACTOR IN A SUPPORTING ROLE: **Ben Johnson**, Jeff Bridges *The Last Picture Show* • Leonard Frey *Fiddler on the Roof* • Richard Jaeckel *Sometimes a Great Notion* • Roy Scheider *The French Connection*
ACTRESS IN A SUPPORTING ROLE: **Cloris Leachman** *The Last Picture Show* • Ann-Margret *Carnal Knowledge* • Ellen Burstyn *The Last Picture Show* • Barbara Harris *Who Is Harry Kellerman, and Why Is He Saying Those Terrible Things about Me?* • Margaret Leighton *The Go-Between*
WRITING (STORY AND SCREENPLAY BASED ON FACTUAL MATERIAL OR MATERIAL NOT PREVIOUSLY PUBLISHED OR PRODUCED): **Paddy Chayefsky** *The Hospital* • Elio Petri, Ugo Pirro *Investigation of a Citizen above Suspicion* • Andy Lewis, Dave Lewis *Klute* • Herman Raucher *Summer of '42* • Penelope Gilliatt *Sunday, Bloody Sunday*
WRITING (SCREENPLAY BASED ON MATERIAL FROM ANOTHER MEDIUM): **Ernest Tidyman** *The French Connection* • Stanley Kubrick *A Clockwork Orange* • Bernardo Bertolucci *The Conformist* • Vittorio Bonicelli, Ugo Pirro *The Garden of the Finzi-Continis* • Peter Bogdanovich, Larry McMurtry *The Last Picture Show*

Golden Globe Awards

BEST MOTION PICTURE – DRAMA: ***The French Connection***
BEST MOTION PICTURE – COMEDY OR MUSICAL: ***Fiddler on the Roof***
BEST FOREIGN LANGUAGE FILM: ***The Policeman* • *Sunday, Bloody Sunday***
BEST DIRECTOR – MOTION PICTURE: **William Friedkin** *The French Connection*
BEST PERFORMANCE BY AN ACTOR IN A MOTION PICTURE – DRAMA: **Gene Hackman** *The French Connection*
BEST PERFORMANCE BY AN ACTRESS IN A MOTION PICTURE – DRAMA: **Jane Fonda** *Klute*
BEST PERFORMANCE BY AN ACTOR IN A MOTION PICTURE – COMEDY OR MUSICAL: **Topol** *Fiddler on the Roof*
BEST PERFORMANCE BY AN ACTRESS IN A MOTION PICTURE – COMEDY OR MUSICAL: **Twiggy** *The Boy Friend*
BEST PERFORMANCE BY AN ACTOR IN A SUPPORTING ROLE – MOTION PICTURE: **Ben Johnson** *The Last Picture Show*
BEST PERFORMANCE BY AN ACTRESS IN A SUPPORTING ROLE – MOTION PICTURE: **Ann-Margret** *Carnal Knowledge*
BEST SCREENPLAY – MOTION PICTURE: **Paddy Chayefsky** *The Hospital*

Cannes International Film Festival

GRAND PRIX: ***The Go-Between***
ACTOR: **Riccardo Cucciolla** *Sacco and Vanzetti*
ACTRESS: **Kitty Winn** *The Panic in Needle Park*

Berlin International Film Festival

GOLDEN BERLIN BEAR: ***The Garden of the Finzi-Continis***
SILVER BERLIN BEAR FOR THE BEST ACTOR: **Jean Gabin** *Le Chat*
SILVER BERLIN BEAR FOR THE BEST ACTRESS: **Shirley MacLaine** *Desperate Characters* • **Simone Signoret** *Le Chat*

1972

British Film Academy Awards

BEST FILM: ***Cabaret*** • *A Clockwork Orange* • *The French Connection* • *The Last Picture Show*
BEST DIRECTOR: **Bob Fosse** *Cabaret* • Peter Bogdanovich *The Last Picture Show* • William Friedkin *The French Connection* • Stanley Kubrick *A Clockwork Orange*
BEST ACTOR: **Gene Hackman** *The French Connection* • **Gene Hackman** *The Poseidon Adventure* • Marlon Brando *The Godfather* • Marlon Brando *The Nightcomers* • George C Scott *The Hospital* • George C Scott *They Might Be Giants* • Robert Shaw *Young Winston*
BEST ACTRESS: **Liza Minnelli** *Cabaret* • Stéphane Audran *Le Boucher* • Anne Bancroft *Young Winston* • Dorothy Tutin *Savage Messiah*
BEST SUPPORTING ACTOR: **Ben Johnson** *The Last Picture Show* • Max Adrian *The Boy Friend* • Robert Duvall *The Godfather* • Ralph Richardson *Lady Caroline Lamb*
BEST SUPPORTING ACTRESS: **Cloris Leachman** *The Last Picture Show* • Marisa Berenson *Cabaret* • Eileen Brennan *The Last Picture Show* • Shelley Winters *The Poseidon Adventure*
BEST SCREENPLAY: **Paddy Chayefsky** *The Hospital* • **Larry McMurtry, Peter Bogdanovich** *The Last Picture Show* • Jay Presson Allen *Cabaret* • Stanley Kubrick *A Clockwork Orange*

Academy Awards

BEST PICTURE: ***The Godfather*** • *Cabaret* • *Deliverance* • *The Emigrants* • *Sounder*
FOREIGN LANGUAGE FILM: ***The Discreet Charm of the Bourgeoisie*** • *The Dawns Here Are Quiet* • *I Love You Rosa* • *My Dearest Señorita* • *The New Land*
DIRECTING: **Bob Fosse** *Cabaret* • John Boorman *Deliverance* • Francis Ford Coppola *The Godfather* • Joseph L Mankiewicz *Sleuth* • Jan Troell *The Emigrants*
ACTOR: **Marlon Brando** *The Godfather* • Michael Caine, Laurence Olivier *Sleuth* • Peter O'Toole *The Ruling Class* • Paul Winfield *Sounder*
ACTRESS: **Liza Minnelli** *Cabaret* • Diana Ross *Lady Sings the Blues* • Maggie Smith *Travels with My Aunt* • Cicely Tyson *Sounder* • Liv Ullmann *The Emigrants*
ACTOR IN A SUPPORTING ROLE: **Joel Grey** *Cabaret* • Eddie Albert *The Heartbreak Kid* • James Caan, Robert Duvall, Al Pacino *The Godfather*
ACTRESS IN A SUPPORTING ROLE: **Eileen Heckart** *Butterflies Are Free* • Jeannie Berlin *The Heartbreak Kid* • Geraldine Page *Pete 'n' Tillie* • Susan Tyrrell *Fat City* • Shelley Winters *The Poseidon Adventure*
WRITING (STORY AND SCREENPLAY BASED ON FACTUAL MATERIAL OR MATERIAL NOT PREVIOUSLY PUBLISHED OR PRODUCED): **Jeremy Larner** *The Candidate* • Luis Buñuel, Jean-Claude Carrière *The Discreet Charm of the Bourgeoisie* • Chris Clark, Suzanne De Passe, Terence McCloy *Lady Sings the Blues* • Louis Malle *Le Souffle au Coeur* • Carl Foreman *Young Winston*
WRITING (SCREENPLAY BASED ON MATERIAL FROM ANOTHER MEDIUM): **Francis Ford Coppola, Mario Puzo** *The Godfather* • Jay Presson Allen *Cabaret* • Bengt Forslund, Jan Troell *The Emigrants* • Julius J Epstein *Pete 'n' Tillie* • Lonne Elder III *Sounder*

Golden Globe Awards

BEST MOTION PICTURE – DRAMA: ***The Godfather***
BEST MOTION PICTURE – COMEDY OR MUSICAL: ***Cabaret***
BEST FOREIGN LANGUAGE FILM: ***The Emigrants* • *The New Land* • *Young Winston***
BEST DIRECTOR – MOTION PICTURE: **Francis Ford Coppola** *The Godfather*
BEST PERFORMANCE BY AN ACTOR IN A MOTION PICTURE – DRAMA: **Marlon Brando** *The Godfather*
BEST PERFORMANCE BY AN ACTRESS IN A MOTION PICTURE – DRAMA: **Liv Ullmann** *The Emigrants*
BEST PERFORMANCE BY AN ACTOR IN A MOTION PICTURE – COMEDY OR MUSICAL: **Jack Lemmon** *Avanti!*
BEST PERFORMANCE BY AN ACTRESS IN A MOTION PICTURE – COMEDY OR MUSICAL: **Liza Minnelli** *Cabaret*
BEST PERFORMANCE BY AN ACTOR IN A SUPPORTING ROLE – MOTION PICTURE: **Joel Grey** *Cabaret*
BEST PERFORMANCE BY AN ACTRESS IN A SUPPORTING ROLE – MOTION PICTURE: **Shelley Winters** *The Poseidon Adventure*
BEST SCREENPLAY – MOTION PICTURE: **Francis Ford Coppola, Mario Puzo** *The Godfather*

Cannes International Film Festival

GRAND PRIX: ***The Working Class Goes to Heaven* • *The Mattei Affair***
DIRECTOR: **Miklos Jancso** *Még Kér a Nép*
ACTOR: **Jean Yanne** *Nous Ne Vieillirons Pas Ensemble*
ACTRESS: **Susannah York** *Images*

Berlin International Film Festival

GOLDEN BERLIN BEAR: ***The Canterbury Tales***
SILVER BERLIN BEAR FOR THE BEST DIRECTOR: **Jean-Pierre Blanc** *La Vieille Fille*
SILVER BERLIN BEAR FOR THE BEST ACTOR: **Alberto Sordi** *Detenuto in Attesa di Giudizio*
SILVER BERLIN BEAR FOR THE BEST ACTRESS: **Elizabeth Taylor** *Hammersmith Is Out*

1973

British Film Academy Awards

BEST FILM: ***Day for Night*** • *The Day of the Jackal* • *The Discreet Charm of the Bourgeoisie* • *Don't Look Now*
BEST DIRECTOR: **François Truffaut** *Day for Night* • Luis Buñuel *The Discreet Charm of the Bourgeoisie* • Nicolas Roeg *Don't Look Now* • Fred Zinnemann *The Day of the Jackal*
BEST ACTOR: **Walter Matthau** *Charley Varrick* • **Walter Matthau** *Pete 'n' Tillie* • Marlon Brando *Last Tango in Paris* • Laurence Olivier *Sleuth* • Donald Sutherland *Don't Look Now* • Donald Sutherland *Steelyard Blues*
BEST ACTRESS: **Stéphane Audran** *The Discreet Charm of the Bourgeoisie* • **Stéphane Audran** *Juste avant la Nuit* • Julie Christie *Don't Look Now* • Glenda Jackson *A Touch of Class* • Diana Ross *Lady Sings the Blues*
BEST SUPPORTING ACTOR: **Arthur Lowe** *O Lucky Man!* • Ian Bannen *The Offence* • Denholm Elliott *A Doll's House* • Michel Lonsdale *The Day of the Jackal*
BEST SUPPORTING ACTRESS: **Valentina Cortese** *Day for Night* • Rosemary Leach *That'll Be the Day* • Delphine Seyrig *The Day of the Jackal* • Ingrid Thulin *Cries and Whispers*
BEST SCREENPLAY: **Luis Buñuel, Jean-Claude Carrière** *The Discreet Charm of the Bourgeoisie* • Kenneth Ross *The Day of the Jackal* • Anthony Shaffer *Sleuth* • Melvin Frank, Jack Rose *A Touch of Class*

Academy Awards

BEST PICTURE: ***The Sting*** • *American Graffiti* • *Cries and Whispers* • *The Exorcist* • *A Touch of Class*
FOREIGN LANGUAGE FILM: ***Day for Night*** • *The House on Chelouche Street* • *The Invitation* • *The Pedestrian* • *Turkish Delight*
DIRECTING: **George Roy Hill** *The Sting* • Ingmar Bergman *Cries and Whispers* • Bernardo Bertolucci *Last Tango in Paris* • William Friedkin *The Exorcist* • George Lucas *American Graffiti*
ACTOR: **Jack Lemmon** *Save the Tiger* • Marlon Brando *Last Tango in Paris* • Jack Nicholson *The Last Detail* • Al Pacino *Serpico* • Robert Redford *The Sting*
ACTRESS: **Glenda Jackson** *A Touch of Class* • Ellen Burstyn *The Exorcist* • Marsha Mason *Cinderella Liberty* • Barbra Streisand *The Way We Were* • Joanne Woodward *Summer Wishes, Winter Dreams*
ACTOR IN A SUPPORTING ROLE: **John Houseman** *The Paper Chase* • Vincent Gardenia *Bang the Drum Slowly* • Jack Gilford *Save the Tiger* • Jason Miller *The Exorcist* • Randy Quaid *The Last Detail*
ACTRESS IN A SUPPORTING ROLE: **Tatum O'Neal** *Paper Moon* • Linda Blair *The Exorcist* • Candy Clark *American Graffiti* • Madeline Kahn *Paper Moon* • Sylvia Sidney *Summer Wishes, Winter Dreams*
WRITING (STORY AND SCREENPLAY BASED ON FACTUAL MATERIAL OR MATERIAL NOT PREVIOUSLY PUBLISHED OR PRODUCED): **David S Ward** *The Sting* • George Lucas, Gloria Katz, Willard Huyck *American Graffiti* • Ingmar Bergman *Cries and Whispers* • Steve Shagan *Save the Tiger* • Melvin Frank, Jack Rose *A Touch of Class*
WRITING (SCREENPLAY BASED ON MATERIAL FROM ANOTHER MEDIUM): **William Peter Blatty** *The Exorcist* • Robert Towne *The Last Detail* • James Bridges *The Paper Chase* • Alvin Sargent *Paper Moon* • Waldo Salt, Norman Wexler *Serpico*

Golden Globe Awards

BEST MOTION PICTURE – DRAMA: ***The Exorcist***
BEST MOTION PICTURE – COMEDY OR MUSICAL: ***American Graffiti***
BEST FOREIGN LANGUAGE FILM: ***The Pedestrian***
BEST DIRECTOR – MOTION PICTURE: **William Friedkin** *The Exorcist*
BEST PERFORMANCE BY AN ACTOR IN A MOTION PICTURE – DRAMA: **Al Pacino** *Serpico*
BEST PERFORMANCE BY AN ACTRESS IN A MOTION PICTURE – DRAMA: **Marsha Mason** *Cinderella Liberty*
BEST PERFORMANCE BY AN ACTOR IN A MOTION PICTURE – COMEDY OR MUSICAL: **George Segal** *A Touch of Class*
BEST PERFORMANCE BY AN ACTRESS IN A MOTION PICTURE – COMEDY OR MUSICAL: **Glenda Jackson** *A Touch of Class*
BEST PERFORMANCE BY AN ACTOR IN A SUPPORTING ROLE – MOTION PICTURE: **John Houseman** *The Paper Chase*
BEST PERFORMANCE BY AN ACTRESS IN A SUPPORTING ROLE – MOTION PICTURE: **Linda Blair** *The Exorcist*
BEST SCREENPLAY – MOTION PICTURE: **William Peter Blatty** *The Exorcist*

Cannes International Film Festival

GRAND PRIX: ***Scarecrow* • *The Hireling***
ACTOR: **Giancarlo Giannini** *Love and Anarchy*
ACTRESS: **Joanne Woodward** *The Effect of Gamma Rays on Man-in-the-Moon Marigolds*

Berlin International Film Festival

GOLDEN BERLIN BEAR: ***Distant Thunder***

1974

British Film Academy Awards

BEST FILM: ***Lacombe Lucien*** • *Chinatown* • *The Last Detail* • *Murder on the Orient Express*
BEST DIRECTOR: **Roman Polanski** *Chinatown* • Francis Ford Coppola *The Conversation* • Sidney Lumet *Murder on the Orient Express* • Louis Malle *Lacombe Lucien*
BEST ACTOR: **Jack Nicholson** *Chinatown* • **Jack Nicholson** *The Last Detail* • Albert Finney *Murder on the Orient Express* • Gene Hackman *The Conversation* • Al Pacino *Serpico*
BEST ACTRESS: **Joanne Woodward** *Summer Wishes, Winter Dreams* • Faye Dunaway *Chinatown* • Barbra Streisand *The Way We Were* • Cicely Tyson *The Autobiography of Miss Jane Pittman*
BEST SUPPORTING ACTOR: **John Gielgud** *Murder on the Orient Express* • Adam Faith *Stardust* • John Huston *Chinatown* • Randy Quaid *The Last Detail*
BEST SUPPORTING ACTRESS: **Ingrid Bergman** *Murder on the Orient Express* • Sylvia Sidney *Summer Wishes, Winter Dreams* • Sylvia Syms *The Tamarind Seed* • Cindy Williams *American Graffiti*
BEST SCREENPLAY: **Robert Towne** *Chinatown* • **Robert Towne** *The Last Detail* • Mel Brooks, Norman Steinberg, Andrew Bergman, Richard Pryor, Alan Uger *Blazing Saddles* • Francis Ford Coppola *The Conversation* • Louis Malle, Patrick Modiano *Lacombe Lucien*

Academy Awards

BEST PICTURE: ***The Godfather, Part II*** • *Chinatown* • *The Conversation* • *Lenny* • *The Towering Inferno*
FOREIGN LANGUAGE FILM: ***Amarcord*** • *Cats' Play* • *The Deluge* • *Lacombe Lucien* • *The Truce*
DIRECTING: **Francis Ford Coppola** *The Godfather, Part II* • John Cassavetes *A Woman under the Influence* • Bob

Fosse *Lenny* • Roman Polanski *Chinatown* • François Truffaut *Day for Night*
ACTOR: **Art Carney** *Harry and Tonto* • Albert Finney *Murder on the Orient Express* • Dustin Hoffman *Lenny* • Jack Nicholson *Chinatown* • Al Pacino *The Godfather, Part II*
ACTRESS: **Ellen Burstyn** *Alice Doesn't Live Here Anymore* • Diahann Carroll *Claudine* • Faye Dunaway *Chinatown* • Valerie Perrine *Lenny* • Gena Rowlands *A Woman under the Influence*
ACTOR IN A SUPPORTING ROLE: **Robert De Niro** *The Godfather, Part II* • Fred Astaire *The Towering Inferno* • Jeff Bridges *Thunderbolt and Lightfoot* • Michael V Gazzo, Lee Strasberg *The Godfather, Part II*
ACTRESS IN A SUPPORTING ROLE: **Ingrid Bergman** *Murder on the Orient Express* • Valentina Cortese *Day for Night* • Madeline Kahn *Blazing Saddles* • Diane Ladd *Alice Doesn't Live Here Anymore* • Talia Shire *The Godfather, Part II*
WRITING (ORIGINAL SCREENPLAY): **Robert Towne** *Chinatown* • Robert Getchell *Alice Doesn't Live Here Anymore* • Francis Ford Coppola *The Conversation* • François Truffaut, Suzanne Schiffman, Jean-Louis Richard *Day for Night* • Paul Mazursky, Josh Greenfeld *Harry and Tonto*
WRITING (SCREENPLAY ADAPTED FROM OTHER MATERIAL): **Francis Ford Coppola, Mario Puzo** *The Godfather, Part II* • Mordecai Richler, Lionel Chetwynd *The Apprenticeship of Duddy Kravitz* • Julian Barry *Lenny* • Paul Dehn *Murder on the Orient Express* • Mel Brooks, Gene Wilder *Young Frankenstein*

Golden Globe Awards

BEST MOTION PICTURE – DRAMA: ***Chinatown***
BEST MOTION PICTURE – COMEDY OR MUSICAL: ***The Mean Machine***
BEST FOREIGN LANGUAGE FILM: ***Scenes from a Marriage***
BEST DIRECTOR – MOTION PICTURE: **Roman Polanski** *Chinatown*
BEST PERFORMANCE BY AN ACTOR IN A MOTION PICTURE – DRAMA: **Jack Nicholson** *Chinatown*
BEST PERFORMANCE BY AN ACTRESS IN A MOTION PICTURE – DRAMA: **Gena Rowlands** *A Woman under the Influence*
BEST PERFORMANCE BY AN ACTOR IN A MOTION PICTURE – COMEDY OR MUSICAL: **Art Carney** *Harry and Tonto*
BEST PERFORMANCE BY AN ACTRESS IN A MOTION PICTURE – COMEDY OR MUSICAL: **Raquel Welch** *The Three Musketeers*
BEST PERFORMANCE BY AN ACTOR IN A SUPPORTING ROLE – MOTION PICTURE: **Fred Astaire** *The Towering Inferno*
BEST PERFORMANCE BY AN ACTRESS IN A SUPPORTING ROLE – MOTION PICTURE: **Karen Black** *The Great Gatsby*
BEST SCREENPLAY – MOTION PICTURE: **Robert Towne** *Chinatown*

Cannes International Film Festival

GRAND PRIX: ***The Conversation***
ACTOR: **Jack Nicholson** *The Last Detail*
ACTRESS: **Marie-José Nat** *Les Violons du Bal*
SCREENPLAY: **Steven Spielberg** *The Sugarland Express*

Berlin International Film Festival

GOLDEN BERLIN BEAR: ***The Apprenticeship of Duddy Kravitz***

1975

British Film Academy Awards

BEST FILM: ***Alice Doesn't Live Here Anymore*** • *Barry Lyndon* • *Dog Day Afternoon* • *Jaws*
BEST DIRECTOR: **Stanley Kubrick** *Barry Lyndon* • Sidney Lumet *Dog Day Afternoon* • Martin Scorsese *Alice Doesn't Live Here Anymore* • Steven Spielberg *Jaws*
BEST ACTOR: **Al Pacino** *Dog Day Afternoon* • **Al Pacino** *The Godfather, Part II* • Richard Dreyfuss *Jaws* • Gene Hackman *French Connection II* • Gene Hackman *Night Moves* • Dustin Hoffman *Lenny*
BEST ACTRESS: **Ellen Burstyn** *Alice Doesn't Live Here Anymore* • Anne Bancroft *The Prisoner of Second Avenue* • Valerie Perrine *Lenny* • Liv Ullmann *Scenes from a Marriage*
BEST SUPPORTING ACTOR: **Fred Astaire** *The Towering Inferno* • Martin Balsam *The Taking of Pelham One Two Three* • Burgess Meredith *The Day of the Locust* • Jack Warden *Shampoo*
BEST SUPPORTING ACTRESS: **Diane Ladd** *Alice Doesn't Live Here Anymore* • Ronee Blakley *Nashville* • Lelia Goldoni *Alice Doesn't Live Here Anymore* • Gwen Welles *Nashville*
BEST SCREENPLAY: **Robert Getchell** *Alice Doesn't Live Here Anymore* • Frank Pierson *Dog Day Afternoon* • Peter Benchley, Carl Gottlieb *Jaws* • Joan Tewkesbury *Nashville*

Academy Awards

BEST PICTURE: ***One Flew over the Cuckoo's Nest*** • *Barry Lyndon* • *Dog Day Afternoon* • *Jaws* • *Nashville*
FOREIGN LANGUAGE FILM: ***Dersu Uzala*** • *Land of Promise* • *Letters from Marusia* • *Sandakan No 8* • *Scent of a Woman*
DIRECTING: **Milos Forman** *One Flew over the Cuckoo's Nest* • Robert Altman *Nashville* • Federico Fellini *Amarcord* • Stanley Kubrick *Barry Lyndon* • Sidney Lumet *Dog Day Afternoon*
ACTOR: **Jack Nicholson** *One Flew over the Cuckoo's Nest* • Walter Matthau *The Sunshine Boys* • Al Pacino *Dog Day Afternoon* • Maximilian Schell *The Man in the Glass Booth* • James Whitmore *Give 'em Hell, Harry!*
ACTRESS: **Louise Fletcher** *One Flew over the Cuckoo's Nest* • Isabelle Adjani *The Story of Adèle H* • Ann-Margret *Tommy* • Glenda Jackson *Hedda* • Carol Kane *Hester Street*
ACTOR IN A SUPPORTING ROLE: **George Burns** *The Sunshine Boys* • Brad Dourif *One Flew over the Cuckoo's Nest* • Burgess Meredith *The Day of the Locust* • Chris Sarandon *Dog Day Afternoon* • Jack Warden *Shampoo*
ACTRESS IN A SUPPORTING ROLE: **Lee Grant** *Shampoo* • Ronee Blakley *Nashville* • Sylvia Miles *Farewell, My Lovely* • Lily Tomlin *Nashville* • Brenda Vaccaro *Once Is Not Enough*
WRITING (ORIGINAL SCREENPLAY): **Frank Pierson** *Dog Day Afternoon* • Federico Fellini, Tonino Guerra *Amarcord* • Claude Lelouch, Pierre Uytterhoeven *And Now My Love* • Ted Allan *Lies My Father Told Me* • Warren Beatty, Robert Towne *Shampoo*
WRITING (SCREENPLAY ADAPTED FROM OTHER MATERIAL): **Bo Goldman, Lawrence Hauben** *One Flew over the Cuckoo's Nest* • Stanley Kubrick *Barry Lyndon* • John Huston, Gladys Hill *The Man Who Would Be King* • Ruggero Maccari, Dino Risi *Scent of a Woman* • Neil Simon *The Sunshine Boys*

Golden Globe Awards

BEST MOTION PICTURE – DRAMA: ***One Flew over the Cuckoo's Nest***
BEST MOTION PICTURE – COMEDY OR MUSICAL: ***The Sunshine Boys***
BEST FOREIGN LANGUAGE FILM: ***Lies My Father Told Me***
BEST DIRECTOR – MOTION PICTURE: **Milos Forman** *One Flew over the Cuckoo's Nest*
BEST PERFORMANCE BY AN ACTOR IN A MOTION PICTURE – DRAMA: **Jack Nicholson** *One Flew over the Cuckoo's Nest*
BEST PERFORMANCE BY AN ACTRESS IN A MOTION PICTURE – DRAMA: **Louise Fletcher** *One Flew over the Cuckoo's Nest*
BEST PERFORMANCE BY AN ACTOR IN A MOTION PICTURE – COMEDY OR MUSICAL: **Walter Matthau** *The Sunshine Boys*
BEST PERFORMANCE BY AN ACTRESS IN A MOTION PICTURE – COMEDY OR MUSICAL: **Ann-Margret** *Tommy*
BEST PERFORMANCE BY AN ACTOR IN A SUPPORTING ROLE – MOTION PICTURE: **Richard Benjamin** *The Sunshine Boys*
BEST PERFORMANCE BY AN ACTRESS IN A SUPPORTING ROLE – MOTION PICTURE: **Brenda Vaccaro** *Once Is Not Enough*
BEST SCREENPLAY – MOTION PICTURE: **Lawrence Hauben, Bo Goldman** *One Flew over the Cuckoo's Nest*

Cannes International Film Festival

PALME D'OR: ***Chronicle of the Burning Years***
DIRECTOR: **Michel Brault** *Les Ordres* • **Costa-Gavras** *Section Spéciale*
ACTOR: **Vittorio Gassman** *Scent of a Woman*
ACTRESS: **Valerie Perrine** *Lenny*

Berlin International Film Festival

GOLDEN BERLIN BEAR: ***Adoption***
SILVER BERLIN BEAR FOR THE BEST DIRECTOR: **Sergei Solovyov** *Sto Dnej Possle Detstwa*
SILVER BERLIN BEAR FOR THE BEST ACTOR: **Vlastimil Brodsky** *Jacob the Liar*
SILVER BERLIN BEAR FOR THE BEST ACTRESS: **Kinuyo Tanaka** *Sandakan No 8*

1976

British Academy of Film & Television Arts Awards

BEST FILM: ***One Flew over the Cuckoo's Nest*** • *All the President's Men* • *Bugsy Malone* • *Taxi Driver*
BEST DIRECTOR: **Ken Kesey** *One Flew over the Cuckoo's Nest* • Alan J Pakula *All the President's Men* • Alan Parker *Bugsy Malone* • Martin Scorsese *Taxi Driver*
BEST ACTOR: **Jack Nicholson** *One Flew over the Cuckoo's Nest* • Robert De Niro *Taxi Driver* • Dustin Hoffman *All the President's Men* • Dustin Hoffman *Marathon Man* • Walter Matthau *The Bad News Bears* • Walter Matthau *The Sunshine Boys*
BEST ACTRESS: **Louise Fletcher** *One Flew over the Cuckoo's Nest* • Lauren Bacall *The Shootist* • Rita Moreno *The Ritz* • Liv Ullmann *Face to Face*
BEST SUPPORTING ACTOR: **Brad Dourif** *One Flew over the Cuckoo's Nest* • Martin Balsam *All the President's Men* • Michael Hordern *The Slipper and the Rose* • Jason Robards *All the President's Men*
BEST SUPPORTING ACTRESS: **Jodie Foster** *Bugsy Malone* • **Jodie Foster** *Taxi Driver* • Annette Crosbie *The Slipper and the Rose* • Vivien Merchant *The Homecoming* • Billie Whitelaw *The Omen*
BEST SCREENPLAY: **Alan Parker** *Bugsy Malone* • William Goldman *All the President's Men* • Lawrence Hauben, Bo Goldman *One Flew over the Cuckoo's Nest* • Neil Simon *The Sunshine Boys*

Academy Awards

BEST PICTURE: ***Rocky*** • *All the President's Men* • *Bound for Glory* • *Network* • *Taxi Driver*
FOREIGN LANGUAGE FILM: ***Black and White in Color*** • *Cousin, Cousine* • *Jacob the Liar* • *Nights and Days* • *Seven Beauties*
DIRECTING: **John G Avildsen** *Rocky* • Ingmar Bergman *Face to Face* • Sidney Lumet *Network* • Alan J Pakula *All the President's Men* • Lina Wertmuller *Seven Beauties*
ACTOR IN A LEADING ROLE: **Peter Finch** *Network* • Robert De Niro *Taxi Driver* • Giancarlo Giannini *Seven Beauties* • William Holden (2) *Network* • Sylvester Stallone *Rocky*
ACTRESS IN A LEADING ROLE: **Faye Dunaway** *Network* • Marie-Christine Barrault *Cousin, Cousine* • Talia Shire *Rocky* • Sissy Spacek *Carrie* • Liv Ullmann *Face to Face*
ACTOR IN A SUPPORTING ROLE: **Jason Robards** *All the President's Men* • Ned Beatty *Network* • Burgess Meredith *Rocky* • Laurence Olivier *Marathon Man* • Burt Young *Rocky*
ACTRESS IN A SUPPORTING ROLE: **Beatrice Straight** *Network* • Jane Alexander *All the President's Men* • Jodie Foster *Taxi Driver* • Lee Grant *Voyage of the Damned* • Piper Laurie *Carrie*
WRITING (SCREENPLAY WRITTEN DIRECTLY FOR THE SCREEN BASED ON FACTUAL MATERIAL OR ON STORY MATERIAL NOT PREVIOUSLY PUBLISHED OR PRODUCED): **Paddy Chayefsky** *Network* • Jean-Charles Tacchella, Danièle Thompson *Cousin, Cousine* • Walter Bernstein *The Front* • Sylvester Stallone *Rocky* • Lina Wertmuller *Seven Beauties*
WRITING (SCREENPLAY BASED ON MATERIAL FROM ANOTHER MEDIUM): **William Goldman** *All the President's Men* • Robert Getchell *Bound for Glory* • Federico Fellini, Bernardino Zapponi *Casanova* • Nicholas Meyer *The Seven-Per-Cent Solution* • David Butler, Steve Shagan *Voyage of the Damned*

Golden Globe Awards

BEST MOTION PICTURE – DRAMA: ***Rocky***
BEST MOTION PICTURE – COMEDY OR MUSICAL: ***A Star Is Born***
BEST FOREIGN LANGUAGE FILM: ***Face to Face***
BEST DIRECTOR – MOTION PICTURE: **Sidney Lumet** *Network*
BEST PERFORMANCE BY AN ACTOR IN A MOTION PICTURE – DRAMA: **Peter Finch** *Network*
BEST PERFORMANCE BY AN ACTRESS IN A MOTION PICTURE – DRAMA: **Faye Dunaway** *Network*
BEST PERFORMANCE BY AN ACTOR IN A MOTION PICTURE – COMEDY OR MUSICAL: **Kris Kristofferson** *A Star Is Born*
BEST PERFORMANCE BY AN ACTRESS IN A MOTION PICTURE – COMEDY OR MUSICAL: **Barbra Streisand** *A Star Is Born*
BEST PERFORMANCE BY AN ACTOR IN A SUPPORTING ROLE – MOTION PICTURE: **Laurence Olivier** *Marathon Man*
BEST PERFORMANCE BY AN ACTRESS IN A SUPPORTING ROLE – MOTION PICTURE: **Katharine Ross** *Voyage of the Damned*
BEST SCREENPLAY – MOTION PICTURE: **Paddy Chayefsky** *Network*

Cannes International Film Festival

PALME D'OR: ***Taxi Driver***
DIRECTOR: **Ettore Scola** *Down and Dirty*
ACTOR: **José Luis Gómez** *Pascual Duarte*
ACTRESS: **Mari Torocsik** *Deryne, Hol Van?* • **Dominique Sanda** *The Inheritance*

Berlin International Film Festival

GOLDEN BERLIN BEAR: ***Buffalo Bill and the Indians, or Sitting Bull's History Lesson***
SILVER BERLIN BEAR FOR THE BEST DIRECTOR: **Mario Monicelli** *Caro Michele*
SILVER BERLIN BEAR FOR THE BEST ACTOR: **Gerhard Olschewski** *Verlorenes Leben*
SILVER BERLIN BEAR FOR THE BEST ACTRESS: **Jadwiga Baranska** *Nights and Days*

1977

British Academy of Film & Television Arts Awards

BEST FILM: ***Annie Hall*** • *A Bridge Too Far* • *Network* • *Rocky*
BEST DIRECTOR: **Woody Allen** *Annie Hall* • Richard Attenborough *A Bridge Too Far* • John G Avildsen *Rocky* • Sidney Lumet *Network*
BEST ACTOR: **Peter Finch** *Network* • Woody Allen *Annie Hall* • William Holden (2) *Network* • Sylvester Stallone *Rocky*
BEST ACTRESS: **Diane Keaton** *Annie Hall* • Faye Dunaway *Network* • Shelley Duvall *3 Women* • Lily Tomlin *The Late Show*
BEST SUPPORTING ACTOR: **Edward Fox** *A Bridge Too Far* • Colin Blakely *Equus* • Robert Duvall *Network* • Zero Mostel *The Front*
BEST SUPPORTING ACTRESS: **Jenny Agutter** *Equus* • Geraldine Chaplin *Welcome to LA* • Joan Plowright *Equus* • Shelley Winters *Next Stop, Greenwich Village*
BEST SCREENPLAY: **Woody Allen, Marshall Brickman** *Annie Hall* • Peter Shaffer *Equus* • Paddy Chayefsky *Network* • Sylvester Stallone *Rocky*

Academy Awards

BEST PICTURE: ***Annie Hall*** • *The Goodbye Girl* • *Julia* • *Star Wars Episode IV: a New Hope* • *The Turning Point*
FOREIGN LANGUAGE FILM: **Madame Rosa** • *Iphigenia* • *Operation Thunderbolt* • *A Special Day* • *That Obscure Object of Desire*
DIRECTING: **Woody Allen** *Annie Hall* • George Lucas *Star Wars Episode IV: a New Hope* • Herbert Ross *The Turning Point* • Steven Spielberg *Close Encounters of the Third Kind* • Fred Zinnemann *Julia*
ACTOR IN A LEADING ROLE: **Richard Dreyfuss** *The Goodbye Girl* • Woody Allen *Annie Hall* • Richard Burton *Equus* • Marcello Mastroianni *A Special Day* • John Travolta *Saturday Night Fever*
ACTRESS IN A LEADING ROLE: **Diane Keaton** *Annie Hall* • Anne Bancroft *The Turning Point* • Jane Fonda *Julia* • Shirley MacLaine *The Turning Point* • Marsha Mason *The Goodbye Girl*
ACTOR IN A SUPPORTING ROLE: **Jason Robards** *Julia* • Mikhail Baryshnikov *The Turning Point* • Peter Firth *Equus* • Alec

Guinness *Star Wars Episode IV: a New Hope* • Maximilian Schell *Julia*
ACTRESS IN A SUPPORTING ROLE: **Vanessa Redgrave** *Julia* • Leslie Browne *The Turning Point* • Quinn Cummings *The Goodbye Girl* • Melinda Dillon *Close Encounters of the Third Kind* • Tuesday Weld *Looking for Mr Goodbar*
WRITING (SCREENPLAY WRITTEN DIRECTLY FOR THE SCREEN BASED ON FACTUAL MATERIAL OR ON STORY MATERIAL NOT PREVIOUSLY PUBLISHED OR PRODUCED): **Woody Allen, Marshall Brickman** *Annie Hall* • Neil Simon *The Goodbye Girl* • Robert Benton *The Late Show* • George Lucas *Star Wars Episode IV: a New Hope* • Arthur Laurents *The Turning Point*
WRITING (SCREENPLAY BASED ON MATERIAL FROM ANOTHER MEDIUM): **Alvin Sargent** *Julia* • Peter Shaffer *Equus* • Lewis John Carlino, Gavin Lambert *I Never Promised You a Rose Garden* • Larry Gelbart *Oh, God!* • Luis Buñuel, Jean-Claude Carrière *That Obscure Object of Desire*

Golden Globe Awards

BEST MOTION PICTURE – DRAMA: ***The Turning Point***
BEST MOTION PICTURE – COMEDY OR MUSICAL: ***The Goodbye Girl***
BEST FOREIGN LANGUAGE FILM: ***A Special Day***
BEST DIRECTOR – MOTION PICTURE: **Herbert Ross** *The Turning Point*
BEST PERFORMANCE BY AN ACTOR IN A MOTION PICTURE – DRAMA: **Richard Burton** *Equus*
BEST PERFORMANCE BY AN ACTRESS IN A MOTION PICTURE – DRAMA: **Jane Fonda** *Julia*
BEST PERFORMANCE BY AN ACTOR IN A MOTION PICTURE – COMEDY OR MUSICAL: **Richard Dreyfuss** *The Goodbye Girl*
BEST PERFORMANCE BY AN ACTRESS IN A MOTION PICTURE – COMEDY OR MUSICAL: **Marsha Mason** *The Goodbye Girl* • **Diane Keaton** *Annie Hall*
BEST PERFORMANCE BY AN ACTOR IN A SUPPORTING ROLE – MOTION PICTURE: **Peter Firth** *Equus*
BEST PERFORMANCE BY AN ACTRESS IN A SUPPORTING ROLE – MOTION PICTURE: **Vanessa Redgrave** *Julia*
BEST SCREENPLAY – MOTION PICTURE: **Neil Simon** *The Goodbye Girl*

Cannes International Film Festival

PALME D'OR: ***Padre Padrone***
ACTOR: **Fernando Rey** *Elisa, Mia Vida*
ACTRESS: **Shelley Duvall** *3 Women* • **Monique Mercure** *JA Martin Photographe*

Berlin International Film Festival

GOLDEN BERLIN BEAR: ***The Ascent***
SILVER BERLIN BEAR FOR THE BEST DIRECTOR: **Manuel Gutierrez Aragon** *Camada Negra*
SILVER BERLIN BEAR FOR THE BEST ACTOR: **Fernando Fernán Gómez** *El Anacoreta*
SILVER BERLIN BEAR FOR THE BEST ACTRESS: **Lily Tomlin** *The Late Show*

1978

British Academy of Film & Television Arts Awards

BEST FILM: ***Julia*** • *Close Encounters of the Third Kind* • *Midnight Express* • *Star Wars Episode IV: a New Hope*
BEST DIRECTOR: **Alan Parker** *Midnight Express* • Robert Altman *A Wedding* • Steven Spielberg *Close Encounters of the Third Kind* • Fred Zinnemann *Julia*
BEST ACTOR: **Richard Dreyfuss** *The Goodbye Girl* • Brad Davis *Midnight Express* • Anthony Hopkins *Magic* • Peter Ustinov *Death on the Nile*
BEST ACTRESS: **Jane Fonda** *Julia* • Anne Bancroft *The Turning Point* • Jill Clayburgh *An Unmarried Woman* • Marsha Mason *The Goodbye Girl*
BEST SUPPORTING ACTOR: **John Hurt** *Midnight Express* • Gene Hackman *Superman* • Jason Robards *Julia* • François Truffaut *Close Encounters of the Third Kind*
BEST SUPPORTING ACTRESS: **Geraldine Page** *Interiors* • Angela Lansbury, Maggie Smith *Death on the Nile* • Mona Washbourne *Stevie*
BEST SCREENPLAY: **Alvin Sargent** *Julia* • Steven Spielberg *Close Encounters of the Third Kind* • Neil Simon *The Goodbye Girl* • John Considine, Patricia Resnick, Allan Nicholls, Robert Altman *A Wedding*

Academy Awards

BEST PICTURE: ***The Deer Hunter*** • *Coming Home* • *Heaven Can Wait* • *Midnight Express* • *An Unmarried Woman*
FOREIGN LANGUAGE FILM: ***Get out Your Handkerchiefs*** • *The Glass Cell* • *Hungarians* • *Viva Italia!* • *White Bim Black Ear*
DIRECTING: **Michael Cimino** *The Deer Hunter* • Woody Allen *Interiors* • Hal Ashby *Coming Home* • Warren Beatty, Buck Henry *Heaven Can Wait* • Alan Parker *Midnight Express*
ACTOR IN A LEADING ROLE: **Jon Voight** *Coming Home* • Warren Beatty *Heaven Can Wait* • Gary Busey *The Buddy Holly Story* • Robert De Niro *The Deer Hunter* • Laurence Olivier *The Boys from Brazil*
ACTRESS IN A LEADING ROLE: **Jane Fonda** *Coming Home* • Ingrid Bergman *Autumn Sonata* • Ellen Burstyn *Same Time, Next Year* • Jill Clayburgh *An Unmarried Woman* • Geraldine Page *Interiors*
ACTOR IN A SUPPORTING ROLE: **Christopher Walken** *The Deer Hunter* • Bruce Dern *Coming Home* • Richard Farnsworth *Comes a Horseman* • John Hurt *Midnight Express* • Jack Warden *Heaven Can Wait*
ACTRESS IN A SUPPORTING ROLE: **Maggie Smith** *California Suite* • Dyan Cannon *Heaven Can Wait* • Penelope Milford *Coming Home* • Maureen Stapleton *Interiors* • Meryl Streep *The Deer Hunter*
WRITING (SCREENPLAY WRITTEN DIRECTLY FOR THE SCREEN): **Nancy Dowd, Robert C Jones, Waldo Salt** *Coming Home* • Ingmar Bergman *Autumn Sonata* • Michael Cimino, Louis Garfinkle, Quinn Redeker, Deric Washburn *The Deer Hunter* • Woody Allen *Interiors* • Paul Mazursky *An Unmarried Woman*
WRITING (SCREENPLAY BASED ON MATERIAL FROM ANOTHER MEDIUM): **Oliver Stone** *Midnight Express* • Walter Newman *Bloodbrothers* • Neil Simon *California Suite* • Warren Beatty, Elaine May *Heaven Can Wait* • Bernard Slade *Same Time, Next Year*

Golden Globe Awards

BEST MOTION PICTURE – DRAMA: ***Midnight Express***
BEST MOTION PICTURE – COMEDY OR MUSICAL: ***Heaven Can Wait***
BEST FOREIGN LANGUAGE FILM: ***Autumn Sonata***
BEST DIRECTOR – MOTION PICTURE: **Michael Cimino** *The Deer Hunter*
BEST PERFORMANCE BY AN ACTOR IN A MOTION PICTURE – DRAMA: **Jon Voight** *Coming Home*
BEST PERFORMANCE BY AN ACTRESS IN A MOTION PICTURE – DRAMA: **Jane Fonda** *Coming Home*
BEST PERFORMANCE BY AN ACTOR IN A MOTION PICTURE – COMEDY OR MUSICAL: **Warren Beatty** *Heaven Can Wait*
BEST PERFORMANCE BY AN ACTRESS IN A MOTION PICTURE – COMEDY OR MUSICAL: **Ellen Burstyn** *Same Time, Next Year* • **Maggie Smith** *California Suite*
BEST PERFORMANCE BY AN ACTOR IN A SUPPORTING ROLE – MOTION PICTURE: **John Hurt** *Midnight Express*
BEST PERFORMANCE BY AN ACTRESS IN A SUPPORTING ROLE – MOTION PICTURE: **Dyan Cannon** *Heaven Can Wait*
BEST SCREENPLAY – MOTION PICTURE: **Oliver Stone** *Midnight Express*

Cannes International Film Festival

PALME D'OR: ***The Tree of Wooden Clogs***
DIRECTOR: **Nagisa Oshima** *Ai No Borei*
ACTOR: **Jon Voight** *Coming Home*
ACTRESS: **Jill Clayburgh** *An Unmarried Woman* • **Isabelle Huppert** *Violette Nozière*

Berlin International Film Festival

GOLDEN BERLIN BEAR: ***Las Truchas* • *Las Palabras de Max***
SILVER BERLIN BEAR FOR THE BEST DIRECTOR: **Georgi Djulgerov** *Avantage*
SILVER BERLIN BEAR FOR THE BEST ACTOR: **Craig Russell** *Outrageous!*
SILVER BERLIN BEAR FOR THE BEST ACTRESS: **Gena Rowlands** *Opening Night*

1979

British Academy of Film & Television Arts Awards

BEST FILM: ***Manhattan*** • *Apocalypse Now* • *The China Syndrome* • *The Deer Hunter*
BEST DIRECTOR: **Francis Ford Coppola** *Apocalypse Now* • Woody Allen *Manhattan* • Michael Cimino *The Deer Hunter* • John Schlesinger *Yanks*
BEST ACTOR: **Jack Lemmon** *The China Syndrome* • Woody Allen *Manhattan* • Robert De Niro *The Deer Hunter* • Martin Sheen *Apocalypse Now*
BEST ACTRESS: **Jane Fonda** *The China Syndrome* • Diane Keaton *Manhattan* • Maggie Smith *California Suite* • Meryl Streep *The Deer Hunter*
BEST SUPPORTING ACTOR: **Robert Duvall** *Apocalypse Now* • Denholm Elliott *Saint Jack* • John Hurt *Alien* • Christopher Walken *The Deer Hunter*
BEST SUPPORTING ACTRESS: **Rachel Roberts (1)** *Yanks* • Lisa Eichhorn *The Europeans* • Mariel Hemingway, Meryl Streep *Manhattan*
BEST SCREENPLAY: **Woody Allen, Marshall Brickman** *Manhattan* • Mike Gray, T S Cook, James Bridges *The China Syndrome* • Deric Washburn *The Deer Hunter* • Colin Welland, Walter Bernstein *Yanks*

Academy Awards

BEST PICTURE: ***Kramer vs Kramer*** • *All That Jazz* • *Apocalypse Now* • *Breaking Away* • *Norma Rae*
FOREIGN LANGUAGE FILM: ***The Tin Drum*** • *The Young Ladies of Wilko* • *Mama Turns a Hundred* • *Une Histoire Simple* • *To Forget Venice*
DIRECTING: **Robert Benton** *Kramer vs Kramer* • Francis Ford Coppola *Apocalypse Now* • Bob Fosse *All That Jazz* • Edouard Molinaro *La Cage aux Folles* • Peter Yates *Breaking Away*
ACTOR IN A LEADING ROLE: **Dustin Hoffman** *Kramer vs Kramer* • Jack Lemmon *The China Syndrome* • Al Pacino *...And Justice for All* • Roy Scheider *All That Jazz* • Peter Sellers *Being There*
ACTRESS IN A LEADING ROLE: **Sally Field** *Norma Rae* • Jill Clayburgh *Starting Over* • Jane Fonda *The China Syndrome* • Marsha Mason *Chapter Two* • Bette Midler *The Rose*
ACTOR IN A SUPPORTING ROLE: **Melvyn Douglas** *Being There* • Robert Duvall *Apocalypse Now* • Frederic Forrest *The Rose* • Justin Henry *Kramer vs Kramer* • Mickey Rooney *The Black Stallion*
ACTRESS IN A SUPPORTING ROLE: **Meryl Streep**, Jane Alexander *Kramer vs Kramer* • Barbara Barrie *Breaking Away* • Candice Bergen *Starting Over* • Mariel Hemingway *Manhattan*
WRITING (SCREENPLAY WRITTEN DIRECTLY FOR THE SCREEN): **Steve Tesich** *Breaking Away* • Valerie Curtin, Barry Levinson *...And Justice for All* • Robert Alan Arthur, Bob Fosse *All That Jazz* • James Bridges, T S Cook, Mike Gray *The China Syndrome* • Woody Allen, Marshall Brickman *Manhattan*
WRITING (SCREENPLAY BASED ON MATERIAL FROM ANOTHER MEDIUM): **Robert Benton** *Kramer vs Kramer* • Francis Ford Coppola, John Milius *Apocalypse Now* • Marcello Danon, Edouard Molinaro, Jean Poiret, Francis Veber *La Cage aux Folles* • Allan Burns *A Little Romance* • Harriet Frank Jr, Irving Ravetch *Norma Rae*

Golden Globe Awards

BEST MOTION PICTURE – DRAMA: ***Kramer vs Kramer***
BEST MOTION PICTURE – COMEDY OR MUSICAL: ***Breaking Away***
BEST FOREIGN LANGUAGE FILM: ***La Cage aux Folles***
BEST DIRECTOR – MOTION PICTURE: **Francis Ford Coppola** *Apocalypse Now*
BEST PERFORMANCE BY AN ACTOR IN A MOTION PICTURE – DRAMA: **Dustin Hoffman** *Kramer vs Kramer*
BEST PERFORMANCE BY AN ACTRESS IN A MOTION PICTURE – DRAMA: **Sally Field** *Norma Rae*
BEST PERFORMANCE BY AN ACTOR IN A MOTION PICTURE – COMEDY OR MUSICAL: **Peter Sellers** *Being There*
BEST PERFORMANCE BY AN ACTRESS IN A MOTION PICTURE – COMEDY OR MUSICAL: **Bette Midler** *The Rose*
BEST PERFORMANCE BY AN ACTOR IN A SUPPORTING ROLE – MOTION PICTURE: **Robert Duvall** *Apocalypse Now* • **Melvyn Douglas** *Being There*
BEST PERFORMANCE BY AN ACTRESS IN A SUPPORTING ROLE – MOTION PICTURE: **Meryl Streep** *Kramer vs Kramer*
BEST SCREENPLAY – MOTION PICTURE: **Robert Benton** *Kramer vs Kramer*

Cannes International Film Festival

PALME D'OR: ***The Tin Drum* • *Apocalypse Now***
DIRECTOR: **Terrence Malick** *Days of Heaven*
ACTOR: **Jack Lemmon** *The China Syndrome*
ACTRESS: **Sally Field** *Norma Rae*
SUPPORTING ACTOR: **Stefano Madia** *Caro Papà*
SUPPORTING ACTRESS: **Eva Mattes** *Woyzeck*

Berlin International Film Festival

GOLDEN BERLIN BEAR: ***David***
SILVER BERLIN BEAR FOR THE BEST DIRECTOR: **Astrid Henning-Jensen** *Vinterborn*
SILVER BERLIN BEAR FOR THE BEST ACTOR: **Michele Placido** *Ernesto*
SILVER BERLIN BEAR FOR THE BEST ACTRESS: **Hanna Schygulla** *The Marriage of Maria Braun*

1980

British Academy of Film & Television Arts Awards

BEST FILM: ***The Elephant Man*** • *Being There* • *Kagemusha* • *Kramer vs Kramer*
BEST DIRECTOR: **Akira Kurosawa** *Kagemusha* • Robert Benton *Kramer vs Kramer* • David Lynch *The Elephant Man* • Alan Parker *Fame*
BEST ACTOR: **John Hurt** *The Elephant Man* • Dustin Hoffman *Kramer vs Kramer* • Roy Scheider *All That Jazz* • Peter Sellers *Being There*
BEST ACTRESS: **Judy Davis** *My Brilliant Career* • Shirley MacLaine *Being There* • Bette Midler *The Rose* • Meryl Streep *Kramer vs Kramer*
BEST SCREENPLAY: **Jerzy Kosinski** *Being There* • Jim Abrahams, David Zucker, Jerry Zucker *Airplane!* • Christopher de Vore, Eric Bergren, David Lynch *The Elephant Man* • Robert Benton *Kramer vs Kramer*

Academy Awards

BEST PICTURE: ***Ordinary People*** • *Coal Miner's Daughter* • *The Elephant Man* • *Raging Bull* • *Tess*
FOREIGN LANGUAGE FILM: ***Moscow Distrusts Tears*** • *Confidence* • *Kagemusha* • *The Last Metro* • *The Nest*
DIRECTING: **Robert Redford** *Ordinary People* • David Lynch *The Elephant Man* • Roman Polanski *Tess* • Richard Rush *The Stunt Man* • Martin Scorsese *Raging Bull*
ACTOR IN A LEADING ROLE: **Robert De Niro** *Raging Bull* • Robert Duvall *The Great Santini* • John Hurt *The Elephant Man* • Jack Lemmon *Tribute* • Peter O'Toole *The Stunt Man*
ACTRESS IN A LEADING ROLE: **Sissy Spacek** *Coal Miner's Daughter* • Ellen Burstyn *Resurrection* • Goldie Hawn *Private Benjamin* • Mary Tyler Moore *Ordinary People* • Gena Rowlands *Gloria*
ACTOR IN A SUPPORTING ROLE: **Timothy Hutton**, Judd Hirsch *Ordinary People* • Michael O'Keefe *The Great Santini* • Joe Pesci *Raging Bull* • Jason Robards *Melvin and Howard*
ACTRESS IN A SUPPORTING ROLE: **Mary Steenburgen** *Melvin and Howard* • Eileen Brennan *Private Benjamin* • Eva Le Gallienne *Resurrection* • Cathy Moriarty *Raging Bull* • Diana Scarwid *Inside Moves: the Guys from Max's Bar*
WRITING (SCREENPLAY WRITTEN DIRECTLY FOR THE SCREEN): **Bo Goldman** *Melvin and Howard* • W D Richter, Arthur Ross *Brubaker* • Christopher Gore *Fame* • Jean Gruault *Mon Oncle d'Amérique* • Nancy Myers, Harvey Miller, Charles Shyer *Private Benjamin*
WRITING (SCREENPLAY BASED ON MATERIAL FROM ANOTHER MEDIUM): **Alvin Sargent** *Ordinary People* • Bruce Beresford, Jonathan Hardy, David Stevens *Breaker Morant* • Tom Rickman *Coal Miner's Daughter* • Christopher de Vore, Eric Bergren, David Lynch *The Elephant Man* • Richard Rush, Lawrence B Marcus *The Stunt Man*

Golden Globe Awards

Best Motion Picture – Drama: ***Ordinary People***
Best Motion Picture – Comedy or Musical: ***Coal Miner's Daughter***
Best Foreign Language Film: ***Tess***
Best Director – Motion Picture: **Robert Redford** *Ordinary People*
Best Performance by an Actor in a Motion Picture – Drama: **Robert De Niro** *Raging Bull*
Best Performance by an Actress in a Motion Picture – Drama: **Mary Tyler Moore** *Ordinary People*
Best Performance by an Actor in a Motion Picture – Comedy or Musical: **Ray Sharkey** *The Idolmaker*
Best Performance by an Actress in a Motion Picture – Comedy or Musical: **Sissy Spacek** *Coal Miner's Daughter*
Best Performance by an Actor in a Supporting Role – Motion Picture: **Timothy Hutton** *Ordinary People*
Best Performance by an Actress in a Supporting Role – Motion Picture: **Mary Steenburgen** *Melvin and Howard*
Best Screenplay – Motion Picture: **William Peter Blatty** *The Ninth Configuration*

Cannes International Film Festival

Palme D'or: ***Kagemusha* • *All That Jazz***
Actor: **Michel Piccoli** *Leap into the Void*
Actress: **Anouk Aimée** *Leap into the Void*
Supporting Actor: **Jack Thompson** *Breaker Morant*
Supporting Actress: **Carla Gravina** *La Terrazza* • **Milena Dravic** *Poseban Tretman*
Screenplay: **Agenore Incrocci, Furio Scarpelli, Ettore Scola** *La Terrazza*

Berlin International Film Festival

Golden Berlin Bear: ***Heartland* • *Palermo oder Wolfsburg***
Silver Berlin Bear for the Best Director: **István Szabó** *Confidence*
Silver Berlin Bear for the Best Actor: **Andrzej Seweryn** *The Conductor*
Silver Berlin Bear for the Best Actress: **Renate Krössner** *Solo Sunny*

1981

British Academy of Film & Television Arts Awards

Best Film: ***Chariots of Fire*** • *Atlantic City, USA* • *The French Lieutenant's Woman* • *Gregory's Girl* • *Raiders of the Lost Ark*
Best Director: **Louis Malle** *Atlantic City, USA* • Bill Forsyth *Gregory's Girl* • Hugh Hudson *Chariots of Fire* • Karel Reisz *The French Lieutenant's Woman*
Best Actor: **Burt Lancaster** *Atlantic City, USA* • Robert De Niro *Raging Bull* • Bob Hoskins *The Long Good Friday* • Jeremy Irons *The French Lieutenant's Woman*
Best Actress: **Meryl Streep** *The French Lieutenant's Woman* • Mary Tyler Moore *Ordinary People* • Maggie Smith *Quartet* • Sissy Spacek *Coal Miner's Daughter*
Best Supporting Artist: **Ian Holm** *Chariots of Fire* • Denholm Elliott *Raiders of the Lost Ark* • John Gielgud *Arthur* • Nigel Havers *Chariots of Fire*
Best Screenplay: **Bill Forsyth** *Gregory's Girl* • John Guare *Atlantic City, USA* • Colin Welland *Chariots of Fire* • Harold Pinter *The French Lieutenant's Woman*

Academy Awards

Best Picture: ***Chariots of Fire*** • *Atlantic City, USA* • *On Golden Pond* • *Raiders of the Lost Ark* • *Reds*
Foreign Language Film: ***Mephisto*** • *The Boat Is Full* • *Man of Iron* • *Muddy River* • *Three Brothers*
Directing: **Warren Beatty** *Reds* • Hugh Hudson *Chariots of Fire* • Louis Malle *Atlantic City, USA* • Mark Rydell *On Golden Pond* • Steven Spielberg *Raiders of the Lost Ark*
Actor in a Leading Role: **Henry Fonda** *On Golden Pond* • Warren Beatty *Reds* • Burt Lancaster *Atlantic City, USA* • Dudley Moore *Arthur* • Paul Newman *Absence of Malice*
Actress in a Leading Role: **Katharine Hepburn** *On Golden Pond* • Diane Keaton *Reds* • Marsha Mason *Only When I Laugh* • Susan Sarandon *Atlantic City, USA* • Meryl Streep *The French Lieutenant's Woman*
Actor in a Supporting Role: **John Gielgud** *Arthur* • James Coco *Only When I Laugh* • Ian Holm *Chariots of Fire* • Jack Nicholson *Reds* • Howard E Rollins Jr *Ragtime*
Actress in a Supporting Role: **Maureen Stapleton** *Reds* • Melinda Dillon *Absence of Malice* • Jane Fonda *On Golden Pond* • Joan Hackett *Only When I Laugh* • Elizabeth McGovern *Ragtime*
Writing (Screenplay Written Directly for the Screen): **Colin Welland** *Chariots of Fire* • Kurt Luedtke *Absence of Malice* • Steve Gordon *Arthur* • John Guare *Atlantic City, USA* • Warren Beatty, Trevor Griffiths *Reds*
Writing (Screenplay Based On Material From Another Medium): **Ernest Thompson** *On Golden Pond* • Harold Pinter *The French Lieutenant's Woman* • Dennis Potter *Pennies from Heaven* • Jay Presson Allen, Sidney Lumet *Prince of the City* • Michael Weller *Ragtime*

Golden Globe Awards

Best Motion Picture – Drama: ***On Golden Pond***
Best Motion Picture – Comedy or Musical: ***Arthur***
Best Foreign Language Film: ***Chariots of Fire***
Best Director – Motion Picture: **Warren Beatty** *Reds*
Best Performance by an Actor in a Motion Picture – Drama: **Henry Fonda** *On Golden Pond*
Best Performance by an Actress in a Motion Picture – Drama: **Meryl Streep** *The French Lieutenant's Woman*
Best Performance by an Actor in a Motion Picture – Comedy or Musical: **Dudley Moore** *Arthur*
Best Performance by an Actress in a Motion Picture – Comedy or Musical: **Bernadette Peters** *Pennies from Heaven*
Best Performance by an Actor in a Supporting Role – Motion Picture: **John Gielgud** *Arthur*
Best Performance by an Actress in a Supporting Role – Motion Picture: **Joan Hackett** *Only When I Laugh*
Best Screenplay – Motion Picture: **Ernest Thompson** *On Golden Pond*

Cannes International Film Festival

Palme D'or: ***Man of Iron***
Actor: **Ugo Tognazzi** *The Tragedy of a Ridiculous Man*
Actress: **Isabelle Adjani** *Quartet* • **Isabelle Adjani** *Possession*
Supporting Actor: **Ian Holm** *Chariots of Fire*
Supporting Actress: **Elena Solovei** *Grouppa Krovi Nol*
Screenplay: **Peter Dobai, István Szabó** *Mephisto*

Berlin International Film Festival

Golden Berlin Bear: ***Deprisa, Deprisa***
Silver Berlin Bear for the Best Actor: **Jack Lemmon** *Tribute* • **Anatoli Solinitsin** *Twenty Six Days in the Life of Dostoevsky*
Silver Berlin Bear for the Best Actress: **Barbara Grabowska** *Goraczka*

1982

British Academy of Film & Television Arts Awards

Best Film: ***Gandhi*** • *ET the Extra-Terrestrial* • *Missing* • *On Golden Pond*
Best Foreign Language Film: ***Christ Stopped at Eboli*** • *Das Boot* • *Diva* • *Fitzcarraldo*
Best Director: **Richard Attenborough** *Gandhi* • Costa-Gavras *Missing* • Mark Rydell *On Golden Pond* • Steven Spielberg *ET the Extra-Terrestrial*
Best Actor: **Ben Kingsley** *Gandhi* • Warren Beatty *Reds* • Albert Finney *Shoot the Moon* • Henry Fonda *On Golden Pond* • Jack Lemmon *Missing*
Best Actress: **Katharine Hepburn** *On Golden Pond* • Diane Keaton *Reds* • Jennifer Kendal *36 Chowringhee Lane* • Sissy Spacek *Missing*
Best Supporting Actor: **Jack Nicholson** *Reds* • Frank Finlay *The Return of the Soldier* • Edward Fox, Roshan Seth *Gandhi*
Best Supporting Actress: **Rohini Hattangady**, Candice Bergen *Gandhi* • Jane Fonda *On Golden Pond* • **Maureen Stapleton** *Reds*
Best Screenplay: **Costa-Gavras, Donald Stewart (2)** *Missing* • Melissa Mathison *ET the Extra-Terrestrial* • John Briley *Gandhi* • Ernest Thompson *On Golden Pond*

Academy Awards

Best Picture: ***Gandhi*** • *ET the Extra-Terrestrial* • *Missing* • *Tootsie* • *The Verdict*
Foreign Language Film: ***Begin the Beguine*** • *Alsino and the Condor* • *Clean Slate* • *The Flight of the Eagle* • *Private Life*
Directing: **Richard Attenborough** *Gandhi* • Sidney Lumet *The Verdict* • Sydney Pollack *Tootsie* • Wolfgang Petersen *Das Boot* • Steven Spielberg *ET the Extra-Terrestrial*
Actor in a Leading Role: **Ben Kingsley** *Gandhi* • Dustin Hoffman *Tootsie* • Jack Lemmon *Missing* • Paul Newman *The Verdict* • Peter O'Toole *My Favorite Year*
Actress in a Leading Role: **Meryl Streep** *Sophie's Choice* • Julie Andrews *Victor/Victoria* • Jessica Lange *Frances* • Sissy Spacek *Missing* • Debra Winger *An Officer and a Gentleman*
Actor in a Supporting Role: **Louis Gossett Jr** *An Officer and a Gentleman* • Charles Durning *The Best Little Whorehouse in Texas* • John Lithgow *The World According to Garp* • James Mason *The Verdict* • Robert Preston *Victor/Victoria*
Actress in a Supporting Role: **Jessica Lange** *Tootsie* • Glenn Close *The World According to Garp* • Teri Garr *Tootsie* • Kim Stanley *Frances* • Lesley Ann Warren *Victor/Victoria*
Writing (Screenplay Written Directly for the Screen): **John Briley** *Gandhi* • Barry Levinson *Diner* • Melissa Mathison *ET the Extra-Terrestrial* • Douglas Day Stewart *An Officer and a Gentleman* • Larry Gelbart, Don McGuire, Murray Schisgal *Tootsie*
Writing (Screenplay Based On Material From Another Medium): **Costa-Gavras, Donald Stewart (2)** *Missing* • Wolfgang Petersen *Das Boot* • Alan J Pakula *Sophie's Choice* • David Mamet *The Verdict* • Blake Edwards *Victor/Victoria*

Golden Globe Awards

Best Motion Picture – Drama: ***ET the Extra-Terrestrial***
Best Motion Picture – Comedy or Musical: ***Tootsie***
Best Foreign Language Film: ***Gandhi***
Best Director – Motion Picture: **Richard Attenborough** *Gandhi*
Best Performance by an Actor in a Motion Picture – Drama: **Ben Kingsley** *Gandhi*
Best Performance by an Actress in a Motion Picture – Drama: **Meryl Streep** *Sophie's Choice*
Best Performance by an Actor in a Motion Picture – Comedy or Musical: **Dustin Hoffman** *Tootsie*
Best Performance by an Actress in a Motion Picture – Comedy or Musical: **Julie Andrews** *Victor/Victoria*
Best Performance by an Actor in a Supporting Role – Motion Picture: **Louis Gossett Jr** *An Officer and a Gentleman*
Best Performance by an Actress in a Supporting Role – Motion Picture: **Jessica Lange** *Tootsie*
Best Screenplay – Motion Picture: **John Briley** *Gandhi*

Cannes International Film Festival

Palme D'or: ***Missing* • *Yol***
Director: **Werner Herzog** *Fitzcarraldo*
Actor: **Jack Lemmon** *Missing*
Actress: **Jadwiga Jankowska-Cieslak** *Another Way*
Screenplay: **Jerzy Skolimowski** *Moonlighting*

Berlin International Film Festival

Golden Berlin Bear: ***Veronika Voss***
Silver Berlin Bear for the Best Director: **Mario Monicelli** *Il Marchese del Grillo*
Silver Berlin Bear for the Best Actor: **Michel Piccoli** *A Strange Affair* • **Stellan Skarsgård** *The Simple-Minded Murderer*
Silver Berlin Bear for the Best Actress: **Katrin Sass** *Bürgschaft für ein Jahr*

1983

British Academy of Film & Television Arts Awards

Best Film: ***Educating Rita*** • *Heat and Dust* • *Local Hero* • *Tootsie*
Best Foreign Language Film: ***Danton*** • *Confidentially Yours* • *Fanny and Alexander* • *La Traviata*
Best Director: **Bill Forsyth** *Local Hero* • James Ivory *Heat and Dust* • Sydney Pollack *Tootsie* • Martin Scorsese *The King of Comedy*
Best Actor: **Michael Caine** *Educating Rita* • **Dustin Hoffman** *Tootsie* • Michael Caine *The Honorary Consul* • Robert De Niro *The King of Comedy*
Best Actress: **Julie Walters** *Educating Rita* • Jessica Lange *Tootsie* • Phyllis Logan *Another Time, Another Place* • Meryl Streep *Sophie's Choice*
Best Supporting Actor: **Denholm Elliott** *Trading Places* • Bob Hoskins *The Honorary Consul* • Burt Lancaster *Local Hero* • Jerry Lewis *The King of Comedy*
Best Supporting Actress: **Jamie Lee Curtis** *Trading Places* • Teri Garr *Tootsie* • Rosemary Harris *The Ploughman's Lunch* • Maureen Lipman *Educating Rita*
Best Original Screenplay: **Paul D Zimmerman** *The King of Comedy* • Bill Forsyth *Local Hero* • Timothy Harris, Herschel Weingrod *Trading Places* • Woody Allen *Zelig*
Best Adapted Screenplay: **Ruth Prawer Jhabvala** *Heat and Dust* • Harold Pinter *Betrayal* • Willy Russell *Educating Rita* • Larry Gelbart, Murray Schisgal *Tootsie*

Academy Awards

Best Picture: ***Terms of Endearment*** • *The Big Chill* • *The Dresser* • *The Right Stuff* • *Tender Mercies*
Foreign Language Film: ***Fanny and Alexander*** • *Le Bal* • *Carmen* • *Entre Nous* • *Job's Revolt*
Directing: **James L Brooks** *Terms of Endearment* • Bruce Beresford *Tender Mercies* • Ingmar Bergman *Fanny and Alexander* • Mike Nichols *Silkwood* • Peter Yates *The Dresser*
Actor in a Leading Role: **Robert Duvall** *Tender Mercies* • Michael Caine *Educating Rita* • Tom Conti *Reuben, Reuben* • Tom Courtenay, Albert Finney *The Dresser*
Actress in a Leading Role: **Shirley MacLaine** *Terms of Endearment* • Jane Alexander *Testament* • Meryl Streep *Silkwood* • Julie Walters *Educating Rita* • Debra Winger *Terms of Endearment*
Actor in a Supporting Role: **Jack Nicholson** *Terms of Endearment* • Charles Durning *To Be or Not to Be* • John Lithgow *Terms of Endearment* • Sam Shepard *The Right Stuff* • Rip Torn *Cross Creek*
Actress in a Supporting Role: **Linda Hunt** *The Year of Living Dangerously* • Cher *Silkwood* • Glenn Close *The Big Chill* • Amy Irving *Yentl* • Alfre Woodard *Cross Creek*
Writing (Screenplay Written Directly for the Screen): **Horton Foote** *Tender Mercies* • Lawrence Kasdan, Barbara Benedek *The Big Chill* • Ingmar Bergman *Fanny and Alexander* • Nora Ephron, Alice Arlen *Silkwood* • Lawrence Lasker, Walter F Parkes *WarGames*
Writing (Screenplay Based On Material From Another Medium): **James L Brooks** *Terms of Endearment* • Harold Pinter *Betrayal* • Ronald Harwood *The Dresser* • Willy Russell *Educating Rita* • Julius J Epstein *Reuben, Reuben*

Golden Globe Awards

Best Motion Picture – Drama: ***Terms of Endearment***
Best Motion Picture – Comedy or Musical: ***Yentl***
Best Foreign Language Film: ***Fanny and Alexander***
Best Director – Motion Picture: **Barbra Streisand** *Yentl*
Best Performance by an Actor in a Motion Picture – Drama: **Tom Courtenay** *The Dresser* • **Robert Duvall** *Tender Mercies*
Best Performance by an Actress in a Motion Picture – Drama: **Shirley MacLaine** *Terms of Endearment*
Best Performance by an Actor in a Motion Picture – Comedy or Musical: **Michael Caine** *Educating Rita*
Best Performance by an Actress in a Motion Picture – Comedy or Musical: **Julie Walters** *Educating Rita*
Best Performance by an Actor in a Supporting Role – Motion Picture: **Jack Nicholson** *Terms of Endearment*

BEST PERFORMANCE BY AN ACTRESS IN A SUPPORTING ROLE – MOTION PICTURE: **Cher** *Silkwood*
BEST SCREENPLAY – MOTION PICTURE: **James L Brooks** *Terms of Endearment*

Cannes International Film Festival

PALME D'OR: ***The Ballad of Narayama***
ACTOR: **Gian Maria Volonté** *The Death of Mario Ricci*
ACTRESS: **Hanna Schygulla** *Storia di Piera*

Berlin International Film Festival

GOLDEN BERLIN BEAR: ***Ascendancy* • *La Colmena***
SILVER BERLIN BEAR FOR THE BEST DIRECTOR: **Eric Rohmer** *Pauline at the Beach*
SILVER BERLIN BEAR FOR THE BEST ACTOR: **Bruce Dern** *That Championship Season*
SILVER BERLIN BEAR FOR THE BEST ACTRESS: **Evgenia Glushenko** *Wljubljon Po Sobstvennomu Zhelaniju*

1984

British Academy of Film & Television Arts Awards

BEST FILM: ***The Killing Fields*** • *The Dresser* • *Paris, Texas* • *A Private Function*
BEST FOREIGN LANGUAGE FILM: ***Carmen*** • *The Return of Martin Guerre* • *Swann in Love* • *Sunday in the Country*
BEST DIRECTOR: **Wim Wenders** *Paris, Texas* • Roland Joffé *The Killing Fields* • Sergio Leone *Once upon a Time in America* • Peter Yates *The Dresser*
BEST ACTOR: **Haing S Ngor** *The Killing Fields* • Tom Courtenay, Albert Finney *The Dresser* • Sam Waterston *The Killing Fields*
BEST ACTRESS: **Maggie Smith** *A Private Function* • Shirley MacLaine *Terms of Endearment* • Helen Mirren *Cal* • Meryl Streep *Silkwood*
BEST SUPPORTING ACTOR: **Denholm Elliott** *A Private Function* • Michael Elphick *Gorky Park* • Ian Holm, Ralph Richardson *Greystoke: the Legend of Tarzan, Lord of the Apes*
BEST SUPPORTING ACTRESS: **Liz Smith** *A Private Function* • Eileen Atkins *The Dresser* • Cher *Silkwood* • Tuesday Weld *Once upon a Time in America*
BEST ORIGINAL SCREENPLAY: **Woody Allen** *Broadway Danny Rose* • Lawrence Kasdan, Barbara Benedek *The Big Chill* • Bill Forsyth *Comfort and Joy* • Alan Bennett *A Private Function*
BEST ADAPTED SCREENPLAY: **Bruce Robinson** *The Killing Fields* • Julian Mitchell *Another Country* • Ronald Harwood *The Dresser* • Sam Shepard *Paris, Texas*

Academy Awards

BEST PICTURE: ***Amadeus*** • *The Killing Fields* • *A Passage to India* • *Places in the Heart* • *A Soldier's Story*
FOREIGN LANGUAGE FILM: ***Dangerous Moves*** • *Beyond the Walls* • *Camila* • *Double Feature* • *Wartime Romance*
DIRECTING: **Milos Forman** *Amadeus* • Woody Allen *Broadway Danny Rose* • Robert Benton *Places in the Heart* • Roland Joffé *The Killing Fields* • David Lean *A Passage to India*
ACTOR IN A LEADING ROLE: **F Murray Abraham** *Amadeus* • Jeff Bridges *Starman* • Albert Finney *Under the Volcano* • Tom Hulce *Amadeus* • Sam Waterston *The Killing Fields*
ACTRESS IN A LEADING ROLE: **Sally Field** *Places in the Heart* • Judy Davis *A Passage to India* • Jessica Lange *Country* • Vanessa Redgrave *The Bostonians* • Sissy Spacek *The River*
ACTOR IN A SUPPORTING ROLE: **Haing S Ngor** *The Killing Fields* • Adolph Caesar *A Soldier's Story* • John Malkovich *Places in the Heart* • Pat Morita *The Karate Kid* • Ralph Richardson *Greystoke: the Legend of Tarzan, Lord of the Apes*
ACTRESS IN A SUPPORTING ROLE: **Peggy Ashcroft** *A Passage to India* • Glenn Close *The Natural* • Lindsay Crouse *Places in the Heart* • Christine Lahti *Swing Shift* • Geraldine Page *The Pope of Greenwich Village*
WRITING (SCREENPLAY WRITTEN DIRECTLY FOR THE SCREEN): **Robert Benton** *Places in the Heart* • Daniel Petrie Jr, Danilo Bach *Beverly Hills Cop* • Woody Allen *Broadway Danny Rose* • Gregory Nava, Anna Thomas *El Norte* • Bruce Jay Friedman, Lowell Ganz, Brian Grazer, Babaloo Mandel *Splash*
WRITING (SCREENPLAY BASED ON MATERIAL FROM ANOTHER MEDIUM): **Peter Shaffer** *Amadeus* • Robert Towne, Michael Austin *Greystoke: the Legend of Tarzan, Lord of the Apes* • Bruce Robinson *The Killing Fields* • David Lean *A Passage to India* • Charles Fuller *A Soldier's Story*

Golden Globe Awards

BEST MOTION PICTURE – DRAMA: ***Amadeus***
BEST MOTION PICTURE – COMEDY OR MUSICAL: ***Romancing the Stone***
BEST FOREIGN LANGUAGE FILM: ***A Passage to India***
BEST DIRECTOR – MOTION PICTURE: **Milos Forman** *Amadeus*
BEST PERFORMANCE BY AN ACTOR IN A MOTION PICTURE – DRAMA: **F Murray Abraham** *Amadeus*
BEST PERFORMANCE BY AN ACTRESS IN A MOTION PICTURE – DRAMA: **Sally Field** *Places in the Heart*
BEST PERFORMANCE BY AN ACTOR IN A MOTION PICTURE – COMEDY OR MUSICAL: **Dudley Moore** *Micki & Maude*
BEST PERFORMANCE BY AN ACTRESS IN A MOTION PICTURE – COMEDY OR MUSICAL: **Kathleen Turner** *Romancing the Stone*
BEST PERFORMANCE BY AN ACTOR IN A SUPPORTING ROLE – MOTION PICTURE: **Haing S Ngor** *The Killing Fields*
BEST PERFORMANCE BY AN ACTRESS IN A SUPPORTING ROLE – MOTION PICTURE: **Peggy Ashcroft** *A Passage to India*
BEST SCREENPLAY – MOTION PICTURE: **Peter Shaffer** *Amadeus*

Cannes International Film Festival

GRAND PRIX: ***Paris, Texas***
DIRECTOR: **Bertrand Tavernier** *Sunday in the Country*
ACTOR: **Alfredo Landa**, **Francisco Rabal** *Los Santos Inocentes*
ACTRESS: **Helen Mirren** *Cal*
ORIGINAL SCREENPLAY: **Theo Angelopoulos**, **Tonino Guerra**, **Thanassis Valtinos** *Voyage to Cythera*

Berlin International Film Festival

GOLDEN BERLIN BEAR: ***Love Streams***
SILVER BERLIN BEAR FOR THE BEST DIRECTOR: **Ettore Scola** *Le Bal*
SILVER BERLIN BEAR FOR THE BEST ACTOR: **Albert Finney** *The Dresser*
SILVER BERLIN BEAR FOR THE BEST ACTRESS: **Inna Tschurikova** *Wartime Romance*

1985

British Academy of Film & Television Arts Awards

BEST FILM: ***The Purple Rose of Cairo*** • *Amadeus* • *Back to the Future* • *A Passage to India* • *Witness*
BEST FOREIGN LANGUAGE FILM: ***Colonel Redl*** • *Carmen* • *Dim Sum: a Little Bit of Heart* • *Subway*
BEST ACTOR: **William Hurt** *Kiss of the Spider Woman* • Victor Banerjee *A Passage to India* • Harrison Ford *Witness* • F Murray Abraham *Amadeus*
BEST ACTRESS: **Peggy Ashcroft** *A Passage to India* • Mia Farrow *The Purple Rose of Cairo* • Kelly McGillis *Witness* • Alexandra Pigg *Letter to Brezhnev*
BEST SUPPORTING ACTOR: **Denholm Elliott** *Defence of the Realm* • James Fox *A Passage to India* • John Gielgud *Plenty* • Saeed Jaffrey *My Beautiful Laundrette*
BEST SUPPORTING ACTRESS: **Rosanna Arquette** *Desperately Seeking Susan* • Judi Dench *Wetherby* • Anjelica Huston *Prizzi's Honor* • Tracey Ullman *Plenty*
BEST ORIGINAL SCREENPLAY: **Woody Allen** *The Purple Rose of Cairo* • Robert Zemeckis, Bob Gale *Back to the Future* • Hanif Kureishi *My Beautiful Laundrette* • Earl W Wallace, William Kelley *Witness*
BEST ADAPTED SCREENPLAY: **Richard Condon**, **Janet Roach** *Prizzi's Honor* • Peter Shaffer *Amadeus* • David Lean *A Passage to India* • Julian Bond *The Shooting Party*

Academy Awards

BEST PICTURE: ***Out of Africa*** • *The Color Purple* • *Kiss of the Spider Woman* • *Prizzi's Honor* • *Witness*
FOREIGN LANGUAGE FILM: ***The Official Version*** • *Angry Harvest* • *Colonel Redl* • *3 Men and a Cradle* • *When Father Was Away on Business*
DIRECTING: **Sydney Pollack** *Out of Africa* • Hector Babenco *Kiss of the Spider Woman* • John Huston *Prizzi's Honor* • Akira Kurosawa *Ran* • Peter Weir *Witness*
ACTOR IN A LEADING ROLE: **William Hurt** *Kiss of the Spider Woman* • Harrison Ford *Witness* • James Garner *Murphy's Romance* • Jack Nicholson *Prizzi's Honor* • Jon Voight *Runaway Train*
ACTRESS IN A LEADING ROLE: **Geraldine Page** *The Trip to Bountiful* • Anne Bancroft *Agnes of God* • Whoopi Goldberg *The Color Purple* • Jessica Lange *Sweet Dreams* • Meryl Streep *Out of Africa*
ACTOR IN A SUPPORTING ROLE: **Don Ameche** *Cocoon* • Klaus Maria Brandauer *Out of Africa* • Robert Loggia *Jagged Edge* • Joseph L Mankiewicz *Forsaking All Others* • Eric Roberts *Runaway Train*
ACTRESS IN A SUPPORTING ROLE: **Anjelica Huston** *Prizzi's Honor* • Margaret Avery (2) *The Color Purple* • Amy Madigan *Twice in a Lifetime* • Meg Tilly *Agnes of God* • Oprah Winfrey *The Color Purple*
WRITING (SCREENPLAY WRITTEN DIRECTLY FOR THE SCREEN): **William Kelley**, **Earl W Wallace**, **Pamela Wallace** *Witness* • Robert Zemeckis, Bob Gale *Back to the Future* • Terry Gilliam, Tom Stoppard, Charles McKeown *Brazil* • Aida Bortnik, Luis Puenzo *The Official Version* • Woody Allen *The Purple Rose of Cairo*
WRITING (SCREENPLAY BASED ON MATERIAL FROM ANOTHER MEDIUM): **Kurt Luedtke** *Out of Africa* • Menno Meyjes *The Color Purple* • Leonard Schrader *Kiss of the Spider Woman* • Richard Condon, Janet Roach *Prizzi's Honor* • Horton Foote *The Trip to Bountiful*

Golden Globe Awards

BEST MOTION PICTURE – DRAMA: ***Out of Africa***
BEST MOTION PICTURE – COMEDY OR MUSICAL: ***Prizzi's Honor***
BEST FOREIGN LANGUAGE FILM: ***The Official Version***
BEST DIRECTOR – MOTION PICTURE: **John Huston** *Prizzi's Honor*
BEST PERFORMANCE BY AN ACTOR IN A MOTION PICTURE – DRAMA: **Jon Voight** *Runaway Train*
BEST PERFORMANCE BY AN ACTRESS IN A MOTION PICTURE – DRAMA: **Whoopi Goldberg** *The Color Purple*
BEST PERFORMANCE BY AN ACTOR IN A MOTION PICTURE – COMEDY OR MUSICAL: **Jack Nicholson** *Prizzi's Honor*
BEST PERFORMANCE BY AN ACTRESS IN A MOTION PICTURE – COMEDY OR MUSICAL: **Kathleen Turner** *Prizzi's Honor*
BEST PERFORMANCE BY AN ACTOR IN A SUPPORTING ROLE – MOTION PICTURE: **Klaus Maria Brandauer** *Out of Africa*
BEST PERFORMANCE BY AN ACTRESS IN A SUPPORTING ROLE – MOTION PICTURE: **Meg Tilly** *Agnes of God*
BEST SCREENPLAY – MOTION PICTURE: **Woody Allen** *The Purple Rose of Cairo*

Cannes International Film Festival

PALME D'OR: ***When Father Was Away on Business***
DIRECTOR: **André Téchiné** *Rendez-vous*
ACTOR: **William Hurt** *Kiss of the Spider Woman*
ACTRESS: **Norma Aleandro** *The Official Version* • **Cher** *Mask*

Berlin International Film Festival

GOLDEN BERLIN BEAR: ***Die Frau und der Fremde* • *Wetherby***
SILVER BERLIN BEAR FOR THE BEST DIRECTOR: **Robert Benton** *Places in the Heart*
SILVER BERLIN BEAR FOR THE BEST ACTOR: **Fernando Fernán Gómez** *Stico*
SILVER BERLIN BEAR FOR THE BEST ACTRESS: **Jo Kennedy** *Wrong World*

1986

British Academy of Film & Television Arts Awards

BEST FILM: ***A Room with a View*** • *Hannah and Her Sisters* • *The Mission* • *Mona Lisa*
BEST FOREIGN LANGUAGE FILM: ***Ran*** • *Betty Blue* • *Ginger & Fred* • *Otello*
BEST ACHIEVEMENT IN DIRECTION: **Woody Allen** *Hannah and Her Sisters* • Roland Joffé *The Mission* • Neil Jordan *Mona Lisa* • James Ivory *A Room with a View*
BEST ACTOR IN A LEADING ROLE: **Bob Hoskins** *Mona Lisa* • Woody Allen, Michael Caine *Hannah and Her Sisters* • Paul Hogan *"Crocodile" Dundee*
BEST ACTRESS IN A LEADING ROLE: **Maggie Smith** *A Room with a View* • Mia Farrow *Hannah and Her Sisters* • Meryl Streep *Out of Africa* • Cathy Tyson *Mona Lisa*
BEST ACTOR IN A SUPPORTING ROLE: **Ray McAnally** *The Mission* • Klaus Maria Brandauer *Out of Africa* • Simon Callow, Denholm Elliott *A Room with a View*
BEST ACTRESS IN A SUPPORTING ROLE: **Judi Dench** *A Room with a View* • Rosanna Arquette *After Hours* • Barbara Hershey *Hannah and Her Sisters* • Rosemary Leach *A Room with a View*
BEST ORIGINAL SCREENPLAY: **Woody Allen** *Hannah and Her Sisters* • Paul Hogan, Ken Shadie, John Cornell *"Crocodile" Dundee* • Robert Bolt *The Mission* • Neil Jordan, David Leland *Mona Lisa*
BEST ADAPTED SCREENPLAY: **Kurt Luedtke** *Out of Africa* • Hesper Anderson, Mark Medoff *Children of a Lesser God* • Menno Meyjes *The Color Purple* • Akira Kurosawa, Hideo Oguni, Masato Ide *Ran* • Ruth Prawer Jhabvala *A Room with a View*

Academy Awards

BEST PICTURE: ***Platoon*** • *Children of a Lesser God* • *Hannah and Her Sisters* • *The Mission* • *A Room with a View*
FOREIGN LANGUAGE FILM: ***The Assault*** • *38* • *Betty Blue* • *The Decline of the American Empire* • *My Sweet Little Village*
DIRECTING: **Oliver Stone** *Platoon* • Woody Allen *Hannah and Her Sisters* • James Ivory *A Room with a View* • Roland Joffé *The Mission* • David Lynch *Blue Velvet*
ACTOR IN A LEADING ROLE: **Paul Newman** *The Color of Money* • Dexter Gordon *'Round Midnight* • Bob Hoskins *Mona Lisa* • William Hurt *Children of a Lesser God* • James Woods *Salvador*
ACTRESS IN A LEADING ROLE: **Marlee Matlin** *Children of a Lesser God* • Jane Fonda *The Morning After* • Sissy Spacek *Crimes of the Heart* • Kathleen Turner *Peggy Sue Got Married* • Sigourney Weaver *Aliens*
ACTOR IN A SUPPORTING ROLE: **Michael Caine** *Hannah and Her Sisters* • Tom Berenger, Willem Dafoe *Platoon* • Denholm Elliott *A Room with a View* • Dennis Hopper *Hoosiers*
ACTRESS IN A SUPPORTING ROLE: **Dianne Wiest** *Hannah and Her Sisters* • Tess Harper *Crimes of the Heart* • Piper Laurie *Children of a Lesser God* • Mary Elizabeth Mastrantonio *The Color of Money* • Maggie Smith *A Room with a View*
WRITING (SCREENPLAY WRITTEN DIRECTLY FOR THE SCREEN): **Woody Allen** *Hannah and Her Sisters* • John Cornell, Paul Hogan, Ken Shadie *"Crocodile" Dundee* • Hanif Kureishi *My Beautiful Laundrette* • Oliver Stone *Platoon* • Richard Boyle, Oliver Stone *Salvador*
WRITING (SCREENPLAY BASED ON MATERIAL FROM ANOTHER MEDIUM): **Ruth Prawer Jhabvala** *A Room with a View* • Hesper Anderson, Mark Medoff *Children of a Lesser God* • Richard Price *The Color of Money* • Beth Henley *Crimes of the Heart* • Bruce A Evans, Raynold Gideon *Stand by Me*

Golden Globe Awards

BEST MOTION PICTURE – DRAMA: ***Platoon***
BEST MOTION PICTURE – COMEDY OR MUSICAL: ***Hannah and Her Sisters***
BEST FOREIGN LANGUAGE FILM: ***The Assault***
BEST DIRECTOR – MOTION PICTURE: **Oliver Stone** *Platoon*
BEST PERFORMANCE BY AN ACTOR IN A MOTION PICTURE – DRAMA: **Bob Hoskins** *Mona Lisa*
BEST PERFORMANCE BY AN ACTRESS IN A MOTION PICTURE – DRAMA: **Marlee Matlin** *Children of a Lesser God*
BEST PERFORMANCE BY AN ACTOR IN A MOTION PICTURE – COMEDY OR MUSICAL: **Paul Hogan** *"Crocodile" Dundee*
BEST PERFORMANCE BY AN ACTRESS IN A MOTION PICTURE – COMEDY OR MUSICAL: **Sissy Spacek** *Crimes of the Heart*

Best Performance by an Actor in a Supporting Role – Motion Picture: **Tom Berenger** *Platoon*
Best Performance by an Actress in a Supporting Role – Motion Picture: **Maggie Smith** *A Room with a View*
Best Screenplay – Motion Picture: **Robert Bolt** *The Mission*

Cannes International Film Festival

Palme d'Or: ***The Mission***
Director: **Martin Scorsese** *After Hours*
Actor: **Michel Blanc** *Tenue de Soirée* • **Bob Hoskins** *Mona Lisa*
Actress: **Barbara Sukowa** *Rosa Luxemburg* • **Fernanda Torres** *Eu Sei Que Vou Te Amar*

Berlin International Film Festival

Golden Berlin Bear: ***Stammheim***
Silver Berlin Bear for the Best Director: **Georgi Schengelaja** *Achalgazrda Kompozitoris Mogzauroba*
Silver Berlin Bear for the Best Actor: **Tuncel Kurtiz** *Hiuh Hagdi*
Silver Berlin Bear for the Best Actress: **Marcelia Cartaxo** *Hour of the Star* • **Charlotte Valandrey** *Rouge Baiser*

1987

British Academy of Film & Television Arts Awards

Best Film: ***Jean de Florette*** • *Cry Freedom* • *Hope and Glory* • *Radio Days*
Best Foreign Language Film: ***The Sacrifice*** • *Jean de Florette* • *Manon des Sources* • *My Life as a Dog*
Best Achievement in Direction: **Oliver Stone** *Platoon* • Richard Attenborough *Cry Freedom* • Claude Berri *Jean de Florette* • John Boorman *Hope and Glory*
Best Actor in a Leading Role: **Sean Connery** *The Name of the Rose* • Gérard Depardieu, Yves Montand *Jean de Florette* • Gary Oldman *Prick Up Your Ears*
Best Actress in a Leading Role: **Anne Bancroft** *84 Charing Cross Road* • Emily Lloyd *Wish You Were Here* • Sarah Miles *Hope and Glory* • Julie Walters *Personal Services*
Best Actor in a Supporting Role: **Daniel Auteuil** *Jean de Florette* • Ian Bannen *Hope and Glory* • Sean Connery *The Untouchables* • John Thaw *Cry Freedom*
Best Actress in a Supporting Role: **Susan Wooldridge** *Hope and Glory* • Judi Dench *84 Charing Cross Road* • Vanessa Redgrave *Prick Up Your Ears* • Dianne Wiest *Radio Days*
Best Screenplay (Original): **David Leland** *Wish You Were Here* • John Boorman *Hope and Glory* • David Leland *Personal Services* • Woody Allen *Radio Days*
Best Screenplay (Adapted): **Gérard Brach**, **Claude Berri** *Jean de Florette* • Hugh Whitemore *84 Charing Cross Road* • Christine Edzard *Little Dorrit* • Alan Bennett *Prick Up Your Ears*

Academy Awards

Best Picture: ***The Last Emperor*** • *Broadcast News* • *Fatal Attraction* • *Hope and Glory* • *Moonstruck*
Foreign Language Film: ***Babette's Feast*** • *Au Revoir les Enfants* • *Course Completed* • *The Family* • *Pathfinder*
Directing: **Bernardo Bertolucci** *The Last Emperor* • John Boorman *Hope and Glory* • Lasse Hallström *My Life as a Dog* • Norman Jewison *Moonstruck* • Adrian Lyne *Fatal Attraction*
Actor in a Leading Role: **Michael Douglas** *Wall Street* • William Hurt *Broadcast News* • Marcello Mastroianni *Dark Eyes* • Jack Nicholson *Ironweed* • Robin Williams *Good Morning, Vietnam*
Actress in a Leading Role: **Cher** *Moonstruck* • Glenn Close *Fatal Attraction* • Holly Hunter *Broadcast News* • Sally Kirkland *Anna* • Meryl Streep *Ironweed*
Actor in a Supporting Role: **Sean Connery** *The Untouchables* • Albert Brooks *Broadcast News* • Morgan Freeman *Street Smart* • Vincent Gardenia *Moonstruck* • Denzel Washington *Cry Freedom*
Actress in a Supporting Role: **Olympia Dukakis** *Moonstruck* • Norma Aleandro *Gaby: a True Story* • Anne Archer *Fatal Attraction* • Anne Ramsey *Throw Momma from the Train* • Ann Sothern *The Whales of August*
Writing (Screenplay Written Directly for the Screen): **John Patrick Shanley** *Moonstruck* • Louis Malle *Au Revoir les Enfants* • James L Brooks *Broadcast News* • John Boorman *Hope and Glory* • Woody Allen *Radio Days*
Writing (Screenplay Based On Material From Another Medium): **Bernardo Bertolucci**, **Mark Peploe** *The Last Emperor* • Tony Huston *The Dead* • James Dearden *Fatal Attraction* • Gustav Hasford, Michael Herr, Stanley Kubrick *Full Metal Jacket* • Pelle Berglund, Brasse Brännström, Lasse Hallström, Reidar Jonsson *My Life as a Dog*

Golden Globe Awards

Best Motion Picture – Drama: ***The Last Emperor***
Best Motion Picture – Comedy or Musical: ***Hope and Glory***
Best Foreign Language Film: ***My Life as a Dog***
Best Director – Motion Picture: **Bernardo Bertolucci** *The Last Emperor*
Best Performance by an Actor in a Motion Picture – Drama: **Michael Douglas** *Wall Street*
Best Performance by an Actress in a Motion Picture – Drama: **Sally Kirkland** *Anna*
Best Performance by an Actor in a Motion Picture – Comedy or Musical: **Robin Williams** *Good Morning, Vietnam*
Best Performance by an Actress in a Motion Picture – Comedy or Musical: **Cher** *Moonstruck*
Best Performance by an Actor in a Supporting Role – Motion Picture: **Sean Connery** *The Untouchables*
Best Performance by an Actress in a Supporting Role – Motion Picture: **Olympia Dukakis** *Moonstruck*
Best Screenplay – Motion Picture: **Mark Peploe**, **Bernardo Bertolucci** *The Last Emperor*

Cannes International Film Festival

Palme d'Or: ***Sous le Soleil de Satan***
Director: **Wim Wenders** *Wings of Desire*
Actor: **Marcello Mastroianni** *Dark Eyes*
Actress: **Barbara Hershey** *Shy People*

Berlin International Film Festival

Golden Berlin Bear: ***The Theme***
Silver Berlin Bear for the Best Director: **Oliver Stone** *Platoon*
Silver Berlin Bear for the Best Actor: **Gian Maria Volonté** *Il Caso Moro*
Silver Berlin Bear for the Best Actress: **Ana Beatriz Nogueira** *Vera*

1988

British Academy of Film & Television Arts Awards

Best Film: ***The Last Emperor*** • *Au Revoir les Enfants* • *Babette's Feast* • *A Fish Called Wanda*
Best Film Not in the English Language: ***Babette's Feast*** • *Au Revoir les Enfants* • *Dark Eyes* • *Wings of Desire*
Best Achievement in Direction: **Louis Malle** *Au Revoir les Enfants* • Gabriel Axel *Babette's Feast* • Bernardo Bertolucci *The Last Emperor* • Charles Crichton *A Fish Called Wanda*
Best Actor in a Leading Role: **John Cleese** *A Fish Called Wanda* • Michael Douglas *Fatal Attraction* • Kevin Kline *A Fish Called Wanda* • Robin Williams *Good Morning, Vietnam*
Best Actress in a Leading Role: **Maggie Smith** *The Lonely Passion of Judith Hearne* • Stéphane Audran *Babette's Feast* • Cher *Moonstruck* • Jamie Lee Curtis *A Fish Called Wanda*
Best Actor in a Supporting Role: **Michael Palin** *A Fish Called Wanda* • Joss Ackland *White Mischief* • Peter O'Toole *The Last Emperor* • David Suchet *A World Apart*
Best Actress in a Supporting Role: **Olympia Dukakis** *Moonstruck* • Maria Aitken *A Fish Called Wanda* • Anne Archer *Fatal Attraction* • Judi Dench *A Handful of Dust*
Best Original Screenplay: **Shawn Slovo** *A World Apart* • Louis Malle *Au Revoir les Enfants* • John Cleese *A Fish Called Wanda* • John Patrick Shanley *Moonstruck*
Best Adapted Screenplay: **Philip Kaufman**, **Jean-Claude Carrière** *The Unbearable Lightness of Being* • Gabriel Axel *Babette's Feast* • Tom Stoppard *Empire of the Sun* • Jeffrey Price, Peter S Seaman *Who Framed Roger Rabbit*

Academy Awards

Best Picture: ***Rain Man*** • *The Accidental Tourist* • *Dangerous Liaisons* • *Mississippi Burning* • *Working Girl*
Foreign Language Film: ***Pelle the Conqueror*** • *Hanussen* • *The Music Teacher* • *Salaam Bombay!* • *Women on the Verge of a Nervous Breakdown*
Directing: **Barry Levinson** *Rain Man* • Charles Crichton *A Fish Called Wanda* • Mike Nichols *Working Girl* • Alan Parker *Mississippi Burning* • Martin Scorsese *The Last Temptation of Christ*
Actor in a Leading Role: **Dustin Hoffman** *Rain Man* • Gene Hackman *Mississippi Burning* • Tom Hanks *Big* • Edward James Olmos *Stand and Deliver* • Max von Sydow *Pelle the Conqueror*
Actress in a Leading Role: **Jodie Foster** *The Accused* • Glenn Close *Dangerous Liaisons* • Melanie Griffith *Working Girl* • Meryl Streep *A Cry in the Dark* • Sigourney Weaver *Gorillas in the Mist*
Actor in a Supporting Role: **Kevin Kline** *A Fish Called Wanda* • Alec Guinness *Little Dorrit* • Martin Landau *Tucker: the Man and His Dream* • River Phoenix *Running on Empty* • Dean Stockwell *Married to the Mob*
Actress in a Supporting Role: **Geena Davis** *The Accidental Tourist* • Joan Cusack *Working Girl* • Frances McDormand *Mississippi Burning* • Michelle Pfeiffer *Dangerous Liaisons* • Sigourney Weaver *Working Girl*
Writing (Screenplay Written Directly for the Screen): **Ronald Bass**, **Barry Morrow** *Rain Man* • Gary Ross, Anne Spielberg *Big* • Ron Shelton *Bull Durham* • John Cleese, Charles Crichton *A Fish Called Wanda* • Naomi Foner *Running on Empty*
Writing (Screenplay Based On Material From Another Medium): **Christopher Hampton** *Dangerous Liaisons* • Frank Galati, Lawrence Kasdan *The Accidental Tourist* • Tab Murphy, Anna Hamilton Phelan *Gorillas in the Mist* • Christine Edzard *Little Dorrit* • Jean-Claude Carrière, Philip Kaufman *The Unbearable Lightness of Being*

Golden Globe Awards

Best Motion Picture – Drama: ***Rain Man***
Best Motion Picture – Comedy or Musical: ***Working Girl***
Best Foreign Language Film: ***Pelle the Conqueror***
Best Director – Motion Picture: **Clint Eastwood** *Bird*
Best Performance by an Actor in a Motion Picture – Drama: **Dustin Hoffman** *Rain Man*
Best Performance by an Actress in a Motion Picture – Drama: **Shirley MacLaine** *Madame Sousatzka* • **Jodie Foster** *The Accused* • **Sigourney Weaver** *Gorillas in the Mist*
Best Performance by an Actor in a Motion Picture – Comedy or Musical: **Tom Hanks** *Big*
Best Performance by an Actress in a Motion Picture – Comedy or Musical: **Melanie Griffith** *Working Girl*
Best Performance by an Actor in a Supporting Role – Motion Picture: **Martin Landau** *Tucker: the Man and His Dream*
Best Performance by an Actress in a Supporting Role – Motion Picture: **Sigourney Weaver** *Working Girl*
Best Screenplay – Motion Picture: **Naomi Foner** *Running on Empty*

Cannes International Film Festival

Palme d'Or: ***Pelle the Conqueror***
Director: **Fernando E Solanas** *Sur*
Actor: **Forest Whitaker** *Bird*
Actress: **Barbara Hershey**, **Jodhi May**, **Linda Mvusi** *A World Apart*

Berlin International Film Festival

Golden Berlin Bear: ***Red Sorghum***
Silver Berlin Bear for the Best Director: **Norman Jewison** *Moonstruck*
Silver Berlin Bear for the Best Actor: **Manfred Möck**, **Jörg Pose** *Einer Trage des Anderen Last*
Silver Berlin Bear for the Best Actress: **Holly Hunter** *Broadcast News*

1989

British Academy of Film & Television Arts Awards

Best Film: ***Dead Poets Society*** • *My Left Foot* • *Shirley Valentine* • *When Harry Met Sally...*
Film Not in the English Language: ***Life and Nothing But*** • *Pelle the Conqueror* • *Salaam Bombay!* • *Women on the Verge of a Nervous Breakdown*
Best Achievement in Direction: **Kenneth Branagh** *Henry V* • Stephen Frears *Dangerous Liaisons* • Alan Parker *Mississippi Burning* • Peter Weir *Dead Poets Society*
Best Actor in a Leading Role: **Daniel Day-Lewis** *My Left Foot* • Kenneth Branagh *Henry V* • Dustin Hoffman *Rain Man* • Robin Williams *Dead Poets Society*
Best Actress in a Leading Role: **Pauline Collins** *Shirley Valentine* • Glenn Close *Dangerous Liaisons* • Jodie Foster *The Accused* • Melanie Griffith *Working Girl*
Best Actor in a Supporting Role: **Ray McAnally** *My Left Foot* • Marlon Brando *A Dry White Season* • Sean Connery *Indiana Jones and the Last Crusade* • Jack Nicholson *Batman*
Best Actress in a Supporting Role: **Michelle Pfeiffer** *Dangerous Liaisons* • Peggy Ashcroft *Madame Sousatzka* • Laura San Giacomo *sex, lies, and videotape* • Sigourney Weaver *Working Girl*
Best Original Screenplay: **Nora Ephron** *When Harry Met Sally...* • Tom Schulman *Dead Poets Society* • Ronald Bass, Barry Morrow *Rain Man* • Steven Soderbergh *sex, lies, and videotape*
Best Adapted Screenplay: **Christopher Hampton** *Dangerous Liaisons* • Frank Galati, Lawrence Kasdan *The Accidental Tourist* • Shane Connaughton, Jim Sheridan *My Left Foot* • Willy Russell *Shirley Valentine*

Academy Awards

Best Picture: ***Driving Miss Daisy*** • *Born on the Fourth of July* • *Dead Poets Society* • *Field of Dreams* • *My Left Foot*
Foreign Language Film: ***Cinema Paradiso*** • *Camille Claudel* • *Jesus of Montreal* • *Waltzing Regitze* • *What Happened to Santiago*
Directing: **Oliver Stone** *Born on the Fourth of July* • Woody Allen *Crimes and Misdemeanors* • Kenneth Branagh *Henry V* • Jim Sheridan *My Left Foot* • Peter Weir *Dead Poets Society*
Actor in a Leading Role: **Daniel Day-Lewis** *My Left Foot* • Kenneth Branagh *Henry V* • Tom Cruise *Born on the Fourth of July* • Morgan Freeman *Driving Miss Daisy* • Robin Williams *Dead Poets Society*
Actress in a Leading Role: **Jessica Tandy** *Driving Miss Daisy* • Isabelle Adjani *Camille Claudel* • Pauline Collins *Shirley Valentine* • Jessica Lange *Music Box* • Michelle Pfeiffer *The Fabulous Baker Boys*
Actor in a Supporting Role: **Denzel Washington** *Glory* • Danny Aiello *Do the Right Thing* • Dan Aykroyd *Driving Miss Daisy* • Marlon Brando *A Dry White Season* • Martin Landau *Crimes and Misdemeanors*
Actress in a Supporting Role: **Brenda Fricker** *My Left Foot* • Anjelica Huston, Lena Olin *Enemies, a Love Story* • Julia Roberts *Steel Magnolias* • Dianne Wiest *Parenthood*
Writing (Screenplay Written Directly for the Screen): **Tom Schulman** *Dead Poets Society* • Woody Allen *Crimes and Misdemeanors* • Spike Lee *Do the Right Thing* • Nora Ephron *When Harry Met Sally...* • Steven Soderbergh *sex, lies, and videotape*
Writing (Screenplay Based On Material From Another Medium): **Alfred Uhry** *Driving Miss Daisy* • Ron Kovic, Oliver Stone *Born on the Fourth of July* • Paul Mazursky, Roger L Simon *Enemies, a Love Story* • Phil Alden Robinson *Field of Dreams* • Shane Connaughton, Jim Sheridan *My Left Foot*

Golden Globe Awards

Best Motion Picture – Drama: ***Born on the Fourth of July***
Best Motion Picture – Comedy or Musical: ***Driving Miss Daisy***
Best Foreign Language Film: ***Cinema Paradiso***
Best Director – Motion Picture: **Oliver Stone** *Born on the Fourth of July*
Best Performance by an Actor in a Motion Picture – Drama: **Tom Cruise** *Born on the Fourth of July*
Best Performance by an Actress in a Motion Picture – Drama: **Michelle Pfeiffer** *The Fabulous Baker Boys*
Best Performance by an Actor in a Motion Picture – Comedy or Musical: **Morgan Freeman** *Driving Miss Daisy*
Best Performance by an Actress in a Motion Picture – Comedy or Musical: **Jessica Tandy** *Driving Miss Daisy*
Best Performance by an Actor in a Supporting Role – Motion Picture: **Denzel Washington** *Glory*
Best Performance by an Actress in a Supporting Role – Motion Picture: **Julia Roberts** *Steel Magnolias*
Best Screenplay – Motion Picture: **Oliver Stone, Ron Kovic** *Born on the Fourth of July*

Cannes International Film Festival

Palme d'Or: ***sex, lies, and videotape***
Director: **Emir Kusturica** *Time of the Gypsies*
Actor: **James Spader** *sex, lies, and videotape*
Actress: **Meryl Streep** *A Cry in the Dark*

Berlin International Film Festival

Golden Berlin Bear: ***Rain Man***
Silver Berlin Bear for the Best Director: **Dusan Hanak** *Ja Milujem, Ty Milujes*
Silver Berlin Bear for the Best Actor: **Gene Hackman** *Mississippi Burning*
Silver Berlin Bear for the Best Actress: **Isabelle Adjani** *Camille Claudel* • **Kaipo Cohen, Gila Almagor** *The Summer of Aviya*

1990

British Academy of Film & Television Arts Awards

Best Film: ***GoodFellas*** • *Crimes and Misdemeanors* • *Driving Miss Daisy* • *Pretty Woman*
Best Film Not in the English Language: ***Cinema Paradiso*** • *Jesus of Montreal* • *Milou en Mai* • *Romuald et Juliette*
Best Achievement in Direction: **Martin Scorsese** *GoodFellas* • Woody Allen *Crimes and Misdemeanors* • Bruce Beresford *Driving Miss Daisy* • Giuseppe Tornatore *Cinema Paradiso*
Best Actor in a Leading Role: **Philippe Noiret** *Cinema Paradiso* • Sean Connery *The Hunt for Red October* • Tom Cruise *Born on the Fourth of July* • Robert De Niro *GoodFellas*
Best Actress in a Leading Role: **Jessica Tandy** *Driving Miss Daisy* • Shirley MacLaine *Postcards from the Edge* • Michelle Pfeiffer *The Fabulous Baker Boys* • Julia Roberts *Pretty Woman*
Best Actor in a Supporting Role: **Salvatore Cascio** *Cinema Paradiso* • Alan Alda *Crimes and Misdemeanors* • John Hurt *The Field* • Al Pacino *Dick Tracy*
Best Actress in a Supporting Role: **Whoopi Goldberg** *Ghost* • Anjelica Huston *Crimes and Misdemeanors* • Shirley MacLaine *Steel Magnolias* • Billie Whitelaw *The Krays*
Best Screenplay (Original): **Giuseppe Tornatore** *Cinema Paradiso* • Woody Allen *Crimes and Misdemeanors* • Bruce Joel Rubin *Ghost* • J F Lawton *Pretty Woman*
Best Screenplay (Adapted): **Nicholas Pileggi, Martin Scorsese** *GoodFellas* • Oliver Stone, Ron Kovic *Born on the Fourth of July* • Alfred Uhry *Driving Miss Daisy* • Carrie Fisher *Postcards from the Edge* • Michael Leeson *The War of the Roses*

Academy Awards

Best Picture: ***Dances with Wolves*** • *Awakenings* • *Ghost* • *The Godfather Part III* • *GoodFellas*
Foreign Language Film: ***Journey of Hope*** • *Cyrano de Bergerac* • *Ju Dou* • *The Nasty Girl* • *Open Doors*
Directing: **Kevin Costner** *Dances with Wolves* • Francis Ford Coppola *The Godfather Part III* • Stephen Frears *The Grifters* • Barbet Schroeder *Reversal of Fortune* • Martin Scorsese *GoodFellas*
Actor in a Leading Role: **Jeremy Irons** *Reversal of Fortune* • Kevin Costner *Dances with Wolves* • Robert De Niro *Awakenings* • Gérard Depardieu *Cyrano de Bergerac* • Richard Harris *The Field*
Actress in a Leading Role: **Kathy Bates** *Misery* • Anjelica Huston *The Grifters* • Julia Roberts *Pretty Woman* • Meryl Streep *Postcards from the Edge* • Joanne Woodward *Mr and Mrs Bridge*
Actor in a Supporting Role: **Joe Pesci** *GoodFellas* • Bruce Davison *Longtime Companion* • Andy Garcia *The Godfather Part III* • Graham Greene *Dances with Wolves* • Al Pacino *Dick Tracy*
Actress in a Supporting Role: **Whoopi Goldberg** *Ghost* • Annette Bening *The Grifters* • Lorraine Bracco *GoodFellas* • Diane Ladd *Wild at Heart* • Mary McDonnell *Dances with Wolves*
Writing (Screenplay Written Directly for the Screen): **Bruce Joel Rubin** *Ghost* • Woody Allen *Alice* • Barry Levinson *Avalon* • Peter Weir *Green Card* • Whit Stillman *Metropolitan*
Writing (Screenplay Based on Material from Another Medium): **Michael Blake** *Dances with Wolves* • Steven Zaillian *Awakenings* • Nicholas Pileggi, Martin Scorsese *GoodFellas* • Donald E Westlake *The Grifters* • Nicholas Kazan *Reversal of Fortune*

Golden Globe Awards

Best Motion Picture – Drama: ***Dances with Wolves***
Best Motion Picture – Comedy or Musical: ***Green Card***
Best Foreign Language Film: ***Cyrano de Bergerac***
Best Director – Motion Picture: **Kevin Costner** *Dances with Wolves*
Best Performance by an Actor in a Motion Picture – Drama: **Jeremy Irons** *Reversal of Fortune*
Best Performance by an Actress in a Motion Picture – Drama: **Kathy Bates** *Misery*
Best Performance by an Actor in a Motion Picture – Comedy or Musical: **Gérard Depardieu** *Green Card*
Best Performance by an Actress in a Motion Picture – Comedy or Musical: **Julia Roberts** *Pretty Woman*
Best Performance by an Actor in a Supporting Role – Motion Picture: **Bruce Davison** *Longtime Companion*
Best Performance by an Actress in a Supporting Role – Motion Picture: **Whoopi Goldberg** *Ghost*
Best Screenplay – Motion Picture: **Michael Blake** *Dances with Wolves*

Cannes International Film Festival

Palme d'Or: ***Wild at Heart***
Director: **Pavel Lounguine** *Taxi Blues*
Actor: **Gérard Depardieu** *Cyrano de Bergerac*
Actress: **Krystyna Janda** *Interrogation*

Berlin International Film Festival

Golden Berlin Bear: ***Music Box*** • ***Larks on a String***
Silver Berlin Bear for the Best Director: **Michael Verhoeven** *The Nasty Girl*
Silver Berlin Bear for the Best Actor: **Iain Glen** *Silent Scream*
Silver Berlin Bear for the Best Joint Performance: **Jessica Tandy, Morgan Freeman** *Driving Miss Daisy*

1991

British Academy of Film & Television Arts Awards

Best Film: ***The Commitments*** • *Dances with Wolves* • *The Silence of the Lambs* • *Thelma & Louise*
Best Film Not in the English Language: ***The Nasty Girl*** • *Cyrano de Bergerac* • *The Hairdresser's Husband* • *Toto Le Héros*
The David Lean Award for the Best Achievement in Direction: **Alan Parker** *The Commitments* • Kevin Costner *Dances with Wolves* • Jonathan Demme *The Silence of the Lambs* • Ridley Scott *Thelma & Louise*
Best Actor in a Leading Role: **Anthony Hopkins** *The Silence of the Lambs* • Kevin Costner *Dances with Wolves* • Gérard Depardieu *Cyrano de Bergerac* • Alan Rickman *Truly Madly Deeply*
Best Actress in a Leading Role: **Jodie Foster** *The Silence of the Lambs* • Geena Davis, Susan Sarandon *Thelma & Louise* • Juliet Stevenson *Truly Madly Deeply*
Best Actor in a Supporting Role: **Alan Rickman** *Robin Hood: Prince of Thieves* • Alan Bates *Hamlet* • Derek Jacobi *Dead Again* • Andrew Strong *The Commitments*
Best Actress in a Supporting Role: **Kate Nelligan** *Frankie & Johnny* • Annette Bening *The Grifters* • Amanda Plummer *The Fisher King* • Julie Walters *Stepping Out*
Best Screenplay (Original): **Anthony Minghella** *Truly Madly Deeply* • Richard LaGravenese *The Fisher King* • Peter Weir *Green Card* • Callie Khouri *Thelma & Louise*
Best Screenplay (Adapted): **Dick Clement, Ian La Frenais, Roddy Doyle** *The Commitments* • Jean-Paul Rappeneau, Jean-Claude Carrière *Cyrano de Bergerac* • Michael Blake *Dances with Wolves* • Ted Tally *The Silence of the Lambs*

Academy Awards

Best Picture: ***The Silence of the Lambs*** • *Beauty and the Beast* • *Bugsy* • *JFK* • *The Prince of Tides*
Foreign Language Film: ***Mediterraneo*** • *Children of Nature* • *Elementary School* • *The Ox* • *Raise the Red Lantern*
Directing: **Jonathan Demme** *The Silence of the Lambs* • Barry Levinson *Bugsy* • Ridley Scott *Thelma & Louise* • John Singleton *Boyz N the Hood* • Oliver Stone *JFK*
Actor in a Leading Role: **Anthony Hopkins** *The Silence of the Lambs* • Warren Beatty *Bugsy* • Robert De Niro *Cape Fear* • Nick Nolte *The Prince of Tides* • Robin Williams *The Fisher King*
Actress in a Leading Role: **Jodie Foster** *The Silence of the Lambs* • Geena Davis *Thelma & Louise* • Laura Dern *Rambling Rose* • Bette Midler *For the Boys* • Susan Sarandon *Thelma & Louise*
Actor in a Supporting Role: **Jack Palance** *City Slickers* • Tommy Lee Jones *JFK* • Harvey Keitel, Ben Kingsley *Bugsy* • Michael Lerner *Barton Fink*
Actress in a Supporting Role: **Mercedes Ruehl** *The Fisher King* • Diane Ladd *Rambling Rose* • Juliette Lewis *Cape Fear* • Kate Nelligan *The Prince of Tides* • Jessica Tandy *Fried Green Tomatoes at the Whistle Stop Cafe*
Writing (Screenplay Written Directly for the Screen): **Callie Khouri** *Thelma & Louise* • John Singleton *Boyz N the Hood* • James Toback *Bugsy* • Richard LaGravenese *The Fisher King* • Lawrence Kasdan, Meg Kasdan *Grand Canyon*
Writing (Screenplay Based on Material Previously Produced or Published): **Ted Tally** *The Silence of the Lambs* • Agnieszka Holland *Europa, Europa* • Fannie Flagg, Carol Sobieski *Fried Green Tomatoes at the Whistle Stop Cafe* • Zachary Sklar, Oliver Stone *JFK* • Pat Conroy, Becky Johnston *The Prince of Tides*

Golden Globe Awards

Best Motion Picture – Drama: ***Bugsy***
Best Motion Picture – Comedy or Musical: ***Beauty and the Beast***
Best Foreign Language Film: ***Europa, Europa***
Best Director – Motion Picture: **Oliver Stone** *JFK*
Best Performance by an Actor in a Motion Picture – Drama: **Nick Nolte** *The Prince of Tides*
Best Performance by an Actress in a Motion Picture – Drama: **Jodie Foster** *The Silence of the Lambs*
Best Performance by an Actor in a Motion Picture – Comedy or Musical: **Robin Williams** *The Fisher King*
Best Performance by an Actress in a Motion Picture – Comedy or Musical: **Bette Midler** *For the Boys*
Best Performance by an Actor in a Supporting Role – Motion Picture: **Jack Palance** *City Slickers*
Best Performance by an Actress in a Supporting Role – Motion Picture: **Mercedes Ruehl** *The Fisher King*
Best Screenplay – Motion Picture: **Callie Khouri** *Thelma & Louise*

Cannes International Film Festival

Palme d'Or: ***Barton Fink***
Director: **Joel Coen** *Barton Fink*
Actor: **John Turturro** *Barton Fink*
Actress: **Irène Jacob** *The Double Life of Véronique*
Supporting Actor: **Samuel L Jackson** *Jungle Fever*

Berlin International Film Festival

Golden Berlin Bear: ***La Casa del Sorriso***
Silver Berlin Bear for the Best Director: **Jonathan Demme** *The Silence of the Lambs* • **Ricky Tognazzi** *Ultrà*
Silver Berlin Bear for the Best Actor: **Maynard Eziashi** *Mister Johnson*
Silver Berlin Bear for the Best Actress: **Victoria Abril** *Lovers*

1992

British Academy of Film & Television Arts Awards

Best Film: ***Howards End*** • *The Crying Game* • *The Player* • *Strictly Ballroom* • *Unforgiven*
Best Film Not in the English Language: ***Raise the Red Lantern*** • *Les Amants du Pont-Neuf* • *Delicatessen* • *Europa, Europa*
The David Lean Award for the Best Achievement in Direction: **Robert Altman** *The Player* • Clint Eastwood *Unforgiven* • James Ivory *Howards End* • Neil Jordan *The Crying Game*
Best Actor in a Leading Role: **Robert Downey Jr** *Chaplin* • Daniel Day-Lewis *The Last of the Mohicans* • Stephen Rea *The Crying Game* • Tim Robbins *The Player*
Best Actress in a Leading Role: **Emma Thompson** *Howards End* • Judy Davis *Husbands and Wives* • Tara Morice *Strictly Ballroom* • Jessica Tandy *Fried Green Tomatoes at the Whistle Stop Cafe*
Best Actor in a Supporting Role: **Gene Hackman** *Unforgiven* • Jaye Davidson *The Crying Game* • Tommy Lee Jones *JFK* • Samuel West *Howards End*
Best Actress in a Supporting Role: **Miranda Richardson** *Damage* • Kathy Bates *Fried Green Tomatoes at the Whistle Stop Cafe* • Helena Bonham Carter *Howards End* • Miranda Richardson *The Crying Game*
Best Original Screenplay: **Woody Allen** *Husbands and Wives* • Neil Jordan *The Crying Game* • Peter Chelsom, Adrian Dunbar *Hear My Song* • David Webb Peoples *Unforgiven*
Best Adapted Screenplay: **Michael Tolkin** *The Player* • Ruth Prawer Jhabvala *Howards End* • Oliver Stone, Zachary Sklar *JFK* • Baz Luhrmann, Craig Pearce *Strictly Ballroom*

Academy Awards

Best Picture: ***Unforgiven*** • *The Crying Game* • *A Few Good Men* • *Howards End* • *Scent of a Woman*
Foreign Language Film: ***Indochine*** • *Urga* • *Daens* • *A Place in the World* • *Schtonk!*
Directing: **Clint Eastwood** *Unforgiven* • Robert Altman *The Player* • Martin Brest *Scent of a Woman* • James Ivory *Howards End* • Neil Jordan *The Crying Game*
Actor in a Leading Role: **Al Pacino** *Scent of a Woman* • Robert Downey Jr *Chaplin* • Clint Eastwood *Unforgiven* • Stephen Rea *The Crying Game* • Denzel Washington *Malcolm X*
Actress in a Leading Role: **Emma Thompson** *Howards End* • Catherine Deneuve *Indochine* • Mary McDonnell *Passion Fish* • Michelle Pfeiffer *Love Field* • Susan Sarandon *Lorenzo's Oil*
Actor in a Supporting Role: **Gene Hackman** *Unforgiven* • Jaye Davidson *The Crying Game* • Jack Nicholson *A Few Good Men* • Al Pacino *Glengarry Glen Ross* • David Paymer *Mr Saturday Night*
Actress in a Supporting Role: **Marisa Tomei** *My Cousin Vinny* • Judy Davis *Husbands and Wives* • Joan Plowright *Enchanted April* • Vanessa Redgrave *Howards End* • Miranda Richardson *Damage*
Writing (Screenplay Written Directly for the Screen): **Neil Jordan** *The Crying Game* • Woody Allen *Husbands and Wives* • Nick Enright, George Miller (2) *Lorenzo's Oil*

• John Sayles *Passion Fish* • David Webb Peoples *Unforgiven*
WRITING (SCREENPLAY BASED ON MATERIAL PREVIOUSLY PRODUCED OR PUBLISHED): **Ruth Prawer Jhabvala** *Howards End* • Peter Barnes *Enchanted April* • Michael Tolkin *The Player* • Richard Friedenberg *A River Runs through It* • Bo Goldman *Scent of a Woman*

Golden Globe Awards

BEST MOTION PICTURE – DRAMA: ***Scent of a Woman***
BEST MOTION PICTURE – COMEDY OR MUSICAL: ***The Player***
BEST FOREIGN LANGUAGE FILM: ***Indochine***
BEST DIRECTOR – MOTION PICTURE: **Clint Eastwood** *Unforgiven*
BEST PERFORMANCE BY AN ACTOR IN A MOTION PICTURE – DRAMA: **Al Pacino** *Scent of a Woman*
BEST PERFORMANCE BY AN ACTRESS IN A MOTION PICTURE – DRAMA: **Emma Thompson** *Howards End*
BEST PERFORMANCE BY AN ACTOR IN A MOTION PICTURE – COMEDY OR MUSICAL: **Tim Robbins** *The Player*
BEST PERFORMANCE BY AN ACTRESS IN A MOTION PICTURE – COMEDY OR MUSICAL: **Miranda Richardson** *Enchanted April*
BEST PERFORMANCE BY AN ACTOR IN A SUPPORTING ROLE – MOTION PICTURE: **Gene Hackman** *Unforgiven*
BEST PERFORMANCE BY AN ACTRESS IN A SUPPORTING ROLE – MOTION PICTURE: **Joan Plowright** *Enchanted April*
BEST SCREENPLAY – MOTION PICTURE: **Bo Goldman** *Scent of a Woman*

Cannes International Film Festival

PALME D'OR: ***Best Intentions***
DIRECTOR: **Robert Altman** *The Player*
ACTOR: **Tim Robbins** *The Player*
ACTRESS: **Pernilla August** *Best Intentions*

Berlin International Film Festival

GOLDEN BERLIN BEAR: ***Grand Canyon***
SILVER BERLIN BEAR FOR THE BEST DIRECTOR: **Jan Troell** *Il Capitano*
SILVER BERLIN BEAR FOR THE BEST ACTOR: **Armin Mueller-Stahl** *Utz*
SILVER BERLIN BEAR FOR THE BEST ACTRESS: **Maggie Cheung** *The Actress*

1993

British Academy of Film & Television Arts Awards

BEST FILM: ***Schindler's List*** • *The Piano* • *The Remains of the Day* • *Shadowlands*
BEST FILM NOT IN THE ENGLISH LANGUAGE: ***Farewell My Concubine*** • *Un Coeur en Hiver* • *Like Water for Chocolate* • *Indochine*
THE ALEXANDER KORDA AWARD FOR THE OUTSTANDING BRITISH FILM OF THE YEAR: ***Shadowlands*** • *Naked* • *Raining Stones* • *Tom & Viv*
THE DAVID LEAN AWARD FOR THE BEST ACHIEVEMENT IN DIRECTION: **Steven Spielberg** *Schindler's List* • Richard Attenborough *Shadowlands* • Jane Campion *The Piano* • James Ivory *The Remains of the Day*
BEST PERFORMANCE BY AN ACTOR IN A LEADING ROLE: **Anthony Hopkins** *The Remains of the Day* • Daniel Day-Lewis *In the Name of the Father* • Anthony Hopkins *Shadowlands* • Liam Neeson *Schindler's List*
BEST PERFORMANCE BY AN ACTRESS IN A LEADING ROLE: **Holly Hunter** *The Piano* • Miranda Richardson *Tom & Viv* • Emma Thompson *The Remains of the Day* • Debra Winger *Shadowlands*
BEST PERFORMANCE BY AN ACTOR IN A SUPPORTING ROLE: **Ralph Fiennes** *Schindler's List* • Tommy Lee Jones *The Fugitive* • Ben Kingsley *Schindler's List* • John Malkovich *In the Line of Fire*
BEST PERFORMANCE BY AN ACTRESS IN A SUPPORTING ROLE: **Miriam Margolyes** *The Age of Innocence* • Holly Hunter *The Firm* • Winona Ryder *The Age of Innocence* • Maggie Smith *The Secret Garden*
BEST SCREENPLAY (ORIGINAL): **Danny Rubin, Harold Ramis** *Groundhog Day* • Jeff Maguire *In the Line of Fire* • Jane Campion *The Piano* • Nora Ephron, David S Ward, Jeff Arch *Sleepless in Seattle*
BEST SCREENPLAY (ADAPTED): **Steven Zaillian** *Schindler's List* • Terry George, Jim Sheridan *In the Name of the Father* • Ruth Prawer Jhabvala *The Remains of the Day* • Bo Goldman *Scent of a Woman* • William Nicholson *Shadowlands*

Academy Awards

BEST PICTURE: ***Schindler's List*** • *The Fugitive* • *In the Name of the Father* • *The Piano* • *The Remains of the Day*
FOREIGN LANGUAGE FILM: ***Belle Epoque*** • *Farewell My Concubine* • *Hedd Wyn* • *The Scent of Green Papaya* • *The Wedding Banquet*
DIRECTING: **Steven Spielberg** *Schindler's List* • Robert Altman *Short Cuts* • Jane Campion *The Piano* • James Ivory *The Remains of the Day* • Jim Sheridan *In the Name of the Father*
ACTOR IN A LEADING ROLE: **Tom Hanks** *Philadelphia* • Daniel Day-Lewis *In the Name of the Father* • Laurence Fishburne *Tina: What's Love Got to Do with It* • Anthony Hopkins *The Remains of the Day* • Liam Neeson *Schindler's List*
ACTRESS IN A LEADING ROLE: **Holly Hunter** *The Piano* • Angela Bassett *Tina: What's Love Got to Do with It* • Stockard Channing *Six Degrees of Separation* • Emma Thompson *The Remains of the Day* • Debra Winger *Shadowlands*
ACTOR IN A SUPPORTING ROLE: **Tommy Lee Jones** *The Fugitive* • Leonardo DiCaprio *What's Eating Gilbert Grape* • Ralph Fiennes *Schindler's List* • John Malkovich *In the Line of Fire* • Pete Postlethwaite *In the Name of the Father*
ACTRESS IN A SUPPORTING ROLE: **Anna Paquin** *The Piano* • Holly Hunter *The Firm* • Rosie Perez *Fearless* • Winona Ryder *The Age of Innocence* • Emma Thompson *In the Name of the Father*
WRITING (SCREENPLAY WRITTEN DIRECTLY FOR THE SCREEN): **Jane Campion** *The Piano* • Gary Ross *Dave* • Jeff Maguire *In the Line of Fire* • Ron Nyswaner *Philadelphia* • Jeff Arch, Nora Ephron, David S Ward *Sleepless in Seattle*
WRITING (SCREENPLAY BASED ON MATERIAL PREVIOUSLY PRODUCED OR PUBLISHED): **Steven Zaillian** *Schindler's List* • Jay Cocks, Martin Scorsese *The Age of Innocence* • Terry George, Jim Sheridan *In the Name of the Father* • Ruth Prawer Jhabvala *The Remains of the Day* • William Nicholson *Shadowlands*

Golden Globe Awards

BEST MOTION PICTURE – DRAMA: ***Schindler's List***
BEST MOTION PICTURE – COMEDY OR MUSICAL: ***Mrs Doubtfire***
BEST FOREIGN LANGUAGE FILM: ***Farewell My Concubine***
BEST DIRECTOR – MOTION PICTURE: **Steven Spielberg** *Schindler's List*
BEST PERFORMANCE BY AN ACTOR IN A MOTION PICTURE – DRAMA: **Tom Hanks** *Philadelphia*
BEST PERFORMANCE BY AN ACTRESS IN A MOTION PICTURE – DRAMA: **Holly Hunter** *The Piano*
BEST PERFORMANCE BY AN ACTOR IN A MOTION PICTURE – COMEDY OR MUSICAL: **Robin Williams** *Mrs Doubtfire*
BEST PERFORMANCE BY AN ACTRESS IN A MOTION PICTURE – COMEDY OR MUSICAL: **Angela Bassett** *Tina: What's Love Got to Do with It*
BEST PERFORMANCE BY AN ACTOR IN A SUPPORTING ROLE – MOTION PICTURE: **Tommy Lee Jones** *The Fugitive*
BEST PERFORMANCE BY AN ACTRESS IN A SUPPORTING ROLE – MOTION PICTURE: **Winona Ryder** *The Age of Innocence*
BEST SCREENPLAY – MOTION PICTURE: **Steven Zaillian** *Schindler's List*

Cannes International Film Festival

PALME D'OR: ***The Piano*** • ***Farewell My Concubine***
DIRECTOR: **Mike Leigh** *Naked*
ACTOR: **David Thewlis** *Naked*
ACTRESS: **Holly Hunter** *The Piano*

Berlin International Film Festival

GOLDEN BERLIN BEAR: ***The Women from the Lake of Scented Souls*** • ***The Wedding Banquet***
SILVER BERLIN BEAR FOR THE BEST DIRECTOR: **Andrew Birkin** *The Cement Garden*
SILVER BERLIN BEAR FOR THE BEST ACTOR: **Denzel Washington** *Malcolm X*
SILVER BERLIN BEAR FOR THE BEST ACTRESS: **Michelle Pfeiffer** *Love Field*

1994

British Academy of Film & Television Arts Awards

BEST FILM: ***Four Weddings and a Funeral*** • *Forrest Gump* • *Pulp Fiction* • *Quiz Show*
BEST FILM NOT IN THE ENGLISH LANGUAGE: ***To Live*** • ***Belle Epoque*** • *Eat Drink Man Woman* • *Three Colours Red*
THE ALEXANDER KORDA AWARD FOR THE OUTSTANDING BRITISH FILM OF THE YEAR: ***Shallow Grave*** • *Backbeat* • *Bhaji on the Beach* • *Priest*
THE DAVID LEAN AWARD FOR THE BEST ACHIEVEMENT IN DIRECTION: **Mike Newell** *Four Weddings and a Funeral* • Krzysztof Kieslowski *Three Colours Red* • Quentin Tarantino *Pulp Fiction* • Robert Zemeckis *Forrest Gump*
BEST PERFORMANCE BY AN ACTOR IN A LEADING ROLE: **Hugh Grant** *Four Weddings and a Funeral* • Tom Hanks *Forrest Gump* • Terence Stamp *The Adventures of Priscilla, Queen of the Desert* • John Travolta *Pulp Fiction*
BEST PERFORMANCE BY AN ACTRESS IN A LEADING ROLE: **Susan Sarandon** *The Client* • Linda Fiorentino *The Last Seduction* • Irène Jacob *Three Colours Red* • Uma Thurman *Pulp Fiction*
BEST PERFORMANCE BY AN ACTOR IN A SUPPORTING ROLE: **Samuel L Jackson** *Pulp Fiction* • Simon Callow, John Hannah *Four Weddings and a Funeral* • Paul Scofield *Quiz Show*
BEST PERFORMANCE BY AN ACTRESS IN A SUPPORTING ROLE: **Kristin Scott Thomas**, Charlotte Coleman *Four Weddings and a Funeral* • Sally Field *Forrest Gump* • Anjelica Huston *Manhattan Murder Mystery*
BEST SCREENPLAY (ORIGINAL): **Quentin Tarantino, Roger Avary** *Pulp Fiction* • Stephan Elliott *The Adventures of Priscilla, Queen of the Desert* • Richard Curtis *Four Weddings and a Funeral* • Ron Nyswaner *Philadelphia* • Krzysztof Kieslowski, Krzysztof Piesiewicz *Three Colours Red*
BEST SCREENPLAY (ADAPTED): **Paul Attanasio** *Quiz Show* • Ronald Harwood *The Browning Version* • Eric Roth *Forrest Gump* • Amy Tan, Ronald Bass *The Joy Luck Club*

Academy Awards

BEST PICTURE: ***Forrest Gump*** • *Four Weddings and a Funeral* • *Pulp Fiction* • *Quiz Show* • *The Shawshank Redemption*
FOREIGN LANGUAGE FILM: ***Burnt by the Sun*** • *Before the Rain* • *Eat Drink Man Woman* • *Farinelli il Castrato* • *Strawberry and Chocolate*
DIRECTING: **Robert Zemeckis** *Forrest Gump* • Woody Allen *Bullets over Broadway* • Krzysztof Kieslowski *Three Colours Red* • Robert Redford *Quiz Show* • Quentin Tarantino *Pulp Fiction*
ACTOR IN A LEADING ROLE: **Tom Hanks** *Forrest Gump* • Morgan Freeman *The Shawshank Redemption* • Nigel Hawthorne *The Madness of King George* • Paul Newman *Nobody's Fool* • John Travolta *Pulp Fiction*
ACTRESS IN A LEADING ROLE: **Jessica Lange** *Blue Sky* • Jodie Foster *Nell* • Miranda Richardson *Tom & Viv* • Winona Ryder *Little Women* • Susan Sarandon *The Client*
ACTOR IN A SUPPORTING ROLE: **Martin Landau** *Ed Wood* • Samuel L Jackson *Pulp Fiction* • Chazz Palminteri *Bullets over Broadway* • Paul Scofield *Quiz Show* • Gary Sinise *Forrest Gump*
ACTRESS IN A SUPPORTING ROLE: **Dianne Wiest** *Bullets over Broadway* • Rosemary Harris *Tom & Viv* • Helen Mirren *The Madness of King George* • Uma Thurman *Pulp Fiction* • Jennifer Tilly *Bullets over Broadway*
WRITING (SCREENPLAY WRITTEN DIRECTLY FOR THE SCREEN): **Quentin Tarantino, Roger Avary** *Pulp Fiction* • Woody Allen, Douglas McGrath *Bullets over Broadway* • Richard Curtis *Four Weddings and a Funeral* • Peter Jackson, Frances Walsh *Heavenly Creatures* • Krzysztof Kieslowski, Krzysztof Piesiewicz *Three Colours Red*
WRITING (SCREENPLAY BASED ON MATERIAL PREVIOUSLY PRODUCED OR PUBLISHED): **Eric Roth** *Forrest Gump* • Alan Bennett *The Madness of King George* • Robert Benton *Nobody's Fool* • Paul Attanasio *Quiz Show* • Frank Darabont *The Shawshank Redemption*

Golden Globe Awards

BEST MOTION PICTURE – DRAMA: ***Forrest Gump***
BEST MOTION PICTURE – COMEDY OR MUSICAL: ***The Lion King***
BEST FOREIGN LANGUAGE FILM: ***Farinelli Il Castrato***
BEST DIRECTOR – MOTION PICTURE: **Robert Zemeckis** *Forrest Gump*
BEST PERFORMANCE BY AN ACTOR IN A MOTION PICTURE – DRAMA: **Tom Hanks** *Forrest Gump*
BEST PERFORMANCE BY AN ACTRESS IN A MOTION PICTURE – DRAMA: **Jessica Lange** *Blue Sky*
BEST PERFORMANCE BY AN ACTOR IN A MOTION PICTURE – COMEDY OR MUSICAL: **Hugh Grant** *Four Weddings and a Funeral*
BEST PERFORMANCE BY AN ACTRESS IN A MOTION PICTURE – COMEDY OR MUSICAL: **Jamie Lee Curtis** *True Lies*
BEST PERFORMANCE BY AN ACTOR IN A SUPPORTING ROLE – MOTION PICTURE: **Martin Landau** *Ed Wood*
BEST PERFORMANCE BY AN ACTRESS IN A SUPPORTING ROLE – MOTION PICTURE: **Dianne Wiest** *Bullets over Broadway*
BEST SCREENPLAY – MOTION PICTURE: **Quentin Tarantino** *Pulp Fiction*

Cannes International Film Festival

PALME D'OR: ***Pulp Fiction***
DIRECTOR: **Nanni Moretti** *Dear Diary*
ACTOR: **Ge You** *To Live*
ACTRESS: **Virna Lisi** *La Reine Margot*
SCREENPLAY: **Michel Blanc** *Grosse Fatigue*

Berlin International Film Festival

GOLDEN BERLIN BEAR: ***In the Name of the Father***
SILVER BERLIN BEAR FOR THE BEST DIRECTOR: **Krzysztof Kieslowski** *Three Colours Blue*
SILVER BERLIN BEAR FOR THE BEST ACTOR: **Tom Hanks** *Philadelphia*
SILVER BERLIN BEAR FOR THE BEST ACTRESS: **Crissy Rock** *Ladybird Ladybird*

1995

British Academy of Film & Television Arts Awards

BEST FILM: ***Sense and Sensibility*** • *Babe* • *The Madness of King George* • *The Usual Suspects*
BEST FILM NOT IN THE ENGLISH LANGUAGE: ***Il Postino*** • *Les Misérables* • *La Reine Margot* • *Burnt by the Sun*
THE ALEXANDER KORDA AWARD FOR THE OUTSTANDING BRITISH FILM OF THE YEAR: ***The Madness of King George*** • *Carrington* • *Land and Freedom* • *Trainspotting*
THE DAVID LEAN AWARD FOR THE BEST ACHIEVEMENT IN DIRECTION: **Michael Radford** *Il Postino* • Mel Gibson *Braveheart* • Nicholas Hytner *The Madness of King George* • Ang Lee *Sense and Sensibility*
BEST PERFORMANCE BY AN ACTOR IN A LEADING ROLE: **Nigel Hawthorne** *The Madness of King George* • Nicolas Cage *Leaving Las Vegas* • Jonathan Pryce *Carrington* • Massimo Troisi *Il Postino*
BEST PERFORMANCE BY AN ACTRESS IN A LEADING ROLE: **Emma Thompson** *Sense and Sensibility* • Nicole Kidman *To Die For* • Helen Mirren *The Madness of King George* • Elisabeth Shue *Leaving Las Vegas*
BEST PERFORMANCE BY AN ACTOR IN A SUPPORTING ROLE: **Tim Roth** *Rob Roy* • Ian Holm *The Madness of King George* • Martin Landau *Ed Wood* • Alan Rickman *Sense and Sensibility*
BEST PERFORMANCE BY AN ACTRESS IN A SUPPORTING ROLE: **Kate Winslet** *Sense and Sensibility* • Joan Allen *Nixon* •

Mira Sorvino *Mighty Aphrodite* • Elizabeth Spriggs *Sense and Sensibility*
BEST SCREENPLAY (ORIGINAL): **Christopher McQuarrie** *The Usual Suspects* • Woody Allen, Douglas McGrath *Bullets over Broadway* • P J Hogan *Muriel's Wedding* • Andrew Kevin Walker *Se7en*
BEST SCREENPLAY (ADAPTED): **John Hodge** *Trainspotting* • George Miller (2), Chris Noonan *Babe* • Mike Figgis *Leaving Las Vegas* • Alan Bennett *The Madness of King George* • Anna Pavignano, Michael Radford, Furio Scarpelli, Giacomo Scarpelli *Il Postino* • Emma Thompson *Sense and Sensibility*

Academy Awards

BEST PICTURE: ***Braveheart*** • *Apollo 13* • *Babe* • *Il Postino* • *Sense and Sensibility*
FOREIGN LANGUAGE FILM: ***Antonia's Line*** • *All Things Fair* • *Dust of Life* • *O Quatrilho* • *The Starmaker*
DIRECTING: **Mel Gibson** *Braveheart* • Mike Figgis *Leaving Las Vegas* • Chris Noonan *Babe* • Michael Radford *Il Postino* • Tim Robbins *Dead Man Walking*
ACTOR IN A LEADING ROLE: **Nicolas Cage** *Leaving Las Vegas* • Richard Dreyfuss *Mr Holland's Opus* • Anthony Hopkins *Nixon* • Sean Penn *Dead Man Walking* • Massimo Troisi *Il Postino*
ACTRESS IN A LEADING ROLE: **Susan Sarandon** *Dead Man Walking* • Elisabeth Shue *Leaving Las Vegas* • Sharon Stone *Casino* • Meryl Streep *The Bridges of Madison County* • Emma Thompson *Sense and Sensibility*
ACTOR IN A SUPPORTING ROLE: **Kevin Spacey** *The Usual Suspects* • James Cromwell *Babe* • Ed Harris *Apollo 13* • Brad Pitt *Twelve Monkeys* • Tim Roth *Rob Roy*
ACTRESS IN A SUPPORTING ROLE: **Mira Sorvino** *Mighty Aphrodite* • Joan Allen *Nixon* • Kathleen Quinlan *Apollo 13* • Mare Winningham *Georgia* • Kate Winslet *Sense and Sensibility*
WRITING (SCREENPLAY WRITTEN DIRECTLY FOR THE SCREEN): **Christopher McQuarrie** *The Usual Suspects* • Randall Wallace *Braveheart* • Woody Allen *Mighty Aphrodite* • Stephen J Rivele, Oliver Stone, Christopher Wilkinson *Nixon* • Joel Cohen, Pete Docter, John Lasseter, Joe Ranft, Alec Sokolow, Andrew Stanton, Joss Whedon *Toy Story*
WRITING (SCREENPLAY BASED ON MATERIAL PREVIOUSLY PRODUCED OR PUBLISHED): **Emma Thompson** *Sense and Sensibility* • William Broyles Jr, Al Reinert *Apollo 13* • George Miller (2), Chris Noonan *Babe* • Mike Figgis *Leaving Las Vegas* • Anna Pavignano, Michael Radford, Furio Scarpelli, Giacomo Scarpelli *Il Postino*

Golden Globe Awards

BEST MOTION PICTURE – DRAMA: ***Sense and Sensibility***
BEST MOTION PICTURE – COMEDY OR MUSICAL: ***Babe***
BEST FOREIGN LANGUAGE FILM: ***Les Misérables***
BEST DIRECTOR – MOTION PICTURE: **Mel Gibson** *Braveheart*
BEST PERFORMANCE BY AN ACTOR IN A MOTION PICTURE – DRAMA: **Nicolas Cage** *Leaving Las Vegas*
BEST PERFORMANCE BY AN ACTRESS IN A MOTION PICTURE – DRAMA: **Sharon Stone** *Casino*
BEST PERFORMANCE BY AN ACTOR IN A MOTION PICTURE – COMEDY OR MUSICAL: **John Travolta** *Get Shorty*
BEST PERFORMANCE BY AN ACTRESS IN A MOTION PICTURE – COMEDY OR MUSICAL: **Nicole Kidman** *To Die For*
BEST PERFORMANCE BY AN ACTOR IN A SUPPORTING ROLE – MOTION PICTURE: **Brad Pitt** *Twelve Monkeys*
BEST PERFORMANCE BY AN ACTRESS IN A SUPPORTING ROLE – MOTION PICTURE: **Mira Sorvino** *Mighty Aphrodite*
BEST SCREENPLAY – MOTION PICTURE: **Emma Thompson** *Sense and Sensibility*

Cannes International Film Festival

PALME D'OR: ***Underground***
DIRECTOR: **Mathieu Kassovitz** *La Haine*
ACTOR: **Jonathan Pryce** *Carrington*
ACTRESS: **Helen Mirren** *The Madness of King George*

Berlin International Film Festival

GOLDEN BERLIN BEAR: ***The Bait***
SILVER BERLIN BEAR FOR THE BEST DIRECTOR: **Richard Linklater** *Before Sunrise*
SILVER BERLIN BEAR FOR THE BEST ACTOR: **Paul Newman** *Nobody's Fool*
SILVER BERLIN BEAR FOR THE BEST ACTRESS: **Josephine Siao** *Xiatian De Xue*

1996

British Academy of Film & Television Arts Awards

BEST FILM: ***The English Patient*** • *Fargo* • *Secrets & Lies* • *Shine*
BEST FILM NOT IN THE ENGLISH LANGUAGE: ***Ridicule*** • *Antonia's Line* • *Kolya* • *Nelly & Monsieur Arnaud*
THE ALEXANDER KORDA AWARD FOR THE OUTSTANDING BRITISH FILM OF THE YEAR: ***Secrets & Lies*** • *Brassed Off* • *Carla's Song* • *Richard III*
THE DAVID LEAN AWARD FOR THE BEST ACHIEVEMENT IN DIRECTION: **Joel Coen** *Fargo* • Scott Hicks *Shine* • Mike Leigh *Secrets & Lies* • Anthony Minghella *The English Patient*
BEST PERFORMANCE BY AN ACTOR IN A LEADING ROLE: **Geoffrey Rush** *Shine* • Ralph Fiennes *The English Patient* • Ian McKellen *Richard III* • Timothy Spall *Secrets & Lies*
BEST PERFORMANCE BY AN ACTRESS IN A LEADING ROLE: **Brenda Blethyn** *Secrets & Lies* • Frances McDormand *Fargo* • Kristin Scott Thomas *The English Patient* • Emily Watson *Breaking the Waves*
BEST ACTOR IN A SUPPORTING ROLE: **Paul Scofield** *The Crucible* • John Gielgud *Shine* • Edward Norton *Primal Fear* • Alan Rickman *Michael Collins*
BEST ACTRESS IN A SUPPORTING ROLE: **Juliette Binoche** *The English Patient* • Lauren Bacall *The Mirror Has Two Faces* • Marianne Jean-Baptiste *Secrets & Lies* • Lynn Redgrave *Shine*
BEST SCREENPLAY (ORIGINAL): **Mike Leigh** *Secrets & Lies* • Mark Herman *Brassed Off* • Joel Coen, Ethan Coen *Fargo* • John Sayles *Lone Star* • Jan Sardi *Shine*
BEST SCREENPLAY (ADAPTED): Anthony Minghella *The English Patient* • Arthur Miller *The Crucible* • Alan Parker, Oliver Stone *Evita* • Ian McKellen, Richard Loncraine *Richard III*

Academy Awards

BEST PICTURE: ***The English Patient*** • *Fargo* • *Jerry Maguire* • *Secrets & Lies* • *Shine*
FOREIGN LANGUAGE FILM: ***Kolya*** • *A Chef in Love* • *The Other Side of Sunday* • *Prisoner of the Mountains* • *Ridicule*
DIRECTING: **Anthony Minghella** *The English Patient* • Joel Coen *Fargo* • Milos Forman *The People vs Larry Flynt* • Scott Hicks *Shine* • Mike Leigh *Secrets & Lies*
ACTOR IN A LEADING ROLE: **Geoffrey Rush** *Shine* • Tom Cruise *Jerry Maguire* • Ralph Fiennes *The English Patient* • Woody Harrelson *The People vs Larry Flynt* • Billy Bob Thornton *Sling Blade*
ACTRESS IN A LEADING ROLE: **Frances McDormand** *Fargo* • Brenda Blethyn *Secrets & Lies* • Diane Keaton *Marvin's Room* • Kristin Scott Thomas *The English Patient* • Emily Watson *Breaking the Waves*
ACTOR IN A SUPPORTING ROLE: **Cuba Gooding Jr** *Jerry Maguire* • William H Macy *Fargo* • Armin Mueller-Stahl *Shine* • Edward Norton *Primal Fear* • James Woods *Ghosts of Mississippi*
ACTRESS IN A SUPPORTING ROLE: **Juliette Binoche** *The English Patient* • Joan Allen *The Crucible* • Lauren Bacall *The Mirror Has Two Faces* • Barbara Hershey *The Portrait of a Lady* • Marianne Jean-Baptiste *Secrets & Lies*
WRITING (SCREENPLAY WRITTEN DIRECTLY FOR THE SCREEN): **Ethan Coen**, **Joel Coen** *Fargo* • Cameron Crowe *Jerry Maguire* • John Sayles *Lone Star* • Mike Leigh *Secrets & Lies* • Scott Hicks, Jan Sardi *Shine*
WRITING (SCREENPLAY BASED ON MATERIAL PREVIOUSLY PRODUCED OR PUBLISHED): **Billy Bob Thornton** *Sling Blade* • Arthur Miller *The Crucible* • Anthony Minghella *The English Patient* • Kenneth Branagh *Hamlet* • John Hodge *Trainspotting*

Golden Globe Awards

BEST MOTION PICTURE – DRAMA: ***The English Patient***
BEST MOTION PICTURE – COMEDY OR MUSICAL: ***Evita***
BEST FOREIGN LANGUAGE FILM: ***Kolya***
BEST DIRECTOR – MOTION PICTURE: **Milos Forman** *The People vs Larry Flynt*
BEST PERFORMANCE BY AN ACTOR IN A MOTION PICTURE – DRAMA: **Geoffrey Rush** *Shine*
BEST PERFORMANCE BY AN ACTRESS IN A MOTION PICTURE – DRAMA: **Brenda Blethyn** *Secrets & Lies*
BEST PERFORMANCE BY AN ACTOR IN A MOTION PICTURE – COMEDY OR MUSICAL: **Tom Cruise** *Jerry Maguire*
BEST PERFORMANCE BY AN ACTRESS IN A MOTION PICTURE – COMEDY OR MUSICAL: **Madonna** *Evita*
BEST PERFORMANCE BY AN ACTOR IN A SUPPORTING ROLE – MOTION PICTURE: **Edward Norton** *Primal Fear*
BEST PERFORMANCE BY AN ACTRESS IN A SUPPORTING ROLE – MOTION PICTURE: **Lauren Bacall** *The Mirror Has Two Faces*
BEST SCREENPLAY – MOTION PICTURE: **Scott Alexander**, **Larry Karaszewski** *The People vs Larry Flynt*

Cannes International Film Festival

PALME D'OR: ***Secrets & Lies***
DIRECTOR: **Joel Coen** *Fargo*
ACTOR: **Daniel Auteuil**, **Pascal Duquenne** *The Eighth Day*
ACTRESS: **Brenda Blethyn** *Secrets & Lies*
SCREENPLAY: **Jacques Audiard** *A Self-Made Hero*

Berlin International Film Festival

GOLDEN BERLIN BEAR: ***Sense and Sensibility***
SILVER BERLIN BEAR FOR THE BEST DIRECTOR: **Ho Yim** *The Sun Has Ears* • **Richard Loncraine** *Richard III*
SILVER BERLIN BEAR FOR THE BEST ACTOR: **Sean Penn** *Dead Man Walking*
SILVER BERLIN BEAR FOR THE BEST ACTRESS: **Anouk Grinberg** *Mon Homme*

1997

British Academy of Film & Television Arts Awards

BEST FILM: ***The Full Monty*** • *LA Confidential* • *Mrs Brown* • *Titanic*
BEST FILM NOT IN THE ENGLISH LANGUAGE: ***L'Appartement*** • *Lucie Aubrac* • *Ma Vie en Rose* • *The Tango Lesson*
THE ALEXANDER KORDA AWARD FOR THE OUTSTANDING BRITISH FILM OF THE YEAR: ***Nil by Mouth*** • *The Borrowers* • *The Full Monty* • *Mrs Brown* • *Regeneration* • *TwentyFourSeven*
THE DAVID LEAN AWARD FOR THE BEST ACHIEVEMENT IN DIRECTION: **Baz Luhrmann** *William Shakespeare's Romeo + Juliet* • James Cameron *Titanic* • Peter Cattaneo *The Full Monty* • Curtis Hanson *LA Confidential*
BEST PERFORMANCE BY AN ACTOR IN A LEADING ROLE: **Robert Carlyle** *The Full Monty* • Billy Connolly *Mrs Brown* • Kevin Spacey *LA Confidential* • Ray Winstone *Nil by Mouth*
BEST PERFORMANCE BY AN ACTRESS IN A LEADING ROLE: **Judi Dench** *Mrs Brown* • Kim Basinger *LA Confidential* • Helena Bonham Carter *The Wings of the Dove* • Kathy Burke *Nil by Mouth*
BEST PERFORMANCE BY AN ACTOR IN A SUPPORTING ROLE: **Tom Wilkinson**, Mark Addy *The Full Monty* • Rupert Everett *My Best Friend's Wedding* • Burt Reynolds *Boogie Nights*
BEST PERFORMANCE BY AN ACTRESS IN A SUPPORTING ROLE: **Sigourney Weaver** *The Ice Storm* • Jennifer Ehle *Wilde* • Lesley Sharp *The Full Monty* • Zoë Wanamaker *Wilde*
BEST SCREENPLAY (ORIGINAL): **Gary Oldman** *Nil by Mouth* • Paul Thomas Anderson *Boogie Nights* • Simon Beaufoy *The Full Monty* • Jeremy Brock *Mrs Brown*
BEST SCREENPLAY (ADAPTED): **Craig Pearce**, **Baz Luhrmann** *William Shakespeare's Romeo + Juliet* • James Schamus *The Ice Storm* • Curtis Hanson, Brian Helgeland *LA Confidential* • Hossein Amini *The Wings of the Dove*

Academy Awards

BEST PICTURE: ***Titanic*** • *As Good as It Gets* • *The Full Monty* • *Good Will Hunting* • *LA Confidential*
FOREIGN LANGUAGE FILM: ***Character*** • *Beyond Silence* • *Four Days in September* • *Secrets of the Heart* • *The Thief*
DIRECTING: **James Cameron** *Titanic* • Peter Cattaneo *The Full Monty* • Atom Egoyan *The Sweet Hereafter* • Curtis Hanson *LA Confidential* • Gus Van Sant *Good Will Hunting*
ACTOR IN A LEADING ROLE: **Jack Nicholson** *As Good as It Gets* • Matt Damon *Good Will Hunting* • Robert Duvall *The Apostle* • Peter Fonda *Ulee's Gold* • Dustin Hoffman *Wag the Dog*
ACTRESS IN A LEADING ROLE: **Helen Hunt** *As Good as It Gets* • Helena Bonham Carter *The Wings of the Dove* • Julie Christie *Afterglow* • Judi Dench *Mrs Brown* • Kate Winslet *Titanic*
ACTOR IN A SUPPORTING ROLE: **Robin Williams** *Good Will Hunting* • Robert Forster *Jackie Brown* • Anthony Hopkins *Amistad* • Greg Kinnear *As Good as It Gets* • Burt Reynolds *Boogie Nights*
ACTRESS IN A SUPPORTING ROLE: **Kim Basinger** *LA Confidential* • Joan Cusack *In & Out* • Minnie Driver *Good Will Hunting* • Julianne Moore *Boogie Nights* • Gloria Stuart *Titanic*
WRITING (SCREENPLAY WRITTEN DIRECTLY FOR THE SCREEN): **Matt Damon**, **Ben Affleck** *Good Will Hunting* • Mark Andrus, James L Brooks *As Good as It Gets* • Paul Thomas Anderson *Boogie Nights* • Woody Allen *Deconstructing Harry* • Simon Beaufoy *The Full Monty*
WRITING (SCREENPLAY BASED ON MATERIAL PREVIOUSLY PRODUCED OR PUBLISHED): **Curtis Hanson**, **Brian Helgeland** *LA Confidential* • Paul Attanasio *Donnie Brasco* • Atom Egoyan *The Sweet Hereafter* • Hilary Henkin, David Mamet *Wag the Dog* • Hossein Amini *The Wings of the Dove*

Golden Globe Awards

BEST MOTION PICTURE – DRAMA: ***Titanic***
BEST MOTION PICTURE – COMEDY OR MUSICAL: ***As Good as It Gets***
BEST FOREIGN LANGUAGE FILM: ***Ma Vie en Rose***
BEST PERFORMANCE BY AN ACTOR IN A MOTION PICTURE – DRAMA: **Peter Fonda** *Ulee's Gold*
BEST PERFORMANCE BY AN ACTRESS IN A MOTION PICTURE – DRAMA: **Judi Dench** *Mrs Brown*
BEST PERFORMANCE BY AN ACTOR IN A MOTION PICTURE – COMEDY OR MUSICAL: **Jack Nicholson** *As Good as It Gets*
BEST PERFORMANCE BY AN ACTRESS IN A MOTION PICTURE – COMEDY OR MUSICAL: **Helen Hunt** *As Good as It Gets*
BEST PERFORMANCE BY AN ACTOR IN A SUPPORTING ROLE – MOTION PICTURE: **Burt Reynolds** *Boogie Nights*
BEST PERFORMANCE BY AN ACTRESS IN A SUPPORTING ROLE – MOTION PICTURE: **Kim Basinger** *LA Confidential*

Cannes International Film Festival

PALME D'OR: ***The Eel*** • ***A Taste of Cherry***
DIRECTOR: **Wong Kar-Wai** *Happy Together*
ACTOR: **Sean Penn** *She's So Lovely*
ACTRESS: **Kathy Burke** *Nil by Mouth*
SCREENPLAY: **James Schamus** *The Ice Storm*

Berlin International Film Festival

GOLDEN BERLIN BEAR: ***The People vs Larry Flynt***
SILVER BERLIN BEAR FOR THE BEST DIRECTOR: **Eric Heumann** *Port Djema*
SILVER BERLIN BEAR FOR THE BEST ACTOR: **Leonardo DiCaprio** *William Shakespeare's Romeo + Juliet*
SILVER BERLIN BEAR FOR THE BEST ACTRESS: **Juliette Binoche** *The English Patient*

1998

British Academy of Film & Television Arts Awards

BEST FILM: ***Shakespeare in Love*** • *Elizabeth* • *Saving Private Ryan* • *The Truman Show*
BEST FILM NOT IN THE ENGLISH LANGUAGE: ***Central Station*** • *Le Bossu* • *Life Is Beautiful* • *Live Flesh*
THE ALEXANDER KORDA AWARD FOR THE OUTSTANDING BRITISH FILM OF THE YEAR: ***Elizabeth*** • *Hilary and Jackie* • *Little*

Voice • *Lock, Stock and Two Smoking Barrels* • *My Name Is Joe* • *Sliding Doors*
The David Lean Award for the Best Achievement in Direction: **Peter Weir** *The Truman Show* • Shekhar Kapur *Elizabeth* • John Madden *Shakespeare in Love* • Steven Spielberg *Saving Private Ryan*
Best Performance by an Actor in a Leading Role: **Roberto Benigni** *Life Is Beautiful* • Michael Caine *Little Voice* • Joseph Fiennes *Shakespeare in Love* • Tom Hanks *Saving Private Ryan*
Best Performance by an Actress in a Leading Role: **Cate Blanchett** *Elizabeth* • Jane Horrocks *Little Voice* • Gwyneth Paltrow *Shakespeare in Love* • Emily Watson *Hilary and Jackie*
Best Performance by an Actor in a Supporting Role: **Geoffrey Rush** *Shakespeare in Love* • Ed Harris *The Truman Show* • Geoffrey Rush *Elizabeth* • Tom Wilkinson *Shakespeare in Love*
Best Performance by an Actress in a Supporting Role: **Judi Dench** *Shakespeare in Love* • Kathy Bates *Primary Colors* • Brenda Blethyn *Little Voice* • Lynn Redgrave *Gods and Monsters*
Best Screenplay (Original): **Andrew Niccol** *The Truman Show* • Michael Hirst *Elizabeth* • Vincenzo Cerami, Roberto Benigni *Life Is Beautiful* • Marc Norman, Tom Stoppard *Shakespeare in Love*
Best Screenplay (Adapted): **Elaine May** *Primary Colors* • Frank Cottrell Boyce *Hilary and Jackie* • Mark Herman *Little Voice* • David Mamet, Hilary Henkin *Wag the Dog*

Academy Awards

Best Picture: ***Shakespeare in Love*** • *Elizabeth* • *Life Is Beautiful* • *Saving Private Ryan* • *The Thin Red Line*
Foreign Language Film: ***Life Is Beautiful*** • *Central Station* • *The Children of Heaven* • *The Grandfather* • *Tango*
Directing: **Steven Spielberg** *Saving Private Ryan* • Roberto Benigni *Life Is Beautiful* • John Madden *Shakespeare in Love* • Terrence Malick *The Thin Red Line* • Peter Weir *The Truman Show*
Actor in a Leading Role: **Roberto Benigni** *Life Is Beautiful* • Tom Hanks *Saving Private Ryan* • Ian McKellen *Gods and Monsters* • Nick Nolte *Affliction* • Edward Norton *American History X*
Actress in a Leading Role: **Gwyneth Paltrow** *Shakespeare in Love* • Cate Blanchett *Elizabeth* • Fernanda Montenegro *Central Station* • Meryl Streep *One True Thing* • Emily Watson *Hilary and Jackie*
Actor in a Supporting Role: **James Coburn** *Affliction* • Robert Duvall *A Civil Action* • Ed Harris *The Truman Show* • Geoffrey Rush *Shakespeare in Love* • Billy Bob Thornton *A Simple Plan*
Actress in a Supporting Role: **Judi Dench** *Shakespeare in Love* • Kathy Bates *Primary Colors* • Brenda Blethyn *Little Voice* • Rachel Griffiths *Hilary and Jackie* • Lynn Redgrave *Gods and Monsters*
Writing (Screenplay Written Directly for the Screen): **Marc Norman, Tom Stoppard** *Shakespeare in Love* • Warren Beatty, Jeremy Pikser *Bulworth* • Roberto Benigni, Vincenzo Cerami *Life Is Beautiful* • Robert Rodat *Saving Private Ryan* • Andrew Niccol *The Truman Show*
Writing (Screenplay Based on Material Previously Produced or Published): **Bill Condon** *Gods and Monsters* • Scott Frank *Out of Sight* • Elaine May *Primary Colors* • Scott B Smith *A Simple Plan* • Terrence Malick *The Thin Red Line*

Golden Globe Awards

Best Motion Picture – Drama: ***Saving Private Ryan***
Best Motion Picture – Comedy or Musical: ***Shakespeare in Love***
Best Foreign Language Film: ***Central Station***
Best Director – Motion Picture: **James Cameron** *Titanic* • **Steven Spielberg** *Saving Private Ryan*
Best Performance by an Actor in a Motion Picture – Drama: **Jim Carrey** *The Truman Show*
Best Performance by an Actress in a Motion Picture – Drama: **Cate Blanchett** *Elizabeth*
Best Performance by an Actor in a Motion Picture – Comedy or Musical: **Michael Caine** *Little Voice*
Best Performance by an Actress in a Motion Picture – Comedy or Musical: **Gwyneth Paltrow** *Shakespeare in Love*
Best Performance by an Actor in a Supporting Role – Motion Picture: **Ed Harris** *The Truman Show*
Best Performance by an Actress in a Supporting Role – Motion Picture: **Lynn Redgrave** *Gods and Monsters*
Best Screenplay – Motion Picture: **Matt Damon, Ben Affleck** *Good Will Hunting* • **Marc Norman, Tom Stoppard** *Shakespeare in Love*

Cannes International Film Festival

Palme d'Or: ***Eternity and a Day***
Director: **John Boorman** *The General*
Actor: **Peter Mullan** *My Name Is Joe*
Actress: **Elodie Bouchez, Natacha Régnier** *The Dream Life of Angels*
Screenplay: **Hal Hartley** *Henry Fool*

Berlin International Film Festival

Golden Berlin Bear: ***Central Station***
Silver Berlin Bear for the Best Director: **Neil Jordan** *The Butcher Boy*
Silver Berlin Bear for the Best Actor: **Samuel L Jackson** *Jackie Brown*
Silver Berlin Bear for the Best Actress: **Fernanda Montenegro** *Central Station*

1999

British Academy Film Awards

Best Film: ***American Beauty*** • *East Is East* • *The End of the Affair* • *The Sixth Sense* • *The Talented Mr Ripley*
Best Film Not in the English Language: ***All about My Mother*** • *Buena Vista Social Club* • *Festen* • *Run Lola Run*
The Alexander Korda Award for the Outstanding British Film of the Year: ***East Is East*** • *Notting Hill* • *Onegin* • *Ratcatcher* • *Topsy-Turvy* • *Wonderland*
The David Lean Award for the Best Achievement in Direction: **Pedro Almodóvar** *All about My Mother* • Neil Jordan *The End of the Affair* • Sam Mendes *American Beauty* • Anthony Minghella *The Talented Mr Ripley* • M Night Shyamalan *The Sixth Sense*
Best Performance by an Actor in a Leading Role: **Kevin Spacey** *American Beauty* • Jim Broadbent *Topsy-Turvy* • Russell Crowe *The Insider* • Ralph Fiennes *The End of the Affair* • Om Puri *East Is East*
Best Performance by an Actress in a Leading Role: **Annette Bening** *American Beauty* • Linda Bassett *East Is East* • Julianne Moore *The End of the Affair* • Emily Watson *Angela's Ashes*
Best Performance by an Actor in a Supporting Role: **Jude Law** *The Talented Mr Ripley* • Wes Bentley *American Beauty* • Michael Caine *The Cider House Rules* • Rhys Ifans *Notting Hill* • Timothy Spall *Topsy-Turvy*
Best Performance by an Actress in a Supporting Role: **Maggie Smith** *Tea with Mussolini* • Thora Birch *American Beauty* • Cate Blanchett *The Talented Mr Ripley* • Cameron Diaz *Being John Malkovich* • Mena Suvari *American Beauty*
Best Screenplay (Original): **Charlie Kaufman** *Being John Malkovich* • Pedro Almodóvar *All about My Mother* • Alan Ball *American Beauty* • M Night Shyamalan *The Sixth Sense* • Mike Leigh *Topsy-Turvy*
Best Screenplay (Adapted): **Neil Jordan** *The End of the Affair* • Oliver Parker *An Ideal Husband* • Ayub Khan-Din *East Is East* • Anthony Minghella *The Talented Mr Ripley*

Academy Awards

Best Picture: ***American Beauty*** • *The Cider House Rules* • *The Green Mile* • *The Insider* • *The Sixth Sense*
Foreign Language Film: ***All about My Mother*** • *Himalaya* • *East-West* • *Solomon and Gaenor* • *Under the Sun*
Directing: **Sam Mendes** *American Beauty* • Lasse Hallström *The Cider House Rules* • Spike Jonze *Being John Malkovich* • Michael Mann *The Insider* • M Night Shyamalan *The Sixth Sense*
Actor in a Leading Role: **Kevin Spacey** *American Beauty* • Russell Crowe *The Insider* • Richard Farnsworth *The Straight Story* • Sean Penn *Sweet and Lowdown* • Denzel Washington *The Hurricane*
Actress in a Leading Role: **Hilary Swank** *Boys Don't Cry* • Annette Bening *American Beauty* • Janet McTeer *Tumbleweeds* • Julianne Moore *The End of the Affair* • Meryl Streep *Music of the Heart*
Actor in a Supporting Role: **Michael Caine** *The Cider House Rules* • Tom Cruise *Magnolia* • Michael Clarke Duncan *The Green Mile* • Jude Law *The Talented Mr Ripley* • Haley Joel Osment *The Sixth Sense*
Actress in a Supporting Role: **Angelina Jolie** *Girl, Interrupted* • Toni Collette *The Sixth Sense* • Catherine Keener *Being John Malkovich* • Samantha Morton *Sweet and Lowdown* • Chloë Sevigny *Boys Don't Cry*
Writing (Screenplay Written Directly for the Screen): **Alan Ball** *American Beauty* • Charlie Kaufman *Being John Malkovich* • Paul Thomas Anderson *Magnolia* • M Night Shyamalan *The Sixth Sense* • Mike Leigh *Topsy-Turvy*
Writing (Screenplay Based on Material Previously Produced or Published): **John Irving** *The Cider House Rules* • Alexander Payne, Jim Taylor *Election* • Frank Darabont *The Green Mile* • Eric Roth, Michael Mann *The Insider* • Anthony Minghella *The Talented Mr Ripley*

Golden Globe Awards

Best Motion Picture – Drama: ***American Beauty***
Best Motion Picture – Comedy or Musical: ***Toy Story 2***
Best Foreign Language Film: ***All about My Mother***
Best Director – Motion Picture: **Sam Mendes** *American Beauty*
Best Performance by an Actor in a Motion Picture – Drama: **Denzel Washington** *The Hurricane*
Best Performance by an Actress in a Motion Picture – Drama: **Hilary Swank** *Boys Don't Cry*
Best Performance by an Actor in a Motion Picture – Comedy or Musical: **Jim Carrey** *Man on the Moon*
Best Performance by an Actress in a Motion Picture – Comedy or Musical: **Janet McTeer** *Tumbleweeds*
Best Performance by an Actor in a Supporting Role – Motion Picture: **Tom Cruise** *Magnolia*
Best Performance by an Actress in a Supporting Role – Motion Picture: **Angelina Jolie** *Girl, Interrupted*
Best Screenplay – Motion Picture: **Alan Ball** *American Beauty*

Cannes International Film Festival

Palme d'Or: ***Rosetta***
Director: **Pedro Almodóvar** *All about My Mother*
Actor: **Emmanuel Schotté** *L'Humanité*
Actress: **Severine Caneele** *L'Humanité* • **Emilie Dequenne** *Rosetta*
Screenplay: **Yuri Arabov** *Moloch*

Berlin International Film Festival

Golden Berlin Bear: ***The Thin Red Line***
Silver Berlin Bear for the Best Director: **Stephen Frears** *The Hi-Lo Country*
Silver Berlin Bear for the Best Actor: **Michael Gwisdek** *Night Shapes*
Silver Berlin Bear for the Best Actress: **Maria Schrader, Juliane Köhler** *Aimée and Jaguar*

2000

British Academy Film Awards

Best Film: ***Gladiator*** • *Almost Famous* • *Billy Elliot* • *Erin Brockovich*
Best Film Not in the English Language: ***Crouching Tiger, Hidden Dragon*** • *The Girl on the Bridge* • *Harry, un Ami Qui Vous Veut du Bien* • *In the Mood for Love* • *Malena*
The Alexander Korda Award for the Outstanding British Film of the Year: ***Billy Elliot*** • *Chicken Run* • *The House of Mirth* • *Last Resort* • *Sexy Beast*
The David Lean Award for the Best Achievement in Direction: **Ang Lee** *Crouching Tiger, Hidden Dragon* • Stephen Daldry *Billy Elliot* • Steven Soderbergh *Erin Brockovich* • Steven Soderbergh *Traffic* • Ridley Scott *Gladiator*
Best Performance by an Actor in a Leading Role: **Jamie Bell** *Billy Elliot* • Russell Crowe *Gladiator* • Michael Douglas *Wonder Boys* • Tom Hanks *Cast Away* • Geoffrey Rush *Quills*
Best Performance by an Actress in a Leading Role: **Julia Roberts** *Erin Brockovich* • Juliette Binoche *Chocolat* • Kate Hudson *Almost Famous* • Hilary Swank *Boys Don't Cry* • Michelle Yeoh *Crouching Tiger, Hidden Dragon*
Best Performance by an Actor in a Supporting Role: **Benicio Del Toro** *Traffic* • Albert Finney *Erin Brockovich* • Gary Lewis *Billy Elliot* • Joaquin Phoenix, Oliver Reed *Gladiator*
Best Performance by an Actress in a Supporting Role: **Julie Walters** *Billy Elliot* • Judi Dench *Chocolat* • Frances McDormand *Almost Famous* • Lena Olin *Chocolat* • Zhang Ziyi *Crouching Tiger, Hidden Dragon*
Best Screenplay (Original): **Cameron Crowe** *Almost Famous* • Lee Hall *Billy Elliot* • Susannah Grant *Erin Brockovich* • David Franzoni, John Logan, William Nicholson *Gladiator* • Ethan Coen, Joel Coen *O Brother, Where Art Thou?*
Best Screenplay (Adapted): **Stephen Gaghan** *Traffic* • Robert Nelson Jacobs *Chocolat* • James Schamus, Wang Hui-Ling, Tsai Kuo-Jung *Crouching Tiger, Hidden Dragon* • D V De Vincentis, Steve Pink, John Cusack, Scott Rosenberg *High Fidelity* • Steve Kloves *Wonder Boys*

Academy Awards

Best Picture: ***Gladiator*** • *Chocolat* • *Crouching Tiger, Hidden Dragon* • *Erin Brockovich* • *Traffic*
Foreign Language Film: ***Crouching Tiger, Hidden Dragon*** • *Amores Perros* • *Divided We Fall* • *Everybody Famous!* • *Le Goût des Autres*
Directing: **Steven Soderbergh** *Traffic* • Stephen Daldry *Billy Elliot* • Ang Lee *Crouching Tiger, Hidden Dragon* • Ridley Scott *Gladiator* • Steven Soderbergh *Erin Brockovich*
Actor in a Leading Role: **Russell Crowe** *Gladiator* • Javier Bardem *Before Night Falls* • Tom Hanks *Cast Away* • Ed Harris *Pollock* • Geoffrey Rush *Quills*
Actress in a Leading Role: **Julia Roberts** *Erin Brockovich* • Joan Allen *The Contender* • Juliette Binoche *Chocolat* • Ellen Burstyn *Requiem for a Dream* • Laura Linney *You Can Count on Me*
Actor in a Supporting Role: **Benicio Del Toro** *Traffic* • Jeff Bridges *The Contender* • Willem Dafoe *Shadow of the Vampire* • Albert Finney *Erin Brockovich* • Joaquin Phoenix *Gladiator*
Actress in a Supporting Role: **Marcia Gay Harden** *Pollock* • Judi Dench *Chocolat* • Kate Hudson, Frances McDormand *Almost Famous* • Julie Walters *Billy Elliot*
Writing (Screenplay Written Directly for the Screen): **Cameron Crowe** *Almost Famous* • Lee Hall *Billy Elliot* • Susannah Grant *Erin Brockovich* • David Franzoni, John Logan, William Nicholson *Gladiator* • Kenneth Lonergan *You Can Count on Me*
Writing (Screenplay Based on Material Previously Produced or Published): **Stephen Gaghan** *Traffic* • Robert Nelson Jacobs *Chocolat* • James Schamus, Wang Hui-Ling, Tsai Kuo-Jung *Crouching Tiger, Hidden Dragon* • Ethan Coen, Joel Coen *O Brother, Where Art Thou?* • Steve Kloves *Wonder Boys*

Golden Globe Awards

Best Motion Picture – Drama: ***Gladiator***
Best Motion Picture – Comedy or Musical: ***Almost Famous***
Best Foreign Language Film: ***Crouching Tiger, Hidden Dragon***
Best Director – Motion Picture: **Ang Lee** *Crouching Tiger, Hidden Dragon*
Best Performance by an Actor in a Motion Picture – Drama: **Tom Hanks** *Cast Away*
Best Performance by an Actress in a Motion Picture – Drama: **Julia Roberts** *Erin Brockovich*
Best Performance by an Actor in a Motion Picture – Comedy or Musical: **George Clooney** *O Brother, Where Art Thou?*
Best Performance by an Actress in a Motion Picture – Comedy or Musical: **Renee Zellweger** *Nurse Betty*

BEST PERFORMANCE BY AN ACTOR IN A SUPPORTING ROLE – MOTION PICTURE: **Benicio Del Toro** *Traffic*
BEST PERFORMANCE BY AN ACTRESS IN A SUPPORTING ROLE – MOTION PICTURE: **Kate Hudson** *Almost Famous*
BEST SCREENPLAY – MOTION PICTURE: **Stephen Gaghan** *Traffic*

Cannes International Film Festival

PALME D'OR: ***Dancer in the Dark***
DIRECTOR: **Edward Yang** *A One and a Two*
ACTOR: **Tony Leung (2)** *In the Mood for Love*
ACTRESS: **Björk** *Dancer in the Dark*
SCREENPLAY: **John C Richards**, **James Flamberg** *Nurse Betty*

Berlin International Film Festival

GOLDEN BERLIN BEAR: ***Magnolia***
SILVER BERLIN BEAR FOR THE BEST DIRECTOR: **Milos Forman** *Man on the Moon*
SILVER BERLIN BEAR FOR THE BEST ACTOR: **Denzel Washington** *The Hurricane*
SILVER BERLIN BEAR FOR THE BEST ACTRESS: **Bibiana Beglau**, **Nadja Uhl** *The Legends of Rita*

2001

British Academy Film Awards

BEST FILM: ***The Lord of the Rings: The Fellowship of the Ring*** • *Amélie* • *A Beautiful Mind* • *Moulin Rouge* • *Shrek*
BEST FILM NOT IN THE ENGLISH LANGUAGE: ***Amores Perros*** • *Amélie* • *Behind the Sun* • *Monsoon Wedding* • *The Piano Teacher*
THE ALEXANDER KORDA AWARD FOR THE OUTSTANDING BRITISH FILM OF THE YEAR: ***Gosford Park*** • *Bridget Jones's Diary* • *Harry Potter and the Philosopher's Stone* • *Iris* • *Me without You*
THE DAVID LEAN AWARD FOR THE BEST ACHIEVEMENT IN DIRECTION: **Peter Jackson** *The Lord of the Rings: The Fellowship of the Ring* • Robert Altman *Gosford Park* • Ron Howard *A Beautiful Mind* • Jean-Pierre Jeunet *Amélie* • Baz Luhrmann *Moulin Rouge*
BEST PERFORMANCE BY AN ACTOR IN A LEADING ROLE: **Russell Crowe** *A Beautiful Mind* • Jim Broadbent *Iris* • Ian McKellen *The Lord of the Rings: The Fellowship of the Ring* • Kevin Spacey *The Shipping News* • Tom Wilkinson *In the Bedroom*
BEST PERFORMANCE BY AN ACTRESS IN A LEADING ROLE: **Judi Dench** *Iris* • Nicole Kidman *The Others* • Sissy Spacek *In the Bedroom* • Audrey Tautou *Amélie* • Renee Zellweger *Bridget Jones's Diary*
BEST PERFORMANCE BY AN ACTOR IN A SUPPORTING ROLE: **Jim Broadbent** *Moulin Rouge* • Hugh Bonneville *Iris* • Robbie Coltrane *Harry Potter and the Philosopher's Stone* • Colin Firth *Bridget Jones's Diary* • Eddie Murphy *Shrek*
BEST PERFORMANCE BY AN ACTRESS IN A SUPPORTING ROLE: **Jennifer Connelly** *A Beautiful Mind* • Judi Dench *The Shipping News* • Helen Mirren, Maggie Smith *Gosford Park* • Kate Winslet *Iris*
BEST SCREENPLAY (ORIGINAL): **Guillaume Laurant**, **Jean-Pierre Jeunet** *Amélie* • Julian Fellowes *Gosford Park* • Baz Luhrmann, Craig Pearce *Moulin Rouge* • Alejandro Amenábar *The Others* • Owen Wilson *The Royal Tenenbaums*
BEST SCREENPLAY (ADAPTED): **Joe Stillman**, **Roger SH Schulman**, **Ted Elliott**, **Terry Rossio** *Shrek* • Akiva Goldsman *A Beautiful Mind* • Andrew Davies, Helen Fielding, Richard Curtis *Bridget Jones's Diary* • Charles Wood, Richard Eyre *Iris* • Fran Walsh, Peter Jackson, Philippa Boyens *The Lord of the Rings: The Fellowship of the Ring*
BEST SCREENPLAY (ORIGINAL): Wes Anderson *The Royal Tenenbaums*

Academy Awards

BEST PICTURE: ***A Beautiful Mind*** • *Gosford Park* • *In the Bedroom* • *The Lord of the Rings: The Fellowship of the Ring* • *Moulin Rouge*
FOREIGN LANGUAGE FILM: ***No Man's Land*** • *Amélie* • *Elling* • *Lagaan: Once upon a Time in India* • *Son of the Bride*
DIRECTING: **Ron Howard** *A Beautiful Mind* • Robert Altman *Gosford Park* • Peter Jackson *The Lord of the Rings: The Fellowship of the Ring* • David Lynch *Mulholland Drive* • Ridley Scott *Black Hawk Down*
ACTOR IN A LEADING ROLE: **Denzel Washington** *Training Day* • Russell Crowe *A Beautiful Mind* • Sean Penn *I Am Sam* • Will Smith *Ali* • Tom Wilkinson *In the Bedroom*
ACTRESS IN A LEADING ROLE: **Halle Berry** *Monster's Ball* • Judi Dench *Iris* • Nicole Kidman *Moulin Rouge* • Sissy Spacek *In the Bedroom* • Renee Zellweger *Bridget Jones's Diary*
ACTOR IN A SUPPORTING ROLE: **Jim Broadbent** *Iris* • Ethan Hawke *Training Day* • Ben Kingsley *Sexy Beast* • Ian McKellen *The Lord of the Rings: The Fellowship of the Ring* • Jon Voight *Ali*
ACTRESS IN A SUPPORTING ROLE: **Jennifer Connelly** *A Beautiful Mind* • Helen Mirren, Maggie Smith *Gosford Park* • Marisa Tomei *In the Bedroom* • Kate Winslet *Iris*
WRITING (SCREENPLAY WRITTEN DIRECTLY FOR THE SCREEN): **Julian Fellowes** *Gosford Park* • Guillaume Laurant, Jean-Pierre Jeunet *Amélie* • Christopher Nolan, Jonathan Nolan *Memento* • Milo Addica, Will Rokos *Monster's Ball* • Owen Wilson, Wes Anderson *The Royal Tenenbaums*
WRITING (SCREENPLAY BASED ON MATERIAL PREVIOUSLY PRODUCED OR PUBLISHED): **Akiva Goldsman** *A Beautiful Mind* • Daniel Clowes, Terry Zwigoff *Ghost World* • Rob Festinger, Todd Field *In the Bedroom* • Fran Walsh, Peter Jackson, Philippa Boyens *The Lord of the Rings: The Fellowship of the Ring* • Joe Stillman, Roger SH Schulman, Ted Elliott, Terry Rossio *Shrek*

Golden Globe Awards

BEST MOTION PICTURE – DRAMA: ***A Beautiful Mind***
BEST MOTION PICTURE – COMEDY OR MUSICAL: ***Moulin Rouge***
BEST FOREIGN LANGUAGE FILM: ***No Man's Land***
BEST DIRECTOR – MOTION PICTURE: **Robert Altman** *Gosford Park*
BEST PERFORMANCE BY AN ACTOR IN A MOTION PICTURE – DRAMA: **Russell Crowe** *A Beautiful Mind*
BEST PERFORMANCE BY AN ACTRESS IN A MOTION PICTURE – DRAMA: **Sissy Spacek** *In the Bedroom*
BEST PERFORMANCE BY AN ACTOR IN A MOTION PICTURE – COMEDY OR MUSICAL: **Gene Hackman** *The Royal Tenenbaums*
BEST PERFORMANCE BY AN ACTRESS IN A MOTION PICTURE – COMEDY OR MUSICAL: **Nicole Kidman** *Moulin Rouge*
BEST PERFORMANCE BY AN ACTOR IN A SUPPORTING ROLE – MOTION PICTURE: **Jim Broadbent** *Iris*
BEST PERFORMANCE BY AN ACTRESS IN A SUPPORTING ROLE – MOTION PICTURE: **Jennifer Connelly** *A Beautiful Mind*
BEST SCREENPLAY – MOTION PICTURE: **Akiva Goldsman** *A Beautiful Mind*

Cannes International Film Festival

PALME D'OR: ***The Son's Room***
DIRECTOR: **Joel Coen** *The Man Who Wasn't There* • **David Lynch** *Mulholland Drive*
ACTOR: **Benoît Magimel** *The Piano Teacher*
ACTRESS: **Isabelle Huppert** *The Piano Teacher*
SCREENPLAY: **Danis Tanovic** *No Man's Land*

Berlin International Film Festival

GOLDEN BERLIN BEAR: ***Intimacy***
SILVER BERLIN BEAR FOR THE BEST DIRECTOR: **Lin Cheng-sheng** *Betelnut Beauty*
SILVER BERLIN BEAR FOR THE BEST ACTOR: **Benicio Del Toro** *Traffic*
SILVER BERLIN BEAR FOR THE BEST ACTRESS: **Kerry Fox** *Intimacy*

2002

British Academy Film Awards

BEST FILM: ***The Pianist*** • *Chicago* • *Gangs of New York* • *The Hours* • *The Lord of the Rings: The Two Towers*
BEST FILM NOT IN THE ENGLISH LANGUAGE: ***Talk to Her*** • *City of God* • *Devdas* • *The Warrior* • *Y Tu Mamá También*
THE ALEXANDER KORDA AWARD FOR THE OUTSTANDING BRITISH FILM OF THE YEAR: ***The Warrior*** • *Bend It like Beckham* • *Dirty Pretty Things* • *The Hours* • *The Magdalene Sisters*
THE DAVID LEAN AWARD FOR THE BEST ACHIEVEMENT IN DIRECTION: **Roman Polanski** *The Pianist* • Stephen Daldry *The Hours* • Peter Jackson *The Lord of the Rings: The Two Towers* • Rob Marshall *Chicago* • Martin Scorsese *Gangs of New York*
BEST PERFORMANCE BY AN ACTOR IN A LEADING ROLE: **Daniel Day-Lewis** *Gangs of New York* • Adrien Brody *The Pianist* • Nicolas Cage *Adaptation.* • Michael Caine *The Quiet American* • Jack Nicholson *About Schmidt*
BEST PERFORMANCE BY AN ACTRESS IN A LEADING ROLE: **Nicole Kidman** *The Hours* • Halle Berry *Monster's Ball* • Salma Hayek *Frida* • Meryl Streep *The Hours* • Renee Zellweger *Chicago*
BEST PERFORMANCE BY AN ACTOR IN A SUPPORTING ROLE: **Christopher Walken** *Catch Me If You Can* • Chris Cooper *Adaptation.* • Ed Harris *The Hours* • Alfred Molina *Frida* • Paul Newman *Road to Perdition*
BEST PERFORMANCE BY AN ACTRESS IN A SUPPORTING ROLE: **Catherine Zeta-Jones** *Chicago* • Toni Collette *About a Boy* • Julianne Moore *The Hours* • Queen Latifah *Chicago* • Meryl Streep *Adaptation.*
BEST SCREENPLAY (ORIGINAL): **Pedro Almodóvar** *Talk to Her* • Steven Knight *Dirty Pretty Things* • Jay Cocks, Steve Zaillian, Kenneth Lonergan *Gangs of New York* • Peter Mullan *The Magdalene Sisters* • Carlos Cuarón, Alfonso Cuarón *Y Tu Mamá También*
BEST SCREENPLAY (ADAPTED): **Charlie Kaufman**, **Donald Kaufman** *Adaptation.* • Peter Hedges, Chris Weitz, Paul Weitz *About a Boy* • Jeff Nathanson *Catch Me If You Can* • David Hare *The Hours* • Ronald Harwood *The Pianist*

Academy Awards

BEST PICTURE: ***Chicago*** • *Gangs of New York* • *The Hours* • *The Lord of the Rings: The Two Towers* • *The Pianist*
FOREIGN LANGUAGE FILM: ***Nowhere in Africa*** • *El Crimen del Padre Amaro* • *Hero* • *The Man without a Past* • *Zus & Zo*
DIRECTING: **Roman Polanski** *The Pianist* • Pedro Almodóvar *Talk to Her* • Stephen Daldry *The Hours* • Rob Marshall *Chicago* • Martin Scorsese *Gangs of New York*
ACTOR IN A LEADING ROLE: **Adrien Brody** *The Pianist* • Nicolas Cage *Adaptation.* • Michael Caine *The Quiet American* • Daniel Day-Lewis *Gangs of New York* • Jack Nicholson *About Schmidt*
ACTRESS IN A LEADING ROLE: **Nicole Kidman** *The Hours* • Salma Hayek *Frida* • Diane Lane *Unfaithful* • Julianne Moore *Far from Heaven* • Renee Zellweger *Chicago*
ACTOR IN A SUPPORTING ROLE: **Chris Cooper** *Adaptation.* • Ed Harris *The Hours* • Paul Newman *Road to Perdition* • John C Reilly *Chicago* • Christopher Walken *Catch Me If You Can*
ACTRESS IN A SUPPORTING ROLE: **Catherine Zeta-Jones** *Chicago* • Kathy Bates *About Schmidt* • Julianne Moore *The Hours* • Queen Latifah *Chicago* • Meryl Streep *Adaptation.*
WRITING (SCREENPLAY WRITTEN DIRECTLY FOR THE SCREEN): **Pedro Almodóvar** *Talk to Her* • Todd Haynes *Far from Heaven* • Jay Cocks, Steve Zaillian, Kenneth Lonergan *Gangs of New York* • Nia Vardalos *My Big Fat Greek Wedding* • Alfonso Cuarón, Carlos Cuarón *Y Tu Mamá También*
WRITING (SCREENPLAY BASED ON MATERIAL PREVIOUSLY PRODUCED OR PUBLISHED): **Ronald Harwood** *The Pianist* • Peter Hedges, Chris Weitz, Paul Weitz *About a Boy* • Charlie Kaufman, Donald Kaufman *Adaptation.* • Bill Condon *Chicago* • David Hare *The Hours*

Golden Globe Awards

BEST MOTION PICTURE – DRAMA: ***The Hours***
BEST MOTION PICTURE – COMEDY OR MUSICAL: ***Chicago***
BEST FOREIGN LANGUAGE FILM: ***Talk to Her***
BEST DIRECTOR – MOTION PICTURE: **Martin Scorsese** *Gangs of New York*
BEST PERFORMANCE BY AN ACTOR IN A MOTION PICTURE – DRAMA: **Jack Nicholson** *About Schmidt*
BEST PERFORMANCE BY AN ACTRESS IN A MOTION PICTURE – DRAMA: **Nicole Kidman** *The Hours*
BEST PERFORMANCE BY AN ACTOR IN A MOTION PICTURE – COMEDY OR MUSICAL: **Richard Gere** *Chicago*
BEST PERFORMANCE BY AN ACTRESS IN A MOTION PICTURE – COMEDY OR MUSICAL: **Renee Zellweger** *Chicago*
BEST PERFORMANCE BY AN ACTOR IN A SUPPORTING ROLE – MOTION PICTURE: **Chris Cooper** *Adaptation.*
BEST PERFORMANCE BY AN ACTRESS IN A SUPPORTING ROLE – MOTION PICTURE: **Meryl Streep** *Adaptation.*
BEST SCREENPLAY – MOTION PICTURE: **Alexander Payne**, **Jim Taylor** *About Schmidt*

Cannes International Film Festival

PALME D'OR: ***The Pianist***
DIRECTOR: **Paul Thomas Anderson** *Punch-Drunk Love* • **Im Kwon-taek** *Chihwaseon (Drunk on Women and Poetry)*
ACTOR: **Olivier Gourmet** *The Son*
ACTRESS: **Kati Outinen** *The Man without a Past*
SCREENPLAY: **Paul Laverty** *Sweet Sixteen*

Berlin International Film Festival

GOLDEN BEAR FOR FILM: ***Bloody Sunday*** • ***Spirited Away***
SILVER BERLIN BEAR FOR THE BEST DIRECTOR: **Otar Iosseliani** *Monday Morning*
SILVER BERLIN BEAR FOR THE BEST ACTOR: **Jacques Gamblin** *Laissez-passer*
SILVER BERLIN BEAR FOR THE BEST ACTRESS: **Halle Berry** *Monster's Ball*

2003

British Academy Film Awards

BEST FILM: ***The Lord of the Rings: The Return of the King*** • *Big Fish* • *Cold Mountain* • *Lost in Translation* • *Master and Commander: the Far Side of the World*
BEST FILM NOT IN THE ENGLISH LANGUAGE: ***In This World*** • *The Barbarian Invasions* • *Belleville Rendez-vous* • *Etre et Avoir* • *Good Bye Lenin!* • *Spirited Away*
THE ALEXANDER KORDA AWARD FOR THE OUTSTANDING BRITISH FILM OF THE YEAR: ***Touching the Void*** • *Cold Mountain* • *Girl with a Pearl Earring* • *In This World* • *Love Actually*
THE DAVID LEAN AWARD FOR THE BEST ACHIEVEMENT IN DIRECTION: **Peter Weir** *Master and Commander: the Far Side of the World* • Tim Burton *Big Fish* • Sofia Coppola *Lost in Translation* • Peter Jackson *The Lord of the Rings: The Return of the King* • Anthony Minghella *Cold Mountain*
BEST PERFORMANCE BY AN ACTOR IN A LEADING ROLE: **Bill Murray** *Lost in Translation* • Benicio Del Toro *21 Grams* • Johnny Depp *Pirates of the Caribbean: the Curse of the Black Pearl* • Jude Law *Cold Mountain* • Sean Penn *Mystic River* • Sean Penn *21 Grams*
BEST PERFORMANCE BY AN ACTRESS IN A LEADING ROLE: **Scarlett Johansson** *Lost in Translation* • Scarlett Johansson *Girl with a Pearl Earring* • Anne Reid *The Mother* • Uma Thurman *Kill Bill Vol 1* • Naomi Watts *21 Grams*
BEST PERFORMANCE BY AN ACTOR IN A SUPPORTING ROLE: **Bill Nighy** *Love Actually* • Paul Bettany *Master and Commander: the Far Side of the World* • Albert Finney *Big Fish* • Ian McKellen *The Lord of the Rings: The Return of the King* • Tim Robbins *Mystic River*
BEST PERFORMANCE BY AN ACTRESS IN A SUPPORTING ROLE: **Renee Zellweger** *Cold Mountain* • Holly Hunter *Thirteen* • Laura Linney *Mystic River* • Judy Parfitt *Girl with a Pearl Earring* • Emma Thompson *Love Actually*
BEST SCREENPLAY (ORIGINAL): **Thomas McCarthy** *The Station Agent* • Denys Arcand *The Barbarian Invasions* • Andrew Stanton, Bob Peterson, David Reynolds *Finding Nemo* • Sofia Coppola *Lost in Translation* • Guillermo Arriaga *21 Grams*
BEST SCREENPLAY (ADAPTED): **Peter Jackson**, **Fran Walsh**, **Philippa Boyens** *The Lord of the Rings: The Return of the King* • John August *Big Fish* • Anthony Minghella *Cold Mountain* • Olivia Hetreed *Girl with a Pearl Earring* • Brian Helgeland *Mystic River*

Academy Awards

BEST PICTURE: ***The Lord of the Rings: The Return of the King*** • *Lost in Translation* • *Master and Commander: the Far Side of the World* • *Mystic River* • *Seabiscuit*

Foreign Language Film: ***The Barbarian Invasions*** • *Evil* • *The Twilight Samurai* • *Twin Sisters* • *Zelary*
Directing: **Peter Jackson** *The Lord of the Rings: The Return of the King* • Sofia Coppola *Lost in Translation* • Clint Eastwood *Mystic River* • Fernando Meirelles *City of God* • Peter Weir *Master and Commander: the Far Side of the World*
Actor in a Leading Role: **Sean Penn** *Mystic River* • Johnny Depp *Pirates of the Caribbean: the Curse of the Black Pearl* • Ben Kingsley *House of Sand and Fog* • Jude Law *Cold Mountain* • Bill Murray *Lost in Translation*
Actress in a Leading Role: **Charlize Theron** *Monster* • Keisha Castle-Hughes *Whale Rider* • Diane Keaton *Something's Gotta Give* • Samantha Morton *In America* • Naomi Watts *21 Grams*
Actor in a Supporting Role: **Tim Robbins** *Mystic River* • Alec Baldwin *The Cooler* • Benicio Del Toro *21 Grams* • Djimon Hounsou *In America* • Ken Watanabe *The Last Samurai*
Actress in a Supporting Role: **Renee Zellweger** *Cold Mountain* • Shohreh Aghdashloo *House of Sand and Fog* • Patricia Clarkson *Pieces of April* • Marcia Gay Harden *Mystic River* • Holly Hunter *Thirteen*
Writing (Screenplay Written Directly for the Screen): **Sofia Coppola** *Lost in Translation* • Denys Arcand *The Barbarian Invasions* • Steven Knight *Dirty Pretty Things* • Andrew Stanton, Bob Peterson, David Reynolds *Finding Nemo* • Jim Sheridan, Naomi Sheridan, Kirsten Sheridan *In America*
Writing (Screenplay Based On Material Previously Produced or Published): **Peter Jackson, Fran Walsh, Philippa Boyens** *The Lord of the Rings: The Return of the King* • Shari Springer Berman, Robert Pulcini *American Splendor* • Braulio Mantovani *City of God* • Brian Helgeland *Mystic River* • Gary Ross *Seabiscuit*

Golden Globe Awards

Best Motion Picture – Drama: ***The Lord of the Rings: The Return of the King***
Best Motion Picture – Comedy or Musical: ***Lost in Translation***
Best Foreign Language Film: ***Osama***
Best Director – Motion Picture: **Peter Jackson** *The Lord of the Rings: The Return of the King*
Best Performance by an Actor in a Motion Picture – Drama: **Sean Penn** *Mystic River*
Best Performance by an Actress in a Motion Picture – Drama: **Charlize Theron** *Monster*
Best Performance by an Actor in a Motion Picture – Comedy or Musical: **Bill Murray** *Lost in Translation*
Best Performance by an Actress in a Motion Picture – Comedy or Musical: **Diane Keaton** *Something's Gotta Give*
Best Performance by an Actor in a Supporting Role – Motion Picture: **Tim Robbins** *Mystic River*
Best Performance by an Actress in a Supporting Role – Motion Picture: **Renee Zellweger** *Cold Mountain*
Best Screenplay – Motion Picture: **Sofia Coppola** *Lost in Translation*

Cannes International Film Festival

Palme d'Or: ***Elephant***
Director: **Gus Van Sant** *Elephant*
Actor: **Muzaffer Ozdemir, Mehmet Emin Toprak** *Uzak*
Actress: **Marie-Josée Croze** *The Barbarian Invasions*
Screenplay: **Denys Arcand** *The Barbarian Invasions*

Berlin International Film Festival

Golden Bear for Film: ***In This World***
Silver Berlin Bear for the Best Director: **Patrice Chéreau** *Son Frère*
Silver Berlin Bear for the Best Actor: **Sam Rockwell** *Confessions of a Dangerous Mind*
Silver Berlin Bear for the Best Actress: **Nicole Kidman, Julianne Moore, Meryl Streep** *The Hours*

2004

British Academy Film Awards

Best Film: ***The Aviator*** • *Eternal Sunshine of the Spotless Mind* • *Finding Neverland* • *The Motorcycle Diaries* • *Vera Drake*
Best Film Not in the English Language: ***The Motorcycle Diaries*** • *Bad Education* • *The Chorus* • *House of Flying Daggers* • *A Very Long Engagement*
The Alexander Korda Award for the Outstanding British Film Of the Year: ***My Summer of Love*** • *Dead Man's Shoes* • *Harry Potter and the Prisoner of Azkaban* • *Shaun of the Dead* • *Vera Drake*
The David Lean Award for the Best Achievement in Direction: **Mike Leigh** *Vera Drake* • Marc Forster *Finding Neverland* • Michel Gondry *Eternal Sunshine of the Spotless Mind* • Michael Mann *Collateral* • Martin Scorsese *The Aviator*
Best Performance by an Actor in a Leading Role: **Jamie Foxx** *Ray* • Gael García Bernal *The Motorcycle Diaries* • Jim Carrey *Eternal Sunshine of the Spotless Mind* • Johnny Depp *Finding Neverland* • Leonardo DiCaprio *The Aviator*
Best Performance by an Actress in a Leading Role: **Imelda Staunton** *Vera Drake* • Charlize Theron *Monster* • Kate Winslet *Eternal Sunshine of the Spotless Mind* • Kate Winslet *Finding Neverland* • Zhang Ziyi *House of Flying Daggers*
Best Performance by an Actor in a Supporting Role: **Clive Owen** *Closer* • Alan Alda *The Aviator* • Philip Davis *Vera Drake* • Rodrigo de la Serna *The Motorcycle Diaries* • Jamie Foxx *Collateral*
Best Performance by an Actress in a Supporting Role: **Cate Blanchett** *The Aviator* • Julie Christie *Finding Neverland* • Heather Craney *Vera Drake* • Natalie Portman *Closer* • Meryl Streep *The Manchurian Candidate*
Best Screenplay (Original): **Charlie Kaufman** *Eternal Sunshine of the Spotless Mind* • John Logan *The Aviator* • Stuart Beattie *Collateral* • James L White *Ray* • Mike Leigh *Vera Drake*
Best Screenplay (Adapted): **Alexander Payne, Jim Taylor** *Sideways* • Christophe Barratier, Philippe Lopes Curval *The Chorus* • Patrick Marber *Closer* • David Magee *Finding Neverland* • José Rivera *The Motorcycle Diaries*

Academy Awards

Best Picture: ***Million Dollar Baby*** • *The Aviator* • *Finding Neverland* • *Ray* • *Sideways*
Foreign Language Film: ***The Sea Inside*** • *As It Is in Heaven* • *The Chorus* • *Downfall* • *Yesterday*
Directing: **Clint Eastwood** *Million Dollar Baby* • Taylor Hackford *Ray* • Mike Leigh *Vera Drake* • Alexander Payne *Sideways* • Martin Scorsese *The Aviator*
Actor in a Leading Role: **Jamie Foxx** *Ray* • Don Cheadle *Hotel Rwanda* • Johnny Depp *Finding Neverland* • Leonardo DiCaprio *The Aviator* • Clint Eastwood *Million Dollar Baby*
Actress in a Leading Role: **Hilary Swank** *Million Dollar Baby* • Annette Bening *Being Julia* • Catalina Sandino Moreno *Maria Full of Grace* • Imelda Staunton *Vera Drake* • Kate Winslet *Eternal Sunshine of the Spotless Mind*
Actor in a Supporting Role: **Morgan Freeman** *Million Dollar Baby* • Alan Alda *The Aviator* • Thomas Haden Church *Sideways* • Jamie Foxx *Collateral* • Clive Owen *Closer*
Actress in a Supporting Role: **Cate Blanchett** *The Aviator* • Laura Linney *Kinsey* • Virginia Madsen *Sideways* • Sophie Okonedo *Hotel Rwanda* • Natalie Portman *Closer*
Writing (Screenplay Written Directly for the Screen): **Charlie Kaufman** *Eternal Sunshine of the Spotless Mind* • Brad Bird *The Incredibles* • Terry George, Keir Pearson *Hotel Rwanda* • Mike Leigh *Vera Drake* • John Logan *The Aviator*
Writing (Screenplay Based On Material Previously Produced or Published): **Alexander Payne, Jim Taylor** *Sideways* • Paul Haggis *Million Dollar Baby* • Richard Linklater, Julie Delpy, Ethan Hawke *Before Sunset* • David Magee *Finding Neverland* • José Rivera *The Motorcycle Diaries*

Golden Globe Awards

Best Motion Picture – Drama: ***The Aviator***
Best Motion Picture – Comedy or Musical: ***Sideways***
Best Foreign Language Film: ***The Sea Inside***
Best Director – Motion Picture: **Clint Eastwood** *Million Dollar Baby*
Best Performance by an Actor in a Motion Picture – Drama: **Leonardo DiCaprio** *The Aviator*
Best Performance by an Actress in a Motion Picture – Drama: **Hilary Swank** *Million Dollar Baby*
Best Performance by an Actor in a Motion Picture – Comedy or Musical: **Jamie Foxx** *Ray*
Best Performance by an Actress in a Motion Picture – Comedy or Musical: **Annette Bening** *Being Julia*
Best Performance by an Actor in a Supporting Role – Motion Picture: **Clive Owen** *Closer*
Best Performance by an Actress in a Supporting Role – Motion Picture: **Natalie Portman** *Closer*
Best Screenplay – Motion Picture: **Alexander Payne, Jim Taylor** *Sideways*

Cannes International Film Festival

Palme d'Or: ***Fahrenheit 9/11***
Director: **Tony Gatlif** *Exiles*
Actor: **Yuya Yagira** *Nobody Knows*
Actress: **Maggie Cheung** *Clean*
Screenplay: **Jean-Pierre Bacri, Agnès Jaoui** *Look at Me*

Berlin International Film Festival

Golden Bear for Film: ***Head-On***
Silver Berlin Bear for the Best Director: **Kim Ki-Duk** *Samaritan Girl*
Silver Berlin Bear for the Best Actor: **Daniel Hendler** *Lost Embrace*
Silver Berlin Bear for the Best Actress: **Catalina Sandino Moreno** *Maria Full of Grace* • **Charlize Theron** *Monster*

2005

Cannes International Film Festival

Palme d'Or: ***L'Enfant***
Director: **Michael Haneke** *Hidden*
Actor: **Tommy Lee Jones** *The Three Burials of Melquiades*
Actress: **Hanna Laslo** *Free Zone*
Screenplay: **Guillermo Arriaga** *The Three Burials of Melquiades*

Berlin International Film Festival

Golden Bear for Film: ***U-Carmen e-Khayelitsha***
Silver Berlin Bear for the Best Director: **Marc Rothemund** *Sophie Scholl – The Final Days*
Silver Berlin Bear for the Best Actor: **Lou Pucci** *Thumbsucker*
Silver Berlin Bear for the Best Actress: **Julia Jentsch** *Sophie Scholl – The Final Days*

Five-star and four-star films

Action

★★★★★

Alien 1979 DVD
Aliens 1986 DVD
Batman 1989 DVD
Crouching Tiger, Hidden Dragon 2000 DVD
Die Hard 1988 DVD
Hero 2002 DVD
Indiana Jones and the Last Crusade 1989 DVD
Mad Max 1979 DVD
The Matrix 1999 DVD
Raiders of the Lost Ark 1981 DVD
Seven Samurai 1954 DVD
Speed 1994 DVD
The Terminator 1984 DVD
Terminator 2: Judgment Day 1991 DVD
Yojimbo 1961 DVD

Action

★★★★

Air Force One 1997 DVD
Alien: Resurrection 1997 DVD
Ashes of Time 1994
Backdraft 1991 DVD
Bad Boys 1995 DVD
Batman 1966 DVD
Batman Begins 2005
Batman Forever 1995 DVD
Batman: Mask of the Phantasm 1993 DVD
Batman Returns 1992 DVD
Battle of the Bulge 1965 DVD
Battle Royale 2000 DVD
A Better Tomorrow 1986 DVD
Beverly Hills Cop 1984 DVD
Black Mask 1996 DVD
The Bourne Supremacy 2004 DVD
The Bride with White Hair 1993 DVD
A Chinese Ghost Story 1987 DVD
City on Fire 1987
Cliffhanger 1993 DVD
Collateral 2004 DVD
Con Air 1997 DVD
Crimson Tide 1995 DVD
The Crow 1994 DVD
Desperado 1995 DVD
Die Hard 2: Die Harder 1990 DVD
Die Hard with a Vengeance 1995 DVD
The Dirty Dozen 1967 DVD
Drunken Master 1978 DVD
Emperor of the North 1973
Enter the Dragon 1973 DVD
Excalibur 1981 DVD
Face/Off 1997 DVD
The Fast and the Furious 2001 DVD
The Fifth Element 1997 DVD
48 HRS 1982 DVD
From Dusk till Dawn 1995 DVD
Full Contact 1992 DVD
Guadalcanal Diary 1943 DVD
Hard-Boiled 1992 DVD
Hard Times 1975 DVD
The Hard Way 1991 DVD
Hooper 1978
House of Flying Daggers 2004 DVD
I, Robot 2004 DVD
In Harm's Way 1965 DVD
Indiana Jones and the Temple of Doom 1984 DVD
Jackie Chan's Who Am I? 1998 DVD
The Jewel of the Nile 1985 DVD
Judge Dredd 1995 DVD
Kill Bill Vol 1 2003 DVD
The Killer 1989 DVD
Kiss of the Dragon 2001 DVD
Kung Fu Hustle 2004
Last Action Hero 1993 DVD
The Last Samurai 2003 DVD
Lethal Weapon 1987 DVD
The Lives of a Bengal Lancer 1935
The Long Kiss Goodnight 1996 DVD
Mad Dog 1976 DVD
Mad Max 2 1981 DVD
The Mask of Zorro 1998 DVD
The Mean Machine 1974 DVD
Minority Report 2002 DVD
Miss Congeniality 2000 DVD
Mission: Impossible 1996 DVD
Mission: Impossible 2 1999 DVD
The Negotiator 1998 DVD
New Jack City 1991 DVD
Ocean's Eleven 2001 DVD
Oldboy 2003 DVD
Once upon a Time in China 1991 DVD
Ong-Bak 2003
Operation Condor: the Armour of God II 1990
Peking Opera Blues 1986
Pirates of the Caribbean: the Curse of the Black Pearl 2003 DVD
Predator 1987 DVD
Princess Mononoke 1997 DVD
Rebellion 1967
The Rink 1916 DVD
Robin Hood: Prince of Thieves 1991 DVD
The Rock 1996 DVD
Ronin 1998 DVD
Runaway Train 1985 DVD
Rush Hour 1998 DVD
The 6th Day 2000 DVD
Southern Comfort 1981 DVD
Spider-Man 2002 DVD
Spider-Man 2 2004 DVD
SPYkids 2: the Island of Lost Dreams 2002 DVD
Strange Days 1995 DVD
Sudden Death 1995 DVD
Sweet Sweetback's Baad Asssss Song 1971
Sympathy for Mr Vengeance 2002 DVD
Three Kings 1999 DVD
Time and Tide 2000 DVD
Tokyo Drifter 1966 DVD
Tokyo Fist 1995 DVD
A Touch of Zen 1969 DVD
True Lies 1994 DVD
Under Siege 1992 DVD
The Warriors 1979 DVD
When the Last Sword Is Drawn 2003 DVD
Where Eagles Dare 1969 DVD
The Wild Angels 1966
X2 2003 DVD
Zatoichi 2003

Adventure

★★★★★

The Adventures of Robin Hood 1938 DVD
The African Queen 1951 DVD
Aladdin 1992 DVD
Antz 1998 DVD
Back to the Future 1985 DVD
Beau Geste 1939
The Black Stallion 1979 DVD
El Cid 1961 DVD
Crouching Tiger, Hidden Dragon 2000 DVD
Dr No 1962 DVD
Don Quixote 1957
ET the Extra-Terrestrial 1982 DVD
The 5,000 Fingers of Dr T 1953
Forbidden Planet 1956
The Four Feathers 1939 DVD
Goldfinger 1964 DVD
The Great Escape 1963 DVD
Gunga Din 1939
The Hidden Fortress 1958 DVD
Indiana Jones and the Last Crusade 1989 DVD
Jaws 1975 DVD
The Jungle Book 1967 DVD
Jurassic Park 1993 DVD
King Kong 1933 DVD
Lady and the Tramp 1955 DVD
Lassie Come Home 1943
The Last of the Mohicans 1920
Lawrence of Arabia 1962 DVD
The Little Mermaid 1989 DVD
The Lord of the Rings: The Fellowship of the Ring 2001 DVD
The Lord of the Rings: The Two Towers 2002 DVD
The Lord of the Rings: The Return of the King 2003 DVD
Lost Horizon 1937 DVD
Mad Max 1979 DVD
The Man Who Would Be King 1975 DVD
One Hundred and One Dalmatians 1960 DVD
The Prisoner of Zenda 1937
Raiders of the Lost Ark 1981 DVD
Romancing the Stone 1984 DVD
Shadowman 1973
Star Trek: First Contact 1996 DVD
Star Wars Episode IV: a New Hope 1977 DVD
Star Wars Episode V: the Empire Strikes Back 1980 DVD
Superman 1978 DVD
The Thief of Bagdad 1940
Toy Story 1995 DVD
Toy Story 2 1999 DVD
The Treasure of the Sierra Madre 1948 DVD
The Vikings 1958 DVD
The Wages of Fear 1953 DVD
You Only Live Twice 1967 DVD

Adventure

★★★★

The Adventures of Baron Munchausen 1988 DVD
The Adventures of Robinson Crusoe 1952
The Adventures of Tom Sawyer 1938 DVD
Aelita 1924
Aladdin and the King of Thieves 1996 DVD
Alone on the Pacific 1963
An American Tail 1986
Anthony Adverse 1936
The Arabian Nights 1974 DVD
The Aristocats 1970 DVD
Around the World in 80 Days 1956 DVD
Atlantis: the Lost Empire 2001 DVD
Back to the Future Part III 1990 DVD
The Beach 2000 DVD
The Bear 1988
The Beast from 20,000 Fathoms 1953 DVD
Beau Geste 1926
The Bedford Incident 1965 DVD
Belleville Rendez-vous 2003 DVD
The Big Blue 1988 DVD
The Big Sky 1952
The Black Pirate 1926
The Black Swan 1942
Blood and Sand 1941
Boom Town 1940
Born Free 1966 DVD
The Brave Little Toaster 1987 DVD
A Bug's Life 1998 DVD
Captain Blood 1935
The Castle of Cagliostro 1979 DVD
Chicken Run 2000 DVD
China Seas 1935
The City of Lost Children 1995 DVD
The Count of Monte Cristo 1934
The Crimson Pirate 1952
"Crocodile" Dundee 1986 DVD
The Dark Crystal 1982 DVD
Desperado 1995 DVD
Dick Tracy 1990 DVD
Die Another Day 2002 DVD
The Dirty Dozen 1967 DVD
The Drum 1938
The Eagle 1925 DVD
Emperor of the North 1973
Enter the Dragon 1973 DVD
Escape from the Planet of the Apes 1971 DVD
Fantastic Voyage 1966 DVD
The Fifth Element 1997 DVD
Finding Nemo 2003 DVD
Fire over England 1937
The Flight of the Phoenix 1965 DVD
Fort Saganne 1984
From Russia with Love 1963 DVD
GoldenEye 1995 DVD
The Guns of Navarone 1961 DVD
Harry Potter and the Chamber of Secrets 2002 DVD
Harry Potter and the Philosopher's Stone 2001 DVD
Harry Potter and the Prisoner of Azkaban 2004 DVD
Hatari! 1962 DVD
The Hitchhiker's Guide to the Galaxy 2005
If I Were King 1938
Ilya Muromets 1956
The Incredible Journey 1963
The Incredibles 2004 DVD
Independence Day 1996 DVD
The Indian in the Cupboard 1995 DVD
Indiana Jones and the Temple of Doom 1984 DVD
The Iron Giant 1999 DVD
Ivanhoe 1952
James and the Giant Peach 1996 DVD
The Jewel of the Nile 1985 DVD
Journey to the Center of the Earth 1959 DVD
Judex 1963
Judge Dredd 1995 DVD
Jumanji 1995 DVD
Kirikou and the Sorceress 1998 DVD
A Knight's Tale 2001 DVD
Ladyhawke 1985 DVD
The Land before Time 1988
Last Action Hero 1993 DVD
The Last of the Mohicans 1992 DVD
The Lion King 1994 DVD
Lion of the Desert 1981 DVD
Live and Let Die 1973 DVD
The Lives of a Bengal Lancer 1935
Lord Jim 1965 DVD
The Lost Squadron 1932
Mad Max 2 1981 DVD
The Mark of Zorro 1940 DVD
The Mask of Zorro 1998 DVD
Master and Commander: the Far Side of the World 2003 DVD
Mulan 1998 DVD
The Muppet Movie 1979
Muppet Treasure Island 1996 DVD
Muppets from Space 1999 DVD
Mutiny on the Bounty 1935 DVD
Mutiny on the Bounty 1962
The Naked Jungle 1953
The Navigator – a Medieval Odyssey 1988
The NeverEnding Story 1984
The New Land 1972
North to Alaska 1960 DVD
Old Yeller 1957
Ong-Bak 2003
Operation Condor: the Armour of God II 1990
Pathfinder 1987
Peking Opera Blues 1986
Perceval le Gallois 1978
Peter Pan 1953 DVD
Pirates of the Caribbean: the Curse of the Black Pearl 2003 DVD
Planet of the Apes 1967 DVD
The Pride and the Passion 1957 DVD
The Princess Bride 1987 DVD
The Prisoner of Zenda 1952 DVD
The Rescuers 1977 DVD
Return from Witch Mountain 1978 DVD
The River Wild 1994 DVD
Rob Roy 1995 DVD
Robin and Marian 1976 DVD
Robin Hood 1922 DVD
Robin Hood 1973 DVD
Robin Hood 1990
Robin Hood: Prince of Thieves 1991 DVD
Rocketeer 1991 DVD
Runaway Train 1985 DVD
Scaramouche 1923
Scaramouche 1952
The Scarlet Pimpernel 1982 DVD
The Sea Hawk 1924
The Sea Hawk 1940
The Sea Wolf 1941
The 7th Voyage of Sinbad 1958 DVD
The Sheik 1921 DVD
The Shiralee 1986
Sholay 1975 DVD
The Silver Brumby 1992
The Son of the Sheik 1926
Spider-Man 2002 DVD
Spider-Man 2 2004 DVD
The Spiders 1919
Spirited Away 2001 DVD
The SpongeBob SquarePants Movie 2004 DVD
SPYkids 2001 DVD
SPYkids 2: the Island of Lost Dreams 2002 DVD
The Spy Who Loved Me 1977 DVD
Stanley and Livingstone 1939
Star Trek II: the Wrath of Khan 1982 DVD
Star Trek IV: the Voyage Home 1986 DVD
Star Trek VI: the Undiscovered Country 1991 DVD
Star Trek: Generations 1994 DVD
Star Wars Episode VI: Return of the Jedi 1983 DVD
Stargate 1994 DVD
Starship Troopers 1997 DVD
The Sundowners 1960
Superman II 1980 DVD
Swiss Family Robinson 1960 DVD
The Tarnished Angels 1957
Tarzan and His Mate 1934
Tarzan, the Ape Man 1932
That Man from Rio 1964
The Thief of Bagdad 1924 DVD
This Island Earth 1955
Three Kings 1999 DVD
The Three Musketeers 1921
The Three Musketeers 1973 DVD
The Time Machine 1960 DVD
Titan AE 2000 DVD
Tom Jones 1963 DVD
Tom Sawyer 1973
Tomorrow Never Dies 1997 DVD
Too Hot to Handle 1938
Trader Horn 1931
The Trap 1966
The 12 Tasks of Asterix 1975
20,000 Leagues under the Sea 1954 DVD
Under Siege 1992 DVD
The War of the Worlds 1953 DVD
Waterworld 1995 DVD
Where No Vultures Fly 1951
The White Dawn 1974
White Hunter, Black Heart 1990
White Mane 1952
The Wind and the Lion 1975
The World Is Not Enough 1999 DVD
X2 2003 DVD
Zatoichi 2003

Animation

★★★★★

Aladdin 1992 DVD
Antz 1998 DVD
Bambi 1942 DVD
Beauty and the Beast 1991 DVD
The Cat Concerto 1947
The Dot and the Line 1965
Duck Dodgers in the 24½ Century 1953
Dumbo 1941 DVD
Fantasia 1940 DVD
Faust 1994
Gertie the Dinosaur 1914
The Jungle Book 1967 DVD
King-Size Canary 1947
Lady and the Tramp 1955 DVD
The Little Mermaid 1989 DVD
Monsters, Inc 2001 DVD
The Nightmare before Christmas 1993 DVD
The Old Mill 1937
One Froggy Evening 1955
One Hundred and One Dalmatians 1960 DVD
Pinocchio 1940 DVD
Snow White and the Seven Dwarfs 1937 DVD

Steamboat Willie 1928
The Three Little Pigs 1933
Toot, Whistle, Plunk and Boom 1953
The Tortoise and the Hare 1935
Toy Story 1995 DVD
Toy Story 2 1999 DVD
What's Opera, Doc? 1957
Who Framed Roger Rabbit 1988 DVD

Animation

★★★★

Akira 1988 DVD
Aladdin and the King of Thieves 1996 DVD
Alice 1988
An American Tail 1986
Animal Farm 1954 DVD
The Aristocats 1970 DVD
Atlantis: the Lost Empire 2001 DVD
Batman: Mask of the Phantasm 1993 DVD
Belleville Rendez-vous 2003 DVD
Birds Anonymous 1957
The Brave Little Toaster 1987 DVD
The Bugs Bunny/Road Runner Movie 1979
A Bug's Life 1998 DVD
The Castle of Cagliostro 1979 DVD
Chicken Run 2000 DVD
Cinderella 1950
The Emperor's New Groove 2000 DVD
Fantastic Planet 1973
Finding Nemo 2003 DVD
The Five Obstructions 2003 DVD
Flowers and Trees 1932
Ghost in the Shell 1995 DVD
The Halloween Tree 1993
The Hunchback of Notre Dame 1996 DVD
The Incredibles 2004 DVD
The Iron Giant 1999 DVD
James and the Giant Peach 1996 DVD
Kill Bill Vol 1 2003 DVD
Kirikou and the Sorceress 1998 DVD
The Land before Time 1988
Lilo & Stitch 2002 DVD
The Lion King 1994 DVD
Little Otik 2000 DVD
Lucky and Zorba 1998
Make Mine Music 1946
A Midsummer Night's Dream 1961
Mouse Trouble 1944
Mulan 1998 DVD
Peter Pan 1953 DVD
The Phantom Tollbooth 1969
The Prince of Egypt 1998 DVD
Princess Mononoke 1997 DVD
The Rescuers 1977 DVD
Robin Hood 1973 DVD
Roujin Z 1991
Shrek 2001 DVD
Shrek 2 2004
South Park: Bigger, Longer & Uncut 1999 DVD
Spirited Away 2001 DVD
The SpongeBob SquarePants Movie 2004 DVD
Titan AE 2000 DVD
Town Rat, Country Rat 1923
Tuck Everlasting 1980
The 12 Tasks of Asterix 1975
Volere, Volare 1991
When Magoo Flew 1955
When the Wind Blows 1986
A Wild Hare 1940
The Wings of Honneamise 1987
Yellow Submarine 1968 DVD

Biography

★★★★★

Amadeus 1984 DVD
Andrei Rublev 1966 DVD
An Angel at My Table 1990 DVD
Before Night Falls 2000 DVD
Bonnie and Clyde 1967 DVD
Born on the Fourth of July 1989 DVD
Chopper 2000 DVD
The Colour of Pomegranates 1969
Dear Diary 1994
The Diary of Anne Frank 1959 DVD
Ed Wood 1994 DVD
Gandhi 1982 DVD
The General 1998
Gods and Monsters 1998 DVD
Heavenly Creatures 1994 DVD
The Insider 1999 DVD
Jacquot de Nantes 1991
Jeanne la Pucelle 1994
The Jolson Story 1946 DVD
The Killing Fields 1984 DVD
The Long Day Closes 1992
The Madness of King George 1995 DVD
Midnight Express 1978 DVD
The Miracle Worker 1962 DVD
The Motorcycle Diaries 2004 DVD
My Left Foot 1989 DVD
Patton 1970 DVD
Prick Up Your Ears 1987 DVD
Quills 2000 DVD
Raging Bull 1980 DVD
Reds 1981 DVD
Schindler's List 1993 DVD
The Sea Inside 2004 DVD
Shadowlands 1993
Shine 1996 DVD
The Straight Story 1999 DVD
10 Rillington Place 1970 DVD
Thirty Two Short Films about Glenn Gould 1993
Topsy-Turvy 1999 DVD

Biography

★★★★

Al Capone 1959
American Splendor 2003 DVD
Anna Boleyn 1920
The Apple 1998 DVD
At Close Range 1985 DVD
The Attic: the Hiding of Anne Frank 1988
Auto Focus 2002 DVD
Awakenings 1990 DVD
Bad Blood 1982
Bandit Queen 1994
The Barretts of Wimpole Street 1934
Beau James 1957
The Believer 2001 DVD
The Best Things in Life Are Free 1956
The Betty Ford Story 1987
Bill 1981
Bird 1988
Birdman of Alcatraz 1962 DVD
Blind Flight 2003 DVD
Born Free 1966 DVD
The Boston Strangler 1968 DVD
Bound for Glory 1976 DVD
Break of Dawn 1988
Brian's Song 1971
The Buddy Holly Story 1978 DVD
Bugsy 1991 DVD
Bukowski: Born into This 2003
Bully 2001 DVD
The Burning Bed 1984
The Burning Season 1994
Calendar Girls 2003 DVD
Captive of the Desert 1990
Caravaggio 1986
Carrington 1995 DVD
Catch Me If You Can 2002 DVD
Chameleon Street 1989
Chihwaseon (Drunk on Women and Poetry) 2002 DVD
Cinderella Man 2005
Coal Miner's Daughter 1980 DVD
Cobb 1994
Confessions of a Dangerous Mind 2002 DVD
The Court-Martial of Billy Mitchell 1955
The Court-Martial of Jackie Robinson 1990
Crime of the Century 1996
Cry Freedom 1987 DVD
A Cry in the Dark 1988 DVD
Dance with a Stranger 1984 DVD
The Day the Sun Turned Cold 1994
Death by Hanging 1968
The Devil and the Nun 1960
Diary for My Children 1982
Diary for My Loves 1987
Dillinger 1945
Dillinger 1973
Docteur Petiot 1990
Dragon: the Bruce Lee Story 1993 DVD
The Eddy Duchin Story 1956
84 Charing Cross Road 1986 DVD
The Elephant Man 1980 DVD
Elvis – the Movie 1979
L'Enfant Sauvage 1970 DVD
The Enigma of Kaspar Hauser 1974
Erin Brockovich 2000 DVD
Escape from Alcatraz 1979 DVD
Europa, Europa 1991 DVD
Evidence of Love 1990 DVD
FairyTale: a True Story 1997 DVD
Farinelli il Castrato 1994 DVD
Fear on Trial 1975
Fear Strikes Out 1957
The Fighting Sullivans 1944 DVD
Finding Neverland 2004 DVD
The Five Pennies 1959
Fly Away Home 1996 DVD
Four Days in September 1997
Fourteen Hours 1951
Frances 1982 DVD
Francis, God's Jester 1950
Frida 2002 DVD
Friday Night Lights 2004
Friendly Fire 1979
Funny Girl 1968 DVD
Geronimo: an American Legend 1993 DVD
Gideon's Trumpet 1980
The Glenn Miller Story 1953
Gorillas in the Mist 1988 DVD
Goya in Bordeaux 1999
Grand Theft Parsons 2003 DVD
The Great Caruso 1951
The Great Moment 1944
The Great Waltz 1938
The Great Ziegfeld 1936 DVD
Gypsy 1962
Heat Wave 1990
Hilary and Jackie 1998 DVD
The Honeymoon Killers 1969 DVD
Hors la Vie 1991
The Hurricane 1999 DVD
I Shot Andy Warhol 1995
I Want to Live! 1958 DVD
I'll Cry Tomorrow 1955
Immortal Beloved 1994
In Cold Blood 1967 DVD
In the Name of the Father 1993 DVD
In the Realm of the Senses 1976 DVD
Indictment: the McMartin Trial 1995
The Inn of the Sixth Happiness 1958 DVD
Innocent Moves 1993 DVD
Interrupted Melody 1955
Intervista 1987
Iris 2001 DVD
Isadora 1968
Journey of Hope 1990
Julia 1977
Kill Me If You Can 1977
The King and I 1956 DVD
Kinsey 2004 DVD
Komitas 1988
The Krays 1990 DVD
Lady Sings the Blues 1972
The Last American Hero 1973
The Last Emperor 1987 DVD
The Last Stage 1947
The Late Shift 1996
Leave 'em Laughing 1981
Lena: My 100 Children 1987 DVD
Let Him Have It 1991 DVD
Let It Be 1970
The Libertine 2004
The Life of Emile Zola 1937
Love Me or Leave Me 1955
Lucky Luciano 1973 DVD
Lust for Life 1956
Mad Dog 1976 DVD
The Magic Box 1951
Man on the Moon 1999 DVD
Mandela 1995
Marie Antoinette 1938
Mask 1985 DVD
Michael Collins 1996 DVD
Mirror 1974 DVD
Mishima: a Life in Four Chapters 1985
Miss Evers' Boys 1997
Missing 1981
Mr Reliable 1996
Mommie Dearest 1981 DVD
Monsieur Vincent 1947
Monster 2003 DVD
Moulin Rouge 1952 DVD
Mrs Parker and the Vicious Circle 1994
Muhammad Ali, the Greatest 1974 DVD
Murder in the First 1994 DVD
My Ain Folk 1973
My Mother's Courage 1995
My Name Is Bill W 1989
My Way Home 1978
Napoléon 1955
The Nasty Girl 1990 DVD
Nazi Hunter: the Beate Klarsfeld Story 1986
Nijinsky 1980
Nixon 1995 DVD
No Regrets for Our Youth 1946
Nobody's Child 1986
Norma Rae 1979 DVD
Les Nuits Fauves 1992
October Sky 1999 DVD
One against the Wind 1991
Out of Africa 1985 DVD
Out of the Darkness 1985
Padre Padrone 1977
Papillon 1973 DVD
The Patricia Neal Story: an Act of Love 1981
The People vs Larry Flynt 1996 DVD
The Pianist 2002 DVD
Playing for Time 1980
Pollock 2000 DVD
The Pride of the Yankees 1942
The Private Life of Henry VIII 1933
A Private Matter 1992
Private Parts 1997 DVD
Promised a Miracle 1988
RKO 281 1999 DVD
Rasputin 1996 DVD
Ray 2004 DVD
Reach for the Sky 1956 DVD
Reversal of Fortune 1990 DVD
Rikyu 1989
The Rise and Fall of Legs Diamond 1960
Rob Roy 1995 DVD
Roberto Succo 2000 DVD
Rosa Luxemburg 1986
Ruby 1992
Salvador 1986 DVD
Salvatore Giuliano 1961
Second Serve 1986
Secret Honor 1984
Sergeant York 1941
Serpico 1973 DVD
Sid and Nancy 1986 DVD
Silkwood 1983 DVD
Sister Kenny 1946
Somebody Up There Likes Me 1956
Something for Joey 1977
The Song of Bernadette 1943 DVD
Sophie Scholl – The Final Days 2005
Stand and Deliver 1988
Star 80 1983
Stavisky 1974
The Story of GI Joe 1945
The Story of Vernon and Irene Castle 1939
Superstar: the Karen Carpenter Story 1987
Surviving Picasso 1996
The Switch 1993 DVD
Tamanna 1997
They Died with Their Boots On 1941
This Boy's Life 1993 DVD
Three Little Words 1950
Till the Clouds Roll By 1946 DVD
Tina: What's Love Got to Do with It 1993 DVD
To Walk with Lions 1999 DVD
Truman 1995 DVD
Tuesdays with Morrie 1999 DVD
24 Hour Party People 2001 DVD
Unconquered 1989 DVD
Unstrung Heroes 1995 DVD
Van Gogh 1991
Veronica Guerin 2003 DVD
Wilde 1997 DVD
With a Song in My Heart 1952
Without Warning: the James Brady Story 1991
The Wonderful, Horrible Life of Leni Riefenstahl 1993 DVD
A World Apart 1987
The Wrong Man 1956 DVD
Yankee Doodle Dandy 1942
Young Mr Lincoln 1939 DVD
The Young Mr Pitt 1942

Comedy

★★★★★

Adam's Rib 1949 DVD
Airplane! 1980 DVD
All about My Mother 1999 DVD
Amarcord 1973 DVD
Amélie 2001 DVD
American Beauty 1999 DVD
American Graffiti 1973 DVD
Annie Hall 1977 DVD
The Apartment 1960 DVD
Arsenic and Old Lace 1944 DVD
Avanti! 1972 DVD
The Awful Truth 1937 DVD
Back to the Future 1985 DVD
Being John Malkovich 1999 DVD
Big Business 1929 DVD
Billy Liar 1963 DVD
Born Yesterday 1950 DVD
Braindead 1992 DVD
Bridget Jones's Diary 2001 DVD
Bringing Up Baby 1938 DVD
Butch Cassidy and the Sundance Kid 1969 DVD
Calamity Jane 1953 DVD
The Cameraman 1928
Capricious Summer 1968
The Cat Concerto 1947
Charade 1963 DVD
City Lights 1931 DVD
College 1927 DVD
Crimes and Misdemeanors 1989 DVD
Day Dreams 1922 DVD
Dear Diary 1994
Destry Rides Again 1939
The Discreet Charm of the Bourgeoisie 1972
Dr Strangelove, or How I Learned to Stop Worrying and Love the Bomb 1963 DVD
The Dot and the Line 1965
Duck Dodgers in the $24\frac{1}{2}$ Century 1953
Duck Soup 1933 DVD
Fargo 1995 DVD
A Fish Called Wanda 1988 DVD
Flirting 1989
4 Clowns 1970
Four Weddings and a Funeral 1994 DVD
The Freshman 1925
The Full Monty 1997 DVD
The General 1927 DVD
Ginger & Fred 1986
Girl Shy 1924
The Gold Rush 1925 DVD
The Graduate 1967 DVD
The Great Dictator 1940 DVD
Groundhog Day 1993 DVD
Hail the Conquering Hero 1944 DVD
Hannah and Her Sisters 1986 DVD
Happiness 1998 DVD
A Hard Day's Night 1964 DVD

Harvey 1950 DVD
Heathers 1989 DVD
Heaven Can Wait 1943
His Girl Friday 1939 DVD
Holiday 1938 DVD
Horse Feathers 1932 DVD
The House on Trubnaya Square 1928
Husbands and Wives 1992 DVD
I Know Where I'm Going! 1945 DVD
I Was a Male War Bride 1949 DVD
I Was Born, but... 1932
I'm All Right Jack 1959 DVD
The Immigrant 1917 DVD
In the Company of Men 1997
It Happened One Night 1934 DVD
An Italian Straw Hat 1927
It's a Gift 1934
Jour de Fête 1947 DVD
The Kid Brother 1927
Kikujiro 1999 DVD
Kind Hearts and Coronets 1949 DVD
The King of Comedy 1983 DVD
King-Size Canary 1947
The Lady Eve 1941 DVD
The Ladykillers 1955 DVD
The Lavender Hill Mob 1951 DVD
Life Is Sweet 1990 DVD
Lola 1960
Lolita 1961 DVD
Lost in Translation 2003 DVD
Love Affair 1939
Love in the Afternoon 1957
Love Me Tonight 1932
The Man in the White Suit 1951 DVD
The Man with Two Brains 1983
Manhattan 1979 DVD
The Marriage Circle 1924
MASH 1969 DVD
The Mask 1994 DVD
Midnight 1939
The Miracle of Morgan's Creek 1944
Mister Roberts 1955
Mr Smith Goes to Washington 1939 DVD
Modern Times 1936 DVD
Mon Oncle 1958 DVD
Monkey Business 1952 DVD
Monsieur Hulot's Holiday 1953 DVD
Monsters, Inc 2001 DVD
The Music Box 1932 DVD
The Naked Gun 1988 DVD
Nashville 1975
A Night at the Opera 1935 DVD
Ninotchka 1939
One Froggy Evening 1955
One Hundred and One Dalmatians 1960 DVD
Our Hospitality 1923
Pack Up Your Troubles 1932 DVD
The Paleface 1921
Perfect Day 1929 DVD
The Philadelphia Story 1940 DVD
Playtime 1967 DVD
The Producers 1968 DVD
Pygmalion 1938
The Quiet Man 1952 DVD
La Règle du Jeu 1939 DVD
Roman Holiday 1953 DVD
Romancing the Stone 1984 DVD
The Royal Tenenbaums 2001 DVD
Ruggles of Red Gap 1935
Sabrina 1954 DVD
Safety Last 1923 DVD
Scream 1996 DVD
Shakespeare in Love 1998 DVD
Shallow Grave 1994 DVD
Sherlock Junior 1924
Show People 1928
Sideways 2004 DVD
Smiles of a Summer Night 1955 DVD
The Smiling Lieutenant 1931
Some Like It Hot 1959 DVD
Sons of the Desert 1933 DVD
Steamboat Bill, Jr 1928 DVD
Stolen Kisses 1968 DVD
The Story of a Cheat 1936
Strictly Ballroom 1992 DVD
Sullivan's Travels 1941 DVD
Swing Time 1936
A Taste of Honey 1961 DVD
This Is Spinal Tap 1984 DVD
The Three Little Pigs 1933
Toot, Whistle, Plunk and Boom 1953
Top Hat 1935
Topsy-Turvy 1999 DVD
The Tortoise and the Hare 1935
A Touch of Class 1973
Toy Story 1995 DVD
Toy Story 2 1999 DVD
Tremors 1989 DVD
Trouble in Paradise 1932
The Trouble with Harry 1954 DVD
The Truman Show 1998 DVD
Twentieth Century 1934
The Two Tars 1928 DVD
Way Out West 1937 DVD
What's Up, Doc? 1972 DVD
When Harry Met Sally... 1989 DVD
Whisky Galore! 1949 DVD
Who Framed Roger Rabbit 1988 DVD
Women on the Verge of a Nervous Breakdown 1988 DVD
You Can't Take It with You 1938 DVD
Zéro de Conduite 1933 DVD

Comedy

★★★★

About a Boy 2002 DVD
About Schmidt 2002 DVD
Accidental Hero 1992 DVD
The Accidental Tourist 1988
Ace Ventura: Pet Detective 1993 DVD
Adaptation. 2002 DVD
The Addams Family 1991
Addams Family Values 1993 DVD
The Adventures of Priscilla, Queen of the Desert 1994 DVD
After Hours 1985 DVD
Un Air de Famille 1996
Alfie 1966 DVD
Alice Adams 1935
All or Nothing 2002 DVD
Almost Famous 2000 DVD
The Ambulance 1990
American Pie 1999 DVD
The American President 1995 DVD
American Psycho 2000 DVD
An American Werewolf in London 1981 DVD
The Americanization of Emily 1964
Analyze This 1999 DVD
And Now for Something Completely Different 1971 DVD
Animal Crackers 1930 DVD
Arachnophobia 1990 DVD
Ariel 1988
Arise, My Love 1940
Arthur 1981 DVD
Artists and Models 1955
As Good as It Gets 1997 DVD
The Assassination Bureau 1969
Auntie Mame 1958
Austin Powers: International Man of Mystery 1997 DVD
Austin Powers: the Spy Who Shagged Me 1999 DVD
An Autumn Tale 1998
The Aviator's Wife 1980 DVD
Babe 1995 DVD
The Bachelor and the Bobby-Soxer 1947
Back to the Future Part III 1990 DVD
Bad 1976
Bad Boys 1995 DVD
Bad Taste 1987 DVD
Bagdad Café 1987 DVD
The Baker's Wife 1938
Ball of Fire 1941
The Ballad of Cable Hogue 1970
The Bank Dick 1940
The Barbarian Invasions 2003 DVD
The Barber Shop 1933 DVD
Barcelona 1994
Barefoot in the Park 1967 DVD
Basket Case 1982 DVD
Bean 1997 DVD
Le Beau Mariage 1982 DVD
The Beautiful Blonde from Bashful Bend 1949
Bedtime Story 1964 DVD
Beethoven 1992 DVD
Beetle Juice 1988 DVD
Being There 1979 DVD
Belle Epoque 1992 DVD
Between the Lines 1977 DVD
Beverly Hills Cop 1984 DVD
Bienvenido Mr Marshall 1953
Big 1988 DVD
The Big Broadcast 1932
Big Daddy 1999 DVD
Big Deal on Madonna Street 1958
The Big Lebowski 1997 DVD
Big Night 1996
The Big Store 1941 DVD
Bill & Ted's Bogus Journey 1991 DVD
Bill & Ted's Excellent Adventure 1988 DVD
Biloxi Blues 1988 DVD
The Bingo Long Travelling All-Stars and Motor Kings 1976
Birds Anonymous 1957
Black Cat, White Cat 1998
The Black Sheep of Whitehall 1941
Blazing Saddles 1974 DVD
Bliss 1985
Blithe Spirit 1945 DVD
Blockheads 1938
Blonde Bombshell 1933
A Blonde in Love 1965
The Blues Brothers 1980 DVD
Blume in Love 1973
Bob Le Flambeur 1955 DVD
Bob Roberts 1992 DVD
Bon Voyage 2003 DVD
Bonne Chance 1935
Bonnie Scotland 1935
The Book of Life 1998
Boudu, Saved from Drowning 1932 DVD
Bowfinger 1999 DVD
Box of Moonlight 1996
A Boy and His Dog 1975 DVD
Brain Damage 1988
Breaking Away 1979
Broadcast News 1987 DVD
Broadway Danny Rose 1984 DVD
Broadway Melody of 1936 1935
Brothers in Law 1956
Buffalo Soldiers 2001 DVD
Bugsy Malone 1976 DVD
Bull Durham 1988 DVD
Bullets over Broadway 1994 DVD
Bulworth 1998 DVD
The 'Burbs 1989 DVD
Bus Stop 1956 DVD
The Butcher Boy 1917
The Butcher Boy 1997
Bye Bye Birdie 1963
Bye Bye Braverman 1968
La Cage aux Folles 1978 DVD
Calendar Girls 2003 DVD
California Suite 1978 DVD
Call Me Madam 1953
Can She Bake a Cherry Pie? 1983
Car Wash 1976 DVD
Career Girls 1997 DVD
Careful 1992
Careful, Soft Shoulder 1942
Carry On Again Doctor 1969 DVD
Carry On Cleo 1964 DVD
Carry On – Don't Lose Your Head 1966 DVD
Carry On Screaming 1966 DVD
Carry On Up the Khyber 1968 DVD
The Cars That Ate Paris 1974 DVD
Casper 1995 DVD
The Castle 1997 DVD
The Cat and the Canary 1939 DVD
Cat Ballou 1965 DVD
Catch Me If You Can 2002 DVD
Chameleon Street 1989
Chasing Amy 1996 DVD
Chicago 2002 DVD
Chicken Run 2000 DVD
Le Chignon d'Olga 2002 DVD
The Children of Heaven 1997
The Children of the Marshland 1998
Children of the Revolution 1996 DVD
Chocolat 2000 DVD
Choose Me 1984 DVD
Chori Chori 1956
A Christmas Story 1983
Chuck & Buck 2000 DVD
Chung King Express 1994 DVD
The Circus 1928 DVD
Citizens Band 1977
City Slickers 1991 DVD
Claire's Knee 1970 DVD
Claudia 1943
Clerks 1994
Closely Observed Trains 1966 DVD
Club de Femmes 1936
Clueless 1995 DVD
Comfort and Joy 1984
The Comic 1969
Les Compères 1983
Confessions of a Dangerous Mind 2002 DVD
Conspirators of Pleasure 1996
The Constant Husband 1955
Les Convoyeurs Attendent 1999
The Cook, the Thief, His Wife and Her Lover 1989 DVD
Cool Runnings 1993 DVD
Le Cop 1985
Cotton Comes to Harlem 1970
The Court Jester 1956
The Courtship of Eddie's Father 1963
Cover Girl 1944 DVD
Crazy from the Heart 1991
Crazy Moon 1986 DVD
The Cremator 1968
Le Cri du Hibou 1987
Le Crime de Monsieur Lange 1935 DVD
Crimes of the Heart 1986 DVD
La Crise 1992
"Crocodile" Dundee 1986 DVD
Cross My Heart 1990
Crossing Delancey 1988
The Cup 1999
The Cure 1917
Daddy Long Legs 1919
Daddy Long Legs 1955
Daisies 1966
Dandin 1988
Dave 1993 DVD
A Day in the Death of Joe Egg 1971
The Day of the Beast 1995
The Daytrippers 1998 DVD
Dazed and Confused 1993 DVD
The Dead and the Deadly 1983
Dead Man's Curve 1997 DVD
Dead Men Don't Wear Plaid 1982 DVD
Dear Heart 1964
Death Becomes Her 1992 DVD
Death by Hanging 1968
Death in Brunswick 1990 DVD
Death Japanese Style 1984
Death of a Bureaucrat 1966
The Decline of the American Empire 1986 DVD
Delicatessen 1990 DVD
The Dentist 1932 DVD
Designing Woman 1957
Desire 1936
Desk Set 1957
Desperately Seeking Susan 1985 DVD
Devils on the Doorstep 2000
Dim Sum: a Little Bit of Heart 1985
Diner 1982
Le Dîner de Cons 1998 DVD
Dinner at Eight 1933
Dinner Rush 2000 DVD
The Dish 2000 DVD
Divorce – Italian Style 1961
Doctor in the House 1954 DVD
Dona Herlinda and Her Son 1986
Don's Party 1976
Down by Law 1986 DVD
The Dream Team 1989 DVD
Drôle de Drame 1937
Drowning by Numbers 1988
Drunken Master 1978 DVD
Dumb and Dumber 1994 DVD
East Is East 1999 DVD
Easy Living 1937
Eat Drink Man Woman 1994
Eating Raoul 1982 DVD
Edtv 1999 DVD
Educating Rita 1983 DVD
8 Women 2001 DVD
El 1953
Election 1999 DVD
Elling 2001
The Emperor's New Groove 2000 DVD
End of a Priest 1969
Enemies, a Love Story 1989
Erotikon 1920
Eternal Sunshine of the Spotless Mind 2003 DVD
An Everlasting Piece 2000 DVD
Everyone Says I Love You 1996 DVD
Evil Roy Slade 1971
Fallen Angels 1995
Family Plot 1976 DVD
The Family Way 1966 DVD
Fast Times at Ridgemont High 1982 DVD
Father Brown 1954
Father of the Bride 1950
Father of the Bride 1991 DVD
Fear and Trembling 2003
The Fearless Vampire Killers 1967 DVD
Ferris Bueller's Day Off 1986 DVD
Fever Pitch 1996 DVD
Fiddler on the Roof 1971 DVD
Finding Nemo 2003 DVD
The First Wives Club 1996 DVD
The Floorwalker 1916
Flowers and Trees 1932
Follow the Boys 1944
Follow the Fleet 1936 DVD
For Heaven's Sake 1926
A Foreign Affair 1948
Forrest Gump 1994 DVD
The Fortune Cookie 1966 DVD
Four Steps in the Clouds 1942
The Fourth Man 1983 DVD
The Freshman 1990 DVD
Fright Night 1985 DVD
The Frighteners 1996 DVD
From Dusk till Dawn 1995 DVD
The Front Page 1974 DVD
Full Moon in Paris 1984 DVD
Funny Bones 1994 DVD
Funny Dirty Little War 1983 DVD
Funny Face 1957 DVD
Galaxy Quest 1999 DVD
Garden State 2003 DVD
The Gay Divorcee 1934
Genevieve 1953 DVD
Gentlemen Prefer Blondes 1953 DVD
Georgy Girl 1966
Get Shorty 1995 DVD
The Ghost Breakers 1940
The Ghost of St Michael's 1941
Ghostbusters 1984 DVD
Gidget 1959
The Girl Can't Help It 1956 DVD
Girl 6 1996
Girlfriends 1978
Girls' Night 1997 DVD
Go 1999 DVD
Go West 1925
Gold of Naples 1954
The Golden Age of Buster Keaton 1975
The Golden Age of Comedy 1958
The Good Companions 1933
The Good Fairy 1935
Good Morning, Boys 1937 DVD
Good News 1947
The Goodbye Girl 1977
The Goose Steps Out 1942
Le Goût des Autres 1999 DVD
Grand Theft Parsons 2003 DVD
Les Grandes Manoeuvres 1955 DVD
The Great McGinty 1940
The Great Race 1965
The Great War 1959
Green for Danger 1946
The Green Butchers 2003
The Green Man 1956 DVD
The Green Ray 1986 DVD

Gregory's Girl 1980 DVD
Gremlins 1984 DVD
Greyfriars Bobby 1961 DVD
The Grinch 2000 DVD
Grosse Pointe Blank 1997 DVD
The Guardsman 1931
Guess Who's Coming to Dinner 1967 DVD
Gumshoe 1971
Guys and Dolls 1955 DVD
Hairspray 1988 DVD
The Half Naked Truth 1932
Hamlet Goes Business 1987
Hands across the Table 1935
Hangin' with the Homeboys 1991
The Happiest Days of Your Life 1950
The Happiness of the Katakuris 2001 DVD
Happy, Texas 1999 DVD
The Hard Way 1991 DVD
Harold and Maude 1972 DVD
Harry and Tonto 1974
Head 1968 DVD
Hear My Song 1991
Hearts of the West 1975
Heaven Can Wait 1978 DVD
Hellzapoppin' 1941
Help! 1965
Henry Fool 1997
Here Comes Mr Jordan 1941
Hi, Mom! 1970 DVD
High Fidelity 2000 DVD
High Hopes 1988
High Society 1956 DVD
Historias Mínimas 2002 DVD
History of the World Part 1 1981
The Hitchhiker's Guide to the Galaxy 2005
Hobson's Choice 1953 DVD
Hold Back the Dawn 1941
Holiday Inn 1942 DVD
Hollywood or Bust 1956
Holy Matrimony 1943
Home Alone 1990 DVD
L'Homme du Train 2002 DVD
Honey, I Shrunk the Kids 1989 DVD
Honeymoon in Vegas 1992 DVD
The Honeymooners 2003 DVD
Hooper 1978
The Hot Rock 1972
House of Angels 1992
House Party 1990
Houseboat 1958 DVD
Housekeeping 1987
How I Won the War 1967 DVD
How to Marry a Millionaire 1953 DVD
How to Murder Your Wife 1965 DVD
How to Succeed in Business without Really Trying 1967
The Howling 1981 DVD
The Hudsucker Proxy 1994 DVD
Hue and Cry 1947 DVD
I ❤ Huckabees 2004 DVD
I Love You Again 1940
I Married a Witch 1942
I Ought to Be in Pictures 1982
IQ 1994 DVD
An Ideal Husband 1999 DVD
The Idiots 1998 DVD
If You Could Only Cook 1935
I'm Going Home 2001 DVD
I'm No Angel 1933
The Importance of Being Earnest 1952 DVD
In & Out 1997 DVD
The Incredibles 2004 DVD
Indian Summer 1993 DVD
Insignificance 1985
The Invitation 1973
Irma la Douce 1963 DVD
Irma Vep 1996
The Iron Petticoat 1956 DVD
Irreconcilable Differences 1984
Isn't It Shocking? 1973
It Should Happen to You 1954 DVD
Italian for Beginners 2000 DVD
It's a Wonderful World 1939
It's Always Fair Weather 1955
It's Great to Be Young 1956
Jackie Chan's Who Am I? 1998 DVD
Jamon Jamon 1992 DVD
Janice Beard 45 WPM 1999 DVD
Jealousy, Italian Style 1970
Jeffrey 1995 DVD
The Jerk 1979 DVD
Jerry Maguire 1996 DVD
Johnny Suede 1991
Jonah Who Will Be 25 in the Year 2000 1976
Judy Berlin 1999
Jumbo 1962
Junk Mail 1997
Keep Cool 1997
Kevin & Perry Go Large 2000 DVD
The Kid 1921 DVD
The Kid from Spain 1932
King of Hearts 1966
King, Queen, Knave 1972
The Kingdom 1994 DVD
Kings & Queen 2004
Kiss Me Kate 1953 DVD
Kitchen Stories 2003 DVD
Kolya 1996 DVD
Kung Fu Hustle 2004
LA Story 1991 DVD
The Ladies' Man 1961 DVD
Lady for a Day 1933
Lady Killer 1933
Lady L 1965
Lady with a Past 1932
The Landlord 1970
Last Action Hero 1993 DVD
Last Life in the Universe 2003 DVD
The Last of the Good Old Days 1989
The Late Shift 1996
Laughter in Paradise 1951
Laurel and Hardy's Laughing 20s 1965
The League of Gentlemen 1960 DVD
La Lectrice 1988 DVD
Leningrad Cowboys Go America 1989
Léolo 1992
Let's Make Love 1960 DVD
Letter to Brezhnev 1985 DVD
Liar Liar 1997 DVD
Libeled Lady 1936
Life Is a Long Quiet River 1988
Life with Father 1947 DVD
Li'l Abner 1959
Lilo & Stitch 2002 DVD
Limelight 1952 DVD
Little Murders 1971
Little Otik 2000 DVD
Little Shop of Horrors 1986 DVD
Little Vegas 1990
Little Voice 1998 DVD
The Little World of Don Camillo 1951
Live Flesh 1997 DVD
Live Now – Pay Later 1962
Living in Oblivion 1995
Local Hero 1983 DVD
Lock, Stock and Two Smoking Barrels 1998 DVD
Lola 1982
Lonely Hearts 1981
Long Live the Lady! 1987
Long Pants 1927
Look at Me 2004
Loot 1970
Love among the Ruins 1975
Love and Death 1975 DVD
Love at First Bite 1979
The Love Bug 1969 DVD
Love in the Afternoon 1972 DVD
Love Is Colder Than Death 1969
The Love Parade 1929
Love with the Proper Stranger 1963
Lovers and Other Strangers 1970
Lucas 1986 DVD
Lucky Break 2001 DVD
Lucky Jim 1957 DVD
The Maggie 1953
Major Barbara 1941
Make Way for Tomorrow 1937
Making Up 1992
The Male Animal 1942
Man about Town 1947
Man Bites Dog 1992 DVD
Man on the Moon 1999 DVD
The Man Who Came to Dinner 1941
The Man without a Past 2002 DVD
Manhattan Murder Mystery 1993 DVD
Man's Favorite Sport? 1964
Margie 1946
Marius et Jeannette 1997
Married to the Mob 1988 DVD
The Marrying Kind 1952
Matilda 1996 DVD
Matinee 1993 DVD
The Mating Game 1959
Me Myself I 1999
Me without You 2001 DVD
The Mean Machine 1974 DVD
Mediterraneo 1991 DVD
Meet the Parents 2000 DVD
Melvin and Howard 1980
Men in Black 1997 DVD
Men o' War 1929 DVD
Mermaids 1990 DVD
The Merry Widow 1934
Mexican Bus Ride 1951
Midnight Run 1988 DVD
A Midsummer Night's Dream 1935
A Midsummer Night's Sex Comedy 1982 DVD
A Mighty Wind 2003 DVD
The Milky Way 1936
Le Million 1931
The Million Pound Note 1953
A Millionaire for Christy 1951
Millions 2004
Miss Congeniality 2000 DVD
Miss Tatlock's Millions 1948
Mr and Mrs '55 1955 DVD
Mr Blandings Builds His Dream House 1948
Mr Deeds Goes to Town 1936
Mr Reliable 1996
Mr Vampire 1986
Mon Père Ce Héros 1991
Monday Morning 2002 DVD
Monkey Business 1931 DVD
Monrak Transistor 2001
Monsieur Verdoux 1947 DVD
Monsoon Wedding 2001 DVD
Monty Python and the Holy Grail 1975 DVD
Monty Python's Life of Brian 1979 DVD
Moonstruck 1987 DVD
The More the Merrier 1943
The Mother 2003 DVD
Motorama 1991
Mouse Trouble 1944
Mousehunt 1997 DVD
Move Over, Darling 1963
Mrs Delafield Wants to Marry 1986
Mrs Doubtfire 1993 DVD
Much Ado about Nothing 1993 DVD
The Muppet Christmas Carol 1992 DVD
The Muppet Movie 1979
Muppet Treasure Island 1996 DVD
Muppets from Space 1999 DVD
Muriel's Wedding 1994 DVD
The Music Man 1962
My Best Friend's Wedding 1997 DVD
My Big Fat Greek Wedding 2002 DVD
My Boyfriend's Back 1989
My Cousin Vinny 1992 DVD
My Favorite Blonde 1942
My Favorite Wife 1940 DVD
My Favorite Year 1982
My Girlfriend's Boyfriend 1987 DVD
My Learned Friend 1943
My Life as a Dog 1985 DVD
My Man Godfrey 1936 DVD
Mystery Train 1989 DVD
Mystic Pizza 1988 DVD
The Naked Gun 2½: the Smell of Fear 1991 DVD
Naked Gun 33⅓: the Final Insult 1994 DVD
The Naked Truth 1957 DVD
National Lampoon's Animal House 1978 DVD
Nationale 7 1999
The Navigator 1924
Neighbors 1920
Never Give a Sucker an Even Break 1941
A New Leaf 1971
Next Stop Wonderland 1998
Night Shift 1982
The Night We Never Met 1993 DVD
No Way to Treat a Lady 1968
North to Alaska 1960 DVD
The Northerners 1992
Not One Less 1999 DVD
Nothing but the Best 1964
Notting Hill 1999 DVD
La Nuit Fantastique 1942
The Nutty Professor 1963 DVD
The Nutty Professor 1996 DVD
O Brother, Where Art Thou? 2000 DVD
O Henry's Full House 1952
Ocean's Eleven 1960 DVD
Ocean's Eleven 2001 DVD
The Odd Couple 1968 DVD
Oh, God! 1977
Oh, Mr Porter! 1937 DVD
Ohayo 1959
The Old Dark House 1932
The Old-Fashioned Way 1934
One Born Every Minute 1967
One, Two, Three 1961 DVD
One Week 1920
Only Two Can Play 1961
Only You 1994 DVD
Operation Petticoat 1959 DVD
The Opposite of Sex 1998 DVD
The Original Kings of Comedy 2000
Orphans 1998 DVD
Our Betters 1933
The Out of Towners 1970 DVD
Overboard 1987 DVD
A Pain in the A...! 1973
The Palm Beach Story 1942
Palooka 1934
Palookaville 1995 DVD
Papa's Delicate Condition 1963
The Paper 1994 DVD
The Paper Chase 1973
Paper Moon 1973
Parenthood 1989 DVD
Parents 1988
Pas sur la Bouche 2003
Passport to Pimlico 1949 DVD
Pat and Mike 1952
Pauline & Paulette 2001 DVD
Pauline at the Beach 1983 DVD
The Pawnshop 1916
La Peau Douce 1964 DVD
The Pentagon Wars 1998
Period of Adjustment 1962
Peter's Friends 1992 DVD
Pillow Talk 1959 DVD
Ping Pong 2002 DVD
The Pink Panther 1963 DVD
Play It Again, Sam 1972 DVD
Playing by Heart 1998 DVD
Pleasantville 1998 DVD
Please Don't Eat the Daisies 1960
Pleasure at Her Majesty's 1976
Poppy 1936
Postcards from the Edge 1990 DVD
Il Posto 1961
Pretty Woman 1990 DVD
Primary Colors 1998 DVD
A Private Function 1984 DVD
Private Parts 1997 DVD
Private's Progress 1956 DVD
Prizzi's Honor 1985 DVD
The Projectionist 1970
P'Tang, Yang, Kipperbang 1982
Punch-Drunk Love 2002 DVD
The Purple Rose of Cairo 1985 DVD
Radio Days 1987 DVD
The Railrodder 1965
Raining Stones 1993 DVD
Raising Arizona 1987 DVD
The Raven 1963 DVD
Ravenous 1999 DVD
Re-Animator 1985 DVD
Red Rock West 1992 DVD
The Red Squirrel 1993 DVD
The Reivers 1969 DVD
Remember the Night 1940
Ride 'em Cowboy 1942
Rien Ne Va Plus 1997
Rififi 1955 DVD
The Rink 1916
Risky Business 1983 DVD
Rita, Sue and Bob Too 1987 DVD
Road to Morocco 1942 DVD
Road to Rio 1947
Road to Utopia 1945 DVD
Robin and the 7 Hoods 1964
Roger Dodger 2002 DVD
A Room for Romeo Brass 1999 DVD
The Roommate 1984
Rose Marie 1936
Rosencrantz and Guildenstern Are Dead 1990 DVD
Roxanne 1987 DVD
Roxie Hart 1942
Rush Hour 1998 DVD
Rushmore 1998 DVD
The Russians Are Coming, the Russians Are Coming 1966 DVD
Ruthless People 1986 DVD
The Rutles – All You Need Is Cash 1978 DVD
A Sailor-Made Man 1921
Salty O'Rourke 1945
Samaritan Girl 2004
Same Time, Next Year 1978
The Scarecrow 1920
Scenes from the Class Struggle in Beverly Hills 1989 DVD
School for Postmen 1947
The School of Rock 2003 DVD
Scorpio Rising 1963
The Scout 1994
Scram! 1932 DVD
Secret Ballot 2001 DVD
The Secret Life of Walter Mitty 1947
The Secret Lives of Dentists 2002
The Secret of Santa Vittoria 1969
The Secret Policeman's Ball 1980 DVD
Send Me No Flowers 1964 DVD
The Seven Year Itch 1955 DVD
Shall We Dance? 1995 DVD
Shaun of the Dead 2004 DVD
She Done Him Wrong 1933
The Sheepman 1958
The Sheriff of Fractured Jaw 1958
She's Gotta Have It 1986
Shirley Valentine 1989 DVD
The Shop around the Corner 1940
A Shot in the Dark 1964 DVD
Shrek 2001 DVD
Shrek 2 2004
Silver Streak 1976
Simple Men 1992
Sing, Baby, Sing 1936
Singles 1992 DVD
Sister Act 1992 DVD
Sitcom 1997 DVD
Sitting Ducks 1979
Six of a Kind 1934
Slacker 1989 DVD
Sleeper 1973 DVD
Sleepless in Seattle 1993 DVD
Slums of Beverly Hills 1998 DVD
The Smallest Show on Earth 1957 DVD
Smokey and the Bandit 1977 DVD
Sneakers 1992 DVD
Soapdish 1991 DVD
Soldier in the Rain 1963
Something Wild 1986 DVD
Son of Paleface 1952
South Park: Bigger, Longer & Uncut 1999 DVD
Spanglish 2004 DVD
Speak Easily 1932
Splash 1984 DVD
The SpongeBob SquarePants Movie 2004 DVD
Stage Door 1937
Stage Fright 1949 DVD
Stardust Memories 1980
Start the Revolution without Me 1970
State and Main 2000 DVD
The Station Agent 2003 DVD
Steel Magnolias 1989 DVD
Stiff Upper Lips 1997
Still Crazy 1998 DVD

Stowaway 1936 DVD
Straight Talk 1992 DVD
The Strawberry Blonde 1941
The Strong Man 1926
Such Good Friends 1971
Sugarbaby 1985
Summer Things 2002 DVD
A Summer's Tale 1996 DVD
The Sunshine Boys 1975
Support Your Local Gunfighter 1971 DVD
Support Your Local Sheriff! 1969 DVD
The Sure Thing 1985 DVD
Sweet and Lowdown 1999 DVD
Sweetie 1989
Swingers 1996 DVD
Take Care of Your Scarf, Tatjana 1994
Taking Off 1971
The Talk of the Town 1942 DVD
The Taming of the Shrew 1967 DVD
Taxi zum Klo 1980
A Taxing Woman 1987
Teacher's Pet 1958
10 1979 DVD
10 Things I Hate about You 1999 DVD
The Tender Trap 1955
That Man from Rio 1964
That Thing You Do! 1996 DVD
Their First Mistake 1932 DVD
Them Thar Hills! 1934 DVD
Theodora Goes Wild 1936
There Was a Crooked Man 1960
There's Something about Mary 1998 DVD
They All Laughed 1981
The Thief of Paris 1967
The Thin Man 1934
Things Change 1988
Things You Can Tell Just by Looking at Her 2000
Thomas Graal's Best Film 1917
Those Lips, Those Eyes 1980
Those Magnificent Men in Their Flying Machines 1965
The Three Ages 1923
Three Coins in the Fountain 1954
Three Colours White 1993 DVD
Three Lives and Only One Death 1996
Three Men and a Baby 1987 DVD
3 Men and a Cradle 1985
Three Men in a Boat 1956 DVD
The Three Musketeers 1973 DVD
Three Smart Girls 1937 DVD
The Threepenny Opera 1931 DVD
Throw Momma from the Train 1987 DVD
Thursday 1998
Time Bandits 1981 DVD
The Time of Your Life 1948 DVD
Tin Men 1987 DVD
Tit for Tat 1934 DVD
Tito and Me 1992
To See Such Fun 1977
Tokyo Chorus 1931
Tollbooth 1994
Tom Jones 1963 DVD
Too Hot to Handle 1938
Tootsie 1982 DVD
Topaze 1933
Topkapi 1964 DVD
Topper 1937
Towed in a Hole 1932 DVD
Trading Places 1983 DVD
Traffic 1970
The Tramp 1915
Tramp, Tramp, Tramp 1926
Travelling North 1986
Trees Lounge 1996 DVD
Trigger Happy 1996
Triple Bogey on a Par Five Hole 1991
Trop Belle pour Toi 1989 DVD
True Lies 1994 DVD
True Love 1989
True Romance 1993 DVD
The Truth about Cats and Dogs 1996 DVD
24 Hour Party People 2001 DVD
Twins 1988 DVD
Two for the Road 1967 DVD
Two Girls and a Guy 1997 DVD
The Two of Us 1967
Two Way Stretch 1960 DVD
U Turn 1997 DVD
Unfaithfully Yours 1948 DVD
An Unmarried Woman 1978
Unstrung Heroes 1995
Up in the Cellar 1970
Used Cars 1980 DVD
Va Savoir 2001 DVD
Vacuuming Completely Nude in Paradise 2001
Valley Girl 1983
The Vanishing Corporal 1962
Very Bad Things 1998
Vessel of Wrath 1938
La Vie de Château 1965 DVD
Les Visiteurs 1993 DVD
Vodka Lemon 2003 DVD
Wag the Dog 1997 DVD
Waltz of the Toreadors 1962 DVD
The War of the Roses 1989 DVD
waydowntown 2000
Wayne's World 1992 DVD
A Wedding 1978
The Wedding Banquet 1993
The Wedding Singer 1998 DVD
Welcome to the Dollhouse 1995
What about Bob? 1991 DVD
What Women Want 2001 DVD
When Ladies Meet 1933
When Magoo Flew 1955
When the Cat's Away... 1996
Where There's Life 1947
Where's Poppa? 1970
While You Were Sleeping 1995 DVD
Whisky 2004
White Men Can't Jump 1992 DVD
The Whole Town's Talking 1935
Wife vs Secretary 1936
Wilbur (Wants to Kill Himself) 2002 DVD
Wild about Harry 2000 DVD
A Wild Hare 1940
Wild Target 1993
Wind with the Gone 1998
Wish You Were Here 1987 DVD
The Witches of Eastwick 1987 DVD
Withnail & I 1986 DVD
Woman of the Year 1942 DVD
The Women 1939
Wonder Boys 2000 DVD
Working Girl 1988
The World of Henry Orient 1964 DVD
The Wrong Arm of the Law 1962 DVD
Xala 1974
Young Frankenstein 1974 DVD
The Young in Heart 1938
The Young Poisoner's Handbook 1994
Yoyo 1964
Zelig 1983 DVD
Zero Effect 1997
Zoolander 2001 DVD

Crime

★★★★★

A Bout de Souffle 1959 DVD
Anatomy of a Murder 1959 DVD
Angels with Dirty Faces 1938 DVD
L'Argent 1983 DVD
The Asphalt Jungle 1950
Atlantic City, USA 1980 DVD
La Bête Humaine 1938 DVD
The Big Sleep 1946 DVD
Blood and Black Lace 1964
Bonnie and Clyde 1967 DVD
Build My Gallows High 1947
Chopper 2000 DVD
City of God 2002 DVD
Cyclo 1995
Dirty Harry 1971 DVD
Double Indemnity 1944 DVD
Farewell My Lovely 1944 DVD
The French Connection 1971 DVD
The General 1998
The Godfather 1972 DVD
The Godfather, Part II 1974 DVD
GoodFellas 1990 DVD
In a Lonely Place 1950 DVD
In the Heat of the Night 1967
Insomnia 2002 DVD
The Killers 1946
Kiss Me Deadly 1955 DVD
LA Confidential 1997 DVD
Laura 1944
The Lavender Hill Mob 1951 DVD
The Long Goodbye 1973 DVD
M 1931 DVD
The Maltese Falcon 1941 DVD
Mildred Pierce 1945
Miller's Crossing 1990 DVD
Odd Man Out 1946 DVD
On the Waterfront 1954 DVD
Once upon a Time in America 1984 DVD
The Postman Always Rings Twice 1946
The Public Enemy 1931 DVD
Pulp Fiction 1994 DVD
Reservoir Dogs 1991 DVD
Scarface 1932
The Shawshank Redemption 1994 DVD
Shoot the Pianist 1960 DVD
A Short Film about Killing 1988 DVD
Sonatine 1993 DVD
The Sting 1973 DVD
The Strange Love of Martha Ivers 1946 DVD
10 Rillington Place 1970 DVD
To Die For 1995 DVD
Touch of Evil 1958 DVD
12 Angry Men 1957 DVD
The Untouchables 1987 DVD
The Usual Suspects 1995 DVD
White Heat 1949 DVD
Who Framed Roger Rabbit 1988 DVD
Witness for the Prosecution 1957 DVD
You Only Live Once 1937 DVD

Crime

★★★★

The Accused 1988 DVD
After Dark, My Sweet 1990
Al Capone 1959
Alphaville 1965 DVD
The American Friend 1977 DVD
The American Soldier 1970
Analyze This 1999 DVD
And Then There Were None 1945 DVD
Angel 1982 DVD
Angel Face 1953
Another Day in Paradise 1998 DVD
Bad Blood 1982
Bad Lieutenant 1992 DVD
Badlands 1973 DVD
The Bait 1995
La Balance 1982 DVD
Bande à Part 1964 DVD
Bandits of Orgosolo 1961
Beyond a Reasonable Doubt 1956
The Big Combo 1955
Big Deal on Madonna Street 1958
The Big Easy 1986 DVD
The Big Heat 1953
The Big House 1930
The Black Bird 1926
Black Sunday 1976
Blood Oath 1990
The Blue Dahlia 1946
The Blue Lamp 1949 DVD
Bob Le Flambeur 1955 DVD
Boomerang! 1947
Borsalino 1970
The Boston Strangler 1968 DVD
Bound 1996 DVD
Brighton Rock 1947 DVD
Bring Me the Head of Alfredo Garcia 1974 DVD
A Bronx Tale 1993 DVD
Brother 1997 DVD
Brubaker 1980 DVD
Brute Force 1947
Bugsy 1991 DVD
Bugsy Malone 1976 DVD
Bullets over Broadway 1994 DVD
Bullitt 1968 DVD
Bus 174 2002 DVD
Cagney & Lacey 1981
Call Northside 777 1948
Carandiru 2003 DVD
Carlito's Way 1993 DVD
Cash on Demand 1961
Casino 1995 DVD
Chaos 1999 DVD
Charley Varrick 1973
The Chase 1946
Choice of Arms 1981
Clean, Shaven 1993
Collateral 2004 DVD
Compulsion 1959
Confessions of a Serial Killer 1987 DVD
The Consequences of Love 2004
Cool Hand Luke 1967 DVD
Le Cop 1985
Cop 1988
Cop au Vin 1984
Cop Land 1997 DVD
Cotton Comes to Harlem 1970
The Court-Martial of Billy Mitchell 1955
Crime and Punishment 1935
Crime and Punishment 1935
Crime in the Streets 1956
Crime of Passion 1957
Criss Cross 1949
Crossfire 1947
Cry of the City 1948
Cutter's Way 1981 DVD
DOA 1988 DVD
Dangerous Female 1931
Darkness in Tallinn 1993
Dead End 1937
Dead Man Walking 1995 DVD
Dead Men Don't Wear Plaid 1982 DVD
Dead Reckoning 1947 DVD
Deep Cover 1992 DVD
The Defiant Ones 1958 DVD
Desperate 1947
Detective Story 1951
Devil in a Blue Dress 1995 DVD
Dick Tracy 1990 DVD
Dillinger 1945
Dillinger 1973
Diva 1981 DVD
Dobermann 1997 DVD
Dr Mabuse, the Gambler 1922 DVD
Dog Day Afternoon 1975 DVD
Donnie Brasco 1997 DVD
The Dragnet 1928
The Driver 1978 DVD
The Element of Crime 1984 DVD
The Enforcer 1951 DVD
Escape from Alcatraz 1979 DVD
Evidence of Love 1990 DVD
The FBI Story 1959 DVD
FX: Murder by Illusion 1985 DVD
Fallen Angel 1945 DVD
Farewell, My Lovely 1975 DVD
Fear in the Night 1947
La Femme Publique 1984
A Few Good Men 1992 DVD
Force of Evil 1948
Fort Apache, the Bronx 1981
The Freshman 1990 DVD
The Friends of Eddie Coyle 1973
Fury 1936
Gang Related 1997 DVD
Gangs of New York 2002 DVD
Garde à Vue 1981
Get Carter 1971 DVD
Get Shorty 1995 DVD
The Getaway 1972 DVD
Ghosts... of the Civil Dead 1988
Gideon's Day 1958
Gideon's Trumpet 1980
The Glass House 1972 DVD
The Glass Key 1942
Go 1999 DVD
Godmoney 1997 DVD
Good Morning, Night 2003 DVD
The Grifters 1990
Gumshoe 1971
Gun Crazy 1949
Hana-Bi 1997 DVD
Hard-Boiled 1992 DVD
Harper 1966
Heat 1995 DVD
Heist 2001 DVD
Hide in Plain Sight 1980
High and Low 1963 DVD
The Hill 1965
The Hitch-Hiker 1953
Homicide 1991 DVD
The Honeymoon Killers 1969 DVD
Honour among Thieves 1954
The Hot Rock 1972
I Am a Fugitive from a Chain Gang 1932
I Wake Up Screaming 1941
I Want to Live! 1958 DVD
In Cold Blood 1967 DVD
Indictment: the McMartin Trial 1995
Infernal Affairs 2002
Inherit the Wind 1960 DVD
Inherit the Wind 1999
Internal Affairs 1990 DVD
It Always Rains on Sunday 1947 DVD
Jackie Brown 1997 DVD
The Jericho Mile 1979
John Grisham's The Rainmaker 1997 DVD
Johnny Angel 1945
Le Jour Se Lève 1939
The Killing of a Chinese Bookie 1976
The King of Marvin Gardens 1972
King of New York 1989 DVD
Kiss of Death 1947
Kiss Tomorrow Goodbye 1950
The Krays 1990 DVD
L.627 1992
The Lady from Shanghai 1948 DVD
The Lady in Red 1979
Lady in the Lake 1947
The Last Run 1971
The League of Gentlemen 1960 DVD
Leave Her to Heaven 1945 DVD
Let Him Have It 1991 DVD
Lift to the Scaffold 1957
Little Caesar 1931
Lock, Stock and Two Smoking Barrels 1998 DVD
The Long Good Friday 1979 DVD
Love Is Colder Than Death 1969
Lucky Break 2001 DVD
Lucky Luciano 1973 DVD
Mad City 1997 DVD
Made in Hong Kong 1997
Madigan 1968
The Man Who Knew Too Much 1934 DVD
The Man Who Wasn't There 2001 DVD
Mapantsula 1988
Marked Woman 1937
The Mattei Affair 1972
Miami Blues 1990 DVD
Midnight in the Garden of Good and Evil 1997 DVD
Mona Lisa 1986 DVD
Monster 2003 DVD
Monster's Ball 2001 DVD
Moonrise 1948
Nada 1974
The Naked City 1948
The Narrow Margin 1952
Natural Born Killers 1994 DVD
Never Steal Anything Small 1959
The New Centurions 1972
New Jack City 1991 DVD
Night and the City 1950 DVD
Nightmare 1956
Nightmare in Chicago 1968
Nine Queens 2000 DVD
Ocean's Eleven 1960 DVD
Ocean's Eleven 2001 DVD
Odds against Tomorrow 1959
One False Move 1992 DVD
Open Doors 1990
The Organization 1971 DVD
Out of Sight 1998 DVD
Out of the Darkness 1985
A Pain in the A...! 1973

Palookaville 1995 DVD
Le Paltoquet 1986
Papillon 1973 DVD
Phantom Lady 1944
Pickpocket 1959 DVD
Pitfall 1948
Pitfall 1962 DVD
The Pledge 2000 DVD
Plein Soleil 1960 DVD
Police 1985
Prescription: Murder 1968 DVD
Primal Fear 1996 DVD
The Prime Gig 2000 DVD
A Question of Silence 1982
A Rage in Harlem 1991
Raw Deal 1948
Razzia sur la Chnouf 1955
Rififi 1955 DVD
Riot in Cell Block 11 1954
The Rise and Fall of Legs Diamond 1960
Road House 1948
Road to Perdition 2002 DVD
The Roaring Twenties 1939 DVD
Roberto Succo 2000 DVD
Rome Express 1932
Roxie Hart 1942
Ruby 1992
Run Lola Run 1998 DVD
The Running Man 1963
Salvatore Giuliano 1961
Scarface 1983 DVD
See How They Fall 1993
Serpico 1973 DVD
Sexy Beast 2000 DVD
Shaft 2000 DVD
Sin City 2005
Sitting Ducks 1979
The Sleeping Tiger 1954
The Sniper 1952
Snow Falling on Cedars 1999 DVD
The Sound of Fury 1950
The Spider and the Fly 1949
State of Grace 1990 DVD
The Street with No Name 1948
Sylvia 1964
T-Men 1947
The Talented Mr Ripley 1999 DVD
Targets 1968 DVD
That Man from Rio 1964
Thérèse Raquin 1953
They Live by Night 1948
Thief 1981 DVD
Thieves like Us 1974
The Thin Man 1934
Things Change 1988
Things to Do in Denver When You're Dead 1995 DVD
Thunderbolt 1929
Thunderbolt and Lightfoot 1974 DVD
Thursday 1998
Time after Time 1979
Time and Tide 2000 DVD
Toni 1935
Topkapi 1964 DVD
Traffic 2000 DVD
Training Day 2001 DVD
Trigger Happy 1996
Le Trou 1959
Trouble in Mind 1985
12 Angry Men 1997
Two against the Law 1973
Two Way Stretch 1960 DVD
Underground 1998 DVD
Underworld 1927
Underworld USA 1961
The Unholy Three 1925
The Unsuspected 1947
Violent Saturday 1955
Wanda 1971
The Watchmaker of St Paul 1973
Where the Sidewalk Ends 1950 DVD
The Whole Town's Talking 1935
Who'll Stop the Rain? 1978 DVD
The Woman in the Window 1945
The Wrong Arm of the Law 1962 DVD
The Wrong Man 1956 DVD
The Yakuza 1975
The Yakuza Papers 1973 DVD
Zero Effect 1997

Disaster

★★★★★

Airplane! 1980 DVD
Testament 1983

Disaster

★★★★

The Day after Tomorrow 2004 DVD
Deep Impact 1998 DVD
Earthquake 1974 DVD
A Night to Remember 1958 DVD
The Poseidon Adventure 1972 DVD
San Francisco 1936
Titanic 1997 DVD
The Towering Inferno 1974 DVD

Documentary

★★★★★

Berlin: Symphony of a Great City 1927
Bowling for Columbine 2002 DVD
The Celluloid Closet 1995
Les Enfants de Lumière 1995
A Great Day in Harlem 1994
Hearts of Darkness: a Film-Maker's Apocalypse 1991
Hoop Dreams 1994 DVD
Hotel Terminus: the Life and Times of Klaus Barbie 1987
Kandahar 2001 DVD
Land without Bread 1933
The Last Waltz 1978 DVD
Man with a Movie Camera 1929
Marcello Mastroianni: I Remember 1997
Martin Scorsese Presents the Blues: Feel Like Going Home 2003 DVD
Night Mail 1936 DVD
Nuit et Brouillard 1955 DVD
People on Sunday 1929 DVD
The River 1937
Roger & Me 1989 DVD
Shoah 1985
Song of Ceylon 1934
The Sorrow and the Pity 1969 DVD
The TAMI Show 1964 DVD
That's Entertainment 1974
The Thin Blue Line 1988
Toot, Whistle, Plunk and Boom 1953
When We Were Kings 1996 DVD
Woodstock 1970 DVD

Documentary

★★★★

ABC Africa 2001
A Propos de Nice 1930
Alexandria Encore 1990
The American Nightmare 2000 DVD
The Battle of Midway 1942
Best Boy 1979
Beyond the Mat 1999 DVD
The Big One 1997
The Big TNT Show 1966
Bodysong 2002 DVD
Bright Leaves 2003
Buena Vista Social Club 1998 DVD
Bukowski: Born into This 2003
Burden of Dreams 1982
Bus 174 2002
Capturing the Friedmans 2003 DVD
Carmen Miranda: Bananas Is My Business 1994
Chang 1927
Charlie: the Life and Art of Charles Chaplin 2003
Chicken Ranch 1983 DVD
Ciao, Federico! 1970
Cinéma Vérité: Defining the Moment 1999
The City 1939
Close-Up 1989
The Clowns 1970
Common Threads: Stories from the Quilt 1989
The Conquest of Everest 1953
Control Room 2004 DVD
Cool and Crazy 2000 DVD
The Corporation 2003 DVD
Crumb 1995 DVD
Dear America: Letters Home from Vietnam 1987
The Decline of Western Civilization 1980
Don't Look Back 1967
Elvis: That's the Way It Is 1970 DVD
Etre et Avoir 2002 DVD
Fahrenheit 9/11 2004 DVD
Festival Express 2003
Fires Were Started 1943
The Five Obstructions 2003 DVD
The Fog of War: Eleven Lessons from the Life of Robert S McNamara 2003
4 Little Girls 1997 DVD
Frank Lloyd Wright 1997
From Mao to Mozart: Isaac Stern in China 1980
Gabbeh 1995
Gallivant 1996
Genocide 1981
Gimme Shelter 1970
The Gleaners and I 2000
God's Country 1985
The Golden Age of Buster Keaton 1975
The Golden Age of Comedy 1958
Grass 1999 DVD
Grass: a Nation's Battle for Life 1925
The Great Rock 'n' Roll Swindle 1979
Hail! Hail! Rock 'n' Roll! 1987
Häxan 1921
Hearts and Minds 1974
Homework 1989
Hostages 1993
The House on 92nd Street 1945
I Am Cuba 1964
In This World 2002 DVD
Intervista 1987
It's All True 1993
Jackie Stewart: Weekend of a Champion 1971
Jimi Hendrix 1973
Le Joli Mai 1962
Joy of Madness 2003
Jungle Cat 1959
The Last Days 1998
Latcho Drom 1993
Let the Good Times Roll 1973
The Living Desert 1953
London 1994 DVD
The Long Way Home 1996
Looking for Richard 1996 DVD
Lost in La Mancha 2002 DVD
The Love Goddesses 1965
Mandela 1995
Martha & Ethel 1993
Martin Scorsese Presents the Blues: Godfathers and Sons 2003 DVD
Martin Scorsese Presents the Blues: The Road to Memphis 2003 DVD
Martin Scorsese Presents the Blues: The Soul of a Man 2003 DVD
Memphis Belle 1943
Microcosmos 1996 DVD
Mr Death: the Rise and Fall of Fred A Leuchter Jr 1999
Moana 1926
Le Monde du Silence 1956
Mondovino 2004 DVD
Monterey Pop 1968
Muhammad Ali, the Greatest 1974 DVD
My Architect 2003
My Voyage to Italy 1999
Le Mystère Picasso 1956
Olympiad 1938
On Any Sunday 1971 DVD
One Day in September 1999
The Original Kings of Comedy 2000
Out of the Present 1995
Paradise Lost: the Child Murders at Robin Hood Hills 1996 DVD
Paragraph 175 1999
Paris Is Burning 1990
Phantom India 1968
Plastic Jesus 1971
Pleasure at Her Majesty's 1976
The Plow That Broke the Plains 1934
Portrait of Jason 1967
Power Trip 2003
Promises 2001
Pumping Iron 1976 DVD
Pumping Iron II: the Women 1984
Punishment Park 1971
The Quince Tree Sun 1991
Riding Giants 2004
Robert Altman's Jazz '34: Remembrances of Kansas City Swing 1996
Robinson in Space 1997 DVD
Salaam Cinema 1995
Salesman 1969
Sans Soleil 1982 DVD
Sergei Eisenstein: Mexican Fantasy 1998
Sick: the Life and Death of Bob Flanagan, Supermasochist 1997 DVD
Silverlake Life: the View from Here 1992
Soul in the Hole 1995
Southpaw 1998
Spellbound 2002 DVD
Stop Making Sense 1984 DVD
The Story of the Weeping Camel 2003 DVD
Strand – Under the Dark Cloth 1989
Super 8 Stories 2001
Super Size Me 2004 DVD
Superstar: the Life and Times of Andy Warhol 1991 DVD
Tales from a Hard City 1994
Tarnation 2004
That's Entertainment, Part II 1976
That's Entertainment! III 1994
Theremin: an Electronic Odyssey 1993
The Times of Harvey Milk 1983
Titicut Follies 1967
Tokyo Olympiad 1965
The Total Balalaika Show 1994
Touching the Void 2003 DVD
Train of Dreams 1987
The Trials of Henry Kissinger 2002
Triumph of the Will 1935 DVD
Tupac: Resurrection 2003 DVD
Uncovered: the War on Iraq 2004
The Undeclared War 1992
Universal Horror 1998
Unzipped 1995
Visions of Light 1992
Wall 2004
The War Game 1965 DVD
War Requiem 1988
The War Room 1993
Wild Man Blues 1997
Winged Migration 2001 DVD
Wisecracks 1991
The Wonderful, Horrible Life of Leni Riefenstahl 1993 DVD
World without Sun 1964
Zoo 1993

Drama

★★★★★

A Bout de Souffle 1959 DVD
Accident 1967 DVD
Ace in the Hole 1951
Aguirre, Wrath of God 1972 DVD
All about Eve 1950 DVD
All about My Mother 1999 DVD
All Quiet on the Western Front 1930 DVD
Amadeus 1984 DVD
Amarcord 1973 DVD
Amélie 2001 DVD
American Graffiti 1973 DVD
Amores Perros 2000 DVD
Anatomy of a Murder 1959 DVD
An Angel at My Table 1990 DVD
Angels with Dirty Faces 1938 DVD
Les Anges du Péché 1943
The Apartment 1960 DVD
Apocalypse Now 1979 DVD
L'Argent 1983 DVD
L'Armée des Ombres 1969
Ashes and Diamonds 1958
Asya's Happiness 1967
L'Atalante 1934 DVD
Atlantic City, USA 1980 DVD
Au Hasard, Balthazar 1966 DVD
The Autobiography of Miss Jane Pittman 1974 DVD
An Autumn Afternoon 1962
L'Avventura 1960
Babette's Feast 1987 DVD
Barry Lyndon 1975 DVD
The Battle of Algiers 1965 DVD
The Battleship Potemkin 1925 DVD
Before Night Falls 2000 DVD
Belle de Jour 1967 DVD
La Belle Noiseuse 1991 DVD
Berlin Alexanderplatz 1980
The Best Years of Our Lives 1946 DVD
La Bête Humaine 1938 DVD
Betty Blue 1986
Bicycle Thieves 1948
The Big Parade 1925
The Big Sleep 1946 DVD
Billy Liar 1963 DVD
Black Narcissus 1946 DVD
Blonde Venus 1932
Body and Soul 1947
Bonnie and Clyde 1967 DVD
Boogie Nights 1997 DVD
Born on the Fourth of July 1989 DVD
Boyz N the Hood 1991 DVD
Breakfast at Tiffany's 1961 DVD
Breaking the Waves 1996 DVD
The Bridge on the River Kwai 1957 DVD
Brief Encounter 1945 DVD
A Brighter Summer Day 1991
Burnt by the Sun 1995 DVD
Butch Cassidy and the Sundance Kid 1969 DVD
Cabaret 1972 DVD
Capricious Summer 1968
Casablanca 1942 DVD
Celine and Julie Go Boating 1974
The Charge of the Light Brigade 1968 DVD
Chariots of Fire 1981 DVD
Chopper 2000 DVD
The Cider House Rules 1999 DVD
Cinema Paradiso 1988 DVD
Citizen Kane 1941 DVD
City of Hope 1991
Cleo from 5 to 7 1961
Close Encounters of the Third Kind 1977 DVD
The Colour of Pomegranates 1969
The Conformist 1969
Crash 1996 DVD
Cries and Whispers 1972 DVD
Crimes and Misdemeanors 1989 DVD
The Crowd 1928
Cyclo 1995
Cyrano de Bergerac 1990 DVD
The Dam Busters 1954 DVD
Les Dames du Bois de Boulogne 1946 DVD
David Copperfield 1935
Day for Night 1973 DVD
Day of Wrath 1943
The Day the Earth Stood Still 1951 DVD
Dear Diary 1994
Death in Venice 1971 DVD
The Deer Hunter 1978 DVD
The Devil Is a Woman 1935
Diary of a Country Priest 1950
Diary of a Lost Girl 1929
The Diary of Anne Frank 1959 DVD

The Discreet Charm of the Bourgeoisie 1972
Dishonored 1931
Distant Voices, Still Lives 1988
La Dolce Vita 1960 DVD
Don Quixote 1957
The Draughtsman's Contract 1982 DVD
Earth 1930
Ed Wood 1994 DVD
8½ 1963
Elmer Gantry 1960 DVD
Eloge de l'Amour 2001 DVD
The End of Summer 1961 DVD
Les Enfants du Paradis 1945 DVD
The English Patient 1996 DVD
Fanny and Alexander 1982 DVD
Far from Heaven 2002 DVD
Farewell My Concubine 1993
Fight Club 1999 DVD
Fires on the Plain 1959
The Fisher King 1991 DVD
Fitzcarraldo 1982 DVD
Five Easy Pieces 1970 DVD
Flirting 1989
The 400 Blows 1959 DVD
The French Connection 1971 DVD
From Here to Eternity 1953 DVD
Full Metal Jacket 1987 DVD
The Full Monty 1997 DVD
Gandhi 1982 DVD
The Garden of the Finzi-Continis 1971
Gate of Hell 1953
The General 1998
Gertrud 1964
Glengarry Glen Ross 1992 DVD
The Godfather 1972 DVD
The Godfather, Part II 1974 DVD
Gods and Monsters 1998 DVD
Gone with the Wind 1939 DVD
Goodbye, Mr Chips 1939 DVD
GoodFellas 1990 DVD
The Gospel According to St Matthew 1964 DVD
The Graduate 1967 DVD
Grand Hotel 1932 DVD
La Grande Illusion 1937 DVD
The Grapes of Wrath 1940 DVD
Great Expectations 1946 DVD
Greed 1925
Hamlet 1948 DVD
Hannah and Her Sisters 1986 DVD
Happiness 1998 DVD
He Who Gets Slapped 1924
Heavenly Creatures 1994 DVD
Heimat 1984 DVD
Heimat 2 1992 DVD
Heimat 3: a Chronicle of Endings and Beginnings 2004
The Heiress 1949
Henry V 1944 DVD
Hope and Glory 1987
How Green Was My Valley 1941 DVD
Howards End 1992 DVD
Hud 1963 DVD
The Human Condition 1958
The Hunchback of Notre Dame 1939
The Hunt 1966
Husbands and Wives 1992 DVD
The Hustler 1961 DVD
I Was Born, but... 1932
The Ice Storm 1997 DVD
Ikiru 1952 DVD
Imitation of Life 1934
The Immigrant 1917 DVD
In the Company of Men 1997
In the Heat of the Night 1967 DVD
In Which We Serve 1942 DVD
The Insider 1999 DVD
Intolerance 1916 DVD
It's a Wonderful Life 1946 DVD
Ivan the Terrible, Part I 1944 DVD
Ivan's Childhood 1962 DVD
Jacquot de Nantes 1991
Jean de Florette 1986 DVD
Jeanne la Pucelle 1994
Jeux Interdits 1953
The Joyless Street 1925
Ju Dou 1990
Jules et Jim 1961 DVD
Julius Caesar 1953
Kameradschaft 1931
Kandahar 2001 DVD
Kes 1969 DVD
Kikujiro 1999 DVD
The Killing Fields 1984 DVD
The King of Comedy 1983 DVD
The Kreutzer Sonata 1987
LA Confidential 1997 DVD
The Last Command 1928
The Last Laugh 1924 DVD
The Last Picture Show 1971 DVD
Last Tango in Paris 1972 DVD
Last Year at Marienbad 1961 DVD
The Leopard 1962 DVD
The Life and Death of Colonel Blimp 1943 DVD
The Life of Oharu 1952 DVD
The Lion in Winter 1968 DVD
Little Dorrit 1987
A Little Princess 1995 DVD
Lola 1960
Lola Montès 1955
Lolita 1961 DVD
Lone Star 1995
The Loneliness of the Long Distance Runner 1962 DVD
The Long Day Closes 1992
The Long Goodbye 1973 DVD
Lost in Translation 2003 DVD
Love Affair 1939
M 1931 DVD
The Madness of King George 1995 DVD
The Magnificent Ambersons 1942
Magnolia 1999 DVD
La Maman et la Putain 1973
A Man Escaped 1956
Marty 1955 DVD
Master of the House 1925
Medium Cool 1969
Men with Guns 1997
Mephisto 1981
Midnight Cowboy 1969 DVD
Midnight Express 1978 DVD
Mildred Pierce 1945
The Milky Way 1968 DVD
Miller's Crossing 1990 DVD
Million Dollar Baby 2004 DVD
Miracle on 34th Street 1947 DVD
The Miracle Worker 1962 DVD
Mister Roberts 1955
Mr Smith Goes to Washington 1939 DVD
Mother 1926
The Motorcycle Diaries 2004 DVD
Mouchette 1966
Mrs Brown 1997 DVD
Mrs Miniver 1942 DVD
My Beautiful Laundrette 1985 DVD
My Left Foot 1989 DVD
My Name Is Joe 1998 DVD
Napoléon 1927
Nashville 1975
Nights of Cabiria 1957
Nil by Mouth 1997 DVD
La Notte 1961
Now, Voyager 1942
The Nun's Story 1959
Odd Man Out 1946 DVD
Oliver Twist 1948 DVD
Los Olvidados 1950
On the Waterfront 1954 DVD
Once upon a Time in America 1984 DVD
One Flew over the Cuckoo's Nest 1975 DVD
Only Angels Have Wings 1939
Ordet 1955
Osaka Elegy 1936
Othello 1952 DVD
The Ox-Bow Incident 1943
A Page of Madness 1926
Pandora's Box 1929 DVD
Les Parents Terribles 1948
Paris, Texas 1984 DVD
Une Partie de Campagne 1936 DVD
A Passage to India 1984 DVD
The Passion of Joan of Arc 1928
Pather Panchali 1955 DVD
Paths of Glory 1957 DVD
Patton 1970 DVD
The Pawnbroker 1965
People on Sunday 1929 DVD
Pépé le Moko 1937 DVD
Performance 1970
Persona 1966 DVD
Philadelphia 1993 DVD
The Piano 1993 DVD
Pierrot le Fou 1965 DVD
Pink Flamingos 1972
Pixote 1981
Le Plaisir 1951
Platoon 1986 DVD
Il Postino 1994 DVD
Prick Up Your Ears 1987 DVD
The Prime of Miss Jean Brodie 1969
Providence 1977
The Public Enemy 1931 DVD
Pulp Fiction 1994 DVD
Le Quai des Brumes 1938
The Quiet Man 1952 DVD
Quills 2000 DVD
Raging Bull 1980 DVD
The Railway Children 1970 DVD
Rain Man 1988 DVD
Raise the Red Lantern 1991
Ran 1985 DVD
Rashomon 1950 DVD
Rebel without a Cause 1955 DVD
The Red Shoes 1948 DVD
Red Sorghum 1987
Reds 1981
La Règle du Jeu 1939 DVD
The Remains of the Day 1993 DVD
Reservoir Dogs 1991 DVD
Ride with the Devil 1999 DVD
Rome, Open City 1945 DVD
La Ronde 1950
Room at the Top 1958 DVD
La Roue 1923
The Round-Up 1966
The Royal Tenenbaums 2001 DVD
Russian Ark 2002 DVD
Salt of the Earth 1954 DVD
Sansho the Bailiff 1954
The Saragossa Manuscript 1964
Saturday Night and Sunday Morning 1960 DVD
Saturday Night Fever 1977 DVD
Scarface 1932
The Scarlet Empress 1934
The Scent of Green Papaya 1993 DVD
Schindler's List 1993 DVD
Scrooge 1951 DVD
The Sea Inside 2004 DVD
Secrets & Lies 1995 DVD
Sense and Sensibility 1995 DVD
Seven Samurai 1954 DVD
The Seventh Seal 1957 DVD
Shadowlands 1993
Shadows of Our Forgotten Ancestors 1964
The Shanghai Gesture 1941
The Shawshank Redemption 1994 DVD
Shine 1996 DVD
Shoeshine 1946
Shoot the Pianist 1960 DVD
Short Cuts 1993
A Short Film about Killing 1988 DVD
Sideways 2004 DVD
Le Silence de la Mer 1947
Sisters of the Gion 1936
The Sixth Sense 1999 DVD
Sonatine 1993 DVD
The Son's Room 2001 DVD
The Southerner 1945
The Spider's Stratagem 1970
The Spirit of the Beehive 1973 DVD
Spring, Summer, Autumn, Winter ... and Spring 2003
Stand by Me 1986 DVD
A Star Is Born 1954 DVD
The Sting 1973 DVD
Storm over Asia 1928 DVD
The Story of a Cheat 1936
The Story of Qiu Ju 1992
Story of the Late Chrysanthemums 1939
A Streetcar Named Desire 1951 DVD
Strictly Ballroom 1992 DVD
Sullivan's Travels 1941 DVD
Summer of My German Soldier 1978
Summer with Monika 1952 DVD
Sunrise 1927 DVD
Sunset Blvd 1950 DVD
Sunshine State 2002 DVD
Sweet Smell of Success 1957 DVD
La Symphonie Pastorale 1946
A Tale of Two Cities 1935
A Taste of Honey 1961 DVD
Taxi Driver 1976 DVD
10 Rillington Place 1970 DVD
Testament 1983
That Obscure Object of Desire 1977
The Thin Red Line 1998 DVD
Thirty Two Short Films about Glenn Gould 1993
This Happy Breed 1944 DVD
This Sporting Life 1963 DVD
Three Colours Blue 1993 DVD
Three Colours Red 1994 DVD
Throne of Blood 1957 DVD
Time of the Gypsies 1988
To Die For 1995 DVD
To Have and Have Not 1944 DVD
Tokyo Story 1953 DVD
Tokyo Twilight 1957
Topsy-Turvy 1999 DVD
Touch of Evil 1958 DVD
Trainspotting 1995 DVD
Tristana 1970 DVD
The Truman Show 1998 DVD
12 Angry Men 1957 DVD
Two Stage Sisters 1964
Ugetsu Monogatari 1953
Umberto D 1952 DVD
The Untouchables 1987 DVD
Viridiana 1961
Vivre Sa Vie 1962 DVD
Walkabout 1970 DVD
Watch on the Rhine 1943
Way Down East 1920 DVD
The Wedding March 1928
Weekend 1967 DVD
Went the Day Well? 1942 DVD
What Ever Happened to Baby Jane? 1962
White Heat 1949 DVD
Wild Strawberries 1957 DVD
The Wind 1928
Witness for the Prosecution 1957 DVD
Woman of the Dunes 1963
The World of Apu 1959 DVD
Wuthering Heights 1939 DVD
Yellow Earth 1984
Yojimbo 1961 DVD
Yol 1982
You Only Live Once 1937 DVD
Zéro de Conduite 1933 DVD

Drama

★★★★

AI: Artificial Intelligence 2001 DVD
About a Boy 2002 DVD
About Schmidt 2002 DVD
Above Suspicion 1943
Accattone 1961
Accidental Hero 1992 DVD
The Accidental Tourist 1988
L'Accompagnatrice 1992
The Accused 1988 DVD
An Actor's Revenge 1963 DVD
The Actress 1953
Adam 1983
Adaptation. 2002 DVD
Adorable Lies 1991
The Adventures of Priscilla, Queen of the Desert 1994 DVD
Advise and Consent 1962
An Affair to Remember 1957 DVD
After Life 1998
Afterglow 1997
The Age of Innocence 1993 DVD
Un Air de Famille 1996
Air Force 1943 DVD
Ake and His World 1984
Al Capone 1959
Alexander Nevsky 1938 DVD
Alexandria Encore 1990
Alexandria Why? 1979
Alfie 1966 DVD
Alice Adams 1935
Alice Doesn't Live Here Anymore 1974 DVD
Alice in the Cities 1974 DVD
All About Lily Chou-Chou 2001 DVD
All Fall Down 1962
All My Good Countrymen 1968
All or Nothing 2002 DVD
All over Me 1996 DVD
All That Jazz 1979 DVD
All That Heaven Allows 1955
All the King's Men 1949 DVD
All the Vermeers in New York 1990
All the Way Home 1963
All This, and Heaven Too 1940
Almost Famous 2000 DVD
Alphaville 1965 DVD
Les Amants 1958
Amateur 1994
The American Friend 1977 DVD
American History X 1998 DVD
American Psycho 2000 DVD
The American Soldier 1970 DVD
American Splendor 2003 DVD
The Americanization of Emily 1964
Le Amiche 1955
L'Amour Fou 1968
Anastasia 1956 DVD
And Quiet Flows the Don 1957
And Quiet Rolls the Dawn 1979
Andaz 1949
Angel Face 1953
Angel Sharks 1997
Angèle 1934
Angi Vera 1980
Aniki-Bobó 1942
The Animal Kingdom 1932
Ankur 1974
Anna Boleyn 1920
Anna Karenina 1935 DVD
Anne and Muriel 1971
The Anniversary Party 2001 DVD
Another Country 1984
Another Day in Paradise 1998 DVD
Another Time, Another Place 1983 DVD
Another Woman 1988 DVD
Anthony Adverse 1936
Antonio das Mortes 1969
Any Given Sunday 1999 DVD
Apa 1966
Aparajito 1956 DVD
Apollo 13 1995 DVD
The Apostle 1997 DVD
L'Appartement 1996 DVD
Applause 1929
The Apple 1998 DVD
The Apprenticeship of Duddy Kravitz 1974
The April Fools 1969
Apt Pupil 1997 DVD
Ariel 1988
As Good as It Gets 1997 DVD
The Ascent 1976
Ashes of Time 1994
Ashik Kerib 1988
Asphalt 1928
The Asthenic Syndrome 1989
At Close Range 1985 DVD
At Five in the Afternoon 2003
Atanarjuat: the Fast Runner 2001 DVD
Attack! 1956 DVD
The Attic: the Hiding of Anne Frank 1988
Au Revoir les Enfants 1987
Auto Focus 2002 DVD
Autumn Moon 1992
An Autumn Tale 1998
Awakenings 1990 DVD
Baadasssss! 2003
The Bachelor Party 1957
Back Street 1941
Back Street 1961
Backdraft 1991 DVD
The Bad and the Beautiful 1952
Bad Blood 1982
Bad Lieutenant 1992 DVD
Bad Timing 1980 DVD
Badlands 1973 DVD
Bagdad Café 1987 DVD
The Bait 1995
Ballad of a Soldier 1959
The Ballad of Narayama 1983
Bande à Part 1964 DVD

- **Bandini** 1963 DVD
- **Bandit Queen** 1994
- **Bandits of Orgosolo** 1961
- **Bang the Drum Slowly** 1973
- **The Barbarian Invasions** 2003 DVD
- **Barbarians at the Gate** 1993
- **Barcelona** 1994
- **The Barefoot Contessa** 1954 DVD
- **The Barretts of Wimpole Street** 1934
- **Barton Fink** 1991 DVD
- **Battle Cry** 1955 DVD
- **Battle of the Bulge** 1965 DVD
- **Battleground** 1949 DVD
- **Bay of the Angels** 1963
- **Beach Red** 1967
- **Beau James** 1957
- **Le Beau Mariage** 1982 DVD
- **Le Beau Serge** 1958
- **Beau Travail** 1999 DVD
- **Becket** 1964
- **Becky Sharp** 1935
- **Before Sunrise** 1995 DVD
- **Before the Revolution** 1964
- **Behind the Forbidden City** 1996 DVD
- **Beijing Bicycle** 2001 DVD
- **The Believer** 2001 DVD
- **Belle Epoque** 1992 DVD
- **La Belle Equipe** 1936
- **Les Belles de Nuit** 1952
- **Benny's Video** 1992
- **Best Intentions** 1992
- **The Best Man** 1964
- **The Best Things in Life Are Free** 1956
- **Betrayal** 1982
- **The Betty Ford Story** 1987
- **Between Two Women** 2000
- **Beyond Rangoon** 1995
- **Beyond the Valley of the Dolls** 1970 DVD
- **Les Biches** 1968 DVD
- **The Big Chill** 1983 DVD
- **The Big City** 1963
- **The Big House** 1930
- **The Big Knife** 1955
- **Big Night** 1996
- **The Big Parade** 1986
- **The Big Red One** 1980
- **Big Wednesday** 1978 DVD
- **Bigger than Life** 1956
- **Bill** 1981
- **Billy Elliot** 2000 DVD
- **Birch Interval** 1976
- **Bird** 1988
- **Birdman of Alcatraz** 1962 DVD
- **Birdy** 1984 DVD
- **Birth** 2004 DVD
- **The Bitter Tea of General Yen** 1933
- **The Bitter Tears of Petra von Kant** 1972
- **The Black Bird** 1926
- **Black** 2004
- **Black Cat, White Cat** 1998
- **Black God, White Devil** 1964
- **Black Rain** 1988
- **Blackboards** 2000 DVD
- **Blanche** 1971
- **Blanche Fury** 1948
- **Bleak Moments** 1971 DVD
- **Blind Flight** 2003 DVD
- **Blind Husbands** 1919
- **Blind Shaft** 2003 DVD
- **Blood Oath** 1990
- **Blood Wedding** 1981
- **Bloody Sunday** 2001 DVD
- **The Blue Angel** 1930 DVD
- **Blue Black Permanent** 1992
- **Blue Collar** 1978
- **The Blue Kite** 1992
- **The Blue Lamp** 1949 DVD
- **The Blue Light** 1932
- **The Blue Max** 1966 DVD
- **Blue Sky** 1991 DVD
- **The Blue Veil** 1951
- **Blume in Love** 1973
- **Bob Le Flambeur** 1955 DVD
- **Boiler Room** 2000 DVD
- **Bombón – El Perro** 2004
- **Le Bonheur** 1965
- **Les Bonnes Femmes** 1960
- **Boom Town** 1940
- **Boomerang!** 1947
- **The Boston Strangler** 1968 DVD
- **Le Boucher** 1969 DVD
- **Bound for Glory** 1976 DVD
- **The Bounty** 1984 DVD
- **The Boy from Mercury** 1996
- **Boycott** 2001 DVD
- **The Boys** 1998 DVD
- **Boys on the Side** 1995
- **Brassed Off** 1996 DVD
- **Braveheart** 1995 DVD
- **Break of Dawn** 1988
- **Breaker Morant** 1979 DVD
- **The Breakfast Club** 1985
- **Breaking Away** 1979
- **Brian's Song** 1971
- **The Bridge** 1959
- **The Bridges at Toko-Ri** 1954 DVD
- **The Bridges of Madison County** 1995 DVD
- **Brighton Rock** 1947 DVD
- **Bring Me the Head of Alfredo Garcia** 1974 DVD
- **Broadcast News** 1987 DVD
- **Broken Blossoms** 1919 DVD
- **A Bronx Tale** 1993 DVD
- **Brother** 1997 DVD
- **The Brothers and Sisters of the Toda Family** 1941
- **The Browning Version** 1951
- **Brubaker** 1980 DVD
- **Brute Force** 1947
- **The Buddy Holly Story** 1978 DVD
- **Buffalo '66** 1998 DVD
- **Buffalo Soldiers** 2001 DVD
- **Bugsy** 1991 DVD
- **Bull Durham** 1988 DVD
- **Bully** 2001 DVD
- **Bulworth** 1998 DVD
- **The Burmese Harp** 1956
- **Burn!** 1970
- **The Burning Bed** 1984
- **The Burning Season** 1994
- **The Butcher Boy** 1997
- **Buttoners** 1997
- **By Love Possessed** 1961
- **By the Law** 1926
- **Bye Bye Braverman** 1968
- **Ca Commence Aujourd'hui** 1999
- **Café Lumière** 2003
- **Cagney & Lacey** 1981
- **Cairo Station** 1958
- **Calendar Girls** 2003 DVD
- **Call Northside 777** 1948
- **Camera Buff** 1979 DVD
- **Camille** 1937
- **The Candidate** 1972
- **A Canterbury Tale** 1944 DVD
- **The Captive Heart** 1946
- **Captive of the Desert** 1990
- **Carandiru** 2003 DVD
- **Caravaggio** 1986
- **Career Girls** 1997 DVD
- **Careful** 1992
- **Careful, He Might Hear You** 1983
- **Careful, Soft Shoulder** 1942
- **Carlito's Way** 1993 DVD
- **Carmen** 1915
- **Carmen** 1983 DVD
- **Carmen Jones** 1954 DVD
- **Carnal Knowledge** 1971 DVD
- **Un Carnet de Bal** 1937
- **Carny** 1980
- **Caroline?** 1990
- **The Carpetbaggers** 1964
- **La Carrière de Suzanne** 1963
- **Carrington** 1995 DVD
- **Carve Her Name with Pride** 1958 DVD
- **Casanova** 1927
- **Casbah** 1948
- **Casino** 1995 DVD
- **Casper** 1995 DVD
- **Casque d'Or** 1952
- **Cass Timberlane** 1947
- **Casualties of War** 1989 DVD
- **Cat on a Hot Tin Roof** 1958 DVD
- **Catch Me If You Can** 2002 DVD
- **Celia** 1988
- **The Cement Garden** 1992 DVD
- **Central Station** 1998 DVD
- **César** 1936
- **C'est la Vie** 1990
- **Chameleon Street** 1989
- **The Champ** 1931
- **Champion** 1949
- **Chance or Coincidence** 1999
- **Chang** 1927
- **Changing Lanes** 2002 DVD
- **Un Chant d'Amour** 1950 DVD
- **The Chant of Jimmie Blacksmith** 1978
- **Character** 1997
- **The Charge of the Light Brigade** 1936
- **Charley Varrick** 1973
- **Charly** 1968 DVD
- **Charulata** 1964
- **The Chase** 1966 DVD
- **Le Château de Ma Mère** 1990 DVD
- **Checkpoint** 1998
- **The Chess Player** 1927
- **The Chess Players** 1977
- **Chicago** 2002 DVD
- **La Chienne** 1931
- **Le Chignon d'Olga** 2002 DVD
- **Chihwaseon (Drunk on Women and Poetry)** 2002 DVD
- **The Children Are Watching Us** 1943
- **Children of a Lesser God** 1986 DVD
- **The Children of Heaven** 1997
- **The Children of the Marshland** 1998
- **Children of the Revolution** 1996
- **The China Syndrome** 1979 DVD
- **Chinese Box** 1997
- **La Chinoise** 1967 DVD
- **Chocolat** 1988
- **Chocolat** 2000 DVD
- **Choice of Arms** 1981
- **Choose Me** 1984 DVD
- **Christ Stopped at Eboli** 1979
- **Christiane F** 1981 DVD
- **Chronicle of a Death Foretold** 1987
- **Chronicle of the Burning Years** 1975
- **Chuck & Buck** 2000 DVD
- **Cinderella Man** 2005
- **The Circle** 2000 DVD
- **Circle of Friends** 1995 DVD
- **Circus Boys** 1989
- **The Citadel** 1938
- **The City and the Dogs** 1985
- **City for Conquest** 1940
- **City Hall** 1996 DVD
- **A City of Sadness** 1989
- **City of Women** 1980
- **The Claim** 2000 DVD
- **Claudia** 1943
- **Clean** 2004
- **Clean, Shaven** 1993
- **Clean Slate** 1981
- **The Clock** 1945
- **Close-Up** 1989
- **Closely Observed Trains** 1966 DVD
- **The Cloud Capped Star** 1960 DVD
- **Club de Femmes** 1936
- **Coal Miner's Daughter** 1980 DVD
- **Cobb** 1994
- **The Cobweb** 1955
- **The Cockleshell Heroes** 1955 DVD
- **Code Unknown** 2000 DVD
- **Un Coeur en Hiver** 1992 DVD
- **Cold Fever** 1994 DVD
- **The Colditz Story** 1954 DVD
- **La Collectionneuse** 1967
- **Colonel Redl** 1984
- **The Color of Money** 1986 DVD
- **The Color of Paradise** 1999
- **The Color Purple** 1985 DVD
- **Come Back, Little Sheba** 1952 DVD
- **Come Back to the Five and Dime, Jimmy Dean, Jimmy Dean** 1982
- **The Comic** 1969
- **Coming Home** 1978 DVD
- **Command Decision** 1948
- **The Commissar** 1967
- **The Commitments** 1991 DVD
- **A Common Thread** 2004
- **The Company** 2003
- **Company Limited** 1971
- **The Company of Strangers** 1990
- **Les Compères** 1983
- **Compulsion** 1959
- **Comrades: a Lanternist's Account of the Tolpuddle Martyrs and What Became of Them** 1986
- **The Conductor** 1980
- **Cone of Silence** 1960
- **Confession** 1937
- **Confessions of a Dangerous Mind** 2002 DVD
- **Confessions of a Serial Killer** 1987 DVD
- **Confidence** 1979
- **Confidences Trop Intimes** 2004 DVD
- **Conflagration** 1958
- **Conquest** 1937
- **The Consequences of Love** 2004
- **Conspiracy of Hearts** 1960
- **Constance** 1984
- **Les Convoyeurs Attendent** 1999
- **The Cook, the Thief, His Wife and Her Lover** 1989 DVD
- **Cool Hand Luke** 1967 DVD
- **The Cool World** 1963
- **The Cooler** 2002 DVD
- **Cooperstown** 1993
- **Cop au Vin** 1984
- **Cop Land** 1997 DVD
- **Countdown** 1968
- **Country Life** 1994
- **The Court-Martial of Billy Mitchell** 1955
- **The Court-Martial of Jackie Robinson** 1990
- **The Courtship of Eddie's Father** 1963
- **Les Cousins** 1959
- **The Cow** 1969
- **The Cracker Factory** 1979
- **The Cranes Are Flying** 1957
- **Crash** 2004
- **Crazy in Love** 1992
- **Crazy Moon** 1986 DVD
- **Les Créatures** 1966
- **The Cremator** 1968
- **Crime and Punishment** 1935
- **Crime and Punishment** 1935
- **Crime in the Streets** 1956
- **Crime of the Century** 1996
- **Crimes of the Heart** 1986 DVD
- **Crimson Gold** 2003 DVD
- **Cromwell** 1970 DVD
- **Cross My Heart** 1990
- **Cross of Iron** 1977 DVD
- **The Crossing Guard** 1995 DVD
- **Crows and Sparrows** 1949
- **The Crucible** 1996 DVD
- **The Crucified Lovers** 1954
- **The Cruel Sea** 1953 DVD
- **Cry Freedom** 1987 DVD
- **A Cry in the Dark** 1988 DVD
- **Cry, the Beloved Country** 1951
- **Cry, the Beloved Country** 1995
- **The Crying Game** 1992 DVD
- **Cuba** 1979 DVD
- **Cup Final** 1991
- **Cutter's Way** 1981 DVD
- **Daddy Long Legs** 1919
- **Daens** 1992
- **Daisy Kenyon** 1947
- **The Damned** 1969 DVD
- **Dance with a Stranger** 1984 DVD
- **Dangerous** 1935
- **Dangerous Female** 1931
- **Dangerous Liaisons** 1988 DVD
- **Danton** 1982
- **Dark Victory** 1939
- **Darling** 1965 DVD
- **Daughters of the Dust** 1991
- **David** 1979
- **The Dawn Patrol** 1938
- **The Dawning** 1988
- **The Day I Became a Woman** 2000 DVD
- **A Day in the Death of Joe Egg** 1971
- **The Day of the Locust** 1975 DVD
- **Day One** 1989
- **The Day the Sun Turned Cold** 1994
- **Daybreak** 2003
- **Days and Nights in the Forest** 1969
- **Days of Being Wild** 1990 DVD
- **Days of Heaven** 1978 DVD
- **Days of Wine and Roses** 1962 DVD
- **Dazed and Confused** 1993 DVD
- **The Dead** 1987
- **The Dead and the Deadly** 1983
- **Dead End** 1937
- **Dead Man Walking** 1995 DVD
- **Dead Poets Society** 1989 DVD
- **The Deadly Affair** 1966
- **Dear Frankie** 2003
- **Dear Wendy** 2005
- **Death and the Maiden** 1994
- **Death of a Cyclist** 1955
- **Death of a Salesman** 1951
- **The Debt Collector** 1999 DVD
- **The Decameron** 1970
- **Deception** 1946
- **The Decline of the American Empire** 1986 DVD
- **Deep End** 1970
- **Deep Impact** 1998 DVD
- **The Defiant Ones** 1958 DVD
- **Le Défroqué** 1953
- **Delbaran** 2001
- **Desert Bloom** 1985
- **Desert Hearts** 1985
- **The Deserted Station** 2002
- **Desperate Living** 1977
- **Les Destinées Sentimentales** 2000 DVD
- **Destiny** 1921
- **Destiny of a Man** 1959
- **Detective Story** 1951
- **Devi** 1960
- **The Devil and the Nun** 1960
- **The Devils** 1971
- **Devils on the Doorstep** 2000
- **Les Diables** 2002
- **Diabolo Menthe** 1977
- **Diary for My Children** 1982
- **Diary for My Loves** 1987
- **The Diary of a Chambermaid** 1964 DVD
- **Diary of a Mad Housewife** 1970
- **Dieu A Besoin des Hommes** 1950
- **Dillinger** 1945
- **Diner** 1982
- **Dinner at Eight** 1933
- **Dinner Rush** 2000 DVD
- **Dirty Dancing** 1987 DVD
- **The Disappearance of Aimee** 1976
- **The Dish** 2000 DVD
- **Distant Thunder** 1973
- **Diva** 1981 DVD
- **Divided We Fall** 2000 DVD
- **Divorce Wars** 1982
- **Djomeh** 2000
- **Do the Right Thing** 1989 DVD
- **Do You Remember Love** 1985
- **The Docks of New York** 1928
- **Docteur Petiot** 1990
- **The Doctor** 1991 DVD
- **Dodes'ka-Den** 1970
- **Dodsworth** 1936
- **Dog Day Afternoon** 1975 DVD
- **Dog Star Man** 1964
- **Dogfight** 1991
- **Dogs in Space** 1986 DVD
- **Dogville** 2003 DVD
- **The Dollmaker** 1984
- **Dolls** 2002 DVD
- **A Doll's House** 1973
- **Dolores Claiborne** 1995 DVD
- **Don** 1998
- **Don Juan** 1926
- **Don Juan DeMarco** 1995 DVD
- **Donnie Brasco** 1997 DVD
- **Donnie Darko** 2001 DVD
- **Don't Move, Die and Rise Again** 1989
- **The Door in the Floor** 2004
- **The Double Life of Véronique** 1991
- **Downfall** 2004
- **The Dragnet** 1928
- **Dragon: the Bruce Lee Story** 1993 DVD
- **The Dream Life of Angels** 1998
- **A Dream of Kings** 1969
- **The Dreamers** 2003 DVD
- **Dreams That Money Can Buy** 1946
- **The Dresser** 1983 DVD
- **The Dressmaker** 1988
- **Driving Miss Daisy** 1989 DVD
- **Drowning by Numbers** 1988
- **Drugstore Cowboy** 1989 DVD

Drunken Angel 1948
Duel in the Sun 1946 DVD
The Duellists 1977 DVD
Duet for One 1986
The Eagle and the Hawk 1933
Eagle in a Cage 1971
An Early Frost 1985
Early Spring 1956
Early Summer 1951
East Is East 1999 DVD
East Lynne 1931
East of Eden 1955 DVD
The Easy Life 1962
Eat Drink Man Woman 1994
L'Eau Froide 1994
The Eclipse 1962 DVD
Ecstasy 1933
The Eddy Duchin Story 1956
The Edge of the World 1937 DVD
Educating Rita 1983 DVD
Effi Briest 1974
8 Mile 2002 DVD
Eighteen Springs 1997
84 Charing Cross Road 1986 DVD
El 1953
The Elephant Man 1980 DVD
Elizabeth 1998 DVD
Elling 2001
Elvis – the Movie 1979
Emma 1996 DVD
The Empty Table 1985
The Enchanted Cottage 1945
End of a Priest 1969
The End of St Petersburg 1927 DVD
The End of the Affair 1954
The End of the Affair 1999 DVD
The End of the Day 1939
Enemies, a Love Story 1989
The Enemy Below 1957 DVD
L'Enfant Sauvage 1970 DVD
Les Enfants Terribles 1949 DVD
The Enforcer 1951
England Made Me 1973
The Enigma of Kaspar Hauser 1974
Equinox 1992
Equinox Flower 1958
Erin Brockovich 2000 DVD
Ermo 1994
Escape from Alcatraz 1979 DVD
Escape from Sobibor 1987
Escape from the Planet of the Apes 1971 DVD
Eskiya 1996
Eternal Sunshine of the Spotless Mind 2003 DVD
The Europeans 1979 DVD
Eva 1962
Everything That Rises 1998
Eve's Bayou 1997
Evidence of Love 1990 DVD
Executive Suite 1954
Exodus 1960 DVD
Exotica 1994
Extension du Domaine de la Lutte 1999
The Exterminating Angel 1962
The FBI Story 1959
The Fabulous Baker Boys 1989 DVD
A Face in the Crowd 1957
The Face of Another 1966 DVD
The Face of Fear 1971
Faces 1968
Fail-Safe 1964
FairyTale: a True Story 1997
Faithless 2000 DVD
Fallen Angels 1995
The Family 1987
Family Viewing 1987
The Family Way 1966 DVD
Fanny 1932
Le Fantôme de la Liberté 1974
Farewell, My Lovely 1975 DVD
Farinelli il Castrato 1994 DVD
Faster, Pussycat! Kill! Kill! 1965 DVD
Fat City 1972
Fear Eats the Soul 1973
Fear of Fear 1976
Fear on Trial 1975
Fear Strikes Out 1957
Fedora 1978
Fellow Traveller 1989
Female Trouble 1974
La Femme Publique 1984
Le Feu Follet 1963
A Few Good Men 1992 DVD
Fiddler on the Roof 1971 DVD
Field of Dreams 1989 DVD
55 Days at Peking 1963
The Fighting Sullivans 1944 DVD
The Final Days 1989 DVD
Finding Neverland 2004 DVD
Fingers 1978
Fiorile 1993
Fire 1996
Fires Were Started 1943
The First Teacher 1965
Fists in the Pocket 1965
5x2 2004
Five Graves to Cairo 1943
The Five Obstructions 2003 DVD
The Five Pennies 1959
The Five Senses 1999
Five Women around Utamaro 1946
A Flash of Green 1984
The Flavour of Green Tea over Rice 1952 DVD
Flesh 1932
Flesh and Bone 1993 DVD
Flesh and the Devil 1926
The Flight of the Phoenix 1965 DVD
The Flower of My Secret 1995
Flowers of Shanghai 1998
Fly Away Home 1996 DVD
A Foreign Affair 1948
Forever and a Day 1943
Forrest Gump 1994 DVD
Fort Apache, the Bronx 1981
49th Parallel 1941 DVD
Four Adventures of Reinette and Mirabelle 1986
Four Daughters 1938
Four Days in September 1997
The Four Days of Naples 1962
Four in the Morning 1965
Four Sons 1928
Four Steps in the Clouds 1942
Fourteen Hours 1951
1492: Conquest of Paradise 1992 DVD
Fox and His Friends 1975
Frances 1982 DVD
Francis, God's Jester 1950
Frankie & Johnny 1991 DVD
A Free Soul 1931
The French Lieutenant's Woman 1981 DVD
Fresh 1994
The Freshman 1990 DVD
Frida 2002 DVD
Friday Night Lights 2004
Friday the Thirteenth 1933
Fried Green Tomatoes at the Whistle Stop Cafe 1991 DVD
Friendly Fire 1979
Friendly Persuasion 1956
The Friends of Eddie Coyle 1973
From the Life of the Marionettes 1980 DVD
The Front Page 1974
The Fugitive 1947
Funny Bones 1994 DVD
Fury 1936
Gabbeh 1995
Gallipoli 1981 DVD
The Gambler 1974
Gang Related 1997 DVD
Gangs of New York 2002 DVD
Garage Olimpo 1999
Garam Hawa 1973
Garde à Vue 1981
Garden State 2003 DVD
Gas, Food, Lodging 1992
Gaslight 1944 DVD
Gate of Flesh 1964 DVD
General Della Rovere 1959
The General Line 1929
A Generation 1954
A Gentle Creature 1969
Gentleman's Agreement 1947 DVD
George Washington 2000 DVD
Georgy Girl 1966
Germany, Year Zero 1947
Ghost 1990 DVD
Ghosts... of the Civil Dead 1988
Giant 1956 DVD
Gideon's Day 1958
Gideon's Trumpet 1980
Girl 6 1996
Girl with a Pearl Earring 2003 DVD
Girl with Green Eyes 1963
Girlfight 2000 DVD
Girlfriends 1978
Girls in Uniform 1931
Girls' Night 1997
The Given Word 1962
The Glass House 1972 DVD
The Glass Menagerie 1987
The Glenn Miller Story 1953
Glory 1989 DVD
Go 1999 DVD
The Go-Between 1971
Go Fish 1994
The Goalkeeper's Fear of the Penalty Kick 1971
Godmoney 1997 DVD
Gohatto 1999 DVD
Going My Way 1944 DVD
Gold of Naples 1954
The Golden Bowl 2000 DVD
Golden Braid 1991
The Golden Coach 1953
Gone to Earth 1950 DVD
The Good Father 1986
Good Morning, Babylon 1987
Good Morning, Night 2003 DVD
Good Will Hunting 1997 DVD
Gorillas in the Mist 1988 DVD
Gösta Berlings Saga 1924
Goto, l'Ile d'Amour 1968
Goya in Bordeaux 1999
Grace of My Heart 1996
Grand Canyon 1991 DVD
Le Grand Chemin 1987
The Great Lie 1941
The Great Moment 1944
The Great Rock 'n' Roll Swindle 1979
The Great Waltz 1938
The Great War 1959
The Greatest Show on Earth 1952
The Green Ray 1986 DVD
Greyfriars Bobby 1961 DVD
The Grifters 1990
Grosse Pointe Blank 1997 DVD
The Group 1966
Guadalcanal Diary 1943 DVD
La Guerre Est Finie 1966
Guess Who's Coming to Dinner 1967 DVD
Gummo 1997
Gunnar Hede's Saga 1922
Guns at Batasi 1964
HM Pulham Esq 1941
La Haine 1995 DVD
The Hairdresser's Husband 1990 DVD
Hamburger Hill 1987 DVD
Hamlet 1964
Hamlet 1990
Hamlet 1996
Hamlet Goes Business 1987
Hana-Bi 1997 DVD
A Handful of Dust 1987 DVD
Hangin' with the Homeboys 1991
Hans Christian Andersen 1952 DVD
Hanussen 1988
Harakiri 1962
Hard-Boiled 1992 DVD
Hard Times 1975 DVD
The Harness 1971
Harold and Maude 1972 DVD
He Got Game 1998
Head On 2004
Hear My Song 1991
The Heart Is a Lonely Hunter 1968
Heart of Glass 1976 DVD
Hearts of the West 1975
Heat Wave 1990
Heaven and Earth 1993 DVD
Heaven Knows, Mr Allison 1957 DVD
Heavy 1995
Hedda 1975
Heimkehr 1928
Heist 2001 DVD
Hell in the Pacific 1968 DVD
Henry Fool 1997 DVD
Henry V 1989 DVD
The Herd 1978
Hester Street 1975
Hide in Plain Sight 1980
High and Low 1963 DVD
High Art 1998
High Fidelity 2000 DVD
High Hopes 1988
Hilary and Jackie 1998 DVD
The Hill 1965
Hiroshima, Mon Amour 1959 DVD
Histoire de Marie et Julien 2003 DVD
Historias Mínimas 2002 DVD
The History of Mr Polly 1948
Hold Back the Dawn 1941
Hold Back the Night 1999 DVD
Holiday Affair 1949
The Holy Mountain 1973
The Home and the World 1984
The Homecoming 1973 DVD
L'Homme du Train 2002 DVD
Honour among Thieves 1954
Hoosiers 1986 DVD
Hors la Vie 1991
Horse Thief 1986
Hostages 1993
Hotel Rwanda 2004 DVD
Hour of the Star 1985
The Hours 2002 DVD
The Hours and Times 1992
House of Angels 1992
House of Flying Daggers 2004 DVD
House of Sand and Fog 2003 DVD
The House on 92nd Street 1945
Houseboat 1958 DVD
Housekeeping 1987
The Hudsucker Proxy 1994 DVD
The Human Comedy 1943
Humoresque 1946
The Hunchback of Notre Dame 1923 DVD
The Hunchback of Notre Dame 1982
The Hunchback of Notre Dame 1996 DVD
Hunger 1966
The Hurricane 1999 DVD
I Am a Fugitive from a Chain Gang 1932
I Am Cuba 1964
I Capture the Castle 2002 DVD
I Confess 1953 DVD
ID 1994
I Even Met Happy Gypsies 1967
I Heard the Owl Call My Name 1973
I ❤ Huckabees 2004 DVD
I Never Promised You a Rose Garden 1977
I Never Sang for My Father 1969
I Remember Mama 1948
I Shot Andy Warhol 1995
I, the Worst of All 1990
I Want to Live! 1958 DVD
I Was Monty's Double 1958
Ice Cold in Alex 1958 DVD
Iceman 1984
The Idiots 1998 DVD
The Idolmaker 1980
If.... 1968
I'll Cry Tomorrow 1955
Ill Met by Moonlight 1956 DVD
Illumination 1972
I'm Going Home 2001 DVD
The Image 1990
Images 1972
Imitation of Life 1959
Immortal Beloved 1994
The Importance of Being Earnest 1952 DVD
The Important Man 1961
An Impudent Girl 1985
In a Year of 13 Moons 1978
In America 2003 DVD
In Casablanca Angels Don't Fly 2003
In Cold Blood 1967 DVD
In Harm's Way 1965 DVD
In My Father's Den 2004
In Search of Famine 1980
In the Bedroom 2001 DVD
In the Gloaming 1997
In the Mood for Love 2000 DVD
In the Name of the Father 1993 DVD
In the Name of the Pope King 1977
In the Realm of the Senses 1976 DVD
In the White City 1983
In This World 2002 DVD
Indecent Proposal 1993 DVD
Indian Summer 1993 DVD
Indictment: the McMartin Trial 1995
Infernal Affairs 2002
Inherit the Wind 1960 DVD
Inherit the Wind 1999
L'Inhumaine 1923
The Inn of the Sixth Happiness 1958 DVD
Innocence Unprotected 1968
Innocent Moves 1993 DVD
L'Innocente 1976 DVD
Insignificance 1985
An Inspector Calls 1954
Interrogation 1982
Interrupted Melody 1955
Intervista 1987
Invaders from Mars 1953
The Invitation 1973
Iris 2001 DVD
The Irishman 1978
Irreconcilable Differences 1984
Irreversible 2002 DVD
Isadora 1968
The Island 1961
It Always Rains on Sunday 1947 DVD
It Came from Outer Space 1953
It Happened Here 1963
It Happened Tomorrow 1944
Italian for Beginners 2000 DVD
It's All True 1993
Ivan the Terrible, Part II 1946 DVD
J'Accuse 1919
Jackson County Jail 1976
Jailhouse Rock 1957 DVD
Jamon Jamon 1992 DVD
Jane Eyre 1943 DVD
Japanese Story 2003 DVD
Je, Tu, Il, Elle 1974
Jealousy, Italian Style 1970
Jeanne Dielman, 23 Quai du Commerce, 1080 Bruxelles 1975
Jericho 1991
The Jericho Mile 1979
Jesus of Montreal 1989 DVD
Jezebel 1938
Jofroi 1933
John Grisham's The Rainmaker 1997 DVD
Johnny Angel 1945
Johnny Belinda 1948
Johns 1995 DVD
The Joke 1968
Le Jour Se Lève 1939
Journey into Fear 1942
Journey of Hope 1990
The Joy Luck Club 1993 DVD
Jubal 1956
Jude 1996 DVD
Judgment at Nuremberg 1961 DVD
Judy Berlin 1999
Julia 1977
julien donkey-boy 1999 DVD
Junior Bonner 1972 DVD
Junoon 1978
Kaagaz Ke Phool 1959 DVD
Kadosh 1999
Kagemusha 1980 DVD
Kanal 1957
Kangchenjunga 1962
Kaos 1984
Ken Park 2002
The Key 1959
The Kid 1921 DVD
Kid Galahad 1937
The Kidnappers 1953
kids 1995 DVD
Kill Bill Vol 1 2003 DVD
Kill Me If You Can 1977
A Kind of Loving 1962 DVD
King Lear 1970
King of Hearts 1966
The King of Kings 1927
The King of Marvin Gardens 1972
King of the Children 1987
King of the Hill 1993

King Rat 1965
Kingdom of Heaven 2005
Kings & Queen 2004
Kings Row 1942
Kinsey 2004 DVD
Kiss of the Spider Woman 1985
Kiss Tomorrow Goodbye 1950
Kitty 1945
Knave of Hearts 1954
Knife in the Water 1962 DVD
Kolya 1996 DVD
Komitas 1988
Kramer vs Kramer 1979 DVD
Krámpack 2000 DVD
The Krays 1990 DVD
Kühle Wampe 1931
The L-Shaped Room 1962 DVD
L.627 1992
The Lacemaker 1977
Lacombe Lucien 1974
The Lady & the Duke 2001 DVD
The Lady from Shanghai 1948 DVD
The Lady in Red 1979
Lady Windermere's Fan 1925
The Lady with the Little Dog 1960
Ladybird Ladybird 1994
Lamb 1985 DVD
Land and Freedom 1995 DVD
The Landlord 1970
Landscape after Battle 1970
The Last American Hero 1973
The Last Days of Mussolini 1974
The Last Detail 1973 DVD
The Last Emperor 1987 DVD
The Last Island 1990
Last Night 1998
Last Orders 2001 DVD
Last Resort 2000 DVD
The Last Run 1971
The Last Samurai 2003 DVD
The Last Stage 1947
Last Summer 1969
The Last Temptation of Christ 1988 DVD
The Last Tycoon 1976
The Last Valley 1971 DVD
The Last Wave 1977
Late Autumn 1960
The Late Shift 1996
Late Spring 1949
Lawn Dogs 1997 DVD
Laws of Gravity 1992
Leave 'em Laughing 1981
Leave Her to Heaven 1945 DVD
Leaving Las Vegas 1995 DVD
The Legend of 1900 1999 DVD
The Legend of the Holy Drinker 1988
Legends of the Fall 1994 DVD
Lena: My 100 Children 1987 DVD
Léolo 1992
Léon Morin, Priest 1961 DVD
Let Him Have It 1991 DVD
The Letter 1940
Letter from an Unknown Woman 1948
A Letter to Three Wives 1949 DVD
Une Liaison Pornographique 1999
The Liberation of LB Jones 1970
The Libertine 2004
Liberty Heights 1999 DVD
The Lie 1992
LIE 2001 DVD
Life and Nothing But 1989
A Life in the Theater 1993
The Life of Emile Zola 1937
Life on a String 1991
Life Upside Down 1964
Lifeboat 1944
Lights of Variety 1950
Lili 1953
Lilies of the Field 1963 DVD
Lilith 1964
Lilya 4-Ever 2002 DVD
Limelight 1952 DVD
Little Caesar 1931
The Little Foxes 1941
Little Man Tate 1991 DVD
The Little Princess 1939 DVD
Little Voice 1998 DVD
Little Women 1933
London 1994 DVD
The Long Absence 1961
The Long Good Friday 1979 DVD
The Long Hot Summer 1958
The Long Journey 1949
The Long Summer of George Adams 1982
The Long Voyage Home 1940
The Longest Day 1962 DVD
Longtime Companion 1990
Look at Me 2004
Look Back in Anger 1959
Looking for Mr Goodbar 1977
Looking for Richard 1996 DVD
Looks and Smiles 1981
Lord of the Flies 1963 DVD
The Lords of Flatbush 1974
The Lost Squadron 1932
The Lost Weekend 1945 DVD
Loulou 1980
Love 1971
Love and Pain and the Whole Damn Thing 1973
Love Field 1992 DVD
Love in the Afternoon 1972 DVD
Love Letters 1983
Love Me or Leave Me 1955
Love on the Dole 1941 DVD
Love with the Proper Stranger 1963
The Lovers of the Arctic Circle 1998 DVD
The Lower Depths 1956
Lucas 1986 DVD
Lucky Luciano 1973 DVD
Lust for Life 1956
Maborosi 1995
Macbeth 1948 DVD
Macbeth 1971 DVD
The McKenzie Break 1970 DVD
Mad City 1997 DVD
Mad Dog 1976 DVD
Madame de... 1953
Madame X 1937
Made in Hong Kong 1997
Mademoiselle Docteur 1936
Madigan 1968
Mado 1976
The Magdalene Sisters 2002 DVD
The Magic Box 1951
Magnificent Obsession 1935
Magnificent Obsession 1954
Make Way for Tomorrow 1937
The Makioka Sisters 1983
The Mambo Kings 1992
Mamma Roma 1962
A Man for All Seasons 1966 DVD
The Man I Love 1946
The Man I Married 1940
Man of Iron 1981
Man of Marble 1977
A Man of No Importance 1994
Man on the Moon 1999 DVD
The Man Who Captured Eichmann 1996
The Man Who Fell to Earth 1976 DVD
The Man Who Knew Too Much 1934 DVD
The Man Who Laughs 1928
The Man Who Played God 1932
The Man Who Wasn't There 2001 DVD
The Man with the Golden Arm 1955 DVD
The Man without a Past 2002 DVD
Mandingo 1975
Mandy 1952
Manon des Sources 1986 DVD
Man's Hope 1945
Mansfield Park 1999 DVD
Map of the Human Heart 1992
A Map of the World 1999 DVD
Mapantsula 1988
Maria do Mar 1930
Marius 1931
Marius et Jeannette 1997
Marked Woman 1937
Marnie 1964 DVD
The Marquise of O 1976 DVD
The Marriage of Maria Braun 1978
The Married Woman 1964
The Marrying Kind 1952
Martha and I 1990
Marvin's Room 1996 DVD
Mary, Queen of Scots 1971
Mask 1985 DVD
The Mask of Dimitrios 1944
Master and Commander: the Far Side of the World 2003 DVD
Mata Hari 1931
Matewan 1987 DVD
Matinee 1993 DVD
The Mattei Affair 1972
Me without You 2001 DVD
Mean Creek 2004
Mean Streets 1973 DVD
Mediterraneo 1991 DVD
Mélo 1986
Melvin and Howard 1980
Memories of Underdevelopment 1968
The Men 1950 DVD
Men Don't Leave 1990
The Merchant of Four Seasons 1971
Merrill's Marauders 1962
Merry Christmas Mr Lawrence 1982 DVD
The Merry Widow 1925
Meshes of the Afternoon 1943
Mexican Bus Ride 1951
Michael Collins 1996 DVD
The Middleman 1975
A Midnight Clear 1991
Midnight in the Garden of Good and Evil 1997 DVD
The Mighty 1998 DVD
The Milagro Beanfield War 1988
Millions 2004
Millions like Us 1943
Mina Tannenbaum 1993
Minor Mishaps 2002 DVD
The Miracle 1990
The Miracle of Bern 2003 DVD
Mirror 1974 DVD
The Misfits 1961 DVD
Mishima: a Life in Four Chapters 1985
Miss Evers' Boys 1997
Miss Julie 1951
Miss Rose White 1992
Missing 1981
Mission to Moscow 1943
Mississippi Burning 1988 DVD
Mississippi Masala 1991
Mr and Mrs '55 1955 DVD
Mr Holland's Opus 1995 DVD
Mr Reliable 1996
Mr Skeffington 1944
Mr Wonderful 1992
The Moment of Truth 1964
Mommie Dearest 1981 DVD
Mona Lisa 1986 DVD
Monday Morning 2002 DVD
Monrak Transistor 2001
Monsieur Vincent 1947
Monsoon Wedding 2001 DVD
Monster 2003 DVD
Monster's Ball 2001 DVD
A Month in the Country 1987 DVD
Moolaadé 2004
Moonlighting 1982
Morvern Callar 2001 DVD
The Mosquito Coast 1986
The Mother 2003 DVD
Mother and Son 1997
Mother India 1957 DVD
Mother Küsters Goes to Heaven 1975
Moulin Rouge 1952 DVD
Moulin Rouge! 2001 DVD
The Mouth Agape 1974
Mrs Doubtfire 1993 DVD
Mrs Parker and the Vicious Circle 1994
Much Ado about Nothing 1993 DVD
Muddy River 1981
Mudhoney 1965 DVD
The Muppet Christmas Carol 1992 DVD
Murder in Mississippi 1990
Murder in the First 1994 DVD
Muriel 1963
Muriel's Wedding 1994 DVD
Music Box 1989
The Musketeers of Pig Alley 1912
My Ain Folk 1973
My Boyfriend's Back 1989
My Brilliant Career 1979 DVD
My Family 1994
My First Wife 1984
My Friend Flicka 1943 DVD
My Friend Ivan Lapshin 1982
My Girlfriend's Boyfriend 1987 DVD
My Life as a Dog 1985 DVD
My Life without Me 2002 DVD
My Love Has Been Burning 1949
My Mother's Courage 1995
My Name Is Bill W 1989
My Night with Maud 1969
My Own Private Idaho 1991 DVD
My Son, My Son! 1940
My Way Home 1978
Mystery Train 1989 DVD
Mystic River 2003 DVD
The Myth of Fingerprints 1996
Nada 1974
Naked 1993
The Naked City 1948 DVD
The Naked Jungle 1953
The Naked Kiss 1964 DVD
Napoléon 1955
The Narrow Margin 1952
National Velvet 1944
Nationale 7 1999
The Natural 1984 DVD
Natural Born Killers 1994 DVD
Nazarín 1958
Nazi Hunter: the Beate Klarsfeld Story 1986
The Negotiator 1998 DVD
Nelly & Monsieur Arnaud 1995
Network 1976 DVD
Never Steal Anything Small 1959
The New Centurions 1972
New Jack City 1991 DVD
The New Land 1972
New York, New York 1977
Newsfront 1978
Next of Kin 1942
Nicholas Nickleby 1947 DVD
Nicholas Nickleby 2002 DVD
Night and Day 1991
Night and the City 1950
'Night, Mother 1986
The Night of Counting the Years 1969
The Night of San Lorenzo 1981
Night Shapes 1999
A Night to Remember 1958 DVD
Nightmare 1956
Nightmare in Chicago 1968
Nijinsky 1980
Nine Queens 2000 DVD
Nineteen Eighty-Four 1984 DVD
1900 1976
Nixon 1995 DVD
No Love for Johnnie 1960
No Place to Go 2000
No Regrets for Our Youth 1946
Nobody Knows 2003 DVD
Nobody's Child 1986
Nobody's Fool 1994
Norma Rae 1979 DVD
El Norte 1983
The Northerners 1992
Nostalgia 1983 DVD
Not One Less 1999 DVD
Not Reconciled, or Only Violence Helps Where Violence Rules 1965
Nowhere in Africa 2001 DVD
Les Nuits Fauves 1992
O 2001 DVD
O Henry's Full House 1952
October Sky 1999 DVD
Odds against Tomorrow 1959
Ode to Billy Joe 1976
Of Human Bondage 1934 DVD
Of Mice and Men 1939
Of Mice and Men 1992 DVD
The Officers' Ward 2001 DVD
The Official Version 1985 DVD
Ohayo 1959
The Old Maid 1939
Old Man 1997
Old Yeller 1957
Olivia 1950
Olivier Olivier 1991
On Golden Pond 1981 DVD
Once upon a Time in China 1991 DVD
Once Were Warriors 1994 DVD
One against the Wind 1991
A One and a Two 1999 DVD
One False Move 1992 DVD
One More Kiss 1999 DVD
One of Us 1989
One Way Passage 1932
The Only Son 1936
Only Yesterday 1933
Open Doors 1990
Open Hearts 2002 DVD
Opening Night 1977
Orders to Kill 1958
Ordinary People 1980 DVD
The Organization 1971 DVD
The Organizer 1963
Orphans 1998 DVD
Orphans of the Storm 1921
Osama 2003 DVD
Ossessione 1942 DVD
Othello 1955
Othello 1965 DVD
Other Men's Women 1931
Our Vines Have Tender Grapes 1945
Out of Africa 1985 DVD
Out of Sight 1998 DVD
Over the Edge 1979
The Oyster Princess 1919
Padre Padrone 1977
A Pain in the A...! 1973
Pakeezah 1971
Palookaville 1995 DVD
Le Paltoquet 1986
Pandora and the Flying Dutchman 1950
The Panic in Needle Park 1971 DVD
Panic in the Streets 1950 DVD
Panic in Year Zero 1962
The Paper 1994 DVD
The Paper Chase 1973
Paper Moon 1973
Papillon 1973 DVD
The Parade 1984
Parineeta 2005
Paris Blues 1961
Paris Nous Appartient 1960
Paris Trout 1991
Park Row 1952
The Party and the Guests 1966
Pascali's Island 1988
Passenger 1963
The Passenger 1975
A Passion 1969 DVD
Passion 1996
Passion Fish 1992
Pastor Hall 1940
Pathfinder 1987
The Patricia Neal Story: an Act of Love 1981
Pauline & Paulette 2001 DVD
Pauline at the Beach 1983 DVD
Payday 1972
Pelle the Conqueror 1987 DVD
Penny Serenade 1941 DVD
The People vs Larry Flynt 1996 DVD
A Perfect World 1993 DVD
Period of Adjustment 1962
Pétain 1992
Pete Kelly's Blues 1955
Peter and Pavla 1964
Peter Ibbetson 1935
Le Petit Prince A Dit 1992
Le Petit Soldat 1960 DVD
The Petrified Forest 1936 DVD
Petulia 1968
Peyton Place 1957 DVD
The Phantom Carriage 1920
Phar Lap 1983
The Pianist 2002 DVD
Pickpocket 1959 DVD
The Picture of Dorian Gray 1945
The Pillow Book 1995 DVD
Pimpernel Smith 1941
Ping Pong 2002 DVD
Pitfall 1962 DVD
A Place for Annie 1994 DVD
A Place in the Sun 1951 DVD
Places in the Heart 1984
Plastic Jesus 1971
Platform 2000 DVD
Playing by Heart 1998 DVD
Playing for Time 1980

Pleasantville 1998 DVD
The Pledge 2000 DVD
Plein Soleil 1960 DVD
The Ploughman's Lunch 1983
Poil de Carotte 1932
The Polish Bride 1998
Pollock 2000 DVD
Pollyanna 1920
Pollyanna 1960 DVD
Polyester 1981
Pork Chop Hill 1959 DVD
Les Portes de la Nuit 1946
A Portrait of the Artist as a Young Man 1977 DVD
Postcards from the Edge 1990 DVD
Il Posto 1961
Powder 1995 DVD
Pressure Point 1962
Pretty Baby 1978
Pretty Village Pretty Flame 1996
Pride and Prejudice 1940
Priest 1994
Primary Colors 1998 DVD
The Prime Gig 2000 DVD
The Prince of Tides 1991 DVD
Prisoner of Honor 1991
Prisoner of the Mountains 1996
Private 2004
The Private Affairs of Bel Ami 1947
The Private Life of Henry VIII 1933
A Private Matter 1992
Le Procès de Jeanne d'Arc 1962 DVD
The Profound Desire of the Gods 1968
La Promesse 1996 DVD
Promise 1986
Promised a Miracle 1988
Proof 1991
Prospero's Books 1991
Pull My Daisy 1959
The Pumpkin Eater 1964
Punch-Drunk Love 2002 DVD
Punishment Park 1971
Pure 2002 DVD
Quadrophenia 1979 DVD
Queen Christina 1933
Queen of Hearts 1989
The Queen of Spades 1948
Quentin Durward 1955
A Question of Silence 1982
The Quiet American 2002 DVD
The Quince Tree Sun 1991
Quiz Show 1994 DVD
RKO 281 1999 DVD
Rachel, Rachel 1968
Rain 2001
Raining Stones 1993 DVD
Raintree County 1957
The Rape of Richard Beck 1985
Rasputin 1996 DVD
Ratcatcher 1999 DVD
Ray 2004 DVD
Razzia sur la Chnouf 1955
Reach for the Sky 1956 DVD
Rebellion 1967
Rebels of the Neon God 1992
Record of a Tenement Gentleman 1947 DVD
The Red Badge of Courage 1951 DVD
Red Beard 1965 DVD
The Red Dance 1928
Red Dust 1932
The Red Squirrel 1993 DVD
Reed: Insurgent Mexico 1971
Regeneration 1915
Regeneration 1997 DVD
Reign of Terror 1949
The Reivers 1969 DVD
La Religieuse 1965
Remember the Night 1940
Les Rendez-vous de Paris 1995
Repentance 1984
Requiem for a Dream 2000 DVD
Resting Place 1986
Restoration 1995
Resurrected 1989
The Return 2003 DVD
Return Home 1989
The Return of Martin Guerre 1982 DVD
Return of the Idiot 1999
Return of the Secaucus Seven 1980
Return to Paradise 1998
Reunion in France 1942
Reversal of Fortune 1990 DVD
Richard III 1955 DVD
Richard III 1995 DVD
Ridicule 1996 DVD
Riff-Raff 1991 DVD
The Right Stuff 1983 DVD
Rikyu 1989
Riot in Cell Block 11 1954
The Ripening Seed 1953
The Rise and Fall of Legs Diamond 1960
The Rise to Power of Louis XIV 1966
The Rite 1969 DVD
The River 1997
A River Runs through It 1992 DVD
River's Edge 1987 DVD
The Road Home 1999 DVD
Road House 1948
Road to Perdition 2002 DVD
Roads to Koktebel 2003 DVD
The Roaring Twenties 1939 DVD
Roberto Succo 2000 DVD
Robinson Crusoe on Mars 1964
Robinson in Space 1997 DVD
The Rocking Horse Winner 1949
Rocky 1976 DVD
Roe vs Wade 1989
Roger Dodger 2002 DVD
Rome Express 1932
Romeo and Juliet 1936
Romeo and Juliet 1954
A Room for Romeo Brass 1999 DVD
A Room with a View 1985 DVD
Rosa Luxemburg 1986
Les Roseaux Sauvages 1994
Roseland 1977 DVD
Roswell 1994
'Round Midnight 1986
Ruby 1992
Rue Cases Nègres 1983
Rumble Fish 1983 DVD
Run Lola Run 1998 DVD
Run Silent, Run Deep 1958 DVD
The Runner 1984
The Running Man 1963
Running on Empty 1988
Rushmore 1998 DVD
The Russia House 1990 DVD
The Saboteur, Code Name Morituri 1965
Sacco and Vanzetti 1971
The Sacrifice 1986 DVD
Sacrificed Youth 1985
[Safe] 1995 DVD
The Saga of Anatahan 1953
Salaam Bombay! 1988 DVD
Salaam Cinema 1995
Salo, or the 120 Days of Sodom 1975 DVD
Salty O'Rourke 1945
Salvador 1986 DVD
The Salvation Hunters 1925
Salvatore Giuliano 1961
Samaritan Girl 2004
Same Time, Next Year 1978
Los Santos Inocentes 1984
Sarraouina 1986
Satyricon 1969 DVD
Saving Private Ryan 1998 DVD
Savior 1997 DVD
Sawdust and Tinsel 1953
The Scarlet and the Black 1983 DVD
The Scarlet Letter 1926
Scenes from a Marriage 1973 DVD
Scent of a Woman 1992 DVD
Scott of the Antarctic 1948 DVD
The Scout 1994
The Sea Wolf 1941
The Search 1948
Second Serve 1986
The Secret Garden 1993 DVD
Secret Honor 1984
The Secret Lives of Dentists 2002
The Secret Nation 1989
The Secret Rapture 1993
Secret Wedding 1989
Secrets of a Soul 1926
See How They Fall 1993
The Seed of Man 1969
A Self-Made Hero 1995
Separate Tables 1958 DVD
September 1987 DVD
Serenade 1956
Sergeant York 1941
The Servant 1963 DVD
The Set-Up 1949
Seul contre Tous 1998
Seven Beauties 1976
7 Women 1966
The Seventh Continent 1989
7th Heaven 1927
sex, lies, and videotape 1989 DVD
Sexy Beast 2000 DVD
Shall We Dance? 1995 DVD
Shame 1968 DVD
Shame 1987
Shanghai Express 1932
Shannon's Deal 1989
The Sheik 1921 DVD
She's Gotta Have It 1986
Shiloh 1996 DVD
The Shiralee 1986
Shock Corridor 1963 DVD
Shoot the Moon 1982
The Shooting Party 1984
Shooting the Moon 1998
The Shop around the Corner 1940
The Shop on the High Street 1965
The Shopworn Angel 1938
Sid and Nancy 1986 DVD
Sidewalk Stories 1989
The Sign of Leo 1959
The Silence 1963 DVD
Silence between Two Thoughts 2003
The Silences of the Palace 1994
Silent Running 1971 DVD
Silkwood 1983 DVD
Simple Men 1992
The Simple-Minded Murderer 1982
Sin City 2005
The Sin of Madelon Claudet 1931
Since Otar Left 2003 DVD
Sink the Bismarck! 1960 DVD
Sister Kenny 1946
Sisters, or the Balance of Happiness 1979
Six Degrees of Separation 1993 DVD
Skokie 1981 DVD
The Sleeping Tiger 1954
Sling Blade 1995
Slums of Beverly Hills 1998 DVD
Small Faces 1995 DVD
Smash Palace 1981
Smilin' Through 1932
Smoke 1995 DVD
Smoking/No Smoking 1993
A Snake of June 2002 DVD
The Snake Pit 1948 DVD
The Sniper 1952
Snow Falling on Cedars 1999 DVD
So Well Remembered 1947
Sokhout 1998
Solaris 1972 DVD
Solas 1998 DVD
Soldier in the Rain 1963
Soldier of Orange 1977 DVD
A Soldier's Story 1984 DVD
Some Kind of Wonderful 1987 DVD
Some Mother's Son 1996
Somebody Up There Likes Me 1956
Somersault 2004 DVD
Something for Joey 1977
Something Wild 1986 DVD
Somewhere beyond Love 1974
Somewhere in Europe 1947
The Son 2002 DVD
A Song for Beko 1992
The Song of Bernadette 1943 DVD
Song of Freedom 1936
Songs from the Second Floor 2000
Sophie Scholl – The Final Days 2005
Sophie's Choice 1982 DVD
Le Souffle au Coeur 1971
Soul Food 1997 DVD
Soul of the Game 1996
The Sound Barrier 1952 DVD
The Sound of Fury 1950
Sounder 1972
Sous le Soleil de Satan 1987
Sous les Toits de Paris 1930
Southern Comfort 1981 DVD
Spanglish 2004 DVD
Spanking the Monkey 1994
Sparrows 1926
Spetters 1980
Spider 2002 DVD
The Spider and the Fly 1949
The Spirit of St Louis 1957
Splendor in the Grass 1961
Spring River Flows East 1947
Springtime in a Small Town 2002 DVD
The Spy Who Came in from the Cold 1965
Stage Door 1937
Stalag 17 1953 DVD
Stalker 1979 DVD
Stand and Deliver 1988
Star 80 1983
A Star Is Born 1937 DVD
Star Maps 1997
Stars 1959
The Stars Look Down 1939 DVD
State of the Union 1948
The State of Things 1982
The Station Agent 2003 DVD
Station Six-Sahara 1962
Stavisky 1974
Stay Hungry 1976 DVD
Steaming 1985
Steel Magnolias 1989 DVD
Stella Dallas 1925
Stella Dallas 1937
Stella Maris 1918
Stepmom 1998 DVD
Stiff Upper Lips 1997
Still Life 1974
The Stolen Children 1992
The Stone Boy 1984
Stones for Ibarra 1988
Stormy Waters 1941
The Story of GI Joe 1945
The Story of Three Loves 1953
La Strada 1954 DVD
Strange Interlude 1932
Strangers Kiss 1983
Street of Shame 1955
Street Scene 1931
Strike 1924 DVD
Strings 2004
The Subject Was Roses 1968
Suddenly, Last Summer 1959 DVD
A Summer at Grandpa's 1984
Summer Interlude 1950 DVD
The Summer of Ben Tyler 1996
A Summer Story 1987
Summer Vacation: 1999 1988
Summertime 1955
The Sun Also Rises 1957
Sunday, Bloody Sunday 1971
Sunday in the Country 1984
Sunday Too Far Away 1974
Sunday's Children 1992
Sunshine 1999 DVD
Sunshine State 2002 DVD
El Sur 1983
Sur 1987
Surviving 1985
Surviving Picasso 1996
Suzhou River 2000 DVD
Swann 1996 DVD
Sweet and Lowdown 1999 DVD
Sweet Emma Dear Böbe 1992
The Sweet Hereafter 1997 DVD
Sweet Hunters 1969
Sweet Sixteen 2002 DVD
Sweetie 1989
The Swimmer 1968 DVD
Swimming Pool 2003 DVD
Swing 1983
Swing Shift 1984
Swingers 1996 DVD
The Switch 1993 DVD
Sylvia 1964
THX 1138 1971 DVD
Taipei Story 1984
Take My Eyes 2003 DVD
Taking Off 1971
Tales from a Hard City 1994
The Talk of the Town 1942 DVD
Talk Radio 1988
Talk to Her 2001 DVD
Tamanna 1997
The Tarnished Angels 1957
Tartuffe 1926 DVD
A Taste of Cherry 1997
A Taxing Woman 1987
Tea and Sympathy 1956
Telling Lies in America 1997
The Tempest 1979 DVD
Ten 2002 DVD
Ten North Frederick 1958
Tender Mercies 1982
A Tender Place 2001
Term of Trial 1962
Terms of Endearment 1983 DVD
La Terra Trema 1947 DVD
The Terrorist 1998 DVD
Tess 1979 DVD
Test Pilot 1938
Le Testament d'Orphée 1960
The Testament of Dr Cordelier 1959
Tex 1982
The Theme 1979
Theorem 1968
The Theory of Flight 1998
There Was a Father 1942
Thérèse 1986
Thérèse Desqueyroux 1962
Thérèse Raquin 1953
These Foolish Things 1990
They Came to Cordura 1959 DVD
They Drive by Night 1940 DVD
They Were Expendable 1945
Thief 1981 DVD
The Thief 1997
The Thief of Paris 1967
Thieves like Us 1974
Things to Do in Denver When You're Dead 1995 DVD
Thirteen Days 2000 DVD
This Boy's Life 1993 DVD
Those Lips, Those Eyes 1980
Those Who Love Me Can Take the Train 1998 DVD
Three 1965
[Three] Après la Vie 2002 DVD
Three Came Home 1950 DVD
Three Colours White 1993 DVD
3-iron 2004
Three Lives and Only One Death 1996
3 Women 1977
Through a Glass Darkly 1961 DVD
Through the Olive Trees 1994
Thunder Rock 1942 DVD
Thunderbolt 1929
Thunderbolt and Lightfoot 1974 DVD
Thursday 1998
Tilaï 1990
A Time for Drunken Horses 2000 DVD
The Time of Your Life 1948 DVD
Time Regained 1999 DVD
The Time to Live and the Time to Die 1985
Timecode 1999 DVD
The Tin Drum 1979 DVD
Tin Men 1987 DVD
Tina: What's Love Got to Do with It 1993 DVD
Titanic 1997 DVD
Tito and Me 1992
To Each His Own 1946
To Kill a Mockingbird 1962 DVD
To Live 1994
To Our Loves 1984
To Sleep with Anger 1990
To the Starry Island 1994
To Walk with Lions 1999 DVD
Tokyo Chorus 1931
Tokyo Fist 1995 DVD
Tol'able David 1921
Tollbooth 1994
Tomorrow 1972
Toni 1935
Topaze 1933
Torch Song Trilogy 1988
The Torrent 1926
Toto Le Héros 1991
A Touch of Zen 1969 DVD
Touching the Void 2003 DVD

Tous les Matins du Monde 1991
Traffic 2000 DVD
Traffic in Souls 1913
The Train 1964 DVD
Train of Dreams 1987
Training Day 2001 DVD
The Traveller 1974
Travelling North 1986
The Travelling Players 1975
A Tree Grows in Brooklyn 1945 DVD
The Tree of Wooden Clogs 1978 DVD
Trees Lounge 1996 DVD
Trial 1955
The Trial 1962 DVD
The Trials of Oscar Wilde 1960
The Trip to Bountiful 1985 DVD
Le Trou 1959
True Love 1989
Truly Madly Deeply 1990 DVD
Truman 1995 DVD
Tuesdays with Morrie 1999 DVD
Tunes of Glory 1960
Turkish Delight 1973 DVD
Turtles Can Fly 2004
The Tuskegee Airmen 1995
12 Angry Men 1997
Twelve O'Clock High 1949 DVD
24 Hour Party People 2001 DVD
21 Grams 2003 DVD
Twice in a Lifetime 1985
The Twilight Samurai 2002 DVD
Twin Peaks: Fire Walk with Me 1992 DVD
Twin Sisters of Kyoto 1963
Two against the Law 1973
Two for the Road 1967
Two Girls and a Guy 1997
The Two of Us 1967
Two or Three Things I Know about Her 1966 DVD
Two Weeks in Another Town 1962
Ulee's Gold 1997 DVD
Ulysses' Gaze 1995
Unbreakable 2000 DVD
The Uncle 1964
Unconquered 1989
Under Fire 1983 DVD
Under the Sand 2000 DVD
Under the Skin 1997 DVD
Underworld 1927
Underworld USA 1961
An Unfinished Piece for Mechanical Piano 1976
An Unforgettable Summer 1994
The Unholy Three 1925
The Unknown 1927 DVD
The Unknown Soldier 1983
Unstrung Heroes 1995 DVD
The Unsuspected 1947
Untold Scandal 2003
Urga 1990
Uzak 2003 DVD
Va Savoir 2001 DVD
Vacuuming Completely Nude in Paradise 2001
Vagabond 1985 DVD
Valley of the Dolls 1967 DVD
Valmont 1989
Les Valseuses 1974
Van Gogh 1991
The Vanishing Corporal 1962
Vassa 1983
Vaudeville 1925
Veer-Zaara 2004
Vendredi Soir 2002 DVD
Vera Drake 2004 DVD
Veronica Guerin 2003 DVD
A Very Long Engagement 2004 DVD
Vessel of Wrath 1938
La Vie de Château 1965 DVD
La Ville Est Tranquille 2000 DVD
Violent Saturday 1955
The Virgin Spring 1960 DVD
The Virgin Suicides 1999 DVD
I Vitelloni 1953
Vive L'Amour 1994
Vodka Lemon 2003 DVD
Voyage to Cythera 1984
WUSA 1970
Waiting for Happiness 2002 DVD
Wake Island 1942
A Walk in the Sun 1945
The Walking Stick 1970
Wall Street 1987 DVD
Walpurgis Night 1935
Wanda 1971
Waqt 1965 DVD
The War Game 1965 DVD
A War of Children 1972
War Requiem 1988
The War Zone 1999 DVD
The Warriors 1979 DVD
The Watchmaker of St Paul 1973
Waterloo Bridge 1940
The Way Ahead 1944 DVD
The Way of All Flesh 1927
The Way to the Stars 1945 DVD
The Way We Were 1973 DVD
We All Loved Each Other So Much 1974
We Don't Live Here Anymore 2003
We Don't Want to Talk about It 1993
We the Living 1942
A Wedding 1978
Welcome to the Dollhouse 1995
Werckmeister Harmonies 2000 DVD
West Beirut 1998
Westfront 1918 1930
Wetherby 1985
The Whales of August 1987
What Price Hollywood? 1932
What Time Is It There? 2001
When Father Was Away on Business 1985
When Ladies Meet 1933
When the Last Sword Is Drawn 2003 DVD
When the Legends Die 1972
When Trumpets Fade 1998 DVD
Where Is My Friend's House? 1987
The Whisperers 1967
Whisky 2004
Whistle down the Wind 1961 DVD
The White Balloon 1995
The White Dawn 1974
White Dog 1981
White Hunter, Black Heart 1990
White Mane 1952
White Men Can't Jump 1992 DVD
White Palace 1990 DVD
Who'll Stop the Rain? 1978 DVD
Who's Afraid of Virginia Woolf? 1966
The Wicked Lady 1945 DVD
The Widow Couderc 1971
Wife vs Secretary 1936
Wilbur (Wants to Kill Himself) 2002 DVD
The Wild Angels 1966
Wild at Heart 1990 DVD
The Wild One 1953 DVD
Wild River 1960 DVD
Wilde 1997 DVD
William Shakespeare's Romeo + Juliet 1996 DVD
The Wind Will Carry Us 1999
Wind with the Gone 1998
Windom's Way 1957
The Wings of the Dove 1997 DVD
The Winslow Boy 1948
The Winslow Boy 1999 DVD
Winstanley 1975
A Winter's Tale 1992
Wish You Were Here 1987 DVD
Wit 2001
The Witches of Eastwick 1987 DVD
With a Song in My Heart 1952
Without Warning: the James Brady Story 1991
Woman in a Dressing Gown 1957
A Woman of Paris 1923 DVD
The Woman on the Beach 1947
A Woman's Face 1938
A Woman's Face 1941
Women in Love 1969 DVD
Wonder Boys 2000 DVD
The Wonderful Lie of Nina Petrovna 1929
Wonderland 1999
The Woodsman 2004 DVD
A World Apart 1987
The World Changes 1933
Woyzeck 1978 DVD
Written on the Wind 1956
The Wrong Man 1956 DVD
Wyatt Earp 1994 DVD
Xala 1974
The Yakuza Papers 1973 DVD
The Year My Voice Broke 1987
A Year of the Quiet Sun 1984
The Yearling 1946
Yesterday Girl 1966
You Can Count on Me 1999 DVD
Young Adam 2003 DVD
The Young in Heart 1938
The Young Ladies of Wilko 1979
Young Mr Lincoln 1939 DVD
The Young Mr Pitt 1942
Z 1968
Zorba the Greek 1964 DVD
Zulu 1964 DVD

Epic

★★★★★

Apocalypse Now 1979 DVD
Ben-Hur 1959 DVD
Ben-Hur: a Tale of Christ 1925
El Cid 1961 DVD
Dances with Wolves 1990 DVD
Doctor Zhivago 1965 DVD
Farewell My Concubine 1993
Gandhi 1982 DVD
Gladiator 2000 DVD
The Godfather 1972 DVD
The Godfather, Part II 1974 DVD
Gone with the Wind 1939 DVD
The Gospel According to St Matthew 1964 DVD
Heimat 1984 DVD
Heimat 2 1992 DVD
Heimat 3: a Chronicle of Endings and Beginnings 2004
The Human Condition 1958
The Iron Horse 1924 DVD
Lawrence of Arabia 1962 DVD
Les Misérables 1934
Once upon a Time in America 1984 DVD
Ran 1985 DVD
Reds 1981
Ryan's Daughter 1970
Sansho the Bailiff 1954
Spartacus 1960 DVD
Star Wars Episode IV: a New Hope 1977 DVD
Star Wars Episode V: the Empire Strikes Back 1980 DVD
2001: a Space Odyssey 1968 DVD

Epic

★★★★

Alexander Nevsky 1938 DVD
Anthony Adverse 1936
The Best of Youth 2003
The Birth of a Nation 1915 DVD
Cabiria 1914
Cheyenne Autumn 1964
Chronicle of the Burning Years 1975
A City of Sadness 1989
Cimarron 1931
The Emperor's Shadow 1996
Exodus 1960 DVD
The Fall of the Roman Empire 1964 DVD
Giant 1956 DVD
The Greatest Show on Earth 1952
How the West Was Won 1962
Ivanhoe 1952
Junoon 1978
The King of Kings 1927
King of Kings 1961
Kingdom of Heaven 2005
The Last Emperor 1987 DVD
The Legend of 1900 1999 DVD
Legends of the Fall 1994 DVD
Little Big Man 1970 DVD
Lloyd's of London 1936
The Loyal 47 Ronin 1941
Marie Antoinette 1938
Les Misérables 1935
Les Misérables 1995
Mughal-e-Azam 1960 DVD
The Nibelungen 1924
1900 1976
October 1928 DVD
The Pride and the Passion 1957 DVD
The Sign of the Cross 1932
Star Wars Episode VI: Return of the Jedi 1983 DVD
Sunshine 1999 DVD
The Ten Commandments 1923
The Ten Commandments 1956 DVD
Titanic 1997 DVD
To Live 1994
The Travelling Players 1975
The Tree of Wooden Clogs 1978 DVD
Ulysses' Gaze 1995
Veer-Zaara 2004
War and Peace 1966
The War Lord 1965
Waterloo 1970 DVD

Experimental

★★★★★

Berlin: Symphony of a Great City 1927
Celine and Julie Go Boating 1974
Un Chien Andalou 1928 DVD
Eloge de l'Amour 2001 DVD
Man with a Movie Camera 1929
Russian Ark 2002 DVD

Experimental

★★★★

A Propos de Nice 1930
Blue 1993
Bodysong 2002 DVD
The Chelsea Girls 1967
La Chinoise 1967 DVD
Close-Up 1989
Conspirators of Pleasure 1996
Cremaster 3 2002
Daughters of the Dust 1991
Dog Star Man 1964
Dreams That Money Can Buy 1946
Eaux d'Artifice 1953
Eraserhead 1976 DVD
Meshes of the Afternoon 1943
Mirror 1974 DVD
Not Reconciled, or Only Violence Helps Where Violence Rules 1965
Out 1: Spectre 1973
Pink Narcissus 1971
Pull My Daisy 1959
The Seashell and the Clergyman 1928
Superstar: the Karen Carpenter Story 1987
Le Testament d'Orphée 1960
Timecode 1999 DVD
Two or Three Things I Know about Her 1966 DVD
War Requiem 1988
Wavelength 1967

Fantasy

★★★★★

Antz 1998 DVD
Batman 1989 DVD
Beauty and the Beast 1991 DVD
Being John Malkovich 1999 DVD
La Belle et la Bête 1946 DVD
Brazil 1985 DVD
Celine and Julie Go Boating 1974
Edward Scissorhands 1990 DVD
Faust 1926 DVD
Faust 1994
The Fisher King 1991 DVD
The 5,000 Fingers of Dr T 1953
Groundhog Day 1993 DVD
Harvey 1950 DVD
Heaven Can Wait 1943
Hero 2002 DVD
It's a Wonderful Life 1946 DVD
King Kong 1933 DVD
A Little Princess 1995 DVD
The Lord of the Rings: The Fellowship of the Ring 2001 DVD
The Lord of the Rings: The Two Towers 2002 DVD
The Lord of the Rings: The Return of the King 2003 DVD
Lost Horizon 1937 DVD
Mary Poppins 1964 DVD
The Mask 1994 DVD
A Matter of Life and Death 1946 DVD
Metropolis 1926 DVD
The Milky Way 1968 DVD
Miracle on 34th Street 1947 DVD
The Nightmare before Christmas 1993 DVD
Orphée 1950 DVD
Pinocchio 1940 DVD
The Saragossa Manuscript 1964
The Sixth Sense 1999 DVD
Snow White and the Seven Dwarfs 1937 DVD
Superman 1978 DVD
The Thief of Bagdad 1940
Time of the Gypsies 1988
The Wizard of Oz 1939 DVD

Fantasy

★★★★

AI: Artificial Intelligence 2001 DVD
The Adventures of Baron Munchausen 1988 DVD
After Life 1998
Akira 1988 DVD
Alice 1988
The Arabian Nights 1974 DVD
Ashik Kerib 1988
Atlantis: the Lost Empire 2001 DVD
Babe 1995 DVD
Babes in Toyland 1934 DVD
Batman 1966 DVD
Batman Begins 2005
Batman Forever 1995 DVD
Batman: Mask of the Phantasm 1993 DVD
Batman Returns 1992 DVD
Les Belles de Nuit 1952
Berkeley Square 1933
Blithe Spirit 1945 DVD
The Bride with White Hair 1993 DVD
Brigadoon 1954 DVD
Casper 1995 DVD
Cinderella 1950
The City of Lost Children 1995 DVD
City of Women 1980
Cocoon 1985 DVD
Conspirators of Pleasure 1996
Cremaster 3 2002
The Crow 1994 DVD
The Curse of the Cat People 1944
Dark City 1998 DVD
The Dark Crystal 1982 DVD
Darkman 1990 DVD
The Dead and the Deadly 1983
Delicatessen 1990 DVD
Destiny 1921
The Devil and the Nun 1960
Dodes'ka-Den 1970
Donnie Darko 2001 DVD
Eaux d'Artifice 1953
The Element of Crime 1984 DVD
Enemy Mine 1985 DVD
Ever After: a Cinderella Story 1998 DVD
Excalibur 1981 DVD
Fantastic Planet 1973
Field of Dreams 1989 DVD
Fireworks 1947
Frequency 2000 DVD
Gabbeh 1995
Ghost 1990 DVD
The Ghost and Mrs Muir 1947 DVD

Ghostbusters 1984 DVD
Goto, l'Ile d'Amour 1968
The Grinch 2000 DVD
The Halloween Tree 1993
Harry Potter and the Chamber of Secrets 2002 DVD
Harry Potter and the Philosopher's Stone 2001 DVD
Harry Potter and the Prisoner of Azkaban 2004 DVD
Hawks and Sparrows 1966
Heaven Can Wait 1978 DVD
Here Comes Mr Jordan 1941
The Holy Mountain 1973
Honey, I Shrunk the Kids 1989 DVD
I Married a Witch 1942
Iceman 1984
Ilya Muromets 1956
The Indian in the Cupboard 1995 DVD
Invention of Destruction 1958
It Happened Tomorrow 1944
James and the Giant Peach 1996 DVD
Johnny Suede 1991
Jumanji 1995 DVD
Kirikou and the Sorceress 1998 DVD
Lady in White 1988
Ladyhawke 1985 DVD
The Last Wave 1977
Life Is a Bed of Roses 1983
Like Water for Chocolate 1993 DVD
Little Otik 2000 DVD
The Living Dead 1932
The Love Bug 1969 DVD
Macario 1960
Malpertuis 1971
Matilda 1996 DVD
Me Myself I 1999
Meet the Applegates 1991
A Midsummer Night's Dream 1935
A Midsummer Night's Dream 1961
The Mighty 1998 DVD
Motorama 1991
The Navigator – a Medieval Odyssey 1988
The NeverEnding Story 1984
The New Gulliver 1935
The Nibelungen 1924
La Nuit Fantastique 1942
Opera do Malandro 1986
Pandora and the Flying Dutchman 1950
Peter Ibbetson 1935
Peter Pan 1953 DVD
The Phantom Carriage 1920
The Phantom Tollbooth 1969
Pink Narcissus 1971
Pirates of the Caribbean: the Curse of the Black Pearl 2003 DVD
Pleasantville 1998 DVD
Powder 1995 DVD
The Princess Bride 1987 DVD
Princess Mononoke 1997 DVD
The Projectionist 1970
The Purple Rose of Cairo 1985 DVD
Q – the Winged Serpent 1982 DVD
The Queen of Spades 1948
Red Balloon 1956
Rocketeer 1991 DVD
Rouge 1987
Satyricon 1969 DVD
The Secret Lives of Dentists 2002
The Secret of Roan Inish 1993
The 7th Voyage of Sinbad 1958 DVD
Shrek 2 2004
Sitcom 1997 DVD
Sleepy Hollow 1999 DVD
Spider-Man 2002 DVD
Spider-Man 2 2004 DVD
Spirited Away 2001 DVD
Splash 1984 DVD
SPYkids 2001 DVD
SPYkids 2: the Island of Lost Dreams 2002 DVD
Strings 2004
Superman II 1980 DVD
Superstar: the Karen Carpenter Story 1987
Suspiria 1976 DVD
The Tale of the Fox 1931
The Tempest 1979 DVD
The Thief of Bagdad 1924 DVD
Thomas the Imposter 1964
Three Lives and Only One Death 1996
Thunder Rock 1942 DVD
Time Bandits 1981 DVD
The Time Machine 1960 DVD
tom thumb 1958
Topper 1937
Tuck Everlasting 1980
Unbreakable 2000 DVD
Les Visiteurs 1993 DVD
Les Visiteurs du Soir 1942
Volere, Volare 1991
Voyage into Prehistory 1955
X2 2003 DVD
Yeelen 1987
Yellow Submarine 1968 DVD
Zu Warriors 1983 DVD

Film Noir

★★★★★

The Big Sleep 1946 DVD
Build My Gallows High 1947 DVD
Double Indemnity 1944 DVD
Farewell My Lovely 1944 DVD
Gilda 1946 DVD
In a Lonely Place 1950 DVD
The Killers 1946
Kiss Me Deadly 1955 DVD
Laura 1944
The Maltese Falcon 1941 DVD
Mildred Pierce 1945
The Postman Always Rings Twice 1946 DVD
The Strange Love of Martha Ivers 1946 DVD

Film Noir

★★★★

Beyond a Reasonable Doubt 1956
The Big Combo 1955
The Big Heat 1953
The Blue Dahlia 1946
The Chase 1946
Crime of Passion 1957
Criss Cross 1949
Crossfire 1947
Cry of the City 1948
Dead Reckoning 1947 DVD
Desperate 1947
Fallen Angel 1945 DVD
Fear in the Night 1947
Force of Evil 1948
The Glass Key 1942
Gun Crazy 1949
The Hitch-Hiker 1953
I Wake Up Screaming 1941
Kiss of Death 1947
Lady in the Lake 1947
Moonrise 1948
Phantom Lady 1944
Pitfall 1948
Raw Deal 1948
T-Men 1947
They Live by Night 1948
Where the Sidewalk Ends 1950 DVD
The Woman in the Window 1945

Historical

★★★★★

All the President's Men 1976 DVD
Andrei Rublev 1966 DVD
The Battleship Potemkin 1925 DVD
The Charge of the Light Brigade 1968 DVD
Chariots of Fire 1981 DVD
El Cid 1961 DVD
Henry V 1944 DVD
Ivan the Terrible, Part I 1944 DVD
Jeanne la Pucelle 1994
Julius Caesar 1953
Lawrence of Arabia 1962 DVD
The Lion in Winter 1968 DVD
Lola Montès 1955
The Madness of King George 1995 DVD
Mrs Brown 1997 DVD
Napoléon 1927
The Round-Up 1966
The Scarlet Empress 1934
Spartacus 1960 DVD

Historical

★★★★

The Alamo 1960 DVD
Alexander Nevsky 1938 DVD
Apollo 13 1995 DVD
Baadasssss! 2003
Barbarians at the Gate 1993
Becket 1964
The Birth of a Nation 1915 DVD
Bloody Sunday 2001 DVD
The Bounty 1984 DVD
Boycott 2001 DVD
Braveheart 1995 DVD
Breaker Morant 1979 DVD
Call Northside 777 1948
The Charge of the Light Brigade 1936
The Chess Players 1977
Comrades: a Lanternist's Account of the Tolpuddle Martyrs and What Became of Them 1986
Conquest 1937
Cool Runnings 1993 DVD
Cromwell 1970 DVD
Danton 1982
The Devils 1971
The Disappearance of Aimee 1976
The Dish 2000 DVD
Downfall 2004
Eagle in a Cage 1971
Elizabeth 1998 DVD
The Emperor's Shadow 1996
Escape from Sobibor 1987
The Fall of the Roman Empire 1964 DVD
Fanfan la Tulipe 1951 DVD
55 Days at Peking 1963
The Final Days 1989 DVD
Fire over England 1937
Fort Saganne 1984
1492: Conquest of Paradise 1992 DVD
Glory 1989 DVD
Gohatto 1999 DVD
Good Morning, Night 2003 DVD
Heartland 1979
Henry V 1989 DVD
Hotel Rwanda 2004 DVD
I, the Worst of All 1990
If I Were King 1938
In the Name of the Pope King 1977
Ivan the Terrible, Part II 1946 DVD
JFK 1991 DVD
Judgment at Nuremberg 1961 DVD
Kingdom of Heaven 2005
The Lady & the Duke 2001 DVD
The Last Valley 1971 DVD
Lloyd's of London 1936
The Loyal 47 Ronin 1941
A Man for All Seasons 1966 DVD
The Man Who Captured Eichmann 1996
Mary, Queen of Scots 1971
Matewan 1987 DVD
The Mattei Affair 1972
Mayerling 1936
The Miracle of Bern 2003 DVD
Monsieur N 2003
Mughal-e-Azam 1960 DVD
Murder in Mississippi 1990
Mutiny on the Bounty 1935 DVD
Mutiny on the Bounty 1962
The Night of Counting the Years 1969
A Night to Remember 1958 DVD
October 1928 DVD
Path to War 2002 DVD
Pétain 1992
Prisoner of Honor 1991
Queen Christina 1933
Quiz Show 1994 DVD
Reed: Insurgent Mexico 1971
Reign of Terror 1949
The Return of Martin Guerre 1982 DVD
Richard III 1955 DVD
Richard III 1995 DVD
Ridicule 1996
The Right Stuff 1983 DVD
The Rise to Power of Louis XIV 1966
Rob Roy 1995 DVD
Roe vs Wade 1989
Sacco and Vanzetti 1971
The Saga of Anatahan 1953
Salvatore Giuliano 1961
Sarraouina 1986
Satyricon 1969 DVD
Scott of the Antarctic 1948 DVD
The Sign of the Cross 1932
Skokie 1981
Soul of the Game 1996
The Spirit of St Louis 1957
Stanley and Livingstone 1939
Thirteen Days 2000 DVD
Tous les Matins du Monde 1991
The Trials of Oscar Wilde 1960
The Tuskegee Airmen 1995
War and Peace 1966
Waterloo 1970 DVD
Winstanley 1975
Zulu 1964 DVD

Horror

★★★★★

The Birds 1963 DVD
The Black Cat 1934
The Body Snatcher 1945
Braindead 1992 DVD
Bride of Frankenstein 1935 DVD
The Cabinet of Dr Caligari 1919 DVD
Carrie 1976 DVD
Dead of Night 1945 DVD
Don't Look Now 1973 DVD
The Exorcist 1973 DVD
Eyes without a Face 1959
Frankenstein 1931 DVD
Halloween 1978 DVD
The Haunting 1963 DVD
Henry: Portrait of a Serial Killer 1986 DVD
Horror of Dracula 1958 DVD
The Invisible Man 1933 DVD
Island of Lost Souls 1932 DVD
Night of the Living Dead 1968 DVD
Psycho 1960 DVD
Rosemary's Baby 1968 DVD
Scream 1996 DVD
The Shining 1980 DVD
The Texas Chain Saw Massacre 1974 DVD
Tremors 1989 DVD
The Uninvited 1944
Vampyr 1932
What Ever Happened to Baby Jane? 1962
The Wicker Man 1973 DVD
Witchfinder General 1968 DVD

Horror

★★★★

The Abominable Dr Phibes 1971 DVD
The Addams Family 1991
Addams Family Values 1993 DVD
Alice, Sweet Alice 1977
Alligator 1980 DVD
Alraune 1927
American Psycho 2000 DVD
An American Werewolf in London 1981 DVD
Anatomy 2000 DVD
Anguish 1986
Arachnophobia 1990 DVD
The Asphyx 1972 DVD
Audition 1999 DVD
The Bad Seed 1956
Bad Taste 1987 DVD
Basket Case 1982 DVD
The Beast with Five Fingers 1946
Beetle Juice 1988 DVD
Black Christmas 1974 DVD
Black Rainbow 1989 DVD
Black Sabbath 1963
The Blair Witch Project 1998 DVD
Blue Sunshine 1976 DVD
Body Snatchers 1993 DVD
Brain Damage 1988
Bram Stoker's Dracula 1992 DVD
The Brides of Dracula 1960
The Brood 1979 DVD
Candyman 1992 DVD
Carnival of Souls 1962 DVD
Cat People 1942
Cemetery Man 1994
Chamber of Horrors 1966
A Chinese Ghost Story 1987 DVD
The Corpse 1969
Creature from the Black Lagoon 1954 DVD
Cronos 1992 DVD
The Curse of Frankenstein 1957 DVD
The Curse of the Cat People 1944
Dark Water 2002 DVD
Darkman 1990 DVD
Daughters of Darkness 1970
Dawn of the Dead 1978 DVD
The Day of the Beast 1995
Day of the Dead 1985 DVD
Death Line 1972
The Descent 2005
Demon Seed 1977
The Devil's Backbone 2001 DVD
Dr Jekyll and Mr Hyde 1931 DVD
Dog Soldiers 2001 DVD
Dracula 1931 DVD
Dracula 1979
Dracula – Prince of Darkness 1965 DVD
Dust Devil 1992
Eraserhead 1976 DVD
The Evil Dead 1983 DVD
The Eye 2002 DVD
The Face behind the Mask 1941
The Fall of the House of Usher 1960 DVD
The Fearless Vampire Killers 1967 DVD
The Flesh Eaters 1964
The Fly 1986 DVD
Frankenstein: the True Story 1973
Freaks 1932 DVD
Freezer 2000 DVD
Fright Night 1985 DVD
The Frighteners 1996 DVD
From Dusk till Dawn 1995 DVD
From Hell 2001 DVD
The Fury 1978 DVD
The Ghost Breakers 1940
The Ghoul 1933 DVD
Ginger Snaps 2000 DVD
Godzilla 1954
The Golem 1920 DVD
Gremlins 1984 DVD
The Hands of Orlac 1960
The Happiness of the Katakuris 2001 DVD
Hardware 1990
Häxan 1921
The Hidden 1987
The Hills Have Eyes 1977 DVD
Histoires Extraordinaires 1967
The Hounds of Zaroff 1932 DVD
House of Dark Shadows 1970
House of Wax 1953 DVD
The Howling 1981 DVD
I Walked with a Zombie 1943
The Innocents 1961
Jeepers Creepers 2001 DVD
The Kingdom 1994 DVD
Lady in White 1988
The Leopard Man 1943
Let's Scare Jessica to Death 1971
Little Shop of Horrors 1986 DVD

The Living Dead 1932
Love at First Bite 1979
Lust of the Vampire 1956
Mad Love 1935
Malpertuis 1971
Martin 1978 DVD
The Mask of Satan 1960 DVD
The Masque of the Red Death 1964 DVD
Mr Vampire 1986 DVD
Monkey Shines 1988 DVD
The Mummy 1932 DVD
Mystery of the Wax Museum 1933 DVD
Nadja 1995
Near Dark 1987 DVD
Night of the Demon 1957
Night of the Living Dead 1990 DVD
A Nightmare on Elm Street 1984 DVD
Nosferatu, a Symphony of Horrors 1922 DVD
Of Unknown Origin 1983 DVD
The Old Dark House 1932
The Omen 1976 DVD
The Other 1972
Parents 1988
The Phantom of the Opera 1925 DVD
The Picture of Dorian Gray 1945
The Pit and the Pendulum 1961 DVD
The Plague of the Zombies 1965 DVD
Poltergeist 1982 DVD
Q – the Winged Serpent 1982 DVD
Rabid 1976 DVD
The Raven 1935
The Raven 1963 DVD
Ravenous 1999 DVD
Re-Animator 1985 DVD
A Reflection of Fear 1973
Ring 1997 DVD
The Rocky Horror Picture Show 1975 DVD
Saw 2004 DVD
Scanners 1980 DVD
Session 9 2001 DVD
Shaun of the Dead 2004 DVD
Shivers 1975 DVD
Sitcom 1997 DVD
Sleepy Hollow 1999 DVD
Son of Frankenstein 1939
The Stepfather 1986 DVD
Suspiria 1976 DVD
Switchblade Romance 2003 DVD
The Testament of Dr Cordelier 1959
The Testament of Dr Mabuse 1932 DVD
The Texas Chainsaw Massacre Part 2 1986 DVD
Theatre of Blood 1973 DVD
The Thing 1982 DVD
The Thing from Another World 1951
The Tingler 1959 DVD
Tokyo Fist 1995 DVD
The Tomb of Ligeia 1964
28 Days Later... 2002 DVD
Videodrome 1982 DVD
Village of the Damned 1960
Waxworks 1924
The Wolf Man 1941 DVD
Young Frankenstein 1974 DVD

Musical

★★★★★

Aladdin 1992 DVD
Annie Get Your Gun 1950 DVD
The Band Wagon 1953 DVD
Beauty and the Beast 1991 DVD
Broadway Melody of 1940 1940
Cabaret 1972 DVD
Calamity Jane 1953 DVD
Carmen 1984 DVD
The Cat Concerto 1947
Easter Parade 1948 DVD
Fantasia 1940 DVD
42nd Street 1933
Gigi 1958 DVD
A Great Day in Harlem 1994
A Hard Day's Night 1964 DVD
The Jolson Story 1946 DVD
Lady and the Tramp 1955 DVD
The Little Mermaid 1989 DVD
Love Me Tonight 1932
Martin Scorsese Presents the Blues: Feel Like Going Home 2003 DVD
Mary Poppins 1964 DVD
Meet Me in St Louis 1944 DVD
My Fair Lady 1964 DVD
The Nightmare before Christmas 1993 DVD
On the Town 1949
Otello 1986 DVD
The Red Shoes 1948 DVD
Saturday Night Fever 1977 DVD
Seven Brides for Seven Brothers 1954 DVD
Show Boat 1936
Show Boat 1951
Singin' in the Rain 1952 DVD
The Smiling Lieutenant 1931
The Sound of Music 1965 DVD
A Star Is Born 1954 DVD
Swing Time 1936
The Tales of Hoffmann 1951
The TAMI Show 1964 DVD
This Is Spinal Tap 1984 DVD
The Three Little Pigs 1933
Top Hat 1935
La Traviata 1982
The Umbrellas of Cherbourg 1964 DVD
West Side Story 1961 DVD
What's Opera, Doc? 1957
The Wizard of Oz 1939 DVD
Woodstock 1970 DVD

Musical

★★★★

All That Jazz 1979 DVD
An American in Paris 1951 DVD
Applause 1929
Artists and Models 1955
Babes in Arms 1939
Babes in Toyland 1934 DVD
The Belle of New York 1952
The Best Things in Life Are Free 1956
The Big Broadcast 1932
The Big TNT Show 1966
Blood Wedding 1981
The Blues Brothers 1980 DVD
Brigadoon 1954 DVD
Broadway Melody of 1936 1935
Broadway through a Keyhole 1933
Buena Vista Social Club 1998 DVD
Bugsy Malone 1976 DVD
Bye Bye Birdie 1963
Cabin in the Sky 1943
Call Me Madam 1953
Camelot 1967 DVD
Carmen 1983 DVD
Carmen Jones 1954 DVD
Carousel 1956 DVD
Casbah 1948
Chicago 2002 DVD
The Commitments 1991 DVD
The Company 2003
Concert for George 2003 DVD
The Conductor 1980
Cool and Crazy 2000 DVD
Cover Girl 1944 DVD
Daddy Long Legs 1955
The Decline of Western Civilization 1980
Dirty Dancing 1987 DVD
Don't Look Back 1967
Earth Girls Are Easy 1988 DVD
8 Women 2001 DVD
Elvis: That's the Way It Is 1970 DVD
Everyone Says I Love You 1996 DVD
Expresso Bongo 1959
Festival Express 2003
Fiddler on the Roof 1971 DVD
The Five Pennies 1959
Flowers and Trees 1932
Follow the Boys 1944
Follow the Fleet 1936 DVD
Footlight Parade 1933
For Me and My Gal 1942
From Mao to Mozart: Isaac Stern in China 1980
Funny Face 1957 DVD
Funny Girl 1968 DVD
The Gay Divorcee 1934 DVD
Gentlemen Prefer Blondes 1953 DVD
Gimme Shelter 1970
The Girl Can't Help It 1956 DVD
The Glenn Miller Story 1953
Going My Way 1944
Gold Diggers of 1933 1933
The Good Companions 1933
Good News 1947
Grace of My Heart 1996
Grease 1978 DVD
The Great Caruso 1951
The Great Ziegfeld 1936 DVD
Guys and Dolls 1955 DVD
Gypsy 1962
Hail! Hail! Rock 'n' Roll! 1987
Hairspray 1988 DVD
Half a Sixpence 1967
Hans Christian Andersen 1952 DVD
The Happiness of the Katakuris 2001 DVD
Head 1968 DVD
Hello, Dolly! 1969 DVD
Help! 1965
High Society 1956 DVD
High, Wide and Handsome 1937
Hit the Deck 1955
Holiday Inn 1942 DVD
Hollywood Revue 1929
How to Succeed in Business without Really Trying 1967
The Hunchback of Notre Dame 1996 DVD
It's Always Fair Weather 1955
It's Great to Be Young 1956
Jailhouse Rock 1957 DVD
Jumbo 1962
The Kid from Spain 1932
The King and I 1956 DVD
King Creole 1958 DVD
Kiss Me Kate 1953 DVD
Lady Sings the Blues 1972
Latcho Drom 1993
Let It Be 1970
Let the Good Times Roll 1973
Li'l Abner 1959
Lili 1953
The Lion King 1994 DVD
The Little Princess 1939 DVD
Little Shop of Horrors 1986 DVD
Love Me or Leave Me 1955
The Love Parade 1929
Make Mine Music 1946
The Mambo Kings 1992
The Man I Love 1946
Margie 1946
Martin Scorsese Presents the Blues: Godfathers and Sons 2003 DVD
Martin Scorsese Presents the Blues: The Road to Memphis 2003 DVD
Martin Scorsese Presents the Blues: The Soul of a Man 2003 DVD
Maytime 1937
The Merry Widow 1934
Monrak Transistor 2001
Monterey Pop 1968
Moulin Rouge! 2001 DVD
Mulan 1998 DVD
The Music Man 1962
Never Steal Anything Small 1959
New York, New York 1977
Oh, Rosalinda!! 1955
Oh! What a Lovely War 1969
Oklahoma! 1955 DVD
Oliver! 1968 DVD
One Hundred Men and a Girl 1937 DVD
One Night of Love 1934
Opera do Malandro 1986
The Pajama Game 1957 DVD
Pas sur la Bouche 2003
Passion 1996
The Pirate 1948
Pleasure at Her Majesty's 1976
Quadrophenia 1979 DVD
Ray 2004 DVD
Ride 'em Cowboy 1942
Road to Morocco 1942 DVD
Road to Rio 1947
Road to Utopia 1945 DVD
Robert Altman's Jazz '34: Remembrances of Kansas City Swing 1996
The Rocky Horror Picture Show 1975 DVD
Rose Marie 1936
'Round Midnight 1986
The School of Rock 2003 DVD
The Secret Policeman's Ball 1980 DVD
Serenade 1956
Sing, Baby, Sing 1936
State Fair 1945 DVD
Stop Making Sense 1984 DVD
The Story of Vernon and Irene Castle 1939
Stowaway 1936 DVD
Strike Up the Band 1940
Summer Stock 1950
Super 8 Stories 2001
Take Me Out to the Ball Game 1949
Thank Your Lucky Stars 1943
That Thing You Do! 1996 DVD
That's Dancing! 1985
Theremin: an Electronic Odyssey 1993
There's No Business like Show Business 1954 DVD
Three Little Words 1950
Three Smart Girls 1937 DVD
The Threepenny Opera 1931 DVD
Till the Clouds Roll By 1946 DVD
Tom Sawyer 1973
tom thumb 1958
The Total Balalaika Show 1994
The Unsinkable Molly Brown 1964
Viva Las Vegas 1964 DVD
When My Baby Smiles at Me 1948
White Christmas 1954 DVD
Wild Man Blues 1997
With a Song in My Heart 1952
Wonder Bar 1934
Yankee Doodle Dandy 1942
Yellow Submarine 1968 DVD
Ziegfeld Follies 1944

Mystery

★★★★★

Blue Velvet 1986 DVD
The Hound of the Baskervilles 1939 DVD
The Hound of the Baskervilles 1959 DVD
Lone Star 1995
Shadowman 1973

Mystery

★★★★

The Adventures of Sherlock Holmes 1939 DVD
And Then There Were None 1945 DVD
L'Appartement 1996 DVD
Birth 2004 DVD
The Bride Wore Black 1967
Caroline? 1990
The Castle of Cagliostro 1979 DVD
The Cat and the Canary 1927
The Cat and the Canary 1939 DVD
The Death of Mario Ricci 1983
The Disappearance of Aimee 1976
Dolores Claiborne 1995 DVD
8 Women 2001 DVD
The Element of Crime 1984 DVD
Flesh and Bone 1993 DVD
The Flower of Evil 2003
The Ghost Breakers 1940
Gosford Park 2001 DVD
The Heart of Justice 1992
In My Father's Den 2004
Judex 1963
Mirage 1965
Monsieur N 2003
Murder on the Orient Express 1974 DVD
Mystic River 2003 DVD
The Name of the Rose 1986 DVD
Night Moves 1975
La Nuit du Carrefour 1932
The October Man 1947
Out 1: Spectre 1973
Paris Nous Appartient 1960
Picnic at Hanging Rock 1975 DVD
Prescription: Murder 1968 DVD
The Private Life of Sherlock Holmes 1970 DVD
The Raven 1943 DVD
Sabotage 1936
The Scarlet Claw 1944 DVD
A Shot in the Dark 1964 DVD
Sleuth 1972 DVD
A Soldier's Story 1984 DVD
The Spanish Prisoner 1997 DVD
Swimming Pool 2003 DVD
Take My Life 1947
Unman, Wittering and Zigo 1971
Vagabond 1985
Whatever Happened to Aunt Alice? 1969 DVD
Young and Innocent 1937 DVD

Period

★★★★★

Aguirre, Wrath of God 1972 DVD
Babette's Feast 1987 DVD
Barry Lyndon 1975 DVD
Ben-Hur 1959 DVD
Ben-Hur: a Tale of Christ 1925
Burnt by the Sun 1995 DVD
Capricious Summer 1968
Crouching Tiger, Hidden Dragon 2000 DVD
Cyrano de Bergerac 1990 DVD
Day of Wrath 1943 DVD
Death in Venice 1971 DVD
The Draughtsman's Contract 1982 DVD
Fanny and Alexander 1982 DVD
Fitzcarraldo 1982 DVD
Gate of Hell 1953
Gladiator 2000 DVD
Gone with the Wind 1939 DVD
Great Expectations 1946 DVD
The Heiress 1949
The Hidden Fortress 1958 DVD
Howards End 1992 DVD
Jean de Florette 1986 DVD
The Last of the Mohicans 1920
The Leopard 1962 DVD
The Life and Death of Colonel Blimp 1943 DVD
The Life of Oharu 1952 DVD
Little Dorrit 1987
A Little Princess 1995 DVD
The Magnificent Ambersons 1942
The Man Who Would Be King 1975 DVD
Miller's Crossing 1990 DVD
Les Misérables 1934
Une Partie de Campagne 1936 DVD
A Passage to India 1984 DVD
The Piano 1993 DVD
The Railway Children 1970 DVD
The Remains of the Day 1993 DVD
Ride with the Devil 1999 DVD
Sansho the Bailiff 1954
Sense and Sensibility 1995 DVD
Seven Samurai 1954 DVD
The Seventh Seal 1957 DVD
Shakespeare in Love 1998 DVD
The Spirit of the Beehive 1973 DVD
The Sting 1973 DVD
Story of the Late Chrysanthemums 1939
A Tale of Two Cities 1935 DVD
Tristana 1970 DVD
Two Stage Sisters 1964
Ugetsu Monogatari 1953
The Vikings 1958 DVD
Wuthering Heights 1939 DVD
Yellow Earth 1984

Yojimbo 1961 DVD

Period

★★★★

The Age of Innocence 1993 DVD
Anastasia 1956 DVD
Anna Karenina 1935 DVD
Anthony Adverse 1936
Ashes of Time 1994
The Assassination Bureau 1969
Bang the Drum Slowly 1973
Barton Fink 1991 DVD
Becky Sharp 1935
Berkeley Square 1933
Big Night 1996
The Bingo Long Travelling All-Stars and Motor Kings 1976
Blanche 1971
Bullets over Broadway 1994 DVD
Burn! 1970
Camelot 1967 DVD
C'est la Vie 1990
Chamber of Horrors 1966
Character 1997
Charulata 1964
The Chess Player 1927
The Children of the Marshland 1998
The Claim 2000 DVD
Colonel Redl 1984
The Color Purple 1985 DVD
The Count of Monte Cristo 1934
Country Life 1994
The Crimson Curtain 1952
The Crucible 1996 DVD
The Crucified Lovers 1954
Cuba 1979 DVD
Daens 1992
Dangerous Liaisons 1988 DVD
Daughters of the Dust 1991
The Dawning 1988
The Dead 1987
The Decameron 1970
Les Destinées Sentimentales 2000 DVD
The Devil's Backbone 2001 DVD
Dieu A Besoin des Hommes 1950
Don't Move, Die and Rise Again 1989
The Dreamers 2003 DVD
Drôle de Drame 1937
The Duellists 1977 DVD
Effi Briest 1974
Emma 1996 DVD
L'Enfant Sauvage 1970 DVD
England Made Me 1973
The Enigma of Kaspar Hauser 1974
The Europeans 1979 DVD
FairyTale: a True Story 1997
Finding Neverland 2004 DVD
The First Teacher 1965
Five Women around Utamaro 1946
Flowers of Shanghai 1998
Forever and a Day 1943
Friendly Persuasion 1956
From Hell 2001 DVD
Gangs of New York 2002 DVD
Gaslight 1944 DVD
Gate of Flesh 1964 DVD
Girl with a Pearl Earring 2003 DVD
The Go-Between 1971 DVD
The Golden Bowl 2000 DVD
The Golden Coach 1953
Gone to Earth 1950 DVD
Good Morning, Babylon 1987
Gosford Park 2001 DVD
A Handful of Dust 1987 DVD
Harakiri 1962
Hard Times 1975 DVD
Heart of Glass 1976 DVD
Hester Street 1975
The Home and the World 1984
House of Flying Daggers 2004 DVD
House of Wax 1953 DVD
I Capture the Castle 2002 DVD
I Remember Mama 1948
An Ideal Husband 1999 DVD
If I Were King 1938
The Importance of Being Earnest 1952 DVD
Indochine 1991 DVD
L'Innocente 1976 DVD
Jane Eyre 1943 DVD
Jude 1996 DVD
Junoon 1978 DVD
Kagemusha 1980 DVD
Kaos 1984
The Kidnappers 1953
Kitty 1945
A Knight's Tale 2001 DVD
Kung Fu Hustle 2004
The Lady in Red 1979
Lady L 1965
The Last of the Mohicans 1992 DVD
The Last Samurai 2003 DVD
The Legend of 1900 1999 DVD
The Libertine 2004
Liberty Heights 1999 DVD
Life and Nothing But 1989
The Little Foxes 1941
Little Women 1933
Lord Jim 1965 DVD
The Lower Depths 1956
Macario 1960
Madame Bovary 1933
The Magdalene Sisters 2002 DVD
Man about Town 1947
The Man Who Laughs 1928
The Man Who Wasn't There 2001 DVD
Mandingo 1975
Manon des Sources 1986 DVD
Mansfield Park 1999 DVD
The Marquise of O 1976 DVD
Martha and I 1990
Master and Commander: the Far Side of the World 2003 DVD
Les Misérables 1935
Les Misérables 1995
Miss Evers' Boys 1997
Miss Julie 1951
My Brilliant Career 1979 DVD
My Friend Ivan Lapshin 1982
My Life as a Dog 1985 DVD
The Name of the Rose 1986 DVD
Nicholas Nickleby 1947 DVD
Nicholas Nickleby 2002 DVD
1900 1976
Nowhere in Africa 2001 DVD
The Old Maid 1939
Old Man 1997
Olivia 1950
The Organizer 1963
Orphans of the Storm 1921
Papa's Delicate Condition 1963
Paper Moon 1973
Park Row 1952
Pascali's Island 1988
Peking Opera Blues 1986
Pelle the Conqueror 1987 DVD
Perceval le Gallois 1978
Persuasion 1995 DVD
The Picture of Dorian Gray 1945
Places in the Heart 1984
Pretty Baby 1978
Pride and Prejudice 1940
The Pride and the Passion 1957 DVD
The Private Affairs of Bel Ami 1947
Quentin Durward 1955
Radio Days 1987 DVD
Raintree County 1957
Ravenous 1999 DVD
Rebellion 1967
Red Beard 1965 DVD
The Reivers 1969 DVD
Restoration 1995
Road to Perdition 2002 DVD
A Room with a View 1985 DVD
Rue Cases Nègres 1983
The Scarlet Pimpernel 1982 DVD
The Secret Garden 1993 DVD
The Secret of Roan Inish 1993
7 Women 1966
The Shooting Party 1984
Sophie's Choice 1982 DVD
Springtime in a Small Town 2002 DVD
Start the Revolution without Me 1970
Stiff Upper Lips 1997
The Summer of Ben Tyler 1996
A Summer Story 1987
Sunday in the Country 1984
Sweet and Lowdown 1999 DVD
Swiss Family Robinson 1960 DVD
Tess 1979
The Tall Target 1951
They Came to Cordura 1959 DVD
The Thief of Paris 1967
Thieves like Us 1974
Tom Jones 1963 DVD
Tom Sawyer 1973
A Tree Grows in Brooklyn 1945 DVD
The Tree of Wooden Clogs 1978 DVD
Triple Agent 2003 DVD
The Twilight Samurai 2002 DVD
An Unfinished Piece for Mechanical Piano 1976
An Unforgettable Summer 1994
Untold Scandal 2003
Up at the Villa 1998
Valmont 1989
Vera Drake 2004 DVD
A Very Long Engagement 2004 DVD
The Virgin Spring 1960 DVD
The War Lord 1965
When the Last Sword Is Drawn 2003 DVD
The White Dawn 1974
The Wicked Lady 1945 DVD
The Wind and the Lion 1975
The Wings of the Dove 1997 DVD
The World Changes 1933
Young Adam 2003 DVD
Zatoichi 2003 DVD

Road Movie

★★★★★

Easy Rider 1969 DVD
The Motorcycle Diaries 2004 DVD
Rain Man 1988 DVD
The Straight Story 1999 DVD
Thelma & Louise 1991 DVD

Road Movie

★★★★

Alice in the Cities 1974
Ariel 1988
Cold Fever 1994
Eureka 2000 DVD
Grand Theft Parsons 2003 DVD
Heaven's Burning 1997
Ikinai 1998
Jump Tomorrow 2001 DVD
Kings of the Road 1976
Motorama 1991
Sitting Ducks 1979
Stranger than Paradise 1984
Sweet Sweetback's Baad Asssss Song 1971
Trans 1998

Romance

★★★★★

A Bout de Souffle 1959 DVD
The African Queen 1951 DVD
Amélie 2001 DVD
Annie Hall 1977 DVD
L'Atalante 1934 DVD
Avanti! 1972 DVD
Breakfast at Tiffany's 1961 DVD
Breaking the Waves 1996 DVD
Bridget Jones's Diary 2001 DVD
Brief Encounter 1945 DVD
Casablanca 1942 DVD
Charade 1963 DVD
City Lights 1931 DVD
College 1927 DVD
Crouching Tiger, Hidden Dragon 2000 DVD
Cyrano de Bergerac 1990 DVD
The Devil Is a Woman 1935
Doctor Zhivago 1965 DVD
The Dot and the Line 1965
The English Patient 1996 DVD
Far from Heaven 2002 DVD
Four Weddings and a Funeral 1994 DVD
Gone with the Wind 1939 DVD
Holiday 1938 DVD
I Know Where I'm Going! 1945 DVD
It Happened One Night 1934 DVD
Lola 1960
Lola Montès 1955
Lost in Translation 2003 DVD
Love Affair 1939
Love in the Afternoon 1957
Manhattan 1979 DVD
Master of the House 1925
A Matter of Life and Death 1946 DVD
Morocco 1930
Notorious 1946 DVD
Now, Voyager 1942
Une Partie de Campagne 1936 DVD
Pépé le Moko 1937 DVD
The Philadelphia Story 1940 DVD
Il Postino 1994 DVD
Le Quai des Brumes 1938
The Quiet Man 1952 DVD
Rebecca 1940 DVD
The Red Shoes 1948 DVD
Roman Holiday 1953 DVD
Romancing the Stone 1984 DVD
Ryan's Daughter 1970
Sabrina 1954 DVD
Sense and Sensibility 1995 DVD
Shadowlands 1993
Shakespeare in Love 1998 DVD
Sideways 2004 DVD
Smiles of a Summer Night 1955 DVD
Stolen Kisses 1968 DVD
Strictly Ballroom 1992 DVD
Summer of My German Soldier 1978
Summer with Monika 1952 DVD
Sunrise 1927 DVD
To Have and Have Not 1944 DVD
A Touch of Class 1973
Trouble in Paradise 1932
When Harry Met Sally... 1989 DVD
Witness 1985 DVD
Wuthering Heights 1939

Romance

★★★★

About a Boy 2002 DVD
An Affair to Remember 1957 DVD
Afterglow 1997
The Age of Innocence 1993 DVD
All That Heaven Allows 1955
All the Vermeers in New York 1990
All This, and Heaven Too 1940
The American President 1995 DVD
Angel Sharks 1997
Anna Karenina 1935 DVD
Anne and Muriel 1971
L'Appartement 1996 DVD
The April Fools 1969
Arise, My Love 1940
As Good as It Gets 1997 DVD
An Autumn Tale 1998
Back Street 1941
Back Street 1961
Barefoot in the Park 1967 DVD
Before Sunrise 1995 DVD
Berkeley Square 1933
Betrayal 1982
The Big Blue 1988 DVD
A Blonde in Love 1965
The Blue Veil 1951
Le Bonheur 1965
The Bride with White Hair 1993 DVD
The Bridges of Madison County 1995 DVD
Brigadoon 1954 DVD
By Love Possessed 1961
Cal 1984
Camelot 1967 DVD
Camille 1937
Cass Timberlane 1947
Chance or Coincidence 1999
Chasing Amy 1996 DVD
La Chienne 1931
Children of a Lesser God 1986 DVD
China Seas 1935
Chinese Box 1997
Chocolat 2000 DVD
Choose Me 1984 DVD
Chung King Express 1994 DVD
Cinderella 1950
Circle of Friends 1995 DVD
The Clock 1945
Clueless 1995 DVD
Conquest 1937
The Cooler 2002 DVD
Cover Girl 1944 DVD
The Cranes Are Flying 1957
Crazy from the Heart 1991
Crazy in Love 1992
The Crimson Curtain 1952
Crossing Delancey 1988
The Crucified Lovers 1954
Daddy Long Legs 1955
Daisy Kenyon 1947
Dear Heart 1964
The Death of Mario Ricci 1983
Designing Woman 1957
Desire 1936
Desk Set 1957
Diabolo Menthe 1977
Dirty Dancing 1987 DVD
Djomeh 2000
Dodsworth 1936
Dogfight 1991
Dolls 2002 DVD
Don Juan 1926
Don Juan DeMarco 1995
Drifting Clouds 1996
The Eclipse 1962 DVD
Eighteen Springs 1997
Emma 1996 DVD
The Enchanted Cottage 1945
The End of the Affair 1954
The End of the Affair 1999 DVD
Erotikon 1920
Eternal Sunshine of the Spotless Mind 2003 DVD
Ever After: a Cinderella Story 1998 DVD
The Fabulous Baker Boys 1989 DVD
Fanfan la Tulipe 1951 DVD
Fear Eats the Soul 1973
Fever Pitch 1996 DVD
First Love 1970
5x2 2004
A Foreign Affair 1948
Four Daughters 1938
Frankie & Johnny 1991 DVD
The French Lieutenant's Woman 1981 DVD
Full Moon in Paris 1984 DVD
Ghost 1990 DVD
The Ghost and Mrs Muir 1947 DVD
Gidget 1959
Girl with Green Eyes 1963
Go Fish 1994
Gone to Earth 1950 DVD
The Goodbye Girl 1977
Grace of My Heart 1996
Les Grandes Manoeuvres 1955 DVD
Grease 1978 DVD
The Great Lie 1941
Gregory's Girl 1980 DVD
The Guardsman 1931
The Harness 1971
Heimkehr 1928
High Society 1956 DVD
Histoire de Marie et Julien 2003 DVD
Hold Back the Dawn 1941
Holiday Affair 1949
Un Homme et une Femme 1966 DVD
Honeymoon in Vegas 1992 DVD
The Honeymooners 2003 DVD
Houseboat 1958 DVD
I Capture the Castle 2002 DVD
I Married a Witch 1942
IQ 1994 DVD
Immortal Beloved 1994
In the Mood for Love 2000 DVD
Indochine 1991 DVD
The Inn of the Sixth Happiness 1958 DVD
Intermezzo 1936
Intermezzo 1939 DVD
The Iron Petticoat 1956 DVD

- It Should Happen to You 1954 DVD
- Italian for Beginners 2000 DVD
- Janice Beard 45 WPM 1999 DVD
- Japanese Story 2003 DVD
- Jeffrey 1995 DVD
- Jerry Maguire 1996 DVD
- Jezebel 1938
- Jump Tomorrow 2001 DVD
- Knave of Hearts 1954
- A Knight's Tale 2001 DVD
- LA Story 1991 DVD
- The Lacemaker 1977
- The Lady from Shanghai 1948 DVD
- Lady with a Past 1932
- Let's Make Love 1960 DVD
- Letter from an Unknown Woman 1948
- Une Liaison Pornographique 1999
- Like Water for Chocolate 1993 DVD
- Lili 1953
- Lonely Hearts 1981
- Love among the Ruins 1975
- Love Field 1992 DVD
- Love Is Colder Than Death 1969
- The Love of Jeanne Ney 1927
- The Lovers of the Arctic Circle 1998 DVD
- Madame Bovary 1933
- Making Up 1992
- Man about Town 1947
- The Man without a Past 2002 DVD
- Marie Antoinette 1938
- Marius et Jeannette 1997
- The Marriage of Maria Braun 1978
- Mayerling 1936
- Maytime 1937
- Me Myself I 1999
- Mélo 1986
- Mermaids 1990 DVD
- The Merry Widow 1925
- A Midsummer Night's Dream 1935
- A Midsummer Night's Dream 1961
- A Millionaire for Christy 1951
- Mississippi Masala 1991
- Mr and Mrs '55 1955 DVD
- Mr Wonderful 1992
- Mon Père Ce Héros 1991
- Monster's Ball 2001 DVD
- Moonstruck 1987 DVD
- Moulin Rouge! 2001 DVD
- Mrs Delafield Wants to Marry 1986
- My Best Friend's Wedding 1997 DVD
- My Big Fat Greek Wedding 2002 DVD
- My Favorite Wife 1940 DVD
- Mystic Pizza 1988 DVD
- Next Stop Wonderland 1998
- Night and Day 1991
- The Night We Never Met 1993 DVD
- Notting Hill 1999 DVD
- One Way Passage 1932
- Only Yesterday 1933
- Only You 1994 DVD
- Open Hearts 2002 DVD
- Out of Sight 1998 DVD
- Overboard 1987 DVD
- The Oyster Princess 1919
- Pakeezah 1971
- Pandora and the Flying Dutchman 1950
- Parineeta 2005
- Paris Blues 1961
- Pas sur la Bouche 2003
- Penny Serenade 1941 DVD
- Persuasion 1995 DVD
- Peter Ibbetson 1935
- Pillow Talk 1959 DVD
- The Polish Bride 1998
- Portrait of Jennie 1948 DVD
- Pretty Woman 1990 DVD
- The Prince of Tides 1991 DVD
- Punch-Drunk Love 2002 DVD
- The Purple Rose of Cairo 1985 DVD
- Queen Christina 1933
- Random Harvest 1942
- The Red Dance 1928
- Red Dust 1932
- Remember the Night 1940
- Les Rendez-vous de Paris 1995
- Reunion in France 1942
- The Rich Are Always with Us 1932
- The Ripening Seed 1953
- Robin Hood 1922 DVD
- Romeo and Juliet 1936
- Romeo and Juliet 1954
- Rose Marie 1936
- Rouge 1987
- Roxanne 1987 DVD
- Same Time, Next Year 1978
- Scaramouche 1923
- Secret Wedding 1989
- Send Me No Flowers 1964 DVD
- 7th Heaven 1927
- Shall We Dance? 1995 DVD
- Shanghai Express 1932
- The Shop around the Corner 1940
- The Shopworn Angel 1938
- Singles 1992 DVD
- Sleepless in Seattle 1993 DVD
- Some Kind of Wonderful 1987 DVD
- Somewhere beyond Love 1974
- Splash 1984 DVD
- Starman 1984 DVD
- Stormy Waters 1941
- The Story of Three Loves 1953
- Straight Talk 1992 DVD
- Strangers Kiss 1983
- The Strawberry Blonde 1941
- Street Angel 1937
- Sugarbaby 1985
- A Summer Story 1987
- A Summer's Tale 1996 DVD
- Summertime 1955
- Sunshine 1999 DVD
- Suzhou River 2000 DVD
- Swing Shift 1984
- Taipei Story 1984
- A Tale of Springtime 1989
- Talk to Her 2001 DVD
- 10 Things I Hate about You 1999 DVD
- The Tender Trap 1955
- Test Pilot 1938
- The Theory of Flight 1998
- There's Something about Mary 1998 DVD
- They Live by Night 1948
- Things You Can Tell Just by Looking at Her 2000
- Those Lips, Those Eyes 1980
- Three Coins in the Fountain 1954
- 3-Iron 2004
- Three Smart Girls 1937 DVD
- Titanic 1997 DVD
- Toni 1935
- The Torrent 1926
- The Trap 1966
- Truly Madly Deeply 1990 DVD
- The Truth about Cats and Dogs 1996 DVD
- An Unfinished Piece for Mechanical Piano 1976
- An Unmarried Woman 1978
- Up at the Villa 1998
- Va Savoir 2001 DVD
- Valley Girl 1983
- Veer-Zaara 2004
- A Very Long Engagement 2004 DVD
- Les Visiteurs du Soir 1942
- Volere, Volare 1991
- Waterloo Bridge 1940
- The Way We Were 1973 DVD
- We All Loved Each Other So Much 1974
- The Wedding Singer 1998 DVD
- What Women Want 2001 DVD
- When the Cat's Away... 1996
- When Ladies Meet 1933
- While You Were Sleeping 1995 DVD
- Whisky 2004
- White Palace 1990 DVD
- The Widow Couderc 1971
- Wild about Harry 2000 DVD
- William Shakespeare's Romeo + Juliet 1996 DVD
- The Wings of the Dove 1997 DVD
- The Winning of Barbara Worth 1926
- A Winter's Tale 1992
- Woman of the Year 1942 DVD
- Wonder Bar 1934
- The Wonderful Lie of Nina Petrovna 1929
- A Year of the Quiet Sun 1984

Satire

★★★★★

- Ace in the Hole 1951
- L'Age d'Or 1930 DVD
- Dr Strangelove, or How I Learned to Stop Worrying and Love the Bomb 1963 DVD
- Fight Club 1999 DVD
- Ginger & Fred 1986 DVD
- The Graduate 1967 DVD
- The Great Dictator 1940 DVD
- The House on Trubnaya Square 1928
- I'm All Right Jack 1959 DVD
- The Man in the White Suit 1951 DVD
- Mon Oncle 1958 DVD
- Monsieur Hulot's Holiday 1953 DVD
- Pink Flamingos 1972 DVD
- The Player 1992 DVD
- Playtime 1967 DVD
- RoboCop 1987 DVD
- Roger & Me 1989 DVD
- Show People 1928
- Sullivan's Travels 1941 DVD
- Sunset Blvd 1950 DVD
- Sweet Smell of Success 1957 DVD
- To Be or Not to Be 1942
- To Die For 1995 DVD
- The Truman Show 1998 DVD
- Viridiana 1961

Satire

★★★★

- About Schmidt 2002 DVD
- Adaptation. 2002 DVD
- Adorable Lies 1991
- American Psycho 2000 DVD
- Animal Farm 1954 DVD
- Barbarians at the Gate 1993 DVD
- Being There 1979 DVD
- Best in Show 2000 DVD
- The Best Man 1964
- Beyond the Valley of the Dolls 1970 DVD
- The Big One 1997
- The Big Picture 1989
- The Book of Life 1998
- Cuba 1979 DVD
- Desperate Living 1977
- Dogma 1999 DVD
- Earth Girls Are Easy 1988 DVD
- Election 1999 DVD
- Ermo 1994
- The Exterminating Angel 1962
- A Face in the Crowd 1957
- Falling Down 1992 DVD
- Family Viewing 1987
- Fanfan la Tulipe 1951 DVD
- Faster, Pussycat! Kill! Kill! 1965 DVD
- Fear and Trembling 2003
- Female Trouble 1974
- The Fireman's Ball 1967
- Freeway 1996 DVD
- The Girl Can't Help It 1956 DVD
- Guelwaar 1992
- Hairspray 1988 DVD
- Hi, Mom! 1970 DVD
- Hollywood Shuffle 1987
- Irma Vep 1996
- Jesus of Montreal 1989 DVD
- Larks on a String 1969
- Leningrad Cowboys Go America 1989
- Life Is a Long Quiet River 1988
- Love and Death 1975 DVD
- Major Barbara 1941
- Male and Female 1919
- Man Bites Dog 1992 DVD
- Mars Attacks! 1996 DVD
- Meet the Applegates 1991
- The Middleman 1975
- A Mighty Wind 2003 DVD
- The Million Pound Note 1953
- The Nasty Girl 1990 DVD
- Network 1976 DVD
- Nothing but the Best 1964
- Oblomov 1980
- Oh! What a Lovely War 1969
- Phantom of the Paradise 1974 DVD
- Polyester 1981
- The President's Analyst 1967
- The Rocky Horror Picture Show 1975 DVD
- Secret Ballot 2001 DVD
- Seven Beauties 1976
- Slaughterhouse-Five 1972
- Smile 1975
- Starship Troopers 1997 DVD
- Strass 2001
- Supervixens 1975 DVD
- The Tale of the Fox 1931
- Tampopo 1986
- Vixen! 1968 DVD
- Wag the Dog 1997 DVD
- Xala 1974
- Zoolander 2001 DVD

Sci-Fi

★★★★★

- Alien 1979 DVD
- Aliens 1986 DVD
- Back to the Future 1985 DVD
- Blade Runner 1982 DVD
- Brazil 1985 DVD
- Close Encounters of the Third Kind 1977 DVD
- The Day the Earth Stood Still 1951 DVD
- Duck Dodgers in the 24½ Century 1953
- ET the Extra-Terrestrial 1982 DVD
- Forbidden Planet 1956
- The Incredible Shrinking Man 1957
- Invasion of the Body Snatchers 1956
- The Invisible Man 1933 DVD
- Island of Lost Souls 1932 DVD
- La Jetée 1962 DVD
- Jurassic Park 1993 DVD
- Mad Max 1979 DVD
- The Matrix 1999 DVD
- Metropolis 1926 DVD
- RoboCop 1987 DVD
- Star Trek: First Contact 1996 DVD
- Star Wars Episode IV: a New Hope 1977 DVD
- Star Wars Episode V: the Empire Strikes Back 1980 DVD
- The Terminator 1984 DVD
- Terminator 2: Judgment Day 1991 DVD
- Them! 1954 DVD
- 2001: a Space Odyssey 1968 DVD
- Le Voyage dans la Lune 1902

Sci-Fi

★★★★

- AI: Artificial Intelligence 2001 DVD
- Aelita 1924
- Akira 1988 DVD
- Alien Nation 1988 DVD
- Alien: Resurrection 1997 DVD
- Alphaville 1965 DVD
- The Andromeda Strain 1970 DVD
- Back to the Future Part III 1990 DVD
- Battle Royale 2000 DVD
- The Beast from 20,000 Fathoms 1953 DVD
- The Blob 1988
- Body Snatchers 1993 DVD
- A Boy and His Dog 1975 DVD
- Brainstorm 1983
- Capricorn One 1978 DVD
- Cocoon 1985 DVD
- Cube 1997 DVD
- Dark City 1998 DVD
- Dark Star 1973 DVD
- Deep Impact 1998 DVD
- Demolition Man 1993 DVD
- Demon Seed 1977
- Encounter at Raven's Gate 1988
- Enemy Mine 1985 DVD
- Escape from the Planet of the Apes 1971 DVD
- eXistenZ 1999 DVD
- The Falls 1980 DVD
- Fantastic Planet 1973
- Fantastic Voyage 1966 DVD
- The Fifth Element 1997 DVD
- The Fly 1986
- Galaxy Quest 1999 DVD
- Gattaca 1997 DVD
- Ghost in the Shell 1995 DVD
- Hardware 1990
- The Hidden 1987
- The Hitchhiker's Guide to the Galaxy 2005
- I, Robot 2004 DVD
- Independence Day 1996 DVD
- Invaders from Mars 1953 DVD
- The Iron Giant 1999 DVD
- It Came from Outer Space 1953
- Journey to the Center of the Earth 1959 DVD
- Judge Dredd 1995 DVD
- The Last Battle 1983 DVD
- Lilo & Stitch 2002 DVD
- Looker 1981
- Mad Max 2 1981 DVD
- The Man Who Fell to Earth 1976 DVD
- The Man with the X-Ray Eyes 1963
- Mars Attacks! 1996 DVD
- Men in Black 1997 DVD
- The Mind of Mr Soames 1970
- Minority Report 2002 DVD
- Muppets from Space 1999 DVD
- Nineteen Eighty-Four 1984 DVD
- Nirvana 1996
- The Omega Man 1971 DVD
- Panic in Year Zero 1962
- Pitch Black 1999 DVD
- Planet of the Apes 1967 DVD
- Planeta Burg 1962
- Predator 1987 DVD
- Quatermass II 1957 DVD
- Repo Man 1984 DVD
- Return from Witch Mountain 1978 DVD
- Robinson Crusoe on Mars 1964
- Roswell 1994
- Scanners 1980 DVD
- Seconds 1966
- The Seed of Man 1969
- Silent Running 1971 DVD
- The 6th Day 2000 DVD
- Slaughterhouse-Five 1972
- Sleeper 1973 DVD
- Solaris 1972 DVD
- Star Trek II: the Wrath of Khan 1982 DVD
- Star Trek IV: the Voyage Home 1986 DVD
- Star Trek VI: the Undiscovered Country 1991 DVD
- Star Trek: Generations 1994 DVD
- Star Wars Episode VI: Return of the Jedi 1983 DVD
- Stargate 1994 DVD
- Starman 1984 DVD
- Starship Troopers 1997 DVD
- The Stepford Wives 1975 DVD
- Strange Days 1995 DVD
- Strange Invaders 1983 DVD
- THX 1138 1971 DVD
- The Thing 1982 DVD
- The Thing from Another World 1951
- Things to Come 1936
- This Island Earth 1955
- Time after Time 1979
- The Time Machine 1960 DVD
- Titan AE 2000 DVD
- Total Recall 1990 DVD
- Trouble in Mind 1985 DVD
- Twelve Monkeys 1995 DVD
- 12:01 1993
- 28 Days Later... 2002 DVD
- The Ultimate Warrior 1975 DVD
- Village of the Damned 1960
- Voyage into Prehistory 1955
- The War of the Worlds 1953 DVD

War of the Worlds 2005 DVD
Waterworld 1995 DVD
Westworld 1973 DVD
The X-Files 1998 DVD

Sports

★★★★★

Body and Soul 1947
Chariots of Fire 1981 DVD
Hoop Dreams 1994 DVD
Million Dollar Baby 2004 DVD
Raging Bull 1980 DVD
When We Were Kings 1996 DVD

Sports

★★★★

Alone on the Pacific 1963
Any Given Sunday 1999 DVD
Bang the Drum Slowly 1973
Beyond the Mat 1999 DVD
Big Wednesday 1978 DVD
The Bingo Long Travelling All-Stars and Motor Kings 1976
Brian's Song 1971
Bull Durham 1988 DVD
The Champ 1931
Champion 1949
Cinderella Man 2005
Cobb 1994
Cool Runnings 1993 DVD
Cooperstown 1993
Fat City 1972
Fear Strikes Out 1957
Field of Dreams 1989 DVD
Friday Night Lights 2004
Girlfight 2000 DVD
He Got Game 1998
Hoosiers 1986 DVD
Jerry Maguire 1996 DVD
Kid Galahad 1937
The Milky Way 1936
The Miracle of Bern 2003 DVD
Muhammad Ali, the Greatest 1974 DVD
The Natural 1984 DVD
Pat and Mike 1952
Phar Lap 1983
Ping Pong 2002 DVD
The Pride of the Yankees 1942
Rocky 1976 DVD
Salty O'Rourke 1945
The Scout 1994
Second Serve 1986
The Set-Up 1949
Somebody Up There Likes Me 1956
Soul in the Hole 1995
Soul of the Game 1996
Southpaw 1998
White Men Can't Jump 1992 DVD

Spy

★★★★★

Dishonored 1931
Dr No 1962 DVD
Goldfinger 1964 DVD
North by Northwest 1959 DVD
The 39 Steps 1935 DVD
Unconquered 1989
You Only Live Twice 1967 DVD

Spy

★★★★

Above Suspicion 1943
Austin Powers: International Man of Mystery 1997 DVD
Austin Powers: the Spy Who Shagged Me 1999 DVD
The Bourne Supremacy 2004 DVD
Carve Her Name with Pride 1958 DVD
The Deadly Affair 1966
Die Another Day 2002 DVD
Foreign Correspondent 1940 DVD
From Russia with Love 1963 DVD
GoldenEye 1995 DVD
The House on 92nd Street 1945 DVD
The Ipcress File 1965 DVD
Journey into Fear 1942
Live and Let Die 1973 DVD
Mademoiselle Docteur 1936
The Mask of Dimitrios 1944
Mata Hari 1931
Mission: Impossible 1996 DVD
Mission: Impossible 2 1999 DVD
Night Train to Munich 1940
Le Petit Soldat 1960 DVD
Pimpernel Smith 1941
The Quiller Memorandum 1966 DVD
The Russia House 1990 DVD
Saboteur 1942 DVD
The Saboteur, Code Name Morituri 1965
Secret Agent 1936 DVD
Spies 1928
The Spy Who Came in from the Cold 1965
The Spy Who Loved Me 1977 DVD
36 Hours 1964
Tomorrow Never Dies 1997 DVD
The World Is Not Enough 1999 DVD

Thriller

★★★★★

Alien 1979 DVD
Aliens 1986 DVD
All the President's Men 1976 DVD
L'Armée des Ombres 1969
The Asphalt Jungle 1950
Blade Runner 1982 DVD
Blood and Black Lace 1964
Blue Velvet 1986 DVD
Charade 1963 DVD
Chinatown 1974 DVD
City of God 2002 DVD
The Conversation 1974 DVD
The Day of the Jackal 1973 DVD
Deliverance 1972 DVD
Les Diaboliques 1954 DVD
Die Hard 1988 DVD
Dirty Harry 1971 DVD
Don't Look Now 1973 DVD
Duel 1971 DVD
Fargo 1995 DVD
Illustrious Corpses 1976
Insomnia 2002 DVD
Invasion of the Body Snatchers 1956
Jaws 1975 DVD
Klute 1971 DVD
The Lady Vanishes 1938 DVD
Leon 1994 DVD
The Manchurian Candidate 1962 DVD
The Matrix 1999 DVD
Memento 2000 DVD
Monsieur Hire 1989 DVD
Mulholland Drive 2001 DVD
The Night of the Hunter 1955 DVD
North by Northwest 1959 DVD
Notorious 1946 DVD
The Parallax View 1974 DVD
Peeping Tom 1960 DVD
Point Blank 1967 DVD
Rear Window 1954 DVD
Rebecca 1940 DVD
RoboCop 1987 DVD
Le Samouraï 1967
Se7en 1995 DVD
Shadow of a Doubt 1942 DVD
The Silence of the Lambs 1991 DVD
Speed 1994 DVD
Strangers on a Train 1951 DVD
The Terminator 1984 DVD
Terminator 2: Judgment Day 1991 DVD
The Third Man 1949 DVD
The 39 Steps 1935 DVD
Twilight's Last Gleaming 1977
The Usual Suspects 1995 DVD
Vertigo 1958 DVD
The Wages of Fear 1953 DVD
Witness 1985 DVD

Thriller

★★★★

Across the Bridge 1957 DVD
After Dark, My Sweet 1990
Air Force One 1997 DVD
Alice, Sweet Alice 1977
Alien Nation 1988 DVD
Alien: Resurrection 1997 DVD
The Ambulance 1990
Amnesia 1994
The Andromeda Strain 1970 DVD
Angel 1982 DVD
L'Appartement 1996 DVD
Arlington Road 1998 DVD
Assault on Precinct 13 1976 DVD
Autobus 1991
Bad Boys 1995 DVD
La Balance 1982 DVD
The Bank 2001
Battle Royale 2000 DVD
The Beach 2000 DVD
Best Seller 1987 DVD
Betrayed 1988 DVD
A Better Tomorrow 1986 DVD
Beverly Hills Cop 1984 DVD
The Big Easy 1986 DVD
The Bird with the Crystal Plumage 1969 DVD
Black Mask 1996 DVD
Black Rainbow 1989 DVD
Black Sunday 1976 DVD
Blood Simple 1983 DVD
Blow Out 1981 DVD
Blue Steel 1990 DVD
Blue Sunshine 1976 DVD
Body Double 1984 DVD
Body Heat 1981 DVD
Boiling Point 1990 DVD
Boiling Point 1993 DVD
Borsalino 1970 DVD
Bound 1996 DVD
The Bourne Supremacy 2004 DVD
Brainstorm 1983
Branded to Kill 1967 DVD
Breakdown 1997 DVD
Bullitt 1968 DVD
Cal 1984 DVD
Cape Fear 1962 DVD
Cape Fear 1991 DVD
Capricorn One 1978 DVD
Cash on Demand 1961
La Cérémonie 1995
Chaos 1999 DVD
City on Fire 1987
The Client 1994 DVD
Cliffhanger 1993 DVD
Collateral 2004 DVD
The Collector 1965
The Colour of Lies 1999
Coma 1977
Con Air 1997 DVD
The Confessional 1995
Cop 1988
Copycat 1995 DVD
Cotton Comes to Harlem 1970
Le Cri du Hibou 1987
Crimson Tide 1995 DVD
Cube 1997 DVD
DOA 1988 DVD
Dark City 1998 DVD
Darkness in Tallinn 1993
Dead Calm 1988 DVD
Dead Ringers 1988 DVD
Death in a French Garden 1985 DVD
Deep Cover 1992 DVD
Defence of the Realm 1985 DVD
Demolition Man 1993 DVD
The Desperate Hours 1955 DVD
Desperately Seeking Susan 1985 DVD
Detour 1945 DVD
Devil in a Blue Dress 1995 DVD
Dial M for Murder 1954 DVD
Die Hard 2: Die Harder 1990 DVD
Die Hard with a Vengeance 1995 DVD
Dobermann 1997 DVD
Dr Mabuse, the Gambler 1922 DVD
Dressed to Kill 1980 DVD
The Driver 1978 DVD
Dust Devil 1992
The Ear 1969
Encounter at Raven's Gate 1988
Enemy of the State 1998 DVD
Europa 1991 DVD
Executive Action 1973
eXistenZ 1999 DVD
The Eye 2002 DVD
FX: Murder by Illusion 1985 DVD
Face/Off 1997 DVD
The Fallen Idol 1948 DVD
Falling Down 1992 DVD
Family Plot 1976 DVD
The Fast and the Furious 2001 DVD
Fatal Attraction 1987 DVD
Father Brown 1954
Felicia's Journey 1999 DVD
La Femme Infidèle 1968 DVD
The Firm 1993 DVD
Foreign Correspondent 1940 DVD
48 HRS 1982 DVD
The Fourth Man 1983 DVD
Frantic 1988 DVD
Freeway 1996 DVD
French Connection II 1975 DVD
Frenzy 1972 DVD
Frequency 2000 DVD
The Frighteners 1996 DVD
The Fugitive 1993 DVD
Full Contact 1992 DVD
Gaslight 1944 DVD
Gattaca 1997 DVD
Get Carter 1971 DVD
The Getaway 1972 DVD
The Ghost of St Michael's 1941
Gloria 1980 DVD
Green for Danger 1946
Guilty Conscience 1985
The Hand That Rocks the Cradle 1992 DVD
Handgun 1983
Harper 1966
The Heart of Justice 1992
Heat 1995 DVD
Heaven's Burning 1997
Hell Drivers 1957 DVD
Hennessy 1975
High Boot Benny 1993
A History of Violence 2005
The Hit 1984
The Hitcher 1986 DVD
Homicide 1991 DVD
House of Games 1987 DVD
The House on Telegraph Hill 1951
The Hunt for Red October 1990 DVD
Hustle 1975 DVD
I, Robot 2004 DVD
In the Line of Fire 1993 DVD
Internal Affairs 1990 DVD
The Interpreter 2005
The Ipcress File 1965 DVD
Isn't It Shocking? 1973
JFK 1991 DVD
Jackie Brown 1997 DVD
Jagged Edge 1985 DVD
Junk Mail 1997
Juste avant la Nuit 1971
Keep Cool 1997
The Killer 1989 DVD
The Killing 1956 DVD
The Killing of a Chinese Bookie 1976
King of New York 1989 DVD
The Kingdom 1994 DVD
Kiss of the Dragon 2001 DVD
Knife in the Head 1978
Lady in White 1988
Lady Killer 1933
Lantana 2001 DVD
Last Embrace 1979
Last Life in the Universe 2003 DVD
The Last Seduction 1993 DVD
The Leopard Man 1943
Lethal Weapon 1987 DVD
Lift to the Scaffold 1957
The Limey 1999 DVD
Live Flesh 1997 DVD
The Lodger 1926 DVD
The Lodger 1944
The Long Kiss Goodnight 1996 DVD
Looker 1981
Lost Highway 1996 DVD
The Lost Honour of Katharina Blum 1975
Love and a .45 1994 DVD
La Madre Muerta 1993
The Man with the X-Ray Eyes 1963
The Manchurian Candidate 2004 DVD
Manhattan Murder Mystery 1993 DVD
Manhunter 1986 DVD
Marathon Man 1976 DVD
Married to the Mob 1988 DVD
Masques 1987
Melancholia 1989
Miami Blues 1990 DVD
Midnight Run 1988 DVD
The Mind of Mr Soames 1970
Minority Report 2002 DVD
The Minus Man 1999
Mirage 1965
Misery 1990 DVD
Mission: Impossible 1996 DVD
Mission: Impossible 2 1999 DVD
Mr Klein 1976
Monsieur N 2003
Mute Witness 1995 DVD
Niagara 1953 DVD
Night Moves 1975 DVD
Night Must Fall 1937
Night Train to Munich 1940
Nightwatch 1994 DVD
Nikita 1990 DVD
Nirvana 1996
No Way Out 1986 DVD
Oldboy 2003 DVD
The Omega Man 1971 DVD
[One] Cavale 2002 DVD
One Deadly Summer 1983 DVD
One Hour Photo 2001 DVD
Open Your Eyes 1997 DVD
Out of the Darkness 1985
Outbreak 1995 DVD
The Outfit 1973
The Pelican Brief 1993 DVD
Pièges 1939
Pin 1988
Pitch Black 1999 DVD
Play Misty for Me 1971 DVD
Point Break 1991 DVD
Police 1985
Predator 1987 DVD
Presumed Innocent 1990 DVD
Primal Fear 1996 DVD
Public Access 1993 DVD
Quai des Orfèvres 1947
Quatermass II 1957 DVD
Que la Bête Meure 1969
The Quiller Memorandum 1966 DVD
A Rage in Harlem 1991
Raising Cain 1992 DVD
The Raven 1943 DVD
The Red Circle 1970 DVD
Red Lights 2004 DVD
Red Rock West 1992 DVD
Repo Man 1984 DVD
Repulsion 1965 DVD
Rien Ne Va Plus 1997
The River Wild 1994 DVD
The Rock 1996 DVD
Romeo Is Bleeding 1992 DVD
Ronin 1998 DVD
Roujin Z 1991
La Rupture 1970
The Russia House 1990 DVD
Sabotage 1936
Saboteur 1942 DVD
The Sadist 1963
Saw 2004 DVD
Scarface 1983 DVD
Sea of Love 1989 DVD
Seconds 1966
Secret Agent 1936 DVD
Serpico 1973 DVD
Session 9 2001 DVD
The Set Up 1995
Seven Days in May 1964
Seven Days to Noon 1950
Seven Minutes 1989
A Shadow of Doubt 1992
Shaft 2000 DVD
The Short Night of the Glass Dolls 1971
Silver Streak 1976
A Simple Plan 1998
Single White Female 1992 DVD
Sisters 1973

The 6th Day 2000 DVD
Sneakers 1992 DVD
Someone to Watch over Me 1987 DVD
Sorry, Wrong Number 1948
The Spanish Prisoner 1997 DVD
Spies 1928
The Spiral Staircase 1946 DVD
Stage Fright 1949 DVD
State of Grace 1990 DVD
The Stepford Wives 1975 DVD
Still of the Night 1982
Strange Days 1995 DVD
Straw Dogs 1971 DVD
The Street with No Name 1948
Subway 1985 DVD
Sudden Death 1995 DVD
Supervixens 1975 DVD
Suspicion 1941 DVD
Switchblade Romance 2003 DVD
Sympathy for Mr Vengeance 2002 DVD
The Taking of Pelham One Two Three 1974 DVD
The Talented Mr Ripley 1999 DVD
The Tall Target 1951
Targets 1968 DVD
Taste of Fear 1961
The Terminal Man 1974
Thieves' Highway 1949
The Third Voice 1960
36 Hours 1964
Three Days of the Condor 1975
Thunderheart 1992 DVD
Tightrope 1984
Time after Time 1979
Time and Tide 2000 DVD
A Time to Kill 1996 DVD
Tokyo Drifter 1966 DVD
Total Recall 1990 DVD
Triple Agent 2003 DVD
Trouble in Mind 1985 DVD
True Romance 1993 DVD
Twelve Monkeys 1995 DVD
12:01 1993
23 Paces to Baker Street 1956
U Turn 1997 DVD
The Ultimate Warrior 1975 DVD
Underground 1998
Up at the Villa 1998
The Vanishing 1988 DVD
Videodrome 1982 DVD
Violent Cop 1989 DVD
Wait until Dark 1967
War of the Worlds 2005
WarGames 1983 DVD
Westworld 1973
Whatever Happened to Aunt Alice? 1969 DVD
Where Eagles Dare 1969 DVD
Wild Target 1993
The Window 1949
The X-Files 1998 DVD
The Yakuza 1975
The Year of Living Dangerously 1982
Zero Effect 1997

War

★★★★★

All Quiet on the Western Front 1930 DVD
The African Queen 1951 DVD
Apocalypse Now 1979 DVD
L'Armée des Ombres 1969
The Battle of Algiers 1965 DVD
The Big Parade 1925
The Bridge on the River Kwai 1957 DVD
The Charge of the Light Brigade 1968 DVD
The Dam Busters 1954 DVD
The Deer Hunter 1978 DVD
Dishonored 1931
The English Patient 1996 DVD
Fires on the Plain 1959
The Four Feathers 1939 DVD
From Here to Eternity 1953 DVD
Full Metal Jacket 1987 DVD
The Garden of the Finzi-Continis 1971
Gone with the Wind 1939 DVD
La Grande Illusion 1937 DVD
The Great Escape 1963 DVD
Hope and Glory 1987
The Human Condition 1958
In Which We Serve 1942 DVD
Ivan's Childhood 1962 DVD
The Killing Fields 1984 DVD
MASH 1969 DVD
Mister Roberts 1955
Mrs Miniver 1942 DVD
Paths of Glory 1957 DVD
Patton 1970 DVD
Platoon 1986 DVD
Ride with the Devil 1999 DVD
Rome, Open City 1945 DVD
Schindler's List 1993 DVD
Summer of My German Soldier 1978
The Thin Red Line 1998 DVD
To Be or Not to Be 1942
To Have and Have Not 1944 DVD
Went the Day Well? 1942 DVD

War

★★★★

L'Accompagnatrice 1992
Air Force 1943 DVD
Alexander Nevsky 1938 DVD
Alexandria Why? 1979
And Quiet Flows the Don 1957
Another Time, Another Place 1983 DVD
Arise, My Love 1940
The Ascent 1976
Attack! 1956 DVD
Au Revoir les Enfants 1987
Ballad of a Soldier 1959
Battle Cry 1955 DVD
The Battle of Midway 1942
Battle of the Bulge 1965 DVD
Battleground 1949 DVD
Beach Red 1967
The Big Red One 1980
Biloxi Blues 1988 DVD
The Black Sheep of Whitehall 1941
The Blue Max 1966 DVD
Bon Voyage 2003 DVD
Breaker Morant 1979 DVD
The Bridge 1959
The Bridges at Toko-Ri 1954 DVD
The Burmese Harp 1956
A Canterbury Tale 1944 DVD
The Captive Heart 1946
Careful, Soft Shoulder 1942
Carve Her Name with Pride 1958 DVD
Casualties of War 1989 DVD
The Charge of the Light Brigade 1936
Checkpoint 1998
Closely Observed Trains 1966 DVD
The Cockleshell Heroes 1955 DVD
The Colditz Story 1954 DVD
Command Decision 1948
Conspiracy of Hearts 1960
Cross of Iron 1977 DVD
The Cruel Sea 1953 DVD
David 1979
The Dawn Patrol 1938
Day One 1989
Destiny of a Man 1959
Devils on the Doorstep 2000
The Dirty Dozen 1967 DVD
Divided We Fall 2000 DVD
The Dressmaker 1988
Downfall 2004
The Eagle and the Hawk 1933
The End of the Affair 1954
The End of the Affair 1999 DVD
The Enemy Below 1957 DVD
Escape from Sobibor 1987
Europa, Europa 1991 DVD
Fires Were Started 1943
Five Graves to Cairo 1943
49th Parallel 1941 DVD
The Four Days of Naples 1962
Four Sons 1928
Funny Dirty Little War 1983
Gallipoli 1981 DVD
General Della Rovere 1959
A Generation 1954
Glory 1989 DVD
The Goose Steps Out 1942
The Great War 1959
Guadalcanal Diary 1943 DVD
The Guns of Navarone 1961 DVD
Hamburger Hill 1987 DVD
Heaven and Earth 1993 DVD
Heaven Knows, Mr Allison 1957 DVD
Hell in the Pacific 1968 DVD
The Human Comedy 1943
I Was Monty's Double 1958
Ice Cold in Alex 1958 DVD
Ill Met by Moonlight 1956 DVD
In Harm's Way 1965 DVD
J'Accuse 1919
Kanal 1957
King of Hearts 1966
King Rat 1965
Lacombe Lucien 1974
Land and Freedom 1995 DVD
Landscape after Battle 1970
The Last Days of Mussolini 1974
The Last Stage 1947
Léon Morin, Priest 1961 DVD
Lifeboat 1944
Lion of the Desert 1981 DVD
The Long Journey 1949
The Long Voyage Home 1940
The Longest Day 1962 DVD
The McKenzie Break 1970 DVD
Mademoiselle Docteur 1936
The Man I Married 1940
Man's Hope 1945
Memphis Belle 1943
Merrill's Marauders 1962
Merry Christmas Mr Lawrence 1982 DVD
A Midnight Clear 1991 DVD
Millions like Us 1943
Mr Klein 1976
My Mother's Courage 1995
My Son, My Son! 1940
Next of Kin 1942
The Night of San Lorenzo 1981
La Nuit Fantastique 1942
The Officers' Ward 2001 DVD
Oh! What a Lovely War 1969
One against the Wind 1991
Operation Petticoat 1959 DVD
Orders to Kill 1958
Pastor Hall 1940
Pétain 1992
The Pianist 2002 DVD
Pimpernel Smith 1941
Pork Chop Hill 1959 DVD
Pretty Village Pretty Flame 1996
Prisoner of the Mountains 1996
Reach for the Sky 1956 DVD
The Red Badge of Courage 1951 DVD
Regeneration 1997 DVD
Reunion in France 1942
Run Silent, Run Deep 1958 DVD
The Saboteur, Code Name Morituri 1965
Salvador 1986 DVD
Saving Private Ryan 1998 DVD
Savior 1997 DVD
The Scarlet and the Black 1983 DVD
Sergeant York 1941
Seven Beauties 1976
Seven Minutes 1989
The Shop on the High Street 1965
The Shopworn Angel 1938
Sink the Bismarck! 1960 DVD
So Well Remembered 1947
Soldier of Orange 1977 DVD
A Song for Beko 1992
Sophie Scholl – The Final Days 2005
Sophie's Choice 1982 DVD
Stalag 17 1953 DVD
The Story of GI Joe 1945
They Were Expendable 1945
36 Hours 1964
Thomas the Imposter 1964
Three 1965
Three Came Home 1950 DVD
Three Kings 1999 DVD
The Tin Drum 1979 DVD
The Train 1964 DVD
The Tuskegee Airmen 1995
Twelve O'Clock High 1949 DVD
The Two of Us 1967
The Unknown Soldier 1983
The Vanishing Corporal 1962
La Vie de Château 1965 DVD
Wake Island 1942
A Walk in the Sun 1945
Waterloo Bridge 1940
The Way Ahead 1944 DVD
The Way to the Stars 1945 DVD
Westfront 1918 1930
When Trumpets Fade 1998 DVD
Where Eagles Dare 1969 DVD
Zulu 1964 DVD

Western

★★★★★

Annie Get Your Gun 1950 DVD
Bad Day at Black Rock 1955 DVD
The Big Country 1958 DVD
Butch Cassidy and the Sundance Kid 1969 DVD
Calamity Jane 1953 DVD
The Covered Wagon 1923
Dances with Wolves 1990 DVD
Destry Rides Again 1939 DVD
El Dorado 1967 DVD
A Fistful of Dollars 1964 DVD
For a Few Dollars More 1965 DVD
Fort Apache 1948 DVD
The Good, the Bad and the Ugly 1966 DVD
High Noon 1952 DVD
The Iron Horse 1924 DVD
The Magnificent Seven 1960 DVD
The Man Who Shot Liberty Valance 1962 DVD
My Darling Clementine 1946 DVD
Once upon a Time in the West 1968 DVD
The Ox-Bow Incident 1943
Red River 1948 DVD
Rio Bravo 1959 DVD
Rio Grande 1950 DVD
The Searchers 1956 DVD
Shane 1953 DVD
She Wore a Yellow Ribbon 1949 DVD
Stagecoach 1939 DVD
3:10 to Yuma 1957 DVD
The Tin Star 1957
The Treasure of the Sierra Madre 1948 DVD
Unforgiven 1992 DVD
Way Out West 1937 DVD
The Wild Bunch 1969 DVD

Western

★★★★

The Alamo 1960 DVD
Apache 1954 DVD
Bad Company 1972 DVD
The Ballad of Cable Hogue 1970
The Beautiful Blonde from Bashful Bend 1949
Bend of the River 1952 DVD
The Big Sky 1952
The Big Trail 1930 DVD
Billy the Kid 1930
Blazing Saddles 1974 DVD
Broken Arrow 1950 DVD
Broken Lance 1954 DVD
Canyon Passage 1946
Cat Ballou 1965 DVD
Cheyenne Autumn 1964
Cimarron 1931
City Slickers 1991 DVD
Comanche Station 1960
The Comancheros 1961 DVD
The Culpepper Cattle Co 1972
A Distant Trumpet 1964
Django 1966 DVD
Doc 1971
Dodge City 1939
Drums along the Mohawk 1939 DVD
Duel in the Sun 1946 DVD
Everything That Rises 1998
Evil Roy Slade 1971
Flaming Star 1960 DVD
The Furies 1950
Geronimo: an American Legend 1993 DVD
The Grey Fox 1982
Gunfight at the OK Corral 1957
The Gunfighter 1950 DVD
The Hanging Tree 1959
Heartland 1979
High Plains Drifter 1973 DVD
High, Wide and Handsome 1937
The Hired Hand 1971 DVD
Hombre 1967
Hour of the Gun 1967
How the West Was Won 1962
Invitation to a Gunfighter 1964
The Jack Bull 1999 DVD
Jesse James 1939
Johnny Guitar 1954 DVD
Jubal 1956
The Last Hunt 1956
Last Train from Gun Hill 1959 DVD
The Last Wagon 1956
The Law and Jake Wade 1958
Law and Order 1932
The Left Handed Gun 1958
Little Big Man 1970 DVD
Lonely Are the Brave 1962
The Long Riders 1980 DVD
McCabe and Mrs Miller 1971 DVD
The Man from Laramie 1955 DVD
Man of the West 1958
Man without a Star 1955
The Missouri Breaks 1976 DVD
No Name on the Bullet 1959
One-Eyed Jacks 1961 DVD
Open Range 2003 DVD
The Outlaw Josey Wales 1976 DVD
Pat Garrett and Billy the Kid 1973
The Plainsman 1936
The Professionals 1966 DVD
The Proud Rebel 1958
Pursued 1947
Ride Lonesome 1959
Ride the High Country 1962
Riders of the Purple Sage 1925
Run of the Arrow 1957
Seven Men from Now 1956
The Sheepman 1958
Shenandoah 1965 DVD
The Sheriff of Fractured Jaw 1958
The Shootist 1976 DVD
Silverado 1985 DVD
Son of Paleface 1952 DVD
The Sons of Katie Elder 1965 DVD
Star in the Dust 1956
Support Your Local Gunfighter 1971 DVD
Support Your Local Sheriff! 1969 DVD
The Tall Men 1955
The Tall T 1957
The Texas Rangers 1936
They Died with Their Boots On 1941
3 Bad Men 1926
Tombstone 1993 DVD
Tribute to a Bad Man 1956
True Grit 1969 DVD
Two Mules for Sister Sara 1970 DVD
Ulzana's Raid 1972 DVD
The Unforgiven 1960 DVD
Vera Cruz 1954 DVD
The Virginian 1929
Wagonmaster 1950
Warlock 1959 DVD
The Way West 1967
The Westerner 1940
When the Legends Die 1972
Wild Bill 1995 DVD
Wild Rovers 1971
Will Penny 1967 DVD
Winchester '73 1950 DVD
Windwalker 1980
The Winning of Barbara Worth 1926
The Wonderful Country 1959
Wyatt Earp 1994 DVD